S0-BYO-013

MARTINDALE-HUBBELL® INTERNATIONAL LAW DIGEST

—•—

ARGENTINA – VIETNAM LAW DIGESTS

—•—

SELECTED INTERNATIONAL CONVENTIONS

MARTINDALE-HUBBELL

WORLD HEADQUARTERS
121 Chanlon Road
New Providence, NJ 07974
U.S.A.
(908) 464-6800
Email: info@martindale.com
World Wide Web: http://www.martindale.com

INTERNATIONAL OFFICE
Halsbury House
35 Chancery Lane
London WC2A 1EL
England
44-171-400-2883
Email: intl-info@martindale.com
World Wide Web: http://www.martindale.com

Published by Martindale-Hubbell®, a member of the Reed Elsevier plc group

Nancy Murray Costa, Publisher, Martindale-Hubbell Law Digest
Carol D. Cooper, Vice President, Associate Publisher
Larry Thompson, Vice President, Marketing
Kevin English, Vice President, Sales
Edward J. Roycroft, Vice President, Sales Support
Dean Hollister, Vice President Database Production
Chuck Doscher, Vice President Production
John R. Agel, Vice President, Ratings
Louis F. Duffy, Vice President, Relations

Important Notices

Martindale-Hubbell has used its best efforts in collecting and preparing material for inclusion in the Martindale-Hubbell Law Directory but cannot warrant that the information herein is complete or accurate, and does not assume, and hereby disclaims, any liability to any person for any loss or damage caused by errors or omissions in the Martindale-Hubbell Law Directory whether such errors or omissions result from negligence, accident or any other cause.

The Law Digests are intended for use as general reference sources for lawyers and are not meant to provide legal opinions or advice, and are not a substitute for the advice of counsel. The Law Digests are not to be used as the basis for advice to clients or applied to particular matters. Local counsel in the applicable jurisdiction should be consulted as to the current law applicable to a particular situation.

International Standard Book Number: 1-56160-250-7 (Set)

Printed and Bound in the United States of America
by R.R. Donnelley & Sons Company
Chicago, Illinois, Willard, Ohio and Lancaster, Pennsylvania

Table of Contents*

*Index and detailed list of contents of each part follows title page of that part.

Detailed Table of Contents

UNITED STATES LAW DIGEST

PART I—DIGESTS OF LAWS OF THE STATES, THE DISTRICT OF COLUMBIA, PUERTO RICO, AND THE U.S. VIRGIN ISLANDS:

* See note at head of respective acts.

† See note at head of Uniform Acknowledgment Act.

†† The Revised Model Business Corporation Act (1984) and the Model Business Corporation Act (1969) were prepared by the Committee on Corporate Law (Section on Corporation, Banking and Business Law) of the American Bar Association. These Model Acts should be distinguished from the Model Business Corporation Act promulgated in 1928 by the Conference of Commissioners on Uniform State Laws as the "Uniform Business Corporation Act." In 1943 the Conference withdrew the Uniform Act and renamed it "Model Business Corporation Act." In 1957 this latter Act was also withdrawn.

* See note at head of respective acts.

PART IV—AMERICAN BAR ASSOCIATION CODES:

Page

INTERNATIONAL LAW DIGEST

PART V—DIGESTS OF LAWS, INTERNATIONAL SECTION:

* See note at head of respective acts.
† See note at head of Uniform Acknowledgment Act.

PART VI—INTERNATIONAL CONVENTIONS

FOREWORD

Welcome to the 1997 *Martindale-Hubbell® Law Digest*. Unequaled in depth and breadth of coverage, this is the legal community's most widely consulted and most respected digest of laws and legal codes in the world. As such, the *Law Digest* parallels the authority and global acceptance of its parent publication, the *Martindale-Hubbell Law Directory*.

The *Law Digest* is an excellent place to begin legal research. Users will find summaries of a vast body of statutory law, compiled by members of prominent law firms and preeminent legal scholars in each jurisdiction.

The scope of the *Law Digest* extends far beyond the borders of the United States. As the number of international legal transactions increases, so does our coverage of international laws. The *International Law Digest* now includes new sections for Latvia, the Slovak Republic, and Vietnam. Clearly, Martindale-Hubbell's international coverage remains unmatched — an invaluable asset to the global legal community.

The *Law Digest* on the LEXIS®-NEXIS® services makes it easier than ever for users to search multiple jurisdictions at one time and search by specific topics to retrieve relevant cases. This valuable online service also gives you access to more than 25 Uniform and Model Acts available in the LEXIS® Model Library.

It is our objective to ensure that Martindale-Hubbell continues to meet the legal community's ever-evolving information needs. We encourage you to contact us with any ideas and suggestions for future editions, and thank you for your support.

Nancy Murray Costa

Nancy Murray Costa
Publisher, Martindale-Hubbell Law Digest

IMPORTANT NOTICE—Since this Directory is produced under a printing schedule requiring early deadlines, it is possible that changes will occur after printing which can only be reflected in subsequent editions. Accordingly, it is suggested that local counsel should be consulted as to the current law applicable to a particular situation.

Preface

For 129 years, the *Martindale-Hubbell Law Digest* has served as the single most useful legal compendium available in the world. Its scope of coverage, which includes all U.S. states and over 60 countries, is matched only by the quality of the thousands of preeminent lawyers around the world who annually update and revise the information contained in each Digest.

The *Law Digest* summarizes the statutory law in each of the United States, the District of Columbia, Puerto Rico and the Virgin Islands, Canada and its provinces, the European Community and its member countries, as well as major countries involved internationally in business and law. Important Uniform Acts promulgated by the National Conference of Commissioners on Uniform State Laws are printed in their entirety, as are Selected International Conventions to which the United States is a party. The Federal Law Digests summarize United States copyright, patent and trademark laws and the American Bar Association section contains the Model Rules of Professional Conduct and the Code of Judicial Conduct promulgated by the Association, as well as other bar association information.

Continuing its tradition of expanding international coverage in areas of the world that are increasing in importance, we are including digests of the laws of Latvia, the Slovak Republic, and Vietnam. As always, users should consult local consul as to current laws applicable to particular situations.

SCOPE AND USE OF THE DIGESTS
UNITED STATES LAW DIGEST

The Domestic Law Digests*

Part I contains comprehensive digests of the laws of each of the fifty states of the United States, the District of Columbia, Puerto Rico and the Virgin Islands. These fifty-three compilations present under almost a hundred principal subject headings (topics) and numerous subheadings (running to a total of as many as five hundred in some of the digests) that portion of the law of the several jurisdictions which well over a century of experience has shown to be most useful to the legal profession.

The uniform arrangement of the material, supported by the abundant citations (including case citations to the National Reporter System), presents the laws in an organized and quickly accessible form. *To obtain the maximum benefit from the digests the user should become familiar with the Topical Index beginning at page XIII of the prefatory material.*

The digests have been compiled and are revised every year by distinguished lawyers and law firms who are acknowledged leaders of the bars of their respective jurisdictions. Every effort is made to insure that the digests reflect the most recent enactments of the legislature and changes in the rules of court.

Attention is directed to the numerous forms of instruments preferred by local usage which appear throughout the digests under the appropriate topics, e.g, forms of acknowledgment under the topic "Acknowledgments," subhead "Forms."

SCOPE AND USE OF THE DIGESTS (Cont.)

The Federal Law Digests

Digests of the Copyright, Patent and Trademark laws of the United States are presented in Part II. The revisers of these three digests are preeminent in their respective fields.

Besides presenting the substantive law controlling the grant of copyright, patent and trademark rights, the digests of these subjects provide information as to the practice to be followed in obtaining, protecting and enforcing such rights, the fee schedules of the respective bureaus, examples of forms in use, and other practical assistance. As in the case of all digests, these are annually revised.

The Uniform Acts

In Part III, the complete texts of many Uniform Acts *including the Uniform Commercial Code and the Uniform Probate Code,* and four Model Acts *including the Revised Model Business Corporation Act* are presented. These Uniform Laws are essential to the legal researcher because they have formed the basis of so much of the statutory law of so many states.

American Bar Association Section

Part IV contains The Model Rules of Professional Conduct of the American Bar Association, The Code of Judicial Conduct and the composition, jurisdiction and rules of procedure of the American Bar Association Standing Committee on Ethics and Professional Responsibility published as a service to the entire Bar of the United States.

---

* The possible impact of Federal law on the laws of the States digested herein must be considered, since that law may override current state legislation in certain areas.

INTERNATIONAL LAW DIGEST

The Law Digests — International Section

Digests of the laws of over 60 countries are supplied in Part V, and, in the case of Australia and Canada, digests of the laws of the States and Provinces of these countries are included with the digest of their Federal Laws. Distinguished lawyers and legal scholars of the respective countries have compiled and annually revise these digests. In some instances, particularly in the case of the Latin-American countries, the digests are revised by authorities resident in this country with the advice and assistance of local experts.

The aim of these digests is to present the points of law most likely to be of assistance to a lawyer with a matter in hand some facet of which is controlled by the law of that country. In addition, descriptions of the governmental and legal systems of the countries are given.

Because of its significance to the laws of a number of European countries, a separate, additional digest is included in this portion of the volume, setting forth European Communities Law.

International Conventions

Part VI sets forth the texts of ten international conventions to which the U.S. is a party. Annotations are included.

Suggestions as to how we can make the materials in this volume of still greater use are invited.

MARTINDALE-HUBBELL®/LEXIS® LEGAL ADVISORY BOARD

The Martindale-Hubbell/LEXIS Legal Advisory Board was formed to ensure that the Martindale-Hubbell Law Directory is responsive to the constantly changing needs of the legal profession. The following lawyers selected from the private, corporate and international sectors of the profession, as well as the legal academic community, comprise the 1996-1997 Board.

VINCENT J. APRUZZESE of Apruzzese, McDermott, Mastro & Murphy, Liberty Corner, NJ. Mr. Apruzzese is a former President of the New Jersey State Bar Association, a former member of the ABA Board of Governors and House of Delegates, and former Chair of the Labor and Employment Law Section of the ABA. Mr. Apruzzese is a Fellow of the American College of Trial Lawyers.

MARTHA W. BARNETT of Holland & Knight, Tallahassee, Florida. Ms. Barnett is the Immediate Past Chair of the House of Delegates of the American Bar Association, the first woman lawyer to be so honored, and serves on the ABA's Board of Governors.

ALLEN E. BRENNECKE of Harrison, Brennecke, Moore, Sasha & McKibben, Marshaltown, Iowa. Mr. Brennecke has served as a Member of the Board of Directors of the National Judicial College, President of the Iowa State Bar Association, a Member of the ABA House of Delegates since 1975 and its Chair, 1984-1986. His prior service to the ABA also includes four years on the Board of Governors and three years as Chair of the IOLTA Commission. He currently serves on the Board of Editors of the American Bar Association Journal and previously served as Chair from 1989 to 1995.

BENJAMIN R. CIVILETTI of Venable, Baetjer, Howard & Civiletti, Baltimore, Maryland. Mr. Civiletti is a former Attorney General of the United States under President Carter, 1979-1981. He has been a Trustee of Johns Hopkins University since 1980. He also serves as Chairman of Venable, Baetjer & Howard. Mr. Civiletti is a Fellow of the American College of Trial Lawyers.

DOUGLAS B. HENDERSON, of Finnegan, Henderson, Farabow, Garrett & Dunner, L.L.P., Washington, D.C. is currently on the Advisory Council for the United States Court of Federal Claims and the Board of Advisors, George Washington University National Law Center. Mr. Henderson was a founder of the ITC Trial Lawyers Bar Association, a founder and former member of the Board of Directors for the Federal Circuit Bar Association and a founder and former member of the Board of Directors of the U.S. Court of Federal Claims Bar Association. He has previously served as Chairman of the Patent Division and as a Member of Council for the Section on Patent, Trademark and Copyright Law of the ABA. He is also a member of the Panel of Arbitrators, American Arbitration Association.

THOMAS G. HEINTZMAN, Q.C., of McCarthy Tétrault, Toronto, Ontario, is a member of the Canadian Bar Association and a Past President (1994-1995). In addition, he is a member of the International Bar Association and serves as the Canadian Delegate to the IBA Council. He is also a member of the Inter-American Bar Association. Mr. Heintzman is a Fellow of the American College of Trial Lawyers and is Chair of its Canadian Judiciary Committee.

THOMAS J. KLITGAARD, fomerly Senior Vice President and General Counsel of Sega of America, Inc., is now in private practice in San Francisco. He is a former Chairman of the California State Bar's Committee on the Maintenance of Professional Competence. Mr. Klitgaard began his legal career as a law clerk to Supreme Court Justice William O. Douglas. From 1963-1985, he was in private practice with the San Francisco law firm of Pillsbury, Madison & Sutro, where he specialized in anti-trust and securities litigation. Since 1979, he has been active in East Asian legal affairs. Fluent in conversational Mandarin Chinese, Mr. Klitgaard is Vice-Chairman of the Shanghai-San Francisco Friendship Committee, and has served as Chairman of the Board of the Chinese Cultural Foundation of San Francisco. He is also a Director of the American Arbitration Association, a Trustee of the University of San Francisco and a member of the Advisory Board for The Southwestern Legal Foundation since 1990.

RALPH I. LANCASTER, JR. of Pierce, Atwood, Portland, Maine. Mr. Lancaster is Past-President of the Maine State Bar Association, and a former member of the House of Delegates of the American Bar Association. He has served as Chairman of the Standing Committee on the Federal Judiciary of the ABA. He is a Fellow of the American College of Trial Lawyers of which he was President, 1989-1990.

JERALYN E. MERRITT, of Denver, Colorado, is an author and frequent lecturer on criminal defense. She was selected by Chairman Bill McCollum, House Judiciary Committee, Subcommittee on Crime, to present oral and written congressional testimony on federal marijuana sentencing laws on behalf of the National Association of Criminal Defense Lawyers (NACDL) on March 6, 1996, in Washington, D.C. She served as Chair from 1995-1996 while a judicially appointed member of the Standing Committee on the Criminal Justice Act for the United States District Court for the District of Colorado from 1994-1996. Ms. Merritt is currently a member of the Board of Directors and Chair of the Advisory Board for the National Association of Criminal Defense Lawyers, the Director of the Cyberspace Bar Association and a member of the Board of Governors for the American Board of Criminal Lawyers.

HARRIET E. MIERS, President of Locke Purnell Rain Harrell, Dallas, Texas, has previously served as President and Director of the State Bar of Texas as well as President and Chairman of the Board of Directors for the Dallas Bar Association. She is currently Chair of the ABA Journal Board of Editors and a member of the House of Delegates for the American Bar Association. Ms. Miers also serves as Chair of the Texas Lottery Commission and as a member of the Board of Directors of the Attorneys Liability Assurance Society.

WILLIAM G. PAUL of Crowe & Dunlevy, Oklahoma City, Oklahoma. Mr. Paul is the former Senior Vice President & General Counsel, Phillips Petroleum Company, Bartlesville, Oklahoma. He has served as President of the Oklahoma State Bar Association, President of the National Conference of Bar Presidents, a Member of the American Bar Association, House of Delegates 1975-1995 and is a Fellow in the American College of Trial Lawyers. In February 1995, he was nominated to the Board of Governors of the American Bar Association to serve a three-year term, 1995-1998.

FERNANDO POMBO, of Gomez-Acebo & Pombo, Madrid, Spain, has contributed to and authored several publications in the field of international commerce. Currently, he is the International Bar Association Secretary (SGP). Mr. Pombo has been a visiting professor at the Institute on International Legal Studies in Salzburg, Austria since 1985. He is also a former President of LES International and a member of the Spanish Arbitration Court. He is fluent in Spanish, English, French and German.

ROBERTA COOPER RAMO, a shareholder of Modrall, Sperling, Roehl, Harris & Sisk in Albuquerque, NM is Immediate Past President of the American Bar Association and currently serves on the ABA Board of Governors. She also served on the Board of the American Bar Retirement Association from 1990-1994 and was Chair of the ABA Council of Section Officers from 1984-1986. She is a former President of the Albuquerque Bar Association (1980) and a member (1988-1994) and President (1991-1993) of the University of New Mexico Board of Regents. Currently, she is a member of the State Bar of Texas, the State Bar of New Mexico, the New Mexico Estate Planning Council, and a Fellow of the American College of Trust and Estate Council. She also serves on the University of Chicago Law School Visiting Committee.

WM. REECE SMITH, JR. of Tampa, Florida, is the senior member of Carlton, Fields, Ward, Emmanuel, Smith & Cutler, P.A., a law firm. A Rhodes Scholar at Oxford University, England, he was later president of The Florida Bar (1972-73), the American Bar Association (1980-81), and the International Bar Association (1988-90). He is a Fellow of the American College of Trial Lawyers and the International Academy of Trial Lawyers and serves on the Council of the American Law Institute. He received the American Bar Association's Gold Medal for "exceptionally distinguished service to the cause of American Jurisprudence."

WALTER H. WHITE, JR. is Managing Director of Steptoe & Johnson International, in Moscow, Russia, and Partner in Steptoe & Johnson L.L.P. in Washington, D.C. Mr. White served as the Wisconsin Commissioner of Securities, 1988-1991. He is a former member of the ABA House of Delegates, and has served on the Board of Milwaukee Foundation and currently is a board member of the Central-Asian-American Enterprise Fund by appointment of President Clinton.

Topical Index

The body of the law suitable for presentation in the Martindale-Hubbell Law Digests of the states of the United States, the District of Columbia, Puerto Rico and the Virgin Islands has been classified under topics or headings, which are uniform in all these Digests. The same classification is followed, as nearly as differing conditions permit, in the Canadian and International Section of the Law Digests.

This Topical Index fulfills, for each Digest, the double object of giving an alphabetical list of the main Digest headings and giving references by which the user may readily ascertain where the particular point which he desires to investigate will be found.

Index headings printed in capitals (**BOLD FACE**, in the actual Digest for each jurisdiction) are the main topics of the Digests, and all references in this Index are to such main topics. References preceded by the words "see also" indicate topics under which may be found matter related to the index heading, but not within it. Each topic is broken down in each of the Digests into appropriate subheads or subtopics (printed in the Digest for each jurisdiction in **Upper and Lower Case, Bold Face**). Where helpful, catchlines (*in italics*) are added under these subheads to further subdivide the law digested.

Forms of many instruments will be found under the appropriate topics, e.g., forms of acknowledgment under topic "Acknowledgments," subhead "Forms."

Uniform and Model Acts promulgated by the National Conference of Commissioners on Uniform State Laws (NCCUSL) in effect in the jurisdiction are listed in each Digest under the topic "Statutes," subhead "Uniform Acts." If the law digested under a specific topic is governed in large part by a Uniform Act, without substantial local deviations, reference to that Act will normally also be made under the specific topic affected, e.g., if the Uniform Commercial Code governs a particular subject, this will be stated, and the reader referred to the topic Commercial Code.

Texts of Selected Uniform and Model Acts promulgated by the NCCUSL which are within the scope of the Martindale-Hubbell Law Digests are supplied in full in **PART III**.

ACKNOWLEDGMENTS

The publishers take pleasure in acknowledging their indebtedness to the following lawyers, legal scholars and law firms, whose interest and untiring efforts in the annual revisions of the Law Digests contained in this volume have made possible the presentation to the legal profession of a vast amount of useful information which could not otherwise have been compiled.

PART I

DIGESTS OF LAWS OF THE STATES, THE DISTRICT OF COLUMBIA, PUERTO RICO AND THE VIRGIN ISLANDS

Alabama:—*Revision by* Bradley, Arant, Rose & White, of Birmingham.

Alaska:—*Revision by* Robertson, Monagle & Eastaugh, A Professional Corporation, of Alaska.

Arizona:—*Revision by* Fennemore Craig, A Professional Corporation, of Phoenix.

Arkansas:—*Revision by* Rose Law Firm, a Professional Association, of Little Rock.

California:—*Revision by* Professor Carol Wilson, University of San Francisco School of Law, of San Francisco.

Colorado:—*Revision by* Holme Roberts & Owen, LLP, of Denver.

Connecticut:—*Revision by* Sorokin, Sorokin, Gross, Hyde & Williams, P.C., of Hartford.

Delaware:—*Revision by* Richards, Layton & Finger, of Wilmington.

District of Columbia:—*Revision by* Margaret L. Moses, of Maplewood, New Jersey.

Florida:—*Revision by* Professor Jarret C. Oeltjen, College of Law, Florida State University, of Tallahassee.

Georgia:—*Revision by* Alston & Bird, Atlanta.

Hawaii:—*Revision by* Carlsmith Ball Wichman Case & Ichiki, of Honolulu.

Idaho:—*Revision by* Merrill & Merrill, Chartered, of Pocatello.

Illinois:—*Revision by* Celeste M. Hammond, Professor, John Marshall Law School, of Chicago.

Indiana:—*Revision by* Ice Miller Donadio & Ryan, of Indianapolis.

Iowa:—*Revision by* Finley, Alt, Smith, Scharnberg, May & Craig, P.C., of Des Moines.

Kansas:—*Revision by* Young, Bogle, McCausland, Wells & Clark, P.A., of Wichita.

Kentucky:—*Revision by* Stites & Harbison, of Louisville, Frankfort and Lexington.

Louisiana:—*Revision by* Phelps Dunbar, L.L.P., of New Orleans and Baton Rouge.

Maine:—*Revision by* Pierce Atwood, of Portland.

Maryland:—*Revision by* Venable, Baetjer and Howard, LLP, of Baltimore.

Massachusetts:—*Revision by* Professor Richard M. Perlmutter, assisted by Bernadette T. Feeley, Colleen Arnott Less and Yvonne A. Tamayo, Instructors, Suffolk University Law School, of Boston.

Michigan:—*Revision by* Miller, Canfield, Paddock and Stone, P.L.C., of Detroit, Ann Arbor, Bloomfield Hills, Grand Rapids, Howell, Kalamazoo, Lansing and Monroe, Michigan; Pensacola and St. Petersburg, Florida; Washington, D.C.; and Gdansk and Warsaw, Poland.

Minnesota:—*Revision by* Faegre & Benson Professional Limited Liability Partnership, of Minneapolis.

Mississippi:—*Revision by* Watkins & Eager PLLC, of Jackson.

Missouri:—*Revision by* Swanson, Midgley, Gangwere, Kitchin & McLarney, LLC., of Kansas City.

Montana:—*Revision by* Crowley, Haughey, Hanson, Toole & Dietrich, P.L.L.P., of Billings.

Nebraska:—*Revision by* Fraser, Stryker, Vaughn, Meusey, Olson, Boyer & Bloch, P.C., of Omaha.

Nevada:—*Revision by* Woodburn and Wedge, of Reno and Las Vegas.

New Hampshire:—*Revision by* Wadleigh, Starr, Peters, Dunn & Chiesa, of Manchester.

New Jersey:—*Revision by* Sills Cummis Zuckerman Radin Tischman Epstein & Gross, P.A., of Newark.

New Mexico:—*Revision by* Rodey, Dickason, Sloan, Akin & Robb, P.A., of Albuquerque and Sante Fe.

New York:—*Revision by* Rogers & Wells, of New York City.
North Carolina:—*Revision by* Womble Carlyle Sandridge & Rice, a Professional Limited Liability Company, of Winston-Salem.
North Dakota:—*Revision by* Nilles, Hansen & Davies, Ltd., of Fargo.
Ohio:—*Revision by* Arter & Hadden, of Cleveland.
Oklahoma:—*Revision by* McAfee & Taft, A Professional Corporation, of Oklahoma City.
Oregon:—*Revision by* Miller, Nash, Wiener, Hager & Carlsen, of Portland.
Pennsylvania:—*Revision by* Ballard, Spahr, Andrews & Ingersoll, of Philadelphia.
Puerto Rico:—*Revision by* McConnell Valdés, of San Juan.
Rhode Island:—*Revision by* Edwards & Angell, of Providence.
South Carolina:—*Revision by* Haynsworth, Marion, McKay & Guérard, L.L.P., of Greenville.
South Dakota:—*Revision by* Davenport, Evans, Hurwitz & Smith, L.L.P., of Sioux Falls.
Tennessee:—*Revision by* Armstrong Allen Prewitt Gentry Johnston & Holmes, of Memphis.
Texas:—*Revision by* Baker & Botts, L.L.P., of Houston, Dallas and Austin.
Utah:—*Revision by* Van Cott, Bagley, Cornwall & McCarthy, A Professional Corporation, of Salt Lake City.
Vermont:—*Revision by* Ryan Smith & Carbine, Ltd., of Rutland.
Virgin Islands:—*Revision by* Grunert, Stout & Bruch, of the Virgin Islands Bar.
Virginia:—*Revision by* McGuire Woods Battle & Boothe, L.L.P., of Charlottesville, Richmond, Norfolk and Williamsburg.
Washington:—*Revision by* Perkins Coie, of Seattle.
West Virginia:—*Revision by* Jackson & Kelly, of Charleston.
Wisconsin:—*Revision by* Quarles & Brady, of Milwaukee.
Wyoming:—*Revision by* Brown, Drew, Massey & Sullivan, of Casper.

PART II

DIGESTS OF UNITED STATES LAWS

Copyright:—*Revision by* Brumbaugh, Graves, Donohue & Raymond, of New York City.
Patent:—*Revision by* Cushman Darby & Cushman, Intellectual Property Group of Pillsbury Madison & Sutro LLP, of Washington, D.C.
Trademark:—*Revision by* Cushman Darby & Cushman, Intellectual Property Group of Pillsbury Madison & Sutro LLP, of Washington, D.C.

PART III

APPENDIX OF UNIFORM ACTS

We are indebted to the National Conference of Commissioners on Uniform State Laws for cooperation in furnishing copies of its Uniform and Model Acts, to the Committee on Corporation Laws of the Section of Corporation, Banking and Business Law of the American Bar Association for the copies of the Model Business Corporation Act and to the National Conference and the American Law Institute for the Uniform Commercial Code, reprints of which appear in this volume.

PART V

DIGESTS OF LAWS—INTERNATIONAL SECTION

Argentina:—*Revision by* Curtis, Mallet-Prevost, Colt & Mosle, of New York City.
Australia:—*Revision by* Arthur Robinson & Hedderwicks, of Melbourne.
Austria:—*Revision by* Zeiner & Zeiner, of Vienna.
Bahamas:—*Revision by* Harry B. Sands & Company, of the Bahamas Bar.

ACKNOWLEDGMENTS

Belgium:—*Revision by* De Bandt, van Hecke & Lagae, of Brussels.

Bermuda:—*Revision by* Appleby, Spurling & Kempe, of Hamilton.

Bolivia:
Brazil: } *Revision by* Curtis, Mallet-Prevost, Colt & Mosle, of New York City

Bulgaria:—*Revision by* Vassil Breskovski, LL.M., in association with Vladimir Petrov, Professor of Law, Sofia University, Bulgaria.

Dominion of Canada:—*Revision by* Borden & Elliot, of Toronto.

Alberta:—*Revision by* Bennett Jones Verchere, of Calgary.

British Columbia:—*Revision by* Davis & Company, of Vancouver.

Manitoba:—*Revision by* Aikins, MacAulay & Thorvaldson, of Winnipeg.

New Brunswick:—*Revision by* Clark, Drummie & Company, of St. John.

Newfoundland:—*Revision by* Lewis, Day, Dawe & Burke, of St. John's.

Nova Scotia:—*Revision by* McInnes Cooper & Robertson, of Halifax.

Ontario:—*Revision by* Borden & Elliot, of Toronto.

Prince Edward Island:—*Revision by* Campbell, Lea, Michael, McConnell & Pigot, of Charlottetown.

Quebec:—*Revision by* McMaster Meighen, of Montreal.

Saskatchewan:—*Revision by* MacPherson Leslie & Tyerman, of Regina.

Channel Islands (Jersey):—*Revision by* Ogier & Le Masurier, of Jersey.

Chile:—*Revision by* Curtis, Mallet-Prevost, Colt & Mosle, of New York City.

China, People's Republic of:—*Revision by* Arnberger, Kim, Buxbaum & Choy, of New York City, Los Angeles, Beijing and Ulaanbaatar.

Colombia:—*Revision by* Curtis, Mallet-Prevost, Colt & Mosle, of New York City.

Costa Rica:—*Revision by* Curtis, Mallet-Prevost, Colt & Mosle, of New York City.

Czech Republic:—*Revision by* Zeiner Golan Nir & Partners in co-operation with Professor JUDr. Zdenek Kucera, of Prague.

Denmark:—*Revision by* Falbe-Hansen, Bruun & Bruun, of Copenhagen.

Dominican Republic:
Ecuador:
El Salvador: } *Revision by* Curtis, Mallet-Prevost, Colt & Mosle, of New York City.

England:—*Revision by* Crockers, of London.

European Union:—*Revision by* De Bandt, van Hecke & Lagae, of Brussels, Belgium.

Finland:—*Revision by* Castrén & Snellman, of Helsinki.

France:—*Revision by* Coudert Brothers, of New York City, and Coudert Frères, of Paris.

Germany:—*Revision by* Boesebeck, Barz & Partner, of Frankfurt/Main.

Gibraltar:—*Revision by* Marrache & Co., of Gibraltar.

Greece:—*Revision by* Dr. Tryfon J. Koutalidis, of Athens.

Guatemala:
Honduras: } *Revision by* Curtis, Mallet-Prevost, Colt & Mosle, of New York City.

Hong Kong:—*Revision by* Robert W.H. Wang & Co., of Hong Kong.

Hungary:—*Revision by* Nagy és Trócsányi, of Budapest, New York, Basel, Switzerland and Stockholm, Sweden.

India:—*Revision by* Mulla & Mulla & Craigie Blunt & Caroe, of Bombay.

Ireland:—*Revision by* Gerrard, Scallan & O'Brien, of Dublin.

Israel:—*Revision by* Yaacov Salomon, Lipschütz & Co., of Haifa and Tel Aviv.

Italy:—*Revision by* Studio Legale Beltramo, of Rome.

Japan:—*Revision by* Blakemore & Mitsuki, of the Tokyo Bar.

Korea:—*Revision by* Kim & Chang, of Seoul.

Latvia:—*Prepared by* Klavins, Slaidins & Loze, of the Republic of Latvia, New York, Connecticut and California.

Lebanon:—*Revision by* Khairallah & Chaiban, of Beirut.

Liechtenstein:—*Revision by* Ritter-Wohlwend-Wolff, of Vaduz.

Luxembourg:—*Revision by* Bonn & Schmitt, of Luxembourg.

Malaysia:—*Revision by* David Chong & Co., of Kuala Lumpur.

Malta:—*Revision by* Rutter Giappone & Associates, of Valletta.

Mexico:—*Revision by* Curtis, Mallet-Prevost, Colt & Mosle, of New York City.
Mongolia:—*Revision by* Arnberger, Kim, Buxbaum & Choy, of New York City, Los Angeles, Ulaanbaatar and Beijing.
Netherlands:—*Revision by* De Brauw Blackstone Westbroek, with offices in Amsterdam, Eindhoven, The Hague, Rotterdam, Brussels, London, New York and Prague.
New Zealand:—*Revision by* Bell Gully Buddle Weir, of Auckland, Manukau and Wellington.
Nicaragua:—*Revision by* Curtis, Mallet-Prevost, Colt & Mosle, of New York City.
Northern Ireland:—*Revision by* C. & H. Jefferson, of Belfast.
Norway:—*Revision by* Advokatfirmaet STABELL DA, of Oslo.
Pakistan:—*Revision by* Surridge & Beecheno, of Karachi.
Panama:—*Revision by* Icaza, Gonzalez-Ruiz & Aleman, of the Panama Bar.
Paraguay:—*Revision by* Peroni-Sosa & Altamirano, of Asunción.
Peru:—*Revision by* Curtis, Mallet-Prevost, Colt & Mosle, of New York City.
Philippine Republic:—*Revision by* Bito, Lozada, Ortega & Castillo, of Manila.
Poland:—*Revision by* Altheimer & Gray, of Chicago, IL and Warsaw in cooperation with Professor Dr. Hab. A. Calus, Chairman, Department of International Law, Central School of Commerce, Warsaw.
Portugal:—*Revision by* Dr. Nuno Telles Pereira, and Luis Miguel Sasseti Carmona, with M.J.H. Reynolds of Lisbon.
Romania:—*Revision by* Hall Dickler Kent Friedman & Wood, Bucharest, Romania, White Plains, NY and Los Angeles, CA.
Russian Federation:—*Revision by* Holme Roberts & Owen, LLC, of Moscow, London, Denver, Boulder and Colorado Springs, Colorado and Salt Lake City, Utah.
Saudi Arabia:—*Revision by* White & Case of New York and Law Office of Hassan Mahassni in Association with White & Case of Jeddah.
Scotland:—*Revision by* Digby Brown & Co., of Glasgow.
Singapore:—*Revision by* David Chong & Co., of Singapore.
Slovak Republic:—*Prepared by* Čechová, Hrbek, of Bratislava.
South Africa:—*Revision by* Cliffe Dekker & Todd Inc., of Johannesburg.
Spain:—*Revision by* J. & A. Garrigues, of Madrid.
Sweden:—*Revision by* Baker & McKenzie Advokabyrå, of Stockholm.
Switzerland:—*Revision by* Pestalozzi Gmuer & Patry, of Zurich.
Taiwan:—*Revision by* Lee and Li, of Taipei.
Thailand:—*Revision by* Tilleke & Gibbins, of Bangkok, and Hanoi and Ho Chi Minh City, Vietnam and Phnom Penh, Cambodia.
Turkey:—*Revision by* Yilmaz Öz, of Ankara.
Ukraine:—*Revision by* Altheimer & Gray, of Chicago, IL and Kiev, Ukraine.
Uruguay:—*Revision by* Curtis, Mallet-Prevost, Colt & Mosle, of New York City.
Venezuela:—*Revision by* Curtis, Mallet-Prevost, Colt & Mosle, of New York City.
Vietnam:—*Prepared by* Tilleke & Gibbins Consultants Limited, of Bangkok, Thailand, and Hanoi and Ho Chi Minh City, Vietnam and Phnom Penh, Cambodia.

PART VI

SELECTED INTERNATIONAL CONVENTIONS

The annotations have been graciously provided by the U.S. Department of State.

Part V

Digests of Laws

INTERNATIONAL SECTION

(For list of digests see next page)

INTERNATIONAL DIGESTS

Note: Abbreviations for page numbers appear in brackets.

ARGENTINA LAW DIGEST REVISER

Curtis, Mallet-Prevost, Colt & Mosle
101 Park Avenue
New York, New York 10178-0061
Telephone: 212-696-6141
Fax: 212-697-1559
*Email:*CMP-NY@mcimail.com

Reviser Profile

The Firm began in 1830 when two practicing lawyers started a long line of lawyers and law firms extending in an unbroken chain up to the present time. In 1897, the firm name became Curtis, Mallet-Prevost & Colt; in 1925 it was changed to Curtis, Mallet-Prevost, Colt & Mosle. The Firm is now made up of approximately 120 lawyers, including experts who have published extensively on such diverse subjects as international money management, transnational contracts, state contracts, litigation against foreign states, sovereign immunity and the act of state doctrine, and the International Court of Justice. Its principal offices are in New York City. There are branch offices in Paris, London, Frankfurt Am Main, Hong Kong, Washington, D.C., Houston, Texas, Newark, N.J., and Mexico City. The Firm has five departments: Corporate and International; Litigation; Real Estate; Tax; and Trusts and Estates. The corporate and international department acts as general counsel to various public and private corporations and individual entrepreneurs. Clients are in the banking, insurance, securities, manufacturing, real estate and oil and gas industries. In addition, the corporate and international department frequently acts as special counsel to domestic and foreign clients, providing assistance in financing, know-how licensing, the negotiation and drafting of all types of contracts and instruments, counselling on all aspects of corporate law, and establishing the vehicles necessary to enable clients to conduct their domestic and foreign business activities. The Firm's international work permeates all areas of its practice and involves questions of private international law, foreign law and an unusual amount of public and quasi-public international law. Traditionally, much of the Firm's international practice has been concerned with Latin America. The Firm maintains its excellence in that area, with its Mexican affiliate, and also through the expertise of Latin American lawyers based in the New York office. The Firm's international practice has undergone a major expansion beyond Latin America to Europe, Africa and the Near and Far East. The Firm's litigation practice includes commercial litigation and arbitration, and white-collar criminal defense. It has substantial experience in civil aviation matters; it also has represented foreign States in transnational litigation and international arbitration arising out of acts of nationalization and alleged breach of economic development or natural resource supply contracts. Among the Firm's clients in real estate matters are institutional lenders and investors, real estate developers, both individual and corporate, foreign and domestic investors and syndicators. The tax department has substantial experience in all aspects of domestic and international business tax matters and real estate taxation. The matters the tax department deals with on a regular basis include: Taxation of foreign investments; the structuring of corporate transactions, including mergers, acquisitions, liquidations and reorganization; federal and state tax litigation; and tax planning for U.S. and foreign individuals. The trusts and estates department engages in general domestic trusts and estates practice and in tax planning for foreign persons wishing to invest in U.S. assets through offshore trusts and corporations. It represents individuals, trust companies, and banks acting as fiduciaries. It works for various charitable organizations, located both in the United States and abroad, including private foundations, museums, universities and hospitals. A group of fiduciary accountants with vast experience in the field assists the lawyers of the trusts and estates department. Curtis, Mallet-Prevost, Colt & Mosle has served as a Reviser for most of Latin American Law Digests since 1930.

ARGENTINA LAW DIGEST

(The following is a list of all Topics, including cross-references, covered in this Digest.)

ARGENTINA LAW DIGEST

Revised for 1997 edition by

CURTIS, MALLET-PREVOST, COLT & MOSLE of the New York Bar.

(C. C. indicates Civil Code; C. Com. indicates Code of Commerce; C.C.P. indicates Code of Civil Procedure.)

ABSENTEES: See topic Death.

ACKNOWLEDGMENTS:

(Law 1184 of July 6, 1934).

According to the system in force generally where the civil law prevails, contracts, deeds and other documents which require authentication by a public official are prepared in Argentina by a notary or other authorized public official, and made a part of his protocol. That is, the original documents are kept in an official register in the office of the notary or official. (See topics Notaries Public ["Escribanos Públicos"] and Public Instruments.) Instruments executed in foreign countries, however, are given full recognition in Argentina if duly acknowledged in the manner required in the country where they were executed, authenticated by a consular or diplomatic agent of Argentina, and the authentication certified to by the Minister of Foreign Affairs of Argentina.

ACTIONS:

Limitation of.—See topic Prescription.

ADMINISTRATION:

See topics Claims Against Decedents' Estates; Executors and Administrators.

ADOPTION:

(Law 19134 of July 21, 1971 as am'd by Law 23264 of Sept. 25, 1985 and Law 23515 of June 8, 1987).

ADVERSE POSSESSION:

See topic Prescription.

AGENCY: See topic Principal and Agent.

ALIENS:

(Law 346 of Oct. 8, 1869 as am'd; Law 23059 of Mar. 22, 1984).

Foreigners enjoy the same civil rights in Argentina as Argentine citizens. They may do business, follow their trade or practice their profession, buy and sell real property, make wills and marry in conformity with the law, and enjoy entire religious freedom. They are not obliged to become citizens or to pay extraordinary taxes.

Naturalization is granted to residents over 18 years of age after two years of continuous residence who meet requirements set forth in Art. 2 of Law 346. Foreigners obtain naturalization or citizenship by submitting written application to federal judge having jurisdiction at their domicile, following corresponding proceedings in accordance with Code of Civil Procedure and Commercial Code.

Foreigners.—Law 22439 of Mar. 23, 1981 as am'd, regulated by Decree 1434 of Aug. 31, 1987 as am'd, and Decree 354 of Aug. 18, 1982 regulate immigration matters (such as admission, entrance, residency and expelling of foreigners). Foreigners may be allowed in country as permanent, temporary or transitory residents. National identity card will only be issued to foreigners who prove their permanent residency.

ATTACHMENT:

(C.C.P. arts. 209-220, 531-558).

The Code of Civil Procedure for Federal Courts is taken as basis for this article.

In order to attach property in an ordinary civil action, one of following conditions must exist: (1) That debtor is not domiciled in Republic; (2) that debt is evidenced by certain written instruments; (3) that in case of an action on a bilateral contract, contract is in writing and complies with certain requirements as to its execution; (4) that debt is evidenced by mercantile books kept in due form; or (5) when debt is subject to a condition, that plaintiff proves that debtor tried to alienate, hide or remove his property or that responsibility of debtor has decreased after obligation was contracted.

An attachment will also issue against specific property which is the object of a possessory action, and in an ordinary action, an attachment will issue at the request of any of the parties when facts are admitted which make out a prima facie case in their favor, or when a favorable judgment has been obtained.

The party who obtains an attachment must give security for costs and damages. Attachments will also issue in the summary actions known as "executory actions."

BANKRUPTCY AND INSOLVENCY:

(Law 24522 of Aug. 7, 1995).

Law is applicable to licensed merchants, private entities and mixed companies.

Reorganization Process.—Reorganization may be to prevent or suspend bankruptcy from time filed at court, before or after bankruptcy proceedings. Reorganization agreement to prevent bankruptcy (concurso preventivo) may be proposed by debtor by filing petition with judge stating his financial conditions and reasons for his petition. Petition itself must comply with specific requirements of form and substance. Debtor must file petition provided no bankruptcy has been declared. Judge of commercial court must rule on petition within five days from its filing date, either rejecting it for failure to meet procedural requirements or declaring opening of preventive proceedings. Ruling of judge opening preventive proceedings identifies petitioner and schedules a hearing for appointment of a receiver and orders publication of notice in order that creditors and interested parties may appear, fixes period for creditors to qualify as such and also orders stay of execution against debtor on claims subject to concurso. Debtor continues to manage business under supervision of receiver, but is prohibited from changing situation of his creditors and judge must authorize payment of salaries and indemnifications for industrial accidents due all employees, subject to receiver's verification of such amounts outstanding. Prior judicial consent must also be obtained for a number of other significant activities undertaken during this period. If debtor fails to obtain such authority, or fails in any other way to observe requirements of receivership, administration of his business can be turned over to a successor by judge. Dismissal of preventive petition may occur when debtor does not observe proper filing requirements or fails to give creditors proper notice of commencement of proceedings. Otherwise, debtor may not voluntarily dismiss action after notices of same have already been properly published.

Creditors must request that receiver verify validity of their claims, indicating amount, substance, and priority thereof and accompanying such written request with all appropriate documentation. Receiver then checks validity of such claims by reviewing books of debtor and, if appropriate, of creditors. Receiver files an individual report on each creditor's claim so presented, but each creditor is permitted to formally object to such report within ten days of its filing and any such objection will be resolved by judge. Judge's decision in this regard is final. Receiver must also file his general report with judge. Such general report contains, among other things, reasons for debtor's financial difficulties, detailed account of assets and liabilities, thorough analysis of debtor's books, statement of when payments technically ceased, formal opinion on viability of proposed agreement, account of debtor's activities during receivership, and, in case of a partnership, whether partners other than debtor have any liability therein. General report may also be objected to by creditors and debtor.

Creditors are grouped into different categories according to nature of their credits; debtor must file payment arrangement to each group of creditors. Payment arrangements must be approved by creditors as stipulated by law and confirmed by judge. After confirmation of same, judge provides for its execution and compliance, dismisses receiver and declares preventive proceedings terminated. If proposed reorganization agreement is rejected by creditors, judge forthwith declares involuntary bankruptcy, which decision may be appealed only for purposes of remanding same. When reorganization agreement is rejected by creditors, in concurso of private entities and mixed companies, creditors, shareholders, employees or third parties may offer to purchase business. Any creditor affected by reorganization agreement may demand its annulment based on causes indicated in law. Decision declaring annulment of agreement must declare bankruptcy of debtor. Bankruptcy is also declared for noncompliance with agreement and by impossibility of debtor to fulfill agreement. Debtor may also enter into out of court reorganization agreement with creditors. Agreement may be confirmed by court decision at request of majority of creditors.

Liquidation Proceeding.—Bankruptcy must be declared at creditor's or debtor's request or in cases indicated above.

Bankruptcy is determined by cessation of payments, which, in turn, may be evidenced by recognition of same by debtor, delay in fulfillment of an obligation, absence of debtor, closing of principal place of business of debtor, delivery or sale of assets of debtor at worthless price, annulment of acts or debtor in defraud of creditors, or by any other fraudulent method utilized by debtor to obtain funds. All assets of debtor are affected thereunder, unless expressly exempted therefrom under law (e.g., non-patrimonial rights, assets not ordinarily attachable, usufruct of assets of minor children of debtor, personal assets of spouse, right to legally defend debtor's assets, indemnifications due debtor for personal injury or mental anguish and all others exempted under other laws). It is not necessary that more than one creditor petition for a declaration of bankruptcy, although creditor must summarily prove that assets of debtor are insufficient to cover his debts. Petitioning creditor may subsequently unilaterally abandon his petition. After creditors have filed their petition and summarily proved debtor's cessation of payments, debtor has a period of five days within which to appear and prove otherwise, after which a judge rules on declaration of bankruptcy. Before any declaration of bankruptcy, if creditors have a good prima facie case, judge may order such precautionary measures as a general inhibition of debtor's assets or a supervised intervention in business in order to protect value of remaining assets of debtor. If debtor himself petitions for a declaration of bankruptcy, he must place his assets in custody of court. He may not subsequently unilaterally abandon his petition unless he can prove prior to first publication that his cessation of payments has terminated.

Formal declaration of bankruptcy deprives debtor of all control over his assets, same being placed under supervision of a receiver for orderly distribution to creditors. Within ten days of last publication, liquidation proceedings may be converted into reorganization proceedings, at debtor's request after complying with conditions stipulated by law. Bankruptcy decree must be published for five days in legal journal and may be appealed by debtor within such period if it was declared upon petition of creditors. Bankruptcy decree also has following impact upon debtor's personal activities: he must fully cooperate with receiver in establishing his net worth; he is not permitted to leave country without court's permission; and he must continue to function in his previous capacity if so requested, unless expressly exempted therefrom. Period between cessation of payments and formal declaration of bankruptcy is designated "period of suspicion," and it is within such period that certain transfers of property by debtor are rendered void or without effect and creditors present their respective claims to receiver.

Once bankruptcy is declared, all claims of creditors become subject to Law of Bankruptcy and may only be satisfied in accordance with provisions of same. Declaration of bankruptcy results in maturity of all debts of bankrupt and all interest on same is suspended, except in case of mortgagees and other secured creditors with liens upon specific property of debtor, who are not prejudiced in their foreclosure remedies and are entitled to receive interest up to amount obtained in liquidation of secured asset. Specific provisions deal with all legal relations previously established by bankrupt (e.g., executory contracts, reciprocal loans, agreements to agree, partnership relations,

BANKRUPTCY AND INSOLVENCY . . . *continued*
debenture agreements, etc.). Under some circumstances, such as where immediate liquidation would cause irreparable harm to interests of some creditors, court may order that business of bankrupt be continued under supervision of receiver. Normally, however, receiver proceeds to an immediate liquidation of debtor's business in accordance with following priorities: (1) Sale of entire business, as a going concern; (2) bulk sale of all assets of business; and (3) sale of all or part of assets of business. Receiver must present his final report and accounting within ten days after last assets have been sold. Once it has been established by judge that a proper and complete liquidation has taken place, all creditors are declared paid in full and bankruptcy proceeding is declared closed. Such declaration may be appealed only by proving that there are new assets of debtor subject to attachment by court.

Foreign reorganization agreement may serve as a basis upon which to open a concurso proceeding in Argentina, upon petition of debtor or of creditor wishing to satisfy claims in country. Notwithstanding international treaties, reorganization agreement may not be invoked against creditors whose claims must be paid in Argentina for purposes of disputing their rights to assets located therein or annulling actions taken by debtor. Those creditors whose claims must be satisfied from assets located in Argentina will take priority over creditors whose claims must be paid exclusively out of assets located abroad, although latter do have rights to claim any residuary assets of debtor after payment of all such domestic claims. In case of single bankruptcy proceedings processed in Argentina, claims payable abroad may be included among local claims, if law of their country of origin provides for same treatment with respect of credits payable in Argentina.

BANKS AND BANKING:

(Law 21526 of Feb. 14, 1977 as am'd, and Law 24144 of Sept. 23, 1992 as am'd). It applies to banks and to other juridical persons, public or private, who mediate regularly between offer and supply of financial resources.

Central Bank supervises compliance with law and authorizes opening of branches of financial institutions. Deposits in Argentine currency are protected in case of insolvency of recipient bank. Central Bank may control financial institutions in danger of insolvency and has enough power to apply consolidation rules to entities that are in danger of insolvency. In such case, entity may enter into agreement for administration with option to be purchased by another entity. If Central Bank considers either that alternative of recuperation has failed or that those for consolidation provided for by such law are not viable or have failed, it may order liquidation of entity with or without revocation of its authorization to operate.

BILLS AND NOTES:

(Decree-Law 5965 of July 19, 1963 as am'd by Law 19899 of Oct. 20, 1972 and Decree-Law 7486 of Sept. 10, 1963).

A bill of exchange must state: (1) that it is to the order or contain the words "bill of exchange" in the language used for the bill; (2) unconditional promise of payment of a specified sum of money, inclusion of interest not being permissible except if the bill is at sight or term after sight and the rate is specified, otherwise the clause is deemed not written; (3) name of drawee who will pay; (4) date of payment or whether payable at sight or at a term after date or after sight or at a number of months after date or sight or at the beginning, middle or end of a month; other periods or successive due dates annul the bill; lack of indication makes the bill at sight; (5) place of payment, otherwise it is payable at place stated beside the name of drawee or at his domicile; (6) name of payee; (7) date of issue and place of same, otherwise deemed issued at place stated beside name of drawer. The bill may be drawn to the drawer's order and for a third party's account. Incapacity of signers, signatures forged or of imaginary persons do not destroy the liability of other obligors under the bill.

The drawer guarantees acceptance unless otherwise stated. He always guarantees payment. An incomplete bill, completed later against agreed conditions creates liabilities in favor of a holder who acquired the bill without bad faith or gross negligence. A bill, to the order or not is endorsable, but if it contains the clause "not to the order" it is only assignable. An endorsement may be made to any person, including drawer or drawee who may re-endorse. Conditions in endorsements are deemed not written and partial endorsements are null and void. An endorsement may be to the bearer, or in blank which is equivalent unless filled in. Endorsers are jointly liable for acceptance and payment unless otherwise stated. They may forbid re-endorsement and thus be free from liability of subendorsers. Endorsements for collection or with similar limitations constitute only an agency; if made "in guarantee" or "pledge" or other expression of suretyship personal defenses against the endorser are not available against a holder without notice. Endorsements after due date are effective, unless after protest for nonpayment or lapse of period therefor, when they constitute assignment which gives the same rights of an endorsement except immunity for personal defenses against endorsers.

Presentment for acceptance may be made on or before due date. Drawer may state the term of presentment for acceptance or forbid it, except if the bill is payable at a term after sight when the period for presentment is one year if not otherwise stated by the drawer, or by endorsers, but the latter may only shorten it. If a bill presented is not accepted drawer may demand to have it presented again the following day. There is no need to leave the bill. Acceptance must be unconditional but it may be limited to a smaller amount. It is signified by the signature alone of the drawee on the note or after the words "accepted" or "seen" or others of similar import, but if a term was established or the bill is payable at a term after sight the acceptance must be dated.

Presentment of a bill payable on a certain date or a period after date or sight may be made on the due date or the two subsequent working days. Presentment to a clearing house is effective. Partial payment may not be rejected. If payable in currency which is no legal tender in the place of payment the bill may be paid in the place's currency at due date exchange rates but in case of arrears holder has option to demand the rate of the actual payment date. When "without protest" clause forms a part of printed text of bill, drawer's signature on bill is sufficient to make clause binding. However, when clause is written in by hand, clause itself must be accompanied by signature of either drawer or endorser. A "without protest" clause, moreover, binds all parties signing bill if placed there by drawer. If placed there by a party other than drawer, however, it binds only that party.

Failure to accept or pay must be established by a protest; if for lack of acceptance, within the period for presentation for acceptance, but if the first presentation was made the last day of the term the protest must be made the subsequent day; if for nonpayment of a bill due on a term after date or sight, the protest must be made within the two days following dishonor and if at sight, within the term for presentation or if presented on the last day, on the following. However, drawer, or an endorser or guarantor, may insert the clause "without protest" or "return without expenses" or other of similar import which if signed relieves holder from protesting but not from presenting the bill. The clause is binding upon the signer and subsequent endorsers.

Protest is made at place indicated for acceptance or for payment, in its case. If no payment place was indicated then at domicile of drawee or of person indicated to pay for him, or other person indicated for the purpose. There are two forms: (a) by a separate notarial document, the notary inserting also a notation in the bill or (b) by mail notice sent by a bank.

The notarial protest contains: date and hour; copy of bill, with acceptances, endorsements, guarantees and other data; demand to drawee or person liable to accept or pay, stating whether he was present or not; reasons for refusal or statement that none was offered; his signature or statement or impossibility of obtaining it or refusal to sign; signature of protesting party or statement of impossibility. The mail notice protest by a bank is made by delivering the bill within two banking days to a bank of the place of the protest. A bank which discounted the bill or advanced funds on it or took it for collection may also act. Within the two subsequent banking days, the bank will send a notice to the drawer or debtor by registered mail, with return receipt requested, demanding acceptance or payment, expenses included, within the banking day following receipt of the notice if within the same village or city or if out of the place within an additional term for the distance as regulated by the Executive Power. Until regulations are issued this kind of protest is not applicable. A certification of the facts including number of the registered mail card, date of delivery of the notice as per returned receipt, that the period to accept or pay has elapsed and whether a counter-protest has been made, giving details of same, shall be issued by the bank, sealed and signed, and delivered with the bill with a notation of the card and receipt, signed and sealed. A counter-protest is an allegation, in protest form, against a mail protest stating reasons for refusal to accept or pay.

Lack of presentation in time or of protest, when necessary, prejudices the bill as against endorsers, drawer and other liable parties, but not the acceptor.

Within four days of a notarial protest or of having received a bank protest certificate or of dishonor of bill, if protest is excused, holder must send notice to his endorser and to drawer and corresponding guarantors. Lack of notice does not prejudice the bill but may create liability for damages to others resulting from negligence. Notice may consist in a letter or the mere sending of the bill, but evidence of the sending is important.

A bill duly protested gives a right to immediate attachment and sale of the assets of persons liable for payment. A bill or its negotiation does not constitute novation, unless so intended, and the original action on the underlying obligation may be brought if the bill is returned and is not prejudiced to the detriment of the defendant.

A bill may be issued in several numbered counterparts. Any holder of a bill may make copies of the same, stating in the copy who holds the original and in the bill up to what point the copy goes. A copy may be endorsed and guaranteed. If the holder of the original refuses to deliver it to the holder of the endorsed copy, latter has action against endorsers and guarantors of the copy, showing the refusal by a protest.

Aval.—An aval is a joint guarantee which may be given by a third party for the drawer or any endorser, by signing on the back of the bill after the words "por aval" or others signifying a joint guarantee or in a separate document.

Promissory notes are governed by the applicable provisions of the bills of exchange. The maker takes the place of an acceptor.

Checks.—(Law 24452 of Feb. 22, 1995). Law governing check is law of domicile of drawee bank. Following data must be inserted for validity of check: (1) Word "cheque," or equivalent in language used, within its text; (2) number, although in international checks it may be omitted; (3) name of drawee and its domicile which is place of payment and which omitted makes check payable at principal place of bank within country; (4) date and place of issue, but latter may be omitted and then domicile of drawer applies; (5) single payment order indicated in writing and in figures; (6) signature of drawer. Checks may be made to specified person to his order or not or to bearer. No insertion of interest is to be made. Invalidity for incapacity or lack of power of drawer does not invalidate liabilities of other signers or endorsers. Drawer cannot exempt himself from liability. Checks issued to specified person are endorsable. Bearer checks are transferred by delivery. Endorsements are subject to rules similar to those applicable to bills of exchange. Checks must be payable at sight. Postdated checks are payable at presentment. Checks made and payable within country are to be presented within 30 days; if issued abroad, within 60. Term may be extended as indicated by law. Bank rejecting payment must state on check reasons and date and hour of presentment and this amounts to protest in which case holder must give notice within two days to drawer and endorsers and these to their corresponding predecessor. Lack of notice does not prejudice actions but endorser who fails to give it will be liable for damages, not in excess of check, to his predecessor. There are provisions on crossed, certified or to be credited in account. Certified checks cannot be issued to bearer, nor for period longer than five days. At expiration of that period, bank shall credit amount to drawer, but check, as such, retains its value. Drawer or endorser may insert statement indicating that check is in payment of specified debt and such statement binds only immediate parties and only creditor of specified debt may then endorse it, negotiability remaining in effect.

Conformed Invoices. (Law 6601 of Aug. 7, 1963).—Sales which are to be paid after more than 30 days, if not to be charged to an account or made against a bill of exchange, note or other commercial document or through a commission merchant or consignee, require an invoice with mention of the words "Original Invoice"; number, page and volume of the entry in the record of invoices which each merchant must keep in book form; date and place of issue; full names and domiciles of seller and buyer; description of merchandise; partial and total prices; and seller's signature. A duplicate

See Topical Index in front part of this volume.

BILLS AND NOTES . . . *continued*
invoice must also be made with mention of the words "Conformed Invoice"; total price in words and numbers and balance due; credits granted; may be either fixed or at a term from sight; place of payment, otherwise the domicile of seller applies. When payment is agreed in installments there shall be issued as many duplicates as installments, with serial numbering and value of all of them, each bearing special mention of its own due date and amount in words and figures, and mention of the registry of the original invoice. Seller must send original and duplicate or duplicates to buyer within 20 days of issue, and 30 days of sale, with a receipt which must be signed by the purchaser. Duplicate must be returned duly signed by purchaser within ten days, and then it constitutes a "Conformed Invoice." If the purchaser had given notice within three days of receipt of packed goods that these were defective or has discovered hidden defects for which seller is liable or if the invoice is wrong or has defects of form invalidating it, he may refuse to "conform" the invoice stating his reasons in the duplicate and returning it to the seller. A conformed invoice must be presented no later than ten days from maturity and is subject to provisions applicable to payment of bills of exchange, being negotiable by endorsement and giving similar rights.

CHATTEL MORTGAGES:

Two kinds of chattel mortgages are recognized: the so-called agrarian pledge (prenda agrarian) and the registered pledge (prenda con registro). Both permit the debtor to retain possession of the article pledged, require the recording of the contract, provide a summary procedure for foreclosure, and forbid stipulations waiving such procedure, except that in certain cases, when the creditor is a government or banking institution, it may itself make the sale. The pledges are effective as towards third parties only from the date of recording. No subsequent pledge affecting the same property may be executed by the debtor, except with the consent of the creditor.

Agrarian pledges (Law 9644 of Oct. 19, 1914 regulated by Decree of Oct. 31, 1914) may affect:(a) machines in general, automobiles, agricultural implements and tools; (b) animals and their products and personal property devoted to rural operations; (c) fruits and crops corresponding to the year in which the pledge is made, whether pending, severed or harvested, and timber, mining products and products of national industries. The lien subsists for two years from date of registration.

Registered pledges (Decree-Law 15348 of May 28, 1946 t.o. 1995) may cover chattels of any nature as well as growing crops, but may be made only in favor of: (a) State, (b) co-operative societies and associations of farmers, stockmen and industrialists, (c) warehousemen of country products, to guarantee credits, (d) merchants and industrialists to guarantee price of merchandise sold, and (e) registered loan establishments. Pledge may be of two kinds: (a) Specific pledge, covering specific articles of any nature, or (b) floating pledge, covering merchandise and raw material in general to guarantee obligations of not over 180 days; this pledge covers the original articles and also those manufactured from them. Pledge contract may be assigned by endorsement, which to be valid against third persons must be recorded. Pledges of motor vehicles are subject to additional registration under Decree-Law 6582 of Apr. 30, 1958 as am'd, regulated by Decree 9722 of Aug. 18, 1960 as am'd.

Personal property such as machinery, cattle, crops, etc., may be included in mortgages on realty whenever such personal property forms an inherent part of the realty. As to ships and aircraft, see topic Mortgages.

Creditors have the right to force the heir to accept or decline the inheritance within a period of not more than 30 days. See topic Descent and Distribution.

CLAIMS AGAINST DECEDENTS' ESTATES:

See topic Executors and Administrators.

COMMERCIAL REGISTER:

See topic Records.

COMMUNITY PROPERTY:

See topic Husband and Wife.

CONDITIONAL SALES: See topic Sales.

CONSTITUTION AND GOVERNMENT:

(Constitution of 1853 as am'd, official text in Law 24430 of Jan. 3, 1995).

Republic of Argentina is a federation composed of provinces and one national territory with Buenos Aires as capital of Republic.

Provinces retain all powers which have not been delegated to Federal Government in conformity with Constitution. Among powers so delegated are those of enacting civil, commercial, penal, labor and mining codes for entire nation. These codes are administered by federal or provincial courts as case may be. Federal Government is also delegated power to enact general laws for whole nation as to naturalization and citizenship, bankruptcy, interstate commerce, defense, customs, banking and currency.

Argentine Republic adopts for its Government federal, republican and representative form. Public acts and judicial proceedings of one Province enjoy full faith and credit in others, also citizens of each province shall enjoy same rights, privileges and immunities of citizens in others. All inhabitants of nation (foreigners and citizens) enjoy following rights among others, in accordance with laws that regulate their exercise: To work and practise any lawful industry, to petition to authorities, to enter, remain and travel throughout Argentine territory, etc. Property is inviolable and no inhabitant of nation can be deprived of it except by virtue of judgment founded on law. Expropriation for reasons of public utility may be authorized by law and must be previously compensated. Federal Government consists of Legislative Power which has two Chambers, one of Deputies of Nation and the other of Senators of Provinces and of Capital. Both chambers shall assemble each year in regular sessions from Mar. 1 until Nov. 30.

Executive Power of the nation shall be vested in a citizen with title of President of Argentine Republic and to be elected President or Vice-President of nation it is necessary to have been born in Argentina and to possess the other qualifications to be senator, among others. Finally, Judicial Power shall be vested in a Supreme Court of Justice and in such lower courts as Congress may establish in territory of Republic.

Law 23968 of Aug. 14, 1991 establishes exclusive economic zone located beyond territorial waters. Economic zone shall be extended to 200 nautical miles counted from baseline. Argentinian Nation enjoys within this exclusive economic zone rights of sovereignty for purpose of exploration and exploitation, preservation and administration of natural resources over seabed including jurisdiction over such matters as sanitation, immigration, customs and taxation.

CONSUMER PROTECTION:

See topic Monopolies and Restraint of Trade.

CONTRACTS:

The nature, form, objects and obligations of contracts are governed generally by the Civil Code. Nevertheless there is a definite class of contracts known as commercial or mercantile contracts, concerning which the provisions of the Civil Code are supplemented by the Commercial Code. The Civil Code, except as modified by the Commercial Code, however, governs mercantile contracts. (Civil Code, arts. 1137-1216).

To constitute a contract there must be an offer and acceptance, express or implied. The offer is void if the offeror dies or becomes incapacitated before the acceptance is received. Offers may be retracted any time before acceptance if the offeror has not renounced his right to retract. Verbal offers must be accepted immediately. A modification of the offer in the acceptance constitutes a new offer. The offeree may retract his acceptance any time before it reaches the offeror. If the offeree has accepted in the ignorance of a retraction by the offeror or of his death or incapacity he is entitled to reimbursement for all losses suffered by him and expenses incurred.

Only those persons having legal capacity may enter into contracts, but only the incapacitated person, his representative and third parties affected may have a contract nullified because of incapacity. Ratification of a contract made in one's name has the same effect as previous authorization.

The objects of a contract must be definite or subject to definite determination. Future inheritances and future hereditary rights cannot be the object of a contract.

Form of contract is determined by place where executed. If executed by various parties in different places, formalities are governed by law of place most favorable to its validity. According to Civil Code following contracts, except when executed at public auction, must be in form of public instruments (see topics Notaries Public ["Escribanos Públicos"] and Public Instruments): contracts regarding real property; extrajudicial partition of inheritances; contracts of incorporation or partnership and extensions of same or when part of capital is real property; contracts of marriage and dower; life annuities; transferring, repudiation or renunciation of hereditary rights; general and special powers of attorney for use in court, for administration of property or which concern a public instrument or execution of one; adjustments with regard to real property; transfer of rights arising from public instruments; acts accessory to contracts which are in form of public instruments; and payments of obligations originating in public instruments, with exception of partial payments, interest and rent.

A contract which should be in the form of a public instrument, but which is drawn up as a private document constitutes an obligation to reduce the same to a public instrument. The same rule applies to verbal contracts. Penalty clauses in contracts are enforceable.

Civil contracts involving more than 10,000 pesos must be in writing and cannot be proved by parol evidence. (See below with regard to modification in mercantile contracts).

Contracts made in Argentina to violate the laws of a foreign country are void. The validity, nature and obligations of contracts to be carried out in Argentina are governed by Argentine laws, whether made in Argentina or in a foreign country, but if they are to be carried out in a foreign country they are governed by the laws of that country. Contracts referring to real property in Argentina, executed in a foreign country, are valid if in the form of public instruments and properly legalized. If they are for the purpose of transferring title to real property the contracts must be protocolized by order of a competent judge.

As stated above the civil law is supplemented by the Commercial Code in respect to mercantile contracts. In general the law of contracts set forth above is generic and applies to all contracts whether mercantile or otherwise. Matters falling within the scope of the Commercial Code are those relating to the transfer of personal property for purpose of obtaining a profit from the same whether in its form when transferred or after changing its form; operations of exchange, banking, or brokerage; negotiations with regard to bills of exchange, checks or other endorsable paper; operations of factories, commercial agents, warehouses and transportation; suretyship and corporate transactions, freight, construction, purchase or sale of vessels, their equipment, provisioning and everything relative to maritime commerce; operations of factors, bookkeepers and other employees of merchants concerning their employers; agreements with regard to salaries of clerks and other employees of merchants; letters of credit, bonds, pledges, etc., and other matters especially treated of in the Code of Commerce. (art. 8, Code of Com). If a contract is commercial as to one party it is deemed commercial as to all parties. Commercial contracts may be evidenced by public instruments; by notations of mercantile agents and certificates of the contents of their books; by private documents signed by the parties or a witness in the contractor's name; by correspondence, telegrams, books of merchants, admission of the parties; by witnesses, and by presumptions. Witnesses may not be used to prove a mercantile contract in matters involving more than m.$n. 200 unless there is some written evidence of the contract. All blank spaces and amendments in mercantile contracts must be authenticated by the signatures of the parties. Telegrams have the same force as letters. Words are understood in their general sense. In case of ambiguity the intention of the parties must be sought and when found outweighs the literal sense. The customs of business are taken into account in interpreting the contract. In general it may be said that contracts governed by the Commercial Code are made with much less formality than those which depend solely on the Civil Code and the methods by which their existence and scope are proved are more numerous. Moreover, in many of the classes of commercial contracts, such as bills of exchange, checks, partnership agreements, etc., special rules are provided in the Commercial Code to govern their

CONTRACTS . . . *continued*
effect and operation. (See topics Bills and Notes; Corporations [Stock Companies]; Partnership.)

CONVEYANCES:

See topic Deeds and Registration.

COPYRIGHT:

(Law No. 11723 of Sept. 28, 1933 as am'd. Argentina subscribed Berne Convention for protection of literary and artistic works by Law 17251 of Apr. 25, 1967).

Copyrights may be obtained for scientific, literary and artistic works, including literary, dramatic and musical compositions, moving picture films, paintings, sculptures, maps, phonograms, software, etc. Privilege pertains to author for life and to his heirs and assigns for 50 years after his death. It is subject to assignment, record of which must be entered in National Copyright Registry. For posthumous works period begins at death of author and continues for 50 years. If there are no heirs or assigns privilege belongs to state. Heirs and assigns cannot object to republication of work if they permit ten years to elapse without publishing it, nor to its translation ten years after author's death; but in such cases they may demand compensation to be determined by experts. Copyrights of anonymous works belonging to corporations last for 50 years. For photographic works, copyright period runs for 20 years from first publication and for moving picture films 50 years from first publication.

For purposes of instruction or scientific purposes, it is allowed to publish commentaries including up to one thousand words of literary and scientific works and the indispensable parts of the text. When the inclusion of other works comprises the principal part of the new work, the courts may determine the amount payable to the authors of the included works. Photographs of a person cannot be published without the consent of such person nor, for 20 years after his death, without the consent of his heirs, except in connection with scientific or other cultural works or matters which happened publicly. Letters cannot be published without the consent of the author or his heirs until 20 years after his death.

Copyrights may be obtained for foreign works with the same rights as for native works except that the privilege does not continue for a longer period than provided in the law of the country where the work was published; if such period be longer than that designated in the Argentine law, the latter prevails.

In order to obtain a copyright three copies of the work must be deposited within three months after its appearance in the National Copyright Registry. For foreign works the period runs from the day the work is offered for sale in Argentine territory. In the case of paintings, sculptures, etc., a sketch or photograph must be deposited with data to permit identification. For moving picture films the deposit consists of an account of the plot and dialogue and photographs of the principal scenes. The National Copyright Registry publishes a daily report in the official newspaper of the works files and if no objection is received within one month the copyright is granted.

Pursuant to Decree 1155 of Jan. 31, 1958, a national license for translating foreign nontranslated works may be granted to Argentina residents seven years after publication.

Under Dec.-Law 1224 of Feb. 3, 1958 regulated by Dec. 6255 of Apr. 28, 1958 as am'd, as implemented by Res. 2460 of July 24, 1963, works becoming of public domain shall nevertheless earn dues for exhibition, performance, reproduction, edition and other uses for benefit of "Fund for the Development of the Arts."

Industrial Models and Designs.—Dec.-Law, No. 6673 of Aug. 9, 1963, regulated by Dec. 5682 of July 20, 1965, grants five year protection to registered industrial models and designs, including foreign ones filed within six months of registration in foreign country.

CORPORATIONS (Stock Companies):

(Commercial Companies Law, "Sociedades Comerciales", Law 19550 of Apr. 3, 1972, t.o. 1984 [D. 841 of Mar. 20, 1984] as am'd by Law 23576 of July 19, 1988 as am'd).

Under Argentina law, stock companies (Sociedades Anónimas) are classed as mercantile companies although they may not have been formed for commercial purposes. They are defined as one or more persons contributing capital for purpose of producing or exchanging assets or services and dividing profits and losses among themselves.

All private securities issued in Argentina (i.e. stocks) shall be nominated and not transferable by mere endorsement.

Corporate Name.—Firm name may include name of one or more persons of visible existence and should contain expression "sociedad anónima", its abbreviation, or "S.A." Use of words "of Argentina" or "Argentina," suggesting ties with foreign corporation requires special authorization.

Organization.—Following conditions are indispensable for formation of a stock company: (1) Capital stock must be totally subscribed; minimum capital is required by law; (2) subscribers must have paid in at least 25% of subscribed capital stock and same must be deposited with official bank; payment of any amount outstanding must be made within two years; (3) proper administrative and judicial authorization must be obtained.

Such authorization will be granted if organization and by-laws of company are in conformity with provisions of law and if its objects are not contrary to public policy.

Articles of incorporation should contain: (1) Name, age, marital status, nationality, profession, domicile and identification of all shareholders; (2) firm name and domicile; (3) precise indication of its purposes; (4) amount of capital, expressed in Argentine currency, setting forth each shareholder's contribution; (5) duration; (6) organization of management, of its supervisory and accounting procedures and of shareholders' meetings; (7) rules regarding distribution of profits and losses; (8) rights and duties of shareholders with respect to each other and to third parties; (9) provisions regarding operation, dissolution and liquidation.

Procedure.—(a) If incorporators of company have subscribed for all requisite capital stock, they may commence business as soon as they have executed articles of incorporation, recorded same and published them together with by-laws, authorization and other fundamental documents. (b) With respect to a public subscription, promoters draw up a prospectus, by public or private instrument, and submit it to administrative authority for approval. Approval is granted within 15 days when all legal and regulatory conditions are duly complied with. Company must then register with Public Commercial Registry within 15 days thereafter. All signatories of prospectus are deemed to be promoters. Decision of Registry is appealable; appellate court may interpose its finding within five days. Prospectus must contain following: (1) Name, age, marital status, nationality, profession, identification and domicile of each promoter; (2) provisions of by-laws; (3) characteristics of shares, amount of planned issuance, conditions for subscription and advance payments; (4) designation of a bank with which promoters must make a contract for purposes of such bank assuming role of representative of future subscribers; (5) advantages and eventual benefits foreseen by promoters. Advance cash subscriptions must not be less than 25% of par value of subscribed shares and term of subscription may not exceed three months.

Organizational meeting must be called and presided over by a representative of administrative authority with intervening bank present. Quorum is constituted by one-half plus one of subscribed shares. Each subscriber has a right to as many votes as he has subscribed and paid-up shares. Decisions are adopted by a majority of subscribers present, representing at least one-third of subscribed capital with a right to vote. First meeting will decide on following matters: (1) Formation of company; (2) action of promoters; (3) by-laws; (4) provisional valuation of non-cash contributions; (5) designation of directors, supervisors (síndicos), and board of overseers (consejo de vigilancia); (6) terms of payment for remaining subscribers; (7) any business presented by bank; (8) designation of two subscribers or representatives who together with president and bank representative shall approve and sign minutes of meeting drafted by administrative authority. Minutes must be published, recorded and approved by administrative and judicial authorities. Funds are then deposited in official bank and documents turned over to board of directors.

Liability of Stockholders and Directors.—During incorporation, promoters and directors are jointly and unlimitedly responsible for any debts. Directors are only authorized to carry out activities related to incorporation and those activities related to company's purpose if they are authorized by articles of incorporation. Once company is constituted, it assumes all responsibilities undertaken in its name and promoters and directors are released from responsibility to third parties, although they may still be held liable to company.

Stockholders who have fully paid for their stock are not liable for obligations of company. All stockholders with interests contrary to that of company have a duty to abstain from voting in any such related matter. If such stockholders do not comply with this provision, they will be responsible for resulting damages or injury, if without such vote there would not have been present the majority vote necessary to adopt such resolution. All stockholders voting in favor of a resolution subsequently declared null shall be unlimitedly and jointly responsible for any consequences resulting therefrom.

Stockholders have a preemptive right with respect to all subsequent stock issues. If such right is violated, stockholders may demand that such issue be cancelled or may initiate a suit against company and its directors for damages not less than three times par value of shares so subscribed.

Directors, supervisors and overseers are unlimitedly and jointly liable for irregularities in public stock offerings and distribution of dividends.

All administrators and representative of the company are subject to a standard of loyalty and diligence; noncompliance resulting in unlimited and joint liability for damages arising therefrom. Director of a company has duty: (1) to reveal any conflict in interest to board of directors and supervisors; (2) to abstain from any related deliberation; and (3) to refrain from competition with company. Directors and supervisors are unlimitedly and jointly liable for negligent performance of their offices, or for violations of law or of by-laws and rules of company. Directors who timely file written protests with supervisors or initiate proceedings against acts of board of directors are exempt from any consequences arising therefrom. Directors and managers may be exonerated from certain acts by a subsequent vote of stockholders. Majority of directors must be domiciled in Argentina and all directors must have special domicile in Argentina.

Company may censure any director and any such resolution results in removal from office of such director.

Management and Supervision.—Active management of stock companies is placed in hands of one or more directors elected by stockholders at general assembly. Directors, who need not be stockholders, may be elected to hold office for a period not exceeding three years, and may be re-elected. Meetings of board of directors are regulated by by-laws. Directors must be present in meeting, teleconferences are not permitted. Directors may receive remuneration, which shall not exceed 25% of profits if dividends are paid, or 5% of profits if no dividends are paid. If there is more than one class of stock, by-laws may provide for election of one or more directors from each such class. Cumulative voting may be authorized for up to one-third of director vacancies to be filled. Executive committee may be constituted by directors for conduct of ordinary business. Stockholders at their annual meeting may elect one or more supervisors (sindicos). Companies subject to permanent state supervision need to appoint supervisors. Other companies only need to appoint supervisors if provided for in by-laws. In this case, if supervisors are not appointed, shareholders have right to exercise individual inspections of company's books.

Supervisors have following general powers and duties: (1) Supervise financial administration of company; (2) verify value of securities; (3) attend all meetings; (4) correct any irregularities; (5) analyze annual report; (6) provide information to stockholders; (7) call special meetings; (8) put important matters on agenda; (9) verify whether company is carrying out law and wishes of its stockholders; (10) supervise liquidation; (11) investigate accusations by stockholders.

By-laws may also provide for a council of overseers (consejo de vigilancia), composed of three to 15 stockholders. Duties of overseers are to: (a) Supervise conduct of board of directors, examine accounting and make cash audits; (b) convoke special meetings; (c) approve certain company business; (d) elect board of directors under some circumstances; (e) report to stockholders on annual report and balance sheets; (f) examine accusations by stockholders; (g) conduct certain other functions of supervisors. If by-laws adopt council, they may dispense with designation of supervisors.

See Topical Index in front part of this volume.

CORPORATIONS (Stock Companies) . . . *continued*

Company is subject to state supervision (fiscalización estatal) in following cases: (1) If it makes a public offer of stocks or debentures; (2) if its capital is greater than certain amount; (3) if it is mixed company of state-private interests; (4) if it engages in investment banking or in public transactions of cash or securities; (5) if it operates public services or concessions; and (6) if it is controlled or controls another company subject to state supervision. Administrative authority can exercise supervisory powers in any other stock companies: (1) If requested to do so by shareholders representing at least 10% of capital stock of company; or (2) when deemed necessary in public interest. In event of any violation of law or of corporate resolutions, administrative authority may issue warnings and fines for each such infraction.

Stockholders' meetings must take place at company headquarters or within its legal domicile, and are either regular (ordinario) or special (extraordinario). Regular meetings are empowered to consider: (1) General balance sheets, annual report, supervisors' report and distribution of profits; (2) designation and removal of directors, supervisors and overseers; and responsibilities of same; (3) any increase in authorized capital up to five times original amount. Special meetings are empowered to consider: (1) Additional increases in authorized capital; (2) reductions and reintegration of capital; (3) redemption, reimbursement and amortization of stock; (4) mergers, dissolutions, liquidations; (5) limitation or suspension of preemptive rights in subscription to new stock issues; (6) issue of debentures and conversions of stock; (7) issue of bonds.

Regular and special meetings shall be held when called by directors or supervisors or by stockholders representing 5% of authorized capital, unless by-laws permit a smaller number.

Notices of meetings are given by means of announcements published for five days at least ten days in advance of date specified for holding of meeting and in such other manner as by-laws may provide. Notices are required to state matter to be considered at meeting. Any action upon matters not specified in notice is void, unless such action: (1) Is approved by unanimous agreement of stockholders representing totality of capital; (2) is expressly exempt under law; or (3) is expressly approved by interested individuals through signatures placed on minutes. Meeting may be recessed and reconvened within 30 days, but only stockholders who participated in first meeting have right to participate in second meeting. In case a meeting cannot be held because a quorum is lacking, another meeting is required to be held within 30 days upon publication of notice three times at least eight days in advance.

Stockholders may be represented at any meeting by a proxy who may not be an officer, supervisor, manager or employee of company. Quorum for regular meetings on first call requires presence of a majority of shares with a right to vote; regular meetings shall be deemed to be constituted on second call regardless of number of shares present. Special meetings require on first call a quorum of 60% of shares with a right to vote, and on a second call a quorum of 30% of voting shares, unless by-laws set a higher percentage. Majority of votes present at regular or special meetings is sufficient to carry a resolution unless by-laws require a higher number. When meeting treats transformation, extension, or dissolution of company, transfer of domicile abroad or any fundamental change in corporate purposes or capital, favorable vote of majority of shares with a right to vote, discounting any plurality of vote, is necessary in order to adopt any resolution related thereto. Such requirement also applies in case of merger, except that absorbing entity is governed by rules applicable to capital increases.

Any resolution affecting one particular class of stock must also be ratified by that class at a special meeting governed by rules for ordinary meetings.

Any resolution adopted at a stockholders' meeting may be challenged by directors, supervisors, overseers, administrative authorities and certain stockholders if such resolution violates law, by-laws or public policy. Minority stockholders dissenting from a decision or from affirmative action regarding matters specified in preceding paragraph may withdraw from company and demand reimbursement of value of stock held by them, as shown by last approved balance sheet of company except in case of dissolution and merger (absorbing entity and publicly traded companies) and capital increase (publicly traded companies). This right of reimbursement, however, must be exercised by those present within five days after termination of meeting, or in case of absent stockholders, within 15 days subsequent to closing of such meeting.

Stocks and Bonds.—Stock certificates must be consecutively numbered and signed by at least one director and one supervisor and must contain: (1) Name of company, its domicile, date and place of incorporation, duration and registration; (2) its authorized capital; (3) number, par value and class of stock which certificate represents and rights embodied therein; (4) if provisional certificates, a notation thereon of amount paid in. Shares of stock are always of equal value and expressed in Argentine currency. Various classes of stock may be established. Certificates may represent one or more shares, which are nominative, negotiable if fully paid. Public companies are authorized to issue global certificates that can be deposited with securities registration systems. Registration of shares is mandatory. Records of shareholdings and stock transfers are kept by local and international clearing houses. Stock Registry Book must be maintained in which information relevant to certificates and their transfer is recorded. Each share of common stock gives holder right to one vote. By-laws may create classes of stock that recognize up to five votes per common share, but only if no public offering has been made. Preferred stock may also be given voting power in certain cases.

Company may issue (1) redemption bonds (bonos de goce) to holders of fully paid-in stock, entitling them to a share of company profits and, in event of dissolution, of proceeds derived from liquidation; and (2) participation bonds (bonos de participación) for amounts which are not capital contributions and which entitle holders to a share of profits in fiscal year. Participation bonds may also be made available to employees in profit-sharing programs and in such case are nontransferable. Modifications of bond conditions require agreement of an absolute majority of bondholders of respective class.

Accounts.—Directors must prepare an annual accounting statement which includes a balance sheet, profit and loss statement and an analysis of same. Annual report must be filed including: (1) Analysis of assets and liabilities; (2) analysis of expenses and profits; (3) reasons for establishing reserves; (4) justification of dividends; (5) estimate of future operations; (6) relations with controlling, controlled and encumbered operations; and (7) amounts not appearing in profit and loss statement.

Financial statements must be approved by stockholders at their annual meeting. Approval does not free directors, supervisors or overseers from their responsibilities of analyzing and reporting on company operations. Certain companies are also subject to state supervision. (See Art. 299.)

Dividends.—No dividend can be declared or distributed to stockholders except out of actual net profits, as per certified balance sheet. Company must set aside at least 5% of its annual net profits for purposes of creating a legal reserve fund until such fund amounts to 20% of its authorized capital. No profits may be distributed until prior losses are covered; nor may they be provisional or anticipatory. Directors, supervisors and overseers are unlimitedly and jointly liable for any unauthorized distributions. Dividends received in good faith are not recoverable.

Issuance of Debentures.—Stock company may issue debentures when permitted to do so by its by-laws. Under Argentine Law debentures are of three classes: (1) Those secured by specific real property, in which case ordinary laws governing execution and filing of mortgages are applicable. Such debentures are termed "Debentures with Special Security" (con garantia especial); (2) those secured by a floating guaranty, such as existing and after-acquired assets or portions thereof. Such debentures are termed "Debentures with Floating Security" (con garantia flotante). Preferred credits existing at time floating security is given and those created during existence of such security, in accordance with general laws, have preference over it; (3) debentures without security (garantia comun). Debenture securities must be of equal value and may be converted into shares and issued in foreign currencies. Coupons may be utilized for interest collection.

Company desiring to issue debentures is required to enter into a contract with a bank (fideicomiso) representing prospective holders of debentures. Requirement that trustee be a banking institution prevails only during period of issuance and subscription. After such period, a meeting of holders of debentures may name any person as trustee. Contract is required to stipulate terms upon which loan is to be made and security, if any, furnished for loan. This document is required to be a public document and to be recorded in Public Registry of Commerce. Before debentures are actually issued, company is further required to publish a prospectus containing certain specified information relative to issue and to record document.

Rights and duties of trustees are prescribed by law, which insures to them, in cases of debentures issued without security or with a floating security, means necessary to keep themselves informed as to condition of company as well as right to demand removal of managing director or board of directors in following cases: (a) When company has lost 25% or more of capital it had on date of issuance of debentures; (b) when 30 days have elapsed since it defaulted in payment of interest or sinking fund requirements; and (c) in case of forced liquidation or bankruptcy of company. Trustee may be removed at any time without cause by meeting of holders of debentures. Such meeting may be called by supervisory authority or by a judge when so requested by 5% of holders of debentures.

Foreign companies that issue debentures with floating security or assets located in Argentina must register contract from which issue of debentures originates, as well as any guarantees related thereto. If it is not registered, debentures shall have no legal effect in Argentina. Every issue of secured debentures which is not limited to specific property susceptible to mortgage shall be deemed an issue with floating security.

Negotiable Bonds.—Corporations and branches of foreign companies are among those authorized to issue negotiable bonds to obtain loans. Such bonds may be traded publicly or privately in local and international capital markets, and issued in local or foreign currency, nominative with different types of repayment guarantees which may be floating, special or common securities over tangible and intangible assets or other types accepted by law.

Dissolution.—Stock company may be dissolved in following cases: (a) At termination of period fixed for its duration; (b) at conclusion of purpose for which it was formed; (c) upon bankruptcy; (d) where it has lost 75% of its capital; (e) where it is shown that company is unable to carry out objects for which it was formed. Where 50% of capital of company has been lost, directors are required to report fact to Court of Commerce and to publish a statement to that effect. Where 75% of company's capital has been lost, company is deemed to be dissolved and directors are made jointly and severally liable to third persons for all obligations which directors have contracted since existence of such deficit came or should have come to their knowledge.

Limited liability companies may be formed for any commercial purpose. Number of members cannot exceed 50; they are liable for amounts stipulated next to their names in company contract. Name of company must be preceded or followed by words "sociedad de responsabilidad limitada." Capital is divided into quotas of equal value of ten pesos or multiples thereof. Twenty-five percent of subscribed quotas must be paid in within two years. Transfer of quotas is not subject to conditions unless otherwise stipulated in by-laws.

Company is managed by one or more managers who have same rights and duties as directors of a corporation. Company may form a supervisory body or a committee of overseers which will be governed by same provisions established for corporations. Committee of overseers is compulsory when company's capital is over 100,000 australes. Modifications of purpose, extensions of duration, transformations, mergers, splits, and all modifications that result in quotaholders having greater responsibilities may only be adopted by vote of 3/4 of company's capital. All other resolutions, such as appointment of managers, may be adopted by majority vote of capital present. Each quota gives its holder right to one vote.

Majority State participation connotes ownership by State or by certain other governmental entities of 51% or more of a company's capital. By-laws may provide for designation of one or more minority directors and supervisors. If extent of private capital is 20% or more, there will be proportional representation on board of directors and minority stockholders will be able to elect at least one supervisor. When minority stockholders exercise this right, public officials may not represent private capital. In all events private capital must be represented on board of directors by at least one director. If charter indicates an intent to maintain State predominance, any stock transaction resulting in a diminution of majority State participation therein must be authorized by law. Company with majority State participation may not be declared

See Topical Index in front part of this volume.

CORPORATIONS (Stock Companies) . . . *continued*
bankrupt. Liquidation proceedings must be conducted by state appointed administrators.

Joint stock company (sociedad en comandita por acciones) is an entity in which active partners incur liability to same degree as active partners of a general partnership and silent partners limit their liability to extent of their subscribed capital. Only capital contributions of silent partners are represented by shares. Unless otherwise provided, joint stock companies are subject to provisions governing stock companies, and, supplementally, to provisions governing general partnerships. Firm name must include words "sociedad en comandita por acciones" its abbreviation, or letters "S.C.A." Administrator shall become jointly liable with company if such words are not included therein. If firm name does not contain names of all partners, words "y compaõnía" or its abbreviation must also appear therein. Administration may be unipersonal and undertaken by an active partner or a third party, whose term of office shall not have any maximum duration. Removal of administrator is governed by same rules pertaining to general partnership, although silent partner may legally request his removal with cause if such silent partner represents at least 5% of capital. Active partner removed as administrator has right to withdraw from company or become a silent partner thereof. Administration must be reorganized within three months if it is incapable of functioning as such, in which case a provisional administrator shall be designated. Meetings of company shall include active and silent partners and administrator shall have a voice, but no vote thereat. Assignment of any active partner's share of capital requires a favorable vote of a majority of shares with a right to vote, without applying thereto provisions governing shares with multiple votes.

Joint Venture.—(a) Business cooperation agreements: Juridical persons organized in country and locally domiciled individuals may organize in group to develop or facilitate certain aspects of business activity of their members or to complete or increase results of such activities. Profits resulting from such activity directly benefit assets of group. Member contributions and property acquired with such contributions form operative common fund of group. Individual creditors of members are unable to enforce their rights over such fund. Members are jointly, severally and unrestrictively liable to third parties on account of obligations assumed by representatives on behalf of entity. Parties may agree by public or private instrument and must register with Public Commercial Registry. (b) Temporary enterprises: Juridical persons organized within country and individuals locally domiciled may agree to temporarily organize as enterprise to develop or perform work, service or supply within or outside country. Except as otherwise provided for in agreement, joint liability of entities is not presumed with respect to acts and transactions developed or performed, or to obligations contracted with third parties. Parties may agree to organize as temporary enterprise by public or private instrument. Foreign companies may participate in such agreements if agreements comply with provisions of law. This enterprise is considered legal entity only for some tax purposes.

Foreign Companies.—(Law 19550, Arts. 118-124, and Law 8867 of Feb. 6, 1912). Company formed abroad and having only occasional dealings in Argentina is governed as to its existence and form by laws of country in which it is legally constituted. It is thus authorized to perform isolated acts in country and to participate in lawsuits. In order to habitually engage in business within scope of its charter, or to establish branches, or any other type of permanent representation in Argentina, a foreign company must comply with following: (1) Certify its existence in accordance with laws of its domicile; (2) establish domicile in Argentina by complying with all local publication and registration requirements; and (3) justify its decision to create such representation and designate a representative to represent it in all civil and commercial matters. Branches must state amount of capital assigned to their operations. If a company is formed in another country with unfamiliar laws, judge of registry will determine formalities to be completed in each case. It is mandatory that foreign company maintain separate accounts in Republic and that it submit to administrative inspection. Normally, corporate papers, by-laws and other documents relative to organization of company are required to be registered in Commercial Registry of place where office or agency has been established. Papers to be forwarded to Argentina should include certified copies of certificate of incorporation and by-laws of parent company and a broad power of attorney authorizing registration of company and empowering representative to conduct business of company in Argentina. If company has a large capitalization it is well to add a certified copy of a resolution of board of directors which indicates amount of capital to be employed in Argentina. This is for purpose of reducing taxes and fees. All of these papers should be authenticated by an Argentina consul. (See topic Acknowledgments.) It is also well to add certified translations of all documents if practicable to avoid great expense of translation in Argentina.

Provision that authorization of executive power is not necessary in cases where same privilege is granted in country of company's origin has caused considerable difficulty in case of American corporations, due to fact that Argentina government is not always disposed to accept proof that reciprocity exists in state of company's origin. Proof of national reciprocity is required, which U.S. Federal Government is not in a position to guarantee. As a result, American corporations registering in Argentina are often subject to considerable delay and embarrassment in obtaining authorization from Executive Power of Argentina. It is always advisable however, in registering an American company to include among papers forwarded, a certificate from a competent state official to effect that Argentina corporations may qualify to do business in state of company's origin, stating formalities which must be complied with.

Service of process on a foreign company may be accomplished as follows: (1) If related to an isolated act, personally on agent who took part in act or contract resulting in litigation; (2) if there exists a branch or other representation, personally on designated representative.

COURTS:

Federal justice is administered by a Supreme Court composed of nine judges and Attorney General, located in City of Buenos Aires; by national courts of appeals in federal capital and provinces as well as courts of first instance and oral courts.

Justice is administered in national capital by following authorities: National Criminal Superior Court, National Courts of Appeals, Oral Courts, national judges of first instance of civil matters. There are likewise judges of misdemeanors, with jurisdiction over minor municipal violations. (Decree Law 1285/58, as ratified by Law 14467 t.o. 1993, as am'd).

Judicial procedure in provincial courts depends upon laws enacted by respective provinces, and federal procedure is governed by federal law. Consequently, though there is legislative unity throughout Republic as to substantive law (civil, penal, commercial, aeronautic and mining codes), adjective laws, or those laws which determine procedure before courts, depend in each case upon such provisions as legislative power of each province may provide. For this reason it is necessary in matters of procedure to examine national or provincial laws as case may be, however great resemblances between them. Acts of an administrative nature are governed by procedures set forth in Law 19549 and Decree 1759 of Apr. 3, 1972, as am'd.

In the provinces there are also Mayors (Intendentes), justices of the peace, judges of first instance (jueces letrados), courts of appeal, and Supreme Courts of the provinces.

CURRENCY:

Monetary unit is peso, which is divided into 100 centavos. (Decree 2128 of Oct. 10, 1991). Only Banco Central de la República Argentina may issue notes and these constitute legal tender for any obligation. (Law 24144 of Sept. 23, 1992).

CUSTOMS:

Customs Code (Código Aduanero) enacted on Mar. 2, 1981 regulated by Decree 1001 of May 21, 1982 as am'd is divided into following 17 sections or chapters: Preliminary Title; Subjects; Control; Importation; Exportation; Common Rules for Importation and Exportation; Special Regimes; Zones Outside the General Customs Territory; Prohibitions of Importation and Exportation; Taxes Ruled by Customs Legislation; Incentives to Exportation; Reciprocity; Penalties; Customs Preference; Procedure; Complementary Rules; Transitory Rules.

Common External Tariff, approved by member countries of southern common market (MERCOSUR) is in effect; each member country has list of goods excluded from common external tariff and subject to their own duty rates. Most goods traded among member countries are not subject to tariff or quota restrictions.

DEATH:

The absence of a person from his domicile or place of abode within the Republic, and where there is no information as to his whereabouts for a period of three years, gives rise to a presumption of death. The absentee's estate is provisionally distributed among his heirs or legatees. After five years from the date of presumption of death, or 80 years from the birth of the absentee, the distribution becomes final. (C. C. arts. 110-125; Law 14394 of Dec. 22, 1954).

Deaths are recorded in the Civil Registry of the Judicial District, of which there are several in each province. Death certificates may be obtained from the official in charge of the Civil Registry Office. Amount of fee is fixed by provincial or local regulations.

Actions for Death.—There is no statute specifically providing for wrongful death action, but this could be supported by the general text of the provisions on torts under which any damage suffered by a person by the fault of another constitutes a tort. There is two year limitation period. However, when a crime is involved, all damages therefrom are determined in the penal judgment as accessory penalty. (C. C. arts. 1109, 1068, 1069, 1110 and 4037).

DECEDENTS' ESTATES:

See topics Claims Against Decedents' Estates; Descent and Distribution; Executors and Administrators; Wills.

DEEDS AND REGISTRATION:

(C.C. arts. 997-1011).

Contracts involving the conveyance, alienation or incumbrance of real property must be in the form of public documents or documents duly authenticated and registered. See topics Acknowledgments; Notaries Public ("Escribanos Públicos"); Public Instruments; Records.

DESCENT AND DISTRIBUTION:

(C. C. arts. 3279-3576, 3585-3595, 3598-3605).

Estates of decedents pass either by will or by operation of law.

A child conceived at the time of the death of the decedent inherits, unless it be stillborn. The following persons are incapable of inheriting: Persons under sentence, as principal or accomplice, for the murder or attempted murder of the decedent, his or her spouse or descendants; heirs who are of age and have knowledge that the death of the decedent resulted from a crime and do not inform the judicial authorities within one month thereafter, unless the crime was committed by an ascendant, descendant, husband, wife, brother or sister of the heir; persons who have accused the decedent of a crime punishable by imprisonment at hard labor for five years or more; persons under sentence for adultery with the wife of decedent; the relatives of the decedent who have found the latter in a demented or destitute condition and have not taken steps to protect him or place him in a public institution; persons who, by force or fraud, have induced the decedent to make or revoke a will or who have concealed a will or have forced the decedent to make certain provisions therein; and natural parent who has refused to recognize or support natural child during his infancy. Wills executed after the person has become disqualified do not preclude him from inheriting by virtue of the will. Three years' possession of an inheritance or legacy cures a previous incapacity to inherit. The children of an incapacitated person are entitled to their shares of the estate in their own right regardless of the incapacity of the parent. Foreigners have the same right to inherit as citizens.

Only part of the decedent's estate may be disposed of freely by will; a certain portion goes to heirs by operation of law, the amount of such portion depending upon the degree of relationship between the decedent and the heirs. Heirs by operation of law and their shares, commonly called "legitimate portions," are briefly as follows:

(1) Children inherit per capita; other descendants per stirpes. When there are children and surviving spouse, latter is entitled to same share as child. Total legal shares of all persons falling within this paragraph is four-fifths of inheritance.

See Topical Index in front part of this volume.

DESCENT AND DISTRIBUTION . . . *continued*

(2) In default of children and descendants, ascendants inherit. Should the father and mother of the decedent survive, they take equal shares. If only one survives he or she will take the entire part of the estate which is inherited by operation of law. In default of surviving father or mother, those ascendants nearest in degree of consanguinity inherit in equal parts. Should there be surviving ascendants and spouse, latter shall inherit one-half of separate property of deceased and one-half of community property belonging to deceased, remaining half of same shall be inherited by legitimate ascendants. Should there be surviving natural parents and spouse, former shall inherit one-half of aforementioned portions otherwise distributable to ascendants.

(3) If there be no descendants, or ascendants surviving, surviving husband or wife has right to one-half of amount of inheritance, and if there survive only husband or wife estate is given to surviving spouse.

Gifts made during the life of the decedent to heirs who are entitled to take by operation of law are charged against their shares of the estate.

In default of heirs by operation of law as stated above, and of a will, inheritance passes to collateral relatives to fourth degree. In this case a full brother excludes a half-brother. Those of equal degree inherit in equal parts. In default of heirs by operation of law, of collateral relatives to fourth degree and of a will, inheritance passes to state.

In order to be entitled to an inheritance, the estate must be accepted by the heir or heirs. The acceptance may be unconditional or subject to the making of an inventory. The heirs accept the estate individually, and the acceptance by one does not affect the rights of any of the others. An unconditional acceptance may be made in writing or may be implied from any act which indicates that the heir has accepted the inheritance. In the case of an unconditional acceptance, the heir is liable for all of the debts of the decedent not only out of the estate which he accepts, but also out of his own property. In other words, the inheritance is merged into his own estate and he takes the place of the decedent with regard to creditors. An acceptance with benefit of inventory must be made expressly before the judge who has cognizance of the estate. In the case of such qualified acceptance, the heir is responsible for the debts of the decedent only out of the estate which he inherits, and his own property is not affected. After making the proper declaration of acceptance with benefit of inventory, three months are allowed in which to make an inventory of the property, and thereafter the heir has 30 days to decide whether he will accept or decline the inheritance.

The heirs, by operation of law, have the right to administer their inheritance but must account to creditors and legatees. Ascendants and descendants who are entitled by operation of law, may take possession without judicial action, but others must prove their right before court. Ascendants or descendants who are out of country at time of death of decedent, must petition court for permission to take their inheritance. Where there are several heirs, no one heir has power to administer estate, and any difference of opinion which arises among heirs regarding administration must be decided by court. Appointment of executor by testator does not deprive heirs by operation of law, of possession of their inheritance, but sufficient property should remain in his possession to pay debts and legacies, unless objection is made to payment of legacies on ground that they prejudice rights of heirs by operation of law.

The partition of an inheritance may be made by the heirs without judicial action when all of them are in possession of their full civil rights. The decision of the majority governs; absentees are cited judicially to appear. Partition must be judicial whenever minors have an interest in the inheritance, when a judicial distribution is requested by interested parties, and when the heirs cannot agree among themselves to make partition out of court. A judicial partition is based on a valuation of the estate made by experts. Before final distribution, sufficient property must be set aside to pay creditors and legatees. The creditors may demand that neither the heirs nor the legatees receive their respective portions until their claims are paid. In case the decedent leaves property both in Argentina and in a foreign country, divisible between foreign heirs and Argentines or foreigners residing in Argentina, the Argentines and the resident foreigners have the right to take from property situated in Argentina a portion equal in value to the property situated in a foreign country from which they may be excluded because of the foreign laws or customs.

DESERTION: See topic Divorce.

DISPUTE RESOLUTION:

(C.P.C. arts. 359-367, 736-773, Law 24573 of Oct. 25, 1995 regulated by Decree 1021 of Dec. 22, 1995 as am'd).

Arbitration.—Any matter on which compromise may be reached is allowed to be submitted to arbitration. There are two types of arbitration: arbitration de jure, in which arbitrators are empowered by parties to decide according to rules of law, and arbitration ex aequo et bono, in which case award is rendered by arbitrators according to their best knowledge and understanding. Arbitration agreement may be in public or private document or act before judge. Number of arbitrators should be three.

Mediation.—Dispute resolution by mediation is mandatory prior to submitting dispute to litigation, except: in criminal matters, matrimonial actions, filiation and child custody (except for monetary aspect of matrimonial actions), declaration of incompetency and rehabilitation, habeas corpus, provisional remedies, reorganization and bankruptcy, labor disputes, discovery before trial, among others. Mediators are elected at random from list of mediators recorded at Registry of Mediators. In order to be registered as mediator, attorney must comply with requirements of law. Registry of Mediators operates under responsibility of Secretariat of Justice. In case of noncompliance with reached agreement, enforcement by judge may be requested.

Conventions.—Interamerican Conventions on Extraterritorial Validity of Foreign Judgments and Arbitral Awards, Montevideo, 1979.

DIVORCE:

(C. C. arts. 64-80; Laws 23515 of June 8, 1987 and 14394 of Dec. 22, 1954 as am'd).

The causes of separation are: Adultery by either spouse; attempt by one spouse against life of other or of their children; provocation by one party to other to commit any crimes; serious offenses; mutual consent, after two years of marriage; and voluntary and malicious abandonment.

After decree of separation spouses may reside in any place.

Divorce dissolving marriage may be granted for: Any reason authorizing separation; separation in fact for three years; and mutual consent after three years of marriage. Divorce decree has same legal effects as separation decree. Spouse may remarry. Support obligation terminates when supported party remarries, lives with someone else without being married or for serious insults by supported party.

Children under five years of age are given to the custody of the wife; those over five years are given to the spouse at court election. If one of spouses has been sentenced to confinement for crime on accusation of other he or she is not given custody of any children unless other consents. Both spouses are obligated to support children.

Spouse who has given cause for divorce or separation is required to support other spouse. In case of necessity, innocent spouse is required to support guilty spouse, if he or she has means.

Pending actions for divorce or separation are terminated, and effects of divorce or separation already granted cease, upon reconciliation of parties. Reconciliation is presumed from cohabitation.

ENVIRONMENT:

(Const. art. 41, Law 24051 of Jan. 8, 1992, regulated by Decree 831 of Apr. 23, 1993).

Constitution establishes legal framework for environmental legislation granting to each person right to enjoy healthy well-balanced environment, suitable for human development, imposing duty to preserve it. Present needs should be satisfied by productive activities without compromising those of future generations. Environmental damage imposes duty to repair damage. Entry of hazardous waste into country, whether actually or potentially dangerous, and of radioactive waste, is prohibited. Law regulates generating, handling and treatment of hazardous waste and considers hazardous waste when it may cause damage, directly or indirectly, to living beings or when it may pollute water, soil, atmosphere or environment. Detailed list of waste and products subject to control are included in law. Law is applicable when hazardous waste is generated or located within areas under federal jurisdiction, when it is located in provincial areas, when it is to be transported between provinces or when it may potentially cause damages beyond provincial boundaries. Provinces may enact their own legislation provided it does not conflict with constitutional principles and regulated matter is not subject to federal jurisdiction. Registration and autorization must be obtained before generating or handling hazardous waste. Generator is responsible for its elimination, including final treatment. Administrative or criminal penalties are imposed for violations of law. Administrative sanctions include fines, suspension or cancellation of registrations, depending on gravity of offense and prior violations. Criminal sanctions include fines and imprisonment as established by Criminal Code and by law. Environmental liability is regulated by general principles of civil code which create obligation to indemnify for causes of damages or to restore environment to previous state. Environmental protection for areas such as zoning, mining, oil, energy, water pollution, and agriculture are regulated by specific legislation.

EXCHANGE CONTROL:

(Law 21382 t.o. 1993, Central Bank Communications of Dec. 18, 1989, Decree 530 of Mar. 18, 1991).

There is unified foreign exchange market free of government intervention and regulations. Unified floating exchange rate is determined by supply and demand. Exporters may keep foreign exchange proceeds.

Remittances abroad of royalties, fees for certain services, principal and interest on loans may be made through purchase of external public debt instruments. Said external public debt instruments are freely convertible into other currencies, and may be discounted on open market, although they may not be traded on Argentine exchanges. Company to which such remittances are being made must agree to accept this means of payment in lieu of regular remittances.

See also topics Foreign Investment; Foreign Trade Regulations.

EXECUTORS AND ADMINISTRATORS:

(C. C. arts. 3844-3874).

A testator may appoint one or more executors. If he does not name an executor the heirs or legatees may by agreement appoint an administrator. If there are neither executors nor administrators, the heirs themselves execute the provisions of the will. The appointment of an executor by a testator must be in one of the forms prescribed for wills (see topic Wills), but need not be in same instrument as will.

A married woman may be appointed executrix and act in that capacity. Heirs, legatees, witnesses of the will, and the notary before whom it was executed may also be executors. A legatee who is named as executor cannot accept his legacy without accepting the duties of executing the will, when the legacy was made in view of the duties imposed upon him as executor. The testator may define the duties of the executor but if he makes no special provisions, the executor has all the powers which are necessary to execute the will. The heirs and legatees may, in case they have justified reason to believe that the executor is not responsible, demand that he give adequate security. When the will is only for the purpose of making legacies and when there are no heirs by operation of law the executor is given possession of the estate.

The executor cannot delegate his authority but may execute his functions through representatives for whose acts he is fully responsible. The testator may give the executor authority to sell his property but the executor may only use this power when it is indispensable for the purpose of executing the will, and by agreement of the heirs or with the authority of a competent judge.

The executor must make an inventory of the estate after citing the heirs, legatees and other interested parties. If there are absent heirs, or persons under guardianship the inventory must be made judicially. The testator cannot excuse the executor from the obligation of making an inventory.

The executor has the right to intervene in any action relative to the validity of the will or any of its provisions.

EXECUTORS AND ADMINISTRATORS . . . *continued*

The heirs may have the executor removed because of incapacity, malconduct or bankruptcy. The executor is required to account to the heirs for his administration although he has not been required to do so by the testator.

When several executors are named the authority is executed by them in the order in which they are named, unless the testator provided that they should act jointly.

The executor is entitled to a commission which is determined according to the importance of his duties and the value of the estate. His expenses are charged to the estate.

Claims Against Decedents' Estates.—(C. C. arts. 3311 to 3381). Creditors of decedents have the right to exact payment of their claims, but the period within which a creditor may enforce this right and the extent of the right depends on whether there has been an unqualified acceptance of the estate by the heirs or an acceptance subject to the making of an inventory (a beneficio de inventario). See topic Descent and Distribution.

In case of unqualified acceptance, the creditor may present his claim at any time after the acceptance of the estate. In this case, the thing inherited becomes an integral part of the estate of the heir and he is obliged with respect to his coheirs, the creditors and legatees, to pay all debts and charges upon it, not only out of the inheritance which he has accepted, but also out of his own property. Creditors of the heir may, in case of a collusive acceptance made fraudulently with creditors of the estate, demand a revocation of the acceptance.

In case of acceptance subject to the making of an inventory, the heir is only obliged to pay the debts of the decedent from the property inherited. He has a period of three months in which to make out the inventory of the property to be inherited, and 30 days thereafter to decide whether he will accept or decline the inheritance. Within this period or during any extension thereof which may be granted by the courts, neither the creditors nor legatees may request payment of their claims. The heir who accepts subject to inventory may abandon all the property to the creditors and legatees, in which case he is entitled to all the assets after the debts are paid, and is not considered as renouncing the inheritance. The heir, if he does not abandon the estate, has the entire administration thereof, but must not prejudice the rights of creditors. The heir must render accountings to the creditors and legatees.

FIDUCIARIES:

See topics Executors and Administrators; Trusts.

FORECLOSURE: See topic Mortgages.

FOREIGN CORPORATIONS:

See topic Corporations (Stock Companies).

FOREIGN EXCHANGE:

See topics Exchange Control; Foreign Investment.

FOREIGN INVESTMENT:

Law 21382 of Aug. 13, 1976, t.o. 1993 and Decree 1000 of Apr. 28, 1983 provide that foreign investors shall have same rights and obligations that Constitution and laws afford to national investors when they invest in economic or productive activities.

Foreign Investment.—(a) Any contribution of capital belonging to foreign investors; (b) acquisition of shares with foreign capital of existing domestic enterprise.

Foreign Investor.—Any person or entity domiciled abroad who owns investment of foreign capital and local enterprises formed by foreign capital.

Domestic Enterprise of Foreign Capital.—Enterprise domiciled within country in which more than 49% of capital is owned by individuals or legal persons domiciled outside country or management is controlled by investors domiciled abroad.

Domestic Enterprise of National Capital.—Any enterprise domiciled within country in which 51% or more of capital is owned directly or indirectly by individuals or legal entities locally domiciled and management control is in hands of investors domiciled in country.

Domicile as defined in Civil Code. (Art. 2).

A foreign investment may be effected in form of:

Freely convertible foreign currency; capital assets, profits or national currency, capitalization of foreign credits in freely convertible foreign currency; intangible assets; and in any other form stipulated in special or promotion regimes (Art. 3).

Foreign investment does not require prior approval. Registration on Registry of Investments of Foreign Capitals is optional.

Registry.—Registry of Investments of Foreign Capital is created under jurisdiction of Subsecretariat of Investment.

Remittances.—Foreign investors may remit abroad net and liquid profits derived from their investments arising from balance sheets adjusted in line to inflation. Such profits may be effected: (1) In same currency in which investment was made or in another foreign currency; (2) in national debt bonds; or (3) in Argentine currency. No prior authorization of Application Authority is necessary to remit profits.

Capital Repatriation.—Foreign capital invested may be repatriated. Foreign investors shall have right to remit proceeds from their investments.

Any form of business organization may be utilized by foreign investors, but in case of corporation, nominative shares must be issued.

Any legal transaction between domestic enterprise and one which controls same or subsidiary of latter is considered as executed between independent parties, when terms and conditions of transaction are according to normal practices between independent parties.

See also topic Licenses.

FOREIGN JUDGMENTS:

(C.C.P. arts. 517-519).

Code of Civil Procedure for federal courts is taken as basis for this article.

Foreign judgments have the force provided by treaty. In the absence of treaty a foreign judgment may be executed if the following circumstances exist: (1) That the judgment was obtained in an action in personam; (2) that the judgment was not entered by default against a defendant who was a resident of Argentina; (3) that the obligation with regard to which the judgment has been issued is valid according to the law of Argentina; and (4) that the judgment was issued in compliance with all the legal requirements of the country where issued and properly authenticated according to the laws of Argentina. A petition for the execution of the judgment must be presented to the judge of first instance. The judgment is translated if in a foreign language and the judge then hears the parties and the District Attorney and decides whether or not it shall be enforced. Foreign judgments are executed in the manner provided for the execution of local judgments. Appeals may be taken from the decisions of the court of first instance.

FOREIGN TRADE REGULATIONS:

(Decree 2868 of Nov. 12, 1979, Law 22374 of Jan. 16, 1981, Law 22415 of Mar. 2, 1981 as am'd, Decree 1001 of May 21, 1982, Decree 155 of Jan. 24, 1983, Decree 2076 of Aug. 11, 1983, Law 23046 of Feb. 8, 1984, Law 23058 of Mar. 30, 1984, Law 23101 of Oct. 19, 1984 as am'd, Decree 4070 of Dec. 28, 1984, Decrees 175, 176 and 177 as am'd of Jan. 25, 1985, Decrees 525 and 526 of Mar. 15, 1985 and Decree 1440 of Aug. 5, 1985).

All importers and exporters must register as such and maintain prescribed books of account. Most importations are subject to system of import duties and ad valorem surcharges, unless expressly exempted therefrom. Import duties and surcharges are subject to constant revision. Special tariff concessions are granted to products originating in member countries of Latin American Integration Association, of South American Common Market and products originating in countries which have signed trade agreements with Argentina.

Exports are also subject to specific incentive and rebate programs. Tax incentives and other benefits are granted to export of services. Countertrade is also regulated.

HOLIDAYS:

(Law 22655 of Oct. 8, 1982, 22769 of Mar. 28, 1983 and Decree 901 of Mar. 23, 1984 and Law 23555 of May 18, 1988 as am'd).

Jan. 1 (New Year's Day); Maundy Thursday*; Good Friday*; May 1 (Labor Day); May 25 (Anniversary of 1810 Revolution); June 10** (Malvinas Isles Day); June 20** (Flag Day); July 9 (Independence Day); Aug. 17** (Death of Gen. San Martin); Oct. 12** (Columbus Day); Dec. 8** (Immaculate Conception); Dec. 25 (Christmas).

Nov. 11 (St. Martin of Tours) is celebrated only in city of Buenos Aires.

*These are movable holidays.

**When fall on Tues. or Wed. are celebrated previous Mon., and when fall on Thurs. and Fri. are celebrated on following Mon.

Note.—Courts are on vacation during whole month of Jan. and during Holy Week. However, urgent business may be transacted during these periods.

HUSBAND AND WIFE:

(C. C. arts. 184-197, 1217-1290; Laws 11357 of Sept. 22, 1926 as am'd by 17711 of Apr. 22, 1968).

Spouses owe each other fidelity, assistance and support. They should live in same house unless relieved by court on special grounds.

Marriage is considered as constituting a partnership in which the property brought into the marriage by the parties is treated separately from that obtained as a result of their industry during marriage.

The wife's dower consists of all the property which she brings into the marriage and which she acquired by inheritance, legacy, or gift thereafter.

Property obtained by the efforts of the parties during the marriage belongs to the marriage partnership, but is administered by the husband.

A prenuptial contract may designate the property which each spouse brings into the marriage and gifts of the husband to the wife, as well as the property which each is to receive at the death of the other.

No contract may be made between husband and wife after marriage. Wife cannot renounce any rights arising out of marriage. While she is a minor, husband must have court authority in dealing with her property and can secure such authority only in case of necessity or manifest advisability.

Wife may obtain a judicial separation of marriage property on ground of maladministration; in such case she has no right to further earnings of husband.

Wife may take part in judicial proceedings without consent of husband.

Woman of legal age possesses full independent legal capacity.

If the husband is under a sentence of imprisonment of two years or over, the wife may with court consent dispose of her husband's property in order to support herself and her children under 18 years. The separate property and the marriage partnership property obtained by her are not liable for the husband's debts, nor are the husband's property and the marriage partnership property administered by him liable for the wife's debts, but there is such mutual liability if the debts were incurred to provide for the needs of the home, the education of the children or the preservation of common property. A wife under age has the same rights as a wife of age except that she can not dispose of her property without her husband's consent, but if he be a minor or refuses consent, she may obtain a judicial authorization.

INCOME TAX: See topic Taxation.

INFANCY:

(C. C. arts. 54-59, 126, 139, 264-310, 377-467, 1045; Laws 10903 of Oct. 21, 1919 as am'd, 11357 of Sept. 22, 1926 as am'd, 14394 of Dec. 22, 1954 as am'd by Decree-Law 5286 of May 20, 1957, and Law 23264 of Sept. 25, 1985, 15244 of Nov. 15, 1959; Decree-Law 5285 of May 20, 1957, 11011 of Sept. 12, 1957 and Decree 1143 of Jan. 28, 1960).

Age of majority is 21. Contracts of minors under 14 are void and over 14 voidable, except some by emancipated children. Ordinarily, minors are subject to parental

See Topical Index in front part of this volume.

INFANCY . . . *continued*
authority of father and mother. Parental authority gives parent usufruct of property, with certain exceptions, owned by minor, as well as its administration. In absence of parents a guardian is appointed but he is not entitled to usufruct. Parents and guardians have limited powers of disposition.

INHERITANCE TAX: See topic Taxation.

INSOLVENCY:

See topic Bankruptcy and Insolvency.

INTEREST:

Obligations may bear interest at any rate which contracting parties stipulate (C. C. art. 621), but in practice courts will not enforce interest rates above those which Argentinian banks are permitted to charge, on ground that usury is against public policy. Interest may not be compounded except by an agreement made after it is due, which authorizes addition of interest to capital, or when a judgment is obtained for principal and interest and debtor defaults in payment. When a debt is past due, interest must be paid at rate agreed upon, or, in absence of an agreement at interest rate established by law, and if no interest rate is established by law, at such rate as court may determine. (C. C. art. 622). Debtor is not in default until demand is made judicially or extrajudicially except when contract provides that default shall occur if debt is not paid at a certain time, or when nature and circumstances of obligation indicate that time is of essence. Interest rate established by courts in case of default varies in different parts of Republic. Code of Commerce (art. 565) provides that in case interest is stipulated but amount is not set, rate established by public banks is intended, and then only in case of default, and that where law or contract speaks of interest at current rate, rate charged by National Bank is understood. Art. 569 of Code of Commerce provides that by means of a judicial proceeding or by private agreement, interest may be earned on arrears of interest. In case of a judicial proceeding, interest must be in arrears for at least one year. Interest is likewise earned on balance due at end of each year pursuant to settlements. It would seem that rate established by National Bank in particular locality is followed generally by courts in fixing rate of interest.

Article (175 bis) of Penal Code provides that if person taking advantage of inexperience, or necessity of another induces him to promise or to give in any way interest or other pecuniary gains that do not reasonably relate to services promised or rendered, or to grant deposits or guarantees that can be deemed extortion, he shall be penalized with imprisonment and with fine. Same penalty is applicable to person who in bad faith acquires, transfers or claims credit bearing usurious interest. Imprisonment and fine shall be increased if person is professional lender or commission merchant who commits acts of usury frequently.

INTESTACY:

See topic Descent and Distribution.

JUDGMENTS: See topic Foreign Judgments.

JUSTICES OF THE PEACE: See topic Courts.

LABOR RELATIONS:

Federal Constitution provides that labor must enjoy protection of law, which must guarantee workers equitable working conditions, limited working day, paid days of rest and vacations, fair remuneration, flexible minimum essential wage, equal pay for equal work, share in enterprises' earnings. Organization of labor and trade unions is guaranteed, to conclude collective bargainings, and right to conciliation and arbitration is consequently protected by Constitution as well as right to strike. Government grants social security benefits which are compulsory and irrenunciable, and flexible retirement pay and pensions. Full protection of family, its welfare and access to decent housing are also expressly contemplated in Constitution among other provisions.

Argentina does not have a labor code. Laws, decrees and regulations have been issued for each specific work or type of work throughout the years.

Law 18204 of May 12, 1969 provides that it is absolutely forbidden to work on Sundays; law allows working in essential services such as transportation, entertainments, hospitals, etc. Law 9511 of Sept. 29, 1914 and Decree 6754 of Aug. 26, 1943 provide that salaries, pensions and certain other compensations cannot be subject of deduction and/or attachment up to certain amount. Law 18204 also provides that it is forbidden to work on Saturdays after 1:00 P.M.; however, certain types of stores such as supermarkets, restaurants, drug stores, etc. are open. Legislation treats, inter alia, medical assistance loans (Laws 18601 and 18980; Decree 4914/71), compensation in event of accident (Law 24557 of Oct. 3, 1995 regulated by Decree 170 of Feb. 2, 1996; contract labor law [Law 20744 of Sept. 11, 1974 t.o. 1976 as am'd] regulated by Decree 2725 of Dec. 26, 1991 as am'd and Decree 739 of Apr. 29, 1992 and Law 21297 of Apr. 23, 1976), and minimum wages (Law 19598). Workers are entitled to paid vacations from 14 to 35 days per year, depending on time of employment. They are also entitled to one salary bonus per year. Hours of labor are limited to eight per day or 48 per week. Overtime is limited to maximum hours per month and per year. There is social security system for retired workers. There are two retirement and pension systems, (1) one in which funds pension benefits to retirees entirely through deductions assessed against salaries and contributions made by employers, and (2) privately-owned and managed pension funds, in which employee's contribution is deposited into personal retirement accounts managed by administrators of pension and retirement funds of their choice. (Law 24241 of Oct. 13, 1993 as am'd and its regulations). Minors under 14 years of age cannot be employed in any kind of activity, whether profit-making or not. Workers may be dismissed only if serious offense is committed. In case of dismissal without justified cause employer must pay to worker indemnity of one month salary for each year of service or any period greater than three months calculated according to formula indicated in law. Unemployment benefits are paid at rate equivalent to last month's pay, for four months to one year after dismissal, to employees dismissed without justified cause, laid off, resignation due to justified cause, bankruptcy, expiration of labor contract, death, retirement or disability of employer, among others. Short-term employment contracts are regulated. Compensation for accidents and injuries is limited by law. There is national workers register which includes work history, registration of employers, pension and medicare contributions.

LICENSES:

Law 22426 of Mar. 12, 1981 and its regulation, Decree 580 of Mar. 25, 1981, govern transfer of technology agreements. Law applies to all onerous juridical acts object of which is transfer of technology or trademarks by persons domiciled outside country to physical or juridical persons domiciled inside country, when said acts produce effects in latter. License Agreements between related parties (such as parent-subsidiary) must be submitted for approval by National Institute of Industrial Technology. License agreements between unrelated parties do not require approval but must be registered with National Institute of Industrial Technology for information purposes only. Agreements covering "military secrets" need not be filed at all. Agreements between related parties must conform to normal commercial practices between independent parties in order to be approved. Application for its approval must be filed within 30 days after execution of agreement. Lack of approval or failure to file application does not invalidate agreement, but any royalty expenses by licensee become nondeductible and fees received by licensor will be taxed at full rate.

LIMITATION OF ACTIONS:

See topic Prescription.

LIMITED LIABILITY COMPANIES:

See topic Corporations (Stock Companies).

LIMITED PARTNERSHIP:

See topic Partnership.

MARRIAGE:

(Laws 23515 of June 8, 1987 and 14394 of Dec. 22, 1954 as am'd; Decree-Law 4070 of Mar. 1, 1956).

The following conditions are a bar to marriage: Consanguinity between ascendants and descendants, brothers and sisters and half brothers and sisters; between those related by adoption; affinity in direct line; fact that woman is under 16 years of age, and man is under 18 years of age; existing prior marriage; fact of having been accomplice in murder of prior husband or wife; and insanity. Minors over 16 years of age in case of women, and 18 years in case of men, may not marry without consent of their parents, their guardians, or court; and deaf mutes who cannot write may not marry unless they can express their concept in other way. Guardian and his descendants who are not emancipated may not marry minor under guardianship until accounts of guardian are settled and guardianship ends.

Consent of the parties expressed before the official in charge of the civil registry is necessary. Persons desiring to marry must appear before officer in charge of civil registry in domicile of either one of them; must state their intention verbally which is reduced to writing and signed by public officer, parties and two witnesses. If parties do not know how to sign another may sign for them. Record must state names of parties, their age, nationality, domicile, place of birth, profession, the names, nationality, profession, domicile of their parents, and whether or not they have been previously married, and if so, name of former spouse, place of marriage and cause of dissolution. Legalized copy of nullification of prior marriage must be presented and also declaration of person whose consent is required if that person is not present and becomes party to proceeding. Two witnesses must certify as to identity of parties and that they believe them to be capable of marrying. Marriage may be opposed on any of grounds of incapacity stated at beginning of this article, either by husband or wife of person who desires to marry another, by ascendants, descendants, brothers and sisters, guardians, and public prosecutor in case he has knowledge of any incapacity. If no objection is made to marriage, or if objection has been resolved in favor of contracting parties, marriage may be performed. Ceremony must take place before officer in charge of civil registry, publicly in his office. Parties may appear personally. There must be two witnesses. If one of parties cannot appear, marriage may be performed in his home. Proceedings are reduced to writing and include declaration that parties have taken each other as husband and wife and that they have been married in name of law. Statement of recognition which parties make of natural children by means of marriage, names, ages, civil status, profession and domicile of witnesses. Record is then signed by all of persons who took part in ceremony and copy of record is given to parties. Proceedings may be shortened when, on petition of physician, it appears that one of parties is in danger of death.

MARRIED WOMEN:

See topics Executors and Administrators; Husband and Wife; Marriage.

MINES AND MINERALS:

The Mining Law consists of the Code of Mines, enacted by Law 1919 of Dec. 8, 1886, amendments thereto and various governmental decrees. Mines, and the buildings, machinery, animals, cars, etc., used in exploiting them are considered real property distinct from the land on which they are located. They may be alienated, leased or mortgaged like any other real property. Mining concessions may be obtained on lands owned by other persons subject in certain cases to prior rights of the owners of the surface.

Mines are divided into three classes:

(1) Mines belonging exclusively to the state, the private ownership of which may be acquired only by virtue of concessions. This class of mines includes all of the precious metals which are enumerated specifically in the Code of Mines, combustibles, such as lignite, anthracite, mineral oils, etc., arsenic, wolframite, mica and precious stones.

Concessions may be obtained by the persons who discover the deposits either as a result of legally authorized exploration or accidentally. In order to make explorations,

See Topical Index in front part of this volume.

MINES AND MINERALS . . . *continued*
a permit must be obtained whether the land is on public or on private property, but the owner of the surface need not obtain a permit to make exploration on his own estate. He cannot interfere, however, with any person who has obtained formal permission to explore his land. A petition containing the information required by the Code of Mines must be presented to the Registrar of Mines who notifies the land owner and records and publishes the petition so that anyone opposing it may appear and object. In the national territory petitions may be presented in sealed envelopes to the postmasters who make a record of their receipt and give a receipt to the petitioner. The envelopes containing the petitions are then forwarded to the proper authorities. If no objection is made, the permission is granted and the place of exploration is then fixed and a record made. The right of exploration gives the grantee the exclusive privilege of exploring and obtaining the concession to work any deposit discovered within the bounds of his grant. The exploration may continue for a definite length of time. The right to explore does not include the right to work mines but includes the right to do the necessary work in connection with the exploration.

The grantee may obtain the right to do formal work necessary to establish the existence of a seam, and to examine its nature and importance. For this purpose, he may have marked out three claims or pertenencias in the area of exploration. When the work is completed a formal concession may be applied for.

In case a discovery is made on land in the course of exploration or accidentally, a formal concession may be obtained. A petition must be presented to the registrar of mines containing the data required by the Mining Code.

The petition is inserted in the protocol of the registrar by order of the court and is duly published. The miner must determine the depth and direction of the deposit by excavations and may take three adjoining claims in the seam which he has chosen. The next step is to have the limits within which the concession may be worked, or the claims, determined. A petition must be presented for the measuring of the claims which must be duly published and the adjoining owners notified. If no objection is presented, the measurement is made by a government official accompanied by an official engineer, the registrar of mines, and a representative or an expert named by any interested party if he so desires. A record is then made of all the proceedings which are signed by the government's representative, the parties and the engineer, and is authenticated by the registrar. It is then recorded and a copy is given to the petitioner as evidence of his title; the grantee must then mark his boundaries and keep them well preserved.

Neither the right to explore nor a formal concession gives permission to occupy the surface of private property under cultivation with works of construction without the consent of the owner, but permission may be obtained from the public authorities to do certain classes of work on cultivated land, such as constructing wells, galleries, etc. The concession of a mine of this class gives a right to purchase the land covered by the claim. If the land is owned by the state or municipality, the grant is gratuitous. If the land is not purchased, the miner has the right to certain established easements provided he pays for the same.

(2) The second class of mines is divided into two subdivisions and comprises those which may be exploited by anyone without concessions and those which are granted preferentially to the owners of the soil. The first subdivision consists of those metallic sands and precious stones which are found in the beds of rivers, running water and deposits along the sides of streams, as well as the workings and wastes of abandoned mines. Anybody may exploit deposits falling within this subdivision unless they are on cultivated lands, but exclusive permission may also be obtained to work them. The second subdivision of this class of mines includes borates, saltpeter, salt, peat, metals not comprised in the first class, and various classes of earths, such as borates, those containing aluminum, phosphates of lime, kaolin, etc. The owner of the surface has a preferential right to the deposits falling within this subdivision but must have his claims marked out officially. A concession may, however, be granted to a person other than the owner of the surface in case a demand is made on the owner to exploit the same and he fails to do so within a specified period. Concessionaries of mines in this class must employ in working them a sum determined by the government within period of four years. (Law No. 10,273 of 1917).

(3) The third class of mines includes deposits of stone and materials which are useful for construction and ornament. They belong to the owner of the surface. In case of lands owned by the state or the municipalities, deposits falling within this class may be worked by virtue of a contract with the government, but in case there is no contract they may be exploited by anyone.

Groups of miners may be formed to work their adjoining claims together on obtaining proper authority. The Code of Mines also provides for a special class of mining companies which may be formed by agreement between two or more persons who have obtained a concession and reduced their contract of association to the form of a public document or who have obtained a concession as a company. The affairs of the company are controlled by a majority vote of the members, one-half of the members forming a quorum, provided that the others have been cited. A representative is appointed to deal with the government and third parties, and an administrator may be appointed to administer the affairs of the company. No member of the company may transfer his rights to a person who is not a member without the consent of all the others.

The right to abandoned and unregistered mines is obtained by prescription by the persons who have exploited them uninterruptedly for a period of three hundred and fifty days. When a person holds a mine by a title apparently good and obtained in good faith, his ownership is complete after two years' occupancy. In other cases other than those above mentioned, the period of prescription is five years.

Geological research as a public service is governed by a chapter added to Mining Code by Dec.-Law 8925 of Oct. 8, 1963. Mines discovered on occasion of geological research become vacant and are so registered two years after discovery, unless granted to a private party, State not being entitled to exploit them, except for reasons of public utility. Law 22259 of July 28, 1980 amends Code of Mines in reference to concessions and legal regime of hydrocarbons and nuclear minerals. In order to promote foreign investment in mining activities, Decree 816 of May 21, 1992 recognizes same rights to foreign investors as to national investors. Law 24196 of Apr. 23, 1993 regulated by Decree 2686 of Dec. 28, 1993 as am'd on investments regime for mining activity grants tax incentives to investors in prospecting, exploration, exploitation and processing of minerals, including tax stability for 30 years from date of presentation of feasibility study.

Hydrocarbons.—Survey licenses, exploration permits and exploitation concessions are granted to privately owned or mixed companies. Survey licenses and exploration permits are awarded through competitive bidding system. Exploration permits are automatically converted into exploitation concessions when discovery of crude oil is declared commercial. Concessionaire has free disposition of hydrocarbons produced thereunder, such right may involve entire production of certain share of production. He may sell his share of production in domestic market or abroad and keep abroad 70% of foreign currency proceeds derived from export; export of hydrocarbons and by-products are exempted from duties, tariffes and withholding. Concessionaire has to pay royalty of 12% and general taxes in effect. Law 17319 of June 23, 1967 as regulated by Law 21778 of Apr. 14, 1978 as am'd and Decree 1443 of Aug. 5, 1985 as am'd by Decree 623 of Apr. 23, 1987, Decrees 1055 of Oct. 10, 1989, 1212 of Dec. 8, 1989, 1589 of Dec. 27, 1989 and 2411 of Nov. 11, 1991 and Law 24145 of Sept. 24, 1992 as am'd.

MONOPOLIES AND RESTRAINT OF TRADE:

(Constitution 1853 art. 10; Law 22262 of Aug. 1, 1980; and Law 22802 of May 10, 1983 as am'd and its regulations, Decree 2121 of Nov. 30, 1994, Law 24240 of Sept. 22, 1993).

Argentine Constitution guarantees free circulation of goods. Law for defense of competition covers monopoly practices in one or more branches of production, industry or transport or in domestic or foreign trade throughout national territory. Law is framed to prevent monopolization of market rather than to cure it. Law defines "dominant position" as question of fact. There is "dominant position" when person for determined product is only one who offers or demands it in national market or where there is no competition. Also, Law refers to "dominant position" when two or more persons do not compete between themselves or with third party.

Acts of monopoly are to fix prices, to limit or control technical development of production of goods or services, to limit distribution, to make exclusive rights agreements to tied-purchasing agreements, to fix resale price below or over cost, destruction of production to increase prices, etc. Law is flexible policy instrument that Government can modulate according to needs of market. For this purpose Law has created public agency in charge of study and repression of monopolization and restrictive business practices.

Local production is protected from unfair practices of international trade by imposition of countervailing duties on import of foreign goods. Dumping and subvention are considered unfair practices. Dumping is defined as import of foreign goods at lower price than normal value of similar or same product in origin or export place in normal commercial transactions. Normal value is determined according to method indicated by law. Subvention is defined as financial assistance from government or public organization in country of origin or exporting country to producer or exporter, such as direct or indirect incentives, premiums, repayment or similar advantages in order to make them more competitive on international market.

Consumer Protection Law.—Law deals with consumer's right to be informed, general representations and warranties, credit operations, lack of performance, services, domiciled sales and mail order and general regulations on subject.

Secretary of Industry and Commerce is in charge of enforcing law.

MORTGAGES:

Mortgages in Argentina, have an effect similar to that of common law, must be recorded to be good as against third parties, and do not pass title to mortgagee with an equity of redemption in mortgagor. Mortgagor retains title subject to lien of mortgage. Mortgages cannot be placed on personal property nor on right of usufruct or use and habitation (see topic Real Property). Mortgages on real property are provided for in C. C. arts. 3108-3203.

A mortgage of real property extends to all accessories, so long as they are united to the property, to all improvements, to buildings erected on vacant land, to the advantages resulting from the extinction of servitudes, to rents, and to the products of insurance. A mortgage is not divisible. All of the properties mortgaged to secure a debt are bound for the whole amount and the creditor may proceed against any or all of them. Mortgages may be subject to any condition. Only the owner of property may mortgage it. Mortgages may be given to secure the debt of a third party. A joint owner of property may mortgage his share, but in case of partition, the mortgage attaches to his share alone.

A mortgage must be in the form of a notarial or public instrument and the contract to which it is an accessory may be in the same document. The instrument may be executed in a foreign country if properly legalized and protocolized (see topic Notaries Public ["Escribanos Públicos"]) by order of court. (C. C. art. 1211). Unless presented for registration within six days after order of protocolization has been issued, mortgages executed in foreign country do not affect third parties until recorded. Mortgages must be accepted by creditor.

The instrument constituting the mortgage must contain the names and domiciles of the debtor and creditor, the date and nature of the contract to which it is accessory and where filed, the situation of the property and its boundaries, and if rural property, the district, and if urban the city or town and street, and the exact amount of the debt. A general designation of property such as "all my property in X City" is not sufficient. The mortgage must be recorded in the mortgage registry. A mortgage is good as against third parties immediately upon execution if recorded within six days thereafter, unless the office of registry is more than two leagues distant from the office of the notary where executed, in which case an additional day is allowed for each two leagues. Otherwise the mortgage does not affect third parties until recorded.

Unrecorded mortgages, however, are good as against those persons who took part in executing them, such as the notary and witnesses. To record a mortgage the first copy must be presented. The expenses of recording are borne by the debtor. Recording may be requested by the grantor, the grantee, the representative of either, and by those interested in the security. A person who mortgages his property a second time before

See Topical Index in front part of this volume.

MORTGAGES . . . *continued*
the first mortgage is recorded is liable for fraud. Mortgages must be re-recorded every ten years to be effective.

The debtor must not decrease the value of the mortgaged property. If he does so, the mortgagee may require a deposit of an amount sufficient to make the security good, and may foreclose the mortgage. The mortgagee may pursue any part of the property mortgaged which has been separated and alienated, into the hands of third parties if that part is realty, but not if it is personal property which is only realty by virtue of its relationships to the estate. In the former case a demand must first be made on the debtor for payment.

Mortgages are foreclosed by executory actions defined in the Code of Civil Procedure.

Mortgages on vessels are governed by Arts. 499 to 514 of Law 20,094 of Mar. 2, 1973. Vessels in excess of ten tons may be mortgaged. Mortgage may be in form of public or private instrument and shall be effective vis à vis third parties only from date of its registration in National Registry of Vessels. Ships under construction may also be mortgaged. Preferential rights among different mortgages are determined by date of registration of contract. Vessels may be mortgaged during a voyage. Mortgages effective outside of country are recorded by Argentine consul who must then communicate existence of said mortgage to National Registry of Vessels. As a rule, mortgages must be renewed every three years. All other naval contrivances can also be mortgaged, subject to aforementioned rules. When Code of Commerce is silent on any given point provisions of Civil Code shall govern maritime mortgages.

Aircraft may be mortgaged for up to seven years under Aeronautics Code. (Law 17, 285 of May 7, 1967 as am'd by Law 22390 of Feb. 6, 1981, regulated by Decree 326 of Feb. 10, 1982).

Motor vehicles may be mortgaged for up to five years. (Decree-Law 15348 of May 28, 1946 as am'd, and Decree-Law 6582 of Apr. 30, 1958, t.o. 1973 as am'd).

Chattel Mortgages.—See topic Chattel Mortgages.

MOTOR VEHICLES:

(Law 24449 of Feb. 6, 1995).

Law 24449 contains complete regulations governing motor vehicles and public ways. License plates are required for all motor vehicles and drivers must obtain license which must be renewed every five years. Minors between 18 and 21 years of age are permitted to operate motor vehicles in special circumstances. In case of traffic accidents, law provides for fines or imprisonment or both depending upon type of violation; imprisonment is applied when driving while intoxicated.

There is National Registry of Motor Vehicles in which detailed information on vehicles and owners of all motor vehicles authorized to use public ways is kept. Registration is compulsory. (Law 22977 of Nov. 16, 1983).

NEGOTIABLE INSTRUMENTS:

See topic Bills and Notes.

NOTARIES PUBLIC ("Escribanos Públicos"):

(Notarial Law 12990 of July 7, 1947 as am'd; C. C. arts. 997-1011).

A notary must be an Argentine citizen, hold a diploma as notary issued by the National University, and be a member of the notarial association called College of Notaries. A notary may not hold any salaried position, public or private, nor engage in commerce or banking, nor in the practice of law, and must reside in the locality where his notarial office is situated. The number of such notarial offices is limited; appointments are made by the Federal Executive from lists of three names submitted by the College of Notaries after competitive examination, but the appointee may designate one or two assistant notaries. Special notaries may be appointed on competitive examination for branches of the Government, municipalities and official banks. Notaries must give bond before entering upon their duties and are subject to the supervision of the courts and of the College of Notaries.

Importance of office is due to fact that all of more important documents which are referred to so often in this digest as notarial documents (escrituras publicas) and which are a class of public instruments (see topic Public Instruments), to have legal effect, must be prepared by a notary or other competent official, and preserved in his record or protocol, which is an official registry kept in manner provided by law and carefully preserved and inspected by public authorities.

Notarial documents must be in the Spanish language. If the person executing the document does not know the Spanish language, the document should be made in the form of a memorandum signed by the parties in the presence of the notary and authenticated by him. If not signed in his presence the genuineness of the signature must be certified to by the notary. It is then translated by an official interpreter. The memorandum and the translation are then placed in the notary's protocol. A notarial document must state its nature, object, the names and surnames of the persons executing it, whether or not they are of age, their family status, domicile or residence, the place, day, month and year when it was signed, which may be a holiday or Sunday. The notary must certify that he knows the persons executing the document, and when completed should read it to the parties, and should at the end certify in his own handwriting to any interlineations, or amendments in the document. The document containing all the conditions, clauses, periods of payment, and a statement of the sums delivered in the presence of the notary which should be written out in full, is then signed by the parties in presence of two witnesses whose names must be stated in the body of the document, and is then authenticated at the end by the notary. If the notary does not know the parties, two witnesses must identify them, and the document must include their names, residence and a certificate that the notary knows them. If the parties are represented by agents, the document must state that the power of attorney has been presented, and it must be transcribed in the notary's register along with the document. If the power has been executed in his own office the notary need only refer to its place of record. Notarial documents which do not state the place and date of execution, the names of the person executing them, their signatures, and which do not include the power of attorney when executed by an agent, and the statement of the presence of two witnesses and their signatures, are void. The absence of other formalities does not vitiate the document but renders the notary liable to fine. Documents are also void which are not found in their proper place in the notary's protocol. The notary must give the parties who request it, an authenticated copy of the document. Subsequent copies may be given also, but in case any of the parties is required by the document to do any act, he may only have a subsequent copy by order of the court. Copies may only be given on citation of the parties in order to give them an opportunity to compare the copy with the original, and in case of their absence a public official is appointed by the court for the purpose.

PARTNERSHIP:

(Law 19550 of Apr. 3, 1972, t.o. 1984).

General partnership (sociedad colectiva) is a partnership of two or more persons with unlimited and joint responsibility, which is formed for commercial purposes under a firm name which must include words "sociedad colectiva" or an abbreviation thereof. If firm name does not contain names of all partners, words "y compañía" or its abbreviation must also appear therein. Partnership agreement regulates administration of company and in absence of any such provision therein any partner may indiscriminately administer company. If certain partners are charged with administration of company without determining their specific roles, or without expressly stating all activities that must be undertaken jointly, they may indiscriminately undertake any administrative act. Administrator, partner or not, even if designated in partnership agreement, may be removed at any time without cause by majority vote of partners, unless otherwise provided. If partnership agreement requires removal with cause, any partner may request a judicial determination thereof. Administrator may resign as such at any time unless otherwise provided, but he remains responsible for any damages resulting therefrom in event his resignation is fraudulent or untimely. All modifications of partnership agreement require unanimous approval of partners, unless otherwise provided, and all other resolutions shall be adopted by majority vote (majority vote herein expressly referring to an absolute majority of capital, unless partnership agreement provides otherwise). Partner cannot undertake acts for himself or for third parties that in any way compete with partnership, except with express and unanimous consent of other partners. Noncompliance with this prohibition authorizes exclusion of partner, reimbursement of all profits derived therefrom and indemnification for all resulting damages.

Limited partnership (sociedad en comandita simple) is a partnership formed for commercial purposes with two or more persons. Active partners have same responsibilities as partners of a general partnership, while silent partners are liable to extent of their capital contribution. Firm name must include words "sociedad en comandita simple" or its abbreviation and names of all active partners should appear therein. Capital contribution of a silent partner is paid-in only by determinate obligations. Administration of a limited partnership is undertaken by active partners or third parties and is subject to same norms as general partnerships. Silent partners may not interfere in business or act as agents of partnership, becoming unlimitedly liable for all such acts, although they may examine books and opine and advise in matters undertaken by partnership. Resolutions are adopted in same manner as general partnership. Silent partners have right to vote in accounting matters and on appointment of administrators. In event of bankruptcy, death, or incapacity of all active partners, silent partner may undertake all urgent acts of partnership until situation stabilizes without incurring liabilities otherwise applicable. Partnership is dissolved if not stabilized within three months. If silent partners do not comply with all legal provisions, they shall be unlimitedly and jointly liable for their conduct.

Partnership of capital and industry (sociedad de capital e industria) is formed by (1) individuals who supply capital and are subject to unlimited liability; and (2) one or more individuals who contribute only their personal services and are not personally liable (although all earnings not received by them may be lost). Firm name must include words "sociedad de capital e industria" or its abbreviation and names of any partners exclusively contributing personal services may not appear therein. Its administration is governed by same rules as set forth for a general partnership, partner providing personal services remaining eligible to become administrator. Voting requirements are same as for a limited partnership, capital of partner providing personal services being deemed to be for such efforts same as capital of active partner with smallest capital contribution. Partnership agreement should contain share of profits to be allocated to partner providing personal services, otherwise such share shall be determined by judicial proceeding.

Cooperative Societies.—Name must be followed by word "limitada." Cannot be restricted as to number of members or shares, capital or duration. Shares must be registered and can be transferred only on conditions expressed in by-laws. Each member has only one vote regardless of total number of shares. Members can withdraw only as specified in by-laws or by law. Of net profits, at least 5% must be allocated to reserve fund and 90% distributed amont members. (Law 11388 of Dec. 20, 1926).

PATENTS:

(Const. art. 17, Law 24481 of May 23, 1995, t.o. 1996, Decree 260 of Mar. 20, 1996).

Constitution provides that inventor is exclusive owner of his work, invention or discovery for period established by law.

Invention Patents.—Any individual or juridical person who invents or discovers or improves something of industrial application may obtain patent. Juridical persons may petition patents for inventions made by persons under their employment. Any invention of products or proceedings in any technology field which is novel, represents inventive step and are susceptible of industrial application is patentable. Invention is novel when it is not within state of art. Discoveries, scientific theories and mathematical methods; scientific, literary and artistic works; diagnostic, therapeutic and surgical methods; computer programs among others are not considered inventions. Invention for which commercial exploitation must be denied in order to protect public policy, morals and people's and animals' health or life, or to preserve vegetation or to prevent serious environmental damages; and natural or artificial, genetic and biological substances are not patentable. Pharmaceutical products are patentable after Oct. 23, 2000, but application for priority may be filed any time before such date. Patents are granted

See Topical Index in front part of this volume.

PATENTS . . . *continued*
for 20 years from filing date. Patent gives exclusive right of exploitation. Patent owner must exploit it, directly or by granting license. Compulsive license may be granted by lack of exploitation within three years after granting date or within four years of filing date, and in case of proof of owner's involvement in anticompetitive practices, such as refusing to supply market in reasonable commercial conditions or fixing excessive prices; and in case of declared emergency or national security reasons.

Utility Models.—New forms of objects or mechanisms, provided they have practical use are registrable. They may be registered as ownership of author if no publicity has been made before filing application. Registration term is ten years from filing date. Provisions regarding patents are applicable to models.

PRESCRIPTION:

(C. C. arts. 3947-4043; C. Com. arts. 846-855).

The acquisition and loss of real and personal rights through the lapse of time is called "prescription." Prescription runs against the state, as well as against private persons, in so far as property of the state which is susceptible of becoming private property is concerned.

Through Law 22488 of Aug. 27, 1981, Argentina has become party to Convention on the Limitation Period in the International Sale of Goods, of 1980.

Prescription in the case of things which are held by force or violence does not begin to run until the illegality of the possession has been cured. Prescription as a general rule does not run against minors nor against persons under guardianship. Prescription does not run between husband and wife, even although the administration of their property may be separated and although they be divorced. When because of difficulties or impossibilities, the bringing of an action has been temporarily prevented, the courts are authorized to free a creditor or proprietor from the consequences of prescription, if, after the difficulty has ceased, the creditor or proprietor has taken immediate advantages of his rights. When prescription is suspended, the time prior to the suspension may be added to the time subsequent in establishing a right of prescription.

Prescription is interrupted when the possessor is deprived of the thing for a year, even though the new possession be illegal or violent. Prescription is interrupted by an action against the possessor although begun before an incompetent judge and although it be void for defects of form or because the complainant has not legal capacity to sue. Prescription is also interrupted by an express or implied acknowledgment by the debtor or possessor of the right of the person against whom prescription is running. When prescription is interrupted the situation is the same as though no part of the period of prescription had run, and thereafter the whole period must elapse before prescriptive title can be obtained.

Title to real property is obtained by ten years' continuous possession, provided possessor holds property in good faith and with a presumptive title. Good faith consists of belief without any doubt on part of possessor that he is exclusive owner of property; and by a presumptive title is meant a title which on its face is valid and sufficient to establish ownership. Formal defects constitute a presumption of bad faith. Ignorance on part of possessor, based on an error of fact is excusable, but ignorance based on an error of law is not excusable. Possession of real property and real rights for a continuous period of 20 years with purpose of holding same in ownership, gives absolute title regardless of whether possessor has a presumptive title or holds in good faith, and regardless of whether rightful owner is present or absent from country.

Actions.—Regarding any kind of actions, mere inaction of creditor for period designated by law, without necessity of a presumptive title or good faith, frees obligee from all obligations. Period of prescription varies according to class of action from two months in case of an action by a husband to declare illegitimate a child born during matrimony, to 20 years in case of an action to partition an inheritance and in other cases enumerated below. In each case not only chapters of Civil Code and Code of Commerce on prescription should be consulted, but also provisions of law with respect to particular subject. Regardless of provisions of Civil Code, Code of Commerce must be carefully consulted in all cases involving commercial and mercantile matters. Enumeration below covers period of prescription in only a few of more important cases covered by Civil Code.

Action to demand partition of an inheritance against a co-heir who has possessed same in whole or in part in his own name, prescribes in 20 years. Action of a debtor to demand restitution of a pledge given as a security of a credit prescribes in same period, if pledge has remained in possession of creditor or his heirs.

Personal actions for debt prescribe in ten years. Right of a minor or his heirs against his guardian for an accounting prescribes in ten years from date of minor's majority or death.

The obligation to pay pensions for support prescribes in five years as also rents and any payment which must be made annually or in shorter periods.

An action to nullify judicial acts for violence, intimidation, error, fraud, etc., prescribes in two years from the date in which the violence or intimidation ceases, or the cause of action is known in case of error, fraud, etc. The obligation to pay the fees of arbitrators, lawyers, and all classes of employees in the administration of justice, notaries, the salaries of agents, and fees of doctors, surgeons and druggists prescribes in two years.

The action of creditors to revoke agreements made by debtors in fraud or prejudice of their rights, prescribes in one year. The obligation to pay for food and lodging, tuition in schools, the wages of servants who are paid annually or oftener and wages of workmen and mechanics prescribes in one year. Actions for libel and slander, for damages caused by animals and for damages as a result of crimes or quasi crimes prescribe in two years.

The action of a purchaser to rescind a contract prescribes in six months.

In mercantile matters the period of prescription is ten years unless a shorter period is provided by the Code of Commerce, the Civil Code or other laws. (C. Com. art. 486). The Code of Commerce has a classification of commercial actions which prescribe in less than ten years. Arts. 847 to 855. For example: The liquidated debt as a result of a sale, interest payable annually or in less periods, and an action to rescind a judicial act of a commercial nature, unless a different period is specifically provided, prescribe in four years; actions regarding improper operations of a company, and actions regarding certain classes of endorsable documents or of documents payable to bearer prescribe in three years; actions arising out of mortgage of ships prescribe in two years; actions arising out of maritime freight contracts, contracts of surety, and the provisioning of vessels prescribe in one year. The articles of the Code of Commerce above mentioned enumerate the periods of prescription in a number of other cases.

PRINCIPAL AND AGENT:

(C. C. arts. 1869-1985; Com. C. arts. 221-281).

Agency may be conferred by public or private instrument or orally. Acceptance may be express or implied. General power of attorney only confers power of administration even though power gives authority to do any act which grantee deems convenient in course of administration. (C. C. art. 1880). Special powers are necessary for following purposes (C. C. art. 1881): To make payments which are not in ordinary course of administration; to make contracts extinguishing obligations which existed at time power was granted; to compromise suit; to arbitrate; to waive jurisdiction; to renounce rights which have been acquired by prescription; to renounce right to appeal; to renounce or remit debts gratuitously, except in case of bankruptcy of debtor; to contract matrimony in name of grantor; to recognize natural children; to make any contract for purpose of obtaining or transferring real property; to make gifts, except in cases of small sums to employees; to loan or borrow money unless business of administration consists of loaning or borrowing, or unless it is absolutely necessary to borrow money to conserve property which is being administered; to lease real property for more than six years; to make grantee bailee, unless power refers to bailments or bailment is made as result of administration of property; to require grantee to perform any sort of personal services; to form company; to make grantee surety; to create incumbrances on real property; to accept inheritances; and to admit obligations existing prior to granting of power.

As general rule anyone capable of contracting may exercise power of attorney. Unless specifically provided to contrary, when power is given to more than one person, it is understood that it is to be accepted by one of them only.

Grantee is required to carry out power within limits of authority given. For instance, special power to sell does not include power to mortgage, nor to receive deferred payments, and power to collect debts does not include power to sue, nor to modify contract or remit debt. Grantee must prefer interests of grantor to his own. He should not carry out power if manifestly injurious to grantor. He must account for all of his operations and deliver to grantor everything received as result thereof, even though received improperly. He is not required to deliver anything obtained as result of illicit transactions, unless power itself has been legal and illicit gains are obtained by abuses of power. Grantee may not sell his own property to grantor or purchase grantor's property without express authority. He may delegate power to another, but is responsible for substitute unless he has been given express authority to substitute, and is always responsible when he has named substitute who is notoriously incompetent or insolvent. Grantee may revoke substitution at any time.

Powers of attorney which are to be presented in court, those for administration of property, and those which concern public instruments or matters which should be in form of public instruments, must themselves be in form of public instruments. (See topic Notaries Public ["Escribanos Públicos"] and C. C. art. 1184.)

Power terminates by revocation, by renunciation on part of grantee, by death of grantee or grantor, or when either of parties has become incapacitated. In case of death of grantor power is not terminated with regard to acts which are to be done after his death, and power also remains in force when its termination would otherwise cause dangerous delays. It is necessary that grantee and third persons know or should have known of termination of power in order to make it ineffective with regard to them. Everything that grantee does while he is justifiably ignorant of termination of power binds grantor. (C. C. arts. 1964-6).

Revocation of power may be express or implied. It is implied when grantor gives new power for same purpose and former grantee has knowledge of subsequent power. (C. C. art. 1971). Granting of special power revokes general power insofar as it affects matters dealt with in special power.

Agent must act within limits of his power but should not do less than what has been entrusted to him. Nature of business determines extent of powers needed to achieve purpose of agency. Agent is not considered to have acted beyond limits of his powers if result has been more advantageous than indicated in agency.

Functions of agent are bestowed on persons holding necessary representation and on persons who through their public office represent specified categories of persons or specified categories of property; on representatives of corporations and of public utility enterprises; on representatives of administration or liquidation of companies in cases so provided by civil or commercial law; on representatives of incompetent persons; on persons acting for another without authority (gestores oficiosos); on procurators; and on executors of estates.

Agent is obligated, by virtue of his acceptance of agency, to comply with terms of agency and he is liable for damages incurred by principal due to partial or total noncompliance, but if he finds it impossible to follow instructions he is not obliged to act without instructions, it being sufficient to take conservation measures indicated by circumstances. He is required to render account of his operations, and to deliver to principal everything he has received under agency, even though it was not owing to principal; latter can even demand any gains resulting from abuse of agent's powers, provided agency was lawful, but he is not entitled to fruits of unlawful agency.

Agent's acts within limits of his authority are deemed to have been done by principal himself; agent cannot enforce them himself, nor is he liable for them. Agent may sign contracts in his own name or in name of his principal. If he exceeds his authority in act that is not ratified by principal, such act is void, provided other contracting party was aware of true extent of agent's authority. Neither would agent be liable in such case, unless he obligated himself personally, or committed himself to obtain ratification. And he would be personally liable if other party was ignorant of his actual authority. Ratification by principal may be tacit, as by his actions, or if he is advised and remains silent. Ratification is retroactive to date of act.

With respect to third parties act is deemed to have been performed within limits of agency if its terms have been carried out, even though agent may have actually exceeded limits of his powers. Third party may not claim that powers have been

PRINCIPAL AND AGENT . . . *continued*
exceeded or that terms of agency have not been observed once principal has ratified action or wishes to ratify whatever has been done by agent.

Agency may be gratuitous or onerous. It is presumed to be gratuitous if there has been no agreement that agent is to receive remuneration for his work. It is presumed to be onerous if it consists of powers or functions conferred on agent by law or when it consists of work connected with lucrative profession or occupation of agent. If agency is onerous, principal must pay agent for his services. Amount of fees may consist of proportion of money or of goods that agent, in carrying out agency, has obtained or administered, except as provided in codes of procedures concerning lawyers and procurators. Principal must also compensate agent for losses he has incurred in carrying out agency without fault on his part.

PUBLIC INSTRUMENTS:

(C. C. arts. 979-996).

The following are public instruments: (1) Notarial documents ("escrituras públicas"), prepared by notaries in their registries ("protocolo") or by other public officers who have the same powers, together with copies of the same made in the manner provided by law; (2) other instruments prepared by notaries or public officers in the form provided by law; (3) entries by brokers in the cases and in the manner provided for in the Code of Commerce; (4) judicial documents made in the records by the clerks of courts and signed by the parties as provided in the laws of procedure, and copies of the same made by judicial orders; (5) bills of exchange accepted by the government or its delegates and credits issued by the Public Treasury; (6) bills of exchange of private individuals made in payment of customs duties with an annotation that they belong to the Public Treasury; (7) registrations of the public debt; (8) shares of stock of companies especially authorized; (9) bills and certificates of credits issued by authorized banks; and (10) records of marriages in the books of the church or in municipal registries and copies thereof.

Public instruments must be signed by the interested parties who appear as having taken part in their execution. Unemancipated minors, insane persons, the blind, nonresidents of the place, those who do not know how to sign, clerks of the office and of other offices authorized to prepare public documents, relatives of the public official to the fourth degree, bankrupts, the clergy, and those convicted of certain crimes, may not be witnesses to public documents.

The class of public instruments included in subdivision (1) above which are referred to as notarial documents ("escrituras públicas") in this digest are of most importance to foreigners. They are fully discussed under topic Notaries Public and referred to from time to time throughout the digest.

REAL PROPERTY:

Practically the same distinction exists in the Law of Argentina between real and personal property as exists at common law. The law governing real or "immovable" property ("inmuebles") is different in many respects from that governing personal or "movable" property ("muebles"). Real property includes land and all solids and liquids thereon and therein whatever the depth, as well as all things of a permanent character fixed to the soil. Personal property which has been made accessory to real property by the owner is also considered realty. Public documents evidencing title to real rights, other than mortgages and anticresis (see below) are also considered realty. (C. C. arts. 2311-4).

The ownership, possession and administration of real property, as well as encumbrances thereon, and its transfer are governed by the provisions of the Civil Code.

Some of the rights in real property other than ownership are as follows:

Usufruct ("usufructo") consisting of the right to use and enjoy property belonging to another, but without changing its substance. This right may also attach to personal property.

Use and habitation ("uso y habitación") consisting of the right to take from land the products which are necessary for the sustenance of a person and his family in the case of use, and the right to occupy a house in the case of habitation.

Servitude ("servidumbre") consisting of a temporary or perpetual right to use real property of another or exercise certain rights thereon, or to prevent the owner from exercising certain rights of ownership.

Mortgage ("hipoteca") see topic Mortgages.

Anticresis, a real right consisting of the possession of realty by a creditor for the purpose of applying the revenues to the interest or to the interest and capital of a debt.

Transfer of real property see topics Deeds and Registration; Records.

RECORDS:

Registry of Real Property.—Law 17801 of June 8, 1968 as am'd by Law 20089 of Jan. 12, 1973 and its regulations, regulates Real Property Registry.

Being a Federal law, registries existing in each province, Federal District and National Territory of Tierra del Fuego, Antártida and South Atlantic Islands are regulated by provisions of present law. Following documents shall be registered: (a) Those that constitute, transmit, declare, modify or extinguish rights upon real estate; (b) those that impose attachments and any other injunctions and (c) those documents established by other national or provincial laws.

To register these documents, certain formalities are required, e.g., to be acknowledged by a notary public or by an administrative or judicial resolution.

Registry is public. Anybody with legitimate interest can investigate legal status of real estate therein registered, and deeds, limitations and attachments recorded. Law does not determine fees for registering documents; its scope covers only general provisions. Fees usually depend upon amount of value of real property registered, capital in mortgages, etc., and vary in each town or province according to their respective laws.

For the law of any particular province the provincial law must be examined.

Registry of Persons.—Law 14586 of June 30, 1958 as am'd by Law 18248 of June 10, 1969, and Decree 3392 of Mar. 31, 1960, regulate provisions for registration of names of physical persons. Right to elect first name can be freely exercised except when names selected are ridiculous or express any particular ideological or political tendency. Foreign names are allowed to be recorded when there is a proper Spanish translation, in which case latter should be used. When foreign name has an easy pronunciation, is also name of parents and there is no translation of it into Spanish, recording officer is permitted to register it. In any case no person is entitled to have more than three initial names. Married women have option to add after their single name their husband's name preceded by preposition "de" (meaning "of"). After judicial separation it would be optional for divorcees to continue using their husband's name.

When foreigners apply for citizenship they may petition authorities to simplify spelling of their names. When pseudonyms have acquired notoriety, they are entitled to same full protection provided by law as real ones.

Law 22435 of Mar. 17, 1981 establishes functions of National Registry of Persons.

A national registry of vital statistics called "National Civil Registry" is regulated by Dec.-Law 8204 of Sept. 27, 1963 as am'd.

Commercial Register.—A public register is maintained by each commercial court for registration of all merchants under its jurisdiction who are required to register their business license and other documents such as articles of incorporation and by-laws in case of a corporation, powers of attorney for managing enterprise granted by merchants to factors or agents and revocation of same. Other acts such as contracts between husband and wife concerning property rights and adjudication of divorce or legal separation are also registered in public commercial register. (C. Com. Arts. 34-42).

Industrial Register.—Law 19961 of Nov. 27, 1972 created "National Industrial Register". All natural and juridic persons whether public or private, national or foreign, which engage in any kind of industrial activity in country must be registered within 30 days of obtaining administrative authorization. Registration must be made for each separate industrial activity on annual basis.

Foreign Investment Register.—See topic Foreign Investment.

SALES:

(Civil Code, arts. 1363-1407).

Sales of real property may be made subject to such conditions as the contracting parties desire to make. A general provision not to resell is void, but a contract not to resell to a specific person is valid.

The law of conditional sales of personal property as known in Anglo-Saxon countries, is not developed in Argentina. It is specifically forbidden to sell personal property with a condition that title shall not pass until the price is paid, or that the vendor may reclaim the property on returning the purchase price, nor may personal property be sold on condition that the sale is void if a purchaser can be obtained who offers a better price.

International Sale of Goods.—United Nations Convention for the International Sale of Goods, in force on Jan. 1, 1988. See topic Treaties and Part VII, Selected International Conventions.

SHIPPING:

Coastwise trade is restricted to national vessels. In order that a vessel may be considered as national: (a) It must be enrolled in the Argentine registry; (b) the captain and officers must be Argentine citizens; (c) at least one-fourth the crew must be Argentinians; (d) the language used in commands and documents must be Spanish. (Decree 19492 of July 25, 1944).

General Navigation Rules are contained in the Maritime, Fluvial and Lacustral Regime approved by Decree 4516 of May 16, 1973, as am'd.

Law 20,094 (Law of Navigation) of Jan. 15, 1973 as am'd and its regulations, contains provisions and regulations governing maritime contracts and liabilities.

Law 17,094 of Dec. 29, 1966 extends national sovereignty up to a distance of 200 marine miles, measured from low tide marks. However, freedom of navigation and aeronavigation is not affected by dispositions of law.

Law 18502 of Dec. 24, 1969 determines that provinces shall have exclusive jurisdiction up to a distance of three marine miles. From that point up to 200 marine miles mentioned above, Federal Government shall have absolute jurisdiction.

Law 18870 of Jan. 7, 1971 as am'd by Law 20395 of May 16, 1973 creates Administrative Court of Admiralty which shall be located in city of Buenos Aires. Court has jurisdiction: (a) Over all navigable waters of nation and states used for interjurisdictional commerce and coasts, as well as over ports under supervision of national jurisdiction; (b) in open sea when accidents have been caused or suffered by national ships or occurred on board. Decisions of court shall be to determine lack of professional skill, inability or negligence of persons directly or indirectly liable for accidents, as well as observance of laws and general regulations in force in each particular case. Court cannot impose civil or penal liabilities; however, if after considering case there is "prima facie" evidence of crime or offense, court must deliver record to competent judge for further proceedings. Court consists of seven members who are designated by Executive Power, and who hold office for two years and may be re-elected. Law sets forth in detail rights and duties of members of court as well as general rules of procedure.

STATUTES:

Spanish and Portugese law is principal source of Argentine legislation. Nevertheless, in compiling civil, commercial, penal, mining and aeronautic codes, laws of several foreign countries were considered. For example, Brazilian "Esbozo" written by Freitas and Napoleon Civil Code of France were taken into account for draftmanship of parts of Civil Code. For this reason French commentators are considered by lawyers and courts as much as, if not more than Spanish commentators. Regarding commercial code, Italian doctrine and legislation has been considered, particularly in such subjects as bills, notes, checks and commercial paper in general. Aeronautic Code is mainly based on international agreements and its provisions are very similar to well-known conventions of Warsaw, Chicago, etc. Mining Code follows old Spanish laws and, finally Penal, Civil and Criminal Procedure Codes have been strongly influenced by Italian doctrine and laws.

TAXATION:

Under national constitution, Congress has exclusive power to levy import and export duties and direct taxes. Power to levy other forms of taxation has been reserved under said constitution to each of the 22 provinces of republic, provisions of whose tax laws are too numerous to be reviewed here.

Internal Revenue Taxes.—There is an internal revenue tax on wines, ciders, artificial beverages, whisky, cigarettes, cigars, tobacco, beers, insurance premiums, steamship passages, alcohol, alcoholic beverages, other alcoholic preparations, imported vermouths, medicinal specialties, natural mineral waters, artificial mineral waters, veterinary specialties, and toilet, cosmetic and sanitary preparations. Amount of internal revenue tax payable in each instance is determined in conformity with provisions of numerous laws, which have been compiled in Decree 2682 of Oct. 23, 1979 as am'd, regulated by Decree 875 of Apr. 25, 1980 as am'd.

Real Property Tax.—All lands and buildings situated in federal district (City of Buenos Aires), states and national territory, are subject to this tax; rates varying according to several factors, such as type of improvements made on land before or after certain periods of time, value of buildings constructed upon land and use of same. In provinces (states) tax is similar to one in force in federal district and rates also vary depending upon type of lands (agricultural lands, forestries, uncultivated lots, etc.), location and improvements.

Municipal taxes also regulate this matter together with provisions regarding taxes for city services such as light, sanitation, water, maintenance of streets and sidewalks, etc. In general, laws and regulations governing this subject are very detailed and are amended often. Surcharges are also imposed from time to time according to type and area of land.

Added Value Tax.—Sales made and personalty located within country, works, insurance, leases, rendering of services and imports of personalty are subject to this tax during final commercialization stage. Tax shall be levied on net price obtained by deducting from amount of invoice discounts or other reductions made according to commercial usage.

Rate is 18%.

Books, newspapers, periodicals, among others, are exempted from this tax.

(Law 23349 of Sept. 19, 1986 as am'd and its Regulations in Decree 2407 of Dec. 23, 1986 as am'd and Decree 769 of June 28, 1988).

Income Tax.—Law 20628 of Dec. 27, 1973, t.o. 1986 as am'd and its regulations in Decree 2353 of Dec. 18, 1986 as am'd imposes "Profits Tax" (Impuesto a las Ganancias).

Any person, corporation or undistributed estate while the will is not probated or the heirs not recognized by judicial decree, resident in Argentina, is subject to tax on worldwide income and when resident abroad is subject to tax on income obtained from sources within Argentina. Export trade benefits related to merchandise produced, manufactured or purchased in Argentina, even those of agencies, branches, representatives or intermediaries. International activities, such as transportation, communications, news services, insurance or reinsurance, movie films distribution and others are made subject to specific percentages in determining that portion of gains which should be Argentine source.

Except when transactions refer to loans or technology contracts, legal acts between local company of foreign capital and its foreign parent company will be considered as effected between independent parties.

Exemptions.—Among others: (1) Income of religious institutions; (2) income of charitable, scientific, artistic and educational membership associations, provided their income is devoted to purpose of their creation; (3) copyrights when received directly by author of work protected by registration; (4) interest of debentures, bonds and other credits issued to finance new works or investments declared of national interest for this purpose by government; (5) premiums on stock issuance; (6) interest paid by national, provincial and municipal agencies as well as interest paid by official banks for loans obtained abroad; (7) interest earned by financial institutions and banks in certain credit transactions.

Basic deduction for individuals residing in country is allowed if resident taxpayer obtains third category income basic deduction may be increased, depending upon exact nature of such third category income.

Dependents.—Taxpayers with dependents residing in Argentina having an income of no more than certain amount from any source are entitled to additional deductions: For spouse, for each infant or incapacitated child, and for each additional dependent authorized by law.

Deductions for Doctor's Fees, Medicine and Funeral Expenses.—Annual deduction per dependent is allowed for medicine; funeral expenses are also allowed up to certain amount.

Community Property.—When a married couple is under system of community property, each spouse is taxed for his or her own income from personal services or work, commerce or industry, and with respect to separate property or property obtained with money from salary or personal fees if, in case of wife, it so appears from proper document of purchase. Husband shall also be charged for community property income, except in case of judicial separation. Companies owned by spouses are not treated as such for tax purposes, being subject to special rules.

Categories.—Gains are divided into four categories: (1) Gains from real property: including rents from rural or urban property, with or without furniture, either in cash or in kind or any other form, and rental value of any property, except his own dwelling, used by its owner, this exemption does not apply for recreational properties; (2) gains from capital: certificates, cedulas, debentures, bonds, credits, loans, rentals of personal property, royalties, periodic payments for good will and similar rights; annuities, benefits or participations in life insurance; amounts received for forbearing from acting, except in commerce, industry, profession or employment; (3) company gains and those earned by certain other types of mercantile entities or persons: corporations' profits, profits earned by other companies or individual proprietorships; profits of brokers; merchants auctioneers, consignees and any other commercial auxilliaries not expressly included in fourth category; profits derived from sale of any real property; any income not included in other categories; (4) profits from personal work: (renta del Trabajo Pesonal): salaries of public employees; income from excercise of professional endeavors; income from activities of brokers, customs expeditors, commercial travelers; income obtained by corporate directors, administrators, attorneys-in-fact, business managers and similar personnel; fees of executors, receivers and trustees; employee's salaries, compensation paid by cooperatives to members for services rendered; pensions and retirement income received as a consequence of personal labor.

Deductible expenses in general are only those made in order to obtain and keep the taxable income, among them: interest on loans or credits and expenses for obtainment, renewal and cancellation thereof; taxes and duties imposed on income-producing property, including penalties for delinquency, except for fraud to the treasury; premiums for insuring income-producing property and for life insurance, with some limitations; gifts to government, provinces, and municipalities; gifts to entities with public and private participation, to extent of such public participation therein up to maximum of 5% of taxpayer's total net income. Also deductible are depreciation and depletion of assets, subject to special provisions; payment of fees or salaries to directors, advisers and organisms of direction acting from abroad; amounts directly invested in mining; amounts invested in housing construction. Fees and other remunerations paid for technical, financial or other types of services performed abroad shall be deductible, as indicated by law. In no category may taxpayer deduct personal expenses, interest and capital of same taxpayer, income tax, and other similar taxes, depreciation of good will, trademarks and similar assets, gifts, except to government, municipalities and certain charitable organizations, net losses resulting from illegal activities and others. From first category income, expenses are deductible for upkeep of real property. From third category income, following are especially deductible: necessary expenses incurred in course of business; depreciation on reserves against bad debts in form approved by Internal Revenue Bureau; organization expenses, which are deductible first year or in first five years, at option of taxpayer; commissions and expenses incurred abroad under certain circumstances and other similar expenses, but legal reserves of corporations are not deductible; depreciation of assets and other similar deductions.

Tax Rates.—Net income of individuals and taxable estates is subject to a progressive tax rate, ranging from 6% to 30%.

Foreign and domestic corporations are subject to 30% tax rate on their taxable income.

Salaries and fees paid to members of board of directors, councils or other organisms of direction and fees or other compensations paid for technical advice, financial or of any other character, when the directors, members or advisers render services from abroad, are subject to a sole and final withholding tax of 30%. 60% of such technical assistance fees and/or salaries is considered net taxable income and 90% of gross payment to nonresident member of board of directors for purposes of said withholding tax.

All income paid or credited to a foreign corporation, any other nonresident beneficiary, or to their attorneys-in-fact, agents or other representatives in Argentina is subject to a withholding tax of 30%. Only 40% of interest on loans obtained abroad is taxed at 30%.

Tax on Real and Personal Property.—(Law 23966 of Aug. 8, 1991 as am'd regulated by Decree 379 of Mar. 2, 1992). Tax is levied on personal and real property of individual or undivided estates, not included in economic process, located in Argentina or abroad and personal and real property of nonresidents, individuals and undivided estates located in Argentina. Tax rate is 0.5% of property value.

Tax on Sale of Real Estate.—(Law 23905 of Feb. 16, 1991). Sale of real estate by individuals and undivided estates is taxed at rate of 1.5% on transfer value.

Tax Evasion.—(Law 23771 of Feb. 22, 1990 as am'd). Imprisonment is imposed for evasion of payment of taxes and social security contributions, including withholding agents for non-deposit of amounts withheld.

TRADEMARKS:

Law 22362 of Dec. 26, 1980 and its regulation, Decree 558 of Mar. 24, 1981, govern matters related to trademarks and tradenames. (Law on Transfer of Technology No. 22426 of Mar. 12, 1981 and its regulations).

Following may be registered as trademarks to distinguish products and services: One or more words with or without conceptual contents, drawings, emblems, monograms, engravings, vignettes, stamps, images, bands, color combinations by which products or packages are distinguished, containers, letters or numbers with special drawing, advertising slogans, and any other sign with distinctive characteristics. Following cannot be used as trademarks: Names, words, and signs which are given to products or services by manufacturer describing its nature, function or qualities; names, words, signs and advertising slogans which have become of general usage before application for registration; form which is given to products; color of products. Following cannot be registered: Trademark identical or similar to another trademark previously registered; national or foreign place names of native country; drawings or expressions contrary to good morals. Trademarks which would produce confusion with other products may not be used. Names and photographs of persons may not be used as trademarks without consent of persons or their heirs; nor can advertising slogans lacking originality be used.

Ownership and exclusive right of trademark is obtained by registration. To have legitimate interest is legal requirement for ownership of trademark or to oppose applications filed by third parties. Protection of trademark lasts for ten years and may be renewed indefinitely for periods of ten years if said trademark has been used within period of five years prior to each renewal in commercialization of product, or rendering of service, or as part of name of activity. Rights to trademarks may be transferred freely to third parties, provided transfer is recorded in National Direction of Industrial Property.

Petition for trademark registration must specify: Name of petitioner, domicile, description of mark and indication of products or services to be identified. Once application for registration has been filed it is published officially. National Direction of Industrial Property must make decision within 30 days. Art. 20 of Law establishes that application for renewal of trademark must be accompanied by sworn statement declaring that trademark has been used within five years prior to renewal, and for at least one of classes of Classification of Products and Services (adopted by Decree 558

See Topical Index in front part of this volume.

TRADEMARKS . . . *continued*
of Mar. 24, 1981), or as tradename. Product, service or activity for which trademark was used will also have to be stated.

Right of ownership of trademark expires by waiver of holder, termination of term of duration or by court order nullifying or cancelling registration. Right of action for nullification prescribes after ten years. Order of nullifying can be obtained against holder of registration that knew or was in condition to know that trademark belonged to third party or when trademark has been registered for purpose of selling it to third party. Judicial cancellation can be requested by legitimate interested party for nonlocal use of trademark in any of classes in which it was registered, within five years prior to date of filing such request.

Misuse of trademarks or commission of acts made illegal by Law is punishable by fine and arrest. Those who commit punishable acts will be liable for from three months to two years imprisonment plus fine. Attachment may be obtained by owner of trademark against articles which bear his trademark illegally.

TREATIES:

Convention on the Limitation Period in the International Sale of Goods, 1980; Montevideo Treaty, 1980 ("Latin American Integration Association"), Asuncion Treaty, Signed on Mar. 26, 1991 creating common market "Southern Common Market" (MERCOSUR); Paris Convention of Mar. 20, 1883 for Protection of Industrial Property; Inter-American Convention of legal regime of powers of attorney to be used abroad; Inter-American Convention on international commercial arbitration; and Inter-American Convention on conflicts of laws concerning bills of exchange, promissory notes, and invoices. Signed at Panama on Jan. 30, 1975. Inter-American Conventions: On conflicts of laws concerning commercial companies, on general rules of private international law, on extraterritorial validity of foreign judgments and arbitral awards, and on execution of preventive measures. Signed at Montevideo on May 8, 1979. International Convention for the Protection of Performers, Producers of Phonograms and Broadcasting Organizations, signed at Rome on Oct. 26, 1961. International Convention on applicable law for Representation and Intermediation Contracts, signed at The Hague on Mar. 14, 1978, Convention on recognition of the legal personality of corporations, associations and foreign foundations, The Hague June 1st, 1956. Multilateral Trade Negotiations, The Uruguay Round, Final Act, Marrakesh, Apr. 15, 1994 and Agreement Establishing the World Trade Organization, Marrakesh, Apr. 15, 1994.

Treaties in force between U.S. and Argentina.—

Agricultural Commodities.—Agreement providing for sale and purchase of cottonseed oil, etc. Signed at Washington Apr. 25, 1955; Agricultural commodities agreement to finance sale to Argentina of edible oils and/or fat. Signed at Buenos Aires Dec. 21, 1955; Agricultural commodities agreement with exchange of notes. Signed at Washington June 12, 1959.

Atomic Energy.—Agreement providing for grant to assist in acquisition of certain nuclear research and training equipment and materials of May 1960. Agreement for cooperation concerning civil uses of atomic energy. Signed June 25, 1969.

Copyright.—Copyright arrangement. (1934).

Economics and Technical Cooperation.—General Agreement for program of technical cooperation. Signed at Buenos Aires June 3, 1957.

Education.—Agreement for financing certain educational exchange programs. Signed at Buenos Aires Aug. 21, 1963.

Extradition.—Treaty on extradition between the two countries. Signed Jan. 21, 1972.

Investment Guaranties.—Agreement relating to investment guaranties under §413(b)(4) of Mutual Security Act of 1954, as am'd. Signed at Buenos Aires Dec. 22, 1959.

Inland Navigation.—Treaty for free navigation of rivers Parana and Uruguay. Signed at San Jose de Flores July 10, 1853.

Postal Matters.—Agreement for exchange of insured parcel post packages. Signed in 1939.

Publications.—Agreement relating to exchange of official publications. Entered into force on Oct. 17, 1939.

Social Security.—Agreement by reciprocal notes concerning payment of social security benefits to citizens of one of parties residing abroad. (1972).

Taxation.—Agreement for relief from double taxation on earnings derived from operation of ships and aircraft (1950).

Tracking Stations.—Agreement relating to co-operative program for optical satellite tracking station at Villa Dolores, Argentina (1962); Agreement by reciprocal notes for installation of OMEGA navigation station in Chubut Province. Signed Dec. 4, 1970.

Trade and Commerce.—Trade agreement and exchanges of notes. Signed at Buenos Aires Oct. 14, 1941; Agreement by reciprocal notes concerning operation of Trade convention of 1941. Signed Aug. 3, 1966.

Visas.—Agreement relating to reciprocal waiver of nonimmigrant passport visa fees (1942).

Bilateral agreements for relief from double taxation on earnings derived from operation of ships and aircraft, with Spain and Israel signed at Buenos Aires on Nov. 30, 1978 and May 19, 1981, respectively. Agreements to avoid double taxation on income tax with Sweden, signed at Buenos Aires on Sept. 3, 1962, Bolivia; signed at Buenos Aires on Oct. 30, 1976; Chile, signed at Santiago on Nov. 13, 1976; Germany, signed at Buenos Aires on July 13, 1978; France and Austria, signed at Buenos Aires on Apr. 4, 1979 and Sept. 13, 1979, respectively; Italy, signed at Rome on Nov. 15, 1979; Brazil, signed at Buenos Aires on May 17, 1980; Spain, signed at Madrid on July 21, 1992 and Canada, signed at Buenos Aires on Apr. 29, 1993.

International Sale of Goods.—United Nations Convention for the International Sale of Goods, in force on Jan. 1, 1988. See topic Sales and Part VII, Selected International Conventions.

TRUSTS:

Trusts as developed by the common law are unknown in the law of Argentina. However, the complete freedom of contracting which exists in Argentina makes it possible, as a practical matter, to constitute a relationship substantially the same as that of trust. Trusts are recognized in the law of debentures (Law No. 8875 of 1912) which provides for the borrowing of money by companies and the issuance of their obligations as security for payment. See topic Corporations (Stock Companies).

WILLS:

(C. C. arts. 3606-3823).

Every person in possession of his mental faculties and capable of manifesting his wish, may dispose of his property by will, unless he is under 18 years of age. Dispositions which are illegal or physically impossible of carrying out or contrary to public policy, are void. The following conditions are prohibited: of dwelling in a particular place or in a place designated by third party; of changing or not changing religion; marrying with a certain person or with the approval of a third person or in a certain place or time; of remaining single, either permanently or temporarily, or of not marrying a certain person; and of divorcing. (C. C. art. 531).

Only a part of the estate may be freely disposed of by will. See topic Descent and Distribution.

The law of the domicile of the testator at the time of making his will determines his capacity to make the will, but the validity of the contents of the will is determined by the law of the domicile of the testator at the time of his death. Capacity to make a will is determined as of the time the will is executed. Insane persons may only make wills during lucid intervals. The law presumes that every person is in his right mind until the contrary is proven. Deaf mutes who can neither read nor write may not make a will. Mutual or joint wills in a single document are prohibited.

The nullity of a will because defective in form nullifies all of the dispositions contained therein, but the nullity of one disposition does not affect the other dispositions of the will. When the signature of the testator is required he must write out his full name without initials, but a signature which is in the form which the person is accustomed to use in signing public and private documents is sufficient. A citizen of Argentina in a foreign country may make a will in the form established by the law of the country in which it is executed. A will made in a foreign country before a minister of Argentina, chargé d'affaires or a consul and two witnesses domiciled in the place where the will is made and containing the seal of the legation or consulate is valid. If there are no such officers in the place, a minister or consul of a friendly nation may exercise the same function. Copies of open wills and of the envelopes containing closed wills, made in foreign countries are sent by the minister or consul to the Minister of Foreign Relations who certifies to the signature of the minister or consul and sends the same to the judge of the last domicile of the deceased in the republic for incorporation in the protocol of the notary of that place.

There are four forms of wills: Holographic wills, open wills or wills in the form of public instruments, closed or sealed wills, and military wills. The law regarding the nature and effect of the dispositions is the same regardless of the class of will. The testator may choose the form of will which he desires to adopt, provided he has the physical and intellectual capacity to execute that class of will.

Holographic Wills.—To be valid a holographic will must be written entirely by the testator, dated and signed by him. Any writing on the will if not in the handwriting of the testator nullifies the will if made by the order or consent of the testator. Holographic wills may be written in any language. The will is not invalid because the place where it has been made is not stated, or because it is erroneously stated. It may be written at different times and in different places. In this case the will may be dated and signed at different times or after it is finally completed. Holographic wills must be separate from other writings and books of the testator. Letters cannot constitute holographic wills. The testator may, if he desires, have the will witnessed and may deposit it with a notary or use any other means he desires to secure it.

Open Wills.—A will in the form of a public instrument or open will is one which is prepared for the testator by a notary. A person who is deaf, dumb or a deaf mute may not make a will in this form, but a blind person may. A notary who is a relative of the testator in the direct line to any degree or in a collateral line to the third degree of consanguinity or affinity may not take part in the preparation of the will. Three witnesses residing in the place are required. The testator may dictate his will to the notary or give it to him already written, or may give the notary the provisions which he desires to make in order that the notary may make the will in the ordinary form. The notary must state in the will the place of execution, the date, the names of the witnesses, their residences and age, and whether he has made the will or has received the provisions already prepared. The will must be read to the testator in the presence of the witnesses and signed by the testator, the witnesses and the notary. At least one of the witnesses must be able to write, and if he signs for any of the other witnesses, the notary must so state. If the testator does not know how to sign or is unable to do so, another person or one of the witnesses may sign for him. In this case two of the witnesses at least must know how to sign. If the testator does not understand the Spanish language, the presence of two interpreters who reduce the will to Spanish is necessary. In this case the will must be written in both languages. The witnesses must understand both languages. Neither the notary nor the witnesses nor their wives or relatives to the fourth degree may take advantage of any disposition under the will.

Closed Wills.—One who does not know how to read cannot execute a closed will. A closed will is signed by the testator, and placed in a sealed package. The will must be delivered to a notary public in the presence of five resident witnesses with a statement that its contents is the will of the testator. The notary certifies as to the presentation on the cover of the will which certificate is signed by the testator and all the witnesses. At least three of the witnesses must be able to sign for themselves. If the testator is unable to sign, another may sign for him. The notary must include in the certificate the name of the testator, his residence, the names and residences of the witnesses and of whoever may sign for the testator, and the place and date. The delivery of the will to the notary and the entries on the cover must be one continuous act. If the testator cannot talk but is able to write, the will must be written and signed in his handwriting and the statement that it is his will must be made by him on the cover. Deaf persons may execute closed wills. If a closed will is not valid for defect of form, it may be valid as an holographic will, if it complies with all the requirements of holographic wills.

WILLS . . . *continued*

Military Wills.—In times of war, sailors on war vessels, and soldiers on military expeditions or in besieged places, or in camp or barracks outside of the republic, and prisoners and camp followers may execute wills before certain specified officers and the required number of witnesses. If the testator dies within 90 days after the situation ceases which permits him to make a military will, his statement is valid.

On the death of the testator holographic wills and closed wills must be presented to the judge of the last domicile of the testator. The judge takes evidence of the handwriting of the testator in the case of holographic wills and if he finds them genuine certifies to each page, and has them recorded. Closed wills cannot be opened by the judge until the witnesses and notary have recognized their signatures and that of the testator. The will is then recorded. If the notary and witnesses cannot appear, the judge receives proof as to the handwriting. Any person who has an interest in a closed will may petition the court to open it.

Witnesses.—Witnesses must have legal capacity to act as such, must be known to the notary or be identified for him, and must understand the language of the testator and the language in which the will is written; they should be residents of the place where the will is executed and must be male and of age. Neither ascendants nor descendants of the testator may be witnesses. Executors and guardians may not be witnesses of the will by which they are appointed. Neither heirs nor the legatees nor anyone who receives a gift from the testator nor the relatives of the notary up to the fourth degree, nor the clerks in his office nor his servants may be witnesses. The blind, deaf, mute and insane cannot be witnesses to wills.

See Topical Index in front part of this volume.

AUSTRALIA LAW DIGEST REVISER

Arthur Robinson & Hedderwicks
GPO Box 1776Q
Melbourne VIC Australia 3001
Telephone: 61 3 9614 1011
Fax: 61 3 9614 4661

Reviser Profile

Introduction: Arthur Robinson & Hedderwicks represents the merger in 1984 of two of Australia's oldest and best known legal firms, Arthur Robinson & Co. and Hedderwick, Fookes & Alston. The founder of Arthur Robinson & Co., Sir Arthur Robinson, KCMG, was prominent in many aspects of Victorian commercial and political life, serving as Attorney-General of the State from 1919 until 1924. Partners of Hedderwick, Fookes & Alston also played a prominent role in Australian public and commercial life, and included Chairmen of some of the nation's major corporations. As of July 1996, Arthur Robinson & Hedderwicks comprised 61 partners and over 150 other lawyers.

Structure and Areas of Practice: Arthur Robinson & Hedderwicks is divided into different specialist departments of lawyers, covering commercial law, commercial litigation, real property work and private client work. The firm's areas of practice comprise: General Corporate Practice, Mergers & Acquisitions, Banking & Finance, Insolvency, Natural Resources, Environmental Law, Governmental Negotiations, Privatisations, Taxation, Trade Practices (antitrust), Aviation Law, Media & Telecommunications, Commercial Litigation, Industrial & Intellectual Property, Sports & Entertainment Law, Real Estate & Property Development, Labor Law and Private Clients.

Each department is distinctive in terms of specialist skills, although in major areas a particular skill may exist in more than one department. Each department is primarily responsible for a number of different corporate clients. However, a department will refer a matter to another department where different specialist skills are relevant to a client's needs.

Client Base: Arthur Robinson & Hedderwicks has been closely identified throughout this century with many of Australia's major mining houses and industrial corporations.

The firm has been particularly prominent in the structuring and financing of many of the largest Australian and Papua New Guinean mineral and petroleum ventures. Projects in which Arthur Robinson & Hedderwicks has acted in a major advisory role include: the Hamersley iron ore project; the Channar iron ore project; the Weipa bauxite project; the Bougainville copper project; the Roxby Downs uranium and copper project; the Ok Tedi gold and copper project; the Mary Kathleen uranium project; the Kidston gold project; the Lihir gold project; the Greenvale nickel project; the Blair Athol, German Creek and Curragh coal projects; the Argyle diamond project; the North-west Shelf domestic gas and liquified petroleum gas projects; the unitization of the Cooper Basin natural gas, petroleum and liquified petroleum gas project; the Jackson to Moonie petroleum pipeline project; and the Alice Springs to Darwin natural gas pipeline project.

The firm also acted for BHP, Australia's largest public company, in its acquisition and restructuring of Utah International's Australian assets—comprising some of Australia's largest coal mines.

Arthur Robinson & Hedderwicks acted as legal advisers for some of Australasia's most significant secondary processing ventures, such as the QAL alumina refinery, the Gladstone aluminum smelter, the Bluff (New Zealand) aluminum smelter and the Portland aluminium smelter.

Support Services: A modern law firm cannot survive and compete without up-to-date research facilities and information systems. Arthur Robinson & Hedderwicks has one of the largest private law libraries in Australia with a comprehensive collection of law reports and legislation from all Australian jurisdictions and Papua New Guinea, and a vast array of texts and journals from all over the world.

With a staff of seven, the library is able to provide our lawyers with up-to-the-minute information from hard copy or computerised information retrieval systems such as LEXIS.

The demands of modern international legal practice also require ever-increasing document production capability both in terms of quality and expedition.

The firm's extensive integrated word processing facilities are operated at least 16 hours per weekday and are also operated on all other days of the year except for Christmas Day and Good Friday.

Printing, photocopying and communications facilities are among the most modern available.

National Legal Federation: In 1987 Arthur Robinson & Hedderwicks joined with the leading legal firms in the capitals of the other Australian mainland States to create an historic national and international legal federation. The Allens Arthur Robinson Group represents the largest, most extensive and most powerful legal network ever established in Australia, with offices in Melbourne, Sydney, Perth, Brisbane, Adelaide and Canberra.

The six firms in the Allens Arthur Robinson Group are: Arthur Robinson & Hedderwicks (Melbourne), Allen Allen & Hemsley (Sydney and Canberra), Parker & Parker (Perth), Feez Ruthning (Brisbane) and Finlaysons (Adelaide).

The Allens Arthur Robinson Group also has offices in London, Singapore, Hong Kong and Port Moresby (Papua New Guinea), has an association with the firm of Wiriadinata and Widyawan in Jakarta, Indonesia, a contact lawyer in Japan and a representative in Shanghai.

Clients of each of the member firms have access to the interstate and international offices of the associate firms, and can draw on the expertise of experienced partners and staff in specialized areas of practice in Australia and overseas.

AUSTRALIA LAW DIGEST

(The following is a list of all Topics, including cross-references, covered in this Digest.)

PART I
THE COMMONWEALTH

PART II
THE STATES

AUSTRALIA LAW DIGEST

Revised for 1997 edition by

ARTHUR ROBINSON & HEDDERWICKS, of Melbourne.

Preliminary Note.—In order to present the law of Australia accurately and clearly, this Digest is divided into two parts: Part I, presenting the laws of the Commonwealth, and Part II, presenting the laws of the several states comprising the Commonwealth. Particular topics will be found in Part I or Part II, or in both parts, according to which law governs the subject.

See topic Statutes.

PART I
THE COMMONWEALTH

ACTIONS:

Foreign claims and foreign law are regarded as matters of fact and must be proved accordingly. However, Commonwealth Constitution provides that full faith and credit must be given throughout Commonwealth to laws, public acts and records and judicial proceedings of every Australian state; and Evidence Acts of the various states direct courts to take judicial notice of Acts of Parliament of U. K., and of certain records, seals and signatures of officials of other Australian states.

Foreign Judgments.—Foreign Judgments Act 1991 enacts statutory system of registration of foreign judgments in Federal Courts or State/Territory Supreme Courts. Act applies to judgments of courts of declared countries that give reciprocal treatment to enforcement of Australian judgments. Upon registration foreign judgment has same force and effect as judgment of court in which it is registered. Requirements for registration and grounds to set aside registration parallel both common law and currently existing State legislation in this area. Act replaces existing common law action on judgment debt in respect of judgments registrable under Act, and now completely replaces State and Territory legislation relating to registration of foreign judgments. Act contains some innovations that do not exist in existing State legislation: including prohibition of enforcement of judgments of declared countries viewed as giving substantially less favourable treatment to Australian judgments, and choice of judgment in foreign currency or converted to Australian dollars at date of application for registration.

Prohibition Orders.—Foreign Proceedings (Excess of Jurisdiction) Act 1984 empowers Attorney-General to make order prohibiting: (a) Production in foreign court or to foreign authority of document located in Australia; (b) doing of act in Australia in relation to document located in Australia with intention or likely result of document or evidence of or information about documents contents being produced in foreign court or to foreign authority; (c) giving of evidence or information in foreign court or to foreign authority by Australian citizen or resident about document located in Australia; or (d) production of document or giving of evidence of or information about document in Australian court or to Austrialian authority for purposes of proceedings in foreign court. Such order only made if Attorney-General satisfied that: (i) Making of order desirable for protection of national interest; (ii) assumption of jurisdiction by foreign court or manner of exercise of jurisdiction is contrary to international law, or is inconsistent with international comity or practice; or (iii) taking or manner of taking of action by foreign authority is contrary to international law, or is inconsistent with international comity or practice. These orders can be enforced by injunction.

Blocking Orders.—Attorney-General may by instrument block foreign antitrust judgments if satisfied that this is necessary for protection of national interest, or that assumption of jurisdiction or exercise of power by foreign court is contrary to international law, or is inconsistent with international comity or practice. In such case defendants in foreign antitrust proceedings can recover damages enforced against them. Attorney-General may declare judgment given by foreign court in antitrust proceedings enforceable if reciprocal agreement with other country. Attorney-General may make order blocking foreign government actions or decisions under laws related to trade or commerce, banking, insurance or external affairs where such action or decision imposes obligation on Australian person to be performed in Australia if such blocking order is desirable in national interest. Attorney-General may make order prohibiting compliance in Australia with certain foreign court judgments relating to trade or commerce, banking, insurance or external affairs where such judgment imposes obligation to be performed in Australia and such blocking order is desirable in national interest.

Penalty for contravention of order: (a) Maximum A$50,000 or 12 months' imprisonment or both for natural person; (b) maximum A$250,000 for corporation.

Foreign Evidence.—Foreign Evidence Act 1994 deals with use of foreign evidence in Australian courts and Australian Evidence in foreign courts. Superior Court may make order if it appears in interests of justice to do so, for examination of person outside Australia. This evidence may be tendered in evidence in proceedings. Attorney-General may request foreign country to provide testimony of person, or exhibit annexed to such testimony, to be used in criminal proceeding or related civil proceeding. Australian Securities Commission may request foreign business authority to provide testimony, or exhibit annexed to such testimony, for use in civil proceedings not being related civil proceedings or proceedings under Corporations Law. Evidence may be taken in Australian courts for use in proceedings instituted in foreign country. Attorney-General may make written order prohibiting production of document or thing or giving of evidence to prevent prejudice to Australia's security.

Superior court means High Court, Federal or Family Court of Australia, Supreme Court of State when exercising federal jurisdiction and Supreme Court of a Territory.

Related civil proceeding means proceeding arising under Proceeds of Crime Act 1987, Customs Act 1901 or proceeding for recovery of tax, duty, levy or charge payable to Commonwealth.

Evidence and Procedure (New Zealand) Act 1994 provides for statutory system for service in Australia and New Zealand of New Zealand and Australian subpoenas, for video link and telephone evidence and special rules for judicial notice of New Zealand laws.

See also Part II—topic Depositions.

ADMINISTRATIVE LAW:

In addition to judicial review of administrative decisions by means of prerogative writs under common law and equitable remedies of injunction or declaration, there are statutory remedies and grounds of review available.

Administrative Appeals Tribunal Act 1975 establishes Commonwealth Administrative Appeals Tribunal to provide for review of certain decisions on their merits. Any person whose interest is affected by certain Commonwealth Government decisions may apply on payment of prescribed fee (if any) to Administrative Appeals Tribunal for such review. Such person may also obtain written statement of reasons for decision from decision-maker. However Attorney-General can certify that certain information is not to be disclosed in reasons of decision-maker, where such disclosure is contrary to public interest. Power to review comes from Administrative Appeals Tribunal Act 1975 and from other Acts which provide that application may be made to Administrative Appeals Tribunal in respect of certain decisions made under those Acts. On reviewing decision, tribunal can exercise all powers and discretions conferred on decision-maker; it can affirm or vary original decision or set aside original decision and either substitute its own decision or remit matter for reconsideration by original decision-maker in accordance with such directions and recommendations as tribunal might give. Appeal from decision of tribunal on question of law lies to Federal Court.

The Administrative Decisions (Judicial Review) Act 1977 provides that person aggrieved by decision made under certain Commonwealth enactments may apply to Federal Court for order of review on certain grounds such as lack of jurisdiction by decision-maker or breach of natural justice. Persons aggrieved by failure to make decision by person with duty to make decision may also apply to Court for order of review. Reasons for decision may be obtained by person who is entitled to make application for review.

Ombudsman.—The Ombudsman Act 1976 provides for complaint to and investigation by Ombudsman in relation to administrative actions. This Act is similar to State Ombudsman Acts—see Part II—topic Administrative Law for description of these Acts.

Freedom of Information.—Freedom of Information Act 1982 gives members of public legally enforceable right of access to government documents unless those documents are exempted from operation of Act. Act applies to most Commonwealth departments and authorities. However, it does not apply to Parliament or parliamentary documents or documents relating to political party matters. Act does not require person to establish any special interest before he is entitled to seek or be granted access to documents. Following categories of documents are specifically exempt from operation of Act: (a) Documents affecting national security, defence, international relations of Commonwealth or which divulge matters communicated in confidence by foreign governments to Commonwealth; (b) documents concerning relations between Commonwealth and States; (c) cabinet and executive council documents; (d) internal working documents; (e) documents affecting enforcement of law and protection of public safety; (f) documents to which secrecy provisions of other laws apply; (g) documents affecting financial or property interests of Commonwealth; (h) documents concerning certain operations of government agencies; (i) documents affecting personal privacy; (j) documents subject to legal professional privilege; (k) documents relating to business affairs; (l) documents affecting national economy; (m) documents containing material obtained in confidence; (n) documents, disclosure of which would be contempt of Parliament or contempt of court; (o) certain documents arising out of Companies and Securities legislation; and (p) electoral rolls and related documents, except that individuals may obtain such documents relating to themselves.

Appeals.—Refusal to grant access is reviewable by internal system of review and by way of application to Administrative Appeals Tribunal. There is right of appeal from Administrative Appeals Tribunal to Federal Court on question of law. Act also allows documents held by government and by agencies in respect of citizen's personal affairs and to which citizen has had lawful access to be amended by citizen where record incorrect. Act can be used in conjunction with other statutory remedies.

Treaties.—High Court has held that signing of treaty could give rise to legitimate expectation that government decision-makers would make decisions consistent with Australia's obligations under treaty, irrespective of whether treaty obligations have been enacted into Australian law. Attorney-General has signalled intention of Commonwealth government to legislate to override its decision.

AIR NAVIGATION:

By Civil Aviation (Carriers Liability) Act 1959, 1929 Warsaw Convention and parts of 1955 Protocol to Warsaw Convention and 1961 Guadalajara Convention have force of law in Australia. By that Act and Air Accidents (Commonwealth Government Liability) Act 1963 liability of domestic carriers for death and or injury caused by air accidents is set at maximum of A$500,000 per person. Maximum for other carriers is

AIR NAVIGATION . . . *continued*
260,000 SDRs and liability of all carriers for loss and injury to registered baggage is maximum of A$900. After expiration of two years from accident carrier's liability under Act is extinguished.

Air Navigation Act 1920 gives Governor-General power to make regulations for purpose of carrying out and giving effect to Convention on International Civil Aviation concluded at Chicago in 1944, and to various Protocols referred to in §3A(2) of Air Navigation Act and for purposes of providing for control of air navigation in relation to trade and commerce with other countries and among states and providing security measures. Foreign aircraft landing in Commonwealth must carry certificates, licenses and log books issued by responsible authority in country to which aircraft belongs. Air Navigation Regulations control flying conditions, fares, timetables, airline licences, use of places as aerodromes, accident enquiries, security measures and similar matters. Civil Aviation Act 1988 (as am'd by Civil Aviation Legislation Amendment 1995) establishes Civil Aviation Safety Authority (CASA) to replace Civil Aviation Authority and operate in connection with Airservices Australia (Air Services Act 1995). CASA has regulatory functions relating to safety of civil aviation. Airservices Australia is government enterprise which provides facilities to permit safe navigation of aircraft, air traffic services, aeronautical information services, search, rescue and fire fighting services, aeronautical communications and oversees regulation of aviation environmental activities. Civil Aviation Regulations complementing Air Navigation Regulations control registration and marking of aircraft, airworthiness, licensing of crew, training, maintenance, defect reporting, air services operation, dangerous goods, log books, radio systems, aerodromes, conditions of flight, rules of air, signals for control of air traffic, safety audit programs and other matters.

Sections 19HE and 19HF Air Navigation Act 1920 provide cockpit voice recording not admissible in court proceedings against crew member, but party seeking damages may apply to court for order that recording be admissible.

Qantas Sale Act 1992 provides for privatisation of Qantas airways, once wholly owned by Commonwealth government. Act repeals Australian National Airlines Act which established Australian National Airlines Commission which operated Australian Airlines, now 100% owned by Qantas. Government sold 25% of its equity in Qantas to British Airways in 1992. Disposed of remainder in public float in 1995. Qantas Sale Amendment Act 1995 limits foreign ownership of Qantas to 49%.

Former "two airlines" policy terminated by Airlines Agreement (Termination) Act 1990.

Federal Airports Corporation Act 1986 establishes Federal Airports Corporation which is responsible for administration and operation of principal Australian airports.

Passenger Movement Charge Act 1978 imposes $27 passenger movement charge.

Hijacking.—Air Navigation Act 1920 and Civil Aviation Act 1988 provide that foreign aircraft not possessing nationality of Contracting State may not make nonscheduled flight over or into Australian territory without permission of Minister and Civil Aviation Authority. Authority may direct path and other matters concerning nonscheduled flight by aircraft possessing nationality of Contracting State, and such aircraft need permission for traffic purposes. Crimes (Hijacking of Aircraft) Act 1972 approves accession of Australia to Convention for Suppression of Unlawful Seizure of Aircraft. Crimes (Protection of Aircraft) Act 1973 provides for ratification by Australia of Convention for Suppression of Unlawful Acts against Safety of Civil Aviation and Supplementary Protocol for Suppression of Unlawful Acts of Violence at Airports Serving International Civil Aviation. Crimes (Aircraft) Act 1963 makes provision with respect to crimes committed in respect of aircraft, aerodromes and air navigation facilities. Crimes (Aviation) Act 1991 relates to crimes and certain other acts committed on or in respect of certain aircraft, aerodromes, airports and air navigation facilities. It also gives effect to certain provisions of Tokyo Convention On Offences And Certain Other Acts Committed On Board Aircraft.

ALIENS:

Aliens Act 1947, which required registration of aliens and penalised failure to do so, repealed by Aliens Act Repeal Act 1984.

See also topics Immigration; Nationality.

Corporations Owned or Controlled by Aliens.—Foreign Acquisitions and Takeovers Act 1975 provides for control of foreign takeovers of Australian businesses through detailed provisions for screening of proposed acquisitions and arrangements giving foreign persons control of Australian businesses and prohibition of takeover proposals determined by Treasurer to be against national interest. Foreign Investment Review Board advises and assists Treasurer in implementation of policy and examining proposals for foreign investment in Australia.

Orders prohibiting proposal may be made where: 1(a) person proposes to acquire shares in prescribed corporation carrying on Australian business (or its holding corporation) or person proposes to acquire assets of Australian business carried on by prescribed corporation, or person proposes to enter into agreement relating to affairs of Australian corporation carrying on Australian business (or its holding corporation) or alter its constituent documents or person proposes to enter into or terminate arrangement in relation to Australian business carried on by prescribed corporation; and (b) result will be that business or corporation will be controlled by foreign persons (or their associates); and (c) result would be contrary to national interest; 2(a) foreign person proposes to acquire interest in Australian urban land, or becomes beneficiary in trust estate (other than deceased estate) that consists of or includes Australian urban land; and (b) result would be contrary to national interest. Orders may be made restoring former control of corporation or ownership of Australian urban land where acquisition or arrangement has been completed.

Controlling Interest.—In determining whether arrangement is within Act, person holds "substantial interest" if that person (with associates) is in position to control not less than 15% of voting power or holds not less than 15% of issued shares in corporation or holds beneficial interest in not less than 15% of corpus or income of trust estate. Two or more persons hold "aggregate substantial interest" where they (with associates) are in position to control not less than 40% of voting power, hold interests in not less than 40% of issued shares in corporation or hold beneficial interest in not less than 40% of corpus or income of trust estate. Such persons are deemed to hold "controlling interest", or "aggregate controlling interest" (as case may be), unless Treasurer is satisfied that in circumstances they (or their associates) are not in position to determine policy of corporation.

Associate of person defined widely to include relatives of person; corporations of which person is officer; where person is corporation, any officer of corporation; employee or employer of person; any other officer of corporation of which person is officer; any corporation in which person holds substantial interest; trustee of trust estate in which person holds substantial interest; where person is corporation, person who holds substantial interest in corporation; where person is trustee of trust estate, person who holds substantial interest in trust estate; any employee of natural person of whom person is employee; any corporation whose directors are accustomed to act in accordance with instructions of person or, where person is corporation, of directors of person; any corporation in accordance with instructions of which, or of directors of which, person is accustomed to act.

Foreign person means: (i) Natural person not ordinarily resident in Australia; (ii) corporation in which natural person not ordinarily resident in Australia or foreign corporation holds controlling interest; (iii) corporation in which two or more persons, each of whom is either natural person not ordinarily resident in Australia or foreign corporation, hold aggregate controlling interest; (iv) trustee of trust estate in which natural person not ordinarily resident in Australia, or foreign corporation, holds substantial interest; or (v) trustee of trust estate in which two or more persons, each of whom is either natural person not ordinarily resident in Australia or foreign corporation, hold aggregate substantial interest.

Prescribed corporation means Australian corporation; foreign corporation (or its holding corporation) holding assets value of which exceeds A$20,000,000 (or, alternatively, is greater than one-half value of total assets of foreign corporation) being assets consisting of land situated in Australia, mineral rights or shares in corporation incorporated in Australia; foreign corporation (or its holding corporation) that is holding corporation of one or more Australian corporation(s) where value of assets held by Australian corporation(s) exceeds A$20,000,000 (or, alternatively, is greater than one-half value of total assets of foreign corporation).

Australian urban land means land situated in Australia that is not used wholly or exclusively for carrying on business of primary production.

Notification.—Person may deliver notice to Treasurer stating that person proposes to acquire shares, assets or interests or to enter into agreement or enter into or terminate arrangement to which Act applies. Treasurer may raise no objection to proposal if Treasurer considers that it will not be contrary to national interest. Where no notice is given to Treasurer, Treasurer may make decision on proposal at any stage.

Urban Land Acquisition.—Foreign person proposing to acquire substantial shareholding in Australian corporation or interest in Australian urban land must notify Treasurer before proceeding with proposal. Failure to do so is offence subject to fine not exceeding A$50,000 or imprisonment for two years in case of natural person or fine not exceeding A$250,000 for corporation.

On receiving notice, Treasurer is required to make decision on proposal within 30 days and to provide person with written advice within ten days after making of decision, or publish order ten days after making of decision. If no advice given or order made, proposal cannot be subsequently questioned. Treasurer may make interin order within 30 days extending period during which order may be made for up to 90 days. Order may completely deprive foreign person of rights gained pursuant to acquisition.

Foreign Investment Proposals requiring Notification.—Under guidelines released by Federal Treasurer in Foreign Investment Policy, Sept. 1992, following types of investment proposals liable to be notified to Treasury: (1) Proposals falling within scope of Foreign Acquisitions and Takeovers Act 1975; (2) proposals for establishment of new businesses with investment of A$10,000,000 or more and proposals for acquisition of existing businesses with total assets valued at more than A$5,000,000; (3) proposals for investment in media irrespective of size; and (4) direct investments by foreign governments or their agencies.

Following types of proposals will be examined: manufacturing, services (excluding urban real estate, banking, civil aviation and media), resource processing, oil and gas, nonbank financial intermediaries, insurance, tourism, rural properties, stockbroking, agriculture and forestry and fishing proposals over A$50,000,000 and will be approved unless contrary to national interest.

Mining.—Proposals for new mining projects with expenditure over A$50,000,000 approved unless against national interest. Plans for value adding activity in Australia must be set out.

Civil Aviation and Newspapers.—Proposals relating to civil aviation and newspapers assessed on individual basis. Proposals for new businesses in civil aviation involving investment over A$10,000,000 or to takeover existing business with over A$5,000,000 in total assets approved unless contrary to national interest. Acquisition by foreign airlines flying to Australia of up to 25% of equity in domestic carrier individually or up to 40% in aggregate approved unless contrary to national interest.

Uranium exploration permitted without Australian participation. Only certain existing development projects permitted to proceed.

See also topic Banking and Currency.

Naturalisation.—Under above guidelines, Government has also instituted system of "naturalisation" for foreign-controlled companies whereby such company will generally be treated as "naturalising" Australian if: (a) It has minimum 25% Australian equity; (b) it amends articles of association to provide that majority of its directors must be Australian citizens; and (c) it publicly commits itself to increase Australian equity to 51% subject to agreed understandings between company, major shareholder interests and Government, and regular discussions are held with Foreign Investment Review Board on progress towards achieving this 51% ownership.

In consultation with companies proposing to naturalise, Government will seek agreed timetable for achieving majority Australian equity subject to provision for adjustment should abnormal circumstances arise.

Once process is complete, company is "naturalised".

Naturalising and naturalised companies not required to notify new projects (except in media, banking, uranium and civil aviation sectors) undertaken on own or in partnership with other naturalised or naturalising companies or Australian companies (i.e. not rearded as foreign interests for purposes of foreign investment guidelines).

See Topical Index in front part of this volume.

ALIENS . . . *continued*

Note: Guidelines do not have direct force of law, although exchange control regulations are administered so as to give practical effect thereto.

See also Part II, topics Aliens; Corporations.

Broadcasting and Television.—Broadcasting Act 1942 largely repealed, now generally only deals with regulation of political broadcasts. Broadcasting Services Act 1992 limits foreign television ownership but, unlike former Act, not foreign radio ownership. Proposals for foreign investment in radio which fall within Foreign Acquisitions and Takeovers Act are considered on individual basis. Television license not to be held by foreign person able to exercise control of license, foreign person with company interests in licensee in excess of 15%, or by two or more persons with company interests in excess of 20% of licensee. Not more than 20% of directors of each corporation holding commercial television broadcasting licence may be foreign persons. "Company interests" defined widely and includes shareholding and voting interests. Subscription television license not to be held by foreign person with company interests in excess of 20%, or by two or more persons with company interests in excess of 35% of license. "Control" widely defined, not only by reference to strict numerical holdings. Tracing rules allow indirect company ownership to be traced for purpose of ascertaining whether "control" exercised. Broadly, foreign person with over 2% interest in Australian company will have interest proportionate to its shareholding in shares held by that Australian company in another Australian company. Transitional provisions apply to changeover to new Act by virtue of Broadcasting Services (Transitional Provisions and Consequential Amendments) Act 1992: (a) Directorship not contravention under 1942 Act not contravention under 1992 Act; (b) periods of grace applying under 1942 Act to excuse contravention carried forward; and (c) contravention of control provisions disregarded if under 1942 Act no contravention, for so long as no change in person's relevant circumstances.

ARRANGEMENTS FOR BENEFIT OF CREDITORS OUTSIDE BANKRUPTCY:

Debtor who desires that his affairs be dealt with under Part X Bankruptcy Act 1966 without his estate being sequestrated may sign authority in accordance with prescribed form authorizing registered trustee (or solicitor) to call meeting of his creditors and authorizing registered trustee to take over control of his property. Upon passing of special resolution at this meeting by those entitled to vote, passage of which resolution requires simple majority in number of creditors present and voting and at least three-quarters in value, debtor may be required to enter into one of following: (i) Deed of assignment in prescribed form—under which debtor disposes, in favour of his creditors, of all property which would have been divisible among his creditors if debtor had become bankrupt; (ii) composition—under which debtor offers to pay sum of money in full satisfaction of his debts; or (iii) deed of arrangement—which provides for arrangement of affairs of debtor with view to payment in whole or in part of his debts e.g. deed of arrangement may contain release of some or all of debtor's debts, assignment of some or all of debtor's property or may be conditional on receipt of undertaking from third parties.

Deeds of Assignment and Compositions.—Deed of assignment or arrangement or composition binds all creditors of debtor and creditor may not present or proceed with creditor's petition or (except in case of deed of arrangement where leave of court must be obtained) enforce any remedy against person or property of debtor or commence or take any fresh step in legal proceedings in respect of provable debt. Deed of assignment or composition has additional effect of releasing debtor from all provable debts other than those that would not have been released by debtor's discharge from bankruptcy if he had been bankrupt.

Trustee of deed is to file deed (except in case of composition) and statement of debtor's affairs with Registrar in Bankruptcy and when he is satisfied that all divisible property of debtor has been realized and final dividend paid he is to provide to debtor, upon his request, certificate of release. Trustee of deed of arrangement, assignment or composition is to be satisfied that terms have been carried out before providing certificate.

Court may declare void any deed of assignment or arrangement or composition where it is not made in accordance with provisions of Act or where debtor has given false or misleading information at meeting of creditors or has omitted material particular from his statement of affairs or has included incorrect material particular in that statement. Court may terminate deed of arrangement or composition on certain grounds including that debtor has failed to comply with or carry out provision of deed or that deed cannot be proceeded with without injustice or undue delay.

Court may set aside composition on certain grounds including that terms of composition are unreasonable or are not calculated to benefit creditors generally.

See also topic Bankruptcy.

ASSIGNMENTS:

See topics Patents, subhead Assignments; Trademarks, subhead Assignments.

ATTACHMENT:

In the High Court a judgment or order for the payment of money into court or for the performance of a judgment, order or writ by which any person is required to do any act, other than payment of money to some person, may be enforced by writ of attachment. Writ of attachment cannot be issued without leave of court applied for on notice to party against whom attachment is to be issued. Failure to observe order or judgment for attachment constitutes contempt of court. See also Part II.

BANKING AND CURRENCY:

Banking Act 1959 provides that banking business shall be carried on only by bodies corporate so authorised in writing by Governor-General in Council. Regulation-making power covers foreign exchange, protection of Australian currency, foreign investment in Australia, Australian investment overseas and prudential supervision of banks, and extends to financial aspects of contracts, acts and transactions between Australian residents and nonresidents. Act also provides for extraterritorial application of Banking (Foreign Exchange) Regulations. Reserve bank empowered to control interest rates.

Foreign Banks.—Foreign bank entry liberalised. Foreign banks may apply to establish authorised branch in Australia to conduct wholesale banking business.

Financial Corporations (Transfer of Assets and Liabilities) Act 1993 facilitates transfer of certain assets and liabilities from foreign bank subsidiaries in Australia to new branches.

Interest withholding tax on money borrowed from overseas is 10%. See topic Taxation.

Distinction between trading and savings banks removed. Reserve Bank has formal authority for prudential supervision of banks. Banks have appointed ombudsman to report to independent council to investigate consumer complaints. Further, financial institutions have implemented self-regulating code of practise concerning operation of electronic banking services.

Banks (Shareholdings) Act 1972 prohibits person from having interest in one or more voting shares of bank if nominal amount of such share or shares exceeds 10% of aggregate of nominal amounts of all voting shares of bank; however exemption is to be granted to allow persons to hold up to 15% of aggregate of nominal amounts of all voting shares of bank (other than Commonwealth Bank) unless such exemption is not in "national interest". Commonwealth Banks Restructuring Act 1990 prohibits person from having interest in one or more voting shares of Commonwealth Bank if nominal amount of that share or aggregate of nominal amounts of those shares, exceeds 5% of aggregate of nominal amounts of all voting shares of Commonwealth Bank.

Commonwealth Banks Act 1959 deals with constitution and operations of Commonwealth banks.

Commonwealth Banks Restructuring Act 1990 converts Commonwealth Bank into public company. Corporations Law applies in relation to Commonwealth Bank's memorandum and articles as if they had been registered as such under that Act. Commonwealth Bank becomes successor in law of State Bank of Victoria.

Commonwealth government announced in 1995 Budget that it intends to sell its remaining 50.4% equity in Commonwealth Bank. Plans to sell by June 1996.

Reserve Bank Act 1959 establishes Reserve Bank of Australia which is required to act as central bank and as bank for Commonwealth. Bank is required to ensure that its monetary and banking policies are directed to greatest advantage of people of Australia and that its powers are exercised in such manner as, in opinion of Board, best contributes to: (i) Stability of Australian currency; (ii) maintenance of full employment in Australia; and (iii) economic prosperity and welfare of Australian people.

In event of any difference of opinion between board or Reserve Bank and Government as to whether monetary and banking policies of Reserve Bank are directed to greatest advantage of people of Australia, Government has ultimate right to direct Bank's policies.

Australian notes are issued by the Note Issue Department of the Reserve Bank, and are legal tender for their face value in the Commonwealth and in all territories under the control of the Commonwealth.

Reserve Bank Act 1959 permits issue of Australian notes in denominations of one, two, five, ten, 20 and 50 dollars, and any other denomination determined by Treasurer. Currency Act 1965 permits issue of coins in denominations of five, ten, 20 and 50 cents, and one, ten, 25, 50, 100 and 200 dollars. Currently in circulation are coins in denominations of five, ten, 20 and 50 cents, and of one dollar, two and 200 dollars, and notes in denominations of five, ten, 20, 50 and 100 dollars. One and two dollar coins have replaced one and two dollar notes. One and two cent coins not reissued after Oct. 1, 1990.

Australian Nugget gold coins issued with nominal face values $100, $50, $25 and $15. Coins are legal tender.

Bank notes do not circulate. Banks may not issue or circulate notes issued by any State, and such notes are not legal tender.

Legal Tender.—Currency Act 1965 provides tender of payment of money is legal tender if made in case of coins of denominations of 5¢, 10¢, 20¢ or 50¢ for payment of amount not exceeding $5; in case of coins of denominations of 1¢ or 2¢ for payment of amount not exceeding 20¢; in case of coins of denomination greater than 50¢ but less than $10 for payment of amount not exceeding ten times face value of coin; in case of coins of denomination of $10 for payment of amount not exceeding $100; in case of coins of another denomination for payment of any amount.

Financial Corporations Act 1974 provides for regulation of non-bank financial institutions. Act applies to corporations such as finance companies, permanent building societies, merchant banks, and money market groups, pastoral finance companies and credit unions. Corporations to which Act applies must register with Reserve Bank, obliged to furnish details of operations. Regulations made under Part IV (not proclaimed) would enable Reserve Bank to control asset ratios, lending policies and interest rates of financial corporations. Part IV unlikely to be proclaimed.

Corporations Legislation Amendment Act 1994 (Cth) seeks to avoid duplication of regulatory burdens imposed on nonbank financial institutions by (a) applying fund-raising provisions of Corporations Law to financial institutions; (b) exposing financial institutions to market offence provisions of Part 7.11 of Corporations Law; and (c) regulating duties of officers, and charges over property of fiancial institutions, through financial institutions legislation.

BANKRUPTCY:

Bankruptcy Act 1966 provides uniform law throughout Commonwealth for insolvency of natural persons.

Federal Court of Australia and Family Court of Australia have jurisdiction in respect to bankruptcy proceedings. (See further topic Constitution and Government, subhead Judiciary.)

Debtor's Petition.—(Pt. IV, Div. 3). In certain circumstances debtor may present to Registrar declaration of intention to present debtor's petition; in such case creditor to whom debtor owes frozen debt cannot apply for issue of enforcement process in respect of debt or enforce remedy against person or property of debtor in respect of

BANKRUPTCY . . . *continued*
debt. Debtor for any amount may become bankrupt on his own initiative by filing petition and statement of affairs in accordance with prescribed form. Once accepted and endorsed by Registrar, debtor is automatically declared bankrupt and bankruptcy dates from date of acceptance of petition by Registrar. Provision is made for presentation of debtor's petition against partnership and by joint debtors. If creditor's petition is pending at time when debtor's petition is presented, Registrar must refer debtor's petition to Court for direction to accept or reject it.

Creditor's Petition.—(Pt. IV, Div. 2). Creditors for aggregate of A$1,500 or more payable as liquidated sum either immediately or at certain future time may petition for sequestration of estate of debtor if within six months of date of petition debtor has committed act of bankruptcy and, if at time of act of bankruptcy, debtor has connection with Australia of specified residential or business kind. Debtor becomes bankrupt upon making of sequestration order. Secured creditor may present such petition as if he were unsecured creditor if he is willing to surrender his security for benefit of all creditors in event of sequestration order being made.

Acts of Bankruptcy.—(a) If in Australia or elsewhere debtor makes a conveyance or assignment of his property for benefit of his creditors generally; (b) if in Australia or elsewhere he makes conveyance, transfer, settlement or other disposition of his property or any part thereof, creates charge over his property or any part thereof, makes payment or incurs obligation that would, if he became bankrupt, be void as against trustee in bankruptcy; (c) if with intent to defeat or delay his creditors he departs or remains out of Australia, he departs from his normal dwelling-house or place of business, he otherwise absents himself or begins to keep house; (d) if execution is issued against him and either property sold or held by sheriff for 21 days or execution is returned unsatisfied; (e) if debtor presents to Registrar declaration of his intention to present debtor's petition; (f) if at meeting of creditors debtor agrees to file debtor's petition and fails to do so within seven days or agrees to appoint registered trustee to take over his affairs yet fails to do so within seven days; (g) if at meeting of creditors he admits to insolvency and fails within seven days at request of majority of creditors to present debtor's petition or to appoint registered trustee; (h) if he fails to comply with bankruptcy notice filed by way of final judgment or order; (i) if he gives notice to any of his creditors that he has suspended or is about to suspend payment of his debts; (j) if he signs authority appointing registered trustee to take over his affairs; (k) if meeting of creditors is called by registered trustee in pursuance of such authority; (l) if he fails to attend such meeting; (m) if he fails to execute deed of assignment or deed of arrangement or to present debtor's petition within specified time having been required by special resolution of meeting of his creditors to do so; (n) if deed of assignment or deed of arrangement or composition entered into with his creditors is declared void; (o) if scheme of arrangement or composition is annulled and before annulment debtor's bankruptcy has been annulled. (§40). Act allows bankruptcy notice to be issued in respect of judgment or order for payment by court exercising bankruptcy jurisdiction.

Act also protects maintenance creditors where orders for arrears of maintenance obtained under Family Law Act 1975 by allowing them to serve bankruptcy notice.

Property divisible amongst creditors includes, subject to many exceptions and protective provisions: (1) All property that belonged to or was vested in bankrupt at commencement of bankruptcy; (2) all property that he acquires or has been acquired for him or devolves or has devolved upon him after commencement of bankruptcy and before discharge; (3) proceeds of certain executions and other proceedings; (4) property disposed of by bankrupt in certain settlements within two years before commencement of bankruptcy; (5) property disposed of by bankrupt with intent to defraud creditors; (6) property transferred to creditors within six months before petition with effect of giving that creditor preference over other creditors. Date of commencement of bankruptcy is defined as date of earliest act of bankruptcy within period of six months preceding presentation of creditor's petition or debtor's petition or application for making of sequestration order or, where no act of bankruptcy committed within six months prior to presentation of debtor's petition, date of presentation of debtor's petition. Act gives Trustee in Bankruptcy power to investigate use of complicated structures to perpetrate insolvency fraud.

See also topic Fraudulent Sales and Conveyances.

Property not divisible amongst creditors includes, subject to many exceptions and protective provisions: (a) Property held in trust for other persons; (b) necessary personal and household effects; (c) ordinary tools of trade, plant and equipment, professional instruments and reference books not exceeding in aggregate A$2,000; (d) property used by bankrupt primarily as means of transport, being property aggregate value of which does not exceed A$2,500; (e) life and endowment assurance policies in respect of life of bankrupt or of spouse and proceeds received therefrom on or after date of bankruptcy up to value of bankrupt's pension; (f) interest in regulated superannuation fund or approved deposit fund and payments received therefrom (not as pension) on or after date of bankruptcy up to value of bankrupt's pension; (g) amounts paid to bankrupt under scheme operated by State or Territory in accordance with agreements between Commonwealth and States and Territories execution of which, on behalf of Commonwealth, was approved by States Grants (Rural Reconstruction) Act 1971; States Grants (Rural Adjustment) Act 1976; States and Northern Territory Grants (Rural Adjustment) Act 1979; States and Northern Territory Grants (Rural Adjustment) Act 1985; States and Northern Territory Grants (Rural Adjustment) Act 1988; and Rural Adjustment Act 1992, being amounts paid by way of grant or loan as assistance for purpose of rehabilitation or household support; (h) property purchased wholly or substantially with protected money; (i) amounts paid under legislation; (j) insurance moneys under contract of insurance against liabilities to third parties; (k) any right to recover damages or compensation for personal injury. (§§116-117).

Debts Provable.—All debts and liabilities, present or future, certain or contingent, to which a bankrupt was subject at date of bankruptcy or to which he may become subject before his discharge by reason of an obligation incurred before date of bankruptcy. (§82). For these purposes "liability" includes: (a) Compensation for work or labour done; (b) obligation or possible obligation to pay money or money's worth on breach of express or implied covenant, contract, agreement or undertaking, whether or not breach occurs, is likely to occur or is capable of occurring before discharge of bankrupt; and (c) express or implied engagement, agreement or undertaking to pay or capable of resulting in payment of money or money's worth, whether payment is: (1) in respect of amount, fixed or unliquidated; (2) in respect of time, present or future or certain or dependent on contingency; or (3) in respect of manner of valuation, capable of being ascertained by fixed rules or only as matter of opinion. Certain sums payable under maintenance agreement or order registered or approved by court are also provable in bankruptcy. Proceeds of Crime Act 1987 provides that pecuniary penalty order or interstate pecuniary penalty order under Act (such order being order that deprives persons of proceeds of and benefits derived from crimes) is provable in bankruptcy.

Order of Payment of Debts.—To extent that security is not relied on, all debts rank equally and if assets are insufficient debts are paid proportionately. (§108). However, there is statutory list of debts whose payment takes priority. See §§109, 109A.

Effect of Bankruptcy.—Present and after-acquired property of bankrupt vests in Official Trustee or registered trustee. No creditor, other than secured creditor, can enforce his debt against debtor or his property. (§58).

Litigation commenced by a bankrupt before bankruptcy is stayed, upon his becoming bankrupt, until trustee makes election to prosecute or discontinue action; however bankrupt may continue in his own name such action where that action is in respect of (i) personal injuries or wrongs done to bankrupt, his spouse or family member or (ii) death of his spouse or of member of his family. Court cannot stay proceedings under Proceeds of Crime Act 1987. (§60).

Where a bankrupt dies before he is discharged from bankruptcy, proceedings in bankruptcy shall, unless court otherwise directs, be continued so far as they are capable of being continued as if he were alive. (§63).

Discharge.—By operation of law, bankrupt is discharged automatically three years from date of bankruptcy (transitional provisions apply if bankrupt before 1 July 1992). (§149). However, extension of time if objection made by Trustee or Official Receiver to Registrar and not cancelled by Inspector-General. (§§149A-Q). Bankrupt may, after six months, apply to Trustee for early discharge. May be discharged in limited circumstances; decision of Trustee reviewable by Inspector-General. (§§149R-ZM).

An order of discharge releases bankrupt from all debts provable in bankruptcy (including secured debts) but excluding those debts incurred by fraud, liability under a maintenance order or agreement (subject to contrary order by Court), debts on recognizance, income contribution amounts payable under Division 4B of Part VI (see subhead Contribution, infra), bail and any liability under pecuniary penalty order or interstate pecuniary penalty order. Discharge of bankrupt does not affect right of secured creditor to realize or otherwise deal with his security if secured creditor has not proved in bankruptcy for secured debt or part thereof, and purpose is to obtain payment of secured debt or part thereof. (§153).

Contribution.—New Division 4B of Part VI of Bankruptcy Act 1966 requires bankrupt to pay to Trustee contribution from income exceeding certain amount. If contribution payable, bankrupt unable to travel overseas. (Division 4C). Bankruptcy Amendment Act 1993 passed to avoid effect of foreshadowed challenge to constitutionality of these provisions.

Examination.—There is provision for examination of trustee of bankrupt's estate or other relevant person about certain matters in relation to trustee. (Division 4A Part VIII; Division 2A Part X).

Aid.—Australian courts will act in aid of Bankruptcy Courts of Canada, New Zealand and U.K. and other prescribed countries and may act in aid of Bankruptcy Courts of non-prescribed countries on letter of request. Australian courts may request courts in other countries to act in their aid. See §29.

BILLS AND NOTES:

Bills of Exchange Act 1909 follows very closely English Bills of Exchange Act of 1882, only minor variations having been made to adapt it to local conditions. See England Law Digest.

Cheques.—Cheques and Payment Orders Act 1986 substantially amends law relating to cheques. Cheque is defined as unconditional order in writing addressed by person to bank, signed by person giving it and requiring bank to pay on demand sum certain in money. Most significant aspect of Act is introduction of new scheme for presentment of cheques whereby cheque need not be physically presented by collecting bank to drawee bank and whereby drawers and indorsers are not liable until presentment. Amendments made by Law and Justice Legislation Amendment Act 1994 remove restrictions imposed by electronic presentment where such presentment occurs within same bank (i.e. internal presentments). Act also modifies previous law in number of ways including following: (i) Increases to 15 months period required before cheque becomes stale cheque; (ii) includes bank cheques and post-dated cheques within Act; (iii) modifies provisions relating to order and bearer cheques; (iv) provides that cheques are negotiable until discharged; (v) modifies provisions relating to dishonour; and (vi) provides new procedure for obtaining replacement for lost or destroyed cheques. Act also provides that certain provisions of Act cannot be altered by agreement between two or more parties to cheque.

Payment order is defined as unconditional order in writing addressed by person to nonbank financial institution (NBFI), signed by person giving it, requiring NBFI to pay on demand sum certain in money, and bearing words "payment order" on front of it. NBFI defined as building society or credit union that is registered corporation within Financial Corporations Act 1974 or other registered corporation within that Act. Provisions of Act applying to cheques generally apply to payment orders—except, for example, provisions relating to presentment (separate presentment procedure is provided for payment orders). Similar duties as imposed on banks regarding presentment and collection of cheques are imposed on NBFIs. Statutory protection also conferred on NBFIs and their customers in relation to agency cheque arrangements between banks and NBFIs.

Bills of Exchange Amendment Act 1986 ensures that Bills of Exchange Act 1909 has no application to cheques.

See also Part II—topic Holidays.

CONSTITUTION AND GOVERNMENT:

Commonwealth of Australia was established on Jan. 1, 1901, by Royal Proclamation dated Sept. 17, 1900, pursuant to Act of British Parliament known as Commonwealth of Australia Act 1900 (63 and 64 Vic, c. 12). Prior to that date colonies of New South Wales, Tasmania, Victoria, Queensland and Western Australia and Province of South Australia, had existed as self-governing colonies of Great Britain; but upon establishment of Commonwealth they became states of Commonwealth of Australia. Australian Constitution is modelled in some respects on that of U.S.A., although American theory of separation of powers only followed in Australia with respect to judiciary.

The Commonwealth government is a government of specified powers, which are for the most part not exclusively within the Commonwealth sphere, but where Commonwealth law conflicts with state law the former is paramount. Matters not specified as subjects upon which the Commonwealth may legislate remain exclusively in the sphere of state legislation except that Commonwealth may legislate through external affairs power to implement bona fide international agreement regardless of subject matter. Queen is represented in Commonwealth by Governor-General, appointed on advice of Commonwealth Government, and in each of six States by Governor appointed on advice of State Government. These officers in general occupy same relative position towards their respective Parliaments as Queen occupies towards British Parliament.

Parliament.—Commonwealth Parliament consists of two Houses: Senate and House of Representatives. Twelve Senators are elected by each State and two Senators by each of Australian Capital Territory and Northern Territory; each State and Territory votes as one electorate. House of Representatives has as nearly as practicable twice as many members as Senate, each representing small electorate. Electorates are distributed amongst States and Territories in proportion to population size. Australian Capital Territory has two members, Northern Territory has one. Cocos (Keeling) Islands Self-Determination (Consequential Amendments) Act 1984 and Christmas Island Administration (Miscellaneous Amendments) Act 1984 extended franchise to inhabitants of external territories of Cocos (Keeling) Islands and Christmas Island. Voting is compulsory for all Australian citizens over 18 years in election of members to both houses. Legislation following referenda conducted May 14, 1977 gives residents of Australian Capital Territory and Northern Territory right to vote in future constitutional referenda. Casual vacancies in Senate are to be filled by appointees of same political party. Casual vacancies in House of Representatives are filled at by-elections.

Commonwealth Electoral Act 1918 establishes Australian Electoral Commission to determine electoral divisions, regulate qualifications for voting, regulate gifts to political parties, report to Minister on electoral matters and generally conduct elections.

The Political Broadcasts & Political Disclosures Act 1991 was controversial legislation prohibiting broadcast of political advertisements during election period. Held unconstitutional (1992) 66 A.L.J.R. 695.

Legislative Powers.—The Commonwealth Parliament has power to make laws for the peace, order and good government of the Commonwealth, with respect to: (1) Trade and commerce with other countries and among the States; (2) taxation, but so as not to discriminate between States or parts of States; (3) bounties on the production or export of goods, but such bounties must be uniform throughout the Commonwealth; (4) borrowing money upon the public credit of the Commonwealth; (5) postal, telegraphic, telephonic and other like services; (6) the naval and military defence of the Commonwealth and of the several States, and the control of the forces to execute and maintain the laws of the Commonwealth; (7) lighthouses, lightships, beacons and buoys; (8) astronomical and meteorological observation; (9) quarantine; (10) fisheries in Australian waters beyond territorial limits; (11) census and statistics; (12) currency, coinage and legal tender; (13) banking, other than State banking; also State banking extending beyond the limits of the State concerned, the incorporation of banks, and the issue of paper money; (14) insurance, other than State insurance, also State insurance extending beyond the limits of the State concerned; (15) weights and measures; (16) bills of exchange and promissory notes; (17) bankruptcy and insolvency; (18) copyrights, patents of inventions and designs, and trademarks; (19) naturalisation and aliens; (20) foreign corporations, and trading or financial corporations formed within the limits of the Commonwealth; (21) marriage; (22) divorce and matrimonial causes, and in relation thereto parental rights and the custody and guardianship of infants; (23) invalid and old age pensions; (23A) the provision of social services (but so as not to authorise any form of civil conscription); (24) service and execution throughout Commonwealth of civil and criminal process and judgments of courts of States; (25) recognition throughout Commonwealth of laws and public acts and records and judicial proceedings of States; (26) people of any race, for whom it is deemed necessary to make special laws; (27) immigration and emigration; (28) influx of criminals; (29) external affairs; (30) relations of Commonwealth with Islands of the Pacific; (31) acquisition of property on just terms from any State or person for any purpose in respect of which Parliament has power to make laws; (32) control of railways with respect to transport for naval and military purposes of Commonwealth; (33) acquisition, with consent of State, of any railway of State, on terms arranged between Commonwealth and State; (34) railway construction and extension in any State with consent of that State; (35) conciliation and arbitration for prevention and settlement of industrial disputes extending beyond limits of any one State; (36) matters in respect of which Constitution makes provision until Parliament otherwise provides; (37) matters referred to Parliament of Commonwealth by parliament or parliaments of any State or States, but so that law shall extend only to States by whose parliaments matter is referred, or which afterwards adopt law; (38) exercise within Commonwealth, at request or with concurrence of parliaments of all States directly concerned, of any power which could, at establishment of Constitution, be exercised only by Parliament of the U.K. or by Federal Council of Australasia; (39) matters incidental to execution of any power vested by Constitution in Parliament or in either house thereof, or in government of Commonwealth, or in federal judicature, or in any department or officer of Commonwealth.

In addition to the above powers, which are not exclusively conferred upon the Commonwealth, but which may be exercised by the States until such time as the Commonwealth overrides them, the Commonwealth Parliament has exclusive power to make laws for the peace, order and good government of the Commonwealth with respect to: (1) The seat of government of the Commonwealth and all places acquired by the Commonwealth for public purposes; (2) matters relating to any department of the public service, the control of which is by the Constitution transferred to the executive Government of the Commonwealth; (3) other matters declared by the Constitution to be within the exclusive power of the Parliament (such as imposition of duties of customs and excise).

Not all the above powers have been exercised, but the most important of the legislation enacted under the above powers is referred to below.

Executive.—In accordance with British practice, the Constitution says very little about the executive. It does not attempt to codify the British Cabinet system, but merely refers to a Federal Executive Council and provides that members of the Federal Executive Council shall administer the departments of state and be Ministers of State, and shall not hold office for a longer period than three months without becoming senators or members of the House of Representatives. Framers of Constitution had British notion of responsible government in mind, and that system is in fact more or less closely followed in Commonwealth.

Judiciary.—The Constitution establishes a Federal Supreme Court, called the High Court of Australia, and vests the judicial power of the Commonwealth in that Court and in such other federal courts as Parliament creates or invests with federal jurisdiction. As in the United States of America, the Constitution does not interfere with the State judiciaries, but provides a federal judiciary capable of pronouncing judgment upon the Commonwealth powers, and protecting the Constitution not only against the States, but against the legislature and executive of Commonwealth.

High Court of Australia.—High Court is in the main a court of appeal (both in constitutional and nonconstitutional matters) from the State courts, but the Constitution confers original jurisdiction upon it in all matters: (1) Arising under any treaty; (2) affecting consuls or other representatives of other countries; (3) in which the Commonwealth, or a person suing or being sued on behalf of the Commonwealth, is a party; (4) between States, or between residents of different States, or between a State and a resident of another State; (5) in which a writ of mandamus or prohibition or an injunction is sought against an officer of the Commonwealth. In addition, Parliament of Commonwealth may confer original jurisdiction upon High Court in relation to certain other matters. Constitution provides that justices of High Court shall be appointed by Governor-General in Council, and shall not be removed except on address from both Houses of Parliament in same session, praying for such removal on ground of proved misbehaviour or incapacity; and that remuneration of Justices of High Court is not to be diminished during their continuance in office. Legislation following referendum of May 14, 1977 provides for retiring age of 70 years for future Justices of High Court and judges in other federal courts.

Appeal to Privy Council.—As Privy Council (Appeals from High Court) Act 1975 provides that, for all practical purposes, no appeals may go from High Court to Privy Council, and as all appeals from Australian superior Courts may go to High Court, usually leave of High Court required, because High Court considers itself ultimate appellate court and has announced that it will no longer regard itself bound by decisions of Privy Council.

Federal Court of Australia.—Parliament has established Federal Court of Australia and conferred on it: (a) Original jurisdiction in matters arising under specified Federal Acts, including those related to income tax, trade practices and industrial property, and (b) certain appellate jurisdiction, including jurisdiction in specified cases to determine appeals from courts exercising Federal jurisdiction, other than Full Courts of State Supreme Courts.

Administrative Decisions (Judicial Review) Act 1977 empowers Federal Court to hear complaints against decisions of ministers and officers acting under Commonwealth laws. Act provides number of grounds for review of decisions to which it applies. Act also applies to omissions to decide. Other rights of review outside Act also preserved. "Order of Review" enables "person affected" by decision to obtain reasons for decision. Certain government decisions exempted from operation of Act. See topic Administrative Law.

Industrial Court of Australia.—Industrial Relations Reform Act 1993 creates Industrial Relations Court of Australia with jurisdiction over matters under Industrial Relations Act and matters remitted to it under §44 Judiciary Act 1903.

Family Court of Australia.—Family Court of Australia (Additional Jurisdiction and Exercise of Powers) Act 1988 extends jurisdiction of Family Court to include proceedings normally brought before Federal Court of Australia by amending following Acts: Federal Court of Australia Act 1976; Family Law Act 1975; Administrative Decisions (Judicial Review) Act 1977; Bankruptcy Act 1966; Income Tax Assessment Act 1936; Trade Practices Act 1974; and Family Law Amendment Act 1987.

Certain non-judicial bodies also exist. For example, Administrative Appeals Tribunal Act 1975 establishes Tribunal to which appeals can be made by person affected by decision, or by special interest association, before decision is made by person under certain Commonwealth Acts, and Ombudsman Act 1976 establishes Ombudsman, who has wide powers of investigation into any matter of administration either on complaint or of his own motion with respect to any department or prescribed authority over which Commonwealth exercises control.

Trade and Intercourse.—The Constitution provides that trade, commerce and intercourse among the states, whether by means of internal carriage or ocean navigation, shall be absolutely free. Freedom of trade and commerce guaranteed by §92 has been interpreted by High Court to be freedom from discriminatory burdens of protectionist kind. Law will violate §92 if on its face protectionist or if law's factual operation produces such result.

Statute of Westminster Adoption Act 1942.—According to the constitutional conventions governing the relations inter se of the members of the British Commonwealth of Nations, the Government of the Commonwealth of Australia has long been completely independent of the Government of Great Britain. This autonomous status has been placed on a legal basis by the adoption by Australia, as from 1939, of the Statute of Westminster, according to which no British statute can extend to the Commonwealth of Australia without the latter's request and consent and Australian Parliament has full power to make statutes repugnant to and amending British law,

CONSTITUTION AND GOVERNMENT . . . *continued*
statutes, regulations or orders in so far as they are part of law of Commonwealth of Australia.

Australia Act 1986 severs all remaining constitutional links between Australia and U.K. It provides that U.K. Parliament shall have no power to make laws for Australia, removes limitations on legislative powers of States and terminates all responsibilities of U.K. government in respect of States.

CONSUMER PROTECTION:

Trade Practices Act 1974 contains certain provisions in Parts IVA, V and VA aimed at protecting consumers from unfair commercial practices engaged in by corporations and, in certain cases, persons other than corporations. Part IVA prohibits corporations in trade or commerce engaging in conduct unconscionable within unwritten laws (i.e. common law and equity) of States or Territories. (§51AA). It also prohibits unconscionable conduct in supply of goods or services to consumers. Among practices specifically prohibited by Division 1 of Part V of Act are misleading or deceptive conduct; making of false or misleading representations or statements concerning certain matters in connection with value, standard, quality, grade, supply or possible supply of goods or services; misleading conduct in relation to sale of land or in relation to employment; offering of gifts and prizes with intention of not providing them as offered; bait advertising, whereby consumers are attracted to trade premises by advertisement of goods at low prices when there is no real intention to have such goods available for sale; referral selling, whereby consumers are offered rebate, commission or other benefit, as inducement to acquire goods or services, for assisting in supply of goods or services to another consumer and where receipt of that rebate, commission or other benefit is contingent on event occurring after consumer's contract of supply entered into; accepting payment without intending to supply as ordered; making misleading statements about profitability, risk or other material aspect of home-operated businesses; physical force, undue harassment or coercion in connection with supply or possible supply of goods or services to consumer or payment for goods or services by consumer; pyramid selling, whereby person who participates in trading scheme is induced to make payments to promoter of scheme by reason of prospect of receiving payments or other benefits in respect of introduction of other persons who become participants in that trading scheme; and assertion of payment for unsolicited goods or services. Division 1A of Part V of Act also provides for prescription of product information, establishment of product safety standards, and recall of products.

Implied Terms.—Division 2 of Part V of Act sets out terms to be implied in consumer contracts for goods and services. These relate to title, supply by description, merchantable quality, fitness for particular purpose, and supply by sample. Important innovation is that terms may not be excluded, restricted or modified except to limit damages for breach of such terms in respect of nonconsumer goods sold for more than A$40,000. Certain credit transactions linked to provision of goods or services are also regulated. Vienna Convention on Contracts for International Sale of Goods prevails over provisions dealing with conditions and warranties in Division 2 to extent of any inconsistency.

Manufacturers and Importers.—Under Division 2A of Part V of Act manufacturers and importers concurrently liable with actual seller of goods in relation to implied conditions and warranties. Part VA makes corporations who supply, in trade or commerce, defective goods manufactured or imported by them, liable for loss suffered as result of defect, whether suffered by injured individual, other individual, other goods, or buildings. Consumer (see definition below) has similar rights against manufacturer or importer as those implied rights which consumer has against seller under Act. Defect in goods may relate to (i) manner in which they are marked; (ii) purposes for which they are marked; (iii) their packaging; (iv) use of any mark in relation to goods; (v) instructions or warnings provided with goods; (vi) what might reasonably be expected to be done with goods; and (vii) time goods were supplied to manufacturer. Consumer has right to compensation from seller, manufacturer or importer where goods: (a) Do not correspond with description under which they are sold; (b) are not reasonably fit for purpose which was known by manufacturer or importer and for which they were acquired by consumer; (c) are not of merchantable quality; (d) are supplied by reference to sample and do not correspond to sample; (e) are supplied by manufacturer or importer which fails to comply with express warranty given in relation to goods; and (f) are supplied by manufacturer or importer which fails to provide reasonable repair and parts replacement facilities.

Consumer.—However, all statutory warranties and conditions under Act arise if, and only if, sale is one to "consumer". Act defines person as consumer if: (a) Price of goods does not exceed prescribed amount (at present A$40,000); or (b) where price exceeds prescribed amount, goods are either of a kind ordinarily acquired for personal domestic or household use or consumption or consist of vehicle acquired for use principally in transport of goods on public roads; and, in either case, (c) goods not acquired for purpose of resupply or use in manufacture, production, repair or treatment of other goods or fixtures to land. But, consumer will only have right of action against manufacturer or importer of goods if goods are of kind ordinarily acquired for personal, domestic or household use or consumption.

Penalties under Act for breaches of Part V are, generally speaking, up to A$200,000 for corporations and A$40,000 for individuals. Courts may grant injunctions and damages or other orders (e.g. corrective advertising orders) may be awarded in favour of party who has suffered loss as result of prohibited practice. Australian Competition and Consumers Commission has power to obtain information, documents and evidence, to inspect documents and to initiate proceedings and intervene.

Competition Policy Reform Act 1995 provides for abolition of Trade Practices Commission and Prices Surveillance Authority merging functions of these into Australian Competition and Consumer Commission (ACCC). Trade Practices Tribunal renamed Australian Competition Tribunal. Competition Policy Reform Act provides for broader application of Part IV Trade Practices Act.

See also Part II—topic Consumer Protection.

COPYRIGHT:

Copyright Act 1968.—Copyright does not exist otherwise than by virtue of this Act. Act extends to every Territory of Commonwealth.

Contravention of Copyright Act may involve penalties up to A$250,000 for body corporate or up to A$50,000 or imprisonment for up to six months for natural person. Courts may order surrender or destruction of infringing material.

Two categories of copyright are set up: (a) Original literary, dramatic, musical and artistic works (which includes building or part thereof) (Literary works include computer programs) (Pt. III); (b) records, films and radio, T.V. broadcasts (including satellite broadcasts where made from place in Australia) and published editions of works (Pt. IV). Circuit Layouts Act 1989 protects original chip layouts and repeals sections of Design Act 1906 and Copyright Act 1968 concerned therewith. Act consistent with draft Treaty on Circuit Layouts developed by World Intellectual Property Organisation. Protects circuit layouts and integrated circuits whether made before or after Act, but action lies only for acts after Act comes into operation. Acts done by Commonwealth for purpose of defence and security of Australia non-infringing.

Copyright Amendment Act 1989 creates unassignable civil rights of action which also have counterpart criminal offences for unauthorised use of performers' performances. Act does not confer copyright protection (i.e. property rights) on performers. Complementary regulations extend operation of new provisions to citizens, nationals and residents of countries members of Rome Convention for the Protection of Performers, Producers of Phonographs and Broadcasting Organisations (1961) and also to performances in those countries, as from 2 Jan. 1992: see Copyright (International Protection) Regulations, reg. 4A. Amendments with other regulations will enable Australia to meet minimum requirements of Rome Convention. Copyright (International Protection) Regulations 1995 extends application of Act to certain performances having connection with World Trade Organisation Countries. Act also permits copying of television broadcasts or works by educational and other institutions. Provisions to allow use of blank tapes for private and domestic copying whilst providing that owners of copyright in recording would receive remuneration through royalty to be levied on blank recording tape held unconstitutional: see (1993) 112 A.L.R. 53. 1989 Act repealed by Copyright Amendment (Reenactment) Act 1993 which reenacts provisions of 1989 Act except those related to blank audio tape royalty scheme.

In relation to the first category (a) copyright is exclusive right to reproduce such a work as referred to, in a material form, to publish it, to perform it in public, to broadcast it, to cause it to be transmitted to subscribers of a diffusion service, or to make an adaptation of it.

Copyright subsists in such a work (a) that is unpublished, author of which was a qualified person, i.e., (1) an Australian citizen, (2) an Australian protected citizen, or person resident in Australia, when work was first published; or, if dead, was so qualified at time of death; (b) until expiration of 50 years from end of year in which author died or, if before death of author work had not been published, until 50 years after end of year in which work was first published. Author of literary, dramatic, musical or artistic work is owner of any copyright subsisting in it, subject to rights of Crown, any assignment of copyright and special provisions regarding contract of service and work under commission.

In relation to the second category (b) copyright subsists for a period of 50 years from expiration of year in which matter was first published or made but copyright in a published edition of such a matter subsists until expiration of 25 years after year in which edition was first published. Person entitled to copyright protection is owner of tape, maker of film, broadcaster, publisher, respectively.

Protection of performers' performance subsists until expiration of 20 years from day when performance was given.

Copyright Act amended by Copyright (World Trade Organisation Amendments) Act 1994, to enable compliance with agreement on trade related aspects of intellectual property rights. Amendments include: (a) grant of rental rights in relation to computer software and sound recordings; (b) extension of scope of performers' protection; and (c) expansion of border enforcement provisions in Act.

Infringement.—Copyright may be infringed by doing acts comprised in copyright, by person who is not owner and without licence of owner. Copyright can also be infringed indirectly in three ways: Importing for sale, distribution etc., copies of category (a) works without license; selling such works when know or ought reasonably to know imported or made in infringement; allowing place of public entertainment to be used for infringing performance. First two types narrowed by Copyright Amendment Act 1991.

It is not infringed by fair dealing for purpose of (a) research or private study; (b) criticism or review; (c) reporting news; (d) judicial proceedings; (e) making back-up copy from non-infringing copy of computer program, to be used if original is lost, destroyed or unusable, provided that owner of copyright may negative this by express direction to owner of copy; (f) inclusion of work in collections for use by places of education; or (g) by reading or recitation of extract of reasonable length from work, either in performance via public media, or by recording it for such performances.

Remedies for Infringement.—(1) Owner may bring action, and court may give relief including injunction and either damages or account of profits; (2) action is given to a person in respect of whom a breach of duty not to attribute falsely the authorship of a work has occurred. (Pt. V).

Designs.—Designs Act 1906 substantially amended by Designs Amendment Act 1981. Design defined as features of shape, configuration, pattern or ornamentation applicable to article, being features that, in finished article, can be judged by eye, but does not include method or principle of construction.

Author of a design is the first owner thereof and the person entitled to make application for registration thereof, unless he makes the design for valuable consideration on behalf of another person, in which case the latter is deemed to be the author of the design.

Registered design may be assigned in writing, and owner of unregistered design may assign whole or part of his interest in design. Initial period of registration is for one year only, this period capable of extension to maximum period of 16 years.

Remedy for infringement of monopoly in registered design is by action for damages, account of profits or injunction.

See Topical Index in front part of this volume.

COPYRIGHT . . . *continued*

Design/Copyright Overlap.—Persons intending to distribute articles in Australia to which registrable design is applied should first seek registration of design. Protection under Copyright Act for published registrable designs is limited.

CORPORATIONS:

Company is separate legal entity from members and can, among other things, initiate or defend legal proceedings and enter into contracts (subject to certain common law and statutory restraints).

Background.—High Court held Commonwealth Parliament does not have constitutional power to legislate with respect to incorporation of trading and financial corporations. Subsequent agreement between States and Commonwealth for new cooperative system, with Commonwealth having larger role in development and passing of legislation and, through Australian Securities Commission, corporate regulation.

National Scheme.—Corporations Act 1989 (Cth) passed for Australian Capital Territory, and adopted as in force for time being by legislation of each State and Northern Territory. Legislation is collectively referred to as "Corporations Law", and prevails over previous cooperative scheme legislation except in relation to matters arising before 1 Jan. 1991.

Corporations Law combines in one piece of legislation four Codes of previous scheme. Australian Securities Commission (established by Australian Securities Commission Act 1989) is sole administrative and regulatory authority, formally responsible to Commonwealth Attorney-General and Commonwealth Parliament. Corporations Law establishes Corporations and Securities Panel to determine applications by A.S.C. for declarations of unacceptable conduct in relation to shares or acquisition of shares. First Corporate Law Simplification Act 1995 attempts to simplify Corporations Law by amending law relating to (among others) share buy-backs, small businesses, proprietary companies and company registers.

Commonwealth has dominant role in amendment of legislation, particularly as to reform proposals relating to national markets (such as takeovers, securities, public fundraising and futures). Ministerial Council (made up of representatives from each State, Northern Territory and Commonwealth) retains consultative role, Commonwealth having four votes and casting vote and each State and Northern Territory having one vote. Commonwealth has right of veto over any reform proposal.

Coverage of Corporations Law is much the same as that of four previous Codes, dealing with wide range of corporate activity: Formation of companies, management of companies, constituent documents of companies and alteration thereof, directors' duties, financing of corporate activities and raising of finance (through share capital and loans), shares and classes of shares, dividends and other types of distribution, and company liquidations and windings up.

Corporations Law c. 6 regulates acquisitions of shares by persons whose holdings are above prescribed percentage (currently 20%) of voting shares of company. Act also extends to acquisitions that would increase person's holding to more than prescribed percentage. "Holding" includes shares over which person can control right of disposal or voting right, and shares of associated person.

Stock Exchange.—Corporations Law c. 7 regulates various aspects of securities industry including Stock Exchange activities, relationship between Stock Exchange and members and between Stock Exchange and bodies that issue securities, and undesirable practices in securities dealings (e.g. insider trading).

Restriction on membership of Stock Exchanges lifted after determination of Trade Practices Commission. Brokers can incorporate and nonmembers of stock exchanges may acquire up to 50% shareholding in broking companies. Overseas entry into Australian exchanges permitted from brokers in countries with reciprocal entry requirements. Corporations can be admitted as members of exchanges and brokers may become members of more than one exchange.

Futures Industry.—Corporations Law c. 8 regulates futures industry. Act follows general format of Securities Industry Act, including prohibition of insider trading and provision for licensing of all futures brokers, advisers and their representatives.

See topic Corporations in Part II.

COURTS:

See topic Constitution and Government, subhead Judiciary.

CURRENCY: See topic Banking and Currency.

CUSTOMS:

Commonwealth Constitution gives exclusive power to impose customs duties to Commonwealth (prohibiting interstate customs duties). Customs Act 1901 deals with general management of customs and collection of customs duty; while Customs Tariff Acts specify what duties are to be collected on particular goods or classes of goods. Customs Act 1901 has been incorporated into Customs Tariff Act 1987 and is to be read as one Act. Customs Tariff Act 1987 applies International Convention on Harmonized Commodity Description Coding System done at Brussels on 14 June, 1983 to Australia. This Act together with Customs and Excise Legislation Amendment Act 1987 results in extensive changes being made to Australian Customs law. Act essentially enacted to implement announcement of Treasurer on 13 May, 1987 relating, inter alia, to: (a) Commonwealth authorities being required to pay duties of customs; (b) revised arrangements governing payments of duty rebates on diesel fuel for eligible purposes. See also Customs and Excise Legislation Amendment Act 1993; and (c) imposition of charge of A$200 (or higher if so prescribed) for processing of applications for refunds of customs duty made after 13 May, 1987. Schedule 3 is principal schedule for customs duties and rates. Entry must be given to Collector of Customs for all imported goods to be unshipped for: (a) Home consumption; (b) warehousing; (c) transshipment or (d) for removal to place specified in entry. Import duties must be paid at rate in force when goods are entered for home consumption. Governor-General empowered to declare certain goods prohibited imports/exports. Importation of some goods requires licence under Customs (Import Licensing) Regulations. Classification (Publications, Films and Computer Games) Act 1995 introduces censorship laws to apply throughout Australia (with cooperation of States). Act establishes Classification Board and Classification Review Board and sets out procedures for classification of publications, films and computer games. Classification decisions are to be made in accordance with National Classification Code and Guidelines to help apply Code. Both Code and Guidelines must be agreed upon by Commonwealth and States. Commonwealth Act will not take effect until complementary State and Territory Acts passed. Customs (Prohibited Imports) Regulations extensively revised 1988; specify goods importation of which absolutely prohibited, or which cannot be imported without ministerial consent, or without complying with specified conditions, e.g. consent of Attorney-General with respect to certain offensive publications. Commerce (Trade Descriptions) Act imposes absolute prohibition on import (or export) of goods having false trade description, or no trade description. §228 Customs Act 1901 provides for forfeiture of boats/ships engaged in smuggling or unlawful importations, or fines up to A$100,000. Protection of Movable Cultural Heritage Act 1986 prohibits unlicensed importing of protected cultural goods exported without permission from a country. Imported Food Control Act 1992 provides for inspection of imported food and drink and monitoring of safety and quality, and allows for treatment, destruction or reexportation of noncomplying items. Act prohibits importation of noncomplying or unsafe food. Strong enforcement provisions. Act does not apply to food imported for private consumption or importation of which forbidden by Customs Act.

The Customs and Excise Legislation Amendment Act 1992 and Customs Legislation Amendment Act 1992 amend Customs Act to increase power of officer of customs. In particular, officer is able to request additional information. Acts also deal with use of computers for import entry and sea cargo purposes. Customs Excise and Bounty Legislation Amendment Act 1995 increases customs officer's power to seize goods and search premises.

The Customs and Excise Legislation Amendment Act 1993 inserts Div. 1A of Part VIII into Customs Act 1901 which refines rules of origin as consequences of 1992 Closer Economic Relations review.

Valuation.—Customs (Valuations) Amendment Act 1981 imposes system for valuing goods for ad valorem duty purposes, where value is aggregate of all payments made in connection with goods by purchaser plus number of specified costs associated with purchase and transport of goods. Under Customs and Excise Legislation Amendment Act 1990, valuation system amended to give greater discretion to Collector of Customs in determining customs value of goods. Purpose to combat minimisation/avoidance of duty through commercial practices understating value. Series of fall-back steps to aid valuation: If Collector can determine transaction value of imported goods, then customs value is transaction value; if not, identical goods value; if not, similar goods value; if not, contemporary sales value, etc. Increased penalty for false documentation (see §§154-161L Customs Act 1901). Customs and Excise Legislation Amendment Act (No. 2) 1989 extends application of excise duties to all government business enterprises.

Customs Tariff Amendment Act 1983 gives effect to Closer Economic Relations Trade Agreement with New Zealand. Through trade agreements, special rates of duty apply to produce or manufacture of New Zealand and Canada; special rates for Papua New Guinea, Forum Island Countries and Developing Countries as defined in First Schedule of Customs Tariff Act. Australia moving towards free trade with New Zealand. Customs and Excise Legislation Amendment Act (No. 2) 1989 extends duty free entry to Australian mainland of goods 50% produced on Christmas Island.

Customs Administration Act 1985 establishes Australian Customs Service and creates office of Comptroller-General of Customs. Commercial Tariff Concession orders may be made. Customs Legislation (Tariff Concessions and Anti-Dumping) Amendment Act 1992 replaces preexisting provisions. Comptroller may give concessions where satisfied no substitutable goods produced or capable of being produced in ordinary course of business in Australia or if importing goods would not be likely to have significant adverse effect on market for Australian produced goods or if in national interest. Orders may be revoked. Goods prescribed in regulations ineligible for consideration.

§268 Customs Act 1901 permits concessional entry where goods re-imported after repairs or renovation where that repair or renovation is not capable of being performed in Australia in normal course of business. Free of duty where repairs made pursuant to specific warranty.

Import Quotas.—Tender schemes for rights to enter goods for home consumption at concessional rates. "Declared period" quotas may be imposed.

Refund, rebate or remission of duty is to be made whenever goods have received damage or been pillaged during the voyage, or have, whilst under Customs control, been damaged, pillaged, lost or destroyed. A refund is also to be made when duty has been paid through manifest error of fact or patent misconception of the law. In general, apart from the cases mentioned above, duty cannot be recovered unless at the time of entering the goods the entry is marked "paid under protest" and a statement of the grounds upon which the protest is made is set out on the entry; and in any subsequent proceedings to recover duty the importer is limited to the grounds so set out. Fee to process such applications for refund is A$200. Usual period for bringing application, within 12 months.

Whenever a new tariff schedule is tabled in Parliament, it is the practice of the department to collect duty at the existing rate or the proposed rate, whichever is the higher. If the new schedule becomes law, it dates back to the date when it was tabled, and if not, a validating act is passed, legalising the collections made under it.

Dumping.—Customs Act 1901 and Customs Tariff (Anti-Dumping) Act 1975 provide for imposition of higher rate of duty on imported goods where: (1) (a) Export price (including charges within exporting country) is less than normal value of goods so exported or (b) direct or indirect assistance has been given to production or export of goods; and (2) (with some exceptions) material injury is caused or threatened to Australian industry producing like goods or another country's trade in Australian market. Types of duty are dumping duty, countervailing duty, third country duty and countervailing third country duty.

Anti-Dumping Amendment Acts from 1983 to 1992 and Anti-Dumping Authority Act 1988 introduce new provisions with respect to anti-dumping and create Anti-

CUSTOMS . . . *continued*
Dumping Authority. Anti-dumping measures have maximum life of five years. However, Customs Legislation (Tariff Concessions and Anti-Dumping Authority) Amendment Act 1992 allows for extension of such measures. Anti-dumping provisions do not apply to goods that are produce or manufacture of New Zealand.

DISCRIMINATION:

Religious Discrimination.—Constitution §116 forbids prohibition of free exercise of religion, and no religious test to be required as qualification for any office or public trust under Commonwealth.

Disability Discrimination.—Disability Discrimination Act 1992 prohibits direct or indirect discrimination against persons with disability, in areas of work, education, access to premises, goods and services, facilities, accommodation, clubs and incorporated associations, sport, administration of Commonwealth laws and programs, and requests for information. Harassment on disability grounds prevented. Victimisation and other acts offences. Area of superannuation and insurace excluded. Various other exemptions, such as for infectious diseases. Act expressed not to cover field; State and Territory Acts may still apply. Action plans, inquiries and civil proceedings all provided for.

See also topics Racial Discrimination, Sex Discrimination.

DISPUTE RESOLUTION:

Mandatory Dispute Resolution.—

Family Law.—Under Family Law Act 1975 once proceedings involving children or property commenced, conciliation conferences are mandatory.

Federal Court may order proceedings or part thereof be referred to mediator pursuant to Federal Court Rules.

Labour Law.—Industrial Relations Commission (established by Industrial Relations Act 1988) attempts to prevent and settle industrial disputes by conciliation and arbitration. See topic Industrial Relations.

Voluntary Dispute Resolution.—

Banking.—Australian Banking Industry Ombudsman Scheme establishes Ombudsman who decides complaints against banks by natural persons or partnerships (not corporations) to A$100,000.

Family Law.—Mediation under Family Law Act 1975 must have agreement by both parties.

Aboriginal Land Rights.—National Native Title Tribunal (established by Native Title Act 1993) can be asked to mediate for parties involving acquisition or receiving grant of interest in land.

Superannuation.—Superannuation Complaints Tribunal (set up pursuant to Superannuation [Resolution of Complaints] Act 1993) deals with superannuation fund complaints by conciliation.

Administrative Law.—Various statutes provide right of appeal to Administrative Appeals Tribunal (established by Administrative Appeals Tribunal Act 1975) for claimant wishing to appeal against administrative decisions.

See also topic Dispute Resolution in Part II.

DIVORCE:

Family Law Act 1975, which regulates divorce throughout Commonwealth, has completely superseded previous divorce procedures by eliminating concept of matrimonial fault.

There is now only one ground for dissolution of marriage, "irretrievable breakdown of marriage," which is only held to be established if parties have been continuously separated for 12 months prior to application. Separation may be effected even though cohabitation was terminated by action or conduct of only one party, and may be held to have continued notwithstanding that parties reside in same residence. No decree will be granted where there is "reasonable likelihood" of cohabitation being resumed.

All proceedings for divorce are instituted by application to Family Court. Proceedings may be commenced if, at time application is filed, either party is Australian citizen, or is domiciled in Australia or has been ordinarily resident in Australia for at least one year.

Act provides for reconciliation procedures through counselling organizations forming part of Family Court structure. Court is given authority to direct parties to attend marriage counsellor where injunction is granted in circumstances arising out of marital relationship. Family Law Reform Act 1995 encourages use of dispute resolution mechanisms instead of courts.

Commonwealth constitutional power allows Family Court jurisdiction in all matrimonial causes including, when at least one party to marriage is party to action, adoption, custody and guardianship of children including ex-nuptial, adopted or foster children and proceedings with respect to property of parties to marriage. However, it is required to take account of certain principles when granting relief, such as need for preservation of institution of marriage, protection of family and protection of rights of children. Proceedings may be brought by person other than party to marriage on behalf of child in relation to custody and maintenance of child. Under Constitution, custody of children other than in matrimonial cause is States matter. See also Part II, topic Guardian and Ward.

No decree absolute may be granted until court is satisfied that proper arrangements have been made for welfare and custody of children. In custodial proceedings court is to consider, inter alia, wishes expressed by child. Act empowers parents to enter into court-registered "child agreement" in relation to custody, guardianship or welfare of or access to child, including ex-nuptial child. Provisions of registered agreement may be varied by court if court considers welfare of child requires it. Child itself may institute proceedings to vary agreement.

Party to marriage is only liable to maintain other spouse so far as he or she is able, and only if other spouse is unable to maintain himself or herself. Both parties are liable to maintain children. Court may also make declarations as to interests of parties in matrimonial property and orders altering their interests in such.

Act deems child born to woman, whilst married to man, as result of artificial insemination or implantation of embryo in woman's body, to be child of man and woman regardless of biological parentage.

Maintenance.—Act extends application to ex-nuptial children within defined limits. Act ensures children receive proper level of financial support from reasonable and adequate share of income, property and financial resources of their parents.

Family Law Amendment Act 1991 gives Court power to grant leave for proceedings to be commenced for adoption of child by: (a) Parent of child; (b) spouse of, or person in de facto relationship with, parent of child; or (c) parent of child and either his or her spouse or person in de facto relationship with parent.

Child Support (Registration and Collection) Act 1988, formerly Child Support Act 1988, provides for collection of certain periodic child and/or spousal maintenance payable under court orders and maintenance agreements. Child Support Register is established and Registrar enters child and spousal support obligations created by court orders or agreements. Once obligation entered becomes debt owed to Commonwealth and amount of debt may be automatically withheld from salary or wages. Entitlement of payee is to receive maintenance from Registrar, Federal Commission of Taxation, which in practice is done by Department of Social Security. By Child Support Legislation Amendment Act 1992, provision is made for: (a) Commonwealth to be sole party in recovering from overseas payers; (b) Registrar to recover from third parties; (c) appropriation of money earned within Australia by person owing child support debt who is outside Australia, to pay debt; and (d) court to set aside transactions designed to defeat child support debt. By Child Support Legislation Amendment Act (No. 2) 1992, penalty interest accrues on late payments.

Objective of reform is to ensure non-custodial parents share costs of supporting their children according to their capacity to pay and that adequate support is available for children of separated parents.

Family Law Act implements Convention on Recovery Abroad of Maintenance signed in New York on 20 June 1956 and Convention on the Recognition and Enforcement of Decisions Relating to Maintenance Obligations signed at The Hague on 2 Oct. 1973. The Family Law Amendment Act 1991 increases powers of court to require provision of information. It also makes provision for situation where member of Court personnel has reasonable grounds for suspecting that child abuse has taken place.

Family Law Reform Act 1995 intends to facilitate greater use of mediation, counselling and arbitration and give greater recognition to rights of children and to remove concepts of "custody" and "access" and replace them with notion of "parental responsibility".

Foreign Divorces.—Dissolution or annulment of foreign marriage or legal separation of parties to marriage effected or deemed to have been effected in accordance with law of overseas jurisdiction is recognized as valid in Australia where: (a) Respondent was ordinarily resident in foreign country at time proceedings were instituted ("relevant date"); (b) applicant was ordinarily resident in foreign country and such residence had continued for not less than a year immediately before relevant date or last place of cohabitation of parties was in that country; (c) applicant or respondent was domiciled in foreign country at relevant date; (d) respondent was national of foreign country at relevant date; (e) applicant was national of foreign country at relevant date and was ordinarily resident there at that time, or had been ordinarily resident there for continuous period of one year falling, at least in part, within two years immediately preceding relevant date; (f) applicant was national of, and present in, foreign country at relevant date, and last place of cohabitation of parties was in country law of which, at relevant date, did not provide for dissolution or annulment of marriage; or (g) dissolution, annulment or legal separation would be recognized as valid under common law rules of private international law. Dissolution or annulment of marriage, or legal separation of parties to marriage, deemed to have been effected in accordance with law of overseas jurisdiction if it was effected in another overseas jurisdiction in circumstances where, at relevant date, it would have been recognised as valid by law of first-mentioned overseas jurisdiction.

Foreign Maintenance Orders.—Family Law Regulations provide for registration and enforcement in Australia of maintenance orders made by courts of reciprocating jurisdictions or of jurisdictions with restricted reciprocity as defined in Act and Regulations. Overseas maintenance agreements from prescribed overseas jurisdictions as defined in Act may also be registered and enforced in Australia.

Foreign Custody Orders.—Regulations provide for registration in courts in Australia of custody orders of prescribed overseas countries, and vice versa.

DOMICILE:

In Australia domicile is basis of determining jurisdiction. It connotes permanent home, place person intends to make home "indefinitely" whether resident or travelling for time being. Any evidence of person's hopes, intentions and behaviour is relevant in aiding court to determine domicile.

Person can only have one domicile at any one time. Rule of law that infant is deemed to have its father's domicile and wife has her husband's domicile has been revoked by Domicile Act 1982 which provides that married woman has independent domicile and child of marriage who is under age of 18 takes domicile of that parent with whom it has its principal home unless child under age of 18 is, or has at any time been, married, in which case it is capable of having independent domicile.

Common law rule of revival of domicile of origin on abandonment of domicile of choice has been revoked by Domicile Act 1982. Act makes provision for dependent domicile of adopted children.

See also this topic under Part II.

ENERGY:

Nuclear.—Atomic Energy Act 1953 (as am'd by Atomic Energy Amendment Act 1987) provides that persons discovering prescribed substance at any place in Australia must report it within one month to Minister. Prescribed substance is defined to mean uranium and other substances used in connection with atomic energy. Any prescribed substance automatically property of Commonwealth. Act also provides that authority may be granted to person or to two or more persons engaged in joint venture to

ENERGY . . . *continued*
undertake operations for discovering, mining, recovering, treating and processing prescribed substances on land in Ranger Project Area on behalf of or in association with Commonwealth.

Environment Protection (Nuclear Codes) Act 1978 empowers Governor-General to approve codes of practice in relation to restoration of environment following nuclear activities.

Australian Nuclear Science and Technology Organisation Act 1987 creates statutory body under that name to undertake research and development into nuclear science and technology and its use in medicine, industry, commerce and agriculture, and to facilitate application of results of such research. Not permitted to work on nuclear weapons or explosive devices. Also to condition, manage and store radioactive materials and waste arising from its and other specified persons' activities, and to make available its knowledge and facilities by training, selling or leasing land or equipment, or as appropriate. Certain laws concerning land and environment do not apply to organisation. Act also establishes Nuclear Safety Bureau to monitor safety of organisation's nuclear plant and advise Commonwealth on nuclear safety issues.

ENVIRONMENT:

Environment Protection (Impact of Proposals) Act 1974 provides for examinations of impact on environment of proposed projects or decisions of or under control of Australian Government. Acts which could threaten with extinction or significantly impede recovery of species listed under Endangered Species Protection Act 1992 are deemed to be acts affecting environment. (§5A).

Environment (Financial Assistance) Act 1977 provides for granting of financial assistance to States in connection with projects related to environment.

Environment Protection (Nuclear Codes) Act 1978 empowers Government to declare national codes of practice to regulate environmental, health and safety aspects of uranium mining and other nuclear activities in Northern Territory, States and Norfolk Island. National Parks and Wildlife Conservation Act 1975 establishes "conservation zones" and places restrictions on mining and other activities in zones and other areas. National Parks and Wildlife Conservation Amendment Act 1992 provides mechanisms for enforcement, giving officers powers of search, arrest, confiscation and enforcement, and providing certain offences.

Great Barrier Reef Marine Park Act 1975 makes provision for Governor-General to declare area within Great Barrier Reef Region as "Marine Park," and prohibits mining in area so declared. Amendment Act 1988 prohibits buildings, pontoons, etc. in certain areas; regulates operation of certain vessels in those areas; prohibits discharge of waste in Marine Park. Great Barrier Reef Marine Park Amendment Act 1990 clarifies and confirms operation of Statutory Marine Park Zoning Plans thereby improving management of Marine Park. Great Barrier Reef Marine Park Amendment Act 1991 introduces scheme of compulsory pilotage on regulated ships within defined area of Great Barrier Reef Region. Amending Acts of 1993 impose charges on commercial users of area to meet costs required to protect it. Environment, Sport and Territories Legislation Amendment Act 1995 regulates discharge of waste and management plans for areas.

Protection of the Sea (Prevention of Pollution from Ships) Act 1983 incorporates International Convention for the Prevention of Pollution from Ships as modified and added to by 1978 Protocol and amendments adopted on 16 Nov. 1990, 4 July 1991 and 6 Mar. 1992. Act relates to protection of Australian waters from pollution by oil and other harmful substances discharged from ships. Transport and Communications Legislation Amendment Act 1994 amends Act to provide for detention of foreign ships which are suspected of, or have committed, act of pollution. Transport and Communications Legislation Amendment Act (No. 2) 1992 inserts prohibition on sewage discharge in Antarctic area (penalty up to A$200,000), and garbage discharge in sea. Defense of "unavoidable leakage" no longer available. Protection of the Sea (Civil Liability) Act 1981 implements provisions of 1969 Civil Liability Convention and 1976 Protocol. Object to ensure adequate compensation where pollution by oil occurs on land or in territorial sea. 1994 Amendment Act gives Maritime Safety Authority statutory right to recover any costs incurred in performing its obligations to combat pollution. Protection of the Sea (Powers of Intervention) Act 1981 implements International Convention Relating to Intervention on the High Seas in Cases of Oil Pollution Casualties 1969, as affected by resolution of Marine Environment Protection Committee adopted 4 July 1991, and subsequent Intervention Protocol 1973. See also topic Shipping. Protection of the Sea (Oil Collection Compensation Fund) Act 1993 and associated taxing Acts require persons who receive into Australia by ship more than 150,000 tons of oil in each year to pay contribution to fund established pursuant to International Convention on Establishment of International Fund for Compensation for Oil Pollution Damage 1971, and amending protocols of 1976 and 1992. Two funds established, 1971 fund and 1992 fund. In addition to compensating for oil spills, 1971 fund available to offset liabilities under Protection of the Sea (Civil Liability) Act 1981.

Hazardous Waste (Regulation of Exports & Imports) Act 1989 regulates export and import of hazardous waste to ensure exported or imported hazardous waste disposed of safely so human beings and environment, within and outside Australia, protected from harmful effects of waste. Act implements Basel Convention on the Control of Transboundary Movements of Hazardous Wastes and their Disposal. Import and export of hazardous waste regulated by import and export permits. Applicants required to have appropriate insurance. Extensive powers of search and seizure vested in inspectors and heavy penalties imposed for offences under Act.

Environment Protection (Sea Dumping) Act 1981 gives effect to 1972 Convention on the Prevention of Marine Pollution by Dumping of Wastes and Other Matter. It is offence for foreign and Australian vessels to dump wastes in Australian waters without permit. Special provisions relate to dumping of radioactive wastes. Environment Protection (Sea Dumping) Amendment Act 1993 implements ratification of one of protocols to Convention for the Protection of the Natural Resources and Environment of the South Pacific Region. Protocol is for protection from pollution by dumping. South Pacific Nuclear Free Zone Treaty Act 1986 effects Treaty in Australia; prohibits dumping at sea of nuclear explosive devices and radioactive materials. Wildlife Protection (Regulation of Exports and Imports) Act 1982 (as am'd by Wildlife Protection [Regulation of Exports and Imports] Amendment Act 1995) deals with obligations to protect and conserve wild fauna and flora in Australia by implementing 1973 Washington Convention on International Trade in Endangered Species of Wild Flora and Fauna.

World Heritage Properties Conservation Act 1983 prohibits acts that might damage or destroy certain property that Australia has identified as "natural heritage" or "cultural heritage" within meaning of Convention for the Protection of the World Cultural and Natural Heritage. High Court has upheld constitutional validity of Act. Amendment Act 1989 extends prohibition to property subject to Commonwealth inquiry or subject to World Heritage List nomination.

Ozone Protection Act 1989, Ozone Protection (Licence Fees—Imports) Act 1989 and Ozone Protection (Licence Fees—Manufacture) Act 1989 implement provisions of Vienna Convention for the Protection of the Ozone Layer as modified and added to by Montreal Protocol on Substances that Deplete the Ozone Layer. Currently updated by Ozone Protection Amendment Act 1995.

Resources Assessment Commission established by Resources Commission Assessment Act 1989 for purpose of inquiring into and reporting on environmental, cultural, social, industrial and economic aspects of resources and their uses; policy for resolving competing claims for use of resources; integrated approach to conservation and development to optimise net benefits to community from nation's resources.

An Intergovernmental Agreement on the Environment was entered into by Commonwealth, States, Northern Territory, Australian Capital Territory and Australian Local Government Association on 1 May 1992. Agreement is basis of National Environment Protection Council Act 1994 (Cth) which establishes National Environment Protection Council to oversee uniform national approach to protection of environment. Council's membership made up of Commonwealth representative and representative from each participating State and Territory. Function is to make national environment protection measures and to assess and report on implementation and effectiveness of such measures.

National Environment Protection Council Act 1994 created National Environment Protection Council which has power to make national environment protection measures relating to air or water quality, noise, site contamination, hazardous wastes and recycling.

Antarctic Territory.—Australia signatory to Antarctic Treaty, adopted into domestic law by various statutes. Antarctic Treaty Act 1960 prohibits nuclear explosion in Antarctica and disposal of radioactive waste material.

Antarctic Treaty (Environment Protection) Act 1980 gives effect to measures of Antarctic Treaty for conservation of Antarctic fauna and flora. Antarctic Treaty (Environment Protection) Legislation Amendment Act 1992 enacts new provisions relating to specially protected species and areas and to historic sites and monuments, provides for environment impact statements and monitoring of proposed activities in area, and prohibits mining in Australian Territory by non-Australian and outside it by Australian. Penalties of up to A$100,000 can be imposed on those in breach. Offences are stated to be indictable. Courts of summary jurisdiction may also hear and determine proceedings. Such courts may impose fine not exceeding A$10,000 in case of individuals, or fine not exceeding A$50,000 in case of body corporate. Act repeals Antarctic Mining Prohibition Act 1991. Antarctic Marine Living Resources Conservation Act 1981 gives effect to Convention on Conservation of Antarctic Marine Living Resources.

Prime Minister announced 22 May 1989 that Australia would not sign Antarctic Mining and Minerals Convention, but would pursue negotiation of comprehensive environmental protection convention for Antarctic within existing treaty.

Mining activity includes activity in connection with recovery or exploitation of minerals, but does not include activity connected with scientific investigation or research.

Endangered Species.—Endangered Species Protection Act 1992 provides for protection of endangered and vulnerable species. Administered by Director of National Parks and Wildlife. Minister may list endangered, vulnerable and presumed extinct species, endangered ecological communities and key threatening processes. Act provides for recovery plans and threat abatement plans. Director may enter conservation agreements and make orders protecting species. Wide powers of officers. Endangered Species Advisory Committee and Scientific Sub-Committee established by Act.

ESTATE TAX: See topic Taxation.

EXCHANGE CONTROL:

Floating Dollar, Reserve Bank Discretionary Power to Trade.—Reserve Bank of Australia is responsible for administering exchange control restrictions under Banking (Foreign Exchange) Regulations made under Banking Act 1959. On Dec. 12, 1983 Australian dollar was floated; however Reserve Bank retains discretionary power to intervene in foreign exchange market. Very few exchange controls now exist—in particular; (i) No restrictions on payment for imports or expenditure of proceeds from exports; (ii) banks free to deal with customers in currencies at negotiated rates; and (iii) financial institutions in Australia permitted to offer foreign currency denominated accounts to clients.

Restrictions on Physically Transferring Notes, Coins and Foreign Currency.—Amount of notes and coins that Australian residents can take with them on departure from Australia and without Reserve Bank approval is A$5,000. Nonresidents (i) can take out any amount in foreign exchange or Australian currency instruments (other than Australian notes and coins) if nonresident brought such amount into Australia and (ii) can bring into Australia any amount of domestic or foreign currency.

Purchasing Foreign Exchange.—Purchases and sales of foreign exchange by residents in exchange for Australian currency have to be made through authorised foreign exchange dealers in Australia. Trading banks and authorised nonbank financial institutions authorised to engage in foreign exchange transactions at mutually negotiated rates. Government has issued over 74 new licences for foreign exchange dealers to nonbank financial institutions since Apr. 10, 1984. These nonbank financial institutions required to apply under Banking (Foreign Exchange) Regulations and must meet following criteria and conditions:

EXCHANGE CONTROL . . . *continued*

(1) Minimum level of shareholders' funds of A$10,000,000; and (2) demonstrated capacity and expertise to carry out foreign exchange dealings. Authorities granted subject to conditions relating to: (1) Observance of certain prudential standards on foreign exchange risk proportions; (2) provision of statistical and other market information; (3) maintenance of acceptable operating standards; (4) observance of requirements associated with monitoring certain transactions for tax screening purposes and government policies requiring supervision of foreign currency transactions. Conditions may be varied from time to time, and authorities withdrawn if conditions not observed.

Tax Evasion Controls on Foreign Exchange Transactions.—Taxation Administration Act 1953 and Banking Act 1959 provide comprehensive legislative basis for tax screening arrangements to prevent evasion or avoidance of Australian tax through transactions with overseas tax havens. Under arrangements: (a) Foreign exchange dealer must receive tax clearance certificate from Australian Taxation Office before undertaking any of following outward foreign exchange transactions: (i) Loan, repayment of loan, payment of consideration for acquisition of securities, land or other property or options thereto other than consideration for purchase through member of Australian stock exchange of listed securities or options, payment of royalty or licence fee, payment for performance of any service, payment to create trust or payment into trust where, as result of transaction, currency transferred to Bahamas, Bermuda, British Channel Islands, British Virgin Islands, Cayman Islands, Gibraltar, Grenada, Hong Kong, Isle of Man, Liberia, Liechtenstein, Luxembourg, Nauru, Netherlands Antilles, Panama, Switzerland or Tonga; (ii) transfer of currency to Vanuatu except where such transfer is one of following kinds: payment for purpose of travel outside Australia, payment relating to life assurance policy, donation or bequest to certain charitable organisations or religious bodies, payment of consideration for purchase of listed securities or option through member of Australian stock exchange, payment of any dividend or interest on listed security which is registered in name of holder with overseas address, or payment of A$200 or less; (iii) transfer of currency by person who has emigrated from Australia within previous 12 months or intends to so emigrate where amount of currency exceeds A$50,000; (b) foreign exchange dealer must send declaration to Australian Taxation Office after undertaking outward foreign exchange transaction where transfer of currency exceeds A$50,000 and transaction comprises direct investment overseas, gift (other than donation by charitable and religious bodies), loan to nonresidents, portfolio investment overseas, repayment of borrowings from overseas, travel expenditure, remittance relating to futures operations overseas, payment of interest or dividend other than on listed security which is registered in name of holder with overseas address, or payment of any service fee or royalty.

Financial Transaction Reports Act 1988 requires reporting of certain currency transfers to and from Australia in excess of A$10,000 to Cash Reports Transaction Agency.

See topics Aliens; Banking and Currency, subhead Banking Act 1959; Taxation.

EXECUTION:

Attachment or execution may issue to enforce a judgment. Attachment of persons can only issue by leave of the court, but execution against land or goods, unless restrained, can issue as of course upon a judgment for a sum of money. There is no equitable relief against execution of a judgment. See also this topic, Part II.

EXPORT CONTROL:

Customs Act 1901 and Export Control Act 1982 provide for regulations to be made controlling, prohibiting or restricting export of prescribed goods, inspection and seizure and associated offences. "Prescribed goods" include food, animal or plants (dead or alive) which are prescribed by regulations made under Act. Certain prohibitions also imposed on exports to countries such as Libya, Iraq, etc. Requirements for export are generally notifying customs and obtaining relevant authority to deal with goods. Customs and Excise Legislation Amendment Act 1989 empowers Minister for Defence to suspend licences and permissions to export goods where in Australia's national interest.

Export control achieved also through provisions of subject-specific statutes, e.g. Wildlife Protection (Regulation of Exports and Imports) Act 1982, Protection of Movable Cultural Heritage Act 1986 and Ozone Protection Act 1989.

FOREIGN EXCHANGE:

See topic Exchange Control.

FOREIGN INVESTMENT:

See topics Aliens; Banking and Currency; Exchange Control; and Taxation.

FOREIGN TRADE REGULATIONS:

Australia is party to Marrakesh Agreement Establishing the World Trade Organisation incorporating General Agreement on Tariffs and Trade and is member of International Monetary Fund, International Labour Organization, United Nations Industrial Development Organisation, A.P.E.C. and O.E.C.D.

See topics Customs; Exchange Control.

See Australian Treaty List, Treaty Series, Department of Foreign Affairs, Canberra, A.C.T.

FRAUDULENT SALES AND CONVEYANCES:

Under Bankruptcy Act 1966 conveyance, transfer or other disposition (including creation) of property that would otherwise have been available to creditors by debtor is void against trustee in bankruptcy. At common law in order to impeach transaction as fraudulent, it is necessary to show fraudulent intent on both sides unless assignee gave no consideration. Under Act it is sufficient to show debtor's main purpose was to prevent or hinder creditors, which can be inferred from circumstances of imminent insolvency. Under Act or at common law there is no time limit prior to date of bankruptcy within which fraudulent disposition must be made before it can be attacked, and there is no time limit after date of bankruptcy in which trustee in bankruptcy must commence actions in respect of transfer to defeat creditors.

IMMIGRATION:

Noncitizen Entry.—Migration Act 1958 says noncitizen must have current visa to lawfully travel to Australia.

Visas.—Noncitizen must have visa. Migration Act 1958 provides for grant of visas to travel to, enter and remain in Australia. Permanent visa is visa to remain indefinitely. Classes of permanent visa include absorbed person visa and ex-citizen visa. Temporary visa is visa to remain for specified period, until specified event happens, or while holder has specified status. Classes of temporary visa include: special category visa, available to New Zealanders and other classes to be prescribed, which does not require authorisation prior to arrival in Australia; criminal justice visa, for noncitizens allowed into Australia in interests of criminal justice; bridging visa; and special purpose visa. Protection visas may be available to refugees. Regulations may prescribe way for making application and allow visa to be granted only in specified circumstances or subject to conditions.

Grant of visa is in discretion of Immigration Minister subject to detailed criteria such as whether applicant accumulates prescribed score based on points given for characteristics (such as employment qualifications, age and language skills). Minister may determine maximum number of each class of visa per year. Minister may cancel visa if: misleading information given by noncitizen when applying; conditions not complied with; or circumstances which permitted grant of visa no longer exist. Before cancellation, noncitizen must be notified and invited to comment.

Detention, Removal and Deportation of Unlawful Citizens.—Immigration officer may ask noncitizen to prove status of lawful noncitizen. Unlawful noncitizens subject to mandatory detention until: (a) removed from Australia; (b) deported from Australia; or (c) granted visa. Detainee may apply for any visa or bridging visa which provides temporary lawful status so detention no longer mandatory. Bridging visa granted if detainee unlikely to abscond.

Unlawful noncitizen, who is without immigration clearance and who has not validly applied for visa other than bridging visa or criminal justice visa, or is detainee whose visa application was rejected, is required to be removed from Australia by immigration officer. Noncitizen deported if: present in Australia for less than ten years and convicted of crime; convicted of serious crime; or is security threat. Noncitizen is liable in debt to Commonwealth Government to pay cost of detention, removal and deportation.

Immigration Assistance.—To assist immigration officers in dealing with unlawful noncitizens, Migration Act 1958 gives officers power to examine and search vessels and aircraft and creates offences for ship owners and masters who carry unlawful noncitizens. Migration Amendment Act (No. 3) 1992 inserts new Part in Migration Act 1958 prohibiting person giving immigration assistance, unless person is: (1) parliamentarian; (2) lawyer giving immigration legal assistance; (3) individual not receiving fee; (4) immigration official; (5) diplomat; or (6) registered migration agent. Penalty for giving immigration assistance is A$5,000. Penalty for person receiving fee for giving immigration assistance or making immigration representations is ten years' imprisonment, unless person is lawyer giving immigration legal assistance or registered migration agent. Individuals apply to Secretary of Immigration Department for registration as migration agent.

Review of Decisions.—Migration Act 1958 provides codes of procedure for decision making. Migration Regulations provide details of codes. There are four tiers of review of decisions: (i) internal review on merits by Department of decisions concerning visas other than protection visas; (ii) review on merits by Refugee Review Tribunal of decisions concerning protection visas and by Immigration Review Tribunal concerning other decisions; (iii) review by Administrative Appeals Tribunal if referred by either Tribunal in (ii); and (iv) appeal on question of law to Federal Court.

See also topic Nationality.

INCOME TAX: See topic Taxation.

INDUSTRIAL RELATIONS:

Commonwealth has power to make laws with respect to "conciliation and arbitration for the prevention and settlement of industrial disputes extending beyond the limits of any one State." As result of machinery set up under this constitutional power and of judicial interpretation it has received, Commonwealth today plays major role in regulating Australian working conditions. Part II of Industrial Relations Act 1988 sets up Australian Industrial Relations Commission "IRC" which has function of preventing and settling industrial disputes by conciliation and arbitration, taking into account among other things public interest and compliance with grievance procedures in any relevant agreement or award.

Part XIV of Act as amended by Industrial Relations Reform Act 1993 confers jurisdiction on Industrial Relations Court of Australia which has jurisdiction to determine appeals from IRC on questions of law referred to it by IRC, appeals from State Courts, validity of State Industrial Relations laws, and to interpret and enforce awards made by IRC.

Part IV of Act sets up Australian Industrial Registry which has number of functions including provision of advice and assistance to organisations regarding their rights and obligations under Act, review of operation of awards, approval of alterations to organisations' rules other than eligibility rules, issuing of certificates as to employers' membership of organisation, and administratively supporting State industrial bodies.

Associations of employers and associations of employees may apply for registration as organisations under Act. Act provides that rules of association applying for registration under Act or organisation registered under Act shall include rules regarding certain matters including democratic control by members, elections, objects, powers and duties, internal management, audit, eligibility for membership, terms of office in organisation and manner of removal of officers.

Further, in order to facilitate participation by members of associated State trade unions in affairs of Federal employee organisations, rules may under certain circumstances authorise organisation to enter into agreement with associated State registered unions with effect that members of State registered unions who are ineligible for membership of Federal associated organisation are eligible pursuant to such agreement to become members of Federal organisation; however, Federal organisation cannot represent such persons in Federal industrial relations system. Hearing of applications

INDUSTRIAL RELATIONS . . . *continued*
for registration of organisations or amendment to eligibility rules of organisations are undertaken by Presidential member of Commission.

Registration provisions have been held sufficient to give organisation legal personality separate from persons who collectively make up its membership, and powers of that separate legal personality are defined by its registered rules which derive their authority from Act. Registered organisation can have powers beyond those necessary for its participation in processes of conciliation and arbitration for settlement of industrial disputes.

Act also provides for supervision of union elections (such elections to be held by secret ballot) and for declarations as to void elections in cases of irregularity. Further provisions regulate loans, grants and donations. Act allows for enforcement of rules directly without need for common law actions.

The Court or Commission has jurisdiction whenever there is industrial "dispute" (which may be of merely formal character, such as making and refusal of claim), or be of more substantive nature, as is case with, for example, demarcation dispute (i.e. dispute as to which organisation of employees has right to represent industrial interests of particular class or group of employees). However, such dispute must extend beyond limits of any one State, which it may do if it exists in more States than one, i.e., particular industry itself may create sufficient nexus between employers to link up into one single dispute, disputes which might otherwise be regarded as series of identical local disputes (as may union between employees). High Court has held Commission has power to order reinstatement of employees. Awards made by IRC bind both present and future members of trade unions and employers associations and also successors, assignees and transmittees (whether immediate or not) to or of business or part of business of employer who was originally party to industrial dispute. Award may settle any industrial matter in dispute and hence may prescribe conditions of employment of nonmembers of trade unions which are before Commission. Under Act it has been possible to provide minimum basic wage and 35-40 hour working week throughout Australia.

Award system now complemented by option available to employees and employers to reach agreement at enterprise level. In National Wage Case in Oct. 1991, Commission used power to certify agreements (see below) to provide for system with enterprise bargaining options. Enterprise level agreements have same legal status as awards, with potential to oust terms of awards. Role of Commission is to conciliate in disputes over enteprise bargains. In Oct. 1991 National Wage Case, Commission also affirmed commitment begun in 1987 to wage increases based on structural efficiency.

Act creates offences where either employer or organisation (registered under Act) takes or organisation advises, encourages or incites person (whether employer or not) to take discriminatory action against employee who refuses or fails to join in industrial action. Act also makes allowance for conscientious objection to membership of organization. All proceedings for offences against Act may be instituted by summons issued on information, without indictment. Penalty for offence by natural person generally A$500 or six months imprisonment or both and for offence by corporation generally A$1,000.

Commission has number of powers including power: (i) To make awards including consent awards (i.e. where parties agree to award) providing that consent award is in public interest; (ii) to prescribe minimum rates of pay; (iii) to include bans clause in award; (iv) to include stand down provisions in award; and (v) to certify agreements. If parties to industrial dispute agree on terms for settlement or prevention of dispute then they may make memorandum of agreed terms and apply to Commission for certification. Commission must certify agreement unless satisfied that agreement disadvantages employees concerned. Terms of certified agreement prevail over terms of award or order of Commission. Parties may vary or terminate certified agreement on application to Commission (to Full Bench of Commission in case of variation).

Another option available to parties is to apply to Commission to approve enterprise flexibility agreement covering enterprise and its employees who are covered by award. Agreement must not disadvantage employees, who must be consulted during negotiations.

Commission has additional powers in relation to industrial disputes in public sector employment. Commission has limited power to dismiss matter without considering merits of dispute.

Commission, comprising of president and such number of vice-presidents and commissioners as are from time to time necessary, also has power, inter alia, to order secret ballot to be held when industrial action is being taken or is threatened, pending or probable. Industrial action means performance of work (which is covered by award of Commission) in manner different from customary performance or adoption of practice in relation to work which leads to restriction or limitation on or delay in performance of work. Also includes ban, limitation or restriction on performance of work or failure or refusal to attend for work. Court has power to cancel registration of organisation on various grounds of misbehaviour e.g. where organisation has or is engaged in industrial action that has had, is having, or is likely to have substantial adverse effect on safety, health or welfare of community or part of community. It is also possible to have partial deregistration i.e. cancellation of right of organisation to represent certain classes or categories of persons. Deregistration powers rarely used. Members of organization at place of work directed by organization to take industrial action can apply for secret ballot and on majority vote not be required to obey direction of organization. Act prevents prescribed persons (persons convicted of crimes relating to fraud, dishonesty, or violence which are punishable by periods of imprisonment of not less than three months or other offences under Act) from holding office in registered organizations unless court grants leave. See also topic Monopolies and Restraint of Trade.

Inspectors (appointed under Part V) investigate observance of Act, regulations and awards and employee safety. Act includes provisions designed to facilitate amalgamation of organizations registered under Act. Applications for approval of amalgamation dealt with by Presidential member who may, on being satisfied (among other things) that amalgamation would further objects of Act and that there is community of interest between organisations amalgamating in relation to their industrial interests, approve ballot on amalgamation by members of amalgamating organisations. In Jan. 1991 amendments were passed to facilitate and encourage amalgamation of organizations, aiming to reduce number of organizations in industry or enterprise. Organizations of employees must now generally have at least 10,000 members to satisfy criteria for registration (previously 1,000); this requirement is to be phased in with reviews of smaller unions every three years potentially leading to their deregistration. Division 7 of Part IX provides speedier procedures for amalgamation. Organizations proposing to amalgamate may apply for registration as federation, which may represent its constitutent members for all purposes of Act (but may not become party to award).

Act contains special provisions relating to Commonwealth and Territory employees.

Federal awards take precedence over State laws, orders and awards. Act also contains provisions to facilitate cooperation and coordination between State and Commonwealth industrial relations system.

Australia has acceded to U.N. Convention on Recognition and Enforcement of Foreign Arbitral Awards. See Part VII of this volume.

Minimum Entitlements.—Industrial Relations Reform Act 1993 in amending Industrial Relations Act 1988 establishes minimum entitlements for wages, equal pay for work of equal value, termination payments, parental leave and compassionate leave.

1995 Amendment Act amends unfair dismissal provisions to provide simpler more effective procedure. Involves beginning with conciliation, moving to consent arbitration, appeal to Full Bench of IRC and ultimately referral to Court.

Workplace Bargaining.—Although Industrial Relations Commission ("IRC") retains its traditional award making function, enabling it to ensure awards maintain fair "safety net" of minimum wages and conditions, Reform Act reflects new emphasis on workplace bargaining. Introduction of enterprise flexibility agreements opens way for workplace deals without prerequisite of union involvement or interstate dispute. With conditions precedent of prior award coverage, no disadvantage to employees and employee consultation and majority agreement, corporation employer may submit enterprise agreement to IRC for certification. Unions may still participate, i.e. represent members if requested or volunteer to be bound by agreement. Union also has right to make submission to IRC. IRC must protect minority interests such as women, young persons and people whose first language is not English.

Immunity from Civil Liability.—Right to strike now recognised in course of bargaining for enterprise agreements. Union taking industrial action is protected from civil liability provided it has given 72 hours' notice to employer, action is duly notified to and authorised by Industrial Registrar and union is negotiating in good faith. Conversely, employer can lock out disputant workers during bargaining period provided it similarly gives 72 hours' notice. Employer cannot discriminate against employees who engage in, or propose to engage in industrial action.

Action in tort against union or members taking industrial action lies only where IRC certifies that conciliation would be unlikely to stop conduct promptly or that it would do substantial injustice to employer to prevent it from taking action or that IRC has not stopped conduct after 72 hours.

Secondary boycotts involving industrial action are exclusively dealt with under Industrial Relations system and are no longer subject of pecuniary penalties of Trade Practices Act 1974. Court proceedings may only be commenced in Industrial Relations Court if IRC has issued certificate.

INSOLVENCY: See topic Bankruptcy.

JUDGMENTS:

If at the trial the judge does not direct judgment to be entered, the plaintiff may set down the cause on motion for judgment. If plaintiff does not do so within seven days, defendant may set down cause on motion for judgment instead. Every judgment is entered by proper officer in book kept for that purpose. Judgment may not be entered by consent unless defendant appears before judge and consents, or solicitor acting for him attests his signature to consent in writing. Procedure exists for plaintiff to enter judgment in default should defendant fail to appear in action or fail to file defence. See also Part II.

Under Foreign Proceedings (Excess of Jurisdiction) Act 1984 Attorney-General may, by instrument, block foreign antitrust judgment if satisfied that this is necessary for protection of national interest, or that assumption of jurisdiction of power by foreign court is contrary to international law, or is inconsistent with international comity or practice. Attorney-General may make order prohibiting compliance with certain foreign court judgments relating to trade or commerce, banking, insurance or external affairs where such judgment imposes obligation to be performed in Australia and such blocking order is desirable in national interest.

Foreign Judgments Act 1991 provides for enforcement of some foreign money judgments where there is substantial reciprocity of treatment in foreign country. Judgment must be final and conclusive. Creditor under foreign judgment must apply to appropriate court in Australia within six years of date of last judgment of proceedings.

See also this topic, Part II.

See also topic Actions.

LAW REPORTS: See topic Reports.

LEGISLATURE:

See topic Constitution and Government, subhead Parliament.

MARRIAGE:

Marriage Act 1961 enacts uniform marriage laws for whole of Commonwealth.

Celebration.—Marriages may be celebrated by authorized or registered ministers of religion or by an authorized celebrant or marriage registrar. Consent of the parents or guardians of any person under age of 18 who is not widow or widower is necessary before marriage of such person to any other person may be solemnized. Where such consent unavailable or refused may apply to judge for consent or for dispensation with consent (see §§15 & 16).

A marriage is not invalid by reason of failure to satisfy requirements of notice or provide declarations of date and place of birth and conjugal status nor on account of any unauthorized person solemnizing the marriage if either party to the marriage at time marriage was solemnized believed that that person was lawfully authorized to solemnize it.

See Topical Index in front part of this volume.

MARRIAGE . . . *continued*

Marriageable Age.—The Marriage Act as amended by Sex Discrimination Amendment Act 1991 provides that marriageable age for both males and females is 18 years (or 16 years if there are exceptional circumstances and Judge or Magistrate gives authorization). This requirement extends to: (a) Marriages celebrated within Australia; (b) marriages celebrated overseas in accordance with provisions of Marriage Act; and (c) marriage of a person domiciled in Australia wherever marriage takes place. Where either party to a marriage is not of a marriageable age marriage is void.

Prohibited Marriages.—A marriage between cousins is not within the prohibited degrees of consanguinity.

Domicile.—The Domicile Act 1982 provides that rule of law whereby married woman has at all times domicile of her husband is abolished.

Marriages solemnized in Australia by foreign diplomats and consular officers of proclaimed countries, according to law or custom of their countries, are valid, provided at least one of parties to marriage is national of proclaimed country and neither party is Australian citizen. Exceptions to validity: One or both already married, not of marriageable age, within prohibited relationship, or lack of consent.

Recognition of Foreign Marriages.—Marriage Amendment Act 1985 gives legislative effect to Hague Convention on Celebration and Recognition of the Validity of Marriages (1978) (Part V A). Foreign marriage valid if: (a) Valid according to law of country of solemnization ("local law"); (b) initially invalid under local law but subsequently valid under that law unless party remarried before subsequent validation of first marriage; (c) solemnized in foreign country by embassy official of other foreign country and recognized as valid by second country and not prohibited by first; (d) as category (c), but only subsequently recognized as valid by second country or (e) not required by (a)-(d) to be recognised as valid, but solemnized in foreign country and recognised as valid under common law rules of private international law. Exceptions to recognition: Parties already married, not of marriageable age (if neither party domiciled in Australia, age qualification is male, 16, female, 14), within prohibited relationship, or lack of consent or subsisting, but voidable, marriage under local law.

See also topics Divorce, and Domicile.

MINES AND MINERALS:

By Seas and Submerged Lands Act 1973 Commonwealth claims sovereignty over territorial sea, its airspace and subsoil and sovereign rights over continental shelf and to recovery of minerals, other than petroleum from seabed, subsoil, and from continental shelf. Exception is made in case of bays, gulfs, estuaries, rivers, creeks, inlets, ports, and harbours which were within limits of States on Jan. 1, 1901 and remain therein. As between Commonwealth and States, validity of Act was upheld by High Court in 1975. However, State law extending to area of Commonwealth sovereignty will apply insofar as it is for peace, order and good government of State and until Commonwealth legislates to contrary.

Maritime Legislation Amendment Act 1994 amends Seas and Submerged Lands Act 1973 to bring Australia's maritime zones into line with those to which Australia is entitled under international law as reflected in 1982 Convention on the Law of the Sea. It declares sovereign rights and jurisdiction in exclusive economic zone and rights of control in contiguous zone. It incorporates new definition of continental shelf and natural resources based on 1982 Convention. Proclamations declaring limits of these zones, continental shelf and territorial seas must be within Convention. Amendment also provides for making of regulations for exercise of Australia's rights under international law in relation to exploration and exploitation of minerals and petroleum as natural resources of continental shelf under primary acts Petroleum (Submerged Lands) Act 1967 and Minerals (Submerged Lands) Act 1981.

Petroleum (Submerged Lands) Act 1967 governs search and production of petroleum in Australia's offshore area. 1980 Amending Act provides that Commonwealth alone will have legislative responsibility for Australia's continental shelf areas beyond three mile territorial seas. Legislation to be administered by joint Commonwealth and State Authorities. Detailed amendments are made in respect of permit terms, renewal conditions, title conditions and suspension of permits in national interest. Petroleum operations permitted on most parts of Australia's continental shelf, except for environmentally sensitive areas such as Great Barrier Reef.

1984 Amending Act establishes enlarged safety zones around offshore installations, and empowers Commonwealth and State Joint Authority to give directions as to rate of petroleum production. 1985 Amending Act provides for granting of retention leases over currently noncommercial discoveries and revises registration provisions. Where competitive bidding applies for offshore tenement, choice, at discretion of granting authority, may be between work program system, cash bonus bidding and royalty bidding, or combination. Exploration title holder who discovers petroleum offshore entitled as of right to grant of production licence in respect of discovery; size limitation; competitive bidding does not apply.

Petroleum (Submerged Lands) Act 1967 and Offshore Minerals Act 1994 provide that where petroleum or minerals are recovered under terms of licences, permits or consents under these acts, ownership of such petroleum or minerals is not subject to rights of other persons such as native title holders, but underlying native title is not extinguished. Amendments under Primary Industries and Energy Legislation Amendment (No. 2) Act 1989 to provisions on grant of access authority and removal of title and repeal of requirement that production licence holders spend $300,000 per block per year or to recover production to that value. Petroleum (Australia-Indonesia Zone of Cooperation) (Consequential Provisions) Act 1990 makes amendments consequent on treaty between Australia and Indonesia (see below) by removing Area A of Zone of Cooperation from operation of Act. The Petroleum (Submerged Lands) Royalty Amendment Act 1991, provides for adjustment of payments of royalties in certain situations and Petroleum (Submerged Lands) Fees Act 1994 prescribes new set of fees for licences.

Offshore Minerals Act 1994 (and various consequential Acts) applies to all minerals other than petroleum. It provides legal framework for exploration for, and production of, minerals on Australia's continental shelf that is under Commonwealth jurisdiction, being area beyond three nautical mile limit from territorial sea base line. (Agreement between Commonwealth and State Governments provides that States will introduce mirror offshore minerals legislation for area within three mile limit establishing common offshore mining code. [See this topic, Part II.].) Principles underlying this regulatory arrangement are: (1) all offshore mineral activity in Commonwealth area adjacent to particular State is governed by joint authority consisting of relevant Commonwealth and State Ministers; (2) joint authorities are responsible for major decisions relating to titles, such as grants, refusals and the like, and in event of disagreement, views of Commonwealth Minister prevail; (3) day to day administration of Commonwealth legislation is carried out by relevant State which is primary point of contact between industry and governments. Act sets up licensing scheme providing for five kinds of authorisation: exploration licences, retention licences, mining licences, works licences and special purpose consents. For each authorization it deals with applications, grants, duration, renewal, obligations of holder and expiry. It also deals with related topics of registration and dealings in licences and administration of licensing system.

Off-shore Installations (Miscellaneous Amendments) Act 1982 extends operation of Australian customs, immigration, quarantine and sales tax laws to ships and installations engaged in exploration for minerals and petroleum in Australian waters. Sea Installations (Miscellaneous Amendments) Act 1987 has similar provisions for certain installations in sea.

Treaty Between Australia And The Republic of Indonesia On The Zone of Cooperation In An Area Between The Indonesian Province of East Timor and Northern Australia, signed Dec. 11, 1989. Treaty expressed to be without prejudice to sovereign rights of both Contracting States to disputed continental shelf boundary between two States. Treaty seeks to facilitate exploration for and exploitation of any petroleum resources which may be in continental shelf within Zone of Cooperation (area to which Treaty applies). Petroleum (Australia-Indonesia Zone of Cooperation) Act 1990 (Cth) enables Australia to fulfil its obligations under Treaty. Act upheld by High Court in 1994.

Coastal Waters (State Powers) Act 1980 provides that legislative powers of each of States extends to territorial sea, being those seas within three miles of low water mark of littoral State.

Coastal Waters (State Title) Act 1980 vests proprietary rights in seabed subsoil, and space above seabed of territorial sea in littoral State.

Petroleum Taxation.—Excise Act 1901 and Excise Tariff Act 1921 impose ad valorem excise upon crude oil recovered. Petroleum Excise (Prices) Act 1987 amended by Petroleum Excise (Prices) Amendment Act 1988 and 1990 amendment establishes mechanism for determining duties of excise, amount depending on whether onshore or offshore and production levels, imposed on certain crude petroleum oil.

Petroleum (Submerged Lands) (Royalty) Act 1967 imposes 10% royalty upon offshore petroleum production beyond territorial sea.

Petroleum Resource Rent Tax Assessment Act 1987 imposes profit based tax upon petroleum projects established after July 1, 1984. Where Resource Rent Tax applies excises and royalties are excluded.

Petroleum Revenue Act 1985 provides that where agreement is reached between State government and producer, and between State government and Federal Government, profits based tax will be applied to exclusion of excises and royalties upon projects otherwise in State jurisdiction.

Uranium.—Control over mining of prescribed substances associated with nuclear production (mainly uranium) governed by Atomic Energy Act 1953. Applies in all States and Territories.

Environmental impact statement pursuant to Environment Protection (Impact of Proposals) Act 1974 must be prepared for all proposed mining. Further special procedures needed in certain areas to satisfy Aboriginal Land Rights. See further Part II, this topic.

MONOPOLIES AND RESTRAINT OF TRADE:

Trade Practices Act 1974 (as am'd by Competition Policy Reform Act 1995) is intended to control restrictive trade practices, promote competitiveness of private enterprise and protect consumers from unfair commercial practices.

Competition Policy Reform Act 1995 represents agreement between Commonwealth, State and Territories to promote national approach to competition policy through adoption of The Competition Code. Provides for abolition of Trade Practices Commission and Prices Surveillance Authority and merger of functions into Australian Competition and Consumer Commission (ACCC). Establishes National Competition Council and renames Trade Practices Tribunal as Australian Competition Tribunal.

From July 1996 there will be broader application of Part IV of Trade Practices Act extending to State/Territory enterprises and local government councils (subject to exemptions).

Part IV of Trade Practices Act prohibits certain restrictive trade practices as follows: (a) Certain agreements and covenants affecting competition, including: contracts, arrangements and understandings or covenants having purpose or effect of substantially lessening competition in market in which corporation party supplies or acquires goods, restrictive covenants running with land with purpose or effect of substantially lessening competition (§45); (b) provisions fixing, controlling or maintaining prices of or discounts, allowances, rebates and credits in relation to goods or services (§45A); (c) "exclusionary provisions" i.e. provisions in contract arrangement or understanding between persons any two or more of whom are competitive with each other which provisions have purpose of preventing, restricting or limiting supply or acquisition of goods or services to or from particular persons; (d) secondary boycotts—this includes (i) actions taken by persons in concert to hinder or prevent corporation in supplying goods or services to, or acquiring goods or services from, third person, with effect or likely effect of causing either substantial loss or harm to business of third person or related body corporate of third person or substantial lessening of competition in any market in which such third person or related body corporate supplies or acquires goods or services where such conduct is engaged in for purpose and would have or is likely to have effect of causing substantial loss or damage to corporation or substantial lessening of competition in any market in which corporation acquires goods or services or (ii) actions taken by persons in concert to hinder or prevent third person in supplying goods or services to, or acquiring goods or services from, corporation, with effect or likely effect of causing either substantial loss or damage to business of corporation or of related body corporate of corporation or substantial lessening of

MONOPOLIES AND RESTRAINT OF TRADE . . . *continued*
competition in any market in which such corporation or related body corporate supplies or acquires goods or services (§45D); (e) misuse of market power including misuse of market power in trans-Tasman market (i.e. market in Australia, New Zealand or Australia and New Zealand for goods or services) (§§46, 46A); (f) resale price maintenance (§48); (g) exclusive dealing (e.g. supplying goods on condition that purchaser will not buy from competitor of supplier) (§47); (h) mergers before 21 Jan. 1993, where result is that corporation likely to be in position to dominate, or increase its power to dominate, market for goods and services. For mergers after 21 Jan. 1993, test is whether acquisition has effect or likely effect of substantially lessening competition in market for goods or services. (§50). Acquisitions outside Australia come within Act if acquisition has effect or likely effect of substantially lessening competition in substantial market for goods or services in Australia. (§50A).

Industrial Relations Reform Act 1993 provides that conduct with ultimate purpose of protecting or advancing interests of person or trade union in relation to industrial matters does not infringe (d) above—secondary boycotts, and is now regulated under Industrial Relations Act 1988 as amended by 1993 Reform Act.

Authorizations under Part VII can be obtained where application is made to ACCC and it is satisfied that (i) in case of contracts arrangements or understandings with anticompetitive effect (except price fixing agreements) and exclusive dealing (except third line forcing)—conduct otherwise in contravention of Act would result or be likely to result in benefit to public which would outweigh any detriment constituted by any lessening of competition resulting or likely to result therefrom; and (ii) in case of exclusionary provisions, secondary boycotts, third line forcing, exclusive dealing and mergers—conduct otherwise in contravention of Act would in all circumstances result in such benefit to public that it should be allowed to take place. Misuse of market power, cannot be authorised, however following Competition Policy Reform Act 1995 price fixing can be. Applications for authorisation may be made public. Commission is deemed to have authorised exclusive dealing, secondary boycotts, exclusionary provisions, or anticompetitive contracts if it does not reject application by corporation within four months.

Penalties under Act for breaches of Part IV before 21 Jan. 1993 are up to A$250,000 for corporations and A$50,000 for individuals. For breaches of Part IV after 21 Jan. 1993, penalties are up to A$10 million for corporations and A$500,000 for individuals. Also, court may impose injunctions (§76), award damages and make other ancillary orders in favour of party who has suffered loss as result of prohibited practice. Trade Practices Legislation Amendment Act 1992 gives Trade Practices Commission power to obtain legally enforceable undertakings. In case of mergers, court may order divestiture of shares or assets illegally acquired. (§81).

Word "corporation" is defined in §4(1) of Act as meaning entity that is: (a) Foreign corporation; (b) trading corporation formed within limits of Australia or is financial corporation so formed; (c) incorporated in internal Territory; or (d) holding company of body corporate of kind referred to in (a), (b) or (c), above.

Part IV does not apply in relation to overseas cargo shipping engaged in by shipowner in pursuance of conference agreement; such agreements are governed by Part X.

Trade Practices (International Liner Cargo Shipping) Amendment Act 1989 effects major changes in regulatory system governing international liner cargo shipping so as to improve competitiveness of this area of activity. Previous exemption from Part IV of Trade Practices Act 1974 for conferences (i.e. shipping cartels) reduced to level necessary for continued provision of rationalised services. Exemption limited to: §45 (anti-competitive agreements) and §47 (exclusive dealing) in Australia's export trades; applied only to specified conduct; and made available for other restrictive conduct but only where there is overall shipper benefit. §46 (misuse of market power) applied to conference operations. Discrimination between similarly situated shippers prohibited. New liner cargo shipping regime under Hamburg Rules to be delayed until 1997.

See also topic Consumer Protection.

NATIONALITY:

Australian Citizenship Act 1948 (substantially amended by Australian Citizenship Amendment Act 1984) recognises status of "Australian citizen".

Following Persons are Australian Citizens: (a) Person born in Australia after Jan. 26, 1949; person born in Australia after Aug. 20, 1986 is Australian citizen only if (i) parent was Australian citizen or permanent resident at time of person's birth, or (ii) if person has throughout period of ten years after birth been ordinarily resident in Australia; (b) person who is adopted under State or Territory law (all of which deal with recognition of foreign orders of adoption) by Australian citizen and who at time of adoption is permanent resident of Australia; (c) person born outside Australia to Australian citizen and whose name is registered at Australian consulate within 18 years of birth, but where parent is Australian citizen by descent that parent must have been lawfully present in Australia before registration of child for aggregate period of two years; and (d) person who has been granted certificate of Australian citizenship.

Australian Citizenship Act 1948 provides that after 18 June 1991 person born outside Australia will only be Australian citizen if: (1) parent is Australian citizen and person's name is registered at Australian consulate as result of application made within 18 years of person's birth to register person's name for those purposes (if person over 18 years of age when applies for registration, then must show acceptable reason for not being registered earlier under Australian Citizenship Amendment Act 1991); or (2) person is born before 26 Jan. 1949, person's natural mother (a) became Australian citizen on 26 Jan. 1949; and (b) was born in Australia or New Guinea; or (c) was naturalised in Australia and person applies to Minister for registration before 18 June 1996. (Minister must be satisfied that person: (a) was present in Australia for any time before 1 May 1987; and (b) is of good character.)

Grant of Certificate of Australian Citizenship.—Minister may, in his discretion, upon application in approved form, grant certificate of Australian citizenship to person who satisfies Minister that he: (a) Is permanent resident; (b) has attained 18 years of age; (c) understands application; (d) has been permanent resident of Australia for aggregate period of at least one year in previous two years and for at least two years in previous five years; (e) is of good character; (f) has basic knowledge of English; (g) has adequate knowledge of responsibilities and privileges of Australian citizenship; and (h) is likely to maintain close association with Australia. Citizenship will only be granted to person who is outside of Australia if person is permanent resident engaged in activities beneficial to interests of Australia.

Exemptions from some of these requirements are available to persons with physical or mental incapacity, persons who have completed defence service, persons formerly Australian citizens or born in Australia, elderly persons, minors, persons applying when minors, and spouse, widow or widower of Australian citizen. If there is significant hardship, minister may treat illegal immigrant's period of stay in Australia as if that person were permanent resident. Minister may include in certificate of citizenship name of child of grantee if at time of application child was under 16 and grantee was responsible parent of child. Restrictions apply regarding grant of certificate to persons subject of criminal proceedings. (§13).

Australian Citizenship Amendment Act 1986 amends oath and affirmation of allegiance to remove requirement to renounce all other allegiances. 1990 Amendment Act replaced oath and affirmation of allegiance with "pledge of commitment as a citizen of the Commonwealth of Australia" which is distinctly Australian in character.

Loss of Citizenship.—Australian citizen who does act, sole or dominant purpose of which is acquisition of nationality or citizenship of foreign country, shall cease to be Australian citizen. Marriage is not regarded as such act. (§17). Where Australian citizen is also citizen of foreign country, service in armed forces of that country at war with Australia may result in loss of Australian citizenship. (§19). Person having grant of Australian citizenship may be deprived by Minister of Australian citizenship if for purpose of Act, person knowingly makes misleading representation or conceals material particular or if, after applying for certificate, person is sentenced by law to death or imprisonment for period not less than 12 months and in either case it would be contrary to public interest for person to remain Australian citizen. (§21). Act provides for resumption of citizenship in some circumstances and extends some protection to children whose parents lose citizenship. (§23). Australian citizenship may in specified circumstances be renounced by declaration. (§18).

NAVIGATION:

See topic Shipping.

NEGOTIABLE INSTRUMENTS:

See topic Bills and Notes.

PATENTS:

Patents Act 1990 provides that invention can be patented if it is (a) manner of manufacture; (b) novel and inventive when compared with prior art base (i.e. public information from acts or documents anywhere in Australia) as it existed before priority date; (c) useful; and (d) has not been secretly used by patentee (or his nominee) before priority date (usually date of filing). Act grants patentee exclusive right, during term of patent, to exploit invention.

Human beings and biological processes for their generation are not patentable inventions. Whether life form or microorganism is patentable is decided according to ordinary principles.

In processing application Commissioner will assess invention for novelty and obviousness against prior disclosures anywhere in world.

Convention applications are basically made and dealt with in same way as other patent applications.

Term.—Standard patent is granted for term of 16 years.

Act allows four year extension where patent is for pharmaceutical substances for human use and there has been delay in marketing substance because of need to obtain government marketing approval. Petty patent (alternative to standard patent with reduced period of protection but obtainable in less time and at reduced cost) can be converted into standard patent but otherwise has maximum term of six years.

Grant.—Pre-grant opposition exists. Patent can be revoked, inter alia, if reasonable requirements of public have not been satisfied. Renewal fees are required for continued valid registration of patent. Act provides for infringement by supply of products if use of products would constitute infringement. Act also provides for obtaining of declarations of non-infringement from persons who wish to exploit invention.

Patents of addition may be granted for further application which constitutes improvement or modification of principal invention. Patent of addition expires at same time as patent for principal invention.

Act has modified application to international applications as defined in Patent Cooperation Treaty signed at Washington on 19 June 1970.

Assignments.—Patents are transferable by making application to Commissioner of Patents to enter proven title in register. Assignments of patent must be in writing and be signed by or on behalf of assignor and assignee. Assignments of patents as well as trademarks and designs are ordinarily by deed. See also topic Trademarks.

PRESCRIPTION:

See topic Limitation of Actions in Part II.

RACIAL DISCRIMINATION:

Racial Discrimination Act 1975 introduces into Australian law obligations contained in International Convention on Elimination of All Forms of Racial Discrimination signed on behalf of Australia on Dec. 21, 1965. Following definition of Convention, Act makes it unlawful for person to act in way involving discrimination based on race, colour, descent or national or ethnic origin which impairs enjoyment of fundamental rights and freedoms. Act also guarantees equality before law and deals with discrimination concerning access to places and facilities, provision of land, housing and other accommodation, goods and services and right to form trade unions. Act establishes Commissioner for Community Relations as independent statutory authority to examine complaints of racial discrimination on systematic basis and settle them by conciliation.

Racial Hatred Act 1995 prohibits certain public conduct involving hatred of people on ground of race, colour or national or ethnic origin. Exceptions exist for certain acts with artistic, academic or scientific purposes.

Australia party to International Covenant on Civil and Political Rights. Human Rights Commission Act 1981 (now repealed, replaced by Human Rights and Equal Opportunity Commission Act 1986) establishes Commission to promote human rights

RACIAL DISCRIMINATION . . . *continued*
and investigate complaints of violations of Covenant. Human Rights and Equal Opportunity Legislation Amendment Act (No. 2) 1992 creates Aboriginal and Torres Strait Islander Social Justice Commissioner with specific responsibility for protecting human rights of Australian Aborigines.

See also topic Discrimination in Part II.

Racial Discrimination Amendment Act 1983 provides that Act is not intended to limit operation of State law furthering objects of Convention and capable of operating concurrently.

Since 1986, Race Discrimination Commissioner is member of Human Rights and Equal Opportunity Commission. See also topic Sex Discrimination.

Equal Employment Opportunity (Commonwealth Authorities) Act 1987 (see topic Sex Discrimination) applicable.

REPORTS:

The official reports of the decisions of the High Court of Australia are entitled Commonwealth Law Reports (C. L. R.).

Australian Law Reports (A.L.R.) contain reports of decisions of High Court, Federal Court, Family Court, and State Supreme Courts exercising Federal jurisdiction. Federal Law Reports (F.L.R.) contain reports of decisions of above courts (except High Court) and Australian Competition Tribunal (formerly Trade Practices Tribunal) and Administrative Appeals Tribunal. Decisions of High Court are also reported in Australian Law Journal Reports (A.L.J.R.). Decisions of Federal Court are also reported in Federal Court Reports (F.C.R.).

RESTRAINT OF TRADE:

See topic Monopolies and Restraint of Trade.

SEQUESTRATION: See topic Bankruptcy.

SEX DISCRIMINATION:

Sex Discrimination Act 1984 (as am'd by Sex Discrimination Amendment Act 1995) gives effect to certain provisions of UN Convention on Elimination of All Forms of Discrimination Against Women.

Act prohibits discrimination on grounds of sex, marital status, pregnancy or potential pregnancy in areas of work, accommodation, education, provision of goods facilities and services, disposal of land, activities of clubs and administration of Commonwealth laws and programs and affirms individual equality before law.

Human Rights and Equal Opportunity Commission Act 1986 establishes Commission to implement objects of Discrimination (Employment and Occupation) Convention 1958. Commission also administers Sex Discrimination Act. Sex Discrimination Commissioner appointed to investigate and conciliate complaints of sexual discrimination. Complaints which cannot be resolved by conciliation dealt with by Commission. Sex Discrimination and other Legislation Amendment Act 1992 provides for more comprehensive regime for representative complaints to Commission and for registration of Commission determinations by Federal Court.

Affirmative Action (Equal Employment Opportunity for Women) Act 1986 requires private sector employers and voluntary bodies with more than 100 employees and higher educational institutions to implement affirmative action programs for employment of women and submit annual progress reports. Act also establishes office of Director of Affirmative Action. Affirmative Action (Equal Employment Opportunity for Women) Amendment Act 1992 establishes Affirmative Action Agency managed by Director of Affirmative Action. Affirmative Action (Equal Opportunity for Women) Amendment Act 1989 removes some of exemptions from principal Act enjoyed by superannuation and life assurance industries.

Equal Employment Opportunity (Commonwealth Authorities) Act 1987 requires certain Commonwealth authorities to develop and implement program to promote equal opportunity in employment.

See also topic Discrimination in Part II.

SHIPPING:

Navigation Act 1912 embraces some 427 sections, and cannot be dealt with in detail here. In the main it applies to ships other than those of defence forces of Australia or another country. Provisions of Act deal with seaworthiness, lifesaving appliances, fire protection, deck and load lines, signals, radio equipment, compasses, collisions, gear, dangerous goods, accidents, prevention of pollution to coast and coastal waters, terms of employment, discipline, crews, qualifications, health, accommodation, survey and safety certificates, passengers, coasting trade, wrecks and salvage, ship owners' liability, legal proceedings and tonnage measurement of ships. Transport and Communications Legislation Amendment (No. 2) Act 1989 amends Act to allow trading ship under State or Territory jurisdiction to be brought under Federal jurisdiction on application by its owner and amends provisions dealing with determination of Marine Council regarding suitability of person for service at sea and with jurisdiction for enforcement of collision regulations. Navigation Act 1912 as amended by Transport and Communications Legislation Amendment (No. 2) Act 1993 provides for making of regulations relating to qualifications, training, standard of competence and licensing of maritime pilots in Australian coastal sea where use of pilots is required. Transport Legislation Amendment Act 1995 amends Act to adopt provisions of 1989 International Convention on Salvage.

Pollution.—Navigation (Protection of the Sea) Amendment Act 1983 provides for issue of construction certificates to ensure tankers are environmentally safe and offences if tankers, including foreign tankers, not certified enter Australian port contrary to direction of Minister. Protection of the Sea (Prevention of Pollution from Ships) Act 1983 implements 1978 Protocol to International Convention for the Prevention of Pollution from Ships (Convention came into force internationally Oct. 2, 1983). Transport and Communications Legislation Amendment (No. 2) Act 1992 amends Act to give effect to Australia's obligations under Annex IV of the Protocol on Environmental Protection to the Antarctic Treaty. Act bestows benefits and imposes liabilities on member States regarding pollution from ships and ship construction. Act amended by various Transport and Communications Legislation Amendment Acts between 1989 and 1992.

Protection of the Sea (Civil Liability) Act 1981, as amended, provides for recovery of amount of any loss, damages, costs or expenses incurred by Australian Maritime Safety Authority in exercising its obligations to combat pollution in maritime environment.

Protection of the Sea (Prevention of Pollution from Ships) Act 1983 as amended by Transport and Communications Legislation Amendment (No. 3) Act 1993 provides for detention of any foreign vessels suspected of causing maritime pollution in port, territorial sea or exclusive economic zone.

Environment Protection (Sea Dumping) Act 1981 amended by 1993 amendment to implement Government's decision to ratify Protocol for Prevention of Pollution of the South Pacific Region by Dumping (SPREP Dumping Protocol) substantively consistent with London Convention 1972 on this matter to which Australia is contracting party.

Various Protection of the Sea Acts of 1993 give effect to International Convention on the Establishment of an International Fund for Compensation for Oil Pollution Damage.

See topic Environment.

Foreign ships which engage in the coasting trade become liable to various provisions of the Act, and, subject to certain qualifications, ship is deemed to be so engaged if she takes on board passengers or cargo at any port in State or Territory, to be carried to and landed or delivered at any other port in same State or Territory or in any other State or Territory. Under Part VI Navigation Act 1912 ships engaged in coasting trade must be licensed (although unlicensed ships may be granted permission to engage in coasting trade), and seamen employed thereupon while so engaged must be paid rates of pay ruling in Australia. In case of ships trading to places beyond Australia, wages to which seaman is entitled must be paid to him before departure of vessel from Australia, and master must produce at last port of departure in Australia evidence of payment. However, Governor-General has power by proclamation to suspend conditionally or unconditionally any of provisions of Part VI as regards any ship or class of ships if he considers it expedient in public interest to do so. General provisions in Act relating to terms of employment, discipline, manning, qualifications, health and accommodation also apply to coastal trade.

Compensation.—Seafarers Rehabilitation and Compensation Act 1992 replaces Seamen's Compensation Act 1911 and establishes new system of compensation and rehabilitation for seafarers injured in course of employment in maritime industry. Act applies to employment of employees on prescribed ship that is engaged in trade or commerce with other countries or among States and Territories. Prescribed ship is ship which is: (a) registered in Australia; (b) engaged in coasting trade; (c) operated by Australian with mostly Australian crew; or (d) trading ship, or off-shore industry vessel, subject to declaration by Australian Maritime Safety Authority. Compensation payable by employer for medical expenses, loss of earning capacity and damage to property. Employer also to pay benefit on death of, or permanent injury to, employee. Employer required to insure for full amount of employer's liability under Act. Rehabilitation provisions designed to get employee back to suitable employment. Act establishes Seafarers Rehabilitation and Compensation Authority to monitor operation of Act.

Shipping Registration Act 1981 requires, subject to certain exceptions, that Australian-owned ships be registered. Previously they were registered as British ships. Ship is defined to mean any kind of vessel capable of navigating high seas. Australian-owned ship is ship majority interest in which is owned by Australian nationals. Fishing vessels, government ships, pleasure craft and ships less than 24 metres in tonnage length are exempt from registration.

Ships (Capital Grants) Act 1987 provides for payments of grants in respect of certain ships providing that such ships meet criteria for eligibility, such criteria relating to ship being or becoming Australian trading ship and having certain crew levels. Transport and Communications Legislation Amendment Act (No. 2) 1989 amends Act by extending availability of grants for new ships to 30 June 1997 and by providing for payment of grants for modifications, completed before 30 June 1992, to existing ships enabling reduction in crew levels and prevents claims for grants where financing arrangements have effect of adding financing and other costs to purchase price of ships.

Naval Defence Act 1910 provides for organization of Australian Navy; appointments, promotion, resignations, enlistment and discharge of officers and sailors in navy; and naval cadets.

STATUTES:

Each Act of Commonwealth Parliament has a short title and Acts are numbered from beginning of each year. Acts Citation Act 1976 provides that Acts may be cited by reference to year in which Act was made without reference to years in which it may subsequently have been amended. Acts and amendments are consolidated periodically and reprinted. Acts Interpretation Act 1901 deals with such matters as commencement, repeal and expiration of Acts; meaning of certain words and references in Acts; construction of powers conferred by Acts; measurement of distance and time; citation of Acts; interpretation of offences and penalties imposed in Acts; construction of rules, regulations, by-laws and instruments and making of regulations; jurisdiction of courts; and application of Acts to coastal sea. Act also deals with construction of Acts—in particular it provides that in interpretation of provision of Act construction that would promote purpose or object underlying Act whether purpose or object expressly stated or not shall be preferred to construction that would not promote purpose or object. Extrinsic material, including reports, journals, speeches and explanatory memoranda of Ministers, Parliament or Commissions may also be used in interpretation of provision of Act.

TAXATION:

Income Tax Framework.—Commonwealth government imposes national uniform income tax regime on all Australian source income and overseas source income with

TAXATION . . . *continued*
Australian connection. States share in national grants from Commonwealth in lieu of imposing own income tax.

What is Income?—Income Tax Assessment Act 1936 (1936 Act) §4B defines taxable income as assessable income less allowable deductions, and Income Tax Rates Act 1986 (as annually amended) imposes liability to pay tax on that taxable income. Assessable income is "ordinary meaning" of income in common usage as interpreted by courts, which includes income from personal services (wages, bonuses, reimbursements) from property (rent, royalties, dividends, interest), and from carrying on business (trade or activity of commercial nature for profit, but not hobby).

1936 Act specifically includes other items in income such as: net capital gains (§160ZO) (see subhead Capital Gains Tax [CGT], infra), benefits received under employee share benefits scheme (§139B inserted by Taxation Laws Amendment Act [No. 2] 1995) and some social security pensions. Retirement and early termination payments are not income.

Capital Gains Tax (CGT).—1936 Act provides that net capital gains realised on assets acquired or deemed to have been acquired after Sept. 19, 1985 are to be included in assessable income. Disposal on death is not taxable but receipt as beneficiary upon death of third person is acquisition subject to tax upon disposal. Tax is levied at ordinary rates of personal and company income tax. Tax applies only upon realisation of assets and only applies to real gains except where assets are acquired and disposed of within 12 months. Gains on taxpayer's principal residence are exempt. Ownership is extended to where person owns licence or right to occupy dwelling such as residential lease.

Definition of asset includes rights which are not forms of property: thus restrictive covenants and trade ties are subject to CGT. Roll-over relief (where imposition of CGT is deferred or pre-CGT status of assets is preserved) is available in certain situations such as transfers of assets between group companies and transfers on marriage breakdown. Group companies need only be related at time of disposal, as opposed to throughout whole year, in order for roll-over relief to be available. Where disposal to related company creates capital loss, there is compulsory roll-over of asset.

Provisions exist to prevent unintended CGT advantages where assets are transferred between companies sharing 100% common ownership and where companies engage in share value shifting arrangements.

Exempt Income.—Certain incomes are exempt from taxation, including income from official salaries of foreign consuls, of Trade Commissioners of any part of British dominions, and of some U.N. officers, income from scholarships, some Defence Force allowances, some pension or social security benefits, bequests under will, child maintenance payments, and overseas continuous employment income.

Tax Deductions.—In general, expenses incurred either in producing assessable income or in carrying on business for purpose of producing such income are deductible. Deduction not permitted to extent to which expenses are of capital, private or domestic nature. Item of expenditure may be apportioned into deductible and nondeductible components.

Entertainment expenses only deductible in very limited circumstances.

Where taxpayer incurs loss, viz excess of allowable deductions over sum of assessable and exempt income, loss can be carried forward and deducted in subsequent income years. Losses incurred pre-1989/90 can only be carried forward for seven years. Losses post 1989/90 can be carried forward indefinitely. Company can only carry forward loss if either there has not been change in majority ownership or company carries on same business.

Development allowance, tax deduction of 10% of cost of capital expenditure incurred in acquiring or constructing eligible property, is available if property is acquired after 26 Feb. 1992 and is ready for use before 1 July 2002 and property is to be used in carrying out large scale projects registered under Development Allowance Authority Act 1992. Expenditure incurred on eligible environmental impact study on or after 12 Mar. 1991 is generally deductible over lesser of ten years or life of project.

Owner-developers of certain public infrastructure projects are able to obtain tax-exempt finance under 1936 Act. For borrowings made after 16 Dec. 1994, borrower must obtain certificate from Development Allowance Authority.

Rebates are subtracted from tax after it has been calculated. Rebates are available to individual taxpayers for dependents, housekeepers, medical expenses and income arrears and are also available to sole parents, low income earners and certain welfare recipients.

R&D Deductions.—1936 Act provides deduction, at rate of 150%, for expenditure on certain research and development activities but only if aggregate expenditure on research and development is over A$20,000 for year of income. For expenditure incurred after 7 Sept. 1989 on core technology, being technology that is basis of research and development project, 100% deduction is permitted. Deduction is available to companies, partnerships of companies and public trading trusts but only if they are residents of Australia. Deduction is only available if body is registered under Industry Research and Development Act 1986.

Investment in Australian Films.—Where resident taxpayer outlays capital expenditure on producing qualifying Australian film and, as consequence, becomes first owner of copyright in film, then 100% of expenditure is deductible if expenditure was incurred under contract entered into after 25 May 1988. Where contract was entered into prior to 24 May 1988, different rates of deduction apply. To be qualifying Australian film, film must be certified by Minister responsible for Arts. Film must be feature film, telemovie, documentary or miniseries made wholly or substantially in Australia. Investor can elect not to use film deduction and, instead, deduct expenditure over two-year period.

Taxpayers.—
Individuals must lodge annual tax return by end of Oct. for previous financial year (ending June 30) if annual income exceeds A$5,400. Income averaging scheme applies to artists, composers, inventors, performers, production associates, sportspersons, writers and primary producers to prevent over-taxing of fluctuating incomes over tax years.

Progressive marginal tax rates apply in bands of taxable income (in A$pa)/marginal rate: up to 5,400/nil; 5,400-20,700/20%; 20,700-38,000/34%; 38,000-50,000/43%; over 50,000/47%.

Medicare Levy Act 1986 requires individuals to pay levy based on taxable income which funds national public health and hospital insurance. Rate is 1.5% for 1995/96 financial year. Low income earners (income below A$12,870 or A$21,718 if married) obtain relief from paying levy.

Tertiary students required to pay levy of A$2,442 (in 1996) per year of full time study under Higher Education Contribution Scheme, which can be paid up-front or at progressive rate from 3-5% of taxable income when income reaches A$27,674.

Partnerships are not taxed, but each individual partner includes that share of partnership income in individual assessable income. Partnership income is determined by lodging tax return for partnership.

Trusts historically used as tax avoidance devices, but 1936 Act now taxes either trustee or beneficiary, depending on who is entitled to trust income.

Companies must file annual return based on self-assessment of tax liability and can carry forward losses from previous year and transfer losses between 100% owned companies in corporate group.

Company Tax Rates.—Between July 1, 1993 and July 27, 1995 tax payable on profits of resident public and private companies was 33%. From July 27, 1995 rate is 36%. Company tax is payable in quarterly instalments.

Dividend Imputation System.—"Imputation" system applies to dividends paid on or after July 1, 1987. System prevents double taxation of company profits by allowing tax credit to shareholders who receive taxable dividends which have been paid out of profits in respect of which income tax has already been paid by company ("franked" dividends). Benefits of these franking credits are only available to resident shareholders. For overseas shareholders, there is also benefit in that withholding tax is not payable on franked dividends.

Taxation of Public Trading Trusts.—Company tax arrangements extend to public unit trusts that carry on trade or business. Taxable income of public trading trust is taxed at company rate. Distributions to unit-holders are taxed at rate applicable to company dividends, subject to imputation system. Limited partnerships established on or after Aug. 19, 1992 also taxed at company rate.

Nonresidents are liable to Australian income tax on all income derived directly or indirectly from all sources in Australia. Income derived by nonresident from sources wholly out of Australia is expressly exempted from Australian income tax. Certain dividends, royalties and interest paid to nonresidents are subject to withholding tax: this tax must be withheld from payment to nonresident and remitted to Australian Tax Office. Amount represents final tax liability on income. Withholding tax on dividends paid by resident company to nonresidents is generally imposed at flat rate of 30%, but where recipient is resident of country with which Australia has double tax agreement, rate is generally 15%. Dividends paid out of profits that have borne company tax ("franked" dividends) are not subject to withholding tax. Withholding tax provisions also apply to royalties. Withholding tax applies where royalties or interest are paid by resident, except where expense of carrying on business outside Australia, or where paid by nonresident and constitute expense of carrying on business in Australia. Rate of withholding tax on royalties is 30%; 10% if recipient is in country with which Australia has double tax treaty. In this latter case, if royalties are connected with nonresident's permanent establishment in Australia, rate is nil. Withholding tax on interest is generally imposed on flat rate of 10%.

Capital gains tax only applies where nonresident disposes of taxable Australian asset acquired on or after Sept. 20, 1985. Generally, "taxable Australian asset" is land or buildings in Australia, asset used in business in Australia, share or interest in share in resident Australian company and interest in resident Australian trust estate.

Taxation of Foreign Sourced Income.—1936 Act contains accruals taxation system which attributes income derived by controlled foreign companies to certain resident Australian controllers ("attributable taxpayers"). Application of system depends upon whether company is resident in "unlisted country" ("tax haven") or "listed country". If income is derived by foreign company resident in listed country or by foreign company resident in unlisted country where company is predominantly engaged in active business, then income is exempted from accruals system. For income subject to system, taxing point for attributable taxpayers is shifted from point at which dividend is paid by foreign company to point at which distributable profits are derived by foreign company.

Accruals system of taxation also applies to foreign source income derived by nonresident trusts in "tax haven" countries where beneficiaries are Australian residents.

Foreign investment funds provisions apply to Australian residents who have interest in foreign company or foreign trust, even though it is not controlled by Australian resident, and Australian residents who have invested in foreign life assurance policy. 1936 Act contains provisions to determine amount of assessable income to be included in such taxpayer's income.

Restriction on Tax Deductions for Interest Payments to Foreign Controllers.—Thin capitalisation rules apply to deductibility of interest paid by Australian company, partnership or trust estate on debts owed to foreign controllers (being entities who hold at least 15% interest in Australian resident). Interest is deductible only to extent that debt to equity ratio does not exceed permitted ratio of foreign debt to foreign equity of 3 to 1. Permitted ratio in case of financial institution is 6 to 1.

1936 Act denies deduction for interest in respect of debt reorganisation through transfer of assets from one related company to another, generally where both buyer and seller at least 50% controlled by nonresident alone or with associates, with limited exceptions. Applies to interest incurred on or after July 1, 1987, unless asset acquired before that date. Where asset acquired before June 20, 1988, applies only where nonresident alone or with associates had 100% interest in both buyer and seller of asset.

International Double Tax Agreements.—Income Tax Convention signed on Aug. 6, 1982 and into force in Australia on Oct. 31, 1983, between Australia and U.S. for avoidance of double taxation and prevention of fiscal evasion with respect to taxes on income. 1983 Convention replaced and extended 1953 Convention.

See Topical Index in front part of this volume.

TAXATION . . . *continued*

Under Convention, income from real property is taxed by contracting state in which it is situated. Business profits of enterprise of one contracting state taxable only in that State unless enterprise carries on business in other contracting state through "permanent establishment" (extensively defined). If there is permanent establishment, only so much of business profits as are attributable to establishment can be taxed by other contracting state. Profits of resident of one contracting state from operation in international traffic of ships or aircraft taxable only in that contracting state. Associated enterprises are taxed as if operating at arm's length.

Dividend, interest and royalties from sources in one contracting state to which resident of other state is entitled may be taxed in other contracting state. May also be taxed in contracting state of source but tax so charged cannot exceed 15% in case of dividends and 10% in case of interest and royalties. Convention also has provisions relating to: income from personal services, entertainers, pensions, annuities, alimony, child support, students and governmental remuneration.

Income Tax Agreement with U.K. has substantially same provisions as Convention with U.S.A. except that tax on dividends paid by company (resident of U.K.) to resident of Australia is exempt from U.K. surtax and dividend paid by company (resident of Australia) to U.K. resident is subject to tax in Australia of half amount normally payable in Australia. Dividends paid by company resident in Australia to company resident in U.K. which is beneficial owner of all shares in Australian company are exempt from Australian tax if U.K. tax is paid on them. In addition remuneration paid by government of one State for official services rendered by one of its officers not normally resident in other State shall be exempt from tax in that other State.

Agreements have been reached with Austria, Belgium, China, Czech Republic, Denmark, Fiji, Finland, France, Germany, Greece, Hungary, India, Indonesia, Ireland, Italy, Japan, Kiribati, Korea, Malaysia, Malta, Netherlands, New Zealand, Norway, Papua New Guinea, Philippines, Poland, Singapore, Spain, Sri Lanka, Sweden, Switzerland, Thailand, UK, USA and Vietnam. Tax agreements prevail over any conflicting provisions in 1936 Act, other than general anti-avoidance provisions or §160AO (which deals with tax credits).

Tax Administration.—1936 Act administered by Federal Commissioner of Taxation supported by Australian Tax Office. Self assessment regime (where taxpayer reports own income deductions) exists with comprehensive penalties and appeal procedures. Penalties of up to 200% can be imposed by Commissioner for breach ranging from understating taxable income to making false or misleading statements or returns. Post assessment of tax returns and auditing of taxpayers are main methods of enforcing 1936 Act.

Tax collected by employers through Pay-As-You-Earn (PAYE) system of deduction direct from employee salaries. Quarterly payment system exists for companies.

System of public (applies to general class of persons) and private (relates only to individual case) rulings introduced in 1992 are binding on Tax Commissioner and set out Tax Office interpretation of particular sections of 1936 Act.

Taxpayer can object to tax decisions, or can appeal Commissioner's decision on objection to Administrative Appeals Tribunal or Federal Court. Some decisions of Commissioner are subject to review under Administrative Decisions (Judicial Review) Act 1977.

Reportable payments system exists under which details of certain payments of income are reported via tax file numbers to Commissioner.

Anti-Avoidance Provisions.—1936 Act contains general anti-avoidance provisions which strike down schemes of artificial or contrived nature that have been entered into for sole or dominant purpose of obtaining tax benefit. Act authorises Tax Commissioner to cancel whole or part of tax benefit and effect tax adjustments. See also topic Statutes.

Financial Transaction Reports Act 1988 requires reporting of certain domestic currency transactions in excess of A$10,000 to Cash Transaction Reports Agency (A$5,000 in case of transfers to and from Australia). Act aims to minimise tax evasion in "cash economy" and to enable easier tracing of assets.

1936 Act contains comprehensive regime to prevent understating of Australian income through intercompany transfer pricing arrangements, such as non-arm's length dealing between companies in two different countries where income and losses can be shifted by internal valuation of assets.

Crimes (Taxation Offences) Act 1980 makes it offence fraudulently to evade income or other taxes, or for company or trustee to enter into arrangement for purpose of ensuring that company or trustee will be or will be likely to be unable to pay tax assessed. Penalty up to ten years' imprisonment or A$100,000 fine (or both) and additional tax penalty.

Taxation (Unpaid Company Tax) Assessment Act 1982 levies tax on vendors and promoters of companies for unpaid company tax. This tax, which is retrospective, evolved from sham sales of companies to bogus shareholders followed by stripping of undistributed profits and disappearance of accounting records. Directors and shareholders could not be traced, so enforcement of tax obligations impossible.

Proposed Changes.—Tax Law Improvement Project aims to rewrite entire 1936 Act and replace it with more user-friendly Act. Aim is not to change substantive law. Four Amending Acts were passed during 1995, and at time of writing one Bill has been introduced in 1996.

Other Taxes.—

Estate Duty and Gift Duty abolished with effect from 1979.

Fringe Benefits Tax.—FBT is payable by employers on total taxable value of benefits provided to employee, or associate of employee, in respect of employee's employment. There are specific rules to determine taxable value of particular benefits, e.g. car benefits. FBT is annual tax. Each FBT year runs from 1 Apr. to following 31 Mar. FBT rate for FBT year commencing Apr. 1, 1996 is 48.5%. From Apr. 1, 1994, tax is calculated under gross-up rules. That is, taxable value is increased by [1/(1-FBT rate)]. The FBT rate is then applied to grossed-up amount to determine tax payable. Income tax deduction is then allowed to employers for amount of FBT paid.

Land tax is imposed only by States.

Petroleum Tax.—The Petroleum Resource Rent Tax Act 1987 ("PRRT") imposes tax on profits of offshore petroleum projects, other than North West Shelf. Rate of tax is 40%. Tax payable is assessed under Petroleum Resource Rent Tax Assessment Act 1987. Exploration expenses can be deducted by company against its PRRT liabilities without limitation by permit area. PRRT is deductible under 1936 Act.

Sales tax is imposed on last wholesale selling price of goods imported or domestically manufactured but not on secondhand goods (see Sales Tax Assessment Act 1992 ["STAA"]). If no wholesale dealing, tax imposed on either retail sale or application of goods to own use, but taxable amount is notional equivalent of wholesale price, or customs value in case of imported goods.

Schedule 1 of Sales Tax (Exemptions and Classification) Act 1992 provides that various business input goods are exempt from sales tax, including goods used in mining, primary production, manufacturing, transport, storage, R&D, etc. Most items require business user to be registered with Tax Office. STAA exempts small businesses with sales tax liability of less than A$10,000 from sales tax on their outputs. Credit system allows reduction in sales tax for various activities, e.g. export, overpaid tax, and leasing of goods.

Stamp duty is imposed only by States and Territories. See Part II (States), topic Taxation.

Superannuation.—Concessional tax rate of 15% applies to all taxable contributions to any net investment income of superannuation funds provided they comply with Superannuation Industry (Supervision) Act 1994 effective July 1, 1994. Noncomplying funds are subject to tax at top marginal rate (47%) on income which includes tax deductible contributions received by fund and realised capital gains. Member contributions would not be taxable because no deduction is allowed to members for contributions to noncomplying fund.

For complying funds, capital gains tax will be imposed on gains arising on disposal of all assets, whenever acquired. These funds can use imputation system and foreign tax credit system to reduce tax liabilities. Investment income, net capital gains, taxable contributions and premium rebates or refunds are generally included in assessable income. Usual range of deductions available to taxpayers under 1936 Act is available to superannuation funds. Expenses for death or disability cover, payments to employer-sponsors, and lump sum payments to deceased member's dependants can also be allowable deductions. Payment of Superannuation Guarantee Charge is not allowable deduction and is treated as taxable contribution. From start of 1994/95 financial year, set dollar limit is imposed on amount of deductible contributions employer can make to complying fund on behalf of each employee. Excess benefits are taxed at top marginal rate.

TRADEMARKS:

Trademark rights can be acquired only by using, and so establishing reputation for, or by registering mark within Australia. Overseas use, reputation or registration is of no assistance and does not bar imitation by Australian entrepreneurs (unless overseas use has created reputation in mark which extends to Australia).

Unregistered Trademarks.—First user of unregistered mark in Australia in any particular trade and area generally prevents others from registering mark or otherwise acquiring exclusive rights in that trade and area, unless first user's rights are abandoned. To acquire exclusive rights, first user must acquire and maintain exclusive reputation for mark, and to prevent others from registering mark, must show their use to be deceptive of public and likely to cause damage to first user.

Rights in unregistered mark cannot be assigned or licensed separately from goodwill of business concerned. Intending users of new marks in Australia are advised to safeguard their position by seeking registration as early as possible, even though registration is not prerequisite to use. Applicants for registration of trademark have priority according to date of application.

Registered Trademarks.—Trade Marks Act 1995 commenced operation Jan. 1, 1996 replacing Trade Marks Act 1994 and Trade Marks Act 1955. 1995 Act implements Australia's obligations under Agreement Establishing the World Trade Organisation.

Registrable trademark is defined broadly as "sign", which (a) includes any letter, word, name, signature, number, device, brand, heading, label, ticket, aspect of packaging, shape, colour, sound or scent; (b) must be used or intended to distinguish goods or services provided in course of trade from other goods and services; (c) must be capable of graphical representation (unclear how this will apply to smells or sounds); (d) must be capable of distinguishing owner's goods or services from others; (e) cannot be deceptively similar to another registered trademark.

Trademark registration is for specific goods or services. Registration gives registered owner exclusive rights to use or authorise use of trademark and to obtain relief for infringement. Registration and renewal procedures simplified.

Trademark can be collective trademark (used to distinguish goods or services provided by association), certification trademark (used to distinguish goods or services certified by owner to be of particular quality, accuracy, origin or materials), or defensive trademark (where registered owner wants to prevent any use of mark on unrelated goods that may suggest those goods are connected to registered trademark goods).

When trademark becomes generic (i.e. generally accepted within relevant trade as sign describing article, substance or service) registered owner no longer has exclusive rights to trademark for such article, substance or service.

Registration of users of trademark is no longer required. Concept of "authorised use" allows authorised user to deal with trademark and bring action for infringement if registered owner does not; and to request Australian Customs Service to seize imported falsely marked goods at point of entry into Australia, if registered owner does not make such request.

Prior Use.—Notwithstanding priority is based on date of application, if person (or predecessor in title) has continuously used in Australia unregistered mark in course of trade starting before registration or use by registered owner, person does not infringe registered trademark by continuing to use trademark. Furthermore, such use will probably (in absence of honest concurrent use by proprietor) allow successful challenge to proprietor's registration.

See Topical Index in front part of this volume.

TRADEMARKS . . . *continued*

Assignments.—Registered trademarks may be assigned or transmitted in whole or in part with or without goodwill of business concerned in goods or services. Restrictions on assignment without goodwill no longer apply under new Act. If registered trademark is assigned or transmitted, registered owner or assignee must apply to Registrar to record assignment in register.

Infringement occurs if person uses sign as trademark that is substantially identical, or deceptively similar to registered trademark, for goods or services covered by registration. Also infringement if such mark used on goods or services "of the same description" or "closely related", unless use is not likely to deceive or cause confusion. Use of trademark well known in Australia is infringement even on unrelated goods or services if it could be taken as indicating connection between goods or services and registered owner.

If notice of prohibition is displayed on goods carrying trademark it is infringement to do certain acts inconsistent with prohibition (e.g. using trademark with altered goods).

No infringement if person in good faith uses own name or place of business, or uses mark as indication of kind, quality, value, origin or intended purpose of goods. Action can be brought in Federal Court or State Supreme Court for injunction and/or damages. Act replaces old strict liability test with new element of fault (requiring that acts be done knowingly or recklessly) to offences of forging, falsifying and falsely applying registered trademarks. Common law action of passing off is expressly preserved.

Removal from Register occurs if: (1) trademark is not renewed within 12 months of expiring (renewal is now standardised at ten years); (2) registration is cancelled by Registrar or Court.

Grounds for cancellation under (2) are (a) applicant had no intention in good faith of using trademark in Australia when application filed, and/or (b) trademark has not been used in good faith in Australia for continuous period of three years. Person aggrieved can apply to Registrar to remove trademark. Registrar can decide or refer matter of nonuse to court, but owner of registered trademark has onus of proof of use. Court retains discretion not to cancel registration even if no such use. Nonuse provisions do not apply to certification marks or defensive marks.

TREATIES:

Australia is party to General Agreement on Tariffs and Trade. It has entered into bilateral preferential trade agreements with Canada, Malaysia, New Zealand and Papua New Guinea. In addition it has concluded bilateral trade agreements with following countries: Argentina, Austria, Bahrain, Brazil, Bulgaria, China, Cyprus, Czechoslovakia, Egypt, German Democratic Republic, Hungary, India, Indonesia, Iran, Iraq, Israel, Italy, Japan, Jordan, Republic of Korea, Latria, Lithuania, Morocco, Nigeria, Oman, Pakistan, Peru, Philippines, Poland, Romania, Thailand, Turkey, U.S.S.R., United Arab Emirates, U.S.A., Venezuela, Socialist Republic of Vietnam and Yugoslavia. See also topics Conciliation and Arbitration; Copyright; Environment; Foreign Trade Regulations; Racial Discrimination; Taxation; Sales (Part II).

Treaties to which Australia is signatory include Patent Co-operation Treaty 1970, Treaty on the Non-proliferation of Nuclear Weapons 1968 and 1974, South Pacific Nuclear Free Zone Treaty 1985, Treaty on Fisheries between the Governments of Certain Pacific Island States and the Government of the United States of America 1987. Australia is party to many International Conventions and agreements.

International Sale of Goods—United Nations Convention on Contracts for the International Sale of Goods, in force on 1 Apr. 1989. See Part II of this Digest, topic Sales and Part VII, Selected International Conventions.

PART II

THE STATES

ABSENTEES:

Generally the position with regard to nonresidents is dealt with under particular topics. There are no provisions specifically directed to protecting absentees' property.

ACKNOWLEDGMENTS:

Where a deed is executed abroad it is advisable it should be acknowledged before a notary public in British possessions, or before the British consul elsewhere.

ADMINISTRATION:

See topic Executors and Administrators.

ADMINISTRATIVE LAW:

All States and Northern Territory have enacted legislation creating office of Ombudsman (Parliamentary Commissioner in Queensland and Western Australia). Ombudsman has extensive powers to investigate any administrative action taken by State Government Departments, Statutory Authorities or Local Government Authorities i.e. by Executive; however, decisions of Ministers and Cabinet are generally not reviewable (in Victoria and South Australia this is result of practice rather than legislation). Ombudsman generally cannot conduct investigation where aggrieved person has right of appeal to tribunal or remedy by way of proceedings in court of law unless such alternative course is unreasonable or immediate investigation is warranted to avoid injustice. Investigation may be conducted either on own motion of Ombudsman or as consequence of written complaint by person affected by decision complained of or on reference by either House of Parliament or committee thereof. If Ombudsman decides to investigate matter he must first inform principal officer of body concerned and outline complaint to him; response of body is communicated to complainant; if complainant still dissatisfied Ombudsman proceeds to investigate. If administrative action of body is defective in one of number of specified ways Ombudsman notifies principal officer that he intends to make adverse finding and notifies him of reasons for adverse finding and recommendations to remedy it. If body does not accept recommendations and Ombudsman dissatisfied with response of body then Ombudsman can send copies of report and body's comments to Governor-in-Council and he may lay such documents before both Houses of Parliament. Any further action is up to Governor-in-Council or Parliament. Parliamentary Committee in NSW exists to monitor and review Ombudsman's exercise of his powers. Committee has power of veto on any proposed appointment or reappointment as Ombudsman. (§§6A, 31BA). See Ombudsman Act 1974 (NSW); Ombudsman Act 1973 (Vic); Parliamentary Commissioner Act 1974 (Qld); Ombudsman Act 1972 (SA); Parliamentary Commissioner Act 1971 (WA); Ombudsman Act 1978 (Tas); Ombudsman (Northern Territory) Act 1978 (NT); Ombudsman Act 1989 (ACT).

Victorian Administrative Law Act 1978 confers specific statutory remedies in relation to taking of administrative action in addition to common law remedies.

Administrative Appeals Tribunal.—Victorian Administrative Appeals Tribunal Act 1984 establishes Victorian Administrative Appeals Tribunal to provide for review of certain decisions upon their merits upon application by person whose interests affected by decision. Such person may also obtain statement of reasons for decision from decision-maker. However Attorney-General or Premier can certify that certain information is not to be disclosed in reasons of decision-maker, in course of tribunal hearing or in decision of tribunal. On reviewing decision, tribunal can exercise all powers and discretions conferred on decision-maker; it can affirm or vary original decision or set aside original decision and either substitute its own decision or remit matter for reconsideration by original decision-maker in accordance with such directions and recommendations as tribunal might give. Substantive jurisdiction of AAT is conferred upon it by wide variety of Acts. Appeal from decision of Tribunal on question of law lies to Supreme Court. ACT also has Administrative Appeals Tribunal and Administrative Decisions (Judicial Review) Act (as to which see this topic, Part I).

Freedom of Information.—Victorian Freedom of Information Act 1982 gives members of public legally enforceable right of access to government documents unless those documents excluded from operation of legislation. Queensland Freedom of Information Amendment Act 1995 also exempts cabinet matters. Applies to most documents of Victorian government, its Ministers and its agencies. Exempted documents include cabinet documents, documents affecting international relations and relations with Commonwealth or other States or Territories, law enforcement documents, documents affecting personal privacy, documents affecting legal proceedings or subject to legal professional privilege, documents relating to trade secrets, documents containing material obtained in confidence, documents affecting economy, certain documents relating to operation of agencies, certain documents arising out of companies and securities legislation, documents to which secrecy provisions of other enactments apply and some internal governmental working documents. Refusal to grant access is reviewable by internal system of review and by way of application to Administrative Appeals Tribunal. There is right of appeal from Administrative Appeals Tribunal to Supreme Court on question of law. Act also allows for documents held by government and agencies relating to citizen to be amended by citizen where record incorrect. Act can be used in conjunction with other statutory remedies. Freedom of Information (Amendment) Act 1993 extends Act to local government, removes exemption on Cabinet documents if solely of technical or statistical nature, but widens definition of Cabinet document in other ways. Amendment Act permits Minister to give unreviewable certificate that document is exempt Cabinet document, and changes fee structure. Repeated request or request which would substantially and unreasonably divert resources may be refused. Freedom of Information Act 1989 (NSW) contains similar provisions to Victorian Act. Freedom of Information (Amendment) Act 1992 (NSW) provides, inter alia, that Ombudsman may recommend release of documents if in overall public interest although exempt documents. See also Freedom of Information Act 1989 (ACT), Freedom of Information Act 1991 (SA), Freedom of Information Act 1991 (Tas), Freedom of Information Act 1992 (Qld) and Freedom of Information Act 1992 (WA). Different Acts have slightly different categories of exempt documents. For example, Tasmania exempts documents communicated by other states and information likely to threaten endangered species, Western Australia exempts documents relating to adoption or artificial conception.

AFFIDAVITS:

Affidavits sworn in and for a particular State must be made before a commissioner for taking affidavits for that State, or in certain circumstances before a justice of the peace for that State. In Victoria, solicitor with current practising certificate under Legal Profession Practice Act 1958 may also take affidavits and interstate residents able to apply for registration as Victorian Commissioner for taking affidavits. Affidavits sworn out of State for use within State must be before notary public, commissioner for that State, Australian consular officer, or diplomatic officer representing any part of British Commonwealth. Provision is generally made for making of affirmations in lieu of swearing affidavits.

For purposes of certain legislation other officials may have affidavits sworn before them.

Generally the person before whom the affidavit is sworn need only add the signature and qualification to each sheet of jurat, which is usually in form:

Form

Sworn at .... on the .... day of .... 19.. before me: .....

Statutory declarations which are used in certain cases in substitution for affidavits, may be made before a wider class of officials. An oath is not administered, but the making of a false declaration will constitute perjury.

AGENCY: See topic Principal and Agent.

ALIENS:

Foreign Ownership of Land Register Act 1988-1989 (Qld) establishes register of details of interests in land in Queensland presently held or acquired by foreign persons. Any person or trustee (including Australian citizen) who acquires legal estate or interest after 17 Apr. 1989 must notify Registrar within 90 days. Person who, as trustee holds equitable interest in land must give details of beneficiary's interest, and whether or not beneficiary foreign person, if requested by person who, as trustee, holds legal estate.

Foreign person defined widely as foreign natural person, foreign corporation, corporation in which foreign natural person or foreign corporation holds controlling interest, or two or more hold aggregate controlling interest. Foreign natural person is person who is not Australian citizen and whose right to reside in Australia is limited to set time imposed by law, or who is not domiciled in Australia.

Foreign corporation means body (incorporated or unincorporated) formed outside Australia and external Territories. Foreign trust means unit trust in which foreign person holds controlling interest, or two or more hold aggregate controlling interest, or trust other than unit trust in which not less than 15% of total income of trust paid to, or applied for benefit of, foreign person, or not less than 40% total income of trust paid to, or applied for, benefit of two or more foreign persons, together with any associate(s).

Substantial interest (person alone or with associate holds at least 15% voting power) deemed controlling interest, aggregate substantial interest (two or more persons with or without associates hold at least 40% voting power) deemed controlling interest, unless Minister declares not in position to determine policy of corporation or unit trust. Tracing provisions apply. Control of voting power defined. Extremely wide definition of associate. "Acquire" includes obtain, gain, receive or acquire by purchase, exchange, lease, will, devolution or operation of law, by grant or gift, by enforcement of security. "Interest in land" includes licences and leases granted under various statutes, but expressly does not include, among others, easements, leases for less than 25 years, most security interests.

Any person, trustee or trust becoming, or ceasing to be, foreign person, trustee or trust must notify Registrar within 90 days. Registrar has broad powers to elicit information. Serious penalties may be imposed for breach of Act, including, ultimately, forfeiture without compensation where foreign person has failed to notify, and not appealed against Minister's determination.

ASSIGNMENTS:

Assignments of debts and other rights are in general effected by deed, but may in many cases be carried out by writing not under seal. As a rule no particular form is required, provided the intention of the parties is clear. In Victoria and Western Australia, assignments of book debts must be registered in order to have legal effect. (Bills of Sale Act 1899-1981 [WA] §51; Instruments Act 1958 [Vic] §84).

Before deed will be admissible in evidence it must bear appropriate stamp duty. (See topic Taxation.)

ASSOCIATIONS:

Unincorporated associations or partnerships of more than 20 persons formed for purpose of acquisition of gain by association or partnership or by individual members thereof are prohibited, but Corporations Law permits partnerships in certain proclaimed professions to consist of more than 20 persons. Limit for accountants and solicitors is 400 persons, for architects, chemists, and veterinary surgeons is 100 persons and for sharebrokers, stockbrokers, medical practitioners and actuaries is 50 persons. Law also makes provision for winding up of associations.

In all States and Territories provision has been made for incorporation of associations not formed for purpose of trading or securing pecuniary benefit to members and which also (for purposes of Tasmania and Northern Territory) have purpose that falls within certain listed purposes (Associations Incorporation Act 1981 [Vic]; Associations Incorporation Act 1984 [NSW]; Associations Incorporation Act 1981 [Qld]; Associations Incorporation Act 1985 [SA]; Associations Incorporation Act 1987

See Topical Index in front part of this volume.

ASSOCIATIONS . . . *continued*
[WA]; Associations Incorporation Act 1964 [Tas]; Associations Incorporation Act 1991 [ACT]; Associations Incorporation Act 1963 [NT]). Incorporated body has power to hold property and deal with it as fully and effectually as natural person and may sue or be sued in its corporate name. Contracts made on behalf of such body may be under common seal or executed by person acting under its express or implied authority and will be effective in law and will bind association and its successors and all other parties thereto. Personal liability of members to creditors of association is limited solely to express provision in rules or trust deed of association. Winding up of incorporated associations is, with necessary modifications, governed by winding up provisions of Corporations Law. In New South Wales, Northern Territory and Victoria, incorporated association may be directed to become registered as company. Acts also deal with other matters, such as required contents of rules of association, voting when interested party, amalgamations, accounts, auditors, meetings, etc.

ATTACHMENT:

Of Persons.—Persons may be attached for contempt of court, and committed to prison; but imprisonment for debt has, for all practical purposes, been abolished. Fraudulent debtors, however, may be examined before a court, and committed to prison in default of payment.

Of Property.—In some States there is procedure where, in relation to cause of action arising in jurisdiction, assets of nonresident defendant can be attached pending resolution of action.

ATTORNEYS AND COUNSELORS:

Legal profession is divided into barristers and solicitors in Queensland only. In Victoria and Australian Capital Territory admission is as both barrister and solicitor, in other jurisdictions, admission as "practitioner".

Each jurisdiction has Acts dealing with matters such as powers and functions of statutory and professional bodies, definitions of legal work and persons permitted to do it, requirements for legal education, admission and practising certificates including fees, regulation of trust accounts, indemnity and insurance, fidelity funds and management and receivership of failed practices, disciplinary offences, procedures and penalties and determination of fee scales and arrangements. See Legal Profession Practice Act 1958 (Vic); Queensland Law Society Act 1952, Legal Practitioners Act Amendment Act 1938 (Qld); Legal Practitioners Act (NT); Legal Practitioners Act 1981 (SA); Legal Practitioners Act 1893 (WA); Legal Practitioners Act 1970 (ACT); Legal Profession Act 1987, Legal Profession Reform Act 1993 (NSW); Legal Profession Act 1993 (Tas). Detailed regulation in statutory rules and rules of professional bodies. In each jurisdiction Legal Societies represent solicitors. Bar Association represents lawyers specialising as barristers. If no formal separation, membership of this is voluntary. Eminent barristers may be appointed Queen's Counsel by Governor-in-Council (appointment is as Senior Counsel in New South Wales). Queen's Counsel are subject to particular rules, for example, in relation to fees or type of work undertaken.

Admission to Practice.—Certain legal work must be conducted by qualified practitioner with current practising certificate if fee to be charged. For admission to legal profession must have recognized legal education, usually graduate law degree. Recognition at discretion of local admission body. Also require post-graduate training in practice or practical institutional course. Applicant must be fit and proper person. Following admission, practising certificate must be obtained on payment of annual fee (except for barristers in Queensland). Mutual recognition legislation makes interstate admission virtually automatic on application. Does not apply in Western Australia. Admission of overseas practitioners governed by Acts and Rules of States and Territories. Preference to practitioners from jurisdictions based on common law, especially New Zealand. Some States have residency requirements. May have to apply for direction that existing qualifications are sufficient for admission in State or Territory. Further study may be necessary. See for example Rules of Council of Legal Education Relating to the Qualification and Admission of Applicants (Vic).

Specialisation Schemes.—Formal accreditation available in Victoria, Western Australia, Queensland and New South Wales, but not necessary as prerequisite to practice in area. Requirements differ but include five years full time practice with substantial involvement in specialty area in preceding period, written assessment and provision of references.

Business Structure.—Practitioners may practise as sole practitioners. Solicitors may practise in partnership or in some jurisdictions as directors of incorporated practice with unlimited liability. Barristers more restricted by rules but varies between jurisdictions. For example, barristers usually must practise as sole practitioners usually in chambers approved by Bar Council, are forbidden from practising with non-barristers (except in Western Australia, South Australia and Tasmania) and prevented from advertising. See topic Associations.

Fees.—Terms of retainer between practitioner and client incorporated by statute or implied by common law. Solicitor has lien over client's documents until all taxed costs paid. Right qualified with respect to third parties. Fee scales influencing fees charged are regulated by professional associations and statutory bodies. Bar Rules prohibit barristers from reducing their fees. Contingency fees on percentage basis prohibited except in South Australia although in some jurisdictions solicitors may agree to be paid normal fee only if client is successful. Barristers cannot enter speculative or contingency fee arrangements. See topic Costs.

Legal professional privilege conferred upon clients to protect confidential communications from disclosure if made for purposes of giving or obtaining legal advice or in contemplation of or for purpose of litigation.

Complaints and Discipline.—Statutory bodies or law societies and bar associations deal with complaints against practitioners for professional misconduct or unprofessional conduct. Systems vary across jurisdictions. Penalties include reprimand, fines, restrictions on right to practice and taking away licence to practice.

Contacts.—The Law Institute of Victoria, 470 Bourke Street, Melbourne, Vic, 3000, (03) 9607 9311. The Law Society of New South Wales, 170 Philip Street, Sydney, NSW, 2000, (02) 9926 0333. The Law Society of the Northern Territory, 18 Knuckey St., Darwin, NT 0800, (08) 8981 5104. Queensland Law Society Incorporated, 179 Anne St., Brisbane 4000, (07) 3233 5888. The Law Society of South Australia, 124 Waymouth Street, Adelaide, SA, 5000, (08) 231 9972. The Law Society of Western Australia, 33 Barrack Street, Perth, WA, 6000, (09) 221 3222. The Law Society of the A.C.T., GPO Box 932, Canberra City, ACT, 2061, (06) 247 5700. The Law Society of Tasmania, 28 Murray Street, Hobart, Tas 7000, (002) 34 4133.

AUTOMOBILES: See topic Motor Vehicles

BARRISTERS AND SOLICITORS:

See topic Attorneys and Counselors.

BILLS OF SALE: See topic Chattel Mortgages.

BUSINESS NAMES:

Any person, company or partnership trading or carrying on business under a name not being his, her, its or their full name or names, must register that name as business name in State or Territory concerned, showing name or names of persons or company so trading or carrying on business, and must register changes of these and other particulars from time to time, and must notify proper officer if business is discontinued. Business names will not be registered if they are deceptive or likely to cause confusion with other business names or company names reserved or registered in State or Territory in question. Australian Securities Commission may act as agent of proper officer.

Business Names Acts do not expressly confer on persons registered any right to enjoin others from misappropriating registered business names, but such persons have usual rights against those who misappropriate distinctive features of their businesses, e.g. action for "passing-off." (See Part I, topic Trademarks, subhead Unregistered Trademarks.)

CHATTEL MORTGAGES:

Mortgages of ordinary chattels, such as household furniture, or trade stock, machinery or plant, are known as bills of sale; but in addition to these, there are farming and pastoral securities, such as liens on crops, liens on wool, and stock mortgages. Provisions are included to protect creditors against unauthorized realization. In all jurisdictions goods mortgages made by company must be registered under Corporations Law. Registration requirements of Bills of Sale Acts then do not apply.

All States and Territories except Victoria have Bills of Sale Acts; under these Acts failure to register relevant instruments will cause mortgage or other security over chattel to be avoided either as against all persons save grantor and grantee (as for example in Queensland) or as against certain nominated persons (for example in South Australia, Australian Capital Territory and New South Wales where bill of sale is avoided only against official receiver or trustee in bankruptcy of grantor, assignee or trustee under any assignment by grantor for benefit of his creditors, sheriff's officer seizing goods of grantor in course of execution, and judgment creditor on whose behalf such execution has been issued) or to be totally void as security (as is case in general in Tasmania, subject to certain qualifications, and in New South Wales in case of trader's bill of sale). Upon registration, effect of instrument dates from time of execution, priority from time of registration. There is no requirement for registration in South Australia if mortgage secures performance of obligations under consumer credit contract within meaning of Consumer Transactions Act 1972-83. These Acts also imply certain powers and covenants into bill of sale e.g. power to seize on default or sell on default (Queensland, South Australia, Western Australia), covenant to keep goods in good repair (except in New South Wales), covenant to pay principal and interest (Queensland, South Australia, Western Australia, Tasmania) and covenants relating to title (Tasmania, Queensland). Assignment of bill of sale need not be registered (Bills of Sale Act 1898 [NSW]; Bills of Sale Act 1899 [WA]; Bills of Sale & Other Instruments Act 1955 [Qld]; Bills of Sale Act 1886 [SA]; Bills of Sale Act 1900 [Tas]; Instruments Act 1935 [NT]; Instruments Act 1933 [ACT]).

In Victoria, Chattel Securities Act 1987 regulates creation and operation of all security interests in goods, and provides for registration of mortgages, hire purchase agreements and leases relating to motor cars and trailers and vessels within meaning of Marine Act 1988. Act makes mortgage, hire purchase agreement or lease interest void against purchaser unless registered. Information relating to goods registered in other States and Territories may be obtained from Victorian register. See also Chattel Securities Act 1987 (WA). The Motor Vehicles Securities Act 1984 (Tas) provides for registration of security interests in motor vehicles and trailers and makes bills of sale relating to these void as against purchaser unless holder of such bills of sale is registered as holder of security interests.

Motor Vehicle Securities Act 1986 (Qld) provides for registration of instruments creating security interests in motor vehicles and trailers and takes such interests outside scope of Bills of Sale and Other Instruments Act 1955. Unregistered interest unenforceable against those not party to it. Two registered interests have priority according to date of registration; unregistered interest loses priority to later registered interest unless notice of it was had. Assignment of interest may be but need not be registered.

Registration of Interests in Goods Act 1986 (NSW) provides for registration of security interests, interest of lessors and interests of owners under Hire Purchase Agreements in motor vehicles and other prescribed goods. By virtue of Bills of Sale (Amendment) Act 1986, such goods do not need to be registered under Bills of Sale legislation. Goods Securities Act 1986 (SA), Registration of Interests in Motor Vehicles and Other Goods Act 1989 (NT) and Registration of Interests in Goods Act 1990 (ACT) are to similar effect.

COLLATERAL SECURITY: See topic Pledges.

COMMERCIAL REGISTER:

See topics Business Names, and Corporations.

CONSTITUTION AND GOVERNMENT:

States continue to retain constitutions which, as colonies, they possessed prior to federation, except as modified by Commonwealth Constitution and as amended by State Parliaments from time to time.

The governors of the States are appointed by the Queen on the advice of the State Government, and occupy a similar position and carry out similar duties to the Governor-General in the Commonwealth and the Queen in England.

Parliament.—Every State has a separate parliament, which, except in State of Queensland, consists of two houses, both being elected.

Statute of Westminster adopted by Commonwealth of Australia (see this topic, Part I) had no application to States. State legislatures had no power to amend or repeal paramount British legislation which had entered into legislation of States. British amending acts would not apply unless clear and unequivocal statement that British parliament intended amending acts to apply to States. However, all States have enacted Australia Acts (Request) legislation which, with Commonwealth Australia (Request and Consent) Act 1985 and identical legislation in U.K. Parliament, remove legal incidents of colonial status from 3 Mar. 1986.

Territories.—Northern Territory (Self-Government) Act 1978 (Cth) substantially grants local autonomy to NT. Act gives NT control over its own treasury as well as general grant of plenary legislative powers to elected unicameral Legislative Assembly. Many South Australian laws passed between 1841 and 1910 still apply in NT

In ACT, Seat of Government (Administration) Act 1910 (Cth) grants power to Governor-General to make Ordinances for government of ACT Under Seat of Government Acceptance Act 1909 (Cth), certain laws of NSW have effect in ACT. Australian Capital Territory (Self-Government) Act 1988 establishes independent Legislative Assembly.

CONSUMER PROTECTION:

All States and Territories have enacted legislation establishing bodies to investigate matters affecting interests of consumers and to make recommendations in relation thereto to respective Governments, to advise and receive complaints from consumers and to conduct research into matters affecting consumers. (Consumer Affairs Act 1972 [Vic]; Fair Trading Act 1987 [NSW]; Fair Trading Act 1989 [Qld]; Fair Trading Act 1987 [SA]; Consumer Affairs Act 1971 [WA]; Consumer Affairs Act 1973 [ACT]; Consumer Affairs and Fair Trading Act 1990 [NT]; Consumer Affairs Act 1988 [Tas]). New South Wales, Victoria, Queensland and Western Australia have enacted legislation establishing Tribunals to deal with consumer claims. (Consumer Claims Tribunal Act 1987 [NSW]; Small Claims Tribunal Act 1973 [Vic]; Small Claims Tribunals Act 1974 [WA]; Small Claims Tribunal Act 1973 [Qld].) A.C.T., South Australia, Tasmania and Northern Territory have provided for small claims proceedings within their existing court systems (Small Claims Act 1974 [ACT]; Magistrates Court [Small Claims Division] Act 1989 [Tas]; Small Claims Act 1974 [NT]; Magistrates Court Act 1991 [SA] Part IV, Div II). Victoria has established Market Court which deals with applications to restrain traders from engaging in undesirable trade practices (Market Court Act 1978 [Vic]). In addition there are various other provisions which differ from State to State but include requirements relating to safe design and construction of goods, product safety and recall, product information standards, dangerous goods, misleading and deceptive conduct, unconscionable conduct, false or misleading representations, offering of gifts and prizes, bait advertising, referral selling, pyramid selling, unsolicited credit and debit cards, unsolicited goods, mock auctions, door to door sales, and unordered goods (some of relevant statutes are Fair Trading Act 1985 [Vic]; Fair Trading Act 1987 [SA]; Fair Trading Act 1987 [WA]; Fair Trading Act 1987 [NSW]; Fair Trading Act 1989 [Qld]; Fair Trading Act 1990 [Tas]; Consumer Affairs and Fair Trading Act 1990 [NT]; Fair Trading Act 1992 [ACT]; Consumer Affairs Act 1973 [ACT]; Sale of Hazardous Goods Act 1974 [Tas]; Mock Auctions Act 1973 [Tas]; Mock Auctions Act 1973 [NSW]; Pyramid Selling Act 1974 [Tas]; Pyramid Selling Schemes [Elimination] Act 1973 [Qld]; Door to Door Sales Act 1967 [NSW]; Door to Door Trading Act 1987 [WA]; Door to Door Trading Act 1986 [Tas]; Door to Door Sales Act 1967 [NT]; Door-to-Door Trading Act 1991 [A.C.T.]; Unordered Goods and Services Act 1973 [Tas]; Unordered Goods and Services Act 1972 [NT]). Some Acts also imply certain terms into sales and/or leases of goods to consumers (e.g. Part IV Goods Act 1958 [Vic]; Consumer Transactions Act 1972-1983 [SA]).

Part V Fair Trading Act 1987 SA, Invasion of Privacy Act 1971 (Qld), Consumer Affairs and Fair Trading Act 1990 (NT) and Credit Reporting Act 1978 (Vic) confer on consumers certain rights in relation to accumulated information that might be used to their detriment, e.g., credit information. In New South Wales similar provisions apply by self-regulation of interested parties. The Privacy Act 1988 (Cth) as amended in 1990 provides for national regulation of consumer credit reporting to prevent privacy abuse and to establish uniformity between States and Territories in this area.

Chattel Securities Act 1987 (Vic) and Chattel Securities Act 1987 (WA) regulate granting and taking of security over goods (see topic Chattel Mortgages). All States and Territories have consumer credit legislation in force, Consumer Credit (Victoria) Act 1995, Consumer Credit (New South Wales) Act 1995, Consumer Credit (Queensland) Act 1995, Consumer Credit (Tasmania) Act 1995, Consumer Credit (Northern Territory) Act 1995, Consumer Credit (South Australia) Act 1995, Consumer Credit Act 1995 (ACT), Credit Act 1984 (WA). Most acts enacted to incorporate Consumer Credit Code, not yet in force but intented to regulate negotiation of credit contracts, interest charges, fees, mortgages, guarantees, related sale contracts, related insurance contracts, advertising. Orders made in each State on 1 Aug. 1993 allow for deregulation of credit cards, removing prohibition on charging fees for credit cards.

See also topic Monopolies and Restraint of Trade.

CONTRACTS:

The law of contracts throughout Australia, especially with regard to the necessity for consideration and the effect of sealing, follows the English law on the subject. Certain contracts require written evidence to make them enforceable. See topic Frauds, Statute of. See also topic Deeds.

Excuses for Nonperformance.—Nonperformance of a contract legal and valid at time of agreement will only be excused if there is a clause specifically excusing performance in the circumstances or if contract has become frustrated. Contract will be regarded as frustrated if there has occurred an event or change of circumstances so fundamental that it strikes at root of contract and is entirely beyond what was contemplated by parties when they entered into agreement. At common law, loss lay where it fell, unless total failure of consideration, when money recoverable. New South Wales, Victoria, South Australia have Frustrated Contracts Acts, to apply subject to express provision in contract for frustrating event. Under Statute, money paid before frustrating event recoverable, whether failure of consideration total or partial. Relief available in certain circumstances involving unjust, harsh or oppressive contracts or unconscionable conduct. See Contracts Review Act 1980 (NSW) and Trade Practices Act 1974 (Cth). Law Reform (Misrepresentation) Act 1977 (ACT) and Misrepresentation Act 1971 (S.A.) generally similar to common law. Funerals (Prepaid Moneys) Act 1993 (Vic) gives certain rights and protections to persons who prepay for funerals.

See also topics Consumer Protection and Interest.

Applicable Law.—Essential validity of a contract is governed by its proper law which, in case of a contract with a private international element, if not expressly specified by parties, is law of country with which contract has most real connection. Capacity to enter a commercial contract is probably governed by proper law. Courts will not enforce a contract which is valid by its proper law but performance of which is illegal by law of place of performance.

Where parties expressly stipulate that their contract shall be governed by a particular law, that law will be proper law of contract provided that selection is bona fide and there is no infringement of public policy, i.e., selecting some other law for purpose of avoiding application of a particular State law.

Legislation in each State and Northern Territory gives effect to United Nations Convention on Contracts for the International Sale of Goods. Convention acceded to on 17th Mar. 1988 and came into force on 1st Apr. 1989.

Government Contracts.—Ordinary law of contract applies.

Sale of Goods.—See topic Sales.

Franchises, Dealerships and Distributorships.—No particular statutes directed at all franchises to regulate their commencement, operation or termination. Petroleum Retail Marketing Franchise Act 1980 (Cth) of narrow application to franchise agreements involving sale of motor vehicle fuel and licensing of trademark. Aims to protect franchisee. All States and Territories have Acts dealing with business franchise licences for tobacco products and petroleum products. Queensland and Western Australian legislation deals only with tobacco products. Franchise interests excluded from definition of prescribed interests and securities in Corporations Law, so that Law has no application to franchises. Various provisions of Trade Practices Act 1974 (Cth) and common law rules against restraint of trade of potential application. See topic Monopolies and Restraint of Trade, Part I. Consumer protection, intellectual property, tax, agency and misrepresentation issues may also arise. Distributors may have to observe fiduciary rules of equity in actions affecting supplier. All States and Territories except Tasmania and Queensland have Acts regulating motor vehicle traders. Acts and regulations made under them deal with licensing, conduct of business, obligations of dealers, rights of buyers and establishment of guarantee fund. See Motor Dealers Act 1974 (NSW); Motor Vehicle Dealers Act 1989 (NT); Sale of Motor Vehicles Act 1977 (ACT); Secondhand Motor Vehicles Act 1983 (SA); Motor Car Traders Act 1986 (Vic); Motor Vehicle Dealers Act 1973 (WA). All States also have Acts regulating secondhand dealers and Acts regulating pawnbrokers. ACT adopts NSW Act. NT has only pawnbrokers Act. For securities dealers, see this Part, topic Corporations.

CONVEYANCES: See topic Deeds.

CORPORATIONS:

Corporations may be created by Act of Parliament or registered under provisions of uniform companies legislation. Incorporation by Act of Parliament is only employed in connection with public trusts or utilities, some government or charitable concerns or activities, or in cases where power which is sought cannot be acquired under companies legislation. All ordinary trading companies are formed under provisions of Corporations Law, uniform companies legislation. See Part I, topic Corporations.

Aim of government is to simplify regulation of companies and reduce burden of compliance, without lowering investor protection. Task Force established to carry out this objective. First Corporation Law Simplification Act 1995 has simplified areas of share buy-backs, regulation and formation of proprietary companies, company registers and plain-English drafting.

Administration.—See this topic, Part I.

Formation.—Prior to formation, list of directors and subscribers and notice of situation of registered office (and where registered office not company's usual place of business consent of person in occupation of office) must be lodged with Australian Securities Commission (ASC). Proprietary companies are no longer required to lodge Memorandum and Articles of Association with ASC if prescribed information is provided on application for registration. Public companies must still lodge Memorandum and Articles. In case of proprietary companies only one subscriber required to Memorandum of Association and in case of public companies five, as well as compliance with other statutory provisions relating to incorporation. Fees payable. Companies incorporated in Australia need only lodge documents in jurisdiction of registration. No need to register in other jurisdictions, but name must be registered in each jurisdiction where place of business established or business carried on.

Terminology.—

Participating State/jurisdiction means all Australian States and Territories.

Home State/jurisdiction is place where company is incorporated.

Company means company incorporated under Corporations Law of given jurisdiction.

Recognized company is company incorporated in another participating State/jurisdiction.

Foreign company means body corporate formed in external Territory or outside Australia (not being corporation sole or exempt public authority) or unincorporated

CORPORATIONS . . . *continued*

body formed in external Territory or outside Australia having capacity under law of its place of formation to sue or be sued and to hold property. Foreign company that registers in one participating State/jurisdiction is known there as registered foreign company.

Limited Companies.—Limited company is company in which liability of each member is limited. There are three types of limited companies: (i) Company limited by shares—maximum liability of member is to contribute amount not exceeding amount of capital unpaid on shares held by member. Trading companies often take this form; (ii) company limited by guarantee—maximum liability of member is to contribute amount not exceeding amount undertaken to be contributed by member in event of company being wound up. Non-trading associations often take this form; and (iii) company limited by shares and by guarantee—hybrid of (i) and (ii). Very rare form of company.

Unlimited Companies.—Unlimited company is company in which liability of each member is unlimited i.e. if company wound up members personally liable for debts of company to extent that assets of company insufficient to pay debts. Unlimited company may or may not have share capital.

"No Liability" Mining Companies.—Corporations Law makes provision for incorporation of "No Liability" mining companies. Acceptance of share in such company, whether by subscription, allotment, transfer or otherwise, is not to be deemed contract on part of person accepting same to pay any calls in respect thereof or to pay any contribution to debts and liabilities of company. No dividends are receivable upon any share in such company upon which call is due and unpaid. When call remains unpaid for prescribed period share is automatically forfeited but can be redeemed upon payment of such call at any time before resale of share.

Public Companies.—Public company is company other than private company.

Private Companies.—Corporations Law makes provision for formation of private companies similar to those permitted under English Acts which companies are not required to comply with all requirements which relate to other companies. These companies are called proprietary companies. Proprietary companies must have share capital and cannot take form of no-liability company; memorandum or articles must also contain specified provisions restricting transfer of shares and number of members (not more than 50) and prohibiting invitation to public to subscribe for shares or to deposit money with company. Exempt proprietary company is proprietary company in which no share is deemed to be held by public company and of which no member is public company; exempt proprietary company need not make annual disclosures of its affairs required of other sorts of companies and also faces less stringent requirements regarding loans to directors and appointment of liquidators and auditors.

With certain exceptions it is possible to convert from one type of company to another type.

On registration under Corporations Law company is given Australian Company Number (A.C.N.), and foreign corporation or registrable Australian body is given Australian Registered Body Number (A.R.B.N.). This number must be displayed after company name when first mentioned on all public documents, and on seal of company.

Foreign Corporations.—Foreign Company must not carry on business in Australia unless registered or has applied for registration. To obtain registration in State or Territory, foreign company must provide, in addition to application for registration, certified copy of its certificate of incorporation or equivalent document, certified copy of its constituent documents, list of directors or other governing persons, appointment of agent authorised to accept service, duly executed memorandum stating powers of directors who are resident in jurisdiction and members of any local boards, documents required to be lodged in relation to any registrable charges, notice of address of registered office in place of formation, notice of address of its registered office in place it seeks registration, and statement of agent in prescribed form. Fees payable. Registration in one participating State/jurisdiction enables foreign company to carry on business in any participating State/jurisdiction.

See also Part I, topic Aliens, subhead Corporations Owned or Controlled by Aliens.

Name.—Search as to availability of proposed company name for registration may be initiated either by letter or by completion and lodgement of form of inquiry as to availability of name. Any person may apply to administering officer for reservation of name for period of two months but no longer compulsory. Period for which any name is reserved may be extended by administering officer for further period of two months if application made during currency of reservation and officer satisfied as to bona fides of application. Name will be available unless it has been registered or reserved in respect of another body corporate, is included on national business names register in respect of another person, or is unacceptable for registration in any of following ways. Generally names suggesting connection with members of Royal Family, Crown, Commonwealth of Nations, Australian Government or State Government, government of foreign country, United Nations, government department or ex-servicemen's organisation are not available. Commission will also refuse to register company with name that is likely to be offensive to members of public or that suggests misleading connection with Sydney 2000 Olympics or Paralympics.

Powers of Company.—Corporations Law gives company rights and powers of natural persons; further, company need not list objects in memorandum.

Subsidiary companies may not own shares in their holding companies.

Raising Capital.—A private company is prohibited from inviting public to subscribe for debentures of, or shares in, company and from inviting public to deposit money with company for fixed periods or payable at call. Public companies, however, may do so. Amendments under Corporations Law 1989 alter prospectus provisions. Any written notice or other instrument offering securities for subscription or purchase or inviting applications to subscribe for or buy securities constitutes prospectus. Part 7.11 creates criminal and civil liability for persons authorizing or causing issue of prospectus which contains false or misleading material statements or material omissions. Further, prospectus complying with requirements of Law will need to be lodged with ASC before any issue, offer or invitation is made, unless issue, offer or invitation falls within categories of exclusion (for example involving listed securities, no consideration, minimum subscription per person of A$500,000, issues of debentures or convertible notes to existing holders, offers to less than 20 persons in any 12 month period, issues to executive officers of corporation, issues to superannuation fund trustees or investment companies, etc.). Prospectus will need to be registered with ASC unless shares or debentures are in class currently listed on Australian stock exchange, or unless allotment, issue, offer or invitation is of shares to existing members of corporation, to exempt recipient (trustee of superannuation fund, investment company, trustee of equity trust, institutional investor, dealer acting as principal), or to employees of listed or approved unlisted corporation of shares in that corporation. Provisions govern form and content of prospectuses that must be lodged or registered; generally it must contain all information reasonably required to enable investors to make informed assessment of corporation and securities. Shares may be issued at premium but not at discount unless resolution of company has court approval, and payments may be made in cash or otherwise.

Most charges and like securities created by corporation require registration in its State of incorporation. Corporations Legislation Amendment Act (No. 2) 1991 renders such registration effective for all other participating States/jurisdictions.

Corporations Law extends registration of charges to foreign corporations. Also provides for priority system of registration of charges. Some equitable charges should be registered.

Alterations to Capital.—Under Corporations Law nominal capital of company may be increased by means of resolution of company to that effect. Reductions of capital, however, require sanction of court although there is provision in all jurisdictions for issue of redeemable preference shares.

Directors.—Corporations Law prescribes that every public company shall have at least three directors (at least two of whom are ordinarily resident in Australia), private company must have at least one director (at least one director must ordinarily reside in Australia). Director must be natural person, not body corporate, of at least 18 years of age (in public company and subsidiary of public company, not over 72 years of age subject to exceptions). Director must not be insolvent, have been convicted of certain criminal offences, have been associated with management of company which has repeatedly breached provisions of Corporations legislation, or have personally breached those provisions on two or more occasions or acted dishonestly or failed to exercise reasonable care and diligence while associated with management of company.

Directors may be required to hold a specified share qualification which must be acquired within a defined period (maximum two months).

Directors must comply with number of common law and statutory duties e.g. (i) directors with interest in any transaction of company must disclose interest to fellow directors; (ii) directors (and other officers) must act honestly and exercise degree of care, diligence and skill not less than reasonably prudent man would exercise in affairs of comparable circumstances; (iii) directors (and other officers) must not make improper use of their position, or improper use of information gained by virtue of such position.

Company other than exempt proprietary company must reveal remuneration of each of its directors. Accounts of company other than exempt proprietary company must state number of directors receiving remuneration in "bands" of A$10,000 (i.e. A$0-A$10,000, A$10,000-A$20,000 etc.). Listed companies and groups of which holding company is listed must also state number of executive officers in each band of A$10,000, starting at A$100,000.

Accounts and Audit.—Every company must keep accounts and records of transactions for period of at least seven years after completion of transaction to which they relate. Annual accounts must be presented to company in general meeting together with directors' report.

Generally large proprietary companies, public companies and small proprietary companies controlled by foreign companies must lay before each annual general meeting: profit and loss account, balance sheet, directors' and auditors' reports. Company's annual return must generally be lodged four months after end of relevant financial year. All companies must appoint auditor except certain small proprietary companies. Small proprietary companies are only required to keep accounting records unless more required by ASC or shareholders. Corporations Legislation Amendment Act 1991 provides that company must make out consolidated profit and loss accounts and balance sheet of economic entity constituted by company and entities (including bodies corporate, partnerships and unincorporated bodies) it controls.

Corporate Law Reform Act 1994 amends Corporations Law to introduce higher standards of continuous disclosure for both listed and unlisted entitles and simplifies prospectus requirements for entities complying with new disclosure regime.

Takeovers.—Corporations Law c. 6 prohibits person who holds between 20-90% of shares in company or whose shareholding in company would be in excess of 20% as result of proposed acquisition from increasing shareholding except as provided in Act, and requires any person who acquires shareholding in excess of 5% in company, either individually or in association with others, to notify company. "Shareholding" includes shares over which person can control right of disposal or voting rights, and shares of associated person. Three methods of increasing shareholding provided in Act: (1) By purchase of up to 3% of target company's voting shares every six months, (2) by making formal takeover offer under Act for all shares in class or uniform proportion thereof, offer being open for at least one month and being attended by certain statements containing information relating to offer, (3) by making takeover announcement on floor of home Stock Exchange of target company unconditionally undertaking to take for one month at specified price all shares offered. If person holds 90% of company's shares, he may (generally speaking) compulsorily purchase remaining 10%. See also Part I, topic Aliens, subhead Corporations Owned or Controlled by Aliens. See also topic Monopolies and Restraint of Trade in Part I.

Insider Trading.—Corporations Law c. 7 severely penalises insider trading in securities of company by person who possesses information which is not generally available with regard to corporation but if it were available would be expected to have material effect on price or value of securities of corporation. Party to such transaction who suffers loss, body corporate that issued securities, or ASC can bring action to recover profits from insider traders.

Winding Up.—Company may be wound up voluntarily following special resolution passed at meeting of members or by court following presentation of petition to wind up company by creditor or member or other specified person.

CORPORATIONS . . . *continued*

Any member of company who believes that its affairs are being conducted in manner oppressive or unfairly prejudicial to, or unfairly discriminatory against, member or members, or in manner contrary to interests of members as whole, can apply to court for order that company be wound up. Court is given wide discretion to make such order or orders appropriate to circumstances.

Exchange Control.—See Part I, topic Exchange Control.

Securities Regulation.—Corporations Law c. 7 gives ASC power to prohibit trading in particular securities on stock market, and powers relating to investigation of securities dealings, insider trading, dealer licences and stock market manipulation.

Under Corporations Law, dealer's representative or investment adviser's representative does not need licence but must hold "proper authority" from his/her principal (who must hold licence). Principals must supervise their representatives and give them adequate training and education, and are liable for conduct of their representatives. ASC has power to ban person from acting as representative.

Corporations Law allows use of Flexible Accelerated Securities Transfer (FAST) system whereby (for example) transferor need not sign transfer form personally, if stamped by designated broker. Corporations Law legalises share buy-backs (previously prohibited) but ASC has power to make orders interfering with transaction or scheme if satisfied that (a) company after transaction or scheme will hold more than 10% voting rights in itself and (b) transaction or scheme would be likely to prejudice company's shareholders or creditors.

Australian Stock Exchange has generally replaced floor trading with screen trading.

Futures Industry Regulation.—Corporations Law changes licensing system applicable to representatives of futures brokers and futures advisers; these changes parallel those for securities industry—see subhead Securities Regulation, supra.

Substantial amendment made by Corporate Law Reform Acts 1992 and 1993. 1992 Act: (a) Clarifies directors' duties; (b) allows civil penalty orders to be made for contravention of many provisions; violation of penalty order renders contravening party liable to compensate company; criminal liability remains possible in relation to these provisions but not in all cases; (c) requires shareholder approval for most transactions of public company giving "financial benefit" to "related party" (generally, director or holding company); (d) simplifies insolvency procedures; (e) provides for system of "administration" for financially troubled company, aimed at reaching agreement with creditors; (f) strengthens powers of liquidator to reverse or recover in respect of antecedent transactions; (g) widens duty of care of liquidators, receivers, etc.; (h) alters priorities of certain unsecured debts; (i) makes assets of related companies available to liquidator of company in certain circumstances if just to do so; and (j) provides for operation of ASX electronic share transfer system, Clearing House Electronic Subregister System (CHESS). Certain entities, including listed companies and most entities whose securities are traded must have half-yearly reports and disclose on ongoing basis any material matter likely to have significant effect on its position.

Corporations Law permits certain types of agreements to be prescribed by regulation and range of provisions of Corporations Law governing securities and futures markets to be applied to such agreements, so as to accommodate trading in new and innovative products in Australian securities and futures markets.

COSTS:

While there is generally no fixed rule in this regard, successful litigant will usually be awarded order for his costs in action on "party and party" basis. Normally this will lead to less than full reimbursement as not all legal costs are covered on this basis.

A plaintiff outside jurisdiction may be required to give security for costs. So may corporations incorporated within Australia.

COURTS:

In each of the States there is a Supreme Court, and there are also subordinate courts, such as county courts, district courts, courts of petty sessions, or magistrates' courts, in addition to special courts, such as courts of marine enquiry, licensing courts, coroners' courts, and industrial courts. By Judiciary Act (Cth) several courts of States are, within their limits of jurisdiction (whether such limits are as to locality, subject matter, or otherwise) invested with federal jurisdiction in all matters in which High Court has original jurisdiction, or in which original jurisdiction can be conferred on it; except that jurisdiction of High Court is exclusive as to matters (other than trials of indictable offences) involving any question, however arising, as to limits inter se of constitutional powers of Commonwealth and those of any State or States, and as to limits inter se of Constitutional powers of any two or more States.

Cross Vesting.—Jurisdiction of Courts (Cross Vesting) Acts 1987 establish system of cross-vesting between Federal, State and Territorial Courts without detracting from existing jurisdiction of any court so as to reduce inconvenience and expense occasionally caused to litigants by jurisdictional limitations in those courts.

Family Court.—Family Court of Australia (Additional Jurisdiction and Exercise of Powers) Act 1988 extends jurisdiction of Family Court—see Part I, topic Constitution and Government.

Appeal to High Court.—Since 1984, Judiciary Act provides that appeals lie from State Courts to High Court only with special leave of High Court, unless provisions of another Act permit appeal. In granting leave to appeal, High Court is required to have regard to questions of law that are of public importance or require resolution of differences between conflicting precedents, provided administration of justice requires that High Court consider question. There is no right of appeal from decision of High Court either in its original or appellate jurisdiction. Australia Act 1986 (Cth) terminates appeals to Privy Council from State Courts, thus effectively making High Court of Australia final court of appeal.

CRIMINAL LAW:

Criminal law of Australia was initially based on common law. Tasmania, Northern Territory, Western Australia and Queensland have subsequently codified law and other States have augmented common law by comprehensive Crimes Acts and Police Offences Acts. NSW Crimes Act is in force in ACT. Few Commonwealth Acts deal with certain national aspects of criminal law such as treason and extradition.

CURTESY:

Abolished.

DAMAGES:

In Australia common law generally prevails. There is however statutory provision in all States which forms an exception to common law rule that no action for damages in respect of death is normally maintainable and allows an action at law to be brought in cases where deceased has left dependants who will suffer pecuniary loss as result of death. See topic Death, subhead Actions for Death.

There is in force in every State and Territory of Australia legislation providing for reduction of damages where victim is guilty of contributory negligence.

DEATH:

No statutory presumption of death of an absentee. Presumption arises at common law if unheard of for seven years by those who would be likely to hear of him if alive. Upon presumption arising at common law, State statutes confer jurisdiction to distribute estate subject to certain safeguards.

Application of rule does not establish death at any particular time; it only produces result that person might be presumed dead at date when question of his death arose in legal proceedings.

§33 Human Tissue Act 1983 (NSW), §41 Human Tissue Act 1982 (Vic), §45 Transplantation and Anatomy Act 1979 (Qld), §2 Death (Definition) Act 1983 (SA), §27A Human Tissue Act 1985 (Tas), §23 Human Tissue Transplant Act 1979 (NT) and §45 Transplantation and Anatomy Act 1978 (ACT) define death to be either: (i) Irreversible cessation of all functions of brain; or (ii) irreversible cessation of circulation of blood in body.

Natural Death Act 1983 (SA) and Natural Death Act 1988 (NT) give legal effect to direction from person of sound mind and at least 18 suffering from terminal illness not to artificially prolong his life. Acts expressly do not affect right of person to refuse medical/surgical treatment generally.

The Rights of the Terminally Ill Act 1995 received assent on 16 June, 1995 but at time of writing has not been proclaimed. Act confirms right of terminally ill person to request assistance from medically qualified person to voluntarily terminate life in humane manner. Provides person rendering assistance with immunity in certain circumstances. Before assistance is given, certain conditions must be met, including: (a) patient has attained 18 years of age; (b) medical practioner is satisfied on reasonable grounds that illness will result in death, does not have a cure and only treatment available is confined to alleviation of pain and suffering; (c) second opinion is obtained; (d) illness is causing patient severe pain and/or suffering; (e) patient has been informed of alternative treatments; (f) patient once informed has decided to end his or her life; (g) medical practitioner is satisfied that patient has considered effect of his or her decision on his or her family; and (h) medical practitioner is satisfied on reasonable grounds that patient is of sound mind and decision was made freely, voluntarily and after due consideration. Other State and Territory governments likely to consider introducing similar legislation.

Medical Treatment Act 1988 (Vic) allows competent patients or their duly appointed agents to refuse medical treatment. Medical Treatment (Agents) Act 1992 (Vic) allows for appointment of alternate agent.

Actions for Death.—No action for damages in respect of death is available under common law.

There is however statutory provision in all jurisdictions which forms exception to above rule and allows action at law to be brought in cases where deceased has left dependants who will suffer pecuniary or quantifiable nonpecuniary loss as result of death. Such action is founded upon negligence of person causing death and is usually brought by executor or administrator of deceased person's estate on behalf of that person's dependants. Damages which can be claimed are for loss of material pecuniary benefit sustained by dependants as result of deceased person's death. Dependents must show that deceased could have sued and recovered against wrongdoer at time of death.

Some States have also made specific statutory provision for damages to be claimed by deceased's estate in respect of funeral and medical expenses occasioned by death. These are only damages which may be claimed where no dependency and pecuniary loss can be proved.

See topic Labour Relations, subhead Workers Compensation.

DECEDENTS' ESTATES:

See topics Descent and Distribution; Executors and Administrators; Wills.

DEEDS:

Execution.—Deeds by individuals are universally signed, sealed and delivered, and attested. Neither signature nor attestation is, however, necessary in all cases, although required by statute for certain documents. The attestation has the value of recording the delivery, which is of importance in the case of deeds by individuals. Gratuitous promises by deed under seal are enforceable notwithstanding the lack of consideration. Delivery means delivered in old legal sense, namely, an act done so as to evince an intention to be bound.

In the case of deeds by corporations, the affixing of the seal imports delivery, and in this case the attestation clause merely records the fact that the common seal was duly affixed. Prima facie, if the common seal of a company appears to have been duly affixed to a deed, it becomes operative; but a corporation may, by express words, suspend the operation of a deed.

Admissibility in evidence of deeds is dependent upon deed bearing appropriate stamp duty, if any.

See also topics Seals; Taxation.

DEPOSITIONS:

In an action in an Australian court the evidence of witnesses abroad may be taken on commission, before a commissioner appointed by the court. The depositions of persons here may also be taken with the object of using them as evidence in foreign courts. But see Part I, topic Actions.

DESCENT AND DISTRIBUTION:

Exact method of distribution on intestacy differs somewhat in particular States. All States and Territories have Administration and Probate Acts except Queensland which has Succession Act 1981, New South Wales which has Wills, Probate and Administration Act 1898 and Western Australia which has Administration Act 1903.

Where deceased leaves surviving spouse and no issue, spouse in Tasmania, New South Wales, Victoria and South Australia is entitled to whole estate, and likewise in Western Australia and Queensland provided there are no near next of kin. If there are near next of kin, then in Western Australia spouse is entitled to household chattels, $75,000 and one-half of remainder of estate, with near next of kin taking (according to specific formula) remaining half; in Queensland spouse is entitled to $50,000 plus one-half of remainder of estate, with rest going to near next of kin. In South Australia and New South Wales specific provision is made for de facto spouses by §4 Administration and Probate Act 1919 and §32G(1) Wills, Probate and Administration (De Facto Relationships) Amendment Act 1984, respectively.

Where deceased leaves surviving spouse and issue: (a) New South Wales: if value of estate (excluding household chattels) does not exceed A$100,000, spouse is entitled to whole estate but if value of estate exceeds that amount, spouse is entitled to household chattels, A$100,000 and one-half of remainder of estate, with issue receiving other half of remainder; (b) South Australia: same provision as for New South Wales, except that value of estate figure is A$10,000; (c) Victoria: same provision as for New South Wales, except that value of estate figure is A$50,000 and spouse is entitled to one-third of remainder of estate; (d) Western Australia: same provision as for New South Wales except that value of estate figure is A$50,000 and spouse is entitled to one-third of remainder of estate (except where there is only one child or issue of one child, in which case spouse gets one-half of remainder); where any issue, parent, brother, sister, child of brother, sister, then spouse has rights in respect of matrimonial home; (e) Tasmania: spouse receives preference of A$50,000, with spouse then receiving one-third and issue two-thirds of residue; (f) Queensland: Spouse receives one-third and issue two-thirds of estate (except where there is only one child, in which case spouse gets one-half of estate). Similar statutory schemes upon intestacy apply in Australian Capital Territory and Northern Territory.

If the deceased leaves neither spouse nor children, in all states except Western Australia, the father and mother are equally entitled to the estate whether there are brothers and sisters or not. In Western Australia, if no brothers or sisters, parents entitled to whole property; if brothers and sisters, parents are entitled to A$6,000 plus half balance. Brothers and sisters, and children of deceased brothers and sisters, are entitled to other half of balance.

See topics Executors and Administrators; Infants; Wills.

DESERTION: See Part I, topic Divorce.

DISCRIMINATION:

Antidiscrimination acts in states prohibit discrimination in areas extending beyond employment, such as education, provision of goods and services and accommodation. Legislative prohibitions on sexual harassment in workplace are in force in Australian Capital Territory, New South Wales, Queensland, South Australia, Victoria and Western Australia.

Each Act prescribes certain exceptions to prohibition against discrimination and establishes procedures by which complaints can be heard and determined.

Commonwealth, New South Wales, Victoria and Western Australia have each legislated to implement affirmative action programs in relation to employment opportunities in public service.

Particular acts in individual states provide as follows:

Victoria.—Equal Opportunity Act 1995 specifies attributes about which discrimination is prohibited. Include age, impairment, industrial activity, sexual activity, marital status, physical features, political belief, pregnancy, race, religion, sex, status as parent/carer or personal association. Act then specifies areas in which discrimination is prohibited including employment, education, provision of goods, services or land, accommodation, clubs, sport and local government.

New South Wales.—Legislation prohibits discrimination on grounds of race, sex, marital status, physical or intellectual impairment, homosexuality and age, HIV/AIDS vilification and compulsory retirement from employment on grounds of age. Prohibition extends to discrimination occurring in employment and other areas (such as membership of clubs, access to places and vehicles, accommodation etc.).

Queensland.—Legislation prohibits discrimination on grounds of sex, marital status, pregnancy, parental status, breast-feeding, compulsory retirement from employment, age, race, impairment, religion, political belief or activity, trade union activity and lawful sexual activity. Extends to discrimination occurring in employment, education, provision of goods and services, superannuation and other areas.

South Australia.—Discrimination prohibited on grounds of sex, sexuality, marital status, pregnancy, race or physical impairment.

Western Australia.—Discrimination prohibited on grounds of sex, marital status, pregnancy, race, religious or political conviction or impairment.

Tasmania.—Sex Discrimination Act 1994 came into force 27 Sept., 1995 and prohibits direct and indirect discrimination on basis of gender, marital status, pregnancy, parental status or family responsibilities in relation to employment and other areas. Act also prohibits sexual and other forms of harassment.

Australian Capital Territory.—Prohibits discrimination on grounds of sex, sexuality, transsexuality, marital status, status as parent or carer, pregnancy, race, religious or political conviction or impairment.

Northern Territory.—Prohibits discrimination on grounds of race, sex, sexuality, age, marital status, pregnancy, parenthood, breast-feeding, impairment, trade union or employer association activity, religious belief or activity, political opinion, affiliation or activity, irrelevant medical record and irrelevant criminal record.

Racial Discrimination.—Each State and Territory (excluding Tasmania) prohibits discrimination based on person's race. High Court held that provisions of Anti-Discrimination Act 1977 (NSW) relating to racial discrimination were invalid as being inconsistent with Racial Discrimination Act 1975 (Cth). However, subsequent enactment of Racial Discrimination Amendment Act 1983 (Cth) removes inconsistency by providing that Commonwealth Act is not intended to limit operation of State law furthering objects of International Convention on Elimination of all forms of Racial Discrimination and capable of operating concurrently. Concurrent operation is ensured by provision that actions or proceedings taken under State law in respect of act or ommission remove entitlement for proceedings under Commonwealth Act. See Part I-topic Racial Discrimination. Equal Opportunity (Amendment) Acts of 1987 and 1993 (Vic) establish Equal Opportunity Commission and enable Commissioner for Equal Opportunity to initiate investigations in certain discriminatory circumstances of serious nature where lodging of complaint by one person only in class or group would be inappropriate. See also Anti-Discrimination Act 1991 (Qld) and Anti-Discrimination Act 1991 (NT).

Physical Discrimination.—Each State and Territory (excluding Tasmania) prohibits discrimination based on person's physical impairment. Guardianship and Administration Board Act 1986 (Vic) and Guardianship and Administration Act 1990 (WA) and Guardian and Administration Act 1993 (SA) establish Guardianship Boards to appoint guardians in respect of persons with disability and to appoint administrators of estates of persons with disability. Acts also create office of Public Advocate to investigate complaints or allegations of abuse of disabled persons and to promote community involvement in provision of services to disabled people. "Disability" encompasses senility and mental and physical impairment. Authority for Intellectually Handicapped Persons Act 1985 (WA) creates authority to protect interests of intellectually handicapped persons. See Part I, topics Racial Discrimination; Sex Discrimination and, topic Guardian and Ward, this part.

DISPUTE RESOLUTION:

Arbitration.—All states and territories have acts to regulate commercial arbitration and arbitration agreements: Commercial Arbitration Act 1986 (ACT); Commercial Arbitration Act 1984 (NSW); Arbitration (Civil Actions) Act 1983 (NSW); Commercial Arbitration Act 1985 (NT); Commercial Arbitration Act 1990 (Qld); Commercial Arbitration Act 1986 (SA); Commercial Arbitration Act 1986 (Tas); Commercial Arbitration Act 1984 (Vic); Commercial Arbitration Act 1985 (WA).

Mandatory Dispute Resolution.—

Victoria.—Rules made under Supreme Court Act 1986 (Vic) provide that judge may order proceeding or part thereof to mediation without consent of parties. County Court may refer civil proceeding to mediation: County Court Act 1958 (Vic). If Employee Relations Commission satisfied that parties to industrial matter unable to reach agreement Commission can attempt conciliation and arbitration; Employee Relations Act 1992 (Vic).

NSW.—Compensation Court and District Court can refer matters to mediation or neutral evaluation: Compensation Court Act 1984 (NSW), District Court Act 1973 (NSW). Industrial Relations Act 1991 enables Industrial Court to refer matters to mediation or neutral evaluation. Farm Debt Mediation Act 1994 (NSW) provides mediation is compulsory between farmer and creditor, where farmer consents.

Northern Territory.—Local Court Act 1989 (NT) provides that court may of its own motion or on application by party refer proceedings to mediation or arbitration conference.

Western Australia.—With some exceptions, parties to actions commenced by writ are required to attend pretrial conference: rules under District Court of Western Australia Act 1969 (WA). For small debts (less than A$3,000) Local Court attempts to bring parties to settlement: Local Courts Act 1904 (WA). Supreme Court Act 1935 (WA) rules provide that Court may direct apointment of mediator.

Voluntary Dispute Resolution.—

Victoria.—Parties may request mediation in civil proceedings before court: Supreme Court Act 1986 (Vic).

Northern Territory.—Local Court Act 1989 (NT) provides that court may of its own motion or on application by party refer proceedings to mediation or arbitration conference.

ACT.—Conflict Resolution Service (non-legislative) is community oriented mediation service.

Queensland.—Dispute Resolution Centres established by Dispute Resolution Centres Act 1990 (Qld). Either party to dispute may initiate conciliation proceedings under Courts of Conciliation Act 1988 (Qld).

NSW.—Community Justice Centres provide mediation services for wide range of complaints: Community Justice Centres Act 1983 (NSW). For local government disputes parties must rely on Land and Environment Court Act 1979 (NSW) or Local Government Act 1993 (NSW) to enter non-litigious processes. Motor Accidents Act 1988 (NSW) established Motor Accident Authority which mediates motor vehicle accident disputes for both claimants and insurers. Land and Environment Court offers mediation of disputes, appeals and applications. Local Courts (Civil Claims) Act 1970 (NSW) enables local courts to refer matters to mediation or neutral evaluaton. Retail Tenancy Disputes Unit (established by Retail Leases Act 1994 [NSW]) facilitates resolution of disputes.

South Australia.—District Court and Magistrates Court may, with consent of parties, appoint mediator to achieve settlement: District Court Act 1991 (SA), Magistrates Court Act 1991 (SA).

Tasmania.—Magistrate in small claims division attempts to bring small claims (under A$2,000) to settlement before making order: Magistrates Court (Small Claims Division) Act 1989.

See also topic Dispute Resolution, Part I.

DIVORCE:

See Part I, topic Divorce.

State Acts in this field have been superseded by Commonwealth legislation. However, New South Wales has enacted De Facto Relationships Act 1984 which covers part of this field giving limited rights to maintenance, and also governing cohabitation and separation agreements. Property Law (Amendment) Act 1987 (Vic) gives some recognition to de facto relationships including property disputes upon breakdown of relationship.

DOMICILE:

In Australia this term has its common law meaning. It connotes "permanent home", the place a man is presumed at the time in question to consider his true home, wherever he may be resident or travelling for the time being. Any evidence of a man's hopes, intentions and behaviour is relevant in aiding a court to establish his domicile.

Each of States and Northern Territory has introduced Acts which revoke rule that wife has husband's domicile and modify rule that infant has father's domicile where parents living separately and apart, in which case infant's domicile is that of parent with which infant lives. Acts also make provision for domicile of adopted children. Northern Territory Act revokes rule that infant has father's domicile. See now Commonwealth legislation (Domicile Act 1982) effecting similar changes, Part I, topic Domicile.

DOWER:

Abolished.

ENERGY:

Increasing awareness of possible energy shortages and prospect and problems of growing uranium mining industry have prompted States to consider energy legislation. In Victoria, privatisation reforms have seen disaggregation of electricity generators and distributors. Privatisation intended to bring about competition reforms.

Nuclear.—Energy Administration Act 1987 (NSW) establishes new Department of Energy to constitute Energy Corporation of NSW. It is empowered (inter alia) to deal with land and enter into contracts in relation to oil, gas, coal and nuclear energy industries and also empowered to acquire and hold shares in company having objects relating to development of energy and energy resources if approval of Governor of State obtained. Nuclear Activities (Prohibitions) Act 1983 (Vic) forbids nuclear reactors and mining, production and enrichment of nuclear material. Nuclear Activities Regulations Act 1978 (WA) allows nuclear activities under ministerial supervision.

Solar.—Renewable Energy Authority Act 1990 (Vic) established Renewable Energy Authority Victoria to encourage and promote research into and development and use of renewable resources and energy conservation measures. This Authority replaces Victorian Solar Energy Council which was established under now repealed Victorian Solar Energy Council Act 1980 (Vic) to promote research into solar energy. Minerals and Energy Research Act 1987 (WA) promotes and co-ordinates development of minerals and energy industries in Western Australia and establishes Minerals and Energy Research Institute of WA.

See Part I, topic Energy.

ENVIRONMENT:

Pollution.—All States have enacted legislation which constitutes environmental control body or bodies. See Protection of the Environment Administration Act 1991 (NSW), Environment Protection Act 1970 (Vic), Planning and Environment Act 1987 (Vic), State Development and Public Works Organization Act 1971 (Qld), Environment Protection Act 1993 (SA), Environmental Protection Act 1986 (WA), Environment Protection Act 1973 (Tas). See also Land (Planning and Environment) Act 1991 (ACT) and Commissioner of the Environment Act 1993 (ACT). Functions of these bodies include environmental planning, surveying and researching pollution problems and making recommendations thereon to government and, in some cases, regulation of environmental hazards. For example, NSW Act establishes Environment Protection Authority to assume general responsibility for environmental protection under wide variety of legislation.

Commonwealth, States and Territories have entered into agreement to create National Environment Protection Council to determine national environment protection measures. Enacted by all States and Territories except WA where Bill has been introduced.

Environment Protection Act 1970 (Vic) contains provisions designed to lower level of disposal of solid wastes. Act creates Recycling and Resource Recovery Council and Waste Management Council, imposes landfill levy and provides for Industry Waste Reduction Agreements.

Land Use Planning and Approvals Act 1993 (Tas), State Policies and Projects Act 1993 (Tas) and Resource Management and Planning Appeal Tribunal Act 1993 (Tas) relate to Tasmania's new Resource Management and Planning System, objective of which is to promote sustainable development of natural and physical resources and maintenance of ecological process and genetic diversity.

Environmental Planning and Assessment Act 1979 (NSW) establishes system of environmental planning and assessment for State with responsibility for administering Act vested in Minister. See also Environmental Assessment Act 1982 (NT). New South Wales has also established Land and Environment Court which handles all proceedings under relevant anti-pollution legislation in that State and all environmental planning appeals and objections: see Land and Environment Court Act 1979 (NSW). See also Environment Resources and Development Court Act 1993 (SA). Environmental Protection Act 1994 (Qld) provides framework for development of environmental strategies.

Legislation in 1990 in New South Wales creates Environmental Research Trust to promote and fund research into environmental problems and to find less harmful methods of operation for industries, Environmental Restoration and Rehabilitation Trust to encourage and support restoration and rehabilitation projects to reduce pollution and environmental degradation, and Environmental Education Trust to promote and fund environmental education programs and increase public awareness of environmental issues.

Commonwealth, SA, NSW and Victoria have each introduced Murray Darling Basin Acts to approve and give effect to new agreement between them to regulate and preserve water and resources of Murray and Darling rivers and basins.

Most States also have specific anti-pollution legislation such as Pollution Control Acts, Litter Acts, Waste Disposal Acts, Acts to protect waters (for example, Pollution of Waters by Oil and Noxious Substances Act 1986 [Vic], Marine Act 1988 [Vic], Environment Protection [Sea Dumping] Act 1987 [Tas]) and Noise Abatement Acts. Environmental Offences and Penalties Act 1989 (NSW) provides for offences and penalties to supplement other environmental legislation of NSW. Environment Protection Act 1970 (Vic) introduces accredited licensee system for corporations, clarifies lenders' liability for contaminated sites and introduces new procedure for impact assessment of State Environment Protection Policies.

Some States provide for protection of ozone in atmosphere, e.g. Chlorofluorocarbons and other Ozone Depleting Substances Control Act 1988 (Tas); Environment Protection Act 1993 (SA); Ozone Protection Act 1991 (ACT); Ozone Protection Act 1989 (NSW); Environmental Protection Act 1994 (Qld); Environment Protection Act 1970 (Vic). Attempts to halt land degradation, particularly salination, in all States.

Legislation in all States and Territories regulates transportation and packaging of dangerous goods directed more at public safety than environmental issues—Dangerous Goods Act 1985 (Vic), Dangerous Goods Act 1984 (ACT), Dangerous Goods Act 1975 (NSW), Dangerous Goods Act 1980 (NT), Carriage of Dangerous Goods By Road Act 1984 (Qld), Dangerous Substances Act 1979 (SA), Dangerous Goods Act 1976 (Tas), Explosives and Dangerous Goods Act 1961 (WA).

Conservation and Preservation.—Most States have shown increasing interest in conservation of significant buildings, works, objects, places (including parks and reserves) and flora and wildlife. Relevant statutes and bills are: Heritage Act 1977, National Parks and Wildlife Act 1974, Wilderness Act 1987, Native Vegetation Management Act 1991, Endangered Fauna (Interim Protection) Act 1991, Historic Houses Act 1980, Rural Lands Protection Act 1989 (NSW); Coastal Management Act 1995, Archaeological and Aboriginal Relics Preservation Act 1972, National Parks Act 1975, Wildlife Act 1975, Historic Buildings Act 1981, Historic Shipwrecks Act 1981, Flora and Fauna Guarantee Act 1988, Heritage Rivers Act 1992 (Vic); South Australian Heritage Act 1978, National Parks and Wildlife Act 1972-1981, Coast Protection Act 1972, Aboriginal Heritage Act 1988, Native Vegetation Act 1991, Wilderness Protection Act 1992, Heritage Act 1993 (SA); Wildlife Conservation Act 1950-1980; Conservation and Land Management Act 1984 (WA); National Parks and Wildlife Act 1970 (Tas); Nature Conservation Act 1992, Aboriginal Land Act 1991, Wet Tropics World Heritage Protection and Management Act 1993, Marine Parks Act 1982 (Qld); Territory Parks and Wildlife Conservation Act 1980-1983 (NT); Nature Conservation Act 1980 (ACT). The Public Land (Administration and Forests) Act 1991 (Tas) establishes Public Land Use Commission to promote balanced use of public land based on evaluation of its potential to fulfill social, economic and environmental needs amongst other objectives.

EVIDENCE: See topic Depositions.

EXECUTION:

Attachment or execution may issue to enforce a judgment. Attachment of persons can issue only by leave of court but execution against land or goods, unless restrained, can issue as of course upon a judgment for a sum of money. Land and goods must be within jurisdiction of court.

There is no equitable relief against execution of a judgment but it is a tort to levy a manifestly excessive execution on debtor's goods, even in absence of malice.

When court official responsible for execution (sheriff) receives notice of presentation of creditor's bankruptcy petition he must refrain from continuing with execution or making payment to any creditor until petition is withdrawn, dismissed or has lapsed.

Where execution has issued both legal and equitable interests pass but title to land passes subject to all registered encumbrances. Equitable interests in general may be seized and sold with following exceptions: Trust properties, even where they are held for benefit of trustee and other beneficiaries; goods held on bailment; goods subject to bill of sale or under hire purchase; patent rights and claims of purely personal nature in tort.

In cases where other forms of execution are inapplicable a receiver may be appointed by way of equitable execution, or a garnishee order may be obtained.

In settlement of debts generally, sheriff apportions them in order in which he receives them. But where writs are issued simultaneously if any step is taken by sheriff under one writ which necessitates a return to such writ for his protection, such return must be made before any step is taken under other writ.

Exemptions from execution limited to tools of trade, clothing and bedding. No exemption in relation to homesteads.

See topic Garnishment and Part I, topic Actions.

Supplementary Proceedings.—See topic Garnishment.

EXECUTORS AND ADMINISTRATORS:

Upon the grant of probate of the will of a deceased person, or letters of administration of his estate, all his property, whether real or personal, devolves upon his executor or administrator. See Administration and Probate Acts in South Australia, Victoria, Tasmania, Northern Territory and Australian Capital Territory, Succession Act (Qld), Wills, Probate and Administration Act 1898 (NSW) and Administration Act 1903 (WA).

Eligibility and Competency.—Any person of full age and capacity may act as an executor, but a company cannot so act unless specially authorised by its incorporating statute. Trustee companies, specially authorised by Act of Parliament to administer estates, are found in all States. Such companies are not required to enter into any bond, even where acting as administrators. Private individuals, however, may be required to enter into guarantees when acting as administrators. Each State has Public Trustee (Vic: State Trust Corporation of Victoria) who/which may act as executor.

See Topical Index in front part of this volume.

EXECUTORS AND ADMINISTRATORS . . . *continued*

Where a will omits to appoint any executor, or the executor appointed has died or is unable or unwilling to act, letters of administration cum testamento annexo may be granted. Where administration has not been completed and there is no one available to complete it, letters of administration de bonis non may be granted.

Resealing.—Probate or letters of administration granted in any State, or in any other part of the British dominions with which reciprocal arrangements exist, may be resealed in any State.

FOREIGN CORPORATIONS:

See topic Corporations.

FRAUDS, STATUTE OF:

Statute of Frauds was originally received into Australia but had been repealed in all States and Territories (except NT and WA). Writing requirements akin to original provisions have been legislatively introduced. At present, certain contracts must either be in writing or be evidenced in writing. Most important category which applies to all States and Territories is contracts for sale or disposition of interest in land. Writing requirements also apply to contracts of guarantee (NT, Qld, Tas, Vic, WA); contracts not to be performed within a year of being made (NT, Tas); sale of goods over A$20 (Tas, WA) or A$50 (NT); agreements in consideration of marriage (NT, Tas) and promises by executor or administrator to answer damages out of estate (NT, Tas).

Contract that does not comply with writing requirements is still valid, but will not be enforced by court or form basis of damages award. However, in some circumstances court will order specific performance or equitable damages if party has sufficiently committed to contract (doctrine of part performance).

Various Credit Acts also require certain guarantees to be in writing (ACT, NSW, Qld, Vic, WA).

Adoption of 1980 United Nations Convention on Contracts for International Sale of Goods (Vienna Convention) by all States alters application of Statute of Frauds in some States. (See topic Sales.)

GARNISHMENT:

Where judgment or order is for recovery or payment of money, party entitled to enforce it may apply to have debtor examined as to whether any and what debts are owing to him; and any debts owing to debtor may be attached in satisfaction of judgment and garnishee order may be obtained requiring person owing money to debtor to pay same to judgment creditor. Enforcement of Judgments Act 1991 (SA) requires consent of judgment debtor before garnishee order made over salary or wages. Debt is bound as soon as order is served on person liable to pay same, but judgment creditor acquires no greater right than judgment debtor possessed. Judgment Debt Recovery Act 1984 (Vic) and Debtors Act 1870 (Tas) allow court to order that judgment debt be paid by instalments and removes imprisonment as penalty for default of payment unless debtor has means to pay and willfully defaults. In Western Australia, Restraint of Debtors Act 1984 provides for arrest of debtors, and restraint of debtor's property in certain circumstances. Debtors Act 1936 (SA) provides for arrest and imprisonment of debtor in limited circumstances. Registered maintenance agreements treated as debts to Commonwealth. See Part I, topic Divorce.

GUARDIAN AND WARD:

Inherent jurisdiction of Supreme Court of each State and Territory includes exercise of parens patriae power for protection of person and property of infants and mentally infirm. Also powers bestowed by relevant Supreme Court Acts; statutory powers do not derogate from inherent powers.

Children.—Under Constitution, guardianship, custody of children other than in matrimonial cause is States' matter. However, revocable reference of certain powers to Commonwealth by all states except WA, so in those States, Family Law Act applies to dispute over guardianship, custody, access or maintenance of child, except where child already subject to State custody or care under State welfare law, or where temporary protective order sought, as under, e.g. Children (Care and Protection) Act 1987 (NSW). All other guardianship powers transferred to Commonwealth by Jurisdiction of Courts (Cross-vesting) Acts of each State. Welfare provisions of Family Law Act cover areas under States' wardship jurisdiction such as medical treatment, blood transfusions and emotional wellbeing of child. In Western Australia, only State law applies to ex-nuptial children. Paramount consideration in all cases is welfare of child. See also Part I, topic Divorce.

Jurisdictional requirement is ordinary residence, though physical presence sufficient territorial connection if protection needed. Child may be ward of person, State or Supreme Court. If ward of Supreme Court, judge awards guardianship to party and can make orders with respect to custody, access, maintenance. Judge retains personal responsibility for child until 18. Ward of Supreme Court may not be removed from jurisdiction, allowed to leave school or marry without judge's permission.

Mental Illness.—Supreme Court has inherent jurisdiction over estate of person with mental illness, and all states have legislation whereby guardian/committee of person and/or administrator of estate may be appointed where person over 18 suffering mental disability (variously defined) and unable to manage own affairs (specific guardianship legislation in ACT, NT, NSW, Vic and WA; guardianship provisions in mental health legislation in Qld, SA and Tas). Views of person to be taken into account in most States. Guardian should be of same sex and reside near patient in same jurisdiction, and is often appointed by Guardianshp Board. Some States include deterioration through age of mental faculties.

Relevant legislation includes: Guardianship and Administration Board Act 1986 (Vic); Guardianship Act 1987 (NSW); Intellectually Disabled Citizens Act 1985 (Qld); Guardianship and Administration Act 1990 (WA); Guardianship and Administration Act 1993 (SA); Guardianship and Management of Property Act 1991 (ACT), Aged and Infirm Persons' Property Act 1979 (NT) and Mental Health Acts of all States and Territories.

Public Trustee (Victoria—State Trust Corporation) may be preferred administrator of estate.

Foreign order of appointment of guardian not regarded as foreign judgment for purposes of law applicable to recognition of foreign judgments in general. Forum itself must make appointment, even if only confirming foreign appointment.

Guardianship orders may be enduring or temporary, plenary or limited, depending on relevant jurisdiction, and appeal and review rights exist in all States.

Medical Treatment.—Consent to major nontherapeutic medical treatment (e.g. sterilisation), usually only with consent of guardian and approval of court. In Victoria, approval of Guardianship and Administration Board is required; in NSW, Mental Health Review Tribunal; in SA, Guardianship Board. Any person aggrieved may challenge decision in court. In Victoria Guardianship and Administration Board Act 1986 established Office of Public Advocate to advocate on behalf of people of all ages with disabilities, defined in Act to include intellectual, psychiatric and physical disabilities, brain damage and senility. Judicial criteria for consent unsettled, but paramount consideration best interests of person.

Power of Attorney by competent donor may continue to operate in some circumstances in event of subsequent incapacity of donor in all States and Territories: Vic: Instruments (Enduring Powers of Attorney) Act 1981, NSW: Conveyancing (Powers of Attorney) Amendment Act 1983, SA: Powers of Attorney and Agency Act 1984, Tas: Powers of Attorney Amendment Act 1987, ACT: Powers of Attorney Act 1956, NT: Powers of Attorney Act 1980, Qld: Property Law Amendment Act 1990, WA: Guardianship and Administration Act 1990.

HEALTH:

All States and Northern Territory have enacted Health Acts and Food Acts and Regulations which prescribe standards for public health. States of Victoria and New South Wales have also enacted provisions restricting sale and advertising of patent medicines.

Statutory control of packaging and marketing of therapeutic goods and cosmetics exists in some States: Therapeutic Goods and Cosmetics Act 1972 (NSW), Therapeutic Goods And Other Drugs Regulations 1982 (Qld), Therapeutic Goods and Cosmetics Act 1986 (NT), Therapeutic Goods Act 1994 (Vic), Therapeutic Goods and Cosmetics Act 1976 (Tas). Therapeutic Goods Act 1989 (Cth) applies in SA, WA and ACT.

States, Territories and Commonwealth have entered National Food Standards Council Agreement established under National Food Authority Act 1991 (Cth). Food Standards recommended by National Health and Medical Research Council apply throughout Australia.

HOLIDAYS:

In all States Jan. 1 (New Year's Day), Jan. 26 (Australia Day), Good Friday, Easter Monday, Apr. 25 (Anzac Day), Queen's Birthday (which is celebrated on proclaimed date), Dec. 25 (Christmas Day) and Dec. 26 (Boxing Day, or Proclamation Day in SA) are public holidays. Labor Day, celebrated on different days in different States, is also a holiday, as is Easter Tuesday (in Tasmania) and Dec. 28 (in South Australia). Some places celebrate public holidays in honour of premier horse race (e.g. in Melbourne only, Melbourne Cup Day—first Tues. in Nov.) or agricultural show (e.g. Brisbane Show Day in Qld, Alice Springs Show Day in NT), Individual States' holidays include Foundation Day (5 June: WA), Hobart Regatta (14 Feb.: Tas), Picnic Day (5 Aug.: NT), May Day (1 May: NT).

Bills of Exchange and promissory notes apparently payable on Sundays or public holidays, may be paid on the day following. In general, no person is compellable to do any act or make any payment on public holiday which he would not be obliged to do or make on Sun. Position with regard to Sun. is governed by statutes in each State regulating particular situations.

In all States and Territories, where last day of period prescribed by statute or ordinance for doing anything falls on Sat., Sun., or public or bank holiday in place where thing is to be done, thing may be done on first day that is not Sat., Sun., or public or bank holiday.

HUSBAND AND WIFE:

See Part I, topics Divorce; Marriage.

On marriage a woman's property remains her own unless she makes disposition of it to the contrary.

Married woman hold and dispose of property, make contracts and carry on business separately from their husbands as if they were single. In all States married women may be liable in respect of any tort, contract, debt or obligation incurred prior to entering marriage and in in New South Wales and Western Australia contractual liability of married woman is limited to her own property. However, distinction of little importance, as married women subject to provisions of Commonwealth Bankruptcy Act 1966. Resulting trust relationship will arise between husband and wife if spouse contributes to joint property. Spouses can sue each other in contract or tort. Married woman no longer acquires domicile of husband, and there is no legal obligation to assume surname of spouse. Husband is generally liable for contracts entered into by his wife for necessaries, but is no longer liable for post nuptial torts in any State or Territory. In ACT, effect of Married Persons' Property Act 1986 is to abolish rule that husband is liable for contracts entered into by his wife for necessaries.

INCOME TAX: See topic Taxation.

INFANTS:

Age of Majority is now 18 years whether male or female, married or not, in all States and Territories.

Contracts.—In general infants have no power to contract except for necessaries (such as food, drink, medicine). Contracts other than for necessaries may be ratified either orally or in writing upon attainment of age of majority. Contracts of minors are voidable at option of minor, but adult cannot plead minor's incapacity to contract as defence, so minor could enforce rights against adult in most cases. Contracts that are unfair or prejudicial to minor may be cancelled by court after looking at whole contract.

INFANTS . . . *continued*

Torts.—In general infants are liable for torts.

Actions.—An infant may sue by guardian, if any, or next friend. A guardian ad litem or next friend may upon request be appointed by court to protect interest of any minor in any suit relating to property in which minor may be or may become interested.

Status of Children.—Legislation passed in all States except WA removes legal disabilities of children born out of wedlock. Relationship between every child and father and mother determined irrespective of whether father and mother are or have been married to one another. Acts apply to every person irrespective of date or place of birth or domicile of father or mother. Child born to woman during her marriage or within ten months after marriage dissolved by death or otherwise shall in absence of contrary evidence be presumed to be child of mother and her husband or former husband. Relationship of father and child for any purpose related to succession to property, etc. recognized only if father and mother of child were married to each other at time of its conception or some subsequent time or paternity has been admitted (expressly or by implication) by or established against father in his lifetime. Methods of establishing paternity also provided for. Western Australian Legitimation Act 1909-1940 has limited operation. Act only legitimatizes children born out of wedlock by subsequent marriage of their parents. Distinction of illegitimacy is now only relevant to guardianship and custody.

Artificial Conception.—New South Wales Artificial Conception Act 1984 and Children (Equality of Status) Amendment Act 1984 provide that where married woman, with her husband's consent, has undergone fertilization procedure resulting in pregnancy (including artificial insemination and in vitro fertilization) husband shall be irrebuttably presumed to have caused pregnancy and be father of child. Similar provisions exist in Status of Children (Amendment) Act 1984 (Vic), Family Relationships Act 1975 (SA) as amended, Status of Children Act Amendment Act 1988 (Qld), Artificial Conception Act 1985 (ACT), Status of Children Amendment Act 1985 (NT), Status of Children Act 1974 (Tas), and Artificial Conception Act 1985 (WA).

Surrogacy agreements prohibited by Surrogate Parenthood Act 1988 (Qld), Family Relationships Act Amendment Act 1988 (SA), Queensland Act applies where offender ordinarily resident in Queensland at time proscribed act occurs, irrespective of where act occurs. Under Infertility Treatment Act 1995 (Vic) surrogacy agreement, whether or not for payment or reward, void; publishing advertisements for surrogacy, and giving or receiving payment for making agreement or acting as surrogate, prohibited. Surrogacy Contracts Act 1993 (No. 4) (Tas) in substantially similar terms to Vic. Act.

Reproductive Technology Act 1988 (SA) establishes South Australia Council on Reproductive Technology which governs artificial fertilization procedures in South Australia. Infertility Treatment Act 1995 (Vic) regulates artificial fertilization procedures, prohibits certain research and establishes Infertility Treatment Authority.

INTEREST:

Usury.—Tasmania and Northern Territory have fully operational Money Lending Acts governing rate of interest which may be charged under money lending contracts—see Lending of Money Act 1915 (Tas) and Money Lenders Act 1903 (NT).

"Money lender" is defined broadly in Acts as meaning person whose business (whether or not he carries on any other business) is that of money lending or who advertises or holds himself out as carrying on that business; but does not include, among other things, person bona fide carrying on business of banking.

Tasmanian and Northern Territory Acts do not prescribe any maximum interest rate.

With introduction of Credit Act 1984 (NSW), Credit Act 1984 (Vic.), Credit Act 1987 (Qld), Credit Act 1984 (WA) and Credit Act 1985 (ACT), Money Lending Acts of those jurisdictions have been repealed except insofar as they relate to contracts entered into prior to introduction of Credit Acts.

Credit Acts govern provision of loan contracts to consumers (excluding corporations) where amount is less than A$20,000 (in Queensland, A$40,000), contracts where goods are provided on credit (i.e. hire purchase); and continuing credit contracts where credit is provided on ongoing basis for goods or services.

New Uniform Consumer Credit Code to be introduced Nov. 1, 1996 in all States (modified version in WA). Code is contained in appendix to Consumer Credit (Queensland) Act 1994 and has been enacted by all States except Tas and WA. Provides for regulation of consumer credit contracts involving restrictions on interest charges and forms of mortgages and guarantees. Extends to housing loans.

There is provision in all States and A.C.T. under above legislation for courts or credit tribunals to reopen transaction where proceedings have been commenced for recovery of any money lent by money lender or credit provider. If court is satisfied that: (a) Interest charged is excessive; or (b) transaction is harsh and unconscionable; or (c) transaction is such that court of equity would give relief, then it is open to court to relieve person sued from payment of any sum in excess of sum adjudged by court to be fairly due in respect of principal.

INTESTACY:

See topic Descent and Distribution.

JUDGMENTS:

Under Service and Execution of Process Act 1992 (Cth), judgment may be registered in court of another State by lodging sealed copy of judgment. Faxed copy may be lodged if sealed copy lodged withing seven days. On registration, judgment has same force and effect and is enforceable as if given by court in which registered, except for interest and stay of proceedings. Interest is assessed on same basis as in court in which judgment given. Court in which judgment registered may stay proceedings to allow judgment debtor to appeal. Rules of private international law about recognition and enforcement of foreign judgments cannot prevent enforcement of judgment under Act.

§118 of Commonwealth Constitution provides that full faith and credit shall be given throughout Commonwealth to laws, public acts and records and judicial proceedings of every State. However due to system of registration described above full faith and credit is not as significant in relation to interstate judgments as it is in U.S.

Foreign Judgments.—Under common law, judgments of foreign courts have been recognized in Australian States under certain conditions, general requirements being as follows: (1) Judgment must be final and conclusive; (2) judgment must be for sum certain (not being tax or penalty); (3) enforcement of judgment would not be contrary to public policy of State in which it is sought to be registered; (4) foreign court must have had jurisdiction, according to Australian rules of private international law (for judgments in personam by presence or residence of judgment debtor in foreign country, or voluntary submission to jurisdiction of foreign court [by appearance or contract], for judgments in rem by situation of property in foreign country); (5) judgment not obtained by fraud; and (6) judgment debtor not denied natural justice.

From 27 June 1993 Commonwealth Foreign Judgments Act 1991 replaced State systems for registration and enforcement of foreign judgments, and in certain circumstances replaced common law action on judgment debt. Act applies to judgments of country if Governor-General is satisfied that substantial reciprocity of treatment assured in that country. As at May 1995 following countries' superior courts are covered: most British Commonwealth countries, including County Courts of UK, Canada, Hong Kong; and also France, Germany, Israel, Italy and Japan; but no US jurisdictions. Act also provides that in respect of all foreign judgments (whether or not registrable under Act) mere appearance to protect seized property, to contest jurisdiction of court, or to invoke court's discretion not to exercise jurisdiction does not constitute voluntary submission to jurisdiction for purposes of recognition or registration.

In South Australia there is provision to register all foreign judgments where jurisdiction of original court is recognised under rules of private international law and judgment is final or conclusive, or where it is seen as just and equitable to enforce judgment.

See Part I, topic Actions.

LABOUR RELATIONS:

States have power to regulate directly labour relations and industrial disputes within territorial limits. Queensland, Western Australia, South Australia, and New South Wales do so by means of conciliation and arbitration: Industrial Relations Act 1991 (NSW); Industrial Relations Act 1990 (Qld); Industrial and Employee Relations Act 1994 (SA); and Industrial Relations Act 1979 (WA). Industrial Relations Amendment Act 1992 (Qld) amends Queensland Act to encourage enterprise bargaining agreements and facilitate amalgamation of unions. Industrial Relations (Miscellaneous Provisions) Amendment Act 1992 (SA) amends South Australian Act to allow for certification of industrial agreements and to regulate family leave and part-time work.

Victoria and Tasmania regulate labour relations by means of arbitral and nonarbitral machinery: Employee Relations Act 1992 (Vic) and Industrial Relations Act 1984 (Tas). Victorian Act provides for employment agreements, either at individual or enterprise level, as well as awards of Employee Relations Commission, which replaces Industrial Relations Commission. Employment agreements must contain minimum terms (e.g. sick leave and annual leave) and dispute-settling procedure. Commission has powers of conciliation and arbitration if employer and all employees consent. Commission also has power to order reinstatement of employee who is subject to harsh, unjust or unreasonable dismissal. Role of unions is reduced under Act, but High Court has held that Federal Industrial Relations Commission could make awards even over employees in State where compulsory arbitration was abolished (i.e. Vic). Industrial Relations (Enterprise Agreements and Workplace Freedom) Act 1992 (Tas) inserts new Part in Tasmanian Act regulating employment agreements at enterprise level.

Workers Compensation is provided for in State legislation which casts obligation on employer to pay compensation to worker who suffers personal injury or death arising out of or in course of his employment. To cover employer's liability to pay compensation legislation compels him to obtain insurance cover for full amount of his liability. Workers Compensation Board is set up to hear compensation claims and make awards: Workers Compensation Act 1987 (NSW); Accident Compensation Act 1985 (Vic); Workers' Compensation Act 1990 (Qld); Workers Rehabilitation and Compensation Act 1986 and WorkCover Corporation Act 1994 (SA); Workers Compensation Act 1988 (Tas); Workers' Compensation and Rehabilitation Act 1981 (WA); Work Health Act 1986 (NT); Workers' Compensation Act 1951 (ACT). Dust Diseases Tribunal Act 1989 (NSW) sets up tribunal in New South Wales to determine claims relating to death or injury resulting from certain dust diseases (e.g. asbestosis).

Accident Compensation Act 1985 (Vic) amended by Accident Compensation (WorkCover) Act 1992 (Vic) and Accident Compensation (WorkCover Insurance) Act 1993. Accident Compensation Commission replaced by Victorian WorkCover Authority. Definition of injury tightened so worker's employment must be significant cause of injury. Journey accidents no longer covered under WorkCover. Benefit structure altered to create incentives for workers to rehabilitate and return to work. Disputes go to conciliation at first, then referred to court if not resolved. Accident Compensation (WorkCover Insurance) Act 1993 (Vic) imposes liability to pay compensation under Act on employers and require employers to insure with authorised insurer against liability.

In all States and Territories there are number of Acts concerning occupational health and safety.

See Part I, topic Industrial Relations.

LAW REPORTS: See topic Reports, infra.

LEGISLATURE:

See topic Constitution and Government.

LICENCES:

Licences may be required in different industries for various activities, such as broadcasting, airlines, provision of consumer credit, banking, dealing in securities or giving investment advice. Individuals may need licence to keep, raise or experiment on animals; shoot game; fish; own or carry gun or other dangerous weapons; and other activities regulated by government. See also topics Air Navigation, Corporations, Banking and Currency, and Shipping in Commonwealth digest (Part I).

LIENS:

Lien is mere right to retain possession of property upon which lien exists, and it cannot as rule be enforced by sale. Lien arises by implication of law or by statute.

Particular Liens.—Particular lien entitles holder to retain property until payment of particular charges incurred in relation to property. Such liens arise, for example: (a) Where creditor is compellable by law to receive goods or to perform certain services to owner of such goods, as in case of common carriers and inn-keepers; (b) where creditor has spent money, skill or labor upon property, as in case of workmen; (c) under maritime law in case of salvage.

General lien entitles holder to retain property as security for payment of full indebtedness of owner no matter on what account charge in relation to property was incurred. Examples of general liens are liens of solicitors, bankers, factors, stockbrokers and insurance brokers. In order to establish general lien by custom of trade, it must be shown that there was certain usage, that such usage is reasonable and not inconsistent with law, and that it was so universally acquiesced in that everybody in trade knew it or ought to have known it. However, in case of above examples, judicial notice has resulted in it being unnecessary to demonstrate actual proof of usage for such liens to be established.

LIMITATION OF ACTIONS:

Various statutory provisions exist in various States for limiting time plaintiff may take to commence action. Actions for torts must generally be brought within six years (three years in NT); actions for simple contract debts generally within six years; actions upon contracts under seal within 12, 15 or 20 years and actions for personal injuries in Qld, SA, Tas and in NSW (arising after 1 Sept. 1990) within three years. May be shorter limits for actions against Crown or public authorities (e.g. in WA).

Cause of action founded on deed generally not maintainable after 12 years. Action to recover land is not maintainable by Crown after 30 years or by any other person after 12 years.

Limitation Act 1974 (Tas) provides that where option to purchase land or right of preemption in respect of land does not provide for time limit for exercise of option or right, action arising out of that option or right must be brought within one year of grant of option or right. Action for contributions between tortfeasors is not maintainable after two years from date cause of action for contribution first accrued and four years after expiration of limitation period for principal cause of action.

Northern Territory Limitation Act 1981 provides that actions based on contract and tort must be brought within three years of date of accrual of action and cause of action founded on deed is not maintainable after 12 years.

Action to recover any tax, fee, charge or other impost paid under authority of any Act must be commenced within 12 months after date of payment: Limitation Act 1935 (WA), Limitation of Actions Act 1958 (Vic) and Limitation of Actions (Recovery of Imports) Act 1963 (NSW), Limitation (Amendment) Act 1993 (ACT); Limitation of Actions Amendment Act 1993 (Qld) and Limitation of Actions (Mistake of Law or Fact) Amendment Act 1993 (SA).

Limitation Amendment Act 1993 (Tas) and Limitation Amendment Act 1993 (NT) same but with six months limitation period.

Time begins to run as soon as the cause of action accrues, which is date it is complete. In an action upon an executory promise the cause of action is the breach, and time runs not from the promise but from the breach. In case of promise to pay on demand time runs from date of promise. In case of contract of indemnity time runs from time when damage was suffered, and not from time when event happened which causes damage.

In relation to personal injuries, action usually accrues at time damage is suffered, but in New South Wales (where cause of action accrued before 1 Sept. 1990), Queensland, Victoria and Western Australia time runs from date when claimant first became aware of facts material to cause of action (in Western Australia—only applies where injuries attributable to inhalation of asbestos and claimant did not become aware of material facts until after Jan. 1, 1984).

Trade-off for three year period is flexibility of court to extend time for up to five years in New South Wales, where cause of action accrues on or after 1 Sept. 1990. If plaintiff was unaware of injury at relevant time court may grant further extension if it decides that it is just and reasonable to do so. In Victoria, South Australia and Tasmania court has discretion to extend limitation period if just and reasonable to do so (in Tasmania—up to maximum of six years).

An action against a statutory body, such as Railway Commissioners, must as a rule be preceded by a notice in writing, to be given within a short period such as three or six months.

Effect of Acknowledgment.—An acknowledgment in writing or part payment of debt provides remedy for recovery thereof, although it had theretofore become barred by limitations. Similarly, written acknowledgment of title to land may extinguish any adverse claim of person making acknowledgment.

Person Under Disability.—Each State and Territory suspends running of limitation period where person to whom cause of action accrues is under disability (infant, mentally deficient, mentally disordered), but usually maximum period 30 years from date cause of action arises.

Forum Shopping.—Various Acts provide that limitation laws to be regarded as substantive law of jurisdiction and thus govern claim brought in another jurisdiction under substantive laws of first jurisdiction. Choice of Law (Limitation Periods) Act 1993 (NSW); Limitation (Amendment) Act 1993 (ACT), Choice of Law (Limitation Periods) Act 1993 (Vic), Choice of Law (Limitation Periods) Act 1994 (NT) and (WA), and Limitations (Amendment) Act 1993 (Qld).

MARRIAGE:

See Part I, topic Marriage.

MARRIED WOMEN:

See topic Husband and Wife; Part I, topic Marriage.

MINES AND MINERALS:

Ownership of Minerals.—Petroleum and natural gas belong to Crown. In South Australia and Northern Territory, all other minerals belong to Crown. In Victoria, Mineral Resources Development Act 1990 provides that Crown owns all minerals except (i) those in respect of which minerals exemption is current; and (ii) those separated from land by holder of licence, miner's right or tourist fossicking authority (royalties are payable to Crown in accordance with licence). In all other States and A.C.T., certain minerals (usually including gold) belong to Crown, whilst rights to other minerals also belong to Crown unless alienated in original Crown grant of land. In Tasmania, effect of Mining Amendment Act 1986 is that all geothermal substances existing above or below ground belong to Crown.

Minerals Exploration.—In most jurisdictions any person may take out miner's right which entitles him to occupy land (with certain exceptions) and to commence mining operations. Miner's right is valid for period of up to five years (depending on jurisdiction) and land so occupied is deemed to be mining land possessed by holder of right.

In return for payment of royalties, lease may be granted to miners. Royalties returned from minerals found on Crown lands remain property of Crown.

Mining lease or licence may be granted upon (generally speaking) presenting application showing reasonable probability of finding minerals on land not occupied by holder of miner's right. Mining Act 1992 (NSW) provides for transfer of parts of leases. Mineral Resources Development Act 1990 (Vic) has repealed most of Mines Act 1958 and replaces license provisions, sets up Mining and Environment Advisory Commitee to advise Minister, and sets up Mining Register. Act provides that licensee must rehabilitate land and compensate owners/occupiers of private land for loss/damage sustained from work done under licence. Licence may be subject to conditions including those concerning protection of environment. All States and Territories have restrictions on mining in public areas, including national parks. Most require consent of Parliament even for prospecting.

Short term titles (usually renewable from year to year on compliance with expenditure conditions) are available for prospecting.

Mine Management Act 1990 (NT) relates to inspection and management of mines. Other States have similar legislation: Mines Inspection Act 1901 (NSW); Mines Safety and Inspection Act 1994 (WA); Mines and Works Inspection Act 1920 (SA); Mineral Resources Development Act 1990 (Vic); Mines Regulation Act 1964 (Qld).

Most jurisdictions also have legislation that deals with particular types of mining such as Coal Mining Act (Queensland) 1925 and Uranium Mining (Environment Control) Act (NT) 1979. Nuclear Activities (Prohibitions) Act 1983 (Vic) prohibits establishment of any nuclear activities, including mining thorium. Also Uranium Mining & Nuclear Facilities (Prohibitions) Act 1986 (NSW); Mining (Precious Stones Field Ballots) Amendment Act 1993 (SA).

Aboriginal Land Rights.—Aboriginal Land Rights (Northern Territory) Act 1976 (Cth.), Aboriginal Land Act 1980 (NT) and Northern Territory Aboriginal Sites Act 1989 qualify position in respect of mining interests and operations in aboriginal land. Other jurisdictions have legislation that gives varying degrees of recognition to aboriginal sacred sites and control of mining and exploration on them.

In important case of Mabo v. Queensland (No. 2) (1992) 175 C.L.R. 1, High Court of Australia held that native title survived European settlement of Australia. Accordingly, Aborigines who can show continuous occupation of land during European settlement can claim native title to land. As result certain titles to land required confirmation. Validation of mining licences and provision of compensation in respect of certain customary titles provided for by: Land Titles Validation Act 1993 (Vic); Land (Titles and Traditional Usage) Act 1993 (WA). Native Title Act 1993 (Commonwealth) provides mechanism for native title claim and determination. This is reflected in Native Title Act 1993 (Qld); Native Title Act 1994 (ACT); Native Title Act 1994 (NSW); and Validation of Titles and Actions Act 1994 (NT).

Environment.—Balance must be struck between mining interests and environmental and conservation interests. Mining (Strategic Prospectivity Zones) Act 1993 (Tas) guarantees mining access to areas of Tasmania with very high potential for efficient mining. See also Mineral Resources Development Act 1990 (Vic) above.

Petroleum Exploration.—Separate legislation deals with petroleum exploration and miners are required to obtain petroleum exploration permit or petroleum prospecting licence (depending on jurisdiction). Permit holder may apply for grant of production licence for petroleum or petroleum mineral lease (again, depending on jurisdiction). States and Commonwealth have also passed legislation for regulation and control of exploration and exploitation of petroleum resources of submerged lands, e.g., Petroleum (Submerged Lands) Act 1982 (NSW), Petroleum (Submerged Lands) Act 1982 (Vic). Vic, NSW and NT legislation has been amended to reflect changes to Commonwealth Act since 1984 including Commonwealth-State cooperative plan of responsibility. See this topic Part I.

Compensation.—Minister may require compensation to be paid to owner of freehold land declared to be mining land. Owner of land is liable in trespass for unauthorised interference with land so declared.

See topics Aliens; Corporations, subhead Terminology, catchline "No Liability" Mining Companies and Part I, topics Aliens; Customs; Mines and Minerals.

MONOPOLIES AND RESTRAINT OF TRADE:

The old common law offences of forestalling, engrossing and regrating, apparently still exist in the Australian States other than Victoria. The repeal of these offences in Victoria still, however, preserves the offence of knowingly and fraudulently spreading or conspiring to spread any false rumour with intent to enhance or decry the price of any goods, wares or merchandise, and the offence of preventing or endeavoring to prevent by force or threat any goods, wares or merchandise being brought to any market.

Several States have enacted laws in area of restrictive trade practices. However, legislation, outlined below, has not been rigorously enforced and is far less significant in area than Trade Practices Act 1974 (Cth) and Competition Policy Reform Act 1995 (Cth).

MONOPOLIES AND RESTRAINT OF TRADE . . . *continued*

New South Wales.—Monopolies Act 1923 defines combination as including any agreement, arrangement or understanding. Act provides that no person shall monopolise, attempt to monopolise, or combine with any other person to monopolise, trade in any commodity or service, with intent to control, to detriment of public, supply or price of commodity or service. Any contract made in contravention of this prohibition is illegal and void; but it is provided that any combination of producers of any commodity which is reasonably necessary for maintenance of industry of such producers, shall not be deemed to be to detriment of public; combination of producers for this purpose is defined as including any association of producers, whether incorporated or unincorporated, and in particular: (a) Any rural society registered under Co-operation, Community Settlement and Credit Act of 1923; and (b) any company under Corporations Law which has objects same as or similar to those of such rural society.

By Part 3 of Act, Industrial Commission is given power, on receiving complaint or on being given reference by Attorney-General, to make inquiry into certain monopolies and combinations, and to report to Attorney-General result of any such enquiry together with any recommendations.

Penalties for offence against Act are maximum of A$1,000 (ten penalty units) for first offence and maximum of A$1,000 or imprisonment for term not exceeding 12 months or both for subsequent offence.

Restraints of Trade Act 1976 states that restraint of trade is valid to extent to which it is not against public policy, whether restraint is in severable terms or not.

Competition Policy Reform (New South Wales) Act 1995 provides that Competition Code (contained in Competition Policy Reform Act 1995 [Cth]) applies as New South Wales law.

Queensland.—Profiteering Prevention Act 1948 deals inter alia with restraint of trade and prohibition of combines and monopolies. (Part IV). It is prohibited for person to hold or buy up goods and store or retain them in his possession or control with intent to corner market or restrain trade therein. Provision is made for Commissioner of Prices under Act to fix maximum prices. Upon report by Commissioner, Minister may, if satisfied that it is expedient to do so to ensure fair distribution of goods amongst all members of community, direct persons to hold goods, which are in their possession or control, on behalf of Crown. It is offence to offer valuable consideration (including rebates, refunds, discounts, concessions, allowances and rewards) to another upon condition that they deal exclusively or principally with person. Restricting dealings against public interest, such as acting under directions regarding sale of goods, entering exclusive dealing arrangements, monopolising goods or fixing price of goods, is offence. Maximum penalty for offence is A$4,000 or imprisonment for two years or both (if natural person) or A$20,000 (if body corporate).

Any association or combination which carries on business or acts in Queensland and has as one of its objects or purposes controlling, determining or influencing of supply, demand, or price of any goods in Queensland is caught by Act.

South Australia.—Prices Act 1948 deals with price control and imposes statutory restrictions on certain trade practices relating to limits on purchases, misleading advertising and attempts to obtain differential terms. Requirements as to price tickets also established.

Western Australia.—Petroleum Products Pricing Act 1983 provides for some enquiry into and control over excessive prices for petroleum products and services.

Victoria.—Under Collusive Practices Act 1965, tendering or bidding, abstaining from tendering or bidding and joint tendering or bidding in accordance with a collusive tendering or bidding agreement are forbidden. Collusive tendering or bidding agreement defined to include agreement which has purpose or effect of preventing or restricting competition among all or any of parties in respect of tendering or bidding. "Tender" is defined as offer for supply or acquisition of goods or services made in response to invitation published for or on behalf of Government of Victoria, Victorian statutory corporation, municipality or certain charitable institutions and hospitals.

"Agreement" includes an arrangement or understanding, formal or informal, express or implied and whether enforceable or intended to be enforceable by legal proceedings or not and whether made within or without Victoria. These practices are punishable by fines or imprisonment or both.

Grocery Prices Act 1987 provides for some control over excessive increases in prices of household groceries.

Competition Policy Reform (Victoria) Act 1995 provides that Competition Code (contained in Competition Policy Reform Act 1995 [Cth]) applies as Victorian law.

Restraint of Trade.—Prima facie, any restraint of trade is void at common law, and the onus is upon the person desirous of supporting the restraint to show that it is reasonable in the interest of the parties and of the public. Question of reasonableness or otherwise is matter of law to be determined by court, and not question of fact for jury; and evidence as to reasonableness cannot be given by persons engaged in trade, or otherwise, but judge will have regard to all circumstances of case, and may hear evidence of nature of business and conditions under which it is carried on.

Consideration of covenants in restraint of trade usually arises out of contracts of employment, or contracts for purchase of goodwill of business, in both of which classes of contracts it may become, and frequently is, necessary to restrain right of vendor or employee, after conclusion of sale or employment, from depriving purchaser or employer of benefit received under contract.

The reasonableness of a contract in restraint of trade is examined in relation to the consideration given, and the time and space for which the restraint extends.

See also Part I, topic Monopolies and Restraint of Trade and Part II, topic Consumer Protection.

MORTGAGES:

See topics Chattel Mortgages and Real Property.

MOTOR VEHICLES:

Motor vehicles must be registered in the State in which they are operated, and bear a distinguishing number of their registration on the front and back of the vehicle. Australian Capital Territory and Northern Territory have their own registration systems. Vehicles may visit from one State to another temporarily, without re-registering. Registration is good for 12 months, and must then be renewed. Driver's licenses must also be obtained for drivers of motor vehicles.

All States and Territories provide for compulsory liability insurance.

Aircraft.—See Part I, topic Air Navigation.

NOTARIES PUBLIC:

Application for appointment as notary public for Victoria must be made to the Dean of the Arches at the Faculty Office, Doctors Commons, London, the faculty itself being issued by the Archbishop of Canterbury. The faculty is usually limited to a defined area or territory within the State. Notice of application for appointment must be served on the Society of Notaries of Victoria, which may caveat against or object to the grant of the faculty. Applicants must show by memorial, supported by affidavit, the need for the appointment. Faculties are usually confined to solicitors, unless exceptional circumstances are shown.

Applications from other States proceed on much same basis. In Western Australia, pursuant to Public Notaries Act 1979, only way of appointing Public Notary is by order of Full Court of Supreme Court. In New South Wales, Public Notaries Act, 1985 provides for appointment of public notaries by New South Wales Supreme Court. Public notaries are similarly appointed in Tasmania and Northern Territory under Notaries Public Act 1990 (Tas) and Public Notaries Act 1992 (NT) respectively.

PARTNERSHIP:

Membership.—See topic Associations.

Liability.—Partners are jointly liable for the debts of the partnership, and may sue and be sued in the partnership name. An order in bankruptcy may be made against a partnership, and operates as a sequestration of the estates of the several partners. Corporations may be partners, provided they have such power under their memoranda of association or other charters or (if pursuant to Corporations Law company chooses not to list any objects) provided such power is not expressly prohibited in those documents. In most States there is statutory provision for limited partnerships whereby some partners may have limited liability: Partnership (Limited Liability) Act 1988 (Qld); Limited Partnerships Act 1909 (WA); Limited Partnerships Act 1908 (Tas); Partnership Act 1892 (NSW); and Partnership Act 1958 (Vic).

Form.—No particular formalities are necessary to constitute a partnership, the contract for which may be either verbal or written, expressed or implied.

Agreement for partnership which is to last for more than a year need not be in writing, if it has been partly performed. Where no fixed term has been agreed upon for partnership, any partner may determine partnership at any time by giving notice to other partners. Partnership will also be dissolved by expiration of time specified in partnership agreement; by death of any one member of partnership, unless there is some agreement to contrary; by bankruptcy of any one partner, unless there is any agreement to contrary; or by happening of any event which renders business of firm illegal. Courts have wide powers to dissolve partnerships.

Relevant Acts are Partnership Act 1892 (NSW); Partnership Act 1958 (Vic); Partnership Act 1891 (SA); Partnership Acts 1891 (Qld); Partnership Act 1895 (WA); Partnership Act 1891 (Tas); Partnership Act 1963 (ACT).

PERPETUITIES:

Future limitations, the vesting of which is postponed beyond lives in being and 21 years afterwards, are void; but this restriction does not apply to charitable bequests, trusts for the accumulation of income for payment of the settlor's debts, and certain other limited cases.

Accumulations must not exceed 21 years from the death of the settlor, or the minority of any person living at the death of the settlor, or the minority of any person who if of full age would be entitled to the income being accumulated; but these restrictions do not apply to provisions for the payment of debts and certain other limited cases.

In Victoria, New South Wales, Queensland, Tasmania, ACT and Western Australia statute reforms rule against perpetuities and abolishes rule against accumulations (except in New South Wales where permitted period for accumulation of income is extended to full period permitted by rule against perpetuities). Reformed rule applies "wait and see rule" and power is given to specify perpetuity period of up to 80 years. In New South Wales, perpetuity period is automatically 80 years.

PLEDGES:

Delivery of possession to pledgee is essential to pledge. Pledge includes lien which may be available when contract is barred by Statute of Limitations. When two or more articles are pledged together, each is security for whole debt. Pledgee must exercise care and is liable for any loss or injury due to negligence; but is not liable if property is stolen without fault or accidentally destroyed. Each State and Territory has Pawnbrokers Act: (Second-Hand Dealers and Pawnbrokers Act 1989 [Vic]; Pawnbrokers Act 1902 [NSW]; Pawnbrokers Act 1984 [Qld]; Summary Offences Act 1953 [SA]; Second-hand Dealers and Pawnbrokers Act 1994 [Tas]; Pawnbrokers and Second-hand Dealers Act 1994 [WA]; Pawnbrokers Act 1980 [NT]; ACT applies NSW statute as amended). Every pawnbroker must be licensed and must keep in book particulars in relation to every pledge received by him. Articles subject of pledge can only be sold in accordance with statutory provisions. Acts also regulate pawnbrokers' business in number of other ways. In Victoria and Tasmania profit or charge which may be made by pawnbroker is limited by law.

PRINCIPAL AND AGENT:

The existence of the relationship of principal and agent is a question of fact, and agency may exist notwithstanding the fact that the agent is described as a buyer, or referred to by some term inconsistent with agency, and vice versa. Relationship of principal and agent may arise (i) by express appointment; (ii) as result of doctrine of estoppel whereby principal represents to third party by conduct or words that person is his agent; (iii) by ratification whereby principal ratifies and adopts contract entered into by professed agent without previous authority; (iv) as result of doctrine of

See Topical Index in front part of this volume.

PRINCIPAL AND AGENT . . . *continued*
necessity; or (v) as result of presumption arising from cohabitation. Agent owes certain duties to his principal including duty to perform and certain fiduciary duties (e.g. to make full disclosure). Third persons dealing with agent may have recourse against principal or agent or both. A del credere agent guarantees to his principal due performance by third persons of contract he enters into on behalf of principal.

Powers of attorney are very strictly construed in Australia, and wide general powers are restricted by the enumeration of more particular powers. An attorney under power has no authority to appoint sub-agents, unless this right is expressly included in his appointment. All States and Territories have Acts that deal with execution and revocation of Powers of Attorney and effect of revocation of Power of Attorney on donee of power and on third party.

Property Law Act 1974 (Qld) §170, Instruments Act 1958 (Vic) Pt. XI, Powers of Attorney and Agency Act 1984 (SA), Powers of Attorney Act 1956 (ACT) as amended by Powers of Attorney (Amendment) Act 1992 §3AA and Conveyancing Act 1919 (NSW) Pt. 16 provide for abridged form of Power of Attorney authorising donee of power to do on behalf of donor all things which donor can lawfully do by attorney.

All States and Territories provide form of power that is not revoked by incapacity of donor of power where such incapacity occurs after execution of instrument creating power. See topic Guardian and Ward. Some States have enactments modelled upon §§126 and 127 of English Property Law Act 1925, providing that powers given for valuable consideration, and expressed in instruments creating them to be irrevocable, cannot be revoked as against purchasers by death, mental disability or bankruptcy of donor: (Powers of Attorney Act 1956 [ACT]; Property Law Act 1969 [WA] Pt. VIII; Powers of Attorney Act 1934 [Tas]; Conveyancing Act 1919 [NSW] Pt. 16). Property Law Act 1974 (Qld), Instruments Act 1958 (Vic) and Powers of Attorney Act 1980 (NT) have similar provisions where Power of Attorney is expressed to be irrevocable and is granted as security. By virtue of Guardianship and Management of Property (Consequential Provisions) Act 1991 (ACT) if guardian is appointed for person who is mentally ill, Tribunal that appointed guardian may make whatever orders it thinks fit regarding continued operation of irrevocable power executed by such person.

Power of Attorney must be registered in Tasmania and, except in Victoria, must be registered in all other States and Territories for certain dealings in relation to land to take effect pursuant to such Power of Attorney.

PUBLICATIONS:

National Classification Code has been enacted by Commonwealth, States and Territories (except Qld and WA). Classification (Publications, Films and Computer Games) Act 1995 (Cth) provides for classification of publications, films and computer games. Classification is based on principles that: (a) adults should be able to read, hear and see what they want; (b) minors should be protected from material likely to harm or disturb them; (c) everyone should be protected from exposure to unsolicited material that they find offensive; (d) consideration should be given to community concerns about depictions of violence particularly sexual violence and portrayal of persons in demeaning manner.

Classification of Publications Act 1991, Classification of Films Act 1991 and Classification of Computer Games and Images (Interim) Act 1995 operate in Queensland, covering classification, demonstration, advertising and supply of publications, films and computer games. Arrangements exist for censorship to be conducted by Commonwealth authorities. In Western Australia Indecent Publications and Articles Act 1902 and Video Tapes Classification and Control Act 1987 apply.

RACIAL DISCRIMINATION:

See topic Discrimination.

REAL PROPERTY:

Most land throughout Australia has been brought under the Torrens system of title registration. In respect of each piece of land under this system Certificate of Title is issued by Government, all original certificates being kept in central office and duplicate being issued to registered proprietor. All dealings with land under this system are carried out by means of simple instruments which to become effective are registered and their details inscribed on certificate. Certificate of Title will thus reveal at any time exact position of land in question, its dimensions, its present owner and any encumbrances to which it is subject. Entry of these facts on Certificate amounts to certification by Government of their accuracy. Certificate is thus conclusive evidence (except in certain limited cases, such as fraud) of truth of matters stated in it so that title search involves no more than examination of original Certificate of Title. Damages for loss arising out of error on register are payable out of Torrens Assurance Fund in New South Wales. Fund financed from fees paid to make and withdraw entries in register and established under Real Property Act 1900 (NSW). Transfer of Land (Computer Register) Act 1989 (Vic) amends Transfer of Land Act 1958 (Vic) to facilitate automation of register and simplify processing of dealings with land titles, as has already occurred in New South Wales.

If owner loses duplicate Certificate of Title new one may be obtained after due precautions have been taken by means of notices and advertisements.

Land not yet under Torrens system is dealt with under old conveyancing system under which title is traced through series of conveyances. Provision is made for recording conveyances in Government Office.

Application may be made to bring any land under Torrens system.

Conveyancers Licensing Act 1992 (NSW) and Conveyancers Act 1994 (SA) provide for licensing and regulation of persons involved in conveyancing legal work in relation to residential property.

There are guidelines for foreign investment set by Commonwealth. Foreign Takeovers Amendment Act 1989 (Cth) controls acquisition of Australian urban land by foreigners. Foreign Ownership of Land Register Act 1988 (Qld) establishes register of details of foreign interests in Queensland land. See also topic Aliens Parts I and II.

In Australian Capital Territory with a few exceptions, land is not freehold but Crown land, leased to tenants usually for a maximum period of 99 years.

Mortgages.—A mortgage under the old conveyancing system takes the form of an actual conveyance of the land to the mortgagee with a right of redemption being reserved to the mortgagor on his repaying the full amount of the loan with interest. Under the Torrens system the mortgage does not take the form of a transfer but is effected by a statutory instrument of mortgage which is registered as an encumbrance on the Certificate of Title and remains there until the loan is repaid at which stage a discharge is in turn noted on the Certificate.

Victoria and Queensland have legislated to provide for operation of secondary mortgage market in each State. While Queensland's market is regulated by board set up under its Mortgage (Secondary Market) Act 1984, Victorian market is regulated by company, National Mortgage Market Corporation Ltd., which has been incorporated specifically for that purpose. Victoria has amended its Trustee Act 1958 to provide guidelines. Stamps (Secondary Mortgage Market) Act 1988 §6, when proclaimed, will repeal those amendments. Other provisions of Act already in force and provide stamp duty exemptions to mortgage-backed securities and give trustee status to mortgage-backed securities. Secondary Mortgage Market (State Equity Participation) Act 1985 (NSW) follows Victorian model with incorporation of First Australian National Mortgage Acceptance Corporation Ltd. Act authorizes Crown and certain statutory corporations to acquire and hold shares in that corporation.

REPORTS:

Principal State Law Reports are: New South Wales Law Reports, South Australian State Reports, Queensland Reports, Tasmanian State Reports, Victorian Reports, Western Australian Reports.

See Part I, topic Reports.

RESTRAINT OF TRADE:

See topic Monopolies and Restraint of Trade.

SALES:

The English Sale of Goods Act 1893 has been generally adopted throughout Australian States. Local Acts are largely uniform and codify principles of law relating to sale of goods which have evolved from court decisions: Sale of Goods Act 1923 (NSW); Goods Act 1958 (Vic); The Sale of Goods Act 1896 (Qld); Sale of Goods Act 1895 (SA); The Sale of Goods Act 1895 (WA); Sale of Goods Act 1896 (Tas); Sale of Goods Act 1972 (NT); Sale of Goods Act 1954 (ACT). Sale of Goods (Amendment) Act 1988 (NSW) reforms and clarifies law in NSW relating to acceptance of goods, enforceability of certain unwritten contracts and rescission of contracts due to misrepresentation.

Stoppage in Transitu.—See England Law Digest.

Notices Required.—No notices required to perfect right of damages or rescission. Identical with English law in this area.

Applicable Law.—See topic Contracts.

Warranties.—Various Acts provide for certain conditions to be implied into contracts for sale of goods including (i) that where goods are bought in circumstances where buyer relies upon description of goods given to him by seller and seller deals in goods of that description (whether manufacturer or not) there is implied condition that goods shall be of merchantable quality, provided that if buyer has examined goods there shall be no implied condition as regards defects which such examination ought to have revealed; (ii) that where buyer expressly or by implication makes known to seller particular purpose for which goods are required so as to show that buyer relies on seller's skill or judgment and goods are of description which it is in course of seller's business to supply (whether manufacturer or not) there is implied condition that goods shall be reasonably fit for such purpose, provided that in case of contract for sale of specific article under its patent or other trade name there is no implied condition as to its fitness for any particular purpose; (iii) that where goods are sold by description there is implied condition that goods shall correspond with description; and (iv) that where goods are sold by sample there is implied condition that bulk shall correspond with sample in quality, that buyer shall have reasonable opportunity of comparing bulk with sample and that goods shall be free from any defect rendering them unmerchantable which would not be apparent on reasonable examination of sample. There is also implied condition that seller has title to sell goods and implied warranties that buyer shall have quiet possession of goods and that goods shall be free from any charge or encumbrance in favour of any third party and not known to buyer at time contract of sale is made.

Such implied conditions and warranties may, however, be excluded by express term in contract of sale.

Part IV Goods Act 1958 (Vic) makes provision for non-excludable terms (similar to those listed above) to be implied in sales of goods and of services (for less than A$15,000 subject to exceptions) and certain leases of goods where cash price of goods or services or rent does not exceed A$20,000 or, if it does exceed that amount, where goods or services are for personal, domestic or household use or consumption. Consumer Transactions Act 1972 (SA) includes similar non-excludable conditions relating to sale of goods and services to consumers. Manufacturers Warranties Act 1974 (SA) and Law Reform (Manufacturers Warranties) Act 1977 (ACT) imply conditions and warranties (equivalent to those given by retailers under Sale of Goods Acts) into supply of goods by manufacturers or importers to consumers despite absence of contractual relationship between them.

Where contract of sale is not severable and buyer has accepted goods or part thereof or where contract is for specific goods, property in which has passed to buyer, breach of any condition to be fulfilled by seller can only be treated as breach of warranty and not as ground for rejecting goods and treating contract as repudiated unless term of contract express or implied to that effect. See Part I, topic Consumer Protection.

International Sale of Goods.—All States and territories have enacted legislation to give effect to United Nations Convention on Contracts for the International Sale of Goods: Sale of Goods (Vienna Convention) Act 1986 (NSW); Sale of Goods (Vienna Convention) Act 1986 (NSW), (WA), (SA), (Qld); 1987 (Tas), (Vic), (NT), (ACT). Convention acceded to on 17th Mar. 1988 and came into force on 1st Apr. 1989.

SALES . . . *continued*

Consumer Protection.—See topic Consumer Protection.

SEALS:

Seals are necessary in execution of deeds, but no particular form of seal is needed, and in Victoria instrument executed by individual and expressed to be sealed takes effect as if it had been sealed. Any mark or wafer intended to stand as seal of party executing deed is sufficient seal. Every company must have common seal, and documents which would require to be sealed by individual, should be sealed by company with its common seal. Document may be treated as deed even though seal has been accidentally torn off. In general contracts under seal are valid, notwithstanding absence of any mutual consideration such as is required in contract without seal. Contract in restraint of trade, however, which would otherwise be void, is not made valid by being executed under seal; and contract under seal may be impeached for absence of consideration if it is fraudulent as against creditors.

STATUTE OF FRAUDS:

See topic Frauds, Statute of.

TAXATION:

Financial Institutions Duty.—All States except Queensland impose duty based on receipts of financial institutions. Rate of tax is 6¢ per A$100 (maximum of A$1,200 per receipt, A$1,500 in NT) in respect of each taxable credit made to taxable account kept with financial institution.

"Financial institution" is defined to include banks authorised to carry on business in Australia, persons whose sole or principal business is borrowing of money and provision of finance, stock brokers, statutory trustee companies, credit providers, and managers of cash management and unit trusts. "Credit provider" is person who provides credit under credit sale contracts, loan contracts or continuing credit contracts (each as defined).

Duty is imposed on loans made on short term money market in Victoria, New South Wales, South Australia, Western Australia, Tasmania, Northern Territory and ACT but at much lower rate.

Debits Tax.—States (except ACT) impose tax on debits made to various debitable accounts. Rates on sliding scale: for debits between A$1-A$100 debits tax is 30¢ (15¢ in NT); A$100-A$500, 70¢; A$500-A$5,000, A$1.50; A$5,000-A$10,000, A$3 and above A$10,000, A$4. See Debits Tax Acts as amended in Vic, NSW, SA and NT. Similar Acts in WA and Tas impose rates at half rate listed above, Qld just above half.

Land Tax.—All States impose land tax upon persons beneficially interested in land.

Income tax is imposed only by the Commonwealth although States too have constitutional power. See Part I, topic Taxation.

Payroll tax is imposed by all States on employers.

Probate or death duties have been abolished in all States.

Stamp Duties.—These are payable on conveyances, transfers, hire purchase agreements, mortgages and other securities, leases, other specified documents and, in some jurisdictions, conduct of credit and rental business.

Gift duty as such is no longer imposed in any State.

TRADEMARKS: See Part I.

TRADENAMES: See topic Business Names.

TRUSTS AND TRUSTEE COMPANIES:

English law is generally applicable. Each State and Territory has Trustee Act (South Australian Trustee Act 1893 applies in that State and Northern Territory).

Trustee companies are in general incorporated under Act of Parliament, with power to act as executors and administrators, and to make charge for their services. Victorian Trustee Companies Act 1984 allows corporations to apply to Victorian Attorney-General for authority to carry on business as trustee company. Tasmanian Trustee Companies Act 1953 allows any company or association to present to Parliament petition to have it declared to be trustee company. Queensland, New South Wales, South Australia, Western Australia and Australian Capital Territory also have Trustee Companies Acts. See also topic Executors and Administrators. Each State has Public Trustee (see e.g. State Trustee [State Owned Company] Act 1994 [Vic]) who/which may act as executor and allow members of public greater access to trustee, administrative and will-making services.

WILLS:

The statutory law relating to wills is embodied in the Wills Acts of the various States: Wills, Probate and Administrations Act 1898 (NSW); Wills Act 1958 and Administration and Probate (Amendment) Act 1994 (Vic); Wills Act 1936 (SA); Succession Act 1981 (Qld); Wills Act 1970 (WA); Wills Act 1992 (Tas); Wills Act 1968 (ACT); Wills Act 1938 (NT). Formal requirements of wills in all States follow English pattern and are as follows:

A will must be in writing and signed at foot (in WA, NSW, SA signature can be anywhere on will) or end thereof by testator (or by some other person in his presence and by his direction), such signature being made or acknowledged by testator in presence of at least two witnesses present at same time; such witnesses must attest and subscribe will in presence of testator. In South Australia, Northern Territory, Western Australia, Tasmania, New South Wales and Queensland document may still be taken as will of deceased notwithstanding that it has not been executed with requisite formalities, provided court is satisfied there can be no reasonable doubt that deceased intended document to constitute his will.

If beneficiary named in will witnesses will, validity is not affected but beneficiary may receive lower amount or may need to satisfy court that gift was given freely (Vic, NSW).

In all States and Territories will may be made by person aged 18 years or over or married person under 18 (NSW, SA, Qld, Tas).

Testators' Family Maintenance.—In each of jurisdictions there are statutory provisions giving spouse and children of testator or intestate right to apply to courts to obtain increased share of deceased person's estate where either will or intestacy provisions (see topic Descent and Distribution) do not make adequate provision. Courts have power to alter provisions to provide for maintenance of applicant.

Foreign Wills.—Generally probate of will of a foreign testator will be granted by State court concerned only if such will complies with law of foreign country in which testator was domiciled at his death or with law of State concerned. In all States and Territories probate will be granted if execution of will conformed to internal law in force in place where it was executed or in place where, at time of its execution or of testator's death he was domiciled or had his habitual residence or in a country of which, at either of such times, he was a national. Probate will also be granted of will executed on board a vessel or aircraft if execution of will conformed to internal law in place with which vessel or aircraft may be taken to be most closely connected. In practice, upon production of an exemplified copy of probate granted by proper court of foreign country where testator died domiciled, Australian court concerned will follow such grant in granting probate in State or Territory upon application before it of executor.

In addition to above rules will, to extent that it disposes of immovables (i.e. in general, land), is valid if execution conformed to internal law in place where property was situated.

See Topical Index in front part of this volume.

AUSTRIA LAW DIGEST REVISER

Zeiner & Zeiner
Schellinggasse 6
A-1010 Vienna, Austria
Telephone: 43 1 512 2364
Fax: 43 1 512 3325

Reviser Profile

Note: The strict standards of lawyers' ethics in Austria prevent us from publishing further information on our Reviser of the Austria Law Digest.

AUSTRIA LAW DIGEST

(The following is a list of all Topics, including cross-references, covered in this Digest.)

AUSTRIA LAW DIGEST

Revised for 1997 edition by

ZEINER & ZEINER, of the Vienna Bar.

(Abbreviations used are: A.B.G.B., Allgemeines Bürgerliches Gesetzbuch, Civil Code; H.G.B., Handelsgesetzbuch, Commercial Code; Z.P.O., Zivilprozessordnung, Code of Civil Procedure; BGBl. RGBl., and St GBl, Bundesgesetzblatt Reichsgesetzblatt and Staatsgesetzblatt, Federal Gazette.)

Austria is member of EU. See European Union Law Digest.

PREFATORY NOTE:

On May 15, 1955 State Treaty was concluded between Austria on the one hand and France, U.K., U.S.A., and U.S.S.R. on the other hand and became effective on July 27, 1955. (BGBl. 152/1955). In compliance with Art. XX of State Treaty, Allies quitted Austria by Oct. 27, 1955, on which day Austria regained her full sovereignty. On July 17, 1989 Austria applied for membership to EU. Treaty of Accession to EU was concluded and approved by referendum in Austria. Membership became effective as of Jan. 1, 1995.

ABSENTEES:

If a person is absent from his permanent residence and of unknown sojourn, or if a person is incapable of action, a guardian may be appointed by the competent District Court for the absentee or person incapable of action, upon motivated request of a third party or ex officio. This guardian is obliged to inform court immediately as soon as place of sojourn of absentee is ascertained or incapacity of action has ceased.

As long as guardianship has not been revoked by court, legal transactions with absentee can only be concluded with guardian of the absentee and have to be approved by guardianship court. In case of a lawsuit being filed against an absentee or a person incapable of action, court where suit is filed has to appoint a guardian on request of suing party for the absentee, but only for this suit.

ACCIDENTS IN TRAFFIC AND TRANSPORT:

See topic Limitation of Actions.

ACKNOWLEDGMENTS:

Form of acknowledgment in use in country where document is executed may be employed. Signatures of parties may be authenticated by Austrian diplomatic or consular officer, or by notary public, his signature finally being acknowledged by Austrian diplomatic or consular officer, unless multilateral or bilateral treaties provide otherwise. (See Part VII of this Volume.)

ACTIONS:

It is permissible to agree upon the application of foreign laws for interpretation of contracts between Austrian citizens and aliens. If an Austrian court is to decide about interpretation of such a contract, it has to apply foreign law agreed upon, so far as its provisions are not against public policy.

See also topics Courts; Limitation of Actions; Contracts.

ADOPTION:

Persons of age are entitled to adopt minor or major persons. Adoption of an adoptee by more than one person is only admissible if adopters are married. (ABGB §§179-186).

Austria is member to Convention on Jurisdiction, Applicable Law and Recognition of Decrees Relating to Adoptions of Nov. 15, 1965 (BGBl. No. 581/1978) and to European Convention on Adoption of Children of Apr. 24, 1967 (BGBl. No. 314/1980).

Consent Required.—Adoptee and adopter must conclude written contract about adoption, which requires permission of Guardianship Court (which is always part of a District Court). Persons under age will be represented in such case by guardian.

Conditions Precedent.—Male adopter must be at least 30 years and female adopter 28 years old. Difference of age between adopter and adoptee must be at least 18 years. If adoptee is relative of adopter or child of one of adopting parents, 16 years difference of age will suffice.

Proceedings.—Permission for adoption is granted by Guardianship Court within its discretion after investigation of domestic situation of adopter(s).

Name.—Adoptee receives surname of adopter.

Effect of Adoption.—Upon conclusion of adoption contract, adoptee obtains same rights against his adopting parents as their legitimate children. On the other hand, in spite of adoption, adoptee retains right of support by true parents and relatives, and adoptee is obliged to support his true parents if necessary. Adoptee has legal right of inheritance from adopting parents.

Setting Aside Adoption.—Under requirements provided by law, court may later revoke or annul adoption retroactively. With annulment or revocation of adoption all rights between adoptee and his true parents revive.

AFFIDAVITS:

Austrian law does not permit substitute evidence by submitting affidavits in court proceedings or before administrative agencies and authorities with exception of proceedings for interlocutory injunctions.

AIR NAVIGATION:

(Law of Dec. 2, 1957, BGBl. No. 253 in wording of BGBl. No. 691/1992).

On principle everybody is free to use the aerial area, unless local or temporary restrictions be made by the pertinent ministry in this respect. A license must be obtained for every air-vehicle; admission of foreign air-vehicles will be acknowledged if reciprocity can be proved. Every pilot must be in possession of a civil pilot's license; foreign pilots' licenses will be acknowledged if reciprocity can be proved. Taking-off and landing of air-vehicles is permitted from and on aviation-fields only. Traffic in air and on ground of any kind of aircraft is regulated by Regulation of Feb. 15, 1967, BGBl. No. 56 in latest wording of BGBl. No. 355/1993.

In Austria air-transportation enterprises are subject to explicit admission, to be granted also to foreign enterprises if reciprocity can be proved. Admitted air-line enterprises have the duty to maintain operation.

All civil aircraft must be appropriately marked pursuant to regulations applicable in that country to which aricraft belongs. Airworthiness of aircraft must be proved and proofs by foreign authorities must be accepted under certain conditions. (Regulation of Traffic Ministry of June 27, 1983, BGBl. No. 415).

Requirements for civil airports are laid down in Regulation of Traffic Ministry of July 1, 1972, BGBl. No. 313.

In case of accidents of foreign aircraft foreign observers can, with consent of Austrian authorities, be sent to place of accident, unless Art. 26 of agreement on international civil air navigation of Dec. 7, 1944, has to be applied. (Law of Mar. 21, 1958, BGBl. No. 68).

Limits of noise of aircraft are determined by Regulation of Ministry of Traffic. (BGBl. No. 700/1986).

On claims for damages caused by accidents in aviation, see topic Limitation of Actions.

Austria is member to Convention on International Civil Aviation of Dec. 7, 1944, (BGBl. 97/1949) in wording of Protocol of Oct. 16, 1974 (BGBl. No. 194/1980), to Protocol on authentic trilingual text of Convention on international civil aviation of Sept. 24, 1968 (BGBl. No. 138/1971), to multilateral agreement of Apr. 30, 1956, on Commercial Rights of Non-Scheduled Air Services in Europe (BGBl. 163/1957), to International Air Services Transit Agreement of Dec. 7, 1944 (BGBl. No. 46/1959), to Convention for unification of rules relating to international carriage by air of Oct. 12, 1929 (BGBl. No. 286/1961) as am'd by Protocol of the Hague of Sept. 28, 1955 (BGBl. No. 161/1971) and to agreement of Apr. 12, 1979 on trade in civil aircraft (BGBl. No. 276/1980) as amended by Protocol of Dec. 2, 1986 (BGBl. No. 83/1988).

ALIENS:

In private and commercial law, aliens have generally same rights as natives. (A.B.G.B. §33).

See also topics Costs, subhead Security for Costs; Immigration; Marriage.

Corporations Owned or Controlled by Aliens.—See topic Foreign Investment.

ALIMONY: See topics Divorce; Infancy.

ARBITRATION:

According to Austrian law (§§577-599 Z.P.O.) every legal dispute which can be decided by a regular court may also be decided by a court of arbitration agreed upon by parties thereto. Every arbitration agreement has to be concluded in writing or by exchange of telegrams or telexes.

Number of arbiters is not limited. If one party does not appoint his arbiter, other party may apply for appointment of an arbiter by court.

Active judges are not allowed to act as arbiters.

Procedure before courts of arbitration is fixed by arbiters, if parties have not yet agreed upon a particular procedure in arbitration agreement.

Court of arbitration may request a regular court having jurisdiction for execution of those measures which court of arbitration, according to law, is not allowed to execute itself.

In case more arbiters are appointed, absolute majority decides upon arbiter's award to be rendered. This award is a basis for execution just as a judicial verdict.

Action for annulment of an award can be brought at competent regular court in specific cases itemized in law.

Foreign Arbitral Awards.—On ground of bilateral treaties awards rendered in following countries can be enforced: Belgium, Federal Republic of Germany, Liechtenstein, Switzerland, Turkey, U.S.S.R. (situation with successor states still unclear), Yugoslavia (applicable to Slovenia pursuant to exchange of diplomatic notes, applicable to Macedonia, situation with successor states still unclear).

On ground of Convention on Recognition and Enforcement of Foreign Arbitral Awards of June 10, 1958 awards rendered in countries listed in Part VII of this volume are enforced.

Geneva Convention of Sept. 26, 1927 on Enforcement of Foreign Arbitral Awards is still in force with following countries: Antigua and Barbuda, Bahamas, Bangladesh, Burma, Croatia, Ireland, Jamaica, Malta, Mauritius, Pakistan, Slovakia, Spain, Yugoslavia (applicable to Slovenia pursuant to exchange of diplomatic notes, applicable to Macedonia, situation with successor states still unclear).

On ground of recognition of reciprocity arbitral awards rendered in British Columbia (Canada) can be enforced. (BGBl. No. 314/1970).

Austria is member of European Convention on International Commercial Arbitration of Apr. 21, 1961 (BGBl. No. 107/1964) and of Convention on the Settlement of Investment Disputes between States and Nationals of other States of Mar. 18, 1965 (BGBl. No. 357/1971).

See Topical Index in front part of this volume.

ASSIGNMENTS:

The assignment of personal property is effected by agreement about the transfer of title to the assignee.

Assignment of claims is, except where claims are transferred by virtue of law or by judicial act, effected by oral or written agreement between assignor and assignee. Notice to debtor is not required for validity of assignment but is advisable to prevent bona fide debtor from discharging his debt by payment to assignor.

For validity of assignments by way of payment between spouses and assignment by way of gift without handing over object, document of notary public is required.

ASSOCIATIONS: See topic Corporations.

ATTACHMENT:

(Law of May 27, 1896, RGBl. No. 79, in wording of Law of July 18, 1956, BGBl. No. 58).

In Austrian law there is no equivalent for attachment in American law. It is possible in form of interlocutory injunction only. Interlocutory injunction is permissible before bringing action or during proceedings, provided that prima facie evidence is furnished for claim and collection of claim would be jeopardized by later enforcement. Latter is assumed, if judgment will have to be enforced abroad.

ATTORNEYS AND COUNSELORS:

No division between barristers and solicitors exists. All Austrian Attorneys at Law are entitled to represent clients before all courts and public agencies throughout Austria. Only in specific cases, are other persons entitled to represent clients before courts and public agencies, namely (a) Patent Attorneys before Austrian Patent Office, (b) specialised jurists of Chamber of Commerce and of Chamber of Labor before first instance Labor and Social Courts and (c) tax advisers and certified public accountants before tax authorities. In very exceptional cases, notaries may also appear before courts.

Every Attorney at Law must be member of local Chamber of Lawyers. Each of the nine federal provinces has its own Chamber of Lawyers. All Chambers of Lawyers form Austrian Lawyers' Diet.

Conditions for becoming Attorney at Law are (a) University degree (Master of Jurisprudence or Doctor of Law), (b) five yars of legal practice of which at least nine months must be served as court clerk (foreign practice may be recognized to certain extent) and (c) passing of special bar examination during five years of practice.

Foreign lawyers from EEA countries may be admitted as resident lawyers in Austria provided that they qualify in their home country and pass additional examination in Austria generally similar to bar examination. Foreign nonresident lawyers may appear before courts in Austria provided that they are accompanied by Austrian Attorney at Law who acts jointly for them (not for client).

Fees of attorneys are regulated as minimum fees by law. Free fee arrangements are possible provided that Attorney at Law gets adequate remuneration for his services. Discounts below legal minimum rates must not be agreed upon in advance with few exceptions like collection cases. Fee arrangements depending on success of litigation are considered unethical and void.

BANKRUPTCY:

(Law of Dec. 10, 1914, in latest wording of BGB1. No. 153/1994).

Bankruptcy proceedings (Konkurs) are ordered by the court in the case of insolvency upon petition made by the debtor or by any creditor, who furnishes prima facie evidence of insolvency of debtor and unsettled claim of at least one further creditor. Suspension of payments is prima facie evidence of insolvency. As regards companies and estates of deceased persons, bankruptcy order can also be obtained if liabilities exceed assets.

When ordering bankruptcy, the court appoints a receiver (Masseverwalter), in whom the bankrupt's assets are vested. He is supervised by the court and may be supervised as well by a committee of the creditors.

All rights of lien or mortgage obtained by way of judicial execution expire on day when bankruptcy proceedings are opened, unless they were established more than 60 days before opening of bankruptcy proceedings. Any other right of lien or mortgage remains unimpaired by debtor's bankruptcy, subject, however, to receiver's right to impugn it. See topic Fraudulent Sales and Conveyances.

In case continuation of bankrupt business would be jeopardized by fulfillment of privileged claim (property right, retainer of title), creditor must not claim fulfillment before expiration of 90 days after opening of bankruptcy proceedings, unless such postponement would cause serious personal or economic disadvantages to creditor.

Distribution of assets by receiver does not effect bankrupt's discharge, but discharge can be obtained by way of judicial composition. Bankruptcy order having been issued, bankrupt may still apply for compulsory composition (Zwangsausgleich), if dividend of at least 20% is offered to normal trade creditors.

Composition with Creditors.—At the request of an insolvent debtor, judicial composition proceedings (Ausgleichsverfahren) may be instituted by the court. Upon institution of such proceedings, rights of lien or mortgage expire to the same extent as in the case of bankruptcy. Minimum dividend to be offered to normal trade creditors is 40% (majority of creditors present at vote and majority of three quarters of unprivileged claims). Privileged creditors must be fully satisfied.

Subject to the court's confirmation, the composition becomes valid (and binding for all creditors) if agreed upon by qualified majority of creditors.

Special regulations are in force with regard to composition proceedings of bankers and banks.

Bankruptcy of Private Persons.—Special debt redemption proceedings which consist of system of payment plans with target of full discharge of debt (minimum payment of 10% within three years), exists for private persons.

Pursuant to bilateral treaties with Belgium, Federal Republic of Germany, France and Italy, effects of insolvency proceedings opened in one country extend to other country.

See topic Fraudulent Sales and Conveyances.

BILLS AND NOTES:

(Law of Feb. 16, 1955, BGBl. No. 49, in wording of Law of June 7, 1978, BGBl. No. 306).

A bill of exchange must contain a statement to the effect that the instrument is a bill of exchange ("Wechsel"). It is usually made payable to order, but this is not essential since a bill payable to a person is presumed to be payable to his order unless it states expressly "not to order."

Bills payable "to bearer" or in which the name of the payee is left blank are not bills of exchange. Promissory notes are treated as a form of bills of exchange.

Bills may fall due at sight, at a certain time after sight, at a certain time after the date of issue, or on a specified day. There are no days of grace. Default of acceptance or of payment must be evidenced by a protest levied by a notary public not later than on second working day following maturity.

Austria is a member of the Convention providing a uniform law for bills of exchange and promissory notes of June 7, 1930, effective since Jan. 1, 1934. (BGBl. No. 289/1932).

Checks.—A check must contain a statement to the effect that the instrument is a check. An acceptance written on a check ("certified check") is of no legal effect. Checks bearing the clause "Payable to account" (often symbolized by a cross drawn across the instrument) are not discharged by payment in cash, but by crediting the sum in question to the payee's bank account.

(Law of Feb. 16, 1955, BGBl. No. 50. in latest wording of Law of June 7, 1978, BGBl. No. 306).

Uniform Law on checks based on the Convention of Mar. 19, 1931, effective in Austria as from Mar. 1, 1959. (BGBl. No. 47/1959 and 246/1959).

CHATTEL MORTGAGES:

There is no equivalent for a chattel mortgage in the Austrian law.

CITIZENSHIP:

(Law of July 19, 1985, BGBl. No. 311 in latest wording of Law of July 3, 1986, BGBl. No. 368).

Austrian citizenship may be obtained by: (a) Origin, (b) written declaration under particular circumstances, (c) grant by government agency and (d) acceptance of position as ordinary or extraordinary professor at Austrian university. Legitimate children obtain citizenship of their father at time of child's birth. Illegitimate children obtain citizenship of their mother at time of child's birth.

Alien woman may obtain citizenship of her Austrian husband by written declaration filed with competent authorities as long as marriage is not dissolved. Austrian citizenship has to be granted to an alien after 30 years of residence in Republic of Austria conditioned upon fulfilment of specific requirements (no sentence, sufficiency of self-support, etc.).

Austrian citizenship has to be regranted to a female alien (1) if she has lost Austrian citizenship by marriage with an alien or by obtention of a foreign citizenship together with her husband during existence of such marriage, (2) if such marriage was dissolved by death of her husband or by divorce and (3) if regranting of Austrian citizenship is applied for within two years after dissolution of such marriage.

Austrian citizenship is generally lost by acquisition of a foreign citizenship. In addition thereto Austrian citizenship is lost by voluntary military service for a foreign country.

Austrian citizenship can be withdrawn from a person in case he or she is employed in administration of a foreign country, if his or her conduct represents considerable damage to interests of Republic of Austria.

Every Austrian citizen may waive his rights of citizenship (1) if he has already obtained a foreign citizenship, (2) if no criminal proceedings are pending against him and (3) if he has fulfilled his duties with respect to Austrian military service.

Record of citizenship is kept by competent community, i.e., (1) in case of birth in Austria, Austrian community of birth place and (2) in case of birth in a foreign country, community of Vienna.

Austria is member of New York Convention on the Reduction of Statelessness of Aug. 30, 1961. (BGBl. No. 538/1974).

COMMERCIAL REGISTER:

Individual firms exceeding volume of small-scale trade as well as partnerships, professional associations, joint stock corporations, limited liability companies, insurance associations, savings banks and other legal entities specifically designated by law must be entered into commercial register (firm book) of High Courts. Juridical persons start their legal existence only upon their entry into commercial register.

Not only establishment of enterprise (firm), but also each branch establishment and any alterations in person of ownership, partners, managers and proxies have to be registered promptly. In case of juridical persons any change of articles of association or by-laws has also to be notified to commercial register and to be made known there. Any such fact has to be reported to competent commercial register by proprietor of enterprise, partners, board of directors of corporation or managers of private limited liability company, respectively. This notification has to be signed by persons named and to be authenticated by notary public. Any failure of registration may be penalized by Commercial Court having jurisdiction.

As long as any factual data are not recorded in commercial register they are not effective to third parties relying in good faith on principle of confidence in such a register.

Commercial registers are maintained by all High Courts acting as Commercial Courts and comprise all enterprises that have their seat or branch establishment in area for which this court is locally competent. Branch establishment has to be registered in both commercial register competent for seat of firm and commercial register competent for branch establishment itself.

CONSTITUTION AND GOVERNMENT:

After World War II, Constitution of Oct. 1, 1920, as am'd in 1929 (BGBl. No. 1/1930 in latest wording of BGB1. No. 268/1994) was reestablished (Law of May 1, 1945, St GBl. No. 4).

The Constitution of 1920 provides that Austria is a democratic, federal republic, with a two-chamber parliament. One chamber is called "Nationalrat" (National Assembly), the other "Bundesrat" (Federal Assembly). The National Assembly is elected by means of general election every fourth year; the members of the Bundesrat are appointed by the Diets of the nine Federal Provinces (Bundeslëander). The nine Federal Provinces (Bundeslëander) that compose the republic are to a comparatively large degree autonomous.

By constitutional Law of Oct. 26, 1955, BGBl. No. 211, Austria by her own will declared her permanent neutrality and undertook not to join any military treaty nor to permit military bases of other countries on her territory.

Political parties are entitled to receive public subsidies, if they have at least five representatives in National Assembly or received more than 1% of votes at last election. (Law of July 2, 1975, BGBl. No. 404 in latest wording of Law of Dec. 17, 1979, BGBl. No. 569).

Austria is member to Vienna Convention on the Law of Treaties (BGBl. No. 40/1980) and to European Charter of Local Self-Government (BGB1. No. 357/1988).

CONTRACTS:

Civil Code (ABGB) contains essential provisions about contracts and their interpretation. There are special regulations in Commercial Code (HGB) with regard to interpretation of contracts between merchants.

Contract infringing statutory prohibition or good morals (public policy) is invalid. (§879 ABGB).

Contracts in favor of third parties are permissible.

An offer must be accepted within period stated by offeror. If no period is stipulated, an offer must be accepted immediately by a person present or within a reasonable period by a person absent. Otherwise offer expires. An offer may also be accepted tacitly by acts permitting such conclusions.

Contracts may be concluded in writing, orally or conclusively. Only in special cases contract in writing is explicitly required.

Excuses for nonperformance.—No consequences for both parties will result from nonperformance, if performance is made impossible for either party by force majeure. Each party is entitled to withdraw from contract, if performance of contract has become impossible through fault of the other party. (§§918-921 ABGB).

Contract Violation.—If performance is not made at stipulated time, place or in stipulated form, other party may either insist on performance and claim damages for bad performance, or may rescind contract upon granting reasonable period of grace for performance. If performance is impossible because of fault of one party, other party may either claim damages or rescind contract. Rescission of contract is not deemed to be waiver of damage claims.

General Business Conditions.—Provision in form contracts or business conditions not relating to main subject matter is void, if it constitutes serious disadvantage for other party. Unusual provisions used therein by one party, which other party could not reasonably expect, do not become part of contract, unless they were specifically indicated to other party.

Applicable Law.—Factual situations comprising links to other jurisdictions are in principle subject to laws of that country to which they are most related. Contracts, however, are subject to that law which parties expressly or conclusively stipulated or which they implicitly considered as governing. Only if applicable law cannot be determined by this test, following rules apply.

Mutually binding contracts under which one party mainly owes money to other party are subject to law of that country where other party has his residence or seat. Unilaterally binding contracts are subject to law of that country where debtor has his residence or seat.

Banking and insurance contracts are subject to law applicable at seat of bank and insurance company, respectively. Stock exchange contracts and contracts concluded at markets or fairs are subject to law applicable at location of stock exchange, market and fair, respectively. Sales at auctions are subject to law applicable at place of auction. Contracts on use of real property are subject to law where real property is situated.

Contracts with party residing in country granting special consumer protection are subject to law of that country if they were concluded by businessman or company in connection with his activity to conclude such contracts in that country. To extent cogent provisions of that law are involved, choice of applicable law to detriment of consumer is excluded.

Contracts on industrial property rights are subject to law of that country for which they are transferred or granted. If more countries are involved, law applicable at place of residence or seat of acquiring party or licensee applies.

Employment contracts are subject to law applicable at place where employee usually works. This law remains applicable even if employee is sent to another country by his principal.

Austria is member to Convention on Contract for International Carriage of Goods by Road (CMR) of May 19, 1956 (BGBl. No. 138/1961) and of Protocol thereto of July 5, 1978 (BGBl. No. 192/1981).

Government Contracts.—There exists no legislation in Austria according to which contracts with governmental bodies must have different wording or contents from contracts between private persons.

CONVEYANCES: See topic Deeds.

COPYRIGHT:

(Law of Apr. 9, 1936, BGBl. No. 111, in latest wording of BGBl. No. 151/1996).

Term of copyright for works of literature, music and fine arts is author's life and 70 years thereafter. Term of copyright for a cinematographic work ends ten years after death of one of following persons, depending on who lives longest: principal director, author of script, dialogues and of especially created work of music. Computer programs are specifically protected.

Encroachments on the copyright can be prosecuted by civil and criminal action.

Austria is member of Berne Convention of Sept. 9, 1886 in Paris wording of July 24, 1971 (BGBl. No. 319/1982 and 133/1985) and of Montevideo Convention of Jan. 11, 1889 (BGBl. No. 75/1924). As to U.S. reciprocity is granted. Austria is member of Universal Copyright Convention in its Paris wording of July 24, 1971. (BGBl. No. 293/1982 as am'd by BGBl. No. 460/1994). Austria has joined International Convention for Protection of Performers, Producers of Phonograms and Broadcasting Organizations of Oct. 26, 1961 (BGBl. No. 413/1973) and Convention for Protection of Producers of Phonograms against Unauthorized Duplication of their Phonograms of Oct. 29, 1971 (BGBl. No. 294/1982). Austria concluded Treaty on Mutual Copyright Protection with USSR on Dec. 16, 1981 (BGB1. No. 424/1983, specifically made applicable by exchange of diplomatic notes to Russian Federation BGBl. No. 257/1995) enhancing protection under Universal Copyright Convention for their nationals.

Pursuant to Agreement between Austria and World Intellectual Property Organization of Oct. 25, 1989 (BGBl. No. 674/1990) International Registry of Audiovisual Works shall be established at Klosterneuburg near Vienna. Details are regulated in further agreement of Dec. 11, 1991 (BGB1. No. 405/1992) which came into force on June 4, 1992. Austria is member to Treaty on the International Registration of Audiovisual Works of Apr. 20, 1989. (BGBl. No. 48/1991).

Industrial Designs.—(Law of June 7, 1990, BGBl. No. 497). Industrial designs can be registered for maximum period of five years starting at date of publication of industrial design and expiring on last day of that month in which five year period ends. Priority under Art. 4 of Paris Union Treaty may be claimed. Registrable industrial designs must be new or are otherwise subject to cancellation. Austria is member to Locarno Agreement of Oct. 8, 1968 establishing International Classification for Industrial Designs. (BGBl. No. 496/1990).

CORPORATIONS:

Austrian law knows two main types of corporations: (1) the Aktiengesellschaft (joint stock corporation) and (2) the Gesellschaft mit beschränkter Haftung (private limited liability company).

Aktiengesellschaften (Joint Stock Corporations).—(Law of Mar. 31, 1965, BGBl. No. 98 in latest wording of BGB1. No. 304/1996). Joint stock corporation must have minimum capital of ATS 1,000,000 divided into shares of at least ATS 100 each. Shares may be issued in form of registered or bearer shares. Registered shares are transferred by endorsement. Rights deriving from registered shares can only be enforced against corporation by owner registered in stock ledger. If according to by-laws approval of corporation is required for transfer of registered shares and corporation refuses such approval approval by decision of court may be obtained, which is of binding force to corporation.

Government permission is required for the formation of an Aktiengesellschaft only if the corporation is to engage in the banking business, and for the establishment in Austria of a branch office of a foreign corporation.

Aktiengesellschaft comes into legal existence by registration in commercial register of the court.

Multiple shares are not allowed in Austria.

Corporation is managed by executive board (Vorstand), which is appointed by the supervisory board (Aufsichtsrat). Appointment of a member of executive board may only hold for maximum period of five years, but may be renewed for further maximum periods of five years each.

Supervisory board is elected by the general assembly. Management of executive board is supervised by supervisory board, which consists of at least three members, but no more than 20 members.

Gesellschaft mit beschränkter Haftung (Limited Liability Company).—(Law of Mar. 6, 1906, RGBl. No. 58, in latest wording of BGB1. No. 304/1996). This corporate form is simpler and widely used. Formation requires one or more founders. Minimum capital is ATS 500,000 of which ATS 250,000 must be paid in. Above that minimum at least one quarter of capital contributions to be made in cash must be paid in. Each share must amount to at least ATS 1,000. Shares are only transferable inter vivos by means of Austrian notarial act.

Company may have one or more managers. Supervisory board is only required if capital exceeds ATS 1,000,000 and number of shareholders exceeds 50 or if company has more than 300 workers and employees. Managers as well as members of supervisory board are appointed by shareholders' meeting.

Genossenschaften (Cooperative Associations).—(Law of Apr. 9, 1873, RGBl. No. 70, in latest wording of BGB1. No. 625/1991). There are several kinds of cooperative associations (Genossenschaften) regulated by special laws. They have no capital stock, but enjoy rights of corporations. Respective shares must have minimum nominal value of ATS 10. Liability of members (whether limited or unlimited) depends upon form of association and provisions of its statutes.

Merger or Change in Status of Corporations and/or Partnerships.—Tax treatment of restructuring of companies and businesses is regulated by Restructuring Tax Act (Umgründungssteuergesetz BGB1. No. 699/1991, in latest wording of BGB1. No. 201/1996). (a) Mergers (Verschmelzungen), (b) transformations (Umwandlungen), (c) contributions of business in kind (Einbringungen), (d) associations in form of partnerships (Zusammenschlüsse), (e) transfer of business property of partnership to successors who were deemed owners (Realteilungen) and (f) spin-offs (Spaltungen) are either not or only partially subject to income tax, corporate income tax and turnover tax. Under certain conditions these transactions are exempted from capital transfer tax and State fees. Hidden reserves shall only be taxed as transfer gains if they would otherwise definitely escape taxation. With few exceptions continuation of book values is compulsory.

Foreign Corporations.—A foreign corporation can found branch offices in Austria, which, before starting business activity, must be entered into commercial register at Commercial Court competent for district in which the office has its seat.

See also subhead Aktiengesellschaften (Joint Stock Corporations), supra.

See also topics Commercial Register; Foreign Investment.

CORPORATIONS . . . *continued*

Taxation.—See topic Taxation.

See also topics Partnership; Licenses.

COSTS:

Party fully defeated at court has to pay to winning party all costs, including attorney's fees according to legal tariff, caused by case. Extent of costs to be paid is determined by court. Award of costs is only effected upon request of litigant parties. Basis for assessment of costs depends on value of litigious matter, as stated by plaintiff in the suit. If plaintiff does not fully succeed with his claim put forward, court may upon its discretion abate costs mutually or award reduced amount of costs to party partially winning.

Security for Costs.—Aliens appearing as plaintiffs before Austrian court have to furnish security upon request of defendant for costs of proceedings, insofar as aliens are not exempted from furnishing security by state treaties. There is no agreement at present between Austria and U.S.A. with regard to exemption from furnishing security. In case of matrimonial suits no such deposit can be fixed.

COURTS:

In Austria District Courts (Bezirksgerichte) are competent for civil law suits, if value of litigious object does not exceed amount of ATS 100,000. If value of litigious object is higher High Courts (Landesgerichte) are competent as courts of first instance. Complaints suitable for issuance of payment order by court may be filed by means of electronic data transmission, but not by telecopy.

Guardianship Courts and Probate Courts are always a part of a District Court.

High Courts (Landesgerichte) act as courts of appeals superior to District Courts (Bezirksgerichte) and Courts of Appeals (Oberlandesgerichte) act as courts of appeals to High Courts.

Supreme Court (Oberster Gerichtshof) in Vienna acts as third instance for lawsuits where value in litigation exceeds ATS 50,000, provided it accepts appeal on basis that important question of law is involved. Important question of law is defined as issue which must be decided for purposes of legal consistency, security or development which is to be assumed, if no relevant jurisdiction of Supreme Court yet exists, or if High Court differed from previous legal approach of Supreme Court. In some specific cases appeal to Supreme Court is generally excluded.

For any litigation with respect to: (a) Paternity of an illegitimate child, (b) any obligation of the illegitimate father towards mother and child, (c) any claim for maintenance and support, which is enforced independent of other titles, (d) any claim in matters of boundary regulations, (e) disturbances of possession, (f) any dispute resulting from lease contracts, (g) any claim of travelers towards transport firms and establishments offering accommodation, independent of the value of the litigious object, the local district court is exclusively competent.

Specialized Labor and Social Courts (Arbeits- und Sozialgerichte) have exclusive jurisdiction beginning from Jan. 1, 1987 for all litigation resulting from employment or similar relationships as well as for all litigation relating to pension and social security matters.

For any litigation with respect to violations of patent rights Commercial Court (Handelsgericht) in Vienna is exclusively competent.

Representation by Austrian Attorney at Law in litigation matters is compulsory except before District Courts in family matters, rental matters and in matters not exceeding ATS 30,000 and before first instance labor costs.

Supreme Constitutional Court decides on constitutionality of laws and regulations and on violations of basic human rights by court or administrative decisions otherwise unappealable. In latter case individual citizens are authorized to appeal to this court.

Supreme Administrative Court decides as last instance on administrative decisions.

CURRENCY:

Monetary unit in Austria is Austrian Schilling (ATS), divided into 100 Groschen.

Austrian National Bank owns monopoly of issuing banknotes. Statutes of Austrian National Bank are regulated by Law of Jan. 20, 1984, BGBl. No. 50 in latest wording of BGB1. No. 697/1991. Under Foreign Exchange Law Austrian National Bank is pertinent foreign exchange authority. (Law of July 25, 1946, BGBl. No. 162, in latest wording of BGB1. No. 34/1992).

Since Nov. 4, 1991, Austrian National Bank approved generally all transactions subject to Foreign Exchange Law provided that certain notification requirements in specific cases are fulfilled.

Austria is a member of O.E.C.D. and of European Monetary Agreement of Aug. 5, 1955.

CUSTOMS:

Austria is Member of EU and therefore EU customs laws and regulations apply with special adaptations. (Law of Aug. 23, 1994, BGBl. No. 659 on Execution of Customs Law of EU).

In addition to duty, on every imported commodity importation turnover tax of generally 20% (in few cases lower rates are applicable) is levied, unless exemptions exist under community law.

For a few other specific goods (liquors, tobacco, etc.) additional duties are levied.

Austria is member to Customs Convention on the Temporary Importation of Private Road Vehicles of June 4, 1954 in latest wording pursuant to BGBl. No. 248/85. If road vehicle is destroyed in Austria by force majeure, Austria will not levy any import duties and taxes.

Austria is member of WTO.

Austria and U.S.A. concluded on Sept. 15, 1976 agreement regarding mutual assistance between their customs services (BGBl. No. 278/1978), Convention on the Harmonization of Frontier Controls of Goods of Oct. 21, 1982 (BGBl. No. 467/1987) and Convention on the Harmonized Commodity Description and Coding System of June 14, 1983 (BGBl. No. 553/1987).

See also topic Foreign Trade Regulations and European Union Law Digest, topic Customs Duties.

DAMAGES:

See topics Death (Presumption of and Actions for); and Limitation of Actions.

DEATH (PRESUMPTION OF AND ACTIONS FOR):

Presumption of Death.—(Law of Dec. 5, 1950, BGBl. No. 23 in latest wording of Law of Feb. 2, 1983, BGB1. No. 135).

Each person's death must be recorded in the Register-Book of Deaths. The entry can be recorded provided there is either a doctor's certificate establishing the death and the reason for it, or a certificate of any foreign official institution.

An official certificate of death may be obtained at registry office of place of death. If such certificate cannot be given it is possible to apply for a declaration of death to High Court of district in which deceased had his last residence, provided certain conditions are met.

Declaration of death is possible ten years after end of that year when person could be proved to have been still alive. Presumption of death is not admissible before end of that year in which that person completed his 25th year of life. Declaration of death may be applied for in case of soldiers or persons officially declared missing one year after end of that year when World War II came to end. Application may be filed by anybody who possesses manifest interest in declaration of death. This court is competent, when person missing was Austrian. Declaration of death with regard to alien can only be issued by Austrian court insofar as this declaration is required for settling of any matter concerning property in Austria of person missing, or if wife of missing person has her permanent residence in Austria.

Probate Proceedings.—In case deceased possessed any estate, "Verlassenschaftsabhandlung" (court proceeding dealing with total property left) must be taken by competent Probate Court (which is always part of District Court) at domicile of deceased. Right of property is transferred from deceased to heirs by virtue of deed, called "Einantwortungsurkunde," to be issued by Probate Court after termination of court proceedings. If alien dies in Austria, court proceedings must be taken as to his real estate left in Austria at local Probate Court competent for matters of real estate.

Movable property left by deceased alien has to be passed to competent authority in native country of deceased for further disposition. If native state of the alien refuses to dispose of movable property of deceased, competent Austrian court must also deal with this estate.

See also topic Descent and Distribution.

DEEDS:

Deeds, in the common law sense, are unknown in Austria. The transfer of real estate is effected by a declaration of both parties before the recording judge or notary and by entry of transfer of title in land register (Grundbuch).

For the validity of certain transactions the establishment of notarized documents is provided by law, e.g., donations between spouses, donations without handing over the object.

DEPOSITIONS:

The Austrian courts will examine witnesses upon direct request of a foreign court if a respective legal aid convention exists or if such request is transmitted through diplomatic or consular officials. Counsel may appear at the examination of witnesses but only in civil suits.

According to Austrian law it is admissible that the court, on demand of party introducing evidence authorizes same to take proofs abroad; however, a public document which must be valid according to laws of the foreign country in question must be drawn up and then be submitted to Austrian court.

DESCENT AND DISTRIBUTION:

An intestate's property, including all his real and personal property, is distributed among his so-called heirs-at-law.

Heirs-at-law are, in the first line, the children of the deceased. A deceased child is represented by his descendants as regards the inheritance. Distribution is made per stirpes. Illegitimate children inherit from their mother as legitimate children. From their father they inherit as legitimate children, if no legitimate children nor mother survive and if it is officially established that intestate is their father.

If the intestate left no issue his parents are heirs in equal shares. If there be but one parent alive the other parent's share devolves on his children (the intestate's brothers or sisters of full or half-blood), previously deceased brothers or sisters being represented by their issue (the intestate's nephews and nieces or as the case may be his grandnephews, grandnieces, etc.). If but one parent or his issue be alive, such parent or his issue (per stirpes) takes the entire estate.

In default of descendants or parents' descendants, the intestate's grandparents are his heirs, previously deceased grandparents being represented by their descendants per stirpes. If there be no issue of previously deceased grandparent, such grandparent's portion falls to portion of other grandparent of same (paternal or maternal) line and of this grandparent's descendants. If there are only paternal or only maternal grandparents or their respective issue surviving, such surviving grandparents or descendants (per stirpes) take whole estate.

In the last resort, the surviving greatgrandparents of the deceased but not their issue, will be his heirs, division in this case being made per capita.

An intestate's surviving spouse succeeds to one-third of his estate if deceased has left descendants. If there be no issue but parents, parent's descendants or grandparents, surviving spouse is entitled to two-thirds. Grandparents' descendants and greatgrandparents are excluded from intestate's succession by his surviving spouse.

If there are neither relatives of above-mentioned degrees nor spouse surviving, intestate's goods escheat to Federal Treasury.

Property left is legally transferred. Any heir is entitled to take possession of property left only by decision of Probate Court.

Except special rules of distribution existing in some provinces about farmers' tenures no distinction is made in the rules of distribution between movable and immovable assets.

DESCENT AND DISTRIBUTION . . . *continued*

Due Portions.—Any testator must bequeath part of his property: (a) To his children and in case he has no children to his parents as well as (b) to his surviving spouse. These persons have right to claim their due portion, which for children and surviving spouse amounts to one-half and for parents to one-third of that share of estate to which they would have been entitled in case of intestacy. Claim for due portion is money claim against heir(s). Surviving spouse is entitled to claim alimony from estate or from heir(s) when lacking sufficient own income. In specific cases (acts of ingratitude, life imprisonment, etc.) due portion can be excluded by last will. If relationship between parent and child was at no time of such nature as it usually exists in family, testator may direct by testament that due portion shall only be 50% of that otherwise due.

Renunciation of Succession.—Rights expectant to succession at law and to due portions can be renounced by agreement to be concluded between the presumptive heir and the still living owner. Such agreement must be filed on the record of a notary public or a court.

Applicable Law.—Succession by inheritance is subject to law of that country of which deceased was citizen. If he had foreign citizenship and Austrian citizenship, Austrian law applies.

DISPUTE RESOLUTION:

As Austrian civil law procedure is considered comparatively fast and efficient, alternate dispute resolution is relevant mainly with respect to international commercial transactions.

See also topic Arbitration.

Mandatory Dispute Resolution.—Certain rental law matters (disputes on amount of rent, etc.) must be filed with conciliation bodies set up at local administrative authorities. Decisions of such conciliation bodies are enforceable as administrative decisions but will cease to be in force if case is brought before court within 14 days after decision has been rendered.

Arbitration Court of Stock Exchange has exclusive competence for disputes arising from stock exchange transactions.

Voluntary Dispute Resolution.—Some courts of arbitration are established under specific laws and set up on permanent basis (i.e. Permanent Aribtration Court of Chamber of Commerce and Arbitration Court of Stock Exchange) and can be made competent by arbitration agreement.

Mediation bodies set up by Professional Associations (doctors, chartered accountants, etc.) may be applied in disputes involving member of respective profession. Involvement of such mediation bodies does not suspend statute of limitations and does not exclude court proceedings. Decisions of such mediation bodies are considered recommendations and are not enforceable.

DIVORCE:

A suit for divorce may be brought before the Austrian courts if (a) at least one spouse is an Austrian citizen; or (b) both parties being aliens, at least one has his permanent residence in Austria; provided, however, that the courts in the husband's home country do not refuse to recognize the validity of an Austrian judgment under such circumstances; or (c) if at least one spouse has no citizenship at all, but one has permanent residence in Austria.

Reasons for divorce are: (a) Adultery; (b) denial of offspring; (c) serious misconduct; (d) mental derangement and illness; (e) serious contagious disease; (f) dissolution of marital community for three years (if defendant objects, court decides on given circumstances but after six years divorce must be granted); (g) agreement between both spouses, provided that marital community has been dissolved for six months and they have concluded or conclude before court written agreement on division of property, on alimony and on relations with minor children. In any case divorce requires court decision.

After divorce property used by spouses during marriage and their savings must be divided. Not subject to this division are: (a) Property which belonged to one spouse already before marriage or which he acquired by inheritance or as gift during marriage; (b) personal property of one spouse or property serving for his profession; (c) property belonging to enterprise; and (d) participations in enterprise unless they are only securities. If spouses cannot agree, court must render equitable decision. If division in kind is impossible court may order compensation payments from one spouse to other. If court decides or spouses agree in divorce procedure that only one of them shall be liable for common bank debts, court must order upon request of either of them that spouse so liable under internal relationship shall be principal debtor and other spouse shall only be conditional guarantor. Such court order is legally effective against creditors.

The divorced wife may resume her maiden name (certain formalities to be observed). If the wife has been declared solely or preponderantly guilty, the husband may prohibit her from continuing to use his name.

Under certain conditions divorce proceedings may be continued, or even started, on anyone's behalf, but this must be done, at the latest, three years after the husband's or wife's decease.

Alimony.—The party who has been declared solely or preponderantly guilty is as a rule required to pay alimony to the other party.

Foreign Divorces.—A divorce granted by a foreign court is valid in Austria only if recognized by the Minister of Justice (Attorney General).

ENVIRONMENT:

General.—Constitutional Act on General Environmental Protection (BGBl. No. 491/1984) makes environmental protection political goal. Act on the Examination of Environmental Compatibility (BGBl. No. 697/1993) is applicable to major construction projects, especially for roads and railways and allows participation of public affected. Trade Act (BGBl. No. 194/1994) regulates basic conditions for construction and restoration of business plants. Austria acceded inter alia to following treaties: Montreal Protocol (BGBl. No. 283/1989 in latest wording of BGBl. No. 846/1993), Basle Treaty on Crossborder Transport of Dangerous Waste (BGBl. No. 229/1993 in latest wording of BGBl. No. 957/1994), Washington Treaty (on trade with endangered species) of Mar. 3, 1973 (BGBl. Nos. 188, 189/1982 in latest wording of BGBl. Nos. 256/1993 and 442/1994).

Waste.—Act on Waste Management (BGBl. No. 325/1990 in latest wording of BGBl. No. 155/1994) and Packaging Regulation (BGBl. No. 645/1992) and Waste Disposal Area Regulation (BGB1. No. 164/1996) regulate avoidance, utilization and disposal of waste as well as export and import thereof. Collection and recycling of household and industrial packaging is managed by private sector under license system (Austria Recycling AG-ARA). Sellers and importers of packaged goods must either prove that they collect and recycle certain percentage of packages themselves—percentages increase every year—or they must participate in nationwide recycling system. Only presently existing system is ARA-system. Households are obligated to separate waste into paper, glass, metal, organic and special waste. Law on the Sanitation of Environmentally Damaged Land (BGBl. No. 299/1989 in latest wording of BGBl. No. 185/1993) is based on principle that such person, which caused damage is responsible for removal of damages (e.g. former dumping sites, oil spills). However, under certain conditions also owners of land can be held responsible. Buyers are not liable if they can prove that damage could not be detected upon due examination of property and register of risk zones.

Water and Air.—Water Act (BGBl. No. 252/1990 in latest wording of BGBl. No. 185/1993) regulates utilization of public and private water, such as rivers and underground water (removal of water, hydroelectric power, channel building, sewage, purification plants). Air pollution control laws for industrial plants, car traffic, heating of private households all contain strict emission standards.

Chemicals.—Chemical Act (BGBl. No. 326/1987 in latest wording of BGBl. No. 759/1992) contains provisions for licensing of new substances, general prohibitions and limitations, duty of care and provision of information, packaging and handling of poison. It is the basis for various regulations e.g. on asbestos, fertilizers, detergents, plant protective agents, formaldehyde.

Nature.—Further provisions on environmental protection in specific cases are contained in Forest Act (BGBl. No. 440/1975 in latest wording of BGBl. No. 970/1993), Plants Protection Act (BGBl. No. 124/1948 in latest wording of BGBl. No. 476/1990), Animal Transport Act (BGBl. No. 411/1994).

EXCHANGE CONTROL:

See topics Currency; Foreign Investment; and also Aliens.

EXECUTIONS:

Execution is granted upon judgments and court settlements (stipulated judgments) as well as on grounds of enforceable document set up before notary public. Movable property must first be seized in order to be realized according to legal regulations. Immovable property can, without previous seizure, be realized by sequestration or public sale.

EXECUTORS AND ADMINISTRATORS:

The function of executor is not provided for by Austrian law. The estate is administered, under the supervision of the court, by the heir or heirs, even though an executor has been appointed by will.

Administrators in the sense of that term in American law are not known in Austrian law, as all the powers and authorities of an administrator (in the common-law sense) are vested in the heir or heirs.

FOREIGN EXCHANGE:

See topic Currency; also topic Aliens.

FOREIGN INVESTMENT:

Foreigners (i.e., physical persons or corporations not considered as residents under Exchange Control Act) may acquire and own individual businesses and companies or participations therein and shares thereof without any restrictions. Participation in foreign companies or businesses by Austrians or Austrian companies is now generally approved. See topic Currency.

Acquisition of real estate by foreigners, foreign corporations and Austrian companies controlled by foreigners is subject to special permission of real estate transfer commissions which are regulated by provincial laws and vary therefore from province to province. Some transactions relating to real property and transfer of funds from abroad are subject to exchange control approval by Austrian National Bank.

Austria concluded treaties for promotion and mutual protection of investments (most favored nation clause, free transfer of proceeds and royalties, retransfer of loans, etc.) with Cape Verde (BGB1. No. 83/1993). People's Republic of China (BGBl. No. 537/1986), Czechoslovakia (BGBl. No. 513/1991 applicable to Slovakia pursuant to exchange of diplomatic notes), Malaysia (BGBl. No. 601/1986), Hungary (BGBl. No. 339/1989), Poland (BGBl. No. 473/1989) and Yugoslavia (BGBl. No. 152/1991), Korea (BGBl. No. 523/1991) and Turkey (BGBl. No. 612/1991), which apply also to Austrian subsidiaries of foreigners. Austria is contributory country to Polish Stabilization Fund.

FOREIGN TRADE REGULATIONS:

On principle import and export of goods is not subject to restrictions in Austria; however, by Foreign Trade Law (Aussenhandelsgesetz 1994, BGBl. No. 172), restrictions can be introduced for export and import of certain groups of commodities. Law is specifically made subject to provisions of EU law. Special commodities may be made subject to approval of Ministry of Economic Affairs, provided that this is not in conflict with EU law if (i) required to prevent serious economic damages; (ii) necessary to prevent or to remove economic emergency situations; (iii) in compliance with international obligations; or (iv) necessary to carry out international measures to restrict commerce with specific countries or areas. Severe restrictions apply to weapons and war material.

See Topical Index in front part of this volume.

FOREIGN TRADE REGULATIONS . . . *continued*

Strict labelling requirements exist especially for foods, pharmaceuticals, chemical products, cosmetics, meat, animal food, wine, etc.

In order to promote exports Minister of Finance is authorized to guarantee in name of Federal Republic performance of foreign partners in transactions with Austrian exporters up to aggregate amount of ATS 420,000,000,000 through Österreichische Kontrollbank AG. (Law of Apr. 8, 1981, BGBl. No. 215 in latest wording of BGBl. No. 733/1995). This authorization will expire on Dec. 31, 2000.

Exportation of objects of historical, artistic or cultural importance needs approval by federal agency of national monuments. Works of living artists until 20 years after their death do not require export approval.

Austria is member of EU.

FRAUDS, STATUTE OF:

While Austria has no statute of frauds, certain contracts must be in writing (e.g., guarantees, arbitration agreements); others must be executed in form of notarial act (e.g., gifts unless actual delivery takes place, contracts between husband and wife, transfer of shares in companies called Gesellschaft mit beschraenkter Haftung, etc.). In some cases notarial certification is sufficient (e.g. some legal documents for joint stock corporations and limited liability companies). All contracts for which law does not specifically require certain form may be executed also orally or conclusively.

FRAUDULENT SALES AND CONVEYANCES:

(Law of Dec. 10, 1914, RGBl. No. 337, in latest wording of Law of June 19, 1968, BGB1. No. 240).

Acts performed by a debtor with the intention to defraud his creditors are voidable by any creditor, who has levied execution without success.

Action for avoiding the fraudulent act must be brought within two years. Similar actions will lie to attack, within two years, any gratuitous conveyance of debtor's property, as well as any act performed by a debtor with an intention, actually or constructively known to the other party, to waste his property.

In case of bankruptcy all those rights of actions are vested in the bankruptcy receiver. In addition, the bankruptcy receiver may attack any act performed by the bankrupt in order to give a preference to one or some of his creditors, provided the creditor or creditors in question had actual or constructive knowledge of such intention and the act was performed within 60 days before the bankrupt's insolvency and no more than a year before commencing bankruptcy proceedings. Moreover, the bankruptcy receiver can attack any act prejudicial to the creditors performed by the bankrupt when already insolvent and not earlier than six months before opening bankruptcy proceedings, provided the person with whom he contracted had actual or constructive knowledge of his being insolvent.

GARNISHMENT:

Attachment of outstanding debts of the debtor is done by decree of court pursuant to which the debt is assigned to the creditor. This decree, together with a garnishee order stating that the debtor's debtor is forbidden to pay to his creditor, must be served upon the debtor's debtor by court. If creditor alleges that debtor has receivables, court must order debtor to specify such receivables under oath with threat of imprisonment.

HOLIDAYS:

(Feiertagsruhegesetz 1957 [Law of June 18, 1957, BGBl. No. 153] in latest wording of Law of June 28, 1967, BGBl. No. 264).

Legal holidays are: New Year's Day; Epiphany (Jan. 6); Easter Monday; Labor Day (May 1); Ascension Day; Whitmonday; Corpus Christi, Assumption Day (Aug. 15); All Saints' Day (Nov. 1); Immaculate Conception (Dec. 8); Christmas Day (Dec. 25); St. Stephen's Day (Dec. 26).

For members of the Protestant Church Good Friday and Oct. 31 are also legally recognized holidays.

For all legal terms and terms of judicial proceedings (except terms relating to bills and checks) as well as for all terms relating to payment of taxes and tax proceedings, all Saturdays and Good Friday are recognized as legal holidays. If the expiration of a term coincides with a holiday, the term expires on the subsequent working day.

Court holidays are from July 15 to Aug. 25 and from Dec. 24 to Jan. 6 of each year. Court holidays only apply to civil cases and no court hearings are to be held at such times with few exceptions. All time limits in civil matters are extended until end of court holidays.

HUSBAND AND WIFE:

Unless otherwise expressly agreed, all property owned by either spouse before marriage, and all property acquired by either spouse after marriage, remains his or her personal property with exception of property used by spouses during marriage. See topic Divorce.

Spouses shall agree, which of them takes care of household and which one earns a livelihood. That spouse who takes care of common household has claim for support against other spouse and represents other spouse in usual transactions for common household, for which other spouse is liable.

Married persons can retain former surname independently of surname of partner or add surname of spouse either to beginning or end of his (her) surname. In absence of agreement common surname is husband's surname. Spouses have to agree on surname of children. Surnames acquired during previous marriages cannot be used as common surname. Either spouse can request change of common residence, if this is justified. Court decides, if spouses do not agree.

Community Property.—Agreements providing for complete or partial community of property may be entered into before or after marriage, before a notary public.

IMMIGRATION:

Aliens are persons not having Austrian citizenship. They need passports and visas for entering, staying in and leaving Austria, unless international treaties provide otherwise, or if they are transit passengers only. Citizens of Afghanistan, Bangladesh, Ghana, Iraq, Iran, Liberia, Libya, Nigeria, Pakistan, Somalia, Sri Lanka and Zaire require even visa for transit. No visa is required for citizens of Andorra, Argentina, Australia, Bahamas, Barbados, Belgium, Bolivia, Brazil, Canada, Chile, Colombia, Costa Rica, Croatia, Cyprus, Czech Republic, Denmark, Ecuador, El Salvador, Finland, France, Germany, Great Britain, Greece, Guatemala, Holy See, Hungary, Iceland, Ireland, Israel, Italy, Jamaica, Japan, Liechtenstein, Luxembourg, Malaysia, Malta, Mexico, Monaco, Netherlands, New Zealand, Norway, Panama, Paraguay, Poland, Portugal, San Marino, Seychelles, Singapore, Slovakia, Slovenia, South Korea, Spain, Sweden, Switzerland, Tobago, Trinidad, Uruguay, USA, and Venezuela. Special permission is required if alien intends to establish regular residence in Austria. Aliens are assumed to have intention to establish regular residence if they stay for more than six months per calendar year in Austria or work in Austria (employed or self-employed).

All aliens other than citizens of countries of EEA intending to take up work in Austria, however, require special visa and work permit. Basis for work permit in Austria is either (a) work permit obtained by and issued to employer for up to one year, or (b) authorization to work obtained by and issued to employee for up to two years, provided that employee has been legally working 52 weeks in Austria during preceding 14 months, or (c) release of work permit requirement obtained by and issued to employee for five years, provided that employee has been legally working five years in Austria during preceding eight years. Total number of employed and unemployed foreigners in Austria must not exceed 8% of total of all employed and unemployed persons (Austrians and foreigners). Applications for work permit must be submitted from abroad before entry into Austria. Extensions can be requested in Austria. (Employment of Foreigners Act, BGBl. No. 218/1975 in latest wording of BGBl. No. 502/1993).

INFANCY:

Minority ends for both males and females on completion of 19 years of age. (§21 A.B.G.B.).

Minors having completed 18 years of age may be released from parental power before completion of 19 years of age, but only with consent of parents and approval of court after pertinent petition has been filed, in which special advantage to person under age has to be justified.

Children under age of 14 years are not subject to any prosecution under penal code. Minors on completion of 14 years and until completion of 18 years are subject to special regulations of penal code. (Juvenile Court Law 1961).

As regards employment in any kind of commercial enterprises minors are subject to special protective provisions.

For marriage, male minors under 19 and female minors under 16 years of age require consent of their parents or guardian. If this consent is refused, it may be replaced upon request by decree of competent Guardianship Court in case of male minors of more than 18 and female minors of more than 15 years of age.

Minor daughters are released from parental power if they marry, and do not return into parental power if divorced during their minority.

Minor children of less than 14 and infants of less than seven years of age are represented by their parents. Each of parents is alone entitled to represent minor child or infant, but for important matters both parents must agree. If one parent is dead, incapacitated or of unknown residence, other parent exercises all parental powers alone. If this applies also to other parent district administration decides, which grandparents shall have parental powers, but guardian is charged with representation of and property administration for minor child or infant.

Person under age can transact business only with consent of his parents or guardian and in important cases also of court, but may freely use earnings acquired by himself.

Before taking any decision regarding custody or education, court shall hear child personally.

Same rules apply to illegitimate children with exception that education and care is exclusively incumbent upon mother.

If person bound to pay alimony and support does not live in common household with minor child and does not pay alimony, advances for such alimony are to be paid by federal agencies, if, upon application, Guardianship Court renders respective decision. Advances paid are to be repaid to federal agencies by person bound to pay alimony and support.

Federal Law of Mar. 1, 1990 (BGBl. No. 160) regulates alimony claims of persons residing in Austria against persons residing in other countries, provided that reciprocity is established by Federal Ministry of Justice. Contrary to claims of other nature, reciprocity exists for alimony claims with most States of U.S. and Australia.

Austria is member to European Convention on the Legal Status of Children Born Out of Wedlock of Oct. 15, 1975 (BGBl. No. 313/1980), to European Convention on Recognition and Enforcement of Decisions Concerning Custody of Children and on Restoration of Custody of Children of May 20, 1980 (BGB1. No. 321/1985) and to Convention of the Rights of the Child of Jan. 26, 1990 (BGB1. No. 7/1993).

Austria acceded to Convention on the Civil Aspects of International Child Abduction of the Hague of Oct. 25, 1980. (BGB1. No. 512/1988; cf. Law of June 9, 1988, BGB1. No. 513).

Adoption.—See topic Adoption.

INSOLVENCY: See topic Bankruptcy.

JUDGMENTS:

Judgments of Austrian courts against which no further appeal lies are enforceable by way of execution. Even if an appeal be admissible, "security" execution may be granted under certain circumstances.

Foreign Judgments are enforceable only if passed by the courts of a country where Austrian judgments are enforceable. A foreign judgment which is not enforceable in Austria is not considered as evidence of the claim of the plaintiff.

Agreements exist on mutual acknowledgment and execution of judgments in general with following countries: Aruba, Belgium, Federal Republic of Germany, France, Greece, Great Britain, Israel, Italy, Liechtenstein, Luxembourg, Netherlands, Norway, Spain, Switzerland, Turkey.

See Topical Index in front part of this volume.

JUDGMENTS . . . *continued*

On ground of Hague Convention of Mar. 1, 1954 on proceedings in civil matters, judgments on law costs rendered in following countries are acknowledged and enforceable: Belgium, Belorussian S.S.R., Croatia, Czech Republic, Denmark, Finland, France, Germany, Holy See, Hungary, Iceland, Israel, Italy, Japan, Lebanon, Lithuania, Luxembourg, Moldavia, Morocco, Netherlands (including Netherlands Antilles), Norway, Poland, Portugal, Romania, Slovakia, Slovenia, Sweden, Switzerland, Spain, Surinam, Turkey, Ukrainian S.S.R., U.S.S.R., Yugoslavia.

On ground of Hague Convention of Apr. 15, 1958 on recognition and enforcement of alimony decisions judgments on alimony claims rendered in following countries are enforceable: Argentina, Belgium, Bosnia-Herzegowina, Croatia, Czech Republic, Denmark, Egypt, Finland, France, Germany, Hungary, Italy, Lebanon, Liechtenstein, Lithuania, Luxembourg, Moldavia, Netherlands (including Netherlands Antilles), Norway, Poland, Portugal, Romania, Russian Federation, Slovakia, Slovenia, Surinam, Sweden, Switzerland, Turkey, USSR, Yugoslavia.

On ground of recognition of reciprocity, judgments in civil and alimony matters rendered in British Columbia, Nova Scotia, Saskatchewan (Canada), Australia and U.S.A. can be enforced. (BGBl. No. 160/1990 as am'd by BGBl. No. 495/1992).

LABOR RELATIONS:

Relations between employers on one hand and employees and workers on other hand are basically regulated by Labor Constitution Act of Dec. 14, 1973, BGBl. No. 22/1974, in latest wording of BGBl. No. 624/1994. Associations representing either workers and employees or employers may be granted power to conclude collective bargaining agreements by public agency set up pursuant to Labor Constitution Act. Collective bargaining agreements are also binding for non-members and only lay down minimum requirements. Changes in favor of employees or workers are always permitted and usual. Matters not regulated by collective bargaining agreements may be regulated by specific agreements between employer and works committee (Betriebsrat).

Number of members of works committee depends on number of workers and employees, begins at five with one member, reaches four members with 100 workers and employees, 13 members with 1,000 workers and employees etc. Office is held for three years. Members of works committee shall supervise compliance with collective bargaining agreements and with other laws for protection of workers and employees. They have no right to interfere with management, but must be heard and periodically informed.

If company has supervisory board, for every two elected members works committee shall appoint one member of its choice.

Legal status of employees is regulated by Law of May 11, 1921, BGBl. No. 292, in latest wording of BGB1. No. 502/1993.

There is only one accredited union of workers and employees, which is entitled to conclude collective agreements with associations of employers, the "Austrian Labor Union" (Österreichischer Gewerkschaftsbund). Although such collective agreement is binding upon any worker and employee, there is no obligation to be a member of "Austrian Labor Union."

Pursuant to Law of Dec. 11, 1969 (BGBl. No. 461 in latest wording of BGBl. No. 446/1994) working time of any employee and worker with a few exceptions is 40 hours per week. Shorter working time applies in some fields of industry on basis of general collective bargaining agreements. Prohibitions and restrictions on work apply to juvenile workers and are defined by regulations of Ministry of Commerce, Trade and Industry.

Any worker and employee is entitled to uninterrupted and paid vacation. (Law of July 7, 1976, BGBl. No. 390 in latest wording of BGB1. No. 502/1993). Generally, with few exceptions, employees with less than 25 years of service are entitled to annual vacation of 30 working days and thereafter to 36 working days. For this purpose Sats. count as working days. Monetary compensation of unused vacation is void by law.

If bankruptcy or judicial composition proceedings are opened against employer, workers and employees are entitled to file claim for salaries and wages not paid by employer during four months after opening of such proceedings with competent labor agency. Necessary means to satisfy these claims are taken from specially created fund. (Law of June 2, 1977, BGBl. No. 324 in latest wording of BGBl. No. 282/1990).

One parent (father or mother) is entitled to maternity leave with job guarantee. He or she receives not salary but support from state.

Special rules on vacation, breaks, severance pay and worker protection apply to night shift workers doing heavy work. Employee Protection Act (BGBl. No. 450/1994) contains provisions on health inspections of employees and for work safety.

Detailed rules on length of permissible overtime, length of required rest for employees and kinds of work permitted on weekends and holidays are contained in Law of Feb. 3, 1983, BGB1. No. 144 as am'd by BGBl. No. 158/1991.

Men and women are to be treated equally regarding salary, fringe benefits and training programs. Unlawful discrimination is defined as adverse differentiation without justification. No job may be offered publicly only to men or only to women, unless sex of employee is unabandonable condition for job. Public employees must not be discriminated against because of their sex.

Retirement age for male employees is 65 years, for female employees 60. Premature retirement is possible, provided employee has worked enough time. Premature retirement age for female employees of presently 55 years will be increased during years 2019 to 2028 by six months annually and regular retirement age for female employees will be increased during years 2024 to 2033 by six months annually, in order to equal retirement status of male and female employees.

Rental of labor is permissible, but restrictively regulated by Law of Mar. 23, 1988, BGB1. No. 196 in latest wording of BGB1. No. 460/1993.

See also topic Infancy.

LAW REPORTS, CODES, ETC.:

See topics Legislature; Reports.

LEGISLATURE:

All Federal laws must be passed by the Austrian Parliament and published in the Federal Gazette. All provincial laws must be passed by the Diet and published in the Provincial Gazette. Each administrative authority can—on the grounds of the law—issue ordinances and regulations within sphere of its activity, which are also published in various official gazettes.

See also topic Constitution and Government.

LICENSES:

Exercise of virtually any trade or industrial activity requires license or, in specific cases, concession to be issued by trade agencies. (Trade Act 1973 of Nov. 29, 1973 BGBl. No. 50/1974 in latest wording of BGBl. No. 29/1993). For obtaining license or concession certain qualifications must be proved (specialized education and experience of certain duration according to kind of activity, residence at place of business, Austrian citizenship, etc.). Only in case of so-called "free trades" registration suffices without proof of education and experience. If reciprocity exists, which is case with Belgium, Federal Republic of Germany, Italy, Netherlands and U.S.A., Austrian citizenship is not required. Citizens of EFTA countries (Iceland, Norway, Portugal, Sweden, Switzerland) and of Finland are only treated like Austrian citizens if goods of EFTA origin are concerned. Citizens of all other countries with exception of nationals of EU require recognition of equal status with Austrian citizens by competent provincial government as condition for grant of license.

Joint stock corporations, private limited liability companies and cooperative associations must nominate person qualifying under Trade Act as holder of license or concession. In partnership at least one general partner must qualify under Trade Act.

LIENS:

Owners of warehouses, carriers and brokers have special liens for their charges. Landlords have a lien on tenants' chattels.

In other cases the law provides for a so-called right of retention which actually nearly amounts to a lien. Thus, a merchant has a right of retention in respect of another merchant's chattels, in order to secure debts arising out of reciprocal business transactions; in case of the debtor's insolvency such right of retention may be exercised even to secure recovery of debts that have not yet become due. Banks have similar rights of retention in respect of securities they are holding for a customer.

LIMITATION OF ACTIONS:

General.—Period of limitation of actions in civil law is not uniform. Most claims in commercial law are barred after three years, same as most claims arising from transactions of "everyday life." Thirty-year period is standard period of limitation if there runs no other. This period governs after judgment has been rendered.

Prescription period is interrupted if claim is expressly or conclusively recognized or if suit is filed and action is duly pursued. If action is rejected, prescription period is retroactively deemed uninterrupted. New prescription period begins upon recognition of claim by debtor. Only if debtor recognizes claim expressly in such way that claim is then based on acknowledgment and not any more on original transaction, then prescription period of 30 years applies.

Railways.—Claims for damages caused by rail accidents: Railroad company is liable for all injuries to property or persons caused by the operation of the railroad, insofar as they are not due to any Act of God or direct fault of person injured.

In case of death of a person reimbursement must be made for cost of medical treatment attempted, the pecuniary damages suffered by loss of ability to earn a livelihood and funeral expenses. In case of physical injury reimbursement has to be made for cost of medical treatment, pecuniary damages caused by the injury and cost of a possible increase in his personal wants resulting from injury. In case of any claims due to the loss or any diminishing of ability to earn a livelihood or increase of personal wants or any claims of third persons for furnishing of support all resulting from the injury, an annuity has to be paid in monthly instalments at beginning of each month. Liability of railroad company for injuries to persons is limited to a total of ATS 1,200,000, or to annuity of ATS 90,000, for each person injured. For cablecars, trolleybuses and private railroads these amounts are limited to ATS 1,200,000 and to annuity of ATS 54,000 respectively. For injuries to property liability of railroad companies amounts to ATS 450,000 of cablecar or trolleybus companies to ATS 270,000 for one accident. If several objects are injured by one accident compensation to be paid is to be distributed proportionally.

Claims for damages are limited to a period of three years after the injury or the name of the person under obligation to reimbursement came to the legitimate claimant's knowledge, or 30 years, regardless of this knowledge. The claimant foregoes any right of claim according to the Railroad-Liability Act, unless he notifies in a written statement the person under obligation to reimbursement within three months after injury and name of the person having caused it came to his knowledge. (Law of Jan. 21, 1958, BGBl. No. 48, in latest wording of Law of Feb. 6, 1968, BGBl. No. 69).

Motor Vehicles.—Claims for damages caused by motor accident: Holder of vehicle is liable for any injuries to property and persons caused by operation of his vehicle, insofar as they are not due to any Act of God or direct fault of person injured. In case of death of a person reimbursement has to be made for cost of medical treatment attempted, for pecuniary damages suffered by loss of ability to earn a livelihood and funeral expenses. In case of physical injury reimbursement has to be made for cost of medical treatment, pecuniary damages caused by injury and cost of a possible increase in his personal wants resulting from the injury. In case of any claims due to loss or any diminishing of ability to earn a livelihood or increase of personal wants or any claims of third persons for furnishing of support, all resulting from the injury, an annuity has to be paid in monthly instalments at beginning of each month. Liability of holder of motor vehicle for physical injuries is limited to ATS 1,200,000 or to annuity of ATS 54,000 for each person injured. Total liability for homicide and injury of one or several persons by one action is limited to ATS 3,600,000. For injuries to property liability of holder of motor vehicle amounts to ATS 270,000 for one accident. If several objects are injured by one accident compensation to be paid is to be distributed proportionally.

LIMITATION OF ACTIONS... *continued*
Foreign insurance companies can be sued on basis of accidents in Austria through Austrian association of insurers before Austrian courts.

Claims for damages are limited to period of three years after injury or name of person under obligation to reimbursement came to the legitimate claimant's knowledge, or 30 years, regardless of this knowledge. Claimant foregoes any right of claim according to Motor Vehicle Liability Act, unless he notifies in a written statement the person under obligation to reimbursement within three months after injury and name of the person having caused it came to his knowledge. (Law of Jan. 21, 1958, BGBl. No. 48, in latest wording of Law of Feb 6, 1968, BGBl. No. 69).

Aircraft.—Claims for damages caused by accidents in aviation:

(a) In case of accidents caused by navigation of aircraft holder of aircraft is liable for injuries as follows: If aircraft does not exceed total weight of 2,500 kilograms maximum liability for injuries to property and persons is ATS 2,250,000. If weight of aircraft exceeds 2,500 kilograms maximum liability goes up to ATS 9,000,000. Liability for each person injured is limited to ATS 1,200,000. If there are injuries to both property and persons two-thirds of amount for which holder injuries to persons is limited to ATS 120,000 for one-third to property injuries.

(b) In case of accidents on board aircraft or on entering or alighting from aircraft holder of aircraft has to reimburse for injuries to persons and property as follows: Extent of liabilities for injuries to persons is limited to ATS 215,000 for each person, regardless of whether that reimbursement is made by one payment or in way of annuity. For injuries to property maximum liability of holder of aircraft amounts to ATS 240 for each kilogram. Moreover, liability for injuries to property of passenger is limited to ATS 4,800 for each passenger and his baggage. In this case liability also covers accidents from time of surrendering baggage to holder of aircraft to time of returning baggage to passenger, regardless of whether accident occurred inside or outside aircraft.

In case injury was caused by wilful action or gross negligence of holder of aircraft or his employees or agents, aforesaid limitations of liability are not applied.

Claims for damages are limited to a period of two years after injury and name of the person under obligation to reimbursement came to the legitimate claimant's knowledge, or 30 years regardless of this knowledge. Claimant foregoes any right of claim according to Aviation Act, unless he notifies in a written statement the person under obligation to reimbursement.

Who May Assert.—Primarily the person injured or in case of his death his heirs by will or heirs-at-law are entitled to assert all aforesaid claims. (See also topic Death [Presumption of and Actions for].)

Court.—For bringing an action for damages, caused by the aforesaid accidents, that court is competent in whose judicial district the accident occurred. All actions may also be filed with court having jurisdiction for sued person's residence.

Aliens.—All aforesaid claims may be asserted in the same way by Austrians and aliens in the competent Austrian court.

Scope of Liabilities for Railways, Motor Vehicles and Aircraft.—These liabilities are based on danger of operating railways, motor vehicles and aircraft and not on fault. If fault of holder or operator of railway, motor vehicle or aircraft can be proved, limits of liability do not apply, but liability covers whole damage caused by accident.

MARRIAGE:

Celebration of marriage must be performed before a civil officer. Celebration before a religious minister is permitted, but no legal significance whatever is attached to it.

Marriage between certain groups of close relatives is prohibited. Prohibited also is marriage between parties who have committed adultery, but an exemption is possible.

Aliens desiring to be married in Austria are required to produce a certificate issued by their home authorities and attesting to their legal capacity of entering into marriage.

Personal relations and property relations between spouses are governed by law of that country to which they both belong or last belonged as citizens; otherwise law of country of their last common residence applies. Property relations between spouses may also be governed by that law on which they expressly agree.

Austria is member to New York Convention on Consent to Marriage, Minimum Age for Marriage and Registration of Marriages of Dec. 10, 1962 (BGBl. No. 433/1969) and to Convention on Issuance of Nubility Certificates of Sept. 5, 1980 (BGB1. No. 417/1985).

See also topics Infancy and Husband and Wife.

MARRIED WOMEN: See topic Husband and Wife.

MONOPOLIES, RESTRAINT OF TRADE AND CARTELS:

For some kinds of trade, public monopolies are established (e.g., the manufacture of cigars, cigarettes and tobaccos, manufacture of salt, etc.).

Nationalized Enterprises.—A number of individual commercial enterprises have been nationalized by law after World War II. Former owners have received indemnification to a certain extent. See Law of July 7, 1954.

Cartels.—(Law of Oct. 19, 1988, BGBl. No. 600 in latest wording of BGB1. No. 693/1993). Cartels are agreements, understandings, harmonized conduct, recommendations and announcements between or by economically independent industrialists for regulation or restriction of competition, particularly in respect of manufacture, distribution or prices. Recommendations of prices are forbidden, unless noncommittal character thereof is specifically referred to, so that any misunderstanding is excluded. Such cartel agreements concluded abroad likewise fall under this law, provided that they affect Austria. Cartel agreements are legally effective only if entered into cartel register. Registration is only possible if cartel is economically justified.

It is also necessary to announce to register those firms which can be considered as "marktbeherrschend" (dominating market). Undertaking is considered as "marktbeherrschend" if (a) it is not exposed to any or only to negligible competition or (b) if its market share exceeds 5% and domestic market is only supplied by two or three companies or it belongs to four largest enterprises which supply together at least 80% of domestic market or (c) if it has outstanding market position as compared with competitors.

Minister of Justice may, upon consultation with Minister of Economic Affairs and with special committee in cartel matters, by means of regulation (a) determine which forms of intercompany cooperation or pricing are not subject to cartel act and may (b) exempt certain groups of cartels from application of cartel act.

Anybody having legal or economic interest may request declaratory decision of Cartel Court whether certain situation is subject to Cartel Act.

Mergers are to be notified to Cartel Court provided that total turnover of merged businesses reached at least ATS 150,000,000 during preceding business year. Mergers of businesses with total turnover of at least ATS 3.5 billion must be published in official gazette. Certain public institutions may request examination of justification of such mergers. If no request is made, Cartel Court must confirm this fact. Otherwise economic justification of merger must be proved. Special rules apply to mergers of mass media businesses.

Restraint of Free Trade.—(Law of June 29, 1977, BGBl. No. 392 as am'd by Law of July 6, 1988, BGB1. No. 424). Upon application of several specified public agencies, suppliers of goods may be forced by Cartel Court to sell to retailers at same conditions. Different conditions are only allowed if justified. Merchants usually supplying retailers may equally be forced to sell to retailer if otherwise requirements of consumers for basic goods cannot be adequately satisfied or if competitiveness of retailer would be jeopardized by nondelivery.

Unfair Competition.—Act Against Unfair Competition (BGBl. No. 448/1984 as am'd by BGBl. No. 227/1993) prohibits various business practices, which are considered to be unfair, mainly (i) violation of good morals in business; (ii) misleading or deceptive statements or advertising; (iii) disparaging of competitors; (iv) infringement of intellectual property rights, (firm) name rights and well-known product get-ups. Competitor may claim (preliminary and/or final) injunction, damages, rendering of account, specific revocation of public statements, removal of illegal situation and publication of judgment. Extensive jurisprudence and literature interprets term "violation of good morals in business", which may consist in breach of contract or conduct independent from any contract. Comparative advertising is permitted in principle, but must not disparage any competitor; in practice comparative advertising is legally only possible in exceptional circumstances. Premiums offered by advertising are generally prohibited and only allowed in few very specific cases.

See also topic Registers.

MORTGAGES:

Mortgages on lands are constituted by having mortgagee's name and sum due entered into land register (see topics Real Property and Registers). Such entry is made either upon a mortgage deed bearing mortgagor's certified signature or by way of execution on a judgment or similar instrument for recovery of a debt. If there are several mortgages their priority depends on day of presenting application for registration.

In case of nonpayment the mortgagee can obtain either the appointment of an official receiver or the public sale of the mortgaged land. The proceeds are distributed among the mortgagees according to their priority, the surplus, if any, being paid over to the mortgagor.

MOTOR VEHICLES:

Indemnification claims after accidents caused by motor vehicles are regulated under Law on Traffic of Railways and Motor Vehicles of Jan. 21, 1959, BGBl. No. 48.

Admission of motor vehicles as well as acquisition of driving licenses for drivers of motor vehicles has been regulated by Motor Vehicle Law 1967 in latest wording of BGBl. No. 743/1994. It defines motor vehicle, prescribes equipment (including quality) required, and regulates operation. Security belts are mandatory.

Motor vehicle traffic has been regulated by Road Traffic Regulation 1960 (Law of July 6, 1960, BGBl. No. 159, in latest wording of BGBl. No. 522/1993), which law contains special regulations for bicycle traffic, coaches drawn by animals and for pedestrians. Besides, this law regulates all activities on public roads. §5 of this law contains special provisions against alcoholized drivers of vehicles; driver's condition is considered impaired if blood alcohol content amounts to 0.8 per mille or more. In this case driving license may be temporarily and, in case of repeated violations, permanently withheld. Police may prevent alcoholized driver from operating his car. In case of accident, blood examination is compulsory if preliminary test shows suspicion of alcoholization.

Austria is a member of the Interstate Convention of Motor Vehicle Traffic, set up in Geneva on Sept. 19, 1949 and/or Sept. 16, 1950.

Austria is member to Agreement of Mar. 20, 1958 concerning adoption of uniform conditions of approval and reciprocal recognition of approval for motor vehicle equipment and parts. (BGBl. No. 177/1971).

If by a motor vehicle a person is injured or killed or damage is caused to objects, both driver and owner of motor vehicle are jointly liable for damage unless either can prove that accident which caused damage was due to force majeure. If damage was at least partially due to fault of injured, parties are liable for damage proportionately to degree of their respective guilt. If this cannot be ascertained, they are liable to equal parts.

Transportation of goods in Austria by domestic and foreign trucks is subject to special duty for maintenance of roads.

Claims for damages caused by motor accidents, see topic Limitation of Actions, subhead Motor Vehicles.

Liability insurance is compulsory and insurance contracts must be concluded pursuant to general terms and conditions of motor vehicle liability insurance as laid down in regulation of Ministry of Finance. Deviations from such terms to detriment of injured third parties cannot be invoked by insurer. Austria is member of European Convention on compulsory insurance against civil liability in respect of motor vehicles since July 9, 1972. (BGBl. No. 236).

NOTARIES PUBLIC:

Notaries public are appointed by the Government. No periodical renewal of license is necessary.

Though appointed for a specific district, a notary public may exercise his functions anywhere in Austria.

PARTNERSHIP:

General Partnership (Offene Handelsgesellschaft).—This is a partnership for the purpose of carrying on a trade or production, under the name of the firm. The name of the firm is registered in the commercial register. The name of the firm must include the name of at least one of the partners and, in addition, some wording that will clearly indicate that the firm is a partnership. However, being once registered the partnership may sell the business to a third person (or to third persons) who may continue to use the original firm name. Each of the partners is jointly and severally liable to creditors of partnership, with all his personal assets; however, fact that name of certain individual person appears in name of firm does not make him liable to creditors of firm unless he was actually still partner at time debt originated.

Limited Partnership (Kommanditgesellschaft).—This is a partnership for the purpose of carrying on a trade or production, under the name of the firm, consisting of two or more persons of whom at least one is liable to the creditors of the partnership with all his personal assets (Komplementaer), while at least one is liable to the creditors of the partnership only to the extent of his contribution to the capital of the partnership (Kommanditist). The name of the latter must not appear in the name of the firm.

Dormant Partnership (Stille Gesellschaft).—This is a partnership only between the partners that does not operate as such against third persons. Only the owner not his dormant partner is liable to creditors.

Professional Association (Erwerbsgesellschaft).—(Law of Apr. 25, 1990, BGBl. No. 257). This is association under common firm name for businesses and other professional activities for which no general or limited partnership can be established. It is general professional association (offene Erwerbsgesellschaft) if liability of none of partners to creditors is restricted, or otherwise limited professional association (Kommandit-Erwerbsgesellschaft). Official abbreviations are OEG and KEG, respectively. This legal form is specifically intended for liberal professions and small businesses. Professional associations must be registered in Commercial Registers at courts. Rules on partnerships shall apply accordingly.

See also topics Licenses; Corporations, subhead Merger or Change in Status of Corporations and/or Partnerships.

PATENTS:

(Patent Act 1970, BGBl. No. 259, in latest wording of BGBl. No. 181/1996).

Patent law protects new inventions, which do not suggest themselves for the expert from state of art and which are susceptible of industrial application. Shall not be considered as inventions: (a) Discoveries, scientific theories, mathematical methods; (b) esthetic design creations; (c) plans, rules and processes for mental activities, for games or business activities and programs for data processing equipment; (d) reproduction of information. Patents shall not be granted: (a) For inventions violating good morals; (b) for processes of surgical or therapeutic treatment and for diagnostic processes; (c) for plant varieties and animal species. Last exception shall, however, not apply to microorganisms, to microbiological processes and to products made by such processes, so that patents may be obtained therefor. Process patents also protect goods manufactured by means of such processes.

Patent applications filed are examined by Patent Office in Vienna as to patentability of invention. Applicant must be given possibility to answer objections of examiner and, if possible, to change and amend patent application. After such examination application is published.

Within four months after publication objections may be filed by third parties. If no objections are filed or if objections are definitely rejected, patent is granted.

Patents are valid for 18 years from date of publication, but not for longer period than 20 years after filing, provided that annual fees are duly paid. Annual fees increase from year to year.

Anybody may file nullity action against granted patent before nullity department of patent office. Upon appeal supreme patent and trademark board decides finally as second instance.

Foreigners have same right to obtain patents as nationals but must act through Austrian patent attorney or attorney at law. Patent attorneys or attorneys at law do not have to submit written powers, but may simply declare their appointment to Patent Office. Power does not terminate upon death of patent owner or change in his legal status.

Patent infringement suits are handled by courts. For civil infringement actions Commercial Court of Vienna has exclusive jurisdiction.

Inventions by employees are those which: (a) Are result of employee's work for employer or which (b) are based on incitements derived from employee's work for employer or which (c) are made by using knowledge or equipment of employer's business. Employed inventor is entitled to adequate compensation from employer for transfer or use of invention, regardless whether invention is patentable or not, unless he is employed as inventor and compensated for this purpose.

European patents under European Patent Convention are protected; they may however be declared void in Austria, if they protect chemical, pharmaceutical or food products as such.

Special law protects topographies of microelectronic semiconductor products. (Law of June 23, 1988, BGBl. No. 372). Protection starts: (a) Upon first public use of topography, provided that application for registration is filed within two years thereafter with Patent Office, or (b) at day of filing with Patent Office, if topography has not been used in public earlier. Protection expires within ten years after beginning of protection. Protection may only be claimed upon registration. Special semiconductor register is kept at Patent Office. Protection is similar to patent. Fee is to be paid at time of filing of application, but no further annual fees. Based on reciprocity, nationals of Belgium, Federal Republic of Germany, Denmark, France, Greece, Great Britain, Ireland, Italy, Japan, Luxembourg, Netherlands, Portugal, Sweden, Spain and U.S.A. are also entitled to file for protection of topographies.

Austria is member of Paris Convention of Mar. 20, 1883 for Protection of Industrial Property in Stockholm wording of July 14, 1967 (BGBl. No. 399/1973 and 384/1984), of Stockholm Convention establishing World Intellectual Property Organization of July 14, 1967 (BGBl. No. 397/1973 and 381/1984), of Strasbourg Agreement Concerning International Patent Classification of Mar. 24, 1971 (BGBl. No. 517/1975 and 125/1984), of Patent Cooperation Treaty of June 19, 1970 (BGBl. No. 348/1979 and 525/1984), of European Patent Convention of Oct. 5, 1973 (BGBl. No. 350, 351/1979 as am'd by BGBl. Nos. 483, 484/1994) and of Budapest Treaty of Apr. 28, 1977 on International Recognition of Deposit of Microorganisms for Purpose of Patent Procedure (BGBl. No. 104/1984). Headquarters of International Patent Documentation Center established in cooperation with World Intellectual Property Organization is located in Vienna. Austria concluded special treaties with USSR (BGBl. No. 194/1982—applicable to Russian Federation pursuant to exchange of diplomatic notes) on legal protection of industrial property.

Utility Models.—(Utility Model Act BGB1. No. 211/1994). Utility models are inventions, which are new and economically applicable. Whether invention is new, including inventive step which is economically applicable, will not be examined in application procedure before Patent Office. Term of protection expires not later than ten years after end of month of filing. Software logic may constitute utility model.

PLEDGES:

Movable objects and assignable claims may be the subject of pledge (Pfand). Movable objects are pledged by actual transfer of possession, where actual transfer of possession is unfeasible, symbolical delivery is necessary (e.g. surrender of documents that will enable the holder actually to dispose of the objects in question).

Remedies of Pledgee.—The pledgee, in order to recover his debt, must sue at law and have the pledge sold by the court at public auction.

PRESCRIPTION:

See topic Limitation of Actions.

PRINCIPAL AND AGENT:

Power of Attorney.—Power of attorney contracts can be made either verbally or in writing. Power of attorney can be general or special. In order to carry out certain business transactions (purchase and sale of articles, loan agreements, carrying on lawsuit, signing settlement, etc.) power of attorney is necessary, which is given expressly for these kinds of transactions. For certain other transactions (gifts, company contracts, etc.) special power of attorney is needed which is given for each separate transaction.

A lawsuit power of attorney must be given in writing; if made out in a foreign country, the court can demand a notarial attestation of the principal's signature.

Speaking generally, the power of attorney expires at the death either of the principal or of the agent; but a lawsuit power of attorney is not withdrawn at the death of the principal, nor a power of attorney made out by a merchant in mercantile trade.

A power of attorney can be withdrawn at all times by either the principal or the agent. The principal is, however, responsible to the agent for all damages incurred by him in consequence of premature withdrawal, and agent is responsible to principal for all damages incurred by him by reason of agent's prematurely ending power of attorney which was given him for purpose of completing transaction entrusted to him.

Where an agent enters into a legal transaction with a third person who is aware that he is acting under a power of attorney all rights and duties thereunder belong to and are imposed on the principal. An agent who exceeds the limits of his power of attorney or one who falsely pretends to act in behalf of a principal (falsus procurator) is responsible to third persons dealing with him in good faith, for all damages sustained, and in commercial transactions he can be compelled by the third person to perform all obligations which he, in virtue of his supposed power of attorney, has incurred in the name of the supposed principal.

Commercial Agents.—Rights and duties of commercial agents are defined by Commercial Agents Act 1993. (BGB1. No. 88/1993). Commercial agents acting in name of principal and receiving commission on one hand and distributors acting in their own name on other hand are strictly differentiated. In case of termination of agreement by principal without fault of other party, only agent is entitled to compensation, maximum amount of which is equivalent of one year's commission based on average of preceding five years. Distributors have no equivalent claim, unless their actual position is equivalent to that of agent in almost all respects, particularly if their gross margin does not exceed commission rate usually paid to agents under comparable circumstances.

REAL PROPERTY:

There are land registers kept by District Courts which keep a record of any real estate within Austrian territory.

The rights in rem referring to each separate parcel of land and the names of the respective beneficiaries appear on the face of the land registers. Rights in rem are ownership, mortgage rights, usufructus, and a limited number of rights resulting from easements, etc. Subject to very few exceptions no such right can be acquired, transferred or extinguished except by obtaining proper entry in the land register which will be granted by the court upon production of a duly certified title deed, a certified copy of such deed being filed in the court's record. The land registers are kept open to the public, and a purchaser in good faith who has acted in reliance upon the land register entries is largely protected against the claims of any former true owner. So the difficulties arising from search of title when acquiring interests in land are unknown in Austrian practice.

An agreement concerning interests in land, entry whereof is not made in the land register, gives but a personal right of action against the parties thereto.

Transfer of real property in rural areas is subject to approval of local real property transfer commission. In absence of such approval contract is null and void.

See Topical Index in front part of this volume.

RECORDS: See topic Registers.

REGISTERS:

The courts keep land registers, registers relating to mining and railway property, commercial registers and ship registers. Trademark register and patent register are kept by Patent Office (Vienna). There exists "Kartellregister" (Cartel Register) at Courts of Appeals in Vienna where all cartels liable to registration must be entered.

Registers of births, marriages and deaths were kept until 1938 by the religious ministers who performed the baptism, marriage or funeral ceremonies; they are since kept by registry offices ("Standesaemter"). Austria is member of Convention of Sept. 8, 1976 on issuance of multilingual extracts from registers of personal status. (BGBl. No. 460/1983).

See also topics Commercial Register; and Monopolies, Restraint of Trade and Cartels.

REPORTS:

There are official reports issued once a year of the more important decisions of the Supreme Court. However, no decision is a binding precedent upon future cases.

SALES:

No particular form is necessary to close contract of sale; sale is completed as soon as parties have agreed upon object of sale and price. However, buyer does not acquire ownership as to object sold until it is delivered. Oral sales contracts are as valid as written contracts. Special rules apply to contracts with consumers.

If a party has delayed fulfilment of the contract, the other party may, at his choice, either demand performance and indemnity for delayed performance, or (after granting a proper period of grace) indemnity instead of performance, or cancellation of the contract.

If buyer is merchant, he must inspect article delivered without delay and notify seller immediately of any defect; otherwise he is considered as accepting article.

Warranties.—Seller warrants that article sold has qualities expressly stipulated or, if no such stipulation took place, qualities usually to be found in article of that kind. If article sold shows a defect that cannot be remedied and which impairs proper use of article, buyer may cancel contract; if, on other hand, defect does not impair proper use of article, or if it can be repaired, buyer may demand a proportionate reduction of price. Strict liability applies to manufacturers or, in case of goods of foreign origin, to domestic importers, if marketed product is defective or does not have qualities usually to be expected of such product. Product Liability Law of Jan. 21, 1988, BGBl. No. 99, in latest wording of BGB1. No. 510/1994, follows closely EEC Directive on product liability.

Notices required.—If object of contract does not correspond to conditions agreed upon or to usual terms of such an object, any claim for the deficiency must be asserted at the court in case of real estate within three years, in case of movables within six months. Otherwise, right to claim expires. Period begins with day of delivery. If deficiency has been advised to supplier of the goods orally or in writing within period mentioned, any claim for damages caused by this deficiency may be raised as defense even after expiration of these periods.

Prices.—(Price Act, BGBl. No. 145/1992). In principle prices for goods and services can be freely determined. However, following exceptions apply: (a) economically justified prices may be fixed for electricity, gas, heating supply and for freely sold pharmaceutical products; (b) for other goods and services Minister of Economic Affairs may only fix economically justified prices in certain cases of emergency determined by regulation of federal government; (c) economically justified prices may also be fixed for goods and related services subject to rationing and control measures pursuant to other federal laws; (d) for maximum period of six months Minister of Economic Affairs may fix economically justified prices if price policy of entrepreneur is found unjustified as result of investigation requested by member of price commission or if abuse of market dominating position has been enjoined by Cartel Court. Members of price commission are: representatives of Minister of Economic Affairs, Minister of Finance, Minister of Agriculture, Minister of Health, Sports and Consumer Protection, Federal Chamber of Commerce, Chamber of Agriculture and Federal Chamber of Labor. Pursuant to Price Labelling Act (BGBl. No. 146/1992) price of goods and services offered to consumers must be marked in Austrian Schilling and in clearly visible form.

International Sale of Goods.—Austria is member to U.N. Convention on Contracts for the International Sale of Goods of Apr. 11, 1980 (BGBl. No. 96/1988 in latest wording of BGBl. No. 420/1995), effective as of Jan. 1, 1989. See Selected International Conventions section.

Applicable Law.—See topic Contracts.

SEALS:

There is no distinction between sealed and unsealed instruments.

STATUTES:

See topic Legislature.

TAXATION:

Land Tax (Grundsteuer).—(Law of July 13, 1955, BGBl. No. 149, in wording of BGB1. No. 201/1996). Land tax has to be paid by proprietor on all plots of land, which tax is different in various communities (approximately 0.8% of standard tax value).

Land Value Tax (Bodenwertabgabe).—(Law of Dec. 15, 1960 BGBl. No. 285, in latest wording of Law of July 10, 1973, BGBl. No. 383). Owners of unused plots have to pay, apart from the land tax, land value tax which amounts to 1% per annum of taxable uniform assessment value.

All plots of land which have not been built up and have a tax value of less than ATS 200,000 are exempt from aforementioned tax.

Land Transfer Tax (Grunderwerbsteuer).—(Law of July 2, 1987, BGBl. No. 309 in latest wording of BGBl. No. 682/1994). All legal transactions inter vivos by which ownership of real property is acquired or which gives right to one party to acquire such ownership of real property (including construction rights on public property and buildings on land owned by third party) are subject to this tax. Rate of tax is 3.5% (2% for transactions between parents and their children and between spouses) of price paid for real property or, in absence of definite price, of actual value of real property. Exemptions mainly relate to acquisitions in course of probate proceedings by heirs and to gifts.

Income Tax (Einkommensteuer).—(Law of July 7, 1988, BGBl. No. 400 in latest wording of BGBl. No. 201/1996). Individuals residing in Austria, regardless of their nationality, are subject to income tax in respect of their entire income, whether derived from sources within Austria or from sources abroad.

Individuals residing abroad are subject to Austrian income tax only in respect of income derived from Austrian real property, from Austrian business enterprises, from licenses in the exercise of industrial property rights, etc. (This rule applies also to Austrian citizens who have no residence in Austria.)

Income tax assessed abroad is not deductible from the Austrian income tax, but is merely considered an expense that reduces the total income subjected to taxation in Austria unless provided otherwise in particular treaties for avoidance of double taxation.

Income tax is assessed on a progressive scale. Tax rate ranges from 10% to 50%. Very small incomes are tax exempt because of deductions which differ in each case. Capital Yields Tax levied on interest, dividends and similar capital yields amounts to 22%. Implementation of Directive of the Council of the EU on taxation of parent and subsidiary corporations of member states allow certain tax reliefs. Workers and employees are subject to corresponding wage tax, which is income tax withheld by employer and paid to tax authorities each month. Rates of wage tax are slightly different.

See topic Treaties, as to double taxation treaties.

Corporate Income Tax (Körperschaftssteuer).—(Law of July 7, 1988, BGBl. No. 401 in latest wording of BGBl. No. 201/1996). Corporations, having their seat in Austria, are liable to pay taxes on their overall profit. Corporate income tax amounts to 34% irrespective of amount of taxable income. Income derived from participations in foreign companies or businesses of at least 25% held not less than 12 months at key date of balance sheet, is exempt from corporate income tax. 12 month term does not apply to shares resulting from capital increase. Minimum tax for corporations amounts to ATS 12,500 per calendar quarter.

Payroll Tax (Kommunalsteuer).—(BGB1. No. 680/1994). Tax basis is total sum of all wages and salaries paid by employer. Tax amounts to 3% of assessment basis.

Added Value Tax (Umsatzsteuer).—(Law of June 15, 1972, BGBl. No. 223 in latest wording of BGBl. No. 201/1996). Most deliveries of goods and services performed by person or company exercising business activity, regardless of legal or operating status, in Austria are subject to this tax. Certain services are deemed to be rendered and are taxable at seat of firm providing services, some where ordering party operates its business. Tax rate amounts in general to 20% and in some exceptions lower tax rates apply. Computation is made in such way, that in principle tax is only paid from added value at each step. This is made by deducting added value tax charged by supplier from amount of tax to be paid. Added Value Tax and special surtax on motor vehicles are not deductible even for entrepreneurs with few exceptions.

Inheritance and Gift Tax (Erbschafts und Schenkungssteuer).—(Law of June 30, 1955, BGBl. No. 141, in latest wording of BGB1. No. 201/1996). Estate of deceased Austrian citizen, except for real property abroad, is subject to Austrian inheritance tax. Estate of alien, wherever he resided, is subject to Austrian inheritance tax only in respect of real estate located in Austria.

Debts due to, or owed by the deceased are considered located at the creditor's place of residence.

Inheritance tax is assessed on a progressive scale, taking into account degree of relationship between deceased and each heir or legatee. Juridical persons are subject to inheritance tax equivalent (Erbschaftssteueräquivalent) assessed on annual basis as surtax on property tax.

Gifts inter vivos are subject to a gift tax equal to inheritance tax.

Stamp Duties.—Most kinds of applications to judicial and administrative authorities as well as most written contracts are subject to highly technical stamp duty rules. Documents drawn up abroad are not subject to stamp duties unless both parties are Austrian persons or companies or document or notarized copy thereof is physically brought into Austria.

Provincial and Communal Taxation.—There are, in addition to the aforementioned taxes, numerous provincial and communal taxes, particularly on real estate.

TRADEMARKS AND TRADENAMES:

Firm Names.—All businessmen whose business exceeds size of small merchants must be registered with their name in commercial register. Registered name of owner of individual firm constitutes firm name. Firm name of partnership must contain at least name of one general partner. Special rules apply to firm names of limited liability companies and joint stock corporations. Registered firm names enjoy broader scope of protection than registered trademarks under unfair competition law. Every new firm name must be easily distinguishable from all other registered firm names within same community. Firm names of foreign companies enjoy protection as unregistered tradenames if they are known to some extent on market. Every businessman and company is free to use certain designation for business or parts of it (unregistered tradename) provided that such designation is not misleading.

See also topic Commercial Register.

Trademarks.—(Trademark Act 1970, BGBl. No. 260, in latest wording of BGBl. No. 773/1992). Trademarks and service marks are protected if entered in trademark register of Patent Office in Vienna. Period of protection is ten years. If renewed in time there is no limit to its prolongation. If application for registration of trademark is filed by alien individual or corporation Austrian attorney has to be named by him. Patent

See Topical Index in front part of this volume.

TRADEMARKS AND TRADENAMES . . . *continued*
attorneys or attorneys at law do not have to submit written powers of attorney, but may simply declare their appointment to Patent Office. Power does not terminate upon death of trademark owner or change in his legal status. Trademarks may be transferred to another owner without business. If trademark has not been used for uninterrupted period of five years it may be cancelled upon application of any third party.

Austria is a member of Paris Convention of Mar. 20, 1883 for Protection of Industrial Property in Stockholm wording of July 14, 1967 (BGBl. No. 399/1973 and 384/1984 as am'd by BGBl. No. 541/1994), of Madrid Agreement of Apr. 14, 1891, on international registration of trademarks in Stockholm wording of July 14, 1967 (BGBl. No. 400/1973 and 123/1984 as am'd by BGBl. No. 541/1994), of Nice Agreement of June 15, 1957 in Geneva wording of May 13, 1977 concerning international classification of goods and services for purpose of registration of marks (BGB1. No. 340/1982 and 124/1984) and of Convention of Stockholm of July 14, 1967 establishing World Intellectual Property Organization (BGBl. No. 397/1973 and 381/1984). Reciprocity for trademark registrations exists with all member countries of Paris Union Treaty and for Afghanistan, Bahamas, Bahrain, Bermuda, Cayman Islands, Chile, China (People's Republic), Colombia, Hong Kong, India, Iran, Jamaica, Korea, Liberia, Malaysia, Panama, Peru, Saudi Arabia, Singapore, Taiwan, Thailand, United Arab Emirates, Venezuela. Austria concluded special treaty with USSR (BGBl. No. 194/1982—applicable to Russian Federation pursuant to exchange of diplomatic notes) on legal protection of industrial property.

TREATIES:

There Exist Conventions between Austria and Following Countries for Avoidance of Double Taxation.—(1) Argentina: Covention of Sept. 13, 1979 for avoidance of double taxation with respect to income and property taxes (BGBl. No. 11/1983); (2) Australia: Agreement of July 8, 1986 for the avoidance of double taxation and the prevention of fiscal evasion with respect to taxes on income (BGBl. No. 480/1988); (3) Belgium: Convention of Dec. 29, 1971 for avoidance of double taxation and for regulation of specific other questions in field of income and property taxes including trade and real estate taxes (BGBl. No. 415/1973 und 216/1974); (4) Brazil: Convention of May 24, 1975 for avoidance of double taxation with respect to income and property taxes (BGBl. No. 431/1976 and 633/1976); (5) Bulgaria: Convention of Apr. 20, 1983 for avoidance of double taxation with respect to income and property taxes (BGB1, No. 425/1984); (6) Canada: Convention of Dec. 9, 1976 for avoidance of double taxation and prevention of fiscal evasion with respect to taxes on income and on capital (BGBl. No. 77/1981 and 318/1982); (7) China: Agreement of Apr. 10, 1990 for avoidance of double taxation and prevention of fiscal evasion with respect to taxes on income and on capital (BGB1. No. 679/1992); (8) Cyprus: Convention of Mar. 20, 1990 for avoidance of double taxation with respect to taxes on income and on capital (BGBl. No. 709/1990); (9) Czechoslovakia: Convention of Mar. 7, 1978 for avoidance of double taxation with respect to income and property taxes (BGBl. No. 34 applicable to Slovak Republic pursuant to exchange of diplomatic notes and to Czech Republic pursuant to decree of Minister of Finances and 484/1979); (10) Denmark: (a) Convention of Oct. 23, 1961 for avoidance of double taxation with respect to income and property taxes (BGBl. No. 126/1962) as am'd by Protocol of Oct. 29, 1970 (BGBl. No. 20/1972); (b) Agreement between Austrian and Danish Ministers of Finance on withholding taxes on dividends (BGBl. No. 172/1972); (11) Federal Republic of Germany: (a) Convention of Oct. 4, 1954 for avoidance of double taxation with respect to income, property, trade and real estate taxes (BGBl. No. 221/1955 as am'd by BGBl. No. 361/1994); (b) Convention of Oct. 4, 1954 for avoidance of double taxation with respect to inheritance taxes (BGBl. No. 220/1955); (12) Finland: (a) Convention of Oct. 8, 1963 for avoidance of double taxation with respect to income and property taxes (BGBl. No. 55/1964) as am'd by Protocol of Sept. 21, 1970 (BGBl. No. 110/1972); (b) Agreement between Austrian and Finn Ministers of Finance on tax relief regarding dividends and interest (BGBl. No. 277/1973); (13) France: (a) Convention of Oct. 8, 1959 for avoidance of double taxation and on mutual assistance with respect to income, property and inheritance taxes (BGBl. No. 246/1961) as am'd by Protocol of Oct. 30, 1970 (BGBl. No. 147/1972 and 387/1973) and by Protocol of Feb. 26, 1986 (BGB1. No. 588/1988); (b) Convention of Mar. 26, 1993 for avoidence of double taxation and prevention of fiscal evasion with respect to taxes on inheritances and gifts (BGBl. No. 614/1994); (c) Convention of Mar. 26, 1993 for avoidance of double taxation and prevention of fiscal evasion with respect to taxes on income and property (BGBl. No. 613/1994); (14) Greece: Convention of Sept. 22, 1970 for avoidance of double taxation with respect to taxes on income and capital (BGBl. No. 39/1972); (15) Hungary: (a) Convention of Feb. 25, 1975 for avoidance of double taxation with respect to taxes on income, proceeds and property (BGBl. No. 52/1976 and 101/1978); (b) Convention of Feb. 25, 1976 for avoidance of double taxation with respect to estate and inheritance taxes (BGBl. No. 51/1976); (16) India: Convention of Sept. 24, 1963 for avoidance of double taxation with respect to income taxes (BGBl. No. 99/1965); (17) Indonesia: Agreement of July 24, 1986 for avoidance of double taxation and prevention of fiscal evasion with respect to taxes on income and on capital (BGB1. No. 454/1988); (18) Ireland: Convention of May 24, 1966 for avoidance of double taxation with respect to income taxes (BGBl. No. 66/1968 and 154/1970) as am'd by Protocol of June 19, 1987 (BGB1. No. 12/1989); (19) Israel: Convention of Jan. 29, 1970 for avoidance of double taxation with respect to taxes on income and capital (BGBl. No. 85/1971); (20) Italy: Convention of June 29, 1981 for avoidance of double taxation and prevention of fiscal evasion with respect to taxes on income and property (BGBl. No. 125/1985) as am'd by Protocol of Nov. 25, 1987 (BGBl. No. 129/1990); (21) Japan: Convention of Dec. 20, 1961 for avoidance of double taxation with respect to income taxes (BGBl. No. 127/1963); (22) Korea: Convention of Oct. 8, 1985 for avoidance of double taxation and prevention of fiscal evasion with respect to taxes on income and on capital (BGBl. No. 486/1987); (23) Liechtenstein: (a) Convention of Nov. 5, 1969 for avoidance of double taxation with respect to income and property taxes (BGBl. No. 24/1971); (b) Agreement of Sept. 27 and Oct. 12, 1971 regarding reimbursement of withholding taxes (BGBl. No. 437/1971); (24) Luxemburg: (a) Convention of Oct. 18, 1962 for avoidance of double taxation with respect to income and property taxes (BGBl. No. 54/1964 as am'd by BGBl. No. 835/1993); (b) Agreement of Mar. 23 and Apr. 10, 1964 on reimbursement of withholding taxes (BGBl. No. 143/1964); (25) Malaysia: Convention of Sept. 20, 1989 for avoidance of double taxation and prevention of fiscal evasion with respect to taxes on income (BGBl. No. 664/1990); (26) Malta: Convention of May 29, 1978 for avoidance of double taxation with respect to taxes on income and on capital (BGBl. No. 294/1979); (27) Netherlands: Convention of Sept. 1, 1970 for avoidance of double taxation with respect to income and property taxes (BGBl. No. 191/1971 and 83/1972) as am'd by Protocol of Dec. 18, 1989 (BGBl. No. 18/1991); (28) Norway: Convention of Feb. 25, 1960 for avoidance of double taxation with respect to income and property taxes (BGBl. No. 204/1960 and 414/1971); (29) Pakistan: Convention of July 6, 1970 for avoidance of double taxation with respect to income taxes (BGBl. No. 297/1971); (30) Philippines: Convention of Apr. 9, 1981 for avoidance of double taxation and prevention of fiscal evasion with respect to taxes on income (BGBl. No. 107/1982); (31) Poland: Convention of Oct. 2, 1974 for avoidance of double taxation with respect to taxes on income and property (BGBl. No. 384/1975 and 472/1977); (32) Portugal: Convention of Dec. 29, 1970 for avoidance of double taxation with respect to income and property taxes (BGBl. No. 85/1972 and 469/1975); (33) Rumania: Convention of Sept. 30, 1976 for avoidance of double taxation with respect to income and property taxes (BGBl. No. 6/1979); (34) Spain: Convention of Dec. 20, 1966 for avoidance of double taxation with respect to income and property taxes (BGBl. Nos. 395/1967, 266/1973 and 21/1995); (35) Sweden: (a) Convention of May 14, 1959 for avoidance of double taxation with respect to income and property taxes (BGBl. No. 39/1960 and 341/1970) as am'd by Protocol of Nov. 5, 1991 (BGB1. No. 132/1993); (b) Convention of Nov. 21, 1962 for avoidance of double taxation with respect to inheritance taxes (BGBl. No. 212/1963); (c) Agreement of Mar. 14 and Apr. 17, 1972 on withholding taxes on dividends and interest (BGBl. No. 298/1972); (36) Switzerland: (a) Convention of Jan. 30, 1974 for avoidance of double taxation with respect to estate and inheritance taxes (BGBl. No. 64/1975 and 161/1995); (b) Convention of Jan. 30, 1974 for avoidance of double taxation with respect to income and property taxes (BGBl. No. 64/1975); (c) Agreement of Dec. 5 and 6, 1974 on dividends, interest and royalties (BGBl. No. 65/1975); (37) Thailand: Convention of May 8, 1985 for avoidance of double taxation and prevention of fiscal evasion with respect to taxes on income and on capital (BGBl. No. 263/1986); (38) Tunisia: Convention of June 23, 1977 for avoidance of double taxation with respect to income and property taxes (BGBl. No. 516/1978); (39) Turkey: Convention of Nov. 3, 1970 for avoidance of double taxation and on other questions regarding income and property taxes (BGBl. No. 595/1973); (40) United Arab Republic: Convention of Oct. 16, 1962 for avoidance of double taxation and prevention of tax evasion with respect to income and property taxes (BGBl. No. 293/1963); (41) United Kingdom: Convention of Apr. 30, 1969 for avoidance of double taxation and prevention of fiscal evasion with respect to taxes on income (BGBl. No. 390/1970, 356/1971, 585/1978, 505/1979 and 835/1994); (42) U.S.A.: (a) Convention of Oct. 25, 1956 for avoidance of double taxation with respect to income taxes (BGBl. No. 232/1957), (b) Convention of June 21, 1982 for avoidance of double taxation and prevention of fiscal evasion with respect to taxes on estates, inheritances, gifts and generation-skipping transfers (BGBl. No. 269/1983); (43) U.S.S.R.: Convention of Apr. 10, 1981 for avoidance of double taxation with respect to income and property taxes (BGBl. No. 411/1982—applicable to Russian Federation pursuant to exchange of diplomatic notes).

There Exist Treaties between Austria and following States about Mutual Legal Aid.—

Multilateral Treaties: (1) Hague Convention of July 17, 1905 on proceedings in civil matters (RGBl. No. 60/1909); (2) Hague Convention of Mar. 1, 1954 on proceedings in civil matters (BGBl. No. 91/1957); (3) Protocol on Arbitration Clauses of Sept. 24, 1923 (BGBl. No. 57/1928); (4) Geneva Convention of Sept. 26, 1927 on enforcement of foreign arbitral awards (BGBl. No. 343/1930); (5) European Convention on international commercial arbitration of Apr. 21, 1961 (BGBl. No. 107/1964); (6) Hague Convention of Sept. 15, 1958 on recognition and enforcement of alimony decisions (BGBl. No. 294/1961); (7) New York Convention of June 20, 1956 on the recovery abroad of maintenance (BGBl. No. 316/1969); (8) European Convention on information on foreign law of Sept. 6, 1968 (BGBl. No. 417/1971), and Additional Protocol of Mar. 15, 1978 (BGBl. No. 179/1980); (9) Convention of Sept. 8, 1967 on recognition of decisions in matrimonial cases (BGBl. No. 43/1978 and 44/1978); (10) European Agreement on the Transmission of Applications for Legal Aid (BGBl. No. 190/1982); (11) European Convention on service abroad of documents relating to administrative matters of Nov. 24, 1977 (BGBl. No. 67/1983); (12) European Convention on calculation of time limits of May 16, 1972 (BGBl. No. 254/1983); (13) various treaties in field of criminal prosecution.

Austria is party to Convention Abolishing the Requirement of Legalisation for Foreign Public Documents. See Part VII of this volume for list of member countries.

Bilateral Treaties: (1) Belgium: (a) Declaration of Dec. 1, 1930 about mutual legal aid in civil and commercial matters (BGBl. No. 358/1930); (b) Convention of Oct. 25, 1957 on mutual recognition and enforcement of court decisions and public documents regarding alimony obligations (BGBl. No. 141/1960); (c) Convention of July 16, 1959 on mutual recognition and enforcement of court decisions, arbitral awards and public documents in the field of civil and commercial law (BGBl. No. 287/1961); (2) Bulgaria: Treaty of Oct. 20, 1967 on legal aid in civil matters and on public documents (BGBl. No. 268/1969); (3) Czechoslovakia: Treaty of Nov. 10, 1961 on communications in civil matters, on public documents and on furnishing of information on legal matters (BGBl. No. 309/1962—applicable to Slovak Republic pursuant to exchange of diplomatic notes); (4) Denmark: Treaty of Nov. 8, 1979, amending Hague Convention of Mar. 1, 1954 (BGBl. No. 41/1981); (5) Federal Republic of Germany; (a) Treaty of Oct. 4, 1954 on legal aid in fiscal matters (BGBl. No. 249/1955); (b) Treaty of June 6, 1959 amending Hague Convention of Mar. 1, 1954 (BGBl. No. 27/1960); (c) Treaty of June 6, 1959 on mutual recognition and enforcement of court decisions, settlements and public documents in civil and commercial matters (BGBl. No. 105/1960); (d) Treaty of Sept. 11, 1970 on legal aid in customs and fiscal matters (BGBl. No. 430/1971); (6) Finland: (a) Convention of Nov. 17, 1986 on recognition and enforcement of decisions in civil matters (BGBl. No. 118/1988); (b) Treaty of Nov. 17, 1986 amending Hague Convention of Mar. 1, 1954 (BGB1. No. 224/1988); (7) France: (a) Treaty of Feb. 27, 1979 amending Hague Convention of Mar. 1, 1954 (BGBl. No. 236/1980); (b) Convention of July 15, 1966 on recognition and enforcement of court

TREATIES . . . *continued*
decisions and public documents in field of civil and commercial law (BGBl. No. 288/1967); (c) Convention of Feb. 27, 1979 on jurisdiction recognition and enforcement of bankruptcy decisions (BGBl. No. 237/1980); (8) Greece: Treaty of Dec. 6, 1965 on mutual legal aid in field of civil and commercial law (BGBl. No. 2/1971); (9) Hungary: (a) Treaty of Apr. 9, 1965 on mutual relations in civil law matters (BGBl. No. 305/1967); (b) Treaty of Apr. 9, 1965 on estate matters (BGBl. No. 306/1967); (10) Iran: Treaty of Friendship of Sept. 9, 1959 (BGBl. No. 45/1966); (11) Israel: (a) Treaty of June 6, 1966 on recognition and enforcement of court decisions in field of civil and commercial law (BGBl. No. 349/1968); (b) Treaty of July 21, 1975 simplifying procedure under Hague Convention of Mar. 1, 1954 (BGBl. No. 225/1982); (12) Italy: (a) Legal Aid Treaty of Apr. 6, 1922 (BGBl. No. 261/1924); (b) Treaty of Apr. 21, 1967 on abolition of legalizations, transmission of legal status documents and simplification of marriage formalities (BGBl. No. 15/1972 and 247/1981); (c) Convention of Nov. 16, 1971 on recognition and enforcement of court decisions in civil and commercial matters, of court settlements and of notarial acts (BGBl. No. 521/1974) am'd by Exchange of Diplomatic Notes of Apr. 7, 1987 (BGBl. No. 472/1989); (d) Convention of June 30, 1975 amending Hague Convention of Mar. 1, 1954 (BGBl. No. 433/1977); (13) Liechtenstein: (a) Treaty of Apr. 1, 1955 on enforcement of decisions in alimony matters (BGBl. No. 212/1956); (b) Treaty of Apr. 1, 1955 on legal aid, attestations, documents and guardianship (BGBl. No. 213/1956); (c) Treaty of July 5, 1973 on recognition and enforcement of court decisions, arbitral awards, settlements and public documents (BGBl. No. 114/1975); (14) Luxemburg: (a) Treaty of Mar. 17, 1972 amending Hague Convention of Mar. 1, 1954 (BGBl. No. 217/1975); (b) Convention of July 29, 1971 on recognition and enforcement of court decisions and public documents in field of civil and commercial law (BGBl. No. 610/1975); (c) Convention of Oct. 16, 1979, on exchange of status documents and waiver of legalization (BGBl. No. 112/1981); (15) Netherlands: Treaty of Feb. 6, 1963 on mutual recognition and execution of court decisions and public documents in the field of civil and commercial law (BGBl. No. 37/1966) extended to Aruba (BGBl. No. 399/1986); (16) Norway: (a) Treaty of May 21, 1984 on recognition and enforcement of decisions in civil matters (BGBl. No. 406/1985); (b) Treaty of May 21, 1984 amending Hague Convention of Mar. 1, 1954 (BGBl. No. 455/1985); (17) Poland: Treaty of Dec. 11, 1963 on mutual relations in civil matters with Additional Protocol, of Jan. 25, 1973 (BGBl. No. 79/1974); (18) Rumania: Treaty of Nov. 17, 1965 on legal aid in civil matters and on public documents (BGBl. No. 112/1969) as am'd by Additional Protocol of Jan. 19, 1974 (BGBl. No. 123/1974); (19) Spain: (a) Treaty of Nov. 14, 1979 amending Hague Convention of Mar. 1, 1954 (BGBl. No. 280/1981); (b) Treaty of Feb. 17, 1984 on recognition and enforcement of court decisions, settlements and enforceable public documents in civil and commercial matters (BGBl. No. 373/1985); (20) Sweden: (a) Treaty of Sept. 16, 1982 amending Hague Convention of Mar. 1, 1954 (BGBl No. 555/1983); (b) Treaty of Sept. 16, 1982 on mutual recognition and enforcement of decisions in civil matters (BGBl. No. 556/1983); (21) Switzerland: (a) Treaty of Dec. 16, 1960 on recognition and enforcement of court decisions (BGBl. No. 125/1962); (b) Treaty of Aug. 26, 1968 amending Hague Convention of Mar. 1, 1954 (BGBl. No. 354/1969); (c) Treaty of May 23, 1979 on reciprocity in official responsibility matters (BGBl. No. 424/1981); (22) Tanzania: Agreement of Nov. 23, 1972 on legal proceedings in civil and commercial matters (BGBl. No. 222/1980); (23) Tunisia: (a) Treaty of June 23, 1977 on legal aid in civil and commercial matters (BGBl. No. 304/1980); (b) Treaty of June 23, 1977 on recognition and enforcement of court decisions and public documents in field of civil and commercial law (BGBl. No. 305/1980); (24) Turkey: (a) Treaty of June 22, 1930 on mutual legal relations in civil and commercial matters and on relations in civil and commercial matters and on enforcement (BGBl. No. 90/1932) (Arts. 18 to 22 are not any longer applicable); (b) Treaty of May 23, 1989 on recognition and enforcement of court decisions and settlements in civil and commercial matters (BGB1. Nos. 571/1992 and 949/1994); (c) Treaty of Sept. 16, 1988 amending Hague Convention of Mar. 1, 1954 (BGB1. No. 570/1992); (25) United Kingdom: (a) Treaty of Mar. 31, 1931 on mutual legal aid (BGBl. No. 45/1932). This Treaty also applies to: Antigua, Australia, Bahamas, Barbados, Botswana, Canada, Cyprus, Dominica, Fidji, Gambia, Ghana, Grenada, Guyana, Jamaica, Kenya, Lesotho, Malawi, Malaysia, Malta, Nauru, New Zealand, Nigeria, St. Christopher-Nevis-Anguilla, St. Lucia, St. Vincent, Sierra Leone, Singapore, Swaziland, Trinidad and Tobago, Tonga, Uganda, West Samoa, Zambia; (b) Convention of July 14, 1961 providing for reciprocal recognition and enforcement of judgments in civil and commercial matters (BGBl. No. 224/1962) as am'd by Protocol of Mar. 6, 1970 (BGBl. No. 453/1971). This Convention also applies to Hong Kong; (26) U.S.A.: Treaty of Friendship, Commerce and Consular Rights of June 19, 1928 (BGBl. No. 192/1931); (27) U.S.S.R.: (a) Treaty of Sept. 19, 1924 on legal aid in civil matters (BGBl. No. 45/1925); (b) Convention of Mar. 11, 1970 on civil law proceedings (BGBl. No. 112/1972—applicable to Russian Federation pursuant to exchange of diplomatic notes); (28) Yugoslavia: (a) Treaty of Dec. 16, 1954 on mutual legal relations (BGBl. No. 224/1955); (b) Treaty of Mar. 18, 1960 on mutual recognition and enforcement of arbitral awards in commercial matters (BGBl. No. 115/1961); (c) Treaty of Oct. 10, 1961 on mutual recognition and enforcement of alimony decisions (BGBl. No. 310/1962).

International Sale of Goods.—United Nations Convention on Contracts for the International Sale of Goods, in force on Jan. 1, 1989. See topic Sales and Part VII, Selected International Conventions.

See also other appropriate topics, e.g., Air Navigation, Arbitration, Constitution and Government, Copyright, Customs, Judgments, Patents, Sales, Trademarks and Tradenames.

TRUSTS:

Trusts within meaning of law of equity are not known in Austrian law, but see topic Monopolies, Restraint of Trade and Cartels.

VITAL STATISTICS: See topic Registers.

WILLS:

It is an axiom of Austrian law that a will, to be valid, must be executed in accordance with law in force at time when, and at place where will has been drafted.

A will may be either holograph or allograph; a holograph testament to be written by the testator in his own hand and signed with his full name, an allograph testament to be signed by the testator and by three witnesses, or else made before a judge or notary public (deposit of the instrument with the court or notary public being optional).

Foreign Wills.—Wills of aliens are valid if executed in accordance with the laws of the country where they were drafted.

Austria is a member of International Convention on Conflicts of Laws relating to form of testamentary dispositions. (BGBl. No. 295/1963).

See Topical Index in front part of this volume.

BAHAMAS LAW DIGEST

(The following is a list of all Topics, including cross-references, covered in this Digest.)

BAHAMAS LAW DIGEST

Revised for 1997 edition by

HARRY B. SANDS & COMPANY of the Bahamas Bar

See topics Law Reports and Statutes.

ABSENTEES:

In absence abroad a person may generally delegate authority to any person of full capacity. Usual instrument is power of attorney, which may be special or general.

Escheat.—Property of deceased person absolutely without an heir according to Bahamian law devolves on Crown i.e. Monarch of British Commonwealth considered as abstract entity rather than physical person.

Legacies unclaimed or refused under terms of will pass into trusts of residue.

See also topic Death.

ACKNOWLEDGMENTS:

An acknowledgment by a witness before a notary public is not sufficient proof of a deed for registration at the Registry of Records. Every deed should be executed before a witness, who should sign as such, and who should make an affidavit before a notary public or other person authorized to take an affidavit. The person executing a deed can make an acknowledgment that he or she executed the same.

Proof by Attesting Witness.—See topics Affidavits; Deeds.

ACTIONS:

By §2 of The Declaratory Act (Bahamas), it is enacted that: Common law of England, in all cases where same hath not been altered by any of Acts or Statutes enumerated in schedule to this Act or by any Act (except so much thereof as hath relation to ancient feudal tenures, to outlawries in civil suits, to wager of law or of batail, appeals of felony, writs of attaint and ecclesiastical matters), is, and of right ought to be, in full force within The Commonwealth, as same now is in that part of Great Britain called England. For action for damages for death of person see topic Death, subhead Actions for Death.

Equity.—By §23 of The Supreme Court Act (Bahamas), law and equity are administered concurrently; and in all matters in which there is any conflict or variance between the rules of law and the rules of equity with reference to the same matter, the rules of equity shall prevail.

Limitation of.—See topic Limitation of Actions.

Foreign Claims and Judgments.—In all cases full information should be provided. See also topic Judgments (The Reciprocal Enforcement of Judgments Act). In any other case person may be sued under judgment obtained in foreign court of competent jurisdiction, or alternatively sued on merits.

ADOPTION:

Adoption of Children Act, 1954, and Rules made under Act provide that order may be given by Supreme Court for adoption of any unmarried infant within jurisdiction provided application made in prescribed manner. Spouses may make joint application; if one spouse applies, order will not usually be made without written consent of other. Consent of parent or guardian required unless such party cannot be found, has neglected or ill-treated infant, or withholds consent unreasonably. Infant should usually be at least six weeks old. Order when given confers on adopter all legal rights and responsibilities of parent vis-a-vis infant, including right to take under dispositions of property made after order.

AFFIDAVITS:

Any deed or document which it is intended to record at the Registry of Records here must have attached thereto an affidavit by an attesting witness. For places outside the Bahamas, following persons are empowered to administer oaths: British or Bahamian consuls, judges, justices of peace, notaries public or other persons legally authorized to administer oaths or take acknowledgments. When such oath or acknowledgment is taken or made in foreign country (except in case of British or Bahamian Consul) official character of officer before whom same was taken or made or official standing of person who attests or certifies official character of such officer must be verified by British or Bahamian consul. Alternatively, Bahamas being signatory to Hague Convention Abolishing the Requirement of Legalisation for Foreign Public Documents procedure set out in Convention may be adopted.

The affidavit is in the first person and the jurat is as follows: Sworn to at the City of ......, this ...... day of ......, A.D. 19...., before me, ...

Notarial decalarations are frequently used for various purposes but cannot be substituted for affidavits of proof.

ALIENS:

The Imperial Statutes, the British Nationality Act, 1948, defines an alien, but such definition was intended essentially as a part of British law and position is now different in the Bahamas, following Independence on 10th July, 1973, (see topic Constitution and Government). Basically, an alien is now anybody who is not a Bahamian, and a Bahamian is essentially a person born in the Bahamas or born elsewhere but of a Bahamian parent. Provisions also exist under constitution for other persons to apply to become Bahamian citizens. Further provisions allow for status of permanent resident, either with or without automatic right to work. This status covers broadly three categories of persons: those who because of their long and close connection with Bahamas were formerly known as "Belongers"; spouses of Bahamian citizens and those who specifically apply for and are granted such status.

Under International Persons Landholding Act (which replaced former Immovable Property [Acquisition by Foreign Persons] Act 1981), acquisitions of real property by foreign persons do not require permit, but must be registered in following circumstances: (1) Where property is to be used by acquirer as single family dwelling and, in case of undeveloped land, does not result in him owning in excess of five contiguous acres; (2) where acquirer is permanent resident; (3) where acquisition is by devise or inheritance. Alien is not eligible to hold any public office or to vote in any election. Company incorporated under Bahamas Companies Act may be composed entirely of foreign shareholders, directors and officers.

Corporations Owned or Controlled by Aliens.—See topic Corporations.

ASSIGNMENTS:

By Choses in Action Act any absolute assignment, by writing under hand of assignor of any debt or other legal chose in action, of which express notice in writing shall have been given to debtor, trustee or other person from whom assignor would have been entitled to receive or claim such debt or chose in action shall transfer legal right to such debt or chose in action from date of such notice.

ASSOCIATIONS: See topics Corporations; Partnership.

ATTACHMENT:

Attachment of debts may be effected by either garnishment or charging order.

ATTORNEYS AND COUNSELORS:

New Legal Profession Act has recently come into force repealing previous Bahamas Bar Act, 1971. Act provides mechanism for regulation of profession's practice conduct etiquette and discipline and lays down that Bahamian subjects may, if duly qualified under Act, apply to Bar Council of Bahamas for admittance to practice, and if successful are admitted by Chief Justice, and have their names enrolled. Twelve month term of pupillage is normally required. Attorneys have lien over their clients' papers for unpaid fees.

Person qualified as a barrister or solicitor in any British Commonwealth country and having right to work in Bahamas may be employed by attorney as associate, and assist generally in attorney's practice. Regulations provide for registration of such persons.

BANKRUPTCY:

The Bankruptcy Act (Bahamas) is virtually a re-enactment of the Imperial Statute, The Bankruptcy Act 1861. (24 & 25 Victoria, c. 134).

By §4 the following are declared to be acts of bankruptcy: (a) That the debtor has made a conveyance or assignment of his property to a trustee for the benefit of his creditors; (b) that the debtor has made a fraudulent conveyance of his property; (c) that the debtor has absented himself; (d) that the debtor has filed a declaration admitting his inability to pay his debts; (e) that execution has been levied, in the case of a trader, by seizure and sale of the goods of the debtor, for a debt of not less than B$200; (f) that debtor has been served with debtor's summons for not less than B$200 three weeks, or in case of trader seven days, prior to petition for adjudication in bankruptcy.

The act of bankruptcy must have occurred within six months of the presentation of the petition and the debt must be liquidated and not a secured debt, unless the creditor agrees to give up his security.

Preferential Payments.—All debts due to Crown and wages or salary of any clerk or servant not exceeding four months and B$200, wages of any labourer or workman not exceeding two months and all contributions payable pursuant to The National Insurance Act, 1972. All other debts are paid pari passu.

Landlord may also distrain for rent with certain limitations and an apprentice or articled clerk may recover certain amounts.

See also topic Fraudulent Sales and Conveyances.

BILLS AND NOTES:

The Imperial Statute, the Bills of Exchange Act 1882 (45 & 46 Vict. c. 61) was extended to the Bahamas by Bahamas Act 5 of 1892 and is Chapter 308 of 1987 Revised Edition of the Statute Law of the Bahamas. See England Law Digest. There have been certain amendments which follow legislation of U.K.

CHATTEL MORTGAGES:

A mortgage of personal property should be by assignment by deed with a proviso of redemption on payment of the principal and interest secured. As recording of any document in the Registry of Records affords priority of charge, all mortgages should be at once lodged for record with the Registrar General, although recording is not essential to validity of a document.

COMMERCIAL REGISTER:

The New Registration of Business Names Act, which came into force on 1st July, 1995, requires every individual, firm and company having place of business in The Bahamas and carrying on business therein to register its business name and every change thereof. Certain exceptions are provided for under said Act.

CONSTITUTION AND GOVERNMENT:

As from 10th July, 1973, when Bahamas became independent, supreme power is vested in parliament consisting of the Queen (i.e., Queen Elizabeth II of U.K.), a Senate and a lower legislative house called House of Assembly; this has 49 members voted in office on franchise system similar to most other countries. Authority of Queen is represented within Bahamas themselves by Governor-General.

CONSTITUTION AND GOVERNMENT . . . *continued*

Head of party put in office by voters is Prime Minister, and he with other ministers forms Cabinet which is main executive organ of state. Judicial authority is vested in a chief justice, assisted by justices and, in lower courts, by magistrates.

Country is fully independent and therefore entirely responsible for running its own affairs, and eligible for membership of various international organizations, including in particular those relating to law of sea.

Integrity of Constitution and its officers maintained by statute law on bribery and disclosure of assets.

Exact meaning of words and phrases explained by Interpretation Act.

CONTRACTS:

Common law of England applies.

Hire-Purchase.—Hire-Purchase Act, 1974 contains lengthy provisions for regulation of Hire-Purchase, credit sale and conditional sale agreements and for purposes connected with these matters. Act generally covers many kinds of purchase and sale including motor vehicles; there are implied warranties as to title; form of agreement and conditions for signature etc. are described, and conditions for cancellation and effective service of notices, including those leading to recovery of possession of article hired or to be sold.

CONVEYANCES: See topic Deeds.

COPYRIGHT:

Provisions of The Imperial Statute, The Copyright Act 1956, extend, with modifications, to the Bahamas with effect from 11 Feb. 1963, except those empowering Governor or Comptroller of Customs to make regulations, which provisions came into effect on 11 Oct. 1962. See England Law Digest. The Bahamas is now member of The Berne Copyright Union and The Universal Copyright Convention.

CORPORATIONS:

On 1st Aug., 1992 new consolidating Companies Act, 1992, came into effect, repealing previous Companies Act, and introducing distinction between private and public companies. Limited companies are incorporated by filing with Registrar General memorandum of association, which is company's charter, and may contain objects for which proposed company is to be establised, but need not, with effect that company has capacity and all rights, powers and privileges of individual of full capacity without legal disabilities. This represents abandonment of "Ultra Vires" doctrine. Fee of B$300 is payable. Although minimum of two subscribers to memorandum are required, once incorporated company can operate with single shareholder. Articles of association, which are by-laws of company, must also be filed with Registrar General. Fee of B$30 is payable upon filing.

Aliens may comprise any or all of shareholders, directors (of which there must be minimum of two) and officers of company, which must have registered office situate within The Bahamas.

In certain circumstances company may purchase or otherwise acquire its own shares.

Directors may conduct meetings by telephone or by certain other permitted electronic means.

Stamp duty payable on Memorandum of Association is: (a) For company limited by guarantee without an authorised capital: B$60; (b) for company formed for charitable purposes; B$5; (c) in every other case, B$60 for first B$5,000 of capital and B$6 for every subsequent B$1,000.

There are no dividend, share certificate or company taxes of any nature, except that fee of B$350 per annum is payable to Registrar General for each company, during month of Jan. in every year. If company is not at least 60% beneficially owned by Bahamian citizens or by another Bahamian company within this definition, annual fee is increased to B$1,000.

For stamp duty on debentures, see topic Taxation, subhead Stamp Duties.

Any corporation carrying on business as bank or trust company or insurance company must be licenced. Additional annual fees are payable in respect of such companies.

Company may hold and deal in lands, personal property, and Bahamian vessels. Foreign-owned Bahamian company acquiring real property in The Bahamas must comply with International Persons Landholding Act. See topic Aliens.

Certain names may be used only with consent of Registrar General, e.g. names which suggest partronage by or proximity to British Royal Family.

Foreign Companies.—A company incorporated abroad before carrying on undertaking in The Bahamas must under Companies Act, 1992 deposit in Registry of Records copy of Act or charter of incorporation of company, and, having complied with certain other requirements set out in Acts. Acquisition of land in Bahamas by foreign companies is subject to provisions of International Persons Landholding Act. See topic Aliens. Stamp duty on Act or charter of incorporation is B$600 and fee of B$50 is payable at Registry of Records.

The International Business Companies Act, 1989 came into operation early in 1990.

It provides for incorporation, registration and operation of international business companies, including Limited Duration Companies, not conducting business with residents of The Bahamas nor owning real estate in The Bahamas or carrying on banking, trust, insurance or reinsurance business or business of providing registered offices of companies. However, such companies may maintain banking accounts in any currency in The Bahamas and lease offices there and generally conduct their corporate affairs from The Bahamas and they may hold shares, debt obligations or other securities of other Bahamian companies.

Shares.—Under Act bearer and no-par value shares are permitted as well as registered shares. Shares may be issued also in fractions, and at less than par value and company may, in certain circumstances, purchase, redeem or otherwise acquire its own shares and may also in certain circumstances reduce its capital without necessity of order of Court. Persons ordinarily residents in The Bahamas may not own shares.

Exemption from Taxes.—Companies incorporated under Act are exempt from all taxes for 20 years.

Confidentiality.—No information of any nature whatever is required to be filed thus ensuring at all times total anonymity of shareholders, officers and directors; such companies are not subject to any exchange control requirement.

Directors and Officers.—Number of directors need not exceed one, officers are optional and no member, officer or director need be Bahamian citizen or resident. Corporations may serve as officers and directors.

Capital of companies incorporated under Act may be expressed in any currency.

How Incorporated and Corporate Documents.—Companies are incorporated under Act by filing Memorandum (Charter) and Articles (Bye-laws) of Association. Subject to any limitation in Memorandum or Articles of Association both documents can be amended following incorporation but Memorandum initially may be drawn in broadest terms so as to include, inter alia, all and any acts and activities not prohibited by Bahamian law. Specific reference to objects and powers, is not, as formerly, now required. "Ultra vires" doctrine is therefore effectively abolished. However, if desired, particular objects may be set out in Memorandum.

Continuation of Existing Bahamian and Other Companies.—Both existing Bahamian company or company incorporated outside The Bahamas which satisfies requirements of Act may, upon filing Articles of Continuation, continue as company incorporated under new Act and company incorporated thereunder may be resolution of directors or members continue as company incorporated under laws of jurisdiction outside The Bahamas in manner provided under those laws.

Merger and Consolidation.—Two or more companies may merge into one or they may be consolidated into new (consolidated) company.

Name.—Any name is permissible which is not identical or too similar to name of company already on Register of Companies but certain words e.g. assurance, bank, imperial, insurance, trust, royal or words conveying similar meaning or suggesting patronage by Her Majesty the Queen or by any member of the Royal Family or by Government of The Bahamas may not be included in name of company. Last word in name of such companies may be limited, corporation, incorporated, societe anonyme or sociedad anonima or abbreviations ltd., corp., inc., or S.A.

Registered Office and Agent.—Companies incorporated under this Act must maintain registered office and registered agent in The Bahamas.

Official Fees.—Official fee initially and annually for company whose authorized capital is B$5,000 or less is B$100 per annum. There is no requirement for capital in excess of B$5,000 but should greater capital be necessary scale of fees is applicable. Fees are payable on merger, consolidation or continuation.

Limited Duration Companies ("LDCs") may be established afresh or converted from IBC. Memorandum (Charter) of LDC limits its existence to 30 years or less and name of LDC must include words "Limited Duration Company" or abbreviation "LDC". LDCs can be utilized, inter alia, in creation of mutual funds and may be preferred to this purpose to IBC. LDCs may be converted to IBCs. In addition to its restricted life LDC need have no directors and may be managed by its members and/or by managing agents removable with or without cause at any time. Articles of company may restrict transferability of share or other interest of member. Winding-up is automatic upon expiry of period fixed for duration of company or upon happening of other events such as, for example, would terminate partnership or upon occurrence of any circumstance prescribed in Memorandum or Articles terminating membership of member of company. Liability of members may be limited or unlimited.

COURTS:

Supreme Court consists of Chief Justice and justices; for lesser matters including civil claims or debts of up to B$3,000 there are several Magistrates Courts in New Providence and one in Grand Bahama.

See topic Constitution and Government.

CRIMINAL LAW:

Other than Dangerous Drugs Act and Firearms Act which are dealt with separately, Penal Code constitutes legislation on all matters concerning crime and criminal jurisdiction, including nature of crimes and whether summary or indictable. Case may commence by summons or by directive of Attorney-General in serious cases; minor matters are usually heard by magistrate in first instance, from whom appeal lies to Supreme Court of Bahamas, and from there to Court of Appeal and in exceptional cases to Judicial Committee of Privy Council in England. Criminal Procedure Code Act, 1968, contains detailed regulations for procedure, arrest, investigations, trial, etc., of accused persons.

It may be noted that use or possession of firearms or drugs are liable to be severely penalised in Bahamas.

CURRENCY:

As from May 25, 1966, currency of Bahamas is expressed in Bahamian dollars, each containing 100 cents and expressed thus: B$1.00. One Bahamian dollar is approximately equal to U.S. $1.

Bank notes are issued in Bahamian currency in denominations of 50= and one, three, five, 10, 20, 50, and 100 dollars.

See also topic Foreign Exchange, Investment and Trade.

CURTESY:

The husband, in the case of intestacy, takes the whole of his wife's lands after her death for an estate for life, provided she was solely seized of an estate of inheritance and issue of the marriage capable of inheriting has been born alive. A married woman can, however, dispose of her land by will and thus defeat an estate by the curtesy.

CUSTOMS DUTIES:

See topics Foreign Exchange, Investment and Trade; Taxation.

DEATH:

There is no statutory presumption of death of an absentee. Seven years continuous absence under certain circumstances is a defence to bigamy. By The Presumption of Death Act it is provided that persons upon whose lives estates depend shall be accounted as naturally dead if they "remain beyond the seas, or elsewhere absent themselves in this realm" for seven years. Evidence that a person has been absent and not heard of for upwards of seven years by those who would be likely to hear of him if living, may raise the presumption that he is dead; but there is no presumption that he died at any particular time. There is no presumption of law as to survivorship among persons perishing by a common calamity, nor that they all died at the same time. The question is one of fact and the evidence may leave the matter in mere conjecture.

Actions for Death.—By Fatal Accidents Act an executor or administrator of a deceased person or other interested party may, for benefit of wife, husband, parent, and child or other near relative bring an action for damages against party causing death of such person. Such action must be brought within six months on behalf of deceased or otherwise within three years of such death. Further, under Survival of Action Act, cause of action survives for benefit of deceased person's estate and damages are recoverable for benefit of estate. Such action, which is in addition to any right of action under Fatal Accidents Act, must be instituted within three years of death of deceased person.

Death certificate may be obtained from the Registrar General, Registry of Records, Nassau, fee, B$10.00.

DECEDENTS' ESTATES:

See topics Curtesy; Descent and Distribution; Dower; Executors and Administrators; Wills.

DEEDS:

Execution.—A deed should be signed, sealed and delivered by the person executing the same in the presence of at least one witness.

Recording of deeds in The Registry of Records is not compulsory but affords priority of title.

To be recorded in The Registry of Records an affidavit of proof has to be sworn to by attesting witness (see topic Affidavits) and stamped, if not stampable under specific head, deeds bear duty of B$10.

Stamp Duty on Conveyances.—Duty is normally payable on ad valorem basis on value of real property and any chattels passing under transaction as follows: Consideration of up to $20,000, 2% of consideration; consideraton of over $20,000 and up to $50,000, 4%; of over $50,000 and up to $100,000, 6%; over $100,000, 8%.

In absence of agreement to contrary, duty to pay stamp duty rests jointly and severally upon parties to instrument or transaction. Where no beneficial interest passes or conveyance is through trust duty may be mitigated.

Short forms of conveyances, mortgages, and other deeds are given in the Schedules to The Conveyancing and Law of Property Act (Bahamas).

DEPOSITIONS: See topic Affidavits.

DESCENT AND DISTRIBUTION:

By The Inheritance Act (Bahamas), inheritance of real estate is traced from the last purchaser; descendants of the purchaser take before any other relation; males take before females in the same degree; and the eldest male is preferred to the younger males in the same degree. If there are no descendants, the nearest male paternal ancestor takes. Female heirs of the same degree take equally as co-parceners.

Surviving Spouse.—By the Imperial Act, the Statute of Distributions, 22 & 23 Charles 11, c. 10, extended to the Bahamas by c. 2 of 1799, if an intestate leaves a widow and children, the widow takes one-third of the personal estate and the children take the remainder. If there are no children, the widow takes a moiety and the residue of the estate is distributed equally among the next of kin of the intestate who are in equal degree and those who legally represent them. The husband is entitled to the personal estate of his wife if she dies intestate.

By The Widows of Intestates Act (Bahamas), if a man dies intestate leaving a widow but no issue, widow is entitled to his real and personal estate if same does not exceed in net value B$200 and if estate exceeds sum of B$150(sic) widow is entitled B$200 and charge for such sum on real and personal estates with interest thereon from date of death of intestate at 4% per annum until payment.

See also topics Absentees, subhead Escheat; Curtesy; Dower.

DISPUTE RESOLUTION:

At present only forms of alternate dispute resolution available to parties are:

(1) Voluntary dispute resolution pursuant to Arbitration Act, c. 168; and

(2) Mandatory dispute resolution under Industrial Relations (Amendment) Act, 1996, whereby responsible minister may, if public interest so requires, refer dispute within Act to industrial tribunal in absence of settlement by parties within 16 days of report of dispute.

DIVORCE:

By The Supreme Court Act (Bahamas), the Chief Justice is the Judge Ordinary of the Divorce and Matrimonial Side of the Court; and subject to any rules made under the Act and to the laws in force in the Bahamas, the jurisdiction of the Court of Probate, Divorce and Matrimonial Causes for the time being in force in England, is deemed to be extended to the Bahamas. (See England Law Digest.) Under provisions of Matrimonial Causes Act, either husband or wife must prove against other since date of marriage either (a) Adultery, (b) cruelty, (c) desertion—two years, (d) separation for continuous period of five years, or (e) homosexuality, sodomy or bestiality. Wife may petition also on ground of rape during marriage. Act contains provisions relating, inter alia, to void and voidable marriages, property settlements, custody maintenance and education of children and for recognition of foreign decrees in certain cases.

DOWER:

Wife is entitled on death of her husband to one-third of her husband's lands for her life provided he was solely seised of an estate of inheritance and issue of marriage capable of inheriting might have been born.

A wife may renounce her dower during her husband's lifetime or release her dower after his death. There is no dower in an equitable estate owned by husband or in a condominium unit. It is possible to prevent dower attaching to land purchased by husband by drafting conveyance to "uses to bar dower."

ENVIRONMENT:

Environmental Health Act provides for regulations to be made by Minister of Health and Environment to give effect to provisions of Act dealing with topics of air and water pollution, sanitation and waste disposal. Act also provides for establishment of Department of Environmental Health Services to implement provisions of Act and Regulations thereunder, and Environmental Health Board to advise on matters concerning environment referred to it by Minister.

EXCHANGE CONTROL:

See topic Foreign Exchange, Investment and Trade.

EXECUTIONS:

Judgments may be enforced by attachment of debts or by writ of fieri facias. The Court has power to appoint a receiver in aid of equitable execution.

EXECUTORS AND ADMINISTRATORS:

An executor is appointed by the will and an administrator by the Court. Probate of a will will not be granted for at least 14 days after the death. Letters of administration are granted after a notice of the application has been published in three successive issues of the official newspaper; the hearing of the application may not be earlier than 14 days from the date of the notice.

The Supreme Court has power to seal with the seal of the probate Probate or letters of administration granted by a court of probate in Great Britain or in any part of British Commonwealth, or in U.S.A.

The Real Estate Devolution Act (Bahamas) vests in the personal representatives, as if it were a chattel real, real estate vested in the deceased without a right in any other person to take by survivorship. One year is usually allowed to personal representatives for winding up an estate. Personal representatives are not liable after public notice has been given of their intention to distribute the estate after a specified date, in respect of any claims of which they have not received notice.

By The Personal Representatives Remuneration Act (Bahamas), executors and administrators are entitled to a commission of 5% on amount of all sums which come into their hands in execution of their trusts.

Probate Duty.—See topic Taxation.

See also topic Death.

EXEMPTIONS:

The wearing apparel and bedding of a person and his family, and the tools and implements of his trade to value of B$100, may not be taken under distress issued by magistrate.

EXPORTS:

The Export Manufacturing Industries Encouragement Act, 1989 makes provision for establishment and development of export manufacturing industries and for matters connected therewith. Export manufacturer is one who annually exports at least 95% of output. Both manufacturer and product require ministerial approval. Raw materials and machinery may be imported free of customs duty under bond by approved export manufacturer.

FOREIGN CORPORATIONS: See topic Corporations.

FOREIGN EXCHANGE, INVESTMENT AND TRADE:

Purchase and conversion of foreign currency and trade are controlled by Central Bank of Bahamas acting in liaison with appropriate Government Ministry. All foreign businesses operating in Bahamas and foreign capital used for investment in Bahamas should be registered with Central Bank of Bahamas and "approved" status for such investment sought. Such status broadly speaking allows repatriation of immediate income and eventual capital proceeds and profit. Such investments, whether or not operated through company or corporation, will receive "resident" or "nonresident" status according to their degree of involvement with Bahamas. Financial transactions of resident businesses, companies etc., should normally be carried out with Bahamian dollars, and vice versa, but exceptions are sometimes made with approval of Controller of Exchange. Persons living but not working in The Bahamas for less than one year from date of arrival are treated as nonresident as are holders of Certificates of Permanent Residence without right to work. Other foreigners living in The Bahamas for less than ten years are treated as temporary residents.

The Bahamas Investment Incentives Act 1991 establishes various zones for "approved developer" or licensee to be granted certain exceptions and fiscal incentives in respect of certain manufacturing, industrial or other business undertakings or enterprises.

In addition Bahamas Government has enacted Investment Programme designed to attract capital and technology. Under this scheme approved persons will be guaranteed tax exemptions and will be granted permanent residence status. It is also designed to attract persons in sphere of the arts. *Note:* This programme is presently under review.

FOREIGN INVESTMENTS:

See topic Foreign Exchange, Investment and Trade.

See Topical Index in front part of this volume.

FOREIGN TRADE REGULATIONS:

See topic Foreign Exchange, Investment and Trade.

FRAUDS, STATUTE OF:

The former English Statute of Frauds, 29 Charles 2, c. 3, is extended to Bahamas by c. 2 of 1799.

FRAUDULENT SALES AND CONVEYANCES:

The Imperial Statute, The Fraudulent Conveyances Act, 27 Elizabeth, c. 4, is extended to the Bahamas by c. 2 of 1799. The Act provides for avoiding mischiefs by fraudulent conveyances of lands. Fraudulent conveyances made to deceive purchasers are declared void as against such purchasers.

By The Voluntary Conveyances Act (Bahamas), voluntary conveyances, if bona fide and without any fraudulent intent, may not be avoided under Act of the Imperial Parliament 27 Elizabeth, c. 4.

By Fraudulent Disposition Act, 1991 any disposition of property made with intent to defraud and at undervalue shall only be voidable at instance of creditor within two years of date of such disposition. Onus of proof of intent to defraud is upon creditor.

GARNISHMENT: See England Law Digest.

HOLIDAYS:

The Public Holidays Act (Bahamas) provides that the following days shall be kept as close holidays in all public offices and banks and in all shops as defined by the Act: Jan. 1, Good Friday, 1st Mon. after Easter, 1st Mon. after Whitsunday, Labour Day (1st Fri. in June), Independence Day (July 10), 1st Mon. in Aug., Oct. 12, Christmas Day, Boxing Day (Dec. 26). Government offices are not open on Saturdays.

If holiday falls on Sunday, following day is usually observed in its place. No concessions are usually made for holiday falling on Saturday.

Bill of exchange falling due on Saturday, Sunday or holiday normally matures on next business day.

Most shops are forbidden to do business on Sundays or holidays.

HUSBAND AND WIFE:

By The Married Women's Property Act (Bahamas), a married woman is capable of holding property and of disposing by will or otherwise of any real or personal property as her separate property in the same manner as if she were a feme sole. The Act provides that a married woman may convey any real estate to her husband, and a husband may convey any real estate to his wife, alone or jointly with another person. The separate property of a married woman which she is restrained from anticipating is not available to satisfy contracts entered into by her.

No community property laws exist.

IMMIGRATION: See topic Aliens.

INFANCY:

Age of majority in most cases is 18 for both sexes. Parents are not normally responsible for torts of their children, who themselves remain liable.

Marriage.—Consent is generally required from parents. See topic Marriage.

Contracts.—By Infants Relief Act, most contracts, except for sale of necessaries are void. Certain other contracts, involving proprietary rights become binding upon majority unless repudiated within reasonable time.

Guardianship.—Guardianship and Custody of Infants Act 1961 governs.

Adoption.—See topic Adoption.

Limitation of Actions.—Infancy is a bar to respective periods of limitation of actions.

See also topic Wills.

INHERITANCE TAX:

None. See topic Taxation.

INSURANCE:

Nation Insurance Act, 1972, lays down provisions for weekly contribution by employers and employees, and self-employed persons, and benefits payable to retired persons, sick or injured persons, widows and women during childbirth.

Motor Cars.—Wide forms of insurance are possible and usual, though only third party risk is compulsory.

INTEREST:

The Money Lending Act gives the Supreme Court or any Magisterial Court, to the extent to which it has civil jurisdiction under any act, power to re-open a transaction which is harsh and unconscionable, and to take an account between the lender and the person sued.

Judgments of Supreme Court bear interest at rate of B$6 per centum per annum.

The Rate of Interest Act provides that maximum permitted rate of interest on any loan of more than B$100 shall be 20% per annum and any loan not exceeding such amount, 30% per annum. Such permitted rate shall not apply to loans in foreign currency or loans made in Bahamian currency by institutions licensed under provisions of The Banks and Trust Companies Regulations Act, 1965. Recent amendment to Act seeks to avoid any question that loan may otherwise be void if there is provision for capitalization of arrears of interest which could result in such maximum rate being exceeded. Privy Council has ruled subsequent to this Amendment that, upon proper construction of Act prior to such Amendment, position was thus in any event. See also topic Corporations.

JOINT STOCK COMPANIES: See topic Corporations.

JUDGMENTS:

Judgment of the Supreme Court, unless otherwise provided by the rules of the Supreme Court, must be obtained by motion for judgment.

Summary judgment may be obtained in Supreme Court when amount sought to be recovered or value of property in dispute exceeds B$3,000.

By means of a specially indorsed writ of summons, summary judgment may be obtained in respect of a claim for a liquidated demand in money.

By The Judgments Act 1931 (Bahamas), all judgments entered up in the Supreme Court bind the real estate of the judgment debtor, and have priority according to the respective days on which they were so filed.

The Reciprocal Enforcement of Judgments Act (Bahamas) is expressed to be an act to facilitate the reciprocal enforcement of judgments, orders and awards in the Bahamas and the United Kingdom and other parts of British Commonwealth.

By The Maintenance Orders Facilities for Enforcement Act (Bahamas), provision is made for the enforcement in the Bahamas of maintenance orders made in England or Ireland.

LABOUR RELATIONS:

Functions are vested in a Minister of Labour and are codified in The Industrial Relations Act, 1970. Act is divided into three main parts: organisation, powers and duties of trade unions; industrial agreements and an industrial relations board; and maintenance of law and protection of private rights. Said Act has now been amended to provide for creation of industrial tribunal, which tribunal shall have power to order reengagement, reinstatment and orders for awards of compensation and damages or payment of exemplary damages.

Fair Labour Standards Act, 1970 deals with such subjects as right of employee to know precise terms of employment; minimum legal wages, holidays etc.

Female Employees (Grant of Maternity Leave) Act, 1988, provides for grant of maternity leave and security of employment during such leave.

LAW REPORTS:

There are some published reports of cases but generally speaking files containing relevant information are open for inspection. English common law decisions are generally binding in Bahamas and are reported in U.K.

LEGISLATURE:

See topic Constitution and Government.

LICENSES:

License is required to carry on businesses of hotels, banking, trusts and insurance. Licenses are also required to operate shop or restaurant or sell liquor; for music and dancing, showing films, acting as auctioneer or as travelling salesman, making beer or spirits, and operating taxi cabs.

Additional license of The Grand Bahama Port Authority is required for all businesses at Freeport, Grand Bahama.

The Business Licence Act provides with certain exceptions that all persons and companies carrying on business or practising profession in Bahamas must obtain business licence annually, cost of which is percentage of gross profits arrived at by reference to scale. Nonresident owned companies pay yearly fee of $100.

LIENS: See England Law Digest.

LIMITATION OF ACTIONS:

The Limitation of Actions Act 1995 came into force on 28th Aug., 1995 and it repeals earlier Limitations of Actions Act. New Act also repeals Real Property Limitations Acts and various other limitation statutes. Actions must be brought within following periods after respective causes of actions accrue.

Twelve Months.—Any action or proceeding against any person for any act, alleged or neglect or default done in pursuance or execution of any statutory duty or any public duty or authority.

Two Years.—Recovery of contribution between tortfeasors.

Three Years.—Personal injuries: negligence, nuisance or breach of duty in respect of; actions for damages in respect of wrongful acts causing death.

Six Years.—Simple contract, actions to recover any sum by virtue of any written law actions to enforce recognisance or judgment, actions for negligence in respect of latent damage not involving personal injuries and generally all torts for which no other period of limitation is provided.

Twelve Years.—Actions upon deeds, actions for recovery of principal moneys secured by mortgage or other charge, recovery of lands: 12 years adverse possession of land defeats title of owner except against persons under disability. Time will run against reversioners of remaindermen only from date of vesting of such estates in possession.

Fifteen Years.—Negligence actions not involving personal injuries.

Exceptions.—Act contains provisions extending prescribed limitation periods in cases involving disability, acknowledgment, part payment, fraud and mistake. Transitional section provides inter alia that no action can be brought which was barred before coming into force of Act by any written law repealed by Act. Furthermore, any action pending at commencement of Act shall be determined in accordance with law in force immediately preceding that commencement.

Act Not Applicable.—1995 Act will not affect equitable jurisdiction of Supreme Court to refuse relief on ground of acquiescence, laches etc. Similarly, Act has no application to any action for which period of limitation is prescribed by some other law (e.g. The Fraudulent Dispositions Act 1991).

See Topical Index in front part of this volume.

LIMITED PARTNERSHIP: See topic Partnership.

MARRIAGE:

Depending on the circumstances persons under age not being widowers or widows must have the consent of both parents or one of them or of a legal custodian or of the surviving parent and guardian or guardian alone; in the event that such consent cannot be obtained of the Chief Justice.

The Marriage Act (Bahamas) provides that marriage may be solemnized under authority of: (1) Registrar's certificate or registrar's certificates; (2) marriage officer's certificate or marriage officer's certificates; (3) license from Registar General. Fee of B$20 is charged for such license.

Prohibited Marriages.—Under provisions of The Marriage Act marriages within prohibited degrees of consanguinity or affinity according to law of Bahamas are null and void. However, no law has been promulgated in The Bahamas setting forth prohibited degrees.

There are no restrictions on marriage with a foreigner.

See also topic Husband and Wife.

MARRIED WOMEN:

See topics Acknowledgments; Descent and Distribution; Dower; Husband and Wife.

MONEY LAUNDERING:

The U.S. Treaty on Mutual Assistance in Criminal Matters, ratified by Government of The Bahamas, has received legal recognition in the The Mutual Legal Assistance Act. The Tracing and Forfeiture of Proceeds of Drug Trafficking Act and Act to Further Facilitate the Combating of the Laundering of the Proceeds of Drug Trafficking (Money Laundering Act) are aimed at tracing assets of drug traffickers and identifying and punishing those facilitating laundering of such assets.

MONOPOLIES AND RESTRAINT OF TRADE:

The common law of England rules.

MORTGAGES:

Registration of mortgages of both real and personal property gives priority of title. An equitable mortgage of real property can be created by deposit of the title deeds with an accompanying memorandum.

First legal mortgage of real property operates to vest legal estate in mortgagee.

Stamp duty on mortgages amounts to 1% of sum assured.

MOTOR VEHICLES:

Driver's license and motor car license are required.

A bona fide visitor may import an automobile into the Bahamas for a period of not more than six months free of duty. However, at their discretion H.M. Customs can require a cash deposit of the amount of the duty which is refundable at the time of exportation within the six months period.

Having entered the Bahamas the automobile should not be driven until it has been licensed. As a prerequisite to being licensed a Certificate of Insurance or insurance clearance must be obtained locally. The minimum insurance required by a resident is unlimited third party (bodily injury) risks but in the case of a bona fide visitor The Road Traffic Authority may exercise a discretion.

The procedure normally followed by visitors bringing automobiles to the Bahamas is to have their own insurance policies endorsed by the insuring companies for the purpose of extending the validity of such policies to the Bahamas. The Road Traffic Authority here in exercise of its discretion referred to earlier may accept such endorsed policies or require a Certificate of Insurance from local Authorized Agents.

License or registration fees are based upon square footage of vehicle, minimum fee being B$75 per annum for automobiles of up to and including 60 square feet. Over 60 square feet, there is a further charge according to size of automobile, maximum fee being B$360. It will be noted that these are annual fees. Annual drivers' license costs B$16.25 throughout Bahamas, as does compulsory Road Traffic Inspection Certificate.

Visitors may use valid American, Canadian and International Drivers licenses (providing holder thereof is not under 17 years of age) until they expire or for three months whichever is the shorter period.

Import Duty.—There is import duty on motor vehicles imported which fluctuates, depending on value of vehicle between 45% and 65%. See topic Taxation, subhead Import Duties. In addition, 7% ad and valorem stamp duty is payable.

See also topics Insurance; Contracts, subhead Hire-Purchase.

NEGOTIABLE INSTRUMENTS:

See topic Bills and Notes.

NOTARIES PUBLIC:

Notaries Public Act, 1971, gives qualifications for being licensed by appropriate Minister to act as notary, viz: (a) any person duly admitted to practise as Counsel and Attorney of Supreme Court of the Bahamas; (b) any person duly admitted as notary when Act came into force; (c) certain government and public officers. Application may be made to Minister by duly qualified persons, who can issue license for up to one year. Complaint as to misconduct or unfitness may be made to Supreme Court.

PARTNERSHIP:

The Partnership Act (Bahamas) declares the law of partnership and deals with the nature of partnerships; the relations of partners to persons dealing with them; the relation of partners to one another; the dissolution of partnerships and its consequences; and provides for the saving of the rules of equity and of common law.

Note: There is presently new draft Partnership Bill under discussion.

Limited Partnership.—The Partnership Limited Liability Act (Bahamas) authorizes the formation of partnerships with limited liability. As greater advantages can be obtained under The Companies Act, limited partnerships are rarely if ever formed.

Exempted Limited Partnerships.—("ELPs") are governed by newly enacted Exempted Limited Partnership Act. Although ELPs are prohibited from carrying on business with "public in The Bahamas", other than as necessary for purposes of carrying on its external business, this term does not include Bahamian registered IBCs or foreign companies. ELPs are exempted from all business licence fees, other taxes such as income, inheritance and stamp tax and exchange control regulations for period of 50 years. Registration and annual fee in respect of ELPs is B$850.

ELPs are created by filing statement with Registrar containing particulars prescribed by Act and consist of one or more general partners and one or more limited partners. Former are liable for debts and obligations of partnership in event of shortfall; latter incur no liability, other than may be provided in partnership agreement, unless such partner takes part in conduct of business of partnership. Partners may be non-Bahamian or domestic corporations or partnerships. ELPs acquire limited liability upon issue of Certificate of Registration by Registrar. ELPs are dissolved by partners subsequent to filing notice of dissolution with Registrar. Provisions of Partnership Limited Liability Act are not applicable to ELPs.

PATENTS:

Under Industrial Property Act 1965 and Industrial Property Rules 1967, Registrar General has power to direct issue of letters patent to an applicant which shall extend to Bahamas.

Application for grant of a patent according to forms in schedule to Act is directed to Registrar General and is accompanied by specifications of invention and filed at Industrial Property Department at Registry of Records.

Every person obtaining letters patent may make, use, exercise, and vend within Bahamas the invention described in specification for a period of four years. Renewal of privileges is annual thereafter for a total period of 15 years.

Act generally consolidates and amends law relating to patents for inventions and trademarks, and provides for protection of industrial designs, and penalizes application of false trade descriptions to goods.

PERPETUITIES:

New Perpetuties Act of 1995 modifies rule against perpetuties to provide that disposition of non-vested interest in property becomes void if interest does not vest within perpetuity period defined by Act, being lives of persons living plus 21 years or, if none specified, 80 years. Act also introduces "wait and see" principle.

PLEDGES: See England Law Digest.

PRESCRIPTION:

See topic Limitation of Actions.

PRINCIPAL AND AGENT:

See England Law Digest.

REAL PROPERTY:

All real property in the Bahamas is held in fee simple, that is to say the freeholder holds feudally of the Crown, who is the supreme owner.

By The Escheat Act (Bahamas), the Crown must establish to the satisfaction of the Court the right of the Crown to escheat property on the grounds alleged in the information.

Property may be conveyed or devised for any interest recognized by the common law or equity. An estate tail is rarely if ever created in Bahamas, and if so created may be enlarged to estate in fee simple by virtue of The Estates Tail Barring Act (Bahamas).

Adverse possession for 60 years against the Crown, and for 20 years, with certain exceptions, against an individual, establishes a good possessory title.

The Imperial Act, the Law of Property Act 1925, is not in effect in the Bahamas.

Condominium Units are governed by Law of Property and Conveyancing (Condominium) Acts.

The Rent Control Act, 1975, applies to any dwelling where value does not exceed B$25,000. Rent payable for any dwelling subject to Act shall not exceed 20% per annum of its value as determined under Act with additional permitted maximum if dwelling is let furnished. Presently, rent payable has been established at 15%.

See also topics Aliens; Corporations, subhead Foreign Companies; and topics Foreign Exchange, Investment and Trade, and Taxation, subhead Real Property Tax.

RECORDS:

All deeds relating to land may, and should, as a matter of course, be recorded in the Registry of Records.

Public Records Act, 1971, provides for official registration and custody of official records, and for appointment of archivist.

REPLEVIN:

The common law applies. By §185 of The Magistrates Act, magistrates have jurisdiction in replevin.

SALES:

The Sale of Goods Act (Bahamas) is virtually a re-enactment of the Imperial Statute, The Sale of Goods Act 1893. See England Law Digest.

Warranties.—There is no special legislation dealing with guarantees of quality. See however topic Contracts, subhead Hire-Purchase.

SEALS: See England Law Digest.

SEQUESTRATION: See England Law Digest.

SHIPPING:

The Merchant Shipping Act, 1976 (Bahamas) as am'd, came into operation on Dec. 31st, 1976. In it provision is made for registration of ships; for control, regulation and orderly development of merchant shipping; for proper qualification of persons employed in sea service; for regulation of terms and conditions of service of persons so employed; and for matters connected with an incidental to foregoing.

The Carriage of Goods by Sea Act (Bahamas) makes uniform the law with respect to the carriage of goods by sea.

The Pilotage Act (Bahamas) regulates the powers and duties of the Pilotage Board and matters relating to pilots and pilotage.

The Bahamas Maritime Authority (Created by The Bahamas Maritime Authority Act, 1995) is responsible, inter alia, for regulation, control and administration of all matters related to merchant shipping as provided for under Merchant Shipping Act (including collection of all registration, annual and other fees and moneys) or any other law. Authority, a corporate body, comprises Chairman, Deputy Chairman and five other members appointed by Minister responsible for maritime affairs. It is presided over by Director of Maritime Affairs (who has general managing direction of authority and superintendance of ships registered in Bahamas), Deputy Directors and staff recruited from without Civil Service, all of whom are employees of Authority. Act prescribes relationship between Authority and Minister.

See also topic Aliens.

STATUTES:

Statute laws are set out in full in the "Statute Law of The Bahamas 1987" as am'd by annual supplements.

TAXATION:

The chief source of revenue is from import duties. See subhead Import Duties, infra.

There are no death duties in respect of real or personal estate and no succession, estate or inheritance duties or taxes of any kind.

There are no income tax, company, dividend, share certificate, or gift taxes of any nature.

Import Duties.—In most cases there is an import duty in accordance with a published scale ad valorem.

Under certain circumstances, chiefly in connection with a business goods may be imported free of duty into Freeport, Grand Bahama.

Real Property Tax.—There is property tax which has been extended to cover all of Bahamas and both developed and undeveloped land; property owned by non-Bahamians is particularly affected. Rate of tax for owner-occupied houses is: (a) On first $500,000 of assessed value on which tax is payable 1% per annum, (b) on assessed value in excess of $500,000, 1½% per annum. Rate of tax for property used for commercial or industrial purpose is: (a) On first $500,000 of assessed value 1% per annum, (b) on assessed value in excess of $500,000 2% per annum. There is exemption for owner-occupation in respect of first $100,000 of assessed value.

Stamp Duties.—In addition to other specific duties (see topics Corporations, Deeds, and Mortgages) various stamp duties are imposed. Duty on debentures is B$4 per B$1,000 assured.

TRADEMARKS AND TRADENAMES:

Trademarks.—The Trade Marks Act (Bahamas) is in effect largely based on the Imperial Trade Marks Act, 1905. The Imperial Trade Marks Act, 1937, has not been extended to the Bahama Islands.

The Trade Marks Amendment Act 1959 (Bahamas) provides in certain instances that a person other than the proprietor of a trade mark may be registered as a registered user thereof in respect of all or any of the goods in respect of which it is registered (otherwise than as a defensive trade mark) and either with or without conditions or restrictions. The Act also provides for defensive registration of well known trade marks consisting of an invented word or invented words.

The Registrar General keeps at the Registry of Records a register of trademarks. Appeals from any decision of the Registrar General lie to the Supreme Court.

Tradenames.—The common law applies. A man is not allowed to use from dishonest motives a tradename used by another.

The Registration of Business Names Act, 1989 has not yet come into operation. It provides for registration of firms, individuals and corporations carrying on business under business names.

See also topic Patents.

TREATIES:

Bahamas is signatory to The Hague Convention Abolishing the Requirement of Legalisation for Foreign Public Documents.

See also England Law Digest.

TRUSTS:

The Imperial Act cited as the Trustee Act 1893 (56 & 57 Victoria, c. 53) is extended to the Bahamas by Bahamas Statute, c. 20, of 1899. The Act provides inter alia for investments, the various powers and duties of trustees, the appointment of new trustees and vesting orders, the payment into Court by trustees, and miscellaneous matters such as the sanctioning of the sale of land or minerals separately.

The Judicial Trustees Act 1969 provides power for Supreme Court to appoint a trustee. The Public Trustee Act 1970 establishes office of Public Trustee.

The Trust (Choice of Governing Law) Act, 1989 provides for choice of governing law in creation of trusts and for matters connected therewith. Settlor, whether or not resident or domiciled in The Bahamas, may expressly declare in trust instrument that laws of The Bahamas shall be governing law of trust. No disposition of property held on trust that is valid under laws of The Bahamas can be set aside by reference to foreign law.

VISITORS:

See topics Currency; Foreign Exchange, Investment and Trade and Motor Vehicles.

WILLS:

The Imperial Acts cited as The Wills Act and The Wills Act Amendment Act 1852 (1 Victoria, c. 26; 15 & 16 Victoria, c. 24) have been extended to the Bahamas by c. 23 of 1841 and c. 21 of 1854, respectively.

Testamentary Capacity.—No will made by any person under age of 18 years is valid.

Testamentary Disposition.—Any property real or personal is capable of being devised or bequeathed by will.

Execution.—A will must be signed by the testator in the presence of two attesting witnesses present at the same time. Exception is made in the case of soldiers and sailors on active service.

Revocation.—A will is revoked by marriage.

Gift to an attesting witness is void.

Construction.—A devise without any words of limitation must be construed to pass the fee simple or the whole other estate or interest in such real estate which the testator had power to dispose of by will, unless a contrary intention appears by the will.

Probate Duty.—Nil. See topic Taxation.

See also topic Absentees, subhead Escheat.

BELGIUM LAW DIGEST REVISER

De Bandt, van Hecke & Lagae
Rue Brederode 13
B-1000 Brussels, Belgium
Telephone: 32 2 517 94 11
Fax: 32 2 517 94 94

Reviser Profile

History: The firm was founded in Brussels in 1969 and has offices in Brussels, Antwerp, New York and London.

Areas of Emphasis and Growth: The firm engages exclusively in a business oriented practice and operates as a full service firm with departmental specialization, including Business and Finance, Corporate, European Community Law, Taxation, Labour, Litigation, Maritime and Transport. The firm consists of 32 partners, 2 counsel and 80 associates, with a support staff of 96 staff members including paralegals.

Client Base: Clients of the firm are predominantly international corporations, a large number of which are operating in Europe from a Belgian base.

Firm Activities: All lawyers of the firm are members of the Brussels, Belgium Bar and three of its partners are also qualified to practice before the Supreme Court of Belgium. Two other partners are members of the New York Bar.

Management: The firm is managed by a committee of partners of varying seniority. The Management Committee monitors performance, client relationship, economic and technological development as well as firm growth and reports to the full Partners Meeting.

BELGIUM LAW DIGEST

(The following is a list of all Topics, including cross-references, covered in this Digest.)

BELGIUM LAW DIGEST

Revised for 1997 edition by

DE BANDT, VAN HECKE & LAGAE, avocats in Brussels.

(Abbreviations used are: C. C., Civil Code; Comm. C., Commercial Code; Const., Constitution; E. E. C., European Economic Community; Hyp., Law on Liens and Mortgages; Cons. Comp., Consolidated Laws on Companies; Jud. C., Judicial Code; R. D., Royal Decree.)

Belgium is member of EU. See also European Union Law Digest.

ABSENTEES:

Absent persons can act through attorney in fact. If whereabouts unknown, court can appoint provisional administrator. (C. C. 112). See topic Death.

ACKNOWLEDGMENTS:

The form of an act is that of the country where it was drawn up. If it is to be used in Belgium, the signature of the foreign officer (e. g., a notary) before whom it was acknowledged must be certified by the authorities of his country, the latter signature then being certified by a Belgian consular or diplomatic officer abroad. This procedure is simplified for public deeds drawn in one of countries having ratified Hague Convention of Oct. 5, 1961. (Belgian Law of June 5, 1975).

ACTIONS:

See topics Aliens, subhead Actions by Aliens; Courts.

Limitation of.—See topic Limitation of Actions.

ADMINISTRATION:

See topic Executors and Administrators.

ADVERSE POSSESSION:

See topic Limitation of Actions.

AFFIDAVITS:

Affidavits, such as provided for by English and Canadian law, do not exist under the law of Belgium. A Belgian lawyer may, however, swear a "Certificat de Coutume" (Declaration as to Custom) before the consul of the country whose court requires to have precisions regarding Belgian law. Moreover pursuant to European convention on information relating to foreign law (signed in London on June 7th, 1968), such information can be obtained through official channels.

AGENCY: See topic Principal and Agent.

ALIENS:

Status and capacity are governed by the alien's national law. (C. C. 3).

Residence.—Under present regulations, before right to live in Belgium more than three months is issued to non-EEC citizens, latter is recommended to have obtained firstly work permit or professional card.

Civil Rights.—The Constitution grants aliens on Belgian soil the same protection as Belgian citizens, both for themselves and their belongings, save a few minor exceptions established by law. (Const. 191). Practically, position of aliens in civil matters is nearly same as that of Belgian citizens.

Real property located in Belgium and owned by aliens is governed by Belgian law. (C. C. 3).

Actions by Aliens.—Aliens suing in Belgium may be compelled at request of Belgian defending party, unless a treaty removes this ability, to give such surety as court may fix, considering costs of suit and amount of damages to which alien plaintiff might be sentenced. (Jud. C. 851-852).

Actions Against Aliens.—Where a foreigner is resident in Belgium civil proceedings can always be commenced against him. There are also numerous cases where a foreigner not resident in Belgium can be summoned to appear before Belgian courts: e. g., where proceedings concern real estate situate in Belgium, contracts entered into or to be performed in Belgium, claims enforced in Belgium, bankruptcy declared in Belgium, choice of forum clause, etc. (Jud. C. 635). Belgian courts also have jurisdiction on basis of plaintiff's residence, unless alien defendant shows that his country's courts would not take jurisdiction in converse situation. (Jud. C. 638 and 636). See also Brussels Convention of Sept. 27, 1968 on jurisdiction and recognition of judgments and bilateral conventions.

Alien Workers and Professional People.—Non-E.E.C. citizens may only work in Belgium if they have first obtained, in case of employees, salesmen or workmen, work permit ("Permis de Travail"—"Arbeidskaart"). In addition, employer who engages aliens must in principle be licensed thereto. Permit is sent to applicant who has to obtain from Belgian embassy or consulate special visa authorizing person in question to reside in Belgium, unless applicant is already residing validly in Belgium at time of application. (R. D. No. 34 of July 20, 1967).

In case of non-E.E.C. subjects who wish to exercise in Belgium independent profession (businessman, lawyer, etc.) they must apply for Professional Card ("Carte Professionnelle"—"Beroepskaart"). Their application must be filed by means of special forms issued by Belgian embassy or consulate of their place of residence or by local authorities, if alien applicant is already residing in Belgium on another basis. Request is examined and thereafter Professional Card is issued; this permits issue of special visa of establishment. (Law of Feb. 19, 1965, R.D. of Aug. 2, 1985).

In case of refusal by the Belgian Authorities to issue either work permit or Professional Card, it is possible to appeal.

Corporations owned or controlled by aliens enjoy same rights as corporations owned or controlled by Belgian citizens, except only with respect to licensing for performance of public works, and flag requirements for aircraft and for ships.

For other provisions relating to aliens, see topics Copyright; Descent and Distribution; Divorce; Marriage.

ALIMONY: See topic Divorce.

ASSIGNMENTS:

In order to be operative against debtor or obligor and against creditors of assignor, assignment or pledge of rights and of debts not embodied in negotiable instrument must be formally notified by bailiff to debtor or obligor or acknowledged by debtor or obligor in public deed. (C. C. 1690).

Business debts evidenced by an invoice can be assigned or pledged to a bank or financial institution by endorsing the invoice.

ASSOCIATIONS:

Nonprofit associations can be incorporated with limited liability by publication of articles.

There is also possible incorporation by Royal Decree for international scientific associations.

ATTACHMENT:

Creditor may, in urgent cases (e. g., when debtor is disposing of his personal property), obtain from court authority to attach debtor's movables. (Jud. C. 1413). Bearer of a bill of exchange protested for default of payment may also obtain permission to attach movables of drawer and endorsers and of a drawee who has accepted bill. (Cons. Laws on Bills of Exch. 94).

Any creditor, if existence of debt is sufficiently established, may obtain authority to attach debts, property or amounts due to his debtor in hands of third persons. (Jud. C. 1447).

Creditor holding prima facie evidence (e.g. acknowledgment by debtor or bill of exchange accepted and protested) may, on that sole title, without any permission of court, attach and issue garnishee order to any third persons holding property of or owing money to his debtor and thus attach all amounts due from them to debtor. (Jud. C. 1445).

Lessors or lessees subleasing have a right, day after summons to pay, to seize tenant's furniture and chattels for unpaid rent. (Jud. C. 1461).

Certain items judged essential for living or for exercising profession, may not be seized; salaries and pensions may be seized only in part.

BANKRUPTCY:

There are three types of bankruptcy in Belgium: (1) ordinary non-dishonorable bankruptcy; (2) bankruptcy resulting from gross extravagance, etc.; (3) fraudulent bankruptcy.

Only traders can be declared bankrupts.

A trader who ceases due payments and whose credit is wavering or who is insolvent is deemed to be in a state of bankruptcy. (Comm. C. 437).

Within three days after cessation of payments, bankrupt must enter at the office of the clerk of the commercial court of his domicile a declaration accompanied by a balance sheet or a note explaining why he cannot deposit his balance sheet and other books which he is under obligation to keep according to merchant law. (Comm. C. 440).

Bankruptcy may also be declared by the commercial court on petition or summons of one or more creditors, or on the court's own motion. (Comm. C. 442).

The court designates one or more sworn trustees, and appoints judicial commissioner to control and supervise liquidation of bankrupt's estate. By same judgment court fixes date of cessation of payments, which must be within six months preceding bankruptcy decree. Latter decree divests bankrupt of administration of his property, and all payments or transactions by bankrupt or to or with him after bankruptcy decree are null and void, as are also following transactions, if carried out by bankrupt after date fixed by court as that of cessation of payments, or within ten days preceding that date: Donations of movables and immovables; transfers of property when consideration is grossly less than real value; payments of debts before maturity; payments of debts at maturity otherwise than in cash or negotiable instruments; mortgages and rights of security created over property of debtor to secure debts previously contracted (Comm. C. 445). All payments of debts at maturity and all other contracts and transfers of property for valuable consideration are voidable if persons receiving payment or dealing with debtor had knowledge of cessation of payments. (Comm. C. 446).

The bankruptcy decree matures all debts owing by the bankrupt. As regards the general body of creditors only, it stops the running of interest on unsecured or non-preferred debts, but not on debts secured by mortgage, pledge or other specific security.

The decree orders creditors to file at the office of the clerk of the commercial court a declaration of their claims and rights within a maximum period of 20 days. Creditors are notified by publications and advertisements, and also by registered letter, as soon as the trustees know their names. The period for declaration is increased in case of creditors domiciled outside of the kingdom.

The declaration must contain full particulars about the creditor, amount of and consideration for the debt and titles and preferential rights if any. This declaration

See Topical Index in front part of this volume.

BANKRUPTCY . . . *continued*
contains a solemn assertion and must be signed by creditor himself or by attorney, in which case stamped and registered power of attorney is filed with the declaration.

The trustees examine all creditors' claims after their declaration, with the help of the bankrupt, if possible, and under control of the judicial commissioner. Claims are either accepted or disputed. Creditors whose claims are disputed are notified, and a new meeting is held at which they are heard. All creditors whose claims are examined or admitted on the balance sheet have a right to attend and defend their claims. Claims insufficiently proved are transferred to court for examination.

After this examination has taken place, a meeting of the ordinary creditors is held, at which the bankrupt may obtain a composition in the event of an ordinary bankruptcy, if his proposals are accepted by a majority in number of the ordinary creditors present, personally or by proxy, representing at least three-fourths of the total amount of the claims admitted by the court. Secured creditors may not vote unless they waive their securities, or sell the same and prove for the balance. (Comm. C. 513). To be enforceable, the composition must be confirmed by the court, and opposition thereto may be made. Only this composition operates as a discharge.

If no composition takes place, the trustees liquidate the estate by selling the property of bankrupt and paying debts. They may, either with consent of judicial commissioner or with confirmation by court, terminate outstanding litigation by agreement.

Assets are equally divided among the creditors, after payment of costs and expenses of bankruptcy, including fees of trustees as determined by royal decree, after deduction of secured debts and necessaries provided for bankrupt, his wife and children, including actual living expenses.

When liquidation is terminated, a new meeting of creditors is held at which trustees make a report upon which court, taking advice of creditors, finds if bankrupt is or is not excusable. If excusable, he may rehabilitate himself. In the event of a fraudulent bankruptcy or a bankruptcy due to gross extravagance, the bankrupt may be tried by a criminal court, and in any event will not be granted the right to a composition.

Particulars regarding bankrupts' estates can be obtained at the registry of the commercial court through a lawyer.

Deeds of Arrangement with Creditors.—A trader can avoid bankruptcy by a prior agreement with his creditors. (Cons. Laws on Judicial Arrangements). To effect this he must enter, at the commercial court of his domicile, a petition with balance sheet and statement of facts on which he bases his request. The court proceeds to a preliminary examination of the case, and if results are favorable, a meeting of creditors is called which votes on the proposed deed.

Provided a majority in number and two-thirds in value of all creditors accept proposal and court confirms it, proposal becomes binding on all creditors. A composition applies only to debts prior to date thereof, and debtor becomes subject to supervision of court. Debts must be paid in full upon return to better fortune. Trader who has obtained deed of arrangement by fraud is deemed to be a bankrupt and is subject to prosecution in criminal courts.

In case of breach of deed of arrangement, or possibly in case of rejection, bankruptcy follows and date of cessation of payments may be carried back to six months before date of petition for such deed.

BILLS AND NOTES:

(Cons. Laws on Bills of Exch.).

A bill of exchange must include the words "bill of exchange." It must be dated and signed and must show amount to be paid, name of person liable to pay, time and place of payment, name of payee (either a third party or the drawer himself), place of drawing and rank of each copy if several are issued. If no date of payment is mentioned, the bill is payable at sight. A bill is always a trading transaction and under the jurisdiction of the commercial court except for bills under Frs.75,000 which are under jurisdiction of Justice of Peace.

The drawer or his agent must provide for payment. This is considered to have been done if, at maturity, the drawee is in possession of goods or funds or is debtor of the drawer or person for whom agent drew bill for at least the amount of bill. Absence of consideration at the date of maturity does not affect the validity of the bill. Negotiability is impaired only if formal rules have not been adhered to or if drawer was not of full capacity.

Acceptance may, at any time before maturity, be required by the holder, who is in certain cases under obligation to require acceptance before a certain date. Holder of a bill payable a certain number of days after presentment must demand acceptance within one year from signature. Failure to observe this period makes bearer lose his right of action against endorsers and drawer. Drawer and endorsers are jointly liable for acceptance by drawee. Acceptor is liable for payment. Acceptance is expressed by the word "accepted" or any equivalent term on the bill. The sole signature of drawee on the front of the bill means acceptance. Bills relating to transactions exceeding the limits of daily management in joint stock companies must bear two signatures for acceptance. Refusal of acceptance is established by a protest drawn up by a public officer.

Bills are transferred, with liens or mortgages attached, by endorsement. Endorsement after maturity is valid provided it takes place before the formal protest of nonpayment. Endorsement should give name of endorsees. Endorsement by means of mere signature of endorser on the back of the bill suffices. Holder may fill in an endorsement in blank. Undated endorsement is held prima facie to have been executed before protest of nonpayment. All who have signed, accepted or endorsed a bill are jointly liable to the holder.

Bills must be paid in the currency indicated therein. Foreign currency is payable in Belgian money at rate of exchange of day of maturity or at rate stipulated in the bill, unless the drawer has expressly stipulated in writing for payment in foreign currency.

Holder of a bill payable on an appointed date must demand payment on day it falls due. Holder of a bill payable at sight must demand payment within one year from signature, unless a shorter period has been indicated. Nonpayment must be established not later than the second day after maturity by a formal protest known as "protest of nonpayment." Failure to observe these periods of limitation and formalities makes bearer lose his right of action against endorsers and also against drawer who can show that he secured consideration. Holder of a protested bill must within four working days notify the last endorser and the drawer of the nonpayment, Every endorser must notify the previous endorser within two working days of the previous notification. Notifications may be effected in any form, even by simply sending the bill back. Holder of a protested bill may enter suit separately against drawer and each of the endorsers, or jointly against drawer and endorsers, on grounds of several or joint liability, and has a preference in respect to the consideration as regards other creditors of the drawer, in case of bankruptcy or insolvency; the action must be brought within one year. Each endorser has the right to enforce the same remedy against drawer and preceding endorsers; the action must be brought within six months.

Formal requirements of acceptance and endorsement are governed by law of place where signature was apposed but capacity is governed by national law. Law of place of signature also governs duties of endorsers but duties of acceptant drawee are governed by law of place of payment. Notifications are governed, as to period, by law of place of issuing bill and, as to form, by law of place of notification.

Novation.—Whether the acceptance of a bill implies novation is decided on a case to case basis according to intention.

"Aval" is the security given by a third party who guarantees acceptance or payment, or both. It is given in writing on the bill or by separate act. This third party becomes jointly liable with party for whom security was given. If party for whom security is given is not specified, aval is held to have been given for drawer.

Check must include the word "check", be payable at sight, be signed by drawer and show day and place of drawing. Checks may be nominative, to order or to bearer and can be transferred by endorsement, even in blank. Payment must be demanded within eight days if drawn in Belgium, 20 days if drawn in Europe including countries bordering Mediterranean, 120 days if drawn outside Europe. Rules governing joint and several liability of all parties to a bill of exchange and those relating to protests apply to checks. Drawing and transfer in bad faith of check without "funds" or with insufficient "funds" are punishable under criminal laws; drawer who knowingly withdraws all or part of the "funds" after drawing a check, or who fraudulently instructs bank not to pay, may be prosecuted criminally.

A crossed check may be presented for payment only through a banker or client of drawee bank. If specific banker is mentioned in the crossing, he alone can cash check. Nonobservance of these rules results in liability for damages not exceeding amount of check.

Drawer or bearer of check may instruct bank not to pay in cash, by writing on the back of the check the words "credit in account" or an equivalent.

Promissory notes come under the same rules as bills of exchange.

BILLS OF LADING: See topic Shipping.

CHATTEL MORTGAGES:

These are unknown in Belgium, save in respect to ships. See topics Shipping; also Sales, subhead Conditional Sales.

A floating charge can be established on the following assets of a business: goodwill, patents, trademarks, lease of premises, business equipment and 50% of inventory, receivables only if specially mentioned. Such charge must be registered in the mortgage registry and can only be established in favor of banks or financial institutions.

COMMERCIAL REGISTER:

All business owners, whether individual or corporate, must register before commencing operations. Operating without registration or outside scope of registration entails fine. Upon motion of defendant suit initiated without proper registration can be dismissed.

For certain types of business registration is conditional on showing that owner or manager meets statutory requirements of education and training.

COMMISSIONS TO TAKE TESTIMONY:

See topic Depositions.

COMMUNITY PROPERTY:

See topic Husband and Wife.

CONSTITUTION AND GOVERNMENT:

Belgium is a hereditary constitutional Kingdom. The Belgian constitution was promulgated Feb. 7, 1831, and has, on various occasions, been amended. It is based on Montesquieu's theory of separation of power and English constitutional tradition.

Since last round of state reforms (1993), Belgium must be considered as a federal state. Belgium consists of three communities and three regions. Communities are competent in educational and cultural matters. Regions are endowed with economic powers.

On federal level, Legislative Power is exercised by Parliament, consisting of Chamber of Representatives, elected by universal suffrage, and federal Senate, which is only partially elected by universal suffrage. Senate has limited legislatory powers. Executive Power is vested in King in ministry.

Each federate entity has its own Legislature, elected by universal suffrage, and its own Executive.

Judiciary.—Judges are appointed by King for lifetime. They are independent of administration and Parliament. Court of Cassation is highest ordinary law court. Judicial review of administrative action is exercised by Council of State. Court of Arbitration is constitutional court with limited powers.

CONTRACTS:

Written contracts are usually made privately, but may be formally made before a notary and so become public deeds. A private written contract must be made in as many copies as there are parties to the agreement having separate interests, and number of copies must be mentioned at foot of contract. (C. C. 1325).

Witnesses to signatures are not required in any event.

CONTRACTS . . . *continued*

Any private agreement or contract which is not contrary to public order or morals can be registered for a small fee, and such registration enables date thereof to be fixed without risk of subsequent contestation. Registration duty is dependent upon object of contract.

Private contracts do not require to be stamped except when registered.

See also topic Seals.

Excuses for nonperformance are admitted with respect to facts or legislation that were unforeseeable and that entail impossibility of performance.

Applicable law is that chosen by parties or, in absence of such choice, law of jurisdiction with which contract is most closely connected. Choice of law with respect to termination of distribution agreements will be disregarded by Belgian courts.

Government contracts are, as a rule, subject to competitive bidding. (Law of July 14, 1976). Special rules covering performance bond, price revision, approval of performance, fines for delay, unilateral termination, limitation of actions are spelled out in Royal Decree of Apr. 22, 1977.

COPYRIGHT:

(Law of June 30, 1994).

The author of a literary or artistic work enjoys the right of reproducing same or authorizing reproduction under any form. This right includes exclusive right to authorize modification, translation, renting and lending out of work. Author also enjoys right of making same known to public. Author also enjoys moral rights, such as right to divulge work, to claim authorship and to oppose any modification. These rights last during author's life and inures to benefit of his heirs or his assignees for 70 years after his death.

No formalities are required for establishment and enjoyment of these rights.

Only economic rights of author are transferable and strict rules apply to transfer of such rights.

Law contains specific provisions regarding copyright to audiovisual works, publishing contract and performance contract. Neighbouring rights are granted to producers of phonograms, to performing artists, to producers of first recording of movies and to radio- and television stations. Computer programs are also granted copyright protection under separate law of June 30, 1994.

Foreigners are given equal rights for the same period, unless their national law limits same to a shorter period, in which case the latter prevails.

Belgium is member of the Bern Union Convention of 1886 and of the Universal Copyright Union.

CORPORATIONS:

See topics Joint Stock Companies; Partnership.

COURTS:

Civil and commercial actions involving less than 75,000 francs (art. 590 C.J.) are dealt with by a justice of the peace (lower judge), with an appeal where value of claim exceeds 50,000 francs (art. 617 C.J.). Actions involving larger sums are dealt with by Courts of First Instance, unless special jurisdiction be granted by law to lower judges (art. 591 C.J.) or to courts such as Commercial Courts, dealing with commercial litigation, or Labor Courts dealing with disputes between employers, employees and workmen. Litigation involving over 75,000 francs (art. 617 C.J.) may go on appeal before Court of Appeal.

In penal matters, the Police Court deals with minor offences, Correctional Tribunal with all other offences or with major crimes when extenuating circumstances have been admitted by prosecutor. Court of Assizes being only court with jury, has jurisdiction over all other crimes, political offences and violations of press laws.

Appeals from the Police Court are dealt with by the Correctional Tribunal and appeals from Correctional Tribunals by Court of Appeal.

The Supreme Court deals only with appeals against judgments on questions of infringement of law or lack of motivation of opinion. If the appeal is allowed the case is remanded.

Arbitration Court decides on possible conflicts between laws enacted by National Parliament and decrees enacted by community or regional councils or between decrees of various community or regional councils, and between these laws and decrees and some constitutional provisions.

Benelux Court gives preliminary ruling concerning interpretation of legal rules made common to Benelux countries.

CURRENCY:

The franc is the monetary unit of Belgium. (Law of Dec. 23, 1988). Belgium is member of International Monetary Fund and of European Monetary System.

The National Bank of Belgium, a private corporation of which the State owns 50%, has the exclusive right to issue banknotes. These are legal tender.

Foreign Exchange.—Exchange control was organized by R. D. of Oct. 6, 1944 on a stringent basis, submitting all payments to and transactions with foreigners to authorization of the Belgo-Luxemburg Exchange Institute. Controls were progressively relaxed and at present liberty of exchange dealings is in practice complete. Certain disclosure requirements still exist concerning nature and currency of payment. Aliens travelling in Belgium may freely import and export foreign or Belgium currency.

See also topic Foreign Trade and Foreign Investment.

CUSTOMS:

As member of European Community ("EEC"), Belgian customs law is largely based on EEC customs legislation. Thus, virtually all Belgian customs duties are established in accordance with Common Customs Tariff, and rules relating to origin, valuation, payment of customs debt, transit procedures, and special customs arrangements such as duty-free import under inward or outward processing regimes are governed by EEC law. Belgian customs law is codified in Customs and Excise Code.

Agents of Customs and Excise Administration are responsible for administering Belgian customs law by, inter alia, collecting customs duties; enforcing import regulations; verifying customs documentation; and engaging in related inspection and investigative activities.

Belgium is member of General Agreement on Tariffs and Trade.

See also European Union Law Digest, topic Customs Duties.

DEATH:

See topic Absentees.

When a person ceases to appear at the place of his domicile or residence and has not been heard of for four years, proceedings may be instituted before the civil tribunal to have the absence established. (C. C. 115). When a judgment declaring the absence has been rendered, the presumptive heirs can be placed in temporary possession of the property which belongs to the absentee. (C. C. 120). If the absence lasts 30 years after temporary possession is granted, the interested parties may apply to the tribunal for a judgment granting final possession. (C. C. 129).

Action for Death.—Surviving spouse, descendants and ascendants, whether nationals or foreigners may claim damages where death is caused by willful deed or negligent conduct. Amount is not limited. It covers pecuniary and nonpecuniary damages.

DECEDENTS' ESTATES:

See topics Descent and Distribution; Wills.

DEPOSITIONS:

Belgian judges may send letters rogatory to foreign courts.

Permission of the Minister of Justice is necessary to execute commissions issued by foreign courts. If given, the permission puts the judges under obligation of proceeding to the hearing. Testimony is taken in the usual form determined by Belgian law. Foreign letters rogatory are transmitted through the diplomatic channels. In urgent cases private transmission by a lawyer may be possible.

DESCENT AND DISTRIBUTION:

The same rules govern succession to movable and immovable property. Relationship is determined by degrees which exist in the direct line, ascending or descending, or in the collateral line. In the direct line, each generation counts for a degree. In the collateral line, the number of generations is counted up to the common ancestor and from him down to the person whose degree of relationship has to be determined. There is no distinction between the sexes and no right of primogeniture.

Heirs at law are of two types: legitimate heirs and Crown. Legitimate heirs are children and direct descendants, surviving spouse, direct ascendants, brothers and sisters and their descendants, and collaterals.

Children and direct descendants exclude all other heirs with exception of surviving spouse who in such case is entitled to usufruct of estate. Direct descendants of child who has predeceased decedent inherit his part by virtue of legal fiction called "representation." If decedent leaves spouse but no children and no direct descendants, and there are other heirs, surviving spouse receives property of estate common to spouses and usufruct of remaining. If decedent leaves brothers and sisters and ascendants other than father or mother, ascendants are excluded. If father and mother survive decedent who leaves brothers and sisters, one-half of estate only goes to latter, other half to parents. If one of parents alone survives, he or she gets one-fourth of estate, remainder being distributed among brothers and sisters.

In case surviving spouse is only heir, he/she inherits all of estate.

Representation in the collateral line takes place only as regards children and descendants of brothers and sisters and of uncles and aunts of decedent.

If decedent leaves no spouse, no descendants, and no brothers and sisters or descendants of same, estate is divided equally between ascendants of both paternal and maternal lines. In each line right to succeed applies to nearest in relationship who, to exclusion of all more distant relations, inherits part coming to his line. Ascendants in one line related in same degree inherit per capita. Collaterals beyond fourth degree do not inherit, except by representation.

In default of legitimate heirs entitled to inherit, estate passes to Crown.

Notarial determination of heirs and successors based on information given by next of kin (acte de notoriété- akte van bekendheid) carries great weight with banks and official agencies.

As regards foreigners, their immovable property in Belgium is governed by Belgian law, but their personal property is governed by the law of their last domicile. Where foreigners and Belgian citizens inherit together and various parts of the estate come under different laws, the Belgian heirs can take compensation on goods situated in Belgium for any amount from which they have been excluded on account of different conflict rules governing the distribution of goods situated outside Belgium. (Law of April 27, 1865).

Forced Heirship.—See topic Wills.

DESERTION: See topic Divorce.

DIVORCE:

Divorce may be for specific cause or by mutual consent. The court of the district of the matrimonial home or of defendant's domicile has jurisdiction.

Aliens will be granted divorce in Belgium only if matrimonial home or defendant's domicile is in Belgium. Petition can only be based on causes recognized by Belgian law. When both parties are alien, no divorce is possible if prohibited by plaintiff's national law.

Divorce for a specific cause may be granted on grounds of adultery, abuse, cruelty or gross insult, actual separation during five years. Conduct which, having regard to social standing of parties, amounts to breach of marriage vows they implicitly or explicitly assumed in marrying is considered as gross insult. Desertion is considered as gross insult, if it is established that plaintiff offered to receive deserter, unless latter can show very serious grounds justifying such desertion.

DIVORCE . . . *continued*

Proceedings begin by petitioner in person, or by special attorney if petitioner resides out of country, lodging request with president of civil tribunal. Wrongs invoked must be enumerated with greatest possible precision regarding time and place. After delivery of this request parties are summoned to appear before president in his office, where he tries to reconcile them. If conciliation fails, he sends parties before court, which fixes time during which proceedings are suspended. This period generally lasts six months but may be reduced to two months. After this period has elapsed, case is recalled at sitting in open court. If plaintiff then produces sufficient evidence of wrongs invoked, court grants "de plano" divorce. Otherwise, plaintiff will be compelled to prove his grievance by hearing of witnesses. After hearings, case is resumed before court, which grants divorce if evidence is sufficient. Belgian law knows no setoff in relation to such offenses. If both parties have good reason to complain, counterpetition will be admitted, and divorce pronounced against either or both parties. Court's decree granting or refusing divorce is appealable to higher court within one month of its notification. After this delay, successful plaintiff must notify judgment to municipal officer who records it.

Alimony and Custody of Children.—After plaintiff has lodged a request, president of civil tribunal makes provision for temporary alimony and for a sum covering indigent spouse's lawsuit costs. Provision is also made for custody of children pendente lite. All these matters are decided according to wishes of parties or, failing agreement, in children's best interests.

When divorce is decreed, provision for custody of children becomes final. When no provision has been made, custody of children is granted to successful party, unless parties have agreed otherwise or Juvenile Court decides otherwise. When divorce is granted on basis of separation of five years, custody is settled in judgment decreeing divorce. Court may also grant successful plaintiff alimony in amount not exceeding one-third of defendant's income. In case of divorce for actual separation of five years, plaintiff may also be ordered to pay alimony even in amount greater than one-third of his income.

Divorce by mutual consent is possible if one of parties is a Belgian national. Both parties must be over 20. Parties must have been married more than two years. Parties must agree on a friendly settlement of their pecuniary interests, on their residences pendente lite, on question of alimony and on custody of children during and after proceedings.

Proceedings are simple. Parties appear three times before president of civil tribunal at intervals of six months. After one year, case is placed on calendar for hearing. Court then grants divorce if all legal requirements have been complied with.

Separation may be petitioned for and granted on same grounds as divorce either for specific cause or by mutual consent. Private separation agreements have no legal value. Legal separation always carries with it separation of property.

Divorce after Separation.—After separation for specific cause has been entered for three years, either party may apply for divorce, which is in discretion of the court. After separation by mutual consent has lasted three years, parties may jointly have separation converted into divorce and either party can request court to do so.

ECONOMIC INTEREST GROUPINGS:

Two new company structures have recently appeared in Belgian law: European Economic Interest Grouping (Law of July 12, 1989) and Belgian Economic Interest Grouping (Law of July 17, 1989).

Economic Interest Groupings can be formed through public or private deed by legal entities or individuals. European Economic Interest Grouping should have members from different EEC-States. Economic Interest Grouping has to be registered with Register of Commerce. It is subject to same accounting requirements as joint stock company. Activity of Economic Interest Grouping should be supportive and ancillary to that of members. Economic Interest Grouping cannot serve as holding.

Economic Interest Grouping has legal capacity. Members are jointly and severally liable for debts of Economic Interest Grouping. Economic Interest Grouping has no capital requirements. Contributions in kind have to be valued by certified auditor. Contributions are not subject to 0.5% registration tax.

Rules on management and membership of Economic Interest Grouping are comparable to those of cooperative company.

Economic Interest Grouping is transparent from direct taxation standpoint. Profits of Economic Interest Grouping are considered profits of its members.

ENVIRONMENT:

Belgian State Structure and Environmental Legislation.—Pursuant to 1980-1988-1993 State reforms, Belgium is federal State composed of three Regions, i.e., Flemish Region, Walloon Region and Brussels Metropolitan Region. Regional authorities have been granted substantial legislative powers over environmental issues. As general rule, Regions are competent for almost all sectors of environmental policy. Federal State retains competence for, inter alia, protection against radiation, transit of waste, adoption of product standards and ecological taxes and protection of North Sea. Existing federal legislation remains applicable insofar as it has not been abrogated or amended by regional legislation.

Environmental Permits.—Industrial activities likely to harm environment are generally not prohibited, but are subject to permit and consequently bound to conditions.

Consequently, companies must apply for several permits in order to perform their activities. Legal framework of environmental permits is quite different in the three Regions.

In the Walloon Region environmental permits are regulated by separate rules, separate application procedures and separate control measures. Basic environmental permit is operating permit. Title 1 of General Regulation on Labor Protection (R.G.P.T.), as enacted by Decree of the Regent, dated Feb. 11, 1946, contains list of activities which are classified as hazardous, harmful or unhealthy. Operation of classified enterprise is subject to prior permit, referred to as operating permit. Operating permit might impose specific conditions for safe and environmentally sound operation of plant (e.g., prevention of noise, air emissions, etc.).

In addition, company might possess waste disposal permit, waste water discharge permit, permit for catchment of groundwater, etc. These permits are governed by separate regulations, which contain conditions holder of permit must comply with.

In Flemish Region, Regional Statute of June 28, 1985 on environmental permit and Decree of the Flemish Government, dated Feb. 6, 1991 on environmental permit (VLAREM I), have introduced one single environmental permit, which is granted for majority of activities likely to harm environment.

However, not all permits have been integrated into environmental permit. Company might thus possess other permits which are governed by separate rules, such as permit for the catchment of groundwater, permit for use and possession of radioactive material, etc.

Decree of the Flemish Government of June 1, 1995 on Flemish Regulations on environmental activities likely to harm environment (VLAREM II) enacts exhaustive list of general (imposed on all industries) and sectoral (imposed on industries of certain sector) standards classified industries must comply with. These standards are intended to prevent air pollution, pollution of surface water, groundwater, noise disturbances, etc.

In Brussels Region regional Statute of July 30, 1992 on environmental permit also provides for one single environmental permit for majority of activities likely to harm environment.

Air.—In Flemish Region VLAREM II details general and sectoral environmental standards for prevention of air pollution.

In Walloon and Brussels Regions atmospheric pollution is primarily fought through operating or environmental permit.

In addition, specific compulsory regulations are provided in connection with air polluting enterprises or activities.

Waste Water.—In Flemish and Brussels Regions environmental permit is required for discharge of cooling water and industrial waste water into surface water or public sewage system on basis of above-mentioned legislation on environmental permit.

In Walloon Region discharge of waste water requires waste water discharge permit (Regional Statue of Oct. 7, 1985 on protection of surface waters against pollution).

Respective regional legislation contains standards relating to composition of discharged water (prohibition to discharge certain substances or maximum level of admitted substances), quantities of discharges and control and measurements of discharges.

Waste.—In Flemish Region, management of waste is governed by Regional Statute, dated July 2, 1981 and its implementing decrees.

According to this Statute, environmental permit is required for disposal or removal of waste. Disposal and removal of waste can be carried out by third parties, provided these have been licensed by provincial government. In that case, generator of waste needs not apply for permit.

It is compulsory for company producing industrial waste to file annual reports on quantities, composition and treatment of waste to Flemish Public Waste Company (OVAM). Company must ensure that any waste is removed properly and in compliance with regulations.

In Walloon Region management of waste is governed by Regional Statute of July 5, 1985 on waste. Brussels Region has adopted Regional Statute of Mar. 7, 1991 on prevention and management of waste.

Pursuant to this legislation, set up and exploitation of waste ground, depot or waste processing installation is subject to prior permit.

Soil Pollution.—In Flemish Region, new Statute of Feb. 22, 1995 on soil clean-up will enter into force on Oct. 29, 1995.

Distinction is made between soil pollution caused after entering into force of Statute and soil pollution having occurred prior to Statute's entering into force (historical pollution). Statute indicates cases for which soil clean-up is required, which part has obligation to clean up site and which party is ultimately liable for costs.

Legislation provides for keeping of register of contaminated soils. No transfer of land will be possible without prior communication to buyer of soil certificate delivered by OVAM on basis of aforementioned register.

Transfer of land on which certain activities have taken place are subject to prior soil investigation and financial bounds.

Implementing decree has been adopted by Flemish Government on Mar. 5, 1996 (VLAREBO).

There does not exist any coherent federal or regional legislation concernng soil pollution in Walloon and Brussels Regions.

General Supervision.—As general rule, authorities competent for delivery of permits are local (provincial and municipal) authorities. In certain cases permits are granted by Minister in charge of environment.

In Flemish Region competent supervising offiers are civil servants of Administration for Environment, Nature and Land Organization of Flemish Ministry of Environment (AMINAL, Belliardstraat 14-18, 1040 Brussels). Officers of Flemish Public Waste Company (OVAM, K. de Deckerstraat 22-26, 2800 Mechelen) have been granted powers in sectors of waste, groundwater and soil pollution.

In Walloon Region competent supervising officers are civil servants of Division of Environmental Police (Division de la Police de l'Environnement, Centre de Mons, Place du Parc 32, 7000 Mons, Centre de Charleroi, Bd. P. Mayence 1, 6000 Charleroi, Centre de Namur, Rue Namur 98, 5000 Namur, Centre de Liège, Rue des Guillemins 26, 4000 Liège).

For Brussels Region reference is made to officers of Brussels Institute for management of environment (I.B.G.E., Gulledelle 100, 1200 Brussel).

ESCHEAT: See topic Descent and Distribution.

EVIDENCE: See topic Depositions.

EXCHANGE CONTROL:

See topic Currency, subhead Foreign Exchange.

EXECUTIONS:

Execution is by way of seizure and public sale of property belonging to debtor. It is possible on basis of either a judgment or a notarially acknowledged debt. Execution is carried out by sheriff ("huissier de justice"—"gerechtsdeurwaarder") at request of creditor.

Seizures can be ascertained at court registry. (Jud. C. 1391).

All other creditors making themselves known are entitled to share in proceeds of sale. (Jud. C. 1627). As incentive for debtor to give performance to judgment, latter can provide for penal sum to be forfeited in case of noncompliance with judgment.

See also topic Attachment.

EXECUTORS AND ADMINISTRATORS:

Executors may be appointed by will but only for a period of one year and one day, and they have only very limited powers, being little more than advisers and arbitrators. They may have the right of seizin over movable property to the extent required to pay any legacies, but the estate devolves directly on the heirs and not on the executors.

Legitimate heirs (see topic Descent and Distribution) can take possession of the estate, whereas Crown has to petition court before taking possession. (C. C. 724). Legatees have to receive possession from heirs, successors or residuary legatee as case may be (C. C. 1010, 1014); residuary legatee from heirs only when they are entitled to a reserved portion (see topic Wills) (C. C. 1004, 1006).

Heirs, successors and residuary or demonstrative legatees are personally liable for estate debts, unless they file a statement with the court and have a notarial inventory of assets and liabilities drawn up.

An administrator can be appointed by the court only where the heirs are undiscovered.

See also topics Descent and Distribution; Wills.

EXEMPTIONS: See topic Attachment.

FOREIGN COMPANIES:

Industrial or financial joint stock companies and all other commercial associations incorporated abroad and having their head office in foreign country may carry on business and enter suit in Belgium. If they have branch or office in Belgium, they must file their deed of incorporation and all changes to it with Commercial Court together with other relevant information regarding foreign company. Such documents must be in French or Dutch, officially translated. They must also deposit their annual accounts and their consolidated accounts prior to opening of branch and thereafter on yearly basis, as approved and filed abroad, within one month from date of such filing. Stationery must indicate name, type, registered address and registration number of foreign company. It must also report Belgian branch's registration number to local Commercial Register and VAT number. Managers of Belgian branches have same liability toward third persons as managers of Belgian corporations.

FOREIGN EXCHANGE:

See topic Currency, subhead Foreign Exchange.

FOREIGN INVESTMENT:

See topic Foreign Trade and Foreign Investment.

FOREIGN TRADE AND FOREIGN INVESTMENT:

International trade policy is within exclusive competence of E.U. authorities. Even though import regimes for certain goods may differ from one Member State to another, rules applicable to imports into and exports from Belgium, including rules relating to anti-dumping and countervailing duties, are laid down in E.U. regulations.

Foreign investment in Belgium is free. However, prior notification to governmental authorities is always required for acquisition of at least 1/3 of capital of enterprises whose activity is taking place on Belgian territory having equity of at least 100,000,000 BF.

Furthermore, any acquisition of voting shares of Belgian companies listed on E.U. Stock Exchange has always to be disclosed to company and Commission for Banking and Finance, if such acquisition results in shareholding of 5% or more of outstanding voting equity as well as any subsequent acquisition which would increase shareholding above further 5% increments (i.e. 10, 15, 20% etc.). Sales of such voting equity causing holder to cross any of these thresholds must be disclosed.

Public bids to acquire Belgian securities made by non-E.U. resident are subject to authorization of Minister of Finance.

Special prospectus and other rules apply on takeover bids and public offers.

Several Acts authorize important incentives to investment by large or small business in certain regions or in accordance with government planning goals. Incentives include interest subsidy, investment premiums, employment premiums and tax exemptions.

Belgium is member of Benelux, European Union and O.E.C.D.

FOREIGN TRADE REGULATIONS:

See topic Foreign Trade and Foreign Investment.

FRAUDS, STATUTE OF:

In civil as distinguished from commercial matters, for claims exceeding 3,000 francs, oral evidence is not admissible. (C. C. 1341).

A private agreement by which one party alone promises to pay a sum of money or a specific thing must be entirely written and signed by the person undertaking the obligation, or, if merely signed, the signature must be preceded by the words "good for" or "approved for" followed by the amount written out in full in the debtor's handwriting. This rule does not apply to traders, artisans, day laborers or farm hands. (C. C. 1326).

GARNISHMENT: See topic Attachment.

HOLIDAYS:

Fixed and regular legal holidays are: New Year's Day; Easter Monday; May 1; Ascension Day; Whit Monday; July 21; Aug. 15; Nov. 1 and 11; Christmas Day.

Saturdays are treated as legal holidays for presentation and protest of bills and for periods for bringing judicial action.

HUSBAND AND WIFE:

Basic Rules.—Husband and wife owe fidelity, help and assistance to one another. Matrimonial residence is chosen by common accord or failing this by court. (C. C. 214).

Each spouse contributes to marriage expenses according to his (her) means. In case this obligation is not met, justice of peace of last common residence may authorize one of spouses to receive other's income, credits, wages, salaries and debts, under certain conditions and to extent specified in his decision. After notification by recorder, decision of judge must be complied with by debtors of spouse. (C. C. 221). Each spouse also has power to engage joint liability of defaulting spouse for household and educational debts. (C. C. 222).

Each spouse may engage upon a business or professional activity but the other spouse may apply to the court for an injunction if he (she) thinks his (her) or the children's interests are thereby adversely affected. Husband and wife may not make use of each other's name in their business or professional transactions without mutual consent. (C. C. 216).

One spouse cannot unilaterally dispose of matrimonial home, unless authorized by court. All notifications concerning lease of matrimonial home have to be addressed to or have to originate from both spouses. (C. C. 215).

Community of Property.—In absence of matrimonial agreement to contrary, community of property comes into being upon marriage. (C. C. 1399-1400). Under legal community rules, each spouse retains ownership of property owned at time of marriage or acquired during marriage either by inheritance or gift as well as other personal property such as clothing, small objects of personal use, (diplomas, decorations, souvenirs), industrial, literary or artistic property rights, damages awarded for personal injuries, mental or physical, pensions and rents. (C. C. 1399, 1403). Income from assets or professional activity of spouses as well as acquisitions made by onerous title during marriage are considered community property. (C. C. 1405).

Debts proper to one spouse, that is incurred for benefit of their personal property or in their exclusive interest, generally encumber their individual property and their income (which is community property). (C. C. 1409).

In contrast, payment of common debts, contracted by both spouses or by one spouse in their common interest, can generally be charged against community property or jointly against all three. (C. C. 1413).

Each spouse manages his own property, his personal income and bank accounts to which he holds title (C. C. 218); each spouse undertakes individually all acts of management necessary for his professional activity (C. C. 1417).

Household expenses and chattel transactions can be carried out by use of community property by either spouse who can individually manage such operations and bind other spouse vis-à-vis such acts. (C. C. 1416).

For more important expenditures, law requires accord of both spouses. (C. C. 1418-1419).

Court can take measures in order to avoid mismanagement by one of spouses. It can also, in case of abuse by one of spouses, set aside such acts. (C. C. 1420-1422).

Community of property rules are rendered inapplicable by death of either spouse, divorce or separation, judicial separation of property, alteration of above rules by contract between parties. (C. C. 1427).

Matrimonial Agreements.—It is customary for people possessing property, who marry in Belgium, to fix their property rights by contract, which must be drawn up by notary. Greatest freedom prevails as to terms of contract, but parties may not depart from basic rules and from rules governing legal powers of parents over children or from rules of inheritance. Marital property agreement can be altered after marriage upon condition of not causing prejudice either to interests of family, or those of children, or rights of third parties. (C. C. 1394-1396).

Spouses can thus adopt either system of community property which is more extensive than that provided by law thus placing all of their property in common or adopt system of complete separation of their property. (C. C. 1466-1469). Under community system, parties cannot depart from rules governing management of personal and community property. Under same system, it is also customary to make allotment of community property in favour of surviving party. Such dispositions are not treated as gifts.

IMMIGRATION: See topic Aliens.

INCOME TAX: See topic Taxation.

INFANCY:

Age of majority is 18 for both sexes. Emancipation is possible at 15 by court order and is automatic upon marriage.

Infants are represented in contracts and court actions by parents. (C. C. 376). For sums owed to infants, courts may establish special conditions governing their use by parents. (C. C. 379).

Mentally deficient persons may be subject to status of prolonged infancy. (C. C. 487 bis e.s.).

INHERITANCE TAX: See topic Taxation.

INSOLVENCY: See topic Bankruptcy.

INTEREST:

At present, legal rate is 8%. Except in few cases determined by law, interest is only due after summons to pay debt, served by bailiff. For trade debts such summons may be given by other means, e.g. registered letter. Interest is due without summons in cases against: (1) Buyer of thing delivered him which yields emblements or any income; (2) guardian, unjustifiably detaining minor's money; (3) principal owing interest to agent on funds advanced by latter.

Usury.—Any rate of interest may legally be agreed on by contract, except in instalment sales where maximum is fixed by decree. Question of a reasonable or maximum rate is one which is decided on merits of each case and is left to entire discretion of court. Broadly speaking anything higher than twice normal commercial or bank rate prevailing would be considered as usury. In most cases, however, deciding factor is question of repetition. One isolated transaction at an extortionate rate between two individuals is looked on with greater leniency than several transactions at a high rate. It is taking of unfair advantage of borrower's necessity which constitutes criminal offense of usury. Court has power, under Civil Code art. 1907 ter, to reduce obligation of debtor to amount actually loaned, plus interest at current legal rate, and such reductions apply to any partial repayments already made, provided application is made within three years from dates of such payments.

INTESTATE SUCCESSION:

See topic Descent and Distribution.

JOINT STOCK COMPANIES: ("Sociétés anonymes" —"Naamloze Vennootschappen"):

Joint stock companies can be formed only by notarial deed filed at Commercial Court. Extract of act is published in Official Journal. This deed of incorporation is not submitted to governmental approval. Joint stock companies have separate legal personality as of date of filing of deed of incorporation. Requirements for formation of joint stock company are: (1) Minimum number of two members, Belgians or aliens, individuals or companies or associations; (2) complete subscription of capital as determined by act of incorporation; (3) actual payment, either in cash or in kind of minimum capital in full and any amounts above that for at least one quarter; (4) minimum subscribed capital of 2,500,000 BEF. Contributions not in cash must be described and valued by chartered public accountant, whose report must be filed with Commercial Court. Articles of association may provide for authorized capital in which case board of directors may within period of five years from incorporation or from time authorized capital was introduced increase capital up to authorized amount by notarial deed filed at Commercial Court. For listed companies, amount of authorized capital may not exceed that of subscribed capital. Authorized capital procedure is not available for capital increases to be effected mainly through noncash contributions by shareholders owning more than 10% of voting rights in company.

At time of incorporation, founding shareholders must furnish notary with financial forecast purpose of which is to assess liability of founding shareholders in event of bankruptcy within three years of incorporation, if capital was obviously insufficient to cover proposed activities for initial period of at least two years.

This type of corporation is characterized by the fact that each member's liability is strictly limited to the amount of his investment determined by his subscription.

If number of shareholders is reduced to one, this sole shareholder after one year becomes jointly liable for obligations of company.

Shares are registered, bearer or dematerialized. Shares must remain registered until fully paid up. Apart from shares representing capital, shares may be issued entitling holder to part of profits, portion being determined by deed of incorporation. Part profit shares must remain deposited with corporation until ten days after publication of second annual balance sheet. Until expiration of aforesaid period, these shares can only be transferred by written contract containing specified information and notified to company within one month of transfer. In listed companies, part profit shares which are subscribed in cash must be fully paid in and are immediately freely transferable.

Founders' shares or other shares entitling holder to part of profits as above may be of unlimited number, but legislation restricts voting rights attached to said shares.

Joint stock companies are managed by a board of at least three directors elected by the general meeting of shareholders. *Note.*—However, board of joint stock company may consist of two directors, if company only has two shareholders. Directors are elected for maximum period of six years. Reelection is permitted. They are subject to removal at any time. Deeds relating to their appointment, resignation, removal and statement of their death are filed at Commercial Court and published in annexes to Official Journal. Managers, officers or other agents may be entrusted with daily management of business and also act as corporation's specific representatives in connection therewith. Such delegation of power is normally filed and published likewise. Directors who have direct or indirect conflict of interest with monetary value in matter submitted to Board must so inform Board and statutory auditors. They may attend and vote at Board, meeting except in listed companies. Board and statutory auditor must report on such matters at next annual general meeting of shareholders. There is also procedure to be complied with in listed companies when board makes decision which might benefit shareholder having major influence on appointment of directors.

Control of company must be entrusted to one or more chartered public accountants, appointed by shareholders meeting for renewable period of three years, if company, meets more than one of following criteria: (1) 50 employees; (2) 100,000,000 BF balance sheet total; (3) 200,000,000 BF turnover or if company employs 100 or more employees. These criteria are not computed on consolidated basis, except for listed companies, some holding companies and companies which are part of group that is required to give consolidated accounts. In all other cases no statutory auditor need be appointed and each shareholder has individual right of control. Shareholder may then be assisted by accountant.

General meeting of shareholders, is held at least once a year on day fixed by deed of incorporation. Board of directors and auditors may call special meeting known as "extraordinary," whenever they deem it necessary. They must call special meeting if requested to do so by number of shareholders representing at least one-fifth of capital. Meetings are convoked by means of press convocations or by registered letter for registered shareholders. General meeting hears report by board of directors (management report) and one by auditors. Balance sheet, profit and loss account are discussed, adopted or rejected; distribution of profits is decided; discharge is given or refused to directors and statutory auditors. Discharge is bar to any later action against directors and statutory auditors by shareholders, except where directors and statutory auditors have acted in violation of articles and approval of that action has not been specifically mentioned in notice. All shareholders may vote, either in person or by proxy. Articles of association may provide for restrictions to voting powers of shareholders. General meeting has power to alter act of incorporation. No change is permitted unless passed on by three-fourths majority. It may only vote on changes of articles of incorporation if shareholders at meeting represent at least one-half of capital. If this quorum is not attained, meeting is adjourned and second one must be called which may then deliberate whatever be proportion of capital represented.

A joint stock company may issue debentures in bearer, registered or dematerialized form.

Dividends may only be distributed out of real profits. Any dividends of which shareholders knew or should have known that they exceeded available profits must be reimbursed. Interim dividends may be distributed out of real profits at most twice a year by decision of board of directors, and if deed of incorporation so provides.

Annual balance, profit and loss account and distribution of profit must be filed with National Bank and are available to public for consultation as is management report either at National Bank or at company's registered office.

Articles of association or shareholders' agreements may restrict share transfers through transfer-blocking and/or preemption clauses provided that (a) they have limited duration and (b) they satisfy corporate interest. Maximum duration for approval and/or preemption clauses is six months.

Joint stock companies may issue voting and nonvoting shares. Nonvoting shares may not represent more than 1/3 of capital and must give right to preferred dividend and preferred right to reimbursement of capital contributions. Holders of nonvoting shares may nevertheless vote their shares under certain circumstances as determined by law.

Joint stock companies may acquire their own shares only under certain conditions as determined by law.

Joint stock companies may not advance funds, extend loans or give securities for purposes of acquisition of their own shares by third party, except under conditions as determined by law.

Cross-participations among affiliated or independent companies may not exceed 10%. Voting rights attached to such shares are suspended. Shares held in excess of this threshold must be transferred within one year.

Under certain circumstances as determined by law, joint stock companies may issue voting shares which are reserved in whole or in part to their personnel.

Minority shareholders owning shares representing at least 1% of voting rights or 50,000,000 BF may sue directors on behalf of company. This minority action ("action minoritaire"/"minderheids-vordering") is somewhat comparable to derivative action under U.S. law.

Voting agreements may be entered into provided that (a) they have limited duration and (b) they satisfy corporate interest. They may not (i) contravene law nor corporate interest nor (ii) provide that shareholder shall exercise his voting rights upon instructions from company.

Procedure aimed at resolving conflicts between shareholders in closed joint stock companies was recently introduced. Procedure allows one or several shareholders owning 30% or more of company's voting rights to force another shareholder to sell them its shares in company. Reverse situation is also covered as any shareholder will be allowed to force other shareholders to buy its shares in company. In both cases, procedure is available only if plaintiffs can prove that their request is supported by good reasons.

Law also authorizes shareholders owning 95% or more of voting rights in joint stock company to squeeze out minority shareholders, even in absence of any conflict between shareholders.

Accounts.—Belgian business and companies must prepare their accounts for publication in accordance with rules of presentation established by Law. Company books have to be kept in accordance with minimum standards fixed in accounting plan defined by Law. (Law of July 17, 1975, as am'd and Royal Decree of 8 Oct. 1976, as am'd).

Loss of Bearer Shares or Debentures.—Person who involuntarily loses possession of share or debenture to bearer must forbid negotiation of same by injunction to National Office of stocks and debentures. (Law of July 24, 1921 as am'd). This injunction is published within two days in special bulletin. All acts of alienation of instrument after day of publication are null and void with regard to person who forbade negotiation. Any one receiving share or dividend warrant under injunction must retain same and warn real owner. If instrument is not found, new one is delivered after publication of injunction in bulletin during four consecutive years. All contestations relating to injunctions must be examined by court.

Private limited companies (sociétés privées à reponsabilité limitée [S.P.R.L.], besloten vennootschap met beperkte aansprakelijkheid [B.V.B.A.]) are authorized by law of July 9, 1935, and correspond to certain degree to private companies as known under English law. Liability of members is strictly limited to amount of their investment by their subscription. Minimum number of members two, Belgian or aliens, individuals or companies or associations. Law of July 14, 1987 authorized private limited companies with only one shareholder.

Minimum capital 750,000 BF of which minimum 250,000 BF paid up in full; minimum one fifth of each share must also be paid up in full; only registered shares.

General management may be entrusted to one or more persons whose period of office and powers are decided by members. Manager nominated in bylaws of company can only be dismissed in accordance with rules relating to modification of bylaws (3/4

JOINT STOCK COMPANIES . . . *continued*
majority and 50% quorum in first meeting). Otherwise manager can be dismissed by simple majority of votes cast. Provisions as to control of company are same as for joint stock companies.

In general, same publication regulations apply as to joint stock companies. Costs of incorporation are slightly lower than those for joint stock companies. Company has separate legal personality as of date of filing of deed of incorporation.

Shares can only be transfered to non-shareholder upon approval of minimum half of shareholders owning minimum three fourths of capital after deduction of shares to be transferred. Law provides for exceptions to this rule but bylaws can provide for even more stringent transfer limitations.

Minority shareholders owning at least 10% of voting rights may sue managers on behalf of company.

Procedure aimed at solving conflicts between shareholders in joint stock companies also applies in private limited companies.

Cooperative companies ("sociétés coopératives"/"cooperatieve vennootschappen") used to be characterized essentially by lack of fixed capital.

Originally designed as vehicle for small cooperative ventures where profits shared in relation to amount of business with company, they are now often used as vehicle for large scale capital ventures. This has been possible because most of rules laid down by Belgian Company Act for cooperative companies could be freely derogated from in deed of incorporation.

Stricter regulations have now been introduced by laws of July 20, 1991, June 29, 1993 and Apr. 13, 1995.

Shareholders can opt for limited liability (to amount of their subscription) or unlimited and joint liability. This choice has to be made in articles of incorporation.

Shares may be transferred under conditions set forth in articles of incorporation.

Minimum number of shareholders is three.

Limited liability cooperative companies must have fixed capital of at least 750,000 BF, of which 250,000 BF has to be fully paid up. Company has separate legal personality as of date of filing of deed of incorporation.

Foreign Companies.—Industrial or financial joint stock companies and all other commercial associations incorporated abroad and having their head office in a foreign country, may carry on business and enter suit in Belgium. If they have branch or office in Belgium; they must file their deed of incorporation and all its changes at Commercial Court and other relevant information regarding foreign company. Such documents must be in French, or Dutch, officially translated. They must also deposit their consolidated and annual accounts prior to opening of branch and, thereafter, on yearly basis. Stationery must indicate name, type, registered address and registration number of foreign company. It must also mention Belgian branch's registration number with local Commercial Register and VAT number, as approved and filed abroad, within one month from date of such filing. Managers of Belgian branch have same liability toward third persons as managers of Belgian corporation.

JUDGMENTS:

Ordinarily, a foreign judgment can be rendered executory only after a procedure of enforcement, in the course of which all the facts and matters are reexamined by the court, where enforcement is requested. This court will also examine: (1) If the decision is not contrary to Belgian public policy; (2) if defendant was given opportunity to set up his defense; (3) if foreign court's jurisdiction was not solely on grounds of plaintiff's nationality; (4) if judgment is final under laws of country where it was rendered; (5) if, under same laws, copy of judgment is official one. (Jud. C. 570).

Enforcement is refused if the court reexamining the case disagrees with the decision or if the answer to one of the five points is negative.

When Belgium has signed a treaty with a country on enforcement of judgments, court limits examination to points covered in treaty and does not reexamine case itself before granting an exequatur.

Brussels Convention of Sept. 27, 1968 on jurisdiction and enforcement of judgments provides for simplified procedure with regard to recognition and enforcement of judgments emanating from French, German, Italian, Luxembourg, Netherlands, British, Irish, Danish and Greek courts.

Arbitration Awards.—Foreign awards are not treated differently from domestic awards. Enforcement order is given by President of Court and can be opposed only if award was rendered ultra vires or if certain specific requirements were not met. (Jud. C. 1723).

LABOR RELATIONS:

Collective and individual labor relations are governed by extensive body of law and regulations, including collective bargaining agreements concluded in various joint (manager-union) committees, set up for virtually every branch of industry and trade. (Law of Dec. 5, 1968).

Minimum pay scales, indexation of salaries, and year-end bonuses are normally determined by collective bargaining agreements.

In companies employing 50 employees or more, health and safety committees must be elected on union sponsored slates. (Law of June 10, 1952 and Royal Decree of Aug. 12, 1994). Election of work council is mandatory as soon as 100 employees or more are employed. (Law of Sept. 20, 1948 and Royal Decree of Aug. 12, 1994). These social elections are organized every four years. Last social elections took place in May 1995.

Union appointed delegates may require formation of union delegations recognized by employer if minimal number of employees fixed by collective agreement is reached. This delegation is competent to negotiate collective agreements in undertaking, supervise respect of regulations by employer and handle grievances. (National Collective Agreement of May 24, 1971).

Union delegates, candidates and delegates to work council and health and safety committees are protected against dismissal.

Termination of blue collar workers can be effected on short notice. Salaried employees are entitled to three months increased with three months per five years seniority, but Labor Courts grant to employees earning 896,000 BEF (as of Jan. 1, 1996) or more per year additional severance pay taking into account seniority, age, position, and salary and abstract chances of reemployment.

In case of dismissal, in addition to severance allowance, sales representatives are entitled to client indemnity if they can evidence that they brought in clients to employer. This indemnity is equal to three months of salary for representatives having one to five years of seniority, plus additional month for each additional period of five-years seniority.

During trial period for salaried employees of maximum six or 12 months depending on whether concerned employee earns less or more than 896,000 BEF (as of Jan., 1996), notice is reduced to seven days. Notice of seven days given during first month of trial period will moreover result in termination at end of first month, at earliest.

Discharge for serious cause is valid if given within three days of full knowledge of facts and if notified by registered letter within three days following discharge.

Social security contributions are levied on salaries and any payments for work performed in subordinate capacity.

Employers' contributions for salaried employees earning 50,000 BF per month total some 17,000 BF, whereas in that case employee's contribution amounts to 7,000 BEF.

Elaborate systems of early retirement have established, charged directly or indirectly to employer.

In case of transfer of enterprise, existing employment contracts are automatically transferred to new employer, with all debts of former employer toward his employees.

For blue collar workers, vacation allowances are included in social security system, but for white collar workers (non-manual workers) extra or double vacation allowance of 89.75% of current monthly salary has to be paid by employer.

LANGUAGE:

Official languages in Belgium are French, Dutch and German. German has official status in one district only. Use of language in labor relations and legally required commercial documents is regulated on basis of place of business.

LAW REPORTS, CODES, ETC.:

See topic Statutes.

Acts of Parliament, Royal and Ministerial Decrees and Treaties are published in official gazette Moniteur Belge, Belgisch Staatsblad. Court opinions are reported and annotated in commercially published legal periodicals.

LEGISLATURE:

See topic Constitution and Government.

LICENSES:

Required, among others, for banks, stockbrokers, instalment financing, insurance, road haulage, transport middlemen.

LIENS:

Liens on realty have to be recorded in mortgage registry. (Hyp. 29).

Most important liens on personalty are: (1) Costs of preservation; (2) freight charges; (3) rents; (4) employee claims for wages and termination compensation; (5) social security contributions. (Hyp. 19 and 20).

Moreover a person holding property under obligation to return it is entitled to a possessory lien ("droit de rétention" — "retentierecht") whereby he may retain property until his charges or claims connected with it have been paid.

LIMITATION OF ACTIONS:

Thirty years is the general period of limitation of actions. However, in matters of realty, time limitation to become the owner of an immovable held in good faith is ten or 20 years, depending on certain circumstances. Numerous civil actions are limited by periods varying from six months to five years (e.g., five years for periodical payments such as interest or rentals).

In mercantile matters also numerous actions are limited by short periods (e.g., three years for action against drawee in respect of bill of exchange) while in labor matters actions are limited by one or five year statute.

LIMITED PARTNERSHIP:

See topics Joint Stock Companies; Partnership.

MARRIAGE:

The minimum age at which a person may lawfully marry is 18, but in exceptional circumstances the court may permit persons under these ages to marry.

Where either party is under age of 18, it is necessary to have consent of both parents. If parents disagree, or are without legal capacity to consent court decides. Consent can also be given by court if it feels refusal is unwarranted.

Marriage is a civil contract and a religious ceremony is accorded no legal recognition. A marriage must be published at the door of the town hall for ten days before celebration. It takes place in public before a municipal officer in the presence of two witnesses. The protocol or "marriage act," aside from the details relating to the marriage itself, must also mention date of marriage contract, if spouses choose to have one, and name of notary who drew up instrument; if these are left out, clauses of contract derogatory to common law will not be effective against third persons.

Foreigners may marry in Belgium after a reasonably short residence.

See also topic Husband and Wife.

MARRIED WOMEN:

See topics Husband and Wife; Marriage.

MONOPOLIES AND RESTRAINT OF TRADE:

Law of Aug. 5, 1991, establishing general competition law, entered into force on Apr. 1, 1993.

Belgian competition law seeks to preserve system of vigorous competition within Belgium. Its territorial scope is Belgian market or any substantial part of it. Law is

MONOPOLIES AND RESTRAINT OF TRADE... *continued*
modelled on EU competition law. Three types of practices are covered: (i) restrictive agreements, (ii) abuses of dominant position, and (iii) mergers and acquisitions ("concentrations").

Belgian competition law is enforced by Belgian courts, and by Competition Council, independent administrative court consisting of six judges and six competition experts. Competition Council will make decisions with regard to restrictive agreements, abuses of dominant position and concentrations (compare with powers of Commission at EU level). Decisions of Competition Council may be appealed to Brussels Court of Appeal. This Court can also give preliminary rulings on issues of competition law pending before Belgian courts.

Law's provisions on restrictive agreements and abuses of dominant position are virtually identical to provisions existing at EU level (see respectively, Arts. 85 and 86 of EC Treaty). Parties can obtain exemption from prohibition on restrictive agreements, provided they establish objective economic advantages which offset any restrictive effect of agreement on competition.

Law institutes merger control system, which closely follows provisions of Council Regulation. (EC No. 4064/89). Decisive test for clearance of concentration is whether concentration has effect of creating or strengthening dominant position on Belgian market or on substantial part of it. Thresholds for notification are: (i) combined aggregate turnover of all parties concerned of at least 3 billion BEF, and (ii) combined market share of at least 25%. Notification must be filed with Competition Service, department of Ministry of Economy. Within one month, Competition Council must make decision. If there is serious doubt as to legality of concentration, Competition Council may order full investigation, which can take up to 75 additional days. In absence of decision within one month, or after subsequent period of 75 days, it can be assumed that Competition Council has no objections.

Restrictive agreements and abuses of dominant position operative on Belgian territory are also prohibited when they infringe Art. 85 or Art. 86 of EC Treaty.

MORTGAGES:

A mortgage gives the mortgagee the right to preference on sale of immovable property.

Mortgages are of three types: legal, by will, or by agreement, and the dominating principle is that of publicity.

Legal mortgages are those given to minors and persons under legal disabilities on their guardians' or curators' immovables, and those in favor of public bodies on property of their accountants. Family council decides on amount of mortgage which must be taken on guardian's immovables as warranty for proper administration.

Mortgages by will are those established by the testator on one or several of his estates specified by will, to secure payment of legacies.

Mortgages by agreement may be granted on real estate only by persons legally capable of alienating same, and unless deposed to before notary and recorded are invalid as against third persons.

Execution and Inscription.—Mortgages may only be granted on immovables specifically described and must be created by a notarial instrument or by a private agreement recognized by judgment. They must be recorded at office of registrar of mortgages in district where immovables are located, and take rank from time of this inscription. Inscription preserves mortgages during 30 years, and may be renewed before expiration of said period.

Whenever requested, the registrar of mortgages must deliver copies of mortgage entries or a certificate stating that no mortgage has been taken on specified immovables.

MOTOR VEHICLES:

Motorists must carry unlimited liability insurance. In all cases of accident, police may be asked to write a report that will carry weight with courts.

NEGOTIABLE INSTRUMENTS:

See topic Bills and Notes.

NOTARIES:

The duties of a Belgian notary are different from those of a notary public as understood in some other countries. He performs many functions more usually associated with solicitors or attorneys.

Belgian notaries are legally trained public officials appointed by the King. They exercise their functions within specific territorial limits. They draw up contracts and agreements to which the parties wish or have to give authentic form or date; they make a record of same and issue certified copies and copies for use in execution. They have also authority to take proof of facts relating to family relationship, ownership, the status of individuals or matters of public interest. Such attestation has the value of prima facie evidence.

They do not do the work of attesting, legalizing and translating documents or such other work as is usually associated with "notaries public" in other countries. Their signatures are not registered at Belgian Consulates abroad.

PARTNERSHIP:

Partnerships may be general, special or by shares. They all have separate legal personality as of date of filing of deed of incorporation.

General partnerships ("société en nom collectif" — "vennootschap onder firma") may be entered into by public deed or ordinary contract in writing. In latter case, contract must be written in as many copies as there are partners with separate interests. Extract of contract, containing names of partners, firm name, names of partners acting as directors and indications of date when partnership begins and ends, must be filed at Commercial Court and published in Official Journal. Name of firm may only include names of partners. Partners are jointly liable for all obligations of firm, even though signed or incurred by one partner only, as long as obligation was taken under firm's name and in accordance with articles of partnership. Liability is unlimited.

Special partnerships ("société en commandite simple" — "commanditaire vennootschap") exist between one or more general partners, whose liability is joint and unlimited, and one or more special partners, who contribute a certain capital. Special partners are liable for partnership debts only to the amount which they have agreed to contribute. They may be compelled by third persons to refund interests or dividends paid on fictitious profits of the partnership. Special partnerships are formed like general partnerships. An extract of articles of association is filed at Commercial Court and published in Official Journal. It must contain same information as for general partnerships in addition to name of each special partner, their respective contributions and extent of their obligations. Name of firm must contain that of one or more general partners, but names of special partners may not appear in same. Special partners may not participate in management or even act as agents of partnership. In case of infringement of this rule, they become jointly liable toward third party with whom they have transacted business for partnership. If special partner allows his name to be used in that of firm or usually participates in management, he will be held jointly liable with general partners.

Partnership by shares ("société en commandite par actions" — "commanditaire vennootschap op aandelen") exist between one or more partners whose liability is joint and unlimited, and one or more shareholders liable only for the amount of their subscription. They are formed likewise by a public act filed at Commercial Court and published in extract in Official Journal. Name of firm must include only name of one or more partners held liable; it may be completed by special denomination or definition of firm's activities, in which case words "commandite par actions" must either precede or follow. Unless there are legal provisions to contrary, rules governing joint stock companies are applicable. Names of partners upon whom directorship is conferred must appear in articles of association and their powers are determined therein. Provisions as to control of company are same as for joint stock companies. Shareholders signing for firm otherwise than by proxy or permitting their name to be used in that of firm become jointly liable. This type of entity is rare in Belgium.

Limited Partnership Companies.—See topic Joint Stock Companies.

Unregistered Partnerships.—Where two or more individuals carry on business under a firm name without registering in any of forms hereinbefore mentioned, their several liability for firm's debts is unlimited. They are deemed to have formed civil company with commercial purpose. Such company has no legal personality.

Clubs and charitable organizations can obtain limitation of personal liability of members, and acquire a Belgian legal entity ("association sans but lucratif" — "vereniging zonder winstoogmerk").

PATENTS:

Belgium is member of the Paris Union Convention of 1883.

As of Jan. 1, 1987, patents are governed by Statute of Mar. 28, 1984.

One of main purposes of this new statute was to bring Belgian legislation on patents in harmony with several international treaties. These treaties are Convention of Strasbourg of Nov. 27, 1963, Convention of Münich regarding the issuance of European Patents, signed on Oct. 5, 1973, and finally Convention of Luxemburg regarding European Community Patent signed on Dec. 15, 1975.

Statute of 1984 has become important and praiseworthy piece of legislation. Statute now contains 78 articles and deals with variety of subjects which until now were not regulated and gave rise to controversies. Statute also explicitly incorporates existing law on right of priority, established by Paris Convention on protection of industrial property.

With respect to what has to be considered as patentable subject matter, law of 1984, adopts basically same broad definition as one which was adopted by old law of 1854. Are considered to be patentable subject matter those "inventions" which are suitable for so-called "industrial" applications. (Art. 2 of Statute of Mar. 28, 1984).

What is new, is that law now explicitly excludes some inventions from legal protection under patent statute. In particular are excluded, among others, discoveries of scientific principles and natural phenomena, mental steps, computer software and so-called biological inventions. (Arts. 3 and 4 of Statute of Mar. 28, 1984). With respect to latter category, however, statute states that inventions in what is called microbiology, contrary to inventions in biology, can be protected under patent.

Under old law question whether invention had to be considered as new, had to be answered in view of those existing inventions which were contained in printed publications or prior patents, as well as those inventions which were already used by third parties on Belgian territory. (Art. 24 of Statute of May 24, 1854). This has now been changed by new law, which provides that novelty has to be determined in view of "state of the art" in general, without having regard to manner in which this "state of the art" has been made accessible to public. (Art. 5, §§1 and 2 of Statute of Mar. 28, 1984). All inventions made accessible to public by whatever means before filing date must be taken into consideration when determining novelty. (Art. 5, §2 of Statute of Mar. 28, 1984).

Requirement of nonobviousness is now formally inserted in statute. To be patentable, invention may not be obvious in view of what person who is skilled in art considers to be normal consequence or application of state of the art. (Art. 6 of Statute of Mar. 28, 1984).

In attempt to revalorize Belgian patent, statute provides for possibility to ask for elaborate novelty and nonobviousness search. (Art. 21, §§2, 5 and 6 of Statute of Mar. 28, 1984).

It has to be emphasized, however, that such search is not mandatory. Applicant who requests search can obtain patent for 20 years. If he does not request search, his patent will only last six years. (Art. 39, §§1 and 2 of Statute of Mar. 28, 1984).

Patent Office cannot refuse to issue patent when in its view search does show that invention is not new or is obvious. Indeed, novelty and nonobvious search is meant only to inform applicant and not to be basis for refusal of patent application. (See Art. 22, §3 of Statute of Mar. 28, 1984.)

Specification and disclosure requirements have also been amended drastically by new statute. Major change is that from now on claims of patent will be decisive. Under old law it was allowed to construe extent of patent protection in view of description in patent application. New Statute of Mar. 28, 1984, however, provides that extent of

PATENTS . . . *continued*
patent protection will only be determined on basis of what is contained clearly and comprehensively in patent claims. (Art. 17, §2 of Statute of Mar. 28, 1984). Description of invention in patent application can, however, still be used to determine meaning of words or terms in patent claims.

In general, patentee can enjoin every third party to exploit invention. Infringing use is defined very broadly. It might be producing, offering, selling, licensing or just having in stock protected product. (Art. 27, §1 of Statute of Mar. 28, 1984). If invention relates to process, patent protection will include not only use of patented process, but also all products which were obtained by using this protected process. (Art. 27, §1[c] of Statute of Mar. 28, 1984).

Noteworthy is that new statute, apart from direct infringement, now also provides for contributory infringement. Contributory infringement is defined as knowingly procuring means necessary for direct infringement. (Art. 27, §2 of Statute of Mar. 28, 1984).

Infringement will result in cease and desist order, as well as in damages, without regard to good faith of infringer. (Art. 52, §4 of Statute of Mar. 28, 1984). If there is bad faith, confiscation may be ordered and patentee can also ask for compensation equal to turnover realised by infringer. (Art. 53 of Statute of Mar. 28, 1984).

With respect to nullity or voidness of patent, Art. 49, §1 of Statute contains limitative list of all causes of nullity. This list refers, among others, to traditional requirements of novelty, nonobviousness, specification and disclosure requirements, as well as some other causes of nullity. Declaration of voidness by court of law will have retroactive effect until day patent was issued. (Art. 50, §1 of Statute of Mar. 28, 1984). Court decisions establishing existence of infringement and assessing damages for patentee, which have res judicata effect and which have been enforced, will, however, not be affected by posterior declaration of voidness. Contracts entered into before declaration of voidness and performed at date of declaration of voidness will not be affected. (Art. 50, §2 of Statute of Mar. 28, 1984).

New law also contains important rules regarding infringement procedure. For instance, statute provides statute of limitations of five years from date of infringement. (Art. 54 of Statute of Mar. 28, 1984).

Most important change with respect to patent litigation, is exclusive jurisdiction of those courts of first instance, which are located at seat of court of appeals. (Art. 73, §2 of Statute of Mar. 28, 1984). This exclusive jurisdiction of court of first instance will not affect, however, possibility to settle basically any patent dispute by way of arbitration. (Art. 73, §6 of Statute of Mar. 28, 1984).

Under Benelux Design and Model Act of Jan. 1, 1975, designs and industrial patterns can be protected when registered.

However, models and designs solely created for achieving certain technical effect may not be registered.

Initial protection under registration is five years and may be extended twice.

Model or design which has not been registered can be protected by Copyright Statute if it embodies "a clear artistic character". (Art. 21 of Benelux Design and Model Act). However, in interpreting this statute, Benelux Court of Justice found that "personal and original" character of product is sufficient. (Benelux Court of Justice, May 22, 1987).

PLEDGES:

Pledges require pledged property to be in possession of creditor or third party agreed upon. In case of pledge of claims, creditor-pledgee acquires possession of pledged claim by entering into agreement and pledge becomes operative against debtor by notification to debtor or acknowledgment by debtor. (C.C. 2075).

Creditor is entitled to preference over unsecured creditors and other liens on proceeds of sale. Sale must be authorized by court. (C.C. 2078 and art. 4, Act 5, May 1872).

See also topic Chattel Mortgages.

PRESCRIPTION:

See topic Limitation of Actions.

PRINCIPAL AND AGENT:

On Apr. 13, 1995, Law on Commercial Agency Agreement ("Law") was enacted. It was published on June 2, 1995 and entered into force ten days after its publication, on June 12, 1995.

Belgian law therefore now distinguishes between agency agreements in general and commercial agency agreements. Commercial agency agreement, within meaning of law, is agreement in which one party, principal, charges other party, commercial agent, on permanent basis and in exchange for remuneration, with negotiation and possible execution of transactions in name and on behalf of principal. Commercial agent acts on independent basis.

Belgian Civil Code provides for general rules applying to agency agreements. In principal, these rules apply to commercial agency agreements to extent that agent is charged with performance of legal actions such as execution of transactions.

Under Civil Code, either general or specific authority can be given. General power of attorney only allows acts of management; for acts of property specific power of attorney is required. Agent cannot bind principal outside scope of his power, except where principal subsequently ratifies acts performed by agent or where there is ostensible authority.

Agent is liable for fraud and negligence (duty of care being however construed less strict if agency is performed for free). Vis-à-vis third parties, agent cannot be sued personally unless he has acted outside scope of his powers.

Agent is required to perform his mandate as long as he has not been revoked. He is liable for any damage caused by his nonperformance.

Principal is required to comply with undertakings entered into by agent within scope of his powers, or when acts are subsequently ratified or where there is ostensible authority. He must reimburse agent's expenses and pay commission if agreed, even in case of failure of agent when such failure is not due to agent's fault. He must indemnify agent for losses incurred when they are not due to any lack of care. He also owes interest on any advances made by agent.

Noncommercial agents are entitled to remuneration or commission only pursuant to specific agreement, except in cases where remuneration is common practice. Contrary to principle of contractual freedom, Belgian case law allows courts to reduce agreed commissions, when excessive.

Revocation of noncommercial agency can be made at any time unless otherwise provided in written power of attorney. Such revocation is effective when notified to persons contracting with agent. Agency is likewise terminated by death, bankruptcy or insanity of either principal or agent.

Law implements EEC Directive No. 86/653 of Dec. 18, 1986 on coordination of laws of Member States relating to self-employed commercial agents. Scope of law is broad. It applies not only to independent commercial agent trading in goods but to any such agent acting as intermediary for transactions. Excluded are commercial agents who do not regularly act as intermediary, contracts signed with their agents by insurance companies, credit institutions and stock brokerage companies and agreements concluded by commercial agents acting on securities exchange, on other regulated securities markets or on commodity exchanges. Except when otherwise provided, law has mandatory character.

Written commercial agency agreements are not required except to enter into commercial agency agreements for definite period. Commercial agency agreements for definite duration which are continued after their expiration are deemed to be agreements for indefinite duration. If commercial agency agreements are for indefinite duration, early termination is possible by either party by giving notice of termination of one month if agreement is in its first year, two months if agreement is in its second year and so on. As of sixth year, notice period becomes six months maximum. Shorter notice periods are not valid. Longer notice periods may be agreed to provided that notice to be served by principal is not shorter than notice to be served by commercial agent. Written notice must indicate beginning and duration of notice period and must be given by registered letter or bailiff writ. If notice is sent by registered letter, it only has effect on third business day as of date of sending.

Commercial agency agreements can be terminated without notice in exceptional circumstances which make any further professional cooperation between principal and commercial agent impossible, or when one party seriously defaults in implementing his obligations. Such termination is only possible during period of seven business days as from occurrence of circumstances or defaults justifying early termination.

Commercial agents may receive fixed remuneration, commissions or combination of both. Parties are free to determine amount of remuneration. In absence thereof, amount is determined on basis of remuneration which is usual for similar transactions in economic sector of location where commercial agent exercises his activity. In absence of such trade custom, commercial agent is entitled to fair percentage as commission. Commissions become due when third contracting party implemented his obligations. Agent can only agree to waive his right to commission in specific cases provided by law.

Law allows that commercial agent guarantees, under certain conditions and within certain limits, obligations of third contracting party.

After termination of commercial agency agreement, commercial agent is entitled to indemnity when he has brought new clients to principal or when he has increased volume of trade with existing clients with substantial advantages for principal after termination (this is presumed when agreement includes noncompetition clause). Indemnity is equal to maximum one year of remuneration calculated on basis of average remunerations for last five years. No indemnity is due when principal terminated agreement for serious fault committed by commercial agent, when commercial agent terminated agreement (unless for cause due to principal or because of his age, invalidity or illness), or when commercial agent or his successors transferred their rights and obligations under agreement to third party. Indemnity must be claimed within one year after termination. If indemnity is not sufficient to cover real damage suffered by agent due to termination of agreement, agent can claim additional damages. Contractual derogations to rules on termination indemnity are only possible after termination.

Law further allows written noncompetition clauses in commercial agency agreement provided they cover type of activities handled by agent, are limited to specific group of clients or specific territory and do not exceed six months after termination. Said clauses do not apply when commercial agency agreement is terminated by principal without cause or by commercial agent with specific cause of termination. Damages in case of violation of noncompetition clause are limited to one-year remuneration unless principal proves higher damage.

Claims resulting from commercial agency agreement expire, pursuant to law, five years after relevent facts and, in any case, one year after expiration of agreement.

Unless international treaties provide otherwise, law applies to any activity of commercial agents having their main establishment in Belgium, Belgian courts having jurisdiction for any dispute relating to such activity.

Law applies to all commercial agency agreements even if they were signed and effective before entry into force of law. It does not apply, however, to obligations resulting from commercial agency agreements submitted to courts before entry into force of law.

Other forms of agents include (i) commission agents acting in their own name and personally liable vis-à-vis third parties; they are also subject to rules of Civil Code described above, (ii) brokers acting as mere intermediaries; insurance brokers are subject to recent law of Mar. 27, 1995 (published on June 14, 1995 and entered into force on Jan. 1, 1996), (iii) stock-broking companies which are also subject to specific regulations and (iv) real estate agents subject to Royal Decree of Sept. 6, 1993.

See also topic Sales.

REAL PROPERTY:

Ownership.—Main principle is that all land is held in private ownership and owner of land is free to dispose of it.

Zoning, Planning and Old Building Protection Regulations.—Right to develop land is, however, strictly regulated by zoning, building and environmental legislation. As Regions (federate entities) have competence in these matters, different regulations and procedures will apply depending on where property is located. There are also protective regulations in relation to historic buildings and sites, for which Regions

REAL PROPERTY . . . *continued*
have jurisdiction. Existence of these regulations may have some bearing on granting of building permits.

Acquisition Regulations and Preemption Rights.—Number of acquisition regulations should be kept in mind. Of particular significance, is right of public entity to buy back industrial land where land was initially acquired from public entity which gave financial help to buyer. In addition, preemption rights of farmer on sale of farming land; and sale of family residence (requiring consent of spouse of owner/seller) and of practical significance.

Right of Surface Ownership ("opstalrecht/droit de superficie").—This is situation where owner grants lease with right to put up buildings on his land. It is horizontal division of ownership rights. Such right is granted for mandatory maximum period of 50 years.

Long Lease ("erfpacht/emphytéose").—This is lease (minimum of 27 years and maximum of 99 years) under which owner of land grants right to use land and buildings on it.

Concession Right ("concessie/concession").—Public entities owning land may grant to private persons or entities right to use land and to build on land by way of concession. One of main characteristics is that public entity is always entitled to terminate agreement if it is in best interest of community.

Usufruct ("vruchtgebruik/usufruit") and Ownership Without Usufruct ("naakte eigendom/nue propriété").—This is division of ownership rights over same property. Usufruct is in essence right to use property or to receive proceeds generated by it. Usufruct can be granted for fixed or indefinite period, but it is always terminated at moment of death of usufructuary. Usufruct in favour of legal entity can only be granted for (mandatory) maximum period of 30 years.

Co-ownership of Apartments.—Legal position of owners of apartments is regulated by Civil Code. In essence, there is co-ownership of common parts such as grounds, roof, corridors, landings, stairways, and private ownership of apartments.

Land Easements.—There are several types of easement ("erfdienstbaarheden/servitudes") under Belgian law. Main division is distinction between legal easements and voluntary easements.

Voluntary easement can be established by contract. This easement must be granted for benefit of one property (as opposed to benefit of particular person) and at encumbrance of another property (as opposed to personal obligation solely borne by particular person). In order to be effective against third parties, easements established by contract must be recorded in Mortgage Register. Voluntary easement can also be established either by continuous use for 30 years or after having been set up by previous owner within his property. Such easements are less common in practice.

Legal easements consist of natural easements and legal easements in strict sense. Natural easements exist because of natural location of properties (e.g. river between two properties). Legal easements in strict sense are concerned with matters such as common walls, right of way, etc. In addition, there are charges of public usefulness, which can be of significance in practice.

SALES:

Contracts of sale may be either oral, implied or written.

The agreement of the parties constitutes the binding sale, the writing is only in the nature of proof, although this may be essential for practical purposes. Special formalities are, however, required for sales of realty.

The seller must specify clearly conditions of sale: if doubt arises, the contract will be construed in favor of the buyer. The seller warrants the buyer against latent defects only, and not against apparent defects such as the buyer could notice. Claims based on latent defects must be brought as quickly as possible, the courts determining the time limit to be permitted for same. On receipt of defective goods, the buyer must either send them back to seller or have them examined by an expert commissioned by the court.

Full expenses are nearly always borne by buyer. Specific performance is granted if such course is feasible.

If the sale price of real estate represents less than five-twelfths of true value, seller may within two years rescind sale, in which case buyer has right to receive back price paid or to avoid rescission by payment of balance of fair value, subject to reduction of one-tenth of total price. (C.C. 1674).

Warranties.—Professional sellers are deemed to know defects of goods sold by them and are liable in damages therefor to purchasers and sub-purchasers.

Notices Required.—On nonconforming delivery buyer should protest to seller (no special form required) and have goods returned to seller or stored in warehouse. If price already paid, he should apply to court for appointment of surveyor.

Applicable Law.—The Hague Uniform Acts on international sale of movables and on formation of international sale contracts of movables of July 1, 1964 are applicable.

Otherwise, applicable law is law explicitly or presumably chosen by parties or, in absence of such choice, law of place where agreement was reached.

Conditional Sales.—Unpaid seller of realty may reserve property and may rescind the sale in case of default provided his lien has been recorded in the mortgage registry. (Hyp. 28-29). Unpaid seller of business equipment has preference over other creditors for five years only if he files invoice with court of purchaser's residence. (Hyp. 20-5·). Reservation of property in personalty is not operative against attaching creditors or trustees in bankruptcy.

Retention of Title Clause.—It is possible for seller to retain property in goods until final payment, but such clause is not opposable vis-à-vis third parties in case of bankruptcy.

Distributorships.—Distributorships, if they are or are deemed to be for unspecified duration and either factually exclusive or coupled with important obligations imposed on distributor, can be terminated by principal only by giving adequate notice or compensation in lieu thereof and additional compensation for goodwill. (Statute of July 27, 1961).

SEALS:

The sealing and delivering of contracts, wills or other documents are unknown in Belgium; the only methods of execution are by simple signature or by public deed before notary.

Joint stock companies do not use a corporate seal, but operate by means of the signatures of the officers authorized by the company's charter.

In case of death of a property owner, if the heirs are minors or absent or if a creditor or interested party requests it, official seals can be attached to any property, and can be broken only in the presence of the notary drawing up the inventory.

Seals are always affixed to deed boxes in banks and safe deposits in case of death.

SHIPPING:

Vessels of twenty-five tons or more ordinarily intended for transportation of passengers, carriage of goods, fishing, towing or any other lucrative occupation at sea are considered as sea ships. (Comm. C., Book II, 1). Vessels of less than 25 tons and vessels ordinarily intended for above mentioned activities in territorial waters are considered as river ships. (Comm. C., Book II, 271).

Ship may be registered at office of registrar of maritime mortgages in Antwerp. Registration can be secured before completion of construction. (Comm. C., Book II, 3).

Certain debts and claims are allowed as liens on ship and freight, in the following order: (1) Court costs and costs spent in common interest of creditors for preservation of ships or up to date of sale; taxes and public charges, costs for dues and maintenance from date of entrance of ship in port; (2) wages of captain and crew and related social contributions; (3) costs and indemnities for salvage and contribution to general average; (4) collision indemnities due for damage caused to other vessels, their cargo or persons on board; (5) necessary costs resulting from act or contract concluded by captain (sea ships only). (Comm. C., Book II, 23).

Ships, including those in process of building, may be mortgaged for a fixed sum. (Comm. C., Book II, 26). Mortgage also covers three years of interest. It must be registered at office of maritime mortgages, and is valid for 15 years. (Comm. C., Book II, 28 and 32).

Shipowners are personally liable for their acts, faults, torts or engagements. They are vicariously liable for the acts of and engagements made by captain within limits of his authority, acts of crew, pilot on board and other agents. (Comm. C., Book II, 46). They can limit their liability in accordance with Treaty of Athens of Dec. 13th, 1974 on Transport of Passengers and Treaty of London of Nov. 19th, 1976 on Limitation of Liability for Maritime Claims (except for art. 2, §1d and e of this Treaty for sea ships). (Comm. C., Book II, 47).

Charterers may limit their liability under same conditions as ship owner.

A law of November 28th, 1928, on bills of lading determines the obligations of the carrier of goods by sea, the indispensable stipulations of bills of lading and the unavoidable liability of carrier and ship according to the so-called "Hague Rules." Law of Apr. 11th, 1989 adapted law of Nov. 28th, 1928 to so-called "Visby Rules". (Comm. C., Book II, 91).

A captain may, in certain extreme cases, hypothecate his ship or sell cargo. He is liable in damages for any negligence on the part of his crew, and for damage to or loss of his cargo. (Comm. C., Book II, 59 and 69).

Sea-going vessels may be arrested after leave of arrest has been granted by Judge of Seizure. Brussels Convention of May 10, 1952 for unification of certain rules relating to arrest of sea-going ships has been incorporated in Jud. C., 1467-1473.

STATUTE OF FRAUDS: See topic Frauds, Statute of.

STATUTES:

Part of Belgian law is codified. Principal code is Civil Code of 1804, which has undergone serious changes by laws of Dec. 16, 1851, on preferential rights and mortgages (Arts. 2092 to 2203), and of July 14, 1976 on matrimonial agreements (Arts. 1387 to 1581).

This code contains three divisions, first relating to persons, second to chattels and real estate, third to different means of acquiring property. There are also codes of commercial law, penal law and criminal procedure, and Judicial Code.

TAXATION:

Income Tax.—

Tax may be either of following: (1) Individual income tax (impôt des personnes physiques—personenbelasting); (2) corporate income tax (impôt des sociétés—vennootschapsbelasting); (3) tax on income of legal entities, being nonprofit organizations (impôt des personnes morales—rechtspersonenbelasting); (4) nonresident income tax (impôt des nonrésidents—belasting der niet-verblijfhouders).

Surcharge.—General surcharge of 3% is due on all income taxes (not on withholding taxes).

Withholding tax (précompte—voorheffing) credited against tax on total income is levied on three types of income: Real property (précompte immobilier—onroerende voorheffing), personal property (précompte mobilier—roerende voorheffing) and compensation (précompte professionel—bedrijfsvoorheffing).

Withholding tax on real property income is levied on assessed rental value (revenu cadastral—kadastraal inkomen). Rate varies according to local taxation. Credit is only granted in respect of individual taxpayer's personal residence and is limited to 12.5% of assessed rental value subject to withholding tax on real property and excess withholding tax is nonrefundable.

Withholding tax on personal property income is levied at 25% or, under certain conditions, at 15% on dividends. Withholding tax of 15% is due on interest from debt securities issued and on income from lease, use or license of personal property. This withholding tax represents final tax for individual taxpayers.

Withholding tax on professional income is levied on salaries, wages, pensions and compensations of employees, of company directors and of active partners in partnerships. It follows progressive rate of individual income tax.

See Topical Index in front part of this volume.

TAXATION . . . *continued*

Corporate Income Tax.—Total corporate income includes: (a) Dividends distributed, retained earnings, and certain nondeductible expenses. As for corporate income, standard rate is 39%. If taxable corporate income is less than Frs. 13,000,000 progressive rates apply (e.g. 28% on net profits below Frs. 1,000,000) (with certain exceptions). Rate is reduced to one-fourth on income from foreign branch if taxed and on income from foreign real property.

Dividends whether domestic or foreign, received by a corporate shareholder are, under certain conditions, excluded from taxable income up to 95% (i.e. intercorporate dividend exemption).

There is tax credit for interest and royalties taxed in source country. Tax credit amounts to 15/85 of net amount of royalties received; for interest, tax credit is calculated according to fraction, numerator of which is equal to foreign tax expressed as percentage of income on which this tax is calculated, limited to 15%, and denominator of which is equal to 100% reduced by amount of numerator. For interests, tax credit thus calculated must be multiplied by coefficient which reflects proportion of total income less movable expences to total income. Income received is grossed up by this tax credit.

Branches (permanent establishments) of foreign companies have to carry separate books and are taxable at 39%.

Capital gains are part of normal income taxed at ordinary rate. Part of capital gains not exceeding monetary depreciation before 1950 is exempt. However any gains (including capital gains) on assets that have been systematically undervalued and capital gains on securities representing recovery of losses previously deducted are taxed at ordinary rate. Capital gains realized on shares are exempt from tax provided dividends on shares qualify for intercorporate dividend exemption.

System of spread taxation is available for voluntary capital gains realized on sale of tangible or intangible fixed assets which are invested in companies for more than five years on condition proceeds of sale are reinvested in Belgium in depreciable tangible or intangible assets. These capital gains are subject to ordinary company income tax in proportion to depreciation accepted on assets acquired as reinvestment (with certain exceptions).

Interest on loans is deductible expense to extent of market rate that would apply under circumstances. Depreciation is admitted according to normal practice (with certain exceptions). Losses including capital losses can be carried forward indefinitely (with certain exceptions).

Individual income tax is progressive to 55% (last bracket starting at Frs. 2,420,000). From 1990 on business income of married taxpayers is taxed separately regardless of amount of their income and both are entitled to tax-exempt amount of Frs. 156,000 (for single taxpayer tax exempt amount raises to Frs. 198,000). Other income items of spouses continue to be aggregated. If only one spouse has earned income, 30% of first Frs. 990,000 (i.e. maximum of Frs. 297,000) of his/her income is attributed to other spouse and both parts of income are submitted to normal tax rates separately. Reductions of income tax are allowed for dependents.

Capital gains on tangible and financial fixed assets, if used by individuals in business activities during more than five years are taxed at reduced rate of 16.5%. Capital gains on nonbusiness assets are tax exempt, except for capital gains on unimproved land if sold within eight years of acquisition (rate 16.5-33%), or capital gains realized on substantial (25%) shareholdings in Belgian companies upon sale to nonresident legal entity (rate 16.5%).

Nonresident individuals and foreign companies are taxable on Belgian source income. In absence of permanent establishment tax liability of foreign companies is limited to withholding tax. If there is permanent establishment Belgian source income is taxed at rate of 39%.

Non-Belgian expatriate executives of multinational enterprises qualify for special deductions and exemption of portion of salary corresponding to work performed abroad.

Commissions paid by individuals to their unidentified brokers or agents are not deductible from taxable income. Payments made by corporate taxpayer to nonidentified persons are subject to special secret commission tax of 300%. Secret commissions as well as special tax are deductible for corporate tax persons.

Special tax status exists for coordination centers being set up within multinational companies as Belgian branch of foreign company or as separate Belgian company under condition that center: (1) Is recognized by royal decree; (2) carries out only certain qualifying activities exclusively for group of companies to which it belongs; and (3) employs at least ten full-time employees.

Tax advantages are for (renewable) ten year period: (1) Lump-sum tax calculated on basis of expenses other than financial and personnel costs; (2) total exemption from 0.5% registration tax on capital contributions; (3) exemption from withholding tax on real property; (4) exemption from withholding tax on dividends, interest and royalties paid by coordination center as well as on interest received on deposits made with banks and other financial institutions. However, annual tax of Frs. 400,000 per full-time employee (with maximum of Frs. 4,000,000) must be paid.

Inheritance Tax.—Net value of worldwide assets of each individual (including aliens) residing at time of his death in Belgium, is subject to inheritance tax. Gross value of real property located in Belgium of nonresident alien is subject to Belgian estate duty at time of his death. Rate of both inheritance tax and estate duty is progressive and varies according to size of estate accruing to each heir, and distance in relationship between deceased and each heir or legatee.

Registration tax is levied on certain types of transactions. Rate is 0.5% on contributions to capital of companies and partnerships (with certain exceptions and exemptions), 12.5% on sales of real estate, 0.20% on leases other than leases exclusively for housing of person or family (duty based on amount of rent for entire period of lease).

Value added tax is levied on goods and services delivered or rendered in exercise of regular business or professional activity. Tax is charged to customer and paid to Treasury by supplier after deduction of any V.A.T. paid by him on deliveries of goods and services. Rates are as follows: 21% general rate; 1% on gold used as investment; 6% on foodstuffs, pharmaceuticals, other necessaries and on certain construction transactions (e.g. repairs with respect to at least 15 year old dwellings; other construction transactions are subject to 21% or 12% V.A.T. rate) 12% on certain other goods and services, including social dwellings and pay television. Zero rate is applicable to exports. Tax exemptions for legal, medical, cultural and social services as well as education.

Excise taxes are levied on use in production of alcohol and alcoholic beverages, sugar, tobacco, mineral oils, as well as on consumption of some nonalcoholic beverages and coffee. Rates vary according to volume, weight, density and alcohol content.

Other taxes are: Tax on automobiles or other motor or steam vehicles; tax on theatres and all public entertainments; tax on gambling and betting; opening tax for bars and cafés.

Local Taxes.—Apart from above-mentioned taxes, in each town, local taxes are payable. Some are levied on same basis as State taxes (real estate tax; surcharge on personal income tax); others are on different basis (e.g., furniture, employees, entertainments).

Avoidance of Double Taxation.—An agreement for purpose of avoiding double taxation has been signed and ratified between U.S. and Belgium, operative for income earned since Jan. 1, 1971. Protocol amending Belgium-U.S. income tax treaty was initiated on Dec. 31, 1987 and has been ratified (entered into effect on Jan. 1, 1988). Among more important of substantive provisions of Convention are following, in summary: (1) Adoption of principles for determining and taxing business income derived by enterprises of one country from permanent establishments within other country; (2) reciprocal exemption from taxation upon certain conditions, of various items of income derived from sources within one country by residents or corporations of other country, including profits from operation of ships and aircraft, royalties, pensions, private pensions and life annuities, and remuneration or payments received by teachers and students; (3) limited reservation by each country of right to tax its own citizens, residents or corporations without regard to provisions of Convention; (4) reciprocal reduction to 15% (as of Jan. 1, 1988 5% provided recipient owns at least 10% of voting stock of company paying dividends) of U.S. and Belgium tax on dividends to shareholder resident in other country; (5) Belgian taxes are allowed as credit against U.S. taxes; income taxed in U.S. and received by resident of Belgium generally is exempted from tax in Belgium but has to be included in order to compute tax rate; (6) as a rule, citizens or corporations of one country, residing in other country may not be subject to heavier tax burden in latter country as citizens or corporations of latter country are subject to; (7) provisions assuring taxpayers right of appeal when they can show that they are taxed contrary to principles of present Convention; (8) provisions for reciprocal exchange of information, subject to certain limitations similar to those provided for in certain other tax conventions of U.S., and for assistance in collection of taxes in certain cases, subject to proviso to ensure that exemption or reduced rate of tax granted by Convention shall not be enjoyed by persons not entitled to such benefits.

Other Conventions exist between Belgium and all Western-European countries except for Iceland, as well as with various other countries, e.g., Brazil, China, India, Indonesia, Israel, Japan, Malaysia, Malta, Morocco and Singapore.

TRADEMARKS AND TRADENAMES:

Statute and Treaties.—Belgium is member, inter alia, of Paris Union Convention of 1883 and of Madrid Agreement.

As of Jan. 1, 1971, trademarks are governed by Benelux Uniform Trademark Act ("BUTA"). Under system implemented by BUTA, Benelux trademark or (as of 1987) service mark registration geographically extends to territory of the three Benelux countries, i.e., Belgium, The Netherlands, and Luxembourg. National courts still have jurisdiction on trademark and service mark (hereafter collectively referred to as "trademark") litigation. However, questions of interpretation of BUTA can, and under certain circumstances must, be referred to Benelux Court of Justice.

Council Directive of Dec. 21, 1988 to harmonize laws of Member States (all three Benelux countries are members of EU) with respect to trademarks should have been implemented by each national government by Dec. 31, 1992. Although the three Benelux governments agreed in 1992 upon necessary changes to BUTA as result of Directive, ratification by respective legislative bodies and subsequent enactment is not expected before Jan. 1996. As Directive is very closely inspired from existing Benelux trademark law, modifications of BUTA will remain limited.

Trademarks.—Any sign which is capable of distinguishing goods or services of one undertaking from those of another undertaking can be registered as trademark. Illustrative list includes words, names, drawings, prints, and even letters, figures, and shapes of goods or of packaging, provided they are distinctive. However, shapes which are determined by very nature of the good, which affect its essential value, or which are functional cannot be protected as trademarks.

Registration.—Exclusive right to trademark is acquired by registration. Unregistered trademarks are not protected under BUTA. Benelux Trademark Office registers applicant's trademark after purely informative examination. When no private search is conducted prior to filing of application, Benelux Trademark Office is requested to carry out official search for prior registrations. Under BUTA, however, Benelux Trademark Office has no authority to reject application due to prior right.

Duration of protection is ten years but can be renewed for successive periods of ten years without any limit, as long as mark remains distinctive.

Infringement.—Based on its exclusive rights, owner of registered trademark can (i) prevent any unauthorized party from using same sign or similar sign in connection with identical or related goods or services and (ii) prevent any third party from using same sign or similar sign in commercial transactions, even in connection with unrelated goods or services, if such use is made without valid excuse and/or under circumstances likely to be prejudicial to trademark owner. Under these circumstances, trademark owner is entitled to damages.

Trademark's scope of protection heavily depends on distinctiveness of trademark, i.e., on its strength, as of time protection is requested. Criteria used by courts to find trademark infringement is very broad. Likelihood of confusion sensu stricto (that is, confusion as to source or origin of goods or services) is not necessary to uphold trademark infringement. Mere likelihood of association (confusion as to sponsorship, endorsement or some other affiliation), even in absence of confusion sensu stricto,

See Topical Index in front part of this volume.

TRADEMARKS AND TRADENAMES . . . *continued*
suffices to consider sign as infringing upon registered trademark. Moreover, trademark protection extends, under certain circumstances, outside markets in which trademark has been registered, used or is known.

Cancellation.—Trademark registrations can be cancelled in court, inter alia, (i) due to prior registration of similar trademark for same kind of goods or services, (ii) when registered sign lacks distinctiveness, (iii) when it is explicitly excluded from trademark protection under BUTA provisions (functional shape, for instance), or (iv) when filing was fraudulent. Such cancellations are effective as of date of filing. Fraudulent filing might result, under circumstances, from prior use of same sign or of similar sign in Benelux, or even abroad, prior to filing date.

Loss of Right.—Registered trademark owner might lose its exclusive rights, inter alia, in case no normal use of trademark has been made either within three years after filing or during uninterrupted period of five years. Loss of right can also result from trademark having become generic due to trademark owner's behavior.

Assignments and Licenses.—To be valid, assignments and licenses must be in writing. To be enforceable towards third parties, they must be recorded in trademark register. Assignment of trademark does not have to be accompanied by assignment of business in which assigned mark was used.

TREATIES:

Self-executing provisions of treaties, if properly approved and published, take precedence over statutes.

Treaty of Friendship, Establishment and Navigation with U.S. is of Feb. 21, 1961.

Belgium is member to European Convention on Human Rights and has accepted right of personal application and jurisdiction of Court of Strasbourg.

See topic Taxation, subhead Avoidance of Double Taxation.

See topic Patents.

See also Selected International Conventions section.

TRUSTS:

Trusts and trustees are unknown.

UNFAIR COMPETITION:

This matter is governed by Law of July 14, 1991 on trade practices and on information for and protection of consumer (hereinafter trade practices and consumer protection act or "T.P.C.P. Act").

New law is, to large extent, restatement of previously existing rules on trade practices. While reinstating old rules, however, some new features have been introduced. These features are sometimes confirmation of case law that has emerged since entry into force of old statute of July 14, 1971 or necessary amendments of or corrections to existing regulations.

Unlike old law, however, new law covers not only relationship amongst business people and corporations. New law indeed contains number of new regulations that will have to be applied in relationship between those business people and corporations, on one hand, and consumer, on other hand.

Indication of Price.—Any product that is being offered to consumer should have price tag mentioning clearly price to be paid. Likewise, fee to be paid for services is always to be indicated in clear and unambiguous way. (art. 2 of T.P.C.P. Act). Any price or fee that is being indicated has to cover full price, covering VAT, any other taxes and mandatory expenses. (art. 3 of T.P.C.P. Act).

Indication of Quantity.—Law also contains number of specific regulations on manner in which weight, contents or, more generally, quantity of particular product is to be indicated on label.

Labeling Regulations.—Any mandatory indication on label, for product or service, is by virtue of art. 13 of law to be mentioned in language or languages of region where product or service is being offered. Apart from this or these languages, use of other complementory languages is allowed.

Denominations of origin are names referring to country, region or any location, such country, region or location playing important if not conclusive role as regards quality or particular characteristics of product. (art. 16 of T.P.C.P. Act). Denomination of origin can only be used for product when such denomination has been formally recognized as such by Royal Decree and when, moreover, product that is being offered for sale under such denomination of origin is fulfilling requirements laid down by said royal decree. Moreover, seller is to be in possession of certificate establishing origin of product, whenever such certificate is being required. (art. 20 of T.P.C.P. Act).

Publicity.—T.P.C.P. Act contains number of new rules with respect to publicity and advertising.

Publicity or advertising governed by law is being defined as any information, of whatever nature, intended either directly or indirectly to promote sale of products or services. (art. 22 of T.P.C.P. Act).

Art. 23 of law contains list of what is considered as unlawful advertising: (a) advertising that is misleading as to characteristics, advantages or conditions of acquisition of particular product; (b) advertising that is misleading as to characteristics, advantages or conditions of acquisitions of particular service; (c) advertising that is misleading as to identity and qualities of seller of product or service; (d) advertising that withholds essential information, with intent to mislead; (e) advertising that cannot be recognized as such at first sight, while not containing clearly visible and unambiguous word "advertising"; (f) advertising that is denigrating vis-à-vis competitor, its products, its services or its activity; (g) comparative advertising that is either deceiving or denigrating, or referring to identity of competitor without any necessity to do so; (h) advertising that may cause confusion with another competitor, its products, its services or its activity; (i) advertising with respect to offer of products or services, while seller does not dispose of stock that is sufficient to meet demand that is to be expected in view of advertising that is being made; (j) advertising that is referring to unauthorized lotteries or sweepstakes; (k) advertising that is referring to comparative tests that have been performed by consumer organization.

Unfair Contractual Clauses.—Any sale of products or services entered into between seller and consumer may not contain one of 21 unfair contractual clauses that are listed in art. 32 of law or, more generally, clause that, when considered as such or together with other clauses, will cause disproportion between obligations of parties. (art. 31 of T.P.C.P. Act).

It is important to stress that for purposes of law seller is being defined as any merchant, craftsman or, more generally, any natural or legal person that is offering for sale products or services in course of business or in order to realize purposes laid down in articles of incorporation. Consumer, on other hand, is being defined as any buyer who is not buying products or services for exclusive professional purposes. (see arts. 1.6· and 7· of T.P.C.P. Act).

Sales as Loss.—It is forbidden to sell at loss. This will be case when product is offered for sale at price which is not at least equal to price against which product has been or will be invoiced upon supply. Any sales with very limited profit margin, taking into consideration price of supply and general expenses is also considered to be sale at loss.

Publicity Relating To Price Deductions or Price Comparison.—When seller is making reference to price deduction, old price referred to has to be price asked for similar products or services in same establishment. This old price must have been used for period of at least one month prior to price deduction. Moreover, deduction of price is to be applied for at least one day. It may not be applied for more than one month. During full period of price deduction date as from which price deduction will be granted is to be indicated. (art. 43 of T.P.C.P. Act).

Tied Offer.—In Belgium tied offers are forbidden. Law defines tied offer as offer of products, services, fringe benefits or titles allowing owner to obtain products, services or fringe benefits, that are tied to acquisition of other yet even similar products or services.

Any such tied offer is not authorized. (art. 54 of T.P.C.P. Act).

Arts. 55, 56 and 57 of T.P.C.P. Act do, however, contain number of exceptions to general prohibition of tied offers.

Unsolicited Goods or Services.—It is prohibited to send to someone, without prior request on his part, any product and invite him to acquire this product against payment of its price, or, in absence thereof, to return it to sender, even at no expense (art. 76 of T.P.C.P. Act). Same rule applies for services.

Sales "at Distance".—T.P.C.P. Act regulates sales of products which are concluded between persons that are not physically present on same location. (art. 77 of T.P.C.P. Act). For such sales sales mechanism is used based on communication methods at distance. In order to protect consumer such sales are concluded only after expiration of consideration period of seven days as of day following day of delivery. No payment nor advances can be asked from consumer before consideration period has expired. Prior to delivery and during consideration period consumer can announce to seller that he will not purchase products. (art. 78 of T.P.C.P. Act).

Sales to Consumer Concluded Outside Seller's Place of Business.—Rules concerning sales concluded outside seller's establishment implement principles of European directive on consumer protection (55/77 of Dec. 20, 1985), in Belgian law.

Dishonest Commercial Practices.—T.P.C.P. Act prohibits, in general way, any act contrary to honest commercial customs whereby seller injures or may injure professional interests of one or several other sellers. (art. 93 of T.P.C.P. Act).

T.P.C.P. Act has also introduced similar catch-all clause in order to protect interests of consumers. (art. 94 of T.P.C.P. Act). Act defines consumer as every physical or moral person which acquires or uses goods or services for nonprofessional purposes only.

In general, acts which fall under no statutory provisions or regulations as well as acts which are regulated by other statutes or regulations may be enjoined on basis of catch-all definition of commercial torts. Professional fault or infringement of statutory provision giving seller advantage to detriment of interests of other sellers or consumers will be considered as dishonest commercial practice.

Sanctions and Enforcement.—Most important sanction is order to cease and desist which may be issued by President of Commercial Court. (art. 95 of T.P.C.P. Act). Procedural rules are those of summary proceedings even though judgment is decision on merits. Such order may be given within few weeks.

In event infringement of T.P.C.P. Act has been brought to attention of Minister of Economic Affairs, he can send warning letter to infringer ordering him to stop his acts. Warning letter must indicate alleged violations and articles which have been infringed upon as well as delay to stop infringement. Further, Minister must reveal if, in event infringer does not react in due course, he will bring action to cease or if he will inform public prosecutor or if he will settle case according to procedure as provided in Act. (art. 101 of T.P.C.P. Act).

Disagreement exists on consequences for potential infringer neglecting warning letter.

Some authors believe that neglecting warning letter is indication that infringer is acting in bad faith, which has to be shown for some infringements to be qualified as penal acts.

WILLS:

To make a will one must be sound in mind. A minor under 16 years of age has no right to make a will. When the age of 16 is attained, a minor may dispose of his property by way of will but only to the extent of one-half of the amount which the law would permit him to dispose of were he a major.

There are three forms of wills:

The holographic will must be handwritten, dated and signed entirely by the testator, but no witnesses are required.

The notarial will is received by a notary to whom testator describes his intentions in the presence of two witnesses, or by two notaries.

The mystic will needs only to be signed by testator who declares it to be his will. It is sealed in the presence of witnesses and deposited in the hands of a notary who

WILLS . . . *continued*
draws up a protocol of the declaration. The protocol is signed by notary, testator and witnesses.

Holographic and mystic wills must be presented to the court who will order them filed with a notary. (C. C. 1007).

Wills can be revoked specifically or by implication. Implied revocation occurs when a subsequent will contains provisions inconsistent with those contained in previous wills. If provisions of a subsequent will are in accordance with those of a previous will not revoked by a specific act, the different provisions are valid and must be executed.

Three categories of legacies are distinguished: specific, residuary and demonstrative (these last being for a portion of the estate).

Forced Heirship.—The general principle is that any person may freely dispose of his property by gift or will, no distinction being made between chattels or immovables. This rule knows but three exceptions: (1) When there are children or representatives of children; (2) when decedent's ascendants are still alive; (3) when there is surviving spouse. If decedent leaves one child, he can only dispose of one-half of his property; if he leaves two, only of one-third; if he leaves three or more, only of one-fourth. Reserved portion goes equally to testator's children. Free portion may be left either to third person or to child he wishes to favour. In absence of children and of surviving spouse, ascendants in both paternal and maternal lines have reserved portion of one-fourth per line. Surviving spouse is entitled to usufruct of half of estate. Usufruct of surviving spouse covers principal family dwelling even if its value exceeds half of estate. This reserved portion of surviving spouse is deducted from reserved portion of children or descendants and from free portion in accordance with their respective sizes.

Foreign Wills.—Will is valid if made either in form prescribed by law of place where drawn or in form prescribed by national law.

BERMUDA LAW DIGEST REVISER

Appleby, Spurling & Kempe
P.O. Box HM 1179
41 Cedar Avenue
Hamilton, Bermuda HM EX
Telephone: 441-295-2244
Fax: 441-292-8666
Email: karenss@novell.ask.bm

Reviser Profile

The present firm was established in 1938 with the late Major Appleby and the late Sir Dudley Spurling as founding partners. Upon Major Appleby's death shortly after the end of the Second World War, the practice was continued by Sir Dudley alone, until he was joined by William Kempe in 1949.

Largely as a result of Bermuda's increasing recognition as an international business centre, the firm has developed substantially over the past 40 years with an international perspective and an ability to meet client needs from offices in Bermuda, Asia and Europe. It is one of Bermuda's largest law firms and has a total complement of over 200 persons, including 40 lawyers, 1 consultant, over 35 company secretaries and a professional librarian.

As a firm of general practitioners, Appleby, Spurling & Kempe can respond to the needs of a diverse local and international clientele with attorneys and administrators specialised in the following principal departments: Company; Litigation; Property; Trusts & Estates; Liquidations & Insolvencies; and Intellectual Property. Complementing the corporate law practice, lawyers and company secretaries provide corporate administrative services to some 2,700 companies which have their registered office at Cedar House.

The firm also encourages its members to serve the local community in other ways. Sir Dudley Spurling had a distinguished parliamentary career extending over 30 years and culminating in his appointment as Speaker of the House of Assembly from 1972 to 1976. Other partners since have served as Members of Parliament, Cabinet Ministers and as Judges of the Supreme Court. Two of the present partners have served as President of the Bermuda Bar Association. Amongst the present partners, there are also those who are or have been involved in politics, on government boards, as members of the Law Reform Committee, as officers of the Bermuda International Business Association, the Bermuda Chamber of Commerce and other service organisations and as directors of leading local public companies and charities.

Responding to the needs of its clients in the Far East and Europe, the firm opened an office in Hong Kong in 1990. Additionally, to complement the activities of European and other clients, the firm established a wholly-owned service company in Guernsey, Channel Islands to provide corporate administrative services. The firm also owns a management company in the British Virgin Islands. The firm's associated company, Harrington Trust Limited has been carrying on a trust business in Bermuda for over 40 years. AS&K Management Services Ltd., which commenced operations in 1992, provides a variety of professional management, consulting and accounting services to its clients. The firm is a member of TerraLex, an international association of law firms, and is represented in the International Bar Association and other international legal organisations.

BERMUDA LAW DIGEST

(The following is a list of all Topics, including cross-references, covered in this Digest.)

BERMUDA LAW DIGEST

Revised for 1997 edition by

APPLEBY, SPURLING & KEMPE, of the Bermuda Bar.

See topic Law Reports, Codes, Etc.

ABSENTEES:

See topics Death; Garnishment; Bankruptcy.

ACTIONS:

Nature of action is defined by Supreme Court Act 1905, as amended, as civil proceedings commenced by writ or in such other manner as is prescribed by statute or by Rules of Supreme Court of Bermuda. Right to bring action and its incidents are determined by English common law and equitable principles, but nature of remedies sought does not affect form of action which is governed by Supreme Court Rules which in turn are largely based upon English Supreme Court Rules.

Mode of Proof of Foreign Claims.—The Evidence Act, 1905, as amended by Evidence Amendment Act, 1984 regulates proof of judgments, judicial proceedings in foreign countries and foreign law; proof of deeds executed abroad is governed by application of English common law.

See also topics Limitation of Actions; Death.

ADOPTION:

Adoption of Children.—Act 1963 No. 151, effective from Jan. 1, 1964, repealed previous Act of 1944. Adoption order may be made by a Special Court in favour of an applicant or two spouses domiciled in Bermuda in respect of an infant (i.e., one under 21 who has not married) who was either born in Bermuda or is child of a person having Bermudian status or is resident in Bermuda with specific permission of Minister for Home Affairs. Condition as to domicile of applicant may be dispensed with where it is shown that under laws of country of domicile of applicant, infant once adopted would be permitted to enter that country. Order may be made in favour of father or mother of infant or of relative (grandparent, brother, sister, uncle, aunt of full or half blood or by affinity) over 21 years of age or other person over 25 years old. Only in special circumstances may sole male adopt female.

Unless one of parents of child is applicant, applicants must register at least three months before application is heard with Department of Health and Welfare which is charged with inquiring and reporting as to facts and suitability of proposed adoption, and (except in cases where one of parents of child is applicant) final order will not be made unless infant has been continuously in care of adopter for three months computed from date not earlier than six weeks after its birth, during which last mentioned time, mother may not consent to adoption. Subject to power to dispense therewith, consent of every person who is parent or guardian of infant and of spouse of proposed adopter must be obtained. Interim order for custody for probationary period not exceeding two years may be made. Appeals from Special Court lie to Supreme Court.

On adoption, adopters acquire same duties, obligations and rights as if child had been born to adopter in wedlock. Unless contrary intention appears, reference express or implied in instruments, executed after date of adoption, to child of adopter includes adopted child, but reference to child of natural parent of adopted child does not include adopted child. However, where natural parent of legitimate child or mother of an illegitimate child dies intestate without other surviving issue, adopted person inherits from such natural parent.

Except with licence from Special Court, it is offence to remove infant from jurisdiction for purpose of adoption abroad.

Registrar-General is charged with maintaining register of adopted persons.

Payment of reward for adoption and advertisement for adoption are prohibited.

ADVERSE POSSESSION:

See topics Limitation of Actions; Real Property.

ALIENS:

An alien is by definition a person who is neither Commonwealth citizen, nor British protected person, nor citizen of Republic of Ireland. British law recognizes concept of plural nationality. Aliens have rights and liabilities of Commonwealth citizens who do not possess Bermudian status: They may not exercise parliamentary or other franchises or hold public offices and are subject to certain other restrictions mostly under Bermuda Immigration and Protection Act, 1956, as am'd.

The British Nationality Act 1981 has made considerable changes in status of British subjects etc.

See topics Immigration; Nationality.

Personal property may be generally acquired and disposed of by aliens, except any share in a British ship, and not more than 40% of issued share capital of any local company may be held by aliens; ownership of share in local partnership is subject to Immigration permission.

Real Property.—Only those houses with Annual Rental Value (A.R.V.) of $43,800 (of which there are approximately 234) and those condominiums with A.R.V. of $15,300 (approximately 418) are available for purchase by "restricted persons". Under Bermuda Immigration and Protection Act 1956, restricted persons i.e. aliens and non-Bermudian Commonwealth citizens may only acquire real property by purchase, gift or inheritance after obtaining sanction of Minister of Labour and Home Affairs. Persons acquiring by devise or inheritance must otherwise dispose of property within three years of death or such extended period as may be sanctioned.

Restricted person may not purchase undeveloped residential land. Houses and condominiums are subject to alien licence fee of 20% of value of house, or 15% of value of condominium. If acquisition is by devise or inheritance or by voluntary conveyance fee payable is $421 (1992).

Application for sanction to acquire or hold real property is made to Chief Immigration Officer, supported by one banker's reference and two personal references. Registration of land acquired by alien must be effected in office of Registrar General within six months, otherwise land will be liable to escheat proceedings, except where real property has passed under conditions mentioned in Washington Convention.

Aliens holding real property may not lease or rent same without permission from Minister of Labour and Home Affairs. The Bermuda Immigration and Protection Amendment Act 1985 by regulations annexed to it entitled The Bermuda Immigration and Protection (Rental Charges) Regulations 1985 levies statutory charge on grant of permit to rent which is $50 or 5% of the rent, whichever is greater.

In theory, alien corporations may, with sanction of Governor, as aforesaid, hold real property but in practice policy of government is to refuse such applications. (See however topics Corporations; Trusts.) It is inadvisable to appoint alien corporation as trustee of real property in Bermuda.

Aliens may acquire leasehold interest in possession in land in Bermuda for terms not exceeding five years without licence from government and, in case of corporation incorporated outside Bermuda, for term specified in licence which cannot exceed 21 years. Such licence would only be granted to such corporation if land is required bona fide for purposes of corporation and if permit has been granted by government enabling corporation to carry on business from Bermuda.

Companies.—Exempted companies may be owned by foreign (i.e. non-Bermudian) companies or persons. Not more than 40% of issued shares of local companies may be held by aliens (or non-Bermudian Commonwealth citizens). Nonresident corporate bodies (those not incorporated in Bermuda) may carry on business from Bermuda, which includes carrying on business abroad from local office, with prior permission of Minister of Finance and upon payment of annual fee to government.

As to banks, see topics Banks and Banking; Corporations.

See also topics Immigration; Real Property; Trusts.

ASSIGNMENTS:

Subject to public policy and contractual or statutory stipulations to contrary, assignments of legal or equitable things are recognised as valid.

By §19(d) of The Supreme Court Act 1905, any absolute assignment, by writing under hand of assignor (not purporting to be by way of charge only), of any debt or other legal chose in action, of which express notice in writing has been given to debtor, trustee or other person from whom assignee would have been entitled to receive or claim such debt or chose in action, shall be, and be deemed to have been, effectual in law (subject to all equities having priority over rights of assignee), to pass legal right to such debt or chose in action.

Such assignments give assignee right to sue in his own name from date of notice. Normally, other assignments can only be enforced by assignee joining assignor in action and notice should be given to preserve priority.

The Life Insurance Act 1978 contains special provisions relating to assignment of life policies.

The Companies Act 1981 and The Exchange Control Act 1972 contain or refer to provisions affecting transfers of shares in Bermuda companies which transfers are also subject to any restrictions in bye-laws.

Assignments by way of security of property in Bermuda or assets of Bermuda companies should be registered to establish priority.

Subject to certain exemptions, assignments are subject to ad valorem stamp duty under The Stamp Duties Act 1976.

See also topics Bills and Notes; Copyright; Patents and Designs; Trademarks.

ASSIGNMENTS FOR BENEFIT OF CREDITORS:

See topic Bankruptcy.

ATTACHMENT:

By Attachment Act, 1874, persons having just cause of action at law for a sum exceeding $14.40 against defendant who has been in Bermuda but is presently absent, having entered action in Supreme Court Registry, filed various documents and given bonded security, may sue out a writ of attachment, inserting as many garnishees in writ as necessary. Only actions of trover or actions founded on contract may be commenced under this Act.

There are penalties for noncompliance by persons served with writ, but if garnishee acknowledges debt in excess of $240 which is less than amount of cause, he may be allowed six months for payment on giving sufficient bonded security. Act provides for liability of garnishees and for their departure from Bermuda, rights of retention and entitlement to costs in certain cases.

Bonded security must be given by plaintiff before suing out execution where defendant has not appeared. Actions are tried in Supreme Court with jury in term in which writ returnable if more than six months since defendant's departure from Bermuda, or if not, at next regular Civil Sessions, but Court has power to grant application to have cause tried in less than six months. No final judgment may be obtained by default.

Goods of defendant in hands of wife, attorney, agent, trustee or servant liable to attachment. Defendant or garnishee has right of appeal similar to defendant in any ordinary suit. (See topic Courts.)

Under Debtors Act 1973 power to arrest any defendant in any action before Supreme Court where plaintiff can show: (1) Good cause of action against defendant (2) who is about to leave Bermuda and (3) whose absence will materially prejudice plaintiff's claim. Under Magistrate's Act, 1948, attachment of earnings order can be made by courts of summary jurisdiction in respect of payments under: (i) Affiliation

See Topical Index in front part of this volume.

ATTACHMENT . . . *continued*

order; (ii) order for maintenance under Matrimonial Proceedings (Magistrates' Courts) Act, 1974; (iii) payments in respect of children made under contribution order under Protection of Children Act, 1943 and payments ordered under Minors Act, 1950; (iv) payment of judgment debt in excess of $25.

Attachment of earnings order is an order directed to employer of debtor and instructs employer to make periodic deductions from debtor's earnings which exceed "protected earnings rate" (rate below which court thinks it reasonable that debtor's earnings should not be reduced), and to pay those deductions to Magistrates' Court Clerk for onward transmission. Duty on employer and debtor to thereafter advise of any change in employment and/or pay.

Attachment of earnings order may be made instead of committal order under §3 of Debtors Act, 1973, and may be varied or revoked in light of material change of circumstances.

Upon satisfying a Supreme Court Judge of expediency, an order of Supreme Court for payment of money may be enforced by way of attachment of earnings. This includes enforcement of maintenance orders made under Matrimonial Causes Act 1974.

Mareva Jurisdiction.—Pre-trial "Mareva" injunction may be obtained preventing foreign defendant removing assets out of country, pending determination of claim justiciable before Supreme Court of Bermuda.

Four basic conditions must be satisfied: (i) Claim is justiciable in Bermudian Courts; (ii) applicant has good arguable case; (iii) it is shown prima facie that there are assets within jurisdiction; and (iv) there is likelihood that they will be removed.

Anton Piller Jurisdiction.—On application of any party to cause or matter, court may make order for detention, custody or preservation of any property which is subject matter of cause or matter, or as to which any question may arise therein, or for inspection of any such property in possession of party to cause or matter. Three preconditions are established for granting of Anton Piller Order: (i) There must be extremely strong prima facie case; (ii) damage, potential or actual, must be very serious to applicant; and (iii) there must be clear evidence that defendants have in their possession incriminating documents or things and that there is real possibility that they may destroy such material before any application inter partes can be made.

AVIATION:

The Aircraft Register.—Governor of Bermuda is required, pursuant to The Air Navigation (Overseas Territories) Order 1989, as amended ("Order"), to maintain Register of Aircraft and to accept applications to register from qualified persons. Primary responsibility for maintenance and operation of Bermuda Register of Aircraft and Flight Crew ("Register") rests with Department of Civil Aviation ("DCA") of Bermuda Government and Director of Civil Aviation acts under powers delegated to him by Governor and Minister of Transport.

Qualified Persons.—Applications to register aircraft on Register must be made by qualified persons which include: bodies incorporated in some part of Commonwealth and having their principal place of business in any part of Commonwealth; Crown; British subjects; citizens of Republic of Ireland; British protected persons and firms carrying on business in Scotland. In practice, most aircraft registered on Bermuda Register are owned by Bermuda exempted companies and it is usual to incorporate Bermuda exempted company specifically for this purpose. Formal applications to register aircraft are made by Bermuda law firms and incorporate technical information in connection with aircraft, usually provided by aircraft maintenance facility.

Certification.—DCA demonstrates flexibility in accepting aircraft, maintenance facilities and crew certified by most major international agencies including Federal Aviation Administration, Civil Aviation Authority and pursuant to Joint Airworthiness Requirements. Certain regulations and directives in connection with operation of Bermuda registered aircraft, modelled to large extent on U.K. requirements, are issued by DCA.

Civil Air Terminal is operated pursuant to provisions of The Civil Airports Act, 1949. Radio and avionic installations subject to provisions of Order and Telecommunications Act, 1986.

Operations.—All aircraft engineers signing certificates for Bermuda registered aircraft and all crew operating such aircraft must have their licenses validated by DCA, pursuant to provisions of Order. Operation of aircraft on Bermuda Register with respect to airworthiness, flight operations and flight crew is regulated by DCA.

As general rule, all aircraft joining or leaving Register are subject to physical survey by DCA together with annual survey prior to renewal of Certificate of Airworthiness.

BANKRUPTCY:

Under Bankruptcy Act, 1989 (operative date 31st Jan., 1990), debtor who has committed "Act of Bankruptcy" may be declared bankrupt, at suit of creditor or creditors, where debt or debts due petitioner or petitioners amount to BDA $5,000 or more.

Acts of bankruptcy may be any of following: That debtor has: (1) made conveyance or assignment to trustee for benefit of his creditors generally; (2) made fraudulent conveyance of his property or any part thereof; (3) with intent to defraud or delay his creditors, departed out of or remained out of Bermuda or from his dwelling house or otherwise absented himself or begun to keep house; (4) suffered execution by seizure of his goods and that goods have either been sold or held by Provost Marshal General (with certain exceptions) for 21 days; (5) filed in Court a Declaration admitting his inability to pay his debts; (6) suffered final judgment and Bankruptcy Notice served upon him and has not within 14 days after service of Notice complied with requirements of Notice or satisfied Court that he has counter-claim, set off or cross demand which equals or exceeds amount of judgment; or (7) given notice to any of his creditors that he has suspended, or that he is about to suspend, payment of his debts.

Debtor may present his own petition for bankruptcy.

Act of Bankruptcy must have occurred within three months before presentation of petition and debt must be liquidated and not secured debt, unless creditor agrees to give up his security.

Preferential debts are confined to municipal rates, land taxes and wages. Absconding bankrupt may be arrested to prevent frustration of bankruptcy proceedings. Debtor may make proposal to his creditor for composition in satisfaction of his debts or scheme of arrangement of his affairs. Creditors at any time after bankruptcy adjudication may accept composition or scheme and Supreme Court may annul bankruptcy adjudication and vest bankrupt's property in him or some other person on such terms and conditions as Supreme Court may declare.

Assignment with intention to prefer creditor by person unable to pay his debts as they become due from his own monies shall, if that person becomes bankrupt within six months of assignment, be void as fraudulent preference. Voluntary settlement made within two years preceding bankruptcy is void; if made within five years preceding bankruptcy it is also void, unless settlor is able to pay all his debts without property settled.

BANKS AND BANKING:

Banking business in Bermuda is primarily regulated by Banks Acts, 1969 which was amended by Banks Act, 1969 Amendments Consolidation Order 1983 ("the Banks Act"). Banks Act provides that no person shall carry on banking business in or from Bermuda other than company or association recognised as company by Companies Act 1981 ("the Companies Act") that is authorised by its Incorporating Act and, inter alia, is licensed by Minister of Finance ("the Minister") to carry on banking business.

"Banking business" is expressly defined in Banks Act to include business of receiving on current, savings, deposit or other similar account, money which is repayable on demand by cheque or order and which may be invested by way of advances to customers or otherwise and nothing in that definition is construed so as to preclude licensed bank from taking time deposits or repaying money otherwise than on demand or, subject to restrictions on certain commercial activities, otherwise conducting business of type and in manner usually carried on by bank. (For restrictions on certain commercial activities of licensed banks see §18 of Banks Act.)

Exempted company, within meaning of Companies Act, if authorised by its Incorporating Act to carry on banking business must be licensed by Minister to carry on such business but is not required to comply with restrictions on Bermudian shareholdings and directors set forth in Part III of Banks Act. (See §4 of Banks Act.)

Companies, other than exempted companies, that are authorised to carry on banking business in their Incorporating Acts (hereinafter called "local banks") must comply with Part III of Banks Act which provides that percentage of Bermudian directors and percentage of shares beneficially owned by Bermudians shall not be less than 60% in each case. In addition, 60% of total voting rights of local bank must be exercised by Bermudians.

Paid up share capital of local bank must be not less than BD$240,000 and all banks require a license from Minister to operate. Minister may, at any time, revoke bank license for any contravention of any provision of Banks Act or any regulation made thereunder or failure by bank concerned to comply with any directive issued by Minister under Banks Act.

Returns.—Licensed banks are required to submit to Minister six monthly statement of assets and liabilities accompanied by statement showing amounts of all outstanding unsecured advances or unsecured credit facilities and return providing analysis of customers' liabilities to bank. This requirement does not include information on affairs of any customer of bank. Any information submitted as aforesaid shall be treated as secret and for official purposes only.

Confidentiality.—Bank Act expressly stipulates that no statement, return or information shall be required to be submitted to Minister with respect to affairs of any customer of bank. With respect to confidentiality, Bermuda banks are under strict duty to keep their customers' affairs confidential.

Stockholders.—Incorporating Act of any licensed bank must provide that in event of assets of such bank being insufficient to meet its engagements, any person who has held shares within 12 months preceding commencement of winding up of such bank shall be deemed to be indebted to such bank in sum equal to aggregate of: (a) Amount unpaid on any shares held by that person during that period; and (b) amount equal to par value of any shares held by him during that period.

Other relevant legislation affecting licensed banks include: Companies Act 1981; Banks and Deposit Companies (Fees) Act 1975; Interest and Credit Charges (Regulation) Act 1975.

BERMUDIAN STATUS: See topic Immigration.

BILLS AND NOTES:

Bills of exchange are governed by Bills of Exchange Act, 1934, which largely adopted law of England. See England Law Digest.

BULK SALES:

See topic Sales.

CHATTEL MORTGAGES:

A chattel mortgage should be a deed in the form of a bill of sale conditioned to be void upon payment of the principal and interest secured, and should be registered in the Registrar General's Office, as priority in registration determines priority of charge. Chattel mortgages may be subject to ad valorem stamp duty.

In the case of a mortgage of stock in trade, the Bulk Sales Act, 1934 may apply. See topic Sales. Also see topic Corporations, subhead Charges.

COMMERCIAL REGISTER:

See topics Corporations; Immigration.

CONSTITUTION AND GOVERNMENT:

Bermuda is administered under the Crown, but by its 1968 Constitution (U.K. Statutory Instrument No. 182 of 1968), as subsequently amended, it has obtained a great measure of internal self-government, with external affairs, defence (including

See Topical Index in front part of this volume.

CONSTITUTION AND GOVERNMENT ... *continued*
armed forces), internal security and police being reserved to Governor ("the reserved matters"). Governor has power to delegate any of reserved matters to Premier.

There is Cabinet which consists of Premier and not less than six other Ministers appointed by Governor on advice of Premier. Governor, acting on advice of Premier, may assign to Ministers responsibility for conduct of any government business or administration (other than in exceptions noted above). Boards which formerly had executive duties are now largely advisory.

There is a Governor's Council comprising Governor (as chairman), Premier and not less than two nor more than three other Ministers appointed by Governor after consultation with Premier. Purpose of Governor's Council is to consider reserved matters and to advise Governor thereon; however Governor is not required to act in accordance with advice of Governor's Council.

Legislative authority is vested in Governor, Senate and House of Assembly. Senate consists of 11 appointed members, five appointed by Premier, three appointed by Opposition Leader and three appointed by Governor in his discretion. House of Assembly consists of 40 members, two from each of 20 electoral districts, elected for maximum term of five years, under system of universal suffrage, with qualifications for voting being either in possession of Bermudian status or being British subject residing in Bermuda and registered as elector as of May 1, 1976.

Premier is member of House of Assembly who leads majority party and Opposition Leader is leader in House of Assembly of any opposition party numerically stronger in numbers than any other opposition party.

1968 Constitution also served to entrench fundamental rights and freedoms which to some extent proscribed legislative authority of Government. All legislation must be consistent with provisions of Constitution.

Legislative Process.—Minister requests Permanent Secretary or Head of Government Department to prepare intent of legislation. Cabinet considers this and Parliamentary Council subsequently drafts Bill which is forwarded to Cabinet for approval. Bill is scrutinized by Government Caucus before going to House for debate.

Special sessions are governed by Rule 64 of Rules of House of Assembly and are rare. Normally, summer recess stands adjourned until formally prorogued by Governor pursuant to formal proclamation under Constitution.

Budget debated during Mar. of each year. Government's financial year ends 31st Mar. and estimates of Government revenue and expenditure considered and approved. Last week in Feb. of each year, Budget Statement read by Minister of Finance. All Members debate on following Fri. Opposition subsequently replies to Statement. In respect of budget, there are seven sittings in each House within period of two weeks.

Throne Speech.—Read by Governor upon reconvening of House of Assembly at end of Oct. Speech outlines Government policy and legislative programme for year.

Senate has no control over any money bills. By precedent independents are chosen as President and Vice-President. At Committee stage, where Bill is scrutinized clause by clause one of independents takes Chair.

Private bills are introduced to House by way of filing of petition and private bill which is subsequently referred to Joint Select Committee which comprises three Members of Senate and five Members of House of Assembly.

Speaker of House has casting vote in case of tie whenever vote is taken. President of Senate, however, has original vote on each occasion vote is taken.

Judicial Authority.—See topic Courts.

CONTRACTS:

Gratuitous promise, even though made in writing, is not enforceable unless it is made in deed under seal. If there has been consideration for promise, i.e. either some right, interest, profit or benefit accruing to promisor, or some forbearance, detriment, loss or responsibility given, suffered or undertaken by promisee it may be enforced if under hand, or frequently, if parol.

Misrepresentation.—A false statement of existing or past fact made by one party to other before or at time of making contract is a misrepresentation.

If misrepresentation is fraudulent, party misled may rescind or repudiate contract. If misrepresentation is made negligently, party misled may institute proceedings in negligence, and if misrepresentation is made innocently, contract may be rescinded by court. Law Reform (Misrepresentation and Frustrated Contracts) Act, 1977, (No. 53) provides that injured party may recover damages as if misrepresentation was fraudulent or that injured party can rescind contract in which case court can, in appropriate circumstances, award damages in lieu of rescission. Act also provides that certain provisions excluding or restricting liability for misrepresentation are of no effect unless allowed by court as fair and reasonable in circumstances.

Excuses for Nonperformance.—A contract which is not capable of performance when made is in general void. Doctrine of frustration operates to excuse further performance where: (i) It appears from nature of contract and surrounding circumstances that parties have contracted on basis that some fundamental thing or state of things will continue to be available or that some future event which forms foundation of contract will take place, and (ii) before breach performance becomes impossible or only possible in very different way to that contemplated without default of either party or owing to fundamental change of circumstances beyond control and original contemplation of parties. To excuse nonperformance, impossibility must be in nature of physical or legal one and not merely relative impossibility, i.e., referable solely to ability or circumstances of promisor.

Act of God or of Queen's enemies may also excuse performance. Act of God is generally an extraordinary occurrence or circumstance which could not have been foreseen or which could not have been guarded against.

A statute may also render performance impossible, which is sufficient excuse.

Rescission.—Contract may be rescinded at instance of party induced to enter it by a misrepresentation of facts made by other party. This is so, even if contract performed. Damages may be ordered by court in lieu of rescission and are also available in addition to rescission (or damages in lieu) where this representation is negligent or fraudulent. These provisions can be excluded only insofar as court deems an exclusion of liability to be fair.

Mistake.—Contract made under fundamental mistake of fact is void. Other less fundamental mistakes will render contract voidable and such contract may be rescinded by court.

Where contract is expressed in writing and there is a mistake in writing, court may rectify writing to express true intention of parties.

Rectification.—Court has power under Human Rights Act 1981 to rectify contract or term in contract so it does not contravene prohibited policies under Act.

Illegality.—An ostensibly valid contract may be rendered void as being contrary to statute or to public policy. These contracts are regarded as illegal and will not be enforced by courts. Contracts falling within this category include: (i) Contract of unlawful gaming; (ii) contracts which are immoral or involve commission of a crime or tort; (iii) contracts which are prejudicial to administration of justice; (iv) contracts which prejudice public service or state in its relation with other states. (See further excuses for nonperformance above.)

Privity.—Person not party to contract cannot sue upon it even if it is for his benefit unless it is insurance policy of vendor of property and he is purchaser, or he is a principal suing on contract made for him by agent, or contract constitutes a trust and person seeking to sue is beneficiary thereunder.

Applicable Law.—Interpretation of contract and rights and obligations of parties are governed, generally, by law which parties agree or intend shall govern it or which they are presumed to have intended, known as proper law of contract. Law expressly stipulated will be proper law of contract provided selection is bona fide and legal and there is no objection on grounds of public policy even where law has no real connection with contract. Where parties make no stipulation courts decide by considering contract as whole and relevant surrounding circumstances and are guided by certain presumptions. Written contracts may also be liable for stamp duty under Stamp Duties Act 1976 and failure to affix appropriate duty may not only result in monetary penalty, but also refusal by Court to admit contract into evidence.

Sale of Goods.—See topic Sales.

Distributorships, Dealerships and Franchises.—In general, franchises etc. are not allowed in Bermuda. Only under strictly controlled circumstances are they permitted.

COPYRIGHT:

The United Kingdom Copyright Act, 1956 (as amended) was extended to Bermuda by Copyright (Bermuda) Order, 1962 and the Copyright (Bermuda) (Amendment) Order, 1985 with certain exceptions and modifications. These Orders provide for copyright in original, literary, dramatic, artistic and musical works and in sound recordings, cinematograph films, broadcast and published editions of such works. 1985 Order made certain modifications to penalties for infringement of copyright. Reference should be made to England Law Digest.

By virtue of Copyright (International Conventions) Order, 1979, Bermuda extends international protection, similar to that which exists in U.K. on all classes of works and subject matter in which copyright subsists, to countries specified in Schedules 1 and 2 of that Order, being countries that adhere to Berne or Universal Copyright Conventions.

The Performers' Protection Act, 1967 gives protection to performers against unauthorized reproductions of their performances and creates criminal offences in respect of such unauthorized reproductions.

(See also topic Patents and Designs.)

CORPORATIONS:

General.—Companies Act 1981 (as am'd) is principal legislation concerning incorporation, management, administration and winding up of companies in Bermuda and is consolidation of law relating to them.

Modes of Incorporation.—Limited liability and unlimited liability companies may be incorporated after prescribed advertisement specifying name of proposed company, stating whether it is to be local or exempted company and summarising its principal objects either by registration under Companies Act, 1981 ("registered company") or by Private Act of Legislature ("statutory company"). Limited liability company can reregister as unlimited liability company.

Statutory or registered company may be either "local" or "exempted." Exempted company is one which, in case of a statutory company, is declared by its incorporating Act to be exempted company or, in case of a registered company, is registered as exempted company. Exempted company is designed for ownership by non-Bermudians and is free from exchange control restrictions, but it is prohibited from trading locally, from holding shares or debentures of any local company and from owning land in Bermuda.

With certain exceptions, Bermuda Monetary Authority must approve all beneficial owners of exempted companies.

General Supervision.—Business of company is managed and conducted by board of directors consisting of not fewer than two persons or such number in excess of two as shareholders may determine. Every exempted company must have sufficient number of directors who are ordinarily resident in Bermuda to constitute quorum of board. Directors are elected annually. Directors of company must, as soon as may be after each annual election, choose or elect one of their number to be president of company and another to be vice-president. Directors must appoint secretary of company and such other officers as may be authorised by bye-laws. Trust companies are also regulated by Bermuda Monetary Authority and will be required to show compliance with Bermuda's Code of Conduct on Money Laundering.

Bye-laws.—Directors may make and amend bye-laws regulating internal affairs of company. All bye-laws and amendments thereto are subject to confirmation by shareholders in general meeting.

Licence to do Business.—No company incorporated in Bermuda can carry on business in Bermuda unless either it is a local company with at least 60% of its shares being beneficially owned by Bermudians and at least 60% of its directors are Bermudians, or alternatively, it is licenced by Minister of Finance under provisions of Companies Act 1981. Foreign company doing business in or from Bermuda will require

CORPORATIONS . . . *continued*
permit from Minister of Finance. Trust companies offering services to public must also be licensed under Trust Companies Act 1991. Private trust companies do not have to be licensed.

Paid in Capital Requirements.—Minimum share capital of exempted company may not be less than Bermuda equivalent of $12,000. Insurance company is required to have minimum authorised and issued share capital of not less than Bermuda equivalent of $120,000, all of which must be paid prior to company's registration as insurer. There are minimum statutory capital and surplus requirements which vary according to class of insurer and type of business. (See topic Insurance for capital requirements.) Trust company licensed under Trust Companies Act 1991 is required to have minimum paid up share capital of $250,000.

Stock.—All shares must have a fixed par value. Par value of local companies must be expressed in Bermudian dollars. Capital of exempted companies must be denominated in other currencies. Registered companies may not issue bearer shares and statutory companies have seldom been permitted to have bearer shares. Subject to Companies Act and authorisation in company's memorandum of association or bye-laws, company may purchase its own shares.

Stockholders Liabilities.—Liability of shareholders of companies (other than banks) is normally limited to amount for time being unpaid on shares respectively held by them.

Dissolution.—Company may be wound up voluntarily if a resolution to that effect is passed at a special general meeting of shareholders held for that purpose, and for which prescribed notice by advertisement has been given. Company may also be wound up by or subject to supervision of Supreme Court of Bermuda if that court, on application of any creditor or shareholder and on its being proved to satisfaction of court that company is unable to pay its debts, or that it is for any other reason just and equitable that it should be wound up, so orders. Companies are wound up under provisions of Companies Act 1981, which largely follows law of England. Court having jurisdiction over winding up is Supreme Court. In addition, Accountant General has statutory authority to dissolve company which he finds is no longer carrying on business or in operation.

Charges.—The Charges Register is voluntary register for all charges by Bermuda companies. Registered charges rank according to date of registration and in priority to unregistered charges. In cases of exempted companies, instrument creating charge is exempt from stamp duty if registered.

Government Fees.—There is no stamp duty payable to Bermuda Government for exempted companies on authorised capital of or on transfer of shares of exempted companies. Stamp duty on transfer of shares in local company ranges from 2%-5% depending on value transferred. There are annual government fees based on "assessable" capital (authorised capital and share premium) of exempted company. Such fees are as follows:

(1) $0-$12,000	-	$ 1,680
(2) $12,001-$120,000	-	$ 3,360
(3) $120,001-$1,200,000	-	$ 5,040
(4) $1,200,001-$12,000,000	-	$ 6,720
(5) $12,000,001-$100,000,000	-	$ 8,400
(6) $100,000,001-$500,000,000	-	$15,000
(7) $500,000,001 or more	-	$25,000
(8) Trust Companies	-	$10,000

Exempted Companies.—Where company's business includes management of unit trusts, $2,365 is payable per each unit trust managed. Exempted companies are entitled to apply for, and ordinarily receive, undertaking from Minister of Finance that, in event of legislation imposing tax on profits, income, etc., such tax shall not be applicable to them for such period as is specified by Minister expiring not later than March 28, 2016.

All companies will be designated as "resident" or "nonresident" for exchange control purposes. Broadly, if designation is "resident," which will only be case if company is controlled by Bermudians, company cannot without consent deal in any currency other than "resident" currency whereas if designation is "nonresident", company can deal in any currency of its choosing other than "resident" currency.

Real Property.—Pursuant to Companies Act 1981, exempted company, unless otherwise authorised (which in practice is seldom granted) does not have power to acquire or hold land in Bermuda other than land required for its business held by way of lease or tenancy agreement for term not exceeding 21 years. Local company, as matter of policy, is only permitted to acquire real property where property is bona fide required for purposes of company's business.

Exempted company may hold in its corporate name mortgage on real and personal property of every description in Bermuda in same manner and in same respects as local company and has as mortgagee all rights that local company would have provided mortgage is in principal sum not exceeding $50,000. Where principal sum exceeds $50,000, exempted company cannot take mortgage without prior consent of Minister of Finance.

See also topics Aliens; Immigration; Taxation; Currency; Exchange Control.

COURTS:

Law administered is common law, law of equity, and statutes. Bermuda is governed by principle of binding precedent. Only English common law, principles of equity, and statues of England up to 1612 are binding in Bermuda except (1) when Queen, by Order in Council, makes later UK Act expressly applicable to Bermuda (list is available in Revised Laws of Bermuda); (2) when Bermuda legislation amends, repeals or supersedes application of pre-1612 English legislation; or (3) by expansion and/or restriction of common law and law of equity by courts and/or legislation. Decisions of English courts after 1612 have persuasive authority in Bermuda.

Law and equity are administered concurrently. In any conflict, rules of equity prevail. Procedure in Supreme Court governed by Rules of Supreme Court 1985, is modelled on rules of High Court of Justice in England.

Supreme Court.—This is superior Court of Record. It consists of Chief Justice appointed by Governor after consultation with Premier; also two-three Puisne Judges appointed by Governor after consultation with Chief Justice.

Admiralty jurisdiction is dependent on Supreme Court Act, 1905. Jurisdiction is similar to that of High Court in England.

Appeals.—In all civil and criminal matters appeal lies to Supreme Court from lower courts. Appeals from Supreme Court lie to Court of Appeal established under Court of Appeal Act 1964. Further appeal lies from Court of Appeal to Privy Council in England under The Appeals Act, 1911, as of right if subject matter is worth $10,000 or more and it is appeal from final decision. Leave is required if matter appealed from is interlocutory or is worth more than above-stated amount. Leave can be sought from Privy Council in event of refusal by Court of Appeal.

Magistrate's courts exercise jurisdiction under statute only in matrimonial and civil claims (jurisdiction up to BD$10,000) as well as minor criminal matters. Procedure governed by Magistrates Court Rules 1973.

See also topics Judgments; Shipping.

CURRENCY:

Bermuda Monetary Authority was established by legislation in 1969, and am'd by an Act of 1973. Principal objects of Authority are to issue and redeem notes and coin, to supervise banks operating in or from Bermuda, to foster close relations between banks themselves and between banks and Government and to advise Government on banking and monetary matters.

Currency of Bermuda is Bermuda dollar which is divided into 100¢. Parity of Bermuda dollar is prescribed by order of Governor, acting in accordance with provisions of Articles of Agreement of International Monetary Fund. Current parity of Bermuda dollar is equivalent to $1 in currency of USA.

See also topic Exchange Control.

CURTESY:

A husband has an estate for his life, expectant on the death of his wife, in the land of which his wife is seized for an estate of inheritance, subject to his having issue by her born alive and capable of inheriting from her. With respect to lands to which a wife is entitled as for her separate property the disposition thereof by the wife will avoid the husband's curtesy, but otherwise the curtesy attaches thereto.

It is thought that an alien husband does not take curtesy in the lands of his wife situate in Bermuda.

Right to Curtesy has been abolished with respect to estate of any person dying after Sept. 1, 1974.

DEATH:

Person of whom nothing has been heard for period of seven years by those to whom such person is likely to have communicated will usually be presumed dead. Proof of these circumstances is defence on charge of bigamy and will also support suit for presumption of death or dissolution of marriage. See also topic Actions.

Records of death (and of births and marriages) are kept in Office of Registrar General at Hamilton. Certificates may be obtained on application to above Office.

Actions for Death.—By Fatal Injuries (Actions for Damages) Act, 1949 (No. 68), in any case where death of person is caused by any act, neglect or default, whether criminal or tortious, then personal representatives or any near relation of deceased has same right of action for damages as deceased if he had survived, provided that not more than one action lies in respect of same subject matter of complaint and any such action must be commenced within three years from date of death or date of knowledge of person for whose benefit action brought, whichever is later, by Limitation Act 1984. Any such action shall be for benefit of deceased's dependents, who may be awarded damages appropriate to actual or reasonably expected pecuniary loss caused to him or to her by reason of death of deceased.

By Survival of Actions Act, 1949 (No. 87), subject to provisions thereof, all causes of actions subsisting against or vested in any deceased person on his death survived against, or for benefit of, respectively, his estate. No cause of action shall be maintained in respect of action in tort which by virtue of this Act has survived against estate of deceased person unless proceedings in respect thereof were pending at time of death, or cause of action arose not earlier than six months before death and proceedings are taken in respect thereof not later than 12 months after death. The Limitation Act, 1984 provides for action for benefit of estate to be taken within three years from date of death or date of estate representatives' knowledge, whichever is later.

Rights conferred by Survival of Actions Act, 1949 for benefit of estates of deceased persons are in addition to those conferred on dependants of deceased persons by Fatal Injuries (Actions for Damages) Act, 1949. Although heads of damages under each Act differ and duplication of damages is not possible, it would seem that provisions of both these Acts apply to all persons.

DECEDENTS' ESTATES:

See topics Curtesy; Descent and Distribution; Dower; Executors and Administrators.

DEEDS:

Any estate or interest in land may be conveyed by deed, which should be signed, sealed and delivered by grantor in presence of one or more witnesses, who should attest execution thereof. See England Law Digest.

Stamp duty is payable on purchase deeds at rate of 2% on consideration up to BD$100,000, 3% where value exceeds $100,000 up to $500,000, 4% where value exceeds $500,000 up to $1,000,000, and 5% on that portion of value which exceeds $1,000,000. Voluntary conveyances bear stamp duty at same rate above mentioned. Conveyances to trusts bear stamp duty at above rates provided trust acquires asset at outset. If asset is subsequently transferred to trust duty rates then payable are nil% on first $50,000, 5% on next $150,000, 10% on next $800,000 and 15% over $1,000,000.

Where deed is executed by attorney, power should be recorded.

See Topical Index in front part of this volume.

DEEDS . . . *continued*

There is no system of land title registration.

DEPOSITIONS:

Local provisions are substantially similar to English law. Application to take evidence by deposition in Supreme Court by application under Order 39 of Rules of the Supreme Court, 1985, including examination of person outside jurisdiction by special examiner. Statutory provision for taking of evidence required for proceedings in other jurisdictions. (The Evidence Act 1905 as am'd).

DESCENT AND DISTRIBUTION:

Substantial changes in law governing intestacy have been made by The Succession Act, 1974 (operative date Sept. 1, 1974) and further by The Succession Amendment Act 1987 (operative date Jan. 1, 1988).

The Inheritance Act, 1835, remains in force for purpose of ascertaining devolution of entailed estates and interests and entitlement thereto but otherwise no longer applies in relation to intestacies.

No distinction is now made between real and personal property which both vest in estate representatives who hold on trust with a power of sale.

Estate representatives must pay all funeral, testamentary and administration expenses, (and pecuniary legacies in case of partial intestacy), debts and property liabilities and residuary estate is then to be distributed or held on trusts according to following rules: (1) surviving spouse (whether husband or wife) is entitled to: (a) personal chattels absolutely, (b) if deceased left issue, 50% of value of residuary estate less personal chattels or BD$100,000 (whichever is greater) with interest at 5% p.a. from end of time allowed for administration (one year from death or six months from grant, whichever is later) until payment, (c) if deceased left no issue, 66⅔% value of residuary estate less personal chattels or BD$150,000 (whichever is greater) with interest at 5% p.a. as above and remainder goes to surviving parents in equal shares or if none, to brothers and sisters per stirpes, (d) if deceased left no issue, no parent, no brother or sister of whole blood or issue of same, residuary estate is held on trust for surviving spouse absolutely; (2) issue are entitled: (a) where deceased leaves surviving spouse, to remainder of residuary estate which is held for them on intestacy trusts, i.e., in trust in equal shares for issue attaining 21 years or marrying thereunder or their issue on same terms, (b) where deceased leaves no surviving spouse, to whole residuary estate which is held on intestacy trusts; (3) if no issue attain a vested interest, then subject to any claim by surviving spouse as above, relatives of deceased are entitled in following order: (a) parents in equal shares absolutely, (b) brothers and sisters per stirpes of whole blood on intestacy trusts, (c) brothers and sisters per stirpes of half blood on intestacy trusts, (d) grandparents in equal shares absolutely, (e) uncles and aunts per stirpes of whole blood on intestacy trusts, (f) uncles and aunts per stirpes of half blood on intestacy trusts, (g) government as bona vacantia. Government has power to make payments out of estate to any dependent of deceased or other person having legal, equitable or moral claim. Any member of one of classes above who attains a vested interest excludes all members of subsequent classes.

Where persons die commorientes, younger is deemed to survive by virtue of §1 of Presumption of Survivorship Act 1956. However, in case of intestacy, where intestate and intestate's spouse are commorientes for purposes of intestate succession spouse shall be deemed not to have survived intestate.

Issue includes illegitimate children as follows: (a) Where father has signed birth certificate; (b) father has sworn affidavit and filed same with Registrar General; (c) father was adjudged to be putative father under The Affiliation Act 1976; or (d) putative father is found to satisfaction of Court (i.e. after death of father).

Application may be made to Court by spouse, former spouse, child or grandchild for provision out of deceased's estate on ground that disposition of estate by will or laws of intestacy is not such as to make reasonable financial provision for applicant. Orders may be made for periodical payments or lump sum provision. Court must have regard to financial needs and resources of applicant and all beneficiaries, obligations of deceased to applicant and beneficiaries, applicant's conduct and other relevant matters.

Application must be made within six months of date of grant, except where Court gives permission to make application out of time. Court has power to make interim orders where there is immediate need and there are assets available to meet such orders. Court has power to take into account property given donatio mortis causa, dispositions made within three years of death (voluntarily or for less than full value of property) or property contracted to be willed. Court must be satisfied that disposition was made with intent to defeat claim under Part III of Act—test being balance of probabilities.

See topics Curtesy; Dower.

DIVORCE:

Jurisdiction.—By Matrimonial Causes Act, general jurisdiction in divorce, judicial separation, nullity and dissolution of marriage on ground of presumption of death was granted to Supreme Court.

Domicile or Residence Requirements.—Jurisdiction for divorce and judicial separation arises where either party (1) is domiciled in Bermuda on the date when proceedings are begun or (2) was ordinarily resident in Bermuda throughout period of one year ending with that date. Jurisdiction for nullity of marriage arises where either party (1) is domiciled in Bermuda on date when proceedings are begun or (2) was ordinarily resident in Bermuda throughout period of one year ending with that date or (3) died before that date and either (i) was at death domiciled in Bermuda; or (ii) had been ordinarily resident in Bermuda throughout period of one year ending with date of death.

Grounds of Divorce.—By §5 it is provided that sole ground for divorce shall be that marriage has broken down irretrievably. §5(2) provides that proof of such breakdown is only afforded if one or more of following conditions are fulfilled: (1) That respondent has committed adultery and in consequence of that adultery petitioner finds it intolerable to live with respondent; (2) that respondent has behaved in such a way that petitioner cannot reasonably be expected to live with respondent; (3) that respondent has deserted petitioner for continuous period of at least two years immediately preceding presentation of petition; (4) that parties to marriage have lived apart for continuous period of at least two years immediately preceding presentation of petition and respondent consents to decree being granted; (5) that parties to marriage have lived apart for continuous period of at least five years immediately preceding presentation of petition.

When Action May Be Started.—Petition for divorce cannot be presented until three years after marriage but judge may grant leave in cases of exceptional hardship suffered by petitioner or exceptional depravity on part of respondent.

Judicial separation may be granted on any of conditions enumerated in subhead Grounds for Divorce (above) and it is not necessary for court to consider whether marriage has broken down irretrievably.

Annulment of Marriage.—See topic Marriage.

Recognition of Foreign Decree.—Recognition of foreign divorces is governed by Recognition of Divorces and Legal Separations Act, 1977, effective as of Aug. 1, 1977. This act adopts Hague Convention of 1968 with minor variations. Overseas divorce or legal separation will be recognised in Bermuda if at date of proceedings (a) either spouse was habitually resident in that country or (b) both spouses were nationals of country or (c) petitioner was national and was either habitually resident there or had been for period of one year within two years immediately preceding institution of proceedings. Further ground for recognition is that petitioner was national of country and was present at date of proceedings and country in which petitioner and respondent last habitually resided did not provide for divorce.

DOWER:

The wife of a decedent is entitled to an estate for her life in one-third part of the freehold estates of inheritance of which her husband was solely seized at any time during the marriage to which her issue by him might by possibility have been the heir-at-law. Dower cannot be defeated by the husband by any disposition by devise or inter vivos, but original conveyance to husband is often in form which bars dower.

Dower does not extend to equitable estates or to real property which is treated in equity as personal property. A widow having dower in any real estate is entitled to have one-third in value thereof allotted to her for her life.

It is questionable whether an alien woman takes dower of real estate in Bermuda.

Proceedings to enforce dower are regulated by the Dower Act, 1866, under which no claim can be made in respect of any arrears arising more than six years prior to the commencing of suit.

Right of dower has been abolished with respect to estate of any person dying after Sept. 1, 1974.

ENVIRONMENT:

Basic Statutes.—Public Health Act 1949 covers water pollution, regulation of operation and maintenance of sewerage systems, drainage of yards, ventiliation of buildings, collection and disposal of house and trade refuse, disposal of human remains and almost all other environmental nuisances. Development & Planning Act 1974 contains provisions enabling regulation of development to protect environment.

Waste and Litter Control Act 1987 provides primarily for control of litter and deposit and collection of household and commercial waste by licensed collection authorities. Criminal penalties and compensatory remedies stipulated.

Recent legislation is Clean Air Act 1991, regulating emission of air contaminants. Provides for granting of construction permits and operating licences to operators of controlled plants. Regulates operation of Bermuda's new incinerator.

Also see: Environment Protection (Overseas Territories) Order 1988 (SI 1988, No. 1084), extending application of certain provisions of (U.K.) Food and Environment Protection Act 1985, in particular provisions relating to deposit or incineration of substances at sea and protection of marine environment; Prevention of Oil Pollution Act 1971 (Bermuda) Order 1980 (SI 1980, No. 1520) extending application of certain provisions of (U.K.) Prevention of Oil Pollution Act 1971, in particular regulation of discharge of oils into sea and keeping of oil record books in ships registered in Bermuda; Fisheries Act 1972, Protection of Birds Act 1975; and Endangered Animals and Plants Act 1976.

General Supervision.—Minister of the Environment; Environmental Authority (established by §3 of Clean Air Act 1991 consisting of not more than seven members appointed by Minister of the Environment, Minister of Health and Minister of Works and Engineering); Minister of Works and Engineering (waste collection; air pollution); Minister of Health (environmental nuisances).

EXCHANGE CONTROL:

Control over foreign currency transactions has existed since 1940 and is now governed by Exchange Control Act, 1972 and Regulations made thereunder and administered by Bermuda Monetary Authority. In general, legislation does not impose restrictions on transactions between residents of Bermuda; it applies mainly to financial transactions between residents of Bermuda and individuals resident in countries outside Bermuda who are termed "nonresidents". For Exchange Control purposes certain persons normally resident in Bermuda have also been designated as nonresident (e.g., non-Bermudian employees of exempted companies).

Exempted companies are also designated nonresident for Exchange Control purposes and consent of Bermuda Monetary Authority is required prior to incorporation of exempted company. Prior consent of BMA is also required to issue or transfer any share, debenture or other security of exempted company. General permission to issue or transfer may be given, for example, in case of public issue of shares or bonds which are to be freely transferable provided necessary supporting documents are previously lodged. Exempted companies are entitled to maintain foreign currency bank accounts and freely to convert such balances into other foreign currencies.

For Exchange Control purposes, currencies of all countries other than Bermuda are "foreign currencies". Restrictions normally affect transactions of capital nature, while current payments (i.e. those relating to normal commercial transactions between residents and nonresidents) are, for most part, subject only to supervision. Recent policy changes mean residents of Bermuda are now allowed to purchase foreign currency, make payments to or place sums to credit of nonresidents, up to equivalent of

EXCHANGE CONTROL . . . *continued*
BD$25,000 per calendar year. No person other than "authorized dealer" may buy, sell, exchange or lend foreign currency or gold (other than dealings in gold coin) without consent of Foreign Exchange Control.

Exchange Control powers under Act and Regulations are broad, but exemptions are granted, either generally or specifically, depending on advantages or disadvantages to economy of Bermuda. Nonresident investment in, and loans to residents of, Bermuda are cautiously welcomed. In case of loans, residents must observe capital repayment allowance in force at that time.

See also topics Corporations; Currency.

EXECUTION:

Judgments are enforceable according to provisions of Rules of Supreme Court 1985. Order 45 Rule 1 of these Rules provides for enforcement of payment of money, not being judgment or order for payment of money into Court; Order 45 Rule 2 provides for enforcement of judgment or order for payment of money into Court; Order 45 Rule 3 regulates enforcement of judgment for possession of land and Order 45 Rule 4 judgment for delivery of goods. Means available include writ of fieri facias, garnishee proceedings, appointment of receiver and writ of sequestration. Power of Court to commit to prison for default in payment is governed by Debtor's Act 1973.

Time for Issuance.—Writ of execution to enforce judgment or order may not issue without leave of Court where six years or more have elapsed since date of judgment or order. Leave is also required where any change has taken place in parties concerned, whether by death or otherwise. Where Court grants leave and writ is not issued within one year, order shall cease to have effect. However, fresh order may be sought. Otherwise, writ of execution may normally be issued immediately after entry of judgment.

Stay.—Party against whom judgment or order has been made may apply to Court for stay of execution or other relief on grounds that: (1) Special circumstances exist which render enforcement inexpedient or (2) unable to pay from any cause.

Lien.—See topic Liens.

Levy.—All land, houses, goods, money, bank notes, cheques, bills of exchange, promissory notes, government securities, bonds, or other securities for money, debts, shares in capital or joint stock of any company and all other property whatsoever, whether movable or immovable belonging to judgment debtor, whether held in his own name or by another person in trust for him or on his behalf, are liable to attachment and sale in execution of judgment.

Return.—Any party at whose instance writ of execution was issued may serve notice on Provost Marshal General requiring him, within such time as may be specified in notice, to indorse on writ statement of manner in which he has executed it.

Sale.—Every sale shall be made under direction of Registrar and conducted according to such order as Court may make on application and shall be made by public auction or in such other manner as Court may order.

EXECUTORS AND ADMINISTRATORS:

Substantial changes in law have been made by Administration of Estates Act, 1974 (operative date Sept. 1, 1974).

Executors take by virtue of appointment in a will, but probate is necessary to enable them to deal fully with estate. In event of an intestacy, administrators are appointed by court in accordance with rules governing order of priority, their powers deriving from grant. Married woman may act as executrix or administratrix, and where infant is absolutely or contingently entitled by will or intestacy, administration shall be granted either to trust corporation with or without individual or not less than two individuals. Court has discretion as to persons to whom administration may be granted and may limit grants as thought fit. Provision is made for distribution of small estates consisting of personalty only not exceeding BD$50,000 without grant.

Both real and personal property of deceased person now vest in his executors, or upon grant by court in event of an intestacy in his administrators. Grant of probate or of administration has effect over both real and personal property unless containing an express limitation and both real and personal estate are made liable for satisfaction of debts of deceased.

Executors and administrators are not bound to distribute before expiration of one year after death or six months from grant (whichever is later). After publishing prescribed advertisements for claims against estate of deceased, they are not liable after distribution for any claims of which they have not had notice, however, creditors retain right to follow distributed property into hands of beneficiaries. Order of distribution of solvent and insolvent estates is similar to that contained in English Administration of Estates Act, 1925. Rule in Allhusen v. Whittell (1867) L.R. 4 Eq. 295 has been abolished unless will shows express contrary direction.

Executor of sole or last surviving executor of testator is executor of that testator. Chain is broken by an intestacy, failure of testator to appoint executor or failure to obtain probate.

Estate representative may agree to remuneration for a trust corporation appointed by him as trustee. Rights of preference and retainer have been abolished.

FOREIGN CORPORATIONS:

See topics Aliens; Corporations; Immigration.

FOREIGN EXCHANGE: See topic Currency.

FOREIGN TRADE REGULATIONS:

See topics Corporations; Currency; Exchange Control; Immigration.

FRAUDS, STATUTE OF:

English Statute of Frauds (29 Car. 2., c. 3) does not extend to Bermuda. Conveyancing Act 1983 provides that contracts for disposition of land be in writing. This provision however does not apply to leases or tenancies for terms not exceeding three years (which period must include options to renew) nor does it affect contract when there has been part performance or sale by court. Law relating to part performance is interpreted in same manner as it was formerly interpreted in courts in England.

FRAUDULENT SALES AND CONVEYANCES:

Conveyances of lands, houses and other hereditaments made with intent to defraud creditors are void. (§3 of Real Estate Assets Act 1787).

Fraudulent or preferential disposals of property may be declared void under Bankruptcy Act, 1876, or under Companies Act, 1981, as appropriate.

By Conveyancing Act 1983, conveyance of property made with intent to defraud creditors or subsequent purchaser is voidable at instance of prejudiced person.

Under Companies Act 1981, any conveyance, mortgage or other act relating to property made or done by or against company within six months before commencement of its winding-up shall, in event of company being wound up, be deemed fraudulent preference of its creditors and invalid if said act had been done by or against individual within six months before presentation of bankruptcy petition on which he is adjudged bankrupt would have been deemed fraudulent preference in his bankruptcy.

Bulk Sales.—See topic Sales, subhead Bulk Sales.

GARNISHMENT:

Cause of action for more than BD$14.40 against person absent from Bermuda but who has been in Bermuda may be enforced by garnishment of that person or corporation subject to action being entered, affidavit of cause of action being filed, security being given with sureties for double amount claimed and writ served on garnishee. Attachment Act, 1874, which provides this remedy, requires trial of action within six months of return date of writ. Anything belonging to such a debtor in hands of his wife, attorney, agent, trustee, clerk or other servant may be garnished.

Other provisions relating to garnishment appear in Supreme Court Rules.

These provisions include means to enforce judgment of Supreme Court.

Application ex parte by affidavit and in first instance there should be show cause hearing after service on garnishee personally and, unless court otherwise directs, on judgment debtor.

HUSBAND AND WIFE:

Law relating to capacity, property and liabilities of married women and liabilities of husbands was amended by Law Reform (Husband and Wife) Act, 1977. Married woman is capable of acquiring, holding and disposing of any property as if unmarried and is similarly liable in respect of tort, contract, debt or obligation and capable of suing and being sued, as well as subject to law relating to bankruptcy and to enforcement of judgments and orders, as if she were unmarried. Restraint upon anticipation is abolished by Act, which also incorporates provisions concerning determinations of questions between husband and wife as to ownership of property, formerly contained in Married Women's Property Act, 1901. Husband's liability for wife's torts and antenuptial contracts, debts and obligations are abolished and parties to marriage now have like right of action in tort against other as if not married.

IMMIGRATION:

Residence.—It is unlawful for any person other than one who possesses Bermudian status (see subhead Bermudian Status, infra) or is special category person (mainly Government employees) or is bona fide visitor to enter and reside in Bermuda without permission of Minister of Labour and Home Affairs. Applicants for such permission may be required to furnish references as to character and means, medical certificates, etc. Bona fide visitors must be in possession of return air ticket on arrival in Bermuda and most visitors are allowed to remain on Island for periods not exceeding three months, permission being required for longer period.

Employment.—It is unlawful for non-Bermudian, other than non-Bermudian spouse of Bermudian, to engage in gainful occupation (which is widely construed) without prior specific permission of Minister, which permission may be subject to conditions and limitations. Permission must be sought by way of application and applicants are required to produce references and evidence of qualifications.

Trading.—Similarly, it is unlawful for companies which are not incorporated in Bermuda to trade in or from Bermuda without permit issued by Minister and payment of annual fee.

Bermudian Status.—The Bermuda Immigration and Protection Act, 1956, as amended ("Act") provides for acquisition of Bermudian status i.e., freedom from immigration regulations, controls entry and residence of non-Bermudians, restricts acquisiton of property by non-Bermudians, and, generally, governs matters of immigration nature. Act is supplemented from time to time by immigration policies promulgated by Minister.

Person is deemed to possess Bermudian status if that person is Commonwealth citizen and: (a) Possessed "domicile" within meaning of Immigration Act, 1937; (b) is born in Bermuda or elsewhere where at time of birth one of his parents possesses Bermudian status and one parent is domiciled in Bermuda (sections of Act relating to acquisitions of status by birth are, subject to certain modifications, applicable to illegitimate children).

Children or adopted children of persons who possess Bermudian status will be "deemed" to possess Bermudian status if child is Commonwealth citizen and under age of 21 years. Child can obtain status in his own right if he makes application to Minister demonstrating he is over 18 and less than 22 years and has been resident continuously for period of five years preceding his application and has been "deemed" for five years immediately preceding application to possess Bermudian status. In absence of such application child will cease to be "deemed" on attaining age of 21 years and, therefore, will be treated as non-Bermudian.

Commonwealth citizen who is spouse of person possessing Bermudian status has special right to status on application to Minister, provided such applicant: (a) Has for period of ten years immediately preceding application been continuously married to Bermudian spouse who throughout that period possessed Bermudian status; (b) has

See Topical Index in front part of this volume.

IMMIGRATION . . . *continued*
been ordinarily resident in Bermudian for seven years immediately preceding application; (c) submits letter from applicant's spouse supporting application. Such application will be approved unless applicant, in Minister's opinion, is estranged from spouse at time of application, has previously been convicted of offence involving moral turpitude, or has otherwise demonstrated bad character or conduct.

Prior to June 1, 1980 British woman married to Bermudian was automatically deemed to possess and enjoy Bermudian status. With passage of amendment act in 1980 this privilege has been withdrawn with effect from May 1, 1980. However, any woman who was deemed to possess and enjoy by virtue of either being married to Bermudian or being widow of Bermudian (provided she is British) continues to possess and enjoy and can make application for grant in her own right after five years provided she meets certain requirements. Finally, it should be noted that in certain circumstances Bermudian status may be lost.

See also topics Aliens; Partnership; Real Property.

INCOME TAX:

None.

See topic Corporations; also topic Taxation.

INFANTS:

Age of majority for each sex is 21 years. Law regarding guardianship custody and property of minors is contained in Minors Act, 1950, and Matrimonial Causes Act 1974 and law for maintenance of children born out of wedlock and other matters connected therewith is contained in Affiliation Act, 1976. Other relevant statutes are Adoption of Children Act, 1963, and Legitimacy Act, 1933.

Contracts.—Contract made by infant, except beneficial contract of service and contract for necessaries, voidable at infant's option.

Actions.—Infants may sue by their next friend according to practice in Chancery Division of High Court of Justice in England and may in like manner defend by guardians appointed for that purpose under provisions of Rules of Supreme Court, 1952.

Parental Responsibility.—Parents are not prima facie liable for torts of infants but may be liable if personally negligent or if infant is servant or agent of parent.

Adoption.—See topic Adoption.

INHERITANCE TAX:

See topic Taxation.

INSOLVENCY—CORPORATE:

Insolvent company can be wound up: (1) by resolution passed at members and creditors meetings or (2) by court order. Members of solvent company can resolve to wind up voluntarily.

Company unable to pay its debts can be wound up by petition to court pursuant to Companies Act 1981 by creditor: (1) proving to court that company cannot pay debts, including prospective and contingent liabilities, or (2) execution or judgment remaining unsatisified, or (3) serving on company demand for payment of debt due exceeding $500 which remains unsatisfied three weeks after service.

Court appoints liquidator, being official receiver in default of other nomination. Liquidator has power to examine persons involved in company or believed to have its property.

After presentation of petition disposition of company property is void; court can appoint Provisional Liquidator to protect assets. Various kinds of antecedent transactions are reversible. After Winding Up Order made actions against company are stayed. Creditors may file proofs in respect of virtually all claims, including contingent and unliquidated claims.

Preferential creditors are Government taxes and rates, wages, holiday pay, employer contributions, workmen's compensation. Otherwise assets are distributed to unsecured creditors on pari passu basis. Set off is broad in scope and mandatory.

Undistributed property of dissolved company passes to Crown; interested party can apply for declaration that dissolution is void within ten years of dissolution.

INSURANCE:

Governing Statutes.—The Companies Act 1981 generally and related Regulations (see topic Corporations) and additional requirements of The Insurance Act 1978, which extend to all insurers, insurance managers and insurance brokers, agents and salesmen.

Supervision By.—Initially, Minister of Finance on recommendation of Insurers Admissions Committee, and thereafter, by Minister of Finance assisted by Registrar of Companies.

Registration.—Any person carrying on insurance business in or from within Bermuda must register.

Conditions of Registration.—Insurer must maintain relevant solvency margin, liquidity and other ratios applicable.

Classes of Insurance Licence.—Minister of Finance has discretion to ascribe insurers to one of four classes of insurance licence, depending on relationship between insurer, its shareholders, its policyholders and type and scope of business. Class 1—pure captive or companies which write coverage for group of affiliates; Class 2—insurers owned by unrelated shareholders who insure themselves and affiliates. May write maximum of 20% third party business; Class 3—catch-all for insurers not falling into other 3 classes; Class 4—large property, catastrophe and excess liability carriers.

General and Long-Term Business.—Any insurer Class 1, 2 or 3 carrying on general business must have minimum authorised share capital in respect of which at least $120,000 has been paid up in cash. Insurer carrying on long-term business must have paid-up share capital of at least $250,000 in cash. Insurers combining both classes of business must have share capital in respect of which at least $370,000 has been paid up in cash. Class 4 general business insurers must have minimum authorised share capital of $1,000,000. Class 4 insurers combining both classes of business must have minimum authorised share capital of $1,250,000.

Principal Representative.—Every insurer must appoint and maintain principal representative and maintain principal office in Bermuda. In most cases insurer's insurance manager will act as principal representative and will provide principal office for insurer.

Accounting Provisions.—Every insurer must prepare statutory financial statements in prescribed form, and these must be audited annually by insurer's approved auditors. Statements and auditors' report must be kept available at insurer's principal office for at least five years. Classes 2, 3 and 4 must file statutory financial statements annually, in addition to statutory financial returns. Class 1 is exempt from filing statutory financial statements, but must file statutory financial returns. Statutory financial returns must be accompanied by business solvency certificates. Class 4 must include schedule of reinsurances. Severe penalty for late filing. Financial return includes three ratios: Premiums to statutory capital and surplus ratio; five year operating ratio; change in statutory surplus ratio.

Loss Reserve Specialist.—Statutory filings must include opinion from loss reserve specialist. This does not apply to Class 1 insurers, but Class 2 must supply opinion every three years. Classes 3 and 4 must supply opinion annually. Where net premiums derived from products liability insurance or professional liability insurance, or from both together, constitute in any relevant year more than 30% of net premiums written by insurer during that year, loss reserves relative to insurance of either or both of these classes must be certified by insurer's Loss Reserve Specialist approved by Minister.

Solvency Margin.—varies in relation to premiums written, but general rule is minimum of: $120,000 for Class 1; $250,000 for Class 2; $1,000,000 for Class 3; $100,000,000 for Class 4.

Premium Writings Restriction.—Maximum premium writings of general business insurer are restricted by operation of solvency margin. Insurer's capital and surplus must be maintained at level calculated by reference to its net premiums written. Basic rule is ratio 1:5.

Restriction on Assets.—Minimum liquidity ratio for general business carriers is that value of its "relevant assets" be not less than 75% of amount of its relevant liabilities. Liquidity ratio does not apply to insurers carrying on long-term business.

Long-Term Business.—Separate accounts must be kept. All receipts must be credited to long-term business fund. No payment may be made directly or indirectly from this fund for any purpose other than in conduct of insurer's long-term business, except to extent that there is surplus certified by approved actuary to be available otherwise than to policyholders. Dividends may only be declared or paid to persons other than policyholders to extent that approved actuary certifies that value of assets in insurer's long-term business fund exceeds liabilities of its long-term business.

Mutual Insurance Companies.—These companies may register in same manner as other companies. Mutual companies will have insurance and reinsurance business as their principal objects. They must maintain reserve fund in lieu of share capital and stipulate that liability of members is limited to amount of their unpaid premiums.

Maintenance of Records in Bermuda.—Certain financial and other business records must be kept in Bermuda. Level of detail varies by class of insurer.

INTEREST:

Part II of Interest and Credit Charges (Regulation) Act 1975 and related Regulations ("Act") provides that where interest is payable under contract governed by Bermuda law or by law and no rate is fixed, rate of interest shall be 5%. Act permits interest to be charged at 7% on unpaid balance of account commencing six months after it was rendered.

The Interest and Credit Charges (Regulation) Amendment Act 1994 suspended application of maximum rate of interest, in relation to contracts to which Part III of Act applies. Bermuda Monetary Authority has power to prescribe maximum rate at any time.

By Part IV of Act, interest accrues at 7% p.a. from date of judgment unless court otherwise directs. In case of action for death or personal injury, court may award interest at 7% for periods prior to judgment.

JUDGMENTS:

Judgments in civil matters may be obtained in Magistrate's Courts on simple summons for amounts not exceeding BD$10,000 and in Supreme Court (without limit) in actions commenced by writ, petition or originating summons.

Supreme Court has power under Judgments (Reciprocal Enforcement) Act, 1958, to permit enforcement in Bermuda of judgment or order of High Court of Justice in U.K. within six years of judgment or order being given. Act has been extended to a number of territories specified in Statutory Instrument made under Act, including, Australia, Hong Kong and most former British colonies in West Indies. Act does not extend to U.S.

Maintenance orders are similarly enforceable under The Maintenance Orders (Reciprocal Enforcement) Act 1974. Execution cannot issue without leave of court after six years from entry of judgment. Reciprocating jurisdictions include U.K., Nigeria, Jersey, Guernsey, Barbados, Hong Kong, and States of California, Missouri, Hawaii, and Florida.

Lien.—A judgment of the Supreme Court for a debt can create a lien or charge on the real estate of the debtor. A judgment more than 20 years old may be presumed satisfied.

LABOUR RELATIONS:

See topic Immigration.

Common law relative to common employment has been repealed; otherwise relation of master and servant (subject to following notes) is governed by common law. Workmen's Compensation Act, 1965, imposes liability upon employers to pay compensation for death or injury of employees arising out of and in course of employment.

See Topical Index in front part of this volume.

LABOUR RELATIONS . . . *continued*

Hospital Insurance Act, 1970, makes provision for both compulsory and voluntary hospital insurance. Every employer of three or more people is required to provide insurance in respect of hospital treatment for both employee and employee's wife if she is not employed. Cost of premiums is shared equally between employer and employee. Both voluntary and compulsory hospital insurance business may be undertaken only by insurer licenced by Government.

The Health and Safety at Work Act 1982 makes provision for securing health, safety and welfare of persons at work by imposing certain statutory duties of care on employers and employees.

Labour Unions.—Trade Union Act, 1965, provides for registration of unions and enacts compulsory rules for them. Certain contracts between members of unions, between unions, collective agreements between unions and employers and other types of contracts are unenforceable although lawful. Trade unions are protected against liability in tort. Labour Relations Act 1975 provides for reference to inquiry settlement and arbitration in event of labour dispute and for establishment of Permanent Arbitration Tribunal and also specially provides for protection of essential services and for conduct of industrial disputes arbitration and other settlement procedures in connection with them. Acts done in contemplation or furtherance of trade disputes which interfere with another person's business are not actionable or punishable. Peaceful picketing is lawful, but intimidation, illegal strikes and lock-outs are punishable criminally. Person who refuses to take part in illegal strikes or lock-outs is protected against any discrimination or disability from within his union. Essential services are protected against strike action.

Labour Relations Amendment Act 1991 further establishes essential industries disputes settlement board to resolve disputes within hotel industry and at Bermuda Civil International Airport, as well as any other industry or business that Parliament may deem to be essential industry in Bermuda. Any award is binding and enforceable in Supreme Court on applications by any party to dispute. Further, Trade Disputes Act 1992 permits Minister responsible for Labour to refer any labour dispute, including any apprehended dispute, in any trade or industry specified in published notice, to tribunal under Act. Any decision or award is binding and tribunal can levy further monetary awards for subsequent noncompliance. Industrial action following referral is unlawful.

See also topic Taxation.

LAW REPORTS, CODES, ETC.:

Considered judgments of Supreme Court are collected in Registry. No recent reports of cases have been published. Law has been codified substantially (i.e., The Criminal Code). Reports of some Bermuda cases in Supreme Court and Court of Appeal are now reported in West Indies Law Reports and Law Reports of Commonwealth. Court of Appeal judgments have been indexed and digest of cases has been prepared and includes index of cases, digest of criminal cases and digest of civil cases. Number of Privy Council decisions have been reported in major British law reports.

LEGISLATURE:

See topic Constitution and Government.

LICENSES:

These are required for many activities including following: To conduct betting office or hold lottery, fly aircraft, sell intoxicating liquors, conduct street trading or hold fair, drive motor vehicle on public road or marry. Term also used to describe certain contractual arrangements, e.g. relating to copyright, patents, trademarks and occupation of land.

See also topic Corporations.

LIENS:

Certain liens, in sense of right to retain possession of property against satisfaction, arise at common law by virtue of usage. They may be general (e.g. banker's lien) or over goods for costs incurred in respect of them (e.g. common carriers particular lien). Similar rights may be created by contract.

Certain equitable liens not founded on possession may arise by virtue of relationship of parties (e.g. partnership or vendor and purchaser) or be created by contract. They are enforceable by sale after judgment.

Certain contractual liens and all equitable liens give rise to charges after possession has passed. Such charges may be registerable. Registration is not necessary to perfect security, but preserves priority.

Maritime liens (e.g. for seamen's wages) are enforceable by action in rem pursuant to §25(3) of Supreme Court Act 1905.

See also topics Sales; Judgments.

LIMITATION OF ACTIONS:

The Limitation Act, 1984, which received legislative assent 17th Dec., 1984, became law on Dec. 1, 1987, consolidating in one Act various limitation provisions, and standardising them, with appropriate exceptions, in respect of all types of actions and proceedings. Readers are advised to consult Act before proceeding.

Some of major provisions:

Actions for debt (on simple contract) and those founded on tort, including negligence, nuisance or breach of duty embracing personal injury claims, must be brought within six years after cause of such action arises.

Actions under Survival of Actions Act 1949 and Fatal Injuries (Action for Damages) Act 1949 are extended from one to three years from date of death or date of knowledge (as defined under Act).

Actions to recover land must be brought within 20 years (if Crown land 60 years) from date when right to action accrued (as defined under Act), conversely title extinguished after adverse possession for 20 years. Note: Crown must bring action within six years.

No action can be brought to recover arrears of rent, or damages in respect to rent arrears, or any distress made, after six years.

Action to recover money secured by mortgage or charge or to recover proceeds from sale of land must be brought within 20 years.

Actions on judgments must be brought within 20 years from date on which judgment became enforceable, and interest in respect of any judgment debt must be recovered within six years from date it became due.

There is provision for extension of limitation period by six years in cases of disability, although ceiling of 30 years is placed on actions to recover land or money charged on land, and ceiling of six years in total in respect of personal injury claims and death.

Court is also given discretion to extend limitation periods in certain circumstances with respect to personal injury claims, and claims under both Survival of Actions Act and Fatal Injuries (Action for Damages) Act, having regard to, inter alia, reason for delay and conduct of defendant.

There can also be postponement of limitation periods in cases of fraud, concealment or mistake.

MARRIAGE:

Regulated by Act 1944, No. 25.

The requisites are: (1) That each of the parties should as regards age, mental capacity and otherwise be capable of contracting marriage; (2) that they should not be within the prohibited degree of consanguinity or affinity; (3) that there should not be a valid subsisting marriage of either of the parties with any other person; (4) that the parties, understanding the nature of the contract, should freely consent to marry one another; (5) that the forms and ceremonies prescribed by the Marriage Act should be observed.

The age of consent is 16 years.

In the case of any person under 21 years of age, not being a widower or widow, the consent of the parents or parent having lawful custody or the lawfully appointed guardian or judicial consent should be obtained.

The ceremony must be performed by a duly licensed marriage officer in the presence of two credible witnesses and either after publication of banns or certificate for marriage by the registrar or by licence of the Governor.

In the case of a marriage in Bermuda between a British subject resident in Bermuda, and a British subject resident in England, Scotland or Northern Ireland a certificate for marriage issued by a Superintendent Registrar in England, or by a Registrar, or a certificate of proclamation of banns in Scotland, or by a Registrar in Northern Ireland, has the same effect as a publication of banns in Bermuda.

Annulment.—*Marriages celebrated prior to December 31st, 1974:*

Marriage is void or voidable for following disabilities, existing at time of ceremony: (1) Existing prior marriage; (2) relationship within prohibited degrees (as defined by English Marriage Acts [see England Law Digest]); (3) insufficient age; (4) mental incapacity or insensibility; (5) lack of consent; (6) incapacity to consummate marriage; and also (7) for certain formal irregularities.

Marriages celebrated after 1st January, 1975:

By §15 of The Matrimonial Causes Act, 1974, a marriage celebrated after commencement of this Act shall be void on following grounds only, that is to say: (a) that it is not a valid marriage under provision of Marriage Act, 1944; (b) that at the time of marriage either party was already lawfully married; (c) that parties are not respectively male and female.

By §16 of The Matrimonial Causes Act, 1974, a marriage celebrated after commencement of this Act shall be voidable on following grounds only, that is to say: (a) that marriage has not been consummated owing to incapacity of either party to consummate it; (b) that marriage has not been consummated owing to wilful refusal of respondent to consummate it; (c) that either party to marriage did not validly consent to it, whether in consequence of duress, mistake, unsoundness of mind or otherwise; (d) that at time of marriage either party, though capable of giving a valid consent, was suffering (whether continuously or intermittently) from mental disorder within meaning of Mental Health Act, 1968 of such a kind or to such an extent as to be unfitted for marriage; (e) that at time of marriage respondent was suffering from venereal disease in a communicable form; (f) that at time of marriage respondent was pregnant by some other person other than petitioner.

MARRIED WOMEN:

See topics Descent and Distribution; Divorce; Dower; Executors and Administrators; Husband and Wife; Marriage; Trusts; Wills.

MONOPOLIES AND RESTRAINT OF TRADE:

There is no statutory regulation of monopolies, but common law rules apply. It is monopoly and against policy of law for any person or group of persons to secure sole exercise of any known trade throughout country. Permitted monopolies may come into being by Crown Grant or statute; i.e. Post Office. Therefore agreement may be void as being monopoly or otherwise as being in restraint of trade at common law. Agreement may be illegal at common law if by causing control over trade or industry to pass into hands of individual or group of individuals it creates monopoly calculated to enhance prices to unreasonable extent. Such agreement is merely unenforceable; it is not illegal in any criminal sense, nor does it give any cause of action to third person. Agreements in restraint of trade are illegal to extent that they are unreasonable.

MORTGAGES:

Legal mortgages of interests in land are effected by transfer of title subject to proviso for redemption. Discharge of security must be by way of transfer back to borrower.

Equitable mortgages of interests in land are recognised and all mortgages of land should be registered in Registrar-General's office as priority in registration determines priority of charge.

Overseas and exempted companies may hold mortgages on Bermuda real and personal property—if principal sum exceeds $50,000 prior consent of Minister of Finance must be obtained and if any overseas or exempted company enters into possession of any land in Bermuda as mortgagee, land shall be sold within five years or within such

MORTGAGES . . . *continued*
further period as Minister may from time to time sanction, and any land which is not sold within that time is liable to escheat.

Mortgages are subject to ad valorem stamp duty.

See also topics Interest; Chattel Mortgages; Assignments.

MOTOR VEHICLES:

Licensing of motor vehicles and drivers and general control by regulation are governed by Road Traffic Act, 1947, and Motor Car Act, 1951 as am'd.

Horsepower and size of vehicles are much restricted. Crash helmets mandatory. Ownership of motor cars restricted to one per household unless medical practitioner. Rental of motor cars not permitted. Ownership of motor-assisted bicycles not restricted; available for rent.

Liability Insurance.—Third party insurance with an approved insurance company is compulsory.

NATIONALITY:

See topics Aliens; Immigration.

NEGOTIABLE INSTRUMENTS:

See topic Bills and Notes.

NOTARIES PUBLIC:

Notaries Public are now appointed by Supreme Court under Commissioners for Oaths and Notaries Public Act, 1972. To be eligible, applicant must be barrister and attorney of at least five years standing and must possess Bermudian status. Certain public officers are ex officio Notaries Public.

PARTNERSHIPS:

Partnerships may be either: (1) general partnerships, which are governed by The Partnership Act, 1902; (2) limited partnerships, which may be formed for any business purpose (except banking or insurance) and which are governed by The Limited Partnership Act, 1883 or (3) overseas partnerships, which are governed by The Overseas Partnerships Act 1995. Exempted partnerships, discussed below, may be general, limited or overseas partnerships.

General Partnerships.—There is no upper limit to number of persons constituting any partnership. Every partner is agent of firm and of his other partners for purpose of partnership business and he is liable jointly with other partners for debts and obligations incurred while he is partner. However, liability is joint and several in respect of certain specified liabilities including torts, frauds and misapplication of money or property received for or in custody of firm. Firm can sue or be sued in its firm name.

Subject to any agreement between partners, every partnership is dissolved by retirement, death or bankruptcy of any partner and may be dissolved by court in certain specified cases. Mutual rights and duties of partners may be varied by unanimous consent which may be express or inferred from a course of dealing.

Limited Partnerships.—They may consist of one or more general partners, who are jointly and severally responsible, and of any other persons contributing cash or other property (but not services) as capital, who are limited partners and, except as provided in 1883 Act, are not liable for any partnership debts.

Overseas Partnerships.—The Overseas Partnerships Act 1995 introduces procedure for partnerships, formed under law of jurisdiction other than Bermuda, to obtain and register permit to do business in Bermuda. Registration of permit will entitle overseas partnership to open office in Bermuda from which to conduct its business. Permits acquired by overseas partnerships will typically restrict ability to conduct trading activities within local economic sector. However, such partnerships will be able to establish place of business in Bermuda from which to conduct their business activities external to Bermuda.

Exempted partnerships are governed by Exempted Partnerships Act, 1992. Act introduced more streamlined approach to registration and more flexible approach to operation and maintenance of exempted partnerships in Bermuda. Usually, where one or more partners does not possess Bermudian status (see topic Immigration) partnership may only carry on business as exempted partnership, i.e., may, upon registration and annual payment of BD$2,000 (reduced by half where registration occurs after 31 Aug.), carry on business outside Bermuda from office in Bermuda. With written permission of Minister of Finance may, however, transact business with another exempted partnership, exempted company or with corporation incorporated abroad but resident in Bermuda. It must maintain resident representative in Bermuda. Applications for establishment of exempted partnerships are subject to approval of Ministry of Finance and Bermuda Monetary Authority has been designated as Minister's representative for receipt of applications.

PATENTS AND DESIGNS:

Patents and industrial designs are governed by Patents and Designs Act 1930.

Any person or persons claiming to be inventor or proprietor of any invention may apply for provisional patent (operative nine months) or full patent which is operative for 16 years and may be extended for further periods of seven years each.

Grantee of patent registered in U.K. may apply within three years for registration in Bermuda.

Patent may be revoked on grounds that: (1) Patent was obtained by fraud; (2) grantee was not true inventor or proprietor of every invention included in his application; or (3) anything claimed by grantee as his invention was publicly manufactured, used or sold in Bermuda before date of patent, or included in some prior patent.

Court may order patentee to grant licences on reasonable terms in certain circumstances.

Priority of assignments and charges are, as regards purchasers for value without notice, determined by priority of registration.

Design is defined as features of shape, configuration, pattern, etc., applied to any article by any industrial process or means, which in finished article appeal to and are judged solely by eye. Author of new or original design is deemed, except in certain circumstances, to be proprietor and can apply for registration. There are 14 different classifications of goods and registration provides initial copyright in design of five years from date of registration, which may be renewed on two occasions for five years each.

Copyright in design may cease in certain circumstances including where design has been published in Bermuda prior to date of registration. There is also provision for granting compulsory licence.

There are penalties specified for infringement of copyright in goods or articles to which registered design has been applied, but these goods or articles must be marked, or no penalty or damages may be recovered unless infringing party is put on notice of existence of copyright in design. Designs registered in U.K. may also be registered and extend to Bermuda like privileges and rights as in U.K. Assignments or all matters affecting proprietorship or validity of patents or designs ought to be registered. Act sets out prescribed forms in respect of various applications.

PERPETUITIES:

Prior to coming into operation on 31st Jan., 1990 of The Perpetuities and Accumulations Act 1989, common law rule against perpetuities applied. Under common law rule, any limitation of real or personal property beyond period of any life or lives in being and 21 years thereafter is void ab initio. Such limitation is invalid if by any possibility this rule may be infringed and it is immaterial that in events which have happened, prescribed period has not been exceeded.

Important exception to common law rule: If there is gift to Charity A, followed by gift over to Charity B upon event which may not happen within perpetuity period, gift over is valid.

The Perpetuities and Accumulations Act 1989 does not apply to instruments taking effect before 31st Jan., 1990 or to exercises of special power of appointment where instrument creating power took effect before that date.

Where Act does apply, settlor or testator may specify period of years not exceeding 100 years as perpetuity period. Act also introduces "wait and see principle" which would determine any questions of validity on basis of actual rather than possible events.

Whether or not Act applies, there is no limit to period during which personalty may be directed to be accumulated, other than relevant limit imposed by controlling rule against perpetuities.

PLEDGES:

Pledge of personal chattels involves delivery of possession by way of security for debt or contract upon terms that pledgee acquires right of sale (but not of foreclosure) on default. General law of contract applies to pledges.

See topics Chattel Mortgages; Liens.

PRESCRIPTION:

See topic Limitation of Actions.

PRINCIPAL AND AGENT:

Common law rules apply. Agency is relationship which arises when one person, principal, authorises another, agent, to act on his behalf, and other agrees to do so. Generally, this relationship arises out of agreement, but there may be agency without agreement.

Types of Principal.—There are two types—disclosed: one of whose existence third party is aware at time of contracting. Undisclosed: one of whose existence third party is unaware at time of contracting.

Rights and liabilities of principal: In general principal can sue third party directly and be sued by third party. However, undisclosed principal's right to sue is limited so as not to prejudice third party who thought he was dealing only with agent, e.g. undisclosed principal can only sue third party subject to defences which third party has against agent; of agent: General rule is that agent is neither liable under nor entitled to enforce contract he makes on behalf of his principal, however, there are exceptions to this rule: where agent intended to undertake personal liability, where principal is undisclosed, where agent purports to act on behalf of principal when he is in fact acting on his own behalf. Agent will also be liable for breach of warranty of authority.

Indemnity.—Agent is entitled to be indemnified by his principal against all liabilities reasonably incurred by him in execution of his authority. He is not entitled to any indemnity in respect of obviously illegal transaction nor in respect of liability due to his own breach of duty.

Duties of Agent.—To act with due care and skill and to carry out instructions. In addition, agent has fiduciary duties: He must not put himself into position where his interests and duty conflict, he must not make secret profit or take bribe and he must not delegate performance of his duties, unless principal expressly or impliedly authorises him to appoint subagent. Agent does not delegate by instructing his own employees.

Termination.—Agent's authority can be terminated by giving him notice, by conduct inconsistent with its continuance, by supervening insanity of his principal or of himself, by his death or by death of his principal. Irrevocable agency is possible where authority is coupled with interest.

REAL PROPERTY:

All tenure is direct of Crown and subject to provisions of Escheats Acts, 1870 and 1871, but original stringencies have been greatly eased by repeal of certain provisions for escheat to Crown for want of heirs.

Any interest in land recognized by the common law and rules of equity may be created or pass by deed of grant under the seal of the grantor, or by will.

An estate tail (i.e., an estate limited to any of the heirs of the body) may be enlarged to an estate in fee simple by executing and recording a disentailing deed.

English legislation has not been followed to any great extent, and in particular the principal Conveyancing Acts, Land Transfer Acts, Settled Land Acts, and Law of Property Acts, have not been adopted in Bermuda. Agreements for sale and purchase

See Topical Index in front part of this volume.

REAL PROPERTY . . . *continued*
of real property since Feb. 9, 1979 are not enforceable unless there is note or memorandum in writing signed by party to be charged; this has been re-enacted in Conveyancing Act 1983 and makes law relating to part performance in England apply to Bermuda.

Conveyancing Act 1983 adopts certain provisions of English land law legislation although primarily to simplify conveyancing practice and to promote consistency in use of forms connected therewith.

No provision has been made for registration of title, or charges, other than mortgages.

In general 60 years title is good against the Crown and 20 years title against all others except persons under disability, remaindermen and reversioners.

Restrictive regulations with regard to development of land, erection of buildings, etc., are authorized by Development and Planning Act, 1974.

Without licence under Act 1956, No. 30, aliens or Commonwealth citizens not possessing Bermudian status (see topic Immigration) may not acquire land (including lease exceeding five years) inter vivos by inheritance or by devise.

See also topics Aliens; Corporations; Curtesy; Deeds; Descent and Distribution; Dower; Husband and Wife; Immigration; Limitation of Actions; Mortgages; Trusts; Wills.

SALES:

Sales are regulated by Sale of Goods Act, 1978 ("SGA").

Unpaid seller is defined as: (a) when whole of price has not been paid; or (b) negotiable instrument has been received as conditional payment and has not been duly met.

Irrespective of rights of unpaid seller by action, he also has right, if title in goods has not passed, to withhold delivery. If title in goods has passed to buyer, seller has: (a) lien on goods for price while he is in possession of them; (b) in case of insolvency of buyer, right of stopping goods in transit after he has parted with possession; (c) right of resale as limited by SGA.

Applicable Law.—See topic Contracts, subhead Applicable Law.

Stoppage in Transitu.—Law on this subject is chiefly governed by SGA by which goods are deemed to be in course of transit from time when they are delivered to carrier (by land or water) or other bailee (for purpose of transmission to buyer) until buyer or his agent in that behalf takes delivery from such carrier or other bailee.

Unpaid seller may exercise his right of stoppage in transitu either: (1) by taking actual possession of goods or (2) by giving notice of his claim to carrier or other bailee in whose possession goods are. Such notice may be given either to person in actual possession of goods or to principal of agent so in possession. To be effectual, notice must be given in sufficient time to enable principal to communicate it to his servant or agent in time to prevent delivery. Where notice is given to ship-owner, it is his duty to transmit it with reasonable diligence to master of ship.

Where document of title to goods has been lawfully transferred to any person as buyer or owner of goods, and that person transfers document to person who takes it in good faith, without notice and for valuable consideration, then that transfer was by way of sale and unpaid seller's right of lien or stoppage in transitu is defeated; if transfer was by way of pledge or other disposition for value, unpaid seller's right of lien, or retention or stoppage is only exercisable subject to rights of transferee. Otherwise, general rule is that unpaid seller's right of lien or stoppage in transitu is not affected by sale or other disposition of goods which buyer may have made, unless seller has assented thereto.

Warranties.—SGA implies following conditions in contracts for sale of goods: (1) seller has right to sell goods and that goods are free from any charge or encumbrance not disclosed; (2) when sale is by description (as defined in SGA) that goods correspond to that description; (3) where goods sold in ordinary course of business, that goods supplied are of merchantable quality except in relation to defects brought to buyer's attention before contract or where buyer examines goods, all defects which that examination ought to reveal; (4) where goods sold in ordinary course of business, that goods are fit for purpose for which they are required provided that buyer impliedly or expressly makes known to seller purpose for which goods are required (except where circumstances show that buyer did not rely, or it would be unreasonable for him to rely, on seller's skill or judgment); (5) where sale is by sample, that bulk corresponds with sample in description and quality and that buyer should have reasonable chance of comparing the two.

Above conditions cannot be excluded by parties to contract in case of "consumer sales" (as defined in SGA) or in any other case where such exclusion would be unfair or unreasonable in accordance with guidelines laid down by SGA. Seller can never exclude warranty of good title. Neither can seller exclude warranties of merchantable quality, fitness for purpose and conformity to description where sale is consumer sale. Consumer sale is sale in ordinary course of business of goods of type ordinarily bought for private use to person who does not buy them in ordinary course of business. Implied warranties may be excluded in all other sales where it is fair and reasonable to do so within guidelines laid down by SGA. Similar provisions apply to hire purchase contracts.

Bulk Sales.—Under Bulk Sales Act 1934, every agreement for sale or transfer of any business or stock in trade in bulk must be in writing, must contain inventory of things sold, must be filed in Registry of Supreme Court within ten days, and purchase price of any part thereof must not be paid or any promissory note or security for purchase price be delivered within 30 days of agreement.

See also topic Liens.

Instalment and Hire Purchase Sales.—By Purchase of Goods by Instalments Act 1943, vendor may not enforce instalment purchase agreement, hire-purchase agreement or guarantee in respect thereof unless agreement: (a) Is executed in duplicate, signed by parties and duplicate delivered to customer; (b) comprises down payment of 25% receipted thereon; and (c) contains provision for payment of balance by equal instalments payable at least monthly over period not exceeding two years. Act requires certain other formalities, and relief may be granted by court in certain cases. When 50% of purchase price has been paid vendor may not recover goods without leave of court. Provisions of Act may not be waived by agreement. In respect of motor cars, principal Act is varied by Purchase of Motor Cars by Instalments Act 1952, so that minimum down payment must be 50% and period of repayment one year.

SHIPPING:

Hamilton, Bermuda is British Registry Port. Ownership, registration and operation of vessels is governed primarily by Merchant Shipping Acts 1930 to 1979 (Bermuda Acts) and those parts of United Kingdom Merchant Shipping Acts 1894 to 1988 (U.K. Acts) in force in Bermuda.

Ownership qualification for registration in Bermuda is governed by U.K. acts as extended to Bermuda. Under Bermuda Acts, Minister has power to direct Registrar of Shipping to refuse to register any ship if, having regard to safety of ship and safety, health and welfare of seamen employed therein, it is detrimental to interests of International Merchant Shipping for ship to be registered in Bermuda.

Merchant Shipping (Demise Charter) Act 1994 provides for registration of vessels on Bermuda Demise Charter Register and vice versa.

Registration of title and mortgages is effected at Hamilton in same way as it is in English ports. Lloyds Register of Shipping and British Committees of Bureau Veritas, Det norske Veritas, Germanischer Lloyd and American Bureau of Shipping are all authorised to issue and renew certain of certificates required in relation to registration and it is not necessary for vessel to visit Bermuda in order to be registered. Bermuda Acts apply provisions of U.K. Acts requiring master, mate, second mate, chief engineer, second engineer and radio officer to be British certificated in relation to vessels registered in Bermuda after Mar. 31, 1980. Minister may by order exempt vessels from these requirements.

Number of subsidiary regulations, modelled to large extent on U.K. regulations, have been implemented under Bermuda Acts.

Following are main International Maritime Conventions/Regulations incorporated into Bermuda law: For unification of certain rules of law relating to Bills of Lading, Brussels, 1924 (plus 1968 Protocol); For the Prevention of Pollution of the Sea by Oil, 1954; For the Safety of Life at Sea, 1974; Relating to the Intervention on the High Seas in cases of Oil Pollution and Collisions, 1972; On Civil Liability for Oil Pollution Damage, Brussels, 1969; On the Establishment of an International Fund for Compensation for Oil Pollution Damage, Brussels, 1971; on Load lines, 1966; Relating to the Carriage of Passengers and their Luggage by Sea, Athens, 1974 (plus Protocol 1976); On Limitation of Liability for Maritime Claims, London, 1976; Collision Regulations 1983 (U.K.); and, Tonnage Regulations (1969 Convention).

The Ports Authority is constituted under Marine Board Act, 1962 (as am'd) with powers in relation to pilot service, berthing, etc. and under Oil Pollution Act, 1973 it is offence to pollute territorial waters.

Under Supreme Court (Admiralty Jurisdiction) Act, 1962 court has jurisdiction to hear wide variety of claims concerning ships and matters incidental thereto by actions both in personam and, where appropriate, in rem.

Under U.K. Maritime Conventions Act, 1911 which applies in Bermuda, actions arising from collisions at sea must be brought within two years.

Under Carriage of Goods by Sea (Bermuda) Order, 1980, which brought into force Convention on Bills of Lading referred to above, both carrier and ship are discharged from all liability in respect of goods unless suit is brought within one year of their delivery or of date when they should have been delivered. In certain circumstances, action for indemnity against third person may be brought after expiration of this period.

TAXATION:

There are no income, profits, capital gains, sale of goods, death or inheritance taxes in Bermuda. Custom duties are chief source of revenue, comprising approximately 32% of total annual public revenues of approximately $390 million. Payroll tax (replacing hospital levy and employment tax) accounts for approximately 21% of annual public revenues with balance of revenues being derived from international business annual fees (approx. 6%), land tax (approx. 6%), passenger tax (approx. 5%), hotel occupancy tax (approx. 3%), foreign currency purchase tax (approx. 1%) and receipts from local company taxes, local stamp duties, vehicle licences, postal services, etc. (together, approx. 26%).

International businesses comprised of exempted undertakings (which include exempted companies, exempted partnerships and exempted unit trust schemes) and permit companies (see topics Corporations and Partnerships) and international trusts are exempt from stamp duty otherwise imposed on instruments and documents under Stamp Duties Act 1976, except for instruments relating to Bermuda property. Local businesses and individuals, estates and trusts continue to be subject to stamp duties on documents relative to wide range of transactions including affidavits of estate value, authorised share capital and share premium, conveyances, mortgages and settlements.

Other than annual fees paid by international businesses and annual tax paid by local companies, there are no corporate fees or taxes in Bermuda. Under Exempted Undertakings Tax Protection Act 1966, Minister of Finance is authorised to give assurance to exempted undertakings that "in the event of there being enacted in these Islands any legislation imposing tax computed on profits or income or computed on any capital asset, gain or appreciation, then the imposition of any such tax shall not be applicable to such entities or any of their operations". In addition, there may be included assurance that any such tax "and any tax in the nature of estate duty or inheritance tax, shall not be applicable to the shares, debentures or other obligations" of such entities. This assurance may be for period not extending beyond 28 Mar. 2016; is applied for as matter of routine by Bermuda attorneys acting in connection with formation of exempted undertakings; and is invariably granted for full period. Application fee for this assurance is $121.

Import duties are imposed by Customs Tariff Act 1970 on nearly all goods imported into Bermuda. Duties are imposed on ad valorem basis, except for duties on fuel, alcohol, tobacco and certain other products which are charged on specific, or per unit, basis. There is also export duty on liquors and other goods taken out of bond. Specific rates and other provisions are specified in such Act.

Effective 1 Apr., 1995, provisions of Miscellaneous Taxes Act 1976, Miscellaneous Taxes (Rates) Act 1980 and respective amendments dealing with hospital levy and

TAXATION . . . *continued*
employment tax were repealed and replaced with Payroll Tax Act 1995. Standard rate of payroll tax is 12% though lesser rates from 9% apply to various classes of employers and self-employed persons, depending on type of business and size of payroll. Employer may recover from employee up to 4.5% of tax payable. Exempted undertakings may elect for all, but not some, of their employees deemed annual remuneration per employee of $66,000, subject to future annual adjustment with reference to Consumer Price Index.

Annual government fee payable by exempted companies and exempted partnerships follows graduated fee structure based on capital calculated as of 31 Aug. of preceding year on authorised share capital and share premium, in case of companies, and on fixed amount of $2,000 in case of partnerships. Under graduated fee structure, exempted company with: Capital not more than $12,000 will pay annual fee of $1,680; capital more than $12,000 up to $120,000—$3,360; capital more than $120,000 up to $1,200,000—$5,040; capital more than $1,200,000 up to $12,000,000—$6,720; and, capital more than $12,000,000 up to $100,000,000—$8,400; capital more than $100,000,000 up to $500,000,000—$15,000; capital over $500,000,000—$25,000. This fee structure applies to all exempted companies (including insurance companies, mutual funds and public finance companies), except for exempted companies whose business includes management of unit trust schemes, which pay additional fee of $2,365 in respect of each unit trust scheme managed, and all exempted partnerships. If company or partnership is formed after 31 Aug. in any year then initial annual fee otherwise applicable will be reduced by one half.

Annual government fee of $1,680 is imposed on permit companies except for insurers, mutual funds and public finance companies which pay annual fee of $3,360. Also any permit company whose business includes management of unit trust schemes pays additional fee of $2,365 in respect of each unit trust scheme managed.

Annual business fee of $1,100 is payable by each exempted insurance company, insurance manager, insurance broker or insurance agent registered under Insurance Act 1978, except for Non-Resident Insurance Undertakings which are required to pay annual fee of $10,000.

Annual fee is imposed on local companies by Companies Act 1981 based on issued capital varying between $525 for issued capital less than $50,000 and $15,000 for issued capital of $10,000,000 or more. Local companies not engaged in commercial enterprise for profit are excluded.

Annual government fees are payable in advance each Jan. except for local and permit companies whose fees are payable in Mar.

Annual land tax is levied under Land Valuation and Tax Act 1967, on private residential real estate on graduated scale by reference to deemed annual rental value and on commercial properties at single prescribed rate. With effect from 1 July 1994, 7% interest is charged on arrears of tax. Also licence fee on real estate sales to non-Bermudians is imposed at 20% (15% on condominiums) of sale price.

Passenger tax is imposed for passengers departing by air at $20 for adults and children over two years; arriving yacht passengers are taxed at $15 each; and cruise ship passengers taxed at $60 each.

There are also taxes under Miscellaneous Taxes Act 1976 in respect of hotel occupancy (charged to hotel proprietor at 7¼% of "rack rate charge" for accommodation), betting transactions (20% on bets made, received or negotiated), timesharing scheme (timesharing occupancy tax charged to developing owner at 10% of purchase price on sale or resale of timesharing interval and timesharing services tax charged to managing agent at 5% of service fee payable by purchaser of timesharing interval), and contract exchanges (5% of trading fee).

Foreign currency purchase tax of 0.25% on dollar is charged generally (there are important exemptions) whenever Bermuda resident buys foreign currency with Bermuda dollars from local bank, pursuant to Foreign Currency Purchase Tax Amendment Act 1994. This tax is also charged where foreign currency is purchased to pay non-Bermuda resident under will or intestacy of deceased Bermuda resident not possessing Bermudian status at time of death.

Bermuda-U.S. Tax Convention signed in 1986 relating to mutual assistance in tax matters and U.S. Federal Income Taxes on business profits of Bermuda insurer and excise taxes on insurance premiums paid to insurer. Convention operative Dec., 1988. Federal income tax part effective for business profits of taxable years beginning 1 Jan. 1988. Excise tax part effective for premiums paid or credited from 1 Jan. 1986. Business profits of Bermuda insurer from insurance business not taxable in U.S. unless insurer trades in U.S. through "permanent establishment". If insurer does so trade, business profits attributable to permanent establishment may be subject to U.S. taxation. Convention applies to Federal excise taxes only where risks covered by insurance premiums are not reinsured with person not entitled to benefits of Convention or any other convention which applies to such taxes. Premiums must constitute income of Bermuda insurance company which is Controlled Foreign Corporation for purposes of §957(a) or (b) of U.S. Internal Revenue Code. Alternatively, premiums must constitute related person insurance income and Bermuda insurer must be Controlled Foreign Corporation subject to relevant provisions of §953(c) of Code. Excise tax exemption ceased effective 31 Dec. 1989. U.S. Government agreed Bermuda is within North American area for convention tax benefits of Code. Treaty provides for exchange of information between U.S. and Bermuda for prevention of tax fraud and evasion of taxes.

TRADE:

See topics Corporations; Immigration.

Trade Unions.—See topic Labour Relations.

TRADEMARKS:

The Trade Marks Act, 1974, operative as of July 1, 1975, brought Bermudian Law closely into line with UK Trade Mark Act, 1938. Provision for registration of service marks was made by Amendment Act of 1993.

Register is divided into two parts: Part A and Part B. For registration in Part A mark must be inherently distinctive and for Part B mark must be found to be capable of distinguishing. Each mark must contain or consist of at least one of following particulars: (a) Name of individual, or firm presented etc. in distinctive manner; (b) signature of applicant; (c) invented word or words; (d) word or words having no direct reference to character or quality of goods, and not being geographical name; (e) any other distinctive mark. Part B, where mark must be capable in relation to goods, of distinguishing goods with which proprietor is connected in course of trade from goods where no such connection exists. Regard is to be had to whether mark is inherently capable of distinguishing and whether, by reason of use of mark or other circumstances, mark is capable of distinguishing.

Chief distinction between Part A and Part B, is that in all legal proceedings relating to mark registered in Part A, original registration is, after expiration of seven years, taken to be valid in all respects unless obtained by fraud or offending against certain provisions relating to deceptive, confusing or scandalous marks.

Registration will be refused of marks likely to deceive, and may be refused of marks containing, e.g., words "registered" or "royal" or representations of flags, arms and seals of Bermuda.

Registration operates for period of seven years, and is capable of renewal for periods of 14 years from expiry. Registration may be effected of parts of marks, and of series of marks and Registrar may in certain circumstances require registration of marks as associated marks. There may be defensive registration of well known trade marks.

Assignment may be effected either in connection with goodwill of business or not. Marks may be removed from register on grounds of nonuse and when mark is in use, but not by its proprietor, registered user may be entered on Register to ensure that there is deemed use by that proprietor.

There are powers of correction and rectification of register. Trade marks registered in U.K. may be registered in Bermuda and if accepted, are registered on same basis and subject to same conditions and limitations as in U.K.

There are prescribed forms and procedures for applications, oppositions and other matters under Act.

TREATIES AND CONVENTIONS:

Bermuda is party to number of treaties and conventions to which U.K. is signatory. These have been extended to Bermuda by Order in Council. See also topics Taxation, subhead Bermuda-U.S. Tax Convention; Trusts, subhead General; United States Bases.

TRUSTS:

General.—Virtually all trusts recognised by English rules of equity may be created and enforced. The Trusts (Special Provisions) Act 1989 validated special purpose trusts but non-charitable purpose trusts are invalid unless they comply with requirements of Act.

With effect from 1st June, 1989, provisions of Hague Convention (Convention relating to law applicable to trusts and their recognition) were extended by order-in-council to Bermuda. The Trusts (Special Provisions) Act 1989 also legislated in respect of capacity to create trust, governing law of trust and circumstances under which Supreme Court may assume jurisdiction.

Trustees are regulated by Trustee Act 1975, statute corresponding in many respects to English Trustee Act 1925. Statute is fairly comprehensive but it may be desirable to confer express powers in trust instrument to give greater flexibility of action. The Trusts (Special Provisions) Act 1989 allows for incorporation by reference of standard administrative provisions into trust instruments.

Trust Companies Act 1991 allows for licensing and regulation of all Bermuda trust companies except private trust companies.

Investment.—In absence of wider or any powers conferred by trust instrument, trustees may invest, amongst other things, in (a) bonds and debentures of or guaranteed by government of Bermuda, any independent member country of Commonwealth, Common Market, U.S.A. or of any province or state thereof, (b) securities issued or guaranteed by International Bank for Reconstruction and Development and (c) bonds, debentures or fully paid shares of a corporation with a fully-paid up capital of at least $3 million whose shares are quoted on a recognised stock exchange.

Remuneration.—In the absence of express provisions in trust instrument, trustees may be allowed remuneration by court.

Variation of Trusts.—Supreme Court may, on behalf of certain specified classes of persons, approve any arrangements varying or revoking trusts of real or personal property or enlarging trustees' powers of administration or management.

Acquisition of Land in Bermuda.—Any conveyance or other assurance of land in Bermuda to a person as trustee for a restricted person (i.e., any British subject not possessing Bermudian status, any person not a British subject or a corporation incorporated outside Bermuda) is void.

Where land in Bermuda is devised by will to a person as trustee for an alien (i.e., any person not a British subject) or for a person under 21 years of age who is child of an alien and who does not possess Bermudian status, vesting of such land is unlawful except under authority of licence granted by Minister of Home Affairs. If such licence is not forthcoming, trustee, or other person having power of sale, must sell land within three years, or such longer period as Minister of Home Affairs may allow, from date of death.

UNITED STATES BASES:

By an Agreement made in 1941 between the Governments of the United Kingdom and the United States of America, bases were released to the United States of America in certain British territories, of which Bermuda is one. The United States Bases (Agreement) Act, 1952 (No. 54), is designed to implement in Bermuda the provisions of the above agreement, dealing primarily with matters of jurisdiction, legal proceedings, and police powers.

Leased Areas comprise number of islands at East-End of Island connected by landfill. Bermuda Civil Air Terminal uses facilities of Base but is not included in Leased Area. Further land was leased at West End as annex of Base. Bases in Bermuda are responsibility of their Commanding Officer.

As part of general winding down of U.S. overseas military installations, U.S. Government withdrew from bases effective 1st Sept. 1995. Leased areas have been returned to Government of Bermuda.

USURY: See topic Interest.

WILLS:

A testator must be of full age and sound disposing mind.

Testamentary Disposition.—All manner of real and personal property may be effectively disposed of by will, but any gift to an attesting witness is void.

Execution.—A will must be in writing and either: (1) entirely in the hand writing of the testator and signed at the foot or end thereof by him; or (2) signed at the foot or end by the testator, or by some other person in his presence and at his direction, and such signature must be made or acknowledged by testator in presence of two or more witnesses present at same time who attest and subscribe will in presence of testator.

Revocation.—Will is revoked by marriage, unless it is made in contemplation of marriage to a named person which thereafter takes place, and may be revoked by subsequent will or codicil or by testator destroying will with intention of revoking same.

Construction and Effect.—Unless a contrary intention appears in the will it is construed to speak and take effect as from the time of the death of the testator.

Unless a contrary intention appears in will, where gift of property is made to any person, being a child or other issue of testator, for an estate or interest not determinable at or before death of such person and such person predeceases testator leaving issue surviving testator, gift does not lapse but takes effect as follows: (a) In respect of wills executed prior to 24th Mar., 1988 as if person had died immediately after testator's death; (b) in respect of wills executed after 24th Mar., 1988 as gift to person's issue per stirpes.

Term "child" in will includes children born out of wedlock for any wills executed after 24th Mar., 1988. Courts have power to determine whether child is child of testatrix after death.

Courts have power to rectify will where testator died after 2nd July, 1986 if it fails to carry out testator's intention because of: (a) Clerical error; or (b) failure to understand testator's instructions.

Court can alter will to carry out testator's intentions. Application for rectification should normally be made within six months of grant of administration.

Extrinsic evidence of testator's intention may be admitted to interpret will where will is ambiguous or part of will is meaningless where testator died after 24th Mar., 1988.

Subject to the provisions of the will a devise of real estate without words of limitation is construed to pass the whole estate or interest of which the testator had power to dispose by will. Where real estate is devised to two or more persons as co-owners it will be construed as devise of tenancy in common in absence of words indicating joint tenancy in any will made after 1st Apr. 1974.

Foreign Probated Wills.—Probate or letters of administration granted in U.K. and colonies, U.S.A. or any Commonwealth jurisdiction may be resealed on production of a copy of will and probate or letters of administration, certified under seal or authority of original court of probate. Before resealing, in case of letters of administration, court must be satisfied that security has been given sufficient to cover property in Bermuda. Court may also require evidence as to domicile of deceased person and adequate security in respect of debts due to creditors in Bermuda. Upon resealing, stamp duty must be paid on so much of estate as consists of real and personal property situated or being in Bermuda.

Under the Evidence Act, 1905, a certified copy of a will and probate granted by any British court or by any competent court in any of the non-British islands of the West Indies or in any part of the United States of America will, on recording the same in Bermuda, be allowed and taken prima facie as good proof of such will in all causes and matters.

Guardianship.—Under the Minors Act, 1950, guardians of minors may be appointed by either parent by will or deed.

BOLIVIA LAW DIGEST REVISER

Curtis, Mallet-Prevost, Colt & Mosle
101 Park Avenue
New York, New York 10178-0061
Telephone: 212-696-6141
Fax: 212-697-1559
Email: CMP-NY@mcimail.com

Reviser Profile

The Firm began in 1830 when two practicing lawyers started a long line of lawyers and law firms extending in an unbroken chain up to the present time. In 1897, the firm name became Curtis, Mallet-Prevost & Colt; in 1925 it was changed to Curtis, Mallet-Prevost, Colt & Mosle. The Firm is now made up of approximately 120 lawyers, including experts who have published extensively on such diverse subjects as international money management, transnational contracts, state contracts, litigation against foreign states, sovereign immunity and the act of state doctrine, and the International Court of Justice. Its principal offices are in New York City. There are branch offices in Paris, London, Frankfurt Am Main, Hong Kong, Washington, D.C., Houston, Texas, Newark, N.J., and Mexico City. The Firm has five departments: Corporate and International; Litigation; Real Estate; Tax; and Trusts and Estates. The corporate and international department acts as general counsel to various public and private corporations and individual entrepreneurs. Clients are in the banking, insurance, securities, manufacturing, real estate and oil and gas industries. In addition, the corporate and international department frequently acts as special counsel to domestic and foreign clients, providing assistance in financing, know-how licensing, the negotiation and drafting of all types of contracts and instruments, counselling on all aspects of corporate law, and establishing the vehicles necessary to enable clients to conduct their domestic and foreign business activities. The Firm's international work permeates all areas of its practice and involves questions of private international law, foreign law and an unusual amount of public and quasi-public international law. Traditionally, much of the Firm's international practice has been concerned with Latin America. The Firm maintains its excellence in that area, with its Mexican affiliate, and also through the expertise of Latin American lawyers based in the New York office. The Firm's international practice has undergone a major expansion beyond Latin America to Europe, Africa and the Near and Far East. The Firm's litigation practice includes commercial litigation and arbitration, and white-collar criminal defense. It has substantial experience in civil aviation matters; it also has represented foreign States in transnational litigation and international arbitration arising out of acts of nationalization and alleged breach of economic development or natural resource supply contracts. Among the Firm's clients in real estate matters are institutional lenders and investors, real estate developers, both individual and corporate, foreign and domestic investors and syndicators. The tax department has substantial experience in all aspects of domestic and international business tax matters and real estate taxation. The matters the tax department deals with on a regular basis include: Taxation of foreign investments; the structuring of corporate transactions, including mergers, acquisitions, liquidations and reorganization; federal and state tax litigation; and tax planning for U.S. and foreign individuals. The trusts and estates department engages in general domestic trusts and estates practice and in tax planning for foreign persons wishing to invest in U.S. assets through offshore trusts and corporations. It represents individuals, trust companies, and banks acting as fiduciaries. It works for various charitable organizations located both in the United States and abroad including private foundations, museums, universities and hospitals. A group of fiduciary accountants with vast experience in the field assists the lawyers of the trusts and estates department. Curtis, Mallet-Prevost, Colt & Mosle has served as a Reviser for most of Latin American Law Digests since 1930.

BOLIVIA LAW DIGEST

(The following is a list of all Topics, including cross-references, covered in this Digest.)

BOLIVIA LAW DIGEST

Revised for 1997 edition by

CURTIS, MALLET-PREVOST, COLT & MOSLE, of the New York Bar.

(Abbreviations used are: C. C. for Civil Code; C. Family for Code of Family; C. Minor for Code of Minor; Com. Co. for Commercial Code; C.C.P. for Code of Civil Procedure; Sup. Dec. for Supreme Decree. All Codes are cited by articles thereof.)

ABSENTEES: See topic Death.

ACKNOWLEDGMENTS:

The American system of acknowledgments is not followed. Formal documents are executed before a notary public who intervenes in the contract and retains the original, issuing certified copies. (See topics Notaries Public; Public Instruments). Instruments executed abroad are accepted if validly executed in accordance with the laws of the foreign country or if executed according to Bolivian law before a Bolivian diplomatic or consular officer. (C. C. 1294). Decree-Law 7458 of Dec. 30, 1965 regulates legalization of signatures of public officers and notaries.

ACTIONS:

Limitation of.—See topic Prescription.

See also topic Death, subhead Actions for Death.

ADMINISTRATION:

See topic Executors and Administrators.

ADOPTION:

(C. Minor Arts. 63-106).

ADVERSE POSSESSION:

See topic Prescription.

AGENCY: See topic Principal and Agent.

ALIENS:

Aliens in general enjoy same civil rights as citizens. Foreign natural or juridical persons can not hold under any title, soil or subsoil within 50 kilometers of national bounderies, except in case of national necessity declared by law. (Const. arts. 18, 19, 23-25; Decree-laws of Aug. 2, 1937 and 13344 of Jan. 30, 1976; Law 1243 of Apr. 11, 1991). Naturalized residents and resident aliens must register and obtain identity card. (Sup. Dec. 10104, Jan. 21, 1972). Aliens whose presence is disturbing may be expelled as well as aliens entering unlawfully; latter may be held within district of country for three years, being otherwise free. (Law of Jan. 28, 1937 and Decree 2369 of Feb. 1, 1951). At least 85% of personnel of any employer must be Bolivians, and 85% of payroll must go to them, with certain exceptions. (Laws Feb. 2, 1937 and Apr. 8, 1942).

See also topics Wills; Real Property.

ASSIGNMENTS:

Title to personal property and rights may be transferred either by public or private instrument. See topics Public Instruments; Sales (Realty and Personalty).

ASSIGNMENTS FOR BENEFIT OF CREDITORS:

An assignment for benefit of creditors may be made by a debtor who cannot pay his debts. It is voluntary when voluntarily accepted by the creditors, in which case the effects are those expressed in the contract. When made judicially its effect is to empower the creditors to sell the property and to receive the income therefrom until such sale. If the property assigned is insufficient to cover all the debts, the debtor continues liable for the balance. If the debtor is a merchant he is adjudged bankrupt. (C. C. 384-403; C. C. P. 584-590. See topic Bankruptcy and Insolvency.)

ATTACHMENT:

(C. C. P. 487; Com. Co. 456).

Attachments may be issued in summary actions based on instruments having executive force such as: (1) Public instruments; (2) acknowledgment of private documents before competent judges; (3) securities and other commercial documents; (4) acknowledgment of bills approved by judicial decisions; (5) credit documents for condominium maintenance fees; (6) credit documents for rent payments; (7) acknowledgment in judicial proceedings; (8) judgments no longer subject to appeal.

Provisional attachments may be granted in certain cases for judicial deposit of property in litigation. Essential elements of mercantile enterprise (as described in art. 449 of Com. Co.) cannot be attached individually by summary actions of creditors, attachment has to be issued on entire enterprise, appointing trustee who will also serve as auditor.

See also topic Mines and Minerals, subhead Mines in General.

BANKRUPTCY AND INSOLVENCY:

(Com. Co. 1487-1692; C. C. P. 562-567; Law Oct. 11, 1924).

Bankruptcy, which relates only to merchants, may be declared if debtor: (1) Defaults on any payment of obligations; (2) absconds; (3) closes his business for more than five working days without prior notice; (4) sells merchandise below market price or conceals same; (5) assigns assets to detriment of creditors; (6) suffers judicial voidance of preferences; (7) takes any fraudulent measure to process funds or avoid compliance with obligations; (8) has nonexistent or insufficient assets to attach; (9) requests insolvency proceedings when not permitted by law or when adjustment with creditors is not reached; (10) defaults on prior insolvency agreement. Bankruptcy is classified as: (1) Fortuitous; (2) with fault; (3) fraudulent.

Declaration of bankruptcy deprives bankrupt of administration and free disposition of his property with exceptions provided by Art. 1584.

A fraudulent bankrupt cannot be discharged and culpable bankrupts can be discharged only after serving their punishment. In order to be discharged bankrupts must show that they have complied with the agreements made with their creditors or have fully paid their obligations.

Insolvency proceedings (concurso de acreedores) are voluntary when requested by the debtor and necessary when demanded by creditors. The claims of the creditors are filed and if no agreement is made with the insolvent his property is sold and distributed.

BANKS AND BANKING:

(Banks and Financial Entities Law 1488 of Apr. 14, 1993 as am'd).

Law regulates Superintendency of Banks and Financial Entities, organization of banks, capital, inspections of banks, administration of banks, reserves on deposits, liquidation, trust sections, and financial entities. Law contains formalities for establishment of bank and opening of branches of foreign banks. Foreign bank doing business in Bolivia is entitled to same rights and privileges and to same rules as domestic banks of same kind. No foreign bank may invoke rights of foreign citizenship in relation to its business in Bolivia. According to Law, financial entities are ones which receive money on deposit and use it, together with their own capital for loans and to purchase or discount promissory notes, drafts and bills of exchange among others.

BILLS AND NOTES:

(Com. Co. 491-738).

Bill of exchange must contain: (1) Indication that it is bill of exchange; (2) place and date of issue; (3) unconditional order to pay sum certain to drawer; (4) name of drawer; (5) name and address of drawer and place of payment; (6) maturity date; (7) signature of drawer, followed by name and address thereof. If any of above requirements is missing, instrument does not produce effects as bill of exchange, with exceptions provided in Code.

Bills payable at fixed date or at fixed period of time after date on sight must be paid on maturity date. Sight bills are payable upon presentment, which must be made within one year following date of bill. Drawer may extend term or prohibit presentment prior to given date but within indicated term.

Endorsements must contain: (1) Name of endorsee; (2) type of endorsement; (3) place and date thereof; (4) signature of endorser. Omission of above has effect as provided in Art. 523. Blank endorsements are valid if they contain signature of endorser. In case of nonacceptance or nonpayment, bills must be protested. Protest must be contained in notarial instrument. Protest for nonacceptance must be made within period established for presentment or before its maturity date; if it is protest for nonpayment, it must be made on third day following its maturity date. Protest should contain: (1) Literal text of bill, all acceptances and endorsements; (2) demand on drawee to accept or pay bill, indicating if such person was present or not at time; (3) grounds for nonacceptance or nonpayment; (4) signature of person to whom protest was made, or indication of impossibility of processing signature or refusal thereof; (5) place, date and hour of protest. Notary must sign protest once above formalities are accomplished.

Promissory notes must be drawn to order of named person. They create same obligations as bills of exchange, except that acceptance is not necessary. Promissory note must contain: (1) Statement that it is promissory note; (2) promise to pay sum certain; (3) name of payee; (4) maturity date or manner of determining same, and place of payment; (5) place and date of execution; (6) signature of maker.

Checks must contain: (1) Printed number and series or code or identification sign; (2) date and place of issue; (3) unconditional order to pay at sight sum certain; (4) name and address of bank; (5) statement whether check is made to order or to bearer; (6) signature of drawer. Checks must be presented for payment: (1) Within 30 days if drawn in Bolivia; (2) within three months if drawn outside of Bolivia and payable thereat. Special checks are: certified, cashiers, crossed, endorsed, checks for payment into account and travellers' checks.

CHATTEL MORTGAGES:

There is no provision for chattel mortgages. See topics Liens; Pledges.

CLAIMS:

See topic Executors and Administrators.

COLLATERAL SECURITY: See topic Pledges.

COMMERCIAL REGISTRY:

This Registry is supervised by Ministry of Industry and Commerce. Natural and juridical persons engaged in commerce must register with Registry. All acts by such persons related to their commercial activities must also be registered, such registration is mandatory and any violations are subject to fines running from 1 to 5% of their working capital. See also topic Corporations.

COMMUNITY PROPERTY:

See topic Husband and Wife.

See Topical Index in front part of this volume.

CONSTITUTION AND GOVERNMENT:

Constitution of Feb. 2, 1967 as am'd.

Bolivia is constituted as unitary republic and all legislative power is vested in Congress. Congress is composed of Chamber of Senators, elected by universal and direct suffrage. (Art. 63). Chamber of Deputies shall be elected by universal and direct voting, by simple plurality of votes, and with proportional representation of minorities. (Art. 60). Senators and Deputies are elected for five years. (Arts. 60, 65). Executive power is exercised by president of republic together with ministers of state. (Art. 85). President is elected for five years and may not be elected again until after expiration of one presidential term. (Art. 87).

For administrative purposes, territory of republic is divided into departments, provinces, provincial sections, and cantons. (Art. 108). Government of a department is entrusted to a prefect who represents executive power, and subordinate to whom are subprefects in provinces and "corregidores" in cantons.

Constitutional Court is independent and subject only to Constitution. Its jurisdiction extends over territory of Republic. It reviews habeas corpus right actions, resolves conflicts among public powers; it has original jurisdiction in certain matters, such as inconstitutionality of laws, decrees, treaties and international conventions.

There is a unified system of courts. See topic Courts.

CONTRACTS:

Nature, form, objects and obligations concerning contracts are generally governed by Civil Code. Nevertheless there are other specific classes of contracts known as commercial or mercantile contracts which are governed by Commercial Code. Labor contracts are regulated by Labor Laws. In those cases, Civil Code acts as a supplement. (Civ. Code arts. 450 to 954).

Civil Code defines a contract as an agreement by which one or more persons bind themselves to another person or persons to give, to do, or not to do, something. Essential elements of a contract are: consent of party to contract, an object, cause, and satisfaction of formalities which may be required. (Art. 452).

Only those persons having legal capacity may enter into contracts. Subsequent ratification of a contract has same effect as its previous authorization. Civil Code specifies which contracts must be formal and which may be informal. Certain contracts must be entered into in compliance with all formalities, such as in case of marriage, gifts, mortgages and company formation. In such cases a written contract is essential and cannot be replaced by any other kind of evidence.

Under Bolivian Commercial Code a contract is commercial or civil, depending on whether it is related to commercial or civil acts. Normally a commercial contract must be concluded by a merchant or between merchants. (Com. Co. arts. 802-1301). Principal commercial contracts are following: company formation, sales, exchange warranties, insurance, commissions and banking operations.

CONVEYANCES:

See topics Deeds; Public Instruments.

COPYRIGHT:

(Decision 351 of Dec. 17, 1993 of Cartagena Commission; Law 1322 of Apr. 13, 1992, regulated by Sup. Decree 23907 of Dec. 7, 1994; Law of Oct. 30, 1945; Decree of June 18, 1945; Sup. Dec. 16762 of July 11, 1979 regulated by Sup. Dec. 18059 of Mar. 4, 1981; and Updated Decree 1068 of Dec. 17, 1971 only on matters not regulated by Decision 351. Law grants certain intellectual, moral and property rights to author, his successors or assignees, regarding scientific, literary and artistic works.)

Author is entitled to: (1) Recognition of his quality as author; (2) right to oppose deformation, mutilation or modification of his work; (3) delayed publication of his work even up to period of 50 years after his death.

Works Protected.—Protection is granted to literary, artistic or scientific work expressed in any form and by any means tangible or intangible, known or actually unknown. Law also protects translations, adaptations, musical arrangements and other transformation of private intellectual works; to protect these copyright works written authorization from original owner of work is necessary. Performers' rights are also protected.

Duration.—Copyrights remain in force: (1) For life and 50 years after author's death. Then, or before if there are no heirs, they become public domain; (2) in case of joint authors, 50-year period begins upon death of last survivor; (3) if author remains anonymous for 50 years from first publication; (4) in case of collective works, photographs, phonograms, radio programs, computer programs, 50 years from publication, exhibition, recording, transmission, or use; if it has not been published, 50 years from creation. After that time, works revert to national patrimony, as well as those art manifestations when their authors are unknown or when they are simply expressions of folklore.

Registration.—Registro Nacional de Derecho de Autor, in which are recorded works submitted by authors, agreements or contracts which in any manner confer, modify etc., patrimonial rights of authors, artists, performers, author's associations. Literary and artistic works, performances and other productions are protected by law without requiring registration.

Law contains provisions regarding publication, as well as for further reproduction and edition of intellectual works and their illegal use and reproduction.

Foreigners in Bolivia enjoy same rights of national authors.

By Decree-Law 6996 of Dec. 10, 1964, textbooks, scientific works and scientific periodicals in foreign languages not registered in Bolivia, can be translated into Spanish by authorization of government.

International Conventions.—Montevideo Convention of 1889, Buenos Aires Convention of 1910, Caracas Agreement of 1911, Washington Convention of 1946, Rome Convention of 1961, Stockholm Convention of 1979.

CORPORATIONS:

Organization.—(Com. Co. Arts. 195-442).

Corporation is designated with name which refers to its principal purpose, and must be accompanied by word "SOCIEDAD ANONIMA", or abbreviation of these words ("S.A."). Name must differ from any existing one. Corporate capital must be divided into shares, responsibility of shareholders being limited to value of their shares. Corporation may be organized as private or by public subscription. If subscription is private, charter must reflect following in addition to requirements established in Art. 127: (1) Minimum of three shareholders; (2) at least 50% of authorized capital must be subscribed; (3) at least 25% of each share value must have been paid-in; (4) by-laws have been approved by shareholders. If subscription is public, founders must submit corporate report for approval of corporation's management, containing: (1) Name, age, marital status, citizenship, profession, residence and identity card of each promoter; (2) type and value of shares; (3) number of promoter shares; (4) draft by-laws; (5) preferences reserved to promoters; (6) term of subscription; (7) contract between bank and promoters to achieve requirements set forth in Art. 224.

Art. 169 provides that in case of "sociedades" (corporations, limited liability companies, etc.) dividends may be paid only from net profits after deducting 5% per annum to set up reserve. Founders will open bank account with their monetary contributions. Property will be contributed to corporation after its organization and, in interim, must be placed in trust with designated bank for subscription. Once organization of corporation has been approved by general meeting of shareholders, all corporate documents must be published.

Shares.—Capital is divided into shares of same value. Par value is 10 bolivianos for multiples of 10. Corporations may not issue shares for price below their par value. Transfers of partly paid shares do not release assigners from liability for unpaid portion. Shares may be transferred freely unless charter establishes conditions (which cannot restrict alienation) on nominative shares.

Shares may be common or preferred. Common shares have right to vote in general stockholders' meetings. Preferred shares may only vote in special meetings, and cannot exceed one half of subscribed capital. Issuance of shares with multiple voting is forbidden. Corporation is prohibited from taking loans, advance payments or negotiations, with guaranty of its own shares.

Stockholders' Meetings.—Constitute primary means for expression of shareholders' will, and may be general or special; unless otherwise provided in by-laws, quorum for general meetings is one half of voting shares; for special meetings quorum is two-thirds. Decisions in general or special stockholders' meetings are taken by majority vote.

Management.—Corporation is administered by board of directors composed of minimum of three members elected by stockholders. By-laws may provide for higher number of directors, which, however, may not exceed 12. Directors need not be shareholders and their services may be remunerated. To guarantee their liability, directors, must produce fiduciary bond. Directors are liable for: (1) Malfeasance; (2) violation of laws, by-laws, regulations or resolutions of meetings; (3) damage caused by willful misconduct, fraud, gross negligence or abuse of power; (4) income distributions in violation of Art. 168. Annual balance sheet or report, indicating dividend payments must be prepared and published.

Internal financial control will be in hands of trustee or trustees (who may be shareholders), with duties indicated in Art. 335. Their services are remunerated and they are liable for noncompliance with their obligations.

Increase and Decrease of Capital.—By resolution of general extraordinary stockholders' meeting, corporate capital may be increased up to amount of authorized capital, with due regard for preemptive rights. Respective resolution must be registered with Commercial Registry. Voluntary decrease of capital must be done by resolution of general extraordinary stockholders' meeting, and must be approved by General Direction of Corporations. Decrease of capitol is obligatory if losses exceed 50% of corporate capital.

Dissolution and Liquidation.—Corporations are dissolved by: (1) Shareholders' agreement; (2) expiration of term; (3) happening of event upon which existence is conditioned; (4) achievement of its purposes or impossibility of attaining same; (5) total loss of capital; (6) declaration of bankruptcy; (7) consolidation or merger; (8) if there is only one stockholder, or less than three for S.A.; (9) in cases provided for in charter. Once corporation has been dissolved, it enters into liquidation.

Conversion, Merger.—Conversion into another form of enterprise requires unanimous consent of stockholders, absent provision to contrary in charter, in which case dissenting shareholders have right to withdraw from company. Resolution approving merger or consolidation must be registered with Commercial Registry and published in local newspaper.

Foreign corporations may obtain authorization of government to do business in Bolivia by filing certified copies, authenticated by Bolivian diplomatic or consular officer, of following documents: (1) Articles of incorporation; (2) by-laws; (3) minutes of organizational meeting setting forth names of directors and certification of amounts paid in on shares; (4) power of attorney of representative. Foreign corporations must establish domicile in Republic and be represented by director or fully authorized representative.

Foreign corporations are governed by laws of their countries of organization with respect to their form and legal existence, but their business operations in Bolivia are governed by Commercial Code and other applicable Bolivian laws.

Mixed economy corporations can be composed of two or more stockholders and are subject to Commercial Code regulations and governed by their by-laws. Private and public sectors of mixed economy companies are liable only up to amount of their subscribed capital and for their contractual obligations.

Limited Liability Companies.—(Com. Co. Arts. 195-216).

Shareholders' liability is limited to amount of subscribed capital, which is divided into shares called "quotas", of 10 bolivianos or multiples of 10. May not have more than 25 members. It must be in name of one or more quotaholders, and must be accompanied by words "limited liability company" (or its abbreviation "Ltda."), otherwise members will be jointly liable as partners. Corporate capital must be fully paid before commencing operations. Quotaholders may agree to increase capital by quotaholders representing ²/₃ of capital. Administration of company is in charge of one

CORPORATIONS . . . *continued*
or more managers elected by members. Meeting must be held at least once a year at which presence of quotaholders representing one half of corporate capital is required to reach legal quorum. Quotaholders have one vote per quota. Dividends may be paid only from net profits after deducting 5% per annum for reserve.

COURTS:

Justice is administered by: (1) A Supreme Court which hears certain classes of appeals from the lower courts and has original jurisdiction in certain matters, such as accusations against high functionaries and questions arising out of government contracts; (2) Superior district courts, which hear appeals from judges; (3) judges, who have original jurisdiction in civil, family, commercial, labor, minors, and criminal cases and misdemeanors. (Judicial Organization Law, 1455 of Feb. 18, 1993).

CURRENCY:

(Law 901 of Nov. 28, 1986 as am'd).

Monetary unit is "boliviano". "Bs." is applicable to designate "boliviano", which is divided into 100 centavos.

CURTESY:

There is no estate by curtesy.

CUSTOMS DUTIES:

See topic Taxation, subhead Custom House Taxes.

DEATH:

An interested party may apply for a declaration of absence after two years from disappearance of absentee. Provisional possession of absentee's property may then be obtained by his heirs upon giving bond. Presumed death of absentee may be declared upon successor's request, five years after last notice of existence. (C.C. 31-51).

Deaths are recorded in the Civil Registry; and death certificates are obtainable from the Chief of the Civil Registry of the district where death occurred. Nominal fees are provided by local regulations.

Actions for Death.—There is no statute dealing with wrongful death actions. However, these could be supported under the few general provisions on torts contained in the Civil Code. Civil liability out of crimes is usually sought within the same criminal procedure. Civil actions out of tort are not usual though, as stated, could be supported under the general statutes on torts.

DECEDENTS' ESTATES:

See topics Descent and Distribution; Executors and Administrators; Wills.

DEEDS:

Transfers of title to real estate must be by public instrument (see topic Public Instruments) and contain a true statement of consideration. They must be recorded in registries of property. Both grantor and grantee must sign deed and both must therefore be present before notary at same time. If one is absent he must be represented by attorney in fact. Original deed, if executed in Bolivia, must remain in files of Bolivian notary, who gives to either party certified copy which has effect of original in courts of law.

DESCENT AND DISTRIBUTION:

(C. C. 1000-1278).

Estates of decedents pass either by will or by operation of law. In default of testamentary provisions estate passes to descendants, ascendants, legal or natural spouse ("convivienta"), collateral kinsmen and state, in order and according to rules established in Civil Code.

(1) Descendants: children and descendants succeed in first order of precedence to inheritance, except as to that part which corresponds as matter of right to legal or natural spouse. Children inherit in equal parts; grandchildren and other descendants, per stirpes.

(2) Ascendants: succeed in absence of any surviving descendants.

(3) Spouse succeeds in event that no descendants or ascendants survive desceased. Natural or common law marriages, recognized under Constitution and Family Code give rise to similar inheritance rights as those created under legal marriage.

(4) Collateral kinsmen: They inherit in absence of surviving descendants, ascendants or spouse.

(5) State: In absence of any heirs State succeeds.

In any case, whether there is a will or not, a certain proportion of the estate goes to the heirs by operation of law. A testator may dispose freely of only one-fifth of his property; the other four-fifths must go to these obligatory heirs. In some special cases proportion will be two thirds.

Inheritances may be accepted expressly or impliedly or may be refused. If accepted the acceptance may be with benefit of inventory, in which case an inventory of the property is prepared and the heir is liable to creditors only up to the amount shown in such inventory, or it may be unconditional, in which case the heir is liable for all debts of the decedent. If there is no one appointed by a testator to make the partition the heirs make the partition themselves, minors and incompetents being represented by their guardians. In case of controversy the judge appoints the partitioner.

Family Code extinguishes difference between legitimate and natural children.

DIVORCE:

(C. Family Arts. 130-157, 399).

Divorce dissolves marriage. It may be granted for: (1) Adultery; (2) conviction of one spouse for having made an attempt against life of other; (3) prostitution of wife by husband, or of children by either spouse; (4) abandonment within six months after demand and refusal to obey judicial demand to return, or after return, new abandonment for two months; (5) cruel treatment; (6) voluntary separation for two years.

Divorce by mutual consent can be demanded only after two years of marriage. Parties must personally appear; judge attempts to reconcile them and if unsuccessful designates a date for another appearance six months later; there is a third hearing after still another six months period, and if parties persist in desiring divorce, same is granted.

Code does not provide any particular length of residence in order to bring an action for divorce.

Judge of last domicile of defendant has jurisdiction of divorce action. He determines amount of alimony to be received by spouse and who is to have provisional care of children. Wife is entitled to alimony unless she is found to be guilty party or unless she has sufficient property of her own. If parties cannot agree on custody of children judge decides; as a rule children under seven years are awarded to mother and others to father, or sons are awarded to father and daughters to mother.

Remarriage.—A divorced wife may remarry after 300 days from the provisional separation or after the birth of a child.

Separation may be granted for: (1) Any cause authorizing divorce; (2) habitual drunkenness, use or trafficking drugs; (3) insanity or chronic contagious disease; (4) mutual consent, but only after two years of marriage.

DOWER:

There is no dower right.

ENVIRONMENT:

(Law 1333 of Apr. 27, 1992 and Sup. Decree 24176 of Dec. 8, 1995).

Law establishes general rules for conservation, protection and improvement of environment to benefit quality of life and establishes principle that present needs should be satisfied by productive activities without compromising those of future generations. Law contains general rules for all productive sectors and considers environment and natural resources as national patrimony to be protected and conserved in social and public interest; and contains such principles as prevention and control of environmental pollution and reparation of damages. Within environmental protection are air, water, hazardous waste and noise pollution. Environmental impact assessments are mandatory for any activity that may damage environment. Entry of hazardous waste into country, whether actually or potentially dangerous and of radioactive waste is prohibited. Administrative or criminal penalties are imposed for violation of law. Criminal sanctions include fines and imprisonment as established by Criminal Code. Law imposes liability on those who cause environmental damage National Secretariat of Environment is responsible of enforcing law.

ESCHEAT: See topic Descent and Distribution.

EXCHANGE CONTROL:

(Sup. Decrees 19893 of Nov. 17, 1983, 20479 of Sept. 16, 1984, 21060 of Aug. 29, 1985 as am'd, 21660 of July 10, 1987 as am'd and 21714 of Sept. 23, 1987).

Foreign exchange auction market is operated by Central Bank. There is one exchange rate that is used for all transactions fixed by Central Bank by auction, except purchase of foreign exchange for overdue loan payments, which are eligible for special rate. Exporters must exchange percentage of foreign currency earnings with Central Bank which authorized foreign exchange for payment for only priority imports. Banks and hotels may buy and sell, dollars, or they may deliver to Central Bank, in exchange for 10% commission. Contracts specifying foreign currency payment or with dollar equivalent clauses are permitted.

EXECUTIONS:

When an order of execution has been issued and property attached, the court designates a day for a public auction. The sale is made on the basis of the appraised value of the property, no bid being accepted for less than three-fourths of such value. Each bidder must make a deposit of 5% of such value. If no bidder appears the appraisement is reduced 10% and there is a new call for bids on this basis. After three 10% reductions the creditor may receive the property at 80% of final basis or take it in pledge subject to further bidding at his request or when another offers 80% of such final basis. There is no right of redemption. (C. C. P. 525-549; Law Dec. 3, 1919).

EXECUTORS AND ADMINISTRATORS:

(C. C. 1220-1278).

If there is no executor appointed by the testator the heirs jointly act as executors, and if they are unwilling or unable to act the executor is appointed by the judge. An executor must conclude his work within one year unless he obtains an extension.

When a person dies intestate his property passes immediately to his heirs and is administered by them. Heir who has accepted inheritance unconditionally is liable for all debts of decedent; if he has accepted with benefit of inventory he is liable only up to value of property received by him. When there are creditors heir who has demanded inventory can sell property of estate only under judicial auspices. Heirs must pay claims as filed insofar as they are liable. Partition is voidable when made under violence or fraud. Suit may be brought within three years from when violence ceased or fraud was uncovered.

EXEMPTIONS:

If debtor shows other assets enough to cover amount claimed, all assets part of commercial or industrial establishment or debtor's household are exempt from attachment and execution. Creditor cannot attach specific assets causing serious detriment to debtor if there exist other attachable assets. (C. C. P. 498; Law Dec. 9, 1941).

FORECLOSURE: See topic Mortgages.

FOREIGN CORPORATIONS:

See topic Corporations.

FOREIGN EXCHANGE:

See topic Exchange Control.

FOREIGN INVESTMENT:

See topic Taxation.

FOREIGN TRADE REGULATIONS:

See topic Exchange Control.

FRAUDS, STATUTE OF:

See topic Public Instruments.

FRAUDULENT SALES AND CONVEYANCES:

Following acts of bankrupt executed up to two years prior to date on which he is deemed to be insolvent are void: (1) Gratuitous contracts or those which should be considered such in view of insufficient consideration; (2) payment of unmatured debts; (3) mortgages or privileges to secure earlier debts; (4) payments, acts or transfer made if debtor's insolvency was notorious or should have been known by transferee; (5) in case of bankruptcy of company any merger, transformation or any amendment to by-laws that could alter responsibility of shareholders. (Com. Co. 1591-1602).

HOLIDAYS:

(Sup. Decree 21060 of Aug. 29, 1985).

Jan. 1 (New Year's Day); Mon., Tues. (Carnival)*; Good Friday*; May 1 (Labor Day); Corpus Christi*; Aug. 6 (Independence Day); Nov. 1; Dec. 25 (Christmas).

Regional holidays: July 16 (La Paz Day) celebrated only in La Paz; Sept. 14 (Cochabamba Day); Sept. 24 (Santa Cruz Day).

* These are movable holidays.

HUSBAND AND WIFE:

(Family Code 96-128).

Husband and wife have same rights and obligations. Both contribute to their common economic needs. Wife has social and economic function in home, protected by law. Community property ("comunidad de gananciales") is created at time of matrimony, as regulated by law. Private agreements with respect thereto are disallowed.

Certain types of property are excluded from community property; property owned at time of marriage, that received by succession, legacy or donation; property title of which passed before marriage; that received for services rendered before marriage; personal property acquired by subrogation, etc.

Spouses can freely and severally administer their individual property. Authorization of other spouse is required in order to effect donation thereof.

Community property ("Bienes comunes") is that property acquired during marriage by reason of work, income from separate property or discovery or by subrogation. Both spouses administer community property.

Community property ceases by death of one of spouses, annulment of marriage, divorce, separation and judicial separation of property.

Married woman of at least 18 years of age may engage in commercial acts, without her husband's authorization and becomes liable with personal property or with her community property. If husband and wife engage in commerce jointly, they will be considered merchants, unless one is dependent on other's commercial activities. (Com. Co. 17-18).

INCOME TAX:

Generally, see topic Taxation. On mining companies, see topic Mines and Minerals.

INFANCY:

(C. C. arts. 3-5 and Family Code 249-275; Law of Oct. 28, 1890; Decrees of Mar. 9, 1950 and 4017 of Apr. 11, 1955).

Age of majority is 21. Infants are not competent to contract, being subject to parental authority. Parental authority includes custody, legal representation and administration of infant's real and personal property, with some exceptions. In absence of parents guardian is appointed. Parents and guardian have restricted powers of disposition.

INSOLVENCY:

See topic Bankruptcy and Insolvency.

INTEREST:

Legal rate is 6%, but parties may agree on any rate. (Law Nov. 4, 1840 and Decree-Law 11552 of June 28, 1975). In addition, various rates are prescribed for different credit institutions and specialized banks.

However, interest on bank loans or discounts may not exceed 15% per year, commissions and additional charges not being permissible; interest on savings accounts must bear a minimum interest of 10% and on deposits at fixed term must bear interest of 8%. (Supreme-Decree 8959 of Oct. 25, 1969 regulated by Supreme-Decree 8986 of Nov. 7, 1969 and Decree-Law 11552 of June 28, 1975).

INTESTACY:

See topic Descent and Distribution.

JUDGMENTS:

Judgments do not constitute a lien on the property of the debtor except as to real property when they are recorded in the registry of real property.

LABOR RELATIONS:

Constitution provides for right to work and a fair remuneration for said work to insure employee and his family proper means of subsistence. Right to social security is also provided for. (Art. 7).

Under General Labor Law of Dec. 8, 1942 as am'd regulated by Sup. Dec. of Aug. 23, 1943 as am'd by several laws, working hours may not exceed eight hours per day or 48 hours a week. Work by minors under 14 is prohibited, except for apprentices. (Arts. 39 to 55). Workers and employees in general are entitled to an annual vacation with full pay according to years of service.

Law of Dec. 14, 1956 as am'd and its regulations Sup. Dec. 5315 of Sept. 30, 1959 established compulsory social security system applicable to all activities with some exceptions which are regulated by special laws.

Women cannot be dismissed during pregnancy and one year after birth. (Law 975 of Mar. 2, 1988).

LEGISLATURE:

Congress meets annually August 6 and remains in session from 90 to 120 days. Special sessions may be called.

LIENS:

Privileged credits in general are as follows in the order stated: (1) Judicial expenses; (2) salaries and wages for past and current year; (3) royalties or fees earned by writers, composers and artists during last 12 months.

The following are liens on specific property: (a) Rentals, as to current crop and personal property of tenant; (b) money lent for purchase of seeds, as to current crop, and money lent for purchase of farming utensils, as to such utensils; (c) unpaid purchase price, as to personal property sold, while in possession of debtor; (d) debts to innkeepers and carriers, as to objects brought into inn or carried; (e) debts secured by pledge, as to article pledged; (f) unpaid purchase price, as to real property sold; (g) money lent to buy real property, as to such property; (h) rights of coheirs, as to real property of estate; (i) debts to architects, builders, masons, etc., as to respective buildings or works. The liens under (f), (g), (h) and (i) above, must be recorded in the public registry. A consignee has a lien on the merchandise received by him for his disbursements on account thereof. (C. C. 1345-1352; M. C. 143-145; Law Nov. 15, 1887. See topic also Pledges.)

LIMITATIONS OF ACTIONS:

See topic Prescription.

LIMITED LIABILITY COMPANIES:

See topic Corporations.

LIMITED PARTNERSHIP:

See topic Partnership.

MARRIAGE:

(Const. Arts. 193, 194; C. Family Arts. 42-67, 73-129; Law Oct. 11, 1911).

The only marriage recognized by law and producing civil effects is the civil marriage, although the parties may thereafter marry by religious rite. The marriage is performed by an official of the civil registry.

The following cannot marry: (a) Males below 16 or females below 14 years of age; (b) ascendants and descendants; (c) collaterals to second civil degree. Parental consent is required for marriage of minors. Marriage by proxy is allowed.

The following are grounds annulling the marriage: (a) If it has not been celebrated by officer of Civil Registry; (b) fact that marriage was performed between two persons of same sex; (c) incapacity due to age, mental health, civil status, consanguinity, adoption, crime against previous spouse, etc.; (d) bigamy; (e) duress, etc. Marriages declared void nevertheless produce civil effects with respect to spouse and children, if they were contracted in good faith.

A marriage is dissolved by death or divorce. After the husband's death the widow cannot remarry until one year has elapsed. A divorced wife may remarry after 300 days from the provisional separation, or after the birth of a child.

MARRIED WOMEN:

See topics Husband and Wife; Marriage.

MINES AND MINERALS:

Provisions relating to mines in general are found in Mining Code, Law 7148 of May 7, 1965, as am'd by Laws 1243 of Apr. 11, 1991 and 1297 of Nov. 27, 1991 as am'd. There is mining control commission and registry of miners. (Sup. Dec. 4892 of Mar. 25, 1958).

State is owner of all mineral substances, on soil and subsoil, whoever may be owner of surface, but State may grant concessions to work them in accordance with Mining Code. Mining concession constitutes right which is distinct from ownership of land, and is indivisible. State may declare certain zones as "reserves" for surveying purposes or for exploitation under special contract, or for reasons of public interest, but rights previously granted shall not be impaired. State participates in operation of mines, through economically self-sufficient entity, Corporación Minera de Bolivia, which is decentralized in four fully-owned subsidiary enterprises which may execute different kinds of contracts such as leasing, operations, service contracts, joint ventures or they may exploit them directly. Joint ventures contract must be granted by bid. Law 373 of Dec. 18, 1967 regulates special companies (Sociedades de economía mixta) which are organized to exploit nationalized mines not under direct exploitation at present by Corporación through its subsidiaries.

Neither foreign states nor Bolivian public officials enumerated in Code can hold any interest whatever in mining enterprises as provided by law. Foreign natural or juridic persons cannot hold mining rights within 50 kilometers of national boundaries, except in case of national necessity declared by law. Before engaging in mining operations, foreign companies are required to prove their legal existence in country of origin, to appoint fully empowered representative and to establish legal domicile in Bolivia.

Unit for a mining concession is "pertenencia," i.e., a pyramid with a square base of 100 meters on each side. No concessionaire may own more than 20,000 "pertenencias" for direct exploitation.

See Topical Index in front part of this volume.

MINES AND MINERALS . . . *continued*

By Supreme-Decree 08339 of Apr. 17, 1968, nuclear minerals such as uranium and thorium, and others that may be selected by Bolivian Nuclear Energy Commission (Comisión Boliviana de Energía Nuclear or COBOEN), are property of State. Exploration, exploitation and fiscalization of such minerals will be undertaken by COBOEN, together with Ministry of Defense. Commercialization of such minerals will be authorized by Executive Power, prior approval necessary in each case of COBOEN and Ministry of Defense.

Mines in General.—Prospecting is free, but prospector is responsible for any damage to private property.

Exploration concessions grant exclusive rights to concessionaire for four years. Renewal of half of original concession may be granted for two years. Concessionaire must begin operations within six months of date of concession and must render report on work progress to Ministry of Mines every six months.

Exploitation concessions grant exclusive rights for indefinite period of time to explore, exploit and process minerals, including gold and precious stones found in area of concession. There are no commercial restrictions on mineral products which may be sold freely in national market or to foreign purchasers.

Mining rights though indivisible, may be leased and transferred with authorization of Government. All contracts concerning operations as well as changes in charter or bylaws of operating concern must be registered in Registro Minero. Exploitation concessions may be mortgaged, but mortgage ceases when concession terminates. Mining rights, as well as industrial installations and mine products are not subject to attachment; intervention is permitted instead.

Jurisdiction.—Petitions for mining concessions are granted by local Superintendent of Mines, one in capital of each Department, who also declares cancellations thereof. An appeal is provided from his decisions before Corte Nacional de Mineria.

Cancellations of Concessions.—Main causes of cancellation are failure to start operations within term prescribed by law (above), nonpayment of amount due for "patente" in two consecutive years, by suspension of work for more than a year, by rescission of contract between two parties, and by judgment in case of legal dispute. When cancellation occurs because violation has been cited by "denouncer" concession may be granted to "denouncer." Concession becomes void when transferred to persons precluded by law to hold interest in mining operations.

Taxes.—(a) An annual "patente," or surface tax, is levied on exploitation concessions. Exploration concessions pay one half rate for exploitation concessions. Payment is made one year in advance. (b) Tax on profits. (Law 843 of May 20, 1986 t.o. 1995 regulated by Sup. Decree 24055 of June 29, 1995). Rate is 25% of annual net income of all companies in mining activity and Complementary Tax equivalent to 2.5% on net sales value. Companies operating in any mining activity are also subject to payment of taxes established by Law 843 of May 20, 1986 as am'd, excepting tax on presumed income and tax on transactions in case of local commercialization of minerals.

All equipment, edifices and materials become property of State at termination of concession.

Petroleum and Gas.—(Law 1689 of Apr. 30, 1996). Hydrocarbon deposits belong to State. Petroleum industry is public utility and of social interest enjoying preferential right to utilize surface with right to expropriation on payment of compensation. State alone has right to explore, exploit, commercialize and transport hydrocarbons and their by-products. These activities are carried out by Yacimientos Petrolíferos Fiscales Bolivianos, State owned corporation or by entering into risk contracts with private entities for certain period of time and under control of Government, national or foreign individuals or juridical persons for maximum period of 40 years. Contract rights may not be alienated, encumbered or rented, except when special permission is granted. Risk contracts are subject to local law and disputes are subject to arbitration. For transportation of hydrocarbons and distribution of natural gas concessions are granted.

Taxes.—All enterprises or companies which contract with Y.P.F.B. for exploration and exploitation as hereinabove described may be subject to tax rate of 11% local, 1% royalty and 19% national of gross oil production at well-head; to tax rate of 25% on net profits; to value added tax, and to other taxes established by Law 843 of May 20, 1986 t.o. 1995 with some exceptions. Refining, industrialization and commercialization are subject to regular tax regime. Export of petroleum, natural gas, and by-products are exempted from taxes, except those on gross oil production at well-head.

MONOPOLIES AND RESTRAINT OF TRADE:

Under Art. 134 of Constitution no form of private monopoly is allowed. State may, however, create monopolies so long as Executive Power obtains legislative approval for certain specified purposes such as exports, provided that needs of country so require. See topic Mines and Minerals.

Local production is protected from unfair practices of international trade, by imposition of countervailing duties on import of foreign goods. Dumping and subvention are considered unfair practices. Dumping is defined as import of foreign goods at lower price than normal price of same or similar goods in place of origin; and subvention as direct or indirect incentives, subsidies, premium or assistance of any kind granted by foreign governments to producers, manufacturers, carriers, or exporters of goods in order to make them more competitive on international market. (Sup. Decree 23308 of Oct. 22, 1992).

Decision 285 of Mar. 21, 1991 of Cartagena Commission is in force.

MORTGAGES:

(C.C. 1360-1397).

Mortgages can be legal, judicial or voluntary. They can affect any private real property, whatever is affixed thereto (which is also considered real property) and some recorded movable assets.

Mortgage must clearly state object and amount it secures. Property located in Bolivia can be mortgaged outside of country.

NOTARIES PUBLIC:

(Notarial Law of Mar. 5, 1858 and Nov. 20, 1950).

Notaries are public officials and, while acting as notaries, are not permitted to exercise any other profession or hold other public office. They are appointed for periods of four years and must pass an examination. They are under the supervision of the courts of their district.

Instruments executed before a notary must be prepared with certain formalities. They must state the names of the parties, their age, occupation, residence and capacity to execute the instrument, also data as to the witnesses. At least two witnesses are required. The instrument must be signed in the presence of the notary and if the parties are unknown to him they must be identified by two witnesses. Notaries cannot act in connection with instruments in which their ascendants, descendants or collaterals to the fourth degree of consanguinity or affinity have any interest. The notary retains the original document and issues to the parties in interest formal certified copies which have the effect of originals and may be used in court. There are special notaries for mining and certain treasury matters.

Notaries must be shown a tax receipt proving that parties to contract, affidavit or other notarial act have paid their taxes before document is executed. (Sup. Dec. 3874, Nov. 11, 1954).

PARTNERSHIP:

(Com. Co. 127; 378; 173-183; 184-194; 356-364; 365-371; C. C. 750-803).

Commercial partnerships are considered as legal entities. They are formed by a public instrument executed before a notary and recorded in the general registry of commerce.

Under supervision of Ministry of Industry, Commerce and Tourism. Partnership agreement must contain: (1) Place and date where entered into; (2) name, age, marital status, citizenship, profession, residence and identity cards of promoters, and name, nature, citizenship and residence of legal entities integrating same; (3) name and address of partnership; (4) nature of business; (5) amount of capital; (6) amount contributed by parties; (7) duration; (8) method of administration and organization; (9) rules to distribute profits or losses; (10) legal reserve; (11) rights and obligations clauses of partners; (12) dissolution and liquidation clauses; (13) arbitration clause if decided upon; (14) other clauses referring to partners' meetings.

Partnership is dissolved by: (1) Decision of partners; (2) termination of its term or of purpose for which it was constituted; (3) happening of event upon which existence is conditioned; (4) total loss of capital; (5) declaration of bankruptcy; (6) merger; (7) if there is only one partner or less than three; (8) clauses set forth in certificate of constitution.

Unlimited partnership (sociedad colectiva) is partnership in usual form in which all partners have unlimited and joint liability. Resolutions require approval of majority of capital with voting rights unless otherwise provided in by-laws. Unless allowed by partnership, partners cannot on their own account engage in same business as partnership.

Limited partnership (sociedad en comandita) is partnership in which one or more of partners are not liable for debts and losses except up to amount of capital they have subscribed, and in which one or more of partners have unlimited and joint liability, whether or not they have subscribed capital. Capital may be divided into shares. Special partner cannot include his name in firm name under penalty of becoming jointly liable with general partners. Special partner cannot perform any act of management, even as attorney in fact of general partners.

Joint stock partnership is partnership in which managing partners have unlimited and joint liability, and special partners are only liable for amount of shares they have subscribed. Rules governing same are set forth in Commercial Code Arts. 356-364.

Accidental partnerships are merely temporary associations whose business is carried on in the name of one of the interested parties. They are not regarded as legal entities. (Com. Co. 365-371).

Civil partnership (sociedad civil) is one which is not formed for commercial purposes. It is governed by the rules of the Civil Code and is distinguished from a mercantile company by being regarded rather as an association of individuals. The partners are not jointly and severally liable for the debts of the partnership.

PATENTS:

(Decisions 344 and 345 of Oct. 29, 1993 of Cartagena Commission; Law of Dec. 2, 1916; Sup. Dec. 4320, Feb. 16, 1956, Law 5470 of May 6, 1960 as am'd by Sup. Decree 21084 of Sept. 28, 1985; Sup. Decrees 9364 of Aug. 27, 1970 and 9673 of Apr. 19, 1971 only on matters not regulated by Decisions).

Any invention of products or proceedings in any technology field which are novel, represent inventive step and are susceptible of industrial application. Invention is novel when it is not within state of art. Discoveries, scientific theories, mathematical methods; scientific, literary and artistic works; therapeutic, surgical and diagnostic methods, among others are not considered inventions. Inventions contrary to public policy, morals and against life or health of people or animals and environment; on animal species and races and biological procedures to obtain them, inventions related to nuclear substances, to pharmaceutical products listed by World Health Organization as essential medicines; and related substances composing human body are not patentable. Patent owner must exploit it, directly or by granting license in any member country of Andean Pact. Industrial production or commercialization of patented product, are considered exploitation of patent. Patent is granted for 20 years from filing date. Industrial designs, any new design which may be applied to industrial object may be registered as ownership of author if no publicity thereof in any form has been made before filing application. Registration is granted for eight years.

Utility models for new forms of objects or mechanism provided they have practical use are registrable. Registration term is ten years from filing date. Law also protects trade secrets and considers them as any confidential information that is valuable and provides competitive or economic advantages to owner. Information considered trade secret must be expressed in tangible form such as documents, microfilm films, laser discs or any other similar means.

Vegetal species are protected when they are novel, homogeneous, distinguishible and stable and generic designation has been assigned to them. When registered certificate of holder is issued for 15 to 25 years, depending on type of vegetal variety.

PATENTS . . . *continued*

Provisions regarding patents are applicable to industrial designs and utility models.

International Conventions.—Montevideo Convention 1889, Buenos Aires 1910, Caracas Agreement 1911.

PLEDGES:

Pledge contracts are not effective unless the pledged object is delivered to the creditor or to a third person agreed upon between the parties. In case of default the creditor may judicially demand that the pledged object be sold or that it be adjudged to him, after appraisal of experts, for account of the debt; any contractual clause exempting him from these formalities is void. If the pledge covers the fruits of real property it must appear in writing. (C. C. 1415-1435).

PRESCRIPTION:

(C.C. 1492-1513; Com. Co. 589-591).

Rights are extinguished by prescription ("prescripción") when not exercised during period of time established by law.

Prescription period begins to run at time right can be enforced or at time exercise thereof has ceased.

Actions.—Prescriptive periods in which right to enforce obligations is lost vary according to nature of obligation. More important are: (1) Proprietary equity, five years, (2) indemnities, three years, (3) rents, salaries and interests, two years, (4) fees of professionals, two years, (5) salary of teachers, price of hotels, one year, etc.

If "executory actions," three years if against acceptor, and one year if in favor of payee.

See also topic Taxation.

PRINCIPAL AND AGENT:

Agency may be express or tacit, if express it may be conferred by public instrument or private writing or orally. It may be general or special. General agency comprises only acts of administration; in order to compromise, alienate or mortgage agency must be express.

Agent must execute agency or else indemnify for damages and must render information and accounts to principal; when acting through substitute agent is liable to principal if he had no right to substitute or if he wrongfully selected substitute. Principal is obliged to pay agent necessary amounts to carry out agency, as well as interest on advances and due remuneration for services rendered. Principal is equally obliged to reimburse agent for losses suffered by reason of agency, if not due to agent's fault. Agency is terminated by: (1) Expiration of term or completion of agency; (2) revocation by principal; (3) resignation of agent; (4) death or incapacity of principal or agent. Principal may revoke agency at any time and compel agent to return documents concerning it. Agency may be irrevocable if specified for special transaction or limited time and if by lawful interest of parties or third person. Agent may resign by notifying principal and if such resignation causes damages to principal he must indemnify him. (C.C. arts. 804-830; Com. Co. arts. 1237-1293).

PUBLIC INSTRUMENTS:

Public instruments are documents executed with all legal formalities. Other documents are private instruments. Public instruments constitute full proof of facts stated therein, as between parties, and as against any party with respect to declarations favoring third persons. Law requires numerous contracts to appear in public instrument, e.g., articles of incorporation or partnership, all documents which are to be recorded in property registry, etc. (C. C. 398-402; C. C. P. 1287-1295).

REAL PROPERTY:

Real property includes land and all solid and liquid matter thereon, at whatever depth, as well as all things of a permanent character fixed to land. Personal property which has been made accessory to real property is also considered real property.

Ownership, possession, and administration of real property, as well as encumbrances thereon, and its transfer is governed by provisions of Civil Code.

Art. 22 of Constitution guarantees right of private property provided that its use is not prejudicial to public interest. Expropiation may be effected for reasons of public benefit or if private property does not fulfill its social purpose, must be authorized by law and must provide for payment of just compensation to owner.

Foreigners may not acquire or possess property located within 50 km. of borders, by means of any title to soil or subsoil, directly or indirectly, individually or as a company, except in cases declared by special law to be of national necessity.

RECORDS:

(Real Property Registry: Law Nov. 15, 1887; Decree Dec. 5, 1888; Mercantile Registry; Com. Co. 26-35; Decree April 28, 1937; Mining Registry: Mining Code; Civil Registry, Law Nov. 26, 1898, regulated by Sup. Decree 22773 of Apr. 8, 1991).

In general all documents transferring, creating, declaring or limiting rights in real property, including leases for over five years, must be recorded in the public registry; also documents declaring bankruptcy or the incapacity of a person, and those limiting the right to dispose of property. The recording of other documents, though not relating to real property, is permissible.

Registrars are semi-judicial officers who do not transcribe the entire document but only the essential details. On receiving an instrument they examine it to ascertain whether it is in legal form. If defects are found a period of one year is allowed to cure them, but in some cases registration may be refused at once. From the registrar's decision an appeal lies to the courts. Registrars are appointed by the President and must give bond.

Besides the registries of property, there are mining registries for mining titles, mercantile registries for recording articles of incorporation and partnership, powers of attorney and other mercantile documents, and civil registries for vital statistics.

REDEMPTION:

See topics Executions; Mortgages.

SALES (Realty and Personalty):

(C. C. 584-650; Com. Co. 824-866).

A sale is perfected and title passes when the vendor and vendee have agreed on the thing sold and the price thereof, though neither has been delivered; but when merchandise is sold by weight or measure the objects sold remain for account of the vendor until weighed, counted or measured. Sales of real property must be recorded. The cost of the instrument of sale and other accessories thereof are for account of the vendee.

The vendor warrants the thing sold and the title thereto. Even if the title warranty be waived he is liable for the price unless the buyer knew the danger or bought at his risk. The vendor is not liable for defects which are visible or could have been ascertained by the buyer. He is liable for hidden defects, but may stipulate that he will not be liable for those not known to him.

If the price is not paid the vendor may ask that the sale be cancelled. The cancellation may be declared at once if the vendor is in danger of losing the thing sold and the price; otherwise the judge may grant the buyer a period for payment.

The right to repurchase cannot be reserved for a longer period than five years.

In sales of real estate rescission may be asked by the vendor within two years if it is found that the price received is less than one-half the value of the property. In such cases the buyer may elect to pay the difference in price and avoid rescission.

In commercial sales, order is considered accepted by vendor if latter does not reject same in ten days. Vendor has obligation to make bill which must contain: (1) Date of sale; (2) names of purchaser and vendor; (3) payment conditions; (4) amount, type, size and weight of merchandise; (5) value of each item; (6) expenses incurred with indication as to whether they are to be paid by purchaser or vendor; (7) number and elements of charter party (contrato de fletamento) and insurance contract if it exists; (8) date of delivery to carrier. Buyer can reject merchandise within ten days after delivery, or otherwise loses his right to make claim. Vendor is liable for hidden defects of merchandise, and can ask for rescission of contract or lowering of price. In any case, there is indemnification for damages suffered by buyer. Statute of limitations for such claim is one year.

SEALS:

Seals are not used in private matters. A document executed before a notary has most of the effects of a sealed instrument in the United States.

STATUTE OF FRAUDS:

See topic Public Instruments.

STATUTES:

Principal codifications are: Civil Code (based largely on the Code Napoleon), Commercial Code, Family Code, Law of Judicial Organization, Code of Civil Procedure, Penal Code, Code of Criminal Procedure, Mining Code, Organic Municipal Law, General Railroad Law and Regulations, Law of Political Organization, Customs Law and Regulations, Labor Code and Social Security Code, Code of Labor Procedure, Aeronautic Code, Tax Code.

TAXATION:

Real Estate Tax.—Local rather than national taxes are levied varying with the region. Including sewage, water and other rates tax can reach 8 per mil of assessed value (Supreme Decrees of Mar. 3, 1953; 5111 of Dec. 10, 1958; and 5312 of Sept. 30, 1959).

Custom House Taxes.—Import tax is regulated by Sup. Decrees 21660 of July 10, 1987, 21910 of Mar. 31, 1988 and 22103 of Dec. 29, 1988, 22753 of Mar. 15, 1991 and 22775 of Apr. 8, 1991. Bolivia adopted Uniform Classification for International Trade.

Value Added Tax and Excise Tax.—(Law 843 of May 20, 1986 t.o. 1995 regulated by 21530 of Feb. 28, 1987 t.o. 1995). Value added tax is applied at rate of 13% to imports, sale of goods, rendering of services and execution of works. Complemented with excise tax which is applied to such goods as perfumes, jewelry, wines, beer, cigarettes, etc. Rate ranges between 10 and 50%.

Tax on Corporate Income.—(Law 843 of May 20, 1986 t.o. 1995 regulated by Sup. Decree 24051 of June 29, 1995). Tax is applied to corporations, whether stock or companies owned by sole individual, branches and subsidiaries of foreign companies on net annual profits of local sources, as per their financial statements prepared according to generally accepted accounting principles. Rate is 25%. Payments to non-domicile recipients are subject to withholding tax of 25% on 50% of amount paid.

Tax on Transactions.—(Law 843 of May 20, 1986 t.o. 1995 regulated by Sup. Decree 21532 of Feb. 28, 1987 t.o. 1995). Tax is applied to individuals and juridical persons on basis of gross income obtained during fiscal year. This tax measures economic capacity of taxpayers on basis of their gross income. Rate is 3% and resulting amount must be paid monthly.

Tax on Gross Income.—(Law 843 of May 20, 1986 t.o. 1995 regulated by Sup. Decree 21531 of Feb. 28, 1987 t.o. 1995). Tax is assessed to individuals and undivided estates on their gross income deriving from Bolivian sources from labor, capital or combination of both. Fixed rate is 13%. Value added tax paid may be taken as tax credit in computing this tax.

Inheritances and Gifts Tax.—(Law 843 of May 20, 1986 t.o. 1995 and its regulations Sup. Decree 21789 of Dec. 7, 1987). Tax is levied on transfers of personal or real property by inheritance or by gift subject to registration. Rates depend on recipient's relationship to deceased: 1% for ascendants, descendants and spouse; 10% for brothers and sisters and their descendants; and 20% for others and donees.

Urban Real Property Tax and Motor Vehicles Tax.—(Law 843 of May 20, 1986 t.o. 1995 regulated by Sup. Decrees 24204 and 24205 of Dec. 23, 1995). All urban real property is subject to tax ranging from 0.35% to 1.5% of fiscal value. Motor vehicles are subject to tax ranging from 1.5% to 5% of value determined as indicated by law.

Investment Law.—(Law 1182 of Sept. 17, 1990). Law provides equal treatment to national and foreign capital, granting them guaranties including free trade, currency

See Topical Index in front part of this volume.

TAXATION . . . *continued*

conversion with exception of those limitations established by law. Foreign investors have no restrictions for repatriation of capital or transfer abroad of profits; only requirement is prior payment of taxes. Disputes related to their investment can be subject to international arbitration except in case of joint ventures that are subject to Bolivian law and must be legally domiciled in Bolivia. All foreign and national investment is subject to tax regime and compliance with all labor and social security laws.

Foreign investment is subject to Decision 291 of Mar. 21, 1991 of Andean Pact on common regime of treatment of foreign capital and of trademarks, patents, licenses and royalties.

Export Tax Incentives.—(D.L. 18829 of Feb. 3, 1982 and D.L. 19048 of July 13, 1982). Some nontraditional products to be exported are exempted from taxes.

Livestock-agricultural Income.—Income from livestock-agricultural production in all the provinces of the Department of La Paz, except Inquisive and Yungas, is subject to a special tax of 2%, for public works. (Law of Dec. 27, 1958).

Mining Taxes.—See topic Mines and Minerals.

Social Security Tax.—Employers must pay to social security 20% of total salaries paid out to its employees. Employees contribute additional 3.5%. (Law 10173 of Mar. 28, 1972 as am'd).

Free Zones.—(Sup. Decree 22410 of Jan. 11, 1990 regulated by Sup. Decree 22526 of June 30, 1990 as am'd; Sup. Decree 22753 of Mar. 15, 1991; Sup. Decree 23574 of July 29, 1993). National or foreign individuals and juridical persons may be authorized to operate in free zones. Law regulates industrial free zones, commercial free zones and warehousing terminals, and temporary entry of goods and draw-back. Industrial free zones are created for manufacture of goods to be exported. Investments in industrial free zones are exempted from real estate taxes, value added tax and excise tax and tax on transactions, tax on business net worth, local taxes and from import duties. Commercial free zones and warehousing terminals are created for storage of goods for unlimited time. Investments in commercial free zones and warehousing terminals are exempted from same taxes and duties as industrial free zones with exception of tax on business net worth. Temporary entry of goods is authorized for assembling, transforming or industrial production of merchandise to be exported. Authorization is granted for two years, and it can renew for additional two years. Importation of goods is duty and tax free, but guarantee must be granted to cover payment of temporary exemption of taxes. All investments are subject to payment of contributions to state social security and to General Labor Law and its regulations.

TRADEMARKS:

Those signs visible and sufficiently distinctive and susceptible of graphic representation can be registered as marks. Trademark is any sign used to distinguish products or services produced or commercialized by one person from same or similar products or services produced or commercialized by another person. Slogans are words, sentences or captions used as supplement to trademark.

The following cannot be used as trademarks: Letters, names or words peculiar to the state; national or foreign arms or flags; phrases or words in general use to describe the article; designs or expressions offensive to persons or institutions; pictures or names of persons without permission of such persons; usual form or color of products; marks which have become public property; those which may be confused with others previously registered; marks contrary to law, those against public policy, denomination of protected vegetal varieties, those identical or similar to registered trade slogans and trade names provided under circumstances public may be confused; those that are reproduction, imitation, translation or total or partial transcription of distinctive signs, locally or internationally, well known, without taking into consideration classification of goods or services concerned; or because of similarity to well-known trademark causes confusion to public independent of classification of goods and services for which registration is applied for. Term of registration is ten years extended for periods of ten years.

Producers or traders associations may register collective marks. Origin denominations belong to State who may grant right to use them for ten years, renewable. Buenos Aires Convention of 1910. Decision 344 of Oct. 29, 1993. Laws of Dec. 2, 1916 and Jan. 15, 1918 and Decree Law 7255 of July 21, 1965 only on matters not regulated by Decision 344.

TREATIES:

Multilateral: Treaty on Civil, Commercial and Procedural Law, signed at Montevideo on Jan 11, 1889; and on Patents and Trademarks of Jan. 16, 1889, approved by Bolivia by Law of Nov. 17, 1903, and ratified with respect to Procedural Law, by Law of Feb. 25, 1904; Convention relative to Rights of Aliens, signed on Jan. 29, 1902, ratified by Bolivia by Law of Feb. 26, 1904; Convention on Inventions, Patents, Designs and Industrial Models signed on Aug. 20, 1910, Buenos Aires; Convention for Protection of Commercial, Industrial, and Agricultural Trademarks and Commercial Names, signed on Aug. 20, 1910; Convention on Literary and Artistic Copyright, signed on Aug. 11, 1910, Buenos Aires; Convention on Pecuniary Claims, signed on Aug. 11, 1910, Buenos Aires; Bustamante Code of Private International Law, Havana, of Feb. 20, 1928 with reservations, ratified by Law of Jan. 20, 1932; International Convention on Telecommuncations, Madrid, of Dec. 9, 1932, approved by Bolivia by R.S. of Jan. 23, 1934; South American Regional Agreement on Radiocommunications, Buenos Aires, of Apr. 10, 1935, approved by R.S. of Dec. 31, 1937. Revised by Agreement of Santiago, Chile, of Jan. 17, 1940, approved by D.S. of Mar. 31, 1942; Convention on International Civil Aviation, Chicago, Dec. 7, 1944, followed by Convention relating to Transit of International Air Services and a Convention on International Air Transportation, ratified by D.S. 722 of Feb. 13, 1947; Inter-American Convention on Rights of Author in Literary, Scientific, and Artistic Works, signed June 22, 1946; International Tin Convention, signed by Bolivia June 3, 1954, and Amendment to Paragraph 22 of Art. IV approved by International Tin Council in Oct. 1956, agreeing with Government of U.K. on reduction in taxes on assets, income, and other property of International Tin Council. Second International Tin Convention, signed in London Dec. 20, 1960, and approved by Bolivia by Law 131 of Dec. 15, 1961; Convention on Regulation of Inter-American Automotive Traffic, Washington 1943, Convention on Highway Transportation and Transportation by Automotive Vehicles, Geneva, 1949. Agreement on Importation of Objects of Educational, Scientific or Cultural Nature, New York 1950; Universal Copyright Convention, Geneva, 1952; Agreement on Andean Subregional Integration, signed at Bogota on May 26, 1969; Panama Treaty of 1975 on establishment of Latin American Economic System (SELA); Montevideo Treaty of 1980 on establishment of Latin American Integration Association (LAIA); Interamerican Convention on the legal regime of powers of attorney to be used abroad, Panama, 1975; Convention on the Recognition and Enforcement of Foreign Arbitral Awards, New York, 1958; Multilateral Trade Negotiations, The Uruguay Round, Final Act, Marrakesh, Apr. 15, 1994 and Agreement Establishing the World Trade Organization, Marrakesh, Apr. 15, 1994.

TRUSTS:

Testamentary trusts are prohibited. (C. C. 1170). There are no provisions regarding other trusts.

WILLS:

(C. C. 36, 443-541, 570-608, 659-661).

Wills may be made by all persons except males under 14 or females under 12 years of age and persons of unsound mind. Males who are of age may be witnesses except the following: Those mentally incapacitated; ascendants and descendants of testator; heirs and other relatives to the fourth degree.

There are two general classes of wills: Solemn wills, which are subdivided into closed and open wills, and privileged wills which require no formalities.

Closed wills are written by the testator or by another person for him and enclosed in an envelope which is delivered to a notary. The latter writes a statement on the envelope and the same is signed by the notary, the testator and seven witnesses, but if any witness cannot write another may sign for him. Deaf and dumb persons require one witness more.

Open wills may be made before a notary and three witnesses who are residents of the locality, or before five witnesses who are residents; if neither a notary nor five residents of the locality can be found, the will may be made before three witnesses who are residents or seven who are not. Blind persons may make open wills before a notary and five witnesses, or before eight witnesses of whom one must write out the will.

Privileged wills.—Indians residing at over one league from their cantons may make wills with only two witnesses. Soldiers may make wills without witnesses if entirely in their handwriting; in time of war they may write on sand, earth or stone, but at least two witnesses must have seen them write.

Oral Wills.—Open wills and privileged wills of Indians may be oral, but the majority of the witnesses must give uniform testimony on all substantial points.

Revocation.—All codicils, changes and revocations must be made with the same formalities required for wills.

Testamentary Disposition.—The testator may dispose freely of his property only in so far as there are no obligatory heirs. (See topic Descent and Distribution.) Legacies may be charged with conditions.

Foreign wills are valid in Bolivia if executed in accordance with the laws of the country where they were made. Aliens making wills in Bolivia in favor of other aliens with respect to property in their country or personal property in their possession or in Bolivia, may follow the law of their country, but if the will relates to real estate in Bolivia it must be in the Bolivian form.

BRAZIL LAW DIGEST REVISER

Curtis, Mallet-Prevost, Colt & Mosle
101 Park Avenue
New York, New York 10178-0061
Telephone: 212-696-6141
Fax: 212-697-1559
Email: CMP-NY@mcimail.com

Reviser Profile

The Firm began in 1830 when two practicing lawyers started a long line of lawyers and law firms extending in an unbroken chain up to the present time. In 1897, the firm name became Curtis, Mallet-Prevost & Colt; in 1925 it was changed to Curtis, Mallet-Prevost, Colt & Mosle. The Firm is now made up of approximately 120 lawyers, including experts who have published extensively on such diverse subjects as international money management, transnational contracts, state contracts, litigation against foreign states, sovereign immunity and the act of state doctrine, and the International Court of Justice. Its principal offices are in New York City. There are branch offices in Paris, London, Frankfurt Am Main, Hong Kong, Washington, D.C., Houston, Texas, Newark, N.J., and Mexico City. The Firm has five departments: Corporate and International; Litigation; Real Estate; Tax; and Trusts and Estates. The corporate and international department acts as general counsel to various public and private corporations and individual entrepreneurs. Clients are in the banking, insurance, securities, manufacturing, real estate and oil and gas industries. In addition, the corporate and international department frequently acts as special counsel to domestic and foreign clients, providing assistance in financing, know-how licensing, the negotiation and drafting of all types of contracts and instruments, counselling on all aspects of corporate law, and establishing the vehicles necessary to enable clients to conduct their domestic and foreign business activities. The Firm's international work permeates all areas of its practice and involves questions of private international law, foreign law and an unusual amount of public and quasi-public international law. Traditionally, much of the Firm's international practice has been concerned with Latin America. The Firm maintains its excellence in that area, with its Mexican affiliate, and also through the expertise of Latin American lawyers based in the New York office. The Firm's international practice has undergone a major expansion beyond Latin America to Europe, Africa and the Near and Far East. The Firm's litigation practice includes commercial litigation and arbitration, and white-collar criminal defense. It has substantial experience in civil aviation matters; it also has represented foreign States in transnational litigation and international arbitration arising out of acts of nationalization and alleged breach of economic development or natural resource supply contracts. Among the Firm's clients in real estate matters are institutional lenders and investors, real estate developers, both individual and corporate, foreign and domestic investors and syndicators. The tax department has substantial experience in all aspects of domestic and international business tax matters and real estate taxation. The matters the tax department deals with on a regular basis include: Taxation of foreign investments; the structuring of corporate transactions, including mergers, acquisitions, liquidations and reorganization; federal and state tax litigation; and tax planning for U.S. and foreign individuals. The trusts and estates department engages in general domestic trusts and estates practice and in tax planning for foreign persons wishing to invest in U.S. assets through offshore trusts and corporations. It represents individuals, trust companies, and banks acting as fiduciaries. It works for various charitable organizations located both in the United States and abroad including private foundations, museums, universities and hospitals. A group of fiduciary accountants with vast experience in the field assists the lawyers of the trusts and estates department. Curtis, Mallet-Prevost, Colt & Mosle has served as a Reviser for most of Latin American Law Digests since 1930.

BRAZIL LAW DIGEST

(The following is a list of all Topics, including cross-references, covered in this Digest.)

BRAZIL LAW DIGEST

Revised for 1997 edition by

CURTIS, MALLET-PREVOST, COLT & MOSLE, of the New York Bar.

ABSENTEES: See topic Death.

ACKNOWLEDGMENTS:

Certificates of acknowledgment in the form customary in the United States are not employed in Brazil. Certain instruments, such as deeds and mortgages, must be "public," i.e., executed on the books of a notary; others may be "private." (See topics Deeds; Notaries Public; Records.) Latter are valid between parties, and constitute full evidence against them if signed by two witnesses, but have no effect as to third persons until recorded.

When instruments are executed before a notary, the equivalent of an acknowledgment is contained in a clause inserted in the body of the document, whereby the notary certifies that the parties are known to the two subscribing witnesses, and (if such be the case) to the notary himself, and that they executed the instrument before him. For a private instrument to be recorded, the signature of the maker must be "recognized" by a notary, i.e., the instrument must have endorsed thereon one of the following statements by a notary: (a) That he recognizes the signature of the maker, which necessitates having the maker's signature registered on the notary's books; or, instead of such "authentic" recognition, (b) by direct guarantee when he certifies that two witnesses personally before him vouch for the genuineness of the signature; or (c) by indirect guarantee when the notary recognizes the signatures of two persons who declare in writing that they recognize the genuineness of the signature in question.

If the document is to be used or recorded in a jurisdiction other than that of the notary who recognized the maker's signature, that notary's signature must in turn be recognized by a notary of such other jurisdiction.

Instruments executed abroad for use in Brazil must be authenticated by a Brazilian consul. This is usually accomplished by having the authority of the notary who takes the acknowledgment certified by the proper court or county clerk, whose signature is in turn certified by the Brazilian consul. Such documents must be translated into Portuguese and recorded. (Decree 84451 of Jan. 31, 1980).

ACTIONS:

Actions for Death.—See topic Death.

Limitation of.—See topic Limitation of Actions.

ADOPTION:

(Law 8069 of July 13, 1990).

Adoption of minors up to 18 years of age is regulated by this law.

Any individual over 21 years may adopt minor under 18 years of age or older if minor is already in custody or guardianship of adopting party and if adopting party is ascendant or brother or sister of adopted party; spouses and common law spouses may adopt when any one is over 21 years of age, and proof of permanent and normal family relation is filed. Adopting party must be 16 years older than adopted party. Adopting parties must have been taking care of minor for term fixed by court, according to each particular case. When adopting party is domiciled abroad, both parties must live locally together at least 15 days when minor is under two years of age and at least 30 days when minor is over two years of age.

Adopted party's consent is necessary when he is over 12 years of age. Adoption extinguishes legal bonds between adopted person and natural family. All adoption proceedings must be made before judge who declares adoption in final decision.

AGENCY: See topic Principal and Agent.

ALIENS:

Aliens are assured equality with Brazilians in the acquisition and enjoyment of civil rights. (C.C. art. 3).

All persons within Brazilian territory, whether Brazilians or aliens, are subject to Brazilian law. The civil capacity and family rights of an alien are governed by the law of his domicile, or, in the case of reciprocal property rights of husband and wife, by the law of the domicile of the couple, or, if they had different domiciles, by the law of their first domicile after marriage. Intestate and testamentary succession is governed by the law of the domicile of the deceased, except when the alien was married to a Brazilian or left children, in which case Brazilian law applies as to property in Brazil unless foreign law is more favorable to spouse or children. (Decree-Law 4657 of Sept. 4, 1942 as am'd).

Aliens are subject to various restrictions in business matters. Concessions of mines, waters and hydraulic energy will be granted exclusively to Brazilians or concerns of national capital organized in Brazil. (Const., art. 176). Coastwise navigation for the transportation of merchandise is restricted to national ships except in cases of emergency; owners, charterers and masters of national ships and at least two-thirds of the crews must be Brazilians. (Const., art. 178).

Foreign enterprises which make agreements raising the sales prices of their products, or restricting the economic freedom of other concerns, or tending to create monopolies, are subject to expropriation with payment in long term bonds. (Decree-Law 7666 of June 22, 1945).

Within 150 kilometers of Brazil's boundaries, alien may not acquire land without previous consent of National Security Council, as such land is considered of national security. Foreigners may be authorized to purchase frontier strip or maritime land, provided land is autonomous unit in condominium, located in urban zone and area sold does not exceed one third of total area. (Decree-Law 9760 of Sept. 5, 1946 as am'd by Law 7450 of Dec. 23, 1985; Decrees 74965 of Nov. 20, 1974 and 87040 of Mar. 17, 1982).

Ato Complementario (Complementary Act) 45 of Jan. 30, 1969 provides that only Brazilians or foreigners resident in country may purchase rural land. Foreigners are considered to be resident when permanently in country. Law 5709 of Oct. 7, 1971 as am'd sets forth amount of land which may be purchased and Law 8629 of Feb. 25, 1993 established that same limitations applied to acquisition of rural land are applied to leasing of rural property by foreigners. Foreign companies and local legal entities controlled by nonresidents may only purchase rural land for attending their purpose. Prior authorization from Ministry of Agriculture and Land Reform through National Institute of Colonization and Agrarian Reform (INCRA) is required in both cases.

Law 6815 of Aug. 19, 1980 as am'd regulated by Decree 86715 of Dec. 10, 1981 as am'd by Decree 1455 of Apr. 13, 1995, and Decree 840 of June 22, 1993, regulates status of aliens in Brazil and National Council of Immigration, related to Department of Labor, in order to direct, coordinate and inspect immigration issues.

For purposes of Law, aliens are divided into transit, tourists, temporary residents, permanent residents, of courtesy, officials and diplomats. Transit visa may be granted to alien who must enter Brazilian territory, in order to reach his destination, for period of ten days. Tourist aliens may enter country for 90 days. No visas are required for foreigners whose country of origin grants reciprocity to Brazilians. Temporary residents are aliens living in Brazil for business or cultural reasons (foreign artists, athletes, technicians, professors and students are included). Permits are granted for period of 90 days, and in certain cases for time deemed necessary in their respective contracts. Permanent residents' permits will only be granted if aliens fulfill all requisites established by National Council of Immigration.

Temporary, permanent, and residents who were granted political asylum, are required to register with Ministry of Justice within 30 days after their arrival. Latter will issue Alien Identification Card. Law also provides grounds for deportation, expulsion and extradition of foreigners. Entering or staying fraudulently in country are causes of deportation; imperiling national security, political or social order, public morals or economy are causes of expulsion, among others. Extradition may be granted to petitioner government if based on treaty or for reasons of reciprocity. Naturalization may be acquired after four years of continous residency in country, provided that all requirements set forth in Art. 111 of Law, are fulfilled. Said term may be reduced to one, two or three years if applicant has Brazilian spouse and/or child; if recommended for his professional scientific or artistic skills or if he has ownership of real estate, industry or shares in corporation aimed at exploration of industrial or agricultural activities.

Law 7180 of Dec. 20, 1983 establishes proceedings to obtain permanent resident status for those foreigners who have temporary registration.

Decree-Law 691 of July 18, 1969 requires that contracts for employment of foreign technicians resident abroad, for performance in Brazil of specialized services on a temporary basis, must establish a fixed period of employment. If contract has a provision for salary in foreign currency, exchange rate of foreign currency salary must be as of date of maturity of obligation. Contractual provision establishing profit sharing by technician with employer is forbidden.

Law 6964 prohibits expulsion of foreigner married to Brazilian for more than five years, if not divorced or separated, or having Brazilian child under his responsibility or giving him economic support.

See also topic Corporations, subhead Foreign Corporations.

ALIMONY: See topic Divorce.

ASSOCIATIONS:

(Const. art. 5 XVII-XXI; Civil Code, arts. 16-23).

Constitution grants full freedom of association for lawful purposes. No one can be compelled to become associated or to remain associated. Civil, literary, religious, moral and scientific companies, public utility associations, foundations and commercial companies are legal entities of private law. Civil associations are nonprofit organizations legally established. They acquire juridical personality through recording of their articles of association in special record in civil registry and published entire or in summary form in official gazette of state in which its headquarters are to be located. Dissolution may be effected by expiration of period agreed upon, if any; by consent of all members; by disappearance of purpose for which association was formed; by loss of all its members or by judicial proceedings brought because of its misconduct.

Collective Bargaining.—Professional associations organized under Cons. of Labor Laws, arts. 511-625 as am'd, have certain rights and duties, most important of which are to represent entire class before Government and bargain collectively. (Const. art. 8 III).

ATTACHMENT:

(Code Civil Procedure, arts. 583-590, 731).

Attachment may be issued in executions based on judgments as well as on certain classes of privileged claims, which include among others following: (a) Debts represented by bills of exchange, promissory notes, checks and trade-bills; (b) debts acknowledged by public or private instruments attested by two witnesses; (c) debts secured by mortgages, pledges, warrants as well as certain insurance claims; (d) claims for leases; (e) tax debts. In such cases attachment will issue unless debtor pays within 24 hours after demand.

See also topic Sequestration.

BANKRUPTCY:

(Law 7661 of June 21, 1945 am'd by Law 6014 of Dec. 27, 1973, Law 7274 of Dec. 10, 1984 and Law 8131 of Dec. 27, 1990).

Only merchants and corporations can be adjudged bankrupt.

The partners personally and jointly liable in a partnership are not covered by its bankruptcy but they are subject to all other effects the bankruptcy may have on the partnership. They have the same duties and rights as the debtor or bankrupt. These provisions apply to those who may have withdrawn and been released by the other

See Topical Index in front part of this volume.

BANKRUPTCY . . . *continued*
partners within two years from date of withdrawal unless such withdrawal was consented to by all creditors existing at the time of such withdrawal, or unless there was novation of contract between such creditors and the remaining partners, or unless the creditors continued to deal with the remaining partners in such manner as to indicate reliance upon their credit alone.

Partners with limited liability who withdraw their funds from the partnership capital are liable up to the amount of such funds for all obligations contracted and losses incurred up to the time of such withdrawal as shown by the commercial registry.

Bankruptcy may be petitioned for by the bankrupt and his heirs or shareholders or by any creditor holding matured, liquid and certain obligation, such as promissory note, accepted draft, judgment, etc.

Grounds for bankruptcy are: (1) Failure to pay at maturity an indebtedness which would give the creditor a right of attachment, or to pay or deposit judicially the amount of a judgment within twenty-four hours after service of execution; (2) resorting to precipitate liquidation or fraudulent or ruinous methods to make payments; (3) calling a meeting of creditors and proposing to them delay, remission of credits or transfer of property; (4) transferring assets to a third party, whether or not a creditor; (5) contracting simulated debts, concealing or diverting property, retarding payments or defrauding creditors; (6) granting mortgages, pledges or other security, preference or privilege in favor of any creditor without retaining free and unencumbered property sufficient to pay all other debts; (7) absenting or concealing oneself without leaving a representative to administer the business and pay creditors.

Besides other defenses which may be offered to bankruptcy proceedings the debtor may set up as a defense a proposal for an agreement with creditors to prevent bankruptcy (see subhead Composition, infra) although not yet in force or he may avoid proceedings by depositing amount due.

During proceedings for adjudication based upon any but the first of the grounds above enumerated, the judge may order the sequestration of the books, correspondence and assets of the alleged bankrupt, and may prohibit any alienation or disposal thereof. After citing the alleged bankrupt and allowing the legal period to answer, the judge must either dismiss the petition or adjudicate the debtor bankrupt. Adjudication order names trustee in bankruptcy (sindico), designates period for proving claims, and may provide for detention of alleged bankrupt upon petition of State Attorney submitting proof of commission of crime punishable under bankruptcy law.

Appeal from bankrupt adjudication does not suspend its effect. Appeal also can be filed from decision dismissing petition in bankruptcy.

Upon adjudication, all debts of the bankrupt immediately mature except obligations subject to condition, the latter being provable but payment being deferred until performance of the condition. Bilateral contracts will not be annulled by the bankruptcy of a party, but may be carried out by trustee or liquidator if to advantage of bankrupt estate. Failure to carry out such contracts will subject bankrupt estate to liability for loss and damage.

Acts specified below are revocable in an action by the bankrupt estate against the party contracting with the bankrupt, whether or not performed with knowledge of the financial condition of the debtor or with intent to defraud the creditors. These acts are: (1) Payment of unmatured debts within the legal period of bankruptcy; (2) satisfaction of matured debts within such legal period by any means other than as provided in the contract; (3) execution by a merchant of mortgages or other real guaranties within the legal period as security for debts contracted prior to such period; (4) donations valued at over specified amount by merchant made within two years preceding adjudication; (5) renunciation of devise, legacy or usufruct within two years preceding adjudication; (6) restitution or delivery of dower before time stipulated in antenuptial contract; (7) registration of mortgages, liens or transfers inter vivos effected after sequestration of bankrupt's property or after adjudication; (8) sale or transfer of business without obtaining consent of creditors; (9) any act performed by debtor with intention of prejudicing his creditors, provided there was fraud on part of other party also.

Trustee and liquidator in bankruptcy (sindico) appointed in order of adjudication is charged with duty to administer, appraise and conserve bankrupt estate, liquidate perishable assets, present detailed report of bankruptcy, including balance sheet of bankrupt and list of all claims against estate; represent estate before courts, and furnish to interested parties information and extracts from books of bankrupt. Trustee is entitled to remuneration determined by judge.

Creditors may intervene in any action instituted by or against the bankrupt estate, examine the books and papers of the bankrupt and the administration of the estate, and institute proceedings tending to benefit the estate or promote the proper execution of the bankruptcy law, costs to be paid by the bankrupt estate when it derives benefit from such proceedings. Absent creditors may be represented by attorneys in fact, who may be authorized by telegraph.

A creditor who fails to prove his claim within the period assigned may nevertheless, subject to loss of right to dividends meanwhile distributed, be admitted as a common creditor at any time before distribution of final dividends.

Claims are classified as follows: claims for damages resulting from accidents at work; other labor claims; tax claims; other claims of fiscal nature; costs and expenses incurred by estate; secured claims; special privileged claims; claims with general privilege and ordinary claims.

Property sequestered or passing to trustee with bankrupt estate may be recovered by owner with proof of ownership or right based on contract. Recovery may be granted even though property has already been transferred by receiver. Articles purchased by bankrupt within 15 days prior to bankruptcy petition may also be recovered if they have not been transferred by bankrupt estate.

Trustee proceeds with the liquidation if the bankrupt has not applied for composition. Trustee or any recognized creditor may bring action for exclusion, rectification, or reclassification of claims, basing such action upon falsity, fraud, deceit, essential mistake of fact, or documents unknown at time of verification of claim.

Reorganization.—With certain exceptions in case of fraud, culpable bankruptcy and failure to comply with requirements of bankruptcy law, bankrupt, after verification of claims, may propose composition agreement requiring suspenson of bankruptcy proceedings. He must offer the common creditors at least 35% of their balance if payment is to be immediate and 50% within two years; two-fifths must be paid in first year.

Exceptions may be taken to the proposed agreement, which will become effective only upon the judge's order after decision on such exceptions. Such order having been made, the bankruptcy proceedings will be terminated. From order of composition appeal will lie. In event of failure to make payment within 30 days after order, composition will be rescinded and bankruptcy will proceed.

Any creditor affected by the agreement may demand its rescission for nonperformance of any of its terms, for abandonment of the assets or their sale for an unreasonably low price making its performance impossible, or in case of condemnation of the bankrupt for fraudulent or culpable bankruptcy or similar crime, or payment of some creditors before maturity resulting in prejudice to the remaining creditors.

Where the bankruptcy proceeds to final liquidation, after distribution of final dividends and presentation of final report and accounts by the receiver, the judge will order the formal closing of the bankruptcy, which should be within two years after adjudication, if not extended for causes beyond the control of the receiver. Such order of the judge does not have the effect of discharging the bankrupt of provable claims, and upon granting the order the judge will issue to creditors requesting it a certificate setting forth the record of the proceedings and the unpaid amount of the debtor's claim as admitted in the bankruptcy. Such certificate will entitle the creditor, until the debt is barred by limitations (interrupted during the bankruptcy proceedings) or until discharge (rehabilitation) of the bankrupt to bring an executive action for the unpaid balance of the debt if the claim was not contested in bankruptcy, or, if so contested, to prosecute such action to recover the unpaid balance as he might have instituted upon the original debt.

The bankrupt may obtain an order of discharge (rehabilitation) if he has fulfilled the terms of his composition agreement, paid his creditors in full both principal and interest or obtained from them full releases, unless convicted of fraudulent bankruptcy or similar crime, in which case he cannot be discharged until five years after serving the sentence therefor.

The bankrupt may be granted a discharge if he pays more than 40% beyond the value of the estate or after five years of the formal closing of the bankruptcy, if he is not convicted of crime. Ten years are required if he is convicted of crime. Discharge completely terminates the effects of bankruptcy.

Reorganization may be to prevent or suspend bankruptcy from time filed at court, before or after bankruptcy proceedings. Reorganization agreement to prevent bankruptcy (concordata preventiva) may be proposed by debtor by filing petition with judge offering to pay his ordinary creditors at least 50% if payment is immediate or 60%, 75%, 90% or 100% within 6, 12, 18 or 24 months respectively, two-fifths of which must be paid in the first year, if payment is made in 18 or 24 months, and stating his financial condition and how he intends to carry out terms of concordata and reasons for it. Debtor must also prove that his assets are worth at least 50% of what he owes to ordinary creditors and that he has been engaged in commerce for more than two years. If petition does not meet all above mentioned requirements, or if debtor's declarations are false or inaccurate, judge opens bankruptcy proceedings. Filing of petition bars bankruptcy proceedings during its pendency, but if concordata preventiva is denied judge declares bankruptcy of debtor.

If the petition is in due form and sets forth the required facts, the judge will order publication of notice in order that creditors and interested parties may appear, will fix a period for creditors to qualify as such, and will also order stay of execution against debtor on claims subject to concordata and appoint commissioner whose duties are similar to those of trustee in bankruptcy, except that commissioner does not take over and administer, but merely supervises administration by debtor of his property, debtor being forbidden to alienate or create lien upon real property or pledge any property without express authorization of judge.

BANKS AND BANKING:

(Law No. 4595 of Dec. 31, 1964, as am'd). Financial institutions are those whose principal or secondary business is collection, brokering or investment of financial resources belonging to themselves or to third parties, in national or foreign currency, and custody of assets belonging to third parties. These financial institutions are controlled by Central Bank of Brazil.

BILLS AND NOTES:

Brazil approved the Geneva Conventions of 1930 and 1931 on forms, taxes and regulations of bills of exchange, promissory notes and checks. (Decree 57595 of Jan. 7, 1966, Decree 54 of Sept. 8, 1964 and Decree 57663 of Jan. 24, 1966).

Bill of exchange is an order of payment containing following requisites: (1) Word "letra" (bill); (2) order to pay a certain amount of money; (3) name of drawee; (4) time of payment; (5) place of payment; (6) name of payee who may be drawer, bearer, a third party or order; (7) date and place where bill is drawn; (8) signature of drawer.

Clause attempting to exclude or restrict responsibility of drawer will invalidate instrument as a bill of exchange. No effect will be given to a clause inserted in a bill of exchange providing for payment of interest unless bill is drawn at sight or at certain period after sight.

The holder is deemed authorized to fill in the date and place of drawing of a bill of exchange in which they are omitted. A bill may be drawn for payment at sight, on a day certain, a certain period after date or a certain period after sight. Bills failing to indicate the date of maturity will be payable at sight.

Title to a bill of exchange may be transferred by endorsement special or in blank. An endorsement "por procuracao" (with power of attorney) or "para cobranca" (for collection) confers upon endorsee powers for presentation, protest, collection, reendorsement or suit upon bill, subject to any restrictions which may be contained in endorsement. Partial endorsement is null and endorsement after maturity produces same effects as endorsement prior to maturity. Endorser is liable for acceptance and payment of bill unless he states otherwise. Endorser may forbid new endorsement and in this case he is not liable for payment to persons to whom bill is later endorsed.

Bills payable certain period after sight must be presented within one year from date of bill unless otherwise specified. Simple signature of bill by drawee will constitute

See Topical Index in front part of this volume.

BILLS AND NOTES . . . *continued*
acceptance. Drawee may limit acceptance to part of amount drawn. Any other modification in acceptance constitutes refusal to accept. Drawee is bound by acceptance to pay bill on due date.

Bill otherwise unmatured falls due (a) for want of acceptance, (b) for bankruptcy of drawee whether he has accepted bill or not, or (c) for bankruptcy of drawer when bill is not acceptable. However, maturity will be deferred until expressed maturity of bill upon acceptance by another person named in bill or upon acceptance for honor when bearer agrees with such acceptance.

Bill must be presented for payment at place therein designated therefor on day it is payable or on one of two following business days. A sight bill should be presented within one year after date of drawing if no other time is specified. Bearer is not obliged to accept payment before maturity. He must accept partial payment if tendered at maturity, but may protest for non-payment of the balance.

Protest is necessary as a means of proof and in order to preserve holder's right of recourse against drawer, prior endorsers and sureties, in following cases: absence, limitation or modification of acceptance; nonpayment; refusal to redeliver a bill tendered for acceptance or payment; insolvency of drawee. Protest is necessary also to entitle holder to interest after maturity. Bill must be delivered for protest to proper official of place of payment on one of two business days following day on which bill is payable, in case of nonpayment; within same period fixed for presentation for acceptance, in case of want of acceptance. Protest official to whom a bill has been delivered must protest it and execute a notice of protest thereof in due form. Notice must contain: date, exact copy of bill, certificate of notification to debtor and his reply or of impossibility of finding debtor, declaration of any intervention for payment or acceptance and of bearer's acquiescence, if obtained, in such acceptance for honor, and signature of protesting officer.

The holder of a protested bill must give advice of such protest to next prior endorser whose address is stated on bill, each endorser so notified to transmit such notice to next preceding endorser. Penalty for failure to give such notice is not loss of recourse against prior endorsers but liability for damages resulting from such failure, enforcible in ordinary action.

Protest may be waived if drawer or endorser inserts in bill a clause "without expenses," or "without protest" or equivalent.

Law 6690 of Sept. 25, 1979 as am'd by Law 7401 of Nov. 5, 1985, provides for cancellation of protest by presentment of protested bill. After cancellation, neither protest nor cancellation will be recorded.

Promissory notes must contain: Words "Nota Promissoria" (promissory note), promise to pay a certain amount of money, time and place of payment, name of payee, date of and place where promissory note is made, and signature of maker. Provisions relating to bills of exchange mentioned above, except those dealing with acceptance, are applicable to promissory notes with necessary modifications, rights and obligations of maker of note are equivalent to those of acceptor of bill of exchange.

Checks must be presented within 30 days after date if payable in place where issued; 60, if issued in other places. Upon failure to make such presentation or to protest for want of payment holder loses his right of recourse in an exchange action against endorsers and sureties and also against drawer in case latter had funds available to meet check at time it should have been presented and such funds ceased to be so available through no cause attributable to drawer. (Decree-Law 7357 of Sept. 2, 1985).

"Duplicatas" (Duplicates).—Law 5474 of July 18, 1968 am'd by Decree-Law 436 of Jan. 27, 1968 provides that when both parties to a sale on credit are domiciled in Brazil, seller may issue invoice in duplicate. Purchaser retains original, but must sign duplicate, formally undertaking to pay amount therein stated at specified time and place, and return it to seller. Duplicate, thus signed, is treated as promissory note.

Rural mortgage cedulas and rural notes and "duplicatas" are treated as negotiable instruments. See topic Chattel Mortgages.

CHATTEL MORTGAGES:

Chattel mortgage of personal property is regulated by Law 4728 of July 14, 1972. (art. 66). Under this Law, title to property is transferred to creditor but debtor holds possession of same. Mortgage must be evidenced by written document which must be registered in special registry. In case of debtor's default, creditor may not retain property but may sell it and apply proceeds of sale to pay his credit delivering any remaining balance to debtor.

There are special provisions regulating chattel mortgages of agricultural implements, crops, farm cattle, motor vehicles and road building machines, and products of pork packing industry.

An agricultural chattel mortgage must be in writing, and to be valid against third parties must be inscribed in the real property registry. (Civil Code, Arts. 781 et seq.; Law 492 of Aug. 30, 1937 as am'd; Decree-Law 2612 of Sept. 20, 1940; Dec. 1003 of Dec. 29, 1938).

A chattel mortgage on cattle is limited to a period of three years, which may be extended for like period. Other agricultural chattel mortgages are limited to period of two years but may be extended for two years. (Civil Code, arts. 782, 788, Law 492 of 1937 and Decree Law 4360 of June 5, 1942).

Mortgage of aircraft may be made under Code of the Air, Decree-Law No. 31 of Nov. 18, 1966.

Rural Credit Cedulas.—Under Decree Law 167 of Feb. 14, 1967, regulated by Decree 62141 of Jan. 18, 1968, in case of agricultural financing, debtor may issue documents of credit known under general name of "rural credit cedulas" which may be "pledge rural cedulas," "mortgage rural cedulas" or "pledge and mortgage rural cedulas," giving a pledge or mortgage or both of rural property, products, machinery, vehicles, etc. used in agricultural endeavor. There are also "rural credit notes" and "rural duplicatas" used in sales of products, without pledge or mortgage but which have certain other privileges. All these documents are negotiable and must be recorded in a special registry.

Industrial Credit Cedulas.—Under Decree Law 413 of Jan. 9, 1969, in case of industrial financing, debtor may issue documents of credit known as "industrial credit cedulas" giving a pledge, chattel mortgage (alienacao fiduciária) or mortgage of industrial buildings and constructions, raw material, machinery, products, vehicles and other items used in industrial enterprises. There are also "industrial credit notes" without pledge or mortgage but which have certain privileges. All these documents are negotiable and must be recorded in real property registry.

See also topics Pledges; Sales.

COLLATERAL SECURITY: See topic Pledges.

COMMUNITY PROPERTY:

See topic Husband and Wife.

CONSTITUTION AND GOVERNMENT:

(Constitution of Oct. 5, 1988 as am'd).

Brazil is Federative Republic formed by union of States, Municipalities and Federal District, under democratic government.

All persons are equal before law without any distinction. Brazilians and foreigners resident in Brazil have guaranteed inviolability of rights to life, liberty, security and property.

Constitution deals with individual and collective rights and duties, social rights, nationality, political rights and political parties. It also regulates economic and financial order and structures financial system; and outlines basic principles of social order based in dignity of labor, and basic regulations on education, security, culture and sports, health, social works, family, childhood, adolescence, old age, Brazilian indians, science and technology, communications and environment.

Constitution establishes jurisdiction of Federative Republic, States, Municipalities, Federal District and Territories with basic general rules for their legislative powers and for imposition of taxes by each of them.

States have their own Constitution based upon Federal Constitution; supplementary laws and ordinary state laws which deal with matters not exclusively subject to Federal law. Municipalities established under Federal Constitution and Organic Law of Municipalities are recognized by state constitutions as territorial units with political, administrative and financial autonomy. Federal District and Territories are subject for their administration and judicial organization to special law.

Legislative power of Republic is exercised by a Congress formed by Chamber of Deputies and Federal Senate. Deputies are elected by direct popular vote in States, Territories and Federal District in proportion to population and Senators are elected, also by direct popular vote, three for each State. Executive Power is exercised by a President elected by direct popular vote. Term of election is four years. President acts with assistance of Ministers of State. Judicial Power is exercised by Supreme Federal Court, Superior Court of Justice, Federal Regional Courts and Federal Judges plus Military. Electoral, and Labor Courts. States have their own judiciary for State matters.

CONVEYANCES: See topic Deeds.

COPYRIGHT:

(Const. art. 5 XXVII, XXVIII; Law 5988 of Dec. 14, 1973 as am'd, Law 7646 of Dec. 18, 1987, Decree 96036 of May 16, 1988).

Free expression of intellectual, artistic and scientific activities and communication is guaranteed by Constitution. Exclusive right of use, publication or reproduction of work belongs to author and it is transferred to his heirs. To safeguard such right, author may file two copies of work in National Library, School of Music or School of Fine Arts of Federal University of Rio de Janeiro according to nature of work. Unauthorized publication of work belonging to another entitles author to confiscate edition and to receive from publisher sale prices of rest of edition. Besides confiscated material, publisher should pay author amount equal to sales price of 2,000 copies when actual number of copies is not known.

When there are several authors of one indivisible work and there is no agreement to the contrary, they will have equal rights therein and if any of them produces the work or authorizes its production without the consent of the others he will be liable to them for damages except when the work in question is to form part of a publication of his complete works.

Computer programs and free commercialization and production of computer programs of national or foreign origin are protected under copyright laws for 25 year period as of date author utilizes program or makes it available to others in any country. Registration or enrollment is not required for protection. However, protection to nonresident foreigners is afforded provided country where computer program originates affords protection to Brazilians and to foreigners resident in Brazil. Brazilian or foreign computer programs must be enrolled with Secretaria Especial de Informática in order to be locally marketed. Imprisonment and fines are provided for infringement of computer programs rights. Contracts of transfer of technology of computer programs must be registered with National Institute of Industrial Property (INPI).

CORPORATIONS:

(Law 6404 of Dec. 15, 1976 as am'd). Corporations may be organized for any object or gain, not contrary to law, public order or good customs.

Organization.—Corporation is designated by name, that must be accompanied by word "companhia" or "sociedade anonima" or abbreviation of these words, except that word "Companhia" must not appear at end of name. Name of founder or other person who has contributed to success of enterprise may appear in corporate name and such name need no longer contain indication of its activity. At least two stockholders are necessary for organization and continued legal existence of corporation. Corporate capital must be divided into shares; responsibility of shareholders being limited to price of their shares. Law makes clear distinction between "open" and "closed" companies. "Open company" is one which has its shares traded in Stock Exchange or in over-the-counter market. "Closed company" is one whose shares are not traded in Stock Exchange or over-the-counter market. Before corporation may be constituted,

CORPORATIONS . . . *continued*
entire capital must be subscribed, at least 10% of price of shares subscribed in money must be paid in, and part of capital subscribed in money must be deposited in Banco do Brasil, S.A. Subscription of capital may be public or private. If public, prior registration of issue with Securities Commission is required, and subscription must be made only through financial institution. After subscription is completed, founders must call organizational meeting which must arrange for appraisal of assets, if applicable, and decide on organization of corporation. Once legal formalities have been observed and there being no opposition from subscribers representing more than half of capital, founder presiding meeting must declare company organized, after which administrators must be elected. If subscription is private, corporation may be constituted by organizational meeting, as in case of public subscription, or through execution of notarial instrument.

To enable corporation to commence operating, its organizational constitution must be filed in Registry of Commerce and published. Registry of Commerce determines whether documents are in proper form and whether legal formalities have been observed, and in such case issues certificate which, with organizational documents of company, must be published in official newspaper. Any amendment of estatutos must be filed and published in like manner.

Corporate capital must be expressed in Brazilian currency and may comprise cash or any kind of property susceptible of valuation in money.

Shares.—Estatutos of company must determine number of shares into which capital is divided, and must stipulate whether shares are with or without par value. Shares may be common, preferred or usufructuary. Common shares of closed corporation as well as preferred shares of any corporation may have one or more classes. Preferred shares may be issued with or without voting rights. Up to two-thirds of issued stock may be composed of preferred shares, without right to vote or subject to restrictions on exercise of such right. Preferred shares may be accorded cumulative or noncumulative dividend preferences and/or preferences upon liquidation. Preferred shares without voting rights or with restricted voting rights will acquire such rights if company, during period stipulated in estatutos, which cannot exceed three consecutive fiscal years, fails to pay fixed or minimum dividends, and will retain this right until payment, if dividends are not cumulative or until overdue cumulative dividends are paid. Shares could be issued in nominative, registered, endorsable or bearer form according to Estatutos, which also provides for their convertibility from one form of shares into another. Estatutos may also authorize creation of "book shares", representing all or part of shares, that will be maintained in deposit accounts in name of their holders, in given financial institution. No certificates are issued for such "book shares". Company may issue at any time type of negotiable security, in nominative form, known as partes beneficiárias, with no par value, and no voting rights, which merely entitle their owners to participate in profits of company. Such participation cannot exceed 10% of net profits. Partes beneficiárias may be issued to founders, shareholders or third parties, as compensation for services rendered to company, or may be sold for cash.

Dividends.—Estatutos regulate policy of dividend distribution. Dividends may be expressed as percentage of net profits, as percentage of corporation's capital or on some other basis. In event that estatutos do not provide for compulsory dividend, stockholders will have right to one-half of net profits of fiscal year. Any amendment to estatutos on compulsory dividends, may not fix such dividends at level below 25% of net profits. In closed companies, stockholders by unanimous vote may approve distribution of dividend smaller than compulsory dividend, or may vote for retention of all profits in company and, if adverse financial situation occurs, declaration of compulsory dividend may be suspended. Such rules do not apply to payment of dividends to preferred stockholders.

Stockholder's meetings must be called by publication in official newspaper and in another newspaper of general circulation, with at least eight days notice in case of first call and five days for subsequent calls. Except in case of force majeure, such meetings must be held in offices of company, and in no case may be held in another city. Save in exceptional cases designated by law, at least one-fourth of corporate voting capital is required to constitute quorum at first call, but any number constitutes quorum on second call. Shareholders without right to vote may nevertheless attend and speak. Shareholders may be represented at meetings by proxy appointed within one year preceding meeting, who may be stockholder, member of administrative body or lawyer.

There must be annual stockholder's meeting to hear report of administrators, discuss accounts of company, vote on allocation of net profit of fiscal year and distribution of dividends, elect administrators and members of audit committee, when applicable, and approve adjustment of monetary expression of capital. At least one month before date of meeting administrators must announce by publication that documents to be considered are at disposal of stockholders and at least five days before meeting such documents must be published in newspapers. Copies of minutes of stockholders' meetings must be filed in Registry of Commerce and published.

Special meetings of shareholders for purpose of modifying estatutos require, at first call, quorum of two-thirds of capital entitled to vote, but any number appearing will suffice for second call. Approval of at least one-half of capital entitled to vote is required for creation of preferred shares, change in their preferences, increase in existing class without retaining proportionality with other classes, except if authorized by estatutos, creation of new and more favorable class, creation of partes beneficiárias, change in compulsory dividend, change in corporate purpose, or merger, consolidation or spin-off of company, dissolution of company or termination of liquidation status, or participation in group of companies. Changes in preferences of preferred shares require approval of more than one-half of capital represented by classes which would be affected.

Stockholders resident or domiciled abroad are required to appoint agent for service of process in Brazil for actions which arise under Corporation Law.

Directors and Administrative Council.—Management of company will devolve upon board of directors and administrative council. Company must have board of directors and (voluntary) administrative council. In open companies and companies with authorized capital existence of administrative council is compulsory. Among others, administrative council has function of electing and removing directors, establishing policies for company, and supervising acts of directors. Administrative council is composed of minimum of three members elected by stockholders for period of three years, but subject to removal at any time. All of its members must be stockholders. In election of members of administrative council, stockholders holding minimum of 10% of voting stock may request adoption of cumulative voting formula, by assigning to each share as many votes as there are members of administrative council to be elected.

Directors are empowered to represent company. Board of directors must be composed of at least two members. Up to one-third of members of administrative council may be elected as directors. Directors need not to be shareholders and will be elected and removed at any time by administrative council, or, in absence thereof, by stockholders.

Members of board of directors and of administrative council must be individuals resident in Brazil. Estatutos must establish rules for replacement of members of board and of administrative council and stockholders will establish their overall or individual remuneration. If estatutos provide for compulsory dividend of 25% or more of net profits, administrators may be granted share in company's profits, provided total thereof does not exceed annual compensation of administrators or 10% of profits, whichever is less.

Audit Committee.—Company must have audit committee composed of minimum of three, and maximum of five members, and equal number of alternates, who must be individuals resident in Brazil. Estatutos must provide for functioning of audit committee which, if not established on permanent basis, may depend, in each fiscal year, on request of shareholders representing at least 10% of voting stock or 5% of nonvoting stock of company.

Holders of preferred stock with nonvoting rights or with restricted voting rights are entitled to elect one member and his alternate of audit committee, same right being granted to minority stockholders holding 10% or more of voting stock. Majority stockholders are entitled to elect as many members as preferred and minority stockholders plus one. Members of audit committee must receive minimum remuneration of 10% of average remuneration paid to directors, excluding participation in profits. Audit committee, among other duties, must supervise administrators and issue opinion on annual report of administration as well as on proposals to amend stated capital, issuance of debentures, subscription bonus, investment plans, budget, distribution of dividends, conversion, merger, consolidation or spin off.

Increase of Capital.—Corporate capital may be increased by adjusting monetary expression of capital's value, through annual compulsory capitalization of monetary correction reserve, by issuance of shares within limits of authorized capital, by new subscription of shares, by conversion of debentures, partes beneficiárias, subscription bonus, stock options, and by capitalization of profits and reserves. Capital may be increased by new subscription after three-fourths of capital has been paid up. Shareholders shall have right of first refusal, in proportion to number of shares they hold, for subscription of capital increase. Estatutos may in certain cases preclude exercise of right of first refusal.

Fiscal Year and Financial Statements.—Company's fiscal year must last one year and closing date must be set in estatutos. By amendment to estatutos or upon organization, fiscal year may be given different duration.

At end of each fiscal year, board of directors must prepare, based on company's business record, balance sheet, accumulated profit and loss statement, statement of results of fiscal year ended, statement of sources and utilization of funds. Financial statement shall be supplemented by explanatory notes which must indicate among others, criteria adopted for appraisal of assets, investments in other companies, when relevant, increased value of assets resulting from revaluation, encumbrances created on assets, guaranties given to third parties and other liabilities, including rate of interest and maturity dates on long term obligations, number, types and classes of capital shares, eventual stock purchase options granted and exercised during year, adjustments from prior fiscal years, as well as any fact that occurred after closing of fiscal year which has, or may have, relevant effect on financial status and results of company.

Dissolution.—Corporations enter into dissolution: (a) On termination of their duration; (b) in cases provided in estatutos; (c) when determined by stockholders; (d) if there is only one stockholder, as evidenced at general meeting, if minimum of two is not re-established prior to following year's meeting, except when corporation's stock is totally owned by Brazilian company; (e) on cessation of authorization to act in cases where such authorization was required. Company enters judicial dissolution: (a) When its constitutive acts are annulled; (b) when shareholders representing at least 5% of corporate capital prove that company cannot fulfill its purposes; (c) in case of bankruptcy. Unless estatutos provide otherwise, general meeting of shareholders determines manner of liquidation and appoints liquidator and fiscal council who act during liquidation.

Bond Issues.—(Central Bank Res. 755 of Aug. 12, 1982). Corporations are authorized to issue debentures, with par value expressed in Brazilian or foreign currency. Debentures may be converted into shares, and may assure their owners fixed or variable interest, monetary correction, participation in profits of company and refund premium. Debentures may also be guaranteed by mortgage or general lien on assets, be divested of right of preference or be subordinated to company's remaining creditors. General lien on assets assures debenture priority on company's assets, but does not preclude sale of properties which constitute such assets. Obligation not to transfer or encumber real property, or other properties subject to title registration, in instrument of indenture can be made binding on third parties, provided it is recorded in appropriate registry office. Indenture must specify majority required, which may not be less than half of outstanding debentures, to approve any modification in debenture's terms and conditions. Holder of debentures may be represented before company by "fiduciary agent". Issuance of debentures abroad by Brazilian companies is conditioned upon prior approval of Central Bank.

Company with authorized but not fully paid up capital, may issue "subscription bonus" which entitles holder to preference in subscription of capital increases up to limit of authorized capital.

See Topical Index in front part of this volume.

CORPORATIONS . . . *continued*

Conversion, Merger, Consolidation and Spinoff.—Conversion of corporation into another form of enterprise requires unanimous consent of stockholders, absent provision to contrary in estatutos, in which case dissenting shareholders have right to withdraw from company.

Merger (*incorporacão*), consolidation (*fusão*) and reorganization (*cisão*), are subject to approval by stockholders of companies involved and dissenting stockholder is entitled to withdraw from company, against reimbursement of value of his shares. Company with outstanding debentures must also obtain prior approval of debentureholders convened in meeting especially called for that purpose.

Mixed economy companies are subject to corporation law and to special federal laws, and are under jurisdiction of Securities Commission. Organization of mixed enterprise requires prior legislative approval and such company may engage only in activities stipulated in laws authorizing its organization. Mixed enterprises cannot be declared bankrupt but their assets are subject to attachment and garnishment and legal entity which controls said companies is subsidiarily liable for their obligations.

Securities Commission issued Ruling 69/87 requiring that information pertaining to acquisition of voting shares in publicly-held company be published in press; any individual or legal entity who comes to hold 10% or more of voting stock in publicly-held company must disclose: Name and identification data, purposes of purchase and quantity involved, number of voting shares acquired as well as of preemptive rights to voting shares of class or kind, already directly or indirectly held by purchaser or persons connected with purchaser; and existence of any contracts or agreements covering exercise of right to vote, purchase and sale of shares or preference in purchasing same, even if such agreements have not been filed at head office of company. Taking into consideration degree of concentration of holdings of shares in company, on request of party, this rule may be waived.

Federal Supreme Court declared that mere presence of public funds in its capital is not sufficient to characterize company as "mixed-economy company"; enterprise must have been created by law.

Controlling, Controlled and Connected Companies.—Company is deemed to be controlled when controlling company, directly or through other controlled companies, owns number of shares which guarantees in permanent manner that it will prevail in corporate decisions and will have power to elect majority of administrators.

Companies are connected when one holds 10% or more of other's capital, without controlling it.

Annual reports and precise financial statements on connected and controlled companies are obligatory and, as general rule, reciprocal stock participation between company and its connected or controlled companies is prohibited.

Controlling corporation and its controlled companies may constitute group of corporations to carry out their respective objectives or towards participation in joint activities or ventures. Contract or agreement which sets up group of corporations must clearly define method for obtaining objectives of group and must be approved in accordance with rules for amending estatutos. Any dissenting stockholder is entitled to reimbursement of his shares. Group of corporations does not constitute legal entity per se, each company retaining its own legal identity and assets. Controlling company must be Brazilian company and must exercise, directly or indirectly, on permanent basis, control over controlled company. Brazilian company is company control of which is in hands of: (a) Individuals domiciled or resident in Brazil; (b) Brazilian government, State, Municipality, or by subdivisions thereof; (c) Brazilian companies controlled directly or indirectly by persons and entities referred to in (a) and (b) above.

Corporations and any other type of legal entity, whether or not under same control, may also establish consortium (consórcio) to carry out specific project. Consórcio, as group of corporations, does not constitute separate legal entity and rights and obligations of each member will be those spelled out in agreement. Agreement and any amendment thereto must be filed with Commercial Registry of place of consórcio's main office, and filing certificate must be published.

Foreign corporations or companies, whatever be their object, require authorization of the Brazilian government to carry on business in the country in their own name or through branches or agencies. They may, however, be shareholders of Brazilian companies except where otherwise provided by law. Petition for authorization must be accompanied by the following documents: (a) proof that the company is constituted in accordance with the law of its country; (b) copy of its articles of incorporation and by-laws; (c) list of shareholders, giving names, professions, domiciles, and number of shares of each, except in case of shares to bearer; (d) copy of minutes of its shareholders' meeting which authorized business in Brazil and stated the capital destined for operations in Brazil; (e) appointment of representative in Brazil who must be authorized to accept conditions under which authorization may be granted; (f) latest balance sheet. These documents must be duly legalized by a Brazilian consul and accompanied by Portuguese translations made by an official translator. The Federal Government in granting authorization may establish such conditions as it may consider advisable in the national interest, including that of requiring shares of the company to be listed in the stock exchange of Rio de Janeiro.

Authorization having been granted, the decree of authorization and the documents on which it is founded must be published in the official newspaper and a copy of the paper must be filed in the Registry of Commerce where the company has its business. The company must also file a certificate of deposit of the part of its capital devoted to its operations in the country, which amount the government will designate in the decree of authorization. (A minimum capital for Brazil is required). Foreign corporations must use same name in Brazil which they had in their country, but may add words "of Brazil" or "for Brazil". They must have permanent representative in country with full power to accept summons and decide any questions which may arise. Any changes in company's corporate documents require approval of Federal Government in order to take effect in Brazilian territory. Foreign companies must, under penalty of losing their authorization to do business, publish in official newspaper of Federal Government or of respective state of Brazil, publications which they are required to make under their national law with respect to accounts and acts of administration. Within 30 days after such publication, copy of official paper must be sent to government statistical service, under penalty of fine or imprisonment for representative of company. Federal Government may at any time withdraw authorization granted to foreign company if it violates law or its corporate objects, or acts in manner harmful to national economy.

Foreign corporations authorized to act in Brazil may, by authorization of the Government, become naturalized and transfer their domicile to Brazil. For that purpose they must file: (a) evidence that they are constituted according to the laws of their country; (b) their articles of incorporation and by-laws; (c) a list of their shareholders with full particulars; (d) their latest balance sheet; (e) proof of payment of their capital; (f) minutes of shareholders' meeting at which such naturalization was determined. The Federal Government may impose such conditions as it may consider advisable in the national interest.

Foreign corporations are subject to the same disabilities to which aliens in general are subject. (See topic Aliens.) When authority to engage in banking operations is included in charter, it is advisable, in order to save time and expense, to file statement that no banking operations will be carried on in Brazil and to petition for registration as ordinary foreign corporation. Foreign participation in insurance companies is restricted to 50% of their total capital and third of their voting capital.

Limited Liability Companies.—See topic Partnership.

Trading Companies.—(Decree-Law 1248 of Nov. 29, 1972 as am'd; Decree 71866 of Feb. 26, 1973; and Portaria 130 of June 14, 1973 as am'd, Minister of Finance).

Organization.—Must be organized as a company issuing shares of stocks. All shares with voting rights must be registered. Up to two thirds of company's capital may be preferred shares; either in registered or bearer form, without voting rights.

Trading company must be registered. Registration may be cancelled in event of nonobservance of law, or of fraudulent practices.

After registration, no transfers of registered shares and no change in capital structure are allowed without prior approval of corresponding governmental office.

Goods covered by law as being objects of trading companies seem to be only "manufactured products." Goods, destined for exportation, will be sent directly by producer-seller to: (a) Port of embarkation to be shipped abroad, on order of trading company; (b) be deposited in special customs warehouses awaiting export by trading company. Decree 71866 of Feb. 26, 1973 created special customs warehouses to permit depsit of goods under fiscal control.

Capital.—Minimum capital, is fixed by National Monetary Council. Fifty percent of minimum capital must be paid in by stockholders at time of registration, and rest within one year of registration date.

Trading company may be controlled by foreign capital although there are special financing arrangements applicable only to trading companies totally controlled by domestic capital.

For incentives granted, see topic Taxation, subhead Income Tax, catchline Major Fiscal Incentives for Producer-Seller and Trading Companies, Under Trading Companies Law.

COURTS:

(Const. arts. 92-126, Law 7746 of Mar. 30, 1989).

The judicial system of Brazil comprises Federal Supreme Court, Superior Court of Justice, Regional Federal Courts and Federal Judges, military courts, labor courts, electoral courts and state courts.

Federal Supreme Court and Superior Courts have jurisdiction over entire territory and have their seat in Federal Capital.

Federal Supreme Court processes and adjudicates, originally among others; Direct actions of unconstitutionality of federal or state law or normative act, and requests for writ of prevention in direct actions of unconstitutionality; litigation between foreign State or international organization and Republic, State, Federal District or Territory; disputes and conflicts between Republic and States, Republic and Federal District, or between one another, including their respective indirect administration entities; extradition requested by foreign State; homologation of foreign court decisions and granting of "exequatur" to letters rogatory, conflicts of jurisdiction between Superior Court of Justice and any other courts, between Superior Courts, or between latter and any other court; and request for "habeas corpus" as indicated by Constitution. Adjudicates, at ordinary appeal level: "habeas corpus", writs of mandamus, "habeas data" and writs of injunction decided in sole instance by Superior Courts, in event of denial; and political crimes; adjudicates, at extraordinary appeal level, cases decided in sole or last instance, when appealed decision: is contrary to provision of Constitution; declares unconstitutionality of treaty or federal law; and considers valid law or local government contested under Constitution.

Superior Court of Justice processes and adjudicates, originally among others: Writs of mandamus and "habeas data" against act of Minister of State or of Court itself; conflicts of jurisdiction between any courts, with some exceptions; criminal reviews of and rescissory actions for its decisions; and conflicts of authority between administrative and judicial authorities of Republic, States and Federal District. Adjudicates, at ordinary appeal level: "habeas corpus" decided by Federal Regional Courts, courts of States, of Federal District and Territories, when decision denies it; writs of mandamus decided in sole instance by Federal Regional Courts or by courts of States, of Federal District and of Territories, when decision denies it; and cases in which parties are foreign State or international organization on one part, and Municipality or person resident or domiciled in Brazil on other part. Adjudicates, at special appeal level, cases decided, in sole instance or last instance, by Federal Regional Courts or by courts of States, of Federal District and Territories, when appealed decision: is contrary to treaty or federal law or denies effectiveness thereof; considers valid law or act of local government, contested in view of federal law; or confers upon federal law interpretation different from that which has been conferred upon it by another court.

Federal Regional Courts process and adjudicate, originally: Federal judges of area of their jurisdiction, including those of Military Courts and of Labor Courts, in common crimes and in criminal malversion, and members of Federal Attorney General's Office, except for jurisdiction of Electoral Courts; criminal review of and rescissory action for their decisions or those of federal judges of region; writs of mandamus and "habeas data" against act of Court itself or of federal judge; "habeas corpus", when constraining authority is federal judge; conflicts of jurisdiction between federal judges subordinated to Court. Adjudicate at appeal level, cases decided by

See Topical Index in front part of this volume.

COURTS . . . *continued*
federal judges and by state judges exercising federal authority in area of their jurisdiction.

Federal judges process and adjudicate among others: Cases between foreign State or international organization and Municipality or person domiciled or resident in Brazil; cases based on treaty or contract of Republic with foreign State or international organization; crimes set forth in international treaty or conventions, when, prosecution having commenced in Brazil, result has taken place or should have taken place abroad, or reciprocally; crimes against organization of labor and, in cases determined by law, against financial system and financial economic order; crimes committed aboard ships or aircraft, except for jurisdiction of Military Courts; crimes of irregular entry or stay of foreigner, execution of letters rogatory after "exequatur", and of foreign court decision after homologation, cases referring to nationality, and to naturalization; and disputes over rights of indians.

Electoral Courts are Superior Electoral Court, Regional Electoral Court and Electoral Boards. Law shall provide for organization an jurisdiction of electoral courts, judges and boards. Decisions of Superior Electoral Court are unappealable, with exception of those which contravene Constitution and those denying "habeas corpus" or writ of mandamus. Decisions of Regional Electoral Courts may only be appealed when: Rendered against express provision of Constitution or of law; there is divergence in interpretation of law among two or more electoral courts; deal with ineligibility or issuance of certificates of election in federal or state elections; annul certificates of election or decree loss of federal or state elective offices; deny "habeas corpus", writs of mandamus, "habeas data" or writs of injunction.

States Courts are organized observing principles established in Federal Constitution. Jurisdiction of courts is defined in Constitution of State.

Military courts decide cases concerning military crimes as defined by law.

Labor courts settle disputes between employees and employers. The highest court of labor disputes is the Tribunal Superior do Trabalho. (Consolidation of Labor Laws, arts. 643-762; Decree-Law 5452 of May 1, 1943).

CURRENCY:

Monetary unit is Real, which is divided into 100 centavos. Only Central Bank may issue notes and these constitute legal tender for any obligation. (Law 8880 of May 27, 1994 and Law 9069 of June 29, 1995).

CURTESY:

No tenancy by curtesy.

CUSTOMS:

Common External Tariff approved by member countries of southern common market (MERCOSUR) is in effect; each member country has list of goods excluded from common external tariff and subject to their own duty rates. Most goods traded among member countries are not subject to tariff or quota restrictions.

DEATH:

When a person disappears a curator may be appointed for him with such powers as the court may determine. If the disappearance lasts two years, or four years if the absentee left a representative, the interested parties may demand that his estate be provisionally distributed among his heirs or legatees, who must give bond. Ten years after decree of provisional distribution, or 80 years after birth of absentee if latest news of him dates back five years, application may be made for definitive settlement of estate and release of bonds. (Civil Code, arts. 463-484).

Deaths must be recorded in the office of the Civil Registry of the judicial district where death occurs. There are several such district offices in each of the larger cities. Death certificates may be obtained by applying to the office of the Civil Registry of the appropriate district. A small fee is charged, the amount being fixed by local regulations.

DECEDENTS' ESTATES:

See topics Descent and Distribution; Wills.

DEEDS:

(Law 4380 of Aug. 21, 1964 as am'd by Law 5049 of June 29, 1966, Law 7433 of Dec. 18, 1985 regulated by decree 93240 of Sept. 9, 1986).

Deeds conveying real property (unless of slight value) must be public instruments drawn up by notary on his books kept as official records, signed by parties, notary and two witnesses, and must be recorded or registered in public registry in order to be valid transfers.

See also topic Husband and Wife, subhead Husband's Consent.

DESCENT AND DISTRIBUTION:

(Const. art. 5 XXX, XXI, Civil Code, arts. 1572-1807, Decree-Law 4657 of Apr. 9, 1942, Law 8971 of Dec. 29, 1994).

Succession may be by testamentary disposition or by intestacy. A decedent survived by lineal descendants or ancestors may validly dispose by testament of only one-half of his individual estate. Order of intestate succession is as follows: (1) Descendants; (2) ascendants; (3) surviving spouse, not judicially separated from decedent at time of his or her death; (4) collaterals to fourth degree; (5) municipality, federal district or union. In case of common law spouses who are single, judicially separated, divorced, widow or widower, with common children or living together for more than six years, intestate succession is as follows: (1) surviving spouse, while he or she does not enter into another relationship (a) usufructs one quarter of estate when descendants are common children or children of decedent, (b) usufructs one half of estate, when there are only ascendants; (2) surviving spouse inherits total estate if there are no descendants and ascendants.

Succession among descendants is per stirpes, the right of representation inuring to those in direct line of descent, but not to those in line of ascent. Capacity to inherit is determined as of the time of the decedent's death. An inheritance may be renounced only expressly by public or judicial act but may be accepted expressly or impliedly. It cannot be accepted partially, conditionally or for a limited period, but a legatee who is also an heir may accept either the legacy or the inheritance, and refuse the other. Creditors prejudiced by renunciation of an inheritance may, with judicial authorization, accept the inheritance, in the name of the renouncing heir, in which case any balance, after satisfaction of the creditors, will be returned to the estate.

Heirs accepting the inheritance are liable for the debts of the deceased to the extent of the assets of the estate. If no inventory has been made, the burden of proof is on the heirs to show that the debts exceed the assets.

See also topic Aliens.

DIVORCE:

(Const. art. 226, §6; Law 6515 of Dec. 26, 1977 as am'd by Law 7841 of Oct. 17, 1989). Marital societies terminate: (a) Upon death of one of spouses; (b) upon nullity or annulment of marriage; (c) upon judicial separation; and (d) upon divorce. Judicial separation ends obligations of cohabitation, fidelity and marital property regime. Separation can occur by mutual consent after one year of marriage.

Special procedure is provided to obtain decree of separation. (Code Civil Procedure, arts. 1120-1124).

Upon separation by mutual consent custody of children will be awarded in accordance with terms of parties' agreement. Upon separation by fault of one party custody of children will be to innocent party. If both parties be at fault, wife will be entitled to custody of minor children unless judge foresees moral damage to them. Woman against whom decree of separation is issued cannot continue to use her husband's name. If she is innocent party right to use husband's name will be optional. Parties having been separated judicially, will have to contribute to support of their children, in proportion to their assets. Judicial separation becomes divorce after one year if declared by court and registered in Public Registry. After two years of de facto separati on divorce proceeding can be initiated.

Law 5478 of July 25, 1968 and Law 8971 of Dec. 29, 1994 regulate alimony actions.

DOWER:

Not recognized in Brazil.

ENVIRONMENT:

(Const. Art. 225, regulated by Law 8974 of Jan. 5, 1995, Law 6938 of Aug. 31, 1981 as am'd, Law 7347 of June 24, 1985, Law 9008 of Mar. 21, 1995, Decree 1306 of Nov. 9, 1994).

Constitution establishes legal framework for environmental legislation granting to all persons right to enjoy ecologically balanced environment, and duty to government and people to defend and preserve it for present and future generations. Among duties set forth for public authorities is preservation and reestablishment of essential ecological processes, definition of territorial areas to be protected, and prior analysis of conditions involving installation and development of any potential activity to determine environmental impact which may be caused. Federal legislation provides for general environmental protection while state and municipal law set forth more specific definition of activities which may be developed within that jurisdiction. Some activities are restricted to exploitation by government or by some state-owned companies, but may be developed by private companies by means of licensing contracts; among such activities are: mining, urban real estate development, transportation of dangerous material, chemical industry, nuclear energy, projects involving use of natural resources. As general rule, polluter has civil liability, independently of existence of fault; once damages are proven, it is enough to evidence its connection with action or omission by agent; not only is polluter subject to liability, but also other individuals and entities that participated in cause which generated environmental damage. Besides civil liability they may be held criminally liable. Federal, state and municipal authorities may impose penalties, such as fines, suspension of activities, cancellation of license to operate. Among main environmental authorities, which form Natural Environment System, are Environment Secretariat, National Council of Environment, Brazilian Institute of Environment and Renewable Natural Resources.

EXCHANGE CONTROL:

Federal Constitution entrusts Union with power to legislate on exchange, foreign trade and transfers of values from country. Laws, decrees and specific instructions bearing on exchange control are numerous. Basis of exchange system is found in Law 4595 of Dec. 31, 1964 as am'd and Law 4131 of Sept. 3, 1962, as am'd by Law 4390 of Aug. 29, 1964 and Law 9060 of June 29, 1995, regulated by Decree 55762 of Feb. 17, 1965.

Under Law 4595, National Monetary Council is entitled to (a) establish general rules of exchange policy, including sale and purchase of gold and of any transactions involving foreign currency; (b) grant to Central Bank monopoly to perform exchange transactions whenever there is a serious imbalance in balance of payments or when there are reasons to anticipate such a situation, and (c) regulate exchange transactions, establishing limits, rates, terms and other conditions. Agencies in charge of carrying out policies and resolutions laid down by National Monetary Council are Central Bank and Bank of Brazil.

All exchange transactions must be performed through duly authorized banks or institutions.

Exchange rate may be negotiated between parties, between limits set forth by Central Bank of Brazil for purchase and sale of foreign exchange. Importation of goods is also transacted in free market exchange and import license is required. Paper or manual exchange, which includes bank notes and traveller's checks is reserved for expenses of travellers who must identify themselves and, is limited up to certain amount.

Central Bank may determine that exchange operations relating to capital movements should be made wholly or partly in financial exchange market, separated from import and export trade operations, whenever exchange situation should warrant it.

See Topical Index in front part of this volume.

EXECUTIONS:

(Code Civil Procedure, arts. 566-795).

After an order of execution has been issued and property attached, the attached property is appraised and thereupon offered for sale on notice published in press which shall also state that if property is not sold for amount superior to appraised value, it shall be sold at any price between tenth and 20th day thereafter. Judge can grant to creditor usufruct of property, if this diminishes burden upon debtor and debt can be effectively satisfied. Judge presides over sale. If property belongs to persons who lack capacity and not more than 80% of appraised value is offered, judge postpones sale for one year.

Before minutes of sale are signed, executing creditor may request that property be adjudged to him for amount of appraisal.

Before sale or adjudication, debtor may at any time redeem property, paying or depositing amount of debt plus interest, costs and attorney fees.

EXEMPTIONS:

(Code Civil Procedure, arts. 648-649).

Property which is considered by law not subject to attachment or garnishment and that which is inalienable, is exempt from execution, particularly: (a) Inalienable property and property voluntarily declared not subject to execution; (b) provisions and combustibles for maintenance of debtor and his family for one month; (c) wedding ring and family pictures; (d) remuneration of judges, teachers and public officers; (e) military equipment; (f) books and utensils necessary for profession; (g) all pensions necessary for support of debtor and his family; (h) materials necessary for work in progress; (i) life insurance.

FIDUCIARIES: See topic Trusts.

FOREIGN CORPORATIONS: See topic Corporations.

FOREIGN EXCHANGE:

See topic Exchange Control.

FOREIGN INVESTMENT:

(Const. Art. 171, Law 4131 of Sept. 3, 1962 as am'd by Law 4390 of Aug. 29, 1964 and Decree-Law 2073 of Dec. 20, 1983 and regulated by Decree 55762 of Feb. 17, 1965; Decree 365 of Dec. 16, 1991). Foreign investors may acquire shares or quotas in Brazilian companies or lend money to local borrowers. Foreign capital (belonging to companies or individuals domiciled abroad) may enter Brazil in form of cash, goods, machinery and equipment, patent and trademark rights and it shall receive same treatment as domestic capital under similar circumstances; any restrictions must be expressly provided for. Foreign capital participation is restricted in areas including mining and exploitation of hydraulic energy resources; transportation; insurance and communication media. All foreign capital entering Brazil, whether in form of investment or loan, must be registered with Central Bank; as well as all contracts which require transfers of funds from Brazil, as dividends, interest amortizations, royalties, technical fees, etc., and all reinvestments of profits and remittances made from Brazil, including repatriation of capital. Registration of foreign capital must be applied for within 30 days of entering country. Companies or individuals desiring to transfer abroad profits, dividends, interest amortizations, royalties, technical fees, etc., must submit to Central Bank contracts and documents necessary to justify remittance. Remittances abroad also depend on registration of company with Central Bank and on proof of payment of any applicable income tax. Registration of foreign capital will be made in currency of country of origin and reinvestments in Brazilian currency, and also in currency of country to which profits could have been remitted. Registration of royalty contracts depends on proof of existence and validity of respective patents or trademarks both in Brazil and in country of origin. Deduction of royalties as operating expense is limited to 5% of gross income from product manufactured or sold. Technical fees may be deducted only during first five years of company's operation or of introduction of special production process. This period may be extended by further five years upon authorization from Conselho Monetario Nacional. Remittance of interest on loans must be at rate stated in contract registered with Central Bank. Any remittance in excess of said rate will be considered amortization of principal. Central Bank will not consider as interest that part in excess of rate obtaining for similar operations in financial market of its origin, at time of negotiation of loan.

Remittances of profits abroad are subject to following restrictions: (a) in case of capital applied in production of goods or services for sumptuary use, to be defined by Executive Decree, remittance will be limited to 8% per year of capital registered with Central Bank. In case of sharp imbalance of foreign trade, Central Bank may limit said remittances, for a temporary period of time, to 10%of registered capital, and stop repatriation of capital. Profits exceeding above limits, if remitted abroad will be considered repatriation of capital and will be deducted accordingly from corresponding registration for purposes of future remittances; (b) in all other cases, remittances will not be limited.

FOREIGN TRADE REGULATIONS:

See topic Exchange Control.

HOLIDAYS:

Jan. 1 (New Year's); Jan. 20 (St. Sebastian, Rio de Janeiro only); Mon., Tues. (Carnival)*; Ash Wednesday (half holiday)*; Good Friday*; Apr. 21 (Tiradentes); May 1 (Labor Day); Corpus Christi*; Sept. 7 (Independence Day); Nov. 2 (All Souls'); Nov. 15 (Proclamation of Republic); Dec. 25 (Christmas).

* These are movable holidays.

HOMESTEAD:

(Civil Code, arts. 70-73).

Homestead exempt from attachment and execution, except for tax debts, comprises dwelling house and furniture, landscaping, equipment and machinery for professional use.

HUSBAND AND WIFE:

(Civil Code, arts. 180-314).

An ante-nuptial agreement may be executed with respect to property, and such agreements must be mentioned in the official record of the marriage. In absence or nullity of such agreement, property of husband and wife will be regarded as partial community ownership. Under this regime, property owned by spouses prior to marriage, or inherited individually after marriage, and in certain other cases, does not constitute community property. However, property acquired after marriage generally constitutes community property, regardless of under which spouses' name such property is registered. Community property will be equally divided when death, divorce or judicial separation terminates marital regime or relationship. Husband is administrator of community property, but he cannot, without wife's consent, alienate or encumber real estate, litigate regarding such real estate, give bond, or make gifts other than of small value. If she refuses without sufficient reason, her consent may be supplied by court, but not with respect to her separate property.

Husband's Consent.—The wife requires the husband's consent for alienating or encumbering the real estate of her separate property, whatever be the system of property management which the parties may have adopted; for litigating with regard to such real estate. In case of his refusal, his consent may in most cases be supplied by court for good reasons. Husband's consent is presumed if wife occupies public office or exercises profession outside of home for over six months. His authorization is also presumed for purchase by her of articles necessary for home and for contracting obligations for industry or profession she exercises with his consent. Federal Supreme Court of Brazil has ruled that husband must obtain his wife's consent before granting surety involving pledge of couple's property, even if property involved only represents what might be considered as his "half" since, under community property regime, that "half" is purely notional. Woman who has not been so consulted may file plea to annul surety. See also topic Divorce.

INCOME TAX: See topic Taxation.

INFANCY:

(C. C. arts. 5-9, 145-158, 379-395, 406-445).

The age of majority is 21. Contracts by minors under 16 are void and if over 16, voidable, except some by emancipated minors. Infants are subject to parental authority of husband, with collaboration of wife, and upon death or impediment of one of spouses, other spouse exercises authority exclusively. Parental authority includes custody, legal representation and administration and enjoyment of minor's real and personal property with certain exceptions. In absence of parents guardian is appointed. Parents and guardian have restricted powers of disposition.

INHERITANCE TAX: See topic Taxation.

INTEREST:

(Civil Code, arts. 1062-64; Com. Code, arts. 248, 254; Decree 22626 of Apr. 7, 1933; Decree-Law 182 of Jan. 5, 1938; Law 1521 of Dec. 26, 1951).

Legal rate, 6%: rates may not be fixed by contract in excess of 12%. Compound interest is not allowed. Defaulted contractual interest may be augmented by 1%. Debtors may pay mortgage or pledge obligations before maturity but creditors may in this case require that payments be not less than 25% of the original amount. Penal clauses are understood to serve the purpose of indemnifying for judicial expenses and fees in collecting debts, and no penalty is demandable when collection is effected without judicial proceedings. Penal clauses in excess of 10% of the obligation are void. Any simulation of the rate of interest is considered usury and punishable by imprisonment and fine.

An agent is liable for interest for any delay in the delivery of funds belonging to the principal, who on the other hand is liable to the agent for interest on sums which the agent may have properly advanced and spent in the fulfilment of the agency.

In obligations which are limited to the payment of a sum certain in money, damages for default are computed at the legal rate of interest unless otherwise stipulated.

Provision for interest in a draft or promissory note being ineffective, the face amount usually includes interest at an agreed rate to maturity. Interest will not run after maturity until the instrument is protested.

INTESTACY: See topic Descent and Distribution.

JUDGMENTS:

Judgments for liquidated amounts are executed by executive mandate, issued by the judge. See topic Executions.

Where it is necessary to reach goods of the judgment debtor in other judicial districts proceedings may be taken and execution issued in such other districts. An unliquidated judgment, before becoming capable of execution, must be liquidated by court proceedings or arbitration under court appointment.

Foreign Judgments.—Judgments of foreign courts are enforceable in Brazil under certain conditions and after they have been "homologated" by the Federal Supreme Court, which "homologation" can be granted only after hearing the parties and the attorney general. Opposition to the enforcement of a foreign judgment may be based on any uncertainty as to the authenticity or meaning of the instrument, that it is not a final judgment, was rendered by a court without jurisdiction, that the parties were not duly served or default not legally proved, or that the judgment contains some provision contrary to public order or law of Brazil. In no event can evidence be introduced respecting the basis of the issues involved. (Decree-Law 4657 of Sept. 4, 1942, C.P.C. art. 584).

See Topical Index in front part of this volume.

LABOR RELATIONS:

(Const. arts. 6-11; Civil Code, arts. 1216-1230; Consolidation of Labor Laws, Decree-Law 5452 of May 1, 1943 as am'd; Law 7783 of June 28, 1989; Law 7998 of Jan. 11, 1990; Law 8036 of May 11, 1990 as am'd).

Employees can opt between two kinds of regimes for protection under labor law, with regard to indemnification and unfair dismissal. Under first and older kind, when no specified term has been stipulated for duration of employment, industrial or commercial employees or workmen are entitled, on dismissal, to bonus of one month's salary for each complete year of work. This compensation as well as notice are required only when there is no just cause for dismissal. Unfaithfulness, carelessness, drunkenness, indiscretion, disobedience, lack of respect towards master and constant gambling are just causes for dismissal. No commercial or industrial employee or workman having more than ten years of employment may be dismissed without just cause proved in thorough inquiry. If employer closes his business for reason other than force majeure, he must pay double compensation. Second option available for employee is Guaranty Fund for Time of Service (FGTS) by virtue of which 8% of monthly salary of employee, which is deposited monthly in separate bank account by employer, can be withdrawn by employee upon unfair dismissal by employer. Upon such dismissal, employer must also pay further 40% of total of such amount to employee.

All employees and workmen are entitled to 30 days vacation per year; duration of holiday's period of time is given in relation to days of absence from work, per year. All workers are guaranteed right to strike. Strike suspends employment contracts. Employers may not rescind such contracts. Payment in event of dismissal is guaranteed. Law requires notification to employers 48 hours in advance of any strike and 72 hours in advance if essential activities are involved.

Hours of labor are limited to eight per day and 44 per week, with certain exceptions. Restrictions are imposed on the employment of women and children. In case of pregnancy, women have 120 days of maternity leave. There is also paternity leave. It is not permitted to pay alien more than Brazilian for same kind of work.

As to restrictions on employment of aliens, see topic Aliens.

Law 7998 of Jan. 11, 1990 as am'd created unemployment insurance to provide temporary financial support to workers, who are unemployed on account of dismissal without just cause, or of total or partial paralization of employer's activities.

There are government pension and retirement funds which retire employees and disabled workmen, and on their death, pension their widows and minor children; employees and workmen must contribute certain amount of their salary to these funds and employers too. (Law 8213 of July 24, 1991 as am'd regulated by Decree 611 of July 21, 1992 as am'd).

Brazil has signed and ratified most of international conventions on subject prepared by International Labor Organization.

For collective bargaining and class representation, see topic Associations, subhead Collective Bargaining.

LAW REPORTS, CODES, ETC.:

See topic Statutes.

LEGISLATURE:

See topic Constitution and Government.

LIMITATION OF ACTIONS:

(Civil Code, arts, 161-179; Com. Code, arts. 441-456).

Prescription does not run between husband and wife during the continuance of the marital union, between parent and child or guardian and ward during the continuance of the parental or tutelary power, against persons absolutely incapable civilly, against persons abroad on national, state or municipal service, or against those serving in the army or navy in time of war.

Prescription is interrupted by personal citation of the debtor or judicial protest (even before a judge not competent in the matter), presentation of claim against an estate, judicial act placing the debtor in default, or by any unequivocal act on the part of the debtor importing an acknowledgment of the cause of action.

After the prescription period has run, the defense may be waived by the debtor, if without prejudice to the rights of third parties, either expressly or by implication from an act incompatible with the claim being unenforceable.

Civil Actions.—As a rule, personal actions are barred by limitation in 20 years; real actions in ten years, between persons present in the same community, otherwise in 15 years unless a shorter period be specifically provided for any particular action.

Among the more important provisions for prescription within a shorter period are the following:

Five years: actions against the federal, state or municipal governments or treasuries, actions to recover rents of real property, to rescind a final judgment, for damage to property rights or to recover interest on obligations when payable annually or at lesser intervals.

Two years: actions for debts of less than 100 cruzeiros, on insurance contracts where the event occurred outside of Brazil, of a husband or his heirs to annul acts performed by the wife without his consent.

One year: action on insurance contracts where the event occurred in Brazil; for the recovery of fees of lawyers, experts in legal causes, physicians and sur-geons; for the recovery of rent, board or tuition by boarding housekeepers and school proprietors.

Six months: actions by purchasers of improved property for abandonment of price by reason of latent defects.

Commercial Actions.—Actions founded on commercial obligations contracted by public or private instrument prescribe in 20 years except where a shorter period is fixed for particular classes of actions, among which are the following:

Five years: executive actions on negotiable instruments against the maker, drawer, acceptor and their sureties; action against former partners who are not liquidators of a dissolved partnership.

Four years: on debts provable by accounts stated or by accounts rendered to a merchant presumed solvent;

Two years: actions for performance of commercial obligations provable only by oral testimony:

One year: actions for wages, services or payments pursuant to contract, unless evidenced by written instruments, executive actions against endorsers of bills and notes:

An action to recover for merchandise entrusted to a merchant without a receipt signed by the defendant is barred in two years if the debtor resides in the same state in Brazil as the creditor, in three years if he resides in a different state and in four years if he resides outside of Brazil.

Actions against the Government.—In the case of debts owing by the Federal Government or by government corporations, prescription can be interrupted only once, and the period remaining can be only one-half the original period. (Decree-Law 4597 of Aug. 19, 1942).

LIMITED PARTNERSHIP: See topic Partnership.

MARRIAGE:

(Const. art. 226; Civil Code, arts. 180-314; Decree-Law 4657 of Apr. 9, 1942).

Marriage is civil ceremony, but may be religious ceremony if celebrated according to law. License to marry within three months is obtained from official of civil registry upon proof of age and residence of parties and other data required by law, including declaration by two witnesses that they know parties and that no impediment to their marriage exists. Notice of intended marriage is given by bulletin posted for 15 days in building where marriages are performed and published, but publication may be dispensed with.

Civil marriages are performed publicly, usually in a court house, at a time previously designated by the judge who is to preside, upon presentation of the license. At least two witnesses must be present. Either or both of the contracting parties may be represented by an agent with special power of attorney.

Marriages between uncle and niece or aunt and nephew are allowed on certain conditions. (Decree-Law 3200 of Apr. 19, 1941, and Law 5891 of June 12, 1973).

Annulment.—Marriages may be declared null if contracted with near relatives, persons already married and in certain other cases.

Marriages are annullable within certain periods where contracted: (1) Under coercion or by persons incapable of consenting, provided action is brought within two years from date of marriage; (2) by a rapist who marries his victim before she has escaped from his power; (3) by a woman under 16 or a man under 18 years of age; (4) by those under guardianship, without the consent of the guardian; and (5) in case of substantial error concerning the person of the other spouse, at the time of consenting. In the first two cases the annulment may be requested by the person incapable of consent or under coercion or by his or her legal representatives; in the third case, by the parties above mentioned or by direct ancestors or collateral relatives to the second degree; in the fourth case above, only upon motion of a guardian who was not present at the marriage. Upon termination of the incapacity the marriage may be formally ratified before the competent authority or impliedly ratified by lapse of time. Marriages cannot be annulled upon the ground of lack of legal age where pregnancy of the wife has ensued.

Upon the ground of substantial error concerning the person of the other spouse annulment may be demanded only by the spouse in error. The Code recognizes as essential error, ignorance at the time of marriage of: (1) Dishonor or bad reputation of the other spouse, subsequent knowledge of which makes the marital union insupportable; (2) conviction for a crime punishable by four years imprisonment or more; (3) irremediable physical defect or grave contagious or hereditary disease exposing to risk the other spouse or children.

Both in the case of declaration of nullity and of annulment, the marriage, if contracted in good faith by both parties, produces all effects of valid marriage including legitimation of children, until such time as it is declared null or annulled. If contracted in good faith by one of parties, it is valid as to that one until annulled or declared null.

MARRIED WOMEN:

See topics Dower; Husband and Wife; Marriage; Divorce.

MINES AND MINERALS:

(Const. arts. 20 VIII, IX, 176; Mining Code, Decree-Law 227 of Feb. 28, 1967, am'd and Laws 6403 of Dec. 15, 1976, 6567 of Sept. 24, 1978 as am'd, 7085 of Dec. 21, 1982, Law 7886 of Nov. 1989, and regulated by Decree 62934 of July 2, 1968 as am'd; Law 7805 of July 18, 1989 regulated by Decree 98812 of Jan. 9, 1990).

Mineral resources and potential hydraulic energy constitute separate property from land for purpose of exploitation and use. They belong to Federal Government which may grant authorizations or concessions to prospect, exploit or use them to Brazilian individuals or Brazilian legal entities.

Authorizations and concessions are granted to Brazilian companies only if production of their mining activities is used in their manufacturing facilities or by their subsidiaries.

Owner of land may use directly, under system of local license, deposits of mineral substances of immediate employment in civil constructions to be used in their natural state, alone or mixed with others or with stones or plasterlike substances, when not used as raw material for industrial transformation. Licensee may request later an authorization and concession. This is mandatory if use of minerals is not as stated.

Normally, minerals must be explored and exploited under an authorization and a concession.

Exploration rights may be granted only to Brazilian natural or Brazilian juridical person or to "mining concerns" by Ministry of Mines after certain proceedings followed by National Department of Mineral Products. Authorization lasts two years extendible for one more, in view of work done, results thereof and proof that exploration is on.

Minerals extracted during exploration may be taken out of area only for analysis and assays and not for sale. At end of exploration a detailed report must be submitted to

See Topical Index in front part of this volume.

MINES AND MINERALS . . . *continued*
Department of Mines. Each authorization must be limited to maximum areas established by regulations and each physical or juridical person may have five authorizations for explorations of deposits of same kind, but no more than 50. Code of Mines requires registration of exploration licenses with National Department of Mineral Production (D.N.P.M.), along with evidence of Brazilian nationality for natural persons and authorization to engage in mining activities in case of juridical persons; also establishes appeal against refusal of exploration license.

Owners of land must be indemnified with a rent for use of land and indemnification for damages. Petitioner must file agreement with owner of land regarding rent and indemnity mentioned above. In its absence, Department of Mines sends record to Court of zone which, after making final determination, orders deposit of equivalent of two years of rent and a security bond for indemnification, after approval of which, Court will order landowner to permit exploration.

Exploration must begin within 60 days after publication of authorization in official newspaper or determination of rent and indemnity by Court, when necessary, and should be suspended for no more than three consecutive months or 120 nonconsecutive days. Any interruption or recommencement must be promptly notified to Department of Mines, as well as any finding of any mineral not included in authorization.

When final report of exploration is filed and approved, explorer has one year in order to request a concession of exploitation. After this period, Government may grant exploitation rights to other petitioners.

Exploitations must be object of a concession which may be granted only regarding an explored area with approved final report. Exploitation area must be adequate to technical and economic requirements of works of extraction and elaboration, always within borders of exploration area.

Only "mining concerns" (see supra, subhead Exploration and infra, subhead Mining Concern) may be concessionaires. There are no restrictions on number of concessions which may be held by one concern. Petition must contain detailed requirements.

Concessionaire must receive possession of mine from Department of Mines, within 90 days after publication of concession in official newspaper, paying fee established by law. Department of Mines will give possession, calling other concessionaires of bordering mines to be present in the act. Markings of limits of concessions must be placed on the points indicated in decree of concession and maintained visible and not changed, except with authorization from Department of Mines.

Concessionaire must commence exploitation works within six months from date of publication of decree in official newspaper, except in case of force majeure qualified by Department; he must work mine pursuant to plans, one of which must be affixed at place of mine; only mineral substance object of concession may be extracted and discovery of another substance must be communicated immediately to Department. Concessionaire must abstain from excessive exploitation which may make impossible further use of mine and he must maintain living quarters in sanitary conditions, prevent loss of waters, pollution of air and waters and comply with several other detailed obligations.

Once exploitation is commenced, works cannot be interrupted for more than six months, except for force majeure. An annual report of works must be filed.

Several concessions of same beneficiary and of same mineral substance, within area of one single deposit or mineral zone, may be joined in a single "mining group." Concessionaire of a mining group when authorized by Department may concentrate his activities in one or several of concessions within the group, provided intensity of work is compatible with importance of total reserve of whole mine.

In zones of National Reserve or in case of a mineral subject to monopoly, Government may permit exploration and exploitation of other mineral substances if works are compatible with reserve or monopoly, under conditions established therefor. Concession may be assigned or encumbered only as a whole to a party with capacity to hold it. When a credit is guaranteed with concession, and this terminates, guarantee ceases but concessionaire continues being liable.

Easements in favor of exploration or exploitation are placed on land and sub-soil where same is located and on bordering lands, insomuch as necessary for construction of offices, installations, living quarters, rights of way, collection of water, conduction of electricity, and similar requirements. Owners of servient lands must be indemnified.

Sanctions may be imposed for failure to comply with obligations resulting from authorization of exploration or concession of exploitation, depending on seriousness of violation.

Authorizations of concessions granted in violation of law may be annulled on authority's own motion or at request of interested party under special proceedings established by law.

"Mining concern" is defined as a Brazilian firm or association or corporation domiciled in Brazil, whatever its legal structure, having within its purposes obtention of benefits from mineral deposits in national territory. Members of firm, association or corporation must be Brazilian or juridical persons specifically named in document of organization. Any individual concern must necessarily be organized by Brazilian citizen. Mining concerns need authorization of Ministry of Mines and Energy in order to exercise mining activities. Petition must be filed with Department of Mines, accompanied with legalized photocopy of registry of firm in Registry of Commerce, in case of individual firms; similar photocopy or second copy of document of organization with proof of registration, in case of limited liability companies and, in case of a corporation, official newspaper where organization was published.

Mining syndicates (Consorcio de Mineraçcao) may be organized by several concessionaires of neighboring mines, open or situated over same deposit or mineral zone. For this purpose they must request permit from Federal Government, showing that productivity of exploitations will be increased thereby. By-laws of proposed syndicate must be filed with plans of works to be realized and statement of benefits required from Government. Syndicate will be subject to conditions fixed by Government, proposed by a committee specifically appointed for purpose.

Special registry will be kept of internal or external trade of precious stones, noble metals and other minerals which may be included by regulations.

Radioactive minerals or materials which may produce nuclear energy may be permitted to be exploited together with other minerals only when latter are of an economic value much higher than former and, then, under special conditions.

Aerial geological prospecting may be made only by mining concerns authorized therefor which prove to have necessary means for the purpose, subject to specific provisions of the law and regulations.

Prior authorizations or concessions granted under prior law and still in effect continue being valid but subject to provisions of new Code.

Prospecting and exploitation on continental shelf and Brazilian waters are regulated by Decree 96000 of May 2, 1988.

Sole Tax on Minerals.—(Decree-Law 1038 of Oct. 21, 1969 as am'd and its regulations Decree 92295 of Jan. 14, 1986). Tax is levied once on extraction, treatment, circulation, distribution, exportation and consumption of minerals. Tax rate ranges from 1% to 15%, depending on kind of mineral, and value of mineral based on value of metric ton set by Government.

See also topic Foreign Investment.

Petroleum and Natural Gas Deposits.—Const. art. 177 establishes petroleum monopoly owned by Federal Government. Law 2004 of Oct. 3, 1953, as am'd and Decree-Law 1288 of Nov. 1, 1973, created a government corporation with a monopoly in all matters relating to petroleum, except for distribution. The Government subscribed 100% of the stock and must retain, at all times, at least 51% of the voting stock. Stock of said company may be sold only to Brazilian individuals, not married to foreigners under the community property system, and to Brazilian companies whose shareholders must all be Brazilians subject to the same limitation. The corporation may organize subsidiaries to carry out particular purposes but the same restriction as to control and nationality must be observed. Existing concessions will not be renewed upon expiration.

MONOPOLIES AND RESTRAINT OF TRADE:

(Federal Constitution art. 173, §4; Law 8884 of June 11, 1994 as am'd, Law 9019 of Mar. 30, 1995, Decree 1488 of May 11, 1995 as am'd, Decree 1602 of Aug. 23, 1995; Decree 1751 of Dec. 19, 1996).

Constitution repressed abuse of economic power in form of acts intended to dominate domestic market, eliminating competition and arbitrarily increasing profits.

Antitrust law purpose is to restrain and prevent infringement of economic policy based on constitutional guarantees of free initiative, free competition, social functions of property, consumer's defense, and restraining abuse of economic power. Law is applicable to individuals and public or private judicial persons, associations of individuals or entities, de facto or legally organized, with or without legal representation, including foreign companies which operate in country through affiliates, agencies, branches, offices, establishments, agents or representatives. Infringement of economic order implicates joint responsibility of enterprise and of its administrators. All acts expressed in any form purpose of which is or may result in limitation or in any harm to free competition or to free initiative; domination of relevant market of goods or services; arbitrary increase of profits or practice of any form of abusive dominant position, constitute infringement of economic policy, regardless of negligence, even if final result is not obtained. Following are practices which are considered infringements of economic policy, among others; price arrangement between competitors, market division, combined bids, refusal to sell, underselling, dumping, imposition of resale prices on distributors, retailers and representatives, retaining of products or consumer goods, excessive increase in price or abusive profits.

Brazilian law is applied by Economic Law Office (SDE) in charge of investigations and by Administrative Board for Economic Defense (CADE) in charge of judicial procedure. Once enough evidence is collected CADE may order end of restrictive practice and also impose fine. Furthermore, all acts and agreements between enterprises are subject to registration and prior approval from CADE when they may limit or in any way jeopardize free competition, or result in domination of relevant market of goods and services.

Brazilian law does not blindly forbid existence of monopolies. Agreements between companies that may reduce market competition are valid if approved by CADE when their purpose is to increase productivity, improve quality or provide technological development.

Antidumping.—Local production is protected from unfair practices of international trade by imposing antidumping and countervailing duties on import of foreign goods to compensate for damages caused to domestic economy by dumping or product subsidies. Dumping is considered unfair practice. Dumping is defined as import of foreign goods at lower price than normal value of similar or same product in origin or export place in normal commercial transactions. Normal value is determined according to method indicated by law. Law contains regulations and administrative procedure in conformity with use of antidumping and countervailing duties approved and adopted by General Agreement on Tariffs and Trade. Protective measures on importation of products may be issued to protect local production of same or similar products.

Consumer Protection Code.—(Law 8078 of Sept. 11, 1990 as am'd regulated by Decree 861 of July 9, 1993). Code deals with: Basic consumer rights; liability and obligations, health and consumer safety protection, misleading advertising, abusive practices, contractual protection and sanctions.

Law 7347 of July 24, 1985, regulated by Decree 92302 of Jan. 16, 1986 and Decree 1306 of Nov. 9, 1994, regulates legal actions and liability for damages caused to consumers, among others.

MORTGAGES:

(Civil Code, arts. 755-767, 809-862, as am'd).

Any real property susceptible of alienation may be mortgaged. Period may not exceed 30 years, but mortgage may be renewed and its prior lien retained by executing a new instrument upon expiration of first 30 years. Mortgages are public instruments drawn up on books of a notary who is charged with duty of seeing that all taxes have been duly paid. All mortgages must be inscribed in registry of place where mortgaged property is located.

MORTGAGES . . . *continued*

Except when the mortgagor is insolvent, a second mortgage cannot be foreclosed, although due, until the maturity of the first mortgage, and failure to pay obligations secured by mortgages subsequent to the first will not cause the mortgagor to be deemed insolvent.

A mortgage may contain provisions for a penalty upon default and for interest at an increased rate thereafter. (See topic Interest.) Such provisions are advisable, since expense of foreclosure proceedings is likely to be rather high.

Under Decree-law No. 70 of Nov. 21, 1966 certain mortgage loans may be represented by "mortgage cedulas." Under Decree-law No. 167 of Feb. 14, 1967 in cases of agricultural financing, "rural mortgage cedulas" may be issued and recorded.

See also topic Chattel Mortgages.

NEGOTIABLE INSTRUMENTS:

See topic Bills and Notes.

NOTARIES PUBLIC:

(Const. art. 236, Law 8935 of Nov. 18, 1995).

Notaries are commissioned by public competitive examination of tests and titles; they must be lawyers of Brazilian nationality with legal capacity and in good standing. Law regulates rights and duties of notaries, disciplinary rules and criminal responsibility. Their activity is supervised by Judicial Power. They keep books in which contracts, deeds, powers of attorney and wills are inscribed and signed, notary thereupon supplying parties with certified copies of document as executed, which copies have force of originals. These books are preserved indefinitely as public records.

Notaries also maintain a registry of signatures and certify, by comparison, the authenticity of signatures on documents. Notaries' records are open to public inspection.

See also topics Acknowledgments; Deeds; Principal and Agent; Records; Wills.

PARTNERSHIP:

(Com. Code, arts. 287-294, 300-353; Civil Code arts. 1363-1409).

Every partnership, whether Brazilian or foreign, in order to carry on business in Brazil, must be evidenced by a written agreement registered in National Department for Trade Registration, when partnership domicile is to be Federal District, or in local commercial registries when it is in any of states. No legal action may be brought against third person without such written evidence of partnership, but suit may be brought against persons as partners who have committed certain acts giving rise to legal presumption that they are partners.

The collective or firm name of a business partnership may include only names of partners who are duly registered merchants and whose liability is not limited.

Special partnerships are permitted in which one or more partners, including at least one registered merchant, are liable as general partners, while the liability of other partners who contribute capital only and are not permitted to act for or be employed by the partnership, even as attorneys-in-fact, is limited to their respective quotas of capital. The quotas of such special partners may be represented by stock.

Decree 3708 of Jan. 10, 1919, permits the formation of limited liability companies by quotas, in which none of the partners is a general partner, the liability of each being limited to the total amount of the capital. The word "Limitada" must appear in the name of such a limited liability company.

Fourth Panel of Federal Appeals Court has ruled that de facto closing of "limitada" company without properly allocating and accounting for its assets constitutes illegal act. Private property of managing partner may be attached if necessary to settle company's tax debts.

PATENTS:

(Const. art. 5 XXIX; Law 9279 of May 14, 1996).

Inventions.—Any invention, whether product or process, in all fields of technology, provided that it is new, involves inventive step and is capable of industrial application, is patentable. Invention is new when it is not within state of art. Inventions contrary to public policy, morals, public health; inventions related to nuclear substances, to plants and animals, except transgenic microorganisms, are not patentable. Patents are granted for 20 years from filing date, but never for less than ten years from granting date. Patent gives exclusive right of exploitation. Law recognizes prior bona fide user rights. Patent owner must exploit it, directly or by granting license. Compulsory license may be granted due to lack of exploitation by patent owner under limited conditions or in case of proof of owner's involvement in abusive practices of economic power.

Utility Models.—New forms of objects or mechanisms, are patentable provided they have practical use and are susceptible of industrial application.

Utility models are new when they are not within state of art. Patents are granted for 15 years from filing date, but never for less than seven years from granting date.

Industrial Designs.—Any new design or model which may be applied to industrial purpose may be registered by its author if it is not within state of art. Industrial designs contrary to public policy, morals, freedom of expression or religious beliefs among others, may not be registered. Registration is granted for ten years from filing date, renewable for three consecutive periods of five years each. Sanctions imposed for infringement of patents rights are imprisonment from three to 12 months or fines. Provisions regarding inventions are applicable to utility models and industrial designs.

Law also deals with unfair competition crimes.

Caveat: Law comes into full effect on May 15, 1997.

See also topic Monopolies and Restraint of Trade.

PLEDGES:

(Civil Code, arts. 755-780; Commercial Code, arts. 271-279).

A pledge may be effected by actual delivery of personal property to the creditor or his representative pursuant to a written instrument specifying the amount of the debt and the articles pledged.

In addition to pledges by agreement, Brazilian law recognizes liens or pledges by operation of law in favor of innkeepers with respect to the baggage, furniture, jewels and money of guests, and in favor of landlords with respect to furniture of tenants, the creditor in such cases being allowed to hold one or more articles up to the equivalent of the debt, thereupon beginning an action to collect the debt.

PRESCRIPTION:

See topic Limitation of Actions.

PRINCIPAL AND AGENT:

(Civil Code, arts. 1288-1323; Com. Code, arts. 140-190, Law 4886 of Dec. 9, 1965 as am'd by Law 8420 of May 8, 1992).

Whenever one person undertakes to act for another in Brazil he should have a formal power of attorney, since few acts can be performed without one. The scope of the powers conferred is strictly construed under Brazilian law, and an instrument in general terms confers only administrative powers, specific authorization being necessary for the attorney to perform many acts, such as to alienate, sell or mortgage property, settle claims, give receipts or releases, sign guaranties, draw, accept or endorse bills of exchange, execute or endorse promissory notes, organize or subscribe for stock in corporations, make loans, open credits, petition for bankruptcy, prove claims in bankruptcy, or substitute the power in favor of another.

Powers of attorney executed in a foreign country in the language and form there employed will be valid in Brazil if duly legalized before a Brazilian consul, and translated by a sworn public translator in Brazil. It is preferable, however, to put such powers in the form customarily used in Brazil.

Powers of attorney are executed in Brazil as public instruments entered by a notary on his books, or as private instruments signed by the grantor who must acknowledge his signature before a notary. See topics Acknowledgments; Notaries Public.

Besides the purpose and extent of the powers conferred, a private instrument should specify the city and state where it is drawn up, the date, the name of the grantor and the name and description of the grantee.

A power of attorney "em causa propria" (i.e., coupled with an interest) is irrevocable.

When the power is granted to more than one person, it will be considered as a successive power, the second grantee being authorized only in case the first named fails to act, unless otherwise specified, i.e., that all are to act jointly, or that any one may act alone.

Agency agreements are governed by Law 4886. Although parties may freely stipulate terms of their agency contracts, provisions must be included on conditions and general requirements of representation, identification of products subject to representation, period of representation, whether definite or indefinite, terms and time of payment for carrying out representation, zone in which representation will be exercised, whether such exclusivity is partially or wholly guaranteed and for what period, and restrictions, if any, to zone exclusivity. Provision for indemnity due to agent upon principal's terminating agreement without just cause is also required. This indemnity must not be less than one-twelfth of compensation earned during representation. Agency agreements may be terminated for just cause. Law 4886 defines just cause to be agent's negligence, agent's breach of contract, acts of agent damaging to principal and conviction of agent for serious criminal offense. Fixed term agreements terminate on date provided; indefinite term agreements are terminable even without just cause after first six months. In all cases, except when other provisions for termination have been agreed upon, service of notice prior to termination is obligatory. If principal fails to serve such notice, compensation is due agent amounting to one third of earnings accrued during last three months just prior to termination. Statute of Limitations for actions arising from this law is five years.

RECORDS:

Many important documents must be in the form of "public instruments," executed upon the books of a notary, which books are public records. In addition to the notarial archives, there are registries in charge of public officials (registrars) for the recording of deeds, mortgages and other documents for authentication and conservation and to establish their validity against third parties.

All deeds and mortgages should be registered, an "extract" being entered on the registrar's books, and many other instruments are sometimes registered, such as leases and powers of attorney.

Law 6015 of Dec. 31, 1965 regulates following registries: (a) Natural persons; (b) juridical persons; (c) deeds and documents; (d) real property. Detailed requirements are provided by law for each of said registries. Documents must strictly comply with legal provisions or will not be recorded by public officer.

Law 8934 of Nov. 18, 1994 regulates Public Registry of Commercial Companies which is in charge of archiving documents related to constitution, amendment, dissolution and liquidation of commercial enterprises and corporations organized according to local laws; and acts related to foreign commercial enterprises authorized to operate in Brazil, and update such information.

SALES:

(Civil Code, arts. 1122-1163; Com. Code, arts. 191-220).

A contract of sale, whereby one party agrees to transfer the title to specified goods in consideration of payment by the other party of a certain price in money, becomes binding as soon as the parties agree on the goods and the price. The determination of the price may be left to third parties or to market quotations at a specified time and place.

As a general rule, the transfer of title is effected upon delivery, actual or constructive. However, where the sale is made subject to the satisfaction of the purchaser, unless stipulated to be an absolute sale subject to revocation, title does not pass with delivery, and the purchaser holds the goods as bailee until he manifests his acceptance thereof or the period for such manifestation expires.

A sale by sample imports a warranty of quality corresponding to sample. A sale of goods which are customarily sampled, tested, weighed or measured before acceptance will be considered a sale to the satisfaction of the purchaser.

See Topical Index in front part of this volume.

SALES . . . *continued*

A contract of sale made with the intent on the part of the purchaser to resell or rent the goods for profit, where one of the parties to the sale is a merchant, or with the intent to use them as supplies in his business, is governed by the Commercial Code, which contains certain special provisions and unlike the Civil Code requires a judicial demand in order to place the purchaser in default. This code recognizes a conditional sales contract wherein title does not pass until performance of the condition. Besides sales by sample, the Commercial Code recognizes a sale by description of goods of standard qualities, questions as to the quality tendered to be decided by arbitration.

Special protection is accorded purchasers of lots on installments. Agreements to sell real estate may be recorded and the courts may adjudicate the property to the purchaser if the seller refuses to execute the final conveyance. (Decree-Law 58 of Dec. 10, 1937; Decree 3079 of Sept. 15, 1938; Code Civ. Proc., arts. 345-359). Likewise there is special protection for sellers of personal property on installments on conditional sales. (Decree-Law 1027 of Jan. 2, 1939; Code Civ. Proc., arts. 343, 344).

SEALS:

Neither individual nor corporate seals are used in Brazil.

SEQUESTRATION:

(Civil Procedure Code, Arts. 813 to 825. See, however, topic Statutes.)

Precautionary measures may be taken to secure the interests of the parties in litigation: such as attachment (arresto) and sequestration (sequestro).

Attachment may be ordered by judge when: (a) Debtor without fixed domicile intends to leave or defaults on his obligations; (b) debtor who has domicile leaves or tries to alienate his property, movable or immovable.

In all cases there must be written proof of such debt.

Sequestration may be ordered by judge on: (a) Movable or immovable property if that property is in litigation; (b) gains of revindicated immovable property if defendant wastes them; (c) community property (bens do casal) in case of separation or annulment if spouse wastes it.

SHIPPING:

Decree 87648 of Sept. 24, 1982 establishes regulations for maritime traffic. Such Decree contains general principles governing ocean, river and lake shipping; it also contains regulations on navigation safety and security in Brazilian waters, registration of vessels.

Decree-Law 1098 of Mar. 25, 1970 extends national sovereignty up to a distance of 200 marine miles, measured from low tide marks. However, freedom of navigation and aeronavigation is not affected by dispositions of law.

Law 7652 of Feb. 3, 1988 regulates registration of maritime property for purposes of establishing nationality, validity, security and disclosure of ownership of vessels, among others. Registration of ownership of vessels is basically granted to Brazilians by birth or companies organized under local law, domiciled in country and managed and controlled by Brazilians by birth, with at least 60% of capital held by Brazilians by birth.

According to law all liens on Brazilian vessels must be registered in order to be valid against third parties.

STATUTES:

The laws of Brazil are based principally upon the Portuguese laws which were continued in force in Brazil in 1822 when the country proclaimed its independence from Portugal and established the Empire of Brazil. The chief codification of these laws was the "Philippine Code," named for Philip II and Philip III of Spain who were also Kings of Portugal when the code was compiled. This code was based largely upon the Roman law.

The Civil Code which became effective on Jan. 1, 1917, continues in force with minor changes, but the Commercial Code adopted in 1850 has been considerably amended and supplemented by a number of special laws.

Other codes include: Code of Civil Procedure (Law 5869 of Jan. 11, 1973); Criminal Code (Decree-Law 2848 of Dec. 7, 1940); Code of Criminal Procedure (Decree-Law 3689 of Oct. 3, 1941); Consolidation of Labor Laws (Decree-Law 5452 of May 1, 1943).

TAXATION:

(Const. arts. 145-162; Tax Code, Law 5172 of Oct. 25, 1966 as am'd).

Constitution and Tax Code control power to raise and collect revenues by Republic, States, Municipalities and Federal District. They allocate different kinds of taxes at each level. Republic has exclusive power to tax importation and exportation of goods, income and earnings of any nature, industrialized products, rural real property, large fortunes, transactions of credit, foreign exchange and insurance, transactions with instruments and securities. States and Federal District may tax property transfers "mortis causa", transactions related to circulation of goods, rendering of services of interstate and intermunicipal transportation and of communication, ownership of motor vehicles, state income tax up to 5% of Republic income tax. Municipalities may tax urban real property, "inter vivos" property transfer, retail sales of liquid and gaseous fuels, except diesel oil, services not taxed by States. Code describes taxes to be imposed by federal, state and municipal jurisdictions, and provides rates of procedure, tax administration and collection.

Tax on Distribution of Goods and Services.—(Const. art. 155-b; Decree-Law 406 of Dec. 31, 1968 as am'd). This State tax is payable at all stages of distribution, from manufacturer to final consumer; basis for assessment is added value with some exceptions. Tax is also payable for rendering of interstate and intermunicipal transportation and communications services. Decree-Law 406 establishes general rules applicable to tax. All states and territories within same economic region are required to agree upon uniform exemptions and tax concessions.

Tax on Industrial Products.—(Const. art. 153, IV, Law 4502 of Nov. 30, 1964 as am'd, and regulations, Decree 87981 of Dec. 23, 1982 as am'd). This Federal tax is levied on numerous national and imported industrial products. Former are taxed upon leaving manufacturing plant; latter upon importation. Rate is ad valorem and varies according to product. There are many exceptions, among them, products for exportation. Tax credit equivalent to excise taxes applicable on exports is allowed against excise tax paid on domestic sales of industrial products. Rebate on income tax applicable to interest, paid abroad by exporter is also allowed. (Law 8402 of Jan. 8, 1992).

Tax on Financial Operations (I.O.F.).—(Decree 1783 of Apr. 18, 1980 as am'd, Law 8033 of Apr. 12, 1990 as am'd). Federal tax levied on credit, insurance, exchange and securities transactions. Rates vary according to transaction.

Income Tax.—(Decree 1041 of Jan. 11, 1994; Law 8981 of Jan. 20, 1995 as am'd, Law 9069 of June 29, 1995, Laws 9249 and 9250 of Dec. 26, 1995). Individuals residing or domiciled in Brazil, individual concerns, and associations and corporations domiciled in Brazil are taxed on their worldwide income. Said concerns and corporations must be registered in special registry kept by Income Tax Bureau and no industrial or commercial establishment may operate if not registered. Individual taxpayers are registered in "Cadaster of Individual Taxpayers." Persons and corporations residing or domiciled abroad not present in Brazil 12 months or residents who are absent for at least 12 months are taxpayers for Brazilian source incomes only. With income return, individual residents must file inventory of their personal and real property.

I. Individual.—Individuals are subject to tax on all income and capital gains. Tax becomes payable on monthly basis, as income and capital gains are received. Gross income does not include insurance and retirement payments, indemnifications, workers compensation, inheritance and donations, among others. Income tax is not collected from retirement gains (inactivity) up to limit when taxpayer is over 65 years of age.

Deductions are allowed monthly and annually; among monthly deductions for withholding tax are: alimony and child support, amount of R$90 (reals) per dependent, social security expenses; among annual deductions for calculating tax are: health and medical expenses, donations and charitable contributions, monthly deductions.

Rates.—Tax on individuals is payable monthly at rates of 15% and 25% on net income.

Withholding.—Payors of salaries in excess of certain amount a month, commissions, brokerage fees and other remuneration for services rendered must withhold certain portions thereof and turn them over to Treasury. Payment will be a credit toward applicable taxes.

II. Juridical Persons and Individual Organized Concerns.—These entities, which include corporations, are subject to tax on gross income less admissible deductions.

Gross income does not include among others, income from certain real property notes of Banco Nacional de Habitacao and real property credit corporations; gains from readjustment of certain Treasury bonds and certain other readjustments; dividends and profits subject to tax in hands of distributing corporations, which then must be kept separate by distributee corporation.

Deductions include among others: taxes actually paid, except income tax; reserve for bad debts, severance pay and indemnities for workmen; certain scientific or technological expenses; payments of royalties; bonuses to employees; payments to private pension funds for employees; certain charitable contributions.

All corporations are required to create Guarantee Fund for severance payments equal to 8% of monthly remuneration paid to employees.

Official Determination.—In case of lack of accounts, or non-reliable accounts, Treasury may calculate profits by establishing percentage of gross income, which can never be lower than 15% of such income, as taxable profits. Such profits are subject to taxation at rate of 25% monthly plus additional 10% rate as stipulated by law, applicable to profits earned over certain annual limit.

Other Rules.—There are special provisions for habitual sales of real property; parcellation of land; agricultural and livestock concerns; exploitation of foreign movie films; insurance and capitalization activities; sea and air transportation concerns and builders.

Social Contributions.—Deductible from taxable income is 18% social contribution.

Participation Fund.—Companies must deposit percentage of their annual gross income plus percentage of their income tax liability in fund administered by Federal Savings Bank.

Rates.—Income tax is calculated on actual or presumed profits as stipulated by law. Corporations and other juridical persons and individual organized concerns pay monthly 15%. Surtax is levied on profits exceeding certain amount at 10% rate, as stipulated by law.

Public utility companies, with profits not in excess of 12% of capital, pay 17%. Agricultural and livestock companies pay taxes at reduced rate of 6%. Certain other public utility companies, engaged in public transportation are also subject to lower 6% tax rate.

Investment Incentives.—For purposes of promoting economic development, country has been divided into several geographic regions, each under supervision of a separate autonomous governmental agency (Superintendencies), in order to implement resource utilization programs, including tax deductions and other incentives to industrial, agricultural, and other concerns operating in region, which are stipulated in laws embodying "development plans," which are revised regularly. For each region, plan in force for particular years should be consulted.

Law 8661 of June 3, 1993 grants tax incentives under industrial and technical development program to industrial companies involved in technical development activities. Law 8685 of July 30, 1993 grants tax deductions for ten years to investments in motion picture productions.

Major Fiscal Incentives for Producer-Seller and Trading Companies, Under Trading Companies Law.—Departure of merchandise from producer-seller establishment under conditions stipulated in Art. 1 of Decree-Law 1248 of Nov. 29, 1972, assures producer-seller right to tax benefits granted by law as an incentive to exportation. (Art. 1 of Decree 8402 of Jan. 8, 1992). These incentives will be calculated using sales price of product, plus freight and insurance costs to warehouse, if producer-seller is responsible for such expenses. (Id., Art. 2).

Trading companies are subject to income tax at rate of 6% on export sales. (Art. 4 of Decree-Law 1248 of Nov. 29, 1972, Decree-Law 2134 of June 27, 1984 and Decree 2413 of Feb. 10, 1988).

TAXATION . . . *continued*

If manufactured products being exported are insured by a Brazilian insurance company or transported by a Brazilian transportation company, cost of such insurance and transportation should be added to export price (thus increasing fiscal incentives given to trading companies). (Art. 4, Para. 2 of Decree-Law 1248 of Nov. 29, 1972 as am'd). Decree-Law 1894 of Dec. 16, 1981 as am'd grants tax incentives for trading companies that export manufactured products of Brazilian manufacture acquired on domestic market, against payment in convertible foreign currency, as follows: Credit for tax on manufactured products levied on acquisition of products and reimbursement of tax on manufactured products paid on domestic market.

Free Zone.—Manaus has been declared a free zone and enjoys exemption from import-export duties under Decree-Law 288 of Feb. 28, 1967 and Regulations issued under Decree 61244 of Aug. 28, 1967. Same Decree-Law creates SUFRAMA (Superintendency of Manaus Free Zone), a governmental agency in charge of administration of installations and services in free zone.

Export Processing Zones.—(D.L. 2452 of July 29, 1988 as am'd regulated by Decree 846 of June 25, 1993). Law authorizes establishment of export processing zones. Such zones are free-trade areas where companies operating there have tax incentives and no control on foreign exchange transactions. Location of each zone depends on interest of States and Municipalities.

III. Individuals or Corporations Abroad.—In general a withholding tax of 15% applies to any taxable income paid or credited to Brazilian residents living 12 months or more abroad. Income and capital gains earned by individuals or corporations residing or domiciled abroad are taxed at source at 15% or 25%, except when double taxation treaty provides for lower rate.

Movie Films.—Revenues derived from exhibition of motion pictures are subject to withholding tax of 15%.

Branches.—In case of branches of foreign corporations, if income is reinvested in Brazil in their industry, increasing corporate capital, withholding tax is 15%.

IV. Interest paid by legal entities to individuals is subject to 15% withholding tax, when those interests exceed minimum designated amount per month, such tax being considered anticipation of tax to be due upon filing of income tax declaration. Rules for withholding and rates of withholding tax may vary depending on type, duration, amount and conditions of loan, in following cases: Income from fixed income securities; bills of exchange with acceptance of financial institutions, fixed from deposit certificates and debentures; interest received by individuals from Treasury Bonds and other public bonds, bank deposits with fixed maturity, debentures and certain other documents.

V. Interest, etc. from Registered Securities Payable to Resident of Country.—When recipient of income from registered documents is a corporation or legal entity, 15% withholding tax applies on distribution of profits and interest on founder's shares.

VI. Income in Foreign Money or in Kind.—Income in kind must be appraised in money as of date of receipt. Income in foreign money must be converted to national currency at rate in effect on date when paid or credited or at rate in which transaction was actually made.

See also topic Foreign Investment.

Inheritance Tax.—States have power to tax transfers of property causa mortis. States cannot establish tax in excess of 4% of value of real property being transferred.

Real Property Transfer Tax.—Taxation of transfer of real property is attribution of States of Federative Republic of Brazil. Individual States must enact laws regulating this matter. Any acquisition of property or right is taxed at rate which varies from 0.5% to 4%. Tax is due from person acquiring property or right.

License taxes are usually collected from offices, shops and factories. In Federal District, tax is imposed at rate of 8% of rental value of premises occupied; for certain types of business, it ranges as high as 14% and for professional offices as low as 4%.

TRADEMARKS AND TRADENAMES:

(Const. art. 5 XXIX; Law 9279 of May 14, 1996).

Those signs distinctive and susceptible of graphic representation can be registered as marks, except those prohibited by law. Following, among others, cannot be registered as marks: national, foreign or international denominations, signs and emblems; expression, figures, designs or any other sign contrary to morals and good habits, freedom of religion, etc; names, signatures, family names and portraits of persons without their consent; title of literary, artistic or scientific works protected by copyright without permission of owner; technical names used in industry, science or art related to product or service to which such names refer; denominations describing products or services that are to be protected by trademarks or their qualities, nature, weight, value, etc., unless they are sufficiently distinctive; colors and their denominations unless they are combined in particular and distinguishing manner; geographical names if their use may suggest origin; imitation or reproduction of collective and certification marks; total or partial reproduction or imitation of trademarks, similar or related goods and services which may be confused or related to it. Protection of well-known registered mark in Brazil is extended to all classes even though there is no special declaration of notoriety. Protection is granted to international well-known marks not registered in Brazil. Law recognizes prior bona fide users right. Registration is granted for ten years from registration date and is renewable. Registration can be cancelled for nonuse for consecutive five year period as indicated by law. Sanctions imposed for infringement of law are imprisonment for three to 12 months or fines.

Caveat: Law enters in force on May 15, 1997.

Franchising.—(Law 8955 of Dec. 5, 1994).

Law regulates business franchising contracts which are defined as system by which franchisor assigns to franchisee right to use trademark or patent and right to exclusive or semi-exclusive distribution of products and services; and in some cases right to use business administration and implementation technology, owned or developed by franchisor without employment link. Assignment is for direct or indirect remuneration.

Information which must be contained in franchise offer is established by law.

TREATIES:

Double Taxation Treaties.—Brazil has signed various treaties for avoidance of double taxation. The National Revenue Code provides, in art. 98, that "the international treaties and conventions revoke or modify the internal tax legislation and must be observed by subsequent internal legislation". Normative Ruling SFR 070 of Oct. 15, 1982 refers to applicability of double taxation treaties with reference to interest payments remitted abroad. Hence, such treaties prevail over internal rules. Treaties are in force with following countries:

Sweden, approved by Legislative Decree No. 33, of Aug. 2, 1966.
Japan, approved by Legislative Decree No. 43, of Nov. 23, 1967.
Portugal, approved by Legislative Decree No. 59, of Aug. 17, 1971.
France, approved by Legislative Decree No. 87, of Nov. 27, 1971.
Belgium, approved by Legislative Decree No. 76, of Dec. 1, 1972.
Finland, approved by Legislative Decree No. 86, of Dec. 5, 1972.
Denmark, approved by Legislative Decree No. 90, of Nov. 28, 1974.
Austria, approved by Legislative Decree No. 95, of Nov. 10, 1975.
West Germany, approved by Legislative Decree No. 92, of Nov. 5, 1975.
Spain, approved by Legislative Decree No. 62, of Aug. 7, 1975.
Italy, approved by Legislative Decree No. 77, of Dec. 5, 1979.
Luxembourg, approved by Legislative Decree No. 78, of Dec. 5, 1979 as am'd.
Norway, approved by Decree-86710 of Dec. 9, 1981.
Argentina, approved by Decree 87976 of Dec. 12, 1982.
Canada, approved by Legislative Decree No. 28, of Nov. 12, 1985.
Ecuador, approved by Legislative Decree No. 4, of Mar. 20, 1986.
Czechoslovakia, approved by Legislative Decree No. 11 of May 5, 1990.
Hungary, approved by Legislative Decree No. 13 of June 22, 1990.
Netherlands, approved by Legislative Decree No. 60 of Dec. 17, 1990.
Philippines, approved by Legislative Decree No. 198 of Oct. 1, 1991.
Republic of Korea, approved by Legislative Decree No. 205 of Oct. 7, 1991.
Republic of India, approved by Legislative Decree No. 214 of Nov. 12, 1991.
People's Republic of China, approved by Legislative Decree No. 85 of Nov. 24, 1992.

Treaties relating to Negotiable Instruments.—Brazil has adhered to Geneva Conventions on uniform laws governing negotiable instruments. (Approved by Legislative Decree No. 54, of Sept. 8, 1964.) There are three conventions which were signed by various States, including Brazil. They are: The Convention relating to the Uniform Law on Bills of Exchange and Promissory Notes; The Convention of Conflict of Laws in relation to Bills of Exchange and Promissory Notes; The Convention on Stamps on Bills of Exchange and Promissory Notes (this latter convention was also signed by U.K.).

Bustamante Code.—Brazil was signatory to Convention on Private International Law, known as Bustamante Code, which was approved by various American states in Havana, Cuba, on Feb. 20, 1928.

Extradition Treaties.—Brazil has signed following bilateral extradition treaties governing extradition of persons wanted for common crimes: Treaty with Bolivia (Decree No. 9,920, of July 8, 1942); Treaty with Chile (Decree No. 1,888, of Aug. 17, 1937); Treaty with Colombia (Decree No. 6,330, of Sept. 25, 1940); Treaty with Ecuador (Decree No. 2,950, of Aug. 8, 1938); Treaty with Italy (Decree No. 21,936 of Oct. 11, 1932); Additional Protocol with Italy (Decree No. 2,574, of Apr. 18, 1938); Treaty with Lithuania (Decree No. 4,528 of Aug. 16, 1939); Treaty with Mexico (Decree No. 2,535, of Mar. 22, 1938); Treaty with Paraguay (Decree No. 16,925, of May 27, 1925); Treaty with Switzerland (Decree No. 23,996, of Mar. 13, 1934); Treaty with Uruguay (Decree No. 13,414, of Jan. 15, 1919); Additional Protocol with Uruguay (Decree No. 4,539, of Feb. 4, 1922); Treaty with Belgium (Legislative Decree No. 26, of June 19, 1956); and Treaty with U.S.A. (Legislative Decree No. 13, of June 18, 1964).

Treaties relating to Aerial and Maritime Navigation.—

Aerial Navigation.—Decree No. 80,977, of Dec. 12, 1977, which brought into effect Agreement on Air Transport with Government of Netherlands; Decree No. 80,486, of Oct. 4, 1977, which brought into effect protocol relating to amendment to Art. 56 of International Civil Aviation Convention, signed in Vienna on July 7, 1971; Decree No. 80,487, of Oct. 4, 1977, which brought into effect protocol relating to amendment to art. 48(a) of International Civil Aviation Convention, signed in Rome on Dec. 1, 1964; Decree No. 76,325, of Sept. 23, 1975, which gave effect to Rules and Recommendations of seventh edition of Schedule 9 of International Civil Aviation Convention, relating to air transport facilities; Decree No. 72,383, of June 20, 1973, which brought into effect Convention for the Repression of Illicit Acts against Security of Civil Aviation; Decree No. 70,218, of Feb. 29, 1972, which brought into effect Agreement on Regular Air Transport with Uruguay; Decree No. 69,210, of Sept. 16, 1971, which gave effect in Brazil to Amendment No. 7 to Schedule 9 of International Civil Aviation Convention, concerning facilities; Decree No. 68,237, of Feb. 15, 1971, which brought into effect Agreement on Air Transport with Switzerland; Decree No. 67,697, of Dec. 3, 1970, which brought into effect Agreement on Air Transport with Mexico; Decree No. 66,520, of Apr. 30, 1970, which brought into effect Convention relating to Offences and Certain Other Acts Committed on Board Aircraft, concluded in Tokyo on Sept. 14, 1963 and signed by Brazil on Feb. 28, 1969; Decree No. 66,237, of Feb. 19, 1970, which brought into effect Agreement on Air Transport with Denmark; Decree No. 66,238, of Feb. 19, 1970, which brought into effect Agreement on Air Transport with Norway; Decree No. 65,813, of Dec. 8, 1969, which brought into effect Agreement on Air Transport with Sweden; Decree No. 64,990, of Aug. 13, 1969, which brought into effect Amendment to Art. 50(a) of International Civil Aviation Convention; Decree No. 64,832, of July 16, 1969, which gave effect to Rules and Recommendations of sixth edition of Schedule 9 to International Civil Aviation Convention, relating to air transport facilities; Decree-Law No. 601, of May 29, 1969, which approved air agreements with Denmark, Norway and Sweden, signed in Rio de Janeiro on Mar. 18, 1969; Decree No. 60,868, of June 16, 1967, which brought into effect Regular Air Transport Agreement with France; Decree No. 60,967, of July 7, 1967, which brought into effect Complementary Convention to the Warsaw Convention for Unification of Certain Rules relating to International Air Transport Effected by

See Topical Index in front part of this volume.

TREATIES . . . *continued*
Non-Contractual Carriers; Decree No. 60,908, of June 30, 1967, which brought into effect Agreement on Regular Air Transport with Argentine; Decree No. 54,203, of Aug. 24, 1964, which gave effect in Brazil to Rules and Recommendations contained in text of Schedule 9 to International Civil Aviation Convention which governs air transport facilities; Decree No. 54,173, of Aug. 21, 1964, which brought into effect Agreement on Regular Air Transport with Federal Republic of Germany; Decree No. 56,463, of June 15, 1965, which brought into effect Protocol amending Convention for the Unification of Certain Rules relating to International Air Transport; Decree No. 225 of Council of Ministers, dated Nov. 24, 1961, which gave effect in Brazil to Rules and Recommendations contained in Schedule 9 to International Civil Aviation Convention which governs air transport facilities; Decree No. 20,384, of Jan. 11, 1946, which brought into effect Provisional Agreement on International Civil Aviation, concluded in Chicago on Dec. 7, 1944 on occasion of International Conference on Civil Aviation, and signed by Brazil in Washington on May 29, 1945.

Maritime Navigation.—Decree No. 80,672, of Nov. 7, 1977, which brought into effect Convention for International Maritime Traffic facilities, signed in London on Apr. 9, 1965; Decree No. 80,106, of Aug. 9, 1977, which brought into effect Agreement on Maritime Transport with Poland; Decree No. 80,068, of Aug. 2, 1977, which brought into effect Convention on International Regulations to Avoid Collisions at Sea, signed in London on Oct. 20, 1972; Decree No. 79,279, of Feb. 15, 1977, which brought into effect Convention on Maritime Transport with German Democratic Republic; Decree No. 78,621, of Oct. 25, 1976, which brought into effect Convention on Maritime Transport with Uruguay; Decree No. 77,630, of May 18, 1976, which brought into effect Maritime Agreement with France; Decree No. 76,566, of Nov. 6, 1975, which brought into effect Convention on Maritime Transport with Mexico; Decree No. 74,999, of Nov. 27, 1974, which brought into effect Convention on Maritime Transport with Peru; Decree No. 74,600 of Sept. 24, 1974, which brought into effect Convention on the Entry of Nuclear Vessels into Brazilian Waters and their Stay in Brazilian ports, entered into with Federal Republic of Germany; Decree No. 72,676 of Aug. 22, 1973, which brought into effect Agreement on Maritime Transport with Soviet Union; Decree No. 66,103, of Jan. 22, 1970, which brought into effect International Convention on Cargo Lines, signed between Brazil and other countries in London on Apr. 5, 1966; Decree No. 65,441, of Oct. 13, 1969, which brought into effect Preliminary Protocol on Permanent Navigation on Bolivian and Brazilian Rivers Forming Part of Amazon River System; Decree No. 19,647, of Sept. 22, 1945, which brought into effect Agreement on Principles relating to Continuation of the Combined Control of the Merchant Navies, signed in London Aug. 5, 1944; Decree No. 351, of Oct. 1, 1935, which brought into effect International Convention for the Unification of Certain Rules relating to Maritime Guarantees and Mortgages, and appropriate Protocol, signed between Brazil and various countries in Brussels on Apr. 10, 1926.

Treaties on Intellectual Property and Industrial Property.—Brazil is Member State of Convention signed in Stockholm on July 14, 1967 under which World Intellectual Property Organization (WIPO) was set up.

Brazil became signatory to Paris Convention Dec. 31, 1929 (by Decree No. 19,056). Brazil signed last revision of this Convention (Stockholm on July 14, 1967) provisionally for five years as from 1970 and only ratified it on Apr. 8, 1975 (by Decree No. 75,572). On finally ratifying Paris Convention, however, Brazil excluded from ratification application of arts. 1 to 12 of Stockholm revision. Accordingly, as far as Brazil is concerned, arts. 1 to 12 of The Hague revision of 1925 remain in force.

The Berne Convention was last revised in Paris on July 24, 1971. Revision was ratified and promulgated in Brazil by Decree No. 75,699 of May 6, 1975.

Brazil has also signed Strasbourg Agreement on International Classification of Patents which sought to harmonize classification of patents to give developing countries easier access to modern technology, and Universal Convention on Authors' Rights, revised in Paris on July 24, 1971, for protection of literary, artistic and scientific works.

Brazil has also signed Patent Cooperation Treaty, main object of which is to permit patent applications to be filed in standard form with automatic and simultaneous validity in some or all countries that have signed Treaty, at option of applicant.

Brazil is member of Multilateral Trade Negotiations, The Uruguay Round, Final Act, Marrakesh, Apr. 15, 1994 and Agreement Establishing the World Trade Organization, Marrakesh, Apr. 15, 1994.

It is also member of Latin American Integration Association (LAIA) 1980 and Latin American Economic System (SELA), created in Panama 1975. Brazil approved Inter-American Conventions: on legal regime of powers of attorney to be used abroad, on international commercial arbitration, on Letters Rogatory, Panama, Jan. 30, 1975. Inter-American Conventions on: proof of and information on foreign law, on conflicts of laws concerning commercial companies, on extraterritorial validity of foreign judgments and arbitral awards, on conflicts of laws concerning checks, Montevideo, May 8, 1979, Asunción Treaty, signed on Mar. 26, 1991 creating southern common market "MERCOSUR."

TRUSTS:

(Civil Code, arts. 1424-1431, 1733-1738).

While Brazilian law does not contemplate trusts of the sort which under English and American law are enforced by courts of equity, the civil code provides that real property or money may be transferred by deed or will to provide for the payment of income to the beneficiary for a specified period. In case the grantee fails to pay, the beneficiary may bring action to obtain instalments in default and security for future instalments under penalty of rescission of the contract. More than one beneficiary may be named and provision may be made that the survivors shall receive the share of a beneficiary who dies. Where the conveyance is made by one person for the benefit of another the payments are exempt from seizure under execution.

The only trust specifically mentioned in Brazilian law is the testamentary trust, comprising the devise of property to one person for life with remainder to another.

USURY: See topic Interest.

WILLS:

(Civil Code, arts. 1626-1769).

With certain exceptions relating to soldiers and sailors, wills must be either public, sealed or private as described below. Joint wills are prohibited, whether simultaneous, reciprocal or otherwise dependent one upon the other.

A public will must be written by a public official upon his records, pursuant to declarations made by the testator in Portuguese before five witnesses, and read in the presence of and signed by or for the testator and by the witnesses and official.

A sealed will must be written by the testator or by another at his request, and signed by the testator or, if he is not able to sign, by the person who wrote the will for him, and delivered by the testator in the presence of at least five witnesses to the official (notary), the testator declaring that it is his will and that he wishes it approved. The official must thereupon, in the presence of all, draw up a note of approval, which must begin immediately after the last word of the will, if space permits, and must be read by the official and signed by him, the witnesses, and the testator if he is able, or for him by one of the witnesses. The notary must then seal and stitch the will after finishing the instrument of approval and deliver it to the testator. A sealed will may be in a foreign language. Such a will cannot be made by a testator unable to read.

A private will must be written and signed by the testator and read to and signed by five witnesses. It may be written in a foreign language understood by the witnesses. At least three of the witnesses must be produced in order to probate a private will.

By a codicil (which in Brazil means a mere memorandum of last wishes), written, dated and signed by the testator, without witnesses, he may make valid provision regarding his burial, charitable gifts of small amount, the disposition of personal furniture, clothing or jewelry of inconsiderable value, and may appoint or substitute executors.

A testator leaving lineal descendants, parents or grandparents cannot dispose of more than one-half of his estate, except in certain special cases, the other half passing to his descendants, or if none, to his other necessary heirs. The testator may, however, provide that the portion of his estate which he cannot alienate shall be converted into property of a different sort, shall not be divided or alienated by the heirs, or that property passing to a female heir shall not be subject to the control of her husband.

Testator may dispose of individual property without providing for surviving wife or husband. (Civil Code, arts. 1721-5).

See also topic Aliens.

BULGARIA LAW DIGEST

(The following is a list of all Topics, including cross-references, covered in this Digest.)

BULGARIA LAW DIGEST

Revised for 1997 edition by

VASSIL BRESKOVSKI, LL.M., in association with VLADIMIR PETROV, Professor of Law, Sofia University, Bulgaria.

(C.P.C. indicates Civil Procedure Code. L.O.C. indicates Law on Obligations and Contracts. L.C. indicates Law on Commerce.)

INTRODUCTION:

Bulgaria was one of first former communist countries in Eastern Europe to adopt new constitution in July 1991. Constitution established principle of separation of powers between legislature, judiciary, executive, and marked beginning of comprehensive market oriented reform of legal system. In 1991, Bulgaria was accepted as member to Council of Europe, and bilateral trade agreement between U.S. and Bulgaria was also concluded. In 1993, Bulgaria and European Union and its member states signed association agreement.

ABSENTEES:

Persons may delegate authority to any person of full capacity. Before court absentee may be represented only by attorney at law, guardian, close family member, or by person who is joint party to absentee in proceedings.

If person domiciled or having property in Bulgaria disappears and is absent from last known residence without being heard from or after diligent inquiry, court must appoint representative to take charge of his or her estate. Petition for appointment of representative may be filed by any person who would be party in interest were absentee deceased or by public prosecutor. If person is absent for more than a year, his or her heirs may ask court to declare him or her missing. See also topic Death (Presumption of and Action of).

ACKNOWLEDGMENTS:

Acknowledgments are to be taken before Bulgarian notary public, whose signature, if document is to be used abroad, must be certified by Ministry of Justice and further by Consular Department of Ministry of Foreign Affairs. Acknowledgment abroad may be taken before Bulgarian consular or diplomatic authorities.

Bulgaria is not party to Hague Convention of 1961 on Abolishing the Requirement of Legalization for Foreign Public Documents, or to Hague Conventions for Civil Procedure of 1905 and 1954.

ACTIONS:

Civil Procedure Code of 1952 sets forth rules for bringing action.

Each person, individual or legal entity may sue and be sued. Bulgarian State does not enjoy jurisdictional immunity within territory of the country. Foreign states and citizens are bound by judgments of Bulgarian courts if they have started case, and if case concerns their enterprises or real property in country. Claims against Bulgarian state are brought against Minister of Finance.

Only one form of civil action exists. All actions are commenced by filing statement of claim with court of justice. Parties are not obliged to be represented by attorney at law. Person without capacity is represented by his or her trustee who exercises his or her powers.

Appropriate Forum.—Appropriate venue or proper district in which to bring action is generally place of residence of defendant: for natural person his or her domicile, and for legal entity—place of seat, i.e. place where its executive office is located. Nevertheless, there are exceptions to general rule, and in certain instances venue might be proper in: judicial district where tort was committed; judicial district where real property that is subject of action is situated; judicial district where corporation's branch is located.

Costs.—Losing party has to bear all costs, including lawyers' fees and reasonable expenses of winning party. Court costs and attorneys' fees are fixed by statute and are in proportion to litigated sum. Persons in difficult financial position may apply for legal aid.

AFFIDAVITS:

Written statement of facts sworn by deponent before authorized person to administer it is unknown in Bulgarian law. However, affidavit taken abroad like any written declaration or statement of facts may be used as evidence before courts.

AGENCY:

Under Bulgarian law representation is concept of acting on behalf and for benefit of principal. Three types of contracts define concept of agency: contract on mandate, contract of agency and contract of sale-purchase on commission.

ALIENS:

Basic human rights guaranteed by Constitution refer to aliens as well. Moreover, aliens have essentially same rights and duties as Bulgarian citizens except in relation to voting rights or free social security. See topics Corporations and Foreign Investment.

ALIMONY:

Spouses have mutual obligation to support each other. In case of divorce, if one of spouses is not able to support herself or himself and is not able to work, he or she has right to separate maintenance payments or alimony.

ANTI-TRUST LAWS:

See topic Monopolies and Trade Restraints.

APPEAL AND ERROR:

Decisions and definitions of trial courts are subject to appeal on legal and factual grounds. Person may also resort to court for purpose of obtaining review of administrative order. However, arbitration awards are not appealable. (art. 36[4] of Law on International Commercial Arbitration).

ARBITRATION AND AWARD:

Parties may agree to submit dispute to arbitration. They cannot take controversies concerning real property rights, alimony or employment relations to arbitration court. Arbitration agreement must be in writing. Arbitration awards are enforced after they have been declared executory by court.

In 1988, Bulgarian Parliament passed Law on International Commercial Arbitration which accepts principles and follows provisions of United Nations Commission on International Trade Law (UNCITRAL) Model Law. Provisions of law apply to arbitration in Bulgaria arising from commercial disputes where at least one of parties has residence in foreign country or is company with foreign participation in Bulgaria.

In 1990, permanent arbitration court at Bulgarian Chamber of Commerce was set up to hear commercial disputes between business entities. Board of Governors of Chamber adopted arbitration rules for court.

Bulgaria is party to New York Convention on Recognition and Enforcement of Foreign Arbitral Awards of 1958 and European Convention on International Commercial Arbitration of 1961 signed in Geneva.

ASSIGNMENTS:

Transfer of interest in right or property from one party to another is effected by agreement.

Assignment of Claim.—Creditors may transfer claims to third parties without consent of debtor unless transfer is contrary to law, contractual stipulation or nature of obligation. Transfer is effective to debtor from time he or she has received notice of assignment. (art. 99 L.O.C.).

ASSOCIATIONS:

Association is nonprofit organization and is differentiated from business organization. Right to association is guaranteed by Constitution.

ATTACHMENT:

Attachment might be granted by court before judgment enters into force. Defendant's property might be taken into legal custody for payment of judgment in event judgment is rendered in plaintiff's favor.

ATTORNEYS AND COUNSELORS:

Lawyers in Bulgaria are attorneys at law or in-house legal counselors. Attorneys at law are fully licensed and can represent clients before courts.

Practicing lawyer must hold Bulgarian law degree. Beside Bulgarian law degree, attorneys at law are required to have at least six months of legal practice, to have passed Bar examination, and to have been admitted by one of Regional Bars.

AUTOMOBILES:

See topic Motor Vehicles.

BANKRUPTCY:

Bulgarian Parliament adopted modern bankruptcy law on July 26, 1994. Law is published in Durzhaven Vestnik No. 63 (1994) as amendment to Law on Commerce and is incorporated as c. 4 (Insolvency) in Law on Commerce of 1991.

Bankruptcy proceedings can be brought by or against state enterprise, as well as private business, but not against individuals in their noncommercial capacity. Law applies to all commercial entities except for certain state monopolies, such as defense plants, banks, insurance companies, State Savings Bank. (Art. 612).

Bulgarian bankruptcy regime follows generally established standards in permitting cases to be started by debtor or creditors. (Art. 625).

Debtor or creditors may initiate proceedings by filing petition in relevant district court where debtor has domicile. (Art. 613). No special bankruptcy courts are set up in Bulgaria.

Debtors must file for bankruptcy within 15 days of being insolvent, i.e. becoming unable to make payments. (Art. 626[1]). If debtor fails to do that, debtor can be held liable for damages caused to creditors because of delay. (Art. 627). Debtor must supplement petition with number of documents including list of creditors, debtor's obligations towards each one of them and estimate of debtor's assets. (Art. 628[1]).

Creditor must support petition with proofs about debtor's insolvency. (Art. 628[2]).

According to Art. 630, court holds hearing in order to decide whether debtor is insolvent and whether to institute bankruptcy proceedings. Decision is publicized through court's register and publication in Durzhaven Vestnik. (Art. 622).

First meeting of creditors is held on date, defined by court. Meeting elects Creditors' Committee and syndic (trustee) and proposes syndic's appointment to court. (Art. 672).

Syndic is responsible for compiling inventory of bankrupt estate and for general management and representation of enterprise under bankruptcy for which syndic receives remuneration. Syndic's obligations are listed in Art. 658 of Law. Syndic is also supposed to perform duties with due diligence. (Art. 660).

See Topical Index in front part of this volume.

BANKRUPTCY . . . *continued*

Creditors are given 30 days after publication of court's decision for commencing bankruptcy proceedings to file claims. (Art. 685). Syndic has 14 days to prepare list of all creditors and their claims. (Art. 686).

Bulgarian law places less emphasis on reorganization than does bankruptcy law of U.S. In this respect, law follows European tradition and even contains provisions allowing court to declare bankruptcy immediately after bankruptcy proceedings have started. (See Art. 630[2]).

Law does not have extensive reorganization provisions.

In Art. 696 Law gives definition of restructuring plan, which may include rescheduling of debts, reorganization of enterprise, way of distribution of assets etc. Such plan can be proposed to court, by debtor, by syndic, by secured creditors holding more than one-third of secured debts, by unsecured creditors holding more than one-third of unsecured debts, by 20% of employees, or by shareholders holding one-third of capital in enterprise. (Art. 697). Plan is considered accepted by class of creditors if more than 50% percent have voted in favor. Court approves plan if it has been accepted by at least two classes of creditors. (Art. 705[2]).

While bankruptcy proceedings are in process, debtor and creditors may conclude compromise agreement, restoring debtor's solvency and terminating whole proceeding. (Art. 740).

If restructuring plan has not been proposed or proposed plan has not been approved, court declares debtor bankrupt. (Art. 710). Declaration of bankruptcy has following effects: control and right to dispose of assets is transferred to syndic; legal proceedings related to liquidation are to be started.

Syndic carries out liquidation pursuant to sections of Civil Procedure Code. (Art. 717). For that purpose syndic conducts sale by public auction.

If bankrupt's estate is liquidated, proceeds, left after satisfaction of secured creditors' claims, are distributed in following order of priority: (1) expenses incurred in administration of bankruptcy proceedings, including state bankruptcy tax, fees for syndic, predetermined support for bankrupt and family; (2) payments accruing from labor relations; (3) unpaid support of third parties; (4) payments to State Social Insurance Fund that have occurred a year before decision to start bankruptcy proceedings came into force; (5) back taxes, duties or other payments due to State. (Arts. 722 and 732).

In case of foreign court's decision declaring bankruptcy, Bulgaria recognizes such decision on basis of reciprocity, if it has been issued by court in country where debtor has domicile. (Art. 757).

BANKS AND BANKING:

Bank system consists of commercial banks formed as joint-stock companies.

Functions of Bulgarian National Bank (BNB) are defined in Law on Bulgarian National Bank passed by Parliament in 1991. Management Board of BNB consists of President and three Vice Presidents. All of them are appointed by Parliament. BNB issues legal tender of Republic of Bulgaria, treasury bills, organizes operations in foreign currency, grants licenses and supervises activities of commercial banks etc.

Law on Banks and Credit was passed by Parliament in 1992. BNB is vested with power to supervise commercial banks. License is needed to undertake banking activities. BNB must give its consent when bank acquires more than 10% of shares of company, when bank wants to open branch abroad or change its license. Law on Banks and Credit defines capital adequacy, liquidity and other requirements concerning banks.

BILLS AND NOTES:

See topic Commercial Paper.

CARTEL LAW:

See topic Monopolies and Trade Restraints.

CHATTEL MORTGAGE:

Equivalent of chattel mortgage in Bulgaria is most frequently used in buying high priced consumer goods such as large appliances and denotes lien on personal property as security for payment of money, or for performance of some other act.

In order to secure credit by banks, pledge on behalf of bank may be instituted on moveable goods purchased by pledgor. Moveable remains in possession of pledgor or third person. Contract should be in written form with notarized date.

Mortgage may also be established on ships. It should be entered in ship register. Maritime mortgage contracts owned by private persons must be in written form and signatures of parties must be notarized.

See also topic Sales, subhead Conditional Sale.

COMMERCIAL PAPER:

Bulgarian law distinguishes between bills of exchange and checks. Provisions on this matter are contained in c. XVIII of Law on Obligations and Contracts.

Bills of exchange are two types: "drawn bill of exchange" and "own bill of exchange" (promissory note).

Every bill of exchange may be transferred by endorsement.

Law of place of payment applies as far as obligations of promisor and maker are concerned. Obligations of other persons signed are determined by place where signatures were affixed.

Own bill of exchange (promissory note) must contain: express designation as "bill of exchange" in any language in which bill is drawn; unconditional promise to pay certain amount of money; time of payment; place of payment; name of payee; date and place of issue; signature of promisor.

Drawn bill of exchange must contain: express designation as "bill of exchange" in any language in which bill is drawn; unconditional order to pay certain amount of money; time of payment; place of payment; name of payee; date and place of issue; signature of maker.

Checks must be drawn on banker, who has funds of issuer on deposit subject to order according to express or implied contract entitling issuer to dispose of such funds through checks. Conflict of laws for checks is governed by same rules as those for bills of exchange.

COMMERCIAL REGISTER:

All business entities and circumstances related to their activities must be registered in one of commercial registers held by District Courts. Registration ends with court decision which has declarative and in some instances constitutive effect for merchants. Some court decision concerning incorporation of limited partnerships and corporations must be published in Durzaven Vestnik.

Commercial register is open to public for inspection.

CONSTITUTION AND GOVERNMENT:

Bulgaria is republic. In 1991, Grand National Assembly adopted new constitution which is based on doctrine of separation of powers.

National Assembly (Parliament).—Legislative power is vested in National Assembly, which consists of one house. Members of Parliament are elected for four year term.

President is highest representative of Bulgarian nation. He or she is elected by popular vote for five year term and can be reelected only once.

Council of Ministers is main governmental body responsible for implementation of domestic and foreign policy. Prime Minister and members of Cabinet are elected by National Assembly.

Judiciary.—Judicial power is vested in courts which are independent of any other authority. Supreme Court of Appeals and Supreme Administrative Court are highest courts in Bulgaria. See also topic Courts.

Constitutional Court consists of 12 judges. It provides interpretation of constitutional provisions and rules on constitutionality of laws and signed international treaties prior to their ratification.

Local Government.—Municipalities are governed by local self-governing bodies which are elected by citizens.

CONTRACTS:

Contract is agreement between two or more parties which creates rights and obligations to act or not to act. Essentials of valid contract are mutual consent, proper subject, parties competent to contract. Consideration is not required for validity of contract.

Contracts may be concluded as result of offer and acceptance. Offeror is bound for period stated by him or her in offer. If no period is stipulated, offers made in presence of another party or by telephone must be accepted immediately. Contract is considered concluded at time when declaration of acceptance reaches offeror.

Contract concluded by person without legal capacity (minors under 14 years of age, persons judicially declared to be fully incapacitated) are invalid. Minors over 14 years and persons with limited capacity may enter into contract with consent of guardian. Under Bulgarian law, legal entities have full capacity. Thus, doctrine of ultra vires liability is unknown.

Applicable Law.—Parties have choice as to applicable law. If parties have not stipulated that in contract following rules may apply: of vendor, donor etc., i.e. law of party whose performance is specific to contract. Bulgarian law is applied in public law interest or when conflict of laws cannot be solved.

Excuses for Nonperformance.—If performance becomes impossible by reason beyond power of one of parties, latter is not liable for breach of contract.

Government Contracts may be concluded only for purposes related to: fulfillment of international obligations; social policy; guaranteeing national security and strategic balances. Achievement of strategic, technological and market goals are also permissible for government contracts. Government contracts cannot exceed two-thirds of firm's capacity.

COPYRIGHT:

As of Aug. 1, 1993, new Law on Copyright and Related Rights (hereinafter "Law") published in Durzaven Vestnik No. 56/2 of June 29, 1993 came into effect. Law follows western European experience and is in conformity with Side Letter of the United States-Bulgarian Trade Agreement of 1991 and with European Union-Bulgaria Association Agreement of 1993.

Object entitled to copyright protection is any literary, scientific or artistic work in any form, including computer programs and data bases. At same time, Law delineates rights that can be exercised: economic and moral rights. Original owner of these rights is natural person who created the work. Copyright protection covers author's life plus 50 years after his or her death. For first time in Bulgarian law, rights of performing artists, of producers of phonograms, of radio and television broadcasting organizations are defined and protected. Law provides for civil and administrative liability if rights of author, performers, producer of phonograms and radio and television organizations are violated. Minister of Culture is authority to impose fines of up to 200,000 leva (US$7,000) for copyright and related rights infringement.

Bulgaria is party to Berne Convention for the Protection of Literary and Artistic Works (Paris Act 1971). In order to provide for better protection of intellectual property rights and to comply with Europe Agreement, in 1995 Bulgaria joined Rome Convention for the Protection of Performers, Producers of Phonograms and Broadcasting Organizations of 1961 and Geneva Phonograms Convention of 1973.

CORPORATIONS:

Bulgarian commercial law recognizes two main types of business corporations, public limited company (company limited by shares or joint stock company or publicly traded corporation) and company with limited liability (private limited company or closed corporation). Cooperatives are corporations like incorporated legal entities with liability limited to their capital. Nevertheless, they are not enumerated under legal notion of "business corporation".

CORPORATIONS . . . *continued*

Domestic legal and natural persons may equally form and participate in corporations. Under Law on Economic Activity and Protection of Foreign Investment of 1992, acquisition of foreign majority or unanimous foreign ownership is subject only to registration and only in few cases to requirement to obtain permission or license.

Corporation may be formed for any lawful business purpose. Though scope of activity for which corporation is formed must appear in articles of incorporation, legal capacity of corporation is unlimited. Thus, contract beyond scope of activity will not be invalid.

Public Limited Company (Aktzionerno drouzestvo "AD") may be promoted by two or more legal or natural persons, or only by State. AD is separate legal entity with liability limited to corporation's capital. Stated capital may not be less than 5,000,000 Bulgarian leva when AD is formed through subscription, and 1,000,000 Bulgarian leva if formed without subscription. Shares have to have nominal value of at least 100 leva and may not be split. There may be common or preferred stock.

Articles of Incorporation of AD must include corporate name, domicile, scope of activity, duration of activity, amount of capital, whether in cash or kind, kind and number of shares, privileges of subscribers, and managing bodies. Moreover, founders are free to resolve any matters related to incorporation, existence and winding up of company in articles of association. Provisions on Law on Commerce are applied, if articles of association are silent.

Public Limited Company comes into existence upon registration in Commercial Register of its domicile. Registration must be accompanied by adopted articles of incorporation, other required documents of procedural nature for appointment of governing bodies. All its stock capital must be subscribed and 25% must have been contributed.

Shares issued by AD may be of following classes: "payable to bearer"; "registered by name". AD will be free to issue preferred stock if expressly mentioned in articles of incorporation.

Bonds may be issued with right to be converted into shares two years from date of incorporation. It is possible to issue bonds earlier if loan is backed by bank or State. Public limited company may not borrow amount which is greater than 50% of its capital. If State holds more than 50% of company, bonds may not be issued.

Increase of capital may occur in three ways: by issuing new shares; by converting convertible bonds into shares; by increasing nominal value of existing shares.

Governance.—Bulgarian Law on Commerce gives discretion to founders of public limited company in setting up corporate governance. They can choose between one-tier system (general meeting of shareholders, board of directors and executive officer) and two-tier system (general meeting of shareholders, board of directors and supervisory board). Members of board of directors are appointed and dismissed by supervisory board (two-tier system) or by general meeting of shareholders (one-tier system). Number of directors may not be more than nine, while number of members on supervisory board may be between three and seven.

Board of Directors (Managers).—Functions are to manage and represent company. In case of one-tier system, board may appoint one or several of its members to be executive officers of corporation. Power of directors' to represent company may be limited internally, but not with effect toward third persons. Any acts of directors which are ultra vires are binding upon corporation. Directors are supposed to act in best interest of company and are jointly and severally liable for any damage caused negligently to it. Directors must deposit guaranty insurance to amount not exceeding three monthly salaries. There is no residence or citizens requirement for directors.

Supervisory Board must exercise monitoring powers and can employ outside experts for this purpose. It appoints and has authority to dismiss members of Board of Directors at any time. Members of Supervisory Board are elected by general meeting of shareholders. Person may not be member of board of directors and supervisory board of one and the same company. Decision making process and operational procedure of Board of Directors must be approved by Supervisory Board.

General Meeting of Shareholders must be convened at least once a year by Board of Directors. Notice must be published in Durzaven Vestnik. Shareholders may vote in person or by proxy. Company is free to establish in its bylaws what constitutes quorum. Resolutions must be adopted by simple majority of shares represented, unless law or articles of incorporation provide otherwise. Two-thirds majority is required to amend articles of incorporation, to reorganize or wind up company, to increase or reduce capital, unless articles of incorporation stipulate something else. Cumulative voting rights are not prohibited by Law on Commerce, but bylaws may be drafted to ban them. Every shareholder is entitled to file suit before District Court against AD. District Court will repeal resolution of general meeting which is unlawful or contravenes to articles of incorporation.

Auditor.—General Meeting of Shareholders must elect auditors who should be certified public accountants. Latter are supposed to carry out audit and ascertain observance of Law on Accountancy and articles of incorporation concerning annual balance sheet.

Annual balance sheet, profit and loss statement, and report of Board of Directors have to be completed by end of Feb. each year. Supervisory Board examines report and balance sheet and upon their approval calls for regular shareholders' general meeting.

Private Limited Company (Drouzestvo s ogranichena otgovornost "OOD").—This corporation form is more convenient type of business organization in cases when capital and number of shareholders are limited. OOD may be formed by one or more persons. Stated capital may not be less than 50,000 leva. At time of registration in commercial register at least 70% of stated capital must be contributed. Stated capital must be divided into several business interests (shares). Minimum par value of each share must be 500 leva. Shares are transferrable only by contract certified by notary public and registered in commercial register. Shares may be transferred freely to other members of OOD, while transfer to third parties require their acceptance as members. As a rule, new members are accepted by resolution of general meeting of members, which must be registered in commercial register.

Certificates for membership, if issued, are not securities.

Members' Meeting is governing body of OOD. It must be convened at least once a year. Meeting is sole authority to decide unanimously on acceptance and dismissal of members, amendments of articles of association, reduction or increase of stated capital, on acquisition of real estate. Decisions to approve company's balance sheet and annual report, distribution of profits, and to appoint managing director may be taken by majority vote, unless articles of incorporation provide otherwise.

Managing Director or directors are elected by Members' Meeting. They are supposed to represent and manage company.

Supervisory Board is optional.

Managing Directors or members of Supervisory Board are liable for any damage caused to company.

Auditors must be elected by Members' Meeting.

COURTS:

Bulgaria has single court system. Courts are divided in courts of general jurisdiction and special jurisdiction.

Regional Courts are courts of first instance for civil and criminal cases (misdemeanors and minor felonies). Courts are composed of one judge and two lay assessors.

District Courts consisting of three judges have exclusive jurisdiction as trial court over matters in which amount of controversy exceeds 100,000 leva, certain matters concerning guardianship law and family law and more serious felonies. District courts are appellate courts for decisions of regional courts.

Supreme Court supervises all courts, ensures uniform interpretation of laws and deals with extraordinary appeal against final judgment. It has three chambers: criminal, civil and military. Constitution of 1991 provides for establishment of Supreme Administrative Court.

Judges are appointed by High Judicial Council. Only Bulgarian citizen, who has completed university legal education and post graduate court training and has passed judicial state examination may be appointed judge.

Enforcement of judgments and other court rulings is performed by special executive judges working for regional courts. Judgments of foreign courts are enforced in same way as judgments of Bulgarian courts.

Exclusive jurisdiction exists in matrimonial matters if one of spouses is Bulgarian citizen or Bulgarian resident, matters respecting adoption of Bulgarian citizen, matters concerning custody and guardianship over Bulgarian citizens, real property rights and possession of real property in Bulgaria, as well as matters relating to alimony if defendant is Bulgarian citizen. Domestic courts have jurisdiction to declare person of Bulgarian nationality presumably dead. See topics Absentees and Death (Presumption of and Action of).

Lack of Jurisdiction.—Bulgarian courts do not have jurisdiction over foreign states. Diplomats enjoy full jurisdictional immunity. Nevertheless, there are exceptions to this rule. See topic Actions.

CURRENCY:

Legal currency of Bulgaria is leva. One lev is divided into 100 stotinki. Bulgarian National Bank (hereinafter BNB) has exclusive authority to issue currency notes.

In 1991, lev became partially internally convertible. BNB has acquired coordinating functions in establishing domestic foreign currency exchange market where commercial banks are main participants. BNB issues official exchange rate of leva toward other currencies every day.

CUSTOMS:

See topic Foreign Trade Regulation.

DEATH (Presumption of and Action of):

Missing person may be declared dead if five years have passed from day of last evidence that he was still alive. One who is reported missing during military actions or other extraordinary event which gives reason to think he or she did not survive may be declared dead after two years after end of military actions or event.

Declaration of death creates presumption that missing person is dead.

Petition for declaration of death must be filed with regional court where missing person has his domicile. Interested people and public prosecutor have right to petition. Court issues judgment that declares death of person. Upon court's judgment estate proceeding may start for distribution of his or her property. Declared dead person's marriage is dissolved.

If person declared dead reappears, he or she may apply for cancellation of court decision and may recover property from heirs. However, his or her marriage remains dissolved.

DEPOSITIONS:

No special rules contained in laws.

DESCENT AND DISTRIBUTION:

Law on Inheritance contains provisions relating to descent and distribution.

Children of deceased and spouse are first entitled to inheritance and inherit in equal shares. If child of deceased did not survive, his share passes to his or her children.

In absence of children or descendants of deceased, his or her spouse and parents are entitled to inheritance. If decedent has been survived only by grandparents and ancestors and brothers and sisters, latter receive two-thirds of inheritance. When spouse inherits with parents and brothers or sisters, he or she collects one half of inheritance if marriage lasted less than ten years, and two-thirds if more than ten years.

If there are no relatives appointed by force of law, entire inheritance passes to surviving spouse. When there are no persons able to inherit, all property of deceased goes to state.

DISSOLUTION OF MARRIAGE:

See topic Divorce.

DIVORCE:

Divorce may be granted only by court. Spouses may demand divorce on grounds of irreconcilable breakdown of marriage.

Divorce is not permissible if demanded solely by party at fault for breakdown of marriage, and other party demands marriage to be preserved. However, important reasons such as adultery and contagious diseases are likely to be considered by court in granting divorce.

In its judgment, court always states which party is at fault for breakdown of marriage. However, court does not decide on fault if both spouses agree on no-fault procedure and present separation agreement which covers all property and personal relations. No-fault procedure can be followed if parties have been married for more than four years.

Court always decides legal custody of common child. It may award custody to only one parent. Children of divorced parents who are pursuing studies may claim support from their parents until 26 years of age.

Divorced spouse may return to his or her surname prior to marriage.

If, after divorce, husband or wife cannot support himself/herself from his or her property and is not able to work, she or he may claim alimony from other. Alimony may not be demanded by spouse who is at fault for breakdown of marriage.

Aliens.—Bulgarian law is applicable if one of spouses is Bulgarian citizen. Bulgarian courts have exclusive jurisdiction if one of parties is Bulgarian citizen. Law of country of which both parties are citizens at time of initiation of divorce proceedings is applicable to divorce. In absence of common national law, applicable law is that which permits divorce. Consequences of divorce are settled by law that is more favorable to children or, if there are no children, to spouse with no fault for breakdown of marriage.

Judgment of foreign court granting divorce may be recognized in Bulgaria. Condition for recognition is that at time when action was filed defendant had domicile in country where judgment was rendered.

EVIDENCE:

There are no limitations on what courts may consider as evidence in civil cases, i.e. witnesses, written documents and expert witnesses. (arts. 127-170 C.P.C.). Courts have authority to collect evidence as well.

EXCHANGE CONTROL:

In general, profits, interests, dividends whether earned in hard currency or in leva (converted into hard currency at prevailing market rate) can be repatriated without limitations.

Foreign citizens may open bank accounts in Bulgarian or in foreign currency. Foreign currency may be purchased by Bulgarian bank for transfer abroad. All taxes have to be paid and one of following conditions must be satisfied: profit must be earned in leva from investment; income must be from sale or liquidation of investment; payments must be in compensation for expropriated property; amount of Bulgarian money received from execution on claim in foreign currency secured by pledge or mortgage.

EXECUTIONS:

Execution is granted in respect to judgments and arbitration awards. In order to execute judgment, plaintiff must obtain official copy with certification of enforceability. Execution can affect both movable and immovable property of debtor on basis of special procedure, which is concluded by public sale of said property.

See topic Courts.

FOREIGN INVESTMENT:

Basic legal act governing foreign investment in Bulgaria is Law on Economic Activity of Foreign Persons and on Protection of Foreign Investment of 1992.

Under art. 3(1), foreign persons may engage in economic activity and acquire shares in companies in same manner as Bulgarian citizens. There is no limit to degree of foreign participation in newly formed or existing companies. Nevertheless, foreign natural person must be permanent resident in order to register as merchant, member of cooperative, partnership or member of unlimited liability of limited partnership.

Foreign investment is defined as investment made by foreign person, merchant, or companies with foreign participation exceeding 50% in: shares registered in Bulgarian companies and partnerships; real property rights; ownership of enterprise; deposits in banks; bonds, treasury bonds and other negotiable instruments issued by State or Bulgarian legal entities; credits granted for term of more than five years.

Foreign investments must be registered in special register held by Ministry of Finance, except deposits in banks.

Permission (license) is required, if foreign person or company controlled by foreign persons wants to engage in: production and trade in weapons; engaging in banking and insurance activity; acquisition of real estate in certain geographic areas; exploration, development or extraction of natural resources from territorial sea, continental shelf or exclusive economic zone. Licenses are granted by Council of Ministers or by Board of Governors of Bulgarian National Bank in case of banking activity.

Law contains provision for priority of international treaties, if they provide for more favorable conditions for economic activity of foreign persons.

Bulgaria has signed bilateral treaties protecting foreign investments with Argentina, Belgium, China, Cyprus, Denmark, Finland, France, Germany, Greece, Italy, Luxembourg, Malta, the Netherlands, Portugal, Russia, Switzerland, Sweden. Agreements provide for national and most favored nation treatment and contain provisions against expropriation or other unreasonable state action by guaranteeing full and effective compensation in hard currencies. Bulgaria and U.S. signed bilateral investment treaty in Sept. 1992, which provides for fair, equitable, and nondiscriminatory treatment of U.S. investment in Bulgaria, free transfers of funds associated with investments, and international arbitration to resolve disputes. Treaty has been ratified by Bulgarian Parliament, and therefore is part of Bulgarian law, and U.S. Senate. Art. I of Treaty sets forth definitions of several important terms, such as "investment", "national", and "company".

Four core articles of Treaty are Art. II, dealing with right to establish investment and treatment to be afforded investment once established; Art. III, imposing conditions on expropriation of covered investment; Art. IV, guaranteeing right to transfer payments related to investment in and out of host country; and Art. VI, creating investor-to-state dispute mechanism. Treaty potentially authorizes investor to invoke any one of four conciliation or arbitration mechanisms: International Center for Settlement of Investment Disputes (ICSID); Additional Facility, which was created by ICSID in 1978 to serve as mechanism for resolving certain types of disputes outside ICSID's jurisdiction under ICSID Convention; ad hoc arbitration under UNCITRAL rules; or ad hoc arbitration under rules of any other arbitral institution mutually agreed upon by parties. It is expected that in future Bulgaria will join Convention on the Settlement of Investment Disputes between States and Nationals of other States (Washington, 1965).

Art. VII gives either party right to submit disputes concerning application or interpretation of Treaty to binding, third party arbitration. Parties have opted out for procedural rules of United Nations Commission on International Trade Law (UNCITRAL) regarding arbitration, which rules indicate Secretary General of Permanent Court of Arbitration to make appointments of arbitrators.

FOREIGN LAW:

Although there is no codification of provisions related to international conflicts of law or such provisions are missing, foreign law may be applied in Bulgaria. International treaties signed and ratified by Bulgaria prevail over its domestic legislation. In case of conflict between treaty and domestic law, court must apply treaty.

Applicable foreign law is verified by courts ex officio. Parties are supposed to assist court in its inquiries about foreign law.

In contracts, parties are free in choice of applicable law.

In case of torts, law where tort was committed is to be applied.

Disputes related to real property, law of place where subject of claim is located applies.

FOREIGN TRADE REGULATION:

Customs rules are generally liberal, but do not permit uncontrolled importation of goods that could injure domestic industries. Customs tariff consists of two columns. First column is applied for products originating from countries to which Bulgaria has offered tariff preferences. Second column is for goods from countries that enjoy most favored nations (MFN) status in their trade relations with Bulgaria. Goods originating from developing countries are exempt from customs duties. Products from countries that do not accord MFN status (these countries are not listed in customs tariff) are levied with retaliatory duty twice as high as average MFN rate.

Tariff schedule's arrangement and classification of commodities is based on Brussels Tariff Nomenclature.

Highest import duties are levied against farm products and food in order to protect domestic producers from foreign competition.

Average level of customs duties for manufactured goods is 18%.

Foreign Trade Regime.—It has been regulated by decrees issued by Council of Ministers which are amended at least twice every year. Trade in almost all commodities can be conducted without specific authorization or restrictions.

Exception is made for some exported and imported goods which are subject to registration. Thus, exports of live animal stock and meat, dairy products, bread grain and animal feed grain, high quality wine, ferrous and nonferrous metals, textiles, tobacco, need to be registered. At same time, exports and imports of tobacco products, coal, oil and liquid fuels and chemical substances under United Nations Convention against Illegal Trafficking of Narcotic Drugs and Psychotropic Substances are also subject to registration.

Licensing requirements are introduced for imports and exports of commodities that are subject to quotas or to international obligations, of military production. In addition, following commodity groups are subject to licensing: endangered species, explosives, precious metals, nuclear materials, hunting and sports weapons, narcotic and psychotropic substances, pharmaceuticals. License is needed for imports of certain tobaccos, natural gas, asbestos, gambling machines, non-bottled alcoholic drinks as well as for exports of works of art and historic treasures and timber. Protective measures as quantitative restrictions on imports of ice cream are established. Quotas are also introduced for textiles in accordance with international agreements signed with Canada, European Union and U.S. and are allocated among Bulgarian producers by Minister of Trade through tenders.

Discriminatory export tax is levied on exports of timber, rawhides, sunflower oil, wool, firewood. Export taxes on grain, flour and animal feed were introduced after Sept. 30, 1994.

List of goods can be imported duty free including equipment for monitoring pollution of environment, equipment for decontamination and treatment of waste waters, vaccines, medical instruments, mining equipment, nuclear fuel.

Quotas for duty free imports exist for seed potatoes, bread wheat, maize, vegetable oils, feed stock for pharmaceutical production and pharmaceuticals for which there is no local substitute, farm machinery. These quotas are supposed to facilitate supply of essential agricultural products and machinery and to encourage development of agriculture.

Finally, commodities received as humanitarian aid, human blood and plasma, unfermented tobaccos, wheat, barley, oats, maize, groats, cereal grains, soya beans cannot be exported.

Decrees Implementing International Agreements.—In 1993, Bulgaria signed Association Agreement with European Union (EU) and Trade Agreement with European Free Trade Association (EFTA) countries.

Interim Trade Agreement with EU, which is part of Association Agreement, was approved in Dec. 1993 by European Union Council of Ministers.

In Jan. 1994, Bulgaria's Council of Ministers adopted Decree 21 (Durzhaven Vestnik No. 12) and Decree No. 22 (Durzhaven Vestnik No. 13) which set up rules for fulfilling obligations arising from Interim Agreement with EU and Trade Agreement with EFTA.

See Topical Index in front part of this volume.

FOREIGN TRADE REGULATION . . . *continued*

Measures Against Dumping and Subsidized Imports.—In 1993, Council of Ministers enacted Decree No. 180 (Durzhaven Vestnik No. 81 [1993]) for adopting safeguard measures against imports. Protective measures may be adopted as matter of urgency where conditions of delivery of imported goods or their quantity is such as to cause or threaten to cause injury to domestic producers of similar goods. Decree is not applicable where international agreements to which Bulgaria is party provide otherwise.

Decree No. 181 (Durzhaven Vestnik No. 81 [1993]) envisages protection of Bulgarian market from goods imported at dumping or subsidized prices. Goods are dumped in Bulgarian market, if their export price is lower than cost for producing them under usual commercial conditions. At same time, goods are deemed to be exported at subsidized prices, if financial support is provided by state organ or social institution in country where goods originated or in country where they were exported from.

Any person may file petition with Minister of Trade alleging dumping or subsidized imports, and that these imports have caused or may cause injury to Bulgarian industry.

Investigation is initiated by decision of Council of Ministers on motion of Minister of Trade. Latter appoints commission which conducts investigation. Investigation can be concluded in three ways. First, procedure is terminated, when there is no sufficient evidence to establish dumping or injury to domestic industry. Second, settlement may be proposed by Minister of Trade or investigated party. However, if Commission findings are dumping or subsidized imports as well as significant injury to Bulgarian industry, Council of Minister imposes antidumping or counterveiling dumping.

Bulgaria is expected to soon become member of World Trade Organization. Bulgaria concluded bilateral trade agreement with U.S.

FOUNDATIONS:

Foundation is legal entity set up by act of donation or by will. It comes into existence upon entry into court's register. Foundation has no members and is governed by board.

Donations to foundations may be deducted from taxable income, if they serve social, educational and charitable purposes.

GARNISHMENT:

Garnishment is statutory remedy consisting of notifying third party to retain something he or she has belonging to defendant (debtor), to make disclosure to court and to dispose of it as directed by court.

HOLIDAYS:

Following days are official holidays in Bulgaria: Jan. 1; Mar. 3 (Anniversary of Independence); May 1-2 (Labor Day); May 24 (Day of Bulgarian Culture and Letters); Dec. 25-26 (Christmas).

HUSBAND AND WIFE:

See topic Marriage.

IMMIGRATION:

Visitors may enter Bulgaria with valid passport and Bulgarian visa. Visas can be obtained at Bulgarian embassies and consulates or at border. There is no visa requirement for U.S. citizens.

INFANTS:

Persons under 14 years are called infants. Persons below 18 are minors. For legal capacity see topic Contracts. Minors can conclude contracts for satisfaction of their everyday needs or to dispose of property acquired by them through work.

INTEREST:

Interest must be lower than official rate stipulated by Council of Ministers.

INVESTMENT PROTECTION:

Law on Economic Activity and Protection of Foreign Investment provides for protection of foreign investments from expropriation. (art. 10). Expropriation may happen by order of Ministry of Finance. Order must be motivated and state important national needs that cannot be met otherwise. Nevertheless, order may be subject to review by Supreme Court. In case of expropriation, compensation equal to market value of property must be paid. See topics Foreign Investment and Exchange Control.

JUDGMENTS:

Judgments of foreign courts are recognized and executed in Bulgaria, if courts of respective foreign country also recognize and execute judgments of Bulgarian courts. Reciprocity is determined by Minister of Justice. Petition for recognition and execution of foreign judgment must be submitted to Sofia City Court. Foreign judgment must have entered into force. Sofia City Court only considers whether judgment contains provisions contrary to Bulgarian laws. Judgment of Sofia City Court recognizing or executing foreign judgments are subject to review by Supreme Court.

Judgment of foreign court is not recognized and not executed in Bulgaria if: (1) dispute concerns rights over real property in Bulgaria; (2) matter belongs to exclusive jurisdiction of Bulgarian court; (3) defendant, Bulgarian citizen, did not take part in proceedings, and there is evidence that he or she has received at least one summons; (4) there is Bulgarian court judgment or there is case pending before Bulgarian court; (5) it is void in country in which it was rendered.

LABOR RELATIONS:

Labor Code in force since 1993 gives more rights to managements and restricts to certain degree activities of trade unions.

Relations between employers and employees are regulated by employment contracts. Provisions of Labor Code and other legislation apply for matters not regulated by contracts.

Law on Economic Activity of Foreign Persons and Protection of Foreign Investment contains provisions concerning relations between foreign persons or companies controlled by foreign persons as employers and their employees.

Labor contracts must follow requirements of Bulgarian legislation concerning: written form of contract; maximum working time; national minimum wage; minimum notice for termination of contract; liability of employer for damages caused by occupational accident; rules on occupational hygiene and safety.

Bulgarian citizens and foreign citizens employed by foreign persons or companies controlled by foreign persons must be insured at expense of employer. All employers must make social security contributions on behalf of their employees. For foreign nationals it is 20% of employees gross monthly salary, while for Bulgarian citizens it is generally 35%.

In Bulgaria, minimum wage is set by Council of Ministers.

Labor disputes are heard by Bulgarian regional courts or by tribunal specified in employment contract.

Legislation is pending in Parliament which would introduce work permits for foreigners with temporary residence in Bulgaria.

LAW REPORTS, CODES:

Bulgaria is governed by statutory law. Case law doctrines of precedent and stare decisis are unknown. However, decisions of Supreme Court are very important because they interpret provisions of laws and are binding on courts. Decisions of higher courts are mandatory and must be followed by lower courts only in cases of appeal.

Bulgarian laws and regulations are published in Durzaven Vestnik.

LEGISLATURE:

See topic Constitution and Government.

LIENS:

Person may have claim upon property of another as security for debt. Lien is right to retain property belonging to another until certain demands have been satisfied. However, lien gives mere right of retainer; there is no right of sale. Retainer has right to be satisfied preferably before other creditors after property was seized by executive judge and was subject to public sale.

LIMITATION OF ACTIONS:

Statute of limitations prevents claimant from enforcing right after certain period of time. Nevertheless, debtor may voluntarily perform obligation or claimant may satisfy claim from security.

Generally, period of limitations of action is five years. Three year limitation applies to many transactions of everyday life, e.g. rents, remunerations. Period in respect of claims for compensation for breach or bad performance of contract is six months.

All agreements altering limitation periods are void. Period of limitation starts running on day on which claim becomes enforceable. Period of limitation for tort claims commences on day claimant learns identity of tortfeasor.

Limitation periods may be suspended and interrupted. After interruption, new period of limitations starts to run. Interruption occurs in following cases: with every act of enforcement of claim; with recognition of claim by debtor; with filing of suit before court. Limitation period is suspended between spouses; between children and parents who exercise parental rights; while case is pending in court.

MARRIAGE:

Bulgarian law acknowledges only civil marriages. Age for marriage is 18 years. In exceptional circumstances, persons of at least 16 years may be allowed to marry. Permission is given by chairman of regional court.

Marriage is prohibited between close relatives, where there is existing marriage, if one person is mentally incapacitated or suffers from serious mental disease or disease dangerous for future generation or other spouse.

Notification of marriage is required. Parties must submit medical certificates and declarations that there are not obstacles for marriage to local municipality. Marriage is concluded in 30 days, or in exceptional circumstances earlier, after notification before municipal council.

Marriage concluded abroad between Bulgarian and foreign citizen will be recognized in Bulgaria, if it follows prescribed form of foreign country's law. Nevertheless, necessary condition of age as well as prohibitions contained in Bulgarian law must be followed.

MONOPOLIES AND TRADE RESTRAINTS:

Law on Protection of Competition was passed in 1991. It regulates both monopolies and unfair competition. Commission on Protection of Competition, with elected members, was set up by Parliament.

Person is in position of monopoly in national market if he or she holds exclusive right to carry on business or has, either alone or with dependent persons, 35% market share. Law contains three prohibitions relating to monopolies. First, government authorities must not take measures establishing monopoly. Second, grouping, subordination or merger of firms is banned if it creates monopoly or results in monopoly. Third, abuses of monopolist position such as hindering others from carrying on business by restricting growth of, or access to, the market; applying distinctly inequitable standards or contract terms; failing to observe common quality standards; creating shortages; imposing tie-ins; resorting to economic constraints to cause other firms to dissolve, split, merge or transform; charging monopoly prices, are not allowed.

Person holding or acquiring monopoly position must give prior notice to Commission and ask for its consent. Decision of Commission is subject to judicial review.

Agreements or decisions whose purpose is to establish monopoly are void.

Exclusive purchasing or distribution agreements are forbidden, if they would restrict competition. Contracts that confine party in its choice of markets, sources of supply, buyers are null unless restriction is justified by specific nature of contract and does not prejudice consumers' interests.

MONOPOLIES AND TRADE RESTRAINTS . . . *continued*

Unfair competition is prohibited. Its definition is behavior contravening bona fide commercial practices that prejudice competitors' interests in relation to each other or to consumers. Unfair competition is damaging reputation of competitors by making false claims; misleading consumers about commodities offered; misusing commercial secrets of others. Employees may not be on governing body of competing firm or be involved in competing business. This restriction extends for three years after employee has left firm.

Commission has authority to collect information. Firms and officials are obliged to provide assistance. Following advice of Commission, Council of Ministers may impose new prices in case of abuse of monopoly position.

Actions for violation of provision of unfair competition law may be brought in district courts by prosecutor, Commission and person whose interests have been endangered or prejudiced. Courts may declare transaction void, impose fines or order activity in question to stop.

MORTGAGES OF REAL PROPERTY:

Mortgage of real property is attached to claim as security. Mortgage is established by entry in land register, based either on contract or on law. It secures only financial claims. Thus, mortgagee has priority for satisfaction before personal creditors after real estate is sold in execution proceedings. Mortgage is established on entire real property and its accessories. If claim expires, mortgage terminates as well.

MOTOR VEHICLES:

Driving license may be obtained upon examination for person of 16 or more. Insurance covering strict liability of owner is required for operation of vehicle. Motor vehicles with foreign registration plate to be used permanently in Bulgaria must be registered. Driving licenses of American tourists are only recognized together with "International License".

NOTARIES PUBLIC:

Notaries public at regional courts act exclusively as such. Their activities include certifying authenticity of signatures and copies of documents, drawing up certain formal declaration and documents, mortgages, wills, acts related to incorporation of companies, transfer of real property. Fees of notaries are regulated by law and grow on progressive base according to amount involved in transaction.

PARTNERSHIP:

According to Bulgarian Law on Commerce, partnership may be general (subiratelno druzestvo) or limited (komanditno druzestvo). Partnerships are legal entities.

General partnership is association of two or more individuals or legal persons to conclude commercial transaction in name of common firm. Liability of partners is unlimited and joint. Name of partnership must contain family names or firm names of one or more partners with word "sudrudzie". Partnership agreement must be in written form and signatures of partners must be certified by notary public. It must contain names, domicile, addresses of partners; firm and domicile of partnership; type and amount of contributions made by each partner; manner of distribution of losses and profits between partners; way of management and representation of partnership. General partnership must be registered in commercial register. Partners may draft agreement to regulate all their relations.

Every partner has right to participate in management of business or represent partnership unless other arrangement made in partnership agreement. However, for transaction involving real property right consent of all partners is needed.

Limited partnership is partnership in which at least one of partners has unlimited liability for all debts and liabilities. Generally, all provisions concerning general partnership apply to limited partnership unless it is indicated otherwise in Law on Commerce. Limited partnership is managed and represented by partners with unlimited liability.

Limited partnership with shares is partnership where shares are held by partners with limited liability.

Civil partnership is general form of partnership which purpose usually is to conduct business activities. It is not legal person and is not supposed to be registered.

PATENTS:

New Bulgarian Law on Patents (hereinafter "Law") entered into force on June 1, 1993. Bulgaria is party to Paris Convention for Protection of Industrial Property and Patent Cooperation Treaty.

Patent is granted for inventions that satisfy internationally recognized standards of novelty, industrial applicability, progress and usefulness. Excluded from patent protection are inventions whose exploitation is contrary to public policy and morals; products obtained by nuclear transformation, designated for military purposes; varieties of plants, animals and biological processes for their production, with exception of microbiological processes and products thereby obtained.

Duration of patent is 20 years from filing date of application. (art. 16). Patent can only be declared null and void on grounds specifically enumerated in art. 26(3): lack of patentability; court has decided patent holder did not have right to patent; insufficient disclosure of invention; subject matter of patent goes beyond its application. Patent expires after 20 years from date on which application was filed, or if patent holder renounces patent in writing, or in case of nonpayment of annual fee six months after due date. Patent holder has exclusive right to use invention for commercial purposes in Bulgaria. (art. 19).

Patent Office has sole authority to grant patents. It maintains patent register.

Procedure Before Patent Office.—Application for patent may be filed by any person, whether citizen or alien, who claims to be true and first inventor of invention, either alone or jointly with another person; legal representative of deceased inventor; employer of inventor or person to whom patent has been assigned. (art. 13). Application must be in writing in form prescribed by rules supported by statutory declaration. Application must be accompanied by drawings and description of invention. If applicant does not in first instance deliver complete specification, he or she must do this within three months. This period may be extended for period not exceeding three months on payment of prescribed fee.

Priority to right to receive patent is determined as of date of filing of application in Patent Office, except in following situation: according to international treaties to which Bulgaria is party, foreign citizens and legal persons have priority to receive patent in Bulgaria as determined by date when they first filed in other country. For that end, they have to file application, and within two months to present declaration of date and country they first filed, and to pay certain fee. They must prove priority to right to receive patent within period of three months after application was filed in Patent Office. (art. 44[2]).

If application has been accepted and has been published in Official Bulletin of Patent Office, invention is provisionally protected. (art. 18).

Licenses to use or deal with patent or application for patent can be negotiated with proprietor in ordinary way. Thus, patent holder can license another party to use invention. According to art. 31(2), there are four types of license agreements: exclusive, non-exclusive, full and limited. In case of exclusive license, granting of license does preclude ability of patent holder to use patent or grant other licenses. Licensee may grant sublicense if he obtains permission from patent holder. Unless specified otherwise, licensor is obligated to give licensee all technical experience necessary for use of patent (full license). Written license agreement registered with Bulgarian Patent Office is valid against third parties from date of registration. (art. 31[4]). There is system of compulsory licensing. Under latter, any interested person may at any time after three years from grant or four years from filing of application apply to Patent Office for compulsory license. Possible grounds for application are: invention is not being used at all or to fullest extent to meet demands of national market, or declared national emergency situation. (art. 32[1]). Compulsory patent can only be non-exclusive. Multilateral or bilateral treaties to which Bulgaria is party can contain other grounds for granting of compulsory license.

PLEADING:

See topic Actions.

PLEDGES:

Pledge is security claim on movable good and may be established by contract between creditor and owner of movable. Object as rule must be delivered to creditor or third person. Creditor is not allowed to use object but has right to satisfy from money received upon its sale. He or she enjoys precedence over personal creditors of owner. Claims may be subject to pledge as well.

PRINCIPAL AND AGENT:

Authorization to act as agent may come from contract, from law, or from statement by principal (power of attorney). In exceptional circumstances, agency is not permitted.

Bulgarian law defines direct and indirect agency.

If agent has not disclosed principal, indirect agency may exist. Relationship is matter only between principal and agent, and does not concern third parties.

Direct agents act on behalf of disclosed principals. Legal transaction concluded by direct agent produces direct consequences for principal.

Written power of attorney may be issued to agent as proof of powers of agent. If particular form is required to make legal transactions valid, power of attorney must be in such form. Death of principal does not necessarily terminate agency.

Law on Commerce defines several kinds of powers of attorney. Special kind of powers of attorney is "prokura". Latter bestows upon agent (procurist) all powers related to conduct of business. Procurist cannot sell business or dispose of real property. Prokura must be entered into commercial register and may be cancelled at any time by principal.

REAL PROPERTY:

Constitution guarantees property rights. Private property is inviolable. Bulgarian nationals may acquire ownership of real property without limitation. Foreign persons (business entities registered abroad or foreign citizens with permanent residence abroad) may acquire ownership over buildings and limited ownership rights over real estate, but may not possess land. Foreign persons may acquire ownership of apartment or house only by exercising right to construct building or by following procedure of law.

Company with foreign participation of more than 50% is not allowed to own agricultural land.

Real property rights as well as mortgages are evidenced by entries in real estate register for each area kept at regional court. Transactions of transfer of real property rights must be done before notary public and become valid upon entry in real estate register.

SALES:

In sale contract, seller is obliged to transfer ownership of object (personal or real property), while buyer must accept object and pay price.

Sales contracts do not require any specific form. Nevertheless, if value of object is above certain amount specified by law, written form is necessary to prove existence of contract before court. Sale involving real property must be in form of notarial deed. Contracts transferring property rights over cars and ships must be in written form and signatures of parties must be certified by notary public.

Warranties.—Seller is liable if sale item has defect decreasing its value, is of insufficient quality, or is delivered to buyer in incomplete state ("physical defects"). He or she is liable if sale item is owned by another person. Seller is not liable if buyer knows of defect at time of delivery.

Notice Required.—Party who is not in default may insist on performance and may renounce sale contract. He or she must notify other party. Notice should be in writing,

SALES . . . *continued*

if contract was concluded in written form. However, if time of performance is specified in advance or time was very important, there is no need for prior notice.

Conditional Sale.—Seller may retain title to movables until full payment of last installment of purchase price. However, risk of destruction of item passes on to buyer upon delivery.

Sale by installments allows buyer to pay seller increments of price over specified period of time.

International Sale of Goods.—Bulgaria has ratified United Nations Convention on Contracts for the International Sale of Goods of 1980.

SECURITIES:

Law on Securities, Stock Exchanges and Investment Companies was passed on June 29, 1995 and was promulgated in Durzhaven Vestnik No. 63 (1995).

Law regulates public offering of securities, operation of intermediaries in selling securities and responsibility of those responsible of regulating market.

Law includes disclosure requirement, capitalization requirement, and rules governing insider trading, antimanipulation, takeovers, tender offers, and licensing of broker-dealers.

Law defines securities as transferable documents and rights, that could be traded publicly. These documents could be shares; bonds; and other documents and rights related to bonds and shares. Investment contracts, as written contracts whereby person invests in common commerical enterprise with expectation of profits derived substantially from efforts of others and that are offered publicly, are explicitly included in definition.

Securities and Stock Exchanges Commission (SEC) controls activities of professional participants in securities market. SEC is de facto state budgetary organization and relies on money from Bulgarian taxpayer. Members of SEC are appointed by Council of Ministers on recommendation of Minister of Finance.

SEC has broad powers and primary responsibility for state regulation of securities market. Some of its functions include: preparation of acts regulating trade in securities which afterwards are adopted by Council of Ministers; licensing brokers, dealers and other intermediaries; registering of stock exchanges; collection and analysis of information concerning activities in securities market.

SEC is in charge of supervisory activities and is empowered to impose measures and sanctions on traders, issuers, and members of stock exchanges. Acts of Commission are subject to judicial review.

Stock exchange must receive license from SEC and be registered in District Court before it starts to operate. Stock exchange must be juridical person operating as joint-stock company with one-tier system of corporate governance (general meeting of shareholders, board of directors and executive officer) and minimum capital requirement of 100,000,000 leva. At least two-thirds of capital must be owned by participants in money, securities, or insurance markets or by state. No stockholder, including state, can possess more than 5% of shares. Shares of stock exchange must be only "registered by name" and be of type "one share—one vote" in accordance with Law on Commerce.

Stock exchange must also set up clearing system of payments for transactions executed on its floor and arbitration court to solve potential disputes.

Law provides for licensing of intermediaries, brokers or dealers to engage in trade in securities. Intermediaries may be banks or joint stock companies and are subject to number of capital requirements defined by SEC and published in Durzhaven Vestnik. Intermediary is held to standard of diligence of ordinary businessman in his/her dealings on behalf of investors.

Regulation of Offering of Securities.—Law contemplates system of public offering of securities under which every offering of securities to general investment public requires filing of prospectus, unless specific statutory exemption is available. Prospectus must include all information needed to make financial assessment of securities. Prospectus must contain information on issue, issuer, its management and main shareholders, business activities. Financial statement certified by public auditor and balance sheet from previous year must be included.

SEC scrutinizes prospectus and may authorize or reject public offering. SEC does not check whether information in prospectus is true and is not liable for any false statements. However, it may ask issuer to provide proof that information is true. Issuer publishes announcement for public offering in two daily national newspapers. Issuer must report and update information contained in prospectus on regular basis every six months or when changes in information might have significant effect on price of securities.

When voting rights of holding held by one person exceed or fall below 10%, company, SEC and stock exchange must be notified.

Anyone who intends to acquire and become holder of 25% or more of votes at company's general meeting must make a full public bid. Acquirer must notify SEC and present draft offer for approval. Notice must be accompanied with evidence that acquirer has necessary money for transaction. Takeover bid can be stopped if Commission for Protection of Competition decides that bid violates provisions of Law on Protection of Competition. Target company is prohibited from carrying out any defensive tactics after commencement of takeover bid.

Insider Trading.—Law prohibits insider trading. Persons ("insiders") who, because of their position with respect to companies which have registered securities, or with respect to securities market in general, have access to inside information, must abstain from trading in securities or revealing this information until information is divulged to investing public. Those who violate rules on insider trading are subject to fines and administrative sanctions.

Inside information is all information for which there is no obligation to be made available to public or which has not yet been disclosed, and disclosure of which might affect significantly price of securities traded.

Persons considered to be insiders are members of supervisory or management boards of issuer, members of boards of companies related to issuer. Those who possess directly or through intermediary 10% or more of issuer's equity and all persons who because of their profession, activity or relationship with issuer or insiders have access to privileged, inside information are subject to provisions of insider trading.

Investment Companies.—Law provides for establishment of investment companies commonly known in other countries as mutual funds or investment trusts. These companies are formed for mutual investment of money in securities. SEC defines minimum requirements for companies, which include minimum capital, capital structure, and liquidity. SEC must be notified by anyone who acquires control of over 10% of votes in investment company.

Investment companies have, as in U.S., corporate structure, and are registered as joint-stock companies. Investment companies can be also of "open-end" or "closed-end" type. Open-end company issues "redeemable" securities; that is, company must repurchase its securities from any owner of its securities who offers them to fund in period of 30 days. Closed-end company does not have such obligation, and its securities trade on stock exchange like securities of any other company.

Investment company must be licensed first by SEC before registration by District Court.

Investment company must issue prospectus which contains much more detailed information than standard prospectus submitted to SEC for listing on stock exchange.

Investment company may acquire shares of another investment company up to limit of 5% of its portfolio. Investment company's shares not traded on stock exchange must not exceed 10%. Investment companies cannot take or give credits, act as bank, insurance company, or investment intermediary.

STATUTE OF FRAUDS:

Bulgaria has no statute of frauds. Certain forms of expression of intention, such as wills, corporate instruments, contracts concerning interest in real property must be in writing and executed before notaries.

See topic Contracts.

TAXATION:

Tax reform is considered priority and following laws have entered into force: Law on Value Added Tax (published in Durzhaven Vestnik No. 90 [1993]), Law on Tax Administration (Durzhaven Vestnik No. 59 [1993]), Law on Tax Procedures (Durzhaven Vestnik No. 61 [1993]), Law on Excise Tax (Durzhaven Vestnik No. 19 [1994]). Draft corporation tax law and draft income tax laws are being discussed in Parliament.

Personal income tax is regulated by Law on the Income Tax. It is direct tax levied on incomes of Bulgarian and foreign nationals earned in Bulgaria. All income is taxable no matter what origin or source is: employment, investment, rents and annuities, transfer of estates, etc. Tax exempt incomes are family allowances; pensions; financial aid in event of death, marriage or injury; interest on bank deposits; scholarship and fellowships; alimony or child support; compensation from insurance; awards from licensed lotteries; salaries of foreign diplomats etc.

Progressive tax rate is applied in two separate schedules to tax base income, i.e. to personal income reduced by exemptions and deductions:

(1) Monthly Salaries of Employees.—Progressive tax rates are applied in nine bands to monthly employment income. Rates start at 20% of amount in excess of 2,500 leva for monthly employment income over 2,500 leva but less than 5,000 leva. For incomes above 320,000 leva, rate is 123,450 leva plus 50% of amount in excess of 320,000 leva. Enterprises are obliged to deduct tax monthly upon payment of remunerations.

(2) Personal Income from Trade, Rent, Free-lance Professions Etc.—Progressive rate is also applied in nine bands to annual income. Rates start at 20% for income over 30,000 leva but below 60,000 leva, and reach 1,477,080 leva plus 50% of amount in excess of 3,840,000 leva for income above 3,840,000 leva. Tax base is decreased by costs. Thus, purchase of bonds, treasury bills or other state or bank securities is deducted. Donations to state, foundations with charitable, health care, cultural or scientific purposes, to scientific, cultural, sport and tourist nonprofit institutions; for scholarships; for scientific research are also deducted up to 20% of taxable income.

Corporate tax is regulated by Decree 56 on Economic Activity. This direct tax is levied on profit of enterprises. All Bulgarian and foreign enterprises that are legal entities and are engaged in economic activity for profit in Bulgaria are subject to corporate tax. Basic tax rate is 40%. However, banks must pay 50%. Tax base is annual profit resulting from difference between gross income and costs and expenditures. Tax base is decreased by depreciation of assets, interest on state loans, payments on investment credit. Losses from past years may be deducted from profit in equal parts over five year period. Companies without state or municipal participation and profits of less than 1 million leva pay tax of 30%.

Legislation suspended tax privileges to foreign companies and divested Council of Ministers of right to grant tax relief in form of rescheduled tax payments. Thus, profits of companies with foreign participation, including those with 100% foreign participation, are taxed at rate of 40% and, provided their annual profit does not exceed 1 million leva, at rate of 30%.

Foreign persons' income from dividends, shares, interest, royalties, remuneration for technical assistance and rent is taxed at same rates that are applied to Bulgarian persons.

Value Added Tax.—Law on Value Added Tax (VAT) was adopted in Oct. 1993 and entered into force on Apr. 1, 1994. Law sets flat VAT rate on transactions in goods and services of 18%. Under Art. 7 of Law, exports are not subject to VAT. Other exempt transactions listed in Art. 9 include: transfer of land ownership; transactions related to performance of financial, medical, or educational services; gambling; rendering of legal services as defined in Law on Advocates; sales of tickets to attend museums, concerts, art galleries; transactions undertaken by nonprofit organization if they involve donations to that organization; rental of land and buildings; transfer of ownership of enterprise, if transaction complies with Law on Privatization.

Group of prime necessities is exempted from VAT taxation for period of three years after Apr. 1994.

Excise Tax Law.—Under Art. 2 of Law on Excise Tax, adopted on Feb. 15, 1994, there are number of goods that are exempted from excise taxes. These are: exported goods, personal consumption of wine and hard liquors produced by physical persons

TAXATION . . . *continued*
within certain limits, goods in duty-free zones, silver hand-made pieces of folk art. With exception of winnings from lotteries and other gambling activities, all other goods and services are subject to both value added tax and excise tax. (Art. 1).

Admission tickets for bars, erotic and other similar forms of entertainment are subject to 50% excise tax. Rates for gasoline vary, depending on quality of gasoline, from 70 to 110%. Coffee and tea are subject to 30% tax; perfumes, 40%; leather and leather clothes, 40%; goods made of precious metals, including jewelry, 20%; erotic publications, 30%; lotteries and other gambling activities, 50%.

Laws on Tax Administration and Procedures.—Law on Tax Administration establishes centralized tax administration and regulates its structure, organization of activity and powers.

Law on Tax Procedures provides for unified tax registration of all taxpayers-business entities and natural persons. Law also lays down procedure for issuance, appeal and execution of acts of tax administration.

Income Tax Treaties.—Bulgaria has not been very active in negotiating new tax income treaties to replace old system of treaties signed mostly in 1980's. However, it is expected that situation will change soon and new wave of treaties will improve climate for foreign investment and contribute to expanded economic activities of foreign companies in Bulgaria. Bulgaria has tax treaties concerning taxes on income and capital with following countries: Austria, Belgium, China, Cyprus, Denmark, Germany, Greece, Luxembourg, Korea, Norway, Russia, Sweden, Switzerland, Zimbabwe. Bulgaria has also signed income tax treaties with Finland, France, India, Indonesia, Italy, Japan, Malta, Netherlands, U.K.

TRADEMARKS:

Law on Trademarks and Industrial Designs of 1967, amended in 1975. Trademarks must be registered with Institute of Inventions and Innovations. Law provides for ten year protection, which may be renewed.

Right of exclusive use of industrial design lasts for five years.

Bulgaria is signatory to Madrid Agreement Concerning International Registration of Marks.

TREATIES AND CONVENTIONS:

Bulgaria is party to United Nations Convention on Recognition and Enforcement of Foreign Arbitral Awards of 1958; European Convention on International Commercial Arbitration of 1961; United Nations Convention on Contracts for the International Sale of Goods of 1980; Paris Convention for Protection of Industrial Property (Stockholm Act, 1967 and am'd in 1979), and to Patent Cooperation Treaty (Washington 1970, am'd 1979 and modified in 1984). See other topics for references to additional treaties and conventions.

VENUE:

See topic Actions.

WILLS:

Person who is 18 years of age or over and has not been fully incapacitated because of mental illness may dispose of his or her property by will. This is also true for married person who is below age of 18. Testator may at any time revoke will.

Holographic Will.—To be valid will must handwritten and signed by testator. Lack of date does not render handwritten will invalid, if it does not give rise to doubts as to testator's capacity to draw up will.

Notarial Will.—Will may be drawn up before notary public. Testator orally states his final will in presence of two witnesses. Protocol is prepared by notary public who affixes date and place of will. Protocol is signed by testator, by two witnesses and by notary public.

Legitimate Portion.—Deceased person cannot deprive descendants, spouse and parents of their compulsory share by will.

CANADA LAW DIGEST REVISER

Borden & Elliot
Scotia Plaza
40 King Street West
Toronto, Ontario M5H 3Y4
Telephone: 416-367-6000
Fax: 416-367-6749
Email: info@borden.com

Reviser Profile

History & Growth: The firm was founded in 1936 by Henry Borden, Q.C. and Beverley V. Elliot, Q.C., two distinguished members of the Ontario bar, whose service in the firm is recognized in its name. Today Borden & Elliot is one of the largest law firms in Canada. There are over 200 lawyers practising in our offices in the Scotia Plaza in downtown Toronto.

In addition, we are a member of Borden DuMoulin Howard Gervais, a four firm national association of leading Canadian law firms founded in October 1990. Our national association includes the law firms of Borden & Elliot in Toronto, Russell & DuMoulin in Vancouver, Howard, Mackie in Calgary, and Mackenzie Gervais in Montreal. There are over 450 lawyers practising in our national association. In June 1993 an international office of Borden DuMoulin Howard Gervais was opened in London, England.

Practice Areas: Borden & Elliot is organized to provide integrated legal services in the following practice areas: Aboriginal; Admiralty & Shipping; Aviation; Banking & Finance; Biotechnology; Capital Markets; Casualty; Commercial Transactions; Communications & Broadcasting; Competition, Marketing & Advertising; Computer & Technology; Construction, Surety & Fidelity; Corporate; Criminal; Defamation; Education; Entertainment & Sports; Environmental; Estates; Expropriation; Family; Franchising & Licensing; Golf Industry; Health; Hospital; Immigration; Insolvency & Bankruptcy; Insurance; Intellectual Property; International Business; Investment Funds; Labour & Employment; Mergers & Acquisitions; Mining & Natural Resources; Municipal, Planning & Public Environmental; Mutual Funds; NAFTA; Pensions; Personal Injury; Personal Services; Products Liability; Real Estate; Regulatory & Criminal Defence; Securities; Taxation and Trusts.

Automation: Borden & Elliot is commited to the use of, and has a significant investment in advanced technology in all practice areas to provide lawyers control and flexibility over their respective practice areas, and facilitate delivery of legal services in an efficient and cost effective manner. All members of the firm are linked by a sophisticated computer network which supports an array of software, including fax and Internet mail to the desktop; document modelling; legal research, dial up and litigation support databases with imaging; and Internet access from personalized accounts. The firm encourages and maintains direct electronic connections of all types with its clients.

Clientele: The firm represents many national and multinational corporations in such business sectors as banking and finance, entertainment, health care, manufacturing, merchandising, mining, oil, gas and other natural resources, pharmaceuticals, publishing, real estate development, securities, service industries of many kinds and transportation. As a result, the firm has wide ranging experience and has developed distinctive expertise in these sectors. Borden & Elliot is responsive and adaptive, designing its services to meet its clients' individual needs in the sectors in which they carry on business.

Borden & Elliot also represents governments (national, provincial and municipal) and government agencies in a wide variety of matters. The firm represents other public institutions including colleges, universities and educational authorities, hospitals and other health care facilities. Business, trade and charitable organizations and associations are also among its clients. Although the majority of the firm's work comes from business or public organizations, the firm maintains its commitment to provide quality legal services to individuals through its Personal Services Group.

Borden & Elliot represents a significant number of national self-regulatory organizations in the important securities sector of the economy. These include the CDS (Canadian Depository for Securities, a computerized Canada-wide clearing house for securities transactions), the Canadian Investors Protection Fund, the Investment Funds Institute of Canada, the Investment Dealers Association of Canada and the Canadian Securities Institute. The firm also acts as special counsel in enforcement matters for the Ontario Securities Commission.

The firm's experience is not confined to Canada. Borden & Elliot has acted in the resolution of international trade disputes; in international banking transactions (including sovereign risk lending); in international insolvencies, liquidations and restructurings; in international business joint ventures, reorganizations and acquisitions; and in international communications networks and commercial contracts of many kinds.

Governance: Borden & Elliot is governed by an Executive Committee of five partners, elected by rotation, working with a number of well-defined practice groups and an administrative staff headed by its chief operating officer. The firm continuously monitors the design and performance of services, client relationships, and legal, economic and technological developments. Borden & Elliot maintains its commitment to planned firm growth.

Professional/Community Activities: The firm encourages its partners and associates to be involved in professional organizations and in community affairs. Lawyers in the firm participate as lecturers and discussion group leaders in the teaching portion of the Bar Admission Course (the final preparatory course for law students prior to admission to legal practice in Ontario). They also lecture at law schools and in continuing legal education programs sponsored by The Law Society of Upper Canada, The Canadian Bar Association and other professional development organizations. Lawyers in the firm have written or contributed to many legal textbooks and periodicals and have served on the executive and legislative review and reform committees of The Canadian Bar Association and its various Sections.

In addition, some lawyers in the firm are members of the International Bar Association, the International Fiscal Association, INSOL, the American Bar Association, the Criminal Lawyers Association, the American College of Trial Lawyers, the American Immigration Lawyers Association, United States Trademark Association, Licensing Executives Society, Patent and Trademark Institute of Canada, the Canadian

Chamber of Commerce, the Metropolitan Toronto Board of Trade, the Toronto Biotechnology Initiative, the Women's Law Association of Ontario and are active in many community and charitable organizations at national, provincial and local levels.

Reflecting the diverse cultural background of Canada, more than 20 languages are spoken at our firm. We have the capacity to provide legal services to our clients, not only in English and French, but also in languages such as Bulgarian, Cantonese, German, Italian, Macedonian, Mandarin, Russian, Slovak, Spanish and Ukrainian.

While Ontario is a common law province, a number of lawyers in the firm are also trained in the civil law tradition, reflecting Canada's heritage of two of the world's major legal systems.

CANADA LAW DIGEST

(The following is a list of all Topics, including cross-references, covered in this Digest.)

CANADA LAW DIGEST

Revised for 1997 edition by

BORDEN & ELLIOT, Barristers, Toronto.

Preliminary Note.—The following is a digest of the federal laws of Canada. The laws of the provinces of Canada are separately digested hereafter under the names of the several provinces. Where digest heading is missing, reference should be had to the appropriate digest of provincial law.

(R. S. C. means Revised Statutes of Canada, 1985; S.C. followed by the year refers to the Annual Statutes; C.R.C. means Consolidated Regulations of Canada, 1978; S.O.R. followed by year and numbers refers to the Regulation as published in the Canada Gazette, Part II.)

ABSENTEES:

See digests of the laws of the several provinces.

ACTIONS:

See digests of the laws of the several provinces.

ADMIRALTY: See topic Shipping.

AFFIDAVITS:

As to affidavits generally see digests of laws of several provinces.

Statutory Declarations.—By Canada Evidence Act (R. S. C., c. C-5), provision is made for taking of statutory declaration in attestation of execution of any writing, deed or instrument or truth of any fact or of any account rendered in writing. Such statutory declarations may be taken before any provincial court judge, notary public, justice of peace, police or stipendiary magistrate, recorder, mayor or commissioner authorized to take affidavits for use in provincial or federal courts or any other functionary authorized by law to administer oath in any matter, and are used in connection with extra-judicial matters. (§41).

Oaths, affidavits, solemn affirmations or declarations may also be administered outside Canada by (a) officers of Her Majesty's diplomatic or consular services, (b) officers of Canadian diplomatic, consular and representative services, (c) Canadian Government Trade Commissioners, Assistant Canadian Government Trade Commissioners and honorary consular officers of Canada, while exercising their functions anywhere outside of Canada. (§§52; 53).

Form

Statutory Form:

I, A.B., solemnly declare that (state the fact or facts declared to), and I make this solemn declaration conscientiously believing it to be true, and knowing that it is of the same force and effect as if made under oath.

Declared before me at
. . . . this . . . . . . day of } . . . .
. . . . 19. . .

AGENCY:

See digests of the laws of the several provinces.

AIRCRAFT:

Regulation of Civil Aviation.—Control of aerial navigation throughout and beyond Canada comes under provisions of Aeronautics Act (R.S.C., c. A-2, as am'd), and Air Regulations (C.R.C. c. 2, as am'd). Administration of Aeronautics Act and Air Regulations is responsibility of Department of Transport (also known as Transport Canada) under leadership of elected Minister of Transport.

Commercial Air Carriage.—National Transportation Agency (formerly known as Canadian Transport Commission) is empowered to inquire into matters relating to transportation and report thereon and make recommendations to Minister of Transport. In particular, National Transportation Agency considers commercial air carriage licence applications and is empowered to approve, reject, cancel or reinstate such licenses. Final decisions of National Transportation Agency may be appealed to Federal Court of Appeal on questions of law or jurisdiction; and Governor in Council may vary or rescind any order of Agency on petition of any party or on own motion. (National Transportation Act, 1987 R.S.C. [3rd Supp.], c. 28, as am'd).

International Air Carriage.—Pursuant to Carriage by Air Act (R.S.C., c. C-26, as am'd) Canada has adopted as law, with some qualification, provisions of 1929 Convention for the Unification of Certain Rules Relating to International Carriage by Air ("Warsaw Convention"), as amended by Hague protocol of 1955. Warsaw Convention addresses, among other things, enforcement of rights and limits of liability in international commercial air carriage. Canada is also signatory of 1944 Chicago Convention on International Aviation (which addresses regulation of international civil air carriage), and is member state of International Civil Aviation Organization (ICAO). In addition, Canada has concluded bilateral agreements with approximately 60 other countries each providing terms of mutual commercial aviation access.

Aviation Claims.—Passenger claims against airlines for losses arising out of international air carriage may be prosecuted pursuant to provisions of Carriage by Air Act. While such claims may be prosecuted in Federal Court of Canada, it is more efficacious and certainly more common for such claims to be prosecuted in superior courts of provinces. Aviation claims arising out of domestic air carriage are not governed by Carriage by Air Act, and are prosecuted in superior courts of provinces.

Aviation Safety and Accident Investigation.—Canadian Transportation Safety Board is established to advance aviation safety in Canada. Board, which is independent from Department of Transport, is responsible for investigating aviation occurrences; where necessary, holding public hearings into contributing factors and causes of aviation occurrences; reporting publicly on results of such investigations; and making recommendations to Minister of Transport on matters relating to aviation safety. Board must submit annual report to Parliament (Canadian Transportation Accident Investigation and Safety Board Act, S.C. 1989, c. 3, as am'd).

ALIENS:

By Citizenship Act (R.S.C., c. C-29) "aliens" means persons who are not Canadian citizens. As to who are citizens see topic Citizenship.

Status of Persons in Canada.—Under Citizenship Act every person who, under enactment of Commonwealth country other than Canada, is citizen or national of that country, has in Canada status of citizen of Commonwealth. For purposes of any law in force in Canada that refers to status of British subject, status so described refers to status of Canadian citizen or citizen of Commonwealth or both as intent of such law may require. Any law of Canada and any regulation made thereunder, unless it otherwise provides, has effect in relation to citizen of Ireland who is not citizen of Commonwealth in like manner as it has effect in relation to citizen of Commonwealth.

Subject to following provisions: (a) real and personal property of every description may be taken, acquired, held and disposed of by person who is not Canadian citizen in same manner in all respects as by Canadian citizen; and (b) title to real and personal property of every description may be derived through, from or in succession to person who is not Canadian citizen in same manner in all respects as though through, from or in succession to Canadian citizen.

Lieutenant Governor in Council of province is authorized to prohibit and annul or in any manner restrict taking or acquisition directly or indirectly of, or succession to, any interest in real property located in province by persons who are not Canadian citizens or by corporations or associations that in opinion of Lieutenant Governor in Council are effectively controlled by persons who are not Canadian citizens. Lieutenant Governor in Council of province may make regulations applicable in province for purposes of determining: (a) what transactions constitute direct or indirect taking or acquisition of any interest in real property located in province; (b) what constitutes effective control of corporation or association by persons who are not Canadian citizens; and (c) what constitutes association.

These provisions do not operate so as to authorize or permit Lieutenant-Governor in Council of province to make any decision or take any action that: (a) prohibits and annuls or restricts taking or acquisition directly or indirectly of, or succession to, any interest in real property located in province by landed immigrant ordinarily resident in Canada; (b) conflicts with any legal obligation of Canada under any international law, custom or agreement; (c) discriminates as between persons who are not Canadian citizens on basis of their nationalities, except insofar as more favourable treatment is required by any legal obligation of Canada under any international law, custom or agreement; (d) hinders any foreign state in taking or acquiring real property located in province for diplomatic or consular purposes; or (e) prohibits and annuls or restricts taking or acquisition directly or indirectly of any interest in real property located in province by any person in course or as result of investment that Minister is satisfied is likely to be of net benefit to Canada under Investment Canada Act.

Person who is not Canadian citizen is triable at law in same manner as if he were Canadian citizen.

Alien does not: (a) qualify for any office or for any municipal, parliamentary or other franchise; (b) qualify to be owner of Canadian ship; (c) qualify to take, acquire, hold or dispose of any property that under or pursuant to any Act of Parliament of Canada may be taken, acquired, held or disposed of only by Canadian citizens; or (d) become entitled to any right or privilege as Canadian citizen except such rights and privileges in respect of property as are expressly given to him. Citizenship Act does not affect any estate or interest in real or personal property to which person has or may become entitled, either mediately or immediately, in possession or expectancy, in pursuance of any disposition made before 4th day of July, 1883, or in pursuance of any devolution by law on death of any person dying before that day.

As to who are citizens, see topic Citizenship.

Corporations Owned or Controlled by Aliens.—See Broadcasting Act, R. S. C., c. B-9; Bank Act, S.C. 1991, c. 46; Insurance Companies Act, S.C. 1991, c. 47; Trust and Loan Companies Act, S.C. 1991, c. 45.

Also see topic Taxation, subhead Income Tax, catchline Nonresidents.

See also topic Corporations, subhead Foreign Investment.

In time of war alien enemies have no right to sue in Canadian courts, but they may appear to defend action brought against them and may appeal from any judgment rendered against them. If alien enemies are within country by licence of Queen to trade therein, they may institute action in Canadian courts to recover money or property.

Immigration into Canada is governed by Immigration Act, R.S.C., c. I-2 and by regulations promulgated thereunder.

Persons who comply with Act and regulations are admissible to Canada except following inadmissible classes which include members of their family: Persons suffering from disease, disorder, disability or health impairment, with likely danger to public health, safety, or likely to cause excessive demands on health or social services; persons unable or unwilling to support themselves and their dependants; certain convicted criminals; persons in respect of whom there are reasonable grounds to believe will commit federal indictable offences, or who may be members of organized crime; persons who have, or persons likely to or who will, engage in acts of crime, espionage or subversion; persons who, while in Canada, will engage in or instigate subversion by force of any government; terrorists; persons who following adjudicative process are found not to be genuine immigrants or visitors; persons previously deported, unless they have obtained consent of Minister to reenter Canada; and persons in respect of whom there are reasonable grounds to believe are war criminals or who have committed crimes against humanity. (§19). Immigration Officers and Senior Immigration Officers

See Topical Index in front part of this volume.

ALIENS . . . *continued*
are empowered to administer Act at ports of entry and are conferred with discretion to grant entry of otherwise inadmissable persons for up to 30 days. Adjudicators conduct hearings at first instance if required by Act. Immigration and Refugee Board empowered to hear and determine certain appeals by immigrants, refugees, persons against whom removal order has been made, and certain sponsors of immigrants. Further restricted appeal to Federal Court of Canada.

Minister of Employment and Immigration may by permit authorize certain persons otherwise inadmissible to enter or remain in Canada. (§37).

Only Canadian citizens and permanent residents may engage in employment in Canada without valid and subsisting Employment Authorization ("work visa"). Except in limited cases, such as intra-corporate transfer of executive and senior management personnel and business persons admissible under provisions of North American Free Trade Agreement ("NAFTA"), employment validation (i.e., "labor certification") from Canadian Employment Commission is pre-condition to obtaining of Employment Authorization. Numerous exceptions to requirement for possession of Employment Authorization are created by regulation (Immigration Regulations, 1978, as am'd §19[1]) including specified short-term business visitors.

Schedule II of Immigration Regulations, 1978 specifies countries whose citizens are exempt from normal entry visa requirements as visitors or otherwise. Visitor status is not normally granted at port of entry for more than 180 days.

As result of North American Free Trade Agreement ("NAFTA"), expedited and preferential treatment has been given to citizens of U.S. and Mexico for business related entries to Canada since Jan. 1, 1994.

Selection of permanent residents is determined in accordance with criteria established by regulation. These criteria are primarily skills and occupation oriented. Preference is given to approved business-class applicants, persons in designated occupations and applicants with close relatives in Canada.

Transportation companies are obliged to return, at own expense to port of departure, persons refused admission to Canada unless such person was in possession of valid and subsisting visa at time of arrival in Canada.

Refugees may apply for status in Canada either abroad or at port of entry. Port of entry refugee determination procedures substantially changed effective Jan. 1, 1989 including expedited preliminary determination in all cases. Limited rights of appeal.

Naturalization is governed by provisions of Citizenship Act., R.S.C., c. C-29.

Alien may obtain certificate of Canadian citizenship from Minister following application for that purpose to citizenship judge, who hears and determines application. Either Minister or alien may appeal decision to Federal Court-Trial Division within 30 days.

Citizenship granted to applicant who: (a) is 18 years of age or over; (b) has been lawfully admitted to Canada for permanent residence and has within four years immediately preceding date of application accumulated at least three years residence in Canada calculated as follows: (i) for every day during residence in Canada before lawful admission to Canada for permanent residence deemed 1/2 day of residence to maximum of one year; (ii) for every day during residence in Canada after lawful admission to Canada for permanent residence deemed one day of residence; (c) has adequate knowledge of French or English language; (d) has adequate knowledge of Canada and responsibilities and privileges of citizenship; (e) is not under deportation order and is not subject of declaration by Governor in Council that to grant him citizenship would be prejudicial to security of Canada or contrary to public order in Canada. (§5[1]).

Minister may in his discretion waive on compassionate grounds: (i) in case of any person, requirements (c) or (d) above; (ii) in case of any person under disability, requirement respecting age set forth in (a) above, requirement respecting length of residence in Canada set forth in (b) above, or requirement that person take oath of citizenship. (§5[3]).

Citizenship also granted to person who: (a) has been lawfully admitted to Canada for permanent residence and is minor child of citizen if application for citizenship is made to Minister by person authorized by regulation to make application on behalf of minor child; or (b) was born outside Canada before Feb. 15, 1977 of mother who was Canadian citizen at time of his birth and was not entitled immediately before Feb. 15, 1977 to become citizen under former Act, if within two years after Feb. 15, 1977 or such extended period as may be authorized by Minister, application for citizenship is made by person authorized by regulation to make application. (§5[2]).

In order to alleviate cases of special and unusual hardship or to reward services of exceptional value to Canada, and notwithstanding any other provision of Act, Governor in Council may, in his discretion, direct Minister to grant citizenship to any person and, where such direction is made, Minister must forthwith grant citizenship to person named in direction. (§5[4]).

Canadian citizen, whether or not he is born in Canada, is entitled to all rights, powers and privileges and is subject to all obligations, duties and liabilities to which person who is citizen under above provisions is entitled or subject and has like status of such person. (§5[5]).

APPEAL AND ERROR:

To Supreme Court of Canada.—By Supreme Court Act, R. S. C., c. S-26, Supreme Court exercises appellate, civil and criminal jurisdiction within and throughout Canada. (§35). Appeal lies to Supreme Court from decision of Federal Court of Appeal in case of controversy between Canada and province or between two or more provinces. (§35.1). Appeal lies to Supreme Court from opinion pronounced by highest court of final resort in province on any matter referred to it for hearing and consideration by Lieutenant-Governor in Council of that province whenever it has been by statutes of that province declared that such opinion is to be deemed judgment of highest court of final resort and that appeal lies therefrom as from judgment in action. (§36). Appeal to Supreme Court lies with leave of highest court of final resort in province from final judgment of that court where, in opinion of that court, question involved in appeal is one that ought to be submitted to Supreme Court for decision. (§37). Appeal to Supreme Court lies on question of law alone with leave of Supreme Court, from final judgment of court of province (other than highest court of final resort therein) judges of which are appointed by Governor-General, pronounced in judicial proceeding where appeal lies to that highest court of final resort, if consent in writing of parties or their solicitors, verified by affidavit, is filed with Registrar of Supreme Court and with registrar, clerk or prothonotary of court from which appeal is to be taken. (§38). No appeal to Supreme Court lies under foregoing from judgment in criminal cause, in proceedings for or upon writ of habeas corpus, certiorari or prohibition arising out of criminal charge, or in proceedings for or upon writ of habeas corpus arising out of claim for extradition made under treaty. (§39). Appeal lies to Supreme Court from any final or other judgment of highest court of final resort in province, or judge thereof, in which judgment can be had in particular case sought to be appealed to Supreme Court, whether or not leave to appeal to Supreme Court has been refused by any other court, where with respect to particular case sought to be appealed, Supreme Court is of opinion that any question involved therein is, by reason of its public importance or importance of any issue of law or any issue of mixed law and fact involved in such question, one that ought to be decided by Supreme Court or is, for any other reason, of such nature or significance as to warrant decision by it, and leave to appeal from such judgment is accordingly granted by Supreme Court. (§40[1]). Supreme Court has jurisdiction as provided in any other Act conferring jurisdiction. (§41). All applications to Supreme Court for leave to appeal are made in writing and determined by quorum of three judges after reading or further oral hearing if they feel it is warranted. (§43).

Procedure in Appeals.—Proceedings on appeal must, when not otherwise provided for by this Act, or by Act providing for appeal, or by general rules and orders of Supreme Court, be in conformity with any order made, upon application by party to appeal, by Chief Justice or, in his absence, by senior puisne judge present. (§56).

Time for Appeal.—Excluding months of July and Aug., applications for leave to appeal must be filed within 60 days after date of judgment appealed from. Where no leave is required, or where leave has been granted, notices of appeal must be filed within 30 days after date of judgment appealed from or granting of leave to appeal, except in case of Criminal Code, Canada Elections Act, Railway Act and Winding-up Act appeals, where different periods are provided for. (§58). 60 day limit may be extended under special circumstances. (§59).

Notice of Appeal and Security.—Appeal is brought by (a) serving notice of appeal on all parties directly affected, and (b) depositing with Registrar security to value of $500 that appellant will effectually prosecute appeal and pay such costs and damages as may be awarded against him by Supreme Court within time prescribed.

Where security deposited is other than money, it shall be to satisfaction of court proposed to be appealed from or judge thereof or to satisfaction of Supreme Court or judge thereof.

Within seven days from deposit of security or security deposited is other than money from later of deposit of security or its approval, appellant must notify all parties directly affected.

Notice of appeal with evidence of service thereof must be filed with Registrar and copy of notice must be filed with clerk or other proper officer of court appealed from within 21 days from time prescribed. (§60).

Whenever error in law is alleged, proceedings in Supreme Court must be in form of appeal. (§61).

Court must be provided with copies of printed or mimeographed record known as Appeal Case and each party must further provide copies of a factum containing arguments to be advanced.

Stay of Proceedings.—Upon the perfecting of security, execution is stayed, except that in certain cases execution will not be stayed until security is given by the appellant that the judgment appealed from will be complied with in case the said judgment is affirmed. (§65).

Extent of Review.—The appeal is in the nature of a review of the judgment pronounced and no new evidence may be produced except in unusual circumstances.

General.—Proceedings in Supreme Court are governed by Rules of Supreme Court of Canada. (SOR/83-74, as am'd).

Courts of Appeal.—See digests of the laws of the several provinces. See also topic Courts, subhead Federal Court of Canada.

ARBITRATION AND AWARD:

See digests of the laws of the several provinces. Also see Expropriation Act R. S. C., c. E-21.

Canada has adopted United Nations Convention on the Recognition and Enforcement of Foreign Arbitral Awards. (S.C. 1986, c. 21). Canada also adopted in 1986 United Nations Convention on the Model Law on Commercial Arbitration.

ASSIGNMENTS FOR BENEFIT OF CREDITORS: See topic Bankruptcy.

BANKRUPTCY:

Law is uniform throughout Canada and is governed by Bankruptcy and Insolvency Act. (R. S. C., c. B-3, as am'd). Extensive amending legislation enacted by Parliament of Canada (S.C. 1992, c. 27) received Royal Assent on June 23, 1992 and came into force on Nov. 30, 1992. Provisions of amending legislation are referenced in text under this heading as "1992 Act".

Applicability of Act.—Act applies to persons, including individuals, partnerships, unincorporated associations, cooperative societies, organizations and corporations incorporated under laws of Canada or province and foreign corporations having office in or carrying on business in Canada, except those corporations which are building societies having capital stock, incorporated banks, savings banks, loan companies, railway companies, trust companies and insurance companies. (§2). Persons engaged solely in farming, fishing, or tillage of soil and wage earners earning less than $2,500 a year and who do not on their own account carry on business, although not subject to provisions regarding involuntary bankruptcy, may make authorized assignments. (§48).

Jurisdiction.—Superior courts of original jurisdiction of the various provinces and territories have jurisdiction in bankruptcy matters with appeal to appellate courts of provinces and territories. Act provides for assignment of special judges, registrars, clerks and other officers in bankruptcy in each province or territory to deal with bankruptcy matters. (§§183-186).

Insolvent person is person (see subhead Applicability of Act, supra) who is not bankrupt, who resides or carries on business in Canada, whose unsecured liabilities to creditors amount to $1,000 and who (a) is unable to meet his obligations as they

BANKRUPTCY . . . *continued*
generally become due; (b) has ceased paying his current obligations in ordinary course of business; or (c) aggregate of whose property is not, at fair valuation, sufficient to pay all his due and accruing due obligations. (§2).

Acts of Bankruptcy.—A debtor commits an act of bankruptcy if he: (1) Makes assignment of his property to trustee for benefit of his creditors generally; (2) makes fraudulent transfer of his property; (3) makes any transfer or charge of his property which would be void under Act as fraudulent preference; (4) leaves or stays out of Canada with intent to defeat or delay his creditors; (5) permits execution to remain unsatisfied until four days before date fixed for sheriff's sale or for 14 days after seizure; (6) exhibits to meeting of creditors statement of assets and liabilities which shows him to be insolvent or presents written admission to meeting of inability to pay his debts; (7) assigns, removes, secretes or disposes of or attempts or is about to assign, remove, secrete or dispose of his goods with intent to defraud, defeat or delay any creditor; (8) gives notice to creditor that he has suspended or is about to suspend payment of his debts; (9) defaults in any proposal made under Act, or (10) ceases to meet his liabilities generally as they become due. (§42).

Involuntary Bankruptcy.—If debtor commits act of bankruptcy, unsecured creditor or creditors that are owed $1,000 may present bankruptcy petition within six months after such act. Secured creditor may present such petition if it states his willingness to give up his security for creditor's benefit if receiving order is made or if it gives estimate of value of his security (in which case, he is treated as petitioning creditor to extent of excess of debt owing to him which must exceed $1,000 over his security's value). Where petition is granted by court, receiving order is made. (§43).

Voluntary Bankruptcy.—Any insolvent person may, before receiving order is made against him, make assignment of all his property for general benefit of his creditors. (§49).

Priorities.—Receiving orders and assignments under Act take precedence over all judicial or other attachments, executions garnishments, judgments and other process against bankrupt's property unless completely executed by payment. Receiving orders and assignments are subject to secured creditors' rights. (§70). Upon receiving order being made or assignment being filed, property of bankrupt becomes vested in bankruptcy trustee subject to Act and to secured creditors' rights. (§71).

Assignments of wages and book debts executed by individual before bankruptcy are of no effect in respect of book debts received after bankruptcy. (1992 Act, §68.1).

See also infra, subhead Proofs of Claims.

Proposals.—Proposal may be made by insolvent person, receiver in relation to insolvent person, liquidator of insolvent person's property, bankrupt or trustee of estate of bankrupt. Special provisions apply to proposal made by consumer debtor (see subhead Consumer Proposals, infra). Proposal must be approved by creditors and by court. Proposal must be made to creditors having claims provable in bankruptcy generally, either as mass or separated into classes as provided in proposal, may also be made to secured creditors in respect of all secured claims of any class or classes of secured claim. Secured claims are included in same class if interests of secured creditors are sufficiently similar to give them commonality of interest, taking into account (a) nature of debts, (b) nature and priority of security, (c) available remedies in absence of proposal and extent to which secured claims would be recovered by exercising those remedies, (d) treatment of secured claims under proposal and extent to which they would be paid under proposal and (e) any further prescribed criteria consistent with those set out in (a) to (d). Court may determine appropriate classes of secured claims and class into which any particular secured claim falls. (1992 Act, §50). Creditors respond to proposal by filing proofs of claim with trustee in manner provided for unsecured creditors and secured creditors. (1992 Act, §§50[1]-[1.7]).

Insolvent person must lodge with licensed trustee, copy of proposal setting out its terms and any proposed security or sureties and statement showing financial position at proposal date. (1992 Act, §50[2]). When filing proposal with official receiver, trustee must also file projected cash flow statement prepared by insolvent person with report by trustee as to reasonableness of statement and report by insolvent person containing representations as to preparation of statement. (1992 Act, §50[6]). Creditors may obtain copy of statement from trustee unless court orders that it not be released because undue prejudice would result to insolvent person and non-release would not result in undue prejudice to creditors. Trustee is not liable for loss resulting in reliance on statement if acted in good faith and took reasonable care in reviewing statement. Trustee under proposal monitors insolvent person's business and financial affairs during period from filing of proposal until court approval of proposal. Trustee must file report on state of business and financial affairs and send report to creditors at least ten days before creditors' approval meeting. (1992 Act, §§50[6]-[10]. Inspectors must first approve filing of proposal by or for bankrupt. (§50[3]).

Trustee must call creditors' approval meeting to be held within 21 days after filing proposal. At meeting, creditors may refuse or accept proposal. (1992 Act, §54[1]). Where creditors refuse proposal, assignment in bankruptcy is deemed to have been made on earliest of filing of date of proposal, of giving notice of intention to make proposal or of filing first petition for receiving order (if any), and trustee must immediately call meeting of creditors of bankrupt estate. (1992 Act, §57). If proposal is accepted by creditors, trustee must apply for court approval within five days after creditor's approval meeting and send notice to every creditor who has proved claim in proposal. (1992 Act, §58).

All proposals must provide that Crown claims for amounts subject to demands under §224(1.2) of Income Tax Act (assessed employee deductions for income tax and Canada Pension Plan and unemployment insurance premiums) be paid in full within six months after court approval of proposal, unless Crown otherwise consents. Proposal cannot be approved by court if (a) any special Crown claims accruing due after filing of proposal or of notice of intention to make proposal have not been paid, (b) proposal does not provide for payment to employees or former employees of amounts of their preferred claims (see subhead Proofs of Claims, infra) immediately after court approval, and (c) proposal does not provide for immediate payment of six months rent in respect of commercial tenancy repudiated by insolvent person. (1992 Act, §60). Court may either approve or refuse to approve proposal. If approved by court, proposal is binding on unsecured creditors and on each class of secured creditors which accepted proposal by majority in number and 2/3 in value of class of secured creditors voting on acceptance resolution. (1992 Act, §62).

Court may annul proposal upon default in performance of any provision, unless default is waived by creditors or remedied by insolvent person within prescribed time. Upon annulment order being made, debtor is deemed to have made assignment in bankruptcy. (1992 Act, §§62.1, 63). Where proposal or notice of intention to make proposal has been filed in respect of insolvent person, no person may terminate, amend or claim accelerated payment under any agreement with insolvent person by reason only of insolvency or that notice of intention or proposal has been filed or, if agreement is lease or licensing agreement, that insolvent person has not paid rent, royalties or other payments of similar nature for period preceding filing of notice of intention or proposal. No public utility may discontinue service to insolvent person by reason only of insolvency or that payment for services rendered or material provided has not been made before filing of notice of intention or proposal. However, creditor may require payments to be made in cash for goods, services, use of leased or licensed property or other valuable consideration provided after filing of notice of intention or proposal, and creditor is not required to make further advances of money and credit. Contractual provisions contrary to these statutory requirements are not enforceable (§65.1).

These requirements do not apply to "eligible financial contracts" including (a) currency and interest rate swap agreements, (b) basic swap agreements, (c) foreign exchange agreements, (d) cap, collar or floor transactions, (e) commodity swaps, (f) forward rate agreements, (g) repurchase or reverse repurchase agreements, (h) commodity contracts, (i) agreements to buy, sell, borrow or lend securities or to clear or settle securities transactions or to act as securities depository, (j) other related derivatives, combinations, options, master agreements and guarantees, and (k) any other agreements of prescribed kind. These requirements do not prevent member financial institution from ceasing to act for insolvent person as clearing agent or group clearer under by-laws and rules of The Canadian Payments Association Act. Court may order that these provisions do not apply to certain contracts. (1992 Act, §65.1).

Any time between filing notice of intention to file proposal and proposal debtor may repudiate commercial leases by paying compensation to landlord immediately after court approval of amount equal to lesser of (a) six months rent or (b) rent for remainder of lease. Landlord may challenge repudiation of commercial lease but if insolvent person shows that proposal would not be viable without repudiation of lease, repudiation will stand. (1992 Act, §65.2).

Insolvent person may file with official receiver notice of intention to make proposal, stating name of licensed trustee who has consented to act and names of creditors with claims greater than $250. Trustee must send notice to every known creditor within five days after its filing. Within ten days after its filing, insolvent person must prepare and file projected cash flow statement and related reports of trustee and insolvent person. If insolvent person fails to file this statement within ten days after filing notice of intention or if proposal is not filed with official receiver within 30 days after filing notice of intention, insolvent person is deemed to have made assignment in bankruptcy on earlier of date of filing of notice of intention or of first petition for receiving order (if any). Official receiver issues certificate of assignment. Trustee must forthwith file prescribed report with official receiver and, within five days after certificate issued, trustee must send notice of first meeting of creditors of bankrupt estate. (1992 Act, §50.4).

After notice of intention is filed, court may grant extensions of original 30-day period for filing proposal, such extensions not to exceed 45 days individually, or five months in aggregate, if satisfied on each extension application that insolvent person has acted and is acting in good faith and with due diligence and would likely be able to make viable proposal if extension granted and that no creditor would be materially prejudiced if extension granted. Court may terminate period for filing proposal upon application of trustee, interim receiver or creditor, if satisfied that insolvent person has not acted or is not acting in good faith and with due diligence or will not likely be able to make viable proposal before period expires or will not be able to make proposal before period expires that will be accepted by creditors or if creditors as a whole would be materially prejudiced. (1992 Act, §50.4).

Consumer Proposals.—Consumer proposal may be made by consumer debtor where aggregate debts, excluding debts relating to principal residence, do not exceed $75,000. Administrator who is licenced trustee or person designated to administer consumer proposals assists consumer debtor in preparing proposal. Administrator must, within ten days after filing proposal, prepare report to be sent to every known creditor and official receiver setting out prescribed information including investigation of debtor's financial affairs and administrator's opinion as to reasonableness of proposal. Meeting of creditors may be requested by official receiver or any creditor. If no request for meeting is made, consumer proposal is deemed to be accepted by creditors. If meeting held, creditors vote to accept or refuse proposal. If deemed accepted or if accepted at meeting of creditors, administrator will either apply to court for acceptance of proposal if requested, or if not requested, consumer proposal is deemed to be approved by court. Once accepted, or deemed accepted by creditors and approved or deemed approved by court, proposal is binding on creditors. Administrator must distribute monies payable to creditors at least once every three months. If default occurs, consumer proposal may be annulled by court. Apart from court application, deemed annulment will occur where payments are in default to extent of three months or more. Assignment of wages made by consumer debtor before filing consumer proposal is of no effect in respect of wages receivable after proposal filing date. Certificate is issued when consumer proposal is fully performed. (1992 Act, §§66.11-66.40).

Stays of Proceedings.—On filing by insolvent person of notice of intention to make proposal (see subhead Proposals, supra), all remedies, actions, executions or other proceedings for recovery of claim provable in bankruptcy are stayed until proposal is filed or until bankruptcy of insolvent person. Stay will not (a) prevent secured creditor who has taken possession of secured property from dealing with property, or (b) prevent from enforcing security, secured creditor who has given notice of intention to enforce security at least ten days before notice of intention to make proposal is filed by insolvent person (see subhead Secured Creditors, infra). Provisions of security rendering insolvent person unable to deal with secured property on insolvency or on filing of notice of intention to make proposal or on default under security are not enforceable. (1992 Act, §69).

See Topical Index in front part of this volume.

BANKRUPTCY . . . *continued*

On filing of proposal (see subhead Proposals, supra), all remedies, actions, executions or other proceedings for recovery of claim provable in bankruptcy are further stayed until proposal has been fully performed or until bankruptcy of insolvent person. Stay will not (a) prevent secured creditor who has taken possession of secured property from dealing with property, or (b) prevent from enforcing security, secured creditor who has given notice of intention to enforce security at least ten days before notice of intention to make proposal (see subhead Secured Creditors, infra), or proposal is filed. If proposal is made to class of secured creditors who vote for refusal of proposal or if proposal is not made to secured creditor in respect of particular security, affected secured creditor is not stayed from enforcing security. Provisions of security rendering insolvent person unable to deal with property on filing of proposal are not enforceable. (1992 Act, §69.1). More limited stay of proceedings exists in cases of consumer proposals. (1992 Act, §69.2).

Upon bankruptcy of debtor, all remedies, actions, executions or other proceedings for recovery of claim provable in bankruptcy are stayed until trustee has been discharged. However, bankruptcy will not prevent secured party from realizing or otherwise dealing with security, unless court otherwise orders. (1992 Act, §69.3). Any creditor affected by any stay of proceedings may apply to court which may order that stay no longer operates in respect of creditor, if continued operation of stay would likely materially prejudice creditor or if it would be equitable on other grounds to so order. (1992 Act, §69.4).

Examinations of Bankrupt and Others.—Bankrupt is examined under oath by Official Receiver as to his conduct, causes of bankruptcy and disposition of his property. (§161). Bankruptcy trustee may examine under oath on creditors' request bankrupt, officers, employees, agents of bankrupt and any person reasonably thought to have knowledge of bankrupt's affairs. (§163). Evidence of any person examined under these provisions must be filed in court. (§163).

Duties of Bankruptcy Trustee.—Trustee must keep books and deposit money in hand in chartered bank in separate trust account in name of estate. (§§25, 26). Trustee must declare and pay dividends to creditors from time to time as required by inspectors. (§148). He must prepare statement of receipts and disbursements before making final dividend payment. (§152). Trustee is not bound to accept appointment but having done so, must perform duties until discharged or replaced. (1992 Act, §14.06). Trustee must provide, or provide for, counselling of individual bankrupt. (1992 Act, §157.1).

Powers of Bankruptcy Trustee.—Trustee has wide powers and may, among other things, do any of following: (a) sell or otherwise dispose of property of bankrupt by public or private sale; (b) carry on business of bankrupt as necessary for beneficial administration of bankruptcy; (c) bring, institute or defend any action or other legal proceeding relating to property of bankrupt; (d) employ solicitor or other agent to take any proceeding or to do any business sanctioned by inspectors; (e) accept purchase money payable in future as consideration for sale of any property; (f) borrow money and give security on property of bankrupt in priority to claims of unsecured creditors; (g) compromise debts, claims and liabilities; (h) divide or distribute any assets in existing form among creditors; (i) lease real property. (§30). In exercising any of these powers, trustee requires permission of inspectors. Trustee may also compel person to deliver or produce property of bankrupt or relevant document concerning estate of bankrupt. (§164).

Environmental Liability of Bankruptcy Trustee.—Notwithstanding any federal or provincial legislation respecting protection or rehabilitation of environment, trustee is not personally liable for any environmental condition or damage that arose before or during his appointment except as resulted from his failure to exercise due diligence. Trustee may have duty under other legislation to report environmental condition or damage. (1992 Act, §14.06).

Interim Receivers.—Where court is satisfied that secured creditor has or is about to send to insolvent person notice of intention to enforce security (see subhead Secured Creditors, infra), court may appoint licensed trustee as interim receiver over all or any part of debtor's property that is subject to security to which secured creditor's notice of intention relates, upon such terms as court may determine. Court must be satisfied that interim receiver is necessary to protect debtor's estate or interests of secured creditor. Interim receiver may be ordered to (a) take possession of debtor's property; (b) exercise control over that property and debtor's business; and (c) take such other action as court considers advisable. (1992 Act, §47).

Court may also appoint interim receiver where insolvent person has filed notice of intention to file proposal (see subhead Proposals, supra), where satisfied that interim receiver is necessary for protection of debtor's estate or interests of one or more creditors or of creditors generally. Where trustee is already named in proposal, court may appoint such trustee, another trustee or trustee under proposal and another trustee jointly, as interim receiver. (1992 Act, §47.1).

Court may, if it is shown to be necessary for protection of estate of debtor, at any time after filing of petition and before receiving order is made, or after filing of proposal, appoint licensed bankruptcy trustee as interim receiver of property and direct him to take immediate possession thereof. Interim receiver may, under direction of court, take conservatory measures and summarily dispose of property that is perishable or likely to depreciate rapidly in value and exercise such control over business of debtor as court deems advisable. (§46).

Upon receiving order being made court appoints licensed bankruptcy trustee as trustee of property of bankrupt having regard to wishes of creditors. (§43). Trustee is, in relation to and for purpose of acquiring or retaining possession of property of bankrupt, in same position as if he were receiver of property appointed by court. (§16).

Meeting of Creditors.—Bankruptcy trustee must, within five days of his appointment (unless time is extended by official receiver), call meeting of creditors, to be held within 21 days of trustee's appointment, to consider affairs of bankrupt and appoint trustee and inspectors. One creditor or representative entitled to vote constitutes quorum for meeting of creditors. All questions at meeting of creditors shall be decided by resolution carried by majority of votes. Votes to be calculated by counting one vote for each dollar of every claim of creditor that is not disallowed. (§§102-115).

Inspectors.—Meeting of creditors must appoint from one to five inspectors to supervise administration by trustee. (§§116-120).

Provable Claims.—All debts and liabilities present or future of bankrupt at date of bankruptcy or filing of proposal or to which he may become subject before discharge by reason of any obligation incurred before date of bankruptcy or filing of proposal are claims provable in proceedings under Act. (§§121, 122). For bankruptcies occurring after proclamation date of 1992 Act, debts provable in bankruptcy will be determined as of date bankrupt becomes bankrupt. (§121). Any contingent or unliquidated claim must be determined as provable claim and valued by court on application of bankruptcy trustee.

A creditor may prove a debt not payable at date of bankruptcy, but in that case must deduct interest at 5% per annum from declaration of a dividend to date when debt would have become payable. (§§121, 122).

Proofs of Claims.—Bankruptcy trustee examines proofs of creditors' claims and may disallow them in whole or in part. His decision may be appealed to court within 30 days. (§135). Subject to rights of secured creditors, claims are paid in following order of priority: (1) funeral expenses, if bankrupt deceased; (2) fees and expenses of trustee and legal costs; (3) levy of Superintendent in Bankruptcy; (4) six months arrears of wages to extent of $2,000 to each employee and disbursements to extent of $1,000; (5) municipal taxes; (6) three months arrears of rent and three months accelerated rent if lease so provides; (7) one solicitor's bill of costs to creditor who has first attached property of bankrupt; (8) for bankruptcies occurring before proclamation date of 1992 Act, indebtedness under any Workers' Compensation Act or Unemployment Insurance Act or under any provision of Income Tax Act creating obligation to pay amounts that have been deducted or withheld; (9) claims resulting from injuries to employees to which Workers' Compensation Acts do not apply; (10) for bankruptcies occurring before proclamation date of 1992 Act, claims of Crown in right of Canada or any Province; (11) ordinary unsecured debts. Subject to Act, all proven claims are paid rateably. Claims in categories (1) to (10) are considered preferred claims. (§136).

Spouse of bankrupt cannot claim as creditor any money in respect of wages, salary, commission or compensation for work done or services rendered in connection with trade or business of bankrupt until all claims of other creditors have been satisfied. (§137). Claims of silent partners for moneys loaned are also postponed. (§139).

Claims of certain close relatives by blood or marriage of individual bankrupt, or officers or directors of bankrupt corporation are not preferred in respect of wages, salary or compensation for work done. (§§138 and 140).

Repossession Right of Unpaid Supplier.—If purchaser of goods supplied for use in purchaser's business is bankrupt or if there is receiver in relation to purchaser, unpaid supplier of goods may, at supplier's expense, have access to and repossess goods by presenting written demand to purchaser, trustee or receiver in prescribed form within 30 days after goods delivered to purchaser. Goods must (a) be in possession of purchaser, trustee or receiver, (b) be identifiable as goods sold, (c) be in same state as they were on delivery, and (d) not have been resold or be subject to agreement for sale at arm's length. Purchaser, trustee or receiver must pay entire amount owing for goods, or release goods to supplier. If portion of goods has been paid for, supplier may repossess portion of goods relating to unpaid amount or may repossess all of goods upon repayment of partial payment to purchaser, trustee or receiver. Repossession right expires if not exercised within ten days after written notice presented to supplier by purchaser, trustee or receiver admitting supplier's repossession right. Supplier's repossession right ranks above every other claim or right against purchaser in respect of goods other than right of bona fide subsequent purchaser of goods for value without notice of supplier's demand for repossession. Supplier who repossesses goods under these provisions is not entitled to be paid for them. (1992 Act, §81.1). There are also special rights for unpaid suppliers who are farmers, fishermen and aquaculturists who deliver products to purchaser within 15 days before purchaser's bankruptcy or appointment of receiver in relation to purchaser. Farmer, fisherman or aquaculturist has statutory charge on all purchaser's inventory for unpaid amounts in respect of such products. (1992 Act, §81.2).

Crown Claims.—With some exceptions, all claims of Crown in right of Canada or province, rank as unsecured claims. Exceptions are claims secured by security or privilege that may be taken by persons other than Crown pursuant to any federal or provincial legislation which does not have as its sole or principal purpose establishing means of securing Crown claims. Other secured Crown claims are valid only if registered before filing date of petition, assignment, proposal or notice of intention to file proposal. (1992 Act, §§86-87).

Secured Creditors.—Subject to restrictions on rights in proposal and stay of proceedings provisions of Act (see subheads Proposals, Stays of Proceedings, supra), secured creditors are generally unaffected by bankruptcy and may (a) realize their security and prove in bankruptcy for balance due after deducting net amount realized or (b) surrender their security and prove whole debt in bankruptcy. (§127). Trustee may require secured creditor to file proof of security upon 30 days' notice. Proof must give full particulars of security, including date on which it was given and its value as assessed by secured creditor. If proof is not filed within 30 days after trustee serves notice requiring proof, trustee may, with leave of court, sell or dispose of secured property, free of secured creditor's security interest. Secured creditor is entitled to receive dividend only on excess over assessed value. Trustee may redeem security on payment of assessed value. (§§128-131).

Secured creditor who intends to enforce security on all or substantially all of inventory, accounts receivable or other business property of insolvent person must send notice of intention to enforce security to insolvent person, and must not enforce security until expiry of ten days after sending such notice, unless, after notice is sent, insolvent person consents to earlier enforcement of security. There is no notice obligation where there is already receiver in respect of insolvent person or in other specified circumstances. (1992 Act, §244).

Receivers.—Within ten days after appointment, receiver in respect of property of insolvent person or bankrupt must send prescribed form of notice of his appointment to Superintendent in Bankruptcy, to insolvent person and to all creditors of insolvent person that receiver, after making reasonable efforts, has ascertained. In case of bankrupt, notice of appointment must also be sent to trustee. (1992 Act, §245). Immediately after taking possession or control of property of insolvent person or bankrupt, receiver

See Topical Index in front part of this volume.

BANKRUPTCY . . . *continued*
must prepare statement containing prescribed information relating to receivership. Receiver must also prepare interim reports relating to receivership and upon completion of duties as receiver must prepare final report and statement of accounts in prescribed forms, and must provide copies of all statements and reports to Superintendent in Bankruptcy, to insolvent person and, in case of bankrupt, to trustee and to any creditor of insolvent person or bankrupt who requests copy at any time up to six months after end of receivership. (1992 Act, §246). Receiver must act honestly and in good faith and deal with property of insolvent person or bankrupt in commercially reasonable manner. (1992 Act, §247). Court may make any order with respect to performance of statutory duties relating to receiverships by secured creditor, receiver or insolvent person or bankrupt, if satisfied that duties are not being performed. (1992 Act, §§244-247, §248).

Fraudulent Preference.—Every transfer of property or charge thereon made, every payment made, every obligation incurred and every judicial proceeding taken by insolvent person in favour of any creditor with view to giving creditor preference over other creditors shall be deemed fraudulent and void as against bankruptcy trustee, if insolvent person becomes bankrupt within three months of date of transaction. (§95). If effect of transaction is to give creditor preference, it is presumed, in absence of contrary evidence, to have been made with view of giving creditor preference over other creditors. (§95). If person to whom preference was allegedly given was related person, applicable period is 12 months. (§96).

Reviewable Transactions.—Certain transactions not at arm's length may be reviewed by court. (§§3, 100). Creditor who entered into reviewable transaction with debtor at any time prior to bankruptcy of debtor is not entitled to claim dividend in respect of claim arising out of that reviewable transaction until all claims of other creditors have been satisfied unless transaction was, in opinion of trustee or bankruptcy court, proper transaction. (§137).

Discharge.—In respect of first-time individual bankrupt, trustee must file prescribed report with Superintendent in Bankruptcy within eight months after date of bankruptcy. Unless opposed by Superintendent, trustee or creditor, bankrupt is automatically discharged on expiry of nine months after bankruptcy date. Trustee must give at least 14 days prior notice of impending discharge to Superintendent, bankrupt and every creditor who has proved claim in bankruptcy. If discharge is opposed, notice of intended opposition must be given within nine months after date of bankruptcy date. Trustee must apply to court for appointment for hearing of opposition to discharge. Bankrupt may apply earlier for discharge. (1992 Act, §168.1). Making of receiving order against, or assignment by, any person (except corporation) operates as application for discharge unless bankrupt files in court and serves on trustee waiver of application. Otherwise trustee, before proceeding to his discharge and not earlier than three months or later than 12 months after bankruptcy, must apply to court on four days notice to bankrupt for appointment for hearing of application by court. Anyone who has waived may at any time at his own expense apply for discharge by obtaining appointment and serving it on trustee who gives notice to creditors. Bankruptcy trustee must prepare and file in court before discharge hearing, prescribed report as to affairs of bankrupt. Corporation may not apply for discharge unless it has satisfied claims of its creditors in full. (§169).

If bankrupt has committed any offence under act a discharge can be refused, suspended or granted on conditions. (§172). Court may either refuse or suspend discharge or grant discharge on conditions if assets are not of a value equal to 50¢ on dollar or if bankrupt among other things: (1) has not kept proper books; (2) has continued to trade knowing himself insolvent; (3) has failed to account satisfactorily for losses or deficiency of assets; (4) has neglected his affairs or speculated; (5) has given undue preferences; (6) has been previously adjudged bankrupt or made proposal to his creditors; (7) has been guilty of fraud or fraudulent breach of trust; (8) has put creditors to unnecessary expense by frivolous defence to proper action; (9) has, within three months prior to bankruptcy, incurred unjustifiable expense by bringing frivolous action; (10) failed to perform his duties under Act; (11) committed offence under Act or other statute in connection with his property in bankruptcy. (§173).

Orderly Payment of Debts.—Insolvent debtor (except corporation) residing in certain provinces (Alberta, British Columbia, Manitoba, Nova Scotia, Prince Edward Island and Saskatchewan), may apply to clerk of court having jurisdiction where he resides for order consolidating payment of claims, demands and judgments not exceeding $1,000 (or greater amount if creditor consents). (§§217-242). These provisions do not prevent debtor from being put into bankruptcy or from making assignment in bankruptcy. (§§217-242).

Companies' Creditors Arrangement Act.-(R.S.C., c. C-36, as am'd).—Where compromise or arrangement is proposed between debtor company (i.e., company, incorporated under laws of Canada or any province of Canada or having assets or doing business in Canada, which is bankrupt or insolvent whether or not proceedings have been taken under Bankruptcy Act or Winding-up Act) and its secured or unsecured creditors or any class of them, court may on application of company, of any such creditor, of trustee in bankruptcy or of liquidator of company, order meetings of such creditors and shareholders of company. (§§4, 5). If majority in number representing three-fourths in value of creditors, class of creditors, present and voting in person or by proxy at meeting or meetings, agree to any compromise or arrangement at any such meeting, court may sanction such compromise or arrangement, which is then binding on all creditors, or such class of creditors, and on company or on trustee in bankruptcy or liquidator and contributories of company, as case may be. (§6).

BANKS AND BANKING:

Banks are governed by Bank Act (S.C. 1991, c. 46, as am'd), federal statute which regulates incorporation, management and manner in which banks may operate.

Banking Corporations.—Minister of Finance may, on application, issue letters patent incorporating bank. (§22). Letters patent incorporating bank shall not be issued to certain bodies, including where bank thereby incorporated would be foreign bank subsidiary, unless Minister is satisfied that it will be capable of making contribution to financial system in Canada and that treatment as favourable for banks to which Bank Act applies exists or will be provided in jurisdiction in which foreign bank principally carries on business of banking. (§24). Bank has capacity, and subject to Bank Act, rights, powers and privileges of natural person. (§15[1]). Bank shall not commence business of banking until Superintendent has, by order, approved commencement and carrying on of business. (§48[1]).

Reserves and Returns.—Since July 1994, banks are not required to hold statutory reserves. (§457).

Interest.—Criminal interest rate provisions may apply to interest or discount on loans or advances made by Bank. See topic Interest, subhead Criminal Code. (R.S.C., c. C-46, §347).

Loans and Advances and Security Therefor.—Bank may not carry on any business other than business of banking and business appertaining thereto. This includes providing any financial service, acting as financial agent, providing investment counselling and portfolio management services, and issuing and operating payment, credit or charge card plan. (§409). Except as authorized by or under Bank Act bank shall not deal in goods, wares or merchandise or engage in any trade or other business. (§410[2]). Directors of bank must establish and bank must adhere to investment and lending policies, standards and procedures that reasonable and prudent person would apply in respect of portfolio of investments and loans to avoid undue risk of loss and obtain reasonable return. (§465). Bank may lend money and make advances on security of hydrocarbons or minerals. (§426). Bank may lend money and make advance to any wholesale or retail purchaser or shipper of, or dealer in, agriculture, aquaculture, forest, quarry and mine, and sea, lakes or river products, or goods, wares or merchandise, on security of such products; to person engaged in business as manufacturer on security of goods manufactured or procured for manufacture by him; to aquaculturist on security of aquacultural stock, equipment or implements, aquatic broodstock or seedstock, pesticides, feed, veterinary drugs, biologicals or vaccines and aquatic plants or animals; to farmer on security of crops, seed grain and seed potatoes, fertilizer, livestock, feed, agricultural implements or equipment; to fisherman on security of fishing vessels, equipment and supplies or products of sea, lakes or rivers; to forestry producer on security of fertilizer, pesticide, forestry equipment, implements or forestry products. (§427). Rights and powers of bank in respect of security obtained under §427 are void against creditors unless notice of intention in prescribed form is registered in appropriate agency of Bank of Canada not more than three years before security was given. (§427[4]).

Deposits.—Bank may accept deposits from any person whether or not person is qualified by law to enter into contracts. Bank may pay deposit to such person unless claimed by some other person in any action to which bank is party and bank has been duly served in respect thereof, or unless prohibited pursuant to injunction made by court. Bank not bound to see to execution of trust, whether express or arising by operation of law, of any deposit. (§437). Where person who made deposit dies, receipt by bank in form satisfactory to it of affidavit in writing signed by or on behalf of person claiming entitlement to deposit and reasons therefor, or where claim based on will or other document of like import, authenticated copy under seal of court or authority having jurisdiction in Canada or elsewhere, or receipt of notarial will or authenticated copy, is sufficient justification for discharge of obligation of bank provided bank is satisfied with such documentation. (§460). Joint deposit given presumption of joint tenancy and beneficial ownership by survivor but presumption may be rebutted.

Unclaimed Deposits.—Where deposit payable in Canada in Canadian currency exists at branch of bank in Canada where no transaction has taken place and no statement has been requested or acknowledged by customer for period of ten years, or where cheque, draft or bill of exchange payable in Canada in Canadian currency has been issued, certified or accepted by bank at branch in Canada and no payment has been made in respect thereof for period of ten years, bank shall pay amount that would be owing in respect of debt or instrument to Bank of Canada, and such payment discharges bank. Claimant may then demand payment from Bank of Canada which must pay out appropriate amount together with interest for period not exceeding ten years. (§438). Sixty days after end of each calendar year, bank must make returns to Superintendent of all such deposits or instruments where no dealings have taken place for nine or more years. (§524). In each year Superintendent shall cause information from such returns to be published in Canada Gazette within 60 days of time provided by Act for providing returns. (§532).

Foreign Banking.—

Status.—Except with consent of Governor-in-Council, foreign banks may not directly or indirectly undertake any banking business in Canada or maintain branch in Canada for any purpose unless authorized to do so under Insurance Companies Act (Canada) or, except as permitted by Bank Act, establish, maintain or acquire for use in Canada automated banking machine or accept data therefrom. (§508[1]). Foreign bank may establish representative office in Canada with approval of Superintendent. Foreign bank may also establish subsidiary in Canada ("foreign bank subsidiary") or locate its head office in Canada. (§509).

Reciprocity.—Foreign bank subsidiary may be established in Canada if its parent country offers reciprocal banking arrangements to Canadian banks and if such establishment is of general benefit to Canada. (§24).

Incorporation under Bank Act.—Any foreign bank subsidiary that wishes to carry on banking business in Canada must be incorporated under Bank Act. (§509). No bank may carry on business until Superintendent has, by order, approved commencement and carrying of business by bank. (§48[1]).

Rights and Powers.—Foreign bank subsidiaries have all powers of Canadian bank subject to following restrictions. Except for bank controlled by NAFTA country resident, beyond head office and one branch, additional branches may be opened with permission of Minister of Finance. (§422.2). At least one-half of directors must be "resident Canadians" (§159[2]). Foreign owned banks will eventually have to conform to same rules as domestic banks regarding share ownership in nonbank companies. At present current holdings will be left undisturbed. (§514[3]).

North American Free Trade Agreement.—Foreign bank subsidiaries controlled by NAFTA country residents may open additional branches in Canada without prior approval of Minister. (§422.2).

The Bank of Canada was incorporated in 1934 by Act of Parliament to function as central bank in and for Canada. Bank is managed by board of directors appointed by

See Topical Index in front part of this volume.

BANKS AND BANKING . . . *continued*
Minister of Finance with approval of Governor-in-Council. See Bank of Canada Act, R. S. C., c. B-2, as am'd.

Canada Deposit Insurance Corporation ("CDIC") was incorporated in 1967 by Act of Parliament (R.S.C., c. C-3, as am'd) insuring Canadian dollar deposits in member institutions up to $60,000. Membership in CDIC is mandatory for banks and federally-owned loan and trust corporations, and optional for provincially-incorporated loan and trust corporations.

Business Development Bank of Canada ("BDBC") was continued in 1995 as successor to Federal Business Development Bank. Purpose of BDBC is to support Canadian entrepreneurship by providing financial and management services and by issuing securities or otherwise raising funds or capital in support of those services. BDBC must give particular consideration to needs of small and medium-sized enterprises. BDBC is agent of Crown and directors are appointed by Designated Minister with approval of Governor in Council. All property, rights and obligations of former Federal Business Development Bank are vested in BDBC. (S.C. 1995, c. 28). See also Farm Credit Corporation Act (S.C. 1993, c. 14) and Export Development Act (R.S.C., c. E-20).

Trust companies may be incorporated by letters patent. Trust company has capacity and, subject to Trust and Loan Companies Act (S.C. 1991, c. 45, as am'd), rights, powers and privileges of natural person (§14[1]). Trust company may not carry on any business other than business generally appertaining to business of providing financial services. This includes acting as trustee, financial agent, receiver, liquidator or sequestrator, providing investment counselling services and portfolio management services, and issuing and operating payment, credit or charge card plan. (§409). Directors of trust company must establish and trust company must adhere to investment and lending policies, standards and procedures that reasonable and prudent person would apply in respect of portfolio of investments and loans to avoid undue risk of loss and obtain reasonable return. (§450). See Trust and Loan Companies Act, S.C. 1991, c. 45, as am'd.

Savings Banks.—Save as to certain provincial government savings banks (see provincial law digests) there are no savings or industrial banks operating in Canada, functions of such banks being performed generally by chartered banks.

BILLS AND NOTES:

Bills of exchange, promissory notes and cheques are governed throughout Canada by Bills of Exchange Act. (R. S. C., c. B-4, as am'd). Generally, Act is similar to U.S. Uniform Commercial Code provisions relating to negotiable instruments and is based on U.K. Bills of Exchange Act, 1882.

Days of Grace.—In the case of bill or note not payable on demand three days' grace are allowed, unless bill or note otherwise provides. When last day of grace falls on legal holiday or Sat. note becomes due next following juridical day. (§41).

Liability of Drawee.—A bill of exchange is not an assignment of funds in hands of drawee and drawee is not liable to holder unless he accepts. (§126).

Interest.—Where interest is payable under bill or note but no rate is fixed by agreement or law, rate is 5% per annum. See Interest Act, R.S.C., c. I-15, §3.

Judgment Notes.—Clause in note providing for confession of judgment thereon if not duly paid is not enforceable, but inclusion of such clause does not invalidate note.

Consumer Bills and Notes.—Rights of holder of such bills and notes, which must be marked "Consumer Purchase," subject to any defence or right of setoff that purchaser of goods would have had in action by seller of goods. (§§188-192).

In case of dishonour the drawer and any endorsers are released from liability unless notice of dishonour has been given and in the case of a foreign bill or note a formal notarial protest is also necessary. Notice of protest or dishonour is sufficient if addressed to the particular party at his address if given, or if not, then at place where instrument is dated. Notice of dishonour or protest must be given not later than next following juridical day. (§§95-125).

Patent Rights.—Every bill or note, the consideration of which consists in whole or part of the purchase price of a patent right, must have upon the face thereof the words "given for a patent right." Without these words the instrument is void except in the case of a holder in due course without notice of such consideration. (§13).

Inland/Foreign Bills.—Rules of common law of England, including law merchant, apply to bills of exchange, promissory notes and cheques in Canada except where such rules are inconsistent with Bills of Exchange Act. (§9). Where bill or note presented for acceptance or payable out of Canada is protested, notarial copy of protest and of notice of dishonour and notarial certificate of service of notice shall be received in courts as prima facie evidence of protest, notice and service. (§11). Holder may treat bill as inland bill unless contrary appears on face of bill. Inland bill is one which is or on face purports to be: (a) both drawn and payable within Canada or (b) drawn within Canada upon some person resident therein. (§24). Where foreign bill appearing to be such has been dishonoured by nonacceptance, it must be duly protested for nonacceptance. (§111). Where foreign bill has been dishonoured by nonacceptance it must be duly protested for nonacceptance, and if not previously dishonoured by nonacceptance but is dishonoured by nonpayment, it must be duly protested for nonpayment, and if accepted only as to part, it must be protested as to balance. Unless these provisions are complied with, drawer and endorsers are discharged. (§111). Inland bills need not be noted or protested in order to have recourse against drawer or endorsers. (§112).

CHARITABLE IMMUNITY:

See digests of the laws of the several provinces.

CITIZENSHIP:

Governed by provisions of Citizenship Act (R.S.C., c. C-29), proclaimed in force Feb. 15, 1977. Person is Canadian citizen if, after Feb. 15, 1977: (a) he was born in Canada; (b) he was born outside Canada and at time of his birth one of his parents, other than parent who adopted him, was citizen; (c) he has been granted or acquired citizenship pursuant to Act and, in case of person who is 14 years of age or over on day that he is granted citizenship, he has taken oath of citizenship; (d) he was citizen immediately before coming into force of Act; or (e) he was entitled, immediately before coming into force of Act, to become citizen under certain provisions of former Act (§3[1]); (a) above does not apply to person if, at time of his birth, neither of his parents was citizen or lawfully admitted to Canada for permanent residence and either of his parents was: (1) diplomatic or consular officer or other representative or employee in Canada of foreign government or employee in service of such person; or (2) officer or employee in Canada of specialized agency of United Nations or officer or employee in Canada of any other international organization to whom there is granted, by or under any Act of Parliament of Canada, diplomatic privileges and immunities certified by Secretary of State for External Affairs.

Person is deemed to be born in Canada if he is born on Canadian ship as defined in Canada Shipping Act, on air-cushion vehicle registered in Canada under that Act or on aircraft registered in Canada under Aeronautics Act and regulations made thereunder.

Person who is lawfully present and entitled to permanently reside in Canada is deemed to have been lawfully admitted to Canada for permanent residence.

Citizenship may be renounced only in accordance with loss of status provisions in Act. Renunciation is accepted only where: (1) citizen is or will become citizen of another country upon renunciation; (2) citizen is of age of majority; (3) citizen is mentally competent; and (4) citizen does not reside in Canada. Renunciation of citizenship must be way of application to Minister on prescribed form and is effective in accordance with issued Certificate of Renunciation.

Subject to judicial review, citizenship may be revoked on notice where permanent resident status or citizenship status prior to naturalization was obtained by false representation, fraud or knowing concealment of material circumstances.

See also topic Aliens, subhead Naturalization.

COMPANIES:

See topic Corporations.

CONSTITUTION AND GOVERNMENT:

Canada was established under Constitution Act, 1867 (formerly British North America Act, 1867) passed by U.K. Parliament. Act united Provinces of Canada, Nova Scotia and New Brunswick. Act created four provinces: Ontario (formerly province of Upper Canada), Quebec (formerly province of Lower Canada), Nova Scotia and New Brunswick. Subsequently, other provinces and territories were admitted to the federation. Canada is now comprised of ten provinces and two territories. U.K. Parliament ceased to have legislative authority over Canada except by consent pursuant to Statute of Westminster, 1931. Canada Act, 1982, which was proclaimed in force on Apr. 17, 1982, formally terminated U.K. Parliament's authority over Canada and provided power to Canada to amend its Constitution. Constitution of Canada which is comprised of Constitution Acts 1867-1982, is supreme law of Canada and any law which is inconsistent with provisions of Constitution is, to extent of inconsistency, of no force and effect.

Federal Parliament.—Parliament consists of Sovereign, Senate and House of Commons. Sovereign appoints Governor General who is Sovereign's representative in Canada. In practice, Sovereign merely formalizes appointment of Governor General who is selected by Prime Minister, leader of governing party.

Senate consists of fixed number of senators who hold office until age 75 as prescribed in Constitution Act, 1867. Each government appoints members to Senate. Senate has technically same powers as House of Commons but it is accepted that role of appointed Senate is subordinate to elected House of Commons.

House of Commons consists of elected representatives of each of provinces and territories. Prime Minister is leader of political party having support of majority of members in House of Commons. Where none of parties forms majority in House of Commons, control of House of Commons may be obtained by one of major parties cooperating with one of minor parties. Prime Minister selects members from House of Commons to form Cabinet and advises Governor General to appoint them as Cabinet Ministers. Cabinet Ministers formulate and carry out all executive policies and administer all government departments.

Constitution Act, 1867 provides that there shall be Queen's Privy Council for Canada to aid and advise government. Cabinet Ministers are all appointed to Privy Council. Since appointments to Privy Council are for life, Privy Council may consist of ministers of past governments. Privy Council also includes persons of distinction who are appointed as an honour. In practice, whole Privy Council does not meet regularly or conduct government business.

Federal Judiciary.—See topic Courts.

Provincial Governments.—Each province has Lieutenant Governor who is nominal Head of State and represents Sovereign in province. Constitution Act, 1867 provides that Lieutenant Governor shall be appointed by Governor General in Council. Lieutenant Governor is actually selected by federal government but Lieutenant Governor is not in practice agent of federal government. Lieutenant Governor acts on advice of provincial Cabinet.

Each province also has Executive Council. Leader of governing political party is President of Executive Council and Premier of Province. Premier makes formal recommendations to Lieutenant Governor on appointment of Cabinet Ministers who comprise Executive Council. Cabinet Ministers head each of departments of government.

Each province's Legislature consists of Lieutenant Governor and Legislative Assembly (in Quebec, known as National Assembly of Quebec) which is composed of all elected representatives of constituencies in province.

Jurisdiction of Federal Parliament.—By Constitution Act, 1867 exclusive legislative jurisdiction over specific subject matters was assigned to Dominion Parliament and Provincial Legislatures. Dominion Parliament has also residuary power to make laws for peace, order and good government of Canada in relation to all matters not coming within classes of subjects assigned exclusively to Provincial Legislatures.

The exclusive legislative authority of the Parliament of Canada extends to the following classes of subjects: (1) amendment of the Constitution, with stated exceptions; (1a) the public debt and property; (2) the regulation of trade and commerce; (2a) unemployment-insurance; (3) the raising of money by any mode or system of taxation; (4) the borrowing of money on the public credit; (5) postal service; (6) the census and statistics;

See Topical Index in front part of this volume.

CONSTITUTION AND GOVERNMENT . . . *continued*

(7) militia, military and naval service and defence; (8) the fixing of and providing for the salaries and allowances of civil and other officers of the government of Canada; (9) beacons, buoys, lighthouses and Sable Island; (10) navigation and shipping; (11) quarantine and the establishment and maintenance of marine hospitals; (12) sea coast and inland fisheries; (13) ferries between a province and any British or foreign country or between two provinces; (14) currency and coinage; (15) banking, incorporation of banks, and the issue of paper money; (16) savings banks; (17) weights and measures; (18) bills of exchange and promissory notes; (19) interest; (20) legal tender; (21) bankruptcy and insolvency; (22) patents; (23) copyrights; (24) Indians, and lands reserved for the Indians; (25) naturalization and aliens; (26) marriage and divorce; (27) the criminal law, except the constitution of courts of criminal jurisdiction, but including the procedure in criminal matters; (28) the establishment, maintenance and management of penitentiaries; (29) such classes of subjects as are expressly excepted in the enumeration of the classes of subjects by this act assigned exclusively to the Legislatures of the Provinces.

Parliament of Canada also has power to make laws in relation to old age pensions and supplementary benefits but no such law affects operation of any law made by provincial legislature governing old age pensions and supplementary benefits.

Parliament of Canada has concurrent powers of legislation with Provincial Legislatures in matters relating to agriculture and immigration into Province. Any law of Provincial Legislatures governing agriculture or immigration is effective as long as it is not repugnant to any statute of Parliament of Canada. Where there is conflict or inconsistency between statute of Parliament and statute of Provincial Legislature, it is federal law which prevails.

Bill of Rights.—On 10th day of Aug. 1960, Federal Parliament enacted a Canadian Bill of Rights (Appendix III to R. S. C.) that affirms rights of individual in a society of free men and free institutions. All Acts passed by Parliament of Canada are subject to rights and freedoms recognized and declared in this Bill.

Discrimination and Human Rights.—By Canadian Human Rights Act ("Act"), R.S.C., c. H-6, race, national or ethnic origin, religion, age, sex, marital status, family status, disability and conviction for which pardon has been granted, are prohibited grounds of discrimination. (§3).

Note: On June 20, 1996, Bill C-33, An Act to Amend the Canadian Human Rights Act, was passed and came into force, adding sexual orientation to above list.

Person discriminated against may institute complaint before Canadian Human Rights Commission or Tribunal appointed by it, under Part III of Act. If complaint substantiated, Commission may order cessation of discriminatory practice or order compensation for complainant. (§53). Commission may also order special compensation up to $5,000 on punitive basis be paid to complainant. (§53[3]).

Each of Provinces has similar statute to federal Canadian Human Rights Act.

Canadian Charter of Rights and Freedoms.—Canadian Charter of Rights and Freedoms (Schedule B to Constitution Act, 1982) sets out those rights and freedoms protected by Canadian constitution. Rights protected include: Fundamental freedoms (§2); democratic rights (§3); mobility rights (§6); legal rights (§§7-14); equality rights (§15); and minority language educational rights (§23). Charter also establishes French and English as official languages of Canada. These languages have equality of status and equal rights and privileges as to their use in all institutions of parliament and government of Canada. (§16).

Charter applies to federal and provincial law and laws inconsistent with its provisions are to extent of inconsistency of no force or effect. (§52). Persons whose rights or freedoms, as guaranteed by Charter, are infringed may apply to court of competent jurisdiction to obtain remedy. (§24). Parliament or legislature of province may avoid provisions of Charter relating to fundamental freedoms or legal rights if legislation expressly declares that it shall operate notwithstanding such provisions. (§33[1]). Notwithstanding anything in Charter, rights and freedoms referred to in it are guaranteed equally to male and female persons. (§28).

Rights of Aboriginal Peoples of Canada.—Constitution Act, 1982 recognizes and affirms "existing" aboriginal and treaty rights of aboriginal peoples. (See R. v. Sparrow, [1990] 1 S.C.R. 1075.)

Constitutional Amendment.—Parliament has power to amend Constitution of Canada where such amendment is authorized by: (1) resolutions of Senate and House of Commons, and (2) accepted by two-thirds of provinces where such provinces have, in aggregate, at least 50% of population of Canada.

Amendments affecting rights or privileges of legislature of province require support by majority of members of each of Senate, House of Commons and legislative assemblies. Where legislative assemblies express their dissent to such amendments by resolution supported by majority of its members, amendment will not have effect in that province.

On Feb. 2, 1996, An Act Respecting Constitutional Amendments came into force, adding further requirement for federal government's exercise of its constitutional amendment authority. Under Act, no amendment may be proposed without consent of Ontario, Quebec, British Columbia, two or more of Atlantic provinces and two or more of Prairie provinces. (S.C. 1996, c. 1).

Jurisdiction of Provincial Legislatures.—The exclusive legislative authority of the Provincial Legislatures extends to the following classes of subjects: (1) the amendment from time to time, notwithstanding anything in this act, of the constitution of the province, except as regards the office of Lieutenant-Governor; (2) direct taxation within the province in order to the raising of a revenue for provincial purposes; (3) the borrowing of money on the sole credit of the province; (4) the establishment and tenure of provincial offices and the appointment and payment of provincial officers; (5) the management and sale of the public lands belonging to the province and of the timber and wood thereon; (6) the establishment, maintenance, and management of public and reformatory prisons in and for the province; (7) the establishment, maintenance and management of hospitals, asylums, charities and eleemosynary institutions in and for the province, other than marine hospitals; (8) municipal institutions in the province; (9) shop, saloon, tavern, auctioneer and other licences in order to the raising of a revenue for provincial, local or municipal purposes; (10) local works and undertakings other than such as are of the following classes: lines of steam or other ships, railways, canals, telegraphs, and other works and undertakings connecting the province with any other or others of the provinces, or extending beyond the limits of the province; lines of steamships between the province and any British or foreign country; such works as, although wholly situate within the province, are before or after their execution declared by the Parliament of Canada to be for the general advantage of Canada or for the advantage of two or more of the provinces; (11) incorporation of companies with provincial objects; (12) solemnization of marriage in province; (13) property and civil rights in province; (14) administration of justice in province, including constitution, maintenance and organization of provincial courts, of both civil and criminal jurisdiction, and procedure in civil matters; (15) punishment by fine, penalty, or imprisonment for enforcing any law of province made in relation to any matter enumerated above; (16) education; (17) generally all matters of merely local or private nature in province; (18) exploration for nonrenewable natural resources and development, conservation and management of nonrenewable natural resources, forestry resources and facilities for generation and production of electrical energy; (19) export from province to another part of Canada of primary production from nonrenewable natural resources, forestry resources, and production from facilities for generation of electrical energy in province provided that such laws may not authorize or provide for discrimination in prices or in supplies exported to another part of Canada.

The Yukon Territory and Northwest Territories are governed by Commissioner and elected council with respect generally to those matters elsewhere within jurisdiction of provincial governments. Yukon Act (R.S.C., c. Y-2) and Northwest Territories Act (R.S.C., c. N-27) provide for government of territories and list classes of subjects in relation to which Commissioner-in-Council may make ordinances. *Note:* Nunavut Act (S.C. 1993, c. 28), which is expected to come into force in Apr. 1999, creates new Territory by severing part of Northwest Territories. This new territory, Nunavut, will have structure and jurisdiction similar to those of other Territories. See topic Public Lands.

CONTRACTS:

See digests of the laws of the several provinces.

Distributorships, Dealerships and Franchises.—Canada has no legislation or special rules governing formation and termination of these types of business arrangements, as they are subject to provincial jurisdiction. See also topic Franchises in Alberta Law Digest.

International Contracts.—See topic Sales.

CONVENTIONS:

Convention on the Service Abroad of Judicial and Extrajudicial Documents in Civil or Commercial Matters (1965). Acceded to by Canada on Sept. 26, 1988 and came into force in Canada on May 1, 1989.

Convention on the Civil Aspects of International Child Abduction (1980). This went into effect in Canada on Apr. 1, 1988.

Convention on the Law Applicable to Trusts and on their Recognition (1985). This Convention has gone into effect in following provinces only: Prince Edward Island (1988), New Brunswick (1988), British Columbia (1989), Newfoundland (1990) Alberta (1990), Manitoba (1993) and Saskatchewan (1994). Partial reservations have been claimed by Alberta with respect to extension to trusts created judicially and to exclude mandatory rules of another state and New Brunswick, Alberta, Manitoba and Saskatchewan with respect to retroactivity.

Convention Providing a Uniform Law on the Form of an International Will (1973). This went into effect in Canada on Feb. 9, 1978. Implementing legislation has been passed in Alberta (1976), Manitoba (1975), Newfoundland (1976), Ontario (1977), Saskatchewan (1981) and Prince Edward Island (1994).

Convention on International Factoring (1988) came into force in Canada on May 1, 1995. Implementing legislation is being drafted.

Convention on International Financial Leasing (1988) came into force in Canada on May 1, 1995. Implementing legislation is being drafted.

Canada-U.K. Convention on the Reciprocal Recognition and Enforcement of Judgments in Civil and Commercial Matters (1984). This is in effect in all provinces of Canada, except Province of Quebec.

See topics Aircraft; Sales; Taxation, subhead Foreign Tax Agreements; Arbitration and Award; Foreign Trade Regulation.

COPYRIGHT:

Copyright in Canada is regulated by Copyright Act. (R. S. C., c. C-42). Amendments to Act bringing Act into conformity with Canada's obligations under Agreement Establishing the World Trade Organization (WTO) came into force in Jan. 1996. Amendments are indicated in text by WTO, Jan. 1996. "Phase II" amendments to Act concerning neighbouring rights, home copying and exceptions to use of works without authorization or remuneration were tabled in 1996.

Copyright subsists in every original literary, dramatic, musical and artistic work if author was at date of making of work British subject, citizen or subject of, or person ordinarily resident in foreign country that is Berne Convention or UCC country or WTO member, or resident within Her Majesty's Realms and Territories (WTO, Jan. 1996) (§5[1]); and if, in case of published work, work was first published within Her Majesty's Realms and Territories or in such foreign country; but in no other works except so far as protection conferred by Act is extended to foreign countries to which Act does not extend (§5[1]).

Minister may certify by notice that any country which has not adhered to revised Berne Convention and grants or has undertaken to grant to citizens of Canada benefit of copyright on substantially same basis as to its own citizens is thereafter for purpose of rights conferred by Act treated as if it were a country to which Act extended. (§5[2]).

Copyright means sole right to produce or reproduce, to perform in public or to publish, work or any substantial part, and includes right to produce, reproduce, perform or publish any translation, to convert dramatic work into nondramatic work or nondramatic work into dramatic work, to make record, cinematograph film or other contrivance for delivery of work, to reproduce, adapt and publicly present original work by cinematograph, and to communicate work by telecommunication. (§3). Performer of

COPYRIGHT . . . *continued*
work has sole right to communicate performer's live performance by telecommunications, to fix performer's performance in sound recording, and to reproduce fixation if made without consent. (WTO, Jan. 1996, §14.1[1]).

Copyright subsists in records, perforated rolls, and other contrivances by means of which sounds may be mechanically reproduced, in like manner as if such contrivances were musical, literary or dramatic works. Copyright means, in respect of any such contrivance, sole right to reproduce any such contrivance or any substantial part thereof in any material form or to publish or rent it. (§5[3]).

Copyright Act provides for computer programs to be protected as literary works. (§2). Computer program is defined as set of instructions or statements, expressed, fixed, embodied or stored in any manner, that is to be used directly or indirectly in computer in order to bring about specific result. (§2). Act permits owner of authorized copy of computer program to reproduce copy by adapting, modifying or converting it, or by translating it into another computer language, if reproduction is essential for compatibility of program with particular computer, if reproduction is solely for person's own use, and reproduction is destroyed when person ceases to be owner of copy of program. In addition, owner of authorized copy of program may make single reproduction for backup purposes if reproduction is destroyed forthwith when person ceases to be owner of copy. (§27[2]).

Copyright is not infringed by fair dealing with any work for purposes of private study, research or for cticism, review or newspaper summary if source and author's name are mentioned. (§27[2]).

Copyright subsists regardless of registration by holder, though there is provision for registration. (§54).

Term.—With certain exceptions copyright subsists for the life of the author and for a period of 50 years from end of calendar year in which author dies. (§6).

Offenses.—Copyright Act provides for substantial penalties for certain acts of copyright infringement. Specifically, any person who knowingly makes for sale or hire, sells or lets for hire, distributes for purpose of trade, exhibits in public, or imports for sale or hire into Canada, any infringing copy of work, is guilty of offence and is liable: (a) on summary conviction, to fine not exceeding $25,000 or to imprisonment for term not exceeding six months, or to both, or (b) on conviction on indictment, to fine not exceeding $1,000,000 or to imprisonment for term not exceeding five years, or to both. Such penalties may also be imposed against person who knowingly makes or possesses any plate for purpose of making infringing copies of any work in which copyright subsists, or who for private profit, causes any such work to be performed in public without consent of copyright owner. (§§42, 43). Same penalties are available against any person who knowingly makes for sale or hire, sells or lets for hire, distributes, exhibits or imports for sale or hire any infringing fixation or infringing reproduction of fixation of performer's performance in respect of which performer's right subsists. (WTO, Jan. 1996, §43.1).

Copyright and Industrial Design.—Copyright Act provides that it is not infringement of copyright to reproduce design applied to useful article where article is reproduced in quantity of more than 50 if reproduction is made by making article or drawing or reproduction in any material form of article. However, this exemption does not apply to artistic work that is used for such purposes as graphic or photographic representation applied to face of object, trademark or label, material having woven or knitted pattern used for piece goods or wearing apparel, architectural work of art that is building or model of building, representations of real or fictional beings applied to article, and other artistic works as set forth in regulations to Act. (§64). It is also not infringement of copyright in work to apply to useful article features that are dictated solely by utilitarian function of article, to make drawing or reproduction of any features of article that are dictated solely by such utilitarian function or to use any method or principle of manufacture or construction. (§64.1). The Industrial Design Act, R.S.C., c. I-9, governs application of designs to useful articles more generally.

Integrated Circuit Topography Act, S.C. 1990, c. 37, protects topographies defined as design, however expressed, of disposition of interconnections and elements for making integrated circuit product or making customization layer or layers to be added to integrated circuit product in intermediate form. (§2[1]). Employer or party contracting for creation of topography is deemed to be creator of topography. (§2[4]). Registration under Act gives creator of topography exclusive right to reproduce topography and to manufacture, import or commercially exploit topography and any integrated circuit product incorporating topography for term of ten years commencing on filing date of application for registration. (§3, 5). Conditions of registration include originality, application for registration before first commercial exploitation in Canada or within two years thereafter and creator's status as Canadian national or individual or legal entity with real and effective establishment for creation of topographies. (§4[1]). Topographies of nationals and legal entities of convention countries, WTO members (WTO, Jan. 1996), countries with real and effective establishments for creation of topographies and countries certified by Minister will also qualify for registration. (§4[1]). Infringement consists in reproduction, manufacture, importation or commercial exploitation of registered topography or integrated circuit product containing registered topography without consent of owner (§6[1]); but there is no infringement by various acts of "fair dealing" (§6[2]). Topographies may be transferred (§7[1]) or licensed (§7[2]).

Administration.—Copyright office is attached to Patent Office and is administered by Commissioner of Patents and Registrar of Copyrights. (§§46, 47). Governor-in-Council is empowered to take such action as may be deemed necessary to secure adherence of Canada to Rome Copyright Convention of 1928. (§71).

See also Cultural Property Export and Import Act, R.S.C., c. C-51.

Act authorizes establishment of Canadian Cultural Property Export Control List which may include, regardless of their places of origin, any objects or classes of objects described in Act, export of which is deemed by Governor in Council to be necessary to control in order to preserve national heritage of Canada. General or specific permit to export objects included in Control List may be issued under Act.

See also Status of the Artist Act, S.C. 1992, c. 33. Act recognizes rights of artists to freedom of association and expression and establishes Canadian Artists and Producers Professional Relations Tribunal to certify artists' associations and govern relations between artists and producers.

CORPORATIONS:

Canadian corporations may be created either by certificate of incorporation issued pursuant to Canada Business Corporations Act (R.S.C., c. C-44) which Act contains general legislation governing corporations, or in special cases by Act of Parliament. Companies incorporated under Part I of Canada Corporations Act (R.S.C. 1970, c. C-32, as am'd) which did not apply for continuance before Dec. 15, 1980 were automatically dissolved as of that date. Companies without share capital with objects of national, patriotic, religious, philanthropic, charitable, scientific, artistic, social, professional or sporting character subject to Part II or Part III of Canada Corporations Act continue to be governed by that Act.

General supervision of incorporation and administration of Canada Business Corporations Act and Canada Corporations Act is performed by Minister of Industry Canada.

Canadian or Provincial Incorporation.—Companies whose operations are to be confined to one province should be incorporated under laws of that province. Companies which carry on business throughout country or in several provinces or in foreign countries should be incorporated under federal laws. Canadian companies are entitled to carry on business throughout country, and no province has constitutional power to impair this right by discriminatory legislation. They are, however, subject to provincial laws of general application, and may be required to obtain extra provincial corporation licences, and licences in mortmain, when operating and owning land in a province which demands such licences.

Canada Business Corporations Act (hereinafter referred to as "Act") came into force on Dec. 15, 1975.

Part I. Interpretation and Application.—

Application.—Act will apply to every corporation incorporated and every body corporate continued as corporation under Act that has not been discontinued under Act.

"Corporation" as defined in Act means body corporate incorporated or continued under Act and not discontinued under Act. "Body corporate" as defined in Act means body corporate wherever or however incorporated.

Exceptions.—Act does not apply to body corporate that is bank, insurance company, trust company or loan company.

Purposes of Act.—Purposes of Act are to revise and reform law applicable to business corporations incorporated for objects other than provincial, to advance cause of uniformity of business corporation law in Canada and to provide means of allowing orderly transference of certain federal companies incorporated under various Acts of Parliament to Act.

Part II. Incorporation.—

Incorporators.—One or more individuals no one of whom: (a) is less than 18 years of age, (b) is of unsound mind and has been so found by court in Canada or elsewhere, or (c) has status of bankrupt, or one or more bodies corporate may incorporate corporation by signing articles of incorporation in prescribed form.

Certificate of Incorporation.—Upon receipt of articles of incorporation in prescribed form Director must issue certificate of incorporation and corporation comes into existence on date shown in certificate of incorporation. Incorporation under Act is matter of right rather than privilege accorded pursuant to government prerogative.

Publication of Name.—Corporation must set out its name in legible characters in all contracts, invoices, negotiable instruments and orders for goods or services issued or made by or on behalf of corporation.

Other Name.—Corporation may carry on business under or identify itself by name other than its corporate name, unless such name is as prescribed, prohibited or deceptively misdescriptive or reserved for another corporation.

Reserving Name.—Director may, upon request, reserve for 90 days name for intended corporation or for corporation about to change its name.

Designating Number.—If requested to do so by incorporators or corporation, Director must assign to corporation as its name designating number determined by him followed by word "Canada".

Personal Liability under Pre-incorporation Contracts.—Subject to certain exceptions including express provision in written contract negating personal liability, person who enters into written contract in name of or on behalf of corporation before it comes into existence is personally bound by contract and is entitled to benefits thereof.

Pre-incorporation and Pre-amalgamation Contracts.—Corporation may, within reasonable time after it comes into existence, by any action or conduct signifying its intention to be bound thereby, adopt written contract made before it came into existence in its name or on its behalf and upon such adoption: (a) corporation is bound by contract and is entitled to benefits thereof as if corporation had been in existence at date of contract and had been party thereto; and (b) person who purported to act in name of or on behalf of corporation ceases, except as court may order on application by any party to contract, to be bound by or entitled to benefits of contract.

Part III. Capacity and Powers.—

Capacity of a Corporation.—Corporation has capacity and, subject to Act, rights, powers and privileges of natural person.

Extra-territorial Capacity.—Corporation has capacity to carry on its business, conduct its affairs and exercise its powers in any jurisdiction outside Canada to extent that laws of such jurisdiction permit.

Part IV. Registered Office and Records.—

Registered Office.—Corporation must at all times have registered office in place within Canada specified in its articles and notify Director within 15 days of any change of address of its registered office.

Corporate Records.—Corporation must prepare and maintain, at its registered office or at any other place in Canada designated by directors, records containing: (a) articles and by-laws, and all amendments thereto, and copy of any unanimous shareholder agreement; (b) minutes of meetings and resolutions of shareholders; (c) copies of all notices of directors or notices of change of directors; and (d) securities register in prescribed form.

Access to Corporate Records.—Shareholders and creditors of corporation, their agents and legal representatives and Director may examine these records during usual business hours of corporation, and may take extracts therefrom, free of charge, and any other person may do so upon payment of reasonable fee.

See Topical Index in front part of this volume.

CORPORATIONS . . . *continued*

Directors Records.—Corporation must prepare and maintain at its registered office or at such other place as directors think fit adequate accounting records and records containing minutes of meetings and resolutions of directors and any committee thereof which records must be open to inspection by directors at all reasonable times.

Retention of Accounting Records.—Subject to other legislation providing for longer retention period, corporation shall retain its accounting records for period of six years.

Records in Canada.—Where accounting records of corporation are kept at place outside Canada, there must be kept at registered office or other office in Canada accounting records adequate to enable directors to ascertain financial position of corporation with reasonable accuracy on quarterly basis.

Shareholder Lists.—Any person, upon payment of reasonable fee and upon sending to corporation or its transfer agent affidavit in prescribed form may upon application require distributing corporation as defined in Act or its agent to furnish within ten days from receipt of affidavit list setting out names of shareholders of corporation, number of shares owned by each shareholder and address of each shareholder as shown on records of corporation.

Use of Shareholder List.—List of shareholders obtained in this manner shall not be used by any person except in connection with: (a) effort to influence voting of shareholders of corporation; (b) offer to acquire shares of corporation; or (c) any other matter relating to affairs of corporation.

Form of Records.—All registers and other records required by Act to be prepared and maintained may be in bound or looseleaf form or in photographic film form, or may be entered or recorded by any system of mechanical or electronic data processing or any other information storage device that is capable of reproducing any required information in intelligible written form within reasonable time.

Corporate seal.—Instrument or agreement executed on behalf of corporation by director, officer or agent of corporation is not invalid merely because corporate seal is not affixed thereto.

Part V. Corporate Finance.—

Shares.—Shares of corporation must be in registered form and must be without nominal or par value.

Transitional.—Where body corporate is continued under Act, share with nominal or par value issued by body corporate before it was so continued is, for purpose of Act, deemed to be share without nominal or par value.

Class of Shares.—Articles may provide for more than one class of shares and, if they so provide, there shall be set out therein rights, privileges, restrictions and conditions attaching to shares of each class.

Class Voting.—Articles must provide for at least one class of shares holders of which are entitled: (a) to vote at all meetings of shareholders except meetings at which only holders of specified class of shares are entitled to vote; (b) to receive any dividend declared by corporation; and (c) to receive remaining property of corporation upon dissolution.

Issue of Shares.—Subject to articles, by laws and any unanimous shareholder agreement, shares may be issued at such times and to such persons and for such consideration as directors may determine.

Shares Nonassessable.—Shares issued by corporation are nonassessable and holders are not liable to corporation or to its creditors in respect thereof.

Consideration.—Share must not be issued by directors until it is fully paid in money or in property or past services that is fair equivalent of money that corporation would have received if share had been issued for money.

Consideration Other than Money.—In determining whether property or past services is fair equivalent of money consideration, directors may take into account reasonable charges and expenses of organization and re-organization and payments for property and past services reasonably expected to benefit corporation.

Property.—For purposes of these provisions, "property" does not include promissory note or promise to pay.

Stated Capital Account.—Corporation must maintain separate stated capital account for each class and series of shares issued, and consideration received by corporation for each share issued must be added to stated capital account maintained for shares of that class or series.

Restriction.—Corporation must not reduce its stated capital or any stated capital account except in manner provided in Act.

Shares in Series.—Articles may authorize issue of any class of shares in one or more series and may authorize directors to fix number of shares in and to determine designation, rights, privileges, restrictions and conditions attaching to, shares of each series, subject to limitations set out in articles.

Series Participation.—If any cumulative dividends or amounts payable on return of capital in respect of series of shares are not paid in full, shares of all series of same class participate rateably in respect of accumulated dividends and return of capital.

Restrictions on Series.—No rights, privileges, restrictions or conditions attached to series of shares authorized under these provisions may confer upon series priority in respect of dividends or return of capital over any other series of shares of same class that are then outstanding.

Pre-emptive Right.—If articles so provide, no shares of class (other than shares to be issued: (a) for consideration other than money; (b) as share dividend; or (c) pursuant to exercise of conversion privileges, options or rights previously granted by corporation) may be issued unless shares have first been offered to shareholders holding shares of that class and those shareholders have pre-emptive right to acquire offered shares in proportion to their holdings of shares of that class, at such price and on such terms as those shares are to be offered to others.

Options and Rights.—Corporation may issue certificates, warrants or other evidences of conversion privileges, options or rights to acquire securities of corporation.

Transferable Rights.—Conversion privileges, options and rights to acquire securities of corporation may be made transferable or nontransferable, and options and rights to acquire may be made separable or inseparable from any securities to which they are attached.

Reserved Shares.—Where corporation has granted privileges to convert any securities issued by corporation into shares, or into shares of another class or series, or has issued or granted options or rights to acquire shares, if articles limit number of authorized shares, corporation must reserve and continue to reserve sufficient authorized shares to meet exercise of such conversion privileges, options and rights.

Corporation Holding Its Own Shares.—Except as provided in Act, corporation must not hold shares in itself or in its holding body corporate and shall not permit any subsidiary corporation to acquire shares of corporation. Corporation shall cause subsidiary body corporate that holds shares of corporation to dispose of them within five years from date became subsidiary or date of continuance under Act.

Corporation may in capacity of legal representative hold shares in itself or in its holding body corporate unless it or holding body corporate or subsidiary of either of them has beneficial interest in shares.

Corporation may hold shares in itself or in its holding body corporate by way of security for purposes of transaction entered into by it in ordinary course of business that includes lending of money.

Acquisition of Corporation's Own Shares.—Subject to Act and to its articles, corporation may purchase or otherwise acquire shares issued by it.

Limitation.—Corporation may not make any payment to purchase or otherwise acquire shares issued by it (other than to satisfy claim of shareholder who dissents following certain actions by corporation or order of court) if there are reasonable grounds for believing that (a) corporation is, or would after payment be, unable to pay its liabilities as they become due; or (b) realizable value of corporation's assets would after payment be less than aggregate of its liabilities and stated capital of all classes.

Alternative Acquisition of Corporation's Own Shares.—Notwithstanding foregoing but subject to its articles, corporation may purchase or otherwise acquire shares issued by it to: (a) Settle or compromise debt or claim asserted by or against corporation; (b) eliminate fractional shares; or (c) fulfil terms of non-assignable agreement under which corporation has option or is obliged to purchase shares owned by director, officer or employee of corporation unless there are reasonable grounds for believing that (d) corporation is, or would after payment be, unable to pay its liabilities as they become due; or (e) realizable value of corporation's assets would after payment be less than aggregate of its liabilities and amount required for payment on redemption or in liquidation of all shares holders of which have right to be paid prior to holders of shares to be purchased or acquired.

Redemption of Shares.—Subject to Act and to its articles, corporation may purchase or redeem any redeemable shares issued by it at prices not exceeding redemption price thereof stated in articles or calculated according to formula stated in articles.

Corporation must not make any payment to purchase or redeem any redeemable shares issued by it if there are reasonable grounds for believing that: (a) Corporation is, or would after payment be, unable to pay its liabilities as they become due; or (b) realizable value or corporation's assets would after payment be less than aggregate of (i) its liabilities, and (ii) amount that would be required to pay holders of shares that have right to be paid, on redemption or in liquidation, ratably with or prior to holders of shares to be purchased or redeemed.

Other Reduction of Stated Capital.—Corporation may by special resolution reduce its stated capital for any purpose including: (a) Extinguishing or reducing liability for amount unpaid on any share; (b) distributing to holder of issued share of any class or series amount not exceeding stated capital of class or series; and (c) declaring stated capital to be reduced by amount not represented by realizable assets, unless with regard to (a) and (b) above there are reasonable grounds for believing that (a) corporation is, or would after reduction be, unable to pay its liabilities as they become due; or (b) realizable value of corporation's assets would thereby be less than aggregate of its liabilities.

Adjustment of Stated Capital Account.—Upon purchase, redemption or other acquisition by corporation under Act of shares or fractions thereof issued by it, corporation must deduct from stated capital account maintained for class or series of shares purchased, redeemed or otherwise acquired amount equal to result obtained by multiplying stated capital of shares of that class or series by number of shares of that class or series or fractions thereof purchased, redeemed or otherwise acquired, divided by number of issued shares of that class or series immediately before purchase, redemption or other acquisition.

Cancellation or Restoration of Shares.—Shares or fractions thereof issued by corporation and purchased, redeemed or otherwise acquired by it shall be cancelled or, if articles limit number of authorized shares, may be restored to status of authorized but unissued shares.

Repayment.—Debt obligations issued, pledged, hypothecated or deposited by corporation are not redeemed by reason only that indebtedness evidenced by debt obligations or in respect of which debt obligations are issued, pledged, hypothecated or deposited is repaid.

Acquisition and Reissue of Debt Obligations.—Debt obligations issued by corporation and purchased, redeemed or otherwise acquired by it may be cancelled or, subject to any applicable trust indenture or other agreement, may be reissued, pledged or hypothecated to secure any obligation of corporation then existing or thereafter incurred, and any such acquisition and reissue, pledge or hypothecation is not cancellation of debt obligations.

Enforceability of Contract.—Contract with corporation providing for purchase of shares of corporation is specifically enforceable against corporation except to extent that corporation cannot perform contract without thereby being in breach of Act.

Commission for Sale of Shares.—Directors acting honestly and in good faith with view to best interests of corporation may authorize corporation to pay commission to any person in consideration of his purchasing or agreeing to purchase shares of corporation from corporation or from any other person, or procuring or agreeing to procure purchasers for any such shares.

Dividends.—Corporation must not declare or pay dividend if there are reasonable grounds for believing that: (a) corporation is, or would, after payment be, unable to pay its liabilities as they become due; or (b) realizable value of corporation's assets would thereby be less than aggregate of its liabilities and stated capital of all classes. Corporation may pay dividend in money or property or by issuing fully paid shares of corporation.

Prohibited Loans and Guarantees.—Corporation or any corporation with which it is affiliated must not, directly or indirectly, give financial assistance by means of loan, guarantee or otherwise: (1) to any shareholder, director, officer or employee of such corporation or affiliated corporation, or associate of any such person; or (2) to any

See Topical Index in front part of this volume.

CORPORATIONS . . . *continued*
person, for purpose of, or in connection with, purchase of share issued or to be issued by corporation other than (a) in ordinary course of business if lending of money is part of ordinary business of corporation; (b) on account of expenditures incurred or to be incurred on behalf of corporation; (c) to holding body corporate if corporation is wholly-owned subsidiary of holding body corporate; (d) to subsidiary body corporate of corporation; (e) to employees of corporation or any of its affiliates (i) to enable or assist them to purchase or erect living accommodation for their own occupation, or (ii) in accordance with plan for purchase of shares of corporation or any of its affiliates to be held by trustee; and (f) in any other case unless there are reasonable grounds for believing that (i) corporation is, or would after giving financial assistance be, unable to pay its liabilities as they become due, or (ii) realizable value of corporation's assets, excluding amount of any financial assistance in form of loan and in form of assets pledged or encumbered to secure guarantee, would after giving financial assistance be less than aggregate of corporation's liabilities and stated capital of all classes.

Shareholder Immunity.—Shareholders of corporation are not, as shareholders, liable for any liability, act or default of corporation except for any money, property or benefits received by them as result of improper reduction of stated capital, liabilities for breach of their duties as directors as result of unanimous shareholders' agreement and judgment against them in representative action brought against them as class.

Part VI. Sale of Constrained Shares.—Part VI regulates sale and transfer of shares that are constrained in order to assist corporation or any of its affiliates or associates to attain specified level of Canadian ownership. Corporation can sell constrained shares to further purposes of constraint upon compensating previous shareholder in form of trust fund comprised of proceeds of sale. Accepted purposes of constraining shares are governed by this Part.

Part VII. Security Certificates, Registers and Transfers.—Part VII of Act represents attempt to achieve two goals (i) to consolidate in one Part of Act all of rules relating to security registers, dealing with security holders and security transfers, and (ii) to introduce concept of Article 8 of Uniform Commercial Code which has effect of making properly endorsed security certificates negotiable instruments between registration dates. Concept of negotiability between registration dates results in security certificate being not merely evidence of legal rights and privileges but embodiment of those rights and privileges which are transferred when security certificate is transferred. Concept of registration assures bona fide purchaser that registered holder is owner of security and gives such purchaser assurance that when registered his ownership of security cannot be impugned.

Negotiable Instruments.—Except where its transfer is restricted and noted on security in accordance with Act, security is negotiable instrument and in case of any conflict with Bills of Exchange Act of Canada Part VII of Canada Business Corporations Act prevails.

"Security".—"Security" or "security certificate" for purposes of this Part of Act is defined to mean instrument issued by corporation that is: (a) in bearer or registered form, (b) of type commonly dealt in upon securities exchanges or markets or commonly recognized in any area in which it is issued or dealt in as medium for investment, (c) one of class or series or by its terms divisible into class or series of instruments, and (d) evidence of share, participation or other interest in or obligation of corporation.

Registered Form.—Security is in registered form if: (a) it specifies person entitled to security or to rights it evidences, and its transfer is capable of being recorded in securities register; or (b) it bears statement that it is in registered form.

Bearer Form.—Security is in bearer form if it is payable to bearer according to its terms and not by reason of any endorsement.

Rights of Holder.—Every security holder is entitled at his option to security certificate that complies with Act or non-transferable written acknowledgment of his right to obtain such security certificate from corporation in respect of securities of that corporation held by him.

Restrictions.—If security certificate issued by corporation or by body corporate before body corporate was continued under Act is or becomes subject to: (a) restriction on its transfer other than restraint on constrained share corporation, (b) lien in favour of corporation, (c) unanimous shareholder agreement, or (d) endorsement that shareholder is dissenting shareholder under Act; such restriction, lien, agreement or endorsement is ineffective against transferee of security who has no actual knowledge of it, unless it or reference to it is noted conspicuously on security certificate.

Securities Records.—Corporation must maintain securities register in which it records securities issued by it in registered form, showing with respect to each class or series of securities: (a) names, alphabetically arranged, and latest known address of each person who is or has been security holder; (b) number of securities held by each security holder; and (c) date and particulars of issue and transfer of each security.

Place of Register.—Central securities register must be maintained by corporation at its registered office or at any other place in Canada designated by directors, and any branch securities registers may be kept at any place in or out of Canada designated by directors.

Dealings with Registered Holder.—Corporation or trustee under trust indenture may as rule treat registered owner of security as person exclusively entitled to vote, to receive notices, to receive interest, dividend or other payments in respect of security, and otherwise exercise all rights and powers of owner of security.

Title of Purchaser.—Upon delivery of security purchaser acquires rights in security that his transferor had or had authority to convey, except that purchaser who has been party to any fraud or illegality affecting security or who as prior holder had notice of adverse claim does not improve his position by taking from later bona fide purchaser. Bona fide purchaser, in addition to acquiring rights or purchaser, also acquires security free from any adverse claim.

Part VII of Act like Part VI of Business Corporations Act, 1982 of Ontario contains elaborate set of provisions governing dealings in corporate securities. Sections in this Part are designed to provide system which would permit fast and reliable securities transactions with minimum of title investigation by securities purchaser. It is anticipated that this rather technical portion of Act would affect comparatively few day-to-day business decisions.

Part VIII. Trust Indentures.—Part VIII of Act sets out specific rules relating to: (a) trust indentures under which debt obligations are issued by corporation in distribution to public and (b) qualifications of trustees appointed under those indentures. Provisions require compliance with expressed statutory standards relating to trustee qualifications, conflict of interest, rights of debenture holders to obtain information, rights of trustee to demand information from issuing corporation and duties of trustee. These statutory standards will apply irrespective of any contradictory or exculpatory clauses in trust indenture. These provisions are substantially same as corresponding provisions of Part V of Business Corporations Act, 1982 of Ontario although there are number of drafting differences which may be found to be of importance.

Part IX. Receivers and Receiver-Managers.—Part IX of Act sets out statutory standards or delegates to court discretion concerning qualifications, functions, rights, powers and duties of receiver and receiver-manager, including his standing with respect to directors, liquidator or trustee in bankruptcy. Provisions of this Part require receiver to submit financial statements in form that directors would have been required to submit to shareholders which reflects fact that receiver-manager assumes management of business and affairs of corporation.

Part X. Directors and Officers.—Subject to any unanimous shareholder agreement, directors must manage business and affairs of corporation.

Corporation must have one or more directors but corporation, any of issued securities of which are or were part of distribution to public, and remain outstanding and are held by more than one person, must have not fewer than three directors, at least two of whom are not officers or employees of corporation or its affiliates.

Affiliated Corporations.—One body corporate is affiliated with another body corporate if one of them is subsidiary of other or both are subsidiaries of same body corporate or each of them is controlled by same person, and if two bodies corporate are affiliated with same body corporate at same time, they are deemed to be affiliated with each other.

Deemed Control.—For purposes of Act, body corporate is deemed to be controlled by person if shares of body corporate carrying voting rights sufficient to elect majority of directors of body corporate are held, directly or indirectly, other than by way of security only, by or on behalf of that person.

Qualifications of Directors.—Following persons are disqualified from being director of corporation: (a) anyone who is less than 18 years of age; (b) anyone who is of unsound mind and has been so found by court in Canada or elsewhere; (c) person who is not individual; or (d) person who has status of bankrupt.

Further Qualifications.—Unless articles otherwise provide, director of corporation is not required to hold shares issued by corporation.

Residency.—Majority of directors of corporation must be resident Canadians.

"Resident Canadian".—"Resident Canadian" is defined in Act to mean individual who is: (a) Canadian citizen ordinarily resident in Canada, (b) Canadian citizen not ordinarily resident in Canada who is member of prescribed class of persons or (c) permanent resident within meaning of Immigration Act, and ordinarily resident in Canada, except permanent resident who has been ordinarily resident in Canada for more than one year after time at which he first became eligible to apply for Canadian citizenship.

Exception for Holding Corporation.—Notwithstanding foregoing, not more than one-third of directors of holding corporation need be resident Canadians if holding corporation earns in Canada directly or through its subsidiaries less than 5% of gross revenues of holding corporation and all of its subsidiary bodies corporate together as shown in most recent consolidated financial statements of holding corporation or most recent financial statements of holding corporation and its subsidiary bodies corporate.

Election of Directors.—Subject to cumulative voting provisions in articles of corporation, shareholders of corporation must, by ordinary resolution at first meeting of shareholders and at each succeeding annual meeting at which election of directors is required, elect directors to hold office for term expiring not later than close of third annual meeting of shareholders following election. It is not necessary that all directors elected at meeting of shareholders hold office for same term.

Appointment of Directors.—Directors may, if articles so provide, appoint one or more directors until next annual meeting of shareholders provided that total number of directors so appointed does not exceed one-third of number of directors elected at previous meeting.

Cumulative Voting.—Articles may provide for cumulative voting at election of directors.

Filling Vacancy.—Subject to articles, quorum of directors may fill vacancy among directors, except vacancy resulting from increase in number or minimum number of directors or from failure to elect number or minimum number of directors required by articles.

Meeting of Directors.—Unless articles or by-laws otherwise provide, directors may meet at any place, and upon such notice as by-laws require.

Quorum.—Subject to articles or by-laws, majority of number of directors or minimum number of directors required by articles constitutes quorum at any meeting of directors, and, notwithstanding any vacancy among directors, quorum of directors may exercise all powers of directors.

Canadian Majority.—Directors, other than directors of holding corporation earning less than 5% of its gross consolidated revenues in Canada must not transact business at meeting of directors unless majority of directors present are resident Canadians.

Participation by Telephone.—Subject to by-laws, director may, if all directors of corporation consent, participate in meeting of directors or of committee of directors by means of such telephone or other communications facilities as permit all persons participating in meeting to hear each other and director in such meeting by such means is deemed for purposes of Act to be present at that meeting.

Delegation.—Directors of corporation may appoint from their number managing director who is resident Canadian or committee of directors and delegate to such managing director or committee subject to limitations set forth in Act, any of powers of directors. If directors of corporation, other than holding corporation earning less than 5% of its gross consolidated revenues in Canada, appoint committee of directors, majority of members of committee must be resident Canadians.

Resolution in Lieu of Meeting.—Resolution in writing, signed by all directors entitled to vote on that resolution at meeting of directors or committee of directors, is as valid as if it had been passed at meeting of directors or committee of directors.

Directors' Liability.—Directors of corporation who vote for or consent to resolution authorizing issue of share for consideration other than money are jointly and severally

See Topical Index in front part of this volume.

CORPORATIONS . . . *continued*

liable to corporation to make good any amount by which consideration received is less than fair equivalent of money that corporation would have received if share had been issued for money on date of resolution. Director is not liable if he proves that he did not know and could not reasonably have known that share was issued for consideration less than fair equivalent of money that corporation would have received if share had been issued for money.

Further Directors' Liabilities.—Directors of corporation who vote for or consent to resolution authorizing: (a) purchase, redemption or other acquisition of shares contrary to §§34-36 of Act, (b) commission contrary to §41 of Act, (c) payment of dividend contrary to §42 of Act, (d) financial assistance contrary to §44 of Act, (e) payment of indemnity contrary to §124 of Act, or (f) payment to shareholder contrary to §196 or §241 of Act; are jointly and severally liable to restore to corporation any amounts so distributed or paid and not otherwise recovered by corporation.

Liability of Directors for Wages.—Directors of corporation are jointly and severally liable to employees of corporation for all debts not exceeding six months wages payable to each such employee for services performed for corporation while they are such directors respectively.

Disclosure of Interested Director Contract.—Director or officer of corporation who: (a) is party to material contract or proposed material contract with corporation, or (b) is director or officer of or has material interest in any person who is party to material contract or proposed material contract with corporation; must disclose in writing to corporation or request to have entered in minutes of meetings of directors nature and extent of his interest.

Time of Disclosure for Director.—Disclosure required by director must be made: (a) at meeting at which proposed contract is first considered; (b) if director was not then interested in proposed contract, at first meeting after he becomes so interested; (c) if director becomes interested after contract is made, at first meeting after he becomes so interested, or (d) if person who is interested in contract later becomes director, at first meeting after he becomes director.

Time of Disclosure for Officer.—Disclosure required by officer who is not director must be made: (a) forthwith after he becomes aware that contract or proposed contract is to be considered or has been considered at meeting of directors; (b) if officer becomes interested after contract is made, forthwith after he becomes so interested; or (c) if person who is interested in contract later becomes officer, forthwith after he becomes officer.

Time of Disclosure for Director or Officer.—If material contract or proposed material contract is one that, in ordinary course of corporation's business, would not require approval by directors or shareholders, director or officer must disclose in writing to corporation or request to have entered in minutes of meetings of directors nature and extent of his interest forthwith after director or officer becomes aware of contract or proposed contract.

Voting After Disclosure.—Director must not vote on any resolution to approve such contract unless contract is: (a) arrangement by way of security for money lent to or obligations undertaken by him for benefit of corporation or affiliate; (b) one relating primarily to his remuneration as director, officer, employee or agent of corporation or affiliate; (c) one for indemnity or insurance under §124 of Act; or (d) one with affiliate.

General notice to directors by director or officer, declaring that he is director or officer of or has material interest in person and is to be regarded as interested in any contract made with that person, is sufficient declaration of interest in relation to any contract so made.

Avoidance Standards.—Material contract between corporation and one or more of its directors or officers, or between corporation and another person of which director or officer of corporation is director or officer or in which he has material interest, is neither void nor voidable by reason only of that relationship or by reason only that director with interest in contract is present at or is counted to determine presence of quorum at meeting of directors or committee of directors that authorized contract, if director or officer disclosed his interest in accordance with Act and contract was approved by directors or shareholders and it was reasonable and fair to corporation at time it was approved.

Duty of Care of Directors and Officers.—Every director and officer of corporation in exercising his powers and discharging his duties must: (a) act honestly and in good faith with view to best interests of corporation; and (b) exercise care, diligence and skill that reasonably prudent person would exercise in comparable circumstances, except to extent that his powers are restricted by unanimous shareholder agreement.

Duty to Comply.—Every director and officer of corporation must comply with Act, regulations, articles, by-laws and any unanimous shareholder agreement.

No Exculpation.—No provision in contract, articles, by-laws or resolution relieves director or officer from duty to act in accordance with Act or regulations or relieves him from liability for breach thereof.

Reliance on Statements.—Director is not liable under above provisions if he relies in good faith upon: (a) financial statements of corporation represented to him by officer of corporation or in written report of auditor of corporation fairly to reflect financial condition of corporation; or (b) report of lawyer, accountant, engineer, appraiser or other person whose profession lends credibility to statement made by him.

Indemnification.—Except in respect of action by or on behalf of corporation or body corporate to procure judgment in its favour, corporation may indemnify director or officer of corporation, former director or officer of corporation or person who acts or acted at corporation's request as director or officer of body corporate of which corporation is or was shareholder or creditor, and his heirs and legal representatives, against all costs, charges and expenses, including amount paid to settle action or satisfy judgment, reasonably incurred by him in respect of any civil, criminal or administrative action or proceeding to which he is made party by reason of being or having been director or officer of such corporation or body corporate, if: (a) he acted honestly and in good faith with view to best interests of corporation; and (b) in case of criminal or administrative action or proceeding that is enforced by monetary penalty, he had reasonable grounds for believing that his conduct was lawful.

Corporation may with approval of court indemnify person referred to in foregoing paragraph in respect of action by or on behalf of corporation or body corporate to procure judgment in its favour, to which he is made party by reason of being or having been director or officer of corporation or body corporate, against all costs, charges and expenses reasonably incurred by him in connection with such action if he fulfils conditions set out in clauses (a) and (b) above.

Right to Indemnify.—Notwithstanding anything contained above, corporation must indemnify any such person who has been substantially successful in defence of any civil, criminal or administrative action or proceeding to which he is made party by reason of being or having been director or officer of corporation or body corporate and who fulfils conditions set out in clauses (a) and (b) above, against all costs, charges and expenses reasonably incurred by him in respect of such action or proceeding.

Directors' and Officers' Insurance.—Corporation may purchase and maintain insurance for benefit of any such person against any liability incurred by him in his capacity as director or officer of corporation, except where liability relates to failure to act honestly and in good faith with view to best interests of corporation.

Part XI. Insider Trading.—

First Insider Report.—Unless he has filed or has been exempted from filing insider report under Canada Corporations Act or regulations, person who is insider or who is deemed by Act to have been insider of body corporate on day on which it is continued as corporation under this Act must, within ten days after end of month in which such day occurs, send to Director insider report in prescribed form, if corporation is distributing corporation. "Insider" in this provision means: (a) director or officer of distributing corporation, (b) distributing corporation that purchases or otherwise acquires, shares (except shares under Act) issued by it or by any of its affiliates, or (c) person who beneficially owns more than 10% of shares of distributing corporation or who exercises control or direction over more than 10% of votes attached to shares of distributing corporation, excluding shares owned by underwriter under underwriting agreement while those shares are in course of distribution to public. "Distributing corporation" means corporation, any of issued securities of which are or were part of distribution to public and remain outstanding and are held by more than one person.

Person who becomes insider shall, within ten days after end of month in which he becomes insider, send to Director insider report in prescribed form.

Subsequent Insider Reports.—Insider whose interest in securities of distributing corporation changes from that shown or required to be shown in last insider report sent or required to be sent by him must within ten days after end of month in which such change takes place, send to Director insider report in prescribed form.

Exemption Order.—Upon application by or on behalf of insider, Director may make order on such terms as he thinks fit exempting insider from any of requirements of this section, which order may have retrospective effect.

Prohibition of Short Sale.—Insider must not knowingly sell, directly or indirectly, share of distributing corporation or any of its affiliates if insider selling share does not own or has not fully paid for share to be sold, unless he owns another share convertible into share sold or option or right to acquire share sold and, within ten days after sale, he: (a) exercises conversion privilege, option or right and delivers share so acquired to purchaser; or (b) transfers convertible share, option or right to purchaser.

Call and Puts.—Insider must not, directly or indirectly, buy or sell call or put in respect of share of corporation or any of its affiliates.

Civil Liability.—Insider who, in connection with transaction in security of corporation or any of its affiliates, makes use of any specific confidential information for his own benefit or advantage that, if generally known, might reasonably be expected to affect materially value of security: (a) is liable to compensate any person for any direct loss suffered by that person as result of transaction, unless information was known or in exercise of reasonable diligence could have been known to that person at time of transaction; and (b) is accountable to corporation for any direct benefit or advantage received or receivable by insider as result of transaction.

"Insider" in this provision means: (a) corporation; (b) affiliate of corporation; (c) director or officer of corporation; (d) person who beneficially owns more than 10% of shares of corporation or who exercises control or direction over more than 10% of votes attached to shares of corporation; (e) person employed or retained by corporation; and (f) person who receives special confidential information from person described in paragraph or paragraph following including person described in this clause (f) and who has knowledge that person giving information is person described in this paragraph or paragraph following including person described in this clause (f).

For purposes of this provision if body corporate becomes insider of corporation, or enters into business combination with corporation, director or officer of body corporate is deemed to have been insider of corporation for previous six months or for such shorter period as he was director or officer of body corporate; and if corporation becomes insider of body corporate, or enters into business combination with body corporate, director or officer of body corporate is deemed to have been insider of corporation for previous six months or for such shorter period as he was director or officer of body corporate.

In paragraph above, "business combination" means acquisition of all or substantially all property of one body corporate by another or amalgamation of two or more bodies corporate.

Part XII. Shareholders.—

Place of Meetings.—Meetings of shareholders of corporation must be held at place within Canada provided in by-laws or, in absence of such provisions, at place within Canada that directors determine.

Meeting Outside Canada.—Meeting of shareholders of corporation may be held outside Canada if all shareholders entitled to vote at that meeting so agree.

Calling Meetings.—Directors of corporation: (a) must call annual meeting of shareholders not later than 18 months after corporation comes into existence and subsequently not later than 15 months after holding last preceding annual meeting; (b) may at any time call special meeting of shareholders; and (c) may fix in advance date as record date for purpose of determining shareholders (i) entitled to receive notice of meeting of shareholders, (ii) entitled to receive payment of dividend, (iii) entitled to participate in liquidation distribution, or (iv) for any other purpose except right to receive notice of or to vote at meeting.

Notice of Meeting.—Notice of time and place of meeting of shareholders must be sent not less than 21 days nor more than 50 days before meeting: (a) to each shareholder entitled to vote at meeting; (b) to each director; and (c) to auditor of corporation.

See Topical Index in front part of this volume.

CORPORATIONS . . . *continued*

All business transacted at special meeting of shareholders and all business transacted at annual meeting of shareholders, except consideration of financial statements, auditor's report, election of directors and reappointment of incumbent auditor, is deemed to be special business.

Notice of Business.—Notice of meeting of shareholders at which special business is to be transacted must state: (a) nature of that business in sufficient detail to permit shareholder to form reasoned judgment thereon; and (b) text of any special resolution to be submitted to meeting.

Shareholder Proposal.—Shareholder entitled to vote at annual meeting of shareholders may: (a) submit to corporation notice of any matter that he proposes to raise at meeting, (hereinafter referred to as "proposal"); and (b) discuss at meeting any matter in respect of which he would have been entitled to submit proposal.

Information Circular.—Corporation that solicits proxies must set out proposal in management proxy circular or attach proposal thereto and, if so requested by shareholder, must include in management proxy circular or attach thereto statement by shareholder of not more than 200 words in support of proposal, and name and address of shareholder.

Nomination for Director.—Proposal may include nominations for election of directors if proposal is signed by one or more holders of shares representing in aggregate not less than 5% of shares or 5% of shares of class of shares of corporation entitled to vote at meeting to which proposal is to be presented, but this provision does not preclude nominations made at meeting of shareholders.

Corporation is not required to set out proposal or supporting statement of shareholder in management proxy circular or attach proposal thereto if: (a) proposal is not submitted to corporation at least 90 days before anniversary date of previous annual meeting of shareholders; (b) it clearly appears that proposal is submitted by shareholder primarily for purposes of enforcing personal claim or redressing personal grievance against corporation or its directors, officers or security holders, or primarily for purpose of promoting general economic, political, racial, religious, social or similar causes; (c) corporation, at shareholder's request, included proposal in management proxy circular relating to meeting of shareholders held within two years preceding receipt of such request, and shareholder failed to present proposal, in person or by proxy, at meeting; (d) substantially same proposal was submitted to shareholders in management proxy circular or dissident's proxy circular relating to meeting of shareholders held within two years preceding receipt of shareholder's request and proposal was defeated; or (e) rights conferred by this provision are being abused to secure publicity.

Notice of Refusal.—If corporation refuses to include proposal in management proxy circular, corporation must, within ten days after receiving proposal, notify shareholder submitting proposal of its intention to omit proposal from management proxy circular and send to him statement of reasons for refusal.

Shareholder Application in Court.—Upon application of shareholder claiming to be aggrieved by corporation's refusal to include proposal in management proxy circular, court may restrain holding of meeting to which proposal is sought to be presented and make any further order it thinks fit.

Shareholder List.—Corporation must prepare list of shareholders entitled to receive notice of meeting arranged in alphabetical order and showing number of shares held by each shareholder.

Examination of List.—Shareholder may examine list of shareholders: (a) During usual business hours at registered office of corporation or at place where its central securities register is maintained; and (b) at meeting of shareholders for which list was prepared.

Quorum.—Unless by-laws otherwise provide, holders of majority of shares entitled to vote at meeting of shareholders present in person or by proxy constitute quorum.

One Shareholder Meeting.—If corporation has only one shareholder, or only one holder of any class or series of shares, shareholder present in person or by proxy constitutes meeting.

Right to Vote.—Unless articles otherwise provide, each share of corporation entitles holder thereof to one vote at meeting of shareholders.

Voting.—Unless by-laws otherwise provide, voting at meeting of shareholders shall be by show of hands except where ballot is demanded by shareholder or proxyholder entitled to vote at meeting.

Resolution in Lieu of Meeting.—Except where written statement is submitted by (a) director who: (i) resigns, (ii) receives notice or otherwise learns of meeting of shareholders called for purpose of removing him from office or (iii) receives notice or otherwise learns of meeting of directors or shareholders at which another person is to be appointed or elected to fill office of director, whether because of his resignation or removal or because his term of office has expired or is about to expire, and submits to corporation written statement giving reasons for his resignation or reasons why he opposes any proposed action or resolution; or (b) by auditor who (iv) resigns, (v) receives notice or otherwise learns of meeting of shareholders called for purpose of removing him from office, (vi) receives notice or otherwise learns of meeting of directors or shareholders at which another person is to be appointed to fill office of auditor, whether because of resignation or removal of incumbent auditor or because his term of office has expired or is about to expire, or (vii) receives notice or otherwise learns of meeting of shareholders at which resolution dispensing with auditor is to be proposed, and submits to corporation written statement, giving reasons for his resignation or reasons why he opposes any proposed action or resolution; (1) resolution in writing signed by all shareholders entitled to vote on that resolution at meeting of shareholders is as valid as if it had been passed at meeting of shareholders; and (2) resolution in writing dealing with all matters required by Act to be dealt with at meeting of shareholders and signed by all shareholders entitled to vote at that meeting satisfies all requirements of Act relating to meetings of shareholders.

Requisition of Meeting.—Holders of not less than 5% of issued shares of corporation that carry right to vote at meeting sought to be held may requisition directors to call meeting of shareholders for purposes stated in requisition.

Court Review of Election.—Corporation or shareholder or director may apply to court to determine any controversy with respect to election or appointment of director or auditor of corporation.

Pooling Agreement.—Written agreement between two or more shareholders may provide that in exercising voting rights shares held by them shall be voted as therein provided.

Unanimous Shareholder Agreement.—An otherwise lawful written agreement among all shareholders of corporation, or among all shareholders and person who is not shareholder, that restricts, in whole or in part, powers of directors to manage business and affairs of corporation is valid. Where person who is beneficial owner of all issued shares of corporation makes written declaration that restricts powers of directors, declaration deemed to be unanimous shareholder agreement.

If reference to unanimous shareholder agreement is conspicuously noted on share certificates, transferee of shares subject to unanimous shareholder agreement is deemed to be party to agreement.

Shareholder who is party to unanimous shareholder agreement has all rights, powers and duties of director of corporation to which agreement relates to extent that agreement restricts discretion or powers of directors to manage business and affairs of corporation, and directors are thereby relieved of their duties to same extent.

Part XIII. Proxies.—Part XII of Act contains substance of proxy rules of Canada Corporations Act while at same time amends some of language and shifts number of minor details with respect to proxy solicitations to regulations.

Appointing Proxyholder.—Shareholder entitled to vote at meeting of shareholders may by means of proxy appoint proxyholder or one or more alternate proxyholders who are not required to be shareholders, to attend and act at meeting in manner and to extent authorized by proxy and with authority conferred by proxy.

Mandatory Solicitation.—Management of corporation must concurrently with giving notice of meeting of shareholders send form of proxy in prescribed form to each shareholder who is entitled to receive notice of meeting unless corporation has fewer than 15 shareholders, two or more joint holders being counted as one shareholder.

Soliciting Proxies.—Person must not solicit proxies unless: (a) in case of solicitation by or on behalf of management of corporation, management proxy circular in prescribed form, either as appendix to or as separate document accompanying notice of meeting, or (b) in case of any other solicitation, dissident's proxy circular in prescribed form stating purposes of solicitation; is sent to auditor of corporation, to each shareholder whose proxy is solicited and, if solicitation other than by or on behalf of management, to corporation.

Copy to Director.—Person required to send management proxy circular or dissident's proxy circular must send concurrently copy thereof to Director together with statement in prescribed form, form of proxy and any other documents for use in connection with meeting and, in case of management proxy circular, copy of notice of meeting.

Upon application of interested person, Director may make order on such terms as he thinks fit exempting such person from any of requirements of Act respecting proxy solicitation which order may have retrospective effect.

Attendance at Meeting.—Person who solicits proxy and is appointed proxyholder must attend in person or cause alternate proxyholder to attend meeting in respect of which proxy is given and comply with directions of shareholder who appointed him.

Duty of Registrant.—Shares of corporation that are registered in name of registrant or his nominee (usually broker) and not beneficially owned by registrant must not be voted unless registrant forthwith after receipt thereof sends to beneficial owner: (a) copy of notice of meeting, financial statements, management proxy circular, dissident's proxy circular and any other documents other than form of proxy, sent to shareholders by or on behalf of any person for use in connection with meeting; and (b) except where registrant has received written voting instructions from beneficial owner, written request for such instructions.

Beneficial Owner Unknown.—Registrant must not vote or appoint proxyholder to vote shares registered in his name or in name of his nominee that he does not beneficially own unless he receives voting instructions from beneficial owner.

Instructions to Registrant.—Registrant shall vote or appoint proxyholder to vote any such shares in accordance with any written voting instructions received from beneficial owner.

Part XIV. Financial Disclosure.—

Annual Financial Statements.—Directors of corporation must place before shareholders at every annual meeting: (a) comparative financial statements as prescribed by Act; (b) report of auditor, if any; and (c) any further information respecting financial position of corporation and results of its operations required by articles, by-laws or any unanimous shareholder agreement.

Exemption.—Corporation may apply to Director for order authorizing corporation to omit from its financial statements any item prescribed, or to dispense with publication of any particular financial statement prescribed, and Director may, if he reasonably believes that disclosure of information therein contained would be detrimental to corporation, permit such omission on such reasonable conditions as he thinks fit.

Consolidated Statements.—Holding corporation may prepare financial statements referred to in Act in consolidated or combined form as prescribed, and in any case corporation shall keep at its registered office copies of financial statements of each subsidiary body corporate.

Examination.—Shareholders of corporation and their agents and legal representatives may upon request therefor examine above statements during usual business hours of corporation and may make extracts therefrom free of charge unless upon application to court, court is satisfied that such examination would be detrimental to corporation or subsidiary body corporate and bars such right or makes any further order it thinks fit.

Approval of Financial Statements.—Directors of corporation must approve financial statements and approval must be evidenced by signature of one or more directors.

Copies to Shareholders.—Corporation must not less than 21 days before each annual meeting of shareholders or before signing of shareholders' resolution in lieu of annual meeting, send copy of financial statements, report of auditor, if any, and any other information required by articles, by-laws or any unanimous shareholder's agreement to each shareholder, except to shareholder who has informed corporation in writing that he does not want copy of those documents.

Copies to Director.—Corporation, any of securities of which are or were part of distribution to public, remain outstanding and are held by more than one person, must before each annual meeting of shareholders or forthwith after signing of shareholders' resolution in lieu of annual meeting, send copy of financial statements, report of auditor,

See Topical Index in front part of this volume.

CORPORATIONS . . . *continued*
if any, and any other information sent to shareholders or to public authority or recognized stock exchange to Director.

Affiliates.—Gross revenues and assets of corporation are deemed by Act to include gross revenues and assets of its affiliates.

Qualification of Auditor.—Unless granted exemption by court order, person is disqualified from being auditor of corporation if he is not independent of corporation, any of its affiliates, or directors or officers of any such corporation or its affiliates.

Appointment of Auditor.—Shareholders of corporation by ordinary resolution, at first annual meeting of shareholders and at each succeeding annual meeting must appoint auditor to hold office until close of next annual meeting unless corporation is eligible to dispense with appointment of auditor or obtains exemption order.

If auditor is not appointed at meeting of shareholders, incumbent auditor continues in office until his successor is appointed.

Remuneration of auditor may be fixed by ordinary resolution of shareholders or, if not so fixed, may be fixed by directors.

Dispensing with Auditor and Exemptions.—Shareholders including shareholders not otherwise entitled to vote may unanimously resolve not to appoint auditor other than corporation and any of securities of which are or were part of distribution to public, remain outstanding and are held by more than one person may not appoint auditor.

Removal of Auditor.—Shareholders of corporation may by ordinary resolution at special meeting remove from office auditor other than auditor appointed by court.

Filling Vacancy.—Subject to articles of corporation, directors must forthwith fill vacancy in office of auditor.

Right to Attend Meeting.—Auditor of corporation is entitled to receive notice of every meeting of shareholders and, at expense of corporation, to attend and be heard thereat on matters relating to his duties as auditor.

Right to Information.—Upon demand of auditor of corporation, present or former directors, officers, employees or agents of corporation must furnish such: (a) information and explanations, and (b) access to records, documents, books, accounts and vouchers of corporation or any of its subsidiaries; as are, in opinion of auditor, necessary to enable him to make examination and report required under Act and that directors, officers, employees or agents are reasonably able to furnish.

Audit Committee.—Unless dispensed with by order of Director, corporation any of issued securities of which are or were part of distribution to public and any other corporation may have audit committee composed of not less than three directors of corporation, majority of whom are not officers or employees of corporation or any of its affiliates. Auditor of corporation is entitled to receive notice of every meeting of audit committee and, at expense of corporation, to attend and be heard thereat.

Duty of Committee.—Audit committee must review financial statements of corporation before such financial statements are approved by directors.

Error in Financial Statements.—If auditor or former auditor of corporation is notified or becomes aware of error or misstatement in financial statement upon which he has reported, and if in his opinion error or misstatement is material, he must inform each director accordingly.

Duty of Directors.—When auditor or former auditor informs directors of error or misstatement in financial statement, directors must: (a) prepare and issue revised financial statements; or (b) otherwise inform shareholders and, if corporation is one that is required to file its financial statements with Director, it must inform Director of error or misstatement in same manner as it informs shareholders.

Qualified Privilege (Defamation).—Any oral or written statement or report made under Act by auditor or former auditor of corporation has qualified privilege for purpose of law of defamation.

Part XV. Fundamental Changes.—

Amendment of Articles.—Articles of corporation may by special resolution be amended to change its name; registered office; restrictions on business; number, classes, designations, rights, privileges and restrictions on its shares; stated capital (if it is set out in articles); number of directors (subject to right of incumbent directors and cumulative voting provisions); restrictions on transfer of shares and any other provision that is permitted by Act to be set out in articles.

Constraints on Share Transfers.—Subject to class voting provisions and reduction of stated capital provisions of Act, corporation any of issued shares of which are or were part of distribution to public may by special resolution amend its articles to constrain issue or transfer of its shares in accordance with regulations: (a) to persons who are not resident Canadians; or (b) to enable corporation or affiliates to qualify under any laws of Canada referred to in regulations (i) to obtain licence to carry on business, (ii) to become publisher of Canadian newspaper or periodical, or (iii) to acquire shares of financial intermediary as defined in regulations.

Proposal to Amend.—Directors or any shareholder entitled to vote at annual meeting may make proposal to amend articles. Notice of meeting of shareholders at which proposal to amend articles is to be considered shall set out proposed amendment and where applicable, shall state that dissenting shareholder is entitled to be paid fair value of his shares in accordance with Act, but failure to make that statement does not invalidate amendment.

Class Vote.—Holders of shares of class or, of series (if such series is affected by amendment in manner different from other shares of same class) are, unless articles otherwise provide in case of amendment referred to in (a), (b) or (e) below, entitled to vote (whether or not shares of such class or series otherwise carry right to vote) separately as class or series upon proposal to amend articles to: (a) increase or decrease any maximum number of authorized shares of such class or increase any maximum number of authorized shares of class having rights or privileges equal or superior to shares of such class; (b) effect exchange, reclassification or cancellation of all or part of shares of such class; (c) add, change or remove rights, privileges, restrictions or conditions attached to shares of such class; (d) increase rights or privileges of any class of shares having rights or privileges equal or superior to shares of such class; (e) create new class of shares equal or superior to shares of such class; (f) make any class of shares having rights or privileges inferior to shares of such class equal or superior to shares of such class; (g) effect exchange or create right of exchange of all or part of shares of another class into shares of such class; or (h) constrain issue or transfer of shares of such class or extend or remove such constraint.

No amendment to articles affects existing cause of action or claim or liability to prosecution in favour of or against corporation or its directors or officers, or any civil, criminal or administrative action or proceeding to which corporation or its directors or officers is party.

Amalgamation.—Two or more corporations, including holding and subsidiary corporations, may amalgamate and continue as one corporation. Each corporation proposing to amalgamate must enter into agreement setting out terms and means of effecting amalgamation.

Shareholder Approval.—Directors of each amalgamating corporation must submit amalgamation agreement for approval to meeting of holders of shares of amalgamating corporation of which they are directors.

Each share of amalgamating corporation carries right to vote in respect of amalgamation whether or not it otherwise carries right to vote.

Amalgamation agreement is adopted when shareholders of each amalgamating corporation have approved of amalgamation by special resolutions of each class or series of such shareholders entitled to vote thereon.

Vertical Short-form Amalgamation.—Holding corporation and one or more of its subsidiary corporations may amalgamate and continue as one corporation without entering into amalgamation agreement and without obtaining shareholders approval if amalgamation is approved by resolution of directors of each amalgamating corporation; all of issued shares of each amalgamating subsidiary corporations are held by one or more of other amalgamating corporations, and resolutions provide that: (a) Shares of each amalgamating subsidiary corporation shall be cancelled without any repayment of capital in respect thereof; (b) except as may be prescribed, articles of amalgamation shall be same as articles of incorporation of amalgamating holding corporation, and (c) no securities shall be issued by amalgamated corporation in connection with amalgamation.

Horizontal Short-form Amalgamation.—Two or more wholly-owned subsidiary corporations of same holding body corporate may amalgamate and continue as one corporation without entering into amalgamation agreement and without obtaining shareholder approval if amalgamation is approved by resolution of directors of each amalgamating corporation and resolutions provide that: (a) Shares of all but one of amalgamating subsidiary corporations shall be cancelled without any repayment of capital in respect thereof, (b) except as may be prescribed, articles of amalgamation shall be same as articles of incorporation of amalgamating subsidiary corporation whose shares are not cancelled, and (c) stated capital of amalgamating subsidiary corporations whose shares are cancelled shall be added to stated capital of amalgamating subsidiary corporation whose shares are not cancelled.

Effect of Certificate of Amalgamation.—On date shown in certificate of amalgamation: (a) amalgamation of amalgamating corporations and their continuance as one corporation become effective; (b) property of each amalgamating corporation continues to be property of amalgamated corporation; (c) amalgamated corporation continues to be liable for obligations of each amalgamating corporation; (d) existing cause of action, claim or liability to prosecution is unaffected; (e) civil, criminal or administrative action or proceeding pending by or against amalgamating corporation or its directors or officers may be continued to be prosecuted by or against amalgamated corporation or its directors or officers; (f) conviction against, or ruling, order or judgment in favour of or against, amalgamating corporation or its directors or officers may be enforced by or against amalgamated corporation or its directors or officers; and (g) articles of amalgamation are deemed to be articles of incorporation of amalgamated corporation and certificate of amalgamation is deemed to be certificate of incorporation of amalgamated corporation.

Continuance (Import).—Body corporate incorporated otherwise than by or under Act of Parliament may, if so authorized by laws of jurisdiction where it is incorporated, apply to Director for certificate of continuance.

Effect of Certificate of Continuance.—On date shown in certificate of continuance: (a) body corporate becomes corporation to which Act applies as if it had been incorporated under Act; (b) articles of continuance are deemed to be articles of incorporation of continued corporation; and (c) certificate of continuance is deemed to be certificate of incorporation of continued corporation.

Rights Preserved.—When body corporate is continued as corporation under Act: (a) property of body corporate continues to be property of corporation; (b) corporation continues to be liable for obligations of body corporate; (c) existing cause of action, claim or liability to prosecution is unaffected; (d) civil, criminal or administrative action or proceeding pending by or against body corporate or its directors or officers may be continued to be prosecuted by or against corporation or its directors or officers; and (e) conviction against, or ruling, order or judgment in favour of or against body corporate or its directors or officers may be enforced by or against corporation or its directors or officers.

Issued Shares.—Share of body corporate issued before body corporate was continued under Act is deemed to have been issued in compliance with Act and with provisions of articles of continuance irrespective of whether share is fully paid and irrespective of any designation, rights, privileges, restrictions or conditions set out on or referred to in certificate representing share; and continuance under this provision does not deprive holder of any right or privilege that he claims under, or relieve him of any liability in respect of, issued share.

Continuance (Export).—Corporation may, if it is authorized by special resolution of shareholders, if it establishes to satisfaction of Director that its proposed continuance in another jurisdiction will not adversely affect creditors or shareholders of corporation and if certain statutory prerequisites are satisfied, apply to appropriate official or public body of another jurisdiction requesting that corporation be continued as if it had been incorporated under laws of that other jurisdiction.

Right to Vote.—Each share of corporation carries right to vote in respect of continuance whether or not it otherwise carries right to vote.

Prohibition.—Corporation may not be continued as body corporate under laws of another jurisdiction unless those laws provide in effect that: (a) property of corporation continues to be property of body corporate; (b) body corporate continues to be liable for obligations of corporation; (c) existing cause of action, claim or liability to prosecution is unaffected; (d) civil, criminal or administrative action or proceeding pending by or against corporation may be continued to be prosecuted by or against body corporate;

See Topical Index in front part of this volume.

CORPORATIONS . . . *continued*
and (e) conviction against, or ruling, order or judgment in favour of or against corporation or its directors or officers may be enforced by or against body corporate.

Borrowing Powers.—Subject to articles, by-laws or any unanimous shareholder agreement, directors of corporation or any director, committee of directors or officer to whom power is delegated, may without authorization of shareholders: (a) borrow money upon credit of corporation; (b) issue, reissue, sell or pledge debt obligations of corporation; (c) except where otherwise prohibited give guarantee on behalf of corporation to secure performance of obligation of any person; and (d) mortgage, hypothecate, pledge or otherwise create security interest in all or any property of corporation, owned or subsequently acquired, to secure any debt obligation of corporation.

Extraordinary Sale, Lease or Exchange.—Sale, lease or exchange of all or substantially all property of corporation other than in ordinary course of business of corporation requires approval of shareholders.

Right to Vote.—Each share of corporation carries right to vote in respect of such sale, lease or exchange whether or not it otherwise carries right to vote.

Shareholder Approval.—Such sale, lease or exchange is adopted when holders of each class or series entitled to vote thereon have approved of sale, lease or exchange by special resolution.

Right to Dissent.—Holder of shares of any class of corporation may dissent if order is made under Act permitting dissent or if corporation resolves to: (a) amend its articles to add, change or remove any provisions restricting or constraining issue or transfer of shares of that class; (b) amend its articles to add, change or remove any restriction upon business or businesses that corporation may carry on; (c) amalgamate, otherwise than amalgamate with holding corporation and one or more of its wholly-owned subsidiaries; (d) be continued under laws of another jurisdiction or another Act of Parliament; or (e) sell, lease or exchange all or substantially all its property.

Payment for Shares.—In addition to any other right he may have, shareholder who complies with this provision is entitled, when action approved by resolution from which he dissents or order becomes effective, to be paid by corporation fair value of shares held by him in respect of which he dissents, determined as of close of business on day before resolution was adopted or order made.

Objection.—Dissenting shareholder must send to corporation, at or before any meeting of shareholders at which resolution referred to above is to be voted on, written objection to resolution, unless corporation did not give notice to shareholder of purpose of meeting and of his right to dissent.

Notice of Resolution.—Corporation must send to each shareholder who has filed objection notice that resolution has been adopted.

Demand for Payment.—Dissenting shareholder must send to corporation written notice containing: (a) shareholder's name and address; (b) number and class of shares in respect of which shareholder dissents; and (c) demand for payment of fair value of such shares.

Suspension of Rights.—After sending notice demanding payment, dissenting shareholder ceases to have any rights as shareholder except right to be paid fair value of shares as determined under this provision except where: (a) dissenting shareholder withdraws notice before corporation makes offer to purchase shares at fair market value; (b) corporation fails to make offer and shareholder withdraws notice; or (c) directors revoke resolution to amend articles, terminate amalgamation agreement or application for continuance, or abandon sale, lease or exchange, in which case rights as shareholder are reinstated as of date notice sent.

Offer to Pay.—Corporation must send to each dissenting shareholder who has sent demand for payment to corporation: (a) written offer to pay for shares in amount considered by directors of corporation to be fair value thereof, accompanied by statement showing how fair value was determined; or (b) notification (see catchline Limitation, infra) that it is unable lawfully under Act to pay dissenting shareholders for their shares.

Same Terms.—Every offer made for shares of same class or series must be on same terms.

Corporation Application to Court.—Where corporation fails to make offer, or if dissenting shareholder fails to accept offer, corporation may, within 50 days after action approved by resolution is effective or such further period as court may allow, apply to court to fix fair value for shares of any dissenting shareholder. If corporation fails to apply to court, dissenting shareholder may apply to court for same purpose within further period of 20 days or such further period as court may allow.

Powers of Court.—Upon such application to court, court may determine whether any other person is dissenting shareholder who should be joined as party, and court must then fix fair value for shares of all dissenting shareholders. Court may in its discretion appoint one or more appraisers to assist court to fix fair value for shares of dissenting shareholders.

If corporation may not make payment to shareholder under Act, dissenting shareholder may: (a) withdraw his notice of dissent, in which case corporation is deemed to consent to withdrawal and shareholder is reinstated to his full rights as shareholder; or (b) retain status as claimant against corporation, to be paid as soon as corporation is lawfully able to do so or, in liquidation, to be ranked subordinate to rights of creditors of corporation but in priority to its shareholders.

Limitation.—Corporation must not make payment to dissenting shareholder under these provisions if there are reasonable grounds for believing that: (a) corporation is or would after payment be unable to pay its liabilities as they become due; or (b) realizable value of corporation's assets would thereby be less than aggregate of its liabilities.

"Reorganization" Defined.—In following provisions, "reorganization" means court order made under: (a) relief from oppression provisions of Act, (b) Bankruptcy Act approving proposal, or (c) any other Act of Parliament that affects rights among corporation, its shareholders and creditors.

Powers of Court.—If corporation is subject to court order made under Part XX of Act with respect to oppressive or unfairly prejudicial act by corporation or its directors, under Bankruptcy Act of Canada approving proposal or any other federal legislation affecting rights among corporation, its shareholders and creditors, its articles may be amended by such order to effect any change that might lawfully be made by amendment of articles under §173 of Act.

If court makes order referred to above, court may also: (a) authorize issue of debt obligations of corporation, whether or not convertible into shares of any class or having attached any rights or options to acquire shares of any class, and fix terms thereof; and (b) appoint directors in place of or in addition to all or any of directors then in office.

Articles of Reorganization.—After such order has been made, articles of reorganization in prescribed form shall be sent to Director together with other documents required by Act, if applicable.

Effect of Certificate.—Reorganization becomes effective on date shown in certificate of amendment and articles of incorporation are amended accordingly.

No Dissent.—Shareholder is not entitled to dissenting shareholders' appraisal remedy if amendment to articles of incorporation is effected under this provision.

"Arrangement" Defined.—Includes amendment to articles, amalgamation of two or more corporations, amalgamation of body corporate with corporation that results in amalgamated corporation, division of business, transfer of all or substantially all property of corporation to another body corporate in exchange for money, property or securities, exchange of securities of corporation held by security holders for property, money or other securities of this or another body corporate that is not take-over bid, liquidation and dissolution of corporation, or combination of foregoing.

Powers of Court.—Corporation may apply to court for order approving proposed arrangement. Court may make any order including order determining notice to be given or dispensed with, order appointing counsel to represent shareholders, order requiring corporation to call, hold and conduct meeting of security, options and rights holders, order permitting shareholder to dissent, order approving arrangement as proposed or amended.

Articles of Arrangement.—After such order made, articles of arrangement in prescribed form shall be sent to Director. Arrangement becomes effective on date shown in certificate of arrangement.

Part XVI. Prospectus Qualification.—

Distribution Document.—Corporation that files or distributes in any jurisdiction prospectus, statement of material facts, registration statement, securities exchange take-over bid circular or similar document relating to distribution to public of securities of corporation must forthwith send to Director, copy of any such document.

Part XVII. Take-over Bids.—Take-over bid means offer, other than exempt offer, made by offeror to shareholders at approximately same time to acquire shares that, if combined with shares already beneficially owned or controlled, directly or indirectly, by offeror or affiliate of offeror on date of bid, would exceed 10% of any class of issued shares of offeree corporation and includes every offer, other than exempt offer, by issuer to repurchase its own shares. Under Act, exempt offer means offer: (a) to fewer than 15 shareholders to purchase shares by way of separate agreements, (b) to purchase shares through stock exchange or in over-the-counter market in such circumstances as may be prescribed by regulation, (c) to purchase shares of corporation that has fewer than 15 shareholders, two or more joint holders being counted as one shareholder, or (d) exempted by court order. Exemption for offers to purchase shares through stock exchange or in over-the-counter market has been limited to transactions carried out as prescribed by regulations.

Every Take-over Bid for Shares.—Whether take-over bid is for all or less than all shares of any class: (a) if terms of take-over bid are amended by increasing consideration offered for shares, offeror must pay increased consideration to each offeree whose shares are taken up pursuant to take-over bid whether or not such shares have been taken up by offeror before amendment of take-over bid and (b) if offeror purchases shares to which take-over bid relates other than pursuant to take-over bid during period of time within which shares may be deposited pursuant to take-over bid, (i) payment other than pursuant to take-over bid of amount for share that is greater than amount offered in take-over bid is deemed to be amendment of take-over bid to increase consideration offered for shares, (ii) offeror must immediately notify offerees of increased consideration being offered for shares, (iii) shares acquired other than pursuant to take-over bid must be counted to determine whether condition as to minimum acceptance has been fulfilled, and (iv) shares acquired other than pursuant to take-over bid must not be counted among shares taken up ratably if take-over bid is for less than all shares and if greater number of shares be deposited pursuant to take-over bid than offeror is bound or willing to take up and pay for.

Exemption Order.—Any interested person may apply to court having jurisdiction in place where offeree corporation has its registered office for order exempting take-over bid from any of provisions of this Part, and court may, if it is satisfied that exemption would not unfairly prejudice shareholder of offeree corporation, make exemption order on such terms as it thinks fit, which order may have retrospective effect.

"Interested Person" Defined.—For purposes of above provision, "interested person" includes: (a) offeree whether or not he deposits shares pursuant to take-over bid; (b) offeree corporation; (c) offeror; and (d) rival offeror.

Right to Acquire.—If within 120 days after date of take-over bid, bid is accepted by holders of not less than 90% of shares of any class of shares to which take-over bid relates, other than shares held at date of take-over bid by or on behalf of offeror or affiliate or associate of offeror, offeror is entitled, upon complying with provisions of this Part, to acquire shares held by dissenting offerees.

Payment.—Offeror must pay or transfer to offeree corporation amount of money or other consideration that offeror would have had to pay or transfer to dissenting offeree if dissenting offeree had elected to accept take-over bid.

Application to Court.—If dissenting offeree has elected to demand payment of fair value of his shares, offeror may, within 20 days after it has paid money or transferred other consideration, apply to court to fix fair value of shares of that dissenting offeree.

Powers of Court.—Upon application to court, court may determine whether any other person is dissenting offeree who should be joined as party, and court must then fix fair value for shares of all dissenting offerees.

Part XVIII. Liquidation and Dissolution.—Part XVIII of Act contains detailed provisions concerning substantive and procedural law on liquidation and dissolution of corporation which is not insolvent within meaning of Bankruptcy Act of Canada. This Part governs, among other things, revival of corporation dissolved under Act, dissolution of corporation that has not commenced business and making of proposal for voluntary liquidation and dissolution of corporation.

Dissolution by Director.—Where corporation: (a) has not commenced business within three years after date shown in its certificate of incorporation, (b) has not carried on its business for three consecutive years, or (c) is in default for period of one year in

See Topical Index in front part of this volume.

CORPORATIONS . . . *continued*

sending to Director any fee, notice or document required by Act; Director may dissolve corporation by issuing certificate of dissolution under Act or he may apply to court for order dissolving corporation.

Grounds for Dissolution.—Director or any interested person may apply to court for order dissolving corporation if corporation has: (a) failed for two or more consecutive years to comply with requirements of Act with respect to holding of annual meetings of shareholders, (b) carried on any business or exercised any power that it is restricted by its articles from carrying on or exercising, (c) denied access to corporate records to persons authorized under Act to have access to same, (d) failed to comply with certain of financial disclosure requirements of Act, or (e) procured any certificate under Act by misrepresentation.

Court may order liquidation and dissolution of corporation or any of its affiliated corporations upon application of shareholder: (a) if court is satisfied that in respect of corporation or any of its affiliates (i) any act or omission of corporation or any of its affiliates effects result, (ii) business or affairs of corporation or any of its affiliates are or have been carried on or conducted in manner, or (iii) powers of directors of corporation or any of its affiliates are or have been exercised in manner; that is oppressive or unfairly prejudicial to or that unfairly disregards interests of any security holder, creditor, director or officer; or (b) if court is satisfied that (i) unanimous shareholder agreement entitles complaining shareholder to demand dissolution of corporation after occurrence of specified event and that event has occurred, or (ii) it is just and equitable that corporation should be liquidated and dissolved.

Application for Supervision.—Application to court to supervise voluntary liquidation and dissolution under this Part must state reasons, verified by affidavit of applicant, why court should supervise liquidation and dissolution.

Part XVIII outlines powers of court upon application to liquidate and dissolve corporation and in connection with dissolution or liquidation and dissolution of corporation.

Appointment of Liquidator.—When making order for liquidation of corporation or at any time thereafter, court may appoint any person, including director, officer or shareholder or any other corporation, as liquidator of corporation.

Part XVIII outlines duties, powers and responsibilities of liquidator in connection with liquidation of corporation under Act.

Continuation of Actions.—Notwithstanding dissolution of corporation under Act: (a) civil, criminal or administrative action or proceeding commenced by or against corporation before its dissolution may be continued as if corporation had not been dissolved; (b) civil, criminal or administrative action or proceeding may be brought against corporation within two years after its dissolution as if corporation had not been dissolved; and (c) any property that would have been available to satisfy any judgment or order if corporation had not been dissolved remains available for such purpose.

Reimbursement.—Notwithstanding dissolution of corporation, shareholder to whom any of its property has been distributed is liable to any person claiming in above civil, criminal or administrative action or proceeding to extent of amount received by that shareholder upon such distribution, and action to enforce such liability may be brought within two years after date of dissolution of corporation.

Part XIX. Investigation.—Shareholder or Director may apply, ex parte or upon such notice as court may require, to court having jurisdiction in place where corporation has its registered office for order directing investigation to be made of corporation and any of its affiliated corporations.

Grounds.—If, upon application, it appears to court that: (a) business of corporation or any of its affiliates is or has been carried on with intent to defraud any person, (b) business or affairs of corporation or any of its affiliates are or have been carried on or conducted, or powers of directors are or have been exercised in manner that is oppressive or unfairly prejudicial to or that unfairly disregards interests of security holder, (c) corporation or any of its affiliates was formed for fraudulent or unlawful purpose or is to be dissolved for fraudulent or unlawful purpose, or (d) persons concerned with formation, business or affairs of corporation or any of its affiliates have in connection therewith acted fraudulently or dishonestly; court may order investigation to be made of corporation and any of its affiliated corporations.

Powers of Court.—In connection with investigation, court may make any order it thinks fit.

Copy of Report.—Inspector appointed by court must send to Director copy of every report made by inspector under this Part.

Power of Inspector.—Inspector has powers set out in order of court appointing him. Provisions of this Part of Act are designed to protect public interest rather than to resolve individual shareholder's grievances.

Part XX. Remedies, Offences and Penalties.—

Commencing Derivative Action.—Complainant may apply to court for leave to bring action in name and on behalf of corporation or any of its subsidiaries, or intervene in action to which any such body corporate is party, for purpose of prosecuting, defending or discontinuing action on behalf of body corporate, except that no action may be brought and no intervention in action may be made unless court is satisfied that: (a) complainant has given reasonable notice to directors of corporation or its subsidiary of his intention to apply to court if directors of corporation or its subsidiary do not bring, diligently prosecute or defend or discontinue action; (b) complainant is acting in good faith; and (c) it appears to be in interest of corporation or its subsidiary that action be brought, prosecuted, defended or discontinued.

"Complainant" means: (a) registered holder or beneficial owner, and former registered holder or beneficial owner, of security of corporation or any of its affiliates, (b) director or officer or former director or officer of corporation or of any of its affiliates, (c) Director, or (d) any other person who, in discretion of court, is proper person to make application under this Part.

Powers of Court.—In connection with such action, court may at any time make any order it thinks fit including, without limiting generality of foregoing: (a) order authorizing complainant or any other person to control conduct of action; (b) order giving directions for conduct of action; (c) order directing that any amount adjudged payable by defendant in action shall be paid, in whole or in part, directly to former and present security holders of corporation or its subsidiary instead of to corporation or its subsidiary; (d) order requiring corporation or its subsidiary to pay reasonable legal fees incurred by complainant in connection with action.

Oppression Remedy.—Complainant may apply to court for order under following provision.

Grounds.—If upon application by complainant to court for order, court is satisfied that in respect of corporation or any of its affiliates: (a) any act or omission of corporation or any of its affiliates effects result, (b) business or affairs of corporation or any of its affiliates are or have been carried on or conducted in manner, or (c) powers of directors of corporation or any of its affiliates are or have been exercised in manner; that is oppressive or unfairly prejudicial to or that unfairly disregards interests of any security holder, creditor, director or officer, court may make order to rectify matters complained of.

Powers of Court.—In connection with such application, court may make any interim or final order it thinks fit.

Duty of Directors.—If such order made by court directs amendment of articles or by-laws of corporation: (a) directors shall forthwith send articles of reorganization in prescribed form and other documents required by Act in connection therewith to Director; and (b) no other amendment to articles or by-laws shall be made without consent of court, until court otherwise orders.

Evidence of Shareholder Approval Not Decisive.—Application made or action brought or intervened in under this Part must not be stayed or dismissed by reason only that it is shown that alleged breach of right or duty owed to corporation or its subsidiary has been or may be approved by shareholders of such body corporate but evidence or (sic) approval by shareholders may be taken into account by court in making order for liquidation or dissolution of corporation, order in connection with derivative action or order concerning oppressive or unfairly prejudicial conduct of corporation.

Court Approval to Discontinue.—Application made or action brought or intervened in under this Part must not be stayed, discontinued, settled or dismissed for want of prosecution without approval of court given upon such terms as court thinks fit and, if court determines that interests of any complainant may be substantially affected by such stay, discontinuance, settlement or dismissal, court may order any party to application or action to give notice to complainant.

Application to Court to Rectify Records.—If name of person is alleged to be or to have been wrongly entered or retained in, or wrongly deleted or omitted from, registers or other records of corporation, corporation, security holder of corporation or any aggrieved person may apply to court for order that registers or records be rectified.

Powers of Court.—In connection with such application, court may make any order it thinks fit.

Application for Directions.—Director may apply to court for directions in respect of any matter concerning his duties under Act and on such application court may give such directions and make such further order as it thinks fit.

Appeal from Director's Decision.—Person who feels aggrieved by decision of Director: (a) to refuse to file in form submitted to him any articles or other document required by Act to be filed by him, (b) to give name, to change or revoke name, or to refuse to reserve, accept, change or revoke name under Act, (c) to refuse to grant exemption under enumerated sections, subsections and regulations, (c.1) to refuse to permit continued reference to shares having nominal or par value, (d) to refuse to issue certificate of discontinuance under Act, (e) to refuse to revive corporation under Act, or (f) to dissolve corporation under Act; may apply to court for order requiring Director to change his decision and upon such application court may so order and make any further order it thinks fit.

Restraining or Compliance Order.—If corporation or any director, officer, employee, agent, auditor, trustee, receiver, receiver-manager or liquidator of corporation does not comply with Act, regulations, articles, by-laws or unanimous shareholder agreement, complainant or creditor of corporation may, in addition to any other right he has, apply to court for order directing any such person to comply with, or restraining any such person from acting in breach of, any provisions thereof, and upon such application court may so order and make any further order it thinks fit.

Offences with Respect to Reports.—Person who makes or assists in making report, return, notice or other document required by Act or regulations to be sent to Director or to any other person that: (a) contains untrue statement of material fact, or (b) omits to state material fact required therein or necessary to make statement contained therein not misleading in light of circumstances in which it was made; is guilty of offence and liable on summary conviction to fine not exceeding $5,000 or to imprisonment for term not exceeding six months or to both.

If person guilty of such offence is body corporate, then, whether or not body corporate has been prosecuted or convicted, any director or officer of body corporate who knowingly authorizes, permits or acquiesces in such failure is also guilty of offence and liable on summary conviction to fine not exceeding $5,000 or to imprisonment for term not exceeding six months or both.

Immunity.—No person is guilty of any such offence if untrue statement or omission was unknown to him and in exercise of reasonable diligence could not have been known to him.

Offence.—Every person who contravenes provision of Act or regulations for which no punishment is provided is guilty of offence punishable on summary conviction.

Order to Comply.—Where person is guilty of offence under Act or regulations, any court in which proceedings in respect of offence are taken may, in addition to any punishment it may impose, order that person to comply with provisions of Act or regulations for contravention of which he has been convicted.

Part XXI. General.—

Notice to Directors and Shareholders.—Notice or document required by Act, regulations, articles or by-laws to be sent to shareholder or director of corporation may be sent by prepaid mail addressed to, or may be delivered personally to: (a) shareholder at latest address as shown in records of corporation or its transfer agent; and (b) director at latest address as shown in records of corporation or in last notice of directors or notice of change of directors.

Notice to and Service Upon a Corporation.—Notice or document required to be sent to or served upon corporation may be sent by registered mail to registered office of corporation shown in last notice of head office.

Certificate of Corporation.—Certificate issued on behalf of corporation stating any fact that is set out in articles, by-laws, unanimous shareholder agreement, minutes of meetings of directors, committee of directors or shareholders, or in trust indenture or

See Topical Index in front part of this volume.

CORPORATIONS . . . *continued*
other contract to which corporation is party may be signed by director, officer or transfer agent of corporation.

Filings with Director.—Notices or documents that are to be sent to Director may be sent in electronic or other form in any manner specified by Director. Director has unqualified discretion to require either original notices or documents or photostatic or photographic copy thereof. Director may exempt such notices or documents or classes of notices or documents containing information already in public domain from provisions of this Act.

Regulations.—Subject to following provisions, Governor in Council may make regulations: (a) prescribing any matter required or authorized by Act to be prescribed; (b) requiring payment of fee in respect of filing, examination or copying of any document or in respect of any action that Director is required or authorized to take under Act, and prescribing amount thereof; (c) prescribing format and contents of annual returns, notices and other documents required to be sent to Director or to be issued by him; (c.1) respecting sending of notices and documents in electronic form; (d) prescribing rules with respect to exemptions permitted by Act; and (e) prescribing that standards of accounting body named in regulations be followed.

Publications of Proposed Regulation.—Minister of Industry shall publish in Canada Gazette and in periodical available to public at least 60 days before proposed effective date thereof copy of every regulation that Governor in Council proposes to make under Act and reasonable opportunity shall be afforded to interested persons to make representations with respect thereof.

Exceptions.—Minister is not required to publish proposed regulation if proposed regulation: (a) grants exemption or relieves restriction; (b) establishes or amends fee; (c) has been published whether or not it has been amended as result of representations made by interested persons as provided in this Part; or (d) makes no material substantive change in existing regulation.

Annual Return.—Every corporation must on prescribed date, send to Director annual return in prescribed form.

Inspection.—Person who has paid prescribed fee is entitled during usual business hours to examine document required by Act or regulations to be sent to Director, except report sent to him by inspector appointed under Part XIX and to make copies of or extracts therefrom.

Authorizing Continuance.—Shareholders of body corporate incorporated by or under Act of Parliament may: (a) by special resolution, authorize directors of body corporate to apply under Act for certificate of continuance; and (b) by same resolution, make any amendment to Act of incorporation or letters patent of body corporate that corporation incorporated under Act may make to its articles.

No Dissent.—Shareholder is not entitled to dissent in respect of amendment made under this provision.

Insolvency and Receivers.—See topic Bankruptcy.

Close Corporations.—Provisions applicable to close corporations include requirement for only one director where securities not distributed to public; certain insider trading provisions do not apply; proxy solicitations not mandatory if less than 15 shareholders; financial statements need not be filed with Director nor is auditor required unless it has distributed its securities to public; take-over bid rules generally do not apply if less than 15 shareholders; trust indenture provisions apply only where debt issued as part of distribution to public; signed resolutions may be used instead of meetings; and shareholders may enter unanimous shareholders' agreement restricting power of directors.

Foreign Corporations.—There are no Dominion licensing requirements applicable to foreign corporations per se, but where business to be carried on is one which may not be purpose of a Dominion company incorporated under Canada Corporations Act, then foreign corporation is subject to statutes governing incorporation for such purposes, for example Insurance Companies Act, or Trust and Loan Companies Act. Foreign companies desiring to carry on business in Canada must obtain a licence in each Province where operations are to be carried on. Fee payable depends upon amount of capital to be employed and corresponds to fee chargeable for incorporation in particular province. See the provincial law digests.

Foreign Investment.—Investment Canada Act (R.S.C. [1st Supp.], c. 28) sets out circumstances in which investments by non-Canadians in new Canadian businesses or acquisitions of control of Canadian businesses will be subject to notice and/or review requirements of Act. For detailed discussion of Act, see topic Foreign Investment.

Taxation.—See topic Taxation, and in provincial law digests.

The Small Loans Act (R.S.C., c. S-11, as am'd) provides for regulation of companies lending money on promissory notes or other personal security and chattel mortgages.

Income tax on corporations, see topic Taxation.

COURTS:

Supreme Court of Canada.—Supreme Court of Canada is constituted by R. S. C., c. S-26, as am'd and exercises appellate jurisdiction both civil and criminal throughout Canada. Supreme Court of Canada has exclusive ultimate appellate civil and criminal jurisdiction. It consists of a chief justice and eight puisne judges. It holds three sessions yearly commencing in Jan., Apr., and Oct. at Ottawa. Procedure is governed by Rules of Supreme Court of Canada, SOR/83-74, as am'd.

See also topic Appeal and Error.

Federal Court of Canada.—Effective June 1, 1971, court of law, equity and admiralty in Canada which existed previously under name Exchequer Court of Canada is continued under name of Federal Court of Canada. (See Federal Court Act, R.S.C., c. F-7.) Court has civil and criminal jurisdiction. Procedure is governed by Federal Court Rules, C.R.C., c. 663. Court consists of two divisions called Federal Court—Appeal Division (also referred to as Court of Appeal or Federal Court of Appeal) and Federal Court—Trial Division. (§4). Principal office of court in Ottawa. Other offices for court in Halifax, Montreal, Toronto, Winnipeg, Regina, Calgary, Edmonton, Vancouver, Quebec City, Fredericton, Charlottetown, St. John's. *Note:* Broad revision of Federal Court Rules is currently being considered.

Court consists of Chief Justice who is President of Appeal Division, Associate Chief Justice who is President of Trial Division and 23 others, ten of whom are appointed to Appeal Division, 13 of whom are appointed to Trial Division.

Jurisdiction.—(A) Trial Division: generally, jurisdiction is in respect to: (1) claims against Crown (§17[1]); (2) claims by Crown where parties consent to jurisdiction (§17[3]); (3) civil claims by Crown (§17[5][a]); (4) claims against or concerning officers or servants of Crown (§17[5][b]); (5) relief by way of injunction, declaration, or writs of certiorari, prohibition, mandamus or quo warranto against federal board, commission or other tribunal (§18[1]); (6) review of decisions of certain federal boards, commissions or other tribunals (§18.1); (7) references from certain federal boards, commissions or other tribunals to determine question of law, jurisdiction or practice (§18.3); (8) interprovincial and federal-provincial controversies (§19); (9) generally industrial property matters (§20) under Copyright Act, R.S.C., c. C-42; Industrial Design Act, R.S.C., c. I-9; Patent Act, R.S.C., c. P-4; Trademarks Act, R.S.C., c. T-13; Integrated Circuit Topography Act, S.C. 1990, c. 37; (10) citizenship appeals (§21); (11) admiralty matters (§22); (12) in all cases where claim for relief made under Act of Parliament and coming within these subjects; bills of exchange and promissory notes where Crown a party, interprovincial works and undertakings, aeronautics (§23); (13) in any case where relief sought under laws of Canada and no other court has jurisdiction (§25); (14) in any case where laws of Canada expressly confer jurisdiction, if such laws confer jurisdiction to court constituted under laws of province (§17[6]); (15) appeals under certain Federal Acts; (B) Appeal Division: generally, jurisdiction is in respect to: (1) appeals from Trial Division (§27); (2) review of decisions of certain federal boards, commissions or other tribunals (§28[1]); (3) reference by certain federal boards, commissions or other tribunals to determine question of law, jurisdiction or practise (§28[2]); (4) appeals from Tax Court of Canada (§27[1.1]).

Appeal lies to Supreme Court of Canada from judgment of Federal Court of Appeal, (1) where Federal Court of Appeal has granted leave (§37.1, Supreme Court Act); (2) where Supreme Court grants leave, whether or not Federal Court of Appeal has refused leave (§40, Supreme Court Act); (3) in case of controversy between Canada and province or between two or more provinces (§35.1, Supreme Court Act). See also topic Appeal and Error.

Commencement of Proceedings.—Proceedings in Trial Division by subject as between subject and subject and by Crown are commenced by filing originating document (statement of claim or declaration Form 11). (Rule 400 of Federal Court Rules). Action against Crown instituted by filing in Registry of Court document set out in Schedule I to Act. (§48). Crown Liability and Proceedings Act gives provincial courts concurrent jurisdiction in actions against Crown in right of Canada except where Federal Court has exclusive jurisdiction; Crown liable for all loss or damage due to illegal wiretap, plus punitive damages not to exceed $5,000 to each person injured (R.S.C., c. C-50). In all actions regular pleadings then follow and provision is made for discovery and production of documents.

Tax Court of Canada.—Constituted as court of record. ((Tax Court of Canada Act, R.S.C., c. T-2). Court consists of Chief Judge of Court, Associate Chief Judge of Court, and 16 other judges. Principal office of Court is in Ottawa. Other offices as may be established by Rules. Court sits regularly in major centres.

Jurisdiction.—Has original jurisdiction on appeals on matters arising from Income Tax Act, Part IX of Excise Tax Act, Canada Pension Plan, Old Age Security Act, Petroleum and Gas Revenue Tax Act, Part III of Unemployment Insurance Act, 1971, and under other statutes where specifically provided. It has powers, rights and privileges of superior court of record.

Commencement of Proceedings.—Appellants may elect informal or formal procedure depending on tax at issue. Informal procedure has relaxed rules of evidence and procedure. Formal procedure follows general rules of practice and procedure. Appeals shall be in writing, setting out reasons for appeal and relevant facts. Appeal under general procedure lies to Federal Court of Appeal (formerly appeal lay to FCTD by way of trial de novo).

See also topic Appeal and Error.

See also digests of laws of several provinces.

CRIMINAL LAW:

Apart from certain incidental penal provisions in provincial statutes, criminal law, including procedure, is within exclusive jurisdiction of Parliament of Canada and has been codified by Criminal Code, R.S.C., c. C-46, as am'd. Criminal Code is based upon English criminal law. Criminal law is under control and administration of provincial courts.

Indictment or Information.—Criminal Code provides for indictable and summary conviction offences. Summary conviction offences are generally less serious offences and proceedings are commenced by laying of information under oath before justice of peace. Indictable offences may be commenced by laying of information or by preferred indictment by provincial Attorney General or his agent, in certain cases federal Attorney General and by grand jury in province of Nova Scotia.

Bail.—Part XVI of Criminal Code governs arrest and bail of accused persons. Generally speaking, these provisions authorize and govern issuance of appearance notices to and interim release from custody of persons suspected of having committed criminal offence and interim release of persons who have been convicted of criminal offence but who have appealed or applied for leave to appeal from conviction or sentence.

Generally speaking, where peace officer arrests person, without arrest warrant, for summary conviction offences and certain less serious indictable offences, peace officer must release person from custody unless he has reasonable and probable grounds to believe that it is necessary in public interest to detain person in custody or that person would not appear in court if released. (§497). Where person has been arrested without arrest warrant for certain indictable offences, officer in charge must release person from custody unless there are reasonable and probable grounds to believe that it is necessary in public interest to detain person in custody or that person would not appear in court if released. (§498). Where accused who is charged with offence other than certain serious indictable offences and who is not required to be detained in custody in respect of any other matter which is taken before justice, justice must, unless plea of guilty by accused is accepted, order accused to be released upon his giving suitable undertaking to appear

See Topical Index in front part of this volume.

CRIMINAL LAW . . . *continued*
in court, without conditions, unless prosecutor shows cause why detention of accused is justified or why conditions should be attached to accused's undertaking. (§515). Detention of accused in custody is only justified if his detention is necessary to ensure his attendance in court or if his detention is necessary for protection or safety of public. (§515).

Where accused is charged with certain indictable offences (for example, murder), only judge of superior court of criminal jurisdiction for province in which accused is charged may release accused before or after committal for trial. Judge must order accused be detained in custody unless accused shows cause why his detention in custody is not justified. (§522).

Criminal Code and Rules of Court enacted pursuant thereto provides complete code of criminal procedure with respect to adult offenders, including bail and other provisions. Criminal procedure for young offenders under age of 18 years, however, is set out in Young Offenders Act, R.S.C., c. Y-1, as am'd, which statute is implemented by youth courts designated by provinces.

See also topic Constitution and Government, subhead Canadian Charter of Rights and Freedoms.

See also Criminal Records Act, R.S.C., c. C-47.

See also topic Extradition.

CURRENCY:

See topic Exchange Control.

DAMAGES:

See digests of the laws of the several provinces.

DEATH:

See digests of the laws of the several provinces.

DEPOSITIONS:

See topic Affidavits.

Compelling Attendance of Witnesses.—Only persons within Canada are compellable witnesses in federal courts. See Criminal Code, R.S.C., c. C-46, §698, Federal Court Act, R.S.C., c. F-7, §333.

DESCENT AND DISTRIBUTION:

See digests of the laws of the several provinces.

DIVORCE:

Subject matter of marriage and divorce is one of subjects which by Constitution Act, 1867 is assigned exclusively to Parliament of Canada, subject to solemnization of marriage being assigned to Provinces.

Divorce throughout whole of Canada is governed by Divorce Act, R.S.C. (2nd Supp.), c. 3.

Jurisdiction.—Appropriate court in province has jurisdiction in divorce proceeding where either spouse is ordinarily resident in province for at least one year preceding commencement of proceeding. (§3). Jurisdiction in corollary relief proceeding arises where court has granted divorce to either or both former spouses (§4), and in variation proceeding if (a) either former spouse is ordinarily resident in province at commencement of proceeding; or (b) both former spouses accept court's jurisdiction (§5).

Divorce.—Court of competent jurisdiction may, on application by either or both spouses, grant divorce on ground that there has been breakdown of their marriage which is established only if (a) spouses lived separate and apart for at least one year immediately preceding determination of divorce proceeding and living separate and apart at commencement of proceeding; or (b) spouse against whom divorce proceeding brought has, since marriage began, committed adultery or treated other spouse with physical or mental cruelty of such kind as to render intolerable continued cohabitation of spouses. (§8). For purposes of calculating one year's separation, period of renewed cohabitation of less than 90 days in length may be ignored, where reconciliation is primary purpose of cohabitation. Subject to certain special circumstances, divorce has legal effect throughout Canada and dissolves marriage of spouses on 31st day after day judgment granting divorce is rendered. (§§12-14).

Corollary Relief.—Court of competent jurisdiction may, on application by either or both spouses, make order or interim order for: Support—payment of support for other spouse and/or any or all children of marriage in amount court thinks reasonable (§15); custody—respecting custody of and/or access to any or all children of marriage (§16); or variation—order varying, rescinding, or suspending, prospectively or retroactively: (a) support order or any provision thereof, or (b) custody order or any provision thereof (§17). Division of property governed by laws of particular provinces. Act to amend Divorce Act, S.C. 1990 c. 18, provides for judicial sanctions against individuals who withhold religious divorce to gain advantage in civil divorce proceedings.

Enforcement.—Corollary relief orders effective throughout Canada and may be registered and enforced according to laws of particular province (§20). To this end, there exists both federal and provincial legislation providing for release of information to assist in locating defaulting spouses, and to assist in enforcement of support orders by garnishment and attachment of moneys payable by either level of government.

Appeals.—From any judgment or order under Act, whether final or interim, as provided by §21.

ENVIRONMENT:

Increasing federal regulation of all aspects of environment, in addition to extensive provincial regulation. Jurisdiction of governments determined according to constitutional law division of powers. Major federal statutes include Transportation of Dangerous Goods Act, S.C. 1992, c. 34 and regulations applicable to all inter-provincial and trans-border shipments of regulated dangerous goods, including hazardous wastes. Labelling, shipping, registration and notification requirements. Canadian Environmental Protection Act, 4th Supp., c. 16, regulates toxic substances, including information disclosure (including extensive new substances notification requirements, and provisions for notification requirements relating to national pollutant release inventory), import and export, spill clean-up; nutrients; international air pollution; ocean dumping. Both statutes set out extensive penalties, including director's liability. The Hazardous Products Act, c. H-3 governs importation, selling or supplying of controlled products as defined in regulations. Labelling and information disclosure provisions; penalties including director's liability. The Canada Labour Code, c. L-2, has special worker information and training provisions in relation to hazardous materials. Exemptions from some information disclosure provisions under Hazardous Materials Information Review Act, 3rd Supp., c. 24. The Bankruptcy and Insolvency Act, c. B-3, contains provisions affecting trustees in bankruptcy in respect of environmental liability.

New legislation includes Canadian Environmental Assessment Act, S.C. 1992, c. 37, to codify requirements for federal environmental assessments and replace existing Environmental Assessment and Review Process Guidelines Order; Energy Efficiency Act, S.C. 1992, c. 36; Northwest Territories Waters Act, S.C. 1992, c. 39 and Yukon Waters Act, S.C. 1992, c. 40.

Other federal legislative sources of environmental regulation include Canada Shipping Act, c. S-9; Fisheries Act, c. F-14; Canada Water Act, c. C-11; Navigable Waters Protection Act, c. N-22.

Information on environmental protection and government restrictions available from Department of the Environment, Ottawa, Canada. Transportation of dangerous goods information from Transportation of Dangerous Goods Directorate, Transport Canada, Ottawa.

ESCHEAT:

See digests of the laws of the several provinces. See also topic Banks and Banking, subhead Unclaimed Deposits.

ESTATE TAX:

See topic Taxation, subhead Income Tax Act, catchline Capital Gains. See also digests of laws of the several provinces, topic Taxation subhead Inheritance Tax.

EXCHANGE CONTROL:

There are at present no restrictions.

EXECUTIONS:

See digests of the laws of the several provinces.

EXECUTORS AND ADMINISTRATORS:

See digests of the laws of the several provinces.

EXEMPTIONS:

See digests of the laws of the several provinces. Also see topic Taxation, subhead Income Tax Act, catchline Exemption From Tax.

EXTRADITION:

Law respecting extradition is governed by Extradition Act, R.S.C., c. E-23, as am'd. Extradition treaties exist between Canada and most principal foreign states. Where there exists extradition treaty or arrangement between Canada and any foreign state, judge of superior or county court or appointed commissioner may issue warrant for apprehension of fugitive on foreign warrant of arrest, upon such evidence or after such proceedings as in opinion of judge would justify issue of warrant if crime of which fugitive is accused or is alleged to have been convicted had been committed in Canada. (§10). Upon arrest, fugitive must be brought before judge who hears case in same manner as if fugitive was brought before justice of peace, charged with indictable offence committed in Canada. (§13). Judge must issue warrant for committal of fugitive to nearest convenient prison until surrender of fugitive to foreign state if there is evidence produced which would prove that fugitive has been convicted of extradition crime and if there is evidence produced which would justify committal of fugitive for trial where fugitive is alleged to have committed extradition crime. (§18). Requisition for surrender of fugitive of foreign state who is or is suspected to be in Canada is made to Minister of Justice by consular officer of foreign state resident at Ottawa or by any minister of foreign state communicating with Minister of Justice through diplomatic representative of Canada in foreign state. (§20).

Minister of Justice may refuse to surrender fugitive where Minister of Justice determines that offence in respect of which extradition proceedings are taken are of political character, proceedings are taken to try to punish fugitive for offence of political character or foreign state does not intend to make requisition for surrender of fugitive. (§22).

Extradition crimes include, among other crimes, following: murder, attempted murder, conspiracy to murder, manslaughter, counterfeiting, forgery, larceny or theft, embezzlement, obtaining money, goods or valuable securities by false pretences, crimes against bankruptcy or insolvency laws, fraud, sexual assault, abductions, child stealing, kidnapping, false imprisonment, burglary, arson, robbery, threats with intent to extort, perjury and piracy. (Schedule I).

Where Canada does not have extradition treaty with foreign state, Governor General may proclaim in force Part II of Extradition Act with respect to that particular foreign state, which would then provide for issuance of warrant for apprehension of fugitive from that particular foreign state. Extradition proceedings and crimes are similar, although not necessarily identical.

Prisoner Transfers.—Where there exists treaty on transfer of prisoners between Canada and foreign state, The Transfer of Offenders Act, R.S.C., c. T-15 allows Canadian citizens imprisoned in foreign states to apply to complete sentence in Canada and foreign citizens imprisoned in Canada may apply to complete their sentences in foreign state. Foreign states include: U.S., Mexico, Peru, France, Spain, Sweden, U.K., Bolivia, Cyprus, Austria, Denmark, Finland, Greece, Luxembourg, Netherlands, Switzerland, Turkey, Thailand and Italy.

FOREIGN EXCHANGE:

See topic Exchange Control.

See Topical Index in front part of this volume.

FOREIGN INVESTMENT:

Foreign Investment Review Act, S.C. 1973-74, c. 46 was repealed effective June 30, 1985, day upon which Investment Canada Act, R.S.C., 1985, c. 28 (1st Supp.), came into effect. Amended by S.C. 1988, c. 65, S.C. 1991, cc. 46, 47, S.C. 1993, cc. 35, 44, S.C. 1994, c. 47 and S.C. 1995, c. 1.

Purpose of Act is set forth in §2 as follows: "Recognizing that increased capital and technology would benefit Canada, the purpose of this Act is to encourage investment in Canada by Canadians and non-Canadians that contributes to economic growth and employment opportunities and to provide for the review of significant investments in Canada by non-Canadians in order to ensure such benefit to Canada."

Foreign investment transactions are dealt with in various ways under Act. Certain transactions, set out in §10, are exempt from both review and notice requirements of Act. Those transactions which involve investments by non-Canadians in new Canadian businesses or non-reviewable acquisitions by non-Canadians of Canadian businesses are notifiable only, unless "cultural heritage or national identity" exception applies, in which case there is reserve power to review transaction. Finally, there are those transactions which are subject to full review under Act and which must pass "net benefit to Canada" test.

Investments requiring review are all "direct" acquisitions by non-Canadians of Canadian businesses with assets of $5,000,000 or more, all "indirect" acquisitions of control of Canadian businesses with assets of $50,000,000 or more and indirect acquisitions of control (see discussion of "control" below) of Canadian businesses with assets between $5,000,000 and $50,000,000 where assets of Canadian businesses represent more than 50% of value of total international transaction. As result of Canada's commitments pursuant to World Trade Organization General Agreement on Trade in Services, effective Jan. 1, 1995, aforementioned thresholds for review of direct transactions involving WTO investors acquiring or divesting control of Canadian businesses has been set at $168 million. It is adjusted annually on formula basis. Industry Canada, which administers Act, has made policy decision not to review indirect investments involving WTO investors in respect of acquisitions or divestitures. Preferential rules do not apply in respect of investments to acquire control of Canadian business engaged in production of uranium, providing any financial service, providing any transportation service or which consists of cultural business (as described below), radio communication intended for public reception, radio, television and cable broadcasting undertakings and satellite programming and broadcast network services.

Control of Canadian business may be acquired through (i) acquisition of majority of voting shares or voting interests of business, (ii) acquisition of more than one-third, but less than majority, of voting shares of business unless it can be established that control is not acquired, and (iii) acquisition of all or substantially all assets of business or group of assets which is considered to be capable of being operated as separate business. "New business" is established where there are employees, place of business and assets used in carrying on business.

Non-Canadians must file notice under Act regarding all non-reviewable transactions or establishments of new Canadian businesses prior to implementation or within 30 days thereafter. Once complete notice has been filed, receipt bearing certified date will be issued to foreign investor. Receipt must advise foreign investor either that investment proposal is unconditionally non-reviewable or that proposal will not be reviewed so long as notice of review is not issued within 21 days of date certified under receipt, pursuant to §15 of Act. Section 15 gives federal cabinet authority to order review of prescribed investments that are related to Canada's cultural heritage or national identity.

If investment is related to Canada's cultural heritage or national identity, it is reviewable if federal cabinet, where it considers it in public interest, on recommendation of Minister, issues order for review within 21 days after certified date on which notice of investment was received under §13. To date only types of business activities which have been prescribed by regulation as related to Canada's cultural heritage or national identity deal largely with publication, film and music industries. Act enables Minister to determine, in cultural heritage and national identity sectors, that entity is not Canadian even though entity otherwise meets required terms in Act on this issue.

Reviewable acquisitions are subject to test of "net benefit to Canada" rather than "significant benefit to Canada" test under previous legislation. Minister responsible under Act for administration of Act and management and direction of Investment Canada determines whether reviewable investment is likely to be of "net benefit" to Canada under Act. Where investment is reviewable non-Canadian investor will be required by §17(1) to file application containing information prescribed by regulation. Generally, favourable decision must be received before investment is implemented. Investment may be implemented prior to decision where Minister permits on basis that delay would cause undue hardship to investor or would jeopardize operation of Canadian business, where investment is indirect or where government determines to review investment in Canadian business having prescribed activities as noted above.

Once application has been filed, receipt will be issued to applicant, certifying date on which it received application. For incomplete applications deficiency notice will be sent to applicant, and if not done within 15 days of receipt of application, it is deemed to be complete as of date it was received.

Within 45 days after complete application has been received Minister must notify investor under §21(1) that he is satisfied that investment is likely to be of net benefit to Canada. If within such 45 day period he is unable to complete his review, Minister has additional 30 days to complete his review, unless applicant agrees to longer period. Within such additional period, Minister must advise either he is satisfied or he is not satisfied that investment is likely to be of net benefit to Canada. If time limits have elapsed, Minister is deemed to be satisfied that investment is likely to be of net benefit to Canada.

Factors to be taken into account by Minister in assessing whether investment is likely to be of net benefit to Canada are as follows: (a) effect of investments on level and nature of economic activity in Canada, including without limiting generality of foregoing, effect on employment, resource processing, utilization of parts, components and services produced in Canada and on exports from Canada; (b) degree and significance of participation by Canadians in Canadian business or new Canadian business and in any industry or industries in Canada of which Canadian business or new Canadian business forms or would form part; (c) effect of investment on productivity, industrial efficiency, technological development, product innovation and product variety in Canada; (d) effect of investment on competition within any industry or industries in Canada; (e) compatibility of investment with national, industrial, economic and cultural policies, taking into consideration industrial, economic and cultural policy objectives enunciated by government or legislature of any province likely to be significantly affected by investment; and (f) contribution of investment to Canada's ability to compete in world markets.

Under Act, "Canadian" means: (a) Canadian citizen; (b) permanent resident within meaning of Immigration Act who has been ordinarily resident in Canada for not more than one year after time at which he first became eligible to apply for Canadian citizenship; (c) Canadian government, whether federal, provincial or local, or agency thereof; or (d) entity that is Canadian-controlled, as determined pursuant to §26, and not determined to not be Canadian-controlled. "Non-Canadian" means individual, government or agency thereof or entity that is not Canadian. "Entity" means corporation, partnership, trust or joint venture.

"Canadian business" means business carried on in Canada that has: (a) place of business in Canada; (b) individual or individuals in Canada who are employed or self-employed in connection with business; and (c) assets in Canada used in carrying on business. "New Canadian business", in relation to non-Canadian, means business that is not already being carried on in Canada by non-Canadian and that, at time of establishment, (a) is unrelated to any other business being carried on in Canada by that non-Canadian; or (b) is related to another business being carried on in Canada by that non-Canadian but falls within prescribed specific type of business activity that, in opinion of federal cabinet is related to Canada's cultural heritage or national identity.

Recent legislation has replaced Investment Canada Agency originally established under Act with Director of Investments under Industry Canada, reorganized federal government department, which will be responsible for administering review and policy functions. Investment promotion functions will be administered by Department of External Affairs.

See also topics Corporations, subhead Foreign Investment; Aliens, subhead Corporations Owned or Controlled by Aliens; Mines and Minerals, subhead Oil and Gas.

FOREIGN TRADE REGULATION:

Canada is signatory to Marrakesh Agreement establishing the World Trade Organization including Plurilateral Trade Agreements. Canada has enacted legislation giving effect to its WTO commitments in Act to Implement the Agreement Establishing the World Trade Organization, S.C. 1994, c. 47.

North American Free Trade (Agreement).—Canada-U.S. Free Trade Agreement Implementation Act (S.C. 1988, c. 65) which gave effect to Canada-United States Free Trade Agreement ("CFTA") between Canada and U.S., and came into force Jan. 1, 1989 has been suspended as result of enactment to North American Free Trade Agreement Implementation Act (S.C. 1993, c. 44; Schedule Parts A-D, S.C. 1993, c. 44) ("NAFTA Implementation Act") effective Jan. 1, 1994. NAFTA Implementation Act amends domestic Canadian legislation and provides for preferential treatment for U.S. and Mexican and "North American" origin goods and investment. Readers from jurisdictions other than Canada, U.S. or Mexico should note that NAFTA establishes preferential trade and investment regime with respect to goods and services, investment (including government procurement). Special rules apply and preferential treatment may be accorded to NAFTA investors, goods and services. In some circumstances non-NAFTA investors can qualify as NAFTA investors through establishment of local presence in NAFTA country, and in addition, non-NAFTA goods may qualify as of NAFTA origin after reprocessing in North America. Substantive provisions of NAFTA have been incorporated into Canadian law and reference also should be made to specific topics. NAFTA has been modelled on prior Canada-United States Free Trade Agreement and like CFTA contemplates gradual elimination of duties and non-tariff barriers as between Canada, U.S. and Mexico. While many provisions of NAFTA are similar to CFTA they are not identical in all respects and new legislation must be referred to. NAFTA provides for gradual elimination of tariffs on goods either immediately or (depending on category) over five or ten or 15 year periods (see topic Taxation, subhead Customs Duties).

Export and Import Permits Act.—Pursuant to Export and Import Permits Act (R.S.C., c. E-19, as am'd) Canada controls certain imports and exports. Canadian government has established export control list of goods ("Export Control List") (§3), "an export control list of countries" ("Area Control List") (§4) and "an import control list of goods" ("Import Control List") (§5). Goods and countries listed in aforementioned lists vary considerable from time to time and must be updated frequently. Under Export and Import Permits Act Canadian government has established export controls over natural resources to encourage further processing in Canada, to limit export of goods in circumstances of oversupply or depressed prices, to restrict export of softwood lumber products, to ensure that there is adequate supply and distribution of certain goods, to give effect to intergovernmental arrangements or commitments, and to ensure that military or strategic goods are not exported to destinations representing strategic threat to Canada.

Under this Act Canada also maintains certain import controls in order to ensure adequate supply and distribution of goods that are scarce in world markets or in Canada; to give effect to Canada's supply management policies in agricultural sector; to restrict importation of certain dangerous arms, ammunitions etc. and to give effect to Canada's commitments pursuant to Agreement on Textiles and Clothing concluded in Uruguay Round of trade negotiations.

Canada's commitments pursuant to Agreement on Agriculture negotiated and agreed to in Uruguay Round are also given effect to under Export and Import Permits Act. In Uruguay Round, Canada committed to moving from quota-based restrictions on imports of sensitive agricultural products to tarrification of imports of sensitive agricultural products. These commitments are reflected in Export and Import Permits Act.

Goods which are regulated under Export and Import Permits Act either require import permit prior to importation or export permit or cannot be imported or exported, depending on the circumstances. Import Control List establishes broad range of goods which cannot be imported into Canada without permit and is used to support action taken under Farm Product Marketing Agencies Act, as well as Farm Income Protection Act, Fisheries Prices Support Act, Agricultural Products Board Act, Agricultural Products

See Topical Index in front part of this volume.

FOREIGN TRADE REGULATION . . . *continued*
Cooperative Marketing Act and Canadian Dairy Commission Act. Special rules apply with respect to restricting imports from NAFTA countries. (§4.1 and following).

Area Control List regulates export of all goods to certain listed countries. As of Apr. 1996, Angola, Libya, Yugoslavia, Rwanda and Bosnia-Herzegovina are on Area Control List. Goods which are exported directly or indirectly to aforementioned countries require export permit and may, depending on goods in question, be prohibited.

Export Control List regulates export of certain goods irrespective of country of destination. In addition, reexport from Canada of goods that are "U.S.-origin" goods is controlled. All nonstrategic U.S.-origin goods require export permit. In most circumstances export of such goods is governed by general export permit. Goods that are further processed or manufactured outside U.S. so as to result in substantial change in value, form or use of goods or in production of new goods are not subject to this restriction. Canada and U.S. recently concluded agreement with respect to export of softwood lumber to U.S. Pending settlement of Canada-United States Agreement on Softwood Lumber effective Apr. 1, 1996, softwood lumber products from Provinces of Ontario, Quebec, Manitoba, British Columbia and Alberta have been placed on Export Control List.

Reexport from Canada of strategic U.S.-origin goods is restricted and general provisions restricting export of strategic goods apply. Canada was member of now dismantled Co-ordinating Committee for Multilateral Strategic Export Controls. However, generally speaking, export controls continue to exist with respect to export of strategic goods and technology and military sensitive goods and technology and equipment. Canada is member of Wassenaar Committee, Zanger Committee and Nuclear Suppliers Group.

Foreign Extraterritorial Measures Act. ("FEMA") (R.S.C., c. F-29 as am'd) permits Canadian government to limit production and disclosure of documents and to block extraterritorial application of foreign legislation or trading directives in circumstances where Canadian trading interests are adversely affected or Canadian sovereignty is infringed; further it enables Canadian government to restrict application of foreign antitrust law.

Where in opinion of Attorney General of Canada, foreign tribunal has exercised, is exercising or is proposing or is likely to exercise, jurisdiction or powers of a kind or in manner that has adversely affected or is likely to adversely affect significant Canadian interests in relation to international trade or commerce involving business carried on in whole or in part in Canada or that otherwise has infringed or is likely to infringe Canadian sovereignty, Attorney General may by order prohibit or restrict production or disclosure of records to foreign tribunal where such documentation is in possession or in control of Canadian citizen or of person resident in Canada. (§§3-5). Attorney General of Canada can thus block application of subpoenas or other orders to produce evidence by foreign tribunals. Under FEMA orders can be made in circumstances where a foreign state or foreign tribunal has taken or is proposing or is likely to take measures affecting international trade or commerce of a kind or in manner that has adversely affected or is likely to adversely affect significant Canadian interests in relation to international trade or commerce involving business carried on in whole or in part in Canada or that otherwise infringe or are likely to infringe Canadian sovereignty. Concurrence of Minister of Foreign Affairs is required to make such order. (§5). Contravention of these provisions of FEMA renders person liable to conviction of indictable offence and/or fine not exceeding Cdn $10,000 or to imprisonment for term not exceeding five years or to both or to conviction of offence punishable on summary conviction and liable to fine not exceeding Cdn $5,000 and/or to imprisonment for term not exceeding two years or both. (§7).

Pursuant to FEMA Canada can restrict application of foreign antitrust laws in Canada. Where foreign court or tribunal has rendered judgment instituted under foreign antitrust law, and Attorney General is of opinion that recognition or enforcement of that judgment in Canada has adversely affected or is likely to adversely affect significant Canadian interest in relation to international trade or commerce involving business carried on in whole or in part in Canada, or otherwise has infringed, or is likely to infringe, Canadian sovereignty, he may declare that judgment will not be recognized or enforceable in Canada. (§8). Where judgment is for specified amount of money, Attorney General may declare that, for purposes of recognition and enforcement of that judgment, amount of that judgment will be deemed to be reduced by amount specified in order. Latter is in response to punitive damages which may be recoverable from Canadian corporations in American civil antitrust actions where treble damages may be awarded. (§9). FEMA also enables Canadian individual or corporation to bring action in Canada to recover from person who has obtained foreign judgment which is subject of subsequent order by Attorney General prohibiting enforcement in Canada of "excessive" amount of foreign judgment. (§9).

Pursuant to FEMA, effective Oct. 9, 1992 Canadian Government promulgated Foreign Extraterritorial Measures (United States) Order, 1992 which blocks extraterritorial application in Canada of U.S. Cuban Democracy Act of 1992. Effective Jan. 15, 1996, Canada expanded scope of 1992 Blocking Order issued pursuant to FEMA. Blocking Order requires Canadian companies to notify Attorney General of Canada of any directive, instruction, intimation of policy or other communication relating to "extraterritorial measure of the United States" from person who is in position to direct or influence policies of Canadian corporation in Canada. Extraterritorial measure is broadly defined to include not only 1992 Cuban Democracy Act but extends now to any statute, regulation, policy, etc. which has trade restricting effect or intent on trade or commerce between Canada and Cuba. Compliance with such intimations of policy by Canadian corporation (including officers, directors and senior management) is prohibited. Blocking Order does not affect Canada's cooperation with U.S. in controlling reexport of U.S. origin goods and technology.

United Nations Act.—Pursuant to United Nations Act (R.S.C., c. U-2) federal government has necessary authority to implement sanctions imposed by United Nations. Countries the subject of UN sanctions change frequently and thus must be updated regularly. As of Apr. 1996, regulations pursuant to UN Act are enforced against Angola, Iraq, Libya, Rwanda and Federal Republic of Yugoslavia (Serbia and Montenegro). Typically, these Regulations restrict export of certain or all products to states named in regulations and reflect position taken at UN Security Council. For example United Nations Iraq Regulations prohibit any person in Canada from knowingly exporting any goods to any person in Iraq and prohibit persons in Canada and Canadians outside Canada from knowingly selling or supplying or attempting to sell or supply any goods that are outside Iraq to any person in Iraq. These Iraq Regulations also prohibit any person in Canada and any Canadians outside Canada from entering into any financial transactions with any person in Iraq. As Security Council Resolution does not prohibit export of food and medical supplies, application may be made for export certificate to export such goods to Iraq. Regulations enacted pursuant to United Nations Act with respect to each of Angola, Federal Republic of Yugoslavia, Libya and Rwanda tend to be sector specific (e.g. aircraft parts, equipment that is of military application) and relate to political unrest in these jurisdictions. Any exports from Canada to jurisdictions subject of UN sanctions and, in some instances, imports, must be carefully reviewed in order to ensure that such actions do not violate United Nations Act and Regulations.

Special Economic Measures Act.—Sanctions can also be imposed from time to time pursuant to Special Economic Measures Act (S.C. 1992, c. 17) (see Customs Duties). As of Apr. 1996, there were no sanctions outstanding pursuant to this legislation.

FRAUDS, STATUTE OF:

See digests of the laws of the several provinces.

GUARDIAN AND WARD:

See digests of the laws of the several provinces.

HOLIDAYS:

Following are legal holidays in Canada: Sundays; New Year's Day; Good Friday; Easter Monday; Victoria Day, being Mon. immediately preceding May 25 in each year; birthday, or day fixed by proclamation for celebration of birth, of reigning sovereign; Canada Day, July 1; Labour Day (first Mon. in Sept.); Remembrance Day, Nov. 11; Christmas Day; any day appointed by proclamation as holiday, e.g., Thanksgiving Day, second Mon. in Oct.; in any province any day appointed by proclamation of Lieutenant Governor of province to be observed as public holiday and any day that is non-judicial day by virtue of Act of provincial legislature. (Interpretation Act, R. S. C., c. I-23, 28[17]).

Legality of Transactions on Holidays.—In general, transactions are not invalidated because done on a holiday. Any contract made on Sunday is invalid, unless made pursuant to a business not prohibited by the Lord's Day Act. (R. S. C., c. L-13, repealed).

See digests of laws of the several provinces.

IMMIGRATION: See topic Aliens.

INCOME TAX: See topic Taxation.

INHERITANCE TAX:

See digests of the laws of the several provinces.

INSOLVENCY: See topic Bankruptcy.

INSURANCE:

Regulated by Insurance Companies Act (S.C. 1991, c. 47) which provides for incorporation and regulation of Canadian companies, including fraternal benefit societies, for regulation of foreign companies and for provincial companies licensed under predecessor federal insurance legislation. Company seeking federal incorporation must apply to Minister of Finance for letters patent. Act contains restrictions on ownership of life companies by nonresidents. Company must obtain order from Superintendent before commencing business. If insurer is owned by "foreign bank" as defined in Bank Act (S.C. 1991, c. 46), consent of Governor-in-Council is also required. Before order can be obtained, certain requirements of Act must be fulfilled including satisfying capital and liquidity standards, participation by life companies in compensation programmes, etc. Minister of Finance must approve transfer of substantial or control blocks of shares as well as transfer of any business or any reinsurance arrangement (other than ordinary course of business reinsurance). Loans, investments and transactions with related parties are regulated. Non-Canadian insurers or exchanges with principal place of business outside Canada that are not authorized to transact insurance business in Canada are subject to 10% premiums tax on Canadian risks.

Supervision by Office of Superintendent of Financial Institutions which is presided over by Minister of Finance; Superintendent of Financial Institutions is deputy head of Office.

Annual return must be filed with Superintendent within 60 days of financial year end (105 days for reinsurers). Superintendent can require additional returns and information and conducts annual investigation of business and affairs of each company.

Policies, Rebates, Liens on Policies, Agents, Brokers, Trade Practices, etc. are regulated by provincial insurance legislation.

Foreign insurance companies must obtain order from Superintendent and be approved by Minister of Finance before commencing business. Before order can be obtained, foreign company must by power of attorney appoint chief agent ordinarily resident in Canada as well as Canadian auditor and actuary. Minister of Finance must be satisfied that applicant foreign company will be able to contribute to Canada's financial system and that Canadian insurers will be treated as favourably in home jurisdiction of applicant. Additional information that must accompany application for approval order includes (a) evidence that applicant is authorized under its home jurisdiction to insure risks, (b) resolution of its Board establishing prudent investment and lending portfolio policy, (c) certified copy of constating documents, (d) evidence of solvency and financial condition, (e) evidence that notice of intention to apply for approval order was published in Canada Gazette as well as in newspaper in general circulation at or near place of proposed chief agency. Except for foreign companies licensed under predecessor federal insurance legislation, new foreign companies cannot insure both (a) risks falling within class of life insurance and (b) risks falling under any other class of insurance, other than accident and sickness insurance. "Grandfathered" foreign insurer

INSURANCE . . . *continued*
transacting life insurance and other classes of insurance must maintain separate fund for its life insurance business. Foreign companies are confined to certain kinds of investments and must maintain in Canada prescribed amounts and kinds of assets to meet Canadian liabilities and such assets must be vested in trust with Canadian trustee under form of trust deed approved by Superintendent. All foreign companies must file annual return with Superintendent within 60 days of financial year end (105 days for foreign reinsurers). Superintendent can require further returns and information and conducts annual investigation of business affairs of foreign company. Foreign company must maintain certain records in Canada and Superintendent's consent is required for processing of Canadian records outside Canada.

Breach of Act.—Any individual found guilty of offence under Act will be liable to fine of up to $100,000 or jail term of 12 months or both; in case of company, maximum fine is $500,000. Court may also issue compliance order requiring person to comply with Act and if offender derived monetary benefit as result of any breach, additional fine in amount of fine can be levied.

See Digests of laws of the various provinces.

See also topics Taxation; Shipping, subhead Admiralty Law, catchline Marine Insurance.

INTEREST:

Except as otherwise provided by Act of Parliament, any rate of interest may be contracted for. (Interest Act, R. S. C., c. I-15, §2).

Banks.—See topic Banks and Banking, subhead Interest.

Criminal Code (R.S.C., c. C-46, §347) establishes as criminal rate of interest effective annual rate that exceeds 60% on credit advanced. Interest includes all charges and expenses (except certain insurance and official fees) payable by or for borrower for advancement of credit. Any person who receives or arranges to receive interest at criminal rate is guilty of: (a) indictable offence and liable to imprisonment for five years, or (b) summary conviction offence and liable to fine of up to $25,000 or to imprisonment for six months or to both.

Judgment Interest.—Under §50 of Supreme Court Act, (R.S.C., c. S-26) unless otherwise ordered by Supreme Court of Canada, judgment thereof bears interest at rate and from date of judgment in same matter in court of original jurisdiction.

Mortgages.—As to interest on mortgages, see topic Mortgages.

See also topic Corporations; see also Digests of laws of various provinces.

JUDGMENTS:

See digests of the laws of the several provinces.

LABOUR RELATIONS:

Canada Labour Code (R.S.C., c. L-2).—Where employment is within federal work, undertaking, or business it comes within federal jurisdiction. Jurisdiction over labour relations primarily falls within provinces' jurisdiction by virtue of Constitution Act, 1867, §92(13). Federal works, undertakings or businesses include: Navigation, shipping, railways, ships, air transportation, broadcasting, banks, or other declared by Parliament to be for advantage of two or more provinces.

Part I—Industrial Relations.—

Basic Freedoms.—Every employee is free to join trade union of his choice and to participate in its lawful activities.

Canada Labour Relations Board.—Board consists of chairperson, vice-chairperson and such additional number of vice-chairpersons, not exceeding four, as is considered advisable. Board has broad powers which include right to establish rules of procedure of its hearings. Board's authority extends to determination of units appropriate for collective bargaining, certification or decertification of trade unions as bargaining agents for unit's employees, conduct of representation votes and determination of evidence as to union membership.

Application for Certification.—Trade union may apply to Board for certification as bargaining agent for unit considered appropriate for collective bargaining. Union must claim to have majority of unit's employees as union members in good standing. Application may be made during certain time periods. Certification may be sought at any time if no collective agreement exists and where no union has been certified to represent proposed unit.

Determination of Bargaining Unit.—Board has exclusive jurisdiction in determining whether or not unit of employees is appropriate for collective bargaining and may include any employees in or exclude any employees from unit proposed by trade union. "Unit" means two or more employees.

Representation Vote.—Board has duty to certify trade union if Board has determined that proposed unit is appropriate and if Board is of opinion that as of date of filing of application for certification, majority of employees in bargaining unit wish to have union represent them as bargaining agent. To find out if employees wish to be represented by particular union, Board can order representation vote.

Successor Rights.—Where employer sells business (a) trade union that is bargaining agent for employees continues to represent them, (b) trade union that applied for certification before sale may be certified by Board to represent employees, and (c) person to whom business is sold is bound by any collective agreement in force at time of sale.

Notice to Bargain.—Trade union certified for bargaining unit has exclusive authority to represent employees in unit. If bargaining agent has been certified but no collective agreement exists, bargaining agent may give employer notice to commence collective bargaining, or vice versa, for purpose of entering into collective agreement.

Duty to Bargain in Good Faith.—Where notice to bargain has been given, bargaining agent and employer, or their representatives, shall meet within 20 days after receipt of such notice and shall begin to bargain in good faith, making every reasonable effort to reach agreement.

Conciliation/Mediation.—Conciliation services are available upon written request of either party where notice to bargain has been given and (a) collective bargaining has not commenced within time fixed; or (b) parties have bargained but have failed to enter into, renew, or revise collective agreement.

Term of Collective Agreement.—If not specified, collective agreement shall be deemed to have minimum term of one year from date on which it comes into force.

First Collective Agreement.—When employer and bargaining agent are negotiating first collective agreement and they have informed Minister that they are at impasse, Minister may, if considered advisable or necessary, direct Board to inquire into dispute and if advisable settle terms and conditions of first collective agreement between parties.

Arbitration.—During term of collective agreement all disputes between parties concerning interpretation, application, administration or alleged violation of agreement shall be submitted to arbitration for final settlement. Powers of arbitrator or arbitration board include right (a) to determine procedure, (b) to exercise power of Canada Labour Relations Board in summoning witnesses, and (c) to determine whether matter referred is arbitrable.

Strikes and lockouts are prohibited while collective agreement is in force. No trade union should declare or authorize strike unless trade union has served notice to bargain collectively, negotiations have failed to produce or revise collective agreement, conciliation procedures have failed, and seven days have elapsed from date on which Minister advised parties of his or her intention not to appoint conciliation officer or board.

Unfair Labour Practices.—No employer shall participate in or interfere with formation or administration of trade union or representation of employees by trade union, or contribute financial or other support to trade union. Employer shall not refuse to employ or suspend, transfer, lay off, intimidate, threaten or otherwise discipline any person because that person participates in promotion, formation or administration of trade union.

Union Duty of Fair Representation.—Trade union and its representatives shall not act in manner that is arbitrary, discriminatory, or in bad faith in representation of any employee in bargaining unit with respect to rights under collective agreement applicable to them.

Complaints.—Written complaints of failure to comply with foregoing provisions may be made to Board not later than ten days from date complainant knew or, in opinion of Board, ought to have known, of action or circumstances giving rise to complaint. Complaints against trade unions respecting grievances must first exhaust union grievance procedure before appealing to Board.

Part II—Repealed.

Part III—Standard Hours, Wages, Vacations and Holidays.—

Hours of Work.—Standard hours of work are eight hours a day, 40 hours a week. Where necessary hours may be averaged over period of two or more weeks. Each employee must have one full day of rest a week. Overtime rate of wages must be not less than 1 and a $^1/_2$ times regular rate.

Minimum Wage.—Every employee 17 and over must be paid $4 an hour or its equivalent if wages paid on basis other than hourly. Persons under 17 may be employed only in occupations and at minimum rate established by regulation.

Equal Wages.—Male and female employees employed in same industrial establishment who are performing similar jobs under similar working conditions requiring similar skill, effort and responsibility must receive equal pay.

Vacations.—Employee is entitled to annual vacation with pay of at least two weeks after each completed year of work with same employer, and after six consecutive years, of at least three weeks with vacation pay in respect of every year of employment by that employer. If any federal work, undertaking, or business is transferred from one employer to another, employee's employment shall be deemed to be continuous. Vacation pay is defined as 4% or, after six consecutive years of work with same employer, 6% of wages during year of employment in which employee is entitled to vacation.

General Holidays.—Every employee is entitled to holiday with pay on each of general holidays falling within any period of employment. General holidays include New Year's Day, Good Friday, Victoria Day, Canada Day, Labour Day, Thanksgiving Day, Remembrance Day, Christmas Day and Boxing Day and includes any day substituted for such holiday.

Maternity Leave.—Employee who has completed six consecutive months of continuous employment with employer is entitled to leave of absence for pregnancy upon presentation of medical certificate and written application submitted at least four weeks before absence is to commence. Period of maternity leave shall consist of period not exceeding 17 weeks. Code also provides that employee who has completed six months of continuous service with employer is entitled to leave of absence for child care purposes up to maximum of 24 weeks.

Notice of Termination.—Code provides that employer must give either two weeks notice of termination in writing, or two weeks wages at regular rate in lieu of such notice where employee has completed three or more continuous months of work and termination is not by way of dismissal for just cause.

Severance Pay.—Under Code, employer who terminates employment of employee who has completed 12 consecutive months of continuous employment by employer shall, except where termination is by way of dismissal for just cause, pay to employee greater of: (a) two days wages at employee's regular rate of wages for regular hours of work in respect of each completed year of employment; and (b) five days wages at employee's regular rate at wages for regular hours of work.

Group Termination.—Notice to Minister of Labour required to be given in writing at least 16 weeks before date of termination by employer of group of employees if group consists of 50 or more employees. Copy of notice must also be given to Minister of Employment and Immigration, Canada Employment and Immigration Commission, and to any trade union representing affected employees. Notice shall contain information prescribed by regulation.

Part IV—Safety of Employees.—Statutory duties are placed on employers and employees in connection with safety with penalties provided for breach. Subject to certain limitations, employees may refuse to work or operate machine or thing if condition exists that constitutes danger to employee.

Employment Equity Act (S.C. 1986, c. 31).—Act establishes process to achieve equality in workplace based solely on ability and to correct conditions of disadvantage in employment experienced by women, aboriginal peoples, disabled persons and persons of visible minority. Act provides employer must prepare yearly plans and timetable to implement employment equity.

See Topical Index in front part of this volume.

LABOUR RELATIONS . . . *continued*

Corporations and Labour Unions Returns Act (R. S. C., c. C-43).—This Act applies to every labour union carrying on activities as such and having local union branch in Canada except labour union having fewer than 100 members resident in Canada at relevant time. (§11). Commencing with reporting period, if any, coinciding with or ending in 1962, every labour union must file return with Dominion Statistician for each reporting period, not later than six months after coming into force of Act or end of that reporting period, whichever is later. (§12). Section A of report is statement setting out name, headquarters address and principal office in Canada, constitution, officers, names and addresses and nationality or citizenship of all officers and employees resident in Canada (other than mere clerical assistants), name and address of each branch and its officers and numbers of its members, particulars of branches under trusteeship, names and addresses of each employer with which union has collective agreement. Section B is comprised of financial statement, including balance sheet and statement of income and expenditure, and in case of union with headquarters outside Canada, particulars of certain payments made to union by or on behalf of members resident in Canada. (§12). Financial statement must be accompanied by auditor's report. (part 13). Union in default in filing returns is liable on summary conviction to fine not exceeding $250 for each day of such default. Any officer, member of executive, or agent being party to offence is also liable on conviction to similar fine, or imprisonment for three months, or to both. (§14). All information, subject to specified exceptions, contained in return filed by corporation or labour union is privileged and no authorized person shall knowingly communicate or allow any person to inspect or have access to information obtained under this Act. No court of law may force any official to produce such privileged information or to disclose statements containing privileged information. However, privileged information may be divulged to authorized person working under Statistics Act.

Unemployment Insurance Act, 1971 (R.S.C., c. U-1).—Repealed by Employment Insurance Act (S.C. 1996, c. 23) which received Royal Assent on June 20, 1996 and is partly in force as of June 30, 1996. Act and regulations establishes contributory system of unemployment insurance and provides for payment of benefits to persons in insurable employment and self-employed fishermen.

Under Act, insurable employment means employment in Canada by one or more employers under an express or implied contract of service or apprenticeship. Contract may be written or not. Employment earnings may be received from employer or some other person and may be calculated by time or by piece, or partly by time and partly by piece, or otherwise. Insurable employment also includes employment in Canada by federal government, service in Canadian Forces or in any police force and employment included in insurable employment by regulation.

Act is not applicable to an employed person who is over 70 years of age, or to whom a retirement pension under Canada or Quebec Pension Plan has become payable. Employment of a person by his spouse, or employment where employee is a dependent of employer is considered to be excepted employment. Employment in Canada (a) under Her Majesty in right of a province, (b) by government of country other than Canada and (c) by international organization are all excluded from coverage. In addition, Act does not apply to certain employment of casual nature, employment that constitutes exchange of work or services, or employment that is excepted by regulation.

Labour Adjustment Benefits Act (R.S.C., c. L-1).—Act establishes payment of benefits to laid-off employees of designated industries where employee has been employed in designated industry at least ten years of 15 years preceding date of his lay-off.

See also Fair Wages and Hours of Labour Act, R.S.C., c. L-4.

See also topic Taxation, subhead Unemployment Compensation Tax.

LAW REPORTS, CODES, ETC.:

See topics Reports; Statutes.

LEGISLATURE:

See topic Constitution and Government.

LICENSES:

Licensing of professions and most commercial activities is under provincial or municipal jurisdiction. See digests of laws of the several provinces, topic Licences.

Commercial activities subject to federal licensing include: aeronautics (R.S.C., c. A-2, as am'd); banking (S.C. 1991, c. 46); broadcasting (S.C. 1991, c. 11); fisheries (R.S.C., c. F-14); insurance (S.C. 1991, c. 47; also under provincial jurisdiction); radio (R.S.C., c. R-2); railways (R.S.C., c. R-3); shipping (R.S.C., c. S-9); telephones (R.S.C., c. R-2; also subject to provincial regulation in some parts of Canada); television (S.C. 1991, c. 11). See also: Animal Disease and Protection Act, R.S.C., c. A-11; Bridges Act, R.S.C., c. B-8; Canada Grain Act, R.S.C., c. G-10; Electricity and Gas Inspection Act, R.S.C., c. E-4; Excise Tax Act, R.S.C., c. E-15; Explosives Act, R.S.C., c. E-17; Feeds Act, R.S.C., c. F-9; Fertilizers Act, R.S.C., c. F-10; Fish Inspection Act, R.S.C., c. F-12; Fisheries Act, R.S.C., c. F-14; Livestock and Livestock Products Act, R.S.C., c. L-9; Small Businesses Loans Act, R.S.C., c. S-11; Timber Marking Act, R.S.C., c. T-11; Trade Unions Act, R.S.C., c. T-14.

Import and export of certain goods is subject to licensing and permit requirements under various statutes including Export and Import Permits Act (R.S.C., c. E-19) and Meat Import Act (R.S.C., c. M-3).

See also topics Insurance; Interest; Shipping; Taxation; Foreign Trade Regulations, subhead Export and Import Permits Act.

LIMITATION OF ACTIONS:

Federal limitation periods are governed by particular statutes. There is no federal equivalent to provincial statutes of limitations. Examples of federal limitation periods: prosecution under Bankruptcy and Insolvency Act, c. B-3, as am'd, within five years of commission of offence if by way of indictment, within three years if by summary conviction; actions and offences under Canada Business Corporations Act, c. C-44, within two years; offences under Canada Water Act, c. C-11, within two years; claim for costs and expenses resulting from release of prohibited substance under Canadian Environmental Protection Act, R.S.C. (4th Supp.), c. 16, two years from later of release or Minister's knowledge thereof; in Federal Court, for cause of action not arising in province, six years (c. F-7); Criminal Code prosecutions by summary conviction, six months (c. C-46). Certain proceedings against Federal Crown require written notice within seven days. (c. C-50). See also Digests of laws of the several provinces.

MARRIAGE:

See digests of the laws of the several provinces.

MINES AND MINERALS:

Mines and minerals within provinces may be subject to both provincial and federal jurisdiction. See topic Constitution and Government, subhead Jurisdiction of Provincial Legislatures.

Licences and leases for mining concessions in Northwest Territories, Yukon, Canadian Arctic and under territorial waters are available and may be granted by Government on application. See topic Public Lands. Mining and control of uranium and certain other prescribed substances under jurisdiction of Atomic Energy Control Board. See Atomic Energy Control Act. (R.S.C., c. A-16).

Administration and disposition of minerals in Canada, except minerals situate in any province or in Yukon Territory, is governed by Canada Mining Regulations under Territorial Lands Act (c. T-7), as administered by either Department of Indian Affairs and Northern Development or Department of Energy, Mines and Resources, depending on specific geographic location of minerals. For Yukon Territory, see Yukon Placer Mining Act (c. Y-3) and Yukon Quartz Mining Act (c. Y-4). See also Yukon Surface Rights Board Act (S.C. 1994, c. 43) re dispute resolution.

Oil and Gas.—Production safety, environmental and employment matters subject to provincial and federal regulation. See Canada Oil and Gas Operations Act. S.C. 1992, c. 35 (formerly Oil and Gas Production and Conservation Act [c. O-7]). Licence issued by National Energy Board required for exports and for imports of natural gas. Under Energy Administration Act, (c. E-6) (formerly: Petroleum Administration Act), Government has power to regulate prices of Canadian crude oil and natural gas that enters international or interprovincial trade. Land tenure in northern and offshore Canada is subject to Canada Petroleum Resources Act, 2nd Supp., (c. 36), as amended, which provides for licensing exclusive exploration and production rights subject to 50% Canadian ownership criterion, which Minister may waive, and for safety, environmental and conservation matters. Subject to this Act, Canada Oil and Gas Regulations provide for exploration agreements with preferential rights to Petro Canada. Various coastal provinces also claim jurisdiction over offshore exploration and federal government is also party to agreements with such provinces.

Petroleum Incentives Program Act (c. P-13), promotes Canadian ownership in oil and gas industry by providing sliding scale of reimbursements for eligible costs. Eligible costs include asset, development and exploration costs as prescribed by regulations. (c. P-13). Percentage of costs reimbursed depends on whether exploration occurs on Canada lands, Canadian control status and rate of Canadian ownership. Canadian lands are northern territories, Sable Island and offshore Canada. (c. P-13). Eligible person applies for certificate stating his Canadian control status and Canadian ownership rate from Department of Natural Resources as prescribed in Canadian Ownership and Control Determination Act. (c. C-20).

See topic Foreign Investment.

Taxes.—Income Tax Act contains provisions relating specifically to exploration and development expenses, falling under headings: Canadian Exploration Expense; Canadian Development Expense; Resource Allowance; Earned Depletion Allowance and Mining Exploration Depletion Allowance (phased out); and Flow-through Shares. Also, under Canadian Exploration Incentive Program Act, qualifying participants are entitled to payments equal to 30% of eligible exploration expenses. Mines and oil and gas wells subject to different royalty rates in each province. Generally, royalties are not deductible for Canadian Income tax purposes. See also Oil Export Tax Act. Energy Administration Act levies special charges on domestic petroleum and amends Excise Tax Act provisions applicable to natural gas. Canada Mining Regulations impose royalty payable to Government calculated on sliding scale based on value of output of mine. Yukon Placer Mining Act imposes royalty on value of gold production. Yukon Quartz Mining Act imposes royalty calculated on sliding scale based on profit.

See also Petroleum and Gas Revenue Tax Act. (c. P-12).

MONOPOLIES AND RESTRAINT OF TRADE:

Section numbers refer to Competition Act, R.S.C., c. C-34, as am'd.

Unlawful Combinations.—It is indictable offence (crime) to conspire, combine, arrange or agree: (1) to limit unduly facilities for transporting, producing, manufacturing, supplying, storing or dealing in any product, (2) to prevent, limit or lessen, unduly the manufacture or production of product, or to enhance unreasonably price thereof, (3) to prevent, or lessen, unduly, competition in production, manufacture, purchase, barter, sale, storage, rental, transportation or supply of product, or in price of insurance upon persons or property, or (4) to otherwise restrain or injure competition unduly, and upon conviction person is liable to imprisonment for five years or fine of $10,000,000, or both. (§45).

This does not apply in respect of combinations or activities of workmen or employees for their own reasonable protection as such workmen or employees, certain contracts between or among fishermen, employers associations for collective bargaining, certain arrangements between underwriters, or arrangements between teams, clubs and leagues pertaining to amateur sport. (§§4, 5 and 6). In establishing that conspiracy, combination, agreement or arrangement is in violation of Act it is not necessary to prove that conspiracy, combination, agreement or arrangement, if carried into effect, would or would be likely to eliminate, completely or virtually, competition in market to which it relates or that it was object of any or all of parties thereto to eliminate, completely or virtually, competition in that market. (§45[2]).

Foreign Directives.—Any company, wherever incorporated, that carries on business in Canada and that implements, in whole or in part in Canada, directive, instruction, intimation of policy or other communication to company or any person from person in country other than Canada who is in position to direct or influence policies of company,

MONOPOLIES AND RESTRAINT OF TRADE . . . *continued*
which communication is for purpose of giving effect to conspiracy, combination, agreement or arrangement entered into outside Canada that, if entered into in Canada, would have been in violation of Act, is, whether or not any director or officer of company in Canada has knowledge of conspiracy, combination, agreement of arrangement, guilty of indictable offence (crime) and is liable on conviction to fine in discretion of court. (§46).

Bid-rigging.—Every one who is a party to bid-rigging is guilty of indictable offence (crime) and is liable on conviction to fine in discretion of court or to imprisonment for five years or to both. This does not apply in respect of agreement or arrangement that is entered into or submission that is arrived at only by companies each of which is, in respect of every one of others, affiliate as that relationship is defined in Act. (§47).

Conspiracy in Relation to Professional Sports.—Every one who conspires, combines, agrees or arranges with another person (a) to limit unreasonably opportunities for any other person to participate, as player or competitor, in professional sport or to impose unreasonable terms or conditions on those persons who so participate, or (b) to limit unreasonably opportunity for any other person to negotiate with and, if agreement is reached, to play for team or club of his choice in professional league, is guilty of indictable offence (crime) and is liable on conviction to fine in discretion of court or to imprisonment for five years or to both. (§48).

Illegal Trade Practices.—It is indictable offence for any person engaged in business to: (1) be party to or assist in any sale that discriminates to his knowledge, directly or indirectly, against competitors of purchaser, in that any discount, rebate, allowance, price concession or other advantage is granted to purchaser over any such advantage available at time of sale to such competitors; (2) engage in policy of selling products in any area of Canada at prices lower than those exacted by him elsewhere in Canada, having effect or tendency of substantially lessening competition or eliminating competitor in such part of Canada, or designed to have such effect; or (3) engage in policy of selling products at prices unreasonably low, having effect or tendency of substantially lessening competition or eliminating competitor, or designed to have such effect. (§50). To be an offence, act must be part of practice of discriminating. Any person guilty of offence under this section is liable for imprisonment for two years. This does not apply to co-operatives. Similar prohibition against discriminatory advertising or display allowances. (§51).

Misleading advertising generally and making of certain representations to public as to testing of performance, efficacy or length of life of product, publishing of certain testimonials with respect to product, double ticketing of products and bait and switch selling are offences (crimes) under Act and are punishable by fines of varying amounts or by imprisonment for varying terms. (§§52-54 and 57). Under Act no person may induce or invite another person to participate in scheme of pyramid selling or referral selling. (§§55 and 56). Act contains similar prohibitions against bait and switch selling and sales above advertised price. (§§57 and 58).

Matters Reviewable by Tribunal.—

Refusal to Deal.—Competition Tribunal, if it finds that: (1) person is substantially affected in his business or is precluded from carrying on business due to his inability to obtain adequate supplies of product anywhere in market on usual trade terms, (2) such person is unable to obtain adequate supplies of product because of insufficient competition among suppliers of product in market, (3) such person is willing and able to meet usual trade terms of supplier or suppliers of such product, and (4) product is in ample supply, may order that one or more suppliers of product in market accept person as customer within specified time on usual trade terms. (§75).

Exclusive Dealing and Tied Selling.—Where Tribunal finds that exclusive dealing or tied selling, because it is engaged in by major supplier of product in market or because it is widespread in market, is likely to: (1) impede entry into or expansion of firm in market, (2) impede introduction of product into or expansion of sales of product in market, or (3) have any other exclusionary effect in market; with result that competition is or is likely to be lessened substantially, Tribunal may make order directed to all or any of such suppliers prohibiting them from continuing to engage in such exclusive dealing or tied selling and containing any other requirement that, in its opinion, is necessary to overcome effects thereof in market or to restore or stimulate competition in market. (§77).

Consignment Selling.—Where Tribunal finds that consignment selling by supplier of product is for purpose of: (1) controlling price at which dealer sells product or (2) discriminating against consignees or dealers, Tribunal may order supplier to cease consignment selling. (§76).

Market Restriction.—Where Tribunal finds that market restriction engaged in by major supplier(s) is likely to substantially lessen competition, Tribunal may prohibit market restriction. (§77).

Abuse of Dominant Position.—Where Tribunal finds that: (1) one or more persons substantially or completely control class or species of business in Canada, (2) they have or are engaging in practice of anti-competitive acts, objects of which are to lessen competition, and (3) practice likely to substantially lessen competition, Tribunal may prohibit such acts. (§79).

Specialization Agreements.—Where Tribunal finds persons to have freely entered into agreement that is likely to bring gains in efficiency that will offset lessening of competition, Tribunal may allow and register agreement. (§§85-90).

Mergers.—Where Tribunal finds merger or proposed merger substantially lessens competition in (1) industry, trade or profession, (2) sources of products, (3) sales outlets, or (4) otherwise, Tribunal may dissolve or prevent merger. (§92).

Resale price maintenance agreements and acts done by dealers in furtherance of resale price maintenance are indictable offences. (§61).

Conviction.—A person convicted of any of offenses in Part VI (§§45-62) from time to time within three years thereafter, may be required to make disclosure of his business to court before which he was convicted. (§35). Any person failing to comply with order of court requiring such disclosure is liable to fine in discretion of court or to two years imprisonment or to both fine and imprisonment.

Customs duties may be reduced or removed from any article imported by a combine which is committing any of the above offences. (§31).

Patents or trade marks may be declared void in whole or in part where they are used to restrain or injure trade or commerce or to restrict competition unduly. (§32).

Damages.—Any person who has suffered damage or loss as result of conduct contrary to Part VI of Act or failure to comply with order of Tribunal or court made under Act may sue for and recover from person who engaged in such conduct or failed to comply amount equal to loss or damage suffered. (§36).

Injunctions may be obtained to restrain anyone convicted of one of the above mentioned offences from continuing or repeating the offence or doing any act directed towards such continuation or repetition. (§34).

Investigations.—Any six persons, being Canadian citizens and resident in Canada, who are of opinion that offence under Act has been or is about to be committed may apply for inquiry by Director of Investigation and Research or such inquiry may be instituted by Director or Minister of Industry. (§§9 and 10). Provision is made for sworn returns, seizure of documents and oral examinations in course of such inquiries. Director may discontinue inquiry if he considers further inquiry to be unjustified. If Director feels that evidence discloses violation, he may inform Attorney-General or apply to Tribunal. (Part VIII and VI). Procedure of Tribunal governed by Competition Tribunal Act, S.C. 1986, c. 26.

MORTGAGES:

Except in the case of real estate mortgages, where interest is made payable at a rate by the day, week, month or any period less than a year, no rate exceeding 5% per annum may be recovered unless the equivalent rate per annum is stated in the contract. (c. I-15, §4). Where principal or interest secured by mortgage on real estate is made payable on sinking fund plan or so that payments of principal and interest are blended, or on plan that involves allowance of interest on stipulated repayments, no interest whatever is recoverable unless mortgage contains statement showing amount of such principal money and rate of interest, calculated yearly or half-yearly not in advance. (§6). No fine or penalty or rate of interest can be exacted on any arrears of principal or interest secured by mortgage on real estate which has effect of increasing charge on any such amount beyond rate of interest on principal not in arrears. (§8). Wherever principal or interest secured by mortgage on real estate is not payable until after five years from date, mortgagor may at any time after five years, tender, in full discharge, amount due up to date of payment together with three months interest. (§10[1]). This, however, does not apply to mortgage on real estate given by corporation or a corporation debenture secured by mortgage on real estate. (§10[2]; Interest Act R.S.C., c. I-15).

Farm Mortgages.—Farm Credit Corporation may grant mortgage credit to farmers. Purpose of Corporation is to enhance rural Canada by providing specialized and personalized financial services to farming operations including family farms and to those businesses in rural Canada, including small and medium-sized businesses, that are related to farming. (Farm Credit Corporation Act, S.C. 1993, c. 14). Corporation has power to make loans or guarantee loans made to persons or bodies for number of purposes. (§4[2]). For protection of income of producers of agricultural products, federal government may enter into agreement with one or more provinces to set up any of following programs: (i) net income stabilization account program; (ii) gross revenue insurance program; (iii) revenue insurance program; and (iv) crop insurance program. (Farm Income Protection Act, S.C. 1991, c. 22). Farm Income Protection Act repeals The Agricultural Stabilization Act, The Crop Insurance Act and Western Grain Stabilization Act.

See also digests of the laws of the several provinces.

MOTOR VEHICLES:

See digests of the laws of the several provinces.

NATURALIZATION: See topic Aliens.

NEGOTIABLE INSTRUMENTS:

See topic Bills and Notes.

PATENTS:

Effective Jan. 1990, Canada satisfied Parts I and II of Patent Cooperation Treaty whereby one form of application filed in Canadian Patent Office gives applicant option of having application deemed to have also been filed in such other member countries as applicant may elect. Amendments to Act to bring it into conformity with Canada's obligations under Agreement Establishing the World Trade Organization came into force in Jan. 1996. These amendments extend treaty benefits to all WTO members. All communications concerning patents are to be addressed to The Commissioner of Patents, Ottawa, Canada. (Rule 5). Models need only be furnished when required by Commissioner. Every model so required must be of convenient size exhibiting its several parts in due proportion and must not exceed 12 inches on its longest side. (§38). Every applicant for patent who does not appear to reside or carry on business at specified address in Canada, must nominate as representative person or firm residing or carrying on business at specified address in Canada. (§29). Applicant's petition must be accompanied by specification. (§27[2]). *Note:* Broad changes to Patent Rules are currently being considered.

Invention is defined as any new and useful art, process, machine, manufacture or composition of matter, or any new and useful improvement thereof. (§§2, 32). Patent claims are allowable for foods and medicines without being limited to process.

Entitlement.—Major amendments to Patent Act came into effect on Oct. 1, 1989, and provide two sets of criteria which govern entitlement to patent.

Applications Filed Prior to Oct. 1, 1989.—Patent granting exclusive property in invention may be obtained and maintained for invention that was not known or used by any other person prior to date of invention, not described in any patent or in any publication printed in Canada or in any other country more than two years before presentation of petition, and not in public use or on sale in Canada for more than two years prior to application in Canada. (§§27, 28 repealed and §§27, 28 Transitional Provision of S.C. 1987, c. 41). Generally, priority is given to first inventor.

See Topical Index in front part of this volume.

PATENTS . . . *continued*

Applications Filed After Sept. 30, 1989.—Patent granting to applicant exclusive property in invention may be obtained and maintained for invention unless patent application describing same invention was filed in Canada by any other person before earlier of date of filing Canadian application or its priority date (generally date of filing foreign application within one year before filing in Canada), patent application describing same invention filed in Canada has earlier priority date, invention was disclosed so as to become available to public prior to earlier of application date or priority date, or invention was disclosed by or through applicant so as to become available to public more than one year before application date. (§§27, 28). Generally, priority is given to first applicant to file rather than to first to invent. Absolute novelty is required with grace period of one year for disclosures directly or indirectly by applicant which become available to public. Priority is determined on basis of subject matter of particular claim rather than entire application. Nonobviousness is expressly required. Public inspection is available 18 months after Canadian filing.

Generally.—Inventor who has applied for patent in any other country before filing application in Canada is not entitled to obtain patent in Canada if patent issues in any other country prior to Canadian filing date, or if Canadian application is filed after issuance of any foreign patent for same invention and more than 12 months after first foreign filing. (§27[2]). No patent may issue for invention which has illicit object in view or for any mere scientific principle or abstract theorem. (§27[3]). Commissioner may refuse to grant patent whenever he is satisfied that applicant is not by law entitled thereto or when it appears that invention has already been patented. (§40). Applicant is allowed to answer Commissioner's objection, or appeal to Federal Court within six months. (§41).

Patent Amendment Act, S.C. 1993, c. 2, now in force, provides full term protection to newly patented pharmaceuticals. Compulsory licenses are abolished retroactive to Dec. 20, 1991. Compulsory licenses granted after that date expire on coming into force of legislation but licenses previously in existence are unaffected. Patented Medicine Prices Review Board continues and is empowered to review and control excessive prices. (§§79-90). Compulsory license may be issued in respect of other patents when patentee fails to work patent in Canada. (§65).

Term.—The term limited for the duration of patent application for which was filed prior to Oct. 1, 1989, is 17 years from date of issue (§45 repealed) and of patent application for which was filed after Oct. 1, 1989, is 20 years from filing date. (§44).

Assignment.—Every invention or patent therefor is assignable in law either as to the whole interest or as to any part thereof by an instrument in writing which shall be registered in Patent Office. (§50). Unregistered assignment is void against any subsequent assignee who registered first. (§51).

Abuse.—It is abuse of exclusive rights under patent to: Fail to work invention in Canada on commercial scale; hinder or prevent working of invention in Canada on commercial scale by importation of patented article from abroad; fail to meet demand in Canada to adequate extent and on reasonable terms; prejudice trade by refusal to grant licence on reasonable terms if it is in public interest that such licence should be granted; or otherwise unfairly prejudice trade in Canada. (§65). Any person may, after expiration of three years from grant of patent, apply to Commissioner alleging that there has been abuse as aforesaid, and if Commissioner is satisfied that case of abuse has been established he may compel grant of licence to applicant or order patent to be revoked. See also topic Monopolies and Restraint of Trade.

Fees.—On filing, by small entity, $150, by other than small entity, $300; on grant, by small entity, $350, by other than small entity, $700; on requesting registration of assignment or any other document, $100 for first, $50 for each additional request; on making disclaimer, $100; on requesting certified copy of document, $35; on requesting photocopy, 50¢ per page. Annuities are payable to maintain issued patents and pending applications. Various fees are provided for other matters.

Government Owned Patents.—Provision is now made for assignment of all benefits arising from certain types of inventions or patents therefor to Minister of National Defence as agent of Crown. This assignment takes place upon requisition by Minister and in case of certain other inventions vital to national defence order may be made by Governor-in-Council to effect that invention, application, etc., shall be treated as if it had been assigned to Minister as above. This latter provision is intended to apply to certain inventions, etc. placed before Atomic Energy Control Board. Persons divulging knowledge of these patents or inventions commit breach of The Official Secrets Act. (§20).

Plant Breeders' Rights Act, S.C. 1990, c. 20, allows plant breeders of new, distinct, uniform and stable varieties to hold exclusive right in such varieties. (§4). Holder of right in variety has exclusive right to produce and sell reproductive material of variety; to use repeatedly variety to produce another variety; to use ornamental plants or parts commercially as propagating material in production of ornamental plants or cut flowers; and to license others to do so. (§5[1]). Duration of right is 18 years, commencing on day certification of registration is issued. (§6). Entitlement to apply for plant breeders' rights requires that breeder did not sell or concur in sale of variety either before prescribed period or before effective date of application inside or outside Canada. (§7[1]). To be eligible to apply for rights, person must be citizen or resident of, or have registered office in, Canada, Union or agreement country. (§8). Priority will be allowed to Union or agreement applicant if application is made under §7 within 12 months of application for same variety in Union or agreement country. (§11[1]). Applicant must claim priority and provide certified documentation of Union or agreement application within three months of application. (§11[2]). Compulsory licences may be granted to ensure that holder of right does not abuse right. (§32[1]). Act and regulations conform to 1978 International Convention for the Protection of New Varieties of Plants. Species (categories) of plants become eligible for protection through regulation. (SOR 91-594, §3). Currently there are 23 categories protected by regulation. Current fees are for filing application, $250; examination of application, $750; registration of grant, $500.

PRACTICE:

See topics Courts and Appeal and Error.

PRESCRIPTION:

See digests of the laws of the several provinces, topic Limitation of Actions.

PRINCIPAL AND AGENT:

See digests of the laws of the several provinces.

PROCESS:

See digests of the laws of the several provinces.

PUBLIC LANDS:

Minister of Public Works has the administration of all lands belonging to federal Crown, except lands specifically under the administration of any other Minister, department, board or agency of Government of Canada.

Minister of Indian Affairs and Northern Development has the administration of all lands in Northwest Territories and Yukon belonging to Crown except lands under management, charge and direction of any other Minister, department, branch or agency of Government of Canada on Oct. 1, 1966 other than Minister or Department of Northern Affairs and Natural Resources.

Pursuant to Nunavut Act, S.C. 1993, c. 28 (in effect Apr. 1, 1999 or such earlier dates as Governor in Council may fix by order), beneficial use, proceeds, management, sale, lease, disposal, administration of control of certain lands in area to be known as Nunavut acquired with funds of Northwest Territories or land administered or controlled by Commissioner of Northwest Territories will be appropriated to Commissioner of Nunavut, subject to laws made by Legislature of Nunavut. Consequential amendments have been made to statutes of general application which refer to Northwest Territories to include references to Nunavut.

For information on subject of public lands communications should be addressed to Department of Indian Affairs and Northern Development.

See Department of Indian Affairs and Northern Development Act, R. S. C., c. I-6; Public Works Act, R. S. C., c. P-38; Territorial Lands Act, R. S. C., c. T-7; Federal Real Property Act, S.C. 1991, c 50.

REAL PROPERTY:

See digests of the laws of the several provinces.

RECEIVERS:

See topic Bankruptcy; also topic Corporations.

REPORTS:

Decisions of Supreme Court are reported in Canada Supreme Court Reports cited "S.C.R." Federal Court decisions are reported in Canada Federal Court Reports cited "F.C." Prior to 1971 Canada Law Reports reported Exchequer Court decisions (cited "EX.C.R") and Supreme Court of Canada decisions (cited "S.C.R."). Decisions which were appealed to Judicial Committee of Privy Council (before appeals to Privy Council were discontinued) are reported in British Law Reports Appeal Cases series cited "A.C."

Other publications of judicial opinions include: Canadian Bankruptcy Reports; Canadian Criminal Cases; Canadian Tax Cases; Dominion Law Reports; Insurance Law Reporter; Tax Appeal Board Cases; Western Weekly Law Reports; Canadian Patent Reporter; Labour Arbitration Cases; Land Compensation Reports; Immigration Appeal Cases; Criminal Reports; Reports of Family Law.

Digests: Canadian Abridgment.

RESTRAINT OF TRADE:

See topic Monopolies and Restraint of Trade.

SALES:

See Digest of laws of the several provinces.

United Nations Convention on Contracts for the International Sale of Goods.—Applicable to contracts of sale of goods between parties whose places of business are in different states if (a) those states have adopted Convention, or (b) rules of private international law lead to application of law of state that has adopted Convention, unless parties expressly agree otherwise. (S.C. 1991, c. 13).

Sales of goods and services are generally regulated by provincial law.

SALES TAX:

See topic Taxation.

See also digests of laws of various provinces.

SECURITIES:

Issue and trade of securities, registration of investment advisers, securities dealers, underwriters, take-over bids, insider trading, proxy solicitations and financial and other disclosure by publicly traded corporations are generally regulated by provincial law. However, take-over bids, insider trading, proxy solicitation and financial disclosure by federally incorporated issuers are also governed by Canada Business Corporations Act, R.S.C., c. C-44, as am'd. See topic Corporations.

SHIPPING:

See in particular the Canada Shipping Act. (R. S. C., c. S-9, as am'd).

Ships are personal property and the general law relating to personal property is in general applicable to them but there is also a comprehensive collection of statutory enactments and customary law exclusively relating thereto.

Purchase.—Ships or shares therein may be acquired by construction, by purchase or by capture in war. The registry enactments make a distinction between purchasers of ship property who are qualified to be owners of a British ship and those who are not. The only persons qualified to hold any legal or beneficial interest in a British ship are British subjects or corporations, and upon the accession of an alien to her proprietary

See Topical Index in front part of this volume.

SHIPPING . . . *continued*
the vessel must be taken off the register and her certificate delivered up. British subjects are defined by British Nationality Act, 1948 as amended, and British corporation is defined as any body corporate incorporated under law of Commonwealth country and having its principal place of business in that country. (§6).

Bill of sale of recorded vessel that is sold must be filed with registrar at port where vessel is recorded and ownership of vessel is deemed unchanged until bill of sale is recorded. (§5).

Registration.—Every ship in theory is divided into 64 shares which may be held by not more than 64 persons. The ownership of any fraction of a share cannot be registered, but any number of persons not exceeding five may be registered as joint owners of a share or shares. (§10). A corporation may be registered as owner by its corporate name. Particulars to be entered on register are following: (1) name of ship; (2) port of registration; (3) tonnage, build and description of ship; (4) time and place of origin; (5) name of owner or owners and extent of interest of each. (§17).

Mortgages.—Except insofar as may be necessary for making the property mortgaged available as security for the mortgage debt, the mortgagee is not by reason of the mortgage deemed to be the owner, nor is the mortgagor deemed to have ceased to be the owner. (§50). Mortgages may be registered on Canadian registered ship. (§45). Registered mortgages have priority according to date registered and registered mortgages have priority over non-registered mortgages. (§49). Builder's mortgages may be registered on recorded vessels. (§§4 and 46). Every mortgagee has power to sell ship or any share therein. Subsequent mortgagee may not sell ship except by court order unless he first obtains concurrence of all prior mortgagees on behalf of ship.

Maritime liens include those in respect of bottomry and respondentia bonds, seamen's and officers' wages, salvage, liabilities and disbursements of the master on behalf of ship, personal injury caused by ship, property damage caused by collision, pilotage, general average and dock, harbour and canal charges. (Federal Court Act, R.S.C., c. F-7, §43).

Statutory Liens.—There exist also certain rights conferred by statute, and therefore known as statutory liens, which are of a lower nature than maritime liens. This term expresses the effect of the arrest of a ship through an action in rem in cases of ownership, possession, building, mortgage, towage, equipping or repairing any ship where ship or proceeds are under arrest of court at time case was instituted; cases of necessaries supplied to foreign ships, or to any ship elsewhere than in port to which she belongs, unless owner is domiciled in Canada; and cases of damage to cargo imported into Canada unless owner is domiciled therein. (c. F-7, §43[3]).

Limitation of Liability.—Shipowner may limit his liability for loss of life, personal injury or property damage caused by his ship if such loss or damage occurs without shipowner's actual fault or privity. Limitation amounts are based on formula involving ship's tonnage. Limitation amounts are tied to IMF's Special Drawing Rights and therefor fluctuate. (c. S-9, §§574-584).

Liability for Ship-Source Pollution.—Part XVI of Canada Shipping Act (R.S.C., c. S-9, as am'd) sets out civil liability for ship-source pollution for vessels carrying pollutants in bulk. Owner is strictly liable for oil pollution damage subject to limited defences. (§677). Shipowner may invoke special limitation of liability where pollution occurs without his fault or privity. (§679). Canada has implemented International Convention on the Establishment of an International Fund for Compensation for Oil Pollution Damage, 1971 and 1976 London Protocol thereto. (§673). It has also implemented International Convention on Salvage, 1989 (§449.1) and International Convention on Oil Pollution Preparedness, Response and Co-operation, 1990 (§660.1-.11).

Ship Safety.—Canadian Transportation Accident Investigation and Safety Board investigates marine occurrences and is granted powers pursuant to Canadian Transportation Accident Investigation and Safety Board Act (S.C. 1989, c. 3, as am'd) to conduct investigations into marine occurrences. Its powers include right to seize and test property and to exclude persons from particular areas. (§19). Board also may hold public inquiries (§21) and make recommendations to Minister of Transport on matters relating to marine safety.

Carriage of Goods.—International Convention for unification of certain rules relating to bills of lading, dated Brussels Aug. 25, 1924, as amended by Protocol signed at Brussels on Feb. 23, 1968, regulates liability of carriage of cargo by water, and these provisions are commonly referred to as "Hague-Visby Rules". These Rules were enacted as part of laws of Canada on May 6, 1993 through amendments to Carriage of Goods by Water Act, R.S.C. 1985, c. C-27 ("COGWA"). Prior to May 6, 1993, COGWA reflected 1924 Brussels Convention without Protocol, and that is commonly referred to as "Hague Rules". See in particular Carriage of Goods by Water Act. (S.C. 1993, c. 21). Canada has just adopted Hague Visby Rules, 1968. New rules apply to shipments: outbound from Canada; inbound to Canada from contracting state; where contract of carriage stipulates that law of contracting state applies; and between Canadian ports where bill of lading is issued. Limitation of liability has been increased to approximately 666.7 SDR's per package or 2 SDR's per kilogram whichever is greater.

Consignee must give written notice of loss or damage to goods within one working day of receipt of goods. Where loss or damage is not apparent, written notice must be given within 15 days of receipt by its consignee.

Action respecting goods must be commenced within two years of date goods were delivered or should have been delivered.

Admiralty Law.—The Federal Court—Trial Division has general jurisdiction in admiralty matters. (Federal Court Act, R. S. C., c. F-7, as am'd). Court's jurisdiction is with respect to: (1) claims as to title of ship or proceeds of sale; (2) claims of co-owners as to possession, employment, earnings, of ship; (3) claims respecting mortgage or charge on ship; (4) claims for personal injury caused by ship or wrongful act or omission of owners; (5) claims respecting loss, damage to goods, personal effects during transit on ship; (6) claims for towage or pilotage; (7) claims for goods, services supplied to (including construction and repair of) a ship; (8) claims by crew for remuneration arising out of employment; (9) claims respecting marine insurance; (10) claims respecting dock, canal, harbour, tolls; (11) claims respecting general average contribution; (12) claims for disbursements or advances made on account of a ship; (13) claims for salvage; (14) claims arising from agreements or charter party of ship; (15) claims for loss of life caused by ship. (§22). It is only court which permits in rem actions. In rem actions may be brought in Federal Court against any ship that, at time action is brought, is beneficially owned by person who is owner of ship which is subject of action. (§43[8]).

Jurisdiction conferred is applicable in relation to all ships, Canadian or not; in relation to all claims whether arising on high seas or within waters of Canada; in relation to all mortgages or charges by way of security on a ship, registered or not, equitable or legal, created under foreign law or not. (§22).

Canada is party to Civil Liability Convention. Where foreign judgment has been rendered, judgment creditor may apply to Federal Court to have foreign judgment registered. On application Court may order that judgment be satisfied. (R.S.C. c. S-9, §688).

Provincial Superior Courts generally have concurrent jurisdiction with Federal Court in maritime matters but they do not possess in rem jurisdiction. As courts of original jurisdiction they also possess jurisdiction for those areas where Federal Court Act does not grant jurisdiction to Federal Court Trial Division. Mareva injunctions can be obtained in Provincial Superior Courts to prevent ships from leaving Provincial Superior Court's jurisdiction where ship's owner has insufficient assets within jurisdiction to respond to claim.

Marine Insurance.—Federal Marine Insurance Act, S.C. 1993, c. 22, was implemented in 1993. It is largely similar to English Marine Insurance Act, 1906.

STATUTES:

Most recent compilation, Revised Statutes of Canada, 1985, came into force on Dec. 12, 1988. Revised Statutes of Canada, 1985 are public general statutes of Canada as of Dec. 31, 1984. Four supplementary volumes contain amendments which came into force from Jan. 1, 1985 through Dec. 12, 1988. Fifth supplement, in force Mar. 1, 1994, contains Income Tax Act. Subsequent statutes are published in annual volumes of Statutes of Canada.

Regulations made under authority of Statutes are consolidated in Consolidated Regulations of Canada, 1978 with amendments published in Canada Gazette, Part II.

See also topic Constitution and Government.

STATUTORY DECLARATIONS:

See topic Affidavits.
See also Federal Court Act, R. S. C., c. F-7.

STAY OF EXECUTION:

See topic Appeal and Error.

TAXATION:

Federal Parliament has power to raise money by any mode or system of taxation. It imposes customs duty, which is not dealt with in this summary, and various taxes and duties which are discussed hereinafter. Provincial legislatures have authority to impose direct taxes within Province in order to raise revenue for provincial purposes.

All provinces and Federal Government have enacted legislation imposing income tax. All provincial income taxes are collected by Federal Government on behalf of provinces except corporation tax in Ontario and Alberta and personal and corporation tax in Quebec. Federal Government grants tax credits in respect of provincial income taxes.

Income Tax Act in effect. (R.S.C. 1985 [5th Supp.], c. 1 and as subsequently am'd).

Liability for Tax.—(Part I, Div. A). Following, among others, are subject to tax: every person resident in Canada at any time in the year; every person who was employed in Canada, carried on a business in Canada, or disposed of taxable Canadian property at any time in the year or a previous year. "Person" includes any body corporate and politic and heirs, executors, administrators and legal representatives of such person but does not include partnership. "Resident" includes among others: Persons who sojourned in Canada more than 183 days; members of Canadian Forces; corporations incorporated in Canada after Apr. 26, 1965; corporations incorporated in Canada before Apr. 27, 1965 and resident or carried on business in Canada in fiscal year or any preceding fiscal year of corporation up to Apr. 26, 1965. Residents of Canada pay income tax on taxable income. Nonresidents pay income tax on taxable income earned in Canada. Taxable income is income less deductions allowed.

Exemption from tax (Part I, Div. H) granted to following: Employee of government of country other than Canada if reciprocal arrangement with such country, and certain members of employee's family; municipal authorities in Canada; corporations of which 90% or more of capital owned absolutely by government of Canada, government of province, Canadian municipal corporation, or wholly-owned subsidiary to such corporation; registered charities; non-profit corporations for scientific research if amounts expended in Canada; agricultural organizations, board of trade or chamber of commerce; certain non-profit non-charitable organizations; Association of Universities and Colleges of Canada; corporations constituted to provide low-cost housing for aged; limited-dividend housing company; labour organizations or fraternal societies; certain mutual insurance corporations; pension trust or corporation; trust under profit sharing plan; trust under registered supplementary unemployment benefit plan; trust under registered retirement savings plan; trust under registered educational savings plan; trust under deferred profit sharing plan; farmers' and fishermen's insurers if over 25% gross premium income in respect of farm property, property used in fishing or their residences; federal or provincial government trust to provide compensation for claims against owner of business where owner unwilling or unable to compensate.

Members of Armed Forces not exempt from income tax but certain travelling and separation allowances received under service regulations as members of Canadian Forces are not included in calculation of income.

Officers or Servants of Foreign Governments.—See catchline Exemption From Tax, supra.

Computation of Income.—(Part I, Div. B). Income of a taxpayer from office or employment is determined under Subdivision a and includes: Salary, wages or other remuneration, including gratuities; plus value of board, lodging (except reasonable allowances at "special work site") and other benefits received or enjoyed in course of such office or employment; directors or other fees; amounts allocated under employees

TAXATION . . . *continued*

profit sharing plan, amounts received in respect of loss of income pursuant to sickness, disability or income maintenance insurance plans; reasonable standby charge for automobile; benefits from salary deferral arrangements and employee benefit plans or trusts; certain loans to officers, employees and shareholders and stock option benefits.

Deductions from Income from Office or Employment.—(Part I, Div. B, Subdivision a). As follows: Certain amounts if taxpayer clergyman, teacher, employee of railway company, salesperson, transport employee; annual dues for membership in professional, union, or public servant organization; interest on borrowed money used to purchase automobile used in performance of duties of employment and that portion of its capital cost as permitted; contributions payable under registered pension fund or plan with limitations; and work space in home.

Deductions in Computing Income (Subdivision e).—Following among others may be deducted in computing taxpayers' income; Capital element of each annuity payment included in computing taxpayer's income; alimony or maintenance payments paid pursuant to court order or written agreement; interest on death duties; premium paid under registered retirement savings plan for taxpayer or his spouse; estate tax and succession duties applicable to certain property; fees incurred in appealing assessment under Income Tax Act, Canada Pension Plan or decision of Unemployment Insurance Commission; certain moving expenses within Canada; certain child care expenses; certain allowances as allowed by regulation in respect of oil, gas well, timber limit; certain special exploration and development expenses incurred by principal-business corporations (corporation carrying on business of production, refining and marketing, petroleum or natural gas, mining or exploring minerals, fabricating metals, operating pipeline, or producing or marketing sodium chloride or potash or business which includes manufacturing products which involve processing sodium chloride or potash); certain exploration and development expenses incurred by individual or corporation other than principal-business corporation.

Tax credits permitted to individual (Part I, Div. E) in computing tax payable. Amounts noted below are 1988 amounts and most are indexed. 1996 index factor is 1.028. Personal tax credits include: Basic personal credit of $1,020. If supporting common-law or married spouse credit of $850, subject to reduction if spouse has income over $500. If no spouse or does not support or live with spouse and is not supported by spouse, spousal credit is available for supported child or certain other dependant living with person. Credit for mentally or physically infirm dependant of $250, subject to reduction if dependant has income over $2,500. Credit for persons over 65 of $550, subject to reduction if person has income over $25,921. Credit of up to $170 for certain pension income. Medical expense credit of 17% of expenses in excess of lesser of $1,500 and 3% of income. Disability credit of $550. Tuition fees credit of 17% of eligible tuition fees paid to qualified institution. Credit of 17% of unemployment insurance premiums and Canada pension plan contributions. Charitable donations credit of 17% of lesser of $200 (unindexed) and individual's total charitable gifts for year plus 29% of total charitable gifts in excess of $200.

Income of taxpayer from business or property is (Division B, Subdivision b) his profit therefrom for year calculated in accordance with ordinary commercial practice, except where specific statutory rules provide otherwise. Individuals generally are taxable on income from property (such as dividends, rents and royalties) on cash basis. Profits from business may be calculated on cash or accrued basis for fishermen and farmers; all other taxpayers calculate profits from business on accrual basis. Special rules apply to interest earned by individuals; with interest earned on contracts entered into or materially changed after 1989 being included in income on accrual basis.

Capital gains realized after Dec. 31, 1971 are taxable. (Subdivision c). For property held on Jan. 1, 1972, in order to not tax capital gains accrued prior thereto, taxpayer's cost base may be measured by either: (1) fair market value on valuation day, or (2) tax free zone method. Valuation day for publicly traded securities is Dec. 22, 1971, for other property, Dec. 31, 1971. Taxable capital gains for year are equal to 3/4 of capital gains. Taxable capital gain included in income. Allowable capital losses for year are equal to 3/4 of capital losses for year. Allowable capital losses are deductible in computing income to extent of taxable capital gains. Capital gain arises on actual or deemed disposition of property. Deemed dispositions include, among others, following events: taxpayer makes gift; taxpayer dies; taxpayer gives up Canadian resident status. Individuals resident in Canada may claim cumulative exemption of up to $500,000 for capital gains realized from qualified small business corporation shares and qualified farm property.

Other Sources of Income (Subdivision d).—Also included in income of taxpayer, following, among others; a superannuation or pension benefit; retiring allowance; death benefit; benefit under Unemployment Insurance Act; under certain conditions a family allowance under Family Allowances Act or equivalent provincial statute; certain benefits paid to persons under Labour Adjustment Benefits Act or Department of Labour Act; certain stock dividends; alimony or maintenance payments, received pursuant to court order or written agreement; annuity payments; proceeds received on cancellation of annuity contract; amounts received under unemployment benefit plan, registered retirement savings plan, deferred profit sharing plan; certain amounts received if insurance interest disposed; legal costs awarded in connection with assessment of income tax or decision of Unemployment Insurance Commission; certain adult training payments; scholarships and bursaries to extent exceeding $500; amounts received for research to extent exceeding expenses incurred; amounts received as repayments of scholarship grants and bursaries; payments from educational savings plans.

Nonresidents pay tax (Part I, Div. D) on generally: their incomes from duties or offices and employments performed in Canada, their incomes from businesses carried on in Canada; their taxable capital gains from dispositions of taxable Canadian property which includes any interest in real property in Canada, any Canadian resource property, any timber resource properties, any income allocated to retiring partner; any other capital property used in business carried on in Canada, any interest in capital stock of public corporation (i.e., corporation resident in Canada) (proposed to limit to shares of class listed on exchange only); any interest in capital stock of other than private corporation resident in Canada if during last five years more than 25% issued shares belonged to, generally, nonresident persons, and interest in partnership under certain conditions, capital interest in a trust resident in Canada, unit of unit trust, unit of mutual trust under certain conditions; less allowable losses from business carried on in Canada; less applicable deductions. If nonresident disposes of any taxable Canadian property, he is required to file notice with Minister setting forth name and address of proposed purchaser, description of property, estimated amount of proceeds and, amount of adjusted cost base (i.e., generally, if depreciable property, capital cost thereof or cost to taxpayer as adjusted under §53) to taxpayer of property. After tax paid or security furnished to Minister certificate will issue. Tax of 25% (unless varied by tax treaties) must be withheld on among others, management or administration fee or charge dividends, interest, rents, royalties, alimony, certain superannuation or pension benefits, registered retirement savings plans, payable by resident of Canada to nonresident, with specified exceptions.

Part time resident may deduct from tax otherwise payable certain taxes paid by him to country other than Canada. (§126).

Rates of tax applicable to individuals on taxable income earned in Canada are graduated. Top marginal rate of federal taxation is 29% on taxable income in excess of approximately $59,000. Federal surtaxes (3% of federal tax plus 5% of federal tax payable in excess of $12,500) and provincial income taxes (except in Quebec) are calculated as percentage of federal tax.

Rate of tax applicable to corporations on taxable income earned in province is generally 28% federal tax plus prevailing provincial tax rate. Corporate surtax of 3% of federal tax payable (proposed to increase to 4% for taxation years after Feb. 27, 1995). Active business income, manufacturing and processing income and certain investment income is taxed at preferential rates. Paid-up capital tax of 2% is levied on taxable capital over $10 million employed in Canada (proposed to increase to 0.225% for taxation years after Feb. 27, 1995). Tax not deductible in computing income but will be reduced by corporate surtax liability on Canadian-source income. Unused surtax liability can be carried forward seven years.)

Basic rate of tax applicable to inter vivos trusts on taxable income or taxable income earned in Canada is 29%.

Returns to be filed with Minister in prescribed form without notice or demand; in case of corporation, within six months from end of their fiscal year; in case of individual on or before Apr. 30 in year following previous calendar year except where individual dies after Oct. and before following June 16; in case of deceased, by legal representative within six months of date of death; in case of estate or trust, within 90 days of year end. Others as required by notice. (§150).

Payment.—Persons paying salary wages or other remuneration, superannuation or pension benefit, retiring allowance, an amount payable on termination payment, or after death in recognition of service, benefit under Unemployment Insurance Act, 1971, amount under supplementary unemployment benefit plan, annuity payment, fees, commissions or other amounts for services, or payment under deferred profit sharing plan, must deduct and withhold prescribed amount and remit to Receiver General of Canada. (§153). Others must pay on or before Mar. 15, June 15, Sept. 15, and Dec. 15 in year amount equal to 1/4 estimated tax for such year. (§156). Farmers and fishermen must remit 2/3 of estimated tax before Dec. 31, remainder before Apr. 30 following year. (§155). If estimated tax payable by individuals, farmers or fishermen in present and previous taxation year did not exceed in aggregate, $1,000, instalment payments are not required. (§156.1). Corporations must pay during 15 months period ending three months after close of their fiscal year either: (1) 1/12 estimated tax before last day of each of first 12 months of such period, (2) 1/12 of its instalment base for immediately preceding fiscal year before last day of each of first 12 months of such period, or (3) 1/12 of its instalment base for second fiscal year preceding before last day of each of first two months in present year and 1/10 of amount remaining before last day of each of ten months remaining; and remainder before last day of period if corporation entitled to small business deduction, otherwise before last day of 14th month of period. (§157).

Penalties.—Persons failing to make a return liable to penalty ranging from 5% of tax unpaid to 50% of tax unpaid if wilfully evading payment.

Refunds may be made without application on any overpayment of tax with interest at a prescribed rate. (§164).

Objections and Appeals.—Taxpayers other than individuals may, within 90 days of mailing notice of assessment, serve Minister with notice of objection to assessment in prescribed form. Individuals may within later of 90 days of mailing notice of assessment or day that is one year after balance due day for individual for taxation year, serve Minister with notice of objection to assessment in prescribed form. Appeals are to Tax Court of Canada with right of appeal to Federal Court of Appeal and limited right of appeal to Supreme Court of Canada.

Foreign Tax Agreements.—The Canada-United States Income Tax Convention (1980) makes provision for avoidance of double taxation and prevention of fiscal evasion of income taxes. Conventions or Agreements of similar nature have been signed with United Kingdom and Northern Ireland, Argentina, Australia, Austria, Bangladesh, Barbados, Belgium, Brazil, Cameroon, China, Cyprus, Czech and Slovak Federal Republic, Denmark, Dominican Republic, Egypt, Estonia, Finland, France, Germany, Guyana, Hungary, India (unratified), Indonesia, Ireland, Israel, Italy, Ivory Coast, Jamaica, Japan, Kenya, Korea, Latvia, Liberia (unratified), Luxembourg, Malaysia, Malta, Morocco, Mexico, Netherlands, New Zealand, Nigeria (unratified), Norway, Pakistan, Papua New Guinea, Philippines, Poland, Romania, Singapore, South Africa (unratified), Spain, Sri Lanka, Sweden, Switzerland, Tanzania (unratified), Thailand, Trinidad and Tobago (unratified), Tunisia, Zambia and Zimbabwe. Treaty with former U.S.S.R. continues to apply to Russian Federation, Ukraine and Belarus. Treaty with Russian Federation signed 1995 but not ratified.

Inheritance Tax.—See digests of the laws of the several provinces.

Estate Tax.—See subhead Income Tax Act, catchline Capital Gains, supra.

See also digests of laws of the several provinces, topic Taxation subhead Inheritance Tax.

Gift Tax.—See subhead Income Tax Act, catchline Capital Gains, supra.

Sales Tax.—

Goods and Services Tax.—The Excise Tax Act (R.S.C., c. E-15, as am'd). GST is form of value added taxation ("VAT") and resembles in many respects VAT applied in most OECD countries.

GST is multi-stage tax levied at each stage in production and distribution chain of most goods and services in Canada. Tax is imposed on recipient of supply but is generally collected from recipient by supplier where supplier is GST registrant. Most

See Topical Index in front part of this volume.

TAXATION . . . *continued*
persons engaged in commercial activity are required to become registrants and collect GST. Commercial activity is defined very broadly and governments, charities and nonprofit organizations are also required to collect and remit GST in certain circumstances.

GST is calculated at rate of 7% of consideration payable for supply. Person who is registrant is entitled to claim offset (referred to as "input tax credit") against tax collected by it for GST paid by it on any property and services used in its commercial activities. Difference between tax collected by registrant and registrant's input tax credits for reporting period is referred to as "net tax". If positive (i.e. tax collected exceeds tax paid) net tax is required to be remitted to Receiver General. Conversely, net tax is refunded to registrant where input tax credits exceed tax collected in reporting period. Purpose of input tax credit mechanism is to ensure that GST applies only on value of final consumer sales and that all business inputs are relieved from tax.

Nonresidents who provide goods or services to Canadians must register for and collect GST if they carry on business in Canada. Nonresidents who register must post security for tax collected equal to one half of one year's estimated GST collectible unless nonresident conducts business from permanent establishment.

GST generally also applies to importation into Canada of goods and certain services and intangible property for use in Canada. GST payable by registrant on imports is eligible for input tax credit mechanism discussed above.

There are two significant categories of transactions which do not attract GST. No GST is payable by purchaser of "exempt supplies". Supplier of exempt supply, however, is not entitled to claim input tax credits in respect of GST paid by it on its purchases to extent that they relate to making of exempt supplies. On "zero-rated supplies" again no GST is payable by purchaser but supplier of zero-rated supply is entitled to claim input tax credits in respect of GST paid on purchases used to provide zero-rated goods or services. Exempt supplies include sales of used residential property, health care services, educational services, child care services, legal aid services, some legal services to nonresidents, financial services including issue of insurance policies and certain supplies made by public sector bodies. It is proposed that most legal services rendered to nonresidents be exempt supplies. Zero-rated supplies include prescription drugs, medical devices, basic groceries, exports, agricultural and fishery products, and certain travel and transportation services.

Rebates of GST are payable to foreign tourists, charities, nonprofit organizations and to certain public sector bodies.

Customs Duties.—Are determined and primarily imposed under two federal Acts, Customs Tariff and Customs Act. Regard must also be had to Special Import Measures Act and Canadian International Trade Tribunal Act.

Customs Act (R.S.C., [2nd Supp.], c. 1, as am'd) sets out basic regulatory framework and requirements for importation or exportation of goods to and from Canada. Customs Tariff (R.S.C., [3rd Supp.], c. 41, as am'd) governs tariff classification and rates of customs duties payable on goods entering Canada.

Part II (§§11-43) of Customs Act imposes certain obligations on importers, including requirement to report goods at customs, declare goods entering Canada and to pay any duties payable. Duties are defined (§2[1]) as including any duties or taxes levied on imported goods under Customs Tariff, Excise Tax Act, Excise Act, Special Import Measures Act or any other law relating to customs. Actual duties and taxes payable are not set out in Customs Act, only requirement to pay such duties and taxes as set out. (§17). Proof of origin and product marking requirements have been enacted pursuant to Customs Act. (§§35.01 and 35.1).

Part III (§§44-72) of Customs Act sets out calculation and value for duty provisions and appeal rules. Value for duty provisions set out in Customs Act (§§44-56) provide for establishment of dollar value of imported goods upon which duty and tax rates are imposed. Valuation provisions of Customs Act are based on transaction value system set out in Agreement on the Implementation of Article VII of the General Agreement on Tariffs and Trade 1994. Primary basis of valuation is transaction value. (§§47 and 48). Transaction value is price paid or payable for goods, as adjusted, when sold for export to Canada. It represents aggregate of all payments made or to be made to purchaser in Canada, whether directly or indirectly, to benefit of vendor. Alternative bases for valuation exist when transaction value cannot be used. These include deductive value calculation and computed value calculation. (§§51 and 52). Origin of imported goods is determined in accordance with §13 and §57.1 of Customs Tariff. Origin of good will determine what tariff rate is applicable. (See separate discussion below with respect to North American Free Trade Implementation Act, consequential amendments to Customs Act and Customs Tariff and special rules of origin).

Tariff classification and value for duty decisions may be appealed in first instance to customs officer and in second instance to Deputy Minister of National Revenue for Customs and Excise ("Deputy Minister"). (§§59-66). Decision of Deputy Minister can be appealed to Canadian International Trade Tribunal ("CITT") (§67); this decision can in turn be appealed to Federal Court of Appeal and thereafter Supreme Court of Canada.

Part IV of Customs Act contains special provisions which deal with abatements and refunds. (§§73-94). Duty relief, including drawbacks and remissions, are addressed in Part II of Customs Tariff.

Minister of National Revenue may grant abatement in whole or in part of duties and taxes to be paid on imported goods where goods have suffered damage or deterioration during shipment or loss of volume or weight while in bonded warehouse. (§73). Refunds of duties and taxes after they have been paid (as distinguished from abatements before duties are payable) may be obtained when goods have been damaged during shipment, when quantity released is less than quantity upon which duties and taxes were paid, or goods are of inferior quality. (§74).

Under Part V of Customs Act goods exported from Canada must be reported. (§§95-97.2). In addition under Export and Import Permits Act special provisions apply with respect to export of certain goods and reexport of U.S. origin goods from Canada. (See discussion subhead Export and Import Permits Act under topic Foreign Trade Regulation.)

Part VI of Customs Act sets out enforcement and offences provisions. (§§98-163). These include powers of search and seizure and forfeiture. In addition contravention of Customs Act is punishable either by way of summary conviction and fines up to $50,000 or by imprisonment for term not exceeding six months or by both fine and imprisonment; or, punishable by way of indictable offence and liable to fines up to $500,000 or by imprisonment for term not exceeding five years or by both fine and imprisonment. Enforcement and offence provisions of Customs Act are used also to enforce other Acts including Customs Tariff.

Customs Tariff.—(R.S.C., c. 41, 3rd Supp.). Governs tariff classification and rates of customs duties payable on goods entering Canada. It must be read in conjunction with Customs Act which imposes obligation to pay customs duty. Customs Tariff is administered by Department of National Revenue. Customs Tariff contains detailed rules of origin, categories of tariff rates and in its schedule sets out tariff items under which goods must be classified and specific rates of duty applicable to such goods. Effective Jan. 1, 1988, Canada adopted in Customs Tariff the Harmonized Commodity Description and Coding System of tariff classification. (§10). Harmonized System of tariff classification for duty purposes is internationally recognized system of tariff classification. Canadian Customs Tariff is governed by Harmonized System General Rules for interpretation of nomenclature, which includes six international rules and three Canadian rules.

Rules of origin determine rate of duty applicable, for example: Most-favoured Nation; United States Tariff; Mexico Tariff; Mexico-United States Tariff; British Preferential Tariff; General Preferential Tariff; Least Developed Developing Country Tariff. Special tariff treatment also exists with respect to goods originating in Australia, New Zealand and Commonwealth Caribbean Countries. (§§47-58).

In Customs Tariff special provision is made for Governor-in-Council to promulgate orders which permit Canada to retaliate against actions of other countries which adversely affect Canadian trade in goods and in services, and for imposition of surtaxes and surcharges. (See §59 and following.) Special bilateral arrangements with respect to agricultural goods, U.S. origin goods, Mexican origin goods, Mexican-U.S. origin goods, fresh fruits and vegetables and textiles and apparel are given effect to in Customs Tariff. (§§60.01-60.5). Customs Tariff and Customs Act also make provision for marking of origin of products imported into Canada. (§§64 and 35.01 and following, respectively). Provision is also made in Customs Tariff for duty deferral, refunds and drawbacks (see §80 and following).

North American Free Trade Agreement Implementation Act (S.C. 1993, c. 44; Schedule Parts A-D, S.C. 1993, c. 44) establishes separate trade and investment regime with respect to goods, services and investments that originate in Canada, U.S. and/or Mexico or deemed to so originate.

Effective Jan. 1, 1994, Canada, U.S. and Mexico have created free trade zone between their respective territories. While NAFTA does not affect external tariff of each NAFTA country, and each of Canada, U.S. and Mexico continue to apply tariff rates negotiated under GATT or other bilateral or multi-lateral agreements to goods imported from third countries, special and different regime applies with respect to goods that are deemed to "originate" within North American Free Trade zone. These rules are detailed in Customs Act and Customs Tariff and regulations enacted pursuant thereto. Rules of origin are complex and must be reviewed with respect to each product to determine whether or not product qualifies as of NAFTA origin within NAFTA rules.

NAFTA rules are separate and distinct from rules established pursuant to Canada-United States Free Trade Agreement ("CFTA"). CFTA has been suspended in Canada and will only be applied in Canada in event that NAFTA is terminated or abrogated. Duty reduction regime negotiated between Canada and U.S. under CFTA will however continue to apply. Specific reference must be had to Customs Tariff with respect to each particular good.

Pursuant to Customs Tariff (§95[2]) and Customs Act (§164[1.1]), NAFTA Rules of Origin Regulations have been enacted. These Regulations reflect Canada's NAFTA commitments with respect to determination of origin of products wholly provided or particularly produced in Canada, U.S. and/or Mexico. Regulations have been developed jointly by the three NAFTA countries and once adopted in final form will be same in all three countries. NAFTA, Regulations and Uniform Rules establish three principal "rules of origin". If a good or product qualifies as of NAFTA origin, preferential duty rates (and in limited circumstances, quota allowances) apply.

Goods wholly obtained or produced entirely in territory of one or more of NAFTA countries qualify as of "NAFTA origin". With respect to manufactured or processed goods, rule of origin is based on changes in tariff classification and/or regional value content. Where each of non-originating materials used in production of a good which undergoes applicable change in tariff classification (as set out in Annex 401 to NAFTA text as incorporated into NAFTA Rules of Origin Regulations) as result of production occurring entirely in territory of one or more of NAFTA countries, or where good otherwise satisfies requirements set out in Annex referenced and no change in tariff classification is required and good satisfies all other requirements under NAFTA Rules of Origin Regulations good will qualify as of "NAFTA origin", good that is produced entirely in territory of one or more of NAFTA countries exclusively from originating materials also qualifies as of "NAFTA origin". Except for certain textile and apparel items, if good is produced entirely in one of NAFTA countries but one or more of non-originating materials provided for as parts under Harmonized System that are used in production of good does not undergo tariff classification because (a) good was imported into NAFTA territory in unassembled or disassembled form but was classified as assembled good pursuant to General Rule of Interpretation under the Harmonized System, or (b) heading for good provides for and specifically describes both good itself and its parts and is not further subdivided into subheadings or subheading for good provides for and specifically describes good itself and its parts, then provided that specified regional value content of good is not less than 60% where "transaction value method is used" or is not less than 50% where "net cost method is used", then that good will qualify as of "NAFTA origin". NAFTA rules of origin are supported by simplified customs procedures including de minimus rule, advance rulings and speedy appeals with respect to NAFTA origin of goods. NAFTA preferential tariff regime is supported through use of certificates of origin which must be supplied.

NAFTA Rules of Origin are supported by Determination of Country of Origin for the Purposes of Marking Goods (NAFTA countries) Regulations. These Marking Rules determine whether or not a good is a good of NAFTA country for marking purposes and accordingly will qualify for preferential tariff treatment. These rules are in addition to existing marking rules. Canada has limited use of these marking rules for tariff preference purposes to agricultural and textile and apparel goods.

See Topical Index in front part of this volume.

TAXATION . . . *continued*

Special Import Measures Act.—Pursuant to Special Import Measures Act (SIMA) (R.S.C., c. S-15, as am'd) proclaimed in force in Canada on Dec. 1, 1984, Canada may impose antidumping and countervailing duties on goods imported into Canada. SIMA replaces Anti-dumping Act and countervailing duty regulations previously enacted pursuant to Customs Tariff. When first enacted, SIMA reflected Canada's obligations under 1979 GATT Codes on antidumping and subsidies and countervailing duties. Today, SIMA gives effect to Canada's commitments under NAFTA and agreements negotiated under Uruguay round of multilateral trade negotiations including Agreement on Subsidies and Countervailing Measures and Agreement on the Implementation of Article VI of the General Agreement of Tariffs and Trade 1994.

SIMA is administered by Department of National Revenue. SIMA provides for imposition of anti-dumping and countervailing duties in circumstances where Deputy Minister of National Revenue ("Deputy Minister") has conducted investigation and determined that dumping or subsidization exists which is not negligible with respect to goods imported. Canadian International Trade Tribunal (CITT) must determine that dumped or subsidized goods imported to Canada have caused, are causing or are likely to cause material injury to domestic industry. (§§5 and 6). SIMA permits Minister to impose provisional duties during period between issuance of Deputy Minister's preliminary determination of dumping or subsidy and finding of CITT. (§8). If CITT determines that no injury has occurred, such provisional duties are subject of refund and where CITT finds duties have been collected in amount greater than final assessment, partial refund will be made. Further, SIMA provides for undertakings by exporters to cease dumping which permits investigations to be terminated. (§49). Antidumping or countervailing investigations must be initiated by Deputy Minister in circumstances where Deputy Minister is of opinion that there is evidence of dumping and/or subsidy and of injury either on Deputy Minister's own initiative or in response to written complaint. (§31). SIMA proscribes what constitutes properly documented complaint (§2[1]) and information to be provided (§37). If Deputy Minister believes that there is no evidence of dumping or subsidization, formal investigation will not be initiated. If Deputy Minister believes that there is evidence of dumping or subsidization but no evidence of "injury", investigation will not be initiated. (§§33 and 34). Matters may be referred to CITT for opinion as to existence of evidence of injury.

Once decision has been made to proceed with investigation, notice therof be published. (§34). Once official notice has been provided, Revenue Canada has 90 days to complete investigation and issue preliminary determination or to terminate investigation. This 90-day period may be extended for additional 45 days. (§§38 and 39). If, as result of investigation, Deputy Minister is of opinion that there is insufficient evidence of dumping or subsidizing, margin of dumping or amount of subsidy is insignificant, actual or potential volume of dumped or subsidized goods is negligible or evidence does not disclose reasonable indication that dumping or subsidization has caused injury or retardation or is threatening to cause injury, investigation must be terminated. (§35). Insignificant or negligible has been defined as margin of dumping of less than 2% of export price or amount of subsidy of less than 1% of export price. Volume of dumped goods is defined to be negligible if volume is less than 3% of total volume of like goods exported to Canada from all countries.

Two-tiered structure for appeals is set out in SIMA pertaining to whether goods are subject to antidumping or countervailing duties or in what amount. Under §61 of SIMA, decisions of Deputy Minister may be appealed; under §59 goods subject to antidumping or countervailing duty orders or findings of CITT or Governor-in-Council made under Act can be appealed.

Special provisions apply as result of North American Free Trade Agreement Implementation Act (S.C. 1993, c. 44, Schedule Parts A-D) to goods imported from Mexico and U.S. to Canada. These include provision that Mexican or U.S. Government as well as Mexican or U.S. producers, manufacturers or exporters may appeal in relation to Mexican or U.S. origin goods, as appropriate, whether or not Canadian importer appeals. Such appeals must address one of following issues: whether imported goods are in fact subject to anti-dumping or countervailing orders; what is proper normal value pertaining to dumped goods or amount of subsidy pertaining to subsidized goods; and proper export price pertaining to dumped goods or amount of export subsidy pertaining to subsidized goods. Appeal to CITT must be made within 90 days after date of Deputy Minister's decision. Decisions of CITT can be appealed to Federal Court.

Under North American Free Trade Agreement Implementation Act special provisions apply with respect to goods originating in Mexico and U.S. These include that certain decisions of Deputy Minister, such as final determinations of dumping or subsidization as well as decisions of CITT, including material injury findings may be reviewed by Bi-National Panel established under c. 19 of North American Free Trade Agreement. Jurisdiction of Panel is limited to determining whether or not decision being reviewed was made in accordance with applicable laws. Decision of panel itself can be appealed by way of extraordinary challenge. Appeal grounds are limited to errors of law or bias on part of member or members of Panel whose decision is being appealed.

Canadian International Trade Tribunal.—CITT was established under Canadian International Trade Tribunal Act. (R.S.C., 4th Supp., c. 47). Main legislative framework governing work of CITT is aforesaid Act and its regulations, special rules and procedures, and Special Import Measures Act, Customs Act, Excise Tax Act, North American Free Trade Agreement Act and World Trade Organization Agreement Implementation Act. (S.C. 1994, c. 47). CITT acts as administrative court in connection with appeals from Revenue Canada rulings and in connection with injury findings and anti-dumping and countervailing duty cases. CITT also has advisory role with powers to conduct research, find facts, hold public hearings and report on broad range of trade-related matters. These programs relate to various import safeguard inquiries and generally inquiries into trade and tariff matters.

Where imported goods are imported in increased quantities and under conditions which cause or threaten serious injury to domestic producers of like or directly competitive goods, safeguard action can be taken under Canadian International Trade Tribunal Act. (§22 and following). There is no requirement that imported goods must be dumped or subsidized prior to safeguard action being instituted. Action can be commenced by filing complaint with CITT which, if it determines that complaint is properly documented, will then conduct inquiry. (§§22-39). Complainant must establish and Tribunal must find that goods subject to complaint are being imported in such increased quantities and under such conditions as to be principal cause of serious injury, or threat thereof to domestic producers of like or directly competitive goods. CITT Act requires that in order for import of goods to be principle cause of serious injuries, it must determine that increased importation of goods is important cause and not less important than any other cause. (§§26 and 27). Where CITT determines that increased volume of imported goods is not principal cause of material injury or that no material injury actually exists, then inquiry is terminated. Where material injury is found, then CITT must report to Governor-in-Council and Minister of Finance. Ministry and Cabinet impose appropriate remedy such as additional customs duties, import quotas or surtaxes. (§§29-30).

Canada's government procurement practices are subject to review under North American Free Trade Agreement and 1994 Agreement on Government Procurement ("WTO Code"). Under North American Free Trade Agreement, Canada reaffirmed its commitment to GATT Procurement Code and established lower thresholds for review of government procurement with respect to goods and services originating from U.S. and Mexico. Review of government procurement procedures is conducted by Canadian International Trade Tribunal established pursuant to Canadian International Trade Tribunal Act. (§30.1 and following). Under NAFTA, government procurements which may be reviewed and which are subject of preferential treatment include contracts with federal government entities that have value in excess of U.S.$50,000 for contracts for goods, services or any combination thereof and U.S.$6.5 million for contracts for construction services; for government enterprises for contracts having value in excess of U.S.$250,000 for contracts for goods and services or combination thereof, and U.S.$8 million for contracts for construction services; different thresholds apply with respect to state and provincial government entities. NAFTA government procurement rules provide review mechanism for prospective bidders from NAFTA countries in circumstances where they have not been provided with opportunity to participate in government contracts or where so-called "national treatment" and "non-discrimination standards" have been violated.

Pursuant to its commitments under WTO Code, Canada has granted access to most federal government departments' and agencies' procurement practices to WTO members. WTO Code thresholds thus apply to contracts for products, services and construction services and purchases of goods and services over $223,000 by federal departments and agencies and purchases of construction services over $8.5 million. State enterprise coverage includes purchases of goods and services over approximately $600,000 and purchases of construction services over $8.5 million. Canada's commitments in WTO Code are given effect to in Canadian International Trade Tribunal Act (see §30.02 and following).

Excess Profits Tax.—No excess profits tax in effect.

Unemployment Compensation Tax.—Unemployment Insurance Act, R.S.C., c. U-1, provides for insurance against unemployment of certain classes of employed persons, with certain exceptions.

Both employers and employees are required to make contributions based on weekly earnings of employees.

Employers must deduct each employee's contribution from his wages and make a contribution equal to 1.4 times employee's contribution to scheme. Employers must deduct and remit employees' premiums and remit employers' premiums together with information return to Receiver General of Canada on or before 15th day of month following month in which employer paid insurable earnings to employee.

Employers must file annual information return for each year on or before last day of Feb. of next following year.

Penalties.—

Income Tax Act.—Where amount of tax paid is less than amount payable, interest at 4% plus prescribed rate (which is adjusted quarterly to reflect prevailing interest rates from previous quarter) is payable on difference of two amounts. In case of tax evasion, taxpayer may be required to pay additional amount and not more than 200% of tax sought to be evaded. (§239). For failure to file annual return when required, penalty equal to aggregate of 5% of tax unpaid, and 1% of tax unpaid for each complete month (up to 12 complete months). (§162[1]). For failure to complete information in annual return, penalty is $100. (§162[5]). Failure to file return by trustee in bankruptcy and others will result in penalty of $10 for each day of default, up to maximum of $50. By §238 fine of up to $25,000 can be imposed on conviction for failure to file return, except that §162 penalty is not then payable, unless penalty was assessed before information or complaint giving rise to conviction was laid.

For penalties in other taxing statutes, see subheads supra and statutes.

TRADEMARKS AND DESIGNS:

Trademarks are governed by Trade-Marks Act, R.S.C., c. T-13. Communications should be addressed to The Registrar of Trade Marks, Ottawa. Amendments to Act to bring it into conformity with Canada's obligations under Agreement Establishing the World Trade Organization came into force in Jan. 1996. Amendments are indicated in text by WTO, Jan. 1996. New Regulations under Trade-Marks Act came into force Apr. 1996.

Trademark Defined.—Trademark means: (1) mark used by person to distinguish wares or services manufactured, sold, leased, hired or performed by that person from those of others; (2) certification mark, which is mark used to distinguish wares or services that are of defined standard with respect to their quality or working conditions, class of persons or area within which they have been produced or performed; (3) distinguishing guise, which is shaping of wares or their containers or mode of wrapping or packaging wares, appearance of which is used by person to distinguish that person's wares or services from those of others; or (4) proposed trademark, which is mark that is proposed to be used by person for purposes mentioned in (1) supra. (§2).

Prohibited Marks.—The use of marks suggesting royal, vice-regal or governmental approval or patronage, the Red Cross, the United Nations' name or emblem, the emblem or mark of any of the Armed Forces, a university or a public authority, the name of, or symbols relating to, the Royal Canadian Mounted Police, international distinctive sign of civil defence, or any matter which may falsely suggest connection with any living individual, is prohibited, unless consent of proper person has been obtained. (§9). No person may use in way likely to mislead any mark that is recognized in Canada as

See Topical Index in front part of this volume.

TRADEMARKS AND DESIGNS . . . *continued*
designating kind, quality, quantity, destination, value, place of origin or date of production of any ware or service. (§10). Nor may denomination used to designate plant variety under Plant Breeders' Rights Act be adopted as trademark in association with plant variety. (§10.1).

Protected Geographical Indications (WTO, Jan. 1996, [2, 11.11-11.2(sic)]). Geographical indication is defined as indication identifying wine or spirit as originating in territory of WTO member where characteristic of wine or spirit is attributable to geographic origin and is protected by law of WTO member, except for indication identifying wine or spirit originating in Canada.

Protected geographical indication means geographical indication kept on prescribed list. Mechanisms are provided for placement of geographical indication on list, for publication and for objection.

Adoption of protected geographical indication in connection with business as trademark or otherwise is prohibited. There are exceptions for use of personal names and in comparative advertising except on labels or packaging.

Use by Canadian of geographical indication is allowed if protected geographical indication was used continuously in good faith before Apr. 15, 1994 or for at least ten years before that date. Use of indication which is common name for wine or spirit or for grape variety is also allowed. Twenty-two specified indications for wines are not protected and 15 specified indications for spiritis are not protected. These unprotected specified indications may be amended by order-in-council.

Registrable Marks.—A trademark is registrable if it is not: (1) the name of an individual who is living or has died within 30 years; (2) clearly descriptive or deceptively misdescriptive in the English or French languages of the character or quality of the wares or services; (3) the name in any language of the wares or services; (4) confusing, as defined in the Act, with a registered trademark; or (5) protected geographic indication for wine or for spirits, in whole or in part (WTO, Jan. 1996). Trademark may be registered notwithstanding (1) and (2) if it has been so used in Canada as to have become distinctive, as defined in Act, on date of application. (§12). Distinguishing guise is registrable only if it has been so used in Canada as to have become distinctive at date of filing and if its exclusive use by applicant is not likely unreasonably to limit development of any art or industry. No registration of distinguishing guise interferes with use of any utilitarian feature embodied in distinguishing guise. (§13).

Persons Entitled to Registration.—Any person may register a trademark which that person has used or made known in Canada in association with wares or services, or which that person has duly registered in his or her country of origin (being member country of Union for the Protection of Industrial Property, as defined in Act, including WTO member [WTO, Jan. 1996]) and has used in association with wares or services, or any proposed trademark, unless, in case of mark previously used in Canada, at date on which that person or his or her predecessor in title first used trademark, or, in case of trademark previously used in foreign country or proposed trademark, at date of application, it was confusing with trademark that had been previously used in Canada or made known in Canada by any other person, or trade mark in respect of which application had been previously filed in Canada by any other person or trade name previously used in Canada by any other person. (§16).

Effect of Registration.—The registration of a trademark gives to the owner the exclusive right to its use throughout Canada in association with wares or services for which it is registered, and right to prevent use of confusingly similar trademarks. Some limited rights exist at common law with respect to unregistered trademarks. (§19).

Certification Marks.—A certification mark may be adopted and registered only by a person who is not engaged in the manufacture, sale, leasing or hiring of wares or the performance of services such as those in association with which the certification mark is used. (§23).

Applications.—The Registrar of Trade Marks, Ottawa, keeps a register of trademarks, transfers, registered users, etc. Applicant for registration of trademark must file with Registrar application containing: (1) statement of wares or services in association with which mark has been or is proposed to be used; (2) date from which applicant has used trademark in Canada or from which it has been made known in Canada and used in country of Union; (3) date of registration in another country of Union; (4) in case of proposed trademark, statement that applicant intends to use trademark in Canada; (5) address of applicant's principal office or place of business in Canada, if any, and, if applicant has no place of business in Canada, address of his principal office or place of business abroad and name and address in Canada of some person or firm to whom any notice may be sent and upon whom service may be made; (6) a drawing of the trademark; (7) statement that applicant is satisfied that he is entitled to use trademark in Canada. (§30).

Foreign Applications and Registrations.—Trademark which applicant has registered in his country of origin, if that country is member of Union, may be registered in Canada if: (1) it is not confusing with registered trademark; (2) it is not without distinctive character; (3) it is not contrary to morality or public order or of such nature as to deceive public; or (4) otherwise prohibited mark. (§14). Certified copy of foreign registration must be filed. (§31). Date of filing application in foreign country will be taken as date of filing in Canada in certain circumstances if application in Canada is made within six months of the foreign application. (§34).

Terms and Renewals.—Any registration made or renewed under the present Trade-Marks Act is subject to renewal 15 years from date of registration or last renewal, and, unless renewed within that period, will be expunged from register. (§46). Provision is made for expunging trademarks for non-user. (§45).

Transfer.—A trademark, whether registered or unregistered, is transferable, and deemed always to have been transferable, either in connection with or separately from the goodwill of the business and in respect of either all or some of the wares or services in association with which it has been used. (§48).

Licensees.—Use of trademark by licensee will have same effect as use by trademark owner provided licence gives owner direct or indirect control of character or quality of wares or services. (§50).

Tradenames.—See digests of the laws of the several provinces.

TREATIES:

Implementing Treaties.—Where treaty made between Canada and foreign country calls for legislative action to implement same, such legislation is generally speaking, to be enacted by Parliament on basis of division of legislative powers between Parliament and Provincial legislatures. Recently there has been obiter dictum (see [1977] 2 S.C.R. 134 and [1982] 2 S.C.R. 112) which appears to raise questions about this rule.

There has been some uncertainty about rule ever since §132 of Constitution Act, 1867 became obsolete, in effect, by virtue of Canada's new status in international affairs after Statute of Westminster. §132 of Constitution Act, 1867 provides that "The Parliament and Government of Canada shall have all Powers necessary or proper for performing the Obligations of Canada or of any Province thereof, as Part of the British Empire, towards Foreign Countries arising under Treaties between the Empire and such Foreign Countries". Power of Parliament to legislate in this connection has been deemed to be unrestricted.

Treaties which are in nature of compacts or bargains which are of such character that it would be vital to security of Canada that they be implemented by Parliament may be so implemented notwithstanding that legislation would trench upon §92 of Constitution Act, 1867. Such treaties entered into for purpose of establishing laws of certain character now, as general rule, contain "federal state" clauses whereby it is accepted that, in face of such international legislative projects, system of distribution of legislative power within federal state remains undisturbed.

Province may not negotiate treaties directly with foreign powers since provinces of Canada in this connection have only such powers as are related to their legislative jurisdiction. Under international law only nations are recognized as international persons with authority to enter into treaties with one another. Province is not such person.

It would appear that only Government of Canada may be party to treaty with foreign sovereign state whether subject matter of treaty is within jurisdiction of Parliament of Canada under §91 of Constitution Act, 1867 or within jurisdiction of Provincial Legislatures under §92. As to income tax agreements and conventions, see topic Taxation, subhead Foreign Tax Agreements. See also Selected International Conventions section. As to Trade see The North American Free Trade Agreement which forms part of federal laws of Canada and is effective Jan. 1, 1994. Canada is member of World Trade Organization and is party to WTO Agreements including Multilateral Agreement on Trade in Goods, General Agreement on Trade in Services, Agreement on Trade-Related Aspects of Intellectual Property Rights, Understanding on Rules and Procedures Governing the Settlement of Disputes, Trade Policy Review Mechanism and Plurilateral Trade Agreement.

UNEMPLOYMENT COMPENSATION:

See topic Taxation, subhead Unemployment Compensation Tax.

See also topic Labour Relations, subhead Unemployment Insurance Act, 1971.

WILLS:

See digests of the laws of the several provinces.

WITNESSES:

Canada Evidence Act, R. S. C., c. C-5 applies to all criminal proceedings and to all civil proceedings respecting which Parliament of Canada has jurisdiction. See also digests of laws of the several provinces.

Husband and Wife.—By Canada Evidence Act, no husband is compellable to disclose any communication made to him by his wife during their marriage and no wife is compellable to disclose any communication made to her by her husband during their marriage. Nonetheless wife or husband of person charged with offence against certain sections of Criminal Code where complainant or victim is under age of 14 years is competent and compellable witness for prosecution without consent of person charged. But where wife or husband of person charged with offence may at common law be called without consent as witness, common law applies. (§4).

Self-Incrimination.—No witness shall be excused from answering any question on ground that answer may tend to criminate him or establish his liability to civil proceeding at instance of Crown or any person. (§5). However, witness who testifies in any proceeding has right not to have any incriminating evidence so given used to incriminate that witness in any proceedings except prosecutions for perjury or for giving contrary evidence. No objection to any question asked or giving of any answer need be made to attract this protection.

See also topic Affidavits.

ALBERTA LAW DIGEST REVISER

Bennett Jones Verchere
4500 Bankers Hall East
855 2nd Street S.W.
Calgary, Alberta T2P 4K7
Telephone: 403-298-3100
Fax: 403-265-7219

Reviser Profile

History: The origins of the firm date back to the 1890's, before the Province of Alberta came into existence, to the Calgary law practice of Sir James Lougheed and The Right Honourable R.B. Bennett, Prime Minister of Canada from 1930 to 1935. The practice was reorganized in 1922 with Bennett, Hannah and Sanford as partners. Today, Bennett Jones Verchere is one of Canada's leading national law firms with over 170 lawyers practicing in its Calgary, Edmonton, Toronto, Ottawa and Montreal offices. The firm is well equipped to serve the changing needs of its clients through continuity of service in all its jurisdictions.

Since its inception, the firm has contributed to and supported the community at large. Our members can proudly display a long and distinguished list of corporate directorships, political appointments, government office positions and senior judicial postings, as well as prominent positions in the cultural, educational, health and sporting arenas. In addition, our lawyers regularly participate in the educational activities of the profession through seminars, public speaking engagements and publication of articles.

Profile of Clients: Bennett Jones Verchere represents a large and diverse group of clients, encompassing industry leaders as well as scores of small and medium-sized businesses involved in virtually all sectors of industry. In addition, Bennett Jones Verchere acts for nonprofit foundations and associations, government and governmental agencies at the civic, provincial and federal levels, and for individuals in attaining their respective business and personal goals.

Areas of Practice: Bennett Jones Verchere's professional practice encompasses virtually every sector of business, industry and government. Supported by the individual and collective resources to offer full-service capability the firm is organized into a number of departments including, corporate/commercial, litigation, energy and natural resources, tax, real estate and estate planning, as well as a legal research group. Spanning these departments are more highly focussed groups that service conventional and emerging industry sectors. These groups include banking, debt-restructuring, securities, mergers and acquisitions, international, intellectual property, environmental, regulatory, labour and employment, and native law. Other interdisciplinary groups focus on transportation, telecommunications, science, technology, health, retail, forestry, utilities, and independent power production.

The corporate/commercial department offers experience and ability to clients ranging from the largest corporations to small businesses and proprietorships. It provides services to a broad range of clients in such areas as commercial transactions, securities, mergers and acquisitions, privatizations, corporate reorganizations and debt restructurings, banking, intellectual property and international trade. A broad base of clients has given the department's commercial lawyers the opportunity to gain experience in commercial transactions and project developments in many different industries and jurisdictions.

The litigation department comprises lawyers with experience in all areas of advocacy. The department's lawyers appear at all provincial and federal court levels, including the Federal Court of Appeal and the Supreme Court of Canada. As well, many of the litigators have substantial practices involving work before regulatory, energy, transportation, competition, telecommunications, utilities and other tribunals.

The energy and natural resources department is among the largest in Canada servicing the needs of suppliers, transporters and buyers in the energy sector. Bennett Jones Verchere has been a part of the development of Canada's natural resources for almost 100 years and our experience in North America's energy and natural resource sectors is both comprehensive and diverse. Our lawyers have developed a comprehensive understanding of all the legal, technical and practical aspects of the industry in which our clients operate.

Bennett Jones Verchere has one of the most comprehensive tax practices in the legal profession in Canada. The department brings together lawyers who are experienced in advisory and transactional work, as well as litigation in every area of federal and provincial tax law. The tax practitioners are noted for their creativity and ability to solve problems rather than create impediments to the completion of transactions.

The firm has a substantial real estate practice. This department acts on behalf of corporations, real estate developers, bankers and other institutional lenders as well as smaller businesses and individuals involved in all types of property transactions. The lawyers in the real estate department have expertise in financing and mortgaging options, and in provincial and municipal legislation, regulations and policies relating to real property and development issues. The department also advises clients with respect to special tax and environmental considerations relating to residential, condominium and commercial property development.

The estate planning department offers assistance to clients in all areas of estate planning, including the drafting of wills and creation of family and business trusts. As well, the lawyers in this department have extensive experience in the creation and administration of charitable foundations and organizations. In conjunction with members of the litigation department, the estate planning lawyers act on behalf of personal representatives and individuals in relation to estate litigation.

The firm employs full-time legal research practitioners to provide opinions on a complete range of legal issues to members of the firm, in-house corporate counsel and other clients. In addition, the department publishes a monthly newsletter for clients on significant cases and legislative changes, including federal and provincial statutes and regulations. The department also maintains a central computerized memo bank which greatly facilitates the timeliness and cost-effectiveness of services provided to our clients.

ALBERTA LAW DIGEST

(The following is a list of all Topics, including cross-references, covered in this Digest.)

ALBERTA LAW DIGEST

Revised for 1997 edition by

BENNETT JONES VERCHERE of the Calgary Bar.

(Citations, unless otherwise indicated, refer to Revised Statutes of Alberta, 1980, Annual Statues of Alberta are cited by year and chapter number; R.S.C. indicates Revised Statutes of Canada, 1985; S.C. indicates Annual Statutes of Canada; A.R.C. indicates Alberta Rules of Court; W.W.R. refers to Western Weekly Reports. See topic Reports.)

ABSENTEES:

Persons resident out of province are under no disability with regard to holding property, but acquisitions are restricted under Investment Canada Act, S.C. 1985 c. 20 and Agricultural and Recreational Land Ownership Act (c. A-9). See also topic Aliens.

Care of Property.—If a resident of province is missing, public trustee may act as custodian of his property. He may mortgage, lease, sell or otherwise dispose of property upon order of a Queen's Bench judge, and has generally all powers of administrator of estate of deceased person. (c. P-36, §§8, 9).

Proceedings are commenced by petition to Court of Queen's Bench by any person interested or by next friend. Notice of every motion or application to court in respect of such person or his property must be served on public trustee. (c. P-36, §5). Does not apply to applications governed by Administration of Estates Act (as of revision date, not yet proclaimed).

Process Agent.—Absentees are not required to appoint agents for service of process (A.R.C. 30); however, absentee plaintiffs and parties entering appearances must provide address for service within 30 kilometres of courthouse where action or proceeding is commenced (A.R.C. 5[1][b]).

Escheat.—The Crown in the right of the Province is entitled to become possessed of bona vacantia quite independently of tenure. See topics Wills subhead Unclaimed Legacies; Banks and Banking, subhead Unclaimed Deposits.

ACCORD AND SATISFACTION:

An accord may be defined as an agreement to accept in extinction of an obligation something different from or less than that which the person agreeing to accept it is entitled.

Part performance of an obligation, either before or after a breach thereof, when expressly accepted by the creditor in satisfaction or rendered in pursuance of an agreement for that purpose though without any new consideration is held to extinguish the obligation. (c. J-1, §13).

A right of action for breach of contract can be discharged by deed or parol agreement with consideration amounting to accord and satisfaction. Part performance is sufficient.

A negotiable note although for a less amount than the debt may be good satisfaction thereof if so taken.

Pleading.—Where a dispute has arisen accord and satisfaction must be specifically pleaded. (A.R.C. 109).

ACKNOWLEDGMENTS:

The form of acknowledgment before a notary public, in common use in the United States, is not sufficient in Alberta, except in the case of a wife who signs a document to bar her dower interest and a person acknowledging his guarantee. (cc. D-38, G-12). Instead of acknowledgment, formal affidavit must be taken by witness or witnesses to document, before proper officer, swearing to due execution of document. See also topic Bonds, subhead The Guarantees Acknowledgment Act.

Fees.—By custom, Commissioner for Oaths may charge 50¢ for administering oath.

Officers Who May Take Affidavits.—See topic Affidavits.

Requisite for Taking.—In all cases the officer must be satisfied as to the identity of the deponent.

Corporations.—No formal proof of execution by a corporate body is generally required where signed by proper officer or officers. (c. B-15, §23[4]; c. C-20, §309).

Married Men/Women.—Spouse signing release or conveyance of his/her dower must appear before proper officer, apart from his/her spouse and acknowledge his/her signature, that he/she understands document and that he/she is not acting under compulsion. (c. D-38, §5[1]). For Form see topic Homesteads.

Authentication.—Documents attested before notary public in Alberta and used in foreign jurisdication may be authenticated by forwarding same to Deputy Provincial Secretary's Office, 9833-109 Street, Room 111, Edmonton, Alberta T5K 2E8, with fee of $5 per document.

Documents attested before a notary public or similar official in a foreign jurisdiction are admissible as evidence in a provincial court if properly sealed and signed, with office shown below signature, without further proof of person's signature, official character or jurisdiction in place where document was completed. (c. A-21, §48).

Alternative to Acknowledgment or Proof.—Person making affidavit or deposition who objects to taking oath may, if objection is based on conscientious scruples, religious belief or he does not regard oath as binding, make affirmation and declaration. (c. A-21, §18).

ACTIONS:

Distinction between law and equity is preserved, but same courts administer both common law and equity and equity rules govern in case of conflict. (c. J-1, §16).

Forms of Action.—Court allows parties greatest freedom in form of their action. As long as necessary facts are pleaded form makes little difference subject only to its being as clear and concise as possible. Amendments are allowed even at trial providing other party is not greatly prejudiced or lawsuit unfairly delayed and then they might be allowed and other party recompensed with costs. (A.R.C. 132). Underlying principle is that parties should not be prevented from obtaining redress simply because of formality. Frivolous, vexatious or scandalous action will be struck out. (A.R.C. 129).

Jurisdiction.—Court of Queen's Bench has jurisdiction over most civil matters. (c. C-29). For many claims in debt not exceeding $4,000 and/or in damages not exceeding $4,000 (Parris v. Reber [1994], 22 Alta. L.R. [3d] 78 [Prov. Ct.]) Small Claims Court is also available and parties are not generally represented by counsel (c. P-20, §36, as am'd).

Commencement.—Except in certain specified cases all actions in Court of Queen's Bench are brought by way of statement of claim, which is merely recital of facts alleged and claim for redress required. (A.R.C. 6, 104). Matrimonial causes other than divorce are included in this general rule. (A.R.C. 578). Claims against Crown or ministers or departments of Crown or government may now be commenced as of right in most cases. (c. P-18). In certain land cases and trust matters, and when seeking declaration settling priority between interests or charges, action is commenced by originating notice which is really notice of application to court for relief claimed. (A.R.C. 410). Application for judicial review of decision of administrative decision maker is also commenced by originating notice. (A.R.C. 753.03). Proceedings for relief offered by statutes, where no procedure is set out may often be obtained by ex parte application with affidavit evidence. (A.R.C. 394-5). Proceedings may be commenced by issue of petition where permitted by statute, there is no person against whom relief is sought, person against whom relief is sought is unknown or unascertained or there are no issues of fact. (A.R.C. 6).

Parties.—Any person may be made defendant by order of court. No person can be added as plaintiff without his consent. (A.R.C. 38). Where proper parties not joined judgment may be rendered saving their rights. (A.R.C. 40). All persons as to whom common questions of law or fact arise may be joined as defendants. (A.R.C. 46). Where action commenced in name of wrong plaintiff proper person may be substituted or added upon such terms as may be ordered by court. (A.R.C. 38[2]).

Joinder and Severance.—Plaintiff may join several causes of action arising out of one transaction or series of transactions (A.R.C. 32), but trustee in bankruptcy suing as such must obtain leave of court to join claim in any other capacity (A.R.C. 33). Where causes are improperly joined or cannot be finally disposed of in one action any cause may, by order, be excluded or tried separately. (A.R.C. 37).

Consolidation.—A multiplicity of actions will not be permitted, but actions will be consolidated in a proper case. (A.R.C. 229).

Abatement.—Action does not abate because of death or insolvency of a party if cause of action survives, nor because of devolution of estate pendente lite. Death of party after hearing of all evidence but before judgment does not cause abatement, whether or not cause of action is one which would survive. (A.R.C. 54, 55).

Limitation of.—See topic Limitation of Actions.

Small Claims.—See topic Courts.

Stay of Proceedings.—Where defendant has paid money into court in satisfaction and plaintiff has accepted it, all further proceedings except as to enforcement are stayed. (A.R.C. 172).

Termination.—Before an action has been set down for trial plaintiff may at any time discontinue his action subject only to being liable to defendant for his costs. After an action is set down for trial plaintiff can only discontinue with leave of court. Defendant may withdraw his opposition to action at any time, with leave of court, thereby allowing plaintiff's claim to succeed. (A.R.C. 225). Actions may terminate by nonprosecution. Where five years have expired from last step that materially advances action, court will dismiss action upon application of defendant. (A.R.C. 244.1[1]). If there has been any delay in prosecution, defendant can apply for dismissal or for directions from court to expedite matter. (A.R.C. 244[1]).

Direct Actions Against Insurer.—See topic Motor Vehicles, subhead Direct Actions.

See also topic Practice.

ADMINISTRATION:

It is function of Ombudsman, to investigate administrative decisions and acts of officials of government and its agencies, either on his own motion or pursuant to a complaint made. His authority is limited to cases where there is no other remedy open to aggrieved person. (c. O-7).

See topic Executors and Administrators.

ADOPTION:

At common law it is doubtful that parents could contract to deprive themselves of custody and control of their children. Adoption is now controlled by statute.

Adult who maintains his usual residence in Alberta or maintained his usual residence in Alberta at time he received custody of child may petition Court for adoption order. (1984, c. C-8.1, §58[1], as am'd).

Consent Required.—Written consent required (unless dispensed with by court) of child if 12 years old or over (1984, c. C-8.1, §56[1], as am'd; §63[4], as am'd), and guardian. Consent executed in province of Canada in form prescribed for consents in that province is as good as if executed in form prescribed in Alberta. (1984, c. C-8.1, §56[2], as am'd).

Proceedings.—Application is by petition which must be presented to Court not later than six months after filing of petition. (1984, c. C-8.1, §58[2], as am'd). Director may

---

See Topical Index in front part of this volume.

ADOPTION . . . *continued*
conduct investigation with respect to proposed adoption and may file report of investigation with Court. (1984, c. C-8.1, §62[1], as am'd). Petitioner and child (if 12 years old or over) entitled to be heard, personally or by counsel, at proceedings before judge. (1984, c. C-8.1, §63[2], as am'd).

Effect of Adoption.—For all purposes including inheritance, adopted child becomes child of adopting parents and ceases to be child of existing parents. However, this does not apply for purpose of law relating to incest and prohibited degrees of marriage. (1984, c. C-8.1, §65, as am'd).

Setting Aside Adoption.—No action to set aside order of adoption can be commenced after expiration of one year from day of order, except on ground that order was procured by fraud and then it may only be set aside if in interests of adopted child to do so. (1984, c. C-8.1, §68[1], as am'd).

Foreign Adoption.—Adoption effected according to law of any other jurisdiction has same effect in Province as adoption under Alberta Act. (1984, c. C-8.1, §65.1, as am'd).

Adoption of Adult Persons.—It is possible to adopt person over age of 18 years. (S.A. 1994, c. A-2.3).

ADVANCEMENTS:

See topic Descent and Distribution.

ADVERSE POSSESSION:

Person who can show actual, open, continuous, peaceful and exclusive possession of lands for ten years may bar right of owner of a registered fee simple Torrens title therein. As against Crown, period appears to be upwards of 60 years. One occupant may assign his rights in lands to another, and latter thereby takes benefit of period of adverse possession of former. (c. L-15, §18; c. L-5, §74, as am'd).

AFFIDAVITS:

In matters in court an affidavit must: be intitulated in cause or matter in which it is sworn, be made in first person and divided into paragraphs and contain full name, occupation, and true place of abode of deponent and be signed by him. (A.R.C. 298, 299, 304). Generally should be confined to statements of fact within knowledge of deponent save on interlocutory matters. (A.R.C. 305).

By Whom Taken.—When sworn to in province it must be sworn to before a judge, clerk of court, or deputy clerk, notary public, justice of peace or commissioner for oaths (A.R.C. 309) and when sworn outside of province before: (a) a judge; (b) a magistrate; (c) an officer of a court of justice; (d) a commissioner for taking affidavits or other competent authority of like nature; (e) a notary public; (f) head of a city, town, village, township or other municipality; (g) an officer of any of Her Majesty's diplomatic or consular services, including an ambassador, envoy, minister, chargé d'affaires, counsellor, secretary, attaché, consul-general, consul, vice-consul, pro-consul, consular agent, acting consul-general, acting-consul, acting vice-consul, and acting consular agent; (h) an officer of Canadian diplomatic, consular or representative services, including, in addition to diplomatic and consular offices mentioned in clause (g), high commissioner, permanent delegate, acting high commissioner, acting permanent delegate, counsellor or secretary, or (i) Canadian Government Trade Commissioner or Assistant Canadian Government Trade Commissioner. (c. A-21, §48[1]).

Formalities.—Every person administering oaths must express date and place of so doing. (A.R.C. 300). All interlineations, alterations or erasures in jurat or in body of affidavit must be initialled by officer taking same. (A.R.C. 308).

Where properly marked exhibit referred to in but not annexed to affidavit, exhibit need not be filed and will be returned on disposal of motion. (A.R.C. 312).

Form of oath must be such as invokes Deity and binds deponent's conscience or it may be administered in such form or in such ceremonies as such person may declare to be binding. Where an oath has been duly administered and taken, fact that deponent had mental reservations or conditions or no religious belief does not affect validity of oath. (c. A-21, §15).

Statutory Declarations.—For certain purposes statutory declarations may be taken instead of affidavits. These are declarations similar in form to an affidavit which are given the force of an affidavit by statute. Strictly speaking they should be used in every case except in the case of court actions where an affidavit is necessary. It is only necessary to declare or affirm the contents instead of swearing.

Authentication.—Any document purporting to have been signed and sworn (with seal attached in case of notary public, etc.) is admissible in evidence without further proof of the fact of seal and signature or official character of person administering oath. (c. A-21, §48[3]).

Filing.—Affidavits upon which a notice of motion or petition is founded shall be filed before service of notice of motion or petition and served with notice of motion or petition. (A.R.C. 310).

Affidavit should commence as follows:

Form

I . . . . . . of the . . . . . . of . . . . . . in the . . . . . . of . . . . . ., ... (occupation) . . . . . . make oath and say: (etc.).

The jurat ordinarily reads as follows:

"Sworn before me at the . . . . . . of . . . . . . in the . . . . . . of . . . . . . this . . . . . . day of . . . . . . A. D. 19. . . . . (officer's signature) . . . . A Commissioner/Notary Public in and for the . . . . of . . . ." etc.

In case of illiterate or blind person, officer administering oath must certify in jurat that (a) affidavit was read in his presence to deponent; (b) deponent seemed perfectly to understand it; and (c) deponent made his signature or mark in his presence. (A.R.C. 302).

Commissioners for oaths and notaries public must print or stamp their names next to their signatures and, if appropriate, date upon which their commission or appointment expires. (c. C-19, §9[1], as am'd; c. N-11, §7[1], as am'd).

Form

Statutory declaration should be entitled "In the matter of . . . . . ." and begin as follows:

I . . . . . . solemnly declare that:

After the contents of the declaration the following is inserted as the last clause thereof.

"And I make this solemn declaration conscientiously believing it to be true and knowing that it is of the same force and effect as if made under oath."

The jurat reads as follows:

"Declared before me at the . . . . . . of . . . . . . in the . . . . . . of . . . . . . this . . . . . . day of . . . . . . A.D. 19. . . . . . etc. (c. A-21, §19).

Alternative to Affidavit.—Person making affidavit or deposition who objects to taking oath may, if objection is based on conscientious scruples, religious belief or he does not regard oath as binding on his conscience, make affirmation and declaration. (c. A-21, §18[1]).

AGENCY: See topic Principal and Agent.

AIRCRAFT: See Canada Law Digest.

ALIENS:

Resident aliens are under practically no disability except as to right to vote in parliamentary elections. They have same exemption (see topic Exemptions) and homestead (see topic Homesteads) rights as citizens but are subject to special registration requirements (see topic Real Property). Acquisitions by nonresidents are subject to restrictions in case of businesses (R.S.C. 1985 [1st Supp.], c. 28) and in case of rural land (R.S.C. 1985, c. C-29, §35 and c. A-9 and Regulations 160/79, 223/79, 31/80 and 236/82).

Nonresident alien may own property and transfer it and deal with it same as resident alien, subject to above restrictions.

See topic Absentees.

ALIMONY: See topic Divorce.

ALLOWANCES:

See topic Executors and Administrators.

APPEAL AND ERROR:

Appeals from decision of judge of Court of Queen's Bench are taken to Court of Appeal. (A.R.C. 505). Notice of appeal should be given within 20 days of entry and service of order or judgment appealed from, but time may be extended by order of court. (A.R.C. 506, 548). Further appeal may be taken from judgment of appellate division to Supreme Court of Canada at Ottawa but only with leave of that Court. (R.S.C. c. S-26, §40, as am'd).

Leave to appeal to appellate division is necessary where amount in question is less than $1,000. (A.R.C. 505).

Review.—Appeal from Court of Queen's Bench is by way of review only. Appeals from Provincial Court Civil Division are heard as appeal on record unless on application by party, Court of Queen's Bench orders appeal to be heard as trial de novo. (c. P-20, §64).

Stay.—An appeal does not per se operate as a stay of enforcement or of proceedings on judgment or order of trial court. (A.R.C. 508).

Bond.—No security for costs required unless special circumstances (A.R.C. 524) but is required in appeal to Supreme Court of Canada (R.S.C. c. S-26, §§60, 61).

ARBITRATION AND AWARD:

Submission.—Parties may agree, or statute require, that specific disputes will be submitted to arbitration pursuant to new Arbitration Act. (c. A-43.1, §2[1]). Agreement may be rescinded in accordance with law of contract. (A-43.1, §5[3]).

Hearing.—Witnesses may be called and evidence taken as in court proceeding. (c. A-43.1, §§29,30). Tribunal is to make decision in accordance with law and equity. (c. A-43.1, §31).

Stay.—Court may order stay of proceedings in court where court believes matter sought to be tried should be tried by arbitration under agreement. No appeal from court decision. (§7).

Enforcement.—Award binds parties, subject to permitted appeal or application to set aside. (§37). Court may enforce tribunal order as if order made by court. (§18).

Appeal.—Award may be appealed to court if agreement so provides. (§44). Court may set aside award, or give directions to tribunal on grounds including invalidity of agreement to arbitrate; procedures improper, party treated manifestly improperly; subject matter may not be arbitrated. (§45).

ASSIGNMENTS:

Choses in Action.—Any chose in action for a debt may be assigned by writing. If assignment is absolute, not being by way of a charge only, and notice in writing has been given to debtor, assignee may bring action in his own name (c. J-1, §21[1]); otherwise document may operate only as equitable assignment and action must be brought in name of original assignor.

Registration.—Personal Property Security Act c. P-4.05 which came into force on Oct. 1, 1990 repealed Assignment of Book Debts Act and consequently references in this section to Assignment of Book Debts Act will no longer be valid after that date.

ASSIGNMENTS . . . *continued*

Personal Property Security Act encompasses what is presently known as "book debt". In Personal Property Security Act book debt is referred to as "account". "Account" means monetary obligation not evidenced by chattel paper, instrument or security, whether or not it has been earned by performance. (§1[1][b]). Primary section under Personal Property Security Act that deals with "accounts" is §41.

Assignment of Book Debts Act required that general Assignments of Book Debts be registered, but did not apply to Assignments of Accounts which are due from specified debtors or growing due under specified contracts. Priority between competing assignees was determined by first assignee to give notice of assignment to account debtor. Under Personal Property Security Act, Assignments of Accounts, whether general or specific, and whether absolute or by way of security, are brought within scope of Act. Priorities are determined by internal priority rules of Personal Property Security Act, and most priority competitions between assignees will be determined by first to register. §4 of Personal Property Security Act excludes limited types of assignments from Act.

Rights of debtor in collateral may be transferred consensually despite agreement between parties but rights of secured party are not to be prejudiced. (c. P-4.05, §33). Assignee's rights are subject to contract between assignor and debtor, and debtor may raise any defence or claim against assignee that could be raised against assignor.

It will still be possible to postpone assignment under Personal Property Security Act. (§40).

Registration of Assignment of Accounts is effected at Personal Property Security Registry. See topic Personal Property Security.

ASSIGNMENTS FOR BENEFIT OF CREDITORS:

Provided the assignor has committed no act of bankruptcy, an assignment to a trustee to pay the debts of the assignor is valid. Bankruptcy, see Canada Law Digest.

ASSOCIATIONS:

Formation.—Five or more persons may become incorporated under Societies Act for any useful purpose, other than for purpose of carrying on a trade or business (c. S-18, §3) by subscribing to declaration of incorporation setting forth objects of society and filing same with Registrar of Companies, together with copy of proposed by-laws of society and information re subscribers (c. S-18, §5).

Liabilities.—No member of an incorporated society is liable in his individual capacity for debts of society. (c. S-18, §17).

Rights and Powers.—No society shall have a capital divided into shares, or declare any dividend, or distribute its property among its members during society's existence. (c. S-18, §4).

Special Associations.—Special legislation governs the formation and operation of religious, agricultural, co-operative, co-operative marketing and building associations.

Unincorporated Associations.—Common law rules apply.

Professional Associations.—See topic Corporations subhead Professional Corporations.

Charitable Immunity.—See topic Damages.

ATTACHMENT:

Claimant may apply to court for attachment order where claimant has commenced or is about to commence proceedings in Alberta or where proceedings commenced before foreign tribunal if award could be enforced in Alberta or defendant has exigible property in Alberta. (c. C-10.5, §17).

Grounds.—Court may grant attachment order if court is satisfied that there is reasonable likelihood claim against defendant will be established and there are reasonable grounds for believing that defendant is dealing with defendant's exigible property, or is likely to deal with that property for purpose outside defendant's reasonable and ordinary business and in manner that would likely seriously hinder claimant in enforcement of judgment against defendant. (c. C-10.5, §17).

Order of attachment is obtained from judge who can impose conditions on use of exigible property. Order shall not attach property that exceeds value of claim, shall cause as little inconvenience to defendant as possible, and shall not be granted unless claimant undertakes to pay any damages or indemnity that court may subsequently decide should be paid to defendant. Applications for attachment order can be made ex parte. (c. C-10.5, §18).

Registration of attachment order takes place at Personal Property Registry or in case of land under Land Titles Act against certificate of title. (c. C-10.5, §22).

Termination.—Attachment order terminates on dismissal or discontinuance of claimant's proceedings or 60 days after claimant receives judgment. (c. C-10.5, §19). Any interested person may apply to court to vary or terminate attachment order. (c. C-10.5, §17[8]).

Personal Property Security.—Under Personal Property Security Act, security interest attaches when value is given, debtor has rights in collateral and except for purpose of enforcing inter parties rights, it becomes enforceable against third parties. Debtor has rights in goods purchased under Agreement to Sell when he obtains possession of them pursuant to sales contract, and in goods leased to him, hired by him or delivered to him under consignment, when he obtains possession of them pursuant to Lease Hiring Agreement or consignment. Debtor has no rights in crops until they become growing crops, young of animals until they are conceived, in oil, gas or other minerals until extracted, or in timber until it is cut. (c. P-4.05, §12).

Concept of attachment denotes time when security interest comes into existence. If security interest is not attached, creditor will have no right to exercise its default rights against collateral, nor will creditor have any right to collateral which can be asserted against other persons who claim property interest in collateral. Generally security interest will not attach until Security Agreement has been executed or secured party has taken possession of collateral or debtor has rights in property claimed as collateral and secured party has advanced money or given binding promise to do so. See topic Personal Property Security.

ATTORNEYS AND COUNSELORS:

These terms are not commonly used in Canada, the terms used being barristers and solicitors, whose rights and duties are, apart from custom, governed by new Legal Profession Act. (c. L-9.1). (Old Legal Profession Act has been largely repealed and replaced with 1990 Legal Profession Act which was, for most part, proclaimed in force May 1, 1991.)

Admission to the bar is governed by regulations of Law Society of Alberta which is a body corporate with continued succession. Detailed information may be obtained from secretary of Society at Calgary. Members of bar are admitted as barristers and solicitors at same time.

Eligibility.—Candidates for admissions as students-at-law must be of good character, and have received degree or completed two years of full program of studies that would entitle them to have studied law at university in Alberta, and degree in law recognized by Co-ordinating Council in Alberta, which evaluates academic qualifications. Every student-at-law must enter into articles of clerkship for continuous period of one year with enrolled barrister and solicitor who is in actual practise, except in case of person enrolled as barrister or solicitor in any Province of Canada but not having practised for period or periods totalling three of last five years immediately before application and members of bar of certain Commonwealth countries who have practised for period or periods totalling three of last five years immediately before application, in which instances period of articles is set by Secretary of Alberta Law Society. Student may article in part under judge. (c. L-9.1, §37). Student may be admitted only if: Canadian citizen; of full age of 18; has served prescribed period of articles; and passed prescribed examinations. Members of bar of any province or territory in Canada may generally be enrolled in Alberta if they have practised for period or periods totalling three of last five years immediately before application and pass prescribed examinations. (c. L-9.1, §§39-42).

Registration as Law Student.—On approval of Education Committee and on payment of proper fees secretary will enter and enrol applicant on his books as student-at-law. No particular time is set for registration but period of articles will be deemed to begin at registration or earlier date approved by secretary. (Rules of Law Society of Alberta, effective Aug. 15, 1994, Part 2, Division 1, §53).

Educational Requirements.—See subhead Eligibility, supra.

Clerkship.—See subhead Eligibility, supra.

Examinations consist of two sets, one in the fall and one in the spring. They are set and conducted by Legal Education Society. Articling students and others may also be required to write any special examinations required by Co-ordinating Council.

Status.—Barrister and solicitor is officer of Court of Queen's Bench and all other courts of record in Alberta. (c. L-9.1, §99). He is ex officio commissioner for oaths for province and is notary public. (c. C-19, §1; c. N-11, §2).

Rights.—A duly enrolled barrister and solicitor is entitled to practice in all Alberta courts and in Supreme Court and Federal Court of Canada.

Compensation.—Fees of members of bar are such as are reasonable having regard to (a) nature of matter; (b) circumstances of person paying; (c) fund from which they are paid; (d) general conduct of proceedings; (e) skill involved; and (f) other circumstances. (A.R.C. 613). They may sue for fees due but no default judgment may be entered and no costs allowed without court order. (A.R.C. 626).

Lien.—A court may, on application, declare a solicitor entitled to lien on property recovered or preserved by his efforts. (A.R.C. 625).

Misappropriation or Conversion.—A barrister and solicitor is not bonded, but there is a special assurance fund for relief of persons who have sustained pecuniary losses by reason of misappropriation or conversion by any member of Law Society of money entrusted to him in his professional capacity. (c. L-9.1, §86).

Disbarment is in control of benchers, who are senior members of profession elected to office and who have absolute discretion, subject only to an appeal to Court of Appeal of Alberta, to disbar members, or prescribe other penalties, for unprofessional conduct. (c. L-9.1, §§51-83).

Unauthorized Practise.—Only active members of Law Society may practise or act as barristers or solicitors, or act as barrister or as solicitor in any court of civil or criminal jurisdiction, commence, carry on or defend actions, or settle claims. This prohibition does not apply, inter alia, to public officers or notary publics acting in course of their duty; or to any person acting on his own behalf; or to any insurance adjuster acting under Insurance Act, or to any person who appears as agent for another when authorized to do so, or to articled student-at-law where he acts as counsel where permitted to do so and if under supervision of member. (c. L-9.1, §103).

BANKS AND BANKING:

Prerequisities to Acting in Fiduciary Capacity.—Registered corporation may engage in provision of real property brokerage services and acquire, hold, maintain, improve, develop, repair, service, lease, dispose of or otherwise deal with real property. Registered trust corporation may offer its services to public as executor, administrator, trustee bailee, agent, custodian, receiver, liquidator, sequestrator, assignee or guardian or trustee of minor's estate, of estate of mentally incompetent person, and carrying on deposit-taking business. However, no registered corporation shall engage in or carry on any business other than business generally appertaining to business of providing financial services. (Loan and Trust Corporations Act, c. L-26.5, §181, 1991).

Reports.—Registered corporation shall prepare annually and send to Minister not later than three months after end of each fiscal year annual return in prescribed form relating to fiscal year. In case of provincial corporation, annual return shall be accompanied by financial statements and report of auditor for fiscal year to which return relates, copy of resolution of directors approving annual return and any other documents and information prescribed by Minister. In case of extra-provincial corporation, annual return shall be accompanied by financial statements and auditor's report on them for fiscal year to which return relates. Where any of required financial statements are in consolidated form, they shall be accompanied by separate audited financial statements in respect of provincial corporation or extra-provincial corporation, as case

BANKS AND BANKING . . . *continued*
may be, where it is holding body corporate or subsidiary. Registered corporation shall also send to Minister copy of every statement of financial nature relating to corporation that is furnished to its shareholders within five days after furnishing of statement to shareholders. (c. L-26.5, §§46-47, 1991).

Investigations.—Minister may, for purpose of inquiring into registered corporation's condition and ability to meet its obligations, conduct of registered corporation's affairs or any complaint made by creditor of registered corporation or person for whom corporation acts in fiduciary capacity, direct corporation, subsidiary of corporation, restricted party of corporation, individual who controls corporation's holding body corporate, or present or former director, auditor, officer, employee, agent, depositor, borrower or creditor of corporation, its subsidiary or its holding body corporate to provide or produce, within reasonable period of time that is stipulated in direction, any information or document. Minister may also periodically examine any aspect of business or affairs of registered corporation or its subsidiaries in order to determine: corporation's condition and ability to meet its obligations, whether corporation is following sound business and financial practices, procedures and standards of management of corporation and whether or not corporation is in compliance with Loan and Trust Corporations Act. Registered extra-provincial corporation must send notice of any change in membership of its Board of Directors within 30 days after effective date of change. Minister may also order that special examination of matter be made by special examiner appointed by Minister. (c. L-26.5, §§270-276, 1991).

Unclaimed Deposits.—Generally speaking ten years after last transaction has taken place in account bank must pay to Bank of Canada an amount equal to amount owing by bank to depositor. Depositor may demand payment from Bank of Canada at any time but will only receive interest on deposit with Bank of Canada for maximum of ten years from day on which payment was received by Bank of Canada. (S.C. 1991, c. 46, §438).

Capital Requirements.—See topic Trust and Loan Corporations.

BONDS:

The Guarantees Acknowledgment Act provides that bonds and guarantees, except bills of exchange, partnership agreements, and bonds given to Her Majesty or to any court or pursuant to any statute or guarantees given on sale of an interest in land or chattels, are invalid unless obligor appears before notary and acknowledges his execution thereof and unless notary issues a statutory certificate that obligor acknowledged and was aware of and understood contents of instrument. Certificate must be attached to or noted upon instrument containing guarantee to which certificate relates. Act does not apply where guarantor is corporation. (c. G-12).

BROKERS:

The Real Estate Act, 1995 (c. R-4.5) has only been partially proclaimed in force. As of Nov. 1, 1995, §§1 to 9, 11 to 16 and 84(1) are in effect. When remainder of Act is proclaimed in force, it will repeal Real Estate Agents' Licensing Act (c. R-5) and Mortgage Brokers Regulation Act (c. M-19) and will bring main elements of real estate trading industry under one Act. Sections of Real Estate Act which are in force establish Real Estate Council in Alberta to set and enforce industry standards and administer Act.

Brokers must be licensed, and no person who is not licensed may act or hold himself out as a real estate broker. (c. R-5, §3). Person wishing to be licensed as agent under Real Estate Act (c. R-4.5) must apply to Superintendent of Real Estate. Superintendent may issue or refuse that person license based on grounds enumerated in Act. (c. R-4.5, §7). Superintendent also has power to suspend license when, inter alia, agent contravenes Act or Regulations. (c. R-5, §8).

Compensation.—Action for services in sale of land or interest therein is not maintainable unless contract to pay or some note or memorandum thereof is in writing signed by party to be charged or his agent lawfully authorized in writing or completed transaction has resulted. (c. R-5, §25).

Cemeteries, etc.—Conduct of cemetery owners and sellers of pre-need funeral services and supplies are limited and supervised by Director. (c. C-2, §60). See also topic Securities.

Foundation.—Alberta Real Estate Foundation is administered by board of governors in accordance with Regulations. Purposes of Foundation are: (a) to promote education law reform and other projects and activities to advance and improve real estate industry; and (b) to undertake projects as directed by Minister. (c. R-5, §15.6).

Funds.—Real Estate Assurance Fund was established for purpose of paying, in whole or in part, judgments against licensed agent or designated representative or salesman of licensed agent based on finding of fraud or breach of trust in respect of trade of real estate. (c. R-5, §14).

Mines and Minerals.—Action for services in sale of oil or gas leases not maintainable unless person bringing action licensed. (c. R-5, §24; [1965] 54 W.W.R 494).

Mortgage brokers must register with Superintendent of Real Estate and are regulated in their advertising and other conduct. Excluded are, inter alia, banks, trust companies, credit unions and insurance companies, and lawyers in course of their practice. (c. M-19).

Sale of Real Estate Located Outside Alberta.—Anyone trading in Alberta in real estate outside Alberta must be licensed, and file prospectus with Superintendent of Real Estate. These requirements do not obtain in respect of isolated trade in real estate when that trade is not part of continued successive transactions of like nature. (c. R-5, §38[2]).

Deposits Regulation.—Only corporations registered under Loan & Trust Corporations Act, or given express authority by statute may engage in deposit-taking business. (c. L-26.5, §182).

CARRIERS:

Dominion railways and provincial railways extending beyond province are governed by Dominion statute and by regulations of Canadian Transport Commission, at Ottawa. Dominion pipelines and provincial pipe lines extending beyond province are also governed by Dominion statute and by regulations of National Energy Board, at Ottawa. Purely provincial railways are governed by Alberta law and by regulations of Public Utilities Board. (c. R-4). Purely provincial pipelines are governed by Alberta law as contained in The Pipeline Act. (c. P-8). In the past, Energy Resources Conservation Board and, if applicable, Public Utilities Board (c. P-37) regulated intraprovincial pipelines. The Alberta Energy and Utilities Board Act (c. A-19.5), which was proclaimed in force on Feb. 9, 1995, established new Board (AEUB) consisting of members of the two aforementioned Boards, with jurisdiction and powers of both. For now, two old Boards remain intact and existing proceedings continued.

Discrimination and excessive rates are prohibited under Public Utilities Board Act and Regulations. (c. R-4, §213; c. P-37, §91).

CERTIORARI:

The proceedings are commenced by originating notice to be served on person from whose decision, act or omission relief is claimed, Attorney General and every person directly affected by proceedings (A.R.C. 753.09) and it is brought on for hearing before judge of Court of Queen's Bench. Common law provides that in absence of privative clause, certiorari will lie, in respect of court or tribunal where, inter alia, there is lack of excess of jurisdiction, where there is error on fact of record, where there has been abuse of jurisdiction or where reasonable apprehension of bias can be shown. Writ of certiorai is not issued but order in nature of certiorari is, containing all necessary provisions. (A.R.C. 738).

Statutory right of appeal may bar certiorari unless exceptional circumstances. ([1971], 5 W.W.R. 89).

CHARITABLE IMMUNITY: See topic Damages.

CHATTEL MORTGAGES:

Subject to certain exceptions, Personal Property Security Act (S.A. 1988, c. P-4.05, §3, as am'd) applies to every transaction that, in substance, creates security interest, without regard to its form and without regard to person who has title to collateral, including chattel mortgages. By reason of Personal Property Security Act, historic forms and concepts of security agreements, such as chattel mortgages, have been discarded in favour of single conceptual basis for all personal property security agreements.

Repeal.—As of Oct. 1, 1990 Personal Property Security Act repealed Bills of Sale Act (R.S.A. 1980, c. B-5), which formerly governed chattel mortgages (S.A. 1988, c. P-4.05, §101).

Transitional.—Chattel mortgage validly registered in accordance with Bills of Sale Act prior to Oct. 1, 1990 shall, upon Personal Property Security Act coming into force, be deemed to have been registered and perfected under Personal Property Security Act, and registered and perfected status of interest created thereby continues for unexpired portion of prior registration, and may be further continued by registration under Personal Property Security Act, provided it could have been perfected by registration if it had attached after Oct. 1, 1990. (R.S.A. 1980, c. P-4.05, §75). See topic Personal Property Security.

COLLECTION AGENCIES:

An official is designated as Administrator under The Collection Practices Act, to supervise licensing of agencies, review records and returns, and approve forms and form letters used by agencies. (c. C-17).

CONSUMER PROTECTION:

See topic Sales.

There is no "plain language" or similar legislation in force in Alberta.

CONTRACTS:

Common Parties Contracts and Conveyances Act has been repealed but relevant provisions still exist governing certain cases such as easements or restrictive covenants in conveyances between common parties. (c. L-5, §§71-72; c. L-8, §§10-13). Contracts otherwise governed generally by common law principles.

Distributorships and Dealerships.—Franchises Act, 1995, c. F-17.1 replaced Franchises Act, R.S.A., 1980, effective Nov. 1, 1995. This new Act requires disclosure document with defined content to be provided to purchaser of franchise 14 days before execution or payment, whichever is first. Lists circumstances where disclosure document is not required. See topic Franchises.

CORPORATIONS:

The Business Corporations Act (1981, c. B-15) was proclaimed in force on Feb. 1, 1982. It is similar to statutes in Manitoba, New Brunswick, Ontario, Saskatchewan and British Columbia and to Canada Business Corporations Act. (R.S.C. 1985, c. C-44). It applies to all new incorporations, aside from loan corporations or trust corporations incorporated under Loan and Trust Corporations Act, S.A. 1991, c. L-26.5, and existing corporations are to be continued under it but until then are governed in part by Companies Act. (c. C-20).

Part 1. Interpretation and Application.—

Application.—Act will apply to every corporation incorporated and every body corporate continued as corporation under Act that has not been discontinued under Act.

"Corporation" as defined in Act means body corporate incorporated or continued under Act and not discontinued under Act. "Body corporate" as defined in Act

CORPORATIONS . . . *continued*
includes company or body corporate wherever or however incorporated. (1981, c. B-15, §1).

Part 2. Incorporation.—

Incorporators.—One or more persons may incorporate by signing articles of incorporation and forwarding same, together with supporting documentation to Registrar of Corporations. (1981, c. B-15, §§5, 7).

Certificate of Incorporation.—Upon receipt of articles of incorporation in prescribed form Registrar must issue certificate of incorporation and corporation comes into existence on date shown in certificate of incorporation. (1981, c. B-15, §§8, 9).

Publication of Name.—Corporation must set out its name in legible characters in all contracts, invoices, negotiable instruments and orders for goods or services issued or made by or on behalf of corporation. (1981, c. B-15, §10[8]).

Other Name.—Corporation shall not have name that is prohibited by regulations or subject to regulations, is identical or similar to name of another corporation if that name is confusing or misleading. (1981, c. B-15, §12).

Designating Number.—If requested to do so by incorporators or by extra-provincial corporation about to continue as corporation, Registrar must assign to corporation as its name designated number determined by him. (1981, c. B-15, §11).

Personal Liability under Pre-incorporation Contracts.—Subject to certain exceptions including express provision in written contract negating personal liability, person who enters into written contract in name of or on behalf of corporation before it comes into existence is deemed to warrant that corporation will come into existence within reasonable time and that contract will be adopted within reasonable time thereafter. Breach of these warranties may result in liability. (1981, c. B-15, §14).

Pre-incorporation and Pre-amalgamation Contracts.—Corporation may, within reasonable time after it comes into existence, by any action or conduct signifying its intention to be bound thereby, adopt written contract made before it came into existence in its name or on its behalf and upon such adoption: (a) Corporation is bound by contract and is entitled to benefits thereof as if corporation had been in existence at date of contract and had been party thereto; and (b) person who purported to act in name of or on behalf of corporation ceases, except as court may order on application by any party to contract, to be bound by or entitled to benefits of contract. (1981, c. B-15, §14).

Part 3. Capacity and Powers.—

Capacity of a Corporation.—Corporation has capacity and, subject to Act, rights, powers and privileges of natural person. (1981, c. B-15, §15[1]).

Extra-territorial Capacity.—Corporation has capacity to carry on its business, conduct its affairs and exercise its powers in any jurisdiction outside Canada to extent that laws of such jurisdiction permit. (1981, c. B-15, §15[2]).

Part 4. Registered Office and Records.—

Registered Office.—Corporation must at all times have registered office in place within Alberta specified in its articles and notify Registrar within 15 days of any change of address of its registered office. (1981, c. B-15, §19).

Corporate Records.—Corporation must prepare and maintain, at its records office or at any other place in Alberta designated by directors, records containing: (a) Articles and by-laws, and all amendments thereto, and copy of any unanimous shareholder agreement; (b) minutes of meetings and resolutions of shareholders; (c) copies of all notices of directors or notices of change of directors; (d) securities register in prescribed form; (e) financial statements; and (f) disclosure information regarding material contracts with directors or officers. (1981, c. B-15, §20[1]).

Directors' Records.—Corporation must prepare and maintain at its registered office or records office or at such other place as directors think fit adequate accounting records and records containing minutes of meetings and resolutions of directors and any committee thereof which records must be open to inspection by directors at all reasonable times. (1981, c. B-15, §20[7]).

Records in Alberta.—Where accounting records of corporation are kept at place outside Alberta, there must be kept at registered office or records office or other office in Alberta accounting records adequate to enable directors to ascertain financial position of corporation with reasonable accuracy on quarterly basis. (1981, c. B-15, §§20[8], 21).

Shareholder Lists.—Any person, upon payment of reasonable fee and upon sending to distributing corporation or its transfer agent statutory declaration in prescribed form may upon application require corporation or its agent to furnish within ten days from receipt of statutory declaration list setting out names of shareholders of corporation, number of shares owned by each shareholder and address of each shareholder as shown on records of corporation. (1981, c. B-15, §21[5]).

Use of Shareholder List.—List of shareholders obtained in this manner shall not be used by any person except in connection with: (a) Effort to influence voting of shareholders of corporation; (b) offer to acquire shares of corporation; or (c) any other matter relating to affairs of corporation. (1981, c. B-15, §21[11]).

Form of Records.—All registers and other records required by Act to be prepared and maintained may be in bound or looseleaf form or in photographic film form, or may be entered or recorded by any system of mechanical or electronic data processing or any other information storage device that is capable of reproducing any required information in intelligible written form within reasonable time. (1981, c. B-15, §22[1]).

Corporate seal.—Instrument or agreement executed on behalf of corporation by director, officer or agent of corporation is not invalid merely because corporate seal is not affixed thereto. (1981, c. B-15, §23[2]).

Part 5. Corporate Finance.—

Shares.—Shares of corporation must be in registered form and must be without nominal or par value. (1981, c. B-15, §24[1]).

Transitional.—Where body corporate is continued under Act, share with nominal or par value issued by body corporate before it was so continued is, for purpose of Act, deemed to be share without nominal or par value. (1981, c. B-15, §24[2]).

Class of Shares.—Articles may provide for more than one class of shares and, if they so provide, there shall be set out therein rights, privileges, restrictions and conditions attaching to shares of each class. (1981, c. B-15, §24[4]).

Class Voting.—If corporation has only one class of shares, rights of holders of those shares are equal in all respects and include rights: (a) To vote at any meeting of shareholders, (b) to receive any dividend declared by corporation, and (c) to receive remaining property of corporation on dissolution. If more than one class of shares, aforementioned rights must attach to at least one class of shares, but all of rights need not be attached to same class. (1981, c. B-15, §24[3][4]).

Issue of Shares.—Subject to articles, by-laws, and any unanimous shareholder agreement, shares may be issued at such times and to such persons and for such consideration as directors may determine. (1981, c. B-15, §25[1]).

Shares Nonassessable.—Shares issued by corporation are nonassessable and holders are not liable to corporation or to its creditors in respect thereof. (1981, c. B-15, §25[2]).

Consideration.—Share must not be issued by directors until it is fully paid in money or in property or past services that is fair equivalent of money that corporation would have received if share had been issued for money. (1981, c. B-15, §25[3]).

Consideration Other than Money.—In determining whether property or past services is fair equivalent of money consideration, directors may take into account reasonable charges and expenses of organization and re-organization and payments for property and past services reasonably expected to benefit corporation. (1981, c. B-15, §25[4]).

Property.—For purposes of these provisions, "property" does not include promissory note or promise to pay given by allottee. (1981, c. B-15, §25; 1983, c. 20, §4[5]).

Stated Capital Account.—Corporation must maintain separate stated capital account for each class and series of shares issued, and consideration received by corporation for each share issued must, with some exceptions, be added to stated capital account maintained for shares of that class or series. (1981, c. B-15, §26; 1983, c. 20, §5; 1987, c. 15, §4).

Restriction.—Corporation must not reduce its stated capital or any stated capital account except in manner provided in Act. (1981, c. B-15, §26[11]).

Shares in Series.—Articles may authorize issue of any class of shares in one or more series and may authorize directors to fix number of shares in each series and to determine designation, rights, privileges, restrictions and conditions attaching to, shares of each series, subject to limitations set out in articles. (1981, c. B-15, §27[1]).

Series Participation.—If any cumulative dividends or amounts payable on return of capital in respect of series of shares are not paid in full, shares of all series of same class participate ratably in respect of accumulated dividends and return of capital. (1981, c. B-15, §27[2]).

Restrictions on Series.—No rights, privileges, restrictions or conditions attached to series of shares authorized under these provisions shall confer upon series greater voting rights than are attached to shares of any other series in same class that are then outstanding or priority in respect of dividends or return of capital over shares of any other series in same class that are then outstanding. (1987, c. 15, §5, repealing and substituting for 1981, c. B-15, §27[3]).

Pre-emptive Right.—If articles or unanimous shareholders' agreement so provide, no shares of class (other than shares to be issued: [a] For consideration other than money; [b] as share dividend; or [c] pursuant to exercise of conversion privileges, options or rights previously granted by corporation) may be issued unless shares have first been offered to shareholders holding shares of that class and those shareholders have pre-emptive right to acquire offered shares in proportion to their holdings of shares of that class, at such price and on such terms as those shares are to be offered to others. (1981, c. B-15, §28).

Options and Rights.—Corporation may issue certificates, warrants or other evidences of conversion privileges, options or rights to acquire securities of corporation; conditions to be set out therein. (1981, c. B-15, §29[1]).

Transferable Rights.—Conversion privileges, options and rights to acquire securities of corporation may be made transferable or nontransferable, and options and rights to acquire may be made separable or inseparable from any securities to which they are attached. (1981, c. B-15, §29[2]).

Reserved Shares.—Where corporation has granted privileges to convert any securities issued by corporation into shares, or into shares of another class or series, or has issued or granted options or rights to acquire shares, if articles limit number of authorized shares, corporation must reserve and continue to reserve sufficient authorized shares to meet exercise of such conversion privileges, options and rights. (1981, c. B-15, §29[3]).

Corporation Holding Its Own Shares.—Except as provided in Act, corporation must not hold shares in itself or in its holding body corporate and shall not permit any subsidiary corporation to acquire shares of corporation. Corporation shall cause subsidiary body corporate that holds shares of corporation to dispose of them within five years from date became subsidiary or date of continuance under Act. (1981, c. B-15, §30, am'd 1987, c. 15, §6).

Corporation may in capacity of legal representative hold shares in itself or in its holding body corporate unless it or holding body corporate or subsidiary of either of them has beneficial interest in shares. (1981, c. B-15, §31[1]).

Corporation may hold shares in itself or in its holding body corporate by way of security for purposes of transaction entered into by it in ordinary course of business that includes lending of money. (1981, c. B-15, §31[2]).

Acquisition of Corporation's Own Shares.—Subject to Act and to its articles, corporation may purchase or otherwise acquire shares issued by it. (1981, c. B-15, §32[1]).

Limitation.—Corporation may not make any payment to purchase or otherwise acquire shares issued by it (other than to satisfy claim of shareholder who dissents following certain actions by corporation or order of court) if there are reasonable grounds for believing that (a) corporation is, or would after payment be, unable to pay its liabilities as they become due; or (b) realizable value of corporation's assets would after payment be less than aggregate of its liabilities and stated capital of all classes. (1981, c. B-15, §32[2]).

Alternative Acquisition of Corporation's Own Shares.—Notwithstanding foregoing but subject to Act and its articles, corporation may purchase or otherwise acquire shares issued by it to: (a) Settle or compromise debt or claim asserted by or against corporation; (b) eliminate fractional shares; or (c) fulfil terms of non-assignable agreement under which corporation has option or is obliged to purchase shares owned by director, officer or employee of corporation unless there are reasonable grounds for

See Topical Index in front part of this volume.

CORPORATIONS . . . *continued*
believing that (d) corporation is, or would after payment be, unable to pay its liabilities as they become due; or (e) realizable value of corporation's assets would after payment be less than aggregate of its liabilities and amount required for payment on redemption or in liquidation of all shares holders of which have right to be paid prior to holders of shares to be purchased or acquired. (1981, c. B-15, §33).

Redemption of Shares.—Subject to Act and to its articles, corporation may purchase or redeem any redeemable shares issued by it at prices not exceeding redemption price thereof stated in articles or calculated according to formula stated in articles. (1981, c. B-15, §34[1]).

Corporation must not make any payment to purchase or redeem any redeemable shares issued by it if there are reasonable grounds for believing that: (a) Corporation is, or would after payment be, unable to pay its liabilities as they become due; or (b) realizable value of corporation's assets would after payment be less than aggregate of (i) its liabilities, and (ii) amount that would be required to pay holders of shares that have right to be paid, on redemption or in liquidation, ratably with or prior to holders of shares to be purchased or redeemed. (1981, c. B-15, §34[2]).

Other Reduction of Stated Capital.—Corporation may by special resolution reduce its stated capital for any purpose including: (a) Extinguishing or reducing liability for amount unpaid on any share; (b) distributing to holder of issued share of any class or series amount not exceeding stated capital of class or series; and (c) declaring stated capital to be reduced by amount not represented by realizable assets, unless for any purpose other than (c) above there are reasonable grounds for believing that (a) corporation is, or would after reduction be, unable to pay its liabilities as they become due; or (b) realizable value of corporation's assets would thereby be less than aggregate of its liabilities. (1981, c. B-15, §36).

Adjustment of Stated Capital Account.—Upon purchase, redemption or other acquisition by corporation under Act of shares or fractions thereof issued by it, corporation must deduct from stated capital account maintained for class or series of shares purchased, redeemed or otherwise acquired amount equal to result obtained by multiplying stated capital of shares of that class or series by number of shares of that class or series or fractions thereof purchased, redeemed or otherwise acquired, divided by number of issued shares of that class or series immediately before purchase, redemption or other acquisition. (1981, c. B-15, §37[1]).

Cancellation or Restoration of Shares.—Shares or fractions thereof issued by corporation and purchased, redeemed or otherwise acquired by it must be cancelled or be restored to status of authorized but unissued shares. (1981, c. B-15, §37[6]).

Repayment.—Debt obligations issued, pledged, hypothecated or deposited by corporation are not redeemed by reason only that indebtedness evidenced by debt obligations or in respect of which debt obligations are issued, pledged, hypothecated or deposited is repaid and those obligations remain obligations of corporation until they are discharged. (1981, c. B-15, §37.1[1], 1983, c. 20, §6).

Acquisition and Reissue of Debt Obligations.—Debt obligations issued by corporation and purchased, redeemed or otherwise acquired by it may be cancelled or, subject to any applicable trust indenture or other agreement, may be reissued, pledged or hypothecated to secure any obligation of corporation then existing or thereafter incurred, and any such acquisition and reissue, pledge or hypothecation is not cancellation of debt obligations. (1981, c. B-15, §37.1[2]).

Enforceability of Contract.—Contract with corporation providing for purchase of shares of corporation is specifically enforceable against corporation except to extent that corporation cannot perform contract without thereby being in breach of Act. (1981, c. B-15, §38[1]).

Commission for Sale of Shares.—Directors may authorize corporation to pay reasonable commission to any person in consideration of his purchasing or agreeing to purchase shares of corporation from corporation or from any other person, or procuring or agreeing to procure purchasers for any such shares. (1981, c. B-15, §39).

Dividends.—Corporation must not declare or pay dividend if there are reasonable grounds for believing that: (a) Corporation is, or would, after payment be, unable to pay its liabilities as they become due; or (b) realizable value of corporation's assets would thereby be less than aggregate of its liabilities and stated capital of all classes. (1981, c. B-15, §40). Corporation may pay dividend in money or property or by issuing fully paid shares of corporation. (1981, c. B-15, §41).

Prohibited Loans and Guarantees.—Corporation or any corporation with which it is affiliated must not, directly or indirectly, give financial assistance by means of loan, guarantee or otherwise: (1) To any shareholder or director of such corporation or affiliated corporation, (2) or associate of any such person, or (3) to any person, for purpose of, or in connection with, purchase of share issued or to be issued by corporation or affiliated corporation other than (a) in ordinary course of business if lending of money is part of ordinary business of corporation; (b) on account of expenditures incurred or to be incurred on behalf of corporation; (c) to holding body corporate if corporation is wholly-owned subsidiary of holding body corporate; (d) to subsidiary body corporate of corporation; (e) to employees of corporation or any of its affiliates (i) to enable or assist them to purchase or erect living accommodation for their own occupation, or (ii) in accordance with plan for purchase of shares of corporation or any of its affiliates to be held by trustee; and (f) in any other case unless there are reasonable grounds for believing that (i) corporation is, or would after giving financial assistance be, unable to pay its liabilities as they become due, or (ii) realizable value of corporation's assets, excluding amount of any financial assistance in form of loan and in form of assets pledged or encumbered to secure guarantee, would after giving financial assistance be less than aggregate of corporation's liabilities and stated capital of all classes. (1981, c. B-15, §42).

Shareholder Immunity.—Shareholders of corporation are not, as shareholders, liable for any liability, act or default of corporation except for any money or property received by them as result of improper reduction of stated capital, liabilities for breach of their duties as directors as result of unanimous shareholders' agreement and judgment against them in representative action brought against them as class. (1981, c. B-15, §43).

Part 6. Security Certificates, Registers and Transfers.—Part 6 of Act (as am'd by 1987, c. 15, §§7 and 8) represents attempt to achieve two goals: (i) to consolidate in one Part of Act all rules relating to security registers, dealing with security holders and security transfers, and (ii) to introduce concept of Article 8 of Uniform Commercial Code which has effect of making properly endorsed security certificates negotiable instruments between registration dates. Concept of negotiability between registration dates results in security certificate being not merely evidence of legal rights and privileges but embodiment of those rights and privileges which are transferred when security certificate is transferred. Concept of registration assures bona fide purchaser that registered holder is owner of security and gives such purchaser assurance that when registered, his ownership of security cannot be impugned.

Negotiable Instruments.—Except where its transfer is restricted and noted on security in accordance with Act, or it is stated conspicuously on certificate that it is nonnegotiable, security is negotiable instrument. (1981, c. B-15, §44[3]).

"Security".—"Security" or "security certificate" for purposes of this Part of Act is defined to mean instrument issued by corporation that is: (a) In bearer, order or registered form, (b) of type commonly dealt in upon securities exchanges or markets or commonly recognized in any area in which it is issued or dealt in as medium for investment, (c) one of class or series or by its terms divisible into class or series of instruments, and (d) evidence of share, participation or other interest in or obligation of corporation. (1981, c. B-15, §44[2]).

Registered Form.—Security is in registered form if: (a) It specifies person entitled to security or to rights it evidences, and (b) either its transfer is capable of being recorded in securities register, or security so states. (1981, c. B-15, §44[4]).

Bearer Form.—Security is in bearer form if it is payable to bearer according to its terms and not by reason of any endorsement. (1981, c. B-15, §44[6]).

Rights of Holder.—Every security holder is entitled at his option to security certificate that complies with Act or non-transferable written acknowledgment of his right to obtain such security certificate from corporation in respect of securities of that corporation held by him. (1981, c. B-15, §45[1]).

Restrictions.—If security certificate issued by corporation or by body corporate before body corporate was continued under Act is or becomes subject to: (a) Restriction on its transfer other than constraint under §168, or (b) lien in favour of corporation, such restriction or lien is ineffective against transferee of security who has no actual knowledge of it, unless it or reference to it is noted conspicuously on security certificate, security certificate contains conspicuous statement it is nonnegotiable or purchaser is not bona fide or is purchaser against whom owner of security may not assert ineffectiveness of endorsement under Act. (1981, c. B-15, §45[8]).

Securities Records.—Corporation must maintain securities register in which it records securities issued by it in registered form for period of time prescribed in regulations, showing with respect to each class or series of securities: (a) Names, alphabetically arranged, and latest known address of each person who is or has been security holder; (b) number of securities held by each security holder; and (c) date and particulars of issue and transfer of each security. (1981, c. B-15, §46, 1987, c. 15, §8).

Dealings with Registered Holder.—Corporation or trustee under trust indenture may generally treat registered owner of security as person exclusively entitled to vote, to receive notices, to receive interest, dividend or other payments in respect of security, and otherwise exercise all rights and powers of owner of security. (1981, c. B-15, §47[1]).

Part 6, Division 3 of Act contains elaborate set of provisions governing dealings in corporate securities.

Title of Purchaser.—Upon delivery of security, purchaser acquires rights in security that his transferor had or had authority to convey, except that purchaser who has been party to any fraud or illegality affecting security or who as prior holder had notice of adverse claim does not improve his position by taking from later bona fide purchaser. Bona fide purchaser, in addition to acquiring rights of purchaser, also acquires security free from any adverse claim; but no rights are conferred on bona fide purchaser unless all necessary endorsements are made by appropriate person as defined in §61. (1981, c. B-15, §56).

Part 7. Corporate Borrowing.—Part 7 of Act (am'd 1983, c. 20, §§7-10, 1988, c. P-4.05, §77) sets out specific rules relating to: (a) Trust indentures under which debt obligations are issued by corporation in distribution to public, and (b) qualifications of trustees appointed under those indentures. Provisions require compliance with expressed statutory standards relating to trustee qualifications, conflict of interest and duties; rights of holders of debt obligations to obtain information; and rights of trustee to demand information and from issuing corporation. Trustee's statutory duties will apply irrespective of any contradictory or exculpatory clauses in trust indenture. These provisions are substantially same as corresponding provisions of Canada Business Corporations Act although there are drafting differences which may be found to be of importance.

Personal Property Security Act (S.A. 1988, c. P-4.05) governs registration of all personal property security interests, including corporate debt obligations. Corporate debt obligations relating to real property must be registered at appropriate Alberta Land Titles Office. Under Personal Property Security Act there is no distinction between corporate debt instruments and other debt instruments. There is no 60 day grace period to register corporate debt instrument. All security instruments are treated in accordance with Personal Property Security Act. "Prior security interest" registered under Act prior to Oct. 1, 1990 is deemed to be valid until Oct. 1, 1993 but may be further continued by registration at Personal Property Registry in accordance with Personal Property Security Act. See topic Personal Property Security.

Part 8. Receivers and Receiver-Managers.—Part 8 of Act (as am'd by 1987, c. 15, §9) sets out statutory standards and delegates to court discretion concerning qualifications, functions, rights, powers and duties of receiver and receiver-manager, including his standing with respect to directors, liquidator or trustee in bankruptcy. Receiver required to submit financial statements in form that directors would have been required to submit to shareholders. Powers of directors that receiver-manager is authorized to exercise may not be exercised by directors until discharge of receiver-manager.

Part 9. Directors and Officers.—Subject to any unanimous shareholder agreement, directors must manage business and affairs of corporation. (1981, c. B-15, §97[1]).

Corporation must have one or more directors but corporation, any of whose issued securities are or were part of distribution to public, and remain outstanding and are

See Topical Index in front part of this volume.

CORPORATIONS . . . *continued*
held by more than 15 persons, must have not fewer than three directors, at least two of whom are not officers or employees of corporation or its affiliates. (1981, c. B-15, §97[2]).

Qualifications of Directors.—Following persons are disqualified from being director of corporation: (a) Anyone who is less than 18 years of age; (b) anyone who is dependent adult as defined in Dependent Adults Act or is subject of certificate of incapacity under that Act, is formal patient as defined in Mental Health Act, is subject of order under The Mentally Incapacitated Persons Act appointing committee of his person or estate or both or has been found to be of unsound mind by court elsewhere than in Alberta; (c) person who is not individual; or (d) person who has status of bankrupt. (1981, c. B-15, §100).

Further Qualifications.—Unless articles otherwise provide, director of corporation is not required to hold shares issued by corporation. (1981, c. B-15, §100[2]).

Residency.—At least one half of directors of corporation must be resident Canadians. (1981, c. B-15, §100[3], 1987, c. 15, §10).

Exception for Holding Corporation.—Notwithstanding foregoing, not more than one-third of directors of holding corporation need be resident Canadians if holding corporation earns in Canada directly or through its subsidiaries less than 5% of gross revenues of holding corporation and all of its subsidiary bodies corporate together as shown in most recent consolidated financial statements of holding corporation or most recent financial statements of holding corporation and its subsidiary bodies corporate. (1981, c. B-15, §100[4]).

Election of Directors.—Subject to unanimous shareholders agreement and articles of corporation, shareholders of corporation must, by ordinary resolution at first meeting of shareholders and at each succeeding annual meeting at which election of directors is required, elect directors to hold office for term expiring not later than close of next annual meeting of shareholders following election. It is not necessary that all directors elected at meeting of shareholders hold office for same term. (1981, c. B-15, §101, 1983, c. 20, §11).

Cumulative Voting.—Articles may provide for cumulative voting at election of directors. (1981, c. B-15, §102).

Filling Vacancy.—Subject to Act, unanimous shareholder agreement and articles, quorum of directors may fill vacancy among directors, except vacancy resulting from increase in number or minimum number of directors or from failure to elect number or minimum number of directors required by articles. (1981, c. B-15, §106[1]).

Meeting of Directors.—Unless articles otherwise provide, directors may meet at any place and upon such notice as by-laws require. (1981, c. B-15, §109[1]).

Quorum.—Subject to articles or by-laws, majority of number of directors appointed constitutes quorum at any meeting of directors, and, notwithstanding any vacancy among directors, quorum of directors may exercise all powers of directors. (1981, c. B-15, §109[2], 1983, c. 20, §12).

Canadian Majority.—Subject to §109(4), directors, other than directors of holding corporation earning less than 5% of its gross consolidated revenues in Canada must not transact business at meeting of directors unless at least one half of directors present are resident Canadians. (1981, c. B-15, §109[3], 1987, c. 15, §12).

Participation by Telephone.—If by-laws provide or all directors of corporation consent, director may participate in meeting of directors or of committee of directors by means of such telephone or other communications facilities as permit all persons participating in meeting to hear each other and director in such meeting by such means is deemed for purposes of Act to be present at that meeting. (1981, c. B-15, §109[9]).

Delegation.—Directors of corporation may appoint from their number managing director who is resident Canadian or committee of directors and delegate to such managing director or committee subject to limitations set forth in Act, any powers of directors. If directors of corporation, other than holding corporation earning less than 5% of its gross consolidated revenues in Canada, appoint committee of directors, majority of members of committee must be resident Canadians. (1981, c. B-15, §110, 1987, c. 15, §12).

Resolution in Lieu of Meeting.—Subject to articles, by-laws or unanimous shareholders agreement, resolution in writing, signed by all directors entitled to vote on that resolution at meeting of directors or committee of directors, is as valid as if it had been passed at meeting of directors or committee of directors. (1981, c. B-15, §112[1]).

Resolution in writing dealing with all matters required by this Act to be dealt with at meeting of directors, and signed by all directors entitled to vote at that meeting, satisfies all requirements of this Act relating to meetings of directors. (1981, c. B-15, §112[1.1], 1987, c. 15, §13).

Directors' Liability.—Directors of corporation who vote for or consent to resolution authorizing issue of share for consideration other than money are jointly and severally liable to corporation to make good any amount by which consideration received is less than fair equivalent of money that corporation would have received if share had been issued for money on date of resolution. Director is not liable if he proves that he did not know and could not reasonably have known that share was issued for consideration less than fair equivalent of money that corporation would have received if share had been issued for money. (1981, c. B-15, §113, 1988, c. 7, §3).

Further Directors' Liabilities.—Directors of corporation who vote for or consent to resolution authorizing: (a) Purchase, redemption or other acquisition of shares contrary to §§32, 33, or 34 of Act, (b) commission contrary to §39 of Act, (c) payment of dividend contrary to §40 of Act, (d) financial assistance contrary to §42 of Act, (e) payment of indemnity contrary to §119 of Act, or (f) payment to shareholder contrary to §184 or §234 of Act, are jointly and severally liable to restore to corporation any amounts so distributed or paid and not otherwise recovered by corporation. (1981, c. B-15, §113[3]).

Liability of Directors for Wages.—Directors of corporation are jointly and severally liable to employees of corporation for all debts not exceeding six months wages payable to each such employee for services performed for corporation while they are directors. (1981, c. B-15, §114[1], 1987, c. 15, §14).

Disclosure of Interested Director Contract.—Director or officer of corporation who: (a) Is party to material contract or proposed material contract with corporation, or (b) is director or officer of or has material interest in any person who is party to material contract or proposed material contract with corporation, must disclose in writing to corporation or request to have entered in minutes of meetings of directors nature and extent of his interest. (1981, c. B-15, §115[1], 1987, c. 15, §15[a]).

Time of Disclosure for Director.—Subject to subsection 2.1, disclosure required by director must be made: (a) At meeting at which proposed contract is first considered; (b) if director was not then interested in proposed contract, at first meeting after he becomes so interested; (c) if director becomes interested after contract is made, at first meeting after he becomes so interested; or (d) if person who is interested in contract later becomes director, at first meeting after he becomes director. (1981, c. B-15, §115[2]).

Proposed Contract Dealt With By Resolution.—Where proposed contract is dealt with by resolution under §112 instead of at meeting, disclosure under above provisions shall be made forthwith upon receipt of resolution or if director was not interested in proposed contract at time of receipt of resolution, at first meeting after he becomes interested. (1987, c. 15, §15[b]).

Time of Disclosure for Officer.—Disclosure required by officer who is not director must be made: (a) Forthwith after he becomes aware that contract or proposed contract is to be considered or has been considered at meeting of directors; (b) if officer becomes interested after contract is made, forthwith after he becomes so interested; or (c) if person who is interested in contract later becomes officer, forthwith after he becomes officer. (1981, c. B-15, §115[3]).

Time of Disclosure for Director or Officer.—If material contract or proposed material contract is one that, in ordinary course of corporation's business, would not require approval by directors or shareholders, director or officer must disclose in writing to corporation or request to have entered in minutes of meetings of directors nature and extent of his interest forthwith after director or officer becomes aware of contract or proposed contract. (1981, c. B-15, §115[4]).

Voting After Disclosure.—Director must not vote on any resolution to approve such contract unless contract is: (a) Arrangement by way of security for money lent to or obligations undertaken by him for benefit of corporation or affiliate; (b) one relating primarily to his remuneration as director, officer, employee or agent of corporation or affiliate; (c) one for indemnity or insurance under §119 of Act; or (d) one with affiliate. (1981, c. B-15, §115[5]).

General notice to directors by director or officer, declaring that he is director or officer of or has material interest in person and is to be regarded as interested in any contract made with that person, is sufficient declaration of interest in relation to any contract so made. (1981, c. B-15, §115[6]).

Avoidance Standards.—Material contract between corporation and one or more of its directors or officers, or between corporation and another person of which director or officer of corporation is director or officer or in which he has material interest, is neither void nor voidable by reason only of that relationship or by reason only that director with interest in contract is present at or is counted to determine presence of quorum at meeting of directors or committee of directors that authorized contract, and director, officer, former director or officer of corporation to whom profit accrues as result of making contract is not liable to account by reason only of holding office, if director or officer disclosed his interest in accordance with Act and contract was approved by directors or shareholders and it was reasonable and fair to corporation at time it was approved. (1981, c. B-15, §115[7]).

Duty of Care of Directors and Officers.—Every director and officer of corporation in exercising his powers and discharging his duties must: (a) Act honestly and in good faith with view to best interests of corporation; and (b) exercise care, diligence and skill that reasonably prudent person would exercise in comparable circumstances, and comply with Act, regulations, articles, by-laws and unanimous shareholder agreement. (1981, c. B-15, §117).

Dissent by Director.—Director present at meeting of directors or committee of directors deemed to have consented to resolution or action taken at meeting unless dissent made as prescribed by Act. (1981, c. B-15, §118[1]).

No Exculpation.—Subject to unanimous shareholders agreement, no provision in contract, articles, by-laws or resolution relieves director or officer from duty to act in accordance with Act or regulations or relieves him from liability for breach thereof. (1981, c. B-15, §117[3]).

Reliance on Statements.—Director is not liable under above provisions if he relies in good faith on: (a) Financial statements of corporation represented to him by officer of corporation or in written report of auditor of corporation fairly to reflect financial condition of corporation; or (b) report of lawyer, accountant, engineer, appraiser or other person whose profession lends credibility to statement made by him. (1981, c. B-15, §118[3]).

Indemnification.—Except in respect of action by or on behalf of corporation or body corporate to procure judgment in its favour, corporation may indemnify director or officer of corporation, former director or officer of corporation or person who acts or acted at corporation's request as director or officer of body corporate of which corporation is or was shareholder or creditor, and his heirs and legal representatives, against all costs, charges and expenses, including amount paid to settle action or satisfy judgment, reasonably incurred by him in respect of any civil, criminal or administrative action or proceeding to which he is made party by reason of being or having been director or officer of such corporation or body corporate, if: (a) He acted honestly and in good faith with view to best interests of corporation; and (b) in case of criminal or administrative action or proceeding that is enforced by monetary penalty, he had reasonable grounds for believing that his conduct was lawful. (1981, c. B-15, §119[1]).

Corporation may with approval of court indemnify person referred to in foregoing paragraph in respect of action by or on behalf of corporation or body corporate to procure judgment in its favour, to which he is made party by reason of being or having been director or officer of corporation or body corporate, against all costs, charges and expenses reasonably incurred by him in connection with such action if he fulfils conditions set out in clauses (a) and (b) above. (1981, c. B-15, §119[2]).

Right to Indemnify.—Notwithstanding anything contained above, corporation must indemnify any such person who has been substantially successful in defence of any civil, criminal or administrative action or proceeding to which he is made party by reason of being or having been director or officer of corporation or body corporate and who is fairly and reasonably entitled to indemnity and fulfils conditions set out in clauses (a) and (b) above, against all costs, charges and expenses reasonably incurred by him in respect of such action or proceeding. (1981, c. B-15, §119[3]).

See Topical Index in front part of this volume.

CORPORATIONS . . . *continued*

Directors' and Officers' Insurance.—Corporation may purchase and maintain insurance for benefit of any such person against any liability incurred by him in his capacity as director or officer of corporation or in his capacity as director or officer of another body corporate if he acts or acted at corporation's request, except where liability relates to failure to act honestly and in good faith with view to best interests of corporation or body corporate. (1981, c. B-15, §119[4]).

Part 10. Insider Trading.—"Insider" in this part means: (a) Corporation; (b) affiliate of corporation; (c) director or officer of corporation; (d) person who beneficially owns at least 10% of voting shares of corporation or who exercises control or direction over at least 10% of votes attached to shares of corporation; (e) person employed or retained by corporation on professional or consulting basis; and (f) person who receives specific confidential information from person described in paragraph or §123 including person described in this clause (f) and who has knowledge that person giving information is person described in this paragraph or §123 including person described in this clause (f). (1981, c. B-15, §121).

For purposes of this part, director or officer of subsidiary body corporate is deemed insider of holding corporation, and person is deemed to own beneficially shares beneficially owned by body corporate controlled by him. (1981, c. B-15, §122).

For purposes of this Part if body corporate becomes insider of corporation, or enters into business combination with corporation, director or officer of body corporate is deemed to have been insider of corporation for previous six months or for such shorter period as he was director or officer of body corporate; and if corporation becomes insider of body corporate, or enters into business combination with body corporate, director or officer of body corporate is deemed to have been insider of corporation for previous six months or for such shorter period as he was director or officer of body corporate. (1981, c. B-15, §123).

In paragraph above, "business combination" means acquisition of all or substantially all property of one body corporate by another or amalgamation of two or more bodies corporate. (1981, c. B-15, §124).

Civil Liability.—Insider who, in connection with transaction in security of corporation or any of its affiliates, makes use of any specific confidential information for his own benefit or advantage that, if generally known, might reasonably be expected to affect materially value of security: (a) Is liable to compensate any person for any direct loss suffered by that person as result of transaction, unless information was known or in exercise of reasonable diligence should have been known to that person at time of transaction; and (b) is accountable to corporation for any direct benefit or advantage received or receivable by insider as result of transaction. (1981, c. B-15, §125).

Part 11. Shareholders.—

Place of Meetings.—Meetings of shareholders of corporation must be held at place within Alberta provided in by-laws or, in absence of such provisions, at place within Alberta that directors determine. (1981, c. B-15, §126[1]).

Meeting Outside Alberta.—Meeting of shareholders of corporation may be held outside Alberta if all shareholders entitled to vote at that meeting so agree. (1981, c. B-15, §126[2]).

Calling Meetings.—Directors of corporation: (a) Must call annual meeting of shareholders not later than 18 months after corporation comes into existence and subsequently not later than 15 months after holding last preceding annual meeting; (b) may at any time call special meeting of shareholders; and (c) may fix in advance date as record date for purpose of determining shareholders (i) entitled to receive payment of dividend, (ii) entitled to participate in liquidation distribution, or (iii) for any other purpose including right to receive notice of or to vote at meeting. (1981, c. B-15, §§127 as am'd, 128).

Notice of Meeting.—Notice of time and place of meeting of shareholders must be sent not less than 21 days nor more than 50 days before meeting: (a) To each shareholder entitled to vote at meeting; (b) to each director; and (c) to auditor of corporation. (1981, c. B-15, §129[1] as am'd).

All business transacted at special meeting of shareholders and all business transacted at annual meeting of shareholders, except consideration of financial statements and auditor's report, fixing number of directors for following year, election of directors and reappointment of incumbent auditor, is deemed to be special business. (1981, c. B-15, §129[6]).

Notice of Business.—Notice of meeting of shareholders at which special business is to be transacted must state: (a) Nature of that business in sufficient detail to permit shareholder to form reasoned judgment thereon; and (b) text of any special resolution to be submitted to meeting. (1981, c. B-15, §129[7]).

Shareholder Proposal.—Shareholder entitled to vote at annual meeting of shareholders may: (a) Submit to corporation notice of any matter that he proposes to raise at meeting (hereinafter referred to as "proposal"); and (b) discuss at meeting any matter in respect of which he would have been entitled to submit proposal. (1981, c. B-15, §131[1]).

Information Circular.—Corporation that solicits proxies must set out proposal in management proxy circular or attach proposal thereto and, if so requested by shareholder, must include in management proxy circular or attach thereto statement by shareholder of not more than 200 words in support of proposal, and name and address of shareholder. (1981, c. B-15, §131[2], [3]).

Nomination for Director.—Proposal may include nominations for election of directors if proposal is signed by one or more holders of shares representing in aggregate not less than 5% of shares or 5% of shares of class of shares of corporation entitled to vote at meeting to which proposal is to be presented, but this provision does not preclude nominations made at meeting of shareholders. (1981, c. B-15, §131[4]).

Corporation is not required to set out proposal or supporting statement of shareholder in management proxy circular or attach proposal or statement thereto if: (a) Proposal is not submitted to corporation at least 90 days before anniversary date of previous annual meeting of shareholders; (b) it clearly appears that proposal is submitted by shareholder primarily for purposes of enforcing personal claim or redressing personal grievance against corporation or its directors, officers or security holders, or primarily for purpose of promoting general economic, political, racial, religious, social or similar causes; (c) corporation, at shareholder's request, included proposal in management proxy circular relating to meeting of shareholders held within two years preceding receipt of such request, and shareholder failed to present proposal, in person or by proxy, at meeting; (d) substantially same proposal was submitted to shareholders in management proxy circular or dissident's proxy circular relating to meeting of shareholders held within two years preceding receipt of shareholder's request and proposal was defeated; or (e) rights conferred by this provision are being abused to secure publicity. (1981, c. B-15, §131[5]).

Notice of Refusal.—If corporation refuses to include proposal in management proxy circular, corporation must, within ten days after receiving proposal, notify shareholder submitting proposal of its intention to omit proposal from management proxy circular and send to him statement of reasons for refusal. (1981, c. B-15, §131[7]).

Shareholder Application in Court.—On application of shareholder claiming to be aggrieved by corporation's refusal to include proposal in management proxy circular, court may restrain holding of meeting to which proposal is sought to be presented and make any further order it thinks fits. (1981, c. B-15, §131[8]).

Shareholder List.—Corporation having more than 15 shareholders entitled to vote must prepare list of shareholders entitled to receive notice of meeting arranged in alphabetical order and showing number of shares held by each shareholder. (1981, c. B-15, §132([1]).

Examination of List.—Shareholder may examine list of shareholders: (a) During usual business hours at records office of corporation or at place where its central securities register is maintained; and (b) at meeting of shareholders for which list was prepared. (1981, c. B-15, §132[4]).

Quorum.—Unless by-laws otherwise provide, holders of majority of shares entitled to vote at meeting of shareholders present in person or by proxy constitute quorum. (1981, c. B-15, §133).

One Shareholder Meeting.—If corporation has only one shareholder, or only one holder of any class or series of shares, shareholder present in person or by proxy constitutes meeting. (1981, c. B-15, §133[4]).

Right to Vote.—Unless articles otherwise provide, each share of corporation entitles holder thereof to one vote at meeting of shareholders. (1981, c. B-15, §134[1]).

Voting.—Unless by-laws otherwise provide, voting at meeting of shareholders shall be by show of hands except where ballot is demanded by shareholder or proxyholder entitled to vote at meeting. (1981, c. B-15, §135[1]).

Resolution in Lieu of Meeting.—Resolution in writing signed by all shareholders entitled to vote on that resolution at meeting of shareholders is as valid as if it had been passed at meeting of shareholders; and resolution in writing dealing with all matters required by Act to be dealt with at meeting of shareholders and signed by all shareholders entitled to vote at that meeting satisfies all requirements of Act relating to meetings of shareholders. (1981, c. B-15, §136).

Requisition of Meeting.—Holders of not less than 5% of issued shares of corporation that carry right to vote at meeting sought to be held may requisition directors to call meeting of shareholders for purposes stated in requisition. (1981, c. B-15, §137).

Court Review of Election.—Corporation, shareholder or director may apply to court to determine any controversy with respect to election or appointment of director or auditor of corporation. (1981, c. B-15, §139[1]).

Pooling Agreement.—Written agreement between two or more shareholders may provide that in exercising voting rights shares held by them shall be voted as therein provided. (1981, c. B-15, §139.1).

Unanimous shareholders agreement may provide for: (a) Regulation of rights and liabilities of shareholders; (b) regulation of election of directors; (c) management of business and affairs of corporation including restriction or abrogation of powers of directors; (d) any other matter permitted under Act. (1981, c. B-15, §140[1]).

If bona fide purchaser without notice acquires shares of corporation which are subject to unanimous shareholders agreement, that person will be deemed to be party to agreement, which issue of shares will not terminate; however, purchaser may: (a) Rescind contract under which shares were acquired from corporation or (b) if share acquired from other than corporation, file notice of objection with corporation. (1981, c. B-15, §140[2][3][4]).

Shareholder who is party to unanimous shareholder agreement has all rights, powers, liabilities and duties of director of corporation to which agreement relates to extent that agreement restricts powers of directors to manage business and affairs of corporation, and directors are thereby relieved of their duties and liabilities to same extent. (1981, c. B-15, §140[7]).

Part 12. Proxies.—

Appointing Proxyholder.—Shareholder entitled to vote at meeting of shareholders may by means of proxy appoint proxyholder and one or more alternative proxyholders who are not required to be shareholders, to attend and act at meeting in manner and to extent authorized by proxy and with authority conferred by proxy. (1981, c. B-15, §142[1]).

Mandatory Solicitation.—Management of corporation must concurrently with giving notice of meeting of shareholders send form of proxy in prescribed form to each shareholder who is entitled to receive notice of meeting unless corporation has fewer than 16 shareholders, two or more joint holders being counted as one shareholder, or if all shareholders entitled to vote at meeting of shareholders agree in writing to waive proxy requirements. (1981, c. B-15, §143).

Soliciting Proxies.—Person must not solicit proxies unless: (a) In case of solicitation by or on behalf of management of corporation, management proxy circular in prescribed form, either as appendix to or as separate document accompanying notice of meeting, or (b) in case of any other solicitation, dissident's proxy circular in prescribed form stating purposes of solicitation, is sent to auditor of corporation, to each shareholder whose proxy is solicited and, if solicitation other than by or on behalf of management, to corporation. (1981, c. B-15, §144 as am'd).

Copy to Executive Director.—Person required to send management proxy circular or dissident's proxy circular must, if corporation is distributing corporation, file concurrently copy thereof with Executive Director together with copy of notice of meeting, form of proxy and any other documents for use in connection with meeting. (1981, c. B-15, §144[3] as am'd).

Exemption Orders.—On application of interested person, Alberta Securities Commission established under Securities Act (Alberta) ("Commission") if corporation is distributing corporation, or court if corporation is not distributing corporation, may

See Topical Index in front part of this volume.

CORPORATIONS . . . *continued*
make order on such terms it thinks fit exempting such person from above requirements respecting proxy solicitation which order may have retrospective effect. (1981, c. B-15, §145 as am'd).

Attendance at Meeting.—Person who solicits proxy and is appointed proxyholder must attend in person or cause alternative proxyholder to attend meeting in respect of which proxy is given and comply with directions of shareholder who appointed him. (1981, c. B-15, §146[1]).

Duty of Registrant.—Shares of corporation that are registered in name of registrant or his nominee (usually broker) and not beneficially owned by registrant must not be voted unless registrant forthwith after receipt of notice of meeting, financial statements, management proxy circular, dissident's proxy circular and any other documents other than form of proxy, sent to shareholders by or on behalf of any person for use in connection with meeting, sends to beneficial owner: (a) Copy of those documents, and (b) except where registrant has received written voting instructions from beneficial owner, written request for such instructions. (1981, c. B-15, §147[1]).

Beneficial Owner Unknown.—Registrant must not vote or appoint proxyholder to vote shares registered in his name or in name of his nominee that he does not beneficially own unless he receives voting instructions from beneficial owner. (1981, c. B-15, §147[2]).

Instructions to Registrant.—Registrant shall vote or appoint proxyholder to vote any such shares in accordance with any written voting instructions received from beneficial owner. (1981, c. B-15, §147[4]).

Part 13. Financial Disclosure.—

Annual Financial Statements.—Directors of corporation, except corporation subject to and that complies with Securities Act (Alberta) provisions regarding placing financial statements before shareholders at every annual meeting, must place before shareholders at every annual meeting: (a) Comparative financial statements as prescribed by Act; (b) report of auditor, if any; and (c) any further information respecting financial position of corporation and results of its operations required by articles, by-laws or any unanimous shareholder agreement. (1981, c. B-15, §§149[1] and 150[1] as am'd).

Exemption.—Distributing corporation may apply to Alberta Securities Commission ("Commission") for order authorizing corporation to omit from its financial statements any item prescribed, or to dispense with publication of any particular financial statement prescribed, and Commission may, if it reasonably believes that disclosure of information therein contained would be detrimental to corporation, permit such omission on such reasonable conditions as it thinks fit. (1981, c. B-15, §150[2] as am'd).

Consolidated Statements.—Corporation shall keep at its records office copy of financial statements of each subsidiary body corporate and of each body corporate the accounts of which are consolidated in financial statements of corporation. (1981, c. B-15, §151[1]).

Examination.—Shareholders of corporation and their agents and legal representatives may on request examine above statements during usual business hours of corporation and may make extracts therefrom free of charge unless on application to court, court is satisfied that such examination would be detrimental to corporation or subsidiary body corporate and bars such right and makes any further order it thinks fit. (1981, c. B-15, §151[2][3]).

Approval of Financial Statements.—Directors of corporation must approve above financial statements and approval must be evidenced by signature of one or more directors. (1981, c. B-15, §152[1]).

Copies to Shareholders.—Corporation must not less than 21 days before each annual meeting of shareholders or before signing of shareholders' resolution in lieu of annual meeting, send copy of financial statements, report of auditor, if any, and any other information required by articles, by-laws or any unanimous shareholders agreement to each shareholder, except to shareholder who has informed corporation in writing that he does not want copy of those documents. (1981, c. B-15, §153).

Copies to Executive Director.—Distributing corporation must at least 21 days before each annual meeting of shareholders or forthwith after signing of shareholders' resolution in lieu of annual meeting and in any event not later than 15 months after last date when last preceding annual meeting should have been held, or resolution in lieu of annual meeting should have been signed, file copy of financial statements, report of auditor, if any, and any other information sent to shareholders or to public authority or recognized stock exchange with Executive Director. (1981, c. B-15, §154 as am'd).

Qualification of Auditor.—Unless granted exemption by court order, person is disqualified from being auditor of corporation if he is not independent of corporation, its affiliates and directors and officers of corporation and its affiliates. (1981, c. B-15, §155).

Appointment of Auditor.—Shareholders of corporation must appoint auditor by ordinary resolution, at first annual meeting of shareholders and at each succeeding annual meeting, to hold office until close of next annual meeting. (1981, c. B-15, §156[1]).

If auditor is not appointed at meeting of shareholders, incumbent auditor continues in office until his successor is appointed. (1981, c. B-15, §156[3]).

Remuneration of auditor may be fixed by ordinary resolution of shareholders or, if not so fixed, may be fixed by directors. (1981, c. B-15, §156[4]).

Dispensing with Auditor.—Shareholders of other than distributing corporation may resolve not to appoint auditor with consent of all shareholders including those not otherwise entitled to vote, but resolution valid only until next succeeding annual meeting of shareholders. (1981, c. B-15, §157).

Removal of Auditor.—Shareholders of corporation may by ordinary resolution at special meeting remove auditor from office except auditor appointed by court. (1981, c. B-15, §159).

Filling Vacancy.—Subject to articles of corporation, directors must forthwith fill vacancy in office of auditor. (1981, c. B-15, §160).

Right to Attend Meeting.—Auditor of corporation is entitled to receive notice of every meeting of shareholders and, at expense of corporation, to attend and be heard thereat on matters relating to duties as auditor. (1981, c. B-15, §162[1] as am'd).

If director or shareholder of corporation, whether or not shareholder entitled to vote, gives written notice to auditor or former auditor at least ten days before shareholders meeting, auditor or former auditor must attend at expense of corporation and answer questions relating to duties as auditor. (1981, c. B-15, §162[2]).

Right to Information.—On demand of auditor of corporation, present or former directors, officers, employees or agents or former auditors of corporation must furnish such: (a) Information and explanations, and (b) access to records, documents, books, accounts and vouchers of corporation or any of its subsidiaries; as are, in opinion of auditor, necessary to make examination and report required under Act and that directors, officers, employees, agents or former auditors are reasonably able to furnish. (1981, c. B-15, §163[1]).

Audit Committee.—Unless dispensed with by order of Alberta Securities Commission, distributing corporation must have and other corporations may have audit committee. Audit committee of distributing corporation shall be composed of not less than three directors of corporation, majority of whom are not officers or employees of corporation or any of its affiliates. Auditor of corporation is entitled to receive notice of every meeting of audit committee and, at expense of corporation, to attend and be heard thereat. (1981, c. B-15, §165 as am'd).

Duty of Committee.—Audit committee must review financial statements of corporation before such financial statements are approved by directors. (1981, c. B-15, §165[4]).

Error in Financial Statements.—Director or officer of corporation must forthwith notify audit committee and auditor of any error or misstatement of which he becomes aware in financial statement that auditor or former auditor has reported on. If auditor or former auditor of corporation is notified or becomes aware of error or misstatement in financial statement upon which he has reported, and if in his opinion error or misstatement is material, he must inform each director accordingly. (1981, c. B-15, §165[7] and [8]).

Duty of Directors.—When auditor or former auditor informs directors of such error or misstatement in financial statement, directors must: (a) Prepare and issue revised financial statement or otherwise inform shareholders; and (b) if corporation is distributing corporation, it must file revised financial statements with Executive Director or must inform Executive Director of error or misstatement in same manner as it informs shareholders. (1981, c. B-15, §165[9]).

Qualified Privilege (Defamation).—Any oral or written statement or report made under Act by auditor or former auditor of corporation has qualified privilege (for purpose of law of defamation). (1981, c. B-15, §166).

Part 14. Fundamental Changes.—

Amendment of Articles.—Articles of corporation may by special resolution be amended to change corporation's name; restrictions on business; number, classes, designations, rights, privileges and restrictions on its shares; change, divide and cancel classes of shares; stated capital; number of directors (subject to right of incumbent directors and cumulative voting provisions); restrictions on transfer of shares and any other provision that is permitted by Act to be set out in articles. (1981, c. B-15, §§36, 167, as am'd).

Constraints on Share Transfers.—Subject to class voting provisions and reduction of stated capital provisions of Act, distributing corporation may by special resolution amend its articles to constrain issue or transfer of its shares in accordance with regulations: (a) to persons who are not resident Canadians; or (b) to enable corporation or affiliates to qualify under any laws of Canada referred to in regulations (i) to obtain licence to carry on business, (ii) to become publisher of Canadian newspaper or periodical, or (iii) to acquire shares of financial intermediary as defined in regulations. (1981, c. B-15, §168[2] as am'd).

Proposal to Amend.—Directors or any shareholder entitled to vote at annual meeting may make proposal to amend articles. Notice of meeting of shareholders at which proposal to amend articles is to be considered shall set out proposed amendment and where applicable, shall state that dissenting shareholder is entitled to be paid fair value of his shares in accordance with Act, but failure to make that statement does not invalidate amendment. (1981, c. B-15, §169).

Class Vote.—Holders of shares of class or, of series (if such series is affected by amendment in manner different from other shares of same class) are entitled to vote (whether or not shares of such class or series otherwise carry right to vote) separately as class or series upon proposal to amend articles to: (a) Increase or decrease any maximum number of authorized shares of such class, (a.1) increase maximum number of authorized shares of class having rights or privileges equal or superior to shares of such class; (b) effect exchange, reclassification or cancellation of all or part of shares of such class; (c) add, change or remove rights, privileges, restrictions or conditions attached to shares of such class; (d) increase rights or privileges of any class of shares having rights or privileges equal or superior to shares of such class; (e) create new class of shares equal or superior to shares of such class; (f) make any class of shares having rights or privileges inferior to shares of such class equal or superior to shares of such class; (g) effect exchange or create right of exchange of all or part of shares of another class into shares of such class; or (h) constrain issue or transfer of shares of such class or extend or remove such constraint. (1981, c. B-15, §170 as am'd).

No amendment to articles affects existing cause of action or claim or liability to prosecution in favour of or against corporation or its directors or officers, or any civil, criminal or administrative action or proceeding to which corporation or its directors or officers is party. (1981, c. B-15, §173[2]).

Amalgamation.—Two or more corporations, including holding and subsidiary corporations, may amalgamate and continue as one corporation. Each corporation proposing to amalgamate must enter into agreement setting out terms and means of effecting amalgamation. (1981, c. B-15, §§175, 176).

Shareholder Approval.—Directors of each amalgamating corporation must submit amalgamation agreement for approval to meeting of holders of shares of amalgamating corporation of which they are directors. (1981, c. B-15, §177[1]).

Each share of amalgamating corporation carries right to vote in respect of amalgamation whether or not it otherwise carries right to vote. (1981, c. B-15, §177[3]).

Amalgamation agreement is adopted when shareholders of each amalgamating corporation have approved of amalgamation by special resolutions of each class or series of such shareholders entitled to vote thereon. (1981, c. B-15, §177[4][5]).

Vertical Short-form Amalgamation.—Holding corporation and one or more of its wholly-owned subsidiary corporations may amalgamate and continue as one corporation without entering into amalgamation agreement and without obtaining shareholders approval if amalgamation is approved by resolution of directors of each amalgamating

See Topical Index in front part of this volume.

CORPORATIONS . . . *continued*
corporation and resolutions provide that: (a) Shares of each amalgamating subsidiary corporation shall be cancelled without any repayment of capital in respect thereof; (b) except as may be prescribed, articles of amalgamation shall be same as articles of incorporation of amalgamating holding corporation, and (c) no securities shall be issued by amalgamated corporation in connection with amalgamation. (1981, c. B-15, §178[1]).

Horizontal Short-form Amalgamation.—Two or more wholly-owned subsidiary corporations of same holding body corporate may amalgamate and continue as one corporation without entering into amalgamation agreement and without obtaining shareholder approval if amalgamation is approved by resolution of directors of each amalgamating corporation and resolutions provide that: (a) Shares of all but one of amalgamating subsidiary corporations shall be cancelled without any repayment of capital in respect thereof, (b) except as may be prescribed, articles of amalgamation shall be same as articles of incorporation of amalgamating subsidiary corporation whose shares are not cancelled, and (c) stated capital of amalgamating subsidiary corporations whose shares are cancelled shall be added to stated capital of amalgamating subsidiary corporation whose shares are not cancelled. (1981, c. B-15, §178[2]).

Effect of Certificate.—On date shown in certificate of amalgamation: (a) Amalgamation of amalgamating corporations and their continuance as one corporation become effective; (b) property of each amalgamating corporation continues to be property of amalgamated corporation; (c) amalgamated corporation continues to be liable for obligations of each amalgamating corporation; (d) existing cause of action, claim or liability to prosecution is unaffected; (e) civil, criminal or administrative action or proceeding pending by or against amalgamating corporation may be continued to be prosecuted by or against amalgamated corporation; (f) conviction against, or ruling, order or judgment in favour of or against, amalgamating corporation may be enforced by or against amalgamated corporation; and (g) articles of amalgamation are deemed to be articles of incorporation of amalgamated corporation and certificate of amalgamation is deemed to be certificate of incorporation of amalgamated corporation. (1981, c. B-15, §180).

Amalgamation with Extra-Provincial Corporation.—Corporation may amalgamate with extra-provincial corporation and continue as one corporation under Act where extra-provincial corporation is authorized to amalgamate both corporations by incorporating jurisdiction and one is subsidiary wholly owned by other. Such corporations must enter into amalgamation agreement as prescribed by Act. Such amalgamation is adopted when: (a) Agreement is approved by directors of both corporations and (b) other corporation has complied with laws of its jurisdiction. (1981, c. B-15, §180.1).

Continuance of Extra-Provincial Corporation in Alberta.—Extra-provincial corporation may, if so authorized by laws of its jurisdiction, apply to Registrar for certificate of continuance. On date shown on certificates: (a) It becomes corporation to which Act applies, (b) articles of continuance are deemed to be articles of incorporation and (c) certificate of continuance is deemed to be certificate of incorporation. (1981, B-15, §181 as am'd).

Continuance (Export).—Corporation may, if it is authorized by special resolution of shareholders, if it establishes to satisfaction of Registrar that its proposed continuance in another jurisdiction will not adversely affect creditors or shareholders of corporation and if certain statutory prerequisites are satisfied, apply to appropriate official or public body of another jurisdiction requesting that corporation be continued as if it had been incorporated under laws of that other jurisdiction. (1981, c. B-15, §182).

Right to Vote.—Each share of corporation carries right to vote in respect of continuance whether or not it otherwise carries right to vote. (1981, c. B-15, §182[3]).

Prohibition.—Corporation shall not be continued as body corporate under laws of another jurisdiction unless those laws provide in effect that: (a) Property of corporation continues to be property of body corporate; (b) body corporate continues to be liable for obligations of corporation; (c) existing cause of action, claim or liability to prosecution is unaffected; (d) civil, criminal or administrative action or proceeding pending by or against corporation may be continued to be prosecuted by or against body corporate; and (e) conviction against, or ruling, order or judgment in favour of or against corporation may be enforced by or against body corporate. (1981, c. B-15, §182[9]).

Extraordinary Sale, Lease or Exchange.—Sale, lease or exchange of all or substantially all property of corporation other than in ordinary course of business of corporation requires approval of shareholders. (1981, c. B-15, §183[1]).

Right to Vote.—Each share of corporation carries right to vote in respect of such sale, lease or exchange whether or not it otherwise carries right to vote. (1981, c. B-15, §183[4]).

Shareholder Approval.—Such sale, lease or exchange is adopted when holders of each class or series entitled to vote thereon have approved of sale, lease or exchange by special resolution. (1981, c. B-15, §183[6]).

Right to Dissent.—Holder of shares of any class of corporation may dissent if order is made under Act permitting dissent or if corporation resolves to: (a) Amend its articles to add, change or remove any provisions restricting or constraining issue or transfer of shares of that class; (b) amend its articles to add, change or remove any restriction upon business or businesses that corporation may carry on; (c) amalgamate with another corporation, otherwise than amalgamation of holding corporation and one or more of its wholly-owned subsidiaries, or with extra-provincial corporation where one is wholly-owned subsidiary of other; (d) be continued under laws of another jurisdiction; or (e) sell, lease or exchange all or substantially all its property. (1981, c. B-15, §184[1] as am'd).

Payment for Shares.—In addition to any other right he may have, shareholder who complies with this provision is entitled, when action approved by resolution from which he dissents or order becomes effective, to be paid by corporation fair value of shares held by him in respect of which he dissents, determined as of close of business on day before resolution was adopted or order made. (1981, c. B-15, §184[3] as am'd).

Objection.—Dissenting shareholder must send to corporation, at or before any meeting of shareholders at which resolution referred to above is to be voted on, written objection to resolution, unless corporation did not give notice to shareholder of purpose of meeting and of his right to dissent, then within reasonable time of learning of resolution and right. (1981, c. B-15, §184[5] as am'd).

Offer to Pay.—Unless otherwise ordered, upon application to fix fair value corporation must send to each dissenting shareholder who has sent demand for payment to corporation written offer to pay for his shares in amount considered by directors of corporation to be fair value thereof. (1981, c. B-15, §184[7] as am'd).

Same Terms.—Every offer made for shares of same class or series must be on same terms and show how fair value was determined. (1981, c. B-15, §184[9] as am'd).

Powers of Court.—Upon such application to court, court may determine whether other dissenting shareholders should be joined as parties, and court must then fix fair value for shares of all dissenting shareholders. Court may in its discretion appoint one or more appraisers to assist court to fix fair value for shares of dissenting shareholders. (1981, c. B-15, §184[12][13] as am'd).

If corporation shall not make payment to shareholder under Act, dissenting shareholder may: (a) Withdraw his notice of objection in which case corporation is deemed to consent to withdrawal and shareholder is reinstated to his full rights as shareholder; or (b) retain status as claimant against corporation, to be paid as soon as corporation is lawfully able to do so or, in liquidation, to be ranked subordinate to rights of creditors of corporation but in priority to its shareholders. (1981, c. B-15, §184[19] as am'd).

Limitation.—Corporation must not make payment to dissenting shareholder under these provisions if there are reasonable grounds for believing that: (a) Corporation is or would after payment be unable to pay its liabilities as they become due; or (b) realizable value of corporation's assets would thereby be less than aggregate of its liabilities. (1981, c. B-15, §184[20] as am'd).

Part 15. Corporate Reorganization.—
"Reorganization" Defined.—In following provisions, order for "reorganization" means court order made under: (a) Relief from oppression provisions of Act, (b) Bankruptcy and Insolvency Act approving proposal, or (c) any other Act of Parliament or of Legislature that affects rights among corporation, its shareholders and creditors. (1981, c. B-15, §185[1]).

Powers of Court.—If corporation is subject to order for reorganization, its articles may be amended by such order to effect any change that might lawfully be made by amendment of articles under Act. (1981, c. B-15, §185[2]).

If court makes order for reorganizations court may also: (a) Authorize issue of debt obligations of corporation, whether or not convertible into shares of any class or having attached any rights or options to acquire shares of any class, and fix terms thereof; and (b) appoint directors in place of or in addition to all or any of directors then in office. (1981, c. B-15, §185[3]).

Articles of Reorganization.—After such order has been made, articles of reorganization in prescribed form shall be sent to Registrar together with other documents required by Act, if applicable. (1981, c. B-15, §185[4]).

Effect of Certificate.—Reorganization becomes effective on date shown in certificate of amendment and articles of incorporation are amended accordingly. (1981, c. B-15, §185[6]).

No Dissent.—Shareholder is not entitled to dissenting shareholders' appraisal remedy if amendment to articles of incorporation is effected under this provision. (1981, c. B-15, §185[7]).

"Arrangement" Defined.—Includes amendment to articles, amalgamation of two or more corporations, amalgamation of body corporate with corporation that results in amalgamated corporation, division of business, transfer of all or substantially all property of corporation to another body corporate in exchange for money, property or securities, exchange of securities of corporation held by security holders for property, money or other securities of this or another body corporate that is not take-over bid, liquidation and dissolution of corporation, or compromise between corporation and its creditors or corporation and its shareholders or holders of debt obligations or any combination thereof. (1981, c. B-15, §186[1]).

Powers of Court.—Corporation or security holder or creditor of corporation may apply to court for order approving proposed arrangement. Court shall, unless it dismisses application, order meeting of shareholders or class or classes of shareholders to vote on proposed arrangement and order meeting of creditors or holders of debt obligation or options or rights to acquire securities or any class of those persons if court considers that those persons are affected by proposed arrangement. Court may, with respect to those meetings, give directions, with respect to calling and notice of meeting, conduct of meeting, requisite majority and any other matter it thinks fit and may make order appointing counsel to represent shareholders. (1981, c. B-15, §186[2][4]).

Articles of Arrangement.—After such order made, articles of arrangement in prescribed form shall be sent to Registrar. Arrangement becomes effective on date shown in certificate of amendment. (1981, c. B-15, §186[10][12]).

Part 16. Takeover Bids.—Takeover bid means offer made to shareholders to acquire all shares of any class of offeree corporation not already owned by offeror, and includes repurchase by corporation of all shares of any class which leaves outstanding voting shares. (1981, c. B-15, §187[g]).

If within time limited by bid or Act, offerees holding 90% or more of shares to which bid relates accept bid, offeror may acquire remaining shares. Notice to remaining holders to be made within 60 days of termination of bid or within 180 days of takeover bid. (1981, c. B-15, §§188, 189). Dissenting shareholders can accept same terms as in takeover bid or demand payment of fair value. Shareholders electing payment of fair value must give notice and make application to court. (1981, c. B-15, §189).

Part 17. Liquidation and Dissolution.—Part 17 of Act contains detailed provisions concerning substantive and procedural law on liquidation and dissolution of corporation which is not insolvent within meaning of Bankruptcy and Insolvency Act of Canada. This Part governs, among other things, revival of corporation dissolved under Act, dissolution of corporation that has not commenced business and making of proposal for voluntary liquidation and dissolution of corporation.

Insolvency.—Proceedings to dissolve or liquidate and dissolve shall be stayed if corporation insolvent within meaning of Bankruptcy and Insolvency Act of Canada. (1981, c. B-15, §200, as am'd).

Dissolution.—Corporation that has not issued shares and has no property or liabilities may be dissolved at any time by all directors. (1981, c. B-15, §203[1]). Corporation that has no property or liabilities may be dissolved by special resolution of

See Topical Index in front part of this volume.

CORPORATIONS . . . *continued*
shareholders. (1981, c. B-15, §203[2]). Corporation ceases to exist on date shown in certificate of dissolution from Registrar. (1981, c. B-15, §203[6]).

Dissolution by Registrar.—Where corporation: (a) Has not commenced business within three years after date shown in its certificate of incorporation, (b) has not carried on its business for three consecutive years, or (c) is in default for period of one year in sending to Registrar any notice or document required by Act; Registrar may dissolve corporation by issuing certificate of dissolution under Act or he may apply to court for order dissolving corporation. (1981, c. B-15, §205 as am'd).

Grounds for Dissolution.—Registrar or any interested person may apply to court for order dissolving corporation if corporation has: (a) Failed for two or more consecutive years to comply with requirements of Act with respect to holding of annual meetings of shareholders, (b) carried on any business or exercised any power that it is restricted by its articles from carrying on or exercising, (c) denied access to corporate records to persons authorized under Act to have access to same, (d) failed to comply with certain of financial disclosure requirements of Act, or (e) procured any certificate under Act by misrepresentation. (1981, c. B-15, §206 as am'd).

Court may order liquidation and dissolution of corporation or any of its affiliated corporations upon application of shareholder: (a) If court is satisfied that in respect of corporation or any of its affiliates (i) any act or omission of corporation or any of its affiliates effects result, (ii) business or affairs of corporation or any of its affiliates are or have been carried on or conducted in manner, or (iii) powers of directors of corporation or any of its affiliates are or have been exercised in manner; that is oppressive or unfairly prejudicial to or that unfairly disregards interests of any security holder, creditor, director or officer; or (b) if court is satisfied that (i) unanimous shareholder agreement entitles complaining shareholder to demand dissolution of corporation after occurrence of specified event and that event has occurred, or (ii) it is just and equitable that corporation should be liquidated and dissolved. (1981, c. B-15, §207).

Application for Supervision.—Application to court to supervise voluntary liquidation and dissolution under this Part must state reasons, verified by affidavit of applicant, why court should supervise liquidation and dissolution. (1981, c. B-15, §208).

Part 17 outlines powers of court upon application to liquidate and dissolve corporation and in connection with dissolution or liquidation and dissolution of corporation.

Appointment of Liquidator.—When making order for liquidation of corporation or at any time thereafter, court may appoint any person, including director, officer or shareholder or any other corporation, as liquidator of corporation. (1981, c. B-15, §213).

Part 17 outlines duties, powers and responsibilities of liquidator in connection with liquidation of corporation under Act.

Continuation of Actions.—Notwithstanding dissolution of corporation under Act: (a) Civil, criminal or administrative action or proceeding commenced by or against corporation before its dissolution may be continued as if corporation had not been dissolved; (b) civil, criminal or administrative action or proceeding may be brought against corporation within two years after its dissolution as if corporation had not been dissolved; and (c) any property that would have been available to satisfy any judgment or order if corporation had not been dissolved remains available for such purpose. (1981, c. B-15, §219[2]).

Reimbursement.—Notwithstanding dissolution of corporation, shareholder to whom any of its property has been distributed is liable to any person claiming in above civil, criminal or administrative action or proceeding to extent of amount received by that shareholder upon such distribution, and action to enforce such liability may be brought within two years after date of dissolution of corporation. (1981, c. B-15, §219[4]).

Part 18. Investigation.—Security holder may apply to court, ex parte or upon such notice as court may require, for order directing investigation to be made of corporation and any of its affiliated corporations. (1981, c. B-15, §223[1] as am'd).

Grounds.—If, upon application, it appears to court that: (a) Business of corporation or any of its affiliates is or has been carried on with intent to defraud any person, (b) business or affairs of corporation or any of its affiliates are or have been carried on or conducted, or powers of directors are or have been exercised in manner that is oppressive or unfairly prejudicial to or that unfairly disregards interests of security holder, (c) corporation or any of its affiliates was formed for fraudulent or unlawful purpose or is to be dissolved for fraudulent or unlawful purpose, or (d) persons concerned with formation, business or affairs of corporation or any of its affiliates have in connection therewith acted fraudulently or dishonestly; court may order investigation to be made of corporation and any of its affiliated corporations. (1981, c. B-15, §223[2] as am'd).

Powers of Court.—In connection with investigation, court may make any order it thinks fit. (1981, c. B-15, §224).

Copy of Report.—Inspector appointed by court shall on request produce to interested person copy of any order made under §§223 or 224(1). (1981, c. B-15, §225[3]).

Power of Inspector.—Inspector has powers set out in order of court appointing him. (1981, c. B-15, §225.[1]).

Part 19. Remedies, Offences and Penalties.—

Commencing Derivative Action.—Complainant may apply to court for leave to bring action in name and on behalf of corporation or any of its subsidiaries, or intervene in action to which any such body corporate is party, for purpose of prosecuting, defending or discontinuing action on behalf of body corporate, except that no such action may be brought and no intervention in action may be made unless court is satisfied that: (a) Complainant has given reasonable notice to directors of corporation or its subsidiary of his intention to apply to court if directors of corporation or its subsidiary do not bring, diligently prosecute or defend or discontinue action; (b) complainant is acting in good faith; and (c) it appears to be in interest of corporation or its subsidiary that action be brought, prosecuted, defended or discontinued. (1981, c. B-15, §232).

"Complainant" means: (a) Registered holder or beneficial owner, or former registered holder or beneficial owner, of security of corporation or any of its affiliates, (b) director or officer or former director or officer of corporation or of any of its affiliates, (c) any other person who, in discretion of court, is proper person to make application under this Part. (1981, c. B-15, §231).

Powers of Court.—In connection with such action, court may at any time make any order it thinks fit including, without limiting generality of foregoing: (a) Order authorizing complainant or any other person to control conduct of action; (b) order giving directions for conduct of action; (c) order directing that any amount adjudged payable by defendant in action shall be paid, in whole or in part, directly to former and present security holders of corporation or its subsidiary instead of to corporation or its subsidiary; (d) order requiring corporation or its subsidiary to pay reasonable legal fees incurred by complainant in connection with action. (1981, c. B-15, §233).

Commencing Oppression Action.—Complainant may apply to court for order under following provision. (1981, c. B-15, §234[1]).

Grounds.—If, upon application by complainant to court for order, court is satisfied that in respect of corporation or any of its affiliates: (a) Any act or omission of corporation or any of its affiliates effects result, (b) business or affairs of corporation or any of its affiliates are or have been carried on or conducted in manner, or (c) powers of directors of corporation or any of its affiliates are or have been exercised in manner; that is oppressive or unfairly prejudicial to or that unfairly disregards interests of any security holder, creditor, director or officer, court may make order to rectify matters complained of. (1981, c. B-15, §234[2]).

Powers of Court.—In connection with such application, court may make any interim or final order it thinks fit. (1981, c. B-15, §234[3]).

Duty of Directors.—If such order made by court directs amendment of articles of corporation: (a) Directors shall forthwith send articles of reorganization in prescribed form and other documents required by Act in connection therewith to Registrar; and (b) no other amendment to articles or by-laws shall be made without consent of court, until court otherwise orders. (1981, c. B-15, §234[5],[6]).

Court Approval to Discontinue.—Application made or action brought or intervened in under this Part must not be stayed, discontinued, settled or dismissed for want of prosecution without approval of court given upon such terms as court thinks fit and, if court determines that interests of any complainant may be substantially affected by such stay, discontinuance, settlement or dismissal, court may order any party to application or action to give notice to complainant. (1981, c. B-15, §235[2]).

Application to Court to Rectify Records.—If name of person is alleged to be or to have been wrongly entered or retained in, or wrongly deleted or omitted from, registers or other records of corporation, corporation, security holder of corporation or any aggrieved person may apply to court for order that registers or records be rectified. (1981, c. B-15, §236[1] as am'd).

Powers of Court.—In connection with such application, court may make any order it thinks fit. (1981, c. B-15, §236[3] as am'd).

Application for Directions.—Executive Director of Alberta Securities Commission may apply to court for directions in respect of matter concerning duties under Act and on such application court may give such directions and make any further order it thinks fit. (1981, c. B-15, §237, as am'd).

Appeal from Registrar's Decision.—Person who feels aggrieved by decision of Registrar: (a) To refuse to file in form submitted to him any articles or other document required by Act to be filed by him, (b) to approve, change or revoke name, or to refuse to approve, change or revoke name under Act, (c) to refuse to permit continued reference to shares having nominal or par value, (d) to refuse to issue certificate of discontinuance under Act, (e) to refuse to revive corporation under Act, (f) to dissolve corporation under Act, (g) to refuse exemption respecting fees for extra-provincial corporation, or (h) to cancel registration of extra-provincial corporation; may apply to court for order requiring Registrar to change his decision and upon such application court may so order and make any further order it thinks fit. (1981, c. B-15, §239, as am'd).

Restraining or Compliance Order.—If corporation or any shareholder, director, officer, employee, agent, auditor, trustee, receiver, receiver-manager or liquidator of corporation does not comply with Act, regulations, articles, by-laws or unanimous shareholder agreement, complainant or creditor of corporation may, in addition to any other right he has, apply to court for order directing any such person to comply with, or restraining any such person from acting in breach of, any provisions thereof, and upon such application court may so order and make any further order it thinks fit. (1981, c. B-15, §240).

Offences with Respect to Reports.—Person who makes or assists in making report, return, notice or other document required by Act or regulations to be sent to Registrar, Executive Director or any other person or filed with Executive Director that: (a) Contains untrue statement of material fact, or (b) omits to state material fact required therein or necessary to make statement contained therein not misleading in light of circumstances in which it was made; is guilty of offence and liable to fine not exceeding $5,000 or to imprisonment for term not exceeding six months or to both. (1981, c. B-15, §243[1], as am'd).

If person guilty of such offence is body corporate, then, whether or not body corporate has been prosecuted or convicted, any director or officer of body corporate who knowingly authorizes, permits or acquiesces in such failure is also guilty of offence and liable to fine not exceeding $5,000 or to imprisonment for term not exceeding six months or both. (1981, c. B-15, §243[2] as am'd).

Immunity.—No person is guilty of any such offence if untrue statement or omission was unknown to him and in exercise of reasonable diligence could not have been known to him. (1981, c. B-15, §243[3] as am'd).

Offence.—Every person who, without reasonable cause, contravenes provision of Act or regulations for which no punishment is provided is guilty of offence. (1981, c. B-15, §244).

Order to Comply.—Where person is guilty of offence under Act or regulations, any court in which proceedings in respect of offence are taken may, in addition to any punishment it may impose, order that person to comply with provisions of Act or regulations for contravention of which he has been convicted. (1981, c. B-15, §245[1]).

Part 20. General.—

Notice to Directors and Shareholders.—Notice or document required by Act, regulations, articles or by-laws to be sent to shareholder or director of corporation may be sent by mail addressed to, or may be delivered personally to: (a) Shareholder at his latest address as shown in records of corporation or its transfer agent; and (b) director

See Topical Index in front part of this volume.

CORPORATIONS . . . *continued*
at his latest address as shown in records of corporation or in last notice of directors or notice of change of directors. (1981, c. B-15, §246[1]).

Notice to and Service Upon a Corporation.—Notice or document required to be sent to or served upon corporation may be sent by registered mail to registered office or post office box designated as address for service by mail, or delivered to registered office. Notice of intent to dissolve corporation may be sent by ordinary mail to registered office or post office box. (1981, c. B-15, §247[1] as am'd).

Certificate of Corporation.—Certificate issued on behalf of corporation stating any fact that is set out in articles, by-laws, unanimous shareholder agreement, minutes of meetings of directors, committee of directors or shareholders, or in trust indenture or other contract to which corporation is party may be signed by director, officer or transfer agent of corporation. (1981, c. B-15, §250[1]).

Regulations.—Subject to following provisions, Lieutenant Governor in Council may make regulations: (a) Prescribing any matter required or authorized by Act to be prescribed; (b) requiring payment of fee in respect of filing, examination or copying of any document or in respect of any action that Registrar is required or authorized to take under Act, and prescribing amount thereof; (c) prescribing format and contents of annual returns, notices and other documents required to be sent to Registrar or to be issued by him; (d) prescribing rules with respect to exemptions permitted by Act; (e) prescribing that standards of accounting body named in regulations be followed; (f) respecting circumstances under which corporation or extra-provincial corporation is prohibited from being incorporated or registered with, having, carrying on business under, identifying itself by or changing its name to specified name or kind of name; (g) respecting form of, period of time for keeping, and disposal of records of corporation; (h) prescribing maximum fee for issuing security certificate pursuant to transfer; and (i) prescribing period of time for which information in securities register must be kept. (1981, c. B-15, §254[1], as am'd).

Annual Return.—Every corporation must on prescribed date, send to Registrar annual return in prescribed form. (1981, c. B-15, §256[1]).

Inspection.—Person who has paid prescribed fee is entitled during usual business hours to examine document required by Act or regulations to be sent to Registrar and to make copies of or extracts therefrom (1981, c. B-15, §259[1]).

Application to Federally-Incorporated Corporations.—The provisions dealing with foreign corporations apply in part only in regard to corporations incorporated under Act of Parliament of Canada. The province has no jurisdiction to enact legislation directed at such federally-incorporated corporations. However, legislation passed by Legislature of Province for other purposes is valid even though it affects federally-incorporated corporations indirectly: Federally-incorporated corporations are compelled to register and to pay annual registration fees and companies engaged in certain businesses are required to obtain provincial licenses.

Continuation.—Alberta company must apply to Registrar for certificate of continuance under new Act. Shareholders, acting by special resolution, must: (a) Adopt articles of continuance, (b) authorize directors to apply for certificate of continuance and (c) may adopt by-laws to become effective upon continuance. Application must be made within three years after last day of anniversary month of company first occurring after Feb. 1, 1982, except for company that applies and qualifies for incentive under Petroleum Incentives Program Act (Canada) and regulations thereunder or Petroleum Incentives Program Act (Alberta) and regulations thereunder in which cases application must be made not later than Dec. 31, 1987. Court can extend period for application. Failure to continue results in dissolution. (1981, c. B-15, §261, as am'd).

Extra-Provincial Registration.—Extra-Provincial corporation is required to register if carrying on business in Alberta as defined in Act. Certain obligations are imposed upon such corporations as to display of name on documents, etc. Disabilities and penalties are set out for failure to register. (1981, c. B-15, Part 21).

Taxation.—See topic Taxation.

Professional Corporations.—If name of corporation in articles of incorporation contains words "Professional Corporation", incorporator must send Registrar evidence of approval of articles by or on behalf of governing body of appropriate profession or occupation. (1981, c. B-15, §7[2]).

COSTS:

Governed by tariff fixed by court rules. Court has discretion, but successful party usually entitled to disbursements and costs based on such tariff. Security for costs may be required of nonresident plaintiff having no property in province, where action is brought by nominal plaintiff or on behalf of class. (A.R.C. 593). Security for costs may be in cash or by bond, application by defendant anytime after service of statement of claim. (A.R.C. 594).

When there has been delay in prosecution of action defendant may be awarded solicitor-client costs or interim costs, plaintiff may be denied costs or be required to post security for costs, and costs may be ordered payable personally by plaintiff's solicitor. (A.R.C. 244.4).

COURTS:

Court of Queen's Bench consists of 65 judges, each of whom has jurisdiction throughout Province, and has original jurisdiction in all civil and criminal matters. (c. C-29). Each judge travels throughout Province and sits alone or with jury to hear and determine cases. In addition, supernumerary judges may be appointed.

Court of Appeal, which is highest court of Province, consists of 14 judges. (c. C-28). In addition, supernumerary judges may be appointed.

Surrogate Courts.—Composed of same judges as Court of Queen's Bench. Jurisdiction over granting of administration and probate. (c. S-28). Surrogate Court Rules. (Alta. Reg. 20/71 repealed and replaced with Alta. Reg. 130/95 eff. June 19, 1995).

Provincial Courts.—Province has single Provincial Court having extensive criminal jurisdiction and limited civil jurisdiction. (c. P-20). Court has jurisdiction over civil claims for debt or damages not exceeding $4,000. (c. P-20). Civil proceedings are informal and parties generally represent themselves.

CREDITORS' SUITS:

Where property cannot be reached under execution there is generally no manner in which a creditor can realize unless he has a lien on goods or lands. In latter case he is generally allowed to proceed against those goods or lands. The Civil Enforcement Act, S.A. 1994, c. C-10.5, consolidates enforcement of money judgments, seizures and eviction procedures within one Act. See also topics Executions; Exemptions.

CRIMINAL LAW: See Canada Law Digest.

CURTESY:

No tenancy by curtesy in Alberta. (c. L-8, §4).

DAMAGES:

Common law generally prevails. See also topic Death.

Comparative Damages.—Where damage is caused by more than one person court may apportion degree of fault and assess damages accordingly. (c. C-23).

Charitable Immunity.—Doctrine of charitable immunity is not recognized in Alberta law.

DEATH:

When a person is not heard of for seven years a rebuttable presumption of death arises for purposes of life insurance. (c. I-5, §278).

Survivorship.—The general rule is that when two persons die under circumstances rendering it uncertain which survived the other the older is presumed to have died first.

In case of a statute or instrument providing for disposition of property operative if designated person dies either before or at time of death of another, or in circumstances rendering it uncertain which of them died first, and designated person does die in those circumstances, then the case for which statute or instrument provides is deemed to have occurred.

Similarly, where a will so designates, then, for purposes of probate the case for which will provides is deemed to have occurred. (c. S-31, §3).

But in case of life insurance, where the insured and the beneficiary die under such circumstances, the beneficiary is presumed to have died first and the insurance money becomes part of the insured's estate, but only if no alternative disposition is provided in the contract or by declaration, and there is no other surviving beneficiary. If there are two or more such beneficiaries, they take in equal shares. (c. I-5, §§263, 284).

Action for Death.—Action for wrongful death may be brought within two years by executor or administrator of deceased. (c. L-15, §53). According to Limitations Act, Bill 205, in force on proclamation, §3(2)(c), personal representative of deceased as successor owner of claim must bring action within earliest of: (a) two years from time deceased owner first knew or ought to have known of conduct giving rise to claim of deceased acquired knowledge more than two years before death; or (b) two years after representative was appointed if he had knowledge of conduct giving rise to claim at time of appointment; or (c) two years after representative first acquired or ought to have acquired knowledge of conduct giving rise to claim if he acquired knowledge after appointment. If there is no executor or administrator or if he does not bring action within one year then action may be brought by beneficiaries (c. F-5, §3[2]) within two year limit. Action is for benefit of surviving husband, wife, cohabitant and children, parent, brother or sister, if any, or of decedent's estate. Cohabitant is person of opposite sex held out to community as deceased's spouse, who has been living with deceased for three years immediately preceding death. In general, only those damages which are not personal losses to deceased are recoverable. Although there are no statutory limitations on amount of damages, sums ranging from $25,000 to $40,000 are prescribed for bereavement damages. (c. F-5, §8[2]). Tort actions survive death of tortfeasor or injured party, if commenced within two years from date of death of person, unless covered by statutory exceptions. (c. L-15, §§53, 57-61; c. S-30). Only those damages that result in actual financial loss to deceased or his estate are recoverable. (c. S-30, §5).

Death Certificate.—See topic Records, subhead Vital Statistics.

DEBT ADJUSTMENT ACT: See topic Actions.

DECEDENTS' ESTATES:

See topics Descent and Distribution; Executors and Administrators; Homesteads; Wills.

DECLARATORY JUDGMENTS:

See topic Judgments.

DEEDS:

Transfers may be of any interest not greater than that owned by the transferor, but the typical titles are fee simple ones from which the minerals have been reserved to the Crown. Land cannot be transferred in fee tail. (c. L-8, §9). See topic Real Property for estates recognized.

Execution.—Land is conveyed by a "transfer." Transfers, etc., shall be witnessed by person who can sign his name and for purposes of registration affidavit of execution must be attached or indorsed. As to who may take affidavit see topic Affidavits. No affidavit of execution is necessary in case of instrument executed by corporation under its corporate seal and no seal necessary if executed by one officer of director who has signature attested to and verifies by affidavit authority to execute instrument. (c. L-5, §152.3). Every instrument affecting registered lands, other than copy of writ of enforcement, must disclose surname, one Christian name and municipal number and street address, if any, of each party to instrument. (c. L-5, §49). See topic Homesteads.

For circumstances in which spouse must join, see topic Dower; also topic Homesteads.

Recording.—Duplicate certificate of title must be surrendered to land titles office when a transfer is registered therewith; new certificate of title is then issued. (c. L-5,

DEEDS . . . *continued*
§§16[6], 50[1]). Where different instruments affecting same estate have been registered they take priority according to serial number assigned on registration rather than date of execution unless question of fraud involved. (c. L-5, §59). In recording any instrument both original and signed duplicate must be produced. Registrar cannot register any transfer or transmission of any estate or interest in land without accompanying declaration under regulations under The Agricultural and Recreational Land Ownership Act (c. A-9, c. L-5, §31) and Citizenship Act (Canada) (§35).

Fees for recording transfers of land or vesting orders are fixed according to value. There must also be paid the assurance fund fee. (c. L-5, §154). See topic Records.

Transfer by Attorney in Fact.—See topic Principal and Agent.

Forms

The following are the principal forms prescribed by the Land Titles Act:

Transfer of Land: I, A.B., being registered owner of an estate (state the nature of estate) subject to registered encumbrances, liens and interests, if any, in all that piece of land described as follows: (here describe land) do hereby, in consideration of (here set out true consideration) transfer to E.F., all my estate and interest in that piece of land. (When a lesser estate describe such lesser estate).

In witness whereof I have hereunto subscribed my name this . . . day of . . . . 19. . . .

SIGNED by the above named)
)
A.B. in the presence of)
) . . . .
. . . .) (Signature)

(Alta. Reg. 538/82, Form 8).

Add affidavit of execution where necessary (see subhead Execution, supra). For form of affidavit see catchline Affidavit of Attestation of Instrument, infra.

For homestead property insert consent of spouse before witness clause and add separate acknowledgment of spouse. (c. D-38). For forms see topic Homesteads.

Every transfer must have oaths or affidavits of value attached by transferor or transferee or their agents. (c. L-5, §154).

Affidavit re Value of Land:

I, A.B., of __________, in the __________ make oath and say:

1. I am (one of) the transferee (or agent of the transferee) named in the within or annexed transfer and I know the land therein described;
2. I know the circumstances of the transfer and true consideration paid by me is as follows:
(Give full details: cash, assumption of mortgage, exchange or other consideration with cash value of same.)
3. The present value of the land, in my opinion, is $________ ("land" includes buildings and all other improvements affixed to the land.)

Sworn before me at the)
__________________)
in the ______________)
this ________ day of) ______________
__________ 19________) Signature

____
(Signature of Commissioner
for Oaths or other officer)

(Alta. Reg. 480/81, Form 32, as repealed and replaced by Alta. Reg. 331/88).

Affidavit of Attestation of Instrument:

I, *A.B.*, of __________, in the __________ make oath and say:

1. I was personally present and did see __________ who is known to me to be the person named in the within *(or annexed)* instrument, duly sign the instrument;
or
I was personally present and did see __________ who, on the basis of the identification provided to me, I believe to be the person named in the within *(or annexed)* instrument, duly sign the instrument;
2. The instrument was signed at __________, in the __________ and I am the subscribing witness thereto;
3. I believe the person whose signature I witnessed is at least eighteen (18) years of age.

Sworn before me at __________)
in the __________)
this ________ day of __________) ______________
19_____ *(Signature)*

Homestead or Dower Affidavit: See topic Homesteads.

Caveat (forbidding registration): Take notice that I (insert name and address of Caveator) claim (specify the nature of the estate or interest claimed and the grounds on which the claim is founded) in the land described as follows: (here describe land) standing in the registrar in the name of . . . .; and I forbid the registration of any person as transferee or owner of, or of any instrument affecting that estate or interest, unless the certificate of title is expressed to be subject to my claim.

I designate the following address as the place at which notices and proceedings relating hereto may be served:

. . . .

. . . .

In witness whereof I have hereunto subscribed my name this . . . . day of . . . . 19. . . .

. . . .
(Signature of the Caveator or his Agent)

(Alta. Reg. 538/82, Form 26)

Affidavit in Support of Caveat:

I, (the Caveator or his Agent), make oath and say (or solemnly declare) as follows:

1. I am the within named caveator (or agent for the caveator).
2. I believe that I have (or the caveator has) a good and valid claim on the land (mortgage or encumbrance), and I say that this caveat is not being filed for the purpose of delaying or embarrassing any person interested in or proposing to deal with it.

Sworn before me at the)
__________ of __________)
in the __________ of __________)
this __________ day of)
__________ 19________) ______________
Signature

____
(Signature of Commissioner
for Oaths or other officer)

(Alta. Reg. 480/81, Form 27, as amended by Alta. Reg. 195/85).

DEEDS OF TRUST:

See topic Mortgages of Real Property.

DEPOSITIONS:

Without the Province.—Where testimony of any person without limits of Alberta is required court may order issue of a commission for examination of such person. (A.R.C. 200 and 270). Such examination must, unless otherwise ordered, be conducted in accordance with practice upon examination of witnesses at trial, so far as is applicable. (A.R.C. 270).

Party having carriage of commission must give notice prescribed by order of intention to despatch commission and order provides for notice of time and place to take examination. (A.R.C. 273). Any party may be represented by counsel at examination. Witness is examined on oath, affirmation, or otherwise in accordance with religion of witness. (A.R.C. 274). Unless otherwise directed, examination of witnesses shall be by oral questions and oral questions and answers thereto shall be reduced into writing and returned with order or commission. (A.R.C. 275). Interrogatories may be used. (A.R.C. 276).

Affidavits obtained abroad may be admitted in the discretion of the court, but are seldom admitted if the facts deposed to are in dispute.

Within the Province for Use Here.—Court may order any party to an action, any officer of a corporate party and any person who has been employed by any party to an action within or without province whether permanently or temporarily to attend and submit to examination on discovery before trial of any pending civil action. (A.R.C. 200, 204). Examination is on notice, and is like examination of witness at trial although broader in scope, and is usually transcribed and can be filed or put before court either during application or at trial. (A.R.C. 212, 214). Any enforcement debtor may be examined in aid of execution. (A.R.C. 372).

Within the Province for Use Elsewhere.—When it is made to appear to a judge that any foreign court or tribunal of competent jurisdiction has duly authorized by commission or otherwise the obtaining of testimony in relation to a matter pending the judge may order that the evidence of any witness within Alberta be taken before the person appointed. (c. A-21, §57).

De Bene Esse.—Depositions may be taken in any action de bene esse on order of court. (A.R.C. 270). Ordinarily depositions made to perpetuate testimony are not of very great value unless they come under category of confessions, admissions against interest, statements re pedigree or etc.

Compelling Attendance of Witnesses.—Provided a witness has been properly served within jurisdiction, his attendance may be procured and his examination conducted in same manner as that of a witness at trial.

DESCENT AND DISTRIBUTION:

Subject to rights of surviving spouse, if any, real and personal property of person dying intestate descends and is distributed as follows, each class of which a member is living taking to the exclusion of subsequent classes: (1) children and/or issue of deceased children per stirpes; (2) parents equally or all to surviving parent; (3) brothers and sisters and/or children of deceased brothers and sisters per stirpes; (4) nephews and nieces in equal shares, no representations being admitted; (5) equally among the next of kin of equal degree of consanguinity to the intestate, no representations being admitted. (c. I-9). Under the Family Relief Act a dependent of deceased may apply to court to vary rules of distribution upon intestacy if there is not adequate support. (c. F-2, §3). See also topic Executors and Administrators.

Surviving spouse takes all if decedent left no issue, one-half if decedent left one child, and one-third if decedent left more than one child. If estate is less than $40,000 widow receives entire estate, or if it is more than $40,000 widow receives $40,000 plus her intestate share of excess. (c. I-9, §23). Rights of surviving spouse are forfeited by living apart from intestate and living in adultery. (c. I-9, §15).

Half Blood.—Whole and half blood share alike. (c. I-9, §9).

Afterborn Children.—Children born within the period of gestation after intestate's death take same as other children. (c. I-9, §10).

Adopted Children.—See topic Adoption.

Illegitimates.—No distinction is made between children born within or outside marriage. (c. I-9, §§13 and 14 repealed).

Advancements are governed by common law rules, except as between spouses. (c. M-9, §36).

Escheat.—Crown in right of Alberta is ultimate heir of every person dying intestate in fact as regards any property situate in Alberta and of every person domiciled in Alberta as regards movables or choses in action wheresoever situate. (c. U-1, §2).

DESERTION:

See topics Divorce; Husband and Wife.

DISPUTE RESOLUTION:

Mandatory Dispute Resolution.—

Pre-Trial Conferencing ("PTC").—In advance of trial, judge meets with disputants to assist in more quickly resolving issues between them. According to Policy Directive Apr. 1, 1995, PTC must be held for: all domestic and matrimonial matters (other than uncontested divorces), any trial set for three days or longer duration, all matters to be tried by civil jury, any case where party requests PTC, or if directed by Rules or Court Order. PTC is primarily oriented towards trial preparation, but can lead to settlement of lawsuit. Judge may issue orders for: exchange of written briefs, costs, civil contempt, and mediation. Judge reviews points of agreement, notes if there are any further admissions, renders opinions on disputed issues when appropriate, and suggests varieties of settlement and extrajudicial procedures for resolution. PTC may be by telephone. Parties can agree to submit to binding PTC. PTC judge shall not preside at trial, unless all parties and Judge consent in writing. (A.R.C. Rule 219). In very long trial action, any case management direction given by Court becomes order of Court whether arising from application of party or from Court on its own motion. (A.R.C. Rule 219.1, Alta. Reg. 277/95).

Financial Consumers Act.—Purpose of Act is to resolve disputes about named financial products efficiently and effectively. (c. F-9.5, §1[d]). Parties must first attempt to resolve dispute over noncompliance with Act themselves. (c. F-9.5, §22). Every agreement between consumers and suppliers, agents and financial planners about named financial products must include provision for arbitration where Arbitration Act will apply unless consumer decides to start court proceedings. (c. F-9.5, §23[1]—awaiting Proclamation). If no such arbitration clause exists, model arbitration clause is in force. (c. F-9.5, §23[2]—awaiting proclamation). Arbitrator must consider certain factors. (c. F-9.5, §27).

Individual Rights Protection Act.—Provides statutory scheme under which Human Rights Commission shall endeavour to effect settlement of complaints of discrimination prohibited by Act. (c. I-2, §20). Commission shall act as both investigator and mediator. Only if Commission is unable to effect settlement of complaint, may Minister direct formal inquiry to be held. (c. I-2, §27).

Insurance Act.—Where contract (other than for hail insurance) provides for appraisal to determine specified matters, and in event of disagreement between insured and insurer, each shall appoint appraiser. If the two appraisers fail to resolve matter, they shall apoint umpire who will decide matter. (c. I-5, §204).

International Commercial Arbitration Act.—Applies to international commercial arbitration agreements and awards. Based upon United Nations Commission on International Trade Law (UNCITRAL) and its set of uniform arbitration rules. Arbitration Act does not apply. (c. I-6.6).

Irrigation Act.—Statutory scheme is provided for resolution of complaints with respect to rates assessments, seepage damage, and other matters arising under Act. (c. I-11).

Labour Relations Code.—Mediation and enhanced mediation is available during collective bargaining process. (c. L-1.2, Part 2, Div. 11).

Voluntary interest arbitration is available to parties in dispute. If there is no settlement within 20 days, arbitrator (one or three member) shall make binding award. (c. L-1.2, Part 2, Div. 15).

Compulsorily Interest Arbitration applies to firefighters who bargain collectively with municipalities, and employers and employees of hospitals. (c. L-1.2, Part 2, Div. 16). Mediator may be requested by parties jointly or Minister. If there is no settlement after 14 days, matter shall be forwarded to compulsorily Arbitration Board. Arbitration Board may select method or combination of methods of arbitration (c. L-1.2, §98) and must consider certain matters (c. L-1.2, §99).

Minister may appoint Disputes Inquiry Board (c. L-1.2, Div. 17) and may create Disputes Resolution Tribunal for purposes of arbitration (c. L-1.2, Div. 20).

Every collective agreement falling within Act shall contain method for settlement of differences between parties bound by collective agreement. (c. L-1.2, Div. 22).

Minister shall refer items in dispute in construction industry labour relations to Disputes Resolution Tribunal if requested to do so by one or more of parties who have not entered into collective agreements, when 75% of sector has entered into collective agreements. Minister may on his own motion refer items in dispute to Construction Industry Disputes Resolution Tribunal. (c. L-1.2, Part 3, Div. 6).

Licensing of Trades and Businesses Act.—Minister may make regulations providing for system of resolving complaints against persons who carry on business to which Act applies. (c. L-13, §4[1][m][iv]).

Marketing of Agricultural Products Act.—Council may in respect of plan administered by Board make regulations regarding arbitration for minimum prices, terms and conditions of agreements, and charges and expenses related to production or marketing of product. (c. M-5.1, §33[1][b]).

Municipal Government Act.—If there is disagreement between Council and person who claims to have incurred damage or loss as result of by-law regarding construction near highways (c. M-26, §258[5]), or with respect to removal of obstructions at road intersections (c. M-26, §259[3][g]), compensation shall be determined by arbitrator under Arbitration Act. If there is complaint about assessments or tax, and complainant indicates that he wishes complaint dealt with by arbitration, designated officer must inform municipality and appoint arbitrator within 30 days of receiving complaint. Arbitrator must be acceptable to both parties, otherwise designated officer must refer complaint to Assessment Review Board for its decision. (c. M-26, §§472, 509).

Oil and Gas Conservation Act.—Minister may make regulations for settlement by arbitration of disputes arising out of ethane supply for straddle plants. (c. O-5, §22.1[5]).

Public Lands Act.—Minister may settle in any manner he considers best all disputes that arise between persons applying for same disposition of public land. (c. P-30, §15). Lieutenant Governor in Council may make regulations authorizing and governing dispositions of public land and provide for arbitration and settlement of any matter relating to dispositions. (c. P-30, §8[1][f]).

Public Safety Services Act.—If any dispute arises concerning amount of compensation payable under this Act, it shall go to arbitration and provisions of Arbitration Act apply. (c. P-30.5, §22). Title and chapter of Act repealed and Disaster Services Act, c. D-36 substituted. (1995, c. 34, §13).

Public Service Employee Relations Act.—Dispute under collective bargaining agreement may be dealt with first by mediation and then by arbitration. (c. P-33, Part 6). Certain things may not be dealt with by arbitration. (c. P-33, §48). Labour Relations Code applies, whereas Arbitration Act does not.

Railway Act.—If landowner or those with interest in land do not give notice to railway company accepting compensation offered for that land or interest, Court on application of company shall appoint arbitrator to decide fair compensation. (c. R-4, §§96, 106-119). If government takes over and acquires railway, and there is no agreement as to compensation, matter shall be determined by arbitration. (c. R-4, §§239-244).

Surface Rights Act.—Surface Rights Board may hold hearing and settle dispute between owner or occupant under lease and owner or occupant under right of entry order, as to amount of compensation for certain damage, loss, or expense not in excess of $5,000. (c. S-27.1, §33).

Ultimate Heir Act.—If person making successful claim and Crown (Alberta) cannot agree as to assets and proceeds to be transferred, matters in dispute shall be settled by Auditor General. (c. U-1, §5[6]).

Water, Gas and Electric Companies Act.—If any company considers it necessary or proper to conduct any of its pipes, wires, or conductors or to carry any of its works through land of any person, and consent of that person cannot be obtained for that purpose, matter must proceed to arbitration under Arbitration Act to determine necessity of carrying on work and appropriate compensation, if it is performed. (c. W-4, §29).

Water Resources Act.—If Minister and licensee are unable to agree on compensation to be paid for works Minister takes over, matter shall be ascertained by arbitration under Arbitration Act. (c. W-5, §45[5]).

Workers' Compensation Act.—Statutory scheme for compensation for workers for earnings lost when they are disabled in course of their employment. Whether or not eligible disabled worker wishes to accept limited benefits available through Act, worker and his family are barred from taking legal action against any employer or worker who is within scope of Act. (c. W-16, §18).

Voluntary Dispute Resolution.—

General.—There are variety of alternative dispute resolution mechanisms and methods. More common ones are: mediation, arbitration, mediation-arbitration, judicial mini-trials, alternative measures (young offenders) and ombudsmen. Other, less common, DR options which are not provided for in any systematic way but are still available include: early neutral evaluation (third party), neutral expert fact-finding (complex, technical issues), private mini-trials (jury composed of executives), summary jury trials (jury composed of public), private judging (rent-a-judge) and circle sentencing (aboriginal bands).

Alberta Family and Social Services.—Custody and Mediation Program: Purpose is to provide expert opinion in certain actions where custody and/or access are in issue. First step is closed mediation, where information from mediation is privileged. If there is no settlement or closed mediation is inappropriate, second step is open assessment where communications are not confidential and are used by assessor to prepare Custody Access Report. Three conditions must be met: (i) Proceedings must be commenced or continued in Queen's Bench or Surrogate Court of Alberta; (ii) both parties to proceedings must reside within boundaries of Province of Alberta; and (iii) both parties must agree to participate.

Arbitration.—See Arbitration Act and Award (which applies to arbitration conducted under arbitration agreement or authorized or required under enactment unless parties exclude it).

There are several types of arbitration. These include: first offer arbitration, revised offer arbitration, modified first offer arbitration, multiple offer selection, issue by issue arbitration.

Final Offer Arbitration (F.O.A.)—arbitrator chooses settlement position of either party and nothing in between.

Modified F.O.A.—if arbitrator dislikes both offers, he can write his own proposal which both parties must accept as solution; otherwise matter returns to arbitrator for choice between original proposals.

Issue By Issue F.O.A.

Repeated Offer Arbitration—if arbitrator considers both offers unreasonable, he can choose neither and require resubmissions.

Multiple Offer Selection—each side submits number (e.g.: three) of optional settlements from which arbitrator chooses best offer; arbitrator discloses which side he has chosen; chosen side then selects one of its submitted options, and this becomes actual award.

Better Business Bureau of Southern Alberta.—Alberta Minister of Justice has authorized BBB to review disputes currently scheduled to be heard in Provincial Court—Civil Division and offer mediation service as alternative. There is no cost for service, and it can only happen if both parties agree to it. Mediation will usually occur within three week period once agreement is in place. Will also mediate disputes between customers and businesses. If mediation is unsuccessful, formal arbitration process is available.

Canadian Dispute Resolution Corporation.—Will mediate personal injury disputes.

Judicial Mini-Trial.—Judge presides and renders nonbinding opinion. Viva voce may be heard. Information is confidential. Briefs must be filed. Clients must appear while lawyers are presenting arguments to judge. No costs are assessed. Will not be same judge at real trial. Held either independently or as part of extended Pre-Trial Conference. Existing practice is for parties to approach Chief Justice or Associate Chief Justice to request mini-trial be held. Another method is for parties to request that Pre-Trial judge schedule Court time to conduct mini-trial.

New Home Warranty Program.—Will provide conciliation, mediation, and arbitration between homeowners and builders.

Other Private DR Agencies.—Alberta Arbitration and Mediation Society, Alberta Family Mediation Society (post-divorce parenting arrangements, child custody and access, child support, spousal maintenance and property disputes), Calgary Community Mediation Service, Edmonton Community Mediation Program.

Rule 403 Referees.—Court has power, upon agreement of parties, to appoint anyone it deems qualified as "referee" to try one or all of issues in action. All Masters in Chambers, Clerks and Deputy Clerks of Court are official referees. Lieutenant Governor in Council may name other referees either on standing or ad hoc basis. Once reference

See Topical Index in front part of this volume.

DISPUTE RESOLUTION . . . *continued*
is concluded, referee will report back to Court which will: confirm report—thereby producing final judgement, vary report and render final judgment, send report back to referee for further clarification, or ignore report and decide question itself.

Agriculture Financial Services Act.—When person applies to Agriculture Financial Service Corporation for insurance, Corporation may provide in its policy method of settling disputes arising out of adjustment of losses. (c. A-12.5, §40[2][o]).

Employment Standards Code.—Officer may mediate between employer and employee for purpose of settling or compromising differences between them. (c. E-10.2, §93[1]). If Officer is unable to mediate, settle or compromise difference between employer and his employee, Officer may (and in certain situations shall) make order to resolve dispute. (c. E-10.2, §94). Director may also attempt to mediate dispute between employer and his employee, and if that fails, then make appropriate order. (c. E-10.2, §95[1]).

Farm Implement Act.—Any dispute between purchaser and dealer, distributor, or manufacturer may, at option of either party, be submitted to two arbitrators under Arbitration Act instead of being settled by action. (c. F-4.1, §18). Inspector may, upon request of purchaser, inquire into attempt to resolve any dispute between purchaser and dealer, distributor, or manufacturer. (c. F-4.1, §19[1]). Where request for disclosure is made as part of inspection, dealer, distributor, or manufacturer must disclose. (c. F-4.1, §19[2]).

Freedom of Information and Protection of Privacy Act.—Commissioner may authorize mediator to investigate and try to settle any matter that is subject of request for review. (c. F-18.5, §65). If matter is not settled under §65 Commissioner shall conduct inquiry and decide all questions of fact or law arising. (c. F-18.5, §66).

Hospitals Act.—Minister may authorize mediation of any dispute that has arisen in course of administration or operation of hospital and may designate mediator, who shall report back to Minister. (c. H-11, §43).

Livestock and Livestock Products Act.—If Minister refuses patron's claim for payment from Fund, patron may within 21 days refer matter to arbitration. (c. L-24, §13.1).

Mines and Minerals Act.—In order to settle any dispute, Minister may direct survey or resurvey be made. (c. M-15, §28).

Ombudsman Act.—Independent, non-partisan third party may investigate complaints of any decision, recommendation, act or omission of Minister or his Department, etc. He may issue nonbinding report and recommendation, as means of correcting organizational abuses and resolving internal disputes. Only available where no other adequate remedy (i.e. appeal) exists. (c. O-6).

Residential Tenancies Act.—Landlord and Tenants Advisory Board will receive complaints and seek to mediate disputes between landlords and tenants of residential properties. (c. R-15.3, §49[2]).

Young Offenders Act.—Alternative measures to judicial proceedings may be used for certain offenses where: youth consents, does not deny his participation in offence, and does not express wish to be dealt with by Youth Court. (c. Y-1, §3). Reconciliation may involve: apology, personal service to victim, compensation if any monetary loss was involved, and/or community service.

DIVORCE:

Note.—Divorce Act, 1985, was proclaimed on June 1, 1986. Changes can thus be expected to Alberta statutes and regulations which make reference thereto.

Either husband or wife may obtain divorce on sole ground of marriage breakdown, established by either one year separation, adultery, or physical or mental cruelty.

Venue.—Court in province has jurisdiction if either spouse was ordinarily resident in province for at least one year immediately preceding commencement of proceedings. (R.S.C. 1985, c. 3, [2nd Supp.], §3).

Proceedings by either husband or wife are begun by petition followed by judgment granting divorce which generally takes effect 31 days later. (R.S.C. 1985, [2nd Supp.], c. 3, §12). Decree nisi and decree absolute have been eliminated under federal statute.

Spousal Support.—Court has jurisdiction to grant either temporary or permanent support to husband or wife, in either lump sum or periodic sums, if either former spouse is ordinarily resident in province at commencement of proceeding or both former spouses accept jurisdiction of court. Interim support is available pending determination of final order. Factors considered are condition, means, needs, other circumstances of each spouse and any dependent child, without regard to conduct including length of cohabitation, functions performed and any agreements or orders. (R.S.C. 1985, [2nd Supp.], c. 3, §4 [as am'd by S.C. 1993, c. 8, §1] and §15). Court has jurisdiction to vary amount or order discontinuance of support at any time upon application by husband or wife. (R.S.C. 1985, [2nd Supp.], c. 3, §17). Order has legal effect throughout Canada (R.S.C. 1985, [2nd Supp.], c. 3, §20[2]) and will be enforced on recipient's behalf by Director of Maintenance in accordance with Maintenance Enforcement Act, S.A. 1985 (c. M-0.5), unless recipient elects to enforce himself. Order may charge real property of payor (c. M-0.5, §§16, 16.1, 17).

Children.—Court may make custody order, either sole or joint or access order, either to spouse or to non-spouse, of either temporary or permanent nature, having regard only to best interests of child and giving effect to principle of encouraging parental contact. (R.S.C. 1985, c. 3, [2nd Supp.], §16). Person other than spouse can apply to vary or discontinue order with leave of court. (§17). Court may order for child support in same manner as spousal support and may be enforced in same way. (§15). Child support is calculated by apportioning parents' pro rata share of child expenses based on their monthly gross income. (4 R.F.L. [4th] 375 [Alta. C.A.]).

Division of Property.—Under Matrimonial Property Act (c. M-9), Court of Queen's Bench may order distribution of property acquired after marriage having regard to earning capacity, duration of marriage, any agreement between parties and contributions of each spouse. (c. M-9, §§7, 8). There are residency rules (c. M-9, §3) and exempt property rules (c. M-9, §7). Application must be made within two years of either divorce or separation. (c. M-9, §6).

Remarriage.—There is no legal restriction upon divorcees remarrying after judgment granting divorce takes effect 31 days later.

Judicial Separation.—Action may be brought by either husband or wife for judicial separation where other has been guilty of adultery, cruelty, desertion without reasonable cause for two years or upwards, failure to comply with judgment for restitution of conjugal rights, or sodomy or bestiality. (c. D-37, §6). Courts have jurisdiction to hear such an action where both parties: (1) Are domiciled in Alberta at time of commencement of action; (2) had a matrimonial home in Alberta when their cohabitation ceased or events occurred upon which their claim for separation is based; or (3) are resident in Alberta at time of commencement of action. (c. D-37, §7). Condonation of offence, collusion with other or connivance at adultery of other party, etc., is absolute bar to action. (c. D-37, §8). Result of judgment for judicial separation is that parties under no obligation to cohabit, wife becomes in fact femme sole, husband and wife are no longer responsible for contracts, wrongful acts, etc. of other. (c. D-37, §§10-12). Order of judicial separation allows spouses to seek matrimonial property order distributing marital assets. (c. M-9, §5).

Separation by Agreement.—Agreement to live apart will be enforced by our courts. If some of the provisions of the contract are illegal they will be struck out and remainder enforced. No consideration other than the mutual agreement to live apart is necessary.

Foreign divorce will be recognized where a decree of divorce is granted by a legally competent authority on basis of parties' domicile. Manner of enforcement of foreign maintenance and custody orders prescribed by statute. (cc. R-7 and M-0.5).

Annulment of Marriage.—See topic Marriage.

DOWER:

All dower rights have been abolished except with respect to the homestead, as to which dower rights of husband and wife are the same. (c. D-38).

Forms under Dower Act.—See topic Homesteads.

Election between dower and testamentary provision, see topic Wills.

EMPLOYER AND EMPLOYEE:

See topic Labour Relations.

ENVIRONMENT:

General Supervision.—Minister of the Environment has broad supervisory powers (c. D-19) and administers principally under Environmental Protection and Enhancement Act ("EPEA"). (c. E-13.3). This Act came into force Sept. 1, 1993 and repeals following statutes: Agricultural Chemicals Act; Beverage Container Act; Clean Air Act; Clean Water Act; Ground Water Development Act; Hazardous Chemicals Act; Land Surface Conservation and Reclamation Act; and Litter Act. Minister also establishes and administers Restricted Developments Areas. (c. D-19, §16).

Release of Substances.—Release of substance into environment, done knowingly or otherwise, is prohibited in amount, concentration or level or at rate of release in excess of what is permitted in regulations (c. E-13.3, §97) or, where no regulations, such as would cause significant adverse effect (§98).

Contaminated Sites.—Site may be designated as contaminated site, where substance that may cause, is causing or has caused significant adverse effect is present. (§110). Environmental protection order to clear-up site may be issued to any person responsible for contaminated site. (§114). Language "person responsible for the contaminated site" is defined broadly and includes present and past owners of site. (§96).

Enforcement.—Investigation must be carried out if two adult persons, ordinarily resident in Alberta, solemnly declare that they believe offence has been committed. (c. E-13.3, §§186-187). Investigator may obtain order for entry and inspection. (§191). Director may obtain enforcement order and suspend or cancel approval or shut down any activity or thing either permanently or for specified period. (§200).

Approval.—No person may commence or continue any activity designated by regulations as requiring approval if appropriate approval has not been obtained. (c. E-13.3, §§58-59). "Activity" includes release of substances likely to have adverse effect, any industrial, manufacturing or processing operation, most energy undertakings, exploration, and any other undertaking or thing defined as activity in regulations. (c. E-13.3, Schedule of Activities). Approval of wide range of activities can be required in Restricted Development Areas. (c. D-19, §16).

Disclosure.—Information provided to Minister for purpose of obtaining approval must be disclosed to public; other information may also be disclosed at Minister's discretion. Confidentiality may be requested. (c. E-13.3, §33).

Penalties.—Failure to comply with numerous requirements of EPEA constitutes offence. Two levels of offence are created - "mens rea" offence and strict liability offence. If individual knowingly contravenes Act, maximum penalty is $100,000 fine or imprisonment for two years or both; for corporation maximum penalty is $1,000,000. Strict liability offence carries fine only - maximum of $50,000 for individuals and $500,000 for corporations. (c. E-13.3, §214).

Environmental Impact Assessments.—Environmental assessment process is established, and any project may be required by Director to undergo process if it warrants further investigation. (c. E-13.3, §39). Process begins with initial review (§42), and may continue with preparation of environmental impact assessment report (§43). Minister may at any time require full impact assessment report if he or she considers it necessary. (§45). Where environmental impact assessment report is prepared, it must be published and otherwise made available in accordance with regulations. (§50).

Other matters covered by EPEA include conservation and reclamation, groundwater and related drilling, potable water, hazardous substances and pesticides, waste minimization, recycling and waste management, and hazardous waste. Regulations in all of these areas came into force Sept. 1, 1993.

Note: Bill 39, Environmental Protection and Enhancement Amendment Act, 1996, has received Royal Assent but is not in force until Proclamation. Bill proposes number of significant changes to current statutory scheme including: right to obtain "conservation easement" to prevent or limit development on easement properties; and insertion of privative clause which limits scope of review against decision of Environmental Appeal Board or of Minister.

See Topical Index in front part of this volume.

EQUITY: See topic Actions.

ESCHEAT:

See topics Absentees, subhead Escheat; Banks and Banking, subhead Unclaimed Deposits; Descent and Distribution, subhead Escheat; Wills, subhead Unclaimed Legacies.

ESTATES: See topics Real Property; Taxation.

EVIDENCE: See topics Depositions; Witnesses.

EXECUTIONS:

Note: Execution Creditors Act, c. E-14, and Seizure Act, c. S-11, repealed by Civil Enforcement Act, c. C-10.5, effective Jan. 1, 1996.

Exemptions.—See topic Exemptions.

Time for Issuance.—Enforcement in respect of money judgment may be issued against personal property only after writ is registered in Personal Property Registry ("P.P.R.") (c. C-10.5, §26[a]) and against land only after writ is registered in P.P.R. and against certificate of title under Land Titles Act, c. L-5.

Life of Execution.—Writ is in force only while judgment is in force, which is ten years unless judgment is renewed or action is brought on judgment within those ten years. Registration of writ in P.P.R. is for two years and may be renewed before that time. (c. C-10.5, §§27, 28). Registration of writ under Land Titles Act is in effect for duration of judgment. (c. C-10.5, §29).

Stay.—Judge may stay enforcement of judgment, or remove or extend stay already granted at or after time of judgment. (A.R.C. 341[1]). Where Judge does so under C.E.A. order may be registered in P.P.R. and, until registered, order is ineffective against those who have no actual knowledge.

Lien.—When registered at P.P.R., writ binds all of debtor's exigible personal property after-acquired. (c. C-10.5, §33[2][a], 33[3]). When registered against certificate of title, writ binds exigible land described in certificate of title. (c. C-10.5, §33[2][b]). Where person furnishes materials or services to goods bound by writ, he takes priority if materials and services are furnished in ordinary course of business and lien does not arise under enactment which provides otherwise. (c. C-10.5, §40).

Levy and sale under C.E.A. must be made through private civil enforcement agencies. (c. C-10.5, §9[1]). For prejudgment relief, Act allows sale of attached property only upon application to court and if likely to depreciate substantially or is expensive to maintain under attachment, or is prudent or necessary for any other reason. (c. C-10.5, §21). For post-judgment relief, if no notice of objection is filed, or court authorizes sale, then agency proceeds with sale. (c. C-10.5, §48[a]). Debtor has 15 days to file objection and agency cannot sell property until permitted by court. (c. C-10.5, §46). Agency can sell by any commercially reasonable method (§48[d]), but duty imposed to act in good faith and in commercially reasonable manner (c. C-10.5, §2[g]). Notice of method of sale must be given to instructing creditor and debtor 15 days befoe sale. (§48[e]). Specific power provided to sell to enforcement creditor by private sale before any other attempt at sale. (§48[f]). Buyer obtains interest of enforcement debtor. Sale is without warranty of title except buyer takes free of any interest subordinate to writ. (c. C-10.5, §48[i]). For sale of land, agency must serve 30 days notice of method of sale on debtor. (c. C-10.5, §74[i]). If notice includes proposed minimum price, any person served may object to price within 30 days and court must approve sale. (§74[3]). If notice excludes minimum price, agency must serve terms of any sale on all parties who must object within 15 days for court to intervene. (§74[4]).

See topic Personal Property Security.

Priorities.—Interest acquired in property after property bound by writ is subordinate to writ. (c. C-10.5, §34). Security interest in personal property not registered or perfected at time property is bound by writ is subordinate to writ. (c. C-10.5, §35). But purchase money security interests have priority over writs, provided security interest registered within 15 days of debtor taking possession of collateral or security interest attaching. (c. C-10.5, §35[3]). Buyer/lessee of nonconsumer goods sold or leased in ordinary course of business of seller/lessor takes free of writ. (c. C-10.5, §36[1]). Buyer/lessee of consumer goods takes free from writ if value given, goods bought/leased without knowledge of writ, and price of goods less $1,000. (c. C-10.5, §36[2]). Where serial numbered goods are bound by writ, but not registered by serial number, buyer/lessee of consumer goods take free of interest as does buyer/lessee of equipment without knowledge of writ. (c. C-10.5, §36[3]). Act provides special priority rules for fixtures and growing crops (§37), negotiable instruments (§38), and market securities (§39).

Claims of Third Parties.—Where claim is made by third party for personal property seized by agency, it must serve on agency written notice setting out claim and address for service. Agency must then give notice of third party claim to instructing creditor. Within 15 days, instructing creditor must give written notice to agency as to whether claim is admitted or disputed. (A.R.C. 457, 458). Where agency has served notice of claim and is satisfied no persons dispute claim, agency may release property from seizure. (A.R.C. 458). Where reasonable grounds exist to believe debtor's exigible personal property is in possession of third party, agency may and, if instructed by creditor, must serve demand on third party requiring delivery of property to agency within 15 days. (c. C-10.5, §44[1]). Third party must either deliver up property, advise agency of place where seizure can be effected, or advise agency that it need not comply with agency's demand because of its right against debtor to retain property or because it is without possession of property. (c. C-10.5, §44[2]). Where demand is not complied with, agency or creditor may apply under §10 to enforce compliance. Where third party complies, agency must compensate for expenses reasonably incurred by third party in compiling with demand. (§44[3]).

Redemption.—There is no provision for redemption of property sold under this Act.

Supplementary Proceedings.—Enforcement creditor may compel enforcement debtor to appear before court and given evidence under oath as to his property, earnings, expenses, etc. (A.R.C. 372). Judgment creditor unable to realize on enforcement because of fraud or attempts to liquidate assets may apply for appointment of receiver, to have necessary inquiries made as to property interest of debtor, or for order for sale of property. (A.R.C. 383, 463-66).

EXECUTORS AND ADMINISTRATORS:

Jurisdiction and Venue.—Administration is granted by surrogate court of judicial district in which decedent resided at time of his death or in which he owned property. (c. S-28, §11).

Time for Application for Probate.—Executors under will of deceased person shall apply as soon as possible for probate of will to court in proper district. Unless court orders otherwise, no grant of probate or of administration with will annexed will be issued until seven days after death, and no other grant of administraton will issue until 14 days after death. (c. A-1, §3). If executor is incompetent or unwilling to act, administration of deceased's property may be granted according to rules of preferring administrators. (c. A-1, §24). If person dies intestate leaving property in Alberta estimated by Public Trustee to exceed $3,000 and no application for letters of administration has been made, Public Trustee may apply for letters of administration after one month's notice to persons in Alberta known to be entitled to apply and who have not renounced rights to do so. (c. P-36, §24).

Preferences in Right to Administer.—Letters of administration are usually granted to surviving spouse or next of kin in order of proximity. (Surr. Ct. R. 11[2]). Preference must be given to applicant for grant of probate or administration with will annexed to personal representative named in will first, then residual beneficiary, then life tenant of residue of will, etc. (Surr. Ct. R. 11[1]).

Eligibility and Competency.—Nonresident or married woman may act as executor or administrator. Minor cannot until becomes adult. (c. A-1, §23).

Qualification.—Administrator or executor out of jurisdiction must give bond with sureties in double value of estate unless otherwise ordered by judge. (c. A-1, §5).

Public Administration.—See supra, subhead Time for Application for Probate.

Advertisement for Claims.—Executors or administrators must publish notice to claimants in newspaper (Surr. Ct. R. 38); claims must be filed within 30 days of publication of last notice. (Surr. Ct. R. 39[1]).

Proof of claims must be made in accordance with Rules. (c. A-1, §41, as am'd by S.A. 1992, c. 21, §47[2]; Surr. Ct. R. 40).

There is no prescribed form of proof of claim in connection with claims against a decedent, but the following is one in common use:

Form

NC 35

ESTATE NAME ____________
DATE OF DEATH ____________
DOCUMENT ____________ Statutory declaration by creditors and claimants

THE DECLARANT SWEARS UNDER OATH OR AFFIRMS THAT THE INFORMATION IN THIS STATUTORY DECLARATION IS WITHIN THE DECLARANT'S KNOWLEDGE AND IS TRUE. WHERE THE INFORMATION IS BASED ON ADVICE OR INFORMATION AND BELIEF, THIS IS STATED.

Declarant

1. The declarant's name and complete address is ________.
2. The declarant makes this claim as a ________.

Amount of Claim

3. The amount claimed against the ________.

Details of Claim

4. This claim is based on ________.

Security for Debt (Creditors only)

5. The declarant holds the following security for this debt ________.
6. The security is owned by ________.
7. The declarant values the security at $ ________.
8. The deceased is ________ liable for this claim.

SWORN OR AFFIRMED BEFORE A COMMISSIONER FOR OATHS AT ________, ALBERTA ON ____________

____________ ____________
Declarant *Commissioner's Name:*

____
Appointment Expiry Date:

____

Notice to Sue.—Personal representative may contest claim in whole or in part, and must do so in accordance with Rules. (c. A-1, §42, Surr. Ct. R. 42, 59, 95).

Payment of Claims.—Any claim which is allowed or is not disputed will be paid pari passu with the other claims if the estate is insolvent, including claims in a foreign jurisdiction. If it appears that creditors in a foreign jurisdiction are being paid an amount in excess of the proper percentage no payment will be made to them until the home creditors have received equal amount. (c. A-1, §§38-45).

Priorities.—All debts are paid pari passu except in case of lien on real or personal estate. (c. A-1, §43).

Accounting.—Executors or administrators must pass their accounts when ordered by court, at instance of court or any application by person interested in estate, creditor or surety, before court. (c. A-1, §46; Surr. Ct. R. 97).

Distribution.—After payment of debts, it is duty of administrator to distribute estate in accordance with law relating to devolution of estates. (See topic Descent and Distribution.). In case of executor, or where property is left by will, it is duty of legal

See Topical Index in front part of this volume.

EXECUTORS AND ADMINISTRATORS . . . *continued*
representative to carry out terms of will and in paying debts and administration costs, residuary estate is first resorted to, unless otherwise provided for in will.

There can be no distribution of estate until debts of estate are disposed of, and where dependants are interested distribution is postponed for six months from date of issuance of probate or administration except where consent of all dependants is given or court order obtained. (c. F-2, §17[2]). Reasonable advances to dependent beneficiaries can be made during delay period.

Allowances.—Upon application to judge, executor or administrator may be directed to pay allowance or lump sum to widow and family, which may be varied from time to time as circumstances require. (c. F-2, §§3, 5, 8).

Compensation.—Executors and administrators are allowed a fee by the court having jurisdiction based on the amount of work involved. (c. A-1, §62; Surr. Ct. R. Schedule #1).

Ancillary Administration.—In the case of a nonresident leaving property in Alberta, ancillary probate or letters of administration may be taken out in this Province. Where nonresident is from Canadian Province or territory, British possession, colony or dependency or member of British Commonwealth, grant may be resealed. (c. A-1, §30).

EXEMPTIONS:

Note: Exemptions Act was repealed by Civil Enforcement Act, c. C-10.5, effective Jan. 1, 1996.

Following property is exempted from writ proceedings: food required by debtor and dependants during next 12 months, clothing less than $4,000, household furnishings and appliances less than $4,000, motor vehicle less than $5,000, medical and dental aids required by debtor and dependants, principal residence where debtor's equity is less than $40,000 (if debtor is coowner of residence, exemption is reduced to amount proportionate to debtor's ownership interest), personal property of less than $10,000 used by debtor to earn income, and for farmers, 160 acres and any personal property necessary for conduct of farming operations for next year. (c. C-10.5, §88).

Debts Against Which Exemptions Not Allowed.—Exemptions do not apply to debtors who are not individuals, writ proceedings on maintenance or alimony judgments, abandoned property, and money judgments arising out of act which debtor has been convicted under Criminal Code. (§93).

Rights of Surviving Spouse and Children.—Where debtor dies, his exempted property remains exempted for period of time property is required for maintenance and support of debtor's dependants. (c. C-10.5, §92).

If debtor owns more than one item of type of exempted property and total value of items exceeds maximum exemption, debtor may select items that will be exempted. (c. C-10.5, §90).

See also topic Garnishment.

FACTORS:

Where a mercantile agent is, with the consent of the owner, in possession of goods or of the documents of title to goods, any sale, pledge or other disposition of the goods made by him to any person in good faith when acting in the ordinary course of business of a mercantile agent is as valid as if he were expressly authorized by the owner of the goods to make the same, and where a person having sold goods continues in possession of the goods or documents of title thereto the delivery or transfer by that person, or by a mercantile agent acting for him, of the goods or documents of title under any sale, etc. to any person receiving same in good faith and without notice of previous sale, is of the same effect as if the person making the delivery or transfer were expressly authorized by the owner of the goods to make the sale. (c. F-1, §§2, 9).

After §81 of Personal Property Security Act, S.A. 1988, c. P-4.05, as am'd, came into force on Oct. 1, 1990, where person obtains goods, or title to goods pursuant to security agreement under new Act, sale, pledge or other disposition of goods does not have same effect as if expressly authorized by owner. See topic Personal Property Security.

Liens.—If owner gives possession of goods to other person for sale or on consignment, or has shipped goods in name of another person and consignee is unaware person is not owner of goods, consignee has same lien on goods as if person were owner and may transfer lien to another person.

FIDUCIARIES:

See topics Executors and Administrators; Guardian and Ward; Trusts.

FORECLOSURE:

See topics Chattel Mortgages; Liens; Mortgages of Real Property.

FOREIGN CORPORATIONS: See topic Corporations.

FRANCHISES:

Note: Franchise Act, R.S.A. 1980, c. F-17, was repealed and replaced by Franchise Act, S.A. 1995, c. F-17.1, which was proclaimed on Nov. 1, 1995. Alberta is only Canadian province which to date has enacted specific legislation dealing with franchises.

Franchise Definition.—Definition of "franchise" expanded from previous Act. Franchise means business in which goods or services distributed under marketing or business plan prescribed in substantial part by franchisor that is substantially associated with trademark, tradename, logotype or advertising of franchisor, and that involves continuing financial obligation to franchisor by franchisee and significant continuing operational controls by franchisor on operation of business or payment of franchise fee. (c. F-17.1, §1[1][d]).

Disclosure Documents.—Franchisor must give every prospective franchisee copy of its disclosure document at least 14 days before signing of any agreement relating to franchise or any payment of consideration. Document must comply with requirements of Regulations, including all material facts, certificate signed by franchisor stating document contains no untrue statement of material fact, etc., financial statements of franchisor for recent fiscal year prepared in accordance with G.A.A.P., and all proposed franchise agreements. (c. F-17.1, §4). Franchisor must provide, in writing, to prospective franchisee description of any material changes. (c. F-17.1, §4[4]). Payment of consideration does not include payment of fully-refundable deposit, defined in Regulations as maximum of 15% of initial franchise fee. (c. F-17.1, §4[6] and Reg. 240/95, §5).

Exceptions.—Franchisor not required to provide financial statements in disclosure document if franchisor has net worth of $5 million, or $1 million if franchisor is controlled by corporation whose net worth is more than $5 million, and if franchisor has at least 25 franchisees conducting business during previous five-year period from disclosure document, has conducted business continuously for at least five years preceding disclosure document date, or is controlled by corporation meeting either of these requirements. (Reg. 249/95, §1).

Exemptions from requirement of franchisor to deliver disclosure document include: sale of franchise by franchisee if he is not franchisor or associate or corporate employee of franchisor, and sale is not effected by franchisor; sale of franchise to officer or director of franchisor who held office for at least six months; sale of additional franchise to existing franchisee; renewal or extension of existing franchise agreement; sale of franchise that has total annual investment not exceeding $5,000 (Reg. 240/95, §6); sale of franchise by executor, receiver, trustee in bankruptcy, etc. on behalf of person other than franchisor; sale of right of person to sell goods/services within retail establishment as department or division of establishment if not required to purchase goods/services from operator of retail establishment; and sale of fractional franchise (defined as franchise granted to person whose sales do not exceed 20% of total sales of business—c. F-17.1, §1[1][c] and Reg. 240/95, §4) (c. F-17.1, §6).

Fair Dealing.—Every franchise agreement imposes on each party duty of fair dealing in its performance and enforcement. (c. F-17.1, §7).

Right to Associate.—Franchisor cannot prohibit or restrict franchisee from forming organization of franchisees or from associating with other franchisees. Franchisor must not directly or indirectly penalize franchisee from engaging in such activities. (c. F-17.1, §8). If franchisor contravenes this provision, franchisee has right of action for damages against franchisor. (c. F-17.1, §11).

Remedies.—If franchisee suffers loss because of misrepresentation contained in disclosure document, franchisee has right of action for damages against franchisor and every person who signed document. If document contains misrepresentation, franchisee is deemed to have relied on it. (c. F-17.1, §9). All parties found liable in action under Act are jointly and severally liable. (c. F-17.1, §12). Act states rights of action conferred by Act are in addition to and do not derogate from any other rights parties have at law. (c. F-17.1, §15). Franchisor not liable for misrepresentation where: it proves franchisee purchased franchise with knowledge of misrepresentation (c. F-17.1, §10[1]); person other than franchisor not liable if person proves disclosure document given without that person's knowledge or consent (c. F-17.1, §10[2]); person other than franchisor not liable unless person did not conduct investigation sufficient to identify misrepresentation or they believed there was misrepresentation (c. F-17.1, §10[3]). Exemptions from liability also provided relating to experts whose reports, opinions or statements were made part of disclosure document. (c. F-17.1, §10[2][b] and [c]).

Recision.—Where franchisor fails to give franchisee disclosure document in accordance with time requirements of Act, prospective franchisee can rescind franchise agreement by giving notice of cancellation no later than 60 days after receiving disclosure document or no later than two years after granting of franchise, whichever occurs first. (c. F-17.1, §13). Notice of cancellation operates to cancel franchise agreement. (c. F-17.1, §14[1]). Franchisor must compensate franchisee within 30 days of receiving cancellation notice for any net losses franchisee has incurred in acquiring, setting up and operating franchised business. (c. F-17.1, §14[2]).

Governing Law, Jurisdiction and Waivers.—Law of Alberta applies to all franchise agreements. (c. F-17.1, §16). Any choice of law or choice of forum clauses in franchise agreements designating venue or law outside Alberta is void. (c. F-17.1, §17). Any waiver or release by franchisee of any rights given under Act or Regulations is void. (c. F-17.1, §18).

Self-Government.—Lieutenant Governor-in-Council can designate one or more bodies to govern franchising and to promote fair dealing among franchisors and franchisees in Alberta, though none has been designated yet. Any such body must be corporation and capable of governing persons involved in franchising. Lieutenant Governor-in-Council can make Regulations dealing with administration, exercise of powers, duties and functions of designated body, and levy of fees. (c. F-17.1, §21).

Other.—Requirement that franchisor delivers disclosure document to franchisee does not apply to sale of franchise if agreement was entered into prior to Nov. 1, 1995, and prospectus or statement of material facts was given in compliance of Act. (c. F-17.1, §22[1]).

FRAUDS, STATUTE OF:

Fourth section of The Imperial Statute of Frauds (29 Car. 2, c. 3) is in force. It is as follows: "That no action shall be brought whereby to charge any executor or administrator upon any special promise to answer damages out of his own estate; or whereby to charge the defendant upon any special promise to answer for the debt, default, or miscarriage of another person; or to charge any person upon any agreement made in consideration of marriage; or upon any contract or sale of lands, tenements or hereditaments, or any interest in or concerning them; or upon any agreement that is not to be performed within the space of one year from the making thereof; unless the agreement upon which action shall be brought, or some memorandum, or note thereof, shall be in writing and signed by the party to be charged therewith, or some other person thereunto by him lawfully authorized." Other provisions in Statute of Frauds are likely in force in Alberta as well. (25 D.L.R. [2d] 760).

Contracts of Sale.—Under the Sale of Goods Act no contract for the sale of goods of the value of $50 or upwards is enforceable unless the buyer accepts part of the goods so sold and actually receives the same, or gives something in earnest to bind the contract or in part payment, or unless some note or memorandum in writing of the contract is made and signed by the party to be charged or his agent in that behalf. (c. S-2, §7).

FRAUDS, STATUTE OF . . . *continued*

Services in Connection with Sale of Land.—There is a further enactment declaring that no action shall be brought to charge any person, either by way of commission or otherwise for services rendered in connection with the sale of land, or interest therein, unless (a) contract or memorandum thereof is in writing, signed by party to be charged or his agent thereunto lawfully authorized in writing or (b) party to be charged has effected sale or lease of land or interest in it as result of services of such agent, or has executed transfer or lease or agreement of sale of land entitling purchaser to possession of land which has been signed by all parties and delivered to purchaser. (c. R-5, §25).

FRAUDULENT SALES AND CONVEYANCES:

Portions of provincial legislation (c. F-18, §3) have been held to be ultra vires because of conflict with exclusive federal jurisdiction over bankruptcy and insolvency ([1965] 50 WWR 155). However, there is now some question as to this authority. ([1977] 2 WWR 111). Other portions of this legislation may continue in effect to void dispositions of property made by persons on eve of insolvency with intent to prejudice creditors.

Remedies.—Any creditor may bring action in proper court to set aside any conveyance on ground of fraud. (c. F-18, §10). Injunction order may be obtained to preserve property until action is disposed of. See also topic Interest, subhead Unconscionable Transactions.

Bulk Sales Act has been repealed by S.A. 1992, c. 21, §5.

GARNISHMENT:

Money owing to a debtor may be garnisheed only after judgment, except with leave. (A.R.C. 470).

Proceedings to Obtain.—The creditor or his agent having obtained leave and having knowledge of the facts must file an affidavit stating nature and amount of indebtedness of debtor and also that in his belief proposed garnishee is indebted to debtor or that monies are accruing due from proposed garnishee to debtor and that proposed garnishee is within Alberta. Affidavit must also set out, to extent that this is within creditor's knowledge, place of business of garnishee through which indebtedness is alleged to be payable, whether alleged debt sought to be attached is for wages or salary, residence of judgment debtor, nature of his service to garnishee and whether judgment was recovered in respect of contract for board or lodging. (A.R.C. 470[3]).

Duties of Garnishee.—Garnishee must file answer to summons disputing liability, stating that money is accruing due but is not yet payable or that debt belongs to third person within ten days or pay into court lesser of amount of money due from him to debtor, or amount sufficient to satisfy claim or judgment and probable costs of creditor. (A.R.C. 475).

Effect of Garnishment.—The garnishee summons when properly served at a time when the money sought to be attached is actually due will bind the debt due or accruing due from the garnishee to the debtor. (A.R.C. 471).

Judgment.—If garnishee does not pay into court or file answer within time limited, judgment may be ordered against him for such amount as court deems proper. (A.R.C. 475[4]).

Earnings.—In case of debt to employee for wages or salary, exemptions of $700 per month in case of married person plus $140 per child or $525 per month plus $140 per child in case of single person are allowed and only excess will be paid in by garnishee. Where such person is paid by periods other than one month he is entitled to pro rata exemption. (A.R.C. 483).

GUARANTEE: See topic Bonds.

GUARDIAN AND WARD:

Ordinarily joint guardians of infant are (a) mother and (b) father if he was married to mother at time of child's birth, his marriage to mother of child was terminated by decree of nullity or divorce not more than 300 days before birth of child, he cohabitated with mother of child for at least one year immediately before child's birth, or he married mother of child after child's birth and has acknowledged that he is father of child. (c. D-37, §47). Court of Queen's Bench may order otherwise, and may also, if it is satisfied that it is in best interests of child and that applicant is willing and able to assume responsibility, appoint person declared to be parent under Part 8 of Domestic Relations Act to be guardian jointly with any other guardian. (c. D-37, §47).

Part 8 of Domestic Relations Act provides that person claiming to be father, mother or child of another person may apply to Court for declaration of parentage, and Court shall decide issue on balance of probabilities. (c. D-37, §64[1]); 1991, c. 11, §1[3]). For all purposes of law in Alberta, there is legal presumption that person is father of child in any of circumstances set out above or if person is registered as father of child as joint request of himself and child's mother under Vital Statistics Act, unless contrary is proven on balance of probabilities. (c. D-37, §63[1]).

Either parent may by will appoint his or her successor as guardian. (c. D-37; §48).

Appointment by Court.—Where the court interferes with the guardianship of an infant or where an infant becomes a ward of the court in some other manner, the court's chief consideration is the welfare of the infant. In appointing guardians the court considers religion, station and ability to care for child chiefly. (c. C-8.1).

Insane Persons.—Upon issuance of certificate of incapacity by Public Trustee, Public Trustee becomes trustee of estate of mentally incompetent person. (c. P-36, §11). Court of Queen's Bench may make orders for committing care and custody of person of unsound mind to plenary or partial guardian or his estate to trustee. Applications must be made in judicial district in which person of unsound mind resides. (c. D-32).

Foreign Guardians.—Adoption orders of any other jurisdiction have same effect as if made in Alberta. (c. C-8.1, §65.1).

Public Trustee appointed under provisions of Public Trustee Act may act as guardian ad litem of infants generally and as trustee of any infant made ward of Province under Child Welfare Act, by provisions of which all neglected children, whether orphans or not may be assigned to public homes. (c. P-36, §4).

HOLIDAYS:

Every Sunday, New Year's Day, Alberta Family Day, Good Friday, Easter Monday, Victoria Day (1st Mon. prior to May 25), Queen's Birthday (fixed by Proclamation), Canada Day (July 1), Labor Day (1st Mon. in Sept.), Thanksgiving Day (Proclaimed by Proclamation), Remembrance Day, Christmas Day, Dec. 26 or when that date falls on Sun. or Mon., then Dec. 27 and any other day which may by proclamation be declared holiday. (c. I-7, §25[1][i.1]). Where time limited for doing anything expires or falls upon holiday, time so limited extends to and thing may be done on first following day that is not holiday. (c. I-7, §22 [1]).

In cases involving documentation with government branches or services, time shall be extended to first following day that office is open. (c. I-7, §22[2]).

Transactions on Sundays or Holidays.—Validity of Sun. observance legislation has been successfully challenged as being violation of Canadian Charter of Rights and Freedoms. ([1985] 1 S.C.R. 295).

HOMESTEADS:

Principle residence of enforcement debtor is exempt from writ proceedings, where enforcement debtor's equity does not exceed $40,000 or such amount proportionate to debtor's ownership in residence. (c. C-10.5, 1994, §§88[g]; Alta. Reg. 276/95, §37[1][e]).

Conveyance or Encumbrance.—Married person may not sell or encumber his or her homestead without written consent of his or her spouse, who must be examined separately and apart from his or her spouse as to such consent: such consent being certified by proper officer. Consent of spouse must be contained in or annexed to instrument disposing of homestead. Judge may by order in certain cases dispense with such consent. (c. D-38).

A person has a life estate in the homestead property of his or her spouse unless that person voluntarily surrenders it. See topic Dower.

Forms

Consent of Spouse.—I, ... being married to the above named . . . . do hereby give my consent to the disposition of our homestead, made in this (or the annexed) instrument, and I have executed this document for the purpose of giving up my life estate and other dower rights in the property given to me by The Dower Act to the extent necessary to give effect to the disposition.

. . . . (Signature of Spouse) (Alta. Reg. 470/81, Form A).

Certificate of Acknowledgment by Spouse.—1. This document was acknowledged before me by . . . . apart from her husband (his wife).

2. . . . . acknowledged to me that she (he):

(a) Is aware of the nature of the disposition (agreement);

(b) Is aware that The Dower Act gives her (him) a life estate in the homestead and the right to prevent disposition of the homestead by withholding consent;

(c) Consents to the disposition (agreement) for the purpose of giving up the life estate and other dower rights in the homestead given to her (him) by The Dower Act, to the extent necessary to give effect to the said disposition (agreement);

(d) Is executing the document freely and voluntarily without any compulsion on the part of her husband (his wife).

Dated at . . . . in the Province of . . . . this . . . . day of . . . . A.D. 19. . . . .

. . . .

A Commissioner for Oaths/Notary etc. (Alta. Reg. 470/81, Form C).

Affidavit.—I,____,
of____
______________________________, ________________________
(occupation)

make oath and say:

1 I am the transferor (or mortgagor, lessor or encumbrancer, as the case may be) (or the agent acting under power of attorney in my favour registered in the Land Titles Office on _______________ 19_____ as instrument number _________ granted by the transferor, mortgagor, or encumbrancer) named in the within (or annexed) instrument.

2 I am (or My principal is) not married.

or

Neither myself nor my spouse (or my principal nor his spouse) have resided on the within mentioned land at any time since our (or their) marriage.

or

I am (or My principal is) married to __________ being the person who executed the release of dower rights registered in the Land Titles Office on ___________ 19____ as instrument number _________.

or

A judgment for damages was obtained against me by my spouse (or my principal by his spouse) and registered in the Land Titles Office on _____________ 19_____ as instrument number _________.

Sworn before me at __________)
in the Province of ____________) ____________________________
this ______ day of ___________)
19___.)

____
A Commissioner, etc. (or as the case may be)

(Alta. Reg. 194/85, Form B).

HUSBAND AND WIFE:

Married person is required to maintain his spouse and criminal information may be made on his failure to do so generally. (R.S.C. 1985, c. C-46, §215).

Actions By or Against Married Women.—A married woman may in all cases sue or be sued without joining her husband to same extent as if she were unmarried. (c. M-

See Topical Index in front part of this volume.

HUSBAND AND WIFE . . . *continued*
7, §1). Action may be brought against any married woman for all civil injuries, and damages may be recovered from her alone and her husband is not responsible therefor unless he would be liable apart from fact of his being her husband. (c. M-7, §6). Married man or woman has same civil remedies against his/her spouse for protection and security of his/her separate property as against other persons. (c. M-7, §2).

Liability of Husband for Debts of Wife.—A husband may be held responsible for the debts incurred by his wife either as his express or implied agent or in cases where the wife would be held to be an agent of necessity, as where the husband has deserted his wife, or in similar circumstances.

Business Dealings of Married Women.—A married woman may carry on business either solely or in partnership with any other person, and her husband will have no interest therein or liability.

Property Dealings of Married Women.—A married woman is capable of dealing in all classes of real and personal property as if she were unmarried. (c. M-7, §3). All property acquired by or devolved upon married woman after Mar. 25, 1936, belongs to her as if she were unmarried and may be so disposed of. (c. M-7, §5).

Right of Husband to Sue for Tort to Wife.—A husband has no right to sue in respect of a tort done to his wife except where and in so far as he has sustained any separate damage or injury. (c. M-7, §4).

Community Property.—There is no community of property in Alberta at present. Under Matrimonial Property Act (c. M-9), upon divorce, separation or period of living separate and apart Court of Queen's Bench may order distribution of property acquired after marriage having regard to earning capacity, duration of marriage, any agreement between parties and contributions of each spouse.

Antenuptial Contracts.—Agreement providing for status, ownership and division of matrimonial property may be entered into by two persons in contemplation of their marriage to each other but is unenforceable until after marriage. (c. M-9, §37[1][2]). Such agreement is unenforceable by spouse if at time of agreement that spouse knew or had reason to believe marriage was void. (c. M-9, §37[4]).

Agreement is enforceable if each spouse or person acknowledged in writing he is: (i) Aware of nature/effect of agreement, (ii) aware of possible future claims to property he has under Act and intends to give up these claims to give effect to agreement, and (iii) executing agreement voluntarily. (c. M-9, §38[1]). Acknowledgment shall be made before lawyer other than lawyer acting for other spouse or person. (c. M-9, §38[2]).

INCOME TAX:

See topic Taxation; also Canada Law Digest, topic Taxation.

INFANTS:

Age of majority 18 both sexes. (c. A-4).

Contracts.—Infant not liable on his contract except for necessaries (c. S-2, §4) or at 16 for life insurance (c. I-5, §271), unless there is ratification.

Property.—Court may make orders respecting real property of infant, and court may order certain settlements. (c. M-16, §2).

Custody, etc.—Court may make orders as to guardianship, custody, maintenance and religious education of infant. (c. D-37, Part 7).

Actions.—Infant sues or counterclaims by next friend and defends by guardian or guardian ad litem. (A.R.C. 58, 59).

Legitimacy.—Child whose parents intermarry after birth is legitimate, as is child of void marriage registered in substantial compliance with relevant law and believed by either of parties to be valid, or child of marriage void because of false presumption of death, or child of voidable marriage annulled by decree. Property interests vested prior to July 1, 1927, not affected. (c. L-11).

Child Welfare Act.—Any person who has reasonable grounds to believe that child is in need of protective services shall report matter to Director. (c. C-8.1, §3). Director may apply to court for Temporary or Permanent Guardianship Order if there are reasonable grounds to believe child's survival, security or development are endangered. (c. C-8.1, Part 3). Court may not appoint guardian if purpose is to facilitate adoption of minor.

Search Agency.—Application may be made to license and search agency for location of family member; or for disclosure of identity and other personal information of applicant to family member or family member to applicant. (c. C-8.1, Part 6).

Wills.—See topic Wills.

Adoption.—See topic Adoption.

INHERITANCE TAX: See topic Taxation.

INJUNCTIONS:

Injunction order may be obtained to prevent disposal of property or doing of any act in all cases in which it may appear to court just or convenient to make such order. (c. J-1, §13[2]). Interim injunction may be granted upon such terms as may appear just to preserve property or interest therein in status quo pending final determination of action. (A.R.C. 383). Except that no injunction before trial shall be granted ex parte to restrain any person from doing any act in connection with strike or lockout. (c. L-1.2, §90). Injunction order is not usually made where damages would be adequate remedy.

INSOLVENCY:

See Canada Law Digest, topic Bankruptcy.

INSURANCE:

Supervision.—The Superintendent of Insurance has general supervision of the insurance business within province. (c. I-5, §3).

License.—Every insurer doing business in the province must take out a provincial license which will be issued only to a corporation, an unincorporated Lloyd's association or certain societies. (c. I-5, §§25, 28).

Real Estate.—Provincial companies licenced under Alberta Insurance Act may hold absolutely such real estate as they require for purposes of transaction of their business and any real property acquired by it by foreclosure or in satisfaction of debt. They may hold for period not exceeding ten years land acquired by them by foreclosure or in satisfaction of debt. (c. I-5, §111).

Investments.—Funds of insurance company must be invested in certain approved ways. (c. I-5, §94).

Fire Insurance.—Under provisions of Alberta Insurance Act, every registered fire insurance company may insure and reinsure any property in which assured has an insurable interest against loss or damage by fire, lightning or explosion. (c. I-5, §30).

No insurer may make a contract covering property outside limits of an incorporated city, town or village for a term exceeding 12 months without a written application signed by applicant or his agent. (c. I-5, §232).

Act provides certain uniform or statutory conditions and no variation therefrom is binding on assured. (c. I-5, §235). If with consent of company, policy is made payable to a mortgagee, policy cannot be cancelled without reasonable notice to mortgagee. (c. I-5, §234).

Life Insurance.—Every life company must register under Federal Act, which provides for deposit of securities with view to secure performance of every life insurance contract (R.S.C. 1985, c. I-12, §§75, 76). Without registration company shall not transact business except as required to protect policy holders. (R.S.C. 1985, c. I-11.8, §§52, 74). Policies of life insurance are also governed by provisions of Alberta Insurance Act, which lays down definite rules as to contents of policy, statutory conditions, nondisclosure, misrepresentation, statements as to age, payment of premiums, when contract takes effect and assignments. (c. I-5, Part 6).

Other Insurances.—In the provisions of the Alberta Insurance Act certain regulations are made in reference to hail, accident, fidelity, guarantee, inland marine, inland transportation, sickness, casualty, automobile, against financial loss, burglary, etc.

Foreign insurance company may do business in the province, provided it obtains a license from the Government and complies with the regulations.

Direct Actions Against Insurer.—See topic Motor Vehicles, subhead Direct Actions.

INTEREST:

Loan Agreements.—Loans, other than those made to a manufacturer, distributor, wholesaler or retailer, in course of business upon security; or by pawnbrokers; or those exempted by regulation; must be evidenced in writing or printing, setting out with respect to loan principal, amount received by borrower, charges, credit charge expressed in terms of money and annual interest, total amount required to be repaid, amount and time of instalments, additional charges for default, and clear and prominent statement of security taken. Duplicate copy must be issued to borrower before money is advanced. Loan agreement or revision thereto must be signed by borrower. Acceleration clause only effective upon written notice to borrower. (c. C-22.5, Part 2). Credit grantor is restricted in amount of interest he may charge. (c. C-22.5, §12). Interest must also be expressed in accordance with Canada Interest Act, otherwise lender is limited to statutory rate. (R.S.C. 1985, c. I-15). Rebates on credit charges in manner required by regulation where payments made before due date. (c. C-22.5). See generally Canada Law Digest.

Unconscionable Transactions.—If a court decides that, by virtue of circumstances, cost of a loan is excessive and transaction is unconscionable court may open transaction and adjust its terms. (c. U-2; §2).

INTESTACY:

See topic Descent and Distribution.

JOINT STOCK COMPANIES:

No statutory provisions. Rules regulating corporations apply.

JUDGMENTS:

When an action is defended, judgment is given by the court in the usual way.

Judgment by Consent.—The defendant may consent to judgment against him. (A.R.C. 329).

Summary Judgment.—After a defense has been entered summary judgment may be obtained in certain cases where the plaintiff can show the defendant has no defense. If there is any possibility of his having a defense the court usually will not deprive him of it. Defendant can now also apply for summary judgment on basis that plaintiff's claim is without merit. (A.R.C. 159).

Declaratory Judgments.—Court has jurisdiction to give declaratory judgments. (c. J-1, §11).

Default Judgments.—After commencement of any action for debt, liquidated damage or recovery of goods or land if defendant does not enter defense within stipulated time, final judgment may be signed against him and executions issued. (A.R.C. 148, 149). In any other kind of action he may be "noted in default" and thereby prevented from entering defense. It is then necessary to have amount of judgment, etc., fixed by judge. (A.R.C. 142, 152). Plaintiff can have vacated its own default judgment to prevent any possible res judicata.

Life of Judgment.—Judgments are valid for ten years. They may be sued upon during that time in which case they are good for ten years again. Once a judgment expires all rights thereunder are lost. (c. L-15, §4, A.R.C. 331). See topic Limitation of Actions.

Opening up Judgment.—Any judgment entered upon default of defense may be opened up upon cause being shown and, usually plaintiff's costs paid. (A.R.C. 158).

JUDGMENTS . . . *continued*

Assignment.—Judgments may be assigned for value and the assignee has all the rights and privileges of the original plaintiff.

Following is per Alberta Court Forms as Satisfaction Piece No. 19.3:

19.3 SATISFACTION PIECE

IN THE COURT OF QUEEN'S BENCH OF ALBERTA
JUDICIAL DISTRICT OF [**DISTRICT**]

BETWEEN

[Style of Cause]

SATISFACTION OF JUDGMENT PIECE

SATISFACTION OF THE JUDGMENT in the within action is hereby acknowledged on behalf of the Plaintiff, and the Plaintiff hereby consents to a Memorandum of Satisfaction being endorsed by the Clerk of this Honourable Court.

DATED at the [**City/Town**] of [**Place**], in the Province of Alberta, this [**Date**].

[**Name of Firm**]

Per: ______________________

Solicitors for the Plaintiff
[Print Name of Lawyer signing]

TO: Clerk of the Court

Foreign judgments may be sued upon in this jurisdiction. They are considered to be simple contract debts or liquidated demands and if not disputed judgment may be entered thereon.

There is a Reciprocal Enforcement of Judgments Act in force in this province by virtue of which judgment may be entered forthwith upon production of a certified copy of judgment obtained in other jurisdiction together with certain affidavits. (c. R-6). This act is only in force at present time with regard to provinces of Saskatchewan, Ontario, Manitoba, British Columbia, North West Territories, Newfoundland, New Brunswick, Nova Scotia, Prince Edward Island, Yukon Territory, and England, Wales, Malta, Isle of Man, Northern Ireland, Papua New Guinea, Barbados, Fiji, State of California, Republic of South Africa, Republic of Singapore, New Zealand, Scotland, Jersey and following states of Australia: Victoria, New South Wales, Queensland, South Australia, Western Australia and Australian Capital Territory.

JUSTICES OF THE PEACE:

Justices of peace exercise limited criminal jurisdiction throughout province in which they reside. (c. J-3).

LABOUR RELATIONS:

Rights and liabilities of employer and employee are regulated by common law supplemented by several provincial statutes.

The Employment Standards Code (c. E-10.2) regulates employment relationship, including records, hours, wages, vacations and holidays with pay and collection of entitlements. Administration of Act is in hands of Director who has recourse to officers to investigate matters under Act and to issue orders. Appeals are to umpires appointed under Act.

Master and Servants Act (c. M-8) applies to contracts or hire of personal service and provides summary machinery for dealing with servants guilty of misconduct and employers failing to pay wages promptly or improperly dismissing employees. It does not affect parties' ordinary civil rights. Act provides that contracts for more than one year must be in writing and signed by both parties. (c. M-8, §2). Act applies in Alberta to contracts made outside of Alberta but to be performed either wholly or in part within province. (c. M-8, §3).

Hours of Labour.—Regulated by The Employment Standards Code. (c. E-10.2). Subject to exceptions in Regulations regular working hours of any employee shall not exceed eight in a day nor 44 in a week. Employer must allow 24 consecutive hours of rest each week or multiple of 24 hours for equivalent multiple of weeks up to four; otherwise overtime must be paid or time off given. (c. E-10.2, Division 5, §27).

Wages.—The Employment Standards Code provides that minimum wages may be fixed by regulation (c. E-10.2, §35) currently Regulation No. 123/92.

Employer is obliged to pay wages owing to each employee within ten days after end of employment period, which period may not exceed one month without approval of Director. (c. E-10.2, §§23, 24).

Act gives employee priority over other claims that are not secured for up to $7,500, and order of officer or umpire covering employee's claim when registered against property of employer becomes secured charge with same priority it would have if it were registered mortgage. (c. E-10.2, §§113, 114).

Child Labour.—No person under 15 shall be employed without written consent of parent or guardian and approval of Director. No person shall during normal school hours employ child required by law to attend school. (c. E-10.2, §75).

Discrimination.—Employers, trade unions and occupational associations forbidden to discriminate because of race, religious beliefs, colour, sex, physical disability, mental disability, marital status, age, ancestry or origin. (c. I-2).

Note: Individual Rights Protection Act is being replaced by Human Rights and Citizenship Act (c. H-11.7, §7[1]) not yet proclaimed but adds "family status and source of income" to prohibited class of discrimination.

Female Labour.—Individual's Rights Protection Act provides that no employer shall pay female employees a lesser wage than male employees employed by employer in similar work. (c. I-2, §6).

Labour Unions.—The Labour Relations Code (c. L-1.2) regulates employment field, except managerial positions and professional members of medical, dental, architectural, engineering or legal professions qualified to practice in Alberta, with respect to certification of unions, collective agreements, mediation, arbitration, strikes and unfair labour practices. Act appoints Labour Relations Board to supervise certification of unions and conduct of strike votes, to investigate and decide labour disputes, and to impose penalties for breaches of Act.

Trade union may be certified as bargaining agent of unit upon showing majority support from members of unit and complying with certification provisions of Code. (c. L-1.2, Part 2, Divison 5). Certified bargaining agent has exclusive authority to bargain collectively on behalf of unit and to bind it by collective agreement. Certification can be revoked upon application of employees in unit or Labour Relations Board's own initiative where no person objects to such initiative. (c. L-1.2, Part 2, Division 8).

Act permits employer organizations in construction industry to bargain collectively on behalf of all employers in territory or trade jurisdiction in respect of whom trade union has right of collective bargaining, where employer organization claims to have majority of employers as members. Employer organization must apply to be registered in manner set forth in Act. (c. L-1.2, Part 3, Division 3).

Labour Disputes.—No employer or employer's organization or its agent can interfere with formation, or administration of union nor can such persons contribute to its support in financial or any other way subject to exceptions contained in Act. Nor may employer exercise any form of restraint or pressure on his employee with regard to his union affairs (c. L-1.2, §§146, 147).

Strike or lockout is illegal during term of collective agreement and up to 30 days after certification of bargaining agent. Legal strike or lock-out requires affirmative vote by majority. (c. L-1.2, Part 2, Division 13). During collective bargaining parties may request or Minister may require appointment of mediator. (c. L-1.2, Part 2, Division 11). Every collective agreement must provide provisions for settling differences. (c. L-1.2, Part 2, Division 22).

Miscellaneous Regulations.—Standards for tools and equipment, washing and sanitary facilities on work site, eating areas and medical facilities on work site may be prescribed by regulation. (c. O-2, §31). Officer has power to inspect for unhealthy or unsafe conditions and stop work if necessary on those sites. Director of Inspection may apply for restraining order where officer's powers are interfered with. (c. O-2, §§6, 7, 9).

Contravention of Safety Standards.—Employer is liable on summary conviction for contravention of safety standards to fine or imprisonment or both. (c. O-2, §32).

Worker's Compensation Act.—(c. W-16) provides machinery whereby worker injured in course of his employment may secure compensation from "accident fund" accumulated and sustained by assessment of employers, in industries coming under provisions of this act.

Act applies to all employers and workers in all industries except those exempted by regulation and may by order extend to persons fighting disasters or emergencies. (c. W-16, §9).

Civil Enforcement Act, c. C-10.5, allows for registration of financing statement to entitle Board to conduct civil enforcement proceedings as if it were enforcement creditor in addition to rights and remedies provided under Act.

Remedy Exclusive.—Provisions of Act are in lieu of all rights of action statutory or otherwise which a workman or his dependents may have been entitled to bring against his employer. (c. W-16, §16).

Unemployment Compensation.—See Canada Law Digest.

LANDLORD AND TENANT:

The ordinary common law rules as to rights and liabilities of landlords and tenants prevail in this province, and are supplemented by Residential Tenancies Act, c. R-15.3, which was proclaimed in force on Aug. 1, 1992.

Leases for more than three years should be in writing under seal, but may be enforced by tenant against landlord and vice versa if there have been acts of part performance, subject to provisions of Land Titles Act, whereby tenant may lose his right as against registered owner if lease is not in writing or lease is not registered. (c. L-5, §98). Court of Queen's Bench of Alberta has power to relieve against forfeiture for breach of covenant in lease. (c. J-1, §10). Where tenant executes residential tenancy agreement in writing landlord must deliver copy to tenant within 21 days of agreement being returned to landlord, otherwise tenant is entitled to withhold payment of rent until served. (c. R-15.3, §15).

When tenant enters into residential tenancy agreement with landlord, landlord shall serve tenant with "notice of landlord" within seven days of tenant taking possession. (§15.1[2]). Landlord must make inspection reports within one week after tenant moves into premises; if no inspection report as per Act, landlord cannot make deduction from security deposit for damages, (§15.2).

Termination of Tenancy.—Weekly or monthly or year to year tenancy may be terminated on either party giving written notice, signed by party or his agent, which designated premises concerned and date that tenancy is to terminate. In case of termination by landlord, landlord must specify reasons for which tenancy is being terminated; landlord's notice is of no effect unless termination is for one or more of prescribed reasons set out in Regulations. (§4.1). Tenant of residential premises may not waive or release rights, benefits or protections provided to him under Act. Except in cases of absence or where service is governed by rules or practice of court, any notice, order or document shall be served personally, by registered or certified mail.

Action for Rent.—Landlord must give tenant written notice of increase in rent; for weekly tenancy—12 weeks, for monthly tenancy—three months, for any other periodic tenancy—at least 90 days. (c. R-15.3, §13). Landlord may sue his tenant for amount of rent but in this case he may lose special rights given to landlord, namely, seizure, priority over most other claims, etc. In case of suit only goods subject to execution are available to satisfy judgment.

Security Deposit.—Landlord of residential premises cannot require security deposit exceeding one month's rent and is regulated as to what can be done with such and when and under what conditions it must be repaid to tenant. Landlord shall not require tenant

See Topical Index in front part of this volume.

LANDLORD AND TENANT . . . *continued*
to pay increase in security deposit. Landlord must place security deposits into interest bearing account and must pay interest annually to tenant, unless otherwise agreed. (c. R-15.3, §§37-40).

Lien.—Landlord has a lien on his tenant's goods for amount of rent owing.

Recovery of Possession.—A landlord may recover possession of his premises in several ways. He may give the tenant notice to quit. He may declare the tenancy forfeited by reason of the breach of covenant in the lease or where the tenant has been convicted of keeping a disorderly house.

Proceedings for recovery where tenant refuses to vacate are commenced by way of originating notice asking for order for possession accompanied by landlord's affidavit attesting to relevant facts as set out in Act. (c. R-15.3). Originating notice of motion may include claim for rent arrears, damages, for use and occupation after expiration or termination of tenancy, and in case of residential tenancy agreement, termination of tenancy by reason of substantial breach. On hearing matter judge may: (a) Give order for possession, (b) give judgment for damages, (c) give judgment for use and occupation by tenant holding over, (d) give order for costs, (e) direct trial of issue, (f) give order for termination of tenancy, or (g) dismiss application.

Proceedings in respect to arrears or compensation can continue even if tenant vacates on service of originating notice. (c. R-15.3, §§20-36).

If tenant commits substantial breach under residential tenancy agreement, landlord may apply to court to determine tenancy with 14 days notice to tenant. This is ineffective if before termination date arrives arrears of rent are paid or tenant supplies written objection.

Distress.—Common law rules and statutes govern distress for rent although goods of strangers are not liable to distress, unless title is derived by purchase, gift, transfer of assignment from tenant or they have security interest in personal property other than Purchase Money Security Interest. The Civil Enforcement Act, c. C-10.5, §§104-105 (proclaimed on Jan. 1, 1996) governs distress for rent. Property claimed by relative of tenant may be distrained, if such relative lives on premises as member of tenant's family. Interest of tenant in property held under conditional sale agreement is also distrainable. No distress may be made after declaration of bankruptcy or winding up order of company. (c. L-7, §2).

Unless otherwise ordered by court, distress can only be made through civil enforcement bailiff. Tenant is given 15 days within which to file notice of objection, failing which goods may be sold by civil/enforcement agency. If notice of objection is filed goods cannot be removed or sold without order from Queen's Bench judge after notice to tenant. (c. C-10.5, §§45-48).

LEASES: See topic Landlord and Tenant.

LEGISLATURE:

The Alberta Act (1905) establishes legislature for province consisting of Lieutenant Governor and single House styled Legislative Assembly of Alberta. (§12). Legislative assembly has exclusive power to make laws in relation to matters of local and private nature and certain other matters enumerated in Constitution Act 1867. (§§92, 92A, 93, 95). Government may call sessions at any time.

LEVY: See topics Attachment; Executions.

LICENSES:

Licensing of Trades and Businesses Act (c. L-13) governs trades, businesses, etc., not licensed or controlled by some other statute. Lieutenant Governor in Council may formulate codes or standards of business ethics, methods, practices, etc., and any business which contravenes such codes or standards may be suspended from operation or be subject to fine of up to $10,000, in case of corporation, or $5,000 in case of individual. Regulatory boards may be established in respect of licensing of particular business. Persons who have suffered loss or damage arising out of operation of licensed business may be compensated out of fund created by regulatory board. Fees payable upon registration cannot exceed $1,000. (§4). Under Municipal Government Act, municipalities are empowered to enact licensing by-laws covering businesses, trade and occupations, etc. (c. M.26.1, §7).

Certain classes of persons and equipment are required to be licensed under statute, regulation or municipal by-law, such as real estate and insurance agents, auctioneers, peddlers, vendors and oil construction and other equipment. See also topic Motor Vehicles. Bona fide commission travelers selling wholesale to retailer are among few exceptions to this requirement.

Federal Government imposes few nominal license fees.

Public Charitable Campaigns.—Provision is made for registration and supervision of public charitable fund-raising campaigns. (c. C-4.5).

LIENS:

Artisan.—Every person who has bestowed money, labour or skill upon any chattel in improving the same and every bailee is entitled to lien and to hold same in his possession and if his lien is unpaid for three months, in the case of a motor vehicle, and, six months, in the case of any other property, may serve notice on the debtor of the amount of his indebtedness, of reasonable time and place for payment, and that in default application will be made at fixed time and place for leave to sell goods. (c. P-13).

Solicitor.—See topic Attorneys and Counselors, subhead Lien.

Vendor of property has a lien charge upon such property unless he has waived his rights.

Lumbering.—Any person engaged in lumbering has a lien upon the logs, etc. (c. W-14).

Warehousemen, wharfingers and bailees are entitled to liens. (cc. P-13, W-3).

Garageman has lien on motor vehicle or farm vehicle for storage, repairs, etc., if he has possession or if before surrendering possession he obtains written acknowledgment of charges signed by person authorizing same. This lien does not depend on continued possession, but claim of lien must be registered with Personal Property Registry within 21 days after termination of storage or service. Lien is postponed to encumbrances on vehicle created in good faith and without express notice before claim of lien is registered. Lien expires unless civil enforcement agency seizes vehicle within six months of registering, or unless order extending time is obtained. If seized, lien holder must enforce his rights and remedies in accordance with provisions of Civil Enforcement Act. (c. G-1).

Registry system and necessary documents fall under Personal Property Security Act regime. See topic Personal Property Security.

Lien on Crops.—Personal Property Security Act allows for registration of security interest in crops. This security interest is enforceable by seizure and removal of growing crops from land. See topic Personal Property Security. (c. P-4.05, §37).

Special Liens.—Certain special liens such as warehousemen's, threshers', woodmen's, livery stable keepers', hotelmen's, etc., are governed by special statutes. In general they are realized upon by sale at public auction after the statutory period (usually one or two months) has elapsed.

Possessory Liens.—All liens not specifically legislated for are governed by the Possessory Liens Act. (c. P-13). See subhead Artisan, supra.

Builders' Lien.—Person who does work upon or supplies materials in respect to an improvement in or on land for owner, contractor or subcontractor has for price of work or materials a lien upon estate or interest of owner of land. Where work done or materials furnished in connection with recovery of minerals then lien does not attach to owner in fee simple of mines and minerals unless that owner expressly requested work or materials. (c. B-12, §4).

Filing and Recording.—Person claiming a lien must register same in appropriate Land Titles Office within 45 days after completion or abandonment, or last furnishing of materials, services or labour. (c. B-12, §30).

Duration of Lien.—Lien ceases to exist unless action is commenced and certificate of lis pendens registered within 180 days from registration of lien. (c. B-12, §32). Trial must be held within two years of registration of certificate of lis pendens, or interested person can apply to have lien discharged. (c. B-12, §33).

Enforcement.—Lien enforced by issuing statement of claim. (c. B-12, §36). On notice other lienholders must prove claim by affidavit or lose lien. (c. B-12, §38). When pleadings close, pretrial application made. (c. B-12, §39).

Mechanics' Liens.—See subhead Builders' Lien, supra.

Lien on Minerals Held from the Crown.—Where lien attaches to estate or interest in minerals held directly from Crown in right of Alberta and estate or interest is less than fee simple estate and not registered under Land Titles Act statement of lien must be registered with Minister of Energy and Natural Resources. (c. B-12, §26.1[1]).

Redemption.—After property covered by a lien has passed by sale or otherwise from the debtor, he cannot redeem. Up to such time he may always redeem upon payment.

Public Works.—General contractor for public buildings or other public works may be required to give satisfactory security for performance of contract and payment of claims for labor and materials. (c. P-38, §10).

LIMITATION OF ACTIONS:

Actions must be commenced within the following periods:

Ten years: On mortgage, agreement for sale of land or domestic judgment. (c. L-15, §§4, 18, 33, 36).

Six years: For recovery of money other than debt charged on land, for fraudulent misrepresentation, for actions grounded on accident, mistake or other equitable ground of relief; registering foreign judgement under Reciprocal Enforcement of Judgments Act. (c. L-15, §§4, 14, 39; c. R-6, §2).

On any other action not specifically provided for in this or any other act. (c. L-15, §4).

Two years: For defamation; trespass to person, assault or battery whether by negligence or otherwise, and including motor vehicle accident cases; false imprisonment; malicious prosecution; seduction; trespass to real property or chattels; conversion. (c. L-15, §51).

On actions by or against decedent's estate within two years of death. (c. L-15, §§5, 53).

Under Fatal Accidents Act where death of person gives cause of action, within two years of death. (c. L-15, §54).

Actions for penalties given by statute to Crown or aggrieved persons. (c. L-15, §4).

One year.—On penal statutes where fine goes to informer (c. L-15, §4); for malpractice or negligence in case of medical and related services (c. L-15, §55); for negligence by approved hospitals (c. L-15, §56).

Absolute Defense.—The statute of limitations is an absolute defense and a person cannot by contract deprive himself of the benefit thereof.

Disability of Plaintiff.—Where person entitled to bring action in tort is under disability at time cause of action arises he may commence action at any time within two years from date he ceased to be under disability except where person under disability is infant in actual custody of parent or guardian or mentally incapacitated person whose affairs are in custody of trustee, guardian or of Public Trustee. (c. L-15, §59).

Absence of Defendant.—When person is out of Province when cause of action arises against him in Province, person entitled to take action may do so within time otherwise limited by Act for bringing of action or within two years after return of person. (c. L-15, §§47, 58).

New Promise or Part Payment.—The running of the statute may be interrupted, or a barred debt revived, by an acknowledgment in writing, containing a clear statement of an intention to be liable for the debt, or by part payment. In such cases the statute begins to run anew from the time of such acknowledgment or payment. (c. L-15, §9).

Pleading.—In order to be available as a defense the statute of limitation must be pleaded. (A.R.C. 109).

LIMITATION OF ACTIONS . . . *continued*

Note: Bill 205, Limitations Act, was passed on Apr. 2, 1996 and will come into force on proclamation. Bill 205 will repeal and supercede Limitation of Actions Act. (c. L-15).

With limited exceptions, Act will apply to any claim if remedial order is sought in court created by Province of Alberta or if claim arose in Alberta and remedial order is sought in court created by Parliament of Canada. (Bill 205, §2).

All actions must be commenced within two years of discovering claim or within ten years of claim arising, whichever is earlier. (Bill 205, §3). Exceptions to ten year limitation period included disability, fraudulent concealment, agreement, acknowledgment and part payment. (Bill 205, §§5, 6, 8, 9).

See also topic Motor Vehicles, subhead Direct Actions.

LIMITED PARTNERSHIP:

See topic Partnership.

LOAN CORPORATIONS:

See topic Trust and Loan Corporations.

MARRIAGE:

Federal Parliament has exclusive right to legislate with respect to capacity of persons to marry. Province has power to make laws relating to "solemnization of marriage".

Minimum age at which males and females may intermarry in this province is 16, unless a doctor certifies that a female under that age is pregnant or the mother of a living child and she has obtained the required consents or order dispensing with same. (c. M-6, §§16, 17).

Consent Required.—Minors under 18 must obtain written consent of parents or guardian. The only exceptions are where the minor's parents are dead, mentally incompetent, and he has no guardian or minor was previously married. Court also has jurisdiction to dispense with consent of parents. (c. M-6, §§18, 19).

Prerequisites.—No marriage may be solemnized in province unless a license has been issued, such license being valid for three months and any person who contravenes this provision is liable to penalties. (c. M-6, §§8, 26). There must be at least two adult witnesses and ceremony must be conducted in understandable language. (c. M-6, §9).

Marriage license may be obtained from the issuer of marriage licenses in the locality in which parties reside. Parties are both required to appear before registrar and answer questions on oath touching matters of name, age, occupation, address, etc., and to swear that they are not aware of any impediment of kindred or alliance or other lawful hindrance to marriage. (c. M-6, §13). Divorced person must submit certified copy of decree absolute or divorce judgment. (c. M-6, §15).

No license will be issued to a person who has obtained a decree of divorce or a declaration of nullity of marriage until 21st day from date of final decree or final declaration and until applicant has filed certificate from Clerk of Court of Queen's Bench that no appeal has been entered from final decree or declaration and that time for appeal has expired. This section does not apply to divorce, petition for which was filed after July 1, 1968. (c. M-6, §14). If one or both of parties are or appear to be under 18 years of age they may be required to adduce other evidence of age or furnish consents of their parents, etc. Penalties are provided for anyone who issues license to person who is mentally handicapped or under influence of alcohol or drugs. (c. M-6, §§17-19, 27).

Ceremony.—No marriage is valid in this jurisdiction unless ceremony is performed by a person authorized by Director for province to perform such ceremonies. These persons are ministers in holy orders and certain persons specially authorized by Director and known as Commissioners. (c. M-6, §§2, 3, 7). Practically all marriages are performed by ministers. Ceremony follows form of particular religion of minister and ceremony is binding although not religion of parties and even though they believe in no religion. Ceremony must take place in presence of two adult witnesses. (c. M-6, §9).

Irregular Marriages.—Where question arises as to inadvertent contravention of Marriage Act application can be made for order declaring marriage duly solemnized. (c. M-6, §23).

Application can also be made for declaration of court that marriage of person under 18 is not valid. (c. M-6, §21).

Common law marriages performed within province are not recognized. As to legal recognition of out-of-province marriages, common law prevails, i.e., lex loci celebrationis governs formal validity of marriage.

Prohibited Marriages.—Express penalties are provided for anyone solemnizing a marriage involving an incompetent, i.e., mentally defective, intoxicated. (c. M-6, §27[4]). No person who has wife or husband living and has not secured valid divorce recognized by our courts may marry. (c. M-6, §§15, 20).

Marriage (Prohibited Degrees) Act, S.C. 1990, c. 46 which repealed Marriage Act, R.S.C. 1985, c. M-2, came into force Dec. 18, 1991, subject to earlier enactment by province. However, Act does not apply to Newfoundland.

Pursuant to Marriage (Prohibited Degrees) Act, marriage by persons related by consanguinity, affinity or adoption are not prohibited or invalid when marrying each other by reason only of their relationship, except if they marry another person related lineally by consanguinity or adoption; as brother and sister by consanguinity, whether by whole blood or by half blood; or as brother and sister by adoption. (c. 46, §2). This Act contains all of prohibitions in Canadian law against marriage by reason of parties being related.

New federal Act contains all prohibitions against marriage by related persons. (c. 46, §4).

Foreign Marriages.—Any form of marriage is recognized if valid according to the law of the country where contracted and of the domicile of the contracting parties. But this does not apply to polygamous marriages.

Annulment.—An annulment may be obtained on grounds of impotence, absence of consent, bigamy or failure to comply with statutory requirements, but unless statute by express word or clear intent renders a marriage void or voidable, marriage will not be set aside.

Our courts have jurisdiction to hear a suit for nullity where the matrimonial residence is within the province. It is not necessary to prove domicile but only that the parties are living within the province at the time of the action.

Record.—See topic Records, subhead Vital Statistics.

MARRIED WOMEN:

See topics Acknowledgments; Dower; Executors and Administrators; Homesteads; Husband and Wife; Marriage; Wills; Witnesses.

MASTER AND SERVANT:

See topic Labour Relations.

MECHANICS' LIENS:

See topic Liens. See also topics Personal Property Security, subhead Registration; Sales, subheads Registration of Contract, Removal of Property into the Province.

MINES AND MINERALS:

All mines and minerals and public lands in the province belong to Her Majesty in right of the Province of Alberta, excepting those which have been alienated by grant or lease or otherwise. Where land is expropriated the Crown does not ordinarily obtain the mines and minerals. (c. M-15, §15).

The Environmental Protection and Enhancement Act (c. E-13.3) may require conservation and reclamation of land used for mining, pipelines, exploration operations or refining. Land must be returned to "equivalent land capability".

A typical land deed does not carry mines and minerals, although some which convey lands which were alienated by Crown in last century do carry mines and minerals. Gold and silver belong entirely to Her Majesty in right of province unless expressly alienated. (c. M-15, §10). Sand and gravel belong to surface owner, as does clay and marl (c. L-8, §§53, 54), which do not include any of substances named to be minerals in Act (c. L-8, §52).

Permits.—Permits and/or licences are required from Energy and Utilities Board to drill well to recover oil and gas (c. O-5, §11), to develop coal mine or commence coal mining operations (c. C-14, §§10, 11), or undertake similar operations. Surface entry may be gained by compulsory acquisition. (c. S-27.1, §12).

Operation of Mines.—The Coal Mines Safety Act regulates working of all coal mines, mine sites and processing plants in Alberta, to persons employed there, and to all coal produced in Alberta. (c. C-15).

Specific sections deal with the operation of the mine, the manner in which shafts shall be sunk, safety devices and precautions, qualifications of various persons working in or about the mines, records to be kept, examination by inspectors, etc.

Oil and Gas.—In Alberta approximately 85% owned in fee simple by Crown (provincial government). Mines and Minerals Act (c. M-15) and regulations thereunder prescribe manner of obtaining, from Crown, and terms and conditions of, leases of such substances. Primary term of leases granted after July 1, 1976 is generally five years which may be extended by production. Gross overriding royalty payable to Crown varies according to whether oil or gas was discovered before or after Apr. 1, 1974. Royalty on oil is calculated on sliding scale of production which increases as production increases. Royalty on production is calculated in accordance with regulations. Simplified natural gas royalty regime has been put in place with royalty liability being triggered at plant gate, except where gas is sold unprocessed. Royalty share of gas is valued at monthly reference price. Regulations under that Act also provide for obtaining by competitive bid on application of "reservations" of large acreages for short-term exploration purposes with subsequent rights to select leases therefrom following test drilling.

Energy and Utilities Board regulates all drilling and production activity in Province, whether on Crown or freehold leases, including quantities of oil and gas which may periodically be produced from each well. (c. O-5). Board also regulates removal of gas or propane from Alberta (c. G-3.1) and National Energy Board at Calgary regulates export of oil and gas from Canada (R.S.C. 1985, c. N-7).

Pricing of natural gas produced in Alberta is no longer regulated by federal/provincial agreement. Deregulation occurred on Nov. 1, 1986. Pricing of gas set by gas contracts between seller and buyer. (c. N-2.8).

Alberta Petroleum Marketing Commission is exclusive agent for sale of Crown's royalty share of crude oil at price that is in public interest of Alberta. (c. P-5, §15).

Action for services in sale of oil or gas leases not maintainable unless person bringing action licensed. (c. R-5; [1965], 54 W.W.R. 494).

Mineral Tax.—Provision is made for annual tax on minerals to be levied by Order of Minister, at rate to be determined therein for each mineral upon or under tract of land. (c. F-19.1, §2). Appeals of assessment under Freehold Mineral Rights Tax Act may be taken to Appeal Board. (c. F-19.1, §§4, 5).

Tax constitutes first charge upon mineral right which is subject to forfeiture to Crown for nonpayment. (c. F-19.1, §§14, 15, 16).

MONOPOLIES AND RESTRAINT OF TRADE:

See Canada Law Digest.

MORTGAGES OF PERSONAL PROPERTY:

See topics Chattel Mortgages; Personal Property Security.

MORTGAGES OF REAL PROPERTY:

Mortgage may be: (1) Common law mortgage, which is transfer of land by way of security; (2) equitable mortgage, which is most commonly created by deposit of title deeds; or (3) statutory mortgage, which is registered charge against lands in statutory form under Land Titles System. Latter form is usual. Mortgagor merely charges his land with debt and remains registered owner and in possession. (c. L-5, §106).

Execution.—A statutory mortgage must be signed by the mortgagor in the presence of a witness who must swear before a proper officer to an affidavit as to the due execution of the instrument. The mortgagor must swear to an affidavit that he or she is

See Topical Index in front part of this volume.

MORTGAGES OF REAL PROPERTY . . . *continued*

not married, if such is the case, or that the lands concerned are not part of his or her homestead. Otherwise the other spouse has a dower interest and must sign a consent thereto and then appear alone before a proper officer and acknowledge that he or she understands the nature of his or her act and that he or she acts of his or her own free will. This dower requirement is not necessary where property is held jointly (as tenants in common or joint tenants). (c. D-38, §25). No witness required where mortgage executed under corporate seal and countersigned by at least one officer of corporation. (c. L-5, §152.3).

Recording.—Every mortgage to be binding on third persons acting bona fide must be registered against the mortgagor's title in the Land Titles office for the district in which the land is situate. If this is done and the mortgaged land is transferred, a covenant is implied between the purchaser and the mortgagee that the purchaser will pay the mortgage and between the purchaser and the original mortgagor that if the latter has to pay the mortgage the purchaser will indemnify him. These covenants may be negatived in the transfer. (c. L-5, §§62, 63, 64).

Recording fees are based on amount secured. There must also be paid assurance fund fee. See topic Records, subhead Assurance Fund. (c. L-5, §154).

Acceleration on Default.—Most mortgages contain an acceleration clause by which the whole amount becomes due immediately upon default being made in any payment.

Attornment clauses are void except for mortgages of business premises, and mortgages in favour of The Canadian Farm Loan Board or Farm Credit Corporation or mortgage secured under National Housing Act or its predecessor and mortgage forms which have been approved by Lieutenant Governor in Council. (c. L-8, §§35, 37).

Foreclosure and Redemption.—If principal and interest are not paid pursuant to the terms of mortgage, then due foreclosure proceedings may be commenced in Court of Queen's Bench. Usually no defense is filed, and order nisi/order for sale is granted giving mortgagee judgment and mortgagor redemption period of six months for urban lands and one year for farm (as specifically defined) lands. Statutory redemption periods are subject to reduction or extension in exceptional circumstances. Unless mortgagor can make payment by that time or show circumstances which will entitle court to grant him further time to redeem, mortgaged lands are advertised for judicial sale. If sale is abortive, mortgagee may then apply for order for foreclosure, vesting title in his name.

Except in case of a mortgage or trust deed executed as security for a debenture issue of a corporation or a mortgage in favour of corporation or National Housing Act mortgages, and rights under attornment clauses above, foreclosure is mortgagee's only remedy and no action can be brought on personal covenant. (c. L-8, §§41, 43).

Restrictions.—Mortgage granted to nonresident of controlled land, which excludes Crown land, urban land and mines and minerals, may be prohibited, or rights granted thereunder may be restricted, by regulations under Citizenship Act (Canada) (R.S.C. 1985, c. C-29, §§34-38) or Agricultural and Recreational Land Ownership Act. (c A-9).

Remedies.—Law of Property Act limits remedy of mortgagee to land itself and action on personal covenant in mortgage is precluded, except in cases of agreement for sale of land to corporation or of mortgages given by corporation or under National Housing Act. However, action on covenant may be pursued against individual who is transferee of land subject to mortgage given by corporation if individual does not use land as his residence or for farming. (c. L-8, §§41, 43, 43.4).

Release.—When mortgage is paid it is released by mortgagee signing a discharge thereof which must be properly witnessed and contain an affidavit of execution. When this is presented to the Land Titles office together with the duplicate mortgage, the encumbrance or charge is cancelled. In cases where the mortgagee cannot be found provision is made for deposit of the moneys owing in a chartered bank. Where the mortgage has been paid but not discharged a judge in proper circumstances may order its discharge. (c. L-5, §108.1).

Trust deeds may be registered against lands by way of caveat, with same effect as ordinary mortgages. (c. L-5, §§130, 135).

Transfer or Release.—A statutory mortgage may be transferred or assigned in whole or as to a certain interest therein. The assignment should be registered in order to protect the holder. (c. L-5, §110). Mortgage may be partially or wholly released and discharged in Land Titles Office as to part released. (c. L-5, §108).

Forms

The following is the usual form of mortgage:

FORM 15

LAND TITLES ACT
(Section 105)

MORTGAGE

I, A.B., being registered owner of an estate (state nature of estate), subject to registered encumbrances, liens and interests, if any, in all that piece of land described as follows: (here describe land) in consideration of (here, set out the amount and particulars of the loan or indebtedness), covenant with E.F., the mortgagee, of (here insert the mortgagee's address):

That I will repay the sum lent to me (or the indebtedness) together with interest thereon as follows: (here set out covenants for repayment of principal and interest and special covenants, if any.)

And for better securing to the mortgagee the repayment in the manner set out above of the principal sum and interest (and other amounts hereby secured), I hereby mortgage to E.F. my estate and interest in the land described above.

In witness whereof, I have hereunto signed my name this . . . . day of . . . . 19. . . .

SIGNED by the above named)
)
A.B. in the presence of) . . . .
) (Signature of mortgagor)
. . . .)

(Alta Reg. 538/82, Form 15)

Discharge: A mortgage may be discharged by the mortgagee executing the certificate of discharge in the following form:

FORM 7

LAND TITLES ACT
(Sections 39, 108)

RECEIPT OR DISCHARGE BY MORTGAGEE OR ENCUMBRANCEE

I . . . ., (the mortgagee, encumbrancee or transferee as the case may be) do hereby acknowledge to have received all the money (or the sum of . . . . . dollars being part of the money) to become due under the mortgage (or encumbrance) made by . . . . to . . . . which mortgage (or encumbrance) was registered in the Land Titles Office for the . . . . Alberta Land Registration District on . . . . as instrument number . . . ., that the mortgage (or encumbrance) has not been transferred; and that the same (or such part of the land as is hereinafter described, that is to say (here give a description of the land to be discharged) is wholly discharged (or discharged as to the sum of . . . . dollars).

In witness whereof I have hereunto subscribed my name this . . . . day of . . . . 19. . . .

SIGNED by the above named)
)
. . . .)
)
in the presence of) . . . . (Signature)
)
)
. . . .)

(Alta. Reg. 538/82, Form 7)

An affidavit of execution is also required. (For form, see topic Deeds subhead Forms, catchline Affidavit of Attestation of Instrument.)

FORM 18

LAND TITLE ACT
(Section 110)

Land Titles Act.—Transfer of Mortgage, Encumbrance, or Lease.

I, C.D., the mortgagee (encumbrancee *or* lessee, *as the case may be*), in consideration of . . . . dollars, this day paid to me by *X.Y.*, of . . . . the receipt of which sum I do hereby acknowledge, hereby transfer to him in the mortgage (encumbrance *or* lease, *as the case may be, describe the instrument fully*), together with all my rights, powers, title, and interest therein.

In witness whereof I have hereunto subscribed my name this . . . . day of . . . . 19. . .

Signed by the said . . . . }
in the presence of } *C.D. (Transferor.)*
. . . . }

(Alta. Reg. 480/81).

This form must be signed by the transferor and by a witness. The witness must then take an affidavit of execution. For form, see topic Deeds subhead Forms, catchline Affidavit of Attestation of Instrument.

Mortgage Brokers.—See topic Brokers.

Chattel Mortgages.—See topics Chattel Mortgages; Personal Property Security.

MOTOR VEHICLES:

Vehicle license or validation marker required annually. One numbered plate must be displayed on rear of all vehicles except truck tractors which require one numbered plate displayed on front. Issued by Motor Vehicles Branch, Department of Solicitor General. Special provision for dealers' plates. Exemption for nonresidents for other than public vehicles for period not exceeding three months, provided displaying current license in accord with laws of place of residence and having financial responsibility card. (c. M-22, §§34, 46-56 inc.).

Operator's License.—Application for operator's license made to Solicitor General in form and content prescribed by Minister. License subsists for five year period. Minimum age for operator's license holders is 16 years and students as defined in Regulations. Exemption from license granted nonresidents remaining in Alberta less than three months, provided authorized by place of residence to operate motor vehicles. Exemption also granted to holder of international driver's license who does not remain in Alberta for more than 12 months. (c. M-22, §§5, 6, 11).

Titles and Sales.—Ownership in motor vehicles passes with change of possession unless otherwise provided, in which case conditional sales agreement must be registered. (See topics Sales and Personal Property Security.) Where ownership passes vehicle registration expires and number plates must be removed and retained in possession of registered owner, but person to whom number plates were issued may apply to Solicitor General to use plates on another vehicle to be registered in his name. Also, when ownership passes in case of certain public vehicles, new owner may apply to Solicitor General to have license plates issued to former owner transferred to him. (c. M-22, §§40, 41).

Garageman entitled to payment of sum for storage, repair or maintenance or price of accessories or parts furnished, has lien on motor vehicle or part thereof for sum entitled to. Garageman must retain possession of motor vehicle from person who authorized storage, repair or maintenance and obtain acknowledgment of indebtedness by requiring person or agent to sign invoice. (c. G-1, §2).

Identification Marks.—Summary conviction offence to deface, or alter operator's license or certificate of registration, permit or number plates or to sell or to have in one's possession motor vehicle or, part of motor vehicle, that does not have serial

MOTOR VEHICLES . . . *continued*
number or other similar identifying mark approved by Solicitor General. (c. M-22, §§25, 42, 55, 84, 85).

Operation prohibited by person under 16 (resident or nonresident) except child 14 or over who has obtained learner's permit which may be issued for maximum period of two years from applicant's next birth date, and is under supervision of holder of valid operator's license, at least 18 years of age, sitting alongside and engaged in driving instruction. Learner's permit for motorcycles, scooters and power bicycles issued under regulations. Special restrictions re operation of tractors and self-propelled implements on highways by persons under 14 years of age. (c. M-22, §§9, 11).

Equipment Required.—Forbidden to occupy house trailer while moving on highway. (c. H-7, §128).

Seat belts are mandatory for all occupants of motor vehicles. Children under age six must be placed in child seating assembly. Failure to wear seat belt or to ensure passenger under age 16 wears seat belt may result in $500 fine to vehicle operator. (c. H-7, §§65, 169).

Lights Required.—Regulated by c. H-7, §§20-42.

Traffic Regulations.—Criminal Code provides sanctions under §§253 and 254, R.S.C. 1985, c. C-46 for impaired driving; driver is liable for minimum suspension of one year from date of finding of guilty. (c. M-22, §109).

Accidents.—Where accident occurs, person in charge of motor vehicle must remain at or immediately return to scene of accident and shall render all reasonable assistance and shall produce in writing to anyone sustaining loss or injury, to any peace officer and any witness his name and address, number of his operator's license, name and address of registered owner of vehicle, registration number of vehicle, and financial responsibility card. When car collides with unattended vehicle or wayside property, person in charge of moving vehicle must notify owner or person in charge of unattended vehicle or property and leave his name and address, number of his operator's license and registration number of vehicle striking unattended vehicle or property. Where accident results in death or injury or damage to apparent extent of $1,000 or more, driver or, where incapacitated, another occupant or owner must submit written report to police. Where vehicle which shows evidence of having been involved in accident causing damage of $1,000 or more or having been struck by bullet is brought into garage for repairs, garage operator must not make repairs until police notified, and must also report vehicles unclaimed for 30 days or more to police. (c. M-22, Part 6).

Owner liable for negligence of person driving motor vehicle and living with and as member of family of owner as well as for negligence of person who is driving motor vehicle and who is in possession of it with consent of owner (see also topic Principal and Agent). Where person sustains loss or damage arising out of operation of motor vehicle upon highway and where that motor vehicle is operated in contravention of any provisions of Highway Traffic Act, 1980, onus of proof in any civil action that loss or damage did not arise by reason of contravention of that Act is upon owner or driver. (c. H-7, §§179, 181).

In some instances, licenses of convicted drivers are automatically suspended for specified periods. (c. M-22, §109).

Financial responsibility card required to be held by owner of motor vehicle. (c. M-22, §70). It is offence for operator, owner or person having care and control of vehicle to fail to produce financial responsibility card, unless vehicle registered outside Alberta or owned by Crown. It is offence to give financial responsibility card to person not entitled to have it and offence not to deliver card to Registrar for cancellation as required. (c. M-22, §72).

Insurance.—Motor vehicles must be insured. Every contract of insurance issued or renewed with respect to vehicle must have minimum $200,000 liability resulting from bodily injury to or death of one or more persons and property coverage. (c. I-5, §312).

No-Fault Insurance.—Not adopted.

General Revenue Fund provides for any injured person who has cause of action against owner or operator of uninsured vehicle for injuries or death occasioned in Alberta, and who is unable to collect from defendant may apply to Administrator of Motor Vehicle Accident Claims Act for payment out of fund. Maximum amount payable out of fund is $50,000 if accident occurred on or after Jan. 1, 1974 and before July 1, 1978 (c. M-21, §11), $100,000 if accident occurred on or after July 1, 1978 and before Jan. 1, 1986, and $200,000 if accident occurred on or after Jan. 1, 1986 (c. M-21, §11), for injury to or death of one or more persons or damage to property arising out of one accident.

Act also covers cases where persons are injured or property damaged in excess of $250 by "hit and run" drivers in Alberta whose names are not ascertainable, provided Administrator is notified in writing within 90 days of accident. (c. M-21, §9).

Administrator of Motor Vehicle Accident Claims Act must be served with notice after any defendant is noted in default, and when served with this notice, he must also be served with copy of statement of claim and every subsequent pleading in action. (c. M-21, §6).

Foreign Vehicles.—If all regulations of place of residence complied with, driver's license and valid financial responsibility card carried and license plates properly displayed, nonresident may drive touring vehicle in province for not more than three months. (c. M-22, §5.)

Nonresident operator licensed in place of residence may operate vehicle registered in place of residence, or vehicle registered in Alberta. Every operator must carry driver's license issued either by his own province or state or by Alberta government.

Action against nonresident, arising out of operation of car, may be commenced by service of process as in any ordinary action.

Direct Actions.—Persons having claim against insured must proceed to judgment against insured and then have insurance money applied towards his judgment, and may sue insurer to have insurance money so applied. Action must be on behalf of all persons having similar claims. Limitation of action against insurer of one year from final determination of action against insured, including appeals, if any. (c. I-5, §320).

Public motor vehicles are regulated by Alberta Motor Transport Board and departmental regulations. By virtue of Motor Vehicle Transport Act, 1987 Board regulates both inter and intra-provincial motor vehicle undertakings within boundaries of Province. (R.S.C., c. 29 [3rd Supp.]).

Aircraft.—See Canada Law Digest, topic Aircraft.

Gasoline Tax.—See topic Taxation.

NEGOTIABLE INSTRUMENTS:

See Canada Law Digest, topic Bills and Notes.

NOTARIES PUBLIC:

Notaries are appointed by Minister of Justice and Attorney General and every member of legislative assembly, house of commons or senate is ex officio notary. (c. N-11, §§1, 4).

Term.—Every barrister and solicitor and student-at-law is notary unless suspended from Law Society of Alberta as are judges of Provincial, Surrogate, Queen's Bench and Appeal Courts and Master In Chambers. (c. N-11, §§2, 3). Commission of other notaries expires two years from Dec. 31 of year of appointment, and such notaries must write or stamp date of expiration of commission on every affidavit, etc. (c. N-11, §§6, 7).

Bond.—Notaries are not required to be bonded.

Name.—Notaries must print or stamp their name on each affidavit, if appointed under §1, date on which appointment expires, etc. attested by them. (c. N-11, §7).

Seal.—Every notary public signing as such must affix his official seal beside his signature, although seal is not necessary for documents used within the province. This seal usually reads ". . . . . ., Notary Public, Province of Alberta" and is usually impressed, although it may be stamped.

Powers.—Every notary has and may exercise power of administering oaths, taking affidavits, drawing, passing and keeping and issuing all deeds and contracts, charter parties and other mercantile transactions in the province, and also of attesting all commercial instruments that may be brought before him for public protestation and otherwise of acting as usual in the office of notary. (c. N-11, §5).

Territorial Extent of Powers.—Authority of notary extends throughout the province.

Diplomatic Representatives.—No longer may act as notaries. (1958, c. 52).

PARTITION:

Proceedings for partition are by action or by Originating Notice in Court of Queen's Bench. If inconvenient to adjust rights by partition, sale will be directed. (c. L-8 Part 3).

PARTNERSHIP:

Partnership Declaration.—All persons associated in partnership for trading, manufacturing, contracting or mining purposes must file with Registrar of Corporations appointed under Business Corporations Act (S.A. 1981, c. B-15) declaration containing names, occupations and residences of each and every partner; name of firm under which they carry on or intend carrying on business; length of time it has existed or is to exist; and declare persons named are sole members of such partnership (c. P-2, §§81, 83). Penalty is provided for nonfiling within six months. Similarly declaration must be filed when change or alteration takes place in membership of partnership, in firm name under which members intend to carry on business or in place of residence of each member of firm and may be filed upon dissolution of partnership. (c. P-2, §§84, 87, 91).

Liability of Partners.—Under a judgment against a partnership, executions may be issued against the partnership or against any member thereof who was served with statement of claim, entered defense, admitted being partner or was adjudged partner. (A.R.C. 82). Each partner is liable jointly for debts of firm incurred while partner, and severally liable for wrongful acts or omissions and misapplication of money or property of third person. (c. P-2, §§11-14). Writ of Enforcement shall not issue against partnership property except on judgment against firm.

Administration of Partnership Property.—On dissolution of partnership each partner entitled as against other partners and persons claiming through them in respect of their interests as partners, to have property of partnership applied in payment of debts and liabilities of firm, and to have surplus assets after that payment applied in payment of what is due to partners respectively after deducting what is due from them as partners to firm. Any partner or his representative may on termination of partnership apply to court to wind up business and affairs of firm. (c. CP-2, §42[1][2]).

Liability of Partners as to Third Parties.—Acts of partner in usual course of business of kind carried on by firm, bind firm and partners unless partner so acting has in fact no authority to act for firm in particular matter, and person for whom partner is dealing knows that partner has no authority, or does not know or believe him to be partner.

Act or instrument relating to business of firm and done or executed in firm name, or in another manner showing intention to bind firm, by person authorized in that behalf, whether partner or not, binds firm and partners. (c. P-2, §§7, 8).

Limited Partnerships.—Limited partnerships may be formed by two or more persons, and, on filing certificate with Registrar of Corporations, must include one or more general partners, who only can transact partnership business and who are generally severally responsible, and partners, who are liable for partnership debts only to extent to which they have contributed or agreed to contribute to capital. There is express provision for registration of foreign limited partnerships. (c. P-2, Part II).

PERPETUITIES:

Common law rule against perpetuities is in force except as provided by The Perpetuities Act. (c. P-4, §2). Common law rule is, briefly, that every interest in property must, to be valid, vest, if at all, within life or lives in being and 21 years. Act creates presumption of validity until actual events establish incapability of vesting within period, in which case interest is void, subject to exceptions created. Act came into force July 1, 1973, and, except as provided, is not retroactive.

See Topical Index in front part of this volume.

PERSONAL PROPERTY SECURITY:

Effective Oct. 1, 1990 Personal Property Security Act 1988, c. P-4.05 (PPSA) came into force. This Act is similar in its scope and operation to statutes of same name already in force in Saskatchewan and Ontario. It applies to every transaction without regard to its form and without regard to person who has title to collateral, that in substance creates security interest, including chattel mortgage, conditional sale, floating charge, pledge, debenture, trust indenture or trust receipt, lease, assignment, consignment or transfer of chattel paper, and, additionally, to assignment of accounts, transfer of chattel paper, consignment, or lease for term of more than one year, notwithstanding that such interests may not secure payment or performance of obligation. It does not apply to statutory or nonconsensual liens, security interests governed by Federal statutes such as Bank Act §§177 and 178, creation or transfer of interest or claim in or under any contract of annuity or policy of insurance that is not indemnity or compensation for loss or damage to collateral, creation or transfer of interests in land, assignments for general benefit of creditors pursuant to Federal statute relating to insolvency, creation or transfers of interests in rights to payment under interests in land, sales of accounts or chattel paper as part of sale of business where vendor loses apparent control of business, creation or transfer of interests in present or future compensation for labour or personal services, transfer of interest in earned right to payment under contract where transferee is to perform contract, transfers of accounts to facilitate their collection, creation or transfer of interests in tort damages. Historic forms and concepts of security agreements are discarded and single conceptual basis for all personal property security agreements is employed. Alberta statute also applies to "corporation securities".

Conflict of Laws.—Basic premise is that law of jurisdiction where collateral is situated when security interest attaches is applicable law for determining validity, perfection and effect of perfection or nonperfection of security interest in such collateral. For intangibles, property normally used in more than one jurisdiction and nonpossessory security interests in securities, instruments, negotiable documents of title, money and chattel paper, law of jurisdction where debtor is located when security interest attaches, governs. Debtor is deemed to be located at his place of business, at his chief executive office if he has more than one place of business and otherwise at his place of residence. For goods brought into Alberta, distinction is made between buyer in good faith of goods brought into province and all other persons. Security interest in collateral already perfected under law of place in which collateral situated when security interest attached and before being brought into Alberta continues perfected in Alberta as against buyer in good faith if perfected in Alberta prior to buyer's acquiring interest in goods and as against all other persons within 60 days after brought into province, or within 15 days after day secured party receives notice that goods have been brought into Alberta, or prior to day that perfection ceases under law of prior jurisdiction, whichever is earliest.

Transitional.—Assented to July 6, 1988 and effective Oct. 1, 1990 Personal Property Security Act causes repeal of Assignment of Book Debts Act, Bills of Sale Act, Chattel Security Registries Act, Conditional Sales Act, Harvesting Liens Act, and amendments to Agriculture Relief Advances Act, Business Corporations Act, Co-operative Associations Act, Crop Liens Priorities Act, Employments Standards Code, Factors Act, Fuel Tax Act, Garagemen's Lien Act, Hotel Room Tax Act, Insurance Act, Interpretation Act, Land Titles Act, Law of Property Act, Livery Stable Keepers Act, Matrimonial Property Act, Mobile Home Sites Tenancies Act, Motor Vehicle Administration Act, Municipal Government Act, Partnership Act, Railway Act, Rural Utilities Act, Sale of Goods Act, Securities Act, Seizures Act, Threshers' Lien Act, Trust Companies Act, and Warehouseman's Lien Act.

Registration under repealed or amended Acts is deemed to be registration under Personal Property Security Act. Question as to priority between security interests validly created prior to coming into force is determined by prior registration law, but priority between prior security interest and security interest validly created after proclamation shall be determined by Personal Property Security Act.

Registration is continued for unexpired portion of filing or registration period under prior law except for registrations under Business Corporations Act which expire on Oct. 1, 1993, unless they were renewed under new Act.

Effectiveness.—Security agreement is effective according to its terms. However, certain terms are prohibited or may be unenforceable. Acceleration clauses are only effective if secured party, in good faith, believes and has commercially reasonable grounds to believe that payment is not going to be made or that collateral is about to be placed in jeopardy. Where debtor reinstates security agreement, operation of any acceleration clause is ineffective.

Enforceability.—No security interest is enforceable against third party unless collateral is in possession of secured party or debtor has signed security agreement that contains description of collateral by item or kind, statement that security interest is taken in all of debtor's present and after acquired personal property, or statement that security interest is taken in all of debtor's present and after acquired property except specified items or kinds of personal property.

Attachment.—Security interest attaches when value is given, debtor has rights in collateral and, except for purpose of enforcing rights between parties, it becomes enforceable against third parties. Debtor has rights in goods purchased under agreement to sell when contract is made and he obtains possession of them, and in goods leased to him, hired by him or delivered to him under consignment, when he obtains possession of them pursuant to lease, hiring agreements or consignment. Debtor has no rights in crops until they become growing crops, young of animals until they are conceived, in oil, gas or other minerals until extracted, in timber until it is cut.

After-acquired Property.—Security agreement may cover after-acquired property and security interest will attach without specific appropriation by debtor.

Future Advances.—Security agreement may secure future advances, which means advances whether or not made pursuant to obligation and includes reasonable costs incurred for protection, maintenance or repair of collateral. If advances are made while security interest is perfected, security interest has same priority with respect to future advances as it has with respect to first advance. Unless parties otherwise agree, obligations owing to debtor to make future advances is not binding on secured party if security interest does not have priority over writ of enforcement with respect to those future advances (§14[2]), as when advances were not made before secured party acquires knowledge of writ (§35[5]; 1996, c. 28, §33).

Perfection.—Security interest is perfected when it has attached and all steps required for perfection required under Act have been completed regardless of order of occurrence. Three methods of perfection are: possession of collateral by secured party or on his behalf; registration of financing statement in Personal Property Registry; and automatic, although temporary, perfection by way of statutory grace periods.

Act also provides specific rules as to perfection with respect to proceeds of collateral. Security interest in collateral extends to proceeds and is perfected if financing statement filed which covered original collateral contains prescribed description, or if proceeds are of type which fall within description of original collateral, or are cash; then, registration perfects security interest in both collateral and in proceeds. Otherwise, security interest in proceeds perfected for only 15 days after debtor receives possession of them.

Purchase money security interest in collateral, other than intangible, that is perfected within 15 days after day debtor or third party at request of debtor obtains possession of where collateral, or collateral is intangible, within 15 days after security interest therein attaches, has priority over any other security interest in same collateral and over interests of debtor's trustee in bankruptcy or liquidator with security interest that is unperfected at date of bankruptcy or winding-up. (1996, c. 28, §33).

Purchase money security interest in collateral or its proceeds, other than intangibles or inventory, that is perfected within 15 days after debtor or another person at request of debtor obtains possession of collateral or in intangible or its proceeds that is perfected not less than 15 days after day security interest in intangibles attaches, has priority over any other security interest in same collateral given by same debtor.

Purchase money security interest in inventory or its proceeds has priority over any other security interest in same collateral given by same debtor if purchase-money security interest in inventory is perfected at time debtor receives possession of it and purchase-money secured party serves notice on secured party who has registered financing statement covering same type of collateral. Exception with respect to sales in ordinary course of business and by virtue of fact that purchase-money security interest in proceeds of inventory does not have priority over prior perfected security interest in accounts receivable given for new value.

Purchasser of goods sold in ordinary course of business of seller takes free of any perfected or unperfected security interest therein given by or reserved against seller, whether or not purchaser knows of it, unless secured party proves that purchaser also knows that sale constitutes breach of security agreement.

Act provides special priority rules between secured and unsecured creditors, and with respect to fixtures, negotiable documents of title, money and securities, chattel paper, future advances, leases, crops, accessions and comingled goods.

Registration.—All registrations under Personal Property Security Act take place at Personal Property Registry. Central Registry and Vehicle Registry are continued as The Personal Property Registry.

Registration of changes on land, though governed by Law of Property Act, also takes place at Personal Property Registry. (c. L-8, §59.2).

Registration of financing statement is effective for length of time indicated in financing statement and may be renewed at any time before document to which it refers expires by registering financing change statement.

Where secured party assigns his interest or subordinates his interest to that of another person, financing change statement in prescribed form may be registered. Registration of such statement is mandatory where debtor transfers his interest in collateral or changes his name.

Search for registrations against name of debtor or against serial number where collateral required by regulation to be described by serial number (i.e., motor vehicles, mobile homes, trailers and airplanes, as defined in regulations) may be obtained, with results given in printed or verbal form.

Time for Registration.—Financing statement may be registered at any time and may be registered before security agreement is made or before security interest attaches. It must be registered prior to expiry of any temporary perfection period (usually 15 days) to continue perfection uninterrupted, and with respect to purchase-money security interest, within 15 days of debtor obtaining possession of collateral.

Rights and Remedies Upon Default.—Part 5 contains code setting out rights, remedies, duties and obligations upon both secured party and debtor many of which, to extent that they give rights to debtor or impose obligation upon secured party, cannot be waived. However all such rights and remedies of secured parties are subject to consumer protection legislation.

PLEADING:

Pleadings in civil actions must be as brief as the nature of the case will admit. Every pleading must contain only plain and concise statement in summary form and in ordinary language of material facts on which party pleading relies for his claim or defense as case may be. Pleadings must not contain evidence. They should be divided into paragraphs and numbered consecutively. All dates, sums and numbers must be expressed in figures and not in words. (A.R.C. 104, 105).

Pleadings Required or Permitted.—The following pleadings are required or permitted in civil actions: Statement of claim; originating notice of motion; notice of motion; petition; statement of defense; reply by plaintiff; reply by defendant; joinder of issue; demand for particulars; reply to demand for particulars; counterclaim; defense to counterclaim; reply to defense to counterclaim; third party notice; defense to third party notice. (A.R.C. 5, 66, 69, 93).

Setoffs and counterclaims are allowed by our courts. (A.R.C. 93).

Writs and Appearances.—Writs of summons are not used to commence actions and appearances are not filed by defendants to action.

Demurrers have been abolished but application may be made to court to dispose of any question of fact or law involved in case (A.R.C. 221[1]) or to strike out pleadings as disclosing no cause of action (A.R.C. 129).

Amendments.—Our courts are very liberal in allowing amendments in actions, and pleadings may be amended even up to the time of trial in proper cases but usually on conditions as to costs. (A.R.C. 132, 133).

See Topical Index in front part of this volume.

PLEADING . . . *continued*

Affidavits of Defense.—Where default judgment was properly obtained, in order to open up default judgment, court will almost always require defendant to file affidavit swearing to facts showing that defendant would have defense on merits at trial. To prevent vacation period for courts from being used in computation of time allowed for obtaining default judgment, and in default of defence being delivered, defendant may file "vacation affidavit" stating that defendant has good defense on merits and intends to defend. (A.R.C. 552, 158).

Statements of defense must be delivered within 15 days of the time of receiving the statement of claim unless a judge otherwise directs. (A.R.C. 85[1]).

Particulars may be asked for at any time to enable a party to plead. (A.R.C. 117).

Claims.—When action is to be commenced on any claim, full information with regard to the cause of complaint should be given to solicitor together with any documents or correspondence in the claimant's possession. Actions on promissory notes, mortgages, agreements, etc., may be commenced upon production of the instrument together with a detailed statement of the amount owing thereunder. Actions for goods sold and delivered may be commenced upon production of statement (preferably in detail) of the account.

Small Claims.—See topics Courts; and Practice.

PLEDGES:

Security interest is enforcible against third parties without registration or agreement in writing signed by debtor where collateral (goods, chattel paper, security, negotiable document of title, instrument, or money) is in possession of secured party and is actually held as collateral but not while it is held as result of seizure or repossession. (c. P-4.05, §§10[1][a], 24).

Pawnbrokers were subject to provisions of Pawnbrokers' Act but it has been repealed. (R.S.C., 1970, c. P-5, repealed 1980-81-82-83, c. 159, Sch. item 12).

PRACTICE:

Practice is governed by rules of court, which are very similar to the English rules of court. Where our rules do not touch upon any point the English rules are usually followed.

In civil actions statement of claim must be served within 12 months after it is issued and statement of claim can only be renewed once thereafter for further period not exceeding three months. (A.R.C. 11).

Discovery.—Any party or employee or officer of corporate party to action who appears to have some knowledge touching question in issue may be orally examined on oath by adverse party without court order. (A.R.C. 200).

Demand for Particulars.—Further and better statement of nature of claim, defence or particulars of any pleading may be ordered within time fixed or eight days. (A.R.C. 117). Any party may by notice demand admission of facts which must be answered within 15 days or they will be deemed admitted. If admission refused unreasonably and fact proved in court, party may be liable for costs of such proof. (A.R.C. 230).

Small Claims Procedure.—Provincial Judge has jurisdiction to try any claim for debt or for damages, including for breach of contract not exceeding $4,000, as well as counterclaims within similar limits. (c. P-20, Part 4). Provincial Judge can try any such matter within Province of Alberta, but action will usually be heard in judicial district where defendant resides or cause of action arose. (c. P-20, §39). Special procedure set out for these claims.

Direct Actions Against Insurer.—See topic Motor Vehicles, subhead Direct Actions.

See also topics Actions; Appeal and Error; Attachment; Depositions; Executions; Garnishment; Injunctions; Judgments; Pleading; and Process.

PRINCIPAL AND AGENT:

Common law rules apply with regard to agency.

Attorney in Fact.—A transfer of land may be executed by an attorney in fact, provided that upon registration of same he must register an original copy of his power of attorney. (c. L-5, §115).

Collection Agencies.—One licensed under Private Investigators and Security Guards Act cannot act as collector of accounts. (c. P-16, §16). Except for lawyers, insurers, bankruptcy trustees, real estate agents, civil enforcement bailiffs realizing on security and other similarly defined categories of persons, no person shall act as collector or carry on business of collection agency without appropriate licence issued pursuant to Collection Practices Act. (c. C-17, §4).

Public Service Vehicles.—In any prosecution under Motor Transport Act owner of public vehicle, not including private passenger vehicle, operated on behalf of person, is liable for acts of operator unless he can prove to satisfaction of court that vehicle was not being operated by him or by any other person with his consent. (c. M-20, §63).

PROCESS:

Action is commenced by issue of statement of claim. (A.R.C., r.6). Actions for claims in debt or damages not exceeding $4,000 may be brought in Provincial Court and then are commenced by civil claim. (c. P-20, §§36, 38).

In certain cases proceedings are commenced by petition or originating notices but the general rules given herein apply to these. See also topic Actions, subhead Commencement.

Service of statement of claim must generally be personal. Orders to serve substitutionally or by advertisement, or otherwise, may be obtained in certain cases upon an affidavit as to facts. (A.R.C. 14, 22, 23).

Service Outside of Jurisdiction.—Order may be obtained allowing service of statement of claim, or concurrent statement of claim out of jurisdiction in certain prescribed cases. Application is supported by affidavit of plaintiff or his agent stating that in belief of deponent applicant has reasonable cause of action, showing in what place or country person to be served is likely to be and giving grounds for application; every order allowing such service shall limit time within which proceedings may be answered or opposed. (A.R.C. 30, 31).

Process is issued by the clerk of the court. (A.R.C. 7).

Who May Serve.—Any one of age may serve the same, although service may be made through sheriff.

Service on an individual is made by leaving with person true copy of original process. Original showing clerk's signature and seal, or certified copy thereof must be shown to him if requested. (A.R.C. 15[4]).

Service on a corporation under either Companies Act or Business Corporations Act may be made by leaving document at or sending it by registered post to registered office of corporation (c. C-20, §308; 1981, c. B-15, §247) or in case of Companies Act by serving any director, manager or other officer of corporation. (c. C-20, §308). Foreign corporation doing business in Alberta must designate an attorney on whom process against it may be served. (1981, c. B-15, §§267, 275).

PROOF OF CLAIMS:

See topics Executors and Administrators; Pleading.

RAILROADS:

See topic Carriers.

REAL PROPERTY:

Every type of estate is recognized in this province except entails. Unless specifically stated otherwise any transfer, etc., of land will convey the fee simple interest thereof or the greatest interest therein which the grantor has. Tenancy by entireties is not recognized as such, but considered joint tenancy. (c. L-8, Part 1).

Sale of Subdivisions Outside Alberta.—See topic Brokers.

Condominiums.—Condominium Property Act provides for condominium ownership of real property in Alberta. (c. C-22).

See also topics Curtesy; Deeds; Dower; Homesteads; Husband and Wife; Landlord and Tenant; Mortgages of Real Property; Partition; Records.

RECEIVERS:

Appointment.—Interim receiver of property or interest therein may be appointed before judgment in proper case (A.R.C. 465) and in bankruptcy by creditor (R.S.C. 1985, c. B-3, §46). Receiver may be appointed under Bankruptcy Act; other court appointments may be under various Provincial Acts for limited purposes. (c. B-12, §40; 1981, c. S-6.1, §38; c. L-8, §45; c. P-2, §§26, 75; c. C-17, §21).

Receivers are appointed by Court of Queen's Bench or by instrument.

Powers.—Receivers exercise such powers as are given them by instrument, court order, or any combination thereof but usually general power of managing and operating business or property taken charge of.

RECORDS:

Records of transfers, mortgages, liens, judgments, and writ of enforcement affecting lands should be filed in designated Land Titles Office. Former Northern and Southern Land Registration Districts have been abolished. (1996, c. 32, §5).

Chattel mortgages, lien notes and other charges on personalty should be registered in Personal Property Registry.

See topic Personal Property Security.

Requisites for Recording.—In recording any instrument both the original and a signed duplicate must be produced. In the Land Titles Office the original is retained and the copy returned. In other cases the original may be returned.

Effect of recording is to fix all parties with statutory notice which in nearly every case prevents bona fide parties from ranking above those already interested.

Torrens System of land registration is in effect in this province.

Assurance Fund.—Any person who suffers damage by reason of mistake or omission or misfeasance in office of Registrar or by reason of deprivation of estate or interest in land by bringing it under Act, by registration of it in another's name or by error, omission or misdescription in certificate of title when deprived person is barred from bringing action for recovery may bring action against Registrar for recovery of damages to be paid out of General Reserve Fund. Former Assurance Fund was abolished effective Mar. 31, 1994 by S.A. 1994, c. 31, §5. (c. L-5, §§158, 171).

Transfer of Decedent's Title.—Where real property is in name of a deceased, duly appointed executor or administrator obtains from court issuing probate or administration, a certified copy of grant. He then applies to have title of deceased registered in his name as executor or administrator. A new title therefor is issued by Land Titles Office and executor or administrator is then in a position to convey property to person legally entitled thereto. (c. L-5, §116). If infants have interest in estate's lands, any transfer requires consent of Public Trustee or court order. (c. L-5, §120).

If real estate in this province, owned by a nonresident, requires transmission as above it is necessary that some person be appointed by the probate court to deal with the estate as above. The original grant of probate or administration may be issued by the Alberta court. If this is not done the grant, if issued within British Commonwealth, may be resealed in this province and person to whom such grant issued then proceeds as above. Resealing requires security to be provided to cover value of property of deceased unless court dispenses with security. (c. A-1, §30; c. L-5, §116).

Vital Statistics.—Records of births, deaths, and marriages are kept by Director of Vital Statistics, Edmonton, but matters of birth, marriage and death may be registered at the office of the district registrars in any city and many towns. (c. V-4, §26). Fee of $20 charged for certificate of birth, marriage or death. (Alta. Reg. 89/90, 195/92).

REDEMPTION:

See topics Executions; Liens; Mortgages of Real Property; Taxation.

See Topical Index in front part of this volume.

REPLEVIN:

In any action for recovery of any personal property, one claiming that such property was unlawfully taken or is unlawfully detained, may after issue of statement of claim obtain order of replevin. (A.R.C. 427).

Proceedings.—Requirements are: affidavit of plaintiff or his duly authorized agent, giving description of goods and value and stating that person claiming goods is rightful owner or entitled to possession thereof; that property was wrongfully taken out of possession of plaintiff or fraudulently removed from his possession or detained within two months next before making affidavit; or, if property was distrained for rent or damage feasant within that period of two months. (A.R.C. 428).

Bond.—Civil enforcement agency will not act on replevin order until plaintiff provides clerk with bond that is twice value of goods or such sum as may be prescribed except where order provides for payment of money into court or dispenses with furnishing of bond. (A.R.C. 432).

Custody of Property.—Civil Enforcement Agency retains goods until ordered by court to return them to plaintiff but shall after 15 days redeliver goods to defendant unless plaintiff serves upon Civil Enforcement Agency order directing otherwise. (A.R.C. 434).

REPORTS:

Important decisions of Courts of Province are covered by Western Weekly Reports, Alberta Law Reports (2nd and 3rd Series) and Alberta Reports. Alberta Law Reports were published until 1932 and then ceased publication until 1977 when Second Series came out. Dominion Law Reports cover all cases of note throughout Canada. Federal Court and Supreme Court of Canada decisions from Province are also found in Canada Federal Court Reports, Canada Supreme Court Reports, National Reporter and Federal Trail Reporter.

There is a Western edition of Canadian Encyclopedic digest.

Alberta Judgments Database on Quicklaw system contains full text of most written Alberta judgments from 1986 on.

RESTRAINT OF TRADE:

See Canada Law Digest, topic Monopolies and Restraint of Trade.

SALES:

The Bills of Sale Act is repealed effective Oct. 1, 1990. Where goods are purchased but left in possession of vendor, purchaser may protect his interest by registering financing statement. (c. S-2, §27[1]; c. F-1, §8[2]). See topic Personal Property Security.

Conditional Sales.—Up to Oct. 1, 1990, conditional sales are governed by Conditional Sales Act. No sale of goods to value of $15 or upwards, conditioned that right of property or possession shall remain in seller, is good as against purchaser or mortgagee from buyer, or against judgments, executions or attachments, unless sale is in writing signed by buyer or his agent, containing description of goods such that they may be known and properly registered. (c. C-21, §2). Also provision for affixing name in lieu of registration. (c. C-21, §11).

Conditional sale agreement need not be acknowledged. Conditional Sales Act is repealed effective Oct. 1, 1990 by Personal Property Security Act. Thereafter, see topic Personal Property Security.

Unconscionable Transactions.—See topic Interest.

Registration of Contract.—Writing or true copy thereof must be registered in Personal Property Registry within 30 days of actual delivery of goods. Conditional sales of motor vehicles, aircraft, trailers or any oil well drilling equipment must be registered within 21 days at Personal Property Registry. (c. C-21, §§3, 4). For registration requirements after Oct. 1, 1990, see topic Personal Property Security.

Registration may be renewed by registering financing change statement at any time before registration expires, and, subject to regulations, period of time for which registration is effective is extended by renewal period indicated on financing change statement, c. P-4.05, §44.

Removal of Property into the Province.—Where motor vehicles, aircraft, oil well equipment or trailers are permanently removed into province, vendor has 21 days from time he first receives notice of removal, to register by filing copy of instrument and related affidavits, etc., by anyone who has compared it with original. As to all other chattels, time limit is 30 days. He then takes precedence over bona fide purchasers, mortgagees, etc., and has a right to sell articles in same manner as in original jurisdiction subject only to complying with our laws. Agreement must give a sufficient description of goods so that they may be readily distinguished. (c. C-21, §14).

If parties to security agreement created in one province agree that goods will be kept in another province and goods are moved to other province before 30 days, security agreement will be governed by laws of other province.

Security interest in goods perfected under law of jurisdiction in which goods are situated at time security interest attaches but before goods are brought into Province continues perfected in Province if it is perfected in Province (a) not later than 60 days after goods are brought into Province; (b) not later than 15 days after day secured party has knowledge that goods have been brought into Province; or (c) prior to date that perfection ceases under law of jurisdiction in which goods were situated when security interest attached, whichever is earliest, but such security interest is subordinate to interest of buyer or lessee of goods who acquires his interest without knowledge of security interest and before it is perfected in Province. (c. P-4.05, §5[2]). See topic Personal Property Security.

Vendor's Remedy.—Vendor may enforce his interest in purchase-money security agreement in one, but not both, of two ways. If goods are surrendered by debtor to secured party with latter's consent, taken into custody and control of receiver or receiver-manager and disposed of, seized and disposed of or retained by secured party, then indebtedness of debtor under purchase money security agreement is extinguished. Alternatively, if vendor brings action on covenant to pay, and goods are seized under writ of execution and sold, then secured party's rights are limited to amount realized from such sale. Any attempted waiver or release protection offered by this legislation is against public policy and void. (c. L-8, §49). These provisions do not apply where, after seizure, goods are destroyed or damaged to such extent that secured party's security is materially impaired either by wilful act of debtor or his neglect or otherwise. (c. L-8, §50).

See topic Personal Property Security for applicable rules after Oct. 1, 1990.

Consumer Credit Transactions.—Time sale agreements and continuous deferred payment plans connected with any consumer sale of $100 or more or consumer loans greater than $50,000 not secured by real property mortgages, such sale not involving use of credit card, must set out in writing and disclose specified information with respect to total cash price, number, amount and due date of installments, description of goods, total amount of credit granted and amount of credit expressed as annual percentage rate. (c. C-22.5, §21).

Bulk Sales.—See topic Fraudulent Sales and Conveyances.

Door to Door Sales.—Direct Sales Cancellation Act provides for cancellation of door to door sales by purchaser within ten days of receipt of copy of contract or in certain circumstances within one year. (c. D-35, §§4, 6).

Product Liability.—Where buyer makes known to seller purpose for which goods are required and relies on seller's or manufacturer's judgment or skill, there is implied condition of fitness for such purpose. If goods are purchased by description from seller or manufacturer who deals in goods of such description, there is implied condition that goods are of merchantable quality. There is no implied condition as regards defects if buyer examines goods. (c. S-2, §17). Manufacturer's liability for defective goods, qua manufacturer, is governed by common law.

Unfair Trade Practices.—Where supplier of goods or services in consumer transaction has committed unfair trade practice or made misleading representation, consumers, consumer organizations and Director of Trade Practices are granted special remedies including punitive damages or injunction. Director may obtain injunction and receivership against suppliers who may be absconding or dissipating assets. (c. U-3). Competition Act (R.S.C., c. C-34 as am'd) purports to provide civil remedy as well as criminal and quasi-criminal remedies.

SALES TAX: See topic Taxation.

SEALS:

In order to create a specialty debt, it is necessary to contract under seal. Seal imports consideration; otherwise as in simple contracts, it is necessary to prove consideration. Words such as "signed, sealed and delivered" are not sufficient and will not suffice in place of seal.

The seal need be of no particular kind. Anything stuck opposite the signature as a seal or any make-shift such as writing "seal" or daubing ink, etc., will be considered as a seal if the parties so intend.

SECURITIES:

The Securities Act (1981, c. S-6.1, now am'd by 1981, c. B-15, 1982, c. 32, 1984, c. 64, 1988, c. 7, 1989, c. 19, 1991, c. 33, 1991, c. L-26.5) was proclaimed in force on Feb. 1, 1982. Act makes Alberta law in this respect similar to Ontario Securities Act.

Licenses.—Under Securities Act, no person may engage in trading of any securities or exchange contracts, acting as underwriter or acting as advisor, without first being registered with Executive Director of Securities. (1981, c. S-6.1, §54). Exemption from registration is available for certain advisors such as financial institutions, insurance companies, lawyers, accountants (c. S-6.1, §64), for trades in securities by executors, administrators, guardians, committees, authorized trustees or assignees, receivers or custodians under Bankruptcy and Insolvency Act (Canada), receivers under Judicature Act, liquidators under Companies Act, Business Corporations Act, Canada Business Corporations Act or Winding-Up Act (Canada), sheriffs or at judicial sale, or trades which are of isolated nature or otherwise limited (c. S-6.1, §65), and for trades in certain specified securities (c. S-6.1, §§65, 66) or exchange contracts (c. S-61, §66.1).

Provincial and foreign companies may be exempted from strict compliance with Act if requirements of jurisdiction in which it carries on substantial part of its business or where its company is incorporated, organized or continued are substantially same as Alberta Securities Act and documents that are filed in foreign jurisdiction are filed in Alberta (c. S-6.1, §184) and Commission assumes extra provincial jurisdiction to extent permitted by foreign jurisdiction (c. S-6.1, §16).

Franchises.—See topic Franchises.

SEQUESTRATION:

Where judgment directs recovery of specific property other than land or money and specified property is not delivered according to writ of delivery that issues, in addition to holding party in civil contempt, judgment may be enforced by writ of sequestration. Where judgment is against corporation, it may be enforced by order holding one or more of its directors or officers in civil contempt or, with leave of court, by writ of sequestration against property of corporation or property of one or more of its directors or officers. (A.R.C 364—366).

SERVICE: See topic Process.

STATUTE OF FRAUDS:

See topic Frauds, Statute of.

STATUTES:

Most recent revision of provincial statutes occurred in 1980 and is cited as RSA 1980. Annual volumes of amendments and new legislation are compiled and published. Amendments and revisions are also compiled in regularly updated looseleaf version of revised statutes. (As to form of citation used herein see note at head of Digest.)

STAY OF EXECUTION:

See topics Appeal and Error; Executions.

SUBMISSION OF CONTROVERSY:

Any bona fide controversy may be brought before the proper court and it will hear it and finally dispose of the same, subject only to appeal. If the parties can agree upon the facts, it will facilitate the disposition of the matter. If matter discloses no cause of action or defence, as case may be, or if it is scandalous, frivolous, vexatious, or otherwise abuse of court, it will be struck out. (A.R.C. 129).

SUPPLEMENTARY PROCEEDINGS:

See topic Executions.

SURETY AND GUARANTY COMPANIES:

No special legislation. See topics Banks and Banking; Insurance.

TAXATION:

There are taxes on real estate, mineral rights, wild lands, a business tax, an income tax, and other taxes imposed for federal, provincial, municipal and educational purposes. No exemptions for members of armed services except as discussed under subhead Income Tax, infra. New Municipal Government Act was proclaimed in force on Jan. 1, 1995. It repeals Municipal Taxation Act, among other legislation, and constitutes complete consolidation of legislation revision governing municipal corporations in Alberta. Taxation powers of municipalities are set forth in Part 10 of Act.

Land taxes are imposed by the city, town, village, county, municipal district, improvement district or special area in which land is situate to raise revenue to be used towards payment of municipality's expenditures, transfers and requisitions. (c. M-26.1, §353). Certain exemptions are available for prescribed taxpayers or types of property. (c. M-26.1, §§361, 362). Such taxes are calculated on basis of assessments prepared by municipality or other authority. (c. M-26.1, §§355, 356). Legislation contemplates tax agreements between certain specified parties and municipalities. (c. M-26.1, §360).

Enforcement.—These taxes may be enforced by action, auction or forfeiture and disposal of lands. (c. M-26.1, Part 10, Div. 8). Taxes are deemed to be in arrears if not paid by Dec. 31 of year in which they are imposed. (c. M-26.1, §326). Municipality must prepare, register with Registrar and post tax arrears list not later than Mar. 31 of each year, and persons liable to pay such tax in arrears must be notified that it has been prepared and registered. (c. M-26.1, §412). Tax recovery notification must be endorsed on certificate of title for each parcel of land shown on tax arrears list. (c. M-26.1, §413). Taxable improvements must not be removed from parcels after endorsement of tax recovery notification upon certificate of title to such parcels. After tax recovery notification has been endorsed upon certificate of title to parcel of land, and until parcel is disposed of by municipality, any person may pay arrears of tax, upon which payment, notification must be removed. (c. M-26.1, §415). Not later than Aug. 1 following receipt of tax arrears list, must notify owner of parcel, taxes for which are in arrears, any person with interest in such parcel, and any encumbrance that if arrears are not paid before Mar. 31 of following year, municipality will offer parcel for sale at public auction, and that municipality will assume ownership immediately after auction if parcel is not sold. Municipality is entitled to possession of parcel from date on which parcel is offered at public auction. Auction must be advertised, copy of which advertisement must be provided to persons with interest in land not less than four weeks prior to auction. (c. M-26.1, Part 10, Div. 8). Person who purchases parcel at public auction takes parcel free of all encumbrances, with certain statutory exceptions. Municipality becomes owner of parcel immediately following auction, if land is not sold at such auction and takes title free and clear of all but certain statutory encumbrances. (c. M-26.1, §§423, 424). Claims of municipality and Crown enjoy priority in distribution of proceeds of sale. Any surplus may be distributed in accordance with order of Court of Queen's Bench. (c. M-26.1, §427).

Redemption.—After municipality assumes ownership of parcel, lands that are not sold or disposed of may be redeemed upon payment of all tax arrears and costs. (c. M-26.1, §426).

Review of Assessment.—Complaints regarding certain matters in relation to assessments or taxes may be brought before assessment review board appointed by by-law. Rules of evidence do not apply to proceedings of assessment review board. Decision of assessment review board may be appealed to Municipal Government Board. Subject to general principles of administrative law, there is no appeal from decision of Municipal Government Board. Alternatively, complaint may be brought before arbitrator chosen by parties and governed by Arbitration Act (Alberta). Decision of arbitrator is final. (c. M-26.1, Parts 11 & 12).

Assessments under Freehold Mineral Rights Tax Act may also be brought before Municipal Government Board. (c. F-19.1, §4).

Income Tax.—For 1987 and subsequent tax years, individuals will pay general rate of 45.5% of federal tax plus 8% surtax of basic tax payable in excess of $3,500 and for 1987 taxation year, 1%, and for 1988 and subsequent taxation years, 0.5% flat tax of Alberta taxable income. Highest combined marginal tax rate for 1986 through 1988 for individuals earning income in Alberta will be 44.93%, and 46.07% for subsequent taxation years, effective July 1, 1989. Large corporations with permanent establishment in Alberta are subject to 14.5% tax in case of manufacturing corporations and 15.5% tax in case of nonmanufacturing corporations, as well as federal capital tax of .2%. (Large Corporations Tax, effective July 1, 1989). Combined federal and Alberta rate of tax for corporations for 1986 and subsequent taxation years will be 36.3% for manufacturing corporations, and 44.3% for nonmanufacturing corporations. Foreign corporations are subject to branch tax under Income Tax Act (Canada) of 25%, subject to reduction under applicable treaty provisions.

Inheritance Tax.—None.

Estate Tax.—None.

Business Tax.—Municipalities may impose business taxes upon persons operating business within municipality. Businesses are assessed for taxation purposes in accordance with certain prescribed criteria. Crown businesses and regional airports are exempt from taxation. (c. M-26.1, Part 10, Div. 3).

Enforcement.—Municipalities seeking to recover business tax arrears may issue distress warrant and seize goods of persons or businesses liable to pay such tax. Goods may also be seized from receivers, trustees in bankruptcy and liquidators of corporations. Seized goods must be auctioned not less than 60 days after seizure. Municipality becomes owner of any goods not sold at auction, whereupon it may sell such goods. Municipality may also bring action for tax arrears before seized goods are auctioned or become property of municipality. (c. M-26.1, Part 10, Div. 9).

Redemption.—Seized goods may be redeemed by any person upon payment of tax arrears at any time before municipality sells goods or takes ownership of them. (c. M-26.1, §443).

Sales Tax.—No provincial sales tax.

Goods and Services Tax.—Federal tax of 7% applies to most goods and services purchased in Alberta, effective Jan. 1, 1991.

Fuel Oil Tax.—Provincial tax of 9¢/litre applies to fuel oils for most fuels consumed in Alberta. (1987, c. F-22.5, §2, as am'd by 1990, c. 16; 1991, c. 15).

Stamp Tax.—Repealed 1953.

Motor Vehicles Tax.—See topic Motor Vehicles.

Mineral Tax.—See topic Mines and Minerals.

Franchise Taxes.—See topic Corporations.

Stock Transfer Tax.—Repealed 1953.

Unemployment Compensation or Social Security Tax.—None imposed by province. As to federal tax, see Canada Law Digest.

TORRENS ACT: See topic Records.

TRADEMARKS AND TRADENAMES:

See Canada Law Digest.

Registration of Trade Names.—Each person or certain partnerships which use business designation or name, must register that name with Registrar of Corporations within six months after its first use, or formation of partnership. (c. P-2, §§81-85).

TRUST AND LOAN CORPORATIONS:

New Loan and Trust Corporations Act (1991, c. L-26.5), was proclaimed in force on Jan. 16, 1992. It repeals previous Trust Companies Act and constitutes complete amalgamation and revision of legislation governing trust and loan companies in Alberta. Several other provinces, as well as federal government, are passing similar legislation to govern trust and loan companies within their respective jurisdictions. It applies to all new incorporations of trust or loan companies and existing trust companies are to be continued under it but until then are governed in part by Trust Companies Act. (R.S.A. 1980, c. T-9).

Part 1. Interpretation and Application.—

Application.—Act will apply to every trust corporation or loan corporation incorporated or continued under Act which has not been discontinued under Act.

"Trust corporation" as defined in Act means body corporate incorporated or operated for purposes of offering its services to public as executor, administrator, trustee, receiver, guardian or trustee of minor's estate or estate of mentally incompetent person, etc., and carrying on deposit-taking business. "Loan corporation" as defined in Act means body corporate incorporated or operated for purpose of carrying on deposit-taking business but does not include bank, treasury branch, trust corporation or credit union. "Body corporate" means any body corporate with or without share capital and wherever or however incorporated. (1991, c. L-26.5 §1[1]).

Part 2. Incorporation.—Loan corporation or trust corporation may be incorporated in Alberta by issuance of letters patent by Lieutenant-Governor in Council on recommendation of Minister (1991, c. L-26.5, §6).

Application for letters patent shall be filed with Minister, and notice of application must be published in Alberta Gazette and in local newspaper. (1991, c. L-26.5, §7).

Conditions for Issuing Letters Patent.—Letters patent shall not issue unless Lieutenant-Governor in Council is satisfied that establishment of additional provincial loan or trust corporation is in public interest, proposed management is fit to manage corporation, proposed capital and share structure are acceptable, any person who will hold or beneficially own 10% or more of any class of shares has adequate financial resources and is fit to hold shares, each proposed director is fit to be director of corporation, depositors of corporation will be adequately protected, proposed plan of operation of corporation is feasible, and corporation intends to offer to public services set out in application for incorporation. (1991, c. L-26.5, §8). Trust or loan corporation will come into existence on date set out in its letters patent. (1991, c. L-26.5, §13).

Capacity.—Subject to Act, loan or trust corporation has capacity and rights, powers and privileges of individual, and may carry on business in any jurisdiction outside Alberta to extent that laws of that jurisdiction permit. (1991, c. L-26.5, §14).

Amendments.—Minister may issue supplementary letters patent to amend letters patent of trust corporation in variety of ways. (1991, c. L-26.5, §17).

Requirements surrounding name of trust or loan corporation and organization and commencement of corporation are similar to those governing corporations incorporated under Alberta Business Corporations Act.

Part 3. Registration.—Trust Corporations Register and Loan Corporations Register are established. (1991, c. L-26.5, §28).

Both Alberta trust and loan corporations, and extra-provincial loan and trust corporations may apply for registration under Act, but application for registration of extra-provincial loan or trust corporation must be accompanied by consent authorizing Minister to conduct examinations at head office of corporation and written undertaking that corporation will provide to Minister any information that Minister requires. (1991, c. L-26.5, §§29-32).

Stated Capital.—In order to be registered, trust corporation which is to be prohibited from carrying on deposit-taking business and which is not fully owned by financial institution, must have stated capital account of at least $2 million. If trust corporation is wholly owned by financial institution, and will be prohibited from carrying on deposit-taking business, stated capital account must be at least equal to amount required by Minister. In any other case, that is, where corporation is going to carry on deposit-taking business, stated capital account of corporation must be at least $3 million in case

TRUST AND LOAN CORPORATIONS . . . *continued*
of loan corporation and $5 million in case of trust corporation, unless greater amount is specified by Minister. Further, corporation must have capital base which is adequate and at least equal to corresponding capital account amount for that corporation. Corporation must also establish, to satisfaction of Minister, that it meets conditions set out above for incorporation of trust or loan corporation. (1991, c. L-26.5, §35). If Minister is not satisfied as to any of or all of matters referred to in §35, or for any other reason, Minister may reject application or approve registration of applicant subject to any terms, conditions and restrictions Minister considers appropriate. (1991, c. L-26.5, §36).

Part 4. Principal Place of Business, Records and Returns.—Requirements imposed on corporation under this part of Act are similar to those imposed on corporations under Alberta Business Corporations Act.

Part 5. Shares and Shareholders.—Requirements in this part of Act are similar to those in corresponding part of Business Corporations Act.

Minister's Consent to Transfer or Issue.—Minister must consent to transfer or issue of voting shares of corporation if transfer or issue would result in person or persons related to that person owning more than 10% of any class of issued and outstanding shares of corporation. (1991, c. L-26.5, §77).

Part 12 of Business Corporations Act and regulations made thereunder, and Part 16 of Business Corporations Act (except §188[3]) apply with respect to loan or trust corporation as if it were corporation within meaning of that Act. Those sections of Business Corporations Act deal with proxies (Part 12) and take-over bids (Part 16). (1991, c. L-26.5, §§99 and 100).

Part 6. Directors and Officers.—Provisions under this part of Act are similar to those in Part 9 of Business Corporations Act, with exception that greater restrictions are placed on persons who may be directors of trust or loan corporation under Act.

Trust or loan corporation must have at least five directors. (1991, c. L-26.5, §101[2]). Individual who is director of affiliated corporation or who has been convicted of indictable offence or offence against Act within last five years is disqualified from being director of loan or trust corporation. (1991, c. L-26.5, §105).

Residency.—At least three-quarters of directors of loan or trust corporation must be ordinarily resident in Canada. (1991, c. L-26.5, §104). Further, no business shall be transacted at meeting of directors unless majority of directors precedent are ordinarily resident in Canada. (1991, c. L-26.5, §122[1]).

Duties and Liabilities of Directors.—Duties and liabilities imposed on directors of trust or loan corporation are similar to those imposed on directors of corporation incorporated under Business Corporations Act. (1991, c. L-26.5, §§130-135).

Part 7. Insider Trading.—Provisions governing insider trading in this part of Act are similar to those governing insider trading in Part 10 of Business Corporations Act.

Part 8. Auditors and Financial Statements.—

Qualifications.—Auditor must be permitted by law to engage in audit that is intended to be relied on by third parties, and must be independent of corporation, its affiliates, and directors and officers of corporation and its affiliates. (1991, c. L-26.5, §142).

Part 8 goes on to set out rights, duties and liabilities of auditor.

Part 9. Restricted Party Transactions.—

Application.—This part does not apply to provincial trust corporation whose registration is subject to term, condition or restriction prohibiting it from carrying on deposit-taking business. (1991, c. L-26.5, §162[1]).

Designation.—Minister may designate any person as restricted party of loan or trust corporation if Minister is of opinion that person is acting or has acted jointly or in concert with restricted party of corporation with respect to entering into transaction, guarantee or investment which would be prohibited if entered into by restricted party or there exists between person and corporation any interest or relationship that might reasonably be expected to affect exercise by corporation of its best judgment with respect to transaction, guarantee, or investment. Further, Minister may designate as restricted parties of corporation two or more persons who have agreed, pursuant to any formal or informal agreement or understanding, to act jointly or in concert in respect of shares of corporation or any entity which own shares or controls entity that owns shares. (1991, c. L-26.5, §163).

Prohibited Transactions.—Except as provided in Act, no provincial corporation shall enter into any transaction with restricted party of corporation, enter into any guarantee on behalf of such restricted party or make investment in any securities of such restricted party. (1991, c. L-26.5, §164[1]).

During 12 month period after person ceases to be restricted party of corporation, corporation may not enter into any transaction with such person unless it has been authorized by board of directors of corporation and is at fair market rate. (1991, c. L-26.5, §165[1]).

Board Approval Required.—With prior approval of board of directors, trust or loan corporation or its subsidiary may enter into contract with restricted party for provision of management services to or by corporation, for lease of real estate or personal property, for pension and benefit plans, stock options, and other reasonable commitments incidental to employment, for provision of goods or services other than management services for term not to exceed five years, for acquisition or sale of prescribed securities, for making of loan to or guarantee of obligations of entity, other than financial institution, in which corporation beneficially owns shares, or for any other transaction permitted by regulations. (1991, c. L-26.5, §167).

Board Approval Not Required.—Without prior approval of board of directors of corporation, trust or loan corporation may enter into new transaction with restricted party for minor or general expenditures, sale of goods or provision of financial services normally sold or provided to public by corporation in ordinary course of business, for taking of deposit from restricted party, or any other transaction permitted by regulations. (1991, c. L-26.5, §168).

Loans.—§169(1) sets out conditions under which corporation or subsidiary may make loan to director, officer, employee or spouse of director or officer.

Financial Institutions.—Loan or trust corporation may make loan to, enter into transaction with, or guarantee obligations of restricted party that is financial institution with prior approval of board of directors of corporation.

No transaction or guarantee or investment under this Part may be in excess of prescribed limits. (1991, c. L-26.5, §171).

Trust and Estate Funds.—Trust corporation shall not enter into transaction with restricted party using funds, other than deposits, held by corporation as fiduciary unless so authorized by court, Act, or regulations. (1991, c. L-26.5, §173).

Where transaction or investment prohibited under this Part takes place, any interested person may apply to court for order setting aside transaction, allowing for damages, or any other order court thinks fit.

Part 10. Capacity and Powers.—

Application.—This part does not apply to provincial trust corporation prohibited from carrying on deposit-taking business.

General Powers.—Subject to Act and regulations, loan or trust corporation shall not engage in or carry on any business other than business generally appertaining to business of providing financial services, with exception that trust corporation may exercise fiduciary powers referred to in Act, and loan or trust corporation may engage in provision of real property brokerage services and acquire, hold, repair, lease, or otherwise deal with real property. (1991, c. L-26.5, §181).

Only registered loan or trust corporation shall engage in deposit-taking business. Only registered trust corporation may offer its services to public as accepting office of executor or administrator or trustee, or guardian or trustee of minor's estate or estate of mentally incompetent person, unless otherwise authorized by other legislation. (1991, c. L-26.5, §183).

No registered loan corporation may carry on business as receiver, liquidator, or sequestrator, or as custodian of property. (1991, c. L-26.5, §184).

Registered trust or loan corporation may not, other than as principal, carry on any securities activities in respect of which filing prospectus or registration under Securities Act is required, but may otherwise carry on securities activities. (1991, c. L-26.5, §186).

Loan or trust corporation shall not engage in any leasing activity that financial leasing corporation within meaning of regulations is not permitted to engage in. (1991, c. L-26.5, §187).

Receiving Deposits.—Loan or trust corporation may, for purposes of investment, receive money repayable on demand or after notice, or repayable on fixed date on expiry of fixed term. Loan corporation may issue debentures or other evidence of indebtedness appropriate to debtor and creditor relationship created by receipt of money, and trust corporation may issue investment certificates or other evidence of receipt of money appropriate to trust relationship created by receipt of money. (1991, c. L-26.5, §188).

Trust corporation receiving money shall earmark in respect of it securities, or cash and securities, equal to full aggregate amount of money received, and shall refer to this as "depositors liability fund". Assets of such funds are held by corporation in trust for benefit of depositors to extent of corporation's liability to them. In order to exercise powers set out in this section, loan or trust corporation must be member of Canada Deposit Insurance Corporation or have its deposits insured by another public agency prescribed by Minister. (1991, c. L-26.5, §188).

Base.—Corporation shall maintain its capital base at not less than levels required by §35(b), and such capital base shall meet leverage ratio and risk rated average ratio requirements set out in regulations. (1991, c. L-26.5, §189).

Loan or trust corporation may borrow money by way of issue of subordinated notes having denomination not less than prescribed amount. (1991, c. L-26.5, §190).

Pledging Assets.—Except as provided in Act, no provincial corporation shall directly or indirectly pledge any part of its total assets, except to Government of Canada with respect to sale of Canada Savings Bonds, borrowing under §188, or in respect of other transactions permitted by regulations. Otherwise, corporation may pledge any of its own assets as security for debt obligation of corporation only if it is in respect of money borrowed to enable corporation to meet short term requirements for liquid funds, and total debt obligation of corporation in relation to which assets are pledged will not exceed 50% of corporation's capital base. (1991, c. L-26.5, §191).

Guarantees.—Loan or trust corporation shall not guarantee on behalf of any person payment or repayment of any sum of money unless it is fixed sum of money, and person on whose behalf guarantee is given has unqualified obligation to reimburse corporation for full amount of payment to be guaranteed. (1991, c. L-26.5, §192).

Limit on Borrowing.—Trust corporation shall not borrow money except from eligible financial institution, bank of Canada or another person approved by Minister unless it is borrowing by way of subordinated notes, or is borrowing as authorized by §191.

Other Prohibited Activities.—No loan or trust corporation shall carry on business as securities dealer, insurer, investment counselling corporation (except insofar as is necessary to exercise fiduciary powers of corporation), portfolio management corporation, mutual fund distribution corporation, information management corporation, or carry on any other prescribed activity. (1991, c. L-26.5, §194). *Note:* Amendment to Act which is not proclaimed in force removes prohibition on loan or trust corporation carrying on business as securities dealer, investment counselling corporation, portfolio management corporation, or mutual fund ditribution corporation. (1996, c. 19, §2).

Part 11. Investments.—

Application.—This Part does not apply to trust corporation prohibited from carrying on deposit-taking business, and this Part does not apply to funds, other than deposits, held by corporation as fiduciary.

Prudent Investment Standards.—Loan or trust corporation shall adhere to prudent investment standards in making investment decisions and in managing its total investments. Prudent investment standards are those which reasonably prudent person would apply to investments made on behalf of another person with whom there exists fiduciary relationship to make such investments without undue risk of loss or impairment and with reasonable expectation of fair return or appreciation. (1991, c. L-26.5, §196).

Liquidity.—Corporation shall at all times keep available in prescribed manner and amount securities of prescribed kind, or cash, or both securities and cash, for liquidity purposes. (1991, c. L-26.5, §198).

Personal Loans.—Corporation may make personal loans to individuals in amounts not exceeding prescribed amounts. (1991, c. L-26.5, §199).

Commercial Loans.—Loan or trust corporation may make commercial loans, aggregate amount of which shall not exceed 5% of total assets of provincial corporation, unless this amount is increased by Minister. Commercial loan does not include residential mortgage loan referred to in §201, mortgage loan on improved real estate in Canada where amount advanced is 75% or less of market value of real estate, acquisition of

See Topical Index in front part of this volume.

TRUST AND LOAN CORPORATIONS . . . *continued*
bankers' acceptances, acquisition of securities that are widely distributed, loans to or fully secured by Government of Canada, government of province, or government that is member of Organization for Economic Cooperation and Development, acquisition of securities that are issued or guaranteed by one of above governments, making of deposits in prescribed financial institution, making of loans to university, municipality, hospital board or school board, acquisition of common shares in body corporate, financing provided to individual up to prescribed aggregate amount, or any other prescribed form of financing.

Mortgage Lending.—Loan or trust corporation may purchase or make loans on security of mortgage on improved real estate in Canada. Where such mortgage is residential mortgage, amount advanced under mortgage must not exceed 75% of market value of real estate unless excess amount is guaranteed or insured by government of province or of Canada, or by insurance policy.

Where corporation acquires improved real estate by means of realizing security held on real estate, real estate may be retained for period not to exceed seven years. (1991, c. L-26.5, §202).

Investment in Real Estate.—Loan or trust corporation may acquire improved real estate in Canada for purpose of producing income or that is or is to be occupied by corporation for its own use, so long as total value of real estate so acquired does not exceed prescribed limits.

Prohibited Investments.—No corporation shall directly or indirectly make loans or other investments in any person or any two or more persons that to knowledge of corporation are connected, in aggregate amount exceeding prescribed amount, unless investment is in securities issued or guaranteed by Government of Canada or province, or mortgages which are insured under National Housing Act or insured by policy of mortgage insurance, or any other prescribed investment vehicles.

Except to protect value of existing asset, no corporation shall acquire assets that are in default because of nonpayment of interest, principal or dividend.

No corporation may beneficially own more than 10% interest in partnership, trust, fund or other unincorporated association or organization unless organization is carrying on business that may be carried on by body corporate referred to in §207(4). (1991, c. L-26.5, §206).

Limitation on Shareholding.—No corporation may beneficially own shares to which are attached more than 10% of voting rights attached to all of issued and outstanding voting shares of body corporate, except for following bodies corporate: loan or trust corporation with approval of Minister, financial leasing corporation, body corporate that is securities dealer, body corporate that is insurer, real property brokerage corporation or real property corporation, factoring corporation, mutual fund distribution corporation, investment counselling corporation, portfolio management corporation, service corporation, information management corporation, bank, or prescribed body corporate. However, notwithstanding above, loan or trust corporation may not own more than 10% of voting shares in body corporate if that body corporate owns more than 10% of voting shares of another body corporate which is not body corporate referred to above. (1991, c. L-26.5, §207).

Divestment Order.—Where corporation owns shares in body corporate as permitted above, and body corporate is carrying on business in unsound manner that imperils corporation's investment or if body corporate, being subsidiary, fails to provide information to Minister, Minister may order that corporation divest itself of all or part of its beneficial ownership. (1991, c. L-26.5, §208).

Collateral Security.—Corporation may take real or personal property as collateral security for any advance or any debt due to corporation, in addition to any other security for advance or debt required under Act. (1991, c. L-26.5, §209).

Common Trust Funds.—Trust corporation may invest money held by it as fiduciary, other than deposits, in one or more common trust funds of trust corporation. (1991, c. L-26.5, §211).

Part 12. Fundamental Changes and Arrangements.—

Amalgamation.—Loan or trust corporation shall not amalgamate with any other corporation except as authorized under this Act. Two or more provincial corporations may amalgamate and continue as one corporation. One or more provincial corporations may, with approval of Minister, amalgamate with one or more extra-provincial corporations and continue as one provincial corporation, or may amalgamate under laws of another jurisdiction for purpose of continuing as one extra-provincial corporation. (1991, c. L-26.5, §214).

Special Approval.—With approval of Minister, body corporate that is not provincial trust or loan corporation may amalgamate with trust or loan corporation and become trust or loan corporation. (1991, c. L-26.5, §215).

Purchaser Sale of Assets.—Loan or trust corporation may sell all or substantially all of its assets to corporation incorporated in Canada, or may purchase all or substantially all of assets of corporation incorporated in Canada if purchasing corporation assumes all or substantially all of liabilities of vendor corporation. (1991, c. L-26.5, §216).

Provisions governing amalgamation agreements and shareholder approvals are similar to those found in Business Corporations Act. However, such agreements must then be approved by Minister. (1991, c. L-26.5, §219).

Corporation may also purchase voting shares to which are attached not less than 67% of voting rights of corporation for purpose of acquiring assets of another corporation in Canada or amalgamating with such corporation. No such purchase shall be made without prior approval of Minister. (1991, c. L-26.5, §222).

Where amalgamation or purchase and sale of assets has been effected, all fiduciary obligations of original corporation are continued. (1991, c. L-26.5, §223).

Arrangements.—"Arrangement" means division of business carried on by provincial corporation, and exchange of securities of provincial corporation held by security holders for property, money or other securities of corporation. Application may be made to court by loan or trust corporation or security holder or creditor for order approving arrangement in respect of corporation. (1991, c. L-26.5, §224).

Part 13. Liquidation and Dissolution.—Dissolution of loan or trust corporation may be effected by issuance of letters patent dissolving corporation as authorized by special resolution of shareholders or resolution of directors if there are no shareholders, where corporation has no property and no liabilities. (1991, c. L-26.5, §226).

Upon such application, Minister may issue certificate of intent to dissolve. (1991, c. L-26.5, §229).

Minister or any interested person may, at any time during liquidation of provincial corporation, apply to court for order that liquidation be continued under supervision of court in accordance with this Part. Court may so order and may make any further order it considers appropriate. (1991, c. L-26.5, §235).

Duties, powers and liabilities of liquidator are also set out in this Part. (1991, c. L-26.5, §§243-249).

Part 14. Administration and Enforcement.—This Part sets out provisions relating to confidentiality of information, indemnity agreements, requirements for approvals and consents of Minister, review of Minister's decisions by review board or by court, Minister's ability to demand information from corporation, Minister's ability to undertake special examination of business or affairs of corporation, compliance orders, suspension and revocation of registration, powers of Minister, and payment of expenses of proceedings.

Dissolution by Court.—Court may on application of Minister or any other interested person make order for liquidation and dissolution of corporation where corporation has contravened Act or regulations and court is satisfied that it is in public interest that corporation be liquidated and dissolved. (1991, c. L-26.5, §289).

Act provides for derivative actions and for relief by court from oppression and unfairness similar to remedies provided by Business Corporations Act.

Part 15. Offences and Penalties.—This Part sets out prohibitions on several actions, such as use of particular names, misuse of confidential information, representations that corporation's solvency or financial standing is vouched for by government or Minister, and false or deceptive statements.

§305 sets out penalties for offences under Act, which are generally fine of $100,000 for first conviction and $200,000 for each subsequent conviction. Where offence is making of false or deceptive statements, person is also liable to imprisonment for not more than two years.

Part 16. General.—This Part deals with priority of government claims, unclaimed deposits, contracts with minors, publication of notices, and regulations.

Part 17. Transitional, Consequential, Repeal and Commencement.—Trust company registered under Trust Companies Act must apply to Minister for letters patent of continuance under new Act by June 25, 1992. (1991, c. L-26.5, §327).

If such corporation, at time letters patent of continuance are issued, is in contravention of prescribed limits with respect to investments referred to in §207, corporation must bring itself into compliance with §207 within five years after date of continuance.

Number of consequential amendments to other Alberta statutes are set out in §335.

TRUST DEEDS:

See topic Mortgages of Real Property.

TRUSTEE PROCESS: See topic Garnishment.

TRUSTS:

Common Law rules govern as to the kinds of trusts recognized in this province, the manner in which they are created, the purposes for which they will be permitted and as to the general rights, duties and liabilities of the trustees and beneficiaries.

Writing Required.—All declarations of trust are required, by the Statute of Frauds, to be in writing, subject to the rules of equity relating to resulting trusts and constructive trusts.

Eligibility and Competency.—No trust company shall be incorporated other than by Act of Legislature. (c. T-9, §7[1]).

Investments.—The Trustee Act (c. T-10, as am'd by 1991, c. L-26.5) regulates conduct of trustees.

Sales.—Where property is held by trustees in trust for infants, the former, by statute, may with leave of the court sell the corpus to maintain and educate the infants. (c. T-10, §36).

The Public Trustee may: (a) Act as guardian ad litem of estate of any minor; (b) act in administration of estates; (c) act as custodian of property of missing persons, convicts and deceased persons; (d) act as judicial trustee of estate of any deceased person upon order of court; (e) act either alone or jointly with any other person or persons, provided he is appointed for that purpose either in instrument creating trust or if appointed after creation of trust he is so appointed with consent of majority of persons beneficially interested therein; (f) act as trustee of estate of any minor made ward of province under provisions of Child Welfare Act; (g) act in such other capacity and do such other acts and matters and things as he is authorized or required to do by rules of court or by judge or by order of Lieutenant Governor in Council or under any act; (h) act as guardian or custodian of estate of any minor or unborn minor who has property vested in him or who is entitled either immediately or after interval either certainly or contingently to any property under intestacy or under will, settlement, trust deed, or in any other manner whatsoever and for whose estate no person has been appointed guardian by issue of letters of guardianship; (i) act as trustee of estate of any mentally incompetent person; (j) if no person has been appointed by court to act for estate of unborn minor, act as guardian or custodian of estate of minor, if minor has or may have property vested in him, or is or may be entitled after certain interval or contingency to property under intestacy, will, settlement, trust deed or other instrument or in any other manner. (c. P-36, §4). *Note:* Certain amendments are made to §4 by c. 28, 1996, §42 but they are not yet in force.

Securities In Name of Nominee.—While no notice of any trust expressed, implied, or constructive shall be entered on the share register and the company is not bound to see to execution of any trust (c. C-20, §72) there is nothing to prevent fiduciary holding securities in name of nominee. Under Business Corporations Act, company is entitled to treat registered owner as person entitled to exercise all rights and powers, and is not required to inquire into performance of any duty owed to another by registered holder. (c. B-15, §47).

See Topical Index in front part of this volume.

TRUSTS . . . *continued*

Accumulations.—Common law rules apply except with regard to trusts of a plan established for purpose of providing pensions, retirement allowances, annuities or similar benefits for employees or their beneficiaries. Perpetuities Act (c. P-4) came into force July 1, 1973, and repealed common law rule; not retroactive.

Perpetuities.—See topic Perpetuities.

Pour Over Trusts.—See topic Wills, subhead Bequests and Devises to Inter Vivos Trusts.

Variation of Trusts.—Subject to trust containing power to revoke or vary, no trust shall be terminated or revoked except with approval of Court of Queen's Bench. (c. T-10, §42).

USURY:

See Canada Law Digest, topic Interest.

VENUE:

Generally economy and convenience determine the place of trial which once settled can be altered only on application showing sufficient cause, e.g.: "local prejudice." (A.R.C. 237).

VITAL STATISTICS: See topic Records.

WAREHOUSEMEN:

Grain elevators, etc., are regulated by Canada Grain Act.

Lien.—Where goods on which lien exists are deposited by any person entrusted with possession thereof, warehouseman must, within two months after deposit, give notice of his lien to owner or person who has security interest in goods registered under provisions of Personal Property Security Act. (c. W-3, §5).

Every warehouseman has a lien on goods deposited with them for storage whether deposited by owner of goods or by his authority or by any person entrusted with possession of goods by owner or by his authority. (c. W-3, §3).

Warehouse Receipts.—A warehouse receipt is a document issued by a person who receives goods for storage for reward, stating that certain goods therein mentioned are deliverable to a person therein named or his assigns by endorsement. Effect of such an endorsement is an authority to receive possession. Endorsee should take prompt steps to receive possession or have warehouseman attorn to him. (c. W-2, §§3, 7).

Security for Loans.—Under provisions of the Bank Act, money may be loaned on security of warehouse receipts, bills of lading, etc. provided certain conditions are met. (S.C. 1991, c. 46).

WILLS:

In view of continued application of previous Wills Act in some cases, both Acts are discussed herein.

Under previous Wills Act any person of age of 21 or a soldier, sailor or other military or naval person of any age on active service, or seaman in course of a voyage, or a minor 19 years of age and married, who is of sound mind, can make a will. (R.S.A. 1955, c. 369, §§4, 6, 7).

Testamentary Disposition.—Under present Wills Act person of age of 18 or person under that age who at time of making will is, or has been, married, is member of component of Canadian Forces referred to in National Defence Act or is on active service under that Act, is mariner or seaman, and is of sound mind, can make will. (c. W-11, §9). Further, person under 18, unmarried but who has children, may make valid will to extent that it is for benefit of children. (c. W-11, §9).

Execution.—No will is valid unless it is in writing. (c. W-11, §4). Except in case of holograph wills or wills of servicemen, will must be signed by testator at foot or end thereof or by some other person in his presence and by his direction. Such signature must be made or acknowledged by testator in presence of two or more witnesses present at same time and such witness must attest and subscribe will in presence of testator. No form of attestation is necessary. Executor may be witness. (c. W-11, §§5-8, 15).

Holographic Wills.—A will wholly in handwriting of testator and signed by him is valid. Fact that it purports to have been witnessed does not invalidate it. (c. W-11, §7).

Noncupative Wills.—No provision.

Revocation.—Will may be revoked or altered by a later will or codicil in proper form, or revoked by either writing declaring intention to revoke or by destruction by testator or at his direction and in his presence where he has intention to revoke. (c. W-11, §16). Marriage revokes will unless it states that it is made in contemplation of marriage or unless it is made in exercise of power of appointment. (c. W-11, §17).

Revival.—Will is revived if re-executed with required formalities or codicil shows intention to give effect to revoked will. (c. W-11, §20).

Testamentary Gifts to Subscribing Witnesses.—A beneficiary, or husband or wife of a beneficiary, who is also a witness to a will cannot take any benefit thereunder unless will was sufficiently attested without his or her signature or required no attestation. But entire will is not invalidated by such attestation. (c. W-11, §13).

Testamentary Guardians.—See topic Guardian and Ward.

Election.—Where the husband clearly indicates in his will that his widow is not to have the benefit of dower she must elect whether she will abide by the terms of the will or will relinquish the testamentary provision, if any, made for her and insist on her dower rights.

Children.—Where a will disposes of entire estate of testator, his children are entitled to nothing more than is given them by will, unless dependents entitled to relief under The Family Relief Act, c. F-2 as am'd.

Probate.—See topic Executors and Administrators.

Support of Dependents Not Adequately Provided For.—Any dependent of a testator (defined as a husband, wife, child under 18 years at time of testator's death, or any child who by reason of physical or mental disability is unable to earn livelihood) may apply to Court for relief if adequate provision for proper maintenance and support has not been made in will. Court will make such order as seems just and equitable under circumstances. This order may take into account their separate estate, if any, and character or conduct of dependent. (c. F-2, §3).

1960 Wills Act.—This Act cited as "The Wills Act", (c. W-11) repeals and replaces "The Wills Act", (R.S.A. 1955, c. 369), with revised Act based on Uniform Act recommended by Conference of Commissioners on Uniformity of Legislation in Canada. Act only applies to wills made on or after July 1, 1960, but wills re-executed or republished or revived by codicil shall be deemed to be made at time at which it was so re-executed, republished or revived. (c. W-11, §2). See also head of this topic.

Foreign Will.—Generally, manner and formalities of making will, and its intrinsic validity and effect as regards interests in land are governed by law at place where land is situated, and as regards interest in moveables by law of place where testator was domiciled at death. But as regards moveables, a will is valid as to manner and formalities if made in accordance with law of place where made, or law of testator's domicile or domicile of origin. Change of domicile does not render will invalid as regards manner and formalities or alter its construction. (c. W-11, Part II). Act adopts convention providing uniform law on form of International Will and Uniform Law on the form of an International Will. (c. W-11, §§45, 46). Minister must establish system of registration or safekeeping of international wills. (c. W-11, §49). Information in registration systems must not be released unless person requesting is testator or person authorized by testator. (c. W-11, §52).

Self-proved Wills.—No provision.

Bequests and Devises to Inter Vivos Trusts.—Provision in a will bequeathing property to inter vivos trust has been upheld on principle of incorporation by reference. Pour-over from will to trust not in existence at time of will, will not be valid.

Unclaimed Legacies.—Where it is brought to attention of Public Trustee that person appears to be missing person, Public Trustee, after it is proved that person is missing, may take possession of lands, money, personal estate and effects of missing person. (c. P-36, §9). Crown in right of Alberta is ultimate heir of any person dying intestate in province with regard to any property situate in province or any moveable property wherever situate, in event of failure of heirs or next-of-kin. Personal representative may transfer estate to Crown in right of Alberta two years after death of intestate and claimant to estate may submit proof of his claim to Crown in right of Alberta. Crown in right of Alberta may admit or reject claim and if rejected claimant must bring action within six years from death of intestate, otherwise Crown in right of Alberta is deemed to be sole heir of intestate. (c. U-1).

Lapse.—Real or personal property comprised in devise that fails because devisee dies in lifetime of testator or devise contrary to law included in residuary bequest unless contrary intention in will. (c. W-11, §23).

Simultaneous Death.—See topic Death, subhead Survivorship.

Testamentary Trusts.—See topic Trusts.

Living Wills.—No legislation.

WITNESSES:

All persons may testify except those of unsound mind or children not of sufficient age to understand the nature of an oath.

Children.—Where a child of tender years is offered as a witness and such child does not, in the opinion of the judge, understand the nature of an oath, its evidence may be received not on oath if, in the opinion of the judge, the child is possessed of sufficient intelligence to justify the receipt of the evidence and understands duty of speaking truth. Corroboration is necessary in such case. (c. A-21, §20).

Interest.—There is no disqualification by reason of previous conviction or interest. (c. A-21, §3).

Affirmation.—Witnesses may affirm. (c. A-21, §18).

Privileged Communications.—Communications between solicitors and clients are privileged, also certain state documents.

Communications between husband and wife are privileged. (c. A-21, §8).

Self-incrimination.—Witness is not excused from answering questions on ground that they may tend to incriminate him, but providing he claims privilege on that ground, while he may be compelled to give evidence to incriminate him, such evidence can not be used against him in any prosecution under an Alberta Act except in prosecution for perjury or for giving of contrary evidence. (c. A-21, §6). Under Canadian Charter of Rights and Freedoms such evidence cannot be used to incriminate that witness in any proceedings, except in prosecution for perjury or for giving of contradictory evidence. (Canada Act, 1982, Part 1, §13).

WORKMEN'S COMPENSATION LAW:

See topic Labour Relations.

BRITISH COLUMBIA LAW DIGEST REVISER

Davis & Company
2800 Park Place
666 Burrard Street
Vancouver, British Columbia V6C 2Z7
Telephone: 604-687-9444
Fax: 604-687-1612

Reviser Profile

History: Davis & Company is one of the largest law firms in Western Canada. The firm was established in Vancouver in 1892 by two lawyers, E.P. Davis and D.G. Marshall. The merger of Davis & Company with another small but prominent law firm in 1958 provided the basis for the subsequent substantial increase in the firm's size and range of services. As of April, 1996 the firm is staffed with 106 lawyers, 12 legal assistants, 15 students and a support staff of 136.

On March 23, 1993 and September 1, 1994, respectively, Davis & Company opened offices in Whitehorse, Yukon Territory and Yellowknife, Northwest Territories, to serve the rapidly growing north.

In 1994, Davis & Company entered into the partnership of Thomas & Davis, with offices in Vancouver and Ottawa. The Thomas & Davis practice focuses on international trade law and international commercial transactions.

Davis & Company is affiliated with Fasken, Martineau, an international partnership with offices in Toronto, Montreal and London.

Areas of Emphasis: Davis & Company provides a full range of legal services. Within the Corporate/Commercial group, the specialized practice areas include: Banking; Securities; Credit Unions and Co-operatives; Natural Resources; Environmental; International Investment; Real Estate Acquisition and Development; Tax; Wills, Trusts and Estates; Intellectual Property; and Computer and Technology Law. In Litigation, the specialized practice areas include: Constitutional and Criminal Law; Insurance; Personal Injury; Immigration; Admiralty Law; Competition Law; and Family and Domestic Relations. Davis & Company also has a very large Employment and Labour Law Practice and Bankruptcy and Realization Department.

Client Base: Davis & Company acts for clients involved in mining, oil and gas, forest products, fisheries and manufacturing areas. The firm also acts for a number of major financial institutions, including one of the five major Canadian chartered banks, one of the world's largest credit unions and various umbrella and regulatory bodies involving credit unions and co-operatives in British Columbia.

In other areas, the firm acts for a number of government bodies, major professional associations and clients in retail, food services, transportation and other service areas. Through its varied client activities, Davis & Company has acquired extensive international experience particularly with Japanese and Chinese clients.

Our People: Of the 106 practising lawyers in Davis & Company 58 are partners. The majority of the firm's lawyers are engaged in corporate/commercial practice or in litigation. Many members have previously practised law in other jurisdictions including Alberta, Quebec, Ontario, New Brunswick, Nova Scotia, Northwest Territories, Yukon Territory, England and Hong Kong. A number of the firm's lawyers have been staff lawyers for major corporations.

While English is the language spoken by all of the firm's lawyers, other languages to be found among some of the members are French, Iranian, German, Japanese, Italian, Russian, Mandarin, Cantonese, Dutch, Hungarian, and Polish.

Activities: Members hold senior positions with the Canadian Bar Association, the Law Foundation of British Columbia, the Vancouver Bar Association and the Canadian Insolvency Association. One of the partners is a Bencher of the Law Society of British Columbia. Others are active participants in the Law Society's Continuing Legal Education programs and some lecture in law at universities in British Columbia.

Serving the community is an important activity for members of Davis & Company. Involvements include, executive positions with Vancouver Hospital, Vancouver Foundation, Vancouver Opera, Big Sisters, Boy Scouts, Downtown Vancouver Association, Heart and Stroke Foundation of B.C. and Yukon and British Columbians for Mentally Handicapped People. A number of lawyers also serve on the boards of charitable trusts, foundations and British Columbia Universities.

Management: Davis & Company is managed by a five person management committee presided over by a managing partner. This management committee continuously monitors lawyer performance, client relationships, economic and technological development and firm growth. Membership on the management committee is determined annually by election among the partners of the firm.

Significant Distinctions: Seven members are Queen's Counsel. Other major distinctions of firm members include: L. Allan Williams, Q.C., Minister of Labour (1975-1979) and Attorney General of British Columbia (1979-1983).

BRITISH COLUMBIA LAW DIGEST

(The following is a list of all Topics, including cross-references, covered in this Digest.)

BRITISH COLUMBIA LAW DIGEST

Revised for 1997 edition by

DAVIS & COMPANY, of the Vancouver Bar.

(References, unless otherwise indicated, are to Revised Statutes, 1979. Subsequent statutes are cited by year and statute number.)

ABSENTEES:

Non-Canadian citizens are under no disability with regard to acquiring and disposing of land viz. Canadian citizens. Person's property rights cannot be disturbed by reason only of citizenship of person from or through whom he derived title. (c. 340, §35).

Care of Property.—Judge of Supreme Court, on application made to Supreme Court, may appoint curator of estate of missing person who owns or is interested in real or personal estate within province where Judge satisfied that it is expedient to do so to deal with property.

An official administrator must be appointed curator except where it is found to the satisfaction of the judge that some other person would be more desirable by reason of personal or business relationship, or other sufficient circumstances. (c. 115, §2). When appointing curator court may impose terms as court thinks proper.

Duties of Curator.—The curator has the custody and management of the absentee's estate as trustee for missing person, but cannot sell or mortgage any portion of estate where value of such portion or amount to be raised by mortgage exceeds $100 in value, except with approval of judge of Supreme Court first had and obtained. (c. 115, §3, §4). Curator may dispose of money coming into curator's hands from missing person's property as directed by court. (c. 115, §4). With sanction of court, curator may sue or be sued in respect of property of missing person. (c. 115, §5).

Process Agent.—Absentees are not required to appoint agents for service of process.

Appearance in Court.—Defendant may appear personally or by counsel or agent, but justice may require defendant to appear personally, and may, if he thinks fit, issue warrant for arrest of defendant, and adjourn trial to await defendant's appearance. (c. 305, §50).

Escheat.—See topic Descent and Distribution.

ACCORD AND SATISFACTION:

Accord may be defined as agreement to accept in extinction of obligation something different from that to which person agreeing to accept it is entitled. Common law doctrine, provides that acceptance of smaller sum of money at same time and place as is required by obligation does not satisfy debt. But debt may be satisfied by payment of smaller sum at earlier time or at different place than that called for. Common law has been superseded by legislative provisions dealing with part performance. Now, part performance of obligation either before or after breach of it, when expressly accepted by creditor in satisfaction or rendered in pursuance of agreement for that purpose, though without any new consideration, shall be held to extinguish obligation. (c. 224, §40).

A negotiable note, although for a lesser amount than debt, may be good satisfaction thereof if so taken.

Pleading.—Accord and satisfaction must be specifically pleaded.

ACKNOWLEDGMENTS:

In British Columbia affidavits may be taken by Commissioners for Taking Affidavits for British Columbia. (c. 116, §66). Ex-officio Commissioners for Taking Affidavits are: all barristers and solicitors of British Columbia, notaries public, judges, justices of peace, court registrars, municipal clerks, regional district secretaries, secretary treasurer of board of school trustees, coroners, government agents, constables holding rank of sergeant or higher and other classes of employment Attorney General prescribes. (c. 116, §67). Also, employees or officers of Province to whom Director of Adoption or director under Guaranteed Available Income For Need Act has delegated powers or duties. (c. 116, §68). Also, any person to whom director under Family and Child Service Act or Community Resource Board Act has delegated powers or duties. (c. 116, §68).

Outside British Columbia affidavits may be taken by any of following: notary public acting within territorial limits of his authority and certified under his hand and official seal, judge or other court officer authorized to administer oaths, mayor of any city, borough or town, certified under seal of city, borough, or town, officer of British, Commonwealth or Canadian diplomatic or consular services exercising his functions in any country other than Canada, Canadian Government Trade Commissioner or Assistant Trade Commissioner in any country other than Canada, or (in another province) Commissioner authorized to take such affidavits by laws of that province. (c. 116, §70).

Others: Commissioned officer of Canadian naval, military and air forces on active service inside or outside Canada. Agents General for British Columbia. (c. 116, §71).

Proof of Execution.—Land Title Amendment Act (1989) (S.B.C., 1989, c. 69) eliminated use of affidavits to prove execution of instruments relating to land and introduces new scheme of officer certification.

Where transferor signature is certified by officer, his signature constitutes certification by him that: (a) transferor appeared before officer and acknowledged that he is person named in instrument as transferor; and (b) signature witnessed by officer is signature of person who made acknowledgment. (c. 219, §43).

Same model applies to execution of instruments by corporation or by individual or corporate attorney on behalf of individual or corporate principal. (c. 219, §§43-46). Officer certification covers circumstances where transferor cannot read English or sign his name in English characters; signature certifies that contents of instrument have been communicated and understood. (c. 219, §47).

Officer certification is required in all cases except where Registrar considers it reasonable to accept affidavit of execution on being satisfied that (1) facts, and (2) testimony by affidavit of other persons stating belief that signature in instrument is signature of named transferor, support such conclusion. (c. 219, §49).

Forms.—(B.C. Reg. 53/90).

STANDARD OFFICER CERTIFICATION

EXECUTION(S):

Officer Signature(s)	Execution Date Y	M	D	Party(ies) Signature(s)
	89	3	15	
Ian Jack Smith 100 Burrard Street Vancouver, B.C. V6C 1A1 Solicitor				John Peter Doe

EXECUTION BY A CORPORATION

EXECUTION(S):

Officer Signature(s)	Execution Date Y	M	D	Party(ies) Signature(s)
	89	3	26	ABC Limited by its authorized signatory
Jim Joe Brown 2500 West Georgia Street Vancouver, B.C. V7L 2P4 Notary Public				John Lee Doe

EXECUTION BY AN ATTORNEY

EXECUTION(S):

Officer Signature(s)	Execution Date Y	M	D	Party(ies) Signature(s)
	89	3	13	JOHN LEE DOE by his Attorney JOHN JOE SMITH
Sue Mary Love 2727-1499 4th Avenue Prince George, B.C. V2L 4Y9 Solicitor				D.F. 667801

See Topical Index in front part of this volume.

ACKNOWLEDGMENTS . . . *continued*

EXECUTION BY A CORPORATE ATTORNEY

EXECUTION(S):

Officer Signature(s)	Execution Date Y	M	D	Party(ies) Signature(s)
	89	3	13	JOHN LEE DOE by his Attorney ABC Limited by its authorized signatory JOHN JOE SMITH
Jane Sue Brown 1700-1250 2nd Avenue Kamloops, B.C. V9C 9Y5 Solicitor				John Joe Smith

EXECUTION BY AFFIDAVIT OF EXECUTION

EXECUTION(S):

Officer Signature(s)	Execution Date Y	M	D	Party(ies) Signature(s)
SEE AFFIDAVIT OF EXECUTION	89	3	13	John Charles Doe

ACTIONS:

Law and equity are conjointly administered.

The Supreme Court Act (1989) merged County and Supreme Courts of British Columbia into one unified Supreme Court of British Columbia. (S.B.C. 1989, c. 40, §17).

Commencement.—Supreme Court is court of original jurisdiction. (S.B.C., 1989, c. 40, §9). Actions or applications commenced by plaintiff or petitioner (party seeking relief), by writ of summons or originating application (petition or praecipe). (Rules of Court, R.8, 10). In Small Claims Court, which is court of limited jurisdiction (S.B.C., 1989, c. 38), actions commenced by Notice of Claim. See topics Courts; Pleading; Process; Depositions; and Canada Law Digest, topic Courts.

Conditions Precedent.—The Municipal Act provides that in some damage claims notice is to be served on the municipality within two months from date on which damage was sustained. (c. 290, §755). Certain municipalities have their own incorporating statutes containing conditions precedent and limitations.

Appearance and Defence.—Defendant resident in British Columbia wishing to contest action in Supreme Court, must enter appearance, and give address for delivery within ten miles of Registry out of which process originated (unless he appears by solicitor) within seven days from service of originating process. (Rules of Court, R.14). Where resident out of province, time limited for appearance is 21 days for person residing anywhere within Canada, 28 days for person residing in U.S., and 42 days for person residing elsewhere (unless shortened by judge on ex parte application). (R.13[6]). Where defendant has entered Appearance, defendant shall file and deliver Statement of Defence and any Counterclaim to plaintiff within 14 days from later of time for Appearance or delivery of Statement of Claim. (R.21[5]). Where plaintiff's claim is solely for recovery of debt or liquidated demand, and defendant has not filed Appearance or Statement of Defence within time allowed, plaintiff may enter final judgment for sum not exceeding that claimed plus interest and costs and may proceed with action against any other defendant. Plaintiff must file proof of delivery of Statement of Claim. Where claim is solely for unliquidated damages, plaintiff may enter judgment for damages to be assessed and costs and proceed with action against any other defendant. (R. 17,25). If defendant appears in any action, plaintiff may, notwithstanding appearance, apply to judge for final judgment, on proving claim by affidavit, and showing that deponent knows of no fact which would constitute defence to whole or part of plaintiff's claim; court may grant judgment, allow defendant to defend claim, or grant any other order it thinks just. Defendant may also apply for summary judgment on ground there is no merit in whole or part of plaintiffs claim and on verifying his contention by affidavit action may be dismissed or court may grant any other order it thinks just. (R.18). If statement of defence filed and triable issue disclosed, plaintiff or defendant may apply to Court to have action decided by summary trial on affidavits. (R.18A). See also topic Judgments.

Parties.—All persons may be joined as plaintiffs in whom the right to any relief claimed is alleged to exist, whether jointly, severally or in the alternative. All persons may be joined as defendants, against whom the right to any relief is alleged to exist, whether jointly, severally, or in alternative. Neither every plaintiff nor every defendant need be interested in whole relief claimed. (Rules of Court, R.5). Court on application by parties may at any time add, substitute or strike out parties, subject to any limitation provisions. (R.15[5]).

Partners may be sued or may sue in firm name (Rules of Court, R.7[1]); service is effected upon firm by serving person who was partner at time cause of action arose or person at place of business of firm who appears to manage or control partnership business (R.7[2]). Person carrying on business in name or style other than his own name may be sued in that name or style. (R.7[10]).

Persons under disability must commence or defend proceedings by their guardian ad litem. (R.6[2]).

Trustees and executors may sue and be sued without joining persons interested in estate. (R.5[17]).

Class Actions.—Where numerous persons have same interest in proceeding, proceeding may be commenced and, unless Court otherwise orders, continued by or against one or more of them representing all. (Rules of Court, R.5 [11]). Court may on application of party appoint one or more defendants or another person to represent one or more of persons having same interest. (R.5[12]). British Columbia resident may commence proceeding in court on behalf of members of class after judge certifies proceeding as class proceeding. Defendant to two or more proceedings may apply to judge for order certifying proceeding as class proceeding. (Class Proceedings Act S.B.C. 1995 c. 21, §§2, 3). Judge must certify proceeding as class proceeding if: pleadings disclose cause of action; there is identifiable class of two or more persons; claims of class members raise common issues; class proceeding would be preferable procedure for fair and efficient resolution of common issues; there is representative plaintiff who fairly and adequately represents interests of class; plaintiff's interests do not conflict with individual interests of other class members; plaintiff has produced workable method of advancing proceeding on behalf of class and of notifying class members of proceeding. (§4). Judge may permit one or more class members to participate in proceeding. (§15). Court may stay any proceeding related to class proceeding. (§13). Members of class may opt in or opt out of class proceeding. (§16). Parties to class have same discovery rights as provided under Rules of Court. (§17). Judgment on common issues binds every member of class, but not parties who opt out of proceeding in future proceedings.(§26). Court may make aggregate awards and may use several methods to ascertain proper allocation of award. (§§31-34). Class proceeding may be settled, discontinued, or abandoned only with approval of court and on terms court deems appropriate. (§35).

Intervention.—Normally intervention in action by person not party not permitted. However, there are certain exceptions:

In probate actions any person interested in estate but not named in estate may, with leave of court, enter appearance and defend action. (Rules of Court, R.62[4]).

At any time before divorce is granted Attorney General may apply to court for leave to intervene in divorce actions for purpose of showing collusion, fraud or bringing evidence before court. (R.60B[34]).

Person registering or filing interest in mortgaged property subject to foreclosure proceedings after Certificate of Pending Litigation may enter appearance. (R.50[4]).

Interpleader.—Where person is sued or expects to be sued in respect of property in his possession or under his control or in respect of proceeds from disposition of property, or receives claim in respect of property or proceeds by or from two or more persons making adverse claims and applicant claims no beneficial interest in property, applicant may apply to court for relief by way of interpleader. (Rules of Court, R.48). Application for interpleader relief may be made ex parte, and court may deal with matter summarily or give directions for service. (R.48[8, 9]).

Joinder of Causes of Action.—Plaintiff may unite in same action several causes of action; court may subsequently order separate trials if actions cannot be conveniently tried together. (Rules of Court, R.5[1], R.5[6]).

Severance of Actions.—Where joinder of several claims or parties in proceeding may unduly complicate or delay trial or is inconvenient Court may order separate trials or make such other order as it thinks just. (Rules of Court, R.5[6]).

Consolidation.—Proceedings may be consolidated at any time by order of court, or may be ordered to be heard at same time or on same day. (Rules of Court, R.5[8]).

Third Party Proceedings.—Provided in following instances: Where defendant entitled to contribution or indemnity, defendant entitled to relief or remedy relating to original subject matter of action and same as relief or remedy claimed by plaintiff, or any issue relating to original subject matter same as issue between plaintiff and defendant and should be determined between all parties. (Rules of Court, R.22). Court may set aside third party notice. (R.22[4]). Third party may enter appearance within seven days of service; appearance must comply with R.14 regarding appearance by defendant. (R.22[5]). If third party wishes to dispute his liability to person issuing third party notice he must file statement of defence within 14 days of entering appearance. (R.22[7]). Defendant issuing third party notice has seven days to file and deliver Reply. (R.22[8]). Where third party has not filed appearance or statement of defence: (a) He is deemed to admit validity of any judgment given, whether by consent or otherwise against party issuing third party notice (R.22[9][a]); and (b) where party issuing third party notice has satisfied judgment against him he may enter judgment against third party to extent of contribution and indemnity claimed in notice, and with leave of court, in respect of any other relief or remedy claimed therein (R.22[9][b]); or (c) where party issuing third party notice has not satisfied judgment against him, he or judgment holder may apply to court for such judgment as nature of case requires, including judgment for judgment holder against third party (R.22[9][c]). Third party who has entered appearance may file statement of defence to plaintiff's statement of claim but defences limited to those open to defendant; third party then treated as if defendant. (R.22[10]). Party affected by third party proceedings may apply to court for directions. (R.22[11]). Plaintiff should not be prejudiced or unnecessarily delayed by third party proceedings and court may impose terms to prevent prejudice or delay. (R.22[12]).

Discontinuance.—Action may be discontinued in whole or in part by plaintiff at any time before action set down for trial, or thereafter with consent of all parties of record or by leave. (Rules of Court, R.36).

See Topical Index in front part of this volume.

ACTIONS . . . *continued*

Stay of proceedings may be ordered by Supreme Court or judge thereof on good cause shown. (Rules of Court, R.54[7, 9], Court of Appeal Act S.B.C. 1982 c. 7, §18).

Abatement.—Cause of action for tort does not abate on death of either party, but action may be continued or brought by or against executor or administrator of decedent. See Estate Administration Act, c. 114, §66(2) and (4) and Family Compensation Act, c. 120, §5. Note: Prior to Oct. 15, 1982 action had to be brought against executor or administrator not later than 12 months after date of death if limitation period had not expired at time of death. Amendment effective Oct. 15, 1982 permits action to be brought against executor or administrator within time otherwise limited for action. (c. 114, §66[4]). CAVEAT: Amendment may have no retroactive effect. If cause of action arose and death occurred before Oct. 15, 1982, may be governed by pre-amendment provision.

Revival of action in which no step has been taken for one year is effected by giving other party 28 days notice. (Rules of Court, R.3[4]). Notwithstanding this rule, defendant or respondent may apply to dismiss for want of prosecution without giving notice. (R.3[5]).

Limitation of.—See topic Limitation of Actions; c. 236; c. 290, §754.

Direct Actions Against Insurer.—See topic Motor Vehicles, subhead Direct Actions.

ADMINISTRATION:

See topic Executors and Administrators.

ADOPTION:

Adoption of children (defined as unmarried person under 19 years) and in some cases adults is governed by c. 4. *Note:* S.B.C. 1995, c. 48 repeals c. 4 and comes into force Nov. 4, 1996. (B.C. Reg. 93/96). See subhead New Adoption Statute, infra.

Who May Apply to Adopt.—Any adult person (including natural parents) or any adult husband and his wife together, may adopt child, or adult husband and his wife together may adopt child of either of them, or adult husband or adult wife may individually apply to adopt child of either of them. (c. 4, §3).

Consent Required.—Generally, private adoptions require written consent of (a) child, if over 12 years; (b) parent(s) of child, or, if child has no parents, child's legal guardian, or, if there is no legal guardian, Public Guardian and Trustee (S.B.C. 1993, c. 64, §30); (c) applicant's spouse. (c. 4, §8). "Parent" under c. 4, §8, does not include all natural fathers, but practice of Supreme Court is to seek consent of all natural fathers, or to require full hearing of petition. (Supreme Court Practice Directive 3.1). Generally, adoptions arranged by Ministry of Social Services require written consent of (a) child, if over 12 years; (b) applicant's spouse; (c) Director of Adoption. (S.B.C. 1994, c. 27, §109). Consents must be verified by affidavits of person consenting and of witness, and content of affidavit is provided for in statute. Written consent of mother not valid unless child ten days old at time of consent. Consent, other than of child, when given may not be revoked unless court satisfied revocation is in best interests of child. Court may dispense with consent in certain instances such as abandonment, neglect, etc. (§8).

Conditions Precedent.—Generally, (a) six months notice of intention to file application; (b) filing of report of Director of Adoption (S.B.C. 1994, c. 27, §111); (c) residence of child with applicant for six months prior to application hearing; (d) conduct of applicant such as to justify order; (e) where one spouse applies to adopt child of other spouse, proof beyond doubt that adoption is in best interests of child. Provision for court to dispense with compliance of length of notice in cases of urgency. (c. 4, §6).

Jurisdiction.—Supreme Court of B. C. (c. 4, §1).

Proceedings.—All adoption applications are commenced in Supreme Court by praecipe and petition. Where all documentation is present, and order is unopposed, adoption may proceed by desk order. Desk order application should be accompanied by supporting affidavits, Registration of Live Birth, Vital Statistics Form HLTH 433 (Identification Particulars), draft order, and report of Director of Adoption.

Name.—Adopted person shall have given names court specifies on adoption order and surname of adoptive parent(s) unless Court otherwise orders. (c. 4, §10).

Effect of Adoption.—(a) For all purposes, adopted child becomes child of adopting parent, and adopting parent becomes parent of child, as if born to adopting parent. (b) For all purposes adopted child ceases to be child of existing parents, and existing parents cease to be his parents. (c) Relationship to one another of all persons determined as in (a) and (b). (c. 4, §11).

Foreign Adoptions.—Adoptions effected according to the laws of any other Province of Canada, or any country or part of it have same effect as adoptions under statute. (c. 4, §12).

New adoption statute provides as follows:

Who May Place Child for Adoption.—Child may be placed for adoption by director of adoption, adoption agency, birth parent or other guardian of child by direct placement, or birth parent or other guardian related to child if child is placed with relative of child. (§4).

Who May Receive Child for Adoption.—Child may be placed for adoption with one adult or two adults jointly, provided that each prospective adoptive parent is resident of British Columbia. (§5).

Consent Required.—Generally, adoptions require consent of (a) child, if 12 years of age or over; (b) birth mother; (c) father; and (d) any person appointed as child's guardian. (§13[1]). For purpose of giving consent to adoption, child's father is anyone who (a) had acknowledged paternity by signing child's birth registration; (b) is or was child's guardian or joint guardian with birth mother; (c) has acknowledged paternity and has custody or access rights to child by court order or by agreement; (d) has acknowledged paternity, and has supported, maintained or cared for child, voluntarily or under court order; (e) has acknowledged paternity and is named by birth mother as child's father; or (f) is acknowledged by birth mother as father and is registered on birth father's registry as child's father. (§13[2]). If child is in continuing custody of director under Child, Family and Community Service Act (S.B.C. 1994, c. 27), or director of adoption is child's guardian under Family Relations Act (c. 121), only consents required are director's consent, and child's consent if 12 years of age or over (§13[3]). If child who has been adopted is to be adopted again, consent of person who became parent at time of previous adoption is required, instead of consent of person who ceased to have any parental rights and responsibilities at that time. (§13[4]). If child has been placed for adoption by extra-provincial agency and law of jurisdiction in which agency is located is that only consent of agency is required for child's adoption, then that consent, and child's consent if 12 years of age or over, are only consents required. (§13[5]). Consent to adoption of child in British Columbia by person resident in British Columbia must be in prescribed form and must be supported by prescribed documents. (§16). Court may dispense with consent in certain instances such as if person whose consent is to be dispensed with has abandoned or deserted child, has not made reasonable efforts to meet their parental obligations to child, is not capable of caring for child, etc. (§17). Generally, person who consented to child's adoption may revoke consent before director of adoption or adoption agency places child for adoption, but only if revocation is in writing, and is received by director or adoption agency before child is placed with prospective adoptive parents. (§18). Birth mother may revoke or consent to adoption within 30 days of child's birth, even though child has been placed for adoption during that period, but only if revocation is in writing, and is received by director or adoption agency before end of the 30 days. (§19). Child may revoke consent to adoption at any time before adoption order is made. (§20). Consent given under law of another jurisdiction to adoption of child in British Columbia may be revoked in accordance with law of that jurisdiction. (§21). After child is placed for adoption, consent to child's adoption may only be revoked by court or in accordance with §§19, 20 or 21. Court may revoke consent if it is satisfied that it would be in child's best interests to do so. (§22).

Conditions Precedent.—Before direct placement, prospective adoptive parents must notify director of adoption or adoption agency of their intent to receive child in their home for adoption. Generally, before placement by director or adoption agency, or as soon as possible after being notified of direct placement, director or adoption agency must (a) provide information about adoption and alternatives to adoption to birth parent or other guardian requesting placement or proposing to place child; (b) obtain as much information as possible about medical and social history of child's biological family and preserve information for child; (c) give prospective adoptive parents information about medical and social history of child's biological families; and (d) make sure that child, (i) if sufficiently mature, has been counselled about effects of adoption, and (ii) if 12 years of age or over, has been informed about right to consent to adoption. For direct placement, director or adoption agency must also prepare pre-placement assessment of prospective adoptive parents, and give copy of pre-placement assessment to prospective adoptive parents and to birth parent or other guardian of child. Before placement by director or adoption agency, director or adoption agency must also (a) if birth parent or other guardian requesting placement wishes to select child's prospective adoptive parents, provide birth parent or other guardian with information about prospective adoptive parents who have been approved on basis of home study completed in accordance with regulations; (b) make reasonable efforts to obtain any consents required; and (c) make reasonable efforts to give notice of proposed adoption to (i) anyone who is named by birth mother as child's birth father if his consent is not required, and (ii) anyone who is registered in birth father's registry in respect of proposed adoption. Director or adoption agency may only place child for adoption with prospective adoptive parents who have been approved on basis of home study. (§§6, 8). Prospective adoptive parents may receive child by direct placement only if they have made reasonable efforts to obtain any consents required, and have made reasonable efforts to give notice of proposed adoption to anyone who is named by birth mother as child's birth father if his consent is not required, and anyone who is registered in birth father's registry in respect of proposed adoption. (§9). Court may dispense with notice of proposed adoption to birth father if it is in child's best interests to do so. (§11).

Name.—Court may change child's given names or family name in adoption order, but only with child's consent, if child is 12 years of age or over, or after considering child's view, if child is at least seven years of age and less than 12. Child's consent to Change of Name is not required if court has dispensed with child's consent to adoption. (§36).

Effect of Adoption.—When adoption order is made (a) child becomes child of adoptive parent; (b) adoptive parent becomes parent of child; and (c) birth parents cease to have any parental rights or obligations with respect to child, except birth parent who remains parent jointly with adoptive parent. (§37).

Adoptions Outside of British Columbia.—Adoption that has, under law of another province or other jurisdiction outside Canada, substantially same effect in that other jurisdiction as adoption under statute has same effect in British Columbia as adoption under statute. (§47).

Adoptions by Aboriginal Custom.—Court may recognize that adoption of person effected by custom of Indian band or aboriginal community has effect of adoption under this Act. (§46).

ADVANCEMENTS:

See topic Descent and Distribution.

ADVERSE POSSESSION:

After registration of indefeasible title no title adverse to or in derogation of title of registered owner shall be acquired by length of possession, but notwithstanding foregoing, first indefeasible title registered is void as against title of any person adversely in actual possession of and rightly entitled to land included in indefeasible title at time registration was applied for and who continues in possession. (Land Title Act c. 219, §23[2] and [3]). All existing methods of obtaining rights over land by prescription abolished and, without limiting generality of foregoing, common law doctrine of prescription and doctrine of lost modern grant are abolished. (§24).

See Topical Index in front part of this volume.

AFFIDAVITS:

Formal Requirements.—Affidavit must be expressed in first person, must show name, address and occupation of deponent, must be signed by deponent (or marked if deponent cannot sign), and must be divided into numbered paragraphs. If deponent is party or solicitor, agent, director, officer or employee of party, affidavit must so state. All alterations in affidavit must be initialed by person before whom affidavit is sworn; if any alterations have not been initialed, leave of court must be obtained before affidavit is used. True reproductions of all documentary exhibits not exceeding five pages must be attached. Other exhibits need not be filed, but must be made available for prior inspection of party, and to court. (Rules of Court, R.51).

Duty of Person Before Whom Affidavit Sworn.—Must sign jurat and identify any exhibits referred to in affidavit by signing certificate in form below. If deponent appears unable to read affidavit, jurat must be certified that affidavit was read to deponent who understood contents. If deponent appears not to understand English language, affidavit must be interpreted to deponent by competent interpreter and endorsement certified on affidavit in form below. (Rules of Court, R.51[6]).

Contents.—Statements made on information and belief may be included in affidavit in interlocutory application or when leave of court is obtained, provided source of information is given. All other affidavits may state only what deponent would be permitted to state in evidence at trial. (Rules of Court, R.51[10]).

Persons Who Can Swear Affidavits.—

In British Columbia affidavits may be taken by Commissioners for Taking Affidavits for British Columbia (c. 116, §66). Ex officio Commissioners for Taking Affidavits are: all barristers and solicitors of British Columbia, notaries public, judges, justices of peace, court registrars, municipal clerks, regional district secretaries, secretary treasurer of board of trustees, coroners and government agents, deputy government agents, provincial or municipal constable holding rank of sergeant or higher, commissioned officers on active service in Canadian Armed Forces, and other classes of office holder or employment Attorney General may prescribe. (c. 116, §67).

Outside British Columbia affidavits may be taken by any of following: commissioners for taking affidavits for British Columbia, notary public acting within territorial limits of his authority and certified under his hand and official seal, judge, magistrate or officer of Court of Justice authorized to administer oaths, mayor of any city, borough or town, officer of Canadian diplomatic or consular services exercising his functions in any country other than Canada, Canadian Government Trade Commissioner or Assistant Trade Commissioner, or Commissioner authorized to administer oaths in Courts of Justice by laws of that province, territory or country. (c. 116, §70).

Use of Affidavits.—Affidavits are normally used to support or oppose interlocutory applications, but with leave of Court obtained either before or at trial, party may present affidavit evidence to prove particular fact or document at trial; unless court orders otherwise, deponent is subject to cross-examination. (Rules of Court, R.40[44]).

Affidavit should have heading setting out name of court, action number, registry where action was commenced and style of cause.

Following jurat clause may be used to witness affidavit sworn in U.S.:

Sworn before me . . . ., a notary public in and for . . . . County, in the State of . . . ., U. S. A., at the City of . . . in the State of . . . ., this . . . . day of . . . ., 19. . . In testimony whereof have hereunto set my hand and affixed the seal of my office.

. . . .,
Notary Public in and for
. . . . .County, in the State
of, ..., U. S. A.
My Commission Expires . . . . [date].

Exhibit Certificate (Rules of Court, R.51[7]).—

This is Exhibit . . . . referred to in the affidavit of . . . . sworn before me the . . . . day of . . . ., 19. . .

. . . .

Form 60 (Rule 51 (2) and (5))
[Style of Proceeding]

AFFIDAVIT

I, *[name, address, and occupation of deponent]*, **MAKE OATH (OR SOLEMNLY AFFIRM) AND SAY THAT:**

1. . . .
2. . . .
3. . . .

SWORN (OR AFFIRMED) BEFORE)
ME in the [city etc.] of ________)
in the Province of British Columbia)
on this _____ day of [month], [year].)
) ____________________
________________________)
A commissioner for taking affidavits
for British Columbia

ENDORSEMENT OF INTERPRETER
[where applicable]

I, *[name, address and occupation]*, certify that:

1. I have a knowledge of the English and languages and I am competent to interpret from one to the other.

2. I am advised by the deponent and verily believe that the deponent understands the language.

3. Before the affidavit on which this endorsement appears was made by the deponent I correctly interpreted it for the deponent from the English language into the language and the deponent appeared to fully understand the contents.

Dated ____________________ ____________________
Interpreter

Alternative to Affidavit.—No statutory provision.

AGENCY: See topic Principal and Agent.

AIRCRAFT:

See Canada Law Digest, topic Aircraft.

ALIENS:

See Canada Law Digest, topic Aliens.

Property.—Aliens have all the rights of citizens as regards holding and disposing of real and personal property. (c. 340, §35).

ALIMONY: See topic Divorce.

ALLOWANCES:

See topic Executors and Administrators.

APPEAL AND ERROR: See topic Courts.

ARBITRATION AND AWARD:

Commercial Arbitration Act S.B.C. 1986, c. 3 applies to "arbitration agreements", including those in commercial agreements. "Arbitration agreement" is defined as written or oral term of agreement present or future to submit dispute to arbitration but does not include agreement to which International Commercial Arbitration Act, S.B.C. 1986, c. 14, applies. May be by any mode agreed upon by parties; otherwise single arbitrator. Where agreement provides for appointment for even number of arbitrators, arbitrators may appoint additional person to act as umpire. In case of failure to appoint arbitrator within seven days notice to do so, Supreme Court Judge may appoint one on application of other party.

Powers of Arbitrators.—Arbitrators may order production of documents, admit evidence and information on oath, subpoena witnesses, make interim order, call witness on own motion, and make order for specific performance for contract for sale of goods.

Enforcement of Award.—Award may, with leave of Court, be enforced in same manner as judgment or order of Supreme Court.

Award Final.—Award is final and binding on all parties to award.

Extent of Judicial Intervention.—Award may be set aside by Supreme Court if it has been improperly procured or there has been arbitral error. Party may appeal award to Supreme Court by consent of all parties or with leave of court. No arbitral proceeding, order, ruling or award can be questioned, reviewed or restrained except as provided for in Act.

International Arbitration.—S.B.C. 1986, c. 14, applies to all international commercial arbitrations, subject to any agreement in force between Canada and any other state, and which applies in British Columbia. Arbitration is international if: (a) parties have at time of agreement places of business in different states; (b) any of following is outside state in which parties have place of business: (i) place of arbitration under agreement, (ii) place where substantial part of obligations to be performed, or (iii) place where subject of dispute is most closely connected; or (c) parties agree that subject of arbitration agreement relates to more than one state.

ASSIGNMENTS:

Written assignment of debt or legal chose in action, of which written notice given to debtor, transfers legal title, subject to equities arising prior to notice of assignment. Assignee may sue in his own name. Debtor or person liable may interplead or pay money into court under and in conformity with provisions of Trustee Act (c. 414) if assignment disputed by assignor or other opposing claim made. (c. 224, §32).

Registration.—Subject to exceptions, when there is transfer of account, transferee is required to register his security interest in personal property registry if he wishes to avail himself of registry's priority system. This system governs rights and remedies of secured parties upon default of debtor. Registration perfects transferee's security interest and places it within priority system according to time of registration (see topic Personal Property Security and S.B.C. 1989, c. 36).

ASSIGNMENTS FOR BENEFIT OF CREDITORS:

See Canada Law Digest, topic Bankruptcy.

ASSOCIATIONS:

(c. 390).

Formation.—Societies may be formed for any lawful purpose or purposes such as national, patriotic, religious, philanthropic, charitable, provident, scientific, fraternal, benevolent, artistic, educational, social, professional, agricultural, sporting, or other useful purposes, but not for purpose of carrying on business, trade, industry, or profession for profit or gain. (§2). May be formed by five or more persons by subscribing constitution and by-laws and forwarding them in duplicate to Registrar of Companies with list of first directors, notice of address of proposed society and prescribed fees. (§3).

Professional associations may be incorporated to promote any object of a professional character, but cannot be incorporated for the purpose of carrying on any trade, industry or business.

Liabilities.—No member of such a society is liable in his individual capacity for its debts. (§5).

Rights and Powers.—There is no share capital (§8) and no dividends and interest is not transferable except as may be provided in by-laws (§9).

Actions.—The society sues and contracts in its own name and may have seal. (§4).

Extra-Provincial Societies.—Extra-provincial society may apply for registration. Any extra-provincial society or agent thereof not registered is incapable of holding any interest in land or maintaining action upon any contract made in whole or in part in Province. Registrar of Companies may require extra-provincial society that carries on insurance business to apply for registration. (§§75, 81).

See Topical Index in front part of this volume.

ASSOCIATIONS . . . *continued*

Cooperative Association Act (c. 66) provides that any five or more persons may, subject to approval of Superintendent of Cooperatives, form association for purpose of carrying on lawful industry, trade or business on cooperative basis, except railway as carrier, unless authorized by Lieutenant Governor in Council, financial services, trust, insurance, or banking business, by subscribing to memorandum and rules and filing them, with list of first directors, address of association, statement outlining services to be provided to members, and required fees with Superintendent of Cooperatives who, upon approval forwards to Registrar of Companies. Registrar of Companies issues certificate of incorporation. Capital consists of unlimited number of shares of such denominations as specified in memorandum and liability of members is limited. Act sets out requirements as to admission, expulsion, dividends, surpluses, administration, directors, auditors, annual reports, dissolution, and the like. Cooperative may contract and sue or be sued in its own name.

ATTACHMENT:

Plaintiff, judgment creditor or person entitled to enforce judgment, may on ex parte application obtain order from judge or registrar that all debts, obligations and liabilities owing, payable or accruing from third person to defendant or judgment debtor be attached subject to certain exceptions with respect to debts due. (c. 75). No attachment of wages permitted prior to judgment. (c. 75, §4).

ATTORNEYS AND COUNSELORS:

(S.B.C. 1987, c. 25).

Designation "counselor" or "counselor at law" is unknown in British Columbia. Legal profession in theory is divided into two branches, barristers and solicitors. Barristers appear in court only. Solicitors do not appear in court. Nearly all lawyers are both barristers and solicitors.

Jurisdiction Over Admission.—The Law Society of British Columbia has jurisdiction over the admission of individuals to the legal profession.

Eligibility.—Applicants must be of good character and repute, have served as articled students to practicing barrister or solicitor, normally for ten months, and complete ten week training course and pass qualification examinations (which requirements may be waived for barristers or solicitors of other Provinces of Canada, but not otherwise).

Educational Requirements.—Graduates of any law school approved by Law Society.

Petition for Admission.—Applications for admission are made to the Secretary of the Law Society.

Examination.—Examinations are conducted by the Law Society, or Examiners appointed by them, at such time and place as are from time to time considered necessary.

Admission Without Examination.—Barristers or solicitors from other Provinces may be admitted upon passing such examinations as Benchers may require.

Unauthorized Practice.—Only members in good standing of Law Society of British Columbia shall engage in practice of law within province, subject to certain provisions allowing others to appear in certain inferior courts and subject to other provisions allowing barrister or solicitor from outside province to act as solicitor or appear as counsel in B.C., or to give legal advice regarding home country.

Licenses.—A certificate is issued annually by the Secretary of the Law Society to all barristers and solicitors upon the payment of dues.

Privileges.—Common law rules apply.

Disabilities.—Common law rules apply.

Liabilities.—Common law rules apply.

Compensation.—A barrister or solicitor may contract with the party for whom he acts, but this contract is subject to review within 90 days of formation of agreement or termination of retainer by registrar of Supreme Court. Any provision in any such contract relieving barrister or solicitor of responsibility for negligence shall be void. Contingent fees are permitted but provision must be made for client to apply to registrar of Supreme Court for review of contract within 90 days from when agreement made or retainer terminated. Any bill for professional services may, under certain conditions, be reviewed upon application of member or party charged by registrar of Supreme Court.

Lien.—A solicitor has a lien for his fees on all property recovered or preserved by proceeding he prosecutes or defends, but may not sue his client for amount of his bill until after 30 days from its delivery.

Disbarment and Suspension.—Members of profession are liable to disbarment or suspension for professional misconduct or conduct unbecoming member of Law Society. Law Society has power to suspend and order retraining of incompetent members.

Professional Associations.—Members may carry on business of providing legal services to public through law corporation if permit to do so has been issued by Law Society. (S.B.C. 1992, c. 74, §21).

Special Fund.—A special fund is administered by Law Society for purpose of partially or fully reimbursing persons by whom pecuniary loss is sustained by reason of misappropriation or wrongful conversion by member of Law Society of money or other property entrusted or received in his or her professional capacity.

AUTOMOBILES: See topic Motor Vehicles.

BAIL: See topic Criminal Law.

BANKRUPTCY: See Canada Law Digest.

BANKS AND BANKING:

See generally Canada Law Digest.

Provincial Trust Companies.—One or more persons may apply to form trust company by subscribing to memorandum, adopting articles specifying rules for company's conduct, and paying prescribed fee. Subscribers must also submit plan to Financial Institutions Commission ("Commission"). In addition to other facts, plan must disclose first directors and senior officers of trust company, and proposed services to be offered to public. (S.B.C. 1989, c. 47, §§12, 18). Trust company shall not carry on business without applying for and receiving business authorization issued by Commission. (S.B.C. 1989, c. 47, §59). Extraprovincial corporation may apply for Certificate of Continuation. (S.B.C. 1989, c. 47, §23).

BILLS AND NOTES: See Canada Law Digest.

BILLS OF LADING: See topic Carriers.

BILLS OF SALE:

See topic Chattel Mortgages; Sales. Act repealed. (c. 48).

BLUE SKY LAW: See topic Securities.

BONDS:

Bond is security of any kind given to ensure performance of obligation. Bond must be payable to Minister, who holds it in trust for persons who establish rights to recover on it. Claim on bond must be brought within two years following end of period during which bond was required to be maintained. (S.B.C. 1993, c. 8).

BROKERS:

Licenses.—Real estate agent must be licensed by Superintendent of Real Estate. (c. 356, §3). Person who is not licensed shall not collect any commission or bring any action in respect thereof. (c. 356, §§30, 37). Unlicensed broker is liable to penalty of not more than $10,000 if corporation and not more than $5,000 if individual. (c. 356, §40, as am'd by S.B.C. 1981, c. 28, §6).

Mortgage Brokers Act (c. 283) provides that persons, their employees, partners or directors who carry on business of lending money, directly, or indirectly, on security of real estate, whether money is his own or that of another person or who holds himself out as, or who by advertisement, notice, or sign indicates that he is mortgage broker, or person who carries on business of dealing with mortgages must register under Act (c. 283, §3). Persons licensed under Real Estate Act or Securities Act shall be deemed to be registered as mortgage brokers. (c. 283, §12). See also topic Mortgages of Real Property.

In addition all agents and brokers, including stock brokers, must be licensed by municipality or city wherein they carry on business.

Insurance companies, savings institutions, solicitors and Crown agencies are exempted from registration requirements. (c. 283, §11).

See also topic Securities.

Bond.—Every real estate broker agent carrying on business may be required to furnish security or proof of financial responsibility.

See also topics Principal and Agent; Securities.

BULK SALES:

See topic Fraudulent Preferences and Conveyances.

CARRIERS:

Except for intra-provincial railways, which are subject to Provincial jurisdiction, all Canadian railways, water carriers and airlines are under control of Canadian Transport Commission and are regulated by Federal statutes and regulations. Intra-provincial trucking and railways are regulated by provincial statutes, regulations and authorities and by law Federal jurisdiction over inter-provincial and international trucking has also been vested in Provincial authorities. Common carriers are bound, unless lawful excuse exists, to carry goods or persons who offer to pay tariff or fare. Rights and duties as between common carrier and those using its facilities are as set forth in contract of carriage including any provisions attached thereto by law.

Transportation of grain for export from Western Canada to lakehead and West Coast ports is now governed by Western Grain Transportation Act R.S.C. 1985 c. W-8 which came into force on 1 Jan., 1984.

Intra-provincial pipelines are subject to Provincial jurisdiction while inter-provincial pipelines are subject to Federal jurisdiction.

Note: National Transportation Act, 1987 R.S.C. 1985 c. N-20.01 (Canada) came into effect Jan. 1, 1988 and substantially deregulates carriage of goods and persons and impacts upon provincial regulations and legislation.

Liability.—Prima facie a carrier is liable as at common law subject to statutory limits. (c. 286, Reg.59/59, §9.2). Such liability can be limited by contract.

Bills of lading of common carriers are governed by common law, subject to applicable statute law. Consignee named in bill of lading and every endorsee thereof to whom goods pass by reason of such consignment or endorsement is vested with all rights of action and is subject to all liabilities in respect of goods as if contract set out in bill of lading had been made with himself. This does not affect vendors right of stoppage in transit or right to claim freight against original shipper or owner. While transferable by endorsement, bills of lading are not negotiable unless in specific form. No endorsee can take better title than his endorsor had.

Lien.—The carrier is not obliged to deliver the goods until the freight is paid as he has a lien for the same.

CERTIORARI:

Judicial Review Procedure Act (c. 209) abolishes writ of certiorari and allows court to grant any relief that applicant would be entitled to under proceeding for relief in nature of certiorari. (§2). Relief can be granted by Supreme Court which reviews proceedings of inferior court or body acting pursuant to statutory power. (§3). Application is taken by way of petition and grounds on which relief is available are absence or excess of jurisdiction (including abuse of discretion and breach of natural justice) and error of law on face of record. (§§2, 3)

See Topical Index in front part of this volume.

CHARITABLE IMMUNITY:

See topic Damages.

CHATTEL MORTGAGES:

Chattel Mortgage Act.—(c. 48). Repealed.

Mobile Homes.—See topic Mobile Homes.

CLAIMS:

See topics Executors and Administrators; Pleading.

COLLATERAL SECURITY: See topic Pledges.

COLLECTION AGENCIES:

See topic Principal and Agent.

COMMISSIONS TO TAKE TESTIMONY:

See topic Depositions.

COMMUNITY PROPERTY:

See topic Husband and Wife.

CONDITIONAL SALES: See topic Sales.

CONSIGNMENTS: See topic Factors.

CONSUMER PROTECTION:

Consumer Protection Act 1967, c. 64. Replaced by Consumer Protection Act. (c. 65). New Act generally affords protections to buyers and borrowers in respect of consumer purchases and credit transactions. Part 1 of Act regulates executory contracts, defined as contracts for sale or lease of goods or services for consideration in excess of $50 and under which delivery, performance or payment is not made at time contract is made. Part 1 regulates referral selling (§11); renders executory contract or contract for future services that direct seller solicits, negotiates, or concludes at place other than his business address unenforceable unless it contains prescribed disclosure of information and particulars, is signed by buyer and copy of it is received by buyer within seven days (§12); gives buyer seven days right to cancel if contract not made at permanent place of business of seller (§13). Provision is made for seller who occasionally does business away from permanent place of business; onus on seller to show such occasions. (§13[1.1], [1.2]). Buyer may cancel time share contract within seven days of receiving copy of contract. (§13.01, S.B.C. 1995, c. 4, §2). Covers when contract must be in writing and what must be contained in it. (§§13.1, 13.2). Buyer may also cancel contract for future services where material change in circumstances of buyer (including death, disability or relocation). (§13[4]). Covers notice of cancellation—when sufficient and when by mail. (§13[5]). Sets out maximum term of two years after date contract was signed by buyer for future services contract. (§19). Provision made for return, retention, and refund of goods upon cancellation. (§§14, 15, 16). Part 1.1 of Act governs direct seller licensing. Part 2 of Act regulates credit transactions. Part 2 requires lenders to disclose cost of borrowing in manner prescribed in Act (§§26, 27); requires lenders who make available variable credit (e.g. credit cards, credit accounts, cyclical accounts or other similar arrangements) to give 30 days prior written notice of increase in cost of borrowing (§28); provides debtors with certain rights of prepayment (§29); provides for regulation of advertising of cost of borrowing in credit transaction and terms of lease or lease to purchase transaction (§30); protects holders of credit cards which have been lost or stolen from liability for any debt incurred with card after notice of loss or theft given to credit card issuer and for any debt in excess of $50 prior to such notice (§31); exempts recipients of unsolicited credit cards or unsolicited goods from any legal obligation for them unless intention to accept is acknowledged in writing (§32); regulates manner of crediting of payments made by debtor to creditor (§34); disentitles lender from collecting any cost of borrowing if lender fails to provide debtor with required disclosure statement or required lending transaction documents (§35); prohibits credit card issuers and others from attempting to influence, discourage or prohibit granting of discounts by seller where buyer makes payment in cash (§36); regulates discounting refunds of income tax and limits maximum discount to 15%. (§37). Part 3 of Act regulates food plan contracts and negative option schemes for selling goods (§39) and services (§39.1). Disclosure notices must be sent to individuals receiving unsolicited services sold by means of negative option offer. (§39.2, S.B.C. 1995, c. 4, §9). Part 4 of Act gives court broad remedial powers to grant relief in respect of unconscionable mortgage transactions (§44). Part 5 gives authorization for director to search and investigate possible complaints. Offences under Act are punishable by maximum $10,000 fine and one year imprisonment if committed by individual and $100,000 fine if committed by corporation. (§58, as am'd by S.B.C. 1993, c. 39, §7).

Trade Practice Act.—(c. 406). Proscribes unconscionable or deceptive acts or trade practices or advertising thereof with respect to any consumer transaction respecting personal property including chattels, services and credit (includes business requiring both expenditure and services in which individual has not been previously engaged, but not securities or contracts of insurance); establishes office of Director of Trade Practices, with authority to, on own behalf, on behalf of consumer or consumers as class, investigate, sue, seek injunctive relief, seek court order to enter and seize evidence, make orders directing person to refrain from dealing with particular assets, receive security bond in lieu thereof, apply to court for appointment of receiver, receiver-manager or trustee of assets, accept from supplier assurance of voluntary compliance on basis of certain undertakings, all with respect to specific breaches; director may also conduct research, hold public hearings, make inquiries and publish studies respecting consumer transactions. Court may declare that act or practice engaged in or to be engaged in deceptive or unconscionable act or practice, issue interim or permanent injunction, and order supplier to advertise particulars of such declaration, order or injunction. (§18). Unconscionable acts or practices in respect of consumer transaction renders that consumer transaction unenforceable by supplier. (§4). Courts may award damages, including punitive and exemplary damages, rescission or restitution, or impose just terms. Offences carry maximum penalty of fine of $5,000 and/or one year's imprisonment for individual, and $100,000 for corporation. (§25). In addition to penalties, court, on convicting defendant, can order defendant to pay compensation to aggrieved consumer. (§25.1). Directors, officers or other persons who authorized, permitted or acquiesced are guilty of offence personally. (§25[4]). Limitation period of two years from date on which subject matter of proceeding arose is imposed. (§27).

Debt Collection Act.—(c. 88). Regulates licencing of debt collection agencies (§§3-5) and manner in which collection agencies can collect debts. Collection agents and bailiffs must be licensed by Director of Debt Collection.(§2). Prohibits collection agencies from engaging in unreasonable collection practices, which includes use of undue, excessive or unreasonable pressure upon debtor or any member of his family or household or his employer. (§14). Unless there is court order to contrary debtor's chattels cannot be removed except during permitted times and in presence of debtor, his spouse, agent or adult resident in his house. (§15). Penalty for contravention of Act or any order of director is minimum fine of $200 and maximum of $5,000 for corporation, and minimum of $100 and maximum of $1,000 for individual, as well as any disciplinary action director sees fit. (§19). Prohibits charging fees to debtor. (§17). There is limitation period of two years from date of offence coming to attention of director to bring proceeding under this Act. (§19). Debtor who suffers damage, loss, abuse or inconvenience as result of contravention of Act has civil cause of action and is entitled to judgment for damages suffered or $100, whichever is greater. (§20).

Credit Reporting Act.—(c. 78). Regulates licencing of credit reporting agencies. (§§2-7). Affects only consumer credit information, not commercial. Registrar of Reporting Agencies is responsible for registration of suitable applicants (§§5, 6) to carry on business as credit reporting agent. Limits manner and content of reports that can be provided about consumer by reporting agencies (§§11, 12) and to whom such information can be given. (§10). Credit agencies may only furnish information under written instructions of consumer in response to court order, or, to person believed intending to use information in relation to: extending credit, loaning money, employment purposes, tenancy agreements, underwriting insurance, determining statutory eligibility, or having direct commercial involvement with consumer. (§10). No person shall obtain report without expressed written consent of consumer, or unless person promptly notifies consumer in writing that report will be obtained. (§12). If user of information denies in whole or part application for credit, or increases cost, because of information received from reporting agency, he must deliver notice of denial or increase to consumer. (§13). User must, on request, supply source of information. Every reporting agency must, on request from person, disclose all information it may have, and names of users to which reports have been sent in last 12 months. (§14). Person may add explanation to any matter contained in information, or he may dispute any information, which agency must then verify. (§§15, 16). Registrar may begin investigation where there are reasonable and probable grounds to believe Act was contravened. (§20). No person shall knowingly supply false information to any agency. (§24). Any person who contravenes Act or director or officer of corporation who authorizes or acquiesces in contravention is subject to maximum fine of $2,000 ($5,000 in case of corporation) and one year's imprisonment. (§25). Consumers who have suffered loss, damage or inconvenience due to contravention have civil cause of action and may obtain judgment for greater of $100 or actual damages suffered. (§26).

Plain Language.—Pending legislation.

CONTRACTS:

Common law principles apply, with some codification, e.g., Sale of Goods Act. (c. 370).

Frustrated Contract Act (c. 144) provides for settlement of losses and claims arising out of frustration of contract not caused by either party, but does not apply to charter parties or contracts of carriage of goods by sea except time charter parties or charter parties by demise, contracts of insurance or contracts entered into before May 3, 1974. Act only applies to extent that contract, on its true construction, contains no provision for consequences of frustration or avoidance. Limitation period for claim under Act shall commence at time of frustration or avoidance. Time limitation period applicable to that of contract applies.

Consumer protection legislation modifies common law principles in consumer contracts. See Consumer Protection Act under topic Consumer Protection.

See also topics Infants; Sales; Seals.

CONVEYANCES: See topic Deeds.

CORPORATIONS: (1979, c. 59).

Types of Companies.—Traditional distinction between public and private companies abolished and replaced by reporting and non-reporting companies. Reporting company defined in Company Act (c. 59) ("Act") as company that: (a) has any securities listed for trading on any stock exchange; (b) previously was public or deemed public company; (c) files prospectus with Superintendent of Brokers with respect to any of its securities; (d) is ordered by Registrar to be so; (e) amalgamated company where one of amalgamating companies was, at time of amalgamation, reporting company; (f) had exemption order under §38A of former Act, unless Registrar otherwise orders. Certain provisions of Act apply to trust companies and insurance companies incorporated under Financial Institutions Act. (c. 131.5).

General Supervision.—Registrar of Companies, 2nd Floor, Waddington Building, 940 Blanshard Street, Victoria, B. C. V8W 3E6 is administrative officer under Company Act.

Purposes.—Memorandum may, but need not, limit business which can be carried on.

Name.—Company must have word "Limited," "Incorporated" or "Corporation" or abbreviations "Ltd.," "Inc." or "Corp." as last word of its name and specially limited company shall also have "Non-Personal Liability" or "N.P.L.". Company may also have "Limitée", "Incorporée" or "Ltée" as last words of its name. Company registered under Small Business Venture Capital Act (c. 386.7) shall have initials "(VCC)" as part of its name. Company licensed under International Financial Business Act (c. 205.7)

See Topical Index in front part of this volume.

CORPORATIONS . . . *continued*
shall have "International Financial Business" or "I.F.B." as part of its name. No company other than company registered under Part 2 of Employee Investment Act (c. 106.4) shall carry on business under name that includes initials "(EVCC)". Company may set out its name in its memorandum in English form, French form, English and French form or combined English and French form. Company may for use outside Canada, set out its name in its memorandum in any language form and it may be designated in that form outside Canada. Registrar can reserve name for 56 days. Registrar can, for good and valid reason, disapprove name. Registrar may order name change if it closely resembles existing company's name.

Term of Corporate Existence.—Subject to company complying with requirements of Company Act, its existence is perpetual. Company incorporated in reciprocating jurisdiction may transfer and continue as B. C. company and with approval of Registrar, vice versa. Company continuing under laws of other jurisdiction ceases to be company under Act.

Incorporators.—One or more individuals (called "subscribers") may form company. Subscribers are first directors. Majority must be ordinarily resident in Canada and one must be B. C. resident.

Proceedings for Incorporation.—Incorporators must subscribe their names to a memorandum in form set out below (except see Act for specially limited company) and file same with Registrar of Companies at Victoria, together with articles which are by-laws by which company intends to be governed, notice of registered and records office (two copies of each), and prescribed fee.

Memorandum and Articles.—Memorandum must be set out in following manner:

Form I
MEMORANDUM

I/We wish to be formed into a company with limited liability under the *Company Act* in pursuance of this memorandum.

[*See* note (*a*)] 1. The name of the company is ". . . . ."

[*See* note (*b*)] 2. The company is restricted from carrying on:— . . . .

[*See* note (*c*)] 3. The company is restricted from exercising the following powers:— . . . .

[*See* note (*d*)] 4. The authorized capital of the company consists of . . . . shares divided into . . . . shares with a par value of . . . . each and . . . . shares without par value.

[*See* notes (*e*) and (*f*)] 5. I/We agree to take the number [and kind] [and class] of shares in the company set opposite my/our name(s).

Full Name(s), Resident Address(es), and Occupation(s) of Subscribers(s)	Number [and Kind] [and Class] of Shares Taken by Subscriber(s)
Total shares taken	

Dated . . . . . [month, day], 19. . . .

[NOTE.—(*a*) *See* section 16.

(*b*) List businesses the company is NOT to carry on. If no restrictions other than those provided by law apply (*see* Part 2), delete this paragraph.

(*c*) List powers the company is NOT to exercise. If no restrictions other than those provided by law are to apply (*see* Part 2), delete this paragraph.

(*d*) In paragraph 4 omit reference to shares without par value if there are only shares with par value; omit reference to shares with par value if there are only shares without par value. If the shares are of both kinds, *see* subsection 19(3) as to their description.

(*e*) Add any additional provisions here.

(*f*) The provisions of the memorandum may only be altered to the extent and in the manner provided by Part 8.]

Articles prescribe rules for conduct of company and company may but need not adopt all or any of sample provisions in Table A of Act together with any other desired provisions.

Filing.—See supra, subhead Proceedings for Incorporation.

Fees.—

1.	incorporation, amalgamation or restoration of a company	$275
2.	registration, amalgamation or restoration of an extraprovincial company	275
3.	conversion of a company pursuant to section 267 or 269	100
4.	filing an annual report	35
5.	changing the name of a company or registering a change of name of an extraprovincial company	100
6.	a certificate of true copy or extract	25
7.	each search conducted through the B.C. OnLine information service using a person's own computer terminal	7
8.	each search conducted by a person using a computer terminal provided by the Province	8
9.	each search conducted by government personnel	10
10.	a copy or extract for any document, .50 cents for every page.	
11.	continuation pursuant to section 36 or 37	275
12.	pre-vetting of documents to be filed with the registrar	100

Certificate of Incorporation.—After memorandum, articles and notice of offices have been registered, Registrar issues a certificate of incorporation and advertises in Gazette notice of incorporation of company.

Specially Limited Companies.—Companies may be specially limited, but business of company is restricted to exploring for, developing, mining, producing, milling (etc.) minerals, coal, petroleum and natural gas and company cannot lend money or guarantee contracts or raise or assist in raising money for or aid any person or corporation.

Shares.—Company's authorized capital may be any amount with shares either with or without par value. Memorandum must state number of shares with and without par value and par value per share, if any. Preferences may be attached to shares and must be set out either in memorandum or articles.

Liability of Shareholders.—Liability of members of a company is limited to amount paid to subscribe for shares. Members have no personal liability for debts of company.

Registered Office and Records Office.—Company must have a registered office and a records office within province which may be at same place.

Alteration of Memorandum/Articles.—Company may by special resolution (3/4 of votes of members) filed with Registrar alter its memorandum to change its name to one approved by Registrar (without affecting any rights or obligations of company or rendering defective any legal proceedings by or against it); to alter any restriction upon its business or powers (except specially limited) subject to statutory rights of dissenting shareholders found in Act. Copy of memorandum as amended by alteration must be filed with certified copy of resolution. Company may alter its articles by filing certified copy of special resolution or resolution passed.

Change of Capital.—Company may by resolution as provided in articles or otherwise by special resolution increase its authorized capital and may by special resolution subdivide and consolidate shares subject to shareholders statutory rights. Company may reduce its capital by special resolution confirmed by court, company may diminish its capital by resolution of directors cancelling unissued shares, surrendered shares, etc. Copy of memorandum as amended by alteration must be filed with certified copy of resolution.

Change of Character of Stock.—If company is incorporated with par value shares it may by special resolution change its unissued or fully paid issued shares with par value into shares without par value. Company may by special resolution change all or any of its unissued shares without par value into shares with par value. Copy of memorandum as amended by alteration must be filed with certified copy of resolution.

Change of Character of Company.—Specially limited company may by special resolution convert itself into a company which is limited only and for that purpose alter its memorandum and articles so as to comply with provisions of Act for such company unless express provision to contrary is contained in memorandum and subject to statutory rights of shareholders. Copy of memorandum as amended by alteration must be filed with certified copy of resolution.

Powers.—Subject to restrictions in its memorandum, company has powers and capacities of natural person except: (a) Operation of railways; and (b) operation of club (without authorization of Minister).

Every company whose articles authorize it may have for use official seal in any other country or province and it may appoint any person to affix same. Company may in writing empower any person to execute documents on its behalf.

Company shall not carry on business without a member. If it does so for more than six months every director and officer during such time is jointly and severally liable for payment of company's debts contracted during that time.

Company shall not give financial assistance directly or indirectly by way of loan, guarantee, provision of security or otherwise: (a) For purpose of purchase or subscription by that person of shares in or debt obligations of company convertible into or exchangeable for shares; (b) upon security of pledge of or charge upon shares of company given by that person to company; or (c) in any other case unless reasonable grounds to believe, or directors are of opinion that, giving of financial assistance is in best interests of company. Notwithstanding above, if authorized by special resolution and reasonable grounds for believing it is in best interests of company, company may: (a) Provide money for subscription or purchase of shares or debt obligations of company by trustees of bona fide employee of company or of affiliate; or (b) provide assistance to full-time employees of company or of affiliate to enable purchase of shares or debt obligations of company to be held beneficially by them. Also, non-reporting company authorized by special resolution may give financial assistance if given in connection with acquisition of shares by person either alone or with his associates and, after acquisition, not less than 90% of issued shares of each class of shares in capital of company will be owned by that person and his associates. Also, can give financial assistance to wholly owned subsidiary, to parent company, to company by another company, where both companies are wholly owned subsidiaries of same parent or are wholly owned by same person, or to sole member of company by that company.

See also supra, subhead Purposes.

Directors and Officers.—Every company shall have at least one director and reporting company at least three directors. Majority of directors shall be persons ordinarily resident in Canada and at least one director shall be ordinarily resident in province. Company must file notice of appointment or election of directors within 14 days after. First directors are subscribers to memorandum and others are appointed or elected in accordance with articles and Act. To be elected or appointed as director person must either consent in writing before meeting electing or appointing him or attend at such meeting and not refuse to act. No person can act as director who is: (a) Under age of 18 years; (b) incapable of managing his own affairs by reason of mental infirmity; (c) corporation; (d) undischarged bankrupt; (e) unless court orders otherwise, was convicted of offence in connection with promotion, formation or management of corporation or involving fraud unless five years have elapsed since sentence was concluded or fine was imposed, or end of period of suspended sentence without sentence or pardoned; (f) in case of reporting company person whose registration under Securities Act or Mortgage Brokers Act or Community Contract Act has been cancelled unless otherwise ordered or five years have elapsed since cancellation. Directors are personally liable for loss or damage to company if they consent to or vote for certain resolutions in contravention of Act.

See Topical Index in front part of this volume.

CORPORATIONS . . . *continued*

Every director who is required by articles to hold a specified share qualification must obtain his qualification within two months after his appointment or time fixed by articles (whichever occurs first). Any director who is interested in a contract in any way, directly or indirectly, with company or has any conflict of interest must declare nature of his interest or conflict of interest at meeting of directors of company. Directors must act honestly in good faith in best interests of company, and exercise care, skill and diligence of reasonably prudent person.

Company may, with court approval, indemnify director or former director under certain circumstances.

Provisions for Accounting.—Reporting company shall, not less than 56 days before any general meeting at which director is to be elected, give advance notice of meeting through various newspapers and regulatory bodies in writing requesting nominations for director by members holding in aggregate not less than 10% of voting shares and that nominations are to be received 35 days before meeting.

Company must keep at its records office a register of directors, which must state their full names, resident addresses, date of appointment, date each former director ceased to hold office as director and name of any office held, date of appointment to such office and date of vacation of such office.

Every company shall have president and secretary, who shall be different persons unless company has only one member. Person not qualified to become director cannot be officer. President and chairman must also be director. Every officer must disclose to president any direct or indirect conflict of interest with respect to his office or property.

Shares and Shareholders.—Company may, where authorized by memorandum or articles pay commission or allow discount when issuing its shares. Except for specially limited company, commission and discount in aggregate shall not exceed 25% of subscription price. Shares without par value can be issued at price or consideration determined by special resolution or where memorandum or articles so permit, at price or consideration determined by directors. No shares can be issued until they are fully paid.

It is illegal to offer shares to public until there has been filed with and accepted by Superintendent of Brokers a prospectus in respect of offering. Concept of series of shares has been added.

Share Certificates.—Every share certificate issued by company shall state on its face: (a) Name of company and words "incorporated in the Province of British Columbia" amalgamated, or continued, as case may be; (b) name of person to whom certificate issued; (c) number and class of shares and that shares are without par value, or if with par value, par value thereof; (d) date of issue; (e) statement of restrictions upon transfer, if any; (f) certificate number. If shares have any special rights or restrictions each certificate shall have attached thereto statement of same or statement referring to same and advising that copy of full text thereof may be obtained from registered or records office of company. Every certificate shall be signed manually by at least one officer, director, registrar or transfer agent of company. Additional signatures may be mechanically reproduced. Where certificate is defaced, lost or destroyed it may be renewed on payment of charge, not exceeding prescribed fee and upon terms as to evidence and indemnity as articles require.

Share Transfer.—Shares are transferrable in accordance with articles but no transfer may be registered unless proper instrument of transfer is delivered to company. Articles may restrict transfer.

Notwithstanding memorandum or articles, guardian, committee, trustee, curator, tutor, personal representative or trustee in bankruptcy of member has rights, privileges and obligations attached to shares held by member upon depositing with company declaration of transmission and share certificate, or security registered in name of deceased or bankrupt, copy of court order, assignment in bankruptcy as case may be, or court certified copy of original grant of probate or letters of administration as case may be (foreign grants may have to be resealed), and otherwise court order or other document appointing him.

Meetings.—Every general meeting of company must be held within province unless Registrar otherwise approves. First annual general meeting of every company must be held within 15 months from date of incorporation, amalgamation or continuance and thereafter annual general meeting must be held at least once in every calendar year and not more than 13 months after holding of last annual general meeting. (Registrar may extend time for holding annual meeting for period of six months.) Provision for deemed meeting of non-reporting company if all members consent in writing.

Not less than 21 days written notice of any general meeting must be given but members may waive or reduce such period by unanimous consent in writing.

Resolutions are either ordinary or special. Ordinary resolution is either resolution passed by company in general meeting by simple majority or resolution which has been submitted to all members of company who would have been entitled to vote thereon and which has been consented to in writing by such members holding shares carrying not less than 3/4 of votes. Special resolution is either resolution passed by majority of not less than 3/4 votes cast by such members of company as vote either in person or by proxy at general meeting of company of which at least 21 days notice specifying intention of proposing resolution as special resolution has been given (unless notice waived) or resolution consented to in writing by all members of company who would have been entitled to vote thereon.

Voting.—Articles may prescribe voting rights and in absence of contrary provisions therein contained each share has one vote except that subsidiary company cannot vote its share in parent company incorporated in province.

Votes may be given either personally or by proxy. Instrument appointing a proxy must be in writing under hand of appointor or of his attorney duly authorized in writing, or if appointor is a corporation, either under hand of an officer or attorney so authorized. Proxy need not be given to member and is good for one specified meeting, and is not valid after one year.

Directors of reporting company may fix time for deposit of proxies not exceeding 48 hours, excluding Sats. and holidays, preceding meeting at which proxy to be used, and in default, instrument of proxy shall not be treated as valid.

Solicitation of Proxies.—Management of reporting company shall concurrently with or prior to giving notice of meeting of shareholders, send by prepaid mail to each member entitled to vote at such meeting form of proxy for use at such meeting unless court otherwise orders.

Unless court otherwise orders and in other special circumstances, no person shall solicit proxies unless: (a) If by management, information circular is sent with notice of meeting to each member whose proxy is solicited; (b) otherwise, person soliciting sends information circular (unless less than 15 proxies solicited).

Acceptable Form of Proxy

I, ... of . . . ., being a member of . . . . Company, Limited, hereby appoint . . . . of . . . ., as my proxy to vote for me and on my behalf at the (annual or extraordinary, as the case may be) general meeting of the Company to be held on the . . . . day of . . . ., 19. ., and at any adjournment thereof.

Signed this . . . . day of . . . ., 19. .

(Signature)

See §181 for contents of special form of proxy for reporting companies.

Books.—Every company must keep at its records office its certificate of incorporation, memorandum and articles, register of members (some exceptions), register of transfers (some exceptions), register of directors, register of debenture holders, register of debentures, register of indebtedness, and register of allotments (some exceptions). Company must also keep minutes of all proceedings of shareholders and directors meetings, copies of all documents filed with and certificates and orders issued by Registrar or Minister, copies of written contracts whereby company has allotted shares for consideration other than cash, copies of all mortgages, copies of all documents approved by directors within preceding ten years, copies of all audited financial statements of company and its subsidiaries, including auditors' reports; where company is an amalgamated company, copies of all documents described above relating to each of amalgamating companies; where company is being wound-up, minutes of every meeting of creditors; copy of every prospectus and take-over bid and information circular issued in preceding ten years, copy of instrument of continuation; and where receiver-manager is appointed under instrument registered in Office of Registrar, name, address, date of appointment and cessation of duties of receiver-manager.

Upon payment of 50¢ (for each document examined) or less as prescribed by company, all records except directors minutes, documents approved by directors, and mortgages, are open for inspection by any person with respect to reporting company and with respect to non-reporting company there is no charge to examine documents and exceptions also include shareholders minutes and financial statements.

Reports and Returns.—Within two months after each anniversary date of incorporation, amalgamation or continuation in province, every company shall file annual report in prescribed form with Registrar as to last anniversary date. Inaccurate information to be corrected on form in space provided and signed by any director or officer. Cheques for fees to be certified.

Certain resolutions must also be filed with Registrar including resolutions changing registered or records offices, appointing receivers or managers, altering memorandum and articles, winding-up. In addition, copies of all mortgages and debentures must be filed with Registrar. Every company incorporated or registered in province shall also file notice of appointment of new directors and any change in number of directors within 14 days thereof.

Taxation.—See topic Taxation.

Amalgamation.—Any two or more companies may amalgamate and continue as one company.

Dividends can be declared as provided in articles but directors who authorize dividends are liable to company if dividends paid when company is insolvent or if payment renders company insolvent.

Sale or transfer of corporate assets need special resolution to approve sale, lease or other disposal of whole or substantially whole of undertaking of company.

Shareholders Actions.—Shareholder can apply to court for relief from oppression and can, with leave of court, bring or defend action in name and on behalf of company.

Dissolution.—Company may be dissolved: (a) Voluntarily; (b) by Lieutenant-Governor in Council; (c) after Registrar strikes it off Register for failure to comply with Act; or (d) in winding-up; including by court order.

Foreign Corporations.—Every extra-provincial company which carries on business in province must register within 30 days after commencing to carry on business in province.

Extra-provincial company does not have to register if its only business is operation of ships provided it does not maintain in province an office, warehouse or place of business under its control or that of a person on behalf of company, provided that every resident agent or representative of such company shall file with Registrar a notice signed by him stating name, chief place of business of company outside province, particulars of his agency and any change of aforesaid. This does not apply to extraprovincial company that (a) is extraprovincial society, as defined in §1 of Society Act, (b) is registered under §62 of Cooperative Association Act, (c) is extraprovincial corporation that is permitted under Financial Institutions Act to carry on in Province any one or more of trust business, insurance business or deposit business.

Registration.—Statement must be filed with Registrar setting out name, place and date of incorporation, business to be carried on in province, address within and without province, name of attorney appointed for British Columbia, details of its charter, shares authorized, issued and owned by corporation, details of directors and officers and a verified copy of corporation's charter and certificate of good standing. In addition, statutory declaration of two directors or officers must be filed declaring that directors are qualified under Act and any details of convictions against company within five years of offence involving fraud and particulars thereof and verifying information in statement.

Process Agent.—Every extra-provincial company (unless head office is within province) must have attorney resident in province to accept service of process in all suits by or against company within province and to receive notices to company.

Reports and Returns.—Annual report in form prescribed must be filed for every extraprovincial company within two months after each anniversary date of its registration in British Columbia.

See Topical Index in front part of this volume.

CORPORATIONS . . . *continued*

Other filings with Registrar consist of changes in attorney, corporate name, address in or out of province, directors, amendments to charter and regulations, and details of all mortgages within province.

Every extra-provincial company shall keep at its head office within province register of directors setting out full names, resident addresses, date of appointment, date on which each former director ceased to hold office, name of any office held by such director and date of appointment and vacation of such office, register of indebtedness of directors and officers (in case of reporting company under Securities Act), copy of mortgages and copy of charter.

Penalties.—Unregistered extra-provincial company may not maintain any suit in any court in province in respect of any contract made in whole or in part within province in course of or in connection with its business, and may not acquire or hold land or any interest therein in province but these provisions do not apply to a federal company. Every extra-provincial company which fails to register as required, is liable to a penalty of $50 per day.

COSTS:

Costs in litigation are governed by tariffs prescribed by Rules of Court. General rule is that costs will follow event unless otherwise ordered by court and they may be either: (1) party and party, or (2) special costs. (Rules of Court, R. 57).

Review.—Solicitor may take appointment with Registrar to review his account 30 days after account has been delivered or sent by post and within one year of delivery. If solicitor delivers unreviewed account, which client feels is excessive, client may, before or within three months after payment and within one year of delivery of account, take appointment with Registrar to have account reviewed. Unless Registrar otherwise orders, if at least one-sixth of account is struck off on review, solicitor shall pay costs of review, but if less than one-sixth of account is struck off costs shall be paid by client. Reviewed solicitor's account is enforceable in same manner as judgment of Supreme Court if filed. (Legal Profession Act, S.B.C. 1992, c. 25).

Security for costs may be ordered in Supreme Court for costs of plaintiff or defendant in matrimonial proceeding. (Rules of Court, R. 60[12]). Security for costs on appeal is set by justice of that court. (Court of Appeal Act, S.B.C. 1982, c.7).

Offers to Settle.—If party delivers offer to settle claim and offer has not expired, been withdrawn or been accepted when party obtains judgment at least as favourable as offer, that party is entitled to receive costs assessed to date offer was delivered and double costs from that date. (Rules of Court, R. 37).

COURTS:

Following civil courts are established by legislature; of this province: (1) Supreme Court, S.B.C. 1989, c. 40; (2) Court of Appeal, S.B.C. 1982, c. 7; (3) Provincial Court c. 341.

Small Claims Division.—See subhead Provincial Court, infra.

County Courts.—Effective July 1, 1990, County Court is merged with Supreme Court. All references to County Court in various provincial legislation are amended to Supreme Court.

The Supreme Court has jurisdiction over all actions, civil and criminal, arising in the province. Courts of assize and nisi prius are held in the various districts at specified intervals, at which civil causes may be tried. Provision is made for attachment of debts due to judgment debtor by third persons, before or after judgment except wages prior to judgment (see topic Garnishment) for examination on oath and discovery by either party before trial; for examination of judgment debtor, after judgment, as to his property and assets, and for his commitment on same grounds as in similar applications in small claims division (see subhead Provincial Court, infra), and for "summary judgment" on affidavit where either party can show that there is no merit to other's case. See topic Actions.

The Supreme Court sits during whole year with exception of months of July and Aug. and from Fri. before Christmas Day until first working day after New Years Day. Certain matters may come before court during vacation periods without consent, and most interlocutory matters may come before court with consent of litigants.

Court of Appeal.—An appeal lies to the Court of Appeal from the Supreme Court and must be brought and served within 30 days commencing on day after order appealed from is pronounced or within any other specified period. Interlocutory appeals require leave to appeal to be applied for within 30 days. Date on which time starts to run is day after day of pronouncement.

Security for the costs of appeal may be ordered. On appeal from money judgment appellant may be ordered to pay amount of judgment into court or post bond in lieu thereof.

In many cases an appeal lies from the judgment of the Court of Appeal to the Supreme Court of Canada at Ottawa.

Executions may be stayed pending appeal on compliance with judgment or order appealed from or on security by bond or otherwise being put up to satisfaction of justice of Court of Appeal.

The hearing before the Court of Appeal is on pleadings filed and evidence taken on trial in court below. Pleadings, exhibits and affidavits, and orders and judgments shall be bound in appeal books.

Family Division.—See subhead Provincial Court, infra.

Provincial Court.—Provincial Court Act (c. 341) establishes Provincial Court having three divisions, Provincial Court, Family Division and Small Claims Division, to handle generally those matters, both criminal and civil, formerly heard by magistrates. Act establishes Judicial Council to consider proposals for improving judicial services, proposed appointments, complaints of judicial misbehaviour or neglect, etc. Act sets out responsibility for salaries of judges of courts, and appointment and jurisdiction of Justices of Peace. Small Claims Act (S.B.C. 1989, c. 38) provides that jurisdiction of Small Claims Division of Provincial Court is limited to disputes where amount claimed is $10,000 or less excluding interest and costs and Provincial Court has no jurisdiction in claims for libel, slander or malicious prosecution.

Federal Court of Canada.—See Canada Law Digest, topic Courts.

CREDITORS' SUITS:

There is no express legislation covering this subject. However, law governing rights of secured creditors is, for most part, governed by Personal Property Security , S.B.C. 1989, c. 36. See topics Chattel Mortgages and Executions, subhead Priorities.

Court Order Enforcement Act (c. 75).—Provides for garnishment, reciprocal enforcement of court orders, foreign judgment registration, and post judgment execution against real and personal property.

Creditor Assistance Act.—(c. 80). Allows execution creditors and other creditors to share rateably money collected by sheriff from debtor, provided creditors' writs or certificates were in hands of sheriff at time he levied money on execution against property of debtor. (§2, 3).

Debt Collection Act (c. 88).—Establishes licensing scheme for collection agents and bailiffs and regulates collection practices.

Debtor Assistance Act.—(c. 89). Establishes Director of Debtor Assistance, with power to assist debtors in dealing with creditors, and may inquire into financial status of debtor, upon request by debtor or court.

Fraudulent Conveyance Act (c. 142).—Provides remedy for creditors of debtor who has disposed of property to delay, hinder or defraud creditors.

Fraudulent Preference Act (c. 143).—Provides remedies to creditors of insolvent person who has disposed of property with intent to defeat, hinder, delay or prejudice creditors and to give one or more creditors preference over other creditors.

CRIMINAL LAW:

Offence Act.—(c. 305). Criminal Law is Federal matter; however, various Provincial statutes and municipal by-laws create "quasi-crimes" which are regulatory in nature. Procedure applicable to these "Provincial offences" is set out in Offence Act (c. 305) and, in general, is same as that for true criminal offences under Criminal Code of Canada. Rules of evidence applicable at true criminal trials are also applied to trials for "Provincial offences". See Canada Law Digest.

Criminal Injury Compensation Act.—(c. 83). Provides compensation (lump sum or periodic) in amounts set out in Act for victims injured or killed by specified crimes, arresting offenders, preventing commission of crimes or assisting peace officers doing so. Application must be made within one year of injury or death to Workers' Compensation Board, who may extend time for application. There need be no conviction of accused nor apprehension of suspect in order for victim to apply.

CURTESY:

Abolished. (c. 114).

DAMAGES:

Common law generally prevails. Negligence Act (c. 298) applies to tortfeasors, and abrogates common law principle that plaintiff's contributory negligence bars recovery.

Charitable Immunity.—Charitable corporations responsible for all negligent actions. (Society Act, c. 390).

Sovereign Immunity.—Subject to some exceptions, Provincial Crown may be proceeded against as if it were person. (Crown Proceeding Act, c. 86, §2[c]).

See also topics Criminal Law; Death, subhead Action for Death; Negligence.

DEATH:

Application may be made to the court for presumption of death in case of a person absent and not heard of from a named day, and not known to be alive, where there is reason to presume death. (Survivorship and Presumption of Death Act, c. 398).

Survivorship.—Where two or more persons die at same time, or in circumstances rendering it uncertain which of them survived other or others, such deaths shall for all purposes affecting title of property be presumed to have occurred in order of seniority, and accordingly younger shall be deemed to have survived older. This provision is modified so that if person whose life is insured under life insurance policy dies in same disaster as beneficiary, former shall be presumed to have survived latter. This is further modified where provision is made in instrument for disposition of property in event of designated person predeceasing other person, dying at same time, or under circumstances rendering it uncertain which of them survived, then if that person dies as provided for in instrument death is deemed to have so occurred. There is similar provision where substituted personal representative is provided for in will.

Action for Death.—Action may be maintained against any person causing death by wrongful act, neglect or default where, if death had not ensued, party injured would have been entitled to maintain action and recover damages. Action shall be for benefit of spouse or common law spouse, parent (includes grandparent or stepparent), and/or child (includes stepchild and person to whom deceased stood in loco parentis), of person whose death has been caused, and shall be brought by and in name of personal representative of deceased. Damages may be given proportioned to injury resulting from death to parties respectively for whose benefit action brought. Damages not limited by any money paid or payable under any contract of assurance or insurance, and may include medical or hospital expenses and reasonable funeral expenses. If person causing wrong dies, action may proceed against his estate. (Family Compensation Act, c. 120). See topic Executors and Administrators, subhead Actions.

Death Certificate.—See topic Records, subhead Vital Statistics.

DECEDENTS' ESTATES:

See topics Descent and Distribution; Executors and Administrators; Homesteads; Wills.

DECLARATORY JUDGMENTS: See topic Judgments.

DEEDS:

Every transfer of estate in fee simple shall be in mandatory form (Form A) prescribed by Land Title Act (c. 219 and amendments), unless (a) another form of transfer is prescribed by another enactment or (b) in opinion of Registrar of Titles, it would be proper to accept another form of transfer. Unless expressly excepted or qualified, every transfer of estate in fee simple for valuable consideration and in prescribed form shall be deemed to be made in pursuance of Land Transfer Form Act (c. 221) Part 1. Where transfer is subject to mortgage there are certain covenants implied by §§19.1 to 20.3 of Property Law Act. (c. 340 as am'd).

Execution.—If spouse has no registered interest in property he or she need not join in instrument unless land has been registered as homestead or entry has been made on title under "Land (Spouse Protection) Act". (c. 223). See topic Homesteads.

Execution of instruments requiring registration must be witnessed by officer who is defined as person before whom affidavit may be sworn under Evidence Act (c. 116, §70). Signature by officer is deemed certification of various matters. Registrar may permit proof of execution by affidavit, for example where execution takes place outside of British Columbia. Corporation shall execute instrument by its authorized signatory. Instrument purporting to transfer, charge or otherwise deal with land need not be executed under seal.

See topic Real Property for types of estates.

Registration.—Except as against person making it, no instrument purporting to transfer, charge, deal with or affect land, or estate or interest in it, is operative to pass any estate or interest, in law or in equity, unless it is registered in compliance with Land Title Act. (R.S. c. 219, §20). Such instruments take effect only upon registration. Priority of registration gives priority of title, irrespective of date of execution, subject to contrary intention appearing in instrument. Subject to fraud in which they have participated, purchasers of registered real estate or interest therein are not affected by notice, express, implied or constructive, of any unregistered interest affecting same, save only interests which have pending registrations, are leasehold interests in possession for term not exceeding three years or involve title of person in adverse possession. Mere want of consideration will not invalidate registered, voluntary conveyance, if executed in good faith.

Application to register transfer in fee simple requires: (i) Documents correctly executed and attested; (ii) statement of new owner's citizenship, Form 16(a); (iii) completed Property Transfer Tax Return (FIN 579); (iv) appropriate fees.

Fees.—Standard fee for Form A transfer of freehold estate and registration is $50. State of Title Certificate is $10. Duplicate Certificate of Title is $45.

Property Transfer Tax.—Subject to certain exemptions, transfers of real property attract tax at 1% of first $200,000 of fair market value and 2% on remaining fair market value. Tax is payable by transferee and must be paid on registration of transfer in Land Title Office.

Goods and Services Tax.—Subject to certain important exceptions, real property transactions subject to G.S.T. in amount of 7%. Circumstances will dictate availability of tax credits and whether purchaser or vendor liable for payment of tax.

Powers of attorney to convey, etc., see topic Principal and Agent.

Prescribed Form of Transfer of An Estate in Fee Simple.—See end of Digest.

DEEDS OF TRUST:

See topic Mortgages of Real Property.

DEPOSITIONS:

Distinction is drawn between obtaining disclosures from opposite party to be used as evidence at trial, and obtaining evidence on oath of some other person prior to trial to be used at trial. Former process is called discovery, and is available to each party as of right. Latter procedure refers to taking of depositions and is available only by order of court or by consent.

Discovery.—Discovery from opposite party is available in six ways as set out below. If party fails to comply with any of these requirements for discovery, except admissions, court may dismiss proceeding or strike appearance or defence. Evidence obtained on discovery may be used against, but never for, party being examined.

Discovery and Inspection of Documents.—Party may require other party as of right to list and produce for inspection all documents not privileged which are or have been in latter's possession or control relating to any matter in question in action. Unless court otherwise orders, party may not put document in evidence or use it for purposes of examination or cross-examination if document has not been produced for inspection when demanded. (Rules of Court, R. 26).

Examination for Discovery.—Party may examine any other party adverse in interest, or director, officer, employee, agent or external auditor, past or present, of such party, as of right. Examining party may select which representative of adverse party is to be examined, but adverse party may apply to court for order that examining party be required to examine some other representative. Party who has examined for discovery any party adverse in interest shall require leave of court to examine agent or employee of adverse party. Party who has examined employee or agent of other party requires leave of court to examine other party. Leave of court is required where party has examined director, officer, agent, employee, or external auditor of party and seeks to examine another director, officer, agent, employee or external auditor of that party. Examination is oral examination in nature of cross-examination and is taken on oath before court reporter. Person being examined must answer any questions within his knowledge or means of knowledge regarding any matter not privileged relating to matter in question in action and is also compellable to give names and addresses of all persons who might reasonably be expected to have knowledge relating to any matter in question in action. Rule applies to persons living outside British Columbia. (Rules of Court, R. 27).

Pre-Trial Examination of Witness.—Where person other than party to action may have material evidence and refuses or neglects upon request to give responsive statement to applicant party, court may order that he be examined on oath prior to trial. Procedures for examination for discovery generally apply to such examination. Expert witness of party may only be examined under this rule if other party seeking to examine has been unable to obtain facts and opinions on subject by other means. (Rules of Court, R. 28).

Discovery by Interrogatories.—Party to action may serve on other party or on director, officer, partner, agent, employee or external auditor of party, written interrogatories relating to matter in question in action. Person to whom interrogatories are directed must deliver answer by affidavit within 21 days. If person later learns that answer is inaccurate or incomplete, person must correct answer by subsequent affidavit. (Rules of Court, R. 29).

Physical Examination.—Court may order person to submit to examination by medical practitioner or other qualified person when person's physical or mental condition is in issue. Court may also order production, inspection and preservation of any property. (Rules of Court, R.30).

Admissions.—In proceeding in which statement of defence, answer or answer and counter petition has been filed, party may request any party to admit, for purposes of proceeding only, truth of fact or authenticity of document. If opposing party does not deny request within 14 days, facts or documents are deemed admitted. At least 45 days before trial date, each party must deliver to other adverse parties notice requesting other parties to admit facts set out in notice and authenticity of documents referred to in notice. Party unreasonably refusing to make admissions on request may be penalized in costs. (Rules of Court, R.31).

Depositions.—Depositions by contrast are available only by order of court (or by consent), and are designed to preserve evidence rather than to permit party to discover other party's case. Deposition evidence will normally be ordered only when it is either impossible or inconvenient for witness to be available at trial, either because of death, infirmity, sickness, absence from jurisdiction or expense. Deposition evidence may be ordered to be taken outside British Columbia but if person to be examined is unwilling to testify or if for any other reason assistance of foreign court is necessary, letter of request must be sent to foreign court through Under Secretary of State for External Affairs for Canada (or if evidence is to be taken in Canada, through Deputy Attorney-General for British Columbia). Deposition evidence must be recorded either by official court reporter, or on videotape or film. At trial, transcript, videotape or film of deposition may be given in evidence by any party and witness may also be called to testify viva voce. (Rules of Court, R. 38, 40).

DESCENT AND DISTRIBUTION:

Law of intestate succession (Estate Administration Act, c. 114, Part 7) applies to realty and personalty alike.

Subject to the rights of the surviving spouse, if any, the entire estate is distributed as follows, each class taking to exclusion of subsequent classes: (1) To issue per stirpes; (2) to parents equally or all to surviving parent; (3) to surviving brothers and sisters per capita, and to children of deceased brothers and sisters per stirpes, but if only children of deceased brothers and sisters surviving then per capita; (4) to nephews and nieces in equal shares with no representation admitted; (5) to other next of kin of equal degree and their representatives, but no representation admitted among collaterals.

Degrees of kindred are computed by counting from intestate up to nearest common ancestor and then down to relatives.

Surviving Spouse.—Where intestate dies on or after Oct. 1, 1983 surviving spouse with no issue takes entire estate. Where intestate leaves spouse and issue, surviving spouse takes household furnishings and life interest in family home plus whole estate up to $65,000; if more than $65,000, where spouse and one child, spouse takes $65,000, plus one-half of residue; where spouse and children, spouse takes $65,000, plus one-third of residue, deceased child leaving issue surviving being counted for purposes of determining share of surviving spouse.

Half Blood.—Kindred of the half blood inherit equally with those of whole blood in the same degree.

Posthumous Heirs.—Descendants and relatives begotten before but born after death of intestate take as though born in intestate's lifetime.

Illegitimates.—As of Apr. 17, 1985 law recognizes no distinction between status of child born inside marriage and child born outside of marriage.

Separated Spouses.—Unless court otherwise orders, on intestacy surviving spouse not entitled if separated for not less than one year with intention of living separate and apart (must apply to court within six months of letters of administration issuing).

Common Law Spouses.—Defined as person united to another by valid common-law marriage or person who has lived and cohabited with another as spouse and has been maintained by that person for not less than two years immediately preceding death. Court may order so much of intestate's estate as it sees fit to be payable for support, maintenance and benefit of common-law spouse (must apply to court within six months of letters of administration issuing).

Adopted Children.—See topic Adoption.

Advancements to children of one dying wholly intestate are taken into account. If equal to or greater than child's share, such child and his descendants are excluded, and otherwise take only so much as will equalize shares.

Escheat.—Where any person dies intestate leaving no lawful heirs any interest of such person in real property situate in province escheats to Crown in right of province. Lieutenant Governor in Council may make assignment to Crown of personal property in such situation. (Escheat Act, c. 111).

Wages.—Up to three months wages owing or accruing due worker in industry within scope of Part I of Workers Compensation Act (1979 c. 437) are payable to widow, widower, or common law spouse, free of debts of deceased, and are not subject to administration on intestacy (Estate Administration Act, §§144, 145, 147).

See also topic Executors and Administrators.

See Topical Index in front part of this volume.

DESERTION: See topics Divorce; Husband and Wife.

DISPUTE RESOLUTION:

Mandatory Dispute Resolution.—Following Statutes contain provisions transferring certain disputes to alternative dispute resolution:

Bee Act, c. 27. Disputes pertaining to application for licences under Act shall be resolved by arbitration in accordance with Commercial Arbitration Act.

British Columbia Railway Act, c. 38. Arbitration provisions of Railway Act apply.

Employment Standards Act, S.B.C. 1995, c. 35. Where collective agreement is in place, grievance procedures of collective agreement regarding hours of work, termination, statutory holidays, and annual vacation, apply for resolving any disputes in application of deemed statutory provisions of Act in these areas (see also topic Labour Relations).

Labour Relations Code.—See topic Labour Relations.

Land Act, c. 214. Disputes relating to price payable for land acquired by one owner from another through resurvey under Act shall be resolved by arbitration, and Commercial Arbitration Act (see subhead Voluntary Dispute Resolution, infra) shall apply.

Mental Health Act, c. 256. Disputes by locality regarding its liability to pay expenses for examinations of patients resident in that locality shall be resolved by arbitration.

Mineral Tenure Act, S.B.C. 1988, c. 5. Disputes regarding occupation and use of land under Act shall be resolved by Mediation and Arbitration Board established under Petroleum and Natural Gas Act (c. 323), if parties to dispute, in consultation with Gold Commissioner appointed under Act, cannot reach settlement.

Mining Right of Way Act, S.B.C. 1989, c. 57. Following disputes shall be resolved by Mediation and Arbitration Board established under Petroleum and Natural Gas Act (c. 323) if parties cannot, in consultation with Gold Commissioner appointed under Mineral Tenure Act, reach settlement: (1) disputes regarding price payable by users of access road to deemed owner of access road for maintenance costs to road, and (2) disputes regarding price payable by recorded leaseholder under Mineral Tenure Act to deemed owner of access road for portion of construction costs of road.

Municipal Act, c. 290. Following disputes under Act shall be resolved by arbitration: (1) disputes concerning agreements between municipal council and owner that fix property values for tax purposes (§403), (2) disputes over accommodation of municipal wires and equipment on poles erected by owner (§627), (3) disputes regarding term for which "latecomer" payments are payable (§990), and (4) disputes regarding regional growth strategies may be resolved by arbitration (§942.22).

Pension Benefits Standards Act, S.B.C. 1991, c. 15. Every pension plan must contain provision for final and conclusive settlement by arbitration or any other method for certain types of disputes arising under plan, as enumerated in §62 of Act. Specific requirements of such provision are set out specifically in Act, as well as particular mechanism that may be followed for arbitrations.

Railway Act, c. 354. Disputes pertaining to compensation payable for land expropriated by railway company or Crown pursuant to Act shall be resolved by Expropriation Compensation Board, established under Expropriation Act, S.B.C. 1987, c. 23.

Residence and Responsibility Act, c. 364. All disputes arising out of application of Act shall be resolved by board of arbitration established pursuant to Act.

Residential Tenancy Act, S.B.C. 1984, c. 15. Landlord and tenant are deemed to have agreed to submit number of types of applications under Act to arbitration, as set out in §13 of Act. Parties may agree in writing that this deemed agreement does not apply.

Small Claims Court Rules, B.C. Reg. 261/93. All actions commenced in Small Claims Court include mandatory Settlement Conference, which is set by Registrar after all of pleadings have been received. Settlement Conference must be attended by all parties to action, with or without counsel, and presiding judge may make any order at conference for just, speedy, and inexpensive resolution of claim, including order giving judgment in matter.

Vancouver Charter, 1-2 Eliz.2 1953, c. 55. Compensation payable by council to property owner for removal or relocation of electrical works in course of exercise of council's powers relating to regulation, placement or maintenance of any electrical works, shall be determined by arbitration.

Water Act, c. 429. Every claim against improvement district arising out of construction or maintenance of dike or out of diversion of water for reclamation or drainage of land in improvement district shall be determined by arbitration.

Voluntary Dispute Resolution.—Various mechanisms and services for alternative resolution of disputes are offered in British Columbia. These include following:

British Columbia Arbitration and Mediation Institute.—Staffed by over 300 arbitrators and mediators with backgrounds in various professions and trades. Also offers training for members to help them become chartered arbitrators or chartered mediators. Institute offers public seminars, provides advice on alternative dispute resolution and recommends persons to arbitrate or mediate in various fields of dispute.

British Columbia International Commercial Arbitration Centre.—Centre provides professional mediators, arbitrators and neutrals for any type of international and domestic commercial/business dispute, as well as physical facilities in which to accommodate settlement. It also administers cases under different rules and procedures for international commercial arbitration, domestic arbitration and commercial mediation. Centre provides following services to Canadian and foreign governments and businesses and their legal counsel operating domestically and internationally: information and advice on alternative dispute resolution, procedural rules for arbitration, mediation and other dispute resolution methods and model contract clauses, administrative services, and training in dispute resolution for lawyers and nonlawyers.

Centre has developed Rules for International Commercial Arbitration and Conciliation Proceedings, which may be used by parties wishing to resolve their dispute in British Columbia, even if they do not wish to use the Centre. These Rules are based upon 1976 UNCITRAL Arbitration Rules and 1980 UNCITRAL Conciliation Rules, although they are adapted to suit particular legislation in British Columbia governing International Arbitration, International Commercial Arbitration Act (see topic Arbitration and Award).

Commercial Arbitration Act and International Commercial Arbitration Act.—See topic Arbitration and Award.

Alternative Supreme Court Proceedings.—Supreme Court Rules, B.C.Reg. 221/90, as amended by B.C. Reg. 95/96, offer following procedures designed to expedite actions and facilitate settlement: (1) Summary Trial or "mini-trial" conducted upon affidavit evidence, evidence from examination for discovery, answer to written interrogatories, and admissions under Rule 31. Judge may decide particular issues or case in its entirety, or make other orders to expedite proceedings. (R.18A). (2) Special Case, where parties may, upon agreement, put any issue of fact or law to court to be decided. Court may also provide relief based upon its decision if parties consent. (R.33). (3) Points of Law arising from pleadings may be put before court, either of its own accord, or by party consent. (R.34). (4) Pretrial Conferences may be ordered by court or requested by parties. Solicitors or parties themselves must attend, and court must examine certain issues at pretrial conference, as set out in R.35. These include simplifying issues, amendments and admissions, quantums, fixing dates, or any other issues that aid in disposition of case. Court may make many orders, including that parties attend mini-trial or settlement conference.

DIVORCE:

Divorce Act, R.S., 1985, c. 3 (2d Supp.) has substantially changed law of divorce in Canada. Grounds for divorce are now: (a) Breakdown of marriage by reason of separation of at least one year, (b) adultery, or (c) mental or physical cruelty. (§8).

Divorce procedure in British Columbia is governed by Rule 60A and Rule 60B of Rules of Court. Uncontested divorces do not require court appearance, and can be proceeded with by way of desk order. In obtaining divorce, where children are involved, British Columbia courts have strictly interpreted §11(1)(b) of Divorce Act, 1985, which impresses duty upon court to satisfy itself that reasonable arrangements have been made for support of any children of marriage prior to granting divorce order.

DOWER:

Abolished. Estate Administration Act. (c. 114, §107).

EMPLOYER AND EMPLOYEE:

See topic Labour Relations.

ENVIRONMENT:

General Supervision.—Ministry of the Environment under Ministry of the Environment Act (1980, c. 30), Environment Management Act (1981, c. 14), Waste Management Act (1982, c. 41), Water Act (c. 429) and Water Protection Act (1995, c. 34).

Prohibited Acts of Pollution.—Discharge of sewage or other effluent to water, of waste on land, or of contaminants to air without permit or temporary approval issued by Director prohibited; any act contrary to Director's orders prohibited. No person may use or offer to sell or package product containers or disposable products contrary to Waste Management Act or its regulations without permit.

Enforcement.—By court action in summary proceedings for offences.

Penalties.—On conviction fine not exceeding $1,000,000, or if offence is of continuing nature (1982, c. 41, §3), fine not exceeding maximum fine for that offence for each day offence is continued (1982, c. 41, §34). Court may in addition, impose fine equal to profit resulting from commission of offence. On conviction for intentionally damaging environment or for showing reckless disregard for lives of others, fine not exceeding $3,000,000 or imprisonment for not more than three years or both. (1982, c. 41, §34.2). Regional Waste Manager may issue pollution abatement orders; Minister may suspend or cancel permit or approval and obtain restraining order from Supreme Court.

Permits and approvals issued by Regional Waste Manager, subject to appeal by interested persons. Cradle-to-grave manifest/permit system for storage and transport of special wastes. Permit and approval not transferable without consent.

In 1988 extensive amendments to Waste Management Act were made and new Special Wastes Regulation was enacted, both of which impose new and extensive licensing provisions in respect of handling, storage, treatment and destruction of hazardous wastes. Also Waste Management Permit Fees Regulation was enacted setting fees in accordance with volumes of waste authorized to be discharged. 1990 amendments to Waste Management Act (1982, c. 41) enact Part 3.1 which provides for Contaminated Site Remediation and issuance of certificates of compliance.

In 1990, provisions were enacted regarding contaminated site remediation.

1992 amendments require municipalities to submit waste management plans which include facilities for recycling and treatment of waste. Also, new regulations enacted on agricultural waste control (Reg. 131/92), gasoline vapour pressure (Reg. 63/92), return of used lubricating oils (Reg. 64/92), storage of recyclable materials (Reg. 133/92), ozone depleting substances (Reg. 53/93) and open burning smoke control (Reg. 145/143).

Water Act.—(c. 429). Regulates use, storage and diversion of water.

Weather Modification Act.—(c. 431). Activity intended to produce changes in composition or dynamics of atmosphere for increasing, decreasing or redistributing precipitation, or for decreasing or suppressing hail, lightning, fog, or cloud, prohibited without first obtaining permit from Minister or designee.

Environment and Land Use Act.—(1979, c. 110). Establishes Environment and Land Use Committee, to foster public concern and awareness of environment and ensure that consideration is given to environmental factors in land use and resource development. Provides that Governor in Council may make orders or regulations respecting environment or land use. Orders made require environmental impact assessment for some developments.

Environment Management Act.—(1981, c. 14). Allows Minister to require preparation of environmental impact assessment, to declare that proposal has detrimental environmental impact and take preventative actions, or to declare that environmental emergency exists and take remedial action.

Ecological Reserve Act.—(c. 101). Permits Lieutenant Governor in Council to establish reserves of Crown land for ecological purposes. Such reserves are unavailable for disposition, and their use, development or occupation may be restricted by regulation.

See Topical Index in front part of this volume.

ENVIRONMENT . . . *continued*

Forest Practices Code of British Columbia Act (1994, c. 41) provides for sustainable forest practices by stringent and comprehensive standards to be included in individual management plans, prescriptions and contracts. Maximum penalties for contraventions of Code are $1,000,000 fine and/or imprisonment of up to three years. Forest Practices Board investigates complaints, conduct, audits, and reports to public. Substantial portions changed by Forest Practices Code of British Columbia Amendment Act S.B.C. c. 6 (1995).

Pesticide Control Act (c. 322) prohibits application and use of pesticides except under terms and conditions of permits issued by Administrator under Act.

Utilities Commission Act (1980, c. 60) requires large scale energy projects to obtain energy project certificates, which may require environmental impact review by Utilities Commission prior to issuance.

Hazardous Waste Management Corporation Act.—Repealed. (1992, c. 6 §1).

See also topics Motor Vehicles; Forestry.

Water Protection Act.—Regulates removal, use and diversion of water sources in B.C. Working in conjunction with Water Act, it requires licenced approval for any large scale water use.

EQUITY: See topic Actions.

ESCHEAT:

See topic Descent and Distribution. See also topic Wills, subhead Unclaimed Legacies.

ESTATES: See topic Real Property.

EVIDENCE:

Common law rules of evidence as modified by Evidence Act (c. 116) and Rules of Court apply in all courts for matters within jurisdiction of British Columbia. For federal matters see Canada Law Digest. See also topics Affidavits; Depositions; Witnesses.

EXECUTIONS:

(Court Order Enforcement Act, c. 75).

Exemptions.—See topic Exemptions.

Types.—There are four types of "writs of execution": seizure and sale (enforcing order of payment of money to person); sequestration (enforcing order to pay money into court or for recovery or delivery of property other than land); possession (enforcing order for recovery or delivery of land); and delivery (enforcing order for recovery or delivery of property other than land). (Supreme Court Rules. R.1[8]).

Effect.—Except as otherwise provided, all goods, chattels and effects of judgment debtor are liable to seizure and sale under writ of execution against goods and chattels. (§49).

Time.—Writs of seizure and sale and of possession may be issued immediately upon judgment. Writ of sequestration may be issued upon proof that order has not been complied with. Depending on order, writ of delivery may be issued immediately upon judgment or upon subsequent order of court.

Stay of execution may issue, at or after time of making order, where appeal is pending, or where judgment has been allowed to go through some error or omission by defendant, usually upon terms of security being given for debt and costs. (R.42[21]).

Duration.—Writs continue in force for one year, but may be renewed for further year. (R.42[15]). Judgments must be registered against interest in land held by judgment debtor (including mortgage, lease, ownership, etc.) to be enforceable against such interest and, once registered, bind interest for two years from time of registration and may be renewed for further periods of two years. (§76). Judgments are enforceable for ten years only, but may be renewed.

Execution Against Land.—Judgment may be enforced against land by first registering judgment against interest in land and then applying to court to call on judgment debtor to show why lands should not be sold to satisfy judgment. (§§79, 84[1]). If court is satisfied that land in question should be sold to satisfy judgment order reference to Registrar of court will be made. (§86). Registrar of court confirms that judgment debtor has interest in land which can be sold and establishes what other interests are on title. Report of Registrar is then referred back to court where order is then made that interest in land be sold. (§88). When one month has elapsed after order for sale is made sheriff may put up land for sale. (§93). Judgment debtor or mortgagee may bid on land. (§96). Money realized from sale of land, after deducting sheriff's fees and incidental expenses, is paid into court and distributed in accordance with priority of claims standing against judgment debtor. Judgment creditor taking proceedings has first claim on money realized for his costs, unless good reason is found to contrary. (§86[3]).

Execution against goods is effected by placing in hands of sheriff, after judgment, writ of execution which is sheriff's authority for seizing sufficient of goods and chattels of judgment debtor to make up amount of judgment and costs, subject to right of debtor to exempt up to $2,000 worth of goods and chattels from seizure within two days of later of seizure or notice of seizure. (§66).

Redemption.—Goods seized under writ of execution can be redeemed by paying to sheriff amount due together with all costs. Redemption can be made at any time before sale. (§53).

Priorities.—When sheriff levies money upon execution against property of debtor, he must forthwith enter in book kept in his office notice stating that such levy has been made and amount thereof and money must be distributed ratably among all execution creditors and other creditors whose writs or certificates were in sheriff's hands at time of levy, or who deliver their writs or certificates to sheriff within one month from entry of notice. (Creditor Assistance Act, c. 80, §§2, 3).

All persons who are at time of seizure by sheriff, in employ of execution debtor have priority claim to unpaid salary or wages not exceeding three months wages or salary, over claims of execution creditor, apart from costs of obtaining judgment and execution. (§46).

Proceedings in Aid of Execution or by Way of Subpoena to Debtor.—When judgment or order has been obtained for recovery or payment of money, and order remains unsatisfied, party entitled to enforce it may examine debtor in aid of execution (Rule 42A) or may issue subpoena to debtor out of court registry in order to have examiner (court, master or designated registrar) examine debtor under oath as to his income and property, debts owing to and by debtor, disposal debtor has made of any property and means debtor has, or has had, or in future may have of satisfying judgment or order (Rule 42[23], 42[26]; Small Claims Rules, R.12). Examiner may order payment by instalments, and imprison debtor for default of payment if it be proved that judgment debtor was able to pay amount ordered to be paid.

EXECUTORS AND ADMINISTRATORS:

(Estate Administration Act c. 114).

Jurisdiction and Venue.—Supreme Court has exclusive jurisdiction in matters of probate and administration of estates.

Administrators.—Administration of intestate's estate may be granted to spouse of deceased or one or more of next of kin or such other person as to court seems expedient. (§7). If no relative in Province entitled to share in distribution of estate of deceased and ready and competent to take out letters of Administration, then Official Administrator may apply. (§46). Where infant (individual under 19 years) is sole executor, administration will be granted to guardian of infant until individual attains 19 years. (§14). Special administration of estate may be granted to creditor, next of kin, or legatee upon application to court if nonresident executor or administrator causes delay. (§10).

Official Administrator.—Public Trustee may be appointed Official Administrator (§39) who may administer estates of persons who die intestate or who have not appointed executor in cases where there are no relatives of deceased within province who are willing or competent (§46). Where all heirs and next of kin in Province competent to take out Letters of Administration renounce or request appointment of administrator of estate, Official Administrator shall make application for and shall be granted administration of estate. (§47).

Qualification.—Administrator must give bond for performance of trust unless this is dispensed with by order of court or judge. Amount is fixed by judge according to size of estate. (§§18, 42). Court may dispense with bond under certain conditions. (§18[2]).

Prior to receiving grant of probate or letters of administration (or resealed grant) executor or administrator must give notice, with will attached, if there is one: to each beneficiary under will; to any person who would be entitled to apply on intestacy or partial intestacy (regardless of whether there is intestacy or partial intestacy); to any person who would be entitled to apply under Wills Variation Act with respect to will; to common law spouse; to surviving spouse separated from deceased for not more than one year; to his committee or to Public Trustee where beneficiary or person entitled may be mentally disordered person; to Public Trustee and guardian or parent where beneficiary or person entitled is minor. Following form is acceptable, with necessary changes (§135):

Form

In the Estate of A.B., of the City of Victoria, in the Province of British Columbia, labourer, who died on the first day of . . . ., 19. . . . .

Take Notice that the undersigned is applying for probate (or letters of administration) of the above estate in the Supreme Court of British Columbia at . . . ., British Columbia

C.D.
Applicant,
1234 Blank Street,
Victoria, British Columbia

Address of Registrar:
Victoria, British Columbia

Notice to Public Trustee must also contain list of names and last known addresses of beneficiaries or persons entitled and be accompanied by copies of all documents filed with court in respect of application for grant. (§135[7]).

Real Estate.—Where real estate is vested in any person without a right in any other person to take by survivorship, then on death, notwithstanding any testamentary disposition, it devolves to and becomes vested in his personal representatives as if it were a chattel real vesting in them. (c. 114, §90).

Claims.—Executor may pay or allow any liability or claim on any evidence executor thinks sufficient. (§71). If personal representative does not admit claim, claimant must commence action in respect of claim within six months of receiving notice in writing of rejection or dispute of claim from executor or claim will be forever barred. (§72[1]).

Actions.—An executor or administrator may continue or bring and maintain action for tort or injury in same manner and with same rights and remedies as decedent might have done if living, but recovery may not extend to damages in respect of physical disfigurement, pain, suffering or death or in respect of possible earnings of decedent had he lived. (§66). This right is subject to provisions of Worker's Compensation Act (see topic Labour Relations and Family Compensation Act) but does not affect right of action for decedent's death (see topic Death).

Distribution of surplus of personal estate should not be made until one year after death of intestate; except where intestate has left dependent or where estate of intestate is being administered by Public Trustee who is satisfied that distribution can be made without prejudicially affecting creditors' rights.

Insolvent Estates.—Where real and personal estate of decedent is not sufficient for payment in full of all decedent's debts and liabilities, executor or administrator shall distribute proceeds of insolvent estate, subject to rights of secured creditors, in accordance with statutory priorities. (§§114-121).

Allowances.—Where deceased was worker employed in industrial occupation, his or her wages earned during three months prior to his or her death and owing or accrued to him are payable to widow or widower, free from all his or her debts. (§144).

See Topical Index in front part of this volume.

EXECUTORS AND ADMINISTRATORS . . . *continued*

When Administration Unnecessary.—Where estate does not exceed $10,000 in value, it is not necessary that administrator be appointed by Court. In such case, Official Administrator or any person competent to take out administration, upon satisfying Registrar of Court, by affidavit filed, that he is competent to take out administration and that value of estate does not exceed $10,000, has same power and authority to administer estate as if he had been appointed by order of Court. (§23).

Estates of Aliens.—Where foreign probate of will has been granted, ancillary probate (or, where jurisdiction is one recognized under Probate Recognition Act, c. 339, resealed grant of probate) or administration may be made to attorney of personal representative appointed by foreign court or to personal representative. (Rules of Court, R.61[48]).

EXEMPTIONS:

Goods and chattels of any debtor, at his option, to value of $2,000, are exempt from forced seizure or sale by any process of law or equity (save distress for rent or sale for taxes) except when stock in trade of his business or when they are taken in satisfaction of debt contracted for or in respect of identical goods or chattels. Works of art or other objects of cultural or historical significance brought into Province for temporary public exhibit and that are not offered for sale are exempt from seizure or sale under any process at law or in equity except execution on judgment respecting contract for transportation, warehousing or exhibition in Province of work or object. (c. 75, §§64–72).

See also topic Garnishment.

Homestead Exemption.—See topic Homesteads.

FACTORS:

Sales.—Nature, rights, and obligations of mercantile agent are defined in Sales on Consignment Act, R.S.B.C. 1960, c. 345. Under this Act, mercantile agent selling certain agricultural products on consignment is required to keep accurate records, report damaged condition of products to its principal, account after sales, disclose fees, commissions etc., and hold sale proceeds in trust and remit them to its principal within set time period. No mercantile agent may purchase consigned products of its principal without prior consent.

Violation subjects individual to fine of not exceeding $10,000 or to imprisonment for not exceeding two years or both, or corporation to fine of not exceeding $100,000.

Good Faith of Purchaser.—Where mercantile agent is, with consent of owner, in possession of goods or documents of title to goods, any sale, pledge or other disposition of same made by him when acting in ordinary course of business of mercantile agent is valid if person taking under disposition acts in good faith and without notice of agent's lack of authority. (Sale of Goods Act, R.S.B.C. 1979, c. 370, §58). This does not apply to consignment to which Personal Property Security Act applies. Lack of substantial compliance with certain provisions precludes mercantile agent from remuneration.

FIDUCIARIES:

See topics Executors and Administrators; Guardian and Ward; Trusts.

FILING FEES:

See topics Corporations; Deeds; Mortgages of Real Property.

FORECLOSURE:

See topics Chattel Mortgages; Liens; Mortgages of Real Property.

FOREIGN CORPORATIONS: See topic Corporations.

FORESTRY:

(Forest Act, c. 140; Forest Practices Code Act, S.B.C. 1994, c. 41).

Tenures.—As of June 15, 1995, substantial portions of Forest Act ("Act") and its accompanying regulations are repealed and replaced by Forest Practices Code Act ("Code") and its accompanying regulations. Remaining provisions in Act, however, continue to regulate tenures granted for harvesting of timber on Crown land in province. Act sets out types of tenures, and procedures for obtaining and renewing these tenures. (§§2-63.1).

Timber Scaling and Marking.—Forest Act regulates marking of timber with timber mark holder's mark and scaling of timber according to its quantity and quality. (§§64-80).

Payments to Crown.—Forest Act regulates royalty and stumpage payments to Crown and annual rent payable for tree farm licences and other licences. (§§81-90.1).

Forest Practices Code.—As of June 15, 1995, Code and its accompanying Regulations are in force. Code replaces repealed portions of Forest Act and implements new statutory provisions concerning previously unregulated aspects of timber harvesting industry. It represents significant change in regulation of timber harvesting on Crown land in province. Code has 12 parts, main ones of which are summarized below. There are also, however, numerous transitional provisions and grandparented forestry plans outlined in Code.

Strategic Planning.—This part of Code outlines objectives for and various standards which must be met in management of tenures. (§§2-9).

Operational Planning Requirements.—This part of Code contains requirements with respect to operational plans for government-industry tenure agreements. (§§10-44).

Forest Practices.—This part of Code outlines practices relating to general forestry, road building, timber harvesting, silviculture, and range which must be included in tenure agreements. (§§45-74).

Protection of Forest Resources.—This part of Code sets out requirements for protecting forests through fire prevention, control and avoidance, and unauthorized timber harvesting and trespass. It also contains provisions regulating botanical forest products and destructive agents such as insects or disease. Finally, it protects recreation resources on Crown land. (§§75-106).

Compliance and Enforcement.—This part of Code contains significantly expanded provisions (as compared to Act) with respect to inspecting, stopping and seizing forest products, and to forfeiture of timber, chattels or livestock. It also sets out offences and vests expanded powers in court to make compliance or enforcement orders. It creates new administrative review procedures for appealing decisions taken by Ministry of Forests officials; Act is also amended to conform with these new procedures. Forest Appeals Commission is established to hear appeals of officials' decisions. Forest Practices Board is established to hear complaints, to do audits, and, ultimately, to draft reports and make recommendations to complainant, to allegedly offending party, and to government. (§§107-159 and §§175-197).

Private Land.—The Forest Land Reserve Act, S.B.C. 1994, c. 40, regulates timber harvesting on certain private land which has been designated as being in Forest Land Reserve. When §47 of Forest Land Reserve Act comes into force by regulation, Code will also apply to land in Forest Land Reserve.

FRANCHISES:

No special legislation.

Public Transportation and Utilities.—Municipal council may enter into agreements for franchise of public transportation or other public utilities, by bylaw adopted with assent of electors and approval of minister. (Municipal Act, c. 290, §646).

FRAUDS, STATUTE OF:

Statue of Frauds, c. 393 has been repealed and replaced by §54 of Law and Equity Act, c. 224, provisions of which are as follows: Contract respecting land or disposition (defined term, excludes creation, assignment or renunciation of interest under trust, testamentary disposition; this provision does not apply to contract or grant of lease of land for three years or less or guarantee or indemnity arising by operation of law or imposed by statute) of land is not enforceable unless in writing or party to be charged has done act or acquiesced in act by other party that indicates existence of contract or disposition not inconsistent with that alleged (including payment or acceptance of deposit or part payment), or person alleging contract or disposition has, in reasonable reliance on it, so changed his position that inequitable result can be avoided only by enforcing contract or disposition. Where court decides alleged contract cannot be enforced it may order either or both of restitution of benefit received and compensation for money spent in reliance on contract. Guarantee or indemnity is not enforceable unless in writing, signed by guarantor or indemnitor or agent or alleged guarantor or indemnitor has done act indicating that guarantee or indemnity consistent with that alleged has been made. Writing can be sufficient even if term is left out or wrongly stated. (c. 224).

FRAUDULENT PREFERENCES AND CONVEYANCES:

Conveyances.—Disposition of property and bond, proceeding or order made, to delay, hinder or defraud creditors and others is void. Act does not apply to disposition of property for good consideration and in good faith lawfully transferred to person not having, at time of transfer to him, notice or knowledge of collusion or fraud. (Fraudulent Conveyance Act R.S.B.C. 1979, c. 142).

Preferences.—Voluntary or collusive agreement to judgment given by person who is insolvent or unable to pay his debts in full, or knows himself to be on eve of insolvency, with intent to defeat or delay his creditors or to give one or more creditors preference, is void against creditors of that person. (Fraudulent Preference Act, R.S.B.C. 1979, c. 143, §2).

Every disposition of property made by person who is insolvent or unable to pay his debts in full or knows that he is on eve of insolvency is, if made with intent to prejudice creditors, or to give any creditor preference, void as against injured creditor. (§3). If action is taken to impeach transaction within 60 days after any document evidencing transaction is registered or, if not registered, within 60 days after date of transaction or where debtor makes assignment for benefit of his creditors within 60 days after disposition same consequence applies without proof of intent. (§4). "Creditor" includes surety and endorser of promissory note or bill of exchange, beneficiary of trust or other person to whom liability is equitable only. (§1).

Disposition is deemed to give preference if creditor is placed in position to realize greater portion of his claim than could be realized for unsecured creditors out of assets left available. (§5). If person to whom disposition of property is made has disposed of or collected property, and that disposition is invalid against creditors, proceeds may be seized or recovered in action by person who would be entitled to do so if property had remained in possession or control of debtor. (§7).

Judgment creditor may apply to Supreme court calling upon debtor and transferee of land or any person who has acquired interest in land to show cause why land or part thereof should not be sold to realize amount of judgment or transfer set aside and property returned or otherwise dealt with and for order that he is entitled to register judgment against interest of debtor or another person's interest. (§9).

Bankruptcy.—Every conveyance or transfer of property or charge thereon made, every payment made, every obligation incurred, and every judicial proceeding taken or suffered by any insolvent person in favor of any creditor or of any person in trust for any creditor with view to giving that creditor preference over other creditors is deemed fraudulent and void as against trustee in bankruptcy if person making, incurring, taking, paying or suffering same becomes bankrupt within three months or makes assignment within three months after date of making, incurring, taking, paying or suffering same. Where creditor is related to insolvent person, period is one year.

If any such conveyance, transfer, payment, obligation or judicial proceeding has the effect of giving any creditor a preference over other creditors, or over any one or more of them, it is presumed to have been made, incurred, taken, paid or suffered with such intent whether or not it was made voluntarily or under pressure and evidence of pressure is not receivable to support transaction. (Bankruptcy and Insolvency Act, R.S.C. 1985, c. B-3, §§95 and 96). (See also Canada Law Digest.)

Bulk Sales.—Sale of Goods in Bulk Act repealed by "Law Reform Amendment Act, 1985" SBC 1985-10-11.

See Topical Index in front part of this volume.

GARNISHMENT:

Court Order Enforcement Act, c. 75. In all courts debts owing to defendant or judgment debtor by third persons may be attached by the plaintiff in action or judgment creditor upon ex parte application, supported by affidavit, by himself or his solicitor, showing that action is pending, amount of debt, and that it is justly due and owing, or that judgment has been recovered and is still unsatisfied, and to what amount, and that any other person is indebted to defendant or judgment debtor and is within jurisdiction of court. Where plaintiff's claim is for debt or liquidated demand, debts owing to defendant may be attached before, as well as after judgment, money attached being paid into court pending judgment in action.

There is no procedure in British Columbia analogous to trustee process except the foregoing. There is, however, procedure to appoint receiver by way of equitable execution to attach funds which cannot be attached by way of garnishing order, and charging order to attach funds which are held in court to credit of judgment debtor. (c. 224, §35).

Earnings.—In all courts 70% of any wages due by employer to employee is exempt from seizure or attachment and exemption shall not be less than $100 per month for person without dependents or pro rata for shorter period, and person with one or more dependents, $200 per month or pro rata for shorter period, subject to debt contracted for board or lodging. No attachment of wages is permitted prior to judgment. Employers cannot dismiss or terminate employment solely by reasons of garnishing orders issued against employee. (c. 75).

The wages of any civil servant in the employ of the provincial government on a wage or salary basis are liable to attachment like any other subject of the Crown. In such case, all process required to be served on garnishee shall be served on Deputy Minister of Finance or if wages usually paid elsewhere, by serving on office through which salary or wages usually paid. It is also possible to attach wages of Federal government employees. There are numerous debts not garnishable.

GUARDIAN AND WARD:

See topic Infants.

Insane Persons.—Patients' Property Act, c. 313, provides for court appointment on application by Attorney General or any other person, of official committee or individuals as committee of estate for person, who is incompetent by reason of mental infirmity. Committee has all rights, privileges and powers to deal with estate as individual would have if of full age and of sound and disposing mind, subject to such direction as court may order, e.g., committee to post security. Act also requires committee to pass accounts before Public Trustee.

HOLIDAYS:

Following are statutory holidays with pay in British Columbia: New Year's Day, Jan. 1; Good Friday; Victoria Day, 1st Mon. preceding May 25; Canada Day, July 1; British Columbia Day, 1st Mon. in Aug.; Labour Day, 1st Mon. in Sept.; Thanksgiving Day, 2d Mon. in Oct.; Remembrance Day, Nov. 11; Christmas Day, Dec. 25. (Employment Standards Act, S.B.C. 1995, c. 38).

See also Canada Law Digest and topic Labour Relations.

HOMESTEADS: (c. 173).

(See also topic Husband and Wife.)

Lands, whether leasehold or freehold, together with erections or buildings, with their rights and appurtenances, may be registered as homestead. To register, owner of property shall register title under Land Title Act, lodge in land title office where land is situated, notice thereof, and declare upon affidavit that he has assets of not less than $2,500 or, where value of homestead is less than $2,500 declare upon affidavit that value of assets does not exceed value of homestead. When so registered, homestead is exempt from seizure or sale under execution (except for taxes) for liability incurred after such registration, or, if value exceeds $2,500 it is exempt to that amount. Any fraud practiced by person effecting registration or on whose behalf homestead is registered in declaration or otherwise, to obtain such registration, will avoid exemption.

Dower and curtesy abolished. (c. 114, §107).

Conveyance or Encumbrance.—Person for whose benefit homestead is registered may, at any time, abandon, alienate, mortgage or otherwise part with, limit or encumber his interest therein. But where homestead owner is married consent of his spouse is necessary if (but not unless) spouse is resident of province. Consent must be given by way of acknowledgment by spouse in same manner as in case of instruments affecting real estate. (c. 173, §7).

Preventing Conveyance by Spouse.—Spouse or person's spouse on person's behalf, may, by statutory declaration, accompanied by affidavit, make application in land title office in district in which land is situate, make application to Registrar for entry on Register that homestead is subject to this Act. Entry on register will prevent spouse holding title from disposing of such land to any other person during lifetime of husband or wife without written consent of said spouse. Registrar of Land Titles may use his discretion in determining if land in question comes within description "Homestead". Where spouses living apart at time of death of his/her spouse under circumstances disentitling alimony, no life estate to vest in surviving spouse, nor shall surviving spouse take any benefit under Act. This Act ceases to apply on decree of dissolution or nullity of marriage. (Land [Spouse Protection] Act, c. 223).

Rights of Surviving Spouse and Children.—Where holder of homestead dies intestate leaving a surviving spouse and minor children, homestead passes to surviving spouse to be held by him or her during minority of children or while surviving spouse remains unmarried and may not be sold during such time for payment of any debt which has been contracted by deceased subsequent to registration of homestead. In case person holding homestead dies intestate leaving surviving spouse and no children, surviving spouse takes homestead absolutely. In case children only survive they take absolutely, in equal shares, divisible on youngest child attaining 19 years. (c. 173, §6).

See topic Deeds.

HUSBAND AND WIFE:

Family Relations Act (c. 121) in force as of Mar. 31, 1979 substantially changed law relating to husband and wife.

Spousal Capacity and Property.—Spouses have independent, separate and distinct legal personalities. There is no difference in law between married women and married men and married person has same legal capacity as unmarried person. Spouse may bring action in tort against other spouse. (c. 224, §55).

Responsibility for Debts of Spouse.—After judicial separation or dissolution of marriage, each former spouse is considered unmarried person in respect of property, right to contract, and rights and obligations in civil proceedings. Former spouses are not liable for other spouse's contracts, wrongful acts or omissions, or for costs incurred in proceeding, except where liability arose during marriage. Former spouse who is in arrears under maintenance order is, however, liable to third party who provides necessaries to child or other spouse who is beneficiary of order. (c. 121, §80).

Nonsupport.—One spouse may be required by court order to support other but spouses or former spouses are otherwise required to be self-sufficient in relation to one another. (c. 121, §57).

Deferred Community Property System.—After separation agreement, declaration in Supreme Court that there is no reasonable prospect of reconciliation, order for dissolution of marriage or judicial separation, or order declaring marriage null and void, spouse is entitled to undivided one-half interest as tenant-in-common in all family assets. Family assets are any assets ordinarily used for family purpose and include one spouse's business where other spouse makes indirect contribution to it. Indirect contributions can include savings through performing household and child-rearing responsibilities. (c. 121, §§43-46). Interest in family assets under this part is subject to: Order of Supreme Court, which has inherent jurisdiction to alter one-half interest if provisions for division of property between spouses would be unfair or if spouses execute marriage agreement or separation agreement. (c. 121, §§48 and 51). Supreme Court has jurisdiction to divide pension earned prior to marriage. (§51[b][2]; §§55.1-55.97 in force July 1, 1995).

Effect of Marriage Agreements on Family Assets.—Spouses can contract out of community property system with marriage agreement or separation agreement but Court can modify agreement on basis of fairness. (c. 121, §§43[3][b], 48[2][b], 51). There are provisions for filing separation or marriage agreements relating to specific land (c. 121, §49) in land titles office.

Husband's/Wife's Protection in Conveyances.—See Homesteads Act (c. 173, §7) and Land (Spouse Protection) Act (c. 223, §3). See topic Homesteads.

INCOME TAX: See topic Taxation.

INFANTS: (c. 196).

Age of majority is 19 for both sexes. (Age of Majority Act, c. 5, §1).

Contracts.—It is enacted that all contracts entered into by infants, other than contracts specified by enactment to be enforceable, affirmed on attaining majority, or performed, partially performed or not repudiated by him/her within one year after attaining majority, are not enforceable against infant. Contracts that are unenforceable against infant are enforceable by infant against adult party as if infant was adult at time contract was made. Infant or adult party to unenforceable contract may apply to court for relief and court shall consider all relevant circumstances in determining whether relief is appropriate. No relief will be granted to person who has acquired right to or interest in property where: That person is not party to contract; and, property has been transferred bona fide and for value to that person or to any of that person's predecessors in title who were not party to contract. Application may be made on behalf of infant to court or to Public Guardian and Trustee in order to be granted contractual capacity or to ratify specific contract. Guarantee of infant's contract is enforceable notwithstanding that contract is unenforceable against infant. Procedures are available for having adult who has entered into contract with infant, one year after that infant attains age of majority, have that infant affirm or repudiate contract. (c. 196, Part 2.1).

Provision is made in certain instances, and in some cases with court approval, for guardians to enter into contracts on behalf of infants.

Actions.—Infants must sue and defend by their guardian ad litem. (Rules of Court, R. 6). In event of judgment in favour of infant, money may be paid into court, and distributed to infant upon reaching age of majority, or as court may order. (c. 196, §33).

Infants Act provides for consent of Public Guardian and Trustee to compromise of infant's action to recover unliquidated demand in money payable to infant or damages for injury to person or property of infant. (c. 196, §31[3] and [6]).

Adoption.—See topic Adoption.

Liabilities.—Infants are not subject to any greater liability than person of full capacity. (c. 196, §16.7[b]). No liability of infant in tort if action in tort is related to contract that is unenforceable against infant. (c. 196, §16.8).

Guardianship.—Where custody granted to other than father or mother, court may direct Superintendent of Family and Child Service to be guardian of person of child or public trustee to be guardian of child's estate. Any court order must be in best interest of child. Guardian over estate or person of child has same authority as testamentary guardian. Subject to guardianship agreement, both parents (while living together) are joint guardians unless a tribunal of competent jurisdiction otherwise orders. After death of either parent, surviving parent is sole guardian unless deceased parent shall have by deed or will, appointed some other person to act, after his or her death, as joint guardian with survivor. Guardians of estate of child may be required to give security for proper discharge of their duty. (c. 121, §§23-31 and c. 196, §40). Note §25[2] and [3]—1987 amendments, not in force. See also Law and Equity Act. (c. 224, §§47, 56).

Protection and Support.—Family and Child Service Act, S.B.C. 1980, c. 11. If Superintendent of Family and Child Service considers child in need of protection, he may without warrant apprehend child. If person has reasonable grounds to believe that child is in need of protection, he must forthwith report circumstances to Superintendent or person designated by Superintendent to receive such reports on warrant granted on ex parte application. Superintendent has right of entry to investigate complaints that child

See Topical Index in front part of this volume.

INFANTS . . . *continued*
is in need of protection. Where Superintendent or police officer has reason to believe child is in immediate physical danger or in need of protection, he may enter premises without warrant, using force if necessary, and apprehend child if he considers it necessary. Where child is apprehended Superintendent has right to custody of child until child is returned to parent apparently entitled to custody, or order terminating Superintendent's custody of child is made under Act. (§§7-10). Putative father of children may be subject to presumptions of paternity as part of proceeding for support and maintenance order for child. (c. 121, §61.2). See also topic Husband and Wife.

Provisions of Hague Convention on child abduction have force of law in B.C., excepting Crown's responsibility for legal costs incurred in enforcing Convention. (Family Relations Act, c. 121, §42.1).

INHERITANCE TAX: See topic Taxation.

INJUNCTIONS:

General equity principles govern. (Law and Equity Act, c. 224, §36). Injunction may be granted by Supreme Court. (Rules of Court, R.45). May be used to prevent disposal and seizure of property and may be granted by court in all cases where it appears just and convenient to such court. Injunction may be granted conditionally or unconditionally. Only granted where no other remedy would suffice.

Interlocutory injunction may be granted pendente lite, and may be made final or removed on final disposition of case. Applicant for interlocutory injunction must show that there is "a fair question" or serious issue to be tried. Injunction will be granted to preserve status quo based on balance of convenience. Integral to balance of convenience test is requirement that applicant show he would suffer irreparable harm not compensable in damages if injunction is not granted. Interlocutory injunction normally only granted on undertaking of applicant to compensate for damages that might result from such injunction. In case of urgency and with leave of court, application for injunction may be made before commencement of proceeding. In provincial labour disputes only Labour Relations Board may enjoin unless there is immediate danger of serious injury to person or actual obstruction or physical damage to property. (Labour Relations Code, S.B.C. 1992, c. 82, §§136, 137). See also topic Labour Relations.

INSOLVENCY:

See Canada Law Digest, topic Bankruptcy.

INSURANCE:

The Insurance Act, except as provided, applies to every insurer that carries on any business of insurance in Province and every contract of insurance made or deemed made in Province. (c. 200, §2). Marine insurance is regulated by Insurance (Marine) Act. (c. 203).

Insurance Corporation Act (c. 201) sets up provincial government operated corporation to engage in business of insurance in all its classes, including operation of plan of universal compulsory automobile insurance. (c. 201, §6). Act generally deals with establishing corporation, borrowing powers, right to contract, limitation period of actions against corporation (generally one year), surpluses, reporting, etc. Provisions of Insurance Act and Finance Institutions Act do not apply to corporation or its classes or plans of insurance except as provided in this Act. (c. 201, §37).

Supervision of Insurance Act is by Superintendent of Financial Institutions.

Carrying on Insurance Business.—No person shall carry on insurance business in province unless authorized. (Financial Institutions Act, S.B.C. 1989, c. 47, §75). No person shall act in Province as insurance agent or insurance salesperson unless person is licensed. (§170[2]).

Insurance Agents, Insurance Salespersons, and Adjusters.—Insurance agents and salespersons must be licensed. (§170[2]). Agent's and salesperson's licenses are of two classes: (a) life insurance, or life insurance together with either or both of accident insurance and sickness insurance, or (b) general insurance. (§173). Adjusters must be licensed. (§179).

Policies.—Insurer may not issue policy of insurance in respect of automobile insurance in form, use application in form, or make advertisement in form, other than form approved by Superintendent of Insurance. (c. 200, §228). Special provisions concerning life, accident, fire, and automobile insurance are contained in Insurance Act. (c. 200).

Statutory Trust.—Preferred beneficiary designation has been repealed. Under policies of life insurance a statutory trust is created by an insured designating an irrevocable beneficiary and insured cannot alter or revoke designation without consent. The insurance monies are not subject to control of insured or his creditors and are not part of his estate. Insured can also designate a beneficiary generally and if he does so he can alter or revoke this designation without consent. (c. 200, §142).

Rebates on premium are prohibited. (S.B.C. 1989, c. 47, §79).

Discrimination.—Discriminative rates are prohibited. (c. 200, §272).

Hospital Insurance.—Subject to the Act, hospital charges of residents at standard rates are paid out of Hospital Insurance Fund. Premiums are paid by Minister of Finance out of Consolidated Revenue Fund. (Hospital Insurance Act, c. 180, §§10-16).

Insurance Premium Tax Act.—Taxpayer other than taxable insurer pays to Minister of Finance 7% of premium payable. (Insurance Premium Tax Act, c. 205, §3.1). Except as stipulated, tax of 3% of gross premiums received or receivable by him on policies insuring B.C. residents and property situate in B.C. is payable by all licensed insurers and insurers permitted to transact business of insurance in province. Tax of 4% of gross premiums will be assessed for any certificate, endorsement or policy relating to motor vehicles issued after Mar. 31, 1988. (c. 205, §3).

Direct Action Against Insurer.—See topic Motor Vehicles, subhead Direct Actions.

Motor Vehicle Insurance.—See topic Motor Vehicles.

INTEREST: See Canada Law Digest.

INTESTACY: See topic Descent and Distribution.

JOINT STOCK COMPANIES: See topic Corporations.

JUDGMENTS:

Order of court be drawn up by any party, and, unless court otherwise directs, must be approved by all parties who appeared or were represented at hearing at which order was made. Order need not be approved by party who has not consented to it and who did not appear or was not represented at trial or hearing. When necessary, terms of order are settled before Registrar, whose decision may be reviewed by court. Court may correct clerical error in any judgment. Judgment is to be dated as of day on which it was pronounced and takes effect on that day, unless court otherwise orders. Default judgments, and all orders of Registrar are dated and effective as of date signed by Registrar. (Rules of Court, R. 41).

Default Judgments.—Judgment may be entered by plaintiff in default of appearance to writ if defendant does not file appearance within time set out in writ, which time limits are governed by Rules of Court. Plaintiff may enter judgment in default if defendant did file appearance but failed to file statement of defence and any counterclaim within 14 days from time limited for appearance or from delivery of statement of claim, whichever is later. Judgment in default is available to defendant with leave of court where plaintiffs fail to file and deliver statement of claim within 21 days after appearance. If defence answers only part of claim, plaintiff may enter judgment with respect to unanswered part with leave of court. Where claim is solely for liquidated amount, judgment may be entered for amount of claim, plus interest and costs. Where claim is for unliquidated damages, judgment may be entered for damages to be assessed and costs. In all cases, affidavit of service or delivery is required but not affidavit of search. Court has jurisdiction to set aside or vary any default judgment. Unless court otherwise orders, where there is counterclaim plaintiff shall not issue execution on judgment obtained under Rule 25(11) until entire action has been disposed. (Rules of Court, R. 17, 20, 21, 25).

Summary Judgments.—Once appearance has been entered, plaintiff may apply to court for summary judgment for all or part of claim upon affidavit setting out facts verifying claim. Affidavit must also state that deponent knows of no fact which would constitute defence to claim, or part of claim, except as to amount. On hearing such application, court may grant or refuse relief requested or may make any other order it thinks just, including giving directions for hearing claim on affidavits at trial and ordering account. Summary judgment given against party who does not appear at hearing of application may be set aside or varied by court. Once appearance has been entered, defendant may, on ground there is no merit in whole or part of claim, apply for summary judgment on affidavit evidence setting out facts demonstrating that there is no merit, and stating that deponent knows of no facts which would substantiate claim. (Rules of Court, R. 18).

Summary Trials.—In action in which defence has been filed, either party may apply for judgment on issue or generally on affidavit, interrogatory or discovery evidence. Court may grant judgment for either party unless it is unable on all of evidence before it to find facts necessary to decide issues of fact or law, or is of opinion that it would be unjust to decide issues on application. Court may grant judgment on terms respecting execution and may award costs. Where court is unable to grant judgment it may order trial of proceeding generally or on issue and give directions to expedite trial. (Rules of Court, R.18A).

Declaratory Judgments.—No proceeding is open to objection, on ground that merely declaratory judgment or order is sought thereby. Court may make binding declarations of right, whether or not any consequential relief is or could be claimed. (Rules of Court, R. 5[22]).

Judgment on Admissions.—A party may apply at any stage of an action for judgment on admissions of fact made by his opponent without waiting for the determination of any other question between parties. (Rules of Court, R. 31[6]).

Consent Order.—Party may consent to judgment against him by signature of his solicitor or, if unrepresented, by his own signature or verbal consent before court or registrar. Term "judgment by confession" is not used in British Columbia. (Rules of Court, R. 41[15]).

Debtor may require judgment creditor to execute, file and deliver Acknowledgment of Payment in Form 50 as condition of paying money judgment. Judgment debtor may also make application for order certifying that judgment has been paid. (Rules of Court, R. 42[19] and [20]). Acknowledgment of Payment Form is as follows:

I acknowledge payment of $. . . . . . . in full (partial) satisfaction of the judgment dated the . . . . . . day of . . . . . ., 19. . . . .

Signed this . . . . . . day of . . . . . ., 19. . . . ., in the presence of

. . . .
(Name)
. . . .
(Address)
. . . .
(Occupation)
Dated . . . .

. . . .
Party receiving payment

Foreign Judgments.—Foreign judgment for payment of money which is obtained in reciprocating jurisdiction within meaning of Court Order Enforcement Act (c. 75, §31) may be enforced by applying within six years of date of judgment to have judgment registered. Registration will be denied if court is satisfied that foreign court acted without jurisdiction or judgment debtor did not submit to jurisdiction of court or would have good defence if action were brought on judgment or if for reasons of public policy cause of action would not be entertained by registering court. Actions on judgments not obtained in such reciprocating jurisdictions are governed by common law and create separate cause of action. Maintenance orders for alimony or maintenance made by court

JUDGMENTS . . . *continued*
in reciprocating state within meaning of Family Relations Act (c. 121, §70.1) may also be registered in British Columbia. Judgment in proceeding outside Canada for loss or injury that arises out of exposure to or use of asbestos mined in British Columbia may not be registered or enforced by court. Where person has cause of action under domestic laws of Province for loss or injury that is suffered outside Canada and arises out of use of or exposure to asbestos mined in Province, he may commence action under domestic laws of Province. (c. 75, §41.1).

Interest on Judgments.—In causes of action arising after May 31, 1974, court in a judgment shall add prejudgment interest as set out in Court Order Interest Act. (c. 76). Every judgment bears interest at an annual rate of interest that is equal to prime lending rate of banker to government calculated every six months on Jan. 1 and July 1. See topic Interest, under Canada Law Digest.

Enforcement.—Judgment may be enforced by delivering to sheriff for execution writ of seizure and sale (for payment of money), of sequestration (for payment into court), of possession (for recovery or delivery of possession of land), of delivery or sequestration (for recovery or delivery of property other than land or money) or by appointment of receiver. (Rules of Court, R. 42[1]-[5]). See generally topic Executions. Judgment creditor may compel attendance of debtor or officer of corporate debtor, for oral examination under oath before court or registrar concerning means debtor has or may have of satisfying judgment. (Rules of Court, R. 42A). Judgment may also be registered in any Land Title Office in Province, as lien and charge against lands of judgment debtor in that district. (c. 219). Other enforcement procedures include garnishment of debts due to judgment debtor. (c. 75).

Limitation Act (c. 236).—Judgment obtained in British Columbia court for payment of money or return of personal property is valid for ten years unless within that period proceedings are brought on that judgment. Judgment may be renewed for further ten year period, prior to expiration of current ten year limitation period. Judgment for possession of land or relating to enforcement of injunction may be enforced at any time. (c. 236). Judgment which has been registered in Land Title Office pursuant to Court Order Enforcement Act must be renewed every two years or statutory charge on judgment debtor's land will lapse. (c. 75, §83). Unexecuted writ of execution expires after one year unless renewed. (Rules of Court, R. 42[15]).

JUSTICES OF THE PEACE:

Are appointed by the provincial government. Justices may exercise all powers and jurisdiction of judge or court when specifically authorized in writing by chief judge.

LABOUR RELATIONS:

Minister of Labour as general executive officer of Provincial Ministry of Labour has general jurisdiction over all labour matters. Employment Standards Act, S.B.C. 1995, c. 38 (repealing S.B.C. 1980, c. 10), consolidates all labour standards legislation administered by Employment Standards Branch of Ministry of Labour. Labour Relations Code (S.B.C. 1992, c. 82) establishes Labour Relations Board. Board has Chair, Vice Chairs, and equal number of employer and employee representatives. Board is divided into two divisions, Mediation Division and Adjudication Division. (§116). Board has exclusive jurisdiction to hear and determine application or complaint under this Code and to make order permitted. This includes exclusive jurisdiction in respect of matters under Code or Regulations, application for regulation, restraint or prohibition of person or group of persons from: ceasing or refusing to perform work or to remain in relationship of employment, picketing, striking or locking out, or communicating information or opinion in labour dispute by speech, writing or other means. (§136). Decisions or orders in respect of which Board has jurisdiction are not open to question or review in any court on any grounds (§138). Public service employees are subject to provisions of Public Service Labour Relations Act, c. 346.

Hours of Work.—Employer must display hours-of-work notices in each workplace in locations where notices can be read by all employees. (c. 38, §31). Employer must pay overtime wages if employer requires or, directly or indirectly allows employees to work over eight hours a day or 40 hours a week. (c. 38, §§40, 41). Employer must ensure that employee working split shift completes within 12 hours of starting work. (c. 38, §33). Despite any provision in Part 4, employer must not require, or directly or indirectly allow employee to work excessive hours or hours detrimental to employee's health or safety. (c. 38, §39). In smelting or coal mining industries (Labour Regulation Act, c. 213, §1) no person shall be employed at coke oven, smelter, concentrator or mineral separation plant for more than eight hours in 24 hours, except that on days when shifts change person may be employed for longer period necessary to make change. Certain tradesmen may work for eight and 1/2 hours. Hours of work legislation is enforced by Employment Standards Branch.

Wages.—Minimum wages throughout province are prescribed by regulations. (c. 38, §16). Minimum wage is currently $7 per hour. Minimum wages for home support worker, resident caretaker and farm workers are different. (Part 4, Employment Standards Act Regulation, B.C. Reg. 396/95). Employment Standards Act prescribes overtime rates after eight hours worked in day or 40 hours worked in week. Employer and employee may apply for variance of certain requirements. (c. 38, §72). Wages must be paid at least semimonthly to employees. (c. 38, §17). Where wages are unpaid, employee may make written complaint to director. (c. 38, §74). Once determination is made requiring payment of wages, employee may commence another proceeding to recover them only if director has consented in writing or cancelled determination. (c. 38, §82). Unpaid wages constitute lien, charge and secured debt in favour of director. (c. 38, §87). Director may file determination in Supreme Court registry, and filed determination is enforceable in same manner as judgment of Supreme Court in favour of director for recovery of debt. (c. 38, §91).

Holidays.—Employees are entitled to annual holiday of at least two weeks after 12 consecutive months of employment and three weeks after five continuous years of employment, (c. 38, §57). Certain days made statutory holidays. Vacation pay must be made in certain cases. (c. 38, §58). See topic Holidays, and also Canada Law Digest, topic Holidays.

Child Employment.—No child under age of 15 years shall be employed without permission of Director of Employment Standards or his authorized representative. (c. 38, §9). Employer and parent are each liable for prosecution for violations of Act. (c. 38, §§9, 125).

Pregnancy Leave.—Pregnant employee who requests leave is entitled to up to 18 consecutive weeks of unpaid leave beginning no earlier than 11 weeks before expected birth date and ending no earlier than six weeks after actual birth date unless employee requests shorter period. Request for leave must be given in writing to employer at least four weeks before day employee proposes to begin leave and if required by employer, be accompanied by medical practitioner's certificate. (c. 38, §50). Employer must not, because of employee's pregnancy, terminate employment or change condition of employment without employee's written consent. (c. 38, §54). See subhead Discrimination, infra.

Parental Leave.—Employee, on written request given at least four weeks before employee proposes to begin leave and if required by employer, production of medical practitioner's certificate or other evidence of his or her entitlement to leave is entitled to parental leave without pay for up to 12 consecutive weeks. (c. 38, §51[1]). If child has physical, psychological or emotional condition requiring additional period of parental care, employee is entitled to up to five additional weeks of umpaid leave, beginning immediately after end of leave taken under subsection 1. (c. 38, §51[2]).

Trade unions are recognized as bargaining agents for purposes of collective bargaining certified by Labour Relations Board. Condition precedent to application for certification is demonstration of support by trade union of at least 45% of employees in that unit. (c. 82, §§18 and 19). If Board is satisfied that on date it receives application for certification not less than 55% of employees in that unit are members in good-standing of trade union, and that union is appropriate for collective bargaining, it will certify that trade union. (§23). Board may refuse to certify in case of domination of union by employer, or violation of Human Rights Act, S.B.C., 1984, c. 22. (§31). Board may require representation vote to be taken to determine if enough employees are members of union. (§§24 to 26). Certification cancellable, if in opinion of Board, trade union has ceased to be trade union, employer has ceased to be employer of employees in unit, or if at least ten months after certification 55% of employees apply and vote for decertification. (§33).

Professional Unions.—Professionals such as architects, accountants, doctors, lawyers, and teachers, etc. may be represented by unions.

Essential Services.—If dispute poses threat to health, safety or welfare of residents of British Columbia, then Minister of Labour may direct Board to designate as essential services those facilities, productions and services that Board considers necessary or essential to prevent such threat. (§§72 and 73).

Labour Disputes.—Every collective agreement shall be deemed to contain provisions prohibiting strikes and lockouts during its term. (§58). Strike and lockout votes are prohibited until collective bargaining has occurred and parties have failed to reach agreement. (§59). Every collective agreement must contain provisions governing dismissal or discipline of employees bound by agreement and for final settlement during term thereof without work stoppage by arbitration or otherwise of all differences concerning interpretation, application, operational or alleged violation of agreement. (§84). If no provision is in agreement, Act prescribes provision for above purpose. Appeal from arbitrator to Labour Relations Board on labour matters or allegations of denial of fair hearing and to Court of Appeal on other matters of general law. (§§99-101). Picketing is lawful in support of lawful strike, or lockout at site of lawful strike or lockout where employees perform work under control or direction of employer and where work is integral and substantial part of employer's operation. Secondary picketing is restricted to locations where struck or locking-out employer is performing work, supplying goods, or furnishing services for its own benefit which except for lockout or strike, would be performed at employer's primary location; or ally is performing work, supplying goods, or furnishing services for benefit of strike or locking-out employer. Secondary picketing requires permission of Board. (§65). During lockout or strike authorized by this Code employer shall not use replacement workers whether paid or not. (§68).

Discrimination as to any term or condition of employment, including wages or as to union membership is forbidden on grounds of race, religion, colour, ancestry, place of origin, political belief, religion, marital status, family status, physical or mental disability, sex, sexual orientation or age (19-65) or because of conviction for criminal or summary conviction charge unrelated to employment. (S.B.C. 1984, c. 22, Index Chapter 185.5, am'd §8[1]).

Employment Standards Act, S.B.C. 1980, c. 10, §7 prohibits assignment of workmen's wages save for certain exceptions. Wage must be paid in Canadian money (c. 10, §6). Notice of termination or severance pay in lieu thereof must be given in most circumstances.

Financial Statements.—Trade union members are entitled to audited annual financial statements. (c. 82, §151).

Workers' Compensation Act.—(c. 437). Workers' Compensation Board has exclusive jurisdiction over all matters in field of compensation to employees or their dependents for personal injury (including industrial diseases) or death arising out of and in course of employment, in multitude of specified industries and in such other industries or occupations as may be determined by Board. (c. 437, §96). When any industry or occupation is brought under Act by determination of Board, it may be brought under on such terms and conditions as Board deems proper.

Part I of Act, which deals with compensation to workers and dependents applies to all employers, as employees, and all workers in British Columbia except employers or workers exempted by order of Board. (c. 437, §2).

In applicable industries, compensation is payable out of Accident Fund administered by Board for personal injury (including disablement or death caused by industrial disease) caused by accident arising out of and in course of employment, (c. 437, §5), and compensation is neither assignable nor attachable except for money advanced by way of financial or other social welfare assistance owing to Province or to municipality, or for money owing to Accident Fund. (c. 437, §15). In these industries if employer is grossly negligent and accident results he may be ordered to reimburse Accident Fund.

LABOUR RELATIONS . . . *continued*
In other industries employer is liable for defective plant or premises, and for negligence of his servants, and knowledge of employee is not bar to recovery. Worker shall not by reason only of his continuing in employment of employer with knowledge of defect or negligence which caused his injury be deemed to have voluntarily incurred risk of injury. (c. 437, §103).

Generally, in regulated industries, employee injured in course of employment may not bring action for damages against employer or worker covered under Act; in actions outside scope of Act, employee may elect within three months or longer period which board allows between action or compensation. (c. 437, §10). Where employee elects compensation, Board is subrogated to his right. Where employee brings action Board must on request of court or party to action determine anything relevant to action within Board's competence. (c. 437, §11).

Accidents Happening Out of Province.—Where accident happens while worker is working elsewhere than in Province, which would entitle him or his dependents to compensation under Act if it had happened in Province, worker (or his dependents) is entitled to compensation under Act if place of business of employer is situate in Province, residence and usual place of employment of worker are in Province, his employment out of Province has immediately followed his employment by same employer within Province and has lasted less than six months, and nature of employment is such that, in course of work or service which worker performs, it is required to be performed within and outside of Province. Otherwise no compensation is payable where accident to worker happens elsewhere than in Province. (c. 437, §8).

Election as to Compensation.—Where by law of country or place in which accident happens worker (or his dependents) is entitled to compensation in respect of it, he is bound to elect whether he will claim compensation under law of that country or place or under Part I, and to give notice of such election within three months after accident or, if it results in death, within three months after death unless Board otherwise allows; and if such election is not made and notice given it is presumed that he has elected not to claim compensation under this Part. (c. 437, §9).

Interjurisdictional Agreements and Arrangements with Canada or Appropriate Authorities of Other Provinces may be made by Board to provide for administrative cooperation and assistance between jurisdictions or to avoid duplication of assessments on workers' earnings. (c. 437, §8.1).

Scale of compensation varies according to degree of disability and is set down within statute. (c. 437, §17).

Limitation.—Claims for compensation must be brought within three months of injury by accident or disablement by industrial disease, or if brought by dependent, within three months after death, or any longer period that Board allows. (§10).

Unemployment compensation is Federal matter.

LANDLORD AND TENANT:

Residential.—Governed by Residential Tenancy Act in force May 1, 1984. (S.B.C. 1984, c. 15 as am'd by S.B.C. 1989, c. 60, and S.B.C. 1993, c. 68). Does not apply to licences, unless it is occupation of room or premises in hotel by hotel tenant (c. 60, §2), cooperatives, tenancy agreement for term exceeding 20 years, except where landlord has prior approval by bylaw to enter such agreement, or where landlord gives notices as required in c. 60, §29(5.1), Tenancy Agreement with Government exceeding three years, or to recreational premises (§2). Principles applicable are based on law of contract rather than traditional concepts of landlord and tenant. Tenant obtains security of tenure by operation of Act. Distress cannot be levied. Right of landlord to receive security deposit is restricted to one-half of one month's rent and to time Tenancy Agreement is entered into. (§15). Landlords are also obligated to make premises reasonably suitable for occupation by reasonable tenant willing to rent it regardless of condition at time of rental. (§8). Act contains statutory duties and prohibitions which are deemed to be covenants in all tenancy agreements. (§3). Exclusive grounds for termination of tenancy are set out in Act. (Part 3). Prescribed forms of notice of termination by landlord must be used. (§33, as am'd by S.B.C. 1993, c. 68, §§7, 14). Landlord is not entitled to forcibly eject tenant but court or arbitrator may issue order for possession which is enforced by sheriff. (§36, as am'd by S.B.C. 1993, c. 68, §§3, 7).

Act administered by court and by arbitration procedure as set out in Act. (Part 4). Where landlord increases rent for residential premises with intent to evict and tenant vacates as result, landlord may be ordered to pay tenant's actual and reasonable moving expenses and other additional expenses. (c. 60, §21). Act contains provisions respecting manufactured home pads.

Human Rights Act (S.B.C. 1984, c. 22 as am'd by S.B.C. 1992, c. 43 am'd to Human Rights Code by S.B.C. 1995, c. 42 effective Oct. 1, 1996) prohibits discrimination in leasing space on grounds of race, colour, ancestry, place of origin, religion, marital status, family status, physical or mental disability, sex, sexual orientation or age (c. 22, §5).

Commercial Leases.—Commercial Tenancy Act (c. 54) governs nonresidential leases. All leases for term exceeding three years should be in writing signed by lessor (Law and Equity Act c. 224, §54), and must be registered in appropriate Land Title Office to have priority over subsequent registered interests. Leases executed by corporations and to be registered in Land Title Office need not be under seal. (§16, Property Law Act, c. 340). Leases for three years or more should be registered, and must be first proved or acknowledged. (Land Title Act, c. 219). Leases whose term exceed 30 years are subject to payment of property transfer tax. (Property Transfer Tax Act, c. 340.5). See topic Taxation, subhead Property Transfer Tax Act. See topics Affidavits; Acknowledgments. Short form of leases (as well as of deeds and mortgages), is provided by statute, and may be used when suitable, though its use is not obligatory, nor always desirable. (Land Transfer Form Act, c. 221).

Rent may be recovered by action or by distress on goods and chattels of tenant. (Commercial Tenancy Act, c. 54, §§1-4).

Distress must be made within six months after determination of lease, and during continuance of Landlord's title or interest, and possession of tenant. (c. 54, §4).

Tenants refusing to give up possession after termination of lease are liable to forfeit double rent during subsequent occupancy (c. 54, §16); or judge of Supreme Court, on application of landlord, may order writ of possession to issue, under which tenant is ejected by sheriff (c. 54, §21).

Subject to court's power to relieve against forfeiture, where rent is overdue for seven days, or tenant is guilty of a breach of any covenant, term or condition of his tenancy, which under terms of tenancy gives landlord a right of reentry, should tenant, on demand in writing, refuse to pay rent or quit possession, landlord may apply to Supreme Court for writ of possession, which will issue unless sufficient cause is shown against it by tenant. (c. 54, §28). If, however, such proceedings are taken only for nonpayment of rent, tenant is entitled to retain possession on payment of arrears, interest and costs. (c. 54, §29[3]).

Occupiers Liability Act.—(c. 303, as am'd by S.B.C. 1989, c. 64, §31). Occupier of premises owes duty to take such care as in all circumstances is reasonable to see that any person and his property will be reasonably safe in using premises. (§3). Such duty relates to condition of premises, and activities on premises and conduct of third parties on premises. (§3). Occupier, however, has no duty of care to person in respect of rights willingly accepted by that person as his own risks or who enters premises that occupier uses primarily for agricultural purposes and who would be trespasser under Trespass Act, other than duty not to create danger with intent to do harm to person or damage to property, or act with reckless disregard. (§3). Occupier is not liable for negligence of independent contractor employed, where former exercised reasonable care in selecting and supervising, and where it was reasonable to engage independent contractor. (§5). Landlord and sublandlord who is responsible for maintenance or repair of premises is bound as occupier. (§1).

If an occupier is permitted by law to exclude, restrict, modify or extend his duty of care by express agreement, or by express stipulation or notice, he shall take reasonable steps to bring that to attention of person affected. (§4).

LEASES:

Personal Property Security Act (S.B.C. 1989, c. 36, as am'd).—Act will apply to lease for term of more than one year notwithstanding that lease does not secure payment or performance of obligation.

See topic Landlord and Tenant.

LEGISLATURE:

(Constitution Act, c. 62; see also Election Act, c. 103).

Legislative Assembly consists of 75 members elected in manner provided for by Election Act. Member represents electoral district in which member was elected. (c. 62, §18 as am'd by S.B.C. 1989 c. 65, §16).

There must be a session at least once every year, so that 12 months shall not intervene between the last sitting of one session and the first sitting in the next. (c. 62, §22).

Public Officials and Government Employees Disclosure.—Financial Disclosure Act (c. 130) requires members of legislature, cabinet, mayors, aldermen, school trustees and certain public employees to disclose their holdings (§§2 to 4). Disclosure statements filed by provincial or municipal officials are made available to public but no such public access is available as to disclosure statements by public or municipal employees except where employee is prosecuted for failing to make or file written disclosure under Act. (§§6 and 12).

LEVY: See topic Executions.

LICENSES:

Are required to be taken out for almost every business or occupation whether the licensee resides in the province or not. In municipalities, license fees are payable to the municipal treasurer; elsewhere to the government agent of the district. Municipalities may require a license fee from persons representing firms or houses not having a permanent place of business in the municipality and selling goods at retail within the municipality, the amount of which is fixed by respective municipalities. See Municipal Act, c. 290. See topics Brokers and Principal and Agent.

Commercial Travellers.—No licenses are required.

LIENS:

Lien rights may be divided into three categories, Common Law, which is generally only possessory in nature, Equitable and Statutory. Common law liens may arise in three ways: by agreement; by trade usage or custom; or by operation of law. Examples of common law liens, subject to judicial decisions, are attorney's lien (see topic Attorneys and Counselors), banker's lien, stockbroker's lien, accountant's lien, etc. Personal Property Security Act (S.B.C. 1989, c. 36, as am'd) provides that lien on goods that arises as result of provision, in ordinary course of business, of materials or services in respect of goods, has priority over perfected or unperfected security interest unless lien arises under enactment that gives priority to security interest. (§32). Equitable liens, which do not require possession, arise to secure performance of obligation or payment of debt and prevent unjust enrichment. Statutory liens are as follows:

Repairer's Lien.—There is possessory lien on chattels (Repairers Lien Act, c. 363) for money, skill or materials bestowed on chattels and in case of nonpayment within 90 days, chattels may be sold to satisfy lien after two weeks advertisement in newspaper (§2). Special provisions exist for lien to continue on motor vehicles, boats and aircraft notwithstanding surrender of possession. (§3, as am'd by S.B.C. 1990, c. 11, §97). Lien will cease after expiry of 21 days unless it is registered in Personal Property Security Registry. (§3, as am'd by S.B.C. 1990, c. 11, §97). Lien expires 180 days from date of registration in Personal Property Registry, unless possession has been retaken or court orders extension and after that period (a) lien ceases to exist, and (b) registration of financing statement is no longer effective. (§7 as am'd by S.B.C. 1990, c. 11, §99).

Builders' Liens.—(Builders Lien Act, c. 40). Worker, materialman, contractor or sub-contractor who does or causes to be done any work upon, or supplies materials for, improvement has lien for wages or price of work or material, or both. (§4).

Trust Funds.—Funds received by a contractor or sub-contractor are trust funds in his hands for benefit of materialmen and workers among others. (§2).

See Topical Index in front part of this volume.

LIENS . . . *continued*

Liens must be registered by filing affidavit of claim in land title office: (1) By contractors or sub-contractors not later than 31 days after contract is completed, abandoned or determined; (2) by materialman not later than 31 days after improvement has been completed or abandoned or contract for improvement has been otherwise determined; (3) by worker within 31 days of last work done by him for which lien is claimed. (§22).

Action to enforce lien and certificate of pending litigation in land title office must be commenced within one year from filing of claim. (§25).

Special provision is made for liens for work done or materials supplied in relation to mine or quarry which lien must be filed within 60 days of completion of work or supply of materials. (§§22-24).

Holdback.—Owners or persons primarily liable under contract may hold back 10% of value of work for 40 days from time contract is completed, abandoned or otherwise determined, and subject to some exceptions, this amount may be paid out to discharge all liens after expiry of the 40 days.

Unpaid Wages Lien.—Employees entitled to wages for labour or services may apply for determination under Employment Standards Act (S.B.C. 1995, c. 38, §§79 and 87); unpaid wages so certified constitute lien, charge and secured debt in favour of director against all real and personal property of obligor in priority to all other claims or rights including those of Provincial Crown and any security interest under Personal Property Security Act (S.B.C. 1995, c. 38, §87) and save for valid prior registered mortgage or debenture interests charging land (S.B.C. 1995, c. 38, §87).

Woodworkers' Liens.—(Woodworker Lien Act, c. 436). Persons performing any labour or services in connection with logs or timber in province have lien thereon and on lumber manufactured therefrom for amount of wages due them, taking priority over all charges except Crown liens or third party tolls thereon. (§2). Such lien must be filed within 30 days after last day such labour or services are performed, and proceedings to enforce same taken in Supreme Court within 30 days after filing lien, or after expiry of period of credit. (§§5-6). In specified circumstances when lien is imperilled by imminent removal of logs or timber from jurisdiction or loss of identifiability of logs and timber by cutting into lumber, writ of attachment may be issued and logs seized and held thereunder, pending judgment, unless security is given or amount claimed is paid into court; failing payment logs or timber may be sold to satisfy lien. (§§12, 16, 24).

Threshers' Liens.—Every thresher who threshes grain has lien on grain for payment of his remuneration for threshing. (Threshers Lien Act, R.S.B.C. 1960, c. 379, §3).

Lien on cattle fed or cared for by another. (Livestock Lien Act, c. 244, §2).

Tugboat worker's lien for services rendered in towage of logs or timber products. (Tugboat Workers Lien Act, c. 417, §4).

Warehouse Lien.—For goods deposited with him for storage. (Warehouse Lien Act, c. 427, §2). Notice must be given to owner and anyone who has registered financing statement under Personal Property Security Act (S.B.C. 1989, c. 36), before warehouseman can sell goods. (Warehouse Lien Act, c. 427, §4).

Tax liens may be imposed under provincial taxation statutes.

Unpaid Seller's Lien.—Unpaid seller of goods in possession entitled to retain possession until payment notwithstanding he is bailee for buyer and goods not sold on credit. (Sale of Goods Act, c. 370, §44). Remedies for unpaid seller of goods on conditional sale are governed by Personal Property Security Act (S.B.C. 1989, c. 36, as am'd) where transaction, in substance, creates security interest. Unpaid seller of goods on conditional sale may, in certain instances, seize or recover possession of goods or sue, except in case of consumer goods where debtor has paid two-thirds of sale price, in which case, seizure is not available. (S.B.C. 1989, c. 36, §58). See topic Sales, subhead Conditional Sales in PPSA.

LIMITATION OF ACTIONS:

Limitation Act, c. 236.

Two Years.—Action for damages in respect of injury to person, excluding sexual assault of minor, or property including economic loss therefrom whether based on contract, tort or statutory duty; for trespass to property; for defamation; for false imprisonment; for malicious prosecution; for tort under Privacy Act; for action under Family Compensation Act (c. 120); for seduction; action in tort under §23.1 of Engineers and Geoscientists Act (c. 109). (c. 236, §3[1]).

Ten Years.—Action against personal representative of deceased person for share of estate; against trustee in respect of any fraud or fraudulent breach of trust to which trustee was party or privy; against trustee for conversion of trust property to trustee's own use; to recover trust property or property into which trust property can be traced against trustee or other person; to recover money on account of wrongful distribution of trust property against person to whom property is distributed or successor; action on judgment for payment of money or return of personal property. (§3[2]).

No Limitation Period.—Action for possession of land where person entitled to possession has been dispossessed in circumstances amounting to trespass; for possession of land by life tenant or remainderman; on judgment for possession of land; by debtor in possession of collateral to redeem that collateral; by secured party in possession of collateral to realize that collateral; by landlord to recover possession of land from tenant who is in default or overholding; action relating to enforcement of injunction or restraining order; action to enforce easement, restrictive covenant or profit a prendre; for declaration as to personal status; for declaration as to title of property by any person in possession of that property (§3[3]); for cause of action based on misconduct of sexual nature; where misconduct occurred while person was minor and for cause of action based on sexual assault (§3[3], as am'd S.B.C. 1994, c. 8, §1).

Six Years.—Matters not specifically mentioned in Limitation Act (c. 236) or any other Act (§3[4]).

Six year limitation period also applies to actions brought by secured party not in possession of collateral to realize on that collateral; by debtor not in possession of collateral to redeem that collateral; for damages for conversion or detention of goods; for recovery of goods wrongfully taken or detained; by tenant against landlord for possession of land, whether or not tenant was dispossessed in circumstances amounting to trespass; for possession of land by person who has right to enter for breach of condition subsequent, or right to possession arising under possibility of reverter of determinable estate. (§3[5]).

Act applies to causes of action arising before July 1, 1975 but nothing in Act revives any action that was statute barred on July 1, 1975. If prior limitation longer than set out in Act and limitation in Act will expire on or before two years from commencement of Act governing limitation period is shorter of two years from July 1, 1975 or previous limitation period. (§14). Prior limitations have no application in cases of sexual misconduct involving minor or sexual assault. (§14[6], as am'd S.B.C. 1994, c. 8, §3).

Foreign Causes of Action.—Where law of foreign jurisdiction applicable and limitation law of that jurisdiction classified as procedural court may apply B.C. limitation law or foreign limitation if more just result produced. (§13[1], as am'd S.B.C. 1993, c. 55, §157). Court must apply B.C. limitation law in cases of sexual misconduct involving minor or sexual assault. (§13[2], as am'd S.B.C. 1994, c. 8, §3).

Disability of Plaintiff.—If person under disability limitation period postponed and does not run until disability removed. Persons under disability if minor or unable to manage his affairs. If person under disability has guardian as defined in Act anyone that person may have action against can serve notice to proceed on guardian and time commences to run as if person ceased to be under disability on date notice delivered. (§7, definition of guardian in §7[5]-[6]).

Postponement of Time.—In most circumstances running of time postponed until plaintiff knows identity of defendant and has sufficient knowledge of facts to be able to bring action. Onus of proving postponement lies on person claiming benefit of same. Statute should be examined to determine if cause of action is of kind that time is postponed. (§6).

Acknowledgment.—If person against whom action lies confirms cause of action during limitation period but prior to its expiry, time prior to confirmation does not count in reckoning limitation period for person having benefit of confirmation. Confirmation must be in writing and signed by maker. (§5).

Ultimate Limitation.—Subject to §3(3) (see subhead No Limitation Period, supra), and notwithstanding provisions dealing with disability, postponement and acknowledgment, no action to be brought 30 years from date right to do so arose, or in action against hospital, hospital employee or medical practitioner for negligence or malpractice, after six years. (§8 as am'd, S.B.C. 1994, c. 8, §2, and see §5 transitional provisions).

Wrongful Death.—Limitation period of two years for action for wrongful death under Family Compensation Act (c. 120). (c. 236, §3[1][g]). One year limitation for application to Workers' Compensation Board for compensation under Criminal Injury Compensation Act, subject to extension by Board. (c. 83, §6).

Pleading.—No express statutory provision requiring pleading limitation defence, but defendant must plead any matter of fact or law that he alleges makes claim not maintainable. (Rules of Court, R. 19 [15]).

LIMITED PARTNERSHIP: See topic Partnership.

MARRIAGE:

Matters concerning formal marriage are governed by Marriage Act, c. 251.

Consent Required.—If contracting party is under 19 years of age, consent of parents, surviving parent, guardian, or Public Guardian and Trustee is necessary; unless, on petition to court, judge of Supreme Court gives declaration that proposed marriage of infant is proper. Lack of proper consent does not invalidate otherwise valid marriage. (§§24 and 26).

License.—Marriage licenses are required. Licenses may be obtained from Director of Vital Statistics. One of parties intending to marry must make affidavit in support of their application for marriage licence.

Marriages may be solemnized at any time within three months after marriage license is issued. (c. 251, §§13, 14).

Reports of Marriage.—See topic Records, subhead Vital Statistics.

Civil Marriage.—A civil marriage may be performed by marriage commissioner if so desired. (c. 251, §17).

Ceremonial Marriage.—Marriages may be solemnized by religious representative (person duly authorized to solemnize marriage according to rites and usages of religious body) registered under Marriage Act.

Common law marriages are now recognized for limited purposes. Family Relations Act, c. 121 defines spouse to include man and woman who, not being married, live together as husband and wife for not less than two years. Either may apply to court within one year of separation for order for custody of children, and maintenance of self and children. Common law spouses are not subject to community property system (see topic Husband and Wife). Part 5 of Estate Administration Act, c. 114, defines common law spouse to mean either person united to another person by marriage valid at common law or persons who have cohabited and been maintained by another for two years preceding death. See topic Descent and Distribution. Validity of out-of-province marriages determined by principles of common law. Formal validity of marriage determined by lex loci celebration is.

Law of England.—In all matters relating to mode of solemnizing marriages, or validity of them, and qualification of parties about to marry, law of England as it existed on Nov. 19, 1858 prevails, subject to Marriage Act and any Act of Canada in force in Province. (§33).

Foreign marriages which are valid according to the law of the country where contracted are recognized, unless bigamous or plural.

Annulment.—Inability to consummate a marriage renders it voidable only and not void. See topic Divorce.

Where order has been granted under Survivorship and Presumption of Death Act (see topic Death) party may apply for and, upon fulfilling certain conditions, obtain marriage licence.

See Topical Index in front part of this volume.

MARRIED WOMEN:

See topics Acknowledgments; Dower; Executors and Administrators; Homesteads; Husband and Wife; Marriage; Wills; Witnesses.

MASTER AND SERVANT:

See topic Labour Relations; also topic Principal and Agent.

MECHANICS' LIENS: See topic Liens.

MINES AND MINERALS:

Mining.—Mineral Tenure Act (S.B.C. 1988, c. 5). "Free miner" is person who holds valid and subsisting free miner certificate. Every person who establishes location must be free miner. (§6[1]). No person shall apply for record of claim unless that person is both locator of claim and free miner. (§6[2]). Before exploring and developing, extracting minerals or placer minerals, locating, recording or acquiring mineral title, executing disposition of mineral title or performing work, person (including company) and his agent must be free miner. Individual applicant must be 18 years of age or older and ordinarily resident of Canada for not less than 183 days in each calendar year or authorized to work in Canada and who demonstrates minimum prescribed knowledge of mineral exploration and integrated resource management principles. (§7[2][a]). Corporate applicant must be incorporated or registered in Province. Free miners certificate is valid from beginning of day on which application was received until end of day expressed to expire and is renewable on application. (§7[3][f]). Free miner may enter Crown mineral lands to explore and locate except land occupied by building, curtilage of dwelling house, orchard land, land under cultivation, land lawfully occupied for mining purposes other than exploring and locating minerals or placer minerals, protected heritage property, or land in park or recreation area (unless authorized by Lieutenant Governor in Council). (§9). Recorded holder of claim entitled to minerals or placer minerals situated vertically downward from and inside boundaries of claim. (§24). Claim is valid for one year after its date of record and may be held thereafter from year to year if, on or before anniversary date holder pays prescribed recording fee and either satisfies gold commissioner that sufficient exploration and development work has been performed, or pays cash in lieu of exploration and development work. (§25). Holder may record excess work done during year and thereby be exempt from doing work for years covered by such excess up to maximum of ten years for mineral claims and five years for placer claims. (§26). Mining leases issued for maximum term of 30 years to holders of mineral claims on application. (§37[4]). Lessee entitled to one renewal for maximum term of 20 years if he complies with Act, regulations and conditions of mining lease. Subject to approval of chief gold commissioner. (§37[5]). Placer leases issued for maximum term of ten years on application. Placer lessee entitled to one or more renewal terms for maximum terms of ten years each on same conditions as for mining leases. (§40). Lease not impeachable except on ground of fraud. (§46). Regulations may cover conveyances to recorded holders of Crown granted two post claims, staking and positioning of posts, disposal of mineral titles which have reverted, escheated, been surrendered or otherwise acquired by Crown, grouping of mineral titles and limitations on numbers that can be grouped, surveying of land covered by placer leases, limiting number of placer claims and leases issued under former Acts that can be consolidated into one placer lease, common anniversary dates for mineral titles and manner they are established, conditions in leases, and establishment and fixing of fees.

Mines Act (S.B.C. 1989, c. 56) which repeals and replaces 1980, c. 28 regulates opening, operation and closing of mine, safety of mine, operation of equipment used in operation of mine, environmental working conditions of exploration and mining, plan for working mine, and reclamation of surface of land and watercourses affected thereby. Waste Management Act (S.B.C. 1982, c. 41) regulates disposal of mine tailings and other waste including air emissions.

Petroleum and Natural Gas Act.—Practically all petroleum and natural gas rights are vested in Crown which grants following interests, terms of which are set forth in Petroleum and Natural Gas Act, R.S.B.C. 1979, c. 323 (as am'd) and regulations thereunder.

Geophysical License.—Permission to conduct geophysical exploration on Crown land, issued on year-to-year basis, but not transferrable. Holder of licence must obtain approval of Commissioner for particular geophysical exploration projects. Geophysical license is not transferable with limited exceptions. Work may be ordered stopped where environmental damage is anticipated. (§§33-35).

Drilling License.—Right, via public tender, to drill on Crown Reserve (lands whose petroleum and natural gas rights are reserved to Crown) and thereby earn lease, as set out in regulation 10/82, as amended by regulations 62/92, 91/92 and 55/94.

Lease.—Grants exclusive right to produce both petroleum and natural gas from location of lease for period of ten years (five in certain cases); term may be extended annually upon application to Commissioner under prescribed conditions for up to three years on penalty payment if lease for ten years; lease of spacing area accommodating well automatically continues indefinitely subject to lessee giving undertaking to drill well within next year.

Leases and exploration permits are each subject to issuance and renewal fees and work obligations (or fees in lieu thereof) specified by regulation 378/82, as amended by regulation 92/92; and holder of lease not less than three years old can be forced to do development drilling or surrender.

Natural gas marketing has been deregulated by Natural Gas Price Act S.B.C. 1989, c. 74, enabling producers to sell to anyone (although export must be authorized by province, and export price by National Energy Board). Petroleum and Natural Gas Act (as am'd) R.S.B.C. 1979, c. 323 imposes royalties on petroleum and natural gas. (§91).

Coal Mining.—Coal Act (c. 51). Before exploring for, developing or producing coal, or acquiring or holding permit, licence or lease, person or company must be free miner (see subhead Mining, supra). Free miner may enter land, except for parks for which special permission is required, in respect of which coal is reserved to Crown, to explore for coal and establish location, being area contained within licence or lease. (§2). Holder of licence may mine and develop coal on location of licence, but not produce for use, marketing or sale unless he first obtains from Minister limited production permit. (§3). Term of licence is one year and is renewable upon, inter alia, satisfaction of work requirements and payment of annual rental and application fee. Licence, permit or lease is transferable and transfer must be in writing and recorded with chief gold commissioner. Holder of lease may explore for, develop and produce coal on location of lease. Term of lease is 30 years and is renewable. Lessee must pay annual rental. Chief gold commissioner appointed under Mineral Tenure Act may cancel free miner certificate if Act, regulations, or protected heritage property contravened.

Mining Tax.—Mineral Tax Act, S.B.C. 1989, c. 55 provides that every operator of mine other than coal mine shall pay tax for each mine equal to aggregate of (a) amount by which 13% of net revenue exceeds aggregate of (i) balance of cumulative tax credit account, (ii) amount of imputed interest for current year; and (iii) 2% of net current proceeds of mine, and (b) 2% of net current proceeds of mine. (§2[1]). Certain deductions are provided for in §§2(2) and 2(3).

Net revenue, net current proceeds and cumulative tax credit account are all calculated by formula specified in Act.

Mineral Land Tax Act.—Under §4 (c. 260, as am'd by S.B.C. 1992, c. 13) of Act every owner of Crown-granted mineral land must pay each year tax at rate of $1.25 per hectare on acreage of less than 20,235 hectares on sliding scale up to $4.95 per hectare on 404,686 hectares or more. Under §5 of Act every owner of designated mineral land situated within production area, definitions of which are set out in Act, must pay tax each year at rate of $4.94 per hectare for each hectare of owner's production area. (in force by B.C. Reg. 434/93).

Royalties at various rates are imposed under Petroleum and Natural Gas Act Regulations as amended.

MOBILE HOMES:

Manufactured Home Act, c. 281 provides registry system for ownership of mobile homes.

Registration of Ownership of Mobile Home.—Registration requirements of Act apply to every transaction, regardless of its form, which has effect of transferring property in mobile home. (§2). Unless mobile home is registered, instrument purporting to transfer property in mobile home will not be effective to transfer property in mobile home except as against person making instrument. Subject to Land Title Act. (c. 219). Act sets out requirements for registering instrument of transfer where property in mobile home is transferred. (§31). Where error has been made in registration of instrument of transfer, Registrar may, on sufficient evidence, correct error. (§37).

Registration of Charges over Mobile Homes.—In order to file charge against mobile home, it is necessary to file financing statement in Personal Property Registry. General rule under Personal Property Security Act, 1989, S.B.C. c. 36, is that as between competing charges, priority is determined according to time of registration.

Moving Mobile Home.—Mobile home may not be moved unless transport permit indicating its destination has been obtained from Manufactured Home Registry and move is made in compliance with §41 of Act.

All registrations and applications for transport permits and identifying decal to be placed upon mobile home must be on prescribed forms, available from Manufactured Home Registry, 2nd Floor, 940 Blanshard Street, Victoria B.C. V8W 3E6 (tel. 604-356-8600).

Residential Tenancy.—The Residential Tenancy Act, S.B.C. 1984, c. 15 applies to mobile homes (see topic Landlord and Tenant).

MONOPOLIES AND RESTRAINT OF TRADE:

This is a Dominion matter. See Canada Law Digest.

MORTGAGES OF PERSONAL PROPERTY:

See topic Personal Property Security.

MORTGAGES OF REAL PROPERTY:

To preserve priority, mortgages should be registered in Land Title Office of that district where land is located. To be registrable mortgage must conform to Land Title Act, c. 219. Mortgage must be in two parts. Part 1 sets out parties, legal description of mortgaged land, signatures of mortgagor and witness (in accordance with Part 5 of Land Title Act), other prescribed terms and conditions, and other prescribed information. Part 2 consists of all other terms of mortgage. These terms may be standard mortgage terms filed by lender at Land Title Office, prescribed standard terms filed by Lieutenant Governor in Council or terms expressly set out in Part 2 of mortgage. If mortgage consists of set of standard mortgage terms, mortgagee or his agent at or before time mortgage is executed must give copy of standard mortgage terms to mortgagor who must acknowledge that he has received same.

Mortgage Broker's Act (c. 283) requires persons, their employees, partners or directors who come within statutory definition of mortgage broker to register with Registrar as broker. Act contains classes of persons exempt from registration and provides penalties for failure to register; but, such failure does not render any mortgage void. Act also requires separate written disclosure for those mortgages requiring repayment of amount in addition to interest, reasonable appraisal, survey and legal fees (viz., bonus). Borrower may rescind this type of mortgage within 48 hours of receipt of written disclosure. See also topic Brokers.

Foreclosure.—The foreclosure of the equity of redemption of a mortgagor is effected by a judgment or order obtained in an action by the mortgagee against the mortgagor in the Supreme Court of British Columbia. In such an action the first order obtained is called an order nisi. It provides for the taking of the accounts between the mortgagor and the mortgagee and the taxation of costs et cetera. Court may order that unless mortgagor, within certain redemption time, usually six months after date of registrar's certificate upon taking of accounts, pays into court or to mortgagee sum so found due, that he be absolutely foreclosed of all right in mortgaged lands, but that upon payment that mortgagee discharge mortgage. Final order is obtained on application to judge and mortgagor may make representations requesting further extension of time for redemption.

MORTGAGES OF REAL PROPERTY ... *continued*

Redemption.—A mortgagor may redeem the mortgaged property at any time before sale or final judgment of foreclosure.

Release of a mortgage should identify mortgaged premises intended to be released, and must be acknowledged. Partial release must specify portion of land intended to be released. If mortgagee will not execute release, after mortgage has been paid in full, action will lie for declaration that mortgage is discharged and satisfied. See also c. 340, §20.2 for extinguishment of residential mortgage.

Trust Deeds.—Debentures and debenture stock are often secured by a trust deed conveying property of the company to trustees in favor of the debenture holders, charging other property and containing a number of ancillary provisions regulating the respective rights of the company and the debenture holder.

Trust deeds must be registered in proper land title office if any real property is charged, in same manner as mortgages. In case of trust deed executed by corporation executed copy must be registered with Registrar of Companies. Trustee appointed under deed need not be resident within province.

Forms.—Land Title (Transfer Forms) Regulation sets out form by which mortgage, transfer, and discharge of mortgage must be filed.

LAND TITLE ACT

FORM C

(Section 219.81)

Province of

British Columbia

GENERAL INSTRUMENT — PART 1 ***(This area for Land Title Office use)*** PAGE 1 **of __ pages**

1. APPLICATION: *(Name, address, phone number and signature of applicant, applicant's solicitor or agent)*

2. PARCEL IDENTIFIER(S) AND LEGAL DESCRIPTION(S) OF LAND:*
(PID) *(LEGAL DESCRIPTION)*

3. NATURE OF INTEREST:*
DESCRIPTION *DOCUMENT REFERENCE* *(page and paragraph)* *PERSON ENTITLED TO INTEREST*

4. TERMS: Part 2 of this instrument consists of (select one only)

(a) Filed Standard Charge Terms ☐ D.F. No.
(b) Express Charge Terms ☐ Annexed as Part 2
(c) Release ☐ There is no Part 2 of this instrument

A selection of (a) includes any additional or modified terms referred to in Item 7 or in a schedule annexed to this instrument. If (c) is selected, the charge described in Item 3 is released or discharged as a charge on the land described in Item 2.

5. TRANSFEROR(S):*

6. TRANSFEREE(S): *(including postal address(es) and postal code(s))**

7. ADDITIONAL OR MODIFIED TERMS:*

8. EXECUTION(S): This instrument creates, assigns, modifies, enlarges, discharges or governs the priority of the interest(s) described in Item 3 and the Transferor(s) and every other signatory agree to be bound by this instrument, and acknowledge(s) receipt of a true copy of the filed standard charge terms, if any.

Execution Date

Officer Signature(s) **Party(ies) Signature(s)**

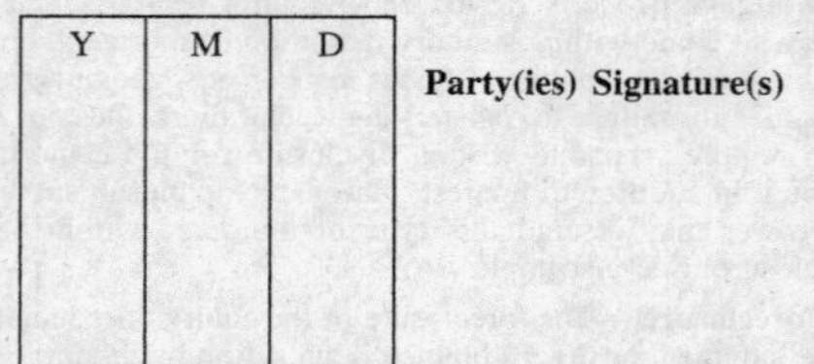

Y	M	D

OFFICER CERTIFICATION:

Your signature constitutes a representation that you are a solicitor, notary public or other person authorized by the *Evidence Act*, R.S.B.C. 1979, c. 116, to take affidavits for use in British Columbia and certifies the matters set out in Part 5 of the *Land Title Act* as they pertain to the execution of this instrument.

* If space insufficient, enter "SEE SCHEDULE" and attach schedule in Form E.

Chattel Mortgages.—See topic Chattel Mortgages.

MOTOR VEHICLES:

Motor Vehicle Act (c. 288).

General regulation of registrations and licenses are under Superintendent of Motor Vehicles.

Vehicle License and Registration.—Shall register motor vehicle, obtain license and obtain certificate of insurance before use or operation on highway. (§§3-3.1). Exception: foreign motor vehicles subject to certain conditions. (§20).

Operators' License.—(See §§22-24.2.) Operator's license of a class appropriate to age of driver and category of motor vehicle driven required and issued after examination, usually for five year periods. (§55). For suspension of licenses see §§82-113. License must be carried while driving and produced to peace officer on demand. (§30). Operators subject to reexamination. (§25). Minors over 16 and under 19 may, on application by parent or guardian, be licensed, but Superintendent may dispense with requirement for application. (§28). Tourists or new residents licensed in place of residence generally exempt for six months. (§31). Point system is in effect allowing suspension of license under certain terms. See subhead Insurance, infra.

Members of Armed Forces.—Motor Vehicle Act provides exemptions from fees for certain disabled past or present members of armed forces. (§3[6]).

Sales.—Notice of transfer must be signed by seller and purchaser in prescribed form and transmitted within ten days of transfer to Superintendent of Motor Vehicles for registration. (§16). Registration of transfer will be refused unless transferee has paid all monies due under Act, Insurance (Motor Vehicle) Act (c. 204) and Social Service Tax Act (c. 388) in respect to every vehicle owned by him. (§16[5]). Bills of sale or chattel mortgages dealing with motor vehicles must be filed. Registration is not proof of ownership. See topic Personal Property Security.

Identification Marks.—Penalty for removal or obliteration of engine or serial number without written permission of Superintendent of Motor Vehicles. Buying, selling, exchanging or dismantling vehicles without legible serial numbers prohibited. (§§53-54).

Operations prohibited by person whose license is suspended or whose blood alcohol level exceeds 80 milligrams per 100 millilitres of blood. (§§88, 92, 92.1, 94, 220.1). See also criminal (federal) provisions which prohibit being in care and control of motor vehicle while over .08.

Size and Weight Limits.—Regulated by Regulations Pursuant to Motor-Vehicle Act, consolidated June 1995.

Lights Required.—Regulated by Regulations Pursuant to Motor-Vehicle Act, consolidated June 1995.

Equipment Required.—Regulated by Regulations Pursuant to Motor-Vehicle Act, consolidated June 1995.

Seat Belts.—With few exceptions, any motor vehicle sold or operated must be equipped with seat belts. Except in very limited circumstances, every person in motor vehicle must wear seat belt. (§217).

Pollution control devices required by regulation on vehicles manufactured after Jan. 1, 1971. (§§45 to 45.3).

Accidents.—Driver must remain at scene, render assistance and give in writing to other driver or those injured and on request to peace officer or witness: name and address of driver and owner, license number of vehicle, particulars of liability insurance or financial responsibility or such information as is requested. (§62). Where unattended vehicle involved driver must leave conspicuous written notice of required particulars. Driver must make reasonable efforts to find and notify owner where property damaged. (§62). Driver must report accident as soon as possible, and at most within 24 hours, to police officer in city municipalities or other municipalities, or if accident did not occur in municipality as soon as possible, and at most within 48 hours to nearest police officer. Such reports are made for police use only and without prejudice in civil actions. (§61).

Owner liable for penalties or fines under statutory regulations governing motor vehicles where vehicle driven by owner or another with owner's permission and is liable for negligence of others who obtain possession of it with consent of owner (consent is deemed in case of family members living together). (§§79 to 81).

Gratuitous Passengers.—Legislation making owner or driver liable for death of, injury to or damage suffered by guest only in event of driver's gross negligence has been repealed. Standard of care now same for all.

Insurance or Proof of Financial Responsibility.—Under Insurance (Motor Vehicle) Act (c. 204) all drivers must have driver's certificate purchased each year, which certificate provides for $200,000 as of Jan. 1, 1985 third party liability and no-fault accident benefits. There is basic licence fee and additional premiums charged where driver has poor record. For vehicle coverage limits and accident benefits refer to Insurance (Motor Vehicle) Act Revised Regulations (1984). For limits of coverage see Schedule 3 of regulations.

No person shall drive a motor vehicle unless insured under valid motor vehicle liability insurance policy or having required proof of financial responsibility. Motor vehicle liability insurance card or financial responsibility card must be carried when driving and produced to peace officer on request.

Amount.—Regulated by regulations pursuant to Insurance (Motor Vehicle) Act.

Reciprocity.—Where the license of a person has been suspended in any part of Canada or the United States under violations analogous to the British Columbia statute, the Superintendent of Provincial Police may suspend any such license issued by the province.

Certain states of the U. S. and provinces of Canada have reciprocal arrangements with British Columbia for filing proof of financial responsibility, and issuance of motor vehicle liability insurance cards.

Insurance.—Valid insurance or financial responsibility card are compulsory. Partial system of accident or "no fault" insurance is compulsory.

New accident benefit provisions for insured in motor vehicle liability policies call for notice to insured's own insurer within 30 days of accident. Statute and schedules should be checked in each instance.

See Topical Index in front part of this volume.

MOTOR VEHICLES . . . *continued*

Insurance (Motor Vehicle) Act, (c. 204) empowers Insurance Corporation of British Columbia (see topic Insurance) to engage in all aspects of motor vehicle insurance including universal compulsory automobile insurance plan. Act provides that all motor vehicles registered or licensed in Province shall be insured under motor vehicle liability policy evidenced by driver's certificate (regs. §§42-51) or owner's certificate (regs. §§3-10). Minimum limits of coverage together with extended coverage and basic premiums together with extra premiums are set by regulations. Method of administration, appointment of agents (§15) and adjustors, claims, limitation of actions (two years generally, one year for claims against Insurance Corporation of British Columbia directly with applicable notification periods), uninsured motorist coverage, hit and run coverage and subrogation are set out in Act.

Act specifies that, before application for a permit or license for a vehicle or trailer, or before application for a driver's license, applicant shall apply for and shall pay for required insurance coverage evidenced by an owner's or driver's certificate (§39). Act also provides penalties, including suspension of vehicle permit or license and suspension of driver's license for failure to comply with Act. Act also provides that insurance coverage ceases on cancellation of permit or licence; e.g., suspension of driver's license on conviction of impaired driving results in cancellation of driver's certificate evidencing motor vehicle insurance coverage (§40).

Insurance (Motor Vehicle) Act, provides for Insurance Corporation of British Columbia to indemnify innocent victims of uninsured or unidentified drivers and Insurance Corporation of British Columbia is then subrogated to rights of person paid and empowered to sue uninsured motorist for amount paid.

Underinsured motorist protection is available to allow injured insured to claim against Insurance Corporation of British Columbia up to insured's own policy limits. Rights may be enforced by arbitration rather than litigation. See §§148.1 to 148.7 of regulations.

Foreign vehicle coming within province must, within 30 days thereafter be registered with Superintendent, or government agent, or person authorized who issues certificate unless used only for touring purposes in which case time limit is six months. This is not required for duly licensed car entering from U.S., where owner obtains, and produces on request, customs permit. Limited to period of reciprocal privileges or as set out in certificate.

Actions Against Nonresidents.—No special provisions with respect to mode of commencement except where proof of financial responsibility has been furnished. See subhead Insurance or Proof of Financial Responsibility, supra.

Direct Actions.—Where plaintiff is successful in action against insured driver he may enforce his judgment directly against defendant's insurer even if insured defendant was in breach of policy at time of accident. If insured was in breach insured is liable to reimburse insurer. (c. 204, §20).

Negligence.—See topic Negligence.

Penalties.—Unless specified in relevant sections, penalties are governed by Offence Act, including fines up to $2,000 and six months imprisonment, or both. However, majority of traffic violations now result in Traffic Violation Report. Reports carry specified demerit points which are registered against driver's license. When driver has accumulated prescribed number of points, Superintendent of Motor Vehicles may suspend license. Reports are served on violator who may dispute allegations. Dispute must be determined by judge. Six month suspension of driver's license is mandatory by superintendent for conviction of impaired driving.

Motor Vehicle Act (c. 288) provides complete code for driving and walking on public highways. Inter alia: Generally pedestrians have right of way in crosswalks; drivers required to give signals as to turns, stops, or decreasing speed; mandatory use of seat belts; speed limits, generally 50 km/h (30 mph) in municipalities and 80 km/h (50 mph) on highways outside municipalities with some 90 and 100 km/h (55 and 60 mph) zones; also provision for school zones, playgrounds, etc.; driving without due care and attention is an offense; traffic on right has right of way at intersection.

Motor vehicle carriers regulated by Minister of Public Works. Under Motor Carrier Act (c. 286) must have special license, and when operated over fixed route must have certificate approving time schedule. Liable for negligent damage to highways. Specific offences listed in §54. Foreign vehicle operating on regular route must have provincial license and permit.

All Terrain Vehicles.—Prohibits operation of all terrain vehicles without certificate of registration. Provides rules for operation, necessary equipment, accident reporting and registration. (c. 289).

Motor Dealers.—Prohibits carrying on business as motor dealer without registration (c. 287, §3). Registrar may refuse to register, cancel, or suspend motor dealers for poor conduct or lack of financial responsibility subject to appeal to commission (§§5-8). Registrar has authority to make orders respecting dealing with assets and to apply for appointment of receiver (§§16, 17).

Aircraft.—See Canada Law Digest, topic Aircraft.

Gasoline Tax.—See topic Taxation.

See also topic Chattel Mortgages.

NEGLIGENCE:

Common law rules apply generally. Modified by Statute as to certain liabilities such as in Good Samaritan Act, c. 155, Motor Vehicle Act, c. 288, Negligence Act, c. 298 and Occupiers Liability Act, c. 303.

Contributory Negligence.—C. 298 provides for apportionment of liability according to degree of fault. "Fault" is not limited to negligence, but includes intentional torts. May also include breach of contract. Unless court otherwise directs, costs follow degrees of liability.

NEGOTIABLE INSTRUMENTS:

See Canada Law Digest, topic Bills and Notes.

NOTARIES PUBLIC: (S.B.C. 1981, c. 23).

Canadian citizen or permanent resident may apply to Supreme Court under applicable rules to be enrolled as notary public. (§4). Number of notaries is limited by district (§5) and applicants may be required to pass examination (§6). Lieutenant Governor in Council may appoint certain other persons notaries during pleasure. (§12). Members of Law Society of British Columbia are ex officio notaries public. (§13).

Powers and Duties.—Notary may: (a) Draw instruments relating to property which are intended, permitted or required to be registered, recorded or filed in registry or other public office, contracts, charter parties and other mercantile instruments in province; (b) draw and supervise execution of wills of following classes: (i) wills by which testator directs his estate to be distributed immediately on death, (ii) wills that provide that where beneficiaries named in will predecease testator there is gift over to alternative beneficiaries vesting immediately on death of testator, (iii) wills that provide for assets of deceased to vest in beneficiary or beneficiaries as members of class not later than date when beneficiary or beneficiaries or youngest of class attains majority; (c) attest or protest all commercial or other instruments brought before him for attestation or public protestation; (d) draw affidavits, affirmations or statutory declarations that may or are required to be administered, sworn, affirmed or made by law of province, another province of Canada, Canada or another country; (e) administer oaths; and (f) perform duties authorized by Act of Legislature. (§15).

Discipline.—§21 creates discipline committee and §17 provides for Special Fund for purpose of reimbursement of pecuniary loss sustained by reason of misappropriation or wrongful conversion by member in his capacity as member. §17.1 provides for annual increase of Special Fund.

PARTITION:

Partition of Property Act. (c. 311, §2). Action of partition in respect of lands lies in Supreme Court. All joint tenants, tenants in common, co-parceners, mortgagees or other creditors having liens and all other parties interested in lands may be compelled to make or suffer partition of land. Court may order partition or division of lands or order sale and division of proceeds among parties entitled, according to their respective interests. (§§2, 6 and 7). Interested parties may, with court approval, bid at such sales. (§10). Court has very wide discretion.

PARTNERSHIP:

General partnerships, limited partnerships and proprietorships come within Partnership Act. (c. 312). Rules of equity and common law continue in force except where inconsistent with Act. (§91).

Formation.—Partnership is relationship which subsists between persons carrying on business in common with view of profit and need not be formed by written agreement. (§2). All persons associated in partnership for trading, manufacturing, or mining purposes must file declaration in prescribed form with Registrar of Companies within three months of formation of firm. (§§81, 82). There is no need to file general partnership agreement. Also see subhead Limited Partnership, infra.

Name.—Registrar of Companies may refuse registration of partnership or proprietorship declaration or limited partnership certificate that contains business name which he disapproves of, or in his opinion is likely to confuse or mislead, and must refuse registration if it is name of corporation, unless corporation consents. (§89). Also see subhead Limited Partnership, infra.

Rights and liabilities of partners inter se may be fixed or varied by agreement, but if not so agreed to are determined by Act. (§27). Partners are required to act in utmost fairness and good faith. (§22). If no fixed term for duration of partnership has been agreed to any partner may by notice determine partnership. (§29).

Rights and Liabilities of Partners as to Third Persons.—Common law rules of agency generally apply as to authority of partner to bind firm. (§7). Every partner is jointly liable for all debts and obligations of firm incurred while he is partner. (§11).

Change in Membership.—Persons dealing with partnership are entitled to continue to treat all apparent members of partnership as partners after change in membership until person has notice of change. Advertisement in B.C. Gazette is notice of change so advertised to persons who had no prior dealings with partnership. (§39). Also declaration is to be filed with Registrar of Companies for each change or alteration in partnership. (§83).

Dissolution.—Act sets out circumstances where partnership will be dissolved subject to agreement. (§35). In certain other circumstances court must or may order dissolution regardless of agreement (§§36-38). Public Notice may be made of dissolution. (§40). Also declaration in prescribed form may be filed with Registrar of Companies. (§86).

Proprietorship.—Every person engaged in business for trading, manufacturing, or mining purposes, who is not associated in partnership but uses some name or designation other than his own as his business name or uses some name indicating plurality of members in his business must file declaration in prescribed form with Registrar of Companies within three months from time name is first used. (§88).

Limited Partnership.—Part 3 sets out comprehensive provisions dealing with limited partnerships. Limited partnership comprising general and limited partners may be formed upon filing certificate with Registrar of Companies complying with §51. Limited partnership in effect prior to Nov. 24, 1978, may be brought within Part 3 upon registration of such certificate, but otherwise shall continue to be governed by Act in force prior to such date. (§79).

Name of limited partnership must end with words "Limited Partnership" in full or French language equivalent and generally may not include corporate name of limited partner. (§53). Limited partnership must maintain registered office within Province where certain records are to be maintained. (§54). Limited partnership formed in any other Province or territory of Canada, State of U. S. A. or U. K. is eligible for registration in British Columbia. (§80 and Reg. 524/78, as am'd).

Actions.—Partnerships and proprietorships may sue or be sued in firm name. (Rules of Court, R.7).

Forms.—See end of Digest.

PERPETUITIES:

Modern rule against perpetuities applies as amended by provisions of Perpetuity Act. (c. 321, §2).

Modern Rule Against Perpetuities.—Common law rule which may be summarized as follows: Every limitation of property must vest, if at all, within life or lives in being plus 21 years plus period of gestation.

Perpetuity Act (c. 321).—Modifies modern rule by: (a) Permitting alternative fixed period not exceeding 80 years (§3); (b) introducing "wait-and-see" rule providing that no contingent interest is void merely because interest may vest beyond perpetuity period (§4); (c) contingent interest capable of vesting within or beyond perpetuity period presumed valid until actual events establish interest is incapable of vesting within perpetuity period, whereupon (subject to §§7 [reduction of age], 8 [exclusion of class members] or 9 [cy-pres]) it becomes void (§5); (d) substituting lower age where gift is contingent on beneficiary attaining age greater than 21 and gift would be void as incapable of vesting within perpetuity period (§7).

Act applies only to instruments taking effect after Act came into force on Jan. 1, 1979, except as provided. (§25).

Options.—Perpetuity period is 80 years. (§18).

Old Rule Against Perpetuities.—Prohibiting disposition, after life interest to unborn person, of interest in property to unborn child or other issue of unborn person. Sometimes called rule against double possibilities or rule in Whitby v. Mitchell is abolished. (§2).

Accumulations Act, 1967.—Repealed with effect from Jan. 1, 1979 by Perpetuities Act. (S.B.C. 1975, c. 53, §24).

PERSONAL PROPERTY SECURITY:

Personal Property Security Act.—S.B.C. 1989 (c. 36) ("PPSA"). PPSA repeals Chattel Mortgage Act, Sale of Goods on Condition Act and Book Accounts Assignment Act and integrates all secured personal property transactions under one statute.

PPSA applies to every transaction that in substance creates "security interest", defined generally in §1 of Act as interest in collateral that secures payment or performance of obligation and to certain others that do not secure payment or performance of obligation. (§3). Security interests are usually created by security agreements signed by debtor. For security interest to be enforceable against third party, collateral must either be in possession of secured party or debtor must have signed security agreement. (§10). Chattel mortgage, to extent that it secures payment or performance of obligation, is clearly within scope of PPSA. (§2).

Registration.—All transactions creating security interests in personal property, including chattel mortgages, may be registered in Personal Property Registry, centralized computerized registry created by PPSA. PPSA creates notice filing system. Rather than filing security agreement itself, secured parties may file financing statement setting out essential details of transaction. (§43). Collateral must be described in accordance with Act and Regulations. Security agreement should be retained by secured party who is required to provide copy of it to debtor or other persons set out in §18 on request.

Chattel mortgages previously registered under Chattel Mortgage Act are deemed to be registered and perfected under PPSA. (§78). Registered and perfected status of such chattel mortgages continues for three years after PPSA comes into force, or for unexpired portion of original registration, whichever period is shorter. (§78). Transition financing statements may be used to re-register chattel mortgages that were previously registered under Chattel Mortgage Act.

There is no time limit for filing financing statement. In fact, financing statement can be filed before security agreement is executed (§43), and can be effective for future financings to same debtor secured by same collateral. Registration fees may be payable. (§43).

Renewal.—Financing statements may be registered for any period of time under PPSA. Registration is effective for period indicated on financing statement and may be renewed by registering financing change statement before registration expires, subject to certain exceptions. (§§35[7] and 44).

Priorities.—Subject to certain exceptions (§§27-32, 34, 36, 39, and 77-78) methods for determining priorities under PPSA are set out in §35. Attachment (§§12, 13) and perfection (§19) are key concepts in determining priorities among secured and unsecured creditors under PPSA. Chattel mortgage like any other security interest may be perfected under PPSA by possession (§24), registration (§25) or temporarily (§§5, 7, 26, 29[4] and 78), and priority generally goes to first party to perfect its security interest.

Remedies.—Part 5 of PPSA deals with rights and remedies of both debtor and secured party in event of default under security agreement. Remedies available to secured party, subject to certain qualifications with respect to consumer goods, include right to seize and sell goods, upon giving proper notice (20 days) to debtor and other interested parties. (§59). Act provides debtor with rights of redemption and reinstatement (consumer goods only) with respect to security agreement. (§62).

If collateral under security agreement is taken in consumer goods secured party may either seize or sue, but not both. (§67). However, secured party cannot seize consumer goods if debtor has paid at least two-thirds of total amount of obligation secured. (§58[3]).

PLEADING:

Pleading is governed by Supreme Court Rules, and is defined in Rules as including statement of claim, statement of defence, reply, counterclaim, statement of defence to counterclaim, third party notice, statement of defence to third party notice and in divorce proceeding, includes petition for divorce, answer and answer and counter-petition. (Supreme Court Rules, R. 1).

Pleadings Generally.—Pleadings must be brief statements of material facts alleged, but not evidence. Alternative allegations are permitted. In pleadings after statement of claim, party shall plead specifically any matter of fact or law that allegedly makes claim or defence of opposite party not maintainable, or might take other party by surprise if not specifically pleaded, or raises issues of fact not arising out of preceding pleading. Particulars of any matter set out in pleading may be requested in writing by any party and if not supplied, may be ordered by court. Any allegation of fact not denied is taken as admitted, except as against infant or mentally incompetent person. (Supreme Court Rules, R. 19).

Statement of Claim.—Statement of claim may be endorsed upon writ of summons or may be delivered as separate document, but must be delivered within 21 days after appearance. Statement of claim must be dated and show relief sought and proposed place of trial. (Supreme Court Rules, R. 8, 20).

Statement of Defence and Counterclaim.—Where appearance entered, statement of defence and counterclaim if any must be filed and delivered within 14 days after time limited for appearance, or from delivery of statement of claim, whichever is later. While general denial permitted, statement of defence must deny specifically some matter of fact in action on bill of exchange, promissory note, cheque or money due under contract. (Supreme Court Rules, R. 21).

Third-Party Procedure.—Where defendant claims indemnity contribution, or other relief relating to original action and substantially same relief claimed by plaintiff or there is issue relating to original subject matter which should also be determined as to plaintiff and defendant and third party, third party notice may be served on that person. (Supreme Court Rules, R. 22). Plaintiff should not be prejudiced by third party proceedings and court may set aside notice or impose terms to prevent prejudice or delay. (Supreme Court Rules, R. 22).

Reply.—Plaintiff may not file reply that is simple joinder of issue, and if no reply filed within seven days after delivery of statement of defence, joinder of issue on that defence is implied. (Supreme Court Rules, R. 23).

Amendment.—Pleading may be amended by party once without leave before notice of trial has been delivered, and at any time by written consent of all parties or with leave of court. (Supreme Court Rules, R. 24).

Striking Out Pleading.—Court may order pleading to be struck out if it discloses no reasonable claim or defence, is unnecessary, scandalous, frivolous or vexatious, may prejudice, embarrass or delay fair trial or is otherwise abuse of process of court. (Supreme Court Rules, R. 19).

Points of Law.—Demurrers have been abolished, but party may raise any point of law in his pleadings, which then may be disposed of on application before trial, or at trial. (Supreme Court Rules, R. 19, 34).

Default of Pleading.—See topic Judgments, subhead Default Judgments.

PLEDGES:

The law relating to pledges is in general governed by common law rules.

The Pawnbrokers Act (c. 314) only applies to transactions in which amount involved is less than $50.

PRACTICE:

Practice is governed by Court Rules Act, Supreme Court Act and Rules, Court of Appeal Act and Rules, Small Claims Act, Provincial Court Act, Criminal Appeal Rules and Adult Guardianship Act.

See topics Actions; Affidavits; Appeal and Error; Attachment; Certiorari; Costs; Courts; Depositions; Executions; Garnishment; Injunctions; Judgments; Motor Vehicles; Pleading; Process; Witnesses.

Discovery.—See topic Depositions.

PRINCIPAL AND AGENT:

In general, and apart from statute, the law of agency is the same as in England and in the United States.

Powers of Mercantile Agent.—Sale or pledge by agent in possession with consent of owner when agent acts in ordinary course of business is valid and binding if purchaser acts in good faith without notice of agent's lack of authority. Disposition of goods or documents of title by agent valid if person taking under disposition did not know of termination of agency. Possession of documents of title to goods pursuant to possession of goods themselves deemed to be with consent of owner. Consent of owner of goods presumed at all times in absence of evidence to contrary. (c. 370, §58). §58 does not apply to consignment to which Personal Property Security Act applies. (§57.1). See also topic Factors.

Real estate agents must be licensed and must plead their license in actions for recovery of commission. Required to keep records of all transactions. Real Estate Council responsible for disciplinary actions. License forfeited if agent does not carry on business for five years. Promises to resell or to purchase or to procure mortgage or loan forbidden unless agent delivers signed statement. Agent must deliver profit/loss statements to purchaser of business. Licensees forbidden to acquire real estate, directly or indirectly for themselves or associated persons, except by way of mortgage, unless full disclosure made to vendor. Payment of commissions to unlicensed agents prohibited. (c. 356).

Insurance agents and adjusters must also be licensed. (c. 200).

Travel Agents.—All travel agents must be registered with Registrar of Travel Services. Money received for prepaid services to be held in trust and paid out only upon service being provided. Money cannot be pledged and is not subject to execution or attachment. Proprietor, at least one partner or one director must be resident in British Columbia. Act establishes "Travel Assurance Board" to regulate industry. Compulsory payments are made by agency into Travel Assurance Fund. Claimants under Act receive money upon Board's recommendation with approval of Minister. (c. 409).

Powers of Attorney.—Attorney's power deemed to continue after termination by revocation or operation of law if such unknown to attorney. Regularizes transactions of persons dealing with attorney even if power revoked provided neither person nor attorney know of revocation. (c. 334). Mental infirmity will be dealt with by Representation Agreement Act when it is proclaimed. (S.B.C. 1993, c. 67). Powers of attorney by which lands are to be affected must comply with following provisions (c. 219) namely:

In every case in which any instrument produced for registration in Land Title Office has been executed by attorney under power of attorney, power of attorney with proof of

See Topical Index in front part of this volume.

PRINCIPAL AND AGENT . . . *continued*
execution, or copy thereof duly certified to be true copy by Registrar, or Registrar of Companies, in whose office original is filed, shall be filed in office of Registrar, and registration of instrument shall not be effected until power of attorney, or duly certified copy thereof, has been delivered to Registrar for filing. (c. 219, §51).

Provided that when the power of attorney has been executed or filed or deposited in any province or country the laws of which require that the original power of attorney shall be filed or deposited with the officer preparing the same or with some other officer or a court, then a copy of the power of attorney accompanied by a certificate or other evidence that the original has been so filed or deposited according to law, and duly certified to be a true copy by the officer under his seal of office, or evidenced as such by the seal of the court, may be filed in lieu of the original. (c. 219, §51).

Every person appointed attorney for execution of any instrument requiring to be registered under Land Title Act must be of full age of 19 years at time of his appointment, and proof of that fact must be made to Registrar at time of filing power of attorney. Land title offices require also statutory declaration by attorney in prescribed form to effect that he had not at time of execution of instrument received any notice or information of revocation of power by death or otherwise. §56(1) of Land Title Act provides that for purpose of Land Title Act power of attorney filed in Land Title Office is not valid after three years after date of its execution. This does not apply to power of attorney executed by corporation, power of attorney referred to in §7(1) of Power of Attorney Act that is filed under §51 of Land Title Act, or to power of attorney which expressly excludes §56(1) of Land Title Act.

Security Businesses.—Persons engaged in security business (i.e., alarm service, armoured car service, locksmith, private investigator, security consultant, or security patrol) and employees must be licensed and carry identification cards. Licensees forbidden to act as debt collectors. Provisions for suspension and cancellation of licenses. Fines and penalties for violations. (S.B.C. 1980, c. 45).

Collection Agencies.—Collection agents, collectors and bailiffs (all defined in Act) are prohibited from acting as agents for collection of debts unless licenced under Act. Terms of application for and granting or refusing to grant licence (subject to appeal) are set out. Audits are mandatory and required records and books are open to inspection under Act. Numerous specified unreasonable collection practices are prohibited and Act provides for prosecution and penalties for failure to comply. Fees and charges are prescribed. (c. 88).

Credit Reporting Act requires all reporting agencies to register with Registrar of Reporting Agencies. Act sets out qualifications for registration and extensive regulations governing furnishing of information and keeping of records. Disclosure required to subject upon written request. Penalties for failure to comply. Subject upon suit recovers statutory minimum of $100. (c. 78).

Employment Agencies.—Any person operating employment agency must be registered under Act. Registration must be renewed annually. Act prohibits charging of fees to persons seeking employment. Agency must maintain specified records. (S.B.C. 1980, c. 10, Part 10).

Inferior Courts.—Agents in certain rare cases and subject to discretion of judge may appear even if not enrolled as barrister provided: (a) Name is on Provincial list of voters; (b) there is not more than one member of Law Society in actual practice in municipality; (c) there is not more than one member of Law Society practicing in court with place of business within eight kilometers of place court sits. (c. 73).

PROCESS:

Service of Writ or Petition.—On individual, must ordinarily be personal (Rules of Court, R.11); where this is impractical substituted service, such as by publication or posting, may be ordered (R.12). Service on corporation may be done by leaving copy with chief officer or agent of corporation, or with city or municipal clerk, or of any branch or agency of corporation in province, or according to Company Act, c. 59, or any act relating to service of process. (R.11). Service on infant according to Infants Act, c. 196. Service on mentally incompetent person by personally serving committee or, if none, person with whom mentally incompetent person is residing, or person caring for mentally incompetent person, or person appointed by Court or Public Trustee. (R.11). Where party is not served and enters appearance, service is deemed as of that date. (R. 11).

Service on party outside Province as of right in circumstances set out in Rules of Court (R.13[1]) or with leave of court otherwise (R.13[3]).

Time of Service.—Service after 4 o'clock in afternoon is deemed effective on next day that is not holiday (R.3[1]).

Times for Appearance.—Seven days for party served in B.C., 21 days in Canada, 28 days in U.S., 42 days elsewhere (R.13[6], 14[3]). Court may shorten time for persons outside of British Columbia if ex parte application (R.13[6]).

Who May Serve.—Generally, process may be served by any person. There may be certain statutory provisions covering certain instances. It would appear that no person should serve process while acting in a judicial capacity.

Proof of Service.—Affidavit of service or delivery shall state when, where, how and by whom service or delivery effected. (R.11[7]).

Nonresident Motorist.—See topic Motor Vehicles.

See also topic Practice.

PROOF OF CLAIMS:

See topics Executors and Administrators; Pleading.

RAILROADS:

Intra-provincial railways governed by provincial law. No company has capacity to operate railway as common carrier except as authorized by provincial cabinet. (c. 59, §21). Railway Act, c. 354 governs intra-provincial railway companies.

See topic Carriers.

REAL PROPERTY:

Torrens System created under Land Title Act. (c. 219). Note also Property Law Act. (c. 339). Real estate industry regulated under Real Estate Act. (c. 356).

Joint tenancy, tenancy in common and leasehold interests are recognized. Tenancy in common is presumed unless the intent to create a joint tenancy is clearly shown (c. 340, §11[1]). Estates tail are abolished. (c. 340, §10).

Rule in Shelley's Case.—Applicability not decided by courts.

Foreign Conveyances or Encumbrances.—If not executed according to Provincial laws may not be capable of registration, although may be valid inter partes.

Condominiums permitted under Condominium Act. (c. 61). Common property, e.g., gardens, hallways, etc., is vested in strata corporation. Common property shall be held by owners as tenants in common in shares proportional to unit entitlement of their strata lots. Share in common property shall not be dealt with separately from strata lot of owner. (§12). Ownership of airspace parcels allowed for, may be dealt with in same manner as other land registered under Land Title Act. (c. 219, Part 9). Strata corporation has certain statutory duties and rights as set out in legislation. (c. 61, §34). Rights and obligations of condominium owners set out in Condominium Act. (§§46, 72).

Zoning.—Lands within municipal or civic boundaries are subject to by-laws of particular city or municipality. Copies of by-laws may be obtained by writing to appropriate governing body.

Province is also divided into "regional districts." Any development of land within such district will require approval of regional district. Regional district may also have by-laws for area, even though it is in rural area. (Municipal Act, c. 290).

See also topics Chattel Mortgages, Deeds, Homesteads, Husband and Wife, Landlord and Tenant, Mobile Homes, Mortgages of Real Property, Partition, Records.

RECEIVERS:

When Appointment Proper.—Receiver or receiver-manager may be appointed under instrument or by court. (Law and Equity Act, c. 224). Court has power to appoint receiver in action to enforce floating charge debenture, foreclosure action, partnership action, on application of interested person under security agreement or in any other case where court is of opinion that property in question will be better conserved or administered by court than by litigants. Also, judgment creditor who has exhausted his legal remedies may apply for appointment of receiver by way of equitable execution.

A receiver of the future earnings of a judgment debtor will not be appointed.

Status, Duties and Powers.—Receiver-manager appointed under instrument is officer of corporation over whose assets appointment extends and not agent of person who appointed him, and he stands in fiduciary relationship to corporation. Receiver or receiver-manager appointed by court is officer of court and not of corporation and must act in accordance with directions of court; he cannot be sued in separate action in respect of acts done as receiver without leave first being obtained.

Bond.—A receiver is generally called upon to put up a bond when he is appointed.

Compensation.—Receiver or receiver-manager is entitled to remuneration; frequently on time basis but ultimately on quantum meruit basis.

Effect of Receivership.—Appointment of receiver does not change owner's interest or title in property. Affairs of owner have simply been taken out of his hands and entrusted to receiver or receiver-manager.

Actions.—Receiver appointed in court should obtain leave before suing or he may be forced to pay costs himself.

RECORDS:

Ownership of land must be registered in land title office in district in which land is situate. Registration is under Torrens system and, except inter partes, legal title is not acquired until actual registration. (Land Title Act, c. 219, §20). Charges take priority according to time of registration subject to contrary intention appearing from instrument. (§28). Judgments, pending litigation and caveats may be registered. All deeds are deposited in title office and retained there. Large majority of titles are now Torrens titles, although some older titles still remain under old system but on any transfer thereof are required to come in under new system.

Where person appears on title as registered owner, province guarantees, subject to certain exceptions, that title is as shown on register, and charge against land must be registered in order to constitute notice. (§§23 and 29 Land Title Act).

See also topic Real Property.

Vital Statistics.—Provision is made for registration of births, deaths, marriages and adoptions with District Registrars and in some cases with the Director of Vital Statistics, Victoria, British Columbia. Certificates generally are obtained from Director. (c. 425).

Fee for each certificate or photo copy issued is $25 per copy including search fee, which covers one three-year period. Fee of $55 is charged when 24 hour search service is offered or requested. All enquiries should be made to offices of Director of Vital Statistics, 818 Fort Street, Victoria, B.C., V8W 1H8, phone: (604)387-0041 or 605 Robson Street, Room 250, Vancouver, B.C., V6B 5J3, phone: (604)660-2937.

See also topic Chattel Mortgages.

REDEMPTION:

See topics Executions; Liens; Mortgages of Real Property; Taxation.

REPLEVIN:

In action for recovery of specific property, other than land, court may, where it considers just and on any terms as to security or otherwise it considers just, order person from whom recovery of property is claimed to surrender it to claimant pending outcome of action. (c. 224, §52 and R. 42).

REPORTS:

Decisions of courts in province are covered for years 1867-1947 inclusive by British Columbia Reports and for years 1977 to present by British Columbia Law Reports; British Columbia cases are also reported (inter alia) in Western Weekly Reports, Dominion Law Reports, Canadian Bankruptcy Reports, Reports of Family Law, and other

See Topical Index in front part of this volume.

REPORTS . . . *continued*
national reports. Summaries of all written decisions since 1972 are provided in British Columbia Decisions, Civil Cases, Criminal Conviction Cases and Criminal Sentence Cases. Most decisions are available through Quicklaw on-line database service. Decisions of many boards, commissions and tribunals are also available through Quicklaw in databases for relevant subject area.

RESTRAINT OF TRADE:

See topic Monopolies and Restraint of Trade.

SALES:

Sale of Goods Act (c. 370) codifies many common law provisions.

Where there is a contract for the sale of specific goods, or where goods are subsequently appropriated to the contract, the seller, may by terms of contract or appropriation, reserve right of disposal of goods until certain conditions are fulfilled. (§24[1]). In such case, notwithstanding delivery of goods to buyer, or to carrier or other bailee for purpose of transmission to buyer, property in goods does not pass to buyer until conditions imposed by seller are fulfilled. (§24[2]). Where goods are shipped, and by bill of lading goods are deliverable to order of seller or his agent, seller is prima facie deemed to reserve right of disposal. (§24[3]). Where seller of goods draws on buyer for price, and transmits bill of exchange and bill of lading to buyer together, to secure acceptance or payment of bill of exchange, buyer is bound to return bill of lading if he does not honor bill of exchange, and if he wrongfully retains bill of lading property in goods does not pass to him. (§24[4]).

Conditions, which are contained in a contract for retail sale of new goods, purporting to negative or diminish conditions or warranties under Act are severable from contract and void, or if collateral or contemporaneous agreement or contract are void. (§20[2]).

Bills of Sale.—Where physical possession is taken by purchaser of any personal property there is no necessity for bill of sale. Where physical possession is not taken bill of sale is taken from vendor and may be registered as set out in Personal Property Security Act, c. 321.5. (§§42-49).

There is no statutory form for a bill of sale.

Product Liability.—Common Law principles apply, privity not required where negligent manufacture and no opportunity for inspection.

Conditional Sales in PPSA.—Conditional sales are regulated by Personal Property Security Act (c. 321.5) which is modelled on Article IX of Uniform Commercial Code. Subject to certain specific exclusions (§4), this Act is applicable to every transaction, without regard to its form and without regard to person who has title to collateral, that in substance creates security interest (§2[l]).

Effectiveness.—Subject to this and any other enactment, security agreement is effective according to its terms. (§9).

Enforceability.—Security interest is only enforceable against third party where collateral is in possession of secured party, or debtor has signed security agreement that contains (i) description of collateral by item or kind, (ii) statement that security interest is taken in all of debtor's present and after acquired personal property or (iii) statement that security interest is taken in all of debtor's present and after acquired property except specified items or kinds of personal property. (§10 [1]).

Registration.—Personal Property Registry established. (§42). Registration is by financing statements (§43), registration may relate to more than one security agreement (§43 [5]). Financing statement can be registered before security agreement is made and before security interest attached. (§43 [4]). As to duration, registration is normally effective for period of time indicated on financing statement by which registration is effected. (§44 [1]). As to renewal, registration may be renewed by registering financing change statement at any time before registration expires, and period of time for which registration is effective shall be extended by renewal period indicated on financing change statement. (§44 [2]). As to amendment, amendment to registration may be made by registering financing change statement at any time during period that registration is effective and amendment is effective from date financing change statement is registered to expiry of registration being amended. (§44 [3]). Where registered security interest is transferred, financing change statement that discloses transfer may be registered. (§45 [1]). If interest in part, but not all, of collateral is transferred, description of collateral must be included in financing change statement. (§45 [2]).

Default.—On default, under security agreement, secured party has right to enforce security agreement by any method permitted by law unless otherwise agreed. (§58 [2][a]). Where collateral is goods of kind that cannot be readily moved, secured party may seize or repossess collateral without removing it from debtor's premises, if secured party's interest is perfected by registration (§58 [2][b]), and may dispose of collateral on debtor's premises without causing any greater inconvenience to person in possession of premises (§58 [2][c]), and if collateral is document of title, secured party may proceed as to document or goods covered by it, and if license, secured party may seize license (§58 [2][d][e]). After two-thirds of contract price has been paid, seller cannot take possession of or seize consumer goods unless court order obtained. (§58 [3][4]).

Bulk Sales.—See topic Fraudulent Preferences and Conveyances.

Retail Credit Sales.—See topic Consumer Protection.

Consumer Protection.—See topic Consumer Protection.

Trade Practice Act.—(c. 406). Defines deceptive and unconscionable acts or practices (§§3 and 4) relating to consumer transactions and permits courts to restrain these practices (§18) and award damages to consumers suffering loss or damages as result thereof (§22). Establishes Director of Trade Practices to investigate consumer transactions, and who may initiate proceedings under act.

Pyramid Sales.—Former Pyramid Distribution Act, now Multilevel Marketing Regulation Act, strictly regulates pyramid-type sales and schemes. There are provisions for inspection of records (§6[2]), appointment of receivers (§10), injunctions and penalties (§§11 and 12). It is administered by Ministry of Consumer and Corporate Affairs. (c. 351).

Mobile Homes.—See topic Mobile Homes.

Trading Stamps.—Offer or use of trading stamps having redeemable value of less than 10¢ is prohibited. (c. 407, §3).

See also topic Contracts.

SALES TAX: See topic Taxation.

SEALS:

Seals not generally necessary, but use advisable. Contract under seal may not need consideration. Corporation may by instrument in writing under its corporate seal, empower person, in respect of specified matter or purpose, as its attorney, to execute deeds or documents on its behalf. (c. 334, §6[1]).

SECURITIES:

Securities Act (c. 380.1 as am'd by S.B.C. 1988, c. 58 and S.B.C. 1989, c. 78, S.B.C. 1990, c. 25, and S.B.C. 1992, c. 52) regulates trading in securities and also deals with takeover bids, trading by insiders, proxies and proxy soliciting, disclosure, and self regulatory bodies and stock exchanges. In this topic "r" means "regulation".

Trading in Securities.—

Registration.—No person (which throughout includes individual, corporation, partnership, party, trust, fund, association, any other organized group of persons, and personal or other legal representative of "person") shall trade in securities, act as underwriter, or advise others regarding trading in securities unless person is registered. (§20, r. 66, 68). Categories of registration are generally dealers and advisors and underwriters. Registrants are further classified within those categories, e.g., as broker—trading in securities as agent or principal; as security issuer—trading in securities of its own issue; as investment counsel—advising others regarding securities, (r. 13, 13.1, 14). Executive Director, being chief administrative officer of Commission (§7) and in some cases delegate of Executive Director, has discretion in granting registration and may refuse where applicant or any of its officers or directors is not resident in B.C. on date of application (§21). Registration may be subject to conditions imposed by Executive Director (§22) and is for period determined by Commission (r. 67). Act grants certain exemptions from registration, e.g., registration as advisor is not required by insurer, savings institution, Federal Business Development Bank or by certain professionals whose performance of services in this area is solely incidental to practice of their profession (§30); trade by executor or like person, authorized trustee, official receiver, receiver, sheriff, isolated trade not made by person whose usual business is trading in securities, trade by Federal Business Development Bank, savings institution or insurer, certain kinds of trade by bank or trust company and other trades which involve specified vendors or purchasers (§31); person may trade in bonds or other evidences of indebtedness guaranteed by government, certain negotiable promissory notes and other specified securities without being registered (§32). In addition, Executive Director may, if not prejudicial to public interest, order that §20 does not apply to any trade in any particular security or by particular person. (§33).

Prospectus.—Unless exempted under Act or regulations, no person may distribute security unless preliminary prospectus and prospectus respecting that security have been filed with, and receipts obtained for them from, Executive Director. (§§42[1], 46). Generally, first trade is distribution. (r. 133, 134). Preliminary prospectus and prospectus shall be in required form and shall provide full, true and plain disclosure of all material facts relating to securities issued and contain specific statements and comply with such other filing requirements as are imposed in discretion of superintendent. (§§42[2], 44, 45). Prospectus shall contain certificate signed by officers, directors, and promoter of issue as specified, and certificate signed by underwriter to knowledge, information and belief, that prospectus contains full, true and plain disclosure. (§§49, 50). In "waiting period", interval between issue of Executive Director's receipt for preliminary prospectus and issue of receipt for prospectus, issuer is limited to specific communications, giving out preliminary prospectus, and soliciting expressions of interest. (§61). From date of issue of receipt for prospectus, only prospectus and any document filed with it or referred to in it or used in §61(2)(a) may be given out. (§65). Similar exemptions to those for registration are granted in respect of filing prospectuses (§55). Executive Director is given power upon application of interested party or on his own motion to exempt from §42 person or class of persons and may also on application order that trade or class of trades is deemed to be distribution. (§59). Act requires person registered to trade in security to deliver latest prospectus to intended purchaser before written confirmation of sale agreement or not later than midnight on second business day after entering agreement but agreement is not binding if dealer receives written notification from purchaser of his intention not to be bound not later than two business days after purchaser's receipt of latest prospectus. (§66). Onus of proving that time for giving notice has expired is on dealer from whom purchaser is purchasing security. (§66[8]). No person shall distribute security under prospectus after 12 months have elapsed from later of date of issue of receipt for preliminary prospectus relating to security or date of last prospectus; this period may be shortened by Executive Director. Distribution may continue if new prospectus is filed and receipt is issued by Executive Director. (§51).

Trading Generally.—Act has broad disclosure requirements and in particular requires continuous disclosure of any "material change" (§67) and full financial disclosure (r. 135-143) subject to exemption order made in discretion of Commission (r. 143). With regard to financial disclosure, foreign companies carrying on business within B.C. are also regulated in this area by Company Act (c. 59) (see topic Corporations). No person may attend at or telephone to any residence for purpose of trading any security. (§34). No person may represent, in order to effect trade, that he will resell, repurchase or refund purchase price of security, give any undertaking with regard to its future price, or that it will be listed on any stock exchange. (§35). No person shall engage in any security transaction which creates misleading appearance of trading or is fraudulent (§41.1).

Take-Over Bids.—Act regulates take-over bids which are defined to mean offer to any person who is in B.C. or to any holder in B.C. of securities to purchase that number of equity or voting securities of class which together with offeror's securities of that class constitute in aggregate 20% or more of outstanding securities of class of securities of company, and includes shares acquired by persons acting jointly or in concert and shares acquired directly and indirectly. (§§74-79). Act sets framework of limitations

See Topical Index in front part of this volume.

SECURITIES . . . *continued*
within which acquisitions and sales of securities during bid may be made (§§83-86) and requires take-over bid circular or issuer bid circular to be sent with offer and directors circular to be sent within specified time and sets minimum contents (§§90-92). Act places further restrictions on acquisitions made by offerors and requires special reporting. (§§93-98). Again some exemptions to these requirements exist in specific circumstances for certain take-over bids (§80) and issuer bids (§81).

Insider Trading.—Act regulates insiders of and other persons having "special relationship" with all domestic companies and generally those foreign companies which either have filed prospectus with Executive Director (see subhead Trading in Securities, supra) or have their securities listed on any stock exchange wheresoever situate. Insider is any director or senior officer of issuer or of person that is itself insider or subsidiary of issuer, or person beneficially holding more than 10% of voting rights attached to issuer's outstanding voting securities. (§1). Senior officer includes all usual named officers of company and five highest paid employees of issuer inclusive of named officers. (§1). Associate includes partner, spouse, or child of, or other relative having common residence with insider or issuer in which insider beneficially owns more than 10% of voting rights attached to all outstanding voting securities. (§1). Further, person in "special relationship" includes insiders and also includes associates of reporting issuer, persons proposing to make takeover bid or specific business combinations, persons who have acquired knowledge through business relationship of material fact, material change, or intention to make take-over bid or issuer bid, and persons who have acquired such knowledge from another person in special relationship. (§3). Insiders are required to file initial report disclosing their beneficial ownership of any securities, such as shares, bonds, debentures, notes, of company within ten days of becoming insider (§70[2]), and thereafter within ten days after end of month in which any change occurs, further report detailing such change (§70[4]). No person in special relationship with issuer nor any person proposing to make takeover bid, to become party to specified business arrangements, or acquiring substantial portion of issuer's property shall make use of knowledge of material fact or material change, or communicate that knowledge (§68), or inform another person of intention to make take-over bid or issuer bid (§68), unless material fact or material change or intention has been generally disclosed. If person does not comply with these provisions, criminal or civil liability may arise (see subhead Miscellaneous, catchlines Enforcement and Liability, infra).

Proxy and Proxy Solicitation.—Act imposes upon all reporting issuers who give notice to security holders, including foreign companies which have filed prospectus with Superintendent (see subhead Trading in Securities, supra) or shares of which are listed on Vancouver Stock Exchange, requirement to send form of proxy and information circular in required form with any notice of meeting of shareholders (§101) and prescribes procedures for voting where proxies involved (§102). That part of Act does not apply if reporting issuer complies with law in jurisdiction where incorporated and that law is substantially similar to requirements in this part but Superintendent may exempt, in whole or in part, person from these requirements if there is conflict or if to do so would not be prejudicial to public interest. (§103). Domestic companies are regulated in this area by Company Act (see topic Corporations). Act makes provisions for holding and issuing of mutual funds and for trading by mutual fund insiders (§§105-113).

Miscellaneous.—

Commission.—Act establishes Commission known as British Columbia Securities Commission which is charged with administration of Act and may review decisions of Executive Director. (§§4, 147[2]).

Investigations and Audits.—Both Commission and Attorney-General may appoint person to make investigation (§§126, 131) and this person is given broad powers of investigation into affairs of any person and may on application to Supreme Court be granted: Power to enter premises, require production of records and property, and remove records and property for purposes of inspection, examination or analysis. (§127). Act also gives Commission following powers: power to order any person having control of safekeeping of any funds or securities of person under investigation to refrain from dealing with such funds or securities in any way; power to register notice against land and mining claims which has same effect as registration of lis pendens (§135); and power to apply to judge of Supreme Court for appointment of receiver, receiver manager or trustee of property of person being investigated (§136). Commission may also appoint person to carry out audit. (§137).

Appeals.—Executive Director or other person acting under authority delegated by Commission, shall notify Commission of decisions made. Commission may review decisions of their own accord, and any person directly affected is entitled to hearing and review upon written application. Further, any person directly affected by decision of Commission, other than decision under §§33 or 59, may appeal to Court of Appeal with leave. (§§147-149).

Enforcement.—Commission or Executive Director has power to order that individual cease trading either generally or in specific securities, resign or be prohibited from acting as director or officer, or order that any or all of exemptions described in §§30-32, 55, 58, 80 or 81 do not apply to person where considered to be in public interest. (§144). Commission or Executive Director has power to order that trading of specified security or exchange contract under specified prospectus be halted or that specific person or persons cease trading in specified security or exchange contract where person has failed to make statutory filings. (§146). Act also provides for criminal penalty for trading under §68, liability for fine of not less than profit made and up to triple profit made or $1,000,000. (§138). Further, upon application by Commission, Supreme Court may make compliance order requested or any order considered appropriate (§140) or Commission may file decision with Supreme Court and on being filed, decision will have effect of judgment of Supreme Court (§144.2). Commission or Superintendent may assess costs incurred by or on behalf of Commission in connection with hearing to those parties whose affairs are subject of hearing. (§154.2).

Liability.—Where prospectus contains misrepresentation, purchaser has right of action for damages or right of rescission against parties specified, including issuer, underwriter, every director of issuer at time prospectus filed and other persons who signed prospectus. (§114). Where bid circular contains misrepresentation, similar rights and liabilities arise. (§115). Where person in special relationship with issuer has knowledge of material fact or material change which has not been generally disclosed and makes use of that knowledge in buying or selling securities of issuer or in communicating material fact or material change, that person may be liable to compensate purchasers or sellers of securities; person will not be liable if he reasonably believed material fact or material change had been generally disclosed or it was known or ought reasonably to have been known by seller or purchaser. These requirements also apply to persons proposing takeover bid, who become party to certain business combinations and who acquire substantial portion of property of reporting issuer. Similar liability arises with respect to premature disclosure of material information. (§119). Where person in special relationship discloses intention to make take-over bid or issuer bid before it is generally disclosed, similar liability arises. (§119).

Local Policy Statements.—In many areas where Executive Director has broad discretionary powers, he issues from time to time statements referred to as blanket orders and rulings, which set out guidelines or framework within which he will either not exercise his discretion or do so favourably. These statements are of substantial assistance in complying with Act although they are not issued under any specific legislative authority.

SEQUESTRATION:

Sequestration is form of equitable execution. Rules of Court provide that order for payment of money into court and order for recovery or delivery of possession of any property other than land or money may be enforced by writ of sequestration. (R.42[2][4]). Writ of sequestration shall be issued only upon filing proof that order sought to be enforced has been served and has not been complied with. (R.42[12]). Writ of execution is defined to include writ of sequestration. (R.1[8] and c. 75, §42). This form of execution is rarely used in British Columbia.

Instead of sequestration, court may make order for detention, custody or preservation of any property that is subject matter of proceeding or to which question may arise and, for purpose of enabling order under this rule to be carried out, court may authorize person to enter upon any land or building. (Rules of Court, R. 46). See also topic Executions.

SERVICE: See topic Process.

STATUTE OF FRAUDS:

See topic Frauds, Statute of.

STATUTES:

Last revision of provincial statutes is Revised Statutes of British Columbia, 1979. Statutes passed at the most recent sittings of the Legislature are published annually.

STAY OF EXECUTION: See topics Courts; Executions.

SUBMISSION OF CONTROVERSY:

Any bona fide or justiciable controversy can be brought before proper court, which will dispose of it subject only to appeal. Frivolous, vexatious or theoretical matters will not be heard by courts.

SUPPLEMENTARY PROCEEDINGS:

See topic Executions.

SURETY AND GUARANTY COMPANIES:

No special legislation.

TAXATION:

The province is restricted to direct taxation. It taxes, with certain exceptions, all income and personal property within province, and all real property within province outside of municipalities.

The municipalities derive their revenue from the imposition of taxes upon land and by the collection of license fees and business taxes. See topic Licenses.

Real estate in unorganized territories coming under the provincial government is liable for sale immediately taxes are in default and the owner has one year from date of sale in which to redeem by payment of arrears and interest.

Real estate within municipalities is governed by the by-laws of each municipality which vary both with regard to when the property is liable to be sold and for how long after sale the property is open for redemption. However, all real estate situate within a municipality may be redeemed by payment of taxes and interest within one year after sale. Assessment of property values in Province provided by Assessment Act R.S.B.C. 1979, c. 21.

Income Tax.—(Income Tax Act, R.S.B.C. 1979, c. 190). Act requires that income tax must be paid for each year by every individual who is resident of British Columbia on last day of taxation year or, who, not being resident in British Columbia on last day of taxation year, had income earned in taxation year in British Columbia as defined by Act. Also, income tax must be paid for each year by every corporation that maintained permanent establishment in British Columbia at any time in year.

It appears that general intent of Provincial Income Tax Act would be to upset by as little as possible procedures and principles of Federal Income Tax Act.

Individual Income Tax.—Nonbusiness income of resident of Canada is taxable under Provincial Income Tax Act if individual resides in B.C. on last day of calendar year, or individual earns income in B.C. during taxation year. Nonbusiness income of nonresident of Canada is taxable under Provincial Income Tax Act if earned in B.C. Earned taxable income in B.C. for nonresidents of Canada is calculated using Federal Income Tax Act definitions. (§§114 and 115). Business income of both residents and nonresidents of Canada will be subject to tax under Provincial Income Tax Act to extent that income can be attributed to permanent establishment located in B.C. Tax payable by individuals on income earned in Province is 52.5% of federal tax payable (for 1993 and subsequent taxation years). For 1993, surtax is 20% of amount by which Provincial Income Tax payable exceeds $5,300, and 10% of amount by which that tax exceeds $9,000 before tax payable is added. For 1994 and subsequent taxation years, respective percentages of high income surtax will be increased to 30% and 20% respectively.

See Topical Index in front part of this volume.

TAXATION . . . *continued*

Corporations.—For 1993 and 1994 taxation years, general rate of Provincial income tax on corporation's taxable income is 16% for that part of taxation year that is on or before June 30, 1993 and 16.5% after July 1, 1993. For 1995 and subsequent taxation years, rate is 16.5%. However, small business rate is provincial tax of 10% on qualifying active business income.

Returns.—Return provisions of Federal Income Tax Act apply to filing of returns for provincial income tax. (§19). Return for each taxation year must be filed: (a) In case of corporation within six months from date of end of fiscal year; (b) in case of individual on or before Apr. 30 in next year; (c) in case of person who had died without making return, by his legal representatives within six months from day of death; (d) in case of estate or trust within 90 days from end of fiscal year.

Payment of Tax, Withholding.—Withholding provisions of Federal Income Tax Act apply to collection of provincial income tax. (§40[1]). Every person paying salary, wages or other remuneration to an officer or employee; or a superannuation or pension benefit; or a retiring allowance; or death benefit; or an amount as benefit under a supplementary unemployment benefit plan; or an annuity payment; or fees, commissions or other amounts for services; or payment under deferred profit sharing plan; or plan referred to in §147 of federal Act as revoked plan; or adult training allowance under National Training Act; or payment out of or under registered retirement savings plan or plan referred to in §146(12) of federal Act as "amended plan"; or amount as, on account or in place of payment of, or in satisfaction of, proceeds of surrender, cancellation or redemption of income averaging annuity contract; or payment out of or under registered retirement income fund, at any time in taxation year must deduct or withhold therefrom such amount as may be prescribed and must at such time as may be prescribed remit that amount to Provincial Minister on account of the payee's tax for year under provincial Act.

Company may be registered as "venture capital corporation", business of which is restricted to making investments in British Columbia in small businesses substantially engaged in manufacturing and processing, research and development, tourism, agriculture, provision of export oriented services or other prescribed business activities. The Small Business Venture Capital Act, §20(3) provides for issue of tax credit certificates to shareholders of venture capital corporations entitling each to tax credit equal to 30% of amount invested. Income Tax Act, c. 190, §8.3 provides for issue of venture capital tax credit certificates to individuals for deduction from tax payable to maximum of $60,000 each year. Corporations are not subject to $60,000 maximum.

Various provisions of Federal Income Tax Act apply mutatis mutandis in respect of payment of tax under Provincial Income Tax Act.

Objections to Assessments.—Taxpayer who objects to an assessment under Provincial Income Tax Act may within 90 days from day of mailing of notice of assessment serve notice of objection in prescribed form in duplicate on Provincial Minister.

Appeals.—Taxpayer who has served notice of objection to an assessment may appeal to Supreme Court of British Columbia to have the assessment vacated or varied after either (a) Provincial Minister has confirmed the assessment or reassessed, within 90 days of notice of confirmation or reassessment; or (b) 90 days have elapsed after service of notice of objection and Provincial Minister has not notified taxpayer that he has vacated or confirmed assessment or reassessed.

By agreement, all matters relating to administration and collection of provincial income tax are carried out by Federal government. One income tax return is made by taxpayer which return is sent to Federal government and indicates separately amounts of provincial and federal taxes.

Farmers and Fishermen.—Provision for averaging.

Capital Tax.—All corporations with paid up capital of in excess of $1.5 million are subject to Corporation Capital Tax. Large banks pay 3%, smaller financial institutions pay 1%, and other corporations (nonfinancial institutions) pay three-tenths of 1% on amount taxable of that corporation.

Returns.—Return for each taxation year must be filed within six months of end of fiscal year. Return must be accompanied by certified financial statement and all documents submitted with Canadian income tax return.

Inheritance Tax.—No succession duties are assessable with respect to deaths occurring after midnight, Jan. 24, 1977. See also Canada Law Digest, topic Taxation, subhead Income Tax Act, catchline Capital Gains.

Probate Fees.—In cases where grant of probate or letters of administration issued before Mar. 12, 1980, in cases where death occurred after Mar. 31, 1947, probate fees are levied under Probate Fee Act (c. 338) on property passing under will or by way of intestate succession. If market value in province is less than $10,000, applicant may file returns without applying for probate or administration. No probate fees are assessable on letters probate issued on or after Mar. 12, 1980. Estate Administration Amendment Act was proclaimed in force Jan. 1, 1982 which, inter alia, repealed Probate Fee Act.

Gift tax is imposed on gifts made since Dec. 31, 1971 and before midnight, Jan. 24, 1977 by resident donors, nonresident owners of real property situate in British Columbia and resident donees on failure of donor to pay tax. By 1977, c. 15, Gift Tax Act was repealed for gifts made after midnight, Jan. 24, 1977.

Insurance Premium Tax Act, c. 205, provides for a Provincial tax of 3% on premium income of insurance companies licensed to conduct business in respect of persons resident and property situated in Province. Rate of taxes 3% generally, 2% for life insurance, sickness insurance, personal accident insurance, and insurance that indemnifies or compensates for loss of salary or wages, 3% on pleasure craft insurance, and 4% on motor vehicle insurance. Person who enters into insurance contract to insure property located in Province with insurer not registered in B.C. must pay tax of 7% on premium.

Motor Fuel Tax Act, S.B.C. 1985, c. 76, levy taxes payable by purchasers on gasoline, coloured fuel, marine diesel fuel, jet fuel, aviation fuel, natural gas, locomotive fuel and marine bunker fuel.

Social Service Tax Act, c. 388 levies 7% tax as of Mar. 20, 1987 on: (a) specified services; (b) purchase price of all tangible personal property including certain fixtures purchased at retail sale in British Columbia; (c) original purchase price of tangible personal property brought into British Columbia for purposes other than resale by any person residing, ordinarily resident or carrying on business in British Columbia; (d) payments under leases of tangible personal property, and levies 10% tax on purchase price of liquor. Variable tax rates for passenger vehicles: 7% of purchase price of vehicle less than $32,000; 8% where over $32,000 but less than $33,000; 9% where over $33,000 but less than $34,000; 10% where over $34,000. Environmental levies of $3 per pneumatic tire and $5 per lead-acid battery apply.

Exemptions from tax include sales or imports of certain food products for human consumption, goods and services in aquaculture industry, medicines, farm and fishing equipment, self-propelled vessels of more than 500 tons gross among others. (§4). Taxable now are hazardous products including disposable diapers. Types of transactions exempt from tax include: (a) Sales of property between parent and subsidiary companies if tax has been previously paid on property and parent subsidiary relationship continues to exist for at least eight months after sale; (b) sales of property between person and corporation wholly owned or controlled by him providing that tax has been paid on property, assets are available to company on first day it commences business and transferor continues to wholly own and control corporation for at least eight months after transfer; (c) sales of property in British Columbia which provide for delivery to buyer outside of British Columbia.

Rateable reduction in tax on purchases of aircraft, trucks, etc., used in interprovincial trade, based on percentage of miles travelled in province to total miles. Persons selling goods at retail sales must collect tax but purchaser is still responsible to pay if they fail to do so. Proceedings for recovery of taxes may be commenced within seven years after date on which tax liability arose. Refunds for overpaid or erroneously paid taxes must be applied for within six years after payment. In respect of taxes paid by mistake of law, proceedings for recovery may be commenced within six years if tangible personal property for personal consumption only. Otherwise, six month limitation period.

Sales Tax.—See subhead Social Service Tax Act, supra.

Stamp Tax.—No provincial stamp tax.

Mining Tax.—See topic Mines and Minerals.

Logging Tax.—(c. 248). Generally 10% of all income derived from logging operations and sale of timber or cutting rights in Province or 150% of credit under §127 Federal Income Tax Act, whichever is lesser.

Horse Racing Tax Act.—(c. 175). Tax equal to 7% of amount deposited with operator at time of making bet collected by Province, and distributed between Province and B.C. Racing Commission in accordance with formula set out in legislation.

Social Security or Unemployment Compensation Tax.—None.

Home-Owner Grant Act, S.B.C. 1980, c. 18, basically provides annual provincial grant to reduce current year property tax of most resident home owners. Basic homeowner's grant is $470 for most homeowners. Homeowners who are seniors, handicapped or recipients of war veterans allowances will receive basic grant of $745. Reduction of homeowner grant with respect to eligible residences, apartments, etc. of residential value in excess of $450,000.

Hotel Room Tax Act.—(c. 183). Provides that purchasers of hotel and motel accommodation are liable to pay tax of 8% of purchase price, to be collected by hotel operators at time of sale. Additional tax may be levied by regulation. Currently, 2% extra tax payable in Vancouver, Victoria, Whistler and other areas.

Land Tax Deferment Act.—(c. 218). Provides that Minister of Finance may enter into agreements with owners of property who are over 60, widows, widowers or handicapped persons, whereby owner may defer payment of all of his real property taxes; eligible property means land with improvements thereon used for residential, farming, commercial or industrial purposes, or vacant land of limited size on which owner certifies he intends to construct single family dwelling as his principal place of residence. Owner must be Canadian citizen or permanent immigrant.

Agreements are registered as note on title, having priority over all other charges.

Agreement will terminate in event of sale of property or after ten years in case of vacant property and deferred tax is then payable together with interest at rate determined by Minister based on prime less 2%.

Owner may prepay deferred taxes at any time without notice or penalty, together with interest at rate fixed by agreement or rate prescribed by Minister based on prime less 2%.

Telegraph and Express Companies.—No special taxes.

Property Transfer Tax Act.—Effective Mar. 23, 1987 property purchase tax is levied on fair market value of conveyances at rate of 1% on first $200,000 and 2% on balance. Tax credits are available.

Penalties.—Generally every taxing or revenue statute has penalties for offences against provisions thereof by way of failing to file appropriate returns or failure to pay taxes due and payable. These offences vary with each statute and it is suggested that reference be made to appropriate statute in each case. Penalty provisions usually provide for fine by way of punishment which may call for imprisonment for nonpayment of fine imposed. Offence Act c. 305, §4 provides general penalty for offence of fine up to $2,000 and/or imprisonment for not more than six months.

TRADE UNIONS:

See topic Labour Relations.

TRADEMARKS AND TRADENAMES:

See Canada Law Digest.

TRUST DEEDS:

See topic Mortgages of Real Property.

TRUSTS: (c. 414).

Writing Requirement.—Trusts need not be in writing. Instruments creating trusts affecting land should be properly acknowledged and registered in land registry office. Such registration is notice to all the world.

See Topical Index in front part of this volume.

TRUSTS . . . *continued*

Interpretations.—Trusts are interpreted and administered in accordance with the principles of equity as varied by the "Trustee Act," which is in effect a reproduction of the English "Trustee Act" of 1850, with its subsequent amendments.

Appointment of Trustee.—Public trustee may be appointed to act as trustee in instrument creating trust, by majority of beneficiaries who are of age of majority, or by court. (c. 348, §6). Where trustee is dead, remains out of Province for more than 12 months, desires to be discharged, refuses or is unfit to act, or is incapable of acting, then person nominated to appoint new trustees, or if there is not such nomination any surviving or continuing trustees or their personal representatives may by writing appoint new trustee. (c. 414, §27). Court may also make order appointing new trustee. (§31).

A married woman may act as a trustee independently of her husband.

Discharge.—The receipt in writing of trustee for money payable to him or her in exercise of trust is sufficient discharge and exonerates the person so paying from seeing to the application thereof (c. 414, §3). Trustees may compromise, compound, abandon or otherwise settle any debt, account or claim relating to trust and may enter agreements for this purpose without being responsible for loss occasioned by such acts done in good faith. (§9).

Authorized trust investments if in all other respects reasonable and proper are: (1) securities of Canada, any province, municipal corporation, the United Kingdom and the United States; (2) securities of which the payment of principal and interest is guaranteed by the above-mentioned governments; (3) securities issued for school, hospital, irrigation, drainage or like purposes secured by or payable out of rates or taxes of any province on property in that province; (4) bonds, debentures, etc., of corporation secured by assignment to trustee of payments payable by Federal or Provincial government; (5) bonds, debentures, etc., of corporation, Federal or Provincial, secured by mortgage, charge upon real estate, its plant or equipment or on indebtedness or shares of class authorized herein; (6) bonds, debentures, etc., of Federal or Provincial corporation with dividend paying record for immediate preceding five years equal to specified rate of preference shares or dividend rate equal to 4% of value of which shares were carried at capital stock account; (7) guaranteed trust or investment certificates of bank, or corporation, Federal or Provincial, authorized to carry on trust business or deposit business; Canadian or Provincial; (8) bonds, debentures, etc., of loan corporation or like corporation with power to lend on mortgages or charges of real estate, paid up capital stock not less than $500,000, reserve fund not less than 25% of capital stock and stock having market value not less than 7% in excess of its par value; (9) preferred shares of corporation, Federal or Provincial, that has dividend payment record for immediate five years preceding equal to specified rate of preference shares or has paid dividend for immediate preceding five years of at least 4% of value of which shares were carried in capital stock account; (10) first mortgages, charges on real estate if loan does not exceed 75% of value of property; (11) securities issued or guaranteed by International Bank for Reconstruction and Development under Bretton Woods Agreement payable in currency of Canada, U.K., British Commonwealth or U.S.; (12) common shares of corporation, Federal or Provincial, that have paid dividend for each of immediate seven years preceding of at least 4% of average value at which shares were carried in capital stock account; (13) deposits in or evidence of indebtedness of Credit Union incorporated in Province. (c. 414, §15). These are in addition to powers conferred by instrument creating trust.

Gifts to Minors.—Public trustee may investigate and audit affairs, dealings and accounts of trust in which beneficiary is minor or mentally disordered. (c. 348, §10).

Trustees may be relieved from liability for breach of trust provided they have acted honestly and reasonably. (c. 414, §98).

Release of Trustees.—Ordinarily speaking, there is no statutory provision for release of trustee, except in case where there are two or more trustees, in which event one of them may be discharged by express agreement under "Trustee Act," executed by co-trustees, and by persons (if any) who are empowered to appoint trustees in respect of particular trust in question. (§28).

Accumulations.—By Perpetuity Act, c. 321 which came into force Jan. 1, 1979 and applies only to instruments taking effect after that date (except as provided) where property is disposed of in such manner that its income must wholly or in part be accumulated, power or direction to accumulate is valid if disposition of accumulated income is or may be valid. (§24). See topic Perpetuities.

Prior to its repeal by Perpetuity Act, Accumulations Act 1967, c. 2 provided that no disposition of any real or personal property shall direct income thereof to be accumulated for any longer period than one of: (a) Life of grantor or settlor, or (b) 21 years from date of making inter vivos disposition, or (c) duration of minority of person living or en ventre sa mere at date of making of inter vivos disposition, or 21 years from death of grantor, settlor or testator, or duration of minority of any person living or en ventre sa mere at death of grantor, settlor or testator, or duration of minority of any person who under instrument directing accumulation would, for time-being, if of full age, be entitled to income directed to be accumulated.

Perpetuities.—See topic Perpetuities.

Securities in Name of Nominee.—Except in case of security that cannot be registered, trustee who invests in securities shall require securities to be registered in his name as trustee for particular trust (c. 414, §20). Trustee engaged in war service and remaining out of province for period exceeding one month may by power of attorney delegate to any person exercise of all his powers and discretions. (§14).

Uniform Simplification of Fiduciary Security Transfers Act not applicable.

Testamentary Trusts.—Trusts may be created inter vivos or by will.

Variation of Trusts.—Supreme Court has jurisdiction to approve variations of trust in interests of beneficiaries and to sanction dealings with trust property. (c. 413, §1).

Pour Over Trusts.—See topic Wills, subhead Bequests and Devises to Inter Vivos Trusts.

USURY:

See Canada Law Digest, topic Interest.

VENUE:

Supreme Court has no local venue for most matters although there are Supreme Court registries throughout Province. Plaintiff chooses and sets out place of trial in statement of claim. (Rules of Court, R. 20[4]). Such place may be changed by court or judge at instance of defendant or plaintiff on grounds of convenience or expense or trial must be heard partly in one place and partly in another. (R. 39[7]).

VITAL STATISTICS: See topic Records.

WAREHOUSEMEN:

The common law rules regarding the liability of a bailee of this class still govern. The depositor is entitled to rely on the skill and care of his bailee. The liability of the bailee may be limited so as not to exceed a fixed amount by the terms of an express contract between him and the bailor, but this limitation will not relieve him if he is acting in violation of the contract.

Bonded warehouses must be open to customs inspection and are subject to excise regulations.

Lien.—By Warehouse Lien Act, c. 427, every warehouseman may have lien on goods deposited with him for storage, for full amount of his charges. (§2). Written notice of lien shall be given to owner of goods and to persons holding security interest in goods registered at date goods were deposited, within two months after warehouseman has knowledge of persons owed notice, where goods are deposited not by owner or his authority, but by person entrusted with possession. (§3). This lien may be enforced by sale by public auction after due notice has been given of intention to sell. (§4) Surplus proceeds of sale are to be paid over to person entitled thereto together with statement of account. (§6).

Warehouse receipts may be either negotiable or nonnegotiable and are governed by Warehouse Receipt Act, R.S.B.C. 1979, c. 428. By §2(4) of this Act, warehouseman may not insert condition in receipt that impairs his obligation to exercise care and diligence in regard to goods or condition contrary to any provision of Act.

WILLS: (c. 434).

Every will speaks from the date of the testator's death (§20[2]), and must be duly proved in court having jurisdiction in probate (see topic Courts) before it can be registered in any land registry office.

Testamentary Capacity.—Person under age of 19 cannot make valid will unless such infant is or has been married or in active military service or mariner at sea. (§7).

Testamentary Disposition.—There is no restriction on the right of a competent person to dispose of property by will, except that where a will does not make adequate provision for the testator's wife, husband or children the court may, on application therefor, order such provision as it deems adequate and equitable to be made out of the estate. Such order is governed by provisions of Wills Variation Act, c. 435, as explained below.

Execution.—A will must be in writing and signed by the testator, or by some other person in his presence and by his direction, and such signature must be made and acknowledged by the testator in the presence of at least two witnesses, present at the same time, who must attest and subscribe in the presence of the testator. (§3-4). No form of attestation is necessary, nor is any publication required. (§9).

A will is not invalid on account of the incompetency of an attesting witness. (§10). Executor may be witness. (§13).

Usual form of attestation clause is as follows:

Form

Signed by the testator in the presence of us, both present at the same time, who at his request and in his presence have subscribed our names as witnesses.

Alteration that is made in a will must be executed in the same way as a will, or signed by the testator and witnesses in the margin or opposite or near to such alterations, or beneath a memorandum subscribed to the will, referring to such alteration. (§17).

Revocation.—Will is revoked by: destruction of will by testator or any other person acting in presence of testator and by his or her direction, with intention to revoke it; subsequent will or codicil or writing declaring intention to revoke and executed in same manner as will; marriage of testator, unless will declares that it is made in contemplation of marriage or in exercise of power of appointment according to which property appointed shall not in default of appointment pass to heir, executor or administrator of testator or persons entitled to estate of testator if he died intestate. (§14-15).

Unless contrary intention appears in will, where after making will but before testator's death: (1) Judicial separation has been ordered with respect to testator's marriage; (2) decree absolute of divorce has terminated testator's marriage; or (3) testator's marriage is found to be void or is nullity, will is to be construed as if testator's spouse (including person considered by testator to be his spouse) had predeceased testator. (§16). Whether or not notice of will has been filed, notice of revocation in prescribed form may be filed with Director of Vital Statistics. (§34).

Registration.—Provision is made for optional registration of wills and for notice of location of wills to be filed with the Director of Vital Statistics. (§33).

Testamentary Gifts to Attesting Witnesses.—A gift to an attesting witness or spouse of attesting witness is void, but does not otherwise affect will, or competency of witness to prove execution. Such gift will not be void, however, if will has been properly executed with at least required number of attesting witnesses who are not recipients of testamentary gifts under will. (§11).

Bequests and Devises to Inter Vivos Trusts.—No statutory provisions in this jurisdiction. Doctrine of incorporation by reference is recognized in the province. Trust instrument should be in existence at date of testator's will.

Unclaimed Legacies.—See topic Descent and Distribution.

Trustee Act (c. 414, §88) provides that any executor or administrator may apply to judge of Supreme Court for opinion, advice or direction on questions respecting management or administration of trust property or assets of any testator or intestate. Acting

WILLS . . . *continued*
upon opinion, advice or direction given, discharges trustee, executor or administrator, unless such opinion, advice or direction is obtained fraudulently. (§89).

Any trustee or majority of trustees having in their hands or under their control, money or securities belonging to a trust may pay same into Supreme Court and a receipt from the appropriate court officer discharges the trustee. (§40).

Any trustee, executor or administrator may apply to any judge of Supreme Court for an order that he be at liberty to distribute proceeds of the estate among the parties entitled thereto having regard only to the claims of such persons as have been ascertained to be entitled. However, this does not prejudice right of any creditor or claimant to follow proceeds into the hands of person or persons who may have received them. (§39).

Lapses.—Unless contrary intention appears by will gifts to siblings, children or other issue, who have died, leaving issue at testator's death, do not lapse, but descend to such issue. (§29). Unless contrary intention appears, gifts of specific property, whether real or personal, which fail to take effect because beneficiary predeceases testator, fall into residue of estate. (§21). Gift of residue that lapses passes on intestacy.

Foreign Wills.—Every will made outside of British Columbia but not in accordance with Wills Act is considered formally valid as regards movables if made in accordance with law in force at time of its making in place where: (a) will made; (b) testator domiciled when will made; or (c) testator had domicile of origin. (§42). Essential validity of will so far as it relates to interest in movables is governed by testator's domicile at time of death. Both essential and formal validity of will relating to immovables is governed by law of place where immovables situate. Ancillary letters probate may be obtained of will probated in foreign country on filing of copy of will and certified copy of probate.

Living Wills.—No legislation.

Wills Variation Act c. 435 provides that when testator has not made adequate provision for proper maintenance of surviving spouse and/or children, Supreme Court may, upon application, vary will accordingly. (§2). Application must be made within six months from issuance of probate in British Columbia. (§10).

Simultaneous Death.—See topic Death, subhead Survivorship.

Testamentary Trusts.—See topic Trusts.

WITNESSES: (See Evidence Act, c. 116.)

A person is not incompetent to give evidence by reason only of interest or crime. (§3). Persons charged with any offence or crime, and their husbands or wives, are competent witnesses. (§6). Parties to civil causes and their husbands or wives are both competent and compellable with certain exceptions. (§7).

Witness is not excused from giving evidence on ground of self-incrimination but may seek protection of Canada Evidence Act or B.C. Evidence Act against use of evidence in any other proceeding.

See also topic Depositions.

Privileged Communications.—A client cannot be compelled, and a legal adviser will not be allowed without the express consent of his client, to disclose oral or documentary communications passing between them in professional confidence. This rule is for the protection of the client and not of the lawyer and is confined to cases of legal advisers.

Expert.—Written expert report is admissable at trial in Supreme Court without proof of signature of expert if copy is given to every part of record at least 60 days in advance. (Rule 40A[2]). However, B.C. Supreme Court Rule 40A provides written statement must be delivered 60 days before expert testifies.

Pre-Trial Examination.—Court may order pre-trial examination of material non-party witness on oath if witness has refused voluntary statement. (Supreme Court Rule 28).

Husband and wife are not compellable to disclose any communications made by one to the other during the marriage. (§8). But, notwithstanding any rule to contrary, husband or wife in any proceedings may give evidence that he or she did or did not have sexual intercourse with other party to marriage at any time. (§7[2]). See also topic Criminal Law, and Canada Evidence Act.

In actions against representatives of deceased persons, the plaintiff's evidence must be corroborated by some other material evidence.

In actions by or against person of unsound mind, evidence of opposite party must be corroborated by some other material evidence. (§9).

See topic Affidavits.

WORKERS' COMPENSATION LAW:

See topic Labour Relations.

See Topical Index in front part of this volume.

This form of declaration required by Reg. 115/93, s.(b).

PARTNERSHIP FORMS
(See topic Partnership.)

524/78

PARTNERSHIP ACT
PARTNERSHIP

APPENDIX
Form 1
[en. B.C. Reg. 115/93, s. (b).]

Province of British Columbia

Ministry of Finance and Corporate Relations
REGISTRAR OF COMPANIES
2nd Floor — 940 Blanchard Street
Victoria, B.C. V8W 3E6

DECLARATION FOR EXTRA-PROVINCIAL LIMITED PARTNERSHIP

NAME APPROVAL NO. IF APPLICABLE N R

DOCUMENT CONTROL NO. **DLP 000000**

OFFICE USE ONLY — REGISTRATION NO.

RETAIN PINK COPY FOR YOUR RECORDS. PLEASE TYPE OR PRINT CLEARLY, AS YOU ARE MAKING THREE COPIES.

SUBMITTING PARTY NAME AND MAILING ADDRESS. PLEASE INCLUDE POSTAL CODE.

NAME ______

ADDRESS ______

CITY/PROV. ______

POSTAL CODE ______

INSTRUCTIONS: Before submitting this form, please ensure the name has been searched for availability for registration. To search a business name write to Name Reservations at the address above. PLEASE NOTE: The registration of a firm name under the *Partnership Act* does not provide any protection for that name.

DETAILS OF NATURE OF DECLARATION

☐ NEW REGISTRATION

☐ AMENDED LIMITED PARTNERSHIP

☐ DISSOLUTION DATE Y M D

QUOTE ORIGINAL REGISTRATION NO. ______

STATE LIMITED PARTNERSHIP NAME IN FULL

MAILING ADDRESS	CITY	PROV.	POSTAL CODE
BUSINESS ADDRESS IN B C - *NOT A P.O. BOX* (☐ SAME AS MAILING ADDRESS OR)	CITY	PROV.	POSTAL CODE

DESCRIBE THE NATURE OF THE BUSINESS

START DATE OF BUSINESS IN B.C. Y M D

BUSINESS TELEPHONE NO.

ADDRESS OF REGISTERED OFFICE IN B.C. - *NOT P.O. BOX*

CITY	PROV.	POSTAL CODE

JURISDICTION WHERE LIMITED PARTNERSHIP FORMED

PROVIDE NAME(S) AND ADDRESS(ES) OF GENERAL PARTNER(S)

CERTIFICATION • I hereby certify that the persons on the attached certificate are the only members of the Limited Partnership.

SIGNATURE OF GENERAL PARTNER OR SOLICITOR

X

RELATIONSHIP TO LIMITED PARTNERSHIP

FIN 780 Rev 93/2/22 WHITE/CANARY: REGISTRAR OF COMPANIES PINK: APPLICANT

This is form of declaration required by §§81, 86, and 88. (Reg. 115/93, s. (b)).

PARTNERSHIP ACT
PARTNERSHIP

524/78

Form 2
[en. B.C. Reg. 115/93, s. (b).]

Province of British Columbia

Ministry of Finance and Corporate Relations
REGISTRAR OF COMPANIES
2nd Floor — 940 Blanchard Street
Victoria, B.C. V8W 3E6

DECLARATION FOR PROPRIETORSHIP OR PARTNERSHIP—REGISTRATION

NAME APPROVAL NO. IF APPLICABLE **N R**

DOCUMENT CONTROL NO. **DP 000000**

OFFICE USE ONLY

REGISTRATION NO.

RETAIN PINK COPY FOR YOUR RECORDS. PLEASE TYPE OR PRINT CLEARLY, AS YOU ARE MAKING THREE COPIES.

1. SUBMITTING PARTY NAME AND MAILING ADDRESS. PLEASE INCLUDE POSTAL CODE.

NAME

ADDRESS

CITY/ PROV.

POSTAL CODE

INSTRUCTIONS: Before submitting this form, please ensure the name has been searched for availability for registration. To search a business name, write to Name Reservations at the address above. PLEASE NOTE: The registration of a firm name under the *Partnership Act* does not provide any protection for that name.

2. NATURE OF DECLARATION

☐ SOLE PROPRIETORSHIP

☐ GENERAL PARTNERSHIP

3. DETAILS OF CHANGE IN NATURE OF DECLARATION - *QUOTE ORIGINAL REGISTRATION NO.*

☐ CHANGE IN NATURE OF BUSINESS

☐ DISSOLUTION DATE Y M D

☐ CHANGE OF BUSINESS NAME - *STATE PREVIOUS BUSINESS NAME*

☐ CHANGE IN MEMBERSHIP OF PARTNERSHIP

A. THIS SECTION MUST BE COMPLETED BY ALL
PROPRIETORSHIP OR PARTNERSHIP NAME

MAILING ADDRESS | CITY | PROV. | POSTAL CODE

BUSINESS ADDRESS IN B C - *NOT A P.O. BOX* ☐ SAME AS MAILING ADDRESS OR | CITY | PROV. | POSTAL CODE

DESCRIBE THE NATURE OF THE BUSINESS | TELEPHONE NO. | START DATE OF BUSINESS IN BC Y M D

B. GENERAL PARTNERSHIP

CERTIFICATION - We hereby certify that the undersigned in Section B, ☐ constitute all of the members in this partnership, as named.

1. PARTNER NAME - *STATE NAME IN FULL* | 1. SIGNATURE OF PARTNER X

RESIDENTIAL OR REGISTERED ADDRESS - *NOT P.O. BOX* | CITY | PROV. | POSTAL CODE

2. PARTNER NAME - *STATE NAME IN FULL* | 2. SIGNATURE OF PARTNER X

RESIDENTIAL OR REGISTERED ADDRESS - *NOT P.O. BOX* | CITY | PROV. | POSTAL CODE

3. PARTNER NAME - *STATE NAME IN FULL* | 3. SIGNATURE OF PARTNER X

RESIDENTIAL OR REGISTERED ADDRESS - *NOT P.O. BOX* | CITY | PROV. | POSTAL CODE

IF ANY OF THE ABOVE PARTNER IS A CORPORATION, STATE PRINCIPAL PLACE OF BUSINESS IN B.C. - *ADDRESS*

C. PROPRIETORSHIP
PROPRIETOR'S NAME - *STATE INDIVIDUAL'S OR CORPORATION'S NAME IN FULL*

RESIDENTIAL OR REGISTERED ADDRESS - *NOT P.O. BOX* | CITY | PROV. | POSTAL CODE

IF A CORPORATION, STATE PRINCIPAL PLACE OF BUSINESS IN B.C. - *ADDRESS*

CERTIFICATION - I hereby certify that no other person is associated with me in this proprietorship.

SIGNATURE OF PROPRIETOR

X

FIN 780 Rev 93/2/24 WHITE/CANARY: REGISTRAR OF COMPANIES PINK: APPLICANT

May 14/93

"The following fee schedule is in force:

General Partnership: $ 30.00
Proprietorship: $ 30.00
Limited Partnership: $165.00

The above includes one certified copy. Additional certified copies are $25.00. There is a $7.00 charge for each search conducted on a person's own on-line computer terminal, or an $8.00 charge using a terminal provided by the provincial government.

Prescribed Form of Transfer of An Estate in Fee Simple

LAND TITLE ACT

FORM A

(Section 181(1))

Province of British Columbia

FREEHOLD TRANSFER

PAGE 1 of ____ pages

(This area for Land Title Office use)

1. APPLICATION: *(Name, address, phone number and signature of applicant, applicant's solicitor or agent)*

2. (a) PARCEL IDENTIFIER AND LEGAL DESCRIPTION OF LAND:*
(PID) *(LEGAL DESCRIPTION)*

(b) MARKET VALUE: $

3. CONSIDERATION:

4. TRANSFEROR(S):*

5. FREEHOLD ESTATE TRANSFERRED:*

6. TRANSFEREE(S): *(Including occupation(s), postal address(es) and postal code(s))**

7. EXECUTION(S):** The transferor(s) accept(s) the above consideration and understand(s) that this instrument operates to transfer the freehold estate in the land described above to the transferee(s).

Officer Signature(s) | Execution Date | Transferor(s) Signature(s)

Y	M	D

OFFICER CERTIFICATION:

Your signature constitutes a representation that you are a solicitor, notary public or other person authorized by the *Evidence Act,* R.S.B.C. 1979, c. 116, to take affidavits for use in British Columbia and certifies the matters set out in Part 5 of the *Land Title Act* as they pertain to the execution of this instrument.

* If space insufficient, enter "SEE SCHEDULE" and attach schedule in Form E.

** If space insufficient, continue executions on additional page(s) in Form D.

MANITOBA LAW DIGEST

(The following is a list of all Topics, including cross-references, covered in this Digest.)

MANITOBA LAW DIGEST

Revised for 1997 edition by

AIKINS, MacAULAY & THORVALDSON, Barristers, etc., Winnipeg.

(C.C.S.M. means Continuing Consolidation of the Statutes of Manitoba; R. S. M. means either Revised Statutes of Manitoba, (1970) or Re-Enacted Statutes of Manitoba (1987 or 1988); S. M. means Statutes of Manitoba; R. S. C. means Revised Statutes of Canada; S. C. means Statutes of Canada; W. W. R. means Western Weekly Reports; Q. B. means Queen's Bench.)

Note: This revision is as of August 9, 1996.

ABSENTEES:

There is no provincial statute with respect to absentees or their estates.

Money paid into Court of Queen's Bench, and remaining unclaimed for six years is paid over to Provincial Treasurer. Limitation of time for making claims is suspended in case of infant or person of unsound mind. (The Suitors' Moneys Act, C.C.S.M. c. S220).

Care of Property.—No provincial statute with respect to care of property of absentees.

Process Agent.—Absentee may authorize agent to accept service of process. Substitutional service of a process may be effected by judge's order.

Escheat.—See topic Descent and Distribution.

ACCORD AND SATISFACTION:

To operate as a bar to an action an accord and satisfaction must be executed. By statute, obligations are satisfied by part performance without new consideration, when expressly accepted by creditor or where rendered pursuant to agreement for that purpose. (The Mercantile Law Amendment Act, C.C.S.M. c. M120, §6).

Pleading.—Must be specifically pleaded.

ACKNOWLEDGMENTS:

Acknowledgments are not ordinarily essential to validity of documents but may be used. See subhead Forms below. (The Manitoba Evidence Act, C.C.S.M. c. E150).

The mere execution of the instrument is sufficient. Any required by statute to be registered, and in ordinary practice most instruments, are executed in the presence of a witness who takes an affidavit, attached to the instrument, of the due execution thereof in the presence of such witness before a commissioner authorized by the province to swear or affirm, or a notary or court officer given similar powers, that the witness was personally present and saw the instrument duly executed.

Foreign Documents.—Proof of documents outside of province may be by acknowledgment before notary public. See subhead Forms below.

Authentication of certificate of acknowledgment not required, whether taken in province or not.

Married Women.—Owner must have consent of spouse to dispose of homestead. Consent must be acknowledged by spouse apart from owner. (The Homesteads, Marital Property Amendment and Consequential Amendments Act, S.M. 1992, C. 46).

Forms

Individual: In Witness Whereof I have hereunto set my hand and seal this . . . . . . day of . . . . . . A. D. 19. .

Signed, Sealed and Delivered in the presence of (Witness). (Signature of Maker)

Corporation: In witness whereof . . . . . . has caused its corporate seal to be hereunto affixed duly attested by the hands of its proper officers in that behalf the day and year first above mentioned (or this . . . . . . day of . . . . . . A. D. 19. .).

(Seal).

(Signatures of signing officers of Corporation).

Dated the . . . . . . day of . . . . . . A. D. 19. . .

. . . .

(Signature).

Certificate as to acknowledgment of maker of instrument:

I hereby certify that, on the day of 19 . . . . who (insert full name of maker of instrument) is personally known to me, (or whose identity has been satisfactorily proved to me by the evidence of . . . . who is personally (name) known to me), appeared before me and that he acknowledged to me that he is the person mentioned in the annexed instrument as the maker thereof and that he duly executed the instrument and that he is the person whose name is subscribed thereto as a party thereto; and that he knows the contents thereof and that he executed the instrument voluntarily and is of the full age of eighteen years.

In testimony whereof I have hereto set my hand and seal of office at . . . . in . . . . this day of 19 .

A Notary Public
in and for . . . .
. . . .
(name of jurisdiction in which notary public is authorized to practise as such.)

(Note: Strike out each of the words in parentheses as are not required)

Certificate as to declaration of party to instrument, etc.:

I hereby certify that, on the day of 19 , ... who (full name of party declaring the facts) is personally known to me, (or whose identity has been satisfactorily proved to me by the evidence of . . . . who is personally (name) known to me), appeared before me and certified and declared that the following matters are true:

(Here set out the facts that would otherwise be required to be proved by the affidavit or statutory declaration of the person so certifying and declaring.)

In testimony whereof I have hereto set my hand and seal of office at . . . . in . . . . this day of 19 .

A Notary Public
in and for . . . .
. . . .
(name of jurisdiction in which notary public is authorized to practise as such.)

(Note: Strike out each of the words in parentheses as are not required)

Alternative to Acknowledgment or Proof.—No statutory provision.

ACTIONS:

Provincial Judges Court.—Provincial Court Act (C.C.S.M. c. C275) provides for provincial judges court with both criminal and family divisions.

Queen's Bench.—Actions must be brought in Court of Queen's Bench, superior court of record with civil and criminal jurisdiction. First statute governing practice in Court of Queen's Bench operational on Oct. 1, 1895. Intention was to make practice as similar as possible to that of superior courts in England and Ontario under Judicature Acts. Separate administration of law and equity was abolished and it was provided that they should be administered concurrently but that in case of conflict, rules of equity should prevail. This rule applies to proceedings in all courts. On Mar. 1, 1989 new Court of Queen's Bench Act (C.C.S.M. c. C280) and new Rules were proclaimed.

Commencement of Actions.—Actions are commenced in the Court of Queen's Bench (Rule 14) by a statement of claim setting out the facts and the relief sought. Defendant, if served in Manitoba, must file statement of defence within 20 days from date of service; if served in any other part of Canada or U.S.A., within 40 days; if served elsewhere, within 60 days from date of service. If the plaintiff does not reside in Manitoba or has insufficient assets in Manitoba to pay costs, court may on motion by defendant make order for security for costs. Service of originating process may be made outside Manitoba in respect of: (a) Real or personal property in Manitoba, or perpetuation of testimony relating to such property; (b) administration of estate of deceased person concerning (i) real property in Manitoba, or (ii) personal property, where deceased person at time of death was resident in Manitoba; (c) interpretation, rectification, enforcement or setting aside of deed, will, contract, agreement or other instrument concerning, (i) real or personal property in Manitoba, or (ii) personal property of deceased person who, at time of death, was resident in Manitoba, (d) trustee in respect of execution of trust contained in written instrument where assets of trust include real or personal property in Manitoba; (e) foreclosure, sale, payment, possession or redemption in respect of mortgage, charge or lien on real or personal property in Manitoba; (f) contract, where (i) contract was made in whole or in part in Manitoba, (ii) contract provides that it is to be governed by or interpreted in accordance with Manitoba law, (iii) parties to contract agreed that Manitoba courts are to have jurisdiction over legal proceedings, or (iv) breach of contract has been committed in Manitoba, even though breach was preceded or accompanied by breach outside Manitoba that rendered impossible performance of part of contract that ought to have been performed in Manitoba; (g) tort committed in Manitoba; (h) loss or damage sustained in Manitoba arising from any cause of action, wherever committed, (i) injunction ordering party to do, or refrain from doing, anything in Manitoba or affecting real or personal property in Manitoba; (j) in respect of claim founded on judgment; (k) in respect of claim authorized by statute to be made against person outside Manitoba by proceeding commenced in Manitoba; (l) person outside Manitoba who is necessary or proper party to proceeding properly brought against another person served in Manitoba; (m) person ordinarily resident or carrying on business in Manitoba; (n) counterclaim, crossclaim or third or subsequent party claim properly brought under rules; or (o) by or on behalf of Crown or municipal corporation to recover money owing for taxes or other debts due to Crown or municipality; (p) family proceeding within meaning of Queen's Bench Act (see Q.B. Rule 17).

Originating process for commencement of application is notice of application. Proceeding may be commenced by application where: (a) Authorized by rules; (b) statute authorizes application, appeal or motion to court and does not require commencement of action; (c) relief claimed is for (i) opinion, advice or direction of court on question affecting rights of person in respect of administration of estate of deceased persons or execution of trust, (ii) order directing executors, administrators or trustees to do or abstain from doing particular act in respect of estate or trust for which they are responsible, (iii) removal or replacement of one or more executors, administrators or trustees, or fixing of their compensation, (iv) determination of rights which depend upon

See note at head of Digest as to 1996 legislation covered.

See Topical Index in front part of this volume.

ACTIONS . . . *continued*
interpretation of deed, will, agreement, contract or other instrument, or upon interpretation of statute, order in council, order, rule, regulation, by-law or resolution, (v) declaration of interest in or charge on land, including nature and extent of interest or charge or boundaries of land, or settling priority of interests or charges, or (vi) approval or arrangement or compromise or approval of purchase, sale, mortgage, lease or variation of trust; or (d) any matter where it is unlikely there will be any material facts in dispute. (See Q.B. Rule 14.)

See topics Pleading; Practice; Process.

Joinder.—Plaintiff may join all claims against opposite party in same proceeding. Court may order relief against joinder where it may unduly complicate or delay hearing or cause undue prejudice to party. (See Q.B. Rules 5.01 and 5.05.)

Parties.—Several persons may join as plaintiffs in same proceeding where represented by same lawyer and they assert claims for relief arising out of same transaction or common question of fact or law may arise, or their joinder would promote convenient administration of justice. Every person whose presence as party is necessary to enable court to adjudicate effectively and completely on issues must be joined as party. Proceedings are not defeated by misjoinder or nonjoinder of any party. Court may order to add, delete or substitute party or correct name of party on such terms as just at any stage of proceedings unless prejudice would result uncompensatable by costs or adjournment. (See Q.B. Rules 5.02-5.05.)

Class Actions.—One or more persons may bring or defend proceeding on behalf or for benefit of numerous persons having same interest. (See Q.B. Rule 12.)

Third Parties.—Defendant may commence third party claim against nonparty to action who is or may be liable to defendant for all or part of plaintiff's claim; is or may be liable to defendant for independent claim arising out of transaction involved in main action or related transaction or event or series thereof; or should be bound by determination of issue arising between plaintiff and defendant. Third party may defend against third party claim by delivering third party defence and, where appropriate, may defend against plaintiff's claim against defendant by delivering statement of defence to main action in which may raise any defence open to defendant. In defending main action, third party has same rights and obligations as defendant and is bound by any order or determination between plaintiff and defendant who made third party claim. (See Q.B. Rule 29.)

Stay of Proceedings.—See subhead Consolidation of Actions, infra.

Consolidation of Actions.—Where two or more proceedings are pending in which there is common question of fact or law or relief claimed arises out of same transaction or occurrence or series thereof, court may order (a) proceedings be consolidated, heard at same time or one immediately after other; (b) any one of proceedings be stayed until any other is determined; or (c) any one of proceedings be asserted by way of counterclaim in any other. (See Q.B. Rule 6.)

Abatement.—If by reason of death (when the cause of action survives or continues) or marriage, or by assignment or conveyance, any estate, interest or title devolves or is transferred, the action may be continued by or against the person to or on whom such estate or title has come or devolved.

Actions and causes of action in tort (except for defamation, malicious prosecution, false arrest, false imprisonment, or loss of care, guidance and companionship) in favour of or against any person do not abate on death but continue in favour of or against personal representative, except that damages for loss of expectation of life are not recoverable in tort action brought by personal representative. (C.C.S.M. c. T160, §53).

Limitation of.—See topic Limitation of Actions.

Small Claims.—Governed by Court of Queen's Bench Small Claims Practices Act. (C.C.S.M. c. C285). May file claim for: (a) amount not exceeding $5,000; or (b) assessment of liability for motor vehicle accident where vehicle of claimant not damaged. Claims commenced by filing simple, signed statement. Act excludes proceedings relating to: (a) ownership of real property; (b) interpretation of testamentary disposition; (c) administration of trust or estate; (d) family proceedings; (e) malicious prosecution, false imprisonment or defamation; or (f) wrongdoing by judges.

Direct Actions Against Insurer.—See topic Motor Vehicles, subhead Direct Actions.

ADMINISTRATION:

See topic Executors and Administrators.

ADOPTION:

Adoption may be private or by way of application to Director or agency. If applicant is married person, spouse must join in application. (C.C.S.M. c. C80).

Consent Required.—If adoption is private, consent must be obtained from natural parent(s) or guardian(s) who have custody of child, or from mother where child is child of unmarried mother, and from child if 12 years of age or older. Father of child of unmarried mother must be served with notice of proceedings. Judge may dispense with consent where person whose consent required cannot be found or where it is in best interests of child. If adoption is through Director or agency, consent must be obtained from same. If child has been living with adopting parents for three years or more, notice only need be given to natural parents. Judge can direct substitutional service or dispense with service where parent cannot be found. If adoption is by spouse of natural parent, notice must be given to parent not party to application.

Conditions Precedent.—Application by other than natural or de facto parent(s) cannot be brought until six months after notice of placement to agency. Person adopting must be older than adoptee.

Jurisdiction.—Adoption hearings are before judge of Court of Queen's Bench who may hear applications by any person resident in Manitoba.

Venue.—Application is heard in Court of Queen's Bench in any judicial centre.

Petition.—Forms of petition, notices, affidavits are supplied by Director of Child and Family Services.

Proceedings are held in camera before judge. An investigation is carried out by Director where adoption is through Director or an agency or where adoption is by de facto parents (where child has lived with adopting parents for three or more years). Where application is by spouse of natural parent or of parent who has sole legal custody no investigation is conducted except on request by judge. No report required in case of previously single parent and spouse. Report of Director is considered along with any other evidence. Unless application is opposed, evidence by applicants is usually by affidavit.

Decree.—All orders of adoption are absolute.

Name.—Adopting parent(s) determines surname of child.

Effect of Adoption.—All rights, duties and obligations between child and his natural parents or his prior adoptive parents and guardians, including rights of inheritance, cease to exist under law. There is provision for registry in which information volunteered by natural and adoptive parents and adult adoptees can be recorded and made available to same. Relationship of child and adoptive parent(s) is for all lawful purposes as if child had been born of adoptive parent(s).

ADVANCEMENTS:

See topic Descent and Distribution.

ADVERSE POSSESSION:

Adverse possession generally gives no title against registered owner of property under Real Property Act (C.C.S.M. c. R30, §61). Under Law of Property Act (C.C.S.M. c. L90, §28) where survey shows that building encroaches upon adjoining land Court of Queen's Bench may: (a) Declare easement to be in existence for life of building, (b) vest title to owner of encroaching building, or (c) order portion of building encroaching to be removed.

Easements.—Proof of uninterrupted use, when such use has been exercised for at least 20 years entitles court to hold that there existed agreement express or implied between predecessors in title and that easement has been established by prescription. (See 1964, 47 W. W. R. 113.)

AFFIDAVITS:

Commissioners for oaths and affidavits within the province, or without the province for use therein, are appointed by the Lieutenant-Governor-in-Council. (The Manitoba Evidence Act, C.C.S.M. c. E150). Commissions expire two years from date of issue, but may be renewed on application to Provincial Secretary before or within one year after expiration.

Within the Province.—Affidavits may be taken within the province by: Commissioner for Oaths; Lieutenant-Governor; Clerk of Executive Council; Justice of the Peace or Police Magistrate; Judge; Master, Referee, Prothonotary, Clerk of the Crown and Pleas, or Registrar of Court of Queen's Bench, or the Deputy of any of them; District Registrar or Deputy District Registrar of Land Titles Office; practising Barrister or Attorney-at-Law; Notary Public; Mayor, Reeve, or Clerk of any Municipality, Resident Administrator of Local Government District, Secretary-Treasurer of School District, School Area or School Division; Post Master of Post Office; Sheriff or Deputy Sheriff of Judicial District; Member of Royal Canadian Mounted Police; practising Land Surveyor; any commissioned officer on full time service in Canadian Armed Forces. (C.C.S.M. c. E150).

Without the Province.—Affidavits may be taken without the province by any of the following exercising his functions or having jurisdiction in the place where the affidavit is taken: Notary Public; Commissioner for taking Affidavit; Judge; Magistrate; Officer of Court of Justice; Head of City, Town, Village, Township or Municipality; Officer of Her Majesty's Diplomatic or Consular Services, including an Ambassador, Envoy, Minister, Chargé d'Affaires, Counsellor, Secretary, Attaché, Consul-General, Consul, Vice-Consul, Pro-Consul, Consular Agent, Acting Consul-General, Acting Consul, Acting Vice-Consul and Acting Consular Agent; Officer of Canadian Diplomatic Consular or Representative Services, including, in addition to the aforementioned diplomatic and consular officers, a High Commissioner, Acting permanent Delegate, Counsellor and Secretary; any commissioned officer on full time service in Canadian Armed Forces. (C.C.S.M. c. E150).

Statutory Declarations.—Statutory declarations in support of writings, deeds, or instruments or of the truth of any fact are provided for in the Evidence Act. (C.C.S.M. c. E150). They are not used in court. Statutory declarations have no force if made outside of Canada.

Forms

Affidavits for use in court are entitled:

In the Court of . . . . . .; and the style of cause is set out immediately below, e.g.,

In the Queen's Bench

Between

. . . ., Plaintiff,

and

. . . ., Defendant.

The jurat is in the following form:

Sworn before me at the . . . .
of . . . . . . in the Province of
. . . . . . this . . . . . . day of . . . ,
A. D. 19. . . } . . . . (Signature of deponent).

A Commissioner for Oaths, etc., or notary public (as the case may be).

Affidavits for other purposes are entitled:

Canada,
Province of Manitoba,
To Wit: } In the Matter of . . . .

If made in pursuance of a statute the name of the statute and the citation should also be given. Jurat as above.

See note at head of Digest as to 1996 legislation covered.

See Topical Index in front part of this volume.

AFFIDAVITS . . . *continued*

Statutory declarations are headed the same as affidavits which are not to be used in court, but the following clause is added at the bottom of the declaration:

"And I make this solemn declaration conscientiously believing it to be true and knowing that it is of the same force and effect as if made under oath."

The jurat is in the following form:

Declared before me at . . . .
the . . . . . . of . . . . . ., in the
Province of Manitoba, this
. . . . . ., day of . . . . . ., 19. . .
. . . . (Signature of declarant).

A Commissioner for Oaths or a notary public (as the case may be).

Where deponent is incapable of reading affidavit or declaration, the form is as follows: Sworn (affirmed or declared) before me at the . . . . . . of . . . . . . in the . . . . . . of . . . . . ., this . . . . . . day of . . . . . ., 19. ., having first been read over and explained by me to the deponent (or declarant) who, being incapable of reading the contents of the affidavit or declaration, appeared to understand the same and (choose one)

(a) signed his/her signature in my presence; or
(b) made his/her mark in my presence; or
(c) verbally indicated his/her understanding of same.

Where deponent is incapable of writing name, the form is as follows: Sworn (affirmed or declared) before me at the . . . . . . of . . . . . ., in the . . . . . . of . . . . . ., this . . . . . . day of . . . . . ., 19. ., by the deponent (or declarant) who made his mark in my presence, being incapable of writing his/her name (choose one)

(a) made his/her mark in my presence
(b) verbally indicated his/her understanding of the affidavit or declaration.

Where interpreter is used, the form is as follows: Sworn (affirmed or declared) before me at the . . . . . . of . . . . . ., in the . . . . . . of . . . . . ., this . . . . . . day of . . . . . ., 19. ., through the interpretation of . . . . . ., of the . . . . . . of . . . . . ., in the . . . . . . of . . . . . ., the said . . . . . . having been first sworn truly and faithfully to interpret the contents of this affidavit (affirmation or declaration) to the deponent (or declarant), and truly and faithfully to interpret the oath about to be administered to him (or declaration about to be taken by him).

Affidavit of Execution of Documents:

Canada,
Province of Manitoba,
To Wit:
(If made outside of Manitoba for use in Manitoba, country, province or state to be substituted).

In the matter of . . . . . .

I (name, address and occupation of deponent), make oath and say:

1. That I was personally present and did see the within instrument (and duplicate thereof) duly signed, sealed and executed by . . . . . . of the parties thereto.
2. That the said instrument (and duplicate) was executed at . . . .
3. That I know the said party and am satisfied that . . . . . . of the full age of eighteen years.
4. That I am a subscribing witness to the said instrument and duplicate.

Sworn before me at the . . . . . .
of . . . . . ., in the . . . . . . of
. . . . .,
this . . . . . . day of . . . . . ., A. D.
19. . .
. . . . (Signature of deponent).

(Commissioner for Oaths or notary public as the case may be).

Alternative to Affidavit.—No statutory provision.

AGENCY: See topic Principal and Agent.

AIRCRAFT:

See Canada Law Digest, topic Aircraft.

ALIENS:

Property.—Ownership of farmland is restricted by The Farmlands Ownership Act. (C.C.S.M. c. F35). Nonresident individuals and corporations, other than family farm corporations, may not acquire any interest in farmland which exceeds ten acres in aggregate. Act does not interfere with farmland held on date on which Act came into force, Sept. 26, 1984. There are no other laws restricting acquisition and holding of property by aliens.

Alien enemies have no privilege in courts, and are liable to be interned. See also Canada Law Digest.

ALIMONY: See topic Divorce.

ALLOWANCES:

See topic Executors and Administrators.

APPEAL AND ERROR:

Court of Appeal.—Appeal lies from final judgment of Court of Appeal to Supreme Court of Canada with leave of latter and in certain other cases with leave of Court of Appeal. (R. S. C., c. S19).

Queen's Bench.—Every rule, order, verdict, judgment or decision rendered by the Court of Queen's Bench except by the consent of parties or on question of costs, which are in discretion of the court, is appealable to the Court of Appeal unless otherwise provided by statute. (C.C.S.M. c. C280).

Notice of appeal to the Court of Appeal does not operate as a stay of proceedings. Judge may order stay unconditionally or on terms. (Q.B. Rules 63.01[1], 63.02[3]).

Provincial Judges.—Decisions are appealable to Court of Queen's Bench, whose judgments on such appeals are final.

ARBITRATION AND AWARD:

There is statutory provision whereby parties may by consent arbitrate their differences out of court, and provision is made for the court to appoint an arbitrator if the parties have agreed to arbitrate, but the arbitrator has refused to act or is incapable of acting, or if a third arbitrator is required, and the parties cannot agree upon a person to act. An arbitrator is given the statutory right to administer oaths and to state a special case for the opinion of the judge. Arbitrator can compel the attendance before him of witnesses. (The Arbitration Act, C.C.S.M. c. A120).

Appointment of Arbitrator.—The court may appoint an arbitrator on application of any party to a submission if the others do not agree or fail to appoint. (§6).

Statutory conditions regulate arbitration unless a contrary intention is shown by the agreement to arbitrate.

Legal proceedings will be stayed unless the defendant has refused to assist towards the arbitration to which he has agreed. (§7).

Submission is irrevocable except by leave of court. (§4).

Award may be moved against in court and may be made a judgment of the Court of Queen's Bench.

See also topic Dispute Resolution.

ASSIGNMENTS:

An equitable assignment of a chose in action requires that notice be given to the party liable.

Earnings.—Assignments of or orders for wages or salary to be earned in future, given in consideration of present advance or loan, in order to be valid against employer, must be accepted in writing by him, except where such assignment is given for indebtedness for necessaries. No assignment made by either cohabiting spouse (married or continuously cohabited for three years or more and one dependent on other or cohabited one year or more and child born of relationship) of wages to be earned by spouse in future without written consent of other spouse. Advance or loan must exceed 95% of wages or salary assigned. (C.C.S.M. c. L90). Portion of wages assigned must not exceed garnishment exemptions. See topic Garnishment.

Book Debts.—See topic Personal Property Security.

ASSIGNMENTS FOR BENEFIT OF CREDITORS:

Practically all such assignments are made under Bankruptcy and Insolvency Act. See Canada Law Digest.

ASSOCIATIONS:

Unincorporated associations are not partnerships in the sense that all members are bound by the acts of other members. An association as such has no power to sue or be sued, and property acquired must be held in the names of trustees chosen by the members.

Statutory provisions are made for cooperative corporations. (The Cooperatives Act, C.C.S.M. c. C223).

ATTACHMENT:

A debtor is liable to have all his property both real and personal, except such as is exempt from seizure under execution, attached for the payment of debts, or for the satisfaction of legal costs of action through a judicial order.

Grounds.—Attachment may be issued where in action in which payment of money is claimed it is alleged that defendant: (1) resides outside Manitoba, or is corporation not registered under The Corporations Act; (2) hides or absconds within Manitoba with intent to avoid service of document; (3) is about to leave or has left Manitoba with intent to change residence, defraud creditor or avoid service of document; (4) is about to permanently remove or has permanently removed property out of Manitoba; or (5) has concealed, removed, assigned, transferred, conveyed, converted or otherwise disposed of property with intent to delay, defeat or defraud creditor, or is about to do so. (C.C.S.M. c. C280, §60[1]).

Affidavit for Attachment.—A judge's order may be made directing the attachment upon the affidavit of the creditor or his agent, stating the facts.

Writ or order is directed to sheriff in Queen's Bench to levy on goods and chattels of debtor for amount mentioned in writ.

Lien.—Every order of attachment at and from delivery to the sheriff binds the goods and chattels of the party against whom the same is issued. To bind lands, a certificate of the issue of such order must be obtained and duly registered in a registry office or land titles office against title to lands of debtor.

Priorities.—Execution creditors share ratably in the proceeds of the property attached and sold.

ATTORNEYS AND COUNSELORS:

Law Society Act (C.C.S.M. c. L100) regulates practice of barristers and solicitors in Manitoba. Two professions of barrister and solicitor are recognized, but all applicants for admission must qualify for both call to bar and admission as solicitor.

Law Society.—The affairs of the Society are regulated by benchers, consisting of elective benchers, life benchers, ex-officio benchers, four appointed benchers who are not Law Society members, a university bencher, a student bencher, faculty bencher and Dean of Faculty of Law of University of Manitoba. Benchers regulate questions of admission to Society, conduct affairs of Society and exercise disciplinary control over members generally.

ATTORNEYS AND COUNSELORS . . . *continued*

Eligibility.—For admission to Law Society as articling student candidate must be graduate of approved law school and produce evidence of good character and repute. Practising barristers, solicitors or advocates from other provinces of Canada who have practiced for three years in preceding five years may be admitted by filing formal application together with evidence of good standing, good character and time during which he has been actively engaged in practice of law and passing such examinations on law and procedure in Manitoba as may be prescribed. See also subhead Examinations, infra.

Registration as Law Student.—Deadline for registration is usually late in June.

Educational Requirements.—Student entering first year law school must have completed at least two years of approved program at University of Manitoba or equivalent. Application forms are obtainable from University of Manitoba Faculty of Law. Enrolment is restricted at discretion of Faculty of Law.

Petition for Admission.—Forms are supplied by Director of Legal Education of Law Society.

Examinations.—Law Society prescribes what examinations must be taken by practicing Barristers, Solicitors or Advocates from other jurisdictions. Law Society conducts examinations for articling students.

Clerkship.—Faculty of Law offers three year full time course of lectures leading to LL.B. degree with 11½ month period of articling following. On completion of degree and articling, which includes bar admission course, candidates will be eligible to be called as Barristers and Solicitors.

Persons from other jurisdictions, otherwise eligible, do not in most cases have to serve any period of clerkship unless they have been in active practice for less than three years. In that event a period of 11½ months must be served. Applicants from other jurisdictions must take examinations in court procedure and statute law as prescribed by examining committee.

Admission without Examination.—See subhead Admission Pro Hac Vice, infra.

Admission Pro Hac Vice.—Benchers have power to admit a lawyer for a particular case. (C.C.S.M. c. L100, §36).

Licences.—Members must have current practicing certificate. Annual fee is set by governing body and must be paid together with an annual assessment to maintain reimbursement fund, as set by governing body, and an annual assessment for professional liability insurance under a Law Society program.

Privileges.—Usual.

Liabilities.—Usual.

Compensation.—Client who disputes account may have it taxed by court officer or if agrees with lawyer, arbitrated through Law Society. Contingency agreements must be in accordance with Law Society Act.

Lien.—Common law lien applies on papers, documents, certificates, etc.

Disbarment or Suspension.—Members may be disciplined, suspended or disbarred by Discipline Committee. Charges laid by Complaints Investigation Committee for infraction of rules of Society or for incompetence.

Unauthorized practice may be enjoined under provisions of Law Society Act. Members cannot incorporate for purposes of practicing law.

Professional Association.—Manitoba Bar Association is Voluntary, unincorporated body. No statutory authorization for formation by lawyers other than Law Society Act. (C.C.S.M. c. L100).

AUTOMOBILES: See topic Motor Vehicles.

BANKS AND BANKING:

See generally Canada Law Digest. Credit unions are Provincially controlled financial institutions governed by Credit Unions & Caisses Populaires Act (C.C.S.M. c. C301).

Trust Companies.—Before a trust company can commence business it must obtain business authorization from Director appointed by Minister of Consumer and Corporate Affairs.

Trust companies which have been approved by order of the LieutenantGovernor-in-Council do not have to give security for the due performance of their duties as executor, administrator, trustee, receiver, liquidator, assignee, guardian or committee. A trust company must not borrow money by issuing bonds or debentures. (C.C.S.M. c. C225).

BILLS AND NOTES:

See generally Canada Law Digest.

Lien Notes.—See topic Liens.

BILLS OF LADING: See topic Carriers.

BILLS OF SALE: See topic Chattel Mortgages.

BLUE SKY LAW: See topic Securities.

BONDS:

Accepted in lieu of cash deposit as security for costs usually in double the value with two sureties, who must furnish affidavits of justification, or by a guaranty company. (Q. B. Rule 56.04).

BROKERS:

The term "broker" is generally applied to those dealing in securities. See topic Securities.

The Real Estate Brokers Act (C.C.S.M. c. R20) provides that no person shall act as broker or salesman in real estate transactions unless duly registered, but this does not apply to lawyers entitled to practice law in Manitoba and certain others. Surety bonds must be filed for $10,000-$100,000 depending on size of broker. Manitoba Securities Commission has powers of investigation.

The Mortgage Dealers Act (C.C.S.M. c. M210) with certain exceptions requires registration of mortgage brokers and mortgage dealers.

BULK SALES:

See topic Fraudulent Sales and Conveyances.

CARRIERS:

Canadian railways have substantial flexibility to operate in competitive transportation environment but are regulated in certain respects by National Transportation Agency under National Transportation Act, 1987, Railway Act and Western Grain Transportation Act. Legislation in various provinces provides for "short-line" railways under provincial jurisdiction.

Some regulatory jurisdiction remains with Agency with respect to rates, conditions of carriage and common carrier obligations, but Canadian railways can now enter into confidential contracts with shippers. Regulatory approval is required for line abandonment, conveyance of lines and joint running rights but shippers may apply to Agency for recourse under various shipper relief provisions contained in National Transportation Act, 1987.

Transportation of "grain" is extensively regulated under Western Grain Transportation Act.

Airline operations have been deregulated as to points served, frequency of service and rates except for "designated area" in northern Canada.

Bills of Lading.—National Transportation Act, 1987 eliminated requirement for uniform rail Bill of Lading. Terms and conditions of carriage including extent of carrier's liability may be negotiated and contained in confidential contract, failing which, in absence of specific order by Agency, carrier's liability is governed by Rail Liability Regulations.

Motor Vehicle Carriers.—See topic Motor Vehicles.

CERTIORARI:

Jurisdiction.—The superior courts exercise jurisdiction in certiorari, and in criminal matters constantly exercise the power of quashing convictions even though a right of appeal exists.

Statutory limitations have from time to time been passed to curtail the operation of certiorari and a great number of our provincial statutes creating offences purport to take away the right. But if there is a lack of jurisdiction or in cases of manifest fraud on the part of the prosecutor or improper conduct on the part of provincial judge certiorari will still lie even though taken away by statute.

Grounds.—The most frequent ground for the issue of the writ is the lack of jurisdiction on the part of a magistrate or inferior court.

CHATTEL MORTGAGES:

See topic Personal Property Security.

CLAIMS:

See topics Executors and Administrators; Pleading.

COLLATERAL SECURITY: See topic Pledges.

COLLECTION AGENCIES:

See topic Principal and Agent.

COMMISSIONS TO TAKE TESTIMONY:

See topic Depositions.

COMMUNITY PROPERTY:

System does not obtain in Manitoba.

CONDITIONAL SALES:

See topic Personal Property Security.

CONSIGNMENTS: See topic Factors.

CONSUMER PROTECTION:

Area governed by The Consumer Protection Act (C.C.S.M. c. C200), The Business Practices Act (C.C.S.M. c. B120), and The Trade Practices Inquiry Act (C.C.S.M. c. T110).

The Consumer Protection Act sets out minimum disclosure requirements in transactions involving borrowing. Right of prepayment on certain transactions. Acceleration of debt on default valid, subject to certain limitations. Time sales must be evidenced by agreement stating, in type not less than ten point in size, that property in goods does not pass on delivery, conditions upon which it does pass and events upon which seller may repossess. Mortgagee of goods may not repossess without leave of court if balance owing is less than 25% of original liability. Implied warranties in every retail sale that goods new and free of encumbrances unless otherwise disclosed, as well as reasonably fit for any purpose disclosed by purchaser. Sales made elsewhere than in vendor's usual place of business may be cancelled within seven days by notice in writing. Consumers Bureau administers Act and receives complaints.

The Business Practices Act sets out specific unfair business practices and provides right of action in court by consumer. Unfair business practices include: (a) doing or failing to do anything which may reasonably deceive consumer; (b) making false claims to consumer; and (c) taking advantage of consumer if supplier should know consumer not able to protect own interests.

See note at head of Digest as to 1996 legislation covered.

See Topical Index in front part of this volume.

CONSUMER PROTECTION . . . *continued*

The Trade Practices Inquiry Act allows complaints to Minister of Consumer and Corporate Affairs by any four residents of Manitoba respecting misleading advertising and unfair or improper charging or dealings. Preliminary investigation by Minister. May recommend inquiry by appointed board who may recommend regulations for price of article or product which is (i) essential to day to day activities of significant number of Manitobans, and (ii) distributed through system limiting competition, and (iii) no reasonable substitute easily available. Criminal penalties for contravention.

Plain Language Statute.—No plain language statute. See, however, The Business Practices Act (C.C.S.M. c. B120) and The Trade Practices Inquiry Act (C.C.S.M. c. T110), supra.

CONTRACTS:

Frustrated Contracts Act (C.C.S.M., c. F190).—Where contract frustrated and parties discharged, sums previously paid are recoverable and sums payable cease to be payable. Court given powers: (1) to allow expenses up to sums paid or payable; (2) to allow for valuable benefit conferred by one party on other or obligation assumed by one for benefit of other; (3) sever contract treating part as not frustrated and part frustrated. Act applies to all contracts governed by Manitoba law except charterparty (except time charterparty or charterparty by demise), contracts for carriage of goods by sea, insurance contracts, sales of specific goods which have perished either before contract or without seller's fault before risk passes to buyer.

Distributorships, Dealerships and Franchises.—No special rules apply.

CONVEYANCES: See topic Deeds.

CORPORATIONS:

The Corporations Act (C.C.S.M. c. C225) applies to all corporations except: (a) Corporation created for government or municipal purpose; (b) bank incorporated under Act of Parliament of Canada; (c) cooperative corporation within The Cooperatives Act (C.C.S.M. c. C223); (d) credit union within The Credit Unions and Caisses Populaires Act (S.M. 1986-87, c. 5) except where The Credit Unions and Caisses Populaires Act indicates provision of The Corporations Act applies (C.C.S.M. c. C225, §3[2][b]).

General Supervision.—Director, Corporations Branch.

Name under which incorporation sought must include "Limited", "Limitée", "Incorporated", "Incorporée", or "Corporation" or abbreviation "Ltd.", "Ltée.", "Inc." or "Corp." as last word of name; may be number name; must not be similar to that of any body corporate, business or association; must not suggest any connection with Crown or government of Canada; unless permitted under Act must not include words "Loan" or "Trust"; must not be objectionable on any public grounds; must not be deceptively misdescriptive or otherwise prohibited by regulation; must be approved by Director. Proposed name stating nature of business may be submitted for approval. Upon application and payment of $30 name may be reserved for 90 days.

Term of Corporate Existence.—May be perpetual. See subhead Dissolution, infra.

Incorporators.—One or more persons or corporations may incorporate corporation. Individual incorporators must be at least 18 years old; must not have been found by court to be of unsound mind; must not have status of bankrupt. No special requirement as to citizenship or residence. Majority of directors must be residents of Canada.

Application.—Articles of incorporation must show name of corporation; place within Manitoba where registered office will be situate; classes and any maximum number of shares that corporation is authorized to issue; preferences or conditions attached to shares, any restrictions on transfer of shares, names in full and residence addresses of all first directors and incorporators. Prescribed forms of articles and affidavits of verification. Articles may set out any provision authorized by Act or by law to be set out in by-laws or unanimous shareholder agreement. First director who is not incorporator must sign consent to act as first director. Signature of each incorporator and fact that each incorporator and first director who is natural person is 18 or over must be verified by affidavit.

Filing of Application.—Filed in duplicate with Director, Corporations Branch.

Issue of Certificate of Incorporation.—If articles are in order and fees are paid, Director must issue certificate of incorporation. Notice thereof is published by Director in Manitoba Gazette. Date of incorporation is that of certificate of incorporation.

Incorporation Fee.—For corporation without share capital, $70; with share capital, $250. In addition there is tariff of fees for services under Act.

Registration.—Manitoba corporations are registered concurrently upon incorporation. Foreign corporations must be registered before carrying on business except federal corporations which must register within 30 days. Foreign corporations must file with Director application in prescribed form in duplicate, power of attorney in prescribed form and any other information Director may require. Fee payable on registration is $250. Reporting requirements are substantially same for foreign and domestic corporations.

Organization.—Incorporators need not be first shareholders or first directors. Any resolution signed by all directors or all shareholders at any time during corporation's existence is as valid as if passed at regular meeting of directors or shareholders. Special resolutions must be confirmed by 2/3 of votes at meeting of shareholders called for that purpose or by written consent of all shareholders entitled to vote at such meeting. By-laws are adopted by shareholder resolution.

Paid-In Capital Requirements.—Shares must not be issued until fully paid.

Amendment of Articles of Incorporation.—May be effected by delivering executed articles of amendment in duplicate to Director along with required fee. Fee is $135 for corporation with share capital, $250 to convert corporation without share capital into corporation with share capital, $35 for corporation without share capital. Amendments require authorization by special resolution (see subhead Organization, supra) and where share rights affected, shareholders entitled to vote separately as class. Shareholders who dissent are entitled to be paid fair value for their shares.

Increase or Decrease of Authorized Capital Stock.—May be effected by articles of amendment. On reduction of capital corporation must not be insolvent.

Shares.—Must be without par value. Unless articles otherwise provide each share entitles holder to vote and to share in distribution of assets upon dissolution. Allotment and issue of shares regulated by directors. Shares must not be issued until fully paid. There are restricted provisions for purchase by corporation of its shares.

Share Certificates.—Every shareholder is entitled to properly signed share certificate stating name of corporation, words to effect that corporation was incorporated under law of Province of Manitoba, shareholder's name, number and class of shares represented thereby and particulars of rights, privileges, restrictions and conditions of shares. Upon demand corporation shall furnish to shareholder full copy of text of share particulars.

Transfer of Stock.—Any restriction on share transfer is ineffective against transferee without actual knowledge unless conspicuously noted on certificate. Transfers of stock must be entered in books of corporation before corporation is bound thereby.

Stock Transfer Tax.—None.

Shareholders.—Elect directors and appoint auditors. Directors are responsible for general supervision of affairs of corporation. If shareholders are dissatisfied they may replace any director before expiration of term. Shareholders may inspect copies of articles, register of security holders and transfer register, and minutes of all shareholders' meetings. Shareholders holding 5% of issued voting shares may requisition meeting of shareholders and may requisition directors to circulate shareholders' resolution to be considered at next shareholders' meeting. Shareholder who dissents from resolution passed by majority to dispose of substantially all assets of corporation, delete share transfer restriction, amalgamate corporation or transfer corporation to another jurisdiction may require corporation to purchase his shares. If wrong is done to corporation such as where: (a) Property or rights of corporation are being appropriated to majority, (b) breach of directors duty to act bona fide in interests of corporation has been condoned by majority, or (c) majority has enacted resolutions which discriminate so as to give majority advantage of which minority is deprived, and majority refuses to cause corporation to take action, derivative suit (class action) may be instituted with leave of court by any shareholder, director or officer, Director or any other person deemed proper by court.

Shareholders' Liability.—Shareholders not liable for corporate debts or obligations. On decrease of issued capital by articles of amendment each shareholder on such date may be individually liable to creditors of corporation for debts due on such date up to amount not exceeding amount of repayment to him. Notwithstanding dissolution of corporation, shareholders among whom its property has been distributed remain liable to its creditors up to amount received by them respectively but action to enforce such liability must be brought within two years of dissolution. Unanimous shareholder agreement imposes on parties liabilities of directors to extent agreement restricts powers of directors to manage.

Shareholders' Meetings.—Annual meetings must be held within 18 months after incorporation and subsequently not more than 15 months after previous annual meeting and in every case within six months of financial year end. Meetings must be held at any place within Manitoba provided in by-laws or if not provided as determined by directors or may be outside Manitoba if articles so provide or all shareholders entitled to vote so agree. Notice of time and place for holding general meetings must unless waived by given at least 21 days and not more than 50 days prior to meeting.

Voting.—Every shareholder is entitled to as many votes as he holds shares unless otherwise provided in articles and may vote by proxy. Nominee appointed by proxy need not be shareholder. Proxy only valid at meeting in respect of which given. Proxy may be revoked by instrument in writing deposited at registered office of company prior to day of meeting or with chairman of meeting on day of meeting. Where articles so provide cumulative voting for directors is permitted. Resolution signed by all shareholders entitled to vote at meeting is as valid as if passed at meeting.

Directors.—Corporation not offering its securities to public must have at least one director; public offering company must have at least three directors of whom at least two shall not be officers or employees of corporation or affilate. Directors need not be shareholders. Generally majority of directors must be Canadian residents. Directors must be individuals over 18 and not undischarged bankrupt or mental incompetent. Directors may be elected for term of up to but not exceeding three years, in rotation or by staggered boards, otherwise election of directors must take place yearly and all directors then in office must retire but if otherwise qualified are eligible for reelection.

Vacancies in board may generally be filled by directors remaining in office provided there is quorum but if no quorum, vacancies must be filled by shareholders.

Directors appoint officers of corporation and may delegate powers to manage. Directors may appoint from their number managing director who is resident of Canada or committee with majority being residents of Canada and, with certain restrictions, may delegate any powers of directors to managing director or committee.

Directors' Meetings.—Business can only be transacted at directors' meeting at which quorum is present and at which majority of those present are Canadian residents. Meetings may be held over conference telephone. Any resolution signed at any time during corporation's existence by all directors is as valid as if passed at meeting. Unless articles or by-laws provide otherwise majority of directors constitutes quorum. Unless articles or by-laws otherwise provide directors may meet at any place and upon such notice as by-laws require.

Powers and Duties of Directors.—Subject to any unanimous shareholder agreement, directors of corporation shall exercise powers of corporation and shall direct management of business and affairs of corporation. Directors may make by-laws which are in force until next general meeting of shareholders when by-laws must be confirmed.

Liabilities of Directors.—Where directors consent to shares of corporation being acquired by it for redemption, purchase or cancellation in contravention of Act or articles, directors are liable to corporation. Directors are jointly and severally liable to corporation for amount of any dividend improperly declared. Directors are jointly and

CORPORATIONS . . . *continued*
severally liable to employees of company for all debts due while they are directors for services performed for corporation up to six months wages.

Powers of Corporation.—Subject to Act and articles corporation has capacity, rights, powers and privileges of natural person. By-law is not necessary to confer any particular power on corporation or directors. No doctrine of constructive notice and no act of corporation is invalid by reason only that it is contrary to articles or Act. There are restrictions on corporation holding shares in itself or parent corporation. Financial assistance by means of loan, guarantee or otherwise to shareholder, director, officer or employee or to any person in connection with purchase of corporation's shares is restricted where corporation would be insolvent after assistance was given. Unless contrary expressly so provided pre-incorporation contract entered into on behalf of proposed corporation personally binds person who enters into it. Upon incorporation corporation may adopt pre-incorporation contract and unless contract provides for joint and several liability person who entered into contract on behalf of corporation ceases to be bound by or entitled to contract. Party to pre-incorporation contract may apply to court for order fixing obligations under contract.

See also topic Aliens.

Dividends.—May be paid in money, property or by issuing fully paid shares in corporation. No dividend can be declared when there are reasonable grounds for believing corporation is insolvent, or when such dividend would render corporation insolvent or diminish its capital.

Sales or Transfer of Corporate Assets.—Sale, lease or exchange of all or substantially all of its property must be authorized by shareholders who have right to dissent and receive fair value for shares.

Books and Records.—Every corporation must keep records containing following information: articles, by-laws and all amendments and copy of any unanimous shareholder agreement; minutes of meetings and resolutions of shareholders; securities register showing for each class names and latest known address of each person who is or has been security holder, number of securities held by each holder and date and particulars of issue and transfer of each security; accounting records and minutes of meetings and resolutions of directors. Various rights of inspection given to shareholders, creditors and others subject in some cases to filing affidavit and payment of reasonable fee where copies furnished.

Reports.—Prospectus must be filed as required by The Securities Act (C.C.S.M. c. S50) upon sale of securities to public.

Annual return must be filed with Director not later than last day of month immediately following month of incorporation. Filing fee is $35 for corporations with share capital, $15 for corporations without share capital, $15 for amendments.

Annual financial statements must be laid before each annual meeting. Corporation which has made distribution to public must send each shareholder interim financial statement in prescribed form not less than 21 days before each annual meeting.

Corporation which has made distribution to public must file with Manitoba Securities Commission comparative financial statements and report of Auditor. (C.C.S.M. c. S50).

Shareholders of corporation which does not make distribution to public may resolve not to appoint auditor.

Corporate Bonds or Mortgages.—See topic Personal Property Security.

Amalgamation.—Two or more Manitoba corporations may amalgamate by statutory procedure. They must enter into amalgamation agreement which is not effective until approved by shareholders of each corporation. Shareholders who dissent are entitled to receive fair value for shares if amalgamation approved.

Continuations.—Corporations incorporated in jurisdictions other than Manitoba, if authorized by laws of that jurisdiction, may on application to Director be continued as if incorporated in Manitoba.

Manitoba corporations if authorized by shareholders and it appears to Director that creditors or shareholders would not be prejudiced may apply to another jurisdiction to be continued as if incorporated under laws of that jurisdiction. Shareholders may dissent and are entitled to be paid fair value for shares upon continuation in another jurisdiction.

Dissolution.—Corporation may liquidate and dissolve by special resolution of shareholders of each class of shares issued whether or not holders are otherwise entitled to vote. Notice of intent to dissolve must be sent to Director in prescribed form and corporation must cease to do business except to extent necessary for liquidation. Director issues certificate of intent to dissolve and corporation must immediately notify each known creditor and publish notice in Manitoba Gazette and in newspaper in place where corporation has registered office and take reasonable steps to give notice in every jurisdiction where it carries on business. After discharging all obligations and other acts required to liquidate business and after proper notice has been given, remaining property is distributed to shareholders, according to respective rights. Articles of dissolution in prescribed form sent to Director and certificate of dissolution issues specifying date corporation ceases to exist.

Court may also order liquidation and dissolution of corporation on application by shareholder. Where corporation dissolved by court order liquidation and dissolution continues under supervision of court.

Director may dissolve corporation after giving 90 days notice: where corporation is two years in default in sending any notice or document to Director; where Director has reasonable cause to believe corporation is not carrying on business; where corporation is in default of sending to Director any fee.

Articles of dissolution may be filed in certain cases of voluntary dissolution as where corporation was never active and never issued shares or where it has no liabilities.

Insolvency and Receivers.—See topic Receivers, and Canada Law Digest, topic Bankruptcy.

Close Corporations.—Act does not provide for private companies. Distinction between corporations which do and do not offer securities to public.

Foreign Corporations.—See subhead Registration, supra.

Taxation.—Corporations must pay income tax of 17% of taxable income earned in Manitoba in year. (C.C.S.M. c. I10). Reduction in rate by 8% is available in respect of active business income subject to small business credit. By Federal-Provincial agreement Canada collects income tax on behalf of Manitoba, so no separate Manitoba tax return need be filed. Insurance Corporations Tax Act (C.C.S.M., c. I50) makes every insurance company liable to tax of 2% of net amount of premiums payable under contracts of accident, life and sickness insurance and 3% under other contracts of insurance on business transacted in Manitoba. Corporation Capital Tax Act (S. M. 1976, c. 68, S. M. 1986-87, c. 18, S. M. 1987, c. 49) requires corporation with permanent establishment in province to pay directly to province each fiscal year 3/10 of 1% of taxable paid-up capital if resident of Canada or of taxable paid-up capital employed in Canada if nonresident. Additional 2/10 of 1% if over $10,000,000 taxable income after June 30, 1987. Deduction of 3/10 of 1% or 2/10 of 1% for total capital over $10,000,000 if corporation outside Manitoba (as defined in Regulations). Tax on banks incorporated under Bank Act (Canada) or Quebec Savings Bank Act for fiscal years ending after June 30, 1986 is 3% of taxable paid-up capital; tax on trust corporations and loan corporations is 3% of taxable paid-up capital. Deduction for bank, trust corporation, loan corporation outside Manitoba of 3% from amount taxable.

Also see topic Deeds, subhead Land Transfer Tax.

Professional Corporations.—Most professions have association created by statute to govern affairs. Professional practice by corporation is permitted only if creating statute allows. (S.M. 1986-87, §15[3]).

COSTS:

Costs are usually given to any party who makes a necessary move and succeeds, but they are in the discretion of the judge in nearly all cases. (The Queen's Bench Act, C.C.S.M. c. C280. See also Q.B. Rules 57 and 58).

Security for costs may be ordered against any plaintiff resident outside of Manitoba without assets in the province sufficient to answer for costs. (See topic Actions.) Such plaintiff may move to have order for security set aside on satisfying court that he has assets in Manitoba, readily available on execution, in excess of amount of security required.

Security may be by bond in such sum as the court orders or by payment into court of one-half the amount of bond ordered. (See topic Bonds.)

Tariffs.—Queen's Bench costs are covered by tariffs.

COURTS:

The Court of Appeal has appellate jurisdiction of civil and criminal appeals from lower courts. (The Court of Appeal Act, C.C.S.M. c. C240). And see topic Appeal and Error.

As to Court of Queen's Bench, Court of Queen's Bench Small Claims Division, and provincial judges courts, see topic Actions.

Long Vacation.—Court of Queen's Bench is closed from July 1 until Sept. 1. During this period no trials are heard unless urgent; but offices of courts are open for transaction of routine business. Short vacation—usually two weeks, at Christmas. Actions may be commenced during vacation and urgent noncontentious motions disposed of.

CREDITORS' SUITS:

A judgment creditor may bring an action on a certificate of judgment which is registered in Land Titles office against debtor's land and have land sold to satisfy judgment; but no proceedings to realize on registered judgment can be commenced until after one year from date of registration. (C.C.S.M. c. J10).

CRIMINAL LAW:

Criminal law and its procedure is regulated by statutes of Canada under constitution. Province only provides courts except for certain provincial penal enactments where province has in conjunction with other jurisdictions, imposed penalties. See Canada Law Digest.

CURTESY:

Curtesy has been abolished by statute, but see topics Homesteads and Descent and Distribution.

DAMAGES:

Common law generally prevails. See also topic Death, subhead Action for Death.

Contributory negligence rules in force. (C.C.S.M. c. T90).

Doctrine of charitable immunity not recognized.

No-Fault Insurance.—See topic Motor Vehicles.

Sovereign Liability.—See The Proceedings Against the Crown Act. (C.C.S.M. c. P140).

DEATH:

Upon application to Court of Queen's Bench, order shall be granted declaring person presumed dead if person absent or not heard of by applicant or any other person, no reason to believe person alive and reasonable grounds for believing dead. (The Presumption of Death Act, C.C.S.M. c. P120).

A written certificate signed by a proper officer of Her Majesty's forces, stating that a named member of such forces is officially reported dead or presumed dead, is sufficient proof of death of such person. (The Manitoba Evidence Act, C.C.S.M. c. E150).

Order of Death.—Except in certain cases under will, and subject to certain provisions of The Insurance Act (C.C.S.M. c. I40), where two or more persons die at same time or under circumstances rendering it uncertain which died first, each, for purpose of disposing of his or her estate, will be deemed to have survived others. (The Survivorship Act, C.C.S.M. c. S250).

DEATH . . . *continued*

Survivorship.—Where two persons die at same time or in circumstances rendering it uncertain which survived, estate of each disposed of as if he had survived. Joint tenants who so die are deemed to have been tenants in common and above rule applies. Where life insured so dies, insurance money payable as if beneficiary predeceased life insured.

Action for death is available to surviving spouse, parents, children, brothers or sisters of deceased if a reasonable anticipation of pecuniary benefit from continued existence of deceased can be established. Action must be commenced within two years after death of deceased. Damages are generally fixed with regard to reasonable expectation of pecuniary benefit on part of person suing, but may include damages for loss of care, guidance and companionship which might reasonably have been expected from deceased; damages are apportioned by judge or jury who tries case. (The Fatal Accidents Act C.C.S.M. c. F50). In specified circumstances, compensation is obtainable under The Criminal Injuries Compensation Act. (C.C.S.M. c. C305). See also topic Actions, subhead Abatement.

DECEDENTS' ESTATES:

See topics Descent and Distribution; Executors and Administrators; Homesteads; Wills.

DECLARATORY JUDGMENTS: See topic Judgments.

DEEDS:

There are two systems by which land is held, mortgaged, or conveyed, called the Old System and the New System.

See topic Real Property for estates recognized.

Old System.—Land held under Old System is regulated by Registry Act (C.C.S.M. c. R30) and is conveyed by means of deed, which usually contains covenants for further assurance on part of grantor and that grantor has done nothing to encumber land mentioned in deed. It is executed under seal in presence of witness who not only signs his name as witness but takes affidavit that he was present at its execution which is attached to or endorsed on deed.

If the grantor is unable to write, his mark is sufficient. His name is written at the foot of the deed and he makes his mark in the presence of two witnesses who subscribe their names opposite as witnesses.

Registration.—Deeds and instruments affecting land are registered in the proper registry office of the district where such land is situate. The registrar of the proper land registry offices abstracts the title to the land the instrument conveys and gives certificates of the abstract and registrations under seal when requisitioned and upon payment of the proper fees. Since priority of registration prevails it is important that deeds be registered to shut out innocent persons who might otherwise become interested in the land.

Fees payable under Old System for registration of deed of land or other instrument affecting title generally $10.

Transfer to New System.—Land under the Old System may be brought under the operation of the Real Property Act (New System) by application to the District Registrar of the Land Titles District in which the land is situated. (C.C.S.M. c. R30).

New System.—The system known as the Torrens or Australian system of land transfer was introduced in 1885. Land Titles Districts have been formed, each presided over by a District Registrar. All lands in each district may be brought under the Torrens System by making application in form prescribed by the statute and a certificate of title issues to the applicant or his directee upon satisfactory proof of his title.

The transfer under the Real Property Act is simply a memorandum describing the transferor; the land; the consideration, and the transferee, accompanied by the affidavit of the transferor that he is the registered owner, the affidavit of the subscribing witness similar to that in deeds, the affidavit of the transferee as to the value of the land together with all buildings and improvements thereon, affidavit of transferor, transferee, or agent as to whether or not land is farm land under The Farm Lands Ownership Act, and consent of spouse under The Homesteads Act if necessary. There must be endorsed on transfer address of transferee. All transfers for registration must be handwritten or printed. Typewritten transfers are accepted if in indelible ink.

The District Registrar may refuse to register a transfer of an undivided fractional interest in the mines or minerals in, under or upon any parcel of land if that fractional interest is less than an undivided one-quarter interest thereof. The District Registrar may also refuse to register a transfer of an interest in mines or minerals if more than four persons are named therein as transferees.

Certificate of Title.—On registration of transfer in Land Titles Office a certificate and duplicate of title issues to transferee.

Every certificate of title, so long as it remains in force and uncancelled, is conclusive evidence at law and in equity as against Her Majesty and all persons whomsoever that the person named in such certificate is entitled to the land described therein for the estate or interest therein specified, subject to certain trifling exceptions mentioned in the statute. Any person aggrieved must look to the assurance fund, which is created by each applicant for title paying a small percentage of the value of his property to the province and which exists for the protection of all Torrens titles.

Fees payable on registration of land transfer, $50, plus applicable land transfer tax. Duplicate certificate of title only issued on owner's request or at discretion of District Registrar. Where land subject to mortgage or encumbrance, duplicate certificate of title, if issued, must be deposited with District Registrar.

Land Transfer Tax.—Formula: Tax = .005 (FMV-$30,000) + .005 (FMV-$90,000) + .005 (FMV-$150,000). Also, change in control of corporation results in purchaser paying transfer tax on fair market value of property corporation has interest in. (The Revenue Act, C.C.S.M. c. R150, §34).

Caveat against a certificate of title may be lodged at any time by any person claiming an interest in the land covered by said certificate, forbidding the issue of a new certificate of title or other dealing with the land except subject to such caveat.

Short forms of deeds, leases and mortgages are provided by "The Short Forms of Indentures Act" (C.C.S.M. c. S120) and "The Real Property Act" (C.C.S.M. c. R30).

Form

Old System Deed:

This Indenture, made (in duplicate) the . . . . . . day of . . . . . ., one thousand nine hundred and . . . . In pursuance of the Act Respecting Short Forms of Indentures between . . . . . . and . . . . . . witnesseth that in consideration of . . . . . . Dollars of lawful money of Canada, now paid by the said part . . . . of the second part to the said part . . . . of the first part (the receipt whereof is hereby acknowledged) . . . . . . the said part . . . . of the first part do . . . . grant unto the said part . . . . of the second part . . . . . . heirs and assigns forever all and singular the lands following, that is to say:

. . . .

To have and to hold unto the said part . . . . of the second part . . . . . . heirs and assigns to and for . . . . . . their sole and only use forever; subject nevertheless to the reservations, limitations, provisos and conditions expressed in the original grant thereof from the Crown.

The said part . . . . of the first part covenant . . . . with the said part . . . . of the second part that . . . . he . . . . ha . . . . the right to convey the said lands to the said part . . . . of the second part notwithstanding any act of the said part . . . . of the first part and that the said part . . . . of the second part shall have quiet possession of the said lands free from all encumbrances. And the said part . . . . of the first part covenant . . . . with the said part . . . . of the second part that . . . . . . will execute such further assurances of the said lands as may be requisite; and the said part . . . . of the first part covenant . . . . with the said part . . . . of the second part that . . . . . . ha. . . . done no act to encumber the said lands and the said part . . . . of the first part release . . . . to the said part . . . . of the second part all . . . . . . claims upon the said lands.

In Witness Whereof, the said parties have hereunto set their hands and seals.

(Signed, sealed and delivered
in the presence of)

(Add consent of spouse, if any, and acknowledgment thereof.)

New System Transfer:

See Form 8 at end of Digest.

See also topics Homesteads; Husband and Wife, subhead Conveyance or Encumbrance of Property.

DEEDS OF TRUST:

See topic Mortgages of Real Property. See also topic Personal Property Security.

DEPOSITIONS:

Oral examination to be held in Manitoba must be held before official examiner of Court of Queen's Bench or person agreed upon by parties. Party to proceeding or person who is to be examined on behalf of party shall be served with notice of examination. Person examined to swear or affirm. (See Q.B. Rules 31 and 34.)

Compelling Attendance.—Where person fails to attend at time and place specified in notice of examination, court may dismiss party's proceedings, make contempt order or make such order as just.

Outside Manitoba For Use Within Manitoba.—Courts may make order respecting where examination to take place, notice provisions, person before whom to take place or any other matter. Where court makes order for examination of party outside Manitoba, order shall, if moving party requests, provide for issue of commission and letter of request of foreign court to issue process necessary to compel person to be examined by Commissioner. Registrar shall issue letter or request and commission. Commissioner shall conduct examination by oral questions in accordance with Manitoba law unless order or foreign law require otherwise. Commissioner shall return commission to issuing registrar with original transcript and exhibits. Form of commission and letter of request are prescribed in rules. (See Q.B. Rule 34.)

Examinations Out of Court.—Party intending to introduce evidence of person at trial may, with leave of court or consent of parties, examine person on oath or affirmation before trial and may tender such testimony as evidence at trial. In granting leave, court will consider convenience of witness, possibility that witness will be unavailable for trial due to death, infirmity, sickness or being beyond jurisdiction of court at time of trial, expense and whether evidence ought to be given in person. Such person may be examined, cross-examined and re-examined in same manner as witness at trial. Any party at trial may use transcript, videotape or other recording of such examination as evidence of person, unless court rules otherwise. (See Q.B. Rule 36.) See subhead Outside Manitoba For Use Within Manitoba, supra.

Interrogatories.—Conducted by serving list of questions to be answered. Are permitted in addition to oral examinations. (See Q.B. Rule 35.)

DESCENT AND DISTRIBUTION:

As of July 1, 1990, former intestate succession regime repealed and replaced by The Intestate Succession Act, C.C.S.M. c. I85, the Dependents Relief Act, C.C.S.M. c. D37, and The Wills Amendment Act, S.M. 1989-90, c. 44.

All property undisposed of by will descends and is distributed as follows (The Intestate Succession Act): (a) If no issue, surviving spouse gets entire estate; (b) if spouse and common issue, entire estate goes to surviving spouse; (c) if surviving spouse and some issue which are not common, surviving spouse receives greater of $50,000 or 50% of estate and one-half of balance, remaining half of balance being divided equally among all of intestate's issue; (d) if no surviving spouse or issue, estate goes to intestate's parents; (e) if no surviving spouse, issue or parent, estate goes to issue of intestate's parents, failing them to issue of intestate's grandparents, or failing them to issue of intestate's great-grandparents; (f) otherwise estate escheats to Crown.

Surviving spouse may make application for accounting and equalization of assets. (S.M. 1992, c. 46). Equalization payment reduced by amount of entitlement of surviving spouse under The Intestate Succession Act. (The Homesteads, Marital Property Amendment and Consequential Amendments Act, S.M. 1992, c. 46).

See note at head of Digest as to 1996 legislation covered.

See Topical Index in front part of this volume.

DESCENT AND DISTRIBUTION . . . *continued*

Distribution at each generation is per capita, not per stirpes.

Posthumous Heirs.—Descendents and relatives of intestate, begotten before his death but born thereafter, inherit as though born in intestate's lifetime.

Adopted Children.—See topic Adoption, subhead Effect of Adoption.

Advancements.—Where in total intestacy intestate has, during lifetime, made advancement to any person, such advancement is included in determination of entire estate and treated as payment toward that person's ultimate share of estate. Onus of proving advancement rests with person asserting.

DESERTION: See topics Divorce; Husband and Wife.

DISPUTE RESOLUTION:

Mandatory Dispute Resolution.—

Labour.—Minister may appoint mediator or conciliation board to facilitate collective bargaining. (C.C.S.M. c. L10, §§95[2], 97[1]). Parties bound to meet and confer. Every collective agreement must have grievance arbitration provision. Where none is provided, deemed grievance arbitration clause. (C.C.S.M. c. L10, §78). Conciliation and Mediation Services (industrial relations) provide (i) mediation and (ii) grievance conciliation; (204) 945-3367.

Voluntary Dispute Resolution.—

Family.—In family division judge or master may at any stage in proceedings refer issue to mediator. (C.C.S.M. c. C280, §47[1]). Family Conciliation provides (i) mediation for custody and access matters, (ii) conciliation counselling for separation and divorce matters; (204) 945-7236.

Labour.—Where collective bargaining has commenced, parties may jointly request minister to appoint mediator. (C.C.S.M. c. L10, §95[1]). If grievance under existing collective agreement, minister may appoint mediator on joint application of parties. (C.C.S.M. c. L10, §129[1]).

Arbitration.—See topic Arbitration and Award.

DIVORCE:

The Court of Queen's Bench for Manitoba has jurisdiction in matters of divorce. An appeal lies to the Court of Appeal.

Grounds.—See Divorce Act, 1985 (S. C. 1986, c. 4), and Canada Law Digest.

Domicile.—See Divorce Act, 1985 (S. C. 1986, c. 4), and Canada Law Digest.

Procedure.—Q.B. Rule 70.

Support.—Provisions for corollary relief and support are in Divorce Act, 1985. (S. C. 1986, c. 4). Provision as to interim disbursements. (See Q.B. Rule 70 and The Marital Property Act, C.C.S.M. c. M45, §18.)

Remarriage.—There is no restriction in regard to either party's right to remarry after decree absolute has been obtained.

Grounds for Legal Separation.—Upon application to court, spouse is entitled to order of legal separation, without need for grounds. Order may include provision for maintenance payable by one spouse to other for support of spouse or child of marriage, non-entry of spouse's residence, nonmolestation, financial disclosure, exclusive occupancy of family residence and postponement of sale of family residence. Spouses have equal obligation to contribute to each other's support, and to support of children under 18 years. (See The Family Maintenance Act, C.C.S.M. c. F20.)

Division of Property of Spouses.—Spouse may apply for accounting and division of family and commercial assets acquired during marriage. Presumption of equal sharing except where grossly unfair. Court may order transfer of asset, payment of monies and/or sale of assets to give effect to accounting and division. (See The Marital Property Act, C.C.S.M. c. M45.)

See also topic Partition.

DOWER:

See topics Homesteads and Descent and Distribution.

EMPLOYER AND EMPLOYEE:

See topic Labour Relations.

ENVIRONMENT:

General Supervision.—Department of Environment and Workplace Safety & Health with assistance of Manitoba Environment Counsel and Clean Environment Commission established by The Environment Act. (C.C.S.M. c. E125). Also The Dangerous Goods Handling & Transportation Act. (C.C.S.M. c. D12).

Prohibited Acts of Pollution.—Discharge or emission of any contaminant or waste products of any kind into air, water or soil without license. Order pursuant to The Clean Environment Act (S.M. 1972, c. F6) (repealed) considered license under new Act.

Enforcement.—Department may deny, withdraw, cancel or suspend license. Environment officer may enter, search and if offence in progress, seize without warrant. Normally, warrant required for seizure.

Penalties.—The Environment Act: For individual—first offence, fine up to $50,000, up to six months imprisonment or both; subsequent offence, fine up to $100,000, up to one year imprisonment or both. For corporation—first offence, fine up to $500,000; subsequent offence, fine up to $1,000,000. Also action to refrain from further offence, clean and restore, pay damage or restitution or additional fine up to monetary benefit received can be ordered plus revocation or suspension of all or some licences if unwilling to remedy. Each day is separate offence. (C.C.S.M. c. E125).

The Dangerous Goods Handling and Transportation Act (C.C.S.M. c. D12).—For individual: First offence, fine up to $50,000, up to six months imprisonment or both; subsequent offence, fine up to $100,000, up to one year imprisonment or both. For corporation: First offence, fine up to $500,000; second offence, fine up to $1,000,000. Each day is separate offence.

Permits.—Licence required.

EQUITY: See topic Actions.

ESCHEAT: See topic Descent and Distribution.

ESTATES: See topic Real Property.

EVIDENCE: See topics Depositions; Witnesses.

EXECUTIONS:

Remedy Against Lands.—There are no writs of execution against lands. The legal remedy is obtained by registering certificate of judgment under the seal of the court in the Land Titles Office or Registry Office of the district in which the lands of the judgment debtor are situated. Such certificates are granted under all judgments exceeding $40 in amount, and, while in force, constitute a lien and charge on the lands of the judgment debtor, which may be sold to satisfy the judgment but only after one year from date of registration. (C.C.S.M. c. J10).

Exemptions.—See topic Exemptions.

Execution Against Goods.—Writs of execution against goods may be issued after judgment has been entered and these bind the goods of the debtor in the Queen's Bench as soon as placed in the sheriff's hands. In Queen's Bench these writs can be issued forthwith after entry of judgment.

Execution can be stayed on a proper case being made, e.g., payment, accord and satisfaction, etc.

Life and Renewal of Execution.—Writ of execution ceases to have force upon expiration of two years from date of issue or renewal, unless renewed before expiration of two years. (C.C.S.M. c. E160). Certificate of judgment remains on title until vacated or discharged. (C.C.S.M. c. J10).

Sale of Lands.—Where a judgment creditor has filed a certificate of judgment to be registered against the land of the judgment debtor, such land may be sold after one year to satisfy judgment by action commenced by judgment creditor for such purpose. Sale is carried on under supervision of court and land may be redeemed at any time until sold upon judgment debtor paying amount of judgment and costs to date.

Sale of Goods.—In the case of goods the amount of the judgment is realized by seizure by sheriff (in Queen's Bench) of judgment debtor's goods after execution has been issued. Sheriff after making seizure must sell goods by public auction duly advertised. After having made money under execution, sheriff must advertise such fact in Manitoba Gazette and hold money for three months and then proceed to distribute same rateably amongst those who have placed executions in his hands.

Redemption of Goods.—Goods seized may always be redeemed by the judgment debtor until sold, by paying to the sheriff amount of judgment and costs, including costs of such sheriff.

Priorities.—There is no priority between writs of execution. Wages for three months take priority over claims of execution creditors, and costs of execution creditors, pro rata, are preferential to dividend upon actual claims.

Supplementary Proceedings.—If execution is returned unsatisfied Queen's Bench Act provides for examination before judge or officer of court of judgment debtor concerning property or means he possessed at time debt was incurred; what disposition he has since made of such property and what estate or means he has for satisfying judgment.

Queen's Bench judges have power to order judgment debtor to make payment, monthly or otherwise, according to his means.

EXECUTORS AND ADMINISTRATORS:

There are two conditions precedent to the grant of probate or of administration, namely, property in this province and death of its owner. (The Court of Queen's Bench Surrogate Practice Act, C.C.S.M. c. C290, §22). These facts must be shown by affidavit of applicant. Grant dates back to death.

Eligibility.—Anyone not under legal disability may act as executor or administrator. Trust company may act, but original letters of administration will not be granted to nonresident of Manitoba.

Preferences in Right to Administer.—The next of kin of an intestate, beginning with the widow, have a prior right to apply for administration of his estate.

Public Trustee of province will act, upon request, where persons interested in estates are unable to arrange for a resident administrator or for bonds.

Effect of Grant of Probate or Administration.—Grant of probate or administration by Court of Queen's Bench effectually protects persons making payments to or dealing with executor or administrator although there may have been defects in preliminaries prior to grant. (C.C.S.M. c. C290).

Renunciation of Probate.—Executors may renounce probate. (C.C.S.M. c. C290).

Bonds.—Security must be given by bond, in double value of estate, to satisfaction of judge, except where applicant is approved trust or guaranty company, Public Trustee, or executor resident of Canada and named in will. One surety required where estate exceeds $50,000, two sureties where estate exceeds $100,000. Judge may dispense with bond or sureties in certain cases. (C.C.S.M. c. C290).

Removal.—Under the Trustee Act, administrators or executors may, on sufficient cause being shown, be removed, and a judicial trustee appointed in their place, to act either with any remaining executor or administrator or as a sole judicial trustee. (The Trustee Act, C.C.S.M. c. T160).

Inventory.—An inventory of the property of the deceased is the first step to be taken by the legal representative. (C.C.S.M. c. C290, §24).

EXECUTORS AND ADMINISTRATORS . . . *continued*

Notice to Creditors.—To avoid personal liability executor or administrator should insert notice in newspaper in district where deceased resided, calling upon all creditors to file their claim within period set by him, usually about four weeks. This notice must be published as well in Manitoba Gazette. (C.C.S.M. c. T160).

Presentation and Proof of Claims.—A claim against the estate is made by the creditor or his agent filing with the executor or administrator full particulars of the claim duly verified by a statutory declaration. (For form, see topic Affidavits.) If particulars are lengthy they may be made an exhibit to the declaration.

After notice has been published, the executor or administrator is entitled to distribute the estate without regard to a claim against the deceased which is not filed in time and of which he has no notice.

Contest of Claims.—In case the executor or administrator disputes any claim, he must notify creditor to that effect and give the creditor an opportunity of proving his claim by court procedure before a distribution of the estate can be had.

Compromises.—The executor or administrator is given power to settle and compromise with creditors of the deceased.

Sales.—In the course of administration the legal representative is authorized to sell real estate for the purposes of paying debts, and a conveyance of real estate sold to provide money for that purpose is good. The representative may also sell real estate for the purpose of distribution on receiving the court's approval.

Allowances.—There is no provision for allowances or exemptions to widows or children in priority to claims of creditors.

Distribution.—After payment of debts, it is the duty of an administrator to distribute the estate in accordance with the law relating to devolution of estates. (See topic Descent and Distribution.) In case of executor, or where property is left by will, it is duty of legal representative to carry out terms of will and in paying debts and administration costs, residuary estate is first resorted to, unless otherwise provided for in will.

There can be no distribution of the estate until the debts of the estate are disposed of, and for that purpose the executor or administrator is given a period of one year.

See also supra, subhead Presentation and Proof of Claims.

Costs of Administration.—Funeral and testamentary expenses and succession duties are proper and necessary expenditures by the legal representative as part of his administration costs. The costs of administration including the money properly paid out for that purpose, and a fair allowance to the legal representative to be fixed and allowed by the court, are a first charge on the estate.

Executors de son Tort.—Executors de son tort may bind the estate by acts of executorship in the course of administration (2 Ellis & Blackburn, p. 630), but the act must have been in the course of administration and the executor must have been carrying on ostensibly as a general executor of the estate. (2 East, p. 500, Reprint).

Accounts.—Before the executor or administrator is discharged from his office he must pass his accounts before Queen's Bench judge and he must produce on hearing accounts and receipts and schedule showing amount paid to discharge debts of estate.

Ancillary probate or administration may be had by producing the foreign probate or administration or court certified copy or exemplification thereof (notarial copy is not sufficient) purporting to be under seal of court by which same has been granted, together with necessary affidavits of applicants for ancillary administration.

Resealing.—Probates or letters from following jurisdictions may be resealed in Manitoba: Other Canadian provinces or territories, Australia, India, Republic of Ireland, New Zealand, Pakistan, The United Kingdom, and the U.S. (C.C.S.M. c. C290, §50).

EXEMPTIONS:

A large number of enumerated articles of personal property, in some cases limited as to value, are exempt from seizure and sale under writs of execution or other process. (The Executions Act, C.C.S.M. c. E160).

See also topic Garnishment.

Partnership firms cannot claim exemption for the several partners, but only one exemption for the firm.

When Exemptions Not Allowed.—No exemptions can be claimed on behalf of a debtor who is in the act of removing from the province, or is about to do so, or who has absconded, taking his family with him. No exemptions as to judgment recovered solely for board and lodging or as to judgments for price of articles seized. (C.C.S.M. c. E160).

Wages.—See topic Garnishment.

In case of death exemption rights pass to dependents. (C.C.S.M. c. E160).

Homestead Exemptions.—See topic Homesteads.

FACTORS:

The Factors Act (C.C.S.M. c. F10) makes valid and binding any disposition of goods by mercantile agent in possession of goods and documents of title relating thereto with consent of owner, which consent may be presumed from possession. Such mercantile agent is deemed to be authorized to dispose of goods in ordinary course of business. If consent of owner has been revoked, disposition of goods by agent thereof to any one with notice of revocation is invalid.

A pledge of goods by a mercantile agent is valid unless given as security for an antecedent debt or without adequate consideration.

A transfer of the documents of title by endorsement or where permitted by delivery alone entitles the bearer to the goods.

FIDUCIARIES:

See topics Executors and Administrators; Guardian and Ward; Trusts.

FILING FEES:

See topics Corporations; Deeds; Mortgages of Real Property; Personal Property Security.

FORECLOSURE:

See topics Liens; Mortgages of Real Property; Personal Property Security.

FOREIGN CORPORATIONS: See topic Corporations.

FRANCHISES:

No special legislation.

FRAUDS, STATUTE OF:

The former English statute of frauds (29 Chas. II, c. 3) was in force in Manitoba until its repeal on July 1, 1983.

Transitional.—Statute continues to apply as if it had not been repealed, in any action based in whole or in part upon acts done, contracts or agreements made, or other claims which arose prior to July 1, 1983.

Statute (§4) provides that no action shall be brought whereby to charge any executor or administrator upon any special promise to answer in damages out of his own estate, or whereby to charge defendant upon any special promise to answer for debt, default or miscarriage of another person, or charge any person upon any agreement made in consideration of marriage (breach of promise excepted) or upon any contract for sale of lands, tenements or hereditaments, or any interest in or concerning them or upon any agreement not to be performed within space of one year from making thereof, unless agreement upon which such action shall be brought or some memorandum or note thereof be in writing, signed by party to be charged therewith or his agent in that behalf.

§17 of the statute of frauds, providing that no contract for the sale of goods of the value of $50 or upwards shall be actionable unless in writing signed by the party to be charged or his agent unless there is acceptance or part payment, is incorporated in the Sale of Goods Act.

Sale of Goods.—A contract for the sale of goods, of the value of $50 or upwards shall not be enforcible by action unless the buyer shall accept part of the goods sold and actually receive the same, or give something in earnest to bind the contract, or in part payment, or unless some note or memorandum in writing of the contract be made and signed by the party to be charged, or his agent for that purpose. This provision applies to every such contract, notwithstanding that the goods may be intended to be delivered at some future time or may not, at the time of the contract, be actually made, procured, or provided, or fit or ready to be delivered. There is acceptance of goods within the meaning of this section, when the buyer does any act in relation to the goods in recognition of the preexisting contract of sale. Salesmen and commercial travelers should therefore note that the signature of the purchaser (or his authorized agent) from them of goods of the value of $50 or more should be affixed to an order of memorandum setting out the parties, description of the goods, the terms of contract, date, etc. (The Sale of Goods Act, C.C.S.M. c. S10). Writing required in contracts involving sale of goods away from vendor's premises or on credit is dealt with in The Consumer Protection Act. (C.C.S.M. c. C200). See topic Sales.

FRAUDULENT SALES AND CONVEYANCES:

Conveyances, or other transfers, of real or personal property with intent to defeat, hinder, delay or defraud creditors or others are void as against such persons except for bona fide transfers for consideration to persons without notice or knowledge of intent. (Fraudulent Conveyances Act [C.C.S.M. c. F160]).

GARNISHMENT:

Prejudgment.—Plaintiff in action for payment of debt or liquidated sum may garnish money in hands of third party except for unpaid wages and application must be accompanied by affidavit stating: (a) Facts showing plaintiff has good cause of action against defendant for payment of debt or liquidated demand; (b) amount of plaintiff's claim, with allowances for all just credits, set-offs and counterclaims known to plaintiff; (c) name and address of each person to whom notice of garnishment is directed; (d) that plaintiff believes those persons are or will become indebted to defendant, and grounds for belief; and (e) such particulars of debts as known to plaintiff.

Court may impose terms requiring plaintiff to post security and promptly prosecute action or pay any damages and costs sustained by reason of prejudgment garnishing order. Payment by garnishee into court is valid discharge by him as against debtor. (Q.B. Rule 46.14).

Post Judgment.—Judgment-creditor may apply for attachment of money in hands of third party ("garnishee"). Application may be ex parte. Application must be accompanied by affidavit stating: (a) That order for payment of money has been made and date of order; (b) date and amount of any payments received; (c) amount payable, including interest; (d) name and address of each garnishee; (e) that creditor believes garnishee is, or will become indebted to debtor and grounds for belief; (f) such particulars of debt as known, including whether or not for wages; and (g) where person to whom notice of garnishment is to be directed is not in Manitoba, that debtor is entitled to sue that person in Manitoba to recover debt, and entitlement to sue in Manitoba. (Q.B. Rule 60.08[3]).

Exemptions from garnishment are: 70% of wages, but at least $350 per month if employer has dependent and debt is not under alimony or maintenance order or agreement; otherwise at least $250 per month. Court may vary or remove exemption in special case such as debt for lodging. Employer must not discharge employee for garnishment. In case of wages earned during period of less than a month, amount of exemption is proportionate to amount of time worked during month.

(See The Queen's Bench Act, [C.C.S.M. c. C280]; see also The Garnishment Act, C.C.S.M. c. G20.)

Public Employees.—Salaries of Federal Government employees may be garnished in accordance with The Garnishment, Attachment and Pension Diversion Act. (S.C. c.

GARNISHMENT . . . *continued*
G2). Those of provincial employees have been made liable by statute. (C.C.S.M. c. G20).

See also topic Labour Relations.

GUARDIAN AND WARD:

Court of Queen's Bench has jurisdiction over guardianship proceedings.

Selection of Guardian.—Court has power to appoint guardians of person of child. Court usually gives effect to testamentary appointment by parent, but in interest of child may refuse to do so and appoint some other person. On proper case being made out court may, on application by adult and upon proper notice to parent, guardian, or child if over 12 years of age appoint some suitable person to be guardian of such child. (The Child and Family Services Act, C.C.S.M. c. C80).

Guardianship of infant's estate granted by Court to parent(s) or other suitable person with consent of parent(s) on application and upon furnishing bond for due administration of estate or Public Trustee may be appointed without bonds. (The Infant's Estates Act, C.C.S.M. c. I35).

Powers and Duties.—Guardian or person of infant has care and control of infant and is responsible for maintenance, education and well-being of infant. (C.C.S.M. c. C80). Guardian of infant's estate entitled to control and management of property, appear in court proceedings and expend monies for benefit of infant where parent(s) unable to do so. (The Infants' Estates Act C.C.S.M. c. I35). (See topic Infants, subhead Termination of Parental Rights.)

Real Estate.—Court has power to permit sale, mortgage, lease or other disposition of land if same is in best interests of infant. (C.C.S.M. c. I35).

Termination of Guardianship.—Guardians are removable for proper cause by Court of Queen's Bench. Guardian may resign with leave of court on terms court deems just. (C.C.S.M. c. I35).

Accounts.—Guardian must post bond and render true account of infant's property as established by Court.

Insane Persons.—Under The Mental Health Act (C.C.S.M. c. M110) Court of Queen's Bench may make orders for committing custody of persons of unsound mind and custody and management of their estates. Public Trustee is committee of estate of every mentally incompetent person who has no other committee and is also committee of person of mentally incompetent who has no other committee whenever appointed by Lieutenant-Governor-in-Council to act as such. (The Trustee Act, C.C.S.M. c. T160).

HOLIDAYS:

See generally Canada Law Digest.

Where the last day for doing any act or taking any proceeding expires on Sunday or other day on which offices of the court are closed, same may be done or taken on next day offices are open. (The Interpretation Act, C.C.S.M. c. I80).

Retail Business.—Certain establishments exempted from holiday closing law. (C.C.S.M. c. R120).

HOMESTEADS:

"Homestead" means, (a) in case of residence in city, town or village occupied by owner and owner's spouse as their home, residence and land on which situated consisting of (i) not more than six lots or, if block is not subdivided into lots, one block, as shown on plan registered in land titles office, and (ii) not more than one acre, if land not described by registered plan; (b) in case of residence outside city, town or village occupied by owner and owner's spouse as their home, residence and land on which situated, consisting of not more than 320 acres or half section, subject to following conditions: (i) if land exceeds 320 acres in same section, 320 acres shall be comprised of quarter section on which residence situated, together with such other lands in that section as owner or owner's personal representative shall designate, (ii) if land in more than one section, river lot or parish lot, homestead shall be comprised of quarter section, river lot or parish lot on which residence is situated, together with other lands in that section or adjacent to or across road or highway from section, river lot or parish lot, but if land so described exceeds 320 acres owner or owner's personal representative shall designate 320 acres of land as homestead including quarter section, river lot or parish lot on which residence situated; (c) unit and common interest within meaning of The Condominimum Act (C.C.S.M. c. C170), occupied by owner and owner's spouse as their home.

Disposition without consent may be set aside if no further disposition to bona fide purchaser for value unless disposition in favour of owner's spouse, spouse released rights in homestead in prescribed form, or spouse has interest in homestead in addition to rights under Act.

When owner dies, surviving spouse entitled to life estate in homestead and any disposition in homestead by owner's Will is subject to this entitlement. (S.M. 1992, c. 46).

Waiver.—Spouse may, in writing in prescribed form and for valuable consideration, release rights under Act. (S.M. 1992, c. 46). Release made before person authorized to take affidavits and includes acknowledgment by owner's spouse, made apart from owner. Acknowledgment that spouse aware of right to life estate and right to prevent disposition of homestead, that spouse aware release gives up these rights, and that spouse executes release freely and voluntarily.

HUSBAND AND WIFE:

Contracts.—No restrictions apply.

Prenuptial contracts can make provisions of The Marital Property Act, C.C.S.M. c. M45 inapplicable but cannot prevent equal division of pension benefits on marriage breakup under The Pension Benefits Act, C.C.S.M. c. P32 or oust court's discretion over child custody and access or prevent support application under The Dependents Relief Act. (C.C.S.M. c. D37).

Conveyance or Encumbrance of Property.—A married woman may convey or mortgage real estate, except the homestead, without the consent of her husband and without examination or acknowledgment.

Husband and wife may transfer real property inter se without intervention or trustee. Restraint upon anticipation by married woman is abolished.

Actions.—Spouse has same remedy for protection and security of property as if unmarried and may sue spouse for tort.

See also topic Divorce.

INCOME TAX: See topic Taxation.

INFANTS:

Infant is any person under full age of 18 years. The Age of Majority Act (C.C.S.M. c. A7) deems all references in Manitoba legislation to age 21 to mean age 18.

Contracts.—Infant over 16 years of age, who has no parent or guardian, or who does not reside with parent or guardian, may enter into an agreement to perform work or service, and is liable upon same and entitled to benefit thereof as if he were of legal age, save that Director of Child and Family Services may declare agreement void on evidence of injustice in case of infant under 18. Otherwise common law with regard to contracts entered into by infants prevails.

The Child and Family Services Act (C.C.S.M., c. C80) and The Family Maintenance Act (C.C.S.M., c. F20) make elaborate provisions for custody, treatment, training and general welfare of infants. And see The Child Custody Enforcement Act (C.C.S.M., c. C360) and Divorce Act, 1985 (S. C. 1986, c. 4).

Termination of Parental Rights.—The Child and Family Services Act (C.C.S.M., c. C80) authorizes Director of Child & Family Services, representative of agency authorized by Act or peace officer to apprehend child they believe is "in need of protection" as defined by Act. Terms and conditions of parental access are determined by judicial order or by agency. Parents can make application for hearing to consider varying access order. Parents can be ordered to pay maintenance.

Adoption.—See topic Adoption.

See also topic Guardian and Ward.

INHERITANCE TAX: See topic Taxation.

INJUNCTIONS:

Injunction may be procured in the Court of Queen's Bench, procedure being regulated by the rules of that court. (C.C.S.M. c. C280).

Interlocutory.—Court may grant restrictive or mandatory interlocutory injunction where it appears just or convenient to do so.

INSOLVENCY:

See Canada Law Digest, topic Bankruptcy.

INSURANCE:

With exception of marine insurance (see The Marine Insurance Act, C.C.S.M. c. M40), all statutes relating to business of insurance in Manitoba are incorporated in Manitoba Insurance Act (C.C.S.M. c. I40). For general information contact Superintendent of Insurance, Legislative Building, Winnipeg, Manitoba.

Licenses.—Every insurer carrying on business in the province must be licensed and license must be renewed annually. Before a license is granted the applicant must file the following material: (1) Certificate of registration under The Corporations Act; (2) certified copy of articles of incorporation, including by-laws; (3) affidavit that insurer is still in existence and legally authorized to transact business under its charter; (4) certified copy of last balance sheet and auditor's report; (5) notice of place of head office, if not in province; (6) notice of place of head office or chief agency in province, if any; (7) statement showing amount of capital stock, number of shares subscribed and amount paid thereon; (8) certified copy of power of attorney to Canadian chief agent if any; (9) notice of appointment of chief agent or resident manager for province; (10) such other evidence as Superintendent of Insurance may require.

Every insurer, before receiving a license, must deposit with the Provincial Treasurer, securities as follows: Life Insurance, $50,000; other classes of insurance, $25,000 if doing business in Manitoba only or $50,000 if doing business both in and outside of Manitoba. Provision is made for reciprocal deposits where a similar provision is made in other provinces.

Contracts.—Part 3 of the Act sets forth the provisions relating to insurance contracts in the province.

Special classes of insurance are regulated by Insurance Act, as follows: Fire, by Part 4, including statutory conditions; Life, by Part 5, which also sets forth law relating to life insurance contracts in province and which corresponds to Uniform Life Act of other provinces; Accident and Sickness, by Part 6; Automobile, by Part 7; Livestock, by Part 8; Weather, by Part 9; Hail, by Part 10; Fraternal Societies, by Part 11; Mutual Benefit Societies, by Part 12; Mutual Insurance Companies, by Part 13; Reciprocal Insurance, by Part 14. Marine insurance is regulated by a separate act. (C.C.S.M. c. I40).

Brokers and Adjusters.—Part 15 of the Insurance Act provides for the licensing and regulation of insurance brokers and adjusters.

Foreign Companies.—The rights of a licensed foreign company are the same as those of a company incorporated in the province.

Service of process in all actions against insurance companies may now be made upon the Superintendent of Insurance and such service is binding upon foreign companies carrying on business in Manitoba.

Taxation.—See topic Corporations, subhead Taxation.

Direct Actions Against Insurer.—See topic Motor Vehicles, subhead Direct Actions.

INSURANCE . . . *continued*

No-Fault Insurance.—See topic Motor Vehicles.

INTEREST:

Judgments.—Quarterly prejudgment interest rate fixed by regulation. Prejudgment interest is paid on principal sum of liquidated claim from date cause of action arose to date of order and for unliquidated claim is paid from date successful party gave written notice of claim to date of order. Prejudgment interest on special damages is paid on such amount incurred by successful party in each six month period following date of notice of claim less amount unsuccessful party's liability is reduced. (The Manitoba Public Insurance Corporations Act, C.C.S.M. c. P215, §38). No prejudgment interest on non-pecuniary damages, rather court makes allowance for lost opportunity to invest. Court may depart from mechanics of act if unfair to either party. The Court of Queen's Bench Act (C.C.S.M. c. C280) fixes net discount rate of 3% to discount value of future damages.

See topic Consumer Protection.

See also Canada Law Digest.

Unconscionable Transactions Relief Act (C.C.S.M. c. U20), provides for court to re-open and alter transaction involving money lent, including real property mortgage and, except where prescribed acknowledgement is obtained by assignee, he is deemed to have full knowledge of transaction.

INTESTACY: See topic Descent and Distribution.

JOINT STOCK COMPANIES:

See topic Corporations.

JUDGMENTS:

Where amount of judgment recovered in Court of Queen's Bench or Federal Court of Canada exceeds $40, certificate of judgment may be registered to form lien and charge in Land Titles Office against Certificates of Title registered in name of judgment debtor. Judgment creditor may proceed upon lien and charge, unless land is exempt under The Judgments Act (C.C.S.M. c. J10), and save for interval of one year. One year interval need not be observed in case of proceeding for sale of land against which judgment for alimony or maintenance is registered and that judgment is in default. Surplus proceeds of sale may be held or invested by court as security for future payments under judgment. Registration of judgment for alimony or maintenance other than for child may be totally or partially discharged or postponed by registration of instrument to that effect by person in whose favour judgment was made. System of General Registry in Manitoba is no longer maintained as of Aug. 19, 1989 and all registrations therein lapse Aug. 20, 1989. (The Real Property Act, C.C.S.M. c. R30).

See topic Executions.

Renewal.—A judgment remains in force for ten years without renewal, and may then be renewed for a further term of ten years by action brought on the original judgment, but no action can be brought upon a judgment recovered on a previous judgment whether in this province or elsewhere. (C.C.S.M. c. J10).

No costs are allowed on reissuing judgment.

Declaratory Judgments.—An action or proceeding is not open to objection on the ground that it is for a declaratory judgment or order only and the court may make binding declarations of right whether or not any consequential relief is or could be claimed. (The Court of Queen's Bench Act, C.C.S.M. c. C280).

Foreign Judgments.—Judgments obtained elsewhere in Canada where there are reciprocal provisions may be registered in province within six years of date when judgment was given. Debtor must be notified of application for registration whenever he was not personally served with process in original action and did not appear, defend, or otherwise submit to jurisdiction of original court. Otherwise registration may be obtained and notice given to debtor within one month. (C.C.S.M. c. J20).

JUSTICES OF THE PEACE:

These are appointed by the provincial government, and have local jurisdiction in criminal and civil matters under the Criminal Code and Q.B. Small Claims Practices Act, two sitting together having authority of magistrate. (The Provincial Court Act, C.C.S.M. c. C275, Part V).

LABOUR RELATIONS:

Employment Standards Act (C.C.S.M. c. E110) deals with wages, hours of work and standards and conditions of employment. Prohibition against discharging employee because employer served with garnishing order. Also: Construction Industry Wages Act (C.C.S.M. c. C190) deals with wages, hours of work and standards for heavy construction workers.

Contracts of service of apprentices must be in writing, for term of no less than two years and in form prescribed by The Apprenticeship and Trades Qualifications Board. Apprentice must be at least 16 years old. (The Apprenticeship and Trades Qualifications Act [C.C.S.M. c. A110]).

Wages.—See The Payment of Wages Act (C.C.S.M. c. P31).

Wages of employees for three months before the date of a receiving order or assignment are a preferred claim against the estate of a bankrupt or insolvent. Directors of employers are personally, jointly and severally liable for six months unpaid wages of employees. (C.C.S.M. c. P31). See also topic Liens, subhead Employees.

Assignment of wages, see topic Assignments, subhead Earnings.

The Minimum Wage Regulations fix standards of minimum wages for employees and hours of employment for every worker employed in any mail order house, office, place of amusement, shop or factory in Manitoba. The board provided for has wide powers of investigation in cases of complaint and every employer is required to keep a register of certain details concerning all employees including their names, addresses and earnings.

The Employment Standards Act (C.C.S.M. c. E110) prevents discrimination between sexes in payment of wages for doing similar work, and provides for paternity and adoption leave as well as maternity leave.

The Vacations with Pay Act (C.C.S.M. c. V20) provides that every employer shall give annual vacation with pay to each of his employees who completes a year's service: two weeks after one year, three weeks after four years.

The Pay Equity Act (C.C.S.M. c. P13) provides for movement toward equal pay for work of equal value for public sector employees.

Discrimination.—The Human Rights Code (C.C.S.M. c. H175) prevents discrimination by employers because of race, nationality, religion, colour, sex, age, marital status, ethnic or national origin, or political beliefs or family status and extends prohibited grounds of discrimination to include sexual harassment, pregnancy, political or religious activity, sexual orientation and gender-determined characteristics and enables government to make affirmative action programs requirement for firms contracting with Province.

Labour Unions.—Union representing majority of employees in unit appropriate for collective bargaining may be certified bargaining agent by Manitoba Labour Board. See subhead Labour Disputes, infra.

Labour Disputes.—Manitoba Labour Board administers Manitoba Labour Relations Act. (C.C.S.M. c. L10). Act sets forth in detail rights of employers and employees, including right of every employee to be member of trade union. Procedure is established for certification of bargaining representatives and negotiation of collective agreements. Every collective agreement must provide for compulsory deduction of union dues whether member of union or not. No strike or lock out while collective agreement in force. Technological change may entitle union to terminate collective agreement. Provision for code of employment in absence of collective agreement. Unfair labour practices are defined. Act provides for conciliation proceedings and also for appointment of mediation board or industrial enquiry commission, where investigation is required. Penalties are established for violation of Act.

Unemployment.—See Canada Law Digest.

Workmen's Compensation.—Workers Compensation Act (C.C.S.M. c. W200), provides for compensation to injured workmen within jurisdiction of Act. Common law remedies of injured party still exist, but if action brought for injury to workmen, application may be made to decide whether action is maintainable or whether injured party is only entitled to compensation from Board. Decisions of Board are final and not subject to review by courts.

LANDLORD AND TENANT:

Residential tenancies are governed by The Residential Tenancies Act (see subhead Residential Premises, infra). Otherwise relations between landlord and tenant are governed by The Landlord and Tenant Act. (C.C.S.M. c. L70). Relationship of landlord and tenant may be created by agreement in writing or oral but if lease for more than three years, agreement must be in writing. In order to affect subsequent purchasers or mortgagees of land caveat must be registered unless lease is for period of less than three years and there is actual occupation of land by tenant.

Termination.—To terminate a lease, a week's notice for a weekly tenancy and a month's notice for a monthly tenancy ending on last day of week or month is sufficient. See subhead Residential Premises, infra.

Holding Over.—Where a tenant holds over after the termination of his term and after notice in writing given for delivering possession thereof by his landlord, he must pay double the yearly value of the land so detained for the time he holds over.

Where a tenant gives notice of his intention to quit the premises at a time mentioned in such notice, and does not deliver up possession thereof at such time, he must from thenceforward pay to the landlord double the rent or sum which he should otherwise have paid, to be levied, sued for and recovered at the same time and in the same manner as the single rent.

Dispossession.—Where a tenant, after notice or demand made upon him in writing to go out of possession, wrongfully refuses or neglects to do so, the landlord may apply upon affidavit to a judge for a writ of possession.

Where a tenant fails to pay his rent within three days of the time agreed upon and wrongfully refuses or neglects upon demand made in writing to pay the rent or to deliver up the premises demised, the landlord may obtain a summons returnable before a judge of Court of Queen's Bench, who must make order for possession unless cause be shown to him by tenant why order should not be made.

Distress.—There are certain limitations on a landlord's right to distrain on the goods of a tenant. No distress may be made for more than three months' arrears of rent where the same is payable quarterly or more frequently or for more than the next preceding one year's rent where the same is payable less frequently than quarterly.

The right to distrain is limited to the goods on the premises of the tenant, or any one claiming by, through or under him by gift, purchase or otherwise, since the commencement of the term. The claim takes priority to any writ of execution or attachment. The Landlord and Tenant's Act specifies the goods and chattels which shall be exempt from seizure under any landlord's warrant of distress. A mortgagee under an attornment clause in a mortgage may only distrain on such goods and chattels of the mortgagor on the mortgaged premises as are not exempt from seizure under execution. The mortgagee may, by notice in writing, served upon the person occupying the land, where such person is not the tenant, require that person to pay to the mortgagee the rental value of the land or so much thereof as has not already been paid and to continue to pay the same from time to time as it falls due. Where a tenant fraudulently removes his goods and chattels to prevent the landlord from distraining the same for arrears of rent, the landlord may, within 30 days next ensuing, seize such goods and chattels wherever found and dispose of the same in the same manner as goods ordinarily distrained for rent. Distress is made under a landlord's warrant of distress and the goods and chattels seized must be appraised by two appraisers and thereafter may be sold for the best price obtainable. Any surplus remaining over and above the amount of rent distrained for and the cost of seizure is returned to the tenant.

LANDLORD AND TENANT . . . *continued*

Where tenant vacates premises, landlord may remove any personal property from premises and store same. If worth of property is less than cost of storage, landlord may dispose of same.

Residential Premises.—Governed by The Residential Tenancies Act. Form of lease for tenancies prescribed by regulations. Any term or condition which contravenes provisions of Act is null and void. Director of Residential Tenancies Branch investigates complaints of breaches of Act, hears applications for orders of possession, regulates rent increases, mediates disputes between landlord and tenant and issues orders. Orders appealable to Residential Tenancies Commission. Security deposit cannot exceed one-half month's rent and tenant must be notified of any claim for damages within 14 days of moving out and application for claim completed within 28 days of end of tenancy.

Rental increases regulated under Act and tenants have right to hearing if increase exceeds regulations. Distress is abolished. Tenants may assign or sublet subject to landlord's consent which cannot be unreasonably withheld.

Notice of termination: from landlord in writing; from tenant in writing or orally but landlord can ask tenant to sign notice. Generally tenant has right to continue occupancy.

Statutory provisions of Act cannot be contracted out of or waived.

LEASES: See topic Landlord and Tenant.

LEGISLATURE:

The legislature meets at the call of the Premier. Either English or French may be used by any person in debates and both those languages must be used in records and journals. (The Manitoba Act 1870, 34-35 Vic. S. C. 1870, c. 28, §23).

See generally Canada Law Digest, topic Constitution and Government. (See also The Legislative Assembly Act, C.C.S.M. c. L110.)

LEVY: See topics Attachment; Executions.

LICENSES:

Transient traders, hawkers, peddlers and persons who go from place to place selling goods, wares and merchandise must obtain license. License required by direct seller under The Consumer Protection Act. (C.C.S.M. c. C200).

Municipalities may license commercial travellers who take orders as well as transient traders and dealers of all kinds who have no place of business therein. They may also license auctioneers, pawnbrokers, public exhibitions, poolrooms, billposters, tobacco stores, scavengers, plumbers, shoe-blacks and a great number of other trades and occupations.

No person may operate any place of amusement or travelling show without a license. (The Amusements Act, C.C.S.M. c. A70).

No person may operate a steam or pressure plant without a certificate of authorization. (The Engineering Profession Act, C.C.S.M. c. E120).

Licenses are required to conduct premises within the province for the sale of liquor. (The Liquor Control Act, R.S.M. 1988, c. L160).

The game laws provide that a license must be taken out to fish or shoot game within the province. The fees payable for such licenses are regulated from time to time by the Minister of Mines and his department, Government Buildings, Winnipeg, Manitoba.

License required to operate day care centre. (Community Child Day Care Standards Act, C.C.S.M. c. C158).

LIENS:

Hotel and boarding house keepers have a lien on the goods and effects of guests, boarders or lodgers, and may detain the same and sell the same to enforce such lien. The lien is for the amount incurred by the person while a guest. (The Hotel Keepers Act, C.C.S.M. c. H150).

Employees have lien and charge on business assets of employer in amount of wages accruing due. Amount of wages due and payable by employer to employee not exceeding $2,000 constitutes first priority lien and charge on property and assets of employer in favour of employee except in some circumstances where property subject to real property mortgage or purchase money security interest. (The Payment of Wages Act, C.C.S.M. c. P31, §7).

Warehousemen have a lien. See topic Warehousemen.

Garage keepers have lien for repairs, painting, storing, or caring for motor vehicle or farm vehicle or any part, accessory or equipment pertaining thereto with priority over all lienholders or mortgagees. Lien remains in effect even when possession is surrendered if garage keeper (1) obtains acknowledgment of owner's indebtedness before surrendering possession and (2) registers claim of lien in Personal Property Registry before or within 20 days of surrendering possession. (The Garage Keepers Act, C.C.S.M. c. G10).

Threshers' Liens.—A thresher may assert a lien by declaring verbally or in writing or doing any act or using language indicating such intention upon a sufficient portion of any grain threshed to net to him the cost of the threshing, provided a set rate was agreed upon. The lien has priority against all other liens (including seed grain liens) and against the owner. The grain may be sold at expiration of five days after written notice to owner and within 60 days after assertion of right of retention, unless owner consents otherwise in writing. Thresher must account to owner within 15 days after sale.

Workmen and persons supplying fuel or repairs may claim against the farmer for money due them by the thresher up to ten days after the machine leaves. Interpleader provision is made for cases where the wages or threshing bill are in dispute. (Threshers' Lien Act [C.C.S.M. c. T60]).

Builders' Liens.—The Builders' Liens Act (C.C.S.M. c. B91) governs any person (except architects and engineers) who does any work or provides any services or supplies any materials to be used in performance of contract or subcontract for construction or for improving land, or for doing of any work or providing of any services in construction or improving land, or for supply of any materials to be used in construction or in improving land has, by virtue thereof, lien for value of such work, services or material upon interest of owner in such land, building, structure, etc., unless owner is Crown, crown agency or municipality, in which case lien constitutes charge on amounts required to be retained under Act, or unless claim for such work, services or materials is less than $300. Person primarily liable for payment under contract under which lien may arise must, as work is done or services are provided or materials are supplied, deduct from any payments to be made by him, and retain for at least 40 days after notice of substantial performance or after completion or abandonment of contract or subcontract, 7.5% of value of work, services and materials actually done, provided or supplied. Sums received by contractor or subcontractor on account of contract price constitute trust fund for benefit of subcontractors, workers, etc. Every agreement contrary to provisions of Act is void.

Registration.—Every claim for lien must be registered in Land Titles Office of district in which subject land is situate, with affidavit of claimant verifying same, within 40 days of substantial performance or abandonment of contract, supplying of last materials, completion of provision of services or doing of last work. Claim for lien may include claims against any number of parcels of land and any number of persons claiming liens upon same land may unite in claim for lien, but where more than one lien is included in one claim for lien, each lien must be vertified by an affidavit, either of claimant or his agent. Any person who registers claim for lien for amount grossly in excess of amount due to him or where he knows or ought to know that he does not have lien is liable to any person who suffers damage as result unless registration made, and amount calculated, in good faith and without negligence.

Actions.—Every lien must be proceeded on by action within two years after date of registration and within 30 days after notice from interested holder in property. In general, provisions of Queen's Bench Act (C.C.S.M. c. C280) and Queen's Bench Rules apply to proceedings to enforce claims for builders' liens. After action is commenced certificate of lis pendens must be filed in Land Titles Office in which lien has been registered. Any claim related to construction or improving land, including claim related to trust fund, may be joined with action to realize lien arising from construction or improving land.

See topic Executions.

Priorities.—Builders' liens have priority over all judgments, executions, assignments, attachments, garnishments and receiving orders, recovered, issued or made or registered in Land Titles Office after such lien arises, and over all payments or advances made on account of any conveyance or mortgage after registration of claim for such lien as provided by Act.

Public Works.—When any public work is being carried out, security must be given by contractor, to and in name of Her Majesty, for due performance of work within amount and time specified for its completion. (The Public Works Act, C.C.S.M. c. P300).

Redemption.—There is no right of redemption of property sold in the enforcement of the aforementioned liens.

Lien Notes.—See topic Personal Property Security.

LIMITATION OF ACTIONS:

Time within which various actions may be brought is limited as follows:

Particular Limitations.—Specific causes of action may be subject to limitation by applicable statutes, as, e.g., two years for malpractice and negligence actions against doctors and physicians (C.C.S.M. c. M90), chiropractors (C.C.S.M. c. C100), naturopaths (C.C.S.M. c. N80); against crown, in respect of highways and drainage works, two years (C.C.S.M. c. P140); against public officials, two years (C.C.S.M. c. P230); against municipal corporations where claim is for return of money paid as taxes at municipality's demand, six months (C.C.S.M. cc. M225, S889); etc.

Statute Limitations.—Actions not limited by particular statute are governed by The Limitation of Actions Act (C.C.S.M. c. L150), under which actions must be brought within following periods after actions accrue:

Ten years: Actions on judgment or order for payment of money.

Six years: Actions for trespass or injury to real property; actions for recovery of money (except debt charged upon land) whether recoverable as debt or damages or otherwise, and whether recognizance, bond, covenant or other specialty, or on simple contract express or implied and action for account; actions for taking away, conversion or detention of chattels; action grounded on accident, mistake, or other equitable ground of relief not otherwise dealt with in Act, as well as any other action for which provision is not specifically made in Act.

Two years: Actions for penalties, damages, or sums of money in nature of penalties given by statute to person aggrieved; actions for defamation; actions for malicious prosecution, seduction, false imprisonment, trespass to person, assault, battery, wounding or other injuries to person; actions for trespass or injury to chattels; actions for violation of privacy of person; actions brought under and by virtue of Fatal Accidents Act.

One year: Actions for penalties imposed by statute brought by informer suing for himself alone or for Crown as well as himself.

Fraudulent Misrepresentation and Mistake.—Actions grounded on fraudulent misrepresentation, accident, mistake or other equitable ground: within six years of discovery of fraud or cause of action.

Any Other Action.—Where provision not specifically made in Act: within six years after cause of action arose.

Foreign Judgment.—The time within which action must be commenced on a foreign judgment is not settled in Manitoba. Such action must certainly be commenced within ten years and possibly within six years. It is uncertain to what extent limitation provisions available in the foreign jurisdiction may be pleaded in Manitoba. (The Court of Queen's Bench Act, C.C.S.M. c. C280). See topic Judgments.

Special Limitations.—Where a statute provides a specific limitation for proceedings thereunder, such provision overrides the general limitations above set forth.

Disabilities of Plaintiff.—In all actions, any time period during which plaintiff is under disability, whether at time cause of action arose or subsequently, is not taken into account when calculating time period in which action must be brought, except that no

LIMITATION OF ACTIONS . . . *continued*
action may be brought after 30 years after act or omission which gave rise to cause of action. However, if other party to action serves notice to proceed, time period in which person under disability must bring action commences to run as if he ceased to be under disability from date of notice.

Absence of Defendant.—If a person be out of the province at the time the cause of action against him arises within the province, the plaintiff may bring action within two years after the return of the defendant to the province, except in the case of penal action and actions for penalties.

Extension of Limitation Period.—Discretionary power to extend period if application made within 12 months of when applicant knew or ought to have known material facts. (C.C.S.M. c. L150).

Acknowledgment, New Promise or Part Payment.—Liability to an action for the recovery of money or on a judgment may be taken out of a statute where the debtor: (1) Promises his creditor in writing to pay such debt; (2) gives a written acknowledgment to his creditor; or (3) makes a part payment on account of the principal debt or interest thereon to his creditor. An action in such case may be brought within six years from such taking out of the statute.

LIMITED PARTNERSHIP: See topic Partnership.

MARRIAGE:

Consent of Family Court Judge is necessary where either party is under 16, unless widow or widower or divorced. Where party between 16 and 18 consent may also be given by parent or guardian. (The Marriage Act, C.C.S.M. c. M50).

License must be obtained or banns published, and marriage must take place within three months from obtaining of license or publication.

Ceremonial Marriage.—Marriage may be solemnized only by person duly authorized. No person under 18 years may solemnize marriage. (C.C.S.M. c. M50).

Irregularities in solemnization do not void marriage, providing parties live together after solemnization as man and wife for one year from date of marriage, validity of marriage is not questioned during that period and neither legally marries another person.

Prohibited Marriages.—A man may not marry his grandmother, mother, granddaughter, daughter or sister.

A woman may not marry her grandfather, father, grandson, son or brother.

Prohibited relationships include half-blood or adoption.

Any such form of marriage would be void and of no effect. (C.C.S.M. c. M50).

Common law marriages are not recognized, although, under certain statutes, individuals living in common law relationship are given rights same as or similar to those legally married.

Annulment.—Expression used in Manitoba is declaration that valid marriage was not effected. Any marriage between persons within prohibited degrees of consanguinity or affinity or related by adoption or which is invalid for any reason may be so declared upon petition to Court of Queen's Bench. Residence in Manitoba confers jurisdiction. Decree in such case is made absolute in first instance. Where either party was under age of 18 at time of marriage and necessary consent of parent or guardian was not obtained, marriage can be validated by cohabitation for one year as man and wife following marriage or until death of one of parties and validity of marriage has not been questioned before expiry of one year and neither party contracts matrimony according to law before expiry of one year. (C.C.S.M. c. M50).

MECHANICS' LIENS: See topic Liens.

MINES AND MINERALS:

The Mines Act. (C.C.S.M. c. M160).

The Oil and Natural Gas Conservation Board has authority to deal with matters regarding extraction of oil and gas and pooling and utilization agreements.

The Mineral Exploration Incentive Program Act.—(C.C.S.M. c. M145).

The Mines and Minerals Consequential Amendments Act.—(C.C.S.M. c. M162) regulates mineral exploration and mining including issuance of prospecting licences and exploration permits as well as manner claims may be staked, mineral leases obtained and minerals mined.

The Mining Claim Tax Act (C.C.S.M. c. M165) imposes tax on owner or lessee of certain mining claim. Amount set by regulation 375/88.

The Oil and Gas Production Tax Act (C.C.S.M. c. O37) provides for tax payable by holders of working interests in well producing oil or gas.

The Mining Tax Act (C.C.S.M. c. M195) imposes tax on profits from mineral processing establishments. It provides for tax holiday for new mines.

The Surface Rights Act (C.C.S.M. c. S235) provides procedure for acquisition and utilization of surface rights, payment of compensation therefor and restoration of land acquired in connection therewith.

The Mining and Metallurgy Compensation Act (C.C.S.M. c. M190) provides for limited liability for persons conducting mining related activities in certain districts. Where damage outside district due to operations within district, Act provides for damages by arbitration.

MONOPOLIES AND RESTRAINT OF TRADE:

See generally Canada Law Digest.

MORTGAGES OF PERSONAL PROPERTY:

See topic Personal Property Security.

MORTGAGES OF REAL PROPERTY:

Old System.—An old system mortgage is simply a deed with a defeasance clause. It is executed in the same manner as an old system deed. See topic Deeds.

New System.—Whenever any land under the Torrens system is to be made security in favor of any mortgagee, the mortgagor must execute a memorandum of mortgage in form prescribed by statute, and if it is subject to any other mortgage or encumbrance the mortgage must so state. A mortgage under the Torrens system does not operate as a transfer of the land charged, but only has effect as security. Mortgages, encumbrances and leases may be transferred by form of transfer provided by statute. If default is made in the payment of principal, etc., and continues for one calendar month, the mortgagee may give written notice to the mortgagor and persons having an interest subject to the mortgage to pay the money then due or to observe the covenants or steps will be taken to remedy default. If default continues for one month from date of service mortgagee may apply for order permitting him to sell land. If sale proves abortive and default continues for six months mortgagee may apply to district registrar for order of foreclosure, and registrar appoints time within which redemption may be made, not less than one month from service of notice to redeem.

Mortgages under this system need not be under seal. The mortgagor in default for payment of principal may within three months, without bonus or notice, pay the same with interest to date of payment; after three months he may pay the same with three months' bonus and interest to date, or he may pay with three months notice, in lieu of bonus, and interest to date of payment fixed by such notice. Mortgage repayable over period greater than five years may be paid off with three months' bonus any time after five years have expired. (C.C.S.M. c. R30).

Fee for registration under new system is $50.

Discharge of Mortgage.—Mortgages are discharged by instruments in writing but not under seal, properly witnessed, with the affidavit of the witness that he is such; that he knows the party executing, whom he knows is of the full age of 18 years and that he saw instrument executed at place of execution. Instrument, duly executed, must be registered in Registry or Land Titles Office in which mortgage is registered. (See Form 12 at end of Digest.) Under Real Property Act memorandum of discharge will be endorsed on certificate of title and duplicate certificate is returned to mortgagor if there are no other encumbrances registered.

Trust deeds are ordinarily used by corporations to secure bond issues. They are charged on real estate and registered in the form of a mortgage in the land titles office of the district in which the land is situated upon obtaining fiat from registrar general. Collateral other than real property should be registered with Personal Property Registry. (C.C.S.M. c. P35).

See topic Personal Property Security.

Foreclosure.—No proceedings against farm property without leave of court. (Family Farm Protection Act, C.C.S.M. c. F15).

Forms are provided by statute, but it is customary to add to the statutory covenants, in both old system and new system mortgages, additional remedies and protection for the mortgagee, especially where a company is mortgagee, and many large law offices have their own forms for this purpose. Statutory forms are as follows:

Forms

Old System Mortgage:

This indenture, made (in duplicate) the . . . . . . day of . . . . . ., one thousand nine hundred and . . . . In pursuance of the Act Respecting Short Forms of Indenture: Between . . . . . . and . . . . Witnesseth that in consideration of . . . . . . Dollars of lawful money of Canada, now paid by the said mortgagee. . . . to the said mortgagor. . . . (the receipt whereof is hereby acknowledged) the said mortgagor. . . . do. . . . grant and mortgage unto the said mortgagee . . . . . . heirs and assigns forever. All and singular th. . . . certain parcel. . . . or tract. . . . of land and premises situate, lying and being . . . . . . (description). Provided this mortgage to be void on payment of . . . . . . dollars of lawful money of Canada, with interest . . . . . . at . . . . . . per cent per annum, as follows: . . . . . . and taxes and performance of statute labor. The said mortgagor. . . . covenant. . . . with the said mortgagee. . . ., that the mortgagor. . . . will pay the mortgage money and interest and observe the above proviso. That the mortgagor. . . . ha. . . . a good title in fee simple to said lands: and that . . . .he. . . . ha. . . . the right to convey the said lands to the said mortgagee. . . . and that on default the mortgagee. . . . shall have quiet possession of the said lands free from all encumbrances. And that the said mortgagor. . . . will execute such further assurances of the said lands as may be requisite. And that the said mortgagor. . . . ha. . . . done no act to encumber the said lands. And that the mortgagor. . . . will insure and keep insured the buildings on the said lands to the amount of not less than . . . . . . currency. And that the said mortgagor. . . . do. . . . release to the said mortgagee. . . . all . . . . . . claims upon the said lands, subject to the said proviso. Provided that the said mortgagee. . . . on default of payment for . . . . . . months may on . . . . . . notice enter on and lease or sell the said lands. Provided that the mortgagee. . . . may distrain for arrears of interest. Provided that in default of payment of the interest hereby secured, the principal hereby secured shall become payable. Provided that until default of payment the mortgagor. . . . shall have quiet possession of said lands.

In witness whereof, the said parties hereto have hereunto set their hands and seals. (Signed, sealed and delivered
in the presence of)

(Add consent of wife, if any, and acknowledgment thereof, affidavit under the Dower Act, and affidavit of witness, for forms of which see topics Acknowledgments; Affidavits).

New System Statutory Mortgage: (See Form 11.2 at end of Digest.)

Old System Assignment:

This indenture, made (in duplicate the . . . . . . day of . . . . . ., one thousand nine hundred and . . . . Between . . . . . ., hereinafter called the assignor, of the first part, and . . . . . ., hereinafter called the assignee, of the second part.

MORTGAGES OF REAL PROPERTY . . . *continued*

Whereas by a mortgage dated on the . . . . . . day of . . . . . ., one thousand nine hundred and . . . . . . and registered in the . . . . . . office at . . . . . . as No. . . . . . ., and made between . . . . . . as mortgagor and . . . . . . as mortgagee the said . . . . . . did grant and mortgage the land and premises therein and hereinafter described to the said . . . . . . heirs and assigns for securing the payment of the principal sum of . . . . . . dollars and interest thereon at the rate of . . . . . . per cent per annum, and there is now owing upon the said mortgage for the principal, the sum of . . . . . . dollars and interest since the . . . . . . day of . . . . . . A. D. 19. . .

Now this indenture witnesseth that in consideration of . . . . . . dollars of lawful money of Canada, now paid by the said assignee. . . . to the said assignor. . . . (the receipt whereof is hereby acknowledged), the said assignor. . . . do. . . . hereby assign and set over unto the said assignee, ... heirs, executors, administrators and assigns, all that the said before in part recited mortgage, and also the said sum of . . . . . . dollars and interest, now owing as aforesaid, together with all the moneys that may hereafter become due or owing in respect of said mortgage, and the full benefit of all powers and of all covenants and provisoes contained in the said mortgage, and also full power and authority to use the name or names of the said assignor, ... heirs, executors, administrators or assigns, for enforcing the performance of the covenants and other matters and things contained in the said mortgage, and the said assignor. . . . do. . . . hereby grant and convey unto the said assignee. . . ., ... heirs, executors, administrators and assigns, all and singular th. . . . certain parcel. . . . or tract. . . . of land and premises situate, lying and being in the Province of Manitoba and being composed of . . . . . . (description).

To have and to hold the said mortgage and all moneys arising in respect of the same and to accrue thereon. And also the said land and premises thereby granted and mortgaged to the use of the said assignee. . . ., ... heirs, executors, administrators and assigns, absolutely forever, but subject to the terms contained in the said mortgage. And the said assignor for . . . . . . heirs, executors, administrators and assigns, do. . . . hereby covenant with the said assignee. . . ., ... heirs, executors, administrators and assigns, that the said mortgage hereby assigned is a good and valid security, and that the said sum of . . . . . . dollars and interest as aforesaid, are now owing and unpaid, and that . . . . . . ha. . . . not done or permitted any act, matter or thing, whereby the said mortgage has been released, assigned, hypothecated, encumbered or discharged, either partly or in entirety and that . . . . . . will upon request do, perform and execute every act necessary to enforce the full performance of the covenants and other matters contained therein.

In witness whereof the assignor. . . . ha. . . hereunto set . . . . . . hand and seal the day and year first above written.

(Signed, sealed and delivered
in the presence of)
(Add affidavit of witness, for form see topic Affidavits).

New System Transfer: (See Form 8.2 at end of Digest.)

Chattel Mortgages.—See topic Personal Property Security.

MOTOR VEHICLES:

Vehicle registration required annually. New resident must register within three months for remainder of year. The Off-Road Vehicles Act (C.C.S.M. c. O31) requires registration of off-road vehicles and imposes other requirements. Antique cars, trucks and motorcycles must be registered. Issued by Registrar of Motor Vehicles. Plate must be displayed on back of vehicle with validation sticker affixed in each year or portion thereof for which new plates are not issued. No exemptions for members of Armed Forces resident in Manitoba.

Operator's License.—Driver or chauffeur must be licensed, carry license on person and produce same when required. Offence to hold more than one driver's license. (S. M. 1985 c. 3). Operator's license issued for one-year period to expire at end of operator's month of birth. Driver's license not issued to anyone under 16. Learner's license may be issued to person under 16 who is 15 1/2 or older, is enrolled in driver education course and has completed four hours of classroom instruction in that course. Chauffeur's license not issued to anyone under 18. No exemptions for members of Armed Forces resident in Manitoba.

Taxicabs.—See The Taxicab Act. (C.C.S.M. c. T10).

Suspension of license and registration may be automatic for failing to prove financial responsibility or for certain offences. License suspension is automatic on conviction for impaired driving or refusal to take breathalyzer test. First conviction: Six months suspension or, where injury to or death of any person or property damage exceeds $1,000, one year suspension. Second or subsequent conviction within five years of first conviction: five years suspension. (S. M. 1985-86, c. 3). For second or subsequent conviction, jail sentence is also automatic. Second conviction: minimum 14 days. Third or subsequent conviction: minimum 90 days. (S. C. 1985, c. 19). License suspension is also automatic for three months upon failure or refusal to take breathalyzer test or give blood sample. (S.M. 1989-90, c. 4 as am'd by S.M. 1989-90, c. 7). License may also be suspended for failure to pay traffic or parking fines. (S. M. 1985, c. 4).

Driving with suspended or cancelled license automatically results in vehicle driven being impounded for 30 days. (S.M. 1989-90, c. 4 as am'd by S.M. 1989-90, c. 7).

Arrest or conviction for any of the above offenses in any other province of Canada or in the United States will have this effect on official notice thereof to the registrar.

Titles.—No requirement to obtain certificate or other evidence of title. Inspection certificate required for transfer of registration where vehicle is of age/class requiring periodic inspection in regulations.

Sales.—New vehicle licence must be taken out by new owner. Registrar may require proof of ownership before registering vehicle.

Liens.—Registration of security interest in motor vehicle may be effected in Personal Property Registry. See topic Personal Property Security.

Identification Marks.—Minimum fine of $50 and maximum fine of $100 and suspension of licence up to six months for defacing, removing or altering manufacturer's serial number. (S. M. 1985-86, c. 3).

Operation Prohibited.—By person under 16 years.

Size and Weight Limits.—Regulated by The Highway Traffic Act (S. M. 1985-86, c. 3) and regulations.

Seat belts must be worn by drivers and passengers. Failure to do so may be contributory negligence. ([1989] 60 Man. R. [2d] 287).

Helmets must be worn by anyone riding on motorcycle.

Equipment Required.—The Highway Traffic Act (S. M. 1985-86, c. 3) requires usual equipment for motor vehicles. Must be two separate means of applying brakes to at least two wheels on same axle. Motor vehicle having width, including load, in excess of 2.05 meters must carry four lighted clearance lamps, one colored green, on each side at front and one colored red on each side at rear. Except for motorcycles of model or make of year 1974 or earlier, and mopeds, automatic turn signal lights required on all motor vehicles. Motor vehicles of year 1968 or later must be equipped at time of sale with seat belts and of year 1971 or later must be equipped with windshield washer. (C.C.S.M. c. H60). Requirements for rear and side view mirror equipment. Frost shields required from Nov. 1 to Mar. 31, both inclusive. Windshield wipers required. Unlawful to operate TV set in front seat of motor vehicle travelling upon highway or drive motor vehicle so equipped upon highway. (C.C.S.M. c. H60).

Lights Required.—Regulated by The Highway Traffic Act. (C.C.S.M. c. H60).

Inspection.—Peace officer may stop and inspect any equipment on vehicle or bicycle on highway. Registrar may require any owner to present motor vehicle for inspection.

Traffic regulations are governed by The Highway Traffic Act and local by-laws.

Accidents.—Driver of motor vehicle involved in accident must stop and give in writing number of his driver's licence, registration no. of vehicle, name of insurer and no. of policy and if he is not registered owner, name and address of registered owner. If there is bodily injury or apparent damage over $1,000 report to local police must be made forthwith and further written report within seven days.

Liability.—Owner liable for negligence of anyone operating car with his consent. Onus on driver to prove not negligent where loss or damage sustained by person by reason of motor vehicle on highway, except in case of collision between motor vehicles or action brought by a passenger.

Actions for damages done by owner or driver of motor vehicle must be commenced within two years after damage sustained.

Guests.—There is no longer any requirement for guest passenger to prove gross negligence in action for damages against owner or operator of motor vehicle. (S.M. 1980, c. 19).

Proof of Financial Responsibility.—Where an owner or driver has failed to satisfy a judgment obtained against him in any Court in Canada or the United States of America within 30 days after rendition thereof, in an action arising out of the operation of a motor vehicle where the cause of action is bodily injury to or the death of another or property damage in excess of $1,000, his license and registration certificate (or in case of nonresident, his privilege of having or using his car within Province) may be suspended and once suspended may not be restored or renewed until he has satisfied judgment at least to extent of $200,000 thereof and furnished proof of financial responsibility.

Proof of financial responsibility must be in an amount of not less than $200,000 (exclusive of interest and costs) with priority of $180,000 for personal injury and $20,000 for property damage, in one of following alternative forms: (a) Written certificate of duly authorized automobile insurance company; (b) bond of guarantee insurance or surety company; (c) certificate of Minister of Finance; (d) motor vehicle liability insurance card. (S. M. 1985-86, c. 3, §160).

After 36 months without accident or conviction and upon judgment being satisfied, person becomes exempt from requirement of proof of financial responsibility.

Insurance.—Must be obtained from Manitoba Public Insurance Corporation. (S. M. 1974, c. 58). Coverage: all perils subject to deductible (generally $400 for private automobile); death benefits calculated based on deceased's income with minimum of $40,000 spousal benefit, and minimum of $19,000 for dependent other than spouse; permanent impairment benefits of not less than $500 and not more than $100,000. "No fault" concept applies to collision (subject to deductible) and death and accident benefits. Insurance certificate obtained upon registration of vehicle. Additional coverage may be obtained from government plan or private insurer.

No-Fault Insurance.—See subhead Insurance, supra.

Foreign Vehicles.—Nonresident owners may operate vehicles in Manitoba without licencing or registration unless vehicle is used to transport merchandise, persons or property for compensation in which case vehicle must be licenced and registered as if owned by resident of Manitoba. Nonresidents, including corporations, carrying on business in province and using motor vehicle in Manitoba must have motor vehicle registered and licenced. Foreign vehicle may be detained by peace officer where offence committed or alleged until final disposition but motor vehicle may be released on satisfactory security. (S. M. 1985-86, c. 3).

Nonresident Operators.—Nonresident operator may drive motor vehicle in Manitoba without being licenced provided he has complied with law of his place of residence relating to licencing of drivers or chauffeurs and does not reside or carry on business for more than three consecutive months in any year. (S. M. 1985-86, c. 3).

Actions Against Nonresidents.—No special provision as to mode of commencement.

Direct Actions.—Direct action against insurer may be maintained only upon recovery of a judgment against insured. Action must be a class action on behalf of all persons who have such judgments. Limitation period of one year following final determination of action against insured.

MOTOR VEHICLES . . . *continued*

Motor Vehicle Carriers.—Highway Transport Board exercises supervision over motor carriers and operators of public service vehicles and commercial trucks and in order to operate a public service vehicle for transportation of persons or property application must be made to that Board for a certificate. Board may specify routes over which carrier may operate, fix maximum or minimum tolls, fares or charges to be made, and regulate and supervise schedules, service, maintenance, equipment, method of operation, etc.

Every vehicle so licensed must be maintained in a safe and sanitary condition and subject at all times to inspection by the Board. Driver must be at least 18 years of age, of good moral character, and competent, and must hold a chauffeur's license and a driver of a passenger-carrying bus must hold a driver's license issued by Registrar of Motor Vehicles. (C.C.S.M. c. H60).

Off-Road Vehicles.—Ownership and operation of off-road vehicles including 3-wheelers and snowmobiles governed by Off-Road Vehicles Act. (C.C.S.M. c. 031).

Aircraft.—See Canada Law Digest, topic Aircraft.

Gasoline Tax.—See topic Taxation.

NEGOTIABLE INSTRUMENTS:

See Canada Law Digest, topic Bills and Notes.

NOTARIES PUBLIC:

May be appointed by minister. Fee $100 with expiration, $150 without expiration and $50 for renewal. Unless appointee is barrister or solicitor, appointment expires two years from date of its issue and date of expiration must be stated connection with signature. Authority extends throughout province and includes administering oaths, attesting of commercial instruments for public protestation, giving of notarial certificates and performing all functions of Commisioner for Oaths. (The Manitoba Evidence Act, C.C.S.M. c. E150).

PARTITION:

(The Law of Property Act, C.C.S.M. c. L90).

Lands held in joint tenancy or tenancy in common are subject to partition. Applicant may proceed by statement of claim or notice of motion in Court of Queen's Bench where land is situate or where related proceedings have been, or may be, instituted. All parties interested in property must be served and brought before court, which will make partition order on ownership being shown.

Where such joint tenant or tenant in common is a married man or a married woman, an action for partition or sale of the land may be brought by or against him or her, and a partition, or a sale thereof in lieu of partition when in the opinion of the court it cannot reasonably be partitioned, may be ordered by the court without the consent of any party to the action, and without the consent of his or her spouse having been obtained as provided in The Homesteads, Marital Property Amendment and Consequential Amendments Act. (S.M. 1992, c. 46).

See topic Homesteads.

The proceedings may be referred to the master to settle the division or for the purposes of sale.

Sale of Property.—If the property is not capable of partition, an order for the sale of the property is made, and the property is sold and the proceeds divided amongst the parties entitled.

PARTNERSHIP:

Law of Manitoba relating to partnership is codified by Partnership Act. (C.C.S.M. c. P30).

Partnership declarations must be registered under The Business Names Registration Act (see subhead The Business Names Registration Act [C.C.S.M. c. B110], infra).

Powers of Partners.—Any partner may bind or pledge the credit of the partnership for any debts incurred in the course of the partnership business.

Partnership Debts.—The assets of the individual members of the partnership may be rendered liable for partnership debts in case of deficiency of partnership assets.

On the principle of "holding out," a person not a partner may be liable as a partner to any one who has given credit to the partnership on the faith of such representation.

Limited Partnership.—General partners are jointly and severally liable, but limited partners are not liable for debts of partnership beyond amount they have respectively contributed to capital. Persons forming limited partnership must register declaration under The Business Names Registration Act (see subhead The Business Names Registration Act [C.C.S.M. c. B110], infra) including names of all general and limited partners and amount of capital each limited partner has contributed.

The Business Names Registration Act (C.C.S.M. c. B110).—Every corporation, and, except for certain professions, every individual carrying on business under name other than its or his corporate name or surname, or in partnership, must register declaration within one month and this is published in Manitoba Gazette. Any changes must be registered and published.

PERPETUITIES:

Common law rule against perpetuities, and accumulations, were both abolished in 1983.

PERSONAL PROPERTY:

No tenancy by the entirety.

PERSONAL PROPERTY SECURITY:

Application.—The Personal Property Security Act was proclaimed in full force Sept. 1, 1978 (C.C.S.M. c. P35) and modelled on Ontario Personal Property Security Act and Article IX of Uniform Commercial Code. It applies to every transaction, without regard to form or person who has title to collateral, that creates security interest, including chattel mortgage, conditional sale, equipment trust, floating charge, pledge, trust deed, trust receipt, assignment (including assignment of book debts), lease or consignment intended as security and every assignment of book debts not intended as security. Manitoba statute also applies to "corporate securities" defined as every security in personal property and fixtures created by corporation and contained in trust deed or other writing to secure bonds, debentures or debenture stock of corporation or of any other corporation, or in any bonds, debentures or debenture stock of corporation as well as in trust deed or other writing securing same, or any trust deed or other writing securing bonds, debentures or debenture stock of any other corporation, or in any bonds, debentures or debenture stock or any series of bonds or debentures of corporation not secured by separate writing.

Transitional.—Proclamation of The Personal Property Security Act caused repeal of The Bills of Sale Act, The Assignment of Book Debts Act, and The Lien Notes Act, and caused amendments to The Garage Keepers Act, (am'd by S.M. 1978, c. 10), The Sale of Goods Act, (am'd by S.M. 1973, c. 6) and The Corporations Act (upon proclamation of §47 of The Personal Property Security Act).

Registration under repealed or amended Acts is deemed to be registration under The Personal Property Security Act. Question as to priorities between security interests validly created prior to Sept. 1, 1978 or between security interest validly created prior to Sept. 1, 1978 and security interest validly created thereafter shall be determined by law as it was prior to that date.

Where there is conflict between provisions of The Personal Property Security Act and The Consumer Protection Act, or The Farm Machinery and Equipment Act, latter Acts prevail.

Registration.—Registration pursuant to The Personal Property Security Act is by way of filing financing statement in form and manner prescribed by Regulations giving notice of security interest in personal property. Security agreement creating security interest does not have to be filed except in case of corporate security where executed copy of trust deed containing security interest, or true copy of bonds, debentures or debenture stock containing security interest, must accompany financing statement. Registration occurs in The Personal Property Registry located in Winnipeg. All registrations made in County Courts or Corporation Branch Mortgage Register prior to Sept. 1, 1978 have been incorporated into The Personal Property Registry.

Security agreement is effective according to its terms between parties to it and against third parties except as otherwise provided by The Personal Property Security Act or any other Act.

Security interest is not enforceable against third party unless collateral is in possession of secured party or debtor has signed security agreement that contains description of collateral sufficient to enable it to be identified.

Registration of financing statement regarding corporate security does not have to be renewed. Registration of financing statement regarding other than corporate security is effective for three years and may be renewed.

The Personal Property Security Act does not require any affidavit of execution or bona fides or any statement of particulars as was case in certain situations prior to Sept. 1, 1978.

There is no time limit to effect registration in order to maintain validity of security agreement. However, timely registration is important in determination of priorities.

Fees.—For filing financing statement in respect of: Security agreement or notice of receivership, $12; garage keepers' lien, $8; corporate security, $200; renewal statements, $12; any other prescribed form, $8.

Attachment.—Security interest attaches when parties intend it to attach, value is given and debtor has rights in collateral. Debtor has no rights in crops until they become growing crops, fish until they are caught, oil, gas or other minerals until they are extracted or timber until it is cut.

After Acquired Property.—Security agreement may cover after acquired property.

Future Advances.—Security agreement may secure future advances or other value whether or not advances or other value are given pursuant to commitment.

Perfection.—Security interest is perfected when it has attached and all steps required for perfection required under Act have been completed regardless of order of occurrence. Possession of collateral by secured party or on his behalf by person other than debtor or debtor's agent perfects security interest in chattel paper, goods, instruments, securities, letters of credit and advices of credit and negotiable documents of title but only during its actual holding as collateral. Registration perfects security interest in chattel paper, goods, intangibles and documents of title, collateral security and floating charge. Security interest in collateral that is dealt with so as to give rise to proceeds continues as to collateral unless secured party expressly or impliedly authorizes such dealing and extends to proceeds.

Priorities.—As general rule, priorities are determined as follows: By order of registration if security interests are registered, by order of perfection if security interests are not registered, and by order of attachment if security interests are not perfected. There are important exceptions to general priority scheme.

Rights and Remedies.—Part V of The Personal Property Security Act sets out certain rights, remedies, duties and obligations upon both secured party and debtor, some of which cannot be waived or released.

PLEADING:

Pleadings are governed by Queen's Bench Rules, which are regulations made under Queen's Bench Act. (C.C.S.M. c. C280).

Pleadings Permitted.—Include statement of claim, statement of defence, reply, counterclaim, defence to counterclaim, reply to defence to counterclaim, crossclaim, defence to crossclaim, reply to defence to crossclaim, third party claim, defence to third party claim, reply to defence to third party claim, petition for divorce and answer.

Statement of Claim.—Generally, action commenced by plaintiff filing statement of claim any time within limitation period. Statement of claim must be served within six months after issue by court. (See Q.B. Rule 14.) Statement of claim must contain

PLEADING . . . *continued*
concise statement of material facts on which party relies and may include claim for relief and conclusion of law if supporting material facts. (See Q.B. Rule 25.)

Statement of Defence.—Shall admit all facts in opposite party's pleading not in dispute and shall plead all matters upon which party intends to rely to defeat claim of opposite party. (See Q.B. Rule 25.) See topic Actions, subhead Commencement of Actions.

Counterclaim.—Defendant may assert, by way of counterclaim in main action, any right or claim he has against plaintiff, and counterclaim is to be included in same document as statement of defence and served within time prescribed for latter. (See Q.B. Rule 27.)

Reply is required (a) when party intends to prove different facts than pleaded in other party's defence and not included in statement of claim; and (b) when party intends to rely on any matter not previously raised which might, if not specifically pleaded take opposite party by surprise. Party must serve reply, if any, within ten days after service of statement of defence, but where other party counterclaims, plaintiff must deliver reply and defence to counterclaim within 20 days after service of defence and counterclaim. (See Q.B. Rule 25.)

Amended Pleadings.—Party may amend pleading without leave, before close of pleadings, if amendment does not cause addition, deletion or substitution of party, or on consent of all parties, or with leave of court. On motion at any stage of action, court will grant leave to amend on such terms as are just, unless prejudice would result that could not be compensated for by costs or adjournments. Form of amendments and service of amended pleadings are prescribed. (See Q.B. Rule 26.)

Particulars.—Rules and contents of pleadings are generally prescribed. Where party demands particulars of allegation in opponent's pleading, and opponent fails to supply within seven days, court may order particulars to be delivered within specified time. (See Q.B. Rule 25.)

Service.—See topics Actions; Process.

Filing.—Originating process may be issued and filed by delivering or mailing original copy to centre in which proceedings are to be commenced, accompanied by prescribed fee.

PLEDGES:

Delivery and retention of possession are essential to a pledge, and if possession is surrendered, the lien which attaches to a pledge is lost. A pledgee is not responsible for the safety of the article pledged if he has exercised reasonable care.

Pawnbrokers are licensed by most municipal corporations and are permitted by the local law to sell the pledges at the expiration of a reasonable time. But they must report all articles pledged and sold by them to the local authority.

PRACTICE:

Practice at common law and in equity in the Court of Queen's Bench and in all other superior courts of record has been completely fused and is governed by the Queen's Bench Act. (C.C.S.M. c. C280).

Language.—Either French or English may be used by any person in any court or other adjudicative tribunal, and on any pleading or process in or issuing from any court or other adjudicative tribunal. Documents emanating from such bodies may be in either language. (The Manitoba Act 1870, 34-35 Vic. S. C. 1870, c. 28, §23).

Direct Actions Against Insurer.—See topic Motor Vehicles, subhead Direct Actions.

See also topics Actions, Appeal and Error, Attachment, Depositions, Executions, Garnishment, Injunctions, Judgments, Pleading, Process.

PRINCIPAL AND AGENT:

Common law rules generally prevail.

A contract of agency may be created verbally or in writing, or may be inferred from a course of conduct. Unauthorized acts may be ratified by the principal, either expressly or by implication.

An agent may be dismissed and his authority revoked at any time, but if the revocation involves a breach of contract he has an action for damages against the principal. Except for power of attorney given for valuable consideration and expressly irrevocable, death of principal revokes agency.

Power of attorney may be given by the registered owner of any land, estate or interest under the Torrens system authorizing any person to act for him in respect of a transfer or other dealing with the land. The power of attorney must be duly executed and attested and verified by affidavit and deposited with the district registrar, and it remains in force until revocation or notice of death is registered. The Powers of Attorney Act (C.C.S.M. c. P97) provides for powers of attorney enduring beyond mental infirmity of donor and irrevocable powers of attorney.

Collection Agencies.—No person not admitted and duly qualified to act as attorney and solicitor may, on behalf of a creditor, write, publish or send any card, letter or notice threatening legal proceedings for the recovery of money or property or intimating that such proceedings will be taken, but such person may threaten or intimate that the matter will be handed to some duly qualified attorney or solicitor for legal proceedings. No person may use in any manner any document or writing which simulates, or is intended or likely to lead any person to believe that it is, a court process or form. (The Law Society Act, C.C.S.M. c. L100).

PROCESS:

Commencement of Proceeding.—Queen's Bench Rules contemplate two types of civil proceedings: Actions and applications. Under Rules, every proceeding must be by action except where statute or Rules provide that proceeding may be brought by application. (See Q.B. Rule 14.)

General Requisites.—Most proceedings commenced in court having jurisdiction by issuance of statement of claim or notice of application. Form and contents of notice and statement are prescribed. (See Q.B. Rule 14.)

By Whom Issued.—All civil proceedings are commenced by issue of originating process by registrar of court in which proceeding is to be commenced, except where statute provides otherwise. Counterclaim that is against present parties to main action, and crossclaim, are commenced by filing and serving of pleading containing counterclaim or crossclaim, and pleading need not be issued. (See Q.B. Rule 14.)

Who May Serve.—Any person.

Personal Service on Individual.—By leaving copy of documents with individual. Original need not be produced.

Personal Service on Minor.—By leaving copy of document with minor and where minor resides with parent or other person having care or lawful custody of minor, by leaving another copy of document with that person, but where proceeding is in respect of minor's interest in estate or trust by leaving copy with guardian of minor's estate, or if no guardian appointed by leaving copy of document bearing minor's name and address with Public Trustee.

Personal Service on Incompetent.—Personal service on person who has been declared mentally incompetent or incapable of managing own affairs is effected by leaving copy of document with committee of person's estate, if one exists or, if not, with committee of person. Personal service on person who is mentally incompetent or incapable of managing own affairs, not so declared, is effected by leaving copy of document with person in whose care incompetent resides and incompetent himself unless attending physician is of opinion that leaving copy with incompetent would cause serious harm.

Personal Service on Partnership.—By service on one or more of partners, or on any person who appears to have control or management of partnership at principal place of business within Manitoba, or where partnership dissolved by leaving copy with every person sought to be made liable.

Personal Service on Domestic Corporation.—By service on officer, director or agent of corporation, or on person at place of business of corporation who appears to be in control or management of that place of business.

Personal Service on Foreign Corporation.—By service on any person having control or management at place of business of corporation within Manitoba.

Substitutional Service.—If it is impractical to effect prompt service of originating process court may make order for substitutional service or dispense with service if it is necessary in interest of justice. Substituted service may include advertising, mailing or posting document.

Personal Service Outside of Manitoba.—See topic Actions, subhead Commencement of Actions.

Proof of Service.—May be affidavit of person who served document.

Nonresident Motorist.—See topic Motor Vehicles.

PROOF OF CLAIMS:

See topics Executors and Administrators; Pleading.

RAILROADS: See topic Carriers.

REAL PROPERTY:

Principal estates in real property recognized in this province are estate in fee simple, estate tail, life estate and leasehold estate. Estate granted to two or more persons is tenancy in common unless expressly declared to be joint tenancy. Every estate vested in executors or trustees is held by them in joint tenancy. (The Real Property Act, C.C.S.M. c. R30). Airspace parcels may be created by registered owner of land with consent of all other parties with claim or interest in land. (S. M. 1986, c. 2).

Condominiums.—Upon registration of declaration and airspace, plan, land and interest appurtenant to land described is governed by The Condominium Act and registrar must: (1) Issue certificate of title in name of condominium corporation thereby created; (2) issue separate certificate of title in name of each owner for each unit described; (3) keep index known as "Condominium Corporations Index"; (4) keep register known as "Condominium Register" of declarations, plans, by-laws, etc. (R. S. M. c. C170 as am'd by S. M. 1987-88, c. 29).

See also topics, Deeds, Homesteads, Husband and Wife, Landlord and Tenant, Mortgages of Real Property, Partition, Records.

RECEIVERS:

Receivers may be appointed in any action, to receive the proceeds of any property of a litigant, either to preserve the property pending litigation or by way of equitable execution to satisfy a judgment. In cases other than receivers by way of equitable execution, no party, attorney or person interested in the action, may be appointed a receiver. Also governed by The Corporations Act (C.C.S.M. c. C225, Part VIII).

Powers.—Receivers may, for the purposes of preserving the property or collecting it, bring and defend actions, receive rents and profits, collect and compromise debts, and make such transfers respecting the property as the court may authorize. Receivers defined under Bankruptcy and Insolvency Act of Canada (Part XI). Act sets out responsibilities and powers of receivers.

RECORDS:

All instruments except wills, sheriffs' deeds, and tax deeds affecting lands in Manitoba, whether there has been a crown grant or not, are deemed fraudulent and void against subsequent purchasers or mortgagees for valuable consideration without actual notice, unless registered in the proper office before the registering of the instrument under which such subsequent purchasers or mortgagees may claim. (The Registry Act, C.C.S.M. c. R50).

RECORDS . . . *continued*

Place of Recording.—Land titles are recorded in the land titles offices of the several land registration districts. Financing statements in respect of chattel mortages are filed in Personal Property Registry in Winnipeg. Letters of probate and administration are filed in Court of Queen's Bench of proper judicial centre and recorded with surrogate clerk at Winnipeg.

Torrens Act.—See topic Deeds.

Vital Statistics.—Records of births, deaths, adoptions, divorces, decrees of nullity of marriage and marriages are kept by Department of Health, Vital Statistics Branch, Winnipeg.

REDEMPTION:

See topics Executions; Liens; Mortgages of Real Property; Taxation.

REPLEVIN:

Where goods, chattels, or other personal property have been wrongfully distrained or wrongfully taken or detained, the owner may bring an action of replevin for their recovery and for damages. (The Queen's Bench Act, C.C.S.M. c. C280, §59; Q.B. Rules, §§44, 60).

Action is commenced in Court of Queen's Bench by statement of claim in same manner as other actions. Order of replevin may then be obtained on motion ex parte. Affidavit in support of application must be filed, setting out facts of wrongful taking or detention, value and description of property and that claimant is owner or is lawfully entitled to possession. Before sheriff executes order he must unless order provides otherwise, take bond from plaintiff with two sureties in double value of property, or money to amount of value of property, as security. Unless otherwise provided goods are then delivered to plaintiff.

After replevin order has been executed, action proceeds like any other action. Where no defence is filed plaintiff may sign default judgment or may sign interlocutory judgment and proceed as in other cases.

REPORTS:

Decisions are reported in Western Weekly Reports, Dominion Law Reports, Manitoba Reports and others.

RESTRAINT OF TRADE:

See Canada Law Digest, topic Monopolies and Restraint of Trade.

SALES:

Law relating to sales of goods has been codified under Sale of Goods Act (C.C.S.M. c. S10), which is substantially same as English Act and Uniform Sales Act formerly in force in many U.S. states.

Act also provides for vendor's lien, and, in cases of insolvency, for stoppage in transit.

Where goods are sold by sample, it is implied that the bulk shall correspond in quality with the sample; that the buyer shall have reasonable opportunity for comparing the bulk with the sample and that the goods shall be free from any defect rendering them unmerchantable, which would not be apparent on reasonable examination of the sample.

The Farm Machinery and Equipment Act (C.C.S.M. c. F40) makes provision protecting purchaser of farm machinery and equipment of all types, and provides for statutory conditions of sale and creates Farm Machinery Board to investigate complaints, establish normal rental rates and recommend safety measures.

Contracts must be in writing in form as in schedule. (§11).

Prices must be listed by vendors with Board and these must be adhered to.

Repossession by vendor may be carried out with consent of purchaser or approval of Board. (§§24-25).

Bills of Sale.—See topic Chattel Mortgages.

Product Liability.—Manufacturer or supplier of goods may be liable to consumer for negligence even where there is no privity of contract. (1932 A. C. 562).

Retail Credit Sales.—See topics Interest; Personal Property Security; and this topic subhead The Consumer Protection Act, infra.

The Consumer Protection Act (C.C.S.M. c. C200) governs form and substance of retail hire-purchases, conditional sales, loans and direct sales and, in some cases, cash sales and chattel mortgages where cost of borrowing does not exceed $10 and purchaser is not corporation. Act provides for licensing of direct sellers and collection agents, sets seven day "cooling off period" in case of sale away from seller's usual place of business. Act also regulates advertising of goods to be sold by time sale. Contract for services must be payable in at least two instalments. No such contract may exceed 12 months' duration. Act provides for mediation of disputes between buyers and sellers and between lenders and borrowers as to terms of any transaction governed by Act. Act requires full disclosure of cost of borrowing in all cases of sales or loans on variable credit.

Trade Practices Inquiry Act (C. C. S. M. c. T110) regulates price of essential products of limited availability. (See topic Consumer Protection.)

The International Sale of Goods Act (S.M. 1989-90, c. 7) incorporates into Manitoba United Nations Convention on Contracts for the International Sale of Goods.

SALES TAX: See topic Taxation.

SEALS:

The common law distinction between sealed and unsealed documents still exists. A sealed document imports a valuable consideration. A wafer or a wax must be attached to the paper, except that in the case of corporations, courts or other bodies the impression of the official seal only upon the paper is sufficient.

SECURITIES:

Sale of securities to public in Manitoba is regulated by The Securities Act. (C.C.S.M. c. S50).

Save as to certain excepted shares and securities such as those guaranteed by any government or those of municipal or public nature or approved as trust investments or those of mining companies when incorporated and mining syndicates when registered no person, firm or corporation may sell or offer for sale in Manitoba any shares, stocks, bonds or other securities issued by any company unless preliminary and final prospectus has been filed with Manitoba Securities Commission. Full disclosure of financial position and all material facts relating to issuing company must be made in prospectus.

Supervision.—Act is administered by Manitoba Securities Commission, 405 Broadway, Winnipeg, Manitoba R3C 3L6. Phone: (204) 945-2548. (§2).

Registration of Dealers.—Under The Securities Act stock brokers and salesmen must be registered with Manitoba Securities Commission and licensed to carry on business in province. Broker must furnish bond to satisfaction of Commission. Commission has power to suspend licenses for violations of certain provisions of Act.

Prevention of Fraud.—Manitoba Securities Commission has power to examine persons to ascertain whether a fraud has been or is about to be committed under The Securities Act and if it so finds it may suspend license to sell shares or on its report Attorney-General may proceed against such person under Act. Commission may suspend any stock exchange from carrying on operations within province for a period not exceeding ten days to prevent such frauds. Attorney-General may give personal or public notice of any fraudulent acts.

SEQUESTRATION:

Order for delivery of possession of property now enforced by writ of possession. Writ obtained by leave of court on motion without notice. Leave granted only where court satisfied all persons in actual possession of land received sufficient notice of proceeding in which order was obtained. (Q.B. Rule 60).

SERVICE: See topic Process.

STATUTE OF FRAUDS: See topic Frauds, Statute of.

STATUTES:

In 1986 Supreme Court of Canada ruled that pursuant to The Manitoba Act 1870, 34-35 Vic. S.C. 1870, c. 28, §23 Statutes and Regulations of Manitoba were required to be passed in both French and English. Revised Statutes of Manitoba, 1970 and amendments passed in English only were granted temporary validity pending translation and re-enactment. Re-Enacted Statutes of Manitoba were passed in 1987 and 1988 containing French translation of Revised Statutes of Manitoba, 1970 and amendments thereto. C.C.S.M. is continually updated looseleaf service of Provincial Queen's Printer encompassing public statutes of Manitoba as amended. Residuary law is that of England on July 15, 1870.

STAY OF EXECUTION:

See topics Appeal and Error; Executions.

SUBMISSION OF CONTROVERSY:

At any stage of an action, the parties thereto may agree on a stated case and submit their rights to the court on such statement, and the court may give judgment as in other actions. (Q.B. Rule 22).

SUPPLEMENTARY PROCEEDINGS:

See topic Executions.

SURETY AND GUARANTY COMPANIES:

See topics Banks and Banking; Bonds; Corporations.

TAXATION:

The revenue for the cities and municipalities in the province is derived largely from taxation of lands situate within the respective city or municipality. The provincial government does not impose any tax on lands but derives its revenue largely from income tax, gasoline tax, mining tax and amusement tax in addition to many others.

Payment.—In municipalities, taxes are payable at par up to and including due date (June 30 in Winnipeg) of year for which levied. As a rule, a discount is allowed for prepayment. Penalty is added to taxes outstanding after due date.

Sales of Land.—Municipal Act (C.C.S.M. c. M225) provides that lands may be sold for taxes due and unpaid for more than one year after 31st day of Dec. in year in which rate was struck. Tax sales must be advertised in Official Gazette and at least one local newspaper. Owner of any lands sold for taxes, or his legal representative, may redeem at any time before title issues to tax sale purchaser by paying taxes, costs, prescribed penalties, and certain bonuses, or by entering into agreement to do so in installments. There are no tax sale deeds but purchaser of lands at sale receives certificate from municipal treasurer to effect that such lands have been sold at tax sale to him. If land be not redeemed tax sale purchaser may at end of one year and must within two years from date of sale, apply for certificate of title under Real Property Act. Notice of such application is then served on all parties interested in land, who are given three months within which to redeem. If land be sold for amount in excess of that due for taxes, surplus must be paid in before expiration of two years from date of sale. District registrar, after appointing three months within which lands must be redeemed and issuing notice to be served upon all interested parties requiring them to redeem and pay arrears of taxes, bonuses and costs incurred, at end of three months, unless lands are before redeemed, will issue indefeasible title to tax sale purchaser. Costs incurred in application are taxed by district registrar whose decision is final. Where value of land sold does not, in his opinion, exceed $10,000 in value, notice may be served by

TAXATION . . . *continued*
registered mail. Enquiries as to lands sold for taxes should be directed to treasurer of municipality in which lands are situated or to district registrar of Land Titles Office in district in which lands are situated.

Oil and Gas Production Tax.—C.C.S.M., c. O37.

Income Tax.—Income Tax Act (Manitoba) (C.C.S.M. c. I10) levies income tax on individuals and corporations. (S.M. 1989-90, c. 86, Part 3). By Federal-Provincial agreements, Canada collects this tax for and on behalf of Province. Rate for individual currently is 52% of tax payable under Federal Income Tax Act plus surtax of 2% of net income. See topic Corporations. See also Canada Law Digest.

Inheritance Tax.—Inheritance tax not levied on estate of person who died after Oct. 10, 1977. (S.M. 1977 [2d], c. 2).

Gift tax not levied on gift made after Oct. 10, 1977. (S.M. 1977 [2d] c. 2).

Sales Tax.—In addition to Federal sales tax (i.e. Goods and Services Tax) (for which see Canada Law Digest) 7% tax on sales is payable by purchasers of tangible personal property and certain services sold and delivered in Manitoba. (The Retail Sales Tax Act, C.C.S.M. c. R130, as am'd by S.M. 1987-88, c. 27).

It is payable to retailer or other supplier by purchaser at time of sale.

Intangible personal property such as insurance policies, bank accounts, mortgages, bonds or shares is not subject to provincial tax.

Sales of real estate subject to land transfer tax (see topic Deeds). Building materials and component parts such as lighting fixtures, cupboards and furnaces are taxable, whether for new construction or for adding to, or improving, house or similar structure on land. Labour charge is tax exempt.

Retailers, storekeepers, suppliers of other services and other vendors are required to collect correct amount of tax at time of sale and remit to government monthly. Amounts so collected are deemed to be held in trust.

Some goods and services are exempt. (The Retail Sales Tax Act, C.C.S.M. c. R130).

Health and Post Secondary Education Tax Levy Act.—(C. C. S. M. c. H24; S.M. 1989-90, c. 86). Employers taxed on 2.25% of remuneration paid to employees at permanent establishment in Manitoba. No tax if remuneration paid is $750,000 or less and if remuneration between $750,000 and $1,500,000, tax is 4.5% of remuneration over $750,000.

The Corporation Capital Tax.—(C.C.S.M. c. C226).

The Insurance Corporation Tax Act.—(C.C.S.M. c. I50).

Amusement Tax.—Municipalities have power to impose amusement tax. (C.C.S.M., c. M225).

Pari-Mutuel Tax.—(C.C.S.M. c. P12).

Gasoline Tax.—(C.C.S.M. c. G40).

Motive Fuel Tax Act.—(C.C.S.M. c. M220).

Tobacco Tax.—(C.C.S.M. c. T80).

Stamp Tax.—None imposed by the province.

Franchise Taxes.—See topic Corporations.

Mining Tax.—See topic Mines and Minerals.

Unemployment Compensation or Social Security Tax.—None.

Utilities Tax.—7% on purchase of electricity, telephone service, gas used as fuel and delivered by pipe, coal and steam or water for heating buildings. There are certain exemptions from this tax with respect to gas, coal, and electricity used to heat domestic dwellings and farm buildings. (C.C.S.M. c. R150, Regulation 74/88).

Penalties.—As to land taxes, see subheads Payment and Sales of Land, supra. As to corportion, income, and estate taxes, see Canada Law Digest.

TORRENS ACT: See topic Deeds.

TRADEMARKS AND TRADENAMES:

See Canada Law Digest. See also topic Partnership.

TRUST DEEDS: See topic Mortgages of Real Property.

TRUSTEE PROCESS: See topic Garnishment.

TRUSTS:

Powers and duties of trustee are defined by The Trustee Act (C.C.S.M. c. T160) which provides for vesting of estates in trustees and makes rules for their guidance in making investments of trust funds, etc., provides for trustee obtaining advice of court in doubtful matters, for their remuneration and for compelling an annual accounting by them. Trustee Act is codification of common law affecting trusts.

USURY: See Canada Law Digest, topic Interest.

VENUE:

Unless otherwise provided by statute, actions in Court of Queen's Bench may be brought in any administrative or judicial centre. Defendant has right to have action transferred to centre nearest to place where cause of action arose, nearest to place where defendant resided at time action commenced, or nearest to place where defendant carried on business at time action commenced.

Change of venue may be ordered if necessary to fair trial or for convenience. (Q.B. Rule 47.02).

VITAL STATISTICS: See topic Records.

WAREHOUSEMEN:

The Warehouse Receipts Act (C.C.S.M. c. W30) defines warehouse receipt as acknowledgment in writing by warehouseman of receipt for storage of goods not his own. Warehouseman means any person who receives goods for storage for reward but does not include express company within legislative authority of Parliament of Canada or railway company or manager or operator of grain elevator. Act provides for form of receipt, its negotiability by delivery and indorsement and rights of person to whom receipt is negotiated. Goods covered by non-negotiable receipt may be transferred by delivery of transfer in writing executed by holder, of which written notice must be given to warehouseman. Indorser of receipt is not guarantor.

Liens.—Warehousemen have a lien on the goods deposited with them for storage, whether deposited by the owner or with his authority or by any person entrusted with the possession of the goods, and the goods may be sold to realize the amount of the storage charges. (The Warehousemen's Liens Act, C.C.S.M. c. W20).

WILLS:

Will may be made by anyone who is over 18, or who is or has been married, or in certain cases, who is member of Armed Forces, provided he or she is of sound mind. (The Wills Act, C.C.S.M. c. W150).

A married woman may devise or bequeath by will, all separate property, real or personal, or any rights she may possess therein whether acquired before or after marriage.

Testamentary Disposition—Dependents' Maintenance.—The Dependents' Relief Act (C.C.S.M. c. D37) provides that where deceased has not made adequate provision for proper maintenance and support of dependent, court may order that adequate support be made out of deceased's estate. Possible dependents includes deceased's spouse, infant children and others substantially dependent on deceased at time of death. Application must be brought within six months of grant of probate. See topics Homesteads; Descent and Distribution.

Execution.—Will must be in writing, signed at the end thereof by the testator and witnessed by two witnesses who must sign at the request of the testator, in his presence and in the presence of each other.

Attestation.—No form of attestation mandated; following is generally used:

Form

Signed, Published and Declared by the Testator . . . . . . as and for his last Will and Testament in the presence of us both present at the same time who, at his request, and in his presence and in the presence of each other, have hereunto subscribed our names as witnesses.

Holographic Wills.—A will wholly written and signed by the testator himself, need not be in any particular form and need not be witnessed.

Nuncupative Wills.—Sailors, soldiers and airmen in actual service or in course of a voyage may make wills without the usual formalities.

Substantial Compliance.—Where document does not comply with formalities of execution required by The Wills Act, judge of Court of Queen's Bench may nevertheless order that it be fully effective as either will of deceased or as revocation, alteration or revival of will of deceased where he is satisfied that such was deceased's intention. (C.C.S.M. c. W150, §23).

Revocation.—Will is revoked by: (a) Marriage unless there is a declaration in will that it is made in contemplation of marriage, (b) later valid will, (c) later declaration of revocation which must be made in accordance with provisions governing making of will, or by (d) burning, tearing or otherwise destroying it with intention of revoking. There is no revocation by presumption of intention based on change in circumstances, except that where subsequent to making of will, testator's marriage is dissolved or declared void, testamentary dispositions or appointments to or of testator's spouse are deemed revoked unless contrary intention is evident in will.

Revival.—Will previously revoked may be revived only by a will or codicil made in accordance with Act showing an intention to revive former will. Mere revocation of subsequent will does not revive former.

Probate jurisdiction is in Court of Queen's Bench. (The Court of Queen's Bench Act, C.C.S.M. c. C280).

Testamentary Gifts to Subscribing Witnesses.—A will is not invalidated by the fact that a witness or the husband or wife of a witness is a beneficiary under the will, but the gift to such person is void unless there are sufficient other attesting witnesses or unless no attestation is required or unless judge of Court of Queen's Bench, on application, is satisfied that neither such person nor his or her spouse exercised any improper or undue influence upon testator.

Bequests and Devises to Inter Vivos Trusts.—No statutory provision.

Testamentary Guardians.—See topic Guardian and Ward.

Contest.—A caveat may be filed in Office of Registrar or in office of Surrogate Clerk, any time after death requiring that nothing be done without notice to caveator. Caveat remains in force for six months. New caveat may be filed. Application may be made to vacate caveat. Application may be made for proof of will in solemn form or for revocation of letters probate. Court issues warning or citation to all parties and after appearances have been entered gives directions for trial of issue. Action is heard by Court of Queen's Bench.

Legacies.—Executor has one year in which to gather assets, pay debts, etc. Thereafter legatee may be entitled to interest.

Unclaimed Legacies.—See topic Descent and Distribution.

Lapse.—Gift by will lapses where donee predeceases testator, except where donee is child or other issue or brother or sister of testator and such donee leaves issue surviving

WILLS . . . *continued*
at time of death of testator. In that event gift does not lapse but goes to issue as if donee had died intestate and without surviving spouse.

Children of the testator, whether born before or after execution of the will, but not mentioned therein, have no right as to property disposed of by the will. But see subhead Testamentary Disposition—Dependents' Maintenance, supra.

Election between Part 4 of The Marital Property Act and testamentary provision, see topic Descent and Distribution.

Foreign Executed Wills.—Valid in so far as the manner and formalities of its making and so far as it relates to an interest in movables, if it is thus valid in place where: (a) Will was made, (b) testator was domiciled at time of making, (c) testator had habitual residence, or (d) testator was a national if one law governed wills of nationals. Intrinsic validity and effect are governed as to interest in movables by law of domicile of testator at time of death. As to interest in land law of succession governs manner and formalities of making of will and its intrinsic validity and effect.

Foreign Probated Wills.—Where probate or letters of administration have been granted elsewhere in Canada, U.K. or any part of British Commonwealth, such grant may be re-sealed in Manitoba on payment of fees, and shall then have like effect as if granted in Manitoba. Ancillary grants may issue upon petition, where probate or administration with will annexed has been granted by court of any other country. The foreign grant may be accepted as proof of death, of execution of will and that it is last will of testator.

International Wills.—Will is valid irrespective of place where made, location of assets, and nationality, domicile or residence if in form of international will.

Simultaneous Death.—See topic Death, subhead Order of Death.

Testamentary Trusts.—See topic Trusts.

Living Wills.—Person who has capacity to make health care decision may make health care directive expressing health care decision to be made if maker is incapacitated or unable to communicate. Person may appoint proxy to make health care decisions on maker's behalf. (The Health Care Directives and Consequential Amendments Act S.M. 1992, c. 33).

WITNESSES:

A person is not incompetent to give evidence by reason of interest or crime. Every person charged with an offense and the wife or husband of such person is a competent witness whether such person is charged solely or jointly with any other person. (The Manitoba Evidence Act, C.C.S.M. c. E150).

Persons under 14 years of age or persons whose mental capacity to give evidence is challenged shall be permitted to give evidence if, after inquiry by court, it is shown that person understands nature of oath or solemn affirmation and is able to communicate evidence. Person who does not understand nature of oath or solemn affirmation but who is able to communicate evidence may testify on promising to tell truth. (C.C.S.M. c. E150).

See also topic Depositions.

Privileged Communications. — A client (whether party or stranger) cannot be compelled, and a legal adviser will not be allowed without the express consent of his client, to disclose oral or documentary communications passing between them in professional confidence. This privilege does not extend to communications made to physicians or clergymen.

Husband and Wife.—Neither husband nor wife is compellable to disclose communications between spouses during marriage. (C.C.S.M. c. E150).

Self-incrimination.—No person is excused from answering any question on ground that it may tend to incriminate him or establish his liability in civil proceeding or by reason of its tending to show he has been guilty of adultery, but no evidence so given may thereafter be received against him in any proceeding against him. (C.C.S.M. c. E150).

WORKMEN'S COMPENSATION LAW:

See topic Labour Relations.

SCHEDULE A
Form 8.2

TRANSFER

Manitoba
Justice
Land Titles

IMPORTANT NOTICE: By virtue of section 194 of The Real Property Act, any statement set out in this document and signed by the party making the statement has the same effect and validity as an oath, affidavit, affirmation or satutory declaration given pursuant to The Manitoba Evidence Act.

District of ______________________

☐ Transfer of Land ☐ Transfer of Mortgage ☐ Transfer of Leasehold Title ☐ Transfer of Encumbrance

1. TRANSFEROR(S) (VENDOR) (include address) AND INTEREST/ESTATE TRANSFERRED

* see schedule ☐

2. LAND DESCRIPTION

TITLE NUMBER(S) MORTGAGE NUMBER(S) * see schedule ☐

3. CONSIDERATION

Receipt of $ is acknowledged.

4. LAND TRANSFER TAX—FAIR MARKET VALUE AND, IF APPLICABLE, EXEMPTION EVIDENCE

1. I certify that the fair market value of the land as a whole with respect to which this transfer is tendered for registration within the meaning of Part III of The Revenue Act is $
2.

* see schedule ☐

DATE
Y M D

....
(Name) (Signature)

5. TRANSFEREE(S) (Purchaser) (True and correct name and address including postal code) AND TENANCY/ESTATE/SHARE ACQUIRED

* see schedule ☐

6. ADDRESS OF TRANSFEREE(S) FOR SERVICE (include postal code)

7. EVIDENCE OF TRANSFEROR(S)

* see schedule ☐

1. I am (one of) the within named transferor(s) and I am of the full age of majority.
2. I am (one of) the (person(s) entitled to be) owner of the within described land.
3. I hereby transfer the land/lease/mortgage/encumbrance to the Transferee(s).
4.
5.
6.

DATE
Y M D

....
Witness (Name) (Signature)

....
Witness (Name) (Signature)

....
Witness (Name) (Signature)

* Attach affidavit of subscribing witness if the witness is other than an officer as defined under ss. 72(4) of The Real Property Act.

See note at head of Digest as to 1996 legislation covered.

See Topical Index in front part of this volume.

8. TYPE OF PROPERTY ☐ Residential ☐ Farm ☐ Commercial

9. EVIDENCE—FARM LANDS OWNERSHIP ACT
1. Declaration under The Farm Lands Ownership Act enclosed; or
2. The within land is not farm land within the definition of subsection 1(1) of The Farm Lands Ownership Act; or
3. The within farm land is exempt by Regulation 325/87 R of The Real Property Act, i.e. it is 5 acres or less; or
4. The within farm land is exempt from The Farm Lands Ownership Act by subsection 85(13) of The Real Property Act.
Particulars:

* *strike out inappropriate statement(s) and initial*

DATE
Y M D

(Name) (Signature)

(Name) (Signature)

Transferee, Transferor or Agent

10/11. HOMESTEADS ACT CONSENT TO DISPOSITION AND ACKNOWLEDGMENT
(Transer of Land or Leasehold title only) (Note: For consent by widow(er) see section 22 of The Homesteads Act)

I, the spouse of the Transferor, consent to the disposition of the homestead effected by this instrument and acknowledge that:
1. I am aware that The Homesteads Act gives me a life estate in the homestead and that I have the right to prevent this disposition of the homestead by withholding my consent.
2. I am aware that the effect of this consent is to give up my life estate in the homestead to the extent necesssary to give effect to this disposition.
3. I execute this consent apart from my spouse freely and voluntarily without any compulsion on the part of my spouse.

DATE
Y M D

(Name of Spouse) (Signature of Spouse)

(Name of Witness) (Signature of Witness)

A Notary Public in and for the Province of Manitoba
A Commissioner for Oaths in and for the Province of Manitoba
My commission expires:
Or other person authorized to take affadavits
under The Manitoba Evidence Act
(Specify)

12. ENCUMBRANCES, LIENS, AND INTERESTS—The within document is subject to instrument No.(s)

13. INSTRUMENT PRESENTED FOR REGISTRATION BY, (include address, postal code, contact person and phone no.)

LTO USE ONLY

FEES CHECKED	REFUND AMOUNT

Certificate of Registration

Registered this date ____________________
as No. ____________________
I certify that the within instrument was registered in the
______ Land Titles Office and entered on
Certificate of Title No. ____________________

Deputy or Assistant
District Registrar

New Certificate of Title No. ____________________

Transfer

See note at head of Digest as to 1996 legislation covered.
See Topical Index in front part of this volume.

SCHEDULE B
Form 11.2

Manitoba
Justice
Land Titles

MORTGAGE

District of ______________ ESTATE AFFECTED ☐ Freehold ☐ Leasehold

☐ Mortgage ☐ Mortgage of Mortgage/Encumbrance ☐ Encumbrance

1. MORTGAGOR/GRANTOR OF ENCUMBRANCE (ENCUMBRANCEE) (include address and postal code)

COVENANTOR (if any) (include address and postal code)

* see schedule ☐

2. LAND (description)

TITLE NUMBER(S) MORTGAGE/ENCUMBRANCE NUMBER(S)

* see schedule ☐

3. MORTGAGEE/ENCUMBRANCER (include address and postal code)

* see schedule ☐

4. NAME AND ADDRESS OF MORTGAGEE/ENCUMBRANCER FOR SERVICE (include postal code)
SAME AS ABOVE OR

* see schedule ☐

5. TERMS
The following terms are incorporated herein:
(a) Standard Charge Mortgage Terms filed as number name
(b) The terms attached hereto as schedule(s) ☐ ☐ ☐ ☐

In this instrument unless otherwise specified, "herein" means this instrument, all schedules to this instrument and the terms referred to in Box 5. Where there is insufficient space in this form for all signatures, one or more Mortgagor or Encumbrancee may sign the schedule identified in Box 7 and attached hereto and/or one or more Covenantor may sign the schedule identified in Box 9 and attached hereto, and such signature or signatures shall bind and obligate the person or persons so signing to the terms herein in the same manner as if such person or persons had signed this form.

6. PAYMENT PROVISIONS * see schedule ☐

a) Principal Amount $				b) Interest Rate % per annum	c) Calculation Period			
d) Interest Adjustment Date	Y	M	D	e) Payment Date and Period	f) First Payment Date	Y	M	D
g) Last Payment Date	Y	M	D	h) Amount of Each Payment Dollars $				
i) Balance Due Date	Y	M	D	Guarantee Mortgage ☐				

Additional Provisions

* see schedule ☐

IMPORTANT NOTICE: The Mortgage Act provides that the Mortgagor can obtain free of charge, from the mortgagee a statement of the debts secured by this mortgage once every twelve months, or as needed for pay off or sale.

LTO USE ONLY

FEES CHECKED	REFUND AMOUNT
Certificate of Registration Registered this date ______ as No. ______ I certify that the within instrument was registered in the ______ Land Titles Office and entered on Certificate of Title No. ______ ______ Deputy or Assistant District Registrar	**Mortgage**

See note at head of Digest as to 1996 legislation covered.

See Topical Index in front part of this volume.

7. SIGNATURE OF MORTGAGOR/ENCUMBRANCEE   * see schedule ☐

** strike out inappropriate statement(s) and initial by party(s) signing*

1. I am/entitled to be an/the owner of the Land/Mortgage/Encumbrance of the Land;
2. As security for performance of all my obligations herein, I hereby mortgage/encumber to the Mortgagee/Encumbrancer my interest in the Land/Mortgage/Encumbrance of the Land;
3. I promise to pay the principal amount and interest and all other charges and money hereby secured and to be bound by all the terms herein;
4. I ackowledge receipt of a copy of this instrument and all of the terms herein;
5. I am of the full age of majority;
6. The within Land is not farm land within the definition of subsection 1(1) of The Farm Lands Ownership Act;
7. The within farm land is exempt from The Farm Lands Ownership Act by subsection 85(13) of The Real Property Act Particulars:
8. My co-mortgagor is my spouse;
9. The person who has consented to this instrument is my spouse;
10.
11.

			DATE Y M D
** Witness	(Name)	(Signature)	
Witness	(Name)	(Signature)	
Witness	(Name)	(Signature)	
Witness	(Name)	(Signature)	

** attach affidavit of subscribing witness if the witness is not an officer under subsection 72(4) of The Real Property Act

8. TYPE OF PROPERTY   ☐ Residential   ☐ Farm   ☐ Commercial

9. SIGNATURE OF COVENANTOR   * see schedule ☐

I acknowledge receipt of a copy of this instrument and all of the terms herein and I agree to perform my obligations herein

			DATE Y M D
Witness	(Name)	(Signature)	
Witness	(Name)	(Signature)	

10./11. HOMESTEADS ACT CONSENT TO DISPOSITION AND ACKNOWLEDGMENT

(Note: For consent by widow(er) see section 22 of The Homesteads Act)

I, the spouse of the Mortgagor/Encumbrancee, consent to the disposition of the homestead effected by this instrument and acknowledge that:

1. I am aware that The Homesteads Act gives me a life estate in the homestead and that I have the right to prevent this disposition of the homestead by withholding my consent.
2. I am aware that the effect of this consent is to give up my life estate in the homestead to the extent necessary to give effect to this disposition.
3. I execute this consent apart from my spouse freely and voluntarily without any compulsion on the part of my spouse.

		DATE Y M D
(Name of Spouse)	(Signature of Spouse)	
(Name of Witness)	(Signature of Witness)	

A Notary Public in and for the Province of Manitoba
A Commissioner for Oaths in and for the Province of Manitoba
My Commission expires:
Or other person authorized to take affadavits under The Manitoba Evidence Act
(Specify)

12. INSTRUMENT PREPARED BY (include address and postal code)

13. ENCUMBRANCES, LIENS, AND INTERESTS - The within document is subject to instrument No.(s)

* see schedule ☐

14. INSTRUMENT PRESENTED FOR REGISTRATION BY, (include address, postal code, contact person and phone no.)

NOTE: SINGULAR INCLUDES PLURAL AND VICE VERSA WHERE APPLICABLE. "I" to be read as including all Mortgagor(s) whether individual or corporate.

IMPORTANT NOTICE: By virtue of section 194 of The Real Property Act, any statement set out in this document and signed by the party making the statement has the same effect and validity as an oath, affidavit, affirmation or statutory declaration given pursuant to The Manitoba Evidence Act.

See note at head of Digest as to 1996 legislation covered.

See Topical Index in front part of this volume.

Form 12

Manitoba
Justice
Land Titles

Discharge

District of ____________________

1. APPLICANTS (include address)

* see schedule ☐

2. NATURE OF APPLICATION

(attach evidence as schedule, if required) ☐

☐ Full Discharge of Instrument no. __________ ☐ Mortgage ☐ Caveat ☐ Other (specify) __________

☐ Partial Discharge of Instrument no. __________ ☐ Mortgage ☐ Caveat ☐ Other (specify) __________

3. LAND (description) Complete **only** for a Partial Discharge. DO NOT Complete for a Full Discharge.

TITLE NUMBER(S)

* see schedule ☐

4. SIGNATURES OF APPLICANTS ** strike out inappropriate statement(s) and initial by party(s) signing*

1. Please discharge the above instrument
IN FULL, all money due or to grow due on same has been paid.
OR
IN PART, only as to the land set out in Box 3,
receipt of $ __________ acknowledged.
2. The above instrument has not been assigned except as follows:

Witness	(Name)	(Signature)	DATE Y M D

* *Complete affidavit of subscribing witness (see reverse) if the witness is other than an officer as defined under ss. 72(4) of The Real Property Act.*

5. INSTRUMENT PRESENTED FOR REGISTRATION BY, (include address, postal code, contact person and phone no.)

Form 12

IMPORTANT NOTICE: By virtue of Section 194 of The Real Property Act, any statement set out in this document and signed by the party making the statement has the same effect and validity as an oath, affidavit, affirmation or statutory declaration given pursuant to The Manitoba Evidence Act.

See note at head of Digest as to 1996 legislation covered.

See Topical Index in front part of this volume.

Back of Form 12

AFFIDAVIT OF SUBSCRIBING WITNESS

I,

of the ______________________________ of ______________________________, in

______________________________ make oath and say:

I am a subscribing witness to the attached instrument and I was present and saw it executed

at ______________________________

by ______________________________

I verily believe that each person whose signature I witnessed is of the full age of majority and is the party of the same name referred to in the instrument.

SWORN before me at the

, in

this day of 19 ________

____

____
A Commissioner for Oaths, etc.

LTO USE ONLY

Certificate of Registration	
Registered this date ______________________________ as No. ______________________________ I certify that the within instrument was registered in the ______________ Land Titles Office and entered on Certificate of Title No. ______________________________ ______________________________ ______________________________ ______________________________ ______________________________ Deputy or Assistant District Registrar	

See note at head of Digest as to 1996 legislation covered.

See Topical Index in front part of this volume.

NEW BRUNSWICK LAW DIGEST REVISER

Clark, Drummie, & Company
Post Office Box 6850 - Station A
40 Wellington Row
Saint John, New Brunswick E2L 4S3
Telephone: 506-633-3800
Fax: 506-633-3811

Reviser Profile

History: Clark, Drummie & Company was formed in 1971 from the merger of two prominent Saint John firms, Drummie, Drummie, Clark & Pappas and Ryan, MacGowan, Higgins & Case, which trace their origins to the early 1920's. It is one of the largest firms in the province. Clark, Drummie & Company is also the member firm for the Province of New Brunswick of Lex Mundi, the world's largest association of independent law firms.

Areas of Practice: Clark, Drummie & Company is a full service law firm which covers a wide range of personal, commercial and business transactions. It offers specialized services in such areas as Administrative Law, Admiralty, Banking, Bankruptcy and Insolvency, Environmental Law, Estates & Trusts, Intellectual Property, Labour & Employment, Personal Injury, Public Utilities, Real Estate, Securities, Transportation, including litigation in these and other areas.

The firm represents a broad range of provincial, national and international clients including banks, trust companies, public and private utilities, insurance companies, protection and indemnity associations, transportation companies and manufacturers.

The firm offers its services in French and English (Canada's official languages).

Firm Activities: Partners and associates of Clark, Drummie & Company are members of the International Bar Association, Canadian Bar Association, the Law Society of New Brunswick and the Saint John Law Society. Its members are regular participants in the Continuing Legal Education program and the Bar Admission Courses of the New Brunswick Law Society, as well as various other public and privately held seminars on legal and business issues. Members of the firm have also held part-time university teaching positions at the University of New Brunswick in courses such as Admiralty, Administrative Law, Business Law and The Canadian Constitution. Former partners in the firm have been appointed to the Court of Queen's Bench and the Court of Appeal. Mr. Drummie is a fellow of the American College of Trial Lawyers. Certain of the partners and associates are members of the Canadian Tax Foundation, International Bar Association, Federation of Insurance & Corporate Counsel, Association of Trial Lawyers of America, Canadian Maritime Law Association, Canadian Board of Marine Underwriters, Canadian Transport Lawyers Association, the Saint John Board of Trade, and are active in many community and charitable organizations at national, provincial and local levels.

NEW BRUNSWICK LAW DIGEST

(The following is a list of all Topics, including cross-references, covered in this Digest.)

NEW BRUNSWICK LAW DIGEST

Revised for 1997 edition by

CLARK, DRUMMIE & COMPANY, Barristers and Solicitors, of the Saint John Bar.

(References, unless otherwise indicated, are to Revised Statutes of New Brunswick, 1973. Later statutes are cited by year and chapter number. References to "R." are to Rules of Court.)

Note: This revision includes all proclaimed and effective legislative changes up to and including the first session, fifty-third legislature.

ABSENTEES:

No specific legislation.

Nonresidents are under no disability with regard to their civil rights including holding of real and personal property. (c. P-19, §10[1]). See, however, as to aliens, topic Aliens.

Property of absconding or absent debtors may be attached by civil process. (c. A-2, §2).

See also topic Death.

Care of Property.—No statutory provisions. See applicable municipal laws.

Process Agent.—Nonresident individuals are not required to appoint agents for service of process. Nonresident corporation doing business in Province must appoint attorney for service pursuant to §197 of Business Corporations Act. (1981, c. B-9.1).

Escheat and Bona Vacantia.—See topics Descent and Distribution, subhead Escheat; Wills, subhead Unclaimed Legacies; and Canada Law Digest, topic Banks and Banking, subhead Unclaimed Deposits.

ACCORD AND SATISFACTION:

Common law principles prevail. Neither the acceptance of nor an agreement to accept a smaller sum of money in the same medium at the same time and place as is required by the obligation, satisfies a debt; but a debt may be satisfied by payment of a smaller sum in the same medium at an earlier time or at a different place than that called for.

Compromise.—No statutory provisions.

Pleading.—No statutory provisions.

ACKNOWLEDGMENTS:

Governing statute is c. R-6 and c. L-1.1.

Before registration of any instrument, its execution must be either acknowledged by person executing same or proved by oath of a subscribing witness. (§44[1]). Under Land Titles Act certificate of execution is required from notary public or execution may be proved by affidavit of attesting witness. (§55).

Within Province.—Officers who may take an acknowledgment or proof by oath are a judge of Court of Queen's Bench; member or ex-member of Executive Council; registrar or deputy-registrar of deeds; notary public. Also in case of proof by oath, commissioner of oaths. (§44[1][a], [c]).

Outside Province.—Officers who may take an acknowledgment are a notary public; mayor or chief magistrate of incorporated municipality; judge of Supreme Court of Judicature of Great Britain or Northern Ireland; Canadian Minister, Ambassador, Consul, Vice-Consul or Consular Agent; Canadian Government Trade Commissioner or Assistant, exercising his functions outside of Canada; judge or Lord of Session in Scotland; judge of court of supreme jurisdiction in any British dominion, colony, province or dependency; British Minister, Ambassador, Charge D'affaires, Consul, Vice-Consul, Acting Consul, Pro-Consul, or Consular Agent of Her Majesty, exercising functions in any foreign place; or Governor of any State. (§44[1][b]).

Officers who may take proof by oath are a commissioner of oaths; notary public; mayor or chief magistrate of any incorporated municipality; judge of Supreme Court of Judiciature of Great Britain or Northern Ireland; judge or Lord of Session in Scotland; judge of a court of supreme jurisdiction in any British dominion, colony, province or dependency; or Governor of any State. (§44[1][d]).

Appointment of nonresident commissioner of oaths shall expire after five years from 31st day of Dec. of year in which Order in Council respecting that appointment was made. (c. C-9, §9[2]).

Persons in or with Canadian Armed Forces.—No statutory provisions. See topic Affidavits, same subhead.

General Requirements as to Taking.—Officer must have knowledge or proof of identity of person acknowledging or proving by oath.

No person who is a party to instrument may take an acknowledgment or proof by oath. (c. R-6, §36).

General Requirements of Certificate.—To be under seal of office, if any, of officer taking. (§44[1]).

Married Woman.—No special requirements.

Attorneys in Fact.—Not applicable.

Corporations.—No formal proof of execution required where corporate seal affixed thereto and attested to by proper officers. Unless instrument is to be recorded in which case affidavit of authorized officer must be attached stating that seal is seal of corporation and that signatures are those of authorized officers. (§43[2]).

Foreign Acknowledgments.—See subhead Outside Province, supra.

Effect of Acknowledgment.—Required before instrument can be registered. (§44[1]).

Proof by Subscribing Witness.—As indicated above, it can be a substitute for acknowledgment.

Authentication.—There is no requirement for authentication of certificate of acknowledgment taken within province. Handwriting and certificate of judge taking acknowledgment or proof by oath outside province must be authenticated under seal of notary public. (§44[1][b] & [d]). There are no other provisions requiring authentication of certificate of acknowledgment either within or without province. No fees are established for any authentication required by law of province or any other jurisdiction, such fees being determined in discretion of person authenticating.

Forms.—Acknowledgment for Individuals:

Province of New Brunswick
County of .....

I, ..., a notary public, duly commissioned, appointed and sworn in and for the Province of New Brunswick, residing and practising at the ..... in the said Province, do hereby certify that on this ..... day of ....., A.D. ....., before me at the (..... name place .....) personally came and appeared ....., and ....., his wife, the Grantors named in the foregoing Deed and severally acknowledged that they signed, sealed, executed and delivered the said deed as and for their respective act and deed to and for the uses and purposes therein expressed and contained.

In Testimony Whereof I, the said notary public, have hereunto set my hand and affixed my notarial seal on the day and year in this certificate written, at the said (..... name place .....).

....
Notary Public, New Brunswick

Validating Acts.—Not applicable.

Alternative to Acknowledgment or Proof.—No statutory provision.

ACTIONS:

Governing statute is c. J-2, and Rules of Court of Queen's Bench enacted pursuant thereto and cited as Regulation 82-73.

Equity.—Concurrent administration of law and equity. In cases of conflict, rules of equity prevail. (§§26, 39).

Forms of Action.—There is but one form of civil action. (§1; R. 1.04).

Conditions Precedent.—Consent of Minister of Justice required before application may be made for injunction which would delay or prevent construction or operation of any manufacturing or industrial plant because discharge from such plant is injurious to some other interest. (§33).

In actions against Crown or Crown Corporation two months previous notice in writing is required to be served on Attorney-General or on Crown Corporation stating name and address of plaintiff, cause of action, and court in which it is to be brought. (c. P-18, §15).

Commencement.—See topics Process; Pleading.

Parties.—Necessary and proper parties to action are plaintiff or applicant and defendant or respondent. (R. 5.02). Joinder of other parties is necessary when plaintiff or applicant claims relief to which other person is jointly entitled. Also everyone whose presence is necessary for effective and complete adjudication of matter must be joined unless ordered by court otherwise.

More than one person may be joined as plaintiff or applicant so long as there is only one solicitor; parties claim relief arising out of same transaction or occurrence; there exists common question of law or fact; or their presence in proceeding promotes convenient administration of justice. (R. 5.03[1]).

Persons may be joined as defendants or respondents where: Relief is claimed against them arising out of same transaction or occurrence; there exists common question of law or fact; there is no doubt about parties from whom plaintiff is entitled to relief; loss to plaintiff has been caused by more than one person; their presence is required for convenient administration of justice. (R. 5.03 [2]).

No proceeding is defeated by misjoinder or nonjoinder of persons, and court may grant leave to add, delete or substitute parties. (R. 5.04).

Parties who are minors, or who are declared to be mentally incompetent of managing their affairs must be represented by litigation guardian; persons whose estates are managed by virtue of Mental Health Act, are to be represented by committee; and person declared to be absentee under Presumption of Death Act is represented by committee. (R. 7.01).

Proceeding may be brought by or against executor, administrator or trustee as representing estate or trust of which he is personal representative or trustee and is representing persons beneficially interested without joining such persons as parties. (R. 10.01).

Court may appoint one or more persons to represent any persons, including unborn persons, unascertained persons or members of class of persons who cannot readily be ascertained, found or served, and who have present, future, contingent or unascertained interest in, or may be affected by, proceeding. (R. 11.01).

In proceeding by assignee of debt or other chose in action, assignor shall be joined as party unless assignment is absolute, and notice in writing has been given to person liable in respect of debt or chose in action. (R. 12.01).

Where assignor is necessary party and does not consent to be joined, he shall be made defendant or respondent unless court orders otherwise. (R. 12.02).

Where, at any stage of proceeding, interest or liability of party is transferred to another person, proceeding shall be stayed until clerk, upon application of party having carriage of proceeding, or some other interested party, orders continuation of proceeding. (R. 13.01).

See note at head of Digest as to 1996 legislation covered.

See Topical Index in front part of this volume.

ACTIONS . . . *continued*

Numerous persons having same interest in cause or matter may be represented by one or more of them, and court may authorize one or more of parties to defend on behalf of all persons so interested. (R. 14.01).

Person who is not party may apply to court by notice of motion for leave to intervene as added party, if such person shows that there exists legal interest in proceedings, or question of fact exists between that person and party to proceeding which is in common with question in issue in proceeding. (R. 15.02).

Court may give leave to person to intervene in proceeding as friend of court for purpose of rendering assistance to court by way of argument, and without becoming party to proceeding. (R. 15.03).

Class or Representative Actions.—See subhead Parties, supra.

Intervention.—See subhead Parties, supra.

Interpleader.—Person under liability for any debt, money, goods or chattels, in respect of which adverse claims have been made against him by two or more persons, may apply to court for relief by way of interpleader. (R. 43.01).

Sheriff may apply for relief by way of interpleader where any real or personal property has been taken, or is intended to be taken in execution of any process against another person, and where person who has claim respecting such property gives notice to sheriff of his claim which is disputed by any other execution creditor. (R. 43.02).

Third Party Practice.—Defendant may issue third party claim against person who is not party to action and who may be liable to him for all or part of claim of plaintiff, or for any other relief relating to subject matter of main action, or should be bound by determination of some issue arising between plaintiff and defendant. (R. 30.01).

Joinder of Causes of Action.—Court may order that two or more pending actions be consolidated or be tried at same time, or one immediately after other, or may order any of them to be stayed until after determination of other of them or asserted by way of counterclaim in any other of them or asserted by way of counterclaim in any other of them. (R. 6.01).

Splitting Causes of Action.—Court may order separate trials or hearings, or require one or more claims to be asserted, if at all, in another proceeding, if joined hearing would unduly complicate or delay trial, or prejudice party. (R. 5.05).

Severance of Actions.—Court may, before or after action is set down for trial, order that different issues be tried at different times. (R. 47.03).

Stay of Proceedings.—Court may stay proceedings to enforce judgment upon such terms as may be just if it is satisfied that events occurring after judgment or other special circumstances render it inexpedient to enforce judgment or judgment debtor is for any reason unable to pay money recoverable under judgment or for any other just cause. (R. 61.16).

Where action has been dismissed for want of prosecution, although not bar to subsequent action unless so provided in dismissal order, judge may stay subsequent action if costs of dismissed action have not been paid. (R. 26.04).

Unless otherwise ordered appeal does not operate as stay of execution or of proceedings under decision or order appealed from, nor does it invalidate any intermediate act or proceeding. Motion for stay of execution or stay of proceedings may be made before judge appealed from, Court of Appeal or judge of Court of Appeal. (R. 62.26).

Abatement and Revival.—Does not apply.

Limitation of.—See topic Limitation of Actions.

Small Claims.—See topic Courts.

Termination of Actions.—Plaintiff or defendant may at any time before action is set down for trial, apply to court to determine point of law raised by pleading in action, and which determination may dispose of action; or to apply to strike out pleading which does not disclose reasonable cause of action or defence; or may apply for judgment of admission of fact in pleadings. Defendant may also apply at any time before trial to have action stayed or dismissed on grounds that court does not have jurisdiction; plaintiff does not have legal capacity to commence or continue action; or another action is pending in same or another jurisdiction between same parties and in respect of same claim (R. 23.01); or New Brunswick is not convenient forum for trial or hearing of proceeding.

Prohibited Actions.—Not applicable.

Administration.—See topic Executors and Administrators.

Direct Actions Against Insurer.—See topic Motor Vehicles, subhead Direct Actions.

Quick Ruling.—Parties to dispute may, any time before pleadings have been closed, including any time before commencement of judicial proceedings, apply to other party to dispute, in writing, for consent to have judge determine dispute upon such stated facts and issues to which parties agree.

Judge may refuse to hear dispute, or may hear it in any manner deemed fair. Decision shall be given at hearing or within 30 days thereafter in respect to whole or any part of dispute, and judge may as well assess damages and order costs.

Although party is not compelled to accept quick ruling (notice must be given of nonacceptance) if determination of issue at trial is same as quick ruling, or less advantageous to party refusing to accept quick ruling, then any costs to which that party is entitled shall be reduced by 50% and any costs ordered to be paid by that party shall be increased by 50%.

Decision of judge under this rule cannot be appealed, and judgment entered under this rule may be appealed only on procedural grounds. (R. 77.04, .05, .06, .07). See also topics Appeal and Error; Attachment; Depositions; Executions; Garnishment; Injunctions; Judgments; Pleading; Practice; Process; Venue.

ADMINISTRATION:

See topic Executors and Administrators.

ADOPTION:

Governing Statute is F-2.2.

Any adult, either alone, if unmarried, or jointly with his spouse, may adopt child; and where adopting child of his spouse, may do so without spouse joining in application. (§66).

Any person wishing to adopt child, whether specific child or not, may apply to Minister. (§67[1]).

Any adult may be adopted where person adopting is older by reasonable number of years than person being adopted and reason for adoption is acceptable to court. (§65[2]).

Consent Required.—No adoption order shall be made without written consent of: (a) Person being adopted if having attained age of 12 years, (b) if person being adopted is under age of majority, parent of child or, Minister if guardianship of adopted person has been transferred to Minister. (§76[1]).

Where child to be adopted is ward, in custody or guardianship of representative of another government, state or other agency, consent of representative, person or agency is required and consent of parent is not required if it was not required if child were to be adopted in that Province or State. (§76[2]).

Court may waive consent required of person, except of person to be adopted, if court is satisfied that person whose consent is to be waived: (a) has abandoned or deserted child, (b) cannot be located, (c) has been incapable of caring for child for period of time of sufficient duration to be detrimental to best interests of child, and remains incapable at time consent is waived, (d) while liable to maintain child has persistently neglected or refused to do so, (e) has not had ongoing parental relationship with child and delay in securing home for child would be detrimental to best interest of child or, (f) in best interests of child, consent should be waived. (§78[1]).

Where child is of age of 12 years or over and is unable to understand or give consent, child's consent may be waived by court. (§78[2]).

Conditions Precedent.—Court shall set time and place for hearing which shall be within five days after application was filed with court (§79[1]), except where application is made to waive consent of person required to give consent in which case hearing shall be delayed accordingly (§79[2]).

Where person, other than Minister applies for adoption order, no application shall be heard by court unless applicant has given written notice to Minister at least 30 days before hearing of his intention to apply for adoption order. (§79[3]).

Applicant shall give Minister notice of time and place set for hearing not later than ten days before hearing date. (§79[4]). Notice to Minister not required under §§79(3), 79(4) and 79(5) with respect to adoption of spouse's child. (§79[6]).

Court shall dispose of application within 30 days after it is made unless court is satisfied that exceptional circumstances require disposition of application be delayed. (§81[2]).

Proceedings.—Applicant presents application and supporting documents to judge of Court of Queen's Bench.

Court may make adoption order, if: (a) Where Minister is applicant, 30 days have elapsed since child was placed for adoption, (b) where applicant has applied to adopt child of his spouse, either 30 days have elapsed since application was made, or, child has resided continuously with applicant for previous six months, (c) in any other case, child has resided continuously with applicant for previous six months. (§83[1]).

All documents must be filed with Registrar in Fredericton upon completion of adoption order.

Effect of Adoption.—Legal relationship between child and adopting parent is same as between child and natural parent, including same rights of inheritance.

Releases natural parents, guardian or custodian from any legal rights or obligations to child, including any right of access that is not preserved by court. Child is similarly freed of rights or obligations to natural parent. Unless preserved in accordance with wishes of natural parent, adoption severs child's right to inherit from natural parent or kindred. Adoption does not affect child's cultural heritage, including aboriginal rights. (§85[2]).

Name.—Unless court orders otherwise, adoptee takes surname of adopting parent. Christian names may also be changed if court satisfied change is in best interests of child, and, where child's wishes can be ascertained, that change is being made with child's knowledge and agreement. Consent of child 12 years of age or over is required for changing his Christian name. (§85[3][4][5]).

Adoption granted according to law of any other Province or State that is substantially similar in effect with law of New Brunswick has same force and effect as if granted in New Brunswick. (§88).

Intercountry Adoption.—1996, Bill 49 adopted: Convention on Protection of Children and Co-operation in respect of intercountry adoption.

Recognizing necessity to take measures to ensure that intercountry adoptions are made in best interests of child and with respect for his or her fundamental rights and to prevent abduction, sale of, or traffic in children.

Requirements for Intercountry Adoptions.—See cc. 2, 3 and 4 of Bill 49.

ADVANCEMENTS:

See topic Descent and Distribution.

ADVERSE POSSESSION:

Common law principles prevail.

Character of Possession.—Continuous, open, visible, exclusive and notorious possession not under a grant or lease and without any active adverse claim by true owner.

Duration of Possession.—Period of 20 years creates prescriptive right against any person except Crown which requires a period of 60 years.

Easements.—Governing statute is c. E-1.

Easements by prescription become absolute after 40 years of uninterrupted enjoyment. After first 20 years enjoyment they cannot be defeated merely by showing they were first enjoyed at some time previous to the 20 years. (§2).

See note at head of Digest as to 1996 legislation covered.

See Topical Index in front part of this volume.

ADVERSE POSSESSION . . . *continued*

No easement to light or air can be acquired subsequent to 1875. (§8). No easement in respect of wire attached to or passing over land can be acquired by prescription. (§9).

Disabilities.—Unless claim is declared absolute and indefeasible, time during which a person against whom a prescriptive right is claimed is mentally incompetent, an infant or a tenant for life, or during which any action is pending, cannot be included in computation of periods. (§6).

AFFIDAVITS:

Governing statute is c. C-9.

Within Province.—All lawyers and other persons either appointed as commissioners of oaths or having similar power pursuant to legislation or by virtue of office may administer oaths required in affidavit, declaration, or affirmation; also justice of peace in and for county where oath is administered unless it is to be used in Court of Queen's Bench or in probate court for any purpose other than swearing of appraisers and attesting to inventories or accounts rendered to executors. Particular legislation often designates who may administer oaths in certain matters.

Outside Province.—Commissioner of oaths for New Brunswick, notary public or commissioner of oaths may administer oaths required in an affidavit, declaration or affirmation. (§11). See topic Acknowledgments, subhead Outside Province.

Persons in or with Canadian Armed Forces.—Commissioned officers in active service with rank of Major or higher in military forces may take oaths required in affidavits, declarations or affirmations to be used within province. (§12).

General Requirements as to Administration.—No statutory provisions.

General Requirements of Jurat.—Commissioner appointed pursuant to §2 must write date on which his appointment expires. (§5). Commissioners by virtue of office must write below their signature "Commissioner of Oaths being a (. . . . . nature of office . . . . .)." (§1[2]). Solicitors enrolled in Court of Queen's Bench must write below their signature "Commissioner of Oaths Being a Solicitor." (§1[1]).

Use of Affidavit.—In Court of Queen's Bench or Probate Courts.

Form.—

SWORN TO in the (. . . . . name city . . . . .) in the County of . . . . . in the Province of New Brunswick this . . . . . day of . . . . ., A.D., 19. . . . .
BEFORE ME:
. . . .
COMMISSIONER of Oaths being a solicitor

Alternative to Affidavit.—Solemn declaration pursuant to §16 of Evidence Act c. E-11.

AGENCY: See topic Principal and Agent.

AIRCRAFT:

See Canada Law Digest, topic Aircraft.

ALIENS:

Property.—Aliens can take, hold, and sell real and personal property, with exception of ships, as if they were native-born citizens. When resident within province and served with process there, an alien may be sued in its courts; or if cause of action arises within province, though alien be not resident or served with process there, he may be sued in its courts. (c. P-19, §10[1]).

ALIMONY: See topic Divorce.

ALLOWANCES:

See topic Executors and Administrators.

APPEAL AND ERROR:

Governing statute is c. J-2 and Rules of Court enacted pursuant thereto.

Court of Appeal has both civil and criminal jurisdiction. Either civil or criminal matters from Court of Queen's Bench may be appealed to Court of Appeal, and criminal matters from Provincial Court may also ultimately be appealed to Court of Appeal. (R. 62, 63, 64).

Supreme Court of Canada.—Appeal may be taken from Court of Appeal to Supreme Court of Canada with leave of either Provincial Appeal Court or Supreme Court of Canada.

See Canada Law Digest, topics Courts, subhead Supreme Court of Canada; and Appeal and Error, subhead To Supreme Court of Canada.

Appeal Bond.—Not applicable.

Stay of Proceedings.—See topic Actions, subhead Stay of Proceedings.

Extent of Review.—To both law and fact. (R. 62.21).

Character of Hearing.—Court has inherent jurisdiction to completely review matter before it. (R. 62.21).

Judgment of Order on Appeal.—Court of Appeal may draw inferences of fact, render any decision and make any order which ought to have been made, and may make such further or other order as case may require. (R. 62.21).

ARBITRATION AND AWARD:

Governing statute is c. A-10.

Submission is a written agreement to submit present or future differences to arbitration, whether an arbitrator is named therein or not. Chapter applies also to every arbitration under any act as if arbitration were pursuant to a submission. (§§1, 3).

Number of Arbitrators.—If no other mode of preference is provided, it shall be to a single arbitrator; if reference is to two arbitrators, they may appoint an umpire at any time within period during which they have power to make an award. If reference is to three arbitrators, award of any two shall be final and binding. (§5).

Court Control.—Proceedings and arbitrators are subject to control by Court of Queen's Bench. Court may remit to arbitrators for consideration, and in event of misconduct by arbitrator or of award being improperly obtained, court may set aside award. (§17).

A final award, not remitted or set aside, may be enforced upon an order from court in same manner as a judgment or decree of court. (§18).

Questions of law can be submitted to Court of Appeal in form of stated case. (§25).

As a general rule awards are final and unappealable except upon errors of law or impropriety; they correspond in effect to a verdict by a jury. (§21).

ASSIGNMENTS:

Debts and Choses in Action.—By statute it is provided that any absolute assignment in writing under the hand of the assignor (not purporting to be by way of charge only) of any debt or other legal chose in action, of which express notice in writing shall have been given to the debtor shall be effectual in law (subject to prior equities) to pass and transfer the legal right from the date of such notice. If the debtor has notice that such assignment is disputed by the assignor, he is entitled to interplead the disputants. (c. J-2, §31).

Assignments of Wages.—Any assignment of wages or any portion thereof and used as security of a debt is invalid. (c. G-2, §31).

Book Debts.—*Note:* C. P-7.1, §75 repealed Assignment of Book Debts Act. See topic Personal Property Security.

Instruments Transferring Title.—Assignments of any mortgage or of any chattel real or of any lease required to be in writing must be by deed. No assignment of any trust shall be valid unless it be in writing, signed by the party assigning the same, or by his last will.

Worker's Compensation Act.—Unless with approval of Board, no sum payable as compensation shall be capable of being assigned.

Notice.—Notice of assignment must be given to debtor before assignee may institute action.

ASSIGNMENTS FOR BENEFIT OF CREDITORS:

Governing statute is c. A-16.

Assignments for general benefit of creditors must be made to the sheriff of the county wherein the debtor resides or carries on business, unless a majority of the creditors having claims of $100 or over have consented thereto, when assignment may be made to any other person in the province. Law as to assignments and preferences applies only so far as not inconsistent with Bankruptcy and Insolvency Act, which is utilized in practice.

ASSOCIATIONS:

There are no restrictions upon associations for any purpose not prohibited by law or contrary to good morals or public policy. Most associations intended to be more or less permanent (excepting some of those for social or recreational purposes) are incorporated under the Companies Act or under special acts.

Special provision is made for the incorporation of cooperative associations for various purposes. (c. C-22.1).

Unincorporated associations, the members of which carry on business in common with a view to profit, are partnerships.

Professional Corporations.—No statutory authority.

ATTACHMENT:

Governing statute is c. A-2.

Actions in Which Allowed.—No attachment of property on commencement of any action. In obtaining judgment order for seizure and sale may issue. See topic Executions.

Courts Which May Issue Order.—Court of Queen's Bench. (§1).

In Whose Favor Order May Issue.—Creditor. No restriction on nonresidents or foreign corporations.

Against Whom Order May Issue.—(1) Person indebted in a sum not less than $50 and departs from or conceals himself within Province with intent to defraud creditors; (2) person jointly or severally indebted not within Province during month next preceding application, and at time of contracting debt or at time fixed for payment thereof not resident in Province; (3) person jointly or severally indebted absent from Province for six months next preceding application and at time of contracting debt not resident in Province but became resident after contracting debt. (§4[1], §2).

Claims on Which Order May Issue.—Debt action and potential debt actions of not less than $50. Order may not issue on unmatured or contingent claims.

Grounds.—See subhead Against Whom Order May Issue, supra.

Proceedings to Obtain.—Order issued to sheriff on affidavit of creditor attesting to indebtedness and departure or concealment of debtor. Departure or concealment of debtor must be verified by affidavit of two witnesses. (§2).

Attachment Bond.—Not applicable.

Levy.—Sheriff can attach real and personal property. (§1).

Indemnity.—Sheriff indemnified out of estate of debtor or to pay costs of wrongful siezure. No action against sheriff unless erroneous taking malicious. (§5[2]).

Lien.—Not applicable.

Priorities.—Over all processes not actually executed. (§2).

Release of Property.—Debtor must satisfy creditors within time limits or pay to creditor amount awarded and costs. If debtor claims setoff, application may be made to judge to adjudicate dispute. (§§10, 11).

See note at head of Digest as to 1996 legislation covered.

See Topical Index in front part of this volume.

ATTACHMENT . . . *continued*

Sale.—If claim not satisfied within time limits sheriff may distribute proceeds of sale of property attached.

Third Party Claims.—All creditors entitled within time limits to file claims verified by affidavit with sheriff and to share in proceeds of sale of property of debtor. (§9[3]).

Vacation or Modification.—Not applicable.

ATTORNEYS AND COUNSELORS:

Attorneys at law are styled "solicitors"; and equivalent of "counselor at law" is "barrister." Solicitors and barristers are officers of Court of Appeal appointed by Court on recommendation of Council of Law Society.

Bar Admission.—Governing statute is Law Society Act, 1986, S.N.B. c. 96.

Eligibility.—Applicants must be British subjects or permanent residents who have declared their intention to apply for Canadian citizenship. A barrister or solicitor must become a Canadian citizen within six years of filing declaration.

Registration as Student-at-Law.—At least four weeks prior to any regular meeting of Council petition must be filed with secretary praying for admission as student-at-law. On approval of Council and on payment of proper fees secretary will admit student-at-law. For fuller particulars apply to Secretary, The Law Society of New Brunswick, Suite 305, 1133 Regent Street, Fredericton, N.B., E3B 3Z2.

Admission as a Solicitor and Barrister on Transfer.—Any person who has been duly called to the bar in any part of Her Majesty's Dominions, or any of Provinces of Canada, and who produces sufficient evidence of such call or admission and satisfactory testimonials of good character, may become a barrister and solicitor of Court of Appeal. For fuller particulars apply to Secretary; see subhead, Registration as Student-at-Law, supra.

Admission for Occasional Appearances.—Member of legal profession outside Province may be admitted to practice for occasional appearances for specified proceedings.

Status.—A barrister and solicitor is commissioner of oaths and notary public.

Privileges.—No barrister or solicitor shall have any privilege as such exempting him from jurisdiction of any court.

Disabilities.—There is no disability upon a barrister or solicitor to act as a surety.

Compensation.—A barrister or solicitor may sue for and recover his reasonable and lawful fees, costs, charges and disbursements. Any bill for fees, costs, charges or disbursements may be taxed before Registrar of Court of Queen's Bench. Contingency fees permitted if client otherwise unable to pay or reasonably forseeable as unable to pay. (c. 32, 1978, §72.1). Local minimum tariffs are recognized for most matters.

Lien.—A barrister or solicitor has a possessory lien on all clients' papers for his fees and disbursements.

Disbarment or Suspension.—Council of Law Society may disbar or suspend from practice of law any barrister or solicitor or expel from society any student who has been guilty of professional misconduct. Such order may be appealed to Court of Appeal of New Brunswick.

Unauthorized Practice.—Persons not admitted to practice law and corporations, etc., may not perform work or services in matters pertaining to law, such as preparing instruments relating to property, petitions, contracts, affidavits, documents relating to incorporation or winding up of companies, etc., except that a justice of peace or notary public may prepare any instrument relating to real estate and a notary public may do any work ordinarily pertaining to his office. Persons violating these provisions may be liable on summary conviction to a fine not exceeding $5,000 or imprisonment for a term not exceeding one year.

Professional Associations.—Law Society of New Brunswick; Canadian Bar Association; Saint John Law Society; York-Sunbury Barristers' Society; Moncton Area Lawyers' Association; l'association du Barreau de Madawaska; Restigouche Barristers' Society; Northumberland Barristers Society; Gloucester Barristers' Society.

AUTOMOBILES: See topic Motor Vehicles.

BAIL: See topic Criminal Law.

BANKS AND BANKING:

See Canada Law Digest, topic Banks and Banking.

Taxes.—See topic Taxation.

BILLS AND NOTES: See Canada Law Digest.

BILLS OF LADING:

See topics Carriers; Factors.

BILLS OF SALE:

Interest of buyer under sale of goods without change of possession is "security interest" under c. P-7.1.

Note.—C. P-7.1, §76 repealed Bills of Sale Act. See topic Personal Property Security.

BLUE SKY LAW: See topic Securities.

BONDS:

Common law applies. Bond of public officer taken in name of Queen. (c. I-13, §25).

Approved trust companies acting in fiduciary capacity not required to file special bonds in each matter.

BROKERS:

See topic Securities.

No regulations as to brokers except those dealing in securities (c. S-6) and real estate (c. R-1).

BULK SALES:

Governing statute is c. B-9.

Sale of stock of merchandise in bulk is deemed fradulent and void as against creditors of vendor unless following requirements complied with. Purchaser must, before paying to vendor any part of purchase price or executing any transfer or giving any promissory note in respect thereof, demand and receive from vendor written statement, verified by vendor's affidavit, showing names and addresses of all creditors of vendor and amount due to each, and vendor must furnish such statement. At time of completion of sale: (a) Claims of all creditors shown on such statement must be paid in full; or (b) vendor must deliver to purchaser written waiver of benefit of Act from creditors representing not less than 60% in number and amount of claims exceeding $50 as shown on statement, or written consent of such number of creditors to sale.

Action to attack sale as violative of bulk sale law must be brought within six months after sale. (§11).

CARRIERS:

Governing statute is c. P-27.

Board of Commissioners of Public Utilities has general supervision of public utilities, including any street railway or any plant or equipment for conveyance of telephone messages or for production, transmission, delivery or furnishing of heat, light, water, gas, or power to or for public, even though such utility is owned, operated, managed or controlled by a city or town. Board may investigate in such manner as it may determine any alleged act or omission by any public utility. (§1).

Bills of Lading.—No special regulations.

Motor Vehicle Carriers.—See topic Motor Vehicles.

CERTIORARI:

Governing statute is c. J-2 and Rules of Court pursuant thereto. Rules of Court in force from time to time respecting judicial review not inconsistent with provision of Criminal Code, or any uniform Rules of Court made by Governor-in-Council under §482(5) of Criminal Code apply to proceedings with respect to mandamus, certiorari or prohibition in matters arising under Criminal Code.

Notwithstanding any Act, remedies formerly obtained by way of certiorari, mandamus, prohibition, quo warranto or notice of motion may now be obtained only on application for judicial review which, subject to any Act, must be commenced within three months from date of order, conviction, commitment, warrant, decision, award or refusal to act which is substance of complaint. (R. 69).

Jurisdiction.—Court of Queen's Bench and Court of Appeal, have authority to supervise decision of any tribunal exercising judicial function.

Grounds.—Judicial review of tribunal's decision will issue wherever tribunal has acted without jurisdiction or transgressed limits of jurisdiction. (R. 69.04).

Proceedings.—Proceedings are commenced by notice of application in accordance with Rule 38 of Rules of Court.

CHARITABLE IMMUNITY: See topic Damages.

CHATTEL MORTGAGES:

See topic Personal Property Security.

CLAIMS:

See topics Executors and Administrators; Pleading.

COLLATERAL SECURITY: See topic Pledges.

COLLECTION AGENCIES:

See topic Principal and Agent.

COMMERCIAL CODE:

Not adopted.

See topics Sales; Chattel Mortgages.

COMMISSIONS TO TAKE TESTIMONY:

See topic Depositions.

COMMUNITY PROPERTY:

Not applicable. See topic Husband and Wife.

CONDITIONAL SALES:

Note.—C. P-7.1, §77 repealed Conditional Sales Act. See topic Personal Property Security.

CONSIGNMENTS: See topic Factors.

CONSUMER BUREAU ACT:

See topic Consumer Protection.

CONSUMER PROTECTION:

Consumer Bureau Act.—(c. C-18). Minister of Justice administers Act which has as its objects: (a) Maintain liason with consumer groups; (b) collect and distribute information to educate and advise consumers regarding, inter alia, lending and borrowing practices, retail sales practices and marketing practices; (c) promote and assist counselling service in respect of consumer protection; (d) receive and investigate complaints of conduct in contravention of any Act which provides for protection of consumers; (e)

See note at head of Digest as to 1996 legislation covered.

CONSUMER PROTECTION . . . *continued*
perform any duty imposed by any other Act; and (f) perform such other duties as are prescribed by this Act or Minister.

Cost of Credit Disclosure Act.—(c. C-28). Governing statute is c. C-28. Act governs investigation of complaints regarding granting of credit or persons engaged in business as lenders, registration of lenders, disclosure of cost of credit and creates offences for failure to comply with Act.

Unless otherwise exempted, only registered lenders may carry on business of extending credit or extend credit in connection with their business.

Before extending credit other than variable credit, lender must make full disclosure of cost of credit including amount of cash received by borrower or actual cash value of goods supplied, amounts allowed for down payment or goods traded in where goods supplied and amounts charged for official fees and insurance premiums. Cost of borrowing must be shown as dollar amount and as annual percentage rate on unpaid balance.

Before extending variable credit, lender must furnish borrower with written statement showing cost of borrowing as annual percentage rate or scale of annual percentages that borrower is required to pay monthly, subject to minimum dollars and cents charged if any. Cost of borrowing must also be expressed in dollars in schedule of amounts and corresponding charges. Borrower must also be furnished at least every five weeks, with statement showing outstanding balance, amount of each extension of credit, total amount credited to borrower, and cost of borrowing expressed in dollars.

Regulations govern collection activities of lenders and prohibits certain collection practices.

Direct Sellers Act.—(c. D-10). Minister of Justice administers Act which has as its objects: (a) Licensing of direct sellers; (b) providing right for buyer to rescind contract for purchase of object; (c) requiring that copy of any written contract for purchase of goods be delivered to buyer and requiring that seller deliver to buyer memorandum setting out seller's address for service within Province; (d) defining direct sellers; and (e) defining types of goods to which Act does not apply.

Unconscionable Transactions Relief Act.—(c. U-1). This Act permits court to investigate into all circumstances surrounding loan of money and if it finds that cost of loan is excessive and that transaction is harsh and unconscionable may grant relief to borrower.

Consumer Product Warranty and Liability Act (c. C-18.1).—

Scope of Act.—Act applies to any consumer product supplied by someone who deals in consumer products of that kind, notwithstanding any other Act or agreement to contrary. (§2).

"Consumer product" is any tangible property (new or used) that is commonly used for personal, family or household purposes. (§1[1][b]).

Parties cannot exclude or restrict any warranty provided by Act except as per §§25 and 26. (§24). Generally, §§25 and 26 permit such restriction except as regards description, agreements which would otherwise be unfair or unreasonable and where liability for "consumer loss" is sought to be refuted or limited.

Act applies to consumer products supplied under: Contracts of sale (including conditional sales contracts); leases; contracts for services or for labour and materials (i.e. applies to product but not services or labour) (see §1, subsection 1, paragraph [b]—definition of "contracts for the sale or supply of a consumer product").

Act applies, in addition, to other rights or remedies available in N.B., except to extent that rights or remedies available are expressly or impliedly contradicted by this Act. (§28).

Warranties.—When "seller" (defined in §1, subsection 1, widely enough to include anyone in chain from manufacturer to consumer) breaches warranty as provided by Act, then any person (regardless of privity) who suffers "consumer loss" is entitled to recover damages reasonably foreseeable at time of formation of contract.

Express warranties include: Any oral statements made by seller in relation to product, unless buyer does not rely on such or it would be unreasonable for him to do so; any such written statement, whether or not buyer relies thereon, unless it would be unreasonable for him to do so; any such statement (however made) to public, unless it would be unreasonable for buyer to rely thereon, whether or not he actually does. (§4, subsection 1). (See also §4, subsections 2 and 4; subsection 4 with respect to when statement is deemed to be that of seller.) Parol evidence is admissible to prove existence of express warranty. (§5).

Contracts for sale or supply of consumer product are subject to implied warranties as to title, quality and fitness. (§8).

Seller is not normally responsible for any defects known to consumer before contract is made; any defect that examination ought to reveal if product is used product and consumer has had chance to examine it before entering contract; or any defect that reasonable examination of sample ought to reveal if sale is by sample. (§10, subsection 2).

All of above warranties operate in favour of all buyers although remedies for breaches thereof differ depending on whether buyer is consumer buyer or business buyer. Business buyer is left to remedies available under Sale of Goods Act and common law. Where seller breaches warranty, buyer must give him reasonable opportunity to rectify breach unless breach is major one or such would create significant inconvenience for buyer. (§14, subsection 1). Damages are those reasonably foreseeable as resulting from breach. (§15). If buyer gives seller opportunity to rectify his breach and seller does not do so, buyer may reject product within reasonable time of discovering breach (and discovery of breach must ordinarily be within 60 days of delivery of product). (§16). When buyer rejects product, he is entitled to refund of purchase price, subject to reduction for use if rejection is not made within ten days of delivery to buyer or, at any time, if consumer is responsible for damage to product. (§17).

Product Liability.—Supplier of consumer product that is unreasonably dangerous to person or property because of defect in design, etc., is liable to any person who suffers "consumer loss" (subject to jurisdictional questions considered in §27, subsection 1) and liability does not depend on any contract or negligence. Seller is not liable for defects not present at time he supplies product or for those which he discloses to person whom he supplies (unless defect breaches Federal or Provincial health or safety standard). (§27).

Plain Language Legislation.—None in force.

CONTRACTS:

Common law applies except where modified by statute.

Capacity.—Married women under no incapacity to contract. (c. M-4).

For capacity of infants see topic Infants.

Acceptance.—In sale of goods buyer loses right to reject after acceptance or he has done any act inconsistent with vendor's ownership except right provided by Consumer Product Warranty and Liability Act. See topic Consumer Protection. (c. S-1).

Consideration.—See topic Consumer Protection, subhead Unconscionable Transactions Relief Act.

See also Small Loans Act. (R.S.C. c. 251).

Distributorships, Dealerships and Franchises.—There are no special rules in relation to these types of business arrangements.

Terms and conditions of some contracts governed by statute as in Insurance Act (c. I-12); Cost of Credit Disclosure Act (c. C-28); Direct Sellers Act (c. D-10).

CONVEYANCES: See topic Deeds.

CORPORATIONS:

Governing statutes are Companies Act C-13 and Business Corporations Act, 1981 c. B-9.1. After Jan. 1, 1982 no further applications for incorporation under Companies Act are accepted except under §16 or §18 which sections permit incorporation of company for such purposes as sporting, literary, charitable etc. However supplementary letters patent with respect to any body corporate referred in subsection 2(8) of Business Corporations Act may be issued after Dec. 31, 1983. (§1 Companies Act).

Companies incorporated under Companies Act could have been continued under Business Corporations Act by application at any time until Dec. 31, 1986 after which all such companies were deemed to be automatically continued. (§2 Business Corporations Act).

For matters relating to companies incorporated under Business Corporations Act or continued or deemed to be continued thereunder see subhead Business Corporations Act, infra.

Companies Act, c. C-13.—

Non-Profit.—§§16 and 18 describe type of corporation which may be incorporated under Companies Act. Companies for charitable, philanthropic, temperance, religious, social, political, literary, educational, athletic or other like purposes may still apply to Minister of Justice for Letters Patent. (§16). These are only types of corporations which may be incorporated under Companies Act.

Incorporation Process.—Incorporation under Companies Act is by Letters Patent. Application must be sent to Minister of Justice indicating reasons for which incorporation is sought and requesting any special provisions which should be included in Letters Patent. Application should also state names, addresses and callings of applicants. Application must be signed by each applicant and witnessed.

Fees.—There is $40 fee for name search and $10 fee for publication of Letters Patent in Royal Gazette. Filing fee is based on real and personal property of company: 0-$25,000 is $50; $25,000-$50,000 is $100; $50,000-$75,000 is $150; over $75,000 is $200.

Annual returns must be filed with Corporate and Trust Affairs, Department of Justice, P.O. Box 6000, Fredericton, New Brunswick, E3B 5H1. There is no annual filing fee.

Continuation.—Companies carrying on business may voluntarily continue under Business Corporations Act. Unless voluntarily continued all such companies shall be deemed to have been continued on Jan. 1, 1987. (Business Corporations Act §2[1]).

Business Corporations Act.—B-9.1 (1981).

Definition.—Corporation means body corporate continued under Business Corporations Act or incorporated under Act, or corporation to which Act applies. (§1[1]).

Application.—Act applies to every corporation incorporated or continued under Act; every body corporate with share capital incorporated under Special Act of Legislature; and every other body corporate with share capital incorporated under General or Special Act of Legislature and every extra provincial corporation doing business in province. (§2).

Act excludes, unless otherwise expressly provided, corporations incorporated under Agricultural Associations Act, Co-Operative Associations Act, Credit Unions Act, Credit Union Federations Act, or Regional Savings and Loan Societies Act. (§2[2]). Body corporate required to be licensed under Trust, Building and Loan Companies Licencing Act; or body corporate having capacity to accept deposits within meaning of Canada Deposit Insurance Corporation Act; to execute office of executor, administrator, guardian of minor's estate or committee of mentally incompetent person; to provide services of fiduciary nature commonly provided by trust company. (§2[8]). Act further excludes insurance companies.

Company under Companies Act may apply for continuation under Business Corporations Act except those companies under Companies Act which have been incorporated by virtue of §§16 or 18 of that Act or to which Part II of that Act applies. Body corporate with share capital and incorporated by Special Act of Legislature may also apply for continuation.

General Supervision.—Minister of Justice, and appointed Director of Business Corporations Act. (§184).

Name.—Word "Limited", "Limitee", "Incorporated", "Incorporee", or "Corporation" or abbreviation "Ltd.", "Ltee.", "Inc.", or "Corp." shall be last word of name of every corporation but corporation may use and may be legally designated by either full or abbreviated form. Director may exempt body corporate continued as corporation under this Act from above mentioned provisions. Either French and English, or French or English, may be used in name of corporation and any corporation may be so legally designated by any such form. Corporation may for use outside of Canada set out its name in its articles in any language and it may be used and legally designated by its name in any such language outside of Canada. Corporation shall set out its name in

CORPORATIONS . . . *continued*
legible characters in all contracts, invoices, negotiable instruments and orders for goods or services issued or made by or on behalf of corporation. Corporation may have registered name under Partnerships and Business Names Registration Act, 1980, c. 39, and use that registered name for purposes of carrying on business. Director may reserve name for intended corporation or for corporation about to change its name, for 90 days. Corporation may have designating number as its name. It may not use name which is deceptively similar to name of another corporation, body corporate registered under Part 17 of Act, company under Companies Act or firm or person that has registered under Partnerships and Business Names Registration Act, limited partnership formed or continued under Limited Partnership Act, or extra-provincial partnership that has filed declaration under Limited Partnership Act. Company may use name that is deceptively similar if such corporation, body corporate, partnership, firm or person consents and, in case of corporation, company under Companies Act, partnership, other than extra-provincial partnership, firm or person, undertakes to change its name within six months of giving its consent. Cannot use name prohibited by regulation or deceptively misdescriptive, or that is reserved for another corporation or intended corporation. Director may order that corporation change its name if it contravenes any of regulations under Act concerning corporate name. Director may also revoke name of corporation and assign to it another name. (§§8, 9, 10).

Powers of Corporation.—Corporation has capacity and subject to Act rights, powers and privileges of natural person subject to Act; as well as capacity to carry on its business, conduct its affairs and exercise its powers outside of New Brunswick. No corporation has capacity to accept deposits within meaning of Canada Deposit Insurance Corporation Act; to execute office of executor, administrator, guardian of minor's estate or committee of mentally incompetent person; to provide services of fiduciary nature normally provided by trust company; to carry on business of building society, trust company, loan company or insurance company, to carry on any business or activity if incorporation for purposes thereof is provided for in any other Act; or to practice profession except as expressly permitted by Act governing that profession. Corporation shall not carry on any business which is restricted by its articles from carrying on nor shall it exercise any of its powers contrary to its articles. No act of corporation including any transfer of property to or by corporation is invalid by reason only that transfer is contrary to its articles or Act. There is no deemed corporate notice by virtue of fact that document has been filed by Director or is available for inspection at office of corporation. Corporation or guarantor of obligation of corporation may not assert against person dealing with corporation, or with any person who has acquired rights from corporation, that: (a) Articles, by-laws and any unanimous shareholder agreement have not been complied with, (b) persons named in most recent notice filed by Director are not directors of corporation, (c) place named in most recent notice filed by Director is not registered office of corporation, (d) person held out by corporation as director, officer or agent of corporation has not been duly appointed and has no authority to exercise powers and perform duties that are customary in business of corporation, (e) document issued by any director, officer or agent of corporation with actual or usual authority to issue document is not valid, (f) financial assistance referred to in Act or sale, lease or exchange of property referred to in Act was not authorized, except where person has or by virtue of his position with or relationship to corporation ought to have had knowledge of facts. (§§13-16).

Incorporators.—One or more persons or corporations may incorporate by signing articles of incorporation complying with relevant sections in Act. Individuals who incorporate must have attained age of 19 years, be of sound mind, and not have status of bankrupt. (§3).

Articles of Incorporation.—Articles of Incorporation shall follow prescribed form and set out: Name of corporation, place within province where registered office is to be, classes and maximum number of shares so authorized to be issued, as well as amount paid for each class, and also rights, privileges and restrictions which pertain to each class of shares or to each series of class of shares. Statement must be given as to par value of each class of shares or, statement that shares are without par value. Articles must also set out restrictions if any in transferring shares, number of directors as well as restrictions if any on businesses that corporation may carry on.

Articles may set out any provisions permitted by Act or by law to be set out in by-laws of corporation or unanimous shareholders agreement. Incorporator shall also send Director notice of location of registered office within New Brunswick as specified in its articles as well as notice of directors of corporation, who are to hold office from issue of certificate of incorporation until first meeting of shareholders, or until successors are elected.

Upon receipt of articles of incorporation Director issues certificate of incorporation which incorporation comes into existence on date shown on certificate. All forms are to be filed in duplicate and fees payable to Minister of Finance sent to Director, Corporate and Trust Affairs, Department of Justice, P.O. Box 6000, Fredericton, N.B. E3B 5H1. (§§4-6).

Incorporation Tax or Fee.—$260 plus $40 name search fee.

License to do Business.—Not required except for extra-provincial corporations. See catchline Foreign Corporations, infra.

Organization.—Organizational meeting must be held after issue of certificate of incorporation. At such meeting directors may make by-laws, adopt forms of share certificates, authorize issue of securities, appoint officers, appoint auditors and conduct such other business as may be pertinent to operation of corporation. However, Incorporators need not be first directors or shareholders. Directors shall then submit such by-laws at annual meeting to be called within 18 months after incorporation. (§§62 and 85).

Paid in Capital Requirements.—Business can be commenced immediately on incorporation without subscription to shares or paying in of any part of its capital.

Amendment of Articles of Incorporation.—Corporation may change or remove any provision that is permitted by this Act to be set out in its articles. Such amendment is made by filing prescribed form in duplicate with Director setting out pertinent amendment. Upon filing appropriate form along with $110 fee Director issues certificate of amendment.

Such amendment may be made by special resolution of shareholders; if particular class or series of class of shares is affected in manner different from other shares of same class then that particular class or series shall vote separately on amendment. Corporation shall not reduce its stated capital if unable to pay its liabilities by so doing, or if value of corporation's assets would be less than amount of its liabilities. Creditor of corporation is entitled to apply to court for order compelling shareholder or other recipient to pay to corporation any financial benefit derived from corporation as consequence of reduction of capital contrary to Act.

Amendment becomes effective on date shown in certificate. Director may order corporation to restate its articles as amended, such restated articles supersede original articles of incorporation and all amendments. (§§113, 115, 116, 118, 119).

Increase or Decrease of Authorized Capital Stock.—May be effected by articles of amendment. (§113). Restricted to corporation in position of solvency before, as well as after reduction of its capital.

May be effected by court order requiring shareholder to pay any liability owing by shareholder to corporation, or requiring corporation to pay shareholder any part of moneys paid by him for shares.

Corporation may also buy back shares issued by it with certain restrictions. (§§31, 32). Corporation may be ordered to buy back shares issued by it. (§166[3][g]).

Shares may be issued with or without par value. If only one class of shares is issued then those shares are equal in all respects. Preferred shares must have preference in some respect over some other class of shares. Shares shall not be issued until fully paid in money or in property or past services. Corporation must maintain separate stated capital account for each class and series of shares it issues, and add to appropriate stated capital account full amount and any consideration received for issue of shares. (§§22, 23, 25).

Share Warrants.—Corporation may if authorized by its articles issue share warrants. Nature of warrant is entitlement to shares therein specified. Warrant entitles bearer to have shares specified. Warrant entitles bearer to have shares specified therein transferred to him by delivery of warrant. (§51).

Share Certificates.—Shareholder is entitled to manually signed share certificate evidencing shares held by him. Such certificate must be signed by proper director or officer, and fee of not more than $3 may be charged by corporation. Certificate shall state on face thereof name of corporation, words "Incorporated under the laws of New Brunswick," name of person to whom it was issued, and number and class of shares, and designation of any series that certificate represents and whether shares are with or without par value, and par value thereof if applicable.

Any restriction, lien, agreement or endorsement which pertains to shares evidenced by certificate is ineffective against transferee thereof unless clearly noted on share certificate, or unless there is actual knowledge of restriction. (§47).

Issuance of Shares.—Allotment and issue of shares is at discretion, and regulated by directors. If, however, corporation does not have its shares listed on prescribed stock exchange, directors are subject to regulations concerning equity shares (§27), articles or by-laws of corporation, or unanimous shareholder agreement. Shares shall be fully paid when issued. (§23).

Transfer of Shares.—Subject to any restrictions placed on transfer of shares by corporation, shareholder may transfer his shares by proper endorsement and delivery of share certificate. Corporation is not required to inquire into existence or observance or performance of any duty owed to third person by registered holder of any of its shares. Provisions are also made for executor, administrator or representative of estate to transfer shares of decreased, upon production of his representative capacity, to corporation, and subject to any applicable law relating to collection of taxes.

Corporation subject to special notice provisions, may treat registered holder of share as person exclusively entitled to vote, to receive notices, to receive any dividend or other payments, and to generally exercise all rights and powers of owner of share. (§§47-49).

Stock Transfer Tax.—None.

Shareholders may vote for directors of corporation, may remove any of such directors when seen fit, have authority to ratify by-laws and amendments to articles, as well as make proposals to make, amend or repeal by-law. (§§61, 64, 67). Proposal may also include nominations for election of directors if such proposal is signed by one or more holders of shares representing at least 10% of shares or 10% of class of shares of corporations entitled to vote at meeting to which proposal is to be presented. Shareholder may apply to court for determination of any dispute concerning proposal made by shareholder. (§89).

Shareholders may also inspect records and register of corporation which include names of shareholders, articles and amended articles of corporation as well as by-laws and minutes of meetings. This is to be available at usual business hours of corporation and without charge. (§§19, 90).

Holders of not less than 10% of issued voting shares of corporation may requisition directors to call meeting of shareholders for purpose stated in requisition. (§96).

Shareholder can also apply to have court determine manner in which requisitioned meeting should take place. (§97). Upon application of shareholder, director or corporation, court may also determine any controversy with respect to election or appointment of director to auditor of corporation. (§98). Shareholders of certain class or series of shares may vote as separate class upon proposed sale, lease or exchange of all or substantially all property of corporation other than in ordinary course of business if sale, lease, or exchange would affect that class or series differently than another class of series. (§130).

Holder of shares of any class of corporation may dissent from proposal of corporation to amend its articles or to amalgamate with another corporation or to divest itself of its property, or to continue under laws of another jurisdiction. Such shareholder has right to be paid by corporation fair value of shares held by him in respect of which he dissents. (§131).

Shareholder may apply to court for leave to bring action in name and on behalf of corporation or any of its subsidiaries for purpose of prosecuting, defending or discontinuing action on behalf of body corporate. (§164). Shareholder, or other complainant by virtue of §163 of Act, may apply to court for determination that shareholder, or other such complainant, has been unfairly treated by corporation, or that acts of corporation or any of its affiliates have been prejudicial to interests of shareholder. Shareholder may

See note at head of Digest as to 1996 legislation covered.

See Topical Index in front part of this volume.

CORPORATIONS . . . *continued*
also request that court make order for dissolution of corporation in such circumstances by virtue of §144 of Act. (§166).

Holders of not less than 10% of issued shares of any class of corporation may apply to court for investigation of corporation or any of its affiliates. Court may order such investigation and make such order as it deems fit. (§§155, 156).

Shareholder's Liability.—Shareholders of corporation are not liable for any liability, act or default of corporation. (§44). Shareholders who are party to unanimous shareholder agreement have all rights, powers and duties of director, can incur all liabilities of director of corporation to which agreement applies, to extent that agreement restricts powers of directors to manage corporation. (§99). Close corporation by-law pursuant to Companies Act shall be deemed unanimous shareholder agreement. (§99). Shareholder may also be liable to creditor of corporation for any liability of shareholder to corporation, that was extinguished or reduced contrary to Act; or shareholder may be forced to deliver or pay to corporation any money or property that was paid or distributed to shareholder as consequence of reduction of capital made contrary to Act. (§35). Such creditor has period of two years within which to commence action.

Corporation may provide through its articles, or its by-laws, that corporation has lien on registered shares in name of shareholder, for debt of that shareholder to corporation. (§44[2]).

Shareholders' Meetings.—Annual meetings must be held within 18 months after incorporation and subsequently not more than 15 months after previous annual meetings. Directors may at any time call special meeting of shareholders. Court may extend time in which first or subsequent meeting may be held. Shareholders may also participate in meetings by way of telephone or other communication facilities, if by-law of corporation so provides or, subject to consent of all shareholders entitled to vote. (§85).

Directors may fix record date for purpose of determining shareholders entitled to receive notice of meeting of shareholders. Record date shall not precede by more than 50 days or by less than 21 days date on which meeting is to be held. If no record date is fixed record date for determination of shareholders entitled to receive notice shall be at close of business on day immediately preceding day on which notice is given or, if no notice is given on day on which meeting is held. (§86). Notice of annual meeting shall be sent not less than 21 days nor more than 50 days before meeting to each shareholder entitled to vote, to each director and to auditor if any. (§87). Failure to receive notice does not deprive shareholder of his right to vote.

Resolution in writing dealing with all matters required by Act to be dealt with at meeting of shareholders, and signed by all shareholders entitled to vote at meeting, satisfies requirements of Act relating to such meetings. (§95). Holders of not less than 10% of issued shares of corporation that carry right to vote at meeting sought to be held may requisition directors to call meeting of shareholders for purposes stated in requisition. (§96).

Subject to articles, each share of corporation entitles holder to one vote, subject to articles of incorporation. (§93). Voting may be done by way of proxy. Body corporate holding shares in corporation holding shareholders meeting, may be represented by any individual authorized by resolution of directors of body corporate. (§93). Voting shall be done by show of hands unless by-laws otherwise provide. (§94).

Voting Trust.—Shareholders may agree in writing to exercise their voting rights as provided by such agreement. (§99[1]).

Directors.—Subject to articles, by-laws and unanimous shareholder agreement, business of corporation shall be managed by one or more directors, other than corporation which has its shares listed on prescribed stock exchange, in which case there must be not less than three directors. Director of corporation is not required to hold shares issued by corporation. (§63). Following are restricted from being directors of corporation: Anyone under age of 19, anyone certified to be of unsound mind, another corporation or person not being individual, bankrupt or someone convicted of offence in connection with promotion, formation or management of corporation, or involving fraud. Each director ceases to hold office at close of first annual meeting of shareholders following his election. (§65). Shareholders entitled to vote for directors may do so by casting all their votes or such that they may have, for one director; or alternatively shareholders may distribute their votes among candidates in any manner. Each shareholder so entitled to vote at election of directors has right to cast number of votes equal to number of votes attached to shares held by him multiplied by number of directors to be elected. (§65).

Director of corporation ceases to hold office when he dies or resigns, or when he is removed from office by shareholders, or if he becomes disqualifed by virtue of §63 of Act. Shareholders may by ordinary resolution remove directors from office, except that where holders of any class or series of shares which have exclusive right attached to them to elect one or more directors, director so elected may only be removed by ordinary resolution at meeting of shareholders of that class. Vacancy created by removal of director may be filled at meeting of shareholders at which director is removed, or alternatively, vacancy may be filled by quorum of directors. (§§66, 67, 69).

Directors meetings shall be held at registered office within Province unless otherwise provided by by-laws and, unless otherwise provided in by-laws, notice of time and place of meeting of directors shall not be less than seven days before meeting. As with shareholders, directors may also participate in meeting of directors or of committee of directors by means of telephone or other communication facility permitting all persons participating to hear, if so provided by by-laws of corporation or, subject to by-laws, all directors of corporation consent. (§72).

Subject to articles or by-laws majority of number of directors required by articles constitute quorum of directors and may exercise all powers of directors. (§72). Resolution signed by all directors is as valid as if passed at meeting of directors. (§75).

Powers and Duties of Directors.—Directors are to manage affairs of corporation subject to articles, by-laws and unanimous shareholder agreements, if any. (§60). Directors may by resolution make, amend or repeal any by-laws that regulate business or affairs of corporation. However, directors must submit by-law or amendment or repeal of by-law to next shareholders meeting for ratification by ordinary resolution. Until such time by-law so made, amended or repealed is effective from date of resolution of directors until it is confirmed or rejected by shareholders. Directors may borrow money upon credit of corporation, issue, re-issue, sell or pledge debt obligations of corporation, give guarantee on behalf of corporation, mortgage, hypothecate, pledge or otherwise create security interest in all or any property as corporation. Directors may also by resolution delegate any or all of their powers listed in previous sentence to director, committee of directors or officer. (§61). Directors may appoint managing director or committee to which they may delegate all powers except those mentioned in §73(2). Directors are also responsible for determining place and time of meetings of directors and shareholders, determining record dates for purpose of shareholder meetings, and administering proposals submitted by shareholders.

Liabilities of Directors.—Acts of directors are valid notwithstanding any irregularity or defect in appointment. (§74). Directors are liable for issuing shares for consideration less than value of shares, and each director is so liable unless that director protests issuance of such shares. Directors are jointly and severally liable for actions contrary to Act and may be forced to contribute their share of judgment satisfied by another director. Directors are also jointly and severally liable, together with corporation, where corporation is taxpayer who fails to pay amount of any tax due and payable or where corporation is collector who fails to remit amount of any tax collected or received. (§23.1[1] Revenue Administration Act). Actions against directors must be brought within two years from date of resolution authorizing action complained of. (§76). Directors are also liable for profits made by virtue of contract in which director was interested, but did not disclose such interest. Court may on application, set aside such contract on such terms as it thinks fit. (§77).

Every director must fulfill his duties in good faith, and no director is relieved of liability for any act unless there is unanimous shareholder agreement. (§§79, 99). Unless there is registered dissent from actions of directors of corporation, all directors present at making of resolution are deemed to consent to such resolution. No director is liable if it is shown that he relied in good faith on financial statements of corporation represented to him by officer of corporation or in written report of auditor; or any report from lawyer, accountant, engineer, appraiser or other person whose profession lends credibility to statement made by him. (§80).

Fact that managing director has been appointed by directors does not relieve directors from liability. (§73).

Officers.—Election of officers of corporation is prerogative of directors. Actions of officer of corporation are valid despite irregularity in his appointment. (§74). Directors may delegate full powers of management to officers of corporation. (§78).

Liability of Officers.—Officers must comply with Act and its regulations in good faith. (§79). Officers must also disclose any material interest which they might have in contract entered into by corporation, and are liable to account for profits made by virtue of such undisclosed interest. (§77). No provision in contract, articles, or by-laws or resolution of corporation relieves officer from any duty to act in accordance with Act, except by virtue of unanimous shareholder agreement.

Indemnification.—Corporation may indemnify directors and officers, as well as all persons who acted at request of corporation as director or officer of body corporate in which corporation held shares, against all costs, charges and expenses reasonably incurred by him in respect of any civil, criminal or administrative action or proceeding to which he is made party by reason of his position with corporation. Corporation may purchase indemnity insurance for benefit of directors and officers of corporation. (§81).

Principal Office.—See catchline Articles of Incorporation, supra. (§17).

Resident Agent.—See catchline Appointment of Attorney, infra. (§197).

General Powers of Corporations.—See catchline Powers of Corporation, supra. (§§13-16).

Dividends.—Corporation may pay dividend in money or property or by issuing fully paid shares of corporation. (§42). Corporation may declare or pay dividend unless there are reasonable grounds for believing that corporation is or would after payment be unable to pay its liabilities as they fall due, or realizable value of corporation's assets would be less than aggregate of its liabilities and stated capital of all classes. (§41).

Sale or Transfer of Corporate Assets.—Sale, lease or exchange of all or substantially all of property of corporation other than in ordinary course of business requires approval of shareholders in accordance with subsections 130(3) and (7). (§130[1]). Approval of shareholders of corporation of sale, lease or exchange, is not effective until holders of shares of each class or series of shares of corporation entitled to vote separately on sale, lease or exchange, have in each case by special resolution approved sale, lease or exchange. (§130[6]).

Books and Records.—Corporation shall prepare and maintain at its registered office or at any other place designated by directors, within Province of New Brunswick, following records: Copies of articles, by-laws and all amendments thereto, as well as copy of any unanimous shareholder agreement; minutes of all meetings and resolutions of shareholders; copies of all notices required to be sent to Director concerning directors of corporation by virtue of §64; share register; and names and addresses of all persons who are or have been directors of corporation with pertinent dates.

Corporation shall prepare and maintain adequate accounting records, and records containing minutes of meetings and resolutions of directors and any committees thereof. Such records shall be kept at registered office of corporation, and shall at reasonable times be open to inspection to directors, shareholders, their agents and legal representatives, as well as Director. (§18).

Reports.—Directors of corporation shall report to shareholders at every annual meeting concerning financial statements relating separately to period not greater than six months before annual meeting of shareholders, and period which began immediately after end of last completed financial year. Also, immediately preceding financial year, as well as report of auditor if any has been appointed and any further information respecting financial position of corporation and results of its operations required by articles, by-laws or any unanimous shareholder agreement. (§100). Directors of corporation shall approve financial statements of corporation. (§102).

Corporation shall also file with Director notices of change in directors, as well as notice concerning change of registered office. (§§71, 17[4]). Corporation shall send to Director without notice annual return in prescribed form on or before last day of month following anniversary month of corporation, and Director shall file it. (§187[1]).

Annual filing fee: $50 regardless of stated capital of corporation.

Corporate Bonds or Mortgages.—Unless articles, by-laws or unanimous shareholder agreement otherwise provide articles of corporation shall be deemed to state that

CORPORATIONS . . . *continued*
directors of corporation may, without authorization of shareholders, borrow money upon credit of corporation, issue, reissue, sell or pledge debt obligations of corporation, give guarantee on behalf of corporation to secure performance of obligation of any person, and mortgage, hypothecate, pledge or otherwise create security interest in all or any property of corporation owned or subsequently acquired, to secure any obligation of corporation. (§61).

Merger and Consolidation.—Two or more corporations including holding or subsidiary corporations, may amalgamate and continue as one corporation. (§120). Each such corporation shall enter into agreement setting out terms and means of effecting amalgamation and, in particular, setting out provisions that are required to be included in articles of incorporation under §4, basis upon which and manner in which holders of issued shares of each amalgamating corporation are to receive securities, money, and securities of any body corporate other than amalgamated corporation, in amalgamation. Agreement shall also state manner of payment of money instead of issue of fractional shares of amalgamated corporation, and whether by-laws of amalgamated corporation are to be those of one of amalgamating corporations, and if not, copy of proposed by-laws, as well as such other details as may be necessary to perfect amalgamation and to provide for subsequent management and operation of corporation. (§121). Directors of each amalgamating corporation shall submit such abovementioned agreement to shareholders of their respective corporations, and to holders of each class or series of such shares. (§122).

After approval of amalgamation by each respective amalgamating corporation, articles of amalgamation in prescribed form shall be sent to Director together with documents required by §§17 and 64 pertaining to registered office in Province as well as names of directors of corporation. (§124). Articles of amalgamation shall have attached thereto statutory declaration of director or officer of each amalgamating corporation that establishes to satisfaction of Director that: There are reasonable grounds for believing that, each amalgamating corporation is and amalgamated corporation will be able to pay its liabilities as they become due and, realizable value of amalgamated corporation's assets will not be less than aggregate of its liabilities and stated capital of all classes and, there are reasonable grounds for believing that no creditor will be prejudiced, and adequate notice has been given to all known creditors of amalgamating corporations and that there are no objections. (§124).

Articles of amalgamation sent to Director shall be in duplicate. (§186).

Continuations.—Body corporate incorporated either in New Brunswick or in jurisdiction other than New Brunswick may, if authorized by laws of jurisdiction in which it is incorporated, apply to Director for certificate of continuance. Duplicate articles of continuation in prescribed form shall be sent to Director together with documents prescribed by §§17 and 64, pertaining to registered or head office of corporation within Province and names of directors of corporation.

Dissolution.—Corporation that has not issued any shares may be dissolved at any time by resolution of all directors. Corporaton that has no property and no liabilities may be dissolved by special resolution of shareholders, or by special resolution of holders of each class of shares whether or not they are entitled to otherwise vote. Corporation that has property or liabilities or both, may be dissolved by special resolution of shareholders or by special resolution of holders of each class of shares whether or not they are otherwise entitled to vote, if by special resolution shareholders authorize directors to cause corporation to distribute any property and discharge any liabilities, and corporation has distributed any property and discharged liabilities before it sends articles of dissolution to Director. (§137).

Articles of dissolution shall be sent to Director in duplicate upon receipt of which Director shall issue certificate of dissolution. Corporation ceases to exist on date in certificate of dissolution. (§137).

Corporation may also be liquidated or dissolved by special resolution of shareholders ratifying proposal by directors. Such statement shall be sent to Director, upon which receipt Director shall issue certificate of intent to dissolve. Where issuance of certificate of intent to dissolve has been sent by Director to corporation, corporation shall cease to carry on business except to extent necessary for liquidation, but its corporate existence continues until Director issues certificate of dissolution.

After issue of certificate of intent, corporation shall cause notice to be sent or delivered to each known creditor of corporation, and forthwith publish notice thereof once a week for four consecutive weeks in newspaper in place where corporation has its registered office and take reasonable steps to give notice in each Province in Canada where corporation was carrying on business, proceed to collect its property or dispose of property not to be distributed to shareholders and to generally do all things required to liquidate its business, and after giving notices required and adequately providing for payment or discharge of all its obligations distribute its remaining property either in money or in kind among its shareholders according to their respective rights. (§138).

Director or any interested person may apply to court for order dissolving corporation if corporation has failed for two or more consecutive years to comply with requirements of Act with respect to holding annual meetings of shareholders, or contravened subsection 14(2) or §§19, 101, or 103; or procured any certificate under Act by misrepresentation. (§140).

Above-mentioned sections deal specifically with corporations carrying on business within their specific powers as allowed by articles of incorporation, allowing directors, shareholders and creditors to examine records and books of company, supplying shareholders at annual meeting with financial statement of company, and abiding by Act and its regulations for any fundamental change to articles of corporation.

Insolvency and Receivers.—Law on insolvency is uniform throughout Canada and is governed by Bankruptcy and Insolvency Act. (R.S.C., c. B-3). See Canada Law Digest (topic: Bankruptcy).

Receiver appointed under instrument shall act in accordance with that instrument and any direction of court. Receiver may pay liabilities connected with property of corporation and realize on security interest of those on behalf of whom he is appointed. Receiver may also, if appointed receiver-manager of corporation, carry on any business of corporation to protect security interest of those on behalf of whom he is appointed. (§§52-57).

Receiver or receiver-manager shall immediately notify Director of his appointment or discharge, and forthwith file with Director notice designating office in New Brunswick where accounts of his administration shall be maintained; as well as take into custody and control property of corporation in accordance with court order or instrument under which he is appointed, open and maintain bank account in his name as receiver or receiver-manager of corporation, keep detailed accounts of all transactions carried on by him as receiver or receiver-manager, keep accounts of his administration that shall be available at office designated, prepare at least once in every six month period after date of his appointment, financial account of his administration, and file copy with Director within 60 days thereafter. Upon completion of his duties receiver shall also render final account of his administration, send copy of such report to Director, and send copy of final report to each director of corporation. (§59).

Close Corporations.—Right to transfer shares may be restricted if in application for incorporation or in articles of amendment.

Appraisal.—Dissenting shareholder who objects to fundamental change in corporation by virtue of §128(4)(d), that affects holder of shares; or if corporation resolves to amend its articles under §113 to alter restrictions on transfer of shares, or to amend its articles to add, change or remove any restrictions upon businesses carried on by corporation, or amend its articles under §113 to provide that meetings of shareholders may be held outside of New Brunswick, or amalgamate with another corporation or be continued under laws of another jurisdiction, or sell, lease or exchange all or substantially all of its property, has right to be paid by corporation fair value of shares held by him in respect of which he dissents, determined as of close of business on day before resolution is adopted or order is made. (§131).

Foreign Corporations.—Extra-provincial corporation shall apply to be registered under Act not later than 30 days after it commences to carry on business in New Brunswick. (§196). Director may exempt extra-provincial corporation from operation of Act with exception of requirements for attorney for service, and filing of annual returns if he is satisfied that it does not carry on business for purpose of gain. (§194). Act does not apply to extra-provincial corporations required to be licensed as insurer under Insurance Act or to extra-provincial corporation to which Foreign Resident Corporations Act applies. (§195).

Extra-provincial corporation shall apply for registration by sending to Director statement in duplicate in prescribed form, accompanied by appointment of individual who is resident in New Brunswick as its attorney for service, prescribed fee which is $210 plus $30 for name search and such other material or information as Director may require. (§197).

Same rules apply to extra-provincial corporation as apply to provincially incorporated company concerning name of corporation. Extra-provincial corporation which is prohibited from carrying on business under its name within province, must register business name in accordance with Partnerships and Business Names Registration Act, c. P-13. (§199).

Director may cancel registration of extra-provincial corporation if: Corporation is in default for one year in sending to Director any fee, notice or document required, in opinion of Director, extra-provincial corporation ceases to carry on business in New Brunswick, extra-provincial corporation has sent notice to Director that it has ceased to carry on business within province, or that it wishes to cancel its registration, extra-provincial corporation has dissolved, extra-provincial corporation does not comply with directive of Director under §199(2) or if extra-provincial corporation has otherwise contravened Part 17 of Act. (§201).

Extra-provincial corporation shall set out its name or name under which it carries on business in province, in legible characters in all contracts, invoices, negotiable instruments and orders for goods or services issued or made by or on behalf of corporation. Whenever extra-provincial corporation which is required to register business name under Partnerships and Business Names Registration Act, sets out its corporate name in contracts, invoices, negotiable instruments or orders for goods or services, extra-provincial corporation shall set out as well in legible characters that business name. (§202).

If attorney of extra-provincial corporation dies or resigns or his appointment is revoked extra-provincial corporation shall forthwith send to Director appointment in prescribed form for individual as its attorney for service and Director shall file appointment. (§203). Service of any process, notice or document in any civil, criminal or administrative action or proceeding shall be deemed to have been sufficiently made upon extra-provincial corporation if made upon attorney as shown in most recent notice on records of Director. (§204).

Registered extra-provincial corporation shall send to Director: Notice of any change in name of extra-provincial corporation resulting from amendment of its charter, notice of any change in address of its principal office in New Brunswick and its head office outside of New Brunswick, membership of its board of directors, board of management or other governing body, within one month after effective date of such. (§206). Registered extra-provincial corporation shall send to Director: Copy of any instrument effecting amalgamation of extra-provincial corporation with one or more other extra-provincial corporations, copy of amalgamation agreement, statement in prescribed form relating to amalgamated extra-provincial corporation and documents referred to in §197 pertaining to appointment of individual who is resident, acting as attorney for service for corporation, prescribed fee, and such other material or information as Director may require. (§207).

If liquidation proceedings are commenced in respect of registered extra-provincial corporation extra-provincial corporation or, if liquidator is appointed, liquidator shall send to Director forthwith after commencement of those proceedings notice showing that proceedings have commenced and address of liquidator, if one is appointed, and shall send to Director forthwith after completion of those proceedings return relating to liquidation. (§208).

Registered extra-provincial corporation shall, in each year on or before last day of month following anniversary month, send to Director annual return in prescribed form or if corporation is incorporated under laws of Canada or province or territory of Canada, annual return required by laws of jurisdiction in which it was incorporated along with filing fee of $200, after which Director shall file return. Where extra-provincial corporation is continued under laws of any jurisdiction other than New Brunswick, Director shall be sent notice. (§209).

CORPORATIONS . . . *continued*

No act of extra-provincial corporation, including any transfer of property to or by extra-provincial corporation, is invalid by reason only that act or transfer is contrary to or not authorized by its charter or internal regulations or any law of jurisdiction in which it is incorporated, or by reason that extra-provincial corporation was not then registered. (§211). No person is affected by or shall be deemed to have notice or knowledge of contents of document concerning extra-provincial corporation by reason only that document has been filed with Director. (§212). Extra-provincial corporation while unregistered, is not capable of commencing or maintaining action or other proceeding in any court in New Brunswick in respect of any contract made in course of carrying on business in New Brunswick while it was unregistered or otherwise in violation of Part 17 of Act. However if corporation registers, after commencement of its action, then proceeding or action may be maintained as if corporation was registered before commencement of action or proceeding. This does not apply to extra-provincial corporation incorporated under laws of Canada. (§213).

Whether or not extra-provincial corporation has been prosecuted or convicted, any director or officer of extra-provincial corporation who knowingly authorizes, permits or acquiesces in failure of corporation to comply with Act commits offence and is liable on summary conviction to fine not exceeding $5,000 or to imprisonment for term not exceeding six months or to both, and in default of payment of fine is liable to imprisonment in accordance with Summary Convictions Act. Extra-provincial corporation which fails to comply with Part 17 of Act is also liable to summary conviction proceedings and to fine of not more than $5,000, and in default of such payment is liable to levy by distress and sale in accordance with §35 of Summary Convictions Act. (§214).

Appointment of Attorney.—When extra-provincial corporation applies for registration within province, statement must be accompanied by appointment of individual who is resident of New Brunswick or corporation incorporated or continued under Business Corporations Act, as its attorney for service, in prescribed form. (§197[2]).

Foreign Resident Corporations.—In time of war or other emergency, foreign corporation may apply to transfer its head office to New Brunswick and become resident there by filing with the Minister of Finance documents including copies of its charter, articles of incorporation or other similar documents, law or decree issued under law which defines terms of creation and legal existence of foreign corporation and copy of law or decree allowing it to its registered office, list of its officers and directors who are to act within New Brunswick, together with their authority and manner of appointment of their successors, address of its proposed registered office in New Brunswick and certificate authenticating same from Ambassador to Canada of country which created it. (Foreign Resident Corporations Act, c. F-19.1).

Corporation Tax.—Tax imposed by Province but collected by Government of Canada. (New Brunswick Income Tax Act c. I-2). See Canada Law Digest. (§§3-5).

Professional Corporations.—See topic Associations, subhead Professional Corporations.

Unclaimed Dividends.—No provincial legislation.

Expropriation.—See topic Real Property, subhead Expropriation.

Claims Against Crown Corporations.—Two months written notice is required to be served on crown corporation stating name and address of plaintiff, cause of action and court in which action to be brought prior to commencement of action. (c. P-18, §15).

COST OF CREDIT DISCLOSURE ACT:

See topic Consumer Protection, subhead Cost of Credit Disclosure Act.

COSTS:

Security for costs.—Plaintiff may be ordered to furnish security for costs if plaintiff is resident out of New Brunswick, costs to be paid by plaintiff in another action remain unpaid, plaintiff is nominal plaintiff, or association or corporation, and it appears that there may not be sufficient assets belonging to plaintiff in New Brunswick to pay costs if so ordered, or if defendant is entitled by statute to security for costs. (R. 58.01).

COURTS:

Court of Appeal.—Governing statute is c. J-2. Court has appellant jurisdiction in both criminal and civil cases. (R. 62, 63 and 64).

Court of Queen's Bench.—This Court consists of two divisions: Trial Division, and Family Division. All causes and matters are proceeded with in Trial Division. Family Division has jurisdiction vested in Trial Division. (§§9, 10, 11).

Small Claims.—Action may be brought in Court of Queen's Bench when debt or damages claimed do not exceed $3,000, or that part of claim exceeding $3,000 is abandoned, and if applicable plaintiff shall so state that fact in claim. Judge conducting hearing is not bound by rules of evidence and may call witnesses and ask questions as deemed fit. Procedure is designed to allow acceptable limit of informality in order to reduce costs and time. (R. 75.12).

Probate Court has power to take probate of wills and grant administration of estates and deal with all related matters. See topic Executors and Administrators.

Provincial Court has all powers, authority, criminal, and quasi-criminal jurisdiction vested in police magistrate or in two or more justices of peace sitting and acting together, under any law or statute of Province.

Judge shall have same protection and privileges as are conferred upon judges of The Court of Queen's Bench of New Brunswick, for any act done or omitted in execution of his or her duty. (c. P-21, §3.1).

Juvenile Courts.—See Young Offenders Act, Statutes Canada, 1980-81-82, c. 110, administered by Provincial Court (see c. J-4), powers to deal with crimes of young offenders, age 12 and over and under age 18. Children under age 12 immune from prosecution.

Ombudsman.—(c. O-5). Ombudsman may investigate administration by a department or agency or officer thereof of any law of New Brunswick, whereby any person is aggrieved or in opinion of Ombudsman may be aggrieved and may request department or agency to notify him within a specified time of steps it proposes to take to give effect to his recommendations and if any department or agency does not act upon recommendation of Ombudsman, refuses to act thereon, or acts in a manner unsatisfactory to Ombudsman, Ombudsman may send a copy of his report and recommendations to Lieutenant-Governor in Council and may thereafter make a report to Legislative Assembly.

CREDITORS' SUITS:

Common law practice prevails.

CRIMINAL LAW:

Governed by Canadian Criminal Code and c. P-22.1.

Bail is contolled by Canadian Criminal Code.

Compensation for Victims of Crime Act (c. C-14) repealed Mar. 31, 1996.

Custody and Detention of Young Persons Act, c. C-40. Young persons have rights and freedoms in their own right, including those stated in Canadian Charter of Rights and Freedoms, and in particular right to be heard in course of, and to participate in, processes that lead to decisions that affect them, and young persons should have special guarantees of their rights and freedoms. (§2).

Lieutenant-Governor in Council may designate places or facilities of classes of places as places of secure custody, open custody or temporary detention. "Youth custodial facility" includes place of open custody, secure custody or temporary detention. (§1). Every young person who is detained in custody in youth custodial facility (a) is subject to rules of conduct and discipline as set out in regulations, and (b) shall participate in programs provided under this Act and regulations. (§10).

CURTESY:

Abolished for property acquired by woman after Apr. 29, 1916. (c. M-4).

DAMAGES:

Contributory Negligence Act (c. C-19), provides that where damage or loss has been caused by fault of two or more persons, court shall determine degree in which each person was in fault. For particular circumstances see Act.

Person who has claim against Crown may enforce it as of right by proceedings against crown in accordance with Proceedings Against the Crown Act, c. P-18 in all cases in which: (a) Land, goods or money of person are in possession of Crown, (b) claim arises out of contract entered into by or on behalf of Crown, or (c) claim is based upon liability of Crown in tort to which it is subject by governing statute. (§3).

No action shall be brought against Crown unless two months previous notice in writing thereof has been served on Attorney-General, or on corporation in case of action to be brought against crown corporation, in which notice, name and residence of proposed plaintiff, cause of action, and court in which it is to be brought shall be explicity stated. (§15).

Service.—Document to be served on Crown shall be served by delivering copy to Attorney-General or Deputy Attorney-General or any barrister or solicitor employed in office of Attorney-General, or to solicitor designated for purpose by Attorney-General; and document to be served on crown corporation shall be served in same manner as upon ordinary corporation. (§12).

Costs are available as against Crown. (§14[1]).

Sovereign Immunity.—See Limitation of Actions Act, c. L-8. No special immunity for Crown; see Proceedings Against the Crown Act. (c. P-18).

Charitable immunity doctrine not recognized.

See topic Death, subhead Action for Death.

DEATH:

Governing statute is c. P-15.1, Presumption of Death Act.

Court of Queen's Bench may order person absent and unheard of to be presumed dead for all purposes or for such purposes as are specified in order. (§2[1]). Where claim is made under insurance policy based on presumption of death of insured, insurer may apply to Court of Queen's Bench or judge thereof for declaration as to presumption of death.

Order made under this Act is not proof of death of person whose life is insured under policy of life insurance for purpose of claiming under that policy. (§5[2]).

Survivorship.—Governing statute is c. S-20. Where two or more persons die under circumstances rendering order of their deaths uncertain, it is presumed, for all purposes affecting title to property, that property is to be distributed on basis that its owner had survived co-decedent. If such persons are insured and beneficiary under life insurance policy and there is no substitute beneficiary, proceeds are paid to personal representative of insured.

Action for death caused by wrongful act, neglect or default may be brought by executor or administrator of decedent for benefit of decedent's wife, husband, parent, child, brother and sister or any of them. Expenses incurred or pecuniary loss sustained by decedent prior to death may also be recovered in such action. Court may apportion amount awarded among beneficiaries of action. Action must be commenced within two years after death. Governing statute is c. F-7.

DECEDENTS' ESTATES:

See topics Descent and Distribution; Executors and Administrators; Wills.

DECLARATORY JUDGMENTS:

See topic Judgments.

DEEDS:

Deeds must be in writing, signed, sealed, acknowledged or proved, and registered.

See note at head of Digest as to 1996 legislation covered.

See Topical Index in front part of this volume.

DEEDS . . . *continued*

Deeds by corporations must be under the corporate seal attested by the proper officer and the seal, signature, and authority to execute verified by affidavit.

Deeds are recorded in extenso in books required kept by registrars of deeds in the various counties. Recording fees are, $30 for all instruments. Deeds must have $1^1/_2$ inch margin on top and left side and if both sides of paper are used, similar margin is required on right side of reverse side. Paper must be white measuring $8^1/_2$ by 14 inches.

See topic Real Property.

Form of Deed.—Mandatory as prescribed by Standard Forms of Conveyance Act. (c. S-12.2). Words and directions which are underscored are not part of form and are inserted for guidance. Parts of form which are enclosed in brackets are optional. Directions printed in square brackets are not part of form.

Form of Deed
Form A13

DEED

Standard Forms of Conveyances Act, S.N.B. 1980. c. S-12.2, s.2
The parties to this deed are:

[ADD ADDITIONAL PARTIES AS REQUIRED]

grantor, of address, occupation or other identification, the "grantor"
and
grantee, of address, occupation or other identification, the "grantee"
(The recitals, affidavits, statutory declarations or other documents attached hereto as Schedule "D" form part of this Deed.)
The grantor conveys (in fee simple, or as the case may be) to the grantee (as joint tenants, or as the case may be) the parcel described in Schedule "A" attached hereto (together with a right-of-way, or as the case may be, as described in Schedule "A") (and) (reserving unto the grantor a right-of-way, or as the case may be, as described in Schedule "A").
(The grantor guarantees title.)
(Covenants and conditions to which this conveyance is subject are attached hereto as Schedule "C").
(The spouse of the grantor joins in this instrument and consents to this disposition for the purpose of complying with Section 19 of the Marital Property Act.)
Dated on month, day, 19__.)
SIGNED, SEALED AND
DELIVERED)
in the presence of:) _____Grantor_____ LS
____

Form of Quit Claim Deed
Form A13.1

QUIT CLAIM DEED

Standard Forms of Conveyances Act, S.N.B. 1980, c. S-12.2, s.2
The parties to this quit claim deed are:

[ADD ADDITIONAL PARTIES AS REQUIRED]

grantor, of address, occupation or other identification, the "grantor"
and
grantee, of address, occupation or other identification, the "grantee"
(The recitals, affidavits, statutory declarations or other documents attached hereto as Schedule "D" form part of this Quit Claim Deed.)
The grantor quits claim to the grantee (as joint tenants, or as the case may be) the parcel described in Schedule "A" attached hereto (together with a right-of-way, or as the case may be, as described in Schedule "A") (and) (reserving unto the grantor a right-of-way, or as the case may be, as described in Schedule "A").
(Covenants and conditions to which this conveyance is subject are attached hereto as Schedule "C".)
(The spouse of the grantor joins in this instrument and consents to this disposition for the purpose of complying with Section 19 of the Marital Property Act.)
Dated on month, day, 19__.)
SIGNED, SEALED AND
DELIVERED)
in the presence of:) _____Grantor_____ LS
____

(Acknowledgment. See topic Acknowledgments.)

Execution.—Deed of land comprising marital home must also be executed by spouse. See topic Husband and Wife.

Taxes.—See topic Taxation, subhead Land Transfer Tax.

DEEDS OF TRUST:

See topic Mortgages of Real Property.

DEPOSITIONS:

By order of court or consent of parties, person may be examined on oath before trial for purposes of having his evidence available to tender at trial, and such witness may be examined, cross-examined and re-examined. Such examination shall be conducted according to R. 33.

Where order is made for examination of witness out of New Brunswick, order shall provide for issuance of commission authorizing taking of such evidence before commissioner, and if necessary issuance of letter of request to appropriate authority in jurisdiction where witness is to be found, requesting issuance of such process as may be necessary to compel witness to attend and submit to examination. (R. 53.01; .02; .03).

DESCENT AND DISTRIBUTION:

Governing statute is c. D-9, Devolution of Estates Act.

Real and personal estate of decedent dying intestate, descends and is distributed as follows (c. D-9):

Entire estate, if there is no spouse, goes to following, each class of which there is a member living taking to exclusion of subsequent classes: (1) Issue, per stirpes; (2) father and mother equally or all to survivor; (3) brothers and sisters equally, issue of deceased brother or sister taking share to which parent would have been entitled if alive; (4) nephews and nieces equally, but no representation allowed among collaterals after children of brothers and sisters; (5) equally among next of kin of equal degree of consanguinity; in no case shall representation be made. (§§23, 25-28).

Degrees of kindred are computed by counting upward from the intestate to the nearest common ancestors and then downward to the relative. (§29).

Kindred of half blood inherit equally with those of whole blood in same degree.

Surviving Spouse.—Subject to rights under Marital Property Act, share of surviving spouse is as follows: If decedent left no issue, whole estate to surviving spouse; if decedent left one child or issue of one child, personal chattels and one-half; if decedent left more than one child, surviving issue of deceased child counting as child, personal chattels and one-third; if decedent left no issue, whole estate.

Husband or wife who has left his or her spouse and is living in adultery at the time of the death of the latter takes no share of the estate. (§37).

Afterborn Children and Relatives.—Descendants and other relatives of the decedent, begotten before his death but born thereafter, take as though born in his lifetime.

Illegitimates.—Illegitimate children inherit from and through the mother as though legitimate. If an illegitimate child dies intestate leaving no spouse or issue surviving, his estate goes to mother if living, otherwise to other children of same mother in equal shares, issue of deceased children taking share to which their parents, if living, would be entitled.

Adopted Children.—See topic Adoption, subhead Effect of Adoption.

Advancements are reckoned as part of the estate, and if an advancement to a child is equal to or greater than his share under the intestate law, he takes no part of the estate. If the advancement is less than such share, the child takes so much of the estate as will, with the advancement, equal the share of each other child.

Election.—None.

Escheat.—If a person dies intestate and leaves no heirs or persons entitled to his real or personal property, it escheats to the Crown.

DESERTION:

See topics Divorce; Husband and Wife.

DIRECT SELLERS ACT:

See topic Consumer Protection.

DIVORCE:

Governing statute is Divorce Act 1985, c. D-3.4, Statutes of Canada and R. 72 governs court procedure and forms.

Grounds for Absolute Divorce.—See Canada Law Digest, topic Divorce.

Grounds for Legal Separation.—Court of Queen's Bench has no jurisdiction to grant decree of judicial separation. Separation agreements in writing entered into by parties are enforceable and may provide for such matters as property division, custody and access to children, support obligations.

Citizenship Requirements.—None.

Residence Requirements.—See Canada Law Digest, topic Divorce.

Jurisdiction.—Court of Queen's Bench, Family Division.

Venue.—Unless ordered otherwise, trial shall take place in judicial district in which one of parties has been ordinarily resident for at least one year immediately preceding commencement of proceeding.

Process.—Petition to be sealed by Registrar of Court of Queen's Bench and to be served within six months of date on which it is filed. Judge may make order for substituted service. Service may be made outside of New Brunswick without leave of Court.

Pleading.—Answer to petition or counter-petition to be served and filed: (a) Within 20 days if petition served in New Brunswick; or (b) within 40 days if petition served elsewhere within Canada or U.S.A.; or (c) within 60 days in all other cases. (R. 20.01).

Judgment or Decree.—If no appeal has been instituted, divorce takes effect on 31st day after judgment granting divorce is given. (§12).

Temporary Alimony.—See Canada Law Digest, topic Divorce.

Allowance for Prosecution of Suit.—Application by way of Notice of Motion to be made to judge by either wife petitioner after service of petition or by wife respondent.

Permanent Alimony.—See Canada Law Digest, topic Divorce.

Division of Property of Spouses.—Divided pursuant to Marital Property Act. (1981, c. M-1.1). See topic Husband and Wife.

Support.—See Canada Law Digest, topic Divorce, subhead Corollary Relief.

Custody of Children.—See Canada Law Digest, topic Divorce.

Remarriage.—No restriction after divorce.

Foreign Divorces.—Decrees granted by a court having jurisdiction in place of domicile of parties, or in place with which parties had real and substantial connection, for example place where marriage was performed, or by court having grounds substantially same as in Divorce Act will be recognized in New Brunswick.

Separation agreements will be recognized and enforced in civil courts to same extent as any private contract. See also topic Husband and Wife.

Annulment of Marriage.—See topic Marriage.

DOWER:

Dower Act, D-13 repealed except where right to dower has vested in possession before Jan. 1, 1981.

EMPLOYER AND EMPLOYEE:

See topic Labour Relations.

ENVIRONMENT:

Generally.—

Provisions.—Governed by Clean Environment Act (c. C-6). Lieutenant-Governor in Council has power to make regulations which prescribe what shall be contaminant or waste under Act. Lieutenant-Governor in Council may establish Regional Solid Waste Commission for region of province (§15.3[1]) for control, reduction, elimination or prevention of contamination or for management of solid waste and operation of solid waste collection and disposal facilities (§15.1[1][a]). Minister of the Environment may issue Ministerial Order to control or stop contamination of environment. (§5). Minister may designate inspectors for purposes of Act. (§23).

Prohibited Acts of Pollution.—No person shall release any contaminant or waste into environment if such act could (a) affect quality or construction of environment, (b) endanger health, safety or comfort of person or animal life, (c) cause damage to property or plant life, (d) interfere with conduct of business or normal enjoyment of life or property. (§5.3).

Enforcement.—On reasonable and probable grounds that contaminant directly or indirectly affects environment, Minister or person designated by him may enter premises, and take all necessary action to control, reduce or eliminate pollution. (§5.01). Minister is liable for unnecessary damages caused by his actions.

Penalties.—Violation of Act or regulation, or noncompliance with Order issued under Act is offence punishable by summary conviction, (a) individual, by fine of $500 to $50,000 and imprisonment on default of payment, (b) person other than individual, fine of $1,000 to $1,000,000. Fine is imposed for each day of violation. (§33).

Water Quality.—

Provisions.—Governed by Clean Water Act, S.N.B. 1989, c. C-6.1. Minister of Environment has authority to supervise discharging, emitting, leaving, depositing, or throwing any contaminant or waste into water. Control of all water in Province is vested, and is deemed to have been vested at all times, in Crown in right of New Brunswick. Lieutenant-Governor in Council may make regulations prescribing what shall be contaminant or waste under Act. (§9).

Advisory Committee.—Land and Water Advisory Committee is responsible for making recommendations to Minister of Environment concerning land and water use policies, and is also charged with reviewing content and operations of Act and its regulations. (§31).

Permits.—Persons planning project that diverts all or part of watercourse shall, before proceeding with project, obtain permit from Minister of Environment. Act requires well-drillers to file report with Minister. Well owners who have had their wells bored, drilled, dug or redrilled are required to have water sample tested for inorganic substances and microorganisms, and to give notice of test results to consumers of water. Every owner of public water system shall have water in public water supply system tested.

Enforcement.—Minister may issue Ministerial Order to control or reduce rate of discharge of contaminants or waste into water, or to stop such discharge either temporarily or permanently. Act confers upon Minister and his designates powers of search and seizure similar to those granted by Clean Environment Act. (§4).

Penalties.—Persons contravening Act may be found guilty on summary conviction. Maximum penalty for individual is fine of $500 to $50,000, or in default of payment, six months in jail. Maximum for corporate offender is $1,000 to $1,000,000 fine. For offences continuing for more than one day, fine payable shall be product of fine imposed under §25(1) and number of days on which violation continues. Notwithstanding maximum fines set out above, where offence was committed for financial advantage or to avoid financial burden of compliance, judge may impose any fine which is appropriate in circumstances.

Prohibited Acts of Pollution.—To be prescribed by regulation. Lt.-Gov. in Council may exempt any person from provisions of Act prohibiting discharge, emission, leaving, depositing or throwing contaminants or waste into air, into or upon soil or water where person authorized by any other Act or agreement prior to coming in force of this Act.

Enforcement.—Minister and other necessary persons may enter upon any land or premises using such force as Minister considers necessary to effect compliance with Ministerial order. Minister may designate any person as inspector for purposes of Act. Inspector may, at any reasonable time upon production of means of identification, for purposes of enforcing Act, enter any area, place or premises, except private dwelling where he reasonably believes any contaminant or waste is being released, and search. May inspect any installation, plant or machinery and test any process of production or manufacture he believes is producing or releasing contaminant or waste and take samples of such. May enter any area, place or premises other than private dwelling, inspect any installation, etc. to determine whether water has been, is being or will be, used or diverted contrary to Act. Minister may designate any person as analyst for purposes of Act. Certificate of analyst of his examination of sample submitted to him by inspector, stating result of examination is admissible in evidence in any prosecution and in absence of evidence to contrary is proof of statements contained without proof of signature or official character of person appearing to have signed.

Injunction.—Without leave of Attorney-General no injunction can be applied for which, if granted, would delay or prevent construction or operation of any manufacturing or industrial plant on ground that discharge from such plant injures some other interest. (Judicature Act, c. J-2, §33).

Endangered Species.—Endangered Species Act (c. E-9.1). "Endangered Species" means any species or subspecies of fauna or flora threatened with extinction by reason of (a) destruction of its habitat or drastic modification or sever curtailment thereof, (b) disease, (c) over-exploitation, (d) predation, (e) use of chemicals, or (f) any combination of foregoing factors, and declared by regulation to be endangered. Lieutenant-Governor in Council may make regulations declaring any species or subspecies of fauna or flora to be endangered.

No person shall kill, injure, harass or interfere with or attempt to kill, injure, harass or interfere with any member of endangered species of fauna. (§4[1]).

No person shall destroy or interfere with or attempt to destroy or interfere with any member of endangered species of flora or habitat of endangered species of flora. (§5).

Person who violates or fails to comply with either of these sections commits offence punishable under Provincial Offences Procedure Act.

Fisheries.—Fish and Wildlife Act (c. F-14.1) applies to all fishing and rights of fishing, and all matters relating thereto, in respect of which legislature has authority to legislate for purposes of this Act, but shall not authorize, lease, license or permit any interference with navigation of navigable waters (c. F-14.1).

Provisions.—Regulates artificial propagation of fish, fishing leases of crown waters, establishment of close seasons, and licensing. Salmon fishing prohibited except by means of fly fishing.

Licenses.—Available from provincial fishery or game warden offices or from most sporting goods stores. No nonresident shall fish for, take or kill any fish with rod and line in any Provincial waters without holding license to do so. Such nonresidents must be accompanied by guide licensed under Fish and Wildlife Act (c. F-14.1), unless authorized by Minister to angle without guide.

Penalties.—Fine depends upon offence and minimum and maximum amounts are set out in Schedule "A" to Act. Imprisonment for term of seven days to two months is mandatory for certain offences. (§104[2]). Illegally used fishing gear is subject to confiscation.

Pesticides.—Governed by Pesticides Control Act. (c. P-8). Regulates sale and application of pesticides within Province. Administered by eight to ten member Pesticides Advisory Board. Vendor's license for one year costs $10; pesticide operator's license valid for one year and costs $10. If Board refuses to issue license, appeal this to Minister of Environment. Permit required to apply pesticide to any body of water.

Penalties.—Breach of any provision is offence punishable on summary conviction to fine not exceeding $50,000 or to imprisonment of not more than one year.

EQUITY: See topic Actions.

ESCHEAT:

See topic Descent and Distribution; also topic Wills, subhead Unclaimed Legacies.

ESTATES: See topic Real Property.

EVIDENCE: See topics Depositions; Witnesses.

EXECUTIONS:

Governing statute is Memorials and Executions Act. (c. M-9 and R. 61).

Superior Courts.—Order of execution includes orders for seizure and sale, orders for possession of land and orders for delivery of personal property. Judgment for money may be enforced by order for seizure and sale. Judgment for payment of money into court may be enforced by order of seizure and sale. Judgment for recovery or delivery of possession of land may be enforced by issue of order for possession of land. Judgment for delivery of personal property, other than land or money, may be enforced by issue of order for delivery of personal property. Judgment requiring any person to do any act other than payment of money, or to abstain from doing anything may be enforced by contempt order.

Exemptions: Furniture, household furnishings and appliances reasonably necessary for debtor and his family; necessary and ordinary wearing apparel of debtor and his family; all necessary food and fuel for debtor and his family for three months; two horses and sets of harness, two cows, ten sheep, two hogs and 20 fowl, and food therefor for six months; any tools, implements and necessities used by debtor in practice of his trade, profession or occupation having cumulative market value of not more than $6,500, and one motor vehicle having market value of not more than $3,000 if required by debtor in course of or to retain employment or in course of and necessary to his trade, profession or occupation, but exemptions provided above do not apply to corporate debtor; seed grain and potatoes required for seedings and planting purposes to following quantities: 40 bushels of oats, ten bushels of barley, ten bushels of buckwheat, ten bushels of wheat and 35 barrels of potatoes; dogs, cats, and other domestic animals belonging to debtor; medical or health aids reasonably necessary to enable debtor or any member of his family to work or to sustain health. (§33).

Interest of annuitant under Government (Canada) Annuity Act is also exempt. (c. M-9, §33[2]).

Expiration.—If order is unexecuted it remains in force for two years, but may, before expiration, be renewed for two years, and so on from time to time.

Issuance.—It may issue at any time within six years from judgment, otherwise, application must be made to the court for leave.

Lien.—Order of seizure and sale, delivered to sheriff to be executed, binds personal property from time of actual levy. Real property is bound by memorial of judgment and is recorded in Registry Office for county in which such real property is situated.

Personal Property.—Includes goods and chattels, the equity of redemption in same (including leasehold interests in any lands), shares and dividends of a stockholder, mortgages, money, bank notes, checks, bills of exchange, promissory notes, etc.

Priority.—Creditors' Relief Act (c. C-33) provides that there shall be no priority among creditors by execution from Court of Queen's Bench. Where sheriff levies money on execution against property of debtor out of Court of Queen's Bench he must enter notice in his books stating that levy has been made, and amount thereof, and money must be distributed ratably among all execution creditors and other creditors whose writs, or certificates, proved under oath, were in sheriff's hands at time of levy, or who shall deliver their writs or certificates to sheriff within one month from entry of

EXECUTIONS . . . *continued*
notice; subject, however, to provisions as to retention of dividends in case of contested claims, and to payment of costs of creditors under whose writ amount was made. This does not apply to money received by sheriff from sale of property by him under interpleader order.

Stay of Execution.—Execution may be stayed by order of court or judge until such time as it or he thinks fit.

Supplementary Proceedings.—A judgment debtor may be examined as to his property and debts owing by and to him.

EXECUTORS AND ADMINISTRATORS:

Governing statute is Probate Court Act. (c. P-17.1).

Jurisdiction and Venue.—Application for probate of estate of deceased person resident in Province at time of his death or for nonresident leaving property in Province may be presented in judicial district in which deceased was resident at time of his death or in which property of deceased is situated. Court has jurisdiction throughout Province. Grant is governed by principles of common law unless restricted by statute or rules. Court has same powers as Court of Queen's Bench of enforcing judgments etc. Practice and procedures of Queen's Bench apply except in contentious matters.

Preferences in Right to Administration.—Upon intestacy, or where executor named in will refuses to prove will, administration may be committed to spouse, to next-of-kin or to spouse of next-of-kin, of deceased as court considers proper. If more than one of next-of-kin who are in equal degrees of kindred to deceased claim administration, it may be committed to such one or more of them as court considers proper.

Eligibility and Competency.—Any resident or nonresident person having reached age of 19 years or any trust company authorized to do business in Province may be appointed as executor or administrator.

Qualification.—No oath required for executor or administrator. Security bond equal to stated value of estate is required before appointment of any resident or nonresident administrator and from any nonresident executor. Spouse of deceased is not required to file administration bond if estate is less than $50,000 and affidavit of debts is filed. Court may under special circumstances reduce amount of, revise conditions of, or dispense with, bond.

Issuance of Letters.—Letters probate of will and letters of administration have effect in all parts of Province and remain in force until revoked. Where minor is named as sole executor under will, administration with will annexed may be granted to guardian of minor or to such other person as court thinks fit until minor has attained age of majority at which time letters probate may be granted to minor. Person entitled to grant of letters of administration may, at discretion of court, take out limited letters. Notarial wills made in Quebec may be admitted to probate in Province.

Public Administrator.—Appointed by Lt.-Gov. in Council. May be contacted c/o Department of Justice, P.O. Box 6000, Fredericton, N. B., E3B 5H1. He may apply for administration of estate of deceased person who dies testate or intestate within Province leaving assets within Province and having no executor, spouse or next-of-kin within Province ready and competent to take out letters of administration. Public Administrator has power to administer estates of less than $3,000 without appointment by court. Public Administrator has authority to administer estate where only pension not exceeding $3,000 is payable. (§20).

Inventory and Appraisal.—Person applying for grant of letters probate of will or letters of administration shall before they are granted deliver to clerk statement verified by oath setting out total value of all property of deceased at time of his death. No statutory provision for appraisal. (§56).

General Powers and Duties.—Common law principles apply as enlarged upon by Executors and Trustees Act (c. E-13) and Trustees Act (c. T-15).

Notice of Appointment.—No statutory requirement.

Notice to Creditors.—No statutory requirement and not usual practice to advertise for creditors.

Presentation of Claims.—No debt to be paid until proven by affidavit presented to personal representative. No statutory form of proof of claim. Usual form of proof of claim is as follows:

Form

IN THE PROBATE COURT
OF NEW BRUNSWICK
JUDICIAL DISTRICT OF ....
IN THE ESTATE OF ...

I, , of in the County of , Province of , (state occupation), make oath and say:

1. That , late of (state occupation of deceased), was during his lifetime and his estate is now indebted to me, this deponent, in the sum of (state general nature of claim, whether for professional services or goods sold and delivered, etc.), performed or delivered, etc., by me to or for the said during his lifetime and at his request according to the statement of particulars of the said account hereunto annexed and marked "A".

2. That I hold no security in respect of the said indebtedness.

SWORN TO AT ...
in the County of ...
and Province of ...
this day of
A.D. 19
A COMMISSIONER OF OATHS
BEING A SOLICITOR
or My Commission Expires ....,
or being a (insert description of office held.)

Approval or Rejection of Claims.—Personal representative if he wishes to contest claim, serves notice thereof on claimant who may then within 30 days apply to court for order allowing his claim and determining amount of it. Court shall hear parties and witnesses and make such order as it considers just. If claimant does not make such application his claim is barred.

Priorities.—In event of deficiency of assets to pay all estate debts and bequests, assets shall be applied in priority as follows: (a) Funeral expenses; (b) probate fees; (c) solicitor's costs; (d) wages given priority by Wage-Earners Protection Act (c. W-1); (e) liabilities incurred by personal representative in respect to administration of estate; and (f) commission allowed to personal representative. If there is still deficiency of assets, all creditors rank equally, but neither rights of Crown or any lien, mortgage nor other security existing during lifetime of deceased on any of his real or personal estate are prejudiced. (§64).

Sales.—All real and personal property devolves upon personal representative and, subject to Devolution of Estates Act (c. D-9), may be sold by personal representative pursuant to terms of will and Executors and Trustees Act (c. E-13). No statutory requirement regarding notice, time or place. Purchaser is not required to see to application of funds.

Actions by Representative.—Causes of action (except for adultery or seduction) vested in deceased survive for benefit of his estate. (c. S-18). Rights are in addition to and not in derogation of any rights conferred by Fatal Accidents Act. (c. F-7).

Actions against Representative.—Causes of action subsisting against deceased survive against his estate. (c. S-18).

Allowances.—None for support of widow and family pending administration.

Widow's Quarantine.—See topic Husband and Wife, subhead Marital Property Act.

Accounting.—Personal representative is not required to account to court other than by inventory of property unless at instance of some person interested in estate or by creditor of deceased. Personal representative may voluntarily pass his accounts in court. At passing of accounts, court has jurisdiction to make full inquiry in such manner as it sees fit. It may also at such time inquire into any complaint or claim of misconduct, neglect or default on part of personal representative occasioning loss to estate and may order personal representative to pay such sum as it considers proper and just. (§69).

Distribution.—Governed by common law principles.

Liabilities.—Liabilities of personal representatives are governed by common law and Trustees Act. (c. T-15).

Compensation of Representatives.—Governed by Trustees Act (c. T-15) and is allowed by court based upon fair and reasonable allowance for his care, pains and trouble, and his time expended in and about estate. There is no specific maximum or minimum fee. Will may specify amount of fee.

Resealing.—Where probate or administration has been granted by court of competent jurisdiction in United Kingdom, or in any province or territory of Canada, or in any country of Commonwealth or in any state or territory of U.S.A., such probate or administration may be resealed by court and has same force and effect as if it had been originally granted in Province. Letters of verification issued in Quebec are deemed to be probate for resealing in Province.

EXEMPTIONS:

See topics Garnishment; Executions, subhead Exemptions.

FACTORS:

Governed by Factors and Agents Act (c. F-1).

A mercantile agent (when acting in ordinary course of his business and with the consent of owner), who is in possession of goods or document of title to goods, may sell, pledge or dispose of same. Pledge of document of title to goods shall be deemed to be pledge of goods. Where mercantile agent pledges goods as security for debt due from him to pledgee, latter acquires no further right to goods than could have been enforced by agent at time of pledge. Consideration necessary for validity of sale or pledge of goods may be either payment in cash, or delivery of other goods, or of a document of title to goods, or a negotiable security; but, where goods are so pledged by agent, pledgee acquires no right in the goods in excess of value of goods or security. Transfer of document of title may be by endorsement or delivery. The term "document of title" as used in this title, includes a bill of lading.

Where the owner of goods has given possession thereof to another person for the purpose of consignment or sale or has shipped the goods in the name of another person and the consignee of the goods has not had notice that such person is not the owner of the goods, the consignee has in respect of advances made to or for the use of such person the same lien on the goods as if such person were the owner of the goods and may transfer any such lien to another person. (§10).

FIDUCIARIES:

See topics Executors and Administrators; Guardian and Ward; Trusts.

FILING FEES:

See topics Personal Property Security; Corporations; Deeds; Mortgages of Real Property.

FORECLOSURE:

See topics Personal Property Security; Liens; Mortgages of Real Property.

FOREIGN CORPORATIONS:

See topic Corporations, subhead Business Corporations Act, catchline Foreign Corporations.

FRAUDS, STATUTE OF:

Governing statute is c. S-14.

See note at head of Digest as to 1996 legislation covered.

See Topical Index in front part of this volume.

FRAUDS, STATUTE OF . . . *continued*

No action shall be brought to charge an executor or administrator upon any special promise to answer damages out of his own estate, or to charge any person upon any special promise to answer for the debt, default or miscarriage of another, or to charge any person upon any agreement made upon consideration of marriage, or upon any contract or sale of lands, or commission for the sale of real estate, or of any interest therein, or upon any agreement that is not to be performed within one year from the making thereof or upon an agreement for a commission for sale of real property, unless the agreement upon which such action is brought, or some memorandum or note thereof, is in writing and signed by the party to be charged therewith or some other person authorized by him. (c. S-14).

FRAUDULENT SALES AND CONVEYANCES:

Governing statute is c. A-16.

Assignments or sales made or confessions of judgment given by any person in insolvent circumstances with intent to defeat or delay creditors, or to give one or more creditors a preference over other creditors, are as against such creditor defeated or declared utterly void, and if any such transaction has effect of giving creditor preference it shall in respect of any proceeding brought within 60 days thereafter to set same aside or any assignment for general benefit of creditors made within 60 days, be presumed to be an unjust preference, whether same made voluntarily or under pressure—i. e., onus is upon debtor and preferred creditor.

Bulk Sales.—See topic Bulk Sales.

GARNISHMENT:

Governing statute is c. G-2.

Where amount unpaid on judgment of Court of Queen's Bench exceeds $80, and is not less than $40 exclusive of costs, any debt due to debtor may be garnished for satisfaction of judgment and collected from garnishee. Wages due judgment debtor for personal labour and services on hiring exempt from garnishment. (c. G-2). See also federal statute: Garnishment, Attachment and Pension Diversion Act, S.C., 1980-81-82-83, c. 100.

Also may obtain payment order for unpaid support orders in family matters. (§125[1]); Family Services Act, S.N.B., c. C-2.1).

Debt due from Crown is not subject to garnishment.

GUARDIAN AND WARD:

Governing statute is c. G-8.

Parents of a child are joint guardians and may jointly appoint in writing another person to be guardian of their child. Parent who has displayed intention to abandon child, however, has no status as guardian.

With respect to the custody, etc., of an infant, the best interest of the infant is the controlling consideration.

Insane Persons.—Governing statute is c. I-8. Court of Queen's Bench has power to appoint committee of person and estate of mentally incompetent person and to empower such committee to do anything in relation to estate that mentally incompetent person could have done if he had remained competent.

Incompetent persons in psychiatric facility have their estates administered by Administrator of Estates subject to provisions of c. I-8. (c. M-10, §§35-58).

Mental incompetence of donor will not terminate authority conferred upon donee by previously created and properly executed power of attorney which expressly allows power to be exercised during such incompetence. (c. P-19, §58.2).

HOLIDAYS:

Governing statute is c. I-13.

"Holiday" includes Sundays, New Year's Day, Good Friday, Easter Monday, Christmas Day, Canada Day, Victoria Day, day appointed for celebration of birthday of Her Majesty, New Brunswick Day (1st Mon. in Aug.), Labor Day (1st Mon. in Sept.), and any day appointed by proclamation of Governor General or Lieutenant-Governor as public holiday, or which by any act of New Brunswick Legislature, or Parliament of Canada is declared to be public holiday within province and whenever holiday other than Sun. falls on Sun., expression "holiday" includes following day. (§38).

HOMESTEADS:

There is no homestead exemption.

HUSBAND AND WIFE:

Subject to Marital Property Act (c. M-1.1), real and personal property belonging to woman before or acquired by her after marriage vests in her, is owned by her as her own separate property, and is exempted from seizure or responsibility in any way for debts or liabilities of her husband. (c. M-4).

Married woman is capable of acquiring, holding and disposing by will, or otherwise, any real or personal property as her separate property, in the same manner as if she were a feme sole. She is capable of entering into and rendering herself liable in respect of, and to extent of her separate property on any contract, and of suing and being sued, in all respects as if she were feme sole, and her husband need not be joined with her as plaintiff or defendant or be made party to any action or other legal proceedings brought by or taken against her; any damages or costs recovered by her in any such proceedings are held to be her separate property, and any damages or costs recovered against her in any such proceedings are payable out of her separate property and not otherwise. (c. M-4).

Contracts.—Every contract entered into by a married woman otherwise than as agent: (a) Is deemed to be a contract entered into by her in respect to and to bind her separate property, whether she is or is not in fact possessed of or entitled to any separate property at the time she enters into such contract; (b) is held to bind all separate property which she may at that time or thereafter be possessed of or entitled to.

Earnings.—Every married woman is entitled to have and to hold as her separate property, and dispose of as such, wages, earnings and property acquired by her in any employment or business and in which her husband has no proprietary interest.

Curtesy.—Husband no longer has curtesy in respect of property acquired by his wife after Apr. 29, 1916.

Dower.—Repealed except where right to dower has vested in possession prior to Jan. 1, 1981.

Remedies for Protection of Separate Property.—She has in her own name against all persons, including her husband, the same remedies for such protection, as if such property belonged to her as a feme sole; a husband has against his wife the same remedies for the protection and security of his property as she has against him for hers; except as aforesaid no husband or wife is entitled to sue the other for a tort.

Marital Property Act (1981, c. M-1.1).—

Division of Marital Property and Debts.—Spouses have equal rights of possession in any property occupied as their family residence, subject to order of court pursuant to §23 or provisions of domestic contract. (§18, Subsection 1). Court may issue §23 order (i.e., order that regardless of ownership, one spouse shall have exclusive possession of matrimonial home) where such is in best interests of child or if other shelter would not be adequate in circumstances. (§23, Subsection 3). §23 order may be merely of temporary nature, pending disposition of another application under Act. (§23, Subsection 2). No spouse may dispose of any interest in marital home without consent or release of other spouse or court order. (§19, Subsection 1). Such disposition may be set aside as per §22 unless person holding interest acquired such for value, in good faith, and without notice that property was marital home. (§19, Subsection 2). Generally, affidavit of spouse not party to disposition, to effect that property is not marital home, deems acquirer of interest to be of good faith and without notice of fact that property is marital home. (§19, Subsection 3).

Spouse, or any person with interest in property, may apply to court and court may make order stating extent, if any, to which such property is comprised of marital home or authorizing disposition notwithstanding lack of consent of non-disposing spouse in certain circumstances. (§22).

Presumption of advancement is abolished insofar as it previously applied to ownership as between husband and wife. Instead, presumption of resulting trust is to apply. Where spouses own property as joint tenants, such is prima facie proof that each is intended to have one-half beneficial interest in property upon severance. Also, funds deposited in joint accounts are deemed to be in names of spouses as joint tenants. (§15, Subsection 1). §15, Subsection 1, applies notwithstanding that events giving rise to presumption occurred before coming into force of this section. (§15, Subsection 2).

Child care, household management, and financial provision are joint responsibilities of spouses and, subject to this Act, fulfillment of these responsibilities entitles each spouse to equal share of marital property and imposes on each spouse burden of equal share of marital debts. (§2). Where decree nisi of divorce is pronounced; marriage declared nullity; spouses apart or marriage broken down and no reasonable prospect of resumption of cohabitation or reconciliation; each spouse, upon application to court, is entitled to have marital property divided in equal shares. (§3, Subsection 1). Where marriage has been annulled, such application must be made within 60 days, subject to court's discretion as per §3, Subsection 4, i.e., court may extend time where applicant not within time limit because of lack of knowledge of granting of divorce or declaration of nullity or for circumstances reasonably beyond his control. Similar limitation period applies where spouse has died. (§4, Subsections 1, 2 and 3). Notwithstanding §2, §3, and §4, court may make division of marital property in unequal shares if it feels that equal division would be inequitable having regard to: Any agreement other than domestic contract, duration of periods of cohabitation and separation, and circumstances related to procurement and maintenance of property. (§7).

§4 permits surviving spouse to apply within 60 days of death of spouse to court for equal division of marital property.

Domestic Contracts.—Spouses (before marriage or while cohabiting) or man and woman not married but cohabiting, may enter into written agreement concerning their respective rights and obligations under marriage or upon separation, dissolution or annulment of marriage or upon death. Specifically, agreement may relate to ownership in or division of property, support obligations, or any other matter in settlement of their affairs except right to custody of, or access to, their children. (§§34 and 35).

Man and woman who cohabited and are living separate and apart or who are cohabiting and who agree to live separate and apart may enter into separation agreement in relation to all matters permissible by §§34 and 35, as well as right to custody of, and access to, their children. (§36). However, court may disregard provisions of this contract relating to custody or access if, in its opinion, it would be in best interests of child to do so. (§38, Subsection 1).

Domestic contracts are to be in writing and signed by parties to be bound and witnessed. (§37, Subsection 1).

Court may disregard any provision of domestic contract if such was made before coming into force of Marital Property Act and not made in contemplation thereof or if spouse challenging provisions entered into contract without having sought independent legal advice. (§41).

General.—Act applies notwithstanding that spouses were married, property in issue was acquired, or proceeding with respect to property rights was commenced but not determined, before Act came into force. (§43).

Community property system does not apply.

Reciprocal Enforcement of Maintenance Order.—Certified copies of maintenance orders made by court in reciprocating state may be transmitted by proper officer of reciprocating state to Attorney General who shall send copy of order to prescribed officer of court in New Brunswick for registration. Such orders of same force and effect as if order originally obtained in court in which it is registered and court has power to enforce order accordingly. (c. R-4.01).

See note at head of Digest as to 1996 legislation covered.

See Topical Index in front part of this volume.

INCOME TAX: See topic Taxation.

INFANTS:

Age of majority is 19 years. (c. A-4).

The rights and liabilities of infants under contract entered into by them during infancy rest upon common law rules which have not been materially affected by statute. An infant may sue in certain courts for wages due him in the same manner as if he were of age. Under Insurance Act (c. I-12), except in respect of his rights as beneficiary, minor who has attained age of 16 years has capacity of person of age of 19 years: (a) To make enforceable contract; and (b) in respect of contract (§§163 & 201[1]). Beneficiary who has attained age of 18 years has capacity of person of age of 19 years to receive insurance money payable to him and to give discharge therefor. (§§164 & 201[2]).

Termination of Parental Rights.—Where security or development of child may be in danger Minister can place child under protective care. (Family Services Act c. F-2.2, §3[2]).

Adoption.—See topic Adoption.

INHERITANCE TAX: See topic Taxation.

INJUNCTIONS:

Request for interlocutory injunction or mandatory order, or for extension thereof, may be made before commencement of proceedings by preliminary motion, and after commencement of proceedings by motion. Subject to §34 of Judicature Act, where motion is made without notice, injunction may be granted for period not exceeding ten days under certain circumstances. Court may extend injunction, but each extension shall be limited to period of 30 additional days. (R. 40.02[3]).

Where person claims monetary relief, court may grant interlocutory injunction to restrain any person from disposing of, or removing from New Brunswick, assets within New Brunswick of person against whom claim is made. In such circumstance, unless otherwise ordered, plaintiff or applicant is deemed to have undertaken to abide by any order as to damages arising therefrom. (R. 40.03, .04).

Procedure for injunction or mandatory order under R. 40 is set out in R. 37 of Rules of Court which stipulate that notice of motion or preliminary motion and affidavits in support thereof shall be served on all parties to proceeding and on any persons who would be affected by order sought. Under certain circumstances court may make order without notice.

On motion or application evidence may be given by affidavit unless directed otherwise by Rules of Court or by order. Affidavit for use on application shall be confined to statements of fact within personal knowledge of deponent, but may contain statements as to his information and belief, if source of his information and his belief therein are specified in affidavit. (R. 39.01).

See topic Environment.

INSOLVENCY:

Governing statute is c. A-16.

Provincial legislation is practically superseded by Bankruptcy and Insolvency Act, R.S. c. B-3.

INSURANCE:

Governed by c. I-12. Inquiries may be directed to Superintendent of Insurance, Centennial Building, P.O. Box 6000, Fredericton, New Brunswick, E3B 5H1.

Marine Insurance is governed by separate Act. (c. M-1). Provincial Marine Insurance Act may be superceded by Federal Marine Insurance Act, passed May 1993.

Licenses.—Every insurer carrying on business in province must be licensed and license must be renewed annually. Before a license is granted applicant must file following material: (1) Certified copy of its Act or charter of incorporation which shall include its regulations verified in manner satisfactory to Superintendent; (2) affidavit or statutory declaration that insurer is still in existence and legally authorized to transact business under its charter; (3) certified copy of its last balance sheet and auditor's report thereon; (4) notice of place where head office of insurer is situate, if without Province; (5) notice of place where chief agency or head office of insurer in Province is to be situate; (6) statement showing amount of capital of insurer and number of shares into which it is divided, number of shares subscribed and amount paid thereon; (7) certified copy of power of attorney to its Canadian chief agent, if any; (8) notice of appointment of chief agent or resident manager for Province; (9) statement in such form as is required by Superintendent of condition and affairs of insurer on 31st day of Dec. then last preceding or up to usual balancing day of insurer or as Superintendent requires; and (10) such other evidence as Superintendent requires. (§27[1]).

Every insurer, before receiving a license, must deposit with Provincial Treasurer, securities as follows: life insurance, $50,000; other classes of insurance, if doing business in New Brunswick only, $25,000; or if doing business both in and outside of New Brunswick, $50,000. Provision is made for reciprocal deposits where a similar provision is made in other provinces.

Contracts.—Part 3 of Act sets forth provisions relating to insurance contracts in province.

Special classes of insurance are regulated by Insurance Act, as follows: Fire, by Part 4, including statutory conditions; life, by Part 5, which also sets forth law relating to life insurance contracts in province and which corresponds to Uniform Life Act of other provinces; accident and sickness, including statutory conditions, by Part 6; automobile, including statutory conditions, by Part 7; livestock, by Part 8; weather, by Part 9; fraternal societies, by Part 10; mutual benefit societies by Part 11; mutual insurance companies, by Part 12; reciprocal insurance, by Part 13; amalgamation, transfer and reinsurance, by Part 14. Marine insurance is regulated by a separate act. (c. M-1).

Brokers and Adjusters.—Part 15 of Insurance Act provides for licensing and regulation of insurance brokers and adjusters.

Foreign Companies.—Rights of licensed foreign company are same as those of company incorporated in province.

Service of process in actions against insurance companies situated outside province may be made by sending copy of notice or process to insurer by registered mail, postage prepaid, addressed to insurer at most recent address filed in Office of Superintendent. Service shall be deemed to have been received by insurer ten days after date of mailing.

Taxation.—See topic Taxation.

Direct Actions Against Insurer.—Where person incurs liability for injury or damage to person or property of another, and is insured against such liability but fails to satisfy judgment against him, person entitled to damages may recover by action against insurer amount of judgment up to face value of policy. (§104). For motor vehicle liability policies, see topic Motor Vehicles, subhead Direct Actions.

INTEREST:

See Canada Law Digest.

Unconscionable Transactions.—See topic Consumer Protection.

INTESTACY:

See topic Descent and Distribution.

JOINT STOCK COMPANIES:

See topic Corporations.

JUDGMENTS:

On hearing motion judge may endorse his disposition on notice of motion or direct successful party to prepare formal judgment for judge's signature. Order disposing of motion takes effect when it is signed. Successful party on motion shall file with clerk endorsed notice of motion or order signed by judge. (R. 60.01).

Where judgment is given at hearing or trial court reporter shall file transcript or copy of order or decision with clerk of judicial district in which proceeding was commenced, and judgment shall take effect from date on which order was given. Where judge gives written order or decision subsequent to hearing or trial, he shall file order or decision with clerk, and judgment shall take effect from date of filing. (R. 60.02).

Party to whom relief has been granted may prepare judgment and present it to clerk to be signed and entered, notwithstanding that costs have not been assessed.

Either before or after judgment party may apply on motion to court to amend or vary decision or judgment respectively. Party may apply on motion to vary judgment where there is clerical error or accidental slip in judgment, or where judgment does not conform to order or decision directing judgment, or if court has failed to specify time for compliance with judgment requiring person to do or abstain from doing act. (R. 60.03).

Clerk may file memorandum of satisfaction of judgment if it is signed by person entitled to benefit of judgment and signature and contents are proven by affidavit, or on motion made to clerk it is shown that notice of motion was served on person entitled to benefit of judgment and judgment has been satisfied. (R. 60.07).

Enforcement of Orders.—Order of court may be enforced in same way that judgment to same effect might be enforced. (R. 61.01).

Declaratory Judgments.—See topic Pleading.

Foreign Judgments.—Foreign judgments may be sued on as such. Jurisdiction of foreign court is admitted only if defendant was ordinarily resident in the country at commencement of the action, or was carrying on business when judgment was obtained, if judgment was obtained in Canada, or if the defendant submitted to the jurisdiction of the foreign court. The foreign court has no jurisdiction if the action involves title to land in New Brunswick or is for damages in respect to land in New Brunswick. If the foreign court had jurisdiction, its judgment is conclusive as to any matter adjudicated in the action. It is a sufficient defense to an action on a foreign judgment that the original court had no jurisdiction, that defendant was not served with process and did not appear, that the judgment is not final, that it was obtained by fraud, is not for a sum certain in money, is for payment of a penalty under the revenue laws of the foreign country or is in respect to a cause of action which for reasons of public policy would not have been entertained in New Brunswick, or that the proceedings in which the judgment was obtained were contrary to natural justice. (c. F-19, c. R-3).

See also topic Limitation of Actions.

LABOUR RELATIONS:

(See Employment Standards Act, c. E-7.2, Industrial Relations Act, c. I-4 and Labour and Employment Board Act, c. L-O.01.)

Common law as to master and servant generally prevails. Minister of Advanced Education and Labour is responsible for general administration of Act. Minister appoints Director from within civil service. Labour and Employment Board established to investigate complaints and conduct hearings as Director deems necessary or as requested in writing. As of Nov. 14, 1994 Labour and Employment Board replaced Employment Standards Tribunal, Industrial Relations Board, Pensions Tribunal and Public Service Labour Relations Board. (c. L-0.01, §24).

Dismissal.—Employer must give employee employed for more than six months and less than five years at least two weeks' written notice when dismissing without cause. In case of employee employed more than five years employer must give at least four weeks' written notice. In lieu of notice employer may pay wages equal to notice period. Common law still prevails. Act only sets out minimum requirements. (§31).

Hours of Work.—No limit on number of hours employee may work. Lt.-Gov. in Council prescribes maximum number of hours employer may require employee to work. Any employee working in excess of prescribed maximum hours must be paid one and one-half times normal wage rate. No employee under 16 is to be employed in place of employment for more than six hours per day except with written authority of Director, for more than three hours on school day, on any day that would require employee to

LABOUR RELATIONS . . . *continued*

spend more than total of eight hours attending school and working, or between 10 P.M. and 6 A.M. (§39).

Terms.—Pregnant employee is to be permitted up to 11 weeks prior to delivery, to take total of 17 weeks of maternity leave. Upon reporting back to work employee must be permitted to resume working in position or equivalent she held before maternity leave with no decrease in pay or loss of seniority or benefits accrued up to commencement of leave. Upon request of employee who is natural parent of newborn or unborn child, or who is adopting child, employer shall grant leave of absence not exceeding 52 consecutive weeks. (§44.02[2] to [8]).

Wages.—Lt.-Gov. in Council makes minimum wage orders on advice of Minimum Wage Board. Priority given in respect of three months' wages over ordinary or general creditors where assignment made for benefit of creditors, where company as employer in process of winding-up, where employer deceased, or where employer execution debtor. Wage claims more than three months same as ordinary creditors. (c. W-1). When employment terminated all wages and salary owed to employee to be paid not later than next regular pay day and never beyond 21 days after last day of employment. (c. E-7.2). Employee vacation pay governed by c. E-7.2. Paid vacation of lesser of two weeks or equal to one day per each calendar month employee worked or in some circumstances 4% of earnings.

No employer may pay employee of one sex at different rate of pay from that which he pays to employee of other sex for work that is performed in same establishment, is substantially same in nature, requires substantially same skill, effort and responsibility, and, is performed under similar working conditions, except where payment is made pursuant to seniority system, merit system, system that measures earnings by quantity or quality of production, or any other system or practice that is not otherwise unlawful. (§37.1). Tips and gratuities (including surcharges paid in lieu of tip or gratuity) are property of employee to whom or for whom they are given and shall not be withheld by employer, notwithstanding any consent given by employee. (c. E-7.2).

Assignments.—See topic Assignments, subhead Assignments of Wages.

Child Labour.—Young persons (under 16) may be prohibited from being employed by Director if he deems employment dangerous or injurious to their health or welfare. Young persons (under 14) may not be employed in specified excluded types of work without written authority of Director. (§§39, 40).

Industrial or occupational safety standards governed by c. O-0.2.

Labour Unions.—Governing statute is c. I-4 for labour relations outside of public sector. Trade unions legal entities capable of suing and being sued. Labour and Employment Board is empowered to certify unions as bargaining agents. Only certified unions have access to conciliation. Time limits introduced in collective bargaining.

Every person has right to join a trade union. Closed shop provisions in agreements allowed. Union cannot refuse membership to anyone who meets terms and conditions applied to other members. (c. H-11). Definition of employee includes professional groups including legal.

Labour Disputes.—Unfair labour practices detailed in c. I-4, §§3-10. Law deals with unfair practices relating to freedom of membership in trade unions and their formation. Provision is made for accreditation of employers organizations.

Where a collective agreement is in operation, no employer may declare lockout and no employee bound by agreement may strike except in accordance with Act.

Workers' Compensation Act.—Compensation for injuries to workers is regulated by Workers' Compensation Act (c. W-13) and Occupational Health and Safety Act (c. O-0.2), and is administered by Workplace Health, Safety and Compensation Commission consisting of those persons who from time to time comprise board of directors (c. w-14, §2).

All employers are classed and assessed according to the nature of the industry carried on. Act applies to employers or workers in or about any industry except: (1) casual employees, (2) persons who play sports as their main source of income, (3) outworkers to whom materials are given to be finished in own home or other noncontrolled premises, (4) family of employer under 16 years and (5) domestic servants. "Industry" is defined to include any operation, undertaking or employment. (§2[3]).

Compensation is payable where the accident or death arises out of and in course of employment except if caused intentionally or wholly or principally due to intoxication or serious or wilful misconduct on part of worker and did not result in death or serious and permanent disability of worker. (§7).

Worker does not forfeit his right of action at common law or by statute against persons other than his employer. Worker may either claim compensation or bring action and if he does not recover by action as much as he would be entitled to under Act he may claim the difference as compensation. Commission on paying compensation is subrogated to rights of worker. (§10).

No compensation is payable unless application made within one year after occurrence of accident or in case of death within six months of time of death except that Commission may pay claim in any event if they decide to do so. (§16). Scale of compensation depends on average earnings and earning capacity calculated by regular remuneration worker was receiving at time of injury, as may appear to Commission best to represent actual loss of earnings, unless worker is under 21 years of age and it is established that under normal conditions his wages will probably increase, in which case increase is considered in arriving at his average earnings or earning capacity which it any case shall not exceed New Brunswick Industrial Aggregate Earnings per year. (§37).

Compensation is payable out of "The Accident Fund" which is created and maintained by annual assessment of the employers in each class rated on the annual payroll. Classification of the industry is at the discretion of the Commission.

Temporary industry may be required to give such security to the Commission as is deemed adequate. If any assessment not paid by employer when due interest at rate prescribed by regulation of Commission may be added and collected as part of such assessment. (§64).

By Part II of the Act if any injury is caused to worker by reason of defect in machinery, etc., or by neglect of employer or any person in his service, worker or his dependents is entitled to recover from employer damages sustained.

Contributory negligence on the part of the worker is not a bar to recovery, but is to be taken into account in assessing damages.

Where employer neglects or refuses to furnish any estimate or information as required is, in addition to any other penalty or liability to which he may be subject, required to pay to Commission full amount or capitalized value of compensation payable in respect of any accident to worker in his employ that happens during period of such default.

The Commission has jurisdiction to inquire into and determine all matters and questions of law and fact and its decision is final and conclusive except upon any question as to its jurisdiction or upon any questions of law, when appeal lies to Court of Appeal, after permission obtained from judge of Court of Queen's Bench. Commission has same powers as Court of Queen's Bench for compelling production of documents and attendance and examining of witnesses. (§§31, 32).

Unemployment Compensation.—See Canada Law Digest.

LANDLORD AND TENANT:

Governing statute is c. L-1 but does not include residential tenancies. See subhead Residential Tenancies, infra.

Form.—Standard forms must be used with respect to any lease intended to be registered in registry office. (c. S-12.2).

Landlord has a right of reentry if the rent reserved or a portion thereof, remains unpaid for 15 days after it is due, unless there is an express agreement to the contrary. (§8).

When a tenant's goods are seized under execution the person making the seizure must pay to the landlord the amount of rent in arrear not exceeding one year.

When lands are let requiring notice to quit, the notice must be as follows: For the year or half year, three months; for the quarter or month, one month; and for the week, one week.

Tenant willfully overholding is liable for double rent or yearly value of premises.

A landlord has the remedy of ejectment where a tenant refuses to deliver up possession of the premises after the expiration of his tenancy or after due notice to quit.

Leases exceeding the term of three years must be in writing and registered. (§19, c. R-6).

Rent may be increased on nonresidential property by amount equal to increase in annual taxes over those of preceding year and must be decreased by amount of any tax decrease notwithstanding any provisions contained in lease, license or permit to contrary. For leases, licenses or permits for nonresidential property executed before 1982 rent may be increasecd by amount equal to increase in annual taxes over amount of taxes paid in 1982. Landlord shall reduce rent by amount equal to any reduction in taxes from those paid in 1982. (§18).

Distress.—Arrears of rent may be distrained for during continuance of landlord's interest and tenant's possession or within six months after termination of lease. No distress may be made between 6 P. M. and 8 A. M., nor may more goods be taken than are necessary to satisfy rent in arrears and costs of distress; but there is no liability for excessive distress if excess is abandoned within seven days. Goods fraudulently or clandestinely removed to avoid distress may be followed and distrained within 30 days and for this purpose doors, locks or other fastenings may be broken or removed. If distress is levied on property of lodger under tenant, such lodger may serve on landlord written notice that tenant has no property or beneficial interest in such property and pay or tender to landlord amount due to tenant and if landlord thereafter proceeds with distress he is liable for illegal distress. Only interest of tenant in goods distrained may be sold.

Residential Tenancies.—c. R-10.2.

Application.—Act applies to all premises used for residential purposes except premises occupied for business purpose with living accommodation attached under single tenancy agreement and further excepts boarding houses and vacation homes.

Rentalsmen.—Appointed by province to administer Act. They will assist both landlords and tenants in such areas as: Education and advice regarding rights and responsibilities of each; mediation and settlement of disputes; and enforcement of rights and responsibilities. (§26).

Lease Form.—Standard form must be used and if not used, it is deemed to apply to tenancy. No part may be altered or deleted. Parties may agree to addition to lease if addition does not alter any right or duty as stated in Act or lease. (§9[1], [3]).

Basic Landlord Responsibilities.—These depend in part on agreement of parties and in part on duties prescribed by law. Standard form leaves it to parties to agree on such things as heat, furniture, electricity, parking, etc. Mandatory responsibilities include: (1) Delivery of premises in good state of repair and fit for habitation and maintenance in same condition; (2) comply with all health, safety, housing and building standards; and (3) keep all common areas in clean and safe condition. (§3[1]).

Basic Tenant Responsibilities.—Mandatory responsibilities include: (1) Ordinary cleanliness of premises; (2) repair damage caused by his wilful or negligent conduct; and (3) conduct himself in manner that will not cause disturbance or nuisance. (§4[1]).

Rent.—Residential Rent Review Act, c. R-10.11 expired Aug. 31, 1985. No statutory provisions regulating rent increases.

Security Deposits.—Lease may provide for security deposit of not more than one week's rent in case of tenancy from week to week and in all other tenancies of not more than one month's rent. Security is to provide for tenant's failure to pay rent or comply with his mandatory responsibilities. Security is held by rentalsman. (§8[1]-[3]).

Entry and Privacy.—Landlord cannot enter premises except: (1) When emergency exists or tenant has abandoned premises; (2) upon seven days notice when normal repairs or redecoration to be carried out; (3) upon 24 hours notice to show to prospective purchasers or mortgagees; and (4) without notice during last rental period and where lease so provides to show prospective tenant. Locks may not be changed without mutual consent or authorization of rentalsman. (§16).

Assignment.—Tenant may assign except where lease prohibits. Where tenant assigns all his rights under lease assignee becomes new tenant for all purposes and assumes all lease obligations. Lease may prohibit assignment or require landlord's consent which he

LANDLORD AND TENANT . . . *continued*
may not arbitrarily withhold. Landlord has option to terminate lease rather than consenting to assignment. (§13).

If landlord transfers his interest he must notify tenant and rentalsman within seven days.

Termination.—Lease for fixed term ends automatically at end of term. Periodic tenancies may be terminated by serving written notice of termination. All notices are effective for last day of periodic term and in case of year to year must be given at least three months prior; in case of month to month must be given at least one month prior; and in case of week to week must be given at least one week prior. Notice period may not be shortened by lease but can be longer if included in lease.

Remedies.—Where tenant is in breach of any obligation, other than payment of rent, landlord may serve notice on tenant stating complaint. Copy must go to rentalsman. If breach not rectified within seven days landlord may give notice to rentalsman who then conducts investigation. Rentalsman may require tenant to fulfill his obligations and if not rectified within time established by rentalsman, rentalsman may serve notice to vacate.

If tenant fails to pay rent on due date, landlord may serve notice on tenant and rentalsman requesting service of notice to quit. Rentalsman will investigate and if he finds rent has not been paid will serve notice to quit on tenant. Tenant may rectify his breach by payment to rentalsman within seven days of receipt of notice to quit. If he fails to pay rent second time and notice to quit is served, he cannot rectify breach.

Distress is abolished.

Landlord must mitigate his damages. (§11[4]).

If landlord is in breach of any of his obligations, tenant may service notice of complaint within seven days (or one day if breach constitutes or involves emergency). If not remedied, tenant may give notice to rentalsman who may conduct investigation. Rentalsman may require landlord to rectify breach and if not so done within time permitted, rentalsman may perform obligation and require future rent payments to be made to him until rentalsman's expenses have been reimbursed.

Services of Notices.—Notices may be delivered personally or sent by ordinary mail to tenant, landlord or rentalsman. Landlord of building containing three or more units and who does not live in building must post conspicuous notice within building or file with rentalsman setting out legal name of landlord or his agent and address for service.

LEASES: See topic Landlord and Tenant.

LEGISLATURE:

Consists of a Lieutenant Governor and one house, styled the Legislative Assembly. Sessions are held annually, ordinarily.

LEVY: See topics Attachment; Executions.

LICENSES:

Licenses are required for: auctioneers, (c. A-17); automobiles and automobile dealers, (c. M-17); billiard saloons and bowling alleys, (c. A-2.1); loan and trust companies incorporated extra-provincially, (c. L-11.2); and brokers, (c. I-12); marriage, (c. M-3); pawnbrokers, (c. M-22); places of amusement, (c. A-2.1); real estate agents or salesmen, (c. R.1); sale of gasoline, (c. G-3). (Note: this list is not all-inclusive.)

Hunting Licences.—Class I licence which authorizes nonresident 18 years of age or over to hunt deer, rabbit, migratory birds is $100.

See also topic Consumer Protection, subheads Cost of Credit Disclosure Act; Direct Sellers Act.

LIENS:

Liens on Goods.—Person has lien on chattel on which he has expended money, labor or skill at request of owner. Wharfinger or gratuitous bailee has particular lien enforceable by sale of chattel if claim is not paid after giving notice to owner if whereabouts known. Jewellers including watchmakers have lien with power of sale. (c. L-6).

Mechanics' Liens.—Governing statute is c. M-6. Anyone who does any work or furnishes material to be used in improvement on land or buildings has lien. Liens are registered in registry office of county where lands affected are situated. They must be registered within 30 days or in some cases 60 days from completion of furnishing materials or labor. Liens for wages can also be registered in like manner. Proceedings to enforce liens must be by action in Court of Queen's Bench, undertaken within 90 days from registration of lien or expiry of period of credit. Action shall be deemed to be discontinued one year after it was commenced unless it has been set down for trial or application has been made to court for order continuing action. (§27).

Woodsmen's lien is given for work on logs or timber. Statement of claim must be filed within 30 days after last work, or 20 days in case of stream driving. (c. W-12).

Redemption.—No right of redemption exists under the various statutes authorizing lienholders to sell property subject to lien, but, generally speaking, lienholder must deliver up property subject to lien to person entitled, on payment, at any time before actual sale, or on expiration of notice required by some statutes to be given, of the debt, interest and all costs, expenses of advertising, etc.

LIMITATION OF ACTIONS:

Governing statute is c. L-8.

Personal.—No action or scire facias upon any judgment (including a foreign judgment), recognizance, bond or other specialty, shall be brought but within 20 years after the cause of action. An action for any sum of money given to any person aggrieved by any act or statute, or for any penalty, must be brought within two years after the cause of action. Actions for assault, battery, wounding, imprisonment, defamation, seduction, and damages arising out of the operation, care or control of a motor vehicle, must be begun within two years after the cause of action. Direct actions by insured against his fire insurer must be brought within one year of accident; actions against car insurer must be brought within two years. Actions grounded on fraud, accident or mistake, or other equitable ground of relief, must be brought within six years after discovery of the cause of action. All other cases must be commenced within six years after the cause of action. See, however, topic Death, subhead Action for Death.

See also topic Corporations, subhead Business Corporations Act, catchline Liabilities of Directors.

Real.—No claim for lands or rent shall be made, or action brought by crown after a continuous adverse possession of 60 years. No person shall make an entry or bring an action to recover any land but within 20 years after the time at which the right to make such entry or bring such action shall have first accrued to such person or the person through whom he claims. When one or more of several persons entitled to any land as co-parceners, joint tenants, or tenants in common, shall have been in the possession or receipt of the entirety or more than his or their undivided share or shares of said land for his or their own benefit, such possession or receipt shall not be deemed to have been the possession or receipt of or by any other person or persons entitled to an interest in said lands.

LIMITED PARTNERSHIP:

See topic Partnership.

LOTTERIES:

Governing statute is c. L-13.1. Crown Corporation known as Lotteries Commission regulates lotteries in Province. Consists of Minister of Finance and two Deputy Ministers. May organize lotteries on behalf of government.

MARRIAGE:

Governing statute is c. M-3.

There is no statutory age under which males or females cannot lawfully marry, therefore, English common law rule of 12 years for girls and 14 years for boys applies. Proper consents must be obtained for children under 18.

Consent Required.—When either party not having been previously married is under 18 years of age, consent of father and mother if both living and not living separate, or guardian is required. Such consent must be verified by affidavit of consenting party before a license is issued or banns allowed. (§19[1]).

Medical Examination.—No statutory provisions.

License and Banns.—Marriage is by license. Application for license by both parties is made to issuer of marriage licenses. Personal attendance of parties before issuer is excused only when undue hardship would occur if personal attendance was required. Application for license is by affidavit of each party stating where marriage is to take place, that there are no bars to marriage and whether parties are bachelors, spinsters, divorced, etc.

Ceremony may be performed by: Any person being resident in province, duly registered under this Act and charged with solemnization of ceremony of marriage by church or religious denomination. No marriage may be solemnized under authority of license unless marriage takes place within three months after day on which license was issued.

A rebuttable presumption of marriage arises where a man and woman have cohabited for such length of time and under such circumstances as to have acquired the reputation of being man and wife. (43 N.B.R. 154).

Proxy Marriages.—Not authorized.

Marriages by Written Contract.—Not authorized.

Annulment.—Court of Queen's Bench may annul any marriage on grounds of impotence or frigidity or consanguinity within degrees prohibited by Act 32 Henry VIII. Such marriage is voidable upon application to court during lifetime of parties thereto but cannot be questioned after death of either party. As to decree, see topic Divorce.

Record.—See topic Records, subhead Vital Statistics.

Common Law Marriages.—Common law applies. No special statutory provisions.

MARRIED WOMEN:

See topics Acknowledgments; Deeds; Dower; Executors and Administrators; Husband and Wife; Marriage; Wills; Witnesses.

MASTER AND SERVANT:

See topics Labour Relations; Principal and Agent.

MECHANICS' LIENS: See topic Liens.

MINES AND MINERALS:

Governing statute is c. M-14.1.

Minister of Natural Resources and Energy has general supervision over mining and mining lands in Province, and establishes mining commissioner who has exclusive jurisdiction to hear and determine all questions, disagreements, matters or claims arising out of application of Act and recorder who shall record all mineral claims and mining leases and all instruments affecting mineral claims and mining leases.

Prospecting Licences.—Any person who is 16 years of age or older, corporation or partnership may apply to recorder for prospecting licence in form prescribed by regulation.

Staking Mineral Claims.—Prospector may stake mineral claim in accordance with regulation.

Mining Leases.—Holder of recorded mineral claim may apply for and obtain mining lease subject to statutory terms and conditions.

Royalties.—Everyone who takes minerals under authority of mining lease shall pay royalties to Crown in accordance with regulations.

Mining Income Tax.—See topic Taxation, subhead Mining Income Tax.

MONOPOLIES AND RESTRAINT OF TRADE:

Provision is made for the investigation of combinations, monopolies, trusts and mergers by Competition Act. (R.S.C. 1985, c. C-34, am'd R.S.C. 1985, c. 19 [2nd. Supp.]). See also R.S.C. 1985, c. T-14, as to trade unions.

MORTGAGES OF PERSONAL PROPERTY:

See topic Personal Property Security.

MORTGAGES OF REAL PROPERTY:

Common law rules govern.

Execution.—Mortgage must be under seal, executed and acknowledged as a deed.

Form.—Standard forms must be used. (c. S-12.2).

Recording.—Mortgages must be recorded in registration district wherein land is situate in order to be effective against third persons. Same provisions as apply to recording deeds apply to mortgages. See topic Deeds.

Recording Fees.—Recording fee is $30. Additional $10 for documents over 15 pages.

Release.—A mortgage is discharged by registration of a certificate signed by the mortgagee, his assignee or representative, stating that the mortgage has been paid, or by the mortgagee signing on the margin of the mortgage registered in the office of the registrar of deeds, and in the presence of the registrar, a receipt for the money due thereon.

Power of sale is procedure most commonly used. Sale under power of sale in mortgage or under Property Act may be used when default occurs. Only power of sale under Property Act permits mortgagee to buy in at sale for his own benefit. Notice of sale is required to be published.

Taxes.—No taxes payable on registration of mortgages.

Future Advances.—Mortgage may cover future advances; however, future advances are subject to any intervening registered charges, encumbrances or liens.

Trust deeds are universally used to secure bond issues. They provide for operation of the property by the mortgagor until default and realization and sale upon and after default.

Assignment.—Made by instrument of assignment executed by mortgagee. When mortgagor is entitled to redeem he may require mortgagee instead of reconveying to assign mortgage debt and convey mortgaged property to any third party. This does not apply if mortgagee is or has been in possession.

Chattel Mortgages.—See topic Personal Property Security.

Debenture.—Standard form of debenture is required. (c. S-12.2).

MOTOR VEHICLES:

Governing statute is c. M-17.

Vehicle License required. Number plate must be displayed in front and rear. Leased vehicles must be registered in both owner's name and lessee's name.

Operator's license required and purchased biannually. No person under age of 16 may be licensed. Members of Armed Forces do not have to be licensed while operating a motor vehicle in service of Armed Forces, but otherwise they must obtain a license on taking up residence in province.

Bills of Sale and Liens.—See topic Personal Property Security.

Operation Prohibited.—By person under age of 16 (except farm tractor) or intoxicated person.

Equipment Required.—Horn or other warning device capable of emitting sound audible under normal conditions for not less than 60 metres; two means of applying brakes; mirror providing unobstructed view of highway for not less than 60 metres in rear; muffler; windshield wiper; speedometer. Cut-out or similar device prohibited.

No person shall ride or operate bicycle on highway unless person is wearing bicycle helmet in accordance with regulations and chin strap of helmet is securely fastened under person's chin. (§177[3]).

Lights Required.—Two in front showing white lights visible a reasonable distance; one in rear throwing white light toward license number and red light directly back; turn indicator and braking indicator lights. Lights not required where vehicle not in motion or parked by side of highway where there is other sufficient artificial light. Spotlight permitted only on right side of vehicle and when so attached as at all times to throw its glare towards right side of road.

Motorcycle or bicycle must have white light or approved reflector visible a reasonable distance in front and red light or approved reflector in rear.

Required lights must be displayed at night time or when there is insufficient light. Lights must be dimmed at least 150 metres before meeting another vehicle or as soon as such vehicle is visible.

Motor vehicle may have not more than two fog lights in front, but such lights may be used only in conjunction with lower or passing beams of head lamps. (§219[2]).

Seat Belts.—Use of seat belts in motor vehicle in which seat belt assembly is provided for, is required except when operator is driving in reverse, holds certificate from medical practitioner certifying operator is unable to wear seat belt or is engaged in work which requires alighting and reentering motor vehicle at frequent intervals and when engaged in such work does not drive at speed in excess of 40 k.p.h. Operator responsible for ensuring passengers under 16 years of age wear seat belts. Penalty is fine of not less than $25 and not more than $100. (§200.1).

Accidents.—In case of accident, operator must stop and give person injured or whose property is injured his name and address and registration number of vehicle. If accident results in personal injury, death or property damage to apparent extent of $400 or more, operator of vehicle, or any person therein at time if operator incapacitated shall immediately notify police of such accident and of his name and address and name and address of owner of car and must upon request of Registrar supply information for accident report. (§130).

Owner is liable for negligence of others operating vehicle with his consent. (§270).

Liability of Parent and Guardian.—Every parent and every guardian is under a legal duty to do everything reasonably within his power to prevent his child or ward from playing on a highway, and every parent and every guardian who fails so to do is guilty of an offence. In the prosecution of a parent or guardian under this section if it is established that a child or ward of such parent or guardian was playing on a highway the court may convict such parent or guardian unless such parent or guardian satisfies the court that he did everything reasonably within his power to prevent his child or ward from playing on the highway.

No parent or guardian of person who is under 16 years of age shall authorize or knowingly permit that person to ride on or operate bicycle on highway unless wearing helmet in accordance with §177(3). (§177[4]).

Financial Responsibility.—The driver's license and every owner's permit of any person who owns or is operating a motor vehicle at the time it becomes involved in an accident resulting in personal or property damage to others in excess of $400, or who is convicted of any one of certain offences involving the operation of a motor vehicle or forfeits bail after arrest on a charge for such an offence, will be suspended until proof of financial responsibility is furnished. The Minister may require proof of financial responsibility before issuing or renewing owner's permit or driver's license to a person under the age of 19 or over the age of 65. Such proof may be by liability insurance, bond or approved guaranty surety company, bond with approved personal sureties or deposit of money or securities in amount or value of $100,000. (Reg. 83-42, §83).

Unsatisfied Judgment Fund.—Applicable only to motor vehicle accidents which occurred prior to Mar. 1, 1990.

Inspections.—Motor vehicles must be safety inspected annually. (Reg. 83-185, §6[4]).

Lieutenant-Governor in Council may make regulations (a) respecting width, height and length of vehicle or any combination or units of vehicles, (b) respecting dimensions within overall size of vehicles or any combination or units of vehicles, (c) respecting extension or overhang of mirrors, other devices or load relative to vehicle, (d) respecting combination of units of vehicles that may be coupled together, (e) respecting exemptions from or exceptions to provisions of regulations made under paragraphs (a) to (d). (§251.1).

Lieutenant-Governor in Council may make regulations respecting dimensions within overall size of trucks, truck tractors, trailers or semi-trailers or any combinations of such vehicles. (§254[4.1]).

Commercial Vehicle Safety requirements are listed in §265.1.

Insurance.—See subhead Financial Responsibility, supra.

Insurance Required.—No person shall operate and no owner shall permit to be operated motor vehicle not covered by policy of insurance. Such policy must cover third party liability to minimum of $200,000 and accident benefits. (§17.1[1]; c. I-12, subsection 243[1]).

Foreign Vehicles and Operators.—A nonresident over the age of 16 years who has in his immediate possession a valid operator's or chauffeur's license issued to him in his own province or country may, without examination or license under the motor vehicle law of this province, drive any motor vehicle for 30 days after he first entered New Brunswick and may drive a motor vehicle registered in the province or country which issued his operator's or chauffeur's license during such period of time and under such conditions that such motor vehicle is exempt from registration in this province by any regulations made under The Motor Vehicle Act, but Registrar may at any time in his discretion cancel privileges granted to any nonresident. (§§46 and 80[2], c. M-17; §§25 and 26, Reg. 83-42).

No person shall have greater right of recovery resulting from negligent operation of motor vehicle in this Province than that person would have in jurisdiction in which he ordinarily resides and in no event any greater right of recovery than person resident in this Province would have in such other jurisdiction.

Actions Against Nonresidents.—No special provision with respect to commencement.

Direct Actions.—An action by an insured against his insurer may be commenced at any time after 60 days from filing of a proof of loss and within two years of arising of cause of action.

When a third party obtains a judgment against an insured and insured does not satisfy same, the third party may then bring an action against insurer for amount of judgment. Insurer has against third party all defences it has against insured over and above the minimum limits. See c. I-12, §250.

Suspension of Drivers' Licenses.—A conviction based on impaired driving, a breathalizer reading in excess of 80 milligrams of alcohol in 100 millilitres of blood, or a refusal to comply with breathalizer demand (where demand has been made because of reasonable and probable grounds to believe accused was impaired), will result in a suspension of driving privileges for a period of 12 months for first offence or 24 months for second or subsequent offence within three years of first offence. License may also be suspended for any conviction under Criminal Code involving use of motor vehicles or for accumulation of motor vehicle offences as listed in §297(2).

Motor-vehicle carriers are regulated by c. M-16.

The members of the Board of Commissioners of Public Utilities and others are constituted a Motor Carrier Board, which exercises jurisdiction over motor vehicle carriers, except as otherwise provided in the Act.

The Board may grant licenses to operate public motor buses or trucks over specified routes and between specified points or generally throughout the province and, except as otherwise provided in the Act, no public motor bus or truck may be operated without a license and a licensed bus or truck may operate only as specified in the license and subject to the Act and regulations adopted thereunder. Licensed carrier may not abandon service without an order of the Board.

MOTOR VEHICLES . . . *continued*

The Board has power to make regulations fixing schedules, rates, fares and charges of licensed motor carriers, prescribe forms, fix fees, require filing of returns, reports and other data and, generally, make regulations concerning motor carriers, public motor buses and public motor trucks.

Act does not apply to any motor vehicle while used or operated exclusively in: Transportation of school children, when maintenance of same is paid for by board of trustees or by province; carrying mails; carrying passengers to or from any train, ship or boat for trips not exceeding 25 kilometres one way; construction of any federal, provincial or municipal work; transportation of mail pursuant to contract with Canada Post Corporation; mineral ore, concentrates, potash or gypsum, coal, salt; bulk milk or cream; grain or any agricultural products in their green or raw form; livestock or poultry; animals used for racing or show purposes; fertilizer, including fertilizer components, peat moss, agricultural limestone; unprocessed forest products, including Christmas trees and related products; pit props; railroad ties; fuelwood, pulpwood, logs, poles, wood chips, bark, shavings, sawdust and hog fuel, but not including any product treated with preservative; horticultural products, including nursery stock, and incidental supplies when carried with such products; any products of sea except those which have been packaged for retail sale; snow, ice or water; buildings with exception of mobile homes, sectional homes and mini homes; any garbage or refuse except for industrial or hazardous waste; any commodity which is bona fide and exclusively property of owner of motor vehicle; or boats that are primarily used for commercial fishing purposes; while used solely: (1) to transport equipment permanently attached to vehicle, (2) to deliver petroleum products to ultimate user thereof, (3) as taxi cab, (4) as tow truck, or as tow-away vehicle. Before any license can be issued liability insurance policy must be filed with Board. (§6).

Aircraft.—See Canada Law Digest, topic Aircraft.

Gasoline Tax.—See topic Taxation.

Size and Weight Limits, Equipment Required, Lights Required.—Governed by c. M-17.

All-Terrain Vehicles.—Governed by c. A-7.11.

NEGOTIABLE INSTRUMENTS:

See Canada Law Digest, topic Bills and Notes.

NOTARIES PUBLIC:

Governing statute is c. N-9.

Notaries public are officials appointed by Lieutenant-Governor-in-Council, under Great Seal of province. While in good standing with Law Society of N.B., all barristers and attorneys are notaries public. Other persons desirous of being appointed as notaries public, are subject to examination in regard to their qualifications for said office by Minister of Justice and no person may be appointed notary public without certificate from Minister of Justice that he has examined applicant, finds him qualified for office, and that he is of opinion that notary public is needed for public convenience in place where such applicant resides and intends to carry on business.

A notary public has authority to draw and prepare any instrument relating to real estate, to attest all commercial instruments that may be brought before him for public protestation, to do any work or perform any acts ordinarily pertaining to his office, and to demand, receive and have all the rights, profits and advantages, rightfully appertaining and belonging to the said calling of notary public during pleasure, and during residence in this province. Every such notary may administer all oaths, affirmations or declarations required to be administered, sworn, affirmed, made or taken under and by virtue of any act of the New Brunswick Legislature, or of the Parliament of Canada or Great Britain or of the legislature of any province or British colony or by the laws of any foreign country, and to attest the same under his hand and notarial seal.

The authority of a notary extends throughout the province. He is not required to append to his signature any statement as to the date of expiration of his commission.

PARTITION:

Proceedings to compel partition or sale of land or of estate or interest therein may be commenced by notice of application. (R. 67.01). In such proceeding court may decide all questions concerning title to lands, order that lands or any portion thereof be partitioned, or that such lands or portion thereof be sold and direct distribution of proceeds of such sale in accordance with interests and priorities of persons having interest in lands, and direct payment of costs from proceeds of sale of lands as may be appropriate. Court may also direct reference upon such terms including directions to sell, as may be necessary. (R. 67.02).

If party has needlessly commenced proceeding for partition, or has without sufficient reason refused to agree to partition, sale or other disposition of property, court may order party to pay all of costs of proceeding or larger proportion of costs than would normally be allowed against such party. Court may also deprive such party of all or part of costs to which he would otherwise be entitled. (R. 67.06[3]).

PARTNERSHIP:

Governing statutes are cc. P-4 and P-5.

Source of Law.—In 1890 common law principles were codified to a large extent in England by Partnership Act of that year. New Brunswick adopted this act verbatim in 1921 and it is now c. P-4. Any standard English textbook on the subject, Lindley for example, is a good reference book for interpretative purposes.

Scope of Act.—Part I deals with the nature of partnership; Part II to the relations of partners to persons dealing with them.

Registration.—Partners of every firm in business of trading, manufacturing and mining must, within two months of commencing business sign certificate of partnership on prescribed form stating names, occupations and residences of partners, firm name and principal place of business. Certificate must be filed with Registrar, Partnership and Business Names, P. O. Box 6000, Fredericton, N. B. E3B 5H1 and advertised in Royal Gazette. Registration must be renewed each five years. Changes in membership or firm name or partnership dissolution are to be filed on prescribed form within two months of happening. Firm name must not be identical or resemble name of other firm or corporation.

Fee for registration of business name and advertising notice thereof is $110. Renewal fee is $50. Fee for registration of partnership and advertising notice thereof is $110. (§12[1] of Reg. 81-35).

Dissolution.—Subject to an agreement between the partners, a partnership is dissolved: (a) By expiration of term fixed for continuance; (b) by termination of venture or undertaking which is sole purpose of partnership; (c) by any partner giving to the others notice of his intention to dissolve partnership entered into for undefined term. (§33).

A partnership may be dissolved by the death or bankruptcy of any partner. (§34).

A partnership is in every case dissolved by the happening of any event which makes it unlawful for the business of the firm to be carried on or for the members of the firm to carry it on in partnership. (§35).

On application by a partner the court may decree a dissolution of the partnership in certain cases in which the partnership is prevented from performing its proper functions. (§36).

On the dissolution of a partnership or retirement of a partner, any partner may publicly notify the same, and may require the other partner or partners to concur for that purpose in all necessary or proper acts, if any, which cannot be done without his or their concurrence. (§38).

After dissolution of partnership, the rights or obligations of partners to one another continue until business is wound up. (§39).

In settling accounts between partners after a dissolution of partnership if the losses or deficiencies go as far as to affect the individual assets, payment must be made by the partners individually in the proportion in which they were entitled to share profits. (§45).

Limited partnerships consist of general and limited partners, liability of limited partners being limited to amount of capital contributed. Prescribed declaration containing full details must be filed with registrar under Partnerships and Business Names Registration Act and copy of certificate must be published in Royal Gazette. (c. L-9.1).

PERPETUITIES:

The rule which is commonly known as the rule against perpetuities forbids any disposition by which the absolute vesting of property is or may be postponed beyond the period of the life or lives of any number of persons living at the date of the disposition, and the further period of 21 years after the death of the survivor.

Under Property Act (c. P-19), no person may by deed, surrender, will or otherwise settle or dispose of any real or personal property so that rents, issues, profits or produce thereof shall be wholly or partially accumulated for longer than one of following periods: (1) Life of grantor or settlor; (2) twenty-one years from death of grantor, settlor or testator; (3) period of minority of any person living or in ventre sa mere at death of grantor or testator; (4) period of minority of any person who, under instrument directing accumulation, would, for time being, if of full age, be entitled to income, rents or profits directed to be accumulated. No accumulation for purchase of land may be directed for longer than period mentioned in (4) above.

In case of violation of the rule against accumulations, the rents, issues and profits go to the person who would have been entitled thereto if no accumulation had been directed.

The foregoing does not apply to accumulations for payment of debts of the grantor or raising portions for any child, etc.

PERSONAL PROPERTY:

Tenancy by entirety does not exist in either real or personal property law. (c. P-19, §19; c. M-4, §§2-3).

PERSONAL PROPERTY SECURITY:

Effective Apr. 18, 1995 Personal Property Security Act. 1993, c. P-7.1 came into force. It applies to every transaction, that in substance creates security interest, including chattel mortgage, conditional sale, floating charge, pledge, debenture, trust indenture or trust receipt, lease, assignment, consignment or transfer of chattel paper, and, additionally, to assignment of accounts, transfer of chattel paper, consignment, or lease for term of more than one year, notwithstanding that such interests may not secure payment or performance of obligation. (§3). It does not apply to statutory or nonconsensual liens, security agreements governed by Federal statutes such as Bank Act security, creation or transfer of interest or claim in or under any contract of annuity or policy of insurance that is not indemnity or compensation for loss or damage to collateral, creation or transfer of interests in land, assignments for general benefit of creditors pursuant to Federal statute relating to insolvency, creation or transfers of interests in rights to payment under interests in land, sales of accounts or chattel paper as part of sale of business where vendor loses apparent control of business, creation or transfer of interests in present or future compensation for labour or personal services, transfer of interest in earned right to payment under contract where transferee is to perform contract, transfers of accounts to facilitate their collection, creation or transfer of interests in tort damages. (§4). Single conceptual basis for all personal property security agreements is employed.

Conflict of Laws.—Law of jurisdiction where collateral is situated when security interest attaches is applicable law for determining validity, perfection of security interest in such collateral. (§5). For intangibles, property normally used in more than one jurisdiction and instruments, documents of title, money and chattel paper, law of jurisdiction where debtor is located governs. (§7[2]). Debtor is deemed to be located at his place of business, at his chief executive office if he has more than one place of business and otherwise at his place of residence. (§7[1]). For goods brought into New Brunswick, distinction is made between buyer in good faith of goods brought into province and all other persons. Security interest in collateral already perfected under law of place in which collateral situated when security interest attached and before

PERSONAL PROPERTY SECURITY . . . *continued*
being brought into New Brunswick continues perfected in New Brunswick as against buyer in good faith if perfected in New Brunswick prior to buyers acquiring interest in goods and as against all other persons within 60 days after brought into province, or within 15 days after day secured party receives notice that goods have been brought into New Brunswick, or prior to day that perfection ceases under law of prior jurisdiction, whichever is earliest. (§7[3]).

Transitional.—C. P-7.1 causes repeal of Assignment of Book Debts Act, Bills of Sale Act, Conditional Sales Act, Corporation Securities Registration Act, Forest Products Loans Act, and amendments to All-Terrain Vehicle Act, Assignments and Preferences Act, Creditors Relief Act, Employment Standards Act, Evidence Act, Factors and Agents Act, Innkeeper's Act, Insurance Act, Limitation of Actions Act, Marital Property Act, Real Property Tax Act, Registry Act, Sale of Goods Act, Statute of Frauds, and Warehouseman's Lien Act. (§§75-79; 1993, c. 36 and 1994, c. 50).

Registration under repealed or amended Acts is deemed to be registration under c. P-7.1. (§73[5]). Question as to priority between security interests validly created prior to coming into force is determined by prior registration law, but priority between prior security interest and security interest validly created after proclamation shall be determined by c. P-7.1.

Registration is continued for unexpired portion of filing or registration period under prior law except for registrations under Corporation Securities Registration Act and Forest Products Loans Act which expire on Apr. 18, 1998, unless they were renewed under c. P-7.1.

Effectiveness.—Security agreement is effective according to its terms. (§9). However, certain terms are prohibited or may be unenforceable. (§10). Security interest attaches, including floating charge, when value is given, debtor has rights in collateral, and except for enforcing inter party rights, it becomes enforceable against third parties. (§12). Security agreement may secure future advances. (§14). Acceleration clauses are only effective if secured party, in good faith, believes and has commercially reasonable grounds to believe that payment is not going to be made or that collateral is about to be placed in jeopardy. Where debtor reinstates security agreement, operation of any acceleration clause is ineffective. (§16).

Enforceability.—No security interest is enforceable against third party unless collateral is in possession of secured party or debtor has signed security agreement that contains description of collateral by item or kind, statement that security interest is taken in all of debtor's present and after acquired personal property, or statement that security interest is taken in all of debtor's present and after acquired personal property except specified items or kinds of personal property. (§10).

Attachment.—Security interest attaches when value is given, debtor has rights in collateral and, except for purpose of enforcing rights between parties, it becomes enforceable against third parties. Debtor has rights in goods purchased under agreement to sell when contract is made and obtains possession pursuant to lease, hiring agreements or consignment. Debtor has no rights in crops until growing crops, young of animals until conceived, in oil, gas or other minerals until extracted, in timber until cut. (§12).

After-acquired Property.—Security agreement may cover after-acquired property and security interest will attach without specific appropriation by debtor. (§13).

Future Advances.—Security agreement may secure future advances. If future advances are made while security interest is perfected, security interest has same priority with respect to future advances as it has with respect to first advance. Future advances will not take priority over interests of person who causes collateral to be seized under legal process, sheriff who has seized, trustee in bankruptcy or representative of creditors who have caused collateral to be seized under legal process, unless advance made before interests of such persons arise, or before secured party receives notice of their interests. Obligation of secured party to make future advances is not binding on creditor if collateral has been seized, attached, charged or made subject to equitable execution and secured party has knowledge of fact before making advances pursuant to obligation unless parties otherwise agree. (§14).

Perfection.—Security interest is perfected when it has attached and all steps required for perfection required under Act have been completed regardless of order of occurrence. (§19). Three methods of perfection are: possession of collateral by third party or on party's behalf (§24); registration of financing statement in Personal Property Registry (§25); and automatic, although temporary, perfection by way of statutory grace periods (§22).

Act also provides specific rules as to perfection with respect to proceeds of collateral. Security interest in collateral extends to proceeds and is perfected if financing statement filed which covered original collateral contains prescribed description, or if proceeds are of type which fall within description of original collateral, or are cash; then, registration perfects security interest in both collateral and in proceeds. Otherwise, security interest in proceeds perfected for only 15 days after debtor receives possession of them. (§28).

Purchase money security interest in collateral, other than intangibles or inventory, that is perfected within 15 days after debtor or third party at request of debtor obtains possession of collateral, whichever is earlier, or intangible, or its proceeds within 15 days after security interest therein attaches, has priority over any other security interest in same collateral given by same debtor. (§34[1]).

Purchase money security interest in collateral as original collateral has priority over purchase money security interest in same collateral as proceeds if perfected in case of inventory, where debtor or third party as request of debtor, obtains possession, whichever is earlier, and in case of collateral other than inventory, within 15 days after debtor or third party at request of debtor obtains possession, whichever is earlier. (§34[5]).

Purchase money security interest in inventory or its proceeds has priority over any other security in same collateral given by same debtor if purchase money security interest in inventory is perfected at time debtor receives possession of it and purchase money secured party serves notice on secured party who has registered financing statement covering same type of collateral. (§34[2]).

Buyer or lessee of goods sold or leased in ordinary course of business of seller takes free of any perfected or unperfected security interest therein given by or reserved against seller, whether or not purchaser knows of it, unless secured party proves that purchaser also knows that sale or lease constitutes breach of security agreement. (§30[2]).

Act provides special priority rules between secured and unsecured creditors, and with respect to fixtures, negotiable documents of title, money and securities, chattel paper, future advances, leases, crops, accessions and commingled goods. (§§30-39). Most priority competitions will be determined by first to register. (§19).

Registration.—All registrations under c. P-7.1 take place by electronic filing in Personal Property Registry.

Registration of financing statement is effective for length of time indicated in financing statement and may be renewed at any time before expiry by registering financing change statement. (§44[2]).

What was known as "book debt" is referred to in c. P-7.1 as "account"—monetary obligation not evidenced by chattel paper, instrument or security, whether or not earned by performance. (c. P-7.1, §1).

Rights of debtor in collateral may be transferred consensually despite agreement between parties but rights of secured party not to be prejudiced. (§33). Assignee rights subject to contract between assignor and debtor, and debtor may raise any defence or claim against assignee that could be raised against assignor. (§41).

Where secured party assigns his interest or subordinates his interest to another person, financing change statement may be registered. Registration of such statement is mandatory where debtor transfers his interest in collateral or changes his name. (§44).

Search for registrations against name of debtor or against serial number where collateral required by regulation to be described by serial number may be obtained, with results given in printed form. (§48).

Time for Registration.—Financing statement may be registered at any time and may be registered before security agreement is made or before security interest attaches. (§43). It must be registered prior to expiry of any temporary perfection period (usually 15 days) to continue perfection uninterrupted, and with respect to purchase money security interest, within 15 days of debtor obtaining possession of collateral. (§22).

Rights and Remedies Upon Default.—Part 5 contains code setting out rights, remedies, duties and obligations upon both secured party and debtor many of which, to extent that they give rights to debtor or impose obligation upon secured party, cannot be waived. However all such rights and remedies of secured parties are subject to consumer protection legislation. (§§55-64).

PLEADING:

Governing statute is c. J-2 and Rules of Court of Queen's Bench. In action, pleadings consist of statement of claim and statement of defence and may include reply; in counterclaim they consist of counterclaim and defence to counterclaim, and reply; in cross-claim they consist of cross-claim, defence to cross-claim, and reply; in third party claim they consist of third party claim, and third party defence, and may include reply. (R. 27.01).

If reply is not filed within time prescribed pleadings are closed and every allegation of material fact made in previous pleading is deemed to be denied. (R. 27.07).

Pleadings shall be divided into numbered paragraphs and each allegation as far as practicable shall be contained in separate paragraph. (R. 27.02).

Every pleading shall be served on opposite party and upon every other person who is, at time of such service, party to action. Where pleading is originating process and is required to be served on party other than opposite party, personal service is not required. (R. 27.03).

Pleadings are deemed to be closed upon noting of default of defendant, upon service of reply, or when time for service has expired as prescribed by R. 16.07 for statement of claim and R. 20.01 for statement of defence. (R. 27.05).

Originating process (notice of action and statement of claim attached) shall contain names of parties and capacity in which they are made parties to proceeding, as well as principal place of residence of party commencing proceeding. (R. 16.06[3]). Upon receiving process and copy along with filing fee, clerk will assign to process court file number, and enface on original and copy number and date of issue. Original will be returned to plaintiff or applicant, or his solicitor and file copy retained by clerk. (R. 16.07). Notice of action with statement of claim attached shall be served, after being issued, within six months. Where action is commenced by issuing notice of action alone, both notice of action and statement of claim shall be served together within six months of issuing of notice of action. (R. 16.08).

Statement of Claim.—Every pleading shall contain concise statement of material facts on which party pleading relies for his claim or defence, but not evidence by which those facts are to be proved. Party may raise any point of law in his pleading. Conclusions of law may be pleaded provided that material facts supporting such conclusions are pleaded. Party need not plead facts presumed in law to be true, unless specifically denied by opposite party. As well, condition precedent to assertion of claim need not be pleaded unless specifically denied by opposite party.

No objection to pleading shall be taken on ground that only declaratory judgment or order is signed, and court may make binding declarations of right whether or not consequential relief is or could be claimed.

If general damages are claimed no amount shall be stated.

Party may plead any fact that has occurred since commencement of action and if fact occurs after filing and serving his pleading, he may apply to court for leave to file and serve amended pleading even if fact alleged may give rise to new claim or defence. Party whose cause of action or defence is founded upon Act, shall plead specific sections on which that party relies. (R. 27.06).

Party shall deny every allegation of fact in pleading of opposite party which is disputed and all other allegations of fact in pleading of opposite party shall be deemed to be admitted unless party pleading alleges that he has no knowledge thereof. However, mere denial of version of facts pleaded by opposite party is not sufficient, but party in defence or reply shall plead his own version of facts as well as every matter upon which it is intended to rely to defeat claim or defence of opposite party, and which if not specifically pleaded might take opposite party by surprise or raise new issue.

See note at head of Digest as to 1996 legislation covered.

See Topical Index in front part of this volume.

PLEADING . . . *continued*

Where contract or agreement is alleged in pleading, bare denial of same by opposite party shall be construed only as denial of making of contract or agreement alleged, or of facts from which same may be implied by law. Denial of legality or validity of contract or agreement shall be specifically pleaded.

In action for damages amount shall be deemed to be in issue unless specifically admitted. (R. 27.07).

Reply and Defence to Counterclaim.—Reply need not be made, but if not filed and served within time prescribed there shall be implied joinder of issue. In counterclaim pleadings consist of counterclaim and defence to counterclaim. (R. 28.01).

Subsequent Pleadings.—Pleadings subsequent to reply shall not be filed and served except with consent in writing of opposite party, or by leave of court. (R. 27.01).

Demurrer.—No demurrer is allowed. Plaintiff or defendant however may at any time before action is set down for trial apply to court for determination prior to trial of any question of law raised by pleading where determination of that question may dispose of action, shorten trial or result in substantial saving of costs, or to strike out pleading which does not disclose reasonable cause of action or defence, or for judgment on admission of fact in pleadings, in examination of adverse party, or answer to request to admit facts. (R. 23.01).

Particulars for purpose of pleading, may be ordered when pleading in question is so vague or ambiguous that opposite party cannot reasonably be required to frame responsive pleading thereto. Where party who has been served with demand for better particulars fails to file such, court may order that particulars be filed and served within specified time. (R. 27.08).

Proof of Claims.—A solicitor should be furnished with the Christian name and surname of the proposed plaintiff and defendant. If the claim is contested it must be proved in the usual way, or by deposition when the witnesses reside abroad.

See also topics Actions; Appeal and Error; Attachment; Practice; Process.

PLEDGES:

Common law rules prevail, except as to pawnbrokers who are regulated by c. M-22.

PRACTICE:

Governing statute is c. J-2 and Rules of Court of Queen's Bench.

Discovery.—Every document which relates to matter in issue in action and which is or has been in possession, custody or control of party or which party believes to be in possession, custody or control of some person not party, shall be disclosed to other party if that other party serves notice requiring affidavit of documents, whether or not privilege is claimed in respect of that document. (R. 31.02; 31.03).

Party to action may examine for discovery, once without leave, any other party who is adverse in interest. (R. 32.02). Examination of plaintiff for discovery may only be initiated after examining party has filed and served statement of defence and if requested has filed affidavit of documents and served it on every other party. Examination of defendant for discovery may be initiated only after defendant has filed and served statement of defence and has filed affidavit of documents and served it on every other party, if requested; or if defendant has been noted in default. (R. 32.03).

Examination for discovery may take form of oral examination or at option of examining party examination by written questions and answers, but not to both forms of examination without consent of opposite party or by leave of court. (R. 32.04).

Court may grant leave to examine for discovery any person who has or is likely to have information relevant to material issue in action where such person was at relevant time employee, agent, partner or spouse of party or was officer, director or auditor of corporate party or is or was at relevant time officer, director or employee of corporation which was at such time subsidiary or affiliate of corporate party, or is potential witness including expert retained by party in preparation for contemplated or pending litigation, unless that party undertakes that he will not call expert as witness at trial, or is person under disability. (R. 32.10).

Direct Actions Against Insurer.—See topic Insurance, subhead Direct Actions Against Insurer.

Request for Admission of Facts.—Either party may issue request. Party on whom Request to Admit Facts is served shall be deemed to admit such facts unless he serves Notice of Refusal within ten days. Court shall take into account refusal in exercising its discretion as to costs.

Small Claims.—See topic Courts.

See also topics Actions; Appeal and Error; Attachment; Depositions; Executions; Garnishment; Injunctions; Judgments; Pleading; and Process.

PRINCIPAL AND AGENT:

Common law rules prevail.

Attorneys in fact are appointed by power of attorney executed by any person able in his own right to do the act for which the appointment is made. Trustees and others in a fiduciary capacity cannot delegate their authority or duties except by express power in their appointment, etc. A power of attorney should be under seal and witnessed; if it relates to any interest in land it should be acknowledged in the same manner as a deed and registered in the same manner. Powers of attorney are revoked by the death, unsoundness of mind or bankruptcy of donor of power except in cases where instrument creating it declares it to be irrevocable and power is given for valuable consideration in which cases, it is irrevocable and all acts under power done by donee at any time are valid.

There is no particular form but the purposes for which it is given and its duration should be set out clearly and the donee should be clearly designated.

Collection Agencies governed by c. C-8.—Must be licensed and notice of license published in The Rōyal Gazette. Doing such business without license subjects to penalty of not less than $50 nor more than $200. Employing unlicensed collection agency subjects to penalty of not less than $10 nor more than $100. Foregoing does not apply to members of bar who carry on collection agencies in their own names, to insurance agents in respect of collection of premiums, nor to any chartered bank or its official servants or agents in respect of business of bank. (c. C-8).

PROCESS:

Originating process shall be served personally unless provided otherwise by Act or Rules of Court, but need not be served on party who has filed and served defence. (R. 18.01). Personal service is effected by service on individual, other than person under disability, by leaving copy of document with him; or if municipality by leaving copy of document with mayor, deputy-mayor, clerk, assistant clerk, or with any solicitor for municipality; or on any other corporation by leaving copy of document with officer, director or agent of corporation or manager who appears to be in control of any office or other place where corporation carries on business in New Brunswick; or service may be effected on board or tribunal by leaving copy of document with secretary or officer or member. If person is out of New Brunswick but carries on business in New Brunswick, service may be effected by leaving copy of document with any person in province appointed as agent for service under Business Corporations Act or carrying on business for party in question in New Brunswick.

Crown in right of Province of New Brunswick is served in accordance with Proceedings Against the Crown Act; and Crown in right of Canada is served in accordance with Crown Liability Act. Attorney General may be served by leaving with him copy of document, or with lawyer employed in Department of Attorney General at Fredericton, N.B.

Minor is served by leaving copy of document with his parent, guardian or other adult with whom or in whose care he resides; if minor is of age of 16 years or over, he may be served personally. (R. 18.02).

Who May Serve.—Service may be effected by any person, and proven by affidavit of that person. Service by sheriff or deputy may be proven by certificate of service. In other cases where solicitor accepts service, admission or acceptance of service is sufficient proof thereof and need not be verified by affidavit. (R. 18.10).

Nonresident Motorists.—See topic Motor Vehicles, subhead Actions Against Nonresidents.

PROOF OF CLAIMS:

See topics Executors and Administrators; Pleading.

RAILROADS: See topic Carriers.

REAL PROPERTY:

Governing statute is c. P-19. Estates tail are abolished and every estate which would hitherto have been adjudged a fee tail is adjudged a fee simple and if no valid remainder is limited thereon is a fee simple absolute and may be conveyed or devised by the tenant in tail or otherwise descends to his heirs as a fee simple. Otherwise all estates recognized at common law are recognized in New Brunswick. Every estate created, granted or devised to two or more persons in their own right is a tenancy in common unless expressly declared to be a joint tenancy, but every estate vested in trustees or executors as such is held by them in joint tenancy.

Rule In Shelley's Case is recognized.

Expropriation.—Governing statute is c. E-14. Interest in land may be taken for public or industrial purposes after procedures set out in Act have been fulfilled.

Condominiums.—Governed by c. C-16. Where land mentioned in description is affected by subdivision bylaw or regulation under c. C-12, description shall not be approved unless such land is certified by development officer appointed under c. C-12 as meeting requirements of c. C-12, §§47(3) and 77(8)(c).

Community Planning.—Governed by c. C-12. Province is divided into seven planning areas to which development officers are designated to administer and control subdividing of real property. Act and regulations govern only where municipal corporate body has not been established. Bylaws of such body govern in such areas.

Power of Attorney.—Governed by P-19 authority conferred upon donee by Power of Attorney is not terminated where donor suffers from mental incompetence after creation of Power of Attorney if Power of Attorney contains provision that expressly allows it to be exercised during such incompetence and is signed by donor, or signed in name of donor by another person in presence and at direction of donor and is witnessed by adult person other than donee (see §§58.1-58.7).

Air Space.—Governed by c. A-7.01. Air space constitutes land and may be dealt with as land.

See also topics Curtesy, Deeds, Dower, Homesteads, Husband and Wife, Landlord and Tenant, Mortgages of Real Property, Partition.

RECEIVERS:

Appointed by court when just and convenient. Court appointed receiver may be required to give security, and must give security duly to account for what he will receive. (R. 41). Some security instruments such as debentures, mortgages, trust deeds, etc., may provide for private appointment of receiver. Receiver appointed for business corporation must give notice of such appointment to Director of Corporations and make periodic reports to such Director, and publish notice in The Royal Gazette. Receiver must also comply with Part XI of Bankruptcy and Insolvency Act. See Canada Law Digest, topic Bankruptcy.

RECORDS:

Governing statute is c. R-6.

All deeds or other documents affecting real estate must be registered at length in office of registrar of deeds for county in which lands lie. Deeds and other documents affecting lands take priority in order in which they are registered.

RECORDS . . . *continued*

All instruments must have 1½ inch margin on top and left side and if both sides of paper are used, similar margin is required on right side of reverse side. Paper must be white measuring 8½ by 14 inches.

Torrens System.—See topic Torrens Act.

Land Titles.—See topic Torrens Act.

Transfer of Decedent's Title.—As all real property of a decedent, testate or intestate, vests in his executor or administrator (see topic Executors and Administrators), transfer of title to devisees or heirs at law ordinarily can be effected only by deed of personal representative, which should be recorded like any other deed. But special provision is made for cases where representative fails to execute such deed when it becomes his duty so to do.

Vital Statistics.—Births, deaths and marriages must be reported to sub-deputy registrar of vital statistics for area in which event occurred. Records therof are kept in office of Registrar General. (Governing statute: Vital Statistics Act, c. V-3).

Fees: $5 for search of records and $15 for each copy. Marriage licence fee $10.

REDEMPTION:

See topics Liens; Mortgages of Real Property; Taxation.

REPLEVIN:

Interim order for recovery of personal property may be obtained on motion by plaintiff supported by affidavit containing description and value of property, statement that plaintiff is owner or lawfully entitled to possession of property, statement that property was unlawfully taken from possession of plaintiff or is unlawfully detained therefrom, and facts of circumstances giving rise to unlawful taking or detention. Unless ordered otherwise notice of motion shall be served on defendant. (R. 44.01).

Court may order security from either plaintiff or defendant, order that property be placed in hands of plaintiff, or remain with defendant, or make such other order as may be just. (R. 44.03).

Where security is required to be paid, condition of security shall be that party providing it will return property to opposite party without delay and pay such damages incurred by opposite party, if ordered to do so by court. (R. 44.04).

REPORTS:

Those recording Canadian cases include: Canada Supreme Court Reports, Canada Exchequer Court Reports, Canada Federal Court Reports, Canadian Criminal Cases, Canadian Railway Cases, Dominion Law Reports, Canadian Bankruptcy Reports, National Reporter, Labour Arbitration Cases, Insurance Law Reporter, Business Law Reports, Dominion Report Service, Reports on Family Law, Land Compensation Reports and in New Brunswick Maritime Province Reports (cited "M.P.R.") and New Brunswick Reports (cited "N.B.R.").

RESIDENTIAL TENANCIES:

See topic Landlord and Tenant, subhead Residential Tenancies.

RESTRAINT OF TRADE:

See topic Monopolies and Restraint of Trade.

SALES:

Governing statute is Sale of Goods Act, c. S-1.

Where a document of title to goods has been lawfully transferred to a person as the buyer or owner of the goods and that person transfers the document to another person who takes it in good faith and for valuable consideration, the latter transfer has the same effect as a transfer of a bill of lading for defeating any vendor's lien or right of stoppage in transitu. (§44).

Bills of Sale.—See topic Personal Property Security.

Conditional Sales.—See topic Personal Property Security.

Bulk Sales.—See topic Bulk Sales.

Product Liability.—Common law of negligence applies. Privity not required if manufacturer negligent and consumer suffers damage due to this negligence. See also topic Consumer Protection, subhead Consumer Product Warranty and Liability Act.

Retail Credit Sales.—See topic Consumer Protection.

Consumer Protection Legislation.—See topic Consumer Protection.

SALES TAX: See topic Taxation.

SEALS:

Common law rules apply.

All orders, writs and decrees issuing from any court must have the official seal of such court affixed thereto. All certified copies of documents issued by officials having an official seal must have such seal affixed thereto. Letters L. S. may be legally substituted on copies only of original document.

Deed must have fixed or impressed upon it seal which has been expressly or impliedly acknowledged by party bound by deed to be his. No particular kind of seal need be used, but it is better that there be either impression or attachment of separate paper or substance.

Corporate Seals.—Power of attorney of a corporation must be under common seal of corporation if it empowers attorney to execute deeds on its behalf. Corporate seal is required for any documents which if executed by an individual would require a seal. Instrument signed by director, officer or agent of corporation is not invalid merely because seal is not affixed.

Effect of Seal.—Undertaking under seal may be enforced even though it is not supported by other consideration.

SECURITIES:

Sale of securities is regulated by c. S-6.

Registration.—No person may: (a) Trade in any security unless he is registered as a broker, or salesman or sub-agent of a registered broker; or (b) act as an official of or on behalf of any partnership or company in connection with any trade in any security by the partnership or company, unless he, or the partnership or company is registered as a broker; or (c) act as a salesman in connection with any trade in any security by a partnership or company, unless he is registered as a salesman of a partnership or company which is registered as a broker. All such registrations must have been made in accordance with the provisions of the Act and Board of Commissioners of Public Utilities may impose such conditions as it deems necessary on any such registration. Any person who sells securities in the province otherwise than as a full-time employee of a registered broker, or who sells securities and at the same time is engaged in some other trade, business, employment, calling, profession or occupation, must be registered as a broker. (§6[1]). Every application for registration must be made in writing on forms provided by Registrar, who is person holding office of Secretary of Board of Commissioners of Public Utilities. Every applicant for registration as broker must, before registration, deliver to Registrar bond of between $1,000 and $5,000 in such form and on such conditions as regulations may prescribe. Board of Commissioners of Public Utilities may examine any person, company, property or thing whatsoever at any time in order to ascertain whether any fraudulent act or any offence against Act has been, is being, or is about to be committed.

Prohibition.—No person registered under the provisions of the Act may sell, offer to sell or directly or indirectly attempt to sell, in the province, any security, other than the securities excepted by §7, or securities approved by Board, or securities listed at time of sale on stock exchange approved by Board, without first obtaining from Board certificate authorizing sale.

Conditions.—Any person desiring to sell securities, before offering or attempting to sell same, must pay to Board such fee as may be prescribed by regulations, and file with Board: (a) Statement showing in full detail plan on which company whose securities it is desired to sell proposes to transact business; (b) copies of all contracts which company proposes to make with its subscribers and of securities it proposes to sell; (c) statement showing name and location of company; (d) itemized account of financial condition, assets and liabilities of company; (e) such other information as Board may require; (f) in case of copartnership or unincorporated association, copy of articles of copartnership or association, and all other papers pertaining to its organization; (g) in case of a company not organized under laws of this province, a copy of laws of state, province, country, territory or government under which it exists or is incorporated, and a copy of its charter, memorandum of association, articles of association, constitution and by-laws, and all other papers pertaining to its organization.

Offenses.—It is unlawful to call at or telephone any residence for purpose of offering securities, other than those mentioned in Act, to public or any member of public for subscription.

No person may print, publish or advertise in a newspaper, magazine, or other periodical printed and published in this province, or otherwise, in this province, issue, put forth or distribute an advertisement, circular letter or other document containing an offer to sell or solicitation to purchase such securities, or broadcast any advertising matter from any public or private radio or television broadcasting station, unless the person offering such securities for sale has been registered as a broker or registered salesman of a registered broker.

The Board may cause to be made a detailed examination of the affairs of any company whose shares it is proposed to sell, such examination to be at the expense of the company or person desiring to sell such securities.

Any person who violates any provision of the Act or regulations or who does any fraudulent act not punishable under the provisions of the Criminal Code of Canada, is liable to a penalty of not more than $1,000 for a first offense or $2,000 for a second or subsequent offense.

SEQUESTRATION:

Judgments or orders generally speaking may be enforced by enforcement orders as follows: For payment of money, by order of seizure and sale; for recovery of possession of land, by order for possession of land; for delivery of personal property, by order for delivery of personal property; and for requiring of doing or abstaining from doing of any act, by contempt order. (R. 61.02).

SERVICE: See topic Process.

STATUTE OF FRAUDS:

See topic Frauds, Statute of.

STATUTES:

Revised Statutes of New Brunswick, 1973, Private Statutes, and annual amendments and new legislation.

Uniform Acts.—No Uniform Acts are in force in Province.

STAY OF EXECUTION:

See topics Appeal and Error; Executions.

SUBMISSION OF CONTROVERSY:

Where parties to proceeding concur in stating, in form of stated case, one or more questions of law for opinion of court, party may apply to court for leave to set stated case down for hearing. This will be done only where court is satisfied that hearing will dispose of proceeding or facilitate determination of matters in issue. (R. 24.01).

SUPPLEMENTARY PROCEEDINGS:

See topic Executions.

See note at head of Digest as to 1996 legislation covered.

See Topical Index in front part of this volume.

SURETY AND GUARANTY COMPANIES:

License may be granted by Superintendent of Insurance to carry on class of insurance described as guarantee insurance. (c. I-12, §23[1]).

Foreign Companies—No prohibition. Must be licensed in same manner as domestic insurance company.

TAXATION:

Real Property Taxable.—Minister of Finance administers assessment of real property; no taxation levied on personal property; Minister of Finance collects tax. (c. R-2).

Exemptions.—Real property of: (1) Churches used only for church purposes or for residence for priest, etc.; (2) cemetery companies not operated for profit; (3) literary and historical societies; (4) institutions, etc. formed for advancement of science or art; and (5) agricultural societies or agricultural fair associations used solely for exhibition purposes. No exemptions for members of Armed Forces. (c. A-14).

Assessment.—Real property is assessed at real and true value except: (1) Freehold timberlands and farm woodlots; (2) property owned and occupied by charitable organization or nonprofit organization; and (3) property occupied by agricultural fair association, racing association or other group and that is used as horse racetrack. Real property includes land and buildings and machinery, etc. providing services to building; also includes trailers used as mobile homes and bunkhouses. Not included as real property are, inter alia: (1) Growing crops; (2) mines below surface of ground; (3) quarries, minerals, gas, etc.; (4) public parks; and (5) railway rights of way.

Business assessment governed by §§5-7, repealed, 1982, c. 7, §§3, 4.

Review of Assessment.—Any person who receives assessment and tax notice may refer any assessment to Executive Director of Assessment within 60 days after mailing of assessment and tax notice. Where assessment has been referred to Director, person making reference may appeal to Regional Assessment Review Board. (§§25-38 of c. A-14).

Rates of Tax.—Each year there shall be tax at rate of $1.50 on each $100 valuation of all real property, used as residence not occupied by owner. Farm woodlots are assessed at value that will realize 80¢ per hectare per year based on combined provincial and municipal rates. Annual rate for other real property is $2.25 on each $100 valuation. Municipal rate fixed by each municipality is payable on all real property. See also §5(4) of c. R-2; c. R-10.

Payment.—Real estate and local service taxes are payable to Minister of Finance and are due on date to be fixed by regulation. If taxes or penalties are unpaid on date to be fixed by regulation penalty is imposed of 1½% per month. Taxes may be prepaid or paid in instalments.

Lien.—Due and unpaid taxes constitute lien on all real property with priority over every claim, lien, privilege or encumbrance of any person and does not require registration or filing to preserve it. There is no lien on personal property for real estate taxes. (§11[1]).

Sale.—Real property may be sold by Department of Municipal Affairs after notice and after Jan. 1 of second year following year in which taxes were imposed. Time, place and terms of sale established by regulation.

Redemption.—Any person may redeem real property sold at tax sale within one year of such sale by paying: (1) 115% of sale price; (2) taxes and penalties remaining unpaid; (3) sums paid by purchaser at tax sale for insurance on property, repairs, taxes and necessary services less any rents received by such purchaser.

Income Tax.—Governing statute is c. I-2. Tax imposed by Province and collected by Federal Government. No municipal income tax. No special provisions for members of Armed Forces while residing in Province. While residing outside Canada, see Canada Law Digest, topic Taxation, subhead Income Tax.

Corporation Taxes.—Tax imposed by Province and collected by Federal Government. See also Canada Law Digest, topic Taxation, subhead Income Tax.

Land Transfer Tax.—Rate is ¼ of 1% of greater of actual consideration or assessed valuation and is payable at time of registration of deed.

Mining Income Tax.—Governing statute is c. M-14.1. See also Metallic Minerals Tax Act. (c. M-11.01). Tax payable is equal to 2% of net revenue after two years of operation and 16% of net profits in excess of $100,000 less credit equal to 25% of eligible exploration expenses and process research expenditures. (§2.1).

Premium Tax.—Every insurance company shall pay to Minister of Finance for provincial purposes tax equal to: (a) 2% of gross premiums that become payable, under contracts of accident, life, and sickness insurance; and (b) 3% of gross premiums that become payable, under any other contract of insurance. No tax payable on premiums received in respect of contracts of marine insurance and contracts providing medical, dental or hospitalization benefits entered into by nonprofit company. (c. P-15).

Inheritance Tax.—None exigible if death occurred after Dec. 31, 1973.

Gift Tax.—None exigible if gift made after Dec. 31, 1973.

Gasoline Tax.—Governing statute c. G-3. Rebates to person validly registered as farmer, fisherman or wood producer under Social Services and Education Tax Act, manufacturers for certain consumption in connection with their callings and certain other commercial users of fuel.

Tobacco tax is imposed by Province at retail sales in respect of consumption of tobacco pursuant to Tobacco Tax Act, c. T-7.

Sales Tax.—Governing statute is c. S-10. Provincial tax of 11% of purchase price of goods purchased plus Goods and Services Tax, is imposed. There are many exemptions such as for food, farm implements, etc. "Goods" includes chattels personal other than things in action and, except where used in §11, includes accommodation, telecommunication service, computer software, dry-cleaning and laundry service. For Federal tax see Canada Law Digest.

Stamp Tax.—No provincial stamp tax imposed on stock transfers or other documents.

Social Security or Unemployment Compensation Tax.—None imposed by Province. See Canada Law Digest.

Penalties.—

Criminal.—See Canada Law Digest.

Failure to Pay Taxes.—Income tax: see Canada Law Digest. Sales taxes: Province has lien upon goods until paid and has lien upon assets used in business for taxes collected and not remitted. Real property taxes: Province may advertise and sell real property after due notice.

Failure to Pay Assessment.—See topic Labour Relations, subhead Workers' Compensation Act.

TORRENS ACT:

Not adopted. Legislation enacted and proclaimed only for Albert County on pilot project basis establishing land titles system to provide for registration of title to land and for guaranteed land title. (1981, c. L-1.1).

TRADEMARKS AND TRADENAMES:

See Canada Law Digest, topic Trademarks and Designs.

Tradenames.—Every person, who is not associated in partnership with any other person but who uses his own name with the addition of "and company" or some other word or phrase indicating a plurality of members, must file a certificate of such with registrar under Partnership Business Names Registration Act. (c. P-5, §9[1]).

As to registration of partnership name, see topic Partnership.

Fees.—Registration fee is $50 and publication fee is $10. See topic Partnership, subhead Registration.

TRUST DEEDS:

See topic Mortgages of Real Property.

TRUSTEE PROCESS: See topic Garnishment.

TRUSTS:

Common law rules govern subject to provisions of Trustees Act. (c. T-15).

Every declaration or creation of any trust in lands must be in writing signed by the party entitled to create the trust or by his last will, except in case of trusts arising by implication or construction of law.

A trustee cannot make a profit out of the trust estate or take advantage of his position for his own pecuniary profit.

Judge may allow remuneration and additional compensation in accordance with §38 of c. T-15 for continued administration of trust.

Investments.—No prohibited investments except that they must be those of a man of prudence, discretion and intelligence.

UNCONSCIONABLE TRANSACTIONS RELIEF ACT:

See topic Consumer Protection.

USURY:

See Canada Law Digest, topic Interest.

VENUE:

Trial of action shall take place in judicial district where proceeding was commenced. However party may apply to court at any time to change place of trial and if so shall show that it would be more convenient to have action tried at place proposed, or that in interests of justice action ought to be tried at that place. (R. 45.02).

VITAL STATISTICS: See topic Records.

WAREHOUSEMEN:

Governing statute is c. W-4.

Every warehouseman has a lien on goods deposited with him for storage for the amount of his charges for storage and preservation of the goods and for money advanced, interest, transportation, labor, weighing, cooperage and other expenses in connection with such goods, which lien may be enforced by sale at public auction after written notice to the debtor, owner and to any person with security interest who has registered financing statement in Personal Property Registry.

Warehouse Receipts.—Governing statute is c. W-3. Banks may acquire and hold warehouse receipt as collateral security for payment of debt incurred in its favor, or as security for any liability incurred by it for any person, in course of its banking business and when so acquired it vests in bank all right and title of previous holder to such warehouse receipt and goods covered thereby or, if warehouse receipt is made directly in favor of bank, all right and title to goods mentioned therein of person from whom bank received such goods. It can only be taken by bank as security for liability contracted at time of acquisition of warehouse receipt or upon written promise to give bank such warehouse receipt, made when liability was incurred. Bank cannot purchase or discount warehouse receipt but can only take it as collateral security. If goods covered by warehouse receipt held by bank are manufactured while so covered products of such manufacturer are property of bank. Bank has claim for amount of its advances secured by warehouse receipt prior to that of unpaid vendor of goods covered by warehouse receipt. There is penalty of two years imprisonment for wilfully making false statement in warehouse receipt given to bank. (R.S.C. 1985, c. B-1, §§186-189).

By c. W-3, "warehouse receipt" means acknowledgment in writing by warehouseman of receipt for storage of goods not his own. Receipt must contain following particulars: (a) location of warehouse or other place where goods are stored; (b) name of person by whom or on whose behalf goods are deposited; (c) date of issue of receipt; (d) statement either: (i) that goods received will be delivered to holder thereof, or (ii) that goods will be delivered to bearer or to order of named person; (e) rate of storage

See note at head of Digest as to 1996 legislation covered.

See Topical Index in front part of this volume.

WAREHOUSEMEN . . . *continued*

charges; (f) description of goods or of packages containing them; (g) signature of warehouseman or his authorized agent; and (h) statement of amount of any advance made and of any liability incurred for which warehouseman claims lien. Where warehouseman omits from negotiable receipt any of above particulars he is liable for damages caused by omission, but no receipt may, by reason of omission, be deemed not to be warehouse receipt. Receipt, when delivered to owner or bailor of goods or mailed to him at his address last known to warehouseman, constitutes contract between owner or bailor and warehouseman; provided that owner or bailor may within 20 days after such delivery or mailing notify warehouseman in writing that he does not accept such contract and thereupon he must remove goods deposited subject to warehouseman's lien for charges and if such notice is not given said warehouse receipt so delivered or mailed constitutes contract. Words in negotiable receipt limiting its negotiability are void. New statute is long and comprehensive in its terms.

WILLS:

Governing statute is c. W-9.

Any competent person of age of 19 years or over may make valid will. Infant cannot make valid will unless he or she is married, is member of active Armed Forces or is seaman. Will may be amended by one or more codicils which, upon death, together with will constitute one instrument.

Execution.—A will must be in writing and signed at the end by the testator or by some one in his presence and by his direction; such signature must be made or acknowledged by the testator in the presence of two or more witnesses present at the same time and who must subscribe their names as witnesses in the presence of the testator and of each other. No particular form of attestation is necessary nor must the will be published to be valid. Alternatively, a testator may make a valid will wholly in his own handwriting and signed by him without witnesses.

An executor is a competent witness, but any devise or legacy to a witness or to the husband or wife of a witness is void, although the execution of the will itself is good.

There is no restriction on gifts.

Nuncupative Wills.—A soldier in actual military service or a marine or seaman at sea may sign his will without witnesses. (§5[1]).

Revocation.—Every will except one in which there is declaration that will is made in contemplation of marriage or one made in exercise of a power of appointment, when estate thereby appointed would not, in default of such appointment, pass to testator's heirs, next of kin or representatives, is revoked by subsequent marriage of testator. Will may be revoked by a writing declaring an intention to revoke same or by testator or some one by his direction and in his presence burning, tearing or otherwise destroying same with intention of revoking it or by another valid will.

Probate proceedings are had in the probate court of Province in venue in which decedent was inhabitant at time of his death. Probate may be opposed by caveat and, after probate, will may be contested by proceedings in probate court, usually called "proof of will in solemn form." See also topic Executors and Administrators.

Self-Proved Wills.—No statutory provision.

Revival can only be brought about by valid will or codicil that shows an intention to give effect to will or part that was revoked. (§19).

Testamentary Gifts to Subscribing Witnesses.—Such gift is void if will is witnessed by beneficiary or spouse of beneficiary.

Lapse will not occur if a person is devised real property in estate tail and dies before or at time of testator's death and leaves issue who would have inherited under entail if that estate existed. If child or other issue, brother or sister of testator is devised or bequeathed interest in real or personal property and dies before testator's death leaving issue surviving testator, no lapse occurs. (§31, c. W-9).

Children, whether living when will is executed or born thereafter, may be disinherited by mere disposition of testator's property to others, without any other indication of intent to disinherit. See subhead Family Support, infra.

Foreign Executed Wills.—In respect of movables, will made out of New Brunswick is valid and admissible to probate if made in accord with law of place where testator domiciled at death, or law in force at time will made in place where will made, or testator's domicile of origin. Change of domicile after will made does not invalidate it. In respect of immovables, law of place where land situate governs formalities of making will.

Foreign Probated Wills.—Where probate has been granted by court of competent jurisdiction in U.K., or in any province or territory of Canada or in any other British possession or any State or Territory of U.S. such probate may be resealed by a probate court in Province. Where probate has been granted elsewhere by a court of competent jurisdiction, ancillary letters probate may be applied for in probate court in venue where New Brunswick assets situated.

Family Support.—Testators Family Maintenance Act (c. T-4) provides that a testator's wife, husband or child may apply to judge of Court of Queen's Bench of New Brunswick for order that such provisions as he deems adequate be made out of estate of testator for proper maintenance and support of applicant or any other dependent of testator, where it is shown that testator did not make adequate provision for his dependents in his will, or, where testator dies intestate as to part of his estate, where operation of Devolution of Estates Act (c. D-9) would not properly provide for dependents. Judge may make order suspending in whole or in part administration of testator's estate. See also topic Husband and Wife, subhead Marital Property Act.

Simultaneous Death.—See topic Death, subhead Survivorship.

Unclaimed Legacies.—Application may be made to Court of Queen's Bench, Trial Division under §90(1) of c. P-17.1 for order permitting executor or trustee to pay money into court in satisfaction of unclaimed legacy.

Marital Property.—(c. M-1.1). Permits surviving spouse to apply within 60 days of death of spouse to court for equal division of marital property.

Living Will.—No legislation.

WITNESSES:

Governing statutes are R.S.C. c. E-10, and R.S.N.B., c. E-11.

Parties to actions, husbands and wives of parties, and persons interested in event of an action are competent witnesses.

Husband and wife are competent for or against each other on any issue in any action in court of divorce and matrimonial causes. In criminal cases, husband and wife are competent for or against each other, except as to confidential communications, but cannot be compelled, to testify.

Any witness may be compelled to answer questions designed to disclose his indebtedness, but may not be compelled to admit adultery.

Person charged with crime is competent, but cannot be compelled, to testify.

See also topic Depositions.

WORKERS' COMPENSATION LAW:

See topic Labour Relations.

See note at head of Digest as to 1996 legislation covered.

See Topical Index in front part of this volume.

NEWFOUNDLAND LAW DIGEST REVISER

Lewis, Day, Dawe & Burke
Suite 600, TD Place
140 Water Street
St. John's, Newfoundland A1C 6H6
Telephone: 709-753-2545
Fax: 709-753-2266
Email: dcdqc@cycor.ca

Reviser Profile

History: Lewis, Day, Dawe & Burke was founded in 1968 by P. Derek Lewis Q.C., a private practitioner active since 1947 in the Law Society of Newfoundland and in the Province's public life. David C. Day Q.C. since 1968, Jean V. Dawe since 1985; and Sandra M. Burke since 1989. The firm has been counsel in many significant civil, constitutional, criminal and family law cases in the Province's Supreme Court and from that Court to the Supreme Court of Canada.

Areas of Emphasis and Growth: Carrying on a general practice in most areas of the law, firm members have particular competence in the following areas of practice: aviation, construction and constitutional, corporate and commercial, criminal, estates and trusts, family, insurance, personal injury, and real estate (including litigation).

Client Base: The firm has a broad client base among private citizens and small businesses throughout the Province. In addition, the firm represents British, Canadian and United States insurers, Canadian trust companies, Canadian branches of an international church, a Canadian church, and several charitable organizations, and residents of Hong Kong, India and the United States.

Firm Activities: All firm lawyers hold membership in the Law Society of Newfoundland and Canadian Bar Association. Several lawyers are members of Canadian, United States and international societies for criminal, family and trial lawyers.

One or another member serves on boards of directors of Canadian corporations and Canadian Research Institute For Law And The Family; national selection boards for awards and scholarships acknowledging legal scholarship and law journalism; editorial boards for Canadian Bar Review; for Thomson Professional Publishing Canada; publications including Reports Of Family Law, Adoption Law and Practice in Canada, Canadian Child Custody Law and Practice, Child Protection Law In Canada, Newfoundland Family Law Statutes and Matrimonial Property Law In Canada; Canadian Family Law and Practice; Consolidated Statutes, and for the Federated Press (Montreal) Litigation Lawyer journals; administrative councils for child protection, family planning, substance addiction treatment, and youth organizations; teaching faculties of National Judicial Institute, Federation of Law Societies of Canada for national criminal and family law programmes, Canadian Police College (Ottawa), The Canadian Institute (Toronto), the School of Social Work and Faculty of Medicine as well as Continuing Studies programmes, at Memorial University of Newfoundland, and the Bar Admission Course and Continuing Legal Education programmes of Law Society of Newfoundland.

David C. Day, Q.C. is author or co-author of books and papers, and a lecturer, on legal and professional responsibility; criminal law; family law; legislation; forensic medicine; social work; advocacy, and legal history.

Significant Distinctions: The firm's senior partner P. Derek Lewis, Q.C. has been a member of the Senate Of Canada since 1978. Mr. Day has served as research assistant to a national water rights study (1967 to 1973), a provincial family law study (1967 to 1973), was counsel to the public inquiry into Mount Cashel Boy's Home and Training School, St. John's, Newfoundland and related matters (1989 to 1991), and, while continuing to practise, will occupy the Milvain Chair in Advocacy at University of Calgary, Alberta, in 1997.

NEWFOUNDLAND LAW DIGEST

(The following is a list of all Topics, including cross-references, covered in this Digest.)

NEWFOUNDLAND LAW DIGEST

Revised for 1997 edition by

LEWIS, DAY, DAWE & BURKE of St. John's, Newfoundland

(Except where otherwise stated references to "court" are to the Supreme Court Of Newfoundland, Trial Division; references, such as "A-3", are to chapters of Revised Statutes Of Newfoundland, 1990 [in force 01 June 1992] as amended; references such as to CNR 750/96 are to consolidated Newfoundland Regulations, publication of which began in 1996; references such as to 222/93 are to Regulations not yet consolidated; and references to "Rule" are to Rules of the Supreme Court [*of Newfoundland*] *1986.)*

ABSENTEES:

Nonresidents are under no disability with regard to holding of real property (by statute [C-11] usually termed "chattels real") or personal property.

Nonresident plaintiff, if (s)he holds no assets within Province or in other circumstances can be required to give security for costs. (Rule 21).

ACCORD AND SATISFACTION:

Common law governs.

ACKNOWLEDGMENT:

(R-10).

Subject to §17, instrument shall, before registration, be proved either (a) by acknowledgment, under oath, by instrument-executing parties, from whom interest passes, of execution of instrument; or (b) by oath of signing witness to instrument, that parties to it, from whom interest passes, executed instrument in his (her) presence. (§13).

Acknowledgment may be taken and oath administered by following officers:

Within Province: (a) Registrar of Deeds; (b) judge of Court of Appeal or Trial Division; (c) officer appointed under R-10; (d) commissioner of Supreme Court; (e) notary public under his (her) official seal; (g) commissioner for oaths in and for province. (§14).

Without Province: (a) judge of court of record under seal of that court; (b) mayor or chief provincial court judge of city or town, under seal of that city or town; (c) notary public, under his (her) official seal; (d) Canadian consul or vice-consul; (e) commissioner for Supreme Court of Newfoundland; (f) commissioner for oaths outside province; (g) commissioner for oaths appointed under law of province in which acknowledgment is taken or oath is administered. (§15).

Authentication of certificate of acknowledgment is not required.

Proof.—Signature of any person from whom interest passes, if not duly acknowledged by him (her), must be proved by oath of subscribing witness, or instrument may not be registered. Proof may be made before any officer who may take acknowledgment. (§16).

Forms.—No prescribed forms.

Alternative to Acknowledgment or Proof.—No legislation.

ACTIONS:

Governed by Judicature Act, J-4.

Equity.—There is no distinction observed between legal and equitable proceedings except that originating application rather than statement of claim is commonly employed to initiate action in certain matters such as construction of instrument, declaration of right, or trusts, as more expeditious method. Question to be determined thereby must be one of law, not fact. Parties sometimes agree upon facts such as in agreed statement or affidavits when proceeding by originating application.

Condition Precedent.—From 01 Apr. 1996 requirement of notice upon municipalities (C-17, §314; M-23, §443) and upon Crown (P-26, §21) before instituting any proceedings against them was repeated (S.N. 1995, c. L-16.1).

Commencement.—See topic Process.

Parties.—Any person having any interest or in any wise affected by cause may commence action by issuing: (1) statement of claim or, (2) originating application or, in limited circumstances (3) petition. Guardians, administrators, executors or trustees shall commence action in representative capacity. In case of guardians ad litem evidence of guardianship shall be filed. In event of death or bankruptcy, action survives against estate whose representative is joined. Order of court is required.

Interpleader.—Where two or more persons claim goods, lands or chattels seized by Sheriff or in custody or control of third party, relief by way of interpleader may be sought by originating application (inter partes) served upon all claimants. Upon hearing application, Court will direct issue between claimants and may make any suitable order in its discretion as to disposition of affected goods, lands or chattels. (Rule 13).

Joinder of Causes of Action.—Subject to (1) where joinder of causes of actions or parties in proceeding may embarrass or delay trial or hearing of proceeding or is otherwise inconvenient or (2) where counterclaim or third party proceeding ought to be disposed of by separate proceedings, party, whether suing in same capacity or different capacities, may join several causes of action in same proceeding. (Rule 7).

Consolidation of Action.—Subject to certain rules of procedure set forth in Judicature Act court has power to consolidate different causes of actions against different defendants. (Rule 18).

Stay of proceedings may be obtained by order of court upon showing cause. (J-4, §95).

Abatement and Revival.—Survival of causes of action is governed by common law rules, as altered by statutes such as Survival of Actions Act, S-32 and Trustee Act, T-10 §22 (see topic Death). When action survives death, if by virtue of death or assignment or conveyance, estate or interest devolves or is transferred, surviving action may be continued by or against person to whom estate has come. Order to continue is necessary.

Termination.—Any time before proceeding is entered for trial or before its hearing is commenced in chambers, plaintiff may discontinue proceeding or withdraw any cause of action against any defendant, or defendant may withdraw his defence or part thereof, without leave, by filing and serving notice of discontinuance or withdrawal on any party concerned. After proceeding is entered for trial or its hearing commenced, plaintiff or defendant may discontinue or withdraw with leave of court, and order may contain provisions as to costs and as to bringing of subsequent proceedings. Party discontinuing proceeding or withdrawing defence must pay costs of any opposing party to date of discontinuance or withdrawal. Subject to terms of court's order, prior discontinuance or withdrawal is not defence to subsequent proceeding for same, or substantially same cause of action. (Rule 19).

Proceedings Against Crown.—Proceedings Against Crown Act, (P-26) governs. Crown in right of Province of Newfoundland may now sue or be sued more or less as any private citizen. From 01 Apr. 1996, requirement of notice upon Crown before institution of proceedings against Crown (P-26, §21) repealed (S.N. 1995, c L-16.1).

Limitation of.—See topic Limitation of Actions.

Direct Actions Against Insurer.—See topic Motor Vehicles, subhead Direct Actions.

Class Actions.—Permitted. (Rule 7.11).

ADMINISTRATION:

See topic Executors and Administrators.

ADOPTION:

(A-3; C-13).

Governed by Adoption of Children Act, A-3 and Children's Law Act, C-13.

Private adoption prohibited.

Definitions.—"Child" means person who is under age of 19. "Minister" means Minister of Social Services.

Consent Required (Written).—(1) Child, where (s)he has attained age of 12 years and is capable of giving informed consent; (2) every parent whose name appears on record of birth of child in jurisdiction where child was born, unless dispensed with by Court; (3) person declared by Court to be parent or who has order for custody of or access to child or who has filed application for declaration of parentage or order of custody or access with court; (4) Director of Child Welfare, where child has been committed to Director's permanent care and custody.

Consent by parent under age of 19 years is valid.

Consent may be cancelled within 21 days by document in writing; otherwise consent shall be irrevocable.

Condition Precedent.—Order of adoption shall not be made unless Director of Child Welfare certifies: that child has resided with applicant for at least six months immediately prior to date of application, under conditions which justify making of order; or that applicant is fit and proper person to have care and custody of child and that, for reasons set out in certificate, period of residence may be abridged or dispensed with.

Jurisdiction and Venue.—Court having jurisdiction to make adoption orders shall be Trial Division or, at option of applicant, but subject to regulations, Provincial Court judge within jurisdiction of which either applicant or child lives at date of application for adoption order (A-3) or Unified Family Court (U-3).

Application under this Act shall be dealt with by judge in chambers and may be heard in private.

For purpose of application under this Act and subject to regulations, court may appoint person or body to act as guardian of child upon hearing of application with duty of safeguarding interests of child before court.

Decisions of Director of Child Welfare may be appealed to Social Services Appeal Board (S-17.1), with further appeal by right to Judge of Trial Division and then to Court of Appeal.

Name.—Adopted child bears surname of adopting parent. Judge may give to adopted child any first name or names requested by applicant. Judge may also order that birth certificate of adopted child shall show some place of birth other than child's actual place of birth. (A-3, §20).

Interim Orders.—Judge may postpone determination of application and may make interim order giving custody of child to applicant for period of not exceeding two years by way of probationary period. (A-3, §21).

Effect of Adoption.—Order of adoption divests natural parent or custodian of adoptee of all legal rights, makes child the child of adopting parent and imposes upon adopting parent all legal obligations incidental to relation of parent and child. (A-3, §20[1]). Adopted child inherits from adopting parent same as natural child (C-13, §91). But adopted child does not lose his (her) right to inherit on intestacy from his natural parents. (I-21, §2).

Registry of adopted children is established at St. John's and adoption order, together with all documents, must be filed with Registrar General of Vital Statistics, responsible for Registry. For pre-adoption records: Post Adoption Services, Div. of Child Welfare, Dept. of Social Services, P.O. Box 8700, St. John's, NF, A1B 4J6.

See Topical Index in front part of this volume.

ADOPTION . . . *continued*

Confidentiality.—Registers, books and indices shall not be open to public inspection or search nor, except under order of court, shall Registrar General provide information from registers or books. (A-3, §26).

ADVANCEMENTS:

See topic Descent and Distribution.

ADVERSE POSSESSION:

Duration of Possession.—Adverse possession of real estate for period of 20 years is capable of giving good title as between parties.

Character of Possession.—Possession must be open, notorious, exclusive and continuous.

Easements may be acquired by prescription in 20 years. (L-16, §§3, 16).

AFFIDAVITS:

(E-16).

Affidavits, oaths, affirmations or statutory declarations may be made before any officer authorized to take acknowledgments (see topic Acknowledgment). Authentication is not required. In addition to above they may be made before following:

Within Province.—Barristers, members of House of Assembly, mayors or chairpersons of municipalities.

Without Province.—Supreme or Provincial Court judge, officer of Court of Justice or commissioner for taking affidavits, with office shown below signature; notary public under his (her) official seal; head of city, town, or other municipality under municipal seal; officer of Canadian diplomatic, consular or representative services, including High Commissioner and Trade Commissioner under his (her) seal or stamp of office, where any such person is authorized to do so in place where carried out.

Armed Services.—Within or without province by commissioned officer on active service in Canadian Forces with rank and unit shown below his (her) signature.

Use of Affidavit.—Affidavits, documents under oath, affirmations and statutory declarations when admissible in legal proceedings may in all cases be made before above-mentioned.

Alternative to Affidavit.—No legislation.

AGENCY:

See topic Principal and Agent.

AIRCRAFT:

See Canada Law Digest.

ALIENS:

Aliens are under no disability as to holding real property in Newfoundland. See Canada Law Digest.

ALIMONY:

See topic Divorce.

ALLOWANCES:

See topic Executors and Administrators.

APPEAL AND ERROR:

Lower Court.—In all civil matters involving amounts not exceeding $3,000 there is right of appeal to Supreme Court, Trial Division from decision of Provincial Court judge provided appellant files and gives notice in writing within 30 days to other party. (P-31.1, §6). In all provincial offence proceedings, person may appeal to Supreme Court, Trial Division from conviction, sentence, or both in accordance with procedure prescribed by Criminal Code (Canada), Part XXVII and, with leave, to Court of Appeal of Supreme Court and thereafter to Supreme Court of Canada.

Supreme Court.—Decision of judge of Supreme Court, Trial Division in civil matter may be reviewed on appeal before Court of Appeal of the Supreme Court. (Rule 57). With leave, there is further appeal to Supreme Court of Canada.

Stay of proceedings may be obtained on motion in discretion of court. Where protection of interests of parties warrants court will order security. (J-4, §95).

Character of Hearing.—Appeal is by way of review, although on application additional evidence may be taken, and extends to questions of fact and law.

Extent of Revision.—Primarily confined to law. Appeal court will not upset finding of fact unless shown to be contrary to evidence.

ARBITRATION AND AWARD:

(A-14).

Parties may, by written agreement, submit any matter of differences, present or future, to arbitration. Arbitrations are governed by terms of submission. (§2). Award may be upset by court or judge because of misconduct of arbitrator, or if award has been improperly procured. (§14).

Recession.—Unless submission expresses contrary intention, submission is irrevocable, except by leave of court, and has same effect as if it had been made order of court. (A-14, §3).

Powers of arbitrators are: (1) to administer oaths; (2) to state award as whole or in part in form of special case for opinion of court; (3) to correct clerical errors unless submission expresses contrary intention. (§10).

Attendance of Witnesses.—Party to submission may swear writ or subpoena ad testificandum or duces tecum. (§34).

Examination of Parties.—Parties of reference and parties claiming through them shall submit to be examined on oath or affirmation by arbitrators and must produce all books, deeds, accounts, writings etc. which are required or called for by arbitrators.

Time for making award may be extended by court. (§31).

Enforcement of Award.—Award may, by leave of court, be enforced in same manner as judgment or order. (A-14, §15).

Setting Aside.—Application in respect of arbitration or award (A-14, §14[2]) may be made to The Supreme Court (Trial Division) within 60 days of receipt of that arbitration or award by parties thereto (§14[2]).

Enforcement of Foreign Arbitral Award.—Foreign arbitral award may be recognized by Trial Division. If recognized, is enforceable in same manner as judgment or order of court. Model Law on International Commercial Arbitration and Convention on the Recognition and Enforcement of Foreign Arbitral Awards are adopted with amendments, as law of Newfoundland.

ASSIGNMENTS:

Any debt or thing in action may be assigned, provided assignment is absolute and in writing and express notice in writing is given debtor or other affected person. Such assignment transfers legal and equitable title.

Actions.—Action may be taken without joining assignor. (J-4, §103).

Filing.—There is no provision for recording of such assignment.

Assignment of wages comes within general provision above summarized except that assignment of wages of civil servants is governed by Public Officials Garnishee Act. (P-41).

Assignment of book debts (A-19) void against persons such as creditors of assignors unless in writing and filed with Registry of Deeds and accompanied by affidavit of certifying witness of execution and by affidavit of assignee or his (her) agent stating assignment was not made to avoid creditors. (A-19, §5).

ASSIGNMENTS FOR BENEFIT OF CREDITORS:

See Canada Law Digest, topic Bankruptcy.

ASSOCIATIONS:

Common law governs.

ATTACHMENT:

Where defendant, or principal shareholder of corporate defendant, (a) resides out of jurisdiction, or is corporation or company that is not registered under Corporations Act or is not corporation created by any statute or other law of province; (b) conceals himself, herself, or itself or absconds within jurisdiction with intent to avoid service on him, her or it of any document; (c) is about to leave or has left jurisdiction with intent to change his or her domicile, defraud his or her creditors, or avoid service of document; (d) is about to remove or has removed his, her or its property or any part thereof permanently out of jurisdiction; (e) has concealed, removed, assigned, transferred, conveyed, converted or otherwise disposed of all or any part of his, her or its property with intent to hinder or delay his, her or its creditors, or is about to do so; or (f) has fraudulently incurred debt or liability in issue in proceeding, plaintiff may, at or after commencement of proceeding and before judgment has been entered and as incident of relief claimed, make application for attachment order.

When plaintiff files affidavit which complies with Rule 28.03 and bond that complies with Rule 28.04, Registrar on ex parte application to him or her shall, unless Court otherwise orders, grant and issue attachment order in Form 28.05A.

When proceeding is commenced for debt or demand not yet due, attachment order may be granted but judgment shall not be entered against defendant until maturity of debt or demand.

Attachment order may be granted, issued, or served on Sat., Sun. or other holiday if affidavit sets out that plaintiff will lose benefit of attachment unless order is granted, issued or served on that day.

Affidavit of plaintiff or plaintiff's agent in support of attachment order shall (a) set out facts showing (i) plaintiff has a good cause of action against defendant whose property is to be attached, and (ii) existence of one or more grounds of attachment; (b) state amount of claim that plaintiff seeks to recover from defendant, including amount of probable costs, after allowing for all just credits, set-offs and counterclaims known to plaintiff; and (c) state plaintiff was advised by plaintiff's solicitor, if any, naming him or her, and verily believes that plaintiff is lawfully entitled to attach property.

Attachment Bond.—Unless court otherwise directs, plaintiff is required to post bond in amount equal to one and one quarter times claim which plaintiff seeks to recover from defendant. This bond must be supported by affidavit of plaintiff and two sufficient sureties or other form of security approved by Registrar of Court. (Rule 28).

Levy.—When plaintiff obtains execution order against defendant whose property has been attached, Sheriff may levy execution against attached property in accordance with Rule 52.

Attachment of Wages.—No debt due or accruing due to employee for or in respect of wages or salary covering any period of one month shall be liable to attachment or execution unless such debt exceeds sum specified in Attachment of Wages Act, A-20 and then only to extent of excess. Judge may make order respecting amount of exemptions. Act does not apply to attachments or executions in respect to financial support orders such as under Family Law Act (F-2) or domestic agreements (such as provided for under Family Law Act, F-2, Pt. IV).

Indemnity.—Sheriff may require indemnity should circumstances so warrant.

Priority.—Attachments rank in order made but judgment creditor attaching under judgment supersedes attachment under warrant of attachment. (Rule 28).

Release of Property.—Defendant may secure release of attached property by furnishing bond to sheriff, to pay any judgment entered; or by payment into court. (Rule 28).

See Topical Index in front part of this volume.

ATTACHMENT . . . *continued*

Sale may be made prior to judgment without order of court or consent of parties. Court may order immediate sale of attached perishable goods.

ATTORNEYS AND COUNSELORS:

(L-9).

Benchers of The Law Society of Newfoundland control admission of persons to practice as barristers and solicitors in province.

Eligibility.—Applicant must be of good character, Canadian citizen resident in province, 19 years of age, have served under articles for 12 months, have passed bar admission examination and have required educational standard. (§39).

Educational Requirement.—Degree in law from university in Canada recognized by Benchers or degree in law accepted as equivalent to degree granted by such university. (§38).

Admission in Special Cases.—Barrister and solicitor from reciprocating province with at least five years standing in previous seven years may be admitted subject to certain circumstances. (§42).

Rights and obligations of barristers and solicitors are governed by Law Society Act.

Lien.—Solicitor has general lien for his fees and disbursements on moneys and papers of his client in his hands. (§67).

Disbarment.—Benchers may disbar or suspend any member who has been guilty of professional misconduct.

AUTOMOBILES:

See topic Motor Vehicles.

BAIL:

See Canada Law Digest, topic Criminal Law.

BANKRUPTCY:

See Canada Law Digest.

BANKS AND BANKING:

Subject to federal legislative jurisdiction: Constitution Act, 1867, S. 91 (head 15); see Canada Law Digest.

Trust Companies and Loan Companies (T-9).—No such company is permitted to carry on business in Province unless it holds valid license issued by Minister of Justice under and in accordance with Trust and Loan Companies (Licensing) Act. No such company will be licensed if its unimpaired paid-up capital and surplus is less than $1,000,000.

Deposit Insurance.—Deposits, within meaning of Canada Deposit Insurance Corporation Act (R.S.C. 1985, c. C-3) shall not be accepted unless company is insured under policy of deposit insurance issued by Canada Deposit Insurance Corporation. (§11).

See also Canada Law Digest.

BILLS AND NOTES:

See Canada Law Digest.

BILLS OF LADING:

See topic Carriers.

BILLS OF SALE:

See topic Chattel Mortgages.

BONDS:

Supreme Court will accept bond of any bonding company licensed by Minister of Finance to do business in Newfoundland.

BROKERS:

(M-18).

Mortgage Brokers.—Must be registered with Registrar of Mortgage Brokers. Mortgage broker and mortgage lender must, 48 hours before lending, disclose to borrower actual amount to be advanced, amount of any bonus, legal fees and disbursements and all other costs. (§8). Lender cannot recover in excess of amount so disclosed. Bonus amount cannot exceed amount set out in regulations. Exemption for loan in excess of $25,000 to corporation.

Insurance Brokers.—See topic Insurance.

Stock Brokers.—See topic Securities.

Real Estate Agents.—See topic Real Property.

BULK SALES:

See topic Fraudulent Sales and Conveyances.

CARRIERS:

(M-19).

Motor Carrier Act applies to all persons and corporations which operate motor vehicle or trailer upon highway for purpose of obtaining fee for transportation of persons and/or freight.

Exemptions.—Act does not apply to: (1) school bus operated by or under contract with school board; (2) vehicle being used exclusively to transport wood products, mineral products, unprocessed farm and fish products; (3) vehicle used to transport personal goods and chattels; (4) municipal vehicle, other than ambulance, being operated by City of St. John's, Corner Brook, Mount Pearl or town, community or region established under Municipalities Act; (5) vehicle exempted by regulations; (6) intercorporate carriage; (7) specific leased vehicles and (8) freight forwarder. (§3).

Certification.—Certificate is granted by Board of Commissioners of Public Utilities for transportation of passengers and parcel express which certificate must be renewed within one year of its issuance. (6).

Residency Requirement.—Certificate holder who does not maintain place of business in province must designate agent in province for purposes of Act and to accept service for and on behalf of certificate holder. (§15).

Performance.—Minister of Works, Services and Transportation shall maintain record on safety performance of all carriers and upon reregistration assign carrier threshold level and safety rating of satisfactory or unsatisfactory as defined by regulations. (Regulation 222/93).

Records.—Every carrier shall keep and maintain at its principal place of business records relating to every driver and commercial vehicle in its employ. Every carrier who fails to maintain required records is subject to fine of not less than $200 nor more than $1,000 (Regulation 222/93).

Bills of Lading.—(M-19, §28[x]). Lieutenant-Governor in Council may make regulations respecting Bills of Lading, uniform or otherwise, and compulsory use of them. (CNR 965/96).

Inspection may take place at any place of business of carrier during normal business hours for purpose of inspecting any records required to be kept under Act. (Regulation 222/93).

CERTIORARI:

Certiorari is governed by Crown Practice Rules in Civil Matters. (R.54). Writ is seldom used. Ordinarily, review of decisions of inferior court is by way of appeal or stated case.

CHARITABLE IMMUNITY:

See topic Damages.

CHATTEL MORTGAGES:

(B-3).

No special form is required.

Registration.—All conveyances, bills of sale and mortgages of personal chattels where actual possession of such chattels continues in grantor or mortgagor, must be registered, upon payment of fees and satisfaction of other requirements. All such conveyances, bills of sale, or mortgages not registered are deemed void as against subsequent purchaser or mortgagee for valuable consideration, who first registers his (her) (its) conveyance, bill of sale, or mortgage; as against any subsequent and actual attachment or execution under process of any court of Province upon such personal chattels; as against trustee of insolvent estate, or as against assignee or trustee under assignment or conveyance for benefit of creditors.

Time within which registration should be made, formerly 30 days after execution, repealed 1996. (§8). Registration cost is $25. Renewal statements must be filed every five years. (§12). Renewal filing cost is $25.

Chattel mortgage registered outside Newfoundland or off-shore area, subject matter of which has been brought to this Province or off-shore area, must be registered in Newfoundland (effective 1996, no time requirement for registration) (§13), in order to have priority as against subsequent purchaser or mortgagee for valuable consideration who shall first register within time allowed; as against attachment or execution under process of law or as against trustee of insolvent estate or assignee for benefit of creditor.

Release.—Mortgagor, upon satisfying indebtedness secured, may demand indenture of release at mortgagor's expense and shall file same. (§17).

Foreclosure.—Chattel mortgage may be foreclosed in same manner as mortgage on realty, by originating application (inter partes) supported by affidavit upon which order may issue. Six months thereafter order absolute is obtainable. Governed by Judicature Act, J-4, Rules 5.02 and 26.

Redemption.—Mortgagor has right to redeem at any time up to obtaining of order absolute.

See also topic Consumer Protection.

CLAIMS:

See topic Executors and Administrators.

COLLATERAL SECURITY:

See topic Pledges.

COMMISSIONS TO TAKE TESTIMONY:

See topic Depositions.

CONDITIONAL SALES:

See topics Consumer Protection; Sales.

CONSTITUTION AND GOVERNMENT:

See topic Legislature.

CONSTRUCTION LIENS:

See topic Liens, subhead Mechanics Lien Act (c. M-3).

CONSUMER PROTECTION:

Consumer protection legislation covers registration and regulation of automobile dealers and sales people (A-21), registration and regulation of collection agencies (C-22), registration and regulation of credit reporting agencies (C-32), registration of conditional sales, bills of sale, collateral mortgages.

See Topical Index in front part of this volume.

CONSUMER PROTECTION . . . *continued*

Consumer Sales.—Conditions and warranties implied under Sale of Goods Act (c. S-6) cannot be excluded from consumer sales. These are sales of goods, made in ordinary course of business to purchaser for his consumption or use, except for resale, for use in business, to association, partnership or corporation. (C-31, §2).

Unsolicited Goods and Credit Cards (U-6).—Persons in receipt of such goods and cards may not be sued for their use, misuse, loss, damage or theft unless they requested or accepted goods or credit cards in writing. Mere receipt of such goods or cards creates no legal obligations.

Direct Sellers.—House to house or telephone salesperson must be registered with Registrar of Consumer Protection and post bond. Direct sales contract is rescinded (1) where purchaser gives notice of rescission of contract within ten days of contract, or (2) where in relation to contract either salesperson not registered or goods not supplied within 120 days, or salesperson fails to observe any term of his (her) license and notice of rescission given within one year to salesperson. (D-24).

Disclosure of Cost of Borrowing.—In case of lending or credit sales, lender must register with Registrar of Consumer Protection. Agreement must be signed by borrower and set out (1) actual amount lent or price of goods or services, down payment or trade-in, amount of official fees, amount of insurance premiums, cost of borrowing, expressed as one sum in dollars and cents and (2) rate of interest charged. Statement of account must be rendered not less than every five weeks. Borrower not liable for costs that exceed that disclosed in statement. (C-31).

Discounting Income Tax Refunds.—Person who in course of business acquires taxpayer's right to refund of various amounts including income tax from federal or provincial government, must specify in writing terms of acquisition and no such acquisition is valid if actual consideration less than 85% of refund of tax, where refund of tax is equal to or less than $300 or is less than $255 plus 95% of any amount by which refund of tax exceeds $300 (Tax Rebate Discounting Act, R.S.C. 1985, c. T-3).

Product Liability.—No legislation; common law governs.

Plain Language.—No legislation.

CONTRACTS:

Common law governs.

Distributorships, Dealerships and Franchises.—No legislation.

Frustrated Contracts Act (F-26).—Where contract frustrated and parties discharged, sums previously paid are recoverable and sums payable cease to be payable. Court given powers: (1) to allow expenses up to sums paid or payable; (2) to allow for valuable benefit conferred by one party on other or obligation assumed by one for benefit of other; (3) to sever contract treating part as not frustrated and part frustrated. Act applies to all contracts governed by province's law other than charterparty (except time charterparty or charterparty by demise), insurance contracts, sales of specific goods which have perished either before contract or, without seller's or buyer's fault, before risk passes to buyer.

CONVEYANCES:

See topic Deeds.

CORPORATIONS:

General Supervision.—Governed by Corporations Act, C-36, including all corporations except government, municipal, agricultural corporations and cooperatives.

Incorporation.—One or more individuals or one or more bodies corporate, including nonresidents, may, by complying with requirements of Corporations Act, form incorporated companies. (§11).

Name or designating number of corporation may not simulate that of another corporation and must be followed by either limited, limitee, incorporated, incorporee, corporation or abbreviation thereof. (§17).

Term of corporate existence is perpetual unless (1) company is removed from province's Registry of Companies (situate at St. John's) by Registrar of Companies for non-filing of share list in which case it is dissolved; or (2) company is wound up.

Escheat.—Upon dissolution all lands, personal property and rights situate in province of incorporation, wherever incorporated, vest in Crown. Crown, if it sees fit, may convey same to person to whom, by reason of dealings or relationship with dissolved corporation or by reason of any other circumstance, such lands, property and rights should be conveyed. (§357).

Articles of incorporation are required to provide concise outline of corporate structure and must contain following particulars: Name of corporation; address of its registered head office; classes and any maximum number of authorized shares; rights, privileges, restrictions and conditions associated with each class or series of shares; any restrictions placed upon share transfer rights; minimum and maximum number of directors; and any restrictions placed upon business of corporation. (§12).

Filing of Articles.—Articles of incorporation must be filed with Registrar of Companies, together with registration fee and filing fee for each document filed. (§14).

Fees payable to Registrar of Companies on incorporation irrespective of capital or number of members.

There is fee for incorporation, for filing annual share list and for registration of any document required or authorized to be registered as set by schedule of prescribed fees. (Corporations Act Schedule of Prescribed Fees).

Certificate of Incorporation.—If application in order and fees paid, certificate is issued by Registrar. (§393). Notice is published in Newfoundland Gazette. Date of incorporation is date shown on certificate of registration. (§16).

Licence to do Business.—No licence required. Certificate of incorporation should be kept in general view at registered office of company.

Amendment of Articles.—Articles may be amended by special resolution which shall be filed with Registrar. (§279). Cannot decrease capital if insolvent or if decrease would render corporation insolvent. (§67[3]). If articles are in order and fees paid, certificate of amendment is issued. Amendment effective from date of issuance.

Shares of corporation are without nominal or par value. Where only one class of shares exists, rights of holders thereof shall be equal in all respects and include right to vote at meeting of shareholders. (§47). Articles may provide for more than one class of shares and rights, privileges, restrictions and conditions attaching to shares of each class shall be set out in shares of that class.

Share Certificate.—Every shareholder is entitled to properly signed share certificate (§88) stating name of corporation, shareholder's name, number and class of shares represented thereby and any preferences, rights, conditions or restrictions or that such exist and that copy of full text is obtainable from corporation on demand (§92).

Share Warrants.—Warrant is any instrument entitling holder to purchase share or debt obligation of corporation. Warrants are dealt with as investment securities. (§121).

Issuance of Shares.—Allotment and issuance of shares is regulated by directors. Shares must not be issued until fully paid (§23) and may not be issued at discount. Share list in form supplied by Registrar must be filed each year by Mar. 31. For failure to file Registrar may have company stricken from Registry.

Share Transfer.—Shares can be transferred by endorsement and delivery by entry of transfer being made on share register. There is no share transfer tax. (Part VI).

Shareholders elect directors (§176) and appoint auditors (§265). If shareholders are dissatisfied with directors, who are responsible for general supervision of affairs of corporation (§171), they may replace board of directors at end of their term or remove any director before expiration of term and elect another to fill vacancy (§179). Shareholders may inspect copies of articles, securities register, minutes of meetings and resolutions of shareholders. (§42). Shareholders holding 5% of issued voting shares may requisition meeting of shareholders (§241) and any shareholder entitled to vote at meeting of shareholders may requisition directors to circulate shareholder's proposal to be considered at next shareholders' meeting (§224). Any shareholder who is entitled to vote at annual meeting of shareholders may make proposal to amend articles. (§§224, 279). Shareholder may apply to court for order calling meeting of shareholders, apply to court to review election or appointment of director or auditor. (§§242, 243). If wrong is done to corporation as where majority has acted to detriment of minority and refuses to cause corporation to take action, with leave of court, any shareholder may institute derivative action. (§369).

Unanimous Shareholder Agreement.—Otherwise lawful written agreement among all shareholders of corporation, or among all shareholders and person who is not shareholder, that restricts, in whole or in part, powers of directors to manage business and affairs of corporation, is valid. (§245).

Shareholders' Liability.—Shareholders of corporation are not liable for default of corporation (except under §§67[4], 245[3] or 335[5]): (a) on decrease of stated capital by special resolution each shareholder may be individually liable to creditors for amount equal to liability that was reduced or amount that was distributed as result of reduction of capital (limitation period two years) (§67[4]); (b) shareholder who is party to unanimous shareholder agreement incurs liabilities of director to extent that agreement relieves directors of liability (§245[3]); (c) notwithstanding dissolution of corporation, shareholders among whom its property has been distributed are liable to its creditors to extent of amount received by them respectively (limitation period within two years of dissolution). (§355[4]).

Shareholders' Meetings.—Statutory meeting must first be held within 18 months of incorporation and not longer than 15 months after last preceding meeting. Company may at any time call special meeting of shareholders. (§221). Requirements of notice set out in Corporations Act must be complied with.

Voting.—Each share has one vote unless articles provide otherwise. Voting at meeting is by show of hands unless ballot is demanded by shareholder or otherwise provided for in articles or by-laws. (§239). Pooling agreements with respect to voting of shares owned by two or more shareholders are permitted. (§244).

Directors.—Subject to unanimous shareholder agreement directors of corporation direct management of business and affairs of corporation. (§167). Majority of directors must be resident Canadians. (§174). Directors must be over 19 and not undischarged bankrupt or mental incompetent. (§172). Directors shall be elected for term expiring not later than close of third annual meeting of shareholders following election. Directors need not hold office for same term. (§175). Where meeting of shareholders fails to elect minimum number of directors, directors elected may exercise powers of directors provided there is quorum. (§175[7]). If no quorum, vacancies must be filled by calling special meeting of shareholders. (§181).

Directors Meetings.—Unless articles or by-laws otherwise provide, directors may meet at any place with required notice. Directors shall not transact business at monthly meeting of directors unless majority of directors present (includes participation by telephone with consent of directors) are resident Canadians. (§§184, 188). Any resolution signed by all directors is as valid as if passed at meeting. (§191).

Powers and Duties of Directors.—Unless articles, by-laws or unanimous shareholder agreement provide otherwise, directors may, by resolution, make, amend or repeal any by-laws that regulate business or affairs of corporation. (§170).

Liabilities of Directors.—Where directors consent to or vote for resolution authorizing purchase, redemption or other acquisition in contravention of Act or articles, directors are jointly and individually liable to corporation. (§193). Where directors consent to: commission, payment of dividend, financial assistance, payment of indemnity, or payment to shareholder contrary to Act, directors are jointly and individually liable to make restitution to corporation. (§193).

Delegation by Directors.—Directors may appoint from their number managing director, who is resident of Canada, or committee of directors and delegate to managing director or committee powers of directors. (§189).

Officers.—Subject to articles, by-laws or any unanimous shareholder agreement, directors may designate officers of corporation, appoint officers, specify their duties

CORPORATIONS . . . *continued*

and delegate to them powers to manage business and affairs of corporation. One person can hold two or more offices. (§202).

Registered Office.—Corporation must have registered office in province in place specified in articles. Notice of registered office in prescribed form shall be sent to Registrar together with articles designating or changing (within 15 days of change) place of registered office of corporation. (§§33, 34).

Powers.—Every company has power to conduct business in accordance with provisions of its articles. In certain cases articles may be changed by special resolutions of company but in such cases permission of judge of Supreme Court (Trial Division) must be obtained. (§27). Provincial company may not conduct banking business and special license is required to conduct insurance business. (Part XXIII).

Books and Records.—Every company must keep share register and file with Registrar annual returns in form provided therefor setting forth names and addresses of its members and directors, number of shares issued and amount called upon each, and number of shares issued for consideration other than cash; must register mortgages on its assets, and must keep such other books as articles of association provide for. (Part III).

Reports.—If offering corporation: (1) financial statements as prescribed by Securities Act, (S-13, §22) must be delivered to Securities Commission of Newfoundland within 140 days from end of last financial year (§79, Securities Act); (2) annual financial statements and auditors' report to be concurrently sent to shareholders (§80, Securities Act); (3) detailed quarterly financial statements must be sent to shareholders and must concurrently be filed by offering corporation with Securities Commission of Newfoundland (c S-13, §78).

If non-offering corporation: annual financial statements and auditor's reports, if any, to be sent to shareholders at least 21 days before annual meeting. (§262).

Audits and Inspections.—If non-offering corporation: shareholders may resolve not to appoint auditor. (§266). Auditors are to be provided with information, explanations, access to records, documents, books, accounts necessary for financial statements, must report annually to shareholders on accounts examined. (§274). Investigation into business and management of corporation may be ordered by court on application by security holder or Registrar. (§359).

Amalgamation.—Two or more corporations, including holding and subsidiary corporations, may amalgamate by statutory procedure. (§288). They must first enter into agreement prescribing terms and means of amalgamation, manner of carrying it into effect, and other details necessary to perfect amalgamation and provide for subsequent management and operation of amalgamated corporation. (§289). This agreement is adopted when shareholders of each amalgamating corporation have approved of amalgamation by special resolution of each class or series of shareholders entitled to vote on it. (§290). New corporation comes into existence on date of certificate of amalgamation with all its property, rights, privileges and subject to all liabilities, obligations of each of companies so amalgamated. (§294).

Continuations.—Corporation incorporated otherwise than under law of Newfoundland may apply to Registrar for continuance. (§295).

Foreign Corporations.—Every corporation having gain for its object or part of its object, which carries on business in province, must register under Corporations Act before commencing business. Application for registration must be made to Registrar of Companies. Fees payable on registration are scaled according to capitalization with minimum fee of $200 for capitalizations up to $500,000 to maximum fee for capitalizations over $1,000,000 of $350 + $0.10/$1,000 over $1,000,000. Additional fee of $10 is payable for each document other than application for registration required by Act to be filed. Such companies may hold title to land and are not otherwise subject to any special tax except income tax. Every such foreign company, except for insurance companies, must in addition file with Registrar not later than Apr. 1st in each year annual return showing share dispositions of company, names and addresses of directors, and other information required by Act, accompanied by annual fee of $200 (subject to certain circumstances). (Corporations Act Schedule of Prescribed Fees).

Franchise Tax.—No annual franchise tax is imposed upon corporations save tax on personal holding corporations, which is in lieu of income tax.

Franchise tax on personal holding corporations is based on authorized capital at following rates: $50 for first $250,000 or less; 10¢ per $1,000 for excess over $750,000 up to $1,000,000; 5¢ per $1,000 for excess over $1,000,000; maximum tax $250. There is also surtax of 50% of amount of tax.

COSTS:

(Rules 21, 55).

Costs are in discretion of court or judge.

Security for costs may be demanded from nonresidents who have insufficient property within province to respond to costs. Bond will be accepted. See topic Bonds.

Liability of Attorney.—Within discretion of court or judge. (Rule 55.14).

COURTS:

(J-4).

Supreme Court of Newfoundland is divided into: Court of Appeal consisting of Chief Justice and five appellate judges sitting only in St. John's; Trial Division consisting of Chief Justice of Trial Division and 17 puisne judges sitting in St. John's, Grand Bank, Gander, Grand Falls, Corner Brook and Happy Valley/Goose Bay; and Unified Family Court consisting of one judge sitting only at St. John's. Trial Division has province-wide unlimited original jurisdiction in all matters. Unified Family Court is territorially limited in its jurisdiction to portion of Avalon Peninsula and matters over which it has jurisdiction specified in Unified Family Court Act, c. U-3.

For purposes of Judges Act (R.S.C. 1985, c. J-1, §32) two additional offices of judge established in 1995 to be filled by person who occupied office of Chief Justice of Supreme Court of Newfoundland (who is also Chief Justice of Court of Appeal) and by person who had occupied office of Chief Justice of Trial Division of Supreme Court of Newfoundland, in event either of such persons elects under Judges Act (Canada) to vacate Chief Justiceship and perform only duties of judge of Court of Appeal or of Trial Division (as case may be) (J-4, §47.1).

Provincial Courts (organized administratively into districts: Regulation 147/87) and every Provincial Court judge of the Court has jurisdiction throughout province. Provincial Court judge (a) shall exercise all powers and perform all duties conferred or imposed upon Provincial Court judge by any of Acts of Legislature or of Parliament of Canada; (b) subject to Young Persons Offences Act, has all power and authority now vested, under any Act of Legislature, in Provincial Court judge, two justices of peace sitting together, or youth court or judge of youth court; (c) may exercise all powers and perform all duties conferred or imposed upon Provincial Court judge or one or more justices of peace under Acts of Parliament of Canada; and (d) is by virtue of office justice of peace.

Provincial Court judge shall be considered to have been specially authorized by terms of his (her) appointment to exercise jurisdiction conferred upon Provincial Court judge under Part XIX of Criminal Code but this does not apply to any number of justices of peace.

CREDITORS' SUITS:

Common law governs.

CRIMINAL LAW:

See Canada Law Digest.

CULTURE:

See topic Tourism.

CURTESY:

Not applicable in Newfoundland.

DAMAGES:

In respect of claims for damages common law prevails.

Fatal Accidents Act, F-6 provides that whenever death of person is caused by any wrongful act, neglect or default entitling any party to damages, action for damages, must be commenced within one year from date of death. Under Limitations Act, S.N. 1995, c. L-16.1, this limitation period does not begin to run against person until he (she) knows or, considering all circumstances of matter, ought to know that he (she) has cause of action. Burden of proving limitation period has been postponed/suspended is on person claiming postponement. Further, subject to principal of confirmation, action must be commenced within ten years of triggering event(s) (except in case of person under disability in which event ten year limitation postponed while person under disability). (§§14, 15). Person under disability includes person under 18 years. (§15). Limitation period may also be extended by operation of principal of confirmation. (§16). Notwithstanding postponement or suspension of limitation and notwithstanding operation of principal of confirmation, action shall not be brought after expiration of 30 years from date on which event which gave rise to cause of action last occurred. (§22). See topic Limitations of Actions.

Under provisions of Contributory Negligence Act, C-33, fault may be apportioned between two or more persons.

Charitable Immunity.—Not applicable in Newfoundland.

DEATH:

Upon originating application (ex parte) to court to be heard after such notice as court deems proper, court if satisfied that person has been absent and not heard of or from by applicant or, to knowledge of applicant, by any other person since day named; and applicant has no reason to believe that person is living; and reasonable grounds exist for supposing that person is dead, may make order that person is presumed to be dead for all purposes or for such purposes only as are specified in order. (P-20).

Survivorship.—Where two or more persons die at same time or in circumstances rendering it uncertain which survived, deaths are presumed to have occurred in order of seniority and accordingly younger is considered to have survived older. Notwithstanding above, for purpose of disposition of property in will, what will provides (whether or not consistent with above) is considered to have occurred. (S-33).

Actions for death resulting from wrongful act, neglect or default of another may be brought by executor or administrator of decedent for benefit of wife, husband, children, grandchildren, parents, stepparents, grandparents or person in loci parentis of decedent. If there be no executor or administrator or executor or administrator does not bring action within six months after decedent's death, action may be brought by any or all of persons entitled to benefit from such action. Action must be commenced within one year after decedent's death (subject to provisions respecting limitations under topic Damages). Judge or, where permitted by Jury Act or other statute, jury may award such damages as deemed proper and apportion same among persons entitled to benefit of recovery. (F-6).

Certificate.—See topic Records, subhead Vital Statistics.

DECEDENT'S ESTATES:

See topics Descent and Distribution; Executors and Administrators; Wills.

DECLARATORY JUDGMENTS:

See topic Judgments.

DEEDS:

(R-10).

All deeds, decrees, judgments and conveyances affecting land in Newfoundland may be registered in Registry of Deeds (situate at St. John's). Deeds may be proven by oath of subscribing witness or by acknowledgment under oath of parties subscribing. Before deed can be registered signature of every person from whom any estate passes must be proven. Registration is not compulsory but is method of protection of purchaser against subsequent purchasers.

See Topical Index in front part of this volume.

DEEDS . . . *continued*

See topic Real Property for estates recognized.

See also topic Husband and Wife.

Execution.—Signature is essential. Seal is necessary in some and advisable in all cases. Witness is not essential but is desirable for purposes of proof for registration as otherwise acknowledgment under oath is required from vendor or transferor. Acknowledgment is not necessary for validity of deed.

DEPOSITIONS:

Depositions are taken by affidavit before persons authorized to administer oaths in accordance with English practice. They are admissible in evidence on proof that deponent is dead, out of jurisdiction, or unable to be present at trial because of sickness or other unavoidable reason. (Rule 47).

Witness.—See S.N. 1991 c. 13, §6.1(b) for definition.

Compelling Attendance of Witnesses.—If witness is within province s(he) may be compelled to attend when order for his (her) examination has been issued. If s(he) is outside province and commission has been issued, commission may be accompanied by letters rogatory addressed to foreign court requesting aid in procuring evidence. (Rule 46).

Examination of Witnesses Out of Court.—Witnesses must be examined on oath, affirmation or otherwise in accordance with law of country in which commission is executed. Examination will normally be upon oral questions to be reduced into writing but it may be upon written interrogatories. Oral examination takes place in presence of parties, their counsel, solicitors or agents (unless otherwise ordered). Witnesses are subject to cross-examination and reexamination. (Rule 46).

Subject to §6.1(6) of Evidence Act (E-16), witness to legal proceeding, defined by §6.1(1)(a), shall not be asked and shall not answer any question or produce any documentation in relation to evidence given previously before either Newfoundland Perinatal Committee or quality assurance or peer review committee of "member" as defined under Hospital and Nursing Home Association Act. (H–8).

DESCENT AND DISTRIBUTION:

(I-21).

Testate Succession.—See topic Wills.

Intestate Succession.—Real and personal estate of intestate dying after June 14, 1951 descends and is distributed as follows:

Entire estate or, if decedent left surviving spouse, excess over share of such spouse, goes to following, each class in which there is member living taking to exclusion of subsequent classes: (1) Issue, per stirpes; (2) father and mother equally or all to survivor; (3) brothers and sisters equally, issue of deceased brother or sister taking share to which parent would have been entitled if alive; (4) next of kin of equal degree and their representatives equally, but no representation allowed among collaterals after children of brothers and sisters.

Degrees of kindred are computed by counting upward from intestate to nearest common ancestors and then downward to relative.

Half Blood.—Kindred of half blood inherit equally with those of whole blood.

Surviving Spouse.—Subject to surviving spouse's rights under Family Law Act, F-2, share of surviving spouse is as follows: if decedent left one child or issue of one child—one-half; if decedent left more than one child, surviving issue of deceased child counting as child—one third; if decedent left no issue, entire estate goes to surviving spouse. (§4).

Afterborn Children and Relatives.—Descendants and other relatives of decedent, begotten before his death but born thereafter, take as though born in his lifetime. (§12).

Illegitimates.—General rules of intestacy govern. For all purposes of law of province, person is child of his (her) natural parents, and his (her) status as their child is independent of whether he (she) is born outside marriage. (C-13).

Adopted Children.—See topic Adoption.

Advancements are reckoned as part of estate, and if advancement to child is equal to or greater than his share under intestate law, he takes no part of estate. If advancement is less than such share, child takes so much of estate as will, with advancement, equal share of each other child.

DISPUTE RESOLUTION:

Mandatory Dispute Resolution.—A-14; C-13; D-10; F-2; I-15; L-1; P-42; T-3; Rules of The Supreme Court (of Newfoundland), 1986 (Rules) 17A; 20A; 39; The Rules of the Unified Family Court, 1979 (U.F.C. Rules) 31-34.

Forms of mandatory dispute resolution include: arbitration; conciliation; conferences; and mediation. Mandatory dispute resolution process may sometimes involve summary, expedited or mini trials.

Arbitration.—Governed by Arbitration Act, A-14 (§§2[d], 17, 19, 20, 25, 30); Department of Employment and Labour Relations Act, D-10 (§6[xvi]); International Commercial Arbitration Act, I-15 (§6); Labour Relations Act, L-1 (§§86, 88-92); Public Services Collective Bargaining Act, P-42 (§§39-41); and Teachers' Collective Bargaining Act, T-3 (§§17, 21-25).

Conciliation.—Governed by Labour Relations Act, L-1 (§§79; 106-121); Public Service Collective Bargaining Act, P-42 (§17); and Teachers' Collective Bargaining Act, T-3 (§§13-14).

Conferences.—Settlement conferences are governed, in Supreme Court of Newfoundland, Trial Division, by Rule 39.05(2); and in Supreme Court of Newfoundland, Unified Family Court, by U.F.C. Rules 31-33. Pretrial conferences are governed, in Supreme Court of Newfoundland, Trial Division, by Rules 39.01-39.04; and in Supreme Court of Newfoundland, Unified Family Court, by U.F.C. Rules 31-33.

Mediation.—Governed by Children's Law Act, C-13 (§37); Family Law Act, F-2 (§4); Labour Relations Act, L-1 (§80); and Public Service Collective Bargaining Act, P-42 (§18).

Special Trials.—In Supreme Court of Newfoundland, Trial Division, summary trials and expedited trials are governed by Rule 17A, and mini trials are governed by Rule 39.05(1). Both Rules are incorporated by reference in The Rules of the Unified Family Court, 1979, under U.F.C. Rule 2(1), and thus apply to Supreme Court of Newfoundland, Unified Family Court.

Voluntary Dispute Resolution.—

Offers to Settle.—In litigation, they are governed, in Supreme Court of Newfoundland, Trial Division, by Rule 20A; and in Supreme Court of Newfoundland, Unified Family Court, by U.F.C. Rule 34.

Others.—Whatever processes are agreed among parties (in litigation) or prospective parties; including aspects of specific mandatory and voluntary dispute resolution procedures.

See topic Arbitration and Award.

DIVORCE:

Substantive law (including sole ground-marriage breakdown) governed by federal Divorce Act. (R.S.C. 1985, 2nd Supp., c. 3).

Procedural law largely prescribed by Province's Divorce Rules of Supreme Court of Newfoundland (separate Rules with same Rule numbering scheme for Trial Division and Unified Family Court Division) with some procedural provisions in federal Divorce Act.

Supreme Court has jurisdiction to hear petition for dissolution of marriage. Ground for dissolution is same as in all other provinces and territories in Canada. See Canada Law Digest.

Process.—Procedure in divorce or corollary relief action governed by and administered by Divorce Rules of Supreme Court of Newfoundland. Divorce action is commenced by issuing petition for divorce. (Rule 4[1]). Marriage certificate must be filed prior to issuing petition, unless petition states that certificate cannot be produced. (Rule 4[2]). Where petition contains claim for support, financial statement in form specified must be filed and served with petition and respondent spouse must deliver financial statements with answer. Petitioner shall be served personally unless otherwise ordered by judge. (Rule 10[1]). Petition must be served by someone other than petitioner. (Rule 10[3]). It is necessary to name, if known, third party alleged to have participated in adultery specie of marriage breakdown ground. (Rule 5[2]).

Proceedings in divorce action consist of petition, answer and reply, if any, contents of which are prescribed, as well as financial statements from both parties in form prescribed by Rules. Where there is child of marriage, financial statement shall be completed, filed and served by all parties no later than day prior to trial. Respondent wishing to oppose claim made in petition must deliver answer, or notice of intent to defend within prescribed time. (Rule 13). Respondent claiming any relief against petitioner other than dismissal of action and costs, must deliver counter-petition, contents of which are prescribed. (Rule 13[6]).

Judgment.—Where divorce is uncontested or undefended, party may move for divorce judgment (which takes effect 31st day after day on which court authorizes divorce judgment).

Interim Relief.—Notice of motion for interim corollary relief (financial support, parenting costs) may be served at same time as, or any time after, petition or counter-petition is served. (Rule 22).

Offers to Settle.—Any party may serve in Form 15, offer to settle any claim raised in petition, answer or notice of motion. (Rule 23[1]). Offer may be accepted in Form 16 before judgment or order. (Rule 23[2]).

Maintenance and Custody of Children.—In divorce proceedings: governed by federal Divorce Act and generally described as corollary relief. Otherwise (such as where husband and wife separate but do not commence divorce proceeding), governed by Province's statute law—primarily, Family Law Act, F-2 and Children's Law Act, C-13—and by common law. Child maintenance is described under Divorce Act as financial support and under Family Law Act, F-2, Pt. III as support.

Maintenance orders of reciprocating jurisdictions may be enforced in Newfoundland. (Reciprocal Enforcement of Support Orders Act, c. R-5, §3). Support or maintenance orders from Newfoundland courts will be enforced by Director of Support Enforcement (1-800-563-1466) pursuant to Support Orders Enforcement Act, 1990, c. S-31, §3 unless recipient spouse elects otherwise.

Act to Amend Divorce Act and Family Orders and Agreements Enforcement Assistance Act, S.C. 1993, c. 8, in force Mar. 25, 1993 except §15, facilitates process of tracing individuals alleged to have abducted child by allowing access to federal information banks.

Governing consideration in custody orders is best interest of children.

Alimony.—Common law term replaced, under Divorce Act, by financial support of spouses (form of corollary relief), and otherwise (such as where husband and wife separate but do not commence divorce proceeding) replaced by support under Family Law Act, F-2, Pt. III.

Grounds for Legal Separation.—No legislation; common law governs.

Division of Property of Spouses.—Governed by Family Law Act, F-2.

See also topic Husband and Wife.

Separation Agreements.—The Family Law Act (especially Pt. IV) provides for domestic contracts. Includes separation agreements, marriage contracts and cohabitation agreements. (c. F-2, §61). Man and woman who cohabitated and are living apart may enter into separation agreement. If in writing, separation agreement signed by parties and witnessed, may provide for ownership in or division of property, support obligations, right to direct education and moral training of children, and any other matter in settlement of parties' affairs. (§64). Written marriage contracts entered into before or during marriage may, upon dissolution of marriage, govern some matters (except custody of or access to children), and possession of matrimonial home. (§62). Court may always disregard provisions governing children (if included in agreement) when children's best interests are not met. (§66).

See also topic Husband and Wife, subhead Domestic Contracts.

See Topical Index in front part of this volume.

DIVORCE . . . *continued*

Foreign Divorces.—Foreign divorce is recognized in province if either former spouse was ordinarily resident in that country or subdivision which granted divorce for at least one year immediately preceding commencement of proceedings for divorce, or, if after July 1, 1968, divorce granted pursuant to law of another country by tribunal or other authority having jurisdiction to do so on basis of wife's domicile determined as if she was unmarried, and if she was minor, as if she had attained age of majority. (Divorce Act, R.S.C. [2nd Supp.], c. 3, §22). It is immaterial that foreign divorce was granted on grounds not recognized in province. For foreign divorce, domicile of wife is that of her husband.

See Canada Law Digest, topic Divorce, subhead Jurisdiction.

DOWER:

Not applicable in Newfoundland.

EMPLOYER AND EMPLOYEE:

See topic Labour Relations.

ENVIRONMENT:

General Supervision.—Department of Environment and Lands Act, D-11, establishes Department and authorizes Minister of Environment and Lands to supervise, control and direct all matters relating to protection and enhancement of quality of natural environment, including water, air and soil quality, conservation, development, control and improvement and proper utilization of water resources of province and management of all crown lands. Waste management is regulated by Waste Material Disposal Act, c. W-4. Water pollution is regulated by Waters Protection Act, c. W-5. Pesticides are regulated by Pesticides Control Act, c. P-8. Danger to public health in general is regulated by Department of Health pursuant to Department of Health Act, c. D-15. Occupational Health and Safety Act, c. O-3, requires extensive disclosure of information and special training for workers exposed to hazardous materials.

Prohibited Acts of Pollution.—Very broad definition of pollution in relation to alteration of natural environment, including adverse effects on health and safety or welfare. Discharges in excess of amounts prescribed by regulation also prohibited. Common law doctrines (nuisance, negligence, strict liability, riparian rights) still apply.

Assessment.—Any undertaking which affects environment is subject to Environmental Assessment Act, E-14. Purpose of Act is to facilitate wise management of natural resources of province and to protect environment and quality of life of people of province through institution of environmental assessment procedures prior to and after commencement of undertaking that may be potentially damaging to environment.

Registration.—Proponent shall before proceeding with final design of such undertaking notify Minister in prescribed form about purpose of undertaking. (§6).

Public Notice.—Proponent will provide public notice at or near geographical area of proposed undertaking with opportunity for public to meet and discuss proposed undertaking and their concerns. (§17).

Exemption.—Minister may with approval of Lieutenant Governor in Council exempt proponent from provisions of this Act.

Packaging Material.—Packaging Material Act S.N. 1993, P-O.1, authorizes Minister to support and encourage programs and research into reduction and/or reuse of packaging waste. (§5). Minister may require corporation, institution or government department to collect and record data on packaging and report to Minister in form prescribed by regulations. (§5). Person who contravenes Act or regulations is guilty of offence and is liable on summary conviction to fine of not more than $250,000. (§7).

EQUITY:

See topic Actions.

ESCHEAT:

See topic Corporations.

EVIDENCE:

In general, common law applies, as altered by statute.

As to competence of child (not defined by statute, probably 14 years at common law) to testify, child is competent if (a) s(he) promises to tell truth and (b) court is of opinion child understands what it means to tell truth and is able to communicate evidence. When necessary to establish whether child competent to give evidence, court may conduct inquiry to determine whether, in its opinion, child understands what it means to tell truth and is able to communicate evidence. If child does not promise to tell truth or if court forms opinion child does not understand what it means to tell truth, child's proposed evidence may still be admitted if court is of opinion it is sufficiently reliable.

Child's evidence need not be corroborated. Judge shall not instruct jury that it is unsafe to rely on child's uncorroborated evidence; provided, however, judge retains discretion to commit on child's evidence. (E-16, §§18; 18.1).

See topics Depositions; Witnesses.

EXECUTIONS:

(Rule 51).

Any party who has obtained judgment may get from Registry of Court execution order under which goods, chattels and effects of debtor may be seized and sold.

Kinds of Execution.—Execution may be obtained by orders of seizure and sale, possession, delivery, attachment or sequestration, by warrants of committal or by garnishee or replevin orders. Warrants may be also placed in hands of any third party having custody or control of any moneys, goods, debts or effects of debtor defendant or plaintiff as case may be, and garnishee proceedings may be taken to examine debtor or third parties alleged to have in their possession property of debtor as in cases of attachment.

Exemptions.—See topic Exemptions.

Time for Issuance/Renewal.—At any time within six years after issue of execution order; leave of court must be obtained after that period. Execution order, once issued, remains in force for six years and may be renewed for such further period(s) as court, upon application, determines.

Levy.—Any real and personal property not exempt may be levied to satisfy judgment.

Priorities.—Executions rank in order of actual seizure.

Sale may be effected by sheriff at public auction, notice of which is published. Costs thereof are first charge upon proceeds.

EXECUTORS AND ADMINISTRATORS:

Jurisdiction relating to all matters affecting letters of administration and letters of probate is vested in Supreme Court. (J-4, §106).

Preferences.—Executor has primary obligation to apply for letters of probate and in event of renunciation application for administration with will annexed shall be made. Granting of letters of administration is in discretion of court. No broad rule may be laid down, but court will be advised by majority of next of kin. (Rule 56).

Eligibility and Competency.—Nonresident (including foreign corporation) will not be appointed administrator(rix) of estate. Non-resident may be appointed executor(rix) if estate will not be prejudiced thereby. (Rule 56).

Qualification.—Administrator or executor (as case may be) must furnish affidavit when applying that s(he) will satisfactorily and fully administer estate and make such returns as by law required. (J-4, §118). In addition, administrator must furnish bond in amount double value of estate (unless Court exempts). (Rule 56).

Issue of Letters.—Application is made by way of petition to Supreme Court Trial Division or one of judges thereof to which is annexed: (1) affidavit of proof of will; (2) bond in case of administration (unless Court exempts); (3) inventory of assets and liabilities; (4) will proved by affidavit witness; (5) oath of administrator or executor. (Rule 56).

Removal.—Executor or administrator may be removed upon same grounds as court may remove trustee and court may appoint some other proper person in his place. (J-4, §121).

Special kinds of administration are with will annexed, durante minoritate (J-4, §124), pendente lite (J-4, §119), temporary and limited.

Public Administrator.—No legislation.

General Powers and Duties.—

Powers.—(1) Bring actions; (2) obtain possession of papers; (3) distrain; (4) assign and make under-leases; (5) collect, realize and distribute estate.

Duties.—(1) Obtain probate; (2) make inventory; (3) collect estate; (4) pay debts; (5) pay legacies; (6) distribute residue; (7) account. (T-10).

Notice to Creditors.—When estate is in position to distribute, in order to protect administrator or executor, notice should be given to creditors, setting time within which claims may be established. (T-10, §24).

Presentation and Proof of Claims.—Proof by affidavit may be required but no special form is legislated. Time may be extended by court on application. If claims not presented within time prescribed or extended estate may be distributed without regard to such claims. (J-4, §128).

Allowances and Widow's Quarantine.—No legislation.

Time Allowed for Administration.—Executor or administrator has one year within which to administer estate and actions against him in that period will be stayed.

Final Accounting.—After year and when estate is administered executor or administrator must file with court (unless exempted): (1) full inventory of value of estate; (2) inventory of estate received in detail; (3) statement of disbursements giving necessary details. (Rule 56).

Compensation.—Trustees, as defined by this Act, shall be allowed, over and above actual and necessary expenses, remuneration that may appear to court or judge of court to be adequate for their services, and court or judge may apportion remuneration among trustees that may appear just, according to labour bestowed or responsibility incurred by them respectively. (T-10, §52).

Where provision is made by will for specific compensation to executor, or deed or other instrument creating trust provides for specific compensation to trustee, compensation shall be full satisfaction for his or her services instead of compensation mentioned in §52 or his (her) share of that compensation, unless executor or trustee by declaration signed by trustee or executor, filed in court, renounces claim to such specific compensation.

Declaration shall be filed before probate or administration taken, or acceptance of office of trustee.

Total remuneration shall not exceed 1/20 of realized value of assets.

Where assets have not been realized court or judge may either order further realization or allow remuneration in respect of unrealized part to sum less than 1/20 of value of assets.

In case of continuing trusts court or judge may allow person entitled to remuneration, annual care and management fee not exceeding 1/250 of average market value of assets under administration. (T-10, §52).

Average market value means monetary value arrived at by ascertaining market value of assets at beginning of period under consideration, adding ascertained market value of assets at end of that period, and dividing by two.

Where estate is less than $1,000 in value, court or judge may allow remuneration that it thinks adequate.

Notwithstanding other provisions of this Act, compensation of Registrar of Supreme Court, when acting as trustee, shall be governed by Rules. (T-10, §53; CNR 972/96).

EXEMPTIONS:

(J-4).

See Topical Index in front part of this volume.

EXEMPTIONS . . . *continued*

Following property is exempt from attachment, execution and distraint: (a) furniture, household furnishings and appliances reasonably necessary for health and welfare of debtor and debtor's family having cumulative market value of not more than $5,000; (b) all necessary food, clothing and fuel for debtor and debtor's family; (c) any tools, implements and necessities used by debtor in practice of debtor's trade, profession or occupation having cumulative market value of not more than $10,000; and (d) one motor vehicle having market value of not more than $5,000, if required by debtor in course of or to retain employment or in course of and necessary to debtor's trade, profession or occupation.

Exemptions provided in (a), (b), (c), and (d) do not apply to corporate debtor.

Amounts set forth in (a), (c) and (d) may be changed from time to time by regulations made by Lieutenant Governor in Council. (J-4, §138).

Homestead Exemption.—See topic Homesteads.

FACTORS:

Common law governs.

FIDUCIARIES:

See topics Executors and Administrators; Guardian and Ward; Trusts.

FILING FEES:

See topic Corporations.

FORECLOSURE:

See topic Mortgages of Real Property.

FOREIGN CORPORATIONS:

See topic Corporations.

FRANCHISES:

No legislation.

FRAUDS, STATUTE OF:

English statute in force.

FRAUDULENT SALES AND CONVEYANCES:

(F-24).

Every charge, mortgage, conveyance, assignment or grant of property of insolvent, and every gift, delivery, or transfer of his(her) goods, and every payment made by him(her) in money, and every cognovit, warrant of attorney, judgment, or other security paid, made, or given by insolvent within two months prior to declaring insolvency and with view to giving undue preference to any creditor, is null and void in case person taking or receiving same had notice of insolvency.

Bulk Sales. (B-11).—"Sale in bulk" means sale (i) out of usual course of business or trade of seller of stock or part of it, (ii) of substantially entire stock of seller, or (iii) of interest in business of seller. (§2).

Application of Act.—This Act applies only to sales in bulk by (a) persons who, as their ostensible occupation or part of it, buy and sell goods, wares or merchandise, ordinarily subject of trade and commerce; (b) commission merchants; (c) manufacturers; and (d) proprietors of hotels, rooming houses, restaurants, motor vehicle service stations, oil or gasoline stations, or machine shops. (§3).

Exemptions.—Nothing in this Act applies to or affects sale by executor, administrator, receiver, assignee or trustee for benefit of creditors, trustee under Bankruptcy and Insolvency Act (Canada), liquidator or official receiver, public official acting under judicial process, or trader or merchant selling exclusively by wholesale or assignment by trader or merchant for general benefit of creditors. (§4).

Notice to Creditors.—Where amount to be realized from proposed sale in bulk is not sufficient to pay in full all creditors of seller, seller shall (a) at least 20 days before sale, send notice by registered mail with postage prepaid, to each of creditors; and (b) publish notice in issue of Newfoundland Gazette, publication date of which is at least 20 days before sale. (§6).

Noncompliance.—Unless this Act is complied with, sale in bulk shall be considered to be fraudulent and void as against creditors of seller, and every payment made on account of purchase price and every delivery of note or other security and every transfer, conveyance and encumbrance of property by buyer shall be considered to be fraudulent and void as between buyer and creditors of seller, but where buyer has received or taken possession of stock in bulk or part of it, buyer is personally liable to account to creditors of seller for the value of it including all money, security or property realized or taken by buyer from, out of or on account of the sale or other disposition of stock in bulk or a part of it. (§11).

Limitation.—No action shall be taken to set aside sale in bulk after six months has expired. (§13).

GARNISHMENT:

(J-4).

Goods, debts or effects of any defendant attached in hands of any third person must be paid into court or delivered to Sheriff as case may be to abide order or judgment of court.

Practice.—For purpose of ascertaining such amount, court or judge thereof may, on application of either party to suit, summon such third person or in event of his (her) absence from province, his (her) agent to appear before such court or judge to be examined on oath under order or commission and thereupon make order for delivery or payment into court of such goods, debts or effects.

Jurisdiction.—Garnishee proceedings may be commenced in Supreme Court before or after judgment.

Inferior court (Provincial Court) has no power to garnishee debts before judgment. After judgment in such court, debts may be attached to answer judgment and garnishee orders made. (S-16).

Judgment.—On application of either party to proceeding Supreme Court may summon third party to appear and be examined viva voce or by way of commission and thereupon make order for: (1) payment into court; (2) delivery to Sheriff; (3) ascertainment and realization by master of court.

GUARDIAN AND WARD:

Supreme Court has power to appoint guardian for persons and estates of infants on petition therefor being presented. Selection of guardians is determined by same rules as those observed by English courts. Failing appointment of suitable near relative as guardian, Court generally appoints Registrar. (C-13, Part IV).

Supreme Court judge on application may appoint guardian for custody and management of estate of mentally incompetent person with such powers as conferred by statute or as directed by judge. (M-10, §3).

Qualification.—Guardian must post bond, with or without sureties, payable for benefit of child in amount that Court considers appropriate. (C-13, §63).

Disposition of Estate.—If it is desired to dispose of estate of infant, application must be made to Supreme Court and directions had therefor. (C-13, §66).

HOLIDAYS:

See Canada Law Digest.

Following are nonobservance days in connection with presentment of bills of exchange, promissory notes, or in calculation of time under court procedure: Sun., Good Friday, Christmas, New Year's, Memorial ("Victoria") Day, Labour Day or day appointed to be kept in its place, any day appointed by proclamation as public feast, thanksgiving day or public holiday and day following Christmas and New Year's, when these fall on Suns. (L-2; Rule 3).

HOMESTEADS:

Not applicable in Newfoundland.

HUMAN RIGHTS:

(H-14).

The Newfoundland Human Rights Code provides for prevention of discrimination with respect to places to which public is customarily admitted, employment, and rates of pay of female employees.

Director appointed by Lieutenant Governor in Council has, subject to Minister of Employment and Labour Relations, wide powers to insure that provisions of Act are adequately enforced.

HUSBAND AND WIFE:

(F-2).

Status.—For all purposes of Newfoundland laws, married person has legal personality that is independent, separate and distinct from that of spouse.

Spouses.—In addition to man and woman married to each other, spouses include persons married by voidable marriage that has not been voided, and persons married in good faith by void marriage who have cohabited within previous year.

Matrimonial Homes.—Notwithstanding that matrimonial home is held by one of spouses, each spouse has one-half interest as joint statutory tenants in matrimonial home owned by either and occupied by them as their family residence, and has same right of use, possession and management as other spouse. (If home held by both spouses and occupied as their family residence, matrimonial home may be owned by spouses as joint tenants or as tenants-in-common.) Where more than one property qualifies as matrimonial home, spouses may designate in writing which property is to be their matrimonial home. Following registration of such designation at Registry of Deeds, any other qualifying property ceases to be matrimonial home. No spouse shall dispose of or mortgage any interest in matrimonial home without consent or release of other spouse or court order. Affidavit of disposing spouse is proof that property is not matrimonial home unless there is actual or constructive notice to contrary. Each spouse is entitled to same right of notice and redemption before any claim may be realized against matrimonial home. Upon application of spouse, court has broad powers to make orders with respect to disposition of interest in or possession of matrimonial home. Statutory joint tenancy creates right of survivorship in surviving spouse and operates to vest beneficial ownership in matrimonial home in surviving spouse without need for probate or administration of estate of deceased spouse and thus matrimonial home is not subject to division upon death as matrimonial asset. (Part I). (Generally, statutory joint tenancy has same characteristics as common law joint tenancy.)

Matrimonial Assets.—They may, upon application of either spouse, be divided equally notwithstanding ownership of these assets. Among circumstances in which such application may be made is by surviving spouse upon death of his or her spouse (but not estate of deceased spouse). Where one spouse has contributed work, money or money's worth to acquisition, management or operation of business asset, court may order upon application that compensation be awarded to contributing spouse. Presumption of advancement is abolished as between spouses and replaced by presumption of resulting trust. (Part II).

Domestic Contracts.—Man and woman may enter into marriage contract either before their marriage or during marriage while cohabiting in which they agree on respective rights and obligations, under marriage, upon separation, upon dissolution of marriage or upon death of one spouse. Man and woman who are not married to one another may enter into cohabitation agreement in which they agree upon their respective rights and obligations during cohabitation, upon ceasing to cohabit or upon death of either of them. Cohabitation agreement may be made which adopts some or all provisions of Family Law Act. Where parties to cohabitation agreement subsequently

See Topical Index in front part of this volume.

HUSBAND AND WIFE . . . *continued*
marry their agreement is deemed to be marriage contract. Marriage contract, cohabitation agreement or separation agreement may include agreement as to ownership or division of property, support obligations, and right to direct education of their children. They may not include provision as to rights to custody of or access to their children. Man and woman who married or who have cohabited, and are living separate and apart may include in agreement all of above-mentioned matters. All domestic contracts are void unless in writing, signed by parties and witnessed. Man and woman may contract out of provisions of Family Law Act by marriage contract, cohabitation agreement (where Act adopted by prior cohabitation agreement) or separation agreement. (Part IV).

INCOME TAX:

See Canada Law Digest: topic Taxation.

INDUSTRY:

(D-15.1).
Department of Industry, Trade and Technology Act, S.N. 1993, D-15.1, establishes Department and authorizes Minister of Industry, Trade and Technology to supervise, evaluate and direct development and promotion generally of growth of manufacturing and technical and service industries of province.

Financial Assistance.—Minister is responsible for evaluating merits of applications for financial assistance from province for establishing or expanding industries. (§6).

INFANTS:

Age of majority is 19. (S.N. 1971, No. 71 as am'd, which survives R.S.N., 1990).

Contracts.—Infant may make valid contract for necessaries and, under Life Insurance Act (L-14), for life insurance (§9). Otherwise, as general rule, contracts made by infant (that is, while under 19 years) are voidable.
This general rule is, however, subject to following from 01 Apr. 1996. Action shall not be maintained for purpose of charging person with respect to promise made after reaching age of 16 years to (a) pay debt or to (b) ratify promise or simple contract, which s(he) contracted or made while still under 16 years, unless promise or ratification is written and signed by that person after s(he) reaches 16. (L-16.1, §25).

Actions.—Infant sues and is sued by guardian ad litem.
Where, at time right to bring action arises, person is under disability, running of time with respect to limitation period under Limitations Act (c. L-16.1) is postponed as long as person is under disability. Person under disability includes person under 18 years. (§18).

Parental Responsibility.—Parent is not liable for tort of child committed without parent's knowledge, participation or sanction, but may be liable for negligence in making it possible for child to cause injury. (Kennedy v. Hanes, aff'd [1941] S.C.R. 384). In action against parent for damage to property or personal injury caused by fault or neglect of minor, onus of establishing that parent exercised reasonable supervision and control is on parent. (c. F-2, §77).

Termination of Parental Rights.—Governed by Child Welfare Act, C-12. Where child is in need of protection and in child's best interests to do so, court may temporarily or permanently commit child to care and custody of Director of Child Welfare or of some suitable person chosen by Director or make child subject to Director's supervision.
Where parent has abandoned or deserted child or where Court is satisfied that parental duties have been neglected, parent loses right to custody of child unless s(he) satisfies Court upon application to Court that s(he) is fit person to have custody.
For more permanent termination of parental rights see topic Adoption, subhead Effect of Adoption.

INHERITANCE TAX:

None.

INJUNCTIONS:

Governed by Judicature Act, J-4.
Injunctions are granted by Supreme Court or judge thereof. Application is made upon affidavit setting forth grounds upon which injunction is claimed. If urgent, application is ex parte.

Interim Injunction.—Court will grant interim injunction where circumstances warrant immediate interference and upon undertaking of applicant that if injunction proves wrongful any losses incurred thereby will be satisfied by him (her).

INSOLVENCY:

See Canada Law Digest: topic Bankruptcy.

INSURANCE:

(L-14).
In general, common law governs.

Life Insurance.—Contract must be in writing (§6) and contain all material terms and conditions (§15). Statements as to age are uncontestable two years after policy has been in force, but provision is made for correcting of premiums where age is misstated. (§17). Contract of insurance is binding upon delivery of policy and payment of first premium. (§11). Period of grace of 30 days is provided for payment of premiums. (§13).
Usual provisions as to insurable interest respecting life insurance apply. Person over 15 years of age may contract insurance on his life and deal with it as person of full age. (§9).
Insurer is entitled to reasonable proof of particulars surrounding maturity of contract, age of insured, beneficiaries and their right as such to receive payment. (§35).
Application may be made to court as to matters arising out of insufficiency of proof or to establish presumption of death. (§41). Thirty days notice is condition precedent. (§40).
Action against insurer for recovery of money must be commenced within one year from furnishing proof of maturity or six years after maturity of contract. (§38). Where order for presumption of death is made court may make order respecting payment of insurance money. (§42).

Life Insurance Companies. (I-9).—Before carrying on business, license must be obtained from Superintendent of Insurance. (§4). It must be renewed each year. (§12). Returns are made to Superintendent of Insurance.

Accident Guarantee or Fidelity Companies.—These must obtain license before carrying on business. License is renewable each year. Fee for license and its renewal is $50. Statement of its affairs must be supplied to Minister of Finance each year.

Fire Insurance Companies.—Annual licence fee of $600 and 2% per annum on gross premiums collected within City of St. John's must be paid by insurer to St. John's Municipal Council. Provincial tax of 12% is charged upon premiums paid by every assured and is collected by insurer if it maintains office in province; otherwise, is payable directly by assured to Minister.

Direct Actions Against Insurer.—See topic Motor Vehicles, subhead Direct Actions.

Licenses (I-10).—No license can be granted to life insurance company unless $500,000 of company's capital has been bona fide subscribed for shares therefor allotted and at least $250,000 of subscribed capital has been paid in cash. In all other types of insurance: where company undertakes insurance in province only, not less than $300,000 of its capital must be bona fide subscribed for and allotted and at least $150,000 paid in cash; where company undertakes insurance elsewhere besides province, amounts are $700,000 subscribed for and allotted and $400,000 paid in cash.
Every insurer must deposit with Minister of Justice approved securities worth, where life insurance company, $200,000; where other types insuring in province, only, $100,000; elsewhere besides province, $200,000.

Brokers.—(I-9). All holders, agents and adjusters must apply to Superintendent of Insurance for licence as defined by §2(h) before commencing employment in or carrying on business in insurance industry.
Superintendent of Insurance may refuse to issue licence or impose such restrictions, limitations or conditions as he (she) considers appropriate. (§6).
Although corporation may apply for licence under this Act, all persons who act under corporation licence must be individually licenced. (§9).
Superintendent of Insurance has power to revoke, suspend or refuse to renew licence issued under Act if, after investigation, there has been contravention of Act or regulations. (§15). Appeal from decision of Superintendent of Insurance is to appeal board consisting of three persons appointed by Lieutenant Governor in Council. (§18).
All licences shall be covered by policy of errors and omissions insurance. (§5). Amount of error and omissions insurance shall be at least $1,000,000 and fidelity insurance in amount of at least $100,000 in respect of any one occurrence. (CNR 989/96).
Licensee shall file annual statement of financial affairs of insurance business with Superintendent of Insurance within three months after fiscal year end of licensee. (§33).
Licensee in contravention of Act or regulations as defined under §45 is guilty of offence. (§46). All prosecutions under Act shall be started within two years of discovery of offence by Superintendent of Insurance. (§47).

INTEREST:

See Canada Law Digest.
(J-2).

Maximum Rate.—Subject to penal provisions of §317 of Criminal Code (R.S.C. 1985, c. C-46) there is no law to prevent parties contracting to pay and to recover any rate of interest, if contracted to be paid under written instrument, but where on suit it appears to court that interest charged is excessive, or that amount paid for expenses, inquiries, fines, bonuses, premiums or any other charge is excessive, or that transaction is harsh and unconscionable, court may reopen transaction and take account between lender and person sued and give equitable relief.

Judgments.—In action on contract, contract rate of interest applies.
Otherwise, as general rule, Judgment Interest Act (J-2) and Judgment Interest Regulations (CNR 16/96) govern. Reg. 2 (authorized by Act) provides that prejudgment and post-judgment interest rate shall be established annually by taking average Bank of Canada rate for period of Oct. and Nov. of each year, rounded to next higher whole number where average Bank of Canada rate includes fraction, minus 1%. Reg. 4 provides that on 01 Dec. or as soon afterwards as possible, in each year, Minister of Justice shall determine following year's prejudgment and post-judgment interest rate, to be effective on 01 Jan. of that following year, and cause its publication in The Newfoundland Gazette.
Effective 01 Jan. 1996 prejudgment and post-judgment interest rate is 6.0%. (CNR 779/96 authorized by Order-in-Council 96-162).

Prejudgments.—See subhead Judgments, supra.

INTESTACY:

See topic Descent and Distribution.

JUDGMENTS:

(J-4).
Generally speaking, common law and practice as to judgments applies to Newfoundland. Since 2 Sept. 1986 "order" has largely replaced "judgment" in Province's judicature.
Except where specifically provided judgment shall be obtained by motion for judgment. It may be interim or final depending upon circumstances, such as necessity for assessment of damages.

JUDGMENTS . . . *continued*

Judgment by Confession.—This procedure is seldom used. Judgments by confession include recognizance (acknowledgment upon record of debt) and cognovit (which is instrument signed by defendant in action already pending). (Rule 33).

Judgment by Consent.—In any cause or matter where defendant has appeared by solicitor no order for entering judgment by consent shall be made by consent unless consent of defendant is given by his (her) solicitor. Where defendant has not appeared he must attend in person in court and give consent unless written consent attested by solicitor is given.

Declaratory Judgments.—Court may make binding declarations of rights whether or not any consequential relief is or could be claimed.

Default Judgment.—Where no appearance or no defence has been entered within required time and claim is for liquidated demand, final judgment may be entered upon affidavit proving claim having been filed. In unliquidated matter judgment may be entered subject to further directions of court or master. In matters which originally could only have been brought before court of chancery plaintiff must proceed as if defendant had appeared. (Rules 16, 17).

Revival.—Judgment which has been dormant for six years may be revived on application supported by affidavit. (Rule 51).

Foreign Judgments (R-4).—Judgments obtained in superior courts in U.K. may be registered in Newfoundland Supreme Court. Permission to register judgments given in superior courts of any country, whether any of Her Majesty's Dominions or foreign country, may be granted by Government of Newfoundland where such superior courts give substantial reciprocity of treatment to judgments of Supreme Court of Newfoundland. Application to register foreign judgments must be made to Newfoundland Supreme Court within six years from date of judgment, or, where there have been proceedings by way of appeal against judgment, within six years after date of last judgment given in those proceedings.

While there is no statute so prescribing, arguably enforcement of foreign judgment would have limitation of 20 years as does local judgment. Whether registered or not foreign judgments may be used by way of defence or counterclaim between same parties in all Newfoundland proceedings founded on same cause of action.

LABOUR RELATIONS:

(L-2).

General law of master and servant as provided for by common law applies. There are also statutory requirements respecting employment standards, human rights, collective bargaining, occupational health and safety. (L-2, H-14, L-1, O-3).

Labour Relations Act (L-1).—Act provides legal framework for acquisition and termination of collective bargaining rights by trade unions, negotiations of collective agreements, resolution of industrial disputes and prohibition of unfair labour practices.

Labour Unions (L-1).—Labour unions are fully recognized. Provision is made for incorporation. Certain enactments have been made for protection of funds of unions. Apart from collective agreements if union can show that it represents majority of employees in unit it may apply to Labour Relation Board for certification as sole bargaining agent in such unit. Union must, when required, file with Minister of Employment and Labour Relations their constitution and list of officers. (§142).

Labour Disputes.—Labour Relations Act, L-1, respecting right of employees to organize and providing for mediation and conciliation of industrial disputes, makes provision for setting up of Conciliation Board and/or Industrial Inquiry Commission to inquire into any labour or industrial disputes referred to it by Minister of Employment and Labour Relations, and to make recommendation thereon. (§98). Labour Relations Board consisting of chairman and four other members, with equal number of members representing employees and employers, is charged with administration of this Act and exercises powers and performs duties imposed therein. (§108).

Labour Standards Act (L-2).—Act provides for minimum standards of conditions of employment in province.

Wages.—Minimum wage for all persons over 16 is $4.75 per hour prior to 01 Sept. 1996; $5 per hour from and including 01 Sept. 1996 to and including 31 Mar. 1997; and $5.25 per hour from 01 Apr. 1997. If employee works more than 44 hours a week (s)he must be paid overtime wages at rate of not less than $7.12 an hour prior to 01 Sept. 1996; $7.50 per hour from and including 01 Sept. 1996 to and including 31 Mar. 1997; and $7.89 per hour from 01 Apr. 1997. (CNR 781/96; NF Reg. 77/96). Minimum rates of wages apply to employee whether he is paid on basis of hourly rate of pay or on basis of fixed wage per week or month or for any part of month and to assistants who are remunerated either wholly or in part on minimum basis. Minister of Employment and Labour Relations has certain powers to make orders respecting special minimum wages for handicapped employees; and to authorize investigations for purpose of determining whether requirements of Act are being observed.

Child Labour.—Between hours of 9 P.M. and 8 A.M. no child under age of 16 may be employed. There is no provision as to wages.

Annual Vacation.—Labour Standards Act, L-2, provides that employees who work 90% of regular working hours in any continuous 12 month period must be given, no later than ten months after 12 month period ends, annual vacation of at least two weeks. (§8). Crown and Crown agencies are bound by this Act but there is provision for making of orders declaring this Act inapplicable in respect to classes of employees set out in such orders. Any person who has worked for less time than that which qualifies him (her) to receive vacation plus vacation pay shall receive equivalent of vacation pay in proportion to time worked. In event of employment terminating before vacation granted employer must pay, in lieu of vacation, 4% of gross pay for period worked in that year. (§9).

Notice of Termination of Employment.—Both employers and employees must give notice of termination of employment, extent of which varies with type of employment and means of payment. (§§52, 53). Prosecution with consent of Minister of Employment and Labour Relations only. Penalties: fine (maximum $100), and employer or employee may be ordered to make payment equivalent to employee's earning during required notice period.

Worker's Compensation Act (W-11).—Worker's Compensation Act provides for Worker's Compensation Board consisting of not less than seven nor more than 11 members appointed by Lieutenant Governor in Council. (§4). This Board administers accident fund from which is paid compensation, medical aid, outlays and other expenses to workers injured in course of their employment or members of family of workers killed in course of employment. This fund is formed by contributions from employers who are classified by Board and required to make annual assessment varying with different classes. (Part VIII). Workers eligible for contribution from fund apply to Board which hears evidence and decides upon amount to be granted applicant and manner of payment. Act sets out fully numerous duties and wide powers of Board which is for purpose of Act judicial body. (Part IV).

Unemployment Insurance Compensation.—Under provisions of Unemployment Insurance Act (R.S.C. 1985, c. U.1) any person employed in Canada in wage earning employment under contract of service is entitled to be insured for Unemployment Insurance benefits.

See also topic Human Rights.

LANDLORD AND TENANT:

(R-14).

Common law applies to landlord and tenant relations, except as modified by Newfoundland legislation including Residential Tenancies Act, R-14.

Kinds of Tenancies.—Tenancy may be at will, at sufferance, for definite period, or as provided for by statute.

Leases.—Unless there has been such part performance as will, in equity, dispense with necessity of writing or memorandum, agreement providing for lease must be in writing and signed by party to be charged or his (her) lawfully authorized agent. While such writing need not be made at time of contract or contained in single document, it must be such as to satisfy requirements of Statute of Frauds and must state parties to agreement, premises to be demised and commencement and duration of term.

Residential Tenancies.—Where written residential lease entered into, landlord must provide copy of lease to tenant or tenant may quit premises at any time after giving written notice. Landlord must in any case provide free copy of Residential Tenancies Act to each tenant. Otherwise tenant is not liable for rent. (§6).

Lease for term not exceeding three years may be made verbally or by writing under hand only. Under Statute of Frauds, all leases of lands, Messages, tenements, hereditaments, etc., must be in writing and signed by parties or their agents lawfully authorized in writing, otherwise they have effect of leases at will only.

Statutory conditions now implied in every landlord-tenant relationship which cannot be waived include: landlord must keep premises fit for habitation, mitigate damages where tenancy terminates, cannot lock or alter locks on premises in control of tenant. Tenant must keep premises clean and fit for habitation. Short of emergency, landlord cannot enter demised premises without tenant's written permission. (§9).

Although rarely done, leases are registrable at Registry of Deeds.

Termination of tenancy must be by notice in writing in time specified by Act; except, where tenant in arrears one rent period, he may be forced to vacate at end of next rent period.

Distress.—All goods on leased premises, except certain personal effects and implements of trade, may be distrained for arrears of rent. Security deposit limited to two weeks rent and landlord must pay interest thereon. (J-4, §135).

Building Leases (L-10).—Every lease made after Aug. 1, 1921 of vacant land in St. John's by which lessee covenants to erect building thereon is subject to condition that lessee or assigns is entitled to purchase, at any time during lease or extension, freehold in land upon payment to lessor or to City of St. John's of sum equal to 20 times amount of annual rental payable under lease. (L-10, §3).

Every lease made after Aug. 2, 1921 of vacant land in St. John's and upon which lessee has erected building is subject to conditions that: (a) where land is not occupied for commercial use lessee is entitled to purchase freehold of land upon payment to City of St. John's of sum equal to 40 times annual rent, (b) where land is being occupied for commercial use lessee is entitled to purchase freehold of land at its fair market value as if it were vacant land or obtain extension of lease at fair rental as if it were vacant. (§§4, 6).

See also topic Human Rights.

Landlord and tenant proceedings dealt with by Residential Tenancies Boards or by Provincial Court in summary manner.

LEASES:

See topic Landlord and Tenant.

LEGISLATURE:

Consists of provincial House of Assembly under provisions of Constitution Act, 1867 as amended (formerly, until 17 Apr. 1982, known as British North America Act).

Sessions.—No statutory provision as to holding of regular or fixed sessions.

LICENSES:

There is municipal tax upon commercial travellers not domiciled in Newfoundland; fire, marine, life and accident insurance companies; telegraph companies; trust companies; loan and investment companies; stockbrokers; transient dealers, auctioneers, junk dealers, peddlers and hawkers; plumbers, and real estate agents.

In case of commercial travellers tax amounts to $200 per annum. If commercial traveller commences business after June 30 in any year, he is liable for half of this tax. Taxes payable by others vary from $5 to $500. (C-17).

The Food and Drug Act, F-21, requires licenses for vending of many food products (§10) and special legislation governs licenses for export of salt fish, which is regulated by province controlled board. (S-7).

Licenses are also required for sale of livestock (L-20, §10); by anyone dealing in salvage and operating salvage yard (S-8, §5), and by persons operating commercial laundries, laundromats and dry cleaning establishments.

See Topical Index in front part of this volume.

LICENSES . . . *continued*

Salesmen.—Door-to-door salesmen and persons who contact occupant of house by telephone for purpose of selling or soliciting orders must register in accordance with Direct Sellers Act, D-24.

Direct sales contracts involving rebate or discounts to purchaser in return for assistance in referral selling of goods and services not binding.

See also topic Banks and Banking.

LIENS:

Major statutory liens are mechanics', builders', suppliers' and workers' (c. M-3); corporations' on shares (c. C-36, §82); innkeepers' (c. I-1, §6); venders' (on chattels) (c. S-6, §§42, 43, 44); lien on timber and trees in favour of Crown (c. F-28, §§31, 69). Major common law liens are: auctioneers', bailees', carriers', solicitors' and vendors' (on land).

Enforcement.—General remedy for enforcement of liens is by retention of property subject thereto, but there are certain statutory powers of sale and remedies with respect to some liens. There is no right of redemption after sale.

Mechanics Lien Act (c. M-3).—Act applies to all contracts, to all subcontracts arising under those contracts and to all services or materials supplied thereunder. Where person who supplies services or materials to be used in making, constructing, erecting, fitting, altering, improving or repairing of land, building, structure or works for owner, contractor, or subcontractor, that person by doing that work or placing or providing those materials, has lien for price of those services or materials upon estate or interest of owner in land, building, structure or works and appurtenances thereto, limited, however, in amount, to sum due to person entitled to lien and sum owing by owner (except, for example, where there is express contract to contrary). (§6). In all cases, person primarily liable upon contract under and by virtue of which lien may arise shall, as work is done or materials are provided under contract, retain for period of 30 days after completion or abandonment of work done or to be done under contract, 10% of value of work and materials actually supplied. (§12). Lien of worker for wages has priority over other liens to extent of 30 days wages. (§16).

Every lien for which claim is not registered expires 30 days following earlier of publication of notice of substantial performance of contract (§12.3), completion or abandonment of contract or subcontract, or date on which claimant last supplied services or materials (§22). Registration must be made against lands on which building or construction is done, and where claim has been registered, lien ceases to exist, unless proceeding is commenced to enforce it within 90 days following earlier of events set out above. (§24). Prior mortgage has priority only to extent of actual value of land and premises at time first lien arose, which value is to be ascertained by judge. (§8).

LIMITATION OF ACTIONS:

(L-16.1).

Numerous statutes of province provide for limitations. Principal limitation of actions statute is Limitations Act, S.N. 1995, c. L-16.1 (in force: 01 Apr. 1996).

Main limitation periods prescribed by Act are as follows:

Following expiration of two years after date on which right to do so arose, person shall not bring action: (a) for damages in respect of injury to person or property (including economic loss arising from injury whether based on contract, tort or statutory duty); (b) for damages in respect of injury to person or property (including economic loss arising from negligent representation and professional negligence whether based on contract, tort, or statutory duty); (c) for trespass to property not contemplated by (a) above; (d) for defamation other than defamation contemplated by Defamation Act §17; (e) for false imprisonment; (f) for malicious prosecution; (g) for conspiracy to commit wrong referred to in (a), (b), (c), (d) and (e) above; (h) which is civil action to recover fine or other penalty and to recover fine or penalty imposed by court "or law"; (i) under Fatal Accidents Act; or (j) under Privacy Act.

Following expiration of six years after date on which right to do so arose, person shall not bring action: (a) for damages for conversion or detention of goods; (b) to recover goods wrongfully taken or retained; (c) for tort committed against that person which is not contemplated by (a) above in previous paragraph; (d) to enforce instrument under seal; (e) to enforce forfeiture of recognizance; (f) to enforce obligation arising from statute; (g) to enforce foreign judgment; (h) to recover debt; (i) by creditor not in possession of collateral, to realize on collateral; and (j) by debtor not in possession of collateral, to redeem collateral. ("Debtor" means person who owes payment or other performance of obligation which is secured; whether or not s(he) owns or has rights in collateral.)

Following expiration of ten years after date on which to do so arose, person shall not bring action: (a) on judgment of court in province for payment of money or recovery of personal property; (b) against personal representative of deceased person for share of estate; (c) against trustee for fraud or fraudulent breach of trust to which trustee was party or privy; (d) against trustee for conversion of trust property to trustee's own use; (e) to recover trust property or property into which trust property can be traced; (f) to recover money on account of wrongful distribution of trust property, against person to whom property is distributed, or successor of such person; or (g) to recover land (other than Crown lands under Lands Act).

As general rule, action for which limiting provision is not included either (a) above or (b) in another statute, shall not be brought after expiration of six years after date on which cause of action arose.

Where person against whom action lies confirms cause of action, time before date of that confirmation shall not count when calculating limitation period for person having benefit of confirmation against person bound by that confirmation. Confirmation must be given before expiration of limitation period for that right of action (where that right of action bound by limitation). Confirmation must be in writing and signed by person against whom cause of action lies or that person's agent. Extensive additional provisions as to confirmation prescribed by §16.

Where cause of action is for damages in which (a) claim involves breach of duty of care founded in contract, tort, or statutory duty and (b) damages claimed involve personal injury or property damage (including economic loss, negligent misrepresentation, or professional negligence), cause of action is considered to arise and limitation period commences to run on date on which damage first occurs.

Furthermore, where cause of action involves (a) personal injury; (b) property damage; (c) professional negligence; (d) relief from consequences of mistake; (e) Fatal Accidents Act; and (f) non-fraudulent breach of trust, limitation period fixed by Act does not begin to run against person until s(he) knows or, considering all circumstances of matter, ought to know that s(he) has cause of action. (Burden of proving that running of limitation period has been postponed or suspended, in any of these circumstances, is on person claiming benefit of postponement or suspension.) Notwithstanding these provisions as to postponement or suspension, action these provisions contemplate shall not be taken after expiration of ten years from later of (a) date of act or omission on which action is based or (b) date of last series of acts or omissions or termination of course of conduct where action is based on series of acts or omissions or continuing curse of conduct.

Disabilities of Plaintiff.—Where at time right to bring action arises, person is under disability, running of time with respect to limitation period under Act is postponed so long as that person is under disability. (Person under disability means person [a] under 18 years; or [b] incapable of management of affairs because of disease or impairment of physical or mental condition; or [c] [for purpose of action for misconduct of sexual nature other than action under §8(2)]; incapable of commencing action due to her[his] mental or physical condition resulting from that sexual misconduct.)

No Limitations.—§8(2), mentioned in subhead Disabilities of Plaintiff, supra, is part of provision listing causes of action not governed by limitation period.

That provision, in summary, provides as follows: §8(1) person not governed by limitation period can bring action (a) relating to enforcement of injunction or restraining order; (b) for declaration as to title to property by person in possession of that property; (c) as mortgagor, to redeem real or personal property in her(his) exclusive possession; (d) as mortgagee, to foreclose or exercise power of sale with respect to real or personal property in her(his) possession; (e) for declaration as to personal status; or (f) to enforce easement, restrictive covenent, profit-a-prendre or other incorporeal hereditament (except action for damages for interference with or breach of that easement, restrictive covenant, profit-a-prendre or incorporeal hereditament); §8(2): where misconduct of sexual nature has been committed against person and that person was (a) under care or authority of or (b) financially, emotionally, physically or otherwise dependent upon, or (c) beneficiary of fiduciary relationship with, another person or organization or agency, there shall be no limitation period and action arising from that sexual misconduct may be brought at any time.

General Provisions.—Notwithstanding that time within which action may, under Act, be taken is extended by virtue of (a) confirmation or (b) postponement or suspension, no action to which Act applies shall be brought after expiration of 30 years from date on which events giving rise to cause of action last occurred; provided, however, that this limitation does not apply to causes of action contemplated under §8(1) and §8(2) summarized above.

Act also contains extensive provisions respecting trusts; recovery of land, and guarantees and sureties.

Act applies to actions in province to exclusion of laws of all other jurisdictions which (a) impose limitation periods for bringing actions or which (b) in another manner prohibit or restrict bringing of action because of lapse of time or delay.

Act applies to causes of action that arose before Act took effect on 01 Apr. 1996 as well as to causes of action that arise after Act took effect.

Nothing in Act revives cause of action in respect of which limitation period has expired before Act took effect.

Where cause of action that arose before Act took effect was not governed by limitation period or limitation period fixed by Act is shorter than limitation period that formerly governed cause of action that arose before Act took effect and, further, limitation period fixed by Act expired before Act took effect or less than two years after Act took effect, applicable limitation period for such cause of action is shorter of following: (a) limitation period that formerly governed, or (b) two years before 01 Apr. 1996 (date Act took effect).

Act repeals considerable number of previously obtaining limitation periods including those under City of St. John's Act and other municipal legislation, under Highway Traffic Act, under Law Society Act, and under Proceedings Against the Crown Act.

LIMITED PARTNERSHIP:

See topic Partnership.

MARRIAGE:

(S-19).

Solemnization of Marriage Act, S-19, governs. No residency requirement. Marriages may be solemnized by clergyman registered under Act or marriage commissioner authorized by Act or by Mayor of City of St. John's, City of Corner Brook, or City of Mount Pearl or by Provincial Court judges. (§§3, 10). Ceremony must be performed in presence of two credible witnesses who are at least 16 years of age. Act sets out form of ceremony required, as minimum, to be used. (§12).

Consent.—Written consent of parents or guardians must be had in circumstances such as where either party is 16 years or over but under full age of 19 years, except where judicially dispensed with, or in case of marriage of expectant mother, or in case of mother of child then living which was born out of wedlock. (§§18, 19).

License.—Ordinarily required to be had and delivered to solemnizer at least four days before solemnization of marriage can take place and no license will be issued to person who is under 16 years old or who is under influence of alcohol or drugs. Person who is under 16 years old who is pregnant may obtain license by court order. License is valid for 30 days after issuance unless issued for 60 day term. (§12). Every application for license must be accompanied by affidavit in prescribed form. (§15).

Proxy marriages are not recognized.

Common law marriages are not recognized.

See Topical Index in front part of this volume.

MARRIAGE . . . *continued*

Annulment.—Grounds for annulment of marriage are same as in most other common law provinces of Canada; being those grounds recognized at common law.

MARRIED WOMEN:

See topics Husband and Wife; Marriage.

MASTER AND SERVANT:

See topic Labour Relations.

MECHANICS' LIENS:

See topic Liens.

MINES AND MINERALS:

(M-12).

License.—No person may search and prospect for minerals without first obtaining miner's license for that purpose. (§20). In case s(he) discovers any deposit of mineral and desires to obtain title thereto, he must first stake location by placing stake consisting of wooden post not less than 1.2 metres above ground and not less than 8.75 centimetres in width and 3.75 centimetres in thickness on vein or deposit of mineral discovered. (Reg. 171/93).

Exclusive Right.—Subject to terms under which license is issued, licensee has exclusive right to explore for minerals in, on or under area of land described in license from date of issuing. (§23).

Limits.—License confers no right to remove minerals except for purpose of sampling, assaying and testing. (§23).

Mineral Holdings Import Act (M-14).—Imposes tax per hectare for 1992 of $8; 1993, $9; 1994, $10; 1995, $11; 1996, $12. For each year after 1996, $12.50. Rentals paid for land and amount expended on lands for exploration may be deducted from impost. Rights to mineral lands will be forfeited for nonpayment of impost. (§7).

Quarry Materials.—The Quarry Materials Act, Q-1, prohibits any person from excavating, digging for, removing or carrying away quarry material except in accordance with provisions of permit or lease issued or continued under Act. (§4). Exclusive exploration licence gives grantee exclusive right in designated area to remove quarry material but only for purpose of sampling, assaying and testing. (§6). Minister of Natural Resources may grant permit to remove quarry material for period not exceeding one year (§7) or grant lease of quarry materials for period not exceeding 20 years (§8). All permits and leases are subject to terms and conditions prescribed in Regulation CNR 804/96 in addition to such other terms and conditions imposed by Minister. Minister may designate areas within province which are exempt from issuance of exploration licences. (CNR 804/96).

MONOPOLIES AND RESTRAINT OF TRADE:

See Canada Law Digest.

MORTGAGES OF PERSONAL PROPERTY:

See topic Chattel Mortgages.

MORTGAGES OF REAL PROPERTY:

(C-34).

Execution.—Mortgagor must sign and seal instrument before witness who, unless authorized by law to witness, must prove same by affidavit for purpose of registration.

Registration is not necessary for validity of mortgage as between parties but is necessary in order to secure priority and charge third persons with notice. Place of registration is Registry of Deeds at St. John's. There is no time limit for registering real estate mortgages.

Registration fee is based on value of money or other consideration (minimum fee: $51).

Future advances must be specifically provided for in instrument, and registration fees are increased accordingly.

Assignment must be by document under seal, proven as in case of mortgage.

Release may be for whole or part of premises. Document of release must be registered to clear title.

Remedies of Mortgagee in Case of Default.—Mortgagee has four courses of action open to him (her) upon default of payment, all or any of which s(he) may resort to, namely: (1) foreclose mortgage (§17); (2) sell property under power of sale (§6); (3) sue mortgagor upon covenant to pay (§5); (4) appoint receiver. S(he) may pursue all remedies concurrently. Mortgagee has power, where mortgage money or interest is one month overdue, to sell mortgaged property. (§6).

Power of sale must be exercised strictly in accordance with its terms.

Redemption.—Mortgagor may redeem property at any time before final order for foreclosure or sale or before sale under power of sale.

Chattel Mortgages.—See topic Chattel Mortgages.

MOTOR VEHICLES:

(H-3).

Vehicle license from Department of Works, Services and Transportation required annually. No exemption for members of Armed Forces. Number plates must be displayed front and rear and must not be defaced or obliterated. (§§30, 31).

Registration and licensing required of motorized snow vehicles and all terrain vehicles.

Operator's license from Department of Works, Services and Transportation required annually for three year term. No exemption for members of Armed Forces. Special regulations exist as to chauffeur's license and snowmobiles. (M-20).

Identification Marks.—License may not be issued for vehicle where manufacturer's serial identification number or mark has been obliterated or defaced.

Sales.—No person may deal in motor vehicles or act as agent for sale thereof unless licensed by Department of Works, Services and Transportation. Dealer in second hand cars must report each sale to Department within six days after made.

Operation Prohibited.—By person under 17 years of age or physically disabled, or if license cancelled. (§48).

Accidents.—Person in charge of car which is involved in accident must remain at scene, render all possible assistance, give to traffic officer and person sustaining injury or loss number of vehicle license, name and address of owner and of operator (if not owner) of car, and show to them his(her) driver's license. Report required, immediately, of accident involving damages over $1,000. Except in case of collision, there is presumption that damage by motor vehicle was due to negligence of operator. (§169).

Seatbelts.—With certain exceptions, use of seatbelts in vehicles driven on highways when vehicle equipped with seatbelts is mandatory. (§178).

Liability of Owner.—Under Highway Traffic Act registered owner liable for damages caused by motor vehicle when driven by any person with his (her) consent. Where Act violated, vehicle owner liable for penalty when violation requires vehicle to be in motion in which event driver liable for penalty.

Guests.—Liability for injury to gratuitous guest restricted to gross negligence or wanton misconduct.

Financial Responsibility.—See topic Insurance.

Insurance.—All drivers must carry public liability insurance of at least $200,000. Judgement Recovery (Nfld.) Ltd. Act, R.S.N. 1990, c. J-3 is repealed and supplanted by Act to Amend the Automobile Insurance Act which took effect July 1, 1994.

Direct Actions.—Under Automobile Insurance Act any person upon obtaining judgment against person insured under policy of automobile insurance has direct cause of action against insurer for amount of judgment and costs within minimum policy limits.

Actions Against Nonresidents.—There are no special provisions with respect to such actions.

Automobile Dealers and Salesmen.—See topic Consumer Protection.

Gasoline Tax.—See topic Taxation.

NEGOTIABLE INSTRUMENTS:

See Canada Law Digest: topic Bills and Notes.

NOTARIES PUBLIC:

(N-5).

Appointed for life by Minister of Justice. Jurisdiction extends over Province of Newfoundland and may witness document brought before him (her) subject to Law Society Act.

PARTITION:

Common law governs.

PARTNERSHIP:

(P-3; L-17).

Law relating to partnership governed by Partnership Act, P-3, and Limited Partnership Act, L-17.

Limited Partnership Formation.—By compliance with Act and recording in Registry of Companies. (L-17, §4).

Limited Partnership Name.—No restriction so long as does not conflict with name of any other limited partnership.

Rights and Liabilities of Limited Partners Inter Se, (L–17).—Governed by agreement or inferred from course of dealing. Joint properties must be held for purposes of partnership. (§3). Absent agreement, partners share equally in capital, profit and liabilities. (§10). Every partner entitled to take part in management. Partners are accountable for all profits. (§29).

Rights and Liabilities as to Third Parties, (L-17).—Every partner is agent of firm and his acts bind firm in absence of notice to third party of lack of authority. (§9). Every partner liable jointly for all debts of firm, torts and misapplication of property. (§11).

Dissolution, (P-3).—If for fixed term, on expiration of term. If for single adventure, on termination of adventure. Where no fixed term, by notice from any partner (§32) or upon death or insolvency of any partner (§33). Court may decree dissolution upon application of any partner in case of mental incompetence or other incapacity, or misconduct of, or breach of partnership agreement by any partner; also where business operating at loss. (§35).

Ex Juris Partnership, (L-17).—Any partnership formed in any other province and there registered as limited partnership may be registered in province and be entitled to same or like limitation of liability in province. (L-17, §4).

PERPETUITIES:

Common law governs.

PLEADING:

Governed by Judicature Act, J-4 and Rules of The Supreme Court, 1986.

PLEDGES:

Rights and duties of pledgor and pledgee are generally governed by common law. Special provisions are contained in Bank Act, S.C. 1991, c. 46.

See Canada Law Digest.

PRACTICE:

In Supreme Court practice is governed by Judicature Act, J-4 and Rules of The Supreme Court, 1986 as well as practices not inconsistent with Act or Rules. These Rules are largely same as English Rules.

Practice in Provincial Court is governed by Summary Proceedings Act, S-30, which in some respects is similar to English Summary Jurisdiction Act.

Direct Actions Against Insurer.—See topic Motor Vehicles, subhead Direct Actions.

See also topics Actions; Appeal and Error; Attachment; Depositions; Executions; Garnishment; Injunctions; Judgments; Pleading; and Process.

PRINCIPAL AND AGENT:

Common law governs.

Collection Agencies.—See topic Consumer Protection.

PROCESS:

(Rules 6 to 10).

Commencement of Proceeding.—Action is commenced in Supreme Court (Trial Division) by statement of claim or originating application requiring defendant to file defence within ten days unless extended by order, otherwise judgment may be given against him (her) by default. In cases of service outside jurisdiction period is extended to such time as court or judge may order. Statement of claim setting forth succinctly grounds and particulars of action must always be served on defendant personally or, with court's leave, substitutionally.

Personal Service on Infant.—Where infant is defendant service on father, mother or guardian or person with whom infant resides, unless court otherwise orders, is good service.

Who May Serve.—There is no special provision in Newfoundland.

Personal Service on Incompetent.—Where person is of unsound mind, service shall be effected on one of committee, person with whom s(he) resides or custodian, unless court orders to contrary.

Partnership.—Service shall be effected upon any one or more partners where action taken against partners as firm.

Corporation-Statutory or Aggregate.—Service upon municipality may be effected upon Mayor or other authorized official. Service upon other corporations may be effected by serving at registered office of company or upon responsible official there.

Foreign Corporation.—If foreign corporation doing business in Newfoundland is represented by agent here, service may be effected by leaving process at agent's office.

Service by Mail or Publication.—On proof to satisfaction of court or judge as to impracticability of personal service of process, it may be by registered post, by advertisement in newspapers, or otherwise as court or judge may order.

Service Outside of the Jurisdiction.—Generally, absent defendant cannot be sued, but court may grant leave to issue statement of claim or originating application against him (her) for service out of jurisdiction whenever: (a) whole subject matter of action is land situate within jurisdiction; or (b) any will, deed, act, or contract affecting land within jurisdiction is sought to be construed; or (c) any relief is sought against any person domiciled or against any ordinary resident within jurisdiction; or (d) action is for administration of estate of deceased resident within jurisdiction or execution of trusts which ought to be administered according to Newfoundland laws; or (e) action is founded on any breach, within jurisdiction, of any contract wherever made, which, according to terms thereof ought to be performed within jurisdiction; or (f) any tort committed within jurisdiction; or (g) any person who is necessary party to action properly brought against some other person duly served within jurisdiction.

Nonresident Motorist.—See topic Motor Vehicles.

PROOF OF CLAIMS:

See topic Executors and Administrators.

REAL PROPERTY:

All lands, tenements and other hereditaments in province which, by common law are regarded as real estate, are held to be "chattels real" and go to executor or administrator of any person or persons dying seised or possessed thereof as other personal estate now passes to personal representatives, notwithstanding any law, usage or custom to contrary. (C-11).

Following estates in real property are recognized: freeholds (i.e., fee simple), leaseholds, life interests, joint tenancy and tenancy in common.

Abandoned lands includes lands granted, leased, or licensed under Part 1 of Lands Act (S.N. 1991) or former Act respecting Crown lands and lands unlawfully occupied that have been for at least 20 years unused and unoccupied by original grantee, lessee or licensee or person in unlawful occupation (§43). Minister may begin proceedings to revest abandoned lands in Crown where no person lawfully entitled to lands or interest in them can be found in province.

Real Estate Agents, (R-2).—No action may be brought to recover commission unless agent is licensed and agreement is in writing signed by party to be charged. (§33). Commission to be charged must be either agreed amount or percentage of sale price or rental. (§44). Every listing agreement must contain provision that is to expire on specified date and copy must be given to party signing it. (§45).

Agents must obtain yearly license from Superintendent (§6) and post bond (§19). Agents must maintain proper books and records and keep trust account for moneys received. (§28). Agent may not him(her)self purchase listed property without full disclosure to listing owner. (§41).

Condominiums, (C-29).—Division of properties into parts that are to be owned individually and parts that are to be owned in common, and their use and management, are provided for in Condominium Act.

See also topics Deeds; Husband and Wife; Landlord and Tenant; Mortgages of Real Property; Partition.

RECEIVERS:

(C-36, Part VIII; Rule 52).

Equitable Execution.—Supreme Court has power to appoint receivers of property by way of equitable execution upon same principles as those followed by English Chancery courts.

Receiver must give security unless otherwise ordered, and receiver's accounts may be referred to master of Supreme Court for inquiry and report.

Registrar of Supreme Court is official receiver of companies wound up by court.

RECORDS:

(C-36; R-10; V-6).

Registrable Instruments.—All deeds, decrees, judgments, conveyances, and other assurances whereby any lands or tenements in Newfoundland may be affected may be registered. All bills of sale, conveyances and mortgages of personal chattels in Newfoundland, where actual possession of such chattels continues in grantor or mortgagor should be registered to maintain priority against subsequent purchaser. Registration is not compulsory but is means of protection against subsequent purchaser.

Place of Registration.—Records of companies are kept in Registry of Companies; records of deeds in Registry of Deeds; records of Crown lands in Department of Environment and Lands, all in St. John's.

Requisites.—To be registered, deed must be proven either (1) by acknowledgment of execution by any person from whom interest passes or (2) by affidavit of witness to execution of any such person made before proper person. (§§17, 18).

See also topic Acknowledgment.

Recording Fees.—Respecting any document filed with Registrar of Companies there shall be paid minimum of $51. Fee commensurate with value of property transferred is payable in respect of mortgages, conveyances and transfers and $51 is charged upon agreements, leases, etc.

Effect of Recording.—Recording does not give any additional rights as admissible evidence. Registration constitutes notice of instrument to all persons claiming any interest in lands subsequent to registration notwithstanding any defect in registration. (§8).

Torrens Act.—Not applicable in Newfoundland.

Transfer of Decedent's Title.—After probate this may be effected by assent or conveyance filed in usual manner upon execution by executor and proven in manner above stated (under subhead Requisites, supra).

Vital Statistics.—Records of births, marriages, deaths, adoptions, and changes of name are kept in office of Registrar General with office at St. John's. Record of birth may be established by production of satisfactory evidence supported by affidavit and filed with Registrar General.

REPLEVIN:

Action not applicable in Newfoundland, except for recovery of chattels wrongfully distrained.

REPORTS:

Reports of many decisions of Supreme Court and Provincial Court are published in Newfoundland & Prince Edward Island Reports and in Atlantic Provinces Reports by Maritime Law Book Ltd., Box 302, Fredericton, New Brunswick, Canada, E3B 4Y9, telephone 1-800-561-0220 (from anywhere in Canada or U.S.A. other than Alaska and Hawaii), telecopier 1-506-453-9525, and all such decisions are procurable from issuing court.

Summaries of reports available monthly from Newfoundland Case Digest, P.O. Box 5835, St. John's, NF, Canada A1C 5X3, telephone 1-709-722-7000; telecopier 1-709-726-1225.

RESTRAINT OF TRADE:

See Canada Law Digest: topic Monopolies and Restraint of Trade.

SALES:

The English Sales of Goods Act is largely replicated in Sales of Goods Act, S-6. International Sales of Goods Act (I-16) was adopted as law of Newfoundland 01 May 1992.

Conditional sales are governed by C-28, similar to Ontario Act. See Ontario Law Digest, topic Personal Property Security. Filing fee is $20. In case of chattels personal capable of being affixed to land, in addition to ordinary filing in Registry of Conditional Sales notice must be filed by seller with Registrar of Deeds not later than 30 days after commencement of affixing of goods to land setting out: name and address of seller and buyer; adequate description of goods; name and address of owner of land to which goods to be affixed; description of land; amount unpaid on purchase price or under terms and conditions of hiring; registration no. of conditional sale in Registry of Conditional Sales. (§15).

Conveyances of Personal Chattels, Other Than Conditional Sales or Bills of Sale.—If possession of chattels remains with grantor, must be registered in accordance with Registration of Deeds Act, R-10, within period of 30 days after execution or be void against subsequent purchaser for valuable consideration or attachment or execution upon chattels which has been registered before conveyance. (R-10, §34).

Consumer Protection.—See topic Consumer Protection.

Bulk Sales.—See topic Fraudulent Sales and Conveyances.

See also topic Licenses.

SALES TAX:

See topic Taxation, subhead Social Security Tax.

SEALS:

Not necessary to validity of documents conveying property except in case of corporation.

SECURITIES:

(S-13).

Registration of Brokers.—Person or company shall not (a) trade in security unless person or company is registered as dealer, or is registered as salesperson or as partner or as officer of registered dealer and is acting on behalf of dealer; (b) act as underwriter unless person or company is registered as underwriter; or (c) act as adviser unless person or company is registered as adviser, or is registered as partner or as officer of registered adviser and is acting on behalf of adviser, and registration has been made in accordance with Act and regulations and person or company has received written notice of registration from director and, where registration is subject to terms and conditions, person or company complies with terms and conditions.

Exempt Transactions.—Registration is not required for trade in security arising from administrator's or executor's or guardian's, etc., sale or isolated sale or where one party is bank. (§§15, 16). Application for registration must be in writing and accompanied by bond in sum prescribed by regulation. (§30). Application may be refused or cancelled or reduced to temporary registration.

Fraudulent Acts.—Where, upon statement made on oath or affirmation, it appears probable to Securities Commission of Newfoundland that person or company has (a) contravened Act or regulation authorized by Act or (b) committed offence under Criminal Code in connection with trade in securities, Commission may, by order, appoint person to make investigation that Commission considers expedient for Act's administration. (Part IV). Act further provides, in circumstances such as where investigation has been ordered, that Commission may order persons and companies, authorized under Act to trade, to curtail their activities in respects and to extent Commission directs.

Voidable Transactions.—Where any person has contracted as broker with customer to buy and carry securities on margin and while contract is in force sells securities for account in which he has any interest, if effect thereof be to reduce their value, contract is voidable at option of customer, which option must be exercised by notice in writing. Securities must be promptly delivered. Minister of Justice may order auditing of any person operating under provisions of Act and upon such audit order any necessary improved system.

Annual Return.—Broker must file annually satisfactory financial statement of his affairs as such. (Part XIV). Power is given to make regulations. (CNR 805/96). There is fine up to $1,000,000 for breaches of Act.

SEPARATION:

See topic Divorce.

SEQUESTRATION:

Supreme Court may issue this writ.

After Judgment on Order.—It is directed to commissioners commanding them to enter lands and take rents and profits and seize goods of person against whom directed.

During Litigation.—It may be issued against defendant who is in contempt by reason of neglect or refusal to appear or answer or to obey decree of court.

SERVICE:

See topic Process.

STATUTE OF FRAUDS:

See topic Frauds, Statute of.

STATUTES:

Following is statute law in force in Newfoundland: (1) English statutory law as at July 26, 1832, date immediately before establishment of first local legislature (so far as such law was applicable to local conditions, which is question to be decided in each case by Newfoundland court); (2) in respect of period 27 July 1832 until British Parliament's Statute of Westminster in 1931 (1931 c. 4 [U.K.]) whereby status of Newfoundland, (Colony since 1826), became dominion: legislation enacted by British Parliament that expressed or necessarily implied intention to apply to Newfoundland (such legislation being infrequently enacted to and including 1907 and, apparently, not since then), e.g. Merchant Shipping Act; (3) statutes of Newfoundland legislature since Newfoundland joined Canada on 31 Mar. 1949 (Newfoundland statutes up to and including 31 Dec. 1990 having been consolidated in Revised Statutes of Newfoundland, 1990, in force from 01 June 1992 and Acts passed by legislature being issued periodically by Queen's Printer, Confederation Building, East Block, St. John's, NF, A1B 4J6, telephone: 1-709-729-3649); telecopier: 1-709-729-1900); (4) Canadian (federal) statutes as they are prorogated in relation to Newfoundland.

SUBMISSION OF CONTROVERSY:

Special Case.—Parties may state any question of law or fact in form of special case for adjudication by court before trial or hearing. (Rule 37.01). Special case to be in prescribed form, including agreed statements of material facts. (Rule 37.02). On hearing case, court may draw from stated facts and documents any inference that might have been drawn if proved at trial or hearing. (Rule 37.04). If parties agree in writing, court may order specific relief to be granted or may enter judgment.

Summary Trial.—Either party may, after defence is filed and before trial, apply to court with supporting affidavit material seeking judgment on or dismissal of all or part of pleading. (Rule 17A.01).

Time of Trial of Questions or Issues.—Court may order any question or issue, whether of fact or law, or partly of fact and partly of law, and whether raised by pleadings or otherwise, to be tried before, at or after trial, and may give directions as to manner in which question or issue shall be stated. (Rule 40.04).

SUPPLEMENTARY PROCEEDINGS:

See topic Executions.

SURETY AND GUARANTY COMPANIES:

(S-13).

Guaranty and surety companies may do business in Newfoundland under Securities Act, S-13.

TAXATION:

Provincial taxation is limited by terms of Constitution Act, 1867, as amended, to direct taxation within province. Chief sources of provincial revenue are federal government subsidies and grants, license fees from motor vehicle owners, gasoline tax, liquor and tobacco sales and minor sums from various miscellaneous sources and retail sales tax.

Municipal Taxation.—City of St. John's, C-17, City of Mount Pearl, C-16 and City of Corner Brook, C-15 under special Acts, and several other incorporated municipalities under Municipalities Act, are empowered to impose property taxes, business taxes, fuel oil and coal taxes, poll taxes and certain license fees.

Sales Tax, (R-15).—Retail sales tax, formerly social security assessment, of 12% is imposed upon every sale of tangible personal property (subject to specified exemptions) purchased for consumption or use and not for retail.

Gasoline and Fuel Oil Tax, (G-1).—No person may offer or keep for sale or sell any gasoline save under and in accordance with authority conferred by provincial license. Tax of $0.165 per litre ($0.150 per litre in Labrador portion of province) is imposed on all grades of gasoline other than propane fuel grades of gasoline. On propane fuel grade of gasoline, tax of $0.07 per litre is imposed, (§3). Gasoline used by aircraft and gasoline purchased in bulk for direct export from Newfoundland and so exported is subject to tax of 7/10 cent/litre. (§3). Gasoline for operation of sea-going vessels or boats (other than pleasure craft) subject to 3.5¢ per litre. Gasoline used by any person for operations which under provisions of any legislation in force are entitled to exemption from taxation or duty of customs on gasoline is not liable to tax.

Income Tax, (I-1).—The Tax Rental Agreement between federal government and province whereby province agreed not to impose income or corporation taxes expired on Dec. 31, 1961 and was not renewed. Province now imposes income tax and this is collected on its behalf by federal government. Tax is percentage (69% in 1996) of tax payable under federal Income Tax Act. Allowances to extent of above percentage will be made on federal Income Tax.

Succession Duties.—None.

Gift Tax.—None.

Stamp Tax.—None.

Social Security Tax (Retail Sales Tax Act, R-15).—Person who acquires tangible personal property whether new or used at retail sale in province shall, in respect of consumption or use of that property, pay to Crown at time of sale tax at rate of 12% of purchase price of property so acquired. Subject to regulations, following tangible personal property is exempt from tax imposed by Act: tangible personal property shipped by vendor for delivery outside province, including ships stores delivered to commercial vessels that normally operate in extraterritorial waters, vessels of more than 300 tons gross used for any purpose; tangible personal property sold at purchase price if less than 26¢, and certain tangible property transferred to corporation.

Sales tax at rate of 12% also applies to federal Goods and Services Tax of 7% where that tax operative.

Exemptions.—There are no exemptions from any of these taxes for members of Canadian Armed Forces.

TECHNOLOGY:

See topic Industry.

TORRENS ACT:

Not adopted in province.

TOURISM:

(D-19.1).

Department of Tourism and Culture Act, D-19.1, establishes Department and authorizes Minister of Tourism and Culture to supervise, control and direct matters relating to promotion, encouragement and development of cultural activities, historic resources and tourist activities in province.

TRADE:

See topic Industry.

TRADEMARKS AND TRADENAMES:

See Canada Law Digest.

TRUSTEE PROCESS:

See topic Garnishment.

TRUSTS:

Governed by common law, as altered by Trustee Act, T-10.

See also topic Banks and Banking.

USURY:

See topic Interest.

See also Canada Law Digest: topic Interest.

See Topical Index in front part of this volume.

VENUE:

Supreme Court may order change of venue within Newfoundland on sufficient cause being shown in civil proceeding (Rule 42.03), or in criminal proceeding under Criminal Code (Canada).

VITAL STATISTICS:

See topic Records.

WAREHOUSEMEN:

Governed by Warehouse Receipts Act, W-1 and Warehousemen's Lien Act, W-2.

Warehouse receipts must be in form prescribed by Warehousemen's Receipts Act, and such receipts are negotiable. (§14). Warehouseman is liable for loss of or injury to goods caused by his failure to exercise such care and diligence in regard to them as careful and vigilant owner of similar goods would exercise in custody of them in similar circumstances. (§14).

Warehousemen's Liens.—Under provisions of Warehousemen's Lien Act, every warehouseman has lien on goods deposited with that person for storage whether deposited by owner of goods or by that person's authority or by any person entrusted with possession of goods by owner or by that person's authority. (§3). In addition to all other remedies provided by law for enforcement of liens or for recovery of warehouseman's charges, warehouseman may, in manner provided by Act sell by public auction any goods upon which that person has lien for warehouseman's charges which have become due. (§5).

WILLS:

(W-10).

Capacity.—No will made by person under age of 17 is valid. Married women may dispose of their property by will (historic common law prohibition on their doing so having been abrogated). Will made by mentally challenged person is invalid and does not become valid by recovery of mental capacity.

Testamentary Disposition.—There is no limitation upon disposition of testator's estate.

Execution.—Will must be signed by testator (testatrix) in presence of two witnesses, who shall sign as witnesses in presence of testator and in presence of each other. If testator is unable to write, will must be read to testator and so noted on will, and such person must make his (her) mark on will and making of mark must be acknowledged. (§2).

Attestation Clause.—Suitable form would be following: "by the testator (trix) as and for his(her) Last Will And Testament in the presence of both of us who, in his(her) presence, at his(her) request, and in the presence of each other, have hereunto subscribed our names as witnesses."

Holographic Wills.—Will wholly in handwriting of testator and signed by him (her), without presence of witnesses, is admitted to probate upon proof of handwriting.

Nuncupative Wills.—Declaration made by testator without writing is invalid excepting such wills of sailors and soldiers made in certain circumstances.

Revocation is effected by: (1) subsequent marriage (with certain exceptions); (2) cancellation; (3) subsequent will; (4) express revocation.

Revival.—Will is not revived by revocation of subsequent will. (§3).

Probate.—Jurisdiction in matters of probate is in Supreme Court. Five clear days notice of application for probate must be posted in Registry. Application is by way of petition supported by affidavit, to which is annexed statement of particulars of estate (inventory and valuation). Provision is made for proof in solemn form by way of originating application to Supreme Court. (J-4, §108).

Contest.—Application for probate may be contested by entry of caveat. (J-4, §112).

Legacies.—Time for payment is within one year of date of grant of probate.

Lapse.—There is no provision against lapse of legacies.

Foreign Wills.—Provision is made for resealing of wills by way of petition. (J-4, §132).

International Wills.—Provided for under Wills Act W-10, Part III which incorporates Convention Providing a Uniform Law on the Form of an International Will.

Land and Movables.—Manner and formalities of making will and its intrinsic validity and effect, so far as it relates to interest in land, are governed by lex situs and so far as it relates to interest in movables by lex domicili at time of death. Wills Act applies to wills made in respect of such land and movables from 01 July 1955 to and including 31 Dec. 1976. (W-10, §29[2]).

Living Wills.—No legislation.

Simultaneous Death.—See topic Death, subhead Survivorship.

WITNESSES:

Common law governs.
See also topic Depositions.

WORKER'S COMPENSATION LAW:

See topic Labour Relations.

NOVA SCOTIA LAW DIGEST REVISER

McInnes Cooper & Robertson
Summit Place
1601 Lower Water Street
Post Office Box 730
Halifax, Nova Scotia B3J 2V1, Canada
Telephone: 902-425-6500
Fax: 902-425-6350
URL: mcrhfx@mcrlaw.com

Reviser Profile

History: McInnes Cooper & Robertson was founded in 1859 by Hiram Blanchard and Jonathan McCully, both prominent in the public life of the Province. Since its establishment, the firm has been involved in many of the important cases which have come before the courts of Nova Scotia and in the industrial and commercial life of the Province.

Areas of Emphasis and Growth: The firm carries on a general practice in all areas of the law. Firm members have expertise in the following areas of practice: Corporate and Commercial, Banking and Finance, Employment and Labour Relations, Environmental, Insurance and Litigation, Public Utilities, Real Estate, Securities, Estates and Trusts, Taxation and Shipping. Lawyers in the firm appear regularly in the Courts of Nova Scotia, the Federal Court, and the Supreme Court of Canada and federal and provincial administration tribunals. The firm has 55 lawyers and approximately 100 support staff including para-legal assistants.

Client Base: McInnes Cooper & Robertson has a broad client base and represents Canadian, American and international corporate and individual clients. Corporate clients include those in banking and finance, insurance, manufacturing, pulp and paper, shipbuilding, mining, fishing, oil and gas and the service industries. The firm also represents a number of universities and other public institutions.

Firm Activities: Lawyers in the firm are encouraged to participate actively in the public life of the Province including professional and charitable organizations, Boards of Directors of public and private companies. All lawyers are members of the Nova Scotia Barristers' Society and the Canadian Bar Association. Some are also members of the Canadian Tax Foundation, the American College of Trial Lawyers, the Federation of Insurance and Corporate Counsel, the International Bar Association and the American Bar Association. A number have been active in politics in both elective and non-elective positions.

Management: The firm's overall management is directed by an executive committee which operates in conjunction with a managing partner. Other committees of the firm are responsible for professional and business development. The members of the executive committee are elected annually by the partners.

Significant Distinctions: Many former members of the firm have been appointed to the bench and have served on the Supreme Court of Nova Scotia and the Supreme Court of Canada.

Members and former members of the firm have held political office. John H. Dickey, Q.C. was a Member of Parliament from 1947-1957. George T.H. Cooper, Q.C. was a Member of Parliament in 1979-1980 and served as Parliamentary Secretary to the Minister of Justice and Attorney General of Canada. Stewart McInnes, P.C., Q.C. was a Member of Parliament from 1984-1988 and was Minister of Supply and Services, Minister of Public Works and Minister responsible for Canada Mortgage and Housing Corporation at various times.

Senior positions in professional organizations have been held by many current and former members of the firm.

NOVA SCOTIA LAW DIGEST

(The following is a list of all Topics, including cross-references, covered in this Digest.)

NOVA SCOTIA LAW DIGEST

Revised for 1997 edition by

McINNES COOPER & ROBERTSON, of the Halifax Bar.

(Citations unless otherwise noted refer to Revised Statutes of Nova Scotia, 1989. Reference to a "Rule" is to the Nova Scotia Civil Procedure Rules, which came into force Mar. 1, 1972. Citation "Judicature Act" is reference to R.S.N.S. 1989, c. 240.)

ABSENTEES:

An absent plaintiff if resident outside of province, may be required to pay money into court. Property of absconding or absent debtors may be attached by civil process in Supreme or county court. If beneficiary under will or administration absent from province, not heard from for ten years, court may order distribution as if absentee were dead.

Process Agent.—Person absent from province may appoint solicitor to act as agent for service of process.

Attachment Against Absentee.—See topic Attachment.

Escheat.—See topic Escheat.

ACCORD AND SATISFACTION:

Common law rules govern.

ACKNOWLEDGMENTS:

Generally, any instrument may be proved by the acknowledgment under oath by the parties executing such instrument of the execution thereof, or by the oath of a subscribing witness to any such instrument that the parties thereto executed it in his presence. (c. 392, §31).

Acknowledgment may be taken by following officers:

Within the province: Judge of the Supreme or county court; notary public; barrister; justice of the peace; commissioner of the Supreme Court. (c. 392, §32).

Without the province: A commissioner appointed to take affidavits without the province for use in the courts of the province; a judge of any court of record; the mayor or recorder of any city or incorporated town; notary public; a minister, consul, vice-consul or consular agent of Her Majesty. (c. 392, §33).

General Requirements of Certificate.—The person taking an acknowledgment either within or without the province must sign a certificate, endorsed upon or attached to the instrument the execution of which is proof of such acknowledgment having been made. (c. 392, §32).

Notary, consul or consular agent must affix seal of office to certificate.

British Acknowledgments.—Acknowledgments made in Great Britain or Ireland or any of Her Majesty's possessions with the forms of proof and authentication legal in those places have the same legal effect in Nova Scotia. (c. 154, §69).

Married Women.—No special form of acknowledgment is required (c. 271, §3), except where woman married prior to Mar. 11, 1898, conveys property acquired by her before that date, in which case the deed must have an acknowledgment, made by her in absence of her husband, that it is her free act and deed, and that she executed it freely and voluntarily without fear, threat or compulsion of, from or by her husband (c. 271, §3).

Effect of Acknowledgment.—Documents properly acknowledged are entitled to be recorded without further proof.

Authentication.—Not necessary if acknowledgment taken within province for use in province.

If required for use out of province, in Canada or U.S., authentication of capacity of notary public provided by Provincial Secretary or Deputy, fee $3; for use elsewhere authentication by Lieutenant Governor, fee $7.50.

Where acknowledgment taken outside province for use within province, no authentication of capacity of notary public is required. (c. 154, §67).

Form of Acknowledgment

Province of . . . ., County of . . . ., ss. I hereby certify that on the . . . . day of . . . ., 19. . . ., at . . . . of . . . ., ..., Grantor, personally known to me, appeared before me, and having been by me duly sworn made oath and said that he is the person mentioned in the annexed instrument as the maker thereof, and that he signed, sealed and delivered the same.

. . . .

(Official Signature).

Form of Proof by Witness

Province of . . . ., County of . . . . ss. On this . . . . day of . . . ., A. D. 19. . . ., before me, the subscriber, personally came and appeared . . . ., a subscribing witness to the foregoing indenture, who having been by me duly sworn made oath and said that . . . . . . the parties thereto signed, sealed and delivered the same in his presence.

. . . .

(Official Signature.)

(Instruments usually proved by oath of witness as above rather than acknowledgment by party. This applies also to corporations.)

Alternative to Acknowledgment or Proof.—No statutory provision.

ACTIONS:

Equity and common law jurisdiction fused by Judicature Act 1972. (c. 240 as am'd by 1989, c. 20; 1992, c. 16 [proclaimed 26 Jan. '93, in force 30 Jan. '93]).

See also topic Death, subhead Actions for Death.

Conditions Precedent.—Generally no actions permitted against units of provincial government unless two months notice of action is given to Attorney General. (c. 360, §18).

Commencement.—See topic Process.

Class Actions.—Permitted (Rule 5.09) but seldom employed.

Joinder and Splitting.—Plaintiff may unite several causes of action, but the court may order separate trials of any of such causes of action as cannot be conveniently tried together. (Rule 5.03).

Parties to an action are plaintiff and defendant. Trustees, executors and administrators may sue and be sued without joining persons beneficially interested. Cause or matter not defeated by misjoinder or nonjoinder of parties. Court may add or strike out or substitute names of parties.

Interpleader is governed by Civil Procedure Rule 50 and Judicature Act c. 240 as am'd by 1989, c. 20; 1992, c. 16 (proclaimed 26 Jan. '93, in force 30 Jan. '93).

Stay of Proceedings.—The Supreme Court of Nova Scotia, or any judge thereof, may direct a stay of proceedings in any action pending before it or him. (Rules 5.02, 6.09, 7.02, 52.09, 53.13, 55.09).

Termination.—Any time before a proceeding is entered for trial or its hearing is commenced in chambers plaintiff may discontinue proceeding or withdraw any cause of action against any defendant, or defendant may withdraw his defense or part thereof, without leave, by filing and serving a notice of discontinuance or withdrawal on any party concerned. After a proceeding is entered for trial or its hearing commenced, plaintiff or defendant may discontinue or withdraw with leave of court, and order may contain provisions as to costs or bringing of subsequent proceedings. Party discontinuing proceeding or withdrawing defense must pay costs of any opposing party to date of discontinuance or withdrawal. Subject to terms of court's order, prior discontinuance or withdrawal is not a defense to a subsequent proceeding for same, or substantially same cause of action. (Rule 40).

Abatement.—Death abates personal actions unless the estate is affected. Abatement does not result from marriage, death or bankruptcy of any of the parties if the cause of action survives or continues. Whether the cause of action survives or not the occurrence of such events between the verdict or finding of the issues of fact, and the judgment, does not abate the action. Party to whom interest passes or estate devolves may continue the action.

See also topics Death, subhead Survival of Actions; Limitations of Actions.

Limitation of.—See topic Limitation of Actions.

Direct Actions Against Insurer.—Direct action may be against liability insurer where tortfeasor is unable to satisfy judgment against him. (c. 231, §28[1]). See topic Motor Vehicles, subhead Direct Actions.

ADMINISTRATION: See topic Executors and Administrators.

ADOPTION:

Children and Family Services Act S.N.S. 1990, c. 5 (as am'd by 1994-95, c. 6) came into force Sept. 3, 1991.

Any person of age of majority may adopt anyone younger than himself or herself. (1990, c. 5, §72).

Consent Required.—Order will not be made except on written consent, of adoptee if over 12 years of age, of spouse if married, of parent or parents if under age of majority. When adoptee given up pursuant to voluntary agreement, child placing agency may give required consent. When adoptee is child in care, Children's Aid Society or Minister may give required consent. (1990, c. 5, §74). In proper cases court may dispense with any required consent (1990, c. 5, §75), but notice must be given to person whose consent is to be dispensed with (1990, c. 5, §75).

Conditions Precedent.—Where adoptee under 16 years of age, adoptee must have resided with petitioner no less than six months; notice must be given to Minister of Social Services at least six months prior to application, or at least one month where one of applicants for adoption is birth parent; notice of hearing and copies of all supporting material to application must be filed with Minister at least one month prior to application. Minister may shorten or dispense with foregoing requirements. If adoptee is child in care of agency, adoption notice must wait for decision of appeals from committal of child to agency. (1990, c. 5, §76, as am'd by 1996, c. 10, §14). Payment in consideration of placing child for adoption or procuring child is illegal. (1990, c. 5, §69).

Jurisdiction.—Court has jurisdiction on basis of residence of applicant, or of proposed adoptee, or domicile of either in Province, or birth of adoptee in Province. (1990, c. 5, §72).

Venue.—If applicant resident, application must be to Family Court of applicant's residence. If applicant not resident in Province, application must be to County Court of district of adoptee's residence. If both applicant and adoptee not resident but domiciled in Province, application to any Family Court. If adoptee born in Province application may be to Family Court of district where born. (1990, c. 5, §72, as am'd by 1992, c. 16).

Petition.—Application must if possible identify adoptee by birth registration number, as evidenced by birth certificate, rather than by name. (1990, c. 5, §77).

Proceedings.—Application and hearing in Chambers; only persons permitted by judge may be present. If adoptee under 16 Minister may make recommendation and/or appear at hearing to assist judge or any party. (1990, c. 5, §77).

See Topical Index in front part of this volume.

ADOPTION . . . *continued*

Decree.—Court must make order granting application if satisfied of ages and identities of parties, that necessary consents obtained or dispensed with, and that adoption proper. (1990, c. 5, §78).

Name.—Unless otherwise ordered, adoptee takes surname of adopter. Court may order such change of name as applicant requests. (1990, c. 5, §78).

Effect of Adoption.—Adoptee is placed in same position for all purposes as if natural child of adopting parent. Except as to incest and consanguinity for marriage purposes, all legal relationship with natural parents or kindred ceases. (1990, c. 5, §80). See topic Infants, subhead Termination of Parental Rights.

Setting Aside Adoption.—Person aggrieved by adoption order may appeal to Supreme Court (Appeal Division). If order made without notice, person aggrieved may apply within one year of date of order to Family Court making order to set order aside; on showing consent obtained by fraud, duress, oppressive or unfair means, court may set aside, and restore adoptee to custody of proper person. (1990, c. 5, §83, as am'd by 1992, c. 16).

Registration.—With Registrar General under Vital Statistics Act. (c. 494, §13).

ADVANCEMENTS: See topic Descent and Distribution.

ADVERSE POSSESSION:

Duration of Possession.—Title may be acquired by adverse possession of real estate for 20 years (40 years as against infants, lunatics or persons absent from the province; 60 years as against the Crown).

Character of Possession.—Possession must be open, adverse, notorious, exclusive and continuous.

Easements may be acquired by prescription in 20 years. (c. 258, §32).

AFFIDAVITS:

May be sworn to: Within the province: before a judge, commissioner, barrister or member of Assembly. (c. 312). Without province: before judge of any court of record; Canadian or British consul, vice consul or consular agent; or notary public. (c. 154, §67).

An affidavit taken before a commissioner or barrister who is a party to the transaction or matter in respect of which it is to be used or who is employed by such party in connection with the transaction, is not evidence on behalf of the person or his employer in any proceedings relating to the transaction except with consent of all other parties to proceedings or on order of the judge or person presiding. (c. 312, §8).

General Requirements.—Affidavits must be entitled in cause in which they are intended to be used. When used on an application, may contain statements as to belief of deponent with sources and grounds thereof. When used on trial, may contain only such facts as deponent can prove of his own knowledge, unless leave granted. Time and place of swearing and person before whom sworn should be stated in jurat of affidavit. Name of person taking affidavit must be printed or typewritten below or adjacent to his signature. (c. 312, §14). Judge taking affidavit must affix seal of court of which he is member; consul, vice-consul, consular agent and notary public must affix seal of office. Affidavits must be in first person, contain full name, residence and occupation of deponent, be divided into paragraphs, numbered, and must be signed by deponent. If two or more deponents, names of each must be inserted in jurat, but if affidavit of all deponents is taken at one time by same officer it is sufficient to state that it was sworn by both (or all) of "above-named deponents." Where deponent is illiterate or blind, jurat should state that affidavit has been read to deponent and that he appeared to understand it and signed it in presence of officer taking affidavit. (Rule 38.06).

Interlineations, erasures and alterations must be initialled by officer taking affidavit.

Exhibits should be certified as being such and identified with affidavit.

Affidavits made out of province before proper officer of foreign jurisdiction have same validity, force and effect in Nova Scotia as if duly made in province and are admitted in evidence without proof of signature or seal or official character of such officer. (c. 154, §67).

Use of Affidavits.—Evidence may be given by affidavit upon any motion, petition or summons, but court may on application of party order attendance of deponent for cross-examination. Affidavits may be used by consent of parties in civil proceedings. May also be used in default actions in rem, and in references in admiralty actions, and in bankruptcy proceedings.

Form of Jurat

Sworn to at . . . . in the county of . . . . Province of . . . . this . . . .
day of . . . . A.D. 19. . . . before me . . . .
(Official Signature)

Alternative to Affidavit.—No statutory provision.

AGENCY: See topic Principal and Agent.

AIRCRAFT: See Canada Law Digest, topic Aircraft.

ALIENS:

Aliens may take, hold, convey and transmit real property situate in Nova Scotia. (c. 385, §2). Aliens may take hold and dispose of personal property, except shares in British ships, in same manner as British subjects. This does not apply to alien enemies.

See topic Real Property, subhead Land Holdings Disclosure Act.

ALIMONY: See topic Divorce.

ALLOWANCES: See topic Executors and Administrators.

APPEAL AND ERROR:

Appeals from orders and judgments of justices of the peace, stipendiary magistrates, city and municipal courts are to Supreme Court judge. Appeals to Supreme Court judge also expressly given by statutes.

Appeals from judge of Supreme Court of Nova Scotia (Trial Division) are to Supreme Court of Nova Scotia (Appeal Division).

Appeals from Supreme Court of N.S. (Appeal Division) are to Supreme Court of Canada.

How Brought.—Appeals to Supreme Court of Nova Scotia (Appeal Division) are brought by notice of appeal (Rules 62.02, 62.05A); to Supreme Court of Canada by notice of motion where leave is required; if no leave is required, notice of appeal is given.

Time.—Notice of appeal to Supreme Court of Nova Scotia (Appeal Division) must be served within 15 days from date of notice of making of order upon decision appealed from in case of appeal from interlocutory judgment or judgment under Divorce Act; within thirty days for other judgments. Court may extend time for appeals from a tribunal authorized by an anactment. If an enactment prescribes how or when appeal should be brought, it will be observed. Appeals to Supreme Court of Canada must be brought within 60 days from date of decision. (July and August are not included in computation of this 60-day period).

Limitations on Right of Appeal.—No appeal as of right to Supreme Court of Canada unless found in some statute. All appeals subject to leave of S.C.C. or S.C.N.S. (A.D.). No appeal from discretionary orders except in equitable matters. Refusal to grant special leave may not be appealed. (R.S.C. 1985, c. S-26, as am'd).

Appeal bond is not required in an appeal to Supreme Court of Nova Scotia (Appeal Division) but is required in appeal to Supreme Court of Canada.

Stay of Proceedings.—Supreme Court of Nova Scotia (Trial Division and Appeal Division) may direct a stay of proceedings in any cause pending before it. Application is made upon motion. Filing of notice of appeal does not operate as a stay of proceedings under order appealed from, unless Appeal Division or a judge thereof, or court appealed from, so orders. (Rule 62.10).

Character of Hearing.—Appeals are by way of rehearing.

See also topic Practice.

ARBITRATION AND AWARD:

Arbitrations are governed by the Arbitration Act (c. 19) which provides for submissions to boards constituted in accordance with act and awards thereby which may be made rule of Supreme Court and which may be set aside for misconduct or because of undue influence. Controversy may be submitted by agreement to a person or persons selected by parties.

Contracts to Arbitrate Future Disputes.—Contracts may contain provisions for arbitration of any controversy arising thereunder.

Rescission.—A submission to arbitration, unless a contrary intention is expressed, is irrevocable and cannot be rescinded except by leave of the court or a judge. (c. 19, §4). Agreement to submit to arbitration may be rescinded by mutual agreement of parties.

Powers of Arbitrators.—Unless a contrary intention is expressed, the arbitrators acting under a submission have power to administer oaths, or take affirmation of parties or witnesses, and to state an award as to the whole or part in the form of a special case for the opinion of the court.

Attendance of witnesses may be compelled by subpoena out of the Supreme Court. (c. 19, §11).

Examination of Parties.—The parties to a reference must submit to be examined on oath or affirmation by the arbitrators and must produce all books, deeds, accounts, writings, etc., which are required or called for by the arbitrators.

Award and Enforcement Thereof.—Unless a contrary intention is expressed, an award on a submission is final and binding on the parties and persons claiming under them. (c. 19, §5).

An award on a submission may by leave of the court or a judge be enforced in the same manner as a judgment or order to the same effect. (c. 19, §17).

Foreign arbitration awards enforceable pursuant to 1958 New York Convention on the Recognition and Enforcement of Foreign Arbitral Awards. (c. 234).

ASSIGNMENTS:

Rights, debts or choses in action are assignable. The assignor may make an absolute assignment of any debt or legal chose in action by writing under his hand.

Notice.—Express notice in writing of the assignment must be given to the debtor, trustee or person from which the assignor would have been entitled to claim the debt or chosen in action. (c. 240 as am'd by 1989, c. 20; 1992, c. 16 [proclaimed 26 Jan. '93, in force 30 Jan. '93]).

Assignment of book debts, to be valid as against creditors of the assignor and subsequent purchasers or mortgagees of such debts, must be in writing and accompanied by an affidavit of the subscribing witness of its due execution, and a further affidavit of the assignee or his agent that the assignment is bona fide and for good consideration. It must be filed in the registry of deeds together with the affidavits within 30 days of its execution. (c. 24).

Assignment of a bill of sale need not be registered, but it may be registered by filing the assignment, accompanied by an affidavit of an attesting witness to the execution thereof, in any office in which the bill of sale is registered. If the chattels are situate partly in two or more registration districts, the assignment and affidavit is filed in one district and duplicate originals or copies thereof certified by the proper officer of that district are filed in the office of the proper office in the other district or districts. (c. 39).

See Topical Index in front part of this volume.

ASSIGNMENTS . . . *continued*

Fees.—For filing assignment of book debts, $30 plus $10 for certification of documents; for filing bills of sale, etc., $30 plus $10 for certification of documents.

Effect of assignment of book debts, bills of sale, etc., is to transfer to assignee title to debt, chattels, etc., covered thereby but subject to equities and obligations between original parties. (c. 92, §25).

ASSIGNMENTS FOR BENEFIT OF CREDITORS:

Authorized assignments may be made under the Bankruptcy Act. See Canada Law Digest. Nova Scotia Assignments and Preferences Act, c. 25 has been held intra vires in so far as not in conflict with Bankruptcy Act. Under this act every assignment for general benefit of creditors not made to official assignee is void. (c. 25, §7). This act is seldom used.

ASSOCIATIONS:

Associations and ordinary clubs and societies, athletic, political, etc., are usually unincorporated without shares of stock; associations of this kind have no legal entity, and cannot sue or be sued on contracts made in their name or on their behalf. Liability rests on person by whom or with whose authority order for goods or work was given. Ordinary principles of agency apply. No statute law.

A Society may be incorporated under the Societies Act to promote any benevolent, philanthropic, patriotic, religious, charitable, artistic, literary, educational, social professional, recreational, sporting, or with any other useful object, but not for the purpose of trade, industry, or business. (c. 435, §3[1]).

Form.—Any five or more persons may incorporate by filing with the Registrar of Joint Stock Companies a memorandum of association and by-laws.

Rights and Powers.—Those necessary to attain objects.

Actions.—May sue or be sued in corporate name.

Resident Agent.—Society must appoint person resident in Province as agent for service. (c. 435 §7).

Dissolution.—By (1) provisions of Companies Winding Up Act (c. 435, §24) or (2) by special resolution (c. 435, §26).

Professional Association.—No statutory authorization.

Co-operative Associations.—See topic Corporations.

Boat-Owner Fishermen.—May join in association to advance common interests including obtaining of collective benefits. (c. 175).

ATTACHMENT:

Attachment order may be granted to attach any real or personal property of a defendant, including debts, rents, shares, bonds, currency, whether due or accruing due, in possession of any person, where defendant resides out of jurisdiction, is a corporation not registered under Corporations Registration Act, or is about to leave or has left jurisdiction with intent to change domicile, defraud his creditors, avoid service, or is about to or has removed property permanently out of jurisdiction, or is about to or has concealed, removed or assigned any property with intent to hinder or delay creditors.

Plaintiff at or after commencement of a proceeding and before judgment and as an incident of relief claimed, may apply by ex parte application for an attachment order which prothonotary will grant and issue unless court otherwise orders. Attachment order may be granted when proceeding is commenced for debt or demand not yet due, but judgment shall not be granted against a defendant until maturity of debt or demand.

Affidavit.—In support of attachment order, plaintiff or his agent must swear out affidavit stating facts giving rise to a good cause of action, amount claimed, including costs after allowance for credits, set-offs and counterclaims, and that solicitor, as named, advised that he is lawfully entitled to attach property.

Bond.—Unless court otherwise orders, prothonotary, before issuing attachment order, shall take a bond from plaintiff in an amount equal to 1¼ times value of claim as stated in affidavit, with two sufficient sureties, or other approved security. Conditions of bond are that plaintiff prosecute without delay, and when ordered by court sheriff shall return attached property or proceeds thereof if sold, and that plaintiff pay defendant damages and costs resulting from wrongful issue of attachment order, wrongful attachment, or if plaintiff fails to recover judgment.

Attachment Order.—Upon application by plaintiff, prothonotary, unless otherwise ordered, issues to sheriff an attachment order directing him within 90 days to attach, hold, evaluate, and otherwise deal with property as provided in order. Order provides full directions to sheriff, and is in standard form 49.04A.

Release of Property.—Defendant, owner, or person entitled to possession of attached property may retain or regain its possession before final judgment or sale under a court order, upon delivery to prothonotary or sheriff of a bond in standard form 49.06A in an amount equal to 1¼ times valuation of attached property, with two sureties, or other security as approved by prothonotary.

Sale.—If agent or debtor does not give security, court may order sale of perishable property, or any attached property which cannot be reasonably retained.

Conflicting Claims on Attachment.—Where there are several orders to attach same property, it is attached in sequence sheriff receives orders. Person not subject to attachment order, claiming an interest in property, or claiming wrongful attachment or issuance of order, may proceed by interpleader or recovery order.

ATTORNEYS AND COUNSELORS:

Attorneys and counselors are known as barristers and solicitors in Nova Scotia. Every solicitor is also a barrister.

Eligibility.—Person seeking to be admitted to bar must comply with requirements as prescribed by Nova Scotia Barristers Society.

Applicant for admission must produce certificate of good moral character from solicitor with whom he was last articled. (c. 30, §4, as am'd by 1990, c. 25, §3).

Registration as law student not required.

Educational Requirements and Clerkship.—Before admission as a barrister an articled clerk must serve under articles of clerkship with one or more practising solicitors for 12 months after receiving degree in law.

Examination.—Applicant must pass examinations required by Bar Society or present certificate of exemption therefrom.

Admission.—Successful applicant is admitted on motion by a member of the Council of the Bar Society (usually the president) made before Judge of Supreme Court (Trial Division).

Admission Pro Hac Vice.—Necessary to have local counsel associated. Barristers of other Canadian provinces may appear without local counsel in certain motor carrier matters. (c. 292, §11 as am'd by 1992, c. 23).

Licenses.—No barrister may practice without holding an annual certificate which is in force. The fee for such certificate is as the Council of the Bar Society from time to time prescribes, and every such certificate expires on June 30 in each year.

Rights and Powers.—Barristers are entitled to practise in all courts in Nova Scotia and in the Supreme Court of Canada and in Federal Court of Canada. Every practising barrister may have one clerk articled to him. Barrister may act as surety. Barristers become notaries upon obtaining, without cost, commission from Lieutenant Governor. (c. 30, §11).

Solicitors may administer oaths to subscribing witnesses to deeds, relative to the execution of the same.

Lien.—Solicitor has a lien on documents in his possession for charges for his professional services.

Suspension and Disbarment.—Barrister and solicitor may be suspended for nonpayment of annual fees, and cannot practise during suspension. Barristers are liable to be struck off the rolls, fined or suspended for misconduct. (c. 30, §32 as am'd by 1992, c. 13). Supreme Court Judge may appoint custodian to manage practice of disbarred or suspended barrister. (c. 30, §35).

Unauthorized Practice.—No corporation may practise law. Fine not exceeding $1,000 for violation. No person not a member of the Bar may practise except articled clerks to a limited extent under supervision of barrister (c. 30, §8[2]), law students in authorized legal aid program (c. 30, §9), and barristers of other non-Canadian jurisdictions in office of practising barristers with permission of Bar Society Council (c. 30, §8[2]).

Professional Association.—No statutory authorization for formation by lawyers.

AUTOMOBILES: See topic Motor Vehicles.

BAIL: See topic Criminal Law.

BANKS AND BANKING:

This matter is not within jurisdiction of the Provincial Legislature. Governed by the Bank Act. See Canada Law Digest, topic Banks and Banking.

See topic Taxation, subhead Corporation Capital Tax Act.

BILLS AND NOTES:

Governed by Bills of Exchange Act. See Canada Law Digest, topic Bills and Notes.

BILLS OF LADING: See topic Carriers.

BILLS OF SALE: See topics Chattel Mortgages; Sales.

BLUE SKY LAW: See topic Securities.

BONDS:

In any case in which security is required by the practice of the court, the bond of an approved guarantee company (see topic Surety and Guarantee Companies) may be accepted without any affidavit of justification. The bond of any such guarantee company may be accepted as security given by a public official and has the same effect as if given by a private individual. Notwithstanding the provisions of any Nova Scotia Act regarding any society or corporation, the bonds or policies of guarantee of any such guarantee company approved by the Governor-in-Council may be accepted instead of or in addition to the bond or security required by such act. (c. 451). No bond given under any statute or rule or order of court or judge for performance of any trust or duty of any kind or for accounting for moneys or property received or to be received will be approved by judge if it contains any provision or condition limiting or impairing the obligation thereof for failure to pay any renewal premium or any condition avoiding or impairing obligation thereof, other than performance of duty or obligation which it is given to secure.

Sureties other than approved guarantee companies may be required to give affidavit of justification showing they are worth or are owners of property of a certain amount depending on amount of the bond.

BROKERS:

See topics Factors; Insurance; Mortgages of Real Property; Principal and Agent; Securities.

BULK SALES: See topic Fraudulent Sales and Conveyances.

CARRIERS:

Carriers are generally under supervision of Board of Commissioners of Public Utilities. Board consists of five commissioners appointed by Governor-in-Council. This board has general supervision of all public utilities and may make orders as to rates, tolls, dividends, etc., but cannot control rates of motor carriers.

Discrimination.—If any public utility gives any undue or unreasonable preference or advantage to any particular firm, person or corporation or subjects them to any unreasonable prejudice or disadvantage, it is deemed guilty of unjust discrimination, which

CARRIERS . . . *continued*
by the act is made unlawful and penalties are provided. (c. 380 as am'd by 1992, cc. 8, 11, 307).

Bills of Lading.—Consignee of goods named in bill of lading and indorsee of bill of lading has vested in him all rights of action and is subject to the same liabilities in respect to such goods as if the contract in the bill of lading had been made to himself. A bill of lading in the hands of a consignee or indorsee for value is conclusive evidence of the shipment as against the person signing the bill, notwithstanding that goods or part of them have not been shipped, unless the person receiving the same had actual notice that goods were not laden on board, or unless there is a stipulation in the bill to the contrary. Person signing same may exonerate himself by showing fraud by shipper or holder or some person under whom holder claims. (c. 38).

Lien.—Carrier has a lien for charges.

Motor Vehicle Carriers.—See topic Motor Vehicles.

Dangerous Goods.—See topic Motor Vehicles.

CERTIORARI:

Order in nature of certiorari may be granted by Supreme Court (Trial Division) or County Court, or with special leave in Supreme Court Appeal Division for purpose of bringing before it, for inspection, examination and determination proceedings of inferior courts and officers who exercise judicial functions. (Rule 56.02).

Grounds.—Writ is directed to judge of inferior court or officer, etc. Certiorari lies unless expressly taken away by statute; but where certiorari is expressly made available by statute it can only be granted subject to restrictions imposed by statute and upon grounds therein set out.

Certiorari lies where a court has acted without jurisdiction, as in case of defect of jurisdiction from the nature of the case, and where the tribunal has a direct interest and is thus biased, as in case of collusion, corruption, fraud, etc.

Proceedings.—Order of certiorari may be granted by court upon application by an originating notice. Such notice must be served upon every person interested or likely to be affected by proceeding, and where certiorari is sought to quash a conviction, warrant or inquiry, such notice must also be served, at least seven days before return date upon Attorney General and person making conviction or order, issuing warrant, or holding inquiry. Originating notice must include endorsement requiring persons served to return to prothonotary all pertinent records. (Rule 58).

Time.—Originating notice for an order in nature of certiorari must be filed and served within six months after conviction, order, warrant or inquiry to which it relates. (Rule 58.06).

Special Statutes.—Many statutes contain provisions regarding certiorari in special cases; e.g., Summary Proceedings Act, c. 450 as am'd by 1990, c. 46;1994-95, c. 18; Probate Act. (c. 359, §141). Certiorari is however governed largely by common law.

CHARITABLE IMMUNITY: See topic Damages.

CHATTEL MORTGAGES:

Common law rules govern as to general nature, incidents, effect and requisites. Statutory enactment is Bill of Sale Act. (c. 39).

Registration.—Every chattel mortgage not accompanied by immediate delivery and actual and continued change of possession of the mortgaged chattels is void as against bona fide creditors and subsequent mortgages or purchasers claiming under or from grantor for valuable consideration and without notice, whose mortgages are valid without registration or have been duly registered, unless such mortgage is evidenced by a bill of sale duly registered. Such bill of sale takes effect only from time of its registration as against said creditors, mortgagees or purchasers. (c. 39, §3).

Bill of sale must be filed within 30 days of its execution, in registry office for registration district where mortgaged chattels are situate at time of execution. Affidavits of attesting witnesses of execution by grantor or grantors identifying the bill of sale and stating date or dates of its execution, and an affidavit of the grantee or of one of several grantees, his or their agent, stating that the bill of sale was executed in good faith, for good consideration, and not for the mere purpose of protecting mortgaged chattels against the grantor's creditors, or to prevent their recovering claims they may have against grantor, must be filed with the bill of sale at same time and place. (c. 39, §§8-10). Upon application county court judge may permit late registration. (c. 39, §25). Chattel mortgages of motor vehicles and other personal property designated by regulation to be registered in Central Designated Personal Property Lien Registry located in Halifax. (1986, c. 15, not yet in force). Mortgages of aircraft governed by Aircraft Securities Interests Act. (1988, c. 3, not yet in force). Act provides that registration of aircraft security interests including chattel mortgages in Central Aircraft Registry established by Central Aircraft Registry Act (Canada) is effective in Nova Scotia. Note as of date of revision no Central Aircraft Registry has been established.

If attesting witness refuses to make or becomes incapable of making such affidavit or dies or leaves the province, a county court judge may order registration of the bill of sale upon such proof of its execution and attestation as he may by his order require. Such order, or a copy thereof, must be attached to and filed with bill of sale.

Where chattels are situate partly in one and partly in another registration district, registration may be effected by filing original documents in one registration district and a duplicate original or copy certified by the registrar in the other registration district. (c. 39, §6).

Removal of Property.—If chattels are permanently removed into a registration district other than that in which they are situate at time of execution of bill of sale, such bill of sale must be registered in the registry office of such district within 30 days after grantee has received notice of place of removal, by filing therein a copy of the bill of sale and of all affidavits and documents accompanying it, or filed on its registration accompanying it, or filed on its registration or renewal, certified as true copies by the registrar of deeds in whose office the bill of sale was registered or last renewed. (c. 39, §12).

If chattels subject to bill of sale executed when they were outside the province are permanently removed into the province, the grantee should file in the registry office of the registration district into which the chattels are moved, within 30 days after receiving notice of place of removal, a copy of the bill of sale and affidavits and all documents accompanying or relating to it. (c. 39, §13).

Renewal.—Bill of sale should be renewed within three years of its registration if registration was previous to June 30, 1983, or within six years if registration was thereafter, by registering renewal statement accompanied by affidavit in registry of deeds for registration district in which bill of sale is registered as regards chattels still situate in that district. Further renewal statement accompanied by affidavit should be registered within three years of registration of first renewal statement, and thereafter within each succeeding period of three years from registration of last renewal. (c. 39), §11).

Fees for registering and filing are: Each bill of sale and accompanying documents, $30; renewal bill of sale, $30; discharge or assignment, $30. Fee for any certificate of registration or discharge is $10.

Assignment.—Bills of sale are assignable. Assignment may, but need not, be registered by filing assignment, accompanied by affidavit of attesting witness of its execution, in any office in which bill of sale is registered. Where chattels are situate partly in one and partly in another registration district, assignments may be registered in various registration districts in same manner as original bills of sale. (c. 39, §15). Assignee takes subject to equities between original parties and to obligations of assignor. (c. 92, §25).

Release or Satisfaction.—Bill of sale may be discharged in whole or in part by registration in office in which it is registered of a certificate of discharge signed by grantee, his executors, administrators or assigns, and accompanied by an affidavit of attesting witness as to execution; but no certificate of discharge by an assignee can be registered until the assignment has been registered in that district.

In the case of chattels situate partly in one and partly in another district or districts registration of discharge may be effected by filing a duplicate or other original of the certificate of discharge and affidavit of execution in office of proper officer in each of the registration districts; or by filing such certificate and affidavit in one registration district and a certificate of entry of the discharge, signed by the registrar of deeds of that district in the registry office of each other district.

Foreclosure.—On default, grantee may foreclose or sell chattels comprised in bill of sale to realize the amount of the debt, interest and costs. Some bills of sale contain a provision empowering grantee in such event to sell by public auction or private sale.

Sale by Mortgagee.—Sale rather than foreclosure is remedy usually employed. Grantee may invoke the assistance of the court in foreclosure and sale, or may proceed on his own responsibility.

Order for Deficiency.—In court action an order against the grantor for any deficiency may be obtained, a right which may be lost if the grantee proceeds without court action.

Redemption of chattels may be effected at any time before foreclosure or sale by payment of debt, interest and costs.

Form.—There is no statutory or general form.

CLAIMS: See topics Executors and Administrators; Pleading.

COLLATERAL SECURITY: See topic Pledges.

COLLECTION AGENCIES: See topic Principal and Agent.

COMMERCIAL CODE:

Uniform Commercial Code not adopted.

COMMISSIONS TO TAKE TESTIMONY: See topic Depositions.

COMMUNITY PROPERTY:

System does not obtain.

CONDITIONAL SALES: See topic Sales.

CONSIGNMENTS: See topic Factors.

CONSUMER PROTECTION: See topics Interest; Sales.

CONTRACTS:

Common law rules govern.

Distributorships, Dealerships and Franchises.—Common law rules govern.

Infants' Contracts.—See topic Infants.

CONVEYANCES: See topic Deeds.

CORPORATIONS:

Nova Scotia corporations may be incorporated under Companies Act (c. 81 as am'd by 1990, c. 15 [proclaimed 9 July '91, in force 15 July '91, except §§3-4]; 1992, c. 10 [proclaimed 12 Jan. '93, in force 12 Jan. '93]) or by special act of legislature.

General Supervision.—Registrar of Joint Stock Companies.

Incorporators; Purposes.—Any one or more persons associated for any lawful purposes, other than banking, loan, trust or insurance company, may form incorporated company with or without limited liability by subscribing names to memorandum of association and otherwise complying with regulations of Companies Act (c. 81 as am'd by 1990, c. 15 [proclaimed 9 July '91, in force 15 July '91, except §§3-4]; 1992, c. 10 [proclaimed 12 Jan. '93, in force 12 Jan. '93]).

Name.—No company may have any name identical with that of any subsisting company or so nearly resemble same as to be calculated to deceive. (c. 81, §16 as am'd by 1992, c. 10). Subject to c. 81, §16 (as am'd by 1992, c.10) a company by special resolution can change its name with approval of Registrar. (c. 81, §18). Name must not

CORPORATIONS . . . *continued*
contain words "Royal" or "Imperial" without consent of Governor-in-Council. (c. 81, §16[1] as am'd by 1992, c. 10). Name in all its language forms may be used but must end with "Incorporated", "Incorporee", "Limited", or "Limitee" (c. 81, §18). Abbreviated term may be used for business purposes.

Term of Corporate Existence.—Perpetual.

Memorandum of association, in case of company limited by shares, must state name of company; restrictions, if any, on objects and powers of company (c. 81, §10); that liability of members is limited; amount of share capital and division into shares; and total number of shares without nominal or par value which company proposes to issue. Memorandum must be signed by each subscriber in presence of at least one witness, who must attest signature. Subscriber must write opposite to his name number of shares he takes, his address and occupation. (c. 81, §10).

Incorporation by Guarantee.—While the above company is the kind usually incorporated in Nova Scotia, companies may be incorporated and limited by guarantee and may also have unlimited company without any limitation on liability.

The memorandum must be filed with the Registrar of Joint Stock Companies. (c. 81, §25).

Articles of Association.—Company may also file articles of association signed by the subscribers to the memorandum and filed with it. If this is not done, the set of articles known as "Table A" apply. The articles usually provide for conduct and calling of meetings of shareholders and directors, etc.—generally the internal management of the company.

Incorporation fees (paid to Registrar of Joint Stock Companies): $327.

Filing Fees.—Certificate of status, $20; change of name, $100; special resolution, no cost; order of court relating to any document, $50; prospectus, $850; where N.S. not principal jurisdiction, prospectus where N.S. principal jurisdiction, $1,250; certified copy of contract under §109, $5; certified copy of resolution distributing dividend or bonus, $5; any other document or notice, $10; appointment of agent, $5; mandatory search of proposed company name, $32.10.

License to do business issued to N.S. company upon incorporation, and to extra-provincial company upon registration under Corporations Registration Act.

Paid-In Capital Requirements.—None.

Amendments.—Companies incorporated prior to Sept. 1, 1982 cannot alter conditions contained in memorandum except by special resolution and for purposes set out in Act. (c. 81, §19). Companies incorporated after Sept. 1, 1982 have same capacity as natural persons and do not alter memorandum for purposes set out in c. 81, §19 applicable to preexisting corporations but, rather, may alter or restrict any restrictions on objects and powers. Preexisting company may alter conditions contained in memorandum to change into company with objects and powers of natural person. (c. 81, §19).

The articles on the other hand may generally be altered by special resolution of the shareholders.

Increase or Decrease of Authorized Capital Stock.—If articles authorize it, company may alter its memorandum so as to increase its share capital by issue of new shares; consolidate and divide its share capital into shares of larger amounts; convert its paid-up shares into stock and reconvert it into paid-up shares of any denomination, except in case of preferred shares; subdivide its shares into shares of smaller amounts; convert any of its unissued share capital into preference shares redeemable or purchasable by company; etc. This must be done by special resolution. (c. 81, §51 as am'd by 1990, c. 15 [proclaimed 9 July '91, in force 15 July '91]). Subject to confirmation of court (if authorized by its articles), company may by special resolution reduce its share capital. (c. 81, §57).

By-Laws.—See subhead Articles of Association, supra.

Stock.—Company may issue preferred, convertible preferred (c. 81, §52), common or no par value shares. Shares of any member are personal property, transferable in manner provided by articles of company. (c. 81, §32). On application of transfer of any share, company enters name of transferee in its register of members. (c. 81, §37).

Stock Certificates.—No statutory regulation of contents of common share certificates; preference share certificates must state terms and conditions of preference. (c. 81, §50[4] as am'd by 1990, c. 15, §3 [not yet proclaimed]).

Issuance of Stock.—Stock may be issued for consideration other than cash or for less than par only on filing with Registrar contract stating consideration. (c. 81, §109). Reasonable commissions and discounts permissible if articles of association allow. (c. 81, §110 as am'd by 1990, c. 15 [proclaimed 9 July '91, in force 15 July '91]).

Transfer of Stock.—A transfer of the share of a deceased member made by his personal representative is a valid transfer although the personal representative is not himself a member of the company. (c. 81, §38).

Uniform Securities Ownership By Minors Act and Uniform Simplification of Fiduciary Security Transfers Act not enacted.

Stock Transfer Tax.—None.

Debentures.—Every company has power to issue debentures secured by mortgage or otherwise. (c. 81, §26[4][m]).

Stockholders' rights and liabilities are determined by articles and common law rules. On winding up stockholders liable to extent of amount unpaid on shares. (c. 81, §135).

Meetings.—The company must hold a general meeting once a year. (c. 81, §83). On requisition of holders of at least one-tenth of issued paid-up capital, directors must convene special general meeting of company. (c. 81, §84). Calling of shareholders and directors meetings, notice required, times and places for holding same and procedure thereat are generally regulated by articles of association.

Voting.—The method of voting, use of proxies, etc., are also generally regulated by articles of association. Ordinarily proxies are permitted.

Voting trusts are governed by articles and common law.

Directors.—Minimum one, no maximum (c. 81, §93); no residence or citizenship restrictions; minimum one qualifying share (c. 81, §94[1] as am'd by 1990, c. 15 [proclaimed 9 July '91, in force 15 July '91]); term of office, method of election and filling vacancies, governed by articles of association, but bankrupt or person who has made authorized assignment cannot act as Director or Manager without order of discharge under Bankruptcy Act (c. 81, §96).

Directors' Meetings.—Time, place, quorum and notice governed by articles of association.

Powers and Duties of Directors.—Governed by articles of association and common law.

Liabilities of Directors and Officers.—Generally governed by common law; full indemnification possible. See topic Environment.

Officers.—President and secretary required.

Principal Office.—No restriction on location of head office, but company must have registered office in Province and file location with Registrar. (c. 81, §79).

Resident Agent.—Company must designate person resident in Province as agent for service. (c. 101, §9).

General Powers of Corporations.—All usual powers given (c. 81, §26[4]) and any specifically provided in memorandum. All companies incorporated after Sept. 1, 1982 have all powers and capacity of natural person. Preexisting companies may by special resolution alter memorandum to convert into company with powers and capacity of natural person. (c. 81, §19).

Company may purchase its own shares if authorized by special resolution provided that thereafter it would still be able to meet liabilities and realizable value of assets would exceed liabilities plus paid up capital. Company may purchase its shares to eliminate fractional shares, settle debts or fulfill employee stock option if authorized by special resolution provided that thereafter it would still be able to meet liabilities and realizable value of assets would exceed liabilities and amount needed to redeem all shares with right to be paid prior to payment of those company seeking to purchase. Company may redeem preference shares without need of special resolution provided it would be able to meet liabilities and realizable value to assets would exceed liabilities and amount needed to redeem all shares with right to be paid prior to or ratably with those company seeking to purchase. (c. 81, §51 as am'd by 1990, c. 15 [proclaimed 9 July '91, in force 15 July '91]). Company may give financial assistance for purchase of its shares provided that thereafter it would still be able to meet liabilities, and realizable value of remaining assets would exceed liabilities plus paid-up capital. (c. 81, §51 as am'd by 1990, c. 15 [proclaimed 9 July '91, in force 15 July '91]).

Dividends.—Common law applies.

Unclaimed Dividends.—No statutory provision.

Sale or Transfer of Corporate Assets.—75% majority of shareholder vote required.

Books and Records.—Register of shareholders (c. 81, §42), and other securities (c. 81, §111) must be kept at registered office; open to inspection by holders only, during usual business hours.

Reports.—Annual statement of resident agent showing names and addresses of directors and officers, and authorized and issued capital must be filed with Registrar. (c. 101, §10).

Corporate Bonds or Mortgages.—If impose fixed or floating charge on assets in Province must be filed with Registrar. (c. 102).

Winding Up.—Companies may be wound up under Companies Winding Up Act. (c. 82). This act provides for winding up where company has passed special resolution requiring company to be wound up or where company, though solvent as respects creditors, has passed extraordinary resolution that it cannot by reason of its liabilities continue its business, etc. (c. 82, §4). Court may also wind up company by order on application of company, contributory, shareholder, or member if it deems it just and equitable. (c. 82, §5). Court may declare that shareholder not party to application for winding up has option to purchase shares of shareholder applying for winding up at price fixed by court. (c. 82, §6). Liquidators are appointed; time is fixed for proving claims by order of court; property is realized on and disposed of, claims gotten in, and affairs all settled; liquidator prepares his account and lays it before meeting of members of company called for purpose, or liquidator may apply to court for order dissolving company. Order must be deposited or reported to provincial secretary within 30 days (c. 82, §67).

Amalgamation.—Upon amalgamation by any two companies the agreement of amalgamation will prescribe the terms and mode of carrying the amalgamation into effect. Upon adoption of the agreement by the two companies, application may be made to court for an order of approval. Dissident shareholders must be notified of time and place of application. The agreement and terms as approved by the court must be filed with Registrar who will issue a certificate of amalgamation. Amalgamated company has all rights and liabilities of the two companies. Memorandum is agreement of amalgamation. Articles may be those of one of amalgamating companies or may be ratified by three quarters of shareholders of amalgamated company. (c. 81, §134).

Private investment holding companies are regulated by c. 357 as am'd by 1990, c. 15 (proclaimed 9 July '91, in force 15 July '91, except §§ 3-4); 1993, c. 36.).

Co-operative associations are regulated by c. 98.

Close Corporations.—No statutory regulation.

Appraisal.—No statutory regulation.

Crown Corporations.—No Crown Corporation may incur any funded obligation without approval of Governor in Council. (c. 365 as am'd by 1992, c. 8; 1994, c. 29).

Foreign Corporations.—A foreign corporation may do business in Nova Scotia on being granted a certificate of registration by the Registrar of Joint Stock Companies of Nova Scotia. Before such certificate will be issued, the foreign corporation must file with the registrar a statement verified under oath, by one of its principal officers showing: Its corporate name; when, where and under what special or general act it was incorporated; situation of its head office; the amount of its capital stock, the amount subscribed or issued, amount paid up (c. 101, §8), and like; nature of each kind of

See Topical Index in front part of this volume.

CORPORATIONS . . . *continued*
business it is empowered to carry on; what kind or kinds of business is or are intended to be carried on in Nova Scotia, and names of its directors and officers. (c. 101, §8). It may not carry on business in name identical to that of other registered corporations, partnerships or individuals without their permission. (c. 101, §6). Foreign corporation must appoint agent resident within province for service of process, etc. Statement showing agent's name and address must be filed with registrar. Agent must in Jan. in every year make and file with registrar statement showing: Names of directors and officers; amount of its nominal capital stock, amount subscribed or issued, amount paid up; amount of rest or reserve fund, and the like; name of recognized agent in Nova Scotia. Or, instead, it may file copy of annual statement filed in jurisdiction of incorporation provided that it contains same information. (c. 101, §10). It must file other statements upon written request from registrar. Upon registration annual registration fee (see infra, subhead Taxes and Fees) must be paid. Penalty for doing business in province without certificate, $50 per day.

A foreign corporation may take, hold, convey and transmit real property situated within the province. (c. 385, §2). See, however, topic Real Property, subhead Land Holdings Disclosure Act.

Continuance.—Foreign corporation may be continued as Nova Scotia corporation on application if no existing corporation and no public interest are prejudiced. Registrar may restrict objects of incoming corporation to conform with Nova Scotia requirements. Nova Scotia corporation may be continued under laws of foreign jurisdiction. (c. 81, §133).

Taxes and Fees.—Every corporation must pay Provincial tax of 16% on taxable income earned in Province for year. (c. 217, §5 as am'd by 1990, c. 10; 1992, c. 15). Annual registration fees are charged on all corporations doing business in province based on nominal capital. (c. 101, §12).

See topic Taxation, subhead Corporation Capital Tax Act.

Professional Corporations.—No statutory authorization.

Deeds.—See topic Deeds.

See topic Environment.

COSTS:

Costs are fixed by Costs and Fees Act (c. 104) which allows fixing of fees by Regulation; party and party costs which are fixed by Party and Party Committee and are published in Royal Gazette (c. 104, §2) and may be taxed by judge of Supreme Court, or by judge of county court as Master of Supreme Court or by Taxing Master at Halifax. Solicitors' bills are taxable by Master. Solicitor may bring proceeding for any costs due to him, but judgment shall not be entered on default, and no costs shall be allowed except upon order of court which may direct taxation of costs. Taxing officer certifies amount of costs taxed by him for and against each party or person, and subject to appeal and terms contained in certificate or order under which taxation has been made, certificate given upon taxation has been made, certificate given upon taxation is final and conclusive as to amounts mentioned against any person who received notice of taxation. (Rule 63.35). Contingent fee agreements permitted, but are subject to taxation and conditions in Rules 63.17-63.20. Costs of and incident to all proceedings in Supreme Court including administration of estates and trusts, are in discretion of court or judge. Costs generally follow event. Costs generally awarded to successful party. If cause is removed from inferior court, costs in court below follow event unless otherwise ordered. If solicitor by neglect causes delay, he must personally pay such costs as court awards.

Security for costs may be ordered where by law or practice a party has heretofore been entitled to obtain such security and also, where plaintiff resides out of province; where he is ordinarily out of province, though temporarily resident within province; where plaintiff has brought another action for same cause, which is pending in province or elsewhere; or where plaintiff has had costs awarded against him which have not been paid; where a proceeding is brought by a nominal plaintiff, or is frivolous and vexatious, and plaintiff does not have sufficient property in jurisdiction to pay costs, or is class action and plaintiff is instigated by others; by enactment; where plaintiff's address not properly given; or where defendant on an ex parte application obtains an order for security of costs. Judge may make such order for security of costs as just. Where security for costs ordered, proceeding is stayed upon service of order until security is given, and upon default, may be dismissed upon ex parte application.

COURTS:

Supreme Court of Nova Scotia exercises original jurisdiction in civil and criminal causes, including divorce, and Nova Scotia Court of Appeal exercises appellate jurisdiction in civil and criminal causes, including divorce. They are courts of common law and equity. No original jurisdiction in actions to recover debt or liquidated demand $5,000 or less (c. 240 as am'd by 1989, c. 20; 1992, c. 16 [proclaimed 26 Jan. '93 in force 30 Jan. '93]).

The Court of Probate has jurisdiction: to grant probate of wills and letters of administration whether general or limited, of estates of deceased persons; to revoke or cancel such probate and letters; to effect and carry out judicial administration of estates of deceased persons through representatives, and to hear and determine all questions, matters and things necessary in relation thereto; and to appoint guardians, (c. 359, §11). Jurisdiction of Supreme Court in these matters is not taken away. (c. 359, §11).

The Divorce Court has jurisdiction over all matters relating to prohibited marriages and may declare any marriage null and void if proper grounds are proved. See topic Divorce.

Family Court Act provides for family courts in areas of Province prescribed by Governor-in-Council, having jurisdiction under Provincial Statutes and certain provisions of the Criminal Code having a family connotation. (c. 159 as am'd by 1994-95, c. 6 [not yet in force]).

Provincial court judges may be appointed by Governor in Council and have jurisdiction throughout Province. Jurisdiction principally confined to criminal matters. (c. 238).

Small Claims Court has jurisdiction in respect of monetary claims up to $5,000 or claims for delivery of property valued at not more than $5,000. No jurisdiction in respect of recovery of land, wills or intestacies, defamation or malicious prosecution, landlord and tenant disputes or claims for general damages in excess of $100. Action commenced by filing claim with court. Service may be personal or by registered mail. Procedure very informal. Evidence may be admitted by adjudicator or court even though not admissible in court except privileged matters. Order of Small Claims Court may be made order of Supreme Court and enforced as such. (c. 430, as am'd by 1992, c. 16; 1994, c. 33).

CREDIT REPORTING AGENCIES:

See topic Sales.

CREDITORS' SUITS:

If a sheriff levies money upon an execution against personal property of a debtor where the amount indorsed to levy is $100 or upwards, he must enter notice of such levy in a book kept in his office. This is open to the public. The money is then distributed ratably amongst all execution and other creditors whose writs or certificates were within the sheriff's hands at the time of the levy or are delivered to him within one month from the entry of the notice. If a further levy is made within the month, it is treated as if levied prior to the entry. Creditor is not entitled to share in distribution unless he has established a claim against the debtor. (c. 112).

Jurisdiction.—Supreme court has jurisdiction. This act does not apply to lands. (c. 112). See also topic Courts, subhead Small Claims Court.

Proceedings.—Sheriff files certificate with prothonotary showing that proceedings have been had against debtor. (c. 112). Creditor files affidavit of claim with prothonotary, and serves duplicate on debtor together with notice of filing duplicate with prothonotary. If claim is not contested, prothonotary after ten days from service, upon application delivers to creditor certificate, in form provided, which must be delivered to sheriff; creditor is then deemed execution creditor. Certificates remain in force only one year unless renewed.

Contested Claims.—Debtor or interested creditor may contest claims. Debtor may file affidavit that he has good defense, and must serve copy on claimant. Contesting creditor may file affidavit that he has reason to believe debt claimed not in good faith due from debtor. Sheriff may continue to levy to meet certificates filed. Claimant may apply to judge for order allowing claim; unless he does so within eight days, he is deemed to have abandoned claim. Judge may try dispute in summary manner. These proceedings apply when debtor allows execution to remain unsatisfied until within two days of time fixed by sheriff for sale, or for 20 days after seizure. (c. 112).

CRIMINAL LAW:

Criminal law and Procedure in Criminal matters is within the exclusive Legislative Authority of the Parliament of Canada (Constitution Act, 1867 §91 [27]). See Canada Law Digest, topic Criminal Law. Provincial legislature may however make laws within specifically named powers set out in §92 of Constitution Act, 1867 for purpose of preventing crime, and may impose punishment by fine, penalty or imprisonment for enforcing any law of province in relation to any matters coming within any of classes of subjects enumerated in that section.

Offences created by provincial laws are "summary offences". (c. 450 as am'd by 1990, c. 46; 1994-95, c. 18). Young Persons Summary Proceedings Act (c. 509) governs prosecution procedure for persons under 16 years of age and determination of place to which 16 and 17 year olds may be committed to custody. Convictions for such offences lapse and cease to have effect after two years although liability for penalties imposed is not affected. Disclosure of lapsed conviction never required. (c. 509). Police are not to be convicted of summary offences under Motor Vehicle Act or Hotel Registration Act if committed during investigation of drug offences. (c. 450, §5).

Compensation.—Subject to certain limitations, compensation may be awarded to individual victims, or their dependants, of certain offences under Criminal Code up to lump sum of $30,000 or periodic payments of $1,000 per month. (c. 83, §29).

CURTESY:

If issue of the marriage born alive, the surviving husband has life estate in real property of which wife died seised.

Curtesy is abolished. (c. 275, §33).

Bar.—The wife may bar her husband's curtesy by will or by deeding or otherwise disposing of her real property. (c. 272, §4) Husband's curtesy may be barred by divorce, if judge so orders.

Release.—Husband may release claim to curtesy by executing a written instrument to that effect.

DAMAGES:

Common law generally prevails. Court may set rate of interest for capitalized value of future damages. (c. 240, §41). Court may award prejudgment interest from date of cause of action to date of judgment. (c. 240, §41).

Comparative Negligence Rule.—Rule adopted. Defendant cannot rely on plaintiff's contributory negligence as complete defence, but court must apportion damages in proportion to degree of fault found against each party. (c. 95).

Charitable Immunity.—Doctrine of charitable immunity not recognised.

Sovereign Immunity.—Lawsuits are permitted against governmental units. Lawsuits governed by Proceedings Against the Crown Act (c. 360 as am'd by 1991, c. 16) or other specific enactment.

Contribution Among Tortfeasors.—Tortfeasors Act (c. 471) governs contribution between and among tortfeasors.

See also topic Death, subhead Actions for Death.

See Topical Index in front part of this volume.

DEATH:

Statutory presumption of death in certain circumstances. (c. 354). Court can make declaration of death where likely person dead and impossible to produce body. Presumption of Death Act prevails when conflict with Insurance Act, c. 231, §212 (where seven years must pass before death presumed).

See also topic Actions, subhead Abatement.

Presumption of survivorship in case two or more persons die at the same time or in circumstances rendering it uncertain which survived is provided for by Survivorship Act. (c. 454). But under Insurance Act where insured and beneficiary die in same disaster, beneficiary is presumed to have died first. (c. 231, §218).

Actions for Death.—Where the death of a person has been caused by a wrongful act, neglect or default of another which would, if death had not ensued, have entitled the person injured to maintain an action and recover damages in respect thereto, the wrongdoer is liable to an action for damages even though the death has been caused under such circumstances as amount to a crime. (c. 163, §3). Damages may be both precuniary and nonpecuniary and may include out-of-pocket expenses incurred for benefit of deceased, travel expenses incurred visiting deceased between time of injury and death, reasonable allowance for value of nursing or housekeeping services provided by claimant, and compensation for loss of guidance, care and companionship. (c. 163, §5). Action is brought in name of executor or administrator of deceased person; but if there is no executor or administrator or if they have not brought action within six months after death of deceased, action may be brought in name or names of spouse (including certain "common law" spouses) (c. 163, §13), parent or child of deceased or any of them (c. 163, §4). Action must be for benefit of spouse (including certain "common law" spouses) (c. 163, §13), any person whom deceased has demonstrated settled intention to treat as his child or parent (c. 163, §12), parent or child of deceased and must be brought within 12 months of death of deceased (c. 163, §10). Amount of damages is discretionary in court (juries though permissible are rarely used), and there is no statutory limitation of amount which may be awarded.

Certificate of Death.—See topic Records.

Survival of Actions.—Where a person dies after Oct. 1, 1954, all causes of action subsisting against or vested in him survive against or, as the case may be, for the benefit of his estate except for adultery and inducing a spouse to leave or remain apart from his or her spouse. (c. 453, §2). Where cause of action survives for benefit of estate of deceased person only damages that have resulted in actual pecuniary loss to estate are recoverable and in no case are damages recoverable for punitive and exemplary matters, loss of expectation of life and pain and suffering. (c. 453, §4). Proceedings are subject to Limitations Act. (c. 453, §5). Ordinary law respecting limitation of actions applies to actions arising after Apr. 1962. (c. 453, §5). Where there is no executor or administrator, court may appoint person to represent estate for purposes of action. (c. 453, §7). Rights conferred by c. 453 are in addition to and not in derogation of any rights conferred by The Fatal Injuries Act.

DECEDENTS' ESTATES:

See Descent and Distribution; Executors and Administrators; Wills.

DECLARATORY JUDGMENTS: See Judgments.

DEEDS:

Deeds must be in writing, signed, sealed and delivered. They should be witnessed; one witness is sufficient. A deed takes effect from the time of its delivery.

Proof of Execution.—Before registration a deed must be proved by the acknowledgment under oath by the parties executing the deed of its execution, or by oath of a subscribing witness. See topic Acknowledgments; also topic Husband and Wife, subhead Conveyances.

Registration is not compulsory, but is necessary to preserve priority as against any person claiming for valuable consideration and without notice under any subsequent instrument affecting title to the same land, and first recorded. (c. 392, §18).

Recording fee for recording a deed $41, plus $1 per page. (c. 104, Sch.pt. 9).

Power of Attorney.—If a deed is executed under a power of attorney, the power of attorney or a deed subsequently confirming it must be registered. (c. 392, §24).

Conveyancing Act (c. 97) authorizes short form of deed, now in general use as follows:

Form of Warranty Deed

This Conveyance made this . . . . . . day of . . . . . ., A.D., 19. . . . .
Between A.B. of . . . . . . in the county of . . . . . . province of . . . . . . hereinafter called the "Grantor" of the One Part
and C.D. of . . . . . . in the county of . . . . . . province of . . . . . . hereinafter called the "Grantee" of the Other Part
Witnesseth, that in consideration of . . . . . . Dollar of lawful money of Canada, and other good and valuable consideration to the Grantor in hand well and truly paid by the Grantee, at or before the ensealing and delivery of these presents, the receipt whereof is hereby acknowledged, the Grantor hereby conveys and grants to the Grantee
All (description) . . . .
The Grantor covenants with the Grantee that the Grantee shall have quiet enjoyment of the lands, that the said Grantor has a good title in fee simple to the lands and the right to convey them as hereby conveyed, that they are free from encumbrances and that the said Grantor will procure such further assurances as may be reasonably required.
In witness whereof the Grantor has duly executed these presents the day and year first above written.

SIGNED, SEALED AND DELIVERED in the presence of } A.B. (L.S.)

(Acknowledgment or proof by witness)

A quit claim deed is practically same as a warranty deed, except that warranties are omitted, and recitals of why quit claim deed is given are usually inserted before granting clause.

Deeds by executors, trustees, etc., are usually made without the covenants in the above form, but contain a covenant by the trustees that they have not done any act to encumber the lands.

Deed Transfer Tax.—See topic Taxation, subhead Real Estate Conveyance Tax.

DEEDS OF TRUST: See topic Mortgages of Real Property.

DEPOSITIONS:

Testimony in judicial proceedings is generally taken by oral examination, but any party may serve on an adverse party or upon any person not a party written interrogatories to be answered by that person. If such person is a body corporate, partnership or association, an officer or agent of corporation shall answer interrogatories. Leave of court not required. (Rule 19.01). In practice it is only in very simple cases that it is done by interrogatories; where case is complex it is advisable to proceed via examination for discovery. (Rule 18).

Commissions.—Any witness who is about to leave province, or is too ill to travel may be examined before a judge or commissioner. Such person may be examined without an order after five clear days notice of time and place of examination has been given person and all other parties.

Outside of Province for Use within Province.—Where a person to be examined resides outside jurisdiction and in a country with a government that allows a person to be examined before a person appointed by court, court may grant an order for examination in prescribed Form 32.01B. Where a person resides in any other country, court may grant an order in prescribed Form 32.01C authorizing issue of a letter of request in Form 32.01D to judicial authorities of country to take, or have taken, evidence of person in that country.

Where order for letter of request is granted, letter is sent by party obtaining order to Under Secretary of State for External Affairs of Canada, and has attached to it pleadings, any interrogatories and cross-interrogatories, names, addresses, and telephone numbers of solicitors or agents of parties, and a copy of each document so attached certified to be a true translation into official language of country where examination is to take place. (Rule 32.02). Party obtaining order must file with Under Secretary of State an undertaking to be personally responsible for Secretary's charges and expenses. (Rule 32.02).

Compelling Attendance of Witnesses.—If any person duly summoned by subpoena and paid or tendered witness fees as provided by Costs and Fees Act (c. 104) to attend for examination refuses to attend, or if, having attended, refuses to be sworn or to answer any lawful question, party requiring attendance of witness may apply to court or judge ex parte or on notice for order directing witness to attend or to be sworn, or to answer any question, or to produce any document. Refusal after this point subjects person to contempt of court charge. (Rule 18). Subpoena may be issued for service in another province of Canada if party issuing subpoena can satisfy judge of Supreme Court of Nova Scotia that witness's presence in Nova Scotia is necessary for due adjudication of proceedings and essential to due administration of justice. (1996, c. 1, §7).

Letters of Request.—In the case of letters of request, notice of motion is given to adverse party, and the application is supported by affidavit showing witness is necessary and why unable to attend that party has on merits a good cause of action or defense and that application is bona fide and not to delay the action. The letters are forwarded by the court through the proper channels, e.g., to Secretary of State for external affairs, to foreign ambassador, etc.

Examination of Witnesses on Commission.—Where such orders for examination of witnesses are made, examination takes place in presence of counsel or agents of parties, and witnesses are subject to cross-examination and reexamination. Unless otherwise directed, witness is examined by oral questions, and answers are reduced to writing and returned with order or letter of request. Deposition is recorded by a reporter. Unless person examined so requests, deposition taken in shorthand need not be read over and signed by him, but must be certified and signed by reporter and examiner. Where deposition not taken down in shorthand, it shall be examined and signed by person examined and examiner, or if person examined refuses to do so, examiner certifies and signs it. Depositions or copies must be sent to prothonotary. Examiner may make a special report to court regarding examination, conduct or ab sence of persons thereat, and court will make an order accordingly. Where a person objects on an examination to answer any question put to him, or objection is taken to any such question, ground of objection and answer to question shall be set out in person's deposition. Court decides validity of objections. Deposition may be used in evidence on trial or hearing if party using it gives other party notice of his intention to do so at least two days prior to trial, rules of evidence are adhered to and it is used to contradict or impeach deponent's testimony as a witness, or where deponent is a party, for any purpose, or where deponent is dead, unable to attend trial, or out of jurisdiction.

Perpetuating Testimony.—Person who desires to perpetuate testimony of himself or any other person regarding any cause of action within jurisdiction of court may apply to court on an originating notice in an intended proceeding to perpetuate any testimony that may be material to establish cause of action. Applicant must swear out affidavit; originating notice must be served on any person expected to become an adverse party. Court to prevent failure or delay of justice, may order deposition to be taken to perpetuate testimony. (Rule 32.15).

DESCENT AND DISTRIBUTION:

Real and personal property in excess of share of surviving spouse, or all property if there is no surviving spouse, descends and is distributed, in case of intestacy, as follows, each class of which a member is living taking to exclusion of subsequent classes: (1) Issue per stirpes; (2) parents equally, or all to survivor; (3) brothers and sisters equally, children of deceased brothers and sisters taking by representation; (4) nephews and nieces equally; (5) next of kin of equal degree except that those claiming through

DESCENT AND DISTRIBUTION . . . *continued*
nearest ancestor take to exclusion of others of equal degree claiming through more remote ancestor. No representation among collaterals more remote than children of brothers and sisters. Degrees of kindred are computed according to civil law rules. (c. 236).

Share of Surviving Spouse.—Real and personal property are combined into one corpus; surviving spouse receives $50,000 or whole of estate if less than $50,000. In addition to $50,000, if one child, one-half residue; if two or more children, one-third residue; if no issue, estate goes to widow. (c. 236).

Half blood inherit equally with the whole blood.

Adopted Children.—See topic Adoption.

Illegitimates.—Illegitimate child treated as if he were legitimate child of his mother. (c. 236, §16).

Child of void marriage deemed to be legitimate child of parents if marriage celebrated at any time in accordance with law of place of celebration and believed by either parent to be valid marriage. (c. 160, §47).

Advancements.—Real or personal property given by an intestate as an advancement to any child or grandchild is considered as a portion of the estate of the intestate and is taken towards such child or grandchild's share. If the advancement exceeds his share he is excluded from any further portion but need not make any refund. If child or grandchild dies before the intestate, leaving issue, the advancement is considered as having been made directly to the representatives of such child or grandchild. Every gift or grant made by an intestate in his lifetime to a child or grandchild is deemed an advancement if so expressed in writing in the grant if charged in writing by the intestate, if acknowledged in writing by the child or grandchild, or if proved so to be evidence before a court or judge, but not otherwise. (c. 236, §13).

Election.—There is no right to dower in an intestacy.

Escheat.—If a person dies intestate and leaves no heirs or persons entitled to his lands, it escheats to the Crown. (c. 151, §2). Same rule applies to personal property. See also topic Executors and Administrators.

DESERTION: See topic Divorce.

DIVORCE:

Governed by Divorce Act (Canada) (Stat. Can. 1986, c. 4). See Canada Law Digest, topic Divorce.

No provincial statutory provision for divorce a mensa et thoro.

Annulment of Marriage.—See topic Marriage.

DOWER:

Note.—Dower is abolished by 1980, c. 9, §33 in force Oct. 1, 1980. When husband died before this date right to dower still applies. Following summarizes applicable law:

Widow is entitled to life estate in one-third of the real estate of which the husband was seised at and after their marriage in which she did not bar dower during his lifetime. Dower extends to equitable estates and rights of entry but not to joint estates or wild land. In case of intestacy widow takes according to provisions of Intestate Succession Act.

Bar and Release.—Dower may be barred by uncondoned adultery or divorce. Wife may release her dower by executing a written instrument to that effect. A bar of dower contained in any mortgage or other instrument intended as security only does not operate to bar such dower to a greater extent than is necessary to give full effect to the rights of the mortgagee or grantee under such instrument.

Election between dower and testamentary provision, see topic Wills.

EMPLOYER AND EMPLOYEE: See topic Labour Relations.

ENVIRONMENT:

Environment Act (1994-95, c. 1) repeals Dangerous Goods and Hazardous Wastes Management Act (c. 118), Environmental Assessment Act (c. 149), Environmental Protection Act (c. 150), Environmental Trust Act (1990, c. 9), Gasoline and Fuel Oil Licensing Act (c. 184), Litter Abatement Act (1989, c. 8), Ozone Layer Protection Act (c. 331), Pest Control Products (Nova Scotia) Act (c. 341), Recycling Act (1989, c. 12), Salvage Yard Licensing Act (c. 410), Transboundary Pollution Act (1993, c. 15). Pursuant to Environment Act undertakings having environmental impacts (to be defined by regulation) will be subject to environmental assessment before work commences. (1994-95, c. 1, §§31-49). Act controls release of substances that have adverse effects on environment (1994-95, c. 1, §§67-74), specifically, hazardous wastes (1994-95, c. 1, §§75-78), pesticides (1994-95, c. 1, §§79-81), and petroleum products (1994-95, c. 1, §§82-84). Minister of Environment is empowerd to set standards for degradability and recyclability (1994-95, c. 1, §100), and to regulate use of packaging in sale of products (1994-95, c. 1, §101). Act promotes stewardship principle that makes producer responsible for its product from point of manufacture to final disposal, and polluter-pay principle that confirms responsibility of polluter to take remedial action and to bear cost therof. (1994-95, c. 1).

Pollution.—Pollution, meaning detrimental alteration of environment, may be forbidden outright or permitted under certain conditions. Control devices may be required. Permits may be altered or cancelled. (1994-95, c. 1). Check regulations.

Penalties.—Orders for elimination of pollution may be made at offender's expense as debt to Crown. (1994-95, c. 1). Corporate directors and officers who authorize offence under Environment Act are liable to be penalized even if corporation is not prosecuted for offence. (1994-95, c. 1, §165).

Water Act gives Environmental Control Council and Minister of Environment (c. 500 as am'd by 1994-95, c. 1) control of all water in province; industrial and commercial users require approval.

Health Act (c. 195)—Sewage disposal system requires Departmental approval.

Beaches.—Beaches are for the benefit, education and enjoyment of Nova Scotians and designated beaches are protected against certain uses without compensation. (c. 32).

Beverage Containers.—Use and control of refillable beverage containers is regulated. (c. 37).

Energy and Mineral Resources.—Energy Board regulates environmental protection in development of energy and mineral resources. (c. 147).

Crown Lands Act (c. 114) provides for regulation of lands owned or controlled by Crown.

Forests Act (c. 179, as am'd by 1992, c. 18) provides for conservation and enhancement of forest resources.

Wildlife Act (c. 504) provides for regulation of hunting and fishing and for management of wildlife and wildlife habitat.

Agricultural Operations Protection Act restricts availability of action in nuisance in respect of farm and agricultural operations. (c. 5).

EQUITY: See topic Actions.

ESCHEAT:

See Escheats Act, c. 151. See also topic Descent and Distribution, subhead Escheat.

ESTATES: See topic Real Property.

EVIDENCE: See topics Depositions; Witnesses.

EXECUTIONS:

Order.—Execution order has replaced writ of execution and orders for garnishee and equitable execution. Equitable execution may be effected by sheriff under execution order (Rule 53) or under receivership order (Rule 54). Sequestration of property and attachment of person have been replaced by contempt order. (Rule 55). Order is granted by prothonotary when a judgment creditor has filed an order for payment or recovery of money in a proceeding.

Issuance.—Prothonotary may grant and issue execution order before costs are taxed, and subsequently a further order to enforce payment of costs; where a party obtains an order for recovery of possession of any property, other than money, prothonotary may issue an execution order to enforce payment of any damages or costs or both, awarded under order. (Rule 53).

Execution order may be issued without leave of court except where six years have elapsed since date of order, a change has taken place in parties entitled or liable under order, goods sought to be received are in hands of a receiver, or where under order a person is entitled to relief subject to fulfillment of a condition which is alleged to have been fulfilled.

Power of Sheriff under Order.—Under execution order (Rule Form 53.02A), sheriff may seize, accept as receiver, hold and sell at public auction, any real or personal property, including any debt, rent, legacy, share bond, debenture or other security, currency or wages due or accruing due, in possession of any person, and disburse proceeds as provided by law.

Any person not being a party to a cause or matter, who obtains an order, or in whose favor an order is made, may obtain execution order as if he were a party.

Sheriff may seize any bond, share, debenture, or other interest of judgment debtor in a body corporate by serving execution order upon body corporate. Order may require employer to pay to sheriff 15% of employee's gross wages, but net wages of employee supporting family may not be reduced below $315 per week, or those of any other employee below $210 per week. (Rule 53.05). Execution order may be issued and enforced against partnership or any partner.

No property shall be seized under execution order after 12 months have elapsed from its issuance, but this does not limit validity of anything previously done under order, or court's power to issue further order.

Full procedural instructions for sheriff's carrying out of order and compliance required are set out in Standard Form Execution Order, Form 53.02A.

Exemptions.—See topic Exemptions.

Stay of Execution.—Execution may be stayed by order of court or judge until such time as it or he thinks fit.

Sale of Perishable Goods.—Perishable goods may be sold by order of court unless security is given for their value. Proceeds retained by sheriff or paid into court to respond the judgment.

Sale of Land.—Land of every judgment debtor may be sold under execution after judgment recorded in the registry of deeds for one year. (c. 409, §4). Sheriff sells without appraisement on receipt of execution. Judgment creditor must cause five consecutive weekly insertions preceding day of sale to be put in newspaper published or circulated in county in which land is situated, containing description of land, that it is to be sold under execution, time and place of sale, at whose suit, name of sheriff, and also of solicitor of judgment creditor. Copies of advertisement must be posted in most public places in district, and mailed to each subsequent encumbrancer at least 20 days before day fixed for sale. Sheriff then sells land at public auction to highest bidder, and executes a deed to him or his nominee, conveying all interest of judgment debtor therein. Grantee under deed may apply to court out of which execution issued for summons calling on judgment debtor and every person in possession of land or any part thereof, deriving title by, through or under the judgment debtor, after registry of judgment, to show cause why writ of possession should not issue to put purchaser in possession. Judge may hear evidence and order writ of possession to issue. If possession not delivered up, sheriff must put purchaser in possession.

Redemption.—There is no right of redemption after an execution sale.

Supplementary Proceedings.—After judgment has been obtained and execution directed against the personal property of the debtor has failed to satisfy it, the judgment creditor may obtain an order for the examination of the debtor. If the judgment was obtained in the Supreme, county or probate court the examination is held before a commissioner of the Supreme Court; if obtained in any municipal court the examination

EXECUTIONS . . . *continued*
is held before the stipendiary magistrate or other officer appointed to preside; if in stipendiary magistrates court, he himself may examine the debtor, and similarly in the case of a justice of the peace. The order is obtained on an affidavit of a creditor, or his agent or solicitor, and must state the judgment, date of its recovery, the amount due thereon, name and residence of debtor. It must also state endeavor and failure to get satisfaction or to find personal property on which to levy, and belief that an attempt to execute on personal property would prove ineffectual. The examiner orders the appearance of the debtor and if it appears to him on examination that the debtor has sufficient income to pay a part or all of the debt, he may order payment by instalments. If the debtor makes default in payment he may be arrested, after examination before a special examiner. This is done by ex parte application to a special examiner supported by affidavit of agent or solicitor, and if it appears to the special examiner that the debtor has refused or neglected to pay without reasonable excuse, he may order his arrest. Examiner after examination of debtor may require debtor to execute assignment of all his real and personal property (except such as is exempt from execution) to creditor in trust for payment due on judgment. If debtor refuses, examiner may order him to appear before special examiner and if he still refuses, this may be taken into consideration in fixing term of imprisonment. If it appears to special examiner that debt was fraudulently contracted, obtained under false pretences, or without reasonable expectation of being able to pay same, or that any fraudulent circumstances have occurred in connection with contracting of debt, or that debtor has made fraudulent disposition of property, he may commit debtor to jail for term not exceeding 12 months. Committal does not take effect until case reviewed by County Court Judge. (c. 76, §§28, 32). Debtors may be fully examined touching matters of inquiry; witnesses may be subpoenaed, sworn, examined and cross-examined. (c. 76, §19).

Arrest to Compel Attendance for Examination.—If defendant is about to leave province after judgment, he can be arrested for purpose of compelling his attendance for examination under the Collection Act. (c. 76, §12). Creditor may obtain warrant for arrest in such case upon application to examiner supported by affidavit of himself or his solicitor setting forth: (1) Judgment and date of recovery; (2) amount due thereon; (3) deponent's belief that debtor is about to leave province, and without stating grounds for belief. Concurrent orders may be issued for arrest in different counties.

EXECUTORS AND ADMINISTRATORS:

Probate or letters of administration are granted by the court of probate for the district in which the testator or intestate had at the time of his death his fixed place of abode; if no such fixed place of abode, or if resident out of the province at the time of his death, the grant may be made by the court of probate for any district in which decedent had property at the time of his death, provided not granted previously by court having jurisdiction in another district. In other cases the grant belongs to the court of probate of any district. (c. 359, §12).

Preferences in Right to Administer.—Probate is granted to the executors named in the will. Administration of the estate of an intestate is granted to one or more of the following persons, who are entitled in the order following: (1) Widow or next of kin or both, as court thinks fit; (2) husband, unless decedent has made some disposition which makes it necessary or proper to appoint some other person; (3) if persons so entitled when so cited do not proceed to take administration within ten days after return day of citation, the court may grant it to one or more of the principal creditors or to any other person upon the application of one or more of the creditors or a person having a cause of action against the estate as the court thinks fit; if no creditor is willing and competent to undertake the trust, then to such person as the court thinks fit; (4) any trust company authorized by statute to act in the administration of estates, if consent in writing is obtained from those entitled in priority. (c. 359, §21).

Eligibility and Competency.—Generally, any person other than an infant or a person of unsound mind may act as an executor or administrator. (cc. 189, 479 as am'd by 1992, c. 8; 1994-95, c. 19). See topic Guardian and Ward. Married woman, alien, corporation sole, or nonresident may act. Corporation aggregate may act if it has such power conferred on it by charter or statute under which it is incorporated.

Qualifications.—Every executor or administrator before entering upon the duties of his office must take an oath for the performance of such duties and must subscribe such oath. (c. 359, §29). Every administrator, before entering upon duties of his office must give bond with two sureties to be approved by court, in such sum as it directs, conditioned for collecting and administering personal property of deceased. If one of such sureties dies or becomes insolvent, court may order administrator to enter into new bond with two sureties to be approved by court, and in such sum as it orders. No bond is required where administrator is public trustee appointed under Public Trustees Act. (1906 England). (c. 359, §30). Court may order an executor wasting estate to give security for performance of his duty. (c. 359, §31).

Removal.—The court may remove an administrator from his office and appoint another person in his place, if it is proved that such administrator has left the province without any apparent intention of returning, or is wasting the estate, or is insolvent, of unsound mind or otherwise incapacitated. (c. 359, §32).

Special Kinds of Administration.—If the executor refuses to act, or if no executor is named in the will, court grants administration with the will annexed to the person or persons entitled to administration if deceased had died intestate. (c. 359, §23). When executor or administrator is out of province, court may appoint any person it thinks fit, to be administrator for limited time, or until administration is revoked on return of any person entitled. (c. 359, §24). Pending any action or contestation touching validity of will of decedent, or for obtaining, recalling or revoking any probate or administration, court may appoint such person as it thinks fit, as administrator of property of deceased. (c. 359, §26). Administrators in these three kinds of administration are subject to immediate control of court and act under its direction. Where there is danger to any part of estate because some of it is perishable or of precarious nature, and persons entitled have not applied for administration and there is likely to be delay, court may grant letters ad colligenda bona to such person as it thinks fit on due security being first taken. (c. 359, §27). Where court of probate in U.K. or in any British province, territory or possession, has granted probate or letters of administration, they may on being produced to and copy thereof deposited with court of probate in this province, be sealed with seal of that court, and then have same force and effect as if granted by court of probate in this province. In case of letters of administration, however, court must first take bond in sum sufficient to cover personal property in Nova Scotia to which letters relate, and may require such evidence as to domicile of deceased as it thinks fit. (c. 359, §34). Duplicate copy or copy or exemplification thereof under seal of court granting them has same effect as original probate or letters of administration. See also infra, subhead Foreign Executors and Administrators.

Inventory.—Every executor or administrator must within three months after grant of probate or letters of administration, or such extended time as the court allows, exhibit and file in the court a full and true inventory upon oath of the real and personal property of the deceased which has come to his possession or knowledge. (c. 359, §38). If any comes to his possession or knowledge after filing such inventory he must file further inventory upon oath within reasonable time.

Notice to Creditors.—Before payment of debts or distribution of estate, executor or administrator must advertise in the Royal Gazette for one month if the estate is under $800, and for six months in all other cases, calling on all persons who have any demands upon the estate to exhibit them within six months from date of advertisement. (c. 359, §43).

Presentation of Claims.—The claimant or, in his absence from the province, his agent must attest such demands when exhibited before the registrar, a commissioner of the Supreme Court or a justice of the peace. After six months from date of advertisement executor or administrator may apply to the court to fix a time for the adjudication of claims, and to grant a citation to creditors to come in and prove them. (c. 359, §43).

When the executor or administrator is a creditor of the estate he must file in the office of the registrar at least one month before distribution of the estate, a correct account of his claim against the estate with dates and items thereof, and all credits to which deceased entitled. (c. 359, §66).

Form of Proof of Claim

County (or district) of . . . . In the court of probate. I, A. B. of . . . . make oath and say that the foregoing paper writing contains a true and correct account of my demands against the estate of . . . . deceased, and that all of the credits to which the deceased was honestly and justly entitled, so far as I believe, have been given on the said account; and that the amount of . . . . . . is justly and truly owing to me and that I hold (or "do not hold," as the case may be) security in respect of the said demand. Sworn before me at . . . . . ., in the County of . . . . . . this . . . . . . day of . . . . . ., A. D. 19. . . .

(Signed). A. B. (c. 359, Sch., Form S).

Payment of Claims.—Every executor or administrator at the expiration of 12 months from the date of probate or letters of administration must pay all legal claims which have been exhibited, so far as estate of deceased will enable him, and must distribute the estate as directed by the will or by the statutes. (c. 359, §68).

Sales, Etc.—If license is granted by the court, executor or administrator may sell, mortgage or let the property for a term not over 21 years. Before the court will issue any license to sell real property of the decedent, the executor or administrator must give a bond to the registrar of probate in such amount as the court directs with two sureties approved by the court, conditioned for the faithful application by him of all moneys received by him under such license and for the due accounting for the same before the court. (c. 359, §§50-63). Auction or private sale of real property may be authorized by Governor in Council when deceased died entitled to real property in province, Probate Act provisions regarding sale to pay debts not applicable, no known heirs, or heirs cannot be found, and it is in their interest to sell or release interest involved. (c. 379, §34).

Actions.—No action can be brought against any executor or administrator except by leave of the court for one year after grant of probate or letters of administration. Filing of copy of claim of creditor with registrar of probate, is equivalent to bringing an action to prevent the operation of any statute of limitations. (c. 359, §43).

Accounts.—At least ten days before time fixed in citation, the executor or administrator must file in the registry of probate his accounts for inspection by any person interested in the estate. (c. 359, §73). Any person interested in estate may contest its settlement and any claim against state which has not been paid. Executor or administrator must produce vouchers on taking of account for all debts and legacies paid, and for all expenses; he may be examined on oath and evidence may be taken regarding property or effects of deceased which have come to his hands or knowledge and disposition thereof. If item of expenditure is proved by sworn statement stating when and to whom payment made, voucher may be dispensed with. (c. 359, §74). Court may appoint one or more auditors to examine accounts and report thereon under oath. Allowance of accounts and final settlement of estate by court of probate, or if appealed, court of appeal, is conclusive evidence against all persons in any way interested in estate upon whom citation has been served either personally by mail, or by publication of following facts: Items in account for moneys paid to creditors, legatees, next of kin, and for necessary expenses are correct; that executor or administrator has been charged all the interest for moneys received by him and embraced in his account for which he was legally accountable; that money stated in such account as collected were all that were collected at the time of allowance of the accounts. (c. 359, §79).

Commissions.—In settlement of any estate, executors or administrators may be allowed a commission not exceeding 5% on the amount received by them over and above all necessary expenses. The court may apportion the commission among the executors or administrators as apperas just according to labor bestowed or responsibility incurred. (c. 359, §76). Specific compensation provided in will, unless renounced, will bar commission.

Allowances.—The widow and family are entitled to such provisions and other articles as are necessary for their reasonable sustenance for 90 days after the death of the husband, and this is omitted from the inventory and not considered as assets. (c. 359, §41).

Insolvent Estates.—The court, in its discretion, upon application of executor or administrator supported by his affidavit that he believes the estate is insolvent, may make an order declaring the estate to be insolvent. If any proceedings against executor

See Topical Index in front part of this volume.

EXECUTORS AND ADMINISTRATORS . . . *continued*
or administrator for any cause accruing against deceased, he may apply to court for stay of proceedings upon the production of a copy of such an order. Judge may order stay or such other order as justice requires. In settlement of insolvent estates, the whole of the real and personal property remaining after payment of necessary attendance on deceased during his last illness, funeral expenses and expenses attendant on settlement of estate must be distributed as follows: wages of clerks, domestics, farm servants and rent must be paid in full for one year preceding death of deceased; any excess on same footing as other claims; all other creditors pro rata. (c. 359, §106). This does not affect mortgage debt or registered judgment or dower of widow.

Settlement of Estate.—After expiration of six months from date of probate or grant of administration, and after any applications made under the Testator's Family Maintenance Act (c. 465) have been disposed of, executor or administrator may, and within 18 months he must, apply to court for citation for settlement of estate. (c. 359, §70). Citation must be addressed to and served upon creditors who have sent in attested claims which have not been paid; legatees who have not been paid; any person interested in estate, including, if court directs, any co-executor or surety.

Any person interested in the estate may attend the settlement thereof and contest the same and any claim against the estate which has not been paid. The allowance of the accounts and the final settlement of the estate by the court of probate, or in case of an appeal, by the court of appeal, is conclusive evidence against all creditors, legatees and all persons in any way interested in the estate upon whom the citation has been served, of the following: (a) That the items in the account for moneys paid to creditors, legatees and for necessary expenses are correct; (b) that the executor has been charged all the interest for moneys received by him and embraced in the account for which he was legally accountable; (c) that the moneys collected were all that were collectable on the debts mentioned in the account when allowed. (c. 359, §79).

Small Estates.—Public trustee will administer certain small estates. (c. 379).

Foreign Executors and Administrators.—Foreign executors may apply to a court of probate in Nova Scotia for probate of a will proved outside the province, the testator having had at time of his death, real or personal property in the province. Whenever administration of estate of any person dying out of the province has been granted in the place in which the deceased was last domiciled out of the province, the foreign administrator may apply to have administration of the property within the province which belonged to the deceased at the time of his death. In either case the court fixes a time for the hearing of the application. Notice of the hearing must be published in three successive issues of the Royal Gazette. Provisions relative to granting of original probate or letters of administration, and security to cover the property within the province apply, except that foreign administrator is preferably entitled to be administrator, and administration granted to him supersedes any other administration granted in respect to such property. (c. 359, §35).

EXEMPTIONS:

Following articles are exempt from seizure under execution: Reasonably necessary wearing apparel, household furnishings and furniture for debtor and his family; all fuel and food reasonably necessary for ordinary use of family; all grain and other seeds and livestock reasonably necessary for domestic use of debtor and family; necessary medical and health aids; farm equipment, fishing nets, tools and other chattels used in debtor's chief occupation in value set by regulation; motor vehicle not to exceed in value $3,000 or amount set by regulation. (c. 240 as am'd by 1989, c. 20; 1992, c. 16 [proclaimed 26 Jan. '93, in force 30 Jan. '93]).

Earnings.—Wages of servant, laborer or workman exempt from attachment up to $210 per week for any other employee and $315 per week for employee supporting family. (Rule 53.05).

FACTORS:

A mercantile agent in the customary course of his business as such agent has authority either to sell goods or to consign goods for the purpose of sale, or to buy goods, or to raise money on the security of goods.

Disposition, sale, etc., of goods by a mercantile agent acting in the ordinary course of his business, when in possession of goods or of the documents of title to goods with the consent of the owner, is as valid as if he were expressly authorized by the owner, provided the person taking acts in good faith and has no notice that the agent has no authority to make such disposition. If the agent had consent the disposition is valid in spite of the termination of the consent by the owner, provided that the person taking had not at the time notice that the consent had been terminated. Where a mercantile agent has obtained possession of any documents of title to goods by reason of his being or having been, with the consent of the owner, in possession of the goods or of any other documents of title to them, the consent of the owner to the possession of all the documents is presumed in the absence of evidence to the contrary. (c. 157, §3).

Pledges of goods by a mercantile agent as security for a debt due from pledgor to pledgee gives pledgee no further right to goods than could have been enforced by pledgor at time of pledge. (c. 157, §5). Where goods are pledged by mercantile agent in consideration of delivery or transfer of other goods or document of title to goods, or of negotiable security, pledgee acquires no right or interest in pledged goods in excess of value of goods, documents or security when so delivered or transferred in exchange. (c. 157, §6).

Redemption by Owner.—The owner of goods pledged by an agent may redeem the goods at any time before sale, on satisfying the claim for which the goods were pledged and paying the agent any money to which he is entitled by way of lien. The owner can recover from the pledgee any balance of money remaining in his hands as the produce of the sale of the goods after deducting the amount of his lien; and can recover from the buyer the price or any part thereof of goods sold by an agent to the buyer, subject to any right of setoff by the buyer against the agent. (c. 157, §11).

Consignments.—Where the owner has given possession of goods to another person for consignment or sale or has shipped goods in the name of another, and the consignee had no notice that such person is not the owner, the consignee in respect to advances made to or for the use of such person has the same lien on the goods as if such person were the owner, and may transfer the lien to another person. (c. 157, §8). Where documents of title to goods have been lawfully transferred to person as buyer or owner of goods, who then transfers it to another who takes them in good faith and for value, latter transfer defeats any vendor's lien previously existing. (c. 157, §9).

FIDUCIARIES:

See topics Executors and Administrators; Guardian and Ward; Trusts.

FILING FEES:

See topics Assignments; Chattel Mortgages; Corporations; Deeds; Mortgages of Real Property.

FORECLOSURE:

See topics Chattel Mortgages; Liens; Mortgages of Real Property.

FOREIGN CORPORATIONS: See topic Corporations.

FRAUDS, STATUTE OF:

Interests in land not put in writing and signed by person making or conveying same or his agent authorized by writing, have force of lease or estate at will only, except leases not exceeding term of three years. (c. 442, §3). Interest in land can only be assigned, granted or surrendered by deed or note in writing signed by party or agent authorized by writing, or by act and operation of law. (c. 442, §4).

Contracts.—No action may be brought to charge any executor or administrator upon any special promise to answer damages out of his own estate, or to charge any person upon any special promise to answer for the debt, default or miscarriage of another person, or to charge any person upon any agreement made upon consideration of marriage, or upon any contract or sale of land or any interest therein, or upon any agreement that is not to be performed within a year from the making thereof, unless the promise, agreement, etc., or some memorandum thereof is in writing and signed by the party sought to be charged or by an agent authorized in writing. (c. 442, §7).

Contract for sale of goods of the value of $40 or over is not enforceable by action unless there is an acceptance and receipt by the buyer of part of them, or unless he gives something in earnest to bind the contract, or in part payment, or unless some note or memorandum in writing of the contract is made and signed by the party to be charged or his agent in that behalf. (c. 408, §7).

FRAUDULENT SALES AND CONVEYANCES:

By the Statute 13 Eliz. c. 5 it is provided that any alienation of real or personal property, made with the intention of delaying, hindering or defrauding creditors is void as against such creditors. But a bona fide purchaser for value who takes an estate or interest from the grantor without notice of the fraud, is protected as against the claims of the creditors, although the intention of the grantor was fraudulent. Such alienations can only be impeached by creditors, who may apply to court to have sale or conveyance set aside.

Conveyances in fraud of creditors are covered by the Bankruptcy Act. See Canada Law Digest, topic Bankruptcy.

Bulk Sales.—Every purchaser of goods or merchandise in bulk, for cash or on credit, before closing such purchase and before paying the vendor any part of the purchase price, must demand and receive from the vendor, and every such vendor must furnish, a written statement, verified by statutory declaration of the vendor or his agent, containing the names and addresses of all the creditors of the vendor, and the amount due, owing, payable, accruing due, or to become due and payable by him to each of the creditors. (c. 48, §3). Any agreement for purchase or sale of goods in bulk must be in writing, contain inventory of goods sold, and must be filed within ten days of its execution in registry office of district where vendor resides, or, if he is nonresident, in registry office of district where property is situate. No part of purchase price is to be paid or any security delivered therefor within 30 days of execution of agreement. (c. 48, §4). If above provisions are not complied with, sale is deemed fraudulent and void as against creditors of vendor, unless proceeds of sale are sufficient to pay creditors in full and are so applied in or towards payment of all creditors pro rata and without preference or priority except as provided by law or previous contract. (c. 48, §5). Any such purchaser must obtain written consent of creditors, or if price is sufficient to pay all creditors, he must pay whole to trustee or trustees for distribution. If purchase price is less than amount due creditors, purchaser must obtain written consent of at least 50% of creditors in number and value, otherwise sale is deemed fraudulent, and is void as against creditors. (c. 48, §6). Any sale out of usual course of business of vendor, or of substantially entire stock in trade or interest in business of vendor is deemed to be sale in bulk. (c. 48, §7). Foregoing does not apply to sales by executors, administrators, liquidators, receivers, assignees for benefit of creditors, or any public official acting under judicial process. (c. 48, §2).

Only creditors of the vendor may attack a sale as violative of the bulk sale law. There is no specific limitation of time within which an action to attack the sale must be commenced.

Form of the statutory declaration above referred to is as follows:

Form

I . . . . . . of . . . . . . in the Province of Nova Scotia, do solemnly declare that the above is a true and correct statement of the names and addresses of all . . . . . . creditors and shows correctly the amount of indebtedness or liability due, owing, payable or accruing due or to become due and payable by . . . . . . to each of said creditors.

And I make this solemn declaration conscientiously believing it to be true, and knowing that it is of the same force and effect as if made under oath and by virtue of the "Canada Evidence Act."

Declared before me at the . . . . . . of . . . . . ., in the Province of Nova Scotia this . . . . . . day of . . . . . ., A. D. 19. . . ..

. . . .

Notary, J. P. or Commissioner.

See Topical Index in front part of this volume.

GARNISHMENT:

Order for garnishee has been replaced by execution order. (Rule 53). See topics Execution; and Attachment.

Wages.—15% of gross wages of employee may be garnisheed provided that when this payment would reduce employee's net wages to amount of $315 per week for person supporting family or $210 per week for any other person, then only difference by which payment of 15% exceeds these amounts, shall be paid to sheriff. (Rule 53.05). These provisions do not apply in cases of garnishee orders pursuant to Family Maintenance Act (c. 160 as am'd by 1990, c. 5; 1994-95, c. 6 [not yet in force]); in which case amount is solely in discretion of Family Court.

GUARDIAN AND WARD:

Jurisdiction with respect to guardianship of minors is in court of probate; of incompetent persons in Supreme Court.

Appointment.—Court of probate may appoint father, mother, person standing in loco parentis or public trustee of infant to be guardian of its estate. (c. 189, §3). Parents jointly or parent with custody can appoint guardian by written instrument until infant reaches age of majority or marries. (c. 189, §4). Surviving parent of infant is guardian unless court of probate otherwise determines. If father or mother does not appoint guardian, or if guardian appointed dies or refuses to act, court of probate may appoint one. Where no guardian appointed for estate of infant who has or is entitled to property, Public Trustee will be guardian. (c. 189, §3).

Eligibility.—Any person of sound mind and of legal age can be a guardian. An infant or partnership cannot be appointed guardian. A nonresident may be appointed, but such appointments are not favoured. The court will not generally appoint as sole guardian a married woman or the solicitor of any of the parties concerned.

Bond.—Every person so appointed as guardian must, before letters of guardianship are issued, to him filed in the court of probate by which he is appointed, a bond made by him to the infant, in such sum and with such sureties as the court directs, conditioned that he will faithfully manage and dispose of to the best advantage the property of the infant committed to his care; that he will not commit waste thereon, and that he will render a true account thereof to the court when required, and to the ward when he becomes of age, and will then deliver and pay over to the ward all the estate then in his hands or under his control, deducting only a reasonable sum for his expenses and charges as guardian. (c. 189, §7).

Powers.—Every guardian so appointed other than a guardian ad litem, has authority to act for and on behalf of his ward; may appear in any court and prosecute or defend any action in his name; and has the charge and management of his real and personal property and the care of his person and education. (c. 189, §8).

Accounts.—The court has jurisdiction to investigate, allow, amend or disallow the accounts of any guardian. (c. 189, §10).

Removal.—Guardian may be removed by the court or probate. (c. 189, §12).

Supreme Court (Trial Division) also has jurisdiction to appoint and remove guardians and to pass accounts of guardians.

Insane Persons.—Guardian for an insane person may be appointed under provisions of Incompetent Persons Act. (c. 218 and Rule 6). On death of incompetent guardian settles with legal representatives of incompetent.

HOLIDAYS:

The legal holidays are: Sundays, New Year's Day, Good Friday, Victoria Day (May 24th), day appointed for celebration of birthday of reigning Sovereign, Canada Day (July 1st), Labor Day (1st Mon. in Sept.), Remembrance Day (Nov. 11th) (c. 396), Christmas Day, and any day appointed by proclamation of Governor-General or Lieutenant Governor. (c. 235, §7). As to Dominion holidays, see Canada Law Digest. Supreme Court of Canada has held that Dominion Lord's Day Act is unconstitutional. Province has responded by enacting Retail Business Uniform Closing Day Act (c. 402 as am'd by 1993, c. 41) which provides with many exceptions that retail business not to be carried on on uniform closing day which is defined to include Sun. Similar legislation in Ontario held by Supreme Court of Canada to be constitutionally valid.

Holiday Falling on Sunday.—If holiday falls on Sunday it is celebrated on Monday.

Legality of Transactions on Holiday.—In general, transactions are not invalidated because done on holiday.

HOMESTEADS:

No provisions.

See also topics Adverse Possession; Curtesy; Deeds; Dower; Husband and Wife; Real Property.

HUSBAND AND WIFE:

Subject to Matrimonial Property Act (see infra, subhead Matrimonial Property Act), married woman can acquire, hold, and dispose of any real or personal property, as her separate property in same manner as if she were feme sole. (c. 272, §4).

Custody of Children.—See topic Infants.

General Rights of Wife.—She can enter into any contract and make herself liable upon the same, to the extent of her separate property, and may sue and be sued in contract, tort or otherwise, in all respects as if a feme sole. Her husband need not be joined in any proceeding brought by or against her. Damages or costs recovered by her are her separate property, against her, are payable out of her separate property only. (c. 272, §13).

Liabilities of Wife.—After marriage, the wife continues to be liable to the extent of her separate property for all ante-nuptial debts, contracts and torts, and she may be sued in respect of such liability, and her separate property is liable therefor, and as between her and her husband, it is primarily liable therefor unless there is a contract between them to the contrary. (c. 272, §19).

Liabilities of Husband.—The husband is only liable for his wife's ante-nuptial contracts and wrongs to the extent of the property of the wife which he has acquired or become entitled to, from or through her. (c. 272, §20). Husband and wife may be sued jointly for her antenuptial contracts or wrongs, but if husband is not liable he gets judgment for costs of his defence. (c. 272, §21). Husband is not merely because of marital relationship, liable for wife's torts committed after marriage. (c. 272, §22).

Husband's interest in wife's realty by virtue of their marriage is not during her life or the life of any of the children subject to his debts. (c. 272, §26).

Conveyances.—A married woman may convey any real property in which she has an interest without her husband joining in the deed or expressing his concurrence by a separate instrument and without any necessity for her to acknowledge that her deed is her free act and deed and was executed freely and voluntarily, without threat, fear or compulsion of, from or by her husband. (c. 271, §3). This does not apply to conveyance by woman married before Mar. 11, 1898, of property acquired by her before that date, as to which former requirements of joinder or consent of husband and special acknowledgment apply. (c. 271, §3).

Wife must join in husband's deed, in order to release dower, unless she is of unsound mind or has been living apart from her husband for two years or more under circumstances which would preclude her getting alimony.

Transfer of property between spouses by way of deed is exempt from land transfer tax. (c. 121, §4 as am'd by 1990, c. 10).

Actions.—The wife may sue in her own name with respect to her separate property. Husband and wife have the same civil remedies against each other, as though unmarried. (c. 272, §18).

Matrimonial Property Act (c. 275).—Regardless of ownership, spouses are equally entitled to possession of matrimonial home. (c. 275, §6). Neither spouse may dispose of any interest in matrimonial home without consent of other. (c. 275, §8). Both spouses are entitled to notice of proceeding to realize security of matrimonial home and have right to redeem. (c. 275, §9).

In event of divorce, annulment, separation or death of spouse, spouse may apply for fair division of matrimonial assets. Equal division is deemed fair unless proved otherwise. Spouse's rights under this Act on death of other spouse are in addition to other rights arising on death. (c. 275, §12). Division of assets will be governed by law of place of last common residence. Ownership of real property is governed by law where situate. (c. 275, §22).

Antenuptial contracts and contracts entered into during marriage are valid, if signed and witnessed by both parties, to determine rights and obligations during marriage or upon separation or divorce. (c. 275, §§23-24). Minor with capacity to marry has capacity to enter into such contract but it must be approved by court either before or after contract entered into. (c. 275, §25). Court may disregard terms which are not in best interests of child (c. 275, §26) and may vary unconscionable, unduly harsh or fraudulent terms (c. 275, §29). On division of property contract not conclusive except where contract entered into before Act came into force. (c. 275, §§5, 13).

Desertion and Nonsupport.—Failure by spouse to provide necessaries to his spouse is offence under Criminal Code of Canada. Adult whose spouse, or child under 19 whose father or mother fails without sufficient cause to provide reasonable maintenance, may obtain maintence order against such spouse or parent for weekly payment. Amount in discretion of court. (c. 160, §§3, 4, 9, 10).

Spouse, who has not married someone else or remarried or lived with someone else as husband and wife, or parent or child may apply to Family Court for maintenance. Maintenance will be based on means and needs, but may be reduced if spouse entitled to maintenance persistently engages in course of conduct that constitutes repudiation of marriage relationship or unreasonably prolongs his or her maintenance requirements. Separation agreements may be varied if not in best interests of any party. Maintenance orders may provide for periodic or lump sum payments or for security and they may be varied on change of circumstances. (c. 160 as am'd by 1990, c. 5). Maintenance orders of jurisdictions according similar treatment to like orders obtained in Nova Scotia may be enforced in Nova Scotia. (c. 268).

Community property system does not obtain.

INCOME TAX: See topic Taxation.

INFANTS:

Nineteen is age of majority for each sex. (c. 4, §2).

Contractual disabilities of infants are governed by common law rules.

Ratification by any person after attaining 19, of any debt contracted during infancy or of any promise or simple contract made during infancy must be in writing and signed by the party to be charged or his duly authorized agent, otherwise no action can be brought thereon. (c. 442, §9).

Actions.—Infants may sue and defend by their guardian ad litem. Infant cannot enter an appearance except by his guardian ad litem; no order for appointment of guardian ad litem necessary, but solicitor applying to enter such appearance must make and file an affidavit that suggested guardian ad litem is a fit and proper person to be such guardian and before a person's name is used as guardian ad litem there must be filed with prothonotary his written consent to be guardian ad litem, or where he has been appointed a guardian or guardian ad litem by court, a true copy of order appointing him. Guardian ad litem of person under disability must act by a solicitor. (Rule 6). Every infant served with a petition, notice of motion, or summons, must appear on hearing thereof by a guardian ad litem in all cases where appointment of special guardian not provided for.

Custody of Children.—Court, upon application, shall enforce and may make such orders as it considers necessary to give effect to, custody order made by tribunal in reciprocating state. Reciprocating state is as declared by Governor in Council for purposes of Act. (c. 387). Hague Convention on Civil Aspects of International Child Abduction adopted, save that Crown is not bound to pay costs of its participation. (c. 67, §4).

INFANTS . . . *continued*

Disposal of Property.—An infant entitled to any leasehold or freehold estate, may by his guardian petition court or judge for an order to let, sell, mortgage or otherwise dispose of such property. If it appears that disposal thereof is necessary for support or education of infant, or that it will substantially promote interests of infant because of property being exposed to waste, dilapidation, or being wholly unproductive, or if there is any other reasonable cause for disposal, court may order disposal on such terms as it thinks fit. Such letting, sale, etc., must be made by guardian or person appointed by court or judge. Where person under disability is an infant over age of 16 years, his consent to sale, etc., verified by solicitor's affidavit, must be filed. Court may order investment, disposal and application of proceeds and of increase and interest arising therefrom for benefit of infant. (Rules 6, 47).

The person appointed by the court must file a bond to Her Majesty, to be approved by the court or judge with such sureties and containing a condition for fulfillment of the directions contained in the order and such other conditions as ordered. No such letting or disposal can be made contrary to any last will or conveyance by which such property or interest was devised or conveyed to the infant unless necessary for the support and maintenance of infant. Any conveyance made by guardian, etc., under such an order has the same effect as if made by the infant and as if he were 19 years of age. Conveyance must refer to the order and the disposal; and the person making the sale must file a report thereof with the prothonotary of the county where lands situated. (Rule 47).

Children and Family Services Act S.N.S. 1990, c. 5 (as am'd by 1994-95, c. 6) came into force Sept. 3, 1991. Supreme Court has broad jurisdiction to make orders under various applications, including adoption (1990, c. 5, §§75-84, as am'd by 1996, c. 10, §14), care and custody (1990, c. 5, §§32-49, as am'd by 1996, c. 10, §§5-8), and child maintenance (c. 160, §§9-12). Parent or guardian may voluntarily agree to place child with agency. (1990, c. 5, §§17, 18). Court may place child with agency if "child in need of protection". (1990, c. 5, §42). Child abuse register kept by Minister of Social Services. (1990, c. 5, §63). Act creates offence for failure to provide information respecting child abuse and to cause or contribute to child being in need of protection. (1990, c. 5, §§23, 24, as am'd by 1996, c. 10, §§2,3). Welfare of child paramount consideration in all actions. (1990, c. 5, §3).

Termination of Parental Rights.—Child in need of protection may be taken into care by agent of Minister of Social Services or peace officer. Child welfare agency has care and custody of child until court otherwise orders. Child in care may, following procedures stated in Act, be placed for adoption. Upon adoption child ceases to be child of person who was parent before adoption order.

Adoption.—See topic Adoption.

INHERITANCE TAX: See topic Taxation, subhead Succession Duty.

INJUNCTIONS:

Supreme Court (Trial Division) has jurisdiction to grant injunctions in all cases in which it appears to it to be just or convenient that such an order should be made. Writs of injunction can no longer be issued, injunctions are granted by order. Court may grant an injunction either before, at or after hearing of any cause or matter, to prevent any threatened or apprehended waste or trespass, whether person against whom it is sought is or is not in possession, and whether estates claimed by either or both parties are legal or equitable. No cause or proceeding at any time pending in Supreme Court can be restrained by injunction. (c. 240 as am'd by 1989, c. 20; 1992, c. 16 [proclaimed 26 Jan. '93, in force 30 Jan. '93]).

Common law rules apply as to cases in which injunctions are granted and also as to prerequisites to the granting injunctions.

Temporary Injunction.—Any party may apply to court or a judge for an interlocutory or temporary injunction. Except in a case of urgency when an application for injunction may be made ex parte, application must be upon notice. In any cause or matter in which an injunction has or might have been claimed, plaintiff may, before or after judgment, apply for an injunction to restrain defendant from repetition of wrongful act or breach of contract complained of, or from committing any act of like kind, relating to same property or right. Interim or interlocutory injunctions cannot be granted to restrain farm or agricultural operations. (c. 5).

See also topic Labour Relations, subhead Labour Disputes.

INSOLVENCY:

This matter is regulated by Dominion legislation. See Canada Law Digest, topic Bankruptcy. See also topic Executors and Administrators.

INSURANCE:

Supervised by Superintendent of Insurance.

Regulated by Insurance Act. (c. 231, as am'd by 1992, c. 20).

Insurance adjusters must be licensed. Superintendent may make regulations respecting qualification and classification; courses of study; examinations, records to be kept by them, their charges. (c. 231, §42).

Insurance companies may be incorporated by special act of the provincial legislature. No insurance company not so incorporated may carry on any part of its business in Nova Scotia unless licensed under the Canadian and British Insurance Companies Act (Canada) or Foreign Insurance Companies Act (Canada). See Canada Law Digest, topic Insurance as to requirements of said acts.

Every automobile insurer is to place authority for settlement of all claims not exceeding $35,000 with person resident in Nova Scotia and is to maintain complete files regarding each such claim in province. (c. 231, §107).

Insurance brokers must obtain a certificate from Superintendant of Insurance and can act only for company or companies named in certificate and for kinds of insurance specified therein. (c. 231, §38).

Taxation.—Every insurance company having an office or place of business in province must pay tax of 3% of gross premiums on life insurance, accident insurance and sickness insurance and 4% of gross premiums on other insurance (c. 232, §3) calculated on gross premium revenue.

Crop & Livestock Insurance Act establishes scheme of crop and livestock insurance. (c. 113).

Direct Actions Against Insurer.—See topic Motor Vehicles, subhead Direct Actions.

INTEREST:

Governed by "The Interest Act" (Canada) and "Money Lenders Act" (Canada). See Canada Law Digest, topic Interest. Interest on Judgments Act stipulates that interest is to be paid from date of judgment until it is satisifed. (c. 233). Interest rate may be set by regulation. (c. 233, §2). Court may award interest from date cause of action arose to date of judgment. (c. 240 as am'd by 1989, c. 20; 1992, c. 16 [proclaimed 26 Jan. '93, in force 30 Jan. '93]).

Unconscionable Transactions Relief Act empowers court to reopen transaction in any proceeding in which amount due in respect of money lent is in question. Court may grant relief to debtor if having regard to all circumstances the cost of the loan is excessive and transaction is harsh and unconscionable. (c. 481).

Consumer Protection Act provides for appointment of Registrar of Credit to supervise granting of credit, conduct inquiries respecting methods of credit grantors, and disseminate information respecting credit granting facilities and practices. Every person who extends credit on sale of goods or services or on lending of money or discounting of income tax and government payments must be registered. (c. 92). Lender must give borrower statement showing amount to be charged for credit in terms of annual percentage rate and in dollars and cents. Lender must disclose on regular basis any changes in interest rate on variable rate loan. (c. 92, §17). Amount of refinanced loan or cost of additional article purchased must be included in "cost of borrowing," and in statement of actual cost given to borrower on completing credit transaction. (c. 92, §17). Disclosure in dollars and cents in continuing or revolving accounts may be expressed in schedule of charges or outstanding balances. Misleading advertising is controlled. Discounters must disclose full cost of transaction in dollar terms and annual percentage 48 hours before transaction completed. (c. 92). Credit grantor limited to recovery of principal and cost of credit properly disclosed. (c. 92). Lender or seller cannot discriminate against women borrowers or buyers. (c. 92, §10). Lender not to extend credit by advancement of money unless previous request made. Repayment of advancement contrary to Act not actionable. (c. 92, §24). No seller shall use negative-option strategy in delivery of service. Where negative-option strategy is used in delivery of service, no action lies for payment of any fee or purchase price for service. (c. 92, as am'd by 1994, c. 16).

Credit Cards.—No action maintainable against recipient of unsolicited credit card unless written acceptance or use by recipient. (c. 92, §23).

INTESTACY: See topic Descent and Distribution.

JOINT STOCK COMPANIES:

No statutory provisions. In this jurisdiction "Joint Stock Company" is obsolete term for normal business corporation. See topic Corporations.

JOINT TORTFEASORS: See topic Judgments, subhead Contribution.

JUDGMENTS:

Judgments may be interlocutory or final. A final judgment determines the principal matter in question. An interlocutory judgment or order is one which does not finally dispose of the rights of the parties. Judgment may be final for one purpose and interlocutory for another.

Judgments by Confession.—Any defendant may confess judgment in an action. This may be done by filing with the prothonotary out of whose office the writ was issued, a signed statement that he cannot deny the action, and that he confesses that he is indebted to the plaintiff for the amount named therein. The prothonotary may then enter the judgment. It may also be done through the defendant's solicitor or agent by filing a warrant of authority to such agent, the agent may then sign the confession and file the same.

Admissions.—Any party may at any stage of a cause or matter, where admissions of fact have been made on pleadings, apply to court or a judge for such judgment as upon such admissions he is entitled to, without waiting for determination of any other question between parties. Court may give such judgment as it thinks fit.

Judgment Preliminary to Trial.—At any time prior to a trial or hearing, on application of any party or on its own motion, court may determine any question of law or fact, or as to admissibility of evidence, give directions as to procedure, or direct parties to define issues, and where in opinion of court, determination of such question or issue substantially disposes of whole proceeding, or any cause of action, ground of defence, counterclaim or reply, court may grant judgment or order as it thinks just. (Rule 25).

Striking out Pleadings.—Court may at any stage of proceeding order any pleading, affidavit or statement of facts to be struck out or amended on ground that it discloses no reasonable cause of action, is false, scandalous, frivolous or vexatious, may prejudice or delay a trial or otherwise is an abuse of court process, and may order proceeding to be stayed or dismissed or judgment to be entered accordingly. (Rule 14.25).

Summary Judgment.—Where defendant has filed a defence or appeared on a hearing under an originating notice, plaintiff may on ground that defendant has no defence to a claim in originating notice except to amount of damages claimed, apply to court for judgment against defendant. On hearing application, court may require examination of witnesses or production of documents; grant judgment for plaintiff on all or part of claim; impose stay of execution or other terms upon plaintiff until determination of defendant's counterclaim or third party proceeding; allow defendant claim unconditionally or on terms relating to giving security, time, mode of trial, or otherwise; order assessment or accounting where defence is to amount only; give directions as to trial or hearing; with consent of all parties dispose of proceeding finally in a summary manner, with or without pleadings or affidavits and without appeal, order delivery of an article; relieve against forfeiture of land; award costs, or grant any order it considers just. (Rule 13). Summary judgment may be granted on an application based on admission of facts

See Topical Index in front part of this volume.

JUDGMENTS . . . *continued*
or documents. Where plaintiff obtains summary judgment, he may continue proceeding in respect of any remaining part of claim, or any other claim, or against any other defendant.

Declaratory Judgments.—No action or proceeding is open to objection on the ground that a merely declaratory judgment or order is sought, and the court may make binding declarations of right whether any consequential relief is or could be claimed or not. Declarations of right may be made on application by originating summons, to determine any question of construction arising under deeds, wills or other written instruments. The jurisdiction of the court to make such declarations is in effect only limited by its own judicial discretion, but it is carefully exercised, and the plaintiff must be entitled to relief.

Default Judgments.—(1) *In default of appearance:* Appearance is no longer used. (2) *In default of pleading:* Where originating notice contains one of claims specified below, and defendant fails to file a defence thereto within ten days of service of notice or such time as court may order, plaintiff may enter judgment against defendant and continue proceeding against any other defendant. Judgment may be for costs, and where a claim is for liquidated demand only, for a sum not exceeding claim, where part of claim is for interest at an unspecified rate, for an additional sum for interest at rate of 6% per annum; where claim is for unliquidated damages, for damages to be assessed; where claim related to detention of goods only, for delivery of goods or their value to be assessed; where claim is for possession of land only, for possession of land provided if there is more than one defendant, judgment shall not be enforced against any defendant until judgment for possession of land has been entered against all defendants. Where interlocutory judgment is entered and damages or value of goods are assessed and costs taxed, a final judgment may be entered. Where originating notice is endorsed with one of above claims together with any other claim, and defendant fails to file a defence or appear on hearing, plaintiff may, after expiration of time limited for defending or appearing, apply to court for judgment. If such claim is against more than one defendant, and any defendant defaults while another defends plaintiff may, if his claims are severable, apply for judgment against defendant in default and continue against any other defendant or set proceeding down for judgment against defendant in default when proceeding is set down for trial against other defendant. Default judgment will not be entered unless an affidavit is filed by plaintiff proving service of originating notice upon defendant, or plaintiff produces originating notice endorsed by defendant's solicitor with statement that he accepts service on defendant's behalf. In lieu of filing defence or appearing on a hearing, defendant may file and deliver a demand notice, and upon receipt of same, plaintiff may proceed as if defendant had failed to file defence or appear on hearing except that defendant shall be entitled to receive notice of all subsequent steps taken in proceeding against him, and final judgment may only be obtained on notice to him. Court may, on such terms as it thinks just, set aside or vary any default judgment. (Rule 12).

Record and Liens.—Every judgment is entered by the prothonotary in a book kept for the purpose, and is dated as of the day it was pronounced, and takes effect from that date. It may by special leave be ante-dated or post-dated. A judgment may be registered in the registry of deeds, and then binds and is a charge upon any land in the registration district of any person against whom it was recovered, whether acquired before or after its registration. (c. 392, §20). Registered judgment also binds interest in land of cestui que trust. (c. 409, §5). If registered and unsatisfied, it continues to be lien on land for 20 years, and for longer period if any payment was made on it.

Assignment.—An absolute written assignment by the assignor of any judgment, of which express notice in writing, is given to the debtor, transfers the legal right to such judgment to the assignee from the date of such notice, and the power to give a good discharge for the same without the concurrence of the assignor. (c. 240, §43 as am'd by 1992, c. 16).

Satisfaction.—If defendant pays amount owing under judgment, it is satisfied or discharged. A satisfaction piece should then be made out stating that it is satisfied; this must be signed by plaintiff or his personal representative or his solicitor or by any other person entitled to benefit thereof who attaches to satisfaction piece an affidavit establishing his entitlement, unless a judge on special circumstances dispenses with such authorization. Form of satisfaction piece is as follows:

Form

19. . . . S. C. No. . . . . . .
In the Supreme Court (Trial Division)
Between A. B. Plaintiff
and
C. D. Defendant

Satisfaction is acknowledged of the order entered by the [Plaintiff] [defendant] against the [plaintiff] [defendant] on the . . . . . . day of . . . ., 19. . . ., for the sum of $. . . . . and costs of $. . . . . Dated at . . . ., Nova Scotia, this . . . . . . day of . . . ., 19. . . ..

(Sgd.) . . . .

Foreign judgments can be enforced only by action thereon. If no defense made in original action any defense which might have been made therein is available in an action on the judgment. A judgment in rem of a foreign court of competent jurisdiction is conclusive as to title in the absence of fraud. A foreign judgment in personam can only be upset by showing fraud or lack of jurisdiction. Reciprocal Enforcement of Judgments Act provides for enforcement by registration. Applies only to reciprocating states. Reciprocating states are United Kingdom and Northern Ireland, and all Provinces of Canada except Quebec. (c. 52). No U.S. states are reciprocating states. Judgment may be registered ex parte if debtor was personally served or submitted to jurisdiction in original proceeding. Other registrations require notice to debtor. No registration if original court lacked jurisdiction, fraud, public policy, appeal pending. Must register within six years of original judgment. Once registered has same effect as N.S. Judgment. (c. 388, §3).

Execution.—See topic Executions.

Contribution.—A joint tortfeasor may recover contribution or indemnity after making a settlement with the injured party. (c. 471).

JUSTICES OF THE PEACE:

Justices of Peace are appointed by Governor-in-Council of province (c. 244, §2 as am'd by 1992, c. 16 [proclaimed 26 Jan. '93, in force 30 Jan. '93]), who may also remove them (c. 244, §8 as am'd by 1992, c. 16 [proclaimed 26 Jan. '93, in force 30 Jan. '93]). Justices of Peace are supervised by Chief Judge of Provincial Court. See topic Courts.

LABOUR RELATIONS:

Occupational Health and Safety Act (1996, c. 7) which enacts comprehensive safety code at workplaces in Nova Scotia. Every "employer", "constructor", "supplier", "contractor", "owner", "architect", "engineer", "provider of occupational health and safety service" to workplace, "employee" and "self-employed person" is subject to duties respecting health and safety. Joint occupational health and safety committees must be established at workplaces where more than 20 persons regularly employed or where Minister of Labour and Manpower designates (1996, c. 7, §29). As of July 1, 1997 occupational health and safety programmes must be established at workplaces where more than 20 persons regularly employed or where regulations require. (1996, c. 7, §28). Employee permitted to refuse to do any act which may endanger his health or safety. (1996, c. 7, §43). Use of hazardous substances is regulated. Inspections and enforcement done by officers of Occupational Health and Safety Division of Department of Labour and Manpower. (1996, c. 7, §§47-57).

Wages.—Labour Standards Code (c. 246 as am'd by 1991, c. 14) provides for establishment of minimum wage rates for all employees except farm labourers and domestic servants. Rates are set by Minimum Wage Board which may make exemptions.

Equal pay to men and women for equal work must be paid. (c. 337, as am'd by 1990, c. 41). Pay Equity Act (c. 337, as am'd by 1990, c. 41) establishes system to increase pay of employees in classes which are predominatly female where determined that by reason of sex discrimination those employees paid less than should be. Act applies only to employees in public sector.

Labour Standards Code (c. 246 as am'd by 1991, c. 14).—Applies to all employees except teachers and as provided in regulations. Wages are to be paid at least semi-monthly unless existing practice, collective agreement or order of director dictates otherwise. Employers must keep prescribed records of employee data for 12 months after termination of employment. Director of Labour Standards must have access to all employees and employer's records. Employee deemed to hold mortgage on assets of employer for accrued vacation pay in priority to all other liens, charges or mortgages except liens for wages due.

Complaints.—Employees may complain personally or anonymously without reprisal from employers. Director can investigate and settle disputes; may refer unsettled complaints to Labour Standards Tribunal for final decision. Appeal from Tribunal to Supreme Court, on law and jurisdiction.

Hours of work may be set by Minister and Minimum Wage Board with some exceptions.

Maternity Leave.—No woman may be laid off due to pregnancy unless unable to fulfill duties. Mothers must take a week post-partem vacation without pay, unless certified fit to work by doctor. Employer must accept woman back with no loss of seniority or benefits.

Children.—Strict provisions concerning employment of children under 16.

Human Rights Act (c. 214 as am'd by 1991, c. 12).—Prohibits discrimination due to race, religion, creed, colour, ethnic or national origin, marital status, sex, sexual orientation, political belief, affiliation or activity, irrational fear of contacting illness or disease, age, or physical or mental disability in housing, employment and access to services and facilities. Prohibits discrimination in housing on basis that applicant for tenancy is recipient of income maintenance. (c. 214, §16 as am'd by 1991, c. 12). Establishes Human Rights Commission to oversee Act and Board of Inquiry which can issue orders. Order can be appealed to Appeal Division. Penalty for violating Act or order is fine not exceeding $500 for individuals or $1,000 otherwise.

Termination of Employment.—Notice required. Time varies with length of employment. Lump sum equal to wages payable in lieu of notice. 4% vacation pay must be paid on termination. Employee of ten years or more not to be discharged or suspended without just cause.

Labour Unions.—Trade Union Act (c. 475) legalizes formation of trade unions and collective bargaining and regulates relations between employers and employees, wage agreements, conciliation preceding strikes or lockouts, etc. Single bargaining unit is only appropriate bargaining unit where there are more than one interdependent manufacturing locations. Labour Relations Board has broad remedial powers regarding violations of Act. (c. 475, §§16-22).

Construction Unions.—Subject to special provisions including preventive mediation, rapid certification and binding arbitration. (c. 475, §§92-107).

Boat-Owner Fishermen.—See topic Associations.

Labour Disputes.—No ex parte injunction may be granted in labour dispute unless actual or apprehended breach of peace, injury to persons, severe damage to property or interruption of essential public service and reasonable attempt to notify union of application. (c. 240 as am'd by 1989, c. 20; 1992, c. 16 [proclaimed 26 Jan. '93, in force 30 Jan. '93]).

Workers' Compensation Act.—(c. 508, as am'd by 1992, c. 35) Part I of Act applies to employees and workers in and about any operations carried on in factory and also in or about enumerated list of about 60 industries which include hazardous or partly hazardous occupations. It may apply to students if so ordered by Governor in Council. (c. 508, §6). It does not apply to traveling salesmen, persons whose employment is of casual nature for purposes other than employer's trade or business, or to outworkers, but includes voluntary fire brigades. If any personal injury occurs to worker by accident arising out of and in course of employment, compensation must be paid to him or his

LABOUR RELATIONS . . . *continued*
dependents, except where it disables him for less than three days from earning full wages at that work, or is attributable solely to his own serious or wilful misconduct, unless injury results in death or serious and permanent disablement. (c. 508, §9, as am'd by 1992, c. 35, §§1, 2). Board arranges for hospitalization and medical attendance free to injured workers, and employer may not take anything from worker either directly or indirectly for any sum which he may become liable to pay into Accident Fund. (c. 508, §22).

Provisions of Part I of Act are in lieu of all rights and rights of action to which workman or his dependents are or may be entitled against employer concerning any accident in which compensation is payable or which arises in course of workman's employment in an industry under Part I at time of accident. (c. 508, §§4-8). Compensation cannot be waived, and any agreement to that effect is void. Compensation is not assignable or liable to attachment. Maximum earnings upon which compensation can be made is $7,000 per year. (c. 508, §49). Where death results from injury compensation is: (a) Necessary burial expenses not over $400 and further reasonable expenses up to $100; (b) where widow or widower is sole dependent, lump sum payment of $500 plus $225 per month (c. 508, §33); (c) where dependents are widow or widower and one or more children, lump sum payment of $500 and thereafter monthly payment of $225 with additional monthly payment of $45 for each child under age of 18 years (c. 508, §33); (d) where dependents are children, monthly payments of $60 to each child under 18 years (c. 508, §33); (e) where no compensation under (b), (c), and (d) and other dependents, sum reasonable and proportionate to pecuniary loss to such dependents occasioned by death of worker, determined by Workers' Compensation Board, but not exceeding $75 per month to any one dependant, and not exceeding in whole $100 per month (c. 508, §33); payments under (e) continue only so long as Board thinks worker would have continued to contribute to support of dependents if he had lived (c. 508, §33). Payments in respect of child cease when it attains age of 18, except that compensation to invalid child continues so long as Board thinks worker would have continued to contribute to its support if he had lived. (c. 508, §57). Where worker dies while receiving compensation, his dependants will receive three times monthly payment in compensation. (c. 508, §36). Where worker dies while receiving compensation for permanent total disability, his dependents will receive nine times monthly payment in compensation. (c. 508, §36). All above amounts may be increased by Governor in Council. (c. 508, §62).

Where permanent total disability results from injury amount of compensation is a weekly payment during his life equal to 75% of his average earnings during previous 12 months, but amounting to at least $225 per month (c. 508, §43) with special provision where dependent child is continuing his education. Same payment is made in case of temporary disability as long as disability lasts provided that compensation shall not be less than $45 per week, or where average earnings are less than $47 per week, amount of such earnings. Allowance not exceeding $300 per month may be made for treatment or services necessary as result of injury (c. 508, §71), and clothing allowance may be paid where prosthetic device causes extra wear on clothing of injured workman. Where permanent partial disability results, compensation is weekly payment of such amount as Board considers represents 75% of difference in worker's earning capacity before and after accident, having regard to degree of disability, age and average earnings of worker, this is payable during lifetime. (c. 508, §45). Minimum presumed earnings are $300 per month. (c. 508, §47). In case of temporary partial disability, compensation is weekly payment of 75% of difference between average earnings of workman before accident and average amount he is earning or able to earn in some suitable employment after accident; payable as long as disability lasts. (c. 508, §38).

Where permanent total disability results from injury, compensation may be paid to dependent children acquired subsequent to injury. (c. 508, §43).

In case of temporary total disability where payments are made for 52 weeks they are indexed every Jan. thereafter as if for permanent total disability. (c. 508, §46).

In computing compensation where recurrence of disability occurs more than one year after original accident, with subsequent return to work, claimant may take into account increase in average earnings between accident and recurrence. This is situation regardless whether recurrence causes temporary or permanent disability. (c. 508, §39).

Where an injured worker who was given permanent disability award dies shortly thereafter and where award is paid on periodic basis, estate shall be paid difference up to 10% of capitalized value of award at time it was made if total payments made to time of worker's death do not equal or exceed 10%. (c. 508, §52).

Appeal from Workmen's Compensation Board decision to Appeal Board must be within one year. (c. 508, §174).

Worker disputing medical opinion on which compensation was based, level of disability found or period of compensation can appeal to Appeal Board. (c. 508, §173).

Part III applies to industries to which Part I does not apply and to workers employed therein. (c. 508, §187). It provides that worker suffering personal injury because of defect in condition or arrangement of machinery, plant, buildings or premises connected with or used in employer's business, or because of negligence of his employer or any person in employer's service acting within scope of his employment, has, or if death results from injury, his legal representatives and any person entitled in case of death has, an action against employer to recover damages sustained or damages as under Fatal Injuries Act as case may be. See topic Death. Same applies where execution of any work is being carried into effect under any contract, and injury is caused by contractor or subcontractor. Contractor or subcontractor is liable, but not so as to enable double damages to be recovered for same injury. Worker is not deemed to have voluntarily incurred risk of injury by reason only of his continuing in employment of employer with knowledge of defect or negligence which caused it. (c. 508, §188). Worker is deemed not to have undertaken risk due to his fellow workers, and contributory negligence by worker does not bar recovery by him or by any person entitled to damages under Fatal Injuries Act, in action for recovery of damages for injury sustained by, or causing death of worker while in service of his employer, for which employer would otherwise have been liable. (c. 508, §189). But contributory negligence is taken into account in assessing damages in such action. (c. 508, §190).

Administration of the act is in hands of Workmen's Compensation Board, which is a body corporate and consists of three or more members.

The Employer's Liability Act, R. S. N. S. (1900, c. 179) was not repealed when revision of statutes was made in 1967, but the subject is mostly covered by Workers' Compensation Act.

Unemployment Compensation.—See Canada Law Digest, topic Labour Relations, subhead Unemployment Insurance Act.

LANDLORD AND TENANT:

Common law rules govern general rights and liabilities arising out of relationship of landlord and tenant, but see subheads Residential Tenancies Act and Rent Review Act, infra.

Kinds of Tenancies.—Tenancies may be at will, at sufferance, from year to year, for a term of years, for a life or lives, or weekly or monthly.

Leases for more than three years must be in writing signed by the lessor or they will have the force of estates at will only. (c. 442, §3). In Halifax, lease for term longer than 21 years is subject to deed transfer tax. (1972, c. 71). See also topic Taxation, subhead Real Estate Conveyance Tax.

Recording.—Leases for over three years must be recorded in the registry of deeds for that district or they will be ineffective as against a person claiming under any subsequent instrument duly registered. (c. 392, §25). Such leases must be proved by acknowledgment of executing parties under oath or by oath of subscribing witness. (c. 392, §31).

Distress.—Landlord may distrain for rent due under the lease upon goods or chattels upon the demised premises, but the following goods are exempt from distress: (1) goods brought into any building used as a market bona fide for the purpose of sale, by any person, not being property in which the tenant has any interest; (2) all articles or goods in possession of tenant under a duly filed agreement for hire, lease, or conditional sale excepting the tenant's interest therein; (3) articles exempt from execution (see topic Exemptions). (c. 464, §9). Where goods are distrained, if tenant or owner of them does not within five days after distress and notice thereof duly served on him, replevy same, landlord may have goods appraised. After appraisal, and five days' notice of sale by handbills in conspicuous places in locality, landlord may sell such goods for best price he can get, and apply proceeds in payment of rent due and expenses incurred; any balance goes to owner of goods. (c. 464, §§3-4). Goods fraudulently removed by the tenant to avoid distress may be seized by landlord within 21 days of such removal, and he may dispose of them as if they had been distrained upon premises, unless sold bona fide for value before seizure. (c. 464, §13). He may distrain on good fraudulently conveyed away and locked up or otherwise secured to prevent distress. In such cases he must call to his assistance constable for city, town or county, in which goods suspected to be so placed or kept, who must help him. They can, in daytime, break open and enter into such place and take such goods. (c. 464, §14). Tenant or person interested in goods may, before sale, commence proceeding for declaration that person other than tenant has interest in goods and judge may stay sale pending determination of interest in goods. (c. 464, §4).

Notice to quit, in tenancies from year to year, must be given at least three months before the expiration of any such lease; from month to month, at least one month before the expiration of any such month; if from week to week at least one week before the expiration of any such week. (c. 464, §18).

Holding Over.—Upon determination of tenancy, landlord, without any demand on tenant, may make a complaint to a magistrate having jurisdiction where land lies. Magistrate may issue a summons directed to tenant stating time and place at which complaint will be heard and determined; a true copy of summons and complaint must be served on tenant at least five days before day of hearing. Magistrate, on hearing parties, makes an order or dismisses complaint. If tenant does not appear, magistrate upon proof of service of summons and complaint may issue an order for possession. An appeal lies to Supreme Court. (c. 329, §10 as am'd by 1992, c. 16 proclaimed 26 Jan. '93, in force 30 Jan. '93).

Residential Tenancies Act (c. 401, as am'd by 1992, c. 31; 1994, c. 5) applies when landlord-tenant relationship exists in respect of "residential premises," meaning places occupied as residences by individuals, including mobile homes and mobile home parks (c. 401 as am'd by 1992, c. 31; 1994, c. 5). Agreement to pay or payment of rent creates landlord-tenant relationship. When Act applies, Overholding Tenants Act and Tenancies and Distress for Rent Act do not apply.

Provisions: (a) Landlord must provide tenant with copy of Act and with respect to written tenancy agreements signed copy of standard form of lease, as prescribed by regulation, within ten days of occupancy or execution. Landlord is entitled to acknowledgment of compliance from tenant; noncompliance allows tenant to vacate within three months without penalty. Standard form of lease is deemed to have been signed by both landlord and tenant whenever oral or written agreement or renewal is entered into otherwise than by signature of Standard Form of Lease (c. 401, §7, as am'd by 1992, c. 31, §3 [not yet in force]); (b) statutory conditions respecting repair and condition of premises, subletting, mitigation of damages on abandonment or termination, entry by landlord, provision of essential services, conduct of tenant, interest on late payment of rent and doorlocks are deemed to be in all leases; (c) notice to quit periods required, with variation if rent is in arrears, for tenant of less than five years; tenant with five consecutive years or more tenancy on or after May 18, 1984 may not be given notice to quit unless one of several statutory exceptions applies. Where tenant's interest is foreclosed or extinguished, tenant may remain in possession until earlier of: (i) expiration of three months from receipt of notice to quit, or (ii) date on which tenancy agreement terminates according to its own terms (c. 401, §8); (d) three months' notice in writing required before rent increase; only one rent increase per 12 month period permitted; (e) "security deposits" defined as money paid in addition to rent must be held in trust by landlord and be deposited accordingly or invested in authorized securities (c. 401, §12, as am'd by 1992, c. 31 §6 [not yet in force]; 1993, c. 40, §11 [in force 22 Feb. '94]); limited to one-half monthly rent and use is restricted; (f) order to comply may be granted by magistrate on complaint. Provision made for enforcing orders; (g) Residential Tenancies Board established with powers, including rent review; (h) Act has restricted application to public housing; (i) landlord may not hold or dispose of tenant's personal property. Interest is to be paid on security deposit. Unlawful for person to

LANDLORD AND TENANT . . . *continued*
stipulate for or accept application fee. (c. 401, §12, as am'd by 1992, c. 31, §6 [not yet in force]; 1993, c. 40, §11 [in force 22 Feb. '94]). Landlord or tenant may apply to Director of Residential Tenancies with respect to disputes. Director of Residential Tenancies is exclusive authority, at first instance, to investigate and mediate settlement. (1992, c. 31, §7 [not yet in force]).

Discrimination.—See topic Labour Relations, subhead Human Rights Act.

Rent Review Act (c. 398). Rents of most residential premises controlled. Administered by Rent Review Commission. Provisions: (a) Landlord must give three months notice of rental increase to tenant and provide Commission with copy of such notice; (b) if increase in excess of limits established by Act (generally 6%) increase is reviewed by Residential Tenancy Officer in light of previous increases in respect of that tenancy, return on investment and effect on landlord's financial position. Officer has power to approve increase, order lessened increase and make consequential orders to pay against landlord and tenant; (c) landlord or tenant may appeal decision to Commission or Commission may review on own initiative; court review limited to questions of law; (d) exemptions include hotels, rooming houses, institutions such as colleges and hospitals, and new residential premises.

Rental Property Conversion Act (c. 399) provides that notice must be given to tenants and Director of Landlord and Tenant Relations of proposal to convert rental property into other use. First offer to tenant to occupy property in converted form must be given. Regulations may prevent conversion of rental property.

LEASES: See topic Landlord and Tenant.

LEGISLATURE:

The Legislature sits every year, generally in the spring of the year. No statutory requirement as to holding regular sessions at any fixed time. Special or extraordinary sessions may be called. There is no provision for the initiative or referendum. (c. 210 as am'd by 1990, c. 21; 1992, c. 21). Conflicts of interest of members governed by 1987, c. 86.

LEVY: See topics Attachment; Executions.

LICENSES:

Special licenses are issued under different statutes. Municipalities, cities and towns are also authorized to license auctioneers, peddlers, markets, billiard rooms, etc.

See also topic Mines and Minerals.

LIENS:

Lien of solicitor for professional services on documents in his possession, lien of warehouseman on goods stored in his warehouse for storage in respect of such goods, innkeeper's lien, carrier's lien, possessory lien of shipwright for work done on ships, maritime liens, liens of vendor and purchaser of land, and other ordinary common law liens are recognized in Nova Scotia.

Artisan's Lien.—Every mechanic or other person who has bestowed money or skill and materials upon any chattel or thing in the alteration and improvement in its properties or for the purpose of imparting an additional value to it, so as thereby to be entitled to a lien on such chattel, has, while such lien exists, in addition to his other remedies, the right to sell the chattel by auction on giving one week's notice in a newspaper published in the county in which the work was done, stating the name of the debtor, the amount of the debt, description of the chattel, time and place of sale, name of auctioneer, and leaving notice at last known residence of owner in the county. (c. 277, §45).

Woodmen's Lien.—Any person performing any labor or service in connection with any logs or timber within the province has a lien thereon for the amount due for such labor. This is a first lien on such logs or timber unless the Crown has a claim on the same. (c. 507, §4). Lien claimant must, within 60 days after last day on which services were performed, file statement, verified by his oath, in office of clerk of county court where labor was performed or where timber drive terminated. (c. 507, §§6-8). Lien ceases unless action to enforce same brought within 30 days after filing of statement or expiration of period of credit. (c. 507, §10). Action to enforce lien must be brought in county court of county where labor was performed.

Liens on Ships.—In the case of ships a statutory lien exists in a case of towage, mortgage, ownership, possession, building, equipping or repairing any ship, if the ship or proceeds are under the arrest of the court when the cause is instituted; of necessaries supplied to a ship; and for damages to cargo imported into Canada, unless owner is domiciled in Canada. This is given in favor of the persons who perform the services, supply the necessaries, etc.

Mechanics' Liens.—Any person who performs any work or service upon or in respect of or places or furnishes any material to be used in making, constructing, fitting, altering, improving or repairing of any erection, building, railway, ship, land, wharf, bridge, vault, mine, excavation, sidewalk, drain, sewer, roadbed, way, etc., or appurtenances to any of them; for any owner, contractor or subcontractor, has by virtue thereof a lien for price of such services or materials upon erection, etc., and land occupied thereby or enjoyed therewith. (c. 277, §6). Lien arises for services done pursuant to rental of equipment. (c. 277, §6). Lien attaches on interest of owner in property. (c. 277, §8). Lien is limited so as not to make owner liable for greater sum than sum payable by owner to contractor. (c. 277, §11). Person primarily liable on any contract under or by virtue of which lien may arise, must deduct from any payment made by him under contract, and retain for 45 days after contract is substantially performed, 10% (c. 277, §13) of value of work, service or materials. Lien is charge on this amount, in favor of subcontractors whose liens are derived under persons to whom such moneys so required to be retained are respectively payable. (c. 277, §13). With respect to amount so retained, mechanics and laborers have, to extent of 30 days wages, priority over all other liens derived through contractor or subcontractor by whom they are employed. (c. 277, §16). Employee deemed to hold mortgage on assets of employer for accrued vacation pay in priority to all other liens, charges or mortgages except liens for wages due. (c. 246, §36).

The lien claimant must register a claim within 45 days after last work performed or last materials placed or furnished. The claim must state the name and residence of the claimant and the owner of the property proposed to be charged, and of the person for whom the work was done or materials supplied, and the time when done; a short description of the work done or materials furnished; the sum claimed; description of the land or property to be charged. The claim must be verified by affidavit of claimant. If claim is not filed within 45 days, lien expires at end of that time, unless an action is begun in the meantime to realize the claim, and a certificate thereof is registered in the registry office in which the claim for lien might have been registered. (c. 277, §§19, 24-25). Taking security or extending time of payment does not waive lien unless agreement in writing by claimant to that effect. (c. 277, §30).

A lien for which the claim is registered expires on expiration of ninety days after work completed or materials furnished, or after period of credit, unless in the meantime an action is begun to realize the claim and a certificate is registered. A lien may be discharged by a receipt signed by the claimant acknowledging payment, and verified by affidavit and registered. May also be discharged by order of court vacating lien. (c. 277, §26).

Mechanics' liens are enforced by action to be brought and tried in Supreme Court of district in which land lies. (c. 277, §34, as am'd by 1992, c. 16). Action is begun by filing statement of claim above referred to in office of clerk of such court. Statement must be served within one month after filing unless time extended by court. Party then applies for appointment fixing day and place of trial, and must, at least eight clear days before day fixed, serve notice of trial upon solicitors of defendants who appear by solicitors, upon all registered lienholders and upon all other persons having any claim on the lands who are not parties or who appear personally in action. Third party proceedings are permitted. (c. 277, §34). Service must be personal unless otherwise ordered. Judge then tries action and gives judgment. (c. 277, §35).

Public Works—There is no requirement that a general contractor for public buildings or other public works shall give bond for faithful performance of the contract and payment of claims for labor and materials going into such buildings or other works.

Redemption.—There is no right of redemption of property sold in enforcement of the liens hereinbefore mentioned.

LIMITATION OF ACTIONS:

Actions must be brought within following times after cause of action arose:

One year: For assault, imprisonment, slander, menace, battery or wounding, assault based on sexual abuse, cause of action for which does not arise until victim becomes aware of injury or harm, and limitation period for which does not begin to run while victim is not reasonably capable of commencing proceeding because of physical, mental, or psychological condition arising from sexual abuse. (c. 258, §2, as am'd by 1993, c. 27).

Two years: For penalties, damages or sums of money given to parties aggrieved by any statute; for damages arising out of motor vehicle accidents (c. 258, §2); for damages for medical or dental negligence or malpractice (c. 258, §2).

Six years: Actions grounded upon contract, lending, award, or for money levied by execution; actions for direct injuries to real or personal property; for the taking away or conversion of property; libel, malicious prosecution and arrest, seduction, criminal conversation, and all actions which would have been brought as trespass on the case; arrears of dower or rent, actions of account; action on foreign judgment. (c. 258, §§2, 25-26).

Twenty years: For recovery of land; for rent upon an indenture of demise, upon a bond or other specialty, upon a judgment or recognizance; for recovery of money secured by mortgage, judgment or lien or otherwise charged or payable out of any land or rent or any legacy. (c. 258, §§2, 10, 23).

Special cases may be provided for in special statutes.

Time commences to run from the time the cause of action accrues. Cause of action in tort generally held to accrue at time plaintiff knew or should have known that he suffered damage or injury.

Disabilities.—Infants, married women, persons of unsound mind, or persons out of the province may bring action immediately disability is removed, and the statute does not run against such person until such removal. Similarly statute does not run in their favor until removal of disability, and action can then be brought against them. (c. 258, §§4-5). Person under disability or person claiming through him is allowed ten years from termination of disability or death of such person to make entry or distress, or to bring action to recover land or rent; but in any case such entry, action, or etc., must be brought within 40 years from time when right frist accrued; in the case of claim of rent by Crown, must be brought within 60 years. (c. 258, §§20-21).

Death.—By the Survival of Actions Act, c. 453, personal rights of action survive, and may be maintained by executors or administrators, if brought within six months after representation is taken out, and in any event, not later than two years after death.

Acknowledgment or promise in writing signed by the party chargeable deprives such party of the benefit of the statute in the case of an action grounded on simple contract; new acknowledgment or promise is also sufficient if in writing. If any acknowledgment has been made either by writing signed by the party liable by virtue of an indenture, or of any specialty or recognizance, or his agent, or by part payment or part satisfaction on account of any principal or interest being then due thereon, the person entitled may bring an action for the money remaining unpaid and so acknowledged to be due, at any time within 20 years after such acknowledgment, part payment or part satisfaction: if the party entitled or the party making the acknowledgment is at the time of making the same, under a disability, then within 20 years after the removal of the disability. Indorsement or memorandum of any payment written or made upon any promissory note, bill of exchange or other writing, by or on behalf of the party to whom such payment was made, is not sufficient proof of such payment so as to take the case out of the operation of the statute. (c. 258, §§8, 9).

Pleading.—Statute of limitations must be specially pleaded. (Rule 14.14).

LIMITATION OF ACTIONS . . . *continued*

Relief.—In cases of limitation periods of less than ten years, except for mechanics liens limitations, court may grant relief from limitation period where equitable within four years from date of expiration of limitation period. (c. 258, §3).

LIMITED PARTNERSHIP: See topic Partnership.

MARRIAGE:

Marriage by persons under 16 years prohibited except where judge of Family or Juvenile Court finds expedient and in interests of parties. (c. 436, §21).

Consent Required.—If either party to an intended marriage (not being a widow or widower or divorcee) is under 19 (c. 436, §20) consent of both parents, if living, where one has not been assigned custody or is otherwise incompetent or surviving parent where one is dead, or if both dead, of guardian, must be obtained before license is issued (c. 436, §20). If father and mother dead or out of province, and no guardian appointed, license may be issued without such consent. (c. 436; §20). Consent of Director of Child Welfare or of Children's Aid Society substituted for consent of father, mother or guardian of ward of Director or Society. Judge of Supreme Court or family court may dispense with consent. (c. 436, §20).

Banns or License.—Marriage is valid if solemnized by person authorized and a license has been obtained for the solemnization. (c. 436, §15).

Proceedings for License.—To obtain license person must make affidavit containing full names of parties, residents, whether bachelor, widow, etc., occupation of applicant and that person making affidavit believes there is no lawful cause or legal impediment to bar or hinder solemnization of marriage, ages of parties, and if any party under 19 (c. 436, §17), facts necesary to enable issuer to determine whether or not consent has been duly given, or whether necessary; if consent in writing it must be annexed to affidavit; divorcee must attach copy of decree absolute (c. 436, §17). Affidavit may be made before issuer, notary public, justice of the peace or commissioner. Licenses are issued by deputy issuers of marriage licenses, appointed by Governor-in-Council. Fee is as determined by Governor in Council by regulation. (c. 436, §18).

Ceremony may be performed by a minister or clergyman of a church or religious denomination or by a commissioner or staff officer of Salvation Army in Canada, male or female, and resident in Nova Scotia, recognized as duly ordained or appointed according to rites and ceremonies of church denomination or society to which he belongs, provided he or she is registered as authorized to solemnize marriage in accordance with Solemnization of Marriage Act. Marriage solemnized according to rites and customs of Religious Society of Friends or of Baha'i Faith (c. 436, §§5, 12, 13) is valid. Judge of family court is authorized to solemnize marriage. (c. 436, §4 as am'd by 1992, c. 16 [proclaimed 26 Jan. '93, in force 30 Jan. '93]). Marriage must be solemnized in presence of at least two witnesses each of whom are at least 16 years of age. (c. 436, §22).

Reports of Marriages.—Every person solemnizing a marriage must make a written record of it in a form prescribed; this must be signed by each of the parties to the marriage, by person officiating, and by at least two witnesses; he must within 48 hours deliver or forward this by registered mail to the issuer of marriage licenses who in turn must on Saturday of every week forward the same to Registrar in Halifax. (c. 436, §§25-28).

Record.—See topic Records, subhead Vital Statistics.

Common law marriage not recognized except under provisions of Family Maintenance Act. (c. 160, as am'd by 1990, c. 5; 1994-95, c. 6 [not yet in force]).

Prohibited Marriages.—Parties are prohibited from marrying because of prior marriage, want of age, idiocy and the like. Marriage contracted while any such impediment exists is void. Relationship within the prohibited degrees is a bar to intermarriage.

Annulment.—The Court for Divorce and Matrimonial Causes may annul any marriage on the grounds of impotence or kindred within the degrees prohibited by 32 Henry 8, c. 38. Such a marriage is voidable upon application to court during life of parties, but cannot be questioned after the death of either. The court has jurisdiction to entertain a suit for nullity, where the marriage was celebrated in Nova Scotia; where the respondent is resident in Nova Scotia not on a visit as a traveler and not having taken up residence for the purposes of the suit; or where the parties to the marriage are domiciled in the province. Issue of an annulled marriage are illegitimate.

Foreign Marriages.—Marriage of foreigners is valid if according to the law of their domicile; provided it was a voluntary union of one man and one woman for life to the exclusion of all others and is not regarded as incestuous by the general consent of Christendom. Where one or both of parties is a British subject, marriage in a foreign country usually recognized as valid in Nova Scotia if celebrated according to form required in such foreign country if there is no lack of capacity of the parties to marry according to the law of their domicil, and if parties not prohibited from marrying by English law because of consanguinity, affinity or a previous marriage.

MARRIED WOMEN:

See topics Acknowledgments; Dower; Executors and Administrators; Guardian and Ward; Husband and Wife; Marriage; Wills; Witnesses.

MASTER AND SERVANT:

See topic Labour Relations; also topic Principal and Agent.

MECHANICS' LIENS: See topic Liens.

MINES AND MINERALS:

Mines and minerals are regulated generally by Mineral Resources Act (1990, c. 18, as am'd by 1992, c. 37; 1994, c. 36) and Coal Mines Regulation Act (c. 73) and Metalliferous Mines and Quarries Regulation Act (c. 284); but some earlier statutes are still in force.

Mineral Resources Act reserves to Crown all minerals except limestone, gypsum and building materials in every grant of Crown land.

Operation of Mines.—Minister of Mines and Energy has general supervision over mines in Nova Scotia. Minister can grant special license allowing entry upon mineral lands and determine amount of compensation to be paid owner. Can also direct upon petition that certain lands shall vest in lessee and fix compensation or submit it to arbitration. Licensing, leasing and royalties are regulated. (1990, c. 18, as am'd by 1992, c. 37; 1994, c. 36).

Petroleum and natural gas are vested in Crown. Exploration and production rights are regulated by Petroleum Resources Act. (c. 342). Offshore areas are regulated by Canada-Nova Scotia Oil and Gas Agreement (Nova Scotia) Act (c. 53) and Offshore Oil and Gas Act (c. 325) which provide for joint federal-provincial administration of offshore areas described in Acts. Administration parallels federal Canada Oil and Gas Act, and is carried out by Canada-Nova Scotia Oil and Gas Board. Canada-Nova Scotia Oil and Gas Agreement (Nova Scotia) Act and Offshore Oil and Gas Act repealed by 1987, c. 3. Regulation of offshore areas to be under Canada-Nova Scotia Offshore Petroleum Resources Accord Implementation (Nova Scotia) Act (1987, c. 3, as am'd by 1988, c. 56; 1992, c. 12; 1993, c. 16), Offshore Petroleum Resources Act (1987, c. 8, as am'd by 1992, c. 12; 1993, c. 16 not yet in force) and Offshore Petroleum Royalty Act (1987, c. 9 proclaimed 4 Jan. '90, in force 5 Jan. '90) which provide for joint federal-provincial administration of offshore areas defined in Acts. Administration parallels federal Canada-Nova Scotia Offshore Petroleum Resources Accord Implementation Act (Canada) and is to be carried out under Canada-Nova Scotia Offshore Petroleum Board. Construction of oil or gas pipelines solely within Province are regulated by Energy Board pursuant to Pipeline Act. (c. 345).

Energy and Mineral Resources Conservation Act (c. 147), set up Energy Board to regulate conservation, safe development and efficient production of energy and mineral resources, and to appraise markets. Conservation, safe development and efficient production of energy resources in offshore areas is regulated under Oil and Gas Production and Conservation (Nova Scotia) Act. (c. 326). Oil and Gas Production and Conservation (Nova Scotia) Act repealed by 1987, c. 3. Conservation, safe development and efficient production of energy resources in offshore areas to be regulated by 1987, c. 10 (not yet in force).

Safeguarding of Employees.—Unless chief inspector in writing otherwise approves, safety lamps shall be used in every mine to which Coal Mines Regulation Act applies. (c. 73, §86). Single gauze safety lamps prohibited. Mine must be equipped with apparatus for testing safety lamps. (c. 73, §86). Mine managers and overmen when underground must carry locked flame safety lamp. (c. 73, §34). No explosive other than a "permitted explosive" can be used for blowing coal or blasting in any mine unless permission is given by chief inspector and deputy inspector of district where mine situated. (c. 73, §68). Suitable apparatus to prevent accidents must be provided at every slope, underground plane and incline. Tops of shafts must be fenced and inspected; tops and entrances of workings, ventilating or pumping shafts must be fenced; safety appliances must be attached to cages. Roof and sides of every traveling road must be made secure, and must be of adequate height and width. (c. 73, §74). There are also similar provisions in Metalliferous Mines and Quarries Regulation Act, e.g., professional engineer must be engaged in supervision of mines of certain sizes and depths. (c. 284).

Gas Storage Exploration Act (c. 181).—Minister of Mines and Energy has general supervision over "gas" which includes any liquid or gaseous material. (c. 181, §2). He may designate Gas Storage Exploration Areas (c. 181, §3) and permit may be issued for exploration in area for five year period (c. 181, §4). Work requirements may be imposed. (c. 181, §5). If exploration indicates "storage area," investigating license may be issued after public hearing of any objection notice. If investigation of storage area shows "storage reservoir," lease may be issued permitting storage of gas in "storage reservoir." (c. 181, §10).

Bituminous Shale Conservation Act (1974, c. 2 unproclaimed).—Reserves to Crown in every grant of Crown lands made after Apr., 1910, all bituminous shale found in land. Provides licensing scheme for any one engaged in development, mining, production, or other dealing with bituminous shale.

Environment Act (1994-95, c. 1, §83). No wholesaler or retailer shall store or sell gasoline or fuel oil without approval issued pursuant to Environment Act. (1994-95, c. 1, §83).

Note: General price regulation by Board of Commissioners of Public Utilities abolished by 1991.

Gas Utilities Act (c. 182).—Governor in Council may grant franchises to distribute gas to public. (c. 182, §8). Energy Board regulates safety, technical aspects of utility. (c. 182, §6). Public Utilities Board set rates. (c. 182, §11).

Petroleum Products Allocation Act (1974, c. 8 unproclaimed) provides that when Governor in Council is of opinion that actual or anticipated shortage of petroleum markets likely to have adverse effect on Province exists, Governor in Council may declare that such shortage exists and implement a mandatory allocation program in respect of petroleum to assure sufficient supply of any or all petroleum products in various parts of Nova Scotia.

Common law rules govern as to general provisions.

MONOPOLIES AND RESTRAINT OF TRADE:

Governed by Combines Investigation Act, Canadian Criminal Code and common law. See Canada Law Digest, topic Monopolies and Restraint of Trade.

MORTGAGES OF PERSONAL PROPERTY:

See topic Chattel Mortgages.

MORTGAGES OF REAL PROPERTY:

Execution.—Mortgage must be in writing, signed, sealed and delivered; should be witnessed, one witness sufficient; takes effect upon delivery.

Recording.—As between parties need not be recorded; but must be recorded in registration district wherein land is situate in order to be effective against other persons. Same provisions as apply to recording deeds (see topic Deeds) apply to mortgages.

Fees.—$41, plus $1 per page.

MORTGAGES OF REAL PROPERTY . . . *continued*

If a mortgage is executed under a power of attorney, such power, or a deed confirming it, must be registered. (c. 392, §24).

Trust deeds are used in Nova Scotia chiefly by corporations; property is mortgaged to trustee (usually a trust company) as security for bond issue of the corporation.

Assignment.—Mortgages may be assigned. Assignment should also be recorded in registry of deeds, as same provisions apply to it as to mortgages, with respect to subsequent instruments affecting title to the same land. Requirements as to execution, same as mortgage.

Satisfaction and Release.—When mortgage is satisfied or paid, a release should be filed in the registry of deeds. Part of the lands may be released by written instrument.

Foreclosure and Sale.—Mortgagee begins action in ordinary way by originating notice and statement of claim. If mortgagor contests action, it is proceeded with like any other action; if he defaults mortgagee proceeds to judgment by default. (Rule 12.04). Mortgagee applies to court or judge for order for foreclosure and sale. Mortgagor in default may apply for discontinuance of foreclosure on condition that arrears and expenses be paid by certain date. If mortgagor fails to meet condition, then foreclosure procedure continues. (c. 240, §42 as am'd by 1992, c. 16 [proclaimed 26 Jan. '93, in force 30 Jan. '93]). Thirty days notice of sale together with copy of foreclosure order is served on all subsequent encumbrancers and on any other person on whom court directs; notice is also posted in county and published in some county newspaper for at least three insertions before date of sale, or as directed by court. Premises are then sold by sheriff at public auction and sold to highest bidder. Sheriff makes deed of land to purchaser. Order is then taken out confirming sheriff's report of sale. All proceedings are in Supreme Court.

Deficiency Judgment.—If proceeds of sale are insufficient to pay what is found to be due to plaintiff, he may have a deficiency judgment when mortgagor is the defendant and such relief has been claimed.

Redemption.—The mortgagor can redeem the mortgaged premises at any time up to the time of the order confirming the sale upon payment of principal, interest and costs.

Brokers and Lenders—Mortgage Brokers and Lenders Registration Act (c. 291).—Must be registered annually with Registrar of Mortgage Brokers. Presumption that person is broker if in one year he lends on security of five or more mortgages or four amounting to $30,000 or more. Every mortgage must state if it can be prepaid and if it can mortgage must state terms of prepayment. If mortgage is silent is may be prepaid without penalty at any time. (c. 291, §23). Governor-in-Council may make regulations relating to registration, records kept, returns to be made by brokers, information given by brokers, cooling-off periods, exemptions of persons or transactions, etc.

Matrimonial Property Act (c. 275) gives spouse to whom Act allows possession of matrimonial home same right to redeem equity of redemption and same right to notice as other spouse. (c.275, §9).

Conveyancing Act (c. 97) authorizes short forms of mortgage, assignment and release, now in general use as follows:

Forms

Mortgage: This Indenture made this . . . . day of . . . . in the year of Our Lord One Thousand Nine Hundred and . . . . . between . . . . . of . . . . . hereinafter called the "Mortgagor" of the One Part and . . . . . of . . . . . hereinafter called the "Mortgagee" of the Other Part.

Witnesseth that the said Mortgagor for and in consideration of the sum of . . . . . of lawful money of Canada, to the said Mortgagor in hand well and truly paid by the said Mortgagee at or before the sealing and delivery of These Presents (the receipt whereof is hereby acknowledged), hath granted, bargained, sold, aliened, enfeoffed, released, remised, conveyed and confirmed and by These Presents doth grant, bargain, sell, alien, enfeoff, release, remise, convey and confirm unto the said Mortgagee, ... and assigns (description)

Together with the buildings, easements, tenements, hereditaments and appurtenances to the same belonging or in anywise appertaining, and the reversion and reversions, remainder and remainders, rents, issues and profits thereof, and all the estate, right, title, interest, claim, property and demand, both at law and in equity of the said Mortgagor of, in, to or out of the same.

To have and to hold the said above granted and described lands and premises, with the appurtenances, and every part thereof, unto and to use of the said Mortgagee . . . . . and assigns forever. And it is hereby agreed and declared that the word "Mortgagor" and the word "Mortgagee," wherever used herein, shall, unless the context otherwise requires, be deemed to and shall include the heirs, executors, administrators, successors and assigns of each of them, and, if there is more than one Mortgagor or Mortgagee named, shall be deemed to and shall include each of such Mortgagors or Mortgagees, as the case may be, their several heirs, executors, administrators, successors and assigns, severally as well as jointly, and any Mortgagee, his executors, administrators, successors or assigns may exercise any of the powers herein conferred upon the Mortgagee. The said words, and all words depending thereon or relating thereto, shall also be deemed to and shall include the feminine and neuter as well as the masculine gender. The amount of principal money advanced on this mortgage is the sum paid to the said Mortgagor as aforesaid and the rate of interest chargeable thereon is . . . . . per centum per annum calculated . . . . . not in advance.

Provided always that if the said Mortgagor do well and truly pay unto the said Mortgagee the full amount of principal money advanced as aforesaid in lawful money of Canada with interest thereon at the rate aforesaid as well after as before maturity and calculated . . . . . not in advance . . . . .

Then these presents shall be void.

Mortgagor hereby convenants, promises, and agrees to and with the said Mortgagee as follows:

(1) That the said Mortgagor shall and will well and truly pay unto the said Mortgagee the full amount of the principal money advanced as aforesaid in lawful money of Canada with interest thereon in the manner after the rate and at the times mentioned in the foregoing proviso;

(2) That the said Mortgagor shall and will pay the said Mortgagee interest at the rate aforesaid on any instalment of interest in arrears from the date that the said instalment shall become due to the date of the payment thereof, the said interest to be compounded on every date when interest is payable hereunder;

(3) That after breach of the foregoing proviso, or in case of the breach or non-performance of any of the covenants or agreements herein contained on the part of the said Mortgagor to be observed or performed, it shall be lawful for the said Mortgagee peacefully and quietly to enter into, hold and enjoy the said granted land and premises, without hindrance or disturbance of, from or by any person or persons lawfully claiming the same or any part thereof;

(4) That the said Mortgagor hath a good, sure, perfect and indefeasible estate of inheritance in fee simple in the said land and premises, and hath good right, full power and lawful authority to grant and convey the same in manner and form aforesaid, according to the true intent and meaning thereof; and will at any time execute or cause to be executed such further and other acts, conveyances and assurances in the law for the better assuring to the said Mortgagee of the lands and premises above described, in manner as above conveyed or mentioned and intended so to be;

(5) That the said Mortgagor the said land and premises unto the said Mortgagee against the lawful claims and demands of all persons, whatsoever, shall and will by These Presents Warrant and Forever Defend;

(6) That until payment shall be made to the said Mortgagee of the principal sum and interest hereby secured the said Mortgagor will keep without intermission insured against casualties by fire the buildings on the said granted lands and premises for a sum not less than the total amount of principal money advanced on this and any other mortgage or mortgages in some good fire insurance office to be selected by and in the name and for the benefit of the said Mortgagee and will deposit with the said Mortgagee all policies and receipts for renewal premiums of such insurance; and that the said Mortgagee may require any insurance on the said buildings to be cancelled and new insurance effected in a company to be approved by "the Mortgagee"; and that in default thereof the said Mortgagee shall and may effect renew and continue such insurance and charge all payments made for or in respect thereof with interest after the rate aforesaid upon the said mortgaged lands and premises or at the said Mortgagee's option may either add all sums of money paid by the said Mortgagee on account thereof to the principal money hereby secured with interest after the rate aforesaid from the time or times when said sums of money are respectively paid, or sue and recover the same from time to time from the said Mortgagor;

(7) That if there shall be any loss by fire, either before or after default shall have been made in payment of the moneys hereby secured or in the doing or keeping or non-observance of any of the covenants or agreements herein contained the said Mortgagee may, at the Mortgagee's option, apply the insurance moneys either towards rebuilding or repairing the property destroyed or in or towards payment of the moneys hereby secured or partly the one and partly the other.

(8) That the said Mortgagor shall and will well and truly pay all taxes, rates, levies, liens, duties, charges, assessments and impositions of every kind and nature whatsoever, which during the kind and nature whatsoever, which during the continuance of this Mortgage shall at any time be rated, taxed, assessed or imposed on or in respect of the said lands and premises or any part thereof, at the times and in the manner required for the payment of such taxes, rates, levies, liens, duties, charges, assessments and impositions; and produce to the said Mortgagee the receipt for the payment of the same and that in default thereof the said Mortgagee may pay and discharge the same or any of them and charge all payments made in respect thereof with interest after the rate aforesaid upon the said mortgaged lands and premises, or at the Mortgagee's option may either add all sum or sums of money paid by the Mortgagee on account thereof to the principal money hereby secured with interest at the rate aforesaid from the time or times the said sum and sums of money are respectively paid, or sue and recover the same from the said Mortgagor.

(9) That the taking of a judgment or judgments on any of the covenants herein contained shall not operate as a merger of the said covenants or affect the right of the said Mortgagee to interest at the rate and times herein provided.

(10) That in case the said Mortgagee shall satisfy any charge or encumbrance on the said lands and premises, the amount paid shall be payable forthwith with interest at the rate aforesaid and become a lien and charge on the said lands and premises and be added to the principal sum due under this Mortgage, and in default of payment the principal sum hereby secured shall immediately become payable; and in the event of the money hereby advanced, or any part thereof, being applied to the payment of any charge or encumbrance the said Mortgagee shall stand in the possession of and be entitled to all the equities and securities of the person or persons so paid.

(11) That in default of payment of any portion of the money hereby secured or the interest thereon at the times and in the manner set forth, or in default of payment of any taxes, liens or charges that may be charged upon the said property, or in case the buildings herein comprised are not kept in good tenantable condition, or in case any waste is permitted on the said lands and premises, or in case the said Mortgagor makes any default hereunder at any time in any of the covenants or agreements herein contained, the whole principal money and interest hereby secured shall at the option of the said Mortgagee immediately become due and payable.

(12) That the amount of principal money advanced on this Mortgage together with any outstanding interest thereon may be repaid by the said Mortgagor at any time after the expiration of one year from the date hereof without notice and without bonus.

In witness whereof the said Mortgagor has duly executed these presents the day and year first above written.

Signed, Sealed and Delivered
in the presence of } . . . .

Assignment: By this Assignment of Mortgage made the . . . . . day of . . . . . 19. . . . . AB hereinafter called the "Assignor" of the one part assigns and conveys to CD hereinafter called the "Assignee" of the second part

In consideration of One Dollar ($1.00) of lawful money of Canada:

1. The mortgage dated . . . . . and recorded in the Registry of Deeds Office at . . . . . as document No. . . . . . for the year . . . . . and made between EF of the one part and AB of the other part to secure repayment of the sum of . . . . . of lawful money of Canada.
2. The land described in the mortgage, but subject to the terms contained in the mortgage.

See Topical Index in front part of this volume.

MORTGAGES OF REAL PROPERTY . . . *continued*

3. The full benefit of all powers and of all covenants and provisoes contained in the mortgage and also the full power and authority to use the name of the Assignor for enforcement of the performance of the covenants and other matters and things contained in the mortgage.

The Assignor covenants with the Assignee that 1. The mortgage hereby assigned is good and valid security and that the principal sum of . . . . . together with interest at the rate of . . . . . per centum per annum from the . . . . . day of . . . . . is now owing and unpaid.

2. The Assignor has not done or permitted any act, matter or thing whereby the mortgage has been released or discharged either partly or entirely.

3. The Assignor will, but at the cost of the Assignee, do and perform every act necessary to enforce the full performance of the covenants and other matters contained in the mortgage.

In witness whereof the Assignor has properly executed this assignment the day and year first above written.

Signed, sealed and delivered
in the presence of: } AB (L.S.)

Release: By this Release of Mortgage made this . . . . . day of . . . . . A. D. 19. . . . . hereinafter called the "Releasor" releases to . . . . . hereinafter called the "Releasee" all the lands mortgaged by a Mortgage made between . . . . . as Mortgagor and the Releasor as Mortgagee which is dated the . . . . . day of . . . . . ., A.D. 19. . . . and registered in the Registry of Deeds at . . . . ., ... in Book . . . . . at page . . . . . the Releasee claiming to be entitled to the equity of redemption in said mortgaged lands and releases also to the Releasee the benefits of the covenants in the mortgage and any bond or security given collateral thereto.

This Release is in consideration of One Dollar ($1.00) and the payment of all amounts of principal and interest secured by the mortgage.

In witness whereof the Releasor ha. . . . duly executed these presents the day and year first above written.

SIGNED, SEALED AND DELIVERED in the presence of . . . .(L.S.)
. . . .
(Witness)

Chattel Mortgages.—See topic Chattel Mortgages.

MOTOR VEHICLES:

Vehicle permit required annually. Number plates issued by Department of Transportation must be displayed one in front and one in rear. (c. 293, as am'd by 1990, c. 36; 1993, cc. 30 and 31; 1994, c. 24 [not yet in force]; 1994-95, c. 12; 1994-95, c. 6 [not yet in force]). No exemption for members of Armed Forces.

Drivers license required; must be renewed every three years. (c. 293, §64). Different classes of drivers licenses prescribed by regulations. (c. 293, §66). Chauffeur must have special license and wear badge assigned by department. Drivers license must be specially endorsed for motorcycle operation. (c. 293, §76). For operator's license must be 16, and for passenger-carrying vehicle for hire, 21; chauffeur's licenses can be granted persons under 18 where vehicles under 7,000 pounds gross weight. (c. 293, §67). No exemption for members of Armed Forces.

Titles and Sales.—Any transfers must be notified to department, and transferee may operate vehicle for 30 days before applying for registration of vehicle provided valid plates assigned to transferee are displayed (c. 293, §23 as am'd by 1994-95, c. 12, §3). If owner transfers registered vehicle, he must endorse name and address of transferee and date of transfer on certificate of registration issued in respect of such vehicle, and must forward same, with vehicle permit, to Department of Transportation. (c. 293, §43). New vehicles sold by dealers must comply with Motor Vehicle Safety Act (Canada). (R.S.C. 1985, c. M-10, as am'd by S.C. 1993, c. 16 [not yet in force]).

Restrictions on Operation.—Persons under 16, insane persons, persons suffering from or afflicted with physical or mental disability or disease so as to prevent exercise of reasonable control over a motor vehicle while operating it, persons who cannot understand highway signs in the English language. Persons whose licenses have been revoked for driving while impaired must apply for restoration after expiration of periods from six months to five years after revocation subject to such conditions and requirements as Registrar of Motor Vehicles deems necessary. (c. 293, §67 as am'd by 1994-95, c. 12, §5). Exception allowed operation of farm tractor on highways by minor 14 yrs. or over. (c. 293, §67). Doctors can report patients with mental or physical infirmities making them unsafe drivers. (c. 293, §279).

Summary Offence Tickets—May be issued for summary conviction offences under Motor Vehicle Act (c. 293) along with others. Procedure under Summary Proceedings Act (c. 450, as am'd by 1990, c. 46; 1993, c. 45; 1994-95, c. 12) allows payment of minimum penalty out of court in lieu of appearance (c. 450, §8 as am'd by 1993, c. 45; 1994-95, c. 18). Accused who fails to make payment or appear will be convicted and receive minimum penalty. (c. 450, §8 as am'd by 1993, c. 45; 1994-95, c. 18).

License Suspension.—A point system based on convictions supplements the various causes of suspension of licenses (c. 293, §282, as am'd by 1994, c. 24 [not yet in force]), including failure to pay sales tax on vehicle (c. 293, §17), and where accident and no insurance (c. 293, §230) and failure to pay fines for offences in relation to motor vehicles (c. 293, §269). Police officer who suspects driver of drunk driving may seize driver's licence immediately and issue temporary licence valid for seven days, after which time order for suspension of driver's licence becomes effective. (c. 293, as am'd by 1994-95, c. 12, §15).

Size and Weight Limits.—Regulated by c. 293, §§189-191, as am'd by 1990, c. 36; 1994-95, c. 12, §§13-14 (not yet in force).

Equipment Required.—Regulated by c. 293, §§174-201, as am'd by c. 12, §§12, 13, 14 (not yet in force). Seat belts must be worn if available by driver and all passengers over age 16. Passengers, under 16, for which child restraint system is prescribed, must be secured in such system while vehicle is being operated; otherwise passengers under 16 must be secured in seat belt if available. Exemptions for: (a) Persons of certain size, build, physical characteristics; (b) medical reasons; (c) peace officer on duty; (d) fireman on duty; (e) taxicab drivers and passengers; (f) public transit bus drivers; (g) medical attendant in ambulance with patient; (h) persons required by job to leave and enter vehicle frequently. (c. 293, §175).

Lights Required.—Regulated by c. 293, §§174-180.

Accidents.—Operator involved in accident resulting in injuries or death to any person, or property damage to an apparent extent of $200 or more must report same within 24 hours to Department of Transportation, or to nearest detachment of Royal Canadian Mounted Police, or to Chief of Police or police officer if accident occurred in city or town. (c. 293, §98). Also has duty to stop, give assistance, show license, etc.

Owner's Liability.—Operator is presumed to be servant of owner acting within scope of his authority and family car doctrine is established. Burden of proving that accident was not entirely due to negligence or improper conduct of operator is on owner or operator, except in case of collision with another motor vehicle and action brought by owner or operator, and except as to guests. (c. 293, §248).

Guests.—Liability for injury to gratuitous passengers is determined according to common law rules of negligence. (Requirement of gross negligence removed by 1983, c. 37.)

Attachment against a motor vehicle may be issued at or after the commencement of an action for injury, loss or damage sustained through negligent operation of such vehicle; but must be issued within 90 days from the day on which such injury, loss or damage was sustained. (c. 293, §250).

The vehicle must be released where defendant is the owner and deposits with the sheriff a certificate under the hand of the Registrar that proof of financial responsibility has been filed by such owner as required by the Motor Vehicle Act or, in case such proof has not been filed or defendant is not the owner, where there is filed with the sheriff a bond in favor of the plaintiff, executed by two sureties satisfactory to the sheriff or by an approved surety company, conditioned for payment of all damages and costs. (c. 293, §253).

Proof of Financial Responsibility.—Driver's license and every owner's permit of any person who owns or is operating a motor vehicle at time it becomes involved in an accident resulting in personal or property damage to others in apparent excess of $200, or who is convicted of any one of certain offences involving operation of a motor vehicle or forfeits bail after arrest on a charge for such an offense, will be suspended until proof of financial responsibility is furnished. (c. 293, §205). Must maintain proof of financial responsibility or face resuspension. (c. 293, §205). Minister may require proof of financial responsibility before issuing or renewing owner's permit or driver's license to person under age of 19 (c. 293, §229) or over age of 65. Proof of financial responsibility must be to extent of at least $200,000 inclusive for personal injury or death or property damage. Such proof may be by liability insurance, bond of approved guaranty surety company, bond with approved personal sureties or deposits of money or securities. (c. 293, §§234, 236). Where proof of financial responsibility is required it must be maintained for period of three years, or such longer period as directed by Minister. (c. 293, §244). Minimum liability insurance is $200,000. (c. 293, §235).

Insurance.—It is an offence not to have liability coverage. (c. 293, §230). See subhead Proof of Financial Responsibility, supra.

Judgment Recovery (N.S.) Limited.—A person who obtains a judgment in an action for damages for bodily injury, death or in excess of $200 for property damage occasioned by or arising out of the ownership, maintenance, operation or use of a motor vehicle within Nova Scotia, may, upon assigning the judgment to Judgment Recovery (N.S.) Limited, receive from it an amount up to a maximum inclusive payment of $200,000 inclusive of interest, plus costs, for personal injury, death or property damage. (c. 293, §213). In hit-and-run case, action may be brought against Registrar where vehicle involved was stolen vehicle and identity of driver cannot be established. (c. 293, §256). No money from fund will be paid to nonresident, unless such person resides in jurisdiction which affords similar relief to Nova Scotian residents. (c. 293, §213). Repayment to fund may be made in instalments. (c. 293, §225).

Foreign Vehicles.—A passenger motor vehicle owned by a person who does not reside or carry on business in Nova Scotia is exempt from registration for 90 days from the date on which it was first operated in Nova Scotia in any registration year, but there can be only one such exemption in the 12 months following such date. A passenger motor vehicle owned by a nonresident and operated within Nova Scotia for the transportation of persons or property for compensation is exempt from registration for 30 days from the date on which it was first operated in Nova Scotia in any registration year, provided no persons or goods are taken on within Nova Scotia, but there can only be one such exemption in the 12 months following such date. A passenger motor vehicle registered in another province of Canada, owned by a nonresident and operated within Nova Scotia for the purpose of providing transportation for commercial travellers or other persons temporarily engaged in business in Nova Scotia and having no fixed place of abode while temporarily in Nova Scotia, may be operated without registration for 30 consecutive days on obtaining from the Registrar a special permit and payment of such fees as the Minister may determine. A commercial motor vehicle owned by a nonresident is exempt from registration for 24 hours from the time it first entered Nova Scotia in any registration year, and the Registrar or any motor vehicle inspector or member of the Royal Canadian Mounted Police may issue a special permit to the driver of such vehicle granting a further exemption of six days under such conditions as may be stated on such special permit. A bus owned by a nonresident is exempt from registration, provided all the passengers brought into the province are taken out of the province in the bus and no passengers are taken on in the province unless the operator is in possession of a special permit issued by the Registrar setting forth the conditions under which such bus may operate without registration in Nova Scotia.

The above exemptions apply only to motor vehicles duly registered in the province or state in which the owner resides, and all requirements of that province or state in regard to the display of number plates and the carrying of permit, registration certificate or registration card must be complied with while the vehicle is operated in Nova Scotia. The exemptions do not apply to any motor vehicle owned by a person residing or carrying on business in any province or state which does not grant substantially similar privileges to vehicles registered in Nova Scotia and where such province or state grants

See Topical Index in front part of this volume.

MOTOR VEHICLES . . . *continued*
a lesser privilege in respect to the operating period or the style of vehicle affected the exemptions are diminished accordingly.

Motor vehicles registered in New Brunswick are entitled to the following exemptions from registration: Passenger motor vehicles, provided the owner does not reside in Nova Scotia; commercial motor vehicles, provided they do not take on any good, wares or merchandise in Nova Scotia to be discharged in Nova Scotia; busses and passenger motor vehicles carrying passengers for compensation, under the conditions stated in a permit issued by the department. This exemption does not apply where any passenger is taken on in Nova Scotia to be set down in Nova Scotia. (c. 293, §25, Regs.).

Nonresident operators, if at least 16 years old and duly licensed in state or province of residence, where examination is required, may operate vehicle exempt from registration without examination or license for 90 days. (c. 293, §65).

Actions Against Nonresidents.—No special provisions as to commencement.

Direct Actions.—Injured person can bring action against insurer upon recovery of judgment against insured. (c. 231, §133). See also topic Actions, subhead Direct Actions Against Insurer.

Motor vehicle carriers governed by c. 292 (as am'd by 1978-79, c. 28 [not in force]; 1990, c. 35; 1992, c. 23 [proclaimed 13 Oct. '92, in force 1 Jan. '93]). Act is administered by Board of Commissioners of Public Utilities. Act does not apply to: Motor carrier with not more than three freight vehicles of which not more than one may be motor vehicle or combination motor vehicle and trailer having more than two axles; vehicles governed by Public Utilities Act; public passenger vehicles from another province or U. S. A. carrying tourists under contracts made outside province, provided all passengers brought into province are taken out; and taxis. Certain other exemptions, acts and regulations also govern license requirements, based on need, quality of service, etc., weight restrictions, insurance, bills of lading and contracts, bonding, construction, maintenance and operation of vehicles, driver requirements, etc. Motor carriers must maintain certain insurance requirements. Every motor carrier must pay seat-mile tax to cities and towns in which operated at rate fixed by town resolution, but not exceeding $^1/_{15}$th of 1¢ per unit of seating capacity for every mile travelled within such town.

The minister may make reciprocal agreements with other provinces concerning registration and licensing of commercial motor vehicles and other related matters.

Moratorium on new bus licences imposed. (c. 200).

Transportation of dangerous goods, as defined in Regulations, prohibited unless prescribed safety standards are complied with, as set out in Regulations. (c. 119). Local authority and provincial traffic authority may designate routes and time for transportation of dangerous goods or prohibit carriage of dangerous goods on designated highways. (c. 293, §191 as am'd by 1994-95, c. 12, §14 [not in force]).

Aircraft.—See Canada Law Digest, topic Aircraft.

Gasoline Tax.—See topic Taxation.

Snow vehicles regulated by c. 323.

Off-highway Vehicles.—Comprehensive regime governing use of all types of off-highway vehicles such as snow vehicles, all-terrain vehicles and motorcycles enacted by c. 323. Persons on roller skates or skate boards not permitted on roadway except while crossing on crosswalk. (c. 293, §172).

See also topics Insurance; Mines and Minerals.

NEGOTIABLE INSTRUMENTS:

See topic Bills and Notes.

NOTARIES PUBLIC:

No bond required. Must affix notarial seal to every document sworn to before him. Provide own seal. Can draw, pass, keep and issue all contracts, charter parties and other mercantile transactions in the province; can attest all commercial instruments brought before them for public protestation, and have other usual notarial powers (c. 312, §3) anywhere in province. No act performed by barrister as notary public valid unless barrister is holder of commission as notary public, issued by Lieutenant Governor. (c. 30, §11).

PARTITION:

Any one or more persons holding land as joint tenants, coparceners, or tenants in common, may bring an action in the Supreme Court for its partition. (c. 333, §5). Such action may be maintained by person who has estate in possession but not by mere remainderman or reversioner. (c. 333, §6). Tenant for term of years, unless 20 years at least remain unexpired, cannot maintain such action against a free-hold tenant (c. 333, §8), but may against tenant for term of years.

Proceedings.—The action is brought in the ordinary way. The statement of claim must set forth the rights and titles, so far as known to the plaintiff, of all persons interested in the land who would be bound by the partition, whether they have an estate of inheritance, for life, years, in possession, remainder or reversion and whether vested or contingent. (c. 333, §9). If any parties are unknown, court may appoint one or more persons to represent them, and judgment or order is binding on such parties. (c. 333, §10). Person not named as party may be joined by leave of court. (c. 333, §13). Defendant in his defense may plead any matter tending to show that plaintiff ought not to have partition either wholly or partially. If defendant fails to appear or to deliver defense or if after trial it appears that partition should be made, court must make order for partition specifying persons entitled and their respective shares. (c. 333, §17). Then unless it appears to court that sale is necessary, it may appoint three commissioners to make partition. (c. 333, §18). Commissioners divide land and allot shares to the persons mentioned in order, designating shares by sufficient monuments. Report of commissioners is valid if two of them concur. (c. 333, §23).

Sale.—Where the land cannot be divided without prejudice to parties entitled, or where any party is because of infancy, insanity, or absence from the province, prevented from accepting such land, the court may order that the land be sold and the next proceeds be divided among the parties entitled. This order may be made in lieu of order appointing commission or after it. Every person interested and every incumbrancer must have at least two days notice of the application for sale; in case of infancy, insanity or absence from the province, court may order notice to be served on guardian or by publication. (c. 333, §28). Sheriff of county in which land lies, or auctioneer or person mentioned in order may make sale and execute deed; or court may make vesting order conveying land to purchaser, who thereby acquires all interest and title, of all persons interested in the land and of all encumbrancers. Where land is subject to dower or encumbrances, or where person entitled to share is unknown, infant, insane or absent from province, and was not personally served, proceeds of sale must be paid into court, or to such persons and according to such priorities, and amounts as court directs. Report of person making sale is subject to confirmation by court. (c. 333, §32).

PARTNERSHIP:

The Partnership Act (c. 334) is very similar to the English Partnership Act, and for most part is declaratory of common law. Partners may sue or be sued in the firm name.

Partnerships and Business Names Registration Act (c. 335, as am'd by 1990, c. 15; 1993, c. 34) applies to every partnership except one whose sole purpose is farming or fishing and also to person who is engaged in business or otherwise for purpose of gain and is not associated in partnership with other person, but uses as his style in connection therewith some name or designation other than his own name or if he uses words "and company" after his name or some other words indicating plurality of persons. Under this Act, every partnership must be registered with Registrar of Joint Stock Companies to carry on business in province. (c. 335, §3). Unregistered partnership cannot maintain suit or action in court in Nova Scotia in connection with contract made in whole or in part in Nova Scotia. (c. 335, §20). Before certificate of registration is issued declaration signed by members must be filed with Registrar stating name and objects of firm, how long it has subsisted and names of members and their residence. Whenever any change or alteration takes place in its membership, name or style, new declaration must be filed and where name of partnership is changed new certificate will be issued. (c. 335, §9). Upon dissolution, any or all of members may sign declaration stating such dissolution. (c. 335, §10). Names of all persons composing partnership must be on all bill-heads and letterheads used by it. Every partnership must file statement appointing resident agent for service of process, writs, notices, etc. (c. 335, §18, as am'd by 1990, c. 15). If partnership merely takes orders for or buys or sells goods by travelers or correspondence, but has no traveler, agent or representative in Nova Scotia, or no office or warehouse in province, it is not deemed to be carrying on business under this act. (c. 335, §21). Penalty for carrying on partnership without certificate is $50 per day. (c. 335, §19).

Rights and liabilities of partners inter sese and as to third persons governed by common law.

Registration Fees.—Set by Governor in Council and published in Regulations. (c. 335, §17).

Limited Partnership.—Limited partnerships may be formed by two or more persons provided at least one is general partner whose liability is unlimited. Formation by registration of certificate with Registrar of Joint Stock Companies. Limited partners are liable only to extent of contribution. (c. 335, §8). Limited partnership registered elsewhere in Canada may be registered by filing with Registrar copy of partnership articles and certificate of original registration. (c. 335, §8).

PERPETUITIES:

No statute. Common law rules apply.

PERSONAL PROPERTY:

Tenancy by the entirety does not exist.

Special Places Protection Act R.S.N.S. 1989, c. 438, as am'd by 1990, c. 45; 1994-95, c. 17 provides for recovery of "historical objects" from designated protected sites. Requires report to Director of N. S. Museum of recovery of such an object. If recovery is reported, object may be acquired by Province and compensation paid. If not reported, object may be seized. Act does not apply to treasure trove.

PLEADING:

Governed by Judicature Act (c. 240 as am'd by 1989, c. 20; 1992, c. 16 [proclaimed 26 Jan. '93, in force 30 Jan. '93]) and Rules of the Supreme Court which have force and effect of statute. Act and rules are modelled from English Act and Rules and are similar.

Pleadings must be as brief as nature of case admits; must contain material facts only in a summary form; a point of law may be raised, but not evidence upon which facts are to be proved; must be concise, precise and clear, but with enough particularity to enable opponent to know case he has to meet. Dates, sums, and numbers may be in figures, not words. Pleadings must be signed by solicitor or party if he sues or defends in person. May be written or printed. Must be filed with prothonotary, with copy served on opposing party. Must have date of delivery marked on face. Subsequent pleadings cannot raise new ground of claim. Answer must not be evasive.

Allegation of performance or occurrence of all conditions precedent for case of a party is implied in his pleading and need not be set out, and when an opposing party intends to contest performance or occurrence of any condition and its nonperformance in his pleading.

Pleadings Required.—Action must be commenced by filing with prothonotary an originating notice with statement of claim attached. Defence must be filed within ten days of service or originating notice. Appearance is no longer used. A pleading subsequent to defence other than counterclaim, defence to counterclaim and third party proceedings, shall not be filed or served without written consent of parties or leave of court. Reply no longer required in most proceedings.

Statement of claim must be attached to and served with originating notice. Must set out to summary form material facts upon which party bases his claim; particulars of any damages, special or general, that are ascertained or capable of being calculated in terms of money, with these damages and amount thereof being claimed as special damages; particulars of any other general damages, but amount thereof need not be stated; any other specific relief or remedy being claimed, but costs need not be claimed.

PLEADING . . . *continued*

Defence.—All allegations in statement of claim are deemed to be denied unless expressly admitted in defence. Party in his defence shall plead his version of facts where he intends to prove a different version than that relied upon by opposing party, specifically plead any matter, e.g., performance, release, payment, statute of limitation, fraud, or any fact showing illegality that might make claim of opposing party not maintainable, surprise opposing party or raise issues of fact not arising out of preceding pleadings. General denial is insufficient. Defence must be filed in prothonotary's office within ten days of service of originating notice with certified copy delivered or mailed to opposing party on day it is received from prothonotary.

Reply.—No longer required in most proceedings. See subhead Subsequent Pleadings, infra.

Subsequent Pleadings.—Rarely used. Can only be filed or served with consent of parties or leave of court. Unless court otherwise orders, pleadings are deemed closed upon filing and service of defence or defence to counterclaim, at which time all material statements of facts in pleading last delivered are deemed to have been denied and put in issue.

Set-off and Counterclaim.—Where a claim by a party to a sum of money, whether amount is ascertained or not, is relied on as a defence to whole or part of a claim made by an opposing party, it may be included in defence and set off against claim, whether or not it is also added as a counterclaim. Where defendant has a claim against plaintiff in any cause of action, he may, rather than bring a separate proceeding, counterclaim. Unless court otherwise orders, defendant must add counterclaim to his defence and file and serve it with defence. Plaintiff must serve and file his defence to counterclaim within ten days from service of defence and counterclaim on him. Unless otherwise ordered, defendant may join a person not yet a party with plaintiff as defendants to counterclaim by adding both names to title of proceedings and with respect to person not previously a party, filing and personally serving an originating notice (counterclaim) in prescribed form 16.02A on him within days from service of originating notice in original proceeding on defendant, or as court orders. Person served with originating notice (counterclaim) becomes a party to counterclaim from time of service, with same rights as any defendant. Counterclaim is separate proceeding and court may proceed with it notwithstanding that judgment is given for plaintiff in original proceeding or that original proceeding is stayed, discontinued or dismissed; pronounce final judgment on both original claim and counterclaim; give judgment for a balance in favour of one party; order counterclaim excluded or tried separately or make such order as is just. (Rule 16).

Demurrers.—No demurrer allowed. Party can raise point of law by his pleading, and on party's application or its own motion, court may determine question prior to trial or hearing or at or after trial. Pleadings may be struck out on ground that they disclose no reasonable cause of action or defence. False, frivolous, and vexatious pleadings may be set aside. These proceedings are in lieu of demurrer. (Rule 14.25).

Amendment.—Party may amend any document filed by him in a proceeding other than an order, once without leave of court, if amendment is made within 20 days from close of pleadings or five days before hearing, or at any other time if written consent of all parties is filed, or otherwise with leave of court. Notwithstanding a period of limitation, court may allow an amendment to correct a name or alter representative capacity of a party. (Rule 15). On such terms as just, court may allow amendment even though its effect will be to add or substitute a new cause of action, if new cause of action arises out of substantially some facts as original cause of action. Amended documents need not be served personally if original was so served, but must be filed with prothonotary and served according to Rule 15.03. Where amended statement of claim, counterclaim or third party notice is served, opposing party may amend defence. Cost occasioned by an amendment is borne by party making it, unless court otherwise orders.

Motion for Judgment.—No longer used. See topic Judgments.

Particulars.—Where party pleading relies on any misrepresentation, fraud, breach of trust, wilful default, or undue influence, or alleges any condition of mind of a person including disorder, malice or fraudulent intent, and in all other cases in which particulars may be necessary beyond usual forms, particulars must be stated in pleading. Further and better statement of defense or further and better particulars of any matter stated in any pleading, may in all cases be ordered. Pleader must give sufficient particulars so opponent will not be surprised.

In forwarding claims to attorneys, Christian and surnames, and residences of proposed plaintiff's and defendant's and itemized particulars of the claim should be given.

PLEDGES:

Only provincial statutory provisions are those contained in Factor's Act. (c. 157). Otherwise common law rules govern. Special provisions are contained in "The Bank Act." See Canada Law Digest, topic Banks and Banking.

PRACTICE:

Common law system in force.

The rules of the Supreme Court govern practice in Supreme Court and Court of Appeal. These rules do not affect procedure or practice in criminal proceedings. Rules for proceedings for divorce or other matrimonial cause are outlined in Rule 57. Party may conduct his own case, otherwise must be conducted by barrister of Supreme Court of Nova Scotia. Articled clerks may conduct cases in smaller courts, but not in Supreme Court.

Discovery.—Oral or written is permitted. (Rule 18).

Demand for admission of facts is permitted. Effect of refusal considered in taxing costs. (Rule 21).

Direct Action Against Insurer.—Direct action may lie against liability insurer where tortfeasor is unable to satisfy judgment against him. (c. 231, §28[1]). See also topic Motor Vehicles, subhead Direct Actions.

Small Claims.—See topic Courts.

See also topics Actions; Appeal and Error; Attachment; Depositions; Executions; Garnishment; Injunctions; Pleading; and Process.

PRINCIPAL AND AGENT:

Common law rules govern, except in case of factors. See topic Factors.

Durable Power of Attorney.—Powers of Attorney Act (c. 352) provides that power of attorney signed by donor and witnessed by person other than attorney or spouse of attorney expressly stating that it may be exercised during legal incapacity is valid and effectual and is not terminated by reason only of legal incapacity of donor. Conduct of attorney subject to control by judge of Trial Division of Supreme Court.

Collection Agencies.—Collection agencies and collectors must hold a license from Registrar of Credit. To obtain and keep a license every collector must represent a licensed collection agency, and collector's license cannot be transferred from one collection agency to another. Decision of Registrar can be appealed to courts within 30 days. Collection agencies must keep proper records. Collection methods are regulated. Any charges incurred in collection of a debt are not recoverable from debtor. Statute does not apply to barristers. (c. 77).

Real estate brokers must be licensed. (c. 384). Real estate assurance fund created for purpose of paying, in whole or in part, any judgment obtained against licensed broker where judgment based on fraud or breach of trust in respect of trade in real estate. (c. 384, §13).

PROCESS:

Civil actions are commenced by filing in prothonotary's office an originating notice (action [prescribed form 9.04A]) with attached statement of claim, stating nature of claim or relief or remedy required. Proceeding in which sole or principal question is one of law, or construction of an enactment, will or other document, in which there is unlikely to be any substantial dispute of fact, or which may be commenced by an originating application, motion, summons, petition or otherwise under an enactment is commenced by filing an originating notice (application inter parties) in prescribed form 9.02A in a proceeding between parties, and by an originating notice (ex parte application) in Form 9.02B in an ex parte proceeding. Originating notice is signed by plaintiff or his solicitor, and must have endorsed thereon address of plaintiff or his solicitor. Prothonotary may issue concurrent originating notice, a true copy of original, at any time while original is valid, which unless renewed pursuant to court order, is for period of six months from date of issue.

Service of notice is by personal service on each defendant by plaintiff or his agent, except on an ex parte application or where a rule otherwise provides. Ex parte application is served by filing notice and affidavit with prothonotary.

Who May Serve.—See subhead Service of Notice, supra.

Personal Service.—Effected on an individual by leaving a true copy of document with him.

Service on Infant or Mentally Incompetent Person.—Effected by leaving a true copy of document with his father, mother or guardian, or if there is no father, mother or guardian with person with whom he resides or in whose care he is, or with a person appointed by court.

Service on Corporation.—Corporation or any society or fellowship may be served by serving principal officer thereof or clerk or secretary. (Rule 10.03). Provincial corporation may also be served by leaving document at or mailing document to its registered office. (c. 81, §154). Any corporation whether domestic, dominion or foreign may be served by service on its registered agent resident within province. (c. 101, §9).

Service on Partnership.—If sued in partnership name, by leaving a true copy of document with one or more of partners, or with a person at principal place of business of partnership who appears to manage or control business there (Rule 10.03) or by service on principal officer, clerk, secretary or registered agent (c. 335, §18 as am'd by 1990, c. 15).

Substituted Service.—If prompt personal service cannot be made, the court may order substituted service or a service by notice or by advertisement. Application for substituted service must be supported by affidavit setting forth grounds on which application is made. There cannot be substituted service where a personal service would not be legally possible. The effect of substituted service is that the judgment is regular and cannot be set aside unless defendant shows he actually received no knowledge of writ and he has a good defense on merits.

Service by publication may be ordered by court where personal service cannot be effected. Same as substituted service.

Service out of the Province.—Originating notice may not be served on person anywhere in Canada or U.S. without first obtaining leave of court. Personal service of documents may be effected by person having authority to serve documents within that jurisdiction. (Rule 10.07).

Where service to be effected outside Canada or U.S., after obtaining leave of court a copy of originating notice certified by prothonotary and a copy translated into language of country in which service is to be effected is sent by prothonotary to Under Secretary of State for External Affairs, with instructions that it be transmitted to government of country in which it is to be served with a request that service be effected and a return be made showing how service has been effected. Prior to transmission of documents to be served, plaintiff's solicitor provides money to answer fees in connection with service. Personal service not required if Nova Scotia rules do not require it, or if it is not practice in foreign country. Proof of service outside Canada or U.S. may be by affidavit or by official return of government official. (Rule 10.08).

Service by Mail.—Document not requiring personal service may be served by leaving document or a copy at person's proper address, mailing it to that address, or in such other manner as court may order. Service is deemed effective on second day following posting where delivery is local and otherwise on day document in ordinary course of post would be delivered. (Rule 10.12).

Proof of Service.—Service may be verified by affidavit of person serving, or written acceptance of service by party's solicitor or agent. (Rule 10.14).

PROCESS . . . *continued*

Nonresident Motorist.—See topic Motor Vehicles, subhead Actions Against Nonresidents.

PROOF OF CLAIMS:

See topics Executors and Administrators; Pleading.

Quieting Titles Act.—See topic Real Property.

RAILROADS: See topic Carriers.

REAL PROPERTY:

All estates tail are abolished. Otherwise all estates recognized at common law are recognized in Noval Scotia. Every estate granted to two or more persons in their own right is a tenancy in common unless expressly declared to be in joint tenancy; but every estate vested in trustees or executors as such is held by them in joint tenancy. No tenancy by entirety. (c. 385, §5).

Rule in Shelley's Case is recognized.

Foreign conveyances or encumbrances must conform to Nova Scotia law to be valid.

Condominiums.—Permitted, subject to c. 85. Conversion of rental property to condominiums must be preceded by three months notice to tenants and Director of Landlord and Tenant Relations. Regulations may determine prerequisites for, or prohibit, such conversion. (c. 399).

Quieting Titles Act.—Persons claiming a property right in land may commence an action where land lies for a certificate of title or may join any other claim in which title to or right to possession of land is in issue. (c. 382).

Vendors and Purchasers Act.—Regulates rights and obligations of vendor and purchaser subject to conditions in contract. Contracts are deemed to provide that vendor will deliver to purchaser a copy of metes and bounds description of land. Purchaser's objections to title must be made within 30 days from date of delivery of description and vendor has 30 days to remove any objection to title; if not done, vendor may cancel contract if purchaser is unwilling to waive objection. Taxes, insurance, rents and interest adjusted as of date of closing. Vendor prepares deed at his expense; purchaser bears expense of registration of deed and mortgage, if any. (c. 487).

Land Holdings Disclosure Act (c. 248).—Nonresidents, and nonresident corporations which are not licenced to carry on business in Province, required to file with Registrar under Act, particulars of holdings of interests (otherwise than as security) in undeveloped land in Province located outside borders of town or city. Failure to comply is offence but does not affect validity of title.

See also topics Curtesy; Deeds; Dower; Environment; Homesteads; Husband and Wife; Landlord and Tenant; Mortgages of Real Property; Partition.

Land Titles Act (1978, c. 8).—Not yet proclaimed. To be brought into operation over number of years. Will introduce "torrens" system of government certified title. Possessory title will be abolished. Coming into force schedule not yet established.

Planning Act (c. 346, as am'd by 1990, c. 19; 1992, c. 11 [as am'd by 1995, c. 7]).—Development, zoning and subdivision must be in accord with regional and municipal development plans. Appeals are heard by Provincial Municipal Board.

Shopping Centre Development Act (c. 427, as am'd by 1992, c. 11 [as am'd by 1995, c. 7]).—Construction of shopping centre facilities in excess of 50,000 square feet may require Provincial Municipal Board approval.

Heritage Property Act (c. 199, in force Aug. 15, 1980, except §20 as am'd by 1991, c. 10).—Exterior appearance of property registered provincial or municipal as heritage property may not be altered without approval of Governor in Council or municipality.

Special Places Protection Act (c. 438 as am'd by 1990, c. 45; 1994-95, c. 17) provides for designation of protected archeological, historical and ecological sites. Protected sites may not be altered without permit.

Protection of Property Act (c. 363) provides for penalties for those who trespass on property of others. Restitution may be ordered to compensate owners of damaged property.

Rental Property Conversion Act.—See topic Landlord and Tenant.

RECEIVERS:

Receiver may be appointed by an interlocutory order of Supreme Court in all cases in which it appears to court to be just or convenient. (Rule 46). Application may be made by any party to action; ex parte or upon notice. Where an order is made directing a receiver to be appointed, person so appointed, unless otherwise ordered, must first give security to account for what he shall receive as such receiver. Unless otherwise ordered, a receiver is allowed a proper salary. Security and form thereof as judge directs. When a receiver is appointed with a direction that he shall pass accounts he must file and pass them within time fixed by court. They must be verified by affidavit. When a receivership is completed, book containing accounts must be deposited in prothonotary's office. In urgent cases, interim receivers are appointed upon ex parte application.

RECORDS:

Registration of Instruments.—Every instrument, conveyance or other document by which the title to land is changed or in any wise affected, and also every writ of attachment, certificate of judgment, lease for term exceeding three years, and vesting order should be registered in the registry of deeds in the district where the land is situated. (c. 392 as am'd by 1992, c. 16 proclaimed 26 Jan. '93, in force 30 Jan. '93).

Upon transfer of any property in City of Halifax, City of Dartmouth, County of Halifax, or other municipality with bylaw to that effect, a deed transfer tax is payable by purchaser within ten days of purchase. See topic Taxation. Failure to register makes instrument ineffective as against any person claiming for value and without noitce under any subsequent instrument affecting title to same land. (c. 392, §20). This does not apply to wills, a grant from Crown or report of partition commissioners.

Bills of sale, conditional sale agreements, chattel mortgages and hire and purchase agreements must be filed in registry of deeds or are void against purchasers and creditors. (c. 39). Assignment of book debts must be filed in registry of deeds or is void as against creditors of assignor and subsequent purchasers or mortgagees of such debts. (c. 24, §§3, 4).

Foreign conveyances or encumbrances must conform to Nova Scotia law to be recorded, but improper certificate will not affect validity of the document as between the parties.

Torrens Act is not in force in Nova Scotia, but see topic Real Property subhead Land Titles Act.

Transfer of Decedent's Title.—Where real estate in the province is devised, probate (or, in a proper case, ancillary probate) of the will must be obtained and a certified copy of the will must then be registered in the registry of deeds for the district where the real estate is situated. (c. 359, §144).

Where the owner of real property (whether resident or nonresident) dies intestate, no documents need be placed on record to show transfer of title to his heirs.

Vital Statistics.—Records of births, marriages and deaths are kept by duly appointed registrars for various districts throughout province. These are all forwarded to Registrar of Vital Statistics in Halifax. Fees: short form, $10, and long form, $15. (c. 494).

REDEMPTION:

See topics Executions; Liens; Mortgages of Real Property; Taxation.

REPLEVIN:

Orders for replevin have been replaced by recovery orders. (Rule 48). Any party or intervenor in a proceeding may apply for an interlocutory order to recover possession of real or personal property that was unlawfully taken or detained from him by any other party, or is held by an officer or under any legal process issued in proceeding. Interlocutory order to recover possession of personal property is issued by prothonotary upon ex parte application, and an interlocutory order to recover possession of real property by court upon ex parte application. When it is sought to enforce an order for recovery of possession of property, a final recovery order may be obtained. (Rule 48.01).

Proceedings.—Before recovery order will be issued affidavit of party applying must be filed describing property, stating its value, that applicant is its owner or entitled to possession, that property was unlawfully taken or detained or is held under legal process, that applicant or his agent has made a demand for property which was refused, and that applicant was advised by his solicitor that he is entitled to recovery of possession of property.

Bond.—Unless court otherwise orders, prothonotary before issuing order takes a bond from applicant in an amount equal to 1¼ times value of property with two sufficient sureties. Conditions of bond are that applicant shall obtain without delay an order settling who is entitled to ownership or possession, return property if he fails to obtain such order and pay costs and damages awarded by court. Bond may be assigned by prothonotary to defendant.

Order.—Recovery order in prescribed Form 48.04A instructs sheriff as to seizure procedure and requires him within 90 days of issuance to report to prothonotary on any action taken. Copy of order must be served upon person from who property is taken. Personal property not delivered on sheriff's demand, may be obtained by forced entry into a building.

Repossession.—Defendant may retain possession on giving security, which may be assigned by prothonotary's endorsement thereon to party entitled.

Special Procedures.—Express provision is made for recovery of shares, bonds, debentures, and other interest in a body corporate. (Rule 48.07). Unique property obtained under recovery order may be ordered kept within jurisdiction. (Rule 48.10). Court may order sale of perishable property recovered. (Rule 48.09).

Final Recovery Order.—Order in prescribed form 48.13A may be granted by prothonotary on an ex parte application supported by an affidavit where applicant seeks to enforce a final order for recovery of possession of property. Sheriff in such a case takes immediate possession of property, and person in possession has no right to retain possession by filing a bond or otherwise. (Rule 48.13).

REPORTS:

Decisions of Supreme Court of Nova Scotia are reported in Nova Scotia Reports (N. S. R.) Vols. 1-60 (1834-1929), Maritime Province Reports Vols. 1-53 (1920-1968), Nova Scotia Reports 1965-69 (5 vols.), and Nova Scotia Reports 2nd Series (NSR [2d]) (1970-. . . . . .); Young's Admiralty Decisions (1865-1881). Nova Scotia cases together with cases from other provinces in Dominion Law Reports (D. L. R.) Vols. 1-70 (1912-1923); 1923-1955 each year containing four volumes; Dominion Law Reports, Second Series (D. L. R. [2d]) Vols. 1-70 (1956-1968); Dominion Law Reports, Third Series (D. L. R. [3d]) Vols. 1-150 (1969-1984). Dominion Law Reports, Fourth Series (D.L.R. [4th]) Vols. 1-. . . . (1984-. . . .). Eastern Law Reports (E. L. R.) Vols. 1-14 (1906-1914) also contain Nova Scotia decisions. Canadian Bankruptcy Reports (C. B. R.) Vols. 1-38 and new series (C.B.R. N.S.) cols. 1-. . . . . ., also contain bankruptcy decisions of Supreme Court of Nova Scotia along with other provinces. Appeals to Supreme Court of Canada are reported in Vols. 1-64 of Supreme Court Reports (S. C. R.), and 1923-1972 Canada Law Reports reporting Supreme Court of Canada, Exchequer Court of Canada and Federal Court of Canada cases. Exchequer Reports of Nova Scotia cases are found in Vols. 1-21 Exchequer Reports of Canada (1878-1927). Reports of Family Law (R. F. L.) Vol. 1 . . . . . . (1971) and Land Compensation Reports (LCR) Vol. 1 (1972) contain report of N.S. cases in these fields.

Digests.—Nova Scotia: Congdon's (1875-1888); Geldert's (1888-1907); Armstrong's (1888-1903); Graham's (1907-1929); digests of cases for all Canadian provinces are contained in Canadian Consolidated Ten Year Law Digest (1911-1929), four volumes, and 1945-1961, 17 volumes; All Canadian Digest (1910-1934 inclusive) and annual volumes thereafter; and Canadian Abridgement Vols. 1-35; Consolidation 1936-1955 and annual volumes from 1955 to present now replaced by Canadian Abridgement, 2d Edition.

RESTRAINT OF TRADE: See topic Monopolies and Restraint of Trade.

SALES:

Regulated by the Sale of Goods Act (c. 408), which is substantially same as English Act.

Bills of Sales.—Governed by Bills of Sale Act. (c. 39). Same provisions apply as in the case of Chattel Mortgages (q.v.).

Products Liability.—Manufacturers or suppliers of defective goods may be liable to consumer for negligence where there is no privity of contract with consumer. Liability is based on the rule in Donoghue v. Stevenson, [1932] A. C. 562.

Conditional sales are governed by the Conditional Sales Act. (c. 84).

A Conditional sale of goods must be evidenced by writing signed by buyer or his agent before or at time of delivery of goods or within ten days. (c. 84, §3). Such writing must state amount of purchase price unpaid or conditions of hiring and must give detailed description of goods. Contract or true copy must be filed within 20 days after signing in registry of deeds for registration district where buyer resided at time of making agreement, or if he lives outside province, in district where goods are delivered; late filing or rectification of filed documents permitted by County Court for sufficient cause. (c. 84, §3). Where goods are delivered in one district and buyer resides in another, original or copy must be filed in both districts. If goods are removed after delivery, seller must file original or copy in registry of district into which they are removed within 20 days after knowledge of removal. Where buyer removes into province goods delivered outside province, original or true copy of contract must be filed in registration district where goods are within 20 days after seller has knowledge of removal. Assignment of conditional sale contract should be filed in same manner as original contract. Conditional sale ceases to be valid as against creditor and subsequent purchaser in good faith for valuable consideration without notice unless renewal statement on prescribed form is registered; within five years, if registration was prior to June 30, 1983, or within six years, if registration was thereafter. Conditional sales of motor vehicles and other personal property designated by regulation to be registered in Central Designated Personal Property Lien Registry located in Halifax. (1986, c. 15, not yet in force).

No limitation on type size in printed contracts.

Licenses.—Sellers who sell or let for hire under conditional sale contracts must have annual license (fee $2) which Attorney General may suspend or cancel. Licenses expire on Nov. 30. (c. 230, §3).

Inspection and Returns.—Affairs of such sellers are subject to inspection, for which purpose statements may be required and inspectors must be allowed free access to books. Annual returns must be made to Attorney General on Sept. 30. (c. 230, §7).

Consumer sales are a contract of sale of goods or services including an agreement of sale as well as a sale and a conditional sale of goods made in ordinary course of business to a purchaser for use or consumption (excludes purchases for resale; purchases in course of purchaser's business; purchases by an association, partnership or corporation; or by a trustee in bankruptcy, receiver, liquidator or person acting under order of a court). Consumer sales are subject to relevant conditions and warranties implied under Sale of Goods Act plus implied conditions that goods, unless otherwise described, are of merchantable quality, new and unused, and durable for a reasonable period of time. Implied conditions or warranties cannot be excluded. Sales involving a rebate or discount contingent on subsequent assistance to seller in making other sales are not binding. (c. 92, §§26-27).

Retail Credit Sales.—No special restrictions, but closely regulated. See topic Interest. In attempting to collect from debtor for debt incurred in purchase of consumer goods, consumer creditors may not overcharge, harass, call collect, abuse, mislead, threaten to contact employer or spouse or impersonate officer of law. (c. 91).

Direct Sales.—Direct selling includes selling or soliciting orders for goods or services other than by a merchant from a recognized retail store. Does not apply to food, drink, newspapers, or to goods or services regulated by federal or provincial statute, sold by Crown owned or controlled corporations or agencies, sold on behalf of a charitable organization, sold to a wholesaler or retailer for resale or for use in business. All direct sellers and salesmen must be licensed, renewable yearly (c. 129, §39), and deliver bond. Direct salesman can only act for direct seller specified in his license and such licenses are nontransferable. Contents of direct sales contracts are regulated and must include clause that cancellation can take place within ten days unless notice of such clause is later personally delivered to purchaser. Direct sales can also be cancelled if seller or salesman not licensed, if goods or services not supplied within 90 days, or if seller or salesman fails to comply with license. No benefits can be offered buyer that are contingent on sale to another person. Any decision of Registrar can be appealed to county court judge within 30 days. (c. 129, §39). Direct sales contract must be signed by salesman at time of sale and his name must be set out below signature. (c. 129, §20).

International Sales.—International Sale of Goods Act (1988, c. 13 proclaimed 7 Apr. '92, in force 1 May '92) adopts United Nations Convention on Contracts for the International Sale of Goods.

Credit Reporting Agencies (c.93).—Credit bureaus must register and meet certain financial and ethical requirements. Director may suspend registration. Use of consumer information is limited to employment, credit, insurance and legal purposes or direct business need. Sources and types of information are restricted. Subject must have access to information on file. Procuring or preparing a consumer reports requires consent of or notice to subject.

Unsolicited Goods.—No right of action for payment. (c. 92, §23).

Credit Cards.—See topic Interest.

Bulk Sales.—See topic Fraudulent Sales and Conveyances.

SALES TAX: See topic Taxation.

SEALS:

Common law rules apply. Not necessary that any particular kind of seal be used provided that there be fixed or impressed something purporting to be a seal. Need not bear any indication that it is the particular seal of the person who affixes it; one person may use another's seal. Circular line enclosing the letters "L.S." does not purport to be a seal.

Corporation Seal.—Company, as a general rule, may contract without a seal; need only affix seal in cases where individuals are required to use a seal. (c. 81, §101). Every company must have common seal, and must have its name engraved in legible characters thereon. (c. 81, §80).

SECURITIES:

Securities industry governed by Securities Act. (c. 418 as am'd by 1990, c. 15).

Supervision.—Responsibility for general administration of Act rests with Nova Scotia Securities Commission. Commission to formulate policies for regulation of securities industry in province and to hear and determine appeals from decisions of Registrar of Securities who will ordinarily make first level administrative decisions on matters of registration of persons and filings of prospectuses and other documents. (c. 418, §5).

Regulatory Powers of Supervising Authority.—See subhead Supervision, supra.

Securities to Which Act Applicable.—Broad definition of security to include among others document or instrument commonly known as security; document evidencing interest in capital assets, property, earnings or royalties of any person or company; document evidencing option or subscription in or to security; bond, debenture note or other evidence of indebtedness, share, stock unit, unit certificate, participation certificate, certificate of share or interest; agreement valued for purposes of conversion or surrender by reference to value of proportionate interest in specified portfolio of assets; subscription agreement; profit-sharing agreement or certificate; certificate of interest in petroleum and mineral lease, claim or royalty voting trust certificate; collateral trust certificate; income or annuity contract not issued by insurance company; investment contract; commodity futures contract or option. (c. 418, §2 as am'd by 1990, c. 15 proclaimed 9 July '91; in force 15 July '91).

Exempt Securities.—Subject to regulations registration not required to trade in inter alia: (a) Bonds, debentures or other evidences of indebtedness (i) of or guaranteed by federal or provincial governments, U.K. or foreign country or political division thereof, (ii) of Canadian municipal corporation, (iii) of or guaranteed by bank, trust company, loan company except where subordinate to payment of deposits held by issuer or guarantor, (iv) of or guaranteed by Asian Development Bank or Inter-American Development Bank if denominated in Canadian or U.S. dollars; (b) certificates or receipts issued by trust company for moneys received for guaranteed investment; (c) securities issued by private mutual fund; (d) negotiable promissory notes or commercial paper maturing within one year of issue and having principal amount of more than $50,000; (e) mortgages or other encumbrances upon real or personal property other than those secured by bond or trust deed if offered for sale by person exempt from registration under Mortgage Brokers and Lenders Registration Act; (f) conditional sales contracts if not offered for sale to individuals; (g) securities issued by certain nonprofit organizations; (h) securities issued by cooperative associations; (i) shares of credit union; (j) securities of private company where not offered for sale to public; (k) securities issued by certain prospectors prospecting syndicates and mining companies; (l) certain variable insurance contracts. (c. 418, §41[2]).

Exempt Transactions.—Subject to regulations registration not required in respect of some 30 categories of trades including: (a) Trade by executor, administrator or guardian, receiver or liquidator, under Bankruptcy Act, Judicature Act, Companies Winding Up Act or Winding-up Act (Canada), or sheriff under Civil Procedure Rules or at judicial sale; (b) isolated trade where not made in course of continued and successive transactions and where not made by person whose usual business is trading in securities; (c) purchase as principal by bank, loan company, insurance company or their wholly-owned subsidiaries, federal or provincial governments, Canadian municipal corporations; (d) purchase as principal by person recognised by Registrar as exempt purchaser; (e) certain trades for purpose of giving security for bona fide debt; (f) trade by pledgee, mortgagee or other encumbrancer for purpose of liquidating bona fide debt; (g) occasional trades by non-trading employees of registered dealer; (h) trade between person and underwriter acting as purchaser or between or among underwriters; (i) trade by person acting solely through agent who is registered dealer; (j) placement with and execution of unsolicited trade through registered dealer by bank or trust company; (k) trade by issuer pursuant to stock dividend, distribution of assets, warrant and rights issues; (l) trade by issuer in security as dividend in specie; (m) trade by issuer as consideration for portion or all of its assets; (n) trade by issuer of securities of its own issue with its employees; (o) certain trades by issuer in securities of its own issue where trade necessary to facilitate incorporation or organization of issuer. (c. 418, §41[1]).

Registration of Securities.—Trading in securities is prohibited unless preliminary prospectus and prospectus have been filed with Registrar. (c. 418, §58). Prospectus must provide full disclosure of all material facts relating to securities issued. (c. 418, §61).

Registration of Dealers.—Subject to certain exemptions no one may trade in securities, act as underwriter, or act as advisor unless registered under Act. (c. 418, §31[1]).

Advertisements.—Registrar has power to investigate use of advertisements and sales literature and may prohibit their use. (c. 418, §56).

Liabilities.—Act provides statutory private right of action for damages in situations in which there has been misrepresentation in prospectus. (c. 418, §137 as am'd by 1990, c. 15 proclaimed 9 July '91, in force 15 July '91).

Tender Offers.—Extensive provisions in Act dealing with take-over bids especially c. 418, §§95-111 as am'd by 1990, c. 15 proclaimed 9 July '91, in force 15 July '91.

SEQUESTRATION:

Writ of sequestration replaced by contempt order issued under Rule 55. Contempt order is used to enforce an order for payment of money, including payment into court, order for possession of real or personal property, or an order requiring person to do or abstain from doing an act. Court must grant party leave to make application for a contempt order; such application must be supported by affidavit describing applicant, person sought to be committed, and facts in support of grounds on which contempt order is sought. On its own motion or application court may order a person to appear to

See Topical Index in front part of this volume.

SEQUESTRATION . . . *continued*
show cause why he should not be held in contempt. Contempt order may order imprisonment, fine and detention of property, and otherwise as deemed just. Contempt proceedings lie against bodies corporate and persons not parties. (Rule 55). See also topics Attachment; Receivers.

SERVICE: See topic Process.

STATUTE OF FRAUDS: See topic Frauds, Statute of.

STATUTES:

Latest official compilation is Revised Statutes of Nova Scotia, 1989. (R. S. N. S.). The laws passed by the Nova Scotia Legislature in each year are published annually and are called "The Statutes of Nova Scotia" for the particular year in which they were passed. The Dominion legislates on matters which are Dominion-wide in scope; the provinces on matters of a local nature. Regulations Act passed but only partly in force requires publication of regulations and provides for public access to all regulations. (c. 393).

Uniform Acts.—No Uniform Acts are in force in Province.

STAY OF EXECUTION: See topics Appeal and Error; Executions.

SUBMISSION OF CONTROVERSY:

Parties to any cause or matter may at any stage or without previous proceedings state any question of law or fact for adjudication by court before trial or hearing. Special case may be set down only with leave of court. Court may draw from stated facts and documents any inference of fact or law that might have been drawn therefrom if proved at trial or hearing. Parties may agree in writing that upon any question in a stated case being answered, court may order specific relief granted or judgment entered. Court itself may state special case for adjudication by Appeal Division. (Rule 27). In addition, court may order any question or issue of fact or law, or partly of fact and law, whether raised by pleadings or otherwise, to be tried before, at, or after trial, and may give directions as to manner in which question or issue shall be stated. (Rule 28.04).

SUPPLEMENTARY PROCEEDINGS: See topic Executions.

SURETY AND GUARANTEE COMPANIES:

These are under the regulation and supervision of the Governor-in-Council.

Bonds or Policies.—When any public officer is required to give security for the performance of his duty or of any obligation undertaken towards the Crown, the bond or policy of any guarantee company may be accepted as such security upon such terms as are determined by the Governor-in-Council. Same provisions apply to this security as if given by individual. (c. 451, §3). Bonds or policies of guarantee of any guarantee company may be taken by judge for due performance of any duty instead of or in substitution for any existing securities of surety or sureties, if judge sees fit to accept such bond or policy and approves of conditions and terms thereof. (c. 451, §5). Bonds or policies of guarantee of any guarantee company may be taken instead of or in substitution for existing securities whereupon existing securities must be delivered up to be canceled. Bonds of surety and guarantee companies of reputable standing and credit may be approved for court proceedings, administration, guardianship, trusts, etc.

Foreign companies may do business in the province, upon taking out certificate and paying taxes.

TAXATION:

The right of the province to tax is restricted by §92 of Constitution Act, 1867 to "direct taxation within the province." Provincial revenue is derived from income tax, mining royalties, federal equalization payments and license fees. Province imposes income tax under authority of the Income Tax Act. (c. 217 as am'd by 1987, c. 3 proclaimed 4 Jan. '90, in force 5 Jan. '90; 1990, c. 10 [proclaimed 12 Jan. '93, in force 12 Jan. '91]; 1992, c. 15; 1993, cc. 3 and 26; 1994, c. 9; 1995, c. 2). Dominion Government revenue is derived chiefly from customs and excise and income tax. Dominion Government may raise money by any mode or system of taxation. Municipal Corporations tax real and personal property on an assessed valuation and may also license occupations, trades, etc.

Taxable Property.—Under Assessment Act (c. 23, as am'd by 1990, cc. 19 & 24; 1992, c. 11 [as am'd by 1995, c. 7]; 1992, c. 11), all real property, including mines, minerals, oil and gas; manufacturing equipment assessed on or before Dec. 1, 1988 (c. 23, §2 as am'd by 1990, c. 19); mobile homes and floating structures used for residential and commercial purposes; and residential and commercial occupancy subject to certain exemptions is liable to taxation. Under Pipeline Valuation Act (1985, c. 4 not yet in force) pipelines for transportation and transmission of hydrocarbons constitute taxable property under Assessment Act.

Assessments.—Occupier of service station, restaurant, hotel, motel, campground, trailer park and car dealer liable for business occupancy assessment equal to 25% of assessed value. Banks, credit unions, loan, investment, insurance or trust companies, investment and mortgage brokers, collection agencies and other financial institutions liable for 75% of assessed value. Occupiers of other commercial properties subject to assessment of 50% of assessed value. Tax apportioned for seasonal, new and terminating business. (c. 23, §11). Council may by by-law set tax on commercial property of nonprofit community, charitable, fraternal, educational, religious, cultural or sporting organization at lower assessment (minimum is residential assessment). (c. 23, §5 as am'd by 1992, c. 11). Property greater than three acres may be assessed at $5 per acre. Property liable to 20% tax upon changing to other than farm land use. All farm land used for agricultural purposes and forest property used for forestry purposes exempt from tax. Farm buildings and residences taxed at residential rate. Tax of 20% of value of farm and forest land upon changing use other than to forest or farm land. (c. 23, §§46, 47 as am'd by 1990, c. 19, 1996, c. 5). Forest property used for forestry purposes and classed as resource property taxed at rate of 25¢ per acre, and 40¢ per acre if classed as commercial property. (c. 23, §47 as am'd by 1990, c. 19).

Exemptions are: (a) All property vested in Crown or any person for Imperial, Federal or Provincial purposes; (b) churches and church property not making income in excess of $100 per year; (c) educational institutions except property used mainly for noneducational purposes; (d) public property; (e) property, occupied or unoccupied, for city, town or municipal purposes except where used to furnish electricity, water or power to public; (f) buildings and land containing fire fighting equipment; (g) property belonging to infant, if his total income in preceding year was under $2,000; (h) property of agricultural society not used for commercial or industrial purposes; (i) rolling stock, tracks, etc. used exclusively for Federal or Provincial railway; (j) property of Royal Canadian Legion, Boy Scouts and Girl Guides (c. 23, §5 as am'd by 1992, c. 11); (k) property of registered charities, if by-law to that effect (c. 23, §5 as am'd by 1992, c. 11); (l) hospital, school and municipal property; (m) property used for village commissioners; (n) property specially exempt by act of legislature; (o) farm land used for agricultural purposes (c. 23, §46 as am'd by 1990, c. 19, 1996, c. 5); (p) growing or unharvested crops; (q) travel and tent trailers; (r) forest property used for forestry purposes (c. 23, §47 as am'd by 1990, c. 19); (s) fruit trees if exempting resolution of Council; (t) municipality may grant further exemptions based on age and marital status by resolution (c. 23, §49); (u) Council may by by-law assess property of nonprofit community charitable, fraternal, educational, religious, cultural or sporting organizations (c. 23, §5 as am'd by 1992, c. 11); (v) members of armed forces living on bases exempt from tax on real and personal property not outside base (c. 23, §8); (w) property of nonprofit organizations where there is by-law to that effect (c. 23, §5 as am'd by 1992, c. 11); (x) property of fire company incorporated under Societies Act or Rural Fire District Act (c. 23, §5 as am'd by 1992, c. 11); (y) property of nonprofit community cemetery; (z) machinery and apparatus installed after Dec. 1, 1988 (c. 23, §43, as am'd by 1990, c. 24, 1996, c. 5).

School rates are governed by Education Act. (c. 136, §42, as am'd by 1990, c. 19; 1991, c. 6; 1992, c. 17; 1993, c. 20). They are recovered (except in Halifax, Sydney and any section whole of which is incorporated town) in school section annually by noting and collecting by area rate of so much on dollar on assessed value of property in area.

Assessors annually send to each person form to be filled out and signed by him or her which must be returned within 30 days after receipt. (c. 23, §20-21). Assessors must set down assessment roll containing location, description, classification and assessed value of lands and name and address of owner. (c. 23, §25). Property of nonresident is assessed as such and so designated. Assessment may be in name of person appearing on record of Registry of Deeds. (c. 23, §38). Occupier of commercial property liable to business occupancy assessment. (c. 23, §11). Property is assessed at actual cash value which is amount assessor thinks it would realize in cash if offered at auction. (c. 23, §42, as am'd by 1996, c. 5). Benefit of easements assessed to dominate tenement. No reduction in assessment due to encumbrances on title. Assessment rolls must be completed by Dec. 31 and assessors must attach signed certificate in prescribed form and send to municipal or town clerk. On completion of assessment, assessor gives notice showing classification and amount of assessment by personally serving person liable, by mailing notice post prepaid to place of business or residence, or by posting notice in conspicuous place on assessed property.

Appeals from valuation, classification or assessment may be brought by property owner, ratepayer, occupier, town or municipal clerk, or any person having interest in property. (c. 23, §62). Notice of appeal must be filed within 21 days after notice of assessment. (c. 23, §63). Appeal is to regional assessment appeal court. Assessor may review and adjust assessment when appeal taken. (c. 23, §68). Appellant upon giving notice may proceed with appeal if adjustment not satisfactory. Decision of assessment appeal court may be appealed to N.S. Municipal Board. (c. 23, §85 as am'd by 1992, c. 11 [as am'd by 1995, c. 7]).

Real Estate Conveyance Tax.—On every deed conveying real property situate wholly or partly within boundaries of City of Halifax, County of Halifax, City of Dartmouth, or municipality having bylaw to that effect, tax is imposed and levied on value of real property conveyed or transferred by deed. In case of Halifax a lease for term longer than 21 years is subject to deed transfer tax. (1972, c. 71). See also topic Landlord and Tenant. If property is situate partly within and partly without boundaries of City, County, or municipality, tax is prorated. Rates: City of Halifax, 1½%; Halifax County and Dartmouth, 1½%; City of Sydney, 1%; Towns of Antigonish, Canso, Truro and Stewiacke, Lockeport and Windsor, Municipalities of Colchester, East and West Hants, Inverness, Lunenburg, Guysborough, St. Mary's, Antigonish, and Queens, ½ of 1%.

Tax is payable by grantee at time of transfer, and immediately after transfer grantee, solicitor or agent, must file with respective Collector affidavit of transfer, in triplicate, setting forth true, complete and actual value thereof, names of parties, location of real property and such other information as required, and at same time pay tax to Collector. Before deed can be recorded, certificate by Collector stating tax paid or no tax payable must be attached.

If not paid, tax, with penalty and interest, constitutes lien on property. Lien attaches when tax due and continues until discharged by payment.

Exemptions.—Generally, no tax is payable in respect of deed that merely confirms, corrects, modifies or supplements deed previously given, if there is no actual consideration paid or payable. No tax payable on real property transferred between parent company and wholly owned subsidiary. No tax payable on transfer of property between spouses or transfer by way of gift. (c. 121, §4 as am'd by 1990, c. 10). Halifax City Charter. (1963, c. 52, §253). Halifax County Deed Transfer Act. (1960, c. 85). Dartmouth City Charter. (1962, c. 67, §224).

Motor Vehicle Carriers.—See topic Motor Vehicles, subhead Motor Vehicle Carriers.

Lien.—Taxes under Assessment Act constitute a first lien on property upon which they are imposed. (c. 23, §134). School rates on real property constitute lien on such property. Lien attaches on date upon which rolls are prepared or rate book approved. Taxes after such time constitute lien upon such property from time they were rated. (c. 23, §§134, 135 as am'd by 1990, c. 19).

Tax Sales.—At any time after Dec. 31, the municipal or town treasurer may upon application supported by affidavit showing that he has fully complied with all requirements with respect to land sought to be sold for taxes, showing amount of arrears,

TAXATION . . . *continued*
unpaid interest, expenses and years in which such lands were rated, obtain a warrant, from warden or mayor directed to such treasurer, for sale of land. (c. 23, §143). Treasurer on receipt of warrant, levies upon and advertises land for sale at public auction at public place in municipality or town. Notice of sale must be published for at least 30 days before sale, in daily or weekly newspaper in municipality or town by one insertion each week. (c. 23, §144). Treasurer sells land at time and place mentioned in notice, deducts amount of rates, taxes, interest and expenses, also any school rates due to secretary of trustees of that school district, and any balance is paid as directed by Supreme Court judge on summary application. (c. 23, §§149, 150 as am'd by 1990, c. 19). Treasurer, within ten days after sale, gives certificate to purchaser stating land sold, description, and price, and that deed will be given to purchaser at expiration of one year and payment of fee set by by-law unless redeemed before such time. (c. 23, §154). If lands not redeemed within one year treasurer on demand of purchaser, his assigns or other legal representatives, at any time thereafter and upon payment of fee set by by-law, must cause deed of land to be made to purchaser in prescribed form and signed by warden or mayor, and treasurer, and under seal of municipality or town. (c. 23, §§157-162 as am'd by 1990, c. 19).

Land Assessed to "Owner Unknown".—Assessor to advise province before any tax sale of "owner unknown land". If province pays taxes land vests in it. Province to advertise such vesting and claimants have one year from vesting date to prove ownership. If claimant does so and pays taxes and expenses, vesting in province ceases. Claimants also have right for up to ten years to apply to Supreme Court for compensation or (if land still vested in province) conveyance. (c. 23, §140).

Redemption.—Taxpayer, his heirs, executors, administrators or assigns may redeem land at any time within the year upon payment to clerk of amount of purchase money with interest at 10% from date of sale (plus amount to cover arrears of taxes if sale price insufficient) and expenses of sale. Clerk then gives him certificate of discharge in prescribed form, vesting in him right, title and interest which he had before sale, subject to lien of purchaser at sale for money which he spent or expenses which he properly incurred in protecting land or rights therein conferred by certificate of sale. Clerk then pays purchase money and interest he receives on redemption to purchaser, who then ceases to have any claim to and except lien above referred to. (c. 23, §§157-162 as am'd by 1990, c. 19).

Income Tax.—*Income Tax Act* (c. 217 as am'd by 1987, c. 3 proclaimed 4 Jan. '90, in force 5 Jan. '90; 1990, c. 10 [proclaimed 12 Jan. '93, in force 12 Jan. '93]; 1992, c. 15; 1993, cc. 3 and 26; 1995, c. 2; 1996, c. 5).—Every individual must pay 59.5% of total amount of tax payable under Income Tax Act (Canada) on: (a) Taxable income if resident within Province; (b) taxable income earned within Province if nonresident. No tax payable on taxable income of corporations carrying on business in offshore until legislature otherwise determines. (c. 217, §58 as am'd by 1987, c. 3, proclaimed 4 Jan. '90, in force 5 Jan. '90). *Note:* Effective July 1, 1997, rate is reduced to 57.5%. (1996, c. 5, §15). Governor-in-Council may make regulations for carrying out efficient administration of Act. Every corporation must pay Provincial tax of 15% on taxable income earned in Province for year. Corporation eligible for small business deduction under Income Tax Act (Canada) pays 10% provincial tax on amount eligible for small business deduction and 16% on remainder. (c. 217, §5 as am'd by 1990, c. 10 [proclaimed 12 Jan. '93; in force 12 Jan. '93] and by 1992, c. 15). Tax credit established for first time buyers of eligible homes. (c. 217, §12 as am'd by 1992, c. 15).

Members of Armed Forces.—No special provision.

Succession Duty (1972, c. 17) repealed by 1974, c. 30 as of Mar. 31, 1974.

Estate Tax.—See Canada Law Digest.

Gift Tax.—Gift Tax Act (1972, c. 9) repealed by 1974, c. 28, as of Mar. 31, 1974. Deed of property by gift exempt from land transfer tax. (c. 121, §4 as am'd by 1990, c. 10).

Sales Tax.—Health Services Tax Act (c. 198 as am'd by 1987, c. 3 proclaimed 4 Jan. '90, in force 5 Jan. '90; 1989, c. 22; 1990, c. 10; 1992, c. 11; 1992, c. 15; 1993, c. 25; 1994, c. 21; 1995, c. 2). Every purchaser must pay at time of making purchase tax at rate of: (a) 10% of purchase price of all tangible personal property including telecommunication services, transient accommodation, repair services and tobacco; (b) 50¢ per month (domestic users), $1 to $30 per month (nondomestic users) on electricity (c. 198, §5 as am'd by 1993, c. 25; 1995, c. 2); (c) 4% of purchase price of tangible personal property used in processing or production of nonrenewable resources (c. 198, §5 as am'd by 1993, c. 25; 1995, c. 2).

Exemptions (c. 198 as am'd by 1987, c. 3, proclaimed 4 Jan. '90, in force 5 Jan. '90; 1989, c. 22; 1990, c. 10; 1992, c. 11; 1992, c. 15; 1993, c. 25; 1994, c. 21; 1995, c. 2).—Food and food products for human consumption off premises; fuels; farm implements, etc.; fishing boats and gear when purchased by commercial fishermen; tangible personal property purchased by volunteer fire department for sole use of fire department; smoke detection equipment; tangible personal property used for pollution control; portable fire extinguishers (c. 198, §12 as am'd by 1990, c. 10; 1992, c. 15 [not yet in force]; 1993, c. 25; 1994, c. 21; 1995, c. 2); transient accommodation purchased by person attending convention of at least 25 participants (c. 198, §12, as am'd by 1990, c. 10; 1992, c. 15 [not yet in force]; 1993, c. 25; 1994, c. 21; 1995, c. 2); water; medicaments, (c. 198, §12 as am'd by 1990, c. 10; 1992, c. 15 [not yet in force]; 1993, c. 25; 1994, c. 21; 1995, c. 2); goods to be incorporated into goods for sale; machinery and equipment used in research and development (c. 198, §12 as am'd by 1990, c. 10; 1992, c. 15 [not yet in force]; 1993, c. 25; 1994, c. 21; 1995, c. 2); fodder, seeds, plants, fertilizer; goods to be shipped by seller outside Province and ship stores delivered to commercial vessels normally operating in extraterritorial waters; railway rolling stock and repairs; tangible personal property costing less than 25¢ (c. 198, §12 as am'd by 1990, c. 10; 1992, c. 15 [not yet in force]; 1993, c. 25; 1994, c. 21; 1995, c. 2); prepared meals costing $2 or less; newspapers; magazines and periodicals purchased by subscription for delivery by mail; property purchased by certain government agencies; aircraft; clothing costing less than $100 per article and footwear costing less than $100 per pair (c. 198, §12 as am'd by 1990, c. 10; 1992, c. 15 [not yet in force]; 1993, c. 25; 1994, c. 21; 1995, c. 2); certain books; explosives used by miners; tangible personal property purchased by and for use of municipality; tangible personal property purchased by commercial concerns for use in pollution control; goods purchased by religious and charitable organizations which enter into capital investment; goods purchased by hospitals, schools, universities which enter directly in construction thereof; tangible personal property except motor vehicles, snow vehicles and beer, liquor and tobacco of Indians on reserves; heat pumps, heat recovery units for extracting heat from waste air or water; time-controlled thermostats for heating systems; devices to recycle heated air; electricity produced or manufactured from excess material and energy of industrial process by corporation for itself; kerosene for domestic purposes; safety equipment (c. 198, §12 as am'd by 1990, c. 10). Tangible personal property received in promotion is exempt to extent fair value exceeds amount paid. (c. 198, §12 as am'd by 1990, c. 10; 1992, c. 15 [not yet in force]; 1993, c. 25; 1994, c. 21; 1995, c. 2). Act does not apply to Nova Scotia offshore area except for tangible personal property purchased on public ferries or vessels transporting persons for or with view to profit; tangible personal property purchased on structures permanently attached to land above low water mark and outside offshore area; tangible personal property purchased for use in respect of submarine mines or mine workings accessible from outside offshore area. (c. 198, §12 as am'd by 1990, c. 10; 1992, c. 15 [not yet in force]; 1993, c. 25; 1994, c. 21; 1995, c. 2). Where exempt property is put to taxable use after acquisition tax is collectible at rate prevailing at time of change of use. (c. 198, §5 as am'd by 1993, c. 25; 1995, c. 2).

Gasoline and Diesel Oil Tax (c. 183 as am'd by 1989, c. 22 [as am'd by 1995, c. 7]; 1992, c. 15; 1993, cc. 23, 24; [proclaimed 13 Feb. '90, in force 1 Mar. '90]; 1990, c. 10; 1992, c. 11) imposes tax on purchaser and consumer. Rate is 20% of average retail price of gasoline and 21% of average retail price of diesel oil. (c. 183, §§3, 5 as am'd by 1990, c. 10).

Gypsum Mining Income Tax.—Imposes tax on mining operation income. (c. 190).

Stamp Tax.—No provincial tax. For Dominion tax see Canada Law Digest, topic Taxation.

Corporation Capital Tax Act (c. 99 as am'd by 1990, c. 10; 1992, c. 15; 1993, c. 17).—Imposes tax on capital, surpluses, reserves and retained earnings of banks, and trust and loan companies allocated to Nova Scotia by regulation.

Franchise Taxes.—See topic Corporations.

Social Security or Unemployment Compensation Tax.—No provincial tax.

Tobacco Tax Act (c. 470 as am'd by 1990, c. 10; 1992, c. 11 [as am'd by 1995, c. 7]; 1992, c. 15; 1994, c. 34 [not yet in force]) imposes tax on tobacco products at rate of 6 8/10¢ per cigarette, 5 1/4¢ per gram of fine cut tobacco, 6¢ per gram of tobacco in tobacco sticks and 50% on purchase price of other forms of tobacco.

Unemployment Compensation Tax.—See Canada Law Digest, topic Taxation, subhead Unemployment Compensation Tax.

Penalties.—

Assessment Act (c. 23, as am'd by 1990, cc. 19 & 24; 1992, c. 11 [as am'd by 1995, c. 7]).—Any person who knowingly makes false statement is liable to fine or imprisonment and loss of right to appeal. (c. 23, §23). Failure to give notice of commencement of business to clerk of district, makes person liable to maximum penalty of $500 or in default to imprisonment for three months. (c. 23, §14 as am'd by 1990, c. 19). If any person fails to pay rates or taxes imposed, his goods may be distrained and sold or in default thereof, debtor may be imprisoned. (c. 23, §§109-112).

Income Tax Act (c. 217 as am'd by 1987, c. 3 [proclaimed 4 Jan. '90, in force 5 Jan. '90]; 1990, c. 10 *[proclaimed 12 Jan. '93, in force 12 Jan. '93]; 1992, c. 15; 1993, cc. 3 and 26; 1994, c. 9; 1995, c. 2).*—Every person who fails to make return as required by c. 217, §23 (as am'd by 1993, c. 26, §9) of Act is liable to penalty equal to aggregate of 5% of unpaid tax when return was required to be filed and sum of 1% of unpaid tax times number of months, to maximum of 12, that return was not filed after it should have been. (c. 217, §23 as am'd by 1993, c. 26, §9). Failure to make return under c. 217, §23 (as am'd by 1993, c. 26, §9) makes person liable to penalty of $25 each day of default to maximum of $100. If information required is not given on prescribed form person is liable to maximum penalty of $100. (c. 217, §23 as am'd by 1993, c. 26, §9). Any person who knowingly or by gross negligence makes statement resulting in failure to pay full tax is liable to penalty of greater of $100 or 50% of amount by which tax payable as calculated in statement is less than tax payable for year. (c. 217, §24 as am'd by 1993, c. 26, §9). Person who wilfully attempts to evade payment of tax for failing to file return as required by c. 217, §23 (as am'd by 1993, c. 26, §9) is liable to penalty of 50% of tax sought to be evaded. (c. 217, §46 as am'd by 1993, c. 26, §18). Burden of proof on Minister of Finance. Minister of Finance and Economics may issue warrant to Sheriff of county where taxpayer's property is located for tax, interest, and penalty which will have effect of Writ of Execution of Supreme Court. (c. 217, §37). Provincial Treasurer may garnishee any payment to be made to taxpayer liable to make payment under Act. (c. 217, §39 as am'd by 1993, c. 26, §16). Goods and chattels of person failing to make payment can be seized and sold at public auction. (c. 217, §38 as am'd by 1993, c. 26, §16). Any person who fails to deduct or withhold tax from amount payable to resident under §10 is liable to penalty of 10% of amount he should have deducted—in any other case, whole amount that should have been deducted plus interest at rate prescribed for purposes of §227(8) of Federal Act. For failure to remit amount deducted or withheld penalty is 10% of amount or $10 whichever is greater, in addition to amount itself, together with interest prescribed for purpose of §227(8) of Federal Act. Every person who fails to comply with regulations made under §117(1) of Federal Act or §23 of this Act is liable to penalty of $10 a day up to $2,500. Failure to file return is offence and taxpayer is liable to fine of not less than 5% of tax owing for year unpaid plus 1% times number of complete months between date return due and date return submitted. Failure to deduct or withhold tax, keep proper records or to comply with c. 217, §42 (as am'd by 1993, c. 26, §16) make person liable to fine of not less than $1,000 nor more than $25,000, or both fine and imprisonment for term not exceeding 12 months. (c. 217, §45 as am'd by 1993, c. 26, §17). Penalty for tax evasion is fine of not less than 50% nor more than 200% of amount of tax that was sought to be evaded, or both fine and imprisonment not exceeding two years. (c. 217, §46 as am'd by 1993, c. 26, §18).

Health Services Tax Act (c. 198 as am'd by 1987, c. 3; [proclaimed 4 Jan. '90, in force 5 Jan. '90]; 1989, c. 22; 1990, c. 10; 1992, c. 11, [as am'd by 1995, c. 7]; 1992 c. 15; 1993, c. 25; 1994, c. 21; 1995, c. 2).—Where person fails to make return or remittance under Act, Commissioner may estimate tax collected by taxpayer and he

See Topical Index in front part of this volume.

TAXATION . . . *continued*
must pay that amount. (c. 198, §19). Commissioner may apply for injunction against vendor found guilty of offence under Act who continues to sell property taxable under Act. (c. 198, §30). Commissioner may assess penalty of 5% of amount due plus interest of 6% against any person failing to remit tax within required time. (c. 198, §32). Every person who fails to collect tax imposed by Act is liable to fine equal to amount of tax including arrears, penalties and interest plus penalty of not less than $100 nor more than $1,000 and in default to imprisonment not exceeding three months. (c. 198, §44). For other offences against Act person is liable to fine of not less than $100 nor more than $1,000 and in default to imprisonment for not more than three months and must pay tax, penalties and interest. (c. 198, §44).

Gasoline and Diesel Oil Tax Act (c. 183 as am'd by 1989, c. 22 [proclaimed 13 Feb. '90, in force 1 Mar. '90]; 1990, c. 10; 1992, c. 11 [as am'd by 1995, c. 7]; 1992, c. 15; 1993, c. 23; 1993, c. 24).—Any person violating any provision of Act or regulation is liable in case of corporation to penalty not exceeding $5,000 and in case of person not corporation to penalty not exceeding $1,000 or in default to imprisonment not exceeding six months. (c. 183, §16). Licenses issued under Gasoline Licensing Act or under Motor Vehicle Act must be suspended for period not exceeding one year.

TORRENS ACT:

Not adopted but see topic Real Roperty, subhead Land Titles Act.

TORTFEASORS ACT: See topic Judgments, subhead Contribution.

TRADEMARKS AND TRADENAMES:

Governed by Trademark and Design Act. See Canada Law Digest.

See also topic Partnership, subhead Partnerships and Business Names Registration Act.

TRUST DEEDS: See topic Mortgages of Real Property.

TRUSTEE PROCESS: See topic Garnishment.

TRUSTS:

The kinds of trusts recognized, the manner of creation, and the purposes for which permitted, and the general rights, duties, and liabilities of trustees and beneficiaries are governed by common law.

The Trustee Act (c. 479 as am'd by 1992, c. 8; 1994-95, c. 19) provides for: Investments in which trustee may invest trust funds unless expressly forbidden by instrument (if any) creating trust; appointment of new trustees; retirement of trustee; powers of court to appoint new trustees and vest property in them; payment into court by trustees of trust money or securities; etc. Trustees are entitled to fair and reasonable remuneration for their care, pains, trouble and time expended in and about estate; judge of Supreme Court may on application to him settle amount, and apportion same where there are several trustees. This does not apply where remuneration is fixed by instrument creating trust. (c. 479, §62). If it appears to court that trustee is or may be liable for any breach of trust, but has acted honestly and reasonably, and ought fairly to be excused for breach, and for omitting to obtain directions of court in matter in which he committed breach, it may relieve trustee either wholly or partly from personal liability for same. (c. 479, §64).

Trust companies approved by the Governor-in-Council may be appointed by the court to execute the office of trustee, executor, administrator, receiver, assignee or guardian of an infant or lunatic; but no company which has issued or has authority to issue debentures can be so approved. Any person having authority may by deed, will or other instrument appoint such a company to execute any such office. (c. 479, §68). Such company may be appointed sole trustee where otherwise it might be necessary to appoint more than one; may also be appointed trustee jointly with any person. It need not give security for due performance of its duty unless otherwise ordered. (c. 479, §72). Governor-in-Council may revoke its approval. Company has same liability and powers as private person. (c. 479, §74).

Trusts in Land.—Declaration or creation of trust in land is not valid unless in writing, signed by the person entitled to create or declare the trust, or by his last will. This does not apply to trust in land arising or resulting by implication or construction of law, or which may be transferred or extinguished by act or operation of law. (c. 442, §5).

Grant or Assignment of Trust.—No grant or assignment of any trust is valid unless it is in writing, signed by the person granting or assigning the same or by his last will. (c. 442, §5).

Variation of Trusts Act.—(c. 486) Provides that Supreme Court may approve variation in trusts on behalf of beneficiaries incapable of assenting or who have contingent interests.

Public Trustee Act (c. 379).—Public trustee may be appointed trustee or guardian under several acts and may have himself appointed under some acts, generally where private parties refuse or are unable to act in public interest.

Accumulations.—See topic Perpetuities.

Perpetuities.—See topic Perpetuities.

USURY: See Canada Law Digest, topic Interest.

VENDORS AND PURCHASERS ACT: See topic Real Property.

VENUE:

Unless court otherwise orders, place of trial of a proceeding, or any question or issue arising therein shall be at place of trial named in statement of claim, or if no place is named, at place where originating notice was issued. Upon satisfying court that he has a good defense and all plaintiffs reside out of jurisdiction or it is just, a defendant may obtain an order changing place of trial to any place within province. When court orders, any proceeding may be tried at any time or at any place in province. (Rule 28). Court at any time may order a proceeding to be transferred to office of another prothonotary (Rule 39.01); where a trial cannot be conveniently heard or completed at a sitting, court may change place of trial, or adjourn trial to another sitting (Rule 30.03). All actions in which title to land is in issue shall be tried in county where lands lie. (c. 247).

VITAL STATISTICS: See topic Records.

WAREHOUSEMEN:

Under The Storage Warehouse Keepers Act (c. 447), keeper of storage warehouse includes proprietor, keeper or manager of warehouse, building, shed, storehouse, yard, wharf or other place for storage of goods, chattels and merchandise delivered to him as bailee for hire, whether he is engaged in other business or not. In addition to his ordinary lien, he has right to sell, at public auction, goods so stored with him, for storage charges in respect of such goods where payment of charges is in arrears, and goods have been in his charge or custody for three months without storage charges, rent or hire having been paid. (c. 447 §§3-4). He must advertise sale for at least one month before the sale by at least three insertions in newspaper in circulation in district where the goods are stored. Advertisement must contain notice of intended sale, short description of goods to be sold, and name of owner or depositor of goods. He must also send notice to last known address of owner or depositor of goods by prepaid registered letter, at least one month before sale. Any surplus after charges, costs and expenses are paid, must be paid to Accountant General of Nova Scotia. Warehouseman must verify by affidavit sale of goods, proceedings, advertisement, sending of notice, amount received, costs, charges, and surplus. (c. 447, §8).

Warehouse receipts are dealt with by The Bank Act; the Cold Storage Act; the Customs Act; the Excise Act; and the Canada Grain Act which deals with grain elevators. See Canada Law Digest.

WILLS:

Any person who has attained age of majority, or who is under age of majority but who is or has formerly been married (c. 505, §4), and who is of sound mind, may dispose of, by will, any real or personal property to which he or she is entitled at time of his death, and which if not so disposed of would devolve upon his or her heirs at law or representatives (c. 505, §3).

Formalities of Execution.—The will must be in writing signed by the testator, or by some other person in his presence and by his direction, at the end or foot thereof. The signature must be made or acknowledged by the testator in the presence of two or more witnesses present at the same time; such witnesses must attest and subscribe the will in the presence of the testator, but no form of attestation is necessary. (c. 505, §5). No appointment made by will is valid unless executed in accordance with proper testamentary formalities. (c. 505, §8).

Witnesses.—No will is invalid on account of incompetency of witnesses to prove its execution. Devise or bequest to an attesting witness or to his or her wife or husband is void, unless there are two other competent witnesses. Creditors, their wives or husbands and executors are competent. (c. 505, §§11, 13).

Holograph wills not recognized.

Living Wills.—No legislation.

Nuncupative Wills.—Soldier in actual military service or any mariner or seaman at sea may dispose of his personal property without formal requisites; this may be by oral will before witnesses. Will of any such person disposing of real estate, who dies after May 17th, 1919, is valid even though he was under 19 (c. 505, §9) when he made will, or even though form was not form required by law (c. 505, §9). Publication is not necessary.

Alterations.—Cancellation by drawing lines through any part of a will, obliterations, interlineations or other alterations made in a will after execution, are invalid unless signature of testator and witnesses is made in the margin opposite or near to such alteration. (c. 505, §20).

Revocation.—Will may be revoked: By another will or codicil duly executed; by a writing declaring an intention to revoke it, and executed in the manner in which a will must be executed; by burning, tearing or otherwise destroying the same by the testator, or by some person in his presence and by his direction, with the intention of revoking it; and by marriage of the testator except in the following cases: (a) Where it is declared in the will that it is made in contemplation of marriage; (b) where the husband or wife elects to take under the will by an instrument in writing signed by him or her within one year after the testator's death and filed in the court of probate; (c) where the will is made in exercise of a power of appointment, and the property thereby appointed would not in default thereof pass to the heir, executor, or administrator or the person entitled as next of kin. A will is not revoked or the construction thereof altered by reason of any subsequent change of domicile of the testator. (c. 505, §§16-19).

Revival.—A revoked will can be revived only by the re-execution or by codicil showing an intention to revive the will. (c. 505, §21).

Probate Jurisdiction.—Probate may be granted by the court of probate for the district in which the testator had at the time of his death his fixed place of abode or in which he had property at the time of his death. As to probate proceedings see topic Executors and Administrators.

Self-proved Wills.—No provision.

Lapses.—A devise or bequest to the testator's child does not lapse if the child dies within the lifetime of the testator leaving issue alive at testator's death, unless there is a contrary provision in the will.

Payment of Legacies.—Executors do not have to pay legacies until accounts are passed and distribution ordered by the court.

Unclaimed Legacies.—Court may order executor to distribute unclaimed legacy if legatee not heard from for ten years and believed dead. (c. 359, §148). See also topic Descent and Distribution, subhead Escheat.

Dependents inadequately provided for can apply for an order for proper maintenance and support. (c. 465, §3). Amount awarded, if any, is in discretion of judge.

WILLS . . . *continued*
Application must be made within six months from grant of probate or of administration with will annexed, but judge may allow an application to be made at any time as to any portion of estate remaining undistributed. (c. 465, §14).

Foreign Wills.—Wills made out of the province, regardless of the domicile of the testator at the time of making or at the time of his death, will, as regards personal property, be held to be well executed for the purpose of being admitted to probate in Nova Scotia, if made according to the forms required, by either: (a) The law of this province; (b) the law of the place where made; (c) the law of the place where testator was domiciled when it was made; or (d) the law then in force in the place where he had his domicile or origin. (c. 505, §15).

The following form of attestation clause is generally used but is not necessary.

Form

Signed, published and declared by the said testator as and for his last will and testament in the presence of us, both present at the same time, who at his request and in his presence and in the presence of each other have subscribed our names as witnesses the day and year last above written.

Simultaneous Death.—See topic Death, subhead Presumption of Survivorship.

WITNESSES:

All persons are competent to testify to give evidence in civil proceedings except lunatics, drunkards, infants and the like, in which case the incapacity is only co-extensive with the defect. If child understands duty to tell truth, his evidence may be admissible even if child does not understand nature of oath, but such evidence shall not determine issue unless corroborated. (c. 154, §63).

No person is incompetent as a witness by reason of conviction of crime or from interest. (c. 154, §44). On trial of any action matter or proceeding, parties thereto and their husbands and wives are competent and compellable to give evidence on behalf of either or any of parties. (c. 154, §45).

See also topic Depositions.

Privileged Communications.—All communications between solicitor and client of a confidential nature and written to the solicitor in his professional capacity for purpose of securing legal advice are privileged, whether or not litigation is contemplated or pending. When litigation is contemplated or pending, communications made between solicitors and third persons are privileged. Communications between a party and a stranger are privileged only if litigation is contemplated or pending, and, if the party is acting for the solicitor, i.e., to help the solicitor prepare his case. Communications between co-plaintiffs and co-defendants are not privileged as such. Privilege does not extend to documents publici juris. Documents relevant to fraud or illegality are never privileged. Client may waive privilege; solicitor cannot.

Witness excused from answering any question as to any proceedings before, or producing any reports or recommendations of, hospital research or peer review committees used in any study, research or program carried on by hospital or for purpose of education or improvement in medical or hospital care or practice. (c. 154, §60).

Husband and Wife.—Parties to an action instituted in consequence of adultery, and their husbands and wives, are competent but not compellable to give evidence; but husband or wife must not be asked, and is not bound to answer any question tending to show that he or she has been guilty of adultery unless he or she has already given evidence in the same action in disproof of his or her alleged adultery or unless permission to ask such question is given by the presiding judge. (c. 154, §46). Husband is not compellable to disclose any communication made to him by his wife during marriage; same applied to wife. (c. 154, §49).

Communications or Transactions With Persons Since Deceased.—In any action or proceeding by or against the heirs, executors, administrators or assigns of a deceased person, an opposite or interested party cannot obtain a verdict, judgment, award or decision therein on his own testimony or that of his wife or both of them, in respect to any dealing, transaction or agreement with the deceased, or in respect to any act, statement, acknowledgment or admission of the deceased unless usch testimony is corroborated by other material evidence. (c. 154, §45).

Self-incrimination.—No witness is excused from answering any question upon the ground that it may tend to criminate him, or may tend to establish his liability to a civil proceeding; but if the witness objects to answer on either of those grounds, then although the witness is compelled to answer, the answer so given cannot be used or received in evidence against him in any criminal proceeding other than a prosecution for perjury in giving such evidence. (c. 154, §59).

WORKMEN'S COMPENSATION LAW: See topic Labour Relations.

See Topical Index in front part of this volume.

ONTARIO LAW DIGEST REVISER

Borden & Elliot
Scotia Plaza
40 King Street West
Toronto, Ontario M5H 3Y4
Telephone: 416-367-6000
Fax: 416-367-6749
Email: info@borden.com

Reviser Profile

History & Growth: The firm was founded in 1936 by Henry Borden, Q.C. and Beverley V. Elliot, Q.C., two distinguished members of the Ontario bar, whose service in the firm is recognized in its name. Today Borden & Elliot is one of the largest law firms in Canada. There are over 200 lawyers practising in our offices in the Scotia Plaza in downtown Toronto.

In addition, we are a member of Borden DuMoulin Howard Gervais, a four firm national association of leading Canadian law firms founded in October 1990. Our national association includes the law firms of Borden & Elliot in Toronto, Russell & DuMoulin in Vancouver, Howard, Mackie in Calgary, and Mackenzie Gervais in Montreal. There are over 450 lawyers practising in our national association. In June 1993 an international office of Borden DuMoulin Howard Gervais was opened in London, England.

Practice Areas: Borden & Elliot is organized to provide integrated legal services in the following practice areas: Aboriginal; Admiralty & Shipping; Aviation; Banking & Finance; Biotechnology; Capital Markets; Casualty; Commercial Transactions; Communications & Broadcasting; Competition, Marketing & Advertising; Computer & Technology; Construction, Surety & Fidelity; Corporate; Criminal; Defamation; Education; Entertainment & Sports; Environmental; Estates; Expropriation; Family; Franchising & Licensing; Golf Industry; Health; Hospital; Immigration; Insolvency & Bankruptcy; Insurance; Intellectual Property; International Business; Investment Funds; Labour & Employment; Mergers & Acquisitions; Mining & Natural Resources; Municipal, Planning & Public Environmental; Mutual Funds; NAFTA; Pensions; Personal Injury; Personal Services; Products Liability; Real Estate; Regulatory & Criminal Defence; Securities; Taxation and Trusts.

Automation: Borden & Elliot is committed to the use of, and has a significant investment in advanced technology in all practice areas to provide lawyers control and flexibility over their respective practice areas, and facilitate delivery of legal services in an efficient and cost effective manner. All members of the firm are linked by a sophisticated computer network which supports an array of software, including fax and Internet mail to the desktop; document modelling; legal research, dial up and litigation support databases with imaging; and Internet access from personalized accounts. The firm encourages and maintains direct electronic connections of all types with its clients.

Clientele: The firm represents many national and multinational corporations in such business sectors as banking and finance, entertainment, health care, manufacturing, merchandising, mining, oil, gas and other natural resources, pharmaceuticals, publishing, real estate development, securities, service industries of many kinds and transportation. As a result, the firm has wide ranging experience and has developed distinctive expertise in these sectors. Borden & Elliot is responsive and adaptive, designing its services to meet its clients' individual needs in the sectors in which they carry on business.

Borden & Elliot also represents governments (national, provincial and municipal) and government agencies in a wide variety of matters. The firm represents other public institutions including colleges, universities and educational authorities, hospitals and other health care facilities. Business, trade and charitable organizations and associations are also among its clients. Although the majority of the firm's work comes from business or public organizations, the firm maintains its commitment to provide quality legal services to individuals through its Personal Services Group.

Borden & Elliot represents a significant number of national self-regulatory organizations in the important securities sector of the economy. These include the CDS (Canadian Depository for Securities, a computerized Canada-wide clearing house for securities transactions), the Canadian Investors Protection Fund, the Investment Funds Institute of Canada, the Investment Dealers Association of Canada and the Canadian Securities Institute. The firm also acts as special counsel in enforcement matters for the Ontario Securities Commission.

The firm's experience is not confined to Canada. Borden & Elliot has acted in the resolution of international trade disputes; in international banking transactions (including sovereign risk lending); in international insolvencies, liquidations and restructurings; in international business joint ventures, reorganizations and acquisitions; and in international communications networks and commercial contracts of many kinds.

Governance: Borden & Elliot is governed by an Executive Committee of five partners, elected by rotation, working with a number of well-defined practice groups and an administrative staff headed by its chief operating officer. The firm continuously monitors the design and performance of services, client relationships, legal, economic and technological developments. Borden & Elliot maintains its commitment to planned firm growth.

Professional/Community Activities: The firm encourages its partners and associates to be involved in professional organizations and in community affairs. Lawyers in the firm participate as lecturers and discussion group leaders in the teaching portion of the Bar Admission Course (the final preparatory course for law students prior to admission to legal practice in Ontario). They also lecture at law schools and in continuing legal education programs sponsored by The Law Society of Upper Canada, The Canadian Bar Association and other professional development organizations. Lawyers in the firm have written or contributed to many legal textbooks and periodicals and have served on the executive and legislative review and reform committees of The Canadian Bar Association and its various Sections.

In addition, some lawyers in the firm are members of the International Bar Association, the International Fiscal Association, INSOL, the American Bar Association, the Criminal Lawyers Association, the American College of Trial Lawyers, the American Immigration Lawyers Association, United States Trademark Association, Licensing Executives Society, Patent and Trademark Institute of Canada, the Canadian

Chamber of Commerce, the Metropolitan Toronto Board of Trade, the Toronto Biotechnology Initiative, the Women's Law Association of Ontario and are active in many community and charitable organizations at national, provincial and local levels.

Reflecting the diverse cultural background of Canada, more than 20 languages are spoken at our firm. We have the capacity to provide legal services to our clients, not only in English and French, but also in languages such as Bulgarian, Cantonese, German, Italian, Macedonian, Mandarin, Russian, Slovak, Spanish and Ukrainian.

While Ontario is a common law province, a number of lawyers in the firm are also trained in the civil law tradition, reflecting Canada's heritage of two of the world's major legal systems.

ONTARIO LAW DIGEST

(The following is a list of all Topics, including cross-references, covered in this Digest.)

ONTARIO LAW DIGEST

Revised for 1997 edition by

BORDEN & ELLIOT, Barristers and Solicitors, Toronto.

(Citations, unless otherwise indicated, refer to chapters (c.) of the Revised Statutes of Ontario, 1990 as am'd. Annual Statutes of Ontario are cited by year and chapter number. Regulations made under authority of Statutes of Ontario are cited R.R.O. followed by the number, and O.Reg. followed by regulation number and year; reference to R.R.O. 1990. R.S.C. indicates Revised Statutes of Canada, 1985. R.P. indicates Rules of Civil Procedure, R.R.O. 1990, Reg. 19 as am'd. Reference to court means Ontario Court [General Division] unless otherwise specified.)

ABSENTEES:

Ontario Court (General Division) may declare person absentee who, having had his usual place of domicile in Ontario, has disappeared, whose whereabouts are unknown, and as to whom there is no knowledge whether he is alive or dead. Application for order may be made by Attorney General; any one or more of next of kin of alleged absentee; spouse of absentee; common law spouse of absentee; creditor or any other person. (c. A.3, §2). If person ceases to be absentee Court may make order so declaring and vacating previous order except as to acts done respecting his estate while such order was in force (c. A.3). See also topic Death.

Property of Foreign Absentees.—Where a person having an interest in land in Ontario, and having his usual place of residence or domicile out of Ontario has been declared to be an absentee by a court of competent jurisdiction, Ontario Court (General Division) may upon being satisfied that person has disappeared, that there is no knowledge of his whereabouts, or whether he is alive or dead, appoint committee with such authority to manage, sell or otherwise deal with his interest in such land as in opinion of court is in best interests of his family. (c. A.3, §8).

Care of Property.—Court may make an order for the custody, due care and management of the property of an absentee and a committee may be appointed with same powers, duties as guardian of property under S.O. 1992, c. 30, §31.

Moneys held on passing of final accounts belonging to a person whose address is unknown must be paid by the personal representative, guardian, or trustee into Ontario Court (General Division) to credit of person entitled to it to be dealt with according to order of Court. (c. T.23, §36).

Process Agent.—None required by nonresidents.

Escheat and Bona Vacantia.—No general statute dealing with disposition of unclaimed property. Any item of tangible personal property other than fixtures left for repair or storage where article unclaimed and unpaid for may be sold or disposed of in certain circumstances, to satisfy repairer or storer's lien. (c. R.25). As to property of person dying intestate without lawful heirs, and property forfeited for any cause to Crown, see topic Descent and Distribution, subhead Escheat and Bona Vacantia. See also topic Wills, subhead Unclaimed Legacies; and Canada Law Digest, topic Banks and Banking, subhead Unclaimed Deposits.

Unclaimed Intangible Property Act, c. U.1.—(Act not yet proclaimed in force.) Act provides procedure whereby, upon expiry of specified time periods, any intangible property including bank deposits, shares, travellers' cheques, and all accretions thereto, which lies unclaimed, will be transferred to Public Guardian and Trustee. Holders of intangible property required to send notice to last address of owner in advance of transfer to Public Guardian and Trustee. Holders also required to notify Public Guardian and Trustee of extent and nature of holdings. Public Guardian and Trustee to deposit and hold funds and to further transfer them to Provincial Treasurer at year end. Persons subsequently claiming interest in intangible property which has been transferred to Public Guardian and Trustee and/or paid out to Provincial Treasurer able to do so by application to Public Guardian and Trustee.

ACCORD AND SATISFACTION:

Part performance of an obligation before or after breach, when expressly accepted by the creditor in satisfaction or rendered pursuant to an agreement for that purpose, though without new consideration, extinguishes the obligation. (c. M.10, §16). Defence of accord and satisfaction must be pleaded. (R.P. 25.07[4]).

In other respects common law rules govern.

ACKNOWLEDGMENTS:

There is no provision in Ontario for the acknowledgment of instruments before a notary.

ACTIONS:

Civil proceedings generally commenced by way of action, with prescribed exceptions for divorce petitions and applications.

Language.—In certain designated counties of Ontario, upon application of party who speaks French language, order may be made that court hearing be before judge and/or jury who speak both French and English. Hearing may be all or partly in French and evidence given in French will be recorded and transcribed in French.

Equity.—Rules of law and equity are concurrently administered in same courts. In cases of conflict or variance rules of equity prevail. (Courts of Justice Act, c. C.43, §96).

Commencement.—See topic Process.

Conditions Precedent.—Several statutes require notice to be given before action can be brought. For example: (1) notice of contest against proposed scheme of distribution to execution creditors of moneys in hands of sheriff within ten days (c. C.45, §32[5]); (2) notice of election to determine date when compensation to be assessed for lands expropriated within 30 days, and notice of injurious affection within one year (c. E.26, §§10[1], [2] and [22]); (3) notice of failure of Department of Highways to keep highway in repair within ten days (c. P.50, §33[4]); (4) notice by landlord of breach of covenant or condition in lease (except rent) and requiring leasee to remedy breach (c. L.7, §19[2]); (5) notice of libel against a newspaper within six weeks (c. L.12, §5[1]); (6) notice of loss by lightning within 30 days (c. L.14, §13[2]); (7) notice of amount due and owing for maintenance of patient in mental hospital quarter-yearly (c. M.8, §20[1]); (8) notice of failure of municipality to keep highway or bridge in repair within ten days in case of county or township and within seven days in case of urban municipality (c. M.45, §284[5]); (9) notice of damage from changeover of electrical utility within 90 days and notice of crop damage within 60 days (c. P.18, §36); (10) notice of certain proceedings against Crown (c. P.27, §7); (11) notice of demand against certain public authorities (c. P.38, §6); (12) notice of damage by public utility within one month after expiration of calendar year in which injury was occasioned (c. P.52, §55[6]); (13) notice of application in respect of voters' list (c. M.53, §28); (14) notice of election under Workers' Compensation Act within three months and notice of accident as soon as practicable after it happens and claim must be made within six months (c. W.11, §§9[2] and 22[1]; §§7[2] and 20[1]); (15) notice of damage in respect of carriage by air within three days of receipt of luggage and within seven days of receipt of goods, or, in case of delay, within 14 days after luggage or goods placed at person's disposal (R.S.C., c. C.26); (16) notice of claim for damages for personal injury caused by snow and ice on sidewalk ten days in case of county or township; within seven days for urban municipality (c. M.45, §§284[5][6]).

Parties.—Action must be prosecuted by real party in interest, but personal representative or trustee may, subject to certain exceptions, sue or be sued without joining beneficiaries. (R.P. 9.01). Assignee of debt or other chose in action must join assignor as party in proceeding unless assignment is absolute and debtor has received written notice of assignment. (R.P. 5.03[3]). Two or more persons represented by same solicitor may join as plaintiffs in same proceeding if they claim relief arising out of same transaction or event, if common question of law or fact may arise in proceeding, or if their joinder may promote convenient administration of justice. (R.P. 5.02[1]). Class Proceedings Act, S.O. 1992, c. 6, legislation allowing for Court certification of class proceedings and dealing with other procedural and substantive matters associated with class proceedings. Persons may be joined as defendants if plaintiff claims relief against them arising out of same transaction or event, if common question of law or fact may arise in proceeding, if there is doubt as to whom plaintiff is entitled to relief from, if plaintiff suffers damage or loss caused by more than one person and there is doubt as to from whom, and for what amount, plaintiff is entitled to relief, or if their joinder may promote convenient administration of justice. (R.P. 5.02[2]). Where there are numerous persons having same interest, one or more may bring or defend proceeding or may be authorized by court to do so on behalf of all. (R.P. 12.01). Generally, every person whose presence is necessary to enable court to adjudicate completely and effectively on issues shall be joined as party to proceedings, and court may order addition, deletion or substitution of any person as party, at any stage in proceeding, on such terms as are just. (R.P. 5.03, 5.04). No person shall be added as plaintiff or applicant without filing of consent. (R.P. 5.04[3]). Where person is required to be joined as necessary party and person will not consent to being joined as plaintiff or applicant, then person shall be made defendant or respondent. (R.P. 5.03[5]).

Interpleader.—Relief by way of interpleader may be granted where two or more persons make adverse claims in respect of personal property, including debt, against person who claims no beneficial interest in property, other than lien for costs, fees or expenses, and is willing to deposit property with court or dispose of it as court directs. Similar relief may be granted to sheriff in respect of both real and personal property or proceeds thereof taken or intended to be taken by sheriff in execution of any enforcement process if sheriff has received claim in respect of that property. (R.P. 43).

Third Party Practice.—(1) Defendant may commence third party claim against any person who is not party to action and who is or may be liable to defendant for all or part of plaintiff's claim; is or may be liable to defendant for independent claim arising out of transaction or event or series thereof involved in main action or related transaction or event or series thereof; or should be bound by determination of issue arising between plaintiff and defendant. (R.P. 29.01). Third party may defend against third party claim by delivering third party defence (R.P. 29.03) or, where appropriate, third party may defend against plaintiff's claim against defendant by delivering statement of defence to main action, in which he/she may raise any defence open to defendant. In defending main action, third party has same rights and obligations as defendant and is bound by any order or determination between plaintiff and defendant who made third party claim (R.P. 29.05); (2) statutory right of contribution or indemnity under Negligence Act is enforced by cross claim against codefendant or by commencing third party claim against nonparty. (c. N.1, §5). No special procedure necessary for persons already parties; (3) see also Insurance Act (c. I.8, §§226 and 258).

Joinder of Causes of Action.—A plaintiff may unite in the same action several causes of action, but if causes of action so joined cannot be conveniently disposed of in one action, or may cause undue prejudice to a party, court may direct that they be tried separately or excluded. (R.P. 5.01, 5.05).

Consolidation of Actions.—Actions may be consolidated by order of the Court. (R.P. 6.01).

Stay of Proceedings may be obtained in proper case on application to court where action pending. (c. C.43, §106; R.P. 21.01[3]).

Abatement and Revival.—Survival of causes of action is governed by common law rules modified by c. T.23, §38 (see topic Estate Trustees). If by reason of death when cause of action survives, or by assignment or conveyance estate or interest devolves or is transferred, pending action may be continued by or against person to whom estate has come. Order to continue is necessary. (R.P. 11.01-11.03).

See Topical Index in front part of this volume.

ACTIONS . . . *continued*

Termination of Actions.—Actions may be terminated by judgment, order or discontinuance. Discontinuance is not a defence to any subsequent action, unless order giving leave to discontinue or consent filed by parties provides otherwise. (R.P. 23.04).

Summary Procedure.—See topic Judgments.

Limitation of.—See topic Limitation of Actions.

Administration.—See topic Estate Trustees.

Direct Actions.—See topic Motor Vehicles, subhead Direct Actions.

Proceedings against the Crown are regulated by c. P.27.

ADMINISTRATION:

See topic Estate Trustees.

ADOPTION:

Adoption is governed by Child and Family Services Act, c. C.11, Part VII. Court may make order for adoption of child resident in Ontario by person resident in Ontario. (§146). Court may make order for adoption if order is in child's best interests, upon application of parent of child, relative of child, or spouse of child's parent. Application may only be made by one individual or jointly by two individuals who are spouses of each other. Court will make order for adoption on application of minor only in special circumstances. (§147). Factors to be considered in determining best interests of child include physical, mental and emotional needs of child, child's cultural and religious background, child's relationship by blood or through adoption order, importance of continuity in child's care, child's wishes if ascertained, effect upon child of delay in disposition of case, and any other relevant circumstances. (§136).

Consents Required.—Spouse of adopter must consent in writing unless it is in best interests of child to dispense with consent. Written consent of every person who is parent or has lawful custody must be obtained after child is seven days old. (§137). Such consent may be cancelled in writing within 21 days or withdrawn later if court satisfied it is in child's best interest, but application to withdraw consent may not be made once child placed for adoption and remaining in that person's care. (§139). Consent of child if age seven is required unless court finds it inappropriate. If child is married, spouse must consent. Consent of Director (defined term in Act) is required only for Crown wards. Each person whose consent is required must be given opportunity to obtain legal advice and counselling before giving consent. Court may dispense with consent of any person other than that of child over seven or Director when it is in child's best interests to do so. (§138). Once notice has been given to person concerned, court must be satisfied that every person consenting understands nature and effect of adopting order. No notice of proposed adoption is given to any person who has consented or whose consent was dispensed with by court or who is parent of Crown ward unless requested by such person.

Conditions Precedent.—Child must have been placed for adoption by adoption agency or licensee, unless applicant is child's relative or spouse of child's parent. (§141). Once child is placed, access orders are terminated. (§143). Where child is under 16, or is 16 years of age or more but has not withdrawn from parental control, Director, pursuant to home study report made by local Children's Aid Society or another approved person, shall file statement in writing that child has resided for six months or more with applicant, dealing with adjustment of child in home, recommending whether or not adoption order should be made, that applicant is to knowledge of Director proper person to have care and custody of adoptee and recommending that period of residence be dispensed with and order for adoption be made. (§149). If Director recommends that adoption order not be made, copy of statement shall be filed with court and served on applicant at least 30 days before hearing. (§149[4]). No report and statement are necessary where application is made by child's relative or spouse of child's parents, unless court so directs. (§149[6]). Offence to give or receive or agree to give or receive direct or indirect payments or reward in consideration of adoption. (§175).

Jurisdiction and Venue.—Family Court in County or District where applicant or child resides, may make adoption order, unless court satisfied preponderance of convenience favours change of venue. (§150). Hearings are held in camera. (§151). Court may appoint litigation guardian if necessary to protect legal interests of child under 18 years of age.

Decree.—Adoption orders are not subject to judicial review but order granting or refusing adoption may be appealed. (§156). Court may postpone application and make interim custody order for one year. (§154). All consents required for adoption order must be filed for interim custody unless dispensed with by court. Where applicant who is given interim custody order subsequently takes up residence outside Ontario, court may make adoption order if Director makes recommendation in favour of order. (§154).

Name.—Court, upon application of adopting parent(s) may order change in adoptee's surname to that surname person would have been given if born to applicant(s). It may also change given name as adopting parent(s) desire. Child age 12 or more must consent to any name change. (§153).

Effects of Adoption.—For all purposes, adoptee becomes child of adopter, adopter becomes parent of adoptee, adoptee ceases to be child of person who was his parent before adoption order was made and that person ceases to be parent of adoptee as if adoptee had been born in wedlock to adopter. Access or visitation by person who was parent before adoption order is prohibited by §160 and case law. Relationship of all persons including kindred of adopter and person who was parent before adoption are determined accordingly. Wills are interpreted accordingly. Adoption does not remove persons from relationships in consanguinity with respect to laws of incest and marriage. (§158).

Confidentiality.—Adoption information shall remain confidential except certain classes of people may request nonidentifying information. (§§165, 167, 168). Identifying information may be disclosed where both parties are registered by Registrar of Adoption Information. (§167[5]).

ADVANCEMENTS:

See topic Descent and Distribution.

ADVERSE POSSESSION:

The general rule is that actual, constant, open, visible and notorious possession for ten years by any person or his predecessors in title by himself or by his tenants or lessees, claiming fee simple to the exclusion of the owner gives good title. (c. L.15). Period as against Crown is 60 years. (c. L.15 §3). Person in possession of any public lands for more than 60 years may obtain quit claim from Crown. (c. L.15). Person claiming title by adverse possession may apply to have his title certified. (c. C.6, §4[2]). No length of possession, however, can defeat title registered under The Land Titles Act after first registration. (c. L.5, §51).

Unimproved Land.—In certain cases of land which is not cultivated or improved, the period is either ten years from the date on which the owner had knowledge of the adverse possession or 20 years from the date of taking such possession, whichever is shorter. (c. L.15, §5[4]).

Easements.—In order to obtain an easement by prescription it must have been enjoyed without interruption for 20 years. Right to easement, once gained, cannot be extinguished by prescription. (c. L.15, §31). No prescriptive right to light or air or in respect of wires or cables can be acquired. (c. L.15, §§33, 35). Continuation of public utility easements of municipality or easements of Ministry of Government Services so that those that existed on July 31, 1981 will continue until Dec. 31, 1999. (c. R .20, §114[2]).

Disabilities.—Special rules apply where the person against whom title is asserted was under one of the following disabilities at the time the right of action accrued: infancy, mental deficiency, incompetency, unsoundness of mind. (c. L.15, §36-39).

AFFIDAVITS:

Affidavits may be sworn or affirmed before following officers:

Within the Province: Commissioners for taking affidavits, notaries public, judges of Ontario Court (General Division) and clerks of courts in which affidavits are required. Members of Assembly, barristers and solicitors, provincial judges and justices of peace are ex officio commissioners. Clerk, deputy clerk, and treasurer of every municipality is ex officio commissioner for that municipality and in case of municipality which is not county, metropolitan or regional municipality for county, regional or metropolitan municipality in which his municipality is situate. Head of every municipal council, reeve of every town, every deputy reeve and every controller and alderman of municipality and certain administrative officials in municipalities having population of 100,000 are ex officio commissioners within their respective counties, districts or regional and metropolitan municipalities. Power to take affidavits may be conferred on certain officers of Canadian and Ontario governments in connection with official duties; on secretary, treasurer, or principal branch officers of corporations and cooperative corporations in connection with corporate affairs; and on certain other persons in connection with court matters. (c. C.17). Such commissions may be limited in time or area. Registrar of deeds and his deputy, in county where lands lie, may take affidavits authorized by Registry Act. (c. R.20).

Outside the Province: A notary public, a commissioner for taking affidavits, an officer of Her Majesty's diplomatic or consular services, an officer of the Canadian diplomatic, consular or representative services, a Canadian trade commissioner, a mayor or chief magistrate of a municipality, a judge of a court of record, a magistrate, an officer of a court of justice, a commissioner authorized to take affidavits in Ontario and, in other provinces of Canada and in the United Kingdom, certain other officials. The official taking affidavits for use in Ontario should sign name, state his or her office below signature and affix official seal, or seal of municipality, consulate, court, etc., if any. (c. E.23, §45).

Armed Services.—Affidavits may be sworn to within or without the province before a commissioned officer on full time service in the Canadian Forces. Rank and unit must be stated below signature.

Authentication.—The signature and official seal of an officer taking affidavits out of Ontario need not be further authenticated in order to be admitted in evidence. The signature and official seal of an officer taking affidavits within Ontario may be authenticated by Provincial Secretary, or in certain cases by clerk of county or district court where the officer resides.

General Requirements.—Every affidavit must be sworn or affirmed by deponent in presence of officer taking affidavit, who must satisfy self of genuineness of signature of deponent, and who must administer oath in manner required by law before signing jurat. Oath may be administered to any person while holding copy of Old or New Testament without requirement to kiss same, or in such other manner and form and with such ceremonies as may be declared to be binding. Where person objects to swearing affidavit on conscientious grounds or for reasons of religious belief, affirmation or declaration is of same effect as oath. (c. E.23, §17). Affidavits must be confined to statement of facts within personal knowledge of deponent or to other evidence that deponent could give if testifying as witness in court (R.P. 4.06[2]) but, in certain cases, may include deponent's information and belief if source thereof and fact of belief is specified in affidavit (R.P. 39.01[4], [5]).

Use of Affidavit.—Use of affidavits is generally confined to judicial proceedings but may be required elsewhere by statute, e. g. Registry Act (c. R.20); affidavit of execution is required for registration of any instrument other than will, grant from Crown, order in council, by-law, or other instrument under seal of any corporation, or certificate of judicial proceedings. Affidavit evidence may, in certain cases, be used in action. Its general use is confined to motions and applications.

Alterations, etc.—Every alteration, interlineation or erasure in body of affidavit or in jurat must be authenticated by initials of person taking same (R.P. 4.06[9]) by placing tick-mark on either side of alteration, etc., and putting initials in margin. Alterations, etc., in body of affidavit should also be initialled by deponent.

See Topical Index in front part of this volume.

AFFIDAVITS . . . *continued*

Form

The affidavit should have a heading containing the name of the court and the title of proceedings. Affidavits must be drawn up in the first person stating the name of the deponent in full, residence and occupation, and must be signed by the deponent. The officer taking the affidavit must indicate the date when officer's commission expires, unless appointment is for life, and must affix seal if any. Officer should type or legibly print his or her name beneath signature. Where exhibit is referred to in affidavit it must be marked by person taking affidavit; where the exhibit is referred to as being attached to affidavit it must be so attached and where practical where the exhibit is a document it must be served with the affidavit. (R.P. 4.06[6]).

Jurat.—The jurat is as follows: Sworn before me at the . . . . . . of . . . . in the . . . . of . . . . ., on . . . . For marksmen, suggested addition following date of jurat is: . . . . . . having first been truly, distinctly and audibly read over and explained to him or her in my presence when he or she appeared perfectly to understand the same and made his or her mark hereto in my presence. Where there are two or more deponents of affidavit there must be separate jurat for each deponent unless all deponents make affidavit before same person at the same time with one jurat containing the words "Sworn (or affirmed) by the above-named deponents". (R.P. 4.06[4]).

AGENCY: See topic Principal and Agent.

AIRCRAFT:

See Canada Law Digest, topic Aircraft.

ALIENS:

Aliens are under no disability as to holding real property in Ontario. (c. A.18). But see Canada Law Digest, topic Aliens.

Agricultural Land.—Nonresidents holding or acquiring interest in aggregate of ten or more hectares of agricultural land must file registration report. (c. N.4, §2).

ALIMONY: See topics Divorce; Husband and Wife.

ALLOWANCES:

See topic Estate Trustees.

APPEAL AND ERROR:

Court of Appeal for Ontario.—Appeal lies to Court of Appeal from: (i) final order of judge of Ontario Court (General Division) except final orders for single payment of not more than $25,000, exclusive of costs, final order for periodic payments that would amount to not more than $25,000, exclusive of costs, in 12 months, or final order dismissing claims of not more than $25,000 exclusive of costs or claims in respect of which judge indicates amount awarded would not have been more than $25,000, exclusive of costs; (ii) order of Divisional Court of Ontario Court (General Division) on question that is not question of fact alone, with leave; and (iii) certificate of assessment of costs issued in proceeding in Court of Appeal.

Divisional Court of Ontario Court (General Division).—Appeal lies to Divisional Court from: (i) final order of judge of Ontario Court (General Division) except those described in Court of Appeal (above); (ii) interlocutory order of judge of Ontario Court (General Division), with leave, and (iii) final order of Master.

Ontario Court (General Division).—Appeal lies to judge of Ontario Court (General Division) from interlocutory order of Master and Certificate of Assessment of Costs issued in proceeding in Ontario Court (General Division).

Procedure.—Law relating to procedure on appeal from both final and interlocutory orders is governed by Rules of Civil Procedure. (R.P. 61-63).

Supreme Court of Canada.—Appeal may be taken to Supreme Court of Canada at Ottawa (subject to leave to appeal being granted) where Court is of opinion that any question involved by reason of its public importance or importance of any issue of law or any issue of mixed law and fact is one that ought to be decided by Supreme Court and in certain other cases by special leave. (R.S.C., c. S-26, §§35-40). Appeals to Privy Council in London, England, were abolished for cases commencing after 1949. (1950, Statutes of Canada, c. 57).

Stay of execution pending appeal, see topic Executions.

ARBITRATION AND AWARD:

Parties may by written or oral agreement submit any matter of difference present or future to arbitration. Such submission, unless contrary intention is expressed therein, may be revoked only in accordance with rules of contract law. (S.O. 1991, c. 17, §5).

Powers of Arbitrators.—Arbitrator has power to administer oaths to parties and witnesses; to request determination of question of law by court (General Division); and to correct any clerical error in award. (c. C.17, §§29, 44).

Enforcement of Award.—An award may, by leave of Ontario Court (General Division) or judge thereof, be enforced in same manner as judgment or order to same effect. (c. C.17, §50).

Enforcement of Foreign Arbitral Award.—Foreign arbitral award may be recognized by Supreme or District Court. If recognized, is enforceable in same manner as judgment or order of court. Model Law on International Commercial Arbitration adopted, with amendments, as law of Ontario.

ASSIGNMENTS:

Any absolute assignment in writing signed by the assignor, not purporting to be by way of charge only, of any debt or other legal chose in action of which express notice in writing has been given to debtor or trustee, transfers legal right to such debt or chose in action from date of such notice together with all legal and other remedies, and power to give good discharge, subject to all equities entitled to priority. (c. C.34, §53).

Equitable assignments are also valid and enforceable in accordance with principles of equity.

Actions.—Assignee of debt or other chose in action may, if assignment is absolute and debtor has received written notice, sue in his own name. Assignee of debt or other chose in action which is not absolute and of which debtor has not received notice must join assignor. (R.P. 5.03[3]).

Assignment of Accounts.—See topic Personal Property Security.

Assignment of Wages.—Any assignment by debtor of any part of his wages to secure payment of debt, except assignment to credit union to which Credit Unions and Caisses Populaires Act applies is invalid. Generally, debtor may assign up to but not exceeding 20% of his wages to such credit union. (c. W.1, §7).

ASSIGNMENTS FOR BENEFIT OF CREDITORS:

See Canada Law Digest, topic Bankruptcy.

ASSOCIATIONS:

Generally speaking, an unincorporated association is not a legal entity and cannot sue or be sued by its society name. See topics Corporations; Partnership. There are various Acts as to specific trade and professional associations. See also topic Labour Relations.

ATTACHMENT:

Where a resident person has departed from the Province with intent to defraud his creditors or to avoid being arrested or served with process, and was, at time of departure, possessed of real or personal property not exempt from seizure, creditor may in a pending action, on application to judge of Ontario Court (General Division), on affidavits showing these facts, obtain order for attachment of all debtor's property not exempt from seizure. (c. A.2, §§2, 3).

Attachment Bond.—No bond is required from creditor unless, at his request, livestock or perishable goods which have been attached are sold by sheriff (c. A.2, §8), or action is taken by sheriff against persons paying debts to debtor after notice of attachment (c. A.2, §14).

Levy.—Attachment is levied by actual seizure of the lands and tangible personalty of the debtor, by giving notice to persons owing debts to the debtor or holding property on behalf of the debtor, and by notifying corporations in which the debtor owns shares.

Release of Property.—The debtor may obtain the release of the property attached by filing sufficient bond in double the appraised value that he will pay into court on order the value of the goods or so much thereof as will satisfy all claims. (c. A.2, §12).

Sale.—Property attached, including debts, may be sold under order of the court. Livestock, perishable goods or other property attached which cannot be safely or conveniently taken care of may be sold by sheriff at auction on request of creditor provided security in double appraised value is given.

Third Party Claims.—Other creditors if they place attachments in sheriff's hands within two months share pari passu with attaching creditor. (c. C.45, §5).

ATTORNEYS AND COUNSELLORS:

Subject to the approval of the Lieutenant-Governor in Council, the Benchers of the Law Society of Upper Canada control the admission of persons to practise as barristers and solicitors in the province. Lawyers are admitted to both professions in Ontario. Lawyers may be admitted as temporary members.

Eligibility.—Applicants must be Canadian citizens and be of good character. (c. L.8, §§27, 28). Temporary members do not have to be Canadian citizens or permanent residents.

Educational Requirements.—An applicant must be Canadian citizen, who has successfully completed at least two years in approved course in approved university. Applicant is required to complete three year course at approved law school. Graduate from such course is eligible for admission to Law Society's Bar Admission Course consisting of 12 months service under articles and four months Bar Admission Course.

Admission in Special Cases.—Barristers and solicitors from other Canadian jurisdictions may be admitted on special application. Canadian members of legal profession from outside of Ontario may, in discretion of Law Society, be admitted for purpose of appearing as counsel in specific proceeding.

Rights and obligations of barristers and solicitors are governed by the Barristers Act, Law Society Act and Solicitors Act. (cc. B.3, L.8, S.15).

Lien.—A solicitor has a general lien for his fees and disbursements on moneys and papers of his client in his hands.

Disbarment.—The Benchers of the Law Society may disbar or suspend any barrister, suspend or strike off the Rolls any solicitor, or expel from the Society any student who has been guilty of professional misconduct or conduct, unbecoming member. (c. L.8, §§34, 37, 38).

AUTOMOBILES: See topic Motor Vehicles.

BANKS AND BANKING:

Subject to exclusive federal jurisdiction under Constitution Act, 1867. (§91, head 15). See Canada Law Digest.

Deposit Insurance.—Ontario Deposit Insurance Corporation incorporated by special act of Ontario Legislature (c. 0.9) for purpose of providing insurance on deposits by public with member institutions. Every loan corporation and trust company incorporated in Ontario and/or registered to do business in Ontario must be member. (§23). All deposits up to $20,000 per person are insured except those not payable in Canada or in Canadian currency or which are covered by federal legislation. (§25). Annual premiums are payable by member institution and are greater of $500 or 1/30 of 1% of deposits on set date. (§29).

BILLS AND NOTES: See Canada Law Digest.

BILLS OF LADING: See topic Carriers.

BILLS OF SALE: See topic Sales.

BLUE SKY LAW: See topic Securities.

BONDS:

The security to be given in civil proceedings where interim order for recovery of personal property is made must either be bond of guarantee company to which Guarantee Companies Securities Act applies or personal bond with sureties who must be approved by court. (R.P. 44.04). As to security for costs, court has discretion. (R.P. 56.04).

BROKERS:

Statutes and amendments thereto regulate activities and licensing of Real Estate and Business Brokers (c. R.4), Insurance Brokers (c. I.8) (see topic Insurance), Stock Brokers (c. S.5) (see topic Securities), Mortgage Brokers (c. M.39) and Motor Vehicle Dealers (c. M.42) (see topic Motor Vehicles).

Real Estate Brokers.—Licensing of real estate and business brokers is governed by special statute. (c. R.4). Amount and form of bonds to be furnished by brokers and salesmen and amount of fees payable upon registration or renewal of registration are governed by regulations issued by Lieutenant-Governor in Council. (c. R.4, §52). Director of Consumer Protection Division of Ministry of Consumer and Commercial Relations is given wide powers to order investigations to be made. (c. R.4, §15). Registrar of Real Estate and Business Brokers subject to giving registrant opportunity to hearing before Commercial Registration Appeal Tribunal may suspend or revoke registration. (c. R.4, §9). Appeal from decision of Tribunal lies to Divisional Court. (c. M.21, §11). No action may be brought to recover commission unless agreement is in writing signed by party to be charged or broker has obtained offer in writing that is accepted (c. R.4, §23), and unless person bringing action was at time of rendering services registered or exempt from registration (c. R.4, §22). Commission provided must be either agreed amount or percentage of sale price or rental. (c. R.4, §34). Every listing agreement must contain provision that it is to expire on specified date and copy of agreement must be delivered to person signing it immediately after execution. (c. R.4, §35). Registered real estate brokers are deemed to be registered mortgage brokers. (c. M.39, §4).

BULK SALES:

See topic Fraudulent Sales and Conveyances.

CARRIERS:

All railways are common carriers. Railways operating beyond the boundaries of the province are subject to the jurisdiction of the Board of Transport Commissioners for Canada. (R.S.C., c. R-3). See Canada Law Digest.

Bills of Lading.—Consignee named in bill of lading and every endorsee thereof to whom the property passes is vested with all rights of action and is subject to all liabilities in respect to the goods as if the contract named in the bill of lading had been made with himself. (c. M.10, §7). This does not affect vendor's right of stoppage in transitu or right to claim freight against original shipper or owner. Although transferable by endorsement, bills of lading are not negotiable. No endorsee can take better title than had his endorser. (cc. M.10, S.1; R.S.C., c. B-5).

Lien.—Carriers have common law possessory lien on goods for freight, storage, demurrage and terminal charges and expenses necessary for preservation of goods carried, and statutory right to sell on nonpayment of such charges. (R.S.C., c. R-3, §311).

Motor Vehicle Carriers.—See topic Motor Vehicles.

CERTIORARI:

Relief formerly given by prerogative writs of mandamus, prohibition and certiorari, applications in nature thereof and applications for declarations or injunctions now generally available through single procedure of Application for Judicial Review. (c. J.1).

Jurisdiction.—Generally Divisional Court but judge of Ontario Court (General Division) with leave of judge thereof in urgent cases. (§6).

Grounds.—Generally as before, but certiorari extended to any decision in exercise of "statutory power of decision" (§2[2]) and court may ignore technical irregularities (§3).

Proceedings.—By notice of application (R.P. 68.01) setting out grounds and nature of relief sought (§9). Notice must be given to attorney general (§9) and decision maker must on notice file record (§10).

Review.—As previously, court may set aside decision (§2) and make interim orders (§4).

CHARITABLE IMMUNITY: See topic Damages.

CHATTEL MORTGAGES:

See topic Personal Property Security.

CLAIMS:

See topics Estate Trustees; Pleading.

COLLATERAL SECURITY: See topic Pledges.

COLLECTION AGENCIES:

See topic Principal and Agent.

COMMERCIAL CODE:

See topic Personal Property Security.

COMMISSIONS TO TAKE TESTIMONY:

See topic Depositions.

COMMUNITY PROPERTY:

System does not exist in Ontario but Family Law Act (c. F.3) provides for adjustment on death or separation of value of property acquired after marriage allowing for certain deductions and exclusions.

CONDITIONAL SALES:

See topic Personal Property Security.

CONSIGNMENTS: See topic Factors.

CONSTRUCTION LIENS: See topic Liens.

CONSUMER PROTECTION:

Registration of Itinerate Sellers.—No person may carry on business as an "itinerate seller" unless registered under The Consumer Protection Act, (c. C.31). "Itinerate seller" means seller whose business includes soliciting, negotiating or arranging for signing by buyer, at place other than seller's permanent place of business, of executory contract for sale of goods or services, whether personally or by his agent or employee. (§1[k]). Every registration and renewal of registration expires on date shown on certificate of registration. Every applicant for registration must state in application address for service in Ontario, and registered itinerate seller must within five days notify Registrar in writing of any change in address for service and of any change in officers or members if registrant is an association, partnership or corporation. (§12). Every application must be accompanied by prescribed bond. (R.R.O. 176, §8).

Form of Executory Contract.—Every executory contract for sale of goods or services where purchase price, excluding cost of borrowing, exceeds $50, other than an agreement involving variable credit, must be in writing and must contain information prescribed by Act and Regulations. Contract is not binding on buyer unless Act and Regulations are complied with and is signed by both parties and duplicate original copy thereof is in possession of each party thereto. (§19[2]). "Executory contract" means contract between buyer and seller for purchase and sale of goods or services in respect of which delivery of goods or performance of services or payment in full of consideration is not made at time contract is entered into. (§1[i]).

Rescission of certain executory contracts, namely those where a seller solicits, negotiates or arranges for signing by a buyer at a place other than seller's permanent place of business, may be rescinded by delivering notice of rescission in writing to seller within two days after duplicate original of contract was delivered to buyer. Delivery of notice of rescission may be personally or by registered mail to seller's address on contract. (§21).

Lien on Other Goods Not Enforceable.—Any provision in executory contract or in any security agreement incidental thereto under which seller may acquire title to, possession of or any rights in any goods of buyer, other than goods passing to buyer under contract, is not enforceable. (§22).

Buyer in Act means person who purchases goods for consumption or services under an executory contract and includes his agent, but does not include (1) person who buys in course of carrying on business, e.g., buying goods or services for purposes of resale in ordinary course of trade or for use in further production of goods and services, (2) association of individuals, (3) partnership, or (4) corporation. (§1[d]).

Pyramidic Sales.—are prohibited in Canada unless they are licensed or permitted by provincial Act. (R.S.C., c. C-34, as am'd). In Ontario referral sales in connection with direct sales by itinerant sellers are expressly prohibited and any contract made in such sale in which buyer is to receive benefit for doing anything that purports to assist seller in finding or selling to another prospective buyer is not binding on purchaser. (§37[2], [3]).

Consumer Sales.—Conditions and warranties implied under Sale of Goods Act (c. S.1) cannot be excluded from consumer sales. These are sales of goods made in ordinary course of business to purchaser for his consumption or use, except for resale, for use in business, to association, partnership or corporation or by trustee in bankruptcy, receiver, liquidator or person acting under court order. (§34).

Assistance in Finding Another Buyer.—If seller holds out to buyer any such advantage, contract not binding on buyer. Buyer here also includes person hiring or leasing with option to purchase or right to become owner. (§37).

Disclosure of Cost of Borrowing.—Every lender must furnish to borrower, before giving credit, a clear statement in writing showing: (1) sum expressed as one sum in dollars and cents actually to be received in cash by borrower, plus any insurance or official fees; (2) where lender is a seller of goods or services, sum, expressed as one sum in dollars and cents, of cash price of goods or services, plus any insurance or official fees; (3) where lender is a seller, amount to be credited to borrower as a down payment or for a trade-in; (4) where lender is a seller, difference between cash price and amount of any down payment or trade-in-allowance; (5) cost of borrowing expressed as one sum in dollars and cents; (6) percentage that cost of borrowing bears to amount actually received in cash by borrower including any insurance or official fees, expressed as an annual rate on unpaid balance of obligation; (7) where lender is a seller, percentage that cost of borrowing bears to amount which is difference between cash price of goods or services and amount of any down payment or trade-in-allowance, expressed as an annual rate on unpaid balance; (8) basis upon which additional charges are to be made in event of a default in payment; (9) amount, if any, charged for insurance or official fees. (§24). See also topic Interest.

Advertising.—If lender or seller orally represents charge for credit by radio, television or otherwise, he is to provide example of calculation of charge and rate it represents. (§29).

CONSUMER PROTECTION . . . *continued*

Credit Cards and Unsolicited Goods.—Recipient of unsolicited credit card or goods has no obligation to sender unless person to whom credit is to be extended requested or accepted credit arrangement and card in writing and obtaining of credit by person named in credit card is deemed to constitute written acceptance. Recipient of unsolicited goods is under no obligation to sender for use, misuse, damage, theft or misappropriation. (§36[3]).

Consumer Reporting.—The Consumer Reporting Act (c. C.33) imposes obligations upon consumer reporting agencies and other persons in connection with applications received from consumer. Consumer is defined as natural person but does not include person engaging in transaction, other than relating to employment, in course of carrying on business, trade or profession. Obligations imposed are with respect to applications received from consumer for: (1) extension of credit to or purchase or collection of debt of consumer; (2) entering into or renewal of tenancy agreement; (3) for employment purposes; (4) underwriting of insurance involving consumer; (5) direct business need in connection with business or credit transaction involving consumer, or (6) up-dating information in consumer report previously given for one of reasons mentioned above. (§8[1]).

Act prohibits any person from knowingly furnishing any information respecting consumer from files of consumer reporting agency except for one of foregoing purposes or in response to court order, order under Act or in accordance with written instructions of consumer to whom information relates. (§8[2]).

All persons (1) when requested by a consumer in writing or personally to do so must inform him whether or not a report respecting him has been or is to be referred to in connection with any specified transaction or matter in which such person is engaged, and, if so, of name and address of consumer reporting agency supplying report; (2) must notify consumer in writing of intention to obtain from consumer reporting agency consumer report (i) containing personal information (which is defined as information other than credit information about consumer's character, reputation, health, physical or personal characteristics or mode of living or about any other matter concerning consumer) or (ii) in considering extending credit to consumer who has not applied for such credit at time such report is requested; such notice must be given before report is requested, and if requested by consumer to do so, person must supply him name and address of consumer reporting agency supplying report; (3) proposing to extend credit to consumer, must notify consumer of intention to obtain from consumer reporting agency report containing only credit information which is defined as information about consumer as to name, age, occupation, place of residence, previous places of residence, marital status, spouse's name and age, number of dependants, particulars of education or professional qualifications, places of employment, previous places of employment, estimated income, paying habits, outstanding debt obligations, cost of living obligations and assets; such notice must be given to consumer at time of application for credit in writing or orally if application is oral; (4) extending credit to consumer persons are prohibited from divulging to other credit grantors or to consumer reporting agencies any personal information except with consent of consumer or on his referral unless person notifies consumer in writing at time of application for credit of intention to do so; (5) denying a benefit to consumer or increasing a charge to consumer either wholly or partly because of information received from consumer reporting agency or anyone else must notify consumer of fact, and consumer is entitled to request person within 60 days thereafter to inform him of nature and source of information or if information is furnished by consumer reporting agency of name and address of such agency. (§10).

No person shall supply list of names and criteria to consumer reporting agency to determine which names meet those criteria, or in any other way obtain information about consumer from consumer reporting agency (except in compliance with [(3)] in paragraph above), without first informing each person named on list that information is being requested. Consumer reporting agencies have reciprocal restrictions. (§11).

At request of consumer, consumer reporting agency shall give to consumer copy of following information: (a) nature and substance of all information in its files pertaining to consumer; (b) sources of credit information; (c) names and addresses of every person on whose behalf file has been assessed; (d) names of recipients of any consumer report relating to consumer furnished within (i) one year if report contained personal information, and (ii) six months if report contained credit information; and (e) copies of any such written reports. Copy of information given to consumer must be in writing and easily readable and information must be in understandable language. (§12).

Unfair Practices.—Under Business Practices Act (c. B.18), any agreement, whether written, oral or implied, entered into by consumer after consumer representation that is unfair practice and that induced consumer to enter into agreement may be rescinded by consumer and consumer entitled to any remedy thereof that is available at law, including damages, or where rescission is not possible because restitution is no longer possible, or rescission would deprive third party of right in subject matter of agreement that he has acquired in good faith and for value, consumer is entitled to recover amount by which amount paid under agreement exceeds fair value of goods or services received under agreement or damages or both. (§4[1]). Punitive damages may be awarded in case of unconscionable consumer representation. Each person making consumer representation is jointly and severally liable with person who entered into agreement with consumer. Remedy conferred may be claimed by giving written notice to each other party within six months of entering into agreement. Notice must be delivered personally or by registered mail. There can be no waiver of rights conferred. (§4[2]-[8]).

"Consumer" means a natural person but does not include a natural person, partnership or association of individuals acting in course of carrying on business. (§1).

"Goods" means chattels personal or any right or interest therein other than things in action and money, including chattels that become fixtures but not including securities as defined in The Securities Act. (§1).

"Services" means services, (i) provided in respect of goods or of real property, or (ii) provided for social, recreational or self-improvement purposes, or (iii) that are in their nature instructional or educational. (§1).

"Consumer representation" means a representation, statement, offer, request or proposal, (i) made respecting or with a view to supplying of goods or services, or both, to a consumer, or (ii) made for purpose of or with a view to receiving consideration for goods or services, or both, supplied or purporting to have been supplied to a consumer. (§1).

Unfair Practices are a false, misleading or deceptive consumer representation including, but without limiting generality of foregoing, (a) (i) representation that goods or services have sponsorship, approval, performance characteristics, accessories, uses, ingredients, benefits or quantities they do not have, (ii) representation that person who is to supply goods or services has sponsorship, approval, status, affiliation or connection he does not have, (iii) representation that goods are of a particular standard, quality, grade, style or model, if they are not, (iv) representation that goods are new, or unused, if they are not or are reconditioned or reclaimed, provided that reasonable use of goods to enable seller to service, prepare, test, and deliver goods for purpose of sale shall not be deemed to make goods used for purposes of this subclause, (v) representation that goods have been used to an extent that is materially different from fact, (vi) representation that goods or services are available for a reason that does not exist, (vii) representation that goods or services have been supplied in accordance with a previous representation, if they have not, (viii) representation that goods or services or any part thereof are available to consumer when person making representation knows or ought to know they will not be supplied, (ix) representation that a service, part, replacement or repair is needed, if it is not, (x) representation that a specific price advantage exists, if it does not, (xi) representation that misrepresents authority of a salesman, representative, employee or agent to negotiate final terms of proposed transaction, (xii) representation that proposed transaction involves or does not involve rights, remedies or obligations if indication is false or misleading, (xiii) representation using exaggeration, innuendo or ambiguity as to a material fact or failing to state a material fact if such use or failure deceives or tends to deceive, (xiv) representation that misrepresents purpose or intent of any solicitation of or any communication with a consumer; (b) an unconscionable consumer representation made in respect of a particular transaction and in determining whether or not a consumer representation is unconscionable there may be taken into account that person making representation or his employer or principal knows or ought to know, (i) that consumer is not reasonably able to protect his interests because of his physical infirmity, ignorance, illiteracy, inability to understand language of an agreement or similar factors, (ii) that price grossly exceeds price at which similar goods or services are readily available to like consumers, (iii) that consumer is unable to receive a substantial benefit from subject-matter of consumer representation, (iv) that there is no reasonable probability of payment of obligation in full by consumer, (v) that proposed transaction is excessively one-sided in favour of someone other than consumer, (vi) that terms or conditions of proposed transaction are so adverse to consumer as to be inequitable, (vii) that he is making a misleading statement of opinion on which consumer is likely to rely to his detriment, (viii) that he is subjecting consumer to undue pressure to enter into transaction. (§2).

No person shall engage in an unfair practice. (§3). Director may order compliance with §3. Fines are provided.

Plain Language.—No "plain language" statute enacted.

CONTRACTS:

Distributorships, Dealerships and Franchises.—Ontario has no legislation or special rules governing formation and termination of these types of business arrangements. Common law of contract will be applied, for example, to require reasonable notice of termination where not expressly limited by contract.

Frustrated Contracts Act.—Where contract frustrated and parties discharged, sums previously paid are recoverable and sums payable cease to be payable. Court given powers: (1) to allow expenses up to sums paid or payable; (2) to allow for valuable benefit conferred by one party on other or obligation assumed by one for benefit of other; (3) sever contract treating part as not frustrated and part frustrated. Act applies to all contracts governed by Ontario law except charterparty (except time charterparty or charterparty by demise), contracts for carriage of goods by sea, insurance contracts, sales of specific goods which have perished either before contract or without seller's fault before risk passes to buyer. (c. F.34).

Gaming Act.—Contains provisions as to illegality of agreements, bills, etc. relating to games and wagers. (c. G.2).

See topics Frauds, Statute of, Infants, Sales and Seals.

CONVEYANCES: See topic Deeds.

CORPORATIONS:

For non-Ontario incorporated corporations doing business in Ontario, see subhead Foreign and Extra-Provincial Corporations, infra; for non-Ontario corporations making take-over bids to Ontario residents or which are listed on Toronto Stock Exchange or which have distributed equity securities pursuant to an Ontario qualified prospectus since Apr. 30, 1967, see topic Securities, subheads Take-Over Bids, Insider Trading and catchline Insider Liability, Proxy Solicitations, and Continuous Disclosure. This topic, except for subheads Foreign and Extra-Provincial Corporations and Taxation, deals solely with Ontario-incorporated corporations.

Corporations with provincial objects may be created by Special Act of Provincial Legislature, but general legislation of Province regulating incorporation of commercial companies is Business Corporations Act. (c. B.16). Business Corporations Act will generally apply to all corporations incorporated under special or general Act of Legislature of Ontario, other than: (i) corporation within meaning of Loan and Trust Corporations Act, (ii) company within meaning of Corporations Act which has objects in whole or in part of social nature, (iii) corporation to which Co-operative Corporations Act applies, (iv) corporation that is insurer within meaning of Corporations Act, (v) corporation to which Credit Unions and Caisses Populaires Act applies, and (vi) non-share capital companies incorporated under Corporations Act. (§2). Corporations are either offering or non-offering or small business development corporations.

Small business development corporation is corporation registered under Small Business Development Corporations Act, (c. S.12). Small business development corporations must comply with provisions of Business Corporations Act, have never previously carried on business, have equity shares without par value that may be issued for

CORPORATIONS . . . *continued*
aggregate consideration not more than $10,000,000 if corporation offering equity shares to public and not more than $5,000,000 in case of corporation not offering its equity shares to public, have objects only to assist in development of small businesses by providing capital through acquisition and holding of securities or providing business and managerial expertise to small businesses and have equity capital of at least $25,000. (c. S.12, §4). Eligible investments for small business development corporation are prescribed in Act. Holder of equity shares in small business development corporation may apply to Minister for grant equal to 25% of money paid by applicant for equity shares issued to applicant. Small business development corporation is largely exempt from payment of capital tax imposed by Part III of Corporations Tax Act. (c. C.40).

General Supervision.—Ministry of Consumer and Commercial Relations.

Name.—Word "Limited", "Limitée", "Incorporated", "Incorporée" or "Corporation" or corresponding abbreviations "Ltd.", "Ltée", "Inc." or "Corp." shall be part of corporation name. (§10). Every corporation assigned corporation number and where no name specified will be assigned number name consisting of corporation number followed by word "Ontario". (§8). Corporation shall not be incorporated with name containing word or expression prohibited by regulations, or name that is similar to name of known body corporate, trust, association, partnership, sole proprietorship, or individual or known name under which any of same identifies itself, if use of that name is likely to deceive, except as provided by regulation. (§9). Corporate name shall not be too general, only descriptive of quality, function or other characteristics of goods or services, primarily name or surname of individual, primarily geographic name, or primarily combination of punctuation marks. (§11, R.R.O. 62). Certain words or expressions are prohibited on public grounds or because they are expressly prohibited by regulation. (§§13-15, R.R.O. 62). Words connoting connection with government or agency thereof or professional association or that business is one of financial intermediary or stock exchange require consent of appropriate body. Words connoting connection with political party or leader thereof where objects political are prohibited. (§16, R.R.O. 62). Name shall not exceed 120 characters in length. Submitted articles must be accompanied by Ontario biased Consumer and Corporate Affairs, Canada name search and any consents required by Act or regulation. (§§18, 21, R.R.O. 62). If not incorporated or if carrying on business in name other than that in articles, cannot use "Limited", "Incorporated" or "Corporation" or abbreviations thereof. (§ 11).

Business name other than corporate name must be registered. See subhead Reports, infra.

Term of Corporate Existence.—May be perpetual. See subhead Dissolution, infra.

Incorporators.—One or more persons or corporations may incorporate a corporation. Personal incorporators must be at least 18 years old and must not be of unsound mind or have status of bankrupt. (§4). There is no special requirement as to citizenship or residence.

Application.—Articles of incorporation must be in prescribed form and must set out name of corporation; address of registered office; minimum and maximum number of directors; names in full and residential addresses of all first directors and whether resident Canadian; restrictions on business or powers of corporation; classes and any maximum number of shares corporation is authorized to issue; rights, privileges, restrictions and conditions attaching to each class of shares; restrictions on issue, transfer or ownership of shares; and names and addresses in full of incorporators. (§5). Articles may set out any provision authorized by Act to be set out in articles or that could be subject of by-law. First director who is not incorporator must sign consent to act as first director.

Filing of Application.—Filed in duplicate with Minister of Consumer and Commercial Relations. (§§6, 273).

Issue of Certificate of Incorporation.—If application is in order and fees are paid articles of incorporation issue automatically. Date of incorporation is that of certificate of incorporation. (§273).

Incorporation Fee.—$315 for all corporations. (O. Reg. 627/93, §10).

License to Do Business.—Ontario incorporated corporations require no such license. For other corporations, see subhead Foreign and Extra-Provincial Corporations, infra.

Organization.—Incorporators need not be first shareholders or first directors. Organization may be completed without any meetings being held because any by-law or resolution signed by all directors or all shareholders at any time during a corporation's existence is as valid as if passed at regular meeting of directors or shareholders. (§§104 and 129). Special resolutions or special by-laws must be passed by directors and confirmed with or without variation by ⅔ of votes at meeting of shareholders called for that purpose or by written consent of all shareholders entitled to vote at such meeting or their attorneys authorized in writing. (§1).

Paid-in Capital Requirements.—Business can be commenced immediately on incorporation. No condition precedent such as subscription and paying up of any part of its capital is imposed.

Amendment of articles of incorporation may be effected by delivering executed articles of amendment in duplicate to Minister along with required fee. (§171). Cannot change name or decrease capital if insolvent or decrease would render it insolvent. For all amendments fee is $130. (O. Reg. 627/93, §10). Amendments require authorization by special resolution. (§§168, 170). Amendments may also be effected by arrangement. (§182). If articles of amendment are in order and fees paid certificate of amendment is issued and amendment is effective upon date of such issuance. (§172).

Increase or decrease of authorized capital stock may be effected by articles of amendment. On a reduction of capital it must be shown that corporation is not insolvent and it may be necessary to show that no creditors object. (§171). There are restricted provisions for purchase by corporation of its own shares. (§§30-31). See also subhead Powers of Corporation, infra.

Shares.—Shares of corporation shall be without par value. Where only one class of shares exists, rights of holders thereof shall be equal in all respects and include right to vote at all meetings of shareholders. (§22). Preference shares may have any of preferences familiar to modern finance such as preferences as regards to dividends and repayment of capital on dissolution or winding up, right to elect stated proportion of board of directors, etc.

Share warrants are dealt with as investment securities. (§§53-91). Warrant is any instrument entitling holder to purchase share or debt obligation of corporation.

Share Certificates.—Every shareholder is entitled to a properly signed share certificate (§54) stating name of corporation, words to effect that corporation was incorporated under law of Province of Ontario, shareholder's name, number and class of shares represented thereby and any preferences, rights, conditions or restrictions or that such preferences, etc. exist and that copy of full text thereof obtainable from corporation on demand (§56). Unless noted conspicuously on share certificate, restriction on transfer of shares and unanimous shareholder agreement is ineffective except as against person with actual knowledge thereof unless reference to it noted conspicuously on share certificate. (§56). Statutory right of corporation to lien on shares must also be noted conspicuously thereon. (§56).

Issuance of Shares.—Allotment and issue of shares is regulated by directors. Shares must not be issued until fully paid. (§23).

Transfer of Shares.—Statute modelled on Uniform Commercial Code, Art. 8. Upon delivery of a security to a purchaser for value in good faith and without notice of any adverse claim purchaser may take free of any adverse claims. (§69). Where security is in registered form it must be properly endorsed and delivered. (§§72-74). Issuer must register transfer if security is properly endorsed, there has been no notice of any adverse claim, and all applicable laws and transfer restrictions have been complied with. (§86). On death of shareholder, capital gains tax is levied on deemed disposition under Canada Income Tax Act. (See Canada Law Digest.) Unless authorized by articles, corporations must not impose restrictions on transfer of shares. (§42).

Stock Transfer Tax.—None.

Shareholders elect directors (§119) and appoint auditors (§149). Directors are responsible for general supervision of affairs of corporation. (§115). If shareholders are dissatisfied they may replace board of directors at end of their term or remove any director before expiration of term and elect another to fill vacancy. (§122). Shareholders may inspect copies of articles, register of security holders, transfer register and minutes of all shareholders' meetings. (§145). Shareholders holding 5% of issued voting shares may requisition meeting of shareholders (§105) and any shareholder entitled to vote at meeting of shareholders may requisition directors to circulate shareholder's proposal to be considered at next shareholders' meeting (§99). Any shareholder who is entitled to vote at annual meeting of shareholders may make proposal to amend articles. (§§99, 169). Shareholder may apply to court for order directing corporation or officers or directors to comply with any provisions of Act, articles or by-laws of corporation. (§253). If wrong is done to corporation such as where: (a) property or rights of corporation are being appropriated to majority, (b) breach of directors' duty to act bona fide in interests of corporation has been condoned by majority, or (c) majority has enacted resolutions which discriminate so as to give majority advantage of which minority is deprived, and majority refuses to cause corporation to take action, derivative action may be instituted with leave of court by any shareholder. (§246).

Unanimous Shareholder Agreement.—Written agreement among all shareholders of corporation and with or without other persons may restrict in whole or in part powers of directors to manage or supervise management of business and affairs of corporation. (§108).

Shareholders' Liability.—Shareholders not liable for corporate debts or obligations. (§92). On decrease of issued capital by articles of amendment each shareholder on such date may be individually liable to creditors of corporation for debts due on such date up to amount not exceeding amount of repayment to such shareholder. (§34). Notwithstanding dissolution of corporation, shareholders among whom its property has been distributed remain liable to its creditors up to amount received by them respectively but action to enforce such liability must be brought within five years of dissolution. (§243).

Shareholders' Meetings.—Annual meetings must be held within 18 months after incorporation and subsequently not more than 15 months after previous annual meeting unless corporation has only one shareholder and necessary action is taken in writing in time. (§94). General meetings may be called either by directors or by holders of 5% of issued voting shares. (§105). Notice of time and place for holding general meetings must, unless otherwise provided, be given at least ten days prior to meeting of non-offering corporation, and 21 days prior to that of offering corporation. (§96). See also subhead Organization supra.

Voting.—Each share of corporation entitles holder to one vote unless otherwise provided, and shareholder may vote by proxy. (§§102, 110). Nominee appointed by proxy need not be shareholder. Proxy ceases to be valid one year from its date. Form and contents of proxy are prescribed. Proxy may be revoked by instrument in writing deposited either at registered office of company at any time up to and including last business day preceding day of meeting or with chairman of meeting on day of meeting. (§110). For proxy solicitation requirements see topic Securities, subhead Proxy Solicitations.

Where articles or by-laws so provide cumulative voting for directors is permitted. (§120).

In connection with shareholders' meetings offering corporations must comply with timing provisions of National Policy Statement No. 41, put out by Canadian Securities Regulators.

Voting Trust.—Agreement by a shareholder to vote in particular manner is legal and trustee may vote shares registered in trustee's name in accordance with such an agreement. (§108).

Appraisal.—Generally, if corporation resolves to (i) amend its articles to add, remove or change restrictions on issue, transfer or ownership of shares, (ii) amend its articles to add, remove or change any restriction on business or powers of corporation, (iii) amalgamate with another corporation, (iv) be continued under laws of another jurisdiction, or (v) sell, lease or exchange substantially all of its property, holder of

See Topical Index in front part of this volume.

CORPORATIONS . . . *continued*
shares of any class or series entitled to vote on resolution may dissent. Shareholder who dissents and complies with statutory requirements is entitled, when action approved by resolution from which shareholder dissents becomes effective, to be paid by corporation fair value of shares held by such shareholder determined as of close of business on day before resolution was adopted. (§185).

Compulsory Acquisitions.—Person who has made issuer bid or take-over bid (offer made to security holders which, taken together with securities currently owned by offeror, its affiliates and associates, will carry, in aggregate, 10% or more of voting rights attached to voting securities of offeree corporation) and who acquires, within 120 days of date of bid, not less than 90% of securities of any class of securities to which bid relates, other than securities held at date of bid by or on behalf of offeror or affiliate or associate of offeror, is entitled, upon complying with Act, to acquire securities held by dissenting offerees. (§188). Where 90% or more of class of securities of corporation, other than debt obligations, are acquired by or on behalf of person, and person's affiliates and associates, then holder of any securities of that class not counted for purpose of calculating such percentage is entitled in accordance with Act to require corporation to acquire holder's securities of that class at their fair value. (§189).

Oppression remedy is available to all existing and former registered or beneficial holders of shares of corporation or any of its affiliates, existing or former directors or officers of corporation or any of its affiliates, any other person who, in discretion of court, is considered proper person to make such application and, in case of offering corporation, Ontario Securities Commission. Where, upon application by any of parties listed above, court is satisfied that in respect of corporation or any of its affiliates, (a) any act or omission of corporation or any of its affiliates effects or threatens to effect result; (b) business or affairs of corporation or any of its affiliates are, have been or are threatened to be carried on or conducted in manner; or (c) powers of directors of corporation or any of its affiliates are, have been or are threatened to be exercised in manner, that is oppressive or unfairly prejudicial to or that unfairly disregards interests of any security holder, creditors, director or officer of corporation, court may make order to rectify matters complained of. (§248).

Directors.—Corporation not offering its securities to public must have at least one director. Offering corporations must have at least three directors of whom at least one-third shall not be officers or employees of corporation or of affiliate of corporation. (§115). Directors need not be shareholders. Majority must be Canadian citizens ordinarily resident in Canada. (§118). Directors must be over 18 and not undischarged bankrupt or mental incompetent. (§118). Directors may be elected for term of up to but not exceeding three years. Terms of directors need not coincide. (§118). At end of term director must retire but if otherwise qualified is eligible for reelection.

Vacancies in board may generally be filled by appointment by directors remaining in office provided there is quorum but if there is no quorum in office, vacancies must be filled by shareholders. (§124). Directors may designate, specify duties and be appointed to any office of corporation. (§133).

Directors' Meetings.—Business can only be transacted at a directors' meeting at which a quorum is present and at which a majority of those present are Canadian citizens ordinarily resident in Canada. (§126). Meetings may be held over conference telephone. (§126). Any by-law or resolution signed at any time during corporation's existence by all directors is as valid as if passed at meeting. (§129). Unless articles or by-laws provide otherwise majority of directors constitutes quorum but quorum must never be less than greater of $^2/_5$ of board or two. (§126). All meetings must be held where registered office of company is situated unless otherwise authorized by by-laws; unless articles or by-laws otherwise provide majority of meetings in any year must be held in Canada. (§126). See subhead Delegation by Directors, infra.

Powers and Duties of Directors.—Unless articles, by-laws or unanimous shareholder agreement otherwise provide, directors may, by resolution, make, amend or repeal any by-laws that regulate business or affairs of corporation. (§116). Such by-laws unless confirmed in meantime or at general meeting, have force only until next annual meeting of corporation. (§116).

Liabilities of Directors.—Where directors consent to shares of corporation being acquired by it for redemption, purchase or cancellation in contravention of Act or articles, directors are jointly and severally liable to corporation. (§130). Directors who consent to dividend improperly declared are jointly and severally liable to corporation for amount of such dividend. (§130). Directors are jointly and severally liable to clerks, labourers, servants, apprentices and other wage earners of company for all debts due while they are directors for services performed for corporation up to six months wages plus vacation pay accrued for up to 12 months. (§131).

See subhead Liabilities of Officers, infra.

Officers.—Subject to articles, by-laws or any unanimous shareholder agreement, directors may designate offices of corporation, appoint officers, specify their duties and delegate to them powers to manage business and affairs of corporation. One person may hold two or more offices. (§133).

Liabilities of Officers.—Directors or officers authorizing or consenting to a loan or to giving of financial assistance in contravention of §20 are jointly and severally liable to corporation for amounts so distributed to corporation and not otherwise recovered by corporation. (§130). Subject to certain exceptions, §20 prohibits loans to shareholders, directors or employees of corporation or to giving of financial assistance to any persons for purchase or subscription of shares of corporation. By-laws may provide that director or officer may be indemnified against any liability and expenses incurred in respect of suit against such director or officer for anything done or permitted by them in respect of execution of duties of their office and against all other expenses incurred in respect of affairs of corporation. Such director or officer is entitled to indemnity from corporation in respect of all expenses reasonably incurred in defence of such actions if substantially successful on merits of defence and fulfils other requirements of Act. (§136).

Insider Trading.—Directors, officers, persons employed or retained by corporation, persons who beneficially own more than 10% of voting securities of corporation, certain tippees and other insiders of both offering and non-offering corporations under Business Corporations Act will have insider liability to third persons and corporation if, in connection with transaction in security of corporation or any of its affiliates, they make use of any specific confidential information for their own benefit or advantage that, if generally known, might reasonably be expected to affect materially value of security. (§138).

Delegation by Directors.—Subject to articles or by-laws, directors of corporation may appoint from their number managing director, who is resident Canadian, or committee of directors and delegate to such managing director or committee any of powers of directors. (§127).

Principal Office.—Corporation must have registered office in Ontario at location specified in its articles or by directors' or special resolution, as applicable. Its location may be changed to another municipality by special resolution or to another address within same municipality by directors' resolution. (§14). Notice of change of address must be filed within 15 days of special resolution or directors' resolution. (Corporations Information Act, c. C.39, §4).

Powers of Corporation.—Corporation has capacity and rights, powers and privileges of natural person. (§15). No act of corporation including transfer of property to or by corporation is invalid by reason only that act is contrary to its articles, by-laws, unanimous shareholder agreement or Business Corporations Act. (§17). In general, subsidiary corporation may not hold shares in parent. (§28). Corporations are, with some exceptions, prohibited from making loans to shareholders, directors or employees or from giving financial assistance for purchase of, or subscription for, their shares. (§20). Pre-incorporation contract will be binding on either corporation for whose benefit it was intended or person who entered into contract on behalf of corporation (contractor) before its incorporation; corporation may obtain benefit of and become liable under such contract by adopting it in which event contractor ceases to have any rights or obligations under contract. Person with whom contractor enters pre-incorporation contract may apply for court order apportioning liability between contractor and corporation whether or not pre-incorporation contract is adopted by corporation. (§21).

Dividends may be paid in cash or property. (§38). No dividend or bonus can be declared or paid when company is insolvent, or when such dividend or bonus would render corporation insolvent or diminish its capital. (§38).

Sale or Transfer of Corporate Assets.—Sale, lease, exchange or disposition of all or substantially all of property of corporation requires approval by special resolution. See subhead Organization, supra. (§184).

Books and Records.—Every corporation must keep books containing following information: copies of all articles, by-laws and special by-laws, resolutions and special resolutions, names, addresses, holdings, etc. of all shareholders and warrant holders, names, addresses, etc. of all directors and record of share transfers. Every corporation must also keep book of accounts containing following information: receipts and expenditures, sales and purchases, assets and liabilities and all other transactions affecting financing position of corporation. Books must also be kept containing minutes of all proceedings and votes of shareholders and of board of directors. (§140). Registers of security holders and transfers must be kept at registered office unless directors otherwise resolve. Branch registrars and transfer agents may be appointed. Various rights of inspection are given to shareholders, creditors and others subject in some cases to filing an affidavit. (§§145, 146).

Reports.—Prospectuses must be filed as required by Securities Act (c. S.5), upon sale of securities in Province.

Initial notice containing prescribed information must be filed with Minister within 60 days of incorporation, amalgamation, continuation or establishing office or carrying on any business activity in Ontario. Notices of change for every change relating to information in initial notice except change of name of Ontario corporation or retirement and subsequent re-election of director, must be filed within 15 days of change. There is no fee for filing initial notice and notices of change. Duplicates of initial notice and notices of change must be kept available for examination at principal office in Ontario. (Corporations Information Act, c. C.39, §§2, 4 and 5). Corporations in default of filings are not capable of maintaining proceedings in Ontario except with leave of court. (c. C.39, §18).

If corporation is to carry on business in Ontario in name other than corporate name, name must first be registered with Minister. Registration is effective for five years and can be further renewed. Generally, corporations must set out corporate and registered name in all contracts, invoices, negotiable instruments and orders. (Business Names Act, c. B.17). Corporations in default of registration are not capable of maintaining proceedings in Ontario except with leave of court and potentially liable to maximum fine of $25,000. (c. B.17, §§7, 10).

Financial statements as prescribed by Securities Act must be laid before each annual meeting if offering corporation. If non-offering corporation, annual financial statements and auditor's report, if any, to be mailed to shareholders at least ten days before annual meeting. (§154). If offering corporation, annual financial statements and auditor's report to be mailed to shareholders at least 21 days before annual meeting. (§154). Such offering company must also mail detailed quarterly financial statements to shareholders. (c. S.5, §77). Annual and quarterly financial statements must be filed by offering corporation with Ontario Securities Commission (O.S.C.) concurrently with mailing to shareholders within set time periods. (c. S.5, §§77-79).

National Policy Statement No. 41 also governs timing of mailings of financial statements for above shareholders' meetings of offering corporations. For insider trading reports, see topic Securities, subhead Insider Trading and catchline Insider Liability.

For take-over bid circulars and directors circulars and filing requirements therefor, see topic Securities, subhead Take-Over Bids.

For proxy solicitation information circulars, see topic Securities, subhead Proxy Solicitations. Certified copies of circulars and copies of proxies must be filed with O.S.C. (c. S.5, §81; R.R.O. 1015, §§180, 181).

For Ontario tax returns, see subhead Taxation—(a) Provincial Tax, infra.

Penalties are provided for cases of default in making any of above reports or returns. See also subhead Dissolution, infra.

CORPORATIONS . . . *continued*

Returns must also be made under Corporations and Labour Unions Returns Act (R.S.C., c. C.43) and federal Income Tax Act. See Canada Law Digest, topics Corporations; Taxation.

Audits and Inspections.—Corporation is exempt from requirements regarding appointment and duties of auditor and annual audit requirements if such corporation is not offering corporation, its assets do not exceed $100,000,000 and its sales or gross operating revenues do not exceed $100,000,000 and its shareholders so consent. (§148; O. Reg. 400/95, §4). Auditors are entitled to right of access at all times to books, accounts and vouchers of corporation and to such additional information as they may require. They must report annually to shareholders on accounts examined. Inspector may be appointed to investigate affairs and management of corporation either by Supreme Court on application by shareholder, or by O.S.C. if offering corporation. (§161).

Corporate Bonds or Mortgages.—Unless articles or by-laws or unanimous shareholder agreement otherwise provide, articles of corporation shall be deemed to state that directors of corporation may, without authorization of shareholders, borrow money upon credit of corporation, issue, reissue, sell or pledge debt obligations of corporation and mortgage, hypothecate and pledge any property of corporation. (§184).

Corporate Securities Registration.—Corporations Securities Registration Act repealed. See topic Personal Property Security.

Amalgamation.—Two or more Ontario corporations may amalgamate by statutory procedure. (§174). They must first enter into agreement prescribing terms and conditions of amalgamation, mode of carrying it into effect and such other details as may be necessary to perfect amalgamation and provide for subsequent management. This agreement is not effective until approved by special resolutions of each of amalgamating corporations. (§176). Executed articles of amalgamation must be delivered in duplicate to Minister. (§178). Fee is $315. (O. Reg. 627/93, §10). New corporation comes into existence on date of certificate of amalgamation with all its property, rights, privileges, and franchises and subject to all liabilities, contracts, disabilities and debts of each of companies so amalgamated.

Continuations.—Corporation incorporated in jurisdiction other than Ontario may, if it appears to Minister to be thereunto authorized by laws of such jurisdiction, file articles of continuance in duplicate continuing it as if it had been incorporated in Ontario. (§180). Fee is $315. (O. Reg. 627/93, §10).

Transfer of Ontario Corporations.—Corporation incorporated in Ontario may, if authorized by special resolution, Minister and laws of other jurisdiction, apply to that jurisdiction for instrument of continuance as corporation incorporated under laws of that jurisdiction if such jurisdiction has laws containing certain specified provisions. (§181). Fee is $315. (O. Reg. 627/93, §10).

Dissolution.—Corporation may be wound up voluntarily where special resolution requiring it to be wound up is passed at general meeting. (§193). Notice of such resolution must be filed within ten days with Minister and published in Ontario Gazette within 20 days. When winding up commences, company must cease to carry on its undertaking except so far as is necessary for winding up, and some transfers of shares or alterations in status of shareholders are void. (§198). Liquidator must apply property of company in satisfaction of its liabilities pari passu and distribute assets. All costs and expenses of liquidation are payable out of assets in priority to all other claims. Liquidators may be empowered to enter into arrangements with creditors. When winding up is complete, liquidator must make report at general meeting and within ten days file notice with Minister. (§205). Corporation is ipso facto dissolved three months after filing of such notice.

Corporation may also be wound up by order of court. (§§207-218). Winding up order may be made on application of corporation or shareholder, or where corporation is being wound up voluntarily, of liquidator or person liable to contribute to property of corporation upon winding up, or creditor with claim of $2,500 or more. Proceedings are same as for voluntary winding up except that all proceedings are subject to order and direction of court.

Corporation may dissolve voluntarily by delivering articles of dissolution to Minister. Where corporation has been active, dissolution must be authorized by shareholders. (§237). Where corporation has not commenced business and has not issued any shares, dissolution may be authorized by incorporators within two years of date on certificate of incorporation. (§237[c]). In both cases, debts must have been satisfied, property must have been distributed, and there must be no court proceedings pending. Dissolution becomes effective on issue of certificate by Minister. (§239). No fee is payable.

Corporation may be dissolved by Minister where sufficient cause is shown. (§240).

Corporation may also be dissolved by Minister for failure to comply with Ontario tax legislation or for failure to file financial statements as required by securities legislation or for failure to comply with filing requirements under Corporations Information Act. (c.C.39). Interested persons can apply to Minister for revival of corporation. (§241).

Insolvency and Receivers.—See topic Receivers, and Canada Law Digest, topic Bankruptcy.

Distribution of Assets Without Winding Up.—No specific provision.

Close Corporations.—Act does not provide for private companies. Distinction between corporations which do and do not offer their securities to public. (§1[6]).

Loan corporation may be incorporated subject to provisions of Loan and Trust Corporations Act. (c. L.25).

Foreign and Extra-Provincial Corporations.—The Extra-Provincial Corporations Act (c. E.27) provides for three classes of extra-provincial corporations: Class 1—corporations incorporated or continued by or under authority of Act of legislature of province of Canada; Class 2—corporations incorporated or continued by or under authority of Act of Parliament of Canada including corporations incorporated under ordinance of Yukon or Northwest Territories; and Class 3—corporations incorporated or continued under laws of jurisdiction outside of Canada (c. E.27, §2). Extra-provincial corporation within class 1 or 2 may carry on any of its business in Ontario without obtaining licence under Act. (c. E.27, §4[1]). No extra-provincial corporation within class 3 shall carry on any of its business in Ontario without licence under Act (licence fee—$315; O. Reg. 626/93, §3) and no person acting as representative for or agent for any class 3 extra-provincial corporation shall carry on any of its business in Ontario unless corporation has licence under Act. (c. E.27, §4[2]). Extra-provincial corporation does not carry on its business in Ontario by reason only that it takes orders for or buys or sells goods, or offers or sells services, by use of travellers or through advertising or correspondence. (c. E.27, §1[3]). Extra-provincial corporation may make application for licence to Director appointed by Minister of Consumer and Commercial Relations. (c. E.27, §5[1]). Director may make licence subject to restrictions on business of corporation and to such other limitations or conditions as are specified in licence. (c. E.27, §5[5]). Every person who, without reasonable cause contravenes Act or regulations or condition of licence is liable to fine of not more than $2,000 or if such person is corporation to fine of not more than $25,000. (c. E.27, §20).

Reporting requirements and taxation of corporate income are substantially same as for domestic companies. See subheads Reports, supra; and Taxation—(a) Provincial Income Tax, infra.

Appointment of attorney for purpose of service of process on a corporation is required for corporation which must be licenced as extra-provincial corporation. (c. E.27, §19).

Taxation—(a) Provincial Tax.—The Corporations Tax Act (c. C.40) levies provincial income, paid-up capital and other special taxes on corporations. Corporations are also subject to federal income tax under federal Income Tax Act. See Canada Law Digest, topic Taxation.

Provincial Income Tax.—Tax imposed on all corporations wherever incorporated that (1) have permanent establishment in Ontario (2) own real property, timber resource property or timber limit in Ontario income from which arose from sale or rental or is royalty or timber royalty, or (3) disposes of taxable Canadian property (as defined in Federal Income Tax Act) situate in Ontario. Relief available in certain circumstances if corporation is resident in country having tax convention with Canada. Corporation must pay for every fiscal year, tax of 15.5% calculated on its taxable income earned or deemed to be earned in Ontario. Tax credit of 2% of corporation's eligible Canadian profits from manufacturing and processing, mining, farming, logging or fishing carried on in Canada is available, resulting in tax rate of 13.5%. Small business rate on first $200,000 per year of active business income of Canadian-controlled private corporation (CCPC) effectively reduces rate to 9.5%, but is "clawed back" by 4% surtax on taxable income of CCPC from $200,000 to $500,000.

"Permanent establishment" includes branches, mines, oil wells, farms, timberlands, factories, workshops, warehouses, offices, agencies and other fixed places of business. Where corporation carries on business through employee or agent who has general authority to contract for corporation, or has stock of merchandise owned by corporation from which employee or agent regularly fills orders which employee or agent receives, such employee or agent is deemed to operate permanent establishment. Where corporation, otherwise having permanent establishment in Canada owns land in province or territory of Canada, such land is permanent establishment. Nonresident corporation which produced, grew, mined, created, manufactured, fabricated, improved, packed, preserved or constructed, in whole or in part, anything in Canada whether or not corporation exported that thing without selling it prior to exportation is deemed to have maintained permanent establishment where it did any of those things. Use of substantial machinery or equipment in particular place constitutes permanent establishment. Corporation with no fixed place of business has permanent establishment in principal place where its business is conducted. Insurance corporation is deemed to have permanent establishment in each jurisdiction in which it is registered or licensed to do business. Where corporation does not otherwise have permanent establishment in Canada it has permanent establishment in place designated in its charter or by-laws as being its head office or registered office.

Taxable income of corporation for fiscal year is its income for that year earned (or deemed to be earned) in Ontario, minus permitted deductions. Generally, provisions of federal Income Tax Act relating to determination of taxable income of corporations are incorporated by reference. See Canada Law Digest, topic Taxation. Exceptions include certain federal provisions relating to: loans to nonresidents; management fees, rents, royalties and similar payments to related nonresidents (deductibility of which is limited so that they are, in effect, subject to Ontario tax at rate of 5%); meal and entertainment expenses deductible only to extent of 50%; rates of capital cost allowance (depreciation) and resource allowance (for petroleum and mineral properties); deductibility of mineral and petroleum royalties; taxability of capital gains on foreign resource properties; treatment of certain unused tax credits as capital losses; deductibility of certain other corporate taxes; and deductibility of certain exploration and development expenses. In addition, number of federal tax preferences or incentive provisions are not carried through for Ontario corporation tax purposes, including provisions which allow depreciation to be taken on 115% of cost of certain assets and provisions relating to international banking centres.

Amounts Not Included in Income.—Amounts received under certain federal development grant programs and amounts referred to in certain exclusions in federal Income Tax Act which are incorporated by reference.

Additional Taxes Imposed.—Paid-up capital tax 3/10 of 1% (1.12% for banks and for corporations registered under Loan and Trust Corporations Act, plus temporary 0.112% surcharge in respect of taxable paid-up capital exceeding $400 million, less tax credit available in respect of certain investments in Ontario small businesses) of taxable paid-up capital is payable annually by corporations having permanent establishment in Ontario and by corporations incorporated outside Canada owning real property, timber resource property or timber limit in Ontario. Exemption for corporations with total assets and gross revenues not exceeding $1 million. Flat rate tax of: (1) $100 where total assets or gross revenues exceed $1 million but taxable capital under $1 million; (2) $200 if total assets and gross revenues less than $1.5 million and taxable capital between $1 million and $2 million; (3) $500 where total assets or gross revenues exceed $1.5 million and taxable capital between $1 million and $2 million. Notch provision for corporations with taxable capital between $2 million and $2.3

See Topical Index in front part of this volume.

CORPORATIONS . . . *continued*
million. Special tax in lieu of paid-up capital tax is imposed on insurance corporations based on gross premiums. Special premiums tax on life insurance companies.

Exemption from income tax is granted to certain types of corporations, primarily governmental and nonprofit organizations (including charities), labour organizations, pension corporations and certain insurers and housing corporations. These generally follow same scheme as federal Income Tax Act, but rule is different for certain nonprofit organizations which are not charities. Generally, corporations which are exempt from income tax are exempt from paid-up capital tax.

Returns.—Corporation must deliver a return to Minister of Revenue within six months of end of its taxation year.

Payments.—Tax must be paid in monthly instalments. If estimated tax payable less than $2,000, may be paid in full by end of second month of next taxation year (or end of third month if CCPC with less than $200,000 of income). There are provisions for interest and penalties in respect of late payment of taxes, payment of instalments and filing of returns. Failure to deliver return, to keep books and records, and contravention of investigation provisions are offences.

Liens.—Taxes, interest and penalties constitute first lien and charge against real property or any interest therein, or against personal property, of corporation upon registration in proper registry office of notice claiming such lien.

Objections and Appeals.—A corporation may object to Minister of Revenue within 180 days from day of mailing of notice of assessment, with a right to appeal to Ontario Court (General Division). Minister may extend time for objection upon application made within one year after mailing date and may extend time for appeal upon application made within 90 days after confirmation of assessment.

Penalties.—For failure to file return: 5% of deficiency in corporation's tax account. Other penalties for false statements, destroying records and evading compliance, failing to comply with written demand from Minister of Finance. Ontario corporation may be dissolved for default under Corporations Tax Act.

Corporate Minimum Tax.—Corporations with gross revenues in excess of $10 million or total assets in excess of $5 million (associated corporations being grouped for this purpose) are required to pay corporate minimum tax (CMT) to extent it exceeds corporate income tax otherwise payable. Starting point for calculation of base on which this tax is imposed is net income after extraordinary items but before tax, as shown on financial statements. This is reduced by: inter-corporate dividends (to extent deductible under federal Income Tax Act); gains on tax-deferred rollovers; and losses carried forward from up to ten prior years (including three years prior to introduction of CMT). If corporation operates outside Ontario, portion of resulting "CMT base" will be allocated to Ontario by formula already used to allocate taxable income of multi-jurisdictional corporations. CMT rate of 4% for 1996 and following years (prorated for tax years that straddle Jan. 1, 1996) will be applied to Ontario CMT base to determine gross CMT. Credits will then be allowed for regular corporate income tax for year and certain foreign taxes on investment income, to arrive at net CMT. Net CMT payable may be carried forward up to ten years and applied as credit against regular corporate income tax. Investment corporations, mortgage investment corporations, mutual fund corporations, nonresident owned investment corporations, communal organizations and income tax exempt corporations are exempt from minimum tax.

Employer Health Tax.—Employer Health Tax Act (c. E.11) requires all employers (corporations and individuals) to remit applicable percentage of annual gross employee wages, salary and other remuneration (.98% of total up to $200,000; graduated rate of total between $200,001 and $400,000; 1.95% of total over $400,000). Remittances required monthly if total annual payroll exceeds $400,000. *Note:* Under proposed legislation, $400,000 exemption is to be phased in starting in 1997.

Taxation—(b) Federal Income Tax.—See Canada Law Digest, topic Taxation.

Taxation—(c) Corporate Property.—See topic Taxation, subhead Property Taxes; see also topic Deeds, subhead Taxes.

Taxation—(d) Corporate Stock.—None.

Taxation—(e) Franchise Tax.—No annual tax on right to do business in Ontario.

Professional corporations may not be incorporated if profession is regulated by a separate Act unless that Act permits incorporation. Professionals in medicine, law, accountancy, and dentistry have not been accorded right to incorporate. Governing legislation for professional engineers, pharmacists and dental technicians permit corporate form subject to specific conditions.

See also topic Securities.

COSTS:

Costs as between party and party in litigation generally follow the event. Award of costs is discretionary and award or refusal will not be lightly interfered with. (c. C.43, §131).

Range of costs awarded is generally fixed by statutory tariff which allows assessment officer discretionary jurisdiction with regard to certain items as circumstances of case require.

Defendant may after appearance make payment into court in satisfaction; if plaintiff does not recover more at trial, judge should, unless there is cogent reason, order plaintiff to pay costs incurred after payment into court.

Costs as between solicitor and his or her client are not fixed by statute but, in default of special agreement, may be assessed by assessment officer at instance of solicitor or client. Fees are fixed having regard to work done, results achieved and skill employed, in accordance with well established practice.

Where plaintiff makes offer to settle at least seven days before commencement of trial, and offer is not withdrawn or accepted by defendant, and plaintiff obtains judgment as favourable as or more favourable than offer to settle, plaintiff is entitled to costs as between solicitor and client from date of delivery of offer to settle. (R.P. 49.10). Where defendant makes offer to settle at least seven days before commencement of trial and offer is not withdrawn or accepted by plaintiff, and plaintiff obtains judgment as favourable as or less favourable than offer to settle, defendant is entitled to party and party costs from date of delivery of offer to settle. (R.P. 49.10).

Security for costs may be ordered, on motion by defendant, i.e. plaintiff will be required to post security in sum equal or proportional to defendant's estimated cost of defending action, where: Plaintiff is ordinarily resident outside Ontario or has another proceeding for same relief pending in Ontario; plaintiff is corporation or nominal plaintiff or there is good reason to believe that action is frivolous and vexatious, and it is reasonable to believe that plaintiff has insufficient assets in Ontario to pay costs of defendant; or where defendant holds unsatisfied order for costs against plaintiff in any proceeding or is entitled by statute to security for costs. (R.P. 56.01). Motion for security for costs available only after defendant has delivered defence, and must be made on notice to plaintiff and every defendant who has delivered defence or notice of intent to defend. (R.P. 56.03). Amount and form of security and time for payment into court are determined by court. (R.P. 56.04). Proceedings, except appeal from order itself, are stayed until security has been given, unless otherwise ordered by court. (R.P. 56.05). Upon default in giving security, action against defendant who obtained order may be dismissed. (R.P. 56.06). Amount of security may be increased or decreased at any time. (R.P. 56.07). Judge of appellate court, on motion of respondent, can make order for security for costs of appeal in certain circumstances. (R.P. 61.05a).

Liability of Solicitor.—A solicitor may be ordered to personally pay costs of his client or any other party to action in certain circumstances (R.P. 57.07), but this occurs rarely.

COURTS:

Court of civil and criminal jurisdiction is Ontario Court of Justice which is comprised of two divisions, Ontario Court (General Division) and Ontario Court (Provincial Division). Ontario Court (General Division) has unlimited monetary jurisdiction combining former jurisdictions of High Court, District Court, Surrogate Court and Small Claims Court. Ontario Court (General Division) sits in each of eight judicial regions of province created in 1990. Divisional Court is branch of General Division having appellate jurisdiction in certain instances. See topic Appeal and Error. Small Claims Court is also branch of Ontario Court (General Division) with monetary jurisdiction of $6,000. Ontario Court (Provincial Division) combines former jurisdictions of Criminal Division and Family Division of Provincial Court as well as provincial Offences Court. General appellate court remains Court of Appeal for Ontario. See topic Appeal and Error.

As a result of reorganization of Ontario court system there are changes in names of various courts. Throughout Ontario Law Digest, references to Supreme or High Court, District Court, Surrogate Court and Small Claims Court are now to Ontario Court (General Division).

Appellate Courts.—See topic Appeal and Error.

CREDITORS' SUITS:

Action (see topic Actions) may be brought by any creditor against debtor or debtor's estate. To expedite proceedings creditor may move for summary judgment (see topic Judgments, subhead Summary Judgment). Where claim has value of $25,000 or less there are cost consequences for not proceeding under applicable rules or in appropriate court.

If debt owing to debtor by third party is ascertained amount such third party can be directed to make payment to sheriff who can then direct payment to judgment creditor, or in Small Claims Court garnishee summons may be issued before judgment in certain circumstances.

See also topics Attachment; Garnishment; Execution; Limitation of Actions.

CRIMINAL LAW:

In addition to procedure set out in Canada Law Digest, Provincial Offences Act, c. P.33 provides that proceedings in respect of summary convictions offences may be commenced by filing certificate of offence.

Compensation may be available to victim (or dependent) of violent crimes under Compensation for Victims of Crime Act, c. C.24.

CURTESY:

Curtesy abolished, effective Mar. 31, 1978.

DAMAGES:

Common law rules generally prevail. Defendant cannot rely on plaintiff's contributory negligence as complete defence in action, but court must apportion damages in proportion to degree of negligence found against each party. (c. N.1). If person is injured or killed by fault or neglect of another where person is or would have been entitled to recover damages, spouse (as defined in Part III Family Law Act), children, grandchildren, parents, grandparents, brothers and sisters of person are entitled to maintain action and to recover their pecuniary loss including expenses incurred for benefit of person injured or killed, funeral expenses, travelling expenses incurred in visiting person during treatment or recovery, claimant's allowance for providing person with nursing, housekeeping or other services, and amount to compensate for loss of care, guidance and companionship. (c. F.3, §61). Action must be brought within two years from time cause of action arose. (§61). In assessing damages any insurance payable for injury must not be considered. (§63). Doctrine of charitable immunity is not part of law of Ontario. Lavere v. Smith's Falls Public Hospital, 35 O.L.R. 98. Court may give guidance to jury and parties may make submissions to jury on amount of damages. (c. C.43, §118).

Sovereign Immunity.—No legislation.

See topic Motor Vehicles, subhead No-Fault Insurance and topic Death, subhead Action for Death.

DEATH:

A person who is absent and unheard from for seven years is presumed to be dead. Where a claim is made under a life insurance policy, based on the presumption of death from absence, the insurer may make summary application to the Court for a declaration as to such presumption. (c. I.8, §209). Where spouse is missing and unheard from for seven years, and reasonable inquiries have been made, married

See Topical Index in front part of this volume.

DEATH... *continued*
person may apply to judge for declaration that spouse is dead to enable applicant to obtain licence to marry. Such declaration has no other effect. (c. M.3, §9).

Survivorship.—Where two persons die at same time or in circumstances rendering it uncertain which survived, estate of each disposed of as if he or she had survived. Joint tenants who so die, are deemed to have been tenants in common and above rule applies. But where life insured so dies insurance money payable as if beneficiary predeceased life insured.

Action for Death.—(a) Where person is killed by fault or neglect of another under circumstances that would have entitled person to recover damages if not killed, spouse (as defined in Part III of Family Law Act), children, grandchildren, parents, grandparents, brothers and sisters of person may recover their pecuniary loss resulting from death, from person from whom person killed would have been entitled to recover. (c. F.3, §61). Damages may include reasonable funeral expenses and other expenses reasonably incurred for benefit of person killed and compensation for loss of guidance, care and companionship. (§61). Action must be commenced within two years after cause of action arose. (§61). Person liable may pay into court sum to be apportioned by court among plaintiffs entitled to recover. (§62). In assessing damages court is not to consider any insurance payable on death. (b) Deceased's right of action in tort (except libel and slander) maintainable by personal representatives or administrator ad litem appointed by judge for benefit of estate within one year of death. No damages for death or loss of expectation of life. (c. T.23, §38).

Gifts of Human Tissue.—See topic Estate Trustees, subhead Human Tissue Gift Act.

Certificate.—See topic Records, subhead Vital Statistics.

DECEDENTS' ESTATES:

See topics Descent and Distribution; Estate Trustees; Wills.

DECLARATORY JUDGMENTS: See topic Judgments.

DEEDS:

Under Land Registration Reform Act (c. L.4) term "deed" is no longer applicable. Term "transfer" is used to cover all conveyances of freehold and leasehold lands. (c. L.4, §1). Transfers required for real property (c. C.34, §§3, 9, 10) and most leases. See topic Landlord and Tenant. No consideration necessary. Recording Acts impose formal requirements. See topic Records. Affidavits under Family Law Act may be replaced by statements contained in body of transfer. (c. L.4). Family Law Act statements may be made by attorney with personal knowledge. (c. F.3, §21[4]). Spouse must consent to transfer of matrimonial home. (c. F.3, §21[1]). See topic Husband and Wife, subhead Status.

Execution.—Common law requirements as to signing, sealing and delivery, as modified by statute. Transfers and charges in statutory form effective without seals. (c. L.4, §13). See topics Husband and Wife, subhead Status; and Real Property.

Recording.—See particular recording requirements under topic Records.

Operation and Effect.—No words of limitation necessary (c. C.34, §5); conveyance passes all estate, etc. (§5), and ancillary rights (§15). Covenants as to title deemed to be included in transfer in prescribed form. (c. L.4, §5). Planning Act (c. P.13, §50) prohibits any transaction dealing with less than whole of lot on plan of subdivision and any transaction in which grantor retains any abutting lands unless transaction fits within Act's exceptions. It prohibits subdivision of land by will as way of avoiding subdivision control requirements of Planning Act and applies where testator dies on or after July 26, 1990. (c. P.13, §50.1).

Taxes.—
Land Transfer Tax Act (c. L.6), payable on purchase of land in Ontario. See subhead Land Transfer Tax under topic Taxation.
Retail Sales Tax.—Payable on valuation of chattels and items of tangible personal property passing with conveyance unless otherwise exempted under statute. See topic Taxation, subhead Sales Tax.

Forms

Transfer.—Transfers under both Registry Act and Land Titles Act shall be in Form 1. (R.R.O. 688, as am'd). See topic Records.
Special Requirements for Particular Parties.—Corporations may execute instrument by signature of authorized person along with either corporation's seal affixed thereto, or person's statement that he or she has authority to bind corporation. Natural persons must be described by surname and by first given name in full, followed by another given name, if any, in full. Married women: No special requirements. Attorneys: Requirement for registration of power of attorney and instrument must refer to registration number and date and state that to best of attorney's knowledge and belief, power of attorney is still in full force and effect and that principal was at least 18 when power of attorney executed.

Condominiums.—See topic Real Property.

DEEDS OF TRUST:

See topic Mortgages of Real Property.

DEPOSITIONS:

Unless Rules of Civil Procedure provide otherwise, witnesses at trial must be examined orally in court and such examination may consist of direct examination, cross-examination and reexamination. (R.P. 53.01[1]). At or before trial, court may make order allowing evidence of witness or proof of particular fact or document to be given by affidavit, unless adverse party reasonably requires attendance of deponent for cross-examination. (R.P. 53.02[1]).

Examinations Out of Court.—Party intending to introduce evidence of person at trial may, with leave of court or consent of parties, examine person on oath or affirmation before trial and may tender such testimony as evidence at trial. In granting leave, court will consider convenience of witness, possibility that witness will be unavailable for trial due to death, infirmity, sickness or being beyond jurisdiction of court at time of trial, expense of bringing witness to trial and whether witness ought to give evidence in person. (R.P. 36.01). Such witness may be examined, cross-examined and reexamined in same manner as witness at trial. (R.P. 36.02). Where court makes order for examination of witness outside Ontario, order shall, if moving party so requests, provide for issue of commission and letter of request enabling assistance of foreign court to be sought to compel attendance of witness. (R.P. 36.03). Any party at trial may use transcript, videotape or other recording of such examination as evidence of that witness, unless court rules otherwise. (R.P. 36.04). Procedures for examination are prescribed by rules. (R.P. 34).

Compelling Attendance of Witnesses.—Party requiring attendance of person in Ontario as witness at trial may personally serve person with summons to witness, which compels person to attend at trial and may also require person to produce at trial documents or such other evidence as specified in summons. (R.P. 53.04). As to compelling attendance of witnesses outside Ontario in Ontario proceedings, see subhead Examinations Out of Court, supra, and R.P. 34.07.

Letters Rogatory.—Court may order letters rogatory to issue in aid of a commission where the assistance of a foreign court is necessary to compel attendance of witness. (R.P. 34.07). Court may render similar assistance to foreign court where in pending action in such court obtaining of evidence of a witness in Ontario has been authorized. Order may be made in proper court in Ontario compelling attendance of witness for examination before appointed person upon payment of conduct money, expenses, etc. (c. E.23, §60).

DESCENT AND DISTRIBUTION:

Succession Law Reform Act (c. S.26) determines devolution of real and personal property of intestate and testate decedent, subject to spouse's entitlement under Family Law Act (c. F.3, §5), rights of surviving owners of joint property and rights of named beneficiaries under Insurance Act (c. I.8, §§190-196). See topics Divorce; Husband and Wife; Estate Trustees, subhead Dependants' Allowances.

Death of Man or Woman.—There is no difference in devolution based on sex but see definition of spouse in subhead Intestate Succession, infra.

Family Law Act, Election.—Surviving spouse can elect Family Law Act entitlement to estate of deceased or to take under will or to receive intestate entitlement. (c. F.3, §§5, 6). If spouse elects Family Law Act entitlement: deemed revocation of gifts to spouse in will unless will provides otherwise; deemed disclaimer of intestate entitlement (c. S.26), and life insurance policies owned by deceased on deceased's life and group insurance and lump sum pension or similar plan amounts to spouse as designated beneficiary credited against Family Law Act entitlement and excess is claim of estate unless designation to contrary. Election and application must be within six months after death (with some rights to extend time) or else deemed election for will or for intestate share. (c. F.3, §6). (See topics Estate Trustees; Wills.)

Testate Succession.—See topic Wills.

Intestate Succession.—Spouses' intestate entitlement is all of estate if no surviving issue of deceased. (c. S.26, §44). Otherwise spouse receives $200,000 (O. Reg. 54/95) and share of residue: 1/3 to spouse and 2/3 equally to children or deceased's more remote issue of nearest degree in which there are surviving issue, with share of any predeceased child or issue in that degree receiving such deceased's share in similar manner (not necessarily per stirpital distribution); if only one child, 1/2 to spouse and 1/2 to child or issue (similar distribution to 2/3 above). If no spouse, children or their issue take all (similar distribution to 2/3 above). If no spouse or issue, estate goes to (in order): Surviving parent(s); surviving brothers and sisters, if any, (children of deceased brother or sister taking parent's share without representation); if no surviving brother or sister, equally to surviving nieces and nephews without representation; next of kin of equal degree without representation. Next of kin determined according to §47. Spouse receives preferential treatment even if deceased leaves infant children of former marriage. (§§45, 46, 47). See topics Divorce; Husband and Wife.

Spouse.—For intestacy is someone married to, or good faith party to void or voidable marriage with, person of opposite sex and can include party to some polygamous marriages. (c. S.26, §1). In wills, spouse is person intended by testator. *Note:* There is some possibility validity of definition might be challenged.

Half Blood.—On intestacy next of kin of half blood take equally with those of whole blood (c. S.26, §47) (note: is some question as to application to classes who take in priority to next of kin). Under wills, gifts to class of persons generally includes those of half blood as well as whole blood, subject always to intent of testator.

Posthumous Children.—On intestacy, children, other descendants and relatives of deceased conceived before and born alive after his death inherit as though born in his lifetime and had survived him. (c. S.26, §47). In wills, gift to class of persons, particularly if described as children, generally includes those conceived before but born after death of testator, subject always to intent of testator.

Illegitimate Children.—Relationships whether by blood or marriage include relationships by births or traced through births outside marriage (c. S.26, §1), subject to contrary intention in will.

Adopted Children.—Treated as natural child and all relationships, whether to family before adoption or to new family, determined accordingly. Applies on intestacy and under will whenever made, subject to contrary intention in will and with some exceptions for interests vested prior to adoption or before Nov. 1, 1985. (c. C.11, §§158-159).

Advancements.—On intestacy, advancements of real or personal property to child, expressed or acknowledged as such in writing, are reckoned as part of parent's estate for purposes of distribution. (Estates Administration Act [c. E.22, §25]). Generally similar principle respecting gifts made after will, including where testator in loco parentis, but subject to intention of testator.

Election.—Family Law Act Election: See subhead Family Law Act, Election, supra. Curtesy: Abolished for deaths on or after Mar. 31, 1978. (c. S.26, §§48, 49). Dower: Abolished, (R.S.O. 1980, c. 152, §70) except for rights to dower vested before Mar.

See Topical Index in front part of this volume.

DESCENT AND DISTRIBUTION . . . *continued*
31, 1978 (S.O. 1978, c. 2, §70[4]), therefore intestate share of wife no longer requires election.

Escheat and Bona Vacantia.—Where person dies in whole or part intestate without lawful heirs, person's real and personal property passing on intestacy vested in Crown in right of Province. (c. E.20, §1 and c. S.26, §47). Person with legal or moral claim may sometimes obtain transfer of property. (c. E.20, §3).

Where person dies in Ontario intestate, leaving no known next of kin in Ontario or where next of kin are minors and no near relative in Ontario willing and able to apply for grant, or to nominate person to apply for grant, Public Guardian and Trustee may obtain appointment as estate trustee for benefit of Her Majesty or such persons as may ultimately appear entitled thereto. (c. C.47, §2). Moneys obtained by Public Guardian and Trustee from such estates and unclaimed for ten years must be paid into Consolidated Revenue Fund. (§10). Any person claiming such moneys may apply to Ontario Court (General Division), and upon proving title thereto is entitled to receive same with interest. (c. C.47, §§11, 12). See also topic Estate Trustees.

See note on Public Guardian and Trustee under topic Estate Trustees, subhead Accounts.

DESERTION: See topic Husband and Wife.

DISPUTE RESOLUTION:

Court-based.—Up until Mar. 1996, pilot project offered as alternative to conventional litigation process in Toronto Region. Pilot project was well-received and successful. Plans are in progress to install on permanent basis some form of court annexed alternative dispute resolution. Particulars, including procedures and rules, are not finalized at date of editing.

Private.—Any time during action, parties may agree to submit to jurisdiction to private judge subject to Arbitration Act, S.O. 1991, c. 17. Binding resolution only achieved by relying on Act. Parties bound by Act including procedure except so far as Act permits variation by agreement. (3). Awards final but appealable to judge of Ontario Court (General Division) subject to contrary agreement. Award enforceable with leave in same manner as court judgment. Nonbinding dispute resolution such as mediation or pretrial available if party's desire on consent.

DIVORCE:

Divorce throughout all Provinces is governed by Divorce Act, R.S.C. (2nd Supp.), c. 3. See Canada Law Digest, topic Divorce. Procedure in divorce or corollary relief action governed and administered by Rules of Civil Procedure.

Process.—Divorce action is commenced by issuing petition for divorce. (R.P. 69.03[1]). Marriage certificate or marriage registration certificate must be filed prior to issuing petition, unless petition states that certificate cannot be produced or that it shall be filed later. (R.P. 69.03[2]). Where petition contains claim for support or division of property, financial statement in form specified must be filed and served with petition, and respondent spouse must deliver financial statement with answer. (R.P. 69.14[1]). Petition may, in addition to personal service, be served by mail with acknowledgment of receipt card or by acceptance of service by solicitor. (R.P. 69.04). Petition must be served within six months after issue (R.P. 69.05) and if served personally must be served by someone other than petitioner (R.P. 69.04[4]). It is not necessary to name other person alleged to have participated in matrimonial offence. (R.P. 69.03[4]).

Pleadings in divorce action consist of petition, answer and reply, if any, contents of which are prescribed (R.P. 69.06), as well as financial statements from both parties whether or not action is contested, in form prescribed by Rules of Civil Procedure, which may be waived by both parties in certain circumstances (R.P. 69.14[3]). Respondent wishing to oppose claim made in petition must deliver answer, or notice of intent to defend, within prescribed time. (R.P. 69.07). Respondent claiming any relief against petitioner, other than dismissal of action and costs, must deliver counterpetition, contents of which are prescribed. (R.P. 69.09).

Children.—Special provisions for process, pleading and practice where child of marriage under 16.

Judgment.—Where divorce is uncontested or undefended, party may move for judgment. Party moving for judgment must file following documents with notice of motion for judgment: Affidavit of evidence, original marriage certificate or certified copy, copies of draft divorce judgments and other documents as prescribed. Documents are to be filed in form of record which must be set down with Registrar of Court. (R.P. 69.19). Registrar will present motion to judge who may or may not grant motion in accordance with draft. (R.P. 69.19[10]-[11]). Certificate of divorce shall be issued when divorce has taken effect where no appeal pending. (R.P. 69.22). Where matter is defended or contested, divorce action continues according to Rules of Civil Procedure governing actions subject to exceptions contained in Rule 69. Fees are payable to Registrar of Ontario Court (General Division) at commencement of divorce action and at times of setting matter down.

Interim Relief for Support, Custody and Disbursements.—Notice of motion for interim relief may be served at same time as, or any time after, petition or counterpetition is served, and court may direct pre-motion with view to settling any or all issues raised by motion or action. (R.P. 69.15). Respondent may serve on petitioner at any time offer to settle any or all claims in petition. (R.P. 49).

Maintenance, Custody of Children, etc.—Maintenance orders of reciprocating jurisdictions may be enforced in Ontario. (Reciprocal Enforcement of Support Act, c. R.7 [§2] and Family Support Plan Act, R.S.O. 1990, c. S.28, am'd by S.O. 1991, c. 5, §3[7]). "Support Deduction Order" made at same time as any support order, and may be sent to payer's employer who must deduct. (c. 5, §§3.1, 3.3). Support or maintenance orders from Ontario courts will be enforced by Director of Family Support Plan pursuant to Family Support Plan Act, §3, unless recipient spouse withdraws order. Custody can be similarly enforced. Bill C-79, Act to amend Divorce Act and Family Orders and Agreements Enforcement Assistance Act, S.C. 1993, c. 8, in force Mar. 25, 1993 except §15, facilitates process of tracing individuals alleged to have abducted child by allowing access to federal information banks. Governing consideration in custody orders is best interests of children. See topic Guardian and Ward, subhead Custody of Infants.

Separation Agreements.—Ontario Court (General Division) has no jurisdiction to grant decree of judicial separation. Family Law Act provides for domestic contracts, which include separation agreements, marriage contracts and cohabitation agreements. (c. F.3, §51). Man and woman who cohabited and are living apart may enter into separation agreement. Agreement, if in writing, signed by parties and witnessed, may provide for ownership in or division of property, support obligations, right to direct education and moral training of children, right to custody of and access to children, and any other matter in settlement of parties' affairs. (§54). Written marriage contracts entered into before or during marriage may, upon dissolution of marriage, govern same matters except custody or access to children and possession of matrimonial home. (§52). Court may always disregard provisions governing children when children's best interests are not met. (§56). Clauses in such agreements making any rights contingent on party remaining chaste are unenforceable, but subsection does not negate contingency upon marriage or cohabitation with another. (§56). See also topic Husband and Wife, subhead Domestic Contracts.

Remarriage.—Domestic contracts may provide that rights of parties are contingent upon no remarriage or cohabitation. (c. F.3, §56). Otherwise there are no restrictions on remarriage of divorced persons. But see topic Marriage, subhead Licence, Banns or Special Permit.

Foreign Divorces.—A foreign divorce is recognized in the Province if either former spouse was ordinarily resident in that country or subdivision which granted divorce for at least one year immediately preceding commencement of proceedings for divorce, or, if after July 1, 1968, if pursuant to law of another country by tribunal or other authority having jurisdiction to do so on basis of wife's domicile determined as if she was unmarried, and if she was minor, as if she had attained age of majority. (Divorce Act, R.S.C. [2nd Supp.], c.3, §22). It is immaterial that foreign divorce was granted on grounds not recognized in Province. For foreign divorce domicil of wife is that of her husband. See Canada Law Digest, topic Divorce, subhead Jurisdiction.

Annulment of Marriage.—See topic Marriage.

DOWER:

Dower abolished effective Mar. 31, 1978. (Family Law Reform Act, S.O. 1978, c. 2, §70).

ELECTION:

See topics Descent and Distribution; Wills.

EMPLOYER AND EMPLOYEE:

See topic Labour Relations.

ENVIRONMENT:

General Supervision.—Extensive regulation by Ministry of the Environment and Energy ("MOEE") under Environmental Protection Act, c. E.19 and regulations in relation to discharges and spills, waste management, motors and motor vehicles, sewage, ozone-depleting substances, PCBs. Waste management also regulated by R.R.O. 347. Water pollution also regulated by Ontario Water Resources Act, c. O.40, and pesticides by Pesticides Act, c. P.11. Dangers to public health in general regulated by Ministry of Health pursuant to Health Protection and Promotion Act, c. H.7. Provincial Occupational Health and Safety Act, c. O.1 requires extensive disclosure of information and special training for workers exposed to hazardous materials. Environmental Assessment Act, c. E.18, for public and designated private undertakings. Other legislative sources of regulation: Environmental Bill of Rights, S.O. 1993, c. 28; Mining Act, c. M.14; Aggregate Resources Act, c. A.8; Dangerous Goods Transportation Act, c. D.1; Gasoline Handling Act, c. G.4; Waste Management Act, 1992, S.O. 1992, c. 1; Planning Act, R.S.O. 1990, c. P.13, as amended by S.O. 1994, c. 23; municipal sewer by-law restrictions.

Prohibited Acts of Pollution.—Very broad definition of "adverse effect" in relation to discharges and spills into natural environment, including impairment of environmental quality, adverse effects on health or safety, or property damage. Discharges in excess of amounts prescribed by regulation also prohibited. Regulations cover all types of pollution. Common law doctrines (nuisance, negligence, strict liability, riparian rights) still apply.

Penalties.—Extensive penalties; fines up to $10,000 on first conviction for each day on which offence occurs; corporations may be subject to fines up to $50,000 per day on first conviction and up to $200,000 per day on first conviction for discharges resulting in actual pollution. Individuals may be subject to prison terms for certain offences.

Liability.—Most offences subject to defence of due diligence. Corporate directors subject to personal duty of reasonable care to prevent corporation from causing or permitting environmental damage. Statutory civil cause of action for spills. Substantial cleanup liabilities for current and previous owners and occupiers of real estate. (c. E.19).

Enforcement.—Where pollutant is spilled, Minister may make order requiring doing of everything practicable to prevent, eliminate and ameliorate adverse effects, and to restore natural environment. (c. E.19, §97). Broad range of administrative orders may be issued by MOEE Director. Extensive powers of investigation.

Permits and Approvals.—Permits required for waste management systems and waste disposal sites, sewage systems, sources of contaminant emission, and development of land on former waste disposal sites.

EQUITY: See topic Actions.

ESCHEAT:

See topics Descent and Distribution; Absentees.

ESTATES: See topic Real Property.

ESTATE TRUSTEES:

Note: Terminology in Rules of Practice changed Jan. 1, 1995. For example, now reference to estate trustee and cetificate of appointment of estate trustee with or without will, rather than to executor or administrator, letters probate or administration, and application procedure substantially amended. (O. Reg. 484/94, 740/94, 69/95, 377/95). But seems terminology in some legislation not changed. In comments in this digest generally terminology in Rules of Practice used.

Estate matters are within jurisdictions of Ontario Court (General Division).

Applications for certificate appointing estate trustee with or without will made to district or county office of Ontario Court (General Division) where deceased had fixed place of abode at death or, if deceased had no fixed place of abode in Ontario at death, to county or district office of such Court where deceased had property at time of death. In other cases application may be made to any district or county office of Ontario Court (General Division). (c. E.21, §7). Notice must be given to all beneficiaries including charities and contingent beneficiaries. (R.P. 74.04, 74.05).

Preferences in Right to Appointment.—Where person dies intestate or estate trustee named refuses to prove will, court may appoint opposite sex spouse (whether or not married) or some one or more of next of kin or both. (§29). (But see topic Descent and Distribution, subhead Spouse, Note on definition of spouse.) In above and other circumstances, persons entitled to appointment may nominate, and court in special circumstances may appoint, another person or trust company to administer any part or whole of property: e.g. creditor of estate. Where several persons are of same degree of entitlement, or if there are persons with prior entitlement, renunciations by those not applying required or order to them to refuse or accept appointment. Consents of beneficiaries wherever resident having majority interest in estate required. (R.P. 74.05). But probably subject to discretion of court. (§29). (See topic Descent and Distribution, subhead Intestate Succession.)

Where infant is sole estate trustee, appointment with will will be granted to guardian of infant or to such person as court may think fit until infant comes of age. (§26).

Other infant executors may apply for appointment at 18 if right reserved to them. (R.P. 74.06). See topic Descent and Distribution, subhead Escheat and Bona Vacantia for appointment on intestacy and minors only next of kin in Ontario.

Competency.—Appointment of estate trustee with will may be granted to individual outside Ontario named estate trustee in will. If not resident in Commonwealth bond is usually required. (§6). Otherwise appointment as estate trustee will not be granted to persons outside Ontario except in certain cases of resealing (§5) (see subhead Resealing, infra). Corporation not both registered trust company and approved cannot obtain grant. (c. L.25, §175[2]).

Sex and marital status do not affect right to appointment except as they relate to definition of spouse. (See topic Descent and Distribution, subhead Spouse, Note on definition of spouse.)

Oath to be taken by estate trustees requires them faithfully to administer property of deceased and to render account of administration when lawfully required. (c. E.21, §39).

Bond.—Appointment of estate trustee granted to estate trustee named in will without bond unless resident outside Commonwealth. (c. E.21, §6). On appointment of estate trustee on intestacy or of estate trustee not named in will bond usually required (§35) but bond may be dispensed with (§37). Some exceptions to requiring bond are: on intestacy where applicant spouse and estate value less than $75,000 if affidavit of debts filed (§36) and Court may require statement in affidavit that debts paid: in those circumstances court likely to waive bond where value less than $200,000—new preferential share for spouse; or registered trust company (c. L.25, §175 [4]). If estate trustees are sole beneficiaries or all beneficiaries are sui juris and consent, usually order waiving bond obtainable if affidavit that all known debts paid or sometimes with undertaking to pay same upon realization of assets. Amount of bond and sureties: double value of estate and more than one bond may be required, amount of each as judge decides, or amount may be reduced (c. E.21, §37); individual sureties give bond for amounts aggregating penalty of bond (R.P. 74.11), usually two individual sureties and each gives bond for value of estate; if value under $100,000, one individual surety; if guarantee company bond, usually one surety for value of estate. Security for succeeding trustee based on value of unadministered estate.

Removal.—Jurisdiction vested in Ontario Court (General Division); grounds for estate trustee same as for other trustee. (c. T.23, §37). Other provisions of Trustee Act may permit appointment of replacements or successors in some circumstances. Provisions of will respecting removal may be applicable.

Special Kinds of Estate Trustees.—Estate trustee with will where estate trustee not one appointed in will (c. E.21, §29); succeeding estate trustee with or without will (R.P. 74.06 and 74.07) including where estate trustee added where right to apply reserved; to call in property of deceased; estate trustee during absence of person entitled to appointment (§14), during minority of person appointed estate trustee by testator (§26), or during litigation with or without will (§28; R.P. 74.10), may be appointed in appropriate circumstances. Appointment without will may be limited to personal property (§31) or appointment with or without will may be limited to part of deceased's estate (§32).

Resealing.—Where estate trustee has been appointed by court of competent jurisdiction in U.K., or in any province or territory of Canada, or in any British possession, such appointment (even if estate trustee not resident in Ontario [§5]) may be resealed at local office of Ontario Court (General Division) and has same force and effect as if it had been originally granted in Ontario. (§52; R.P. 74.08). Bond required in same circumstances as if original appointment based on value of assets over which jurisdiction is sought in Ontario unless sufficient security given to Court of original grant. (§52[3]; R.P. 74.11). (See subhead Bond, supra.) Appointment of estate trustee of notarial will made in Quebec may be made in Ontario. (§15). Letters of verification issued in Quebec are deemed certificate of appointment of estate trustee for resealing in Ontario (§52).

Ancillary Appointments.—Where estate trustee with will appointed by any other court of competent jurisdiction ancillary appointment with will may be obtained in Ontario, probably in county or district where decedent had assets. (R.P. 74.09). No ancillary appointment with no will obtainable: original appointment in Ontario required unless resealing available. (See subhead Resealing, supra.) (See R.P. 74.05 for requirement of renunciations and consents.) Bond required in same circumstances as for original grant but based on value of assets over which ancillary estate trustee seeks jurisdiction in Ontario (R.P. 74.11)(see subhead Bond, supra).

Inventory.—Statement of value required on application for appointment as estate trustee must set forth total value of property affected by grant (§32[3]), verified by oath of applicant. Certain property including joint property passing by survivorship, insurance payable directly to beneficiary and realty outside Ontario may be excluded. Real estate is valued net of encumbrances—see application forms. Amounts payable to named beneficiaries of pensions and some other plans ordinarily excluded.

Fees.—On application for appointment as estate trustee with or without will: $5 per $1,000 of value on first $50,000; $15 per $1,000 on excess. (O. Reg. 293/92). Value for calculating fees generally same as for inventory but some uncertainty whether value for fees confined to property affected by appointment. (§§32[3] and 53). Fees are payable on application for appointment on value or on estimated value (R.P. 74.13) with undertaking to pay on any additional value.

General Powers and Duties.—With some exceptions, common law rules as to administration of personalty govern. (c. E.22, §§3-5, 7). There are also several special provisions governing realty. (§§9, 15, 16, 17). Powers can also be provided by will. Most property of deceased vests in estate trustee (§2) but some exceptions for jointly held property, proceeds of insurance where named beneficiary and some difference in treatment of certain plans where named beneficiary: may sometimes be dealt with without involving estate trustee, although sometimes such plans may be collected by estate trustee to satisfy creditors. See also subhead Distribution infra as to vesting of realty in beneficiary after three years. See c. T.23 as to some other powers and duties.

Notice to Creditors.—Estate trustees should consider advertising for creditors for their own protection. (c. T.23, §53). See also c. E.22, §26 respecting no distribution on intestacy within one year and repayment in certain circumstances, subject to advertising provisions. (c. T.23, §53). Advertisement published three times in newspaper where deceased resided and/or carried on business usually leaving one month from first appearance date before date when ad states distribution will take place with regard only to claims then known to executor/administrator is considered sufficient. (See also subhead Distribution, infra.)

Proof of Claims.—Claims against estates of deceased persons are usually given by submitting to personal representative particulars of claim and any documentation supporting claim verified by statutory declaration within time limited by advertisement.

For notice of claim following form might be used (see subhead Enforcement of Claims, infra, and form of claim under c. E.21, §47 and also subhead Approval or Rejection of Claims, infra, when claim under c. E.21, §44 or 45 contested):

Form

Canada
Province of . . . .

In the Estate of . . . .
And in the Claim of . . . .

I, ..., of the City of . . . . . ., in the State/Province of . . . . . ., (Occupation), do solemnly declare that

1. I am the above-named claimant (or as the case may be).
2. (Name of deceased) late of, etc., (occupation), was at the time of his death and his estate still is indebted to me in respect of (nature of claim) in the sum of $. . . . . .
3. The following are the particulars: . . . . . .
4. I hold no security for the said debt, nor have I received any satisfaction therefor save and except the following: . . . . . .

And I make this solemn Declaration conscientiously believing it to be true, and knowing that it is of the same force and effect as if made under oath, and by virtue of the "Canada Evidence Act." . . . .

Declared before me at the . . . . of . . . . .
in the . . . . of . . . . this . . . . day of
. . . ., A. D. 19. . .

. . . . A Notary Public.

Claims against estates which are being wound up under the direction of the court, or by a trustee, for the benefit of creditors, may usually be proved by affidavit evidence, unless the claims are contested, and any claims which are contested will have to be proved by oral evidence in court or by evidence taken under commission. The form of affidavit is similar to the above form. There are special forms and procedures for claims if estate being administered by trustee in bankruptcy. See also payment of debts, evidence of debts, settling claims and procedure where deficiency of assets, including valuation of security. (c. T.23, §§48-59).

Approval or Rejection of Claims.—For certain claims estate trustee wishing to contest claim, may serve notice thereof on claimant, who may then apply to judge of Ontario Court (General Division) for order allowing claim and determining amount of it. Parties and their witnesses are heard and claim is dealt with by court. (c. E.21, §§44, 45, R.P. 75.08). Other claims may have to be dealt with in same manner as if claim not against estate.

Enforcement of Claims.—Certain claims against estates of deceased persons may be enforced by action against estate trustee. (c. T.23, §§38, 39; c. F.3, §§61, 62, 63). *Note:* can be special limitation periods; also special limitation periods where notice of claim giving full particulars of claim verified by affidavit filed with estate trustee. (c. E.21, §47). If no estate trustee appointed, may apply to Court for appointment of litigation administrator. (R.P. 9.02). Creditor may also obtain appointment as estate trustee. All creditors, other than secured, rank pari passu. (c. T.23, §50). Some preference may be given for funeral and testamentary expenses. May be some differences if estate is administered by trustee in bankruptcy.

See Topical Index in front part of this volume.

ESTATE TRUSTEES . . . *continued*

Dependants' Allowances.—Where deceased, whether testate or intestate, has not made adequate provision for proper support of dependants, application may be made to Ontario Court (General Division) (c. S.26, §58) for order charging estate with payment of such support. Application must be made within six months after issue of certificate of appointment of estate trustee, or later if court considers proper against any part of estate that remains undistributed. (§61). Court may take into account certain property not part of estate and impose charge on it for payments to dependants. (§72). Support may be by lump sum, periodic payments or certain other means. Court may make interim order and vary orders. (§§ 64, 65).

Spouses' Right of Possession.—Occupying spouse has right to possession rent free of matrimonial home for 60 days after death of spouse who had interest in matrimonial home. (c. F.3, §26). Surviving spouse who has not been adequately provided for by deceased spouse and is dependant may make application described under subhead Dependants' Allowances, supra.

Accounts.—Of estate trustees filed and passed before judge of Ontario Court (General Division) in office which granted certificate of appointment on notice to all parties interested. Where infants are interested and in some circumstances where incapable persons have interest, notice of passing must be given to Children's Lawyer. Where charities or certain incapable persons have interest, Public Guardian and Trustee must be served. (c. E.21, §49). Accounts must contain specified information and are filed with local registrar and are open for inspection by interested parties. (R.P. 74.16 to 74.18). Persons interested in property of deceased may require accounting in Court by estate trustee with or without will. (c. E.21, §§48, 50, R.P. 74.15[1][h]). If beneficiaries all adults and otherwise fully capacitated, accounts may be approved by them and estate trustee released without passing accounts in court.

Note: Effective Apr., 1995 Public Trustee became Public Guardian and Trustee and Official Guardian became Children's Lawyer (although it seems this change not made to all legislation).

Distribution.—If a claim is not presented within the time limited in advertisement, estate trustee may distribute estate without being personally liable for debts of which he had no knowledge, but any right of creditor to follow assets is not prejudiced. (c. T.23, §53). Real estate is subject to deceased's debts (c. E.22, §2), but purchaser in good faith, for value, without notice from estate trustee under express power of sale in will is free of debts. In other cases, purchaser in good faith, for value, without notice is usually free of debts, whether real estate validly sold by estate trustee (§19) or beneficiary (§§21 and 23). However, if estate trustee transferred real estate to beneficiary within three years after death, purchaser from beneficiary in that period not free of debts until three years have passed, and then only if no creditor has in that period registered pending action or caution. (§17[8]). Exception: purchaser will be free if judge allows transfer within the three years. (§21). Purchaser not free of debts may have claim against beneficiary or estate trustee. (§17[8]). If purchaser free of debts, creditor may have claim against same persons. (§§20 and 23). Real estate automatically vests in beneficiaries three years after death (§9), but no automatic vesting if will gives real estate to estate trustee or gives express or implied power of sale over real estate to estate trustee. Estate trustee can register caution to prevent vesting or may reverse it. (§§9 and 11).

Personal property, other than money, having value of over $5,000, or any bequest of money cannot be distributed to foreign beneficiary in designated country without court order. (c. E.22, §20). No country yet designated.

Upon death of spouse there may be valuation of net family property. If value of net family property of deceased spouse exceeds that of surviving spouse, surviving spouse is entitled to half of difference. (c. F.3, §§4, 5). See topic Descent and Distribution, subhead Family Law Act, Election. Entitlement of surviving spouse has priority over all gifts under will (except for value of consideration given) or entitlement on intestacy or dependant's allowance order except for deceased's child. (§6). No distribution of estate allowed for six months unless written consent of spouse or court authorizes distribution. (§6).

Compensation.—No specified legal rate of compensation for estate trustees. Entitled to fair and reasonable allowance in discretion of court for efforts. Same as for trustee. See topic Trusts, subhead Compensation.

Public Guardian and Trustee is corporation sole under that name with perpetual succession and official seal, and may sue and be sued under above name. (c. P.51, §1). See topic Descent and Distribution, subhead Escheat and Bona Vacantia re Public Guardian and Trustee administering estates. Public Guardian and Trustee may become guardian of incapable person (S.O. 1992, c. 30), may represent mentally incapable persons and charities in certain circumstances (e.g. see subhead Accounts, supra, and c. E.22, §17), and may administer any charitable or public trust (c. P.51, §12). With his consent in writing, Public Guardian and Trustee may be appointed trustee of any will or settlement or other instrument creating trust. (§7).

Human Tissue Gift Act. (c. H.20).—Consents are required for inter vivos gifts for transplants and postmortem gifts for transplants and other uses. Consent may be given on death in some circumstances by spouse or other family members or person lawfully in possession of body. Sale of tissue prohibited and any such dealing invalid. (§10). See Coroners Act, c. C.37, §29 respecting removal of pituitary gland for use in treatment of growth hormone deficiency.

EVIDENCE: See topics Depositions; Witnesses.

EXECUTIONS:

Judgments or orders for payment or recovery of money or for recovery of personal property may be enforced by writs of execution, garnishment or appointment of receiver. Order requiring person to do any act, other than payment of money, or to abstain from doing any act, may be enforced by contempt proceedings. (R.P. 60).

Kinds of Execution.—Execution may be obtained by writs of seizure and sale, possession, delivery, attachment or sequestration, by warrants of committal or by garnishee or replevin orders.

Exemptions.—See topic Exemptions.

Time for Issuance.—Execution may be issued without leave at any time within six years from date of judgment, but leave is required after six years has elapsed or if enforcement of order is subject to fulfilment of term or condition. (R.P. 60.07[2]). It may be renewed before its expiration six years from issuance for further period of six years (R.P. 60.07[6]–[19]) and succeeding renewals in like time may extend force of judgment even after 20 years.

Stay.—On delivery of notice of appeal from any order, final or interlocutory, other than order for injunction, mandatory order, or order awarding support, maintenance, custody or access, order is automatically stayed until disposition of appeal, unless appeal judge orders otherwise. (R.P. 63.01). Any order, including exceptions above, may be stayed by order of court whose decision is to be appealed, subject to expiry, or by order of judge of appeal court. (R.P. 63.02). Generally, where order is stayed, no steps may be taken under order or for its enforcement, but stay does not prevent issue or filing of writ of execution. (R.P. 63.03).

Lien.—Lands of defendant are bound from moment of delivery of writ of execution to sheriff of county or district in which lands are situated, or, in case of lands under Land Titles system, upon filing in appropriate land titles office and satisfying proper master of titles that name of execution debtor and name of registered owner as it appears in records of land titles office represent same person. Personal property except as to bills of sale, chattel mortgages, is bound only as against persons with actual notice that writ of execution has been delivered to sheriff and is unexecuted. (c. E.24, §9).

Levy.—Execution issued to enforce any judgment affects real and personal property of defendant in county or union of counties or district over which sheriff to whom it is directed has authority. Included with lands of the defendant subject to seizure are lands held in trust for him and any interest of his in lands held in joint tenancy.

Priorities among execution creditors have been abolished. (c. C.45, §3).

Claims of Third Persons.—Creditors Relief Act (c. C.45) abolishes priority among creditors with judgments; proceeds of any execution distributed rateably among creditors who have filed executions with Sheriff; there is similar procedure for garnishments affecting Small Claims Court judgments.

Sale.—Real and personal property of debtor may be sold by sheriff to satisfy judgment. Where personal property is seized under writ of seizure and sale, sheriff must, upon request of debtor, deliver inventory of property seized before, or within reasonable time after, removal from premises. Personal property not to be sold unless notice of time and place of sale is mailed to both creditor and debtor at least ten days before sale and is published in local newspaper. No sale of land may be held until six months after filing of writ with sheriff, and until 30 days notice of sale has been given to debtor, creditor and public. (R.P. 60.07[14]–[23]).

Supplementary proceedings are available for purpose of working out relief which should flow from a judgment or order which has already been given or granted. The judgment debtor may be examined once a year (unless court orders otherwise) as to estate and effects of debtor, and as to property and means he had when debt or liability was incurred, and as to property or means he still has of discharging judgment, and as to disposal he has made of any property since contracting debt or incurring liability, and as to any and what debts are owing to him; and if it is ascertained that judgment debtor has fraudulently disposed of any of his property for purpose of defeating his creditors, transfer or conveyance of such property may be set aside and property itself made exigible in execution. So also any debts which may be owing to debtor may be garnisheed. Where difficulty arises concerning enforcement of order, court may permit such examination of person other than debtor who may have knowledge of matters set out above.

If judgment debtor, upon his examination fails to make satisfactory answers, he is liable to be committed to jail for any term not exceeding 12 months, and if, upon his examination he discloses that his property has been concealed or made away with to defeat claim, he will be liable to committal. (R.P. 60.18).

Equitable Execution.—Provision is made for the appointment of a receiver after judgment by way of equitable execution. (c. L.2, §19).

EXECUTORS AND ADMINISTRATORS:

See topic Estate Trustees.

EXEMPTIONS:

Following chattels are exempt from seizure under any writ issued out of any court and claims of creditors after death: (1) necessary and ordinary wearing apparel of debtor and his family not exceeding $1,000 in value; (2) equipment, food and fuel that are contained in and form part of permanent home of debtor not exceeding $2,000 in value; (3) in case of debtor not engaged solely in tillage of soil or farming, tools and instruments and other chattels ordinarily used by debtor not exceeding $2,000 in value; if chattels so used exceed $2,000 in value, they may be sold and first $2,000 of proceeds must be paid over directly to debtor; (4) in case of a person engaged solely in tillage of soil or farming, live stock, fowl, bees, books, tools and implements and other chattels ordinarily used by debtor not exceeding $5,000 in value; in lieu of retaining above chattels, debtor may ask to have them sold and receive first $5,000 of proceeds; (5) in case of a person engaged solely in tillage of soil or farming, sufficient seed to seed all his land under cultivation, not exceeding 100 acres, as selected by debtor, and 14 bushels of potatoes, and, where seizure is made between first day of Oct. and 30th day of Apr., such food and bedding as are necessary to feed and bed live stock and fowl that are exempt under this section until 30th day of Apr. next following. Above exemptions are not available to corporate debtors. (c. E.24, §§2, 7).

Debts Against Which Exemptions Not Allowed.—No article, except beds, bedding, and necessary wearing apparel, is exempt from seizure in satisfaction of a debt contracted for purchase of such article. (c. E.24, §7). Only exemptions for tools and instruments used by debtor in ordinary course of business apply in respect of debt for maintenance of spouse or child. (§7).

Earnings.—Except for purposes of support order (c. W.1,. §7), 80% of wages are exempt from seizure or attachment, provided that judge upon hearing of matter may reduce or increase percentage of exemption. Debtor may apply to judge for release of

EXEMPTIONS . . . *continued*
garnishment. (c. W.1, §7). Only valid wage assignment is to credit union for portion of wages not exempt. (c. W.1, §7). See topic Assignments, subhead Assignment of Wages.

Homestead Exemption.—See topic Homesteads.

FACTORS:

Factors are governed by the Factors Act. (c. F.1). Sale or pledge in ordinary course of business by mercantile agent who is in possession of goods with owner's consent; is valid if made to person who has no notice that agent is without authority to make such sale or pledge.

The consignee acquires no property in the goods consigned but the title remains in the consignor till the goods are sold to a purchaser. The consignee has a lien on the goods for his charges only, and failure to account for goods in excess of the amount of same renders him criminally liable. He may sue in his own name for the purchase price.

FIDUCIARIES:

See topics Estate Trustees; Guardian and Ward; Trusts.

FOREIGN CORPORATIONS:

See topics Corporations; Insurance; Mines and Minerals.

FRANCHISES:

Ontario has no equivalent to American Uniform Franchise and Business Opportunities Act. In Ontario, law of franchises is essentially matter of contract between parties. See topic Contracts.

FRAUDS, STATUTE OF: (c. S.19).

Contracts.—Unless the agreement or some memorandum or note thereof is in writing, signed by the party to be charged, or one lawfully authorized by such party, no action shall be brought to charge any person upon: (a) promise of executor or administrator to answer for damages out of his own estate; (b) promise to answer for debt, default or miscarriage of another; or (c) any contract for sale of lands or interest therein. (c. S.19, §4).

Such contracts not in form required by c. S.19 are unenforceable. Equitable doctrine of part performance may be set up against defence under c. S.19. Promise to pay debt contracted during infancy or ratification thereof; representation concerning character, conduct, credit, etc., of another made with intent that such other person may thereby obtain credit, money or goods (§§7, 8), and agreement to pay commission for sale of real property must be in writing (c. R.4, §23).

Sale of Goods.—It is no longer legal requirement that contract for sale of goods be in writing.

Real Property.—All estates, interests of freehold, term of years and all uncertain interests in real property must be granted, assigned or surrendered by deed or note in writing signed by grantor, assignor or person surrendering, or authorized agent. Leases (except where term does not exceed three years and rent amounts to at least two-thirds of improved value), and certain other interests (c. C.34, §9) are void if not by deed (c. S.19, §§1-3). Declarations or creations of trusts of lands, or assignment or surrender thereof, except trusts created, transferred or extinguished by operation of law must be in writing. (§§9-11).

FRAUDULENT SALES AND CONVEYANCES:

Every conveyance of real or personal property made with or without consideration with intent to defeat or delay creditors is void against creditors or others, and their assigns except where person to whom such property is conveyed took bona fide upon good consideration without notice or knowledge of the intent. Every conveyance of real property with intent to defraud purchaser is deemed void only against purchaser, assigns or those claiming under him. Exception: a conveyance bona fide upon good consideration. (c. F.29).

Creditors' remedies are by way of action to set aside conveyance, or, if debtor in bankruptcy, by motion in bankruptcy court by trustee in bankruptcy.

Bulk Sales.—In a "sale in bulk," defined as "a sale of stock in bulk out of the usual course of business or trade of the seller," (§1) statutory requirements protect trade creditors of seller, except where sale in bulk is by executor, administrator, committee of estate of incompetent person, secured creditor, receiver, trustee or public official under judicial process (§2). Sale in bulk is voidable at suit of creditor or trustee in bankruptcy of seller unless buyer complied with Act. If sale set aside buyer personally liable for value of stock in bulk. Before sale, buyer must obtain from seller statutory declaration giving names and addresses of all creditors. Before obtaining such declaration, buyer may pay seller sum not exceeding 10% of purchase price which is subject to statutory trust. When declaration is obtained sale may then be carried through if claims of all secured trade creditors and unsecured trade creditors each do not exceed $2,500, or if all such creditors have been paid in full, or if adequate provision has been made for payment upon completion of sale to all such creditors who have not submitted waivers. "Creditors" here only includes those of whom buyer has notice. Otherwise, proceeds of sale must be delivered by buyer to trustee, consent to sale obtained from 60% of unsecured creditors with claims of $50 or more and affidavit produced by seller stating that all creditors have received copy of sale contract, list of trade creditors, and statement of affairs. Bankruptcy Act of Canada governs priority of distribution of proceeds by trustee. Within five days after completion of sale, buyer's affidavit together with copies of all documents must be filed at Ontario Court (General Division) with local registrar where stock located at time of sale. No actions can be taken to avoid sale after six months from date of this filing. Seller may apply to district court judge to exempt sale from Act where it will not impair his ability to pay creditors. Statute prescribes forms for seller's statement of creditors, waiver, consent and statement of affairs. (c. B.14). Every person purchasing stock through sale in bulk must obtain from vendor duplicate copy of certificate furnished under §6(1) of Retail Sales Tax Act. (c. R.31).

GARNISHMENT:

Creditor may enforce order for payment or recovery of money by garnishment of debts payable by other persons to debtor. Creditor must file requisition for garnishment, copy of order, any other evidence establishing amount awarded and creditor's entitlement, and prescribed affidavit evidence relating to amount owing to creditor and names and addresses of those persons who are or will become indebted to debtor. Upon filing, registrar issues notices of garnishment which must be served on debtor and each garnishee by ordinary mail or by personal service or alternative thereto.

Once served garnishee is liable to pay to sheriff all such debts, up to amount shown in notice, within ten days of later of time of service or time debt becomes payable. Garnishment applies to debts payable within six years after service of notice. Payment to sheriff discharges debt. If garnishee makes payment to any other person garnishee remains liable to pay debt in accordance with notice. Garnishee may dispute garnishment by filing garnishee statement with court and serving it on creditor and debtor within ten days after service of notice. (R.P. 60.08).

Eighty percent of debtor's wages exempt from garnishment, except for purposes of support order. (c. W.1, §7). See topic Exemptions, subhead Earnings. Where in personal account other than joint account, funds of debtor in bank account may be attached either by way of garnishment or by writ of seizure and sale directed to sheriff in district in which account located.

GUARDIAN AND WARD:

Ontario Court (Provincial Division), Unified Family Court or Ontario Court (General Division) may make order for custody of or access to child and may, on application by parent of child or any other person, appoint guardian of property of child. (c. C.12, Part III).

Bond.—The guardian is required to give a bond payable to minor in the amount and with such sureties as court may direct except where parent of child is appointed and Court is of opinion that bond is not required. (c. C.12, §55).

Powers and Duties.—Unless otherwise limited, the guardian has authority to act for and on behalf of the infant and has charge and management of his estate, real and personal, and the custody of his person and the care of his education.

Accounts.—Guardian may be required to account, or may voluntarily pass accounts, in respect of care and management of property of child (c. C.12, §52) and is required to transfer all of child's property to child when child attains age of 18 years (c. C.12, §53).

Management of Assets of Ward.—The guardian may apply to Ontario Court (General Division) for opinion, advice or direction of court on any question respecting management of assets of his ward and in acting upon such opinion, advice or order will be deemed to have discharged his duty as guardian. (c. T.23, §60).

Termination of Guardianship.—Testamentary guardians and guardians appointed by a court may be removed by the Supreme Court or by the surrogate court for the same causes for which trustees are removable and such guardian may by leave of the court resign his office. (c. C.12, §57).

Custody of Infants.—Custody, access and guardianship now dealt with under Children's Law Reform Act. (c. C.12, Part III). Order regarding custody of child and right of either parent to access to child, made on basis of best interests of child. Court may appoint person who has technical or professional skill to assess needs of such child. (§30). Court may also order support of child by parent pursuant to Family Law Act. (c. F.3, §33). Child and Family Support Act provides for appointment of Director of Family Support Plan capable of enforcing Ontario orders, as well as orders made in other jurisdictions, on behalf of dependents. Act requires "income source" (defined term) of "payee" (defined term) to deduct amount of support obligation from payee's income to maximum of 50% of net amount owed to payee by income source, and forward to Director on ongoing basis until Order terminates, is varied, or withdrawn from Director on payment of four months' support. Father and mother of child are equally entitled to custody of child. (c. C.12, §20). Where parents of child are separated and child lives with one of them with consent, implied consent, or acquiescence of other of them, right to exercise incidents of custody, but not entitlement to access, are suspended until separation agreement or order provides otherwise. (§20[4]).

Neglected and Abused Children.—Judge of Ontario Court (Pension Division) or Unified Family Court may, upon finding child to be in need of protection, order psychological or social assessment made of child and parent; child returned to parent or other person subject to supervision by Children's Aid Society; child made ward of Children's Aid Society for period not exceeding 24 months; child made ward of Crown until wardship is terminated or expires. Parent or child if age 12 may, after six months, apply for termination; Children's Aid Society having care of child, foster parent, parent or child may apply for court review. Every wardship terminates when child marries or attains age 18 but Crown wards may be provided for until 21 if student or incapacitated. Such judge may also make order regarding access to any child and order for payment by parent or estate where child is committed to care or another person or society. Every person with reasonable grounds to suspect in course of professional or official duties that child has suffered abuse from person with charge of child required to report it to society. (Child and Family Services Act, c. C.11, Part III).

Children's Lawyer in Toronto is guardian of property of all infants in Province not having a guardian appointed by court.

Insane Persons.—Ontario Court (General Division) may upon application, where it is satisfied beyond reasonable doubt, declare person mentally incompetent and appoint committee of person or of estate of person, or both, and propound scheme for management of estate. (Mental Incompetency Act, c. M.9). Finding of mental incompetency means that person has such condition of arrested or incomplete development of mind whether arising from inherent causes or induced by disease or injury, or is suffering from such disorder of mind that he requires care, supervision, control for protection of person and property. Powers and duties of committee of mentally incompetent persons are provided by statute. Where person is not found mentally incompetent but incapable of managing his affairs through mental infirmity arising from disease, age, habitual drunkenness, use of drugs, or other cause, a committee may be appointed to manage his estate. Such committee exercises its power subject to jurisdiction and authority of Court as if committee of mentally incompetent person. (c. M.9, §35). On death of mentally

See Topical Index in front part of this volume.

GUARDIAN AND WARD . . . *continued*
incompetent persons, probate of will, providing it was made when maker had testamentary capacity, or administration is proceeded with in normal way and any committee previously appointed, or Public Guardian and Trustee if incompetent dies while a patient in a mental hospital, remains in control of estate until executors or administrators are appointed by order of Surrogate Court. *NOTE:* Legislation passed but not yet proclaimed in force will substantially revise this subhead.

HOLIDAYS:

See Canada Law Digest.

Sunday.—No document may be served and no order executed on Sun., except with leave of court. (c. C.43, §124).

Holiday.—Where time for doing act or taking proceeding expires on a holiday, act or proceeding may be done or taken on next juridical day. (R.P. 3.01[1][c]). Where time limited for act expires on holiday, time extended to next day not holiday. Holiday: Sun. (c. I.11).

Retail Businesses.—Certain establishments exempted from Sun. closing law. (c. R.30).

HOMESTEADS:

There is no exemption of real property from execution on the ground that it is a homestead.

HUSBAND AND WIFE:

Status.—For all purposes of Ontario law, married person has legal personality that is independent, separate and distinct from that of his/her spouse. Married person has legal capacity for all purposes as if unmarried, and has right of action in tort against spouse. (c. F.3). Spouse defined as either of man and woman who are married to each other or have entered into void or voidable marriage in good faith. Marriage that is actually or potentially polygamous is valid for purposes of Family Law Act if celebrated in jurisdiction where it is valid. (§1).

Family Law Act provides for deferred community of property system. During marriage, net family property owned by spouse with title. Net family property defined as "value of all property, except property which is excluded that a spouse owns on the valuation date (see below), after deducting the spouse's debts and other liabilities, and the value of property, other than a matrimonial home, that the spouse owned on the date of the marriage, after deducting the spouse's debts and other liabilities, calculated as of the date of the marriage". Each spouse makes separate calculation. Property means any interest, present or future, vested or contingent, in real or personal property and includes property over which, whether alone or in conjunction with another person, there is power of appointment exercisable in favour of himself or herself, property disposed of by spouse but over which spouse has power to revoke disposition or disposal of property, and in case of spouse's right under pension plan that has vested, spouse's interest in plan including contributions made by other persons. Excluded from net family property calculations are: (1) property, other than matrimonial home, that was acquired by gift or inheritance from third person after date of marriage; (2) income from such gifts or inheritances if donor or testator has expressly excluded it from donee's net family property; (3) damages or right to damages for personal injuries, nervous shock, mental distress, or loss of guidance, care and companionship, or settlement representing those damages; (4) proceeds of life insurance policies; (5) property other than matrimonial home, into which property referred to in paragraphs 1 to 4 can be traced; (6) any property excluded by domestic contract between spouses. Onus of proving deduction or exclusion from net family property is on party claiming same. (c. F.3, §4). All net family property of spouses is valued on earlier of following valuation dates: (1) decree nisi of divorce is pronounced; (2) marriage is declared nullity; (3) spouses have separated with no prospect of resumed cohabitation; (4) death of spouse; (5) spouses cohabiting but serious danger one spouse may improvidently deplete net family property. (c. 4, §4). Upon valuation date, spouse whose net family property is lesser of two net family properties is entitled to one half of difference between them. (c. 4, §5). Court has discretion to vary equalization of net family property if equalization would be unconscionable given: (1) One spouse's failure to disclose to other spouse debts and liabilities existing at date of marriage; (2) one spouse incurred debts recklessly or in bad faith thereby reducing net family property; (3) part of value of net family property consists of gifts from other spouse; (4) spouse's intentional or reckless depletion of net family property; (5) amount spouse would receive is disproportionately large in relation to period of cohabitation less than five years; (6) one spouse has incurred disproportionately larger amount of debts and liabilities than other spouse for support of family; (7) written agreement between spouses that is not domestic contract; or (8) any other circumstance relating to acquisition, disposition, preservation, maintenance or improvement of property. (§5).

Spouses have equal rights of possession of matrimonial home regardless of who holds title, as against each other. (c. F.3, §19). Matrimonial home is property in which person has interest and is, or if spouses are separated, was at time of separation ordinarily occupied by person and spouse as family residence. (§18). Court can make order for exclusive possession of matrimonial home taking into account, among other things, best interests of children affected, financial position of both spouses, availability of other suitable and affordable accommodation and any written agreement between parties. (§24). Property can be designated by registered instrument as matrimonial home by one spouse or both spouses. If only one spouse registers designation, any other property qualifying as matrimonial home remains matrimonial home. If both spouses register designation, any other undesignated matrimonial home ceases to be matrimonial home. (§20). No spouse may dispose of or encumber any interest in matrimonial home without consent or release of other spouse or court order. (§21). Statement by person making disposition or encumbrance, or by person's attorney based on personal knowledge, that person is not spouse or that property is not matrimonial home is sufficient proof of such unless person to whom disposition or encumbrance is made has notice to contrary. (§21). Spouse with right to possession of matrimonial home has right to redeem or to relief against encumbrancers and is entitled to notice respecting claim and its enforcement or realization. (§22).

Issues of ownership of property between husband and wife are governed by rule of resulting trust except that property taken in name of spouses as joint tenants is prima facie proof of intent that each spouse has one-half beneficial interest on severance, and money on deposit in bank or similar financial institution in name of both spouses is deemed to be held by them as joint tenants. (c. F.3, §14). Common law rules govern with respect to constructive trust. (Rawluk v. Rawluk [1990], 23 R.F.L. [3d] 337 [S.C.C.]).

Support Obligations.—Every spouse has obligation to provide support for self and other spouse, in accordance with need, to extent that he or she is capable of doing so. (c. F.3, §30). For support purposes, definition of spouse includes unmarried man and woman who have cohabited continuously for three years or more or are in relationship of some permanence and are natural or adoptive parents of child. (§29). Spouse, dependent, or social welfare agency making payments to spouse may apply to court for support order against other spouse. Support order should recognize both spouses' contribution to relationship and economic consequences of relationship on spouse, share economic burden of child support equitably, assist spouse receiving support to become able to contribute to own support and relieve financial hardship not relieved by equalization of net family property and orders regarding matrimonial home. Factors court considers in awarding support are set out. (§33). Conduct of either spouse has no effect on obligation to support, but conduct of spouse so unconscionable as to constitute obvious and gross repudiation of relationship may be considered by court in fixing amount of support. (§33). Court may make support order for periodic payments or lump sum (§34), may vary support order (§37), may index support order (§34), may order employer of party to application for support to provide court written return showing party's remuneration (§42), and may imprison or fine spouse absconding from support order (§§43, 49). While cohabiting spouse may pledge credit of self and other spouse jointly for necessaries except where express withdrawal of authority by other spouse. (§45). See also topic Divorce, subhead Maintenance, Custody of Children, etc.

Domestic Contracts.—Family Law Act provides for domestic contracts which are paternity agreements, separation agreements, marriage contracts and cohabitation agreements. (c. F.3, §51). Domestic contracts must be written, signed by both parties and witnessed. (§55). Any agreement affecting children is subject to court determination of best interests of children. (§56). Provisions requiring party to remain chaste are void. Domestic contracts may be set aside as unconscionable if one party failed to disclose significant assets, debts or other liabilities to other when contract entered, if one party did not understand nature and consequences of contract, or otherwise in accordance with common law. (§56). Provisions for support in domestic contract or paternity agreement may be set aside by court if it results in unconscionable circumstances, if person receiving or waiving support qualifies for public assistance, or if there is default in provision of support under agreement. (§33). Man and woman who are not spouses may enter into paternity agreement for payment of expenses of child's prenatal care and birth, support of child, or funeral expenses of child or mother. (§59). Party to domestic contract may file it with court and court may enforce it. (§35).

Marriage Contracts.—Husband and wife may enter marriage contract before or during their marriage agreeing on their respective rights and obligations under marriage, or on separation, annulment or dissolution of marriage, or upon death, including ownership of property, support obligations, education and moral training of children and any other matter in settlement of their affairs except custody or access to children. No such agreement may alter rights of equal possession in matrimonial home. (c. F.3, §52). See also topic Divorce, subhead Separation Agreements.

Cohabitation Agreements.—Man and woman who are cohabiting or intend to cohabit and who are not married to each other, may enter into agreement in which they agree on their respective rights and obligations during cohabitation, or on ceasing to cohabit or on death, regarding same matters as marriage contracts. (c. F.3, §53).

Antenuptial or Prenuptial Contracts.—Marriage contracts or cohabitation agreements made in contemplation of marriage are synonymous terms for antenuptial or prenuptial contracts and latter are governed by statutory provisions of former.

Actions.—Each spouse has like right of action in tort against other as if not married. (c. F.3, §64).

See also topics: Marriage; Death, subhead Action for Death; Damages; Infants, subhead Maintenance.

INCOME TAX:

See Canada Law Digest, topic Taxation.

INFANTS:

Age of majority is 18 for both sexes. However, minimum age for purchasing, obtaining or consuming liquor is 19. (c. L.19, §30). See also topics Marriage, subhead Consent Required; Wills.

Contractual disabilities of infants are governed by common law rules. See, however, subhead Ratification of Contracts, infra.

Ratification of Contracts.—No action may be maintained to charge a person upon a promise made after full age to pay any debt contracted during infancy or upon any ratification after full age of any promise or simple contract made during infancy unless the promise or ratification is in writing signed by the party to be charged or his duly authorized agent. (c. S.19, §7).

Actions.—Any proceeding involving minor must be commenced, continued or defended by litigation guardian. (R.P. 7.01[a]). Qualifications for and duties of litigation guardian are prescribed. (R.P. 7.02-7.09). Actions between parent and child are permitted. Actions for prenatal injuries are permitted. Money payable to infant may be paid into court. (c. T.23, §36).

Parental Responsibility.—Parent is not liable for tort of child committed without parent's knowledge, participation, or sanction, but may be liable for negligence in making it possible for child to cause injury. (Thibodeau v. Cheff, [1911] 24 O.L.R. 214 [C.A.]; Kennedy v. Hanes, aff'd [1941] S.C.R. 384). In action against parent for damage to property or personal injury caused by fault or neglect of minor, onus of establishing parent exercised reasonable supervision and control is on parent. (c. F.3, §68).

See Topical Index in front part of this volume.

INFANTS . . . *continued*

Maintenance.—Every parent has obligation to provide support, in accordance with need, to unmarried child who is minor or is enrolled in full time program of education, to extent parent is capable of doing so, unless child age 16 or over and has withdrawn from parental control. (c. F.3, §31).

Adoption.—See topic Adoption.

Legitimacy.—For all purposes of law of Ontario, person is child of natural parents and status as their child is independent of whether child born within or outside marriage. Distinction at common law between status of children born in wedlock and born out of wedlock abolished, and relationship of parent and child and kindred relationships flowing therefrom determined for purposes of common law accordingly. (c. C.12, §1[4]). Unless contrary intention appears, reference in instruments and legislation to persons described in terms of blood relationship or marriage to another construed to refer to person who comes within description by reason of relationship of parent and child as determined above. (§2).

Custody.—Where order is made for custody of or access to child court may order supervision of custody or access and may make order restraining person from harassing applicant or child. (c. C.12, §§34, 35). Court may also make orders where there are probable grounds to believe person proposes to remove child from Ontario contrary to court order. (§36). Courts generally do recognize extra-provincial orders for custody of or access to child or may in certain circumstances supersede extra-provincial order. (§40). See also topic Guardian and Ward, subhead Custody of Infants.

INHERITANCE TAX: See topic Taxation.

INJUNCTIONS:

An injunction may be granted where it appears to court to be just or convenient that such order should be made, and any such order may be made upon such terms and conditions as court may deem just. It is provided as extraordinary remedy granted only where no other remedy would adequately meet case. Special provisions exist in respect of labour disputes. (c. C.43, §§101, 102).

Jurisdiction.—Injunctions may be granted by Ontario Court (General Division) and by Unified Family Court provided action or subject matter of dispute is within jurisdiction, monetary or otherwise, of court. (§101).

Interim Injunction.—An interim injunction pendente lite may be granted. Such an injunction is only granted on undertaking of applicant to pay any damages suffered which in opinion of court he ought to pay. Interim injunction in labour dispute shall not be for period longer than four days. (§102[5]; R.P. 40).

INSOLVENCY:

See Canada Law Digest, topic Bankruptcy.

INSURANCE:

Insurance companies may be incorporated under Corporations Act (c. C.38, Part V), but all insurers, wherever incorporated or established, undertaking insurance or carrying on business in Ontario are governed as well by Insurance Act (Ontario) (c. I.8) which includes specific provisions regulating fire, guarantee, life, automobile, accident and sickness, livestock and weather insurance contracts; fraternal societies, mutual benefit societies, pension fund associations, reciprocal and inter-insurance exchanges, agents, brokers and adjusters and licencing thereof, rating bureaux, unfair and deceptive practices, investments, reserves, deposits, capital requirements and amalgamation, transfer and reinsurance. (c. I.8). Marine insurance is regulated by c. M.2. Ministry of Financial Institutions through Ontario Insurance Commission has general supervision of business of insurance within Province with offices located at 5160 Yonge Street, Box 85, North York, Ontario M2N 2L9. Commission, comprising Commissioner, Superintendent and Director of Arbitration administer and enforce Insurance Act and other insurance legislation. Ontario Health Insurance Plan, established by government and mandatory for all employees. Plan is financed by employer payroll tax.

Licences.—Every insurer undertaking insurance in Ontario shall obtain licence from Commissioner.

Brokers.—No person can act as insurance broker unless person is registered broker under Registered Insurance Brokers Act. (c. R.19). Act contains restrictions on ownership of broker by nonresidents. Act establishes complaints committee and discipline committee. Where discipline committee finds member guilty of misconduct or incompetence, it may suspend or revoke certificate of member. Decisions of discipline committee are subject to appeal to Divisional Court. (c. R.19).

Agents.—No person can act as agent dealing in life insurance or accident and sickness insurance and no person can act as adjuster unless licensed under Insurance Act. (c. I.8, Part XIV).

Investments.—See c. I.8.

Rebates on premiums are prohibited. (c. I.8).

Premium Tax.—Insurance companies are liable to tax of 2% calculated on gross premiums payable under contracts of accident insurance, life insurance and sickness insurance, and 3% calculated on gross premiums payable under any other contract of insurance in respect of business transacted in Ontario during calendar year. (c. C.40, §74). In addition, additional tax of one-half of 1% is payable on premiums received for property insurance. Tax is in lieu of capital and place of business tax. If another jurisdiction imposes higher taxes on Ontario-based insurers than on local insurers, Province may require insurers from such jurisdictions to pay additional taxes. (c. C.40). Tax of 3% on automobile insurance revoked. (S.O. 1990, c. 2, §83).

Annual statements must be filed with Superintendent on or before last day of Feb. (Mar. 15 for reinsurers).

Foreign insurance companies may obtain licence to carry on business in Ontario under Insurance Act. (c. I.8). Foreign insurer must satisfy Superintendent that it can meet policy obligations and must appoint resident chief agent to receive service of process, etc. Regulation of foreign insurers similar to that of domestic insurers.

Direct Actions Against Insurer.—See topic Motor Vehicles, subhead Direct Actions.

No-Fault Insurance.—See topic Motor Vehicles, subhead No-Fault Insurance. See Canada Law Digest, topic Insurance.

INTEREST:

See Canada Law Digest, topic Interest.

Where court finds cost of money lent excessive in all the circumstances, and transaction harsh and unconscionable, it may reopen transaction and take account between creditor, debtor; or reopen any account taken and relieve debtor from payment of any sum exceeding fair one; or order repayment of such excess; or set aside in whole or part or revise or alter security given or loan agreement or where creditor has parted with security, order indemnity of debtor. Cost of loan means whole cost and includes interest, bonus, commission, etc. except express necessary disbursements. Powers exercisable in action by creditor or debtor, or on application by debtor to Ontario Court (General Division). (c. U.2).

Every person who extends credit on sale of goods or services or by advancement of money must furnish to person receiving credit written statement disclosing full cost of borrowing computed in accordance with Consumer Protection Act and regulations. (c. C.31).

INTESTACY: See topic Descent and Distribution.

JOINT STOCK COMPANIES:

There are no joint stock companies distinct from partnerships and incorporated companies, though provision is made for limited partnerships. (c. L.16). See topic Partnership.

JUDGMENTS:

Orders include judgments, and may be interlocutory or final. Prejudgment interest is recoverable at bank rate prevailing at end of first day of last month of quarter prior to that in which proceeding was commenced plus 1% except where prejudgment interest is claimed at rate as prescribed by some other right, e.g. by contract. Post-judgment interest is chargeable on all judgments and costs at bank rate prevailing for quarter preceding that in which order is given, plus 1%. Judicial discretion to disallow prejudgment and post-judgment interest, to alter rate and to alter period for which interest is payable. (c. C.43, §§127-130).

Judgment by Confession.—There is no judgment by confession in Ontario.

Judgment on consent may be entered in all cases except matrimonial causes.

Default Judgments.—Plaintiff, upon filing prescribed documents, may require registrar to note defendant in default where defendant fails to deliver statement of defence within prescribed time, or has statement of defence struck out without leave to deliver another or, with leave, fails to deliver another within prescribed time. (R.P. 19.01). Defendant noted in default is deemed to admit all allegations of fact in statement of claim, may not deliver defence except with leave of court or consent of plaintiff, and generally is disentitled to further notice in proceedings. (R.P. 19.02). Having noted defendant in default, plaintiff may obtain judgment as follows: (1) where claim is for debt or liquidated demand, for recovery of land or chattels or for foreclosure, sale or redemption of mortgage, by having registrar sign default judgment (R.P. 19.04); (2) where registrar has not signed default judgment or where claim is for unliquidated damages, by moving for judgment (R.P. 19.05); and (3) where motion for judgment refused, by proceeding to trial (R.P. 19.06). Same rules apply with necessary modifications to counterclaims, crossclaims, and third party claims. (R.P. 19.10).

Summary Judgment.—After delivery of statement of defence, either party may move, with supporting affidavit material or other evidence, for summary judgment on all or part of claim. (R.P. 20.01). Contents of factum and affidavit to be served on other party are prescribed. (R.P. 20.02, 20.03). Each party entitled to cross-examine upon any affidavit of opposing party after delivery of own evidence. (R.P. 39.02). Where satisfied there is no genuine issue for trial with respect to claim or defence, court shall grant summary judgment; where only issue is question of law, court may decide question and grant judgment accordingly; and where only issue is amount to which plaintiff entitled, court may order trial of that issue or grant judgment with reference. (R.P. 20.04). Where summary judgment refused or granted only in part, court may nevertheless specify what facts are not in dispute, define issues to be tried, and order speedy trial. (R.P. 20.05). Cost sanction imposed for improper use of this procedure. (R.P. 20.06). Procedure also applies to counterclaims, crossclaims and third party claims. (R.P. 20.09).

Declaratory judgments may be obtained in appropriate cases.

Lien.—Judgment is not ordinarily a lien on land but execution thereon may be. See topic Executions. Judgment may affect subsequent purchaser with notice of it or if execution registered against land.

Satisfaction.—Party may acknowledge satisfaction of order in document signed by party before witness, and document may be filed and entered in court office where order entered. (R.P. 59.07).

Actions on judgments must be brought within 20 years but an acknowledgment in writing or a part payment within the limitation period provides a new starting point for the running of the limitation period. (c. L.15).

Foreign Judgments.—Foreign judgments may be sued on in this province where according to rules laid down by Ontario courts, foreign court had jurisdiction in matter.

Foreign judgments, being treated by case law as simple contract debts, must be sued upon within six years of date of judgment. See topic Limitation of Actions, subhead Statute of Limitations.

Statutory provision is made for reciprocal enforcement in Ontario, subject to certain restrictions, of judgments of courts of reciprocating states provided judgment creditor applies to Ontario Court (General Division) at any time within six years after date of judgment to have judgment registered in that court. "Judgment" means judgment or order of court in any civil proceedings whereby any sum of money is payable and includes award in proceedings on arbitration if award is enforceable in same manner as

JUDGMENTS . . . *continued*

judgment in that jurisdiction. All provinces and territories within Canada are reciprocating jurisdictions except for Quebec. (c. R.5).

Statutory provision is made for reciprocal recognition and enforcement of judgments in civil and commercial matters between Canada and United Kingdom. Ontario designated as province to which convention extends. (c. R.6).

Statutory provision is also made for reciprocal recognition and enforcement of maintenance orders between provinces, various American states and other specified countries. (c. R.7). Statutory provision is also made for recognition and enforcement of commercial arbitration awards; see topic Arbitration and Award.

Judgment Notes.—See Canada Law Digest, topic Bills and Notes.

JUSTICES OF THE PEACE: (c. J.4).

Appointment and Removal.—Justices of peace are appointed by provincial government (c. J.4, §2). They can only be removed from office by executive order based on evidence of incapacity or failure to perform duties. (§8). Review Council monitors appointment and conduct of justices of peace (§§9-11).

Powers and Jurisdiction.—All judges are justices of peace. (c. J.4, §5). Justices of peace have jurisdiction throughout Ontario. (§17[1]). They shall perform duties and exercise powers conferred upon them by federal or provincial statute. (§22).

See also topic Affidavits.

LABOUR RELATIONS:

Relationship of employer and employee is governed by common law rules relating to employment contract. There are extensive statutory regulations including minimum employment standards, human rights, pay equity, collective bargaining, and health and safety legislation. (cc. E.14, L.2, E.12, O.1, W.11, H.19, P.8, H.4, P.7).

Labour Relations Act (S.O. 1995, c. 1, Sch. A).—Act provides legal framework for acquisition and termination of collective bargaining rights by trade unions, negotiation of collective agreements, resolution of industrial disputes and prohibition of unfair labour practices. Certification process is provided to govern acquisition of bargaining rights by trade unions. Conciliation and mediation procedures are provided to assist in negotiation of collective agreements between employers and trade unions once bargaining rights have been secured by trade union. Act also provides for first agreement interest arbitration.

During term of collective agreement, grievances must be resolved by binding third party arbitration and not through resort to strikes/lockouts. There are successor rights provisions that cause flow-through of bargaining rights upon sale of business. Business is deemed to have been sold in certain circumstances, such as when contractor of specified site services is replaced by another contractor. Employers who operate through more than one legal entity may be found to be one employer for purposes of Act to maintain bargaining rights over employees engaged in same economic activity under common direction and control.

Ontario Labour Relations Board has developed large body of case law through its administrative decisions under legislation. Board has major role in development of labour relations policy in Ontario.

Employment Equity Act, S.O. 1993, c. 35.—*Note:* Repealed by S.O. 1995, c. 4. Transitional provision in place; final repeal not in force at Apr. 30, 1996.

Employment Standards Act (c. E.14).—Act provides for certain minimum standards of employment. Employee cannot waive his or her rights under Act.

Hours of Work.—Employee must not work more than eight hours a day or 48 hours in a week, except in case of accident or injury. Director of Employment Standards may approve regular work day of more than eight hours but not in excess of 12 hours, where employees and employer jointly agree on arrangement. Employee may not work more than five consecutive hours without receiving at least one half-hour eating period. (c. E.14, §§17-20).

Public Holidays.—Subject to certain exceptions, employees are entitled to eight public holidays with pay: New Year's Day, Good Friday, Victoria Day, Canada Day, Labour Day, Thanksgiving Day, Christmas Day and Boxing Day. Employer, with employee's consent, can substitute another working day for public holiday. If public holiday falls on nonworking day employee shall be given another working day off with pay or, if employee agrees, employer will pay employee regular wage for public holiday. Employee who works on public holiday must be paid premium rate of at least one and one-half times regular rate for those hours worked, in addition to employee's regular day's pay for that public holiday. (c. E.14, §25).

Overtime Pay.—After 44 hours of work per week overtime rate of pay is one and one-half times regular rate of pay. Regular rate is wage rate per hour of work in regular non-overtime work week. This does not apply to employees engaged in specified industries and professions or to employees whose only work is supervisory or managerial. (c. E.14, §24).

Vacation Pay.—After one year of service employee is entitled to two weeks vacation with pay. Vacation pay must be equal to at least 4% of total wages for year. Employee who terminates before having completed one full year of service must receive minimum of 4% of total wages calculated from first day of employment. (c. E.14, §§28 and 30).

Pregnancy and Parental Leave.—Female employee is entitled to at least 17 weeks unpaid leave of absence for pregnancy if she has been employed at least 13 weeks immediately preceding estimated date of delivery. Leave may commence at any time during 17 weeks prior to estimated date of delivery. Employee entitled to such leave is required to give two weeks' notice in writing together with medical certificate estimating date of delivery, to employer when applying for leave of absence due to pregnancy. In addition, 18 weeks of unpaid parental leave can be taken by each parent who has been employed at least 13 weeks before birth of child or 13 weeks before child came into parent's custody, care and control for first time. For natural mother, parental leave commences when pregnancy leave ends or when baby first comes into custody, care and control of parent. For fathers and adoptive parents, parental leave commences within 35 weeks after birth or after child first comes into custody, care and control of parent. Employer must reinstate employee to same or comparable job at same wages with seniority and benefits accrued as of date of leave. Employer is not required to pay wages to employee while employee is on pregnancy or parental leave. (c. E.14, §§34, 37, 38 and 40).

Equal Pay for Equal Work.—Employer must not differentiate between male and female employees by paying employees of one sex less for substantially same kind of work in same establishment, performance of which requires substantially same skill, effort and responsibility and which is performed under similar working conditions, except where such payment is made pursuant to seniority system, merit system, system that measures earnings by quantity or quality of production, or differential based on any factor other than sex. (c. E.14, §32).

Notice of Termination.—Employer is required to give written notice of termination ranging from one to eight weeks, depending on length of employee's service. Only after written notice has been given and time of notice has expired can employee be terminated. During notice period, all benefits must be maintained. If employer terminates employee without notice, employer must provide pay in lieu of notice and maintain benefits for prescribed notice period. Full vacation pay entitlement must also be paid to employee for prescribed notice period. (c. E.14, §57). These statutory rules set out minimum standards; courts frequently award substantially higher amounts for termination without adequate notice, based on various factors including age, service, experience, expertise, likelihood of finding alternative employment, and character of employment.

Severance Pay.—Where employer's annual payroll is $2.5 million or more, terminated individual employees with five or more years of employment are entitled to severance pay. Where payroll is less than $2.5 million, severance pay must be paid when 50 or more employees are terminated in six-month period owing to permanent discontinuance of all or part of business at establishment. Severance pay is calculated as one week's pay per year of employment, to maximum of 26 weeks' pay. Severance pay is payable in addition to any right employee may have to notice of termination or pay in lieu of notice. (c. E.14, §58).

Payments on Termination.—Any monies to which employee is entitled upon termination, other than pay in lieu of notice of termination and severance pay, must be paid within seven days of termination. Pay in lieu of notice of termination and severance pay are allocated to first two weeks following termination and must be paid in two installments, one in each of first two weeks. (c. E.14, §7).

Director's Liability.—Workers whose employers are insolvent, have gone bankrupt, abandoned business, or have failed to pay wages or other monies, will be able to recover up to $5,000 for unpaid wages, vacation and holiday pay, and termination and severance pay. Employees must file claim for compensation with Employment Standards Branch of Ministry of Labour. If funds cannot be recovered from employer, Branch can attempt to collect them from directors. (c. E.14, §§58.4, 58.8 and 58.19). (*Note:* New legislation which is at Third Reading Stage has been proposed that will amend various provisions in Employment Standards Act.)

Human Rights Code, 1981 (c. H.19).—Code provides that every person has right to equal treatment with respect to employment without discrimination because of race, ancestry, place of origin, colour, ethnic origin, citizenship, creed, sex, age, record of offences, marital status, family status, sexual orientation or handicap. (c. H.19, §5). Ontario Human Rights Commission administers Code. Its duties include promoting understanding of Code, inquiring into incidents regarding prohibited ground of discrimination, initiating investigations and enforcing provisions of Code and orders of boards of inquiry.

Harassment.—Code forbids harassment of employees by employer or anyone acting on employer's behalf, or by co-worker, on grounds of race, ancestry, place of origin, colour, ethnic origin, citizenship, creed, sex, age, record of offences, marital status, family status or handicap. Harassment is defined as course of vexatious comment or conduct that is known or ought reasonably to be known to be unwelcome. (c. H.19, §5).

Sexual Harassment.—Employees have right to freedom from harassment in workplace because of sex. Every employee has right to be free from unwelcome sexual advance made by person in position to grant or deny benefit or advancement to another. Employees also have right to be free from reprisal or threat of reprisal for rejection of sexual solicitation or advance where reprisal is made or threatened by person in position to grant or deny benefit or advancement. (c. H.19, §7).

Handicap.—Discrimination because of handicap is prohibited in all areas protected by Code. Except where handicap renders person incapable of performing essential duties of job, employer can not discriminate because that person has, or used to have, handicap. Under Code, handicap includes any degree of physical disability or disfigurement caused by injury, illness or birth defect; learning disability; or injury for which benefits were claimed or received under Workers' Compensation Act. (c. H.19, §10[1]). It is not contravention of Code to discriminate against person if handicap, which cannot be accommodated by employer without undue hardship, renders person unable to perform essential duties of job. (c. H.19, §17).

Employment Advertising.—Employment advertising may not directly or indirectly classify or indicate qualifications on basis of any of prohibited grounds of discrimination. (c. H.19, §23).

Application Forms.—Under Code, right to equal treatment with respect to employment is infringed where employment application forms are used, or written or oral inquiries are made of applicant, that directly or indirectly classify or indicate qualifications on basis of any prohibited grounds. (c. H.19, §23).

Employment Interviews.—Code permits greater latitude on employment interviews than on application forms. It is permissible to ask questions concerning prohibited ground of discrimination at interview, provided Code permits discrimination on that ground. (c. H.19, §23).

Occupational Health and Safety Act (c. O.1).—Act is designed to protect workers against health and safety hazards in workplace. Act requires creation of health and safety committees in all workplaces with 20 or more employees. It provides for regular compulsory inspection of workplace by employee representative and entitles employees to refuse work where their health and safety is in danger. Act regulates identification and manner of use of hazardous substances. It also provides for investigative and enforcement powers and procedures. Act requires company directors and officers to take all reasonable care to ensure company complies with Act and Regulations, orders and requirements of inspectors and orders of Minister.

See Topical Index in front part of this volume.

LABOUR RELATIONS . . . *continued*

Pension Benefits Act, 1987 (c. P.8).—Every employer who establishes pension plan must register plan with Pension Commission of Ontario and maintain plan's qualifications for registration while it is in force. In addition, plan must be approved under Income Tax Act of Canada. Pension Commission administers Act and its regulations and promotes establishment and improvement of pension plans in Ontario.

Pay Equity Act, 1987 (c. P.7).—Act is designed to redress systemic gender discrimination in compensation for work performed by employees in female job classes. All employers in public sector and private sector firms with 100 employees or more are required to develop, post and implement one or more pay equity plans. Private sector firms with ten to 99 employees can choose to develop and post plans but they are not required to do so under Act. However, they are still required to achieve pay equity and may be subject to complaints from their employees if they do not. In unionized workplace, bargaining agent and employer are required to jointly negotiate pay equity plan. Maximum of 1% of establishment's previous years payroll must be set aside to upgrade compensation of certain female employees until pay equity is achieved. Pay Equity Commission provides information to employees on job-evaluation schemes, offers approval for implementation of schemes and investigates inequities.

Workers' Compensation Act (c. W.11).—Awarding of compensation to injured worker is under jurisdiction of Workers' Compensation Board. Personal injury by accident arising out of, and in course of employment is covered, unless attributable solely to serious and wilful misconduct of worker (except injuries resulting in death or serious disablement). Industrial disease due to nature of employment is covered regardless of earning capacity. Common law remedies of injured party still exist, but if action is brought at law in respect of injury to worker, upon application of any party to action, Board has jurisdiction to determine whether same is maintainable, or whether injured party is only entitled to compensation from Board, and, if so, may order action forever stayed. Compensation in form of monthly payments or whatever Board may decide, based on 90% of average earnings of injured worker is payable by Board out of accident fund formed by annual assessment on employers.

Employer Health Tax.—Each employer in Province of Ontario is required to pay Employer Health Tax (EHT) based on annual payroll. EHT is applied as follows: rate of 1.95% of payroll for employers with annual payrolls over $400,000; rate of .98% for employers with annual payrolls of $200,000 and under; and graduated rates for employers with $200,001 to $400,000 in annual payroll. Employers paying over $400,000 in remuneration annually to employees are required to make monthly instalment payments. Other employers are to make quarterly instalment payments or monthly instalments if they wish.

Unemployment Compensation.—See Canada Law Digest, topic Taxation, subhead Unemployment Compensation Tax.

LANDLORD AND TENANT:

In general, common law rules govern, as supplemented by Landlord and Tenant Act, c. L.7; Ontario Human Rights Code (c. H.19) prohibits discrimination. Conversion of rental housing to other uses restricted by Rental Housing Protection Act, c. R.24. Rent Control Act, S.O. 1992, c.11, continues rent controls and provides for registration of rents for residential premises.

Leases.—A lease for a period of three years or more must be by deed or note in writing. (c. S.19, §§2, 3). If it is in writing but not sealed, it may nevertheless be enforceable as agreement for lease. If it is not in writing and tenant enters and pays rent by year, it becomes tenancy from year to year.

Registration.—Need not be registered if not more than seven years, under Registry System, or three years, under Land Titles System. Effect of nonregistration in other cases, see topic Records.

Termination.—Common law rules apply except as to residential tenancies.

Relief Against Forfeiture.—Courts have power to relieve against forfeiture for breach of any covenant in lease and may grant such relief as thinks fit on such terms as to payment of rent, costs, expenses, damages, compensation, penalty or injunction to restrain future breaches as deemed just. (c. L.7, §20). Tenant must be given notice and opportunity to remedy breach first (c. L.7, §19).

Insolvent Tenant.—The right of the landlord to rent on the insolvency of a tenant is restricted to arrears of rent due during the three months next preceding the assignment and rent for the three months following, and thence as long as the assignee retains possession, but any payment to be made to the landlord in respect of accelerated rent must be credited against the amount payable by the assignee for the period of his occupation. (c. L.7, §38[1]). Landlord may not terminate lease of insolvent person by reason only that insolvent person is insolvent, or notice of intention or proposal has been filed or that insolvent person has not paid rent. (Bankruptcy and Insolvency Act, R.S.C., B-3, §65.1). Insolvent commercial tenant may repudiate lease on 30 days notice, subject to landlord's right to challenge such repudiation. Upon repudiation, landlord is entitled to compensation equal to lesser of six months rent under lease and rent for remainder of lease from date repudiation takes effect. §65.2).

Dispossession.—Where a tenant overholds after expiry of his lease or where for any other reason an existing lease may be terminated, landlord or tenant (if applicable) may make summary application to Ontario Court (General Division) judge for writ of possession. Overholding tenant may be liable for double rent. (c. L.7, §§58, 59).

Distress.—Common law as modified by c. L.7 applies.

Residential Tenancies.—Tenant's obligations cease unless executed copy of lease delivered to him 21 days after execution by him (c. L.7, §81); security deposits prohibited except for last months rent, 6% interest payable on security deposits (§82); distress prohibited (§84); doctrine of frustration applies (§86); covenants interdependent (§87); right to assign protected (§89); statutory obligation on landlord to repair (§94); other tenant protections; special provisions as to notices to quit; unless tenant has vacated or abandoned, no repossession except pursuant to court order; special rules as to service of notices (c. L.7). Person who becomes mortgagee in possession of residential premises is deemed to be landlord subject to tenancy agreement and provisions of Landlord and Tenant Act that apply to residential premises. However, mortgagee in possession of single family home or other residential premises may obtain possession where it enters into binding agreement of purchase and sale and purchaser requires premises for purposes of its own occupation. (Mortgages Act, c. M.40). Procedures have been established to control rent on residential premises. (Rent Control Act, S.O. 1992, c. 11 as am'd by S.O. 1994, c. 2, §§8-30).

Condominiums.—See topic Real Property.

LEASES: See topic Landlord and Tenant.

LEGISLATURE:

Province is divided into electoral districts with each district electing one member to sit in Legislative Assembly.

LEVY: See topics Attachment; Executions.

LICENCES:

Professions.—Licensing of most professions is carried out by self-regulating bodies under authority of provincial legislation: accountants (c. P.37); architects (c. A.26); dentists (c. H.4); doctors (c. H.4); lawyers (c. L.8); nurses (c. H.4); optometrists (c. H.4); pharmacists (c. H.4); professional engineers (c. P.28); psychologists (c. P.36).

Businesses and Trades.—Licensing of most businesses and trades, where applicable, is carried out directly by provincial or municipal public officials.

Provincial: auto and other mechanics (c. T.17); bailiffs (c. B.2); carpenters (c. T.17); collection agencies (c. C.14); electricians (c. T.17); dealers in livestock and livestock products (c. L.22); insurance brokers (c. R.19); insurance companies (c. I.8) (also under federal jurisdiction); itinerant sellers (i.e., door to door salesmen) (c. C.31) (see also topic Consumer Protection); loan and trust companies (c. L.25); mortgage brokers (c. M.39); motor vehicle dealers (c. M.42); pawnbrokers (c. P.6); plumbers (c. T.17); private investigators and security guards (c. P.25); sale of liquor (c. L.19). See also topic Brokers.

Municipal: Licensing requirements vary by municipality and may include many common commercial activities including: amusement places; billiard parlours; bowling alleys; carnivals; cigarettes; circuses; gas stations and garages; hairdressing shops; massage parlours; movie theatres; parking lots; public baths; public halls; restaurants; retail stores.

Federal Undertakings.—Licensing of certain commercial activities is carried out by federal public officials including aeronautics; banking; insurance (also under provincial jurisdiction); railways; shipping; telecommunications. See Canada Law Digest, topic Licenses.

LIENS:

Major statutory liens are: Builders', suppliers' and workers' (c. C.30); corporations' on shares (c. B.16); innkeepers' (c. I.7); vendor's (chattels) (c. S.1); and forestry workers' lien for wages (c. F.28).

Major common law liens are: Auctioneers', bailees', carriers', solicitors', and vendors' lien (land).

Enforcement.—The general remedy for enforcement of liens is by retention of the property subject thereto; but there are certain statutory powers of sale and remedies with respect to some liens. There is no right of redemption after a sale.

Construction Lien Act (c. C.30).—Act applies to all contracts and subcontracts for supply of labour or materials to be used in any alteration, addition or repair to, or any construction, erection or installation on any land, building or structure, including demolition or removal (referred to herein as "improvement"). Person who supplies has lien on interest of owner in amount of lesser of amount earned but unpaid under claimant's contract or subcontract, and claimant's pro rata share of holdbacks required to be maintained by contractual payer of claimant's defaulting contractual payer's. Act defines "owner" to include any person with interest in improved premises at whose request (broadly speaking) supply was made, and includes tenant. Said holdbacks are equal to 10% of value of services and materials supplied under each contract or subcontract under which lien may arise ("statutory holdback") plus amount of any lien of which payer has received written notice from claimant, from time to time ("notice holdback"), which must be deducted from any payments to be made by payer and retained until liens which may be claimed against said holdbacks expire, have been satisfied, discharged, or vacated upon posting of security. Except where preserved as described below, lien for services or materials supplied under contract (between claimant and owner of improved premises) or subcontract (between claimant and any other person supplying improvement) expires 45 days after: (i) in case of contract, completion or abandonment of contract; (ii) in case of subcontract, date on which claimant last supplies services or materials to improvement pursuant to subcontract, or on which said subcontract is certified as complete in accordance with terms of Act; (iii) in either case, date of publication of certificate of substantial performance called for in contract in respect of improvement to which claimant supplied, but where contract calls for certification of substantial performance, said holdbacks must only be retained in respect of labour and materials supplied prior to date that substantial performance is actually certified, and separate holdback, statutory holdback and notice holdback must be retained in respect of remaining services or materials actually supplied. Lien may be preserved by registering claim for lien in prescribed form prior to expiry in proper land registry office. Preserved lien must be perfected within 45 days after deadline for its preservation. Preserved lien may be perfected by issuing and registering certificate of action issued from Ontario Court (General Division) in applicable land registry office. Where lien is in respect of improvement to land of which Crown is owner, or of public street or right-of-way owned by municipality, or of railway right of way, lien may be preserved by giving copy thereof to owner in manner specified in Act prior to expiry, and it may be perfected by commencing action to enforce lien as above, but without requirement of obtaining or registering certificate of action. Lien may be vacated by posting of security with Court as described in Act (§44), including security for costs. Perfected lien expires immediately after second anniversary of commencement of action that perfected lien, unless, on or before that anniversary, any lien action in which lien

See Topical Index in front part of this volume.

LIENS . . . *continued*
may be enforced (including any lien extant, whether or not vacated, in respect of same lands) is set down, or order is made for trial thereof. (S.O. 1994, c. 27, §42).

Owner is trustee, and contractor is beneficiary of trust fund made up of following: all amounts received by owner other than Crown or municipality, that are to be used in financing of improvement; all amounts certified as payable under contract, or unpaid value of substantially performed portion of contract, which is in owner's hands or later comes into owner's hands; and net sale proceeds of improved premises. Contractor or subcontractor ("trade trustee") is trustee of all amounts owing to or received by trade trustee, on account of contract or subcontract price of services or materials supplied by trade trustee to improvement; beneficiaries of said trust fund are all persons who have supplied services or materials to improvement pursuant to subcontract with trade trustee. Trustee under Act is not allowed to appropriate or convert to its own use or to any use inconsistent with trust any portion thereof unless and until all beneficiaries of trust have been paid in full. Directors, officers and other persons controlling relevant activities of trustee under Act, who assent to or acquiesce in actions that they know or ought to know amount to breach of trust are liable for damages for breach.

Subject to certain exceptions stated below, liens arising from improvement have priority over mortgages affecting owner's interest in premises. Mortgage registered prior to time first lien in respect of improvement arises has priority in respect of liens arising from improvement, to extent of lesser of actual value of premises at time when first lien arose and amount advanced prior to that time. In addition, mortgage advance which is made after first lien arises, but prior to receipt of written notice thereof, or preservation or perfection thereof, or subsequent to time that all such liens have been discharged or vacated, takes priority over all liens in respect of improvement. Where mortgage is registered after first lien arises in respect of improvement, or where mortgage is taken for purpose of financing making of improvement, liens arising from improvement have priority over said mortgage at least to extent of any deficiency in holdbacks required to be retained by owner under Act, and where, prior to making of any advance, mortgagee has received written notice of lien in respect of improvement, or where such lien has been preserved or perfected and not discharged or vacated, said advance and all subsequent advances lose priority to all liens arising from improvement. Lien arises when claimant commences supplying services or materials, not when its lien is preserved.

Repair and Storage Liens Act (c. R.25).—Act sets out rights of repairer or storer to claim lien against article (defined as item of tangible personal property, other than fixture) which has been repaired or stored. Repair includes altering, restoring or improving article and transporting for purpose of making repair. Storer is person who receives any article for storage, repair or both in understanding that he will be paid, while repairer is one who repairs on understanding he will be paid. Repairer or storer has lien for amount which customer agreed to pay for services, or for fair value of service where no amount agreed upon. Repairer or storer can retain article until paid and further, Act creates nonpossessory lien rights which permit repairer or storer to retain lien rights even where article restored to customer.

Possessory lien rights permit claimant, after 60 days, to dispose of article in accordance with Act's redemption and sale provisions. Rights of possessory lien claimant have priority over all other interests in article, including any nonpossessory lien claimant. Nonpossessory lien claimants must register financing statement in Personal Property Security Act registration system to ensure lien enforceable against third parties.

Act provides procedure for distributing proceeds of any sale in accordance with specified priorities.

Carrier's Lien.—See topic Carriers.

Execution Lien.—See topic Executions.

Judgment Lien. See topic Judgments.

Solicitor's Lien.—See topic Attorneys and Counselors.

Tax Liens.—See topic Taxation.

LIMITATION OF ACTIONS:

Particular Limitations.—Specific causes of action may be subject to limitation by applicable statutes, as, e.g., malpractice actions, one year (1991, c. 18, Sched. II, §89[1]); actions for personal injuries and property damage occasioned by motor vehicle, two years (c. H.8, §206[1]); actions by family for death or injury to member, two years (c. F.3, §61[4]); actions against public authorities, six months (c. P.38, §7[1]); against public hospitals, two years (c. P.40, §31); against municipal corporations for nonrepair of highways, three months (c. M.45, §284[2]) with notice to be given within seven days (§284[5]); etc.

Statute of Limitations.—Actions not limited by particular statute are governed by The Limitations Act (c. L.15) under which actions must be brought within following periods after respective causes of action accrue:

Twenty Years.—An action for rent upon an indenture of demise, an action upon a bond or other specialty, an action upon a recognizance or a judgment (other than a foreign judgment).

Ten Years.—An action upon a covenant contained in an indenture of mortgage or any other instrument to repay the whole or part of any moneys secured thereby or alternatively, if under a mortgage, within ten years after the person liable on the covenant transferred his interest, whichever is the later; an action by a mortgagee against a grantee of the equity of redemption, an action of dower, an action to recover land or rent.

Six Years.—An action for trespass to goods or land, simple contract or debt grounded upon any lending or contract without specialty, debt for arrears of rent, detinue, replevin or upon the case other than for slander; an action for money levied on execution; an action upon an award where the submission is not by specialty; an action for an escape; an action upon a foreign judgment, which by case law is treated as a simple contract debt (Stewart v. Guibond [1903], 6 O.L.R. 262; Rutledge v. U.S. Savings and Loan Company [1906], 37 S.C.R. 546).

An action for personal injuries will generally be an action upon the case and not subject to four year period below, but see special periods, especially for motor vehicle injuries, under subhead Particular Limitations, above.

Four Years.—An action for assault, battery, wounding or imprisonment.

Two Years.—An action for a penalty, damages, or a sum of money given by any statute to the Crown or the party aggrieved, an action for slander.

One Year.—An action for a penalty imposed by any statute brought by any informer suing for himself alone or for the Crown as well as himself.

Concealed Fraud.—In the case of concealed fraud in actions for recovery of land or rent, time runs from time fraud is discovered or might have been discovered by reasonable diligence. (c. L.15).

Disability of Plaintiff.—If the plaintiff is under disability owing to infancy, insanity, etc., the statutory period does not begin to run until disability is removed.

Absence of Defendant or Plaintiff.—If defendant is out of Province, statutory period (under c. L.15) begins to run from time defendant returns. In no case is extension of time allowed by reason of absence of plaintiff.

Interruption of Statutory Period.—The statutory period (under c. L.15) begins to run anew from time of payment on account or acknowledgment of indebtedness in writing. But in case of action upon covenant contained in mortgage made on or after July 1st, 1939, part payments or acknowledgments made by person other than person liable, will not interrupt statutory period.

Pleading.—Any statutory limitation should be pleaded specifically. (R.P. 25.07[4]).

Foreign Causes of Action.—Action must be commenced within limitation period applicable under Ontario Limitations Act. However if Ontario courts characterize limitations legislation of jurisdiction of proper law as being substantive rather than procedural, action must also be within that time period as well. (Traders Finance v. Casselman, [1960] S.C.R. 242).

LIMITED PARTNERSHIP: See topic Partnership.

MARRIAGE:

Governed in Ontario by Marriage Act. (c. M.3).

Consent Required.—Consent in writing of both parents is required before marriage license may be issued to minor who is of age of 16 or more, except where one of parents is dead or both parents are living apart, in which case consent may be given by parent having actual or legal custody of minor. Prescribed form of consent. (c. M.3, §5).

Licence, Banns or Special Permit.—Marriage licences which remain valid for three months may be issued for a fee by office of Minister of Consumer and Commercial Relations and by clerk of every city, town, or village. (c. M.3, §§3 and 11). Alternatively, marriage may be solemnized under authority of publication of banns or in certain cases under authority of special permit. (§§9, 10 and 17). When one party to intended marriage applies for licence, he or she must personally make affidavit stating amongst other things, that there is no lawful cause or legal impediment to prevent marriage and must produce to issuer official copy of registration of birth of other party to marriage or deposit affidavit by such other party or member of his or her family stating age, date and place of birth of such other party. Where both parties to intended marriage attend before issuer it is sufficient if each of them makes required affidavit. No medical examination required. No marriage may be solemnized earlier than third day after date of licence or fifth day after banns published.

Where a previous marriage of the applicant has been dissolved or annulled in Canada, no licence will be issued unless certified copy of final decree or judgment deposited. Where dissolved or annulled outside Canada, written authorization of Minister is required before licence will be issued. (c. M.3, §8). See also topic Death.

Ceremonial Marriage.—Marriages may be solemnized by the duly appointed ministers and clergymen of every denomination, if they are residents of Ontario and have been registered by Minister as authorized to solemnize marriage. Judge or justice of peace may solemnize marriages in their chambers or offices between hours of nine o'clock in morning and five o'clock in afternoon. Fee is payable.

Records of Marriages.—Every issuer of marriage licences must keep a record of the licences which he has issued and any person may have a search made of any licence issued within the three preceding months.

Common Law Marriages.—Marriages by cohabitation and repute are not formally recognized in Ontario but where man and woman have cohabited continuously for not less than three years, or have cohabited in relationship of some permanence and are natural or adoptive parents of child, they are considered spouses for purposes of support obligations. (c. F.3, §29). Common law marriages, if constituted in jurisdictions which recognize them, may be regarded as formally valid in Ontario. (Forbes v. Forbes, 20 O.W.R. 924).

Proxy marriages are not authorized.

Marriages by written contract are not authorized.

Prohibited Marriages.—A man may not marry his grandmother, grandfather's wife, wife's grandmother, aunt, wife's aunt, mother, stepmother, wife's mother, daughter, wife's daughter, son's wife, sister, granddaughter, grandson's wife, wife's granddaughter, niece or nephew's wife. A woman may not marry her grandfather, grandmother's husband, husband's grandfather, uncle, husband's uncle, father, step-father, husband's father, son, husband's son, daughter's husband, brother, grandson, granddaughter's husband, husband's grandson, nephew or niece's husband. The prohibitions include all such relationships, whether by the whole or half blood and whether legitimate or illegitimate.

MARRIED WOMEN:

See topics Dower; Estate Trustees; Husband and Wife; Marriage; Wills; Witnesses.

MASTER AND SERVANT:

See topic Labour Relations.

MECHANICS' LIENS: See topic Liens.

MINES AND MINERALS:

Ministry of Northern Development and Mines of Ontario has general supervision over mining and mining lands in province, and maintains inspectors to enforce requirements of Mining Act (c. M.14) made thereunder with respect to mining operations in province, and health and safety of employees.

Aggregate Resources Act, (c. A.8) governs licensing and operation of pits and quarries, including rehabilitation and abandonment.

Prospector's Licence.—No person or company may prospect for minerals upon Crown lands or land of which mining rights are in the Crown without a prospector's licence. Licences are valid for five years. Licence is not required to hold mining claim.

Prospecting.—The Mining Act stipulates requirements as to proper staking of claims, recording of staked claims, recording of required work on claims and acquisition of mineral and/or surface rights by patent, lease or licence of occupation. For administration of Act, Province divided into Mining Divisions with a Recorder in each. Patented property and leaseholds are administered under land titles and land registry systems. See topic Records.

Operation and Inspection of Mines, and Safeguarding of Employees.—Detailed provisions governing these matters are set out in Mining Act (c. M.14) and Occupational Health and Safety Act (c. O.1) and Regulations thereunder. See topic Labour Relations.

Development and Environmental Protection.—Part VII of Mining Act (as am'd) governs these matters. Advanced exploration (as defined) requires prior written notice to Director of Rehabilitation. Public notice and closure plan or financially assured closure plan may be required. Annual reports indicating changes to project, mine life expectancy and projected rehabilitation work are required. See also Industrial and Mining Lands Compensation Act. (c. I.5). Also see topic Environment.

Refining of Metals.—All lands, claims or mining rights leased, patented or otherwise disposed of under any Act or any authority are subject to condition that all ores or minerals raised or removed therefrom be treated and refined in Canada so as to yield refined metal or other product suitable for direct use in arts without further treatment. In default, Lieutenant-Governor in Council may declare lease, patent or other form of title to be void whereupon said lands revert to and become vested in Her Majesty, freed and discharged of any interest or claim of any other person or persons whomsoever. Lieutenant-Governor in Council may exempt any lands from operation of this provision for such time as he may deem proper.

Mineral Exploration.—Where person or corporation who is resident of Ontario proposes to carry out program of mineral exploration in Ontario, he may apply to have program designated under Ontario Mineral Exploration Program Act. (c. O.27). Upon application by person Minister may pay grant to person (if not corporation) exploration expenses incurred by such person. Where applicant is corporation Minister may issue certificate that such corporation is entitled to tax credit up to prescribed percentage of exploration expenses incurred by corporation.

Foreign mining companies desiring to operate in Ontario must obtain an Ontario licence for that purpose. License not required for ownership of mining properties. See topic Corporations, subhead Foreign and Extra-provincial Corporations.

Mining Court.—Abolished. Jurisdiction formerly exercised by it to determine claims arising under Mining Act is exercised by Mining and Lands Commissioner.

Oil and Gas.—See Energy Act (c. E.16) as to handling of hydrocarbons; O. Reg. 72/93 under Mining Act for leases for production of petroleum and natural gas from Crown lands under water; Petroleum Resources Act (c. P.12), licence required to explore for oil or gas, lease oil or gas rights except from Crown, produce oil or gas and permit required to drill etc., issued by Minister of Consumer and Commercial Relations subject to reference to Ontario Energy Board; Ontario Energy Board Act (c. O.13); Gas and Oil Leases Act (c. G.3), termination of leases for default; Gasoline Handling Act (c. G.4); Gasoline Tax Act (c. G.5), as amended by Gasoline Tax Amendment Act, 1992, S.O. 1992, c. 9 (including re: exports); Fuel Tax Act (c. F.35).

Taxation.—Mining Tax Act (c. M.15) imposes tax on annual profits at rate of 20% of amount by which operator's profit, as calculated by given formula for given year, exceeds amounts outlined in Act. Minister may deem companies associated and combine profits. Tax is lien on mine, leases, rights and machinery. Mining Act (c. M.14) imposes annual acreage tax at rates prescribed by regulation. See also provisions contained in Income Tax Act (Canada). See Canada Law Digest, topic Mines and Minerals.

MONOPOLIES AND RESTRAINT OF TRADE:

See Canada Law Digest.

MORTGAGES OF PERSONAL PROPERTY:

See topic Personal Property Security.

MORTGAGES OF REAL PROPERTY:

In general common law rules govern, supplemented by statutes. (Land Titles Act, c. L.5, Mortgages Act, c. M.40, Registry Act, c. R.20, Land Registration Reform Act, c. L.4, Family Law Act, c. F.3). Under Land Registration Reform Act, c. L.4, term "mortgage" replaced by term "charge" and common law concept of conveyance of fee simple to mortgagee is abolished. (§6). Charges in statutory form deemed to include covenants listed in c. L.4 (§7). Standard charge terms filed under c. L.4 (§8) may be incorporated in charge by reference (§9). Affidavits required under Family Law Act may be replaced by statements contained in body of transfer. Family Law Act statements may be made by attorney with personal knowledge. (c. F.3, §21[4]). Spouse must consent to charge of property occupied as family residence (matrimonial home). (c. F.3, §21[1]). See topic Husband and Wife, subhead Status.

Execution.—Charges in statutory form effective without seals. (c. L.4, §13). Copy of mortgage must be delivered by mail by mortgagee to mortgagor or agent within 30 days after execution. (c. M.40, §4).

Recording.—Necessity for and validity without, see topic Records.

Trust deeds are ordinarily used to secure issues of bonds or debentures. They must be registered same as ordinary mortgages to charge lands and filed with Ministry of Consumer and Commercial Relations under Personal Property Security Act (c. P.10) to charge tangible or intangible personal property.

Future Advances.—Mortgage may secure future advances but see topic Records.

Priorities.—Common law rules modified by recording statutes. See topic Records.

Assignment.—Charge may be assigned by attaching executed Assignment (Registry Act) or Transfer (Land Titles Act).

Discharge or Satisfaction.—Registered charge is discharged by registration of discharge in prescribed form by chargee, his assignee or representative entitled to money. Discharge must include registration date and number of charge and all assignments or other documents relating to charge. Execution of discharge is same as for transfer or charge.

Duplicate of mortgage and any assignments must be produced with the discharge and cancelled by registrar. If duplicate is lost, loss must be proved by declaration filed. Where assignment includes other mortgages, its production is not required. (c. R.20).

An executor or administrator of the mortgagee may discharge any mortgage on payment of the debt. It is not necessary for spouse of mortgagee to join in discharge of any mortgage.

Instead of the statutory discharge, a release and reconveyance may be given. In the case of a bond mortgage, the latter course is followed.

Release of Part of Property. —Same form as discharge except that lands to be released are specifically described.

Foreclosure and Sale.—Every mortgage contains either an express power of sale or an implied power, which is inserted therein by statutory provisions. (c. M.40, §24). Upon default of payment, mortgagee may realize, either by sale, under such power of sale, or by proceedings for foreclosure and sale in Ontario Court (General Division), or in district courts if sum claimed to be due does not exceed $15,000.

Although mortgage provides for exercise of power of sale on default without notice to mortgagor or subsequent encumbrancers, notice must be given in all proceedings under powers of sale, unless and to extent only that notice is ordered dispensed with by judge under §39. Notice may only be given after at least 15 days default, and sale shall not be made for at least 35 days after notice. (§32). Manner of giving notice is prescribed. (§33). These provisions do not apply to bond mortgages or debentures. (§41).

The mortgagee may recover personal judgment on the covenant contained in the mortgage. In case the lands are sold pursuant to a power of sale in the mortgage or pursuant to judgment in an action for foreclosure and sale, and there is a deficiency, the same may be recovered on such personal judgment.

Where default under the mortgage accelerates principal and interest, relief from sale or action by the mortgagee will be given upon the mortgagor remedying the default, excluding payment of monies not payable by reason only of lapse of time. (§23).

Redemption.—Every mortgagor, after default in payment of his mortgage, may redeem the mortgaged property at any time before his right is barred under the statute of limitation where the mortgagee is in possession, or under a final order of sale, or final order of foreclosure made by the court, or before the lands are sold under the power of sale contained in the mortgage, on payment of the amount due, with interest and costs.

A mortgage for more than five years, except one given by corporation, may be redeemed at any time after five years on payment of principal and interest to date of payment and on three months further interest in lieu of notice. (c. M.40, §18).

Forms

Charge.—Charges under both Registry Act and Land Titles Act shall be in Form 2. (R.R.O. 688, as am'd).

Discharge.—Discharges under both Registry Act and Land Titles Act shall be in Form 3. (R.R.O. 688, as am'd).

Assignment.—Under Registry Act there is no statutory form.

Chattel Mortgages.—See topic Chattel Mortgages.

MOTOR VEHICLES:

Registrar of Motor Vehicles, acting under instructions of Minister of Transportation and Communications has general supervision over all matters relating to highway traffic. (c. H.8, §3).

Vehicle licence is required annually. No registration fee is payable for military, governmental or diplomatic vehicles in Ontario. Number plates must be attached on the front and back of every motor vehicle in a conspicuous position and on the back of every trailer. New residents are exempt from registration and plate requirements for 30 days if complied with requirements of former jurisdiction. See subheads Proof of Financial Responsibility and Insurance; Foreign Vehicle. Motorized snow vehicles must be registered and owners must obtain permits. (c. M.44).

Driver's licence required. Licence issued on anniversary of birth date of driver; duration of licence, three years unless issued to probationary driver. Members of Armed Forces driving military vehicles on duty do not require licence. Person under 16 years old may not be licenced. Licences must be carried when driving and produced on demand. No owner of motor vehicle shall operate motor vehicle or cause or permit motor vehicle to be operated on highway unless motor vehicle is insured under contract of automobile insurance. (c. M.25). Classes of licences governed by regulation. See subhead Nonresident Operator, infra.

Instruction permits available, limited in time. Driving instructors must be licensed and are governed by regulations under Act.

Titles and Sales.—Notice must be given on prescribed form by forwarding same to Ministry of Transportation and Communications by both vendor and purchaser within six days of sale. Safety standards certificate must be obtained or vendor may forward to Ministry required notice together with current number plates and vehicle licence. (c. H.8, §60).

Liens.—See topic Personal Property Security.

See Topical Index in front part of this volume.

MOTOR VEHICLES . . . *continued*

Identification Marks.—It is an offence to deface or remove vehicle identification numbers or other identification marks of manufacturer of motor vehicle or knowingly to deal with or possess a motor vehicle on which they have been altered. (c. H.8, §60).

Restrictions on Operation.—May not be operated by person without driver's licence, by person under age of 16 or by intoxicated or disqualified person or for any illicit trade or transportation. Statutory regulations are in force governing weight of vehicles varying in accordance with type of vehicle, width of tire and season of year. Regulated by c. H.8 and Regulations thereunder. Certain prescribed vehicles will be prohibited from operating on highway unless displaying vehicle inspection sticker. Regulations may be made with respect to types of vehicles requiring sticker, procedures relating to use or issue of stickers, and intervals of inspection. Regulations may also be made prescribing that specified classes of vehicles have covered loads if travelling on certain types of highways. No person shall transport any dangerous goods in vehicle on highway unless all prescribed safety requirements are complied with and vehicle and all containers and packaging comply with prescribed safety standards and marks. Exception exists if under direction of Minister of National Defence for Canada or permit has been obtained. (c. D.1).

Equipment Required.—Regulated by c. H.8 and Regulations thereunder.

Lights Required.—Regulated by c. H.8, §62 and Regulations thereunder.

Inspection.—No regular inspection required but spot-checks and certificates thereof are authorized. It is offence to refuse to submit vehicle for examination on request. Licence plates of vehicle found in dangerous or unsafe condition may be seized until remedied. (c. H.8, §82). Restrictions are placed on form and manner in which safety standard certificates are issued. Dump trucks registered in another jurisdiction will not be issued permit or number plates unless they have safety standard certificate. (c. H.8). Inspector may stop and inspect vehicle and its load if he believes dangerous goods are being transported. (c. D.1).

Traffic regulated by stop signs and 3-phase lights, slow signs, flashing amber (slow and proceed) and flashing red (stop and proceed) lights and stop and yield-right-of-way signs, pedestrian cross-walks marked "X." Passing on right permitted under certain limited conditions. Right turns permitted at stop signs and red lights after stopping.

Impounding.—Where vehicle is driven by intoxicated person or by person whose permit or licence has been suspended or revoked, and in certain other cases, vehicle may be impounded for three months, unless vehicle is not owned or is held under lease that has less than three months to run by person convicted and person convicted is not principal driver. Court has discretion not to impound if order would cause hardship to another person with interest in vehicle. (c. H.8, §220). See topic Environment, subhead Enforcement.

Accidents.—Person in charge must stop, give assistance if necessary, give in writing his name and address and that of owner and number of permit if demanded. If accident results in personal injuries or if apparent damage to property exceeds $700 (c. H.8, §199; R.R.O. 596, §11), person in charge of vehicle must report accident to nearest police officer. Must also report damage to property on highway such as poles, lights, signs and sod. (c. H.8, §201).

Seatbelts.—With certain exceptions, use of seatbelts in vehicles driven on highways when vehicle equipped with seatbelts is mandatory. Driver of vehicle commits offence if he drives vehicle on highway without requiring child between two and 16 to wear seatbelt. Passengers in vehicle driven on highway who are 16 years of age or over commit offence if they fail to use seatbelt. (c. H.8, §106).

Motorcycles.—When on highway, motorcycle must carry lighted white lamp on front and lighted red lamp on rear. (c. H.8, §104). Drivers and passengers must wear helmets when motorcycle in operation. (c. H.8, §44).

Liability of Owner and Driver.—Owner is liable for loss or damage to any person by reason of negligence in operation of the vehicle unless it was, at the time, in possession of person other than owner or his chauffeur without his consent. If vehicle leased, consent of lessee is deemed consent of owner. (c. H.8, §192).

There is statutory onus on owner and driver to disprove negligence when loss or damage is sustained by any person (pedestrian) by reason of motor vehicle on highway. This does not apply in cases of collision between motor vehicles (including streetcars), or to action brought by passenger in motor vehicle. (c. H.8, §193).

After June 22, 1990 and before Jan. 1, 1994 neither owner or operator of automobile are liable in action in Ontario for loss or damages from bodily injury arising out of use or operation of automobile, operated in Canada or U.S. unless injured person has died or has sustained: (a) permanent serious disfigurement; or (b) permanent serious impairment of important bodily function caused by continuing injury which is physical in nature. (c. I.8, §266).

This "threshold" prohibition of right to sue applies to all persons, commencing action in Ontario, no matter where they are resident or domiciled.

After Jan. 1, 1994, neither owner nor operator of automobile are liable in action in Ontario for pecuniary loss or damage from bodily injury arising out of use or operation of automobile operated in Canada or U.S.

Owner or operator of automobile will only be liable for non-pecuniary loss or damages from bodily injury arising out of use or operation of automobile in event that injured person has died or has sustained: (a) serious disfigurement or (b) serious impairment of important physical, mental or psychological function. (c. I.8, §267.1.

Non-pecuniary damages awarded for bodily injury arising out of motor vehicle accidents occurring after Jan. 1, 1994 are subject to deductible of $10,000. Deductible is to be adjusted from year to year. (c. I.8, §267.1)

Damages awarded for non-pecuniary loss under Family Law Act for motor vehicle accidents occurring after Jan. 1, 1994 are subject to deductible of $5,000. Deductible is to be adjusted from year to year. (c. I.8, §267.1).

Actions for damages occasioned by motor vehicle must be brought within two years from time damages were sustained. (c. H.8, §206). Limitation period does not run as against parties under disability such as minors and mental incompetents until person is freed of disability. (Murphy v. Welsh). Limitation period may also be extended in case where it is not discovered until some time after fact that injuries are permanent and serious. (Peixeira v. Haberman).

Driver is liable, owner not liable for penalties for moving violations of Act such as speeding, careless driving, etc.

Guests.—Statute section limiting liability of owner to guests repealed.

Proof of Financial Responsibility and Insurance.—Act to provide for temporary automobile insurance entitled Compulsory Automobile Insurance Act, c. C.25. Every owner of motor vehicle who operates, or causes or permits operation of motor vehicle not insured under contract of insurance, is liable to fine of not less than $500 and not more than $2,500 and, in addition his driver's license may be suspended for one year.

Operator of motor vehicle shall have motor vehicle proof of insurance that motor vehicle, or operator is insured under contract of insurance at all times. Agent, within meaning of Insurance Act, shall provide to owner of motor vehicle, who is resident in Ontario, application for automobile insurance, when requested to do so.

Facility Association of insurers is established to provide plan of operation for providing contract of automobile insurance to owners and licenced drivers of motor vehicles who would be unable to obtain such insurance, but for plan.

Contract of insurance that has been in effect for more than 60 days can be terminated only for specified reasons, such as nonpayment of premium, or misrepresentation by insured in application for insurance.

No-Fault Insurance.—From Jan. 1, 1972, every automobile policy issued in Ontario must provide no-fault accident benefits in a statutory form as Schedule B to policy.

Benefits payable were substantially increased as result of S.O. 1990, c. 2 and O. Reg. 273/90. Benefits payable were further increased as result of S.O. 1993, c. 10.

Benefits are payable to any occupant of automobile in respect of accidents in Ontario and to named insured, his or her spouse and any dependent relatives while occupant of any other automobile, or involved in any automobile accident, or who is not involved in accident but who suffers physical, psychological or mental injury to close relatives.

Benefits include: Weekly indemnity benefits for loss of income of up to $600 per week; weekly indemnity benefits of $185 per week for persons without income e.g. students, homemakers; death benefits of $25,000 in event of death of insured or spouse, and $10,000 per dependent; funeral expenses up to $3,000; supplementary medical and rehabilitation benefits not covered by O.H.I.P., up to $500,000 per person; ongoing care benefits, up to $500,000 per person, to maximum of $3,000 per month.

Enforcement Proceedings.—Notice of claim within 30 days; complete application within 120 days; thereafter mediation of disputes is compulsory. If mediation fails insured can elect to arbitrate or bring action in Court. Action must be commenced within two years after insurer's refusal to pay.

All benefits paid or available for accidents occurring before Jan. 1, 1994 reduce any claim person may have in tort against wrongdoer.

Benefits paid for accidents occurring after Jan. 1, 1994 are not deductible in tort action against wrongdoer.

Motor Vehicle Accident Claims Fund.—A fund from which claims arising out of certain automobile accidents may be paid has been established by statute. Claims may be made where alleged personal or property damage caused by uninsured motor vehicle, or motor vehicle insured by insolvent or recalcitrant insurer, in certain cases where judgment obtained for personal or property damage and judgment debtor unable to satisfy judgment, or where identity of vehicle or driver, or both, causing personal injury cannot be established. Payments are limited to $200,000 exclusive of costs, for all damage to persons or property arising out of one accident, occurring after Mar. 1, 1981. Where claim against uninsured vehicle, or motor vehicle insured by insolvent or recalcitrant insurer, direct application for payment may be made to Minister of Consumer and Commercial Relations without action. Claim is settled and payment from Fund is made unless owner or driver of uninsured vehicle disputes liability in which case action and judgment for claimant is prerequisite to application for payment from Fund. No interest is payable out of Fund. Where accident has been caused by a vehicle or driver whose identity cannot be established, an action may be brought against Superintendent of Insurance, and payment of damages made from Fund. Person resident outside Ontario may claim from Fund only where his own jurisdiction has similar legislation available to Ontario residents. (c. M.41).

Direct Actions.—Third party liability actions for property damage against owner or driver of Ontario insured automobiles are prohibited. Instead, Ontario insured motorists have recourse against their own insurers for property damage, and fault principles apply to such claims.

Non-Ontario insured motorists have tort right to recovery for property damage against at fault motorist.

Direct actions against automobile insurers are permitted for no-fault benefits and for claims arising from uninsured or unidentified vehicles, and for claims arising from inadequately insured motorists, pursuant to S.E.F. 44.

Foreign Vehicle.—Owner who is at least 16 years old and resides in foreign country is exempt from necessity of obtaining licence plates and permit to operate in Ontario for three months in year if jurisdiction of residence grants similar privileges to residents of Ontario but certain vehicles owned by nonresidents must be registered if operated in Ontario for more than 30 days in a calendar year. (c. H.8, §15). Owner residing in another province of Canada and not carrying on business in Ontario is exempt for six consecutive months if he has complied with requirements of his province of residence and such province grants similar privileges to Ontario residents. (c. H.8, §15).

Nonresident operator who is at least 16 years old and has complied with licencing law of home state or province may operate without Ontario licence if: (a) he is resident of foreign country and does not reside in Ontario for more than three months in any one year, (b) he is resident of another province of Canada and has complied with law of province in which he resides regarding drivers of motor vehicles, or (c) he is holder of valid International Driver's Permit. Upon becoming resident he is exempt from licencing requirements for 30 days if he has complied with laws of jurisdiction in which he previously resided. (c. H.8, §32).

Action against nonresident operating or responsible for operation of motor vehicle in Ontario, arising out of accident in Ontario, may be commenced by service of process on the Registrar of Motor Vehicles, who is constituted agent of such nonresident for such purpose and who forwards the process to the defendant in accordance with statutory provisions. A bond in the sum of $200 must be left with the Registrar to

MOTOR VEHICLES . . . *continued*
reimburse defendant his expenses should plaintiff not succeed in the action. (c. H.8, §194).

Motor Vehicle Carriers.—Governed by Truck Transportation Act (c. T.22) and Public Vehicles Act (c. P.54). First applies to commercial motor vehicles and dual purpose vehicles operated for transportation of goods for compensation and not confined to one zone. Second applies to all motor vehicles except taxicabs operated for transportation of passengers and express freight for compensation and not within municipality and car pool vehicles. First also applies to "freight forwarders." Both Acts supervised by Ministry of Transportation and Communications. Municipalities also have supervisory functions. Cc. T.22 and T.54 require operators to hold operating and vehicle licences and freight forwarders to hold freight forwarders' licences.

C. T.22 prescribes minimum terms for bills of lading and requires carriers to carry bills for all goods shipped to be produced on request for inspection.

Under both Acts the Highway Transport Board's certificate of public necessity and convenience must be obtained before an operating licence will be issued. Board and Ministry in operating licences may prescribe terms of licences. C. T.22 requires filing of tariffs of tolls and regulates contents of bills of lading and transportation contracts. C. P.54 requires notices of discontinuance of services, filing and approval of tariffs of tolls.

Licensed persons must carry a bond of insurance, a certificate of which must be filed with the Department.

Sale of Motor Vehicles.—No dealer shall sell a motor vehicle manufactured after June 26, 1970 that does not conform to standards required under Canada Motor Vehicle Safety Act and bears National Safety Mark. (c. H.8, §105).

No person may carry on business as a motor vehicle dealer nor act as a salesman of a motor vehicle dealer unless registered under The Motor Vehicle Dealers Act. (c. M.42). Every dealer in used motor vehicles must give to purchaser, on delivery of vehicle, safety standards certificate issued on inspection completed not more than 30 days before delivery. (c. H.8).

Gasoline and Diesel Fuel Taxes.—See topic Taxation.

Off-road Vehicles.—Provisions dealing with issuance of licences to drive off-road vehicles e.g. motorcycles, farm equipment. (c. O.4).

NEGOTIABLE INSTRUMENTS:

See Canada Law Digest, topic Bills and Notes.

NOTARIES PUBLIC: (c. N.6).

Bond.—No bond is required.

Powers.—A notary has the power of drawing, passing, keeping and issuing all deeds and contracts, charter-parties and other mercantile transactions in the Province, of attesting all commercial instruments, taking affidavits and otherwise of acting as is usual in the office of notary.

Territorial Extent of Powers.—A person other than a barrister or solicitor who is appointed a notary public may be limited by his commission as to the territory in which he may act. Otherwise he may act anywhere in the Province.

Commission of every notary public, other than a barrister or solicitor, expires after three years. Commissions are renewable for successive three year terms. Notaries with limited commissions must indicate under their signatures date upon which their commissions expire and territory in which they may act.

Seal on Affidavits.—When notary public administers an oath or takes an affidavit or declaration, it is not necessary to validity of such oath, affidavit or declaration that he affix his seal thereto, but it is customary for him to do so.

PARTITION:

Any one or more of several joint tenants or tenants in common and other parties interested in any land in the Province may apply to Ontario Court (General Division) for partition or sale of property. (c. P.4, §3; Rule 66). Where joint tenants are spouses, see topic Husband and Wife, subhead Status.

Proceedings.—Application is by originating notice served on one or more of persons entitled to a share in common property. All parties must be served personally unless a court order dispenses with personal service. Court must proceed in least expensive and most expeditious manner for partition or sale, adding of parties, ascertainment of rights of various persons interested and taxation and payment of costs.

Persons Under Disability.—Notice must be given to Children's Lawyer where infants are interested and mentally incompetent person must be served personally unless otherwise ordered. Application for partition may be made on behalf of infant by his guardian or next friend with sanction of judge to be first obtained upon notice to Children's Lawyer.

Sale may be ordered by the court when it is considered to be more advantageous to the parties interested than partition.

Condominiums.—See topic Real Property.

PARTNERSHIP:

The law relating to partnership is in part codified in Partnerships Act (c. P.5) which is similar to English Act. Limited partnerships are dealt with in Limited Partnerships Act, (c. L.16) and registration of partnerships is dealt with in separate statute (Business Names Act, c. B.17).

Name.—Persons associated in partnership must not carry on business before registering. (c. B.17, §2). Form is provided for such registration and required information includes names and addresses of partners, name of partnership, date of birth of partners under 18 years of age, etc. If partner is corporation, name, Ontario corporation number, if any, and address for service must be set out. (O.Reg. 121/91, §2).

Penalties provided for failure to file registration or amended registration or for making false statement in such registration. Failure to register precludes partnership from maintaining proceeding in Province without first seeking leave of court. Contravention, without reasonable cause also carries fines. (c. B.17).

Change in Partnership.—Amended registration must be filed within 15 days after change in initial registration. (c. B.17, §4).

Cancellation of registration also effected by filing Form. (c. B.17, §4).

Fee.—Filing fee is payable for any registration required under foregoing paragraphs.

Renewal.—Registrations expire five years after filing; new declarations must then be filed.

Limited partnerships, in which liability of one or more partners is limited to amount of capital contributed, may be formed. (Limited Partnerships Act, c. L.16). Such partnership is formed when declaration is filed with Registrar appointed under Business Names Act and need only be signed by general partner. Declarations expire five years after date of filing unless declarations are cancelled by filing declaration of dissolution or replaced by filing new declaration before that date. General partner must maintain current record of limited partners at principal place of business. Restrictions are placed on withdrawal of capital by and interest paid to limited partners and also on limited partner's ability to be involved in business of partnership. Special provisions apply to extra-provincial limited partnerships.

PERPETUITIES:

Perpetuities.—Future interest in property is void from outset if it is incapable of vesting within perpetuity period. This is period of lives of certain persons who are living when interest is created, plus 21 years. However, even if interest would be void because it may possibly vest outside period, Perpetuities Act (c. P.9, §4) may make it valid if it in fact vests within "wait and see" period. These rules may apply whenever interest in property vests on event which may or may not happen, such as option.

Accumulations.—The Accumulations Act (c. A.5) provides that direction to accumulate income of property is void as far as period of accumulation goes beyond certain periods (generally not more than 21 years).

Mortmain.—Formerly, law of mortmain prevented corporation from holding land without license or statutory power. Law of mortmain no longer applies, but some corporations still need extra-provincial licenses to hold land in Ontario.

PERSONAL PROPERTY SECURITY:

Personal Property Security Act (c. P.10) modelled on Article IX of Uniform Commercial Code. It applies to every transaction without regard to its form and without regard to person who has title to collateral, that in substance creates security interest, including chattel mortgage, conditional sale, equipment trust, debenture, floating charge, pledge, trust indenture or trust receipt, assignment (including assignment of accounts or chattel paper), lease or consignment that secures payment or performance of obligation and every assignment of accounts or chattel paper that does not secure payment or performance of obligation. (§2). Major exceptions are for some statutory liens and deemed trusts and for creation or assignment of interest in real property other than fixtures or assignment of right to payment under mortgage, charge or lease where assignment does not convey or transfer assignor's interest in real property. (§4).

Conflict of Laws.—Applicable law is generally determined by jurisdiction where collateral is situated at time security interest attaches. Security interest in collateral already perfected under law of place in which collateral was when security interest attached and before being brought into Ontario, continues perfected in Ontario, if financing statement is registered before goods are brought into Ontario or if perfected in Ontario by earliest of (i) 60 days from entry, (ii) 15 days after secured party receives notice of entry, or (iii) date on which perfection ceases under law of other jurisdiction. Security interest that has ceased to be perfected may thereafter be perfected in Ontario, but is only effective from date of perfection. Security interest not perfected under law of place in which collateral was when security interest attached and before being brought into Ontario, may be perfected under Act, in which case perfection dates from time of perfection in Ontario. (§5).

Effectiveness.—Except as otherwise provided, security agreement is generally effective according to its terms between parties and against third parties. (§9).

Enforceability.—Security interest is not enforceable against third party unless it has attached. (§11).

Attachment.—Security interest attaches when, (a) secured party or person on behalf of secured party other than debtor or debtor's agent obtains possession of collateral or when debtor signs security agreement that identifies collateral, (b) value is given, and (c) debtor has rights in collateral, unless parties have agreed to postpone time for attachment. Debtor has no rights in crops until they become growing crops, fish until they are caught, young of animals until they are conceived, minerals or hydro carbons until they are extracted, or timber until it is cut. (§11).

After Acquired Property.—Security agreement may cover after acquired property. (§12).

Future Advances.—Security agreement may secure future advances. (§13).

Care of Collateral.—Secured party shall use reasonable care in custody and preservation of collateral in its possession, and, unless otherwise agreed, in case of instrument or chattel paper, reasonable care includes taking necessary steps to preserve rights against prior parties. Secured party is liable for any loss or damage caused by failure to meet this obligation, but does not lose security interest. Within certain limits secured party may use collateral but is liable for any loss or damage by its use of collateral otherwise than within such limits and is subject to being restrained. (§17).

Statement of Account.—Debtor, judgment creditor or person having interest in collateral, by notice in writing, may require secured party to furnish statement in writing of amount of indebtedness and terms of payment as of date specified; statement in writing approving or correcting as of date specified statement of collateral or part thereof as specified in list; statement in writing approving or correcting as of date specified statement of amount of indebtedness and terms of payment thereof; true copy of security agreement; or sufficient information as to location of security agreement or true copy so as to enable inspection. Secured party to answer notice within 15 days of receipt and secured party liable for loss or damage caused by failure to do so or for incomplete or incorrect answer. Where person receiving notice no longer has interest in

See Topical Index in front part of this volume.

PERSONAL PROPERTY SECURITY . . . *continued*
collateral, he shall, within 15 days of his receipt of notice, disclose name and address of latest successor in interest known to him. (§18).

Perfection.—Security interest is perfected when it has attached and all steps required for perfection required under any provision of Act have been completed regardless of order of occurrence. (§19). Possession of collateral by secured party or on his behalf by person other than debtor or debtor's agent perfects security interest in chattel paper, goods, instruments, securities, negotiable documents of title and money but only while it is actually held as collateral. (§22). Registration perfects security interest in any type of collateral. (§23). Where collateral gives rise to proceeds, security interest therein continues as to collateral unless secured party expressly or impliedly authorized dealing with collateral and extends to proceeds. (§25). Buyer of goods from seller who sells goods in ordinary course of business takes them free from any security interest therein given by seller even though it is perfected and buyer knows of it unless buyer also knew that sale constituted breach of security agreement. Lessee of goods from lessor who leases goods in ordinary course of business holds goods to extent of lessee's rights under lease free from any security interest therein given by lessor even though it is perfected and lessee knows of it unless lessee also knew that lease constituted breach of security agreement. Purchaser of chattel paper who takes possession of it in ordinary course of business has to extent that purchaser gives new value priority over any security interest in it that was perfected by registration if purchaser did not know at time of taking possession that chattel paper was subject to security interest or that has attached to proceeds of inventory whatever extent of purchaser's knowledge. (§28).

Priorities.—In general, following priority rules apply to security interests in same collateral. Where priority is to be determined between security interests perfected by registration, priority shall be determined by order of registration regardless of order of perfection. Where priority is to be determined between security interest perfected by registration and security interest perfected otherwise than by registration, (i) security interest perfected by registration has priority over other security interest if registration occurred before perfection of other security interest, and (ii) security interest perfected otherwise than by registration has priority over other security interest if security interest perfected otherwise than by registration was perfected before registration related to other security interest. Where priority is to be determined between security interests perfected otherwise than by registration priority shall be determined by order of perfection. Where priority is to be determined between unperfected security interests, priority shall be determined by order of attachment. Purchase-money security interest is security interest taken or reserved in collateral to secure payment of all or part of its price or security interest taken by person who gives value for purpose of enabling debtor to acquire rights in or to collateral to extent that value is applied to acquire rights. (§30). Purchase-money security interest in inventory has priority over any other security interest in same collateral given by same debtor if purchase-money security interest was perfected at earlier of time debtor or third parties at request of debtor obtained possession of inventory; before debtor receives possession of inventory secured party gives notice in writing to every other secured party who has registered financing statement in which collateral is classified as inventory before date of registration by secured party; and notice referred to states that person giving it has or expects to acquire purchase-money security interest in inventory of debtor describing such inventory by item or type. Purchase-money security interest in collateral or its proceeds other than inventory or its proceeds has priority over any other security interest in same collateral given by same debtor if purchase-money security interest in case of collateral other than intangible was perfected before or within ten days after earlier of debtor or third party at request of debtor obtained possession of collateral or in case of collateral in intangible was perfected before or within ten days after attachment of purchase-money security interest in intangible. Where more than one purchase-money security interest is given, purchase-money security interest of seller has priority over any other purchase-money security interest given by same debtor. (§33). Subsequent purchaser for value of interest in real property or creditor with prior encumbrance of record on real property to extent that he makes subsequent advances has priority to security interest in goods that attached to goods that are or become fixtures if subsequent purchase or subsequent advance under prior encumbrance of record is made or contracted for without knowledge of security interest and before notice of it is registered in proper land registry office. Otherwise security interest in goods that attached before goods became fixture has priority as to fixture over claim of any person who has interest in real property and also security interest in goods that attached after goods became fixture has priority as to fixture over claim of any person who subsequently acquired interest in real property, but not over any person who had registered interest in real property at time security interest in goods attached and who has not consented in writing to security interest or disclaimed interest in fixture. (§34). Security interest in right to payment under lease of real property, to which Act applies, is subordinate to interest of person who acquires lessor's interest in lease if interest, or notice thereof, of person is registered in proper land registry office before interest, or notice thereof, of secured party is registered in proper land registry office. Security interest in right to payment under mortgage or charge of real property, to which Act applies, is subordinate to interest of person who acquires mortgagee's or chargee's interest in mortgage or charge if interest is registered in proper land registry office before notice of security interest is registered in proper land registry office. (§36). Secured party may subordinate his security interest to any other security interest and such subordination is effective according to its terms. (§38).

Registration.—Registration system, including central office and branch offices, is maintained for purposes of Act and Repair and Storage Liens Act. Central office located at City of Toronto. (§41). Registration by notice filing and is effected by filing financing statement, or, if by electronic transmission, data, in prescribed form. Financing statement may be tendered for registration by delivery to any branch office or by mail addressed to Personal Property Security Registrations, Central Registrations Branch, Box 21100, Postal Station, "A", Toronto, Ontario, M5W 1W6. Financing statement that is data in prescribed format may be tendered for registration by above means (if information capable of being read by registration system computer), or, if tendered by authorized person, by direct electronic transmission to registration system database. (§46). Except where collateral is consumer goods, financing statement may be registered before or after security agreement signed, and one financing statement may perfect one or more security interests created or provided for in one or more security agreements between parties. (§45). Financing statement may be registered for perpetual period or for such period of years as is set out in financing statement. (§51). Registration may be renewed. (§52). Assignments of security interests may be registered. (§47). Where financing statement or financing change statement is registered secured party to deliver copy (or verification statement, if registration done electronically) to debtor within 30 days. $500 fine payable to debtor for failure to do so. (§46). Certificate setting out whether there are registrations affecting debtor in registration system can be obtained. (§43). Notice may be registered in prescribed form in proper land registry office where collateral is or includes fixtures or goods that may become fixtures or crops, or minerals or hydro carbons to be extracted, or timber to be cut or security interest is security interest in right to payment under lease, mortgage or charge of real property to which Act applies. (§54).

Default.—Upon default under security agreement secured party has, unless otherwise agreed, right to take possession of collateral by any method permitted by law, if collateral is equipment and security interest has been perfected by registration, secured party may, in reasonable manner, render such equipment unusable without removal thereof from debtor's premises and secured party may dispose of collateral on debtor's premises. (§62). Proceeds of disposition are to be applied consecutively to: (i) reasonable expenses of secured party, including cost of insurance and payment of taxes and other charges incurred in retaking, holding, repairing, processing, and preparing for disposition and disposing of collateral and, to extent provided for in security agreement, any other reasonable expenses incurred by secured party and (ii) satisfaction of obligations secured by security interest of party making disposition. (§63). Secured party shall account for and pay over any surplus consecutively to (i) any person who has security interest in collateral that is subordinate to that of secured party and whose interest was perfected by possession, continuance of which was prevented by secured party who took possession of collateral or was immediately before disposition, perfected by registration, (ii) any other person with interest in surplus who has delivered written notice to secured party of interest before distribution of proceeds and (iii) debtor or any other person who is known by secured party to be owner of collateral. Where there is question as to who is entitled to surplus, secured party may pay surplus into Ontario Court (General Division) and surplus shall not be paid out except upon application to court. (§64). Unless collateral is perishable, if secured party believes on reasonable grounds that collateral will decline speedily in value, collateral is of type customarily sold on recognized market, cost of care and storage of collateral is disproportionately large relative to its value, Ontario Court (General Division) on application made without notice is satisfied that notice of disposition is not required, after default every person entitled to receive notice of disposition consents in writing to immediate disposition, or receiver and manager disposes of collateral in course of debtor's business, secured party shall give not less than 15 days notice in writing containing brief description of collateral, amount required to satisfy obligation secured, amount of applicable expenses in realizing on collateral or reasonable estimate thereof, statement that upon receipt of payment payer will be credited with any rebates or allowances to which debtor is entitled by law or under agreement, statement that upon payment of amounts due any person entitled to notice may redeem collateral, statement that unless amounts due are paid collateral will be disposed of and any debtor may be liable for any deficiency, and date, time and place of any public sale or date after which any private disposition of collateral is to be made, to debtor who owes payment or performance of obligation secured, every person who is known by secured party before date notice is served on debtor to be owner of collateral or obligor who may owe payment or performance of obligation secured, every person who has security interest in collateral and whose security interest was perfected by possession continuance of which was prevented by secured party who has taken possession of collateral or is perfected by registration before date notice is served on debtor, and every person with interest in collateral who has delivered written notice to secured party of interest in collateral before date that notice is served on debtor. (§63). Notice to be served personally or by registered mail addressed at last known address. (§68). Where collateral is disposed of as provided, disposition discharges security interest of secured party making disposition and, if disposition is made to buyer who buys in good faith for value discharges any subordinate security interest and terminates debtor's interest in collateral. Special rules govern collateral which is consumer goods. (§65). Where conflict exists, Consumer Protection Act prevails (see topic Consumer Protection). (§73). Application may be made to Ontario Court (General Division) to ensure compliance with Act or to recover compensation for any loss or damage suffered because of failure to discharge duties or obligations imposed by Act. (§67).

PLEADING:

Pleadings are governed by the Rules of Civil Procedure, which are regulations made under Courts of Justice Act. (c. C.43).

Statement of Claim.—Generally, action is commenced by plaintiff having court issue statement of claim any time within limitation period. (R.P. 14.03[1]). If insufficient time to prepare statement of claim, plaintiff may issue notice of action and must then file statement of claim within 30 days. (R.P. 14.03[2], [3]). Statement of claim must be served, together with notice of action where applicable, within six months after being issued. (R.P. 14.08).

Statement of Defence.—Defendant must deliver statement of defence within 20 days after service of statement of claim if served in Ontario, within 40 days if served elsewhere in Canada or U.S., or 60 days if served anywhere else. (R.P. 18.01). Alternatively, defendant may deliver notice of intent to defend within prescribed time, thereby gaining additional ten days to file statement of defence. (R.P. 18.02). In defence, defendant must admit every allegation of fact in statement of claim that defendant does not dispute, and all allegations of fact not denied in defence, except as to question of damages, shall be deemed to be admitted unless defendant pleads no knowledge in respect of that fact. (R.P. 25.07).

Counterclaim.—Defendant may assert, by way of counterclaim in main action, any right or claim he or she has against plaintiff, and counterclaim is to be included in same document as statement of defence and served at same time. (R.P. 27.01-27.04).

See Topical Index in front part of this volume.

PLEADING . . . *continued*

Reply.—Plaintiff must deliver reply, if any, within ten days after service of statement of defence, but where defendant counterclaims, plaintiff must deliver reply and defence to counterclaim within 20 days after service of defence and counterclaim. (R.P. 25.04[3]). Reply to defence to counterclaim, if any, must be delivered within ten days after service of defence to counterclaim. (R.P. 27.06). Pleadings are closed when plaintiff has delivered reply to every defence or time therefor has expired, and every defendant in default in delivering defence is noted in default. (R.P. 25.05). Defendant may crossclaim against co-defendant who is or may be liable to defendant for all of plaintiff's claim, is or may be liable to defendant for independent claim arising out of situation giving rise to main action or related situation or who should be bound by determination of issue between plaintiff and defendant. Crossclaim to be included in same document as statement of defence and to be delivered within time allowed for delivery of statement of defence. (R.P. 28).

Third Party Claim.—Defendant may commence third party claim against nonparty in circumstances where crossclaim could be issued if nonparty already co-defendant. Rules respecting defence to third party claim and reply to defence to third party claim substantially same as for defence and reply in main action. Where appropriate, third party may defend plaintiff's claim against defendant in main action by delivering statement of defence in main action raising any defence that would be open to defendant in main action. (R.P. 29).

Amended Pleadings.—Party may amend pleading without leave, before close of pleadings, if amendment does not cause addition, deletion or substitution of party, or on consent of all parties, or with leave of court. (R.P. 26.02). On motion at any stage of action, court shall grant leave to amend on such terms as are just, unless prejudice would result that could not be compensated for by costs or adjournment. (R.P. 26.01). Form of amendments and service of amended pleadings are prescribed. (R.P. 26.03-26.06).

Particulars.—Rules for and contents of pleadings are generally prescribed. (R.P. 25.06-25.09). Where party demands particulars of allegation in opponent's pleading, and opponent fails to supply within seven days, court may order particulars to be delivered within specified time. (R.P. 25.10).

Service.—Notice of action, statement of claim, counterclaim against person not already party to main action or other originating process must be served personally or by prescribed alternative to personal service. (R.P. 16.01). Any other document may be served on solicitor of record for party by mailing copy to solicitor's office, leaving copy with solicitor or employee in his office by telephone transmission or as otherwise prescribed. (R.P. 16.01; 16.05).

Filing.—Every pleading must be filed, marked on the face with the date of filing, the title of the action, the description of the pleading and the name, address and telephone number of solicitor filing same. (R.P. 4.02).

Foreign Claims.—In giving instructions to institute proceedings in the Province, the full names and places of residence of the proposed plaintiffs and defendants should be given, together with complete details of the claim, including all requisite dates and figures.

PLEDGES:

The rights and duties of pledgor and pledgee are generally governed by common law.

Pawnbrokers are subject to special legislation. (c. P.6). No person may carry on trade of pawnbroker without license obtained from municipality where that person is to carry on such trade. License fee is $60 or such sum set by municipality and $2,000 security for due observation of Act must be given. If pledge is destroyed or damaged by fire or other defined peril pawnbroker is nevertheless liable to pay value of pledge after deducting sum lent, interest and charges on application within time in which pledge is redeemable. Pledge becomes absolute property of pawnbroker unless: (a) where sum lent is $15 or less, it is redeemed within one year; (b) where sum lent is more than $15 and not more than $30 and pledge has been in pawn for more than a year, it is redeemed within 15 days after notice by mail to pawner; (c) where sum lent is more than $30 and pledge has been in pawn for more than a year, it is redeemed within 15 days after notice by publication in newspaper, which notice may be published 15 days after notice mailed to pawner. No pawnbroker may deal with person who appears to be under 18 years of age.

PRACTICE:

Most of law relating to practice is contained in Courts of Justice Act, 1984 (c. C.43), and in Rules of Civil Procedure, which are regulations made under that Act.

Case Management.—In effort to speed up litigation process, case management pilot projects have been introduced in Toronto, Windsor and Sault Ste. Marie. Rules relating to case management in each area differ. Pilot projects are presently temporary in nature but it is expected that province wide case management program establishing deadlines for occurrence of certain events in litigation process will be instituted in near future.

See also topic Dispute Resolution.

Commercial List.—To facilitate hearing specified eligible commercial law litigation matters in Toronto, unique commercial list was established. There are special rules to expedite hearing and determination of these matters. It is still in development stages and only available in Toronto.

Simplified Procedure.—Generally, all claims $25,000 or less governed by new Simplified Procedure in attempt to expedite such claims. No oral discovery and provision for summary trial. (R.P. 76).

Discovery.—Generally, examination for discovery may be by oral examination or, at option of examining party, by written questions and answers, but examining party not entitled to subject person to both forms without leave. (R.P. 31.02). Procedures for both oral and written examinations are prescribed. (R.P. 34, 35). Party is entitled to examine for discovery any party adverse in interest once, or more than once with leave, and party may examine individuals on behalf of corporation, partnership, sole proprietorship, person under disability, assignee, trustee in bankruptcy, or nominal party. (R.P. 31.03). Generally, party being examined must answer, to best of person's knowledge, information and belief, any proper question relating to matter in issue or matter made discoverable by Rules. (R.P. 31.06). Where party, or person examined on party's behalf, refuses to answer proper question, and has failed to furnish information in writing within ten days after trial date is set, party may not introduce that information at trial, except with leave. (R.P. 31.07). Discovery of nonparties generally unavailable but court may grant leave to examine any nonparty who there is reason to believe has information relevant to material issue, other than expert engaged by or on behalf of party in preparation for litigation. (R.P. 31.10). At trial, party may read into evidence any evidence given on examination for discovery of adverse party or person examined on behalf or in place of, or in addition to, adverse party, if that evidence is otherwise admissible unless trial judge orders otherwise. (R.P. 31.11). Procedure available for examining person residing outside Ontario. (R.P. 34.07).

Other forms of discovery include discovery of documents (R.P. 30), inspection of property in certain proceedings (R.P. 32), and medical examination of any party whose physical or mental condition is in question in proceeding (R.P. 33). Discovery against Crown regulated by c. P.27. In proceedings against Crown rules of court in which proceedings are pending as to discovery and inspection of documents and examination for discovery apply in same manner as if Crown were corporation, except that Crown may refuse to produce documents or answer questions on ground that production or answer would be injurious to public interest.

Request for Admission of Facts.—At any time, party may serve request to admit on any other party, requesting admission, for purposes of proceeding only, truth of fact or authenticity of document. Party has 20 days after service to respond to request or is deemed to admit. Cost consequences may flow from denial of or failure to admit anything that should have been admitted. (R.P. 51, 57.01). See also topic Pleading concerning deemed admissions of allegations not denied in statement of defence.

Direct Actions Against Insurer.—See topic Motor Vehicles, subhead Direct Actions.

See also topics Actions, Appeal and Error, Attachment, Depositions, Dispute Resolution, Executions, Garnishment, Injunctions, Judgments, Pleading and Process.

PRINCIPAL AND AGENT:

Common law rules generally apply.

General Powers of Attorney.—Powers of Attorney Act, c. P.20 (substantially repealed by S.O. 1992, c. 32) permits general powers of attorney for property and gives some protection where good faith action taken without notice of revocation, termination or invalidity of power.

Continuing Power of Attorney for Property.—Continues in effect after donor mentally incapable if donor expresses intention that it may be exercised during donor's incapacity to manage property or if it states it is continuing power of attorney. Donor may give attorney power to do anything donor can do when fully capable except make will. Governed by Substitute Decisions Act, 1992, S.O. 1992, c. 30, in force Apr. 3, 1995 and substantially amended by S.O. 1996, c. 2 in force Mar. 28, 1996, which sets out detailed provisions for giving or revoking such power of attorney and conduct, resignation (§11), replacement of attorney and termination (§12) of power of attorney. Some protection for actions in good faith without knowledge after termination or invalidity of power. (§13). Act gives attorney several powers where donor incapable, e.g. to provide for donor's dependants, gift or lend from donor's estate. (§37). Donor may by power of attorney restrict or deny most such powers. Power can be effective immediately or upon specific date or happening of event. (§7[7]). Attorney must be at least 18. (§5). May appoint more than one attorney. May appoint substitute attorneys. (§§7, 11).

Execution/Revocation of Continuing Power of Attorney and Capacity to Give.—Must be in writing signed before two witnesses. Certain people cannot be witnesses. Some power to validate improperly executed powers. (§10). Donor must be at least 18. Kind of capacity required to give continuing power of attorney outlined in Act and not necessarily same as capacity to manage property. (§§8, 9). Power revocable while donor has similar level of capacity. (§8[2]). Revocation must be by writing executed in same way as continuing power of attorney. (§12[2]).

Compensation and Passing of Accounts.—Act provides for voluntary and required passing of accounts of attorneys or statutory guardians acting under continuing power of attorney. (§42). Attorney for property may receive compensation as provided by regulation (or in power of attorney). (§§40, 90, O. Reg. 26/95).

Statutory Guardian.—Public Guardian and Trustee can become statutory guardian of person who is incapable, where donor certified in psychiatric facility replacing attorney under continuing power of attorney. (§15). Named attorney can terminate statutory guardianship of Public Guardian and Trustee (§16.1) or apply to replace Public Guardian and Trustee as statutory guardian (§17): on refusal of Public Guardian and Trustee to issue certificate of appointment of statutory guardian to named attorney, procedure available for court application (S.O. 1992, c. 30, §18). On application to replace Public Guardian and Trustee, security from attorney may be required by Public Guardian and Trustee subject to waiver by court. (§17). Act provides when statutory guardianship terminated. (§§16.1, 20 and 20.3).

Statutory Guardian Where No Continuing Power of Attorney and Court Appointed Guardians of Property.—Substitute Decisions Act, 1992, also provides for appointment of statutory guardian of incapable person where no continuing power of attorney. If Public Guardian and Trustee is statutory guardian, incapable persons' spouse, partner, certain relatives or trust company may apply to Public Guardian and Trustee to replace him or her. (§§15 and 17).

Court may appoint guardian of property whether or not there is continuing power of attorney. (§22). Some restrictions on who may be appointed. (§24).

Personal Care Power of Attorney.—Now effective and governed by Substitute Decisions Act, 1992 (S.O. 1992, c. 30) in force Apr. 3, 1995, and substantially amended by S.O. 1996, c. 2 in force Mar. 28, 1996, whether executed before or after that date. Can appoint attorney to make decisions for personal care. Personal care includes health care, including giving consent under Health Care Consent Act, 1996, S.O. 1996, c. 2, nutrition, shelter, clothing, hygiene or safety. Some powers may have to be specified in

See Topical Index in front part of this volume.

PRINCIPAL AND AGENT . . . *continued*
power of attorney—e.g. giving of consent under Health Care Consent Act, 1996, (§20, S.O. 1992, c. 30, §49); use of force in carrying out authority given (S.O. 1992, c. 30, §50). (See also topic Wills, subhead Living Wills.) Attorney must be at least 16. (§44). Certain people cannot be attorneys. (§46). May appoint more than one person as personal care attorneys and substitute attorneys. (§§46 and 52).

Power effective only when donor loses capacity to make decisions with respect to one or more aspects of personal care or when attorney has reason to believe donor lacks capacity to make decision (although power of attorney may require lack of capacity to be proved) and then only for that decision. (§49). Registration by donor while fully capable may be prerequisite to exercise of some powers, e.g. authorized use of force. (§50). Act sets out certain duties of attorney and attorney may apply to court for directions. (§§66, 67, 68). Provisions for assessment of donor by assessors qualified under Act. (§§20.1, 49, 50, 51 and 78).

Detailed provisions in Act for giving or revoking personal care power of attorney and conduct, resignation (§52) of attorney and termination of power (§53).

Execution/Revocation of Personal Care Power of Attorney and Capacity to Give.—Must be in writing signed before two witnesses. Certain persons cannot be witnesses. Some power to validate improperly executed power. (§48). Donor must be at least 16. (§43). Kind of capacity person requires to give personal care power outlined in Act (§47) and may differ from capacity for personal care. Power revocable if donor has similar level of capacity (§47) and if revocation in writing executed as required to give power (§53). See also §50(4) for use of force provisions.

Records of Attorney and Compensation.—Obligations of personal care attorney to maintain records and compensation for personal care attorney as prescribed by regulation. (§§66 and 90 and O. Reg. 99/96).

Court Appointed Guardians of Person.—Court may appoint guardian of person whether or not person has given personal care power of attorney. (§55). Some restrictions on who may be appointed. (§57).

Land Registry.—No instrument affecting land purporting to be signed or executed by person by attorney may be registered unless at or before time of registration original power of attorney or copy thereof certified for registration is itself registered in same registry office. (c. R.20, §46; c. L.5, §70; Reg. 690, §41).

Collection Agencies.—Must be registered. Payment of fee and posting of bond prescribed in regulations required on registration. Statutory provisions and regulations govern information to be filed on application for registration, books and records to be kept, banking, collection methods, returns to be made, etc. (c. C. 14; Reg. 74).

Real Estate Agents.—See Real Estate and Business Brokers Act, R.S.O. 1990, c. R.4.

Insurance Agents.—See topic Insurance, subhead Agents.

Securities Agents.—See topic Securities, subhead Registration of Dealers, Advisers, etc.

PROCESS:

Commencement of Proceeding.—Rules of Civil Procedure contemplate two types of civil proceedings: Actions and applications. Generally, application is summary proceeding in which judge is asked to determine questions of law where there are no material facts in dispute. Under Rules, every proceeding must be by action except where statute or Rules (R.P. 14.05) provide that proceeding may be brought by application. Examples of proceedings commenced by application are where executor or trustee asks court for directions or where determination of rights depends on courts interpretation of will, contract, deed or other instrument.

General Requisites.—Most proceedings commenced in court having jurisdiction by issuance of statement of claim, notice of application, or by notice of action followed by such statement. Form and content of notice and statement are prescribed. (R.P. 14).

By Whom Issued.—All civil proceedings are commenced by issuance of originating process by registrar of court in which proceeding is to be commenced, except where statute provides otherwise. Counterclaim or counterpetition that is only against present parties to main action, and crossclaim, are commenced by delivery of pleading containing counterclaim, counterpetition or crossclaim, and need not be issued. (R.P. 14.01). Originating process is issued by registrar's act of dating, signing and sealing pleading with court seal and assigning to it court file number. (R.P. 14.07).

Who May Serve.—Service may be effected by any literate person.

Personal service on individual is effected by delivering to and leaving with the person to be served a true copy of the process to be served. The original need not be produced. (R.P. 16.02[2]).

Personal service on minor is effected by leaving copy of document with minor, and where minor resides with parent or other person having care or lawful custody of minor, by leaving another copy of document with that person, but where proceeding is in respect of minor's interest in estate or trust, minor shall be served by leaving copy of document bearing minor's name and address with Children's Lawyer.

Personal Service on Incompetent.—Personal service on person who has been declared mentally incompetent or incapable of managing own affairs is effected by leaving copy of document with committee of person's estate, if one exists or, if not, with committee of person. Personal service on person who is mentally incompetent or incapable of managing own affairs, not so declared, is effected by leaving copy of document bearing person's name and address with Public Guardian and Trustee and leaving another copy with person.

Personal service on partnership is effected by service on one or more of the partners or at the principal place within the Province of the business of the partnership, on any person having the control or management of the partnership business there.

Personal service on domestic corporation is effected by service on an officer or agent of corporation, or with person at any place of business of corporation who appears to be in control or management of that place of business.

Personal service on foreign corporations is effected by service on any person having the control or management of the business of the corporation within Province.

Personal Service Outside Province.—Service of originating process or other document outside Ontario in state that is contracting state to Convention on Service Abroad of Judicial and Extrajudicial Documents in Civil or Commercial Matters (the Hague, 1965) to be served in manner provided for in convention. Otherwise service of originating process or other documents to be made in manner set out in Rules of Civil Procedure or in manner provided by law in jurisdiction where service to be made if service in such manner could reasonably be expected to come to notice of person to be served. Under Rules of Civil Procedure, party to action or proceeding may be served out of Ontario where action or proceeding consists of claim for or in respect of real or personal property in Ontario or administration of estate of deceased person in respect of real property in Ontario; where action is in respect of personal property in Ontario or administration of personal property in Ontario of deceased person who at time of death was domiciled in Ontario; where will affecting real or personal property in Ontario or personal property of deceased person who at time of death was domiciled in Ontario is sought to construed; where action is against trustees in respect of execution of trusts of property within Ontario; where action is upon mortgage, charge or lien on property within Ontario; where action is founded on breach of contract or tort committed within Ontario; where parties to a contract have agreed that courts of Ontario are to have jurisdiction; where damages are sustained in Ontario arising from a tort or breach of contract committed elsewhere; where an injunction in respect of things done in Ontario is sought; where action is a matrimonial cause, or an action to declare a marriage void, or claim is for custody, maintenance or access to an infant; where any relief is sought against any person domiciled or ordinarily resident in Ontario; where person to be served is necessarily or properly a party to an action properly brought against another person duly served within Ontario; where action is founded on judgment; where by statute claim may be made by action commenced in Ontario; and, where claim is for contribution, indemnity or other relief over in respect of any claim made against defendant in action commenced in Ontario. (R.P. 17.02). Party to action or proceeding may be served outside of Ontario with leave of court for circumstances falling outside of R.P. 17.02. (R.P. 17.03).

Party who has been served out of Ontario, may, within time limited for delivering defence, notice of intent to defend or notice of appearance, apply for order setting aside service or, in alternative, for order staying proceedings. (R.P. 17.06).

Nonresident Motorist.—See topic Motor Vehicles, subhead Action Against Nonresident.

Substituted service by advertisement or otherwise may be ordered when the person to be served is evading service. (R.P. 16).

Proof of service by manner set out in Rules of Practice, by law of jurisdiction where service is made or in accordance with Convention on the Service Abroad of Judicial and Extrajudicial Documents in Civil or Commercial Matters (The Hague, 1965). Generally service proven by affidavit of person making service setting out date and manner of service, person served, identifying document served and address where service made.

PROOF OF CLAIMS:

See topics Estate Trustees; Pleading.

RAILROADS: See topic Carriers.

REAL PROPERTY:

The estates recognized in Ontario include estates in fee simple, for life, pour autre vie, for years, at will, at sufferance, by entireties, tenancy in common and joint tenancy. Estates in fee tail can no longer be created. Limitation in conveyance or will that before May 27, 1956 would have created estate tail, is construed as estate in fee simple. (c. C.34, §4). Estate granted to two or more persons is tenancy in common unless expressly declared to be joint tenancy, but every estate vested in executors or trustees is held by them in joint tenancy. (§13).

A body corporate can hold real or personal property in joint tenancy like an individual.

Warranties.—Ontario New Home Warranties Plan Act (c. O.31) applies to all new homes or condominiums sold in Ontario after Jan. 1, 1977. Act implies warranty for one year for minor defects but warranties regarding major structural defects continue for up to seven years depending upon date upon which new home was constructed. Statute administered by nonprofit corporation which must establish warranty fund or purchase insurance to be used to compensate owners whose homes are defective. Disputes between vendors and purchasers resolved by arbitration. (c. O.31, §17[4]). All vendors and builders must register under statute. (c. O.31, §6).

Condominiums.—Condominium Act (c. C.26) governs properties which are divided into parts that are to be owned individually and parts that are to be owned in common. Prescribed information must be registered in appropriate registry division (§§3, 4, 5), creating corporation whose members are owners of individual units. Provisions regarding governing of corporate business by board of directors confirmed by owners. Corporation must maintain insurance for both units and common elements. (§27). Owners must contribute to common expenses of property (§32), part of which must be put in reserve fund for major repairs (§36). Mandatory annual audit. (§35). Unless otherwise provided, corporation must maintain common elements and repair and maintain common elements and units after damage. Owners must maintain their units. (§41). Where there has been substantial damage to 25% of building, owners may vote to terminate corporation. (§§43 and 42). Protection of original purchasers provided by implied covenants in agreements of purchase and sale, prescribed duties of original owner of property (§51) and mandatory disclosure of information prior to binding agreement (§52).

Trespass.—Trespass to Property Act (c. T.21) makes it offence to enter premises or engage in activity on premises without occupier's express permission (§2). Persons committing offence under this Act are subject to arrest (§9) and may be fined up to $2,000. Act also requires convicting judge to make award of damages not in excess of $1,000 to compensate person who has suffered loss caused by convicted person if prosecutor requests and person suffering loss consents. (§12). If award is not made under Act, person suffering damage may claim damages in civil courts.

See Topical Index in front part of this volume.

REAL PROPERTY . . . *continued*

Occupiers' Liability.—The Occupiers' Liability Act, c. O.2 determines standard of care owed by occupiers of premises. Act does not relieve occupier from higher liability or higher standard raised by virtue of any statute or rule of law imposing special liabilities or standards of care on particular classes of people. (§9). Act does not affect rights or liabilities of persons in respect of causes of action arising before Sept. 8, 1980. (§11).

Occupier of premises owes duty to take such care as in all circumstances of case is reasonable to see that persons and property brought on premises are reasonably safe while on premises. (§3). Duty of care may be modified by contract. (§5[2]). Landlord owes same duty of care as occupier. (§8). Duty may be modified with respect to persons who are willing to assume risks, with respect to persons who enter with intention of committing criminal acts, and with respect to certain classes of property. (§4).

Rule in Shelley's Case is recognized and applies to both wills and deeds and to the creation of both legal and equitable interests.

See also topics Curtesy, Deeds, Dower, Homesteads, Husband and Wife, Landlord and Tenant, Mortgages of Real Property, Partition, Records.

RECEIVERS:

In Ontario Court (General Division) or Unified Family Court receiver or receiver and manager may be appointed by interlocutory order where it appears just and convenient to do so by virtue of order made pursuant to other Courts of Justice Act and Rules of Civil Procedure. (§41). Order appointing receiver shall name person appointed, specify amount and terms of security, if any, to be furnished by receiver for proper performance of his duties, state whether receiver is also appointed as manager and, if necessary, define scope of his or her managerial powers and contain such directions and impose such terms as are just. (§41.03). Receiver may obtain directions at any time on motion to judge. (§41.05). Receiver may be discharged only by order of judge. (§41.06).

Proceedings.—A receiver may be appointed by interlocutory order of the court, such order to be made either unconditionally or upon such terms and conditions as the court may deem just.

Equitable Execution.—Receivers may be appointed by way of equitable execution as a means of enforcing judgments and reaching property not capable of being seized under an execution.

See Canada Law Digest, topic Bankruptcy, subheads Receivers; Secured Creditors.

RECORDS:

Land registrars of various divisions have charge of records for land under both Registry Act (c. R.20 as am'd, dealt with below) and Land Titles Act (c. L.5, see subhead Land Titles or Torrens System, infra). As to records of personal property, see topics Chattel Mortgages; Sales, subheads Bills of Sale and Conditional Sales; Assignments; Corporations, subhead Corporate Securities Registration; Personal Property Security.

Registerable Instruments.—In general, all instruments affecting land may be registered including: Crown grants, orders-in-council, deeds, conveyances, mortgages, assignments of mortgages, notices of sale by mortgagee, certificates of discharge of mortgages, assurances, leases, bonds, releases, discharges, powers of attorney, agreements for sale or purchase of land, wills, probates of wills, grants of administration, cautions or renewals thereof, municipal by-laws, certificates of proceedings in any court, judgments or orders of foreclosure, certificates of payment of taxes, sheriffs' and treasurers' deeds of land sold, bankruptcy and insolvency orders, plans of survey or subdivision of land.

Place of Recording.—In various registry divisions established by regulation. (R.R.O. 996 as am'd).

Requisites of Registration.—Instruments must generally contain description on land conforming to Act and regulations.

Effect of Registration.—An instrument affecting land is void as against any subsequent purchaser or mortgagee for value without actual notice, unless it has been registered before the registration of the instrument under which the subsequent purchaser or mortgagee claims. Exceptions are leases in possession for seven years or less and certain municipal by-laws. Registration constitutes notice to all persons claiming any interest in land subsequent to registration, provided instrument is recorded in abstract index for that land. Priority of registration prevails unless before prior registration there has been actual notice of prior instrument by person claiming under prior registration.

Land Titles or Torrens System.—A system of land titles has been set up in Province under Land Titles Act (c. L.5) which exists concurrently with Registry Act system in all districts and some counties or other areas of Ontario and may be extended to other areas by regulations made by Lieutenant Governor in Council. Once land has been brought under land titles system, provisions of Registry Act no longer govern it. Act establishes clear title to land by declaring under guarantee of indemnity that it is vested in named person. Entries in Land Titles register are binding when signed by Land Registrar and accuracy of entries is guaranteed by Assurance Fund. Exceptions to title guarantee set out in §44 include taxes, easements, leases in possession for three years or less, dower, expropriation, statutory liens (including liens for corporations and retail sales taxes), municipal by-laws and invalidity by reason of Planning Act (see topic Deeds, subhead Operation and Effect). Assurance Fund indemnifies certain persons wrongfully deprived of land. Place of recording: various divisions established by regulation. (R.R.O. 691 as am'd).

Certification of Titles to Land.—Owner of land or any person claiming estate in fee simple may apply under Certification of Titles Act (c. C.6, §4) to have title to any land under registry system investigated and certified. Upon registration of Certificate of Title, certificate deemed conclusive evidence that owner has absolute title subject to exceptions set forth in certificate. (§14).

Assurance Fund available to persons who may be wrongfully deprived of land or some estate or interest therein by reason of land being brought under The Land Titles Act (c. L.5, Part V, §§54-59) or being certified under The Certification of Titles Act (c. C.6, §§1, 15, 16, 18[7]).

Transfer of Decedent's Title.—Conveyances by personal representatives to beneficiaries must be registered if made within three years of death. See topic Deeds.

Vital Statistics.—Records of births, marriages deaths, divorces, adoptions and changes of name are kept in office of Registrar-General, Macdonald Block, Queen's Park, Toronto M7A 1Y5. Father and mother may register child's surname as being both their surnames connected by hyphen. Birth records may be altered to reflect result of transsexual surgery. (c. V.4).

Forms.—Under Land Registration Reform Act (c. L.4, §3) and R.R.O. 688 as amended, documents shall not be registered under Registry Act or Land Titles Act unless they are in one of prescribed forms, or attached to Document General (Form 4).

REPLEVIN:

Where goods, chattels, deeds, bonds, debentures, promissory notes, bills of exchange, books of account, papers, writings, valuable securities or other personal property or effects have been wrongfully distrained or wrongfully taken or detained, the owner or person lawfully entitled to possession of property may bring action requesting order for recovery of personal property and for damages. (c. C.43, §104).

Proceedings.—Action is commenced like any other action and, after statement of claim is issued, interim order for recovery of personal property may be obtained on motion, in urgent cases ex parte. Such motions must be accompanied by supporting affidavits. Court may grant interim order for recovery of personal property: (1) subject to posting of security by plaintiff in amount twice the value of property, or any amount in its discretion; and (2) directing sheriff to take property, detain it or deliver it to plaintiff. Alternatively, court may order defendant to post security and direct that property remain in possession of defendant. Security may be by bond. (R.P. 44).

Repossession.—The defendant may apply to the court to discharge, vary or modify the order or to stay proceedings, or for any other relief with respect to the return, safety or sale of the property. (R.P. 44.05).

Execution of Order.—Order of recovery is executed by sheriff who must: (1) ascertain that security is given before executing order; (2) serve defendant with order when property recovered or soon thereafter; and (3) report to plaintiff after attempt to enforce or within ten days of service of order on defendant. (R.P. 44.07).

Judgment.—After recovery order has been executed or denied, action proceeds like any other action and security secures any judgment which defendant or plaintiff may recover.

Small Claims Court Cases.—Where value of goods detained does not exceed $6,000, replevin suit may be brought in small claims court.

REPORTS:

Decisions of the superior courts of the Province are reported by authorized reporters who are appointed by the Law Society. Until 1901, there were three series of authorized reports: The Ontario Appeal Reports containing decisions of The Court of Appeal, Ontario Reports and The Ontario Practice Reports containing decisions of the high court. In 1901, The Ontario Law Reports series was commenced containing decisions of all superior courts. In 1931, it was succeeded by The Ontario Reports series.

The most important Ontario reports are as follows: Upper Canada Queens Bench (U.C.Q.B.) 1844-1882; Upper Canada Common Pleas (U.C.C.P.) 1850-1882; Grants Chancery Reports (Gr.) 1849-1882; Ontario Reports (O.R.) 1882-1900; Ontario Appeal Reports (A.R.) 1876-1900; Practice Reports (P.R.) 1850-1900; Ontario Law Reports (O.L.R.) 1901-1931; Ontario Weekly Reporter (O.W.R.) 1902-1915; Ontario Weekly Notes (O.W.N.) 1909-1962; Ontario Reports (O.R.) 1931-1973; Ontario Reports 2nd Series (O.R. [2d]) 1974-1990; Ontario Reports 3rd Series (O.R. [3d]) 1991. . . .

RESTRAINT OF TRADE:

See Canada Law Digest, topic Monopolies and Restraint of Trade.

SALES:

Law relating to sale of goods is codified in Sale of Goods Act (c. S.1) which follows English Act.

Contracts of Sale.—See topic Frauds, Statute of.

Bills of Sale.—Bills of Sale Act repealed.

If price of goods is in excess of $50, and buyer is person who purchases goods for consumption (excluding [1] persons who buy in course of carrying on business, e.g., buying for purposes of resale in ordinary course of trade or for use in further production of goods and services, [2] associations of individuals, [3] partnerships, and [4] corporations), agreement must meet additional requirements imposed by The Consumer Protection Act. (c. C.31). See topic Consumer Protection.

Conditions and Warranties.—Following conditions are implied: that seller has right to sell the goods, that goods sold by description will correspond with description or if sold by sample will correspond with sample, and in certain circumstances that they will be reasonably fit for purpose for which they are to be used and of merchantable quality. There is an implied warranty that buyer will have and enjoy quiet possession and that goods will be free of any undeclared charge or encumbrance in favour of a third party. (c. S.1, §§13-16). Implied conditions and warranties can be excluded by contract except in consumer sales. (c. C.31, §34).

Product Liability.—Manufacturer or supplier of defective goods may be liable to consumers for negligence where there is no privity of contract with the consumers. Liability is based on the rule in Donoghue v. Stevenson, [1932] A.C. 562.

Transfer of title of specific or ascertained goods takes place when the parties intend it to. (c. S.1, §18). When no intention is expressed, statutory rules apply for ascertaining intention of parties. Generally speaking, property passes when contract of sale is concluded provided that it is not subject to conditions and goods are in deliverable state. Prima facie risk passes to buyer when title passes. (c. S.1, §21).

Delivery.—Prima facie delivery is the seller's responsibility, the place of delivery is his place of business and he must bear the expense of putting the goods in a deliverable state. (c. S.1, §§26-28).

See Topical Index in front part of this volume.

SALES . . . *continued*

Stoppage in Transitu.—If the buyer becomes insolvent the unpaid seller has the right of stopping the goods in transitu and after recovering possession may retain them until payment or tender of the price. The right may be exercised by taking actual possession of goods or by giving notice to carrier who must then redeliver goods according to directions of seller and seller is responsible for expense of such redelivery. (c. S.1, §§42-44).

Remedies of Seller.—If property has passed the seller may sue for the price. If the buyer refuses to accept the goods the seller may sue for nonacceptance; the measure of damages is the estimated loss directly or naturally resulting, which generally will be the difference between the market and the contract price. (c. S.1, §§47-48).

Remedies of Buyer.—The buyer may sue for damages for nondelivery, with the same measure of damages as applies in the case of a seller's action. Specific performance may be ordered if the court thinks fit. (c. S.1, §§49-52).

United Nations Convention on Contracts for the International Sale of Goods.—Applicable to contracts of sale of goods between parties whose places of business are in different states if (a) those states have adopted Convention, or (b) rules of private international law lead to application of law of state that has adopted Convention, unless parties expressly agree otherwise. (S.C. 1991, c. 13; R.S.O. c. I.10).

Conditional Sales.—See topic Personal Property Security.

Consumer Protection.—See topic Consumer Protection.

Retail Credit Sales.—See topic Consumer Protection.

Bulk Sales.—See topic Fraudulent Sales and Conveyances.

Sales of Motor Vehicles.—See topic Motor Vehicles.

SALES TAX: See topic Taxation.

SEALS:

Certain transactions must be by deed rather than written or oral agreement. Deed may be used for other transactions. Generally, deed must bear seal of person executing it. However, courts will treat writing as deed if it was intended to be sealed. Usually, attached wafer of printed impression is used. Person is bound by agreement in deed even though he received no consideration for agreement. Deeds are mainly required for real property transactions, but seals are no longer required for transfer, mortgage or discharge of mortgage. (c. L.4, §13).

Corporate Seals.—Corporations formerly had to have corporate seal capable of making impression on paper, but this is no longer required.

SECURITIES:

Law relating to issue and trade of securities in Ontario, registration of investment advisers, securities dealers, underwriters, take-over bids made to shareholders in Ontario, insider trading, proxy solicitations, and financial and other disclosure by publicly traded corporations is governed by Securities Act, (c. S.5, as am'd). Law relating to take-over bids made to shareholders in Ontario, insider trading, proxy solicitations and financial disclosure by federally incorporated issuers is also governed by Canada Business Corporations Act, R.S.C. c. C-44, as am'd. (See Canada Law Digest, topic Corporations.) Law relating to proxy solicitation by Ontario public corporation is also governed by Business Corporations Act (c. B.16, as am'd), as is financial disclosure of Ontario corporation which is not "reporting issuer". Reporting issuer is Securities Act term meaning issuer that has issued voting securities on or after first day of May, 1967 in respect of which prospectus has been filed and receipt obtained or in respect of which securities exchange take-over bid circular has been filed; whose securities have been at any time since Sept. 15, 1979 listed and posted for trading on any stock exchange in Ontario recognized by Ontario Securities Commission (O.S.C.); is governed by Business Corporations Act and is offering its securities to public within meaning of Business Corporations Act; that is amalgamated, merged or continued company where one of prior companies has been reporting issuer for at least 12 months.

Enforcement of securities legislation is responsibility of O.S.C. Executive Director is appointed to act as chief administrative officer of O.S.C. All powers and duties of O.S.C. except those of certain administrative proceedings and reviews and investigation of offences may be assigned to Executive Director, or to another Director of O.S.C. (§6). Decisions of Director may be reviewed by O.S.C. at request of affected person (§8) and appeal lies from most O.S.C. decisions to Divisional Court (§9).

Regulatory Powers of O.S.C.—O.S.C. has authority to make rules that have force of regulations. (§143). O.S.C. also may issue policy statements as guidelines that do not have force of laws. (§143.8). See also subheads Distribution of Securities to Public; and Registration of Dealers, Advisers, etc., infra.

Investigation by O.S.C.—O.S.C. may appoint any person to carry on such investigations as it deems expedient for due administration of Ontario securities law or regulation of capital markets in Ontario or to assist in due administration of securities laws or regulation of capital markets in another jurisdiction. Any person so appointed is given same power to summon and enforce attendance of witnesses, and compel them to give evidence under oath and to produce documents and things as is vested in Ontario Court (General Division) in trial of civil actions. Person giving evidence at such investigation may be represented by counsel. Investigator may apply to judge of Ontario Court (Provincial Division) for order authorizing investigator or other person to enter any building or place and search for and seize specified items.

Distribution of Securities to Public.—Securities Act contemplates closed system. Under this system every distribution of security to general investing public requires filing of prospectus, unless specific statutory exemption is available; and every distribution of security acquired pursuant to prospectus exemption to general investing public requires filing of prospectus unless specific exemption is available. Exemptions may be available where securities have been held for certain periods of time, and issuer is reporting issuer, no unusual efforts have been made to prepare market and no extraordinary commission or consideration is paid or where issuer of securities is and has been for at least 12 months reporting issuer in compliance with public disclosure requirements. (§§53 and 72). Similarly, all trades in securities must be made by entity (e.g. registered dealer) registered under Securities Act to trade in securities, unless specific statutory exemption from registration requirements is available. (§25). See subhead Registration of Dealers, Advisers, etc., infra.

Prerequisites to Sales or Offerings.—No "distribution to the public" of any security is permitted until there has been filed with O.S.C. both "preliminary prospectus" and "prospectus" in respect of offering and receipts therefor obtained from Director. (§53). "Distribution" of security includes trades in securities of issuer not previously issued; re-issue of such securities that have been redeemed or purchased by or donated to that issuer; trades in previously issued securities by person or company or combination of persons or companies holding sufficient number to affect materially control of issuer, provided that holding in excess of 20% of outstanding voting securities of issuer deemed, in absence of evidence to contrary, to affect materially control of issuer; and trade in securities previously acquired pursuant to prospectus exemption (such as re-sale by underwriter or private placement investor) unless that trade is also exempt, meets certain conditions and hold periods or ruling obtained that such trade would not be prejudicial to public interest. (§§72 and §74). Distributions that are exempt from prospectus requirements include following trades (§72): Principal purchaser is Canadian bank, Federal Business Development Bank, credit union, loan, trust or insurance company, federal, provincial, territorial or municipal government or any municipal corporation or public board or commission in Canada; isolated trade by or on behalf of issuer in security of own issue; principal purchaser recognized as exempt purchaser; purchaser purchases as principal and trade is for aggregate acquisition cost not less than $150,000; trade by controlling person to creditor for purpose of giving collateral for bona fide debt; trades by issuer where no commissions or remuneration paid except for professional services or services of registered dealer: (i) in own security distributed as stock dividends; (ii) in securities distributed to security holders pursuant to winding up or reorganization; or (iii) trades in securities issued through exercise of right to purchase, convert or exchange previously granted by issuer; trade by issuer in security of reporting issuer held by it that is distributed by it to holders of its securities as dividend in kind; rights issue and securities issued on exercise of rights previously granted by issuer where same is approved by O.S.C.; exchanges of securities in connection with statutory amalgamation, arrangement or other procedure; exchange of securities in connection with take-over bid; trade in security to person in connection with take-over or issuer bid made by that person; trade by issuer in security of its own issue as consideration for portion or all of assets of any person or company, if fair value of assets so purchased is not less than $150,000; trade by issuer in security of its own issue in consideration of mining claims where vendor enters into such escrow or pooling agreement as Director considers necessary; trade by issuer in securities of its own issue with its employees or employees of affiliate who are not induced to purchase by expectation of employment or continued employment; trade by issuer on incorporation or organization of issuer where trade is necessary to facilitate incorporation or organization is for nominal consideration and is to not more than five shareholders; trade by issuer in securities of its own issue where solicitations are made to not more than 50 prospective purchasers resulting in sales to not more than 25 purchasers and where all sale agreements are concluded within six months of solicitation and each purchaser has access to substantially same information found in prospectus, each purchaser is informed investor purchasing as principal or is senior officer or director of issuer or his/her spouse, parent, brother, sister or child, there is no advertisement or promotional expense in connection with trade and no promoter of issuer, other than registered dealer, has acted as promoter of any other issuer which has traded in securities of its own issue pursuant to this exemption within previous 12 months, but issuer may only rely on this exemption once; trade is between registered dealers where registered dealer purchasing is acting as principal; trade is to underwriter or between underwriters; or trade in commodity futures option or commodity futures contract where such trade is that of hedger through dealer within meaning of Commodity Futures Act. (c. C.20).

Prospectus Requirements.—Prospectus (including preliminary prospectus) must contain full, true and plain disclosure of all material facts relating to securities issued and must set forth information prescribed by Securities Act, and Regulations thereto. (§56). Where material adverse change occurs prior to completion of distribution amendment must be filed to prospectus. (§57). Chief executive officer, chief financial officer, and on behalf of board of directors, any two directors of issuer, other than foregoing, and any promoter of issuer (§58) must certify prospectus constitutes full, true and plain disclosure of all material facts relating to securities offered by prospectus. Underwriters must certify that to best of their knowledge, information and belief, prospectus constitutes full, true and plain disclosure of all material facts relating to securities offered by prospectus. (§59). Where company has only three directors, two of whom are chief executive officer and chief financial officer, certificate may be signed by all directors of company. Audited financial statements required by Securities Act must accompany and form part of prospectus. Preliminary prospectus may exclude auditors report, information on price to underwriter and offering price to public. Certain qualifying senior issuers (12 month reporting issuer history and public float valued at Cdn $75 million or, for debt issues, compliance by issuer or guarantors with certain investment grade tests) may distribute pursuant to short form prospectus which incorporates by reference information contained in "annual information form" filed by such senior issuers and continuous disclosure filings. (Blanket Ruling under §74 and National Policy 47 Prompt Offering Qualification System). Such senior issuers may also make continuous or delayed offerings of debt or equity under short form prospectus legended as shelf offering prospectus. Maximum quantity of securities which may be qualified under shelf prospectus is amount of securities issuer or selling security holder reasonably expects to sell within two years of date of filing prospectus. Shelf prospectus also incorporates by reference prospectus supplement (which is not reviewed) relating to each tranche. (Blanket Ruling under §74 and National Policy 44-Shelf Prospectus Offerings and Post-Receipt Pricing System). U.S. issuers may distribute securities, including debt or preferred shares with approved rating or rights immediately exercisable for such securities, by prospectus under Multijurisdictional Disclosure System (MJDS) (National Policy 45 MJDS) provided distribution complies with U.S. law where, in case of debt, preferred shares or rights exercisable therefor, (i) issuer has securities registered pursuant to Securities Exchange Act of 1934 ("1934 Act") or files reports under 1934 Act; (ii) issuer filed with Securities and Exchange Commission material required under 1934 Act for 12 months preceding filing of prospectus; (iii) issuer not investment company under Investment Company Act of 1940; (iv) issuer not commodity pool issuer; and (v)

SECURITIES . . . *continued*
securities must be either: (a) not convertible; or (b) if convertible, only convertible one year after issue into securities with public float of U.S.$75,000,000. In case of equity securities, U.S. issuer must satisfy requirements (i)-(iv) and have minimum public float of U.S.$75,000,000.

Renewal.—If distribution is in progress 12 months, new prospectus and receipt therefor must be obtained from Director within 20 days from expiration of 12 month period from date of preliminary prospectus or previous prospectus in order to continue distribution. (§62). For shelf offering prospectus there must be filed new preliminary prospectus within 20 business days, and new final prospectus within five business days prior to expiration of two-year term of prospectus, and receipt must be obtained by expiration date, in order to continue distribution. (National Policy 44).

Waiting Period.—Director issues receipt for preliminary prospectus immediately upon filing. Minimum ten day waiting period before receipt for prospectus may be issued. During waiting period it is permissible to advertise security, in limited manner, distribute preliminary prospectus, and solicit expressions of interest. (§65). Record of distribution of preliminary prospectus must be kept. (§67).

Final Receipt.—Issuing of receipt for prospectus is in discretion of Director. O.S.C. has adopted selective review system for prospectuses and certain other documents. Under selective review system, incoming documents are subjected to initial screening process that applies both objective and subjective selection criteria. Documents are then selected for full review, issue oriented review or no review. Securities Act, §61(2) sets out list of items resulting in non-issue of receipt.

Cease Trading Order.—Where it appears to O.S.C., after filing prospectus and issuing receipt therefor, that any circumstance set out in §61(2) exists, O.S.C. may order distribution of securities to cease. (§70).

Delivery of Prospectus.—It is mandatory for dealer to deliver prospectus to purchaser. No agreement for purchase of securities during distribution is binding on purchaser until midnight of business second day after receipt by purchaser of prospectus. (§71).

Rescission and Civil Liability.—Purchaser of security during period of distribution has right of damages for misrepresentation (including by omission) contained in prospectus, on which there is deemed reliance against issuer; selling security holder on whose behalf distribution is made; each underwriter required to sign certificate by §59; every director of issuer at time prospectus or amendment to prospectus was filed; every person or company whose consent was filed under regulations but only with respect to reports, opinions or statements that have been made by them; and every person or company who signed prospectus or amendment other than persons listed above. Such persons are liable jointly and severally. (§130). Parties other than issuer or selling security holder have available due diligence defence, and underwriters not liable for more than total public offering price of underwritten portion. (§130[5] and [6]). Alternatively, purchaser has right to rescind purchase.

Limitation Periods.—No action may be commenced to enforce right of action, in case of rescission, 180 days after date of transaction giving rise to cause of action or, in any other case, earlier of 180 days after plaintiff first had knowledge of facts giving rise to cause of action or three years after date of transaction giving rise to cause of action. (§138). Except as otherwise provided, proceeding cannot be commenced later than five years from date of occurrence of last event on which proceeding is based. (§129.1).

Penalties.—Noncompliance is offence punishable by fine of not more than $1,000,000 and/or two years in prison. Directors and officers who authorize, permit or acquiesce in commission of offence by company also may be punishable by fine of not more than $1,000,000 and/or two years in prison. (§122).

Securities Affected.—"Security" includes any document, instrument or writing commonly known as security; any document constituting evidence of title to or interest in capital, assets, property, profits, earnings or royalties of any person or company or association of legatees or heirs; any document constituting evidence of option, subscription or other interest in or to security; any bond, debenture, note, share, stock, unit, unit certificate, participation certificate, certificate of share or interest, pre-organization certificate or subscription, other than contract of insurance issued by insurance company or evidence of deposit issued by Canadian bank or loan or trust corporation; any agreement under which interest of purchaser is valued for purposes of conversion or surrender by reference to value of proportionate interest in specified portfolio of assets, except certain contracts issued by Canadian insurance companies; any agreement providing that money received will be repaid or treated as subscription to shares, stock, units or interests at option of recipient or of any person or company; any certificate of share or interest in trust, estate or association; any profit-sharing agreement or certificate; any certificate of interest in oil, natural gas or mining lease, claim or royalty voting trust certificate; any oil or natural gas royalties or leases or fractional or other interest therein; any collateral trust certificate; any income or annuity contract not issued by insurance company or issuer within meaning of Investment Contracts Act (c. I.14); any investment contract other than investment contract within meaning of such Act; any document constituting evidence of interest in scholarship or educational plan or trust; and any commodity futures contract or commodity futures option that is not traded on commodity futures exchange registered with or recognized by Commission under Commodity Futures Act (c. C.20) or form of which is not accepted by Director (§1[1]).

Registration of Offerers.—See subhead Registration of Dealers, Advisers, etc., infra.

Registration of Securities.—Securities per se are not registered. However, prospectus must be filed for any distribution of securities (unless exemption is available) and annual information form kept current for most reporting issuers. Securities remaining unsold at expiration of two-year term of shelf offering prospectus must be qualified under new prospectus prior to being sold. See subhead Distribution of Securities to Public, catchlines Prerequisites to Sales or Offerings and Prospectus Requirements, supra.

Registration of Underwriters.—See subhead Registration of Dealers, Advisers, etc., infra.

Registration of Dealers, Advisers, etc.—No person or company may trade in security unless registered as dealer or as salesperson, partner or officer of registered dealer. No person may act as underwriter or as adviser unless registered as underwriter or adviser. (§25). Registration as adviser is not required by, among others, Canadian banks, Federal Business Development Bank, Canadian trust or insurance companies, lawyers, accountants, engineers, teachers, registered dealers or partners or employees thereof, publishers of news in each case where such service is incidental to adviser's principal business. (§34). Underwriter does not include Canadian bank with respect to certain securities and banking transactions. (§1[1]). Registration is not required in case of trades and securities specified in §35(1) Securities Act. However, regulations under Securities Act provide for "universal registration" which requires registration by market intermediaries in respect of many trades specified in §35(1). Definition of market intermediary is broad and includes any person or company engaged in the business of selling securities (R.R.O. 1015, §204).

Security Holder.—Registration is not required for trade in security by person or company acting through agent who is registered dealer. (§35[1], item 10).

Registration.—Registration must be made in accordance with Securities Act and regulations. Written notice of registration must be received from Director and if subject to terms and conditions, such terms and conditions must be complied with. (§25). Director may restrict registration, including duration of registration and may restrict registration to trades in certain securities. (§26). Applicant must state address for service in Ontario in application (§30) and Director may require one year's residence within Canada prior to date of application (§32). O.S.C. will permit nonresident adviser to register as adviser in Ontario if adviser complies in all respects with regulatory requirements applicable to advisers and satisfies O.S.C. that appropriate level of proficiency is met. O.S.C. also will permit nonresident advisers to obtain adviser registration to advise certain sophisticated clients including banks, loan, trust or insurance companies, federal or provincial government of Canada, pension funds having assets of at least $100 million, registered charities having assets of at least $5 million, high net worth individuals or certain mutual funds. (O.S.C. Policy 4.8). Termination of employment of salesperson operates as suspension of registration until notice in writing has been received by Director from another registered dealer of employment of salesperson and reinstatement of registration has been approved by Director. (§25[2]). Registered dealer must notify Director within five business days of change of address. (§33).

Take-Over Bids.—Take-over bid is defined in Part XX of Securities Act as offer to acquire voting or equity securities made to security holders in Ontario, where, together with offeror's securities, such securities constitute 20% or more of outstanding securities of that class at date of offer. (§89[1]). Subject to regulations, take-over bid is exempted from Part XX if: bid is made through facilities of approved stock exchange; bid is for not more than 5% of outstanding securities of class and acquisitions do not aggregate more than 5% of securities within 12 months and price paid does not exceed market price at date acquired; bid is offer by private agreement with five or fewer security holders at price not exceeding 115% of market price; offeree issuer is not reporting issuer, published market does not exist for issuer's securities, number of security holders is not more than 50, exclusive of employees and former employees of issuer or issuer's affiliate; and number of holders in Ontario subject to bid is less than 50, securities held constitute less than 2% of outstanding securities of class, bid is made in compliance with laws of jurisdiction recognized by O.S.C. and all bid material is sent to security holders in Ontario. (§93[1]). O.S.C. may exempt any person or company from Part XX if not prejudicial to public interest. (§104[2]). Every offeror that acquires ownership of, or power to control or direct, or securities convertible into, voting or equity securities of any class of reporting issuer that, together with offeror's securities of that class constitutes 10% or more of outstanding securities, must issue press release forthwith and file report disclosing intention with O.S.C. within two business days. (§101). Take-over bids for securities of U.S. issuers may be made under Multijurisdictional Disclosure System (MJDS) provided they comply with U.S. law where (i) bid is subject to U.S. law; (ii) bid made to all security holders in Canada on same terms and conditions as in U.S.; and (iii) less than 40% of securities subject to bid are held in Canada. Material provided to U.S. security holders must also be provided to holders in Canada. Material must disclose bid made in accordance with U.S. law. (National Policy 45 MJDS).

Issuer Bid.—Issuer bid is defined in Part XX of Securities Act as offer to security holders in Ontario by issuer to acquire or redeem any securities of issuer, other than nonconvertible debt securities. Issuer bid is exempted from Part XX of Act if: securities are purchased, redeemed or otherwise acquired in accordance with terms attaching thereto; purchase, redemption or acquisition required by instrument creating securities or by statute under which issuer incorporated; securities carry right of owner to require issuer to redeem or repurchase securities and are acquired through such right; securities acquired from current or former employee of issuer or issuer's affiliate, and if there is published market for securities, price paid does not exceed market price at date acquired and aggregate number of acquisitions does not aggregate more than 5% of class within 12 month period; issuer bid is made through approved stock exchange; issuer publishes notice in form prescribed by regulation and purchases securities in normal course in open market through stock exchange, if aggregate acquisitions in any 12 month period does not exceed 5% of securities of class sought; issuer is not reporting issuer, published market does not exist for issuer's securities, number of security holders is not more than 50 exclusive of employees and former employees of issuer or issuer's affiliate; number of holders in Ontario subject to bid is less than 50, securities held constitute less than 2% of outstanding securities of class, bid is in compliance with laws of jurisdiction recognized by O.S.C., and all bid material is sent to security holders in Ontario; or bid is exempt by regulations.(§93[3]).

Unless exempt, take-over bid or issuer bid circular must accompany any such bid. In take-over bid made through facilities of approved stock exchange, bid must be for cash only and only conditions that may be attached to bid are: (i) maximum number of shares that offeror will take up and (ii) no action be taken under provisions of Competition Act (Canada) within periods specified in that Act.

Directors' circular of directors of offeree company must be sent to each offeree within ten days of take-over bid which must include either recommendation to accept or reject take-over bid and reasons therefor or statement unable to make or not making recommendation and if no recommendation made, reasons therefor. (§99).

Time Periods.—Period for deposit of securities must be minimum of 21 days. Securities deposited may not be taken up and paid for by offeror until expiration of 21 days from date of bid and offeree may withdraw securities within 21 days of date of bid. If

SECURITIES . . . *continued*
bid is for less than all of class of securities sought and where greater number were deposited, offeror must take up securities pro rata. (§95).

Filing.—Securities Act requires take-over bid material to be filed with O.S.C. (§100, R.R.O. 1015, §203).

Penalties.—Every person or company who makes misrepresentation in take-over or issuer bid circular or contravenes Securities Act is liable to fine of not more than $1,000,000 and/or imprisonment for two years. (§122).

Rescission and Civil Liability.—Where take-over or issuer bid circular or any notice of change in respect thereof contains misrepresentation, every offeree is deemed to have relied on such misrepresentation and may elect to exercise right of action for rescission against offeror or damages against offeror and every director of offeror at time circular signed; every person or company whose consent was filed under regulations but only with respect to reports, opinions or statements made by them; and every person who signed certificate in circular or notice other than person listed above and such persons are liable jointly and severally. (§131[1] and [8]). Similar right also exists against directors who sign directors' circular or notice of change in respect thereof containing misrepresentation. (§131[2]). Parties other than offeror have available due diligence defence and where securities offered by offeror, persons not liable for damages that do not represent depreciation in value of security offered because of misrepresentation. (§131[6] and [9]). See subhead Distribution of Securities to Public, catchline Limitation Periods, supra.

Proxy Solicitations.—Solicitations of proxies by management of reporting issuers is mandatory, if notice of shareholders meeting is given, or intended to be given. (§85). This also applies to Ontario corporation "offering its securities to the public". (Business Corporations Act, c. B.16, §111). Form of proxy must be sent to security holders, whose address in books of reporting issuer is in Ontario, and to nonregistered holders pursuant to National Policy 41. Form of proxy is prescribed for Ontario corporations and must state on whose behalf it is solicited, provide space to name nominee of shareholder's choice and provide "for and against" ballot. (R.R.O. 162). Form of proxy for reporting issuer is prescribed by regulations. (§85).

Information circular, contents of which must set out prescribed information (§84) must accompany proxy solicitation (§86[1]). Information circular not required if, among other things, solicitation, otherwise than by management, is for proxies of not more than 15 security holders (§86[2]). Companies may apply for exemption from all or some of requirements. (§88[2]). Information circular must be filed with O.S.C. (§81).

Insider Trading.—

Reporting.—(Part XXI, Securities Act). Person or company who becomes insider of reporting issuer must file report within ten days after end of month of becoming insider. (§107[1]). Person or company who has filed or is required to file insider report must report any changes of direct or indirect beneficial ownership of securities within ten days of end of month in which change takes place. Special provisions apply to mutual funds and management companies. (§§110-121). O.S.C. summarizes insider reports and publishes monthly periodical which is available to public for fee. (§120). O.S.C. may make order exempting person or company from requirements of Part XXI. (§121 [2]).

"Insider" or "insider of reporting issuer" means: every director or senior officer of reporting issuer; every director or senior officer of company that is itself insider or subsidiary of reporting issuer; any person or company who beneficially owns directly or indirectly or who exercises control or direction over more than 10% of voting securities of reporting issuer; reporting issuer where it has purchased, redeemed, or otherwise acquired its securities. "Senior officer" means chair or vice-chair of board of directors, president, vice-president, secretary, treasurer or general manager of company or individual who performs similar functions and each of five highest-paid employees including senior officers previously mentioned. (§1[1]). Company is deemed affiliate of another company if one is subsidiary of other or both are subsidiaries of same company or each is controlled by same person or company. Company is deemed controlled by another if other holds more than 50% of votes for election of directors, and votes are entitled, if exercised, to elect majority of board of directors. Company is deemed subsidiary of another if controlled by other, or others controlled by that other, or is subsidiary of company that is that other's subsidiary. Person is deemed to own securities beneficially owned by company controlled by person or by affiliate of such company and company is deemed to beneficially own securities beneficially owned by its affiliates. (§1[2]-[6]).

Extent of Disclosures.—Insider must disclose any direct or indirect beneficial ownership, control or direction over securities of reporting issuer as required under regulations in prescribed form.

Insider Liability.—Every person or company in "special relationship" with reporting issuer who sells or purchases securities with knowledge of, or who informs another person or company of, "material fact" or "material change" not generally disclosed is liable to compensate purchaser or vendor for damages. (§134). Person or company in "special relationship" means (a) person or company that is insider, affiliate or associate of (i) reporting issuer, (ii) person or company making take-over bid for securities of reporting issuer, (iii) person proposing to become party to reorganization, amalgamation, merger or arrangement or similar business combination with reporting issuer or to acquire substantial portion of its property; (b) person or company engaged in or proposing to engage in business activity with reporting issuer or person or company in (a) (ii) or (iii); (c) person is director, officer or employee of reporting issuer or of person or company in (a) (ii) or (iii) or (b); (d) person or company that learned of material fact or change regarding reporting issuer while person or company described in (a), (b) or (c); (e) person or company that learned of material fact or change regarding reporting issuer from person or company that was itself in special relationship with reporting issuer who knew or ought reasonably to have known other person or company was in such relationship. (§76[5]). Insider must also account to reporting issuer for any benefit or advantage received. (§134[4]). Such trading or informing is also offence subject to penalty of not less than profit made or loss avoided and not more than greater of $1,000,000 and triple profit made or loss avoided and imprisonment for up to two years.

Continuous Disclosure.—Every reporting issuer must file annual and quarterly financial statements with O.S.C. (or in case of mutual funds, annual and semi-annual financial statements), and concurrently send copies to all security holders resident in Ontario, and to unregistered security holders as prescribed in National Policy 41. (§§77-79). If reporting issuer subject to corresponding requirement by laws of jurisdiction where incorporated, continued compliance with such requirement sufficient. (§§79, 82). Provisions for exemption from filing requirements. (§80). Where "material change" or "material fact" occurs in affairs of reporting issuer press release disclosing nature of change must be issued and filed with O.S.C. forthwith, and report of such material change shall be filed with O.S.C. within ten days of date on which change occurs. (§75[1] and [2]). Where such disclosure unduly detrimental to interests of reporting issuer or disclosure to be confirmed by directors of reporting issuer and no use made of knowledge in dealings with securities, reporting issuer may file report marked "confidential" with written reasons for nondisclosure. (§75[3]). No person or company in special relationship with reporting issuer may buy or sell its securities with knowledge of "material fact" or "material change" not disclosed, or inform another of such undisclosed fact or change until generally disclosed. (§76). See subhead Insider Trading, catchline Insider Liability, supra. Any material information concerning affairs of issuer also must be disclosed immediately through news media. (National Policy 40, Timely Disclosure).

SEQUESTRATION:

Property may be taken into legal custody to preserve it during litigation or to compel compliance with a judgment or order.

During Litigation.—Court may make interim order for custody or preservation of any property in question in proceeding or relevant to issue therein, and for that purpose may authorize entry on or into any property in possession of either party or nonparty. Where property is perishable or likely to deteriorate or for other reasons ought to be sold, court may order sale. Where right to specific fund is in question, court may order funds paid into court or posting of security therefor. (R.P. 45.01[1], [2], 45.02).

After Judgment or Order.—Writ of sequestration, directing sheriff to take possession, and hold property, of person against whom order has been made, and to collect and hold any income from that property until person complies with order, may be issued only with leave of court, which is to be obtained on motion. Court may grant leave only where satisfied that other enforcement measures are likely to be ineffective, and may order that writ be enforced against all or part of person's real and personal property. (R.P. 60.09). Where corporation is in contempt of order, judge may grant leave to issue writ of sequestration against any officer or director of corporation. (R.P. 60.11[6]).

SERVICE: See topic Process.

STATUTE OF FRAUDS: See topic Frauds, Statute of.

STATUTES:

Latest revision is Revised Statutes of Ontario, 1990. Subsequent acts are in annual Statutes of Ontario. Regulations made under authority of statutes are consolidated in Revised Regulations of Ontario 1990, with amendments published in Ontario Gazette.

STAY OF EXECUTION: See topic Executions.

SUBMISSION OF CONTROVERSY:

Special Case.—Where parties to proceeding concur in stating question of law in form of special case, any party may move before judge to have special case determined, which judge may hear and determine, if satisfied that determination of such question may dispose of all or part of proceeding, substantially shorten hearing, or result in substantial cost savings. (R.P. 22.01). Special case to be in prescribed form, including agreed statements of material facts and relief sought. (R.P. 22.04). On hearing case, court may draw any reasonable inferences from facts and may, on determination of question of law, make order or grant judgment accordingly. (R.P. 22.05).

Determination of Issue Before Trial.—Either party may move before judge before trial for determination of any question of law raised by pleading where outcome may dispose of all or part of action, substantially shorten trial, or result in substantial costs saving. Either party may move before judge to strike pleading as disclosing no cause of action or defence. No evidence is admissible on such motions, but parties are required to deliver factums containing concise statements of facts and law to be relied on. (R.P. 21.01-R.P. 21.03).

Construction of Contract.—Where the rights of the parties depend upon the construction of any contract or agreement or where it is unlikely there will be any material facts in dispute, such rights may be determined upon notice of application. Contract or agreement may be construed before there has been breach thereof. (R.P. 14.05[3]).

SURETY AND GUARANTY COMPANIES:

Surety and guaranty companies are subject to the laws applicable to companies generally.

Rights and Powers.—Before it can give bonds as security in cases where security is ordered to be given by the court or by statute, a guaranty company must be approved as such by an order-in-council. The bond, policy or guaranty contract of an approved company may be taken in lieu of security by bond with sureties. The guaranty company is not bound to justify. (c. G.11).

TAXATION:

The Minister of Finance has general supervision of administration of all provincial tax laws. All public moneys must be paid to credit of Minister of Finance of Ontario.

Exemptions—Armed Forces.—Unless otherwise specified, members of armed forces enjoy no exemptions from taxation.

Property taxes are of three kinds: (1) general realty tax levied by municipalities on owners of land and based on assessment; (2) business taxes levied by municipalities on occupiers of premises for business purposes and generally based on assessment plus a percentage varying with business; and (3) taxes levied by government in unorganized territories under Provincial Land Tax Act (c. P.32) based generally on assessment. See also occupancy reduction under subhead Income Tax, infra.

Development Charges Act (c. D.9) has three operative parts. Part I establishes statutory scheme for imposition of municipal lot levies on new development. Part II

TAXATION . . . *continued*
provides for "front-ending agreements" between municipalities and landowners for installing services, under which landowners who are not parties can be required, as condition of any development of lands within benefiting area, to pay proportionate share of costs. Part III is statutory scheme for collection of lot levies on new development by school boards and is in essence form of taxation.

Commercial Concentration Levy.—Now repealed.

Assessment.—At market value, by provincial Assessment Commissioners for land within municipalities. Assessment Roll is prepared annually and notice of any changes given at least 14 days prior to completion of roll.

Review of Assessments.— Appeal from municipal assessment lies to local Assessment Review Board, and from its decision to Ontario Municipal Board. On questions other than those of wrongful placing on or omission from roll and amount of assessment, appeal to judge with further appeal to Divisional Court.

Times for payment, discounts and penalties are fixed by the municipalities subject to statute.

Lien and Sale.—Unpaid municipal taxes on lands form a charge upon the lands, and they may be collected by seizure of personal property of person taxed, if on lands or elsewhere within county or district, or by action. Where, after two years in case of improved land and one year in case of vacant land, arrears are still owing, treasurer of municipality may register tax arrears certificate against title to land in respect of which arrears are owing, indicating that land will be sold by public sale if cancellation price (tax arrears plus interest, penalties and collection costs) is not paid within one year following date of registration of certificate. (Municipal Tax Sales Act, c. M.60).

Income Tax.—(a) Individuals (including estates and trusts): Ontario income tax payable under Income Tax Act (c. I.2) by Ontario residents and, on income earned in Ontario, by non-Ontario residents. Tax is 58% of basic federal tax payable on such income. Under proposed legislation, rate reduced to 56% for 1996 and 49% for 1997 and subsequent years. No tax payable (unless federal alternative minimum tax rules apply) where individual's tax otherwise payable is less than $205 (plus $395 for each dependent who is child age 18 or under, or disabled). Surtax is payable at rate of 20% on personal income tax between $5,310 and $7,635 and at rate of 30% on personal income tax above $8,000. There is special deduction in respect of occupancy cost of principal residence. Under fiscal agreements, tax is collected by federal government and combined returns are filed. Every person who fails to file return as and when required is subject to prescribed penalties. As tax is percentage of federal income tax, see Canada Law Digest, topic Taxation. (b) Corporations: See topic Corporations, subhead Taxation, catchline Provincial Income Tax.

Health Tax.—All self-employed individuals with net annual income in excess of $40,000 are required by Employer Health Tax Act (c. E.11) to pay levy on excess. Rate is 78% of following: .98% on income between $40,000 and $200,000 plus 2.726% on income between $200,001 and $400,000, if income is over $400,000, rate is 78% of 1.95% on full amount of excess over $400,000. *Note:* Under proposed legislation, this tax would be phased out between 1997 and 1999.

Inheritance Tax.—For death occurring after Apr. 10, 1979 no inheritance tax on property passing on death.

Estate tax is levied in form of income tax on deemed dispositions at death under federal Income Tax Act. See Canada Law Digest, topic Taxation.

Gift Tax.—None.

Sales Tax.—Retail Sales Tax Act, c. R.31—8% retail sales tax is levied on purchaser of tangible personal property which is used or consumed within Ontario, on certain leases and rentals of such property, on some services (telecommunications, maintenance and repair of personal property, warranties, parking charges and on most insurance premiums) and on restaurant meals over $4. Tax is 5% on hotel rooms and other transient accommodation and on auto insurance premiums, 10% on entertainment admissions over $4 and on alcoholic beverages sold in licensed premises (bars and restaurants), and 12% on alcoholic beverages sold in retail stores. Exemptions include most foodstuffs, fuel, drugs and medicines, prescription goods, newspapers, subscription magazines, and manufacturing equipment. Vender of taxable tangible personal property must obtain permit.

Penalties are provided for failing to collect tax imposed (amount of tax plus 10% up to $1,000); failing to file return (10% of tax payable up to $1,000).

Tobacco tax imposed by Tobacco Tax Act. (c. T.10).

Stamp Tax.—See Corporations, subhead Stock Transfer Tax. There are no other stamp taxes.

Gasoline tax imposed on gasoline and aviation fuel by Gasoline Tax Act. (c. G.5). Fuel tax imposed on motor fuel (other than gasoline and aviation fuel) by Fuel Tax Act (c. F.35).

Land Tax.—Land in territory without municipal organization is liable to assessment and taxation under Provincial Land Tax Act. (c. P.32).

Land Transfer Tax.—Land Transfer Tax Act (c. L.6) imposes tax on registration of conveyances of land calculated upon total consideration paid for land and buildings conveyed in instrument tendered in registration. Attached to every instrument is affidavit setting out consideration. Where land other than land zoned or assessed as commercial, industrial or residential or land assessed for or actually used as farm, agricultural woodlands, recreational land or as orchard, is conveyed to nonresident of Canada, tax is 20% of value of consideration. All other conveyances, tax is 1/2 of 1% of value of consideration up to $55,000, 1% of value between $55,000 and $250,000, and 1 1/2% of value of remainder, additional tax of 1/2% applies to amount above $400,000 for certain single family dwellings. Under proposed legislation, temporary refund of tax (up to $1,725) is available to first time home buyers who agree to purchase newly-constructed home before Mar. 31, 1997 and who acquire home between May 8, 1996 and June 30, 1997. Nonresident, subject to 20% rate, may apply to Minister for deferral or rebate if nonresident undertakes to develop and sell land for residential, commercial or industrial purposes within five years, or to establish, relocate or expand business within five years, or if nonresident is Canadian citizen and undertakes to become resident within five years, or if land is acquired at arm's-length by way of foreclosure or default and nonresident undertakes to resell within five years, or if non-Canadian citizen undertakes to become resident within two years. Minister may also grant cancellation of tax if land is acquired by nonresident Canadian citizen for his principal residence or by nonresident employer for use by his employees. Certain other classes of conveyances, such as those to family farm or business corporations and leaseholds for 50 years, may be exempted from high rate or from entire tax by regulations.

Tax is also imposed on most unregistered transfers of beneficial interests in real property on same basis as registered transfers. Exceptions include transfers by operation of law which arise on death, transfers to provide security for debts and transfers by way of lease for less than 50 years. Minister may also grant deferral of tax (which may ultimately result in cancellation of tax) for transfers within related corporate group if security for tax is given to Minister and transferor undertakes to hold unregistered property interest for three years.

Nonresident person broadly defined. Includes Canadian corporations where nonresidents own more than defined levels and types of shares or where nonresident directors control corporation. See definition in §1 of Act.

Corporation Tax.—See topic Corporations, subhead Taxation, catchline Taxable Income.

Mines and Natural Gas Tax.—See topic Mines and Minerals.

Social Security Tax.—No social security or unemployment compensation tax is imposed by the Province of Ontario. See Canada Law Digest, topic Taxation.

Penalties.—See subheads detailing particular taxes, supra.

TORRENS ACT: See topics Deeds; Records.

TRADEMARKS AND TRADENAMES:

See, generally, Canada Law Digest.

As to registration of partnership or person doing business under a name other than his own, see topic Partnership.

TRUST DEEDS:

See topic Mortgages of Real Property.

TRUSTEE PROCESS: See topic Garnishment.

TRUSTS:

Trusts are interpreted and administered in accordance with the principles of equity as varied by the Trustee Act. (c. T.23).

Kinds.—Express trusts for any legitimate purpose including testamentary trusts and trusts arising by implication of law including resulting and constructive trusts. Trusts also arise under statutes; sometimes special statutory provisions apply to them.

Variation.—Generally, if all interested persons ascertained and with legal capacity, on their consent; and with consent of court for minors, other persons incapable or unborn or for persons, ascertained or not, with certain possible future interests. (c. V.1). Provisions for amendment in trust document may apply. Rule in Saunders & Vautier, (1841) 49 E.R. 282, applies generally to possible early wind-up of trust where all possible beneficiaries adult and otherwise fully capacitated. Case law should be carefully considered before proceeding.

Removal of Trustee.—The court may remove trustees or appoint substitute or new trustees. (c. T.23, §5). Limited provisions for other removal, replacement and appointment of trustees, for personal representatives of last deceased or sole trustee to act or for such trustee to appoint replacement by will. (§§2, 3, 4, 6). Provisions of instrument creating trust may provide for same.

General powers and duties of trustees usually defined by instrument creating trust, but equitable doctrines applicable to supplement or qualify these powers and duties. Also, trustees have by statute (c. T.23) some powers or extended powers, including powers respecting sale, renewing leases, mortgaging, investment in specified classes of securities. Trustees may apply to court in summary manner for opinion, advice or direction of court on administration of trust, interpretation of trust instrument, determination of rights of beneficiaries and certain other matters. (§60; R.P. 14.05[3]).

Liabilities of Trustee.—A trustee is liable for damages if he fails to carry out terms of trust or is negligent. Court may relieve trustee from personal liability for technical breaches of trust. (c. T. 23, §35). Certain additional relieving provisions or indemnities in Trustee Act. (§§30—34). Provisions for exoneration or indemnity of trustees in trust instrument may apply.

Investments.—Trust funds may be invested in the types of property permitted in trust instrument, failing which, in securities set out in Trustee Act. (c. T. 23, §§26 and 27). See Haslam v. Haslam (1994), 3 E.T.R. (2d) 206 and subsequent cases on investment in mutual funds.

Accounting.—By estate trustees: see topic Estate Trustees, subhead Accounts. Other trustees file and pass accounts in office of Ontario Court (General Division) of county or district where trustee resident or part of trust estate situate. (c. T.23, §23). For procedure on passing of accounts, see R.P. 74.16, 74.17, 74.18. Action for accounting may be brought against trustee.

Compensation.—Where compensation not fixed by the trust instrument, it may be fixed by judge of Ontario Court (General Division) upon passing of accounts or otherwise. Amount such as is allowed by judge as fair and reasonable. (c. T.23, §§23, 61). Certain percentages of amounts of receipts and disbursements and of value of property for management fees usually allowed. Trustee may take reimbursement out of trust for expenses incurred administering trust. Beneficiaries, if all adult and otherwise fully capacitated, may agree to compensation. Taking compensation without such consent of beneficiaries or Court approval improper in most circumstances.

USURY:

See Canada Law Digest, topic Interest; also topic Interest, of this Digest.

See Topical Index in front part of this volume.

VENUE:

In statement of claim, plaintiff must name as place of trial place where court normally sits in county in which plaintiff proposes that action be tried, but where statute requires trial in particular county, plaintiff must name as place of trial place where court normally sits in that county. (R.P. 46.01). Special rules govern venue in divorce actions and family law proceedings. (R.P. 69.17; 70.05). Trial is held at place named in statement of claim unless court makes order changing venue. (R.P. 46.02).

Change of Venue.—Where plaintiff named venue other than that required by statute, court will order, on motion by any party, that trial be held at place required. In addition, court will order, on motion by any party, that trial be held at place other than that named in statement of claim if satisfied that balance of convenience substantially favours holding of trial at another place, or that it is likely that fair trial cannot be held at place named by plaintiff. (R.P. 46.03). Where party moves to change venue, prior agreement as to place of hearing is not binding, but may be considered by court. (c. C.43, §114).

VITAL STATISTICS: See topic Records.

WAREHOUSEMEN:

The business of warehousemen as bailees for reward is regulated by rules of common law as amended by statutes. A warehouseman is liable for loss of or injury to goods caused by his failure to exercise such care and diligence in regard to them as a careful and vigilant owner of similar goods would exercise in the custody of them in similar circumstances. (c. W.3).

Bonds and Licences.—Warehousemen are not required by provincial law to post bonds or obtain licences before carrying on their business.

Warehouse Receipts.—A warehouse receipt is an acknowledgment in writing by a warehouseman of the receipt for storage of goods not his own. The form of the receipt, the conditions of its negotiability, and other matters relating to it are governed by The Warehouse Receipts Act (c. W.3) and by The Mercantile Law Amendment Act (c. M.10).

Liens.—Person who receives article for storage or storage and repair has lien against article for amount equal to amount agreed upon for storage or storage and repair or where no such amount has been agreed upon, fair value of storage or storage and repair including all lawful claims for money advanced, interest on money advanced, insurance, transportation, labour, weighing, packing and other expenses incurred in relation to storage or storage and repair of article. Storer may retain possession of article until amount is paid. In addition to other remedies provided at law, lien claimant may sell by public or private sale provided he observes statutory provisions governing such sales. (c. R.25).

WILLS:

Capacity.—Persons under 18 years cannot make valid will, except certain members of Canadian Forces, sailors in certain circumstances, or persons who have been or are married or who are contemplating marriage, but will must name person testator intends to marry and is invalid if marriage does not take place (c. S.26, §8). Persons lacking requisite mental capacity cannot make valid will. Sex and, except for persons under 18, marital status irrelevant.

Testamentary Disposition.—Every person may by will dispose of all real and personal estate which without will would devolve upon his heirs, executors or administrators. This is subject to some limitations: where adequate provision for dependant not made court may make order therefor against estate; Family Law Act entitlement of spouse (c. F.3, §5), (see topics Descent and Distribution; Estate Trustees, subhead Distribution); rights of surviving owners of jointly owned property and rights of beneficiaries under unrevoked or irrevocable designations noted below. Person may designate beneficiary: under certain plans providing benefits, including profit sharing and pension plans, for employees and some other persons or of some (usually tax sheltered) individual retirement or savings plans, in will or in signed document as permitted (c. S.26, §§50, 51); or of proceeds of life or accident insurance (c. I.8, §§190, 313). Some designations, e.g. of life or accident insurance, protect proceeds from creditors. (§§196, 317). Provisions for gifts of human tissue are contained in c. H.20. (See topic Estate Trustees, subhead Human Tissue Gift Act.)

Execution.—Will must be in writing, signed at foot or end by testator or by some other person in presence and by direction of testator. Signature must be made or acknowledged by testator in presence of two or more witnesses present at same time, and such witnesses must subscribe will in presence of testator and each other. (c. S.26, §4). No seal is required. Certain armed forces members on active duty or sailor in certain circumstances may make will by writing signed by or at direction of that person and no witness required.

Attestation Clause.—While no form of attestation is necessary the following form is customarily used.

Form

Signed by the testator, (Name), as his last Will, in the presence of us, both present at the same time, who at his request, in his presence and in the presence of each other have hereunto subscribed our names as witnesses.

Living Wills.—Provision often included in personal care power of attorney (see topic Principal and Agent) but legal effect beyond ability to have personal care attorney refuse or consent to treatment as provided in Substitute Decisions Act, 1992, S.O. 1992, c. 30, in effect Apr. 3, 1995 and Health Care Consent Act, 1996, S.O. 1996, c. 2, in effect Mar. 28, 1996, is uncertain. Also, see Malette v. Shulman (1990), 72 O.R. (2d) 417.

Holograph Wills.—Any testator may make valid will wholly by own handwriting and signature without witness or further formality. (c. S.26, §6).

Appointment of Estate Trustee of Holograph Will.—Applicant must submit affidavit attesting that entire will, including signature, in handwriting of deceased. (R.P. 74.04). (*Note*: See reference to change in terminology at beginning of topic Estate Trustees.)

Revocation.—Will may be revoked by subsequent valid will, by writing declaring intention to revoke, executed in manner required for valid will; or by burning, tearing or otherwise destroying same by testator or person in presence and by direction of testator, with intent to revoke. (c. S.26, §15). Will also revoked by marriage of testator except: where will declares it made in contemplation of such marriage; where spouse of testator elects to take under will by writing filed within one year after death in office of Estate Registrar for Ontario; or where will made in exercise of power of appointment and property appointed would not in default of appointment pass to testator's personal representatives. (§16). Will not revoked by presumption of intention on ground of changed circumstances except: if testator after making will becomes divorced or marriage declared nullity, will construed as if former spouse predeceased testator, subject to contrary intent in will. (§17).

Revival.—No revoked will revived except by re-execution or duly executed will or codicil showing intent to revive. Subject to contrary intention, revival of will wholly revoked does not extend to part revoked prior to revocation of whole. (c. S.26, §19). Will deemed to be made at time revived. (§21).

Testamentary Gifts to Subscribing Witnesses.—Beneficiary or spouse of beneficiary under will is competent witness and may sign will on behalf of testator, but gifts or appointments (except direction to pay debts) to that witness, person signing or such spouse or to any person claiming under any of them are invalid unless court finds no exercise of improper or undue influence on testator by such witness, person signing or spouse. If more than two witnesses and at least two not beneficiaries or their spouses, or if no attestation required, no such forfeiture of gifts. (c. S.26, §12). Both executor and creditor whose debt is charged on property by will or their spouses are competent witnesses. (§§13, 14). Direction or charge for payment of debts specifically excepted from gifts that are invalid. No similar specific exception for any provision for gift or compensation to executor.

Certificate of Appointment.—Jurisdiction to appoint estate trustee with will lies in Ontario Court (General Division). Application to be filed in its office in county or district in which deceased had at time of death fixed place of abode. If deceased had no fixed place of abode in or resided out of Ontario at death application may be made in such Court's office in any county or district in which deceased had property at death. In other cases application may be filed in such Court's office in any county or district. (c. E.21, §7). Usual application for appointment as estate trustee with will on affidavit evidence with notice to all parties entitled to share in estate but without appearance. Forms provided. (R.P. 74.04). Estate trustee or person with financial interest may apply for formal proof. (R.P. 75.01). Lost or destroyed will may be proved on affidavit evidence without appearance or as Court directs. (R.P. 75.02). (See also topic Estate Trustees.)

Notice of Proceeding.—Person with financial interest can receive notice of commencement of proceeding in estate until certificate appointing estate trustee issued. (R.P. 74.03).

Contest.—Proceedings to contest application for appointment as estate trustee with will commenced by filing notice of objection with Estate Registrar for Ontario or local registrar of Ontario Court (General Division) for county or district. (c. E.21, §21; R.P. 75.03). For application to revoke appointment of estate trustee with will or order to return certificate of appointment to Court, see c. E.21, §§23, 24 and R.P. 75.04, 75.05. Grounds for contesting appointment or to revoke appointment of estate trustee can include, as applicable, lack of testamentary capacity; undue influence; invalid execution; discovery of subsequent will or codicil; appointment made without jurisdiction, in irregular manner, or to person not lawfully entitled; or certain other grounds.

Self-proved Wills.—No provision.

Legacies.—If no direction on time of payment in will, with few exceptions, legacy payable within year of death of testator. If not paid by that time, legacy bears interest at legal rate unless contrary intention appears in will. (Interest Act, R.S.C., c. I-15, §3).

Unclaimed Legacies.—Money in hands of estate trustee on final passing of accounts of estate, which belongs to person whose address unknown, or who is minor or mentally incapable person, must be paid into court to credit of person entitled or to Public Guardian and Trustee if guardian of such person's property. Money paid into court subject to order of court. (c. T.23, §36). See topic Absentees, subhead Escheat and Bona Vacantia.

Lapse or Ademption of Legacies and Devises.—Generally, any devise of realty or bequest of personalty fails if beneficiary dies before testator, subject to contrary intention in will. Some exceptions: Unless contrary intention by will, if such beneficiary is child, grandchild, brother or sister of testator, and beneficiary leaves issue or spouse surviving testator, gift takes effect as if made to persons who would receive beneficiary's estate if dies intestate immediately after testator, without debts (such persons include beneficiary's spouse, except no $200,000 preferential share for spouse). (c. S.26, §31); if gift is to class or is joint gift, lapse is avoided. (See Dodge [Litigation Guardian of] v. Dodge Estate [1993], 15 O.R. [3d] 422 on contrary intention in will.) Generally, if property devised or bequeathed does not belong to deceased at death, gift fails. Exceptions to this general rule of ademption include statutory exceptions: if testator conveys or deals with property by contract or otherwise, or if property destroyed or damaged or expropriated, or receives mortgage or other security interest on sale of property, beneficiary of property entitled to testator's rights and interest under contract, proceeds of insurance or expropriation or to mortgage or other security interest. (§20). And where guardian of property disposes of property under Substitute Decisions Act, 1992, S.O. 1992, c. 30, beneficiary of that property acquires interest in proceeds. (S.O. 1992, c. 30, §36). Guardian also subject to restrictions on disposition of property that is subject of specific testamentary gift. (§35.1). Unless contrary intention in will, any devise or bequest which fails by death of beneficiary before testator or by being disclaimed or contrary to law or otherwise incapable of taking effect is included in any gift of residue (§23) and gift of all or any portion of residue which fails passes as on intestacy, subject to some exception in favour of appointed executor. (§33).

Children.—Will need not show affirmatively intention to disinherit children or their issue, whether living when will executed or born later. Gifts to children and some others may be saved from lapse if donee predeceases testator (see subhead Lapse or Ademption of Legacies and Devises, supra) and children may be able to obtain support under

WILLS . . . *continued*
Succession Law Reform Act. (c. S.26, §58). (See topic Estate Trustees, subhead Dependants' Allowances.) For meaning of children or issue, see topic Descent and Distribution, subheads Adopted Children, Illegitimate Children.

Election.—See topic Descent and Distribution, subheads Family Law Act, Election, and Election on abolition of curtesy and dower.

Foreign Executed Wills.—In respect of moveables or land, will made anywhere is as to manner and formalities valid and admissible on application for appointment of estate trustee if made in accord with law where will made, where testator was then domiciled, where testator then had habitual residence or where testator was national if one law for wills there. (c. S.26, §37). Reference also to laws of situs of land and domicile at death of testator respecting moveables as regards essential validity and effect and also as to manner and formalities. (§36). Also some special situation provisions. (§37[2]). Will executed in accordance with Hague Convention on International Wills is valid as to form. (§42, Convention Schedule, Art. 1).

Foreign Certificates of Appointment of Estate Trustee.—Where appointment of estate trustee with will made by Court of competent jurisdiction in U.K., or any province or territory of Canada or any other British possession, certificate may be resealed by Ontario Court (General Division). (c.E.21, §52; R.P. 74.08). Where appointment with will made elsewhere by Court of competent jurisdiction, ancillary appointment of estate trustee may be applied for to Ontario Court (General Division) in county or district where Ontario assets situate. (§7; R.P. 74.09).

See also topic Estate Trustees.

Simultaneous Death.—See topic Death, subhead Survivorship.

Testamentary Trusts.—See topic Trusts.

WITNESSES:

In civil actions no person is incompetent to give evidence by reason of being interested as party or otherwise or by reason of conviction of crime. (c. E.23). This heading applies to civil actions and other proceedings within jurisdiction of provincial legislature. Criminal actions are governed by Canada Evidence Act, R.S.C., c. C-5. See also topic Depositions.

Privileged Communications.—Generally, common law rules apply as to privileged communications, but certain statutory privileges exist with reference to documents in official possession of governmental departments, and with reference to information required by law to be disclosed to administrative officials.

Husband and Wife.—Husbands and wives of parties to an action are competent and compellable to give evidence on behalf of any of the parties, but no husband or wife may be compelled to disclose any communication made by one to the other during marriage. (c. E.23, §§8, 11). Husband or wife may in any action give evidence that he or she did or did not have sexual intercourse with other spouse at any time or within any period before or during marriage. (§8). In proceedings instituted in consequence of adultery no party or spouse of any party is bound to answer any question tending to show that he or she is guilty of adultery unless such witness has already given evidence in same action in disproof of his or her alleged adultery. (§10).

Communications or Transactions with Persons Since Deceased or Incompetent.—In actions by or against the representatives of a deceased person in respect of any matter occurring before the death of the deceased and in actions by or against mentally incompetent persons, etc., an opposite or interested party may not obtain a verdict or judgment upon his or her own evidence unless it be corroborated by some other material evidence. (c. E.23, §§13, 14).

Self-incrimination.—A witness is not excused from answering any question upon the ground that the answer may tend to incriminate or establish liability to civil proceeding. But if witness objects to answer such question and is compelled to do so, answer may not be used against witness in any other civil proceeding. Witness who testifies in any proceeding has right not to have any incriminating evidence used to incriminate witness in any other proceeding, except prosecution for perjury or for giving contradictory evidence, and it is not necessary for witness to object to obtain such protection.

Compelling Attendance.—See topic Depositions.

WORKERS' COMPENSATION LAW:

See topic Labour Relations.

PRINCE EDWARD ISLAND LAW DIGEST

(The following is a list of all Topics, including cross-references, covered in this Digest.)

PRINCE EDWARD ISLAND
LAW DIGEST

Revised for 1997 edition by

CAMPBELL, LEA, MICHAEL McCONNELL & PIGOT, of the Charlottetown Bar.

(Statute citations, unless otherwise indicated, refer to 1988 Revised Statutes of Prince Edward Island.)
Note: Legislative Assembly in recess at time of going to press. This revision incorporates 1996 Acts passed by the Assembly and in force as of June 15, 1996.

ABSENTEES:

There is no general statute respecting absentees or care of their property, but a judge may order payment and distribution of moneys in court to the credit of a person absent from the province and whose address or place of residence is unknown and who has not been heard of for seven years. Payment and distribution may be made to the persons who would be entitled to the personal property if the absentee has died intestate at time of application for distribution. See also Death.

ACCORD AND SATISFACTION:

This is a defence whether the cause of action arises out of contract or tort, but must be specifically pleaded. It is a good equitable answer to an action for a specialty debt, but as against joint creditors it is only a defence against the creditor who was a party to the accord and satisfaction. An accord and satisfaction releasing one of two joint debtors without any reservation of rights against the other may be successfully pleaded by the latter. Payment of a lesser sum in satisfaction of a greater cannot be a satisfaction for the whole, but where the cause of action is for an unascertained sum or a disputed debt, an agreement to accept a sum certain in satisfaction, smaller than the amount claimed, would be binding. The promise or performance of something different from, not being merely a part of, what would have been due under the obligation discharged by the accord and satisfaction, is binding. An agreement by a number of creditors with the debtor that each will accept a composition in satisfaction of his debt will be effective to discharge their several debts. Payment of a smaller sum by a negotiable instrument will be effective if the bill or note is actually given as satisfaction and accepted as such.

ACKNOWLEDGMENTS:

Documents affecting title of land must, before registration in land registry office, be proved for registry.

Execution Within the Province.—If executed within the province this may be done either by personal acknowledgment of the party executing the document or by oath of a subscribing witness, taken before the registrar or a commissioner appointed to take such proof.

All notaries are attorneys, and appointed for life. Minister of Justice authenticates appointment.

Execution Without the Province.—If executed without the province proof may be given in like manner before the mayor of a city, borough or town corporate, certified under the common seal of the city, borough or town corporate, or before any British ambassador, envoy, minister, chargé d'affaires or secretary of embassy or legation exercising his functions in any foreign country, any British consul-general, consul, vice-consul, acting consul, pro-consul, or consular agent exercising his functions in any foreign place, or before a judge of a court of record within the British Empire, or before a notary public, certified under his official seal, or before a commissioner authorized by the laws of this province to take, in such place, affidavits in and for any of the courts of record of the province, or acknowledgments or proof of the execution of deeds or mortgages for registry in the province.

Alternative to Acknowledgment or Proof.—No statutory provisions authorizing statement in lieu of acknowledgment or proof.

ACTIONS:

Actions are commenced by filing notice of action or statement of claim.

Direct Actions Against Insurer.—See topic Motor Vehicles, subhead Direct Actions.

See also topics Courts; Limitation of Actions; Pleading; Practice; Process.

ADMINISTRATION:

See topic Executors and Administrators.

ADOPTION:

Any person 18 years of age may apply to adopt younger person. Joint application for adoption is only permitted for married couples. Competent person over 18 years may be adopted.

Consent Required.—No order for adoption shall be made without consent within year preceding hearing of (a) child, if 12 years of age or more, or if court believes it appropriate in any other case; (b) mother of child unless guardianship has been legally transferred from her permanently or, if temporarily, with her clear knowledge that adoption was purpose or likely to occur; (c) father of child, if (i) he is married to mother, (ii) he is registered as father in accordance with Vital Statistics Act or corresponding legislation of another jurisdiction, or (iii) his paternity has been legally established under Child Status Act or corresponding legislation of another jurisdiction, unless guardianship has been legally transferred from him permanently or, if temporarily, with his clear knowledge that adoption was purpose or likely to occur; (d) legal guardian; and (e) Director of Child Welfare, if (i) there is no other person entitled to give or withhold consent, or (ii) applicant resides out-of-province.

Form of consent may be prescribed by regulations or court. Consent must state that it is freely and voluntarily given and effects of consent and adoption have been fully explained and understood. For valid consent person to be adopted must be at least 14 days old at time of execution of consent. Consent may be effectively withdrawn within 14 days of giving it by written statement to person to whom it was given and Director.

Court may dispense with consent (except consent of child where required and Director) where satisfied that (a) person does not have clear entitlement to give consent; (b) person cannot competently make decision to consent; (c) person does not wish to exercise entitlement to consent; (d) person has not demonstrated responsibility or clear intention to contribute to care and well-being of child; (e) person cannot be contacted, despite reasonable efforts; or (f) best interests of child should override entitlement to consent.

Placement.—No one may place child for adoption except Director of Child Welfare, agency approved by Director and person holding license/permit. No one may receive child except from foregoing. Person placing child must comply with standards prescribed by regulations. No child may be placed out-of-province except with permission of Director. Director must be notified of all placements with particulars. Person placing child must provide summary of nonidentifying information on child's background. Parents (birth and adoptive) may arrange for continuing contact but only if recorded in formal written agreement, reached after parties have had independent legal advice and copy deposited with Director. During period between placement and adoption order custody is with receiving persons. It is offence to receive payment or reward for procuring or assisting in procuring placement.

Conditions Precedent.—Adopted person must have been placed with applicant at least three months before application unless authorized by Director, agency or court or applicant is stepparent.

Jurisdiction.—Supreme Court Trial Division makes adoption order. Court must hear application at least three months after application submitted.

Application For Adoption.—Subject to court order, application must include (a)(i) birth certificate, or (ii) where required to keep surname or parentage of child secret, then (A) number of birth registration, given name, sex, date and place of birth, and (B) sealed and not disclosed to applicant, certified copy of or extract from birth record, permitting identification of surname or parentage; (b) marriage certificate for joint applicants; (c) decrees of divorce where either applicant or parent divorced; (d) agreement or court order regarding custody or guardianship of child; (e) information about applicant, including name, age, marital status and relationship to child; (f) description of placement circumstances and length of time in placement; (g) consents required; (h) agreement about continuing contact.

Director of Child Welfare.—Administers Adoption Act S.P.E.I. 1992 Cap-1. Exercises standards/control to protect rights of those involved in placements/adoptions. Provides authorizations, permissions and consents required by Act. Assists applicants, appears and may be heard on court applications. Prepares pre-hearing study where required.

Proceedings.—Hearing is in private. Persons having interest are entitled to be heard. Court must inquire into child's capacity to understand application and consider child's views.

Decree.—Court issues Adoption Order.

Name.—Where child's previous identity or parentage has been kept secret, adoption order may not show previous name but rather child's given name followed by number or code referring to child's birth registration. Adoption order shall show surname child is to have. Child must consent to surname if over 12 and subject to consultation by court if under 12.

Effect of Adoption.—Notwithstanding hereditary, social, emotional and other forms of relationships, adoption order has effect as follows: (a) for all purposes of law, adopted child becomes child of adopting parent and adopting parent becomes parent of adopted child; (b) for all purposes of law, adopted person ceases to be child of person who was parent prior to adoption order, except that parent who is spouse of adopting parent continues to be parent; (c) previous relationships to other relatives prior to adoption cease and new relationships have effect on date of adoption order in accordance with relationships of adopting parent. In will, conveyance or other such document whether make of will or document is alive, reference to person or group or class of persons described in terms of relationship by blood or marriage to another person is deemed to refer to or include person who comes within description as result of adoption, unless contrary is expressed. Adoption order does not affect interest in property that has vested before order made.

Records.—Adopted Children Register kept by Director of Child Welfare records adoptions. Records and documents of Director, agency or court re: placement/adoption are confidential annd kept secure. Information may not be disclosed except where Act provides or court orders. Director, agency or Director of Vital Statistics may allow access or disclosure of information for purposes of genealogical/historical research if all parties to adoption have been deceased for at least 20 years and there is no reason to believe that access or disclosure will be harmful to other living persons.

Disclosure Nonidentifying Information.—Agency, person who places child, Director of Child Welfare or court may provide to any party to placement/adoption information concerning background of child adopted, except in case where secrecy is kept under Act, any information which would establish child's previous identity or

ADOPTION . . . *continued*
parentage. Director, agency or person who placed child or court may provide to health professional health-related information concerning child for purposes of child's care.

Disclosure Identifying Information-Reunion.—Director of Child Welfare shall keep reciprocal Search Register for purpose of matching and assisting persons who have significant relationships affected by adoption and valid reason to seek information or make connection. Adult shall apply as regulations prescribe or Director requires naming person sought. If there is match Director shall (a) inform each party of match; (b) attempt to ensure that adoptive parent informed; (c) provide for exchange of current nonidentifying information; (d) determine whether there is mutual agreement to proceed further. If there is mutual agreement, Director shall provide further information, including identity and if jointly wanted facilitate meeting of parties. If either party requests discontinuance of process, Director shall not proceed. If Director considers provision of information or contact between parties is likely to reveal identity of birth parent against their probable wishes, Director shall obtain approval of birth parent before proceeding. Notwithstanding foregoing if Director believes that approval of birth parent insignificant to action on request or not feasible to obtain, Director may decide to act on match.

Adult adopted person seeking identity of or identifying information concerning or to make contact with birth parent or sibling of that person, shall make request to Director/agency. Director/agency shall attempt to ensure adoptive parents are consulted concerning search. Director/agency shall search records pertaining to placement/adoption and ascertain requested information and make contact on confidential basis with person about whom request made. If person contacted gives permission, Director/agency shall release to person making request identity or information requested and if person making request wishes contact, arrange contact between parties. If Director/agency cannot contact person about whom request made, of if person is found to be incompetent to give permission, Director/agency may, considering wishes of person making request and probable wishes or interests of person sought, and reasons therefor, decide on whether to provide requested information. If person about whom request was made deceased, Director/agency shall provide person making request with requested information unless reason to believe that significant harm would result. Director/agency may refuse to disclose identifying information or facilitate reunion if determined that it is not feasible to do or that it would be likely to have harmful results for persons involved in placement/adoption. Where person about whom request was made is contacted but unwilling to have identifying information released or contact arranged with person making request, Director/agency shall not proceed.

Adopted person who is minor, with written consent of parent or guardian of minor, or parent or guardian with written consent of minor, may apply if Director or agency believes that result is significant to health or well-being of adopted person. If person fails to obtain consent required that person may apply and application may be acted upon if Director determines that consent cannot practically be obtained or unreasonably withheld and adopted person would suffer seriously harmful consequences if action not taken.

Intercountry Adoption (Hague Convention) Act.—Convention in effect since July 14, 1994, S.P.E.I. 1994, c. 28.

ADVANCEMENTS:

See topic Descent and Distribution.

ADVERSE POSSESSION:

Twenty years adverse possession bars recovery of land unless person entitled is under disability such as infancy, etc., or absent from the province, in which case action must be commenced within six years after disability removed.

Possession must be open, notorious, exclusive and continuous.

Title to easements (e.g., ways, light, air, lateral support, etc.) may be acquired by continuous and uninterrupted use and enjoyment for such period and under such circumstances as will result in implication of a lost grant.

AFFIDAVITS:

Affidavits to be used in legal proceedings must be entitled in the court and in the cause or matter in which they are sworn or in which they are to be used. Deponent's full name, address and occupation should be set out.

Affidavits made within the province must be sworn before a commissioner of the court in which they are to be used or before commissioned officer of Canadian Forces on full-time service.

Affidavits Made Without the Province.—Oaths, affidavits, affirmations or statutory declarations administered, sworn, affirmed or made in any other province or territory of Canada or any country other than Canada before: (a) Judge, magistrate or officer of court of justice or commissioner authorized to administer oaths in courts of justice of province, territory or country; (b) commissioner appointed under §6 Affidavits Act; (c) officer of Her Majesty's diplomatic or consular services exercising functions in country other than Canada, including ambassador, envoy, minister, charge d'affairs, counsellor, secretary, attache, consul general, consul, vice consul, proconsul, consular agent, acting consul general, acting consul, acting vice consul and acting consular agent; (d) officer of Canadian diplomatic and consular service exercising functions in country other than Canada, including, in addition to diplomatic and consular officers mentioned in clause (c), high commissioner, permanent delegate, acting high commissioner, acting permanent delegate, counsellor and secretary; (e) Canadian government trade commissioner and assistant Canadian government trade commissioner while exercising functions in country other than Canada; (f) notary public acting within territorial limits of his authority, and certified under his hand and official seal; (g) commissioner authorized by laws of province to take affidavits are as valid and effectual, and are of same force and effect, for all purposes as if oath, affidavit, affirmation or statutory declaration had been administered, sworn, affirmed or made in province before commissioner for taking affidavits or other competent authority of same nature; or (h) commissioned officer of Canadian Forces on full-time service.

Absence of Official Seal.—If affidavit be sworn without the province before a person not having an official seal, signature of such person must be attested under the hand and official seal of some other person authorized as above to take such affidavit.

Authentication not required in province. Clerk of court authenticates for use in other provinces.

Erasures and interlineations in affidavit or jurat should be initialed by official taking the oath, who should also identify and initial any documents annexed which are referred to in the affidavit.

Jurat should contain date and place and county wherein sworn, and when sworn by more than one deponent their names should appear in the jurat, e.g.:

Form

The above-named deponents, A. B. and C. D. were severally sworn at . . . . . in the County of . . . . . . on the . . . . . . day of . . . . . ., 19. . . ., before me, C. C., a commissioner (etc., as the case may be).

Solemn declarations in attestation of execution of any writing, deed or instrument, or of truth of any fact, or of any account rendered in writing may be made in following form:

Form

I, A. B., do solemnly declare that (state fact or facts declared to), and I make this solemn declaration conscientiously believing it to be true, and knowing that it is of the same force and effect as if made under oath, and by virtue of The Canada Evidence Act. (Signature).

Declared before me at . . . . . . this . . . . . . day of . . . . . ., A.D. 19. . . . (Signature of officer).

Alternative to Affidavit.—No statute allowing statement in lieu of swearing before notary or proper officer.

AGENCY: See topic Principal and Agent.

AIRCRAFT: See Canada Law Digest.

ALIENS:

Aliens may hold, transmit by descent or convey real and personal property, subject to same limitations set forth under topic Real Property, subhead Ownership. They are not eligible for public office.

APPEAL AND ERROR:

Appeal lies to Supreme Court from judgment or order of Provincial Judge, except where otherwise expressly provided. Judgment, order or decision of a judge of Supreme Court, sitting in chambers or in court (with or without a jury), is appealable to Supreme Court Appeal Division. Notice of appeal must be filed and served within 15 days after date of judgment or order, unless time is enlarged by order.

Appeal from any official act, decision, decree or order of the probate court may be taken to Supreme Court within ten days, on giving notice and $100 security for costs of appeal.

Appeal from final judgment of highest court of final resort in the province goes to Supreme Court of Canada.

ARBITRATION AND AWARD:

A submission of, or written agreement to submit, present or future differences to arbitration, whether or not an arbitrator is named therein, is, unless a contrary intention is expressed therein, irrevocable, except by leave of the court or a judge, and has same effect as if made an order of court. On default in appointing an arbitrator or umpire the court has power to appoint. The court may stay proceedings if party to submission, or person claiming through or under him, commences an action against any other party to submission in respect of a matter agreed to be referred. An award may, by leave of the court or a judge, be enforced in same manner as a judgment or order to same effect.

ASSIGNMENTS:

An absolute assignment by writing under the hand of the assignor, not purporting to be by way of charge only, of a debt or other legal chose in action, of which express notice in writing is given to the debtor, transfers the legal right to such debt or chose in action and all legal and other remedies for the same and the power to give a good discharge for the same without concurrence of the assignor.

Assignment of book debts made by a person or corporation engaged in trade or business is void against existing and subsequent creditors of assignor, unless in writing and registered within thirty days of its execution with an affidavit by attesting witness as to its execution by assignor, identifying the assignment and stating date of execution, and with an affidavit by assignee or his agent that assignment was executed in good faith and for valuable consideration and not for mere purpose of protecting the book debts against assignor's creditors or preventing them from recovering claims against assignor.

Affidavit on renewal must be made and registered within five years of registration of assignment; otherwise assignment will thereafter be void as against creditors, and as against subsequent purchasers whose assignments have been registered or are valid without registration. Affidavit on renewal must be made by assignee or by one of assignees, or by his or their agent, and must state that assignment is valid and subsisting, and is not being kept in force for any fraudulent purpose or to defeat, delay or prejudice assignor's creditors. Affidavit must be filed within 30 days of its making.

Similar affidavits on renewal must be registered within five years after registration of last preceding affidavit, if validity of assignment is to be preserved as against such creditors or purchasers.

See note at head of Digest as to 1996 legislation covered.

See Topical Index in front part of this volume.

ASSIGNMENTS . . . *continued*

Requirement of registration does not apply to an assignment of book debts made by a corporation engaged in a trade or business within the province, contained in a trust deed or other instrument of the corporation or of any other corporation to secure bonds, debentures or debenture stock nor to such bonds, debentures or debenture stock, nor to an assignment of book debts then due from specified debtors, or growing due under specified contracts, nor to an assignment of book debts included in the transfer of a business made bona fide and for value, nor to an assignment of book debts in any authorized assignment under the Bankruptcy and Insolvency Act.

See also topic Corporations.

ASSIGNMENTS FOR BENEFIT OF CREDITORS:

Assignments for benefit of creditors are governed by the Bankruptcy and Insolvency Act of Canada. See Canada Law Digest.

ASSOCIATIONS:

There are no restrictions upon associations for any purpose not prohibited by law or contrary to good morals or public policy. Most associations intended to be more or less permanent (excepting some of those for social or recreational purposes) are incorporated under The Companies Act or under special acts for particular societies or types of businesses such as rural creameries, rural fairs, horse racing associations, etc.

Special provision is made for incorporation of cooperative associations for various purposes.

Incorporated associations, members of which carry on business in common with a view to profit are partnerships.

Professional Associations (i.e., regulation by statute of entire profession) include lawyers, doctors, dentists, architects, nurses, land surveyors, engineers, pharmacists, dietitians, occupational therapists, optometrists, agrologists, physiotherapists, social workers, etc.

A Society may be incorporated under provisions of Part II of The Companies Act which provides for incorporation of a company without share capital for purpose of carrying on in Prince Edward Island, without pecuniary gain to its members, objects of a patriotic, religious, philanthropic, charitable, scientific, artistic, social, professional or sporting character, or the like.

See topic Corporations; also topic Partnership.

ATTACHMENT:

Property of a resident debtor, except debts due to him (as to which see topic Garnishment), cannot be seized until after judgment.

Absent Debtors.—The property of an absent debtor may be attached on an affidavit of debt, setting out the fact and that the debtor is an absent or absconding debtor from the province.

Summons may be served on agent or person in possession of property of defendant which binds property in his hands.

Lien.—Writ does not bind defendant's lands as against purchasers, mortgagees or other encumbrancers unless certificate of pending litigation is issued by Supreme Court and certificate registered in proper land registry office identifying lands to be affected.

Collection of Debts.—Sheriff is empowered to collect all debts due to defendant to abide event of suit.

Rehearing.—Defendant may obtain rehearing any time within three years.

Pre-execution Security.—Plaintiff, before he has execution, must give security to repay judgment and costs in case it should be reversed on rehearing.

Time of Trial.—Absent debtor suits cannot be brought on for trial until three months after issue of writ.

Sale.—Goods must be appraised before sale. Perishable property may be ordered to be sold unless security for its value is given within eight days after attachment.

ATTORNEYS AND COUNSELORS:

Attorneys and counselors are known as barristers and solicitors in Prince Edward Island. Every solicitor is also a barrister.

Eligibility.—Person seeking to be admitted to bar must comply with requirements as prescribed by Law Society of Prince Edward Island. Applicant must be Canadian citizen or permanent resident of Canada and 18 years old.

Applicant for admission must produce certificate of good moral character from solicitor with whom he was last articled. He must be at least 18 years of age.

Registration as law student not required (except as hereinafter stated).

Educational Requirements and Clerkship.—Applicant for admission must hold degree in law from law school recognized by Society, must serve term of articles under practicing barrister qualified to engage articled clerk of no less than 12 months and must complete prescribed bar admissions course. Barrister and solicitor who has been in active practice in another Province of Canada (except Quebec) for at least three years of previous ten years, must serve term of articles of six months. Barrister and solicitor from other provinces who has been in active practice for at least five years of previous seven years, may be approved for admission if successfully examined in statutes, procedures and practices of Prince Edward Island law. Further details available from Secretary of Law Society of Prince Edward Island in Charlottetown.

Licenses.—No barrister may practice without holding an annual certificate which is in force. Fee for such certificate is as Council of the Law Society from time to time prescribes, and every such certificate expires on last day of June of each year.

Rights and Powers.—Barristers are entitled to practice in all courts in Prince Edward Island and in Supreme Court of Canada. Barristers become notaries upon obtaining, without cost, a commission from Lieutenant-Governor.

Solicitors are empowered to take acknowledgments of deeds.

Occasional Appearances.—Subject to compliance with regulations barrister/solicitor of another Canadian jurisdiction may act or appear as attorney in a matter.

Lien.—Solicitor has lien on documents in his possession for charges for his professional services. Lien extends to property recovered or preserved as result of proceeding.

Suspension and Disbarment.—Barrister and solicitor may be suspended for non-payment of annual fees, and cannot practice during suspension. Barristers are liable to be struck off rolls or suspended for misconduct.

Unauthorized Practice.—No corporation may practice law. Fine not exceeding $20,000 for violation by corporation and not exceeding $2,000 for violation by non-member. No person not member of bar may practice.

Professional Association.—There is no statutory authorization for formation of by lawyers, except that Law Society of Prince Edward Island is a professional society which governs conduct of its own members.

AUTOMOBILES: See topic Motor Vehicles.

BANKRUPTCY: See Canada Law Digest.

BANKS AND BANKING:

The Parliament of Canada has exclusive legislative jurisdiction on the subject of banks and banking. See Canada Law Digest.

As to business tax on banks and trust companies, see topic Taxation.

As to trust and loan companies, see topic Corporations, subhead Foreign Corporations, catchline Trust and Loan Companies.

BILLS AND NOTES:

See Canada Law Digest.

BILLS OF LADING: See topic Carriers.

BILLS OF SALE:

See topics Sales and Chattel Mortgages.

BLUE SKY LAW: See topic Securities.

BONDS:

Security for the performance of duties pertaining to office of administrator, guardian, committee, receiver, curator, trustee, municipal or public officer or other fiduciary, is frequently given by bond with personal sureties, but may be given by the bond of a surety company qualified to act as surety or guarantor and holding certificate from Director of Corporations setting forth such qualification and authority to do business.

BROKERS:

As to information to be filed by stockbrokers before selling securities, see topic Securities.

As to business license taxes on brokers, see topic Taxation.

See topic Real Property, subhead Real Estate Agents.

BULK SALES:

See topic Fraudulent Sales and Conveyances.

CARRIERS:

A bill of lading representing goods to have been shipped on board a vessel or train is, when held by a consignee or endorsee for valuable consideration, evidence of the shipment as against the master or other person signing it, although the goods may not actually have been shipped, unless the holder of the bill of lading, when he received it, had actual notice that the goods were not in fact put on board, or unless the bill of lading contains a stipulation to the contrary. The master or person signing the bill of lading may, however, exonerate himself by showing that the misrepresentation was caused without any default on his part and wholly by the fault of the shipper or holder of some person through whom the holder claims.

Bills of lading of goods carried on ships from one port to another in Canada, or from a port in Canada to a port outside of Canada, are subject to the provisions of the Carriage of Goods by Water Act, Revised Statutes of Canada, 1985, c. C-27.

As to business taxes on carriers, see topic Taxation.

Motor Vehicle Carriers.—See topic Motor Vehicles.

CERTIORARI:

In civil cases where appeal to Supreme Court lies, certiorari will be granted only for special cause shown on affidavit and must be applied for within a month after making of the judgment, order or other proceeding in the court below. No certiorari is allowed where an appeal has been taken. Certiorari now deemed to be application for judicial review under Supreme Court Act, Cap. S-10.

CHARITABLE IMMUNITY: See topic Damages.

CHATTEL MORTGAGES:

A sale or mortgage not accompanied by immediate delivery and an actual and continued change of possession of the chattel sold or mortgaged is void as against creditors and subsequent purchasers or mortgagees claiming from or under the grantor in good faith, for valuable consideration and without notice, whose conveyances or mortgages have been duly registered or are valid without registration, unless the sale or mortgage is evidenced by a bill of sale duly registered; and the sale or mortgage and the bill of sale, if any, evidencing the sale or mortgage shall, as against creditors and such subsequent purchasers or mortgagees take effect only from the time of the registration of the bill of sale.

CHATTEL MORTGAGES . . . *continued*

Registration is effected by filing the bill of sale with the proper officer in the registration district where the goods are situated, within 30 days of its execution. If the goods or chattels comprised in the bill of sale are located in more than one registration district, registration may be effected by filing the bill of sale in one registration district and a duplicate original or a certified copy in the other districts.

A judge of the Supreme Court, if satisfied that omission to register a bill of sale or renewal statement was accidental or due to inadvertence or impossibility or other sufficient cause, may extend the time for registration. No defect or irregularity in a bill of sale or renewal, being of a clerical nature, will invalidate the bill of sale or renewal, unless in the opinion of a Court or Judge, the error has misled some person whose interests have been affected by the bill of sale.

Fees for registering and filing are: Each bill of sale and accompanying document, $15; renewal of bill of sale, $15; assignment of bill of sale, $15; certificate of discharge, $5; and for any certificate of registration or discharge or other certificates, $5.

Affidavits.—The affidavit of an attesting witness must accompany every bill of sale presented for registration (except if grantor is corporation). Such affidavit must identify bill of sale, stating date of execution by grantor or respective dates of execution by grantors if there be more than one.

A bill of sale given to secure the grantee repayment of advances made under an agreement therefor or against loss or damage by reason of the endorsement of a bill of exchange or other liability incurred by the grantee for the grantor or to be incurred under an agreement must set forth clearly the terms or substance of the agreement, a copy of the bill or note and endorsements and the nature and extent or terms or substance of the agreement respecting the liability. It must also when presented for registration, be accompanied by an affidavit of the grantee or his agent verifying such matters, and stating that the bill of sale truly sets forth the extent or amount of the liability incurred or to be incurred and secured, and that it was executed in good faith and for the purpose of securing the grantee and not to protect the chattels from the grantor's creditors or to prevent such creditors from recovering their claims against the grantor.

If an attesting witness dies or leaves the Province or refuses to make or becomes incapable of making an affidavit of execution of a bill of sale, a Supreme Court Judge may order registration of the bill of sale upon such other proof of its due execution and attestation as the judge may, by his order require. The order so made by the judge must be attached to and filed with the bill of sale.

Affidavits may be sworn before any one authorized to take affidavits within the Province and may be made before a solicitor of one of the parties to the bill of sale or before the partner of such solicitor. An affidavit required of the grantee may, after his death, be made by his executor or administrator or his agent or by any of the next of kin of the grantee. Where a grantee or assignee is a corporation, the affidavit may be given by any officer or employee or agent of the same, and in all cases, the deponent must state that he is aware of the circumstances connected with the bill of sale or with its renewal and has a personal knowledge of the facts deposed to. Where a bill of sale, certificate of discharge or assignment is executed by a corporation, no affidavit of attesting witness is required. In the case of a bill of sale being given to the Crown, no affidavit of bona fides nor renewal statement is required.

Renewal.—After five years from registration, a chattel mortgage ceases to be valid as against creditors and subsequent purchasers or mortgagees in good faith, for valuable consideration and without notice, whose conveyances or mortgages have been registered or are valid without registration, unless before the expiration of that period a renewal statement in a prescribed form is filed accompanied by an affidavit in verification made by or on behalf of the mortgagee. A further renewal statement with affidavit must be filed within five years from the registration of the first renewal statement, and thereafter within each succeeding five year period, otherwise the bill of sale becomes void as against such creditors, purchasers and mortgagees.

Removal of Chattels.—Where chattels, before discharge of a mortgage or bill of sale, are permanently removed to another registration district, registration must be effected in that district by registering a certified copy of the original, together with affidavits, with the proper officer, within 30 days after the grantee has received notice of the place to which the chattels have been removed, otherwise the bill of sale will not be valid as against creditors and subsequent purchasers or mortgagees claiming under the grantor in good faith, for valuable consideration and without notice, whose conveyances or mortgages have been registered or are valid without registration.

Assignment.—An assignment of a bill of sale need not, but may be, registered by filing the assignment, together with the affidavit of an attesting witness of its execution; in the office where the bill of sale is registered. Where the goods are located in more than one registration district, duplicate originals of the assignment and affidavit, or a copy certified by the registration officer, may be registered in the district where any of the goods are located.

Satisfaction or Discharge.—A bill of sale may be discharged by filing with the proper officer in the district where the bill of sale is registered, a certificate of discharge, together with an affidavit of an attesting witness of execution; but no discharge certificate by an assignee may be registered unless the assignment has been registered in that office. If the chattels are situate in more than one registration district, registration of discharge may be effected by filing a duplicate or other original of the certificate of discharge and affidavit of execution in the office of the proper officer in each of the registration districts or by filing such certificate and affidavit in one registration district and a certificate of entry of the discharge therein signed by the proper officer of that district in the registry office of each other district. A Judge of the Supreme Court, if satisfied that the debt has been satisfied, may make an order declaring the bill of sale to have been discharged, and when the order or a copy is registered, an entry of the discharge must be made by the registration office.

Foreign Mortgages.—If chattels held under a chattel mortgage outside the province are removed permanently into the province, registration must be effected in the registration district into which they have been moved within thirty days after the grantee has received notice of the place to which the chattels have been removed. Registration is effected by filing, with the proper officer, a copy, properly verified by affidavit of the mortgagee, together with all affidavits or documents relating to or accompanying it.

Special Legislation.—The Potato Crop Mortgages Act, Cap. P-12 makes mortgages or charges against potato crops invalid except where given to secure: (1) Price of potatoes sold, fertilizer or spray, (2) performance of agreement to sell said articles, or (3) bank or credit union loan.

COLLATERAL SECURITY: See topic Pledges.

COMMERCIAL CODE:

No uniform commercial code has been adopted.

COMMISSIONS TO TAKE TESTIMONY:

See topic Depositions.

CONDITIONAL SALES: See topic Sales.

CONSIGNMENTS: See topic Factors.

CONSUMER PROTECTION:

See topic Sales, subhead Consumer Protection Legislation.

CONTRACTS:

Common law rules govern.

Distributorships, Dealerships and Franchises.—No special rules or legislation applicable to formation or termination of these types of business arrangements. Common law applies.

Infants' Contracts.—See topic Infants.

CONVEYANCES: See topic Deeds.

CORPORATIONS:

Act governing incorporations generally is Companies Act. Company may be incorporated by statute, or by issue of letters patent under Companies Act.

General Supervision.—Director of Corporations, P.O. Box 2000, Charlottetown, Prince Edward Island, Canada, CIA 7N8.

Purposes.—Company may be incorporated for any business or nonprofit purpose.

Name must be cleared through Director of Corporations.

Term of Corporate Existence.—Perpetual.

Incorporators.—At least one incorporator is required. There are no restrictions on residency or citizenship of incorporators.

Certificate or Articles of Incorporation.—Application for issuance of letters patent must be prepared in duplicate, addressed to Minister of Justice and delivered to Director of Corporations. Application must include: (1) Name, address, occupation of incorporators, (2) company name, (3) whether company is private or public, (4) specific restrictions on share transfers where desired, (5) purposes of incorporation, (6) address of registered office in Prince Edward Island, (7) amount of authorized capital and its division in classes of shares (no minimum is required).

Incorporation Tax or Fee.—Fee is $200.

Paid in Capital Requirements.—None.

Amendment of Certificate or Articles.—Supplementary letters patent must be applied for if additional purposes or objects are required. Fee for application is $200. Amendments to letters patent must be approved by resolution passed by vote of at least two-thirds in value of total shareholders at special general meeting called for purpose.

Increase or decrease of authorized capital stock requires passing of by-law sanctioned by vote of not less than two-thirds in value of shareholders at general meeting called for considering same and confirmation by supplementary letters patent.

Shareholders' Liabilities.—None beyond payment of shares.

Shareholders' Meetings.—Annual meetings required held at some place in province and at such time as letters patent or by-laws prescribe, at which meetings directors are elected.

Directors.—Private Corporation requires minimum of one director, no maximum; public corporation requires minimum of three directors, no maximum. Unless letters patent otherwise provide, director not required to hold shares. Directors elected annually at general meeting of shareholders. Number of directors may be increased or decreased by by-law sanctioned by vote of not less than two-thirds in value of shareholders at general meeting called for considering same and filed with Director of Corporations.

Books and Records.—Must be kept at head office; may be inspected by any shareholder or creditor during reasonable business hours.

Reservation of Corporate Name.—Company incorporated in any Province of Canada, on payment of $25 fee to Director of Corporations, may register name of that company, and, on such registration, no other company may be incorporated by that name in Province.

Annual Statement.—Every provincially incorporated company is required to file with Director of Corporations annual statement together with fee, such statement to contain names and addresses of directors, officers, shareholders, authorized capital, shareholder holdings per class of share and amount and location of lands held or leased in province.

See note at head of Digest as to 1996 legislation covered.

See Topical Index in front part of this volume.

CORPORATIONS . . . *continued*

Transfer of Stock.—No share of stock is transferable until all previous calls thereon have been fully paid and the directors of a company may decline to register any transfer of shares belonging to any member who is indebted to the company. All transfers of stock with the date and other particulars of such transfer and the date of the entry thereof must be registered in a book to be kept by the company. The transfer of a share of a deceased member may be made by his personal representatives.

Corporation Securities Registration.—In order to be valid as against creditors and as against subsequent bona fide purchasers or mortgagees, it is necessary that a mortgage or charge, whether specific or floating, of chattels in the Province, created by a corporation, and that an assignment of book debts, whether by way of specific or floating charge, made by a corporation engaged in a trade or business in the Province to secure bonds, debentures or debenture stock, be registered with Director of Corporations within 30 days from its execution, accompanied by proof of execution and affidavit of bona fides. When so registered, it need not be filed as bill of sale nor as assignment of book debts under laws relating to those securities. No renewal of security is required.

Close Corporations.—See subheads Certificate or Articles of Incorporation; and Directors, supra.

Foreign corporations may acquire and hold real estate, without restriction as to either original acquisition or length of time of holding provided they can otherwise hold real property in Province. See topic Real Property, subhead Ownership.

Every foreign corporation carrying on business in this province having gain for its purpose or object must, subject to penalty on default, before beginning business in this province, transmit to Director of Corporations statement showing: (a) Corporate name of company; (b) how incorporated; (c) place of company's head office; (d) amount of authorized capital stock; (e) amount of stock issued and amount paid up; (f) nature of each kind of business company is empowered to carry on and what kind or kinds of business are carried on in Prince Edward Island; Such company must also transmit to Director of Corporations of each year statement showing all changes during preceding year.

All foreign corporations doing business in Province are subject to a license fee (minimum $200; maximum $1,200). License fee depends on type of business carried on.

Trust and loan companies must deposit insurance with Canada Deposit Insurance Corporation, or with Province to an amount approved by Director of Corporations as reserve for protection of depositors and investment certificate holders.

Foreign Resident Corporations Act.—Foreign corporation, company organized under laws of jurisdiction other than Prince Edward Island and which has determined to protect its interests in time of war or other emergency as defined by Act to transfer its registered office to Prince Edward Island, may apply to Minister of Justice to operate within Prince Edward Island as foreign resident corporation provided original jurisdiction does not expressly prohibit such transfer. Upon receipt of proper certificate from Minister company, may operate from this jurisdiction.

Non-profit corporation excludes any person other than existing universities from being known as university or granting academic degrees. See also topic Associations.

Professional Corporations.—Generally permitted, but special statutory authorization for optometrists (Optometry Act, Cap. O-6), pharmaceutical chemists (Pharmacy Act, Cap. P-6), and agrologists (Agrologists Act, Cap. A-10). See, however, topics Associations; Attorneys and Counselors.

Deeds.—See topic Deeds.

Model Non-Profit Corporation Act not adopted.

Taxation.—See topic Taxation.

COSTS:

Costs as between party and party in litigation generally follow event. Their award is, however, discretionary and award or refusal will not lightly be interfered with. (Supreme Court Act, §§53, 55).

Range of costs awarded is fixed by statutory tariff which allows assessment officer discretionary jurisdiction with regard to certain items as circumstances of case require.

Defendant may after appearance make payment into court in satisfaction; if plaintiff does not recover more at trial, judge should, unless there is cogent reason, order plaintiff to pay costs after payment.

Costs as between solicitor and his client are not fixed by statute but, in default of special agreement, may be assessed by assessment officer at instance of solicitor or client. Fees are fixed having regard to work done, results achieved and skill employed, in accordance with well established practice.

Where plaintiff makes offer to settle at least seven days before commencement of trial, and offer is not withdrawn or accepted by defendant, and plaintiff obtains judgment as favourable as or more favourable than offer to settle, plaintiff is entitled to costs as between solicitor and client from date of delivery of offer to settle. (R. 49.10). Where defendant makes offer to settle at least seven days before commencement of trial and offer is not withdrawn or accepted by plaintiff, and plaintiff obtains judgment as favourable as or less favourable than offer to settle, defendant is entitled to party and party cost from date of delivery of offer to settle. (R. 49.10).

Security of costs may be ordered, on motion by defendant, i.e. plaintiff will be required to post security in sum equal or proportional to defendant's estimated cost of defending action, where: Plaintiff is ordinarily resident outside P.E.I. or has another proceeding for same relief pending in P.E.I.; plaintiff is corporation or nominal plaintiff or there is good reason to believe that action is frivolous and vexatious, and it is reasonable to believe that plaintiff has insufficient assets in P.E.I. to pay costs of defendant; or where defendant holds unsatisfied order for costs against plaintiff in any proceeding or is entitled by statute to security for costs. (R. 56.01). Motion for security for costs available only after defendant has delivered defence, and must be made on notice to plaintiff and every defendant who has delivered defence or notice of intent to defend. (R. 56.03). Amount and form of security and time for payment into court are determined by court. (R. 56.04). Proceedings, except appeal from order itself, are stayed until security has been given, unless otherwise ordered by court. (R. 56.05). Upon default in giving security, action against defendant who obtained order may be dismissed. (R. 56.06). Amount of security may be increased or decreased at any time. (R. 56.07). Judge of appellate court, on motion of respondent, can make order for security for costs of appeal in certain circumstances. (R. 61.15).

Liability of Solicitor.—Solicitor may be ordered to personally pay costs of his client or any other party to action in certain circumstances (R. 57.06), but this occurs relatively rarely.

COURTS:

Supreme Court has original and appellate jurisdiction in all matters and may give equitable relief.

Provincial Court exercises jurisdiction over offences under Criminal Code, Federal and Provincial Statutes.

CREDITORS' SUITS:

There is no general statute authorizing creditors' suits for general discovery and in aid of common law execution, but a creditor may file a bill in equity for administration of a deceased debtor's estate. See also topics Executions, subhead Supplementary Proceedings; Fraudulent Sales and Conveyances.

CRIMINAL LAW:

No provincial criminal law. See Canada Law Digest.

CURTESY:

Curtesy is abolished, effective Dec. 31, 1978.

DAMAGES:

Common law generally prevails. Contributory negligence governed by Contributory Negligence Act.

Charitable Immunity.—Liability of charities for damages is governed by common law and is not abrogated by statute.

Sovereign Immunity.—Crown immunity abrogated by Crown Proceedings Act (effective July 1, 1973). Crown liable in tort for: (a) Tort committed by officers or agents, (b) breach of employer-related duties to servants and agents, (c) breach of duties attaching to ownership or possession of property, (d) breach of statute, regulation or by-law.

Law relating to indemnity and contribution enforceable by/against Crown.

In suit against Crown for injunction or specific performance court may not so grant but will grant order declaratory of rights.

Act does not authorize proceedings in rem against Crown nor seizure, attachment, detention or sale of Crown property.

In proceedings against Crown, trial without jury.

For limitation of actions and notice requirements, see topic Limitation of Actions, subhead Proceedings Against Crown.

Volunteers Liability Act.—S.P.E.I. 1994. Volunteers who render emergency assistance to person or provide assistance to protect endangered property are not liable for injury/death to person or damage to property in absence of gross negligence.

See also topic Death, subhead Action for Death.

DEATH:

A person who has not been heard of for seven years by those who, if he had been alive, would be likely to have heard of him, and as to whom such inquiries and searches as circumstances suggest have been made, is presumed to be dead. See also topic Absentees.

Survivorship.—Where two or more persons die in circumstances rendering it uncertain which died first, the usual presumption is that the younger survived the older, but as between a person whose life was insured and the beneficiary under the policy it is presumed that the beneficiary died first.

Action for Death.—Where death of a person has been caused by the wrongful act, neglect or default of another, action for damages may be brought against the wrongdoer. Subject to certain exceptions, action must be in name of executor or administrator of decedent. Action is for benefit of dependents as defined in Fatal Accidents Act, Cap. F-5 and damages are proportioned to injury to such persons by reason of death. Reasonable funeral expenses of decedent may be awarded. Insurance moneys may not be considered in assessing damages. Compensation for loss of guidance, care, companionship available.

DECEDENTS' ESTATES:

See topics Descent and Distribution; Executors and Administrators; Wills.

DEEDS:

Deeds of conveyance of real property are effective to pass the legal estate only when executed under seal. No more than one witness to execution of deed is necessary, unless deed is executed in pursuance of a power of appointment specially directing more than one witness to be necessary. Under Family Law Act, spouse must consent to transfer of property occupied as family residence (matrimonial home). (Family Law Act, Cap. F-3, §36). See topic Husband and Wife, subhead Status.

Registration.—To be effective against subsequent grantees or incumbrancers for valuable consideration without notice, deed must be registered in duplicate in office of registrar of deeds in county in which land is situated. Execution of deed must be proved before registry by acknowledgment of grantor or by oath of a witness before proper officer. See topic Acknowledgments.

DEEDS . . . *continued*

Powers of attorney authorizing another to convey land must describe land to be conveyed with certainty.

Recording Fees.—Cost of registration of documents is as follows: (a) Deeds—from $25 to $125 depending on consideration for transfer; (b) mortgage—from $25 to $125 depending on mortgage amount; (c) satisfaction of mortgage—$10; and (d) any other document—$25.

DEEDS OF TRUST:

See topics Corporations; Chattel Mortgages; Mortgages of Real Property.

DEPOSITIONS:

Evidence of witnesses unable to attend trial may be taken by commissioners, under order of court, on application of any party. To perpetuate testimony, a suit may be brought in Supreme Court, and evidence taken and enrolled.

Witness Outside of Province.—Witnesses absent from province may be examined under a commission issued for the purpose, and depositions of such witnesses may be given in evidence at the trial upon terms of the order and subject to proper objections.

Compelling Attendance and Testimony of Witnesses.—Witnesses within the province, unless ill or infirm or unable to travel, may be compelled to attend court and give viva voce evidence at the trial upon being served with a subpoena. If the witness is ill or infirm or unable to travel or is about to leave the province, an order may be obtained requiring the witness' evidence to be given before a judge or commissioner, and permitting the deposition so given to be put in evidence at the trial. Witnesses absent from the province may be examined under a commission issued for the purpose, and depositions of such witnesses may be given in evidence at the trial upon the terms of the order and subject to proper objections.

Examination on discovery of a party litigant or of any witness may be ordered before trial; and a party or witness who has made an affidavit to be used in an action may be subpoenaed to attend for cross-examination upon such affidavit.

DESCENT AND DISTRIBUTION:

In the distribution of the estates of persons who died intestate on or after Mar. 17, 1944, the following rules apply to realty and personalty alike.

The estate in excess of the share of the widow or surviving husband (as to which see subhead Surviving Spouse, infra), or the entire estate if there be no surviving spouse, descends and is distributed as follows: each class of which a member is living taking to the exclusion of subsequent classes; (1) children and/or descendants of deceased children per stirpes; (2) parents equally or all to surviving parent; (3) brothers and sisters equally, children of a deceased brother or sister taking the share to which their parent would be entitled if living, provided that where the only persons entitled are children of deceased brothers and sisters they take per capita; (4) nephews and nieces; (5) next of kin of equal degree of consanguinity to the intestate.

Kindred of the half blood inherit equally with those of the whole blood of same degree.

Surviving spouse takes as follows: (a) one-half if decedent left only one child or only issue of one deceased child; (b) one-third if decedent left more than one child, one child and issue of one or more deceased children, or issue of two or more deceased children. If an intestate dies leaving a widow but no issue, his estate shall go to his widow.

If at the time of the death of a husband or wife the other spouse is living apart and in adultery, the survivor takes no part of the estate of the deceased spouse.

Illegitimate children and their issue inherit from the mother and as representative of the mother, as though legitimate. The estate of an illegitimate child dying intestate, without spouse or issue, goes to the mother if living, otherwise to other children of the same mother or their representatives.

The estate of an illegitimate child dying intestate leaving no issue, goes, subject to the right of his widow, to his mother if living, and if she is dead, then equally to the other children of the same mother; and if any child is dead, the children of the deceased child take the share as if the parent were living. If the only persons entitled are children of the deceased children of the mother, they take per capita; but if the mother is dead and there are no other children of the same mother or children of a deceased child or children of the same mother, the whole estate goes to his widow.

Adopted Children.—See topic Adoption.

Advancements.—If any child has any estate by settlement from the decedent or has received advancements from the decedent during his lifetime, the value of such estate or advancement must be deducted from such child's share of the personalty. The same rule applies to settlements or portions received during descedent's lifetime, which must be deducted from the child's share of the realty.

Escheat.—Where the intestate left no heirs, his property escheats to the province.

DISPUTE RESOLUTION:

Mandatory Dispute Resolution.—None.

Voluntary Dispute Resolution.—For any matter falling under Family Law Act (pre-divorce issues of support, custody and property division) court on parties mutual consent appoints mutually selected mediator. Mediator confers with parties and children and prepares and files full or limited report as required by parties. Full report includes anything said by parties and anything mediator considers relevant. Limited report gives only conclusion of agreements reached or that no agreement was reached. No evidence of anything said or of any admission/communication made during mediation is admissible in proceeding if limited report requested except with parties' consent. Parties pay mediators' fees and expenses.

DIVORCE:

See Canada Law Digest. Procedure regulated by Rules of Supreme Court. Grounds for divorce governed by Laws of Canada.

Apart from grounds for divorce stated in Canada Law Digest, there may be a decree of judicial separation or divorce from bed and board under authority of Provincial Statute (5th William IV) and amendments thereto in so far as that statute was not repealed by Dominion Act. There may also be a decree of nullity which is not covered by Dominion legislation.

See topic Husband and Wife for division of spousal property.

DOWER:

Dower is abolished effective Dec. 31, 1978, except in respect of right to dower that has vested before Dec. 31, 1978.

EMPLOYER AND EMPLOYEE:

See topic Labour Relations.

ENVIRONMENT:

Environmental Protection Act, Cap. E-9 governs protection of environment. Purpose of Act is to manage, protect and enhance environment.

General Supervision.—Minister of Environment designated by Lieutenant-Governor-in-Council.

Function.—Minister of Environment may take such action as he considers necessary in order to manage, protect or enhance environment including (a) investigating and inquiring into any activity or situation that causes, appears to be cause of, or may cause contamination of environments; (b) coordinating work and efforts of public departments, boards, commissions, agencies and interest groups in Province respecting management of environment; (c) preparing and publishing policies, strategies, objectives and standards; (d) planning, designing, constructing, operating and maintaining works and undertakings; (e) exercising exclusive control over quality, use, protection or alteration of surface, ground and shore waters and all beaches, sand dunes and wetlands and allocating use of water; (f) entering into agreements; (g) delegating any of his functions under Act or Regulations; (h) performing such other functions as may be assigned to him by Lieutenant Governor in Council.

Environmental Impact Assessment.—No person shall initiate any undertaking unless person has filed written proposal with Department of Environment and obtains from Minister written approval to proceed with undertaking. "Undertaking" is broadly defined as any construction, industry, operation or other project which in any way significantly or detrimentally effects environment.

Watercourses.—No person without permit from Minister may alter watercourse, wetland, or any part thereof or water flow therein.

Sand Dune and Beaches.—No person without written permission of Minister may operate motor vehicle on beach or sand dune, carry out any activity that will or may interfere with natural supply or movement of sand to or within beach or sand dune or alter, remove or destroy natural stabilizing features, including vegetation, of beach or sand dune.

Penalties.—For individual, minimum $200 maximum $10,000 or 90 days imprisonment; for corporation, minimum $1,000 maximum $50,000 per day of noncompliance. Officer, director or agent of corporation may be personally liable for offences of corporation if directed, authorized, assented to, acquiesced in, or participated in unlawful activity.

EQUITY: See topic Actions.

ESCHEAT: See topic Descent and Distribution.

EVIDENCE: See topics Depositions; Witnesses.

EXECUTIONS:

Execution may issue on judgment of the Supreme Court as soon as the money or costs are payable. It remains in force for one year but may be renewed from time to time. It is a lien on defendant's goods and chattels from time of its delivery to sheriff.

Exemptions.—See topic Exemptions.

Time for Issuance.—In the Supreme Court execution may issue at any time within ten years without affidavit; after ten years, or when any change has taken place by death or otherwise in the parties entitled or liable to execution, the party entitled to execution may apply for leave to issue execution or to amend any execution already issued.

Property situated on leased premises may not be taken under execution unless, before removal of the property, the party at whose instance execution was issued pays to the landlord all arrears of rent, not exceeding one year in the case of rental terms of less than one year, and rent for two years in all other cases. Rent so paid may be added to amount of execution.

Sales.—Lands may be seized and advertised for sale by sheriff and after two months' notice may be sold to the highest bidder. The sale will be confirmed absolutely on application to the court. Eight days' notice of sale of chattels is given by sheriff.

Stays.—The court or judge may at or after time of giving judgment stay execution until such time as it or he thinks fit.

Supplementary Proceedings.—Upon plaintiff's affidavit setting out that his judgment stands unsatisfied a judge will issue an order for the examination of defendant. Third persons can also be subpoenaed as witnesses. Defendant must disclose all his property and assets. If he conceals same or refuses to answer he may be committed to jail.

EXECUTORS AND ADMINISTRATORS:

The sole jurisdiction for granting letters probate or letters of administration is vested in Supreme Court Trial Division, Estates Section.

Preferences and Right to Administer.—In case of intestacy preference is given to applicants for administration in following order: (1) Husband or wife; (2) next of kin; (3) creditors. Creditors are not appointed without first citing next of kin and their refusal.

Eligibility and Competency.—A married woman or an infant may be appointed executor, and a married woman may act as administrator, but the court would refuse to appoint an infant as administrator. There is nothing to prevent a nonresident or foreign corporation from acting as either executor or administrator but absence from the jurisdiction would doubtless prevent the court from appointing a foreign corporation as administrator.

Qualification.—No bond is required from an executor on his appointment as executor but an oath of office is required. An administrator is required to give a bond with sureties, usually in double the value of the estate, and is required to take an oath of office.

Issuance of Letters.—These are issued by the court after filing an inventory.

Removal.—Probate may be issued in common form in the first instance but the executor may afterward be cited by the next-of-kin to prove the will per testes or in solemn form. If upon such citation the executor does not prove the will, the probate may be revoked. The court has also power to remove an administrator on sufficient grounds shown for the revocation for instance, if he is acting in an irregular manner.

Special Kinds of Administration.—Administration may be temporary; limited; de bonis non; cum testamento annexo; ad colligendum; ad litem; and ancillary.

Interim Administrator.—Pending litigation about the validity of a will, granting or revocation of probate or grant of administration, an interim administrator may be appointed with limited powers.

Public Administrators.—Where the decedent left no known relatives living within the Province, or a known relative living elsewhere who cannot readily be communicated with, the court may grant administration to the Attorney-General for the use of Her Majesty, or for the use of such persons as may ultimately appear to be entitled to the use of the estate. No security is required from the Attorney-General upon his appointment. After a year, the decedent's land may be sold upon authorization of the Lieutenant-Governor-in-Council. If the husband, widow, next-of-kin or heir of the decedent should claim administration, or if a will of the decedent is proved, letters of administration or letters of probate will be granted accordingly, and the Attorney-General in such case, must surrender his letters and file an account under oath. Upon application for the purpose, a court may direct an inquiry as to whether or not Her Majesty is entitled to any portion of the estate, as on an escheat.

Inventory and Appraisal.—A sworn inventory must be filed before letters of probate or administration are granted. The actual market values at the time of the death must be given, but no other appraisal is necessary, the sworn statement of the applicant for letters of administration being accepted. A notice of the granting of probate must be served upon each beneficiary within a month from the granting of probate or administration.

General Powers and Duties.—The real property of the deceased devolves at his death upon and becomes vested in his personal representatives who hold the property as trustees for the persons by law beneficially entitled thereto. If eight months expire from the date of the letters of probate or administration without the personal representative having conveyed the property to the persons beneficially entitled, an application may be made to the court to have a conveyance ordered and in default for a vesting order. The personal representative may convey the real property to the persons beneficially entitled and may make the conveyance either subject to a charge for the payment of any money the personal representative is liable to pay or without such charge.

As to the decedent's property other than real estate, the personal representative has an absolute power of disposal.

Notice of Appointment.—See subhead Inventory and Appraisal, supra.

Notice to Creditors.—A notice to creditors to present claims is required to be inserted in the Royal Gazette within a month from the granting of probate or administration. If the estate is under $800 the notice should be inserted for a month, in other cases for three months. By this notice all persons having any demands on the estate are to have their demands duly attested within six months from the date of the advertisement.

Presentation of Claims.—Creditors of the estate, who fail to present a claim to the personal representative before the passing of the accounts by the court and the making of a final decree for distribution, are barred from enforcing or collecting their claim.

Proof of Claims.—No specific form required. (The affidavit may be made by the creditor or by an agent of the creditor who swears to a knowledge of the facts.)

Approval or Rejection of Claims.—Upon making a final decree for distribution and passing the accounts, the Judge has a discretion to preserve the rights of a creditor or claimant whose claim may not have been admitted or proceeded with to judgment. The personal representative may require a creditor to commence an action and proceed to trial. If the creditor fails to commence the action within three months from the giving of notice, he shall be barred.

Payment of Claims.—If, after the publication for six months in the Gazette of a notice of a personal representative to creditors requiring them to present claims duly attested, the personal representative applies the assets to the payment of debts of which he had notice, and a creditor afterwards brings an action for a demand against the estate, it shall be a good defense to the action that the assets have been so applied before the personal representative had notice from the creditor.

Priorities.—No preference may be given in payment of any debt over any other debt of same class whether by specialty or simple contract, legal or equitable, nor shall debt due and payable be entitled to preference over debt not due. If assets are insufficient to pay all debts in full, payment must be made in following order: (a) mortgages on real or personal property and liens including judgment and execution liens as against property on which they severally attach; (b) funeral expenses in amount not exceeding $1,500; (c) expenses of administration or probate, including any allowance to personal representative; (d) medical and nursing expenses of last illness but not exceeding last one month's such expenses; (e) all other debts pari passu including balance of funeral expenses and balance of medical and nursing expenses (if any).

Sales of real property for purpose of distribution only are not valid as respects any person beneficially interested unless he concurs therein or unless where adult beneficiary declines to concur, or where under will there are contingent interest or interests not yet vested, or where persons who may be beneficiaries are not yet ascertained, application may be made to Supreme Court for authority to make sale. Personal representative may sell real property for purpose of paying debts.

Before granting of letters probate or of administration verified inventory of assets, with market values and information as to names, addresses and relationship to deceased of beneficiaries, must be filed.

Accounts of executors and administrators may be allowed and passed by the probate court any time after six months from the grant of letters, after giving due notice to creditors.

Compensation.—Executors and administrators may be allowed a commission not exceeding 5% of estate.

Letters of ancillary probate or administration may be granted where probate or administration has been granted by a court of competent jurisdiction in the United Kingdom or in any province of Canada, or in any other British province, the applicant in such case to give security or produce satisfactory evidence that security was given in the court of original jurisdiction covering assets within the province.

Distribution if Abroad.—There is no special provision for disposition of funds payable to a distributee to whom it is not feasible or permissible to make payment for some reason, such as residence abroad or behind the Iron Curtain.

See also topic Wills.

EXEMPTIONS:

The following articles only are exempt from seizure under execution: Necessary wearing apparel, beds and bedding of debtor and his family; household furniture, utensils, equipment, food and fuel contained in permanent home of debtor not exceeding $2,000; for non-farmer debtor, tools, instruments and chattles used by debtor in business, trade or calling not exceeding $2,000; for farmer debtor, livestock, fowl, agricultural machinery and equipment used by debtor in operation not exceeding $5,000 and sufficient seed to cultivate 100 acres; motor vehicle owned by debtor not exceeding $3,000.

If debtor is married person, a widow or widower supporting one or more children under 16 years of age or unable from physical or mental disability to support themselves, not less than $10 per week of his or her wages is exempt from garnishment, value of board and wages supplied to debtor by employer being considered as part of wages paid.

Designation of Beneficiaries Under Benefits Plans Act.—Where designation under prescribed pension plans is spouse, child, grandchild or parent of participant, assets, rights and interests in plan are exempt from execution and seizure.

See also topic Garnishment.

FACTORS:

Where a mercantile agent, in the ordinary course of his business, sells, pledges or assigns goods in his possession as such agent, such sale, pledge or assignment is as valid as though expressly authorized by the owner of the goods. The owner of the goods may, however, recover from the buyer the agreed price or any part thereof, subject to any right of set-off on the part of the buyer against the agent.

FIDUCIARIES:

See topics Executors and Administrators; Guardian and Ward; Trusts.

FORECLOSURE:

See topic Mortgages of Real Property.

FRANCHISES:

No special legislation.

FRAUDS, STATUTE OF:

Contract for sale of any goods of the value of $30 or upward is not enforceable unless buyer accepts part of the goods sold and actually receives the same or gives something in earnest to bind the contract or in part payment or unless some note or memorandum in writing of the contract is made and signed by the party to be charged or his agent in that behalf.

To convey freeholds a deed is required; as, also for all leases upwards of three years.

Contracts of executors or administrators to answer damages out of their own estate, contracts to answer for the debt or default of another, contracts concerning land or any interest therein, contracts not to be performed within a year, contracts in consideration of marriage, and ratification to take debt out of statute of limitations, must all be in writing and signed by party to be charged.

The modifications of the Statute of Frauds effected in England by Lord Tenterden's Act (9 George IV, c. 14), and by the English Mercantile Law Amendment Act, 1856, have been adopted by provincial enactment. Consideration need not be stated in written memorandum of promise to answer for debt, default or miscarriage of another person.

FRAUDULENT SALES AND CONVEYANCES:

Any transfer of property, gift, conveyance, assignment, delivery over or payment of goods, chattels or effects, bills, bonds, notes, shares, dividends, premiums or any other property real or personal made by a person in insolvent circumstances or unable to pay his debts in full or who knows that he is on the eve of insolvency, with intent to defeat or delay the claims of creditors or a particular creditor, are void as against the creditor or creditors injured, delayed or prejudiced, whether made voluntarily or under pressure.

All bills of sale or writings purporting to transfer the property in chattels absolutely and unconditionally are fraudulent and void, except as between grantor and grantee, unless grantee, forthwith on execution thereof, takes actual possession of the chattels.

Proceedings to annul fraudulent conveyances may be taken by bill in equity.

Bulk Sales.—The Bulk Sales Act defines a sale in bulk as any sale, transfer, conveyance, barter or exchange of a stock or part thereof out of the usual course of business or trade of the vendor, or a sale, etc., of substantially the entire stock of the vendor or of an interest in his business, or an agreement so to sell, etc.

Purchaser must, before closing the purchase, obtain from the vendor a statutory declaration giving the names and addresses of the vendor's creditors, with the amount due to each, and may pay the vendor not over $50 on account of the purchase price. After such statement is furnished no creditor can obtain any preference as to the property sold or the proceeds thereof.

At the time of completion of the sale the claims of all creditors of the vendor, as shown by the aforementioned written statement, must be paid, or the vendor must produce and deliver to the purchaser a writing from creditors representing not less than 60% in number and amount of claims over $50 waiving the provisions of the statute or consenting to the sale. In case of consent to the sale the entire proceeds must be paid to trustees of the creditors.

In case of noncompliance with the statute, the sale is deemed fraudulent and void as to creditors of the vendor, but the purchaser continues to be indebted for the purchase price, which may be attached by the vendor's creditors, and the purchaser is a trustee of the property for the vendor's creditors and personally liable to account to them for all moneys or security realized or taken by him from out of or on account of the sale or other disposition by him of such stock or any part thereof.

Proceedings to attack a sale as violative of the statute must be commenced within four months from the date of the sale.

GARNISHMENT:

A garnishee order may be obtained in Supreme Court, either before or after judgment, on affidavit of debt, and disclosing some money due and owing to debtor.

Exemptions.—There shall be exempt from garnishment on wages due or accruing due, to any debtor for his personal labour and service, sums in such amounts and for such purposes as shall be more particularly set forth in regulations approved by Lieutenant-Governor-in-Council, provided always that total exemptions hereunder shall in no case be less than amount which debtor would receive under provisions of Welfare Assistance Act of Province, and regulations approved pursuant thereto. (1972, c. 18).

Future Accruing Wages.—If a debtor is in receipt of a regular salary or wages, a judge may make an order for attachment of future accruing wages after making statutory exemptions and for payment into court of such wages and salary as and when same become due.

GUARDIAN AND WARD:

Provision is made for appointment of guardians for infants in proper cases.

A parent or next of kin may assign all rights of guardianship over infants, to be binding on them until 18 years of age. Committees and managers or orphans' homes or other charitable institutions having care of orphans may transfer all rights of guardianship over any orphans under their care, and transferee is bound to fulfill all duties imposed by laws on a parent or guardian.

HOLIDAYS: See Canada Law Digest.

HOMESTEADS:

No homestead law in the province.

See Curtesy; Deeds; Dower; Husband and Wife; and Real Property.

HUSBAND AND WIFE:

Status.—For all purposes of law, married person has legal personality that is independent, separate and distinct from that of spouse. Married person has legal capacity for all purposes as if unmarried, and has right of action in tort against spouse. Spouse defined by Family Law Act, Cap. F-3, as either man and woman who are married to each other or have entered into void or voidable marriage in good faith on part of person asserting right. Marriage that is actually or potentially polygamous is valid for Act purposes if celebrated in jurisdiction where it is valid.

Act provides for deferred community of property system. During marriage, net family property owned by spouse with title. Net family property defined as value of all property, including income from property, that spouse owns on valuation date (see below), after deducting spouse's debts/disabilities on valuation date, value of property spouse owned on marriage date less spouse's debts/liabilities on marriage and value of following property acquired by spouse after marriage and owned by spouse on valuation date: (1) property acquired by gift or inheritance from third person; (2) damages or right to damages for personal injuries, nervous shock, mental distress, or loss of guidance, care and companionship, or settlement representing those damages; (3) proceeds of contract of life, accident or sickness insurance policies; (4) property into which property referred to in (1) to (3) can be traced; (5) any property excluded by domestic contract between spouses. Onus of proving deduction from net family property is on party claiming it. Each spouse makes separate calculation. Property means any interest, present or future, vested or contingent, in real or personal property and includes property over which, whether alone or in conjunction with another person, there is power of appointment exercisable in favour of himself or herself, property disposed of by spouse but over which spouse has power to revoke disposition or disposal of property, and pension benefits whether vested or not. All net family property of spouses is valued on earliest of following valuation dates: (1) date of separation; (2) date divorce granted; (3) date marriage declared nullity; (4) date spouse commenced action for improvident depletion of property which is subsequently granted. Upon valuation date, spouse whose net family property is lesser of two net family properties is entitled to one half of difference between them. Court has discretion to vary equalization of net family property if equalization would be inequitable because of substantial change after valuation date in value of property included as net family or if equalization would be unconscionable given: (1) one spouse's failure to disclose to other spouse debts and liabilities existing at date of marriage; (2) one spouse incurred debts recklessly or in bad faith thereby reducing net family property; (3) part of value of net family property consists of gifts from other spouse; (4) spouse's intentional or reckless depletion of net family property; (5) amount spouse would receive is disproportionately large in relation to period of cohabitation less than five years; (6) one spouse has incurred disproportionately larger amount of debts and liabilities than other spouse for support of family; (7) written agreement between spouses that is not domestic contract; or (8) any other circumstance relating to acquisition, disposition, preservation, maintenance, improvement, deterioration, destruction, division or transfer of property.

Spouses have equal rights of possession of family home regardless of who holds title, as against each other. Family home is property in which person has interest and is, or if spouses are separated, was at time of separation ordinarily occupied by person and spouse as family residence. Court can make order for exclusive possession of family home taking into account, among other things, best interests of children affected, financial position of both spouses, availability of other suitable and affordable accommodation, any written agreement between parties and violence committed against one spouse. Property can be designated by registered instrument as family home by one spouse or both spouses. If only one spouse registers designation, any other property qualifying as family home remains family home. If both spouses register designation, any other undesignated family home ceases to be family home. No spouse may dispose of or encumber any interest in family home without consent or release of other spouses or court order. Affidavit by person making disposition or encumbrances, or by person's attorney based on personal knowledge, that person is not spouse or that property is not family home is sufficient proof of such unless person to whom disposition or encumbrance is made has notice to contrary. Spouse with right to possession of family home has right to redeem or to relief against encumbrancers and is entitled to notice respecting claim and its enforcement or realization.

Issues of ownership of property between husband and wife are governed by rule of resulting trust except that property taken in name of spouses as joint tenants is prima facie proof of intent that each spouse has one-half beneficial interest on severance, and money on deposit in bank or similar financial institution in name of both spouses is deemed to be held by them as joint tenants. Spouse not entitled to equitable remedy, including constructive trust, with respect to property owned by his or her spouse as restitution for contribution to acquisition, maintenance, preservation or improvement of property. Spouse not entitled to equitable remedy, including resulting trust, with respect to property owned by his or her spouse based on common or presumed intention of spouses regarding his or her contribution to acquisition, maintenance, preservation or improvement of property.

Support Obligations.—Every spouse has obligation to provide support for self and other spouse, in accordance with need, to extent that he or she is capable of doing so. For support purposes, definition of spouse includes unmarried man and woman who have cohabited continuously for three years or more or are in relationship of some permanence and are natural or adoptive parents of child. Spouse, dependent, or social welfare agency making payments to spouse may apply to court for support order against other spouse. Support order for spouse should (a) recognize any economic advantages or disadvantages to spouses arising from relationship or its breakdown; (b) apportion between spouses any financial consequences arising from care of child of relationship over and above obligation apportioned between spouses; (c) relieve any economic hardship of spouses arising from breakdown of relationship; and (d) promote economic self-sufficiency of each spouse within reasonable period of time. Support order for child should (a) recognize that parents have joint financial obligation to maintain child; and (b) apportion that obligation between parents according to abilities to contribute to performance of obligations. Factors court considers in awarding support are set out. Conduct of either spouse has no effect on obligation to support. Court may make support order for periodic payments of lump sum, may vary support order and may index support order. Support order binding on estate. While cohabiting spouse may pledge credit of self and other spouse jointly for necessaries except where express withdrawal of authority by other spouse.

Domestic Contracts.—Family Law Act provides for domestic contracts which are parental agreements, separation agreements, marriage contracts, cohabitation agreements and domestic contracts. Domestic contracts (marriage contract, separation agreement or cohabitation agreement) must be written, signed by both parties and witnessed. Any agreement affecting children is subject to court determination of best interests of children. Provisions requiring party to remain chaste are void. Domestic contracts may be set aside as unconscionable if one party failed to disclose significant assets, debts or other liabilities to other when contract entered, if one party did not understand nature or consequences of contract, or otherwise in accordance with law of contract. Party to domestic contract may file it with court and court may enforce it.

Marriage Contracts.—Husband and wife may enter marriage contract before or during their marriage agreeing on their respective rights and obligations under marriage, or on separation, annulment or dissolution of marriage, or upon death, including ownership in or division of property, support obligations, education and moral training of child and any other matter in settlement of their affairs except custody or access to children. No such agreement may alter rights of equal possession in family home.

HUSBAND AND WIFE . . . *continued*

Cohabitation Agreement.—Man and woman who are cohabiting or intend to cohabit and who are not married to each other, may enter into agreement in which they agree on their respective rights and obligations during cohabitation, or on ceasing to cohabit or on death, regarding same matters as marriage contracts. Cohabitation agreement deemed to be marriage contract upon marriage of parties to cohabitation agreement.

Parental Agreements.—Man and woman who are not spouses may agree on payment of expenses of child's prenatal care and birth, support of child or funeral expense of child or mother. Agreement may be incorporated in court order and enforced.

Actions.—Each spouse has like right of action in tort against other as if not married. See also topics Death, subhead Action for Death; Dispute Resolution.

INCOME TAX: See topic Taxation.

INFANTS:

Age of majority is 18. (Age of Majority Act, Cap. A-8). No statutory exceptions to age of majority.

All persons under 18 are incapable of making valid contracts or conveyances. But their marriage contract and their contract to pay for necessaries purchased is good. On coming of age may ratify a contract previously entered into.

Questions relating to custody of infants are determined by Supreme Court. By statute, father and mother of infant are joint guardians and are equally entitled to custody, control and education of infant. Custody Jurisdiction and Enforcement Act allows for greater recognition and easier enforcement of extra-provincial custody orders.

Adoption.—See topic Adoption.

Termination of Parental Rights.—By Family and Child Services Act, Cap. F-2 state may intervene in family relations, apprehend child and through court order sever parent/child relationship forever where level of care of child falls below standards acceptable by members of society.

Tobacco Sales to Minors.—No person shall sell to, or purchase for use of, minor (under 19 for this purpose), tobacco. Fines for offenders range from $2,000 to $10,000 to loss of vendor's license.

INHERITANCE TAX: See topic Taxation.

INJUNCTIONS:

Supreme Court may grant injunction by interlocutory order, or provisional or perpetual injunction.

INSOLVENCY:

Subject to Canadian Bankruptcy and Insolvency Act (see Canada Law Digest).

INSURANCE:

Insurance companies are subject to general corporation law and to certain license fees. (See topic Taxation.) Special provisions are made by The Insurance Act with respect to life, accident, fire and other insurance.

Direct Actions Against Insurer.—See topic Motor Vehicles, subhead Direct Actions.

Plain Language.—See topic Sales, subhead Consumer Protection Legislation.

INTEREST:

Open accounts do not carry interest, unless an agreement to pay interest can be proved. Bills, notes and cheques carry interest at 5% per annum, unless otherwise specified in document itself.

Judgment and Prejudgment.—Person entitled to order for payment of money is entitled to claim and have included in order award of interest at prejudgment interest rate, calculated from date cause of action arose to date of order. Rate of interest on damages for non-pecuniary loss in action for personal injury is discount rate determined by Rules of Court. If order includes amount for past pecuniary loss, interest calculated on total past pecuniary loss at end of each six-month period and at date of order. Interest not awarded (a) on exemplary or punitive damages; (b) on interest accruing under statute; (c) on award of costs in proceeding; (d) on that part of order that represents pecuniary loss arising after date of order and that is identified by finding of court; (e) with respect to amount of any advance payment that has been made towards settlement of claim, for period after advance payment has been made; (f) where order is made on consent, except by consent of debtor; or (g) where interest payable by right other than under statute. Court may, where just disallow interest, allow interest at rate higher or lower than prescribed or allow interest for period other than prescribed. Court will take into account (a) changes in market interest rate; (b) circumstances of case; (c) fact that advance payment was made; (d) circumstances of medical disclosure by plaintiff; (e) amount claimed and amount recovered in proceeding; (f) conduct of any party that tended to shorten or lengthen unnecessarily duration of proceeding; and (g) any other relevant consideration.

INTESTACY: See topic Descent and Distribution.

JOINT STOCK COMPANIES:

See topic Corporations.

Professional Associations.—See topics Associations; Corporations.

JUDGMENTS:

Judgments in Supreme Court bind real estate of party on minute of judgment being filed in office of prothonotary.

Judgment Notes.—These have no legal existence in this province.

Satisfaction.—Sufficient that party acknowledging sign before prothonotary or practicing attorney attending at plaintiff's request. If signed abroad signature must be acknowledged before a person authorized by the law of this province to take affidavits.

Canadian Judgments.—By Canadian Judgments (Enforcement) Act, S.P.E.I. 1994 final judgments of court or tribunal of another Canadian jurisdiction may be registered by paying fee and filing with Supreme Court certified copy of court/tribunal judgment. Registered judgment, subject to statutory exceptions, may be enforced to same extent as local judgment.

Foreign Judgments.—Are not conclusive proof of debt, but correctness of same may be disputed, and defendant may inquire into, contest and dispute all or any of the facts upon which said judgment is founded, or were the cause of action in the suit in which such judgment was given.

JUSTICES OF THE PEACE:

Justices of the peace have no jurisdiction in civil cases, but try cases of petty misdemeanors, breach of the peace, and the preliminary hearing in criminal cases is sometimes taken before them.

LABOUR RELATIONS:

Rights of employer and employee are as at common law except as varied by statute. Labour relations are governed by Labour Act, Cap. L-1 which among other things, legalizes formation of trade unions and collective bargaining and regulates relations between employers and employees, wage agreements, conciliation and mediation preceding strikes, lockouts, unfair labour practices, employment standards, including minimum wages for men and women, vacation pay, etc.

Employment Standards Act (Cap. E-6.2).—Act provides for certain minimum standards of employment.

Exempt Employees or Provisions.—Except for provisions relating to payment and protection of payment, Act does not apply to commission salespersons and farm labourers. Minimum wage and hours of work provisions do not apply to persons employed for sole purpose of caring for children, handicapped or aged persons and employees of nonprofit organizations who live at facility operated by organization. Act does not apply to employees covered by collective agreement except provisions relating to parental, maternity and adoption leave, to sexual harassment and to payment and protection of pay, payroll records and notice of prosecution.

Hours of Work.—Standard work week is 48 hours. Employment Standards Board may approve longer week.

Paid Holidays.—Subject to certain exceptions, employees are entitled to five holidays with pay: New Year's Day, Good Friday, Canada Day, Labour Day and Christmas Day. If paid holiday falls on nonworking day employer shall grant employee holiday with pay on either working day immediately following holiday or day immediately following employee's vacation or grant employee another day agreed upon by employee and employer before date of next annual vacation of employee. Where employee is required to work on paid holiday employer shall pay employee at rate at least equal to one and one-half times employee's regular rate for time worked on that day in addition to one days pay at employee's regular rate or pay that employee regular rate of wages for time worked on that day and grant employee holiday with pay on another day agreed to between employer and employee before date of next annual vacation of employee.

Overtime Pay.—After 48 hours or such other standard week as approved by Board, employee must be paid at rate of one and one-half times regular rate.

Vacation Pay.—After one year of service employee is entitled to two weeks vacation with pay. Employee is entitled to vacation pay of 4% of total wages for year or time in service. Every employer is deemed to hold vacation pay in trust for employee and amount of vacation pay is charge upon assets and estate of employer and has priority over claims of all other persons.

Minimum Wage.—Board with government approval by regulation fixes minimum wage of employees and may exempt certain employees from minimum wage provisions.

Parental, Maternity and Adoption Leave.—Female employee is entitled to maternity leave for period not exceeding 17 weeks during period of 11 weeks immediately preceding estimated date of birth, if employee has been employed at least 20 weeks. Maternity leave is without pay. Employee entitled to such leave is required to give four weeks notice with medical certificate estimating date of delivery. Same provisions apply to adoptive parent or male employee becoming natural father of child. Employer granting maternity leave must permit employee to resume work in position occupied by employee at time leave commenced or if position no longer exists in comparable position but not less than at same wages and benefits employee would have received if employee had not been granted maternity leave and in either case with no loss of seniority or pension benefits.

Bereavement Leave.—Employer shall grant employee leave of absence without pay up to three consecutive calendar days on death of member of employee's immediate family.

Sexual Harassment.—Every employee is entitled to employment free from sexual harassment meaning conduct, comments, gesture or contact of sexual nature that is likely to cause offence or humiliation to employee or that might on reasonable grounds be perceived by employee as placing condition of sexual nature on employment or on any opportunity for training or promotion. Every employer is required to have policy statement concerning sexual harassment. Employee's right of redress for violation of provision is through Human Rights Act.

Notice of Termination.—Unless employee has not been employed continuously for at least six months or employer has just cause, employer is required to give written notice of termination ranging from two to four weeks depending on length of employee's service. Only after written notice has been given and time of notice has expired can employee be terminated. Notice of termination is not required if employee

LABOUR RELATIONS . . . *continued*

is required to be discharged or laid-off for reasons beyond control of employer or because of labour disputes, weather conditions or actions of any governmental authority that directly affects operations of employer. Statutory rules set out minimum standards and courts frequently award substantially higher amounts for termination without adequate notice based on various factors such as age, service, experience, expertise, likelihood of finding alternaive employment and character of employment.

Unpaid Pay.—Unpaid pay set out in Determination made by inspector under Act constitutes lien, charge and secured debt in favour of inspector against all real and personal property of employer and has priority over all liens, judgments, charges or other claims or rights of any person and has priority over any assignment, mortgage, debenture, contract, accounts receivables, insurance claim whether made or created before or after date wages were earned or became due.

Workmen's Compensation Act.—Cap. W-7 applicable to workmen, but not to farm labourers or domestic or menial servants, or others exempted by Regulation, provision is made for compensation in respect of accidents and industrial diseases, fatal or non-fatal, occurring in the course of their employment. Employers are required to contribute towards fund to be administered as system of state insurance by Workmen's Compensation Board appointed by Provincial Government. Payroll assessments are made upon employers and Provincial Government also contributes to fund. Scale of compensation varies according to nature of injury and wages of workman. Claims for compensation under Act may not be assigned and are not subject to attachment.

LANDLORD AND TENANT:

A lease for three years or less need not be under seal, or even in writing. A lease for more than three years is void at law unless made by deed under seal, although it may be effective as an agreement for a lease. A lease must be recorded or registered in order to protect lessee's interest against subsequent purchasers or mortgagees from lessor.

Tenant's assignee for creditors, or tenant company's liquidator in winding-up proceedings, may elect to retain leased premises for unexpired term of lease, or on payment of rent then due may assign lease if proposed assignee is approved by a judge of the Supreme Court.

Increases in rent by landlord are governed by Rental of Residential Property Act, Cap. R-13.1.

Distress for Rent.—Arrears of rent for which distress may be made are limited to six years. The right of distress against goods and chattels which are claimed by a person other than the tenant by virtue of an execution against the tenant or by virtue of a purchase, gift, transfer or assignment from the tenant, whether absolute, in trust, by way of mortgage or otherwise, is limited to the rental due for one year in the case of rental terms of less than one year, and to the rental due for two years in all other cases.

Certain articles are exempt from distress.

Where the tenant makes an assignment for benefit of creditors or becomes bankrupt, or where a tenant corporation is being wound up under Winding-up Act, landlord's right to distrain or to continue distress proceedings ceases, but in distribution of tenant's property landlord has priority as to arrears or rent due at time of assignment or commencement of bankruptcy or winding-up proceedings equal to three terms or times of payment, if payments are due weekly, monthly or quarterly, or one year's rent if times of payment are more than three months apart, with costs of proceedings, if commenced.

Not available for residential tenancies except where tenant abandons premises.

Termination of Tenancy.—As regards residential tenancies, landlord-tenant relationship is one of contract and common law rules apply. Common law rules respecting effect of breach of material covenant and frustration, given statutory confirmation. Tenant may terminate rental agreement by serving lessor Notice of Termination as prescribed by Rental of Residential Property Act, Cap. R-13.1. Notice for fixed term agreement is two months, for month to month rental is one month and for week to week rental is one week. Landlord may not terminate rental agreement other than for cause as set out in Act. Cause includes nonpayment of rent; breach of statutory condition incorporated in rental agreement; damages to rental property; where lessor in good faith seeks to have possession of premises for himself or to convert premises for other than residential use; etc.

As regards commercial tenancies, subject to express agreement to contrary (in which case common law rules apply), landlord or tenant can statutorily terminate weekly, monthly and yearly tenancy, upon giving week's, month's and three months' notice respectively; six months' notice required in cases of agricultural land leased on yearly basis.

LEGISLATURE:

Legislature holds its regular sessions in Parliament Buildings in Charlottetown.

Legislature is composed of Lieutenant-Governor and Legislative Assembly of 32 members, a session being held at least once in every year, so that twelve months shall not intervene between last sitting in one session and first sitting in next. Ordinarily session is called in March, but special sessions may be called at any time. Assembly may be summoned and called from time to time by Lieutenant-Governor by instrument under Great Seal of Province.

Distribution of legislative powers between provincial Legislature and Parliament of Canada is specifically set out in British North America Act 1867. See Canada Law Digest, topic Constitution and Government.

LEVY: See topics Attachment; Executions.

LICENSES:

Licenses are required for various occupations, but there are no restrictions on commercial travellers soliciting orders for goods from wholesale trade.

See topic Principal and Agent, subhead Collection Agencies; topic Real Property, subhead Real Estate Agents.

See also topic Taxation.

LIENS:

The general law of liens is in accordance with the common law of England and the statutes dealing with particular cases.

Garage Keepers' Lien.—Garage Keepers' Lien Act provides that a garage keeper shall have a lien on every motor vehicle left with him for services rendered upon it by garage keeper. Garage keeper may detain motor vehicle and right of detention has priority over and is not subject to any lien, lien note, chattel mortgage, bill of sale or other charge or encumbrances upon or in receipt of motor vehicle existing at time of detention and garage keeper may sell vehicle by public auction in accordance with terms of Statute.

Mechanics' Liens.—A person who does or causes to be done any work upon or in respect of any improvement to land, or furnishes any material to be used in an improvement to land, for an owner or for a person having an interest in land, or for a contractor or sub-contractor, has a lien for wages or for the price of the work or material, upon the estate or interest of the owner of the land so improved, but the lien does not make the owner liable for a greater sum than the amount he may owe the contractor. Liens must be registered in the registry office of the county within which the land is situated within 60 days from the performance of the work or services or the furnishing of the last material the price of which is claimed for. If no action to enforce the lien is commenced within 30 days the lienholder may then be required to commence an action within 30 days to enforce the lien, otherwise the lien ceases. The lien may be enforced by action brought in the Supreme Court. To meet any such lien, the owner liable on a contract where a lien may arise must deduct and retain, for 60 days after the completion of the work, 20% of the value of the work and material, but if the value of the work and material exceeds $15,000 the amount to be deducted and retained is 15%. Provincial Crown lands can be liened.

A lien has priority over judgments, executions and other legal proceedings recovered or issued after the lien arises as well as over claims under conveyances, mortgages and other charges and agreements for sale of the land, whether registered or unregistered, which are made by the owner after the lien arises, but a mortgage or conveyance registered after a lien for material arises but before the registration of the lien, has priority over the lien to the extent of payments or advances made in good faith before the person making the payments or advances has knowledge of the lien. Securities registered before the lien arises have certain limited priorities over the lienholder.

LIMITATION OF ACTIONS:

Governed by Statute of Limitations.

Action to recover money on any bond, recognizance or specialty may be brought within 20 years after the cause of action accrued.

On all contracts not under seal suit must be begun within six years after cause of action accrued. Action on a judgment or order for the payment of money must be brought within ten years after cause of action arose. Action to recover possession of land must be brought within 20 years after right accrued, except when claimant is under disability of infancy, coverture, lunacy or absence beyond seas, when six years are allowed from ceasing of such disability, but whole time not to exceed 30 years. Special limitation periods in actions against insurer by insured under Insurance Act.

Torts.—Actions on the case, with some exceptions, must be brought within six years after cause of action arises. Action for libel, slander, assault, battery, wounding, false imprisonment, malicious prosecution or seduction must be brought within two years.

Proceedings Against Crown.—Protection of Statute of Limitations extends to Crown. Crown further protected by Crown Proceedings Act (CPA) as follows:

(1) No action shall be brought against Crown to enforce claim for damages caused by accident arising from condition of highway including sidewalk, or from presence of nuisance on highway or sidewalk, unless: (a) Notice in writing of accident indicating place where it occurred and cause thereof is given to Deputy Minister of Transportation and Public Works within 90 days of happening thereof and (b) action is brought within two years after date of accident.

(2) No action shall be brought against Crown to enforce claim for damages sustained in respect of drainage works unless it is brought within two years after date on which damages sustained. Where death results from accident mentioned in (1), want of notice is not bar to action; and in all other cases want or insufficiency of notice is not bar to action, if court considers that there was reasonable excuse for want or insufficiency.

(3) No person may avail himself: (a) Of any set-off or counterclaim in proceedings by Crown for recovery of taxes, duties, or penalties; or (b) in proceedings of any other nature by Crown, of any set-off or counterclaim arising out of right or claim to repayment in respect of taxes, duties or penalties.

(4) No proceedings shall be brought against Crown under Act in respect of any act or omission, transaction, matter or thing arising, occurring or existing before July 1, 1973.

No proceedings shall be commenced against Crown under CPA unless 90 days notice served on Crown with details of facts supporting claim.

See also topic Damages, subhead Sovereign Immunity.

MARRIAGE:

Marriage of a person under 16 years of age is forbidden except in case of a female who is either pregnant or mother of a living child, and consent of parents or guardian is obtained. If either of applicants under age of 18 years, license will not be issued unless consent of parents or guardian of such applicant is obtained. In certain circumstances, consent may be dispensed with by order of Supreme Court Judge.

Consent Required.—Consents required are stated above; consent is evidenced by writing in form of affidavit of consenting parent or guardian. Such affidavit is filed with licencing officer.

MARRIAGE . . . *continued*

Medical Examination.—Certificate of pre-marital health is required to be filed with licencing officer.

License.—Marriage licenses are issued by a person appointed by Lieutenant-Governor in Council, known as an "Issuer." Both parties must apply for a license and must appear in person before licencing officer; a pre-marital health examination must show that applicants are free from venereal disease; in case of divorced applicant, license will not be issued until 14 days after date of final decree, and applicant must furnish certificate that no appeal has been taken against final decree or that where there is an appeal, it has been disposed of; in ordinary cases, there is a waiting period of five days from filing of all necessary affidavits and certificates, and date of issue of marriage certificate.

Waiting Period.—None.

Ceremonial Marriage.—No person is authorized to solemnize a marriage except a Supreme Court judge, or a "registered clergyman." Director of Vital Statistics maintains a record showing name and religious affiliation of every registered clergyman. Marriage may not be solemnized except under authority of a marriage license, and within three months of date of license, and in presence of parties and at least two credible adult witnesses.

Report of Marriages.—Every issuer of marriage licenses must keep a record of licenses which he has issued and any persons may have a search made of any license issued. Record of marriages is kept in Department of Vital Statistics.

Record.—See topic Records.

Common law marriages are not recognized.

Proxy marriages are not authorized.

Marriages by written contract not authorized.

Prohibited Marriages.—Marriages between persons who are insane, or mentally ill, are prohibited. Pursuant to Regulations published under authority of Marriage Act (Cap. M-3), following are degrees of affinity and consanguinity which, under statutes in that behalf, bar lawful solemnization of marriage: Man may not marry his: grandmother, grandfather's wife, wife's grandmother, aunt, uncle's wife, wife's aunt, mother, stepmother, wife's mother, daughter, wife's daughter, son's wife, sister, granddaughter, grandson's wife, wife's granddaughter, niece, nephew's wife, wife's niece or brother's wife; woman may not marry her: grandfather, grandmother's husband, husband's grandfather, uncle, aunt's husband, husband's uncle, father, stepfather, husband's father, son, husband's son, daughter's husband, brother, grandson, granddaughter's husband, husband's grandson, nephew, niece's husband, husband's nephew or husband's brother.

Relationships set forth include all such relationships whether by whole or half blood, and whether legitimate or illegitimate.

However, by Revised Statutes of Canada, 1985, M-5, §2, it is enacted that "A marriage is not invalid merely because the woman is a sister of a deceased wife of the man, or a daughter of a sister or brother of a deceased wife of the man."

Also, by Revised Statutes of Canada, 1985, M-5, §3, it is enacted that "A marriage is not invalid merely because the man is a brother of a deceased husband of the woman or a son of a brother or sister of a deceased husband of the woman."

Prohibited marriages are void. Children of prohibited marriages are illegitimate.

Foreign Marriages.—Any form of marriage is recognized if valid according to domicile of parties and jurisdiction where ceremony was performed.

Annulment.—Supreme Court may annul a marriage on grounds of impotence or kindred within degrees prohibited by statute. Such marriage is voidable upon application to court during life of parties, but cannot be questioned after death of either.

MARRIED WOMEN:

See topics Acknowledgments; Dower; Husband and Wife; Marriage; Witnesses.

MASTER AND SERVANT:

See topic Labour Relations; also topic Principal and Agent.

MECHANICS' LIENS:

See topic Liens.

MINES AND MINERALS:

There are no mines in this province, but provisions are made by statute for granting of licenses to search for oil and natural gas and granting of leases subject to royalty. Provisions are also made by statute governing minerals other than oil and natural gas. (Oil and Natural Gas Act, Cap. O-5).

MORTGAGES OF PERSONAL PROPERTY:

See topic Chattel Mortgages.

MORTGAGES OF REAL PROPERTY:

Mortgages must be signed, sealed and delivered, as deeds. May be released as to part of mortgaged property by mortgagee executing deed of release to which the mortgagor is also a party. Restriction placed on ability to encumber matrimonial home. See topic Husband and Wife.

When the mortgage money is wholly paid, all that is necessary is for the mortgagee to sign a certificate of satisfaction in the form provided by statute.

The usual mode of foreclosure is by sale under power contained in mortgage after giving notice for time and in manner specified in mortgage.

Chattel Mortgages.—See topics Chattel Mortgages; Corporations, subhead Corporation Securities Registration.

MOTOR VEHICLES:

Note: Law relating to motor vehicles, their registration, licensing, operation, rules of traffic, etc., is codified in Highway Traffic Act, Cap. H-5.

Vehicle license and trailer license required annually. Number plate must be displayed on front and back of motor vehicle unless otherwise ordered and on back of motorcycle, trailer, semi-trailer, pole-trailer and on front of trailer tractor. (Highway Traffic Act, §§20, 21, 22, 23, 24).

Operator's license issued by Registrar of Motor Vehicles, required annually before last day of anniversary month of licensee's month of birth. Minimum age of operator's license holders is 16 years, except farm tractors for which minimum age is 14 years. Minimum age for chauffeur's license is 18 years. No exemption for members of Armed Forces.

Titles, Sales and Liens.—Title to or interest in vehicle must be registered with Registrar of Motor Vehicles, who must be notified of sales and transfers. Lien must be registered with Prothonotary of Supreme Court.

Identification Marks.—Must not alter or remove serial numbers or other identification marks of maker or knowingly deal with or possess car so altered.

Operation Prohibited.—By a person under age of 16 (resident or nonresident) unless operating a farm tractor: by a chauffeur, by a driver of a vehicle weighing over $2^1/_2$ tons, unless over the age of 18 years; by intoxicated persons; by person suffering from disease or physical disability likely to render his operation of vehicle dangerous.

Size and Weight Limits.—Regulated by Highway Traffic Act, §§216-221 and under Roads Act of Prince Edward Island, Cap. R-15.

Equipment Required.—Bell, gong or horn audible for 200 feet; adequate brakes; rear view mirror. Cutouts prohibited.

Seat-Belt Legislation.—Children under age of 12 years must be restrained by prescribed child restraint system in private passenger vehicles. Driver and passengers must wear seat belt except if person: (a) Is unable for medical reasons to wear seat belt and holds medical certificate; (b) is unable to wear seat belt because of person's size, build or physical characteristic; (c) is peace officer transporting prisoner; (d) is fireman on fire-fighting vehicle; (e) is taxi cab driver; (f) is medical attendant in ambulance; (g) is driver of registered commercial vehicle.

Lights Required.—Two in front showing white light only, visible from not less than five hundred feet and such as to render a person clearly discernible at a distance of 500 feet, and lamp at back casting red light only, clearly visible for like distance in rear of vehicle. Additional approved clearance lamps or reflectors required on left side of vehicles wider than 86 inches. Trailer to carry reflector or red light. (Highway Traffic Act, §§96-115).

Accidents.—In case of personal injury, or property damage over $500, or if a vehicle involved in accident remains stationary on highway, person in charge of vehicle who is directly or indirectly a party to accident, must forthwith report accident to a member of Royal Canadian Mounted Police nearest scene of accident and as soon as possible furnish a written report to such police, setting forth all material facts, number of driver's license, and registration numbers of all motor vehicles involved. Supplementary reports may be required by police.

Attachment against a motor vehicle may be issued before or after commencement of an action for injury, loss or damage sustained through negligent operation of such vehicle. Such vehicle may be released upon owner depositing security to answer such damages.

Owner liable for negligence unless vehicle at time of accident in possession of some person other than the owner or his chauffeur without the owner's consent. Any member of the family of the owner living with him deemed to be agent or servant of owner.

Guests.—Ordinary rules of negligence apply.

Insurance.—Motor vehicle must be insured motor vehicle under Highway Traffic Act before Registrar of Motor Vehicles shall license same. Must be insured for minimum of $200,000 public liability and property damage. Insured motor vehicle may be liability insurance, bond of approved guaranty surety company, bond with approved personal sureties, or deposit of money or securities in amount or value of $11,000. (Compulsory Third Party Insurance Highway Traffic Act, Part X, §§299-313, proclaimed effective Jan. 1, 1976).

Judgment Recovery (P.E.I.) Limited.—Person who obtains judgment in action for damages for bodily injury, death or in excess of $200 for property damage occasioned by or arising out of ownership, maintenance, operation or use of motor vehicle within Prince Edward Island which occurred after Jan. 1, 1965, may, upon assigning judgment to Judgment Recovery (P.E.I.) Limited, receive from it amounts up to $200,000, exclusive of interest and costs for loss or damage resulting from bodily injury to or death of one or more persons and damage to property, and where in any one accident loss or damage results from bodily injury or death and loss or damage to property, any claims arising out of bodily injury or death shall have priority over claims arising out of damage to property to an amount of $190,000, and any claims arising out of damage to property shall have priority over claims arising out of bodily injury or death to an amount of $10,000, plus one-half solicitor's taxed costs. No money will be paid from fund to nonresident, unless such person resides in jurisdiction which affords similar relief to Prince Edward Island residents. Repayment to fund may be made in installments.

Foreign vehicle registered in home state or province and displaying license plates required by laws of home state or province may operate without license or registration for current year, except that where foreign vehicle is used for transportation of merchandise or of persons or property for compensation regular fee must be paid regardless of registration elsewhere. Nonresidents, including foreign corporations, must register motor vehicle or trailer if used in carrying on business in the province.

Nonresident operator licensed in home state or province may operate vehicle registered in home state or province for private use but not any other vehicle without domestic license.

Actions Against Nonresidents.—No special provisions as to mode of commencement.

MOTOR VEHICLES . . . *continued*

Direct Actions.—Under Insurance Act, Cap. I-4 statutory conditions are implied in all contracts of motor vehicle insurance providing no-fault benefits for loss of wages (max. $140 per week), medical expenses (max. $25,000) and funeral expenses for injury or death of person injured in motor vehicle accident. Person injured or estate of deceased person has direct action against insurer of vehicle causing damage or vehicle in which injured person was passenger. To claim in excess of no-fault benefits against insurer of person at fault for motor vehicle accident, injured person must first obtain judgment against person at fault before suing insurer.

Motor Vehicle Carriers.—Highway Safety Division must issue operating authority to applicant upon filing of application and prescribed fee.

Gasoline Tax.—See topic Taxation.

Garage Keepers' Lien.—See topic Liens.

NEGOTIABLE INSTRUMENTS:

See Canada Law Digest, topic Bills and Notes.

NOTARIES PUBLIC:

Appointed for life or during good behavior by Lieutenant Governor in Council. Jurisdiction extends throughout province. No bond required. Usual for them to use seal.

PARTITION:

Partition proceedings in this province are now brought in Supreme Court and general law and practice is same as courts in England exercising equitable jurisdiction. Court has power to order a sale when circumstances of case would make a sale more beneficial to parties than a partition among them, and court will order sale on application of any of parties interested in property to extent of one-half. All sales are made under direction of court, and proceeds paid into court, and subsequently divided among parties in proportion to their interests in property.

The compulsory partition of lands among joint tenants, tenants in common and coparceners may also be effected by suit brought in the Supreme Court by way of petition.

Personal representatives of an intestate may, with concurrence of persons beneficially interested, partition the estate among the heirs.

PARTNERSHIP:

Partnership must be registered with office of Director of Corporations. Failure to register guilty of offence subject to fine not less than $100 or more than $500 or in default to imprisonment for not more than 30 days. Any individual doing business under joint or firm name must also register same with Director of Corporations in same manner as partnership and subject to same penalty. Partnership and business name registered by filing prescribed statutory declaration with filing fee of $25.

General law of partnership governed by English common law and Partnership Act, Cap. P-1.

Limited partnership can be formed under Limited Partnership Act, Cap. L-13. Limited partnership (LP) may carry on any business unlimited partnership does. LP formed upon filing prescribed declaration with Registrar. Declaration expires after five years but expiration does not dissolve partnership. Any contribution by limited partner must be money or property; not services. Limited partner's liability limited to contribution stated in declaration unless he takes part in control of business over/above rights granted by Act. Retirement, death or incompetence of general partner or dissolution of corporate general partner dissolves LP unless business is continued by remaining general partners pursuant to right to do so in partnership agreement and all partners consent. Such partnership formed elsewhere in Canada may be registered here and partner thereof maintains same degree of limited liability as before in accordance with law of province limiting liability.

PATENTS: See Canada Law Digest.

PERPETUITIES:

Period during which existence of a future estate or interest in any hereditament, right, profit, easement or other property, real or personal, may be suspended, and during which rents, revenues, profits or income thereof may be allowed to accumulate, in whole or in part, may extend to, but must not exceed, the life of a person or of the survivor of several persons born or en ventre sa mere at the time of the creation of the future estate or interest and ascertained for that purpose by the instrument creating the same, and 60 years, to be computed from the dropping of such life or lives and ascertained for that purpose by such instrument. Time of death of testator is deemed to be time of creation of estate or interest created by will, and time of execution of instrument creating power is deemed to be time of creation of estate or interest created by execution of a power not tantamount to absolute ownership.

PLEADING:

Pleadings are governed by Rules of Civil Procedure, which are regulations made under Supreme Court Act.

Statement of Claim.—Action is commenced by plaintiff filing statement of claim any time within limitation period. (R. 14.03). If insufficient time to prepare statement of claim, plaintiff may issue notice of action and must then file statement within 30 days. Statement of claim must be served, together with notice of action where applicable, within six months after issue of statement or notice. (R. 14.08).

Statement of Defence.—Defendant must deliver statement of defence within 20 days after service of statement of claim if served in P.E.I., or 40 days if served elsewhere in Canada or U.S.A. or 60 days where served elsewhere. Defendant may deliver notice of intent to defend within prescribed time, thereby gaining additional ten days to file statement of defence. (R. 18.02). In defence, party must admit every allegation of fact in opposite party's pleading that party does not dispute, and all allegations of fact not denied in defence, except as to question of damages, shall be deemed to be admitted unless party pleads no knowledge in respect of that fact. (R. 25.07).

Counterclaim.—Defendant may assert by way of counterclaim, any right or claim he has against plaintiff, and counterclaim is to be included in same document as statement of defence and served within time prescribed for latter. (R. 27.01-27.04).

Reply.—Plaintiff must deliver reply, if any, within ten days after service of statement of defence, but where defendant counterclaims, plaintiff must deliver reply and defence to counterclaim within 20 days after service of defence and counterclaim. (R. 25.04). Reply to defence to counterclaim, if any, must be delivered within ten days after service of defence to counterclaim. (R. 27.06). Pleadings are closed when plaintiff has delivered reply to every defence or time therefor expires, and every defendant in default in delivering defence is noted in default. (R. 25.05).

Amended Pleadings.—Party may amend pleading without leave, before close of pleadings, if amendment does not cause addition, deletion or substitution of party, or on consent of all parties, or with leave of court. (R. 26.02). On motion at any stage of action, court will grant leave to amend to such terms as are just, unless prejudice would result that could not be compensated for by costs or adjournment. (R. 26.01). Form of amendments and service of amended pleadings are prescribed. (R. 26.03-26.06).

Particulars.—Rules and contents of pleadings are generally prescribed. (R. 25.06-25.09). Where party demands particulars of allegation in opponent's pleading, and opponent fails to supply within seven days, court may order particulars to be delivered within specified time. (R. 25.10).

Service.—Notice of action, statement of claim, counterclaim against person not already party to main action or other originating process must be served personally or by prescribed alternative to personal service. (R. 16.01). Any other document may be served on solicitor of record for party by mailing copy to solicitor's office, leaving copy with solicitor or employee in his office or by telephone or as otherwise prescribed. (R. 16.01-16.05).

Filing.—Every pleading must be filed, marked on face with date of filing, title of action, description of pleading and name and address of solicitor filing same. (R. 4.02).

PLEDGES:

Common law rules apply.

PRACTICE:

Most of law relating to practice is contained in Supreme Court Act and in Rules of Civil Procedure which are regulations made under that Act.

Discovery.—Generally, examination for discovery may be oral examination or, at option of examining party, by written questions and answers, but examining party not entitled to subject person to both forms without leave. (R. 31.02). Procedures for both oral and written examinations are prescribed. (R. 34, 35). Party is entitled to examine for discovery any party adverse in interest once, or more than once with leave, and party may examine individuals on behalf of corporation, partnership, sole proprietorship, person under disability, assignee, trustee in bankruptcy, or nominal party. (R. 31.03). Generally, party being examined must answer, to best of his knowledge, information and belief, any proper question relating to matter in issue or matter made discoverable by Rules. (R. 31.06). Where party, or person examined on his behalf, refuses to answer proper question, and has failed to furnish information in writing within ten days after trial date is set, party may not introduce that information at trial, except with leave. (R. 31.07). Court may grant leave to examine any nonparty who there is reason to believe has information relevant to material issue, other than expert engaged by or on behalf of party in preparation for litigation. (R. 31.10). At trial, party may read into evidence any evidence given on examination for discovery of adverse party or person examined on behalf or in place of, or in addition to, adverse party, unless trial judge orders otherwise, if that evidence is otherwise admissible. (R. 31.11). Procedure available for examining person residing outside P.E.I. (R. 34.07).

Other forms of discovery include discovery of documents (R. 30), inspection of property in certain proceedings (R. 32), and medical examination of any party whose physical or mental condition is in question in proceeding (R. 33).

Request for Admission of Facts.—In defence, party must admit every allegation of fact in opposite party's pleading that party does not dispute, and all allegations of fact not denied in defence, except as to quantum of damages, shall be deemed to be admitted unless party pleads no knowledge in respect of that fact. (R. 25.07). At any time, party may serve request to admit on any other party, requesting admission for purposes of proceeding only, truth of fact or authenticity of document. Party has 20 days after service to respond to request or is deemed to admit. Cost consequences may flow from denial of or failure to admit anything that should have been admitted. (R. 51, 57.01).

Direct Actions Against Insurer.—See topic Motor Vehicles, subhead Direct Actions.

See also topics Appeal and Error, Attachment, Depositions, Executions, Garnishment, Injunctions, Judgments, Pleading and Process.

PRINCIPAL AND AGENT:

Common law rules govern.

Agents for parties abroad who are sued here as absent debtors may be summoned and made to disclose the property of their principals.

Auctioneers' charges or commissions, when not a matter of contract, are governed by the rule of quantum meruit. Auctioneers must be licensed before conducting auction.

Attorneys in Fact.—Attorneys may be given power to do on behalf of donor anything donor can lawfully do. Power affecting real property must specify property

See note at head of Digest as to 1996 legislation covered.

See Topical Index in front part of this volume.

PRINCIPAL AND AGENT . . . *continued*
and power registered in registry office. Power may be exercised during legal incapacity (save death) of donor if power so provides; execution of such power must be witnessed. Powers of Attorney Act applies.

Collection Agencies.—No person shall within Province engage in or advertise himself as engaged in business of a collector of debts due, or alleged to be due, to any other person or in any way hold himself out as so engaged, without obtaining license from Registrar of Collection Agencies. Business of collector of debts includes business of purchasing or taking of assignments of debts. Collecting agency must deposit collections in trust accounts in chartered banks, keep proper accounts and without any notice must, within seven days after end of month in which it has collected any money, account to person entitled for money received. Lieutenant-Governor-in-Council may from time to time make regulations for carrying out of provisions of this statute. Act does not apply to barristers, sheriffs, banks, trust companies or credit unions. License to be obtained annually and applicants for original license must provide a bond prescribed by Act. (Collection Agencies Act, Cap. C-11).

PROCESS:

Commencement of Proceeding.—Rules of Civil Procedure contemplate two types of civil proceedings: actions and applications. Generally, application is summary proceeding in which judge is asked to determine questions of law where there are no material facts in dispute. Under Rules, every proceeding must be by action except where statute or Rules (R. 14.05) provide that proceeding may be brought by application. Examples of proceedings commenced by application are where executor or trustee asks court for directions or where determination of rights depends on court's interpretation of will, contract, deed or other instrument.

General Requisites.—Most proceedings commenced in court having jurisdiction by issuance of statement of claim, notice of application, or by notice of action followed by such statement. Form and contents of notice and statement are prescribed. (R. 14). See topic Pleading.

By Whom Issued.—All civil proceedings are commenced by issuance of originating process by registrar of court in which proceeding is to be commenced, except where statute provides otherwise. Counterclaim or counterpetition that is only against present parties to main action, and crossclaim, are commenced by delivery of pleading containing counterclaim, counterpetition or crossclaim, and pleading need not be issued. (R. 14.01). Originating process is issued by registrar's act of dating, signing and sealing it with seal of court and assigning to it court file number. (R. 14.07).

Who May Serve.—Service may be effected by any literate person.

Personal service on minor is effected by leaving copy of document with minor if over 12, and where minor resides with parent or other person having care or lawful custody of minor, by leaving another copy of document with that person, but where proceeding is in respect of minor's interest in estate or trust, minor shall be served by leaving copy of document bearing minor's name and address with Official Trustee.

Personal Service on Incompetent.—Personal service on person who has been declared mentally incompetent or incapable of managing his affairs is effected by leaving copy of document with committee of person's estate, if one exists or, if not, with committee of person. Personal service on person who is mentally incompetent or incapable of managing his affairs, not so declared, is effected by leaving copy of document bearing person's name and address with Official Trustee and leaving another copy with person.

Personal service on partnership is effected by service on one or more of partners or at principal place within Province of business of partnership, on any person having control or management of partnership business there.

Personal service on domestic corporation is effected by service on officer or agent or corporation, or with person at any place of business of corporation who appears to be in control or management of that place of business.

Personal service on foreign corporation is effected by service on any person having control or management of business of corporation within Province.

Personal Service Outside Province.—Under Rules, party to action or proceeding may be served out of P.E.I. where action or proceeding consists of claim for or in respect of real or personal property in P.E.I. or administration of estate of deceased person in respect of real property in P.E.I.; where action is in respect of personal property in P.E.I. or administration of personal property in P.E.I. of deceased person who at time of death was domiciled in P.E.I.; where will affecting real or personal property in P.E.I. or personal property of deceased person who at time of death was domiciled in P.E.I. is sought to be construed; where action is against trustees in respect of execution of trusts of property within P.E.I.; where action is upon mortgage, charge or lien on property within P.E.I.; where action is founded on breach of contract or tort committed within P.E.I.; where parties to contract have agreed that courts of P.E.I. are to have jurisdiction; where damages are sustained in P.E.I. arising from tort or breach of contract committed elsewhere; where injunction in respect of things done in P.E.I. is sought; where action is matrimonial cause, or action to declare marriage void, or claim is for custody, maintenance or access to infant; where any relief is sought against any person domiciled or ordinarily resident in P.E.I.; where person to be served is necessarily or properly party to action is founded on judgment; where by statute claim indemnity or other relief over in respect of any claim made against defendant in action commenced in P.E.I. (R. 17.02). Party to action or proceeding may be served outside of P.E.I. with leave of court for circumstances falling outside of R. 17.02.

Substituted service by advertisement or otherwise may be ordered when person to be served is evading service.

Proof of service may be by affidavit which must state date on which document was served and endorsed by person serving it.

REAL PROPERTY:

All estates tail are abolished. Otherwise all estates recognized at common law are recognized in Prince Edward Island. Every estate granted to two or more persons in their own right is a joint tenancy unless expressly declared to be a tenancy in common; and every estate vested in trustees or executors as such is held by them in joint tenancy. No tenancy by the entirety.

Ownership.—By Lands Protection Act, Cap. L-5 nonresident person or corporation cannot acquire aggregate land holding (includes any interest whatsoever in real property except any parcel less than one acre situate in city or town existing on May 1, 1995 and except interest acquired by bank, financial institution or trust company in ordinary course of business as security for debt/obligation) in excess of five acres or having shore frontage in excess of 165 feet unless Cabinet permission is first given.

No person or corporation shall acquire aggregate land holding in excess of 1,000 and 3,000 acres respectively. Natural person's land holding includes land holdings of person's minor children and land holdings of corporation in which person or his minor children hold more than 5% issued and voting shares. Where person/corporation has aggregate land holding in violation of Act, Minister may by order require (a) reduction of land holding, (b) application for permit, (c) evidence of no violation. Failure to comply with order may result in Court Order (a) declaring null and void any document by which land holding is in violation of Act, (b) for sale of said land, (c) cancelling of registry record, (d) to return consideration for acquisition, (e) for possession of land, (f) to pay costs. Fines may be imposed up to $250,000 and two years jail for violation. Officer, director or agent of corporate violator who directed, authorized, assented to, acquiesced in or participated in offence, liable to same punishment.

By said Act any person exceeding limit must by June 1, 1996 submit land holding disclosure statement to responsible Minister and apply for permit to hold excessive land holding. Permit may allow excessive land holding and attach conditions.

Quieting Titles Act.—Persons claiming a property right in land may commence an action where land lies for a certificate of title or may join any other claim in which title to or right to possession of land is in issue.

Real Estate Agents.—No person shall within Province engage in or advertise himself as engaged in business of trading in real estate as an agent unless he holds a license under The Real Estate Trading Act. Business of trading in real estate includes: (1) Disposition or acquisition of or transaction in real estate by sale, purchase, agreement for sale, exchange, option, lease, rental or otherwise; (2) any offer or attempt to list real estate for purpose of any such disposition, acquisition or transaction; and, (3) any act, advertisement, conduct or negotiation, directly or indirectly, in furtherance of any such disposition, acquisition, transaction, offer or attempt.

Salesmen acting for real estate agents must also be licensed. Real estate agents must maintain permanent office in Province. Licenses are granted by Registrar upon application. Real estate agents must keep proper books and accounts and must maintain trust account for every person from whom trust monies are received and must also maintain trust account in chartered bank or loan company in which all trust monies must be deposited. Act does not apply to any person acting under any statute of Canada or of Province, person acting under order of any court, administrator of estate or trustee selling under terms of will, marriage settlement or deed of trust, bank, loan trust or insurance company, person not ordinarily trading in real estate, or barrister of Supreme Court. Licenses are obtained annually and applicants for original license must provide bond in form prescribed by Act. Lieutenant-Governor-in-Council may from time to time make regulations for carrying out of provisions of this statute. Persons failing to comply with provisions of Act are guilty of offence and liable to fine not exceeding $1,000 for first offence and $2,000 for each subsequent offence.

Condominiums.—Permitted, Condominium Act, Cap. C-16.

See also topics Curtesy, Deeds, Dower, Husband and Wife, Landlord and Tenant, Mortgages of Real Property, Partition, Records.

RECEIVERS:

Appointed according to usage and practice of courts of equity.

In cases of insolvent companies, or corporations ordered to be wound up under the Winding Up Act, a liquidator is appointed.

RECORDS:

Deeds and other documents affecting title to land should be registered in duplicate in office of registrar of deeds; otherwise they may be void as against subsequent purchasers or incumbrancers whose conveyances or incumbrances are registered. Bills of sale and chattel mortgages may be filed with prothonotary or deputy prothonotary in county in which grantor or mortgagor resides.

Torrens system of land registration not adopted.

Vital Statistics.—Records of births, deaths and marriages are filed with Registrar General.

Fees for obtaining certificates of birth, etc., are $10, obtainable at office of Department of Health and Social Services.

REPLEVIN:

Orders for Replevin have been replaced by Recovery Orders. (Rule 48). Any party or intervenor in proceeding may apply for interlocutory order to recover possession of property that was unlawfully taken or is unlawfully detained from him by any other party, or is held by officer under any legal process issued in proceeding. This action may be maintained in Supreme Court.

Before recovery order is issued, prothonotary shall take from plaintiff bond with sureties in amount equal to $1^1/_4$ times value of property sought to be recovered. Bond is assignable to defendant on request.

REPORTS:

Reports of decisions of courts of province are published in Newfoundland & Prince Edward Island Reports, P.E.I. Reports and Dominion Law Reports.

See note at head of Digest as to 1996 legislation covered.

See Topical Index in front part of this volume.

SALES:

The Sale of Goods Act of the province is substantially the same as the English Sale of Goods Act 1893. See England Law Digest.

Seller's Lien.—Unpaid seller, while in possession of goods sold, has lien on them where sale was made without any stipulation as to credit, term of credit has expired or buyer has become insolvent.

Contracts of Sale.—No statutory limitation exists as to type size in printed contracts.

Bills of Sale.—Bills of sale are not required. See topic Chattel Mortgages.

Conditional Sales.—Where possession of property is delivered to a buyer thereof, any agreement that title shall remain in the seller is void as against subsequent bona fide purchasers or mortgagees from the buyer without notice, creditors of the buyer without notice and any assignee or trustee in insolvency or bankruptcy of the buyer unless such agreement is in writing, describing the property and stating amount unpaid and conditions of hiring, signed by the buyer or his agent prior to, at the time of or within ten days after delivery of the property and such writing, or a true copy thereof, is filed, within 20 days after the signing thereof, with the prothonotary of the registration district where the buyer resides or, if the buyer is a nonresident, where the property was delivered. If buyer resides in one district and property was delivered in another, filing in both districts is necessary. If property is removed from district where delivered or property subject to a conditional sale agreement made outside of the province is brought into the province, the agreement or a copy thereof must be filed in the district into which the property is removed within 20 days after the seller has knowledge of such removal.

If seller retakes possession, he must retain the property for 20 days, during which time purchaser may redeem by paying balance of purchase price and costs. If there is no redemption within such time, seller may sell the property at private sale or public auction, at any time thereafter. Notice of sale must be given to the buyer, or person guaranteeing payment, personally or by registered mail, and may be given during the 20 days allowed for redemption. If price exceeds $30 and seller intends to look to buyer, or person guaranteeing payment, for any deficiency on a resale, the notice must contain: (a) A description of the property; (b) an itemized statement of balance of price and costs; (c) a demand that amount stated be paid not less than five days from personal delivery of notice or not less than seven days from mailing of notice; (d) a statement that unless such payment is made the property will be sold at private sale or advertised and sold at public auction.

No statutory limitation as to type size in Conditional Sales Contracts.

Retail Credit Sales.—No special restrictions. Rates of interest are governed by Interest Act (Canada).

Bulk Sales.—Bulk sales are governed by provisions of Bulk Sales Act. See also topic Fraudulent Sales and Conveyances.

Consumer Protection Legislation.—

Business Practices Act.—(Cap. B-7). Director of Consumer Services administers act which has as its primary objective protection of consumer from unfair business practices as same are set out in Act. Person who is ordered to cease unfair practice by Director, is entitled to hearing by Minister. Any party to proceedings before Minister may appeal from his decision or order to Supreme Court in accordance with rules of court.

Unconscionable Transactions Relief Act.—(Cap. U-2). This Act permits court to investigate into all circumstances surrounding loan of money and if it finds that cost of loan is excessive and that transaction is harsh and unconscionable may grant relief to borrower.

Consumer Protection Act.—(Cap. C-19). Consumer loan, credit or borrowing agreements must be approved by Ministry of Community Affairs. Agreements not in compliance with Act cannot be sued upon.

Consumer Reporting Act.—(Cap. C-20). Consumer reporting agency and personal information investigator must be licensed.

Direct Sellers Act.—(Cap. D-11). Direct selling means selling, offering for sale or soliciting of orders for sale of goods or services by: (1) Going from house to house, (2) telephone, (3) mail. Direct sellers must be licensed. Direct sale may be rescinded by purchaser by notice to seller within seven days of purchase where seller is licensed. Direct sale is also cancelled where (i) goods/services not supplied within 30 days of contract, (ii) vendor/salesman breaches term of license; or (iii) vendor/salesman is not licensed; and purchaser serves written notice of cancellation within one year of contract.

Plain Language.—No "Plain Language" statute.

Energy-Efficient Appliances.—Designated appliances must meet prescribed efficiency standards. No person may offer for sale, sell or lease new designated appliances that do not meet efficiency standards (not yet in force).

International Sale of Goods Act makes applicable "United Nations Convention on Contracts for the International Sale of Goods".

SALES TAX:

See topic Taxation, subhead Sales Tax.

SEALS:

All deeds must be under seal. Mark or scroll not sufficient.

SECURITIES:

Securities Act, Cap. S-3 governs all matters of trading in securities. Trading and securities are broadly defined. No person may trade in security, except exempted securities, without being registered as broker or salesman. Registration is made on prescribed forms and requires placement of bond. No trading by registered brokers is permitted without filing prospectus unless prospectus filing is exempted by Act. Registrar of Securities administers Act and has power to exempt trades from broker registration and prospectus filing and power to investigate any actions of broker or person trading in securities.

Regulatory Powers of Supervising Authority.—Sale of securities within Province is subject to provisions of statute referred to above.

SERVICE: See topic Process.

STATUTE OF FRAUDS:

See topic Frauds, Statute of.

STATUTES:

Revised Statutes (1988) comprise 272 Acts.

STAY OF EXECUTION: See topic Executions.

SUBMISSION OF CONTROVERSY:

No statutory provision.

SUPPLEMENTARY PROCEEDINGS:

See topic Executions.

SURETY AND GUARANTY COMPANIES:

Surety and guaranty companies are allowed to sign the bonds of public and municipal officials and surety bonds required from their servants by corporations, banks, etc., and also to be taken as surety on bonds required by the courts to be filed in various cases, provided they are authorized under the law of the province or state where incorporated.

They must comply with the laws of this province respecting corporations, and must have a paid up capital of at least $250,000, and good available assets exceeding their liabilities, and a premium reserve at the rate of 50% of the current annual premium on outstanding bonds. They must file with Director of Corporations application to do business, and each year file statement under oath of their paid up capital with full particulars, and amount of annual premiums and of outstanding obligations. They must appoint attorney here upon whom process may be served. Upon complying with these requirements Director of Corporations will issue certificate permitting company to do business for ensuing year. There is license fee or tax of $25 per year.

TAXATION:

Business License Taxes.—There is imposed upon following corporations and persons license fees hereinafter specifically set forth, which license fees each of such corporations and persons are required to pay annually to Minister of Finance: Accident insurance companies, guarantee insurance companies, accident and guarantee insurance companies, fees set by regulation; banks, finance companies, loan companies or trust companies, $1,200; corporations operating chain store, branch chain wholesale store, branch chain theater, $600; light and telephone companies, $600; oil and gas companies based on litres; all other nonresident corporations, $200. Licensing fees are payable annually on June 1.

Domiciled Companies License Tax.—Corporations known as "domiciled companies" are subject to an annual license or registration fee of $25, and are not subject to any other provincial tax or license.

Environment Tax.—Tax of $2 per tire imposed on new tires.

Gasoline Tax.—Tax of 12¢ and 12.5¢ per litre for gasoline and diesel oil respectively is payable.

Stamp Tax.—No such tax imposed.

Financial Corporation Capital Tax.—Financial corporation (bank, trust company, loan company) having permanent establishment in P.E.I. pays capital tax of 3% of paid-up capital allocated to province.

Sales Tax.—Provincial Sales Tax of 10% of fair value of goods sold at retail is imposed. There are many exceptions, including food, gasoline, agricultural goods as defined by Minister, commercial fishing equipment, agricultural feeds, seeds, fertilizers, etc., newspapers when purchased by subscription for delivery by mail, children's clothing, etc. There is no tax on sales under 26¢. This tax is in addition to Dominion Sales Tax.

Real Property Tax.—(Real Property Assessment Act, Cap. R-4 and Real Property Tax Act, Cap. R-5). Provincial Department of Finance administers assessment of real property and collection of taxes thereon; no taxation levied on personal property; business property subject to taxation.

Exemptions.—Real property of (1) churches used for church purposes only, (2) nonprofit cemeteries, (3) public squares and parks, (4) Crown and Crown corporations and agencies, except within a municipality and then only subject to municipal tax thereon, (5) purification systems buildings and equipment, (6) University of Prince Edward Island and Holland College used for educational purposes, (7) Province or municipality for purpose of a public institution of learning and education.

Assessment.—Real property is assessed at real and true market value except for farm property. Not included as real property are: (1) growing and unharvested crops, (2) mines below surface of ground, (3) land used as a public right-of-way.

Business Assessment.—Business property is assessed on a percentage of real property assessment fixed by Lieutenant-Governor-in-Council.

Review of assessment made first by Minister and then may be referred to appeals board.

Rates of Tax.—Uniform rate of $1.50 per $100 assessed valuation is levied and payable by owner of real property. Additional rate of $1.50 per $100 assessed valuation levied on business property and payable by occupier of portion of business property occupied. Foregoing is subject to reduction of 10¢ per $100 of assessment on

TAXATION . . . *continued*
that portion of taxable real property assessed as residential property. Local municipal levy to be determined annually is also payable by owner and occupier of real property and business property. Resident of P.E.I. entitled to tax credit of 50% of assessed value of noncommercial property.

Payment.—Real estate, business and municipal taxes are payable to Minister of Finance and are due on date to be fixed by regulation. If taxes unpaid on due date a penalty of 3/4 of 1% per month. Taxes may be prepaid by installments.

Lien.—Taxes and interest thereon constitute a first lien on all real property and does not require registration or filing to preserve it.

Sale.—Real property may be sold by Minister of Finance after notice where taxes in arrears. Time, place and terms of sale established by regulations. Deed in fee simple to real property and may not be redeemed after sale.

Personal Property Tax.—None.

Income Tax.—By agreement with Dominion of Canada, personal and corporation income taxes are imposed by provinces and collected by Government of Canada. Province imposes an income tax. Rate of this tax for individuals is 58% for 1991 and 59.5% for 1992 of tax payable under Federal Income Tax Act (See Canada Law Digest.) Rate for corporations is 15% of income earned within Province. By agreement, Dominion is given right to collect this tax at same time tax under Federal Act is collected, and for administration purposes, one return is used.

Tobacco Tax.—A tax is imposed on the price to the consumer on all tobacco sold within the Province. Every consumer of tobacco purchased at retail sale in Province must pay tax at following rates: (a) 5.675¢ per cigarette; (b) 125% of retail price of each cigar; (c) 3.01¢ on every gram or part thereof of tobacco, other than cigarettes or cigars, where mass of tobacco is expressed on package or container in metric measure; (d) 4.46¢ per tobacco stick.

Liquor Tax.—Tax of 25% is levied on retail price of all intoxicating liquor sold by retail vendors.

Amusement tax is collected on admission to places of amusement, the amount being not less than 1¢ and not more than 50¢.

Social Security or Unemployment Compensation Tax.—None.

Succession Duty.—None. 1972, c. 45 imposing such a tax repealed. (1973, c. 34). Amounts collected thereunder refunded.

Exemptions.—Charitable institutions are generally exempt from taxation in the jurisdiction.

Inheritance Tax.—There is no Provincial inheritance tax.

Gift Tax.—None. 1972, c. 19 imposing such a tax repealed. (1973, c. 9). Amounts collected thereunder refunded.

TRADEMARKS AND TRADENAMES:

See topic Partnership, and Canada Law Digest.

Tradenames.—Every person engaged in business not associated in partnership with another person who uses as his business style some name or designation other than his own name or who in such business uses his own name with addition of "and Company" or some other word or phrase indicating a plurality of members shall cause to be filed statutory declaration of fact in writing signed by such person. Declaration must contain name, surname and residence of person and name, style or firm name under which he carries on or intends to carry on business. Declaration filed in Office of Director of Corporations; filing fee $25.

TRUSTEE PROCESS: See topic Garnishment.

TRUSTS:

The law of trusts is based on the general equity jurisprudence of England. All declarations or creations of trusts of any lands and all grants or assignments of any trusts must be manifested by some writing signed by the party declaring or assigning the same or by his last will. Trusts arising or resulting by implication or construction of law, or transferred or extinguished by an act or operation of law need not be in writing.

International Trusts Act makes applicable Hague "Convention on the Law Applicable to Trusts and on Their Recognition".

Variation of Trusts Act (Cap. V-1) provides that Supreme Court may approve variation in trusts on behalf of beneficiaries incapable of assenting or who may have contingent interests.

USURY: See Canada Law Digest, topic Interest.

VENUE:

County where cause of action arose or where some of parties reside. May be changed by judge on application.

VITAL STATISTICS: See topic Records.

WAREHOUSEMEN:

Warehouseman has a lien for his charges on goods deposited for storage and, on nonpayment of charges, may sell goods at public auction, after notice. Where deposit was not made by owner of goods or by his authority, but was made by a person entrusted with possession of the goods, notice of the lien must be given to owner or grantee of goods within two months after the deposit.

WILLS:

With the exception stated infra as to nuncupative wills, a person under the age of 18 cannot make a valid will. Married woman may dispose of her property by will.

Living Wills.—No legislation.

Execution.—Will must be in writing and signed at end by testator or some person in his presence and by his direction. Must be acknowledged or made in presence of two witnesses who must attest will in presence of testator.

Holographic Wills.—Document in testator's handwriting and signed by him may be admitted to probate if Supreme Court satisfied document intended to constitute will and testamentary intentions.

Nuncupative Will.—Soldier in actual military service, or seaman or mariner at sea may dispose of personal property by nuncupative will, even though under the age of 18.

Devise to attesting witness or his or her wife or husband void, but witness may prove will.

Revocation.—Will is revoked by marriage, by another will or codicil duly executed by some writing declaring an intention to revoke the same and executed in same manner as a will or by destruction of the same by the testator or some person in his presence or direction with the intention of revoking the same.

Probate.—The executors must prove and file will in the court within 30 days after death of the testator, under heavy penalties.

Self-Proved Wills.—No statutory provision prohibiting same. Wills have been admitted to probate on strength of testators' acknowledgment and affidavit of witness which were executed prior to testator's death.

Dependants inadequately provided for can apply for an order for proper maintenance and support. Amount awarded, if any, is in discretion of court. Application must be made within six months from grant of letters probate or letters of administration. (Dependants of a Deceased Person Relief Act, Cap. D-7).

Lapse.—Where there is a devise or bequest to a child or other issue of testator and the devisee or legatee dies before the testator, leaving issue who survive the testator, such issue of the devisee or legatee take as though the devisee or legatee had survived testator and died after testator's death, unless the will shows a contrary intent.

Unclaimed Legacies.—Escheats Act, Cap. E-10 allows Crown to revest property in persons legally or morally entitled thereto where same has escheated to Crown.

Simultaneous Death.—See topic Death, subhead Survivorship.

International Wills.—Province has adopted Unidroit Convention Providing a Uniform Law on Form of an International Will in Probate Act, Cap. P-21, Part VII.

WITNESSES:

All persons are competent as witnesses. Husband and wife may give evidence for or against each other. Communications between husband and wife during marriage privileged.

See also topic Depositions.

WORKMEN'S COMPENSATION LAW:

See topic Labour Relations.

See note at head of Digest as to 1996 legislation covered.

See Topical Index in front part of this volume.

QUEBEC LAW DIGEST REVISER

McMaster Meighen
1000 de La Gauchetière Street West
Suite 900
Montréal, Québec H3B 4W5
Telephone: 514-879-1212
Fax: 514-878-0605
Email: message@mcmastermeighen.com

Reviser Profile

History: McMaster Meighen was founded in Montreal in the year 1823 by the Honourable William Badgley, Q.C. and included among its early partners Sir John J.C. Abbott, the third Prime Minister of Canada. With a view to offering its clients a national service the firm formed an affiliation in late 1990 with Fraser & Beatty. As a result, the firm's clients have access to legal services in Montreal, Toronto, New York, Ottawa and Vancouver.

The history of McMaster Meighen is interwoven with the economic and industrial development of Canada. Members of the firm acted as solicitors during the formation of the Canadian railway system and played a vital part in the founding and growth of several of Canada's major companies involved in transportation, finance and trade, as well as its oldest banking institution, today a major Canadian chartered bank.

Areas of Practice: The firm provides services in both the English and French language and is comprised of lawyers versed in common and civil law. McMaster Meighen presently carries on a broadly-based domestic and international practice and continues the tradition set by its founders of providing professional expertise to a wide range of clients. The firm's finance and admiralty practice is particularly international in scope and involves regular activities in the major business and financial centres around the world. Within Canada the firm offers specialized services in the fields of admiralty, banking, corporate, commercial, computer technology, insurance, finance, securities, tax, estates and trusts, pensions, bankruptcy, receivership, insolvency, real estate, municipal, environmental, administrative and labour law, including litigation with respect to all of these matters.

The firm has developed well established and close informal links with other leading firms in Canada and throughout the world. In 1990, McMaster Meighen formed an affiliation with Fraser & Beatty, another of Canada's leading law firms, and is thus well equipped to advise on a wide spectrum of legal matters, both nationally and internationally.

The firm's clients rely on the support of over 60 lawyers, all of whom provide legal services in both the French and English languages with some also offering services in Spanish, Greek, Italian and German.

Client Base: The firm has a large client base made up of individuals, partnerships, associations and corporations and includes a Canadian chartered bank, a major Canadian trust company, a major public utility, domestic and international financial institutions, insurance underwriters, protection and indemnity associations, textile companies, real estate developers, food producers, transportation companies, universities, hospitals and municipalities.

Firm Activities: McMaster Meighen encourages its partners and associates to participate in professional and business associations, continuing legal education programs and community organizations. All partners and associates are members of the Canadian Bar Association, the Quebec Bar Association and/or the Ontario Bar Association with some sitting on the executive and section committees of these Associations. Certain of the partners and associates are members of the Canadian Tax Foundation, the International Bar Association, The Association of Trial Lawyers of America and Canadian Maritime Law Association.

QUEBEC LAW DIGEST

(The following is a list of all Topics, including cross-references, covered in this Digest.)

QUEBEC LAW DIGEST

Revised for 1997 edition by

McMASTER MEIGHEN, Advocates, Barristers and Solicitors of the Montreal Bar.

(C. C. indicates Civil Code of Lower Canada; C. C. Q. indicates new Civil Code of Quebec (see topic Statutes); C. P. indicates Code of Civil Procedure; R. S. Q. indicates Revised Statutes of Quebec; S. Q., followed by the year, indicates an annual statute of Quebec; R.R.Q. indicates Revised Regulations of Quebec 1981; O. C. Q., followed by the number and date, indicates an Order of the Lieutenant-Governor in Council. Citations refer to articles of the codes and to chapters and sections of statutes. See topic Statutes.)

Note: Legislature still in session at time of going to press. This revision covers Acts of 1996 adopted and approved by the Parliament of Quebec up to Chapter 38.

ABSENTEES:

Definition.—Those who, having a domicile in Quebec, have ceased to appear without advising anyone, and of whom it is unknown whether they are still alive. (C.C.Q. 84). Absentee is presumed to be alive for seven years following his disappearance, unless proof of his death is made before then. (C.C.Q. 85). See topic Death.

Care of Property.—If necessary to provide for administration of property of absentee tutor may be appointed by court on advice of tutorship council. Court fixes amounts for expenses of marriage, for maintenance of family or for payment of obligation of support. (C.C.Q. 87s.).

Succession to Property.—Spouse or tutor may, after one year of absence, apply to court for liquidation of patrimonial rights of spouses. Tutor may obtain court authorization to accept/renounce partition of acquests of spouse of absentee or otherwise decide on rights of absentee. Tutorship terminates upon return of absentee, appointment by absentee of administrator, by declaratory judgment of death or upon proof of death. Declaratory judgment may be pronounced seven years after disappearance or where death is certain when it is impossible to draw up attestation of death.

Absentee may inherit. (C.C.Q. 617).

Escheat.—See topic Descent and Distribution, subhead Irregular Successions; also topic Wills, subhead Unclaimed Legacies.

ACCORD AND SATISFACTION:

By a contract known as "Transaction," parties may terminate law suit already begun or prevent future litigation by means of concessions or reservations made by one or both of them. Transaction has, between parties, authority of final judgment but except for error of law, it may be annulled for same causes as contracts generally. Transaction is not subject to compulsory execution until it is homologated. (C.C.Q. 2631s.).

Dation en paiement (giving in payment) is contract by which debtor transfers ownership of property to his creditor who is willing to take it in place and payment of sum of money or some other property due to him. (C.C.Q. 1799). It is subject to rules pertaining to contracts of sale and makes party giving it liable to same warranties as seller. (C.C.Q. 1800).

ACKNOWLEDGMENTS:

Instruments not executed in authentic form (i.e., before notary of Province) are normally proved by affidavits of subscribing witnesses. Courts of Justice Act (R. S. Q. c. T-16) states that such affidavits may be taken by following officers:

Within the Province.—Persons appointed by Minister of Justice as Commissioners for Oaths for a particular district; prothonotaries or clerks of a court of justice or their deputies; mayors, councillors and clerks or secretary-treasurers of every municipality; pastors or ministers of religion authorized to solemnize marriages in any territory not erected into municipality; practising advocates and notaries; and justices of peace.

Without the Province.—Persons appointed by Minister of Justice as Commissioners for Oaths for Province of Quebec; before head of post, delegate or delegate general of Quebec; notaries public under their hand and official seal; mayors or chief magistrates of any city, town or borough under seal of such city, town or borough; judges of superior court in any province of Canada, or in any other British territory; any consul, vice-consul, temporary consul, pro-consul or consular agent of Canada or of Her Majesty.

Commissioner for Oaths.—Commissioners for Oaths for particular judicial district or for Province of Quebec are appointed for term of three years. Commissions may be renewed. Persons administering oaths in capacities similar to Commissioners for Oaths retain their powers while holding their office or while practising their profession, as case may be. (O.C.Q. 493-82, 1982).

Married Women.—There are no special requirements concerning acknowledgments by married women.

Effect.—Instrument acknowledged or proved according to law may be read in evidence and used in any court of province. See topics Deeds; Records.

Alternative to Acknowledgment or Proof.—No statutory provision.

Authentication.—See topic Notaries.

Fees.—Customary fee for certificate of Chambres des notaires authenticating signature of notary of province, $10.

Forms.—None prescribed. The following may be used:

Forms

Individual:

I, ..., residing at No. . . . . Street, in the City of . . . . . ., in the State of . . . . . ., do solemnly declare; I was present and did see . . . . . . of . . . . . . to me personally known to be the person described in and who executed the within (deed, power of attorney, etc.), sign and execute the same. The signature . . . . . . is in the handwriting of the said . . . . . . and was subscribed to the within . . . . in my presence and in that of the other subscribing witness.

And I have signed . . . .

Solemnly declared before me at . . . . . . this . . . . . . day of . . . . . . 19 . . . . .

(Signature and title of officer administering oath).

Corporation:

I, ... of . . . . . . do solemnly declare I was present, and did see . . . . . . of . . . . . . the president, and . . . . . . of . . . . . . the secretary of (name of corporation), to me personally known to be the persons described in and who executed the within (deed, power of attorney, etc.) on behalf of the said company, sign and execute the same and affix thereto the seal of the company. The signatures . . . . . . and . . . . . . are in the handwriting of the said . . . . . . and . . . . . . respectively, and were subscribed to and the seal of the said company was affixed to the within . . . . . . in my presence and in that of the other subscribing witness.

And I have signed . . . .

Solemnly declared before me at . . . . . . this . . . . . . day of . . . . . . 19 . . . . .

(Signature and title of officer administering oath).

ACTIONS:

There has never been any distinction between law and equity in Quebec; civil action is purely and simply judicial prosecution of legal civil right.

Commencement.—Except in certain specified cases, action is instituted by means of writ of summons in name of Sovereign, prepared by plaintiff or his attorney, endorsed by clerk upon payment of judicial stamps. Causes of demand must be stated in writ or in a declaration annexed thereto. Ordinarily, defendant has ten days from date of service to appear. (C. P. 110s.). Certain actions against cities or municipalities are subject to prior notice being given before instituting action.

Parties.—Any inhabitant of Quebec may be sued in its courts for fulfillment of obligations contracted by him at home or abroad. (C.C.Q. 3134). Subject to ordinary rules of jurisdiction (C. P. 68s.), aliens, although not resident in Quebec, may be sued in its courts for fulfillment of obligations contracted by them even in foreign countries. Correlative right of appearing as plaintiffs is conferred upon nonresidents by C. P. 57, 58.

Whoever brings an action at law, whether for enforcement of right which is not recognized or is jeopardized or denied, or otherwise to obtain judgment upon existence of a legal situation must have sufficient interest therein and free exercise of his rights. Person who has not free exercise of his rights must be represented in manner provided by laws which govern his status and capacity or by Code of Civil Procedure. Irregularity resulting from failure to be so represented can be remedied retroactively at any stage of case even in appeal. (C. P. 55s.).

Class Actions.—When several persons have a common interest in a dispute, any one of them may appear in judicial proceedings on behalf of them all, if he holds their mandate. (C. P. 59). Any group of persons associated for pursuit of a common purpose which does not possess a civil personality and is not a partnership within meaning of civil code may defend an action at law taken against it and may also, if it is an association of employees within meaning of labor code, institute legal proceedings. (C. P. 60).

By Act respecting Class Action (1978 S.Q., c. 8) Code of Civil Procedure amended by adding Book Nine (arts. 999 to 1051). Class action may be brought in any matter which is not small claim and Superior Court has exclusive jurisdiction. Bringing of class action requires authorization of court obtained on motion. Applicant must, inter alia, establish that persons on whose account he acts have in common identical, similar or related questions of law or fact to bring and court must ascertain that person to whom it ascribes status of representative is in position to represent members of group adequately. Judgment on motion describes members of group, identifies questions to be dealt with collectively. Notice to members published and delay provided for members to advise they wish to be excluded from group. Action must be brought within three months of authorization. Decision binding on members of group who did not give notice of exclusion. Pleno jure appeal lies to Court of Appeal.

Act also creates "Fonds d'aide aux recours collectifs" fund to ensure financing of class actions. Contains rules for granting of assistance, rights and obligations of fund and recipients, right of appeal from refusal to grant assistance to Court of Quebec.

Intervention.—There are two types of intervention, voluntary and forced.

Voluntary intervention occurs when any person interested in action between other parties or whose presence is necessary to represent incapable party, may intervene therein at any time before judgment, by means of declaration served on all parties. Voluntary intervention is termed aggressive when third party asks for acknowledgment of right against other parties; it is termed conservatory when third party wishes to represent or to assist one of parties in his action. (C.P. 208s).

Forced intervention occurs when party in case impleads third party whose presence is necessary to permit complete solution of action, or against whom he claims to exercise recourse in warranty. This intervention is effected by service of writ of summons on third party and other party within five days of judgment authorizing it, together with declaration annexed thereto setting forth grounds for intervention and copy of principal demand. (C. P. 216s).

See note at head of Digest as to 1996 legislation covered.

See Topical Index in front part of this volume.

ACTIONS . . . *continued*

Joinder of Causes of Action.—Several causes of action may be joined in same suit, provided they are not incompatible or contradictory, that they seek condemnations of like nature, that their joinder is not prohibited by some express provision, and that they are susceptible of same mode of trial. (C.P. 66).

Two or more persons whose claims have same juridical basis or raise same points of law and facts may also join in same suit. (C. P. 67).

Splitting Causes of Action.—See subhead Joinder of Causes of Action, supra.

Consolidation of Actions.—Two or more actions between same parties, in which questions at issue are substantially same, or for matters which might properly be combined in one action, may be consolidated by order of judge upon such terms as are deemed proper. (C. P. 270). Court may also order several actions between different parties to be tried at same time and decided on same evidence, or evidence in one action to be used as evidence in another. (C. P. 271).

Stay of Proceedings.—Defendant may stay suit by dilatory exception on various grounds, e.g., when he wishes to implead third party against whom he claims to have recourse in warranty or when writ or declaration is affected by irregularity prejudicial to his interest. (C. P. 168). Nonresident plaintiff must give security for costs of his suit if required to do so by defendant. (C. P. 65). Defendant may, within five days of his appearance, apply to judge or prothonotary to delay contestation of action until security for costs has been given. (C. P. 152).

Abatement.—Where case is not ready for judgment, trial not having been completed, all proceedings had subsequently to notice given of death or change of status or cessation of functions of parties are null; and suit is suspended until its continuance by those interested, or until latter have been called in to continue. But where case is ready for judgment, it cannot be retarded. (C. P. 254s).

Revival.—Continuance of suit is effected by serving on all parties an appearance and an affidavit containing reasons therefor. Right to continue suit may be contested within delay of ten days from date of appearance. (C. P. 258).

Termination.—Actions may terminate by discontinuance by plaintiff at any time before judgment (C. P. 262) or by acquiescence in demand by defendant (C. P. 457); by peremption, when no proceeding has been had during one year (C. P. 265); by transaction (C.C.Q. 2631); and, of course, by final judgment.

Limitation of.—See topic Limitation of Actions.

Small Claims.—See topic Courts, subhead Court of Quebec, catchline Small Claims.

Direct Actions Against Insurer.—See topic Motor Vehicles, subhead Direct Actions Against Insurer.

See topic Language.

ADMINISTRATION OF PROPERTY OF OTHERS:

Any person charged with administration of property or patrimony that is not his own assumes office of administrator of property of others. Rules governing administrators of property of others apply to every administration unless another form of administration applies under law, constituting act, or due to circumstances. (C.C.Q. 1299). Curators, tutors, trustees and liquidators are all administrators of property of others. Administrator entitled to remuneration unless administration gratuitous. (C.C.Q. 1300). Administrative expenses are borne by beneficiary or trust patrimony. (C.C.Q. 1367).

Types of Administration.—Administration is either simple or full. Simple administrators are required to maintain and preserve property for use for which it was ordinarily destined. (C.C.Q. 1301). Full administrators are expected to preserve property and make it productive, increase patrimony or appropriate it to purpose in interest of beneficiary or of trust. (C.C.Q. 1306). Tutors to persons of full age and liquidators have simple administration of property of others. (C.C.Q. 208, 802). Curators to persons of full age and trustees have full administration of property of others, except Public Curator, who has simple administration. (C.C.Q. 282, 1278, 262).

Administrator charged with simple administration is bound to collect fruits and revenues and pay debts of property under his administration and exercise rights pertaining to property, such as voting, conservation or redemption rights attached to securities. He must continue use or operation of property which produces fruits and revenues without changing its destination, unless he is authorized to make change by beneficiary or by court. He must invest sums of money under his administration in accordance with rules governing presumed sound investments. See subhead Investments, infra. He may also change any investment made before he took office or that he has made himself. With authorization of beneficiary or of court, simple administrator may alienate or mortgage property if necessary to pay debts, maintain use for which property is ordinarily destined, or preserve its value. He may alienate without authorization any property that is perishable or likely to depreciate rapidly. (C.C.Q. 1301s.).

Administrator charged with full administration may alienate property, charge it with real right or change its destination in order to perform his obligations. He may perform any other necessary or useful act, including any form of investment. (C.C.Q. 1307). Curators, however, must make presumed sound investments. (C.C.Q. 282). In full administration, there is implicit recognition of even-hand rule. (C.C.Q. 1317, 1340).

Rules of Administration.—Administrator must comply with obligations imposed by law and by constituting act, and must act within powers conferred on him. He is not liable for loss of property resulting from superior force or from its age, perishable nature or normal and authorized use. He must act prudently, diligently, honestly and faithfully, in best interests of beneficiary or of object pursued. He cannot act in his own interests or place himself in conflict of interest. If administrator is beneficiary, he must exercise his powers in common interest. He must declare any potential conflict of interest he has in enterprise without delay. During his administration no administrator may become party to contract affecting administered property or acquire other than by succession any right in property or against beneficiary, unless authorized to do so by beneficiary or court. Administrator must not mingle administered property with his own property. He cannot use for his benefit property he administers or information obtained by reason of his administration without authorization from beneficiary, from law or from constituting act. He may not dispose of administered property gratuitously, unless it is in very nature of his administration to do so, except for property of little value disposed of in interest of beneficiary or of object pursued. No administrator may, except for value, renounce any right belonging to beneficiary or forming part of patrimony administered. (C.C.Q. 1308s.).

Accounts.—Administrator must establish revenue and capital accounts. Revenue account generally debited for insurance premiums, cost of minor repairs and other administrative expenses, half of remuneration of administrator and his reasonable expenses, taxes payable on administered property, cost paid to safeguard rights of beneficiary of fruits and revenues and half costs of judicial rendering of account, amortization of property, except property used by beneficiary for personal purposes. (C.C.Q. 1346).

Capital account generally debited for expenditures not debited from revenues, including expenses pertaining to capital investment, alienation of property and safeguard of rights of capital beneficiary or right of ownership. (C.C.Q. 1347). Taxes on gains and amounts attributable to capital are generally debited from capital account. (C.C.Q. 1347[2]).

Summary account is prepared and given to beneficiary at least once a year. (C.C.Q. 1351). This annual account must be sufficiently detailed to allow verification. (C.C.Q. 1352). Administrator must allow beneficiary to examine books at all times. (C.C.Q. 1354).

Beneficiary of fruits and revenues entitled to net income of administered property from date determined in act giving rise to administration or from beginning of administration or death which gave rise to it. (C.C.Q. 1348). Fruits and revenues payable periodically are counted day by day. (C.C.Q. 1349).

At end of administration, final account must be rendered. See subhead End of Administration, infra.

Inventory.—Administrator not bound to make inventory unless so required by law, by act, or by court order. Administrator who is bound to make inventory must enumerate all administered property. Inventory includes: description and value of immovables and movables, description of currency and other securities, listing of valuable documents, statement of liabilities, and recapitulation of assets and liabilities. Where inventory contains personal effects of holder or deceased, general description of items over $100 each is sufficient. (C.C.Q. 1324s.).

Inventory made by notarial act en minute, or by private writing before two witnesses. (C.C.Q. 1327). Administrator must furnish copy of inventory to person who entrusted him with administration and all other known interested persons. Where required by law, he must publish inventory in Register of personal and real rights and in newspaper. See topic Executors and Administrators of Estates, subhead Inventory. Any interested person may contest inventory. (C.C.Q. 1330).

Investments.—Presumed sound investments include: (a) Immovable property; (b) bonds or other evidence of indebtedness issued by prescribed governments or corporations; (c) debts of company secured by first-ranking hypothec on immovable property, approved securities or equipment; (d) debts secured by hypothec on immovable in Quebec, if payment guaranteed by prescribed governments, if amount of debt not more than 75% of value of immovable; (e) fully paid preferred shares issued by company whose common shares are presumed sound investments or which, during last five financial years, has distributed stipulated dividend on all its preferred shares; (f) common shares issued by company that for three years has been meeting timely disclosure requirements deemed in Quebec Securities Act; (g) shares of mutual fund and units of unincorporated mutual fund or of private trust, provided that 60% of its portfolio consists of presumed sound investments and fund complies with Quebec Securities Act. (C.C.Q. 1339).

Administrator decides on investments, working toward diversified portfolio producing both fixed income and variable revenues. He may not acquire more than 5% of shares of same company nor acquire shares, bonds or other evidences of indebtedness of legal person or limited partnership which has failed to pay prescribed dividends on its shares or interest on its bonds or other securities, nor grant loan to that legal person or partnership. Administrator may deposit sums of money with bank, savings or credit union or other financial institution, if deposit is repayable on demand or 30 days' notice, or for longer term if repayment is fully guaranteed by Régie de l'assurance-dépôts du Québec or if he receives court authorization. (C.C.Q. 1340, 1341).

Liability.—Administrator may sue and be sued in respect of anything connected with his administration. He may also intervene in any action respecting administered property. (C.C.Q. 1316). Joint administrators are solidarily liable, unless duties have been divided by law, act or court order. (C.C.Q. 1334).

Where administrator binds himself, within limits of his own powers, in name of beneficiary or trust patrimony, he is not personally liable towards third persons with whom he contracts. He is liable to them if he binds himself in his own name, subject to any rights they have against beneficiary or trust patrimony. Where administrator exceeds his powers, he is liable towards third persons with whom he contracts unless these persons were sufficiently aware of fact or unless beneficiary tacitly or expressly ratified obligations contracted. (C.C.Q. 1319, 1320). Administrator who exercises alone powers that he is required to exercise jointly with another person exceeds his powers. He does not exceed them if he exercises them more advantageously than required. (C.C.Q. 1321).

Beneficiary or trust patrimony is liable for damage caused by fault of administrator to extent of any benefit he derived from act. (C.C.Q. 1322). Where person fully capable of exercising his civil rights has given reason to believe that another person was administrator of property, he is liable towards third persons who in good faith have contracted with that other person, as though property had been under his administration. (C.C.Q. 1323).

Administrator acting in accordance with provisions relating to sound investments is presumed to act prudently. Administrator who makes unauthorized investment is, by that very fact and without further proof, liable for loss resulting from it. (C.C.Q. 1343). See subhead Investments, supra.

Administrator not bound to take out insurance or furnish other security unless so required by law, act or court order. (C.C.Q. 1324). He may insure property entrusted to him against ordinary risks at expense of beneficiary or trust. He may also take out

---

See note at head of Digest as to 1996 legislation covered.

See Topical Index in front part of this volume.

ADMINISTRATION OF PROPERTY OF OTHERS . . . *continued*

insurance guaranteeing performance of his obligations. If administration is gratuitous, such insurance is at expense of beneficiary or trust. (C.C.Q. 1331).

Administrator may delegate duties only for specific acts, not for general administration. He is accountable to person selected by him if, among other things, he was not authorized to make selection. If he was so authorized, he is accountable only for care with which he selected person and gave him instructions. (C.C.Q. 1337).

Obligations contracted by administrator unaware that his administration has terminated are valid and bind beneficiary or trust, as do obligations contracted with third persons who were unaware that administration had terminated. (C.C.Q. 1362).

End of Administration.—Duties of administrator terminate upon his death, resignation, replacement, bankruptcy or placement under protective supervision. Administration also terminated by extinction of right of beneficiary in administered property, by expiry or fulfilment of stipulated term or condition, or by achievement of object of administration or disappearance of its cause. Administrator may resign upon written notice to beneficiary, any co-administrators, any supervisory person or body designated by law or failing these, Public Curator. Beneficiary who has entrusted administration of his property to another may replace his administrator, particularly by exercising right that property be returned to him on demand. Any interested person may apply to replace administrator who fails to fulfil his obligations. (C.C.Q. 1355s.). Resignation or replacement binds beneficiary or trust to pay administrator his expenses and any remuneration he has earned. (C.C.Q. 1367).

Final account must be rendered in sufficient detail to allow verification. (C.C.Q. 1363). Administrator owes interest on balance of property administered from closing of final account or from formal notice to produce it. (C.C.Q. 1368). Administrator must deliver over administered property, and all that he has received in performance of his duties. Administrative expenses, including those related to account and delivery of property, are borne by beneficiary or trust patrimony. (C.C.Q. 1365, 1367). Where there are several beneficiaries, their obligation toward administrator is solidary. (C.C.Q. 1370).

ADOPTION:

Adopters.—Any person of full age may adopt child alone or jointly with another. (C.C.Q. 546). Adopter must be at least 18 years older than adoptee unless adoptee is child of spouse of adopter or unless court dispenses with this requirement. (C.C.Q. 547).

Adoptees.—Person of full age may be adopted only by person who had adopted him in loco parentis when minor unless court dispenses with this requirement. (C.C.Q. 545). No minor child may be adopted without consent of father and mother or tutor unless judicially declared eligible. (C.C.Q. 544). Following may be judicially declared eligible: (1) Child over three months if no paternal or maternal filiation established; (2) child whose care, maintenance or education not taken in hand by mother, father or tutor for at least six months; (3) child whose parents have been deprived of parental authority if child has no tutor; (4) child who has no parents or tutor. Motion for eligibility may only be made by ascendant of child, collateral relative to third degree, spouse of such ascendant or relative, child himself if 14 years, or director of youth protection. (C.C.Q. 559-560).

Consent Required.—Consent of adoptee if ten years of age or older is required unless impossible to express will; if adoptee under 14 years of age refuses to give consent court may defer adoption or grant adoption notwithstanding refusal (C.C.Q. 549); refusal to consent by child of 14 is bar to adoption (C.C.Q. 550). Adoption must take place with consent of any parents unless deprived of parental authority or unless his filiation with child is not established, or any tutor of child if there be one. Consent may be withdrawn within 30 days from its date. (C.C.Q. 557). Consents must be in writing before two witnesses. (C.C.Q. 548). In case of adoption of child domiciled outside Quebec, rules respecting consent to adoption and eligibility for adoption are those provided by law of his domicile. Effects of adoption are subject to law of domicile of adopter. (C.C.Q. 3092).

Conditions Precedent.—No placement for adoption without court order and not until 30 days after consent to adoption. Unless court decides otherwise, no adoption granted unless child has lived with adopter for six months before adoption order granted. (C.C.Q. 566s.).

Jurisdiction.—Court of Quebec, Youth Division. (C.P. 36.1).

Venue.—District of domicile of child or plaintiff or, if child has no domicile in Quebec or if adopters consent, district where director of youth protection last to have charge of adoptee exercises his functions. (C.P. 70).

Effects of Adoption.—From judgment granting adoption: (a) Court assigns adoptee given names and surname chosen by adopter unless adoptee or adopter request keeping original names (C.C.Q. 576); (b) adoption confers on adoptee filiation which replaces his original filiation and creates same rights and obligations as filiation by blood; (c) effects of preceding filiation cease except regarding parent if adoption by spouse of such parent; (d) tutor loses rights and duties except to render account (C.C.Q. 577s.). Judicial and administrative files of adoption confidential. Adoptee of full age may have access to find his parents if they previously consented thereto, similarly for parents if adoptee consented once of full age. (C.C.Q. 582, 583).

Application.—Application for placement presented by adopter and, unless case of special consent, by director of youth protection. If child not domiciled in Quebec, application by adopter and person or agency legally qualified to act as intermediary in adoption. If child ten years or older, must receive notice of application. If mother, father or tutor gave consent to adoption during year preceding adoption, must receive notice from director of youth protection. Joint application if proposed adoption by two persons. (C.P. 825s; Youth Protection Act, R.S.Q. c. P-34.1, §§72.2, 72.3).

Decree.—Clerk of Court that has rendered judgment of adoption gives notice of judgment to Registrar of civil status. (C.C.Q. 129).

Setting Aside Adoption.—Appeal to Court of Appeal from any judgment or order rendered in matter of adoption and, with leave, from interlocutory judgment of Youth Court in matter of adoption. (C.P. 25s).

ADVANCEMENTS:

See topic Descent and Distribution, subhead Advancements.

ADVERSE POSSESSION: called acquisitive prescription in Quebec.

Both movables and immovables may be subject to adverse possession, called acquisitive prescription in Quebec.

Character of Possession.—Possession is exercise of real right by person having detention of property with intention of acting as holder of that right. (C.C.Q. 921). Possession must be peaceful, continuous, public and unequivocal. (C.C.Q. 922). Person who detains on behalf of another or with acknowledgment of superior domain over property, as does, for example, lessee, is presumed to continue to detain it in that quality unless nature of his possession is formally changed on basis of unequivocal facts. (C.C.Q. 923, 2914) Possessor is presumed to hold real right he is exercising. Person contesting that presumption has burden of proving his own right and, as case may be, that possessor has no title, defective title, or defective possession. (C.C.Q. 928).

Duration of Possession.—Possession vests possessor with real right he is exercising if he complies with rules on prescription. (C.C.Q. 930).

Possessor in good faith of movable property acquires ownership in three years, running from dispossession of owner. Until expiry of that period, owner may revendicate movable property, unless it has been acquired under judicial authority. (C.C.Q. 2919).

Person who has for ten years possessed, as owner, immovable that is not registered in land register may acquire ownership of it only upon judicial demand. Possessor may, under same conditions, exercise same right in respect of registered immovable where owner of immovable is not identified in land register; where owner is dead or absentee at beginning of ten-year period or where land register indicates that immovable has become thing without owner. (C.C.Q. 2918).

Easements.—Rights of servitude (easements) cannot be established by possession alone but are extinguished by nonuse during ten years. (C.C.Q. 1181, 1191).

Disabilities.—For above purposes prescription does not run against unborn persons or minors. (C.C.Q. 2905). Spouses cannot prescribe against each other during cohabitation. (C.C.Q. 2906).

Things Imprescriptible.—Generally, property of State cannot be appropriated by prescription. (C.C.Q. 916).

AFFIDAVITS:

Before Whom Taken.—Affidavit taken outside Province of Quebec must be made before an agent-general or delegate-general of Quebec; before notary public under his hand and official seal; before mayor or chief magistrate of any city, town or borough under seal of such city, town or borough; before judge of a superior court in any province of Canada, or in any other British territory; before any consul, vice-consul, temporary consul, pro-consul or consular agent of Canada or of Her Majesty; or before Commissioner for Oaths authorized to receive oaths for use in Courts of Quebec. (R. S. Q. c. T-16).

Affidavit intended for use in Quebec made before notary public in U.S. must have attached to it a certificate of clerk of court of district to effect that notary public is, in fact, a notary public for district in question, duly commissioned and authorized to take affidavits. (C.C.Q. 3109).

Form.—There is no prescribed form required for affidavit, but it should be divided into paragraphs, numbered consecutively, and so far as possible only one principal statement should be contained in each paragraph. Name, occupation, and exact address of deponent should be mentioned. Date when and place where it was sworn must be inserted in jurat. (C. P. 91). Following form may be used:

Form

—I, William Penn, engineer, residing at No. . . . . street, in the . . . . city of Philadelphia, in the State of Pennsylvania, one of the United States of America, being duly sworn do depose and say:

1. (Here set forth the facts as clearly as possible).

And I have signed. . . . .

Sworn to before me at Philadelphia, this . . . . . . day of . . . . . ., A. D. 19. . .

. . . .

Alternative to Affidavit.—Person who objects to taking oath because to do so would be contrary to his religious beliefs may make solemn affirmation. (C. P. 299). See topic Acknowledgments.

AGENCY: See topic Principal and Agent.

AIRCRAFT:

See Canada Law Digest, topic Aircraft.

ALIENS:

See topic Immigration and see Canada Law Digest.

Aliens may acquire and transmit by gratuitous or onerous title as well as by succession or by will any property in the Province and may sue and be sued in courts of Province. (C.C.Q. 3134).

See also topic Real Property, subhead Land Transfers to Nonresidents.

ALIMONY: See topic Divorce.

ALLOWANCES:

See topic Executors and Administrators.

APPEAL AND ERROR:

Appeals Proper.—Appeal lies to Court of Appeal from: (1) Any final judgment of Superior Court or Court of Quebec in which value of object in dispute is at least $20,000; (2) any final judgment of Court of Quebec where that Court has exclusive jurisdiction under any Act other than Code of Procedure; (3) judgment or order on noncontentious matters; (4) with leave of judge of Court of Appeal, from final judgment of Superior Court or Court of Quebec when matter at issue is one which should be submitted to Court of Appeal; (5) any final judgment rendered in matters of contempt of court when no other recourse exists; (6) any judgment or order rendered in matter of adoption (C.P. 26). With leave of Court of Appeal or that of Supreme Court of Canada, judgments of Court of Appeal can be carried to Supreme Court of Canada. Procedure in such final appeal governed by federal statutes and regulations. (C. P. 24). See Canada Law Digest.

Security on Appeal.—No security for appeal is generally required. However, judge of Court of Appeal may, upon motion, when appeal appears dilatory, or for some other special reason, order appellant to furnish security for costs of appeal and amount of condemnation, within fixed delay and under penalty of dismissal of appeal. (C. P. 497).

Remedies Against Judgments of All Courts.—Besides appeals proper, two following remedies may be available:

1. *Revocation of Judgment.*—If party was prevented from filing his defence by surprise, fraud, or any other reason considered sufficient, and was condemned by default to appear or plead, or when no other useful recourse is available against judgment in seven special cases, he may request that judgment be revoked. Revocation of judgment is sought by motion stating both grounds for revocation and defence to action. Motion must be served upon all parties concerned and filed within 15 days from day when remedy became available. Nevertheless, if not more than six months have elapsed since judgment, court may upon motion, relieve party from consequences of his default. (C. P. 482s).

2. *Opposition by Third Persons.*—Every person whose interests are affected by judgment rendered in suit in which neither he nor his representatives were summoned, may, by motion, demand that it be revoked insofar as it prejudices his rights. (C. P. 489).

Remedies Against Proceedings and Judgments of Inferior Courts.—See topic Certiorari, subhead Evocation.

ARBITRATION AND AWARD:

C.P. 940-952 apply to all arbitrations where parties have not made stipulations to contrary, except for articles which are peremptory.

Where action brought on dispute in matter where parties have arbitration agreement, court must refer them to arbitration on application of either of them unless case inscribed on roll or it finds agreement null. (C.P. 940.1). Judge or court may grant provisional measures before or during arbitration proceedings on motion of one of parties. (C.P. 940.4).

Each party appoints arbitrator, these appoint third. (C.P. 941). Order of arbitration proceedings in C.P. 944-944.11. Arbitrators determine procedure. Party intending to submit to arbitration must notify other party of his intention specifying matter in dispute. Witnesses summoned in accordance with C.P. 280-283. Arbitrators administer oaths, receive solemn affirmations.

Award must be made by majority of arbitrators. (C.P. 945.2). Copies of award remitted to each party. Execution of award against condemned party made under authority of competent court upon motion for homologation. (C.P. 946-946.6).

Generally, court cannot refuse homologation except on proof that: One of parties not qualified to enter arbitration agreement; arbitration agreement invalid under law elected by parties or under laws of Quebec; party against whom award invoked not given proper notice of appointment of arbitrator or arbitration proceedings or otherwise unable to present his case; award deals with dispute not contemplated by or within arbitration agreement or contains decisions on matters outside agreement; mode of appointment of arbitrators or applicable arbitration procedure not observed. (C.P. 946.4). Court cannot enquire into merits of dispute. (C.P. 946.2). Award may be annulled for reasons set out above.

Certain matters may be referred by court to arbitration by advocates or to investigation by accountants or other experts. Procedure in such cases is governed by different rules. (C. P. 382s, 414s).

Mandatory Arbitration.—See topic Labor Relations, subhead Collective Agreements.

See topic Language, subhead Labor Relations.

ASSIGNMENTS:

Principles governing sales also govern assignments. See topic Sales, subheads Sale of Incorporeals, Sale of Rights of Succession, Sale of Litigious Rights.

Instrument Transferring Title.—No particular form is required for assignment except where property is transferred by way of gift, then transfer must be by published authentic (notarial) act, except for gifts of movables accompanied by delivery and immediate possession. (C.C.Q. 1824).

Assignments for Benefit of Creditors.—See Canada Law Digest, topic Bankruptcy, subhead Acts of Bankruptcy.

Filing, Recording and Notification.—Must file and record assignments of immovables. Assignment of claim is perfected against debtors and third parties as soon as debtor has acquiesced in or received evidence of deed of assignment or upon publication of notice thereof in newspaper if debtor not found in Quebec. (C.C.Q. 1641). Same formalities apply to assignment of universality of claims which must also be registered in Register of personal and movable real rights. (C.C.Q. 1642). However, assignment of claim secured by hypothec must be published at appropriate land registry office if hypothec securing claim is immovable hypothec or in Register of personal and movable real rights if hypothec securing claim is movable hypothec. Certified statement of registration must be furnished to debtor. (C.C.Q. 3003). See topics Deeds; Motor Vehicles, subhead Title and Sales.

Effect.—Assignments have same effect as sales except if by way of security when they are called movable hypothecs on claims. See topics Sales; Mortgages of Personal Property, subhead Movable Hypothecs, catchline Hypothecs on Claims.

ASSIGNMENTS FOR BENEFIT OF CREDITORS:

See Canada Law Digest, topic Bankruptcy, subhead Acts of Bankruptcy.

ASSOCIATIONS:

Certain associations may be incorporated, notably: cooperative agricultural associations (R.S.Q. c. C-67.2); dairy associations (R.S.Q. c. S-23); musical associations, recreational, social, educational and amusement clubs (R.S.Q. c. C-23); benefit societies (R.S.Q. c. S-31). Incorporation is achieved by recording articles of association for authorized purposes, or by special act of Legislature. Number of members necessary to form association varies according to its category. After being legally formed, association has most rights and obligations of ordinary incorporated company, but will usually be exempt from taxation.

In most cases, notice of formation or dissolution of association must be given to clerk of Superior Court and recorded with registrar of district where head office of association is or ceases to be located. In number of instances notices and reports must be filed with government department regulating business or activities carried on by association.

Enterprise.—Persons carrying on organized economic activity, whether or not commercial in nature, consisting of producing, administering or alienating property, or providing service, carry on enterprise. (C.C.Q. 1525). See topic Mortgages of Personal Property, subhead Movable Hypothecs, catchline Movable Hypothecs Without Delivery.

Formation.—By written or verbal contract whereby parties agree to pursue common goal other than making of pecuniary profit. (C.C.Q. 2186, 2267). Created upon formation of contract if no other date indicated therein. (C.C.Q. 2187). No obligation of registration. (An Act respecting the legal publicity of sole proprietorships, partnerships and legal persons, S.Q. 1993 c. 48).

Contract governs object, function, management and other terms and conditions. Contract presumed to provide for admission of members other than founders. Failing special rules, directors elected from association members. (C.C.Q. 2268-2269).

Actions.—Directors are mandataries of association, and may sue or be sued to assert association's rights. (C.C.Q. 2271). Association may also sue and be sued in own name. (C.C.P. 60, 115).

Rights and Powers.—All members entitled to participate in collective decisions, which are taken by majority vote of members unless otherwise stipulated in contract. Member has right to consult all books of association. Member can withdraw or be excluded from association.

Liabilities.—Where property of association insufficient, directors and administrating members solidarily or jointly liable for debts resulting from decisions they approved, whether or not incurred by enterprise of association. Liability of non-administrating member limited to promised contributions to association. (C.C.Q. 2272-2276).

Dissolution.—When contract of association terminated, liquidator named by directors or court. After debts paid, remaining property devolves as per contractual rules; failing rules, members share equally. Notwithstanding any stipulation to contrary, any property derived from third persons devolves to association, legal person or trust sharing objectives similar to association's; if this is not possible, property goes to State. (C.C.Q. 2278, 2279).

See also topics Corporations; Language; Partnership.

ATTACHMENT:

Writ may issue before judgment upon authorization of judge, to attach property of debtor, if there is reason to fear that debt would not otherwise be recovered. (C. P. 733). Creditor may without such authorization attach movable property which he has right to revendicate in his capacity as owner, pledgee, depository, usufructuary, institute, substitute or unpaid vendor; motor vehicle which has caused him damage; movable property upon price of which he is entitled to be collocated by preference and which is being used to jeopardize his prior claim; and movable property which provision of law permits him to seize to conserve his rights. (C. P. 734). Spouse in suit in nullity of marriage, payment of compensatory allowance, separation of property or bed and board or divorce may also seize before judgment his own movables and, with leave, property of his spouse in which he would be entitled to share if matrimonial regime dissolved. (C.P. 734.0.1).

Levy in all above cases is made by bailiff. Writs are issued upon written application supported by affidavit indicating facts giving rise to seizure, and served upon defendant. If declaration is not served on defendant with writ of seizure it must be filed in court within five days from service, with copy for defendant. (C. P. 735s).

Lien.—Attachment binds on attached goods from time of levy but does not in itself constitute prior claim or lien.

ATTORNEYS AND COUNSELORS:

Under name of "Barreau du Québec," advocates, barristers, legal counsel, attorneys and solicitors of province, generally called "advocates," form professional corporation governed by provisions of its charter, rules and regulations subject to Professional Code. (R. S. Q. c. B-1).

Requirements for admission to Bar of Province of Quebec are: (a) Canadian citizen (b) age of majority; (c) degree recognized as valid by Government or considered equivalent by General Council; (d) professional training under conditions prescribed by by-law; (e) take oaths of allegiance and office prescribed by act and by-laws; (f) pay exigible contributions.

Under provisions of Professional Code, Bar must issue permit to persons who meet said requirements. Bar cannot issue permit except to persons whose knowledge of

ATTORNEYS AND COUNSELORS . . . *continued*
French is appropriate to practice of profession. Person is deemed to have appropriate knowledge if: (a) Has received at least three years secondary or post-secondary instruction in French; (b) has passed fourth or fifth year secondary level examinations in French as first language; or (c) from and after school year 1985-86, he obtains secondary school certificate in Quebec. Restrictive permit valid for maximum one year can be issued to persons from outside of Quebec who are otherwise qualified.

Requirements in Special Cases.—Special requirements affect attorneys from other provinces who seek admission to Bar as practising advocates and lesser requirements govern admission of such attorneys as solicitors who by Bar Act are precluded from exercising certain prerogatives of practising advocates. Professors in law faculties subject to special provisions concerning admission to Bar as solicitors. (R. S. Q. c. B-1).

Disabilities.—Advocates cannot be notaries, nor can they become bondsmen or other legal sureties. They cannot purchase litigious rights.

Lien.—See topic Principal and Agent, subhead Obligations of Principal.

Taxed costs in a suit or action are fixed by law.

Legal Aid.—Persons having insufficient means to obtain legal counsel or to exercise rights before the courts or other tribunals are provided with gratuitous services of advocates and notaries. (R. S. Q. c. A-14).

AUTOMOBILES: See topic Motor Vehicles.

BAIL: See topic Bonds.

BANKRUPTCY: See Canada Law Digest.

BANKS AND BANKING:

See Canada Law Digest.

BILLS AND NOTES:

See topic Consumer Protection. See also Canada Law Digest.

BILLS OF SALE: See topic Sales.

BLUE SKY LAW: See topic Securities.

BONDS:

Bail may be given by one or more solvent bondsmen in civil or criminal matters. Bondsmen must have sufficient property in Quebec to answer obligation and must be domiciled in Canada. (C.C.Q. 2337). Guarantee company approved by Lieutenant-Governor in Council may be legal surety.

The bondsmen or sureties are liable only upon the default of the debtor. (C.C.Q. 2346).

BROKERS:

Agent and Principal.—See topic Principal and Agent.

Factors.—See topic Principal and Agent.

Insurance Brokers.—See topic Insurance.

Real Estate Brokers.—No person shall act as broker or real estate agent unless he holds permit. (Real Estate Brokerage Act R.S.Q. c. C-73.1). Act governs issuing of said permits and contents of brokerage contracts.

Investment Brokers.—See topic Securities, subhead Registration of Dealers and Advisers.

BULK SALES:

See topic Fraudulent Sales and Conveyances.

CARRIERS:

Jurisdiction.—Modes of transportation extending beyond province generally fall within federal jurisdiction and are governed by federal statutes and regulations of National Transportation Agency.

In broad terms, all carriage within province, by land, water or air must conform with essential provisions of Quebec law as contained in C.C.Q. 2030-2058. Other special rules govern carriage by water (C.C.Q. 2059-2084) and number of special provincial statutes may also apply, such as Quebec Railway Act (R.S.Q. c. C-14), and Truck Transportation Act (R.S.Q. c. C-5.1) and various regulations of Commission des Transports.

Categories of Carriers.—Carriage is either gratuitous or for consideration. Gratuitous carrier is obliged to exercise due care. Other carriers are liable unless they prove "superior force", inherent defect in cargo or fault of shipper or passenger.

Carriage is either successive, effected by several carriers in succession using same means of transportation, or combined, in which several carriers use different means of transportation. (C.C.Q. 2031). Sub-carriers are deemed to be party to original contract. (C.C.Q. 2035).

Carrier is not liable for loss of documents, money or other property of great value unless he agreed to carriage after nature or value was declared. He is not liable for hand luggage or other effects remaining in passenger's possession unless fault is proven. (C.C.Q. 2038).

Carriage of cargo by water is closely linked to Hague-Visby Rules.

Liability for Delay.—Carriers are liable unless they prove "superior force". (C.C.Q. 2034).

Limitations of Liability.—Carrier may not exclude or limit liability except as authorized by law. (C.C.Q. 2034). When so entitled, limitation by truck is $4.41 per kilo. Liability of water carriers is limited in accordance with Hague-Visby Rules. Liability for personal injury may not be limited. (C.C.Q. 1474).

Lien.—Carriers may exercise possessory lien until freight and other charges are paid. Carrier who accepts shipment C.O.D. has no claim against shipper. (C.C.Q. 2057-2058). See Canada Law Digest, topic Shipping, subheads Maritime Liens; Statutory Liens; Admiralty Law.

Rights of Action.—Actions to enforce personal rights generally carry three-year time bar. (C.C.Q. 2925). Actions against water carriers, and by water carriers against shippers, are prescribed one year after delivery of cargo or date it should have been delivered. (C.C.Q. 2079). However no action is admissible against carrier unless notice in writing was given within 60 days of delivery, or if cargo was not delivered, within nine months from shipment. Law suit within those time frames satisfies notice requirement.

Motor Vehicle Carriers.—For special provisions see topic Motor Vehicles.

CERTIORARI:

There is no writ of certiorari. However, remedy known as evocation lies against proceedings and judgments of inferior courts.

Evocation.—When there is want or excess of jurisdiction, Superior Court may evoke before judgment a case pending before court subject to its superintending and reforming power, or revise judgment already rendered. Similarly, evocation lies if judgment of court seized with proceeding is not susceptible of appeal and when enactment upon which proceedings have been based or judgment rendered is null or of no effect, or when proceedings are affected by some gross irregularity and there is reason to believe that justice has not or will not be done, or when there has been a violation of law or abuse of authority amounting to fraud and of such a nature as to cause flagrant injustice. (C. P. 846s). See topic Appeal and Error, subhead Remedies Against Judgments of All Courts.

CHARITABLE IMMUNITY:

See topic Damages.

CHATTEL MORTGAGES:

See topic Mortgages of Personal Property.

CLAIMS:

See topics Executors and Administrators; Pleading.

COLLATERAL SECURITY: See topic Pledges.

COLLECTION AGENCIES:

See topic Principal and Agent.

COMMERCIAL CODE:

Uniform Commercial Code not applicable.

COMMISSIONS TO TAKE TESTIMONY:

See topic Depositions, subhead Rogatory Commission.

COMMUNITY PROPERTY:

See topic Husband and Wife.

CONDITIONAL SALES: See topic Sales.

CONSIGNMENTS: See topic Principal and Agent.

CONSUMER PROTECTION:

Governed by C.C.Q. 1384, 1435-1437 and by Consumer Protection Act (R.S.Q. c. P-40.1). Latter governs contracts for goods and services between consumer and merchant in course of business including contracts of credit as well as certain particular contracts and business practices. Consumer defined as natural person, except merchant who obtains goods and services for purposes of business. Stipulation whereby merchant liberated from consequences of own acts or acts of representative prohibited.

Contracts.—No offer, promise or agreement prior to contract binding on consumer unless confirmed in contract in accordance with Act. Contract must be legibly drawn in duplicate. Must be in French unless parties expressly agree otherwise. Merchant must sign copy of contract and give sufficient delay to consumer to examine it. Complete upon signature of both parties. Merchant bound by signature of his representative. Consumer bound upon receipt of signed duplicate of contract. See also topic Contracts.

Unconscionable Transactions.—Consumer may demand nullity of contract or reduction of obligations where disproportion between respective obligations of parties is so great as to amount to exploitation of consumer or where obligation of consumer is excessive, harsh or unconscionable.

Warranty.—Merchant must warrant that goods sold are unencumbered, fit for intended purpose, durable for reasonable period; must also warrant against latent defects. Form of warranty prescribed. Merchant bound by warranty as advertised. Goods and services must conform to advertised description, merchant bound by description. Warranty transferable to subsequent purchaser.

Contracts of additional warranty offered by third parties also regulated.

Recourse against merchant or manufacturer for latent defects and against manufacturer, wholesaler, retailer, distributor or supplier, by consumer or third parties, for safety defects. (C.C.Q. 1468).

Itinerant merchant is one who personally or by representative, elsewhere than at his address, solicits particular consumer for purpose of making contract or makes contract with consumer. Contract must be in writing and duplicate furnished consumer. Consumer may cancel contract within ten days of receipt of duplicate.

CONSUMER PROTECTION . . . *continued*

Contracts of credit include contracts for loan of money, contracts extending variable credit, instalment sales and other contracts involving credit. Contracts of credit, except for loan of money, payable on demand must be evidenced in writing. Act contains provisions with respect to writing and statements to be furnished to consumer, method of computing credit rate. Contracts for loan of money and contracts involving credit may be cancelled by consumer within two days of receipt of duplicate contract.

No merchant may refuse to enter into contract with consumer on pretext that latter refuses to subscribe, through him, to insurance policy.

Contract extending variable credit is contract by which credit is extended in advance by merchant to consumer who may avail himself of it, in whole or in part, from time to time, in accordance with terms and conditions of contract, and includes what are commonly called credit cards, credit accounts, budget accounts, revolving credit accounts, marginal credit and credit openings.

Provision in contract which requires consumer in default to pay all or part of balance of his debt before maturity is clause for forfeiture of benefit of term. Clause takes effect only after 30 days from receipt of written notice and statement of account from merchant. After 30 days balance becomes payable unless upon motion by consumer court changes terms and conditions of payment or authorizes consumer to return goods to merchant and thus extinguish obligation.

Merchant required to place in trust account moneys received pending his performance of contract. Consumer Protection Office may make exemptions from trust account requirement.

Merchant outside province soliciting Quebec consumers prohibited from asking consumer to send money before merchant performs its obligation. Exemption may be obtained on posting security and compliance with certain requirements.

Particular Contracts.—Particular contracts governed by Act include contracts for long-term lease of goods, sale, repair and long-term lease of used automobiles and motorcycles, for repair of household appliances and for lease of service involving sequential performance. These latter defined as contracts object of which is to obtain instructions, training or assistance for purpose of developing, maintaining or improving health, appearance, skills, qualities, knowledge or intellectual, physical or moral faculties of person or to assist person in establishing, maintaining or developing personal or social relations. Special provisions govern contracts entered into with physical fitness studios.

Prohibited business practices include various forms of false advertising and misrepresentation of goods and services, pyramid sales, alteration of automobile odometer, use of commercial advertising directed at persons under 13 years of age. Unless exempt by regulation, sales prices must be clearly and legibly marked on goods or wrappings.

Advertising regarding terms and conditions of credit or of long-term lease of goods prohibited unless information prescribed by Act and regulations is disclosed.

Permits must be held by itinerant merchants, merchants making contracts for loan of money or operating physical fitness studio or offering or making contracts of additional warranty. Application for permit made in form and with accompanying documents prescribed by regulations. Permits are valid for two years.

Office de la Protection du Consommateur set up to supervise application of Act, receive consumer complaints, educate public, evaluate goods and services.

Plain Language.—No statute in force.

Personal Information.—An Act respecting the protection of personal information in the private sector (S.Q. 1993 c. 17) governs collection and communication of personal information, and provides for confidentiality of information acquired through operation of enterprise. Consumers must be given valid opportunity to refuse that personal information be used or conveyed to third parties for purposes of commercial or philanthropic prospection, such as compilation of mailing list. See topics Associations, subhead Enterprise and Human Rights, subhead Reputation and Privacy.

CONTRACTS:

General.—Contracts generally regulated by C.C.Q. which states that parties must act in good faith when obligation is created, performed and extinguished. Consent alone of parties constitutes contract. Contracts pre-determined by one party, contracts containing printed standard clauses, and printed order forms, invoices and receipts must be drawn up in French; however customer or person acceding to contract may require it in English. Subject to certain exceptions contracts formed in Quebec by public administration and related sub-contracts must be in French.

Requisites.—Parties legally capable of contracting, their consent legally given, prestation which forms its object and lawful cause or consideration. (C.C.Q. 1385).

Form.—No special forms dictated unless parties require contract to take form of solemn agreement or in certain specific contracts such as conditional sales contracts.

Nullity.—Contracts may be annulled as a result of error, lesion or fear (C.C.Q. 1399); lesion is cause of nullity available only to minors and persons of full age under protective supervision (C.C.Q. 1405). C.C.Q. defines classes of contracts including contracts of adhesion, in which essential stipulations are imposed by one of parties or on their behalf or instructions and are not negotiable, and consumer contracts. C.C.Q. defines external, illegible and incomprehensible clauses which may be annulled, and abusive clauses, which may be reduced or annulled, where these clauses are contained in contract of adhesion or consumer contract. See also topic Consumer Protection.

Interpretation.—When meaning of parties in contract is doubtful, intention determined by interpretation rather than by adherence to literal meaning. C.C.Q. contains other rules of interpretation. (C.C.Q. 1425-1432).

Effects of Contract.—Contracts generally have effect only between contracting parties; party may bind himself that another shall perform an obligation. (C.C.Q. 1440-1443).

Effect of Obligations in Contract.—C.C.Q. contains detailed provisions regulating effect of various types of obligations such as obligations with term, alternative obligations, solidary obligations, divisible obligations, penal clauses, payment, subrogation, etc. (C.C.Q. 1497-1552).

Specifically Regulated Contracts.—C.C.Q. and Consumer Protection Act also contain provisions governing certain specific contracts such as sale, lease and hire, mandate, loan, etc. See appropriate topic.

Equity in Contracts.—No provisions to relieve or modify contractual relationships on basis of equity except that court may pronounce nullity of contract, order reduction of obligations arising from contract or reduce monetary obligations under loan of money if having regard to risk and other circumstances involved, one of parties has suffered lesion. (C.C.Q. 2332). Small claims may be decided on equity. See topic Courts, subhead Court of Quebec, catchline Small Claims.

Distributorships, Dealerships and Franchises.—No special legislation. Issues of intellectual property regulated by federal law. See topic Principal and Agent.

See topic Language.

CONVEYANCES: See topic Deeds.

CORPORATIONS:

The Quebec Companies Act (R.S.Q. c. C-38—"Act") applies to all companies incorporated in province except railway, telephone, telegraph, banking, loan, insurance and trust companies. Provincial corporations are constituted by articles or, in exceptional cases, letters patent.

General Supervision.—Minister of Finance is responsible for administration of Act while Inspector General of Financial Institutions is responsible for carrying out administration.

Purposes.—Provincial corporations (except railway, telephone, telegraph, banking, loan, insurance and trust companies) may be incorporated by articles issued in virtue of Act. As of Apr. 1, 1990, Letters Patent no longer granted under Part 1 and as of Sept. 1, 1990, Supplementary Letters Patent only granted in special circumstances.

Name.—Regulations govern corporate names available to companies incorporated under Parts I and IA and corporations incorporated under Part III; generally, proposed name must not be that of any other known company, incorporated or unincorporated, unless with consent of latter, or any name liable to lead to confusion with another person, partnership or group in Quebec or otherwise objectionable. Corporate name must end in either "ltee" or "inc." or include word "corporation" and must be French name which may be accompanied with version in another language. Family names, place names, expressions formed by artificial combination of letters, syllables or figures and expressions taken from other language may appear in firm names subject to government regulations. Companies may use another name other than their corporate name except on certain specified documents. See topic Language. Corporate name may be reserved under various circumstances upon application and payment of fee.

Term of Corporate Existence.—Perpetual.

Incorporators.—Articles of incorporation under Part IA must be signed by one or more persons who are not less than 18 years of age. They need not be either Canadian citizens or residents, but they must not be civilly incapacitated or undischarged bankrupt.

Application for Incorporation.—Incorporation under Part IA made by one or more incorporators filing two copies of articles with Inspector General. Articles must set out corporate name, judicial district of head office in Quebec, details of authorized capital, restrictions if any on activities or transfer of shares and number or maximum and minimum number of directors. Articles must be filed with notices of head office address and first directors, all in duplicate.

Legislative charters may also be procured from the Legislature by special Acts for all purposes within the powers of the Provincial Legislature. Once incorporated, such special corporations are governed, for all matters not covered by their act of incorporation, by Part II of Act.

Federal and provincial charters carry the same rights in province.

Fees payable on application for supplementary letters patent are as follows: (1) In instances not provided for hereinafter, $300; (2) in case of change of name, $150 with certain specified exceptions; (3) in case of increase in capital stock, fees computed by considering increase as proposed capital on application for letters patent; (4) in case of subdivision of no par value shares, fees computed as on application for letters patent on total consideration for which new unissued shares can be issued, or if consideration is not mentioned, on valuation of $100 for each new share; (5) in cases of several purposes in one application, only largest fee is payable.

Fees payable under Part IA (incorporation and filing of articles), excluding taxes, on issuance of certificate of incorporation are $356. Other Part IA fees include: (1) Any and all certificates of amendment, $164; (2) upon issuance of certificate of amalgamation, $603; (3) upon issuance of certificate of continuance, $246.

When incorporation is obtained by special Act, costs are usually much heavier and vary according to circumstances.

Powers.—Provincial companies legally incorporated can carry on business outside of the Province of Quebec and even in foreign countries. (R. S. Q. c. P-16).

Amendment of Charter.—Under Part I on petition and under special circumstances supplementary letters patent may be obtained modifying powers of company or any provisions of its charter. Under Part IA articles may be amended by filing articles of amendment with Inspector General.

Increase or Decrease of Authorized Capital Stock.—By-laws increasing or decreasing the authorized capital stock require (1) the approval of at least two-thirds in value of the shares represented at a special general meeting and (ii) supplementary letters patent in case of Part I company or articles of amendment in case of Part IA company.

By-laws.—Under Part I directors may make by-laws providing for: (a) Shares of more than one class and for preferred or special rights, conditions or limitations attaching to each class of shares; and (b) conversion of shares of any class into shares of another class. Such by-laws require: (1) Approval of at least two-thirds in value of

CORPORATIONS . . . *continued*
shares represented at special general meeting; and (2) confirmation by supplementary letters patent. Under Part IA all amendments to articles must be by by-law, approved by at least two-thirds of votes cast by shareholders at special general meeting.

The directors may make by-laws for the following purposes: allotment of stock, calls and payment, registration of stock certificates, transfer of stock, forfeiture of stock for nonpayment; declaration and payment of dividends; number of directors, term of service, qualification and remuneration; appointment, functions, duties and removal of all agents, officers and servants, their remuneration, and security to be given by them; holding of annual meetings, calling of meetings, regular and special, of board of directors and of company, quorum, proxies; delegation of powers; penalties and forfeitures; conduct in all other particulars of affairs of company. Amendments to such by-laws may be adopted by directors, but such by-laws and amendments (except those concerning agents, officers and servants) have effect only until next annual meeting of company, unless confirmed in meantime at special general meeting.

Stock.—A corporation may issue common stock with or without par value, but under Part I only stock preferred as to capital or redeemable must have par value.

Stock certificates evidencing the stockholders' ownership of stock in the corporation may be issued under corporate seal duly attested by proper signing officers, usually President or Vice-President and Secretary.

Whole text of the preferred or special rights, conditions and limitations attaching to preferred shares must be a part of every certificate for such shares, unless a summary is inscribed thereon with a statement that text thereof will be furnished free of cost on demand.

Share warrants may be authorized by the charter with respect to fully paid-up shares.

Issuance of Stock.—Shares with par value shall not be issued as fully paid, save for a consideration payable in cash to total par value of shares so issued, or for a consideration payable in property or services which directors determine by resolution to be the fair equivalent of cash to total par value of shares so issued. Unless letters patent, articles or by-laws of company provide to contrary, shares without par value may be issued for such consideration, payable in cash, property or services, as may be fixed by directors; and all shares so issued shall be deemed fully paid upon receipt by company of consideration for their issue.

Transfer of Stock.—The provisions regulating companies incorporated in Quebec in this connection are practically identical with those regulating companies incorporated by federal charter, that is to say, briefly:

No share can be transferred until all previous calls thereon have been paid; nor can any share be transferred, until it has been fully paid-up, without the consent of the directors of the company.

Except as regards the rights of the parties inter se, no transfer will be complete, unless made by sale under execution or by order of the court, until it has been entered in the register of transfers.

In the case, however, of the stock of any company listed and dealt with on a recognized exchange, by means of scrip, the usual endorsement and delivery will constitute a valid transfer, except for the purpose of voting at meetings of the company.

Any transfer of shares of a deceased shareholder made by the personal representative of latter is valid upon production of evidence of transmission.

Stock Transfer Tax.—Stock transfer tax repealed effective Apr. 19, 1972. (S. Q. 1972, c. 27).

Shareholders.—They elect directors, appoint auditors, consider approval of annual financial statements and of by-laws, vote at general meetings personally or by proxy, receive payment of dividends when declared and payable, appoint liquidators in case of voluntary winding up. Upon dissolution surplus is distributed among shareholders.

Shareholders' Liabilities.—Their liability is limited to any unpaid balance on their shares.

Shareholders' Meetings.—Annual meeting of the company must be held in Quebec. Unless otherwise provided by letters patent, articles or by-laws, ten days notice of any general meeting must be given to each shareholder by registered letter, and in two newspapers (one in English and one in French).

At annual meeting, a balance sheet, statement of income and expenditures and auditors' report thereon are submitted; directors are elected for ensuing year; and auditors are appointed. Shareholders of Part IA corporations may by unanimous resolution in certain cases decide not to appoint auditors.

Shareholders holding one-tenth of the subscribed shares of the company may, by written requisition, call special meetings of the company for the transaction of any business specified in the notice convening the meeting.

Voting.—Shareholders may be represented by proxy at a general or special meeting. Proxy need not be shareholder. A proxy is revocable. Subject to letters patent, articles or by-laws, every shareholder is entitled to one vote per share, but one cannot vote if he is in arrears in respect of any call. For Part IA corporations written resolution signed by all shareholders able to vote has same effect as if passed at shareholders' meeting.

Directors.—Under Part I affairs of corporation must be managed by board of not less than three directors. They need not be either Canadian citizens or residents. No person shall be elected or appointed director of company unless he or any other company of which he is officer or director is shareholder and, if by-laws of company so provide, unless he owns shares of company absolutely in his own right or in right of such other company to required amount and provided that he is not in arrears in respect of any calls thereon. Any person holding shares of company in capacity of testamentary executor, tutor, curator or trustee may also be elected or appointed director. In absence of any special provision, minimum qualification is one share. Under Part IA corporation may have only one director if it has not issued securities to public; directors need not be shareholders. Notice of any change of directors must be given within 15 days thereof by filing declaration to that effect under Act respecting the legal publicity of sole proprietorships, partnerships and legal persons. (R.S.Q. c. P-45).

The directors are elected at a general meeting of the shareholders for such term not exceeding two years as set by letters patent, articles or by-laws. In absence of such other provisions, directors are elected annually by ballot. Retiring directors are reeligible and they continue in office until their successors are elected. Any vacancy may be filled, for remainder of term, by directors.

The directors elect from among themselves a president and, if they see fit, a chairman of meetings and one or more vice-presidents and may also appoint all other officers.

Directors' Meetings.—The calling of directors' meetings, their place and the quorum required are determined either by letters patent, articles or by-laws. Directors may agree to hold meetings by verbal means of communication such as telephone. Written resolutions signed by all directors have same effect as if passed at actual meeting.

Powers and Duties of Directors.—The directors administer all the affairs of the company. They may make or cause to be made in its name any kind of contract which it may lawfully enter into. They may make by-laws for the purposes already indicated. See subhead By-laws, supra. They issue the stock of the company, declare dividends, appoint, supervise and remove the agents, officers and servants of the company. They cause the proper books to be kept by the Secretary. See subhead Books and Returns, infra. They cause the returns and notices required by law to be prepared and filed or published. They approve the financial statements to be submitted to annual meetings. They take steps for calling of annual meetings and special meetings of the shareholders. For Part IA corporations shareholders by unanimous written agreement may restrict powers of directors.

They may submit to the shareholders a resolution to wind up voluntarily the company and in case of such a winding up, the directors may pass by-laws for distributing the surplus assets among the shareholders. Generally, it is the duty of the directors to protect the interests of company.

Liabilities of Directors.—Directors are solidarily liable if (1) they declare and pay any dividend when company is insolvent or which impairs capital; (2) they make loans to any shareholder. Directors of Part IA corporations solidarily liable in cases of reduction of capital and granting of financial assistance to designated persons in breach of specified tests.

Directors are solidarily liable to company's employees for wages, not exceeding six months, for services performed while they were directors, provided (1) company is sued within one year after wages became due and writ of execution is returned unsatisfied in whole or in part, or (2) during such delay, winding-up order is made against company or it becomes bankrupt and claim for such wages is filed in its bankruptcy.

Liabilities of Directors and Officers.—A director or officer is liable for damages, and also to a penalty of $100 for each offense, if he refuses to exhibit the books which must be kept by the company (see subhead Books and Returns, infra), or knowingly makes or assists in making any untrue entry or fails to make any proper entry in such books.

A general penalty of not more than $200 or two months of imprisonment or both is enacted against directors or officers who fail to comply with any provisions of the Quebec Companies Act.

Directors, officers or attorneys of companies who order, authorize or advise commission of offence under Act respecting the legal publicity of sole proprietorships, partnerships and legal persons (R.S.Q. c. P-45) are guilty of offence and liable to fine of not less than $200 and not more than $2,000. Fines doubled for subsequent offenses.

Head Office.—Company is obliged to have head office in Quebec; it is its legal domicile. Notice of address of all establishments and designation of principal office and of any change therein must be given by filing declaration to that effect in accordance with Act respecting the legal publicity of sole proprietorships, partnerships and legal persons.

Resident Agent.—Under Act respecting the legal publicity of sole proprietorships, partnerships and legal persons (R.S.Q. c. P-45), companies or partnerships without domicile or establishment in Quebec must designate attorney residing in Quebec. See subhead Reports, infra.

General Powers of Company.—Part I sets forth powers of corporation. Rights which corporation may exercise, besides those specially conferred by its charter, or by general laws applicable to its particular kind, are all those which are necessary to attain object of its creation; thus it may acquire, alienate and possess property, sue and be sued, contract, incur obligations and bind others in its favor. Under Part IA corporation has full enjoyment of civil rights.

Dividends.—Under Part I no dividend may be declared which would impair capital of company; annual dividend may however be paid out of reserve fund. Under Part IA declaration and payment of dividends is subject to meeting solvency tests. Directors may declare stock dividends.

Mining companies or companies whose assets consist of goods consumed when used, may declare and pay a dividend out of the funds derived from such use. Such companies may pay dividends in species or in kind. Amounts due for calls may be deducted from the dividends of a shareholder.

Sale or Transfer of Corporate Assets.—Directors have power to authorize sale of any corporate assets without reference to the shareholders; but approval of the shareholders should be obtained for the sale of all the assets and undertaking of the company or of property constituting the major portion of its assets.

Books and Returns.—Corporation must cause to be kept at its offices a book or books comprising a copy of charter and by-laws of company, names of shareholders, address and calling of each, number of shares of stock held by each shareholder, amounts paid in and remaining unpaid on such stock and names, addresses and calling of directors and dates on which each became or ceased to be such director and also a book called "register of transfers" containing particulars of every transfer of stock of company. Books must also be kept showing (a) receipts and disbursements and matters to which they relate; (b) financial transactions; (c) credits and liabilities. Minute books for meetings of shareholders and of directors and under Part I register of mortgages must also be kept. Such books are to be open for inspection during ordinary hours at

CORPORATIONS . . . *continued*
head office of company and are subject to inspection by shareholders and creditors of company and judgment creditors of shareholders, who may take extracts therefrom.

Reports.—Under An Act respecting legal publicity of sole proprietorships, partnerships and legal persons (R.S.Q. c. P-45) main provisions of which came into force on Jan. 1, 1994, every company constituted under laws of Quebec and every company not constituted under laws of Quebec if domiciled in Quebec or carrying on activity in Quebec or possessing immovable real right, other than prior claim or hypothec, in Province of Quebec must register declaration of registration in register created under said Act.

Companies and partnerships constituted in virtue of laws other than those of Quebec who commence carrying on activity in Quebec in 1994 and Quebec companies and partnerships which come into existence in 1994 must file declaration of registration under said Act. In case of companies incorporated under laws of Quebec after Jan. 1, 1994 Inspector General of Financial Institutions will deposit company's constituting documents in register automatically. Quebec companies in existence prior to said Act and companies constituted under laws other than those of Quebec carrying on activity in Quebec prior to new legislation had until Dec. 31, 1994 to file declaration of registration. All companies, partnerships and individuals subject to Act must file annual declaration for purposes of updating information contained in declaration of registration originally filed. In case of companies annual declaration must be filed between Aug. 1 and Oct. 31 each year. In addition to annual declarations all companies, partnerships and individuals subject to Act are required to file amending declaration as certain changes of information occur. Inspector General has right to strike from register company, partnership or individual who has failed to file annual declaration for two consecutive years. In case of company constituted under laws of Quebec this will entail dissolution. New Act replaces Companies and Partnerships Declaration Act and Companies Information Act and repeals Extra-Provincial Companies Act. As to other returns required, see Canada Law Digest, topic Corporations.

Merger and Consolidation.—Under Part IA, subject to solvency tests two or more Part I or Part IA companies may amalgamate by agreement. Agreement must prescribe terms of amalgamation, name of new company, names of future directors, manner of converting capital of old companies into that of new. Agreement is approved by by-law, all shares are voting shares for purposes of adopting by-law, class and series votes may be required and articles of amalgamation and notices of address of head office and directors must be filed with Inspector General in duplicate. Corporation under its new name possesses all property, rights, privileges and franchises of companies so amalgamated and it is subject to all their liabilities, contracts, disabilities and duties.

Part I and Part IA corporations may amalgamate subject to meeting specified solvency test. Simplified procedure for amalgamation between corporation and its subsidiary and between subsidiaries of same corporation.

Continuation.—Corporations governed by Part I with certain exceptions may continue themselves under Part IA by by-law enacted by directors and ratified by two-thirds of votes cast at special general meeting of shareholders. Upon applying for continuation corporation may change its name, reduce its issued share capital and otherwise modify its charter subject to certain limitations. If rights attaching to issued shares are affected, all shareholders including those not otherwise carrying voting rights must consent.

Dissolution.—Company constituted under laws of Quebec may be struck from register created under An Act respecting the legal publicity of sole proprietorships, partnerships and legal persons (R.S.Q. c. P-45) by order of Inspector General for failing to file annual declaration two consecutive years. Striking entails dissolution of company. Copy of Inspector General order is sent to registrant.

Company may be dissolved voluntarily if company proves to satisfaction of Inspector General: (1) That it has no debts or obligations; or (2) that it has parted with its property, divided its assets rateably amongst its shareholders and has no debts or liabilities; or (3) that its debts and obligations have been provided for or protected or that creditors consent. Notwithstanding dissolution of company, directors, at that time, remain solidarily liable for debts of company except in case of good faith.

Insolvency and Receivers.—See Canada Law Digest, topics Bankruptcy; Corporations.

Close Corporations.—Act does not provide for private companies. Distinction between corporations which do and do not offer their securities to public.

Appraisal.—No statutory provisions.

Corporation Taxes.—Taxation Act (R. S. Q. c. I-3) imposes following taxes on corporations:

(1) Tax on Paid-up Capital.—See topic Taxation, subhead Tax on Capital.

(2) Tax on Profits.—See topic Taxation, subhead Income Tax, catchline Corporation.

See topics Language; Taxation.

COSTS:

Losing party must pay all costs unless for special reasons court reduces or compensates them or orders otherwise. (C. P. 477). Costs bear interest from date of judgment granting them (C. P. 481) and are set out in fixed tariff.

Security for Costs.—Nonresident plaintiffs must give security for costs, if required to do so by defendant. (C. P. 65). Amount required varies according to amount involved in action.

COURTS:

Courts which have jurisdiction in civil matters in province are as follows (R. S. Q. c. T-16; C.P. 22s).

Superior Court has original jurisdiction in all matters except those exclusively under jurisdiction of Court of Quebec and Federal Court of Canada (C.P. 31).

Court of Quebec, saving right of evocation in certain matters, has jurisdiction in all suits for amounts less than $30,000 except suits for alimentary allowances and those reserved for Federal Court, and ultimate jurisdiction, to exclusion of Superior Court and irrespective of amount claimed, in suits for municipal and school taxes and to set aside valuation roll of immovables taxable for municipal or school purposes.

Small Claims.—Natural or legal person with no more than five employees with claim which does not exceed $3,000 due by debtor residing or having place of business in Province including any motion for dissolution, rescission or cancellation of contract where value of contract does not exceed $3,000, can recover same before Court of Quebec through simplified procedure not involving pleadings where judge assists each party to ensure respect for law and equity. Advocates are not allowed to act in that capacity in such claims except in certain cases involving complex question of law. (C.P. 953s).

Court of Quebec, Youth Division.—Exclusive jurisdiction in matters respecting adoption and other jurisdiction determined by special Acts. (C.P. 36.1).

Federal Court of Canada has exclusive jurisdiction in matters specifically assigned to it by federal statutes and concurrent jurisdiction with Superior Court in other special matters within powers of Federal Parliament such as infringements of patents, maritime claims, etc. See Canada Law Digest, topic Courts.

Other Tribunals.—In addition, there are other inferior courts of local jurisdiction such as Municipal Court (R. S. Q. c. C-72), over which Superior Court has superintending and reforming power (C. P. 33).

There are no courts of equity in province.

Appeal Courts.—Appeals in civil matters are heard by Court of Appeal (R. S. Q. c. T-16) sitting in appeal and finally by Supreme Court of Canada. See topic Appeal and Error.

See topic Language, subhead Legislature and Courts.

CREDITORS' SUITS:

If creditor's claim is certain, liquid and exigible, he may exercise rights and actions of debtor where debtor refuses or neglects to exercise them to prejudice of creditor. Creditor may not exercise rights strictly personal to debtor, such as right to damages for libel, slander, or personal injuries. (C.C.Q. 1627).

CRIMINAL LAW:

See Canada Law Digest, topic Criminal Law. See also topic Labor Relations, subhead Workmen's Compensation.

CURTESY:

Unknown to Quebec law.

DAMAGES:

Comparative Negligence.—No statutory rule of comparative negligence, plaintiff even when in part at fault may recover damages at civil law in proportion to degree of defendant's fault.

Charitable Immunity.—No statutory provisions.

No-Fault Insurance.—See topic Motor Vehicles, subhead No-Fault Insurance.

Sovereign Immunity.—Crown can generally be held liable for its actions.

See topic Offences and Quasi-offences.

DEATH:

After seven years have elapsed, absentee is reputed to be dead from date of disappearance or latest intelligence received. Succession opens by death. (C.C.Q. 613). Successor is entitled to have heirship recognized at any time within ten years from opening of succession or from day right arises. (C.C.Q. 626). Even before lapse of these periods, tutor (if one is designated) may administer property of deceased. (C.C.Q. 86s.). See topic Absentees.

Survivorship.—Persons deemed to have died at same time if impossible to determine who died first and at least one of them is called to succession of other. Succession of each devolves to persons who would have received in their place. (C.C.Q. 616s.).

Action for Death.—Subject to three-year prescription period for actions to enforce personal rights. Obligation exists to indemnify dependents of workman under Industrial Accidents and Occupational Diseases Act (R.S.Q., c. A-3.001), where amount of indemnity is fixed but is owing independently of any fault on part of employer. See topic Labor Relations, subhead Workmen's Compensation.

Declaratory judgment of death may be obtained on application of any interested person seven years after disappearance. Declaratory judgment of death is obtainable before that time where death presumed certain and (1) death occurs in Quebec or (2) death is of person domiciled in Quebec. Date of death is either date occurring on expiry of seven years since disappearance or earlier date if death presumed certain at that date. Registration of judgment in Register of Civil Status equivalent to Act of Death issued by Registrar. (C.C.Q. 92s.).

Certificate.—Acts of death are authentic acts of civil status. See topic Records, subhead Vital Statistics. Attestations of death may be obtained, in applicable cases, from physicians or peace officers.

Anatomical Gifts.—In absence of knowledge of wishes of deceased, physician may remove part of remains, with consent of person who can give consent to care or who could have given it. Consent not necessary when two physicians attest in writing impossibility of obtaining it in due time, urgency of operation and serious hope of saving human life or appreciably improving its quality. Death of donor must be ascertained by two physicians not participating in removal or transplantation before removal of parts. (C.C.Q. 42s.).

DECEDENTS' ESTATES:

See topics Descent and Distribution; Executors and Administrators; Wills.

See note at head of Digest as to 1996 legislation covered.

See Topical Index in front part of this volume.

DECLARATORY JUDGMENTS:

Declaratory judgments may be requested by any person who has interest in having determined immediately his rights, powers or obligations under contract, will, or any other written instrument, statute, order in council, or resolution or by-law of municipal corporation. Application is made by motion to court supported by affidavit setting forth matter in dispute and interest of applicant in obtaining immediate decision. It must be served on all interested parties at least ten days before presentation. (C. P. 453s).

See topic Language.

DEEDS:

Executed Within the Province.—Deeds may be either in authentic or notarial form, or in private writing.

Authentic Deed.—Makes proof against all persons of juridical act which it sets forth and declarations of parties which directly relate to act. (C.C.Q. 2818, 2819). Executed by all parties before practising notary. (C.C.Q. 2813, 2814). See topic Notaries. Such deed cannot be contradicted and set aside as false, in whole or in part, except upon improbation. (C.C.Q. 2821). As general rule, notarial instrument received before one notary is authentic if signed by all parties, and no witnesses are required; though if party is unable to sign, it is necessary that his declaration of consent be given before witness who signs. (C.C.Q. 2819). Notarial will is signed before notary in presence of one witness. (C.C.Q. 716). However it must be signed before notary and two witnesses if testator cannot sign. (C.C.Q. 719). See topic Wills.

Certain deeds must be in notarial form, including: (1) renunciation to succession except if made by judicial declaration which is recorded (C.C.Q. 646); (2) donations inter vivos, except gifts of movables accompanied by delivery and immediate possession (C.C.Q. 1824); (3) marriage contracts (C.C.Q. 440); (4) immovable hypothecs (C.C.Q. 2693); declaration of co-ownership (C.C.Q. 1059).

The original of the authentic deed remains of record in the office of the notary and constitutes part of his repertory as a public officer. Copies attested by notary are issued as required and are also considered authentic. (C.C.Q. 2815). Notarial deed transferring immovable property must be attested by notary who received it in order to permit its registration in land register. (C.C.Q. 2988). See topic Records.

Power of attorney under private writing made outside Quebec makes proof against all persons where it is certified by competent public officer who has verified identity and signature of mandator. (C.C.Q. 2823).

Though the majority of deeds do not require the notarial form, the advantages which attach to the notarial instrument for the obtention of true copies and for registration or recording purposes in addition to facility of proof, make this form desirable when important transactions are involved, especially in connection with immovables or real rights.

Private Writings.—Deeds which by law need not be in notarial form may be validly drawn in any form which expresses intention of parties. No other formality is required other than signature of parties. (C.C.Q. 2826s.). These may be signed before subscribing witnesses in order to facilitate proof thereof, if required. Deed under private signature transferring immovable must be attested by notary or advocate and must respect certain formalities in order to permit its registration. (C.C.Q. 2291, 2981s.). See topic Records.

Deeds executed outside Province are valid as to form if executed in accordance to lex loci. (C.C.Q. 3109).

Act may be made outside Quebec before Quebec notary if it concerns real right the object of which is situated in Quebec or if one of parties is domiciled in Quebec. (C.C.Q. 3110).

See topic Language.

DEEDS OF TRUST:

See topic Mortgages of Personal Property, subhead Movable Hypothecs, catchline Movable Hypothecs Without Delivery.

DEPOSITIONS:

When proof and hearing are necessary, and defendant has not appeared, witnesses may be heard out of court; but if defendant has appeared witnesses can only be heard out of court with permission of court or consent of parties and provided all parties are present or duly summoned. However, in applications for separation from bed and board, in nullity of marriage or for divorce, evidence of plaintiff must be given in court. (C. P. 196, 404).

Outside of Province for Use within Province.—See infra, subhead Rogatory Commission.

Rogatory Commission.—Court may, upon application of any party appoint commissioner to receive testimony of any person residing outside province or in place too far distant from place where case is pending and to report thereon. Any party may be represented at examination and commissioner may put, and must allow parties to put, any questions relevant to case. (C. P. 426s.).

Compelling Attendance of Witnesses.—Witnesses are summoned at diligence of parties, by writ of subpoena issued by judge, clerk or lawyer, copy of which is served upon them at least five clear days before date fixed for appearance. In cases of urgency judge can reduce delay for service but not for less than 12 hours before date fixed for appearance. In case of minister or deputy-minister of Quebec government, delay is ten days. (C. P. 280).

See topic Witnesses.

DESCENT AND DISTRIBUTION:

When there is no will, the succession passes to the lawful heirs in the order established by Civil Code of Quebec; in default of such heirs it devolves to State. (C.C.Q. 653). As there is in Quebec freedom of testamentary disposition (see topic Wills), it must be clearly noted that following conditions and rules are applicable only in case of intestacy.

Lawful heirs are the surviving spouse, descendants of deceased, and ascendants and collateral relations in order and according to Rules of Intestacy hereinafter laid down. (C.C.Q. 666s.).

Children and Descendants.—No distinction between legitimate and illegitimate children. Rights of children depend on whether filiation is established. Filiation proved by act of birth, presumption or acknowledgments and may be contested or disavowed. (C.C.Q. 523s.).

Ascendants comprise privileged ascendants, who are the father and mother of deceased, and ordinary ascendants, being all others.

Collaterals comprise privileged collaterals, who are the brothers and sisters and nephews and nieces in the first degree of the deceased; and ordinary collaterals, being all other relations.

Adopted Children.—See topic Adoption.

Rules of Intestacy.—If the deceased leaves:

1. Descendants and spouse: two-thirds of estate devolves to descendants (sharing equally) and one-third to spouse. (C.C.Q. 666).

2. Descendants but no spouse: descendants take entire succession. (C.C.Q. 667).

3. Spouse but no descendants: spouse takes all if there are no privileged ascendants and no privileged collaterals. (C.C.Q. 671).

4. Spouse, privileged relations, no descendants: spouse takes two-thirds, privileged ascendants one-third; if only privileged collaterals, spouse takes two-thirds and privileged collaterals one-third. (C.C.Q. 672, 673).

5. Privileged relations only: privileged ascendants take one-half, privileged collaterals other half, sharing equally among themselves. (C.C.Q. 674). Where there is only one privileged ascendant, he takes share that would have devolved to other. Where there are no privileged ascendants, privileged collaterals inherit entire succession and vice-versa.

6. Ordinary relations: These will succeed only in default of privileged relations. (C.C.Q. 677). Certain particular rules must also be observed between them. Further, division between paternal and maternal lines is ordered, and it is only in default of relations within heritable degree in one line that relatives of other line will inherit whole. (C.C.Q. 679, 682).

Acceptance of Succession.—Succession devolving to unemancipated minor, to protected person of full age under tutorship or curatorship or absent person is accepted by representative of successor with authorization of tutorship or curatorship council. Succession devolving to emancipated minor or person of full age requiring assistance, is deemed accepted by successor himself, assisted by his tutor or adviser. In no case is successor liable for payment of debts of succession amounting to more than value of property he receives. (C.C.Q. 638).

Irregular Successions.—Relations beyond eighth degree do not inherit. (C.C.Q. 683). In default of spouse and descendants or relations within heritable degree in both paternal and maternal lines, State succeeds. (C.C.Q. 696). See topic Wills, subhead Unclaimed Legacies.

Legal Seizin.—If the decedent has left no will, his legal heirs upon his death become legally seized of his patrimony. If legal heirs comply with rules of administration, they are not liable to greater extent than value of property they receive, and retain right to demand payment of their claims. They are seized also of rights of action of deceased against any person for breach of his personality rights. (C.C.Q. 625).

Representation takes place without limit in the direct line descending. It is allowed whether children of deceased compete with descendants of represented child, or whether, if all children of deceased are dead or unworthy, descendants of these children happen to be in equal or unequal degrees of relationship. (C.C.Q. 661). It does not take place in favor of ascendants; nearest in each line excluding more distant. (C.C.Q. 662). In collateral line, representation takes place in favor of nieces and nephews of deceased, whether or not they compete with their parents, and in favor of other descendants of brothers and sisters of deceased in other degrees, whether they are in equal or unequal degrees of relationship to each other. (C.C.Q. 663). No person who has renounced succession may be represented, but person whose succession has been renounced may be represented. Partition is effected by roots. If one root has several branches, subdivision also made by roots in each branch, and members of same branch share among themselves by heads. (C.C.Q. 664, 665).

Advancements are known as "returns". With view to partition, each coheir must return to mass only what he has received from deceased by gifts or by will under express obligation to return it. Successor who renounces succession has no obligation to make any return. (C.C.Q. 867). Person who represents another must return what person represented would have had to return, in addition to what he is bound to return in his own right. Return is due even if person who represents other has renounced succession of person represented. (C.C.Q. 868). Return is made only to succession of donor or testator. It is due only from one coheir to another, not to legatees or creditors. Return is made by taking less, not in kind unless so elected by heir and property not charged with real right. (C.C.Q. 870). Value of property returned is reduced by increase in its value resulting from initiative and disbursements of person returning it, or increased by decrease in value due to actions of person returning it. (C.C.Q. 874).

Alimentary Support Creditors of support include spouses and relatives in direct line, and divorced spouses. (C.C.Q. 585, 688). All creditors of support, including heirs or legatees, and those who did not exercise right to support before date of death, may claim financial contribution from succession within six months of death. (C.C.Q. 684). Right does not exist in favor of person unworthy of inheriting.

Former spouses of deceased in receipt of support at time of death may claim equivalent of 12 months' support. Claims of other creditors of support determined according to new rules in C.C.Q. (C.C.Q. 688).

Surviving spouse may apply for allowance as compensation for his contribution in goods and services to patrimony of deceased spouse, payable as agreed between parties or as determined by court. (C.C.Q. 809, 823; C.P. 827.1). Application must be brought within one year of death. (C.C.Q. 2928).

See topic Husband and Wife, subhead Family Patrimony.

DESERTION:

See topic Husband and Wife.

DISPUTE RESOLUTION:

No special legislation.

Mandatory Dispute Resolution.—None.

Voluntary Dispute Resolution.—Parties to action before small claims court may seek mediation of dispute. Also available in family matters. Commercial contracts may specify arbitration clause. See topics Arbitration and Award; Courts, subhead Court of Quebec.

DISSOLUTION OF MARRIAGE:

See topic Divorce.

DIVORCE:

Superior Court of Province of Quebec has jurisdiction in matters of divorce in virtue of provisions of Federal Divorce Act (S.C. 1986, c. 4) as proclaimed by Lieutenant-Governor in Council of Quebec. C.C.Q. contains articles dealing with provisional measures for family residence and interim support. (C.C.Q. 500, 502, 503). For grounds and procedure, see Canada Law Digest, topic Divorce.

Temporary Alimony.—See Canada Law Digest, topic Divorce, subhead Corollary Relief.

Permanent Alimony.—See Canada Law Digest, topic Divorce, subhead Corollary Relief.

Allowance for Support of and Custody of Children.—See Canada Law Digest, topic Divorce, subheads Corollary Relief; Enforcement.

Recovery of Support Payments.—Collector of support payments appointed by Minister of Justice empowered to seize movable or immovable property effected on behalf of creditor. (C. P. 659.1). Collector may also act for foreign creditor when foreign judgment executory in Quebec after filing or registration. (C. P. 659.3). Court may order person to furnish creditor with information on place of residence or work of debtor. (C. P. 546.1). Arrears of support prescribed after three years. (C.C.Q. 2925).

Joint Property.—If divorced parties hold property in community, under partnership of acquests or as joint owners, community or partnership is dissolved by divorce, and either party may demand partition of the joint property (C.C.Q. 845, 1030).

Division of Property of Spouses.—Division of property depends on family patrimony and marital regime governing spouses at date of dissolution of marriage. For details see topic Husband and Wife.

Foreign Decrees.—Generally divorces granted in foreign countries recognized and enforceable by Québec authorities if granted in accordance with federal Divorce Act (S.C. 1985, c. 3 2d supp.). (C.C.Q. 3155).

Separation as to Bed and Board.—See topic Husband and Wife, subhead Separation as to Bed and Board.

Annulment of Marriage.—See topic Marriage, subhead Annulment.

DOWER:

Legal or customary dower no longer applicable to marriages entered into after July 1, 1970. Legal and conventional dower established before July 1, 1970 remain subject to former provisions of Civil Code and consist of usufruct for wife and ownership for children of one-half of immovables which belong to husband at time of marriage and of one-half of those which accrue to him during marriage from his father, mother and other ascendants unless marriage contract provides otherwise. (S. Q.1969, c. 77, former text of C. C. 1426-1435).

ELECTION:

See topic Wills, subhead Election.

EMPLOYER AND EMPLOYEE:

See topic Labor Relations.

ENVIRONMENT:

General Supervision.—Under Environment Quality Act (R. S. Q. c. Q-2), Minister of Environment responsible for implementing policy of protection of environment. Minister has power of supervision and control over quality of environment. Advisory Council on the Environment advises Minister on studies pertaining to quality of environment and makes recommendations based on petitions made under Act.

Matters Regulated.—Emission, deposit, issuance or discharge into atmosphere, water or soil of any contaminant in greater quantity or concentration than that provided for by government regulation. Act has special provisions regarding water quality, management of waste water, depollution of atmosphere, waste management, sanitary conditions of public buildings and places, rays and other energy vectors, and limits of excessive noise.

Depollution Attestation.—Applies to pulp and paper manufacturers. No manufacturer shall emit, deposit, release or discharge any contaminant if Minister has refused to issue depollution attestation which sets out contaminant levels relative to industrial production and methods and equipment required to minimize contaminant levels. Applicant must comply therewith, and may have to submit waste management plan. Attestation does not apply to discharge of contaminants contemplated by municipal by-law approved by Minister. (R.S.Q. c. Q-2, §31.10s).

Municipal Corporations.—Under Cities and Towns Act, Municipal Code and special charters of cities, municipal corporations have power to adopt by-laws regulating emission of smoke and other forms of air pollution and forcing use of smoke abatement devices, regulating sewerage in municipalities as well as drains and water courses, preventing pollution of waters within or adjacent to municipalities, regulating garbage, cesspools and other unsanitary conditions. (R. S. Q. c. C-19).

Other Acts.—Other provincial legislation provides some control of environment: use of forests and wildlife conservation (Forest Act, R.S.Q. c. F-4.1, Parks Act, R.S.Q. c. P-9, Tree Protection Act, R.S.Q. c. P-37, Act respecting conservation and development of wildlife, R.S.Q. c. C-61.1, Act respecting ecological reserves, R.S.Q. c. R-26), water quality (Act respecting the Société d'assainissement des eaux, R.S.Q. S-18.2.1), preservation of waterways (Watercourses Act, R. S. Q. c. R-13), prohibition of roadside dumps and advertising (Roads Act, R. S. Q. c. V-8, Roadside Advertising Act, R.S.Q. c. P-44), regulation of transportation of poisonous, infectious and radioactive substances (Highway Safety Code, R. S. Q. c. C-24.2), regulation of pesticides (Pesticides Act, c. P-9.3), and recycling (Act respecting the Société québécoise de récupération et de recyclage, R.S.Q. c. S-22.01).

Penalties.—For individuals, fines not exceeding $20,000 for first offence and $40,000 for subsequent offence or up to one year imprisonment or both. For corporations, fines not exceeding $250,000 for first offence and $1,000,000 for subsequent offence. Every director or officer of corporation who, by means of order or authorization or through his advice or encouragement, leads corporation to contravene Act is personally liable to same penalties. Minister may take measures to clear, collect or contain contaminations that are or that are likely to be emitted, deposited, etc. into environment where he considers such measures necessary to avert or diminish risk of damage to public or private property and may claim direct and indirect costs from any person or municipality who has custody or control over contaminants and from any person or municipality responsible for their emission, deposit etc. Where offence is continued for more than one day, it constitutes separate offence for each day. Minister may order demolition of any works done in contravention of Act and may force works or improvements to be carried out in accordance with Act. Municipal corporations may assess penalties for violation of their environment by-laws and regulations.

Permits.—Sewer systems, waterworks, intakes or outlets, water purifying or treating systems, commercial deep water drilling, pesticide distribution and manufacturing, waste management systems, amusement or camp grounds and public beaches require permit from Minister. Industrial activities require certificates of authorization from Minister. Permit required for activities involving hazardous materials may necessitate security deposit or civil liability insurance. Municipal corporations also may require permit issued upon submission of plans.

EQUITY: See topic Actions.

ESCHEAT:

See topic Descent and Distribution, subhead Irregular Successions; also topic Wills, subhead Unclaimed Legacies.

ESTATES: See topic Real Property.

EVIDENCE: See topics Depositions; Witnesses.

EXECUTIONS:

Creditor may seize and sell movable property of his debtor which is in possession of latter, that in his own possession and that in possession of third parties who consent thereto. Similarly he may seize in execution, immovable property of which debtor is or is reputed to be in possession as owner. (C. P. 569).

Real Actions.—When party condemned to deliver or surrender property, movable or immovable, fails to do so within prescribed delay, plaintiff may be placed in possession in virtue of writ ordering that defendant be expelled or that property be taken from him, as case may be. (C. P. 565).

Personal Actions.—Judgments containing condemnation are executed by bailiff, sheriff or sheriff's officer by means of writ issued upon written requisition. Movable property must first be exhausted before real estate can be sold. (C. P. 572).

Exemptions.—See topic Exemptions.

Stay of execution is granted until expiry of delays for appeal. Saving cases where provisional execution is ordered, appeal suspends execution of judgment. (C. P. 497). In case of opposition to seizure by debtor or by third party having right to revendicate, execution is stayed until such time as opposition is disposed of. (C. P. 596, 597, 673). Bankruptcy also operates stay of execution unless otherwise ordered by court.

Levy.—Seizure of property subject to execution is made by bailiff in case of movables or sheriff in case of immovables.

Liens.—Execution per se does not create a lien on proceeds of sale except as to law costs.

Sale under execution cannot take place, in case of movables, until ten days after publication of notice in local newspapers. (C. P. 594). Real estate cannot be sold until 30 days after publication of notice in Quebec Official Gazette and in local newspapers. (C. P. 670, 671).

Effect of Sheriff's Sale.—Property is discharged from all real rights not mentioned in conditions of sale, with only few exceptions. (C. P. 696).

Redemption.—Real estate sold under execution is not subject to redemption.

Supplementary Proceedings.—By application to court, judgment debtor may be ordered to appear to be examined as to all property he possesses or has possessed since incurring of obligation which was basis of judgment, as to his sources of revenue and may be ordered to produce books or documents. (C. P. 543s).

Execution by garnishment is allowed. See topic Garnishment.

EXECUTORS AND ADMINISTRATORS OF ESTATES:

Appointment.—Executors are known as liquidators. Any person designated by testator as administrator of property of another, executor or liquidator is governed by rules on liquidators. Testator may designate one or several liquidators and determine mode of

EXECUTORS AND ADMINISTRATORS OF ESTATES . . . *continued*
their replacement; otherwise, office of liquidator devolves to heirs who, by majority vote, may designate liquidator and mode of replacement. (C.C.Q. 786, 785). Failing agreement, or if it is impossible to replace liquidator, court may designate one. (C.C.Q. 788). Liquidators are charged with simple administration. See topic Administration of Property of Others.

Eligibility and Competency.—Any person fully capable of exercising his civil rights, or any legal person authorized by law to administer property of others, may be liquidators. All restrictions concerning married women eliminated effective July 1, 1970. (C.C.Q. 783, S. Q. 1969, c. 77). Nonresident may act as liquidator.

In case no liquidators are appointed and no heirs renounce or claim estate, six months after death Public Curator is seized of property in same manner as heir. Seizin vests for ten years. Public Curator acts as liquidator and makes account to Minister of Finance. After account, Public Curator administers succession for ten years from date of opening or until heir presents himself or petition of inheritance decided. (C.C.Q. 697s.).

Replacement.—Any interested person may apply to court for replacement of liquidator who is unable to assume responsibilities or who neglects duties and obligations. (C.C.Q. 791).

Inventory.—Liquidator must make inventory of succession, in manner of administrator of property of others. Must publish notice of closure of inventory identifying deceased and indicating place where inventory may be consulted by interested persons. Notice of closure published in Register of personal and movable real rights as well as in local newspaper. Liquidator informs heirs, successors, legatees and creditors of registration of notice of closure and of place where inventory may be consulted. These persons may contest inventory. Liquidator may be exempted from making inventory and publishing notice of closure, but only with consent of all heirs and successors. Heirs and successors become liable for debts of succession in excess of value of property they take if (1) they consent to exemption from making inventory, (2) if they neglect making of inventory for 60 days after expiration of six month period for deliberation, or (3) they mingle succession's property with their personal property before inventory, unless such property was already mingled. (C.C.Q. 794s.). See topic Administration of Property of Others, subhead Inventory.

Seizin and Powers.—Testator is at liberty to define, extend or limit duties of his liquidators. Liquidators have seizin of property and may claim possession of it against heirs and legatees.

If liquidation exceeds one year, liquidator shall, at end of first year and at least once a year thereafter, render annual account of management to heirs, creditors and legatees who have not been paid. Likewise, administrator renders summary account of his administration to beneficiary at least once a year. (C.C.Q. 777, 806, 1351).

Form for Proof of Claim.—See subhead Claims, infra.

Claims.—Creditors' claims against debtor's succession are not affected by debtor's death nor are they outlawed or barred by creditors' failure to exercise same within any specified delay, except that they become extinguished by expiration of delay of prescription applicable to any such claim in same way as if debtor were still alive. When estate has been accepted, claims may be brought against liquidators or heirs in usual manner. Form for proof of claim may be that of ordinary affidavit. See topic Affidavits.

Creditors may, if liquidator unknown or cannot be found within reasonable period of time, sue heirs or legatees collectively without mentioning their names or residences. Process may be served at last domicile which deceased had in province. If same is not in Quebec, is closed or is no longer occupied by any member of deceased's family, service may be made upon one of heirs or legatees by particular title. Service on liquidator is made at his domicile, residence or business office, or, if outside Quebec or unknown, on one of heirs. (C.P. 116, 133).

When succession opens outside province, any immovable action relating to his estate may be taken against heirs collectively who have not registered declaration of transmission by succession of such property, and in such case heirs and legatees may be served upon authorization by public notice, in district in which immovable in dispute is situated. (C. P. 116, 133, C.C.Q. 2998). All obligations contracted by deceased continue in existence after his death except those which on account of their nature have become impossible of performance due to his decease.

Payment of Debts.—Liquidator pays debts by realizing property of succession to extent necessary. He may alone sell movables which are perishable or expensive to preserve; he may sell other property with consent of heirs or court. (C.C.Q. 804).

Acceptance of Succession.—Acceptance by heirs is express or tacit, and may also result from law. Acceptance is express when successor formally assumes title or quality of heir. It is tacit where successor performs act that necessarily implies his intention of accepting. (C.C.Q. 637). Successor who renounces can accept for ten years from day right arose if it has not been accepted by another person. (C.C.Q. 649). Renunciation is tacit if successor unaware or has not made it known for ten years from day right arose. (C.C.Q. 650).

Investments.—Unless will otherwise provides, liquidators may only invest moneys held by them in presumed sound investments. See topic Administration of Property of Others, subhead Investments.

Distribution.—Before distributing property under his control, every assignee or other person, with exception of trustee in bankruptcy, who winds up, administers or controls property, business, succession, income or commercial activities of another, must give notice of intention to distribute to Minister of Revenue. Minister advises of duties, interest, and penalties exigible or which will so become within 12 months under any fiscal law. Distribution cannot be made until certificate received from Minister establishing that no amount is exigible, that sureties for payment accepted or that no creditor has priority of rank over Crown. Distribution made without obtaining said certificate renders person making distribution personally liable up to amount of property he has distributed. In case of succession, property up to value of $6,000 can be distributed prior to giving notice to Minister. (R.S.Q. c. M-31, §14).

Insolvent Estates.—Where succession not manifestly solvent, liquidator may not pay debts of succession or legacies until expiry of 60 days from registration of notice of closure of inventory or from exemption of making inventory. Liquidator may pay ordinary public utility bills and debts in urgent need of payment if required.

If property of succession insufficient, liquidator may not pay any debt of legacy before drawing up statement thereof, giving notice to interested persons and homologating payment proposal in court. In accordance with proposal, liquidator first pays hypothecary or preferred creditors; next other creditors, except for creditors of support; next creditors of support; finally, legatees by particular title. Liquidator may alienate property bequeathed as legacies if necessary to pay creditors. If property insufficient to pay legatees by particular title, liquidator, in accordance with proposal, first pays those having preference under will and then legatees of individual property. (C.C.Q. 810s.).

Allowances.—There is no provision for allowances for creditors of support pending administration, but if application for support is made against estate, provisional support may be awarded for duration of proceedings, and to cover cost of proceedings. (C.C.Q. 588). Creditors of support include spouses and relatives in direct line, and divorced spouses. (C.C.Q 585, 688). See topic Descent and Distribution, subhead Alimentary Support.

Remuneration.—Liquidator is entitled to reimbursement of expenses, and to remuneration if he is not heir. If heir, he may be remunerated if will so provides or heirs so agree. Remuneration is fixed by testator, heirs, or court where there is disagreement. (C.C.Q. 789). Liquidator not bound to take insurance or furnish security unless testator or majority of heirs demand it, or upon court order. (C.C.Q. 790).

Small Estates.—No simplified procedures are available for administration of small estates.

Foreign Liquidators and Administrators.—Any person who, under law of foreign country, is empowered to represent person who died or made his will there and left property in province, may be party in that capacity to proceedings before any court of Quebec. (C. P. 58).

Anatomical Gifts.—See topic Death, subhead Anatomical Gifts.

EXEMPTIONS:

Following are exempt from seizure: Consecrated vessels; family papers and portraits, medals and other decorations; property declared by donor or testator to be exempt from seizure, which may however be seized by creditors posterior to gift or to opening of legacy with permission of judge and to extent that he determines; alimentary allowances and alimony; books of account, titles of debt and other papers in possession of debtor, except currency, bonds, debentures, promissory notes, and other instruments payable to order or to bearer; contingent emoluments and fees due to ecclesiastics and ministers of religion and income of their clerical endowment; pensions granted to employees out of retiring or pension funds, as well as instalments paid or to be paid to form such funds; salaries and wages to extent of 70% of excess of following: $180 per week plus $30 per week for each dependent in excess of two if debtor is supporting his spouse, has dependent child or is main support of relative; and $120 per week in all other cases; reimbursement of expenses and periodic disability benefits under contract of accident and sickness insurance; property of person that he requires to compensate for handicap; works of art or historical property brought to Quebec to be placed on public exhibit. In calculating salaries and wages, account must be taken of any remuneration in money, kind or services, paid for services rendered under contract of employment, of enterprise, for services or of mandate, excepting: contributions of employer to pension, insurance or social welfare funds; value of food and lodging supplied or paid for by employer on occasion of travelling while carrying out work; passes given by transportation undertaking to its employees. Also anything declared unseizable by law. In case of alimentary debt, 50% of pensions, salaries or wages are seizable. (C. P. 553).

Debtor may select and withdraw from seizure certain categories of articles including household furniture, utensils and other things of general use to value of $6,000 as well as food and fuel required by him and his family and instruments of work needed for personal exercise of his professional activity. (C. P. 552).

FACTORS:

See topics Principal and Agent, Mortgages of Personal Property and Assignments.

FIDUCIARIES:

See topics Executors and Administrators of Estates, subhead Investments; Trusts.

FILING FEES:

See topics Corporations, subhead Fees; Records, subhead Registration Charges.

FISH AND GAME:

Persons are required to hold licence in order to hunt, trap or fish in province. (Act respecting the conservation and development of wildlife, R.S.Q. c. C-61.1). Fees for licence established by regulation. Government may grant lease of exclusive hunting, trapping or fishing rights on all or part of Crown lands. Rental and other terms and conditions of lease determined by regulation. Seasons for fishing certain species of fish and possession limits and for hunting set by regulation. Penalties provided for contravention of Act and regulations. Act also governs outfitting operations for practice of fishing, hunting or trapping activities.

For further particulars apply directly to Department of Tourism, Fish and Game.

FORECLOSURE:

See topics Liens; Mortgages of Personal Property, subhead Hypothecs Generally.

FOREIGN CORPORATIONS:

See topic Corporations, subhead Resident Agent.

FRANCHISES:

No special legislation.

FRAUDS, STATUTE OF:

There is no real equivalent to Statute of Frauds. General rule is that all evidence of any fact relevant to dispute is admissible and may be presented by any means. (C.C.Q. 2857). Proof of juridical act set forth in writing or content of writing is made by production of original or copy which legally replaces it. Party unable to produce original of writing or copy which legally replaces it may, however, make proof by any other means where he is acting in good faith and with dispatch. (C.C.Q. 2860).

Proof of juridical act permitted by testimony in cases where value in dispute is less than $1,500 except: (1) if there is commencement of proof in writing or by material thing, or (2) if proof is being made against person of legal act he executed in ordinary course of business of enterprise—then testimonial proof can be made regardless of value in dispute. (C.C.Q. 2862).

FRAUDULENT SALES AND CONVEYANCES:

Any conveyance which is shown to be simulated can be set aside by any interested party.

Creditor who suffers prejudice through juridical act of his debtor in fraud of his rights, particularly act designed to render debtor insolvent or to prefer another creditor, may obtain declaration that act may not be set up against him. (C.C.Q. 1631).

Presumptions of Fraud.—A gratuitous contract or payment is deemed to be made with fraudulent intent, even if the contracting party or creditor was unaware of the facts, where debtor was or became insolvent at time of making it. (C.C.Q. 1633).

An onerous contract or payment made by debtor to person who knows him to be insolvent or knows that debtor thereby becomes insolvent, is deemed to be made with fraudulent intent. (C.C.Q. 1632).

Limitation of Actions.—Action in avoidance is forfeited unless brought within one year from day on which creditor obtained knowledge of injury resulting from act which is attacked or, in case of bankruptcy, from date of appointment of trustee. (C.C.Q. 1635).

Bankruptcy.—Additional special rules are contained in federal bankruptcy statutes. See Canada Law Digest, topic Bankruptcy.

Bulk Sales.—In Quebec, called sale of enterprise. Transfer of whole or substantial part of enterprise made outside ordinary course of business of seller is sale of enterprise. Sale made by: prior or hypothecary creditor in exercise of his rights, person charged with administration of property of others for benefit of creditors, or public officer acting under judicial authority, is not sale of enterprise.

Before paying price, buyer must obtain sworn statement from seller containing names and addresses of all creditors, nature and amount of their claims and security attached thereto. Buyer must give notice of sale to each prior and hypothecary creditor listed in this statement, with request to indicate within 20 days amount of their claim and value of any security. Where cash sale proceeds are sufficient to pay all creditors, no notice of sale required, but buyer must pay all creditors.

Person designated to distribute sale price is bound to prepare distribution statement and give copy to creditors. Creditors have 20 days to contest. Buyer and seller are liable for failure of designated person to distribute sale price in accordance with prescribed formalities but buyer's liability limited to value of property he has bought.

Where buyer has observed prescribed formalities, creditors of seller have no right against buyer or sold property but retain recourse against seller. Where prescribed formalities not observed, sale of enterprise may not be set up against creditors of seller who have claims prior to date of conclusion of sale. Fact that sale not opposable may be invoked within one year of day on which creditor becomes aware of sale and, in any case, within three years from act of sale. (C.C.Q. 1767s.).

Unconscionable Transaction.—See topic Consumer Protection.

GARNISHMENT:

Execution on sums and effects due or belonging to debtor in the hands of third party, known as garnishee, is effected by service thereon and on judgment debtor or writ of seizure by garnishment which orders garnishee to appear on day and at hour fixed to declare under oath what sums of money he owes to debtor or will have to pay him and what movable property he has in his possession belonging to him, and not to dispossess himself thereof. Garnishee's declaration may be made before day mentioned in writ by giving notice to judgment debtor and to seizing creditor. When corporation, partnership or group of persons associated for pursuit of common purpose in province but without civil personality is garnishee, declaration must be made by person so authorized by general or special power of attorney. (C. P. 625s).

Garnishee's declaration may be contested and garnishee who fails to make declaration may be condemned personally to pay seizing creditor's claim. Upon payment of costs incurred by his default, garnishee may obtain leave to make his declaration at any time. (C. P. 634, 635).

Adverse Claims.—In case of several seizures by different unsecured creditors in hands of same garnishee, each seizure has preference over subsequent seizures according to date of service on garnishee, unless debtor's insolvency is alleged, in which case all creditors are collocated pro rata. (C. P. 640). In cases of seizure of salaries or wages, any creditor may file sworn claim so long as garnishment remains binding.

Voluntary Deposit by Debtor.—No creditor may garnish salary or wages of his debtor, who, having produced in Court of Quebec, declaration under oath containing designation of his employer, amount and date of his remuneration, his family responsibilities, list of his creditors with their addresses and nature and amount of their claims, thereafter deposits regularly seizable portion of his remuneration (see topic Exemptions) within five days following each payment. Compliance with these requirements also protects debtor against seizure of furniture in his residence, except in exercise of privilege or right of recovery. (C. P. 652, 653).

GUARDIAN AND WARD:

Supervision of Minors.—

Tutors.—Tutorship is conferred by Court, on advice of tutorship council unless it is applied for by director of youth protection. (C.C.Q. 205). Generally, tutorship council is composed of three persons designated by meeting of relatives, persons connected by marriage or friends. (C.C.Q. 222).

Eligibility and Competency.—Tutorship is personal office open to every natural person capable of fully exercising his civil rights and who is able to assume such office. (C.C.Q. 179).

Duties.—Tutor acts as administrator entrusted with simple administration of property of minor. (C.C.Q. 208). See topic Administration of Property of Others.

Within 60 days of institution of tutorship, tutor shall make inventory of property administered. (C.C.Q. 240). Tutor is bound to invest sums of money under his administration in accordance with rules relating to presumed sound investments. (C.C.Q. 1304).

He cannot renounce or accept successions which have fallen to the minor without the advice of tutorship council. (C.C.Q. 638). See topic Descent and Distribution, subhead Acceptance of Succession.

Actions belonging to the minor are brought in the name of the tutor. (C.C.Q. 159).

At the end of the tutorship the tutor is bound to render an account of his administration. (C.C.Q. 247).

Before contracting substantial loan in relation to patrimony of minor, offering property as security, alienating important piece of family property, immovable or enterprise, or demanding definitive partition of immovables held in co-ownership, tutor must obtain authorization of tutorship council or Court. (C.C.Q. 213).

Emancipation.—Court after obtaining advice of tutor and, where applicable, of tutorship council, may emancipate minor. (C.C.Q. 168). Tutor is accountable for his administration to emancipated minor; he continues, however, to assist him gratuitously. (C.C.Q. 169).

Foreign Guardians.—If minor or protected person of full age is domiciled outside Quebec but possesses property in Quebec or has rights to be exercised and law of domicile does not provide for him to have representative, tutor or curator may be appointed to represent him in all cases where tutor or curator may represent minor or protected person of full age under laws of Quebec. (C.C.Q. 3085).

Protective Supervision of Persons of Full Age.—Protective supervision of person of full age is established in his interest to ensure protection of his person, administration of his patrimony and exercise of his civil rights. (C.C.Q. 256).

Appointment.—May be sought at initiative of person requiring protection or someone close to such person, or at initiative of director general of health or social services establishment, through Court in jurisdiction which person requiring protection had domicile or residence. Mandatary designated by person or Public Curator may also apply for institution of protective supervision. (C.C.Q. 268-269). Judgments establishing protective supervision reviewable any time. (C.C.Q. 277).

Powers and Duties.—Tutor or curator must be appointed to represent, or advisor to assist, person of full age unable to care for himself or to administer his property by reason of illness, deficiency or debility due to age impairing mental faculties or physical ability to express will. (C.C.Q. 258).

Tutor or curator so appointed responsible for custody and maintenance and moral and physical well being of person of full age, based on consideration of several factors. (C.C.Q. 260).

Advisors.—Appointed to person of full age, generally and habitually able to care for himself and administer property, requiring for certain acts or certain time, assistance or advice regarding administration of property. Advisor does not have administration of property. (C.C.Q. 291).

Tutors.—Appointed to person of full age if established that inability to care for himself or to administer property partial or temporary. (C.C.Q. 285). Tutor has simple administration of property, exercised in same manner as tutor to minor, unless Court decides otherwise. (C.C.Q. 286).

See topic Administration of Property of Others.

Curators.—Appointed to person of full age if established that inability to care for himself or administer property total and permanent. (C.C.Q. 281). Curator has full administration of property exercised according to rules of administration of property of others. (C.C.Q. 282).

Termination.—By judgment of release; death of protected person or upon expiry of period for contesting report attesting cessation of inability. (C.C.Q. 295).

Investments.—See topic Administration of Property of Others, subheads Types of Administration and Investments.

Public Curator.—Appointed by Lieutenant-Governor in Council. Supervises administration of private tutorships and curatorships, above. Assumes provisional simple administration of certain properties and assumes tutorship to property of minors and tutorship or curatorship to persons of full age not already provided with such. (R.S.Q. c. C-81). Public curator does not have custody of protected person of full age when he serves as tutor or curator, unless Court entrusts to him where no other person can assume role. Under most circumstances, public curator may do what is necessary for simple administration of property without judicial authorization.

Termination.—Administration ceases upon appointment of private tutor or curator; when testamentary executor or heirs of person represented by public curator accept duties or succession following death of person represented, or upon cessation of need for protective supervision.

See topics Administration of Property of Others, Descent and Distribution, subhead Irregular Successions; Wills, subhead Unclaimed Legacies; Principal and Agent, subhead Power of Attorney.

Power of Attorney.—See topic Principal and Agent, subhead Power of Attorney.

HOLIDAYS:

Following are holidays and non-juridical days in Province of Quebec: Sundays; 1st of Jan.; 2d of Jan.; Good Friday; Easter Mon.; 24th of June; 1st of July, Canada Day, or 2d of July when 1st is Sun.; first Mon. of Sept., Labor Day; 2d Mon. of Oct.; 25th of Dec.; 26th of Dec.; day fixed by proclamation of Governor-General for celebration of birthday of Sovereign; any other day fixed by proclamation of Government as public holiday. Sat. only considered non-juridical for purposes of computing delays. (C.P. 6, 8).

HOMESTEADS:

No homestead exemption.

HUMAN RIGHTS:

By act entitled Charter of Human Rights and Freedoms (R. S. Q. c. C-12) basic human rights and freedoms are given statutory recognition. Charter also recognizes certain political, judicial, economic and social rights and sets out a number of prohibited acts related to violations of said rights and freedoms.

Basic human rights and freedoms, political and judicial rights including prohibitions related thereto are stated to prevail over provisions of any subsequent act inconsistent therewith unless subsequent act expressly states that it applies despite Charter. Charter binds Crown in matters under legislative authority of Quebec.

Commission named "Commission des droits de la personne" established to receive complaints and generally assist in promotion, understanding and acceptance of Charter. Penalties are provided for contravention of certain prohibitions and right to obtain cessation of interference with rights or freedoms as well as compensation for resulting prejudice, including exemplary damages, given statutory recognition.

Affirmative action programmes upon recommendation of Commission statutorily recognized and regulated covering equality in employment, educational services available to public, health and public services.

For Canadian Charter of Rights and Freedoms enacted by Constitution Act, 1982 see Canada Law Digest.

Reputation and Privacy.—C.C.Q. prohibits invasion of person's privacy or reputation. (C.C.Q. 35 to 41). These provisions are completed by Act respecting the protection of personal information in the private sector (S.Q. 1993, c. 17), which applies to all private enterprises which, directly or indirectly, gather, hold, use or convey personal information to third parties.

Person collecting personal information for purpose of establishing file on another person can collect only information necessary to attain object of file. Information must be collected from person concerned unless person concerned consents to collection from third persons. Consent to communication or use of personal information must, in order to be valid, be manifest, free, enlightened and given for specific purposes.

Persons operating enterprises are required to ensure that any personal information on others that they hold or use remains confidential. Employee on whom personal information is requested has right to be informed of object of file, of categories of persons who will have access to file and place where file will be kept.

Finally, Act also establishes specific rules pertaining to agents who establish files on other persons on commercial basis and prepare and communicate credit reports to third persons. Such agents will be required, in future, to register with Commission and make their activities known to public by means of notices published periodically in press. Act prescribes penal sanctions and insures concordance of its provisions with legislation currently in force.

HUSBAND AND WIFE:

By S. Q. 1969, c. 77 relationships between husband and wife, property rights, capacity of wife, basic marital regime and immutability of matrimonial regime were changed with effect from July 1, 1970.

Rights and Duties of Spouses.—Husband and wife mutually owe each other respect, fidelity, succour and assistance. Spouses must live together but may have separate domiciles without prejudice to that rule. (C.C.Q. 82). Each spouse retains own surname and given names and exercises civil rights under these names. Persons married before Apr. 2, 1981 have option of using surname of spouse. Spouses contribute towards expenses of marriage in proportion to their respective means. Each spouse may make contribution by activity within home. (C.C.Q. 392, 393, 396).

Residence.—Spouses choose family residence together. Neither spouse may alienate or encumber residence without consent of other. Similar provision for household furniture. If residence is leased, spouse who is lessee may not sublet or transfer or terminate lease without consent of other. Declaration of residence may be published. (C.C.Q. 395, 401s.).

Family Patrimony.—By R.S.Q. 1989, c. 55 legislation enacted establishing family patrimony, effective July 1, 1989, which applies to couples married after this date, as well as to spouses married before July 1, 1989 unless they declared wish to be exempted therefrom within 18 months of date of effect. Operates in addition to matrimonial régime to favor economic equality between spouses.

Marriage establishes family patrimony of certain property of spouses regardless of which of them holds right of ownership. (C.C.Q. 414). Composed of principal residence and secondary residence of family or rights conferring such uses and household furniture used to furnish same; vehicle used for family travel and benefits accrued during marriage under various retirement plans. Excludes property devolved to spouse by succession, legacy or gift before or during marriage. (C.C.Q. 415).

In event of separation as to bed and board or dissolution or annulment of marriage, value of family patrimony divided equally between spouses or between surviving spouse and heirs. (C.C.Q. 416). May be effected by giving in payment or by payment of money. (C.C.Q. 419). Court may order compensatory payment where property alienated to detriment of spouse prior to need for partition. (C.C.Q. 421).

Spouses cannot, by way of marriage contract or otherwise, renounce rights in family patrimony; but spouse may renounce such rights by notarial deed, from death of spouse or from judgment of divorce, separation or nullity. Renunciation entered in register of personal and movable real rights. Failing registration within one year of right to partition, renouncing spouse deemed to have accepted. (C.C.Q. 423). Action for annulment of renunciation of family patrimony or partition of acquests must be commenced within three years from act. (C.C.Q. 2925).

Spousal Allowance.—Court, in declaring separation, divorce or annulment may order either spouse to pay to other, as compensation for latter's contribution, in property or services, to enrichment of patrimony of former, allowance based on consideration of advantages of matrimonial régime and of marriage contract. Award may include right in family residence, household furniture or retirement benefits. Same applies in case of death, based on advantages of succession to surviving spouse. (C.C.Q. 427). See topic Descent and Distribution, subhead Alimentary Support.

Antenuptial Contracts.—Basic marital regime is partnership of acquests (replacing prior basic regime of community of property). (C.C.Q. 432). However, spouses may by notarial marriage contract entered into prior to marriage modify basic regime or establish another regime such as community of movables and acquests or separation of property. (C.C.Q. 431-437). Spouses may also after marriage modify or change their marital regime by notarial deed homologated by court provided rights of family and creditors are not prejudiced. (C.C.Q. 438).

Partnership of Acquests.—Spouses married on or after July 1, 1970 who have not entered into special agreement by marriage contract are subject to regime of partnership of acquests. (C.C.Q. 432).

Acquests falling into partnership consist of all properties not declared by law to be private property and in particular: (1) Proceeds of spouse's work during marriage; (2) all fruits and revenues which fall due or are received during marriage. (C.C.Q. 449).

Following are private property of each spouse: (1) Property owned or possessed on day of marriage; (2) property acquired during marriage by succession or gift, fruits and revenues therefrom if testator or donor so provided; (3) property acquired in replacement of private property; (4) clothing, personal papers, wedding ring, decorations and diplomas; (5) rights or benefits devolving to spouse as subrogated holder or specified beneficiary under retirement plan or other annuity or insurance; (6) instruments required for spouse's occupation. (C.C.Q. 450).

In partnership of acquests each spouse has administration, enjoyment and free disposal of his private property and acquests but cannot, without concurrence of other spouse, dispose of acquests by gratuitous title inter vivos with exception of small sums and customary presents. (C.C.Q. 397-398). Property with respect to which neither spouse can establish exclusive ownership is deemed to be acquest held in undivided ownership. (C.C.Q. 459-460). This does not limit right to name third person beneficiary of annuities, retirement pensions or life insurance policies. (C.C.Q. 461-463).

Partnership of acquests is dissolved by death of one of spouses, by conventional change of matrimonial regime, by judgment pronouncing divorce, separation from bed and board or separation of property or nullity of marriage and by absence of one of spouses after a certain period. (C.C.Q. 465).

Community of Property.—Spouses married before July 1, 1970 in legal community of property or who before Apr. 2, 1981 were governed by community regime, legal or contractual, are now governed by rules concerning community of movables and acquests or terms of their marriage contract. Regime of community of movables and acquests otherwise abolished. (S. Q. 1980, c. 39, s.66).

Community of movables and acquests consists of: (1) All movable property which spouses possess at time of marriage and also all which they acquire afterwards except property coming to them by gift or legacy under terms of which it is excluded from community; (2) proceeds of work of spouses during marriage, subject to provisions relating to reserved property; (3) all fruits and revenues arising from private property if they fall due or are received during marriage; (4) immovable property they acquire during marriage. (C. C. 1272).

Husband alone administers property of community, but he cannot sell or mortgage any immovable property of community without concurrence of wife. Nor can husband dispose by gift any property of community except small sums of money and customary gifts without concurrence of his wife. This does not limit his right to name a third party beneficiary of annuities, retirement pensions or life insurance policies. Husband may nevertheless without concurrence of his wife sell or pledge any movable property of community other than a business or household furniture in use by family. (C. C. 1292).

Proceeds of personal work of wife common as to movables and acquests, savings therefrom, movables or immovables she acquires by investing them are reserved to her administration and she has enjoyment of free disposal of them. She cannot alienate them by gratuitous title, nor alienate or hypothecate immovables, nor alienate or pledge stock in trade and household furniture in use by family without husband's concurrence. (C. C. 1425).

Community is dissolved for same reasons as partnership of acquests.

Wife may carry on trade or calling, without her husband's consent. However, if she is common as to property and carries on trade despite husband's opposition, she does not bind community beyond amount of benefit community derived from such trade or calling. Wife common as to property who carries on trade or calling with husband's consent obligates community for all that relates to such trade or calling.

After dissolution by death of partnership of acquests or community of movables and acquests and in absence of any will to contrary, surviving spouse has enjoyment of acquests or of property of community coming to children from deceased spouse; usufruct lasts as to each child until he reaches age of 18 years old or until he is emancipated. (C. C. 1426).

Separation as to Property.—Spouses may by simple declaration in marriage contract retain exclusive rights of administration, enjoyment and disposal of their property. Property over which neither spouse is able to establish exclusive right of ownership is presumed held by both in undivided ownership, one-half by each. (C.C.Q. 485-487).

Disability of Married Women.—Spouses have identical rights and obligations in marriage. Powers may be limited by marriage regime.

Separate Property.—Compensation received by spouse after marriage as damages for moral or corporal injury as well as right to such compensation are private property of spouse if partners as to acquests and individual property if in community. (C.C.Q. 454). See subheads Partnership of Acquests; Community of Property, supra.

Contracts.—Husband and wife have full capacity to contract with each other and confer benefits inter vivos upon each other during marriage. Wife is no longer prohibited from binding herself for her husband with respect to her personal property.

Actions.—See subhead Disability of Married Women, supra.

Agency.—Each spouse may give other mandate to represent him or her in exercise of his or her rights and powers under their matrimonial regime. Each spouse may bind other for current needs of family. (C.C.Q. 397-398).

See topic Principal and Agent, subhead Power of Attorney.

See note at head of Digest as to 1996 legislation covered.

See Topical Index in front part of this volume.

HUSBAND AND WIFE . . . *continued*

Desertion and Non-Support.—In separation action based on desertion or other grounds, either spouse may demand alimentary pension and/or lump sum payment. Children entitled to maintenance from parents according to their needs and means of parents. This obligation reciprocal. In all cases amount of maintenance fixed by court unless parties agree. (C.C.Q. 585s.).

Community Property.—See subheads Partnership of Acquests; Community of Property, supra.

Separation as to Bed and Board.—Application for separation as to bed and board may be granted by court of district of common domicile or, if no common domicile, domicile of either spouse. (C.P. 70). It is granted when will to live together is seriously damaged. (C.C.Q. 493). Court may grant it without disclosure of grounds if draft separation agreement is submitted and court considers it sufficiently preserves interests of spouses and children. (C.C.Q. 493, 495). Judgment releases obligation to live together and carries with it separation of property but does not dissolve marriage. In pronouncing separation, court may order either spouse to pay support to other. (C.C.Q. 507s.). Separation as to bed and board produces same effect towards children as divorce. (C.C.Q. 513, 514s.).

See also topic Substitution.

IMMIGRATION:

Pursuant to series of Federal-Provincial agreements on the subject, jurisdiction over selection of immigrants seeking to reside in Quebec is, with certain exceptions, exclusively within jurisdiction of Province. In order to attain landed status, applicants must obtain "Certificate of Selection" from Province. Province alone is responsible for establishing applicable selection criteria.

Except in cases where alien has been granted Employment Authorization by Federal government on grounds that employment of person will not have adverse affect on employment opportunities for Canadian citizens or permanent residents in Canada, applicants for Employment Authorization must first obtain "Certificate of Acceptance" ("CAQ") issued by Province. CAQ's are also required for aliens seeking to obtain student authorization in order to study in Quebec as well as for aliens seeking medical treatment at Quebec hospital.

INCOME TAX: See topic Taxation.

INFANTS:

Age of majority is 18. (C.C.Q. 153).

Incapacity of Minors.—Act performed alone by minor or his tutor without authorization of tutorship council may not be annulled or obligations reduced unless minor suffers damage. (C.C.Q. 163). Minor may, within limits imposed by his age and power of discernment, enter into contracts alone to meet his ordinary and usual needs. Minor 14 years of age or over is deemed to be of full age for all acts pertaining to his employment or to practice of his craft or profession. In judicial matters minors generally represented by tutor. (C.C.Q. 155).

Emancipated Minor.—Minor can obtain simple emancipation if 16 years of age or over with approval of tutorship council or court. (C.C.Q. 167-168). Emancipation enables him to perform all acts of simple administration provided minor does not notably reduce his capital. (C.C.Q. 172).

Full emancipation is obtained by marriage and enables minor to exercise his civil rights as if he were of full age. (C.C.Q. 175-176).

Support of Minor.—Father and mother must maintain their children. (C.C.Q. 599). Spouses contribute to expenses of marriage in proportion to their respective means which contribution may be made by activity within home. (C.C.Q. 396).

Parental Responsibility.—Father and mother exercise parental authority together except in cases where Code otherwise provides. (C.C.Q. 394, 600). Person having parental authority is responsible for damage caused by child subject to such authority. Responsibility attaches unless person with parental authority can prove that he or she did not commit any fault with regard to custody, supervision or education of child. (C.C.Q. 1459).

Termination of Parental Rights.—Youth Protection Act (R.S.Q. c. P-34.1) establishes agency entitled "Comité de la protection de la jeunesse" entrusted with right to intervene between child and parents in order to prevent situations threatening security and development of child such as where parents deceased, lack of appropriate care, lack of necessary material conditions of life, custodian's way of life creates risk of moral or physical danger, child forced to act unacceptably for his age, sexual abuse, or where serious behavioral disturbances not remedied by his parents.

Social Service Centres with directors established under Act. Director may, where urgent measures necessary, immediately remove child from environment and entrust child to appropriate centre. Measures applied without need of parental consent for 24 hours. Longer periods require court permission.

Young Offenders Act (S.C. 1982, c. 110) governs arrest, detention, trial, and sentencing of minors in criminal matters. Youth court established under Act may dispense with consent of parents normally required in order for youth to be detained for treatment of physical or mental disorder, if it appears that parents not available or not taking active interest in proceedings.

Adoption has effect of conferring parental authority on adopter. (C.C.Q. 556,559).

Generally, courts may for serious cause and in interest of child limit or terminate parental authority. (C.C.Q. 606).

INHERITANCE TAX:

See topic Taxation, subhead Succession Duties.

INJUNCTIONS:

Injunction may be demanded by way of action and granted by Superior Court, or judge thereof, enjoining person, his officers, agents, or employees, not to do or to cease doing, or, in certain cases to perform particular act or operation. At commencement of or during suit, interlocutory injunction may be granted when it is considered to be necessary in order to avoid serious or irreparable injury to applicant, or factual or legal situation is of such nature as to render final judgment ineffectual. Application for interlocutory injunction is made by written motion, supported by detailed affidavit affirming truth of facts alleged and served upon opposite party with notice of presentation. In cases of urgency, judge may grant application perfunctorily before it has been served, for maximum period of ten days. Application for interlocutory injunction may not be presented before writ of summons issues unless writ has not been issued in due time. If granted, order is attached to and served with writ. If application is granted prior to issuance of writ, judge may permit application to be served without writ and fix delay for service of writ. Unless judge otherwise decides for good reason, party demanding injunction must give satisfactory security for loss or damage to which opposite party may be subject.

Any person who knowingly contravenes terms of injunction may be condemned to fine not exceeding $50,000, with or without imprisonment for term not exceeding one year, without prejudice to opposite party's claim for damages. (C. P. 751s).

INSOLVENCY:

See Canada Law Digest, topic Bankruptcy.

INSURANCE:

Regulated by Act respecting insurance (R. S. Q. c. A-32), by C. C.Q. 2389-2628, and also by federal legislation. See Canada Law Digest, topic Insurance.

Supervision.—Inspector General of Financial Institutions is responsible for supervision of insurance business.

Annual Statements.—Insurer before Mar. 1 of each year must prepare and file with Inspector General statements of operations for preceding year.

Policies.—Form and content of insurance policies are regulated generally by C.C.Q. 2389 to 2628, and as consumer contracts or contracts of adhesion by C.C.Q. 1435, 1436-1437. See topic Contracts, subhead Nullity.

Rebates prohibited whether direct or indirect.

Agents, Brokers and Claims Adjusters.—Regulated by and licensed under Act Respecting Market Intermediaries. (R.S.Q. c. I-15.1).

Process Agents.—Insurer not having head office in province must designate chief representative in province when applying for license. Chief representative must under power of attorney be authorized to act as process agent.

Investments.—Title IV, Chapter III of act respecting insurance governs investments, assets and reserves of insurers.

Foreign Insurance Companies.—May be licensed by Inspector General subject to certain specified requirements. See also special statutory provisions governing foreign insurance companies, Canada Law Digest, topic Insurance, subhead Foreign Insurance Companies.

Taxation.—Governed by Taxation Act. See topic Corporations, subhead Corporation Taxes, and topic Taxation, subheads Corporation Taxes, Sales Tax.

Direct Action Against Insurer.—Injured third person may bring action directly against insured, insurer or both. (C.C.Q. 2501). See topic Motor Vehicles, subhead Direct Actions Against Insurer.

No-Fault Insurance.—See topic Motor Vehicles, subhead No-Fault Insurance.

INTEREST:

Maximum Rate.—No maximum rate.

Legal rate is 5% per annum. (R.S.C. I-15).

Judgments.—Legal rate in absence of agreement to contrary, to which may be added indemnity equivalent to difference between such rate and rate fixed by §28 of Act respecting Ministère du Revenu. (R.S.Q. c.M-31). Interest runs from institution of action except, if judgment for nonpayment of sum of money, from default. (C.C.Q. 1618, 1619, 1600, 1617). Monetary obligations under loan of money may be reduced or annulled if court finds, having regard to risk and circumstances, that one of parties has suffered lesion. (C.C.Q. 2332).

INTESTACY:

See topic Descent and Distribution.

JOINT STOCK COMPANIES:

Joint stock companies are formed either under the authority of a charter, or of act of legislature, and are governed by their charter and Part II of Companies Act. See topic Corporations.

JUDGMENTS:

Judgments by Acquiescence.—At any stage of proceedings, defendant may file in office of court acquiescence in all or part of any demand, except in most family matters. If acquiescence is not for whole demand and is refused by plaintiff, case proceeds but if court decides refusal unjustified, cost limited as if acquiescence had been accepted. (C. P. 457, 460).

Judgments on Pleadings.—Court cannot adjudicate beyond conclusions in pleadings. (C. P. 468).

Default Judgments.—As soon as default to appear or to plead recorded, case may be inscribed for judgment, notice of inscription must be given in case of default to plead. Party may be relieved of default at any time before judgment is entered. (C. P. 192, 193). It takes about one month depending on district in which action is taken to obtain judgment if action not contested.

Offer of Judgment.—See subhead Judgments by Acquiescence, supra.

See note at head of Digest as to 1996 legislation covered.

See Topical Index in front part of this volume.

JUDGMENTS . . . *continued*

Actions.—Judgments are good for and can be executed any time within ten years. Rights resulting from judgment are prescribed after ten years if not exercised and cannot be revived. (C.C.Q. 2924).

Liens.—Registration of judgment against immovable property operates as hypothecary claim thereon in creditor's favor; otherwise judgment creditor has no priority unless seizure made. (C.C.Q. 2724).

Declaratory Judgments.—See topic Declaratory Judgments.

Foreign Judgments.—Decisions rendered outside of Quebec are recognized by Quebec authorities and are declared enforceable except (1) when authority of country where decision was rendered had no jurisdiction; (2) decision is subject to ordinary remedy or is not final or enforceable where it was rendered; (3) decision was rendered in violation of fundamental procedural principles; (4) identical dispute between same parties is pending in Quebec; (5) outcome of foreign decision is manifestly against public order as understood in international relations; (6) decision enforces obligations arising from taxation laws of foreign country. (C.C.Q. 3155).

Payment of Maintenance.—Judgments rendered in another province of Canada, ordering the payment of maintenance, may be executed in Quebec provided they conform to the rules of public order of this province, especially those relating to marriage. A certified copy of the judgment, along with the depositions or stenographic transcript of testimony, is transmitted to the Attorney-General who in turn transmits same to the prothonotary of the Superior Court of the district where the defendant has his residence. Defendant may file an opposition to execution on ground that judgment is incompatible with rules of public order of the Province and in such case judgment becomes executory only after confirmation, upon petition, by the Superior Court of the district. The Court may either confirm, modify or quash the extra-provincial judgment. There is an appeal from this judgment. A judgment of maintenance obtained in Quebec against a person not domiciled there may be transmitted by the Attorney-General to the Department of Justice of the province where the debtor has his domicile to be executed according to the laws of that province. (R. S. Q. c. E-19).

See also topic Language, subhead Legislature and Courts.

LABOR RELATIONS:

Contract of Employment.—C.C.Q. governs "Contract of employment" (C.C.Q. 2085 to 2097), whereby person/employee, undertakes for limited period to do work for remuneration, according to instructions and under direction or control of another person/employer (C.C.Q. 2085). Contract of employment is for fixed or indeterminate term. (C.C.Q. 2086).

C.C.Q. also provides essential obligations of employee and employer to each other during contract of employment. (C.C.Q. 2087-2088). Parties may stipulate in writing that even after termination of contract, employee may neither compete with employer nor participate in enterprise which would compete with employer. Stipulation must be limited as to time, place and type of employment, to whatever is necessary for protection of legitimate interest of employer. (C.C.Q. 2089). Stipulation of noncompetition cannot be invoked by employer who has resiliated contract of employment without serious reason or if employer has given employee serious reason for resiliating contract. (C.C.Q. 2095).

C.C.Q. also provides how contract of employment for indeterminate term is tacitly renewed (C.C.Q. 2090) or terminated by giving reasonable notice (C.C.Q. 2091). One of parties may unilaterally resiliate contract of employment without prior notice but only for serious reason. (C.C.Q. 2094). Where insufficient notice of termination is given or where manner of resiliation is abusive, employee may not renounce his right to obtain compensation. (C.C.Q. 2092).

Contract of employment is not terminated by alienation of enterprise or any change in its legal structure by way of amalgamation or otherwise and is binding on representative or successor of employer. (C.C.Q. 2097).

Labor Code (R.S.Q. c. C-27), is principal statute concerning labor relations. It protects right of association, provides for certification of labor unions, establishes certain rules, procedures and delays for negotiation of labor agreements and establishes labor court to decide on disputes arising out of interpretation or application of Labor Code. Labor Court has jurisdiction in appeal from decisions of labor commissioners and in first instance on any penal proceedings under Labor Code.

Other legislation covers minimum wage and vacations, hours of work, disputes between public services and their employees, and discrimination in employment, collective bargaining in construction industry and extension of principal terms of a collective agreement in a given trade to all employees in that trade in a given area.

Labor Unions.—Every employee has right to belong to an association of employees of his choice and to participate in activities and management thereof. Any association of employees comprising absolute majority of employees of an employer is entitled to be certified and may apply for certification by petition made to labor commissioner general appointed under Labor Code who investigates representative character of petitioning association and its right to be certified. Where more than one union is seeking certification, labor commissioner may certify union with most votes after one or several ballots, even if such union does not have absolute majority of votes. Starting with certification and as long as same not revoked employer bound to deduct from salary of employees covered by certification amount equal to dues fixed by union and remit same monthly to union. (R.S.Q., c. C-27).

An employer is prohibited from hindering, dominating or financing formation or activities or any association of employees and from participating therein.

Collective Agreements.—Employer and union must negotiate in good faith. Conciliation services may be requested by either party from Minister of Labor who may appoint conciliator even without request. If no collective agreement concluded right to strike or lock-out acquired 90 days after notice to other party of demand to commence negotiations or if no notice given, 90 days after certification or expiry of last collective agreement. Special rules govern negotiations and right to strike in public and parapublic sectors. Collective agreements must be for minimum one year. Grievances (disagreement respecting interpretation or application of collective agreement) must be submitted to arbitration which is binding on parties and not subject to appeal. (R.S.Q., c. C-27).

Anti-discrimination.—It is unlawful for an employer to refuse to hire, to discharge or to discriminate against an individual on basis of race, age, colour, religion, ethnic or national origin, or social condition, sex, sexual orientation, pregnancy, handicap, language, political convictions or civil status, nor may he require information on these matters in connection with hiring of employee. See topic Human Rights.

Workmen's Compensation.—Industrial Accidents and Occupational Diseases Act (R.S.Q., c. A-3.001) provides compensation for injuries resulting from industrial accident or occupational disease. Compensation includes provisions for necessary care for consolidation of injury, physical, social and vocational rehabilitation of worker, payment of income, replacement indemnities, compensation for bodily injury, and death benefits.

Act applies to every worker who has industrial accident in Quebec or contracts occupational disease in Quebec whose employer, when accident happens or disease contracted, has establishment in Quebec. Act also applies, under certain conditions, to worker, domiciled in Province, when industrial accident or occupational disease contracted outside Province. Act does not apply to cases where injury or disease arises solely as result of gross and willful negligence of worker who is victim unless ends in his death or causes severe permanent physical or mental impairment.

Worker is defined as natural person who does work for remuneration under contract of hire or personal services and includes under certain conditions, independent operators, students, volunteers, and persons given employment by government, such as persons detained in house of detention. Independent operators, domestics' employers and directors of companies may register under Act to be entitled to benefits if suffer employment injury. Special rights for construction workers.

Employment injury means injury resulting from industrial accident or occupational disease. Industrial accident means sudden and unforeseen event, attributable to any cause, which happens to person, arising out of or in course of his work and resulting in employment injury. Occupational disease is disease contracted from work or in course of work and characteristic of that work or directly related to risks peculiar to that work. Special provisions apply to occupational lung diseases.

Worker who suffers employment injury is entitled to income replacement indemnity equal to 90% of net income worker derives annually from employment, if becomes unable to carry on employment by reason of injury. Is entitled to indemnity until returns to employment or similar work or until refuses without valid reason to do so.

Act also provides for compensation for bodily injury proportional to permanent physical or mental impairment calculated according to factors set out in Schedule to Act. Indemnity is paid in form of pension every two weeks.

Death of worker entitles spouse to lump sum indemnity in excess of $50,000 determined with reference to gross annual income of worker and factor set out in Schedule to Act. Spouse also receives 55% of income replacement indemnity which worker entitled to at death, paid monthly for period established according to age of spouse. Special indemnity of $1,000 also paid to spouse or failing same to dependents in equal shares. If no dependents father and mother of worker entitled to $3,000 indemnity each. Children of worker entitled to $250 monthly and if attending school full time to lump sum of $9,000. Special provisions if beneficiary invalid at time of worker's death. Other indemnities include $1,500 for funeral expenses and cost of transportation of body.

Worker who has suffered employment injury has right to rehabilitation, either physical, social or professional depending on worker's needs. Physical rehabilitation includes treatment deemed necessary by physician. Social rehabilitation programs include implementation of means to provide worker with residence and vehicle adapted to residual capacity. Vocational rehabilitation programs include assistance in finding employment and payment of subsidies to employer to favor employment of workers who have sustained permanent physical or mental impairment.

Worker who has suffered employment injury is entitled to medical aid required by his condition resulting from injury. Act imposes duty on employer to immediately give first aid to worker who suffers employment injury in establishment.

Act gives worker right to be reinstated in former employment in preference to others, provided worker is able to carry on employment. Worker continues to accumulate seniority within meaning of collective agreement applicable to him.

No employer may dismiss, suspend or transfer worker or impose any sanctions because he has suffered employment injury or exercised any rights conferred upon him by Act. Any sanction imposed within six months of date of which worker has suffered employment injury gives rise to presumption sanction was imposed because of employment injury. Burden then on employer to prove sanction was imposed for another good and sufficient reason. Complaints under this rule must be filed within 30 days of knowledge.

Act is administered by Commission de la santé et de la sécurité du travail (Occupational Health and Safety Commission). Commission pays out indemnities to workers and collects from employers sums required for administration of Act. Commission assesses annually every employer according to type of economic activity carried on in their establishment. Employers must pay assessment within 30 days. Certain employers operating interprovincial or international railway transport or shipping firms are personally liable for payment of benefits awarded by Commission.

Commission has exclusive jurisdiction to decide any matter or question contemplated in Act and to reconsider decision it has rendered, if decision has not been subject of decision by review office, in order to correct error. Decision of Commission has immediate effect notwithstanding application for review unless decision awards compensation for bodily injury or lump sum death benefit. Person believing wronged by decision may apply to Review Office for review. Decision of Review Office may be appealed to Board of Appeal (Commission d'appel en matièere de lésions professionnelles). Commission, Review Office and Board of Appeal may conciliate parties in pending litigation.

Worker's rights vested without regard to personal liability, no worker or beneficiary may institute civil liability action against employer as result of employment injury or death. Beneficiary can not bring civil liability action against employer other than

LABOR RELATIONS . . . *continued*
worker's employer or against worker or mandatory of employer except in limited circumstances.

Worker can exercise rights even if employer does not fulfill obligations. In case of transfer of establishment new employer assumes obligations of old employer towards worker and Commission.

In case of accident worker must notify superior immediately and medical certificate given to employer. Employer notifies Commission in prescribed form attaching medical certificate. Claim must be filed with Commission within six months of injury or death.

Act provides transitional provisions relating to claims and obligations under old Workmen's Compensation Act.

Province through Commission pays victims of certain criminal offences compensations provided by Act for persons killed or injured in course of their work. (R.S.Q. c. I-6).

Occupational Health and Safety Act.—(R.S.Q. c. S-2.1). Object of Act is to eliminate dangers to health, safety and physical well-being of workers. Act declared to be of public order. Act established Commission de la santé et de la sécurité du travail to prepare, propose and implement policies respecting workers' health and safety. Commission which replaces Workmen's Compensation Board empowered to carry out inquiries and inspections of work sites. Act provides offences and penalties.

Act establishes general principle that worker is entitled to proper working conditions defined in Act. Worker may refuse to work when he has reasonable grounds for believing performance of work would endanger his health, safety or well-being or expose another to similar danger. Worker not entitled to refuse to work where his refusal would endanger another person, or where conditions complained of are ordinary conditions in his kind of work. Worker may in certain circumstances request protective reassignment. Act also provides for reassignment of pregnant worker. If reassignment not made immediately, pregnant worker may stop working until reassignment or until date of delivery. Worker placed under obligation to cooperate in all respects with object of Act.

Act obliges employer to take necessary measures to protect health and ensure safety and physical well-being of worker. Employer entitled to counselling services to assist in carrying out that obligation. If required by regulation, employer must supervise prevention program in its establishment. Act provides for worker participation in health and safety committees (when more than 20 workers are employed and enterprise is designated by regulation). Safety representative may be appointed. Construction sites governed by special provisions.

Act provides for involvement of community health services in preparation and implementation of health programs. Act provides for Health and Safety Committees in certain establishments.

Act provides comprehensive transitional provisions relating to other statutes and regulations (see subhead Workmen's Compensation, supra).

Labor Standards.—Regulated by Labor Standards Act. (R.S.Q. c. N-1.1).

Labor Standards Act establishes Commission to supervise implementation and application of labor standards. "Employee" defined to include domestics. Commission may hear and determine employee's complaint, and may exercise claim on behalf of employee. Commission may also conduct its own inquiry and may enter employer's establishment to examine registers, books and other documents.

Labor Standards Act regulates payment of wages, hours of work, statutory holidays and nonworking days with pay, annual leave with pay, rest periods and miscellaneous leaves, including maternity and parental, prior notice of termination and work certificate upon termination.

Employee may not be dismissed by reason of exercise of rights under Act, by reason of having given information or evidence to Commission relating to application of labor standards, on ground of seizure by garnishment of employee wages, on ground that employee is pregnant, for purpose of evading application of Act, or on ground that employee refused to work beyond regular hours due to child care requirement. Act provides offences and penalties.

Unemployment Compensation.—Governed by Federal legislation.

See topic Language, subhead Labor Relations.

LANDLORD AND TENANT:

C.C.Q. contains rules applicable to all leases (C.C.Q. 1851-1891) and special provisions governing leases of dwellings (C.C.Q. 1892-2000).

Principal obligations of landlord are to: (1) Deliver leased property in good state of repair in all respects; (2) give peaceable enjoyment of property throughout term of lease; (3) warrant tenant that property may be used for purpose for which it was leased; (4) maintain property for that purpose throughout term of lease. (C.C.Q. 1854). Principal obligations of tenant are to: (1) pay rent; (2) use property with prudence and diligence; (3) upon termination of lease, surrender property in condition in which he received it, except for changes resulting from aging or fair wear and tear or superior force. (C.C.Q. 1855, 1890). Tenant cannot disturb normal enjoyment of other tenants (C.C.Q. 1860).

Form.—No special form set by law for lease which need not be in writing. See topic Records for formalities required if lease to be registered. See also subhead Lease of Dwellings, infra for special mandatory clauses.

Security Deposits.—No prohibition except for leases of dwellings where security deposit prohibited. (C.C.Q. 1904).

Registration.—Lease of movable property may be registered in register of personal and movable real rights. Lease of immovables may be registered in land register. Registration in land registry office against immovable affected by lease results in tenant being better protected against resiliation of lease as result of change in ownership of immovable. (C.C.Q. 1887). For registration purposes, which may be by deposit or summary, lease must be in writing and must meet special registration requirements. See topic Records.

Rent not controlled by law except in certain cases applicable only to leases of dwellings. See subhead Lease of Dwellings, infra. Tenant may demand reduction of rent if landlord fails to execute his obligations. (C.C.Q. 1863). If landlord does not make repairs to which he is bound tenant may apply to tribunal to obtain permission to withhold rent in order to proceed to repairs. (C.C.Q. 1867).

Lien of Landlord.—Effective Jan. 1, 1994 privilege of landlord on tenant's movable effects in leased premises abolished. For leases signed prior to this date, transitional measures to C.C.Q. preserve landlord's claim for maximum of ten years provided landlord complied with renewal requirements by Dec. 31, 1994.

Termination.—Lease for fixed term terminates of right at expiry of term. (C.C.Q. 1877). Lease for indeterminate term may be resiliated by either party on one month or one week notice if rent payable by month or week and if rent is payable according to another term notice must be equal to such term or if more than three months within three months. (C.C.Q. 1877, 1882). For lease of movable property, notice is ten days. (C.C.Q. 1882). Lease is not resiliated by death of either party. (C.C.Q. 1884). Voluntary or forced alienation of property affected by lease or extinction of landlord's title does not terminate lease. If lease with indeterminate term not registered may be cancelled upon new owner giving required notice. (C.C.Q. 1886-1887). In case of lease of immovable with fixed term and if more than 12 months remain from date of alienation or extinction of title, lease may be resiliated by new landlord upon expiry of 12 months unless lease is registered at registry office before deed of alienation or act by which title is extinguished was registered. (C.C.Q. 1887). Expropriation of thing leased results in resiliation of lease or reduction of rent in case of partial expropriation. (C.C.Q. 1888).

Holding Over.—Lease is tacitly renewed on same conditions for one year or for same term if it was originally less than one year where after expiry of lease with fixed term, tenant continues to occupy premises for more than ten days without opposition by landlord. Renewed lease is also subject to renewal. (C.C.Q. 1879).

Dispossession.—Landlord may obtain eviction of tenant who continues to occupy premises after expiry of lease or after date agreed upon during term of lease. For movable property, landlord may, upon termination of lease, obtain handing over of property. (C.C.Q. 1889).

Sublease or Assignment.—Tenant cannot sublet all or part of leased property or assign lease without consent of landlord who cannot refuse without serious reason. If landlord refuses, he is bound to inform tenant of reasons for refusal within 15 days after receiving tenant's request, otherwise, he is deemed to have consented. (C.C.Q. 1870-1871). Assignment of lease releases former tenant of his obligations, unless, where lease is not lease of dwelling, parties agree otherwise. (C.C.Q. 1873).

Lease of Dwellings.—Special rules apply to dwellings. Dwelling is defined to include mobile home placed on chassis or land intended for emplacement of mobile home and, except in certain instances, a room. (C.C.Q. 1892). Landlord must deliver dwelling in good livable condition and thereafter maintain that condition. (C.C.Q. 1910-1911). Tenant must keep dwelling in clean condition. (C.C.Q. 1911). Landlord and tenant must comply with other specified obligations. If landlord fails to fulfil his obligations, tenant has following recourses: deposit rent at tribunal upon notice of ten days or withhold rent with authorization of tribunal, demand specific performance (where possible), damages, reduction of rent or cancellation of lease if serious prejudice. If tenant fails to fulfil his obligation, landlord may demand: specific performance (where possible), damages, cancellation of lease if serious prejudice to landlord or other tenants. (C.C.Q. 1863, 1907).

Extension.—Lease for fixed term of 12 or more months extended as of right for one term of 12 months and if for less than 12 months extension of right for same term as original term. (C.C.Q. 1941). Parties may agree to different extension term. (C.C.Q. 1941). Landlord wishing to avoid extension or to increase rent or change other conditions must give notice in writing within stipulated delays. (C.C.Q. 1942 to 1944). Tenant who objects to the modification proposed by landlord or wishes to avoid extension must give similar notice. (C.C.Q. 1945, 1948). Where tenant objects to modification, landlord may apply to court within one month of receiving notice of objection, for fixing of rent or ruling on other modification of lease (C.C.Q. 1947); otherwise lease renewed on same conditions. Alienation of immovable within which leased dwelling located does not affect rights and obligations of tenant. (C.C.Q. 1937). Spouse of tenant or person who has been living with tenant for at least six months, being concubinary or blood relative of tenant or person connected to tenant by marriage, is entitled to maintain occupancy if he continues to occupy dwelling after cessation of cohabitation and gives notice to landlord within delay of two months after cessation. Person living with tenant at time of death may have benefit of lease if he notifies landlord within two months after death. (C.C.Q. 1938). Except when person living with tenant has given said notice to landlord, heirs of deceased tenant may cancel lease on three months notice given within six months of death. (C.C.Q. 1938-1939). Landlord may avoid extension if tenant has sublet dwelling for more than 12 consecutive months by notifying tenant and subtenant. (C.C.Q. 1944).

Resiliation.—Landlord may demand resiliation of lease for nonpayment of rent for more than three weeks or when tenant frequently delays payment of rent such as to cause serious prejudice. (C.C.Q. 1971). Tenant may obtain resiliation of lease if dwelling is unfit for habitation. (C.C.Q. 1913 to 1917 and 1975). Tenant may resiliate his lease if he is moving into dwelling in designated low rental housing or if tenant is no longer able to occupy his dwelling because of handicap or, in case of elderly person, if he is admitted permanently to residential and long term care centre. (C.C.Q. 1974). If tenant leaves dwelling before expiry of lease taking his movable effects, lease is cancelled of right, save damages. (C.C.Q. 1975).

Prohibitions.—In leases of dwellings: exacting payment of rent in advance for more than first payment period (C.C.Q. 1904); clause forfeiting term for payment of rent (C.C.Q. 1905); requesting cheque or other postdated instruments for payment of rent (C.C.Q. 1904); in lease for fixed term of 12 months or less clause providing for adjustment of rent during term; in lease for fixed term of more than 12 months clause providing for adjustment of rent during first 12 months of lease or more than once during each 12 month period (C.C.Q. 1906); clause exonerating or limiting liability of landlord, clause rendering tenant liable for damages caused without his fault (C.C.Q. 1900); clauses providing for penalty which exceeds damage actually sustained by landlord or imposing obligation on lessee which is unreasonable in circumstances

LANDLORD AND TENANT . . . *continued*

(C.C.Q. 1901); clause providing for altering rights of tenant by reason of increase in number of occupants, unless size of dwelling warrants it; clause limiting right of tenant to purchase goods or to obtain services from persons of his choice and on such terms and conditions as he sees fit (C.C.Q. 1900); changing of locks to premises without consent of other party (C.C.Q. 1934); stipulation whereby tenant acknowledges dwelling is in good condition (C.C.Q. 1910); leasing dwelling declared unfit for habitation by competent authority (C.C.Q. 1913); refusing to make lease with or maintain person in his or her rights solely because person is pregnant or has children, unless refusal justified by limited space of dwelling (C.C.Q. 1899); clause limiting right of tenant of land used for installation of mobile home to alienate or lease his mobile home (C.C.Q. 1998).

Lease.—Landlord must, before making lease, give tenant copy of rules he has established which then are deemed to form part of lease. (C.C.Q. 1057, 1894). Within ten days of making of lease, landlord must give tenant copy of written lease or, if lease is oral, writing indicating name and address of landlord and reproducing mandatory particulars prescribed by regulation, in form indicated therein. (C.C.Q. 1895). Lease, mandatory writing and rules must be drawn up in French but may be in another language if parties so choose. (C.C.Q. 1897).

Rental Control.—Régie du logement created by R.S.Q. c. R-8.1 has jurisdiction in matters respecting lease of dwellings when amount of application does not exceed jurisdiction of Court of Quebec (see topic Courts, subhead Court of Quebec). Régie empowered to fix or revise rent, rule on changes to lease and to control certain acts in respect of dwelling which would have effect of evicting lessee, namely: Retaking of possession by landlord for himself or relative, division or changing of destination of immovable, demolition, alienation of immovable situated in housing complex and registration of declaration of co-ownership. Certain categories of buildings are exempt from application of provisions respecting extension of lease and increase and fixing of rent.

See topic Language.

LANGUAGE:

General.—By Charter of French Language (R. S. Q. c. C-11) French declared official language of Quebec. Charter sets out certain fundamental language rights.

Legislature and Courts.—Legislative bills printed, published, passed and assented to in both French and English; regulations and other similar acts to which §133 of Constitution Act, 1867 applies shall be passed, printed and published in both French and English; both versions of said texts to be equally authoritative. French version of regulation or other similar act to which §133 of Constitution Act, 1867 does not apply prevails over English version if discrepancy exists. Either language to be used by any person in, or pleading in, or process issuing from, any court of Quebec. All judgments and decisions rendered by courts or quasi-judicial bodies shall be translated into French or English at request of parties, by civil administration.

Civil Administration.—Special provisions regulate mandatory use of French in government, government departments and other agencies of civil administration. Contracts entered into by civil administration and related sub-contracts must be drawn up in French except when administration enters into contracts with parties outside of province.

Semi-public Agencies.—Public utility firms, professional corporations and their members must make services available in French. Notices, communications and printed matters intended for public must be in French. Communications with artificial persons and civil administration must be in French. Charter provides other mandatory uses of French for such semi-public agencies.

Labor Relations.—Employer's written communications to staff must be in French as well as offers of employment or promotions. Collective agreements must be in French. Arbitration awards shall be translated into French or English at parties' request and expense. Dismissals, lay-offs, demotions or transfers for sole reason of being exclusively French speaking or insufficient knowledge of language other than French prohibited. Other provisions govern cases where requirement of knowledge of other language permitted and provide specific remedies for breaches of above requirements and prohibitions.

Commerce and Business.—Inscriptions on products, containers, wrappings, leaflets, brochures or cards supplied with product including directives for use and warranties must be in French but may be accompanied by translation in other language but not more prominently displayed than French. Catalogues, brochures, folders, commercial directories and similar publications may be in two separate versions, French only, and another language only provided French version as accessible. Contracts predetermined by one party, contracts containing printed standard clauses and related documents must be drawn up in French but may be drawn up in another language at express wish of parties. Application forms for employment, order forms, and releases must be drawn up in French. Save for certain exceptions, public signs and posters and commercial advertising must be in French. They may be in French and another language provided that French has much stronger visual impact (defined by regulations). Firm name may be accompanied with version in another language than French, provided French version is as prominent. (§68). Firm names must be in French. Companies to be incorporated must have French name. Family names, place names, expressions formed of artificial combination of letters, syllables and figures and expressions taken from other languages may appear in firm name. Business firms employing 50 or more must hold francization certificate issued by Office de la langue Françcaise commencing with date fixed by Office; certificate attests that firm is applying program approved by Office or that French already enjoys status that such programs are designed to ensure. Business firms employing 100 or more must form francization committee; representation on committee set out in Act. Office may suspend or revoke certificate if use of French is no longer generalized at all levels of firm.

Education.—Instruction in kindergarten, elementary and secondary schools in French except for: (1) child whose father or mother is Canadian citizen and received elementary instruction in English in Canada, provided that instruction constitutes major part of elementary instruction received in Canada; (2) child whose father or mother is Canadian citizen and has received or is receiving elementary or secondary instruction in English in Canada, and brothers and sisters of that child, provided that instruction constitutes major part of instruction received by child in Canada; (3) child whose father and mother are not Canadian citizens, but whose father or mother received elementary instruction in English in Quebec, provided that instruction constitutes major part of elementary instruction received in Quebec; (4) child who, in his last year in school in Quebec before 26 Aug. 1977, was receiving instruction in English in public kindergarten class or in elementary or secondary school, and brothers and sisters of that child; (5) child whose father or mother was residing in Quebec on 26 Aug. 1977 and had received elementary instruction in English outside Quebec, provided that instruction constitutes major part of elementary instruction received outside Quebec.

Miscellaneous.—Where Act does not require use of French only, French and another language may be used together. Health and social services must be available in English for anglophones in Province. Various bodies set up for purposes of Act such as Office de la langue Françcaise, Commission de Toponymie, Conseil de la Langue Françcaise. Fines and penalties provided for breach of Act.

LEASES: See topic Landlord and Tenant.

LEGISLATURE:

Powers conferred on Legislature of Quebec exercised by Parliament of Quebec, which is composed of National Assembly and Lieutenant-Governor. Legislature has term of not more than five years and session to occur at least once in every year.

See Canada Law Digest, topic Constitution and Government.

LEVY: See topics Attachment; Executions.

LICENCES:

Certain businesses are required to be licensed. The fees therefor are paid to the province and/or the municipality concerned. The amount of such fees is fixed by special laws, and varies according to the kind of business.

LIENS:

Innkeeper is entitled to lien on effects and baggage brought into hotel by guests for cost of lodging and services rendered. If amount remains unpaid for 90 days, effects may be sold. (C.C.Q. 2302 and 2303). Mechanics and others who hold property for repairs or for service have lien on articles taken for price of services performed. (C.C.Q. 1592). Workmen are compensated directly by Workmen's Compensation Board. In admiralty, maritime and statutory liens exist in usual cases. See topic Carriers, subhead Lien.

Mechanics' Liens.—Laborers, workmen, builders, building suppliers, architects and engineers acquire legal hypothec on immovable for additional value given by their work or by their materials. (C.C.Q. 2726). Legal hypothec is preserved by publication of notice indicating amount of claim and describing immovable charged. Notice is served on owner within 30 days of end of work. (C.C.Q. 2727). Legal hypothec is extinguished on failure to publish action against owner of immovable or to register prior notice of exercise of hypothecary right within six months after end of work.

Persons having participated in construction or renovation of immovable who did not contract directly with owner have lien under same conditions for value of their work after notification in writing to owner of immovable of contract with builder. (C.C.Q. 2728).

Attachment Lien.—See topic Attachment.

Attorney's Lien.—See topic Attorneys and Counselors.

Collateral Security Lien.—See topic Pledges.

Judgment Lien.—See topic Judgments.

Liens on Exempt Property.—See topic Exemptions.

Real Estate Mortgage Lien.—See topic Mortgages of Personal Property, subhead Legal Hypothecs.

Tax Lien.—See topic Taxation.

Enforcement.—Liens are enforced by means of ordinary action at law except that of innkeeper who can sell property without judicial intervention.

No right of redemption exists with regard to property sold under lien.

LIMITATION OF ACTIONS:

Prescription is governed by law applicable to merits of dispute. (C.C.Q. 3131).

One Year.—The following actions are prescribed by one year: (1) For slander or libel, reckoning from the day that it came to the knowledge of the party aggrieved; (2) for bodily injuries; (3) contracts entered into by debtors in fraud of their creditors cannot be set aside at suit of latter, unless action is brought within a year from discovery of injury resulting from fraud; (4) applications by surviving spouse for compensation for his contribution to enrichment of patrimony of deceased spouse. (C.C.Q. 2928-2929).

Three Years.—Unless provided otherwise, action to enforce personal right or movable right. (C.C.Q. 2925). Where right of action arises from moral, corporal or material damage appearing progressively or tardily, period runs from day damage first appeared. (C.C.Q. 2926).

Arrears of municipal taxes are prescribed by three years save if there is a special statute. (Municipal Taxation Act R.S.Q. c. F-2.1, art. 251).

Actions in restitution of minors for lesion, in rectification of tutors' accounts and for rescission of contracts for cause of nullity. (C.C.Q. 2927).

Five Years.—Actions against architects and contractors based on their warranty of work they have done are prescribed by five or eight years according to circumstances. (C.C.Q. 2118, 2925).

LIMITATION OF ACTIONS . . . *continued*

Ten Years.—All rights and actions the prescription of which is not otherwise regulated by law. (C.C.Q. 2922). See topic Judgments.

LIMITED PARTNERSHIP:

See topic Partnership.

MARRIAGE:

Generally persons under 16 years of age may not lawfully marry. (C.C.Q. 373).

Consent Required.—Where either party is under age of 18, consent of person having parental authority or tutor is necessary. (C.C.Q. 373).

Publication of banns is a prerequisite, except where a dispensation or license is obtained from competent authority; publication is by posting of notice 20 days prior to marriage. (C.C.Q.368s.).

Ceremonial Marriage.—May be solemnized by designated clerks or deputy clerks of Superior Court and every minister of religion authorized by his religious society and by Minister of Justice. (C.C.Q. 366).

Marriages by written contract are not recognized. As to antenuptial marriage contracts see topic Husband and Wife, subhead Antenuptial Contracts.

Common law marriages within or without the province are not recognized under Quebec law.

Foreign Marriages.—Validity of marriage governed by law of place of its solemnization or by law of country of domicile or of nationality of one of spouses. (C.C.Q. 3088).

Prohibited Marriages.—Officiant may not solemnize marriage if either spouse is, in relation to other, ascendant, descendant, brother or sister. (C.C.Q. 373).

Annulment.—Any interested person may apply to have any marriage not solemnized in accordance with C.C.Q. declared null. No action lies after lapse of three years from solemnization, except where public order is concerned. (C.C.Q. 380).

Application for nullity made by declaration. If defendant is absent he may be summoned by notice in newspaper. Attorney General must be served and may intervene. (C.P. 813s).

Marriage, although declared null, produces civil effects with regard to husband and wife if contracted in good faith. If good faith exists on part of one of parties only, marriage produces civil effects in favor of such party alone. Nullity does not deprive children of advantages secured to them by law or by marriage contract and rights and duties of fathers and mothers towards their children are unaffected by nullity. (C.C.Q. 381s.).

MARRIED WOMEN:

See topics Dower; Husband and Wife; Marriage; Witnesses.

MASTER AND SERVANT:

See topics Labor Relations; Principal and Agent.

MECHANICS' LIENS: See topic Liens.

MINES AND MINERALS:

Granting of mining rights pertaining to mineral substances and underground reservoirs in public domain are governed by Mining Act which is administered by Minister of Energy and Resources. (R. S. Q. c. M-13.1).

Quebec Mining Companies Act, R. S. Q. c. C-47, contains provisions for incorporation and administration of companies operating mines and privileges granted to companies incorporated for purpose of operating mines.

Also regulates activities and legal publication of mining companies incorporated outside Québec.

Operation of Mines.—See topic Labor Relations, subhead Occupational Health and Safety Act.

Safeguarding of Employees.—See topic Labor Relations, subhead Occupational Health and Safety Act.

Inspection of Mines.—See topic Labor Relations, subhead Occupational Health and Safety Act.

Oil and Gas.—See subhead Petroleum and Natural Gas, infra.

Petroleum and Natural Gas.—Exploration for and production of petroleum and natural gas can be done only under exploration and operating licences granted by Minister of Energy and Resources. In certain circumstances special licences required for exploration and development of other mineral substances.

Duties.—Mining Duties Act imposes duties on annual profits of operators of mines less certain deductions. (R.S. Q. c. D-15).

Taxes.—See subhead Duties, supra.

MONOPOLIES AND RESTRAINT OF TRADE:

See Canada Law Digest.

MORTGAGES OF PERSONAL PROPERTY:

Hypothecs Generally.—In Province of Quebec, general regime for security on movable property and on immovable property is hypothec. There are rules of law which determine what property is movable and what is immovable. Generally, movable property is charged by way of movable hypothec and immovable property is charged by way of immovable hypothec. By exception, hypothecs on present and future rents produced by immovable and on indemnities paid under insurance contracts covering these rents are considered immovable hypothecs, even though such rents and indemnities are themselves movable. Pledge is form of movable hypothec.

There are some general rules which apply to all hypothecs, whether they are movable or immovable, whether they are on present or future property, whether they are on specified property or on universality of property. However, there are different rules which affect to greater or lesser extent different types of hypothecs on different types of property. Certain features are common to all hypothecs, such as following: (1) Hypothec can be given to secure any obligation. It is accessory right and therefore survives only as long as obligation whose performance it secures continues to exist. (2) Property charged by hypothec can be one or more specified properties or all property included in universality of assets. (3) Amount of hypothec must be stated in hypothec. This stated amount is not necessarily related to amount of debt, but it establishes amount up to which creditor can claim against hypothecated property as secured creditor. (4) All hypothecs must be published in order to be opposable to third parties. Publication refers to requirements which must be respected in order that hypothec become effective as against third parties. Publication also establishes rank of rights. Generally, earlier ranking creditors taking priority over later ranking creditors when exercising hypothecary rights. (See subhead Ranking of Hypothecary Rights Generally, infra.) Immovable hypothecs and movable hypothecs (other than pledges) are published by registration in appropriate government register. See topic Records. Pledges are published by delivery and holding of property pledged. (5) Other than personal recourses and certain provisional measures, hypothecary creditors have only four hypothecary recourses available to them for enforcement and realization of their hypothecs, namely: taking possession for purposes of administration, taking in payment, sale by creditor or sale by judicial authority. Recourses of taking possession for purposes of administration and of sale by creditor are only available on property of enterprise. Before creditor may exercise its hypothecary recourses, appropriate prior notice must be served and registered. Notice period is 20 days for movables or 60 days for immovables, or ten days in case of taking of possession for purposes of administration.

Ranking of Hypothecary Rights Generally.—As a rule, rights rank according to date, hour and minute of their registration in appropriate register. Rights in virtue of pledge rank according to time at which property or title is delivered to creditor. Hypothec affecting universality of immovables ranks in respect of each immovable only from time of registration of hypothec against each specific immovable in appropriate register. Hypothec affecting universality of movables ranks in respect of each movable in universality from due registration of hypothec in appropriate register. Registration of notice of crystallization determines rank of floating hypothec. (See subhead Floating Hypothecs, infra.) There are many detailed rules as to ranking or preservation of hypothecs in particular circumstances such as vendors' hypothecs, hypothecs on future property, hypothecs on property that is transformed, hypothecs on property which changes in nature, hypothecs on property represented by bill of lading or other negotiable instrument or on claims, or hypothecs on property subsequently sold. Further, there are transitional rules applicable to security taken prior to Jan. 1, 1994.

Movable Hypothecs.—Movable hypothec can be created with or without delivery of property hypothecated. When it is created with delivery it may also be called a pledge.

Movable Hypothecs With Delivery.—See topic Pledges.

Movable Hypothecs Without Delivery.—Generally, these may only be given by persons carrying on enterprise and by certain corporations which are not carrying on enterprise. If given by individual carrying on enterprise, only assets of enterprise can be charged with movable hypothec without delivery. Movable hypothec without delivery must, on pain of absolute nullity, be in writing. Hypothec securing payment of bonds or other titles of indebtedness issued by trustee, limited partnership or legal person authorized to do so shall, on pain of absolute nullity, be granted by notarial deed in favor of person holding power of attorney of creditors. See topic Associations, subhead Enterprise.

Movable hypothec without delivery must be published in public register kept for that purpose, called Register of personal and movable real rights. Publication is effected by registering application for registration which must contain sufficient description of hypothecated property or, if universality is hypothecated, nature of universality. For purposes of registration specific government form must be completed (Form "RH"). In this form following information must be set out in prescribed manner: names and addresses of parties, date and place of birth of individual who is party, complete description of property hypothecated, amount of hypothec, date on which registration ceases to have effect (no later than ten years) and date and place security document was signed. Only those rights which are set out in application and entered into register are published.

Generally, so long as hypothec continues to subsist, registration has effect until date it ceases to have effect as indicated in application, which cannot be more than ten years after registration. Registration can be renewed prior to expiry. Other or further registrations may be required to preserve rights against hypothecated property.

Hypothecs on Claims.—Hypothec on claim or claims is form of movable hypothec; it charges one or more receivables. There are special rules which apply to these hypothecs. Hypothec on claim will rank against other hypothecs on same claim from date it is registered, however it is not opposable against debtor of hypothecated claim unless that person has been individually served with appropriate notice of hypothec. If claim is itself secured by hypothec, there are further requirements as to service of notice.

By law, hypothecary creditor has right to collect claims hypothecated, even prior to default, and to apply them to his debt. However, hypothecary creditor can in deed of hypothec authorize person who granted hypothec to continue to collect claims until such time as creditor withdraws such authority by giving and registering appropriate notice to this effect.

Floating Hypothecs.—Hypothec is floating hypothec when some of its effects are suspended until, after default, creditor provokes its crystallization by serving notice of default and crystallization on debtor or grantor and registering notice. Registration of this notice determines rank of floating hypothec for most purposes. Only person or trustee who carries on enterprise may grant floating hypothec on property of enterprise. This type of hypothec can charge both immovable and movable property. Floating character of hypothec must be expressly stipulated in act. Property affected by hypothec is determined at time of crystallization. There are other specific rules relating to floating hypothecs.

MORTGAGES OF PERSONAL PROPERTY . . . *continued*

Legal Hypothecs.—Legal hypothec is not granted by contract by debtor to creditor, but rather it arises by law in respect of certain types of claims against property and having rank established by law.

There are four kinds of claims which give rise to legal hypothecs in Province of Quebec: (a) claims of State for sums due under fiscal laws, and certain other claims of State or of legal persons established in public interest, under specific provision of law; these can affect movable or immovable property and take effect from their registration; (b) claims under judgment; these can affect movable or immovable property and take effect from registration; (c) claims of persons having taken part in construction or renovation of immovable; these may affect immovable in question only to extent of added value; they have to be registered within certain delays to preserve legal hypothec, however they may rank above other hypothecs registered prior to registration of legal hypothec; and (d) claim of syndicate of co-owners for payment of common expenses and contributions to contingency fund; these can affect only fraction of co-owner in default and have effect only from registration. (C.C.Q. 2644 to 2802, 2934 to 3075).

MORTGAGES OF REAL PROPERTY:

For general rules regarding hypothecs see topic Mortgages of Personal Property, subheads Hypothecs Generally and Ranking of Hypothecary Rights Generally.

Hypothecs on immovable property, as well as hypothecs on present and future rents produced by immovable and hypothecs on indemnities paid under insurance contracts covering rents, are immovable hypothecs.

Requisites of Instrument.—All immovable hypothecs in Province of Quebec must be granted by deed in notarial form and executed before Quebec notary. In addition, in order that rights created be registrable, there are further requirements as to form, content and certification. Rules which govern form of document include size and weight of paper. With respect to content, application for registration in land register must contain all of particulars prescribed by law, but no more than those which are prescribed. Content requirements vary depending on rights created by deed but generally deed and application for registration must contain following information, all in prescribed manner: date of deed and place it was signed, name and address of parties to deed and quality in which they are acting, date and place of birth of parties who are individuals, complete legal designation of property, characterization of right whose registration is being applied for, amount for which hypothec is granted and indication of legal text on which right is based. (Provisional Regulation Regarding the Land Register R-1, §32). Also, notary who receives notarial deed by which immovable hypothec is granted must certify that he has verified identity, quality and capacity of parties, that document represents will expressed by parties and, where applicable, that title of grantor or last holder of right concerned has been previously and validly published.

Registration.—In order to be opposable to third parties, immovable hypothecs must be registered in land register of registry office in land registration division in which immovable is situated. There are three ways in which immovable hypothec can be registered: by presenting deed itself or by presenting notarial extract of deed, in each case if they contain only prescribed information, or by means of summary which sets out particulars prescribed by regulation. Application must be in prescribed form, including requirements as to size and weight of paper and presentation of text. If registration is made by way of summary, applicant must also present deed itself, extract of deed or any document summarized in extract or summary for conservation and consultation and summary must be accompanied by certificate of notary, and must state that summary is accurate. Regardless of which means of registration is used, application may only contain information prescribed by law. Only those rights set out in application and entered into register are published. (C.C.Q. 2644 to 2802, 2934 to 3075).

MOTOR VEHICLES:

Vehicle License.—Owner must register vehicle (unless exempted) in accordance with formalities determined by Société de l'assurance automobile du Québec ("Société") and upon payment of prescribed fees. Société may refuse to register vehicle where government regulations are not met. Registration is valid for period determined by regulations. Registration certificate must contain all information required by regulations and be signed by its holder. Registration plate is also issued bearing assigned registration number and must be attached at rear of vehicle. Registration of vehicle requires proof of minimum insurance for public liability. See subhead Financial Responsibility, infra.

Drivers' permits are issued upon payment of prescribed fees in accordance with formalities, terms and conditions established by Société. Proficiency and medical or optometric examinations may be required by Société. Permits valid for period determined by regulations. Drivers' permits issued outside Quebec recognized only for 90 days after holder settles in Quebec.

Every person driving vehicle must produce for police registration certificate, his driver's permit and certificate of insurance required by Automobile Insurance Act. Must inform Société of any change of address within 30 days of change.

Title and Sales.—When ownership of vehicle is transferred owner must apply to Société for transfer by remitting license plate and endorsed certificate. Purchaser must then apply for new registration. When there is exchange between parties each owner must remit endorsed certificate and apply for new registration. Where vehicle is transferred to dealer and new vehicle is being purchased, transferor retains license plate but must apply to Société for certificate corresponding to new vehicle. If no new vehicle being purchased, transferor must remit license plate to Société and endorse certificate to dealer.

Liens.—Any sum due to Crown under Highway Safety Code constitutes preferred debt upon motor vehicles.

Identification Marks.—It is offence to deface, alter, make illegible, replace or remove identification number of vehicle or bicycle. No alterations to chassis, body or other mechanism likely to affect stability of braking or change type of motor vehicle or alterations not meeting requirements of Motor Vehicle Safety Act (R.S.C. 1985 c. M-10) without prior authorization of Société.

Operation Prohibited.—No person may drive motor vehicle on public highway unless holds driver's license of appropriate category and class designated by regulations or learner's license. Person holding learner's license must be accompanied by person holding driver's license. Intoxicated or drugged person may not operate car or have charge of car stopped on highway. Occupant may not drink alcohol inside vehicle on highways, roads, and places where public traffic permitted.

Equipment.—Required on public highways: Tires conforming to standards prescribed by regulations; horns in good working order; two brake systems sufficiently powerful to stop vehicle in emergency; exhaust system in conformity with noise level regulations; mudguards; two rear view mirrors; odometer and speedometer; safety glass windows and windshield; windshield wipers and any other accessories or equipment prescribed by regulations. Radar warning devices are prohibited.

Seat Belts.—Driver and passengers in front and back seats of passenger vehicle must wear seat belts subject to certain exceptions.

Lights Required.—Two white headlights, two amber or white parking lights on front, two red parking lights at rear, two red reflectors at rear, two red stop lights at rear, two amber or white turn-signal lights on front, two red or amber turn-signal lights at rear, one amber side marker lamp and one amber side reflector on each side, one red side marker lamp and one red side reflector on each side, white back-up light at rear, white light illuminating rear registration plate. Cars manufactured after Jan. 1, 1987 must have third red stop light at rear. Front lights must enable driver to discern person, object at 150 m. All lights must be visible at distance of not less than 150 m.

Speed limits as follows: (a) Autoroutes: 60 km/h minimum, 100 km/h maximum; (b) hard surface public highways: 90 km/h maximum; (c) gravel highways: 70 km/h maximum; (d) cities, towns, villages, when children enter or leave school: 50 km/h maximum. Minister of Transport may fix different speed limits.

Traffic Regulations.—On two way roadway, driver of vehicle must signal intention to pass and may pass only after ascertaining that he may do so without risk to vehicle being passed. No lane hopping is permitted. On two lane road every vehicle must drive in right hand lane except to pass. Cannot pass vehicle on right. Must comply with all traffic control devices. Must not pass vehicle using lane reserved for ongoing traffic on curve, on crest or at crest of grade if visibility insufficient, or at intersection. Before turning, changing lane, making u-turns or returning to road from shoulder or parking area must signal intention by means of turning signals. If not equipped with turning signals must signal manually as follows: Left turn, extend arm horizontally; right turn, extend forearm upwards; stops or slowing down, extend forearm downwards.

Accidents.—Driver must stop and give name and address of owner, driver, driver's license number, certificate of insurance and license plate number to police or person having sustained loss. Driver must remain at scene of accident and give necessary assistance to any person injured.

Owner liable for any violation of Highway Safety Code committed with vehicle unless he proves that at time of accident vehicle was in possession of third party without his consent. Person who leases vehicle for more than one year is considered owner.

Guests.—There is no statute restricting liability for injury to guest.

Insurance.—See subhead Financial Responsibility, infra.

Financial Responsibility.—Under Automobile Insurance Act (R. S. Q. c. A-25) owner of automobile must, subject to certain exceptions, have minimum $50,000 liability insurance for property damages resulting from accidents occurring in Canada or U.S. and for bodily injuries resulting from accidents outside of Quebec but within Canada or U.S. Indemnity fund also set up under Act and, subject to certain exceptions, persons having obtained final unsatisfied judgment for property damages (and bodily injuries in certain cases) resulting from automobile accident may within one year make claim to have judgment satisfied by fund up to $50,000. If more than one claim results from same accident claimants share pro rata.

Foreign vehicle validly registered by law of place of residence or place of business is exempt from registration in Quebec for six months from date of arrival in Quebec.

Bicycles.—Motorized bicycles or three-wheel vehicles having piston displacement of not over 50 c.c., and mass of 60 kg. or under and automatic transmission are deemed to be mopeds. In general, bicycles may not be used on public highways where maximum speed more than 50 km/h. Driver of moped or motorcycle must keep white headlight on at all times. Every person riding moped, motorcycle or sidecar must wear protective helmet which meets requirements of regulations. No person may drink alcoholic beverages while riding bicycle.

No-Fault Insurance.—By Automobile Insurance Act (R. S. Q. c. A-25) victims of bodily injuries resulting from automobile accidents are indemnified by Automobile Insurance Board on no-fault basis. All rights, recourses and rights of action in respect of bodily injuries resulting from automobile accidents are replaced by indemnities under Automobile Insurance Act, Workmen's Compensation Act or Criminal Victims Compensation Act, subject to certain exceptions.

Indemnification available to all victims of automobile accidents occurring in Quebec whether or not resident of Quebec. Indemnification available to Quebec resident whether accident occurred in or outside Quebec. If automobile registered in Quebec and is involved in accident in Quebec, owner, driver and passengers deemed resident in Quebec. Nonresident victims compensated to extent they are not responsible for accident. Right to indemnification prescribed by three years from date of accident, manifestation of injury or death, subject to extension by Société.

Indemnities are: (i) Income replacement indemnities in cases of incapacity to continue to hold employment, quantum established in accordance with provisions of Act, (ii) death benefits in favor of spouse and dependents and based on percentage of income replacement indemnity, (iii) indemnification for particular injuries by way of lump sum plus medical expenses.

Board decides on right and quantum of indemnity. Appeal lies to Commission des Affaires Sociales from decision of Board or of its officers.

See note at head of Digest as to 1996 legislation covered.

See Topical Index in front part of this volume.

MOTOR VEHICLES . . . *continued*

Compensation for Property Damage.—Recourse of owner of vehicle for damages to such vehicle can only be exercised against his insurer to extent that direct compensation agreement is established by Groupement des assureurs automobiles, made up of representatives of authorized insurers. Owner if not satisfied with settlement made in accordance with said agreement may sue insurer before civil courts. Insurer has no right of subrogation against insured or against person whose liability covered by insurance contract except when insurer pays indemnity which it was not bound to pay under insurance contract. Except as above stated victims of property damage caused by automobiles are compensated in accordance with ordinary rules of law subject to presumptions of liability mentioned under subhead Owner Liable, supra.

Pedestrians.—Must comply with pedestrian lights or, if there are none, traffic lights.

Nonresident operator may drive vehicle for six months if holds valid driver's permit issued by another government authorizing holder to drive category of vehicle he is driving in Quebec, if other government grants reciprocal right to Quebec drivers.

Outsized vehicles, loads must hold special permit. No person may drive on public highway vehicle carrying load which is not solidly attached, secured and covered so as not to intervene with driver's vision and so as not to detach itself from vehicle. Special permits required for carrying loads in excess of width of vehicle, or in excess of length of vehicle by more than one metre in front or two metres in rear.

Actions Against Nonresidents.—There is no special provision with respect to commencement of such actions.

Direct Actions Against Insurer.—Subject to amount and conditions of insured's contract of insurance, insurer is responsible directly to third parties, but insurer cannot be sued by third parties until they have obtained against insured final judgment which is executory.

Motor Vehicle Carriers.—Under Transport Act R.S.Q. c. T-12 and regulations thereunder and under Highway Safety Code, public vehicles, in addition to registration, must obtain travel permit monthly. Special provisions respecting chauffeurs, operation and equipment of buses and transportation of hazardous substances and permits re: transport brokerage.

Aircraft.—See Canada Law Digest, topic Aircraft.

Gasoline Tax.—See topic Taxation.

NEGOTIABLE INSTRUMENTS:

See Canada Law Digest, topic Bills and Notes.

NOTARIES:

Notaries are public officers whose chief duty it is to draw up and execute deeds and contracts to which the parties desire to give the character of authenticity. Such deeds make proof of the facts attested by the notary, assure the date thereof, and the originals are preserved in the office of the notary. (C.C.Q. 2814, 2818, 2819).

Notaries are represented and governed by the Order of Notaries of Quebec, a body politic, possessing full power to make and amend the tariffs of notarial fees, and rules and regulations for the due management of all matters regarding the profession subject to Professional Code which also contains provisions for disciplining members of the order. (R. S. Q. c. C-26 and N-2).

Only Canadian citizens are admitted to the profession, and no advocate can be a notary. Notaries are appointed for life, subject to good behavior. Their jurisdiction extends throughout the province and even outside of the province in certain cases. (C.C.Q. 3110)

Copy of a notarial deed, certified by the notary to be a true copy, is authentic and proves its contents. (C.C.Q. 2815, 2820). For use outside of Quebec, signature of notary is authenticated by Chambre des notaires.

Fees.—See topic Acknowledgments.

OFFENCES AND QUASI-OFFENCES:

Every person endowed with reason has duty to abide by rules of conduct which lie upon him, according to circumstances, usage or law, so as not to cause injury to another. (C.C.Q. 1457). He is responsible for any injury he causes to another and is liable to reparation for bodily, moral or material injury which victim proves he has suffered. Degree of prudence, skill and care required depends on circumstances of case. Person cannot exclude or limit liability for bodily or moral injury. (C.C.Q. 1474). Contributory negligence is not bar to recovery but damages may be reduced in proportion to respective share of responsibility. (C.C.Q. 1478).

Person is also responsible for act or fault of person under his control or thing under his care. (C.C.Q. 1459 to 1465). Manufacturer of product is liable for safety defect in product. (C.C.Q. 1468) Person is not liable for damages caused by superior force unless he has undertaken to make reparation for it. (C.C.Q. 1470). Accidents resulting in death of victim give right of action to any person who can prove direct damages caused by death.

Prescription in cases of offenses and quasi-offenses is three years. (C.C.Q. 2925).

PARTITION:

Undivided ownership (indivision) arises from contract, succession or judgment or by operation of law. (C.C.Q. 1012). Partition may be requested in various circumstances, unless it has been postponed by agreement, testamentary disposition, judgment, operation of law or unless it has become impossible because property has been appropriated to durable purpose. (C.C.Q. 1030).

Partition of Successions.—Partition may not take place or be applied for before liquidation is terminated. (C.C.Q. 836). Testator may order partition wholly or partly deferred for limited time. (C.C.Q. 837). To avoid loss, court may continue undivided ownership for five years. (C.C.Q. 843, 844). Undivided ownership may also be continued in case of family enterprise (C.C.Q. 839), family residence or movable property serving for use of household (C.C.Q. 840).

Court may order partition where causes that justified continuance of undivided ownership have ceased or where undivided ownership has become intolerable or presents too great a risk for heirs. (C.C.Q 845).

Form of Partition.—If all heirs agree, partition may be effected as proposal appended to final account of liquidation; otherwise, partition is made as heirs see best. If heirs disagree, partition effected in accordance with prescribed rules and in forms required by Code of Civil Procedure. (C.C.Q. 838).

Undivided Co-ownership of Mainly Residential Immovable.—Notwithstanding any agreement to contrary, partition may be demanded by three-quarters of undivided co-owners representing 90% of shares of mainly residential immovable property in order to establish divided co-ownership of it. (C.C.Q. 1031). Undivided owners may satisfy those who object by apportioning their share to them in money; share of each undivided co-owner is then increased in proportion to his payment. (C.C.Q. 1031).

PARTNERSHIP:

Formation.—Commercial partnerships may be general, limited or undeclared. (C.C.Q. 2188s.). Limited partnerships must consist of one or more general partners and one or more special partners. Special partners make contributions to common stock by money or other property. Partnerships are formed in accordance with C.C.Q. 2186s. and must be registered under An Act respecting the legal publicity of sole proprietorships, partnerships and legal persons. (R.S.Q. c P-45). Limited and general partnerships share many attributes of legal persons. See topic Corporations.

Undeclared partnerships may arise from written or verbal contract or overt act indicating intent to form undeclared partnership. Each partner contracts in his own name and is alone liable towards third parties, unless he acts in quality of partner, to knowledge of third party. Partners are solidarily liable for debts contracted for use or operation of common enterprise and cannot limit their liability toward third parties. (C.C.Q. 2250-2266).

Rights and Liabilities of Partners as to Third Persons.—In general partnerships, partners are jointly liable for obligations contracted by partnership in respect of third parties, but solidarily liable if obligations were contracted for service or operation of enterprise of partnership. (C.C.Q. 2221). General partners are solidarily liable on their personal property to full extent of firm's obligations. (C.C.Q. 2246). Special partners are liable only to amount they agreed to contribute but if name of special partner appears in firm name he is liable as general partner unless status as special partner clearly indicated. Only general partners authorized to administer business of partnership. (C.C.Q. 2244).

Partnership Declaration.—Within 60 days of its formation, every general and limited partnership must file declaration with clerk of Superior Court stating: (1) its name and any other business name it uses, (2) its legal form, (3) its domicile, (4) its object, (5) its establishments in Quebec, (6) two main sectors in which it does business, (7) number of its employees in Quebec, (8) its termination date (if it has one), (9) name and domicile of all partners, (10) indication that no other person is member of partnership. Declarations must be filed annually and updated regularly. (An Act respecting legal publicity §26s, C.C.Q. 2190, 2194). Declaration of limited partnership shall additionally (1) distinguish general from special partners, (2) name special partner who is greatest contributor, (3) state that it is limited partnership, (4) indicate place where register containing up-to-date information on special partners and their contributions to common stock may be consulted. (An Act respecting legal publicity §34, C.C.Q. 2239). Partnership formed on date when contract of partnership signed, unless other date stipulated therein. (C.C.Q. 2187).

Partnership Name.—No partnership, either local or foreign, may be registered if its name includes prohibited expression, is immoral or offensive, falsely suggests nonprofit status, is same as that of partnership previously registered or is liable to mislead third persons in whatever manner. Firm name must be French, may be accompanied by English version. Family names, place names, expressions formed by artificial combination of letters, syllables or figures and expressions taken from other language may appear in firm names subject to regulations of Government. See topic Language. General partnership's name must include words "Société en nom collectif" or "S.E.N.C."; limited partnership's name must include words "Société en Commandite." or "S.E.C." (Regulation respecting the application of the Act respecting legal publicity of sole proprietorships, partnerships and legal persons).

Foreign partnerships and unincorporated firms may do business in the province without a special license, but must register under An Act respecting the legal publicity of sole proprietorships, partnerships and legal persons. (R.S.Q. c. P-45).

Dissolution.—Upon dissolution of general or limited partnership, property must be liquidated as provided in C.C.Q. 357-364. Involves filing notice of dissolution and naming liquidator, and filing notice of closure. Liquidator pays debts and divides assets between partners in proportion to their rights. (C.C.Q. 361).

PERPETUITIES: See topics Substitution and Trusts.

PLEADING:

General Procedure.—Defendant must appear either in person or by attorney within ten days from date of service of writ, and plead within ten days from expiry of time in which to appear. (C. P. 119, 149, 173). Plaintiff may then file answer within same delay. Subsequent written pleadings must be authorized by judge in chambers. (C. P. 182). Apart from these ordinary pleadings, preliminary exceptions or inscriptions in law may be filed in certain cases. (C. P. 159).

Form.—In their written pleadings, parties state facts that they intend to invoke and conclusions which they seek. Such statement must be frank, precise and brief; it shall be divided into paragraphs numbered consecutively, each paragraph referring so far as possible to one essential fact. (C. P. 76).

Every fact of such a nature as to take opposite party by surprise if not alleged, or to raise issue not arising from pleadings already filed, must be expressly pleaded. (C. P. 77).

See note at head of Digest as to 1996 legislation covered.

See Topical Index in front part of this volume.

PLEADING . . . *continued*

Except when otherwise provided, silence of a party in respect of a fact alleged by opposite party must not be interpreted as admission of truth of such fact. (C. P. 86).

Party may allege in his defence or answer any material facts, even those which have arisen since institution of action, and may take any conclusions necessary to defeat a ground set up by opposite party. (C. P. 183).

Counter Claim or Set-Off.—Defendant may in pleading constitute himself cross-plaintiff to urge against plaintiff any claim arising from same source as principal demand or from related source. Court remains seized of cross-demand irrespective of outcome of principal demand. (C. P. 172).

Inscription for Hearing.—As soon as issue is joined, either party may inscribe case for proof and hearing. Before case be put on role plaintiff must produce declaration attesting that: All interrogatories and documents to be produced as proof have been filed at court, all incidental proceedings have been tried and all expert testimony has been produced. This declaration is served upon defendant, who must produce similar declaration within 60 days. At least ten days before trial date each party must produce brief summary of issues and list of jurisprudence and authorities. Prothonotary sends notice of trial to parties at least 30 days and not more than 60 days prior. (C.P. 274, 278, Rules of Practice, §§15, 18). Chief Justice may determine cases in which pretrial conference to be held to determine questions of fact and questions of law to be argued. (Rules of Practice, §18.1).

Amendments.—Writ of summons, declaration, defence and other pleadings may be amended with or without leave of judge according to rules of Code of Civil Procedure and Rules of Practice. (C. P. 199s).

Party may amend in order to modify, correct or complete allegations or conclusions of original pleading, to invoke facts which have occurred during suit, or to assert a right accrued since service of action and connected with right originally claimed. (C. P. 202).

Proof of Claims.—Actions for sum of money in which defendant has failed to appear or plead, and founded upon authentic deed or private writing, verbal agreement to pay specific sum of money, or detailed account for services rendered or goods sold and delivered, may be proved by affidavit.

All other actions must be inscribed for proof and hearing before court. In cases where defendant is in default to appear, witnesses may be heard out of court. When defendant has appeared, witnesses can only be heard out of court with permission of court or consent of parties. (C. P. 192s).

In all cases where oral evidence is permitted, proof may be adduced by one witness; subject, however, to rule of Code of Civil Procedure regarding testimony of a child. Testimony given by party, on his own behalf or at instance of another party, may serve as commencement of proof in writing against him. (C. P. 293s).

See topic Language.

PLEDGES:

Pledge is form of movable hypothec, otherwise called movable hypothec with delivery.

For general rules regarding hypothecs see topic Mortgages of Personal Property, subheads Hypothecs Generally and Ranking of Hypothecary Rights Generally.

Movable hypothec with delivery is granted by delivery of property or title to creditor (or third person with consent) or, in case property is already held by creditor, by his continuous holding of it with grantor's consent, in each case to secure creditor's claim.

Movable hypothec with delivery is published by creditor's continuous holding of hypothecated property or title. Movable hypothec granted with delivery may also be published by registration at later date, provided publication is not interrupted. Where title is negotiable by endorsement and delivery, or delivery alone, its remittance to creditor takes place by endorsement and delivery, or delivery alone. Rights in virtue of pledge rank according to time at which property or title is delivered to creditor, subject to exceptions. (C.C.Q. 2644 to 2802, 2934 to 3075).

Special rules govern certain pledges taken by banks as security for loans. See Canada Law Digest, topic Banks and Banking.

PRACTICE:

General.—Practice in civil matters is governed by Code of Civil Procedure and by rules of practice established by specific courts and districts. See topics Actions, Appeal and Error, Attachment, Depositions, Executions, Garnishment, Injunctions, Judgments, Pleading, Process.

Discovery.—Defendant before filing defence may summon plaintiff or his agent, employee or officer and other persons in specified cases for examination on discovery. Examination may relate to all facts of action and allows defendant to obtain communication of any document relating thereto. After defence filed, any party may summon any other party or his agent, employee or officer and other persons in specified cases for examination on all facts relating to issues between parties or to give communication and allow copy to be made of any document. Examining party may file all or part of deposition into Court record. (C.P. 397, 398, 398.1).

Demand for Admission of Facts.—After defence filed party may call upon other party to admit genuineness or correctness of any document, plan, photograph or other material thing produced in evidence. Admission is deemed made unless within ten days or other delay fixed by judge, other party serves solemnly affirmed statement denying or setting out reasons why he cannot admit. Unjustified refusal to admit may result in condemnation to consequent costs. (C.P. 403).

Direct Actions Against Insurer.—See topic Motor Vehicles, subhead Direct Actions Against Insurer.

Small Claims.—See topic Courts, subhead Court of Quebec, catchline Small Claims.

PRINCIPAL AND AGENT:

The contract of agency, known in Quebec as "mandate", may be either special for particular business or general for all business of mandator (principal). When general it includes only acts of simple administration. Power to perform other acts is conferred only by express mandate. (C.C.Q. 2135). Agent cannot go beyond authority given or implied by mandate and he cannot, if employed to buy or sell a thing, be buyer or seller on his own account, unless principal authorizes it. (C.C.Q. 2130, 2135, 2136, 2147).

Obligations of Agent.—The agent is bound to execute the mandate which he has accepted and must act with prudence and diligence in performing it. (C.C.Q. 2138). He is obliged, upon termination of mandate, to do whatever is necessary consequence of his acts and to complete business which cannot be deferred without loss or injury. (C.C.Q. 2182).

Sub-agency.—The agent is answerable for the person whom he substitutes in the execution of the mandate when he is not empowered to do so and if the principal be injured by reason of such substitution, he may repudiate the acts of the substitute. (C.C.Q. 2141 and 2161).

Joint Agency.—When several agents are appointed together for the same business, mandate has effect only if accepted by all. Agents are solidarily liable towards principal unless it is otherwise stipulated or implied. (C.C.Q. 2144).

Liability of Agent.—An agent acting in the name of his principal and within the bounds of his mandate is not personally liable to third persons with whom he contracts. An agent who acts in his own name is liable to third persons without prejudice to the rights of the latter against principal. He is also liable toward third persons when he exceeds powers of his mandate unless he has given party with whom he contracts sufficient communication of such powers or unless principal has ratified acts performed by agent. (C.C.Q. 2157-2158).

Liability of Principal.—As regards third persons the principal is bound by all acts of his agent done in execution and within powers of mandate and also for acts which exceed such powers if ratified by him either expressly or tacitly. (C.C.Q. 2160). Principal is also liable to third persons who, in good faith, contract with person not his agent under belief that he is so when principal has allowed such belief. (C.C.Q. 2163).

Obligations of Principal.—The principal is bound to discharge agent for all obligations contracted by him towards third persons and to reimburse expenses and charges which agent has incurred in execution of his mandate. (C.C.Q. 2150, 2152). Agent is entitled to deduct what principal owes him by reason of mandate from sums he is required to remit. He may also retain what was entrusted to him by principal for performance of mandate until payment of sums due to him. (C.C.Q. 2185). If mandate be given by several persons, their obligations towards agent are solidary. (C.C.Q. 2156).

Revocation.—The agency may be revoked, but the principal will still be bound toward third parties who have not been notified of the revocation. (C.C.Q. 2181). Appointment of new agent for same business has effect of revocation of first appointed from day on which first agent has been notified of new appointment. (C.C.Q. 2180). Death, institution of protective supervision in certain circumstances or bankruptcy of either principal or agent terminates mandate. (C.C.Q. 2175).

Collection Agencies.—Act Respecting the Collection of Certain Debts (R.S.Q. c. R-2.2) regulates activity of collection of debts including activities of collection agents who must hold permit issued by Consumer Protection Office established under Consumer Protection Act, R.S.Q. c. P-40.1. Application for permits must be accompanied with requisite security in amount and form prescribed by regulation and ranges from $10,000 to $25,000. See topic Human Rights, subhead Reputation and Privacy.

Power of Attorney.—Mandate for eventuality of mandator's incapacity to take care of himself or administer his property may be given for administration of person or his property. Must be executed by notarial deed or in presence of witnesses. Performance of mandate subordinate to occurrence of person's inability and acknowledgment of mandate by Court. (C.C.Q. 2166). If mandate proves inadequate for representation, some form of protective supervision may be required. (C.C.Q. 2169). If assumed by public curator, mandatary may be designated private tutor or curator. Mandate functions as long as mandator unable to take care of himself or administer property and may be revoked upon application to Court. (C.C.Q. 2172). See topic Guardian and Ward, subhead Protective Supervision of Persons of Full Age.

PROCESS:

Service of summons is effected by serving defendant personally, or by leaving copy at his domicile with reasonable person residing therein. (C. P. 123). In case of commercial firms it is sufficient to leave copy at their usual place of business, and with corporations to leave copy with any one of their officers at their place of business. (C. P. 129, 130).

If circumstances so require judge or prothonotary may authorize different mode of service such as by mail or public notice. Unless judge decides otherwise public notice is by way of summons order published only once; publication either: (a) In newspaper, designated by judge or prothonotary, circulated in locality of last known address of defendant or, if no newspaper circulated in that locality, in locality where he is required to appear, or (b) in Gazette Officielle du Québec, in accordance with terms and conditions prescribed by Lieutenant-Governor in Council.

If circumstances so require, judge may order publication by other appropriate means, in particular by letter, or by advertisement on radio or television.

Service by one publication is complete and is deemed to have taken place on date of such publication; in other cases, service is complete only when all prescribed publications have been made, but deemed to have been made on date of first publication. (C. P. 139).

Writ is prepared in duplicate by plaintiff or his attorney; one original is deposited in court and other is numbered, signed, sealed, and issued by court upon payment of judicial stamps. (C. P. 111). In cases of urgency, writs may be issued outside office hours and on non-juridical days, without seals or judicial stamps. (C. P. 112).

Plaintiff is not bound, before date of hearing, to return to court original of writ and declaration and proof of their service, unless defendant or another party to case requests him in writing to do so. (C. P. 148). Judgment cannot be rendered against defendant who has not appeared if plaintiff has not previously filed original of writ and declaration and proof of their service. (C. P. 198). Object of demand and causes thereof must be stated in writ or in a declaration annexed to it. (C. P. 117).

PROCESS . . . *continued*

Long Arm Statute.—No specific provisions respecting service outside Canada but such may be made by notices in local newspapers or by mail, upon order of Court. (C. P. 138s). Service upon party domiciled or ordinarily residing in another province may be made by any person of legal age, who must make certificate of service. (C. P. 137).

Who May Serve.—Service is made by sheriff or bailiff. (C. P. 120). Where there is no sheriff or bailiff in District, service may be made by any person of legal age there residing. (C. P. 122).

Nonresident Motorist.—See topic Motor Vehicles.

PROOF OF CLAIMS:

See topics Executors and Administrators; Pleading.

RAILROADS: See topic Carriers.

REAL PROPERTY:

Emphyteusis.—Right established by contract or will which grants person full benefit and enjoyment of immovable owned by another provided that he does not endanger its existence and undertakes to make constructions, works or plantations thereon that durably increase its value. (C.C.Q. 1195).

Immovable may be conveyed by emphyteusis for term not less than ten and not more than 100 years. (C.C.Q. 1197). Emphyteutic lessee has all rights in property that are attached to quality of owner subject to certain restrictions in C.C.Q. and in constituting deed, is liable for partial loss of immovable and all real property charges affecting it. (C.C.Q. 1200, 1202, 1205).

Easements.—Servitude is charge imposed on immovable in favor of another immovable belonging to different owner. Under charge, owner of servient land is required to tolerate certain acts of use by owner of dominant land or himself abstain from exercising certain rights inherent in ownership. Servitude extends to all that is necessary for its exercise. Servitudes remain attached to property through changes of ownership, subject to publication of rights. (C.C.Q. 1177, 1182). Servitude is established by contract, by will, by destination of proprietor or by effect of law. It cannot be established without title, and possession, even immemorial, is insufficient for that purpose. (C.C.Q. 1181). Servitude by destination of proprietor is made in writing by owner of land who, in contemplation of its future parcelling, immediately establishes nature, scope and situation of servitude on one part of land in favor of other parts. (C.C.Q. 1183). Servitudes are extinguished by nonuser for ten years and other causes. (C.C.Q. 1191-1194).

Foreign Conveyances.—If no law is designated by parties, sale of immovable property is governed by law of country where it is situated. (C.C.Q. 3114). Conveyance may be made outside Quebec before Quebec notary if it pertains to real property situated in Quebec or if one of parties is domiciled in Quebec. (C.C.Q. 3110).

Condominiums.—Governed by provisions of C.C.Q. entitled: Divided Co-ownership of Immovables. (C.C.Q. 1038 to 1109).

See also topics Deeds, Husband and Wife, Landlord and Tenant, Mortgages of Personal Property, Mortgages of Real Property, Partition, Records.

Preservation of Agricultural Land.—By Act to preserve agricultural land (R.S.Q. c. P-41.1) effective from Nov. 9, 1978, certain limitations on use of specified lands enacted to secure preservation of province's agricultural land. Act provides for creation of "Commission de protection du territoire agricole du Québec" to oversee administration of Act.

Act involves three basic steps: firstly, government may, by decree, identify any part of province as designated agricultural region. Decree contains list of municipalities affected and summary plan of territory. Copies sent to registrar of registration districts concerned and to municipal corporation. Act itself lists as designated agricultural regions over 600 municipalities.

Once decree in force, subdivision, alienation, construction and other specified uses of any lot in designated agricultural region without authorization of Commission is prohibited subject to certain exceptions.

Second step involves designation by Minister of Agriculture of reserved areas in municipality situated in designated agricultural region subject to procedure set out in Act permitting submission to be made prior to such designation. Once reserved area established restrictions above cease to apply to lands situate outside reserved area.

Third step is establishment of agricultural zone plan for municipality by Commission and municipal corporation. Failing agreement between Commission and municipal corporation, zone plan prepared by Commission and submitted to government for approval and becomes effective by decree which is published and registered. After decree restrictions outlined above cease to apply to any land not within zone.

Act contains provisions for submission to have lot included in or excluded from agricultural zone to municipal corporation and Commission.

Rights and hypothecs created by or resulting from any deed contravening Act may be cancelled by order of Superior Court. Lots must be restored to their previous condition.

Fines between $250 and $6,075 for first offence and $500 and $12,150 for second offence committed within two years provided for violation of Act; corporations liable to fines between $750 and $36,425 for first offence and $1,475 and $72,850 for second offence committed within two years.

Lands situate in agricultural zone used for nonagricultural purposes when Act became applicable to it may continue to be used for such purposes with authorization of Commission.

Farm Lands.—By Act respecting acquisition of farm land by nonresidents (R.S.Q., c. A-4.1) nonresidents require authorization of Commission de Protection du Territoire Agricole du Québec to acquire directly or indirectly farm lands. Act defines farm lands as land used for agricultural purposes having area not less than four hectares consisting of one lot or several contiguous lots or several lots which would be contiguous if not separated by public road. "Resident in Quebec" for individual means person who has resided at least 366 days in 24 months preceding acquisition. Special rules govern residence of corporations and individuals occupying designated functions. Act does not apply north of 50th parallel nor to lands excluded from agricultural zone enacted under Act to preserve agricultural land. Certain other exceptions. Authorization obtained by application to said Commission.

Commission may issue order enjoining person to cease contravention of Act or conditions of authorization and failing compliance with such order attorney general or Commission may obtain order from Superior Court. Acquisitions contravening certain provisions of Act may be annulled. Fines ranging from $200 to $5,000 for natural persons and from $600 to $30,000 for artificial persons may be imposed for contravention of certain provisions of Act. Contravention of other sections of Act result in fines ranging from 10% to 20% of value of land acquired in contravention of Act.

RECEIVERS:

See Canada Law Digest, topic Bankruptcy.

RECORDS:

Rights published by registration in register of personal and movable real rights or in land register. Province is divided into registration divisions, each having office where register is kept for registration of rights affecting immovable property. (C.C.Q. 2969). Publication of rights concerning immovable is made in land register of registry office of division in which immovable is situated. (C.C.Q. 2970). As soon as cadastre or official plan of any territory comes into force in order to affect immovable therein, deed must describe immovable under its official number. (C.C.Q. 3030).

Personal and movable real rights published in register of personal and movable real rights. One central register kept for entire province.

Registerable Deeds.—Acquisition, creation, recognition, modification, transmission or extinction of immovable real right requires publication. Renunciation of succession, legacy, community of property, partition of value of acquests or of family patrimony, and judgment annulling renunciation, also require publication. (C.C.Q. 2938). Restriction on right to alienate, other than purely personal restrictions, and clauses of resolution, resiliation or eventual extinction of any right which shall or may be published, and any transfer or transmission of such rights themselves shall or may be published. (C.C.Q. 2939).

Personal rights and movable real rights require publication to extent prescribed or expressly authorized by law. Modification or extinction of published right shall also be published. (C.C.Q. 2938[3]).

Requisites for Registration.—Applications for registration in land register or in register of personal and movable real rights must be in required form and identify holders and grantors of rights, state nature of rights, describe property concerned and any other facts prescribed by law or by regulation. (C.C.Q. 2981). Name, address and date of birth of natural persons and name, juridical form, jurisdiction of incorporation and local citation, address of head office and where applicable, name and address of establishment directly concerned of legal persons required. For registration in land registry application may be made by presenting deed itself or authentic extract of deed or by summary. (C.C.Q. 2982). Special rules determine which method should be used and form thereof. Notaries and attorneys receiving or drafting deeds concerning registration of rights in land register must certify having verified identity, quality and capacity of parties, that document represents will expressed by parties, that title of grantor or last holder of right previously and validly published. Exceptions provided for leases of immovables. (C.C.Q. 2988, 2991). No certification required for register of personal and movable rights. (C.C.Q. 2995).

As with all conveyance deeds of immovable, every transfer by legal or testamentary succession of immovable must be registered. In addition, declaration made by notarial act en minute is also registered. (C.C.Q. 2998). Declaration sets forth name and last domiciliary address, date and place of birth and of death, nationality and civil status, and matrimonial regime, if any, of deceased. It also sets forth whether succession is legal or testamentary, quality of declarant as heir, legatee by particular title or spouse, degree of relationship between each of heirs and deceased, any renunciations, description of property and of persons concerned, and right of each in property. (C.C.Q. 2999).

Effect of Registration.—Registration of rights allows them to be set up against third persons, establishes their rank and, where law so provides, gives them effect. (C.C.Q. 2941).

Registration of right in register of personal and movable real rights or land register carries simple presumption of existence of that right. (C.C.Q. 2944[2]). Registration does not interrupt prescription. However, publication of right of ownership in immatriculated immovable property interrupts acquisitive prescription of that right as long as publication subsists. (C.C.Q. 2957). See topic Adverse Possession.

Registration Charges.—Schedule of charges are obtainable from registry offices.

Registration Taxes.—See topics Taxation, subhead Land Transfer Duties, and Real Property, subhead Land Transfers to Nonresidents.

Vital Statistics.—Registrar of civil status is sole officer of civil status and he is responsible for drawing up and altering acts of birth, marriage and death; also responsible for keeping and custody of register of civil status and for providing access to it. (C.C.Q. 103). Notice of every contract of marriage shall be entered in register of personal and movable real rights at requisition of receiving notary. (C.C.Q. 442).

REDEMPTION:

See topics Executions, Sales, Taxation.

REPLEVIN:

In Quebec, called seizure before judgment, where plaintiff has right to revendicate. Used to claim possession of movable property withheld by defendant. Writ issued upon written requisition supported by affidavit affirming existence of debt and facts giving rise to seizure and, if based on information, indicating sources thereof. (C.P. 734[1], 735).

Unpaid vendor's right to revendicate is subject to four conditions: Sale must not have been made with term and buyer must be in default; thing must still be entire and in same condition; thing must not have passed into hands of third person who has paid for it or of hypothecary creditor who has obtained surrender thereof; it must be exercised within

REPLEVIN . . . *continued*
30 days after delivery. Where buyer is in default to pay price and property meets conditions prescribed for resolution of sale, seizure of property by third person not bar to rights of seller. (C.C.Q. 1741).

Defendant may prevent removal of property or have same returned after its seizure by giving seizing officer security equal to amount claimed or to market value of property. (C. P. 739).

REPORTS:

Judicial decisions in Quebec now reported by Société Québécoise d'Information Juridique (SOQUIJ), provincial Crown Corporation, in: Recueils de jurisprudence du Québec; Recueil de droit de la famille; Recueil de droit immobilier; Recueil en responsabilité et assurances; Recueil de droit fiscal québécois; Jurisprudence Logement. SOQUIJ also provides access to on-line data bases. Wilson & Lafleur, private publisher, publishes La revue légale and Revue de droit judiciaire. Editions Yvon Blais, private publisher, Bulletin de droit immobilier, Bulletin de droit de l'environnement, Bulletin de droit de la santé.

Previous decisions found in: Rapports judiciaires officiels du Québec, Cour supérieure; Rapports judiciaires officiels du Québec, Banc du Roi/Reine; Recueils de jurisprudence du Québec, Cour supérieure; Recueils de jurisprudence du Québec, Cour d'appel; Recueils de jurisprudence du Québec, C.P., C.S.P., T.J.; Quebec Appeal Cases; Bulletin de droit immobilier; Lower Canada Jurist; Lower Canada Reports; Montreal Law Reports; Perrault's Quebec Reports; Pykes Reports; Quebec Law Reports; Quebec Practice Reports; Ramsay's Appeal Cases; Stuart's King Bench Reports; Revue de jurisprudence; Revue de législation et de jurisprudence; Revue critique.

Digests: Annuaire de jurisprudence du Québec; Jurisprudence Express; Droit fiscal québécois Express; Droit du travail Express; Accès à l'information Express; Droit disciplinaire Express; Quantum; La Presse Juridique.

RESTRAINT OF TRADE:

See Canada Law Digest, topic Monopolies and Restraint of Trade.

SALES:

The contract of sale is completed by the consent of the parties, although the thing sold not then delivered. (C.C.Q. 1385, 1454 and 1708). When property determined only as to kind is sold, sale is not perfect until property is certain and determined and buyer has been notified. (C.C.Q. 1453).

A promise of sale with delivery and actual possession is equivalent to sale unless intention of parties to contrary is expressed. Any amount paid on occasion of promise of sale is presumed to be deposit on price unless otherwise stipulated in contract. (C.C.Q. 1710-1712).

Sale of Another's Property.—The sale of property by person other than owner or than person charged with its sale or authorized to sell it may be declared null. Sale may not be declared null, however, if seller becomes owner of property. True owner may apply for annulment of sale and revendicate property sold from buyer unless sale was made under judicial authority or unless buyer can set up acquisitive prescription. (C.C.Q. 2919). If property is movable sold in ordinary course of business of enterprise, owner is bound to reimburse buyer in good faith for price he has paid. Buyer as well may apply for annulment of sale; he may not do so, however, where owner himself is not entitled to revendicate property. (C.C.Q. 1713-1715). See topic Associations, subhead Enterprise.

Warranty by Seller.—Every contract of sale carries with it warranty of quality as well as warranty of ownership by which seller warrants buyer that property is free and clear of all rights except those declared at time of sale. Such warranties may be specifically excluded by agreement except for warranty against seller's personal acts. (C.C.Q. 1723s., 1726s., and 1732s.).

Sale of Incorporeals.—Sale of debts and rights of actions against third parties is perfected between seller and buyer, but buyer has no possession available against debtor and third persons until debtor has acquiesced in it or received copy or pertinent extract of act of sale or any other evidence of sale which may be set up against seller. Where debtor cannot be found in Quebec, sale may be set up upon publication of notice in newspaper of locality of last known address of debtor or, if he carries on enterprise, in locality where principal establishment is situated. Sale of universality of claims may be set up against debtors and third persons by registration, provided that other formalities whereby sale may be set up against debtors who have not acquiesced in sale have been accomplished. (C.C.Q. 1637-1650). Every transfer of hypothecary claim must be registered in registry office in which title creating debt has been registered. (C.C.Q. 2956). See topic Assignments.

Sale of Rights of Succession.—Person who sells rights of succession without specifying property affected warrants only his quality as heir. (C.C.Q. 1779).

Every person who is not heir but to whom another heir transferred his right in succession may be excluded from partition, either by all co-heirs or by one of them on being reimbursed value of right at time of redemption and his disbursements for costs related to transfer. (C.C.Q. 848).

No one can accept or renounce succession of living person or make any stipulation with respect thereto. (C.C.Q. 631).

Sale of Litigious Rights.—When litigious right is sold, person from whom it is claimed is wholly discharged by paying to buyer price, costs related to sale and interest on price computed from day buyer paid it. (C.C.Q. 1784).

Sale of Residential Immovables.—Sale of residential immovable is particular contract defined as sale of residential immovable to natural person for own occupation. Obligatory preliminary contract with option to withdraw promise to buy, and containing information regarding price and execution. Special rules for immovables under divided co-ownerhip or forming part of development. (C.C.Q. 1787-1792). Purchaser may demand nullity of sale not preceded by preliminary contract upon demonstration of serious prejudice suffered.

A right of redemption stipulated by the seller entitles him, after giving buyer, and any subsequent acquirer if right of redemption has been published, required notice of his intention, to take back property free of any charges which buyer may have laid upon it provided right of redemption was published, upon restoring price of it and reimbursing to buyer expense of sale, and costs of all necessary repairs, and of such improvements as have increased value of thing, to amount of such increased value. Right of redemption of property acquired for service or carrying on of enterprise may not be set up against third persons unless it is published. Buyer may retain possession of thing until seller has satisfied all these obligations. Right of redemption cannot be stipulated for term exceeding five years. (C.C.Q. 1753).

Instalment Sales.—Goods may be sold on condition that property does not pass until goods are paid for. Reservation of ownership of property acquired for service or carrying on of enterprise must be published to be opposable to third persons. Instalment sales contracts need not meet special requirements save for contracts between merchant and consumer which are subject to following provisions of Consumer Protection Act. (R. S. Q. c. P-40.1).

When seller repossesses thing sold for noncompliance with contract, notice must be sent to buyer who may remedy such noncompliance during such delay (20 days for movable property, 30 if sale to consumer, and 60 days for immovable). If buyer has paid one half of total sale price of thing sold, seller must obtain court permission to repossess goods sold to defaulting consumer. (C.C.Q. 1749 and 2778). See topic Consumer Protection.

Bills of Sale.—A bill of sale will not avail against third parties or against seizing creditors, provided the goods be not actually transferred, or provided they are not represented by a warehouse receipt which is transferred.

Sale of Enterprise.—See topic Fraudulent Sales and Conveyances.

Product Liability.—See subhead Warranty by Seller, supra.

Retail Credit Sales.—See subhead Instalment Sales, supra.

Consumer Protection.—See topic Consumer Protection.
See topic Language.

SALES TAX: See topic Taxation.

SEALS:

Except for certain corporate documents, it is not necessary for validity of a document that seals be affixed. Documents executed elsewhere are recognized as valid if executed in form prescribed by law applicable to content of act, by law of place where property which is object of act is situated when act executed, or by law of domicile of one of parties when act executed in accordance with rule locus regit actum. (C.C.Q. 137, 3109).

SECURITIES:

Provincial Blue Sky Law.—Securities Act. (R.S.Q. c. V-1.1, as am'd [up to and including S.Q. 1996, c. 2]).

Supervision.—Quebec Securities Commission composed of not more than seven members appointed by Government, including chairman and two vice-chairmen, exercises supervision and control over trading in securities. In addition to powers mentioned in subsequent subheads, function of Commission is to: (a) Promote efficiency in securities market; (b) protect investors against unfair, improper or fraudulent practices; (c) regulate information that must be disclosed to security holders and public in respect of persons engaged in distribution of securities and of securities issued by these persons; (d) define framework for professional activities of persons dealing in securities, for associations of such persons and for bodies entrusted with supervising securities market. Commission may appoint experts to assist it, order investigations to aid in administration of and repression of contraventions to Act, regulations or securities legislation of another legislative authority, institute proceedings under Act, make orders prohibiting disposition or withdrawal of funds, securities or other assets, or recommend appointment of provisional administrator, winding-up of property of person or winding-up of company. Commission may exempt person from requirements of Act or regulations where it considers exemption not to be detrimental to protection of investors and Commission may deny benefit of exemption contained in Act or regulations where it considers it necessary to do so to protect investors. Commission may review its decisions at any time, except in event of error in law. Decisions of Commission, except those granting exemptions, are subject to appeal to three judges of Court of Quebec whose decision can be appealed to Court of Appeal by special leave.

Securities to which Act Applicable.—Subject to exceptions set forth therein, Act applies to: (a) Any security recognized as such in trade, more particularly, share, bond, capital stock of incorporated entity, subscription right or option to purchase; (b) instrument, other than bond, evidencing loan of money; (c) deposit of money, except deposit received by Government of Quebec, Government of Canada, or one of their departments or agencies; (d) option or negotiable futures contract pertaining to securities, or Treasury bond futures contract; (e) option on commodity or financial instrument futures contract; (f) share in investment club; (g) investment contract; (h) any option negotiable on organized market; (i) other form of investment designated by regulation.

Distribution of Securities to Public.—

Prospectus Requirements.—Subject to exceptions (see catchline Exempt Securities, infra), distribution of securities to public is not permitted unless prospectus containing information and certificates prescribed by regulation and disclosing all material facts likely to affect value or market price of securities to be distributed has been filed with Commission and receipt therefor has been issued by Commission. Provision is made for filing "shelf" prospectus or simplified (short form) prospectus by "seasoned" reporting issuers. Where material change occurs in relation to information presented in prospectus, amendment to prospectus must be made. If distribution of securities is to continue for more than 12 months from date of receipt for prospectus, new prospectus must be filed with Commission and receipt therefor obtained from Commission.

See note at head of Digest as to 1996 legislation covered.

See Topical Index in front part of this volume.

SECURITIES . . . *continued*

Rescission.—Person who has subscribed for or acquired securities in distribution effected with prospectus containing misrepresentation has right to have contract rescinded or price revised, without prejudice to any claim for damages.

Exempt Securities.—No prospectus is required for distribution of following securities: (a) debt security issued or guaranteed by Government of Canada or any Canadian province; (b) debt security issued or guaranteed by certain municipal, hospital and educational bodies in specific circumstances; (c) security issued by closed (private) company, provided it is not distributed by way of public distribution; (d) security issued by nonprofit legal person, provided that distribution entails no remuneration; (e) various securities issued by certain institutions provided for in Savings and Credit Unions Act (Quebec), provided applicable criteria are met; (f) share in cooperative or cooperative federation, issued to member or prospective member thereof, or debt security issued only to member, provided subscription was neither solicited nor received by remunerated salesman or canvasser; (g) share in mutual insurance association as defined in Act respecting insurance (Quebec), issued to member or prospective member; (h) instrument evidencing debt and issued in settlement of credit sale or conditional sale, as long as it is not transferred to natural person; (i) instrument evidencing debt, provided issue and transfer constitute, for issuer as well as for subscriber and any subsequent purchaser, isolated transactions; (j) deposit of money within meaning of Deposit Insurance Act (Quebec), provided it is received by person duly registered under that Act or by duly registered bank or savings bank; (k) credit balances in accounts of securities dealer's clients; (l) share in mutual fund and units of unincorporated mutual fund, provided fund established and administered by duly licensed trust company, securities of fund are distributed by trust company and assets of fund are composed exclusively of unsolicited funds received from trustees and other such administrators of property of others; (m) share of investment club that has no more than 50 members, does not issue debt securities or pay any remuneration to securities advisers or brokers, except normal brokerage fees, all of whose members are required to make contributions, in proportion to their shares, for financing of its operations; (n) insurance or annuity contract issued by duly licensed insurer, except individual variable contract that is not individual variable life annuity or that does not guarantee payment, at maturity, of at least 75% of premiums paid before age 75; (o) debt security issued or guaranteed by duly registered bank or savings bank, except one that confers right of payment ranking lower than deposit described in (j) and entrusted to issuer or guarantor thereof; (p) debt security issued or guaranteed by International Bank for Reconstruction and Development, Asian Development Bank or Inter-American Development Bank, if payable in Canadian or American currency; (q) promissory note payable in one year or less and evidencing, if distributed to natural person, debt for sum of $50,000 or more; and (r) any security distributed without advertisement where total cost to purchaser acting as principal is at least $150,000 and where notice in prescribed form is filed with Commission within ten days.

Exempt Distributions.—Subject to filing of notice in prescribed form with Commission within ten days, no prospectus is required where distribution of securities is made to Government of Canada or to Government of any Canadian province or to any of their departments or agencies or is made to sophisticated purchaser and offer is made without advertisement. Sophisticated purchaser is defined to include following: (a) Company all of voting securities of which are owned by Government of Canada or by Government of any Canadian province or by one of their departments or agencies; (b) bank to which Bank Act (Canada) applies or any wholly-owned subsidiary thereof; (c) loan and investment society; (d) federation of savings and credit unions; (e) Caisse centrale Desjardins du Québec; (f) trust company or any wholly-owned subsidiary thereof; (g) insurance company or any wholly-owned subsidiary thereof; (h) certain municipal and educational bodies and public agencies established pursuant to Act of Government of Canada or of Government of any Canadian province; (i) securities dealer or adviser registered under Act; (j) pension fund with assets of over $100,000,000; (k) such other persons designated by order of Commission. Subject to filing of offering notice in prescribed form with Commission, or giving Commission information required by regulation, issuer is not required to prepare prospectus in connection with following: (a) Distribution to holders of its securities of exchange, conversion or subscription rights relating to its securities, as well as securities issued on exercise of such rights; (b) distribution of securities through dividend reinvestment or stock dividend distribution plan; (c) distribution of securities to its shareholders through subscription plans; (d) distribution of permanent shares or preferred shares by savings and credit union to members who already hold such shares through subscription plans; (e) distribution of portfolio securities issued by reporting issuer to permit exercise of exchange, conversion or subscription right previously granted by issuer; (f) distribution of securities of its own issue to its employees and senior executives or those of affiliate who are not induced to purchase by expectation of employment or continued employment.

No prospectus is required for alienation of securities of reporting issuer purchased pursuant to exempt distribution where initial purchaser and subsequent purchasers entitled to such exemption have held securities for required period immediately preceding alienation and if reporting issuer has complied with applicable disclosure requirements during same period.

Disclosure Requirements.—

Reporting Issuer.—Defined as issuer that has made distribution of securities to public. Reporting issuers are subject to disclosure requirements of Act.

Timely Disclosure.—Where material change occurs that is likely to have significant influence on value or market price of securities of reporting issuer and is not generally known, reporting issuer must immediately prepare and distribute press release disclosing substance of change, unless senior management has reasonable grounds to believe that disclosure would be seriously prejudicial to interests of reporting issuer and that no transaction in securities of reporting issuer has been or will be carried out on basis of information not generally known. Copy of press release must be filed immediately with Commission.

Financial Disclosure.—Within 140 days from end of financial year every reporting issuer must file detailed annual financial statements with Commission and send to every registered holder of its securities (other than debt securities) and to Commission annual report containing annual financial statements and auditors' report together with such other information as required by regulation. Within 60 days from end of each of first three quarters of its financial year every reporting issuer must file with Commission quarterly financial statements in form determined by regulation and send copy of same to every registered holder of its securities (other than debt securities).

Proxy Solicitation.—Management of reporting issuer is required to send proxy in prescribed form with notice of meeting sent to holders of voting securities. Every person who solicits proxies for meeting of holders of voting securities of reporting issuer is required to send to such holders and to Commission circular prepared in prescribed form.

Insider Trading and Reporting.—Insiders of reporting issuer are defined to be: (a) Issuer itself, its subsidiaries, its senior executives and those of its subsidiaries; (b) any person who exercises control over 10% or more of class of voting securities of reporting issuer; (c) senior executives of person contemplated in paragraph (b). Senior executives means any person exercising functions of director, or of president, vice-president, secretary, treasurer, controller or general manager, or similar functions. Act contains provisions prohibiting insider having privileged information on reporting issuer from trading in securities of issuer unless he is justified in believing that information is generally known or he avails himself of plan for acquisition of securities established before he learned of information. Person who becomes insider of reporting issuer must disclose to Commission his control over securities of reporting issuer within ten days in prescribed form and must disclose any change in his control over securities of issuer in prescribed form within ten days of event. Except for purchase made as part of take-over bid or issuer bid pursuant to provisions of Act, person who becomes owner of securities carrying 10% or more of voting rights attached to outstanding securities of reporting issuer shall file report in prescribed from within two business days and file further reports within two business days upon acquisition of securities carrying additional 2% of voting rights.

Take-Over Bid and Issuer Bid.—Take-over bid provisions apply where offeror intends to obtain or increase interest of 20% or more of class of voting securities from at least one security holder in Quebec. Take-over bid is exempt from requirements of Act where purchase is of not more than 5% of securities of class over 12 month period and is on recognized stock exchange, subject to conditions fixed by rules of that stock exchange. Commission may exempt offeror from take-over bid requirements when it considers exemption not to be detrimental to protection of investors.

Issuer bid provisions apply where issuer intends to acquire securities issued by it other than debt securities not convertible into securities representing interest in its share capital. Issuer bid exempt from requirements of Act where: (a) Securities are acquired in accordance with conditions in writing at time of issue or determined subsequently consistent with constituting Act; (b) issuer acquires less than 5% of class of securities over 12 month period, following publication of notice of intention in prescribed form.

Take-over bid or issuer bid circular in prescribed form must accompany bid sent to security holders and be filed with Commission. Directors circular of offeree issuer in prescribed form must be sent to security holders, addresses of whom are in Quebec, within ten days from date of take-over bid and may include recommendation to accept or reject offer. Period for deposit of securities must be at least 21 days. It is offence to make misrepresentation that is likely to affect value or market price of security in take-over bid or issuer bid circular. Offender, including every senior executive or employee thereof who authorizes or permits offence, is liable to fine of $5,000 to $1,000,000.

Registration of Dealers and Advisers.—No securities dealer or adviser or representatives thereof may carry on business in Quebec unless registered with Commission. Commission may revoke or suspend rights granted by registration or impose restrictions or conditions on their exercise where, in its opinion, registrant fails to comply with Act or regulations or where protection of investors requires it. Act sets forth certain investigative powers with respect to registered dealers and advisers and certain exemptions from registration requirements.

Offences and Penalties.—Act contains detailed provisions defining offences, including offences pertaining to false or misleading information, and provides for heavy penalties to curb unfair and fraudulent practices.

Franchising, Pyramid Sales, Etc.—For prohibitions on pyramid sales to consumers, see topic Consumer Protection.

Language.—All securities offering documents, including prospectus, offering notice and permanent information record, and take-over bid and issuer bid documents must be in French or in French and English. See also topic Language.

SEQUESTRATION:

Court may order sequestration of movable or immovable when protection of rights of party so requires. May be ordered by trial judge when case in appeal.

A sequestrator is bound to apply to the safekeeping of the things seized the care of a prudent administrator. He is in general subject to the duties and obligations imposed upon guardians in seizures under execution.

Conventional Sequestration. — Sequestration may also take place by agreement when two or more persons deposit a thing in dispute in the hands of a third person who obliges himself to restore it after the termination of the contest to the person to whom it may be adjudged. (C.C.Q. 2305).

SERVICE: See topic Process.

STATUTE OF FRAUDS:

See topic Frauds, Statute of.

STATUTES:

Civil and Commercial Law of Quebec is governed by Civil Code of Quebec, which replaced Civil Code of Lower Canada on Jan. 1, 1994. For convenience of reference in digest, provisions of Civil Code of Lower Canada are cited C.C. and Civil Code of Quebec are cited C.C.Q. Transitional provisions governing application of the two codes are set out in An Act respecting the implementation of the Civil Code. (S.Q. 1992, c.

STATUTES . . . *continued*
57). Note that C.C.Q. has no retroactive effect but does affect prescription periods already running.

Practice and procedure in civil matters by Code of Civil Procedure (1897) (cited C.C.P.) which was extensively amended in 1994 by S.Q. 1992, c. 57. Small letter "s." after citation is first letter of French word "suivants" (in English: "and following"). French text of statutes of Quebec prevails over English text where a discrepancy cannot be satisfactorily resolved by ordinary rules of interpretation. (R.S.Q. c. C-11).

Exclusive right to legislate on certain subjects is vested in Parliament of Canada. Only laws uniformly applicable to all provinces are those passed by that Parliament. See Canada Law Digest, topic Constitution and Government.

STAY OF EXECUTION:

See topic Executions.

SUBMISSION OF CONTROVERSY:

Persons who are at variance upon question of law but in agreement as to facts, may submit matter for decision of court on filing joint factum containing statement of question of law, facts which gave rise to it, and conclusions of each party. Decision rendered by court has same force and effect as judgment in ordinary action. (C. P. 448s).

SUBSTITUTION:

Substitution permits donor or testator to pass property on to more than one rank of beneficiaries. First beneficiary, institute, receives property with obligation of delivering it to subsequent beneficiary, substitute, after certain time. (C.C.Q. 1218, 1219). There can be at most two ranks of beneficiaries exclusive of initial institute. Accretion between co-institutes upon death of one of them, where it is stipulated that his share passes to surviving institutes, is not considered to be made to subsequent rank. (C.C.Q. 1221).

Substitution is established by gift or by will. It must be evidenced in writing and published in registry office. (C.C.Q. 1218). Opening of substitution takes place at death of institute unless earlier time fixed by grantor. Where institute is legal person, substitution may not open more than 30 years after gift or opening of succession, or after day legal person's right arises. Where it is stipulated that share of institute passes, on his death, to surviving institutes of same rank, opening of substitution takes place on death of last institute, unless prejudicial to substitute who would have received but for stipulation. Only person having required qualities to receive by gift or by will at time substitution opens may be substitute. Where there are several substitutes of same rank, only one need have required qualities to receive to protect right of all other substitutes to receive. (C.C.Q. 1240s.).

Obligations and Rights of Institute.—Until substitution opens, institute is owner of substituted property which forms within his personal patrimony separate patrimony intended for substitute. During this time, institute may exercise all rights of ownership, including alienation, hypothecation and leasing of property. Rights of acquirer, creditor or lessee are unaffected by substitute's rights at opening of substitution. (C.C.Q. 1229).

Within two months after gift or legacy, institute, in manner of administrator of property of others, must make inventory of property at his own expense, after convening substitute. Where institute refuses or fails to make inventory, substitute may do so at expense of institute, after convening institute and other interested persons. On each anniversary of date of inventory, institute must inform substitute of any change in general mass of property and of reinvestments of any proceeds from alienation. (C.C.Q. 1224, 1236, 1231).

In administering property, institute must act with prudence and diligence in view of rights of substitute. Institute must maintain and preserve property. He pays all charges and debts due before substitution opens and collects claims, gives acquittance therefor and exercises all judicial recourses relating to property. He must insure property against ordinary risks unless premium is too high in relation to risks. Any proceeds of alienation must be reinvested in accordance with provisions relating to presumed sound investments. See topic Administration of Property of Others. If constituting act of substitution provides therefor, institute may dispose of substituted property gratuitously or not reinvest it. He has no right to bequeath property. Institute may, before substitution opens, renounce his rights in favor of substitute and deliver over substituted property to him in anticipation. (C.C.Q. 1223s.).

Institute must take out insurance or furnish security to guarantee performance of his obligations if required by act creating substitution or by court order. If institute fails to perform obligations or endangers rights of substitute, court may deprive him of fruits and revenues, require him to restore capital, declare his rights forfeited in favor of substitute or appoint sequestrator. (C.C.Q. 1237, 1238).

Opening of Substitution.—Rules on successions, particularly those relating to right of option or to testamentary dispositions, apply to substitution from time it opens, whether created by gift or will. (C.C.Q. 1222). See topic Executors and Administrators of Estates.

Substitute is seized of ownership of property upon opening of substitution. Institute must render account to substitute and deliver to him substituted property, whatever has been acquired through reinvestment of said property, or value of property at time of its alienation. Institute liable for any loss caused by his fault or not resulting from normal use. Where substitution affects only residue of property, institute delivers only property remaining and price still due on alienated property. (C.C.Q. 1244s.).

Institute is entitled to reimbursement, with interest accrued from opening, of capital debts and expenses generally debited from capital incurred by reason of substitution. Institute is also entitled to reimbursement, in proportion to duration of his right, of expenses generally derived from revenues for any object that exceeds duration, and for any useful disbursements, subject to rules applicable to possessors in good faith. (C.C.Q. 1247, 1248).

Opening of substitution revives claims and debts that existed between institute and grantor and terminates confusion, in person of institute, of qualities of creditor and debtor, except in respect of interest accrued until opening. Institute may retain substituted property until payment of what is due to him. Institute's heirs have same rights and obligations as institute. They must continue anything that necessarily follows from acts performed by institute or that cannot be deferred without risk of loss. (C.C.Q. 1249s.).

Lapse of Substitution.—Lapse of testamentary substitution with regard to institute does not give rise to representation and benefits his co-institutes or, in absence of co-institutes, substitute. Lapse of testamentary substitution with regard to substitute benefits his co-substitutes, if any; otherwise, it benefits institute. Donor may revoke substitution with regard to substitute, as long as it has not been accepted by substitute. In respect of donor, substitute is deemed to have accepted where he is child of institute or where one of co-substitutes has accepted substitution. Revocation of substitution with regard to institute benefits any co-institute; otherwise it benefits substitute; revocation with regard to substitute benefits any co-substitute; otherwise, it benefits institute. Grantor may reserve for himself prerogative of determining share of substitutes or confer that prerogative on institute. Exercise of prerogative by donor does not constitute revocation of substitution even if in effect it completely excludes substitute from benefit of substitution. (C.C.Q. 1252s.).

SUPPLEMENTARY PROCEEDINGS:

See topic Executions.

SURETY AND GUARANTY COMPANIES:

Such companies must be licensed and registered under An Act Respecting Insurance (R.S.Q. c. A-32) and are usually required to make deposit with Minister of Finance of Province. Foreign companies must also be licensed under Foreign Insurance Companies Act (Revised Statutes of Canada, 1985, c. I-13) and make deposit with Receiver General of Canada. See Canada Law Digest, topic Insurance.

In order to act as surety in judicial proceedings, a company must also obtain a license to that effect from Superintendent of Financial Institutions.

Such company must: (1) deposit with Superintendent of Financial Institutions certified copy of its charter; (2) establish that it is incorporated in this province with power to produce sufficient security or is empowered to grant security bonds and is licensed by competent authority to carry on business of surety or guaranty in Province; (3) deposit in office of Superintendent of Financial Institutions if its head office be outside Province power of attorney constituting agent in Province; and (4) establish its solvency to satisfaction of Superintendent of Financial Institutions.

TAXATION:

Caveat.—Certain provisions incorporated in this text reflect some proposed amendments which are currently being applied although enabling legislation is not yet in force.

Administration.—Most provincial taxes are payable to Minister of Revenue. Other taxing authorities within province, such as municipalities and school corporations, attend to their own collections.

Taxable property may be movable or immovable and of any description, provided it is within the province and imposition of the tax is direct. Under the Constitution, the provinces have powers of direct taxation only, within their boundaries and for provincial purposes.

Exemptions.—No special exemptions for members of the armed forces.

Real estate taxes are imposed on immovable or real property within their respective limits by city, town and rural municipalities as their chief source of revenue.

School commissioners and trustees empowered to levy taxes on taxable real property in school municipality for payment of expenses not covered by government grants and subsidies. Rate of school assessments shall be uniform upon all taxable property in school municipality and assessment based on standardized assessment of taxable property. (Education Act, R. S. Q. c. I-14 as am'd by Act respecting municipal taxation R.S.Q. c. F-2.1).

Land Transfer Duties.—Municipalities must, under law, levy duty on transfer of immovables at rate of 0.5% on portion of consideration (or of municipal valuation if higher) which does not exceed $50,000, 1% on portion of consideration which exceeds $50,000 up to $250,000 and 1.5% on excess. Transfer includes lease of immovable if for more than 40 years. Transferee is liable for duties which are payable upon registration of deed of transfer. Special rules govern transfers of immovables situated in more than one municipality. Farm lands exempted. Transfers to lending institutions to secure payment of debt or to extinguish debt secured by immovable also exempt. Certain other exemptions provided. (An Act respecting duties on transfers of immovables, R.S.Q. c. D-15.1). (See also topic Real Property, subhead Land Transfers to Nonresidents.)

Valuation of immovable property for taxation by such local public corporation is determined in accordance with An Act respecting municipal taxation (R. S. Q. c. F-2.1) by assessors duly appointed.

Lien.—Municipal taxes are prior claims with respect to immovable properties.

Rates of tax and assessments are fixed by the municipalities themselves, within the terms of their respective charters or incorporating acts, or in conformity with the Cities and Towns Act (R. S. Q. c. C-19), or Municipal Code, or Education Act (R. S. Q. c. I-14) as case may be.

Redemption.—Under Municipal Code, real estate sold for municipal or other local assessments may be redeemed by former owner or any person having interest therein at any time within two years after date of adjudication upon reimbursing to secretary-treasurer of corporation of county where immovable situated, amount paid for property, plus 10% thereof for interest and costs. In certain localities, redemption period is shortened to one year. Similar but not identical provisions under Cities and Towns Act. (R. S. Q. c. C-19).

Business taxes have been replaced in some cities by surtax on all nonresidential immovables, payable by owner but may be passed on to tenants. Surtax declared unconstitutional in judgment rendered by Superior Court of Quebec in 1993. Quebec

TAXATION . . . *continued*
Government is appealing judgment. In interim, statute has been amended to create new tax on nonresidential immovables akin to surtax but without elements held unconstitutional in judgment of Superior Court.

Corporation Taxes.—Corporations and joint stock companies doing business within province must pay provincial taxes on paid-up capital and also on profits. See subhead Tax on Capital, infra.

Income Tax.—Income tax imposed on individuals and corporations by Taxation Act, R. S. Q. c. I-3.

Individual.—Individuals resident in province on last day of taxation year, individuals deemed resident in province and individuals not resident in Canada at any time in taxation year but who carried on business in province, were employed in province or disposed of taxable Quebec property during taxation year or previous taxation year are subject to income tax on income earned in province during year. Taxable income for resident individuals is income from all sources in Canada or elsewhere plus net taxable capital gains less allowable deductions. For nonresident individuals carrying on business in province, taxable income is profits of business calculated according to regulations. Nonresident individuals employed in province pay tax on income reasonably attributable to their employment or office in province. For nonresidents disposing of taxable Quebec property, see catchline Capital Gains, infra.

See Canada Law Digest, topic Taxation, subhead Income Tax Act, for rules governing computation of taxable income, amounts included and excluded, and various deductions which in most cases are same as under Taxation Act.

Tax on taxable income of individuals is graduated and ranges from 16% for taxable income not exceeding $7,000 to $10,550 plus 24% of amount exceeding $50,000 plus surtax equal to 5% of tax in excess of $5,000 and an additional 5% of tax in excess of $10,000.

Special rules govern income of farmers, fishermen, professionals, prospectors and trusts.

Corporation.—Taxable income from business or property is corporation's profits therefrom. If corporation carrying on business in province also carries on business outside of province, tax is payable in proportion that profits earned in province bears to its profits earned within and without province, calculated according to regulations. Subject to detailed provisions in Taxation Act, general tax rate (with surtax) for corporations is 8%. Tax rate on eligible or active business income for corporations qualifying for Canadian small business deduction is 5%. Investment income taxed at 16.25%. See Canada Law Digest, topic Taxation, subhead Income Tax Act for rules governing computation of income and deductions allowed which, in most cases, are same under Taxation Act. Special rules govern insurance corporations and savings and credit unions.

Capital Gains.—After Dec. 31, 1971 one-half of capital gains for year less one-half of allowable capital losses from disposition of any property is taxable as income. For 1988 and 1989, 2/3, and since 1990, 3/4, of capital gains less same respective percentage of allowable capital losses, would be taxable as income. Disposition of property includes: Transactions or events entitling to proceeds of disposition of property; redemption or cancellation of share, bill of exchange, promise of sale, debt or interest therein; conversion of share pursuant to amalgamation; expiry of option on property; transfer of property to trust or from trust to beneficiary. Excluded are: Transfer for purpose of securing debt and release of such transfer; issue by corporation of bonds, debentures or bills of exchange or making by it of hypothec or mortgage; issue by corporation of shares of its capital stock and other transactions provided by regulations. Only net capital gains accrued and realized since Jan. 1, 1972 subject to tax. Gains are excess of proceeds of disposition over cost or deemed cost adjusted in accordance with Taxation Act and regulations. Special rules govern deemed realizations when Quebec taxpayer abandons Canadian resident status and deemed acquisitions when taxpayer assumes Canadian resident status in Quebec.

Tax on Capital.—Tax is imposed on paid-up capital of corporations with establishments in Quebec. General paid-up capital is computed by reference to corporation's paid-up capital, retained earnings and other sources of capital, with reduction granted to corporations which carry on business both within and outside Quebec. Rate is 0.64% of its paid-up capital (minimum $250) for corporations other than mining corporations, insurance corporations and banks, loan corporations, trust corporations etc.

Exemptions and Credit for Foreign Taxes.—For exemptions, see Canada Law Digest, topic Taxation, subhead Income Tax Act. Resident taxpayer who has paid to foreign countries or political subdivisions thereof income tax of same nature as provided by Part I of Taxation Act may deduct from tax otherwise payable amount established in accordance with regulations.

Return and Payment.—Individuals must file return on or before Apr. 30 in each year, corporations within six months of end of their fiscal year. Employees earning salaries, wages or other remuneration from office or employment subject to withholding by employer as prescribed by regulations, balance if any payable on Apr. 30 following taxation year. Certain individuals must make quarterly payments on 15th day of Mar., June, Sept. and Dec. on estimate of income and pay balance on Apr. 30 following. Corporations pay tax monthly on last day of month according to provisions set out in Act.

Assessment and Appeal.—Minister of Revenue examines each return and assesses any tax payable and notifies taxpayer. Taxpayer may file objections to assessment with Minister within 90 days of mailing of assessment (this period may be extended if taxpayer was physically unable to act). For 1991 and subsequent taxation years, individual taxpayer and testamentary trust may file objections in year following expiry of delay to file income tax return or within 90 days of mailing of assessment, whichever is latest. Taxpayers may appeal from Minister's decision on objections to Quebec Court. Appeal provided to Court of Appeal of Quebec from decision of Quebec Court. In certain circumstances individual who is not mandatory of Minister of Revenue may bring summary appeal before Small Claims Division of Quebec Court.

Succession Duties.—The Succession Duties Act (R. S. Q. c. D-16) replaced by Succession Duty Act, R.S.Q. c. D-13.2, passed Dec. 22, 1978. Act applies to successions opening after Apr. 18, 1978. Provisions of Act levying duties repealed for successions opening after Apr. 23, 1985. Succession Duty Act was entirely repealed for successions opening after May 27, 1986.

Estate Tax.—No statutory provisions.

Apportionment Against Inter Vivos Dispositions.—No statutory provisions.

Inter-Province Co-operation.—No longer applicable as all provinces have abandoned succession duty field.

Gift Tax.—Provisions of Taxation Act levying tax on gifts repealed May 27, 1986 for gifts made after Apr. 23, 1985.

Sales Tax.—The Retail Sales Tax Act (S.Q. 1990 c. 60) has been replaced by An Act respecting the Québec Sales Tax (R.S.Q. c. T-0.1) to reflect newly introduced federal Goods and Services Tax (G.S.T.) (Part IX of Excise Tax Act R.S.C. 1985, c. E-15), by increasing scope of taxable goods to include most of those subject to G.S.T., with one notable exception being books. As result of this increase in scope, rate of Quebec Sales Tax (Q.S.T.) has been lowered from 9% to 8%, and effective May 13, 1994 to 6.5%. Furthermore, starting on July 1, 1992, most services, incorporeal movable property (e.g. royalties) and commercial and new residential immovables are taxable at rate of 4% and effective May 13, 1994, 6.5%. Q.S.T. legislation is harmonized with federal G.S.T. legislation, subject to certain adjustments. For example, financial services are zero-rated as opposed to exempt under federal G.S.T.

Q.S.T. of 6.5% of purchase price is exigible at time of making purchase which as defined in Act includes other forms of transfer or lease at retail in province of property (except certain exceptions detailed in Act) including gas, electricity, telephone service and lighting service, meals and hotels. Those exceptions will be phased out on Aug. 1, 1995 for small businesses and for large businesses on Nov. 30, 1996 (taxable supplies in excess of $6,000,000). No person, including contractors, manufacturers, importers and wholesalers carrying on business in province, may sell any movable property in province at retail sale, unless he has obtained registration certificate under Q.S.T. legislation and unless such certificate is in force at time of sale. Person who has neither residence nor place of business in province cannot institute or continue any proceedings in province for recovery of debt arising from sale or delivery of property to person who resides or carries on business therein, unless he holds registration certificate under said legislation. Sales tax of 9% (5% in case of automobile insurance) exigible on payment of premiums for insurance for life, health or physical integrity of persons and risks in province but not exigible on premiums for individuals' life, accident and sickness insurance. (R. S. Q. c. T-0.1).

For federal sales tax, see Canada Law Digest, topic Taxation, subhead Sales Tax.

Telecommunications Tax.—Imposed by R. S. Q. c. T-4. *Note:* This tax repealed on July 1, 1992 as part of reform on sales tax.

Gasoline Tax.—Imposed by R. S. Q. c. T-1.

Stamp Tax is imposed on certain legal documents filed at court house and on deeds entered at registry office. In practice this tax is invariably paid by lawyers or notaries taking proceedings and included in their charges. See topic Records, subhead Registration Charges.

Real Estate Conveyance Tax.—See subhead Land Transfer Duties, supra; also topic Real Property, subhead Land Transfers to Nonresidents.

Tobacco Tax.—Imposed by R. S. Q. c. I-2.

Amusement Tax.—Imposed by R. S. Q. c. D-14. *Note:* This tax repealed on July 1, 1992 as part of reform on sales tax.

Meals and Hotels Tax.—Imposed by R. S. Q. c. T-3. *Note:* This tax has been repealed by S.Q. 1990 c. 60 as of Jan. 1, 1991.

Stock Transfer Tax.—See topic Corporations, subhead Stock Transfer Tax.

Unemployment Compensation Tax.—See Canada Law Digest, topic Taxation, subhead Unemployment Compensation Tax.

Health Insurance Contributions.—Every employer must make contributions equal to 4.26% of salary paid to any employee who reports for work in establishments in province of Quebec or whose salary is paid from establishments in province of Quebec. (R. S. Q. c. R-5).

Penalties.—Following penalties may be imposed for violation of certain taxing statutes, more particularly:

Taxation Act.—Person who fails to make return of income when required is liable to penalty of 5% of tax unpaid when return was required to be filed and when taxpayer is not individual 1% of unpaid tax for each complete month not exceeding 12 months with interest at rate fixed by regulation without necessity of demand. For tax returns filed, which should have been filed before but not filed after, June 30, 1992, additional penalty of 1% will also be applicable to individual taxpayer. Starting after Sept. 30, 1992, recovery charge of 10% of unpaid balance of debt will be levied if Minister of Revenue exercises recovery measure or recourse before court. Person who fails to complete on prescribed form information as required, is liable to penalty of 1% of tax payable but, whether he is taxable or not, not less than $25 or more than $100, or in case of individual, such lower amount as Minister of Revenue may fix. If taxpayer knowingly or by circumstances equivalent to gross negligence makes declaration or omission in return which results in lesser assessments than would otherwise be case, he is subject to penalty of 25% of difference. Every person who wilfully evades or attempts to evade payment, collection or remittance of amount prescribed by fiscal law incurs penalty of 50% of amount of such payment, collection or remittance. Every person who wilfully makes statement or omission which results in lesser payment of taxes is subject to penalty of 50% of difference. Every person who makes false return or allows deceptive entries to be made in material records, or wilfully evades or attempts to evade compliance with Act is liable on summary conviction to fine of not less than $200 and not more than $10,000 and/or imprisonment for maximum term of two years. If additional tax is payable, fine must be at least equal to amount of taxes that should have been

TAXATION . . . *continued*

payable plus 25% of such amount but not exceeding double the amount (R. S. Q. c. M-31).

Succession Duty Act.—Provisions of Act imposing penalties repealed for all successions opening after May 27, 1986.

Sales Tax.—Penalty provisions of Act Respecting Ministére du Revenu (R.S.Q. c. M-31) apply to matters contemplated by any fiscal law.

Tobacco Tax Act.—Person who buys tobacco without paying tax is liable, in addition to payment of tax and costs, to fine of between $200 and $5,000.

TORRENS ACT: See topic Records.

TORTS:

See topic Offences and Quasi-Offences.

TRADEMARKS AND TRADENAMES:

As to trademarks see Canada Law Digest, topic Trademarks and Designs.

Tradenames.—No partnership or corporation may be registered which bears name of existing partnership or corporation or one so similar that public may be misled. Person in business alone who uses tradename or designation other than his own personal name, and partnership or corporation carrying on business under tradename in addition to its legal designation, must register said tradename(s) pursuant to Act Respecting the Legal Publicity of Sole Proprietorships, Partnerships and Legal Persons. See topic Corporations, subhead Reports.

See topic Language, subhead Commerce and Business.

TRUST DEEDS:

See topic Mortgages of Personal Property, subhead Movable Hypothecs, catchline Movable Hypothecs Without Delivery.

TRUSTS:

Creation.—Trust results from transfer of property from patrimony of settlor to that of trust created by him for particular purpose, and which trustee undertakes to hold and administer. Trust is established by contract, onerously or gratuitously, by will or by operation of law. Where authorized, it may be established by judgment. (C.C.Q. 1261, 1262). It is constituted upon acceptance of trustee. If object of trust by onerous title is to secure performance of obligation, trustee shall, in case of default by settlor, follow rules applicable to exercise of hypothecary rights. See topic Mortgages of Personal Property, subhead Hypothecs Generally.

Kinds.—Trusts are constituted for personal purposes or for private and social utility. Provided it is designated as trust, trust may be identified by name of grantor, trustee or beneficiary, or, in case of trust constituted for purposes of private or social utility, by name which reflects its object.

Personal trust is constituted gratuitously for purpose of securing benefit for determinate or determinable person. If constituted for benefit of several persons successively, it may not include more than two ranks of beneficiaries of fruits and revenues exclusive of beneficiary of capital; it is without effect in respect of any subsequent ranks it might contemplate. Accretions of fruits and revenues between co-beneficiaries of same rank are subject to rules of substitution relating to accretions between co-institutes of same rank. See topic Substitution. Right of beneficiaries of first rank opens not later than 100 years after trust is constituted, even if longer term is stipulated. Right of beneficiaries of subsequent ranks may open later but solely for benefit of those beneficiaries who have required quality to receive at expiry of 100 years after creation of trust. In no case may legal person be beneficiary for period exceeding 100 years, even if longer term is stipulated. (C.C.Q. 1266s.). Administration of trust is subject to supervision of settlor or his heirs, and of beneficiary, even future beneficiary. Rights of beneficiary, if he is not yet conceived, are exercised by person who, designated by settlor as curator, accepts office, or, failing him, by person appointed by court or by interested person. Public Curator may be designated to act. (C.C.Q. 1287, 1288).

Private trust is trust created to erect, maintain, or preserve thing or to use property appropriated to specific use, for indirect benefit of person or in his memory, or for some other private purpose. Trust constituted by onerous title, particularly one created to allow making of profit by means of investments, provisions for retirement or procuring another benefit for settlor or persons he designates or members of partnership, company or association, or employees or shareholders, is also private trust. (C.C.Q. 1267, 1268).

Social trust is trust constituted for purpose of general interest, such as cultural, educational, philanthropic, religious or scientific purpose. It does not have making of profit or operation of enterprise as its main object. (C.C.Q. 1270).

Private or social trust may be perpetual. (C.C.Q. 1273). In cases provided for by law, private or social trust may be subject to supervision of persons or bodies designated by law. Where such is case, trustee must file with person or body statement indicating nature, object and term of trusts and name and address of trustee, must allow trust records to be examined and must furnish any account on request. (C.C.Q. 1287, 1288). Where trust has ceased to meet first intent of settlor, court may terminate trust or, in case of social trust, substitute another closely related purpose for original purpose. If trust continues to meet settlor's intent but changes would allow more faithful compliance therewith, court may amend provisions of constituting act. (C.C.Q. 1294).

Beneficiaries.—Only person having qualities to receive by gift or will at time his right opens may be beneficiary of trust constituted gratuitously. Where there are several beneficiaries of same rank, it is sufficient that one of them have such qualities to preserve right of others if they avail themselves of it. (C.C.Q. 1279). For limitations on beneficiaries of personal trusts, see subhead Kinds, supra.

Appointment of Trustee.—Any natural person having full exercise of his civil rights, and any legal person authorized by law, may act as trustee. Settlor or beneficiary may be trustee but shall act jointly with trustee who is neither settlor or beneficiary. Settlor may appoint one or several trustees or provide mode of their appointment or replacement. (C.C.Q. 1276). Court may appoint trustee where settlor has failed to do so or where it is impossible to appoint or replace trustee. (C.C.Q. 1274s.).

General Powers and Duties of Trustees.—Trustee must preserve property and make it productive, increase patrimony or appropriate it to purpose, where interest of beneficiary or pursuit of purpose of trusts requires it. (C.C.Q. 1306). Trustee has control and exclusive administration of trust patrimony, and titles relating to property are drawn up in his name; he has exercise of all rights pertaining to patrimony and may take any proper measure to secure its appropriation. Trustee acts as administrator of property of others charged with full administration. (C.C.Q. 1278). See topic Administration of Property of Others.

Unless administration of trust is gratuitous according to law, act or circumstances, administrator is entitled to remuneration fixed in act, by usage or by law, or to remuneration established according to value of services rendered. (C.C.Q. 1300).

Investments.—To fulfil duties trustee may perform any necessary or useful act, including any form of investment. (C.C.Q. 1307). See also topic Administration of Property of Others, subhead Rules of Administration.

Powers and Liabilities of Trustees.—Where trustee binds himself, within limits of his powers, in name of beneficiary or trust patrimony, he is not personally liable towards third parties with whom he contracts. He is liable towards them if he binds himself in his own name, subject to their rights against beneficiary or trust patrimony. (C.C.Q. 1319).

Settlor, beneficiary or any interested persons may take action against trustee to compel him to perform his obligations or perform any act necessary for trust, or impugn acts performed by trustee in fraud of trust patrimony or rights of beneficiary. (C.C.Q. 1290).

When there are several trustees, the majority may act, saving a stipulation to contrary in act or in law. (C.C.Q. 1332).

Upon death of trustee or his being placed under protective supervision, liquidator of his succession or his tutor or curator must give notice of death or protective supervision to beneficiary and to any co-administrators and do all that is immediately necessary to prevent loss; he must render account and deliver property over to those entitled to it. (C.C.Q. 1361).

Distribution.—See topic Executors and Administrators of Estates, subhead Distribution.

Removal of Trustees.—Any interested person may apply for replacement of trustee who is unable to discharge his duties or does not fulfil obligations. (C.C.Q. 1360).

Securities in Name of Nominee.—Titles relating to property of trust are drawn up in trustee's name. He has exercise of all rights pertaining to patrimony and may take any proper measure to secure its appropriation. (C.C.Q. 1278).

Uniform Simplification of Fiduciary Security Transfers Act.—No such statute in this Province.

Accumulations.—No rule against accumulations. While trust is in effect, beneficiary has right to require, according to constituting act, either provision of benefit granted to him or payment of both fruits and revenues and capital or of only one of these. (C.C.Q. 1284).

Perpetuities.—Private or social trust may be perpetual. (C.C.Q. 1273). Personal trust limited to two ranks of beneficiaries whose quality to receive comes into existence within 100 years of creation of trust. Legal person cannot be beneficiary for more than 100 years. (C.C.Q. 1271s.).

Pour Over Trusts.—See topic Wills, subhead Bequests and Devises to Inter Vivos Trusts.

Termination of Trusts.—Trust is terminated by renunciation or lapse of right of all beneficiaries, both of capital and of fruits and revenues. Trust is also terminated by expiry of term or fulfilment of condition, by attainment of purpose of trust or by impossibility of attainment as confirmed by court. At termination, trustee delivers over property to those entitled to it. Where there is no beneficiary, property devolves to settlor or his heirs. Property of social trust that terminates by impossibility of fulfilment devolves to trust, to legal person or to group of persons devoted to similar purpose as designated by court on recommendation of trustee and advice of any person or body designated by law to supervise trust. (C.C.Q. 1296s.).

Foundations.—Foundation is appropriation of property for socially beneficial purpose. Its main object cannot be making of profit or operation of enterprise. Foundations consist either of autonomous patrimony, in which case they are governed by provisions on social trusts (see subhead Kinds, supra) or patrimony of legal person, in which case they are governed by laws applicable to legal persons of same kind. Foundation created by trust is established by gift or by will in accordance with rules governing those acts. Unless otherwise provided for in constituting act of trust foundation, initial property of trust foundation or any property substituted therefor or added thereto shall be preserved and allow for fulfilment of purpose, either by distribution only of those revenues that derive therefrom or by use that does not appreciably alter substance of initial property. (C.C.Q. 1256s.).

USURY:

See Canada Law Digest, topic Interest, subhead Criminal Code.

VENUE:

In personal actions, defendant may be summoned before court: (1) Of his domicile, real or elected; (2) of his ordinary residence, or of place where his property is situated, or of place where action is personally served upon him, when defendant is not domiciled in province but resides or possesses property therein; (3) of place where whole cause of action has arisen, or, if it concerns suit for libel publication in newspaper, of district where plaintiff resides if newspaper is circulated therein; (4) of place where contract was made. (C. P. 68).

In real or mixed actions, defendant may be summoned before court of his domicile or of district where property in dispute is situated. (C. P. 73).

See note at head of Digest as to 1996 legislation covered.

See Topical Index in front part of this volume.

VENUE . . . *continued*

If there are several defendants in personal or mixed action residing in different districts they may all be brought before court of district in which any one of them may be summoned, but in case of real action, must be court of place where object of dispute situated. (C. P. 75).

Action based upon contract of insurance taken against insurer may be instituted before court of domicile of insured; in case of insurance of property, it also may be instituted before court of place where loss occurred. (C. P. 69).

Applications in most family cases are before court of common domicile of parties or, failing such domicile, that of either party. Opposition to marriage, applications for certain dispensations regarding age or intellect for marriage are taken where marriage to be solemnized or domicile of minor or person of full age under tutorship. (C. P. 70).

Contract Provisions.—Parties may by agreements fix a venue but this would not deprive courts from exercising jurisdiction they would otherwise have.

VITAL STATISTICS: See topic Records, subhead Vital Statistics.

WAREHOUSEMEN:

Some must be licensed under various federal provisions. The general principles of civil law regarding liability for loss or damage of deposited goods apply. (C.C.Q. 2280s.).

WILLS:

Testamentary Capacity.—Capacity of testator considered relatively to time will is made. Minor may not dispose of property by will, except articles of little value. Persons of full age under curatorship may not make will. Person of full age provided with advisor may make will without assistance. Will made by person of full age under tutorship may be confirmed or not according to circumstances and nature of dispositions. Tutor, curator or adviser may not make will on behalf of person whom he represents, either alone or jointly with person. (C.C.Q. 707-711).

Forms.—Only Forms of wills are (1) Notarial, made in presence of notary, en minute, and witness, or in certain cases notary, en minute, and two witnesses. (2) Holograph, written entirely by testator and signed with own hand. (3) In presence of two witnesses of full age, written by testator or third person, signed by testator and witnesses. (C.C.Q. 712s.). Notarial will makes complete proof (C.C.Q. 2814[6]); holograph and witnessed will must be probated (C.C.Q. 2826s.).

Witnesses.—Any person of full age may witness notarial will, except employee of attesting notary who is not himself notary. (C.C.Q. 725).

Testamentary Gifts to Subscribing Witnesses, Etc.—Legacies made in favor of the notaries or to spouses or relatives in first degree of any such notaries are void, but do not affect other provisions of will. (C.C.Q. 759). Legacies to witnesses, even supernumeraries, are null, but do not affect other dispositions of will. Same applies to liquidator or administrator of property designated by will if such person acts as witness, to extent legacy exceeds his remuneration. (C.C.Q. 760).

Bequests and Devises to Inter Vivos Trusts.—Any person may increase trust patrimony by transferring property to it by contract or by will in conformity with rules applicable to constitution of trust. (C.C.Q. 1293). See topic Trusts, subhead Creation. Trustee may receive legacy intended for trust or legacy to be used to accomplish objective of trust. (C.C.Q. 618).

Revocation of will is express or tacit. Tacit: (1) Legacy to spouse before divorce or nullity of marriage is revoked unless testator stipulates against this presumption in will. Revocation of legacy entails revocation of spouse as liquidator of legacy. (2) Bequest of property revoked if property alienated during testator's life. Express: (1) Made by subsequent will expressly declaring change in intention. (2) By means of deliberate destruction, tearing or erasure of holograph will, or of that made in presence of witnesses, deliberately effected by testator, with intention of revoking it, or by reason of destruction of will becoming known to him, and failure to replace it. If owing to circumstances unforeseeable at time of acceptance of legacy, execution of charge becomes impossible or too burdensome for heir or legatee by particular title, court may revoke or change it. (C.C.Q. 763s.).

Following persons are unworthy of inheriting by operation of law: (1) persons convicted of making attempt on life of deceased, (2) persons deprived of parental authority over child while child is exempted from obligation of support in respect of child's succession. Persons may be declared unworthy of inheriting if (1) they were guilty of cruelty or seriously reprehensible behavior towards deceased, (2) they concealed or destroyed in bad faith will of deceased, (3) they hindered writing, amendment, or revocation of deceased's will. Heir will not be declared unworthy if deceased knew of his unworthiness and made bequest anyway. Any successor may, within one year of opening of succession or becoming aware of unworthiness of heir, apply to court to have heir declared unworthy if not already by operation of law. Spouse in good faith inherits if marriage declared null after death. (C.C.Q. 620s.).

Probate.—Wills in notarial form do not require probate. Probating of other two forms of wills is done on application to Superior Court where testator had his domicile, or, if had no domicile in Quebec, before court of district in which he dies or left property. Supported in case of witnessed will by affidavit of one of subscribing witnesses, or, if neither of them is available, affidavit of one or more other persons who knew testator and can identify his signature and, in case of holograph will, by affidavit of one or more persons who are familiar with testator's handwriting and can swear that will was wholly written and signed by him. (C. P. 887).

Self-proved Wills.—Notarial wills are self-proved and require no probate. For probate of wills made before witnesses and holograph wills, affidavit of witness or other person normally sufficient for probate and can be executed at same time as will or while testator is alive. Affiant need not testify in person before court unless probate contested by interested person.

Contest.—Notwithstanding probate, will may be afterward contested by action by any interested person who did not oppose application for probate or who, having opposed it, raises grounds which he was not in position to urge. (C.P. 891).

Unclaimed Legacies.—Where deceased leaves no spouse or relatives within degrees of succession, or where all successors have renounced or where no successor is known or claims succession within six months of death, State is seized in same manner as heir of property situated in Quebec. Any testamentary disposition which renders this right nugatory without otherwise providing for devolution of property is without effect. (C.C.Q. 696, 697).

Lapses.—Legacies lapse when testator survives legatee or when legatee refuses legacy, is unworthy or dies before fulfilment of suspensive condition of purely personal nature. Legacies also lapse if thing bequeathed perished totally during testator's lifetime or before opening of legacy made under suspensive condition. If loss of property occurred at death of testator or opening of bequest or subsequently, insurance indemnity substituted for property. Legacy made to liquidator lapses if he refuses office. (C.C.Q. 750s.).

Election.—The distribution of the estate of the deceased is unalterably governed by the terms of will, subject to survival of obligation of support. See topic Descent and Distribution, subhead Alimentary Support. Legatees have no right of election between testamentary provision and dower or distribution under intestate law.

Children, whether living when the will is executed or born thereafter, have no rights in the estate except such as are given them by the will. They may be disinherited by mere implication arising from failure to mention them.

Foreign Wills.—Wills executed outside the limits of the Province of Quebec are valid if made according to the forms required by the law of the country where they were executed and foreign executors and trustees may exercise their functions in this province under such wills and may appear in judicial proceedings before any court in the province. (C.C.Q. 3109 and C. P. 58).

Simultaneous Death.—See topic Death, subhead Survivorship.

Living Wills.—Provided for by rules governing mandate by person given in anticipation of incapacity to care for himself or to administer his property.

Mandate must be made by notarial act en minute or in presence of two witnesses. If given in presence of witnesses, mandate must be written by mandator or by third person. Witnesses must have no interest in act and be in position to ascertain whether mandator is capable of acting. Mandator: (1) declares nature of act but need not disclose its contents, (2) signs act or recognizes his signature, (3) may also have third person sign writing for him in his presence and according to his instructions. Witnesses then sign mandate. (C.C.Q. 2166s.).

Performance of mandate is subordinate to incapacity and to homologation by court, at mandatary's request. (C.C.Q. 2166). Acts performed before homologation may be annulled or resulting obligations reduced, on mere proof that mandator's incapacity was notorious or known to other party at time acts were entered into. (C.C.Q. 2170).

Where scope of mandate in doubt, mandatary interprets it according to rules respecting tutorship to persons of full age. (C.C.Q. 2168). See topic Guardian and Ward. Mandatary cannot renounce mandate unless he has previously provided for his replacement or applied for institution of protective supervision. (C.C.Q. 2174).

Mandate ends when court ascertains that mandator is again capable, when mandator revokes mandate, when mandatary renounces mandate, or when either party dies. (C.C.Q. 2172, 2175). If mandate is not faithfully performed, any interested person may apply to court for revocation of mandate and institution of protective supervision. (C.C.Q. 2177).

WITNESSES:

All persons are competent to testify except those who because of physical or mental condition are not in fit state to report facts of which they have knowledge. Any person competent to testify may be compelled to do so. Any person who has taken oath to tell the truth, the whole truth and nothing but the truth, may testify. If oath is contrary to his religious beliefs, witness can only testify if he has made a solemn affirmation. Testimony of witness is not disallowed by reason of his relationship to interested party.

Husband and wife cannot be compelled to testify against each other.

One witness is sufficient to prove a fact. (C. P. 293s).

WORKMEN'S COMPENSATION LAW:

See topic Labor Relations.

See note at head of Digest as to 1996 legislation covered.

See Topical Index in front part of this volume.

SASKATCHEWAN LAW DIGEST REVISER

MacPherson Leslie & Tyerman
1500-1874 Scarth Street
Regina, Saskatchewan 54P 4E9
Telephone: 306-347-8000
Fax: 306-352-5250
Saskatoon Office: 1500-410-22nd Street East, S7K 5T6. *Telephone:* 306-975-7100 *Fax:* 306-975-7145

Reviser Profile

History: MacPherson Leslie & Tyerman continues a Saskatchewan legal tradition that dates from 1920 when the firm was founded by Murdoch Alexander MacPherson at the City of Regina.

M.A. MacPherson, Q.C. was joined in the practice in 1925 by Everett Clayton Leslie and in 1929 by David McIntyre Tyerman. Also in 1929, M.A. MacPherson, Q.C. became Provincial Treasurer and Attorney General of the Province of Saskatchewan. The firm took its present name in 1951 and in the period since that time, it has grown from six lawyers to more than 40 lawyers with offices in Saskatchewan's two major cities, Regina and Saskatoon.

Areas of Practice: MacPherson Leslie & Tyerman carries on a full service practice in all areas of the law. The firm is organized into integrated practice areas which include corporate and commercial law, labour and administrative law, litigation, and land resources.

A large part of the firm's practice is dedicated to satisfying the needs of corporate and commercial clients in a broad range of areas such as project development, corporate finance, acquisitions, mergers and tax law. The firm's corporate and commercial lawyers have extensive experience in the design and establishment of joint venture enterprises and in large scale resource sector acquisitions, share issues and financing transactions. In addition, they have had a significant role in advising regarding drafting legislation such as *The Securities Act, The Co-Operatives Act, The Personal Property Security Act* and *The Community Bonds Act,* among others.

MacPherson Leslie & Tyerman also represents employers in all aspects of employment and labour relations matters. The practice of the firm's labour and administrative group includes collective bargaining, grievance arbitrations, collective agreement administration, labour relations board practice, construction industry labour relations, labour injunctions, advising on administrative law issues, and appearing before all manner of administrative tribunals. The labour and administrative law group also provides employment law advice and counseling in wrongful dismissal litigation, employer/employee claims, occupational health and safety matters, human rights matters, employment agreements, employment practices, and regarding employee benefit plans and labour standards.

The litigation department comprises a significant part of the firm's practice and extends to both civil and criminal matters. The members of this group practice before all Courts of Saskatchewan, the Federal Court of Canada and the Supreme Court of Canada. Matters handled by the litigation group range across environmental law cases, constitutional challenges, criminal price fixing conspiracies, challenges to store hour bylaws, shareholder derivative actions, defamation actions, contractual disputes, construction law suits, insurance litigation and claims involving large commercial undertakings. As well, the group handles tort actions including negligence relating to automobile accidents, airplane accidents, products liability and medical, dental, architectural, engineering, legal and accounting malpractice cases.

The firm's real estate practice is varied. The land and resources group represents real estate developers and subdividers, real estate brokerage firms, commercial and residential lenders including banks, insurance companies and corporate and individual purchasers and sellers. The land and resources practice area also maintains an active oil, gas and resources group which handles a wide range of transactions, primarily for larger resource sector companies. In addition, the firm has always played an active role in providing legal services to the developers and operators of Saskatchewan's uranium and potash industries and continues to act for a number of the largest mine and mill facilities in the Province.

Client Base: The firm has a broad and varied client base which includes firms which are leaders in their respective industries in Saskatchewan and elsewhere such as Ipsco Inc., Saskoil, The Toronto-Dominion Bank, Weyerhauser Canada Limited, Cogema Resources Inc., Saskatchewan Motor Club, Uranerz Exploration and Mining Limited, TransCanada PipeLines Limited, Producers Pipelines Inc., Canada Safeway Limited, Hudson Bay Company and many other national and international corporations. The firm also represents a number of small and medium size businesses and acts for individuals in a range of personal, professional and commercial matters.

Other Activities: It is a firm policy to encourage its partners and associates to become involved in the Law Society and Bar organizations. All members of the firm belong to the Canadian Bar Association and the Law Society of Saskatchewan. A number of partners hold and have held senior posts in the Canadian Bar Association, the Law Society of Saskatchewan, and in the American College of Trial Lawyers. A number of the firm's litigators belong to the Saskatchewan Trial Lawyers Association. In the past, partners of the firm have served as Benchers and as President of the Law Society of Saskatchewan, Chairman of the Law Foundation of Saskatchewan, and President of the Canadian Bar Association, Saskatchewan Branch.

It is also an important policy of the firm to encourage all lawyers to contribute personally to the community. Its lawyers are engaged in a wide range of volunteer and service activities ranging from charitable to political.

Significant Distinctions: The firm's founding partner, M.A. MacPherson, Q.C., was Attorney General of Saskatchewan from 1927 to 1934. The late E.C. Leslie, Q.C. was President of the Canadian Bar Association from 1957 to 1958. A total of ten former partners of the firm have been appointed to the Provincial Court, Court of Queen's Bench, and Saskatchewan Court of Appeal. Donald K. MacPherson, who joined the firm in 1951, was appointed Chief Justice of the Court of Queen's Bench in 1989. Existing partners have served as President, Saskatchewan Branch of the Canadian Bar Association and the Law Society of Saskatchewan.

SASKATCHEWAN LAW DIGEST

(The following is a list of all Topics, including cross-references, covered in this Digest.)

SASKATCHEWAN LAW DIGEST

Revised for 1997 edition by

MacPHERSON, LESLIE & TYERMAN, of the Regina and Saskatoon Bars.

(R.S. indicates Revised Statutes of Saskatchewan, 1978; Annual Statutes of Saskatchewan are cited by year and chapter number; R.C. indicates Rules of Court of Saskatchewan, 1961, as am'd.)

Note: Legislative session just concluding at time of going to press. This revision covers the session laws assented to and proclaimed in force by the Lieutenant Governor up to May 31, 1996.

ABSCONDING DEBTORS:

Under Absconding Debtors Act (R. S., c. A-2) it is permissible to attach debtor's property after commencement of suit in which claim is over $50. Grounds for attachment are that defendant: (1) Is about to abscond or has absconded leaving personal property liable to seizure, (2) has tried to remove such property out of province or to dispose of same to defraud creditors or plaintiff, or (3) keeps concealed to avoid process.

Act provides for commencement of proceedings by writ, method of seizure by sheriff, return of property upon giving security, length of time property to be held, and procedure for quashing writ by judge on affidavit that plaintiff had no grounds for same. This act is intended only to protect creditors' interests in debtor's property until such time as action is properly concluded, so after attachment, action must continue in normal way.

ABSENTEES:

Nonresidents have, generally, the same civil and property rights as residents.

Creditors or next-of-kin may apply to Court of Queen's Bench to have a person whose where-abouts cannot be ascertained declared an absentee, and an order may then be made with respect to disposition of absentee's property in Saskatchewan. (The Absentee Act, R. S., c. A-3).

In certain cases nonresidents claiming an interest in land are required to name agents within the province for service of statutory notices.

See also topic Costs.

Escheat.—Any money remaining unclaimed under control of any court for six years is paid to Minister of Finance. (R. S., c. C-43.1). Owner may, on application recover it.

Any balance remaining unclaimed for three months after sale under lien of a carrier is deposited with the Dominion Minister of Finance for the public uses of Canada. Owners may recover without suit, at any time within six years from the date of such deposit.

Unclaimed Bank Deposits.—See Canada Law Digest.

ACCORD AND SATISFACTION:

The part performance of an obligation, either before or after a breach thereof when expressly accepted by the creditor in satisfaction or rendered in pursuance of an agreement for that purpose, though without any new consideration, will extinguish the obligation. (R. S., c. Q-1 §45, para. 7).

ACKNOWLEDGMENTS:

Apart from a wife's acknowledgment pursuant to The Homesteads Act, 1989 (R.S., c. H-5.1) (see topic Homesteads) and execution of guarantee governed by The Saskatchewan Farm Security Act (R.S., c. S-17.1); there is no provision in Saskatchewan for acknowledgment of instruments before notary. Instead, witness to execution of documents must take formal affidavit, before proper officer, swearing to due execution of document.

Corporations.—Documents executed by corporations to which corporate seal is affixed, need not be witnessed, and no proof of execution is required.

Officers Who May Take Affidavits.—See topic Affidavits.

Fees for Taking.—No set fees are prescribed.

General Requirements as to Taking.—Officer taking must be satisfied as to identity of deponent.

Forms.—Form of affidavit of execution in general use is that prescribed by Land Titles Act (R. S., c. L-5) for transfers of land. See topic Real Property, subhead Forms.

Alternative to Acknowledgment or Proof.—No statutory provision.

ACTIONS:

Equity.—There is concurrent administration of law and equity. In cases of conflict, rules of equity prevail. (R. S., c. Q-1).

Forms of Action.—There is only one form of civil action, formal distinctions between actions at law and suits in equity having been abolished.

Conditions Precedent.—In actions against cities, towns, or villages for damages arising out of non-repair of highways, notice of claim must be given within 14 days and action brought within three months. (R. S., c. U-11, §314). In certain other cases action must be commenced within statutory period.

Commencement.—Except as noted hereafter, all actions are commenced by issue of statement of claim. (R.C. 13). Following applications may be commenced by originating notice: construction of documents; appointment of new trustee; vesting order; applications by executors or others interested in estates for determination of many questions involving the estate. (R.C. 452). See topics Process; Pleading.

Joinder and Severance.—The plaintiff may join in the same action several causes of action, and actions may be consolidated in the discretion of the court. Separate trials may be ordered by the court should it appear more convenient. An action for the recovery of land may not have any other joined with it unless by leave or it is of a similar nature. Motion for judgment on pleadings may be made and judgment may be entered for amount admitted due and trial proceed as to balance. On setoff judgment may be entered for any amount so allowed and cause continued as to remainder. On payment into court of any money admitted to be due by defendant, plaintiff may accept it as satisfaction in full or in part and continue as to remainder.

Parties.—An action or suit is not defeated by misjoinder or nonjoinder, but parties may be added or dropped at any stage by order of court.

Appearance.—Defendant who intends to defend shall serve and file statement of defence. Ordinary time for service and filing of statement of defence is 20 days; if out of Saskatchewan but within Canada or U.S., 30 days; if elsewhere, 40 days. (R. C. 100).

Stay of Proceedings.—The court has power to stay either generally or so far as may be necessary for the purposes of justice. A stay may be granted where the action is frivolous or vexatious; if the costs of a former action in which the cause of action was substantially the same have not been paid; pending the decision of a point of law; where partner plaintiffs do not comply with demand for names and places of residence of persons constituting firm; where the solicitor whose name is endorsed on statement of claim declares it was not issued by him.

Abatement will not be caused by marriage, death or insolvency of any of parties. Between verdict and judgment it does not result whether cause of action survives or not. Where defendants are liable jointly only the cause of action survives against surviving defendants, if any, and personal representative of deceased defendant cannot be added.

Limitation of.—See topic Limitation of Actions.

Direct Actions Against Insurer.—See topic Motor Vehicles, subhead Direct Actions.

Actions Respecting Land.—An action for foreclosure of a mortgage or cancellation of an agreement for sale respecting land cannot be commenced without leave of Court of Queen's Bench, on special application therefor unless mortgagor is corporation which has waived necessity of application. Application for appointment for hearing of application for leave must be preceded by 30 clear days written notice to Provincial Mediation Board of intention to do so. Fifteen days notice of appointment must be given to mortgagor or purchaser. Judge has wide discretion on application for leave. Application is pursuant to Land Contract (Actions) Act. (R. S., c. L-3). Mortgage securing National Housing Act Loan (R. S., c. H-13) and mortgage given after Oct. 1, 1975 to secure Federal Business Development Bank Act loan (1976-77, c. 37) are exempt from above provisions. Corporate body which is mortgagee or purchaser under agreement for sale of land may contract out of above mentioned provisions. (R. S., c. L-3).

See topics Moratorium; Mortgages, subhead Foreclosure.

Provincial Mediation Board Act (R. S., c. P-33) established Provincial Mediation Board, which on written request of debtor or creditor, endeavours to bring about amicable arrangement. Such board may intervene in tax sales and stay same.

ADMINISTRATION:

See topic Executors and Administrators.

ADOPTION:

Married adults jointly, unmarried adults, stepparents, or any other person that court may allow having regard to best interests of child, may petition judge of Court of Queen's Bench (Family Law Division) to adopt unmarried child under age of 18. Applicant must be resident of Saskatchewan, unless requirement waived by court. Where applicable, following persons must consent to adoption: birth mother; birth father; in case of Crown ward, appropriate minister; where guardianship vested in agency, agency; where no birth parent alive, guardian; and child being adopted, if over 12 years old. Court may dispense with requirement of consent. Consent of birth mother, birth father or guardian must be accompanied by affidavit of execution, certificate of independent legal advice and certificate of counselling.

Petition for order of adoption to be heard by judge in chambers without presence of public. Application and required materials must be served on director 30 days prior to filing application in court. Court may interview child, require presence of applicant or any other person or direct formal hearing be held.

No person may give or receive any payment for any purpose related to adoption. (1989-1990, c. C-7.3).

Legal effect of adoption order is to divest natural parents of all legal rights and responsibilities in regard to child and to transfer those rights, obligations, and responsibilities to the adopting parents. Surname of adoptive parent becomes surname of child unless court orders otherwise. Upon request, court may change given names of child. Child becomes heir of adoptive parent as if natural child. Appeals may be made to Court of Appeal by applicant, person whose consent is required but was not obtained and not dispensed with, or minister.

See also topic Courts, subhead Court of Queen's Bench.

ADVANCEMENTS: See topic Descent and Distribution.

ADVERSE POSSESSION:

No title to real estate can be acquired by adverse possession since 1913 where the land is under the Land Titles system, which is almost universally the fact. In other cases the period of adverse possession in which to obtain title to real estate is ten years.

Easements can only be acquired by express grant or statutory authority, but not by prescription.

AFFIDAVITS:

An affidavit may be made:

Within the province before a judge, clerk of court or deputy clerk, notary public, justice of the peace or commissioner for taking affidavits. A member of the Legislative Assembly may take an affidavit anywhere.

Without the province and within any British possession, before any judge of a court of record or notary public under his hand and seal or before a commissioner appointed for taking affidavits outside the province to be used within the province, or before any officer of the Canadian diplomatic or consular service, or before the mayor of any city or town.

In any foreign state, before any British consul or vice consul or before a judge of a court of record or a notary public under his hand and seal or before a commissioner appointed for taking affidavits outside the province to be used within the province or before any officer of the Canadian or British diplomatic or consular service, or the mayor of any city or town.

In the N. W. or Yukon territories, before a Magistrate or member of the R. C. M. P., a notary public or the mayor of any city or town.

Before a Military Officer.—Any person holding a commission in the permanent naval, military or air forces, if he holds the rank of lieutenant in the naval forces, captain in the army or flight lieutenant in the air forces, or a higher rank, may take an affidavit or administer an oath at any place.

General Requirements as to Administration.—Officer taking must be satisfied as to identity of deponent, and must administer an oath, form of which invokes the Deity or otherwise binds deponent's conscience.

General Requirements.—In matters in court an affidavit must be intituled in the cause or matter in which it is sworn, be made in the first person and divided into paragraphs numbered consecutively and contain description and true place of abode of deponent and be signed by him. (R.C. 322). Every person administering an oath must express time and place of so doing. All interlineations or alterations in jurat or in body of affidavit must be initialed by officer before whom sworn. Documents referred to in affidavit must be referred to as exhibits and not as annexed and must be signed by officer.

General Requirements of Jurat.—Every person administering oaths must express time and place in jurat. (R.C. 321). A Commissioner must write or stamp below his signature on each jurat completed by him: "A Commissioner for Oaths in and for Saskatchewan," and date on which his appointment expires, unless he is a Saskatchewan solicitor, in which case, he must insert the phrase "being a solicitor." A Notary Public must affix his notarial seal to his signature in each case and, unless he is a Saskatchewan solicitor, he must also insert date on which his commission expires.

Use.—Affidavits are used only in court proceedings or where authorized by statute. Otherwise, where required, statutory declaration is necessary. See Canada Law Digest, topic Affidavits.

Form

Affidavits.—Style of cause, giving Court, name of parties, etc.

I, A. B., of the . . . . of . . . ., in the Province of . . . ., (occupation), make oath and say:

(1) That . . . . .

Sworn before me at the . . . . of . . . . . in the Province of . . . .
(Signature of Affiant) this . . . . day of . . . ., 19. .
(Signature of Officer)

Alternative to Affidavit.—No statutory provision.

AGENCY: See topic Principal and Agent.

AIRCRAFT: See Canada Law Digest.

ALIENS:

Personal Property.—Same rights to acquisition, transmittal, and disposition as Canadian citizens. See Canada Law Digest.

Real Property.—Nonresident persons, except those who were resident farmers of land during any five years, shall not have aggregate land holding with assessed municipal tax value in excess of $15,000 excluding assessments for improvements. Nonresident with holdings in excess of this amount has five years to reduce holdings to permitted amount. Some exceptions if transferor was close relative and is or was resident farmer. (The Saskatchewan Farm Security Act 1988-89, c. S-17.1).

Amendments limit nonresident persons to 160 acres and $15,000 assessed value. Exception to 160 acre limit if land acquired prior to Sept. 15, 1977. Certain sections of amendments retroactively in force as of Sept. 15, 1977. (1988, c. S-17.1).

Amendments retroactively in force as of May 6, 1980, provide that no nonresident person shall, after that date, have aggregate land holding in excess of ten acres or $15,000 assessed value. Exception where acquired prior to that date, in which case Act as unamended applies, or where nonresident person was resident and farmed land during any five year period. "Resident person" means individual who resides in Saskatchewan for at least 183 days in any year. Nonresident with excess holdings and not within exception has five years to reduce holdings to permitted amount. Nonresident may apply to Farm Land Security Board for exemption.

Most nonagricultural corporations are also prohibited from holding in excess of ten acres, but certain ones are permitted to hold 320 acres. Nonagricultural corporation may hold land in excess of these limits with written consent of Farm Land Security Board. To qualify as agricultural corporation, corporation must be primarily engaged in farming and be corporation of which majority of issued voting and nonvoting shares are owned by resident farmer.

No person shall acquire land on behalf of nonresident person or nonagricultural corporation in excess of limits for such person or corporation.

ALIMONY:

See topics Divorce and Other Matrimonial Causes; Husband and Wife.

ALLOWANCES:

See topics Executors and Administrators, subhead Dependents' Relief Act; Wills.

APPEAL AND ERROR:

Appeals from Unified Family Court and Queen's Bench Court lie to Court of Appeal. Notice of appeal from interlocutory orders must be given within 15 days; in other cases within 30 days. In Queen's Bench Court actions appeal lies from court of appeal to Supreme Court of Canada at Ottawa. Any such appeal is limited to review only.

Appeals from surrogate court lie, if amount involved exceeds $300, either to a Judge of the Court of Queen's Bench within 15 days with a further appeal to the Court of Appeal, or direct to the Court of Appeal within 30 days.

Appeals from police magistrates and justices are governed as to procedure by the criminal code, a federal statute. When from justices, they are hearings de novo and lie to Queen's Bench judge. When from magistrates they are usually to the Court of Appeal on the trial evidence.

Leave to Appeal.—Appeals are as of right; leave is not required except in appeals to Supreme Court of Canada. In the latter case leave will only be given if the question involved is one of public importance, or the amount involved is large and the decision doubtful.

Stay of Proceedings.—Except in award of mandamus, injunctions, alimony or maintenance for child or spouse, execution of judgment shall not be stayed on appeal or by Judge of Court of Appeal. Executions are stayed in all other cases unless ordered otherwise by Judge of Court of Appeal.

Appeal Bond.—No bond is required except on appeal to Supreme Court of Canada but otherwise security for costs of an appeal may be ordered on ground of appellant's poverty and that his appeal is unlikely to succeed.

ARBITRATION AND AWARD:

Any controversy may be submitted to arbitration by agreement of parties. Arbitration agreement may be rescinded only in accordance with law of contract.

An award, by leave of the court, may be enforced in the same manner as a judgment. The award may be attacked for misconduct of the arbitrators or where the arbitration or award has been improperly procured.

Arbitration agreements may be entered into as at common law. (R. S., c. A-24.1).

ASSIGNMENTS:

Pursuant to Choses in Actions Act (R. S., c. C-11), any chose in action, including bona fide insurance policies, may be assigned, and assignee or beneficial owner may sue thereon subject to rights of defendant acquired before notice. Assignee of lender subject to same liabilities as assignor, limited to balance owing on contract at time of assignment. Assignment of wages or any portion thereof made to secure debt is invalid except where made to credit union organized by employees of employer to whom assignment is directed. (Assignment of Wages Act, R. S., c. A-30).

Assignment of accounts and most assignments for security purposes are within Personal Property Security Act (R. S., c. P-6.1) and its system of registration and priorities. See topic Personal Property Security.

ASSIGNMENTS FOR BENEFIT OF CREDITORS:

See Canada Law Digest, topic Bankruptcy.

ASSOCIATIONS:

The organization of unincorporated associations is not regulated by statute. An association consisting of more than 20 persons formed for the purpose of carrying on any business for gain must be incorporated.

Unincorporated associations may sue and be sued in names of some members on behalf of all members.

ATTACHMENT: See topic Absconding Debtors.

ATTORNEYS AND COUNSELORS:

These terms are not commonly used in Canada, the terms used being barristers and solicitors, whose rights and duties are, apart from custom, governed by the Legal Profession Act. A barrister and solicitor is in effect an officer of the court and his fees are governed largely by a tariff fixed by rules of court. Apart from custom, his conduct is regulated by Legal Profession Act, 1990, c. L-10.1.

Admission to Bar.—Applicant must be permanent resident of Canada or Canadian citizen and must have conformed to rules of Law Society of Saskatchewan respecting apprenticeship and legal education. Provision is made for admission of any person who has been admitted to practice as legal practitioner in any other country of British Commonwealth or U.S.A.

See note at head of Digest as to 1996 legislation covered.

See Topical Index in front part of this volume.

ATTORNEYS AND COUNSELORS . . . *continued*

Inquiries regarding conditions of admission to bar or relating to professional conduct should be directed to Secretary, Law Society of Saskatchewan, 201-2208 Scarth Street, Regina, Saskatchewan, S4P 2J6.

Disabilities.—A practitioner is exempt from jury duty and is prohibited from acting as surety on administration bonds.

Liens.—A solicitor is entitled to a common law lien for his charges upon documents in his possession belonging to his clients, and also to a lien of an equitable nature upon the fruits of judgments or orders obtained by him for his clients, in the suit in which he was employed, for his costs in that suit.

Compensation.—A client can always have his solicitor's bill taxed by the clerk of the court.

The Legal Aid Act provides for legal aid representation in certain civil and criminal matters. (R. S., c. L-9.1).

AUTOMOBILES: See topic Motor Vehicles.

BAIL: See topic Criminal Law.

BANKRUPTCY: See Canada Law Digest.

BANKS AND BANKING:

See Canada Law Digest.

BILLS AND NOTES: See Canada Law Digest.

BILLS OF LADING: See topic Carriers.

BILLS OF SALE: See topic Sales.

BLUE SKY LAW: See topic Securities.

BONDS:

Bonds in legal proceedings are generally payable to the party entitled to the benefit thereof. In estate matters bonds are payable to the surrogate court judge, and in lunacy matters, generally, to the local registrar of the court. Where bonds of guaranty companies are submitted, only the bonds of companies approved by the provincial secretary will be accepted by the court. Other sureties on bonds must justify. Bonds can be enforced only by suit in the usual way.

BROKERS:

Brokers must be registered pursuant to Securities Act, 1988 (1988-89, c. S-42.2), and are subject to audit and investigation by Securities Commission, as well as other control on their activities. Insurance brokers must be licensed pursuant to Saskatchewan Insurance Act (R. S., c. S-26), and must give bond for $10,000 in cities of Regina and Saskatoon, $5,000 in other cities and $2,000 in towns. See also topic Securities.

BULK SALES:

See topic Fraudulent Sales and Conveyances.

CARRIERS:

Generally railways and carriers are under the jurisdiction of Canadian Transport Commission.

Bills of Lading.—Consignee named in bill of lading and every endorsee thereof to whom the property passes is vested with all rights of action and is subject to all liabilities in respect to the goods as if the contract named in the bill of lading had been made with himself. This does not affect the vendor's right of stoppage in transitu or the right to claim freight against the original shipper or owner. While transferable by endorsement, bills of lading are not negotiable. No endorsee can take a better title than his endorser had. (R. S., c. F-1).

Liens.—A carrier has a lien on goods for freight, storage demurrage and terminal charges and expenses necessary for preservation of goods. Provision is made for sale of goods on non-payment of charges.

Motor Vehicle Carriers.—See topic Motor Vehicles.

Pipe lines are subject to Pipe Lines Act. (R. S., c. P-12).

CERTIORARI:

Order in nature of certiorari issues out of Court of Queen's Bench or Court of Appeal. Application for must be made within six months from date of judgment, conviction or order. Application for certiorari is directed to judge or other officer of inferior court of record, or to persons or bodies who are by statute or charter intrusted with judicial functions out of ordinary course of legal procedure, but within general scope of common law. Grounds and extent of inquiry are generally as at common law. Application for certiorari may be made available or be taken away by statute. Generally certiorari does not lie as substitute for appeal.

Applicant must give security for costs unless court orders otherwise.

CHARITABLE IMMUNITY:

See topic Damages.

CHATTEL MORTGAGES:

See topic Personal Property Security.

CIVIL RIGHTS:

Every person has right to freedom of conscience, of expression, of association, of religion, from arbitrary arrest or detention. Every person has right to employment, to own or occupy property, of access to public places, to join professional and trade organizations, and to education, without discrimination on basis of race, creed, religion, colour, sex, sexual orientation, family status, marital status, disability, nationality, ancestry, place of origin or receipt of public assistance. (R. S., c. S-24.1). Human Rights Commission administers these rights.

Ombudsman for Saskatchewan has duty and power to investigate any decision or recommendation made or any acts done or omitted relating to a matter of administration and affecting any person or body of persons in his or its personal capacity in or by a department or agency of government or by any officer, employee, or member thereof in exercise of any power, duty or function conferred upon him whereby any person is or may be aggrieved. Investigation may be taken, upon written complaint by any person or ombudsman's own motion. Complaint to ombudsman must be made by a person who is a resident of Saskatchewan. (R. S., c. O-4).

The Victims of Domestic Violence Act (1994, c. V.6.02) provides victim of domestic violence with right to apply to court for relief including compensation, exclusive possession or use of residence or other property and restraining orders.

CLAIMS:

See topics Executors and Administrators; Pleading.

COLLATERAL SECURITY: See topic Pledges.

COLLECTION AGENCIES:

See topic Principal and Agent.

COMMISSION TO TAKE TESTIMONY:

See topic Depositions.

COMMUNITY PROPERTY:

System does not obtain in Saskatchewan. But see topic Husband and Wife, subhead Matrimonial Property.

CONDITIONAL SALES:

See topic Personal Property Security.

CONSIGNMENTS: See topic Factors.

CONSUMER AFFAIRS: See topic Sales.

CONSUMER PROTECTION:

Under Consumer Products Warranties Act (R. S., c. C-30), promise, representation, affirmation of fact or expression of opinion that can reasonably be interpreted by consumers as promise relating to quality, condition, performance of efficacy made verbally, in writing, or through advertising deemed express warranty if it would usually induce reasonable consumer to buy product whether or not consumer actually relies on it.

Statutory warranties in retail sales include that: Retailer has right to sell products; product free from encumbrances; product corresponds with description or sample (if sale by description or sample); product is of acceptable quality; product is fit for purpose if consumer makes known to seller any particular purpose for which product being bought; and product and its components are reasonably durable and spare parts and repair facilities are reasonably available for reasonable length of time after sale.

If seller in breach of warranty, seller must make good breach free of charge if breach remedial. If breach is substantial, consumer has option to have breach remedied by seller or reject product and recover purchase price. There can be no contracting out of Act. Parol evidence admissible in consumer action to establish express warranty even if it modifies written contract.

Notwithstanding lack of privity, consumer has action against manufacturer who is deemed to have given same deemed statutory warranties as seller.

No "Plain Language" statute.

See topic Sales.

CONTRACTS:

Distributorships, Dealerships and Franchises.—No special legislation.

CONVEYANCES: See topic Deeds.

CORPORATIONS:

Business Corporations Act (R. S., c. B-10), modelled upon Canada Business Corporations Act, governs since 1977. Corporations incorporated under previous Companies Act required to be continued by filing articles of continuance by Dec. 31, 1980.

Formation.—One or more persons can incorporate corporation by signing and delivering articles of incorporation to Director of Corporations, 1871 Smith Street, Regina, Sask. Articles of incorporation must set out name of corporation, municipality within Saskatchewan where registered office is to be, classes and any maximum number of shares corporation authorized to issue, any restriction on right to transfer shares, number of directors, and any restriction on business corporation may carry on.

Fee for incorporation is $250, payable to Minister of Finance.

Restoration of company after Dec. 31, 1980.—Fee of $250 for certificate of continuance, payable to Minister of Finance.

Name.—Word "Limited", "Limitee", "Incorporated", "Incorporee", "Corporation" or abbreviations thereof must be part of name of every corporation. No corporation name shall be same as or similar to name of another firm, suggest connection with Crown or federal or provincial governments, or suggest connection with any political

CORPORATIONS . . . *continued*
party. Where name has not yet been cleared with Director it is possible to incorporate by designating number assigned by Director.

Powers.—Corporation generally has capacity and powers of natural person. No requirement of reciting objects.

Directors.—Only one director needed except that distributing corporation (one that distributes securities to public) must have at least three directors. Except if articles provide for cumulative voting, no requirements of fixed number of directors; may have minimum and maximum number of directors.

Majority of directors must be resident Canadians. No requirement that directors hold shares issued by corporation, unless articles so require. Quorum for directors meeting is majority of directors or majority of minimum number of directors if articles provide for minimum and maximum number.

Directors chosen by ordinary resolution of shareholders. If no expressly stated term director ceases to hold office at close of first annual meeting following his election. Generally, directors may be removed by ordinary resolution at special shareholders meeting.

Liabilities of Directors and Officers.—Must act honestly and in good faith with view to best interests of corporation and exercise care, diligence and skill of reasonably prudent person. Directors who consent to illegal corporate action such as payment of illegal commissions, prohibited dividends, prohibited financial assistance, or prohibited shareholders payments must indemnify corporation for any loss suffered thereby. Directors liable to employees for all debts to employees for services while they were directors. Directors are liable for unremitted revenue taxes of corporation, subject to due diligence defence. (The Revenue and Financial Services Act, 1994, c. R-22.0).

Stockholders (Shareholders) Rights.—Holders of not less than 5% of voting shares may require directors to call meeting of shareholders for particular purposes. Fundamental changes to corporation require special resolution of shareholders (i.e. 2/3 of votes cast). Shareholder may dissent if corporation resolves to amend articles, vary restrictions on shares, vary restrictions upon business of corporation, amalgamate, or dispose of substantially all of its property. Dissenting shareholder, if action from which he dissents is approved, entitled to be paid fair market value for shares. Shareholders may apply to court to have corporation investigated.

Shareholders may apply for leave to bring action in name of corporation, thus allowing shareholders to bring derivative action against directors and majority shareholders for oppression.

Stock.—Shares must be no par value shares only. Corporation may have unlimited share capital; therefore no requirement of authorized share capital and maximum consideration.

Corporation required to maintain separate stated capital account for each class or series of shares issued. Consideration received for shares to be added to appropriate stated capital account which may only be reduced by special resolution and in circumstances which, generally stated, indicate that corporation will remain solvent.

Meetings.—Directors must call annual shareholder meetings within 18 months of formation and subsequently within 15 months of last preceding annual meeting. Notice of shareholders meeting must be sent to all directors and shareholders within 21 and 50 days before meeting.

Records.—Corporation must maintain at its registered office in Saskatchewan or at any other designated place in Saskatchewan, records containing articles, by-laws, amendments, minutes of meetings, and shareholders resolutions. Shareholders and creditors of corporation can examine records during usual business hours.

Dissolution.—Corporation with no property and no liabilities may be dissolved by special resolution of shareholders and upon filing "articles of dissolution" with Director. Director of Corporations may cause corporation to be dissolved if failure to restore name of corporation to Register within two years after having been struck off, failure for two or more consecutive years to hold annual shareholders meetings, or failure to forward financial statements to shareholders.

Cooperative associations may be formed by six or more persons or by amalgamation of two or more cooperative associations for any cooperative business, with some exceptions. Capital may be limited or unlimited and divided into shares or without share capital. Each member has one vote and cannot vote by proxy. (R. S., c. C-37.1).

Credit Unions.—Ten or more residents in the province may incorporate as a credit union to receive savings from and make loans to its members and with other general powers. (R. S., c. C-45.1). Privilege of joining credit union is extended to another credit union, cooperative association, municipal body, labor organization or fraternal society and other organizations where no part of income goes to personal benefit of member.

Foreign Companies.—Every extra-provincial company carrying on business in Saskatchewan must be registered within 30 days after commencing business.

Information to Be Filed.—Every extra-provincial company must, before registration, file with the registrar a certified copy of its charter and by-laws, the petition and statutory declarations in stated form, and a duly executed power of attorney, under its common seal, empowering some person named therein and residing in a city, town or village in Saskatchewan, to act as its attorney for the purpose of receiving service of process in all suits and proceedings against the company in Saskatchewan and of receiving all lawful notices.

Fee for registration of extra-provincial corporation is $250.

Annual returns to be filed in prescribed form and notice of changes of head office address, power of attorney, or his address, directors and amendments to articles affecting change of name, amalgamation or continuance under another jurisdiction.

Property Rights.—See topic Aliens.

For Dominion companies, banks, etc., see Canada Law Digest.

Crown Corporations.—Provincial Government has established Crown Investments Corporation of Saskatchewan as holding company for Crown corporations. It will perform supervisory and coordinating functions for all Crown corporations. Provincial Government by Order-in-Council, may create Crown corporation to operate any industrial, commercial, financial or public utility enterprise on behalf of Province. Crown corporation has power to borrow money and make loans and advances to Crown Investments Corporation of Saskatchewan. Crown corporations may sue and be sued in contract or in tort. (1993, c. C-50.101).

Taxation.—See topic Taxation.

Non-Profit Corporations now governed by Non-Profit Corporations Act (R.S., c. N-4.1) modelled on Business Corporations Act. Corporations are deemed to be charitable corporations (and therefore subject to some special rules under Act), if they solicit donations or other gifts, receive government grants or property in excess of 10% of income during any fiscal year and if they are registered as charities under Income Tax Act (Canada).

Other corporations are membership corporations which are incorporated for benefit of their members.

Trade Names or Styles.—Pursuant to Business Names Registration Act (R. S., c. B-11), every person (including corporations, partnerships, joint ventures, etc.) carrying on business under business name, name to be registered under Act. Registrar can reject registration of certain objectionable or confusing names. Records are kept by Director of Corporations.

COSTS:

The costs of proceedings and actions in court are governed by the tariff of costs fixed by rules of court. Generally they are at the discretion of the court, but usually a successful litigant is entitled to his proper disbursements and certain costs based upon this tariff, which are recoverable against the opposite party. There are certain costs which are not taxable against the opposite party, commonly known as solicitor and client costs.

Security for costs may be required from non-resident plaintiff who has no property within the province and where the defendant prima facie has a good defence.

COURTS:

Court of Appeal has no original jurisdiction except in contempt, mandamus, certiorari, prohibition, quo warranto and habeas corpus. It has appellate jurisdiction by appeal from Court of Queen's Bench in both civil and criminal matters and from Unified Family Court. Court consists of seven judges. Court sits at both Regina and Saskatoon at such times as may be fixed annually by court. (R. S., c. C-42). See topic Appeal and Error.

Court of Queen's Bench has jurisdiction in all cases, except where excluded by statute. It sits on rotating basis at each judicial centre. Number of judges is 31. Family Law Division of Court of Queen's Bench has jurisdiction in family matters pertaining to adoption, infants, illegitimate children, juvenile delinquents, deserted wives' and children's maintenance, married and common law women's property rights including homesteads, and solemnization of marriage. Number of Family Law Division judges is six. (R. S., c. Q-1).

Judges of provincial court adjudicate claims brought under Small Claims Act which provides expeditious procedure to try claims for debt, damages, and recovery of goods or chattels, up to maximum amount or value of $5,000. (1988-89, c. S-50.1).

Justice of the Peace has jurisdiction in minor criminal matters, and may conduct preliminary hearing of most criminal charges.

CREDITORS' SUITS:

See topic Fraudulent Sales and Conveyances.

CRIMINAL LAW:

Criminal law is within the jurisdiction of the federal parliament. (See Canada Law Digest.) The provincial legislature has power to impose a fine and imprisonment for breach of its statutes.

Bail is entirely in the discretion of the court.

CROP PAYMENTS ACT:

In case of lease, agreement for sale or mortgage where payment is to be by share of crop not exceeding 50%, such payment has priority over everything except seed grain chattel mortgage, and the right vests as soon as the crop is sown. (R. S., c. C-48). See also Saskatchewan Farm Security Act (1988-89, c. S-17.1) for exceptions.

CURTESY:

No tenancy by curtesy.

DAMAGES:

Common law generally prevails. In damages for negligence, Contributory Negligence Act (R. S., c. C-31) applies. Doctrine of charitable immunity is not recognized in Saskatchewan.

Where contract does not contain provisions for consequences of frustration and contract is frustrated, parties are relieved from their accrued obligations, liable for consequential losses, entitled to restitution of benefits and may have lost expenses apportioned. (The Frustrated Contracts Act, 1994, c. F-22.2).

Privacy.—Violation of privacy of another person is tort actionable without proof of damage. (R. S., c. P-24).

See also topic Death, subhead Actions for Death.

DEATH:

Common law presumption of death after seven years absence.

Survivorship.—Where two or more persons die at same time, or within period of five days, property of each person is to be disposed of as if that person survived other persons, except where such persons hold title to property jointly, title to property is deemed to have been held as tenants in common in equal shares unless contrary

DEATH . . . *continued*
intention appears in written agreement between such persons. Where two or more persons die in circumstances rendering it uncertain who died first, these deaths are presumed to occur at same time. However, insured under life insurance policy is presumed to survive beneficiary, and wills that dispose of property or appoint executor to be operative in event of such circumstances, case for which will provides is deemed to have occurred. (1993, c. S-67.1).

Actions for death may be maintained by personal representative, or child, or spouse, or common law spouse, or parent of decedent. Action must be brought within two years after death. Damages are apportioned among those who have suffered financial loss by the death. There is no statutory limit of amount recoverable. (R. S., c. F-11).

Death Certificate.—See topic Records, subhead Vital Statistics.

The Human Tissue Gift Act regulates inter-vivos and post-mortem disposition of human tissue. All transplants or dispositions of body, organs, or other human tissue, except as otherwise provided in statute, prohibited. Death defined according to medical practice. (R. S., c. H-15).

See also topics Marriage, subhead Presumption of Death of Absent Spouse; and Wills, subhead Living Wills.

DECEDENTS' ESTATES:

See topics Descent and Distribution; Executors and Administrators; Homesteads; Wills.

DECLARATORY JUDGMENTS: See topic Judgments.

DEEDS:

The ordinary common law rules as to deeds apply, the seal being the essential thing but this does not extend to documents under the Land Titles Act.

Execution.—For circumstances in which spouse must join, see topic Homesteads, subhead Alienation or Encumbrance; also Real Property, subhead Forms.

For deeds and documents relating to real property, see topic Real Property.

DEEDS OF TRUST: See topic Mortgages.

DEPOSITIONS:

Depositions in any cause or matter pending in court may be taken out of the province under commission. The application for same is made on motion before a judge in chambers.

The requisites of a deposition are not prescribed.

Outside of Province for Use within the Province.—Court may make any order for examination upon oath before any person at any place, of any witness or person, and may empower any party to give such deposition in evidence therein, on such terms as court may direct. (R.C. 289). Copy of pleadings or copy of documents necessary to inform examiner so appointed of questions at issue, shall be furnished to him. (R.C. 291). Examination takes place in presence of parties and their solicitors or agents, or such of them as may think fit to attend. Witnesses are subject to cross-examination and reexamination. (R.C. 292). Depositions may be taken in shorthand by the commissioner, an official court reporter, or a duly sworn shorthand writer, or they may be taken in longhand in presence of examiner, and signed either by witness or examiner. If witness refuses to attend at examination, or to be sworn, or to answer any lawful question, court may issue a warrant for immediate arrest of the witness, to be brought before court, or examiner. (R.C. 296). In addition, court may order witness to pay any costs occasioned by his refusal. (R.C. 297). When examination has been concluded, original deposition authenticated by signature of examiner, shall be transmitted by him to local registrar of the court, and shall be filed by him. (R.C. 298). Depositions, taken in accordance with Rules, may be given in evidence at trial without proof of signature of person taking examination. (R.C. 300).

To Perpetuate Testimony.—Any person claiming any property, interest or office in the future may commence proceedings to perpetuate material evidence and have such evidence taken under the direction of the court and filed with the court.

Compelling Attendance of Witnesses.—Witness within province may be compelled to attend for examination on order of court called subpoena. Failure to attend can result in court ordering his arrest and deliverance for examination.

Commission or Letters Rogatory.—Upon application to a judge in chambers by person duly authorized by a foreign tribunal showing that such tribunal desires to obtain the testimony of any person within the jurisdiction respecting any civil, commercial or criminal matter, an order may be obtained giving effect to such request.

DESCENT AND DISTRIBUTION:

(R. S., c. I-13).

In case of intestacy, the entire estate, real and personal, or the excess over the share of the surviving spouse, if any, descends and is distributed as follows, each class of which a member is living taking to exclusion of all subsequent classes: (1) Children and issue of deceased children, per stirpes; (2) parents equally or all to surviving parent; (3) brothers and sisters equally, children of deceased brother or sister taking share to which their parent, if living, would be entitled; (4) if no brother or sister survive, nephews and nieces per capita; (5) next of kin of equal degree. No representation among collaterals further removed than children of brothers and sisters.

Surviving Spouse.—Share of surviving spouse is entire estate of decedent up to net value of $100,000, and, of residue over that sum, as follows: Entire residue if decedent left no issue; one-half of residue if decedent left only one child or only issue of one deceased child; one-third of residue in all other situations.

Surviving spouse who has left decedent and is living in adultery at the time of decedent's death takes no share in the estate.

Half Blood.—Kindred of the half blood inherit equally with those of the whole blood of same degree.

Posthumous Heirs.—Descendants and relatives begotten before decedent's death but born thereafter take as though born in his lifetime.

Illegitimate children are entitled to same rights in property of their mother as if legitimate.

Illegitimate child treated as if were legitimate child of his mother. (R.S., c. I-13).

Illegitimate child of a male person entitled to share in estate of same whether under will or intestacy in same manner as a legitimate child provided that court of competent jurisdiction satisfied that during deceased's lifetime deceased acknowledged that he was father of child, or that deceased was living with mother of child at child's birth and appeared to accept child as his own. (R. S., c. I-13).

Where illigitimate child has died intestate father of same takes entire estate if otherwise estate would escheat to Crown and above provision satisfied. (R. S., c. I-13).

Adopted Children.—See topic Adoption.

Advancements of real or personal property to a child are reckoned as part of the estate of the parent for purposes of distribution.

Escheat.—In default of heirs, all property escheats to the Crown. (R. S., c. E-11).

DESERTION:

See topics Divorce and Other Matrimonial Causes; Husband and Wife.

DISPUTE RESOLUTION:

General.—The Queen's Bench Act (R.S., c. Q-1) provides for mediation as aspect of civil proceedings in Court of Queen's Bench for both family and nonfamily matters in designated judicial centres. Number of other statutes provide for mediation of claims or disputes arising in respect to particular subject matter governed by statute.

Mandatory Mediation.—On commencement of family law proceeding, action cannot proceed until parties have met and discussed possibility of mediation with mediator. Mediator will meet with each party individually to present overview of mediation process and to assist parties in assessing whether or not mediation is best option available for resolution of dispute. After mediation session, parties may continue with mediation or any party may discontinue mediation and continue with legal proceedings. (R.S., c. Q-1).

At close of pleadings in nonfamily proceeding, action cannot proceed without parties attending mediation session. Mediator will meet with each party individually to discuss dispute and meet with parties jointly to discuss mediation process and its appropriateness for resolution of dispute. After mediation session, parties may continue with mediation or any party may discontinue mediation and continue with legal proceeding. (R.S., c. Q-1).

The Saskatchewan Farm Security Act (R.S., c. S-17.1) requires mediation upon commencement of any action in court with respect to farmland by mortgagee for foreclosure, sale or possession of farmland or related relief before action may proceed. If mortgagee fails to participate in mediation process in good faith, court may supervise mediation.

Voluntary Mediation.—Claimants of personal injury benefits in automobile accidents may request mediation of claim for benefits. (R.S., c. A-35).

Employee may request Director of Labour Standards to negotiate and settle any difference between employee and employer or corporate director. (R.S., c. L-1).

In application pursuant to The Children's Law Act (1995, c. C-8.1) pertaining to custody and access of children, court may appoint person to mediate matters at issue between parties.

In application pursuant to Family Maintenance Act (1994, c. F-6.1), court may appoint person to mediate any matter that is dealt with in application and that is at issue between parties.

Owner or occupant of surface land who filed complaint with Surface Rights Arbitration Board concerning operations of person and/or company that has acquired right to mineral thereunder may request that complaint be referred to mediation. Further, where there is matter in dispute pending determination by Surface Rights Arbitration Board, board and owner of surface land may request to have matter referred to mediation. (R.S., c. S-65).

Also see topic Arbitration and Award.

DIVORCE AND OTHER MATRIMONIAL CAUSES:

Governed by Federal Divorce Act. See Canada Law Digest.

Grounds for legal separation are adultery, intolerable physical or mental cruelty or intentionally living separate and apart for one year. Court of Queen's Bench (Family Law Division) has jurisdiction to hear matter when parties are domiciled or had matrimonial home in province. See Queen's Bench Act, R. S., c. Q-1.

Annulment of Marriage.—See topic Marriage.

Presumption of Death.—See topic Marriage.

Family Maintenance Act.—Court may order person to pay maintenance for spouse and/or children. Court can also make order restraining person from wasting of assets that would impair claim under Act. No limitation period operates to bar claim under Act. (R.S., c. F-6.1).

DOWER: There is no dower.

ELECTION: See topic Wills.

EMPLOYER AND EMPLOYEE:

See topic Labour Relations.

See note at head of Digest as to 1996 legislation covered.

See Topical Index in front part of this volume.

ENVIRONMENT:

Administration of The Environmental Management and Protection Act (R.S., c. E-10.2) assigned to Department of Environment and Public Safety, 3085 Albert Street, Regina, Saskatchewan, S4S 0B1. Department coordinates activities, policies and programs of government agencies and advises government with respect to management protection and use of environment. Where pollutant is present in environment or being discharged in circumstances harmful to environment, Minister may make orders to protect or restore environment. (§4). Any person subject to such order can appeal to Court of Queen's Bench within 30 days. (§10). Owner of pollutant civilly liable to third parties for damages caused by discharge of pollutant or neglect or default in execution of duty imposed by Act without proof of fault, negligence or willful intent. (§13). Minister has general supervision of all matters concerning water quality and its impairment by pollution. (§14). Government can make regulations controlling disposal of solid wastes into environment, controlling activities affecting water courses, classifying manufactured products and requiring that any class of product be reused, prescribing place and manner in which solid, liquid or radioactive wastes may be disposed of, controlling use and application of chemicals, describing duties of any person conducting operations affecting surface of land and controlling noise levels. Contravention of regulation may result in fine being imposed. No permit or approval to discharge wastes into environment is valid unless approved by Minister of Department. (§39).

The Public Health Act, 1994 (1994, c. P-37.1) empowers local authorities to order removal or remedy of any health hazard.

Parks Act (R. S., c. P-1.1) provides for certain offences and penalties for pollution, contamination, litter, waste, or destruction of or on any provincial park, recreation site, historic site or protected area as defined by Act.

Use and protection of Crown Land and resources found therein and thereon is governed by Provincial Lands Act. (R. S., c. P-31).

Water Pollution.—Government is empowered to prohibit by order discharge of any substance which may in its opinion cause water pollution and to revoke previous governmental approval or permit for discharge of substance in question. Government can do all things necessary to bring about compliance with water pollution legislation at cost of delinquent party. (Ground Water Conservation Act, R. S., c. G-8; Water Corporation Act, R. S., c. W-4.1).

Litter Control.—No person shall abandon, upon land owned by others or Crown or into water, a manufactured article, processed material or any waste. This prohibition does not apply to disposal in a proper receptacle. Contravention of prohibition is an offence. Minister may establish policies and programs in respect to waste minimization. (Litter Control Act, R. S., c. L-22).

Pesticides.—Certain prohibitions have been set up as to selling pesticides that do not meet certain standards, as to use of a pesticide and as to applying of pesticides to an open body of water, without a permit. There are also prohibitions as to keeping pesticides in certain containers and as to disposal of pesticides and containers. Where government is of opinion that any plant, animal or water is contaminated, it may prohibit sale or use, or order destruction. Compensation is payable. (Pest Control Act, R. S., c. P-7).

Air Pollution.—Clean Air Act (R.S., c. 12.1), prohibits operation of industrial source unless permit obtained from Department. Minister can issue control orders directing that person refrain from emitting air contaminant. Contravention of order constitutes offence which could result in fine of not more than $1,000,000, imprisonment for not more than three years, or both. Ozone-depleting Substances Control Act, 1993 (1993, c. O-8.1) regulates or prohibits manufacture, sale and consumption of certain ozone-depleting substances and products. Contravention of Act could result in fine of not more than $1,000,000, imprisonment for not more than three years, or both.

Chemical Pollution.—Environment Spill Control Regulations under Department of Environment Act requires reporting of spills of chemicals.

Environmental Assessment.—The Environmental Assessment Act (R. S., c. E-10.1) provides that no person shall proceed with development until he has received ministerial approval. "Development" is defined as any project, operation or activity, or any expansion thereof which is likely to have effect on any unique, rare or endangered feature of environment, cause emission of any pollutant, cause widespread public concern because of potential environmental changes, involve new technology that is concerned with resource utilization and that may induce significant environmental change, that substantially utilizes any provincial resource so as to preempt use of that resource for any other purpose, or that will have significant impact on environment. However, proponent may conduct feasibility study, including research and exploration, prior to obtaining approval to proceed with development.

Act sets out Assessment and Review Procedure in which proponent of development must participate. Normally public will be notified of assessment in manner to be prescribed in regulations. Minister may require public information hearing to be held, or appoint persons to conduct inquiry, prior to reaching his decision with regard to development. Developments may only proceed in accordance with terms of ministerial approval, if granted. Minister has power to conduct investigation where, in his opinion, terms and conditions of approval are not being complied with. Where any person proceeds with unauthorized development, he is liable to any other person who suffers loss, damage or injury as result of development.

EQUITY: See topics Actions; Practice.

ESCHEAT:

See topics Absentees; Descent and Distribution; Wills.

ESTATES: See topic Real Property.

EVIDENCE: See topics Depositions; Witnesses.

EXECUTIONS:

(R. S., c. E-12).

Execution on a judgment may issue at any time while judgment is in force, and is good for ten years after which an alias writ may issue. Executions against land expire ten years after date of judgment.

Exemptions.—See topic Exemptions.

Lien.—Execution against goods binds the goods from the date of delivery to the sheriff, subject to the rights of a bona fide purchaser from the debtor, who, without notice of execution obtains and continues in actual possession.

Where an execution against goods has been issued judgment creditor may issue execution against lands at any time provided at least $100 remains unpaid. (R. S., c. E-12).

Execution against lands binds all lands of the debtor within the judicial district of the sheriff to whom the writ is directed from the time of filing a certified copy of such execution in the proper Land Titles Office.

Stays.—Execution may be stayed on motion to a judge, showing special grounds, and on such terms as the judge may impose. See topic Moratorium.

Levy and Sale.—All sales of property seized under execution are by public auction, after advertisement and notice. There is no right of redemption from execution sales. Immediately he receives the execution the sheriff makes seizure of sufficient goods of the debtor to satisfy the debt.

Should there not be sufficient goods, lands, although meanwhile subject to execution, may not be sold thereunder until at least expiration of one year from time of receipt of execution by sheriff and only then with leave of Queen's Bench Court.

Priorities.—The creditor at whose instance and under whose execution the seizure was made has a priority for the costs of his action but otherwise the proceeds of the sheriff's sale are divided rateably between all the execution creditors having executions in the sheriff's hands within two months of the time of the sheriff's levy, except where the amount is realized from the sale of the article for the purchase price of which judgment was obtained or is upon a judgment for alimony or under a separation agreement. (R. S., c. C-46).

Supplementary Proceedings.—If execution returned unsatisfied, debtor may be examined as to property or means he had when debt incurred, what disposition made thereof, and what means he has for satisfying judgment.

EXECUTORS AND ADMINISTRATORS:

The authority of a personal representative to administer property situate in the province can only be granted by Court of Queen's Bench. Appointment of executors and administrators is under The Queen's Bench Act. (R.S., c. Q-1). Matters relating to powers and authority of trustees and executors and administration of estates are found in The Trustee Act, R. S., c. T-23, and Devolution of Real Property Act, R. S., c. D-27.

Jurisdiction and Venue.—Petition for letters probate or letters of administration may be made to court at any judicial centre, if deceased had estate or effects in Saskatchewan.

Eligibility and Competency.—Married woman or nonresident may petition. Although infant may be appointed, he cannot act until 18 years of age. A nonresident executor is usually granted probate as a matter of course. Letters of administration can be granted to nonresident petitioner but usual practice is to have a resident apply under power of attorney from non-resident entitled to administration.

Preferences in Right to Administration.—Widower or widow or next of kin in order of nearness.

Official Administrator.—Public official, usually Public Trustee for Saskatchewan; powers, duty and authority provided by Queen's Bench Act. On notice such official administrator will take possession of neglected property of deceased and may apply for administration of estate if no application for probate or administration is made within 30 days of death of deceased. Appointment of official administrator, so made, may be revoked in discretion of judge and appointment given to individual ordinarily entitled to apply for same.

Bonds.—No bond is required for probate. Petitioner for letters of administration must furnish bond to value of estate if by guaranty company or double value of estate if a private bond. Private sureties must justify. Court may dispense with bond in certain cases.

Claims.—Claim of creditor against the estate must be brought to attention of executor or administrator. Executor advertises for creditors in the locality where deceased lived and general practice is to prove claims by a statutory declaration certifying as to the claim, stating nature thereof and what, if any, security is held and placing a value on such security. Form of claim is as follows:

Form

Proof of Debt.—In the Matter of the Estate of . . . . Late of the . . . . of . . . ., in the Province of . . . ., ..., Deceased.

I, ..., of the . . . . of . . . . in the . . . . of . . . ., (occupation), do solemnly declare and say:

1. That I am the undermentioned creditor (or the . . . . of the undermentioned creditor) and have knowledge of all the circumstances connected with the debt hereinafter referred to.

2. That the said . . . ., deceased, was at the time of his death, and his estate still is, justly and truly indebted to me in the sum of . . . . ($. . . .) Dollars, as shown by the account hereunto annexed and marked "A."

3. That I have not, nor has any person by my order to my knowledge or belief, for my use had or received any manner of satisfaction or security whatsoever save and except the following:

And I make this solemn declaration conscientiously believing it to be true and knowing that it is the same force and effect as if made under oath and by virtue of the Canada Evidence Act.

Declared before me at the . . . . of . . . . in the . . . . of . . . . this . . . . day of . . . . A. D. 19. . . . .

See note at head of Digest as to 1996 legislation covered.

See Topical Index in front part of this volume.

EXECUTORS AND ADMINISTRATORS . . . *continued*

. . . .

(A Commissioner for Oaths (or Notary Public).

If the creditor holds any security for his claim or part thereof, he should give full particulars of the same, and if the security is on the estate of the deceased, a specified value should be placed thereon, and the creditor ranks as a general creditor only for the excess.

After due advertising for creditors, the executor may distribute the assets having regard only to claims of which he then has notice. However, unpaid creditors may still realize by following the assets into the hands of beneficiaries receiving same. If the creditor holds any security for his claim or part thereof, he should give full particulars of the same, and if the security is on the estate of the deceased, a specified value should be placed thereon, and the creditor ranks as a general creditor only for the excess. See topic Limitation of Actions.

Priorities.—The property of the testator is distributed rateably among all creditors of the testator, whether specialty or simple contract creditors. Funeral and testamentary expenses are preferred claims.

Sale of Estate Assets.—No restriction on sale of personal property, but unless power of sale is given in will consent of beneficiaries should be obtained. No consent of beneficiaries to sale of real or personal property is necessary if sale is made for purpose of paying debts of the estate. If infants interested in estate, no sale of real property is valid unless consent of Public Trustee or court order approving sale is obtained. (Devolution of Real Property Act, R. S., c. D-27). See also topic Real Property, subhead Title of Deceased Owner.

Accounts.—Executors and administrators required to pass accounts to satisfaction of the court unless the court dispenses with same by order.

Dependents' Relief Act (R. S., c. D-25) gives to wife, husband, certain common law spouses or dependent child of decedent, whether testate or intestate, domiciled in Saskatchewan right to apply, within six months after decedent's death, to Court of Queen's Bench (Family Law Division) for order making reasonable provision for applicant's maintenance. Court, if of opinion that decedent has not made reasonable provision for dependent, may make order in such manner as it deems sufficient to provide reasonable maintenance. Wide discretionary power is given to court which takes into consideration all circumstances of estate and relations of parties; no dependent may contract himself out of statute.

No executor or administrator shall distribute assets of an estate within six months from grant of probate or administration without consent of all beneficiaries or without court order so as to allow dependents sufficient time to make application. (R. S., c. D-25).

Compensation to executor or administrator is in discretion of court, usually 5% or less, on amount realized. Sometimes an annual fee is allowed where estate runs a number of years.

Ancillary Administration.—A nonresident executor or administrator, whose appointment has been confirmed in a foreign jurisdiction, will be appointed as a matter of course by the Saskatchewan courts on application for the resealing of the foreign letters probate or administration. No security is required of a foreign executor, and a foreign administrator must give security only to the extent that the foreign security does not cover the Saskatchewan assets. Same effect is given to resealing as to original grant of letters. See topic Wills.

EXEMPTIONS:

A number of enumerated articles of personal property and certain real property up to 160 acres, in some instances limited as to value, are exempt from seizure and sale under execution. (R. S., cc. E-14, S-17.1).

Substitution.—A debtor who does not possess articles specifically exempted is not entitled to hold money or other property exempt in lieu thereof.

Debts Against Which Exemptions Not Available.—There is no exemption where the claim is for board and lodging or hospital expenses or is upon judgment for maintenance or under separation agreement.

No property is exempt from seizure under an execution on a judgment for the purchase price thereof.

Loss of Exemption.—There are no exemptions where the debtor absconds leaving no family behind.

Death of Debtor.—Exemption extends to the debtor's family on his death.

Wages.—No debt due or accruing due to a mechanic, workman, laborer, servant, clerk or employee, for wages or salary is liable to attachment or garnishment except to extent of excess thereof over $500 plus $100 for each dependant he supports. Above has reference to monthly earnings, and if less than month it must be computed on above proportional basis. (R. S., c. A-32). See also topic Garnishment.

Homestead Exemption.—See topic Homesteads.

FACTORS:

(Factors Act, R. S., c. F-1).

Sale, pledge, or other disposition to bona fide purchaser without notice in ordinary course of business by mercantile agent who is, with consent of owner, in possession of goods or documents of title, is as valid as if he were authorized to do so. This does not apply to consignments covered by Personal Property Security Act, but it applies to sellers remaining in possession of goods and any mercantile agent acting on behalf of such seller. Registration of buyer's interest under Personal Property Security Act prevents seller in possession from passing good title. See also topic Brokers.

Consignments.—Where the owner of goods delivers to another for consignment or sale or has shipped in the name of another the consignee, not having had notice of the real owner's interest, has a lien upon the goods to the extent of any advances made to the nominal consignor and may transfer such lien.

Agricultural Machinery.—A special act deals with the sale of agricultural machinery, particularly large implements and provides for filing of a list of implements with full particulars thereof and prices and repairs with the Minister of Agriculture, with forms of contract. Applies only to manufacturers and dealers. (R. S., c. A-10).

FIDUCIARIES:

See topics Executors and Administrators; Guardian and Ward; Trusts.

FILING FEES:

See topics Chattel Mortgages; Corporations; Deeds; Mortgages.

FISHERIES:

Property in all wild fish is in province; persons only acquire property therein by obtaining possession pursuant to license.

The Province controls the fishing industry and requires a license for every fisherman, fish dealer, processing or packing plant or exporter, and restricts purchase except from licensed dealer. (1994, c. F-16.1).

FORECLOSURE:

See topics Chattel Mortgages; Liens; Moratorium; Mortgages.

FOREIGN CORPORATIONS: See topic Corporations.

FRANCHISES:

Pursuant to The Pyramid Franchises Act (R.S., c. P-50), any person selling pyramid franchise must be licenced under Act. Pyramid franchise is defined as arrangement to sell or distribute goods and recruit persons to do likewise under marketing system organized and controlled by franchisor.

FRAUDS, STATUTE OF:

The former English statute of frauds is in force. The fourth section is as follows: "That no action shall be brought whereby to charge any executor or administrator upon any special promise to answer damages out of his own estate; or whereby to charge the defendant upon any special promise to answer for the debt, default or miscarriage of another person; or to charge any person upon any agreement made in consideration of marriage, or upon any contract for sale of lands, tenements or hereditaments, or any interest in or concerning them; or upon any agreement that is not to be performed within the space of one year from the making thereof, unless the agreement upon which action shall be brought, or some memorandum or note thereof, shall be in writing and signed by the party to be charged therewith or some other person thereunto by him lawfully authorized."

Sales of Goods.—The 17th section is practically reenacted in The Sale of Goods Act. It applies to the sale of any goods of the value of $50 or upwards. See topic Sales. (R. S., c. S-1).

FRAUDULENT SALES AND CONVEYANCES:

Pursuant to Fraudulent Preferences Act (R. S., c. F-21), any creditor may bring action to set aside any conveyance made in fraud of creditors or having effect of giving preference. Certain transactions are deemed preferential regardless of innocent intent of debtor and regardless of pressure exerted by any creditor. In case of gift conveyance, etc., of any property which is in law invalid against creditors where such property has been sold or disposed of by transferee, money or other proceeds may be followed and transferee held liable for value thereof.

GARNISHMENT:

(R. S., c. A-32).

Where a debt is on a judgment, or is for a liquidated amount, money owing to the debtor, except for wages, may be garnished either before or after judgment upon an affidavit being filed, of the creditor or his agent, or solicitor, who can swear to the indebtedness of the debtor and also that, to the best of his information and belief, the proposed garnishee is indebted to the debtor. The garnishee may pay the money into court.

Money due for wages cannot be attached or garnished before judgment, except that by virtue of special order of court, which may be obtained ex parte. Wages due or payable within five days after service may be attached.

Wages of members of provincial public service and of provincial Crown Corporation employees may be attached.

Employers may not discharge employee by reason only of fact that garnishee proceedings taken against him. (R. S., c. L-1).

Exemption of wages or salary, see topic Exemptions.

GUARDIAN AND WARD:

Parents are joint custodians of infant child and joint guardians of infant child's property with equal powers and duties. On death of either parent, survivor is custodian and guardian subject to agreement between parents authorizing deceased parent to appoint custodian of child and guardian of child's property. If no agreement between parents to contrary, surviving parent can appoint custodian of child and guardian of property to take effect on death of surviving parent. When granting custody of child, court is to consider only best interests of child and, where court considers appropriate, wishes of child. Nonresident can be custodian of child or guardian of property. Custodian of child or guardian of property may be changed or removed by court for cause. (1990, c. C-8.1).

Investments.—(R. S., c. T-23). See topic Trusts.

Accounts.—Guardian of property of child must have accounts passed by court.

GUARDIAN AND WARD . . . *continued*

Insane Persons.—Interested person or designated corporation or agency may apply to Court of Queen's Bench to become personal guardian or property guardian, or both, with respect to "dependent adult", as defined. (R.S., c. D-25.1).

See topic Infants.

HOLIDAYS:

The following are holidays: every Sunday, 1st of January, Good Friday, Easter Monday, Victoria Day (Mon. prior to May 24), Dominion Day (July 1), Labor Day (1st Mon. in Sept.), Thanksgiving Day (proclaimed by proclamation), Remembrance Day, Christmas Day and any other day which may by proclamation be declared holiday.

If a holiday other than a Sunday or Remembrance Day falls on a Sunday, the following Monday is a holiday.

See topic Labour Relations.

For bank holidays, see Canada Law Digest.

HOMESTEADS:

A homestead personally occupied to the extent of 160 acres, or the house and buildings occupied by a debtor with the lot or lots on which situated to the value of $32,000, is exempt from seizure and sale under execution except under judgment for purchase price thereof. Exemption extends to debtor's family on his death. (R. S., c. H-5.1; R. S., c. E-14; R. S., c. A-32; R.S., c. S-17.1).

Alienation or Encumbrance.—(R.S., c. H-5.1). Every transfer, agreement for sale, lease, mortgage, or other instrument intended to convey or transfer interest in homestead (defined as property that is or has been occupied by both spouses as family home at any time during their marriage) to any person other than nonowning spouse of owning spouse must be accompanied by consent of nonowning spouse together with certificate of independent legal advice. (§§5, 7). Consent may be dispensed with by court. (§11). Every instrument not so executed must be accompanied by affidavit of each signator of disposition swearing that subject land is not his or her homestead or he or she has no spouse or his or her spouse is registered owner of subject land and co-signator of disposition. (§8). Caveat may be filed by nonowning spouse to protect his or her homestead rights. (§14).

HUSBAND AND WIFE:

Antenuptial Contracts.—Where spouses have entered into interspousal contract that deals with possession, status, ownership, etc. of matrimonial property, including future matrimonial property, and contract is in writing, signed and properly witnessed, it is binding despite lack of valuable consideration. Each party must sign acknowledgment as to nature and effect of agreement before own lawyer, and lawyer signs certificate as to execution by party. Contract may provide for distribution at time of separation and may be made in contemplation of marriage. Any provision of contract that is void or voidable is severable. (R. S., c. M-6.1, §38).

Separate Property.—Neither spouse has any interest in property of the other spouse during the latter's lifetime, except that a wife has certain rights in her husband's homestead. See topic Homesteads.

Carrying on Business by Married Woman.—A married woman may carry on business either solely or in partnership with any other person and her husband will have no interest therein or liability therefor.

Liability of Husband for Debts Incurred by Wife.—A husband may be held responsible for debts incurred by his wife either as his express or implied agent or in cases where the wife would be held to be an agent of necessity, as where the husband has deserted his wife or in similar circumstances.

Liability of Husband for Torts of Wife.—Husband is not, merely by reason of marriage relation, liable for wife's torts, and cannot be joined in an action against the wife for her torts.

Actions.—A married woman may in all cases sue or be sued without joining her husband to the same extent as if she were unmarried. Action may be brought against any married woman for all civil injuries and damages be recovered from her alone, and her husband is not responsible therefor unless he would be liable apart from the fact of his being her husband.

Maintenance.—By statute court may make order directing person to pay maintenance to spouse or children. (R.S., c. F-6.1).

Foreign Maintenance Orders.—Provision is made for reciprocal enforcement in Saskatchewan of maintenance orders made elsewhere, and for enforcing orders elsewhere when made in Saskatchewan.

Community property system does not exist in Saskatchewan. See, however, subhead Matrimonial Property, infra.

Matrimonial property means real or personal property and is to be distributed equally by court upon application by spouse. Court distributions subject to equitable considerations and to interspousal contract in writing dealing with distribution of matrimonial property including future claims. (1979, c. M-6.1 in force).

INCOME TAX: See topic Taxation.

INFANTS:

The usual rules of common law apply to contracts of infants. They become of age at 18, regardless of sex or marriage. Legal drinking age is 19.

There is an official guardian of infants for the province whose consent is required in most matters concerning infants' estates. (R. S., c. P-43.1). Infants sue as plaintiffs by their next friends and in like manner defend by their guardians. Guardian ad litem may for this purpose be appointed by court.

Court of Queen's Bench (Family Law Division) has control of custody of infants and may deal with same in actions for divorce or alimony or on special application. Welfare of infant is determining factor. (1990, c. C-8.1).

See also topic Guardian and Ward.

INHERITANCE TAX: See topic Taxation.

INJUNCTIONS:

An injunction order may be obtained in the Court of Queens' Bench to prevent the disposal of property, or the doing of any act, in all cases in which it may appear to the court just or convenient to make such order.

An interim injunction may be granted on such terms as may appear just to preserve the property or other matter in statu quo, pending a final determination of the action.

An injunction order is not usually made where damages could be an adequate remedy.

Bonds may be ordered. Usually the party applying, by his solicitor undertakes to the court to abide by any order as to damages the court may make should the court thereafter be of the opinion the defendant has sustained any by reason of the order.

INSOLVENCY:

See Canada Law Digest, topic Bankruptcy. Orderly payment of debts procedure, Part 10 of The Bankruptcy Act, S.C. 66, c. 32, is in force in Saskatchewan and is administered by Provincial Mediation Board.

INSURANCE:

(R. S., c. S-26).

Fire Insurance.—The Saskatchewan Insurance Act provides for certain uniform or statutory conditions and no variation therefrom is binding on the assured unless evidenced by the addition to the policy of such variations printed in conspicuous type in red ink and then only so far as such variations shall be held by the court to be just and reasonable to be exacted by the insurance company. If with the consent of the company the policy is made payable to a mortgagee, the policy cannot be cancelled without reasonable notice to the mortgagee. Notwithstanding the terms of a mortgage or agreement for sale, the mortgagor or purchaser can place any necessary fire insurance in any company doing business in the province.

Life Insurance.—This is chiefly governed by the provisions of the Dominion Insurance Act, which provides for the deposit of securities with a view to securing the performance of each life insurance contract upon an actuarial basis; also providing for the nonforfeiture of any policy so long as the reserve shall be sufficient to pay the accruing premium. Provision is made under the Insurance Act for insurance for the benefit of wife and children, the apportionment thereof and the variation of such apportionment. Any beneficiary so named may enforce direct his rights under the policy as they exist at the maturity of the policy. A minor of 16 may effect life insurance as if he were of age.

Children's Insurance.—There is a limit on insurance on children under five. It is $200 for children under one year and increases $200 a year to $1000 for children in their fifth year.

Other Insurances.—Certain regulations are made in reference to hail, accident, fidelity, guaranty, sickness, casualty, loss, etc., etc., insurance.

Motor Insurance.—See topic Motor Vehicles.

Automobile Accident Insurance.—On registration of a motor vehicle and upon issuance of a chauffeur's or operator's license, applicant is automatically given certain insurance coverage under Saskatchewan Government Insurance Plan. Protection against damage from bodily injury while driving or riding in or colliding with or being struck by moving motor vehicle in Saskatchewan are covered to extent, and insured and any passenger domiciled in Saskatchewan are further protected from bodily injury while riding in car driven by insured operator in any place in Canada or U.S. Amount of liability is fixed and scaled and amount, as specified in regulations, is deductible. If other insurance is carried, liability is determined by type of insurance; if standard policy, Government Insurance Plan takes effect to cover excess liability; if extension policy, Government Insurance Plan takes effect first and extension policy covers excess liability. This insurance also covers property damage and fire and theft with limitations as to amounts. See also topic Motor Vehicles, subhead Insurance.

Municipal Hail Insurance is provided by an Association consisting of representatives from the municipalities which have entered the association, and which provides for a levy by way of taxes on all lands in the municipality except where the owner has withdrawn his land, which he may do. The rates are fixed by the Association. (R. S., c. M-29).

Tax on Income from Insurance Premiums.—A 2% tax is imposed with respect to gross premiums received during each year by every insurance company transacting business in Saskatchewan. (R. S., c. I-10).

Further 1% tax imposed on income from motor vehicle insurance to finance a program of driver training. (R. S., c. M-23).

Direct Actions Against Insurer.—See topic Motor Vehicles, subhead Direct Actions.

INTEREST:

Interest is governed by Federal Law (see Canada Law Digest) but ordinarily is matter of contract. Under Unconscionable Transactions Relief Act (R. S., c. U-1), debtor is entitled to ask court to reopen or set aside transaction in which having regard to circumstances at time loan was made, cost of his loan was excessive or transaction was harsh and unconscionable.

Cost of Credit Disclosure Act (R. S., c. C-41), requires lenders to provide debtor with clear statement in writing showing particulars of cost of borrowing. This does not apply to transactions on security of real property or inventory.

Judgments.—Pre-judgment Interest Act (R. S., c. P-22.2) permits interest before judgment on certain causes of action arising after Jan. 1, 1986.

INTESTACY: See topic Descent and Distribution.

JOINT STOCK COMPANIES:

See topic Corporations.

JUDGMENTS:

A judgment, even if not proceeded on, is good for ten years. See also topic Executions.

Declaratory Judgments.—No proceeding is open to objection on the ground that a merely declaratory judgment or order is sought thereby, and the court may make binding declarations of right whether or not any consequential relief is or can be claimed. (R. S., c. Q-1).

Liens.—In itself a judgment, generally, does not create any lien. An execution or some proceeding in the nature thereof must be taken to enforce the judgment.

Foreign Judgments.—Foreign judgments may be sued on as such. Jurisdiction of foreign court is admitted only if defendant was ordinarily resident in the country at commencement of the action, or was carrying on business when judgment was obtained, if judgment was obtained in Canada, or if the defendant submitted to the jurisdiction of the foreign court. The foreign court has no jurisdiction if the action involves title to land in Saskatchewan or is for damages in respect to land in Saskatchewan. If the foreign court had jurisdiction, its judgment is conclusive as to any matter adjudicated in the action. It is a sufficient defense to an action on a foreign judgment that the original court had no jurisdiction, that defendant was not served with process and did not appear, that the judgment is not final, that it was obtained by fraud, is not for a sum certain in money, is for payment of a penalty under the revenue laws of the foreign country or is in respect to a cause of action which for reasons of public policy would not have been entertained in Saskatchewan, or that the proceedings in which the judgment was obtained were contrary to natural justice. (R.S., c. F-18).

See also topic Limitation of Actions, subhead Six Years.

JUSTICES OF THE PEACE: See topic Courts.

LABOUR RELATIONS:

A hiring or contract for personal service for more than one year is void unless in writing and signed by both parties.

Under Labour Standards Act (R. S., c. L-1) persons who perform entirely managerial services may be defined as employees respecting employees wages and recovery, annual holidays, and female labour, but not respecting hours of work and minimum wage. See subheads Priority of Wages; Recovery of Wages; Annual Holidays; and Female Labour.

The Labour Standards Act (R. S., c. L-1) sets up board called Minimum Wage Board which makes orders fixing minimum wages and maximum hours of labor in wholesale and retail establishments, mail order houses, fuel, lumber and building supply yards, warehouses, draying, cartage, transfer and delivery businesses, hotels, restaurants, beauty parlors and barber shops, theatres and dance halls.

The Board may fix the public holidays for which the employee shall be paid, whether he works or not, and the rate, and may fix the amount to be charged where the employer furnishes board or lodging.

Priority of Wages.—The Labour Standards Act (R. S., c. L-1) grants priority to employees' wage claims not exceeding three month's wages as against rights of Crown, assignee of monies due or accruing due on specific contracts, assignee of book debts, assignee for general benefit of creditors, trustee under Bankruptcy Act, liquidator of company under winding-up legislation, and any other person claiming against employer. Employee has security interest in wages due from employer. (R. S., c. L-1).

Recovery of Wages.—Employer deemed to hold all wages accruing due to employee in trust for employee, such amount is charge on assets of employer or his estate and has priority over all other claims. Where employer has not held wages in trust and employer's assets insufficient to pay in full trust monies owing, employees shall share assets on pro rata basis. Employer cannot set off cost of merchandise purchased by employee in any action against him for payment of wages. (R. S., c. L-1).

Where employee has not been paid: (1) Employee may lay a charge for nonpayment of wages before a magistrate, who may discharge employee from his contract and order employer to pay wages not exceeding $500 and costs including a solicitor's fee. Payment may be enforced by distress and sale of chattels not exempt from seizure under execution. Appeal lies to Queen's Bench Court and trial de novo takes place. That Court's decision is final, certiorari does not lie. Time limit six months. (R. S., c. W-1).

(2) The Labour Standards Act (R.S., c. L-1) empowers Director of Labour Standards, where he apprehends that employer has failed or may fail to pay wages, to issue wage assessment against employer or corporate director for amount of wages due. Employer or employee has 21 days to appeal wage assessment to adjudicator, 21 days to appeal adjudicator on legal point to court and 30 days to appeal court on legal point to appeal court. If wage assessment is not appealed or upheld on appeal director may issue certificate of wages and director's fees which are owing, which may be entered as judgment against employer or corporate director. Director may negotiate and settle any difference between employer and employee. Act further provides that corporate director's liability to employees is joint and several for up to six months' wages.

Female Labour.—Employment of employee cannot be terminated solely on grounds she is pregnant or is temporarily disabled because of pregnancy. Maximum of 18 weeks maternity leave is provided without pay after at least 20 weeks employment during immediately preceding 52 weeks and under certain conditions. Law protects all benefits and return of employee to same or comparable job. (Reg. 226/79).

Paternity Leave.—Employee who has been employed for at least 20 weeks during immediately preceding 52 weeks and applies for leave at least four months prior to commencement of leave, is entitled to not more than 12 weeks paternity leave to be taken in any combination during the months before or eight months following estimated date of birth of child.

Adoption Leave.—Employee who has been employed for at least 20 weeks during immediately preceding 52 weeks and applies for leave at least four weeks prior to adoption of child, is entitled to not more than 18 weeks adoption leave.

Trade Unions.—Employees and/or dependent contractors may form or join trade union and bargain collectively with their employer. Members of trade union may bargain through their officers, and any agreement with employer to contrary is void. Once trade union and employer have entered into collective bargaining agreement, terms thereof may only be varied by further agreement between parties. It is offense to intimidate any person in order to coerce him to join or refrain from joining trade union. (R. S., c. T-17).

Employer who proposes to introduce technological change which is likely to affect terms, conditions or tenure of employment of a significant number of employees shall give notice of technological change to trade union representing employees and to minister. Notice must be at least 90 days. Trade union may within 30 days from receipt of notice give notice to commence collective bargaining for purpose of revising agreement relating to terms, conditions or tenure of employment or relating to provisions to assist employees adjust to effects of technological change. Employer or trade union may, within 45 days of notice of technological change, request minister to appoint conciliator to assist parties in collective bargaining. If trade union gives notice, employer must not introduce technological change unless he receives order from Labour Relations Board relieving him from collective bargaining with union, or until he reaches agreement with trade union. (R. S., c. T-17).

Strikes and lockouts during term of collective bargaining agreement are prohibited. No strike may commence subsequent to strike vote without giving employer 48 hours notice and notifying Minister. No employer may lock out employees unless union is given 48 hours notice and Minister notified. Where strike is continued for 30 days, union, employer or employees representing 25% of bargaining unit can apply to Labour Board for vote among striking employees to determine whether majority are in favour of accepting employer's final offer and returning to work. Only one vote per strike. Employee cannot withdraw offer after acceptance by vote. At conclusion of strike or lockout, employees are to be reinstated.

The Trade Union Act is administered by a Labour Relations Board whose orders are final and conclusive with no right of appeal and can be only attacked by certiorari. The act is very wide and the powers granted to the Board very extensive. The court is bound absolutely by the findings of the board and is required to make all necessary orders to see that every person complies with the board order. If an employer discharges an employee and the union alleges unfair labour practice, the onus is on the employer to rebut such presumption. The board may appeal from any decision of any court affecting the Board's orders. If the employer is convicted, he is liable to a penalty of $50 per day if an individual or $250 a day if a corporation, while the default continues.

The Labour Relations Board may direct a vote of employees by ballot to ascertain what union shall have the right to bargain for them with employers.

Upon request of certified union specified union security clause must be included in any collective agreement, and must be complied with by employer even if no collective agreement is in force, under which all union members must maintain membership as condition of employment and all new employees must, within 30 days of hiring, apply for and maintain membership as condition of employment.

Construction Industry.—Unionized employers are required to bargain through representative organizations. Labour Relations Board also has authority to declare that associated or related construction companies constitute one unionized employer. (1992, c. C-29.11).

Electrical work must be done by a licensed mechanic. Exception is made for the owner in respect to his own domestic domicile with certain qualifications. (R. S., c. E-7.1).

Apprentices in certain skilled trades in cities and towns have qualifications, hours, and rates controlled by regulation. (R. S., c. A-22.1).

Hours of Work.—No employer can require any employee to whom Labor Standards Act (R. S., c. L-1) applies, to work for more than eight hours a day or 40 hours a week (32 hours in weeks in which holidays occur) without payment at overtime rates for excess, nor can employer require more than 16 hours in 24 hour period nor 40 hours in any week without employee's consent. Act applies to all employees in or within radius of five miles of any city or in any office or shop in Province to which Labor Standards Act applies, and any factory, exceptions being made for agricultural employees, domestic servants, janitors and caretakers in residential blocks, members of employer's family, foremen and business managers. Certain circumstances are provided under which employees may be required to work for ten hours in day or for more than eight hours per day.

For employees employed 20 hours or more per week, rest period of one day in every seven days must be granted, except in retail trade in which two consecutive days off, one of which is to be Sun., must be granted in establishments with more than ten employees.

Annual Holidays.—An employee is entitled after each year of his employment with any one employer to an annual holiday of three weeks with pay during first ten years, and of four weeks with pay thereafter. (R. S., c. L-1).

Actions.—The common law rules prevail except that in an action against an employer for damages for the injury or death of an employee, the negligence of an employee engaged in a common employment with the one injured is not a good defense. Legislation similar to the English Lord Campbell's act is in force providing for damage actions against an employer where the employee has been killed. The action must be brought within two years from time of death and is for benefit of immediate relatives who have suffered financial loss. (R. S., c. F-11).

Workers' Compensation.—A special act (1979, c. W-17.1) extends to nearly all industries, which contribute to fund administered by board which supervises medical attention of all workmen, pays compensation during "functional impairment", and

LABOUR RELATIONS . . . *continued*
where worker totally unable to work due to injury occurring on or after Jan. 1, 1980, minimum compensation of one half of average wage in June of previous year or where average earnings are less than that amount, amount of actual earnings. Compensation is payable irrespective of fault of either party. Worker includes executive officer of corporation if on payroll as well as apprentice but does not include school teacher, farmer, household servants or casual employees.

Worker may sue where entitled to legal action against someone other than employer in addition to collecting compensation, but compensation board is subrogated to such right of recovery to extent of payments made for compensation. Board may bring separate action in own name or join with worker in action for recovery of damages. Where board or worker intends to bring action it shall give notice to other, but lack thereof shall not affect defendant. Any sum recovered applied firstly to costs of action, secondly to board for repayment of compensation already made, and thirdly to worker or dependents.

Industry or worker not within scope of Act may be admitted by ruling of board on application of employer with consent of union. Board may levy against employers to cover cost of industrial safety program under The Occupational Health and Safety Act. (R. S., c. O-1). Neither act extends to farming. When workman is killed his widow and children under 18 get monthly allowance depending in part on number of children.

Unemployment insurance is a matter of Dominion legislation.

LANDLORD AND TENANT:

Renting of residential premises under Residential Tenancies Act (R. S., c. R-22) not lease under meaning of Landlord and Tenants Act or Land Titles Act. Agreement to rent residential premises deemed to contain number of statutory conditions. (R. S., c. R-22). No increase in rent of residential premises except through rentals-man. Residential Tenancies Rent Review Board may vary or disallow proposed rent increases. No appeal from decision of Board. General relations between landlord and tenant are governed by Landlord and Tenants Act. (R. S., c. L-6).

Leases for the period of three years or upward should be in writing under seal, but may be enforced by the tenant against the landlord and vice versa if there have been acts of part performance, subject to the provisions of the "Land Titles Act" whereby the tenant may lose his rights if the lease is not in writing or the lease is not registered. The Queen's Bench Court has power to relieve against the forfeiture for breach of a covenant in a lease.

See also topic Real Property.

Notice to Quit.—A week's notice or a month's notice to quit is sufficient in case of weekly or monthly tenancy.

Holding Over.—Respecting Landlord and Tenants Act, tenant overholding after notice to quit is given to or by him is liable to proceedings in Queen's Bench Court to place landlord in possession. Such proceedings must be brought by notice of motion. Provincial Mediation Board can make order prohibiting proceedings for possession.

Distress.—Landlord's right of distress on goods of his tenant abolished with respect to renting of residential premises under Residential Tenancies Act. (R. S., c. R-22). Respecting other leases covered by Landlord and Tenant Act (R. S., c. L-6) landlord's right of distress fixed by statute and is about same as that of execution creditor. See topic Executions.

Among other things, distress is permitted upon growing crops, loose grain, hay and straw, and gives the landlord a preference over execution creditors for arrears of rent not exceeding one year.

Distress must be made during the tenancy or within six months thereafter if the tenant is still in possession.

Dispossession.—Respecting residential premises application for order of possession must be made to magistrate. Appointment for hearing will be granted which must be served on tenant at least ten days before day appointed. Application must be heard at nearest judicial centre to premises. No costs allowed to any party in these proceedings. (R. S., c. R-22).

Either landlord or tenant may apply to Provincial Mediation Board to mediate dispute as alternative to procedure before magistrate. Board will appoint time for hearing and notify parties not less than five days before day appointed. Where board unable to settle dispute landlord may proceed as above noted before magistrate. (R. S., c. R-22).

Landlord and tenant may agree in writing that board should arbitrate dispute. When this agreement is filed with board a time for hearing is appointed and each party served with notice by board. Decision of board upon arbitration is final and when copy of award is filed in district court at nearest judicial centre such award has force of judgment of court. (R. S., c. R-22).

See also topic Crop Payments Act.

LEASES: See topic Landlord and Tenant.

LEGISLATURE:

One elected body of representatives, called the Legislature, which must have one session per year, usually commencing in February.

LEVY: See topics Attachment; Executions.

LICENSES:

Various persons are required to obtain licenses, such as peddlers, petty chapmen and various other classes of persons under municipal regulation. Auctioneers, liquor vendors, operators of gaming establishments, electrical contractors and journeymen, agricultural implement dealers, collection agents, dairy manufacturers, motor dealers, ophthalmic dispensers, embalmers, seed cleaners, and plumbing contractors are some of trades or callings that are required to be licensed, and in many cases bonded, under statutes governing each such trade. As to insurance, investment, real estate and mortgage brokers, see topic Brokers.

In most cases, direct (door-to-door) sellers are required to obtain both provincial and municipal licenses.

Any business that depends upon training others in any activity or skill for a fee must be licensed under Sale of Training Courses Act. (R. S., c. S-3).

Direct Sellers.—Persons going from door to door offering goods for sale or soliciting orders, are required to be licensed. Registrar has power to grant, suspend or cancel licenses. License valid for period of five years. Persons may be required to post bond. (Direct Sellers Act, R. S., c. D-28). See topic Sales.

Pyramid Franchises.—One must be or be employed by a licensed franchisor before he can sell a pyramid franchise. Registrar may refuse to issue a license where, inter alia, inadequate provision is made for financial protection of franchisee. He has broad powers of suspension and cancellation. (Pyramid Franchise Act, R. S., c. P-50).

Credit reporting agencies must be licensed under Credit Reporting Agencies Act. (R. S., c. C-44). License shall expire five years from issue. Registrar has broad power of issuance and suspension. Credit reporting agency cannot divulge contents of file or furnish credit report to anyone other than to person requiring information to make decision on consumer's application for credit, insurance, employment or tenancy, any agency of government or police officer, or consumer who is subject of credit report. Certain items cannot be contained in credit report: bankruptcy which occurred more than 14 years prior to making of report; information regarding writs issued more than 12 months prior to making of credit report if status of present action is not ascertained; information regarding writs, judgments or debts which are statute barred; and any other information more than seven years old unless voluntarily given by consumer. Credit reporting agency must take reasonable steps to insure accuracy of its information. Credit reporting agency must upon request of consumer disclose nature and substance of all information in his file respecting consumer but it need not disclose source of investigative information.

LIENS:

There are statutory liens of garage keepers, solicitors, threshers, woodsmen, hotel keepers, warehousemen and corporation's lien on shares of shareholders.

Artisan.—Every person who has bestowed money or skill upon any chattel in improving the same is entitled to lien and to hold same in his possession, and, if his lien is unpaid for three months, has power to sell on one month's notice in a newspaper stating the amount of his indebtedness, description of the chattel, time and place of sale, etc., and on notice to the debtor. (Mechanics' Lien Act, R. S., c. M-7).

Garage Keepers.—Liens must be filed pursuant to Personal Property Security Act to maintain beyond 45 days after giving up possession of vehicle. (Garage Keepers Act, R. S., c. G-2).

Vendor of real or personal property has a lien upon such property for unpaid purchase money unless he has waived his rights.

Builders' Liens.—All sums received by contractor or subcontractor on account of contract price constitute trust fund and contractor or subcontractor shall not appropriate funds to his own use until all workmen and all persons who have supplied materials or surfaces, are paid. All sums received by owner to be used in financing, constitute trust fund in hands of owner. Every person for whose benefit trust is created, has lien upon trust fund for value of work done. Every lien is charge upon amount directed to be retained in favor of lien holders. Contractor or subcontractor shall distribute money from time to time among persons for whose benefit trust is created on pro rata basis. Persons primarily liable under contract, shall as work is done, retain for statutory period, 10% of value of work done. Every owner, contractor or subcontractor is deemed to have notice of lien upon trust fund in his hands. Persons who do work or provide services for improvement have lien against estate or interest of owner in land occupied by improvement. Lien under this Act has priority over all judgments, executions, attachments and receiving orders made after lien arises. Lien of labourer for 40 days wages has priority over any other lien. Lien can be assigned by instrument in writing. Claim for lien on land can be registered in Land Titles Office. Lien relating to mines or minerals can be filed with Department of Energy and Mines. Lien must generally be registered within 40 days of completion of work. Where there is dispute over trust fund, work to be done, services rendered, or amount due, person can apply to Court of Queen's Bench to settle dispute in summary way. Action shall be brought within one year after contract completed or abandoned. (Builders' Lien Act, R. S., c. B-7.1).

Public Works.—Crown now bound by builders' lien procedure as set out above, except that no writ may be registered against Crown property at Land Titles Office. Instead lien claim notices should be served on appropriate Crown agency thus preserving builders' lien on trust fund created by 10% holdback of value of work done. (§26).

Enforcement.—The general remedy for enforcement of liens is by sale of the property subject thereto: but there are certain statutory remedies with respect to some liens. There is no right of redemption from lien sales.

See also topic Crop Payments Act.

LIMITATION OF ACTIONS:

Actions must be commenced within the following periods after the cause of action accrued:

Ten years: On domestic judgment; to recover possession of land; to recover money secured by mortgage or charged against land; to recover legacy or distributive share of personalty of an intestate.

Six years: On foreign judgment; to recover money on contract; for arrears of rent or mortgage interest; in cases not otherwise provided for.

Two years: For defamation; for trespass to the person (excluding sexual or domestic assault in which case there is no limitation period); for penalty.

Motor Vehicle Accidents.—See topic Motor Vehicles.

LIMITATION OF ACTIONS . . . *continued*

Claim against or on behalf of deceased person's estate may be brought within time otherwise limited for bringing of action or within one year after death, whichever is longer. (1990, c. S-66.1).

Interruption of Statutory Period.—Written promise to pay or acknowledgment of debt to the creditor, or part payment on account by the debtor or his agent, interrupts the running of the statute and the period begins to run anew from time of such promise, acknowledgment or payment.

Pleading.—Statute of limitations must be specially pleaded.

LIMITED PARTNERSHIP: See topic Partnership.

LIQUOR:

The sale of liquor is controlled entirely by the Province, which operates liquor stores and grants licenses for various types of outlets. Minors are not admitted to any of these outlets. There are statutory restrictions as to where liquor may be consumed. (R. S., c. A-18.01).

MARRIAGE:

(R. S., c. M-4).

Solemnization of marriage in the Province may be performed by clergy and marriage commissioners registered under Marriage Act.

Prerequisites to Marriage.—Minors not previously married must have written consent of parents or a judge's order except in special cases. Statutory declaration must be made by parties separately before issuer of license, negativing consanguinity and need of parental consent. License shall become effective day after day statutory declaration filed. In exceptional circumstances license may become effective on day statutory declaration filed.

License must be obtained from marriage license issuer and marriage must take place within three months of issuance of license.

Previously married parties must submit proof to clergy who is to solemnize marriage and to issuer of license that marriage was properly dissolved or annulled. Proof must consist of court certified copy of decree dissolving or annulling previous marriage with proof that time for appeal from such decree has expired. If previous spouse of party is deceased, then proof of death of that spouse must be submitted by way of death certificate or affidavit of some person knowing facts.

Health certificate of each party signed by qualified medical practitioner and dated within 30 days of the marriage must be presented to the person solemnizing the marriage.

Ceremony of Marriage.—Person solemnizing the marriage may do so according to the rites of his church but not until the above prerequisites have been fulfilled. The person solemnizing the marriage must duly register same and furnish each party with a marriage certificate. Two adult credible witnesses are required at every marriage. The issuer of a marriage license may not solemnize the marriage. Marriage may not be solemnized between 10 p.m. and 6 a.m. or if either party is under influence of alcohol or drugs, or has specified communicable disease. Civil marriage may be performed by marriage commissioner in his office in accordance with statutory form and manner.

Common law marriages, regardless of where they are initiated, are not recognized.

Prohibited marriages not allowed between parties where statutory degree of consanguinity exists.

Annulment of Marriage.—Jurisdiction to annul marriages is in Court of Queen's Bench (Family Law Division). It will assume jurisdiction where husband is domiciled in Saskatchewan at commencement of action or if marriage was celebrated in Province and one of parties is there resident. Residence alone as basis of jurisdiction in annulment is uncertain. Annulment may be granted (1) where parties are within forbidden degrees of consanguinity; (2) for bigamy or impotence; or (3) where form of marriage is gone through between persons either of whom is under age of 18 without consent required by The Marriage Act, and marriage has not been consummated (before or after ceremony), and parties have not since ceremony cohabited as husband and wife and plaintiff is person who was under age of 18 at time of marriage.

Presumption of Death of Absent Spouse.—Queen's Bench Court (Family Law Division) may grant leave to petitioner to presume his or her spouse to be dead and to remarry upon producing evidence that for more than seven years spouse has been continually absent and petitioner has made reasonable inquiries and has no reason to believe that other party has been living within that time. Marriage following such presumption is, however, invalid if missing spouse turns up.

MARRIED WOMEN:

See topics Deeds; Dower; Executors and Administrators; Homesteads; Husband and Wife; Marriage; Wills; Witnesses.

MECHANICS' LIENS: See topic Liens.

MINES AND MINERALS:

See Canada Law Digest. The actual operation of coal and other mines is governed by Occupational Health and Safety Act, 1993, c. O-1 and regulations passed thereunder whereby stringent provision is made for making and filing of plans and as to operation of mines with view to prevention of accidents. Companies Act has provisions for issue by mining companies of shares without personal liability.

Mineral rights are divided into two classifications: (a) those owned by individuals; and (b) those owned by the Province. The reason for the two classifications is that prior to the year 1890, Crown Government grants of land to individuals and corporations included mineral rights, whereas after that date the mineral rights were reserved to the Crown. The majority of the mineral rights are owned by the Crown in the right of the Province, with the individually-owned mineral rights being scattered throughout the settled portion of the Province. Mineral rights which are individually owned are real property and may be dealt with as set forth under the topic Real Property. Minerals owned by the Province are administered by government department called Saskatchewan Energy and Mines, which also regulates all mining and the drilling of oil and gas wells. (The Crown Minerals Act, R. S., c. C-50.2, and Oil and Gas Conservation Act, R. S., c. O-2). Dispositions of Crown minerals are subject to Mineral Dispositions Regulations, which also provide for Crown royalties and detailed royalty schemes for uranium and graphite. Subsurface minerals such as potash and coal are subject of separate topical regulations under Mineral Resources Act.

Some minerals are owned by the Government of Canada, e.g., Indian lands, and are administered by various agencies of that Government.

Mineral Tax.—Mineral Taxation Act, 1983, proclaimed in force on Jan. 1, 1984. Tax imposed based on production of those minerals referred to in schedules to Act. In addition, subject to certain exceptions, every owner of mineral rights is liable to pay each year tax in amount of $960 for each section of aggregate area of all mineral rights owned by him that year plus pro rata share of any mineral rights owned by him that are not full nominal section. (R. S., c. M-17.1).

Petroleum and Natural Gas.—

Tax.—Freehold Oil and Gas Production Tax Act, R. S., c. F-22.1, has been in force since Jan. 1, 1983 and supersedes Oil Well Income Tax Act, R. S., c. 0-3.1. Latter Act applies to period from Dec. 31, 1973 to Dec. 31, 1982 (see infra).

Pursuant to Freehold Oil and Gas Production Tax Act, taxes paid by holders of working interests on freehold oil and gas produced. Tax payable is proportionate to working interest.

Well operators are designated agents of Crown for purpose of collecting and remitting taxes. Money held for remittance to Crown is held by operator in trust. Failure by operator to deduct as required makes him personally liable for amount of tax. As well, operator is to advise Crown as soon as possible when well is producing. If tax from income has not been withheld by operator, owner of working interest must remit.

Crown has certain powers to enforce Act, including right to access premises to review records, to apply to Queen's Bench Judge for injunction where payment of future tax endangered or to obtain order for production of records or, in case of default, to collect taxes, interest and penalty by distraining. Tax and interest owed constitute first lien on entire interest of person liable to pay.

Act provides for exemptions from payment of tax for owners of producing tracts where aggregate of their interest does not exceed 640 acres. Also exempt is oil and gas produced from lands vested in Crown and administered by Federal Government for purposes of Canada, including lands on Indian Reserves.

Offences include failure to make return required by Act or to complete information with fines ranging from $10 to $50 per day. Knowingly failing to complete any information, or to deliver return may result in fine of not less than $1,000 and not more than $10,000 and/or imprisonment of up to six months. Willful attempt to evade taxes may amount to fine of not less than 25% nor more than double amount of taxes sought, and/or six months imprisonment. Penalty for contravention of Act not otherwise provided for shall not be less than $100 and no more than $5,000 and/or not more than six months imprisonment.

Oil Well Income Tax Act is still in force but administration of it is largely restricted to reassessment of tax returns.

MONOPOLIES AND RESTRAINT OF TRADE:

See Canada Law Digest.

MORATORIUM:

Saskatchewan Farm Security Act, 1988-89, c. S-17.1, places severe restrictions on enforcing security against farmers, farmland and farm machinery.

There is moratorium on all foreclosure actions on farmland. With respect to mortgages executed prior to coming into force of Act on homestead, Court must adjourn any foreclosure application for three years where farmer has been making sincere and reasonable effort to make payments. With respect to other farmland, mortgagee may apply to Court for order exempting application of Act. Farmland Security Board must be given notice and provided with report, and mortgagee must prove, inter alia, that mortgagor has no reasonable possibility of meeting his obligations under mortgage and that he is not making reasonable and sincere effort to meet the obligations. Farmland Security Board will meet with mortgagee and mortgagor prior to exemption application being heard by Court and prepare and submit report to Court respecting mortgagor's reasonable possibility of meeting his obligations. If mortgagee does not participate in mediation in good faith, farmer may request Court supervised mandatory mediation. If mortgagee does not negotiate in good faith, mortgagee's application may be adjourned for further period and mortgagee may have costs awarded against it. Where mortgagee obtains final order of foreclosure, farmer is entitled to right of first refusal to repurchase land. These provisions of Act also extend to sale of farmland pursuant to writ of execution. Operation of final order of foreclosure, insofar as it effects homestead, is stayed for as long as homestead continues to be such.

Personal guarantees and acknowledgments relating to obligations incurred by farmer must be executed before lawyer or notary public who issues certificate in prescribed form indicating that guarantor understands same.

Secured party intending to take possession of farm implement must serve notice, and farmer in response thereto may apply for hearing by Court. Court may make any order it considers just. No seizure may be made until after notice is served. Notice must also be given after repossession and farmer may apply for hearing after such repossession. Secured party must keep implement for at least 40 days.

MORTGAGES:

Mortgage may be under "Land Titles Act," and will take priority according to date of registration. "Land Titles Act" mortgage does not operate as transfer of title but only as security. Common law mortgage may still be effected by transfer of title to mortgagee, with caveat of mortgagor against mortgagee's title, but is rarely done.

When land is transferred, subject to a mortgage, a covenant is implied between the transferee and the transferor, that the former will indemnify the latter.

See note at head of Digest as to 1996 legislation covered.

See Topical Index in front part of this volume.

MORTGAGES . . . *continued*

When a mortgage provides for a share of the crops to be delivered, the mortgagee takes such share in priority to mortgagor or any person claiming through him.

Mortgage money overdue may be paid at any time before final order of foreclosure. Mortgagee cannot add to mortgage debt life insurance premiums due on collateral policy, nor hail insurance premiums without written consent in the year.

Person who carries on business of dealing in mortgages or lends money on security of land or interest in land must be licenced. Exceptions amongst others: Chartered banks, credit unions, federal and provincial corporations. (R. S., c. M-21).

Registration Fees.—(a) Where principal sum secured is less than $1,000, $20; (b) where principal sum secured exceeds $1,000, $20 plus (i) for each $1,000 or fraction thereof over $1,000, but less than $1,000,000, $2, (ii) for each $1,000 or fraction thereof over $1,000,000, $1.

Distress.—Where mortgage provides that mortgagee may distrain for payments in arrears, such distress may take place in usual way as under The Landlord and Tenant Act, provided mortgage was given to lender and not vender. Exemptions from seizure under execution are good as against mortgagee distraining.

The right of a mortgagee or vendor of land or of a crop-share lessor collateral to a mortgage or agreement for sale, is limited to one-third of the crop, less one year's taxes if the crop is less than ten bushels per acre, except where he has supplied the seed or pays a share of the threshing or binder twine, in which case he is limited to one-half of the crop. This share of the crop is subject to abatement when necessary to meet the cost of harvesting and a living allowance for the debtor and family until the following harvest.

Foreclosure.—Limitation of Civil Rights Act (R. S., c. L-16) may restrict creditor to realization of security to recover his arrears and prevent any suit against debtor on personal covenant. See also topics Sales; Pledges. Court has wide discretionary powers in actions on mortgages and agreements for sale of land. Only action under mortgage in default is against land itself and not on personal covenant or under power of extrajudicial sale. Before commencing foreclosure action leave must be obtained from Queen's Bench judge. (R. S., c. L-16; R. S., c. L-3). After such leave granted them mortgagee may take proceedings in ordinary way by issue of Writ of Summons and proceed to obtain order nisi and final order of foreclosure resulting in title vesting in mortgagee or vendor. See also topics Actions; Moratorium.

Deficiency and Personal Liability.—The taking of a final order for foreclosure of a mortgage on land operates in full satisfaction of the debt secured by the mortgage provided debtor is not corporation which waived application of Limitation of Civil Rights Act.

Redemption.—Every mortgagor in default may redeem by payment of arrears and costs until final order of foreclosure or sale issues. Even after final order has gone he may still redeem should the mortgaged property not have been alienated by the mortgagee and providing the delay is satisfactorily explained.

The following is the statutory form of mortgage:

Form

"I, ..., A. B., ..., being registered as owner of an estate (here state nature of interest) in that piece of land described as follows (insert description), containing . . . . . . acres, more or less (here state rights of way, privileges, easements, etc., if any), in consideration of the sum of . . . . . . dollars lent to me by . . . . . . E. F. . . . . . . of . . . . . ., the receipt of which sum I hereby acknowledge, covenant with the said E. F.:—firstly, that I will pay to him the said E. F. the above sum of . . . . . . dollars on the . . . . . . day of . . . . . .; secondly, that I will pay interest on the said sum at the rate . . . . . . on the dollar in the year, by equal amounts, on the . . . . . . day of . . . . . . and on the . . . . . . in every year; thirdly, (here set forth special covenants, if any). And for the better securing of the said E. F. the repayment in manner aforesaid of the principal sum and interest, I hereby mortgage to the said E. F. my estate and interest in the land above described. In witness, etc." There must be an affidavit of execution. For form see topic Real Property.

Discharge of Mortgage.—A mortgage may be discharged by the mortgagee executing a certificate of discharge in the following form:

Form

"Land Titles Act"—Discharge of mortgage. To the registrar of the . . . . . . land registration district. I, ... of . . . . . ., in the province of . . . . . ., do hereby certify that . . . . . . of . . . . . . in the . . . . . . has satisfied all moneys due or to grow due on a certain mortgage . . . . . . made by . . . . . . to . . . . . ., which mortgage bears date the . . . . . . day of . . . . . . A. D., 19. . . ., and was registered in the land titles office for the . . . . . . land registration district on the day of . . . . . ., A. D., 19. . . ., as number . . . . That the said mortgage has . . . . . . been assigned. And that I am the person entitled by law to receive the said money, and that the said mortgage is therefore discharged.

In witness whereof I have hereunto set my hand at the . . . . of . . . . in the . . . . this . . . . day of . . . . 19. . . . .

Signed by the said . . . .
. . .

In the presence of

An affidavit of execution is also required. For form see topic Real Property. Discharge of mortgage must be deposited in proper land titles office.

There is also provision for obtaining a judge's order directing the discharge where the mortgagee is absent from the province or mortgage has been lost or other unusual occurrence of similar nature.

Trust Deeds.—Under the Land Titles Act no certificate of title may have endorsed thereon any notice of any trust, and the registered owner is considered the absolute owner, subject to registered encumbrances, subsisting leases, taxes, etc. If land is to be transferred to a person upon a trust, the land is transferred in the usual way and the cestui qui trust may protect his interest by registering a caveat. Trust mortgages are registered in the usual way, the terms of the trust being set out therein. If such trust mortgage covers chattels or book debts, registration thereof in the land titles office is not sufficient and the mortgagee will have to protect himself by registration under personal property security legislation.

Chattel Mortgages.—See topic Personal Property Security.

See also topic Moratorium.

MOTOR VEHICLES:

Vehicle License.—No person residing in Saskatchewan for more than 90 days shall permit his vehicle to be operated in Saskatchewan unless such vehicle is registered with Highway Traffic Board, who shall issue a certificate of registration. License plates are issued at same time and must be displayed on front and rear of vehicle when it is in use. Registration renewed annually and annual validation stickers applied to original plates. License plates can be used for five year period. (Highway Traffic Act, R. S., c. H-3.1).

Snowmobiles unless operated on private property must be registered with Highway Traffic Board. Following provisions apply to snowmobiles by provisions of Snowmobile Act except where stated. (R. S., c. S-52).

Operator's License.—No person residing in Saskatchewan for more than 90 days shall drive a vehicle in Saskatchewan unless he holds a subsisting chauffeur's, instructor's, learner's or operator's license, issued to him by Highway Traffic Board. Said license is required annually. Applicants for instructor's or chauffeur's licenses must be 18 years and applicants for other licenses must be 16. (Vehicle Administration Act, R. S., c. V-2.1). No exemptions for members of Armed Forces, except general exemption that above provisions do not apply to person while operating motor vehicle in service of Government of Canada.

Operator of snowmobile must be at least 16 years old and properly licensed by board, or at least 12 years old and accompanied on snowmobile by person holding valid snowmobile license. Operators license under R. S., c. V-2.1 deemed to be proper license under Snowmobile Act, and provisions of Vehicle Administration Act (R. S., c. V-2.1) respecting registration and licensing, financial responsibility, and enforcement apply mutatis mutandis (R. S., c. S-52).

Titles, Sales and Liens.—Bill of sale not necessary on sale of any car for cash. Lien on or interest in vehicle must be recorded in Personal Property Registry, Regina. Dealers in motor vehicles must be licensed and bonded. (R. S., c. M-22). See also topic Sales.

Operation Prohibited.—By unlicensed or intoxicated person.

Equipment Required.—Adequate brakes, suitable horn, exhaust-pipe, muffler, rear-view mirror, and shatter-proof windshield. To be prescribed for snowmobiles by regulation. (R. S., c. S-52).

Lights Required.—Two in front, of equal power enabling operator to see any substantial object at 100 metres on high beam and 30 metres on low beam. Dimming or deflecting beams necessary for meeting other vehicles at night. One light in rear showing red visible for distance of 200 metres and throwing white light on number plate. Where load overhangs any vehicle red light by night and red flag by day required. Where vehicle extra wide four clearance lamps or reflector necessary, one amber on each side at front, red on rear. Vehicle other than motor must carry white light or reflector in front and red light in rear visible at distance of 200 metres. Motor vehicles must have adequate signal and brake lights. To be prescribed for snowmobiles by regulation. (R. S., c. S-52).

Seatbelts.—If seatbelt assembly available it must be used by operator and all passengers while motor vehicle is operated on public highway. (R. S., c. H-3.1).

Accidents.—Where motor vehicle accident results in personal injuries or property damage apparently over $500, driver must report accident to nearest peace officer, otherwise must notify owner of damaged property of his name and address, driver's licence number, vehicle registration number and insurance particulars. (R.S., c. H-3.1, §83).

Actions as a result of death or damages caused by a motor vehicle (R. S., c. H-3.1) or snowmobile (R. S., c. S-52) must be commenced within one year after date of accident.

Onus of Proof.—Where damage or injury occurs by reason of accident involving motor vehicle or snowmobile, unless such damage or injury sustained by passenger or by collision with another motor vehicle or snowmobile, onus of proof that damage or injury did not solely arise by negligence of owner or operator of motor vehicle or snowmobile is on owner or operator of motor vehicle or snowmobile. (R. S., c. H-3.1, R. S., c. S-52).

Contributory Negligence.—Where damage results from the negligence of two or more, the liability to make good the damage is in proportion to the degree in which each person was at fault and the costs are in the same proportion. If it is not possible to determine the different degrees of fault, the liability is divided equally. (R. S., c. C-31).

Liability for damage from negligence extends to owner as well as operator unless car was stolen or wrongfully taken from owner. Action for such damage must be commenced within one year.

Guests.—No limitation.

Government Insurance.—See topic Insurance.

Financial Responsibility.—Motor vehicles or snowmobiles involved in accidents resulting in personal injury or property damage exceeding $500 are impounded until evidence of financial responsibility is produced. (R.S., c. V-2.1, §68).

See also subhead Insurance, infra.

Insurance.—Owners and operators of snowmobiles must comply with Automobile Accident Insurance Act (R. S., c. A-35) before licence will be issued to them (R. S., c. S-52). Under that Act, Saskatchewan motorist is covered for loss arising out of his liability to pay for bodily injury to, or death of, others and damages to property of

MOTOR VEHICLES . . . *continued*
others, up to limit of $200,000 regardless of number of claims arising from any one accident. Coverage does not extend to injuries to insured or his spouse, children, parents, brothers, sisters, or gratuitous guests (if spouse or child of insured), unless these two categories of guest risk are specifically included in policy. See also topic Insurance, subhead Automobile Accident Insurance.

Nonresidents.—Nonresident may use his motor vehicle or trailer for touring purposes unconnected with business for 90 days in any year, if he has complied with the laws of his place of residence and carries its certificate and number plates.

Nonresident chauffeur driving visiting car exempt from registration, provided he wears badge assigned him in place of residence.

Actions Against Nonresidents.—No special provisions as to commencement.

Direct Actions.—No action against insurer by injured person is allowed, except in hit-and-run accident where identity of vehicle cannot be ascertained.

Motor Vehicle Carriers.—Highway Traffic Board has power to make regulations governing security to be furnished by all carriers, nature of merchandise carried, routes, car capacity, maximum weights permitted, rates, schedules, tickets, uniform bill of lading, etc. No person can operate a public service vehicle on a public highway without a permit, and without furnishing security covering injury to passengers or property and payment of all funds payable. The ordinary liability of a common carrier attaches. Proper books of account open to inspection by the Board must be kept. Provision is made to secure the safety, health and convenience of passengers and safety of baggage and freight. (Motor Carrier Act, R. S., c. M-21.2).

Aircraft.—See Canada Law Digest, topic Aircraft.

Gasoline Tax.—See topic Taxation.

MUNICIPALITIES:

The province is divided into cities, towns, villages, rural municipalities and local improvement districts, each of which has a separate Act, and each of which has its own local government, the officers all being elected, franchise being extended to all 18 years of age or over. Service Districts composed of two or more municipalities may be established by order. (Service Districts Act, 1996, c. S-47.2). On money by-laws each individual owning property has one vote.

NEGOTIABLE INSTRUMENTS:

See Canada Law Digest, topic Bills and Notes.

NOTARIES PUBLIC:

Minister of Justice may appoint any Canadian or British subject 18 years of age residing within province notary public.

A notary public may do certain conveyancing such as drawing contracts, deeds, etc., may attest commercial instruments brought before him for public protestation, and otherwise act as is usual in office of a notary. He may act officially anywhere in province. Every commission issued, unless it is to a solicitor, or to a person who afterwards becomes a solicitor, expires at end of five years. Notary whose commission expires must show date of expiration on every affidavit, declaration or certificate taken or given by him and his notarial seal should be impressed. (R. S., c. N-8).

Commissioners for oaths are appointed by Minister of Justice with power to take affidavits, declarations and affirmations either within or without Saskatchewan according to their appointment. Appointments are valid until end of fifth calendar year and date of expiry of commission must appear on document taken except in case of Saskatchewan solicitors in good standing who have authority as long as they are such. Solicitor merely adds, after his name, "Being a Solicitor." (R. S., c. C-16).

PARTITION:

Real Property.—Actions for partition may be brought only in Queen's Bench Court. Court may either order partition or if partition is not the proper remedy, then a sale under court supervision.

Personal Property.—When an equal division of goods and chattels cannot be made in kind among those entitled thereto, the court may direct the same sold and distribute the proceeds.

PARTNERSHIP:

All persons associated in partnership which carries on business under business name are required to cause that name to be registered under Business Names Registration Act. (R. S., c. B-11). Partnership is required to file in office of Corporation Branch declaration signed by all of partners containing names and residences of every partner and name or style of firm under which they carry on or intend to carry on business, nature and date of commencement of business and that there are no other members of partnership. Similarly, declaration must be filed upon dissolution of partnership.

Subject to agreement between partners death, bankruptcy or authorized assignment under Bankruptcy Act (Canada) of any partner automatically dissolves partnership.

Limited partnerships under which special partner's liability is limited to capital he contributes may be formed. Any number of persons may join a limited partnership.

Limited partnership is formed when business name is registered with Director of Corporations, 1871 Smith Street, Regina, Saskatchewan. Declaration signed by all partners containing business name, nature of business and name and places of residence and other matters must be filed with application for registration. (R. S., c. B-11).

No extra-provincial limited partnership shall carry on business in Saskatchewan unless registered under Business Names Registrations Act. (R.S., c. P-3, §75.1). Laws of jurisdiction pursuant to which extra-provincial limited partnership is formed govern its formation, internal affairs and limited liability of limited partners. (R.S., c. P-3, §75.2).

PERPETUITIES:

Common law rule in force.

PERSONAL PROPERTY SECURITY:

The Personal Property Security Act (R. S., c. P-6.1) applies to every security agreement without regard to its form, or to person who has title to collateral, that creates security interest, including chattel mortgage, conditional sale, floating charge, pledge, debenture, trust indenture or trust receipt, lease, assignment, consignment or transfer of chattel paper, and to assignment of accounts, transfer of chattel paper, consignment, or lease for term of more than one year, notwithstanding that such interests may not secure payment or performance of obligation. Historic forms and concepts of security agreements are discarded and single conceptual basis for all personal property security agreements is employed. Saskatchewan statute also applies to "corporation securities".

Conflict of Laws.—Basic premise is that law of jurisdiction where collateral is situated when security interest attaches is applicable law for determining validity, perfection and effect of perfection or non-perfection of security interest in such collateral. For intangibles, property normally used in more than one jurisdiction and nonpossessory security interests in securities, instruments, negotiable documents of title, money and chattel paper, law of jurisdiction where debtor is located when security interest attaches, governs. Debtor is deemed to be located at his place of business, at his chief executive office if he has more than one place of business and otherwise at his place of residence.

For goods brought into Saskatchewan, distinction is made between buyer in good faith of goods brought into province and all other persons. Security interest in collateral already perfected under law of place in which collateral situated when security interest attached and before being brought into Saskatchewan continues perfected in Saskatchewan as against buyer in good faith if perfected in Saskatchewan prior to buyer's acquiring interest in goods and as against all other persons within 60 days after brought into province, or within 15 days after day secured party receives notice that goods have been brought into Saskatchewan, or prior to day that perfection ceases under law of prior jurisdiction, whichever is earliest.

Transitional.—Proclamation on May 1, 1981 of Personal Property Security Act caused repeal of Assignment of Book Debts, Bills of Sale Act, Conditional Sales Act, Corporations Securities Registration Act and amendments to Agricultural Implements Act, Creditors Relief Act, Distress Act, Executions Act, Exemptions Act, Garage Keepers Act, Sales of Goods Act and Limitations of Civil Rights Act.

Registration under repealed or amended Acts is deemed to be registration under The Personal Property Security Act. Question as to priority between security interests validly created prior to coming into force is determined by prior registration law, but priority between prior security interest and security interest validly created after proclamation shall be determined by The Personal Property Security Act.

Registration is continued for unexpired portion of filing or registration period under prior law except for registrations under Assignment of Book Debts Act and Bills of Sale Act which expired on May 1, 1984, unless they were renewed under new Act.

Effectiveness.—Security agreement is effective according to its terms. However, certain terms are prohibited or may be unenforceable. For instance, any prohibition against assignment of account or intangible or against sale in ordinary course of business will be unenforceable and acceleration clauses will be ineffective due to redemption provisions.

Enforceability.—No security interest is enforceable against third party unless collateral is in possession of secured party or debtor has signed security agreement that contains description of collateral which enables type or kind of collateral taken under security agreement to be distinguished from types or kinds of collateral which are not collateral under security agreement, and, in case of security interest taken in all of debtor's present and after-acquired property, statement indicating that security interest has been taken in all of debtor's present and after-acquired property is sufficient.

Attachment.—Security interest attaches when value is given, debtor has rights in collateral, and, except for purpose of enforcing inter partes rights, it becomes enforceable against third parties. Debtor has rights in goods purchased under agreement to sell when he obtains possession of them pursuant to sales contract, and in goods leased to him, hired by him or delivered to him under consignment, when he obtains possession of them pursuant to lease, hiring agreement or consignment. Debtor has no rights in crops until they become growing crops, young of animals until they are conceived, in oil, gas or other minerals until extracted, in timber until it is cut.

After-acquired Property.—Security agreement may cover after-acquired property and security interest will attach without specific appropriation by debtor.

Future Advances.—Security agreement may secure future advances whether or not advances are made pursuant to obligation in security agreement. If future advances are made while security interest is perfected, security interest has same priority with respect to future advances as it has with respect to first advance. Future advance will not take priority over interests of person who causes collateral to be seized under legal process, sheriff who has seized, trustee in bankruptcy or representative of creditors who has caused collateral to be seized under legal process, unless advance made before interests of such persons arise, or before secured party receives notice of their interests.

Perfection.—Security interest is perfected when it has attached and all steps required for perfection required under Act have been completed regardless of order of occurrence. Three methods of perfection are: Possession of collateral by secured party or on his behalf; registration of financing statement in Personal Property Registry; and automatic, although temporary, perfection by way of statutory grace periods.

Act also provides specific rules as to perfection with respect to proceeds of collateral. Security interest in collateral extends to proceeds and is perfected if financing statement filed which covered original collateral contains prescribed description, or if proceeds are of type which fall within description of original collateral, or are cash, then registration perfects security interest in both collateral and in proceeds. Otherwise

PERSONAL PROPERTY SECURITY . . . *continued*
security interest in proceeds perfected for only 15 days after debtor receives possession of them.

Purchase money security interest in collateral or its proceeds other than inventory, that is perfected within 15 days after day debtor obtains possession of collateral, or collateral is intangibles or its proceeds, within 15 days after security interest therein attaches, has priority over any other security interest in same collateral or its proceeds given by same debtor.

Purchase-money security interest in inventory or its proceeds has priority over any other security interest in same collateral given by same debtor if purchase-money security interest in inventory is perfected at time debtor receives possession of it and purchase-money secured party serves notice on secured party who has registered financing statement covering same type of collateral. Such notice covers collateral of which debtor receives possession in two year period following notice. Exception with respect to sales in ordinary course of business and by virtue of fact that purchase-money security interest in proceeds of inventory does not have priority over perfected security interest in accounts receivable given for new value.

Purchaser of goods sold in ordinary course of business of seller takes free of any perfected or unperfected security interest therein given by or reserved against seller, whether or not purchaser knows of it, unless secured party proves that purchaser also knows that sale constitutes breach of security agreement.

Act provides special priority rules between secured and unsecured creditors, and with respect to fixtures, negotiable documents of title, money and securities, chattel paper and future advances.

Registration.—Registration system to be known as Personal Property Registry, is established. Registration is by notice filing and is effected by filing financing statement in prescribed form. Financing statement or financing change statement may be tendered for registration by personal delivery or by mailing to Personal Property Registry, 3rd Floor, 1874 Scarth Street, Regina, Saskatchewan, S4P 3V7.

Registration of finanacing statement is effective for length of time indicated in financing statement and may be renewed at any time before document to which it refers expires by registering financing change statement.

Where secured party assigns his interest or subordinates his interest to that of another person, financing change statement in prescribed form may be registered. Registration of such statement is mandatory where debtor transfers his interest in collateral or changes his name.

Search for registrations against name of debtor or against serial number where collateral required by regulation to be described by serial number (i.e., motor vehicles, mobile homes, trailers and airplanes, as defined in regulations) may be obtained, with results given in printed or verbal form.

Time for Registration.—Financing statement may be registered at any time and may be registered before security agreement is made or before security interest attaches. It must be registered prior to expiry of any temporary perfection period (usually 15 days) to continue perfection uninterrupted, and with respect to purchase-money security interest, within 15 days of debtor obtaining possession of collateral.

Rights and Remedies Upon Default.—Part V contains code setting out rights, remedies, duties and obligations upon both secured party and debtor many of which, to extent that they give rights to debtor or impose obligations upon secured party, cannot be waived. However, all such rights and remedies of secured party are subject to consumer protection legislation.

PLEADING:

Every pleading must contain a statement in a summary form of the material facts on which the party relies for his claim or defense, as the case may be.

As a rule there are not more than two pleadings in any action, a statement of claim by the plaintiff and a statement of defense by the defendant. A defendant may set up a counterclaim, which is in the nature of a cross action and to this the plaintiff must deliver a special reply stating his answer to the counterclaim.

Amendments of pleadings may be allowed at any stage of the action, by the court, on such terms as may be just, for the purpose of determining the real questions in controversy. Plaintiff may amend once without leave before replying or time therefor gone.

Verification.—Ordinarily an affidavit is not required to be delivered with any pleading. It is required, however, when commencing an action for divorce and in divorce actions verifying the defence where it is not merely a general denial.

Demurrers.—No demurrer is allowed.

Time Requirements.—Statement of claim expires after six months unless served or renewed. Defendant must usually file and serve statement of defence within 20 days. Time for filing may be extended by court.

PLEDGES:

Pledge is deposit of personal property as security for certain sum and is governed by personal property security legislation and valid without registration. Distinction between pledge and mortgage of personal property is:

(1) That in former title is retained by pledger, while in latter it passes to mortgagee.

(2) That delivery of possession of property to pledgee is absolutely essential to pledge being valid between parties. Such delivery is not necessary to validity of mortgage. Property delivered to pledgee to secure debt may be sold by latter and good title passes.

Pawnbrokers are subject to the provisions of the "Pawnbrokers Act" (Dominion), which limits the rate chargeable.

PRACTICE:

Most of the law relating to practice is contained in the Queen's Bench Act (R. S., c. Q-1) and in rules of court which have force of statute. Except as so modified practice is governed by rules of common law. Law and equity are administered by court and in all cases of variance rules of equity prevail.

Discovery.—Parties and relevant documents. (R.C. 222).

Demand for Admission of Facts.—Any party may by notice before trial call upon any other party to admit any specific fact. Costs of proving unadmitted facts awarded against party unreasonably refusing to admit. (R.C. 244).

Direct Actions Against Insurer.—See topic Motor Vehicles, subhead Direct Actions.

Small Claims.—See topic Courts, subhead Judges of Provincial Court.

Jury.—The number is 12. In criminal cases they must be unanimous. In civil cases ten may render a verdict. Juries may be demanded only in Queen's Bench cases. Party demanding jury must advance its costs which are usually fixed at $1,200. Civil Cases: number is six, five may reach verdict. Civil juries may be demanded as of right in actions for libel, slander, seduction, malicious harassment, malicious prosecution or false imprisonment and where claim amount exceeds $10,000. Party demanding jury will pay jury costs whether or not successful in action, except in aforesaid actions and in personal injury action for claimed damages in excess of $10,000 whereby trial judge has discretion to make appropriate order as to jury costs. Criminal Cases: Act will apply to criminal jury trials except where inconsistent with Criminal Code (see Canada Law Digest).

See also topics Absconding Debtors; Actions; Appeal and Error; Depositions; Executions; Garnishment; Injunctions; Judgments; Pleading; and Process.

PRINCIPAL AND AGENT:

An agent properly authorized may do any act which his principal might do, except that to which the latter is bound to give his personal attention. The principal is liable for the act or neglect of his agent while in the course of his duty as agent. In the absence of legislation, common law rules apply.

Collection agencies must be licensed by province and bonded. (Collection Agents Act, R. S., c. C-15).

Real Estate.—Agents must be licensed by province and bonded. (Real Estate Brokers Act, 1987, R.S., c. R-2.1).

PROCESS:

Service of statement of claim must generally be made personally on defendant. Exceptions: (1) On infant by serving minor, father, mother, guardian or person under whose care he is; (2) on lunatic by serving guardian or person under whose care he is; (3) on partnership by serving any of partners, or anyone having management of partnership business, at principal place of business within jurisdiction; (4) on corporation by service on officer, clerk, agent or representative of corporation or any branch in Saskatchewan; (5) on absent defendant having agent or representative in Saskatchewan by service on such agent or representative. (R.C. 22). Service is permitted outside province; in certain cases an order being necessary. (R.C. 31-33). Service must be effected within six months after issue of Statement of Claim. (R.C. 16).

Who May Serve.—Any literate person other than plaintiff may serve writ. (R.C. 19).

Substituted Service, Etc.—Orders to serve substitutionally or by advertisement or otherwise may be obtained in certain cases upon an affidavit as to facts. Service of statement of claim out of jurisdiction is permitted in most cases without order.

Service by Mail.—In claim for custody or access of infant, maintenance, matrimonial cause other than divorce, claim under The Matrimonial Property Act, or action for liquidated damages, service of originating documents may be made by registered mail or certified mail. (R.C. 19).

Nonresident Motorist.—See topic Motor Vehicles.

PRODUCT LIABILITY: See topic Consumer Protection.

PROOF OF CLAIMS:

See topics Executors and Administrators; Pleading.

RAILROADS: See topic Carriers.

REAL PROPERTY:

The Torrens system of land registration is in effect in this province. Matters relating to title to land, registration of documents pertaining to land, etc., are provided for by The Land Titles Act. (R. S., c. L-5). For purposes of administration province is divided into eight land registration districts each with its own Land Titles Office in which all documents pertaining to land situate within particular land registration district must be filed.

Ownership.—The registered owner of land is regarded as the absolute owner. Ownership by two or more parties is regarded as tenancy in common, but joint tenancy is recognized if duly created. When land is transferred to a man and his wife the transferees take according to the tenor of the transfer and do not take by entireties unless it is so expressed in the transfer. Ownership of land may or not include mines and minerals. See topic Mines and Minerals.

Foreign Ownership.—See topic Aliens.

Registration.—Only those documents prescribed by The Land Titles Act may be registered and then only in the form prescribed. Interests in land in form or of a nature not registerable may be protected by registration of a caveat, the form of which is prescribed and which is a short statement of the interest claimed setting forth description of the land with respect to which the interest is claimed and signed by the claimant or its agent and verified by affidavit. Registration of such caveat protects the interest of the caveator against all subsequent dealings with the land.

See note at head of Digest as to 1996 legislation covered.

See Topical Index in front part of this volume.

REAL PROPERTY . . . *continued*

Priorities of Interests.—Where different instruments affecting the same estate have been registered they take priority according to time of registry and not according to date of execution.

Transfers of Land.—Each parcel of land is represented by a title issued by and kept in the Land Titles Office. Land covered by title or portion thereof is conveyed by registered owner executing "transfer" in proper statutory form. Owner must sign transfer and witness must also sign and complete affidavit of execution. (See below and see topic Affidavits for persons who can take affidavit, oath.) Corporations must execute transfer by signatures of authorized officers under corporate seal and no affidavit of execution required. Where there are two or more transferees and they are to take as joint tenants then transfer must so state, otherwise title will issue to them as tenants in common. After transfer is executed it must be delivered to Land Titles Office. Land Titles Office then registers transfer, cancels old title and issues new title to the transferee. Mortgages to be registered as such must be in statutory form.

Leases.—Owner of leasehold title for term exceeding ten years may obtain certificate of title for his leasehold estate. (R. S., c. L-5).

Title of deceased owner can only be dealt with by authorized personal representative. (See topic Executors and Administrators.) Application must be made to the Land Titles Office for the district in which the land is situate for transmission into the name of personal representative. Application must be accompanied by original and certified copy of letters probate or administration (resealed in Saskatchewan, if originals granted outside Saskatchewan) and duplicate certificate of title and prescribed fee. New title is then issued in the name of the executor or administrator as such executor or administrator. He may then deal with the land as an owner in fee simple subject to certain restrictions as in the case of infants being interested in the estate a consent of the official guardian of infants to any further disposition of the lands or where no infants interested a certificate of the official guardian to that effect.

Forms prescribed by the Land Titles Act for transfers of land are as follows:

Forms

Transfer

I, ..., being registered owner of an estate in fee simple in that piece of land described as . . . ., do hereby in consideration of the sum of . . . . dollars paid to me by . . . ., the receipt of which sum I hereby acknowledge . . . ., transfer to the said . . . . all my estate and interest in the said piece of land.

In witness whereof . . . . have hereunto subscribed . . . name this . . . . day of . . . ., 19. . . . . Signed by the said . . . .

In the presence of

Affidavit as to Marital Status and Homestead

Where land is not homestead, transfer must be accompanied by transferor's affidavit as follows (R.S., c. H-5.1):

I, ... of . . . ., make oath and say that:

1. I am the/a transferor (lessor, mortgagor or as the case may be) or . . . . (state capacity in which person acts on behalf of the owner, e.g. agent acting under power of attorney).

2. My spouse and I (or The transferor, lessor, mortgagor or as the case may be and his or her spouse) have not occupied the land described in this disposition as our (or their) homestead at any time during our (or their) marriage.

-or-

2. I have (or The transferor, lessor, mortgagor or as the case may be has) no spouse.

-or-

2. My spouse (or The spouse of the transferor, lessor, mortgagor or as the case may be) is a registered owner of the land that is the subject matter of this disposition and a co-signator of this disposition.

-or-

2. My spouse and I (or The transferor, lessor, mortgagor or as the case may be and his or her spouse) have entered into an interspousal agreement pursuant to The Matrimonial Property Act in which my spouse (or his or her spouse) has specifically released all his or her homestead rights in the land that is the subject matter of this disposition.

-or-

2. An order has been made by Her Majesty's Court of Queen's Bench for Saskatchewan/Unified Family Court pursuant to The Matrimonial Property Act declaring that my spouse (or the spouse of the transferor, lessor, mortgagor or as the case may be) has no homestead rights in the land that is the subject matter of this disposition and (the order has not been appealed and the time for appealing has expired) or (all appeals from the order have been disposed of or discontinued).

-or-

2. My Spouse (or The spouse or the transferor, lessor or mortgagor or as the case may be) is the transferee (or lessee, mortgagee or as the case may be) named in this disposition.

Sworn before me at . . . .)
in the Province of . . . .)
this . . . . day of . . . .)
19 . . . .)
. . . .

Consent of Non-Owning Spouse

Where land is transferor's homestead, transfer must be accompanied by consent signed by non-owning spouse and certificate signed by practicing solicitor:

I, ..., non-owning spouse of . . . ., consent to the above/attached disposition. I declare that I have signed this consent for the purpose of relinquishing all my homestead rights in the property described in the above/attached disposition in favour of . . . . to the extent necessary to give effect to this . . . . (type of document).

. . . .

Signature of Non-owning Spouse

I, ..., ... (indicate capacity), certify that I have examined . . . ., non-owning spouse of . . . ., the owning spouse, in the above/attached . . . . (type of document) separate and apart from the owning spouse. The non-owning spouse acknowledged to me that he or she:
(a) signed the consent to the disposition of his or her own free will and consent and without any compulsion on the part of the owning spouse; and
(b) understands his or her rights in the homestead.
I further certify that I have not, nor has my employer, partner or clerk, prepared the above/attached . . . . (type of document) and that I am not, nor is my employer, partner or clerk, otherwise interested in the transaction involved.

. . . .

Signature

Affidavit of Execution

Province of Saskatchewan,
To Wit:

I, A.B., of (insert address and occupation), make oath and say:

1. That I was personally present and did see . . . . named in the within instrument, who is personally known to me to be the person named therein, duly sign and execute the same for the purposes named therein;

2. That the same was executed at the . . . . of . . . ., in the province of . . . ., and that I am the subscribing witness thereto;

3. That I know the said . . . . and he is in my belief of the full age of eighteen years.

Sworn before me at the . . . .
of . . . . in the province of . . . .
this . . . . day of . . . . A.D. 19 . . . . . } . . . .
(Signature)

. . . .

A commissioner for oaths in and for the province of Saskatchewan (or notary or other officer).

If affidavit of execution does not show date of execution, or if transfer is not presented for registration within three months after execution, transfer must be accompanied by an affidavit, made at time of presentation for registration, showing whether transferor is then alive or dead. This does not apply if the registered owner is a nonresident of the province.

Affidavit of Value

[must accompany transfer]

Canada, Province of Saskatchewan, To Wit:

I, ..., of the . . . . of . . . ., in the province of . . . . (occupation) make oath and say:

1. That the within described parcel of land, together with all buildings and other improvements thereon, is in my opinion of the value of . . . . dollars and no more.

Sworn before me at the . . . .
of . . . . in the province of . . . .
this . . . . day of . . . ., A. D. 19 . . . . . } . . . .

A commissioner for oaths or other officer.

Form of Caveat

Province of Saskatchewan. The Land Titles Act. To the Registrar of the . . . . Land Registration District. Take notice that I . . . . of the . . . . of . . . . claiming an interest as (purchaser, or as the case may be. Give details as to right under which interest is claimed) in the following land, that is to say: (describe property) forbid the registration of any transfer or other instrument affecting such land or the granting of a certificate of title thereto except subject to the claim herein set forth. My address is . . . . and my address for service of notices and processes in Saskatchewan is . . . . . Dated the . . . . day of . . . ., A.D. 19. . . . .

. . . .
Signature of Caveator or his agent

I, the above named . . . . (or . . . . agent for the above . . . .) of (residence and description) make oath and say:

1. That the allegations in the above caveat are true in substance and in fact, to the best of my knowledge, information and belief;

2. That the claim mentioned in the above caveat is not to the best of my knowledge, information and belief founded upon a writing or a written order, contract or agreement for the purchase or delivery of any chattel or chattels within the prohibition contained in section 151 of The Land Titles Act.

Sworn before me at
. . . . in the . . . . this . . . .
day of . . . ., A.D. 19 . . . .
. . . . } . . . .
Signature

Fees for registration of land transfers are fixed according to value of the land, as follows: For first $1,000, $20; for each $1,000 or fraction over $1,000, but not exceeding $1,000,000, $2; for each $1,000 or fraction over $1,000,000, $1.

Recovery of Possession of Land.—Where a person not an overholding tenant refuses or fails to cease using or occupying land wrongfully or without lawful authority, the person entitled to possession may apply on affidavit to judge of Court of Queen's Bench of district where land is situated for possession, and right thereto is summarily disposed of, and any order made is duly enforced. Appeal lies to the Court of Appeal. (R. S., c. R-7).

Condominiums are permitted in Saskatchewan, and requirements with respect thereto are set out in Condominium Property Act, 1993, c. C-26.1.

See note at head of Digest as to 1996 legislation covered.

See Topical Index in front part of this volume.

REAL PROPERTY . . . *continued*

See also topics Curtesy; Deeds; Dower; Homesteads; Husband and Wife; Landlord and Tenant; Mortgages; and Partition.

RECEIVERS:

Receivers may be appointed before judgment in a proper case upon application of either party when he establishes an apparent right to property or on the winding up of a partnership or where it is necessary to preserve property in its original condition; also in mortgage actions or vendor and purchaser actions.

Bonds.—Where an order is made appointing a receiver, in almost all cases the person appointed must first give security to be approved by the court or a judge.

RECORDS:

Statutory provision is made for the recording and registration of security interests, lien notes, crop liens, hire receipts, minerals (including oil and gas) interest in Crown and freehold lands, certificates of partnership, trade names, etc. Effect of recording, generally, is to give notice and preserve prior rights.

Only certain documents affecting land can be registered. See topic Real Property.

Vital Statistics.—Records of births, deaths, marriages and dissolutions of marriages are kept by Minister of Public Health, Regina.

Certificates for birth, marriage and death obtainable from Division of Vital Statistics, 3475 Albert Street, Regina. Fee: $15 each certificate, except marriage certificate which will change from time to time as prescribed by regulation.

Statistics.—Director of Statistics, plans, promotes and develops integrated social and economic statistics relating to province and government. It collects, compiles, analyzes, abstracts and publishes statistical information relating to commercial, industrial, financial, social, economic and general activity and condition of province and persons in province. (R. S., c. S-58).

REDEMPTION:

See topics Executions; Liens; Mortgages; Taxation.

REPLEVIN:

The plaintiff in any action for the recovery of any personal property, claiming that such property was unlawfully taken or is unlawfully detained, may after the issue of statement of claim obtain writ of replevin. Application must be supported by affidavit of plaintiff or his duly authorized agent, stating judicial district in which goods are, giving description of goods and value and stating that person claiming goods is rightful owner or entitled to possession thereof; that property was taken under color of distress damage feasant or for rent, if such is case, or time and particulars of wrongful or fraudulent taking out of his possession, and such facts as show that plaintiff is entitled to goods. He must also furnish to sheriff bond equal to value of goods. Sheriff retains goods till ordered by court to return them to plaintiff, except that in all cases but cases of distress, defendant can retain possession upon giving bond.

REPORTS:

Official reports are Saskatchewan Law Reports, now discontinued. Private publications are: Western Weekly Reports, Saskatchewan Reports and Dominion Law Reports.

Digest.—Canadian Abridgement.

RESTRAINT OF TRADE:

See Canada Law Digest, topic Monopolies and Restraint of Trade.

SALES:

The law relating to the sale of goods is codified in "The Sale of Goods Act" under which contracts for the purchase of goods of the value of $50 or upwards require part acceptance, part payment or writing to be enforceable by action. All other contracts are governed by common law as modified by statute. (R. S., c. S-1).

Bills of sale no longer required to be registered but interest of purchaser must be registered pursuant to Personal Property Security Act to prevent vendor left in possession of goods from conveying clear title to third parties.

Product Liability.—See topic Consumer Protection.

Retail Credit Sales.—Every lender of money or seller of goods or services on credit must provide to borrower or purchaser a clear statement in writing showing actual sum borrowed or cash price, plus official fees and insurance fees, amount of down-payment or trade-in, if any, cash difference, cost of borrowing expressed in cash and as an annual percentage and, in default, cost of borrowing is not recoverable from buyer as borrower. Similar disclosure must be made in advertisements. (Cost of Credit Disclosure Act, R. S., c. C-41).

Credit Cards.—Recipients of unsolicited credit cards or goods have no legal obligation to sender unless recipient expressly acknowledges in writing his intention to accept them. (Unsolicited Goods and Credit Cards Act, R. S., c. U-8).

Conditional Sales.—See topic Personal Property Security.

Sales of Farm Implements.—Every contract made by a manufacturer or dealer for sale of any farm implement or machine of the selling price of $1,000 or more (except to persons carrying on implement business) is governed by The Agricultural Implement Act (R. S., c. A-10) and generally contract must be in writing or is presumed to be in form prescribed in Act. Dealers are required to furnish to government lists of implements and repairs carried and prices charged therefor. In case of repossession provision is made for arbitration in fixing value should vendor and purchaser not agree thereon. Certain restrictions are imposed on vendor's right to repossess. (*Note:* The Agricultural Implements Amendment Act.—Effect: Implement dealer who assigns security interest remains agent of financial institution [assignee] for purpose of receiving payment from buyer until notice of assignment given to buyer. Notice to be sent separately from security agreement. If financial institution accepts payment from dealer, once again agent until financial institution sends new notice to buyer.)

Consumer Affairs.—Department of Consumer and Commercial Affairs has general supervision of all consumer and commercial affairs. It can enter into inquiries as to consumer and commercial affairs legislation in Canada and make recommendations for changes in Saskatchewan's consumer and commercial affairs legislation. It can investigate complaints respecting contraventions of consumer and commercial affairs legislation or respecting practices which are contrary to interests of consumers. Minister may, where in his opinion it is in public interest, order person to cease using particular form of advertisement which is in contravention of Cost of Credit Disclosure Act, using particular form of contract in selling of goods or services, selling or distributing any goods in any business undertaking. Such order expires within five days after its making. Minister can apply to Court of Queen's Bench to have order extended past five days. (R. S., c. C-29.2).

Bulk Sales.—See topic Fraudulent Sales and Conveyances.

Closing-Out Sales.—Where a municipality has passed a general by-law to that effect, no closing-out sale (e.g., bankruptcy, insolvency, assignee's, trustee's, executor's, jobber's, fire, smoke, water, etc.) can be advertised or conducted unless licensed by an inspector to whom is furnished full particulars showing details and bona fides of sale. Period of sale must be not less than 30 days nor more than 90 days and only one license can be issued to any one person in a period of 12 months. Only regular stock-in-trade can be sold at such sale. (Closing-out Sales Act, R. S., c. C-13).

Door-to-Door Sales.—Where a sale is made at a person's home, by a direct seller, buyer has four days within which to rescind contract, or if goods are not delivered within 120 days he can rescind. Buyer is entitled to a true copy of sales contract at time of execution. (Direct Sellers Act, R. S., c. D-28). See topic Licenses.

SALES TAX: See topic Taxation.

SEALS:

In order to create a specialty debt, it is necessary to contract under seal which imports a consideration; otherwise, in simple contracts, consideration must be proved.

SECURITIES:

Law relating to securities is governed by Securities Act 1988-89, (R.S., c. S-42.2) and to lesser extent by Business Corporations Act (R. S., c. B-10).

Supervision.—The powers under the Act are exercised by a Commission consisting of Chairman and not more than six other members with Chairman having right to exercise powers subject to review of Commission.

Regulatory Powers of Supervising Authority.—No person or company shall trade in any security unless such person or company is registered with the Commission. Commission has wide discretion in deciding whether application for registration should be granted or denied, including regard for the public interest.

Prerequisites to Sales or Offerings.—Before primary distribution to the public may be made of a security, a prospectus must be filed and a receipt issued therefor. The Act lays down detailed requirements of the contents of prospectuses for various types of companies and requires that they be fully executed accompanied by balance sheets and engineering reports in case of oil and gas and mining companies.

Securities to Which Act Applicable.—The word "security" has a wide definition covering many types of documents other than those ordinarily known as securities and documents so designated by the Commission by regulation. It also includes oil and gas leases so that mineral lease brokers buying and selling oil and gas leases must register under Act.

Exempt Securities.—Government securities; certificates issued by licenced trust corporations for guaranteed investment; commercial paper maturing within one year; variable insurance contracts; private issuer securities not offered for sale to public; private mutual fund securities; co-operative or credit union securities; mutual fund securities administered by licenced trust corporation; mortgage of real or personal property; conditional sales contracts; and other stated securities. (§39[2]).

Exempt Transactions.—Trades by executor, trustee, receiver, or sheriff in certain circumstances; isolated trades; purchaser is bank, trust company, federal or provincial government, crown or municipal corporation; private placement; trades to settle debts of issuer; security to lender as collateral for debt; stock dividends, distributions on winding-up, distributions effected through exercise of warrants, conversion or exchange privileges and securities of another reporting issuer distributed as dividend in specie; rights issue; exchange of securities upon mergers, amalgamations, reorganizations or arrangements; trades pursuant to takeover bid; trades pursuant to redemption or repurchase; trades by issuer in own security for consideration of at least $150,000; trades to employees; trades necessary to facilitate incorporation; trade by issuer to or between promoters; trade by issuer in own security in return for resource assets; trades by registered real estate brokers in course of listing; trades by issuers in own security to raise seed capital; trades in government incentive securities; trades by issuer with close friends and business associates; and certain other trades and discretionary exemptions. (§39[1]).

Registration of Brokers, etc.—Underwriters, brokers, investment dealers, mutual fund dealers, scholarship plan dealers, real estate securities dealers, exchange contracts dealers, financial advisors, investment counsel, portfolio managers and securities advisors must apply for registration on prescribed form and must normally be bonded. Registration expires with calendar year.

Investigations by Commissions.—Wide powers of investigation are conferred on the Commission for a person appointed by it to investigate improper acts or transactions and to refer matters to the courts.

Residential and Telephone Calls.—The Commission may prohibit a person from calling at a residence or telephoning from within Saskatchewan to any residents within or without Saskatchewan for the purpose of trading subject to certain minor exceptions.

SECURITIES . . . *continued*

Verbal Misrepresentations.—Securities Act provides for civil liability for verbal misrepresentation made to prospective purchaser of security. (Part XIX).

The Personal Property Security Act provides for registration of debentures, trust deeds and the like. (R. S., c. P-6.1). See topic Personal Property Security.

SEQUESTRATION:

If any judgment or order against a corporation be wilfully disobeyed, the plaintiff may obtain a writ of sequestration against its property. If a person is taken into custody under a writ of attachment without obeying the judgment, upon the sheriff's return to that effect, the opposite party is entitled to a writ of sequestration against the estate and effects of disobedient person. If the person refusing or neglecting to obey the judgment cannot be found the writ of sequestration may issue without a writ of attachment having first been issued.

SERVICE: See topic Process.

STATUTE OF FRAUDS:

See topic Frauds, Statute of.

STATUTES:

Statutes are consolidated in Revised Statutes of Saskatchewan, 1978. Subsequent statutes are the annual sessions laws.

STAY OF EXECUTION:

See topics Appeal and Error; Executions.

SUBMISSION OF CONTROVERSY:

No statutory provisions.

SUPPLEMENTARY PROCEEDINGS:

See topic Executions.

SURETY AND GUARANTY COMPANIES:

Surety and guaranty companies are required to become registered in the province. Every company becoming registered is required to appoint a resident attorney for service of process.

TAXATION:

Exemptions.—The following property is exempt: property owned by the Crown including local government property; church property; burial grounds; educational institutions; libraries and charitable institutions, not for profit; and certain memorial societies. Local bonds may be exempted from local taxes by the issuing authority. Members of Armed Forces and veterans are not, by virtue of this fact alone, exempt from income tax.

Local Taxes.—Local municipal authorities are given right to impose taxation and to make assessments and arrange for collections. Land valuations must be at fair value and buildings must not be assessed at more than 60% of fair value. (See Urban Municipality Act and Rural Municipality Act, R. S., c. U-11; R. S., c. R-26.)

Tax Enforcement.—Land is no longer offered for sale to realise arrears of taxes, but eventually passes to municipality in default of payment of taxes. When whole or any portion of taxes on land is unpaid for more than six months after Dec. 31 of year in which rate was struck, treasurer prepares a list and publishes same in The Saskatchewan Gazette with a notification that unless arrears and costs are paid treasurer will, at expiration of 60 days, proceed to register a tax lien. Tax lien is registered in Land Titles Office and after expiration of one year from date of filing tax lien municipality may apply for title to any parcel of land affected. Upon receipt of an application for title treasurer must send out notices to parties interested and after expiration of six months from date of service of last notice required to be served registrar, failing redemption and on request of municipality, issues a certificate of title to municipality. Owner may redeem at any time before title is lost.

Income Tax.—Province imposes an income tax. Rate of this tax for individuals is percentage of tax payable under Federal Income Tax Act (see Canada Law Digest). Rate is 50% for 1987, and subsequent years plus flat tax of 2% of net income plus surtax of 15% on provincial income tax in excess of $4,000. General corporate income tax rate is 17% for 1994 and subsequent years, with resource corporations liable for Corporation Capital Tax subject to further surcharge of 3.6% on value of their production. By agreement, Dominion collects this tax at time tax under Federal Act is collected, and then pays over to Province. For administration purposes, one return is used. Members of armed forces and veterans are not, by virtue of this Act alone, exempt from taxation. (Income Tax Act, R. S., c. I-2).

Inheritance Tax.—None imposed by this province.

Estate Tax.—None imposed by this province with exception of property passing or deemed to pass upon death of any person after Dec. 31, 1971 and prior to Jan. 1, 1977 for which Succession Duty Act is then deemed to be in force. (S. S. 1940, c-50).

Corporation Capital Tax.—Taxable paid-up capital of corporations resident in Canada and taxable paid-up capital employed in Canada of nonresident corporations subject to tax which is payable in monthly instalments by all corporations having permanent establishment within Canada, other than credit unions, cooperatives, family farm corporations, insurance corporations and corporations exempt from income tax federally. Rate of tax is 0.6% of taxable amount except for banks for which rate is 3.0% and trust or loan corporations for which rate is 3.0%.

Paid-up capital for corporations other than banks and trust and loan corporations is aggregate of paid-up capital stock plus earned, capital and other surpluses, plus reserves, plus sums advanced or loaned by shareholders or other corporations, plus all indebtedness of corporation. Special computation for determining paid-up capital employed in Canada of nonresident corporation.

Taxable paid-up capital for resident corporations equals paid-up capital minus $10,000,000 and minus other specified deductions for good will, discounts on share sales, Canadian exploration and development expenses and investment allowance.

Resource corporations may be required to pay additional tax depending upon their level of sales.

Stamp Tax.—No provincial stamp tax. For Dominion stamp taxes see Canada Law Digest.

Sales Tax.—In addition to Goods and Services Tax (see Canada Law Digest) there is provincial sales tax of 9.0% imposed on retail purchases within province of tangible personal property, except for liquor which is taxed at 7%, and tobacco taxed at 8.0¢ per cigarette and at least 17¢ per cigar; tobacco taxed at 5.3¢ per gram.

Exemptions.—Tax is not imposed on farm machinery, implements, and commodities, including gasoline; drugs, medicines, and medical appliances; chemicals; water; food and drink (apart from liquor); books, magazines and periodicals; newspapers; items of clothing under $300; and other specified items. (R.S., c. E-3).

Gasoline Tax.—There is fuel tax of 15¢ per litre on gasoline and diesel fuels, 7¢ per litre on aviation fuels and 9¢ per litre on propane. Saskatchewan farmers and individual primary producers are exempt from tax on commercial purchases from bulk fuel dealers. All heating fuels are exempt.

Mineral Tax.—See topic Mines and Minerals.

Petroleum and Natural Gas Tax.—See topic Mines and Minerals.

Hospitalization Tax.—None.

Medical Care Insurance Tax.—None

School tax provided by Education Act. (R. S., c. E-0.1). This declares that each property whether business or residential in city, town, village or rural municipality within each school division is assessed tax calculated by percentage rate, set by school board for division of estimated value in order to obtain operating funds.

Persons 65 and over are eligible to rebates of up to $510 on principal residence, including trailer resident. (The Senior Citizens Heritage Rebates Act, R.S., c. S-46.1).

Unemployment Compensation or Social Security Tax.—None imposed by this province.

Penalties.—Following penalties may be imposed upon persons for default under Saskatchewan taxation statutes:

Property Taxes.—If property taxes are unpaid after Dec. 31 in year of assessment, penalty of 5% of arrears of taxes is added for each year that default continues. Land taxes form special lien upon property involved, and are collectible by action or distress in priority to all claims except those asserted by Crown. Municipal authorities have broad powers to distrain upon goods and chattels of assessed person in respect of tax arrears wherever such goods and chattels may be found in municipal unit involved.

Income Tax.—Apart from penalties imposed by Dominion legislation (see Canada Law Digest), Saskatchewan statute provides its own penalties. In event of underpayment of tax, interest from expiration of time within which return must be filed to date of payment of correct amount of tax is chargeable at 6% per annum on underpayment. If return is not filed, penalty of 5% of tax unpaid when return was required to be filed is levied, if tax payable was less than $2,000. If tax payable was over $2,000, penalty is $100. Failure to file information returns invokes penalty of 1% of tax payable, but not less than $25 nor more than $100. If person knowingly or negligently misstates his income thereby reducing tax payable, penalty of 25% of amount by which tax is reduced is payable. In addition, criminal penalties are provided by statute. In event of failure to file return, person is subject to minimum fine of $25 for each day default continues. Employers failing to submit returns, to keep accurate records, or to withhold tax are liable to fine from $200 to $10,000, together with possible jail term of up to six months. Any person participating in falsification of returns or in evading or willful avoiding of tax is liable to fine from $25 to $10,000, together with, in an appropriate case, an amount not exceeding double amount of tax that should have been shown to be payable or that was sought to be evaded, and, alternatively, fine as mentioned above together with imprisonment for up to two years may be imposed.

Corporation Capital Tax.—For failure to file returns, fine is up to $100 per day. Wilful understating of value of amount taxable or overstating deductions, penalty is up to 50% tax sought to be evaded. Offences for contravention of Act can attract fines up to $1,000 per day.

Sales Tax.—Vendor failing to forward tax collected is subject to penalty of 10% of amount of tax so retained, together with other penalties imposed by statute. Interest is chargeable on amount required to be paid over by vendor at 6% per annum from date when vendor was required to make payment. If vendor fails to make required returns, government may estimate amount of tax collected by him and unaccounted for, and may require such amount to be paid over by vendor. Any violation of Act, including providing false returns, may result in fine from $25 to $500 and, in default of payment thereof, imprisonment of up to three months.

Mineral Tax.—Mineral Taxation Act, 1983, provides that taxes payable under it for first charge on all mineral rights owned by taxpayer and in case of mineral production tax, on interest of taxpayer in any mineral and mineral rights. Government may seize and sell estate to which first charge attaches to cover taxes.

TORRENS SYSTEM:

See topics Records and Real Property.

TRADEMARKS AND TRADENAMES:

See Canada Law Digest.

See note at head of Digest as to 1996 legislation covered.

See Topical Index in front part of this volume.

TRANSIENT TRADERS: See topic Licenses.

TRUST DEEDS: See topic Mortgages.

TRUSTEE PROCESS: See topic Garnishment.

TRUSTS:

Rules of equity and common law rules generally govern creation and kinds of trusts and appointment, eligibility, competency, qualification and removal of trustees. All declarations of trust are required by statute of frauds to be in writing subject to rules of equity relating to resulting trusts.

Trust and Loan Corporations Act (R. S., c. T-22.1), governs registration and operation of such bodies in Province.

Trustee Act (R. S., c. T-23) regulates investment of trust funds sales, and vesting orders relating to title to property, and generally sets forth powers and duties, rights and liabilities of trustees, executors and administrators.

The Trusts Convention Implementation Act (1994, c. T-23.1) specifies Law applicable to trusts and governs their recognition.

USURY:

See Canada Law Digest, topic Interest.

VENUE:

Except in cases covered by special provisions, venue is within the jurisdiction where the cause of action arose or the defendant resides. By contract the venue may be anywhere within the province. Court may order change of venue to insure fair trial or to suit balance of convenience.

VITAL STATISTICS: See topic Records.

WAREHOUSEMEN:

(R. S., c. W-3).

Under the Warehousemen's Lien Act a warehouseman means a person lawfully engaged in the business of storing goods as a bailee for hire. The warehouseman is given a lien on goods stored by him for storage charges, money advanced, interest, labor, transportation, etc. A written notice of the lien must be given to the owner within two months from deposit of goods where the deposit is not made by the owner or by his authority. In case warehouse charges remain unpaid, on notice and advertisement the warehouseman may sell the goods and any surplus realized must be paid into court if not demanded by the person entitled thereto.

Warehouse Receipts.—The endorsee of a warehouse receipt should take prompt steps to receive possession, or to have the warehouseman attorn to him.

WILLS:

Any person of the age of 18, or any married infant, if of sound mind can make a will. (R.S., c. W-14).

Testamentary Disposition.—The testator has complete power of disposition over his estate except he cannot deprive his widow of her homestead rights nor his widow and children of their rights under the Dependents' Relief Act, and where his life insurance was in his lifetime payable to one of his preferred beneficiaries he cannot take his life insurance out of that class.

Execution.—No will, except that of a soldier or sailor on active service, is valid unless it is in writing. It must be signed by the testator or by some other person in his presence and by his direction and must be apparent on face of will that testator intended to create will. Such signature must be made or acknowledged by testator in presence of two or more witnesses, present at same time, and such witnesses must attest and subscribe will in presence of testator. Executor may be witness.

Attestation Clause.—Two witnesses as are present at the time the testator makes or acknowledges his signature must attest and subscribe the will in the presence of the testator, but no form of attestation is necessary. The following is used in practice:

Form

Signed, published and declared by the said testator, (name), as and for his last will and testament, in the presence of us, both present at the same time, who at his request, in his presence and in the presence of each other, has hereunto subscribed our names as witnesses.

Nuncupative Wills.—Nuncupative wills are abolished except as regards a soldier in actual military service, or mariner or seaman at sea.

Holograph will, wholly in handwriting of testator and signed by him, may be made without any further formality, or any requirement as to the presence of, or attestation or signature by any witness.

Testamentary Gifts to Subscribing Witnesses.—Except in the case of a charge for the payment of a debt, a testamentary gift to a witness, or the husband or wife of a witness, is void; however gift may be validated if it is proven within six months that such person did not exercise any improper or undue influence on testator.

Probating.—Executors may apply for probate to Court of Queen's Bench at any judicial centre if deceased left estate or effects within Saskatchewan.

If the subscribing witnesses are dead or if no affidavit can be obtained from any of them, due execution of the will may be shown by proof of the handwriting and signatures of the witnesses or testator or from those present at the execution of the will but who did not sign as witnesses.

Self-proved Wills.—No provision.

Living Wills.—No legislation.

Unclaimed legacies lapse and fall into residue, ultimately to escheat to Province if no heirs or next of kin. (R. S., c. E-11).

Lapse.—Unless a contrary intention is expressed in the will a bequest to a child or other issue or brother or sister of testator does not lapse on death of legatee in testator's lifetime, if legatee leaves spouse or issue living at testator's death, but bequest takes effect in all respects as if legatee had died intestate, without debts, immediately after death of testator, except that surviving spouse is not entitled to usual preferential share of $100,000.

Revocation.—A will is revoked by subsequent marriage of the testator unless it was made in contemplation of marriage. (*Note:* The Wills Amendment Act, proclaimed in force Oct. 8, 1982. Effect: Where marriage of testator is terminated by decree absolute, divorce or nullity, devise or bequest to spouse or appointment of spouse as executor or trustee or general power of appointment conferred on spouse in will is revoked.) Otherwise no will or codicil may be revoked except by another will or codicil executed in manner required for will or by some writing declaring intention to revoke same and execute in manner in which will is required to be executed, or by burning, tearing or otherwise destroying same by testator, or by some person in his presence and by his direction, with intention of revoking same.

Foreign will is well executed as regards personal property for purpose of probate here if it is made according to form required, by either: (1) The law of this province; (2) the law of the place where the testator was domiciled when the will was made; or (3) the law of the place where the will was made; or (4) by the law then in force in that part of Her Majesty's Dominions where the testator had his domicile of origin.

Wills executed outside of Saskatchewan must, as regards real property in Saskatchewan, be executed according to the form required by the law of this province.

Resealing of Foreign Grants.—Application is made to Court of Queen's Bench at any judicial centre.

Simultaneous Death.—See topic Death, subhead Survivorship.

International Will.—Will made in accordance with rules as set out in "Convention Providing a Uniform Law on The Form of an International Will". Convention between Government of Canada and U.S. effective date: six months after day on which Government of Canada submits to U.S. government, declaration that Convention extends to Saskatchewan. Provides for safekeeping and registration of international wills. (The Wills Amendment Act, proclaimed in force Oct. 8, 1982).

WITNESSES:

Children under 14 or person whose mental capacity is challenged, may testify under oath or solemn affirmation if court determines that person understands nature of oath or solemn affirmation and is able to communicate evidence. Where such person does not understand nature of oath or solemn affirmation but can communicate evidence, they may testify on promising to tell truth. Where such person does not understand nature of oath or solemn affirmation and is not able to communicate evidence, they cannot testify. There is no disqualification by reason of interest or criminality. No witness shall be excused from answering any question on ground that his answer may tend to criminate him or establish civil liability. Where witness objects to answer on ground that his answer may tend to criminate him or establish civil liability, although he is compelled to answer, answer may not be used against him in other civil proceedings.

Communications between solicitors and clients, certain state documents and communications between husband and wife are privileged. (R. S., c. S-16).

See also topic Depositions.

WORKMEN'S COMPENSATION LAW:

See topic Labour Relations.

CHANNEL ISLANDS (JERSEY) LAW DIGEST

(The following is a list of all Topics, including cross-references, covered in this Digest.)

CHANNEL ISLANDS (JERSEY) LAW DIGEST

Revised for 1997 edition by

OGIER & LE MASURIER, of the Jersey bar

ACTIONS:

Generally, any person may sue or be sued in Jersey Royal Court ("Royal Court"), subject to jurisdictional requirements and Rules of Procedure framed by Royal Court. Questions relating to evidence are generally decided by lex fori as well as questions of admissibility, competence and compellability of witnesses, mode of trial and nature of plaintiff's remedies. Foreign law is matter of evidence which must be pleaded and proved. Proof of foreign law may be made by properly qualified experts. Plaintiff resident abroad is normally ordered to pay into court sum by way of security for costs, to ensure defendant's legal costs will be met by plaintiff if plaintiff's action fails. Sum is refunded if plaintiff succeeds. In most cases, court documents must be served by Royal Court's executive officer, Viscount. Royal Court has extensive and well developed powers to order preemptive seizure of assets (including documents) and, in some cases, arrest of person. Royal Court will assist foreign courts to obtain evidence in both civil and criminal matters. Summary judgment may be available when plaintiff is able to show defendant has no defence to action.

ADMINISTRATOR (FOR ABSENTEES FROM THE ISLAND):

Administrator may be appointed to have control and administration of property of individual absent from the Island. Absentee who reappears is repossessed of all property. Administrator may be appointed at instigation of relative or other person interested in absentee's property. Absentee's seven closest relatives, friends or neighbours attend in Royal Court and elect one of their number as administrator. If absentee is away for less than a year and a day action may be brought against him in his own name or administrator may be appointed; if for more than a year and a day, it is necessary to appoint administrator. Royal Court can order appointment of administrator at any stage in proceedings. In addition, administrator can be appointed for company.

AFFIDAVITS:

Affidavit is written statement of fact sworn by deponent before person authorised to administer oaths, such as notary.

Form.—Affidavit is commenced with title of action, e.g.:

FILE NO: 95/123

IN THE ROYAL COURT OF THE ISLAND OF JERSEY

(............ Division)

BETWEEN	**XXXXXXXXXXXX**	**PLAINTIFF**
AND	**YYYYYYYYYYYY**	**DEFENDANT**

AFFIDAVIT

[Deponent's full name, true place of residence and occupation must then be stated. Then set out facts deposed to in first person in paragraphs numbered consecutively. Affidavit must be confined to facts within deponent's own knowledge, except on interlocutory applications where statements as to his belief, with sources and grounds thereof, may be admitted.

Affidavit is formally concluded by attestation being memorandum of place, time and person before whom it is sworn. Full address, sufficient for identification, must be given and attestation should follow, immediately after end of text.]

Form:

SWORN by the deponent)
.... (name))
at .... in the) (Signature of deponent)
country of .... on the)
.... day of .... 199..)

BEFORE ME ....
(SEAL)

....
Signature of Officer
Title of Officer

On front page of affidavit and on back sheet one must state: (i) Party on whose behalf it is filed; (ii) initials and surname of deponent; (iii) number of affidavit in relation to deponent; and (iv) date when sworn (e.g. Defendant: J. Smith (No.): 1st June 1995).

Affirmation, instead of oath, may be made where it is not reasonably practicable to arrange for oath to be administered or where deponent is atheist.

Exhibits.—Any document may be referred to in body of affidavit, as exhibit, thus: "the said letter is now produced and shown to me marked ('AB')" (deponent's initials are generally used). Where there is more than one exhibit best course is to use, as exhibit marks, deponent's initials followed by consecutive numbers, as thus: ("AB1"), ("AB2") etc. By this means, exhibits to affidavits of several witnesses are readily identified. Every exhibit referred to in affidavit must be marked with short title of cause, or matter, as set out for affidavit, and various certificates signed by officer before whom affidavit is sworn.

Form

[Title to the Action]

This is the exhibit marked ("AB") or ("AB1") referred to in the affidavit of XY sworn in this action this day of 199 before me ....
(name and title of officer).

ALIENS:

Nationality is covered by British Nationality Act 1981 as extended to island of Jersey by Immigration (Jersey) Order 1993; order of Her Majesty in Council. In British Nationality Act 1981 definition of United Kingdom ("UK") includes Channel Islands. Alien is person who is not British citizen, British dependent territories citizen, British overseas citizen, British subject, British protected person, Commonwealth citizen or citizen of Republic of Ireland. (See England Law Digest.)

Property.—Prior to coming in force of Wills and Succession (Jersey) Law 1993 on 1 Sept. 1993, inheritance of realty by alien was subject to certain restrictions. These restrictions have been abolished on estates of such persons dying after commencement of law.

ASSIGNMENTS:

Assignments (other than by way of security—see subhead Assignments for Benefit of Creditors, infra) similar to position under English law.

Assignments for Benefit of Creditors.—Security assignments relating to intangible moveable property in Jersey are governed by Security Interests (Jersey) Law 1983, as amended ("Law"). Law sets out specific requirements for creation of security under Jersey law in respect of intangible movable property other than leases (leases of more than nine years being regarded as immovable property which may be mortgaged). Assets capable of assignment under Law include cash in bank account, shares, life insurance policies and other contractual rights and benefits.

ATTACHMENT:

Any Royal Court judgment may authorise plaintiff to distrain on defendant's goods. Viscount sells goods at public auction, or privately under Royal Court Rules. Distraint order will last for ten years. Person may also be imprisoned for nonpayment of judgment debt. Judgement creditor must pay standard charge to maintain debtor in prison. Imprisonment may be for up to one year and judgment debtor will remain liable for debt. Acte of Court can also be obtained from Royal Court authorising distraint on wages. (See topic Actions in relation to preemptive remedies.)

ATTORNEYS AND COUNSELLORS (LAWYERS):

Jersey lawyers may either be advocates or "écrivins" (Jersey solicitors). Jersey Law Society governs conduct of advocates and rules relating to qualification and admission of advocates and "écrivins" are set out in Advocates (Jersey) Law 1968 and Solicitors (Jersey) Law 1971. Advocates have full rights of audience before Petty Debts Court, Royal Court, Police Court, Youth Court, Court of Appeal and ultimately Privy Council. "Écrivins" have audience only in Petty Debts Court.

BANKRUPTCY:

Corporate Bankruptcy.—Bankruptcy (Désastre) (Jersey) Law 1990 together with provisions set out in Part XXI of Companies (Jersey) Law 1991 set out appropriate methods of dealing with corporate bankruptcy.

Individual Bankruptcy.—Various methods of realising assets of debtor for benefit of creditors are available under Jersey law. These are: (i) "Dégrèvement"; (ii) "Remise de biens"; (iii) declaration of "désastre" under Bankruptcy (Désastre) (Jersey) Law 1990.

Procedure of "dégrèvement" is set out in Loi (1880) sur la Propriété Foncière as amended. Any dégrèvement must be commenced by "cession" or after Royal Court has made order at instance of judgment creditor that goods of debtor be adjudged renounced following his failure to pay judgment debt.

"Cession" is voluntary renunciation by debtor of his moveable and immoveable property. It is privilege granted by Royal Court and not a right. It operates as complete discharge of all debts existing at time it is granted. "Cession" will not be granted unless debtor is "malheureux" and acts in good faith. Loi (1832) sur les décrets provides that before "cession" can be made debtor must be imprisoned and reduced to short rations, or must have obtained Acte of Court 15 days prior to cession announcing his intention to do so, which acte is posted at Royal Court and in Jersey Gazette. "Cession" is not selling procedure and, if granted, Royal Court will, on application of creditor, order "dégrèvement" of immoveables or "réalisation" of moveables, as appropriate.

Loi (1832) sur les décrets had introduced concept of adjudication of renunciation enabling compulsory "dégrèvement" to be applied for by creditor over debtor's assets. Creditor obtains judgment of Royal Court and after period of three months, if debtor does not satisfy creditor's claim, immoveable and moveable property of debtor is adjudged renounced.

See Topical Index in front part of this volume.

BANKRUPTCY . . . *continued*

Function of "dégrèvement" is to find creditor willing to take on debtor's property and pay off superior ranking creditors, thereby discharging immoveable property from all encumbrances. First persons to whom property is offered are unsecured creditors and, if none of them take property as "tenant après dégrèvement", property is offered to secured creditors in turn in reverse chronological order.

Loi (1839) sur les remise de biens introduced system whereby Royal Court, if satisfied debtor has sufficient property prima facie to discharge all secured debts, allows debtor to place his affairs into Royal Court's hands, normally for period of six months, during which period two jurats of Royal Court appointed to examine merits of original application will attempt orderly discharge of debtors' liabilities. It is because "remise" realises only sufficient assets to satisfy creditors, that it is more equitable system than "dégrèvement". If there is surplus this will be returned to debtor. If "remise" pays off all creditors, then it operates as complete discharge. If it fails, placing of property in hands of Royal Court acts as "cession" and "dégrèvement" of immoveable property and "réalisation" of movables will follow.

In order to simplify various procedures available for bankruptcy, Bankruptcy (Désastre) (Jersey) Law, 1990 was introduced. Declaration "en désastre" had previously been means of realising debtor's movable property only for benefit of all his creditors.

Désastre may be declared in respect of assets of debtor (which can be either individual or company) which: is (or was within 12 months preceding application) ordinarily resident in Jersey; or carries on (or has in three years preceding application) business in Jersey; or has immovable property in Jersey; or is or was Jersey incorporated company.

Application can be made by creditor with liquidated claim exceeding £1,000 or by debtor. If Royal Court is satisfied that "désastre" application is made in proper form, (with supporting affidavit) Royal Court will make declaration of "désastre" and all property will vest in Viscount (executive officer of Royal Court). Viscount will take steps to realise assets of debtor and apply proceeds of sale in satisfaction of creditor's claims. Viscount will manage "désastre" giving notice to creditors and will pay off debts in order set out in law. Any excess will go to debtor. 1990 law deals with transactions at undervalue and preferences. Viscount may set aside transactions made by debtor two years prior to declaration of "désastre" if made at undervalue. If debtor was insolvent at time of transaction or became insolvent as result of transaction, then relevant period is five years. If debtor prefers one creditor over another at time when he is insolvent or becomes insolvent as result of giving preference, Viscount may set aside any preference made less than one year prior to declaration of désastre. Customary law in Jersey also recognises "actions pauliennes", whereby transaction may be set aside if debtor has transferred property to another with intention of fraudulently defeating his creditor's claims. These may be alienations for value or alienations to volunteer. If transfer is to mere volunteer it is voidable if debtor alone has intention to defeat his creditors, but if it is made for value, then both debtor and transferee must be aware of intention to defeat creditors.

BILLS AND NOTES:

Cheques, demand drafts and certain other specified instruments are governed by Cheques (Jersey) Law 1957. This confers protection on bankers paying unindorsed or irregularly indorsed cheques where banker acts in good faith. It also protects bankers collecting payment of cheques in good faith and without negligence where customer has no title or defective title to instrument.

Law relating to bills of exchange and promissory notes is similar to that of English law.

CONTRACTS:

Much of Jersey law of contract is based on customary law of Duchy of Normandy, of which Channel Islands historically formed a part. Framework of customary law as set out in medieval "Grand Coûtum" ("Ancienne Coûtum") and "Coûtum Reformée" of late 16th century. Royal Court looks to its own precedents (perforce limited in number) and to many commentators on Coûtumes and, where appropriate, Court may look for guidance to modern French law where this has evolved from customary origins. However, in some areas of law (e.g. misrepresentation, mistake and assessment of damages) where principles of civil law have much in common with law of England, Royal Court has had regard to English common law. As far as principles relating to remoteness of damage and categories of damage are concerned (both in contract and in tort) English law is generally followed.

Formation of Contract.—There must be agreement between parties intending to create legal relationship based upon offer and acceptance of terms with "cause" (form of consideration) moving between promisee and promisor. Maxim "la convention fait la loi des parties" (agreement between parties makes law) is guiding principle of Jersey law of contract. If contract is tainted by "vice de consentement" (by error, violence or fraud) contract is null. In addition, contract that lacks "cause" or is uncertain is null. In principle, contract which is null is without effect ab initio and each party must make restitution of what he has received.

Breach of Contract and Consequences.—When party does not fulfil his contractual obligation, there are various remedies available to other party. Injured party can act in justice to force offending party to fulfil contract (specific performance) save that he cannot force defaulting party to transact in relation to any hereditary interest in immovable property. In such case, however, and in all cases where aggrieved party does not seek specific performance, courts may order defaulting party to pay damages and interests. In some circumstances, defaulting party may be exonerated: e.g. force majeure. "Force majeure" refers to events which make performance impossible, not merely to events which only make it more onerous and is regarded as being more restrictive than English doctrine of frustration. With exception of personal contracts, impossibility must be absolute. Impediment must have been unforeseeable and irresistible. If proved, "force majeure" will release contracting party from his obligations.

Applicable Law.—Rights and obligations of contracting parties and interpretation of contract are governed by law which parties agree or intend shall govern it or which they are presumed to have intended, which is known as "proper law" of contract. Proper law may be ascertained by express intention with express words, providing that choice is bona fide and legal and there is no reason for avoiding choice on grounds of public policy. Where there is no express indication of proper law, intention must be inferred from terms and nature of contract, and general circumstances of case. If choice of proper law is neither expressed or capable of being inferred, contract will be governed by system of law which Royal Court determines has its "closest and most real connection". In reaching its determination, Royal Court will ascertain how reasonable person would have regarded issue and what intention prudent person would have been likely to have had in mind, if his mind had been directed to issues. Principal matters to be considered are any choice of jurisdiction or arbitration clauses, form of contract, places of contracting, place of performance, place of residence or business of parties and nature and subject matter of contract.

COPYRIGHT:

UK Copyright Act 1911 was extended to Jersey by Loi (1913) au sujet des droits d'auteur. It covers original, artistic, dramatic, literary and musical works. Musical copyright is also protected by The Musical (Summary Proceedings) Copyright Act 1902 and Musical Copyright Act 1906 which are also extended to Jersey. UK Copyright Act 1956 has not been fully extended to Jersey.

Patents are governed by Patents (Jersey) Law 1957 which is reregistration law permitting grantee of patent in UK, or person claiming rights from such grantee, to register patent in Jersey.

Registered Designs.—Designs are governed by Registered Designs (Jersey) Law 1957 which is reregistration law permitting proprietor of design registered in UK, or person entitled to rights of such proprietor, to register design in Jersey.

Trademarks and Service Marks are governed by Trade Marks (Jersey) Law 1958 and Trade Marks (Jersey) Rules 1986. Trade Marks (Jersey) Law 1958 is reregistration law which permits proprietor of trademark or service mark registered in UK, or person entitled to rights of such proprietor, to register trademark or service mark in Jersey.

CORPORATIONS:

Charges.—Law does not require company to maintain register of charges and there is no public register of charges in Jersey, save for charges secured on immovable property which are recorded in Public Registry of Royal Court.

Dissolution.—Company may be dissolved by special resolution of its shareholders, by court in certain circumstances, on expiry of its period of existence (if any) as stated in its Memorandum of Association (if any) or consequent on certain insolvency procedures, as to which see topic Insolvency.

General.—The Companies (Jersey) Law 1991 ("Law") governs incorporation, management, administration and dissolution of limited liability companies in Jersey.

Government Fees.—Capital duty at rate of 0.5% is payable on authorised share capital of company, subject to minimum of £50. There is no stamp duty or other fees payable in Jersey on transfer of shares in Jersey company.

Incorporation.—Any two persons (including bodies corporate) (or single subscriber in case of wholly owned subsidiary) may form company by signing and delivering to Registrar of Companies Memorandum of Association, containing certain prescribed information, together with Statement of Particulars setting out address of registered office, whether company is private or public company and whether Standard Table Articles of Association set out in Companies (Standard Table) (Jersey) Order 1992 are to be adopted by company. It is normal practice for Articles of Association to be submitted to Registrar of Companies with incorporation documents and in absence of this Standard Table will be deemed to constitute Articles of Association of company.

Doctrine of ultra vires has been abolished by Law which provides that capacity of company is not limited by anything in its Memorandum or Articles of Association. In view of this, it is no longer standard practice to include long-form objects clause.

Law provides for two types of limited liability companies, public companies and private companies. Public company is one which has more than 30 members (excluding directors, employees and former directors and employees) or which states in its Memorandum of Association that it is public company. All other companies are private companies. Public company may, unlike private company, circulate prospectus, and must, unlike private company, appoint auditors to audit its financial statements.

Issue of Shares and Securities.—The Control of Borrowing (Jersey) Order 1958 provides that company may not issue shares or securities without obtaining prior consent of Finance and Economics Committee of States of Jersey, who delegate their responsibilities in this regard to Financial Services Department. In view of this requirement, it is normal practice for general consent to issue of shares to be obtained on incorporation of company by submission of application form containing prescribed information, which includes names and addresses of ultimate beneficial owners of company.

Share capital of company may be denominated in any currency. Law permits issue, subject to certain conditions, of fractions of shares and of redeemable shares. Shares may not be issued at no par value or at discount.

Licence to Carry on Business.—Like an individual company which trades in Jersey, such that it occupies office space or retains employees in Jersey, requires consent to carry on business under Regulation of Undertakings and Development (Jersey) Law 1973, unless business has been carried on at same premises since date prior to 1 Jan. 1974.

Management and Directors.—Management of company is governed by its Articles of Association which will usually provide that directors have general management and control of company. Private company needs only one director but public company must have at least minimum two directors. Body corporate may not be director.

Prospectuses.—Circulation of prospectus by company (other than open-ended collective investment fund which is regulated under collective investment funds legislation) is regulated by Companies (General Provisions) (Jersey) Order 1992 which provides that certain information must be contained in prospectus and requires that consent of Registrar of Companies be obtained prior to circulating prospectus. For these purposes prospectus means invitation to public to acquire or apply for any securities in company.

See Topical Index in front part of this volume.

CORPORATIONS . . . *continued*

Reports and Registers.—Company must file each year annual return with Registrar of Companies containing certain limited prescribed information concerning its issued shares and shareholders as at 1 Jan., together with requisite fee. Public companies must also file audited accounts.

Certain registers, including register of shareholders and directors must be maintained by company at its registered office.

COURTS:

Civil.—Royal Court, as civil court is regulated primarily by Royal Court (Jersey) Law 1948 as amended. Royal Court is divided into Héritage Division, Matrimonial Causes Division, Probate Division and Samedi Division. Essentially Héritage Division deals with immoveable property. Matrimonial Causes Division deals with family law matters. Probate Division deals with probate and administration and testamentary causes in relation to movables. Samedi Division deals with anything not within jurisdiction of other three divisions. Appeals are to Court of Appeal.

Court of Appeal.—This court (criminal and civil) consists of three judges selected from panel. They can sit ad hoc but usually hear cases in Island during four week-long sessions each year. Panel consists of Bailiffs and Deputy Bailiffs of Jersey and Guernsey and usually about ten eminent English QCs. On most occasions Court comprises three of those QCs and it has not yet sat in Jersey with more than one of Channel Islands judges. Appeals from Court of Appeal are to Privy Council.

Criminal.—Royal Court may sit as Inferior Number, Superior Number or as Assize. Inferior Number consists of Bailiff (chief judge) together with two Jurats (lay magistrates who decide questions of fact, unless there is Assize, and sentencing); Superior Number which consists of Bailiff and at least five Jurats; Assize which consists of Bailiff, at least three Jurats and jury of 12 members of public. In latter case, jury will decide verdict, Jurats, sentence and Bailiff will advise on questions of law. Procedure for Assize is dealt with by Loi (1864) réglant la procédure criminelle. Assizes are held six times a year if need be, and, if need be, there can be supplementary sittings. Appeals are to Court of Appeal.

Judicial Committee of Privy Council.—This consists of Lord Chancellor of England and Wales, Lords of Appeal if Privy Councillors, and other members of Privy Council who have held high judicial office in UK or colonies.

Petty Debts Court is governed by Loi (1867) sur la cour pour le recouvrement des menues dettes. Its jurisdiction includes claims for liquidated sums up to £2,500 and cases of eviction of tenants. It also has limited jurisdiction in making of separation and maintenance orders. Court usually sits only once a week. It is presided over by one of judges of Police Court. Appeals from Petty Debts Court are to Royal Court.

Police Court.—This is governed by Loi (1853) établissant la cour pour la repression des moindres délits, Loi (1864) réglant la procédure criminelle and Police Court (Miscellaneous Provisions) (Jersey) Law 1949.

Almost all criminal cases are initially brought before Police Court. It is presided over by single stipendiary magistrate or his deputy (who are legally qualified) or, exceptionally, by Jurat. Judge has limited powers of sentencing. He may commit to Royal Court for trial and/or sentence.

Royal Court.—See subheads Civil and Criminal, supra.

Youth Court and Youth Appeal Court.—These are governed by Criminal Justice (Young Offenders) (Jersey) Law 1994.

Youth Court deals with young persons under age of 18.

CURRENCY:

Finance & Economics Committee of States of Jersey has exclusive right to issue and redeem notes and coins. Currency of Jersey is Jersey Pound which is divided into 100p.

Jersey Pound is equal to one Pound Sterling and can be exchanged for Pounds Sterling freely. By Bank Notes (Jersey) Law 1955 English bank notes are legal tender in Jersey.

DEATH (PRESUMPTIONS OF AND ACTIONS FOR):

Presumption of Death.—Individual is presumed dead if absent from island for seven years without news.

Where applicant for grant of probate or administration of estate who is unable to furnish evidence of death of person in respect of whose personal estate application is made, Royal Court will convene applicant and such other persons as it may deem fit and make declaration of presumption of death if it is satisfied beyond all reasonable doubt that death has occurred.

Registration.—All deaths must be registered.

Actions for Causing Death.—Fatal Accidents (Jersey) Law 1962 provides that if death is caused by wrong which would be actionable if deceased had survived, action may be brought by relative. Every action must be brought by executor/administrator save that if he fails to bring action within six months, relatives can bring action. Any action must be brought within three years of death.

Customary Law Amendment (Jersey) Law 1948 states that all actions for or against deceased survive death, except defamation, seduction, adultery or enticement away of spouse. Actions in tort can only be brought if proceedings were pending at death, or are brought within six months of probate. If person dies before or at same time as damage he causes, cause of action will deem to have existed at time of death.

DEPOSITIONS:

Civil.—Service of Process and Taking of Evidence (Jersey) Law 1960 governs obtaining of evidence in Jersey in respect of foreign civil proceedings. Upon Royal Court receiving letters of request from foreign court for disclosure, Royal Court may make provision for examination of witnesses, either orally or in writing, for production of documents, or for inspection, photocopying, preservation, custody or detention of any property. However, no evidence may be obtained which could not be obtained by ordinary rules of discovery of civil proceedings in Royal Court. Application for taking of evidence may be heard by judge in chambers to preserve confidentiality.

Criminal.—Evidence (Proceedings in Other Jurisdictions) (Jersey) Order 1983 governs obtaining of evidence in respect of criminal proceedings in other jurisdictions. Application must be made by court or similar tribunal outside Jersey in respect of criminal proceedings which are not of political nature and which have actually been instituted. Royal Court can order examination of witnesses or production of documents. Royal Court cannot require steps to be taken which could not be taken in criminal proceedings in Jersey. (See also Investigation of Fraud (Jersey) Law 1991 and Drug Trafficking Offences (Jersey) Law 1988.)

DISPUTE RESOLUTION:

Mandatory Dispute Resolution.—There are no local statutes or court rules of general application requiring that litigation within Island be transferred to alternate dispute systems such as fact finding, mediation, arbitration or minitrials. However, Royal Court has recognised arbitrations on principle that "la convention fait la loi des parties", agreement makes law between parties, (see topic Contracts, subhead Formation of Contracts). Thus, where litigation arises out of contract and which incorporates arbitration clause then Royal Court may stay action commenced before it unless all parties agree for arbitration requirement to be waived. Although Royal Court claims inherent jurisdiction to set aside arbitration awards it will only interfere with arbitration award if it has not been regularly made. Royal Court will not interfere with finding of fact by arbitrator properly arrived at and will only interfere with mistake of law if there has been manifest error.

Voluntary Dispute Solution.—See subhead Mandatory Dispute Resolution, supra.

EXCHANGE CONTROL:

There are no restrictions on transfer of funds into or out of Jersey save where Jersey is party to or otherwise affected by international protocols.

EXECUTIONS:

Any Royal Court judgment may authorise plaintiff to distrain on defendant's goods (with exceptions being made for workmen's tools, books of profession etc). Viscount will then sell goods distrained at public auction or privately. Distraint order lasts for ten years. In addition, individual may be imprisoned for nonpayment of judgment debt.

FOREIGN EXCHANGE:

There are no restrictions on foreign exchange. See topic Exchange Control.

FOREIGN INVESTMENT:

No restrictions. See topic Exchange Control.

FRAUD:

Investigation of Fraud (Jersey) Law 1991 has provided wide powers to Attorney General to investigate fraud. Attorney General's powers are exercisable where there is suspected offence involving serious or complex fraud, wherever committed, and there is good reason to do so for purposes of investigating affairs of any person. Attorney General may, by notice in writing, require person whose affairs are to be investigated, or any other person who he has reason to believe has relevant information, to answer questions or otherwise furnish information. Attorney General may also, by notice in writing, require any person under investigation to produce documents. Also, Attorney General, on application to Bailiff, may issue warrant to search premises and take possession of documents.

Fraudulent Sales and Conveyances.—In certain circumstances, transfers of property may be set aside or declared void. Generally, all transactions relating to immoveable property (except leases of up to nine years duration) must be passed before court and registered in Public Registry or will be void. Once documents are registered in public records they acquire prima facie validity and will stand until they fall by "moyen de nullité" (means of nullity e.g. error, violence etc.—see topic Contracts). Conveyances may be void where person lacks legal capacity, where contract is against public policy or where it lacks formality. In addition, customary concept of "déception d'outre moitié" states that, where property is disposed of for less than half of its value, it is voidable at instance of injured party. (See topic Bankruptcy for description of fraudulent transactions and preferences.) (See also topic Contracts generally.) Individual (e.g., creditor) has right to lodge opposition, in writing, with Royal Court against alienation of property of debtor. Royal Court Rules provide that any contract of alienation passed while caveat or injunction is in force, is absolutely void. Caveat against passing of contract of alienation remains in force for six months but may be renewed from time to time.

GARNISHMENT:

(See generally topics Attachment and Executions.)

INSOLVENCY:

(See generally topic Bankruptcy.)

INTEREST:

Interest is payable either by agreement between parties or when allowed by specific legislation (for example, where late payment of income tax is made) or may be allowed by Court on judgment debt for such period and at such rate or rates as Court may deem fit.

There is no specific law against usury but Court may refuse to enforce extortionate interest claims. Whether or not something is extortionate will depend on circumstances. There is no statutory definition of the term.

JUDGMENTS:

Any actionable wrong can be rectified by judgment or order of Royal Court. In cases of liquidated demands, sued for in Royal Court, summary judgment may be obtained where it is clear that there is no prima facie defence. Judgment in default can be entered

JUDGMENTS . . . *continued*
where defendant does not acknowledge order of justice or summons, does not file defence, or fails to heed court order.

Foreign judgments can be enforced by action at common law in Jersey courts and underlying issues cannot normally be reopened, provided defendant was present in jurisdiction of foreign court when proceedings were begun, or submitted to jurisdiction. Judgments (Reciprocal Enforcement) (Jersey) Law 1960 applies to foreign judgments of Superior Courts of England, Wales, Scotland, Northern Ireland, Isle of Man and Guernsey and may be used in respect of judgments that are final and conclusive for payment of liquidated sum of money. Law does not apply to matrimonial matters, administration of estates, bankruptcy, winding-up and lunacy or guardianship of infants. Application must be made within six years of judgment. Foreign court must have jurisdiction and judgment may be set aside in certain circumstances. Maintenance Orders (Facilities for Enforcement) (Jersey) Law 1953 provides for reciprocal enforcement of maintenance orders between certain jurisdictions.

LAWS, REGULATIONS, LAW REPORTS, CODES, ETC.:

States of Jersey is legislative body of the Island. Since 1771 all "lois" have been published in volumes of "Recueils des Lois". Volumes of subordinate legislation (Regulations and Orders) have been published since 1939.

Since 1950 reasoned judgments of Royal Court have been given, most important of these having been published in series called "Jersey Judgments". New commercial series of reports called "Jersey Law Reports" was first published in 1987. Code of 1771 provides consolidation of preexisting legislative process. Recourse is also had to Norman customary law and Jersey and Norman commentators, particularly in areas of succession and land law. (See also topic Contracts.)

LAWYERS:

See topic Attorneys and Counsellors (Lawyers).

LIMITATION OF ACTIONS:

40 Years: Action to prove title in relation to land must be brought within 40 years.

Ten Years: Simple contracts and judgments of Royal Court and Petty Debts Court. "Droit de suite" of judicial and legal hypothecs is prescribed after ten years with certain exceptions.

Six Years: Registration of foreign judgment. (See topic Judgments.)

Three Years: Torts—three years from date on which cause of action accrued or three years from date of death (see topic Death [Presumptions of and Actions for]).

A Year and a Day: Action on agreement for sale. Rectification of contract. Action to annul contract (except in cases of "deception d'outre moitie" [where property is disposed of for less than half its value]). Action to nullify will of realty (from date of registration of will). Action to nullify will of personalty (from date of probate). Actions to regain possession of land.

Six Months: See topic Death (Presumptions of and Actions for). See also topic Fraud, subhead Fraudulent Sales and Conveyances.

40 Days: Landlord's right to follow moveables for rent to third party may not be exercised against bona fide purchaser after 40 days.

NOTARIES PUBLIC:

See topic Affidavits.

PARTNERSHIPS:

Partnerships may be either ordinary partnerships established under common law or limited partnerships established under Limited Partnerships (Jersey) Law 1994.

Limited partnerships are governed by Limited Partnerships (Jersey) Law 1994. Limited partnership must comprise at least one general partner and one limited partner, although there is no restriction on number of partners. There is no requirement that any of partners, including general partners, be resident in Jersey, although partnership must have registered office in Jersey.

Limited partnership is formed by declaration in prescribed form being registered with Registrar of Limited Partnerships. Creation of partnership interests may require consent of Finance and Economics Committee of the States of Jersey (who delegate their responsibility in this regard to Financial Services Department) under Control of Borrowing (Jersey) Order 1958. Although general partner is liable for all debts of partnership, liability of limited partners is restricted to amount agreed to be contributed to partnership by them, unless limited partner participates in management of partnership, in which case he may incur liability as general partner.

Ordinary Partnerships.—There is no limit on number of persons who may constitute partnership. Each partner impliedly confers on his partners apparent authority to incur debts on behalf of partnership and to bind all partners. Partnership has no legal personality distinct from partners comprised in it.

PLEDGES:

Pledge of personal chattels is transfer, by delivery of immediate possession, by way of security for performance of obligation, pledger remaining owner of chattels but pledgee acquiring right to sell (but not foreclose), in event of default. In respect of intangible moveable property, reference must be had to Security Interests (Jersey) Law 1983. (See topic Assignments.)

PRESCRIPTION:

See topic Limitation of Actions.

STATUTES:

Sources of law in Jersey are primarily Acts of the States of Jersey ("States") sanctioned by English Crown in Council (Lois), triennial regulations passed by States, prerogative orders of English Crown in Council and Acts of Parliament of the UK which apply expressly to Jersey. (See also topic Laws, Regulations, Law Reports, Codes, Etc.)

CHILE LAW DIGEST REVISER

Curtis, Mallet-Prevost, Colt & Mosle
101 Park Avenue
New York, New York 10178-0061
Telephone: 212-696-6141
Fax: 212-697-1559
Email: CMP-NY@mcimail.com

Reviser Profile

The Firm began in 1830 when two practicing lawyers started a long line of lawyers and law firms extending in an unbroken chain up to the present time. In 1897, the firm name became Curtis, Mallet-Prevost & Colt; in 1925 it was changed to Curtis, Mallet-Prevost, Colt & Mosle. The Firm is now made up of approximately 120 lawyers, including experts who have published extensively on such diverse subjects as international money management, transnational contracts, state contracts, litigation against foreign states, sovereign immunity and the act of state doctrine, and the International Court of Justice. Its principal offices are in New York City. There are branch offices in Paris, London, Frankfurt Am Main, Hong Kong, Washington, D.C., Houston, Texas, Newark, N.J., and Mexico City. The Firm has five departments: Corporate and International; Litigation; Real Estate; Tax; and Trusts and Estates. The corporate and international department acts as general counsel to various public and private corporations and individual entrepreneurs. Clients are in the banking, insurance, securities, manufacturing, real estate and oil and gas industries. In addition, the corporate and international department frequently acts as special counsel to domestic and foreign clients, providing assistance in financing, know-how licensing, the negotiation and drafting of all types of contracts and instruments, counselling on all aspects of corporate law, and establishing the vehicles necessary to enable clients to conduct their domestic and foreign business activities. The Firm's international work permeates all areas of its practice and involves questions of private international law, foreign law and an unusual amount of public and quasi-public international law. Traditionally, much of the Firm's international practice has been concerned with Latin America. The Firm maintains its excellence in that area, with its Mexican affiliate, and also through the expertise of Latin American lawyers based in the New York office. The Firm's international practice has undergone a major expansion beyond Latin America to Europe, Africa and the Near and Far East. The Firm's litigation practice includes commercial litigation and arbitration, and white-collar criminal defense. It has substantial experience in civil aviation matters; it also has represented foreign States in transnational litigation and international arbitration arising out of acts of nationalization and alleged breach of economic development or natural resource supply contracts. Among the Firm's clients in real estate matters are institutional lenders and investors, real estate developers, both individual and corporate, foreign and domestic investors and syndicators. The tax department has substantial experience in all aspects of domestic and international business tax matters and real estate taxation. The matters the tax department deals with on a regular basis include: Taxation of foreign investments; the structuring of corporate transactions, including mergers, acquisitions, liquidations and reorganization; federal and state tax litigation; and tax planning for U.S. and foreign individuals. The trusts and estates department engages in general domestic trusts and estates practice and in tax planning for foreign persons wishing to invest in U.S. assets through offshore trusts and corporations. It represents individuals, trust companies, and banks acting as fiduciaries. It works for various charitable organizations located both in the United States and abroad including private foundations, museums, universities and hospitals. A group of fiduciary accountants with vast experience in the field assists the lawyers of the trusts and estates department. Curtis, Mallet-Prevost, Colt & Mosle has served as a Reviser for most of Latin American Law Digests since 1930.

CHILE LAW DIGEST

(The following is a list of all Topics, including cross-references, covered in this Digest.)

CHILE LAW DIGEST

Revised for 1997 edition by

CURTIS, MALLET-PREVOST, COLT & MOSLE, of the New York Bar.

(Abbreviations used are: C. C.—Civil Code; C. C. P.—Code of Civil Procedure; C. Com.—Code of Commerce; L. C.—Labor Code; L. J. O.—Law of Judicial Organization; t.o.—compiled text.)

ABSENTEES: See topic Death.

ACKNOWLEDGMENTS:

(L. J. O. 419-421, C. C. 1699, C. C. P. 345).

According to the system in force generally where the civil law prevails, contracts, deeds and other documents which require authentication by a public official are prepared by a notary or other authorized officer and made a part of his protocol; that is to say, the original documents are kept in an official registry in the office of the notary or official. (See topics Notaries Public and Public Instruments.) However, private documents may be acknowledged before a notary. Documents executed abroad, in conformity with law of country where executed, are entitled to recognition in Chilean courts with same force as in country where executed, if duly authenticated by consular or diplomatic agent of Chile or of country where executed, and authentication is certified to by Minister of Foreign Affairs of Chile. Legal effect which in U.S. is secured by seals and acknowledgments is obtained in Chile by having document executed before notary in form known as public instrument.

ACTIONS:

Limitation of.—See topic Prescription, subhead Actions.

ADMINISTRATION:

See topic Executors and Administrators.

ADOPTION:

(Law 18703 of Apr. 26, 1988).

There are two types of adoption: Partial adoption (adopción simple) and full adoption (adopción plena).

Partial Adoption.—Individuals of legal age and capacity may adopt minor under 18 years; adopting party must be 15 years older than adopted party, and must have been taking care of minor at least six months before adoption. Partial adoption does not extinguish legal bonds between adopted person and his natural family but suspends parental authority of his natural parents. Partial adoption ends by legal age of adopted party, by court sentence or by another adoption.

Full Adoption.—Spouses married for at least four years, over 25 years and under 60 years of age (and in certain cases widows and widowers) may adopt minor under 18 years of age; except with judge's approval or when adopting party is related to minor adopting parties must be 20 years older than adopted party; adopting parties must have been taking care of minor at least one year before adoption.

Full adoption extinguishes legal bonds between adopted person and natural family. Full adoption is irrevocable but may be declared invalid by court sentence. All adoption proceedings must be made before judge of same domicile as adopting parties. Minors to be adopted abroad can leave country only with Court's authorization. Adoption in these cases is governed by law of country where adoption is effected.

ADVERSE POSSESSION: See topic Prescription.

AGENCY: See topic Principal and Agent.

AIRCRAFT: See topic Motor Vehicles.

ALIENS:

Foreigners need a passport with a visa for entering in Chile, but tourists need no visa and are permitted to remain up to a 90 day period, renewable once. There are special visas for "residents under contract", "resident students", "temporary residents", and "political refugee residents". There are besides diplomatic and official visas. There are special provisions for sailors and persons in tourist ships. Undesirable foreigners or foreigners entering illegally are subject to deportation. Permanent residence may be obtained after a determined period of stay or residence, according to category of the applicant. Immigrants may apply for permanent residence after two years.

Immigrants must have an Immigration Card. All foreigners over 18, except tourists, must hold a "Personal Identification Card" and request registration within 30 days after arrival in the Special Registry of Foreigners kept by the Service of Investigation.

There are numerous laws governing these matters, including Decree with force of Law 69 of Apr. 27, 1953, Decree-Law 1094 of July 14, 1975 am'd.

ASSIGNMENTS:

Title to personal property may be transferred either by public or private instrument. See topics Deeds; Public Instruments; Sales (Realty and Personalty).

ASSIGNMENTS FOR BENEFIT OF CREDITORS:

A debtor who is not a merchant may assign all his property for the payment of his debts if conditions are not such as to warrant a declaration of bankruptcy. If there is but one creditor the assignment is made to him; if there are more, it is made to the official receiver of the district. The creditors may object and if their objections are sustained by the court, the debtor is declared a bankrupt. (C. C., arts. 1614-1627; Law 18175 of Oct. 13, 1982, arts. 241-255).

ASSOCIATIONS:

Benevolent associations are governed by special provisions of Civil Code. They must be authorized by a special law or have approval of President of Republic. (C. C. arts. 545-564 Decree 110 of Jan. 17, 1979). Special laws govern workmen's associations (Labor Code) and cooperative associations. (Sup. Decree 502 of Nov. 9, 1978).

ATTACHMENT:

Attachments are granted only in the summary actions known as executory actions or in the execution of judgments, but the following "precautionary measures" are available in other suits: (1) The judicial deposit of personal property which is the object of the suit and which is in danger of being lost; (2) the appointment of supervisors for real or other property and the retention of the income therefrom, if there is danger that the rights of the plaintiff may be injured; (3) the retention of monies or personal property if the defendant has insufficient property to guaranty the results of the suit or there is reason to believe that he will conceal his assets; (4) the prohibition to act or contract with respect to property which is the object of the suit, or in other cases when the assets of the defendant are insufficient to guaranty the results of the suit. (C. C. P. arts. 290-302).

AUTOMOBILES: See topic Motor Vehicles.

BANKRUPTCY AND INSOLVENCY:

(Bankruptcy Law 18175 of Oct. 13, 1982 as am'd).

Person may be declared bankrupt on his own behalf or on application of creditor. Person dedicated to commercial, industrial, mining or agricultural activities has duty of filing bankruptcy petition within 15 days after defaulting in payment of mercantile obligation. Creditors may make application: (a) When debtor is person dedicated to commercial, industrial, mining or agricultural activities and defaults in payment of any mercantile obligation; (b) when debtor against whom three or more overdue documents are outstanding on which summary executive actions might be based and against whom two such actions have actually been instituted, does not within four days satisfy claims; (c) when debtor has absconded; and (d) when settlement made by him with his creditors is annulled.

There are official receivers appointed by Government. Upon declaration of bankruptcy local receiver takes charge of assets and business, collects sums due bankrupt and notifies creditors to file their claims in 30 days; foreign creditors have additional time designated in notice. Receiver reports on such claims and makes list of creditors. Meetings of creditors are held on dates and times fixed by first creditors' meeting and when requested by receiver, bankrupt, or creditors representing one-fourth of liabilities. On declaration of bankruptcy all debts of bankrupt fall due. Receiver makes distribution of assets whenever sums available amount to 5% of liabilities.

Bankruptcy may be: (1) Fortuitous; (2) culpable; or (3) fraudulent. In latter two cases bankrupt is subject to criminal prosecution and cannot be discharged until he has served his sentence and unless all his liabilities are paid.

The bankruptcy proceedings are suspended when the assets are insufficient to pay the costs of the proceedings; during the period of suspension the creditors may bring individual actions against the debtor. Bankruptcy proceedings are terminated and the debtor is discharged: (a) Upon agreement of the creditors; (b) when all claims are paid or bond is given for their payment; (c) upon the expiration of two years after approval of the final report of the receiver, provided the bankruptcy was fortuitous and the debtor has not been convicted of fraud.

Offers of composition made before the bankruptcy declaration require the consent of all creditors. Those made afterwards can be considered after the receiver has filed a list of recognized credits and provided the debtor was not guilty of fraud. In such case a meeting of creditors is called and the composition is accepted if agreed to by the debtor and two-thirds of the creditors present, such majority representing three-fourths of all the liabilities. Objecting creditors may appeal to the court against the composition. Foreign creditors who have not yet appeared are considered as objecting.

See also topic Fraudulent Sales and Conveyances.

BILLS AND NOTES:

(C. Com., arts. 620-781; Law 18092 of Dec. 23, 1981; Law 18155 of Aug. 4, 1982).

Bills of exchange must show following: (1) Statement that document is bill of exchange in same language as entire document; (2) place and date of issue; if place is not indicated, domicile of drawer will be considered as place of issue; (3) unconditional order to drawee to pay certain amount of money; (4) name of payee; (5) name and address of drawee; (6) place and date of payment; if place is not indicated payment must be done at domicile of drawee; if date of payment is not indicated, bill is payable at sight; (7) signature of drawer. If bill lacks any of these requisites it is considered as simple promise to pay. If bill contains phrase "value received" consideration is understood to have been cash.

Endorsements must set forth signature of endorser and may have place and date and name of endorser. Endorsement with statement "value in collection" is merely collection fee. Endorsement in blank, with or without date, transfers ownership and authorizes endorsee to fill in requirements of endorsements. Additional clauses aimed to encumber legal effects of endorsements are invalid. Endorsement of matured drafts has effect of mere assignment.

Drafts at period after sight must be presented for acceptance within one year. Drafts drawn for payment within fixed period after date must be presented for acceptance

See Topical Index in front part of this volume.

BILLS AND NOTES . . . *continued*
within such period. Those in which payment date is designated also need to be presented for acceptance before designated date.

Acceptance is signified by writing the words "I accept" or "Accepted" or similar words, with the signature of the acceptor, or the mere signature, and if payable at a period after sight the date of acceptance must be added. Acceptance may be for a smaller amount not less than one-half the par value of the draft, but if a conditional acceptance is admitted, the holder assumes all the risks of the draft. Acceptance imposes on the acceptor the obligation of paying at maturity unless he proves that the bill was a forgery. If acceptance is refused, the bill must be protested.

Bills whether accepted or not must be presented for payment on their due date, or if that be holiday, Sat. or Dec. 31, on following working day. There are no days of grace.

In case of nonacceptance, bills must be protested. In case of nonpayment they must also be protested, even though previously protested for nonacceptance. The obligation to protest is not removed by the death, interdiction or bankruptcy of the drawee. In case of his bankruptcy protest may be made before the due date.

Upon protest, the holder, by the first or second mail, must advise his assignor of the protest. Such assignor in turn must advise his assignor, and so on until the drawer is reached. The holder must demand payment or acceptance from the person designated by the drawer or endorsers. Failure to protest causes the holder to lose his rights against the drawer and endorsers, unless the drawee or acceptor becomes bankrupt before the date of maturity.

The proper time for making protests is before 3 P. M. on the day following that on which acceptance or payment was refused. The protest will be cancelled if the amount of the draft and the expenses of the protest are paid before sunset on the same day. A protest must be made before a notary public and must appear on back of document or in additional paper. Protested drafts bear interest at current rate from day of protest provided there is not agreement in matter.

Promissory notes, payable to order, should contain: (1) Statement that document is promissory note in same language as entire document; (2) unconditional promise of payment of certain amount; (3) place and date of payment; (4) name of payee; (5) place and date of issue; (6) signature of maker. They are generally subject to law governing bills of exchange. If not payable to order they are subject to rules of Civil Code regarding transfer of credits.

Checks, in addition to stating whether they are to bearer or drawn to the order of a particular person, may contain only: (1) Name of drawee; (2) date and place where drawn; (3) amount in words and figures; (4) signature of drawer. They must be presented within 60 days if drawn in the place where they are payable, within 90 days if drawn elsewhere in Chile, and within three months if drawn outside the country. Failure to present within these periods causes holder to lose right of action against endorsers, and also against drawer if payment becomes impossible through fault of drawee. After said periods drawee may refuse to honor check. Duplicate checks are forbidden, unless payable abroad. In case of loss of a check, holder must notify drawee, publish loss in a newspaper for three days and advise drawer and endorser, or apply to court and give bond. Checks may be crossed and in that case are payable only to a bank. Checks may be protested for non-payment, in which case an executory suit and criminal action may be brought thereon within one year after protest; otherwise, payment can be enforced only by an ordinary suit. (Decree with force of Law 707 of July 21, 1982 as am'd).

CHATTEL MORTGAGES:

Chattel mortgages, except the special contracts known as agrarian and industrial pledges, and the special lien in instalment sales, are unknown to the law of Chile. In general mortgages may be placed only on real property and real estate rights. Personal property such as machinery, pictures, statuary, etc., is included in mortgage on realty when it forms an inherent part of the realty.

Agrarian pledges may cover: (1) Animals and their products; (2) machinery and tools; (3) seeds, crops and fruits; (4) lumber. They must appear in a public instrument (q. v.) and be recorded in a special registry in office of real property registrar. In suits for their enforcement only a limited number of defenses is allowed. (Law 4097 of Sept. 24, 1926 as am'd, and its regulations Decree 1511 of Sept. 29, 1927, Decree with Force of Law 251 of Mar. 30, 1960).

Industrial pledges may cover industrial and mining installations, machinery, tools and products. In general they are subject to the same rules as agrarian pledges. (Law 5687 of Sept. 16, 1935 as am'd; Regulations decree 1274 of Apr. 5, 1928).

Instalment sales are authorized in which the unpaid part of the price is secured by a chattel mortgage on the object sold. Such contracts may cover most non-fungible identifiable chattels. The contract must be made before a notary or an official of the civil registry and recorded in a special registry. (Law 4702 of Dec. 6, 1929 as am'd. Regulations by Decree 2836 of Dec. 31, 1929).

CLAIMS:

See topic Executors and Administrators.

COLLATERAL SECURITY: See topic Pledges.

COMMERCIAL REGISTER: See topic Records.

COMMUNITY PROPERTY:

See topic Husband and Wife.

CONSTITUTION AND GOVERNMENT:

Decree 1150 of Oct. 21, 1980 as am'd approved and promulgated Constitution in effect. State of Chile is unitary, its territory is divided into regions. Law will endeavor to get decentralized administration. Government of Chile is democratic republic. Chileans are: Those born in territory of Chile; children of Chilean father or mother born in foreign territory, if serving Republic, or when said children live in Chile for more than year; foreigners may obtain letters of naturalization according to law, upon express renunciation of former nationality. However, renunciation of foreign nationality shall not be required from persons born in foreign country which, by virtue of international treaty, grants same right to Chilean. Chilean nationality is lost: By naturalization in foreign country, except in cases where Chilean nationality has not been lost due to international treaty; by cancellation of letters of naturalization and by lending aid during war to enemies of Chile or their allies; by judicial sentence due to crime against country or against interest of state. Chileans who have attained 18 years of age, have not been condemned to corporal punishment, and are inscribed in electoral registry are citizens with right of suffrage. Same applies to foreigners residing in country for more than five years. Citizenship is lost: When nationality is lost, by sentence of corporal punishment or terrorist crimes.

C. III of Constitution contains constitutional guaranties and bill of rights. C. IV regulates Executive Power and Ministers of State as well as general bases for administration of state and state of emergency in case of war, emergency or public calamity. C. V contains powers and limitations of National Congress which is composed of two branches: House of Representatives and Senate. Former is composed of members elected by electoral districts by direct vote and in manner prescribed by electoral law. It is renewed every four years. Latter is composed of members elected by direct ballot for each regional group. Each group is entitled to elect two senators, which will be elected for eight years and renewed every four years. Congress alone has power to legislate. Judicial Power shall be vested in Supreme Court of Justice and in such lower courts established by law. Independently there are special courts such as: Constitutional Court, Elections Court, and Military Courts. C. XII provides that Central Bank, technical and independent agency, is prohibited from extending loan guaranties to financial public or private institutions. Republic of Chile is divided for governmental purposes into regions. These into provinces, these into communes. Executive head in region is Intendente, in province Governor, in commune Major and Communal Council. Each region will have council for regional development provided by Intendente and composed of Governors of respective Provinces. C. XIV contains special provisions for amendment of Constitution.

CONVEYANCES: See topic Deeds.

COPYRIGHT:

(Code of Intellectual Property, Law 17336 of Aug. 28, 1970 as am'd; regulated by Decree 1122 of May 17, 1971 and Law 17773 of Oct. 18, 1972).

Copyrights may cover any form of intellectual expression, whether scientific, artistic or musical. Books, pamphlets, articles, lectures of any kind including encyclopedias, dictionaries, and all type of digests are included in law. Plays, either dramatic or musicals, choreographies, ballets, photographs, lithographs, movie scripts, architectural projects, maps (of any type), paintings, sculptures, videos, software, "diaporama", and any other manifestation of intellectual production are covered by provisions set forth in sections of law. Owner of intellectual property has exclusive right to reproduce it in any manner; such ownership remains in his control for life and then to his heirs, legatees or assignees for 50 years only. However, in case of surviving spouse, or single or widowed daughters, right to ownership will also be for lifetime.

After that time, works revert to national patrimony, as well as those art manifestations when their authors are unknown or when they are simply expressions of folklore such as legends, dances and popular songs.

In case of several authors, 50 year term starts to run after death of last surviving co-author.

Works must be recorded in National Register of Intellectual Property, in case of sculptures, engineering projects, paintings, etc., a photograph of same is sufficient provided it accurately shows its details, attached to a writing specifying personal data of author, co-authors, collaborators, authors using pseudonyms, if any, etc. Regarding motion pictures or plays, it is enough to deposit copy of plot, scenario and script.

Law also contains detailed provisions regarding first publication, as well as for further reproduction and editions of intellectual works and their illegal use and reproduction.

Chile ratified Inter-American Treaty on copyright signed in Washington in 1946. In effect by Decree 74 of Feb. 16, 1955 and Universal Convention signed in Geneva by Decree 75 of July 26, 1955. Also by Decree 121 of Mar. 20, 1973, Chile ratified Berne Agreement of Sept. 9, 1886, as revised in Brussels on June 26, 1948 for protection of Literary and Artistic Works. Also ratified Convention signed in Geneva, Oct. 29, 1971 for protection of record player manufacturers.

CORPORATIONS:

Corporations are governed by Laws 18046 of Oct. 21, 1981 as am'd, 18045 of Oct. 21, 1981 as am'd by Law 18482 of Dec. 27, 1985 and its Regulations, Decrees 587 of Aug. 4, 1982 as am'd, 4657 of Sept. 24, 1929, 6156 of Jan. 13, 1938, 16394 of Dec. 18, 1965, Decree-Law 251 of May 20, 1931, all of these as am'd. Agrarian Law 16640 of July 28, 1967, forbids corporations to be formed for purposes of agricultural exploitations or cattle raising. Corporations are also forbidden to purchase rural lands, with certain exceptions. Corporations can be formed for purposes of personal business.

Corporations may start operations after extract of public instrument executed before notary public containing charter and by-laws are registered at Registry of Commerce and published in official gazette. Any amendment of by-laws must be filed and published in like manner.

Corporations are formed without special governmental authorization. Corporations dedicated to banking, insurance, reinsurance, mutual funds, stock exchange, and other corporations regulated by special laws require governmental authorization.

Organization.—Corporations are designated by name accompanied by words "Sociedad Anónima" or abbreviation "S.A." At least two stockholders are required for organization and continued legal existence of corporation. There is no restriction as to nationality or residence of incorporators. Foreigners who act as incorporators, must appear in person before notary, unless they are represented by duly empowered agent. Chilean corporations may be organized outside of Chile. Corporate capital is divided into shares. Responsibility of shareholders is limited to their shares. One third of authorized capital shall be subscribed and paid in on incorporation. Unless subscription and payment of capital balance is made within three years, capital is reduced by

See Topical Index in front part of this volume.

CORPORATIONS . . . *continued*
operation of law to amount paid-in. There are "open" and "closed" corporations. "Open corporations" are: (1) Those which have their shares traded in Stock Exchange; (2) have at least 500 stockholders; (3) at least 10% of their subscribed capital belongs to no less than 100 stockholders. Open corporations should be registered at National Securities Registry and comply with special regulations. "Closed corporations" are those which do not fulfill any of above requirements.

Documents of incorporation should contain: (1) Name, profession, and domicile of incorporators; (2) name and domicile of corporation; (3) object; (4) duration; (5) capital, kind, number, value of shares, manner and time of payment and value given to consideration given for stock if other than money; (6) organization, administration and control by stockholders; (7) time when inventory and balance sheet should be drawn and regular meetings of stockholders held; (8) distribution of dividends; (9) liquidation; (10) arbitration; (11) temporary board of directors; (12) and any other agreement such as management, eligibility, liability and powers of directors, stockholder's meetings, etc.

Personal Liability.—Stockholders are liable for unpaid portion of their stock. In case corporation is declared null and void stockholders are unlimitedly liable. Joint owned stock results in joint liability of owners.

Management.—Corporations are managed by board of directors. Board of closed corporations must have minimum of three directors. Board of open corporations must have minimum of five directors who are elected by stockholders for maximum period of three years. Directors may be reelected indefinitely and need not be shareholders. Absent and/or incapacitated directors are replaced by their deputies. In case vacancy cannot be filled by deputy new board of directors should be appointed. By-laws may provide special rules for shares of different types. Directors may be remunerated as provided in by-laws. Matters in which directors have personal or third party interest should be called to attention of board and resolutions taken must be reported to next annual meeting of stockholders. Board of directors and manager, if appointed, represent corporation. Directors of open corporations cannot be managers. Stockholders' meetings are ordinary or extraordinary, and should be held at corporate domicile. Ordinary meetings are held at least once a year within four months of balance sheet date. Ordinary meetings should receive report of inspectors and auditors, discuss accounts of corporation, vote on allocation of net profit for fiscal year, distribute dividends and elect board of directors. Extraordinary meetings may be held at any time to decide on matters specially enumerated by law, such as modification of articles of incorporation, dissolution, issuance of bonds, sale of corporation's business, etc. Stockholders' meetings are called by board of directors. Notice must be published as stipulated in by-laws. In open corporations mail notice should be given to Superintendency of Values & Securities and to all stockholders within 15 days before meeting. Notice must contain agenda or statement of matters to be discussed. These requisites may be omitted if all shares are represented. Stockholders may be represented by proxies.

Superintendency of Values & Securities investigates open corporations and may send representative to stockholder's meetings. Subject to certain legal limitations dissident stockholders have right to withdraw from corporation.

Stock.—Capital and numbers of shares must be specified, and whether shares are with or without par value. Shares may be common or preferred. Preferred shares may be issued with or without voting rights or restricted voting rights. Otherwise, each share has one vote. All shares must be nominative. If any share is paid for otherwise than in money, such contribution must be evaluated by experts and submitted to stockholders' meeting for approval. Portions of shares not fully paid can be registered and shall be transferred by recording in stockholders' registry. If corporation acquires its own shares, those shares cannot be voted nor receive dividends, and should be sold on stock market within a year, otherwise capital is reduced by operation of law. Amount of corporate capital and value of shares may be increased or reduced by modification of articles of incorporation; also, corporation can modify its capital through stockholders' meeting approval of its balance sheet. Corporations are authorized to issue debentures which may be converted into shares or into promises to issue shares.

Fiscal Year and Financial Statements.—At annual meeting of stockholders of "closed corporation" two inspectors of accounts should be appointed to examine corporation's accounts, inventories, financial statement, and to file report at next stockholders' meeting. "Open corporations" shall appoint independent external auditors to examine corporation's accounts, inventories, financial statement and report at next stockholders meeting. Dividends may be declared only from profits shown by inventories and balance sheets approved by meeting of stockholders. Open corporations must distribute dividends in cash and at least 30% of profits, except when there is stockholders' agreement to contrary. In case of closed corporations dividends are distributed in accordance with by-laws.

Corporation's fiscal year ends Dec. 31, unless otherwise provided in by-laws. At end of each fiscal year, board of directors is required to submit to annual stockholders' meeting statement of results for fiscal year then ended, balance sheet, profit and loss statement and report filed by external auditors or inspectors. Financial statements of open corporations must be published before such meeting.

Dissolution.—Corporations are dissolved: (1) By expiration of term; (2) when all shares are owned by one person; (3) by resolution of stockholders; (4) by judicial order; (5) by governmental order; (6) by provision of by-laws. After declaration of dissolution, liquidation of corporate assets is entrusted to liquidators appointed by stockholders' meeting.

Controlled and Connected Corporations.—Corporation may be controlled (filial-matriz) directly or through another corporation, more than 50% of whose capital is owned by controlling corporation or when controlling corporation has power to elect majority of directors. Corporations are connected (coligadas) when, in absence of control one corporation holds 10% or more of other's capital. Controlled and connected corporations are required to prepare annual consolidated financial reports. Corporations that are controlled or connected cannot buy stock of controlling or connecting corporation.

Foreign Corporations.—Foreign corporation may be authorized to do business in Chile through registered branch upon compliance with following requisites: (a) Agent or representative must appear before notary public and incorporate into public document, following documents: (1) proof that corporation was constituted in accordance with laws of its country of origin, and certificate of its continued existence, (2) copy of by-laws, (3) power of attorney appointing and authorizing agent to act for corporation, accept judicial service and exercise full powers in connection with litigation, also it shall include proof of authority of corporate representative granting power. All documents must be legalized and translated into Spanish; (b) when appearing before notary agent must declare: (1) name under which corporation will act in Chile and its object, (2) that corporation is acquainted with Chilean laws and regulations which are to govern its agencies, acts, contracts, and obligations, (3) that corporation's property is subject to Chilean laws, (4) that corporation shall have enough assets in Chile to respond for its obligations, (5) amount of capital set aside for branch in Chile and date and form of payment thereof, (6) address of principal office. Extracts of public documents should be recorded in Registry of Commerce and published in official gazette. Branches of foreign corporations must publish annually branch balance sheet.

See also topic Exchange Control.

COURTS:

Justice is administered by: (1) law judges, at least one in each department, with original jurisdiction in civil, commercial, mining, and treasury matters whatever amount involved, and in criminal and labor matters; (2) courts of appeals, each with appellate jurisdiction in appeals from law judges and arbitrators, and administrative supervision over judges of their territory; (3) Supreme Court at Santiago, which hears appeals for errors of law from decisions of courts of appeals. (Law 7421 of Judicial Organization of June 15, 1943 as am'd).

CURRENCY:

Monetary unit is Peso, which is divided into 100 centavos. (Decree-Law 1078 of June 25, 1975 as am'd and Decree-Law 1123 of July 30, 1975 as am'd by Law 17996 of May 12, 1981). Only Banco Central may issue notes and these constitute legal tender for any obligation.

CURTESY:

No such right.

CUSTOMS:

Common External Tariff, approved by countries member of southern common market (MERCOSUR) is in effect; each member country has list of goods excluded from common external tariff and subject to their own duty rates. Most goods traded among member countries are not subject to tariff or quota restrictions.

DEATH:

Death of a person is presumed from his disappearance without knowledge of his whereabouts. Such presumption must be declared by judge of last domicile in Chile, upon proof that, after due efforts made, there has been no knowledge of whereabouts of person for at least five years, or six months in case of disappearance in loss of ship or aircraft and one year in earthquake. (C. C. arts. 80-94).

Deaths must be recorded in the Civil Registry. Death certificates are issued by the official in charge of the Civil Registry upon payment of the tax for stamped paper and a nominal local fee.

Actions for Death.—There is no specific wrongful death statute but the corresponding action may be supported by the general language of provisions on torts (C. C. 2314 et seq.). Some court decisions have granted damages for wrongful death to relatives who had a right to be supported or who were actually supported by decedent. Action is limited to four years.

DECEDENTS' ESTATES:

See topics Descent and Distribution; Executors and Administrators; Wills.

DEEDS:

(C. C. 686, 1801-1807, L. J. O. 403-439).

All transfers of title to real estate must be by public instrument (q. v.) and must contain a true statement of the consideration, since the state tax on transfers of title is based on the real consideration involved. The tax must be paid at the time the document is executed before the notary, or, if executed in a foreign country, at the time it is authenticated in Chile. Deeds must be recorded in the registries of property.

Both grantor and grantee must sign the deed and both must therefore be present before the notary at the same time. If one is absent he must be represented by an attorney in fact. The original deed, if executed in Chile, must remain in the files of the Chilean notary who gives to either party a certified copy which has the effect of an original in courts of law. If the deed is executed abroad, it must be authenticated by a Chilean consul or diplomatic agent.

DESCENT AND DISTRIBUTION:

(C. C. arts. 951-1385).

Estates of decedents pass either by will or by operation of law. The rights are transmitted from the moment of the decedent's death. The law designates various acts which render guilty parties incapable of inheriting, such as having committed a crime against the deceased, etc.

In default of testamentary provisions the bulk of the estate passes to the following in the order named: (1) Legitimate descendants; (2) ascendants; (3) legitimate and in some cases also natural brothers and sisters; (4) the spouse and natural children; (5) collaterals to the sixth degree; (6) the state. In the first three cases the spouse has a varying interest and in the second and third cases, the natural children. The shares of descendants and of brothers and sisters may pass to their heirs per stirpes.

Only part of the decedent's estate may be disposed of freely by will; a certain portion goes to the heirs by operation of law. Such "asignaciones forzosas" or "forced

DESCENT AND DISTRIBUTION . . . *continued*
legacies" are: (1) The support owed by the decedent to certain persons; (2) the conjugal portion which varies but never exceeds one-fourth of estate; (3) "legítimas" or "legal portions" pertaining to obligatory heirs; and (4) "mejoras" or "betterments."

Obligatory heirs are the descendants and ascendants. One-half of the estate must be divided among them in accordance with the rules relating to intestate succession; this half makes up the legal portions. If there are no legitimate descendants, the testator may freely dispose of the remaining half. If there are such descendants he must give one-fourth of his estate known as "betterments" to spouse or to one or more descendants and may freely dispose of only the remaining fourth. Obligatory heirs may be disinherited for certain reasons, such as having committed a crime against the testator, etc.

In order to be entitled to the inheritance, the heir must accept the same, and the acceptance may be unconditional or subject to the making of an inventory. If some heirs desire an inventory and others do not, all are obliged to accept subject to inventory. Acceptance may be express or implied. In the case of an unconditional acceptance the heir is liable for all the debts of the decedent, not only out of the estate which he accepts but also out of his own property. An acceptance with benefit of inventory or after the making of a formal inventory renders the heir responsible for the debts of the decedent only to the extent of the amount which he inherits and does not affect his own property.

If a testator has not appointed anyone to partition the estate the partition may be made by the heirs when all of them are capacitated to dispose of their property. Otherwise the partitioner is appointed by the judge. The partitioner must effect the partition within two years.

DESERTION: See topic Divorce.

DIVORCE:

Divorce does not dissolve the marriage bond but merely effects the separation of the spouses. It may be temporary, not exceeding five years, or permanent. It may be granted for the following causes: (1) Adultery; (2) serious and repeated ill treatment by deed or word; (3) commission or attempted commission of a crime against the property, honor or life of the other spouse; (4) attempt of one spouse to prostitute other spouse; (5) avarice of one spouse to point of depriving other of necessities; (6) refusal of one spouse without legal cause to follow other spouse; (7) abandonment or unjustified refusal to comply with conjugal obligations; (8) unjustified absence for over three years; (9) inveterate vice of gambling, drunkenness or dissipation; (10) conviction for crime; (11) corruption or attempted corruption of children; (12) ill treatment of children to point of endangering their life. Causes numbered 5, 6, 7, 8 and 12 cannot be grounds for permanent divorce. Divorce and its effects cease if parties consent to live together again, except in cases numbered 4 and 12 above. Public prosecutor is party in divorce actions.

The competent court is the court of the domicile of the defendant; the wife's domicile is the same as that of the husband while he lives in Chile.

The marriage bond will be definitely dissolved if one of the spouses has disappeared for 15 years, or has disappeared for five years and would be seventy years old or older. (Law Jan. 10, 1884 as am'd).

DOWER:

No dower right.

ENVIRONMENT:

(Basic Environmental Law, Law 19300 of Mar. 1st, 1994 as am'd, Regulations 86 of May 8, 1995, 93 and 94 of May 15, 1995).

Law regulates right to live in nonpolluted environment, environmental protection, preservation of nature and conservation of environmental patrimony. Law contains basic principles for interpretation of existing environmental regulations and for development of implementation laws. Environmental impact statements are mandatory for projects having environmental impact, such as, dams, thermoelectric and hydroelectric plants, nuclear plants, mining, oil, gas, airports, highways and roads, ports, real estate developments in congested areas, water pipelines, manufacturing plants, forestry projects, sanitary activities; production, storage, recycling toxic, inflammable and hazardous substances, among others. Other projects must file sworn environmental impact declaration that project or activity does not affect environment and does not violate environmental legislation. All projects must be approved by regional or national environmental commission. Law imposes liability to those who knowingly or negligently cause environmental damage. Liability includes payment for clean-up of environmental damage and indemnification according to law. Failure to comply with obligation to prevent damage to environment, clean-up plans and with legal provisions are sanctioned with warnings, fines, temporary or permanent closure of facilities or immediate suspension of activity causing damage.

EXCHANGE CONTROL:

(Law 18840 of Oct. 4, 1989 as am'd).

Banco Central de Chile regulates export and import trade and foreign exchange transactions, including commissions, insurance, freight balances, profits etc. earned abroad. There are two foreign exchange markets: Mercado Cambiario Formal and free market. Banco Central fixes exchange rate within Mercado Cambiario Formal. Export and import trade are free, except when forbidden or restricted by general provision of Treasury Department, but exporters shall turn proceeds over to authorized bank. Banco Central is empowered to reject imports under certain conditions.

Foreign capital coming to Chile can also be registered under Decree 600, of July 11, 1974 (see topic Foreign Investment), as am'd, called Foreign Investment Statute.

Debts in foreign money are subject to special rules.

Rules regarding foreign exchange operations, indicating markets, their revenues and disbursements and establishing penalties for violations thereof, issued at frequent intervals by Central Bank are to be taken into consideration.

EXECUTIONS:

(C. C. P. arts. 231-241, 434-544).

Judgments for payment of money are carried into effect by attaching property of the debtor. Personal property is sold at auction by a public auctioneer and commercial securities are sold by a broker. Real property is valued, unless a valuation has been agreed upon, and advertised for sale. The sale is held by the judge.

Bidders must file a bond for 10% of the valuation of the property. No bid is accepted which is less than two-thirds of the valuation. If there are no bidders, the creditor may ask for the adjudication of the property to him at two-thirds of the valuation, or request that a new sale of the property be advertised with the valuation reduced by not over one-third. If still no bid is obtained, the creditor may ask for adjudication to him at two-thirds of such new valuation, or for a third sale at any valuation the court may fix, or for the delivery of the property to him to collect and apply the income. In the last case, there may at any time be a further sale of the property at the request of the creditor or debtor, or the debtor may redeem the property. After any sale there is no equity of redemption.

Third parties may intervene to allege preferential rights, but the sale is not stayed unless the intervenor claims ownership based on a public instrument of earlier date than the execution.

EXECUTORS AND ADMINISTRATORS:

(C. C. arts. 1222-1385; C. C. P. arts. 858-888).

A testator may appoint one or more executors. The office of executor cannot be held by various classes of persons whose disabilities or occupations might interfere with their duties, such as minors, incapacitated persons, illiterates, blind or dumb persons, persons of notorious bad conduct, persons residing out of the country, priests and military men in active service. A married woman may be an executrix with the consent of her husband or the authorization of a court. The office is voluntary, but the executor who declines or resigns without serious cause loses whatever legacy or bequest may have been made him, except such as pertain to him as an obligatory heir.

With the consent of the heirs present, an executor may sell personal property at a public sale and also real property, if there is not sufficient ready money to pay the debts or legacies, but the heirs may prevent the sales by advancing the necessary money. The testator may provide that all or part of the estate be taken in custody by the executor. The heirs or legatees may ask that the executor be required to give bond.

The executor must conclude his labors within the time determined by the testator, or, if no time is determined, within one year, but the period may be extended by the judge. His compensation is such as may be determined by the testator or, in default of such determination, by the judge. If for any reason there is no executor the heirs are charged with the execution of the testator's wishes.

Upon the death of a decedent, whether testate or intestate, any party in interest may ask that the personal property of the estate be taken into custody. If within fifteen days the estate or part of the same has not been accepted by the heirs and there is no executor designated to take over the estate, the judge may, upon the petition of an interested party, appoint a curator for the estate. The heirs obtain the administration of the estate as and when they accept the inheritance.

Creditors.—Executors are obliged to publish notices to creditors and upon a partition of the estate, set aside a sufficient amount to pay the known debts.

Creditors of decedents have the right to exact payment of their claims, but the period to enforce the right and the extent of the right depend on whether there has been an unqualified acceptance of the estate by the heirs or an acceptance subject to the benefit of inventory. (See topic Descent and Distribution.)

In case of unqualified acceptance, the creditor may present his claim at any time within the period of limitations. In this case the heir is obliged to pay all debts and charges on the property he inherited, not only out of the accepted inheritance but also out of his own property; he is, however, liable only for his proportionate share of such debts and charges. In case of acceptance subject to the benefit of inventory, the heir is obliged to pay the debts of the decedent only up to the value of the property inherited.

Creditors may at any time demand the separation of the inherited property from the other property of the heir, so that their credits may have preference as against such inherited property over the other debts owing by the heir. Such separation can be demanded at any time within the period of limitations unless the creditor has already recognized the heir as debtor or the property inherited has been alienated by the heir or becomes confused with his other property.

EXEMPTIONS:

The following are exempted from attachment and execution: (1) Salaries and pensions paid by the state and municipalities, except that for maintenance ordered by a court one-half of such salaries and pensions may be attached; (2) social benefit funds of laborers and employees; wages and salaries, including commissions, participations, etc., but only up to a monthly amount not exceeding six monthly cost-of-living salaries. In cases of support and maintenance, of fraud, embezzlement or larceny, etc. against the employer, and of failure of the employer to pay his employees or laborers only an amount equal to three monthly cost-of-living salaries is exempt; (3) maintenance allowances required by law; (4) periodical income due to the liberality of another, so far as necessary for the maintenance of the debtor and his family; (5) deposits exempted under the national savings bank law; (6) life insurance policies and payments, but no premiums; (7) sums paid to contractors for public works while the work is going on, unless the suit was instituted by workmen or laborers or by creditors for materials supplied for the respective work; (8) beds and clothing of the debtor, his wife and children; (9) and (10) professional books and instruments up to 900 pesos; (11) uniforms and equipment of military men; (12) objects required for the work of artists and artisans and animals and equipment required by farmers, up to 400 pesos; (13) household utensils and food and fire material required by the debtor and his family for one month; (14) property held in a fiduciary capacity; (15) rights entirely personal, such as use and habitation; (16) real property donated or bequeathed as not attachable up to the valuation made at the time of delivery; (17) properties required for a public service but not the income therefrom; (18) other properties declared exempt by special laws. (C. C. P. art. 445).

FIDUCIARIES:

See topics Executors and Administrators; Trusts.

FORECLOSURE: See topic Mortgages.

FOREIGN CORPORATIONS:

See topic Corporations.

FOREIGN EXCHANGE:

See topic Exchange Control.

FOREIGN INVESTMENT:

Decree 600 compiled by Decree 523 of Sept. 9, 1993 governs foreign investments, and prohibits discrimination as between foreign and local investor. However, Chilean Government does reserve right to limit access of foreign investors to local credit.

Foreign investment is defined as any investment made with freely-convertible foreign exchange; new and used foreign capital goods; various forms of capitalized technology and credits related to foreign investment. Foreign investors can negotiate guarantees against changes in tariffs and indirect taxes on importation of capital equipment and machinery, during amount of time it takes to set up investment viz.: (A) Three years extended up to eight years in investment over US$50,000,000, (B) eight years in mining, extended to 12 years upon application to Foreign Investment Committee.

Decree-Law 2349 of Oct. 13, 1978 establishes that international agreements for public sector can be subject to foreign law.

Remittance of Profits.—Convertibility of profits will be made at most favorable exchange rate prevailing.

Repatriation of Capital.—Will be tax-free up to amount of original investment. Companies can liquidate assets after one-year period and repatriate original capital investment.

Tax Regime.—Investors have following choices: 42% corporate income tax; or 40% rate on normal income but if profits remitted abroad exceed 40% of average capital level invested during preceeding five years, additional 30% must be paid; both choices have ten year stability period extended up to 20 years in investments over US$50,000,000, or rate paid by Chilean firms (48%) with no guarantees of stability.

Approval of Foreign Investment Committee (CIE) is necessary for investments over $5,000,000 and involving media, public services or other activities normally carried out by government or participation by foreign government or public entity. If less than that sum, investments will only require approval of committee's executive secretary.

Foreign Capital Investment Funds.—Law authorizes establishment of foreign capital investment funds to be used for purchase of long-term securities and financial instruments issued in Chile. Such funds must be administrated by Chilean corporation. Capital can be repatriated after five years and profits are taxed at 10%.

FOREIGN TRADE REGULATIONS:

See topic Exchange Control.

FRAUDS, STATUTE OF:

See topic Public Instruments.

FRAUDULENT SALES AND CONVEYANCES:

(C. C. arts. 2465-2470; law 18175, arts. 74-79).

Acts and contracts executed in bad faith to defraud creditors may be rescinded provided action is brought within one year.

Gifts are void as against creditors if made after the cessation of payments or within ten days prior to such cessation, or one hundred and twenty days if made to relatives to the fourth degree. In case of a merchant the following are also void if executed after the cessation of payments or within ten days before such cessation: (1) Payments of debts in advance of maturity; (2) payments of matured debts if made otherwise than as stipulated, but payment in merchandise is considered equivalent to payment in money; (3) mortgages or pledges to secure debts arising before the said ten days. Other payments and contracts made between the cessation of payments and the declaration of bankruptcy may be annulled if the third party was aware of the cessation of payments. Mortgage registrations made after the tenth day prior to the cessation of payments may be set aside if the time between the date of the mortgage and its registration is over fifteen days plus an additional period allowed for the distance to the place of recording.

GARNISHMENT:

See topics Attachment; Executions; Exemptions.

HOLIDAYS:

Jan. 1 (New Year's); Good Friday*; May 1 (Labor Day); May 21 (Navy Day); Corpus Christi*; June 29 (St. Peter & St. Paul); Aug. 15 (Assumption of the Virgin); Sept. 11; Sept. 18-19 (Independence Day); Oct. 12 (Columbus Day); Nov. 1 (All Saints); Dec. 8 (Immaculate Conception); Dec. 25 (Christmas). (Law 2977 of Jan. 28, 1915 as am'd).

*These are movable holidays.

HUSBAND AND WIFE:

(C. C. arts. 131-178, 1715-1792; C. Com. 11-17; Decree 2200 of Apr. 29, 1949).

The husband and wife are obliged to live together and mutually help each other.

Unless otherwise provided in a prenuptial agreement, marriage is considered as a copartnership covering the following property: (1) Salaries and compensation of all kinds earned by each spouse during the marriage; (2) the fruits and revenues of all the property of the marriage partnership and of each spouse; (3) money or personal property contributed by either spouse to the marriage partnership, but with the obligation to restore the value of the same; (4) all property acquired by either spouse for a valuable consideration during marriage. Property belonging to either spouse before marriage and not contributed to marriage partnership continues to be separate property of such spouse. Money, credits and similar property are presumed to belong to community unless proved to be separate property.

The marriage partnership property is liable for: (1) Pensions and interest owing by partnership or either spouse and originating during marriage; (2) debts and obligations contracted during marriage by husband, or by wife with authorization of husband or court, unless they are personal as, for instance, debts contracted to set up children of a former marriage; (3) personal debts of either spouse, debtor being obligated to compensate partnership for amounts so taken; (4) maintenance charges of property of either spouse; (5) maintenance of spouses, maintenance, education and establishment of children and other family charges.

The husband is chief of the marriage partnership and as such may fully administer the community property and the separate property of his wife, but the wife may administer the proceeds of her professional or industrial labor. Third persons may regard the community property as though it formed part of the husband's patrimony and it is therefore liable for his debts, though he is considered obligated to compensate the marriage partnership to that extent. Debts made by the wife with the husband's consent are regarded as debts of the husband. The wife's property is not liable for any such debts unless shown to have been contracted for the personal benefit of the wife, as for the payment of debts existing before marriage. The husband cannot alienate or encumber the separate property of the wife except with her consent or judicial authorization, if she is unable to express her will; judicial approval is always required in the case of the sale of real estate. The husband cannot, without the wife's consent or judicial authorization, lease the wife's rural real property for over eight years nor her urban real property for over five years.

In case of the husband's incapacity or his prolonged absence, the wife may be appointed curator of her husband, or of his property and, in such case, she has the administration of the community property. She cannot, however, alienate or encumber real property forming part of community property without judicial authorization, and restrictions on her right to lease are similar to those of husband with respect to lease of wife's property.

The marriage partnership is dissolved by dissolution or annulment of the marriage, by permanent divorce, by the presumption of death of one of the spouses, or by an agreement of separation of property. Upon such dissolution there is a liquidation and division of the community property.

Separation of property during the marriage may be determined by agreement of the parties, or in certain cases by provision of law, or decreed by the judge in case of the insolvency or fraudulent administration of the husband. In such case the wife may dispose of her property and appear in court without her husband's consent. It may also be stipulated that the wife may freely dispose of specified sums. Persons married in a country where the laws do not provide for marriage community property, who become domiciled in Chile, are considered as married with separation of property unless they agree on it and register their marriage in Chile.

Parties may agree on regime of participation of increase of value of their property. During marriage separation of property of parties is maintained, each spouse administers, enjoys and freely disposes of his property. When this regime ends either by death or presumption of death of either spouse, declaration of annulment of marriage, divorce or separation judgment or separation of property judgment, increased value of their property is divided into equal parts.

Married woman may freely engage in business or follow profession or employment. In such cases husband and wife are considered separated as to property in connection with her business and its proceeds, and her acts do not affect husband nor is her separate business property liable for his debts unless his obligation was contracted for her benefit and that of family. However, while under 21 years of age she requires judicial authorization to alienate or encumber real property.

INCOME TAX: See topic Taxation.

INFANCY:

(C. C. arts. 26, 219-292, 338-544, 1447, 1682; Law 14,908 of Sept. 14, 1962 as am'd and 16618 of Mar. 8, 1967, and Decree 2531, Dec. 24, 1928 as am'd).

The age of majority is 18. Contracts by males under 14 or females under 12 are void and if over those ages are generally voidable. Minors are subject to parents' custody. The legitimate father or legitimate mother, exercises parental authority over nonemancipated minor. Parental authority includes legal representation, administration and enjoyment of usufruct of infant's real and personal property, with certain exceptions. Minors not under parental authority are given guardian who has administration of property and may have custody. Parents and guardians have restricted powers of disposition.

INHERITANCE TAX: See topic Taxation.

INSOLVENCY:

See topic Bankruptcy and Insolvency.

INTEREST:

Parties may agree to any rate not exceeding 50% of current banking interest, as determined every month by Central Bank. (C. C. arts. 2205-2209; Laws 4694 of Nov. 29, 1929, 11234 of Sept. 7, 1953, 16464 of Apr. 25, 1966, Law 18010 of June 23, 1981 and several resolutions of Central Bank of Chile).

INTESTACY:

See topic Descent and Distribution.

See Topical Index in front part of this volume.

JUDGMENTS:

Judgments do not constitute a lien on the property of the judgment debtor as against third persons, except as to real property, when they are recorded in the registry of property.

Foreign Judgments.—Foreign judgments have the force provided by treaty or, in the absence of treaty provisions, the force which in the foreign country is given to Chilean judgments. If the courts of the foreign country refuse to carry out Chilean judgments, the judgments of that country have no force in Chile. If the foregoing rules cannot be applied, the foreign judgment will be enforced in Chile if: (1) It contains nothing contrary to the laws of Chile; (2) it does not conflict with national jurisdiction; (3) it was not rendered by default; (4) it is in form ready for execution, in accordance with the laws of the country where rendered. The Supreme Court decides whether or not a foreign judgment should be executed by the courts of Chile. (C. C. P. arts. 231-251).

LAW REPORTS, CODES, ETC.:

See topic Statutes.

LEGISLATURE:

The Chilean Congress, which is composed of a Senate and a Chamber of Deputies, meets in regular session annually from May 21 to Sept. 18, but it may be called in special session by the President or by the President of the Senate on request of a majority of either house.

LIENS:

(C. C. arts. 2465-2491; C. Com. arts. 218, 1084-1135).

Credits are divided into five classes: (1) Those for judicial costs in matters favoring all creditors, necessary funeral expenses, expenses of sickness beyond six months to amount under control of judge, salaries of employees and workers and family allowances, taxes and payments of social security agencies and accrued withholding or surcharge taxes, necessary family subsistance items, for last three months, legal and contractual labor indemnification of employees and workers, other taxes including accrued municipal taxes; (2) those of innkeepers, carriers and pledgees, which are liens on property brought by guest into inn and articles carried or pledged; (3) those of mortgage creditors, which are liens on property mortgaged; (4) those of government against tax collectors and administrators, of municipalities, churches and educational and charitable establishments, against collectors and administrators of their funds, married woman for her property administered by husband, as against his property, and of children and wards for their property administered by parents, guardians or curators as against properties of such persons; and (5) those of common creditors.

The credits of the second and third class constitute a lien on the specific properties to which they refer. In case of insolvency, however, those of the first class are preferred to all others if the other property of the debtor is not sufficient to pay them. See also topic Sales (Realty and Personalty).

In commercial matters the consignee has a lien similar to that of the carrier against the articles received by him. Likewise, in maritime matters the provisions of law relating to average designate the classes of credits which constitute a lien against the vessel.

Mechanics' Liens.—There are no special provisions corresponding to mechanics' liens.

LIMITATION OF ACTIONS:

See topic Prescription.

LIMITED PARTNERSHIP:

See topic Partnership.

MARRIAGE:

(Law of Jan. 10, 1884 as am'd; C. C. arts. 98-130).

The following are incapacitated to marry: persons who are: (1) Already married; (2) below the age of puberty; (3) permanently and incurably impotent; (4) unable to express their will clearly in word or writing; (5) demented.

The following cannot contract marriage with each other: (1) Ascendants and descendants by consanguinity or affinity; (2) collaterals by consanguinity to the second degree; (3) the surviving spouse and the principal or accomplice in the murder of the deceased spouse; (4) spouse convicted of adultery, with other party to offense for period of five years from judgment.

The authorities are not allowed to perform the marriage ceremony for a widower unless a curator has been appointed for the property of his children by the former marriage, nor for a woman previously married before the birth of her child if she was pregnant, or before 270 days have elapsed since the dissolution or annulment of the former marriage, but the latter period may be shortened upon proof that she was separated from her husband. Minors under 18 years require consent of their father, mother, ascendant or curator. Minors marrying without such consent may be disinherited and, in case of intestate succession, have their shares reduced by one-half. There is no action for breach of promise to marry, such promise being regarded as entirely matter of honor and conscience.

The only marriage recognized by law and producing civil effects is the civil marriage, although the contracting parties may in addition marry by any kind of religious rite. Persons desiring to marry must apply to the official of the civil registry of the domicile or residence during the last three months of either of the parties, and present two witnesses to prove the facts stated in their application. The marriage ceremony may be performed at any time within 90 days thereafter. It is performed by the official of the civil registry in the presence of two witnesses, and recorded in the civil registry.

Marriages performed in a foreign country in accordance with the laws thereof are valid in Chile, but if one of the parties was a Chilean and the marriage is a forbidden marriage under the laws of Chile, it will have the same effect as if performed in Chile.

Annulment.—The following marriages may be annulled: Forbidden marriages (see supra); marriages not performed by the proper civil registry official or at which the requisite number of witnesses was not present; and marriages in which free consent was lacking by reason of error, duress or abduction.

The action of nullity may be brought by the parties, their ascendants and the public prosecutor, but an action founded on error or duress must be brought by the party suffering the error or duress. In the case of death-bed marriages, the action of nullity may be brought by the heirs of the deceased spouse.

MARRIED WOMEN:

See topics Dower; Executors and Administrators; Husband and Wife; Marriage.

MINES AND MINERALS:

(Mining Code, Law 18248 of Sept. 26, 1983 as am'd and its regulations Decree 1 of Jan. 3, 1987, Law 18097 of Jan. 7, 1982 on mining concessions as am'd.)

The state is the owner of all mineral and fossil substances, whoever may be the owner of the surface, but private persons may obtain concessions to work them in accordance with Mining Code. Such concessions are transferable, mortgageable and irrevocable and are regulated by same civil law rules that regulate real estate and fixed assets. Mine is property distinct from that of surface and its owner may occupy as much of surface as is necessary, upon payment of proper indemnity.

Prospecting is allowed on any lands not cultivated or enclosed and the right to prospect on other lands can also be obtained. All persons except certain government officials and incapacitated persons may obtain mining concessions. Exploration concessions are granted for two years which may be extended for two years; maximum area allocated for each concession is 5,000 hectares. Exploitation concessions do not have fixed time period and area allocated per concession is limited to maximum of ten hectares. Discoverer of mine makes his application to law judge of department, who orders publication; applicant must erect location monument, file plan and demand survey; there is another publication and official survey; such survey when approved and recorded constitutes title of mine. Law establishes that mining assets are not subject to attachment.

Mines may be owned by individuals or by companies formed under the general law or under the special rules of the mining code. When a mine is registered as belonging to more than one individual a mining company is deemed to exist, with a capital stock of 100 shares, and whose shareholders are not personally liable.

Petroleum.—(Const. art. 19). State reserves to itself exploitation of petroleum wherever situated.

Hydrocarbon deposits may not be subject of concession for exploration or exploitation.

Pursuant to Decree with Force of Law 2 of Dec. 4, 1986, State may enter into special operation agreements (contratos especiales de operación) which are those by virtue of which contractor binds by itself private individual or legal entity national or foreign to carry out, on behalf of State, exploration, exploitation and processing activities on hydrocarbon deposits.

Contractor commits himself to turn over to State total output of hydrocarbons obtained. According to Art. 1, consideration received by contractor as compensation for his services may be arranged for in national or foreign currency. If payment is stipulated in foreign currency, Central Bank of Chile shall grant required currencies for which effect operation agreement must register with said institution. State is authorized to pay all or part of consideration in hydrocarbons, which may be exported without being subject to regulations for controlling exports.

State guarantees contractor free use of foreign currency obtained as result of hydrocarbon exports received in payment.

Upon expiration of agreement, contractor, in addition to turning over to National Petroleum Company oil wells and related facilities, must transfer to said enterprise equipment, tools, machinery, etc. purchased during last five years of contract's enforcement, with prior payment of its residual value.

Art. 9 provides for specific oil work agreement whereby contractor of special operation agreement engages third party as subcontractor for carrying out determined service on specific work.

Said contractor is subject to tax assessed directly on value of consideration as defined above, equivalent to 50% of said consideration or, as elected by President of Republic, tax regime of income tax law (Ley de la Renta) may be applicable. Nevertheless, President of Republic is empowered to grant tax deductions, irrespective of tax system chosen, ranging from 10% to even 100% when circumstances so warrant it: e.g., nonexistence of double taxation agreements between two countries involved. Law provides for further tax exemptions.

State is required to withhold and deduct amount due for taxes upon payment of agreed consideration.

Copper.—Law 17450 of July 15, 1971 nationalized large copper mining enterprises (Gran Minería del Cobre). Law 19137 of May 6, 1992 authorizes copper exploration and exploitation by government enterprise in joint venture with private interest.

Taxes.—Mines pay annual tax per hectare. In case of failure to pay tax concession is offered at public auction, at which each bidder must deposit amount of unpaid tax and no bid of less than such amount is admissible. Purchaser receives mine with outstanding liens. Owner of mine cannot be bidder but may avoid sale by paying double amount of tax. Any surplus over tax due and costs is paid to former owner. Sale does not include buildings and accessories of mine unless former owner fails to remove them within one year. If there is no bid concession becomes void. It also becomes void if for any reason sale was not held and tax has not been paid for two years. See also topic Taxation, subhead Some Special Tax Provisions and Treatment.

MONOPOLIES AND RESTRAINT OF TRADE:

(Decree 511 of Sept. 17, 1980 as am'd).

Law is based on concept of free competition and market structure. It promotes and protects free competition, prohibits monopolistic practices and any other unfair practice that may limit economic freedom. Law is applied to individuals and private

MONOPOLIES AND RESTRAINT OF TRADE . . . *continued*
juridical persons engaged in economic activities. Law prohibits any practices, arrangements or agreements that limit or restrict free competition such as manipulation of production or distribution of goods; economic concentration leading to domination of part or whole market; abuse of dominant position in market. Acts restricting free competition are permissible in principle where they are necessary for stability of growth of national investment. Fines and imprisonment may be imposed for infringement of law and dissolution of juridical persons can be declared.

MORTGAGES:

(C. C. arts. 2407-2434, C. Com. 839-881).

Mortgages must be executed before a notary in the form of a public instrument (q. v.) and recorded in the mortgage registry. Their date and effect are counted only from the date of recording. Mortgages made in foreign countries on property in Chile are valid if recorded in the proper registry in Chile. Each party must be present before the notary. The instrument should describe the property in detail and state at what amount the parties value each parcel mortgaged.

Only real property possessed under ownership or usufruct title can be mortgaged. The mortgage covers movable property permanently belonging to the soil, such as machinery, implements and animals on farms, etc., as well as the increases or improvements of the mortgaged property, unharvested crops and unpaid rents and insurance, unless there is an agricultural lien. Mortgages are foreclosed by an executory suit.

Ship mortgages are governed by Code of Commerce.

MOTOR VEHICLES:

(Law 18290 of Jan. 30, 1984 as am'd).

Law contains complete regulations governing motor vehicles and public ways. License plates are required for all motor vehicles and drivers must obtain license, which is granted for indefinite period of time, while all requirements fulfilled. Minors between 18 and 21 years of age may get driving license of type indicated by law. In case of traffic violations, including driving while intoxicated, law provides for fines and suspension or cancelation of driving license, depending upon type of violation.

A license tax on automobiles for the benefit of the respective municipalities and a surcharge for the state's treasury are collected annually.

Aircraft.—(Law 18916 of Jan. 19, 1990). National aircraft must be registered and owners thereof must be Chilean citizens. If owner is corporation majority of corporate capital must belong to Chileans and president and majority of board of directors must be Chileans. Lease and encumbrance of aircrafts and maximum carrier's liability in case of accidents and loss or damage to baggage and freight is fixed. Aircraft flying over Chile must have navigation certificate from home country, registration certificate and certain other documents relating to crew, passengers and cargo. Only in case of necessity can aircraft alight elsewhere than at national or private airfields. Chile has ratified Pan American Commercial Aviation Convention signed at Havana in Feb., 1928, and International Aerial Navigation Convention signed at Paris Oct. 13, 1919.

See also topic Death.

NEGOTIABLE INSTRUMENTS:

See topic Bills and Notes.

NOTARIES PUBLIC:

(L. J. O. arts. 399-445; Decree-Law 407 of Mar. 19, 1925).

Notaries are public officials whose duties are more important than those of notaries under the American law. They are appointed on examination and must be lawyers, but while acting as notaries can practice law only in personal affairs. They must give bond and cannot leave the town of their residence without leave of absence from the proper judge or from the President of the Republic. They are under the supervision of the courts of appeals having jurisdiction over the respective departments.

Instruments executed before notaries must be prepared with certain formalities. Name, status, nationality, occupation, identification or passport number and residence of parties must be stated; unless parties agree otherwise notary must read instrument to them; and instrument must be signed in his presence. If parties are unknown to notary their identity must be certified under oath by two witnesses known to him. All public instruments executed before notary must have at least two witnesses. Notary retains original document and issues to parties in interest formal certified copies which have effect of originals and may be presented in court. At intervals records of notaries are forwarded to keeper of archives of department. Notaries may legalize signatures to private documents.

Law 16250 of 1965 empowered Executive to fix notarial tariff and to modify it according to living cost fluctuations.

PARTNERSHIP:

(C. C. arts. 2053-2115; C. Com. arts, 348-423, 470-511; Law 3918 of Mar. 7, 1923 as am'd by Laws 6156 of Jan. 13, 1938 and 12588 of Oct. 21, 1957).

Partnerships are considered as legal entities and may be formed by two or more persons. Before a mercantile partnership can do business, the partnership agreement must be drawn up in a public instrument executed before a notary, and within 30 days an abstract thereof must be recorded in the registry of commerce.

Unlimited Partnerships.—An unlimited partnership ("sociedad colectiva"), is a partnership in the usual form in which all partners have unlimited and joint liability. Such a partnership must act under a firm name which must include the names of all the partners, or of one of them followed by the words "y Compañía," generally abbreviated to "y Cía." The name of no person not a partner, can appear in the firm name.

The partnership agreement must express: (1) The name and domicile of the parties; (2) the firm name; (3) the names of the managing partners who may use the firm name; (4) the amount of the capital contributed by each partner; (5) the nature of the firm's business; (6) the share of profits and losses pertaining to each partner; (7) when the partnership is to begin and end; (8) the amount annually allowed each partner for his private expenses; (9) the manner of liquidation and division; (10) whether differences between the parties are to be submitted to arbitration and, if so, how the arbitrators are to be appointed; (11) the domicile of the firm; (12) any other lawful agreements.

The management of the business may be placed in the hands of one or more partners; otherwise, all may use the firm name. The use of the firm name may also be granted by power of attorney to a third person. Partners cannot on their own account engage in the same kind of business as the partnership.

Limited partnerships ("sociedad en comandita"), is a partnership in which one or more of the partners are subject to unlimited and joint liability for the partnership obligations, and one or more are not responsible for debts and losses except up to the amount of the capital they have subscribed.

The name of a special partner cannot appear in the firm name. The firm name is generally followed by the words "Sociedad en Comandita," commonly abbreviated to "S. en C." The special partners have no participation in the management of the company and cannot be attorneys in fact of the same, but they may attend the meetings of the other partners and express their opinion. The capital belonging to the special partners may be represented by shares. Many of the provisions relating to unlimited partnerships are applicable to limited partnerships.

Limited company ("sociedad con responsabilidad limitada"), is generally subject to the rules applying to unlimited partnerships, except that the liability of all members is limited. The number of members cannot exceed fifty and the firm name must be followed by the words "Limitada."

Civil partnership ("sociedad civil"), is one which is not formed for commercial purposes. It may have the form of an unlimited or limited partnership or of a corporation. It is governed by the rules of the Civil Code and is distinguished from a commercial company by being regarded rather as an association of individuals: thus, an obligation assumed by an unlimited civil partnership does not render the partners jointly liable, unless they have all subscribed to it in person or by attorney in fact.

Foreign partnerships may do business in Chile upon registering and publishing their partnership agreements in the same manner as Chilean partnerships. For tax purposes they may set aside a limited amount of capital for the use of their business in Chile.

PATENTS:

Any invention considered to be new, which results from inventive activity and is susceptible to industrial application is patentable in accordance with terms of law. Patents cannot be granted, among others, for inventions already existing in theory or nature, items against morality, law and public policy, economic, financial or commercial systems or plans. Novelty is destroyed by printed or oral publication, or public use of invention in any country. Application of foreign inventions must be filed within one year from date of filing application in country of origin. If invention is improvement on patent in force in Chile, patent on such improvement will be granted to original patentee for unexpired period of his patent, but to third persons only with permission of original patentee to use original invention in connection with improvement; or if such permission be refused, from date of expiration of original patent.

Patents are granted for 15 years from filing date.

Patents on foreign inventions are granted for same term granted in country of origin provided they do not exceed 15 or eight years, respectively. Compulsory licenses must be granted in case of monopoly abuse as determined by Government. Law contains provisions on penalties in case of illegal use of patents. Patented product or its container must be marked with the number and date of the patent. (Law 19039 of Jan. 24, 1991 regulated by Decree 177 of May 6, 1991).

Revision of Paris Convention of Mar. 20, 1883, for protection of industrial property, done at Stockholm July 14, 1967, as am'd on Oct. 2, 1979 and to Agreement on Trade-Related Aspects of Intellectual Property Rights, Marrakesh, Apr. 15, 1994.

Vegetal species are protected when they are novel, distinguishable, homogenous and stable and generic designation has been assigned to them. When registered at Registry of Protected Varieties, certificate of holder is issued for 18 years for trees and vines, and 15 years for other species. (Law 19342 of Oct. 17, 1994; International Convention for the Protection of Vegetal Species, Paris, Dec. 2, 1961, as am'd).

PLEDGES:

(C. C. arts. 2384-2406; C. Com. arts. 813-819; Decree-Law 776 of Dec. 19, 1925; Law 4287 of Feb. 22, 1928; Law 18112 of Mar. 23, 1982).

Pledge contracts are not effective unless the object pledged is delivered to the creditor or, in the case of commercial contracts, to the creditor or a third party agreed upon by debtor and creditor. Except in case of bank pledges, the document constituting the pledge must be a public instrument or a private instrument protocolized by a notary, and must contain a description of the objects pledged so that the creditor may have a privilege above other creditors. If payment is not made at maturity, the creditor may ask that the object pledged be sold at public auction under judicial auspices.

Law 18112 regulates pledge only when object pledged is not delivered to creditor. Document constituting this type of pledge must be public instrument executed before notary public and must contain description of objects pledged; extract of such document must be published in official gazette.

As to agrarian and industrial pledges, see topic Chattel Mortgages.

PRESCRIPTION:

(C. C. arts. 2492 to 2524; C. Com. arts. 761 to 764, 822, 1313 to 1318).

The acquisition of property or rights by virtue of possession and the extinction of obligations by failure to require performance is called prescription. Prescription can be expressly or tacitly waived as far as it has run, but no waiver can be made of future prescriptive periods.

In order to acquire by prescription, possession must be uninterrupted. Natural interruption exists: (1) When possession of the property becomes impossible by a natural cause, as by inundation, in which case the period of interruption is deducted; or (2) when a third person enters upon the property, in which case the entire previous prescriptive period is not counted unless possession is regained by legal proceedings. Civil interruption is produced by judicial demand.

PRESCRIPTION . . . *continued*

Against a title recorded in the registry of property the prescriptive period does not run except by virtue of another recorded title. Ordinary prescriptive period is five years for real property and two years for personal property. Prescriptive period is suspended in favor of persons who are minors, demented, deaf and dumb, wards or married women; it is always suspended between spouses.

Real property can be acquired by extraordinary prescription by possession for ten years; in such case no title need be shown and there are no suspensions in behalf of incapacitated persons.

Actions.—Prescriptive periods in which right to enforce an obligation is lost vary according to nature of action. More important are: (1) Actions to recover an inheritance, ten years; (2) ordinary suits in actions in which no special period is fixed, five years; (3) executory suits in actions in which no special period is fixed, three years; (4) actions between drawers and acceptors of bills of exchange, actions based on marine loans or insurance, four years; (5) actions to recover compensation due to attorneys, physicians, teachers and other professional men, two years. There are also special provisions for actions that prescribe in a shorter period of time.

Many of the above periods of prescription of actions are suspended in favor of incapacitated persons, but after ten years no suspension is taken into account.

Prescription of actions is interrupted by express or tacit recognition of the debt by the debtor and by judicial demand.

PRINCIPAL AND AGENT:

(C. C. arts. 2116-2173; C. Com. arts. 233-247).

An agency may be written or verbal, but for most purposes powers of attorney should appear in public instruments executed before a notary and should be detailed and explicit regarding the powers conferred. Powers of attorney should be drawn up with great care and the authority of the person granting the same must clearly appear.

A general power of attorney merely covers acts of administration. In order to buy, alienate or encounter real estate, make compromises or perform any other act outside the ordinary course of administration, the power to do so must be specifically granted. An agency is not perfected until accepted, but the acceptance may be express or tacit. An agent is required to adhere strictly to the instructions of the principal. He may delegate his powers if not expressly prohibited from doing so, but is liable for the acts of the substitute if there was no authority to make the delegation or if his appointee is notoriously incompetent.

The principal must reimburse the agent for his expenses, pay him the stipulated or customary compensation and indemnify him for losses suffered by reason of the agency. The agent may retain goods of the principal as a pledge for such payments.

Powers of attorney are terminated by: (1) The expiration of the term or business for which the power was granted; (2) revocation by the principal; (3) resignation of the agent; (4) death, bankruptcy, insolvency or loss of civil rights of principal or agent; (5) marriage of female agent; (6) cessation of powers of principal if the agency was constituted by virtue of such powers. In case of resignation the agent must continue acting for a reasonable time until the principal can make other arrangements.

Persons presuming to act for others without authority place themselves in the position of an agent but they are entitled to no compensation and are liable for damages if their administration is bad.

PUBLIC INSTRUMENTS:

(C. C. arts. 1698-1711; C. C. P. arts. 342-355).

A public instrument is one written by a notary in his protocol book from which he issues certified copies. Private documents may be given the effect of public for certain purposes by acknowledgment of its signatures before a notary.

As towards third parties a private instrument is considered as executed only from the death of one of the signers or from the date on which it was recorded or inventoried by a competent official or on which it was presented in court or acknowledged.

The law designates numerous acts or contracts which must appear in a public instrument, among them being the conveyance of real property and easements, the creation and assignment of mortgages, marriage settlements, contracts modifying a public instrument, powers of attorney for most purposes, promises to contract, the emancipation of minors and others.

RECORDS:

(C. C. arts. 686-697; L. J. O. arts, 361-388; Real Property Registry Regulations of June 24, 1857; Fees Decree 254 of May 20, 1931 as am'd; C. Com. arts. 20, 21; Commercial Registry Regulations of August 1, 1866; Civil Registry Law 4808 of Jan. 31, 1930 am'd and its regulations D. F. L. 2128 of Aug. 10, 1930).

The following must be recorded in the registry of properties: documents conveying or declaring the ownership of real estate and real rights; documents constituting, conveying, modifying or renouncing rights of usufruct, mortgage and certain other rights in real estate; and judgments declaring the ownership of real property, the definitive possession of the property of absent persons, the loss of civil rights, the rehabilitation of demented persons and spendthrifts, and the separation of property of married persons. Until such documents are presented for record the tradition of the property is not deemed affected. Other documents relating to real property or rights therein, such as leases, attachments, etc., may be recorded so as to constitute notice to third parties.

The registrars are semi-judicial officers who do not transcribe the entire document but only the essential details. On receiving an instrument they examine it to ascertain whether it is in legal form and whether the grantor is the owner of record and his right to execute the document appears sufficiently. If defects are found, a period of time is allowed to cure them, and in some cases registration may be refused at once. From the decision of the registrar a summary appeal lies to the courts. Registrars are appointed by the President and must give bond. Their fees are reasonable and are fixed by law.

Besides the registry of real property, there are commercial registries where certain instruments and data relating to merchants, corporations, etc., must be recorded; mining registries for the recording of mining titles, mortgages and transfers; and civil registries for the recording of births, marriages, deaths and other personal data. The notarial records are also preserved.

SALES (Realty and Personalty):

(C. C. arts. 1793, 1896; C. Com. arts. 130-160; Decree 3 of Feb. 12, 1931).

A sale is perfected and binding when the vendor and vendee have agreed upon the thing sold and the price thereof, though neither has been delivered; except that the sale of real property and rights and of an inheritance is not perfect until a public instrument is executed, but this exception does not apply to the sale of trees and pending fruits, building materials, etc. The determination of the price cannot be left to one of the parties.

The fiscal fees and the expenses of execution of the instrument of sale are payable by the vendor unless agreed otherwise. Sales of real property must be recorded. In the absence of an agreement to the contrary, the vendor warrants the thing sold and the title thereto; and in any case he is liable for hidden defects in the thing sold if known to him and not called to the buyer's attention. If the buyer does not pay the price at the time stipulated, the vendor may institute suit for the price or may, within four years after the date of the contract, ask for the rescission of the same.

In private sales of real property rescission may be asked within four years by the vendor if it is found that the price received is less than one-half the just value of the property, and by the buyer if the value is less than one-half the price paid. If a sale of real property is made at a certain price for a unit of area, the vendor must, if the area is found to be less than that stipulated, make up the difference or refund part of the price paid; if the area is found greater, the buyer must pay more; but in either cases if the difference exceeds 10% the sale may be annulled.

In commercial sales if the vendor does not deliver the goods at the time stipulated, the buyer may demand the fulfillment or rescission of the contract with damages in either case. He is not obliged to receive part of the merchandise purchased, but if he accepts partial delivery, the sale is consummated with regard to the goods received. If the purchaser refuses without just cause to receive the goods bought the vendor may demand the rescission of the sale, with damages, or the payment of the price and interest, but in the latter case he must deposit the merchandise to the order of the court for sale at public auction for account of the buyer.

Sales of bonds and shares for future delivery are prohibited.

Instalment Sales.—See topic Chattel Mortgages.

International Sale of Goods.—United Nations Convention on Contracts for the International Sale of Goods, in force on Mar. 1, 1991. See topic Treaties and Part VII, Selected International Conventions.

SEALS:

Seals are not used in private matters. Public instruments executed before notaries have most of the effects of sealed instruments in the United States.

SHIPPING:

Principal provisions with regard to shipping are to be found in Navigation Law (Decree-Law 2222 of May 21, 1978 as am'd by Law 18680 of Dec. 22, 1987 and Law 18892 of Dec. 22, 1989), and in Book III of Code of Commerce. Owners of Chilean vessels must be Chilean citizens or companies. For purposes of registration are considered Chilean companies those which principal domicile and real and effective seat is Chile, its chairman, manager and majority of directors are Chileans and majority of its capital belongs to Chilean individuals or entities. Crew of Chilean vessels must be Chilean citizens. Chilean vessels must be registered in office known as "Registro de Matrícula". Captains must be Chileans. Coastwise traffic is restricted to Chilean vessels. Export and import trade with countries served by Chilean navigation lines is reserved to Chilean vessels in proportion of at least 50%, for which special regulations of maritime companies in general are established. (Laws 6415 of Sept. 15, 1939; 12041 of June 26, 1956 as am'd; regulated by Decree 78 of Feb. 11, 1975).

There are special laws for national and foreign fishing vessels.

STATUTE OF FRAUDS:

See topic Public Instruments.

STATUTES:

Most of the legal provisions are codified. The first code, the Civil Code, took effect Jan. 1, 1857, and is based largely on the Spanish laws and on the Civil Codes of France, Austria and Louisiana. Other important codifications, most of which have been extensively amended, are the Code of Commerce which took effect Jan. 1, 1867; the Penal Code, effective Mar. 1, 1875; the Law of Judicial Organization, promulgated June 15, 1943; Code of Civil Procedure, effective Mar. 1, 1903; Code of Penal Procedure, effective Mar. 1, 1907; Labor Code, Law 18620 of May 27, 1987; Code of Waters, Decree with Force of Law 1122 of Aug. 13, 1981; Municipal Law, Law 18695 of Mar. 29, 1988 as am'd; Customs Ordinances of Oct. 13, 1982 t.o. 1993 as am'd; Fiscal Code, Decree-Law 830 of Dec. 27, 1974; Aeronautic Code, Law 18916 of Jan. 19, 1990.

TAXATION:

Taxation Code providing for administration, supervision and payment of taxes, except Custom House duties, was enacted by Decree-Law 830 of Dec. 27, 1974, as am'd and Decree 824 of Dec. 27, 1974 as am'd.

Real Estate Tax.—Law 17235 of Nov. 10, 1969, as am'd established single rate of 13.5 per mil of assessed value of real property as overall national and municipal territorial taxes, including charges for public light, pavement of streets and certain municipal loan services. Value assessments are made every five years or more and at least once every ten years. Property of less than legal amount in most cases is exempted.

Decree-Law 824 of Dec. 27, 1974 also imposes a tax on real estate. Real estate used in agricultural activities is taxed at rates which vary from 4% to 10% on appraised valued while other real estate is taxed at a flat 7%.

Real Estate Transfer Tax.—See subheads Stamp Taxes; and Inheritance and Gift Tax, infra.

TAXATION . . . *continued*

Stamp taxes are payable by the use of stamped paper on which certifications, documents, receipts proceedings, etc. must be written or by affixing revenue stamps to same.

Some documents, acts or contracts pay a percentage in consideration to value involved. Other documents as in case of checks, promissory notes, bills of exchange, etc., pay a fixed rate. Incorporation of companies, shares of stock, transfer of patents and licenses are also subject to stamp taxes. Such fixed rates vary frequently. (Decree 3475 of Aug. 29, 1980 as am'd).

Income Tax.—(Decree-Law 824 of Dec. 27, 1974 as am'd). Any person domiciled (residence plus intention to stay, C.C. art. 59) or residing (more than six months) in Chile is subject to tax on incomes derived from sources within or outside country. Nonresidents are taxed on income from Chilean sources. However, if foreigner takes domicile in Chile, he will be subject to tax on income from Chilean sources only, during first three years, which term can be extended by fiscal authority. Payments for severance or retirement, living allowances and pensions even from foreign sources are not treated as income. Undivided estates are taxed for no more than three years as if deceased were alive. Descendants must file their separate returns after that term has elapsed.

Basic Tax.—Incomes are divided in two categories: (1) Income of capital and enterprises: all incomes, except salaries and some professional fees, are first category income, and are taxed at general rate of 15%, including any income of corporations; income from real property, it being presumed that a house inhabited by its owner renders 7% of its fiscal value, with some exceptions, income from invested capital such as interest, annuities, certain dividends (see infra catchline Tax on Dividends), it being presumed that noncommercial credits or credits secured with mortgage, pledge or collateral signature earn at least 10%; income from commerce and industry, including mining, fishing and other extractive activities; fees of brokers, commission merchants, auctioneers, builders, custom house agents, shippers and other agents intervening in maritime commerce and nonindividual insurance agencies; income of small artisan miners, street merchants, owners of artisan workshops; and (2) salaries and professional fees not included above. Decree 824 of Dec. 27, 1974 does not distinguish between blue collar workers ("obreros") and white collar workers ("empleados"). It imposes tax according to graduated scale on all income over ten monthly tax units ("unidad tributaria").

Rates.—See also catchline Adjustment of Rates, below.

Individuals and associations are subject to (a) 15% on income of first category; for artisans, and merchants, industrialists and farmers rate is: 3.5%; (b) at progressive rate of from 5% to 45% on salaries including gratuities per diem and other similar payments on second category income. When associations which are not corporations render services through their members or through other nonmember professionals hired by association, association itself is subject to second category tax rate of 12%.

Corporations are subject to 15% first category income tax.

Complementary Tax.—This tax applies to individuals having domicile or residing in Chile on sum of their incomes, including dividends in cash or property. Rate is progressive, first ten yearly tax units are exempted, it being 5% on amounts up to 30 yearly tax units; 10% on any excess up to 50 yearly tax units; and so on until rate is 45% on excess over 120 yearly tax units. Credit of 10% of one tax unit is granted to each taxpayer. Credit is granted at same rate as dividends were taxed at corporate level for dividends paid out of income already subject to corporate tax. Ocean freights, commissions or participations in ocean freights originating or destined to Chilean ports and other income for services to ships and cargo at local or foreign ports which must be rendered to maritime transport, also are subject to this complementary tax. Rate is 5% and it taxes shipowners, agents, consignees and forwarders. Tax is not applicable when income is generated by foreign ships, provided that countries where those ships are registered, do not have similar tax, or if they have it, exemptions are granted to Chilean shipping companies.

Tax on Dividends.—Dividends distributed to registered shareholders by corporations subject to tax are not taxable as category income (but see catchlines Complementary Tax, supra, and Additional Tax, infra); dividends of foreign corporations not doing business in Chile are taxable when distributed to shareholders residing or with domicile in Chile. Dividends paid to resident legal entities by Chilean corporations or limited partnerships are exempted from taxes.

Additional Tax.—A tax of 35% called "additional" applies to: (1) Foreign individuals with no residence or domicile in Chile and to corporations organized abroad and having establishment, branch, agent or representative in Chile, on all incomes received from Chilean sources; (2) dividends or profits distributed by Chilean corporations or "sociedades en comandita" to nonresidents without domicile in Chile, regardless of nationality, except if in form of stock dividends or increases of par value of outstanding shares or distribution of stock of company formed with part of assets of distributing company, and except also in case of liquidation of company. Credit is granted at same rate as dividends were taxed at corporate level for dividends paid out of income already subject to corporate tax. For copyrights exploitation rate is 15%. Rate is 35% for: Royalties, participations or other similar amounts paid to recipients with no domicile or residence in Chile for use of trademarks, patents, know-how, or similar items; certain royalties and technical assistance, qualified as unproductive or not necessary for national development, are subject to tax rates up to 80%; interest paid to creditors with no domicile or residence in Chile, except, (a) if paid to international banks or foreign public finance institutions, (b) interest on bonds or debentures issued by Chilean corporations for improvement of production or increase of capitalization, and (c) interest payable by reason of imports with deferred payments, (d) interest on local bank deposits and bank accounts on foreign exchange. Rate is 4% on interest under (a) and (c) when Central Bank authorized them; any compensation for services rendered abroad payable to nonresidents, except for freight, commissions, insurance and similar services and for melting or refining or other processes to which Chilean products are subjected abroad. Tax when applicable, is sole tax on said royalties, interest or compensations, in spite of name "additional".

Rate shall be 20% for wages or salaries originating exclusively from skilled or unskilled labor of natural foreign persons and only when these have been realized in Chile in connection with scientific, cultural or sportive activities.

All Chileans not domiciled in Chile shall pay an additional tax of 35% upon aggregate of their taxable income derived from different categories.

Capital Gains.—Gains are taxed as ordinary income. In addition decree also provides exclusive list of gains and benefits which unless derived from habitual activities are to be excluded from income. Among excluded gains and benefits are those derived from alienation or assignment of shares in corporation, alienation of bonds and debentures, inheritance awards, etc.

Capital gains are not subject to other income taxes except when distributed by corporations to residents or domiciliaries, who must declare them for complementary tax purposes.

Adjustment of Rates.—When payments are made by installments, tax is readjusted to reflect 100% of variation of consumer price index.

Some Special Tax Provisions and Treatment.—Law 16528 of Aug. 9, 1966 as am'd regulated by Sup. Decree 1270 of Sept. 27, 1966 grants tax exemptions to production of goods to be exported.

Decree-Law 889 of Jan. 30, 1975 as am'd regulated by Sup. Decree 274 of Apr. 14, 1975 establishes special tax incentives to promote economic development of northern and southern regions of country. Law 18392 of Jan. 10, 1985 grants income tax and import duties exemption up to 50 years to industrial and mining companies; companies dedicated to exploitation of sea resources, and transportation and tourist companies located in southern part of country.

Decree-Law 3059 of Dec. 21, 1979 as am'd grants tax exemptions to national companies dedicated to navigation, lighter service and docks.

Persons or concerns dedicated to parcelation of rustic lands may enjoy certain benefits if development plans are subject to specific requirements and are approved by Corporation of Agrarian Reform. (Art. 156 of Law of Agrarian Reform of July 28, 1967 extending effects of Decree-Law 14 of Mar. 1, 1963).

Special tax treatment for automotive industry is established by Law 18483 of Dec. 27, 1985 which grants fiscal credits until Dec. 31, 1995.

Mining enterprises may be subject to the following treatment:

(a) Law 13,305 of 1959, in Art. 256 provides that small and medium sized mining concerns located in Antofagasta which mine copper for exportation shall enjoy same benefits which Law 16528 of 1966 (above) grants to industries in other Departments; same benefit was extended to similar enterprises and other industries in Atacama by Law 15564 of 1964; (b) Law 16624 of May 15, 1967 as am'd establishes that large copper mining enterprise is one producing blister, fire refined or electrolytic copper in amounts not less than 75,000 metric tons a year, mixed mining enterprise is any with government participation over 25% and small mining enterprise is any concern dedicated to mining belonging to individual owners or to mining company (sociedad minera), excepting some corporations.

Mining industry is subject to income tax law. (D.L. 824 of Dec. 27, 1974 as am'd). See also topic Foreign Investment.

Special Taxes.—

Sales and Services Tax.—By Decree-Law 825 of Dec. 27, 1974 as am'd, Decree-Law 1606 of Dec. 3, 1976 as am'd and its regulations, Sup. Decree 55 of Feb. 2, 1977, sale of personal tangible property is subject to tax as well as services rendered in national territory, regardless of other laws which impose special taxes on sale, production or import of goods or performance of services. General tax rate is 18% on total value of sale or service; sale of foreign currency, 50%, etc. There are many exemptions, such as sale of raw material for goods to be exported, certain types of investments and corporations which do business in areas of communication (radio or television), transportation and education.

Salaries and Payroll Taxes.—Salaries and wages are subject to several taxes, some of them for social benefits.

Inheritance and Gift Tax.—(Law 16,271 of July 10, 1965 am'd by Decree-Law 3545 of Dec. 16, 1980). Inheritances and gifts are subject to sliding scale tax, depending on relationship and amount involved.

Rates applicable to inter vivos gifts or transfers by inheritance, legacy or bequest to spouse, and first degree relatives or ascendants or descendants are 1% on amounts of corresponding share up to 80 yearly minimum salaries; 2.5% on excess up to 160 salaries; 5% on excess up to 320 salaries and so on until rate is 25% on amounts in excess of 1,200 minimum salaries. For collaterals of 2d, 3d, and 4th degree same rate applies with surcharge of 20% of tax; more remote relatives and strangers are subject also to same rate, with surcharge of 40%.

Property situated abroad is taxable but if the decedent or donor is a foreigner its inclusion takes place only regarding property acquired with resources obtained from Chilean sources. The foreign tax is a credit but this cannot effect a reduction of the tax otherwise applicable to Chilean assets alone.

Gifts made during life are includable as part of estate but gift tax constitutes a credit against inheritance tax.

Shares of stock transferred during life of the holder who dies before registration in the corporation register is petitioned, may not be registered without consent of Director of Internal Revenue who will scrutinize the transaction.

TRADEMARKS AND TRADENAMES:

Trademarks may be registered in Office of Industrial Property. The following cannot be registered as trademarks: (1) Flag or coat-of-arms, names or signs of any country or international organization; (2) scientific or technical denominations; (3) name, picture or signature of individual without his consent or that of his heirs, except names of historic personages 50 years after their death; (4) form or color of article or its containers; (5) common expressions indicating nature, origin or qualities of article; (6) misleading expressions; (7) marks similar to others already registered; (8) expressions commonly used to designate article; (9) marks showing medals or diplomas granted; (10) marks contravening morals or public order. Term of registration is ten years and may be renewed. Notice of registration is given by stamping words "Marca Registrada" or letters, "M. R." on trademark. Transfers of trademarks must be made in writing and recorded in respective registry.

Industrial designs may be registered for ten years. Phonograph records and motion picture films may be registered without prejudice to the rights of the owners of the

See Topical Index in front part of this volume.

TRADEMARKS AND TRADENAMES . . . *continued*
copyright. (Sup. Dec. 897 of Oct. 13, 1971; Dec. 675 of Nov. 2, 1972; Law 19039 of Jan. 24, 1991 regulated by Decree 177 of May 6, 1991).

TREATIES:

Bilateral Treaties.—
With European Countries:
Austria.—Commercial Agreement, Feb. 24, 1955.
Belgium.—Agreements Concerning Commercial Air Services of Nov. 5, 1966.
Bulgaria.—Commercial Agreement, Nov. 5, 1968; Credit Agreement, June 2, 1971.
Denmark.—Treaty of Commerce and Navigation, of Feb. 4, 1899; Additional protocol of Nov. 30, 1905.
Finland.—Treaty of Commerce of Mar. 1, 1935.
France.—Financial Protocol, Nov. 5, 1968.
Germany, Federal Republic of.—Basic Agreement on Economic and Technical Cooperation, Oct. 18, 1968.
Hungary.—Commercial Agreement, Nov. 10, 1967; Copper Industry and Trade Act, July 13, 1968; Commercial Agreement, June 6, 1971; Economic Cooperation Agreement, June 29, 1971.
Norway.—Treaty of Commerce and Navigation and Additional Protocol, Feb. 9, 1927; Agreement Amending Treaty of Commerce and Protocol of Aug. 5 and 26, 1937.
Poland.—Commercial Agreement, June 9, 1971.
Portugal.—Commercial Modus Vivendi, of Feb. 2, 1960.
Romania.—Commercial Agreement, Oct. 21, 1968; Basic Agreement on Economic and Technical Cooperation, Oct. 1, 1968.
Spain.—Commercial and Payments Agreement of Aug. 9, 1950; Supplementary Agreement to Foregoing, Nov. 5, 1953; Agreement on Joint Production of Cinematographic Works, Mar. 31, 1970; Agreement on Taxation of Railway Personnel, Nov. 6, 1974; Commercial Air Transport Agreement, Santiago, Dec. 17, 1974.
Sweden.—Treaty of Commerce and Navigation of Oct. 30, 1936; Commercial Agreement of May 28, 1950.
Switzerland.—Treaty of Commerce, Oct. 31, 1897; Supplementary Commercial Agreement, June 17, 1955.
Yugoslavia.—Commercial and Payments Agreement, Aug. 2, 1954; Final Act of Conversations on Commercial Interchange, May 28, 1965.
With American Countries:
Argentina.—Labor Agreement, Antofagasta, Oct. 17, 1971; Treaty for Judicial Solution of Disputes, Buenos Aires, Apr. 5, 1972.
Bolivia.—Treaty of Economic Complementation of Jan. 31, 1955; Supplementary Protocol to Treaty, and Clarifying Exchange of Notes, of Oct. 14, 1955; Commercial Agreement of Nov. 10, 1955; Payments Agreement of Nov. 10, 1955.
Brazil.—Treaty of Commerce and Navigation of Mar. 1, 1943; Cotton Textiles Agreement of Dec. 30, 1946; Additional Protocol to Treaty of Commerce and Navigation of July 4, 1947; Exchange of Notes Relating to Additional Protocol of July 4, 1947; Agreement on Brazilian Coffee, of Apr. 13 and May 3, 1954; Exchange of Notes Concerning Nitrates of Aug. 27, 1955; Payments Agreement of Sept. 10, 1958; Agreement on Joint Production of Cinematographic Works, Mar. 18, 1966; Agreement on Maritime Transport, Brasilia, Apr. 25, 1974; Agreement on Technical and Scientific Cooperation, Santiago, June 19, 1974.
Canada.—Commercial Agreement Oct. 10, 1941.
Colombia.—Treaty of Commerce and Navigation of Dec. 27, 1936; Agreement Amending Treaty of Commerce and Navigation of June 14, 1950; Agreement on Technical and Scientific Cooperation, Bogota, May 8, 1971.
Cuba.—Agreement Relating to Commercial Air Transport Services, Feb. 25, 1971.
Dominican Republic.—Basic Agreement on Technical and Scientific Cooperation, Santo Domingo, Sept. 12, 1975.
Ecuador.—Commercial Agreement, of Aug. 4, 1949; Payments Agreement of Dec. 30, 1957; Amendment to Payments Agreement of June 30, 1958; Final Act of VIII Regular Meeting of Permanent Committee on South Pacific, Oct. 17, 1964.
Mexico.—Commercial Modus Vivendi of June 23 and July 1, 1954.
Paraguay.—Agreement to Establish in Antofagasta a Free Deposit and Free Trade Zone for Exports and Imports through Paraguay, Aug. 19, 1968; Free Zone Agreement, Santiago, Sept. 19, 1974.
Peru.—Treaty of Commerce and Additional Protocol of Oct. 17, 1974; Exchange of Notes Amending Treaty, dated Aug. 7 and Sept. 7, 1950; Final Act of VIII Regular Meeting of Permanent Committee on South Pacific, Oct. 17, 1964.
United States.—Agreement on International Air Transport Services, Chicago, Dec. 7, 1944; Air Transport Agreement and Exchange of Notes, signed at Santiago, May 10, 1947; Agreement Relating to Passport Visas for Nonimmigrants, Exchange of notes at Santiago Aug. 29, 1950; Agreement Relating to Informational Media Guaranty Program in Chile (1955); Agreement Relating to Investment Guaranties under Mutual Security Act of 1954, as am'd, Exchange of notes at Santiago July 29, 1960; Agreement on double air taxation, Exchange of notes, Santiago, 1975.
Uruguay.—Basic Agreement on Scientific and Technical Cooperation, Santiago, Sept. 20, 1975; Agreement on free transit of tourists, Santiago, Sept. 20, 1975; Agreement on economic, scientific and technological cooperation, Santiago, Sept. 20, 1975.
Venezuela.—Conversations on Economic Complementation, Apr. 1, 1966.
With Asian Countries:
China, People's Republic of.—Commercial Agreement, Apr. 20, 1971; Agreement on merchandise credit, Peking, June 8, 1972.
Fiji.—Agreements on Air Transport Services, Santiago, July 9, 1973.
Japan.—Exchange of Notes on Credits, Feb. 24, 1971.

Multilateral Treaties—Agreement on Waterborne Transportation of LAFTA, Dec. 10, 1966, at Montevideo; Protocol for Settlement of Disputes, Dec. 2, 1966, at Montevideo; Protocol on Transit of Persons, Dec. 12, 1966, at Montevideo; Andres Bello Agreement on Educational, Scientific and Cultural Integration of Andean Region, Bogota, Jan. 31, 1970; Uniform Regime of Multinational Enterprises, Dec. 18, 1971.

Chile has also signed following: Convention on Suppression of Illicit Drug Traffic, Geneva, June 26, 1936, and New York, Dec. 11, 1946; Intergovernmental Maritime Consultative Organization, Geneva, Mar. 6, 1948; Equal Pay for Male and Female Workers, June 6, 1951; Convention Concerning Customs Facilities for Touring, New York, June 4, 1954; Discrimination in Employment, June 4, 1958; Convention on the Recognition and Enforcement of Foreign Arbitral Awards, New York, June 10, 1958; Inter-American Convention on Facilitation of International Waterborne Transportation, Mar del Plata, Argentina, June 14, 1963; Agreement Establishing Internal Agreements for Global Commercial Communications Satellite System, Aug. 20, 1964, Washington, D.C.; Convention on Registration of Vessels in Internal Trade, Geneva, Jan. 25, 1965; Convention on Transit Trade of Landlocked States, New York, July 8, 1965; International Telecommunications Convention, Montreux, Switzerland, Oct. 21, 1965; Agreement on International Juridical Persons of Permanent Commission of South Pacific, Lima, Jan. 14, 1966; Convention on Measurement of Vessels Navigating Internal Waters, Geneva, Feb. 15, 1966; Treaty for Prohibition of Nuclear Weapons in Latin America, Mexico, Feb. 14, 1967; Convention on International Land Transport between Argentina, Brazil, Uruguay and Chile, Apr. 28, 1967; Convention on International Hydrographic Organization, Monaco, May 3, 1967; Agreements on Exploitation and Conservation of Maritime Resources of South Pacific, signed by Ecuador, Peru and Chile, at Quito, Ecuador, May 30, 1967; Intergovernmental Council of Copper Exporting Countries, June 8, 1967; Adherence to Convention Establishing World Intellectual Property Organization, Stockholm, June 14, 1967; Berne Convention for Protection of Literary and Artistic Works, revised at Stockholm, July 14, 1967; Stockholm Act of Paris Convention for Protection of Industrial Property, adopted at Stockholm, July 14, 1967; Agreement on Taxation of Railway Personnel, Nov. 6, 1967; International Conference on Load Lines, London Apr. 5, 1968; Brussels Customs Agreement, June 11, 1968; Agreement on Road Signs, Vienna, Nov. 8, 1968; Conservation of Vicuna, La Paz, Aug. 16, 1969; Universal Postal Union, Vienna, July 10, 1964, and Tokyo, Nov. 14, 1969; Statutes of World Tourism Organization, Mexico City, Sept. 27, 1970; Convention for Suppression of Unlawful Seizure of Aircraft, The Hague, Dec. 16, 1970; International Telecommunications Satellite Organization (INTELSAT) Washington, Aug. 20, 1971; Agreement for Suppression of Unlawful Acts Against Safety of Civil Aviation, Montreal, Sept. 23, 1971; International Cacao Agreement, New York, Jan. 12, 1973; Convention on International Trade in Endangered Species of Wild Fauna and Flora, Washington, Mar. 3, 1973; Latin American Energy Organization, Lima, Nov. 2, 1973; International Sugar Agreement, Geneva, Oct. 24, 1968 and Dec. 6, 1971; World Food Program, Santiago, Apr. 2, 1974; Inter-American convention on conflict of laws concerning bills of exchange, promissory notes, and invoices, Panama, Jan. 30, 1975; Inter-American convention on conflict of laws concerning checks, Panama, Jan. 30, 1975; Inter-American convention on international commercial arbitration, Panama, Jan. 30, 1975; Inter-American convention on letters rogatory, Panama, Jan. 30, 1975 and its protocol; Inter-American convention on taking of evidence abroad, Panama, Jan. 30, 1975; Inter-American convention on legal regime of powers of attorney to be used abroad, Panama, Jan. 30, 1975.

Convention on Private International Law (Bustamante Code) Havana 1928, Asuncion Treaty, signed on Mar. 26, 1991 creating common market "Southern Common Market" (MERCOSUR), Montevideo Treaty, 1980 (Latin American Integration Association); United Nations Convention on Recognition and Enforcement of Foreign Arbitral Awards, 1958; Multilateral Trade Negotiations, The Uruguay Round, Final Act, Marrakesh, Apr. 15, 1994 and Agreement Establishing the World Trade Organization, Marrakesh, Apr. 15, 1994. See topic Copyright.

International Sale of Goods.—United Nations Convention on Contracts for the International Sale of Goods, in force on Mar. 1, 1991. See topic Sales (Realty and Personalty) and Part VI, Selected International Conventions.

TRUSTS:

Trusts as developed by the common law are unknown to the law of Chile. The freedom of contract which exists in Chile makes it possible as a practical matter to constitute a relationship substantially the same as in the case of a trust, and various such similar relationships are expressly recognized in the Civil Code. (C. C. arts. 732-763, 1079, 1164-1166). A similar result may also be obtained under the banking laws, since mortgage and commercial banks are authorized to act as trustees and to perform the duties of agents, bailees, receivers in bankruptcy, executors, administrators and the like. (D.F.L. 252 of Mar. 30, 1960 as am'd and Decree-Law 1097 of July 16, 1975 as am'd).

USURY: See topic Interest.

WILLS:

(C. C. arts. 999-1316).

Wills may be made by all persons, except those under the age of puberty, mentally incapacitated, civilly dead, or unable to express their will clearly. Wills are opened and published in the court of the last domicile of the testator.

Forms.—With respect to form, wills are either (a) solemn or (b) privileged. Solemn wills are: (1) Open, also called nuncupative or public; (2) closed or secret. Privileged wills are: (1) Oral; (2) military; or (3) naval.

Witnesses.—The following cannot be witnesses to solemn wills executed in Chile: Minors below 18, persons mentally incapacitated, or blind, or deaf, or dumb, or convicted of certain crimes, clerks of the officiating notary, foreigners not domiciled in Chile and persons not understanding the testator's language. At least two witnesses must be residents of the Department, and one in three or two in five must know how to read and write.

In cases of privileged wills, any person of sound mind over eighteen who sees, hears and understands the testator can be a witness, provided he has not been convicted of certain crimes and can read and write.

Open Wills.—Open wills are executed before a notary and three witnesses or before five witnesses. They must express the name, birthplace, nationality and residence of the testator, and that he is of sound mind, the names of the persons whom he has married and of his children, stating whether they are living or dead, the names and

See Topical Index in front part of this volume.

WILLS . . . *continued*
residences of the witnesses, the name of the notary, and the place and date of execution of the will. The will must be read aloud by the notary or a witness, to the parties assembled, and all must sign. Blind persons can execute only open wills.

Closed Wills.—Closed wills are privately prepared and signed by the testator and enclosed in a sealed envelope which the testator must, in the presence of a notary or judge of first instance, declare to contain his will. On the envelope the notary makes a minute of such declaration and the same must be signed by all the parties assembled. Persons who cannot understand or be understood in conversation can make only closed wills.

Oral Wills.—Oral wills may be made in the presence of three witnesses by a person in imminent danger of death. They are not valid if the testator survives for over 30 days, or if not reduced to writing by the witnesses before a judge of first instance within 30 days after the testator's death.

Military Wills.—Military wills may be made in time of war by military men, hostages, and prisoners, before certain army officers.

Naval Wills.—Naval wills may be made on the high seas before the commander or lieutenant commander of a Chilean man of war or before the captain, mate or pilot of a Chilean merchant vessel.

Revocation.—Wills validly executed are rendered invalid by revocation by the testator. Revocation may be total or partial. A later will which does not expressly revoke a former will leaves in force all the provisions of the former will which are not in conflict with the later one.

Testamentary Disposition.—The testator may dispose freely of his property only in so far as there are no forced heirs. (see topic Descent and Distribution). Legacies may be charged with conditions. Testamentary provisions are void if made in favor of the notary or witnesses before whom the will is signed, or in favor of their wives, ascendants, descendants, brothers or sisters, brothers or sisters in law, or servants.

Foreign Wills.—Foreign wills are valid in Chile if executed in accordance with the laws of the country where made. Wills may be made abroad in the form provided by the Chilean law for solemn wills, if: (1) The testator is a Chilean or a foreigner domiciled in Chile; (2) the witnesses are Chileans or domiciled in the city of execution; (3) the will is executed before a Chilean diplomatic official or consul; and (4) the signature of the Chief of the Chilean Legation appears on the will, if open, or the envelope, if closed.

See Topical Index in front part of this volume.

CHINA LAW DIGEST REVISER

The International Law Firm of
ARNBERGER, KIM, BUXBAUM & CHOY
Suite 2518, China World Trade Center
No. 1, Jian Guo Men Wai Avenue
Beijing, China
Telephone: 86 1 6505-2288 Ext. 2523
Fax: 86 1 6505-2638
New York Office: 100 Maiden Lane, 16th Floor, Suite 1600B, New York, 10038.
Telephone: 212-504-6109. Fax: 212-412-7016.
Los Angeles Office: 515 South Flower Street, Suite 3500, Los Angeles, California, 90071-2201.
Telephone: 213-236-4355. Fax: 213-426-6222.

Reviser Profile

ARNBERGER, KIM, BUXBAUM & CHOY is an international law firm with offices on the east and west coasts of the U.S.A. (New York City, Los Angeles and San Francisco) and in Hong Kong, China and Mongolia. The Firm's international division maintains five offices inside China, including the capital at Beijing and the cities of Guangzhou (Canton), Shanghai, Shenzhen, and Xiamen. Each of the Firm's partners are recognized international practitioners, several of whom are prominent in their respective legal fields and some of whom have extensively published and frequently lectured on current legal issues. The Firm's attorneys include several prominent American, Asian and European-trained attorneys, along with attorneys who are of counsel to the Firm and assist it from associated offices in Tokyo, Seoul, Taipei, Bangkok, Jakarta and Sydney.

Established in 1969 the Firm traces its roots in Asia to 1972, when one of its attorneys became the first American attorney to represent foreign parties in China. It has since become one of the largest American firms in East Asia. The Firm's international practice is also supported by experienced attorneys in the Firm's state-side offices, who provide expertise and work closely to coordinate overseas representations with client management and in-house counsel in North America and Europe. The Firm opened the first foreign law office in Mongolia in 1992, and is active in legal work, including arbitration, in Russia and some Eastern European countries. The Firm's legal prominence in Northeast Asia is recognized in its appointment as the official Reviser of Martindale-Hubbell's *China* and *Mongolia Law Digests.*

The Firm's attorneys have handled challenging cross-border cases and international transactions, ranging from leading copyright infringement and antipiracy victories in China on behalf of foreign software and literary publishers, through the negotiation of natural resource concession rights in Myanmar (Burma), to obtaining one of the largest product liability settlements in the Commonwealth of the Northern Marianna Islands on behalf of Japan's largest construction contractor. The Firm undertakes numerous major transactional matters including drafting the first insurance joint venture contracts in China; establishing major power plant contracts, handling major loan agreements and leasing transactions and assisting in public offerings. The Firm handles numerous transactions on behalf of major international banks. The Firm also handles all corporate work and other legal work on behalf of overseas divisions of European, Asian and American corporations.

The Firm is active in the representation of parties in the U.S.A., including foreign parties doing business in the U.S. Attorneys in the American offices actively handle all aspects of domestic-based litigation, complex business transactions and corporate matters, securities and commodities, admiralty law, employment law and intellectual property transactions. Attorneys in the Firm's U.S. offices also routinely counsel businesses and entrepreneurs in their investment matters and day-to-day corporate and business activities. Attorney's in the Firm's U.S.-based litigation division routinely handle a variety of cases, including securities and commodities, breach of contract, employment discrimination, insurance disputes, marine law, product liability, unfair competition, and intellectual property infringement litigation. The Firm has handled appeals all the way to the U.S. Supreme Court, including a successful landmark case (*Butz v. Economou* 438 US 478, 1978). The Firm's U.S.-based attorneys are frequently called upon to represent clients in significant transactions, example of which includes the US$60 million acquisition of America's third largest ski resort by a major foreign investor and the first ever negotiated license of patent rights between the National Institute of Health and a major Japanese manufacturer. The Firm has been very active in securities and commodities compliance and litigation, as well as public offerings in the U.S.A.

The Firm's partners and associates bring extensive international and domestic legal experience that few firms of its size can equal. The Firm therefore offers the expertise and diversity of a big-firm, while simultaneously providing the personalized service and responsiveness found in smaller firms. The Firm has thus been favored with a broad client base comprised of many of the world's foremost multinational companies from the U.S., Canada, Asia and Europe. Various attorneys of the Firm are admitted to practice in New York, California, and other U.S. jurisdictions, as well as in foreign jurisdictions such as China, Mongolia, Hong Kong, Japan, Korea, Thailand, Indonesia and Australia. In addition to English, attorneys of the Firm are fluent in numerous foreign languages, including Mandarin, Shanghainese, Hokkien, Cantonese and other Chinese dialects, Japanese, Thai, Indonesian Bahasa, Korean, French, Spanish and Swedish.

PEOPLE'S REPUBLIC OF CHINA LAW DIGEST

(The following is a list of all Topics, including cross-references, covered in this Digest.)

PEOPLE'S REPUBLIC OF CHINA LAW DIGEST

Revised for 1997 edition by

ARNBERGER, KIM, BUXBAUM & CHOY, of the New York & California Bars.

PRELIMINARY NOTE:

Standing Committee of Fifth National People's Congress, 12th Meeting, on Nov. 29, 1979 adopted resolution reaffirming as remaining in full force all laws and decrees enacted since founding of People's Republic of China, except those abrogated by subsequent legislation. This resolution clarified condition of legislation enacted since 1949, some of which had not been applied during period of so-called "Cultural Revolution" 1966-1976. With enactment of Common Program in 1949 laws in existence prior to establishment of People's Republic of China on Oct. 1, 1949 were essentially abrogated. Active promulgation of substantial legislation and drafting of much new legislation to be promulgated has taken place in China since 1979. Resolution of Nov. 29, 1979 reaffirmed approximately 1,500 laws, decrees and administrative regulations. There are presently lacunae in law pending promulgation of various draft legislation and some legislation is in conflict with other laws, thus State Council ordered 31 ministries, commissions and bureaus under its jurisdiction to compile all laws and regulations issued since founding of People's Republic of China so they may be revised and where valid, reissued. On Apr. 24, 1987 State Council announced five year program to draft 50 new laws and 300 administrative regulations to be submitted to National People's Congress from 1987 to 1990, to help perfect legal system. Major areas were designated, namely: Giving enterprises more authority, perfect market system, development and indirect control of foreign economic relations; copyright legislation; and company law were to be drafted.

Recent Developments: Government policy of developing socialist market economy continued in 1995, though at slower pace. Tensions between development of market economy and problems of inflation caused Chinese government to intrude into free market areas in attempt to control inflation.

ABSENTEES:

See topic Civil Code.

Chinese nationals living abroad who acquire foreign nationality lose their Chinese nationality. (The Nationality Law of the People's Republic of China, Art. 8). Persons may, under certain circumstances, be represented in judicial proceedings by counsel, without being present themselves. (Provisional Regulations Concerning Attorneys, Art. 7, Code of Criminal Procedure, etc.).

ACCOUNTING:

See topic Joint Stock Companies.

Accounting Law was adopted by National People's Congress on Jan. 21, 1985, effective as of May 1, 1985, and was amended by National People's Congress on Dec. 29, 1993, effective as of Jan. 1, 1994. Law is applicable to state organs, state-owned enterprises, institutions and individual household enterprises.

Accounting Practices.—Following items must be audited: (1) receipts and payments of money and negotiable securities; (2) receipts, dispatch, appreciation or depreciation and use of property; (3) occurrence and settlement of credits and debits; (4) increase or decrease of capital and funds and receipts and expenditures; (5) computation of income, expenses and costs; (6) computation and handling of financial revenue; and (7) other items needed to go through accounting procedures and accounting practices. (Art. 7). Accounting documentation, accounting books, accounting statements and other accounting data must conform to provisions of national unified accounting system. (Art. 10). There must be no forgery and alteration of accounting documentation and accounting books and no submission of false accounting statements. (Art. 10). Where computers are used in accounting practices, software applied and accounting documentation, accounting books, accounting statements and other data generated by software shall meet requirements of financial department of State Council. (Art. 10). Original voucher must be submitted to accounting organizations, which must check and verify them and use verified original voucher to maintain accounts. (Art. 11). Accounting voucher, accounting books, accounting statements and other accounting data must be properly kept; period and procedures for destruction must be determined by financial department of State Council together with relevant departments. (Art. 15). Fiscal year starts from Jan. 1 and ends on Dec. 31 on Gregorian Calendar. (Art. 8). Reporting currency shall be Renminbi. (Art. 9). Where entity mainly uses foreign currency in their routine receipts and payments it may choose one foreign currency as reporting currency, however foreign currency must be converted into Renminbi in compiling accounting statements. (Art. 9).

Accounting Supervision.—Accounting organizations and accounting personnel of all entities must supervise accounting of respective entities, refuse to accept false or illegal original voucher and return inaccurate and incomplete original vouchers for correction. (Arts. 16, 17). Where accounting organizations and accounting personnel find any records of accounting books not being tallied with objects or funds, they must handle them according to relevant regulations. Should they not be empowered to handle them, they shall report to their heads immediately and request investigation and handling of matter. (Art. 18). Accounting organizations and accounting personnel must refuse to accept illegal receipts and payments. Where they deem receipts and payments to be illegal, they must correct them. Should they fail to stop and correct them, they shall file written reports to heads of their entities, requesting matter be handled. Heads of entities shall make written decisions within ten days after receipt of allegedly illegal matters and bear responsibility for their decisions. Where accounting organizations and accounting personnel fail to correct illegal receipts and payments and report to heads of their entities, they shall bear liability. (Art. 19). Where receipts and payments seriously violate law and harm interests of state and public, accounting organizations and accounting personnel shall report to competent departments of financial, auditing or tax authority, which is responsible for handling cases after receipt of said reports. (Art. 19).

Accounting Organizations and Accounting Personnel.—All entities shall set up their own accounting organizations or appoint accounting personnel in relevant organization and designate accounting personnel in charge according to requirements of their accounting affairs. (Art. 21). Should entity not have said conditions, it may entrust accounting consultancy and service organizations established legally to keep accounts on its behalf. Large- and medium-sized enterprises and institutions may appoint chief accountant, whose post shall be held by personnel with at least qualification of chartered accountant. (Art. 21). Accounting organizations should establish auditing system. (Art. 21). Cashiers shall not concurrently take charge of auditing, maintain accounting records or register income, expenses and credits and liabilities. (Art. 21). Major authority of accounting organizations and accounting personnel are as follows: (1) carry out accounting practices; (2) exercise accounting supervision; (3) draft specific procedures for handling accounting matters in their own entities; (4) participate in drafting of economic plan, business plan and assess and analyze implementation of budgets and financial plan; and (5) undertake other affairs related to accounting. (Art. 22). Accounting personnel should have qualified professional knowledge. (Art. 23). Appointment and removal of head of principal accounting personnel in accounting organization of state-owned enterprises and institutions should obtain approval of competent departments. (Art. 23).

Penalties.—Where heads of entities, accountants or their people forge, alter or deliberately destroy accounting vouchers, accounting books, accounting statements and other accounting data, or evade taxes or harm interests of state and public by using false accounting vouchers, accounting books, accounting statements and other accounting data, such cases shall be handled by financial, auditing or tax authorities within their respective authority prescribed by law and administrative decree. Should case be serious enough to constitute crime, criminal liabilities must be imposed. (Art. 26). Where accounting personnel accept untrue or illegal original vouchers or fail to file written reports to heads of their entities regarding illegal receipts and payments or fail to report to competent departments or financial, auditing or tax authorities regarding receipts and payments seriously harming interests of state and public, and cases are serious, administrative disciplinary actions shall be imposed. (Art. 27). Should they cause serious losses to public and private property and are serious enough to constitute crime, criminal liabilities must be imposed. (Art. 27). Where heads of entities and other persons retaliate against accounting personnel who perform their duties according to law, administrative disciplinary actions shall be imposed. Should they be serious enough to constitute crime, criminal liabilities shall be imposed. (Art. 29).

Enterprises Accounting.—Standards of conduct of Enterprises Accounting approved by State Council and promulgated by Ministry of Finance Nov. 30, 1992, effective July 1, 1993, applicable to all enterprises created in China.

Enterprises shall only account for business transactions which have actually taken place and report financial situation and business operation results accurately. (Art. 19). Enterprises shall adopt credit and debit accounting method (Art. 8) and maintain accounting books using accrual method (Art. 16). Enterprises shall match income with related expenses. (Art. 17). Assets and materials of enterprises shall be accounted for at historical cost. Where prices fluctuate, enterprises shall not adjust carrying value at own discretion unless otherwise provided by state. (Art. 19). Reporting currency of enterprise accounting shall be Renminbi. Where foreign currency main sources of enterprise income and expenses, enterprise may choose specific foreign currency as reporting currency and convert into Renminbi when compiling statements. (Art. 7). Standards require accounting records and statements be clear and distinct for easy understanding and utilization. (Art. 15).

Accounting Regulations of Enterprises Experimenting with Share-Holding System (hereinafter "Share-Holding Enterprises") promulgated by Ministry of Finance and State Economic Restructuring Commission May 23, 1992, retroactively effective Jan. 1, 1992, applicable to Share-Holding Enterprises having legal approval. Regulations provide substantially same principles as aforementioned standards. Differences: reporting currency shall be Renminbi. Where Share-Holdings Enterprises receive foreign currency, shall be converted into Renminbi in maintained accounts and account for amount of foreign currency and conversion ratio. (Art. 7). Share-Holding Enterprises shall adopt double entry accounting method. (Art. 8).

Accounting Regulations of Foreign Investment Enterprises (hereinafter "FIE") adopted by Ministry of Finance June 24, 1992, effective July 1, 1992, applied to Chinese-foreign equity joint ventures, contractual joint ventures, wholly foreign owned enterprises. Regulations provide substantially same principles as aforementioned Standards and Regulations. Regulations afford FIEs more autonomy: FIEs may maintain accounts in Renminbi or foreign currency chosen by enterprises. FIEs engaged in multi-currency financing or finance leasing may maintain Renminbi accounts according to actual need. (Art. 13). FIE accounts shall be kept in Chinese or both Chinese and foreign language. (Art. 14). In contractual joint ventures where parties thereto pay taxes separately, combined accounting books shall be kept in respect of assets, liabilities, income, expenses commonly shared and borne by parties. Parties shall also keep own relevant accounting books. (Art. 17). Where FIEs use software to maintain accounting books, software shall conform with relevant requirement and possess functions for ensuring security and confidentiality. Data stored on magnetic or other media shall be supported by back-up files; hard copies shall be printed on regular basis. (Art. 18).

Chartered Accountants Law was adopted by National People's Congress on Oct. 31, 1993, effective as of Jan. 1, 1994. Law replaced Chartered Accountants Regulations promulgated by State Council on July 3, 1986.

Qualification of Chartered Accountants.—Candidates passing qualification examination of chartered accountants organized by China Chartered Accountants Association, and having two years or more experience in auditing business, must submit registration application through accounting firm which they intend to join, to Chartered

See Topical Index in front part of this volume.

ACCOUNTING . . . *continued*

Accountants Association at provincial level for approval. (Arts. 7, 9). Their applications shall be approved, provided that none of following situations exist: (1) have not obtained full competence; (2) criminal liabilities have been imposed, and it is within five years from date of completion of criminal penalties to date of application; (3) administrative disciplinary action or discharge from post imposed due to serious wrongs in work in finance, accounting, auditing, enterprise management or other economic management, and it is within two years from date of imposition of disciplinary action decision to date of application; (4) credentials of chartered accountants was revoked and it is within five years from date of revocation decision to date of application; and (5) other situations that bar candidates' registration pursuant to provisions of financial department of State Council. (Arts. 10, 11). Those approved by aforesaid Associations are chartered accountants and are given uniform credentials of chartered accountants. (Art. 12). Chartered accountants shall practice services in accounting firm (Art. 3) and conduct their practices independently according to law (Art. 6).

Scope of Services.—Chartered accountants render two categories of services: (1) auditing, particularly audit accounting statements and issuing auditing report; verify paid-in capital of enterprises and issue capital verification report; handle auditing affairs in enterprise merger, dissolution, or bankruptcy liquidation and issue relevant report and other auditing affairs provided for by law and administrative decrees; (2) accounting consultancy and accounting services. (Arts. 14, 15). When chartered accountant practices services, commission contract will be executed by and between accounting firm he/she joins and principals(s). (Art. 16). Accounting firm shall assume civil liabilities for business handled by its chartered accountants. (Art. 16). Chartered accountants must maintain secrecy of trade secrets that they acquire in process of conducting business. (Art. 19). Where chartered accountant has conflict of interest with principal, he/she shall recuse himself/herself or principal is entitled to have such chartered accountant removed. (Art. 18). Chartered accountant shall refuse to issue relevant reports under any of following situations: (1) principal requests chartered accountant issue untrue or improper certificate; (2) principal fails to provide relevant accounting data deliberately; or (3) chartered accountant cannot make correct statements regarding major financial and accounting practice in report, since principal has unreasonable requests. (Art. 20).

Accounting Firm.—Chartered accountant may employ partnership to organize accounting firm, in which each partner shall assume joint and several liability for obligations of accounting firm. (Art. 23). Where accounting firm meets all following requirements, it may be qualified as legal person assuming limited liabilities: (1) have registered capital of RMB 300,000 or more; (2) have certain number of professionals, with at least five chartered accountants; and (3) service scope and other requirements are those provided by financial department of State Council. (Art. 24). Accounting firm may set up branch office which shall be subject to approval of provincial financial department where branch office is intended to be established. (Art. 27). Accounting firm shall pay taxes according to law. (Art. 28).

Foreign Accounting Firm.—Foreign nationals may apply to participate in national unified examination organized by China Chartered Accountants Association in spirit of reciprocity treatment. (Art. 44). Foreign accounting firms may establish representative offices in China which shall be subject to approval of financial department of State Council. (Art. 44). Where foreign accounting firm and Chinese accounting firm enter into joint venture accounting firm, approval must be obtained from competent department of Foreign Economic Relations and Trade of State Council, or financial department of State Council after initial approval of other authorized departments of State Council and provincial government. (Art. 44). Where foreign accounting firm intends to handle ad hoc business in China, approval must be secured from provincial financial department. (Art. 44).

Penalties.—Where chartered accountant violates mandatory provisions of law, competent financial department shall impose warning, fines, temporary cessation of practice or revocation of credential of chartered accountants depending upon it seriousness, or referral to judicial organs to bring violators to justice where they are serious enough to constitute crime. (Arts. 39, 40). Where principals and other interested persons suffer damages due to violation of law, accounting firm shall compensate losses therefrom. (Art. 42).

Interim Provisions of Chartered Accountants for Rendering Services to Enterprise Experimenting with Share-Holding Enterprise promulgated by Ministry of Finance and State Economic Restructuring Commission Sept. 17, 1992, effective upon promulgation.

Chartered accountants and accounting firms desiring to render services to corporations issuing stocks to general public and listed on stock exchange shall satisfy separate requirements provided by provisions, in addition to requirements provided by aforesaid Chartered Accountants Regulations, and are subject to Ministry of Finance for approval. (Arts. 4, 5). Chartered accountants working in accounting firm approved to conduct aforementioned services move to another accounting firm without aforesaid qualification shall return license and cease to conduct services. (Art. 5). Where chartered accountants without approval and non-chartered accountants render auditing service for Share-Holding Enterprises, they are not binding. (Art. 5).

Scope of Services.—Main areas of service chartered accountants may render for Share-Holding Enterprises include: (1) asset evaluation; (2) audit results of assets evaluation for newly-created or reorganized Share-Holding Enterprises; (3) verify paid-in capital of Share-Holding Enterprises; (4) audit accounting statements and other annual financial data of Share-Holding Enterprises; (5) verify prospectus of share limited corporation; (6) assist in financial and accounting affairs for Share-Holding Enterprises to be listed, including A-shares listings, B-shares listing, foreign listing; (7) assist in affairs concerning merging and dissolution of Share-Holding Enterprises, including compiling accounting statements and other financial data; (8) assist in financial and accounting affairs related to share transfer of Share-Holding Enterprises; (9) assist in handling termination, liquidation of Share-Holding Enterprises, including checking assets, creditors right and obligation, verifying liquidation report and vouchers, books and statements of liquidation period; (10) accept entrustment of board of supervisors of Share-Holding Enterprises, reexamine accountant report, business operation report, profits distribution plan and other financial data; (11) offer relevant management consultancy and other services requiring entrustment to chartered accountants. (Art. 6).

Share-Holding Enterprises desiring to issue B-shares shall entrust Chinese chartered accountants to audit public accounting statements and provide auditing report. Where outside shares sole distributor bank requires entrustment to outside accounting firm having resident representative office in China for auditing, permission from competent authorities of prospective listed corporation shall be obtained and auditing fees borne by distributor. (Art. 10). Chinese chartered accountants and outside accountants may cooperate in auditing accounts, each shall issue respective auditing report. Regarding annual accounting statement made public after issuance of B-shares, where outside security exchange regulators deem necessary to employ outside accounting firm to audit accounts, listed corporations may directly employ such and bear auditing fees, in addition, accounts must be audited by Chinese chartered accountants issuing auditing report. (Art. 10). Regarding enterprises listed outside of China, where local security exchange regulators provide mandatory requirement concerning accountants conducting such services, enterprises may directly entrust local accountants and bear auditing fees, in addition, accounts must be audited by Chinese chartered accountants. (Art. 10).

Penalties.—Chartered accountants shall not only follow provisions, codes of conduct and proceedings, but also assume legal liabilities for work results and issued reports, including economic compensation, economic sanction, warning, temporary cessation of practice and revocation of credentials. (Art. 14). Those committing crime shall be referred to judicial organs and brought to justice. (Art. 14).

ACKNOWLEDGMENTS:

See topic Notaries Public.

ACTIONS:

See topics Arbitration and Award; Contracts; Environment; Foreign Trade; Libel; Torts; Trademarks; Civil Code.

Citizens' rights to lodge administrative complaints against malfeasance or to initiate legal proceedings to protect their rights are safeguarded by Constitution and Administrative Law. (Art. 41). In addition, international contracts may specify tribunal having jurisdiction over dispute, normally arbitration tribunal, and law that will govern any disputes. Said tribunal and law need not be local but may be non-Chinese. Agreement on Trade Regulations signed on July 7, 1979 between U.S. and China specifically provides that arbitration is permitted and provides that competent authorities in each jurisdiction will enforce arbitration awards. Treaty also expresses intent of parties to be bound by customary international trade practices. In addition, Foreign Trade Arbitration Commission established in China on May 6, 1954 provides for arbitration of disputes arising from foreign trade. By decision of State Council of Feb. 26, 1980 Foreign Trade Arbitration Commission was renamed Foreign Economic and Trade Arbitration Commission, and its jurisdiction enlarged to include taking cognizance of international disputes such as those arising from joint ventures with foreign firms, foreign investment disputes and disputes over credit and loans between Chinese and foreign banks, etc. Obviously, this tribunal's jurisdiction depends initially upon agreement between parties. Arbitral panels have been established in Shenzhen, which include Hong Kong barristers and solicitors.

Art. 8 of Environmental Protection Law, adopted on Sept. 13, 1979 confers upon Chinese citizens right to commence lawsuit against organization or individual that violates provisions of this draft Act.

Organic Law of People's Courts promulgated on July 1, 1979 (C. I, Art. 5) specifies that Chinese citizens, regardless of race, sex, occupation, social status, religion, education, economic circumstances or length of residence will be treated equally before law. There is no specification in this statute that foreigners may have access to courts, or that they are denied access to courts, but in fact cases initiated by foreigners have been brought in courts and Chinese courts have accepted jurisdiction over said proceedings. Furthermore, Code of Civil Procedure, Part IV, provides that foreigners have access equal to Chinese citizens to courts for purposes of civil and commercial litigation, so does Administrative Law.

Code of Civil Procedure, promulgated initially in 1982, revised effective Apr. 9, 1991, containing 270 articles covering major areas of civil procedure. Part IV, Arts. 237-270 contains Special Regulations of Civil Procedure Concerning Foreign Matters.

General Principles.—Part I, which deals with general principles of Code, states that it is based upon Constitution (Art. 1), and purpose of Code is to ensure that courts clearly examine facts, clearly differentiate truth from falsity, properly apply law, promptly try civil cases, and affirm relationship between rights and duties in civil matters; to punish acts that violate law in civil matters; to protect rights and interests of nation, collective organizations and individuals, and to instruct citizens in conscientious observance of law (Art. 2). All civil proceedings commenced within territory of China must observe provisions of this Code. (Art. 4).

Authority to decide civil cases must be exercised by courts, which must, pursuant to provisions of law, independently decide civil cases without interference from administrative organizations, mass organizations, or individuals. (Art. 6). In trying civil cases, court must use facts as basis and law as standard. (Art. 7). Foreign nationals, stateless persons, foreign enterprises and organizations have same procedural rights and obligations as Chinese citizens, legal persons and organizations. (Art. 5).

Where foreign courts impose limits on citizens, enterprises or organizations from China, courts will implement principle of reciprocity regarding that country's nationals, enterprises and organizations. (Art. 5).

In civil litigation, parties have equal rights at trial. (Art. 8). In trying civil case, court should safeguard litigants in exercising their rights at trial, and apply law equally to all parties. (Art. 8).

In trying civil cases, courts should attempt voluntary conciliation in accord with legal principles. But if conciliation ineffective, should then render judgment. Civil cases should be handled on basis of legal regulations providing for: Two levels of courts with court of second instance being court of last resort; trials open to public; collegiate system, and system of not allowing those with relationships with parties to handle cases. (Art. 10). Citizens of each nationally have right to employ language and script of their nationality in civil proceedings. (Art. 11). In minority areas or areas

See Topical Index in front part of this volume.

ACTIONS . . . *continued*
where many minority members reside alongside one another, civil court should employ commonly spoken and written language of said nationalities in trial proceedings and issuance of legal documents. Civil courts should provide translators for local nationality litigants who have different written and spoken languages in common use that are not mutually understood by each litigant. (Art. 11).

Parties to civil litigation have right to argue issues in dispute (Art. 12), and have right, within ambit provided by legal regulations, to restrict their own civil litigation rights (Art. 13). People's Procuratorate has authority to legally monitor courts during trial of civil matter. (Art. 14). Government and mass organizations, enterprises and institutions may support suits in court brought by individuals or units damaged by acts that impaired civil rights and/or interests of individuals, collectives, or state. (Art. 15). Conciliation committees are organizations of mass character, under direction of basic level governments and courts to conciliate disputes among people. Conciliation tribunals undertake conciliation work according to legal regulations, based upon principle of voluntary participation. Parties should abide by agreements reached through conciliation. Those unwilling to conciliate may commence suit in court, and suit may be commenced if conciliation unsuccessful or if party violates conciliation agreement. Courts should revise those decisions reached following conciliation by conciliation tribunals that violate policy or law. (Art. 16).

Congresses and standing committees of nationality minority self-governing areas can establish several adaptations or supplemental regulations, based on principles of Constitution and this statute, and also based on specific circumstances of local nationality peoples. Regulations of self-governing districts (qōu) should be reported for record to Standing Committee of National People's Congress. Regulations of self-governing prefectures (zhoōu) and counties (xiòan) should be reported for approval to standing committee of provincial congress or self-governing district, and should be reported for record to Standing Committee of National People's Congress. (Art. 17).

Part IV. Special Regulations on Civil Procedure Concerning Foreign Matters.—

Chapter XXIV. General Principles.—Civil litigation concerning foreign matters in China must utilize regulations of this Part. If regulations of particular Part do not govern disputes, other relevant provisions of statute will govern dispute. (Civ. Pro. Code, Art. 237).

Those foreign persons and organizations, or international organizations, which give rise to civil litigation, but enjoy exemption from legal process, are to be handled by courts according to laws of China, or treaties entered into by China, or regulations provided in international conventions entered into by China. (Civ. Pro. Code, Art. 239). Where treaties of China or international agreements to which China is signatory have provisions different from those provided in this statute, provisions of international agreement should be applied, except where China has reserved its rights in provision of said agreement. (Civ. Prop. Code, Art. 238).

When court tries case concerning foreign matters, written and spoken language normally used in China should be utilized. If parties request interpreter, such can be provided, but said party must be responsible for paying fees of interpreter. (Civ. Pro. Code, Art. 240). Foreign nationals, stateless persons, foreign enterprises and organizations that bring or respond to suits, and those who need to entrust attorneys to represent them in litigation, must employ attorneys of China. (Art. 241). Foreign nationals or stateless persons who do not reside in China and foreign enterprises and organizations who entrust attorneys to represent them in litigation, must have powers of attorney notarized in country where they reside and obtain Chinese embassy or consulate attestation thereto or verification through procedures provided in relevant treaty between China and foreign entity's country of origin who mail to Chinese attorneys or Chinese citizens powers of attorney must, in order for said powers to have legal effect, have such powers of attorney documented by notary public in nation where they reside and have Chinese embassy or consulate attestation thereto. (Civ. Pro. Code, Art. 242).

Regarding disputes arising from contract or other property rights and interests in which respondents not domiciled in China, where contract is signed or performed in China, or subject matter of suit located in China, or respondents have property in China which may be distrained, or respondents have resident representative office in China, People's Court may exercise jurisdiction where contract signed or performed, subject matters of suit located, property which may be distrained located, infringing act committed, or resident representative office located. (Art. 243). Parties to disputes involving foreign contract or other property rights, may agree in writing to choose litigation forum. Where parties choose Chinese court as forum, mandatory provisions concerning jurisdiction by court hierarchy and exclusive jurisdiction of Code shall be observed. (Art. 244). Where respondents do not file opposition regarding jurisdiction of People's Court and respond to suit, respondents deemed recognizing People's Court jurisdiction. (Art. 245). Suits arising from dispute involving performance of Chinese-foreign equity joint ventures, contractual joint ventures and Chinese-foreign cooperative exploration and development of natural resources, under jurisdiction of People's Court. (Art. 246).

Where final judgment, or order rendered by foreign court requires recognition and (or) enforcement by Chinese court, may directly apply to Intermediate People's Court having jurisdiction for recognition and (or) enforcement, or may request foreign court apply to People's Court for recognition and (or) enforcement in accordance with provisions of international treaties concluded or acceded to by China and country where judgment or order rendered, on reciprocity principle. (Art. 267). Where People's Court deems judgment order does not violate fundamental principles of Chinese law, national sovereignty, security and social interest, it shall order recognition of validity of judgment or order, and issue execution order, which will be enforced according to relevant code provisions. (Art. 268). Regarding award rendered by foreign arbitral tribunal requiring recognition and enforcement of Chinese court, parties shall apply directly to Intermediate People's Court where person against whom award will be enforced has domicile or property is located. Chinese court shall handle enforcement in accordance with international treaties concluded or acceded to by China or on reciprocity principle. (Art. 269).

Opinions Regarding Several Questions on Enforcing the Law of Civil Procedure was promulgated by Supreme People's Court July 14, 1992. C. XVIII, Arts. 304-320 contains special provisions of civil procedure involving foreign matters. Foreign parties to civil procedure may entrust citizens of home country or attorneys of home country to appear in court without utilizing attorney's title, as agent ad litem. (Art. 308). Officials from foreign embassy, consulate to China may personally act as agent ad litem on behalf of citizens of their countries, however they do not enjoy diplomatic privileges and immunities. (Art. 308). Where nationals of foreign countries are parties to suit and do not reside in China they may, under name of diplomatic personnel ret ain, Chinese attorneys or Chinese citizens as agents ad litem for nationals of foreign countries. (Art. 309).

ADMINISTRATIVE LAW:

Administrative litigation law of China was adopted on Apr. 4, 1989 at second session of seventh national Congress. Since citizens have authority to sue government, this statute ensures courts try administrative cases correctly and promptly, so as to protect legitimate rights of citizens, legal persons and other organizations, and ensure administrative organizations exercise powers in accordance with law.

Citizens, legal persons or other enterprises and organizations whose legitimate rights are infringed by concrete actions of administrative organization and their staff have rights to bring suit against said organizations. (Art. 2).

In administrative proceedings, courts utilizes system of collegiate bench, public trial and two levels of appeal in accordance with law. (Art. 6). Mediation is generally not utilized. (Art. 50).

Courts shall accept litigants for following concrete administrative actions: (1) contesting administrative punishments as detention, fine, revoking business license, instructions to stop production or operations, confiscating capital, etc.; and (2) contesting such forcible administrative measures as limit of personal freedom or in sealing up, distraining, freezing assets; and (3) infringement on decision-making power in operations and management by (4) administrative organizations and staff; and administrative organizations failure to issue business license or to reply to persons who conform to lawful provisions for application for licenses; and (5) refusal to perform or failure to reply to applications to administrative organization for liability for personal rights, property rights and the like; and (6) failure to pay pensions for disabled or for family of deceased; and (7) illegally requiring parties to undertake liability for matter they have no responsibility for; and (8) infringement on personal rights and property rights. (Art. 11).

Courts are directed not to take cases concerning national defense, diplomatic affairs, and rules or regulations and concrete administrative acts where administrative organizations have final decision making authority pursuant to law.

Foreigners, stateless persons, foreign enterprises and organizations within territory of China can all undertake suit except those actions governed by other laws. (Art. 70). Foreigners enjoy same rights and obligations as citizens and organizations of China in commencing administrative action. (Art. 71).

Court is to apply principle of reciprocity to right to administrative proceedings by citizens, enterprises and organizations of those countries that impose restrictions on rights of administrative proceedings by citizens, enterprises and organizations of China. (Art. 71).

Where provisions of international treaties, which China has concluded or to which China is party are different from those of this law, former shall be applicable, except as to clauses where China has declared reservation. (Art. 72).

Citizens, legal persons or other enterprises and organizations have rights to claim for compensation when their legitimate rights are infringed upon and they suffer loss as result of actions by administrative organizations or staff. In case of claims for compensation only, disputes shall be decided first by administrative organization. Litigant contesting decision rendered by administrative organization may bring action against administrative organization. Mediation may be applied to proceedings for compensation. (Art. 67).

This law contains all chapters, 75 Articles and is effective as of Oct. 1, 1990.

Regulation of Pharmaceuticals.—(Approved by State Council on Dec. 12, 1992 and promulgated by Decree No. 12 of State Pharmaceutical Administration on Dec. 19, 1992.)

These Regulations are formulated with view to expanding economic and technological cooperation and exchange with foreign countries and providing administrative protection for lawful rights and interests of owners of exclusive right of foreign pharmaceuticals. Pharmaceuticals as mentioned in these Regulations refer to medicines for human beings. Enterprises and other organizations or individuals from any country or region which has concluded bilateral treaty or agreement with People's Republic of China on administrative protection of pharmaceuticals may apply for administrative protection of pharmaceuticals in accordance with these Regulations. (Arts. 1–3).

ADOPTION:

Art. 20 of revised Marriage Law of People's Republic of China, promulgated on Sept. 10, 1980, effective as of May 11, 1981, provides for adoption of children and considers adopted child to have same rights and duties in adopted home as natural child. Legal relationship with natal home is considered terminated upon adoption. Arts. 20 & 21 of Marriage Law, as revised, provide for protection of adopted children.

See topics Civil Code; Infants.

Adoption Law was adopted during 23rd meeting of Standing Committee of Seventh National People's Congress on Dec. 29, 1991, promulgated by Order No. 54 of Chairman of People's Republic of China on Dec. 29, 1991, and effective as of Apr. 1, 1992. Adoption Law was enacted to protect lawful adoptive relationships and to safeguard rights of parties involved in adoptive relationships. (Art. 1).

Adoption shall be in interest of upbringing and growth of adopted minors, in conformity with principles of equality and voluntariness, and not contravene social morality (Art. 2) nor contravene laws and regulations on family planning (Art. 3).

Minors under age of 14, enumerated below, may be adopted: (1) orphans bereaved of parents; (2) abandoned infants, or children whose natal parents cannot be ascertained or found; or (3) children whose natal parents are unable to rear them due to unusual difficulties. (Art. 4).

ADOPTION . . . *continued*

Following citizens or institutions shall be entitled to place children for adoption: (1) guardian(s) of orphan; (2) social welfare institutions; or (3) natal parents unable to rear their children due to unusual difficulties. (Art. 5).

Adopting parents shall simultaneously meet following requirements: (1) shall be childless; (2) shall be capable of rearing and educating adoptee; and (3) shall have reached age of 35. (Art. 6).

Adopting parents may adopt only one child, either male or female. Orphans or disabled children may be adopted irrespective of restrictions that adopter shall be childless, be more than 35 years of age and shall adopt only one child. (Art. 8).

Where male person without spouse adopts female child, age difference between adopter and adoptee shall be no less than 40 years. (Art. 9).

Where natal parents intend to place child for adoption, they must act in concert. If one parent cannot be ascertained or found, other parent may alone place child for adoption. Where person with spouse adopts child, husband and wife must adopt child in concert. (Art. 10). Adoption of child and placing of child for adoption shall both take place on voluntary basis. Where adoption involves minor of age ten or more, consent of adoptee shall be obtained. (Art. 11).

If both natal parents of minor are persons without full civil capacity, guardian(s) of minor may not place minor for adoption, except when natal parents may impose serious harm upon minor. (Art. 12).

Whoever adopts abandoned infant, or child whose parents cannot be ascertained or found, or orphan in care of social welfare institution, shall register adoption with Civil Affairs Department. Apart from above, written agreement on adoption shall be executed by adopter and person placing child for adoption, in accordance with regulations on adoption and on placing child for adoption, provided by Adoption Law. Adoption agreement may also be notarized. If adopter or person placing child for adoption wishes that adoption agreement be notarized, adoption agreement shall be notarized. (Art. 15).

Orphans, or children whose parents are unable to rear them, may be supported by relatives or friends of parents. Adoptive relationship shall not apply to relationship between supporter and supported. (Art. 16).

Where spouse places minor child for adoption after death of other spouse, parents of deceased spouse shall have priority in rearing child. (Art. 17).

Persons having placed child for adoption may not bear any more children, bearing of which would violate regulations on family planning. Placing child for adoption terminates one's freedom to have any more children. (Art. 18).

It is strictly forbidden to buy or sell child outright, or to do so under guise of lawful adoption. (Art. 19).

Foreigners may adopt Chinese children, either male or female, in People's Republic of China. With respect to adoption by foreigner in People's Republic of China, papers certifying certain particulars regarding adopter, such as age, marital status, profession, property, health and record of past criminal convictions and punishments, shall be provided. Such certifying papers shall be notarized by notarial agency or notary of country of which adopter is citizen. Notarization shall be authenticated by Embassy or Consulate of People's Republic of China located in that country. Adopter shall execute written agreement with person placing child for adoption, register adoption agreement in-person with Chinese Civil Affairs Department and complete procedure for notarizing adoption agreement at designated notarial agency. Adoptive relationship shall be established as of date of notarization. (Art. 20).

When adopter and person placing child for adoption wish to keep adoption strictly confidential, other persons shall respect their wishes and shall not make disclosure thereof. (Art. 21).

Rights and duties pursuant to relationship between adopted child and natal parents and other close relatives shall terminate simultaneously with establishment of adoptive relationship, to which new relationship they will apply. (Art. 22).

Adopted child may adopt adoptive father's or adoptive mother's surname, and may also retain original surname, if agreed pursuant to consultation between parties concerned. (Art. 23).

Any act of adoption in contravention of Adoption Law or deemed invalid by People's Court shall have no legal affect. Invalidity of act of adoption shall date back to commencement of act. (Art. 24).

No adopter may terminate adoptive relationship before adoptee reaches age of majority except when adopter and person having placed child for adoption agree to terminate relationship. If adopted child reaches age of ten or more, child's consent shall be obtained. Where adopter fails to perform duties of rearing adoptee, or engages in mistreatment, abandonment, or other acts which encroach upon lawful rights of minor adopted child, person having placed child for adoption shall have right to demand termination of adoptive relationship. Where adopter and person having placed child for adoption fail to reach agreement, suit may be brought in People's Court. (Art. 25).

Where relationship between adoptive parents and adult adopted child deteriorates to such degree that their living together in same household becomes impossible, they may terminate adoptive relationship by agreement. In absence of agreement, suit may be brought in People's Court. (Art. 26).

To terminate adoptive relationship, parties concerned shall execute written termination agreement. Where adoptive relationship was established through registration with Civil Affairs Department, parties shall complete procedure for registering termination of adoptive relationship at Civil Affairs Department. Where adoptive relationship agreement was notarized, parties shall also have termination agreement notarized at notarial agency. (Art. 27).

Upon termination of adoptive relationship, rights and duties pursuant to relationship between adopted child and adoptive parents and close relatives shall also terminate. Rights and duties pursuant to relationship between child and natal parents and close relatives shall be restored automatically. However, with respect to rights and duties in relationship between adult adopted child and natal parents and close relatives, restoration may be decided upon pursuant to consultation between parties. (Art. 28).

Upon termination of adoptive relationship, adult adopted child who has been reared by adoptive parents shall provide money to support adoptive parents who have lost ability to work and are left with insufficient source of income. If adoptive relationship is terminated on account of mistreatment or desertion of adoptive parents by adult adopted child, adoptive parents may demand appropriate amount of compensation from natal parents of adopted child for living and education expenses paid during period of adoption. However, if adoptive relationship is terminated on account of mistreatment or desertion of adopted child by adoptive parents, no compensation may be demanded. (Art. 29).

Whoever abducts child or engages in illegal trafficking of children, under guise of legal adoption, shall be investigated to determine their possible criminal liability. Whoever abandons infant shall pay fine of not more than 1,000 yuan to, and imposed by, Public Security organ. If circumstances are so flagrant as to constitute criminal action, offender shall be investigated for his criminal liability. Whoever sells his or her own child shall be punished as above. (Art. 30).

On Aug. 30, 1984 Supreme Court issued Opinion Related to Several Problems of Enforcing the Civil Law. Adoption relationship agreed upon by natal parents and foster parents having gone through legal formalities shall be legally protected. (para. 27).

Where either of natal parents refuses to give up child for adoption no adoption can take place; but when one natal parent knows that other is sending their child to be adopted, and says nothing, their consent will be implied.

Where one of adopting parents does not, at time of adoption, agree with adoption, but relationship persists during prolonged period, adoption shall receive legal recognition.

Where legal procedures have not been followed at time of adoption, but relationship generally acknowledged, testified to by relevant person, and subsisted for long time it should be treated as if had gone through proper legal procedures. (para. 28).

Where either natal or foster parents attempt to alter adoption, Court shall examine record and decide on basis of best interests of adopted child. Adoption of someone as grandchild is lawful.

Where foster parents discover that their adopted children had physiological defects or diseases and ask to terminate adoption, this will not be permitted, unless natal parents deliberately withheld information on child's infirmity. (para. 30).

This Law is effective as of Apr. 1, 1992. (Art. 33).

ADVERTISING:

See topic Sales.

AFFIDAVITS:

Affidavits in China may be sworn and signatures acknowledged by notaries public.

AIRCRAFT:

U.S. and China entered into agreement relating to civil air transport on Sept. 17, 1980 and agreement relating to reciprocal issuance of visas to crew members of aircraft and vessels on Jan. 7, 1981. On Mar. 5, 1982 U.S. and China agreed to mutual exemption from taxation of transportation income of shipping and air transport enterprises. Income and profits derived from operation of ships or aircraft, including rental income of those operated in international traffic (Art. II[1][b]); rental income incidental to operation of ships or aircraft in international traffic (Art. II[1][c]); income and profits from rental or use of containers (Art. II[1][d]) and related equipment for transportation of containers (Art. II[1][d]) taxable only by contracting state (Art. I). Salaries of crew members of said vessels operated in international traffic exempt from tax in other contracting state. (Art. V). International traffic defined in Agreement to mean any transport by ship or aircraft except that solely between places in other contracting state. (Art. I[2]).

Interim Provisions Concerning Compensation of Personal Injuries of Passengers on Domestic Airways was initially promulgated by State Council on Jan. 3, 1989, and amended by State Council on Nov. 29, 1993. Domestic passenger transportation refers to transportation whose departure and destination are in territory of China. (Art. 2). Carrier shall compensate losses of passengers' death or injuries occurred in aircraft or in course of getting on or off board. (Art. 3). Maximum of compensation shall be RMB 70,000. (Art. 6). Should carrier prove that death or injuries of passengers are caused by force majeure or their own health condition, liability shall be exempted. If they are caused by negligence or willful acts of passengers, liabilities may be mitigated or exempted. (Arts. 5, 6). If passengers purchase insurance against personal accidents in air from insurance company, they are entitled to get insurance compensation without prejudice to their compensation to be obtained from carrier. (Art. 7). Compensation received by foreigners, overseas Chinese and compatriots from Hong Kong, Macao and Taiwan may be converted into foreign currency of their respective country or region according to exchange rate of date of compensation payment quoted by national exchange administration in China. (Art. 8).

ALIENS:

Regulations Governing Entry, Exit, Transit, Residence and Travel of Aliens were originally promulgated by State Council in China on Apr. 13, 1964. Law on Control of Entry and Exit of Aliens was adopted by Standing Committee of National People's Congress and promulgated on Nov. 22, 1985 effective as of Feb. 1, 1986. Aliens, pursuant to these latter regulations, must have prior permission of competent Chinese agencies for their entry, exit, transit, residence and travel in China. (Art. 2) viz. Ministry of Public Security and Foreign Affairs and agencies in China handling entry and exit of aliens (Art. 25). Chinese diplomatic and consular missions abroad handle applications from aliens for entry, exit and travel in China (Art. 6), as authorized by Ministry of Foreign Affairs, as does China Travel Service in certain locations such as Hong Kong. Diplomatic, consular and other officials of foreign diplomatic and consular missions who apply for entry, transit or exit from China are processed by Ministry of Foreign Affairs or local bureaus of foreign affairs.

Visas are required by aliens to enter, exit and transit in China (Art. 6) except when they are covered by agreements between states for mutual exemption from visas (Art. 6). Residency in China requires application and residence registration, normally with local public security organs. (Art. 13). Aliens who are defendants in criminal cases, or criminal suspects confirmed by public security organ, procurator or court, or who

See Topical Index in front part of this volume.

ALIENS . . . *continued*
through court notification are involved in unresolved civil cases, can be denied exit from China. (Art. 23).

Regulations Governing Aliens Traveling in China promulgated on 9 Oct., 1982 by Ministry of Public Security.

General Ministry of Staff of Foreign Affairs and State Travel Bureau classify travel areas into four types: (a) 29 specified cities where aliens can travel without credentials, or any advance notice (Art. 3[1]); (b) areas opened to aliens or where aliens may travel with travel permits routinely granted (Art. 3[2]); (c) non-open areas where aliens may go with travel permits for investigation, scientific exchange, construction or other official business (Art. 3[3]); and (d) all areas except aforesaid three types of areas where aliens are not permitted travel until host organization obtains agreement of said province's autonomous region's government or great military region, then makes application to security unit for traveling permit.

Aliens marrying Chinese citizens are governed by various procedures, some of which originally varied from province to province. For example, Guangdong province on Aug. 7, 1979 promulgated certain procedures (see South China Daily of said date) whereby foreign persons marrying Chinese nationals proceed according to Chinese Marriage Law. Both parties must in person go to institutions that register marriages, fill out application forms and respond to inquiries of said units. Special regulations exist for persons of Chinese origin from Hong Kong and Macao who marry Chinese citizens in China. Foreigners residing in China must have notarized evidence of their status as single persons and Ministry of Foreign Affairs certification (Art. 7), as well as local health examinations prior to registration of said marriage (Art. 10). On Aug. 26, 1983 National Regulations on Chinese Marriages to Foreigners promulgated. If wedding takes place on Chinese soil, and complies with Chinese marriage laws, and does not involve Chinese diplomatic, public security, military personnel, or those involved in confidential work or work considered important, or those serving prison sentences or receiving labor reform reeducation, then approval may be granted within one month of application. Foreign partner must produce passport, residence permit, and certificate of marital status issued by notary in home area.

Provisional Regulations for Handling of Long Term Representatives of Foreign Enterprises were promulgated on Oct. 30, 1980 by State Council. These representative offices must, pursuant to regulations (Art. 2), apply for long term status, obtain approval and be registered. Different organizations in China are afforded authority to approve these applications. Thus, Ministry of Foreign Trade would handle applications from foreign trading organizations, transportation companies, factories, etc. (Art. 4[1]), while insurance companies would apply to Bank of China (Art. 4[2]). Within 30 days of approval of application foreign firm must register with Office of General Administration for Industry and Commerce (Art. 5), and thereafter employees of said enterprise must apply to local public security office for residence permits in China (Art. 6). Hiring local personnel to assist in said office must proceed through appropriate Chinese government offices. (Art. 11).

Subsequent to promulgation of these regulations, various localities promulgated detailed procedures for implementing these rules. Thus, on May 11, 1981 Guangdong province published procedures for registration of foreign corporations on long term basis in Guangdong and on July 21, 1981 Bureau of Labor of Guangzhou city published procedures for hiring local personnel by said foreign entities. Shanghai is about to publish detailed procedures for registering foreign corporations on long term basis, at time of this writing, while Beijing's (Peking) rules have been in force for some time.

Consular Relations Agreement of Jan. 31, 1979 between China and U.S. provides that U.S. citizens having visas to China are insured consular access and protection. (Art. 3). Similarly, if American citizen is arrested in China, consular or embassy notification must be without delay. (Art. 5).

Regulations Governing Foreign Journalists and Permanent Offices of Foreign News Agencies to promote international communications and dissemination of information were adopted by State Council on Jan. 11, 1990, promulgated by State Council on Jan. 19, 1990 and became effective as of date of promulgation.

Present regulations apply to resident foreign correspondents, foreign reporters for short term news coverage (referred to as "foreign journalist") and permanent office of foreign news agencies. (Art. 2).

Chinese government shall protect legitimate rights and interests of foreign journalist and of permanent offices of foreign news agencies according to law. Government shall provide them with facilities for their normal journalistic activities. Foreign journalists and news agencies must abide by laws and regulations of China. (Art. 3).

Ministry of Foreign Affairs of China is competent authority in charge of affairs concerning foreign journalist and news agencies in China. (Art. 4).

Foreign news agency wishing to send resident correspondent to China shall file application with Information Department of the Foreign Ministry. Application must be signed by head of its headquarters and contain following particulars: (1) basic facts about news agency; (2) name, sex, age, nationality, position, curriculum vitae and place of intended residence of correspondent to be sent; (3) professional correspondent certificate of correspondent. (Art. 5).

Upon approval of application, resident foreign correspondent to be sent shall, within seven days of arriving in China, register with Information Department and obtain Foreign Journalist Identity Card. (Art. 6).

Foreign news agency shall apply to Information Department with following particulars: (1) basic facts about news agency; (2) name of office to be set up in China, place of intended residence, business scope, number of staff as well as name, sex, age, nationality, position and curriculum vitae of head of office and other members; (3) copy of registration certificate of news agency issued in China. (Art. 7).

Resident foreign correspondent shall apply to Information Department or authorities entrusted by it for examination and renewal of his Foreign Journalist Identity Card annually. (Art. 10).

Foreign reporter or journalist group wishing to come to China on short-term basis shall file application with Chinese embassy or consulate abroad as well as involved governmental department in China after approval. Individual shall go through procedures for visas at Chinese embassy or consulate abroad or visa-issuing organization authorized by Foreign Ministry. (Art. 12).

Foreign journalist or news agency shall conduct journalistic activities within scope of its registered business or within that of mutually agreed to plan for news coverage. They must observe journalist ethics and may not distort fact, fabricate rumors or carry out news coverage by foul means, and may not engage in activities incompatible with their status or nature of profession, or detrimental to China national's security, unity or social and public interests. (Art. 14).

Foreign journalist shall apply for approval through Information Department for interviewing top leader of China, and shall apply to relevant foreign affairs departments for approval for gathering news from China's governmental departments or other institutions. Foreign journalists shall obtain permission in advance from relevant provincial foreign affairs office, autonomous region or municipality directly under central government for news coverage in open areas in China. They shall submit written application to Information Department for approval. If they intend to cover news in non-open areas in China, they shall go through formalities for travel certificates at relevant public security organization for approval. (Art. 15).

Foreign journalists and news agencies may not install transceivers or satellite communications facilities within China. They shall apply to competent telecommunications department for approval if they are to use walkie-talkies or telecommunication facilities within China. (Art. 17).

In case of violation of these regultions by foreign journalist or news agencies, Information Department may, on merits of each case, give warning, suspend or cancel their journalistic activities in China, or revoke their foreign journalist cards or certificates for permanent office of foreign news agency. (Art. 19).

APPEAL AND ERROR:

According to Organic Law of Courts (C. I, Art. 12), after decision and judgment of basic level courts, parties, including procurator in criminal action, can according to law appeal decision one level. Appellate decisions of middle level courts, high courts and Supreme Court are final decisions and have legal effect, as does decision of first impression of Supreme Court. Chief judges of each level court have duty, if they discover errors of fact or law in judgments rendered within their courts, though said judgments have legal effect, to bring it to attention of trial committee of court for disposition. (C. I, Art. 14). Higher level courts have authority if mistakes are discovered in lower level decisions and judgments which have legal effect, to review matter themselves or order retrial by lower courts. (Art. 14). All courts have responsibility to diligently handle matters where effective legal decisions and judgments have been rendered but where parties raise issues for review. (Art. 14). Higher level procurator also has certain powers pursuant to procedures to resist decisions of lower level courts in criminal matters.

ARBITRATION AND AWARD:

Arbitration Law of China was adopted by National People's Congress on Aug. 31, 1994, effective as of Sept. 1, 1995.

Scope of Arbitration.—Contract disputes and other disputes regarding property rights and interests between civil subjects with equal status, including individuals, legal persons and other entities, may resort to arbitration. (Art. 2). Disputes concerning marriage, adoption, guardianship, fosterage and inheritance, and administrative disputes which should be handled by administrative agencies shall not resort to arbitration. (Art. 3).

Where parties intend to resort to arbitration, they must reach agreement of their own accord. In absence of such agreement, arbitration commission must refuse to accept case if one party applies for arbitration. (Art. 4). Where parties have reached arbitration agreement and one party initiates lawsuit in court, court must reject lawsuit. (Art. 5). If one party brings lawsuit without stating that effective arbitration agreement has been reached, but other party submits arbitration agreement before first hearing, court should dismiss lawsuit. If other party does not take objection, court will resume trial. (Art. 26). Arbitration commission is selected by parties concerned through consultation. Jurisdiction by level and by region does not apply to arbitration. (Art. 7). Arbitration should be conducted independently according to law, free from any interference of any administrative institutions, social organizations or individuals. (Art. 8). Arbitration awards binding and final. After making such awards, arbitration commissions and courts must refuse to accept same cases if parties submit them for re-arbitration or institute lawsuit. (Art. 9).

Arbitration Commission.—Arbitration commissions may be established in centrally directed municipalities, and provincial cities, and autonomous regions. Other cities, if deemed necessary, may also have arbitration commissions. (Art. 10). Arbitration commissions must register with judicial administrative authorities. (Art. 10).

Arbitration commission should have one chairperson, two-four deputy chairpersons, and 7-11 members. (Art. 12). Chairperson and deputy chairpersons must be selected from experts in law, economy and trade and those having practical experiences. Number of experts in law, economy and trade must not be less than two-thirds of total. Arbitrators engaged by arbitration commissions must be just and have moral integrity. They must satisfy one of following requirements: (1) engaged in arbitration work for at least eight years; (2) as lawyers at least eight years; (3) as judges at least eight years; (4) engaged in law research or teaching and have senior titles concerned; or (5) possessing legal knowledge and having been engaged in economic or trade work with senior titles or same qualification.

Arbitration commission should have list of arbitrators in different specialties. Arbitration commissions must be independent from administrative authorities; they must not be subordinate to administrative authorities nor to each other. (Art. 14).

China Arbitration Association is social association having legal person status. All arbitration commissions are its members. Articles of Association of said association should be adopted by national conference of said association. China Arbitration Association is self-disciplinary organization of arbitration commissions. It is empowered to exercise supervision over malpractice of arbitration commissions and their members as

ARBITRATION AND AWARD . . . *continued*
well as arbitrators according to its articles. China Arbitration Association should formulate arbitration rules in accordance with law. (Art. 15).

Arbitration agreement includes arbitration clause specified in contract and other written agreements for arbitration reached before or after occurrence of dispute. (Art. 16). Arbitration agreement must have following contents: (1) willingness to resort to arbitration; (2) scope of arbitration; and (3) selected arbitration commission. Arbitration agreement should be null and void if one of following circumstances arises: (1) matters for arbitration have gone beyond scope of arbitration as stipulated by law; (2) arbitration agreement signed by any persons having no civil competence or limited civil competence; or (3) arbitration agreement reached by coercive means by one party to another. (Art. 17).

Arbitration agreement should be independent, and its effect should not be affected by any modification, termination or invalidation of contract concerned. Arbitration tribunal is entitled to determine effect of contract. (Art. 18). Where parties concerned have objections to effect of arbitration agreement, they may petition to arbitration commission or apply to court. If one party petitions to arbitration commission for decision, but other to court for adjudication, court should adjudicate it. Parties concerned should put forward their objections before first session of arbitration tribunal. (Art. 20).

Application and Acceptance.—In applying for arbitration, following requirements must be met: (1) having arbitration agreement; (2) having specific request, facts and reasons for arbitration; and (3) issue shall be within scope of arbitration. (Art. 21). Parties must submit to arbitration commission arbitration agreement, petition and their duplicates. Petition must include following: (1) name, sex, age, profession, working unit and domicile of each party concerned; names and addresses of legal persons or other organizations; and names and titles of their legal representative or principal leaders; (2) claims and facts as well as reasons on which claims are based; and (3) evidence and its sources, and names and domicile of witnesses.

Arbitration commission must accept case and inform applicant within five days from receipt of petition, if petition meets requirements of arbitration. If not, it must reject and inform applicant within same time limit. (Art. 24). Applicants may waive or modify their claims. Respondent may accept or rebut arbitration claims, and may also institute counterclaims. (Art. 27). Parties and agents ad litem may entrust attorneys or other agents to represent them. Entrusted attorneys or agents must produce power of attorney before arbitration commission. (Art. 29).

Arbitration tribunal may consist of three arbitrators or one sole arbitrator. There must be chief arbitrator for three-arbitrator tribunal. (Art. 30). Where parties agree that arbitration tribunal should be composed of three arbitrators, each of them should select one arbitrator or entrust chairperson of arbitration commission to appoint arbitrator for them respectively. Third arbitrator should be selected by parties jointly or by chairperson of arbitration commission entrusted by parties. Third should be chief arbitrator. Where parties agree that tribunal should be composed of one sole arbitrator, arbitrator should be selected by parties jointly or by chairperson of arbitration commission entrusted by parties. (Art. 31). Where parties fail to reach agreement on composition of arbitration tribunal or fail to select arbitrator, chairperson of arbitration commission should decide composition of tribunal as well as arbitrators. Arbitration commission should inform parties in writing about formation of tribunal. (Art. 33).

Tribunal Session.—Arbitration should be conducted by tribunal sessions. If parties agree that it may be conducted without such sessions, arbitration tribunal may make arbitration decision according to petition and defense as well as other materials concerned. (Art. 39). Arbitration tribunal sessions should not open to public. Where parties agree that tribunal sessions should open to public, tribunal session may open to public, provided it does not involve State secrets. (Art. 40).

Arbitration commission should inform parties of dates for opening of tribunal sessions within time limit prescribed by arbitration rules. Parties, if they have justifiable reasons, may request tribunal session be postponed, which is subject to approval of tribunal. (Art. 41). Applicants who are informed in writing of tribunal session but fail to appear at tribunal session without justification or leave tribunal in middle of tribunal session without permission should be deemed to have withdrawn arbitration claims. Arbitration tribunal may make decision despite absence of respondent when he or she is informed in writing of tribunal session but fails to appear at tribunal without justification or leave in middle of tribunal session without permission from tribunal. (Art. 42). Parties should produce evidence for their claims. Arbitration commission may collect evidence at its own initiative if it is necessary. (Art. 43).

Parties have right to argue for their own claims.

Awards.—Arbitration tribunal may settle dispute by mediation before making award. Tribunal should mediate dispute if parties are willing to do so. Arbitration tribunal should make award promptly if mediation fails. Arbitration tribunal should make mediation document or arbitration adjudication according to agreement when mediation agreement has been reached. Mediation document has same legal effect as arbitration award. Mediation document should include claims for arbitration and results agreed upon by parties concerned, and should be signed by arbitrators and bear seal of arbitration commission. Then document should be delivered to parties concerned. Mediation document should take effect after being signed by parties. If parties go back on agreement before document is signed, arbitration tribunal should timely make award. (Art. 52). Arbitration award should be made according to majority vote of arbitrators. Dissenting opinions of minority arbitrators must be recorded in minutes. If there is no majority opinion on arbitrated issue, arbitration award should be made according to chief arbitrator's opinions. (Art. 53). Claims for arbitration, facts, reasons for arbitration, result of arbitration, payment of arbitration fees, and date for making award should be included in arbitration award. If parties concerned agree, facts and reasons for arbitration award may be omitted from award. Arbitration award should be signed by arbitrators and bear seal of arbitration commission. Those arbitrators who hold dissenting opinions on arbitration award may sign document at their own discretion. (Art. 54). Arbitration award will take effect immediately after it is made. (Art. 57).

Annulment of Arbitration Award.—Where parties concerned provide evidence and show that arbitration award was made under one of following circumstances, they may submit application to intermediate court at location of arbitration commission for annulment of arbitration award: (1) there exists no arbitration agreement; (2) issues arbitrated are beyond scope of arbitration or beyond jurisdiction of arbitration commission; (3) composition of arbitration tribunal and arbitration procedure are against procedure stipulated by law; (4) evidence on which arbitration award is made is fabricated; (5) one party has concealed evidence, which is serious enough to affect fair arbitration; or (6) arbitrators have done such malpractice as asking for and taking bribes or obtaining personal gains.

Court should organize collegiate bench to investigate whether arbitration award is related to one of circumstances mentioned above. If one of above circumstances is involved, court should set aside award. If court decides that arbitration award is against public interest, it should also set aside award. (Art. 58). Parties should submit application for annulment of arbitration award within six months from date they received arbitration award. Court should make decision whether to set aside award or reject application within two months from date when application was received. (Art. 60).

Execution of Awards.—Parties concerned should perform arbitration award. One party may apply to court for execution of award in line with provisions of Civil Procedure Law, in event other party does not perform award. Court accepting such application should enforce award. Where respondent provides evidence and shows that arbitration award involves one of circumstances prescribed by Art. 217 of Civil Procedural Law, collegiate bench organized by court should reject execution of award after examination and verification. (Art. 63). When one party applies for execution of arbitration award while other party applies for revocation of award, court should suspend execution of award. Court should terminate execution of arbitration award, if it has already made ruling to revoke award. If court rejects application for revocation of award, it should resume execution of award. (Art. 64).

Arbitration Involving Foreign Interests.—Foreign arbitration commission must be organized by Chinese Chamber of International Commerce. It must have one chairperson, several deputy chairpersons and several members, as may be engaged by Chinese Chamber of International Commerce. (Art. 66). Foreign arbitration commissions may select arbitrators from foreign personnel possessing knowledge of law, economy and trade, and science and technology. (Art. 67). Where any party to arbitration involving foreign interest applies for preservation of evidence, arbitration commission should submit such application to intermediate people's court having jurisdiction over area where evidence is located. (Art. 68). Foreign arbitration commissions may keep minutes of their tribunal sessions or just keep record of key points of sessions. Record of key points may be signed or sealed by parties and other participants. Where parties provide evidence and show that arbitration awards involve one of circumstances specified in Art. 260 of Civil Procedure Law, collegiate bench of court may revoke such awards after examination and verification. (Art. 70). Where parties concerned apply for execution of arbitration award with legal effect made by foreign-related arbitration committee, they should directly apply to foreign court concerned for recognition and execution of arbitration award if person subject to execution or his or her property is outside territory of China. (Art. 72). Arbitration rules may be made by Chinese Chamber of International Commerce in accordance with law. (Art. 73).

Numerous contracts with American and other foreign firms provide for arbitration outside China according to foreign laws and procedures. For some time, Stockholm, Sweden had been favored locus of arbitration in accordance with Swedish Arbitration Procedures and with reference to Swedish arbitration laws. Switzerland, and in past Holland, were also typical third nations chosen for locus of arbitration. Arbitration in respondent's country is another typical clause in Chinese contracts with foreigners. Chinese presently do not object to having arbitration in U.S. pursuant to A.A.A. rules on some sort of reciprocal basis. Contracts specifying arbitration in Hong Kong are becoming more common. China has acceded to United Nations Convention on the Recognition and Enforcement of Foreign Arbitral Awards, effective as of Apr. 22, 1987.

With respect to maritime arbitration, China adopted Rules of China Maritime Arbitration Commission on Sept. 12, 1988 at third session of China Council for Promotion of International Trade. These rules are similar, but there are differences.

See also topic Labor Relations, subhead Labor Disputes.

ASSIGNMENTS:

See topic Civil Code.

Chinese law at present does not prohibit assignments of claims of creditor to another person, unless contrary to contractual provisions.

ASSOCIATIONS:

Constitution of 1978 provides citizens with freedom of association (Art. 45), freedom to believe in religion (Art. 46), freedom to engage in scientific research, literary and artistic creation, and other cultural activities (Art. 52). On Sept. 10, 1980 third session of Fifth National People's Congress revised Art. 45 of Constitution. While retaining freedom of speech, correspondence, press and assembly, it eliminated terms which gave citizens right to speak out freely, air their views fully, hold great debates and write big character posters. Constitution promulgated on Dec. 4, 1982 provides that citizens have freedom of association, procession and demonstration (Art. 35), freedom of religious belief (Art. 36), nondiscrimination on basis of religion (Art. 36) and also that religious affairs may not be dominated by foreign country (Art. 36). Right to engage in scientific research, literary and artistic creation and other cultural pursuits preserved. (Art. 45). Freedom and privacy of correspondence, except in cases of state security or investigation of criminal offenses preserved. (Art. 40).

There are numerous government sponsored associations in China, as well as religious and other organizations, that have quasi-governmental status. Cooperative societies also receive government blessing, particularly in agricultural and small business areas. Often one of cooperative parties in cooperative venture is state.

Foreign Chambers of Commerce.—Several nations have established chambers of commerce in China. Provisional regulation concerning administration of foreign chambers of commerce were promulgated on Apr. 28, 1989. Foreign chambers of commerce

See Topical Index in front part of this volume.

ASSOCIATIONS . . . *continued*
refer to nonprofit making bodies established in China by foreign business organizations and individuals. Foreign chamber of commerce in China shall not engage in business. (Art. 2).

Chamber must establish articles of association, select chief officers, establish fixed office and have legal source of income. (Art. 4). Chamber may have organizations and individuals as members. (Art 5). Such chamber should be established under name of country whose citizens it represents and word "China" must be added. (Art. 6). Written application must be made to China Foreign Economic and Trade Bureau through China International Chamber, along with articles of association, list of members, resumés of chairman, vice-chairman and staff members, for permission to establish chamber.

China Foreign Economic and Trade Bureau will examine each case to determine which applicants meet criteria and issue approval certificates. (Arts. 7, 8). China Civil Administration Department is responsible for registration of foreign chambers of commerce. (Art. 9).

Chamber should set up books of account in place where its office is located. (Art. 10). Annual report of activities shall be submitted for examination and registration to authorities through China International Chamber in Jan. of each year. (Art. 11).

Registration authority has access to several means of sanctioning chamber for wrongdoing which range from admonishment, fines, cancelling activities, revoking registration, or instructing culpable chamber to wind up operations in China. (Art. 13). China International Chamber will supply consultation services to foreign chambers engaging in activities and will assist them in establishing contacts with appropriate Chinese authorities. (Art. 11).

ATTACHMENT:

See topic Civil Code.

Once civil proceedings are commenced party can make application to have its claim secured prior to issuance of judgment, and courts presently have authority to attach property to secure civil claim. (Code of Criminal Procedure, Art. 53).

Attachment can be commenced by application of one of parties prior to court adjudicating claim if there is reason to believe that it will be difficult or impossible to make execution after adjudication because of acts of one of parties or for some other reason. Normally, court would be concerned with sale, transfer or secreting of property in question. Under extraordinary circumstances court should provide written decision within 48 hours from party's application for preservation of certain property, and should commence immediate execution on said property. Application to preserve property in question, provides scope of relief that may be granted, unless it is property which is subject matter of litigation in which case said property determines scope of relief. If after application for relief, party is not satisfied with decision, application can be made for reconsideration, but during reconsideration original decision stands.

Court can use numerous means of preserving property including: Attaching or sealing property, distraining property or freezing asset (Code of Civil Procedure, Arts. 251-256). Latter form of freezing asset is normally applied to monies or property in bank, or cooperative trust, etc. Sealing involves placing notice of sealing where property is located or property can be moved to another location. If property is distrained, said property can be placed in other persons hands for safe keeping or if property is perishable it can be sold.

In addition court can request guarantee such as deposit of money in bank, bond, etc.

In disputes involving foreign property or foreign parties, courts have same authority to act on petition of party to preserve property. Provisional attachment is available where monetary claims or claims for property are made, or claims are made that can be converted into monetary claims.

Courts in which litigation is taking place, normally basic level courts, or economic trial courts of intermediate level courts, have jurisdiction to act on provisional attachments, etc. If property to be attached, distrained or sealed is not in courts jurisdiction, court where property is located, at behest of trial court, shall act to attach property pursuant to order of trial court.

ATTORNEYS AND COUNSELORS:

See topic Civil Code.

Attorneys Law.—On May 15, 1996 the Standing Committee of the Eighth People's Congress promulgated the "Attorneys Law".

Attorney is defined as one who provides legal services to society with attorney's license. (Art. 2). Attorneys should possess credentials and have license to practise law. (Art. 5). Person who has specialized in study of law for minimum of two years as well as four-year university graduate in any discipline may become attorney through passage of National Uniform Attorney Qualification Examination. (Art. 6). Law college graduate with experience in law teaching or research may become attorney through passage of Ministry of Justice examination. (Art. 7). Those who support PRC Constitution and meet following requirements may apply for attorney license: (a) possession of law credential; (b) one year of practice in law firm; and (c) good behaviour. (Art. 8). Following people are ineligible to apply for attorney license: (a) Those who have not yet reached age of civil capacity or are mentally incompetent; (b) those who have received criminal penalty, except for criminal negligence; and (c) those who have been discharged from public employment or whose attorney license has been previously revoked. (Art. 9). Practice in two or more law firms concurrently is not allowed (Art. 12), but attorney's practice is not restricted by region (Art. 12). Those without attorney's license cannot practice law under auspices of attorney. (Art. 14).

Law firm should conform to following specifications: (a) have its own name, office and bylaws; (b) have assets of RMB 100,000 or more; and (c) have attorneys in accordance with law. (Art. 15). Law firms are classified into three categories: (a) state-owned law firms; (b) cooperative law firms; and (c) partnership law firms. Former two kinds of firms bear liability for their debts limited to total assets of firm, partnerships bear unlimited joint and several liability. (Arts. 16—18). Law firms may set up branch offices, and must bear their branch's debts. (Art. 20).

Attorney's primary responsibilities include: acting as counsel to individuals, corporations and other organizations; accepting civil, criminal and administrative cases and making court appearances in relation thereto; drafting legal complaints, briefs and other legal documents; furnishing general legal advice; acting as accusorial agent in private prosecutions; posting of bail; and management of non-litigation matters such as conciliation and arbitration. (Art. 25). Termination of established attorney-client relationship may be effected by client at will with or without cause, while termination by attorney must be for good cause only. (Art. 29).

Attorneys have right to investigate their client's case and collect relevant materials pertaining thereto, meet and communicate with persons in custody. (Art. 30). No attorney may represent opposing parties in same case. (Art. 34).

Following conduct is forbidden: establishment of attorney-client relationship outside sponsorship of law firm; exploitation of attorney representation for personal profit; meeting with judges, government attorneys or arbitrators involved in attorney's current case, bribing or solicitation of judges, government attorneys or arbitrator; presenting false evidence; and disturbing order of court. (Art. 35).

Citizens who are involved in support of their parents, workplace injury, criminal litigation and State compensation, have right to obtain legal aid even if they cannot afford it. (Art. 41). Penalties for violating law governing attorneys include warnings, suspension of business activities from three months to one year, confiscation of illegal income, maximum fines of RMB 5,000 or five days' detention, revocation of license to practice and, in criminal cases, determination of criminal responsibilities. (Arts. 44-46).

Penalties for violating law governing firms include confiscation of illegal income, fines of one to five times amount of illegal income, suspension of business or revocation of business license. (Art. 47). Firms damaging clients due to illegal practices or professional negligence must compensate client. Firm involved may then seek compensation from attorney involved. Attorneys and law firms cannot avoid or limit their liability due to illegal practices or professional negligence. (Art. 49).

Attorney Association is organization which governs attorneys. (Art. 37).

Foreign nationals, foreign enterprises and foreign organizations seeking counsel to represent them in litigation in China must employ attorney of People's Republic of China, or can entrust private persons to represent them.

China Law Society active in sending and welcoming legal specialists.

Foreign attorneys recognized by Chinese arbitral law, etc. and in practice foreign firms have been permitted to utilize their counsel in China during business negotiations. American attorneys have offices in Beijing, Shanghai and Guangzhou, etc. Certain American law firms have agreements with local Chinese law firms, which are approved by Provincial Bureau of Justice, for cooperation in legal matters both in China and elsewhere.

Interim Provisions Governing Foreign Law Firms Establishing Offices in China promulgated by Ministry of Justice and State Industrial and Commercial Administration May 26, 1992. Where foreign country permits Chinese law firm to establish office in its territory, in reciprocity China allows foreign law firm from said country to establish office in China according to provisions. (Art. 6). Office of foreign law firm including its members shall observe Chinese laws and regulations, and shall not injure national security of China, social interest and legal interest of Chinese citizens and legal persons. (Art. 4).

Establishment and Termination.—Foreign law firm shall file with Ministry of Justice written application directly or refer to Ministry of Justice through Judicial Department (Bureau) at provincial level where prospective office to be located. (Art. 7). Ministry of Justice shall examine application, decide within 60 days whether to approve or reject application and notify applicant. (Art 7.). Applicant shall obtain Certificate of Approval in place and time designated by Ministry within 60 days following date applicant received notice. (Art. 9). Applicant shall register with State Industrial and Commercial Administration within 30 days when Certificate of Approval has been issued. (Art. 9). Where applicant fails to register within designated period, Certificate of Approval shall automatically be nullified. (Art. 9). Office of foreign law firm shall be titled as XX Law Firm XXX (name of city) Office. (Art. 10). Duration of foreign law firm office shall be five years commencing from date when registration certificate is issued, which may be renewed after expiration. (Art. 11). Foreign law firm shall assume immediate liability for taxes and debts of its Chinese office. (Art. 14).

Scope of Services.—Foreign law firm, including its members, may render three categories of service (Art. 15): (1) consultancy to clients on law of country where admitted to practice law and relevant international custom and practices; (2) entrustment of legal work by clients or Chinese law firms undertaken in country where admitted to practice law; (3) act as agent for foreign client, and employ Chinese law firms to handle legal affairs in China. Office of foreign law firm including its members shall not act as agent in Chinese legal affairs, interpret Chinese laws and regulations for clients and perform other services that Chinese law prohibits foreigner to engage in. (Art. 16). Foreign law firm shall not employ Chinese attorneys. (Art. 17). Legal fees for services rendered in China shall be settled in China. (Art. 18). Standard legal fees and billing methods shall be filed with approval authority and registration authority. (Art. 18).

Penalties.—Ministry of Justice and its authorized departments (bureaus) or provincial levels may impose warnings, cessation of practice or revocation of approval, etc. in light of seriousness of offense. (Art. 23). State Industrial and Commercial Administration and its authorized local authorities may impose fines, confiscation of illegal income or revocation of registration etc. according to relevant laws and regulations regarding industry and commerce administration. (Art. 23).

BANKRUPTCY:

See topics Civil Code; Joint Stock Companies.

Introduction.—With exception of certain local trial regulations, those of Shenyang being most prominent, China enacted no bankruptcy legislation until latter part of 1986. On Nov. 29, of that year Standing Committee of Guangdong Provincial Congress enacted bankruptcy regulations for companies with foreign participation in Shenzhen Special Economic Zone (hereinafter "SEZ Bankruptcy Law") and on Dec. 2, 1986, Standing Committee of Sixth National People's Congress enacted, for trial implementation, Enterprise Bankruptcy Law of China, effective as of 1 Nov. 1988.

SEZ Bankruptcy Law only has effect in Shenzhen and is only applicable to corporations in Shenzhen having foreign equity participation (Art. 2), whereas Enterprise

See Topical Index in front part of this volume.

BANKRUPTCY . . . *continued*
Bankruptcy Law is applicable only to state owned enterprises in all of China (Art. 3). Nevertheless these are first serious statutes to deal with bankruptcy matters.

C. XVIV of Law of Civil Procedure, Arts. 199-206, contains provisions governing bankruptcy applicable to all enterprises, legal persons other than state-owned enterprises, including collective enterprises with status of legal person, jointly operated enterprises, private enterprises, and Chinese-foreign equity joint ventures, contractual joint ventures and wholly foreign-owned enterprises in China. Where all parties to jointly operated enterprises are state-owned enterprises, Enterprise Bankruptcy Law of China applies instead of chapter governing enterprises bankruptcy proceedings.

Definition.—Both regulations define bankruptcy as inability to repay debts as they fall due. (Art. 3 of both statutes).

Intermediate court in Shenzhen handles all bankruptcy matters and determines bankruptcy (Arts. 7, 3) as do state courts pursuant to Enterprise Bankruptcy Law (Art. 5).

Petition for Bankruptcy.—In Shenzhen creditors of bankrupt and debtor itself may petition court, but debtor's petition requires resolution of its shareholders or board of directors. (Art. 8). In national legislation creditors may petition for bankruptcy (Arts. 3, 7) or debtor may petition after approval of senior department in charge of enterprise (Art. 8).

Creditor's Meeting.—Enterprise Bankruptcy Law provides that creditors of bankrupt may hold meeting in which all unsecured creditors have right to vote and court has power to appoint chairman of creditors' committee. (Art. 13). Creditors' committee adopts resolutions by majority vote of those attending, so long as they represent more than half of unsecured debt. (Art. 15). If there is agreement between creditors and bankrupt this can be approved by court and bankruptcy proceedings suspended or terminated. (Art. 19).

In SEZ Bankruptcy Law, court can appoint liquidation committee, to be paid by debtor, which acts under court supervision and in turn convenes and presides over creditors' meetings. (Arts. 12, 13, 14). Creditors' committee itself elects representatives to work with liquidation committee and represent creditors. (Art. 16). Similarly decisions are made at creditors' committee by majority of members present at meeting who represent more than half of unsecured creditors. (Art. 18). Agreement between creditors and bankrupt can be approved by court. (Art. 18).

Bankruptcy Declaration.—SEZ Bankruptcy Law provides that upon adjudication of bankruptcy, court shall make public announcement specifying time limit for creditors to register their claim, providing date for first creditors' meeting, etc. (Art. 27). Enterprise Bankruptcy Law provides after declaration by court of bankruptcy (Arts. 23 and 3) court shall appoint liquidation committee (as in SEZ Bankruptcy Statutes), who shall appraise and allot assets of bankrupt (Art. 24). Under Enterprise Bankruptcy Law, liquidation committee, which is responsible to court, is to be appointed from senior general agency in charge of bankrupt, Ministry of Finance and related departments. (Art. 21).

Bankrupt's Assets.—Assets of bankrupt are defined in both statutes. SEZ statute lists assets as all property belonging to bankrupt at time of bankruptcy declaration, other rights to property, rights to assets surrendered by bankrupt within 180 days of declaration of bankruptcy that should not have been released (e.g. advance payments of certain debts, etc.). (Arts. 31, 11).

Enterprise Bankruptcy statute defines assets of bankrupt to include all assets of bankrupt at time of declaration of bankruptcy and those acquired prior to liquidation, as well as other rights and interests of bankrupt. (Art. 28). Statute also gives liquidation committee authority to determine whether or not to perform contracts of bankrupt not yet performed. (Art. 26). Enterprise statute also has provision for recalling assets wrongfully released within six months of bankruptcy. (Art. 25).

Non-Bankrupt Assets and Unacceptable Claims.—SEZ Bankruptcy Law provides that debts occurring after declaration of bankruptcy are not normally part of claims that can be made (Art. 34); Enterprise Bankruptcy Law has similar provision (Art. 30). Both statutes deny creditors fees for participation in bankruptcy proceedings as claims against bankrupt estate. (Enterprise Law, Art. 30; SEZ Law Art. 34[2]).

Priorities.—SEZ statute provides that secured debts shall have prior claim up to amount of debt or if value of asset securing debt is less than claim than up to value of asset. (Art. 35). Enterprise Bankruptcy statute provides priority to secured assets (Art. 32) pursuant to similar terms.

Enterprise Bankruptcy Law provides that bankruptcy fees are to be first appropriated from bankrupt estate, then salaries of staff and workers, labor insurance fees, tax payments, and unsecured debts are to have priority in that order. If assets do not suffice to cover debts then they are to be paid off proportionately. (Art. 37).

Similarly SEZ regulations provide that bankruptcy fees including legal costs have certain priority; thereafter salaries, labor insurance, national taxes and unsecured debts, in that order, have priority.

Subsequent Legislation.—Statutes will have to be supplemented by detailed legislation and administrative rules. National legislation, affecting as it does only state owned enterprises, is naturally very carefully drawn so as not to appear too harsh or hasty. Thus there are provisions making this law only trial legislation, for short period, with steps for trial implementation to be separately stipulated. (Art. 43). Declaration of bankruptcy requires acquiesence of superior government agency in charge (Art. 3), state is to arrange jobs for employees thrown out of work as result of bankruptcy (Art. 4), government organizations are encouraged to subsidize state enterprises in financial difficulty having significant national importance (Art. 1) etc. Law has yet to be implemented.

SEZ Bankruptcy statute only applies to enterprises in Shenzhen partially or fully owned by non-Chinese interests, thus it is less tentative and immediately effective.

National legislation applicable to enterprises without qualification of legal person, industrial and commercial households, rural lease holding households, individual partnership may be promulgated in future.

BANKS AND BANKING:

See topic Currency.

China has two primary banking systems, viz. Bank of China handling foreign currency and international transactions, and Industrial and Commercial Bank and Agricultural Bank which handles ordinary domestic, commercial and retail transactions aside from financing agriculture. Banking is state monopoly, although foreign banks have maintained offices in China since 1949. For example, Standard Chartered Bank and Hong Kong Shanghai Bank, both English banks, have maintained branch offices in Shanghai for many years and perform certain international banking functions. Recently several foreign banks have been permitted to open branch offices in Shanghai such as Japanese bank Sanwa that also has branch in Shenzhen. At least 48 American banks have full correspondent relations with Bank of China, and some maintain representative offices in Beijing. Bank of China handles accounts for foreign corporations as well as letters of credit and other normal commercial transactions. In Shenzhen SEZ foreign banks are permitted to provide range of branch services. Joint venture bank has been established in Xiamen, and another such bank has been recently approved. Branches of foreign banks are permitted and have been established in Shenzhen, and in Hainan Province. In general opening of branch offices of foreign banks in China is proceeding rapidly.

Banking Laws and Related Legislation.—With development of China's financial system reform, series of statutes, regulations, and rules have been adopted and promulgated by both State Council and Central Bank (People's Bank of China). Following is list of relevant laws related to banking in China:

Financial Entity Laws.—The Temporary regulations on the People's Bank of China (Promulgated by State Council on Jan. 7, 1986); Regulations of China Governing the Administration of Foreign-Invested Financial Entities (Promulgated by State Council on Feb. 25, 1994); Regulations of China Governing the Adminstration of Financial Entities (Promulgated by People's Bank of China on Aug. 5, 1994); Measures on the Administration of the State Treasury in the People's Bank of China (Promulgated by State Council on July 27, 1985); Temporary Regulation of the Verification of People's Bank of China (Promulgated by People's Bank of China on July 5th, 1985); Notice Regarding the Assets Balance System Regulation in the Commercial Banks (Promulgated by People's Bank of China); Regulations of the Urban Credit Unions (Promulgated by People's Bank of China on July 17, 1986); Temporary Regulation on the Credit Union in the Countryside (Promulgated by the People's Bank of China on Oct. 12, 1990); Temporary Regulation on the Financial Trust & Investment Entities (Promulgated by People's Bank of China on Apr. 26, 1986); Notice Regarding the Regulation on Pawn-Brokering (Promulgated by People's Bank of China on Aug. 19, 1993).

Financial Transaction Laws.—Temporary Regulation on Credit Loans (Promulgated by People's Bank of China on Feb. 15, 1994); Temporary Regulation on Commercial Banks (Promulgated by People's Bank of China on Mar. 3, 1993); Temporary Regulation on the Assets of the Trust & Investment Entities (Promulgated by State Council on Dec. 24, 1986); Regulation on Deposits (Promulgated by State Council on Dec. 11, 1992); Measures on Loan Contracts (Promulgated by State Council on Feb. 28, 1985); Temporary Regulation on Banking Interest (Promulgated by People's Bank of China on Dec. 11, 1990); Regulation System Regarding the Credit Loan on Special Projects (Promulgated by People's Bank of China on Dec. 24, 1980); Regulation on the Use of the International Business Loan (Promulgated by State Council on Jan. 12, 1989); Measures on the Inter-Bank Loans (Promulgated by People's Bank of China on Mar. 8, 1990); Regulation on Working-Capital Loans to State-Owned Industry and Transportation Entities by the Industry and Commercial Bank of China (Promulgated on Aug. 25, 1986); Loan Legislation by the Agricultural Bank of China (Promulgated on Jan. 23, 1990); Regulation on Short-Term Foreign Exchange Loans by the Bank of China (Promulgated on Aug. 30, 1980); Regulation on Loans to Foreign Invested Enterprises by the Bank of China (Promulgated on Apr. 24, 1980); Regulation on Bank Accounts (Promulgated by People's Bank of China on Dec. 9, 1994); Penalty Measures on Violations of the Banking System (Promulgated by People's Bank of China on Oct. 9, 1994); Law of the People's Republic of China regarding People's Bank of China. (Detailed information described hereinafter); Law of the People's Republic of China on Commercial Banks (Detailed information described hereinafter).

Currency Laws—Ren Men Bi (RMB).—Temporary Regulation on the Currency Issuance System by the People's Bank of China (Promulgated on Mar. 30, 1988); Regulation on the Cash Deposit of the Commercial Banks (Promulgated by People's Bank of China on Dec. 9, 1985); Cash Regulation Measures (Promulgated by State Council on Sept. 8, 1988).

Foreign Exchange Laws.—Temporary Rules on the Foreign Exchange Regulations (Promulgated by State Council on Dec. 18, 1980); The Detailed Penalty Rules on Violations Related to Foreign Exchange (Promulgated by State Administration on Foreign Exchange on Jan. 11, 1993); Regulations on the Foreign Exchange Transaction in the Non-Banking Financial Entities (Promulgated by State Administration on Foreign Exchange on Jan. 1, 1993); Notice on Further Control of Foreign Exchange System (Promulgated by People's Bank of China on Dec. 28, 1993); Temporary Regulation on Foreign Exchange Accounts (Promulgated by People's Bank of China on Apr. 1, 1994).

Gold and Silver.—Regulation on Gold and Silver (Promulgated by People's Bank of China on June 15, 1983); Regulation on Import and Export of Gold and Silver (Promulgated by People's Bank of China and China General Customs on Feb. 1st, 1984).

Policy Banks.—China's banking system is under major reform. On Dec. 25, 1993, State Council adopted Decision Governing Restructuring Banking System. Ultimate goal of restructure is to separate policy finance from commercial finance and commercialize its existing specialized banks. To that end, State Council decided to set up policy banks, namely State Development Bank, Agricultural Development Bank of China and Import & Export Loan Bank of China.

State Development Bank was approved by State Council on Mar. 17, 1994. Main function of bank is to establish long term stable capital sources and capitalize funds for and lead social funds to state capital construction. Bank is based in Beijing and will administer People's Construction Bank of China and state investment organizations.

Import & Export Loan Bank of China was approved by State Council in Apr. 1994. Major functions of bank are to implement state industrial policy and foreign trade

BANKS AND BANKING . . . *continued*
policy, provide policy finance support for import and export of machinery and equipment and complete plant transfer, provide export credit insurance, export loan guaranty and import and export insurance, issue negotiable securities abroad, handle foreign exchange business and provide consultancy for import and export business and project appraisal. Funds of bank will be allocated by Ministry of Finance. Bank is based in Beijing, will not set up branch offices, however, may establish representative offices in some large cities.

Agricultural Development Bank of China undertakes to provide policy loans for national cereal, cotton and oil reserves, agricultural products purchase and agricultural development, allocate aid-agriculture funds and supervise their uses. Bank will establish branch offices in major agricultural province.

People's Bank of China.—Law of the People's Republic of China on the People's Bank of China was promulgated by National People's Congress on Mar. 18, 1995, effective as of date of its promulgation. People's Bank of China (hereinafter "People's Bank") is central bank of People's Republic of China (Art. 2) and it shall be under direction of State Council (Art. 3). It must perform following functions: (1) to formulate and implement monetary policies; (2) to issue Renminbi (RMB) and control its circulation; (3) to approve, supervise and administer financial institutions; (4) to supervise and control financial markets; (5) to promulgate ordinances and rules concerning financial administration and business; (6) to hold, administer and manage State's foreign exchange reserve and bullion reserve; (7) to act as fiscal agent for State; (8) to maintain normal operation of payment, clearing and settlement systems; (9) to be responsible for statistics, investigation, analysis and forecasting for financial industry; (10) to engage in relevant international financial activities in capacity of central bank of China; and (11) other functions assigned by State Council. (Art. 4). People's Bank must report its decisions concerning annual supply of bank notes, interest rates, foreign exchange rates and other major issues specified by State Council for approval before implementation, while other decisions on matters concerning monetary policies must be immediately implemented by People's Bank. (Art. 5). People's Bank of China must submit work reports to Standing Committee of National People's Congress on matters concerning monetary policies and its work of supervision and control over financial industry. (Art. 6). People's Bank must independently implement monetary policies, exercise its functions and carry on its operation according to law. (Art. 7). Entire paid-up capital of People's Bank is allocated by State and owned solely by State. (Art. 8).

Institutional Structure.—People's Bank must have one governor and a number of deputy governors. Person for Governor must, nominated by Premier of State Council, be decided upon by National People's Congress (NPC); and when NPC is not in session, determined by NPC Standing Committee and appointed or removed by President of P.R.C. (Art. 9). Governor, deputy governors and other staff must refrain from holding posts concurrently in any other financial institutions, enterprises or foundations (Art. 13) and must keep secrets of State, financial institutions and clients under their supervision and control (Art. 14). People's Bank must establish monetary policy committee (Art. 11) and its branches as its representative organs (Art. 12).

Renminbi.—Legal tender of P.R.C. is Renminbi (RMB). (Art. 15). Renminbi must be printed, minted and issued solely by People's Bank. (Art. 17). Any counterfeiting or altering of RMB is prohibited. Selling, buying, transporting, possessing or using counterfeit or altered RMB is prohibited. It is illegal to destroy RMB intentionally. Illegal use of RMB on propaganda material, publications and other commodities is prohibited. (Art. 18). No organization or individual is allowed to print or issue coupons as substitutes of RMB for circulation. (Art. 19). People's Bank must establish RMB issue treasury, and its branches must establish subsidiary treasuries. No organization or individual can use issue fund in violation of relevant regulations. (Art. 21).

Business Operation.—Aim of monetary policies is to maintain stability of value of currency and thereby promote economic growth. (Art. 3). People's Bank may, for purpose of implementing monetary policies, apply following monetary policy measures: (1) to require financial institution to place deposit reserve fund at required ratio; (2) to fix basic interest rates; (3) to provide rediscount business for financial institutions having current accounts in People's Bank; (4) to provide loans for commercial bank; (5) to buy and sell state bonds and other government bonds and foreign exchange in open market operation; and (6) other monetary policy instruments defined by State Council. (Art. 22).

People's Bank must act as fiscal agent for State. (Art. 23). People's Bank may organize financial institutions in issuing and cashing state bonds and other government bonds on behalf of financial department of State Council (Art. 24); may open accounts for financial institutions as needed, but may not provide financial institutions with overdraft facilities (Art. 25); may determine amounts, duration, rate of interest and form of loans to commercial banks, but duration must not exceed one year (Art. 27); and People's Bank must organize or assist in organizing financial institutions in settling interinstitutional accounts, coordinating such activities and providing such services (Art. 26). People's Bank may not provide State with overdraft facilities, may not directly subscribe and underwrite state bonds and other government bonds (Art. 28); and may not provide loans to local government or governmental departments at all levels, or to financial institutions other than banks, other organizations or individuals, except special financial institutions other than banks to which People's Bank may provide loans as determined by State Council (Art. 29). People's Bank may not act as financial guarantor for any organization or individual. (Art. 29).

Supervision over Financial Institutions.—People's Bank must approve establishment, changes, termination and business scope of financial institution. (Art. 31). People's Bank has power to audit, check and supervise at any time deposits, credits, settlements, bad loans and other business affairs of financial institutions (Art. 32); has power to check and supervise raising or lowering of interest rates on deposits or loans by financial institutions in violation of regulations (Art. 32); has power to demand financial institutions to submit balance sheets, statements of profit and loss and other accounting reports and materials pursuant to regulations (Art. 33). People's Bank must guide and supervise business operation of state banks responsible for implementing state policies. (Art. 35).

Financial Accounting.—People's Bank must exercise independent control over its financial budget, and budget must be incorporated into central budget. (Art. 37). People's Bank must turn over to State Treasury entire net profit after deducting annual expenditures from annual income and drawing funds for its general reserve at proportion determined by financial department of State Council; losses sustained by People's Bank must be offset by State Treasury. (Art. 38).

Legal Liabilities.—Penalties for violating law include detention of no more than 15 days, fine of RMB5,000-200,000, giving administrative sanctions and, if case constitutes crime, being investigated for criminal responsibilities. (Arts. 41-50).

Commercial Banks.—Commercial Banking Law of People's Republic of China was promulgated by National People's Congress on May 10, 1995, effective as of 1 July 1995. Commercial banks refer to corporate legal persons established in accordance with this law and Company Law of P.R.C. to receive money deposits from public, extend loans, provide settlement services and do other relevant businesses. (Art. 2). Commercial bank may engage in some or all of following businesses: (1) receiving money deposits from public; (2) extending short, medium and long-term loans; (3) providing domestic and international settlements; (4) handling cashing of bills and notes; (5) issuing financial bonds; (6) acting as agent in issuing, cashing and underwriting government bonds; (7) dealing in government bonds; (8) interbank call-money business; (9) dealing or acting as agent in foreign exchange transactions; (10) providing L/C service and guarantee; (11) acting as agent in collection and payment and insurance business; (12) providing safe deposit box service; and (13) other businesses approved by People's Bank of China. (Art. 3). Commercial bank operates independently and must assume civil responsibilities independently with its entire assets as legal person. (Art. 4). Commercial bank must abide by principle of equality, voluntariness, fairness, honesty and good faith in doing business with its clients. (Art. 5). In doing credit business, commercial bank must strictly examine credibility of borrower and persist in extending loans against collateral in order to ensure recalling loans on time. (Art. 7). Commercial bank is protected by law to retrieve principal and interests of loan from borrower. (Art. 7). Commercial bank must refrain from unfair competition and be subject to supervision and administration by People's Bank of China. (Art. 10).

Establishment and Organization.—Establishment of commercial bank requires examination and approval by People's Bank. No organization or individual can receive money deposits from public or do any business of commercial bank or use title of "bank" without approval of People's Bank. (Art. 11). Establishment must satisfy following requirements: (1) having its rules and procedures in compliance with this law and Company Law; (2) having minimum registered capital defined by this law; (3) having chairman of directors (president), general manager and other senior managerial personnel with expertise and professional experience required by their positions; (4) having complete organization and management system; and (5) having up-to-standard business site, safety measures and other facilities relevant with business. (Art. 12). Minimum registered capital for commercial bank is RMB1,000,000,000; RMB 100,000,000 for city cooperative commercial bank; and RMB50,000,000 for agricultural village cooperative commercial bank. People's Bank can adjust registered minimum capital based on economic development. (Art. 13). Approved applicants must register and obtain business licenses from Industrial Commercial Administration Department. (Art. 16).

Company Law is applicable to form and structure of organization of commercial bank. (Art. 17). Commercial bank solely owned by State must have board of supervisors, which must be composed of representatives of People's Bank and governmental departments, experts from other relevant departments, and representative of staff of bank. Board of supervisors must exercise control of solely state-owned commercial banks over quality of credit funds, ratio of assets to liabilities, hedging and appreciation of state-owned assets, etc., and behavior of its high-ranking managerial personnel violating law, administrative decrees, or rules and procedure, or committing acts damaging interests of bank. (Art. 18). Commercial bank may set up its branches within and outside territory of P.R.C. Total sum of working capital to be allocated to all branches must not exceed 60% of total capital of commercial bank proper. (Art. 19). Commercial bank must apply to its branches financial system of unified accounting, centralized fund allocation and level-by-level management. (Art. 22). Branch of commercial bank must not be qualified as legal person and must do business within scope authorized by headquarters which will assume civil responsibilities. (Art. 22).

When commercial bank or its branch has not started for over six months from date of being granted business license or has automatically suspended operation for over six consecutive months after starting its operation, People's Bank must revoke its banking permit and make public announcement. (Art. 23). Anyone who has one of following backgrounds must not hold high managerial positions in commercial bank: (1) having once been sentenced to imprisonment or deprived of political rights on account of graft, bribery, illegal possession of property, embezzlement of public property or disruption of social economic order; (2) having served as director of board of directors, director or manager of company which went bankrupt because of mismanagement and having been personally responsible for bankruptcy; (3) having been legal representative of company whose business license has been revoked on account of violation of law and having been personally responsible thereof; and (4) having failed to repay fairly large debt already due. (Art. 27). Any organization or individual intending to buy more than 10% of shares of commercial bank must obtain approval from People's Bank. (Art. 28).

Protection of Depositors.—Commercial bank in its savings deposit business must abide by principle of voluntariness in depositing, freedom of withdrawal, interest on every deposit and keeping secrets of depositor. With regard to savings deposits of individuals, commercial bank has right to reject demand of any department or individual to investigate, freeze, or withhold and transfer savings deposit, unless otherwise specified by law. (Art. 29). With regard to deposits of any organization, commercial bank has right to reject demand of any other organization or individual for investigation, unless otherwise specified by laws or administrative decrees; it has right to reject demand of any other organization or individual for freezing, or withholding and transferring such deposit, unless otherwise specified by law. (Art. 30). Commercial bank must fix its interest rates for deposits pursuant to ceiling and floor of interest rates defined by People's Bank and make public announcement thereof. (Art. 31). Commercial bank must place required reserve with People's Bank and keep adequate

See Topical Index in front part of this volume.

BANKS AND BANKING . . . *continued*
stand-by reserve in accordance with stipulations of People's Bank (Art. 32). Commercial bank must guarantee payment of principal and interest of every deposit and must not delay or refuse payment. (Art. 33).

Basic Principles for Loans and Other Businesses.—Commercial bank must conduct strict examination of usage, capability and form of repayment as well as other relevant matters of borrower in order to extend loan. Examination and actual extending of loan are conducted by separate departments, and examination and approval of loan are conducted at different levels. (Art. 35). Commercial bank must extend loan against security, and conduct strict examination of repaying capability, ownership and value of mortgage or pledge, and feasibility of realization of mortgage or pledge. Borrower may be exempted from providing security after commercial bank has conducted examination and found it to have high credit rating and capability of repayment. (Art. 36). Commercial bank must sign written contract with its borrower to extend loan. Contract must specify category, usage, amount, rate of interest, date and form of repayment, default liabilities and other matters deemed as necessary by parties. (Art. 37).

Commercial bank in its loan business must abide by regulations on ratios of assets and liabilities listed below: (1) capital adequacy rate must not fall short of 8%; (2) ratio of outstanding balance of loans to that of deposits must not exceed 75%; (3) ratio of outstanding balance of liquid assets to that of liquid liabilities must not fall short of 25%; (4) ratio of outstanding balance of loans to one borrower to that of capital of bank must not exceed 10%; and (5) other stipulations of People's Bank. (Art. 39). Commercial bank must not extend unsecured loans to related persons and must not provide related persons with secured loans on conditions more favorable than those to borrower of similar loan. Related persons refer to: (1) members of board of directors, member of board of supervisors, managerial personnel and staff of credit business department of commercial bank, and their close relatives; and (2) company, enterprise or other economic organization wherein aforesaid persons having made investment or assumed senior managerial positions. (Art. 40). Commercial bank has right to refuse any organization's or individual's demand for loan or guarantee. Commercial bank owned solely by State should provide loans for special projects approved by State Council. Losses resulting from such loans must be compensated with appropriate measures taken by State Council. (Art. 41).

Borrower must repay principal and interest of loan on schedule. When borrower fails to repay secured loan, commercial bank has right to be repaid principal and interest of loan or priority of getting paid with collateral thereof. Commercial bank must dispose of real estate or stocks on mortgage or pledge within year from date of obtaining. Borrower must assume responsibility in accordance with contract for failure to repay unsecured loan falling due. (Art. 42). Commercial bank must not engage in trust investment or stock business, nor invest in real estate not for its own use. Commercial bank must not invest in nonbank financial institutions or enterprises within P.R.C. (Art. 43). Commercial bank, in handling settlements such as acceptance, remittance and collection, must make timely cashing and entries pursuant to relevant provisions without detaining bills or instruments, nor dishonouring them in violation of regulations. Relevant provisions for time limit for bill acceptance and entries in accounting books should be made public. (Art. 44).

Commercial bank must apply for approval for issuing financial bonds or seeking loans outside China in accordance with law and administration decrees. (Art. 45). Interbank loan must be subject to time limit determined by People's Bank and maximum time for such financing must not exceed four months. It is prohibited to use call money to extend loans on fixed assets or to make investment. Call money for lending must be only idle fund after depositing required reserve, leaving adequate stand-by reserve and repayment of loans falling due to People's Bank. Call money for borrowing must be used to meet position shortage in interbranch settlement and interbranch remittance, and temporary needs for turnover of funds. (Art. 46). Commercial bank must not receive money deposits or extend loans by raising or lowering interest rates or by other unjustifiable means in violation of regulations. (Art. 47).

Enterprise or undertaking may open principal account with commercial bank of its own choice for day-to-day transfer and settlement of accounts and cash receipt and payment, but it cannot open two or more principal accounts. (Art. 48). Commercial bank must collect commission fees on handling business and providing services in accordance with stipulations of People's Bank. (Art. 50). Staff of commercial bank must not commit following wrongs: (1) taking advantage of their positions to demand or accept bribes, or accept commissions or service fees under any pretext; (2) taking advantage of their positions to commit graft, embezzlement or unlawful possession of funds of bank or of banks; (3) providing loans or guarantee to relatives or friends in violation of regulations; (4) holding positions concurrently at other economic institution(s); (5) other acts in violation of law, administrative decrees, and rules of business management (Art. 52); and (6) disclosing State or commercial secrets which come into possession during their service in bank (Art. 53).

Financial Accounting.—Commercial bank must truthfully record and comprehensively reflect its business activities and financial position, produce its annual financial accounting report, and timely submit its financial statements to People's Bank and treasury department. Commercial bank must not establish accounting books other than those legally specified. (Art. 55). Commercial bank must publish its business performance and audited statement of previous fiscal year within three months after end of every fiscal year in accordance with stipulations of People's Bank. (Art. 56). Commercial bank must retain reserve against bad and doubtful accounts and write off bad debts pursuant to relevant State regulations. (Art. 57).

Supervision and Administration.—Commercial bank must periodically submit to People's Bank balance sheets, profit and loss statements and other financial statements and information. (Art. 61). People's Bank is authorized to examine and supervise deposits, loans, settlements and doubtful accounts of commercial bank. (Art. 62). Commercial bank is subject to audit control by auditing authorities in accordance with audit law and regulations. (Art. 63).

Takeover and Termination.—When commercial bank is in or is likely to be in credit crisis, thus seriously threatening interest of depositors, People's Bank may take over said bank. (Art. 64). Debtor-creditor relationship of commercial bank existing before takeover remains unchanged. (Art. 64). People's Bank must determine takeover and organize its implementation. (Art. 65). On expiration of term of takeover, People's Bank may determine to prolong takeover, but term must not exceed two years. (Art. 67). Takeover may be terminated in any of following cases: (1) term or prolonged term of takeover expires, (2) prior to expiration of term of takeover, commercial bank has recovered its capacity of normal operation, or (3) prior to expiration of term of takeover, commercial bank has been merged or declared bankrupt. (Art. 68). Commercial bank must be dissolved with approval from People's Bank. Liquidation group must be formed to conduct liquidation, and repayment of principals and interests of deposits must be made in time according to plan for liquidation when commercial bank is to be dissolved. People's Bank must oversee liquidation process. (Art. 69). When commercial bank is closed down on account of its banking permit having been revoked, People's Bank must immediately form liquidation group to conduct liquidation. (Art. 70). When commercial bank is incapable of repaying its mature debts, it may, with consent of People's Bank, be declared bankrupt by People's Court. People's Court may organize People's Bank and other relevant departments and personnel to form liquidation group to conduct liquidation. (Art. 71). At time of bankrupt liquidation, commercial bank must give priority to paying principal and interest of savings deposits after paying liquidation fees and its staff wages and labor insurance fees in arrears. (Art. 71).

Legal Liabilities.—Penalties for violating law include confiscation of illegal income, fines of RMB10,000-500,000, revocation of business license and cessation of business operation, depending on severity of case, and if case constitutes crime, being investigated for criminal responsibilities. (Arts. 73-86).

Agricultural Bank of China, separated from People's Bank since Apr. 1, 1979, is, like People's Bank, directly under State Council. It has about 23,000 branches which extend agricultural loans and undertake normal rural retail banking transactions.

Construction Bank of China, also directly under State Council, as part of its responsibilities invests funds provided by Ministry of Finance, either in form of loans or grants, in major capital construction projects approved by State Capital Construction Commission. It has also begun to extend certain short-term loans for renovation. It has approximately 2,500 branches and pursuant to Provisional Regulations for Granting Capital Construction Loans of Nov. 1979, has been making loans on local level to enterprises having independent accounting systems for periods of from five to 15 years. Recipients of loans must assume complete responsibility for their own economic performance. Tourism, light industry and textiles are areas of loan emphasis by Construction Bank.

State Administration of Foreign Exchange Control now reports to People's Bank of China. Handles planning of foreign exchange control policies, implements foreign exchange rules and regulations and sets foreign exchange rates. Is closely tied to Bank of China.

Ministry of Finance authorizes capital construction, is in charge of annual and long-term planning of State budget and is in charge of fiscal policy.

Bank of China, in existence since 1912, has approximately 77 domestic branches and overseas branches in Hong Kong, London, Singapore, Luxembourg, Tokyo and New York. Bank of China monopolizes foreign exchange transactions and has been very active in loans for joint ventures. See topics Currency; Foreign Trade.

China Investment Bank ("CIB") authorized to raise construction funds from abroad, formed in Dec. 1981, acts as intermediary of World Bank. Head offices in Beijing with seven branches in Hubei, Jiangsu, Hebei, Fujian, Liaoning, Tianjin and Shanghai.

Regional Banks.—By middle of 1992, China has launched at least four regional banks such as Shanghai Development Bank, Guangdong Development Bank, Fujian Investment Bank and Shanghai Development Bank. Shenzhen Development Bank adopted shareholding system, but it will not issue its shares to individual investor nor list its shares in local securities exchange.

Other banks such as Communications Bank and CITIC Industrial Bank have rather broad authority in banking field but as yet are limited in size and branches.

Foreign Banks.—Since China opened its door to outside world, many foreign banks have opened branches in China. At least 40 foreign-funded banks and financial institutions and 220 foreign bank representative offices have been established in China by end of July 1992, most are opened in the five special economic zones and eight coastal cities. Shanghai will be opened for Renminbi business to foreign-funded financial institutions shortly.

Shanghai is one of central regions for foreign financial investment. In order to enhance investment by foreign financial institutions, People's Bank of China, with approval of State Council, promulgated Measures for the Administration of Foreign-capital Financial Institutions and Chinese-Foreign Equity Joint Financial Institutions in Shanghai on Sept. 8, 1990.

Term "foreign capital financial institutions and Chinese-foreign equity joint financial institutions" denotes following institutions: (1) foreign-capital banks with their head offices established in Shanghai (foreign bank); (2) branches of foreign banks established in Shanghai (foreign branch bank); (3) banks established in Shanghai with joint capital and operation by foreign financial institutions and Chinese financial institutions (joint bank); (4) financial companies established in Shanghai with joint capital and operation by foreign financial institution and Chinese financial institution (joint financial company). (Art. 2).

People's Bank of China is competent authority in charge of examining and approving, administering, and supervising foreign-capital financial institutions and Chinese foreign joint financial institutions. People's Bank of China authorizes its Shanghai Branch to exercise day to day administration and supervision. Any party applying for approval to set up foreign bank must satisfy following requirements: (1) investor is financial institution; (2) applicant has representative office of more than three years standing inside China; (3) applicant possesses total assets of more than US$10 billion at end of year prior to submission of its application. (Art. 5).

Regulations of China Governing the Administration of Foreign-Funded Financial Entities was promulgated by State Council on Feb. 25, 1994, effective as of Apr. 1, 1994. Regulations superseded Regulations Regarding Administration of Foreign Banks and Joint Venture Banks in Special Economic Zones promulgated by State Council on Apr. 25, 1985 and Regarding Administration of Foreign Financial Entities and Joint Venture Financial Entities in Shanghai approved by State Council on Sept. 7,

See Topical Index in front part of this volume.

BANKS AND BANKING . . . *continued*

1990 and promulgated by People's Bank of China on Sept. 8, 1990. Foreign-funded financial entities refers to following entities approved to set up and handle business in China and in accordance with relevant laws and regulations: (1) wholly foreign-owned banks whose headquarters are located in China (hereinafter "foreign-owned banks"); (2) branches in China established by foreign banks (hereinafter "foreign branches"); (3) joint venture banks in China established jointly by foreign and Chinese financial entities (hereinafter "joint venture banks"); (4) wholly foreign-owned financial companies whose headquarters are located in China (hereinafter "foreign-owned financial companies"); and (5) joint venture financial companies established jointly by foreign and Chinese financial entities (hereinafter "joint venture financial companies"). (Art. 2). Areas where foreign-funded financial entities may be set up will be separately determined by State Council. (Art. 2). Foreign-funded financial entities must follow laws and regulations of China and must not harm social and public interests of China. (Art. 3). People's Bank of China is competent department in charge of administration and supervision of foreign-funded entities and branches of People's Bank of China, and branches of People's Bank of China undertakes to administer and supervise routine affairs of said entities in their respective jurisdictions. (Art. 4).

Formation.—Minimum registered capital for foreign-owned banks and joint venture banks must be convertible foreign currencies on par with RMB 300 million, and minimum registered capital for foreign-owned financial companies and joint venture financial companies on par with RMB 200 million, whose paid-in capital must not be less than 50% of registered capital. (Art. 5). Working capital of foreign branches provided by their headquarters must not be less than convertible foreign currencies on par with RMB 100 million. (Art. 5). In applying for foreign-owned bank or foreign-owned financial company, applicant must meet following requirements: (1) being financial entity; (2) having representative office in China for two years or more; (3) having total assets of no less than US$10 billion at end of first preceding year of application; and (4) having complete financial supervision and control system in its home country or region. (Art. 6). In applying for foreign branch, applicant must meet following requirements: (1) having representative office in China for two years or more; (2) having total assets of no less than US$20 billion at end of first preceding year of application; and (3) having complete financial supervision and control system in its home country or region. (Art. 7). In applying joint venture bank or joint venture financial company, applicant must meet following requirements: (1) all partners must be financial entities; (2) foreign partner has set up representative office in China; (3) total assets of foreign partner must be no less than US$10 billion at end of first preceding year of application; and (4) foreign partner has complete financial supervision and control system in its home country or region. (Art. 8).

Foreign financial entity must capitalize in full paid-in capital or working capital which must be verified by chartered accountants of China, and transfer into China within 30 days after receipt of approval issued by People's Bank of China, and go through registration procedures with industrial and commercial authorities and tax authorities. (Art. 15). Foreign entity shall obtain "Foreign Exchange Business License" from State Administration of Exchange Control within 30 days after approval of People's Bank of China. (Art. 16).

Scope of Business.—Foreign-owned banks, foreign branches and joint venture banks in China may handle partial or whole of following business to be approved by People's Bank of China: (1) foreign exchange deposit; (2) foreign exchange loan; (3) foreign exchange bill discount; (4) approved foreign exchange investment; (5) foreign exchange remittance; (6) import and export settlement; (7) foreign exchange guarantee; (8) foreign exchange transactions for currencies and foreign exchange bills; (9) payment for foreign exchange credit card on commission basis; (10) safe-keeping; (11) credit rating and consulting; and (12) standard currency business and other foreign exchange business approved. (Art. 17). Foreign-owned financial companies and joint financial companies may handle partial or whole of following business to be approved by People's Bank of China: (1) foreign exchange deposit with each deal no less than US$100,000 and with term of no less than three months; (2) foreign exchange loan; (3) foreign exchange bill discount; (4) approved foreign exchange investment; (5) foreign exchange guarantee; (6) foreign exchange transaction for themselves or for their clients; (7) credit rating and consulting; and (8) standard currency business and other foreign exchange business approved. (Art. 18). Foreign exchange deposit includes following deposits in foreign currencies: (1) interbank deposits inside and outside China; (2) non-interbank deposits outside China; (3) deposits of foreigners inside China; (4) deposits of overseas Chinese and compatriots from Hong Kong, Macao and Taiwan; (5) deposits of foreign-funded enterprises; (6) redeposits of loans of foreign-funded financial entities to non-foreign-funded enterprises; and (7) other deposits in foreign exchange to be approved. (Art. 19).

Supervision and Administration.—Interest rate for deposits and loans and commission fees must be determined by foreign-funded financial entities according to relevant regulations of China. (Art. 22). In handling deposits foreign-funded financial entity must pay reserves against deposits to branch of People's Bank of China in its locality, with ratio to be determined and adjusted by People's Bank of China, which will bear no interest. (Art. 23). Thirty percent of working capital of foreign branch must be interest-bearing assets designated by People's Bank of China, including bank deposits designated by People's Bank of China. (Art. 24). Total assets of foreign-owned bank, joint venture bank, foreign-owned financial company or joint venture financial company must not exceed 20 times sum total of paid-in capital and reserves. (Art. 25). Loans to one specific enterprise and its correlated enterprises by foreign-owned bank, joint venture bank, foreign-owned financial company or joint venture financial company must not exceed 30% of sum of its paid-in capital and reserves, unless otherwise permitted by People's Bank of China. (Art. 26). Total investment by foreign-owned bank, joint venture bank, foreign-owned financial company or joint venture financial company must not exceed 30% of sum of its paid-in capital and reserves, excluding those investments to financial entity with approval of People's Bank of China. (Art. 27). Total fixed assets of foreign-owned bank, joint venture bank, foreign-owned financial company or joint venture financial company must not exceed 40% of sum of its paid-in capital and reserves. (Art. 28). Foreign-funded financial entities must ensure fluidity of its assets, specific measures for which shall be separately formulated by People's Bank of China. (Art. 30). Total amount of deposits inside China in foreign-funded financial entity must not exceed 40% of total assets of said entity. Foreign-funded financial entity must set aside reserves against bad debts in accordance with law. (Art. 31). Where paid-in capital of foreign-bank, joint venture bank, foreign-owned financial company, or joint venture financial company is less than its respective minimum registered capital, it must draw 25% of its post-tax profits to replenish deficiency until sum of its paid-in capital and reserves equals registered capital. (Art. 32). Foreign-funded financial entity must recruit at least one Chinese citizen as senior management officer. (Art 33). Foreign-funded financial entity must employ chartered accountant of China, which is subject to approval of branch of People's Bank of China in said locality. (Art. 34). People's Bank of China and its branch offices are entitled to check and verify operations, management and financial situation of foreign-funded financial entities. (Art. 37).

Dissolution and Liquidation.—Should foreign-funded financial entity terminate its operations it must submit written application to People's Bank of China 30 days prior to termination, and must dissolve and liquidate after approval of People's Bank of China. (Art. 38). Should foreign-funded financial entity become insolvent, People's Bank of China may order it to cease operation and wind up within prescribed time limit. (Art. 39). Should it become solvent in course of winding up and need to restore operation, it must file application with People's Bank of China. Should it fail to restore solvency after prescribed time limit, it must carry out liquidation. (Art. 39). After liquidation, foreign-funded financial entity must go through cancellation registration procedures with its original registration authority within time limit prescribed by law. (Art. 41).

Penalties for violation of law include warning, confiscation of illegal incomes, fines of RMB 3,000-100,000, revocation of business license and cessation of business operation, depending on severity of cases. (Arts. 42-46).

BILLS AND NOTES:

See topics Securities; Negotiable Instruments Law.

Bills of exchange and promissory notes were not used in China until 1980s when checks began to be recognized and used widely. In 1980s, bills of exchange and promissory notes, together with checks, began to appear in some regulations concerning clearing forms in banks. Clearing Forms in Bank, regulation law promulgated by People's Bank of China in Dec. 1988, says bills of exchange, promissory notes and checks can all be used as clearing forms. From then on, they became important instruments of payment and credit. In China, bills of exchange, promissory notes, and checks are generally referred to as negotiable instruments. Idea of making general rule on negotiable instruments was proposed by State Council, and People's Bank of China started process in 1986. Resulting document, Negotiable Instruments Law of the PRC was adopted by 13th Session of Standing Committee of the National People's Congress on May 10, 1995 and is effective as of Jan. 1, 1996.

Negotiable Instruments Law is applicable to bills of exchange, promissory notes and checks. (Art. 2). Drawer should have his signature or seal on negotiable instrument in legal way and bear liability of payment. (Art. 4). Agent may, within scope of power of agency, have its signature or seal in place of its principal, but agency relationship must be indicated on negotiable instrument. (Art. 5). Signature or seal by person having no or limited capacity for civil conduct is ineffective, but it does not lead to ineffectiveness of rest of signatures or seals on negotiable instrument. (Art. 6). Corresponding consideration is required in exchange for negotiable instrument, except if negotiable instrument was acquired by tax, inheritance or gift, which makes consideration unnecessary. (Arts. 10, 11). Any counterargument of debtor of negotiable instrument against drawer or holder's predecessor cannot be applied as evidence against holder unless holder clearly knows about it. (Art. 13). Loser of negotiable instrument has right to inform payer of losing negotiable instrument and prevent payer from paying to anyone else, and loser can also apply for procedure of presentment and information or bring suit in court. (Art. 15). Holder's right to negotiable instrument will not be protected if holder does not exercise its rights within statutory term: term for drawer's and acceptor's right to negotiable instrument is two years from due date; term for bill of exchange or promissory note payable at sight is two years from date of issue; term for right of drawer of check is six months from date of issue; term for recourse to predecessor is six months from day when payment was refused; and term for second recourse to predecessor is three months from day of payment or day when case was brought in court. (Art. 17).

Issue of Bills of Exchange.—Bills of exchange can be divided into bank drafts and commercial drafts. (Art. 19). There should be real relationship of entrustment of payment between drawer and payer, and drawer should have reliable capital sources. (Art. 21). Bills of exchange without consideration, intended to cheat banks or other persons concerned, not allowed to be issued. (Art. 21). Following items must be recorded on bill of exchange: words "bill of exchange" or the like, entrustment of payment without any conditions, fixed amount of money, name of payer, name of payee, date of issue, and signature or seal of drawer. (Art. 22). In terms of date of payment, bill of exchange may be payable at sight, on specific date, after sight, or after fixed date. (Art. 25).

Issue of Promissory Note.—Promissory note refers to cashier's check. (Art. 73). Drawer should have reliable capital sources to ensure payment. (Art. 74). Following items must be recorded on promissory note: words "promissory note" or the like, promise of payment without any conditions, fixed amount of money, name of payee, date of issue, and signature or seal of drawer. (Art. 76).

Issue of Check.—Drawer of check should open checking account and deposit certain amount of money into that account. (Art. 83). Checks can be used to obtain cash or transfer funds between accounts. (Art. 84). Following items must be recorded on check: word "check" or the like, entrustment of payment without any conditions, fixed amount of money, name of payer, date of issue, and signature or seal of drawer. (Art. 85). Amount of money drawn on check cannot be more than monetary total in checking account. (Art. 88).

Endorsement.—Negotiable instrument is transferable unless drawer clearly states that it is not. (Art. 27). Holder's endorsement is required for transferring negotiable instrument. (Art. 27). Endorsement must include signatures or seals of endorser and endorsee, and date of endorsement. (Arts. 27, 29). Every successor of negotiable instrument should make sure that contents of its direct predecessor's endorsement are

See Topical Index in front part of this volume.

BILLS AND NOTES . . . *continued*
true. (Art. 32). Endorsement with any kind of condition is ineffective, and endorsement by which money is only partially transferred or money is transferred to two or more persons is also ineffective. (Art. 33). Negotiable instrument can also be used as mortgage, which must be recorded on it. (Art. 35). If negotiable instrument is dishonored or term for presentment expires, it can no longer be transferred. (Art. 36).

Acceptance.—Provisions on acceptance apply only to bills of exchange. (Arts. 38, 81, 94). Holder of bill of exchange payable on or after fixed date should present bill of exchange to payer and ask for payment before date. (Art. 39). Holder of bill of exchange payable after sight should present it to payer and ask for payment one month after date of issue. (Art. 40). Holder of bill of exchange payable at sight is exempt from requirement of presentment. (Art. 40). Payer should agree or refuse to accept bill of exchange presented to it within three days after presentment. (Art. 41). Acceptance must not be attached with any conditions, or else it is considered refusal of bill of exchange. (Art. 43).

Warranty.—Provisions on warranty apply only to bills of exchange and promissory notes. (Arts. 45, 81). Liability of bills and notes can be warranted by anyone except debtor of bill or note. (Art. 45). Following items must be recorded on bill or note: words like "bill of exchange" or "promissory note", name and domicile of warrantor, name of warrantee, date of warranty, and signature or seal of warrantor. (Art. 46). Warranty cannot be attached with any conditions, and any condition attached to warranty will not affect liability of warranty. (Art. 48). Warrantor and warrantee share joint and several liability to holder of bill or note. (Art. 50). After discharging debt, warrantor has recourse to warrantee and its predecessors.

Payment.—Holder of bill of exchange payable at sight should present bill of exchange to payer and ask for payment within one month, and holder of other bills of exchange should make presentment within ten days after due date. (Art. 53). Payer must pay fully on day of holder's presentment. (Art. 54). Drawer of promissory note must pay holder, not more than two months after date holder presents promissory note. (Art. 78). Holder of promissory note will be deprived of recourse to all predecessors except drawer if it does not present promissory note according to this law. (Art. 80). Check is payable at sight and any payment date included is ineffective. (Art. 91). Holder of check should present check to payer and ask for payment within ten days from date of issue. (Art. 92). After payment, negotiable instrument should go to payer. (Art. 55). Before payment, payer should examine endorsements, holder's legal identification or other effective certificates. (Art. 57). After payment, all liabilities of negotiable instrument are canceled. (Art. 60).

Recourse.—If past due negotiable instrument is dishonored, holder can have recourse against endorser, drawer, and other debtors of negotiable instrument. (Art. 61). Holder should provide protest or other documents verifying protest. (Art. 62). If holder is not able to provide protest or other legal documents when it is refused payment, it will lose recourse to its predecessors, but acceptor and drawer will still bear liability of negotiable instrument. (Art. 65). Holder should inform its predecessor of reasons for being refused within three days after protest, and holder's predecessor has same obligations to own predecessor. (Art. 66). Drawer, endorser, acceptor and warrantor bear joint and several liability to holder. (Art. 68). However, if holder is also drawer, it has no recourse to predecessors; and if holder is also endorser, it has no recourse to successors. (Art. 69). Holder can require monetary total refused by payer, and interests and expenses spent on obtaining protest and on informing. (Art. 70).

Applicable Law of Negotiable Instruments Involving Foreign Elements.— Negotiable instrument involving foreign elements refers to negotiable instrument where some of elements—issue, endorsement, acceptance, warranty and payment—take place in China and some in foreign country. (Art. 95). Where there are conflicts between this law and treaties which China has concluded or acceded to, provisions of treaty will prevail, unless reservations to treaty have been made. (Art. 96). If there are no provisions in either this law or treaties to which China is party, then customary international practice will be applicable. (Art. 96). Civil capacity of debtor of negotiable instrument is subject to its country's law. (Art. 97). Required items recorded on negotiable instrument are subject to law of country where it is issued, and required items recorded on check may be subject to law of country where payment takes place if parties agree. Endorsement, acceptance, payment, and warranty of negotiable instrument are subject to law of country where they take place. (Art. 99). Term for recourse is subject to law of country where negotiable instrument is issued. (Art. 100). Term for presentment, form of protest, and term for providing protest are subject to law of country where payment takes place. (Art. 101). When negotiable instrument is lost, application for preservation of negotiable instrument right is subject to law of country where payment takes place. (Art. 102).

Legal Liability.—Person who breaches law may be administratively or criminally liable. (Arts. 14, 103-107).

Supplementary Provisions.—Terms in this law should be calculated according to provisions in General Rules of Civil Law. (Art. 108). People's Bank of China will provide unified forms, printing procedures, and management procedures of negotiable instruments. (Art. 109). Rules for the Implementation of the Negotiable Instruments Law will be made by People's Bank of China and approved by State Council. (Art. 110).

CIVIL CODE:

General Rules of Civil Law ("Civil Law") were adopted by Sixth National Peoples Congress on Apr. 12, 1986, effective as of Jan. 1, 1987. Chinese law is held applicable to civil activities in China, as is Civil Law, which is applicable to foreigners, stateless persons and citizens unless otherwise specified. (Art. 5). Opinion of Supreme Court adopted on 26 Jan. 1988 provides details regarding Civil Law. See subhead The Opinion of the Supreme Court on Several Problems of Enforcing the General Rules of Civil Law (Trial Implementation), infra.

Civil Rights and Capacity of Natural Persons.—Civil Law provides that natural persons have equal civil capacity and rights (Art. 10), normally enjoyed from birth until they die (Art. 9); capacity to act civilly is acquired at age of 18, however one who is earning own livelihood can acquire such capacity at 16 years of age (Art. 11); person of ten years of age has limited civil capacity, and one under ten years of age no civil capacity but must act through legal representative (Art. 12), as must mental patient unable to act (Art. 13).

Residence of person is place where household registration is maintained, unless they frequently reside elsewhere. (Art. 15).

Parents are guardians of children unless deceased or lacking capacity, in which case guardians are grandparents, elder siblings and other close relatives or friends willing to undertake guardian roles; latter requiring consent of unit or resident or village committee of infant. (Art. 16). Guardians must deal with property of persons they are responsible for, in interests of said persons and must protect said persons, their property and lawful rights and interests. (Art. 15).

If person's whereabouts unknown for two full years, those concerned with his interests may apply to court to declare him missing person, except during time of war, when said time is to be computed from time war ends. (Art. 20). Property for missing persons will be managed by one's spouse, parent, adult children or other close relatives. (Art. 21). If person's whereabouts not known for four years, or for two years from occurrence of accident, he may be declared dead by application by person concerned with his interests, to court. (Art. 23).

Individual may register sole proprietorship for industrial or commercial business (Art. 26) and rural collectives engaged in sales of commodities may register rural contracting operations (Art. 27), but individuals are responsible for debts of said business (Act. 29).

Partnership may be formed on basis of agreements for capital contribution, distribution of profits, termination, withdrawal, etc. (Art. 30); property accumulated by partnership is jointly owned (Art. 32); each partner is responsible for debts in accordance with partnership agreement, but joint and several liability exists. However, where one assumed greater share of debts than provided in partnership agreement they can look to other partners for contribution. (Art. 35).

Civil Rights and Capacities of Legal Persons.—Entity which has civil rights and capacities, enjoys those rights from time of establishment of said legal person (Art. 36); to be considered legal person entity must have its own name, structure, premises, property, be established according to law and able to independently undertake civil liability (Art. 37). Legal representative of legal person is person designated by law or articles of association of said legal person to act on behalf of said legal person. (Art. 38). Legal person is considered resident of location of its major office. (Art. 39).

In order for enterprise to obtain status of legal person, if it is Chinese-foreign joint venture, cooperative venture, or wholly owned foreign entity, it needs government approval and registration with relevant division of General Administration of Commerce and Industry. (Art. 41).

As for state enterprises and collective enterprises, who meet capital requirements, have articles of association, premises, organizational structure, and ability to undertake civil liability, they will obtain status of legal person upon approval of organization in charge and registration. (Art. 41).

Scope of business operations of enterprise is operational limits approved for its registration (Art. 42), and it shall operate through its legal representative or other personnel (Art. 43). If enterprise merges, or branches split off, separate registration is required (Art. 44), and if it terminates operation it must go through termination procedures to revoke its registration (Art. 46). In cases of dissolution, bankruptcy, and like, enterprise shall establish organized group to liquidate all accounts under jurisdiction of relevant department of court or organization in charge of enterprise. (Art. 47).

Social organizations, groups and governmental organizations having their own independent funds have status of legal persons from time of their establishment, except for those social organizations and groups required to register, whose status as legal person shall only commence after approved registration. (Art. 50).

Civil Law Acts and Agency.—Act in civil law is defined as one where person establishes, alters or terminates civil rights and obligations (Art. 54), provided person has capacity to act, manifests said act factually, and act is not in violation of law or public interest (Art. 55).

Unless law prescribes specified form, oral or written forms may be adopted to undertake civil act. (Art. 56).

Civil acts in excess of one's capacity, or undertaken by fraud or coercion, or in violation of public interest, or for unlawful purpose, or economic contracts in violation of state plan's instructions, or acts detrimental to state, cooperative or third party's interest, are void ab initio. (Art. 58). Where party had serious misunderstanding as to nature of act or it is manifestly unfair, party can make application to court or arbitral tribunal to have it altered or set aside and if set aside shall be void ab initio. (Art. 59).

Where portion of civil act lacks effectiveness, but it does not affect rest of act that is effective, then remaining portion shall continue in force and effect. (Art. 60).

If civil act is set aside or found without effect, property shall be returned to any party suffering loss and if one party is at fault then said party shall compensate other party for its losses, but if both parties are at fault they shall undertake to make good on their respective liabilities. (Art. 61).

Principal and Agent.—Agent may within scope of its authority undertake legal act in name of its principal. (Act. 63). Agents include those entrusted with certain acts, statutory agents and designated agents. Designated agents are those designated either by courts or designating unit. (Art. 63). Where agent is entrusted with specific acts, document shall specify agent's name, items upon which he will act, limits of his authority and time period within which document has effect. (Art. 65).

If document authorizing agency of entrustment is unclear then principal and agent shall have joint liability to third parties (Art. 65); principal is only responsible for acts exceeding document granting agency if he retroactively ratified or acknowledges said acts, or, if principal knows another is acting in his name, and does not renounce said act such scheme shall be deemed to be consented to (Art. 66). Agent is liable for acts he is entrusted with if he knows said acts are in violation of law. (Art. 67). Where agent entrusted with task must in turn entrust another person, he must obtain consent of his principal (Art. 68), else, save in emergency, agent shall be liable for acts of subsequent agent (Art. 68).

Termination of agency of entrustment occurs where either principal or agent dies, or either principal or agent terminate agency, or agent loses his capacity to act civilly or period of agency expires or acts to be performed by agent are completed. (Art. 69).

See Topical Index in front part of this volume.

CIVIL CODE . . . *continued*

Relation of statutory or designated agents with their principal terminates if either dies, agent loses its capacity to act civilly, principal on whose behalf agent acts loses capacity to act civilly or court or organization designating agent cancels appointment. (Art. 70).

Ownership of property is defined to mean that owner enjoys right to occupy, use, benefit from and dispose of property in accordance with law. (Art. 71). Except where separately provided ownership of property occurs when property is delivered. (Art. 72).

Property includes: (1) State property defined as that owned by all people (Art. 73); (2) property of collective organizations including land, forests, mountain ranges, pastures, wasteland and beaches specified in law to be collectively owned; including buildings, reservoirs, farms and water conservancy facilities and facilities for education, science, culture, hygiene and physical education. Collectively owned land is that collectively owned by villagers and farmers and operated and managed by village committees or village agricultural production cooperatives. (Art. 74). Personal property includes houses, lawful income, savings, articles of daily use, cultural relics, livestock, books, trees, and productive materials permitted by law and other legal property. (Art. 75). Citizens have right to inherit property pursuant to law. (Art. 76). Lawful property of social groups, including religious groups, is protected by law. (Art. 77).

Property may be owned by two or more citizens or legal persons. Two types of joint ownership are joint ownership pursuant to shares and common joint ownership. Where joint ownership is pursuant to shares person enjoys rights and benefits of that ownership relative to respective shares owned, and has right to subdivide or transfer said shares, though other joint owners have preemptive rights on same terms and conditions offered third parties. (Art. 78).

State owned land may be used according to law by collective units and state units. Rights of citizens or collectives to contract for state owned or collective land is protected by law. Rights and obligations of parties shall be specified in contract. (Art. 80). Similarly citizens or groups can contract to operate forests, mountain ranges, grasslands, wastelands, beaches and waters, which are owned collectively or state owned but used by collective. Rights and obligations of parties shall be specified in contract. (Art. 81). However, state owned mineral and water resources, or state owned and legally protected collectively owned waters, forests, mountain ranges, grasslands, wastelands and beaches shall not be bought, or sold, rented or mortgaged or illegally transferred. (Art. 81). Citizens rights, pursuant to law, to excavate mineral resources owned by state are protected by law. (Art. 81).

Adjoining real estate parcels should in spirit of reasonableness, fairness, mutual cooperation, unity, convenience, and profitable production deal with matters of water drainage, water interception, natural lighting, access, ventilation, etc. (Art. 83).

Creditor's Rights.—Debt is specific relationship of rights and obligations created between parties pursuant to contract or by law. (Art. 84). Person enjoying such rights is creditor, person having obligation is debtor, and creditor has right to demand debtor's performance pursuant to contract or provisions of law. (Art. 84).

Contract is agreement where parties establish, alter or terminate civil relationships (Art. 85); parties to contract should fully perform their obligations in accordance with contractual terms (Art. 88); where terms of contract are not clear and parties cannot reach agreement through negotiations regarding quality, time limits, location or cost then as to: (1) Quality, contract will be performed in accordance with national quality standards, but if there are none then pursuant to usual standards; and (2) time limit, debtor can perform at any time and creditor can demand performance at any time, giving debtor necessary time to prepare performance; and (3) location of performance, unless otherwise indicated, party making payment shall make it in location where party receiving payment is located; and (4) cost, if not clearly specified, payment shall be made pursuant to state specified prices, or if there are none then with reference to market prices or standard prices for similar type goods or remuneration for similar work (Art. 88).

Where contract contains no arrangement as to right of application for patent, party making invention or creation enjoys that right. (Art. 88).

Debts may be guaranteed in following manner: (1) Guarantor may give creditor assurance that debtor will fulfil debt obligation, and where debtor fails to do so, pay said debts and thereafter look to creditor for reimbursement, or (2) debtor or third person may provide certain property as pledge, and pursuant to law creditor shall have right to value of pledge or money from sale of pledge, or (3) party may pay deposit to another party and if one paying deposit does not fulfil its debts, then it may not ask for return of deposit, or if party receiving deposit does not fulfil its obligation then it must return twice value of deposit; or (4) where party pursuant to contract occupies property of other party, and latter party does not make timely payment of its obligations, person in control of property has lien on said property which it can levy upon. (Art. 89).

Transfer of portion of or all of rights and obligations under contract to third party, except where contract or law otherwise provides, requires consent of other party and approval of state organization that approved initial contract. (Art. 91).

If person is unjustly enriched without lawful basis and causes losses to others, he shall return said unjust enrichment to person suffering said loss. (Art. 92). Where person undertakes services or management without legal obligation to do so, to prevent loss to others, he shall be entitled to obtain repayment from beneficiary for necessary expenditures. (Art. 93).

Intellectual Property.—Copyright, patent, trademark and discoveries are all protected by law. (Arts. 94, 95, 96, and 97).

Personal Rights.—Citizens enjoy right to life and health (Art. 98), right to one's given name and surname, and to change said name pursuant to law and to forbid others to interfere with one's name (Art. 99); citizen's likeness shall not be used for profitable purposes without citizen's consent (Art. 100); and citizens and legal persons enjoy right to their reputation and honor (Art. 102); and right to choose their own spouse (Art. 103); and women enjoy equal rights with those of men (Art. 105).

Civil Liability—General.—Persons who breach contracts and those who trespass on other's property are civilly liable (Art. 106), except if due to force majeure (Art. 107). Debts shall be repaid in full, and only with consent of creditor or by court ruling can debt be repaid in late installments. (Art. 108).

Civil Liability—Breach of Contract.—Where party fails to perform or its performance does not conform to contractual terms, other party has right to demand performance or to take remedial measures and demand compensation for any losses. (Art. 111). Compensation for breach of contract should make injured party whole (Art. 112), though parties may have liquidated damages clause in contract or may specify means of computing loss for breach (Art. 112). Where there is breach of contract by both parties they should separately undertake civil liability for their own breach. (Art. 113). Party must promptly attempt to mitigate its damages if other party breaches contract. (Art. 114). Where losses are caused by one party breaching because of acts of higher level organization, contracting party is liable under contract for its breach but it may claim compensation from higher level organization. (Art. 116).

Tortious Conduct.—Those who trespass on state, collective or other property should return said property or compensate owner at market price. (Art. 117). Similarly, those who damage property shall either repair it or compensate injured party at market prices for damage. (Art. 117). For other special losses as result of trespass tortfeasor shall make compensation for loss suffered. (Art. 117).

If plagiarism, infringement, and like occur with regard to copyright, patents, trademark or discoveries then injured party may demand cessation of such tortious conduct and compensation for loss. (Art. 118).

Where there is battery, tortfeasor must pay medical costs, income loss, funeral expenses if death ensued and support those who were dependent upon deceased. (Art. 119).

Where there has been infringement of use of person's name, image, or defamation, then person has right to stop such tortious conduct, eliminate its effect, obtain apology and demand compensation for loss. (Art. 120).

Where persons or property have been damaged by product's quality not meeting standards, manufacturer and distributor of product are both liable for damages. Where storage or transportation groups are responsible for damage product manufacturer and distributor have right to demand compensation from these parties. (Art. 122).

Those who violate environmental protection regulations shall have civil liability pursuant to law. (Art. 124).

Those who properly defend themselves are not liable for damages unless defense goes beyond necessary limits causing injuries. (Art. 125). Where person to avoid dangerous situation caused by others, cause damage, person creating dangerous situation shall be liable. (Art. 129).

If two or more parties commit tort they have joint liability (Art. 130) and if injured party contributed to damage then defendant's liability will be proportionately reduced (Art. 131).

Statute of Limitations.—Civil case to enforce civil rights must be brought within two years unless otherwise specified in law. (Art. 135). Following cases have one year statute of limitations: (1) Where there is demand for compensation for bodily injury; and (2) where commodities, not up to standard are sold without notice of said fact; and (3) where there is delay or refusal to pay rents; and (4) where property in storage has been lost or damaged.

Calculation of commencement of (Art. 136) running of statute of limitations commences from time infringement of rights was or should have been known (Art. 137). Where there is agreement to perform obligations which are subject of suit, period of limitations shall be suspended and only commence again if there is failure to perform. (Art. 140).

Civil Relations Involving Foreign Parties.—Where there are conflicts between treaties to which China is participant and civil law, unless reservations to said treaty have been made, provisions of treaty prevail. (Art. 142). If there are no provisions in either domestic Chinese law or in treaties to which Chinese are parties then customary international practice shall prevail. (Art. 142).

Law of country wherein real estate is located shall be applicable to issues relevant to ownership of real estate. (Art. 144). Unless law otherwise provides, parties may choose law applicable to contract disputes, involving foreign party, or if they do not so choose, national law having closest link to contract shall apply. (Art. 145).

Where application for damages for tortious conduct is made, law of country where such acts occur shall apply (Art. 146), but if both parties reside in same country or have same nationality, national laws or laws of country of residence shall also be applicable (Art. 146). Where Chinese law does not deem act occurring outside its territory as tortious act, it shall not be determined as tort. (Art. 146).

For marriage between citizen of China and foreigner, law of country where marriage is concluded shall be applicable (Art. 147) and as for divorce law of country where court handles said case shall be applicable (Art. 147). For adoption law having closest link with person being raised shall apply. (Art. 148).

For inheritance of property, laws of country of residence upon deaths of testator or intestate shall be applicable to movable property and laws of country where immovable property is located, shall be applicable to immovable property. (Art. 149).

Where foreign or international law is applicable pursuant to this chapter it shall not violate social or public interest of China. (Art. 150).

Supplementary Principles and Definitions.—Force majeure referred to herein refers to objective circumstances which are unforseeable, irrevocable, and unsurmountable. (Art. 153).

Periods referred to in this Civil Law shall be computed pursuant to hour, day, month and year of Gregorian calendar. (Art. 154). Where period specified is to be computed according to hours, it shall be computed from commencement of specified time. Where it is to be computed according to day, month or year, day of commencement shall not be counted, but period shall commence from next day. (Art. 154). Where last day of period falls on Sun. or holiday, day following holiday shall be considered as last day. (Art. 154). Closing time for last day of period is 24:00 hour. If business hours are specified, time business activities cease shall be closing time. (Art. 154).

For enterprise existing prior to this law coming into force, of state organization, approved by department in charge above level of province, autonomous region or city

See Topical Index in front part of this volume.

CIVIL CODE . . . *continued*
directly under control of central government, already registered with General Department of Commerce and Industry, no additional registration is necessary to be classified legal person. (Art. 152).

The Opinion of the Supreme Court on Several Problems of Enforcing the General Rules of Civil Law (Trial Implementation) was adopted on 26 Jan., 1988. It contains 200 articles providing substantial details regarding Civil Law matters.

Natural persons who are citizens enjoy civil rights from birth. Date of birth is taken from household registration certificate, or if there is none then from birth certificate issued by hospital or is taken from other evidence. (Art. 1).

Natural persons over 16 but not more than 18 years old who maintain themselves by their own work have capacity to enter civil transactions. (Art. 2).

Legal effect of civil acts of minors over ten years old depend on their age, intelligence, connection of their action and their livelihood, whether they can comprehend consequences of their acts. (Art. 3).

Legal consequences of civil action of mental patients depends upon whether they can understand consequences of their acts. (Art. 4).

In civil litigation proceedings when party or closely related person asserts that one of parties is mentally ill court should determine whether said person has capacity to proceed, and degree of capacity. (Arts. 7, 8).

Where citizen leaves domicile and continues to reside for over one year in new location (except in hospital) that new location becomes domicile. If move is not permanent then citizen's domicile shall remain at location of household register.

Guardian's duties include caring for health, managing and protecting property, acting as agent in civil proceedings, managing and educating, acting as agent for benefit of person over whom they have guardianship. (Art. 10).

Close relatives defined by General Principles of the Civil Law include spouse, parent, children, brothers and sisters, grandparents, grandchildren.

If whereabouts of one is unknown reference is made to circumstance of disappearance without communication after citizen left final domicile, to determine if person is alive for civil law purposes.

Person who is in Taiwan or abroad who cannot be contacted should not be declared dead.

Court shall determine time of declaration of death according to special procedure of civil law of civil procedure. (Art. 34).

When court hears case of declaration of death, court should search out property of one declared missing, appoint provisional manager, take preservative measures, or send announcement to find missing person; period of announcement is half year.

At expiration of announcement period, court should make declaration of missing person or ruling terminating suit according facts.

If person was declared missing by decree, property agent of missing person shall be appointed at same time. (Art. 34).

If property agent of missing person shall apply for changing property agent by reason of lack of ability to proceed with duty, court should try case according to special procedures.

If property agent of missing person does not proceed with duties or infringes on property of missing person, person with beneficial relationship to missing person may appeal to court to claim civil liability for agent. In case person aforesaid appeals to court for change of agent at same time, court should hear this independently according to special procedures. (Art. 35).

Date of court announcement of decision is date of death of person who is so declared. Court's verdict should announce place where person who is declared dead is located and place where court is located.

If date of declaration of death and natural death do not coincide, legal result of declaring one dead still valid. If civil action is completed before natural death, does not coincide with result of declaration, civil action is binding. (Art. 36).

In civil proceedings, industrial and commercial households with shops should appoint head of household in business's license as agent for legal proceedings. (Art. 41).

Industrial and commercial individual households or those contracting to manage rural operations shall apply for registration by use of individual citizens.

When investing common property of family or investing main benefits of enterprise supporting family, then debts should be paid off by family's common property. (Art. 42).

During period that relationship of husband and wife exists, earnings of individual manager or contract manager of household enterprise, run by one of spouses, belongs to their common property, and debts should be paid off by said common property. (Art. 43).

If debts of industrial and commercial individual household enterprise or contract management countryside enterprise is paid from family common property, necessities and essential work tools of members of family shall be preserved. (Art. 44).

During civil proceedings individual partnerships of shops should appoint responsible partner as representative of partnership for acts of partnership. (Art. 45).

Enterprises that are legal persons and other employers shall operate as legal persons and where others suffer economic losses as result of their actions, enterprise shall assume responsibility for said losses. (Art. 58).

Questions as to applicability of substantive law, where conflicts of law matters arise involving foreign parties, are to be determined by c. 8 of General Principles of Civil Law. (Art. 178).

COMMERCIAL CODE:

No actual commercial code exists but commercial transactions are widespread. Some commercial transactions will be covered by Civil Code now in draft form, some are governed by private international law and custom (see topic Actions), some by specifics of approved contracts and Economic Contracts Law (see topics Contracts; Joint Stock Companies) and some by specific legislation such as Joint Venture Law. See topic Joint Stock Companies.

COMMERCIAL REGISTER:

See topics Aliens; Corporations; Joint Stock Companies.

CONFLICTS OF LAW:

See topics Contracts; Joint Stock Companies; Civil Code.

International contracts can and do specify which law is to govern particular transaction, and where they fail to so specify, then unless otherwise provided in Chinese law, e.g. contracts pursuant to Joint Venture Law are by statute governed by Chinese law, then law of country most closely related to contract will apply. (Foreign Economic Contracts Law, Art. 5, Maritime Law, Art. 269). Inheritance of property within China is governed by Chinese law; however, wills may be governed by law of decedent's domicile. Some of these conflicts questions have yet to be resolved in statutory law or by judicial fiat, but contracts themselves can specify governing law except when in conflict with Chinese laws or regulations.

CONSTITUTION AND GOVERNMENT:

Structure of Chinese government is determined by Constitution of Mar. 5, 1978 as am'd. (See topic Associations.) Committee for Constitutional Revision was selected by National People's Congress on Sept. 10, 1980 and is composed of 103 members, Head, Yeh, Jianying and two Assistant Committee Heads, Sung, Chingling (deceased) and Peng Zhen. Fifth People's Congress, 3d Session, accepted recommendations of Central Committee of Chinese Communist Party to establish said Constitutional Revision Committee and to present draft Constitution to be promulgated by National People's Congress for discussion among peoples and nationalities in China and based on these discussions, to present revised version of Constitution to Fourth Session of National People's Congress.

On Apr. 21, 1982 draft of Revised Constitution of China approved by Constitutional Revision Committee and thereafter submitted to nation for discussion. On Dec. 4, 1982 new constitution was adopted by Fifth National People's Congress.

Seventh National People's Congress adopted amendments containing two articles to 1982 Constitution Apr. 12, 1988 and Eighth National People's Congress adopted amendments containing nine articles to 1982 Constitution Mar. 29, 1993.

Highest organ of Chinese state pursuant to Constitution is National People's Congress. Congress elected for term of five years by people's congresses of provinces, autonomous regions, municipalities directly under central government, and by People's Liberation Army. (New Const. Arts. 57-60). Congress normally holds one session per year. According to Constitution National Congress has power to amend Constitution, promulgate laws, supervise enforcement of laws and Constitution, select Premier of State Council, upon recommendation of Central Committee of Communist Party, and to select other members of State Council, upon recommendation of Premier. National People's Congress also has power to elect President of Supreme People's Court and Chief Procurator of Supreme People's Procuratorate, as well as authority to examine and approve state budget, decide on questions of war and peace, etc. (Art. 62). Permanent organ of National People's Congress is its Standing Committee, latter responsible to and accountable to Congress. Constitution states Congress must make and amend basic laws concerning criminal offenses, civil affairs, structure of state, etc. (Art. 60[3]), while Standing Committee may enact and amend other laws (Art. 67[2]) and partially amend and supplement basic laws enacted by Congress when latter not in session (Art. 67[3]).

Standing Committee of National People's Congress, elected by Congress, has numerous important functions. For example, Standing Committee conducts election of deputies to Congress (Const. Art. 59), convenes sessions of Congress (Const. Art. 61), enacts decrees and interprets laws and Constitution, supervises work of State Council, Supreme People's Court and Supreme People's Procuratorate (Const. Art. 67[1, 3, 4]), alters improper decisions of lower organs, viz. provinces, autonomous regions, and municipalities directly under central government, decides on appointment of ambassadors abroad, decides on ratification and abrogation of treaties (Const. Art. 67 [7, 13]), and decides on proclamation of war when Congress not in session, etc. (Const. Art. 67[18]).

State Council highest executive organ of state power, but responsible to National People's Congress or, when latter not in session, to its Standing Committee. (Const. Arts. 85, 92). State Council composed of Premier, vice premiers, ministers and commission heads. Its powers permit it to formulate administrative actions; issue decisions and orders; propose laws to Congress or its Standing Committee; lead ministries, commissions, local organs of state administration; draw up and put into effect budget; appoint and remove administrative personnel; maintain public order and safeguard citizens' rights, etc. (Art. 32). Standing Committee of National People's Congress May 4, 1982 approved plan whereby State Council has been streamlined and original 53 ministries and commissions reduced to 41.

Constitution reinstitutes position of President and Vice-President of China, former, who would in effect be head of state, to be elected by National People's Congress (Const. Arts. 79, 83) for no more than two consecutive five-year terms (Const. Art. 79).

Supreme People's Court highest judicial organ, with authority to supervise work of all other courts. Court responsible to National People's Congress and its Standing Committee. (Const. Arts. 127, 128). Constitution specifies that courts "shall exercise judicial authority independently according to . . . law and are not subject to interference by administrative organs, public organizations or individuals." (Const. Art. 126). While higher courts exercise administrative supervision over lower courts (Const. Art. 127), and courts at each level are responsible to congress of same level (Const. Art. 128), courts to be independent in their decision making. Pursuant to Constitution Standing Committee of National People's Congress, which supervises work of Supreme People's Court (Const. Art. 67[6]), has authority to amend orders, administrative rules, statutes and decisions of State Council and provincial level authorities that contravene Constitution, or state laws or decrees (Const. Art. 67[7],[8]). No laws, decrees or statutes may contravene Constitution. (Const. Art. 5).

Supreme People's Procuratorate ensures observance of Constitution and law by all departments under State Council, local organs, personnel of state and ordinary citizens. Supervises work of local people's procuratorates. Responsible to National People's Congress and its Standing Committee, while local people's procuratorates, like local people's courts, responsible to and accountable to local people's congresses. (Art. 130). Pursuant to Constitution, Supreme People's Procuratorate exercises its

See Topical Index in front part of this volume.

CONSTITUTION AND GOVERNMENT... *continued*
authority independently, according to law, and is not subject to interference by any administrative organization or individual. (Const. Art. 131).

Communist Party of China is referred to in Preamble to Constitution as having under its leadership formed " ... a broad patriotic united front ... composed of democratic parties and people's organizations ... " embracing all patriots who support socialism and all socialist working people. (Art. 2). Constitution states that: "All power in ..... China belongs to the people," and said power is exercised through National People's Congress and local congresses (Art. 2). Constitution states China is socialist state. (Art. 1).

Local government in China consists of 23 provinces (including Taiwan, considered by People's Republic to be part thereof), five autonomous regions, and three cities directly under central government (Beijing, Shanghai, Tianjin) at highest, provincial level. Former divided into 220 cities, 29 autonomous prefectures, 170 districts, one administrative area and nine leagues. Below this level are 2,137 county level organizations. Large cities divided into prefectures and counties. People's congresses established in provinces, municipalities directly under central government, counties, cities, municipal districts, townships, nationality townships and towns. (Const. Arts. 30, 95). Under new Constitution, political power removed from communes and granted to towns, etc. (Const. Art. 95).

Regional Autonomy in China for ethnic minorities living in compact communities is governed by Statute on Regional Self-Government for [Minority] Nationalities, effective Oct. 1, 1984. This statute, once it comes into effect, pursuant to Const., Art. 4, provides these minority districts, counties, etc. with political authority (Art. 4) and authority to carry out national law and policy based on actual circumstances of locality (Art. 4). People's Congresses of self-governing regions have authority, on basis of localities' special cultural, political and economic circumstances, to promulgate rules and regulations of self government. (Art. 19). These rules and regulations effective upon approval of Standing Committee of National People's Congress. (Art. 19). Self-governing counties must obtain approval of their regulations from standing committee of People's Congress of province or self-governing region. Similarly, regulations, orders, decisions and notices of superior government agencies, if not compatible with actual circumstances of self-governing locality, can, on application and approval of superior government agency, be altered. (Art. 20). Freedom to use native languages, preserve customs and protect religious freedom is granted (Arts. 10, 11); however, religion must not be used to destroy social order or injure citizens' health, or harm national educational system (Art. 11), nor become subject to foreign domination (Art. 11).

Deputies to People's Congress of provinces and centrally directed municipalities, counties, cities, municipal districts are elected for five-year term. (Art. 11, Amendment to Constitution). Deputies to People's Congress of townships, national townships and towns are elected for three-year term. (Art. 11, Amendment to Constitution). Deputies to congress of province, centrally directed municipalities and cities divided into districts are elected by next lower level. (Constitution Art. 97). However, deputies to congress of counties, cities not divided into districts, townships, national township and towns are directly elected by voters. (Constitution Art. 97). Local congresses have parallel authority in their jurisdiction with National People's Congress in its area, and local people's governments have same type of executive authority within their jurisdiction as does State Council on national level. Local authority expanded as China decentralized its governmental organization and thus provinces and local authorities given jurisdiction in most areas, up to specific financial amounts, to approve joint commercial undertakings with foreigners, without need for central government approval.

Constitution provides for Central Military Commission to lead armed forces of China (Const. Art. 93), which has Chairman who is responsible to National People's Congress, or its Standing Committee when former not in session. (Const. Art. 94).

Bill of Rights and Duties.—Constitution specifies certain rights and duties of citizens (see topic Associations). Thus, citizens have right to vote when they reach age of 18 (Const. Art. 34), enjoy freedom of speech, correspondence, press, assembly, association, procession, demonstration (Art. 35) (see topic Associations), and freedom of religious belief (Art. 36). Citizens' equality before law added as fundamental right (Const. Art. 33). Freedom of religion enhanced in Constitution to include prohibition against state or individual discriminating against anyone for their religious beliefs or lack thereof. (Const. Art. 36). Constitution does specify that religious affairs may not be dominated by any foreign country. (Const. Art. 36). Freedom of persons and freedom in their homes is held inviolable (Const. Arts. 37, 39); arrest requires decision of people's court or sanction of people's procuratorate; arrest is to be made by public security organ (Const. Art. 37). There have been limitations placed on writing of big character posters, etc. (see topic Associations), religion is in part regulated, although there is definite policy to restore houses of religious worship confiscated during cultural revolution, to practitioners thereof and to permit free worship. Nevertheless, foreign propagation of religion and outside control, such as that of Catholic church of Rome over Chinese Catholics, is frowned upon and prohibited. Protestant churches have been amalgamated under Three Self Patriotic Movements Committee of Protestant Churches. Chinese Patriotic Catholic Association maintains its independence from Rome. Similarly, Buddhist, Taoist and Islamic Associations maintain some control over religious practices although there is no question that religion is, relatively speaking, flourishing in China at present, compared to period of cultural revolution. Churches, temples and mosques are being restored to parishioners. Property, including homes illegally confiscated during cultural revolution, and salaries of those wrongfully dismissed from positions are being restored, and compensation is being paid.

In addition to these traditional rights, Constitution provides right and duty to work (Const. Art. 42), to rest (Const. Art. 43), to material assistance in old age or in case of illness or disability (Const. Art. 45), to education (Const. Art. 46) and freedom to engage in scientific research or artistic creation (Const. Art. 47). Women enjoy equal rights with men and equal pay for equal work. (Const. Art. 48). In fact, factories and other organizations often have specific quotas of women that must be hired to meet this provision of Constitution. Citizens can lodge complaints against government organs or personnel without retaliation. (Const. Art. 41). Revised Constitution provides additional rights, such as compensation for loss for those whose rights infringed by organs of state or functionaries. (Const. Art. 41). Insult or slander against citizens prohibited by Constitution. (Const. Art. 38). State's interest in protecting legitimate rights and interests of Chinese residents abroad explicated in Const. (Art. 50).

Citizens must protect public property, observe labor discipline, public order, respect social ethics and safeguard state secrets. (Const. Art. 53). Labor discipline, not strictly enforced for many years because of concept of not firing laborers who do not work, so-called "iron rice bowl" policy, now undergoing some resurgence, with emphasis upon enterprises being profitable. While exercising their freedom and rights, citizens must not infringe upon state interests, those of society of collective, or those of other citizens. (Const. Art. 51). Constitution requires support of security, honor and interests of motherland (Const. Art. 54) and stipulates duty to maintain state secrets (Const. Art. 53). Citizens obliged to perform military service (Const. Art. 55), although military presently recruited on voluntary basis. Work is both duty and right, and state said to combine moral encouragement with material reward. (Const. Art. 42).

Nationalities have freedom to use and develop own languages, to preserve or reform their customs and to have some regional autonomy where they reside in compact neighborhoods. (Const. Art. 4).

China deemed socialist state. (Art. 1). State sector of economy, viz. socialist sector, deemed by Constitution to be leading force in economy (Art. 5, Amendment to Constitution), although private sector increasingly encouraged recently. Nonagricultural laborers can engage in individual labor (Constitution Art. 11; Amendment to Constitution Art. 1), and small restaurants, dressmakers, handicraft shops, repair shops, etc. under private ownership have appeared in many cities. Collective members permitted to farm private plots of land for personal needs, engage in household sideline production, and raise privately owned livestock (Art. 6, Amendment to Constitution). In fact, agricultural production for private use, so-called free market, increasing in importance, and more and more farmers come to cities to sell their products in free markets which exist in most cities and many rural areas. Role of commune has been substantially reduced. State protects right of citizens to own lawfully earned income, savings, houses, and other lawful property. (Const. Art. 13). In addition, Constitution states that state protects, by law, right of citizens to inherit private property. (Const. Art. 13). While emphasizing socialist economy, Constitution affirms that state protects lawful rights and interests of individual economy, private economy. (Constitution Art. 11; Amendment to Constitution Art. 1). Private ownership of homes in China is widespread, as are private bank accounts and other private property. Leading capitalists have been called back into service, including some in very high positions, to help development of commerce, industry and agriculture.

All organs of state are required by Constitution to maintain close contact with people, rely on them, heed their opinion, accept their supervision and work hard to serve them. (Const. Art. 26).

Rule of Law, as denominated in Constitution, holds Constitution as paramount law of land. No laws, decrees or statutes may contravene Constitution. (Const. Art. 5). All organs of state, armed forces, all political parties, public organizations, enterprises and institutions must abide by Constitution and law, and no organization or individual enjoys privileges that transcend law or Constitution. (Const. Art. 5).

All citizens of China equal before law. (Const. Art. 33). Right of citizens to criticize any organ of state or functionary, to complain, appeal or report any transgressions of law or neglect of duty by any organ of state or functionary, unless by deliberately false charges, protected by Constitution. (Const. Art. 41). No one may suppress such appeals, complaints or reports, or retaliate against citizens making them. (Const. Art. 41). People suffering loss through infringement of their rights as citizens by organs of state, or functionaries, have right to compensation according to provisions of law. (Const. Art. 41). Freedom of person held inviolable (Const. Art. 37), as are homes of citizens (Const. Art. 39), and as is privacy and freedom of correspondence (Const. Art. 40). Arrest of citizen can be made only by decision of court or sanction of procuratorate. (Const. Art. 37). Extralegal detention, restraints on freedom of person, and searches prohibited. (Const. Art. 37).

Mass Organizations played major role in Chinese political activity since 1949. Their role has dwindled but they still are of some significance. Communist Youth League, All China Federation of Trade Unions, National Women's Federation, Federation of Returned Overseas Chinese, Chinese People's Association of Friendship with Foreign Countries, etc., all play role in quasi-government activity. Most importantly in international trade, Chinese Council for Promotion of International Trade, State-Owned Trading Corporations and China Export Commodities Fair ("Canton Fair") all play significant roles in trade.

Organizations denominated Democratic Parties exist in China and play small role in political process. Since Constitution provides that Communist Party is leading organ of politics, these other organizations have obviously smaller role to play. Nevertheless, organizations such as Chinese Democratic League, Revolutionary Committee of the Chinese Kuomintang, China Association for Promoting Democracy, China Democratic National Construction Association, Chinese Peasants and Workers Democratic Party, China Zhi Gong Dang, Jiusan Society, Taiwan Democratic Self-Government League and All-China Federation of Industry and Commerce all play some small role in political process. Constitution, while stating China is socialist state (Const. Art. 1), no longer states Communist Party core of leadership of whole Chinese people. Role of Communist Party de-emphasized, except in Preamble to Constitution. These so-called democratic parties have members elected to various people's congresses at all levels and to Chinese People's Political Consultive Congress ("PPCC") at all levels.

CONSULS:

U.S. and China have signed consular relations agreements, initially on Jan. 31, 1979 whereby they agreed to establish consular relations, open consular offices by each in other's territory, promote well being of each country's citizens in other's territory, foster family reunion, tourism, commercial, scientific, technological, cultural and other relations between peoples of both nations. China, pursuant to these agreements has consulate in Houston, New York and San Francisco and embassy in Washington, D. C., while U.S. has consulates in Guangzhou, Shenyang and Shanghai and embassy in Beijing. Other consulates will be opened by both countries in future.

See Topical Index in front part of this volume.

CONSULS . . . *continued*

Parties to consular agreements, if disagreements arise, undertake to resolve them by spirit of mutual understanding, drawing on principle of customary international law embodied in Vienna Convention on Consular Relations of 1963.

Aside from agreeing to process all applications to facilitate family reunions as quickly as possible, governments agreed to facilitate travel between their countries of those claiming dual nationality. Chinese Nationality Law, however, does not recognize dual nationality. Nevertheless, U.S. citizens who enter China with Chinese visas are to be considered U.S. nationals for purpose of ensuring consular protection and access, regardless of whether they may also be regarded as citizens of China. Chinese citizens enjoy same rights in U.S. Citizens of each country arrested or detained in other have right to have their consular post or embassy notified without delay and are permitted access to consular officer.

The Standing Committee of the People's Congress enacted Diplomatic Privileges and Immunities Regulations in 5 Sept., 1986. Rules are in accord with Vienna Consular Convention, effective on 19 Mar., 1967, of which China is signatory.

Territorial independence of foreign embassies in China is assured (Art. 4); they are essentially free from taxes (Art. 5), their files are sacrosanct (Art. 6). Foreign representatives enjoy diplomatic immunity from civil or criminal action, except where acting in personal capacity, e.g. as heir to property or personal business. (Art. 14).

If there are conventions or treaties to which China is party, said international treaties or conventions take precedence over these Regulations.

Regulations Governing Consular Privileges and Immunities were adopted at 16th Meeting of the Standing Committee of the Seventh National People's Congress on Oct. 30, 1990, promulgated on Oct. 30, 1990 and became effective as of date of promulgation.

Under these regulations, consular officers shall be of nationality of sending State. Chinese, foreign nationals who are or permanent residents of China or nationals of sending State may be appointed only with consent of competent Chinese authorities.

Consulate and its head shall have right to use national flag and emblem of sending State on premises of its Consulate, on residence of head of its Consulate and on his means of transport when used on official business. (Art. 3).

Premises of Consulate shall be inviolable. (Art. 4). Premises of Consulate and residence of its head shall be exempt from dues and taxes other than such as payment for specific services rendered. (Art. 5). Archives and documents of Consulate shall be inviolable. (Art. 6).

Members of Consulate shall enjoy freedom of movement and travel within Chinese territory except for prohibited areas or areas restricted by regulations of Chinese Government. (Art. 7). Consulate may, for official purposes, communicate with its Government and diplomatic mission and other Consulates of sending State freely. In so doing, it may employ all appropriate means, including diplomatic couriers or consulate couriers, diplomatic bag or consulate bag or messages in code or cipher. (Art. 8).

Consulate may install and use wireless transmitter-receiver only with consent of Chinese Government. (Art. 9). Consulate bag shall not be opened or detained. (Art. 10).

Consulate officer shall enjoy diplomatic rights and privileges. Chinese authorities concerned shall take appropriate measures to prevent any attack on his personal freedom and dignity. Consulate officer shall not be liable to arrest or detention, except that arrest or detention is executed in case of grave crime and in accordance with legal procedures. Consulate officer shall not be committed to prison save in execution of judicial decision of final effect. (Art. 12).

Residence of consulate officer shall be inviolable. His papers and correspondence shall be inviolable. His property, except as provided in Art. 14 of present Regulations, shall be inviolable. (Art. 13).

Consulate officers and members of administrative and technical staff of Consulate shall enjoy immunity from judicial and administrative jurisdiction in respect of acts performed in exercise of acts other than those performed in exercise of their functions in accordance with bilateral treaties and agreements between China and country concerned or on principle of reciprocity. (Art. 14).

Consulate officers and members of administrative or technical staff of Consulate shall be excepted from all dues and taxes, except: (1) dues and taxes of kind which are normally incorporated in price of goods or services; (2) dues or taxes on private immovable property situated in territory of China, excepting those used in Consulate premises; (3) estate, succession or inheritance duties, except movable property left in China by deceased Consulate officer shall be excepted therefrom; (4) dues and taxes on private income with its source in China; or (5) charges levied for specific services rendered. Members of service staff of Consulate shall be excepted from dues and taxes on wages which they receive from their service in Consulate. (Art. 17).

Members of Consulate shall be exempted from all personal and public services as well as military obligations. (Art. 18).

Imported articles for Consulate's official use, personal use of Consulate officers, personal use of members of administrative or technical staff of Consulate, including articles intended for their establishment, imported within six months of time of installation shall, in accordance with their relevant regulations of Chinese Government, be exempted from customs duties and all other related dues and taxes with exception of charges for storage, cartage and similar services. (Art. 19).

Following persons shall enjoy necessary immunity and inviolability during their transit through or sojourn in China: (1) Consulate officer stationed in third State who passes through China together with his spouse and minor children forming part of his household; and (2) visiting foreign Consulate officer who has obtained diplomatic visa from China or who holds diplomatic passport of State with which China has agreement on mutual exemption of visas. (Art. 23).

Persons enjoying consulate privileges and immunities under present regulations shall: (1) respect Chinese laws and regulations; (2) not interfere in internal affairs of China; and (3) not use premises of Consulate and residence of members of Consulate for purposes incompatible with exercise of Consulate functions. (Art. 24).

Consulate officers shall not practice for any professional or commercial activity outside his official functions for personal profit within Chinese territory. (Art. 25).

Where international treaties to which China is contracting or acceding party provided for, otherwise, in respect of consular privileges and immunities, such provisions shall prevail, with exception of those to which China has declared reservations. Where bilateral treaties or agreements between China and other countries provided for, otherwise, in respect of Consular privileges and immunities, such provisions shall prevail. (Art. 27).

CONSUMER PROTECTION:

Goods sold by state organizations, as well as those imported, are subject to inspection by Import and Export Commodity Inspection Bureau. There are 29 bureaus in all provinces except Taiwan, municipalities directly under central government (Beijing, Shanghai, Tienjin) and autonomous regions. Role of Bureau is to undertake inspection of goods being exported and imported to ensure quality control, so that goods meet national standards and conform to contractual specifications. There is Bureau of Weights and Measures that inspects imported weighing and measuring apparatus. In addition, there is Animal and Plant Quarantine Center for quarantine of imported plants and animals. Ministry of Health is responsible for inspecting imported foodstuffs and drugs and Ship Inspection Bureau is responsible for inspecting ships, etc. Import and Export Commodity Bureau has right to inspect certain commodities specified in "List of Commodities Subject to Inspection", 196 in number, as well as right to inspect animal products and foodstuffs subject to inspection. If contracts require certificate of inspection from Bureau, it obviously has right to inspect said products. Inspection of other foodstuffs and drugs involves quality, specifications and packing conditions, and where satisfied, certificate is issued releasing goods from Customs. Provisional Regulations Governing Inspection and Testing of Import and Export Commodities were promulgated as of Jan. 3, 1954. State Council replaced said Regulations on Jan. 28, 1984 with Regulations on Inspection of Import and Export Commodities. These latter regulations were also later replaced by Laws on Inspection of Import and Export Commodities, adopted on Feb. 21, 1989, effective Aug. 1, 1989.

According to latest Regulations, State Council will establish Inspection of Import and Export Commodities Department. (Art. 2). Violators of regulations will be fined by Commodity Inspection Organization; in cases resulting in serious loss, responsible party will be penalized according to Art. 187 of Criminal Code. (Art. 26). In addition to this Bureau there is National Bureau of Standards whose work is being expanded to include development of standards at each level of production pursuant to Regulations Governing Standardization promulgated by State Council on July 31, 1979.

Foreign inspection institutes which invest in Chinese territory to set up import/export commodity inspection organizations must obtain approval by China National Commodity Inspection Bureau. Without such approval, relevant economic and trade departments and other organizations will not handle examination procedures. Administrative department of industry and commerce will not handle registration for organizations of Import/Export Commodity Inspection without getting such approval.

Product Quality Law adopted by National People's Congress Feb. 22, 1993, effective Sept. 1, 1993. It prohibits falsification or passing off such quality marks as authentication mark, well-known mark and top-quality mark (Arts. 4, 19, 26), and origin of products, factory name and address (Arts. 4, 18, 25). It also prohibits mixing impurities or false materials in products, assuming false as genuine, inferior as superior. (Arts. 4, 20, 27). Manufacturers shall be responsible for quality of products produced by themselves. (Art. 14). Sellers shall repair, replace or return goods not possessing functions which they should have and sellers fail to declare, or do not conform with product standard described in technical manuals or package, or do not conform with quality indicated by technical manuals, samples etc. (Art. 28). If users or consumers suffer any damages, sellers liable for damages thereupon. (Art. 28). Sellers may seek recourse from manufacturers or their wholesale seller, if they are liable for defective goods. (Art. 28). Manufacturers are liable for damages to persons or other properties incurred by defective products, unless they show any of following circumstances which they shall be exempted from liabilities, i.e. products are not put into market, defects do not exist when they are put into market, defects not discoverable by level of science and technology when they are put into market. (Art. 29). Sellers are liable for damages to persons, other properties incurred by defects of goods due to faults of sellers. (Art. 30). Sellers failing to show manufacturers of defective goods or supplier of defective goods shall be liable for damages. (Art. 30).

Penalty.—Manufacturers and sellers producing or dealing in goods involving human health and safety of human body and property, failing to meet standard of state or specific sector of trade, shall cease to produce or sell products or have confiscation of lawful products and income, and concurrently be fined amount of one-five times unlawful income. (Art. 37). Manufacturers and sellers mixing product with impurities or false materials, assuming false as genuine, inferior as superior, non-qualified as qualified, shall cease to produce or sell, have confiscation of unlawful income, and concurrently be fined amount of one-five times unlawful income. (Art. 38).

Manufacturers and sellers falsifying origin of products, falsifying or passing off factory names, factory addresses, and quality marks shall have confiscation of unlawful income and may concurrently be fined. (Art. 41). Any of above cases constitutes crime, violators shall be penalized according to criminal code. (Arts. 37-41).

Supplementary Provisions Concerning Punishing Criminal Activities of Counterfeiting Registered Trademarks was adopted by National People's Congress Feb. 22, 1993, effective July 1, 1993. Those using trademark identical with registered trademark on same product without permission of exclusive rights owner and obtaining relatively large income or willfully dealing in product with counterfeiting registered trademark and obtaining relatively large income, shall be imprisoned three years or less, or detention; in cases where violators obtain huge income, imprisonment of three-seven years shall be imposed. (Art. 1).

Law Concerning Protection of Consumer Rights and Interests was adopted by National People's Congress on Oct. 31, 1993, effective as of Jan. 1, 1994.

Consumers' Rights.—Consumers may enjoy right to protect their personal and property safety from injuries in course of purchase and use of commodities and acceptance of services. (Art. 7). Consumers are entitled to request operators to provide commodities and services in conformity with requirements of personal and property safety protection. (Art. 7). Consumers may enjoy right to have access to true conditions of commodities purchased or used or services accepted. (Art. 8). Consumers are

See Topical Index in front part of this volume.

CONSUMER PROTECTION . . . *continued*

entitled to choose commodities or services at their own discretion. (Art. 9). Consumers enjoy right to fair dealing. (Art. 10). Consumers may obtain such transaction term as quality warranty, reasonable price and correct measures and reject unilateral mandatory transaction in purchase of commodities or acceptance of services. (Art. 10). Consumers may obtain compensation according to law should their body or property be injured in course of purchasing or using commodities or acceptance of services. (Art. 11). Consumers may acquire knowledge regarding consumers and consumers' rights and interests protection, and establish social associations designed to protect their legal rights and interests according to law. (Arts. 12, 13). Consumers are entitled to respect for their dignity or national custom in course of purchasing or using commodities or acceptance of services. (Art. 14). Consumers are entitled to supervise work of consumers' rights and interests protection and commodities and services. (Art. 15).

Obligations of Operators.—Operators shall provide consumers products or services in conformity with requirements provided for by product Quality Law and other laws and regulations, as well as agreements reached between operators and consumers. (Art. 16). Operators shall ensure their products or services are in conformity with personal or property safety standard. (Art. 17). Should their products or services be likely to endanger personal or property safety, they shall make true instructions and obvious warnings to consumer, and explain and indicate correct methods to use products or services which will likely result in injuries to personal or property safety of consumer even though consumers use them correctly. They shall immediately report to relevant administrative departments and consumers, and take preventive measure to avoid injuries. (Art. 18). Operators shall provide accurate information regarding their products or services to consumers and must not make misleading advertisements. (Art. 19). Operators must indicate their true names and marks. (Art. 20). Operators must ensure their products or services possess reasonable quality, features, purposes and periods of use in cases where they are normally used or accepted, except where consumers have knowledge of defects prior to purchases of products or acceptance of services. (Art. 22). Should operators indicate quality conditions of their products or services in advertisements, instructions or samples or any other means, they must ensure actual quality of their products or services is in conformity with stated quality. (Art. 22). Operators must undertake to repair, replace or return products or services in accordance with provisions of State or agreements reached between operators and consumers, and must not deliberately delay or unreasonably refuse. (Art. 23). Operators must not specify unfair or unreasonable provisions or exempt or mitigate their civil liabilities by way of standard contracts, notice, statement or placard; such clauses are null and void and of no effect. (Art. 24). Operators must not insult or libel consumers, search bodies of consumers and their personal articles and infringe upon personal freedom of consumers. (Art. 25).

Dispute Settlement.—Consumers may resolve their disputes in following manner: (1) discuss with operators; (2) apply for mediation to Consumers Association; (3) complain to relevant administrative departments; (4) submit to arbitration tribunal in accordance with arbitration agreement; and (5) initiate litigation in court of law. (Art. 34). Where consumers suffer injuries to their legal rights and interests in purchasing or using commodities, they are entitled to claim damages against sellers. (Art. 35). Should liabilities be attributable to manufacturers or other sellers at upper level, they may have recourse against manufacturers or other sellers at upper level. (Art. 35). Where consumers or other victims suffer injuries to body or property due to defective commodities, they may claim damages against sellers or manufacturers. (Art. 35). Should manufacturers compensate consumers first and sellers are found liable, they may have recourse against seller or vice versa. (Art. 35). Should consumers suffer injuries to their legal rights and interests in acceptance of service, they may claim damage against service suppliers. (Art. 35). Where operators use business license of others to provide commodities or services illegally and cause harm to consumers' rights and interests, consumers may claim damages against said operators or license holders. (Art. 36). Where consumers purchase commodities or accept services in exhibitions and trade fairs or leased counters, and suffer injuries to their legal rights and interests they may claim damages against sellers or service suppliers. Should exhibitions and trade fairs close or period of counter lease expire, they may claim damages against holders of exhibitions and trade fairs or counter lessor, who may have recourse against sellers or service suppliers. (Art. 38). Where consumers suffer injuries to their legal rights and interests due to false advertisement of operators, they may claim damages against operator. (Art. 39). Where advertisement dealer disseminates false advertisement and fails to provide true names and addresses of operators of goods, advertisement dealer shall assume compensation liability. (Art. 39).

CONTRACTS:

See topics Joint Stock Companies; Trade Zones; Civil Code; Sales.

Traditional Chinese law, as reflected by law and practice of last imperial dynasty, Ching (1644-1911), permitted extensive scope for freedom of contract. Ching code itself was addressed in only small part to civil law matters, and civil contracts were butressed by customary law and practice.

In international trade, contracts and tribute dominated commercial practice. Transactions in People's Republic of China, particularly in international field, have until recently been relatively unfettered by domestic regulations and thus contracts determined not only normal rights and obligations of parties, but also provided for things such as patent protection, etc. Contracts thus at times established law to govern particular transaction.

Chinese publicists have for some time recognized importance of contracts. Chinese authors have recognized that in order to have binding contract there must be mutuality of interest, and recognize that legal consequences of contract are those parties intend. Chinese authors of legal texts have recognized that parties to contract have equal status, and those who breach contracts will be liable for damages flowing therefrom. Chinese recognize need for offer, and acceptance within terms of said offer, in order for there to be standard contract. Chinese legal experts hold that contracts must be based on free intention of parties and yet state that contracts should be fair and reasonable. If portion of contract is unreasonable it may be deemed void. Under Joint Venture Law contracts must be reviewed by certain Chinese government agencies and most complicated international agreements made at local level must be approved by provincial authorities which to some extent examine said contracts for reasonableness.

Chinese authorities have recognized sales contract as being bilateral contract, consensual in nature, and being non-gratuitous.

Chinese international contracts normally contain force majeure provision. Chinese international contracts are frequently denominated in hard currencies. Contracts are often in English or Chinese and English, although not infrequently executed only in Chinese language.

Joint Venture Law, Environmental Protection Law, Trademark Law, Patent Law, tax laws and other recent legislation limit ability of parties in international transactions to freely contract.

China has promulgated legislation directly concerned with contract law e.g., Government Administrative Council on Sept. 27, 1950 promulgated Provisional Rules for Contracts by Organizations, National Enterprises and Cooperative Societies. It provided for type of arrangements in which contracts were necessary, including sale and purchase of goods, loans, rental agreements, joint ventures, etc. Rules also provided for responsibility of guarantors of contracts; thus, e.g., if contract for bank loan is involved, there must be guarantor, in principle goods themselves acted as guarantors, but if there were no such goods lending unit, superior organization or principal organization was to guarantee loan. When signing contract there should be person, normally in superior organ, who undertakes to review contractual terms. Contract must be executed by legal entity, since individual cannot undertake to execute or guarantee contract if organization he represents refuses to execute contract.

Once contract is executed both sides must undertake to carry out their duties pursuant to its terms, and if for some reason one side or other cannot conform to its terms, any changes must be made with consent of other side to have legal effect. If one side is damaged by failure of other side to perform its terms, then they must be compensated by other side for damage; guarantor also has such obligation. If contracts are between domestic entities in China, administrative units can be utilized to compel performance of contractual terms and if that is ineffective, then one can bring judicial proceedings before court.

On Nov. 10, 1963 State Council promulgated Rules Regarding Strictly Implementing Economic Contracts which concerned strict adherence to said contractual terms, including time of delivery, quantity and quality of goods, time of payment, etc. Those failing to adhere to said contracts would have economic responsibility for losses of other side.

In 1963 National Economic Committee promulgated Provisional Regulations Regarding Basic Provisions of Contracts for Purchase of Industrial and Mining Products. These regulations also call for strict performance of contracts. They provide that contracts should include specific technological standards for products and packing which is subject matter of contract, viz., name, specification, measurements, amount, packing standard, weight, shipping instructions, time of delivery, price calculations and economic responsibility. Latter is in nature of penalty clause to ensure performance.

Various governmental commercial agencies in China also promulgated their own regulations to ensure performance of contracts and meeting of national plans. E.g., Ministry of Textile Industry on Oct. 17, 1953; and on Apr. 11, 1955 Ministry of Heavy Industry, promulgated regulations regarding contracts. Primary intent of these provisions was to ensure meeting of goals embodied in national plan. These contracts call for inclusion of provisions making reference to national plan, employees, wages, incentives, etc.

Different regulations relating to insurance contracts were also promulgated in China, including marine insurance, railroad insurance, property insurance, aviation insurance, and insurance of citizens' property.

Economic Contract Law was adopted by National People's Congress on Dec. 13, 1981, effective as of July 1, 1982 and amended by National People's Congress on Sept. 2, 1993. Law is applicable to contracts specifying rights and obligations by and between subjects with equal civil status, namely legal persons, other economic entities, individual industrial and commercial households and rural households of contracting operation, in order to realize specific economic goals. (Art. 2). "Economic Contracts" refers to purchases and sales contracts, construction and projects contracts, transportation contracts, processing contracts, supply and use of electricity contracts, storage and warehouse agreements, property lease agreements, loan agreements, property insurance contracts and other economic contracts unless otherwise provided for by law. (Art. 8). In executing economic contracts, one must follow laws and administrative decrees of State and in no way to use them to engage in illegal activities, disrupt economic order, impinge upon interests of State and interests of public or to seek illicit income. (Art. 4). In execution of economic contracts, principles of equality and mutual benefit and unanimity through consultation must be adhered to (Art. 5). No one party may force other party to accept its intention and no entity or individual may illegally interfere. (Art. 5). After execution, economic contracts shall bind parties concerned who shall perform their overall obligations specified in contract and not unilaterally modify or terminate contract. (Art. 6).

Formation.—In general, contracts should be made in written form. (Art. 3). Documents, telegrams and charts regarding amendments to contracts agreed upon by parties concerned through consultation shall be indispensable parts of contracts. (Art. 3). Contracts are formed when principal clauses are agreed unanimously through consultation by both parties according to law. (Art. 7). Principal clauses of contracts refer to following: (1) subject matter (goods, labor services, construction projects, etc.); (2) quality and quantity; (3) price or remuneration; (4) time limit, place and method of performance; and (5) liabilities for breach of contract. (Art. 12). Terms provided for by law or necessitated by nature of said contracts or requested by one party to be included are also principal clauses. (Art. 12). Where contracts are concluded by agents, they are binding upon principal regarding rights and obligations therefrom only when agents have proxy from principal and sign contracts in name of principal within entrusted authority. (Art. 10). Should enterprise be imposed with state mandatory plans, such contract should be concluded in accordance with rights and obligations provided for by relevant laws and administrative decree. (Art. 11).

Invalid contract refers to following: (1) contract in violation of laws and administrative decree of State, (2) contract made by fraud, duress or other such means; (3)

CONTRACTS . . . *continued*
contract executed by agents in excess of their authority; or (4) contract which violates interests of State or public. (Art. 7). Authority to affirm invalid contract is held by courts of law and arbitration tribunals. (Art. 7). Should clause be severable from contract and it is declared null and void, other clauses remain valid. (Art. 7). Should contract be declared null and void, parties concerned shall return to each other any property acquired pursuant to contract. Should one party be at fault, it shall compensate other party for losses incurred therefrom. Should both parties be at fault they assume liabilities proportionate to their respective faults. (Art. 16). Where both parties are found to have acted deliberately to harm interests of State or public, they must turn over properties acquired or which they have agreed to acquire pursuant to contract, to State Treasury. (Art. 16). Where only one party is found to have acted deliberately, said party must return to other party any property acquired from other party; party being not at fault must turn over any property acquired from said party to State Treasury. (Art. 16).

Performance.—In performance of obligations under contract, Renminbi must be used in computation of price and payment unless otherwise provided for by law or administrative decree. (Art. 13). Accounts shall be settled through bank account transfer or bills, unless it is otherwise permitted by State to use cash. (Art. 13). One party may pay deposit to other party which must be returned or set off against price after performance. (Art. 14). Should party having paid deposit fail to perform contract, it does not have right to claim return of deposit. Should party having received deposit fail to perform contract, it shall return twice amount of deposit. (Art. 14). Where one party requests guarantee, it may be provided by guarantor. Should guaranteed party fail to perform contract, guarantor must perform or assume joint and several liability pursuant to guaranty agreement. (Art. 15). In sales contract, matters regarding quantity, quality, package quality and prices of product and time limit for delivery shall be fixed as follows: (1) terms of product quantity shall be fixed through consultation of parties. Provisions of State shall govern measurements; in absence of such provisions, methods agreed upon by parties shall apply; (2) quality of products and package must not be lower than State mandatory standard or specialized standard if any; in absence of such standard, qualities shall be fixed through mutual consultation between parties; (3) product prices shall be fixed through mutual discussion unless it is otherwise required to follow State regulated prices; where State regulated prices apply, if such prices are adjusted within time limit of delivery prices at time of delivery apply. Should delivery be delayed, original price applies when price has gone up; new price applies when price has dropped. Should taking delivery or payment be delayed, new price applies when price has gone up and original prices applies when price has dropped; and (4) should one party request advance or delay in delivery or taking of goods, price agreement shall be reached. (Art. 17).

Alteration/Cancellation.—Contract may be altered or cancelled in any of following cases: (1) Both parties reach agreement and alteration or cancellation does not harm interests of State or public; (2) all obligations in contracts cannot be performed due to force majeure; and (3) any one party fails to perform contract in time limit provided for by contract. Should one party merge or split, party or parties resulting from change shall undertake to perform contract and enjoy its respective rights. (Art. 26). Notices or agreements for alteration or cancellation must be in written form including documents, telegrams and other like materials etc. Prior to new agreement, original contract shall remain binding except that all obligations provided for in contract cannot be performed due to occurrance of force majeure or any one party fails to perform contract within time limit provided. (Art. 27). After execution of contract, it must not be altered or cancelled due to changes in legal representative or person in charge. (Art. 28).

Breach of Contract.—Where contract cannot be performed due to fault of one party, said party is liable for breach of contract; should both parties be at fault, each party must assume corresponding liabilities according to actual circumstances. (Art. 29). If major accident or serious losses occur as result of wrong doing or illicit contract, criminal liabilities may result. (Art. 29). Should one party break contract it shall pay contractual breach damage to other party. Should losses caused by breach exceed amount of contractual breach defaulter shall pay compensation to make up deficiencies. Where other party requests continued performance, defaulter shall continue to perform. (Art. 31). Contractual breach money or compensation must be paid within ten days after liabilities are clearly affirmed. Otherwise payment is deemed overdue. (Art. 32). Should one party be unable to perform contract due to force majeure, it must promptly notify other party of reasons why it cannot perform or why it needs extension of time to perform. When it has obtained relevant evidence of an occurrance which delays performance, it must be allowed to defer performance, perform partially, or not perform and it may be fully or partially exempted from liabilities for breach of contract depending upon circumstances. (Art. 30).

Dispute Settlement.—Should disputes be unable to be resolved by consultation or mediation, any party may submit to arbitration within two years of discovering breach, or may directly commence litigation. (Arts. 42, 43). Awards rendered by arbitration tribunals are binding and any party must perform them voluntarily. Should any party refuse to perform within prescribed time limit, other party may apply for compulsory enforcement in court of law. (Art. 42).

Law on Technological Contracts was adopted by National People's Congress June 23, 1987, effective Nov. 1, 1987. Law supersedes Economic Contract Law in area of technological contract including technology development, technology transfer, technology consultancy and technology service contract. (Art. 53).

Formation.—Technological contract should be in written form (Art. 9), formulated when parties to contract sign or seal on contract; in cases which require approval from relevant authorities, shall come into force when it is approved (Art. 10). Technological contract drawn according to law is legally binding and cannot unilaterally be terminated or modified. (Art. 11). Technological contract should, in general, include following clauses: name of project; content, scope and requirement of subject matter; plan, schedule, time, place and means of performance; confidentiality of technological information and materials; allocation of risks; attribution and share of technical results; standard and means of inspection; price or reward and payment terms; liquidated damages or calculation method of damages; means of dispute settlement and definition of terminology. (Art. 15). Technological contract violating law or injuring interests of state or society, unlawfully monopolizing technology and impeding technology development, injuring legal rights and interests of others or formulated through fraud or coercion, are null and void.

Alteration/Cancellation.—Technological contract may be altered and or canceled when agreed by mutual consultation, through written novation (Arts. 23, 9); in cases contract has been approved by relevant authorities, permission should be obtained from such. Where one party fails to honor contract, or force majeure occurs or technology as subject matter of technology development contract has entered into public domain resulting in impossible or unnecessary performance, other party may notify party to cancel contract. (Art. 24). Parties entitled to claim damages may recover damages, after contract alteration or cancellation. (Art. 25).

Breach.—Where on party fails to honor contract or performance fails to conform with contract requirement, other party entitled to demand remedial measures or claim actual compensation foreseeable at time when contract formulated. (Art. 17). One party should mitigate damages when confronted with breach of contract of other party. (Art. 17). Where both parties have faults, each should bear its responsibilities proportionate to respective faults. (Art. 18). Where faults of breach on part of breaching party are attributed to its superior competent authority, breaching party must compensate other party or take remedial measures according to contract. (Art. 19).

Dispute Settlement.—If disputes cannot be settled by mutual consultation, any party may apply to arbitral tribunal for arbitration according arbitration clause in contract or subsequent arbitration agreement. (Art. 51). Arbitration award is binding and enforceable by court. (Art. 51). In absence of arbitration clause or agreement, any party may petition to People's Court for litigation. (Art. 51).

Shenzhen S.E.Z. Foreign Economic Contract Regulations.—On Feb. 7, 1984 Guangdong government promulgated Shenzhen SEZ Regulations Concerning Foreign Economic Contracts, which had been approved by Standing Committee of People's Congress of Guangdong province on Jan. 11, 1984.

Scope of these contractual regulations encompasses: (1) Agreements between: Chinese enterprises or other organizations in SEZ and foreign enterprises, economic organizations or individuals, entered into in order to develop economic and technical cooperation in SEZ, that have agreements under Chinese law establishing relationships of mutual rights and obligations; and (2) between following entities which execute agreements to be undertaken in SEZ: foreign and Chinese-foreign joint venture or joint agreement enterprises registered and doing business in SEZ; SEZ enterprises and foreign enterprises or other economic organizations or individuals; and SEZ enterprises and Chinese enterprises or other economic organizations established in SEZ. (Art. 2).

Approvals Required.—These contracts must have approval of SEZ government or its authorized representative (Art. 5), and applications for approval to be determined within three months of submission (Art. 5). Those contracts in violation of Chinese law, or doing damage to Chinese sovereignty or social public interests, or employing fraud or coercion are null and void ab initio; however, if portion of confirmed contract which does not influence efficacy of remainder is null and void, rest of contract still has effect. (Art. 5).

Elements of Contract.—Contracts must be in written form, clearly specify parties' rights and obligations and be signed by parties or their authorized agents. Cables, letters, or telexes sufficient to provide written form of contract if both parties agree not to execute formal contract. (Art. 7).

Authority to Contract and Guarantee.—Parties executing contract should present following documents to each other for examination: (1) Copies or photocopies of documents of registration with local or other governmental agency; (2) evidence of financial status re responsibility; (3) notarized documents of guarantee; and (4) documents evidencing authority of agents. (Art. 9).

Parties to contract should provide guarantees, which can take following form: (1) Deposit of cash; or (2) pledge of property; or (3) bank guarantee; or (4) corporate or enterprise guarantee; or (5) other guarantee. (Art. 12).

Provisions of Different Forms of Contracts.—

Joint venture is contract or written agreement whereby both parties invest, and divide profit or losses in proportion to said investment, in limited liability entity. Such contracts should contain following elements: (1) Names of parties, registered address, legal address and name of legal representative, nationality; (2) name of joint venture enterprise, address, scope of its activities and size, amount of land to be used; (3) total amount of investment, registered capital, each party's contribution to capital, form of contribution to capital, and provisions for time period to pay in said capital; (4) important equipment and technology to be used for production, and its origins; (5) means of purchase of raw materials and sales of products; (6) each party's responsibility for preparatory work, construction, production, operations, etc.; (7) time limit of joint venture, procedures for computation and windup, division of capital on termination of venture; (8) principles of accounting, auditing and finance; (9) provisions of labor management, salaries, social benefits, labor protection and insurance, etc.; (10) organization, duration of office and responsibilities of board of directors; (11) means of selecting general and assistant general manager, personnel organization and their responsibilities and authority; (12) limitations of liability and division of profits and losses; (13) guarantees and responsibility for breach of contract; (14) arbitration agreement or other means of resolving disputes; (15) time and place of execution of contract; and (16) other provisions parties deem necessary. (Art. 15).

Cooperative venture is written contract for venture in which SEZ party provides use of land, buildings, labor, labor services, authority to exploit resources, and foreign party provides capital, equipment, materials, technology, etc. Contract also provides for cooperation in production or operations, etc., and specifies each party's share of profits or products, and each party's assumption of risk, etc. Essential contents of this type of contract similar to joint venture. (Art. 16).

Compensation Trade (Art. 17) and Assembly and Work-Added Contracts (Art. 18) also outlined by statute. Contracts for wholly-owned foreign entities (Art. 19), and contracts for land use, labor, importation of technology, leasehold pledges or mortgages, etc. are not outlined by this statute, but reference made to other unspecified regulations of SEZ. Contracts for sales of goods, utilities products, insurance, construction, and transportation are not outlined by statute, but reference made to unspecified Chinese national statutes. (Art. 19).

See Topical Index in front part of this volume.

CONTRACTS . . . *continued*

Breach of Contract and Dispute Resolution.—Shenzhen city Bureau of Industry and Commerce designated as supervisory agency for contracts, and after approval of said contracts, copy should be sent by parties to this agency for registration, as well as to tax bureau. (Art. 31). This agency can supervise contracting parties, conciliate disputes, restrain parties from unlawful acts, and can fine parties for serious violations. (Art. 32). When entering into joint ventures, cooperative ventures, cooperative ventures to exploit natural resources, and contracts closely connected with matters of Chinese sovereignty, parties must apply Chinese law in resolution of disputes through arbitration. (Art. 35). Arbitration of these contracts should take place in China, but need not utilize arbitral organization in SEZ if parties agree to another arbitral body. (Art. 36). If contract has no arbitral provision, parties can bring suit in Chinese courts having jurisdiction over said disputes. (Art. 36). There are also various specific penalty provisions for breach of certain contracts; thus, where there is failure to ship goods on time, in addition to breaching party's responsibility to compensate plaintiff for its losses, statute requires breaching party to pay for each day's delay one-thousandth of value of goods that were to be shipped on said day. (Art. 21). Statute also contains force majeure provision (Art. 24) permitting avoidance of liability if breach caused by war, serious natural disaster, or other force majeure specified in contract, etc.

Technology Transfer, etc. Contracts.—Shenzhen SEZ also has Temporary Regulations for the Importation of Technology, promulgated by Standing Committee of People's Congress of Guangdong on Feb. 8, 1984, covering all importation of technology from abroad by enterprises, etc. in SEZ. (Art. 2). These contracts for technology transfer must be in writing (Art. 4), and said technology must be modern, all clearly economically effective. Scope of technology covered includes patented technology, patent-pending technology and trade secrets. (Art. 5). Shenzhen city Scientific Technology Development Center, or other Chinese national scientific research organization, can verify level of modernity or important economic effectiveness of technology; thereafter, tax bureau, land bureau, etc. must approve in order to obtain special advantageous provisions for importation of such technology. (Art. 6). If technology has already been patented or is pending patent approval, evidence of such approval must be proffered. (Arts. 7, 8). Those involved in technology transfer of trade secrets must proffer evidence, including designs, forms, samples, models, etc. (Art. 9). Party applying for technology transfer should: (1) Provide Shenzhen city government with application, letter of intent, and feasibility study report; (2) after approval of project application, application for technology transfer should be obtained, contract signed, and application for approval of contract made to Shenzhen city government. (Art. 15). Said contract in triplicate, together with application for technology transfer in triplicate, evidence of lawful status of parties (each in triplicate), and purchaser's operations license in triplicate should all be submitted to Shenzhen city government for approval. (Art. 15). Decision on approval should be made within three months of application and once said contract is approved, it is effective as of date of approval. (Art. 16). Thereafter, said contract must be submitted to Shenzhen Bureau of Commerce and Industry and to tax bureau for registration. (Art. 16). Contract should include following important provisions: (1) Name of project, parties, and their addresses; (2) definition of key terms; (3) scope and contents of technology; (4) trademark used; (5) technological training and technological service to be undertaken; (6) operational plans; (7) guarantees of technology; (8) secrecy agreement; (9) provisions for rights and duties of the parties; (10) means of calculating value of technology; (11) breach provisions; (12) force majeure clause; (13) arbitration or dispute settlement clause; (14) time period of contract; (15) location of execution of contract; (16) means of calculating royalty and payment rights and duties of parties, and other provisions parties deem necessary. (Art. 17). Statute further provides that other than for investment purposes, these contracts normally do not exceed five years, but they can be extended with approval of Shenzhen city government, provided application made within six months of expiry of contract, and decision made within one month of submission. (Art. 19). Transfer of patented technology must not exceed period of validity of patent, unless contributed as investment. (Art. 19). If technology invested in joint venture, its value should not exceed 20% of registered capital of joint venture. (Art. 23).

Regulations on technical imports to Xiamen S.E.Z. promulgated Feb. 24, 1985. These regulations are applicable to imports of technology from abroad or from Hong Kong, Macau or Taiwan where payment is made to foreign entity concerned. (Art. 2). Technology must be practical, advanced, have clear economic benefit and includes technology: (1) With valid patent rights; (2) with patent pending; and (3) proprietory technology. (Art. 3).

Forms of contracting include licensing, consultancy or service contracts, investment of proprietory technology, coproduction, compensation trade, turnkey projects and other forms. (Art. 5).

Domestic organization acquiring technology will enjoy benefits provided by S.E.Z. including possibility of receiving low interest loan or other financial assistance from domestic bank in S.E.Z. if: It is of world advanced level as certified by state scientific organizations; it can markedly improve competitiveness of products in international market; it will markedly improve economic results of existing local enterprise, or S.E.Z. city government recognizes its special need for technology. (Art. 6).

Procedures to go to contract involve submitting letter of intent and feasibility study to S.E.Z. city government; once approved parties may go to contract. Approval of contract should be within 44 days of submission. (Art. 7).

Contracts are to include: Definition of terms, subject and scope of technology, list of technical information, date of delivery, implementation plan, technical service and training provisions, use of trademark, warranty and acceptance of technology procedures, rights and obligations of parties to improve technology, secrecy clause, means and amount of payment, responsibility for breach of contract. (Art. 8).

Provisions of Contracts for Purchase and Sale of Industrial and Mineral Products were promulgated by State Council pursuant to Economic Contract Law on Jan. 23, 1984, effective as of promulgation. These Provisions cover both industrial and mineral products used in production and for human consumption. (Art. 1). These Provisions cover contracts for sale of industrial and mineral products between all enterprises having status of legal persons, rural communes and brigades, national organizations, commercial and noncommercial units, and social organizations, etc. (Art. 2). Individual households and rural commune members, specialist households and important households must, when signing contracts with legal persons for purchase or sale of mineral products do so with reference to these regulations. (Art. 2). Principles of contracting require parties contracting for essential supplies to emphasize Economic Plan first and free market as supplementary. (Art. 3). Except where urgent necessity to wind up activities of one party, contracts must be in writing and signed or sealed by person with legal authority to represent party, and sealed with official seal, or seal used for contracts by parties. (Art. 4).

Essential elements of said contracts include: Name, type, specifications, article numbers, technical standards and specifications, quantities, packaging, shipping specifications, date of shipment, inspection methods, price, bank, responsibility for breach and other agreed-upon matters. (Art. 6). Each of these items spelled out in some detail in statute.

Regulations of property insurance contracts promulgated on Sept. 1, 1983 pursuant to Economic Contracts Law. This statute is particularly relevant to various types of insurance concerning property and other interests. Liability of insurance company is for actual loss at time of occurrence as limited by coverage of policy. (Art. 16). Property insurance contracts involving foreign parties are to apply these regulations by reference.

Regulations of construction, installation engineering contracts promulgated Aug. 5, 1983 by State Council pursuant to Economic Contract Law. These contracts which must be in writing (Art. 3), are to include documents for design and agreed design alteration, data, charts, negotiating records all of which are components of this contract (Art. 3). Said contracts shall include limits of contents of project, commencement and termination dates, quality guarantees, costs, terms of payment, methods of inspection and approval, dates for providing design, budget and technical data, provision for material and equipment, delivery schedule, and responsibilities for breach. (Art. 6).

Regulations of survey and design engineering building contracts promulgated by State Council Aug. 5, 1983 pursuant to Economic Contract Law require affixing of seals of parties to be valid. (Art. 6). Deposit is required, either 30% of survey fee or 20% of design fee. (Art. 7).

Foreign Economic Contract Law promulgated by Standing Committee of People's Congress on Mar. 21, 1985 effective as of July 1, 1985 is now paramount piece of legislation regarding foreign contracts. This statute is applicable to economic contracts between Chinese enterprises or other economic organizations and foreign enterprises, institutions or individuals. (Art. 2).

Law permits parties choice of law in dispute settlement (Art. 5) or if they make no choice law of country most closely related to contract shall apply (Art. 5), except for those joint, cooperative or prospecting contracts operating within boundaries of China to which Chinese law is applicable (Art. 5). International customary rules may be applied where Chinese law lacks provisions.

Compensation for breach of contract should be actual compensation foreseeable at time contract was made (Art. 19), though parties can limit their liability for breach (Art. 20). One must mitigate damages (Art. 22), when confronted with breach of contract.

Dispute settlement by arbitral tribunal agreed to by parties is acceptable. (Art. 38). Statute of limitations for commencing action is four years from knowledge of or when one should know of breach of contract for contracts concerning purchase and sale of commodities. (Art. 38). Other limitations for bringing action to be provided in separate legislation.

Joint venture, cooperative venture, joint exploration contracts undertaken within China with approval of relevant Chinese government authorities can be governed by provisions of approved contract even if there is subsequent intervening legislation. (Art. 40).

On 19 Oct., 1987 Supreme Court issued Notice Regarding Answers to Several Problems in Application of Foreign Economic Contract Law.

Notice pointed to broad scope of use of Foreign Economic Contract Law (Art. 1[a][b]), but stated that in China, for contracts between Chinese entities and joint ventures, applicable statute is Economic Contract Law (Art. 1[c]). Joint ventures, cooperative ventures, joint exploration agreements in China, must apply Chinese law and their domestic contracts cannot select foreign law for dispute settlement. (Art. 2[c]). See further Art. (2)(f)(i)ff for various conflicts of laws application.

Regulations on Administration of Contracts for Acquisition of Technology, promulgated by State Council May 24, 1985. These regulations apply to acquisition of technology from abroad (Art. 2), including contracts for licensing of or transfer of patents or other industrial property rights (Art. 2[1]); supply of technical knowhow in form of management, quality control, or through supply of drawings, technical materials, technical specifications, etc. as to provide product design, formulae or process specifications (Art. 2[2]) or supply of technical services (Art. 2[3]).

Acquired technology must be advanced, applicable (Art. 3) and should conform to at least one of following: (1) Development and production of new products; (2) improve quality and performance of products, reduce cost and consumption of energy or materials; (3) maximize use of Chinese resources; (4) increase exports of product and foreign currency earnings; (5) benefit environmental protection; (6) improve production safety; (7) improve management operations; or (8) assist in raising scientific technology standards. (Art. 3).

These contracts must be approved by Ministry of Foreign Economic Relations and Trade or its designated agency, which contracts must be acted on by said agencies in 60 days or they shall be regarded as approved. (Art. 4).

These contracts must specify content, scope and description of technology and list of patents and trademarks, technical goals to be reached within specified time period and means of achieving said goals, and means of payment. (Art. 5).

Supplier should guarantee that it owns technology, that it is complete, without faults, effective and able to meet objective specified in contract. (Art. 6). Purchaser shall within scope and time period agreed to by parties maintain secrecy of confidential portion of technology. (Art. 7).

See Topical Index in front part of this volume.

CONTRACTS . . . *continued*

These contracts shall not be longer than ten years without special approval of approving authority. (Art. 8). In addition, following restrictions require special permission of approving recipient: Restrictions on freedom of choice to purchase raw material, intermediate products or equipment from different sources; restrictions on purchaser developing or improving technology; restrictions on requisition of similar or competing technology; nonreciprocal exchange of improvements of technology; restrictions on volume, variety or sales price of products produced; unreasonable restrictions on sales channels or export markets; restrictions on use of technology after expiration of contract or requiring recipient to take or pay for patents that will not be used or have expired. (Art. 9).

Model Contract, Oil Exploration.—Chinese have prepared model contract for offshore oil and gas exploration. More than 18 foreign corporations have signed varied versions of this contract which is based on Law on Exploration of Offshore Petroleum Resources in Cooperation with Foreign Enterprises (see topic Joint Stock Companies). Model contract contains 30 articles plus annexes. Chinese oil company is contracting partner, which enters into agreement with foreign parties based on award systems made on discretionary basis. Fifty percent of total production is allocated to cover costs of exploration and development; price of oil is determined by negotiations or if parties fail to agree weighted average of crude oil produced offshore China and sold to third parties in specific calendar quarter shall determine price. Foreign partner's proposal will prevail if there is disagreement about exploration activities. Arbitration is only dispute settlement means provided for in model contract. Model contract was revised in 1991 eliminating or spreading out initial payment requirement and permitting geological studies by foreign firms prior to entering into commitment to drill.

Thus China has promulgated several sets of regulations concerning contracts, and Chinese legal experts have written about contracts. Many of these regula-tions emphasize domestic contracts although they embrace concepts applicable to private international agreements. Trade Agreement of July 7, 1979 between China and U.S. calls for commercial transactions to be concluded on basis of customary international trade practice and commercial considerations. Contracts approved by proper legal authorities at times contain provisions contrary to statutes. For example, tax relief may be granted by contract despite statutory provisions for standards of payment. See also topic Joint Stock Companies.

COPYRIGHT:

See topic Civil Code.

Trade Agreement of July 7, 1979 between China and U.S. requires parties to insure mutual copyright protection for citizens of other party. China is in process of implementing these treaty provisions and General Rules of Civil Law provide such protection.

In July 1985, State Council established State Copyright Administration to supervise Chinese copyright activity.

Chinese copyright law was enacted in Sept., 1990 effective as of 1 June, 1991.

Irrespective of whether their works are published or not, Chinese citizens, legal persons, units with legal personality have copyright protection pursuant to this law. (Art. 2).

Foreigners have copyright protection according to this law if their works were published in China first. (Art. 2). Foreigner's books that are published out of China enjoy copyright protection pursuant to agreements executed between their country and China or international conventions. (Art. 2).

Works protected by this statute include literature, art, natural science, social science and technical engineering work including written works, oral works, music, drama, opera, fine art, dance, arts and crafts, photographs of film, television, video, engineer designs, production designs, papers, illustrations, maps, sketch maps, computer software, other works protected by law and administrative principles. (Art. 3).

According to law, works prohibited publication are not protected by this law. (Art. 4).

Protective measures for copyright of folk literature and art will be separately provided by State Council. (Art. 6).

Scientific technical works that should be protected by patent law, technical contract law, etc. are protected by applicable provisions of said statutes. (Art. 7).

Copyright administrative management department of State Council is in charge of national copyright administrative management. Copyright administrative management bureau of province, autonomous region and municipality are in charge of copyright administrative management of own administrative region. (Art. 8).

Those with copyright protection enjoy right to publish work or determine whether or not to license protected work to others. (Art. 10).

Right to copyright extends to life of individual plus 50 years. (Art. 21).

Registration of work is not required, and legal protection is afforded by statute, which provides for redress in courts or if provided for by contract in arbitration tribunals, and there can be resort to administrative sanctions.

Regulations for the Protection of Computer Software were promulgated by State Council on June 4, 1992 and became effective on Oct. 1, 1992. Computer software stated in these regulations shall refer to computer programs and their related documents. (Art. 2).

Chinese citizens and units shall be entitled to copyright of software that they develop in accordance with these regulations, without regard to whether or where such software rights have been issued.

Foreigners are entitled to copyright protection in accordance with these regulations if their software is first registered in China.

Software registered outside China by foreigners entitled to copyright protection in accordance with agreements concluded between their respective countries and China or international treaties that their respective countries have entered into with China shall be protected by these regulations. (Art. 6). See subhead Conventions, catchline Foreign Works, infra.

Software owner is entitled to right to issue, disclose developer's identity, usage, license and receive remuneration, and transfer of software. (Art. 9).

Software copyright protection period is 25 years, terminating on 31 Dec. of 25th year after first registration of software. Prior to expiration of protection period, owner may apply for extension of another 25 years. However, maximum protection period shall not be longer than 50 years.

As for inventor's right of disclosing his identity, there is no limitation for such protection period. (Art. 15).

Within software copyright protection period, software copyright owner or assignee has right to permit other people to exercise right of usage specified in Item (3) under Art. 9 of these regulations. Copyright owner or assignee may charge fee in accordance with their agreed terms when permitting other people to exercise right of usage.

Right to license software copyright shall be exercised by concluding and executing written contract in accordance with relevant provisions of China. Licensee shall exercise such right in accordance with forms, conditions, scope and time as specified by such contract.

Valid period of contract on licensing shall not be longer than ten years, but it can be renewed upon its expiration.

If licensed software copyright has not been specified as exclusive in contract, such right shall be regarded as non-exclusive.

Above licensing activities do not change software copyright ownership. (Art. 18).

Limited number of software reproductions can be used for noncommercial purposes such as classroom teaching, scientific research and performance of official duties required by State organizations without consent of software copyright owner or his assignee and no remuneration shall be paid to them. Nevertheless, in using such copies, name of software and its inventor shall be indicated, and other rights belonging to copyright owner or his assignee in accordance with these regulations shall not be infringed. Such copies shall be properly kept, recalled or destroyed after being used and shall not be used for any purposes other than those stated above, nor shall they be provided to any other users. (Art. 22).

Application for registration of software after promulgation of these regulations may be submitted to Software Registration Administration. Once application is approved, registration certificate shall be issued and announcement of such approval shall be made to public. (Art. 23).

When Chinese nationality license software copyright owner transfers copyright of his software that he has invented in China to foreign user, he shall apply for approval of appropriate competent department under State council and report such transfer to software registration administration for recording. (Art. 28).

Disputes concerning software copyright infringement may be settled through mediation. In case mediation fails, or one of parties repudiates agreement reached through mediation, suit may be filed with People's Court. If party objects to settling dispute through mediation, it may file suit directly with People's Court. (Art. 34).

Conventions.—China joined Berne Convention for the Protection of Literary and Artistic Works and Universal Copyright Convention on July 1, 1992, pursuant to decision of Standing Committee of National People's Congress, effective Oct. 1, 1992. China also acceded to Geneva Convention for Protection of Producers of Phonograms Against Unauthorized Duplication of their phonogram. Works of foreigners from countries acceded to above-mentioned conventions to enjoy corresponding protection under Chinese Copyright Law in accordance with conventions. American works shall also enjoy copyright protection under Chinese Copyright Law in accordance with Memorandum Concerning Intellectual Property Protection concluded by and between governments of U.S.A. and China Jan. 1992.

Foreign Works.—On Sept. 25, 1992, Provision on the Implementation of International Copyright Treaties was promulgated by Decree No. 125 of State Council of People's Republic of China. This provision, which became effective on Sept. 30, 1992, covers protection of foreign works.

"International copyright treaties" mentioned in this provision refer to Berne Convention for the Protection of Literary and Artistic Works and bilateral agreements on copyrights which China has concluded with certain foreign countries. (Art. 3).

Regarding protection of foreign works, Copyright Law of PRC, Regulations for the Protection of Computer Software and this Provision apply. (Art. 2). Foreign works include: (1) works of which author or one of coauthors or other owner of copyright or one of co-owners of copyright is national or permanent resident of country that is party to international copyright treaties; (2) works of which author is not national or permanent resident of country that is party to international copyright treaties but which have been first published or published simultaneously in country that is party to international copyright treaties; (3) works created by others by commission from Chinese-foreign entity joint venture, Chinese-foreign contractual joint venture or foreign-capital enterprise which, by virtue of contract, is owner or one of co-owners of copyright of work. (Art. 4).

Arts. 20 and 21 of Copyright Law refer to term of protection for unpublished foreign works. These articles apply to term of protection for unpublished foreign works. (Art. 5).

Regarding foreign works of applied art, term of protection is 25 years commencing from creation of work. This does not apply to fine art works, including designs of cartoon characters, used on industrial goods. (Art. 6). Foreign computer programs are protected as literary works and are not subject to registration. These enjoy 50 year term of protection that commences from end of year of their first publication. (Art. 7). Foreign works which, at date on which international copyright treaties entered into force in China, had not fallen into public domain in their countries of origin are protected until expiration of protection term as is prescribed in Copyright Law and this provision. This does not apply to uses of foreign works that had taken place before international copyright treaties entered into force in China. (Art. 17).

Foreign works created by compiling non-protected materials are protected, provided that originality is shown in selection and arrangement of such materials, in accordance with provisions of Art. 14 of Copyright Law. Such protection does not preclude others from using same materials to create compilation work. (Art. 8). Foreign video recordings are protected as cinematographic works to extent that international copyright treaties treat them as such works. (Art. 9). Prior authorization of copyright owner is required if published foreign work, created in Chinese, is to be translated into and published in language of minority group. (Art. 10). Such authorization is also required for newspapers or periodicals to reprint foreign works. This does not include reprinting of articles on current political, economic and social topics. (Art. 13).

COPYRIGHT . . . *continued*

Copyright owners of foreign works have right to authorize others to publicly perform their works in any manner and by any means or to communicate publicly performance of their works. (Art. 11). Owner of foreign cinematographic works or works of television or video-recordings has right to authorize others to publicly perform those works. (Art. 12).

Copyright owners of foreign works may authorize or prohibit rental of copies of their works after authorizing others to distribute such copies. They also have right to prohibit importation of following types of copies of their work: (1) infringing copies; (2) copies coming from country where their works are not protected. (Arts. 14 and 15). Chinese citizen or legal person who owned and used particular copy of foreign work for particular purpose before international copyright treaties came into effect in China may continue to make use of that copy of work without liability. However, such copy may not be reproduced nor used in any manner that may unreasonably prejudice that legitimate rights and interests of copyright owner. (Art. 17).

CORPORATIONS:

See topics Aliens; Foreign Trade; Joint Stock Companies; Civil Code; Trade Zones.

Office of General Administration for Industry and Commerce has broad responsibilities over private and public enterprises. On Dec. 30, 1950 General Administrative Council promulgated Provisional Regulations for Private Enterprise. These regulations provided for private enterprises' forms of organization, labor regulations, registration of said enterprises, and scope of authority and business activity of said entities. On Mar. 30, 1951 Government Administrative Council promulgated Rules for Implementing Provisional Regulations of Foreign Enterprise, which provided for approval and registration of companies, including limited liability companies, joint venture companies, limited liability stock companies (corporations), joint venture stock companies, etc. On July 15, 1950 General Administrative Council issued Notice Concerning Problems of Private Corporate Responsibility. On Dec. 22, 1950 Government Administrative Council promulgated Rules for Reevaluating Revised Capital of Private Enterprises. On Dec. 1, 1962 State Council promulgated trial Rules for Registration of Commercial and Industrial Enterprises. These rules were in force until July 7, 1982, when Standing Committee of State Council approved and promulgated Regulations for the Handling of Registration of Industrial and Commercial Enterprises, which superseded original regulations. (Art. 22).

Regulations on Registration of Legal Representative of enterprise were adopted on May 13, 1988. Administration of Commerce and Industry is responsible for handling said registration (Art. 4) and its Registration Authority must decide, within 30 days of receiving application, whether or not to approve registration (Art. 14).

Steps for implementation of aforementioned Regulations were adopted on Nov. 3, 1988. Accordingly, all state enterprises, collectively owned enterprises, private enterprises, jointly operated enterprises, and enterprises having foreign investment in China (including Chinese-foreign joint ventures, Chinese-foreign cooperations and enterprises operated exclusively with foreign capital) must register with Administration of Commerce and Industry. (Art. 2). Foreign representative offices must also register. (Art. 5).

Enterprise having foreign investment must also register legal representative with Administration of Commerce and Industry. (Art. 7). Said registration requires enterprise having foreign investment to demonstrate properly authorized and approved name, location, contract and Articles of Association; their equipment, working capital, scope of business and employees must be registered and approved, and it must use authorized system of finance and accounting, etc. (Art. 16). Similarly, aforementioned approvals are required for said enterprise to obtain business registration. (Art. 17).

Specifically, enterprises having foreign investment must use system of unified accounting. (Art. 17). They must register name, location, identity of individual in charge, etc. (Art. 18). Name of enterprises must include name of firm, line of business (or feature of business) and form of organization. (Art. 24). Said name must be approved before enterprise may sign contracts or obtain Articles of Association. (Art. 25).

Regulations for Registration of Enterprises Having Foreign Investment requires submission of following documents: Application duly signed by chairman and vice-chairman of Board of Directors; contract; Articles of Association approved by proper authority; project proposal; preliminary feasibility study with certified documents; license to conduct commercial business; certified approval of all assets; list of board members; certified approval of appointing members of board, general manager and vice-general manager; names of all Chinese employees; and any other relevant documents and certifications. (Art. 35).

Registration of commercial business requires submission of following: Application to conduct commercial business, evidence of approval of operation capital, credentials of individual in charge, certified approval to use operation site and any other relevant documents and certified statements. (Art. 36).

Registration of branch or office requires submission of following documents: Application signed by chairman of board; evidence of approval and notice from original registration authority; decision by Board of Directors to establish branch or office; copy of business license; evidence of certification of individual in charge; and any other relevant documents and certified statements. (Art. 37).

If application meets aforementioned regulations, then certified business license and registration, etc., will be issued. These can be used to open bank accounts, obtain official seal, and conduct other relevant business activities. (Arts. 38, 39). To change registration, application signed by legal representative of enterprise, and all other relevant documents, must be submitted. (Art. 40). Upon receipt of said documents from applicant, registration authority must, within 30 days, approve or deny request. (Art. 49).

Foreign investment enterprise must apply to cancel its registration within three months from expiry date of business term, which is when all business ceases, business certification becomes automatically invalid and original examination authority approves decision to terminate contract. (Art. 51).

Regulation of Enterprise Registration Fee Standards and Range, promulgated by State Administration for Industry and Commerce, Ministry of Finance and State Price Authority on Dec. 22, 1988. Registration fee for commercial business is 0.1% of all registered capital. If this amount is greater than RMB 10 million, 0.05% of sum exceeding RMB 10 million must be paid. If this amount exceeds RMB 100 million, registration fee is not levied on sum exceeding RMB 100 million. Registration fee shall not be less than RMB 50. State Administration of Industry and Commerce will stipulate fee for change of registration and annual examination. (Art. 1[1]).

Sanctions.—Registration authority may administer one or more of following sanctions, depending on circumstances, for violation of aforementioned regulations: Admonishment, fine, notification to enterprise's bank to cease payments, temporary closing of business for modifications, permanent closing of business, revoking business license, confiscating all illegal income, etc. (Art. 66). Violations include: Commencing business without proper authorization; concealing factual circumstances or blatant deception upon registration; illegally changing enterprise's name, address, nature of business, legal representative, director or amount of business capital; operating beyond permitted scope of business; forging, altering, leasing, lending, transferring, selling, or illegally copying business license; unlawfully protecting against examination by registration authority, etc. (Art. 66). In cases of criminal law violations, violator must be sent to judicial branch for punishment. (Art. 68).

Hong Kong, Macau and Taiwan enterprises or those of overseas Chinese and compatriots from Hong Kong, Macau and Taiwan who establish either joint ventures or enterprises operated exclusively with their own capital must also register pursuant to aforementioned regulations. (Art. 72).

Regulations Governing the Administration of the Registration of Enterprise Name was promulgated by State Administration for Industry and Commerce on July 22, 1991 and became effective on Sept. 1, 1991.

All enterprise names are required by Name Regulations to be written in Chinese characters and all foreign names shall be consistent with their Chinese names and duly registered with registration authorities. Registration authorities are State Administration for Industry and Commerce and its local administration bureaus at all levels. (Art. 4).

Name Regulation provides that no enterprise name can include word "China" or "International" unless enterprise involved has nationwide operations or is large import-export enterprise approved by State Council or its authorized agencies. (Art. 13). Moreover, enterprise name may not contain names of foreign countries, international organizations, political parties or any other contents or words that may deceive or mislead public, Chinese phonetic alphabet (except for those used in foreign language name) or figures, or other elements prohibited by laws or administrative regulations.

In case enterprise established is branch, name of enterprise and its branch shall meet following requirements: (1) when "head office" is contained in name of enterprise, it must have established at least three branches; (2) when branch cannot assume civil liability independently, its name shall be preceded by name of enterprise which it is under and followed by words such as "branch company", "branch factory", or "branch shop"; (3) when branch can assume civil liability independently, it shall use independent name; (4) when branch that can assume civil liability independently established sub-branch, enterprise name of that sub-branch established shall not contain name of head office. (Art. 14).

Enterprise name shall be composed of business name (or trade name), line of trade or specialties in business and form of organization. Enterprise name shall be preceded by name of administrative division of province, municipality or county where enterprise is located. Upon approval by State Administration for Industry and Commerce, name of following enterprises do not have to be preceded by name of administrative division where they are located: (1) enterprises listed in Art. 13 of these regulations; (2) enterprises that have long history and whose business names are well-known; (3) foreign investment enterprise. (Art. 7).

Foreign investment enterprise shall apply in advance for registration of its name only after approval of its project proposal and feasibility study report, but prior to approval of its contract and article of association. Foreign investment enterprise can apply to registration authorities for registration of only its enterprise name even before commencement of business. Registration authorities must decide within ten days of receiving application whether or not to approve registration. If approved, registration authorities will issue Enterprise Name Registration certificate and name will be reserved for one year. (Arts. 17, 18, 19).

Name Regulations also provide for various penalties and sanctions to deal with violation of provision of Name Regulations. These penalties and sanctions include closure of business of unregistered enterprise, confiscation of illegal income and/or monetary fines. (Art. 26). Furthermore, where enterprise uses another enterprise's registered enterprise name without approval or infringes upon another enterprise's exclusive right to use its enterprise name, registration authorities have power to order infringer to cease and desist and make compensation to infringed party. Registration authorities also have power to confiscate infringer's illegal income and impose fine. Infringed party is also given right to bring law suit in People's Court against infringer. (Art. 27).

Regulations Governing Company Registration was promulgated by State Council on June 24, 1994, and effective as of July 1, 1994. This set of regulations serves to acknowledge company's enterprise legal person qualification and regulate company registration. (Art. 1).

Incorporation, transformation and termination of limited liability company and joint stock limited company must be registered according to regulations. (Art. 2). Companies must be qualified as enterprise legal persons after their applications for registration have been examined and approved by authorities in charge of company registration, and have received business licenses for enterprises. (Art. 3).

Company registration is handled by Administration for Industry and Commerce. (Art. 4). State Administration for Industry and Commerce is responsible for registration of following companies: (1) joint stock limited companies approved for incorporation by departments authorized by State Council; (2) companies authorized by State Council to invest; (3) organizations authorized by State Council to invest, or limited liability companies solely or jointly invested by departments; (4) limited liability companies invested by foreign business people; and (5) other companies required by law or State Council's regulations. (Art. 6). Administration for Industry and Commerce of provinces, autonomous regions and municipalities under central government

See Topical Index in front part of this volume.

CORPORATIONS . . . *continued*
are responsible for registration of following companies: (1) joint stock limited companies approved for incorporation by governments of provinces, autonomous regions and municipalities under central government; (2) companies authorized by governments of provinces, autonomous regions and municipalities under central government to invest; (3) organizations authorized by State Council to invest, or limited liability companies jointly invested and established by department and investor; (4) organizations authorized by governments of provinces, autonomous regions and municipalities under central government to invest, or limited liability companies solely or jointly invested by departments; and (5) companies authorized by State Administration Industry and Commerce to be registered thereof. (Art. 7). Registration of other companies is responsibility of Administration for Industry and Commerce of cities or counties. (Art. 8).

Items of Registration.—Items to be registered for company are: name, residence, legal representative, type of enterprise, scope of business, duration of operation, names of shareholders of limited liability company or sponsors of joint stock limited company. (Art. 9). Company must use only one name and one residence, which must be in area under registration authority's jurisdiction. (Art. 12).

Incorporation of Registration.—To incorporate company, applicant must first apply for examination and approval of name. (Art. 14). To incorporate limited liability company, applicant for name approval and registration must be representative appointed by all shareholders or agent (attorney) jointly authorized by shareholders. (Art. 15). To obtain approval of name, following documents should be submitted: (1) application for advanced approval of company name signed by all shareholders of limited liability company and all originators of joint stock limited company; (2) certificate of legal person qualification of shareholders or originators, or certificate of identify of natural person; and (3) other documents required by company registration department. (Art. 15). To incorporate state-owned company, applicant for registration must be organization authorized by State to invest or department authorized by State. (Art. 17).

To apply for incorporation of limited liability company or joint stock limited company, following documents must be submitted: (1) application for incorporation registration signed by chairperson of board; (2) certificate of representation or agency (only for limited liability company); (3) relevant documents approved by government or department authorized by State Council and minutes of inaugural meeting (only for joint stock limited company); (4) articles of association; (5) certificate of verification of capital; (6) certificate of legal person qualification of shareholders or originators, or certificate of identity of natural person; (7) report of financial audit in preparation for incorporation (only for joint stock limited company); (8) documents recording names and residence of directors, supervisors and managers, and certificates indicating that they are appointed, voted and employed; (9) document of appointment and certificate of identity of legal representative; (10) notice of advanced approval of company name; and (11) certificate of company residence. (Arts. 17, 18). When company has been examined and approved by registration authority and Business License for Enterprise as Legal Person has been received, company is considered established. (Art. 22).

Change in Registration.—Company must apply for change in registration from former registration authority and submit following papers: (1) application for change in registration signed by legal representative of company; (2) decision of change made according to company law; and (3) other documents required by registration authorities. (Arts. 23, 24). When company needs to change its name, legal representative, scope of business, and shareholders, it must apply for change in registration within 30 days after decision of change was made.

Cancellation of Registration.—In one of following situations, liquidation committee must apply for cancellation of registration within 30 days after completion of liquidation: (1) company declared bankrupt according to law; (2) term of operation as stipulated by articles of association of company expires or other reasons for dissolution occur; (3) shareholders' meeting resolved to dissolve company; (4) dissolution due to merger or division of company; and (5) company instructed to close. (Art. 36). Following papers must be submitted when company applies for cancellation of registration: (1) application for cancellation of registration signed by person in charge of liquidation committee; (2) ruling of bankruptcy made by court, decision made by company, or document of closing ordered by administrative decree; (3) liquidation report confirmed by shareholders' meeting or relevant department; (4) Business License for Enterprise as Legal Person; and (5) other documents required by laws and administrative regulations. (Art. 37).

Registration of Branch of Company.—Branch of company must not be qualified as legal person. (Art. 39). While company establishes branch, it must apply for registration from registration authority. Branch will receive business license after application is approved. (Art. 40). Items to be registered for branch of company are: name, site for business operation, person in charge, and scope of business. (Art. 41).

Procedure of Registration.—Company authority must issue notification of acceptance of company registration after receiving all papers, and make decision to approve registration or not within 30 days after issuance of notification of acceptance. Company registration authority must issue, exchange, or get back Business License for Enterprise as Legal Person or Business License within 15 days after examination and approval for registration. (Art. 45). Company must pay registration fee of one thousandth of total registration capital for Business License for Enterprise as Legal Person; if total registration capital is greater than RMB 10 million, 0.05% of sum exceeding RMB 10 million must be paid; if amount exceeds RMB 100 million, registration fee is not levied on sum exceeding RMB 100 million; pay RMB300 for Business License; and pay RMB100 for change in registration. (Art. 46).

Regulation Governing the Registration of Resident Office of a Foreign Enterprise was approved by State Council on Mar. 5, 1983, and became effective Mar. 15, 1983. State Administration for Industry and Commerce of China is organization for registration of resident offices for foreign enterprises. It shall empower administrative departments for industry and commerce in provinces, autonomous regions and municipalities directly under Central Government to handle registration procedures. (Art. 4).

Main items to be registered for resident office of foreign enterprise are: name of office, address of residence, number of representatives and their names, business scope and period of residence. (Art. 5). Foreign enterprises and other economic organizations shall go through prescribed registration procedure at administrative Department of Industry and Commerce in provinces, autonomous regions and municipalities directly under Central Government where said offices are to be located within 30 days from date of their applications for setting up resident offices within China are approved by authorities. (Art. 6).

Foreign enterprise or economic organization shall submit following documents applying for registration of resident office: (1) approval document issued by appropriate authorities; (2) documents and data as listed in Art. 3 of Interim Provisions. (Art. 7).

If documents submitted by foreign enterprise or economic organization for registration are established as conforming to these measures through examination, registration office shall grant permission to registration and issue certificate of registration and certificates for representatives after registration fee is paid. Resident office of foreign enterprise shall, on strength of approval document, certificate of registration and certificates for representatives, register with public security organization, banks and customs and tax authorities and other departments for residence permits and other related matters. (Art. 8).

Resident office of foreign enterprise is deemed as formally established from date of its registration and legitimate activities of said office and its representatives shall thereafter be protected by laws of China. Resident office that has not been approved and registered shall not proceed with its business activities. (Art. 9).

Registration certificate for resident office of foreign enterprise is valid for period of one year. Said office must, upon end of period, renew aforesaid document if it wishes to continue its residence. To renew its registration, resident office of foreign enterprise must, within 30 days before date of expiration submit to registration authorities annual report of its business operations and application for renewal. In case renewal of resident office is approved, document of approval for renewal issued by same authorities must also be submitted at time of renewing registration of office, original certificate shall be turned in and new certificate of registration shall be issued. (Art. 11).

If resident office of foreign enterprise desires to terminate its business operations upon or before expiration of term of residence, or enterprise represented by office declares bankruptcy, it shall go through deregistration procedure at registration office. In going through deregistration procedure, documents issued by tax authorities, banks and customs to certify clearing up of taxes, liabilities and other related matters shall be produced before approval is granted for deregistration and cancellation of certificate of registration. Should said office leave any matter unsettled, foreign enterprise or economic organization office represents shall be held responsible for settlement of that matter. (Art. 13).

Corporate Trial Code and Regulations.—These trial codes and regulations governing shareholding organization including Company Law, corporate entities drafted by five central departments with State Economic Restructuring Commission as leader, was incorporated in 15 different documents and fall into three categories. First, overall policy document entitled "Trial Implementation of Shareholding Enterprises" sets forth overall purpose, principles and requirements of shareholding system. Second, two "Prescriptive Opinions", Prescriptive Opinions of Share Limited Company (hereinafter SLC) and Prescriptive Opinions of Limited Liability Company (hereinafter LLC), which are legislative code-like documents, set forth in detail organization of SLC and LLC. Last, set of temporary regulations governing 12 aspects of operation of corporations, including macro-management, accounting system, labor and wage administration, taxation, auditing, financial management, materials distribution and like.

In Guangdong province, Corporation Regulations of Guangdong Province (hereinafter GD Regulation) was adopted by Standing Committee of Provincial People's Congress May 14, 1993, effective Aug. 1, 1993. GD Regulations superseded Corporation Regulations involving foreign interests in Special Economic Zones of Guangdong province adopted Oct. 20, 1986. GD Regulation sets forth major areas of SLC, LLC and branches of foreign corporations.

SLC Regulations of Shenzhen Special Economic Zone (hereinafter SLC of SEZ) and LLC Regulations of Shenzhen Special Economic Zone (hereinafter LLC of SEZ) adopted by Shenzhen People's Congress Apr. 26, 1993, effective Oct. 1, 1993 and July 1, 1993, respectively. SLC and LLC of SEZ contain substantially same provisions concerning SLC and LLC as central legislation.

Limited Liability.—Both LLC and SLC are legal persons, shareholders of which assume limited liability only for amount of capital invested. (SLC, Art. 1; LLC Art. 1; GD Regulation, Art. 3; SLC of SEZ, Art. 2; LLC of SEZ, Art. 2). Both LLC and SLC shall not become unlimited liability shareholder of other economic entities or partners of partnership. (SLC, Art. 4; LLC, Art. 6; GD Regulations, Art. 11; SLC of SEZ, Art. 9; LLC of SEZ, Art. 9).

Method of Capitalization.—Shareholders of LLC shall subscribe corporate capital completely only once. (LLC, Art. 11; DG Regulations, Art. 19). In Shenzhen SEZ, partial contribution of capital is allowed, but initial investment shall be 50% of total capital or more. (LLC of SEZ, Art. 19). SLC capitalizes through initiators' subscription, in which initiators shall subscribe to all shares of prospect corporation, or stock issuance to general public, in which initiators shall subscribe to at least 30% of total shares. (SLC, Arts. 7, 8; GD Regulation, Art. 67; SLC of SEZ, Art. 15).

Shareholders of LLC and SLC may make investment in cash, in kind, land-use rights, industrial property or know-how. In cases where investment made in kind, land-use right, industrial property or know-how, they shall be evaluated by asset evaluation agency and value of industrial property and know-how shall not exceed 20% of corporate registered capital. (SLC, Art. 22; LLC, Art. 12; GD Regulation, Art. 18 and 69; LLC of SEZ, Art. 2; SLC of Shenzhen, Art. 20).

Number of Shareholders.—SLC: minimum of three initiators is required with no maximum requirement. (SLC, Art. 9). However, in GD and Shenzhen SEZ, minimum of five initiators required, among which at least one initiator shall have domicile in GD or Shenzhen SEZ, respectively. (GD Regulation, Art. 66; SLC of SEZ, Art. 16). Initiators shall be legal persons created in China, excluding private enterprises and wholly foreign-owned enterprises. (SLC, Art. 10; SLC of SEZ, Art. 16). Natural persons can become stockholders. (SLC, Art. 7; SLC of SEZ, Art. 15).

LLC.—Minimum of two shareholders required with maximum of 30 shareholders allowed, or up to 50 shareholders with special approval. (LLC, Art. 9). However, in GD and Shenzhen SEZ, maximum of 50 shareholders is allowed without special government approval. (GD Regulation, Art. 15; LLC of SEZ, Art. 15).

See Topical Index in front part of this volume.

CORPORATIONS . . . *continued*

Minimum Capitalization.—For SLC, minimum registered capital required is RMB 10,000,000 for general SLC, and RMB 30,000,000 for SLC with foreign investment. (SLC, Art. 12). In GD, minimum registered capital required is RMB 10,000,000 for SLC generally, those issuing stocks to general public required to have minimum capitalization of RMB 30,000,000. (GD Regulation, Art. 68). In Shenzhen SEZ, those created through subscription of initiators required to have minimum capitalization of RMB 10,000,000, those created through issuing stocks to general public are required to have minimum capitalization of RMB 50,000,000. (SLC of SEZ, Art. 19).

For LLC, minimum capitalization varies with trade sector namely, manufacturing and distribution is RMB 500,000, commercial retailing is RMB 30,000, and service oriented businesses are RMB 100,000. (LLC, Art. 10). In GD, minimum capitalization is RMB 300,000 in general, and specific amounts for different trade sector shall be formulated by provincial government. (GD Regulations, Art. 16). In Shenzhen SEZ, minimum capitalization of RMB 100,000 required in general, and specific amount for different trade sectors shall be separately formulated. (LLC of SEZ, Art. 18).

Shareholders Meeting.—For SLC, shareholders meeting is supreme authority of corporation which ratifies all major issues of corporation. (SLC, Art. 43; GD Regulation, Arts. 98, 99; SLC of SEZ, Art. 81). For LLC, corporation may, at its own discretion, decide to have or not have shareholders meeting, where shareholders meeting absent, functions and powers shall be assumed by all shareholders jointly. (LLC, Art. 22; GD Regulation, Art. 29; LLC of SEZ, Art. 42).

Use of Foreign Investors.—LLC not applicable to foreign investment enterprises, which are governed by different set of laws and regulations. (LLC, Art. 78). Foreign investors may invest in SLC via holding B-shares, or enter into equity joint venture with Chinese venturer and transform joint venture into SLC subject to government approval. (SLC, Arts. 10, 13).

Company Law was adopted by National People's Congress on Dec. 29, 1993, effective as of July 1, 1994. Law is applicable to limited liability company (hereinafter "LLC") and company limited by shares (hereinafter "CLS"). (Art. 2). See also topic Securities, subhead Securities Market of P.R.C.

Both LLC and CLS are enterprise legal persons. (Art. 3). LLC bears liability for its debts with all its assets, and its shareholders assume liability within limit of amount of investment made by shareholder. (Art. 3). CLS bears liability for its debt with all its assets, and shareholders assume liability to CLS within limit of amount of shares they hold. (Art. 3). Company is entitled to enjoy civil rights, and rights over all its property formed by shareholders' investment and assume civil liabilities. (Art 4). Ownership of state-owned property in company is held by State. (Art. 4). Company shall operate independently with all its assets and be responsible for its own profits and losses. (Art. 5). Company may invest in other LLC or CLS and bear liability to company in which it has invested, in proportion to its investment shares. (Art. 12). Except for investment companies and holding companies, as specified by State Council, should company invest in other LLC or CLS, aggregate amount of investment may not exceed 50% of its net assets excluding capital gains it obtains from invested company. (Art. 12). Company may set up branches, without status of legal persons and parent company is responsible for their civil liabilities. (Art. 13). Company may set up subsidiaries which are independent enterprise legal persons and responsible for their own civil liabilities. (Art. 13).

Formation.—LLC shall meet following requirements: (1) number of shareholders must be at least two and not more than 50, except that investment entities or departments authorized by State may set up solely state-owned LLC; (2) minimum amount of registered capital must be at least: (a) for LLC mainly engaging in production and operation, RMB 500,000, (b) for LLC mainly engaging in wholesales, RMB 500,000, (c) for LLC mainly engaging in retail sales, RMB 300,000, and (d) for LLC engaging in technology development, consultancy and services, RMB 100,000. Where minimum amount of registered capital of LLC in specific trade must be higher than that specified above, it shall be separately determined by law or administrative decree; (3) shareholders jointly formulate articles of association, (4) LLC has suitable name in which words "limited liability" shall be included and organizational set-up complying with legal requirements; and (5) LLC possesses production, or operation site(s) and necessary conditions for production or operations. (Arts. 9, 19, 20, 23).

CLS shall meet following requirements: (1) there should be at least five promotors half of which must have domiciles in China. For CLS reorganized from state-owned enterprises, number of promoters may be less than five, however, it should capitalize through public offering; (2) minimum amount of registered capital of CLS is RMB 10,000,000. Where minimum amount of registered capital must be higher than that specified above, it must be provided by law or administrative decree; (3) issuance of stocks and relevant preparatory matters conform to provisions of law; (4) articles of association are formulated by promoters and adopted by establishment meeting; (5) CLS has name which shall clearly indicate CLS and organizational set-up meeting requirements of law; and (6) CLS possesses fixed production or operational site(s) and necessary conditions for production or operations. (Arts. 9, 73, 75).

Method of Capitalization.—Shareholders of LLC shall subscribe corporate capital completely only once. (Art. 25). Shareholders may make their investment in cash, in kind, in industrial property rights, in non-patented technology or land use rights. Investments in kind, industrial property rights, non-patented technology and land use rights should be correctly assessed and verified in terms of value without any over valuation or under valuation. (Art. 24). Appraisal of land use rights shall be made according to law or administrative decrees. Amount of industrial property or non-patented technology in value shall not exceed 20% of LLC's registered capital, unless otherwise provided for by State for high and new technology. (Art. 24). Should investment be made in cash, contribution in cash shall be deposited in full into temporary bank account of LLC; should investment be made in kind, industrial property rights, non-patented technology or land-use rights, property rights shall be transferred to LLC according to law. (Art. 25).

CLS may capitalize through promotion and public offering. (Art. 74). Promotors shall subscribe to shares due to them according to law and be responsible for preparations of CLS. (Art. 76). Promotors may make investment in cash, in kind, in industrial property rights, non-patented technology and land-use right. Investment in kind, industrial property rights, non-patented technology and land-use rights should be assessed in value and converted into shares according their assessed value without over valuation or under valuation. (Art. 80). Value assessment of land-use rights shall be conducted according to law or administrative decrees. Industrial property rights or/and non-patented technology in value shall not exceed 20% of CLS's registered capital. (Art. 80). Should CLS capitalize through promotion, promoters should subscribe in writing amount of shares provided for in articles of association in full and make immediate payment. Where investments are made in kind, industrial property rights, non-patented technology and/or land-use rights, property rights shall be transferred to CLS. (Art. 82). If CLS capitalizes through public offering, amount of shares subscribed by promoters may not be less than 35% of CLS's total shares. (Art. 83). Promoters must publish prospectus which should include following items: (1) number of shares subscribed by promoters; (2) par value and issuance price of each share; (3) total number of non-registered shares to be issued; (4) rights and obligations of subscribers; and (5) time limit for public offering and notification that subscribers may revoke their subscription of shares if offering is under-subscribed at close of offer. (Art. 87).

Articles of Association.—Both LLC and CLS must formulate articles of association which bind company, shareholders, directors, supervisors and managers. (Art. 11). For LLC, its articles of association shall clearly specify following: (1) name and address of LLC; (2) scope of business; (3) names of shareholders; (4) registered capital of LLC; (5) rights and obligations of shareholders; (6) forms and amount of investment made by shareholder; (7) conditions for shareholders to transfer their investment; (8) organizations of LLC and method of establishment, their powers and functions and procedures for meetings; (9) legal representative; (10) grounds for dissolution and liquidation method; and (11) other matters deemed necessary by shareholders. (Art. 22). Shareholders shall sign and seal articles of association. (Art. 22).

For CLS, its articles of association must define following items: (1) name and address of CLS; (2) scope of business; (3) method of establishment; (4) total shares, par value of each share and amount of registered capital; (5) names of promoters and shares subscribed by them; (6) rights and obligations of shareholders; (7) composition, powers and functions, term of office and rules of procedures of board of directors; (8) legal representative; (9) composition, powers and functions, term of office and rules of procedures of supervisory board; (10) method of profit distribution; (11) grounds for dissolution and liquidation method; (12) method of issuing public notices or announcements; and (13) other matters deemed necessary by shareholders' meeting. (Art. 79).

Shareholders' Meeting.—For LLC, shareholders' meetings comprised of all shareholders are supreme authority and may exercise at shareholders' meeting following powers and functions: (1) decide upon operation policies and investment plans; (2) elect and replace directors and decide matters regarding remuneration of directors; (3) elect and replace supervisors who represent shareholders and decide on payment to supervisors; (4) examine and approve reports of board of directors; (5) examine and approve reports of supervisory board or individual supervisors; (6) examine and approve annual financial and budget plan and financial accounting plan; (7) examine and approve plans of profit distribution and loss recovery; (8) to adopt resolutions on increase or decrease of registered capital; (9) adopt resolutions on transfer of investment from shareholders to persons other than shareholders; (10) to adopt resolutions on bond issuance; (11) adopt resolutions on matters regarding merger, division, changes in corporate form, dissolution and liquidation and other affairs related; and (12) revise articles of association. (Art. 38). Resolutions on increase or decrease of registered capital, merger, division, dissolution, change of corporate form or revisions in articles of association shall be adopted by two thirds vote or more by shareholders with voting rights. (Arts. 39, 40). Shareholders exercise voting rights in proportion to their investment in LLC. (Art. 41). Shareholders' meetings include regular meetings and irregular meetings. Irregular meetings may be convened by shareholders representing one-fourth or more of voting rights or by one-third or more of directors or supervisors. (Art. 43).

For CLS, shareholders' meetings are supreme authority. (Art. 102). Following powers and functions may be exercised at shareholders' meetings: (1) determine operation policies and investment plans; (2) elect and replace directors and decide upon matters regarding their remunerations; (3) elect and replace supervisors representing shareholders and decide on matters regarding their remunerations; (4) examine and approve reports by board of directors; (5) examine and approve reports by supervisory board or individual supervisors; (6) examine and approve CLS's proposed annual financial budget and final accounts; (7) examine and approve CLS's profit distribution plan and loss recovery plan; (8) adopt resolutions on bonds issuance; (9) adopt resolutions on merger, division, dissolution and liquidation and other related matters; (10) adopt resolutions on increase or decrease of registered capital; and (11) amend articles of association. (Art. 103). Shareholders' meetings include annual meetings and interim meetings. Interim meeting shall be held under any of following situations: (1) number of directors is less than two-thirds of number of directors as required by law or articles of association; (2) uncovered losses reach one-third of total share capital; (3) request of shareholders holding 10% or more of total share capital; (4) board of directors deems necessary; (5) at request of supervisory board. (Art. 104). Every share has vote at shareholders' meetings. Resolutions regarding merger, division or dissolution must be adopted when two-thirds or more voting rights are present at meeting. (Art. 106). Resolution on amendment to articles of association must be adopted when two-thirds or more of voting rights are held by shareholders present at meeting. (Art. 107). Shareholders are entitled to examine articles of association, minutes of shareholders' meetings and financial and accounting statements and put forward proposals or inquiries in respect to operation of CLS. (Art. 110). Should resolutions of shareholders, meeting or board of directors violate law or legal rights and interests of shareholders, shareholders concerned may sue in court of law to have such acts enjoined. (Art. 111).

Board of Directors.—LLC shall have board of directors consisting of three to 13 persons. (Art. 45). Chairman of board of directors is legal representative of LLC. (Art. 45). Board of directors exercises following powers and functions: (1) convene and report work to shareholders' meeting; (2) execute resolutions adopted by shareholders' meeting; (3) decide on business operation and investment plans; (4) formulate annual financial budget and finance accounts; (5) formulate profit distribution and loss recovery plans; (6) formulate plans regarding registered capital increase or decrease; (7) draft plans regarding merger, division, change of corporate form and corporate dissolution; (8) decide on organizational set-up; (9) appoint or dismiss manager or deputy manager and financial officers according to recommendation by manager and decide

CORPORATIONS . . . *continued*

on their remuneration; and (10) formulate basic management systems. (Art. 46). Term of office for directors shall be specified in articles of association and their maximum length shall not exceed three years. (Art. 47). Directors may be reelected to serve another term upon expiration of prior term. (Art. 47). Shareholders' shall not dismiss director from his/her post before expiration of term without justifiable reason. (Art. 47). Chairman convenes and presides over meeting of board of directors. (Art. 48). Should Chairman be unable to perform his/her duty due to special reasons, vice-chairman or director designated by chairman shall convene and preside over meetings. (Art. 48). Meeting of board of directors may be convened upon motion by at least one-third of directors. (Art. 48). Method of discussion and procedures for voting at meeting of board of directors shall be defined in articles of association except otherwise provided for by law. (Art. 49). Board of directors shall keep minutes of meetings which directors present should sign. (Art. 49).

CLS must have board of directors consisting of five to 19 members. (Art. 112). Term of office for directors must be specified in articles of association, maximum length of which shall not exceed three years. (Art. 115). Directors may serve another term of office upon reelection after expiration of former term. (Art. 115). Meeting of board of directors shall be held at least twice a year. (Art. 116). All directors shall be notified of meeting ten days before meeting. (Art. 116). Meeting of board of directors shall be held only when at least half of directors are present, and resolutions of board require approval of at least half of directors. (Art. 117). Board of directors shall maintain minutes of meetings for decisions on matters discussed, and directors present at meeting and person recording minutes shall sign minutes. (Art. 118). Board of directors shall be responsible for shareholders' meeting and exercise following powers and functions: (1) convene shareholders, meeting and report work to meeting; (2) decide on matters regarding business set-up; (3) execute resolutions of shareholders' meeting; (4) formulate annual financial budget and accounts; (5) formulate plans for profit distribution and losses recovery; (6) formulate plans for registered capital increase or decrease and plan for bond issuance; (7) draft plans for merger, division or dissolution; (8) appoint or dismiss manager or deputy manager and financial officers according to recommendation by manager and decide on their remunerations; (9) formulate basic management systems and (10) decide on organizational set-up. (Art. 112). Board of directors must have one chairman and one or two vice-chairmen, who must be elected by majority vote of directors. (Art. 113). Powers and functions of chairman are as follows: (1) preside over shareholders' meeting and convene and preside over meetings of board of directors; (2) examine implementation of resolutions of board of directors; and (3) sign shares and bonds issued by CLS. (Art. 114). Vice-chairman must assist chairman of board of directors. Should chairman be unable to perform his/her duty, he/she may designate vice-chairman to act on his/her behalf. (Art. 114).

Manager.—LLC must have manager, subject to appointment or dismissal by board of directors. (Art. 50). Manager is responsible to board of directors and exercises following powers: (1) direct business operation and management, and organize implementation of resolutions of board of directors; (2) implement annual business operations and investment plans; (3) formulate internal organizational system; (4) formulate basic management system; (5) formulate detailed rules and regulations; (6) nominate and recommend dismissal of deputy managers and financial officers; (7) appoint or dismiss management officers other than those required to be appointed or dismissed by board of directors; and (8) other powers authorized by articles of association and board of directors. (Art. 50).

CLS, powers and functions of manager are identical to LLC. (ART. 119). Persons within any of following categories may not serve as manager in LLC and CLS: (1) persons without civil competence or with limited civil competence; (2) persons having committed crimes of embezzlement, bribery, infringement of property, misappropriation, sabotaging social and economic order in which criminal penalties were imposed within past five years; (3) persons who are former directors or managers of company or enterprise which has become bankrupt and has been liquidated within three years from time when bankruptcy and liquidation were completed and for which they are personally liable; (4) persons who are legal representatives of company or enterprise whose business license was revoked due to violation of law within past three years commencing from date license was revoked and for which they are personally liable; (5) persons having relatively large amount of debts due and outstanding; and (6) civil servants of State. (Arts. 57, 58, 123). Managers shall follow articles of association, perform their duties faithfully and safeguard interests of LLC and CLS, and shall not take advantages of their position and powers for personal gain. (Arts. 59, 123). Managers are not allowed to take advantage of their positions to accept bribes or other illegal income, seize property or misappropriate funds of LLC or CLS. (Arts. 59, 60, 123). Managers may not deposit assets of LLC or CLS in their own or other personal bank accounts and provide assets of LLC or CLS as guarantee for debts of shareholders of said LLC or CLS or others. (Arts. 60, 123). Managers may not engage on their own behalf of on behalf of others in any business that is same as LLC or CLS, activities that are harmful to LLC or CLS; proceeds from such activity which shall belong to LLC or CLS. (Arts. 61, 123). Unless otherwise provided for by law or with prior consent of shareholders' meeting, managers may not divulge secrets of LLC or CLS. (Arts. 62, 123). Where managers violate law or articles of association in performing official duties which result in injuries to said LLC or CLS, they shall compensate those losses. (Arts. 63, 123).

Supervisory Board.—LLC with relatively large scale operations must have supervisory board consisting of at least three members, and LLC with relatively small number of shareholders and small operations may simply have one or two supervisors. (Art. 52). Supervisory board must include representatives of shareholders and certain proportion of representatives from staff, which must be specified in articles of association. (Art. 52). Directors, managers and financial officers must not concurrently serve as supervisors. (Art. 52). Term of office for supervisor is three years, and supervisor may be reelected and serve another term upon expiration of prior term. (Art. 53). Supervisors must attend meetings of board of directors as nonvoting members. (Art. 54). Supervisory board exercises following powers and functions: (1) review of financial affairs; (2) supervise activities of directors and managers which violate laws and regulations or articles of association; (3) request directors and managers to remedy their activities whenever such activities harm interests of their company; (4) propose interim shareholders' meeting; and (5) other powers authorized in articles of association. (Art. 54).

CLS shall have supervisory board consisting of at least three supervisors. (Art. 124). Directors, managers and financial officers may not serve concurrently as supervisors. (Art. 124). Supervisory board must include representatives of shareholders and appropriate proportion of representatives from workers and staff which must be specified in articles of association. (Art. 124). Term of office and powers and functions of supervisory board are identical with that of LLC. (Art. 125, 126). Supervisors faithfully must perform their duties according to law and articles of association. (Art. 128).

Financial Affairs and Accounting.—LLC and CLS must establish financial and accounting systems. (Art. 174). Company must submit financial and accounting reports at end of each fiscal year, which are subject to examination and verification. (Art. 175). Financial and accounting report shall contain following accounting statements and schedules: (1) balance sheets; (2) profit and loss statement; (3) statement of financial changes; (4) statement of financial conditions; and (5) statement of profit distribution. (Art. 175). LLC must submit financial and accounting report to shareholders within time limit prescribed in articles of association and CLS must file financial and accounting statements at said CLS for inspection by shareholders at least 20 days prior to annual shareholders' meeting. (Art. 176). CLS created through public offering must make public its financial and accounting statements through announcement. (Art. 176). In distributing each years' post-tax profits, company must set aside 10% as statutory reserve funds until aggregate balance of account is 50% or more of companies registered capital and 5 to 10% as statutory public welfare funds. (Art. 177). Where aggregate balance of statutory reserve funds is insufficient to cover losses sustained in previous years, current year's profit shall be used to cover losses before statutory reserve funds and statutory public welfare funds are set aside. (Art. 177). Company may set aside discretionary common reserve funds subject to resolution of shareholders' meeting when it has set aside statutory reserve funds from post-tax profits. (Art. 177). Profits remaining shall be distributed to shareholders proportionate to their capital contribution in LLC or number of shares held by shareholders in CLS, when losses have been covered and statutory reserve and statutory public welfare funds have been set aside. (Art. 177). Should shareholders' meeting or board of directors distribute profits before losses are recovered and statutory reserve and statutory public welfare funds are set aside, distributed profits must be returned to company. (Art. 177). Premium obtained by CLS by offering shares at price over par value and any other income designated by competent financial department of State Council must be allocated to company's capital common reserve funds. (Art. 178). Company's common reserve funds must be used to recover for losses, expand production and operations or transfer as capital increases. (Art. 179). Statutory public welfare funds should be used for collective welfare of workers and staff. (Art. 180). Company may not maintain accounting books and records other than those provided for by law and assets of company may not be deposited in accounts opened under individual's name. (Art. 181).

Merger and Division.—Merger or division is subject to resolution adopted by shareholders' meeting. (Art. 182). Merger or division of CLS must have approval of competent department authorized by State Council or provincial level government. (Art. 183). Merger may be made by means of absorption or creation. (Art. 184). Merger by absorption means company absorbs one or more other companies by dissolution of absorbed company(s). (Art. 184). Merger by creation means unification of two or more companies by dissolution of existing one(s) and creation of separate new company. (Art. 184). In case of merger, merger agreement must be executed by and between parties concerned and balance sheets and list of assets must be compiled. (Art. 184). Companies concerned shall notify their creditors within ten days from date when merger resolutions are adopted and announce in newspapers at least three times within 30 days. (Art. 184). Creditors are entitled to request payment of debts or provide corresponding guarantees within 30 days after they receive notification or within 90 days from date of first announcement should they not have received notification. (Art. 184). Merger may not be carried out without clearing debts or providing guarantees. (Art. 184). Survival companies after merger or newly-created companies shall bear credits and debts of parties to merger. (Art. 184). In case of division, assets of company shall be divided accordingly. (Art. 185). Company shall compile balance sheet and list of assets, and notify creditors within ten days from date when resolutions of division are adopted and announce in newspapers at least three times within 30 days. (Art. 185). Creditors are entitled to request payment of debts or provide corresponding guarantees within 30 days when they have received notification. (Art. 185). Division of company may not be carried out without clearing debts or providing guarantee. (Art. 185). Debts of company before division shall be borne by companies after division according to their prior agreement. (Art. 185). In case of merger or division, company must change its registration with registration authority, should there be changes in registered items; cancel registration should company be dissolved; or register for new company should new company be created. (Art. 188).

Bankruptcy, Dissolution and Liquidation.—Should company become insolvent, court may declare bankruptcy according to law and organize liquidation group composed of shareholders, relevant departments and specialized professionals which will conduct liquidation. (Art. 189). Company may dissolve under any of following cases: (1) term of operation prescribed in articles of association expires or other conditions for dissolution as provided for in articles of association; (2) resolution for dissolution is adopted by shareholders' meeting; and (3) dissolution is necessitated by merger or division. (Art. 190). Company must dissolve if it is ordered to close down for violation of law and in which case competent department shall organize liquidation group composed of shareholders, relevant departments and professionals. (Art. 192). Liquidation group shall exercise following powers and functions during period of liquidation: (1) carry out clearance of assets and compile balance sheets and list of assets; (2) to notify creditors or make public announcement; (3) to handle remaining businesses; (4) to pay overdue taxes; (5) to clear credits and debts; (6) to dispose of remaining assets when all debts are paid off; and (7) to participate in civil proceedings on behalf of company. (Art. 193). Liquidation group shall notify creditors within ten days from its establishment and make public announcement in newspaper at least three times within 60 days. (Art. 194). Creditors shall demand payment from liquidation group within 30 days from date they received notification or within 90 days from date of first announcement should they not have received notification. (Art. 194). When creditors

See Topical Index in front part of this volume.

CORPORATIONS . . . *continued*
demand payment, they must specify relevant matters and produce evidence. (Art. 194). Liquidation group shall register outstanding debt. (Art. 194). Liquidation group shall formulate liquidation plan and submit to shareholders' meeting or competent department for approval, after clearing assets, and compiling balance sheet and list of assets. (Art. 195). Where assets of company are sufficient to pay debts, assets shall be used respectively to pay liquidation fees, wages and labor insurance fees of workers and staff, overdue taxes and debts of company. (Art. 195). Remaining assets after liquidation will be distributed to shareholders proportionate to their investment in LLC or shares held. (Art. 195). In course of liquidation, company shall not engage in new business activities. (Art. 195). Upon completion of liquidation, liquidation group shall formulate liquidation report and submit to shareholders' meeting or competent department for approval, and submit to registration authority for cancellation of registration and make public announcement regarding termination of company. (Art. 197). Otherwise registration authority may revoke its business license and make public announcement regarding matter. (Art. 197). Members of liquidation group shall be loyal to their duties and perform their liquidation duties according to law. (Art. 198). Members of liquidation group shall not take advantage of powers and functions to accept bribes or other illegal income or convert property of company into their own. (Art. 198). Members of liquidation group shall compensate losses suffered by liquidated company or creditors due to their deliberate acts or serious negligence. (Art. 198).

Foreign Company.—Companies incorporated outside China under laws of foreign countries are "foreign companies". (Art. 199). Foreign companies may set up branches to engage in production and business operation inside China according to law. (Art. 199). Foreign companies are legal persons of foreign countries and their branches are not legal persons in China. (Art. 203). Foreign companies shall assume civil liabilities for business activities of their China branches. (Art. 203). In establishing branch, foreign company must file application with Chinese competent department and produce its articles of association, registration certificate issued by original country of registration and other relevant documents. (Art. 200). Foreign company must appoint representative or agent in charge of branch in China and appropriate necessary funds compatible with its business operations. (Art. 201). Branch of foreign company shall follow law of China and shall not harm social and public interests. (Art. 204). Legal rights and interests of branch of foreign company shall be protected by law of China. (Art. 204). Before closing its branch in China, foreign company shall clear debts of its branch according to law and conduct liquidation. (Art. 205). It shall not transfer assets of branch out of China before debts are fully paid. (Art. 205).

COURTS:

See topics Actions; Constitution and Government. Organic Law of People's Courts promulgated on July 1, 1979 am'd on Sept. 2, 1983, by National People's Congress clearly determines structure and composition of court system in China. Three judicial levels include local people's courts and higher level courts, viz., basic level, middle level and high level courts; special courts, including military courts, railroad shipping courts, maritime courts, forestry courts and other special courts, and Supreme Court. (Art. 2). Business of courts is to decide civil and criminal cases according to Constitution and laws. (Art. 3). Courts decide cases independently only, conforming to law (Art. 4), and do not discriminate on basis of status, sex, nationality, religion, education, or property. Courts apply law equally to all persons. (Art. 5). Trials are normally held in public, except when concerned with state secrets, crimes of infants, and private confidential matters. (Art. 7). Criminal defendants have right to counsel, including state-provided counsel. (Art. 8). Each level court must establish trial committee whose responsibilities include summarizing court's experience, discussing important or difficult cases and other trial problems. Members of trial committee are appointed on recommendation of court head by Standing Committee of People's Congress of same level, which has authority to appoint or remove said members. (Art. 11). Parties to case have power to apply to have judge or assessor recuse himself if party feels said judicial officer has such close personal relationship with case that cannot decide it fairly. Decision on this application is made by court head. (Art. 16).

Each level court has responsibility and must report to People's Congress and its Standing Committee on corresponding level. Superior courts supervise lower level courts. (Art. 17). Citizens eligible to vote and be elected who are 20 years of age can be selected as judicial officers (Art. 34), or serve as assessors (Art. 38). Latter have same authority as judges during trial.

Basic level courts include counties (xian) and urban courts, self-governing district courts, and districts under jurisdiction of cities. Courts at this level have head and assistant head of court and several judges. These courts have authority to establish civil, economic and criminal sections, and to appoint section heads and assistant section heads. Such courts, depending upon population in area and circumstances of their case load, can set up several sections. These sections, or tribunals, are organs of basic people's courts and decisions and judgments of said sections are those of basic level courts. (Arts. 18, 19, 20). Normally, absent legal provisions to contrary, these basic level courts have jurisdiction over trial of civil and criminal cases of first instance. (Art. 21). If, however, said basic level courts regard case as particularly serious they can request that it be handled by higher level court. (Art. 21). Aside from decisions or judgments, basic level courts handle minor criminal cases and civil disputes not requiring trial, instruct personnel of mediation committees and administer judicial work within their area of responsibility. (Art. 22).

Middle or intermediate level courts include those prefectures under provincial level, self-governing areas, in cities directly under central government jurisdiction; in cities under provincial or self-governing area jurisdiction and in self-governing prefectures. (Art. 23). Much of structure of these courts is similar to that of basic level courts but those in urban areas also have, by law, in addition to civil and criminal tribunals economic tribunals that handle most commercial cases and have jurisdiction over major disputes involving foreign matters or persons. (Civ. Pro. Code, Art. 19). These middle level courts handle cases of first instance that are specially designated by law as being within their jurisdiction, or those sent up to them for trial from basic level courts, or appeals from basic level courts, or those matters brought before them by Procuratorate pursuant to supervisory procedures. Middle level courts also have authority, when presented with difficult cases, to request that higher level courts handle matter. (Art. 25).

High Level Courts.—There are 29 (30 including Taiwan province) high level courts, in provinces, self-governing areas and those cities directly under Central Government control. As minimum they are composed of civil, criminal and economic tribunal. (Art. 26). They handle special cases of first instance designated by law as within their jurisdiction cases of difficulty sent to them by lower level courts, appeals from lower level courts and appeals from Procuratorate. (Art. 28). Specialty courts are established pursuant to regulations issued by Standing Committee of National People's Congress. (Art. 29).

Supreme Court has supervisory jurisdiction over all lower level courts, criminal, civil, economic and other tribunals, jurisdiction over cases of first instance specially designated by law as being within its jurisdiction, appellate authority over decisions and judgments of high level courts and specialty courts, and cases presented by Chief Procuratorate pursuant to supervisory procedure. (Art. 32). Supreme Court, when deciding case where there are substantive legal problems will undertake explanation thereof. (Art. 33).

Maritime courts were established in 1984 in Shanghai, Qindao, Tianjin and Dalian, regarded as intermediate courts and take cognizance of domestic and foreign maritime cases. Courts are bound by law of civil procedure.

Substantive laws applicable to maritime courts are: General Principles of Civil Code, Law of Maritime Traffic Safety, Law of Maritime Environment Protection, Fishing Law, Regulations Controlling Prevention of Pollution of Sea Areas by Vessels, Regulations Concerning Control of Dumping of Waste at Sea, Regulations Concerning Environmental Protection in Offshore Oil Exploration, etc. Maritime Law of China was adopted by National People's Congress Nov. 7, 1992, effective July 1, 1993. Said law with 278 articles contains all major areas of admiralty.

Trial Organization.—In trial of civil cases in court of first instance, judges and assessors together may comprise collegiate bench for trial, or judges themselves may comprise collegiate bench. Members of collegiate bench at trial must comprise odd number. Judicial personnel of courts must have adequate knowledge of law. (Civ. Pro. Code, Arts. 40, 41). Simple civil cases can be tried by single judge. Assessors, when undertaking reponsibilities in court, have equal authority to that of judges. (Civ. Pro. Code, Art. 40). When court adjudicates second level civil case, judges comprise collegiate bench, and said collegiate bench must comprise odd number of judges. (Civ. Pro. Code, Art. 41). When second level court sends case back for retrial, original trial court should, according to procedures of first instance trial court, convene another collegiate bench for retrial. (Civ. Pro. Code, Art. 41). If case being retried was originally of first instance, then trial bench separately constituted according to procedures of courts of first instance; if case was originally of second level, another collegiate bench should be reconstituted according to procedures of second level courts. (Civ. Pro. Code, Art. 41).

Person responsible as head judge in collegiate panel will be appointed by head of court or head section (or tribunal) of court. If either head of court or of one of its tribunals sits on collegiate panel, said person assumes responsibility as head of panel. (Civ. Pro. Code, Art. 42). When collegiate panel considers case, it should implement principle of minority subordinate to majority. Written record should be made of deliberations and should be signed by members of collegiate panel. Differences of opinion in deliberations must be entered into record strictly according to facts. (Civ. Pro. Code, Art. 43).

Recusal and Removal for Potential Prejudice.—Under following circumstances judicial official must recuse himself; party to litigation also has authority to make formal application, either orally or in writing, to have such judicial official removed: (1) Being party to case or close relative of party; (2) having interest in outcome of litigation; (3) having some other relationship with party to litigation that may influence impartial consideration of case. These rules also applicable to translators, clerks of court, and expert witnesses. (Civ. Pro. Code, Art. 45).

When parties apply for removal, they should state reasons clearly, and raise these when case commences. If reasons for removal become known or arise after commencement of trial of case, they can be raised in court prior to final argument. (Civ. Pro. Code, Art. 46). Those about whom application is made for removal should temporarily cease undertaking their responsibilities, except in cases where necessary to take emergency measures. (Civ. Pro. Code, Art. 41). If head of court sitting as head of panel and application made for his recusal, trial committee should decide matter; regarding removal of one of adjudicators from trial panel, court head should decide matter. Recusal or removal of others should be decided by head of trial panel. (Civ. Pro. Code, Art. 47). Decisions by court regarding applications for removal or recusal can take either oral or written form. If party making application not satisfied with decision, may apply once for reconsideration, but trial of case must not cease during reconsideration.

Judges Law (adopted at Twelfth Standing Committee of the Eighth People's Congress on Feb. 28, 1995, effective as of July 1, 1995). Judges are judicial officers who legally exercise judicial authority; serving as: deputy directors, vice-directors or members of adjudication committees; presidents or vice presidents of chambers; judges or deputy judges of Supreme People's Court, local people's courts at different levels, military courts, or other special people's courts. (Art. 2). Judges must undertake following obligations: to strictly observe constitution and other laws (Art. 7.1); to hear cases on basis of fact and law (Art. 7.2); to legally protect parties' procedural rights (Art. 7.3); to lawfully defend rights and interests of citizens, legal persons and other organisations, along with interests of State and public (Art. 7.4); to maintain ethical standards, be devoted to one's duty, and obey judicial discipline (Art. 7.5); to protect secrets of State and Administration of Justice (Art. 7.6); and to accept supervision where necessary (Art. 7.7). Judges possess following rights: to certain powers as judicial officers; proper working conditions (Art. 8.1); to hear cases without being interfered with by bureaucracy, social organisations or individuals (Art. 8.2); to not be relieved, demoted, dismissed, or punished unless pursuant to statutory reasons and procedures (Art. 8.3); to obtain payment for labour; to be given insurance, along with other material benefits (Art. 8.4); to have person, property and domicile be legally

COURTS . . . *continued*
protected (Art. 8.5); to be trained (Art. 8.6); and to resign (Art. 8.8). To qualify as judge one must meet following requirements: Chinese nationality; over 23 years old; has upheld constitution; high level of political and professional competence; healthy; obtained Master of Law or Doctorate of Law, or otherwise obtained either Bachelor of Law with one year experience in legal field, or to have at least two years experience working in legal field. (Art. 9). Rank of judge has 12 separate levels, ranging from judge, senior judge, justice to Director of Supreme Court (Chief Justice). (Art. 16). People's Court has established judicial assessment committee to monitor judiciary. (Art. 46).

CRIMINAL LAW:

On July 6, 1979 Standing Committee of National People's Congress promulgated Criminal Code and Code of Criminal Procedure, both of which were to become effective as of Jan. 1, 1980. Pursuant to recommendation of Supreme People's Court and Procuratorate, which was made because of lack of trained personnel, etc., in judicial organs as result of anti-legal policies of leaders of Cultural Revolution, Standing Committee of National People's Congress determined that all cases filed on or before Dec. 31, 1979 wherein no judgments have yet been rendered are to be handled by prior procedures. Cases accepted as of Jan. 1, 1980 shall, where possible, be handled by Code of Criminal Procedure, although standing committees at each level were given authority, if personnel remained short, to present application to extend time-limit for handling case until end of 1980.

Pursuant to Resolution on Planned Enforcement of Law of Criminal Procedure courts, procuratorates, public security organs, etc., were required to draw up specific plans to enforce Code of Criminal Procedure (also called Law of Criminal Procedure).

Criminal Code (also called Criminal Law) has been supplemented by certain statutes for offenses, such as those against public order. Thus Supplementary Decision on Reeducation of Offenders Through Labor was approved by Standing Committee, and two statutes promulgated in 1957 were republished, viz., Decision on Reeducation of Offenders Through Labor and Regulations Governing Offenses Against Public Order. Work study schools, where corporal punishment is prohibited, have been established for youngsters who have committed petty offenses as form of semi-compulsory or compulsory reeducation. In Aug. 1983 department for reform and reeducation of criminals through labor transferred from Public Security organs to judiciary.

Furthermore, in order to strengthen public security, and in accordance with recognition given to validity of prior legislation, following rules were republished: Organic Rules of Neighborhood Offices, Organic Rules of Urban Residents Committees, tentative Organic Rules of Public Security Committees and tentative Rules for Organization of People's Mediation Committees. In addition on Feb. 23, 1979 Regulations on Arrest and Detention were approved by Standing Committee of National People's Congress.

Arrest and Detention.—Regulations on Arrest and Detention were promulgated pursuant to Art. 18 of old Constitution, which provides for punishment of counter-revolutionary activity, treason, and bad elements etc., but also is based on Art. 37 of Constitution which protects citizens in their homes and from arbitrary arrest. (Art. 1). Arrest cannot take place without obtaining court order or approval of procuratorate. (Art. 2). Arrests are to be made immediately where facts of criminal activity have been carefully investigated and possibility exists of punishment worse than imprisonment, and arrest seems necessary and court has so decided or procuratorate has approved. (Art. 3). Exceptions to immediate arrest exist for criminals subject to arrest who are seriously ill, or are pregnant women, etc., who can be subject to household supervision, etc. (Art. 3). Arrest after necessary procedures is to be made by relevant public security organization. (Art. 4). Public security organs must have warrant at time of arrest and inform arrested party of said warrant. Aside from very special circumstances, within 24 hours of arrest public security organ, procuratorate or court should inform family of arrested party of fact of arrest, reason for arrest and location of party arrested. (Art. 5).

Rules permit public security organ to detain certain serious criminal elements etc. under special circumstances, such as when criminal act is in preparation, is being committed or just completed and it is discovered, or when injured party or one who personally saw crime points out criminal, or where someone has evidence of crime on their person or in their residence, etc. (Art. 6). There are special provisions for citizen arrests where they catch culprit in act, etc. (Art. 7).

Where detention is made by public security organ and person should be formally arrested, then within three days of detention, or seven under special circumstances, facts of crime and evidence thereof should be brought to local procuratorate, who within three days after said notification should determine whether or not to formally arrest said person. If approval for arrest is not granted party should be freed immediately and given evidence of his release. (Art. 8). See also Code of Criminal Procedure Arts. 38-52.

Code of Criminal Procedure.—Code provides that responsibility for different aspects of criminal cases shall be divided among different government units. Thus, investigation, preliminary detention and preliminary questioning in criminal case is responsibility of public security unit. Approving formal arrest, undertaking procuratorial work (including investigation), and deciding on whether to indict and bring to trial is responsibility of Procuratorate. Courts are responsible for trial of all cases. No other governmental agencies, groups or individuals have authority to undertake any of these responsibilities, all of which must strictly be undertaken according to Code of Criminal Procedure and other relevant laws. (Art. 3).

Right of defendants to counsel in criminal cases made explicit by Code. (Art. 8). No special privilege permitted any person and law equally applicable to all persons. (Art. 4). Cases normally to be adjudicated in public. (Art. 8). Procedural safeguards to be guaranteed and litigants and other participants in crimi-nal proceedings have right to bring complaints against personnel in judicial, procuratoral, or investigatory organizations who violate their procedural rights. (Art. 10).

Jurisdiction.—Criminal cases are normally tried in first instance at basic court level (Art. 14), but middle level courts have jurisdiction over first trials for counter-revolutionary crimes, crimes where death penalty or life imprisonment is asked for, crimes committed by foreigners and crimes by citizens against foreigners (Art. 15). Major criminal cases affecting entire province, self-governing area (provincial equivalents) or city directly under central government are handled by high courts as courts of first instance. (Art. 16). For crimes that affect entire nation, Supreme Court can be trial court. Normally venue is located in area where crime was committed, although if more convenient it can be located at defendant's residence. (Art. 19).

Recusal.—Code makes provision for withdrawal or removal of judges, assessors, procurators, and investigators who might be prejudiced by prior relationship, etc. (Art. 23) and Code gives parties right to seek withdrawal of such persons (Art. 23).

Counsel.—Code provides that aside from attorney, other individuals may assist defendant, such as those recommended by people's organizations, defendant's unit, or other citizens with court's permission, or those having close familial relationship with defendant, etc. (Art. 26). Court has power to appoint counsel for those without legal assistance in cases where public prosecutor appears in court to commence prosecution. (Art. 27). Counsel has right to review case materials, understand circumstances of case, can visit defendant in place of detention and correspond with him. (Art. 29). Defendant has right to discharge counsel during proceedings and to employ other counsel. (Art. 30).

Evidence, such as tangible things, written evidence, testimony of witnesses (including victims) and defendant, expert opinion and records of examination or analysis or physical evidence, etc. must be examined for probity, etc., in order to be admitted as evidence in case. (Art. 31). Prosecutors etc. must prove their case with objective evidence, obtained strictly according to legal procedures; use of torture, threat, enticement, deceit, or other illegal methods of obtaining evidence is prohibited. (Art. 32). Public security organ's warrant of arrest, prosecutor's indictment, court's decision, all must be based on fact. If there is deliberate hiding of factual matters, persons responsible should be investigated and punished. (Art. 33). Courts, procuratorate and public security organ all have authority to obtain evidence from all government agencies, enterprises, service organizations, communes, people's organizations, and citizens. (Art. 34). Falsification of evidence, hiding or destruction of evidence are all punishable offenses irrespective of who commits these offenses. (Art. 34). In all cases emphasis must be placed on evidence and investigatory material, and oral testimony not to be lightly accepted. (Art. 35). If only testimony is that of defendant, and there is no other evidence, then defendant cannot be convicted of crime; however, if solid evidence of guilt but no testimony of defendant, defendant can be convicted of crime. (Art. 35). Evidence of witnesses must be presented in public prosecution, injured party, defendant and counsel have right to examine testimony, evaluate evidence, and only thereafter is it admissible evidence. (Art. 36). Anyone with knowledge of facts of case has duty to be witness. (Art. 37).

Supplemental Civil Proceedings.—Party injured by criminal activity can, during said criminal proceedings, commence civil proceedings, and if state property involved, or that of collective organization, procuratorate can also bring suit for damages during said criminal proceedings. Court has authority to have defendant's assets frozen or distrained. (Art. 53).

Entire Code of Criminal Procedure contains 164 articles and deals with numerous matters in great depth.

Criminal Code.—Criminal Code went through numerous drafts commenced prior to Cultural Revolution before it was promulgated. 22d draft was completed in 1957 and 33d draft in 1963. It had as its basis prior legal experience in China, including numerous court cases. Criminal Code has 192 Articles and together with Code of Criminal Procedure is substantial body of legislation.

Criminal Intent.—If one knows that his or her acts will result in social harm and hopes for result or disregards consequences, and thereby does commit crime, this is intentional criminal act and bears criminal responsibility. (Art. 11). Code also makes provision for negligent criminal conduct which bears criminal responsibility only where there is special statutory provision. (Art. 12). If injury is caused without intent or criminal negligence and one could not foresee consequences of act, then there can be no criminal responsibility. (Art. 13). Person 16 years of age has criminal responsibility, as does someone 14 years of age but not 16 if he commits serious crimes such as murder, arson, etc. but those from 14 years of age but less than 18 years of age should receive comparatively lighter or reduced sentences. In case of someone who, because less than 16 years of age, does not receive criminal punishment, head of household of said youth can be ordered to increase his supervision and education, or government can undertake education of said offender. (Art. 13).

Forms of Punishment.—Various forms of punishment for criminal acts are provided by Code, including death penalty, life imprisonment, imprisonment for fixed periods, limited detention, public supervision, fines, confiscation of property, loss of political rights and, for foreigners, deportation. (Arts. 28, 29, 30). Criminals can be required to compensate victims for economic loss. (Art. 31). Minor offenses can result in admonishment, or order to provide written undertaking of responsibility and repentance, or to make apology, or to make compensation for losses suffered, or to be subject to administrative sanctions by responsible department. (Art. 32).

Categories of Crime.—Code provides for several categories of crime, including counterrevolutionary activity, endangering public safety, sabotaging socialist economic order, violation of citizens' personal rights, violation of citizens' political or democratic rights, crimes against property, impairing socialist management order, crimes against marriage and family, and crimes of dereliction of duty.

Specific crimes under these general categories are explicated in Code, e.g., counterrevolutionary activity generally defined as acts endangering nation, or acts designed to overthrow political powers of dictatorship of proletariat and socialist system. (Art. 90). Code provides specific punishment for specific acts, such as combining with foreign nations to endanger national sovereignty, territorial integrity and security, punishable by terms of imprisonment from ten years to life. (Art. 91). If, with counterrevolutionary intent, one undertakes any of following destructive acts, then punishment will, unless circumstances minor, be imprisonment from ten years to life: Cause fires, set explosives, cause floods, use technology or other means to destroy military equipment, communications equipment, construction materials and other enumerated items, including hijacking ships, airplanes, trains, streetcars or motor vehicles. (Art. 100).

Endangering public safety defined in part as causing fire, explosions or floods or employing other dangerous means to destroy factories, mines, oil fields, ports, rivers, water sources, warehouses, homes, forests, agricultural areas, pastoral areas, valleys, major pipelines, public buildings or other public or private property; for above acts

See Topical Index in front part of this volume.

CRIMINAL LAW . . . *continued*
threatening public peace, which did not have serious consequences, Code provides imprisonment from three to ten years. (Art. 105). Where some of same acts caused serious injury to persons or property, Code provides for up to life imprisonment or even death penalty. (Art. 106).

Sabotaging socialist economic order includes criminal violation of customs laws, engaging in smuggling, and violating following laws: Foreign currency, financial, gold and silver, or Industrial and Commercial Administration. Code provides for punishments ranging from fines to maximum three years imprisonment for certain offenses.

Protection of citizens' personal or political rights and other rights so that no person or organization illegally violates said rights is one's duty to state. Those directly responsible who, in contravention of law, seriously violate said rights will be punished according to Criminal Code. (Art. 131). Intentional murder punishable by death penalty, or life imprisonment, or imprisonment for more than ten years. (Art. 132). Under minor circumstances punishment can be from three to ten years imprisonment. (Art. 132). Those who intentionally inflict physical injury on others can be punished with three years or less imprisonment (Art. 134) or more, depending on severity of injury. Code provides more severe punishment, e.g., if said injury led to death, punishment can be from seven years to life imprisonment. (Art. 134). If employee of state violates prohibition against compelling testimony in criminal cases, can be imprisoned for up to three years. (Art. 136). If said official caused serious bodily injury during said act, punishment to be heavier pursuant to other parts of statute. (Art. 136). Strictly prohibited to use any means or method to falsely accuse and charge cadres or citizens with offenses. If one does commit this offense, even against one in prison, will be punished according to nature, seriousness and consequences of act of accusation; one will be criminally punished more strictly if said false accuser is employee of national government. (Art. 138). If said accusation, though false, is not intentionally so, but is brought through error or is erroneous presentation of non-factual material, then this provision of law is inapplicable. (Art. 138). Numerous other provisions provide criminal punishment for rape, compelling prostitution, violation of election regulations, obstructing free exercise of elections, unlawful detention, deprivation of freedom of person, unlawful search of person or residence, serious public defamation, use of public office for private gain, depriving citizens of freedom of religious belief, intentionally testifying falsely about significant matters, unlawfully opening, concealing or destroying private mail, infringing on citizen's freedom of correspondence, etc. Also covered by this category of crime are offenses of concealing stolen goods, destroying evidence of crime, resisting arrest (Art. 153) and blackmail to extort property (Art. 154).

Crimes against property include corruption. For example, pursuant to Code, if employee of state uses facilities of his official position to corruptly expropriate public property, then punishment will be from detention to five years imprisonment. (Art. 155). If circumstances especially serious, punishment can be life imprisonment or even death penalty. (Art. 155). Penalty herein can include confiscation of property, or require restitution and/or compensation for said property. (Art. 155). Most offenses against property in this portion of Code are traditional offenses of robbery, embezzlement, criminal fraud, etc., and criminal taking of private or public property. (Arts. 150-154).

Impairing socialist management order includes offenses such as threatening officials so as to obstruct them from their duty according to law (Art. 157), failure to carry out final judgment of courts (Art. 157), or after being sentenced to imprisonment, to flee or escape (Art. 161). Numerous offenses against lawful order at docks, public airports, markets, parks, movie theatres, exposition halls, athletic fields, etc., are also covered in this section. (Art. 159). Other acts covered by this section include harboring of counterrevolutionary or other criminal elements (Art. 162), violation of grain control legislation (Art. 163), sale of bogus medicine harmful to health (Art. 164), posing as state personnel for fraudulent purposes (Art. 166), forging, altering, stealing or forcibly seizing or destroying official documents or seals (Art. 167), assembling, for profit, group to gamble or making occupation of gambling (Art. 168), selling pornographic literature for profit (Art. 170), manufacturing, selling or transporting narcotics (Art. 171), concealing or distributing goods known to have been stolen (Art. 172), violation of laws on protection of cultural relics (Arts. 173), violation of quarantine and health regulations at boundaries, and violation of laws, and regulations on entering and leaving China (Art. 176).

Offenses against marriage and family include use of force to interfere in other persons' marital freedom (Art. 179), bigamy (Art. 180), criminal mistreatment of family members (Art. 182), failure to undertake responsibilities for nurture of old, young and infirm (Art. 183), and abduction of minor from his home or guardian (Art. 184).

Crimes of dereliction of duties comprise use of one's official position to damage proper activities of governmental organization. Thus receipt of bribes or tendering of bribes to those in official positions is punishable (Art. 185), as is release of secret state information in violation of law (Art. 186).

Death penalty, which is provided for in Code, is only to be imposed on offenders committing most heinous crimes, and two-year reprieve from execution can be granted to see if defendant can be reformed through labor. (Art. 43). Code also has statute of limitations (Art. 76) which is tied to penalties for offense. Thus, prosecution is prohibited: (1) After five years for offenses for which maximum prescribed penalty is imprisonment for below five years; (2) after ten years for offenses for which maximum prescribed penalty is imprisonment for not less than five but below ten years; (3) after 15 years for offenses for which maximum prescribed penalty is imprisonment for not less than ten years; and (4) after 20 years for offenses for which prescribed penalty is life imprisonment or death, unless Supreme Procuratorate approves extension of latter period. (Art. 76). Extradition to U.S. is not provided for by treaty.

Economic Crimes.—On Mar. 8, 1982, Standing Committee of People's Congress approved regulations amending Criminal Code, in view of what was termed rampant cases of smuggling, illegal currency transactions, speculation and profiteering, attempts to obtain exorbitant profits, stealing of public property, stealing and selling of valuable cultural objects, and giving and receiving of bribes, etc. Criminal Code amended to increase maximum penalties in particularly serious cases of so-called economic crimes, such as found in Arts. 118, 153, 171 and 173, from ten years or more in prison, to life sentences or death penalty and confiscation of property. Where government officials used their official position to commit crimes specified above and circumstances are particularly serious, they are to be punished by imposition of aforesaid severe penalties.

CURRENCY:

See topic Banks and Banking.

Currency in China is denominated either as people's currency (renminbi) or yuan, and comes in denominations of 50, 10, 5, 1, 0.50, 0.10, .05, .02 and .01. Value of currency has varied since 1972 from about four renminbi (or ¥) per U.S. $1 to less than 1.5 renminbi per U.S. dollar. In Aug. 1981 exchange rate was approximately 1.78 renminbi per U.S. $1; in 1991 exchange rate fluctuated at more than 5 renminbi and less than 6 per U.S.$1; in 1995 rate was about 8.3 renminbi per U.S.$1. It is prohibited to take Chinese currency out of China. Foreign exchange certificates were abolished. In Shenzhen Special Economic Zone Hong Kong currency and other non-Chinese currencies may be used in ordinary purchases and sales. Commercial transactions of international type are normally handled with hard currency such as U.S. dollars, Japanese yen, Swiss francs, English pounds, German marks, etc. Foreign currency bank accounts and domestic currency bank accounts (to be withdrawn in foreign exchange certificates) are permitted for foreign companies, and individuals frequently in or resident in China.

Measures Forbidding State Currency to Cross Border promulgated 6 Mar., 1951 still remain in force.

State currency as defined in this measure refers to currency issued by People's Bank of China and local currency issued with special permission of Central Government. (Art. 2).

State currency may not cross border, and if carried, transported or mailed across territory privately, will be confiscated (Art. 3), and prosecution can be affected (Arts. 4, 5).

In fact, Chinese currency can be purchased at exchange centers in Hong Kong and there are limited overseas transactions in purchase and sale of reminbi.

Temporary Rules on Management of Cash promulgated by State Council on 16 Aug. 1988, provides for control of cash accounts in banks. (Art. 2). Rules encourage interaccount transfers and decrease in use of cash (Art. 3); similarly detailed Provision for Carrying out Temporary Rules of Cash Management were promulgated by central bank on 12 Sept. 1988. These provide that central bank is in control of cash and banks holding cash accounts. (Art. 3). On 19 Sept. 1988, central bank promulgated method of Computation by Banks pursuant to Bank Management Regulations.

Bank of China operates in and out of China and has branches abroad in New York, Singapore, etc. International Department of bank is in charge of its relationship with its numerous correspondent banks and Joint Operations Department of bank coordinates foreign exchange earnings retained by local governmental units, including provinces and enterprises. It recommends to General Administration of Exchange Control amounts of foreign exchange available for use by local authorities. Clearing house of Bank of China is foreign exchange department, which is responsible for daily balancing of international accounts, for transferring funds between accounts, for raising funds from abroad, for buying and selling foreign exchange, etc. Credit department of bank handles project financing in China. There are other departments, most important of which is banking department, which handles banking transactions including issuance of foreign exchange certificates.

Provisional Foreign Exchange Control Regulations promulgated by State Council on Dec. 18, 1980, governing all foreign exchange income and expenditure, issuance and circulation of all payment instruments in foreign currency and dispatch and carriage into and out of China of foreign exchange and precious metals. (Art. 1). Pursuant to Approval of State Council of July 19, 1983, State Administration of Foreign Exchange Control on Aug. 1, 1983 promulgated Detailed Rules for Implementation of Foreign Exchange Controls ("Rules"). Foreign exchange defined to include, aside from banknotes, currency and coins, securities in foreign currency (broadly defined) and instruments payable in foreign currency, including bills, drafts, checks, bank deposit certificates, etc. (Art. 2). State General Administration of Exchange Controls ("SGAEC") is in charge of exchange control. Foreign exchange bank in China is Bank of China, only banking institution authorized to engage in foreign exchange business in China without consent of SGAEC. (Art. 3). Use of foreign currency in China prohibited, except in Shenzhen Special Economic Zone ("SEZ"), pursuant to Art. 32, where particularly Hong Kong dollars are in circulation. Chinese and foreign organizations and individuals, unless otherwise stipulated, must sell their foreign exchange to Bank of China. (Art. 4). Foreign exchange income of domestic organizations is regulated, although permitted to retain portion of their foreign exchange receipts in accordance with regulations (Art. 5), which funds must be placed in foreign currency accounts with Bank of China (Art. 9). Use, possession, deposit abroad, borrowing and offset of foreign exchange by domestic organizations must be approved by SGAEC. (Art. 6). Securities cannot be issued by domestic organizations with foreign exchange values inside or outside China unless approved by State Council. (Art. 7). Foreign loans to domestic institutions are made according to plans submitted to SGAEC and Foreign Investment Control Commission for examination and to State Council for approval. (Art. 8). Individuals in China receiving foreign exchange must sell it to Bank of China (Art. 13), except that kept in their own possession (Art. 14). Foreign exchange receipts of enterprises with foreign capital must be deposited with Bank of China and these enterprises, including joint venture enterprises, must submit periodic reports to SGAEC, enjoined to inspect activities of said institutions. (Art. 22). Periodic reports submitted to SGAEC by these enterprises must include balance sheet, profit and loss statement, statement of receipt and payments of foreign exchange for prior calendar year and audit reports for prior year, and must be submitted by Mar. 31 each year. (Rules 91). Budget of foreign exchange receipts and disbursements for coming year must be submitted by Dec. 1 each year. Foreign firms may applyto Bank of China to remit net profits after taxes, and other legitimate earnings. (Art. 24). Individual foreigners can remit up to 50% of their net wages and other legitimate earnings in foreign currency. (Art. 25).

There are no restrictions on amount of foreign exchange, precious metals and objects made from precious metals carried into China, but declaration must be made to Customs. (Art. 27). Said foreign exchange and precious metals can also then be carried

CURRENCY . . . *continued*
out of China. (Art. 27, 28). There are provisions for enforcing these regulations which include fines, confiscation or punishment by judicial organs pursuant to law. (Art. 31). (See also topic Criminal Law.) Exchange control regulations for special economic zones, such as Guangdong province, Fujian province, Shunjen, Zhuhai, Xiamen and Shantou are to be formulated by those governments in spirit of these regulations and in light of specific local conditions. (Art. 32). These regulations came into force as of Mar. 31, 1981. (Art. 34).

Swap Centers.—Numerous swap centers have been established in China to help facilitate exchange of local currency (either reminbi or FEC) for foreign currency. While initially designed to assist entities in China with foreign investment who had excess local currency, in fact both foreign and Chinese entities in China use these exchanges. First quasi-official swap center was located in Shenzhen, thereafter official foreign currency exchanges were established in Shanghai, Beijing, Fujian and elsewhere. Unofficial or quasi-official exchanges have operated in several Chinese cities. See State Rules of People's Bank of China for Adjustment of Retained Foreign Exchange, for some of regulations relating thereto, and Regulations for Encouragement of Foreign Investment, promulgated on 11 Oct., 1986. In some exchanges, e.g., Shanghai, exchange acts as medium for transaction, rather than direct transaction between buyer and seller. Various local rules have been promulgated, e.g., Interim Measures of Beijing City on Administration of Foreign Exchange of Foreign Investment Enterprises, 1988, which requires participating foreign enterprises to be members of exchange. These centers have helped reduce black and grey market sale of foreign currency and discrepancy between official exchange rate and market rate.

Announcement on Further Reforming the Foreign Exchange Administration System was promulgated by People's Bank of China on Dec. 28, 1993. Announcement provides that issuance of foreign exchange certificates shall be stopped starting from Jan. 1, 1994, and foreign exchange certificates in circulation may continue to be used until they are formally phased out which essentially has been accomplished.

Administration of foreign exchange in bonded areas was promulgated by State Administration of Exchange Control on 29 June, 1991.

Rule empowered State Administration of Exchange Control ("SAEC") or its branch office to supervise enterprise in bonded areas whose business involves receipt and expenditure of foreign exchange.

Bonded goods shall be valued in foreign currency upon their entering or leaving bonded areas, whilst nonbonded goods shall ve valued in Renminbi in such circumstances. (Art. 4).

Enterprises in bonded areas have to deposit all their foreign exchange income gained from their export of commodities, labor, services into their foreign exchange account, maintained with local banks. (Art. 6). Domestic Chinese enterprises are allowed to keep part of their foreign exchange income as working capital. (Art. 7).

Operation of foreign exchange business by banks and nonbank financial institutions and their branches in bonded areas shall be subject to approval by SAEC or local exchange control branch office. (Art. 8).

Enterprises outside bonded areas may use either foreign currency or Renminbi in investing in bonded areas. Foreign investors who wish to establish enterprises in bonded areas may do so but subject to state regulation on foreign exchange control relating to foreign funded enterprises. (Art. 10). Enterprises in bonded areas are allowed to raise funds from foreign banks and Chinese foreign joint venture banks subject to state regulations relating to control of foreign debts. (Art. 12).

Buying and selling foreign exchange by enterprises in bonded areas at foreign exchange adjustment centers within or outside bonded areas shall be subject to relevant regulation on foreign exchange adjustment. (Art. 13). Entry into or exit from China of Renminbi, foreign exchange, notes, and certificates, and precious metals must also be done in accordance with relevant state regulation. (Art. 14).

SAEC is empowered to deal with violation of foreign exchange control regulations, and to impose sanctions in accordance with those regulations.

Administration of Foreign Exchange Guarantee issued by Resident Institution in China.—On Feb. 20, 1987, Provisional Rules Governing the Foreign Exchange Guarantee Supplied by Resident Institution in China were issued by People's Bank of China. Based on it, People's Bank of China approved Rules on Foreign Exchange Guarantee Supplied by Resident Institution in China on Aug. 1, 1991, strengthening administration of foreign exchange guarantee business.

Rules apply to foreign exchange guarantee or counter-guarantee that resident institutions issue to foreign creditors, foreign capital banks, joint Chinese-foreign banks and joint Chinese-foreign nonbank financial institutions in China, including: (1) loan guarantee; (2) financial lease guarantee; (3) performance guarantee for compensation trade; (4) debt guarantee for external project contract; and (5) other guarantee. (Arts. 2, 14).

Institutions that can issue foreign exchange guarantee are: (1) financial institutions which have been approved to be entitled to operate foreign exchange guarantee business; and (2) nonfinancial corporations which have source of foreign exchange income.

Government and institutions are not permitted to operate foreign exchange guarantee business. (Art. 3).

Limits of Foreign Exchange Guarantor.—For financial institution, remaining sum of foreign exchange guarantee and of foreign debt should not exceed 20 times foreign exchange fund it has; for nonfinancial institution, remaining sum of foreign exchange guarantee should not exceed foreign exchange fund it has. Guarantor should not issue foreign exchange guarantee for registered capital of foreign investor. (Art. 5).

Jurisdiction and Limits of Examination and Approval of Foreign Exchange Guarantee.—Foreign exchange guarantee that is issued to local institution should be examined and approved by local foreign exchange control office; guarantee that is issued to Chinese corporation abroad should be examined and approved by State foreign exchange control authority. (Art. 6). Loan guarantee issued by Industrial and Commercial Bank of China, Agricultural Bank of China, People's Construction Bank of China, Investment Bank of China, Communications Bank and Industrial Bank of Cities and foreign exchange guarantee issued by other financial institutions except above-mentioned banks and nonfinancial enterprises should be examined and approved. (Art. 7).

Foreign Exchange Guarantee's Procedure.—For examination and approval, guarantee should totally or partly supply following materials: (1) documents approving feasibility study of guarantee project and other documents of approval; (2) certificate of guarantor's foreign exchange fund; (3) documents of guarantor's foreign debt and guarantee; (4) letter of intention of guarantee contract; (5) debt contract under guarantee or letter of intention and other documents concerned; (6) document of counter-guarantee; and (7) certificate that foreign institution or foreign capital enterprise mortgages foreign exchange asset to guarantor if guarantee is issued to foreign institution or foreign capital enterprise. (Art. 8). Guarantor should go to local foreign exchange control authority for registration after issuing guarantee, nonfinancial institution should go to local foreign exchange control authority to fill in form of registration of foreign exchange guarantee and obtain certificate of registration of foreign exchange guarantee within ten days after issuing guarantee, financial institution should fill in form of feedback of changes of foreign exchange guarantee and report debt guarantee changes of last month within 15 days of preceding month. (Art. 10). Guarantor should apply to local foreign exchange control authority for approving extension 15 days before deadline of debt if extension of foreign exchange guarantee is necessary. (Art. 11). If debt under guarantee matured, and what may make guarantee contract end has happened, nonfinancial institution guarantor should return certificate to foreign exchange control authority to cancel guarantee, and financial institution should cancel guarantee monthly. (Art. 12).

Guarantor's Rights and Obligations.—Guarantor's rights include: (1) supervise condition of debtor's fund and assets; (2) cancel guarantee if creditor and debtor modify contract without its agreement or approval of authority, or creditor does not perform contractual obligations; (3) ask creditor to pay relevant compensation for nonperformance of contractual obligations; and (4) require debtor to issue counter-guarantee or mortgage, and collect guarantee fee from debtor. Guarantor's obligations include: (1) supply financial reports, balance sheet and other material concerned to creditor; and (2) perform guarantee obligation if debtor does not perform its obligation before maturity of contract. (Art. 9).

Legal Liabilities.—If guarantor violates this regulation, foreign exchange control authority should warn, circulate notice, suspend or cancel foreign exchange guarantee business of guarantor, and punish guarantor according to penal provisions for violation of exchange control regulations. (Art. 13).

Interim Provisions Governing Administration of Foreign Exchange Settlement, Sale and Payment were promulgated by People's Bank of China effective as of Apr. 1, 1994. Provisions are applicable to all enterprises, institutions, state organs and social associations inside China (hereinafter "domestic entities").

Foreign Exchange Settlement.—Foreign exchange of domestic entities within any of following categories must be sold to authorized banks: (1) foreign exchange derived from export, transit trade with payment before receipt and other trading activities; (2) foreign exchange derived from winning international bidding for items under loan outside China; (3) foreign exchange derived from supply of goods or services in areas of transportation including all means of transportation, including seaports and airports, posts and telecommunications excluding international remittance, tourism, advertising, consulting services, exhibitions, consignment sales, maintenance and repairs, and various agency service; (4) foreign exchange derived from operation of bonded goods under supervision of customs inside China; (5) fees, fines and confiscations in foreign exchange collected by administrative or judicial organs; (6) foreign exchange derived from transfer of land-use rights, copyright, trademark, patent, non-patented technology, goodwill and other intangible assets; (7) foreign exchange derived from sales of real estate and other property to foreigners; (8) profits in foreign exchange remitted back to China by Chinese-owned enterprises abroad; (9) foreign exchange derived from compensation claimed abroad and guarantee money refunded from abroad; (10) foreign exchange derived from insurance in foreign exchange by insurance entities; (11) foreign exchange derived from operation of foreign exchange business by financial entities with foreign exchange license; (12) foreign exchange derived from donations, aid and support from abroad; and (13) other foreign exchange income to be decided by State Exchange Control Administration. (Art. 4).

However, domestic entities may apply to State Exchange Control Administration or its branches for opening foreign exchange accounts with authorized banks with respect to their foreign exchange falling into following categories: (1) foreign exchange obtained by companies in process of contracting for engineering projects and provision of labor, technical cooperation and other services abroad; (2) foreign exchange obtained by foreign agencies and overseas organizations; (3) foreign exchange payable or saleable including bid bonds, contract performance bonds, transit trade with receipt before payment, international foreign exchange remittance handled by posts and telecommunications departments, advance payment collected by first class travel agencies from foreign tourism organizations, foreign exchange collected by railway departments in handling foreign guarantee transportation business and guarantee money and mortgages collected by Customs; and (4) foreign exchange premiums collected by insurance entities in handling foreign exchange insurance, reinsurance abroad or premiums pending settlement. (Art. 5). Foreign exchange falling within any of following categories may not be sold but should be deposited in foreign exchange account opened with authorized banks: (1) foreign exchanges approved by State and verified by foreign exchange administration to be used specially to repay debts at home and abroad; (2) donations in foreign exchange to be used abroad as prescribed by donation agreement; (3) foreign exchange derived from foreign loans, issuance of bonds or stocks in foreign currencies; (4) foreign exchange remitted into China as investment by foreign legal persons or natural persons; (5) foreign exchange held by foreign embassies and consulates, international organizations and representative office of foreign legal persons in China; (6) foreign exchange of foreign-funded enterprises; and (7) foreign exchange held by Chinese citizens and foreign nationals in China. (Art. 6).

Sale of Foreign Exchange.—When domestic entities need foreign exchange for trade and non-trade international payments, they may acquire foreign exchange from authorized foreign exchange banks by presentation of valid commercial bills of payment and other valid documents including: (1) import licenses issued by competent departments and corresponding import contracts with respect to foreign exchange used to purchase goods under quota control or special products import control; (2) corresponding registration documents and import contracts with respect to foreign exchange

CURRENCY . . . *continued*
used to purchase goods under automatic registration system; (3) import contract merely for foreign exchange used to purchase other goods conforming to State import control regulations; (4) valid documents prescribed in Items 1 through 3 for foreign exchange used to purchase goods in bonded areas, or bonded warehouses or exhibits held by foreigners in China; (5) import contracts or agreements for foreign exchange used to import patent, copyright, trademark, computer software and other intangible assets; (6) exchange settlement certificates, compensation agreements, claim settlement certificates and exchange refund certificates for foreign exchange used to refund or compensate foreigners for exported item; and (7) bidding documents for foreign exchange used in bid bonds for contracting for engineering projects abroad and relevant contracts for foreign exchange used in performance bonds or advance payments for engineering projects. (Art. 8). Authorized banks may pay foreign exchange in first instance upon presentation of payment list and thereafter make subsequent verification for international payments to be used in following trade or non-trade business: (1) import of materials and components used for processing goods for reexport upon presentation of processing contracts approved by foreign economic cooperation and trade authority; (2) import of duty-free goods within business scope of duty-free goods companies approved by State Council; (3) international through-transport charges, equipment maintenance and repairing fees, station and harbor use fees, fuel supply fees, insurance fees, nonfinancing leasing fees and other service commissions to be paid abroad by civil aviation, shipping and railway transport entities; (4) foods and other allowance paid to personnel engaging in international operations by civil aviation, shipping and railway transport entities; and (5) international postage and telecommunication fees paid by posts and telecommunications organizations. (Art. 9).

Payment.—Should entity have foreign exchange account, it must first use its balance in foreign exchange account to make payment; should balance be insufficient or if there is no foreign exchange account, it may purchase foreign exchange from authorized banks. (Art. 18). All payments must be made according to date specified in contract or settlement method and any payments abroad in advance are not permitted. (Art. 20). Where principal and interests of foreign debt requires repayment in advance, approval should be obtained from Foreign Exchange Control Administration. (Art 21.).

CURTESY:

This institution is unknown in law of China.

CUSTOMS (DUTY):

General Administration of Customs, directly under highest administrative organ, State Council has approximately 93 branches in China. All cargo and vessels must pass through Customs and be released by Customs when entering or existing from China. Foreign trade organs issue import and export licenses against which Customs officials check cargo. Customs officials also check for damage to cargo. Cargo can be examined either at warehouses, wharves and the like under Customs control, or at ultimate destination of cargo if Customs so permits. In addition, Customs officials have responsibility for preventing smuggling or illegal transportation of precious metals and foreign currency. (See topic Currency). Customs officials have authority to confiscate goods that are brought into China illicitly, to impose fines, not exceeding value of said goods, and/or send offender to judicial authorities for punishment.

Customs Law was passed at 19th Session of Standing Committee of Sixth National People's Congress on Jan. 22, 1987 and became effective as of July 1, 1987.

Customs Department of China shall be state organization responsible for supervision and control over everything entering and leaving territory. Customs Department shall, in accordance with this law and other related laws and regulations, exercise supervision and control over transport, goods, travellers, luggage, postal items and other articles entering or leaving territory, collect customs duties, and other taxes and fees, uncover and suppress smuggling, work out customs statistics and handle other customs operations. (Art. 2).

State Council must set up General Customs Administration which must exercise unified administration of customs establishment throughout country. State must set up Customs Office at ports open to foreign countries and regions and at place with concentrated customs operations of supervision and control. Subordination of one customs establishment to another must not be restricted by administrative divisions. (Art. 3).

All import and export of goods and articles by any means of transportation must pass through Customs Office. (Art. 5).

All imported and exported goods must have declared value and duties must be paid by declaration enterprise registered with customs or by enterprise entitled to engage in import and export business. (Art. 6).

Inward and Outward Means of Transport.—When means of transport arrives at or departs from customs, person in charge of that means of transport must make truthful declaration to Customs Office, submit relevant papers for examination and accept customs control and examination. (Art. 8).

Inward means of transport from countries or regions outside territory or outward means of transport of units or enterprises within territory shall not be transferred or devoted to other uses prior to completion of customs formalities and payment of customs duties. (Art. 13).

Inward and Outward Goods.—Consignee for import goods and consignor for export goods must make accurate declaration and submit import or export license and relevant paper to customs for examination. In absence of import or export license, goods whose importation or exportation is restricted by State must not be released. Declaration of import goods must be made to Customs Office by consignee within 14 days of declaration of arrival of means of transport, declaration of export goods must be made by consignor 24 hours prior to loading. (Art. 18).

Inward and Outward Article.—All inward and outward articles must be accurately reported to Customs Office by owner and must be subjected to customs examination. (Art. 29).

Customs duties must be levied according to import and export tariff on goods permitted to be imported and exported and articles permitted to enter and leave territory. (Art. 35).

Consignee of Import Goods.—Consignor of exporter and owner of inward and outward articles must be declared on required customs duty paper. (Art. 36).

Duty-paying value of import item must be its normal CIF price. Approved by customs, duty-paying value of export items must be its normal FOB price, approved by customs, minus export duty. (Art. 38).

Duty reduction or exemption must be granted for following list: (1) adverstising items and trade samples of no commercial value; (2) material presented free of charge by foreign government and international organizations; (3) goods to which damage or loss has occurred prior to customs release; (4) article of quantity or value within fixed limit; (5) other goods and articles specified by law as items for duty reduction or exemption; (6) goods and articles specified as items for duty reduction or exemption by internationl treaties to which China is either contracting or acceding party. (Art. 39).

Duty reduction or exemption may be granted for imports and exported goods of SEZ and other specially designated areas; specific enterprises, such as Chinese-foreign equity joint ventures, Chinese-foreign contractual joint venture and wholly foreign-owned enterprise; goods devoted to specific purposes; and material donated for use for public welfare undertaking. (Art. 40).

Where obligatory customs duty payer is involved in dispute over duty payment with customs, he must first pay duties and may, within 30 days of issuance of duty memorandum, apply to customs in writing for reconsideration of case. Customs must reach decision within 15 days of receipt of application. If payer refuses to accept decision, he may apply to General Customs Administration for consideration of case within 15 days of receipt of decision. If payer does not accept decision of General Customs Administration, he may file suit in People's Court within 15 days of receipt of decision. (Art. 46).

Tonnage dues on foreign vessels, Chinese vessels under foreign charter and Chinese or foreign vessels chartered by joint foreign-Chinese corporations and calling at Chinese ports are levied by Customs officials under Provisional Rules Governing Levying of Tonnage Dues of Customs, approved by Financial and Economic Committee of Government Administrative Council on Sept. 16, 1952, effective as of Sept. 29, 1952. Vehicle and shipping license fees are not required. Tonnage fees vary with tonnage from, e.g., ¥0.30 per ton for under 50 tons to ¥1.80 per ton for tonnage above 5,001 tons for motor-vessels including steamers and tugs. Said fee are for three-month periods. (Art. 2). Thirty day tonnage dues are at half this rate. (Arts. 2, 3). Tonnage certificates must be produced when applying to enter ports, as must certificates of nationality of vessel. (Art. 4). Certain vessels used by diplomatic missions, entering solely for purpose of shelter or repair, vessels under charter to central or local people's government and vessels exempt by Art. 27 of Provisional Customs Laws, are exempt from tonnage dues. (Art. 11).

Civil aircraft are governed by certain Customs rules promulgated by Ministry of Foreign Trade on Oct. 1, 1974 entitled "Rules Governing the Supervision and Control of International Civil Aircraft by the Customs Agency". Term "international civil aircraft" is defined to include any civil aircraft entering or leaving Chinese territory while engaged in international air traffic, except any special plane carrying heads of state or other governmental leaders. (Art. 2). Said aircraft must notify Customs two hours prior to landing or take-off. (Art. 3). Loading and discharging of cargo, mail, luggage, etc., and embarking or disembarking of passengers all require permission, supervision and control of Customs authorities. (Art. 4). Pilot must present passenger and cargo manifest and crew list to Customs (Art. 5), including crew's list of personal effects, currencies and gold and silver (Arts. 5, 6) upon landing or take-off. International aircraft are subject to Customs inspection. (Art. 9). Passengers, their luggage and articles entering or leaving China, must first pass through Chinese formalities (Art. 11) as must crew members (Arts. 17, 18, 19). Customs also has authority to examine and seal fuel, oil, spare parts, equipment, stores, gold and silver, foreign currencies and other articles on board aircraft. (Art. 20).

Goods for exhibitions are governed by Rules Governing Supervision and Control of Importation of Goods for Exhibitions by Customs, promulgated by Ministry of Foreign Trade on Nov. 3, 1975. Under said rules organization responsible for reception of incoming foreign exhibitions shall present copies of authorizing documents to Customs. (Art. 3). Customs formalities must be adhered to, but said goods are essentially exempt from customs duties, except for those sold in China, for which foreign trade control organs must grant import license and duties must be paid. (Art. 15).

Import duties on passenger baggage are governed by Rules Governing Levying of Import Duty on Articles in Passengers' Baggage and Personal Postal Parcels approved by State Council on June 16, 1978 and promulgated by Ministry of Foreign Trade on Aug. 1, 1978. These rules provide for ad valorem duties, assessed on c.i.f. value, or where not ascertainable, domestic price (Art. 5), and run as high as 100% on foodstuffs, beverages, clothing made of cotton or linen, radio sets and record players (Art. 3). Wristwatches, tobacco, wine, spirits, and cosmetics are taxed at 200%. (Art. 3). Appeals as to levy can only be made after paying duty. (Art. 6). Passengers entering China as tourists or for brief visits are not subject to these levies pursuant to regulations, unless they are carrying unusually large quantity of items beyond what appears to be normal personal usage. See Provisional Customs Regulations for Supervision and Control over Baggage and Articles Accompanying Incoming and Outgoing Overseas Chinese and Other Passengers, promulgated by Ministry of Foreign Trade on Apr. 5, 1978. See also Customs Guide for Passengers Entering and Leaving China, which provides that articles and baggage carried by incoming passengers, in reasonable quantities for personal use, shall be released duty free, but there are limits on certain articles, e.g. wristwatches, bicycles and radios, which are to be limited normally to one per person.

Regulations Governing Import and Export Tariff of China was promulgated by State Council on 7 Mar., 1985, amended and promulgated by State Council on 12 Sept., 1987. Second amendment was promulgated by State Council on 18 Mar., 1992.

All goods are permitted to import or export through Customs Office but shall be subject to levy of customs duties on imports and exports according to "Customs

See Topical Index in front part of this volume.

CUSTOMS (DUTY) . . . *continued*
Import and Export Tariff" of China. Goods which were originally produced or manufactured in China but were purchased out of customs territory and then imported shall be subject to levy of import duty according to "Customs Import and Export Tariff". (Art. 2).

Tariff Commission established by State Council is responsible for formulating guidelines, policies and principles for drafting and/or amending "Regulations on Import and Export Duties" and "Customs Import and Export Tariff" to examine draft of amendments of Tariff, to set temporary tariff rate and to examine and to approve partial adjustment of tariff rate. (Art. 3).

Both consignee of imports and consignor of exports are persons obligated to pay customs duty. (Art. 4).

Tariff rates on imports fall in two categories: general tariff rate and minimum tariff rates. General tariff rate shall apply to imports originating in countries with which China has not concluded any trade treaties or agreements with reciprocal favorable tariff clauses therein. Minimum tariff rates shall apply to imports originating in countries with which China has concluded trade treaties or agreements with reciprocal favorable clauses therein. Special duty may be imposed on goods imported from any country or region which imposes discriminating duty or other forms of discriminating treatment in respect to imported goods originating in China. (Art. 6).

Import and export of goods shall be classified under appropriate heading or subheading in light of Interpretation Rules set forth in "Customs Import and Export Tariff" and, for purpose of taxation, tariff rates applicable shall be applied accordingly. (Art. 7).

Duty-paying value of goods to be imported shall be assessed according to CIF price based on normal transaction value as verified by Customs Office. (Art. 10).

Duty-paying value of goods to be imported for sale shall be identical with FOB price of goods with export duties deducted. (Art. 16).

Consignee or consignor or his agent shall pay customs duties at designated bank within seven days (excluding Sun. and national holidays) after day of issuance of duty memorandum by customs. In case of any payment in arrears, 1% of total amount of overdue customs duties shall be charged as fee on delayed payment per day from eighth day to date of fulfillment of payment. (Art. 22).

Duty-paying value of imported goods shall include payments for charges and fees made to parties out of customs territory in regards to patents, copyrights, know-how, computer software and information relative to goods imported for purpose of their production, use, publication or circulation in customs territory. (Art. 15).

Customs duties shall be reduced or exempted on goods and articles in accordance with relevant provisions of international treaties, to which China is contracting or accepted party. (Art. 29).

See also topic Trade Zones.

Import and Export Commodity Inspection.—China's State Council has established Administration for Import and Export Commodity Inspection, which performs inspection of import and export commodities throughout country in accordance with Law of China on Import and Export Commodity Inspection, adopted at sixth session of Standing Committee of Seventh National People's Congress on Feb. 21, 1989, and effective as of Aug. 1, 1989.

State Administration for Import and Export Commodity Inspection (SAIECI) must formulate, adjust and publish list of Import and Export Commodities subject to inspection by Commodity Inspection Authorities (hereinafter List of Commodities). (Art. 4). Inspection of imports and exports by Commodity Inspection Authorities covers: (1) inspection of import and export commodities included in list of commodities; (2) hygiene inspection of foods for exports; (3) testing and inspection of performance and use of packages and containers for dangerous export goods; (4) cargo worthiness inspection on such means of transportation as vessels, holds and containers for carrying perishable foods and frozen goods for exports; (5) inspection of imports and exports to be contacted by Commodity Inspection Authorities according to relevant international treaties; etc.

No permission will be granted for sale or use of import commodities specified in List of Commodities until they have undergone inspection; and no permission will be granted for export of commodities specified in List of Commodities until they have been found to be up-to-standard through inspection. (Art. 5). Inspection of import and export commodities must cover quality, weight, packing and requirements for safety and hygiene. Import and export commodities governed by compulsory standards or other inspection standards which must be complied with as provided for by laws or administrative rules and regulations must be inspected in accordance with such inspection standards. In absence of such stipulations, import and export commodities must be inspected in accordance with inspection standards agreed upon in foreign trade contracts.

Inspection of Import Commodities.—For import commodities which are subject to inspection, consignee must register them with Commodity Inspection Authorities located at port of discharge or station of arrival. Import commodities which are included in List of Commodities must be checked and released by customs upon presentation of seal of Commodity Inspection Authorities affixed to customs declaration. (Art. 9). Consignee must apply to same authorities for inspection in places and within time limit specified by them. Commodity Inspection Authorities must accomplish procedure for inspection and issue inspection certificate within period of validity of claim prescribed in foreign trade contract. (Art. 10).

Inspection of Export Commodities.—For export commodities which are subject to inspection by Commodity Inspection Authorities, consignor must apply to same authorities for inspection in places and within time specified by them. Commodity Inspection Authorities must accomplish procedure for inspection and issue certificate without delaying prescribed time for shipment. Export commodities which are included in list of commodities must be checked and released by customs upon presentation of seal of same authorities affixed to customs declaration. (Art. 13). Export commodities which have been inspected and passed and for which inspection certificate or paper for release has been issued must be declared for export and shipped out of country within time limit specified by Commodity Inspection Authorities. Failure to meet time limit will entail reapplication for inspection. (Art. 14).

DAMAGES:

See topics Arbitration and Award; Contracts; Environment; Shipping; Civil Code.

Concept of damages for breach of contract is known, understood and not infrequently explicated in Chinese contracts, including international contracts which may have penalty clauses or clauses that call for compensation for breach thereof. In addition, certain statutes provide for damages. Thus statute promulgated on Aug. 17, 1959 by Government Administrative Council entitled Provisional Regulations for Protection of Inventions, Patent Rights and Patents, provided in para. 3 of Art. 7 that those who do not obtain permission of patent holder, may not use invention, and those who violate this provision will according to law compensate patent holder for his loss. On Oct. 15, 1959 Ministry of Communications promulgated Several Rules Concerning Compensation for Loss at Sea, whereby negligent acts of ship employees resulting in loss require owners of said ocean vessels to make compensation; if cause of loss is carrier, however, then carrier should be responsible for compensation. Similarly, Art. 32 of trial Law on Environmental Protection provides that organizations or individuals who violate provisions of law may be called upon to make compensation for losses.

DECEDENTS' ESTATES:

See topics Descent and Distribution; Executors and Administrators; Civil Code.

DEEDS:

See topic Property.

Chinese use of official seals, individual seals and organizational seals on documents, including conveyances, is common, generally required as only effective means of making document, like conveyance, legally binding.

DEPOSITIONS:

See topic Criminal Law.

DESCENT AND DISTRIBUTION:

See topics Property; Civil Code.

Art. 9 of Constitution provides that state protects right of citizens to own lawfully earned income, savings, houses and other means of livelihood. Art. 18 of Marriage Law, as am'd on Sept. 10, 1980, provides that husband and wife have right to inherit each other's property, and that parents and children have right to inherit each other's property. In addition, there have been other statutes that mention inheritance. For example, Provisional Regulations for Protection of Patent Rights and Patents of 1950 (Art. 6, para. 2), states that if one inherits patent rights and thereby is entitled to awards, then these awards shall be given to those so inheriting. State Council notified Ministry of Justice on Mar. 29, 1958 that, with regard to private property of members of agricultural cooperatives who die, if they have wills property passes pursuant to will and if not, property becomes that of cooperative. Thus, there are two means of inheritance by law in China, intestate succession and by will.

Inheritance Law was passed by People's Congress on Apr. 10, 1985 effective as of Oct. 1, 1985. Supreme Court Opinion on Several Problems of the Inheritance Law, issued on 11 Sept., 1985 deals with statute (hereafter "Opinion").

Property that citizens may inherit includes real property (houses, buildings), household articles, funds, woods, animal husbandry, poultry, art objects, books, tools for production, rights to authorship, economic benefit of patents, and other lawful property (Art. 3), including securities, evidence of debt (Opinion Art. 3).

Inheritance can be by will or bequest or by intestate succession. (Art. 5). One can lose ones right to any bequest by intentional murder of person from when he is to inherit; in disputed inheritance matter to murder one of contesting parties; abandonment of testator or intestate, serious mistreatment of testator; serious forging, alteration or destruction of will. (Art. 7).

Statute of limitations for disputes concerning matters of inheritance are two years from time party knew or should have known of infringement of his rights but in any case not more than 20 years from occurrence of event of inheritance. (Art. 8). Male and female have equal rights to inherit (Art. 9); order of interstate succession is: First order: spouse, children, parents; second order: brothers, sisters, grandparents. If those in first order inherit then no one in second order will inherit. Children are defined to include those born in and out of wedlock and adopted children and stepchildren reared by parent. (Art. 9). Similarly, parents are defined to include natal parents and parents who adopted child and steparents who reared child. Brothers and sisters are defined to include full and half brothers and sisters, those related by adoption, and stepbrothers and sisters. (Art. 9).

Persons who have special difficulties or lack ability to labor, should be specially considered in allocating heritable property. (Art. 13). Normally, however, those of same order of inheritance, inherit equally. Those who assisted in rearing party whose property is being distributed or resided with him can receive larger portion of property.

Formalities of will include one testator himself wrote, which should be signed and dated; if prepared by others, two or more witnesses must attest to will, all of whom together with scriviner and testator must sign will. Oral wills which also require at least two witnesses are permitted in times testator is in danger. (Art. 17). Those to whom bequest is directed cannot be witnesses. (Art. 18). Will should consider those lacking in ability to labor or who have no source of livelihood. (Art. 19).

Many problems of inheritance are obviated by Chinese social practice. There is quite often division of household property that takes place while parents are yet alive. If there is one son with whom parents reside, who has not separated and divided his share of family property, then home in which he resides will, on death of both parents devolve upon said son. Daughters who marry out of family household, having equal rights to inherit with brothers who remain at home, may waive said rights. In final analysis distribution of estate pursuant either to intestacy or will depends in part upon law or will and, in part, upon social and economic facts relevant to intestate or testator and heirs.

If foreign matters of inheritance are involved, then matters of personal property will be determined by law of domicile of decedent or law of his last residence. (Opinion Art. 63).

See Topical Index in front part of this volume.

DISPUTE RESOLUTION:

Various means of dispute resolution exist in China; there are forms of mediation, both institutionalized mediation and that carried on by Courts and the like. Arbitration and adjudication are well utilized means of dispute resolution.

DISSOLUTION OF MARRIAGE:

See topic Divorce.

DIVORCE:

See topic Civil Code.

Marriage Law as am'd on Sept. 10, 1980 specifies that divorce is granted when husband and wife both desire it. (Art. 24). Application can be made for dissolution at marriage registration office, which has responsibility of determining that divorce is desired by both parties, and that appropriate measures have been taken for care of children and disposition of property. (Art. 24). Upon ascertaining these facts, divorce certificate should be issued without delay. (Art. 24).

If only one party insists upon divorce, relevant government agency may try to effect reconciliation between parties. Party can directly petition court for divorce, and court should try to reconcile parties. (Art. 25). In cases of complete alienation of mutual affection, and when mediation has failed, divorce should be granted. (Art. 25). If spouse of member of armed services insists on divorce, consent must be obtained from member of armed services. (Art. 26).

Husband may not apply for divorce when his wife is pregnant or within one year after birth of child, unless court deems it absolutely necessary to agree to deal with said divorce application by husband. (Art. 27). Wife may apply for divorce at any time. (Art. 27). Both parties can remarry each other after divorce. (Art. 28).

After divorce, irrespective of which party has custody of children, they remain children of both parties (Art. 29) and both parents have right and duty to rear and educate their children (Art. 29). Guiding principle, in determining custody on divorce, is to give mother custody of breast-fed infant until weaning. (Art. 29). After weaning if there is custody dispute, then court should decide in accordance with rights and interest of child and circumstances of both parties. (Art. 29). Parties, where one has custody, and other is responsible for all or part of necessary cost of education and maintenance, should agree as to amount of cost and duration of payment. Failing such agreement court should make decision on these matters. (Art. 30). Despite agreement, or court judgment, child can make reasonable request, where necessary, for either parent to increase amount decided upon. (Art. 30).

In case of divorce, disposition of joint property, where parties fail to agree, should be determined by court, taking into consideration actual state of family property and rights and interests of wife and children. (Art. 31). Debts incurred jointly during marriage should be paid out of this joint property, and where said property is insufficient, and parties fail to agree, court should make judgment as to how joint debts should be paid. (Art. 32). Separate debts incurred by parties should be paid by responsible party. (Art. 32).

If either party to divorce has difficulty in maintaining self, then other party should render appropriate financial assistance (Art. 33), and if they fail to agree then court should make determination as to said maintenance (Art. 33). Where party refuses to pay maintenance, costs of rearing or support, pursuant to court orders, or fails to carry out orders regarding division of property, court has power to enforce its orders and organizations concerned have duty to assist such execution. (Art. 35). Persons violating Marriage Law can be subject to administrative disciplinary sanctions or legal sanctions according to law, depending upon particular circumstances. (Art. 34).

1982 census samples showed only 0.59% of divorcees remained single in Chinese population over age 15; 63.67% of population had spouses; 7.18% widows and widowers.

Supreme Court (on Nov. 11, 1989) issued concrete opinion on how to decide complete alienation of mutual affection. According to said opinion, divorce should be granted, if husband and wife live apart for three years because of alienation of mutual affection and it is found impossible to resume affection, or live apart for one year after divorce is not granted by court and do not carry out duties of husband and wife.

DOWER:

This institution is unknown in contemporary Chinese law.

ENVIRONMENT:

See topics Joint Stock Companies; Trade Zones.

Constitution provides that state protects and improves environment, ecology, prevents and eliminates pollution and other hazards to public. State organizes and encourages people to grow and protect forests. (Const. Art. 26). Also provides that state protects places of scenic or historical interest and cultural relics, etc. (Const. Art. 22).

China has promulgated series of regulations on environmental protection since 1979, such as Standing Committee of Fifth National People's Congress' adoption, pursuant to Art. 11, of Environmental Protection Law for Trial Implementation in 1979, Marine Environmental Protection Law in 1982, Law on the Prevention and Control of Water Pollution in 1984, Law on the Prevention and Control of Air Pollution in 1987, Regulations for the Prevention of Pollution of Sea Areas by Ships in 1983, Regulations for the Management and Protection of Environment for the Exploration and Exploitation of Offshore Petroleum in 1983, Regulations on the Prevention and Control of Noise Pollution in 1989, Law on Water and Soil Conservation in 1991.

On Dec. 26, 1989, 11th Session of Standing Committee of Seventh National People's Congress of China adopted revised Environment Protection Law. This law is applicable within China and sea areas under jurisdiction of China. (Art. 3). Term "environment" is broadly defined by statute to include air, water oceans, and mineral resources, forests, grasslands, wild organisms, natural historical remains, relics of civilization, natural preservation regions, scenic and historical spots, cities and rural village, etc. (Art. 2).

Administrative department of State Council in charge of environmental protection shall implement unified supervision and administration of environmental protection work in entire nation. (Art. 7).

Administrative department of State Council in charge of environmental protection shall formulate state quality standards for environment. (Art. 9).

Administrative department of State Council in charge of environmental protection will formulate state standards for discharge of pollutants in accordance with state environmental quality standard and economic and technological conditions of state. (Art. 10).

In construction of projects that pollute environment, contractor must comply with state provisions concerning administration of environmental protection for construction projects.

Environmental impact report for construction projects must make appraisal of pollutants and effects on environment by construction project, and formulate measures for prevention and control, and, after advance review by department in charge of project and in accordance with stipulated procedures, shall be submitted to administrative departments in charge of environmental protection for approval. Planning departments may only approve design task report of construction projects after approval of environmental impact report. (Art. 13).

Units that engender environmental pollution and other forms of pollution must incorporate environmental protection work into their plans, establish responsibility system for environmental protection, and adopt effective measures to prevent and control pollution and harm to environment by waste gas, waste water, waste residue, dust, foul-smelling gases and radioactive materials, as well as noise, vibration and electromagnetic radiation engendered in course of production and construction or other activities. (Art. 24).

Pollution prevention and control facilities in construction projects must be designed, constructed and their use started up at same time as principal project. Pollution prevention and control facilities must have been inspected and found qualifying by original administrative department in charge of environmental protection that examined and approved environmental impact report before such construction projects may start up production or use. (Art. 26).

Administrative departments in charge of environmental protection or other departments that exercise administrative authority for environmental supervision in accordance with provisions of law shall impose fines on enterprises and institutions that cause environmental pollution in violation of provisions of this Law in accordance with harmful consequences caused; when circumstances are relatively serious, administrative sanctions shall be imposed on relevant responsible personnel by their units or government authorities in charge. (Art. 38).

When international treaties concerning environmental protection concluded or joined by China have different provisions from laws of China, provisions of international treaties shall apply, with exception of articles to which China has expressed reservation. (Art. 46).

Industrial Wastes and Pollutants.—Pursuant to National Standard GBJ4-73, effective Jan. 1, 1974, amended 1984, 1987, trial standards enacted for release of three industrial wastes, which standards designed to prevent pollution caused by industrial gas, water and water residues. (Art. 1). All factories, mines and other enterprises required to diminish or eliminate these three pollutants. Industrial noxious water and gas which cannot be re-used must proceed to purification and recovery treatment pursuant to national standards of release. (Art. 3). All plans for new construction, expansions or reconstruction projects for factories, mines or other enterprises must incorporate purification installations for three waste products. Such installations must meet national standards and be put into operation concurrently with primary project. Existing factories, mines and other enterprises causing pollution must provide plan of elimination of said pollution within approximately five years, depending on severity of pollution. (Art. 4). All relevant industrial departments required, pursuant to standards of these draft regulations, to lay down design criteria for enterprises and administrative norms for consumption of raw materials and fuels, as well as water to be discharged. (Art. 5).

Environmental monitoring organizations in all areas must assist factories, mines and enterprises in monitoring release of three waste products and are responsible for enforcement of standards. (Art. 6). Regulations on radioactive protection provide standards for discharge of radioactive three waste products. (Art. 7). Local environmental protection agencies must, together with other local organizations, formulate local standard s for discharge of these three industrial wastes in accordance with principles of these standards and said local regulations must be submitted to province, etc.

Standards provide specific criteria for discharge of noxious substances. Thus, for example, following industrial gases covered by Art. 10 of regulations: Sulphur dioxide, carbon disulphide, hydrogen sulphide, fluoride converted into F, nitrogen oxide converted into NO2, Chlorine, Chlorine Hydride, Carbon Monoxide, sulphuric acid, lead, mercury, Beryllium compound converted into Beryllium, dust and powder dust. In each case, different types of industry are provided with standards for releasing these noxious substances. Thus, for example, in discharging sulphur dioxide powder, metallurgical and chemical engineering plants, depending on kg. per hour discharge, are provided with specified stack heights for discharge pipes. For example, power plant discharging 1,200 kg. of sulphur dioxide per hour must have discharge stack of 100 meters, while chemical engineering enterprise discharging 280 kg. per hour of sulphur dioxide must have discharge stack of 100 meters. (Art. 10).

Industrial waste water may not pollute sources of drinking water and water at scenic sightseeing locations. (Art. 11). Fishery and agricultural water must be designed to maintain lives of animals and plants and prevent toxic remains beyond edible standard from remaining in their bodies. (Art. 11). Two classes of industrial waste water, first class being those noxious substances that accumulate in environment of bodies of animals and plants and have long term deleterious influence on human health. (Art. 12). For example, law permits maximum concentration for discharge of .05 mg. per litre of discharge of mercury and mercury's inorganic compounds, and 1 mg. per litre of lead and its compounds.

With regard to second class industrial waste water, following examples of certain maximal concentration standards for discharge: Cyanide 0.5 mg. per litre, Organic Phosphorous 0.5 mg. per litre, Petroleum 10 mg. per litre. Industrial water may not drain into any public health protection zones of source of drinking water in any town or city or scenic sightseeing location. (Art. 13). To safeguard subsoil water resources

ENVIRONMENT . . . *continued*
against pollution, drainage of noxious industrial waste water by penetrating pit, penetrating well, or slow-flow methods is prohibited. (Art. 13). Ministry of Agriculture and Forestry responsible for setting standards for waste water used to irrigate farms. (Art. 15). Waste residues which contain soluble poisons such as cadmium, arsenic, mercury, lead, cyanide, yellow phosphorous, etc. must have waterproof and leakproof measures to prevent them from being discharged into surface waters, and may not be buried in ground.

In addition to national regulations, provincial and local regulations have been enacted. Thus, for example, Guangdong province has promulgated provincial regulations governing elimination of smoke and dust, which provide that Environmental Protection Bureau of province has authority to interpret these regulations. (Art. 14). Bureau has right to issue warnings and critical circulars, order compensation for damage, impose fines and in serious cases, propose disciplining of leaders of offending departments or complain to relevant judicial organizations. (Art. 14). Bureau can issue orders halting production and orders requiring elimination of pollution and during period prior to actual elimination, order that those in charge of eliminating smoke and dust in offending organization receive reduced wages as penalty. (Art. 14). Regulations provide that discharge of smoke, dust, sulphur dioxide and other noxious substances must not exceed limitations provided in rules on three waste products. (Art. 1).

Standards for Discharge from Boilers and Kilns.—Shade of smoke discharge classified into five grades and law prohibits normal discharge of smoke thicker than first grade, or intermittent and shorter discharge of smoke thicker than second grade. (Art. 1). New construction, reconstruction or extensions of furnaces and kilns must be designed to eliminate smoke and dust and be operational at completion of main project or construction and production will be prohibited. (Art. 2). Newly produced boilers must also have installations qualified to eliminate smoke and dust or their sale will be prohibited. Existing furnaces and kilns should be technically reformed according to local conditions in accordance with following standards: (1) Small boilers with evaporation volume of no more than one ton per hour must proceed to reformation by integration of simple reforms, burning of natural gas and dust elimination; (2) boilers having evaporation volume of more than one ton per hour must gradually replace manual coal feeding operations with mechanical burning operations and installation of dust eliminator; (3) large capacity boilers, such as pulverized fuel boilers, etc. must have high efficiency eliminator installation for smoke and dust and if wet process is adopted, waste water produced from this method must proceed to treatment and coal ash utilized; (4) metallurgical furnaces, furnaces or kilns for porcelain clay and heating furnaces must be provided with means to eliminate dust, and oil furnaces must adopt fuel injector operations and mechanized, automatic operations. (Art. 5).

Non-polluting or less polluting energy sources such as natural gas, liquefied gas, methane gas, solar energy and geothermal energy must be developed and utilized. (Art. 6). Specific standards enacted providing for maximum allowable concentrations of harmful gases, vapors and dusts in factories, shops and dwellings and in surface waters, as of Apr. 1, 1963.

Enforcement.—Mar. 1981, State Council adopted decision "On Strengthening the Work of Environmental Protection in the Period of Economic Readjustment" which requires departments of environmental protection and capital construction to halt construction of any projects under way whose use of resources and energy is seriously wasteful, as well as projects that would cause serious pollution. Decision requires that environmental protection agencies pay particular attention to impact on environment of large water conservancy and water consumption projects before construction commences.

Tentative Regulations on Charging Beijing's Units Discharging Waste Water provide that all units discharging water containing poisonous substances will be fined according to type and consistency of noxious substance, from five fen to six yuan per cu. mtr. of waste water. Those units continuing to discharge waste water containing noxious substances in excess of state standards after Jan. 1, 1983 will be fined additional 30% per year. Double fines will be levied for all discharge of waste water through seepage pits or wells, which is banned. In addition, Tentative Regulations on Management of Boilers and Kilns provide that units whose boilers or kilns emit soot and smoke at density exceeding 200 mg. per cu. mtr. will be fined 2.5% to 10% of their fuel fees, and units producing or selling boilers or kilns without pollution withdrawal items will be fined 10% of price of boilers or kilns.

People's Government in Shandung province, June 1980, issued Tentative Regulations on Collecting Fines from Enterprises and Establishments Discharging Harmful Waste Water. As of Jan. 1981, 4,430,000 yuan have been collected from 164 enterprises. Throughout nation, more than 1,500 industrial enterprises fined for effuent discharge in excess of permitted levels by Jan. 1981, and by May, 1981 nearly 10,000 enterprises fined for pollution. Numerous plants threatened with shutdowns; at Dongfang Chemical Works in Beijing's eastern suburbs, construction work terminated due to danger to ground water, although construction had begun and contracts signed with foreign firms.

Seas and Oceans.—On Aug. 23, 1982 Standing Committee of State Council promulgated Law of Environmental Protection of the Seas and Oceans.

Jurisdiction.—This law, effective Mar. 1, 1983 (Art. 48), covers all sea waters under jurisdiction of China, including inland seas and territorial waters (Art. 2), and covers virtually all activities of shipping, underwater and aviation apparatus, platforms, including scientific research, production, exploration, development, navigation, and any other activities of commercial and noncommercial enterprises and individuals (Art. 2). Sea waters outside jurisdiction of China, where there is discharge of noxious substances, or dumping of discarded materials that damage seas under Chinese jurisdiction are covered by this statute. (Art. 2).

Duties and Responsibilities.—All units and individuals entering sea waters within Chinese jurisdiction have responsibility to protect environment of these oceans, and have duty to control their actions and report offenses to authorities. (Art. 3).

Governmental Jurisdiction.—Provincial level governments bordering on ocean can, with State Council approval, establish special protected and nationally protected ocean areas. Scenic tourist areas can also be established by said governments. (Art. 4).

Oil Exploration.—Enterprises or other responsible units involved in developing offshore oil projects should, in front of prepared written report of their planned assignment, submit written report on impact of said assignment on environment of oceans, including effective steps to prevent harmful pollution of ocean's environment. (Art. 10). This should be submitted to relevant environmental protection units of State Council for approval. (Art. 10). When offshore oil exploration or other ocean activity requires blasting operations, effective measures should be taken to protect fishery resources. (Art. 11). Oil used during development of oil exploration should be handled with enhanced care, in order to prevent leaks. Remaining oil and waste oil should be recovered, and it is not permissible to cast it out to sea. (Art. 12). Accumulated sewage and oily mixtures contained in offshore oil well drilling ships, and platforms and oil extraction platforms, cannot be directly discharged, but must first be processed and reclaimed, and then discharged. Oil content cannot exceed national standards. (Art. 13). When disposing in ocean of oil, accumulated industrial garbage or other industrial garbage, ships and platforms referred to in Art. 13 must not create pollutants in commercial fishing waters or shipping lanes. (Art. 14).

Pesticide Registration.—Pursuant to Environmental Protection Act regulations were promulgated, effective Oct. 1, 1982, requiring registration of all technical and formulated products of chemical pesticides and biological pesticides used to control plant diseases, insects, pests, weeds, and other harmful living beings in agriculture, forestry and animal husbandry. (Art. 2). Regulations prohibit production, distribution or use of pesticide without registration. (Art. 4). Even pesticides used for demonstration purposes must apply for temporary registration. (Art. 4[3]). In addition to providing samples for registration (Art. 6), regulations require four copies of information on toxicology, residues, effect upon environment, products standard, application technique, production technique and description of product (Art. 5). Pesticides produced by foreign companies must be registered before marketing (Art. 7), but information on techniques of production need not be provided. Registration requires certification by relevant authorized organizations of Ministries of Chemical Industry, Public Health, Urban and Rural Construction and Environmental Protection, Agriculture, Animal Husbandry and Fishery.

Ministry of Commerce may set packaging standards, and Evaluation Committee on Pesticide Registration shall make overall evaluation and certificate shall be issued by Ministry of Agriculture, Animal Husbandry and Fishery. (Art. 6).

Comprehensive program to reduce pollution and protect environment announced by Environmental Protection Bureau in Nov. 1982 so that by turn of century: Industrial dust pollution at 8.5 million tons (62% reduction), total sulphur dioxide discharge controlled at 23.5 million tons; over 80% factory water recycled; sewage treatment rate over 75%; utilization rate of industrial residue over 50%; forests enlarged to 20% of Chinese territory (now 12%); garbage and human faeces purified and utilized; soil erosion and desertification brought under control.

Forest protection provided by statute, National Forestry Law (1984), and Detailed Regulations for Carrying Out National Forestry Law (1986); including local regulations—e.g. Provincial Methods for Protection and Management of Forest Resources in Beijing Rural Areas, promulgated by Beijing Standing Committee Municipal People's Congress, effective Mar. 1, 1984. Regs. prohibit livestock grazing and fuel gathering in young forests, forests of special economic value, and those on hillsides set aside for natural propagation. Banned activities include timber felling, hunting, wasteland reclamation, excavating sand and earth, etc. Trees for personal use around dwellings, on spare land or hillsides are private property and can be inherited, though other trees property of state.

ESCHEAT:

See topic Descent and Distribution.

EXCHANGE CONTROLS:

See topic Currency.

EXECUTIONS:

Pursuant to Trade Agreement between U.S. and China certain foreign arbitral awards and judgments embodying said awards can be enforced in Chinese courts. See topic Arbitration and Award.

Legally effective decisions, judgments, orders, and conciliation agreements concerning property are to be executed by court of first instance. (Code of Civil Procedure). Courts having jurisdiction can also enforce arbitral awards. (Code of Civil Procedure, Art. 217). If property to be executed upon is outside jurisdiction of court, court where property is located can be entrusted with execution of said judgment, which should commence within 15 days of receipt of petition and should not be refused. (Code of Civil Procedure, Art. 210).

Marshall of court should undertake enforcement of judgment. Compulsory execution commences with service of process by marshall of document of execution. Record should be made of circumstances of execution and someone at location, etc. should sign or place his seal on said record, as witness thereto. (Art. 209). Where notarial offices have legal authority and undertake execution on behalf of creditors they may do so but if there is resistance to execution, application to basic level court can be made for enforcement of said document reflecting indebtedness. (Code of Civil Procedure, Art. 218). If both parties are natural persons they have one year in which to apply for execution, while if both parties are legal persons they have six months to apply for execution. Time for execution is calculated from last day of time limit specified in legal document upon whose provisions execution is sought. (Code of Civil Procedure, Art. 219).

Where courts determine to levy on savings deposits or on salary of one subject to execution, pursuant to civil judgment, organizations served with said levy must conform to its provisions. Court, in making such levy, should leave sufficient income or assets to provide individual and his family with essential living expenses. (Code of Civil Procedure, Art. 221).

Where courts distrain, confiscate, freeze or sell-off property of defendant pursuant to execution, they should not levy on essential tools needed by said person and his family for his livelihood. (Code of Civil Procedure, Art. 172).

Party upon whose property execution is to take place by sealing or distraint should be notified or adult of his family should be notified to appear at location of execution.

EXECUTIONS . . . *continued*
Their failure to appear will not delay execution. In addition work unit and basic governmental organization where property is located should also send representative to location. List of property executed upon must be made and one on location should sign or put his seal on list, and thereafter said list should be given to person upon whose property execution has taken place. (Code of Civil Procedure, Art. 173). Marshall should notify person whose property was distrained or sealed that he has specific time to meet legal obligations provided in court decision. When time expires property is to be turned over for sale. (Code of Civil Procedure, Art. 175).

If there is execution on realty (land or buildings), then person on whose property execution is to take place should be given notice, and if he fails to perform within that time marshall should use compulsory process to compel performance. (Code of Civil Procedure, Art. 172).

Tools needed for work and goods and income needed for essential livelihood of individual and his family are exempt from execution. Individual himself is also exempt.

EXECUTORS AND ADMINISTRATORS:

Testator may appoint executor of his estate by will, but if one dies intestate, then where necessary court will make disposition of estate pursuant to law. If will fails to name executor, court may appoint one. See topic Descent and Distribution.

EXPROPRIATION:

Constitution provides that state may in public interest requisition by purchase, or take over for use, land under conditions prescribed by law. (Const. Art. 10). In fact expropriation is not common means of obtaining land for state projects in China, since normally organization or individuals in lawful possession of land must be compensated for said land use, and often must be provided with acceptable alternative sites for their own use.

FACTORS:

No private commission merchants function publicly. State stores provide outlets for citizens' used items, particularly antiques, jewelry and precious metals.

FISHING ZONE:

In 1977 Chinese government announced that it intended to establish 200 nautical mile economic and fishing zone and Chinese authorities have gradually been working toward that goal, although they have yet to fully implement this policy. Chinese have given support to present Convention on Law of Sea and if said convention eventuates, that would naturally affect their policy toward this fishing and economic zone. Within South China sea Chinese lay claim to large area, including Paracel Islands and much of Spratly Archipelago, consisting of approximately 33 islands, etc. permanentaly above sea level, over area of 180,000 sq. km. Latter claim is disputed in part by Hanoi, and more recently by Philippines and Malaysia. China's basis for this claim is Chinese presence since Sung dynasty. Nevertheless, Chinese have done little to enforce their claim. Potential petroleum resources in shallow waters of this area make it source of potential dispute.

FOREIGN INVESTMENT:

See topic Foreign Trade.

FOREIGN TRADE:

See topics Advertising; Arbitration and Award; Contracts; Copyright; Corporations; Customs (Duty); Joint Stock Companies; Taxation; Trade Zones.

Foreign Trade Law was promulgated and adopted by National People's Congress on May 12, 1994, and became effective on July 1, 1994.

Significance.—As viewed from domestic perspective, for more than 40 years in China, foreign trade has been chiefly administered by direct administrative measures. This method was necessary for planned economy and was effective as China's foreign trade was then limited. However, after about 12 years of reform and opening up to other countries, enormous change has taken place in foreign trade. Imports and exports totaled US$195.72 billion in 1993, 172 times 1950 sum of US$1.135 billion and 9.5 times 1978 total of US$20.638 billion. China maintains trade ties with over 180 countries and regions. There are 180,000 Chinese enterprises across the country directly engaging in import and export operations. It is increasingly difficult for administrative measures to effectively regulate such emerging and large scale economic activities. Tremendous growth in trade has led China to increasingly sober understanding: to develope national economy it is necessary to put national economy, including foreign trade, onto correct legal track.

Opening up to other countries is fundamental State policy. Foreign trade accounted for merely 4.7% of GNP in 1978, only 10.8% in 1988 and as high as 38% in 1993. Further opening up will increasingly bring China's economy closer to world's economy. Most importantly, China will utilize generally accepted international practices such as GATT trade rules. As early as 1986, China applied for resumption of its contracting party status in GATT. Basic GATT requirement is unified and transparent trade system, which is inconceivable without Foreign Trade Law. Promulgation of Foreign Trade Law represents vital step in effort to link China's economy to world economy.

General Principles.—Foreign Trade Law is made to develop foreign trade, defend foreign trade order, and promote healthy development of socialist market economy. (Art. 1).

"Foreign trade" in this Law means import and export of goods and technologies, and trade in international services. (Art. 2).

State Council's competent Department of Foreign Economic Cooperation and Trade is in charge of whole country's foreign trade business. (Art. 3).

Principles of Chinese foreign trade are equality and mutual benefit. (Art. 5).

Foreign Trade Operator.—"Foreign trade operator" refers to legal persons or entities engaging in foreign trade according to law. (Art. 8).

Foreign trade operator shall meet following requirements and obtain license from department in charge of foreign economic cooperation and trade under State Council: (1) have its own name and organizational set-up; (2) have clearly defined scope of foreign trade business; (3) have site, funds and professional personnel necessary for carrying out foreign trade; (4) import and export business handled through agencies must reach prescribed merits or have necessary sources of goods for import or export; and (5) meet other conditions as required by other laws and regulations. (Art. 9).

Foreign-invested enterprises (hereinafter called "FIE") are exempted from aforesaid license when they import nonmanufactured goods for their own use, equipment, or raw or other materials needed for their own production, and export their own products. (Art. 9).

Establishment and business operation of international trade enterprises and organizations shall obey this Law and other relevant laws and shall administer other regulations. (Art. 10).

Foreign trade operators operate their businesses independently and are responsible for their own profits and losses. (Art. 11). While foreign trade operator engages in foreign trade business operation, he shall adhere to contracts, ensure commodity's quality, and perfect sold services. (Art. 12).

Entity without foreign trade license may entrust foreign trade operator as agent to handle ad hoc transactions within ad hoc scope of business. (Art. 13). Foreign trade operator acting as agent shall provide appropriate information to principal. (Art. 13). Principal and agent must enter into contract which defines rights and obligations of each party. (Art. 13).

Foreign trade operator shall submit related files and materials in foreign trade business operation to concerned department. Concerned department shall keep business operations secret. (Art. 14).

Import and Export of Goods and Technologies.—China allows free import and export of goods and technologies, unless otherwise provided by Law. (Art. 15).

China may restrict import or export of goods or technologies if: (1) necessary because of national security and public interest; (2) necessary to restrict export of because of deficient supply at home or domestic resource is in danger of being exhausted; (3) under restriction of import in importing country or region due to its limited market capacity; (4) necessary to restrict import of by State in order to protect smooth or accelerated development of particular industries at home; (5) agricultural, animal husbandry and fishery products in any form for which it is necessary to restrict import by State; (6) necessary to restrict import of by State in order to maintain certain international financial position or to ensure balance of international payment; or (7) necessary to restrict import and export of pursuant to international treaties or agreements signed or acceded to by China. (Art. 16).

China may bar import or export of goods or technologies which are: (1) dangerous to national security or public interest; (2) necessary to bar import of in order to protect life or health of people; (3) dangerous to ecological environment; or (4) necessary to restrict import of pursuant to international treaties signed or acceded to by China. (Art. 17).

Goods whose import or export is restricted must be subject to quota or license control. Technologies whose import or export is restricted shall be subject to license control. (Art. 19). Goods and technologies subject to quota or license control can be imported or exported only when approval is obtained from department in charge of foreign economic cooperation and trade or together with other concerned departments under State Council. (Art. 19). Import and export quotas must be allocated by department in charge of foreign economic cooperation and trade or together with other concerned departments under State Council within their authority on basis of principles of efficiency, justice, and open and fair competition. (Art. 20).

Cultural relics, wild animals, plants and their products, whose import or export are restricted or banned pursuant to laws and regulations, must be restricted or banned in import or export accordingly. (Art. 21).

International Services Trade.—China encourages progressive development of international services trade. (Art. 22). China grants market access or national treatment to other parties with whom China has jointly acceded or entered into international treaties and agreements. (Art. 23).

China may restrict international services trade due to following reasons: (1) safeguarding national security or public interest; (2) protection of ecological environment; (3) safeguarding smooth or accelerated development of particular services trade domestically; (4) ensuring national balance of international payments; or (5) other grounds as provided for by law. (Art. 24).

China must ban international services trade under any of following circumstances: (1) danger to national security or public interest; (2) inconsistentcy with international obligations undertaken by China; or (3) ban by other laws and regulations. (Art. 25).

State Council's competent Department of Foreign Economic Cooperation and Trade and concerned departments of State Council can manage international services trade pursuant to this Law and other applicable laws and relevant regulations. (Art. 26).

Foreign Trade Order.—Foreign trade must be undertaken in compliance with law under principle of fair competition. (Art. 27).

Following acts are strictly prohibited: (1) to forge, modify or trade certificates of origin and import/export licenses; (2) to infringe upon intellectual property rights protected by laws of China; (3) to expel competitors by resorting to unjustifiable means of competition; (4) to obtain export tax refund from State by deception; or (5) acts in violation of other laws and regulations. (Art. 27).

Foreign exchange must be appropriately cleared and used according to law. (Art. 28).

Should normal production of domestic goods be greatly harmed, or under great threat of harm due to increasing imports of similar kinds of goods, State may take any countermeasures to expel or mitigate such harm or threat of harm. (Art. 29).

Should well-established or fledgling industry at home be in substantial harm, or under threat of harm due to import of relevant goods under normal value, State may take any countermeasures to expel or mitigate such harm or threat of harm. (Art. 30).

Should well-established or fledgling industry at home be in substantial harm, or under threat of harm due to import of goods that are exported under certain kinds of subsidies of exporting country or region, State may take any countermeasures to expel or mitigate harm or threat of harm. (Art. 31).

FOREIGN TRADE . . . *continued*

Foreign Trade Promotion.—China will set up and improve special financial institutions to serve foreign trade, and establish foreign trade development fund and risk fund. (Art. 33).

China uses import and export credits, export drawbacks and other ways to develop foreign trade. (Art. 34).

China will employ various promotional measures to develop foreign trade including issuance of import/export credits and setting up of export refunds. Foreign trade operators may establish or participate in any import/export chamber of commerce lawfully established. (Art. 35).

Organization for Promotion of International Trade will develop contacts with overseas businesses, hold exhibitions, provide information and consulting services, and engage in other foreign trade promotional activities according to articles of association. (Art. 36).

China supports and promotes national autonomous regions and underdeveloped areas in order to develop foreign trade. (Art. 37).

Others.—Separate customs territory in People's Republic of China is not controlled by this Law. (Art. 43).

Trade Agreement of July 7, 1979 between U.S. and China expresses intent of contracting parties to expand trade primarily by contracts between companies. Said contracts are to be concluded on basis of commercial considerations and customary international trade practice. Each country must afford other most-favored-nation treatment on products originating from other. Quantitative restriction on certain products applied by either contracting party shall be applied on equitable basis, with other countries so restricted. Parties expressed their intent to reciprocate satisfactory concessions with regard to tariff and non-tariff barriers to trade. Agreement declares intent of parties to promote visits by commercial persons, to support holding of fairs, exhibits and technical seminars, to permit and facilitate stationing of representatives or establishment of business offices by firms and corporations of party trading in other party's territory. Art. V of Trade Agreement provides that there are to be no restrictions, except in time of declared national emergency, on payments or transactions to be effected in freely convertible currencies mutually acceptable to parties executing contracts or otherwise agreed by parties. Industrial property rights including patents, trademark and copyright are to be protected.

Textile agreements were originally executed between China and U.S. on July 23 and 25, 1980 by exchange of letters, and Sept. 17, 1980 by executed Agreement. July exchange of letters proposed visa system for textiles, which Chinese accepted, for cotton, wool and man-made fiber textiles and textile products from China. Each commercial shipment of said products from China is to be accompanied by export visa issued by official of Chinese government. Said visa, stamped in blue ink on customs invoice Form 5515 or commercial invoice will have visa number and date. Agreement of July 23, 1980 reaffirmed Agreement on Trade Relations (Art. 1) which provided for three-year agreement from Jan. 1, 1980 through Dec. 31, 1982 (Art. 2) and provides for categories of goods (Art. 3 and Annex. A) with restrictions on exports from China to U.S. in certain categories (Art. 4 and Annex. B). There is provision for exceeding specific limits by stipulated percentage in any year provided said expansion is compensated for by equivalent decreases in one or other specific limit for that Agreement year. (Art. 5). China is to use its best efforts to space exports, within each category, evenly throughout year, taking into consideration normal seasonal factors. (Art. 6). If government of U.S. believes that imports from China in any category not covered by specific limits are, due to market disruption, threatening to impede orderly development of trade between two countries, then consultations, based on detailed factual statements for reason for same, may be requested by U.S. (Art. 8). Contracting parties agree to supply each other with data of imports and exports in categories for which levels have been established. (Art. 10). Annex. B contains specific limits on cotton gloves, knit shirts and blouses, non-knit blouses, trousers and sweaters. This Agreement successfully renegotiated in early Aug. 1983; and renegotiated again in 1990.

Investment guarantees was subject matter of Agreement between U.S. and China effected by Exchange of Notes signed in Beijing on Oct. 30, 1980, and related Letter and Statement signed in Beijing on Oct. 7, 1980. Agreement relates to investment insurance, including reinsurance, and investment guarantees administered by Overseas Private Investment Corporation (OPIC). Coverage for loss from political risks on any investment guarantee provided by OPIC for projects in China is subject matter of Agreement. (Art. 1). Agreement provides that insofar as OPIC makes payment to any American investor, Chinese government shall recognize said payment, and succession of OPIC to rights, title, claim and cause of action of said investor. (Art. 3[a]). While OPIC cannot assert right greater than investor, U.S. reserves right to assert claim in its sovereign capacity under international law. (Art. 3[b]). Government of China also agreed to make appropriate arrangements for another entity to succeed to rights of American investor if OPIC cannot pursuant to law acquire any interest in property in China. (Art. 4). Disputes under Agreement, not resolvable by negotiation shall be resolved by arbitration, where each government selects arbitrator and two arbitrators select third-country president of said tribunal. (Art. 6). Constitution permits foreign investment and economic cooperation by foreign persons pursuant to Chinese law, and protects these lawful foreign rights and interests. (Const. Art. 18).

In July, 1980 legislation authorizing OPIC operations in China was passed. On Aug. 8, 1980 President Carter determined that it was in national interest for OPIC to do business with China. Agreement of Oct. 30, 1980 provides final link in preliminary procedures necessary for OPIC to commence activity regarding China projects; thus, OPIC has now started its China activity. OPIC insurance, loan guarantees, direct loans, pre-investment assistance, construction insurance and insurance for contractors' guarantees are all theoretically available for China projects. In addition, Ex-Im Bank has full authority to institute its programs in China, but will only finally approve project after it has been approved by Bank of China. Treaty on investment protection still under discussion between U.S. and China although China has signed treaties on promotion and protection of investment with Sweden, Belgium, West Germany, Luxemburg and Romania.

Export Administrative Regulations in U.S. were am'd in May, 1980 creating new group category (Group P) for China, permitting more liberalized policy toward China than other non-market economies. On Sept. 12, 1980 U.S. Department of Commerce announced guidelines for export licenses to China for commodities and technical data controlled by Department for national security purposes. Department indicated willingness to approve cases for some military end-users, for example, if data or equipment could be used in design, development or manufacture of tactical military items, licenses may be approved. Nor would licenses be disapproved merely because equipment incorporates some advanced technology appropriate for end-use (see Office of Munitions Control Newsletter 81, Mar. 1980). On Nov. 23, 1983 China was removed from Country Group P to Group V under Export Administration Regulations, U.S. Department of Commerce emphasizing that sales to China should be on similar basis as most other friendly nations. On Dec. 27, 1985 export control regulations were further amended (50 FR 52900–01) to require end user's certificates from technology import-export department of MOFERT.

International Trade Commission (ITC) held public hearings in Apr. 1981 on issue of whether to grant China preferential tariffs under U.S. Generalized System of Preferences (GSP). Normally GSP status requires recipient to participate in General Agreement on Tariffs and Trade (GATT) which China, as of this writing, has yet to do. In addition, U.S. Trade Representative at ITC on July 1, 1981 was to advise it as to whether granting duty-free treatment of designated nonsensitive goods from China would harm domestic manufacturers and U.S. economy. U.S. Trade Representative in turn will advise President on what action he should take.

Foreign firm's activity in China is governed by Trade Agreement and applicable Chinese law. Upon receipt of visas issued by Chinese embassy in Washington, or any Chinese consulate, embassy or related institution elsewhere, representatives can proceed to China to negotiate, execute and carry out agreements. Permanent offices in China require application by foreign firms active within country. U.S. citizens in China for extended periods and companies having long-term representative offices are subject to Chinese tax laws.

Grain Agreement.—On Oct. 22, 1980 China and U.S. entered Agreement on Grain Trade whereby China agreed to purchase, and U.S. agreed to sell, at least 6,000,000 metric tons of wheat and corn annually over period Jan. 1, 1981 until Dec. 31, 1984 through normal private commercial organizations in accordance with normal commercial terms and prices then prevailing. Approximately 15-20% of purchase was corn. If China intends to buy more than 9,000,000 metric tons of wheat and corn it shall give prior notice to U.S. government. China has not renewed grain agreement to date but continues to purchase U.S. grain. Export enhancement subsidy program has been utilized by Chinese from time to time.

Atomic Energy.—On Jan. 1, 1984 China became member of International Atomic Energy Agency (IAEA) after admission by resolution adopted at 27th Conference of IAEA on 11 Oct. 1983 and depositing of acceptance of organization's statute with depository state, U.S. government. China's Agreement with U.S. on nuclear energy is entitled: "Agreement for Cooperation between the Government of the United States of America and the Government of the People's Republic of China concerning peaceful uses of Nuclear Energy" signed in Washington July 23, 1985 during Pres. Li Xiannian's visit to U.S.

Parties in preamble affirm their support for objectives of Statute of the International Atomic Energy Agency (IAEA), parties agree to cooperate in use of nuclear energy for peaceful purposes and agree that they may not invoke provisions of their domestic law as justification for failure to perform this treaty. (Art. 2[1]). Transfer of sensitive nuclear technology or facilities or major critical components require additional amendments to treaty. (Art. 2[4]).

Any special nuclear material to be transferred under this treaty is to be low enriched uranium (Art. 4[1]) except small quantities of special nuclear material may be transferred for use as samples, standards, detectors, targets, radiation sources, and for such other purposes as parties may agree (Art. 4[4]).

Parties agree that they have no plans to enrich to 20% or greater, to reprocess or alter in form or content material transferred pursuant to this treaty. (Art. 5[2]). Parties also agree that they have no plans to change location for storage of plutonium, uranium 233 (except as contained in irradiated fuel elements) or high enriched uranium transferred pursuant to this treaty or used in or produced through use of any material or facility transferred by this treaty. (Art. 5[2]). In event party changes its mind then parties will promptly hold consultations and agree to mutually acceptable arrangement. Such activities are to be solely for peaceful purposes.

Material, facilities or components transferred pursuant to this treaty or products thereof are not to be used for any nuclear explosive device, for research on or development of any nuclear explosive device or for any military purpose. (Art. 5[3]). Security is to be maintained as provided for in Annex II.

After ratification of this treaty U.S. is able to compete in sale of nuclear power plants to China from which it had been excluded in past.

Assessment of Foreign-Invested Property.—Regulations Governing Assessment of Foreign-Invested property was issued by State Administration of Import and Export Commodity Inspection and Ministry of Finance on Mar. 18, 1994, effective as of May 1, 1995, governing assessment of properties invested in or bought in China by foreign (including Hong Kong, Macao and Taiwan) companies, enterprises, economic entities, individuals (foreign businesses); foreign-invested enterprises in China; and foreign investors involved in compensatory trade or trustees of foreign-funded firms. (Art. 2). State Administration of Import and Export Commodity Inspection (SAIECI) is responsible for assessment of foreign-invested properties in China. Local branch of SAIECI is responsible for assessment of foreign-invested properties in locality. (Art. 3). Ministry of Finance is in charge of capital certification of foreign-invested properties in China and their related financial affairs. (Art. 4). Assessment of foreign-invested properties includes appraisal of variety, quality, quantity, value, and losses of properties invested in by foreign businesses. Assessment of variety, quality, and quantity involves check-ups on name, model, quality, quantity, specifications, trademark, condition, date of production, country of production and producer of such properties. (Art. 6). Local administrative organs of Import and Export Commodity Inspection issue property assessment certificates to investors after conclusion of property assessment. Certificates are effective documents certifying value of property invested by parties concerned. (Art. 7).

See Topical Index in front part of this volume.

FOREIGN TRADE . . . *continued*

Assessment of foreign-invested properties should adhere to principle of being authentic, fair, scientific and feasible. Assessment process should be in line with methods and standards stipulated by State, with proper regard to international conventions. (Art. 5). Assessment should be conducted in light of realistic conditions of such properties, time already used, functions, technical indicators, cost of replacement and profit earning capacity. (Art. 10). Assessment of foreign-invested properties should proceed in following order: (1) applicant files application for property assessment; (2) assessment agency conducts preliminary examination of relevant materials and accepts application; (3) appraiser compiles assessment program; (4) assessment agency examines papers and information provided by applicant and conducts related investigation of both home and overseas market; (5) assessment agency makes on-the-spot survey; (6) assessment agency chooses correct approach to conclude final assessment; and (7) assessment agency issues property assessment certificate to applicant. (Art. 15). When applicant files application for assessment of foreign-invested property, it should fill out application form, stating purpose, objects and requirements of such assessment, as well as submitting related property list, customs declarations, contracts, invoices, insurance policy, maintenance cost report, technical documents of related equipment and other relevant information. (Art. 16).

Military Embargo.—After 4 June 1989, Presidential Directive was issued embargoing sales of all military equipment to China and effectively terminating military cooperation between two countries, since then there has been some relaxation of this provision.

FOREIGN TRADE REGULATIONS:

See topic Foreign Trade.

FRAUDS, STATUTE OF:

Contracts may have to be notarially certified where title to buildings, or building rights are conveyed, and will have to be registered with local authorities. Normally all international commercial contracts are evidenced by writing as matter of practice.

FRAUDULENT SALES AND CONVEYANCES:

Sale concluded under influence of fraud is generally regarded by Chinese legal authorities as invalid, with wrongdoer being required to return what was received under contract. (See topics Contracts; Criminal Law; Civil Code.) Details of Chinese concepts of fraudulent sales will be further explicated in Civil Code when said draft is promulgated.

GARNISHMENT:

See topics Divorce; Civil Code.

In certain cases, such as marital disputes, Marriage Law calls for various means for enforcing payment of maintenance and child support, and requires cooperation of other agencies including, presumably, those paying spouse who is in arrears, his or her salary. Presumably under such circumstances said salary could be garnished. (See topic Criminal Law.) Courts also have power to tailor their judgments so as to garnish salary in civil and criminal cases.

Code of Civil Procedure (Arts. 222, 223) provides that if various forms of property do not meet debts of debtor, then salary of debtor can be garnished, but sufficient funds for essential livelihood of debtor and his family must be allowed debtor.

GUARANTY LAW:

General.—Guaranty Law was promulgated on June 30, 1995, effective as of Oct. 1, 1995, governing relationship between creditor and debtor where debtor or third party deposits something of value with creditor to assure fulfillment of obligation. Guaranty agreement and subsequent changes should be in writing with consent of all related parties, pursuant to principles of fairness and good faith, whereby third-party guarantor may ask creditor for counter-guaranty. (Arts. 3, 4, 13, 38, 64, 90). Guaranty agreement becomes void as main contract becomes unenforceable. (Art. 5).

Third Party Guaranty.—Guaranty governs relationship between creditor and third-party guarantor in that guarantor assures creditor to undertake debtor's obligation in event of debtor's default. (Art. 6). While any legal persons, including legal organizations or citizens, can act as guarantors, government organizations serving to benefit general public may not. (Arts. 7-9). No person can compel banks or financial organizations to act as guarantors, and such financial entities may refuse to grant guaranty. (Art. 11). Should there be more than one guarantor, each guarantor is responsible for its share of obligations pursuant to guaranty agreement. (Art. 12). If agreement fails to indicate individual responsibility, each guarantor can be held responsible jointly and serverally. (Art. 12). Creditor and guarantor may specify guaranty agreement for single debt or for sequence of borrowing with cap amount within specified period. (Art. 14). Agreement should stipulate type and amount of main debt, type of guaranty (general guaranty or joint guaranty), time frame within which debtor must fulfil obligation, scope of guaranty, and guaranty period. (Art. 14).

In general guaranty agreement, guarantor takes over whole debt at debtor's default. In joint guaranty agreement, creditor can hold both guarantor and debtor liable, jointly or individually. (Arts. 17, 18). If agreement is ambiguous, law deems it joint guaranty agreement. (Art. 19). Guarantor can be held liable for full debt if agreement fails to indicate guarantor's obligation. (Art. 21). Creditor may assign debt with guaranty with written consent from guarantor. (Arts. 22, 23). Sequence guaranty agreement without specific time frame permits guarantor to avoid obligations for future borrowing by giving written notice to creditor. (Art. 27). Guarantor has legal rights to seek reimbursement from debtor for guaranty payment made to creditor. (Art. 31).

Mortgage refers to legal pledge of property or real estate to creditor as security for payment of loan or other debt without surrendering possession of property. In event of debtor's default, creditor has right to auction or sell property pursuant to this chapter. (Art. 33). Property can be used to secure various debts, provided that sum of debt does not exceed value of property. (Art. 35). Mortgage must be in writing, specifying type and amount of main debt; time frame within which debtor must fulfil obligation; name, quantity, condition, location, ownership and usage right of property; and scope of guaranty. (Arts. 38, 39). Mortgage takes effect upon proper registration. (Art. 41).

Mortgagor must notify mortgagee with respect to subsequent transfers or sales of registered mortgaged property; failure to give proper notice nullifies transaction. (Art. 49). Proceeds from sales of mortgaged property will be applied to fulfill mortgage obligation, and debtor remains responsible for any deficiency or surplus. (Art. 51). Priority of creditors corresponds to order of registration, and creditors with same priority share proceeds proportionally. (Art. 54).

Pledge of mobile property refers to debtor or third party allowing creditor to take possession of mobile property as security to guaranty payment of debt. (Art. 63). Pledge agreement takes effect upon pledger's delivery of possession of property to creditor. (Art. 64). Pledge agreement may not stipulate that pledger will transfer ownership of property to creditor in event of debtor's default at expiration of pledge period. (Art. 66). Creditor may, however, auction or sell secured property pursuant to pledge agreement. (Arts. 63, 71). Creditor has duty to safeguard property and will bear civil liability for loss of value due to mismanagement. (Art. 69). Pledge of intangibles refers to security interest created by using drafts, checks, cashier's checks, bonds, bills of lading, transferable stocks, trademarks, monopoly rights, and other pledges permitted by law. (Art. 75).

Lien under Guaranty Law refers to creditor's right arising under safekeeping agreements, transportation agreements and subcontracting agreements, to appraise, auction or sell property of debtor. (Arts. 82, 84). Lien agreement should indicate that debtor must fulfill obligation within two months from lien attachment. (Art. 87). If lien agreement fails to specify, creditor should assure time frame no less than two months and notify debtor to fulfil obligation within that period. (Art. 87).

Down Payment.—Party may make deposit, no more than 20% of main debt, to another party to guaranty repayment of debt. (Arts. 89, 91). Should debtor default, person who places deposit has no right to get deposit back. If person who receives deposit defaults, he must return twice amount of deposit to other party. (Art. 89). Deposit agreement takes effect upon making of deposit. (Art. 90).

HEALTH REGULATIONS:

On Nov. 19, 1982 Trial Regulations on Foodstuffs Sanitation were promulgated effective as of July 1, 1983. These regulations, which cover all persons engaged in production of foodstuffs, provide for enforcement measures ranging from providing time limit in which to come up to standards, to confiscation, loss of health certificate, fines up to ¥30,000, etc. (Art. 37). Any individual may bring complaint against violator. (Art. 3). Specific requirements are provided for production and supply of foodstuffs (Art. 6) and restrictions are enumerated (Art. 7) applying not only to all food items but also to materials, tools, equipment, location, environment, packing, containers, and additives (Art. 3). These regulations are comprehensive, providing standards, inspection, regulations concerning additives and packaging, and enforcement.

HOLIDAYS:

Nonworking days for urban workers are normally Sundays, Spring Festival (Chinese lunar calendar New Year) for three days, normally in Feb., June 1 for young students, May 1 (International Labor Day), Mar. 8 (Woman's Day) for women only, May 8 (middle level students and above), Aug. 1 (Military Holiday for soldiers) and Oct. 1 (Independence Day) for two days, May 4 (Youth Day, 1/2 day); Jan. 1 (New Year).

HOMESTEADS:

See topics Property; Civil Code.

Families may, and most do, construct privately owned dwellings and farm buildings. Private plots are allocated to farmers and usufruct of this land may be consumed or sold by said farmers.

HUSBAND AND WIFE:

See topic Aliens.

Husband and wife have equal status in home. (Marriage Law, Art. 9). Both husband and wife have right to use their family names. (Marriage Law, Art. 10). Both husband and wife have freedom to work, study and participate in social activities, and neither is permitted to restrain or interfere with other. (Marriage Law, Art. 11). Both husband and wife are under duty to practice family planning. (Marriage Law, Art. 12). Said duty is encouraged by benefits that accrue to those who adhere to state policy of having only one child per family. Normally individual receives cash award, plus medical care, and school costs for child are free. If three children are born then extra grain rations, etc. can be denied family for new child.

Property acquired during marriage is joint property, unless there is agreement between parties to contrary. (Marriage Law, Art. 13). Husband and wife enjoy equal rights to possession and management of said property. (Marriage Law, Art. 13).

Husband and wife have duty to support and assist each other. (Marriage Law, Art. 14). If one party fails to support and assist party in need, then party in need has right to legally demand such support and assistance (Marriage Law, Arts. 14, 35), which demand can be enforced by court (Marriage Law, Art. 35). Both husband and wife have duty to rear and educate their children, and children duty to support and assist parents. (Marriage Law, Art. 15). Children who are minors and incapable of maintaining themselves can demand that their parents pay for their care (Marriage Law, Art. 15), and parents who have lost ability to work or have difficulties in providing for themselves, have right to demand that their children pay for their support (Marriage Law, Art. 15). Parents have right and duty to protect their children and subject them to discipline. When children who are minors cause harm to state, collective or other person, parents must make compensation for economic loss. (Marriage Law, Art. 17).

IMMIGRATION:

See topic Aliens.

INCOME TAX:

See topic Taxation.

INFANTS:

See topics Adoption; Criminal Law; Descent and Distribution; Husband and Wife; Civil Code.

Children may adopt either their father's or their mother's name. (Marriage Law, Art. 16). Children born out of wedlock enjoy same rights as children born in wedlock and father of said child is responsible for part or all of cost of child's support until child is self-supporting. (Marriage Law, Art. 19). Adoption relationships protected by state, are governed by same laws that govern relationships between parents and children they conceived. (Marriage Law, Arts. 20, 21). Rights and duties in relationship between adopted children and their natural parents are terminated upon adoption. (Marriage Law, Art. 20). When parents are deceased or incapacitated grandparents or older brothers or sisters having capacity to bear relevant costs are responsible for support of said children.

INHERITANCE TAX:

See topic Taxation.

INSOLVENCY:

See topic Bankruptcy.

INSURANCE:

See topic Contracts.

Insurance Law was adopted by National People's Congress on June 30, 1995, effective as of Oct. 1, 1995. This law applies to all insurance activities within territory of China, as well as to establishment of insurance companies with foreign investment, or branch companies of foreign insurance companies within territory of China. (Arts. 3, 148). This law is also applicable to marine insurance, if Maritime Law does not have relevant provisions. (Art. 147). All insurance business must be handled by insurance companies created according to this law. (Art. 5). If legal persons and other entities located in China need to purchase insurance, they must do so through insurance companies within China. (Art. 6).

Insurance contract is agreement defining rights and obligations between insurer and insured. (Art. 9). Insured must have insurable interests towards subject matter of insurance, or insurance contract will be invalid. (Art. 11). It should be made in writing, including insurance policy, other insurance certificate and other written documents. (Art. 12). It must include following minimal terms: (a) name and domicile of insurer; (b) name and domicile of insured, and name and domicile of beneficiary to life insurance; (c) subject matter; (d) liabilities of insurance and their exemptions; (e) insurance period and commencement of insurance liability; (f) insurable value; (g) insured amount; (h) premium and its method of payment; (i) insurance compensation and its payment; (j) liabilities for breach of contract and dispute settlement; and (k) time of execution of contract. (Art. 18).

Insured must pay premium as specified in contract, and insurer must assume insurance liability from time specified in contract. (Art. 13). Insured may discharge insurance contract unless otherwise provided by law or insurance contract. (Art. 14). Insurer must not discharge insurance contract unless law or contract provides otherwise. (Art. 15). Insurer must inform insured of terms and conditions of insurance contract, and may ask for information and data about subject matter or insured; insured must tell truth. (Art. 16). Should insured conceal facts wilfully and fail to perform disclosure obligations, or fail to do so due to negligence, which is sufficient to influence insurer to decide on whether to accept such application or increase rate of premium, insurer is entitled to discharge insurance contract. Should insured wilfully fail to perform disclosure obligations, insurer will not assume compensation or insurance liability for insurance accident which occurred before discharge of contract, and should not refund premium. Should insured fail to disclose due to negligence, thus seriously affecting occurrence of insurance accident, insurer may refund premium, but will not assume compensation or insurance liability for insurance accident occurred before discharge of contract. (Art. 16). Insurer must expressly inform insured of exemption clauses; otherwise, they are null and void. (Art. 17). During term of contract, it may be modified through consultation and agreement between insurer and insured. (Art. 20). If agreement to modify has been reached, written agreement should be made, or insurer should note changes in original contract. (Art. 20).

Insured and beneficiary must promptly notify insurer of insurance accident, when they have knowledge about such accident. (Art. 21). In claiming insurance compensation, insured must provide to insurer certification and materials related to nature and causes of insurance accident and degree of damage. (Art. 22). Should insurer deem certification and materials provided by insured incomplete, insurer should notify and request insured or beneficiary to provide supplementary certification and materials. (Art. 22). After receiving request for payment of insurance compensation from insured or beneficiary, insurer must promptly examine case. Insurer must pay insurance compensation to insured or beneficiary within ten days from date they reached agreement. If insurance contract contains fixed amount of insurance compensation or designates specific time for payment, insurer must pay same to insured or beneficiary as specified in contract. (Art. 23). Should insurer fail to provide insurance compensation, it must compensate resulting losses incurred by insured or beneficiary, in addition to payment of insurance compensation. (Art. 23). No entity or individual is allowed to interfere with insurer's obligations to pay insurance compensation, and to restrict insured's rights to obtain insurance compensation. (Art. 23). If insured's request does not fall within insurance coverage, insurer must notify insured in writing of refusal of payment. (Art. 24). If insurer cannot decide on amount of compensation within 60 days from receiving insured's request and supporting certification and materials, it must prepay minimum amount which can be determined according to foregoing certification and materials. (Art. 25). When amount of compensation is finally determined, insurer must pay balance to insured. (Art. 25). In nonlife insurance, insured or beneficiary must exercise rights to claim insurance compensation within two years beginning from date when it had knowledge of occurrence of insurance accident; while in life insurance, insured or beneficiary must do so within five years commencing from date when it had knowledge of occurrence of insurance accident. (Art. 26).

Insurer may assign in part its insurance business that it has underwritten to other insurers, which is called "reinsurance". At request of reinsurer, assigner must disclose to reinsurer relevant information about original insurance and its obligations. (Art. 28). Reinsurer must not request insured of original insurance to pay premium. Insured or beneficiary of original insurance contract must not claim insurance compensation against reinsurer. (Art. 29). Assigner must not refuse to perform or defer to perform original insurance liability under excuse that reinsurer has not performed reinsurance obligations. (Art. 29). Insurer or reinsurer must keep confidential relevant information about business and property of insured or assigner. (Art. 31). When insurer has disputes over contents of insurance contract with insured or beneficiary, court and arbitration commission must make interpretations favorable to insured or beneficiary. (Art. 30).

Property Insurance Contract.—Subject matter of property insurance contract must be property and its relevant interests. (Art. 32). If subject matter is transferred, insured must notify insurer. If insurer agrees to continue to underwrite new subject matter, contract must be modified, with exception of carriage of goods insurance contract, or insurance contract provides otherwise. (Art. 33). In insurance contracts regarding carriage of goods and voyage of transport vehicles, if insurance liabilities have started, parties must not discharge contract. (Art. 34). Insured should comply with regulations on fire prevention, safety, production and operation, and labor safety, and maintain safety of subject matter. (Art. 35). As per contract provisions, insurer may check and inspect safety conditions of subject matter, and put forward written proposal regarding non-safety factors. (Art. 35). Should insured fail to perform such safety obligations toward subject matter, insurer may request insured to increase premium or discharge contract. (Art. 35). In order to maintain safety of subject matter, insurer may, after obtaining consent from insured, adopt preventive measures. (Art. 35). Should degree of danger of subject matter increase during term of contract, insurer may request insured to increase premium or discharge contract. (Art. 36). Should insured fail to notify insurer of foregoing increased danger, insurer must not assume liability of compensation for insurance accident which occurred due to increased danger. (Art. 36). If degree of danger of subject matter substantially reduces or insurable value markedly decreases, insured may request insurer to reduce premium or refund relevant premium. (Art. 37).

After occurrence of insurance accident, insured must take measures to attempt to mitigate losses. (Art. 41). Insurer must assume reasonable and necessary cost for foregoing measures. (Art. 41). If subject matter suffers damage in part, insured may terminate contract within 30 days from payment of compensation by insurer. Unless otherwise provided in contract, insurer may terminate contract. (Art. 42). After occurrence of insurance accident, if insurer has paid compensation in full, and insured value is equivalent to insurable value, remaining rights of damaged subject matter must belong to insurer. (Art. 43). If insured value is lower than insurable value, insurer must enjoy rights in ratio of insured value to insurable value. (Art. 43). Should insurance accident be caused by third person, insurer is entitled to subrogation right against such third party from date when it has paid insurance compensation to insured. (Art. 44). After occurrence of insurance accident, if insured has obtained damages from such wrongdoer, insurer may deduct that sum in calculation of insurance compensation. Should insured waive rights to claim damages against such third party, before insurer pays insurance compensation, insurer will be exempted from insurance liabilities. Should insured do so after receiving insurance compensation, such act of insured is null and void. (Art. 45). Unless family members of insured wilfully cause insurance accident, insurer must not exercise subrogation rights against family members of insured. (Art. 46). Insured must provide necessary documents and relevant information within its knowledge to insurer so as to support insurer exercising subrogation rights against third person. (Art. 47).

Life Insurance Contract.—Subject matter of life insurance contract must be life and body of human being. (Art. 51). Insurance purchaser has insurable interest towards following persons: (1) self, (2) spouse, children and parents, and (3) other family members and close relatives. In addition, if insured agrees to have insurance purchaser to purchase life insurance for him or her, it is deemed that purchaser has insurable interests toward insured. (Art. 52). If age of insured disclosed by insurance purchaser is not true, and actual age does not conform to age restriction as specified in contract, insurer may discharge contract and refund premium after deduction of various costs, within two years from execution of contract. (Art. 53). Should foregoing untrue age result in less premium paid by insurance purchaser, insurer may request foregoing purchaser to make up balance. (Art. 53). Insurance purchaser must not purchase life insurance on persons without civil competence contingent upon insured's death, and insurer must not underwrite such insurance. (Art. 54). However, parents may do so for their minor children. (Art. 54). Life insurance contract contingent upon death must not be valid unless insured has agreed in writing and confirmed insured value. (Art. 55). Policy of foregoing insurance must not be transferred or mortgaged in absence of written consent of insured. (Art. 55). After execution of contract, purchaser may pay premium by one lump sum or by instalments as specified in contract. (Art. 56). Insurer must not resort to litigation to request purchaser to pay premium of life insurance. (Art. 59). Beneficiary may be designated by insured or purchaser. When purchaser designates beneficiary, consent must be obtained from insured. (Art. 60). Should insured be person without civil competence, or with limited competence, person's guardian may designate beneficiary for insured. (Art. 60). If death, injury, or disease of insured is caused by wilful act of beneficiary or purchaser, insurer shall be exempted from insurance liabilities. If purchaser has paid premium for two years or more, insurer may refund cash value of policy to other beneficiaries. (Art. 64). For contract contingent upon death, should insured commit suicide, insurer will be exempted from insurance liabilities, but must refund premium paid by purchaser. (Art. 65). However, if such contract has reached two years or more, insurer must pay insurance compensation as specified in contract, despite insured's suicide. (Art. 65). Should insured's intentional crime result in death or injuries of insured, insurer must not assume insurance liabilities. (Art. 66). If purchaser has paid in full premium for two years or more, insurer must refund its cash value as specified in contract. (Art. 66).

Insurance companies must take one of following forms: (1) corporations limited by shares and (2) wholly state-owned companies. (Art. 69). Insurance company must be subject to approval of financial supervision department. (Art. 70). To create insurance

See Topical Index in front part of this volume.

INSURANCE . . . *continued*

company, following requirements must be met: (1) articles of association in conformity with insurance law and company law; (2) minimum registered capital as required by insurance law; (3) senior officers having professional knowledge and practical experiences; (4) having complete organizational set-up and management system; and (5) having business sites in conformity with requirements and other necessary facilities. (Art. 71). Minimum registered capital of insurance company must be RMB200 million. (Art. 72). In applying for insurance company, following documents and materials must be submitted to financial supervision authorities: (a) application specifying name, registered capital and scope of business for prospective company; (b) feasibility study report; and (c) other documents and materials as required by financial supervision authorities. (Art. 73). Financial supervision authorities must decide on approval or disapproval within six months from receipt of foregoing materials. (Art. 75). Upon approval of financial supervision authorities, insurance company may establish branches at home and abroad. Branches do not have separate legal identity; civil liability must be borne by head company. (Art. 79).

If any of following circumstances occurs, insurance company must secure approval from financial supervision authorities: (1) change in name; (2) change in registered capital; (3) change in business sites of insurance companies and their branches; (4) adjustment in scope of business; (5) merger or division; (6) amendments to articles of association; (7) change of capital investors or shareholders holding 10% of shares or more; and (8) other changes as provided by financial supervision authorities. (Art. 81). Organizational set-up must be governed by company law. (Art. 82). If insurance company becomes insolvent, court may declare bankruptcy, after obtaining consent from financial supervision authorities. (Art. 86).

Guidelines for Insurance Operation.—Scope of business of insurance company is: (1) property insurance business including property damage insurance, liability insurance, credit insurance, etc.; and (2) life insurance including life insurance, health insurance, accidental injuries insurance, etc. One insurance company is not allowed to engage in both property insurance and life insurance. (Art. 91).

Upon approval of financial supervision authorities, insurance company may engage in reinsurance business. (Art. 92). Apart from life insurance, other insurance businesses must set aside liability reserve funds from retained premium of insurance company, which must be equivalent to 50% of retained premium. For life insurance, liability reserve funds must be equivalant to net value of all valid life insurance policies. (Art. 93). Insurance company must set aside pending compensation reserve funds, according to insurance compensation being claimed or paid, or insurance accident having occurred, but insurance compenstion has not been claimed. (Art. 94). In addition, insurance company must also set aside statutory reserve funds in accordance with relevant laws, regulations and financial and accounting system. (Art. 95). Retained premium by property insurance company must not exceed four times its actual capital and statutory reserve funds. (Art. 98). Liability assumed by insurance company for maximum damage of each possible insurance accident must not exceed 10% of its actual capital and statutory reserve funds. Part in excess of 10% will be subject to reinsurance. (Art. 99). Reinsurance business of insurance company must offer priority to domestic insurance companies. (Art. 102). Financial supervision authorities entitled to restrict or prohibit insurance company from assigning reinsurance to insurance company abroad. (Art. 103). Funds of insurance company must be confined to bank deposits, government bonds, financial bonds and other uses as provided by State Council. Funds of insurance company must not be used to create securities dealer or to invest in enterprises. (Art. 104).

Supervision and Administration.—Basic terms and conditions of primary commercial insurances and rate of premium must be formulated by financial supervision authorities. Terms and conditions and rate of premium for other insurances may be formulated by insurance company, which must be submitted to financial supervision authorities for record. (Art. 106). Financial supervision authorities may examine and check business situation, financial condition and capital utilization of insurance company, and may require it to submit relevant written reports and materials within prescribed time limit. (Art. 107). Financial supervision authorities may at their descretion select professional insurance personnel and designate relevant personnel in said insurance company so as to organize reorganization group which will reorganize insurance company. (Art. 109). Reorganization group may supervise day-to-day business of insurance company. Responsible persons and relevant officers must exercise their duty under direction of reorganization group. (Art. 110). Insurance company must submit annual business report, annual financial statement and relevant reports to financial supervision authorities within three months after preceding fiscal year ended. (Art. 117). Insurance company must submit statistics statement to financial supervision authorities at end of each month. (Art. 118). Insurance company must properly keep complete accounting book, original voucher and relevant data for at least ten years from termination of insurance contract. (Art. 121).

Agent and Broker.—Agent must represent insurer within authority as entrusted by insurer and charge fees from insurer. (Art. 122). Broker must represent insurance purchaser, enter into contract on behalf of purchaser, and charge commission from said purchaser. (Art. 123). Insurer will be liable for acts of agents. Life insurance agent must not represent two or more insurers at same time. (Art. 124). If insurance purchaser and insured suffer any losses due to fault of broker, broker must assume liability of compensation. (Art. 125). Agent and broker must not take advantage of administrative authority, or favorable position of profession, and not resort to undue means to coerce or lure others to enter into insurance contract. (Art. 126). Agent and broker must have their own business sites and accept supervision of financial supervision authorities. (Art. 128). Insurance company must have book listing its agents. (Art. 129).

INTEREST:

Interest is charged by Bank of China and all other Chinese banks on loans they extend, and interest is given to those maintaining savings accounts with relevant banks in China. Chinese organizations borrowing money from foreign banks likewise pay interest, often at commercial rates.

INTESTACY:

See topic Descent and Distribution.

INVESTMENT INCENTIVES:

See topics Joint Stock Companies; Taxation; Trade Zones.

Regulations for Encouragement of Investment were promulgated by State Council on Oct. 11, 1986.

These regulations covered corporations whose products are primarily for export, which have net foreign exchange surplus, or which have advanced technology supplied by foreign investor to develop new products or upgrade existing products to either increase foreign exchange or act as import substitutes. (Art. 2). Companies meeting these standards are termed Export Enterprises or Technically Advanced Enterprises. Regulations provide exemption of said enterprises from certain subsidies payable to staff, special land use fees outside busy urban centers, e.g. 5-25 RMB per square meter per year were development and end use fee is computed together, and not more than 3 RMB per square meter per year where development fee is chargeable on one time basis. (Art. 4). Exemption from said fees may also be granted. (Art. 4).

Said enterprises are also given priority in obtaining utilities and communication and transportation facilities and fees are to be same as local enterprises (Art. 5), as well priority for short term working capital, bank loans and credit (Art. 6). Remittance of profits abroad are exempt from tax (Art. 7), and after initial tax holiday Export Enterprise exporting 70% or more of products in year may pay enterprises income tax at one half rate specified. Where said tax in SEZ is 15%, it shall be reduced to 10%. (Art. 8). Similarly after initial tax holiday Technically Advanced Enterprises may extend for three years payment of enterprise income tax at half specified rate. (Art. 9).

Export products of enterprises, except for crude oil or oil products, are exempt from Consolidated Industrial and Commercial Tax. (Art. 11). Equipment, raw materials, vehicles etc. used in production by these enterprises are exempt from requirement for import licenses. (Art. 13).

Ministry of Finance on 31 Jan., 1987 promulgated Method of Carrying Out Provision for Preferential Tax Treatment ("Method"), pursuant to State Council Regulations for Encouragement of Investment.

Method does not apply to joint oil exploration agreements and major natural resource enterprises. (Art. 6). Method permits corporations with foreign investment to enjoy tax benefits of either export company or modern technology enterprise but not both at once. (Art. 5). Though after enjoying three year tax benefits as being modern technology enterprise, corporation can then apply for export corporation tax benefits. To obtain return of tax monies paid by foreign enterprises for profits earned that are reinvested, these must be reinvested in China. (Art. 4).

JOINT STOCK COMPANIES:

See topics Advertising; Corporations; Statistics, Standards and Quality Control; Taxation; Trade Zones.

Law on Joint Ventures Using Chinese and Foreign Investment (Joint Venture Law of China) was adopted by National People's Congress on July 1, 1979, and amended on Apr. 4, 1990 by 3rd Session of 7th National People's Congress and permits foreign companies to enter into joint ventures with Chinese companies or other entities, subject to authorization by Chinese government. (Art. 1). Statute provides that Chinese government protects resources invested by foreign investor, as well as any profits due. (Art. 2). State shall not nationalize or expropriate assets of joint venture. Under special circumstances, where public interest calls for action, State may exercise expropriation through legal procedures and appropriate compensation shall be made. (Art. 2). Parties to joint venture originally to apply to appropriate authorities of Foreign Economic Relations and Trade of China and Foreign Investment Commission in China for approval of agreements and contracts between parties, and articles of association. (Art. 3). Commission had three months to reject or approve these documents, and if approved, joint venture shall register with General Administration for Industry and Commerce (GAIC) and pursuant to license obtained, commence operations. (Art. 3). This has been modified by Regulations for the Implementation of the Law on Joint Ventures Using Chinese and Foreign Investment ("J.V. Implementation Regs."), promulgated by State Council on Sept. 23, 1983. These Regulations formulated with view to facilitating implementation of Joint Venture Law. (J.V. Implementation Regs. Art. 1). Pursuant to said Regulations promulgated subsequent to Joint Venture Law, joint venture is normally subject to approval of Ministry of Foreign Economic Relations and Trade ("MOFERT"), which issues certificate of approval. (J.V. Implementation Regs. Art. 8). However, MOFERT can and does designate government organizations of provinces, autonomous regions, and municipalities directly under central government, or relevant ministries or bureaus under same Council, to examine and approve establishment of joint ventures complying with certain specific conditions. Chinese partner to joint venture submits to its department in charge project proposal and preliminary feasibility report of joint venture which, on approval of department in charge, must be submitted to approval authority for final approval. Thereafter, work can be commenced on relevant feasibility study and joint venture agreements based on such preliminary feasibility report. (J.V. Implementation Regs. Art. 9[1]).

Regulations on Registration of Joint Ventures Using Chinese and Foreign Investment ("Joint Venture Registration Regulations") approved by State Council on July 26, 1980 provide that joint venture should within one month of receiving Foreign Investment Commission approval register with GAIC. (Joint Venture Registration Regulations, Art. 2). Local administrative bureaus of industry and commerce are authorized to register joint ventures, but licenses shall be issued only after examination by GAIC. (Joint Venture Registration Regulations, Art. 2).

Joint venture is limited liability company, in general foreign partner contributing not less than 25% of registered capital, wherein parties share profits and risk of loss in proportion to their registered capital. (Joint Venture Law, Art. 4). Investment of party may be cash, capital goods, industrial property rights, use of site, etc., but technology and equipment contributed by any foreign partner "shall be truly advanced and appropriate to China's needs." (Joint Venture Law, Art. 5). Joint venture's board of directors shall have chairman appointed by Chinese participant and one or two vice-chairmen appointed by foreign participants, amended on Apr. 4, 1990 to allow foreign

JOINT STOCK COMPANIES . . . *continued*
party to provide Chairman of Board of Directors. If one party to joint venture assumes position of board chairman, then vice-chairman of board of directors shall be assumed by other party (Art. 6), thus no longer requiring Chinese party be chairman of board. Board is empowered to discuss and take action, pursuant to articles of association, on all venture's fundamental issues, viz., budget, production programs, business programs, distribution of profit, pay scales, termination of business, expansion projects, appointment and hiring of president, vice-president(s), chief engineer, treasurer and auditors, as well as their functions, power and remuneration, etc. (Joint Venture Law, Art. 6). President, vice-president(s), general manager and assistant-general manager(s) in factory shall be chosen from among parties to venture. (Art. 6). Within scope of joint venture contract, articles of association, and Chinese laws and decrees, joint venture has right to do business independently. (J.V. Implementation Regs. Art. 7). However, governmental department in charge of Chinese participant in joint venture will be in charge of joint venture and responsible for guidance and assistance, and will exercise supervision over joint venture. (J.V. Implementation Regs. Art. 6).

Length of Term of Joint Venture.—Contract term of joint venture shall be decided according to its particular line of business and circumstances. Some lines of business of enterprise with foreign investment shall provide term of joint venture, some may or may not provide term of joint venture. Those enterprises with foreign investment which have decided term of joint venture, if parties have agreed to extend term, shall apply to examination and approval authority six months before expiration of term of joint venture. Upon receipt of application for extension of contract, examination and approval authority shall, within one month decide whether to approve or disapprove it. (Art. 12). Pursuant to Interim Provisions governing length of terms of Joint Venture (promulgated by Ministry of Foreign Economic Relations and Trade on 22 Oct., 1990) enterprises must provide following terms of joint venture: (1) type of trade, such as hotels, apartment, office building, recreation and entertainment, catering trade, taxi service, development and printing of color films and photos, maintenance, business consultancy; (2) joint ventures engaged in land development and real estate; (3) joint venture engaged in prospecting and development of natural resources; (4) joint venture engaged in projects subject to investment restriction as stipulated by state; (5) joint ventures for which contact period shall be decided through consultation, as prescribed by other laws and regulations of state. Before expiration of joint venture contract in cases of heavy losses aside from failure of party to fulfill obligations prescribed by contract and articles of association, force majeure etc., contract may be terminated through consultation and agreement by parties to joint venture, subject to approval by authority in charge of national foreign economic trade and to registration with General Administration for Industry and Commerce. In case of losses caused by breach of contract financial responsibility shall be borne by party that breaches contract. (Art. 13).

Balance of Foreign Exchange Receipts and Disbursements.—Ministry of Foreign Economic Relations and Trade promulgated Measures Concerning the Purchase of Domestic Products for Export by Enterprises with Foreign Investment to Balance Foreign Exchange Receipts and Disbursements on Jan. 20, 1987. In principle, enterprises with foreign investment shall achieve balance of foreign exchange receipts and disbursements through export of products of such enterprises.

With regard to production enterprises with foreign investment for which temporary difficulties exist, they may, within fixed period of time, apply to purchase domestic products (except commodities subject to unified control according to state regulations) for export so as to balance foreign exchange receipts and disbursement of such enterprises. (Art. 2). If enterprise with foreign investment, meeting requirements of Art. 2 herein, needs to purchase domestic products for export to balance foreign exchange receipts and disbursements, it shall file application in advance with foreign economic relations and trade department at provincial level in locality where enterprise is located. (Art. 3). Quantity of domestic products for export approved for purchase by enterprise with foreign investment shall be limited to amount required in that year to make up for foreign exchange required for production and operation of enterprises and remittance of profits to foreign party, or foreign exchange required to be remitted upon winding up and liquidation of enterprise. (Art. 4). Domestic products approved for purchase by enterprise with foreign investment to balance foreign exchange receipts and disbursement must be transported out of Chinese territory for distribution and sale and shall not be resold within Chinese territory. (Art. 6).

Swap centers have helped relieve problem of currency exchange.

Labor Regulations promulgated on Nov. 26, 1986 by Ministry of Labor and Personnel limit autonomy of enterprises having foreign investment in hiring personnel, setting wages and paying insurance and welfare expenses of employees.

Enterprise having foreign investment may, according to its production and operational needs, independently determine its organizational structure and personnel system and, with assistance from local Department of Labor and Personnel, it may recruit and select employees using its own criteria. (Art. 1[a]).

Senior management personnel selected by Chinese party in enterprise for work in said enterprise must be capable of grasping concepts, be knowledgeable about technology, have management skills, be innovative and able to cooperate and work with foreign investors. Supervisors in their respective departments must support said senior personnel in their position and generally not transfer them during their term of office. If said transfer becomes necessary, Board of Directors must consent. (Art. 1[c]).

Enterprises having foreign investment may dismiss those employees who prove unqualified for their posts after probationary or training period or who have been rendered unnecessary by changes in technology or new methods of production. Employees who violate regulations of enterprise with damaging consequences may be sanctioned accordingly, with maximum sanction being discharged. (Art 1[d]).

Wages of employees of enterprise having foreign investment will be set by its Board of Directors but may not be less than 120% of average wages paid workers of state-owned enterprises with similar conditions, in same field and in same area; said level must be adjusted periodically, mainly in response to improved economic performance of enterprise. (Art. 2[a]).

Enterprise having foreign investment must pay retirement and pension funds and employment insurance premiums for Chinese employees according to regulations of local People's Government. Insurance and welfare plans must also meet government requirements set for state-owned enterprise and must be funded strictly by said enterprise. (Art. 2[b]).

Enterprise having foreign investment must pay housing subsidy funds according to regulations of local People's Government. Chinese party to enterprise shall apply said funds to expenses incurred in building and purchase of housing for employees of said enterprise. (Art. 2[c]).

Labor Relations.—Contract between parties shall, pursuant to law, cover employment and discharge of workers and staff members. (Joint Venture Law, Art. 6). On July 26, 1980 State Council approved Regulations on Labor Management in Joint Ventures Using Chinese and Foreign Investment ("Joint Venture Labor Reg."). Regulations require that labor contracts be signed either collectively with trade union, or if venture is small, with individual members of staff and laborers, specifying conditions of employment, dismissal, resignation, production tasks, other work, wages, awards, punishment, working hours, vacations, labor insurance, welfare insurance, labor protection and labor discipline. (Joint Venture Labor Reg., Art. 2). This contract must be submitted to labor management department of province, autonomous region or municipal people's government for approval. (Joint Venture Labor Reg., Art. 2). Where there are surplus workers as result of changes in production and technical conditions of joint venture, said workers, pursuant to labor contract, can be discharged, but enterprise must compensate these workers. (Joint Venture Labor Reg., Art. 4). Workers violating rules and regulations of enterprise with resulting bad consequences can be discharged, but such discharge must be reported to authorities having jurisdiction over joint venture, and to labor management department for their approval. (Joint Venture Labor Reg., Art. 5). Trade union can object to dismissal or punishment of workers and staff, and send representatives to board of directors for consultation. (Joint Venture Labor Reg., Art. 6). If said consultation fails, then either party can seek to have matter arbitrated by labor management department of people's government of province, autonomous region or municipality where venture is located, and if arbitration decision is not acceptable either party can file lawsuit. (Joint Venture Labor Reg., Art. 14). Wage level of workers and staff members in joint venture will be determined at 120% to 150% of real wages of workers and staff members in state-owned enterprises of same trade in locality. (Joint Venture Labor Reg., Art. 8). Joint venture must pay for Chinese workers' labor insurance, cover their medical expenses and provide various kinds of subsidies in line with prevailing standards in state-owned enterprises. (Joint Venture Labor Reg., Art. 11). Joint ventures are also required to implement relevant rules and regulations of Chinese government regarding labor production to ensure safe and civilized production. (Joint Venture Labor Reg., Art. 13). Labor management department of Chinese government is authorized to supervise and inspect implementation of these rules. (Joint Venture Labor Reg., Art. 13).

Loans from Bank of China.—Bank of China promulgated regulations on Apr. 24, 1987, concerning loans to enterprises with foreign investment. In granting loans, Bank of China must sign loan agreements with borrowing enterprise. (Art. 4). Bank of China grants following types of loans to enterprises: (1) Fixed asset loan, which may be medium or short-term, on buyer's credit, syndicated or for project financing; (2) working capital loan, in form of production reserves and revolving funds, temporary credit or overdraft limit on current account; (3) Renminbi loan against mortgage; (4) stand-by credit loan. (Art. 5).

Loan may be provided in Renminbi or foreign currencies such as US dollar, British pound, Japanese yen, Hong Kong dollar, German mark and other convertible currencies acceptable to Bank of China. (Art. 6).

Enterprise is qualified to apply for loan from Bank of China if following conditions met: (1) It has business license issued by Administration of Commerce and Industry and at least one account with Bank of China; (2) it has fully paid in its registered capital according to contractual obligations and relevant regulations; (3) it has both power of attorney and permission from its Board of Directors to make such application; (4) planning authorities have approved its capital construction project; (5) it has ability to repay said loan and can provide reliable security for repayment of principal plus interest. (Art. 7).

Term of loan begins on effective date of loan agreement and ends on date specified in said agreement, at which time principal plus interest and any charges must be paid in full. (Art. 8). Term of fixed asset loan is maximum of seven years but may be extended, pending approval by Bank of China, provided said extended term ends not later than one year before expiry of business license of enterprise. (Art. 9). Term of working capital loan may not exceed 12 months. (Art. 10).

If required, enterprise must provide Bank of China with security which Bank approves. (Art. 15). Said security may be either guarantee or mortgage. Acceptable collateral includes: House property; machinery and equipment; marketable goods in stock; deposits or certificates of deposit in foreign currencies; negotiable securities and bills; and equity shares and other transferable rights and interests. (Art. 16). When enterprise mortgages its property for loan, said enterprise must sign mortgage agreement with Bank of China, duly notarized by Chinese notary office. Mortgaged property will be insured by People's Insurance Company of China. (Art. 17).

Bank of China reserves right to supervise utilization of loan by enterprise. (Art. 22). Bank of China may invoke against enterprise which violates provisions of loan agreement, according to seriousness of case, one or more of following sanctions: Demanding enterprise rectify its error within given time period; suspending disbursement of loan; recalling loan before maturity; calling on guarantor to perform obligations. (Art. 20). In the event that enterprise fails to repay principal plus interest (and any other monies in case of guaranteed loan), Bank of China may legally recover principal, interest and other outstanding monies by disposing of collateral at discount value or selling it at auction. Interest may be charged, in addition to interest charged as per loan agreement, on overdue loan at rate of 20 to 50% as from due date. (Art. 21).

Branches of Bank of China in Special Economic Zones may formulate and execute detailed rules of their own according to their business needs, subject to approval of Head Office. (Art. 26).

Net profit of joint venture shall be distributed between parties to venture in proportion to their respective shares in registered capital, after paying joint venture income tax on gross profits pursuant to China's tax laws, and after deducting, as stipulated in articles of association, monies for reserve funds, bonus and welfare funds and expansion funds. (Joint Venture Law, Art. 7). Said net profit received by foreign participant, funds received when joint venture terminates, and other funds may be remitted abroad

See Topical Index in front part of this volume.

JOINT STOCK COMPANIES . . . *continued*

through Bank of China, in currencies specified in contract. (Joint Venture Law, Art. 10). Applications for income tax reduction by joint ventures having up-to-date technology for first two or three profit-making years may be made, as can application for restitution of portion of taxes paid be made by foreign entity which reinvests any part of its share of net profit in China. (Joint Venture Law, Art. 7). Joint ventures exempt from customs duty and Industrial and Commercial Consolidated Tax on certain imported materials, such as raw materials, auxiliary materials, components, parts and packing materials imported by joint venture for production of export goods, machinery, equipment, parts and other materials imported with funds which are part of joint venture's total investment or are part of foreign partner's shares of investment according to provisions of contract. (J.V. Implementation Regs. Art. 71).

Settlement in Foreign Currency.—Regulations promulgated by State Administration of Exchange Control, effective Mar. 1, 1989, were attempt to control use of foreign currency by foreign investment enterprises to settle debts in China and to assist said enterprises in their balance of payments in foreign currency.

Foreign investment enterprises who wish to sell products for foreign currency in China must apply to State Administration of Exchange Control or one of its branches. (Art. 1).

Enterprises having foreign investment which meets following requirements may apply for permission to do business in foreign currency: (1) Whose products are necessarily imported based on government plan; (2) whose products are marketed in Special Economic Zones, Economic and Technical Development Zones and to other foreign investment enterprises; (3) materials and parts of whose products must be imported by Chinese manufacturing enterprises. (Art. 2).

To apply for permission to do business in foreign currency, enterprise must submit application report including reasons for request, name of product, quantity sold, total amount, term requested, certificate of approval of capital issued by registered accounts office, and any other documents required by State Administration of Exchange Control. (Art 3.).

Investment Certificates, Contributions to Capital, Registered Capital, etc.—Joint venture corporation empowered to issue investment certificates to parties who invest in joint venture. (J.V. Implementation Regs. Art. 32). In order for party to assign all or part of its investment to third party, other party to joint venture has preemptive rights, and must consent to such assignment if not to itself. (J.V. Implementation Regs. Art. 23). Thus, investment certificates not negotiable documents. Contributions to joint venture can be in cash, buildings, premises, materials, industrial property, know-how, right of use of site, etc. (J.V. Implementation Regs. Art. 25). Investment of know-how or industrial property rights must be verified by documentation and serve as annex to joint venture contract. (J.V. Implementation Regs. Art. 29). Joint Venture bank accounts are to be opened with Bank of China or bank approved by Bank of China, although in business operations venture can obtain funds directly from foreign banks. (Joint Venture Law, Art. 8). Insurance appropriate to joint venture shall be furnished by Chinese companies. (Joint Venture Law, Art. 8). In its purchase of required raw and semi-processed materials, fuels, auxiliary equipment, etc., joint venture should give first priority to Chinese sources, but may also acquire them directly from world market with its foreign exchange funds. (Joint Venture Law, Art. 9). Said venture can market its produce in and out of China, and it may set up affiliates outside of China. (Joint Venture Law, Art. 9). Contract period of joint venture may be agreed between parties, and may be extended by agreement between parties and application, six months prior to expiration, to Foreign Investment Commission. (Joint Venture Law, Art. 12). Termination of joint venture can take place before expiration date if there are heavy losses, or if any party fails to execute its obligations under contract, or by force majeure, etc. (Joint Venture Law, Art. 13). Parties must agree to said early termination and obtain authorization of Foreign Investment Commission. (Joint Venture Law, Art. 13).

Law On Chinese Foreign Contractual Joint Ventures.—Law on Contractual Joint Ventures, promulgated on 13 Apr. 1988, provides for establishment of terms of joint venture including distribution of profit on basis of agreement of parties rather than by operation of law. (Art. 2). Contractual joint venture entity can acquire status of independent legal person under Chinese law. (Art. 2). These agreements must be approved by relevant government examination and approval authority within 45 days of receipt of application (Art. 5); modification requires same approval procedure as does assignment. Board of directors or management committee shall be established to manage venture pursuant to contract and/or articles of association. (Art. 12). Hiring and firing of staff shall be specified in contracts with said employees (Art. 13) though union can be established (Art. 14). Contractual joint ventures permit foreign parties to recover their investment on priority basis prior to payment of income tax, provided such is approved by financial and tax authorities. (Art. 27).

Dispute Resolution and Legal Status.—Validity, interpretation, formation and execution of contract, as well as settlement of disputes under joint venture contract, governed by Chinese Law. (J.V. Implementation Regs. Art. 15). Joint venture contract, articles of association and amendments to either come into force after approval by examination and approval authorities. (J.V. Implementation Regs. Art. 17). Disputes between parties to joint venture may be settled through conciliation or arbitration by Chinese arbitral body or through arbitral body agreed upon by parties. (Joint Venture Law, Art. 14). In cases of losses caused by breach of contract by party to venture, financial responsibility shall be borne by said party. (Joint Venture Law, Art. 13).

Expropriation.—Joint Venture Law of China was amended on Apr. 4, 1990. Amendments provide China will not nationalize and requisition enterprises with foreign investment. In case of special circumstances according to demand of social public interest, enterprises with foreign investment may be requisitioned by legal procedures; corresponding compensation will be granted. (Art. 2).

Law on Wholly Foreign Owned Enterprise.—Sixth National People's Congress of China adopted Law on Wholly Foreign Owned Enterprise on 12 Apr., 1986 to encourage international economic cooperation and technological exchange and promote development of China's national economy. State Council also adopted Implementation of the Law of China on Wholly Foreign Owned Enterprise on 28 Oct., 1990. Under these regulations, China permits foreign enterprises and other economic entities or individuals (foreign investor) to establish wholly foreign owned enterprise within China and protect its legal rights and interests.

Wholly foreign owned enterprise as referred to in this law means enterprise established in China in accordance with relevant laws of China, whole capital of which is invested by foreign investors. Such enterprises do not include branch office established by foreign enterprises and other economic entities in China. (Art. 2).

Establishment of wholly foreign owned enterprise must be beneficial to development of China's national economy and such enterprise shall have at least one of following conditions: (1) enterprise is to adopt advanced technology and equipment, engage in development of new products, conserve energy and raw materials, involve upgrading of products and replacement of old products with new ones which can be used in place of similar imported goods; (2) annual output value of export products exceeds 50% of its annual output value of all products thereby realizing balance between revenue and expenditures in foreign exchange or with surplus. (Implementation Art. 3).

No foreign capital enterprise shall be established in following areas: (1) press, publication, broadcasting, television and movies; (2) domestic commerce, foreign trade and insurance; (3) postal and telecommunications; (4) other trades in which establishment of foreign capital enterprise is forbidden by Chiness government. (Implementation Art. 4).

Establishment of foreign capital enterprise shall be restricted to (1) public utilities; (2) communication and transportation; (3) real estate; (4) trust investment; (5) leasing. Application for establishment of wholly foreign capital enterprise shall be submitted to Ministry of Foreign Economic Realtion and Trade for China for approval except as otherwise provided by China's laws and regulations. (Implementation Art. 5). Examination and approval authorities shall decide to approve or disapprove within 90 days from date of receiving application. (Art. 6).

Wholly foreign capital enterprise must abide by China's laws and regulations and not harm social and public interests of China. (Art. 4).

State shall not nationalize or expropriate any wholly foreign capital enterprises. Under special circumstances, State, based on need of social and public interests, may expropriate wholly foreign capital enterprise according to legal procedures and pay commensurate compensation to owner. (Art. 5).

Wholly foreign owned enterpirse that meets requirements regarding legal persons under laws of China shall obtain status of Chinese legal person. (Art. 8).

Foreign investors shall, within 30 days from receiving of approval certificate, apply for registration with administration authorities of Industry and Commerce and to obtain business license, date of issuance of business license shall be date of establishment of enterprise. (Art. 7).

Foreign owned enterprise shall, within 30 days after its establishment, go through procedures for taxation registration with tax authorities. (Implementation Art. 13).

Split-up, merger, or other important changes of wholly foreign owned enterprise shall be submitted to authorities for examination and approval and shall go through procedures of administrative authorities of Industry and Commerce for change in registration record. (Art. 10).

Production and operating plan of wholly foreign owned enterprise shall be submitted to department in charge of record. No interference shll be allowed in operation and management activities if enterprise conducts its business according to its approved articles of association. (Art. 11).

Wholly foreign owned enterprise must keep its account books in China and carry out independent accounting, submit accounting statement according to regulations and accept supervision by finance and tax authorities. (Art. 14).

Supplies such as raw materials and fuel needed by enterprise within approved scope of business may be purchased in China or in international market; if terms are same, it shall give priority to purchase same in China. (Art. 15). Enterprise employing Chinese staff and workers shall enter into contracts according to law and shall specify in contract provisions relating to matters of employment, dismissal renumeration benefits, labor protection, and labor insurance. (Art. 12).

Staff and workers of enterprise shall establish trade union according to law, carry on trade union activities, and protect lawful rights and interests of staff and workers. (Art. 13).

All items of insurance on enterprise shall be insured with insurance company within China. (Art. 16).

Enterprise shall pay taxes in accordance with relevant tax regulations of State and may enjoy preferential treatment in tax reduction and exemptions. (Art. 17).

Foreign exchange matters of enterprise shall be handled in accordance with Foreign Control Regulations. Enterprise shall resolve balance between its foreign exchange income and expenditure by itself. If products of enterprise are sold on Chinese market with approval of relevant authorities, it shall be responsible for resolving any imbalance. (Art. 18).

Lawful profits and other lawful income obtained by foreign investor from enterprise and funds they receive may be remitted abroad. Salary and other lawful income of foreign staff and workers may be remitted abroad after payment of individual income tax according to law. (Art. 18).

Written application for establishment of foreign owned enterprise shall include following: (1) name or designation, residence and place of registration of foreign investor, and name, nationality, and position of statutory representative; (2) name and residence of foreign owned enterprise; (3) scope of business operations, varieties of products, and scale of production; (4) total amount of investment, registered capital, source of funds, and method of investment contribution and operation period; (5) organizational form and organization, and statutory representative of foreign capital enterprise; (6) primary production equipment to be used and degrees of depreciation, production technology, technological level and their sources; (7) sales orientation and areas, sale channels and methods, and sales proportion between China's market and foreign markets; (8) arrangements for revenue and expenditures in foreign exchange; (9) arrangement for establishment of relevant organization and authorized size of working personnel, engagement and use of workers and staff members, their training, salaries, and wages, material benefits, income and labor protection; (10) degrees of probable environmental pollution and measures for tackling pollution; (11) selection of sites and area of land to be used; (12) funds, energy resources, raw and processing materials needed in capital construction and in production and business operations and

See Topical Index in front part of this volume.

JOINT STOCK COMPANIES . . . *continued*
solution thereof; (13) progress plan for construction of project; (14) period of business operations of foreign owned enterprise to be established. (Implementation Art. 15).

Application for establishment of enterprise shall be submitted to Ministry of Foreign Economic Relations and Trade. After examination and approval, certificate of approval shall be issued by Ministry. State Council shall, under following circumstances, authorize government of relevant province, autonomous region, municipality directly under Central Government, municipality separately listed on state plan, or special economic zone, to issue certificate of approval after examining and approving application; (1) total amount of investment within limits of powers for examination and approval of investments stipulated by State Council; (2) proposed enterprises do not need raw and processed materials to be allocated by State, or do not influence unfavorably national comprehensive balance of energy resource communication and transportation, as well as export quota for foreign trade. (Implementation Art. 8).

Foreign investor shall prior to filing of application, submit report to local people's government at or above county level where proposed enterprise is to be established. Report shall include: (1) aim, scope and scale of business operation; (2) products; (3) technology and equipment; (4) proportion of sales of product between domestic market and outside market; (5) area of land to be used; (6) conditions and quantities of water, electricity, coal, coal gas, and other forms of energy resource required; and (8) equipment of public facilities.

Wholly foreign owned enterpirse shall be limited liability company. Liability of foreign investor to enterprise shall be limited to approval amount of investment subscribed and contributed to enterprise by investor. Enterprise may also take any other form of liability. Liability of foreign investor to enterprise shall be dealt with in accordance with provisions of Chinese law and regulations. (Implementation Art. 19).

Foreign investors may use convertible foreign currencies for contribution of investment, or use as their investment, machinery and equipment, industrial property rights, and proprietary technology that are assigned fixed price. Foreign investor may, after approval by relevant organization, use, as their investment, their profits in Renminbi (RMB) earned from other enterprises with foreign investment establised within China. (Implementation Art. 26).

Foreign capital enterprise shall, in accordance with Chinese law, set up financial and accounting systems, and file with financial departments and tax authorities at place where enterprise is located. (Implementation Art. 59).

Reserve funds, bonus and welfare funds for workers and staff members shall be withdrawn from profits after foreign capital enterprise has paid income tax in accordance with Chinese tax law. Proportion of reserve funds to be withdrawn shall not be lower than 10% of total amount of profits after payment of tax, withdrawal of reserve funds may be stopped when total cumulative reserve has reached 50% of registered capital. Proportion of bonus and welfare funds for workers and staff members to be withdrawn shall be determined by foreign owned enterprise. (Implementation Art. 6).

In case that foreign capital enterprise employs workers and staff members within China, both enterprise and workers and staff shall, in accordance with Chinese law and regulation, sign labor contract and such matters as employment, dismissal, salaries, and wages, welfare, labor protection and labor insurance shall be clearly stated in contract. (Art. 67).

Workers and staff of enterprise shall have right to set up grass-roots trade union, organization and carry out trade union activity in accordance with provisions of Trade Union Law of China. (Art. 69).

Law on Exploitation of Offshore Petroleum Resources in Cooperation with Foreign Enterprises.—On Jan. 13, 1982, Standing Committee of State Council promulgated Regulations for Joint Exploitation of Offshore Petroleum Resources, which permits foreign enterprises to participate in exploitation of Chinese offshore petroleum resources. (Art. 1). Statute provides that government of China will protect foreign investments, foreign shares of profit and other legitimate rights in these cooperative enterprises. (Art. 3). Ministry of Petroleum in charge of exploitation of offshore resources in cooperation with foreign enterprises (Art. 4), and China National Offshore Oil Corporation (CNOOC), state corporation, responsible for working with foreign enterprises to exploit said resources (Art. 5). CNOOC has authority to enter into contracts with foreign enterprises, which contracts subject to approval of Foreign Investment Commission of People's Republic of China. (Art. 6).

It is envisioned that foreign investor will normally provide investment, operations, and bear all exploration risks. Upon discovery of commercially viable oil or gas field, both CNOOC and foreign contractor will jointly invest in development of said field. Initially, envisioned that foreign contractor will be responsible for development and production operations, but after period of time specified in contract, CNOOC will take over production and operations. Foreign contractor, in addition to recovering its investment and expenses out of production will, pursuant to contract, receive remuneration out of petroleum product. (Art. 7). Pursuant to tax laws, taxes must be paid by foreign corporation and its employees to People's Republic of China (Art. 9), but equipment and materials imported to implement petroleum contract either exempt from customs duty or such duty levied at reduced rate (Art. 10). Foreign investor obliged to transfer technology and pass on its experience to Chinese personnel (Art. 12), and preference to be given to Chinese personnel in employment, and percentage of Chinese personnel employed must steadily rise (Art. 12). Foreign contractor required by law to establish subsidiary branch or representative office in China and to fulfill registration requirements. (Art. 14).

Preference must be given to Chinese equipment and material, to Chinese subcontractors, manufacturers and engineering companies in implementing petroleum contract, provided only that Chinese goods and services are competitive. Operators and subcontractors must carry out petroleum explorations in compliance with laws and rules of environmental protection and safety of People's Republic of China, and with reference to international laws to protect fish and other natural resources, and prevent air, sea, rivers, lakes and land from being polluted or damaged. (Art. 24). Dispute settlement provided for in Regulations by mediation or arbitration (Art. 27), and Ministry of Petroleum Industry has authority to regulate operator or subcontractor who violates Regulations in conducting petroleum operations. If violations serious, judicial action may be taken. (Art. 28).

Accounting Regulations for Joint Ventures Using Chinese and Foreign Investment were promulgated on Mar. 4, 1985. These regulations, applicable to all Chinese-foreign joint ventures established in China (Art. 2), can be supplemented by public finance bureaus of provinces, etc. (Art. 3). Joint ventures must have separate accounting offices; if large or medium size, controller and auditor which offices and persons are to fulfill their responsibilities with care, make accurate calculations, reflect faithfully actual conditions, and strictly supervise all economic transactions. (Art. 7).

Joint ventures are to adopt debit and credit double entry bookkeeping (Art. 11) and books of account and accounting statements are to be prepared accurately and promptly (Art. 12), to be kept in Chinese language and if parties wish concurrently in foreign language (Art. 13).

Accrual basis of accounting is to be used; all revenues realized and expenses incurred during current period shall be recognized in current period. (Art. 15). Assets are to be stated in their original costs and accounting methods are to be consistent from one period to other, changes to be submitted to local tax authorities. (Arts. 17, 19).

JOINT VENTURES:

See topic Joint Stock Companies.

JUDGMENTS:

See topics Arbitration and Award; Courts.

Enforcement of Foreign Judgments, Court Orders, etc.—On basis of treaties or international conventions to which People's Republic of China is signatory, on principle of reciprocity Chinese and foreign courts can mutually entrust each other to undertake certain litigation action. Where matter foreign court wishes to entrust is incompatible with sovereignty or security of People's Republic of China, it should be rejected; where it is not within scope of authority of court, reasons should be clearly explicated and matter returned to foreign court. (Civ. Pro. Code, Arts. 262-267). Chinese courts have discretion to enforce foreign judgment in China.

Where court of People's Republic of China is presented with judgment having legal effect, or definitive decision of arbitration tribunal and petitioner wishes to compel enforcement thereof, and said petition involves property which is not in Chinese territory, court can, pursuant to treaties or international conventions to which China party, or in accordance with principles of mutuality, entrust foreign court to assist in execution of said judgments, etc. (Civ. Pro. Code, Arts. 262-270). With regard to judgments and final arbitral decisions which foreign courts authorize Chinese courts to enforce, Chinese courts should, according to treaties and international conventions to which China signatory, or on basis of principle of mutuality, commence examination of said judgment and if they consider it does not violate basic principles of laws of People's Republic of China or China's social interests, and ascertain that said decision has validity, execute judgment according to procedures provided in this statute. If these conditions not met, then matter should be referred back to foreign court. (Civ. Pro. Code, Arts. 262-270).

Documents of foreign courts entrusting courts of People's Republic of China to assist in execution, or to represent said foreign court in delivery, and documents entrusting Chinese court to undertake specific legal action, must have appended Chinese translation. Documents of courts of China entrusting foreign court to represent it in serving papers or assist in execution of Chinese decree, etc. and document wherein China entrusts foreign court to undertake specific legal action, must have appended foreign language translation. (Civ. Pro. Code, Arts. 262-270).

China became signatory on 2 Dec., 1986 to Convention on the Recognition and Enforcement of Foreign Arbitral Awards, agreed to in New York on 10 June, 1958. See topic Arbitration and Award.

LABOR RELATIONS:

See topics Aliens; Associations; Constitution and Government; Joint Stock Companies; Trade Zones.

Labor Law of China was passed on July 5, 1994 by Standing Committee of Eighth National People's Congress, and came into force on Jan. 1, 1995. This is first code of labor law since 1949. It plays important role in protecting lawful rights of workers and adjusting labor relationships.

Labor Law applies to all enterprises and individual businesses (hereinafter "employing units") established in China and laborers who form labor relationship with employing units. State organs, institutions, and social organization, as well as laborers who form labor contract relationship therewith must follow this law. (Art. 2).

Workers have right of equal opportunity to work and choose work, right of remuneration, right to rest, right to labor protection, right to occupational training, right to social insurance and welfare, and right to request handling of labor dispute. Workers have duty of fulfilling labor assignments, improving professional skills, implementing rules on safety and health at work, and abiding labor discipline and professional morality. (Art. 3).

Labor contract between workers and employing unit must be concluded when labor relationship is to be established. (Art. 16). Labor contract must be concluded in writing and include following terms: (1) duration of labor contract; (2) contents of work; (3) labor protection and working conditions; (4) remuneration; (5) labor discipline; (6) conditions for termination of labor contract; and (7) liability for breach of labor contract. (Art. 19). Duration of labor contract must be divided into fixed term, indefinite term, and certain term for finishing particular assignments. (Art. 20). Parties may agree on other optional terms in labor contract, such as probation period which must not be longer than six months, and obligation of workers to keep trade secrets of employing units. (Arts. 21, 22). Labor contract can be terminated upon expiry of contract term, or when conditions of termination agreed by parties present. (Art. 23). Labor contract may be revoked by agreement between parties through consultation. (Art. 24).

Employing unit may revoke labor contract without notice while worker is in any of following situations: (1) not meeting employment conditions during probation; (2) serious breach of labor discipline or rules and regulations of employing units; (3) serious neglect of duties, engaging in malpractice for selfish ends, and causing grave

See Topical Index in front part of this volume.

LABOR RELATIONS . . . *continued*
damage to employing units; (4) having committed criminal offenses. (Art. 25). Labor contract can also be revoked by employing unit with 30 days prior written notice while worker is in any of following situations: (1) inability to work due to sickness or nonindustrial injuries after medical treatment has expired; (2) incompetence to work despite training or reallocation of job; (3) performance of contract is impossible because of great changes in objective conditions under which contract was made, and parties could not reach agreement to modify terms. (Art. 26). In case of restructuring of enterprises on verge of insolvency or grave difficulties occurring to enterprises' production, employing units can reduce workers after reporting to trade union or all workers and labor administration department at least 30 days in advance. (Art. 27).

In following situation, it is illegal for employing units to dismiss workers: (1) workers incapable of work due to occupational disease or industrial accidents; (2) during recovery period for sickness or nonindustrial injuries; (3) women workers during pregnancy, childbirth or breast-feeding period; and (4) other situations stipulated by law and administrative rules and regulations. (Art. 29). Workers can request unilaterally to revoke labor contract with 30 days prior written notice (Art. 31), or at any time in following cases: (1) during probation; (2) under forced labor due to employing units using force, oppression, or illegal imprisonment; and (3) employing units failing to pay remuneration or to provide working conditions according to labor contract (Art. 32). Labor contract will be void in following situations: (1) contract concluded in violation of laws or regulations and (2) contract concluded by resorting to such measures as cheating and intimidation. (Art. 18).

Collective Contract.—Workers may conclude collective contract with enterprise on matters relating to remuneration, working hours, rest and vacations, occupational safety and health, and insurance and welfare. Draft collective contract must be submitted to congress of workers for discussion and adoption. Collective contract must be concluded by trade union on behalf of workers with enterprise (Art. 33) and submitted to labor administration department for approval (Art. 34).

Working Hours, Rest and Vacations.—Labor Law prescribes standard working hours as follows: no more than eight hours a day and no more than 44 hours a week. In Mar. 1995, State Council promulgated Provisions on Work Hours for Staff and Workers, which changed 44-hour work week to 40 hours. Labor Department and Personnel Department also promulgated implementation rules. Under these rules, 40 hours a week is prescribed for state organs, institutions and social organizations, starting from 1 May 1995, but no later than Jan. 1, 1996. Same requirement applies to enterprises located in China, starting from May 1, 1995, no later than 1 May 1997.

Employing unit may extend working hours due to requirements of its production or business after consultation with trade union and workers, but in general overtime work for day must not exceed one hour; for special reasons, it must not exceed three hours a day, Total overtime in month must not exceed 36 hours. (Art. 48). Employing units must pay workers remuneration for overtime work as follows: (1) no less than 150% of normal wages if extension of working hours is arranged; (2) no less than 200% of normal wages if extended hours are arranged on rest days; and (3) no less than 300% of normal wages if extended hours are arranged on statutory holidays. (Art. 44).

Employing unit must guarantee that its workers have at least one day off a week. (Art. 38). Statutory holidays are: New Year Day, Spring Festival, International Labor Day, National Day, and other holidays prescribed by laws, rules and regulations. (Art. 40). State must practice system of annual vacation with pay; workers who have worked for one year and more are entitled to annual vacation with pay.

Remuneration.—Employing unit must independently determine its form of wage distribution and wage level according to law and based on characteristics of its production and business and economic results. (Art. 47). State is to implement system of guaranteed minimum wages. Specific standards on minimum wages will be determined by governments of provinces, autonomous regions or municipalities directly under control of central government and be reported to State Council for record. (Art. 48). Determination and readjustment of standards on minimum wages must be made with reference to following factors: (1) lowest living expenses of workers themselves and average living expenses of family members they need to support; (2) average wage level of society as whole; (3) productivity; (4) situation of employment; and (5) different levels of economic development between regions. (Art. 49). Wages must be paid monthly to workers in form of currency. (Art. 50). Employing unit must pay wages according to law to workers who observe statutory holidays, take leaves during periods of marriage or funeral, or participate in social activities in accordance with law.

Labor Protection.—Employing unit must strictly comply with rules and standards of State on safety and health at work (Art. 52), and provide workers with safety and health conditions in accordance with provisions of State and necessary articles of labor protection (Art. 54). Workers have right to refuse to operate if management personnel command operation in violation of rules and regulations or force workers to take risk. Workers must have right to criticize, report or file charges against acts endangering their life, safety and health. (Art. 56). State provides female workers and juvenile workers with special protections. (Art. 58). No female workers or juvenile workers can be hired to engage in work in pit of mines, or work with Grade 4 physical labor intensity, or perform other work that they should avoid. (Arts. 59, 64). Employing unit is strictly forbidden to employ any child workers under 16 years old. Female workers, after childbirth, are entitled to no less than 90 days of maternity leave with pay. (Art. 62). Female workers during pregnancy must not carry out work with Grade 3 physical labor intensity. Those pregnant for seven months or more must not work overtime or on night shifts. (Art. 61).

Social Insurance and Welfare.—China's social insurance system was established as early as 1951. Government Administrative Council promulgated Labor Insurance Regulation on Feb. 26, 1951. But this regulation is inadequate and outdated due to China's economic system reforms. Recently, Chinese government has focused on social insurance reform and asked expert to establish perfect social insurance system. According to Labor Law, workers must enjoy social insurance benefits under following circumstances: (1) retirement; (2) sickness or injury; (3) disability due to industrial accident or occupation disease; (4) unemployment; and (5) childbearing. Survivors of insured worker are entitled to subsidies for survivors. (Art. 73). State set up social insurance funds, and sources of social insurance funds are determined according to categories of insurance; employing unit and workers must participate in social insurance and pay premiums. (Art. 72). State encourages employing unit to set up supplementary insurance for workers and workers to maintain savings accounts as personal insurance. (Art. 75). State develops social welfare projects, constructs public welfare facilities, and provides workers with conditions for taking rest, recuperation and rehabilitation. (Art. 76).

Labor Disputes.—In early 1950's, China had system of settling labor disputes. Later, however, organizations which settled labor disputes were abolished as country nationalized its economy, in which workers and staff members were guaranteed their wages and salaries that were divided into several grades. Thus, few labor disputes occurred. As country's economic reforms progress, China has begun to reform its labor system to enable enterprises to punish or even discharge workers and to pay workers according to their contributions. Many enterprises also have recruited contractual workers. Subsequently, number of labor disputes has grown dramatically. In 1987, State Council promulgated Interim Provisions of the State-Owned Enterprises on the Handling of the Labor Disputes. In 1993, State Council reissued Regulation Governing the Settlement of Labor Disputes in Enterprises. According to Labor Law, if labor disputes arise, parties concerned may apply to labor dispute mediation committee of their unit for mediation; if mediation fails or one party requests arbitration, that party may apply to labor dispute arbitration committee for arbitration. Either party may also directly apply for arbitration. If one party is not satisfied with arbitration decision, it may file lawsuit. (Art. 79). Labor dispute mediation committee may be established inside employing unit which should be composed of representatives of workers, representatives of enterprises, and representatives of trade union. (Art. 80). Labor dispute arbitration committee must be composed of representatives of labor administration department, representatives of trade union, and representatives of employing unit. (Art. 81). Party that requests arbitration must file written application with arbitration committee within 60 days from date of occurrence of labor dispute; arbitration committee should make decision within 60 days. (Art. 82). If one party is not satisfied with arbitration decision, it may bring lawsuit in court within 15 days from date of receiving decision. If one party does not comply with arbitral decision, other party may apply to court for compulsory implementation. (Art. 83).

Foreign Investment Enterprise Labor Management Regulations.—This set of regulations was promulgated by Labor of Ministry and Ministry of Foreign Trade and Economic Cooperation on Aug. 11, 1994. It applies to Chinese-foreign equity joint ventures, Chinese-foreign cooperative joint ventures, wholly foreign-owned enterprises, and Chinese-foreign companies limited by shares, and their staff and workers. (Art. 2).

With respect to recruitment, enterprise can autonomously determine time, terms and conditions, methods, and number of staff and workers in accordance with relevant laws and administrative regulations. (Art. 5). When enterprise recruits staff and workers, it may recruit through employment agency recognized by labor department where it is located. It may also recruit directly and outside its areas with approval of local labor administration department. (Art. 5). Enterprise must not recruit staff and workers whose employment relationship with current employer has not dissolved, nor employ child labor. (Art. 5). When enterprise recruits staff and workers, it must be Chinese staff and workers within China. (Art. 6). If it needs to recruit foreign personnel or personnel from Taiwan, Hong Kong, and Macao, it must obtain approval of local labor administration department and apply for employment certificates, etc. (Art. 6). Enterprise should establish occupational training system; staff and workers who will be engaged in technical work or be required to possess special technical skills must receive training and be certified before assuming posts. (Art. 7).

Labor contracts should be made in writing. (Art. 8). For matters concerning remuneration, working hours, leave, safety and health, insurance, and benefits, unions (worker representatives if there is no union) may represent staff and workers to negotiate with enterprises and to conclude collective contracts. (Art. 8). Labor contracts should be submitted to local labor department for certification within one month, and collective contracts should be submitted to local labor administration department for record. (Art. 9). Collective contracts become effective if local labor department does not raise objections within 15 days of receipt. (Art. 9).

In following situations, enterprise or worker (staff) may terminate labor contract: (1) parties to labor contract have reached agreement; (2) employment conditions were not met during probation, worker failed to perform labor contract, worker has seriously violated labor discipline and enterprise rules which are established in accordance with laws, or worker received labor education or was sentenced to imprisonment; or (3) enterprise uses violence, threats, imprisonment, or other means restricting liberty to force labor, failed to perform labor contract, or violated laws and administrative regulations, thus infringing upon lawful rights and interests of staff and worker. (Art. 11). However, enterprise should solicit opinion of labor union and give 30 days' written notice before terminating labor contract if: (1) worker cannot resume original position or engage in other work arranged by enterprise after medical treatment period for illness or nonwork injuries has expired, (2) worker is not qualified after receiving training or being transferred to another position, (3) changes in objective circumstances under which labor contract was entered have made it impossible to perform labor contract, and parties were unable to reach agreement to modify contract, and (4) other situations determined by laws and administrative regulations. (Art. 12). Enterprise may not terminate labor contract if: (1) worker has contracted occupational disease or has sustained on-the-job injuries and lost part or all of work ability, (2) sick worker is recovering during medical treatment period, (3) female worker is in pregnancy, childbirth, or nursing period. (Art. 13).

Wage levels of staff and workers should be determined through collective bargaining and in accordance with guidelines set by local people's government or labor administration department; wage levels should be increased annually in accordance with enterprise's economic development. (Art. 14). Enterprise must participate in pension, unemployment, medical, work injury, and maternity insurance, etc. in accordance with relevant State regulations, and must pay social insurance premiums on time to social insurance organizations. (Art. 17). Enterprise must pay lump-sum living subsidy to staff or worker whose labor contract is terminated due to mutual agreement or forced labor, or who is terminated by 30-day prior notice. (Art. 19). If labor contract

See Topical Index in front part of this volume.

LABOR RELATIONS . . . *continued*
is terminated due to worker's inability to work after medical treatment period has expired, medical subsidies should be given in addition to living subsidies. (Art. 19). Living subsidies should be one month's actual wages per year of service; medical subsidies should be three months' actual wages for workers who have worked for less than five years and six months' actual wages for workers who have worked for five years or more; workers who have worked for six months or more but less than one year considered having worked for one year. (Art. 20). Fringe benefits of staff and worker should be determined in accordance with State regulations. (Art. 22). Enterprise must set housing fund for Chinese staff and workers in accordance with local people government's regulations. (Art. 23).

Local labor administration department may impose various fines if rectification is not made after warning is given. (Arts. 28-33). In case of conflict between previous regulations regarding labor management in foreign investment enterprises and this set of regulations, latter will prevail. (Art. 36).

Trade Union Law was adopted at Fifth Session of the Seventh National People's Congress on 3 Apr., 1992. It replaces Trade Union Law promulgated in 1950.

New Trade Union Law in 1992 applies to all State-owned firms, collectively run firms, private businesses and foreign investment enterprises. Under new Trade Union Law, all laborers who are wage earners in China, regardless of nationality, race, sex, profession, religion, education, have right to organize and join trade unions. (Art. 3).

Local trade union committee may be established in enterprise, institution, or organization in which there are 25 or more members of trade union. Different levels of general trade union may be established in counties, municipalities, and provinces. National or local industrial unions may be established in same industries or related industries. All China Federation of Trade Unions was established nationwide. (Art. 12).

All China Federation of Trade Unions, local general trade unions and industrial unions are entitled to status of legal persons. Local trade union meeting requirement of legal person under General Principles of Civil Law may obtain status of legal person as social organization. (Art. 14).

Trade unions have right to represent workers and staff members to conclude collective contracts with administration of enterprises and institutions. (Art. 18).

When state-owned enterprise holds meeting discussing worker and staff matters, such as workers' wages, welfare, safety, production, labor insurance, etc., there must be representative from trade union. (Art. 32).

Chinese-foreign equity joint ventures and Chinese-foreign contractual joint venture must receive input from trade union in matters concerning wages, welfare, safety, production, labor protection, and labor insurance, etc. Trade union of foreign-capital enterprises may make proposals concerning wages, welfare, safety, production, labor protection and labor insurance, etc. (Art. 33).

Labor Insurance Regulations promulgated Feb. 26, 1951, and Jan. 2, 1953, by Government Administrative Council, applied initially to state, joint state-private, private, or cooperatively owned factories and mines employing more than 100 workers and staff; railway, water, air transport, post, telecommunications enterprises; capital construction units of factories, mines and transport enterprises, and state-owned building companies. Management, or owners of enterprises, must bear in full various labor insurance expenses. (Art. 7). Said management, or owners of enterprises, must pay to labor insurance fund each month amount equal to 3% of total payroll of workers and staff members of enterprise concerned, which must not be separately collected from staff members or workers. (Art. 8). Payment to be made to All-China Federation of Trade Unions in first two months. Commencing from third month, 30% to be deposited in account of All-China Federation and 70% to People's Bank of China. (Art. 9). People's Bank of China entrusted by aforesaid Federation to take custody of all labor insurance funds. (Art. 11).

If worker is injured or disabled while at work, he must be treated at clinic or hospital of enterprise concerned, or one designated by enterprise; if enterprise unable to provide treatment, worker must be sent to another hospital. Management provides all expenses for treatment, including meals and travel expenses, and wages must be paid in full throughout period of treatment. Workers or staff members disabled as result of injuries sustained while at work must be paid monthly allowances from labor insurance fund, depending on circumstances. Thus, e.g., worker with partial disability paid between 10% and 30% of his wages prior to being disabled but total, together with his new wages, must not exceed wages prior to being disabled. Worker completely disabled and needing persons to take care of him will receive life pension amounting to 75% of his wages. (Art. 12).

In case of sickness, injury or disablement not sustained at work, enterprise still responsible for total cost of treatment, operation, hospitalization and ordinary medicines. Expensive medicines, meals and travelling expenses must be borne by patient. However, if such worker in financial straits, allowance may be obtained from labor insurance fund. Those absent from work due to illness or injury not sustained at work will, according to duration of employment in enterprise, be paid by management of enterprise from 60% to 100% of original wages, providing period of absence does not exceed six consecutive months. (Art. 13). For periods exceeding six months, similar relief benefits to be paid from labor insurance fund. Lineal dependents of worker or staff member also partially covered for up to half cost of operation fees and ordinary medicines and may receive free treatment at clinic. (Art. 13).

Death benefits, including funeral expenses, provided for in labor insurance regulations (Art. 14), and provisions made for old-age pensions (Art. 15). Old-age pensions range from 50% to 70% of wages, depending on length of time worked, normally calculated after 25 years employment. (Art. 15). Male workers may retire once have attained age of 60, worked five years for enterprise concerned and 25 years in all. Female workers, upon attaining age of 50 and having worked 20 years, including five years in enterprise concerned, entitled to old-age pension. (Art. 15). Special provisions made for early retirement by those working in mines or certain dangerous extracting or manufacturing industries. (Art. 15[c][d]).

On Feb. 6, 1958 State Council enacted provisional regulations concerning granting of home leave to workers and staff members and wages during such leave. These regulations, of substantial importance, apply to persons living away from parents or spouses whom they cannot visit on prescribed holidays. (Art. 2).

Work Safety.—China also has statutes regulating safety at work, e.g., Industrial Factories Safety and Health Regulations. On Feb. 22, 1991, State Council promulgated Provisions on Reporting Handling of Accident-Related Deaths and Casualties Incurred by Workers and Staff in Enterprises. It replaced Workers and Office Workers' Injuries Accident Reports promulgated in 1956.

Regional Laws.—Provinces, municipalities, and special economic zones have also promulgated regulations on labor relations.

LANDLORD AND TENANT:

See topic Civil Code.

Most urban citizens obtain local housing from government or entity-owned units at fixed rentals which are quite low. Private owners of dwellings or apartments may lease them, and under special circumstances, occupants of public housing may sublease. Foreign diplomats and consuls obtain premises through negotiations, with approval and assistance of relevant Foreign Affairs offices and Ministry of Foreign Affairs. Foreign commercial personnel lease residences and offices through individual negotiations with hotels, private parties, or with assistance of sponsoring agency.

LAW REPORTS, CODES, ETC.:

See topics Constitution and Government; Courts.

There are compilations of law decisions and judgments made by each court and general compilations of law decisions that have heretofore been circulated domestically among those in legally related positions, but not circulated for public distribution. With advent of new legal system and consequent activity, future of law reports has not been clarified, but at least domestic circulation among specialists will likely continue. Publication of all statutes and administrative regulations as revised may be accomplished after their compilation.

All laws promulgated by Central Government or local governments are published either in State Council Bulletin if national regulation, or in local newspapers, etc., if local law.

Legislative Affairs Commission of Standing Committee of National People's Congress of China has commenced publication in Chinese and English of laws adopted by Congress or its Standing Committee from 1979 to 1986, and thereafter. Supreme Court has commenced publication of Supreme Court Bulletin which includes regulations, instructive cases, and reports of work. National Congress and many localities have their own official bulletins to make legislation public.

LEGISLATURE:

See topic Constitution and Government.

LIBEL:

See topics Criminal Law; Civil Code.

Intentionally false criminal accusations, even if made against criminal, are prohibited by Criminal Code. (Art. 138). Pursuant to Code of Criminal Procedure (Art. 53), those injured by criminal acts can make civil claims during criminal proceedings against criminal defendant. Court has authority to enforce civil judgment against defendant's assets. (Code of Criminal Procedure, Art. 53).

LICENSES:

See topics Contracts; Corporations; Joint Stock Companies; Patents.

LIENS:

See topics Guaranty Law; Husband and Wife; Property; Attachment; Executions.

LIMITATION OF ACTIONS:

See topics Criminal Law; Civil Code.

LIMITED PARTNERSHIP:

See topics Partnerships; Civil Code.

MARITIME LAW:

Maritime Law of China adopted by National People's Congress Nov. 7, 1992, effective July 1, 1993. Law sets forth in detail all major aspects of admiralty, including vessels, mariners marine cargo transport contract, passenger transport contract, charter, collision at sea, marine towage, marine salvage, general average, limitation on maritime damages claim, marine insurance contract, prescription and applicable law. Where international treaties concluded or acceded to by China contain provisions different from Chinese law, treaties shall prevail, unless otherwise reserved by China. (Art. 268). Where there are no relevant provisions in Chinese law and international treaties concluded or acceded by China, international custom and practices may be applied. (Art. 268).

Vessel.—Law governs all ocean vessels and other moving installations at sea, excluding vessels for military uses and government official operation, and small vessels of less than 20 gross tons. (Art. 3). Acquisition, transfer and loss of ownership of vessel should be registered with vessel's registration authority, in cases registration is absent, shall not defend against third party. (Art. 9). Transfer of vessel ownership should be transacted through written contract. (Art. 9). Vessel owner or designated persons of vessel owner may mortgage vessel to mortgagee for debts, and in case mortgagor fails to honor debts falling due, mortgagee may apply to auction off vessel and be satisfied with vessel prices with priority. (Arts. 11, 12). Vessel's mortgage shall be conducted through written contract and registered with vessel registration authority, where registration is absent, it shall not defend against third party. (Arts. 12, 13). Vessels under construction may be mortgaged, vessel building contract must be filed with registration authority. (Art. 14).

Regarding claims due to any and all of following situations, vessel priority which should be satisfied with priority to maritime lien and mortgage emerges: (1) salaries, other labor remuneration, mariners dispatch money and social insurance fees of Captain, mariners and other staff pursuant to labor law or labor contracts; (2) damages for

See Topical Index in front part of this volume.

MARITIME LAW . . . *continued*
personal injuries due to vessel operation; (3) vessel tonnage dues, pilotage dues, port dues and other statutory fees; (4) salvage proceeds of marine salvage; (5) property damages due to tortious act during voyage of vessel. (Arts. 21, 22, 25). Vessel priority must be executed through court of law which enforces it by distraining vessel. (Art. 28).

Marine cargo transportation contract defined as contract in which carrier charges freight fee and transports cargo from one port to another. (Art. 41). Carrier or consignor may request contract be formulated in writing, however, voyage charter must be in written form. (Art. 43). Telegram, telex and facsimile are considered as authentic as original. (Art. 43). Contract or Bill of Lading (B/L) as evidence of contract shall not contain clauses in violation of mandatory provision of said law. (Art. 44). Partial invalidity does not affect validity of remaining parts. (Art. 44). Clauses in which insurable interest of cargo is transferred to carrier or similar clauses are null and void. (Art. 44).

Consignor may rescind contract before vessel leaves loading port, however should pay half of freight fee to carrier, where cargo has been loaded on board, consignor bears cost of loading, unloading and relevant fees, unless otherwise provided in contract. (Art. 89). Both parties may rescind contract and be exempted from liabilities to each other, in cases where force majeure occurs or contract unable to be performed due to causes not attributable to consignor and consignee. (Art. 90). Unless otherwise provided in contract, carrier shall refund freight fee to consignee where fee paid; consignor shall bear unloading charges when cargo loaded; consignor return B/L to carrier where B/L issued. (Art. 90). Where vessel cannot arrive at designated destination due to force majeure or other cause not attributable to carrier and consignor, Captain entitled to unload cargo at safe port or point neighboring to destination and contract deemed honored, unless otherwise provided in contract. (Art. 91).

Responsibilities of Carrier.—For container transport, responsibility begins from acceptance of cargo at loading port and ends with delivery of cargo at discharging port, entire period cargo under carrier's control. (Art. 46). For non-container transport, responsibility begins from loading cargo on board and ends with unloading cargo, entire period when cargo under carrier's control. (Art. 46). During this time, carrier liable for losses and damages to cargo, unless carrier not culpable. (Art. 46). In following situations, carrier exempted from liabilities for losses and damages to cargo: (1) faults of Captain, mariners, pilots or other employees of carrier in course of piloting or administering vessel; (2) fire, excluding those due to faults of carrier; (3) natural disaster, dangers or accident at sea or other navigable waters; (4) wars or armed conflicts; (5) action, quarantine or judicial distraining enforced by government or competent authorities; (6) strike, shipping service or labor obstruction; (7) salvage or attempt to save life or property at sea; (8) act of consignor, owner of cargo or agent; (9) natural features or inherent defects of cargo; (10) improper packaging or unclear signs; (11) potential defects of vessel not discovered through prudent management; (12) other causes not attributable to carrier, employees or carrier's agent. (Art. 51). Law allows carrier to assume other responsibilities and obligations through mutual consultation with consignor, in addition to those provided by law. (Art. 45).

Bill of Lading.—At consignor's request, carrier shall issue B/L after acceptance or loading of cargo by carrier, which evidences transportation contract, testifies acceptance or loading of cargo and acts as carrier's guarantee of delivery. (Arts. 71, 72). B/L may be issued by designated person of carrier; in cases B/L issued by Captain is deemed issued by carrier. (Art. 72). B/L should contain: (1) description of cargo and declaration of hazardous cargo; (2) carrier's name and principal place of business; (3) vessel's name; (4) consignor's name; (5) consignee's name; (6) loading port and date of cargo acceptance; (7) unloading port; (8) multimodal transport B/L shall add place where cargo is accepted and delivered; (9) date, place of issuance of B/L and copies; (10) freight fee payment; (11) signature of carrier or representative. (Art. 73). Absence of one or more items above does not affect nature of B/L. (Art. 73). Straight B/L shall not be transferred, order B/L may be transferred through straight endorsement or endorsement in blank, and open B/L may be transferred without endorsement. (Art. 79).

Delivery of Cargo.—Where carrier delivers cargo to consignee and consignee fails to notify in writing situations of damages to or losses of cargo, delivery is deemed prima facie evidence that cargo delivered according to requirements of transport documents and cargo in good condition. (Art. 81). Where loss or damage to cargo is nonobvious and consignee fails to file written notice within seven consecutive days from day after cargo delivered, and 15 consecutive days from day after cargo delivered for container transport, delivery deemed duly honored. (Art. 81). Where consignee and carrier inspected cargo jointly in course of delivery, is unnecessary to file written notice concerning damage or loss of cargo. (Art. 81). Carrier exempted from liabilities, where carrier does not receive written notice cllaiming economic loss from late delivery within 60 consecutive days from date cargo delivered. (Art. 82). Where cargo not accepted for delivery or consignee defers to or refuses to take delivery of cargo at discharging port, Captain may unload cargo and store in warehouse or other proper places. Risks and fees incurred therefrom borne by consignee. (Art. 86).

Collision at Sea.—Where one vessel collides with another, Captain of colliding vessel must with best endeavors rescue damaged vessel and people, provided it does not endanger safety of his vessel and crew. (Art. 166). Captain of colliding vessel shall notify counterparty with name of vessel, port of registration, port of departure and destination. (Art. 166). In cases in which collision due to force majeure, or other causes not attriutable to either party or causes not identifiable, each party to collision free from liabilities to each other. (Art. 167). Where one party at fault, such party liable for damages. (Art. 168). Where both parties at fault, each party shall assume liabilities proportionate to respective faults, where faults of each are equal, or proportion of faults is not determinable, liabilities equally allocated. (Art. 169). Damages to properties of third parties due to collision where each party culpable, each party bears liabilities proportionate to faults; where personal injuries to third party due to collision and is attributable to each party, each assumes joint and several liability. (Art. 169).

Marine salvage contract formulated when salvor and salvaged reach agreement concerning terms and conditions of marine salvage. (Art. 175). Captain of vessel in danger may enter into salvage contract on behalf of vessel owner, and Captain or owner of vessel in danger may enter into salvage contract on behalf of owner of property on board. (Art. 175). Where contract is formulated under undue influence or dangerous situation and terms of contract obviously unfair; or fee for salvage obviously higher or lower than salvage services rendered actually by salvor, any party may apply to court or arbitration agency to modify contract. (Art. 176). Salvor must render salvage with due care and prevent or reduce environment pollution. (Art. 177). Salvor may seek assistance from other salvors where reasonably necessary. (Art. 177). Code adopts old and widely accepted principle of "NO CURE, NO PAY". (Art. 179). Salvage pay allocated among salvaged vessel and owners of other properties proportionate to respective salvaged value. (Art. 183). Salvor saving life shall not claim pay from salvaged people, however, may obtain reasonable proportion of pay from salvage pay of other salvors saving vessel or other properties, or preventing or reducing environment pollution. (Art. 186). Salvaged shall provide reasonable guarantee for salvage pay at request of salvor, and owner of salvaged vessel shall try to request owners of cargo to provide reasonable guarantee for salvage pay of their corresponding salvaged value. (Art. 188).

General Average.—Where vessel, cargo and other properties confronted with common perils on same voyage, special losses and special charges due to reasonable measures deliberately adopted for common safety are defined as General Average. (Art. 193). Losses due to delay of vessel or cargo on voyage or after voyage, including losses of charter period, freight rate and other indirect losses, are not General Average. (Art. 193). For accident resulting in special losses and special charges of General Average, where caused by faults of one party on voyage, party with faults may request General Average be shared, however, other non-fault parties or party with fault may claim damages due to faults or defend against claim. (Art. 197). Party requesting General Average be shared shall produce evidence testifying that losses be listed as General Average. (Art. 196). General Average to be shared by beneficiary parties proportionate to corresponding Allocation Value. (Art. 199). Allocation Value of vessel is total value of vessel after voyage by deducting losses beyond General Average, or actual value after voyage by adding losses of General Average. (Art. 199). Allocation Value of cargo is value of cargo at time of boarding including insurance premium and freight by deducting losses beyond General Average and freight which risks should be borne by carrier; in cases where cargo is resold before arriving at destination port, Allocation Value is net income by adding losses of General Average. (Art. 199). Allocation Value of freight is freight for which carrier assumes risk and entitled to charge after voyage by deducting expenses to complete voyage after General Average accident by adding losses of General Average. (Art. 199). Undeclared cargo or cargo given false information shall share General Average, however losses should not be listed as General Average. (Art. 200). Where declared value unduly lower than actual value, General Average shall be shared according to actual value, where General Average occurs thereto, losses calculated according to declared value. (Art. 200). Baggage and private articles of passengers shall not share General Average. (Art. 199).

Marine Compensation Responsibilities Limitation.—Vessel owner including charterer, vessel manager, and salvor may limit compensation responsibilities for personal injuries or damages or losses of properties on board or related to vessel operation or salvage operation, or compensation claims caused by late delivery of cargo or delay of passengers and their baggage, or compensation claims caused by infringement of non-contractual right related to vessel operation or salvage operation, or further damages resulting from measures taken by other persons to avoid or reduce damages of responsible parties whose compensation may be limited according to law. (Arts. 204, 207). Salvage pay or General Average allocation claim, compensation claim of oil pollution damages pursuant to International Convention on Civil Liabilities of Oil Pollution acceded to by China, compensation claim of nuclear damages pursuant to International Convention or Limitation of Liabilities of Nuclear Damages, compensation claims of nuclear damage caused by nuclear vessel, shall not be limited. (Art. 208). In compensation claim for damages caused by knowingly willful or negligent act or omission by party, responsible party's liability may not be limited. (Art. 209). Law sets forth separate limitations on claim for personal injuries and nonpersonal injuries, adopting standard of International Convention on Limitation of Liabilities of Vessel Owner. (Art. 210).

Marine Insurance.—According to Maritime Code of the People's Republic of China, with marine insurance contract insurer undertakes to indemnify itself from loss of insured subject matter. In addition, insurer indemnifies itself from liability caused by perils of insured against payment of insurance premium by insured. Definition of maritime "perils" are to be agreed upon by insurer and insured. Perils include those occurring on inland rivers or on land which is related to maritime adventure. (Art. 216).

Subject matter of marine insurance includes (1) ship; (2) cargo; (3) income from operation of ship, including freight, charter lines and passenger fares; (4) expected profit on cargo; (5) crew wages and other remuneration; (6) liabilities to third parties; (7) other property that may sustain losses from maritime peril and liabilities and expenses arising therefrom.

Insurer may reinsure insurance of subject matter. In such case, original insurance is not entitled to benefit of subsequent insurance unless specifically agreed to in contract. (Art. 218).

Insurer and insured determine insurable value of insured subject matter. If no insurable value has been agreed upon, it is calculated in following manners: (1) For ship. Value of ship at time when insurance liability commences. This includes total value of ship's hull, machinery, equipment, fuel, stoves, gear, provisions and fresh water as well as insurance premium; (2) Goods. Aggregate of invoice value of cargo or actual value of non-trade commodities at place of shipment, plus freight and insurance premium when insurance liability begins; (3) Freight. Sum of freight value, payable to carrier, and insurance premium when insurance liability commences; (4) Other subject matter. Aggregate of actual value of insured subject matter and insurance premium when insurance liability commences. (Art. 219).

If insured amount exceeds value of subject matter, portion in excess is negated. (Art. 220).

Before conclusion of contract, insured shall inform insurer of material circumstances of his ordinary business practice which he knows of or should have known of. Circumstance is material if it may have bearing on insurer's decisions as to (1)

See Topical Index in front part of this volume.

MARITIME LAW . . . *continued*
whether or not to insure and (2) amount of premium. If insured intentionally fails to inform about material circumstance then insurer may terminate contract without refunding premium. Furthermore, insurer will not be liable for any losses arising from perils that occur before contract termination. If failure to inform was unintentional then insurer may terminate contract or demand corresponding increase of premium. However, insurer will be liable for losses arising out of perils which occur prior to termination of contract.

When contract concludes, if insured knows or should have known that subject matter suffered loss due to peril then insurer is not liable for indemnification but has right to premium. If insurer knows or should have known that peril, related to loss to subject matter, is impossible, then insured may recover paid premium.

Where insured concludes contracts with several insurers regarding identical subject matter against same risk and insured amount exceeds insured value then insured may demand indemnification from any of insurers. Total amount to be indemnified may not exceed value of loss suffered by subject matter, unless otherwise agreed to in contract. Liability of each insurer will be proportional with amount insured bears versus total of insured amounts by all insurers. Any insurer, who has paid indemnification in excess of that for which he is liable, may inquire as to reasons why other insurers have failed to pay amounts for which they are liable. (Arts. 221-225).

Prior to commencement of insurance liability, insured may terminate insurance contract. In such case, insured must pay insurer's handling fees. Insurer must refund premium. Neither party may terminate contract once insurance liability begins unless otherwise stated in contract. If insured wishes, following contract specifications, to terminate agreement after insurance liability commences, then insurer may retain portion of premium. Payable premium is calculated from day of liability commencement to that of contract termination. If insurer wishes to terminate contract, he also retains premium from period beginning with contract termination and ending with insurance period expiration. However, insured may not demand termination of cargo or voyage insurance contracts after liability begins. (Arts. 226-228).

Marine insurance contracts for transport of goods by sea may be assigned by insured through endorsement and other methods. Rights and obligations under contract are assigned accordingly. If premium remains unpaid up to time of contract assigment then assignee and insured will be held jointly and severally liable. If contract is assigned because of change in ownership of insured ship, then insurer consent must be obtained. If insurer consent is lacking, contract terminates from time of ship ownership transfer. If ownership transfers during voyage, contract will terminate when voyage ends. (Arts. 229-230).

Insured may employ open cover with insurer for goods to be shipped or received in batch within given period. Open cover is evidenced by open policy issued by insurer. Insurer, at request of insured, must issue insurance certificates separately for cargo shipped in batches, according to open cover. These certificates prevail if they vary from open policy. Insured, immediately upon learning that cargo that has been issued under open cover has been shipped or has arrived, must notify insurer. This notification must include name of carrying ship, voyage, value of cargo and insured amount. (Arts. 231-233).

Marine insurance contract formulated when underwriter agrees to accept insurance and reaches agreement concerning terms of insurance between underwriter and assured. (Art. 221). Contract shall include names of underwriter, assured, subject matter insured, insurance value, insured amount, insurance responsibilities and exemptions, insurance period and premium. (Art. 217). Vessel, cargo, vessel operation income, estimated profits of cargo, salaries and other labor remuneration of mariners, liabilities to third party and other responsibilities and charges that insurance accident may incur, may become subject matter of insurance contract. (Art. 218). Insurable value of subject matter may be consulted and insured amount may also be consulted by and between underwriter and assured, howver insured amount shall not exceed insurable value. (Art. 220). Assured shall disclose such important information to which insurer will take into account in deciding premium rate or whether to accept insurance; where assured fails to disclose, underwriter entitled to cancel contract without refunding premium, and may be exempted from compensation if insurance accident ocurs. (Arts. 222, 223). When contract formulated, if assured knows or should have known insurance accident has occurred, assured is free from compensation and entitled to charge premium; where underwriter knows or should have known insurance accident is impossible to occur, assured is entitled to premium refund. (Art. 224).

Before commencement of insurance responsibility, assured may request contract cancellation and premium refund, however assured shall pay underwriter fee. (Art. 226). Unless otherwise agreed in contract, assured and underwriter shall not cancel contract after commencement of insurance liability. (Art. 227). For cargo transport and voyage insurance, insured shall not rescind contract after commencement of insurance responsibility. (Art. 228).

Contract may be transferred through indorsement of assured or other means, and right and obligation shall be transferred correspondingly. (Art. 229). If premium not paid at time contract transferred, assured and transferee shall assume joint liability to pay. (Art. 229). If contract transferred with assignment of vessel, permission shall be obtained from insurer. (Art. 230).

When insurance accident takes place, underwriter may request assured to produce evidence and materials related to nature and degree of damage before insurer pays insurance compensation. (Art. 251). Where damages within coverage caused by third party, claim against such shall be transferred to underwriter from date underwriter pays insurance compensation. (Art. 252); assured obliged to provide necessary documents and other information and try to assist underwriter to recover damages from third party (Art. 252). Where assured abandons claim to third person without permission of underwriter, or through its own fault makes recovery from third party impossible, underwriter may deduct corresponding amount from insurance compensaton. (Art. 253). Underwriter may deduct corresponding amount from insurance compensation which assured acquires from third party and assured shall refund underwriter amount exceeding insurance compensation. (Art. 254). Underwriter may abandon rights over subject matter and pay all insurance compensation agreed in contract to relieve it from obligation, where accident occurs. (Art. 255). Where insured subject matter suffers total loss, underwriter obtains all rights over it when insurance compensation completely paid. (Art. 256). Where insured amount is less than insurance value, underwriter may obtain partial right over it in proportion of insurable value to insured amount. (Art. 256).

Applicable Law of Relationship Involving Foreign Interest.—Unless otherwise provided by law, parties to contract may choose governing law for contract, where parties fail to choose, law most closely connected with contract applies. (Art. 269). For acquisition assignment and loss of vessel ownership and vessel mortgage, law of flag applies. (Arts. 270, 271). For vessel priority, law of court where case is accepted. (Art. 272). For damage claim from vessel collision, law of location of tortious act applies. (Art. 273); where collision occurs on high sea, law of court where case accepted applies; where collision with vessel of same nationality, law of flag applies (Art. 273). For General Average adjustment, law of country where adjustment conducted applies. (Art. 274). For marine compensation claim limitation, law of court where case is accepted applies. (Art. 275). Where foreign law or international custom and practices apply, they shall not harm social interests of China. (Art. 276).

MARRIAGE:

Marriage status exists in Chinese law after issuance of marriage license (Marriage Law, Art. 7) which is issued when marriage is registered. Marriage can be registered if registration office finds proposed marriage to be in conformity with provisions of Marriage Law. (Art. 7). Marriage Law requires that marriage be based on complete willingness of parties (Marriage Law, Art. 4), that it not be contracted before man has reached 22 years of age and woman 20 years of age (Marriage Law, Art. 5); it is prohibited where man and woman are lineal relatives by blood or collateral relatives by blood (up to 3d degree of relationship) (Marriage Law, Art. 6[1]); and is prohibited where one party is suffering from leprosy or from such other disease regarded as rendering person unfit for marriage by medical science (Marriage Law, Art. 6[2]).

See topic Civil Code.

MARRIED WOMEN:

See topics Descent and Distribution; Divorce; Husband and Wife; Marriage.

MASTER AND SERVANT:

See topics Contracts; Joint Stock Companies; Labor Relations.

MEDIATION:

See topics Arbitration and Award; Courts; Divorce; Foreign Trade.

Mediation is preferred means of resolving civil and commercial disputes in China. Organizations that handle mediation are numerous. Departments responsible for certain work are encouraged to mediate. Courts have responsibility to attempt to mediate prior to undertaking formal civil litigation or granting divorce. Mediation was locally organized in 1949 and on Feb. 25, 1954 Government Administrative Council promulgated Provisional General Rules for Organization of People's Mediation Committees, providing unified principles of organization and work for entire nation's mediation tribunals. Pursuant to decision of People's Congress, Standing Committee, reaffirming validity of laws and decrees enacted since founding of People's Republic of China, following laws were republished in Dec. 1979: Provisional General Rules for Organization of People's Mediation Committees ("Mediation Committee's Rules"), Organic Rules of Urban Neighborhood Offices ("Neighborhood Office Rules"), Organic Rules of Urban Residents' Committees ("Urban Residents' Committees' Rules"), and Provisional Organic Rules of Public Security Committees ("People's Security Committees' Rules"). Part of stated reason for reemphasis on these rules and organizations according to report of National People's Congress Standing Committee of Aug. 26, 1980, is to reactivate and strengthen grass roots organizations and implement mass basis for maintenance of good public order.

Organization of Mediation Committees is designed to handle civil and minor criminal disputes. (Mediation Committees Rules, Art. 1). Mediation committees have nature of organization of masses and they operate under direction of basic level people's government and court. (Mediation Committees Rules, Art. 2). Normally these committees, composed of from three to 11 members, operate in district police or public security offices or in street units and, in countryside, in village units. (Mediation Committees Rules, Art. 4). Pursuant to clarification of Art. 4 of Mediation Committee Rules by Ministry of Justice on Jan. 16, 1980, in view of changes in rural administrative districts since 1954, in rural areas mediation committees can be set up in large production brigades, or in areas of lesser population in production teams. Work of mediation committees must follow principles of: (1) Undertaking mediation on basis of governmental policy and law; (2) obtaining consent of parties and not compelling mediation; and (3) understanding that mediation is not procedure litigant must pass through, and because one has not yet gone through mediation procedures, or mediation was unsuccessful, people cannot be prevented from commencing litigation in courts. (Mediation Committees Rules, Art. 6). Mediation committees are prohibited from receiving fees corruptly, punishing or detaining any of parties to mediation and using any forceful action against any of parties. (Mediation Committees Rules, Art. 7). Mediation committees should operate during non-working hours, listen to ideas of parties, investigate facts in depth, clearly understand circumstances of case, maintain friendly and patient attitude, and reason things out. (Mediation Committees Rules, Art. 9). After case has been mediated, it should be recorded and, where necessary, parties should be given mediation agreement. (Mediation Committees Rules, Art. 8). Where handling of mediated case violates government policy or law, court should correct it or revoke proceeding. (Mediation Committees Rules, Art. 9). Basic level courts and governments should supervise and instruct mediation committees and assist their work. (Mediation Committees Rules, Art. 10).

Urban Residents Committees Rules, originally promulgated on Dec. 31, 1954, provide that one of responsibilities of said committee is to mediate disputes between residents. (Urban Resident Committee Rules, Art. 2[5]).

Ministry of Justice in Apr. 1954 issued Explanation Regarding the Mediation Committee Rules which is found in Handbook on People's Mediation Work. Ministry

See Topical Index in front part of this volume.

MEDIATION . . . *continued*
explained that relatively serious cases, and cases where circumstances are more complicated, or where impact of case is relatively large, irrespective of whether civil or criminal matter is involved, are all to be handled directly by courts. On Mar. 10, 1982 Zhang You yu, vice-president, Chinese Academy of Social Sciences stated that mediation committees in 1981 handled 12.8 times as many civil and minor criminal cases as did basic level courts. He asserted 90% of civil cases had been handled by mediation. In 1982, 860,049 mediation committees resolved 8,165,763 civil cases. In rural areas 691,029 of 714,638 production brigades had mediation committees and in urban areas 56,793 of 62,871 residents' committees had such committees. In addition, 112,227 industrial enterprises have mediation committees. Nevertheless civil disputes accepted by courts in 1982 up 17% over 1981.

MILITARY SERVICE:

China has adopted Military Service Law.

MINES AND MINERALS:

See topic Property.

Mineral resources are owned by state (Const., Art. 9) and are exploited by state enterprises or jointly with foreign enterprises.

MONOPOLIES AND RESTRAINT OF TRADE:

Tobacco Monopoly.—China also has established monopolies including monopoly in tobacco pursuant to regulations such as The Tobacco Monopoly Law of China, adopted at 20th Session of the Standing Committee of the National People's Congress on June 29, 1991. Tobacco monopoly includes cigarettes, cigars, pipe tobacco, fluecured tobacco, tobacco leaf, cigarette paper and filters, cigarette manufacturing equipment, etc. (Art. 2).

State monopolizes production, sale, import and export of tobacco industry. It carries out licensing system for tobacco monopoly. (Art. 3). Tobacco Monopoly Administration Management Bureau under State Council is responsible for work of tobacco monopoly on national level. (Art. 4).

Any enterprise which intends to engage in production must obtain license for tobacco production after approval by competent department of tobacco monopoly under State Council, and must register with Administrative Department for Industry and Commerce after examination. (Art. 12).

Any enterprise which intends to engage in wholesale tobacco business shall obtain wholesale license for sales after approval by competent department for tobacco monopoly under State Council or in relevant province, and must register with Administrative Department for Industry and Commerce after examination. (Art. 15).

It is prohibited to broadcast or print any advertisement involving tobacco products. (Art. 19).

Enterprise shall apply to register trademark if they produce cigarettes, cigars, and pipe tobacco with packing. It is prohibited to produce and sell tobacco products using falsely registered trademarks. (Art. 20).

Competent department for tobacco monopoly under State Council governs business of import and export and foreign economic technology cooperation in tobacco industry. (Art. 28).

Any enterprise which engages in business of import and export for tobacco production, consignment for sale of foreign tobacco products, and buying and selling foreign tobacco products in regions supervised and managed by customs, shall obtain management license for special tobacco monopoly. (Art. 29).

Economic Combination and Socialist Competition.—Provisional Regulations Concerning the Promotion of Economic Combination, adopted by State Council on July 1, 1980, designed to encourage certain types of economic combination. These Regulations, particularly applicable to state enterprises, encourage voluntary participation in economic combinations. Combination of various enterprises not restricted by trades, territory or ownership, or relationship of subordination. (Prov. Regs. Promotion Economic Combination, Art. 1). Combination of producers and processors of raw material promoted. (Art. 3). Combined enterprises may obtain raw materials, for example, directly from enterprises with which it combined, bypassing intermediate supply and marketing distribution departments. Combination agreement normally executed contract. Breach of contract settled through mediation between parties, under jurisdiction of department in charge, or if that fails, by arbitration by court.

On the other hand, Provisional Regulations Concerning the Development and Protection of Socialist Competition, adopted by State Council on Oct. 17, 1980, obviously designed to promote competition. To that end, these Regulations provide that enterprise must be granted greater power to make its own decisions (Art. 2) without interference of local authorities or departments in rights to which enterprise entitled by law, particularly regarding production, supply and marketing, personnel, finance and materials. Agreements and contracts between enterprises must be honored by both parties and protected by laws of state. Party breaching contract held legally and economically responsible for said breach. (Art. 2). Clause three states that in economic activities no monopoly of commodity allowed, other than those State has specified to be handled exclusively by certain departments and units. While Regulations give priority to production for Plan targets, enterprises may market products in excess of Plan targets for those allocated for state use. (Art. 4). Departments not permitted to forbid sale of outside products in own locality or department, and regional monopoly should be restrained. (Art. 6). Compensation should be made for transfer or possession of important technological achievements to encourage technological innovation and inventions. (Art. 7).

Thus, Chinese policy and law provide dual goals for both combination and competition. In licensing joint ventures, or other entities including foreign participants, Chinese at times offer to protect market for new joint venture, and in licensing other ventures with similar technology or products are sometimes careful to protect existing enterprises.

Anti-unfair Competition Law was adopted by National People's Congress on Sept. 2, 1993, effective as of Dec. 1, 1993. Said law requires business operators to firmly adhere to principles of voluntariness, equality and fairness, honesty, keeping one's word and observing commonly accepted commercial ethics in conducting business transactions. (Art. 2).

Unfair Competition.—Business operators are not allowed to employ any of following unfair means which will harm competitors in conducting market transaction: (1) copy other's registered trademarks; (2) use, without prior permission same or similar names, packages, decorations of well-known products to disguise products as original to confuse and mislead buyers; (3) use, without prior permission, names of other enterprises to mislead buyers; (4) forge or use without prior permission identification marks, marks for quality and other quality marks in commodities or falsify places of origin and use other false indicators to mislead with regard to quality. (Art. 5). Public utility enterprises or other certified monopolized business operators must not press buyers to buy from operators designated by them so as to squeeze out their competitors. (Art. 6). Government and its auxiliary departments may not abuse administrative powers to make others buy commodities handled by operators designated by them, create obstacles to fair business activities of other operators, and they may not abuse administrative powers to reject entry of any commodities from other places into local markets or prevent local commodities from flowing out to markets in other places. (Art. 7). Business operators may not resort to bribery means in selling or buying commodities. Any rebates given to units or individuals undercover without entry into account are deemed bribery, acceptance of which by any unit or individual is deemed as acceptance of bribery. (Art. 8). Where business operators are permitted to give discount to buyer or commissions to middleman in express manner, amount of such discount or commission must be entered into account. Where business operators are allowed to accept such discount or commission, amount concerned must also be entered into account. (Art. 8). Business operators may not mislead public in advertisements or other means with regard to quality, composition, property, purposes, producers, validity period and places of origin of commodities; advertisers may not design, produce, publicize or act as agent for any advertisements which they knew or should have known were false. (Art. 9). Business operators may not infringe upon trade secrets by employing following means: (1) obtain trade secrets of other proprietors by theft, inducement, coercion or other illegal means; (2) disclose, use or allow others to use trade secrets obtained by aforesaid illegal means; (3) disclose, use or allow others to use trade secrets of other proprietors in their possession by breach of agreement or requirement of owners regarding maintaining secrecy. (Art. 10). Where third person knew or should have known trade secrets were illegally obtained by aforesaid means; or obtains, uses or reveals said trade secret, it is deemed infringement of trade secrets. (Art. 10). Business operators may not sell products at lower-than-cost prices aimed at defeating competitors except when (1) selling goods at seasonally adjusted prices; (2) selling goods at reduced price due to clearance of debts, shifting to other products or business closure. (Art. 11). In selling commodities, business operators may not tie in other goods or demand unreasonable terms and conditions aganst will of buyers. (Art. 12). Business operators may not engage in following prize sale promotions: (1) lie about prize; wilfully let internal personnel win prize; (2) use prize sales to promote goods of poor quality at higher price; (3) offer highest prize exceeding RMB 5,000. (Art. 13). Business operators may not fabricate or spread false information to harm competitors, commercial credit and creditability of competitors' commodities. (Art. 14). Tenderers shall not collude with one another to push up or push down offer price for bid; tenderers and tenderees may not collude to harm fair competition of competitors. (Art. 15).

Penalties.—Business operator must pay compensation when it has caused damage to other operators due to committing unfair competition and if damages are incalculable, amount of profits obtained by infringer during period of infringement should be paid, with reasonable fees arising from investigation. (Art. 20). Businesses being infringed may file suit when their legal rights and interests have been infringed by acts of unfair competition. (Art. 20). Where business operator fakes registered trademarks of others, uses without prior permission, names of other enterprises, forges or infringes identification marks, marks for quality products and other quality marks on commodities or falsifies place of origin, commits other actions to mislead people with regard to quality, it may be dealt with according to provisions of Trademark Law and Law of Product Quality. (Art 21). Where business operator uses, without prior permission, special names, packages and decoration identical to those of well-known commodities to create confusion and mislead buyers, supervision and examination departments order it to stop offense, confiscate illicit proceeds, impose fine more than twice but less than three times amount of illegal proceeds depending on severity of case. Where case is serious, business license may be revoked. Where selling inferior or fake goods constitutes crime, criminal responsibility must be prosecuted according to law. (Art. 21). Where business operator sells or buys commodities by resorting to bribery and other means sufficient to constitute crime, criminal responsibility must be prosecuted according to law. Where case does not constitute crime, fine amounting to more than RMB 10,000 but less than RMB 200,000 shall be imposed, in addition to confiscation of illegal proceeds. (Art. 22). Where public utility enterprise or certified monopolized business operator forces others to buy commodities handled by operators it has designated, so as to keep other operators from fair competition, supervision and examination departments at provincial level order it to terminate offense and impose fine of more than RMB 50,000 but less than RMB 200,000 depending on severity of case. Where operator sells goods of inferior quality for higher price or indiscriminately collects fees, supervision and examination departments must confiscate their proceeds and impose fines more than twice but less than three times amount of illegal proceeds depending on severity of case. (Art. 23). Where business operator misleads public regarding his products by using advertisements or other means, supervision and examination departments must order it to terminate offense, eliminate influence and impose fine of more than RMB 10,000 but less than RMB 200,000 depending on severity of case. (Art. 24). Where business operator infringes upon trade secret, supervision and examination department must order it to terminate offense and impose fine of more than RMB 10,000 but less than RMB 200,000 depending on severity of case. (Art. 25). Where business operator engages in premium sale which falls within category of unfair competition, supervision and examination departments must order it to terminate offense and impose fine of more than RMB 10,000 but less than 200,000 depending on severity of case. (Art. 26). Where tenderers collude to push up price or push down offer price for bid or if tenderers collude to squeeze competitors out of fair

See Topical Index in front part of this volume.

MONOPOLIES AND RESTRAINT OF TRADE . . . *continued*

competition, bid won must be invalidated. Supervision and examination departments must impose fine of more than RMB 10,000 but less than RMB 200,000 depending on severity of case. (Art. 27). Where business operator offends provisions regarding order to stop selling, transferring, concealing or destroying money or materials related to act of unfair competition, supervision and examination departments must impose fine more than twice but less than three times amount of prices of materials sold, transferred, concealed or destroyed depending on severity of case. (Art. 28). Where party concerned refuses to accept punishments imposed by supervision and examination departments, it may apply for review with departments at next higher level within 15 days beginning from date when punishment decision was received. If it refuses to accept decision under review, it may institute litigation before court within 15 days from date review decision was received. Party concerned may also bring case directly before court. (Art. 29). Where government or its auxiliary department forces buyers to buy commodities handled by operators it has designated, or restrict other business operators in their legitimate business activities or restrict normal circulation of commodities among regions, departments concerned at higher-level must order it to cease this pressure. Where case is very serious, departments concerned at same or higher level must impose sanctions on person(s) directly responsible. Where designated operator takes advantage of such opportunity to promote sale of goods of inferior quality at higher price or indiscriminately collects fees, supervision and examination departments must confiscate illegal proceeds and impose fine more than twice but less than three times amount of illegal proceeds depending on severity of case. (Art. 30).

MORTGAGES:

Both Shenzhen and Guangzhou have enacted legislation to provide procedures for mortgages on real property. Guangzhou City Law on Handling of Mortgages of Real Property, enacted and effective as of June 6, 1990 provides regulations for handling mortgages in City of Guangzhou (Canton); and requires domestic mortgage lender to be licensed by central bank. (Art. 2). Mortgages and mortgage agreements must be notarized and registered with city land bureau.

See topic Guaranty Law, subhead Mortgage.

See also topic Liens.

MOTOR VEHICLES:

Consuls, long term business representatives and other foreign residents in China may purchase automobiles from abroad and bring them to China for use and take them out of China or sell them in China when they wish. Duties that must be paid, if any, and ease of obtaining access depend in part on location of one's home or office, since regulations vary in different localities even within same city. Additionally, vehicles can now be driven from Hong Kong into China, to Guangzhou and Shenzhen, etc., in Guangdong province but procedures, including Hong Kong procedures, are as yet cumbersome. Temporary tax Regulations for Licenses to Use Vehicles and Boats promulgated Sept. 13, 1951 by Government Administrative Council. This tax, in essence license fee, depending on local rules, paid quarterly, semiannually or annually. (Art. 5). For example, in Guangdong province said fees for motor vehicles paid quarterly (Jan., Apr., July, and Oct.), while fees for bicycles and pedicabs paid annually. (Art. 5, Guangdong Regulations). Regulations exempt certain vehicles from these fees, such as fire engines, ambulances, sanitation trucks, sprinkler trucks, and vehicles used in suburbs by peasants. (Art 6[1]; 6[5]). Passenger cars taxed at quarterly rate of 15-80 yuan; truck carrying cargo, at rate of 4-15 yuan per net ton capacity, per quarter. (Art. 7). Provincial and urban governments have authority, within these amounts, to determine fees. (Art 9). Thus, in Guangdong province passenger vehicle with ten or less seats pays only 40 yuan per quarter.

Regulations provide for fines of up to three times license fees for failure to report, register, pay fees or obtain licenses. (Art. 15). While Guangdong regulations presumably cover all cities and counties in Guandong, nevertheless Guangzhou has its own regulations. Thus, passenger vehicle with ten seats must pay 50 yuan per quarter license fee in Guangzhou, while passenger vehicle with seven seats or less pays 40 yuan per quarter.

Rules of road and road markings on major roads are those of International Convention, but many roads are small, narrow and cluttered.

NATIONALITY:

See topic Aliens.

Nationality Law was adopted at Third Session of Fifth National People's Congress, promulgated by Order No. 8 of Chairman of Standing Committee of National People's Congress on Sept. 10, 1980 and has been effective since that date.

Nationality Law is applicable to acquisition, loss and restoraton of person's recognition as citizen of People's Republic of China. (Art. 1). It specifies People's Republic of China is unitary multinational state. Persons belonging to any nationality in China shall have Chinese nationality. (Art. 2). People's Republic of China does not recognize dual nationality for Chinese nationals. (Art. 3).

Person born in China whose parents are both Chinese nationals, or one of whose parents is Chinese national, shall be Chinese national. Person born abroad whose parents are both Chinese nationals, or one of whose parents is Chinese national, shall be Chinese national. (Art. 5). Person born in China whose parents are stateless, or of uncertain nationality and have settled in China, shall be considered Chinese national. (Art. 6). However, person whose parents are both Chinese nationals and have settled abroad, and one who has acquired foreign nationality at birth, shall not be considered Chinese national. (Art. 5).

Foreign nationals or stateless persons who are willing to abide by China's Constitution and laws, and who meet one following conditions, may be naturalized upon approval of their applications: (1) are near relative of Chinese nationals; (2) have settled in China; or (3) have other legitimate reasons. (Art. 7). Persons who apply for naturalization as Chinese national shall acquire Chinese nationality upon approval of their applications. Persons whose applications for naturalization as Chinese national have been approved shall not retain foreign nationality. (Art. 8).

Chinese national who has settled abroad and who has been naturalized as foreign national, or who has acquired foreign nationality of his own free will, shall automatically lose Chinese nationality. (Art. 9). Chinese nationals who meet one of following condition may renounce Chinese nationality: (1) are near relative of foreign nationals; (2) have settled abroad; or (3) have other legitmate reasons. (Art. 10). Persons who apply for renunciation of Chinese nationality shall lose Chinese nationality upon approval of their applications. (Art. 11). However, state functionaries and military personnel on active service shall not have Chinese nationality renounced. (Art. 12).

Foreign nationals who once held Chinese nationality may apply for restoration of Chinese nationality if they have legitimate reasons. Those whose applications for restoration of Chinese nationality have been approved shall not retain foreign nationality. (Art. 13).

Persons who wish to acquire, renounce or restore Chinese nationality, with exception of cases of automatically losing Chinese nationality, shall go through formalities of application. Applications of persons under age of 18 may be filed on their behalf by parents or legal representatives. (Art. 14). Nationality applications in China shall be handled by Public Security Bureaus of municipalities or counties where applicants reside. Nationality applications abroad shall be handled by China's diplomatic representative agencies and consular offices. (Art. 15). Applications for naturalization of Chinese nationals and for renunciation or restoration of Chinese nationality are subject to examination and approval by Ministry of Public Security of People's Republic of China. Ministry of Public Security shall issue certificate to person whose application has been approved. (Art. 16).

Nationality status of persons who have acquired or lost Chinese nationality before promulgation of Nationality Law shall remain valid. (Art. 17).

Nationality Law is effective as of Sept. 10, 1980. (Art. 18).

NEGOTIABLE INSTRUMENTS LAW:

See topic Bills and Notes.

NOTARIES PUBLIC:

See topics Descent and Distribution; Property.

Notaries public existed in China before "Cultural Revolution" and have been gradually restored to active role in legal system. As of Feb. 1984, 2,267 notarial offices and 6,600 notaries public in China under administration of Ministry of Justice in 28 provinces, municipalities and autonomous regions. Both Chinese citizens and persons from abroad made use of notaries public in 1950's and are now looking to these offices for various purposes. Notarial work encompasses not merely attestation of signature, but also evidences legality of document or act. It is based on application by party and evidence brought forth and examined. At times special forms and careful examination of law are required for notary seal to be properly affixed. Notarized documents have many applications, but not meant to be used to resolve legal disputes that should be settled in court of law, but rather to lessen need for litigation.

On Apr. 13, 1982 State Council promulgated Temporary Regulations for Notaries Public, consisting of six chapters and 30 regulations. Regulations also apply to foreign citizens living in China (Art. 28), as well as applications by Chinese citizens to Chinese embassies and consulates abroad (Art. 15). Notarial duties undertaken only upon application of party to evidence, according to law, legal act, fact or document. (Art. 1). Fourteen separate duties conferred upon notaries by Art. 4 of Regulations, including those of evidencing: Contract, will or trust; power to inherit; gift or division of property; adoption; familial relations; status, educational degrees, work records; birth, marital status, whether someone dead or alive; that signature or seal on document correct, and that copies, photocopies, portions or translations of document identical with original document. Also, notarial office can evidence that document reflecting compensation due on debt or for goods is undoubtedly authentic, and that it can be compulsorily enforced; can evidence that something is to be preserved and can maintain wills or other documents; can represent party in drafting application to have document notarized. Notarial office can also, upon application and in accordance with international custom, handle other notarial responsibilities.

Notaries public are Chinese citizens with rights to vote and having legal education or training (Art. 4), who should not act as notary to close relations (Art. 17). Notaries must examine applicant's status and capacity and factual and legal basis of application and documents submitted. (Art. 18). They must maintain confidentiality of notarial work. (Art. 19). Where notary public has determined pursuant to Art. 4(i) that document reflecting debt, etc. can be enforced by compulsory process, if necessary, party can then apply to basic level court having jurisdiction for enforcement. (Art. 24).

Where notarial evidence denied, reasons for denial should be communicated, either orally or in writing, to petitioner. (Art. 24). Party may appeal denial of notarial evidence to higher judicial administrative organization. (Art. 25). Where application for notarization is to be used outside China, aside from procedures in this statute, matter should be submitted to Ministry of Foreign Affairs or foreign affairs office of province, self-governing area, or city under direct jurisdiction of central government and Chinese embassy or consulate in country in question, unless there are different regulations in nation where document to be used or parties agreed that embassy or consulate unnecessary.

OFFSHORE OIL EXPLOITATION:

See topic Joint Stock Companies.

PARTNERSHIPS:

See topics Contracts; Corporations; Joint Stock Companies; Civil Code.

Since domestic private enterprises exist, and cooperative ventures with foreign entities can be with individual foreign person(s), partnerships can exist. Small private partnerships in urban areas would have to be registered and licensed for certain purposes, such as establishing restaurant. Foreign ventures with local entities also must be licensed but are unlikely to be partnerships in that other than partnerships between two entities, viz., joint ventures, partnerships with individual Chinese persons will not be common in normal international transactions.

PATENTS:

In 1984 China signed Paris Convention for the Protection of Industrial Property and in 1983 joined World Intellectual Property Organization. China was accepted as International Examining Authority under patent cooperation treaty.

On Mar. 12, 1984 Standing Committee of People's Congress promulgated China's Patent Law ("Law"), effective Apr. 1, 1985. Chinese patent law was amended Sept. 4, 1992 by National People's Congress.

On Jan. 19, 1985 State Council promulgated Implementing Regulations of the Patent Law ("Regs").

Inventions, utility models and exterior designs may be patented. (Law. Art. 2).

Invention is defined as any new technical solution relating to product, process or improvement thereof (Regs 2); utility model is any new technical solution relating to shape, structure or combination for product fit for practical use (Regs 2); and design means any new design of shape, pattern, color or their combination of product, which creates aesthetic feeling and is fit for industrial application (Regs 2).

Unpatentable subject matters include: (1) scientific discoveries; (2) rules and processes of mental activities; (3) methods of diagnosis or treatment of diseases; (4) animal and botanical varieties; (5) substances derived by means of nuclear transformation. (Law Art. 25). However, processes of item (4) are patentable. (Law Art. 25). All chemical inventions including pharmaceutical and agricultural chemicals, whether products or processes, are patentable under new patent code.

Microbiological processes, products thereof and microorganisms will be patentable (Regs 25 and 26), and computer software while not clearly excluded by statute, is said by some officials to be covered by forthcoming legislation and if software is closely related to operation of hardware for which patent application is made then software may now be patentable.

Authority to examine patent applications and issue patents is held by Patent Office. (Art. 3). China has established Patent Office, which is reported to have staff of several hundred persons, including attorneys, examiners and administrators. This office has headquarters in Beijing and offices throughout China. By end of 1992, China established approximately 500 patent agencies, trained and registered 5,000 agents, and assembled library of 30 million patent documents from 20 countries. Patent application by nonresident foreigners or foreign businesses without offices in China is to be made either to Patent Agency of China Council for the Promotion of International Affairs, Hong Kong based China Patent Agent (HK) Ltd. or Shanghai Patent Office. Foreign persons resident in China can make patent application through local patent offices where they have residence. Chinese have also established offices in New York and California to assist in registration in China.

Patent Office shall maintain Patent Register (Regs Art. 80) and publish Patent Gazette (Regs Art. 81) containing abstract of invention or utility model, and information on all proceedings by Patent Office regarding application, e.g. approval, registration, request for examination, etc. China Patent Agent (HK) Ltd. will publish bilingual quarterly entitled China Patents and Trademarks.

Within six months of first application for exterior design, and 12 months of first application for invention or utility model in foreign countries, applicant may enjoy preemptive right for application in China for same subject matter under Chinese patent code in accordance with international treaties concluded or acceded to by China and said foreign countries or on principal of reciprocity. (Law Art. 29). Within 12 months of first application for invention or utility model in China, applicant may enjoy preemptive right for its application for same subject matter in China. (Law Art. 29).

Said inventions and utility models must have characteristics of newness, originality and practicality. (Law Art. 22). Newness is defined as where prior to date of patent application no similar invention or practical new model has been published or otherwise made known either in China or in foreign countries. Originality of utility model means it must have substantial distinguishing features and represent improvement, while originality of invention is defined as it having substantial distinguishing features and representing marked improvement over prior inventions. Practicality is defined to mean utility model or invention can be made to produce effective results. Any exterior design to be patentable, must not be identical with or similar to any design published in foreign or Chinese publications or publicly used in China prior to date of application to be patentable. (Law Art. 23).

No other entity or individual may exploit patent after issuance of patent without authorization of patentee. Patent marking can be placed on patented products.

From third year of application for patent of invention where application has not yet been granted, applicant must commence paying maintenance fee, said fee payable annually is 100 yuan (100 renminbi). In addition, once patent has been issued annual fee shall be paid. For inventions said fee varies according to years, thus from first to third year it is 200 yuan, 300 yuan from fourth to sixth year, 600 yuan from seventh to ninth year, 1,200 yuan from tenth to 12th year and 2,500 yuan from 13th to 15th. Utility model patents annual fees start at 100 yuan per year and go to 200 yuan from fourth to fifth year and 300 yuan from sixth to eighth year. Exterior design patents start at 50 yuan, go to 100 yuan from fourth to fifth year and 200 yuan from sixth to eighth year.

Where two or more applicants file applications for patents for identical inventions, utility models or exterior designs, patent right shall be granted to applicant whose application was first filed, though if both file on same day inventors may negotiate mutual agreement as co-inventors. Exhibition of patentable product, six months prior to application at international exhibition sponsored or recognized by Chinese government, at prescribed academic or technical meeting or disclosure without consent of applicant, shall not result in loss of novelty. Receipt of priority shall be counted from date above events occurred for patent on invention or utility model. Where foreign applicant filed application in China within 12 months from first filing in foreign country (or within six months for exterior design) pursuant to reciprocity or treaty, priorty date will be date application first was made in foreign country. Claim of priority by filing in foreign country requires applicant to within 15 months of said filing submit filing number in China.

Entity capable of exploiting invention or utility model failing to obtain license from patent holder with reasonable terms and conditions within reasonable time, Patent Office may issue compulsory license for invention or utility model at request of entity. (Law Art. 51). Person receiving compulsory license cannot license others and shall not have exclusive right to exploitation of patent. Award of compulsory license can be appealed to courts within three months of notification of decision.

Patent Office, within 18 months of date of filing of patent for invention, or earlier at request of applicant, if after preliminary examination finds application in conformity with law, shall publish application. Substantive examination can be made within three years from date of filing, provided that request is made by applicant; failure of applicant without justified reason to make such request in three year period will result in application having been deemed withdrawn. Patent Office can on its own initiative proceed to examine any application of invention for substance. If, in application for patent for utility model or exterior design, Patent Office upon preliminary examination finds it in conformity with patent law, it shall immediately so announce.

Within six months following patent granting, any entity or individual deeming patent not in conformity with patent code may apply to Patent Office to revoke patent. (Law Art. 41). Patent Office examines application and decides whether to maintain or reject patent. (Law Art. 42). Applicant and patentee may appeal to Patent Re-examination Board which decides to maintain or revoke patent. (Law Art. 43). Applicant or patentee may file suit with court of law against decision within three months from receipt of decision (Law Art. 43), however decision of Board regarding utility model and exterior design are final (Law Art. 43).

Applications must be submitted in duplicate. Invention and utility model applications require abstract on main points, description and claims and title, name of inventor, name and address of applicant and description in manner sufficiently clear to permit person skilled in relevant technology to carry it out. Where necessary, drawings should be provided. Applications for exterior design require drawings or photographs of design; statement as to class to which product belongs shall also be included. Relevant materials about priority of earlier applications should be included.

Normally as to invention or utility model following should be provided: Title, technical field, description of relevant prior art, task it is to perform, its merits compared to prior art, description in drawings, best mode for carrying it out, claims in clear and precise manner explaining protection sought, dependent or independent nature of claim, if involving microbiological process or product thereof, deposit sample shall be provided.

Drawings or photographs that must be submitted shall be no longer than 19 cm by 27 cm and no smaller than 3 cm by 5 cm. Where necessary Patent Office may require application for patent design to submit sample or model of product incorporating design, and if design seeks protection of colors drawing or photograph in color and black and white shall be submitted.

Inventor or creator may apply for patent as individual or entity or if discovered in course of duty or during work entrusted to said person by entity for whom he works, then entity may make application. Right to apply for patent can be assigned, pursuant to written contract, though assignment of right to apply by Chinese entity or individual to foreigner must be approved by relevant Chinese government authorities.

Duration of patent for inventions is 20 years and patent for utility model and exterior design is ten years from date patent application filed with Patent Office. (Law Art. 45). Patentee shall pay maintenance fee from year granted. (Law Art. 46).

Patent Agency.—Regulations on Patent Commissioning promulgated by Decree No. 76 of State Council of People's Republic of China on Mar. 4, 1991, and effective as of Apr. 1, 1991. These regulations contain all chapters, 28 articles.

For purpose of these regulations, term "Patent Commissioning" means handling by patent application or other patent-related matters in name of commissioning party. (Art. 2). Term "patent agency" refers to service organ which, on accepting commission of comissioning party, applies for patent or handles other patent-related matters within authorized scope of its commission. Patent agencies shall include: (1) patent agencies which handle foreign-related patent work; (2) patent agencies which handle domestic patent work; (3) law firms which handle domestic patent work. (Art. 3).

Patent agency may undertake following work: (1) providing patent-related consultancy; (2) preparing, on commission, patent application documents and filing patent applications; handling matters related to requests for substantive examination or reexamination; (3) handling matters related to filing oppositions and requesting announcement of patent right invalidation; (4) handling matters related to assigning of patent application rights or patent rights, as well as patent licensing; (5) accepting invitations and appointing patent agents to serve as patent advisers. (Art. 8).

Patent agency shall, when it accepts commission and undertakes work, have letter of appointment signed by commissioning party stating clearly commissioned items and extent of authority of commission. Patent agency shall, after accepting commission, be prohibited from accepting commission of any other commissioning party in relation to patent work of same content. (Arts. 9, 10).

Term "patent agent" as in these regulations refers to person having "Patent Agent Qualification Certificate" and "Patent Agent Work Permit". (Art. 14). Patent agency shall engage as patent agents those persons with "Patent Agent Qualification Certificate". Employment procedures shall be completed for patent agents engaged, and patent agency shall issue "Patent Agent Work Permit" to them and report to Patent Office of PRC for record. (Art. 11).

Where patent agency changes its name, address or person in charge, it must make report to Patent Office of People's Republic of China to register changes. Only after it is subject to approval and registration is change effective. Where patent agency ceases its operations, it must, after appropriately handling all unfinished matters, make report to its original examination authority, and this authority shall report to Patent Office of PRC for completing relevant procedures. (Art. 12). Where, due to change in circumstances, approved patent agency no longer meets requirements stipulated in Art. 4 of these Regulations and will still be unable to meet these requirements within one year, original patent administration authority which approved its establishment shall suggest to Patent Office of PRC to cancel that patent agency. (Art. 13).

Any Chinese citizen who upholds constitution of PRC and satisfies following requirements may apply to be patent agent: (1) is at least 18 years of age with full capacity for civil actions; (2) is graduate of institution of higher learning in science or engineering (or having equivalent educational level) with command of one foreign language; (3) is well-versed in patent law and related legal knowledge; and (4) has worked for at least two years in scientific, technical or legal field. (Art. 15).

See Topical Index in front part of this volume.

PATENTS . . . *continued*

Patent agent shall only handle patent commissioning work assigned by its patent agency, and may not accept commissions directly. Patent agent may not undertake patent commissioning work in two or more patent agencies simultaneously. Patent agent must, before he is transferred from patent agency, make appropriate arrangements for all uncompleted commissions. (Arts. 17, 18).

"Patent Agent Qualification Certificate" automatically ceases to be valid if holder fails to engage in any patent commissioning work or patent administrative control work over five-year period. Patent agent may apply for patent while engaged in patent commissioning work or within one year of ceasing involvement with such work. (Arts. 19, 20).

Staff of State authorities may not work for any patent agency in part-time manner or engage in any patent commissioning work. Patent agent has responsibility to keep secret content of any invention-creation which, in course of his commissioning work, he may become aware of except those in patent applications that have already been published or announced. (Arts. 22, 23).

If patent agency does not agree with penalty decision made by Patent Office of PRC on canceling its status as patent agency, or patent agent does not agree with penalty decision on revoking his "Patent Agent Qualification Certificate", application for reconsideration of case may be lodged with Patent Office of PRC. Where aforesaid agency or agent still disagrees with reconsidered decision, legal proceedings may be initiated with People's Court within 15 days from date of receiving notice of reconsidered decision.

Patent Office of People's Republic of China responsible for interpretation of these regulations. These regulations enter into force as of Apr. 1, 1991. Interim Provisions on Patent Agency, approved by State Council on Sept. 4, 1985 and promulgated by Patent Office of PRC on Sept. 12, 1985 shall be annulled as of same date.

Adjudication of Patent Disputes.—Measures of Patent Administrative Authorities on Adjudicating Patent Disputes have been implemented effective as of Dec. 4, 1989. Patent administrative authorities shall mediate and adjudicate following patent disputes: (1) patent infringement; (2) license fees for use of invention or creation between time of publication of patent application for invention or public announcement of patent application for utility model or design and time when patent is granted: (3) right to apply for patent and disputes over ownership of patent; and (4) other patent disputes which may be mediated or dispose of by patent administrative authorities. (Art. 5). Disputes over right to apply for patent and disputes over ownership of patents shall be mediated and adjudicated by patent administrative authorities where respondents are located. (Art. 7). If any party to dispute has instituted proceedings in court, patent administrative authorities shall not accept petitions for mediation and adjudication. (Art. 12[4]). In mediating and adjudicating patent disputes, patent administrative authorities shall abide by principle that matter once decided shall not be subject to readjudication. (Art. 4). If party is not satisfied with decision of patent administrative authorities, then institution of proceedings in court can be commenced within three months after receipt of such decision. Where no proceedings have been instituted upon expiry of this time limit, decision shall become effective immediately. (Art. 24).

See topic Civil Code.

PERPETUITIES:

No limitation on disposition of property comparable to common law rule against perpetuities exists in China. Land usage can be assigned in perpetuity or for fixed term of years.

PERSONAL PROPERTY:

See topic Property.

PLEDGES:

See topics Guaranty Law; Liens; Civil Code.

PRESCRIPTION:

See topics Limitation of Actions; Property.

PRINCIPAL AND AGENT:

See topic Civil Code.

Representation by agent is generally permitted and some standard form Chinese contracts are drafted with agent as executing entity. Agent may not be bound if he clearly is not principal to contract. Power of attorney must be in writing and may have to be notarized at times before Chinese entity like embassy or consulate.

Power of Attorney.—To entrust another to represent one in litigation, one must present written power of attorney to court, containing signature or seal of individual entrusted. Power of attorney must specify matter and scope and time limit of such authority. Specific authority required for attorney in fact to conciliate, counterclaim, admit, abandon litigation or alter its object. (Civ. Pro. Code, Art. 59). Power of attorney to represent citizens of China living out of China must be attested to by Chinese embassy or consulate in that country or, if none, by patriotic overseas Chinese organization. (Civ. Pro. Code, Art. 59). Parties required to inform court in writing of any alterations or termination in power of attorney and through court inform other parties. (Civ. Pro. Code, Art. 60). Divorce cases require presence of parties even though power of attorney issued, unless special circumstances. (Civ. Pro. Code, Art. 62). Foreign nationals or stateless persons not residing in China who mail Chinese attorneys powers of attorney must have said power of attorney documented by notary public in their country and attestation by local Chinese embassy or consulate. (Civ. Pro. Code, Art. 242).

PRIVATE ENTERPRISE:

Provisional Regulations were promulgated on June 25, 1988, by State Council, effective as of July 1, 1988, where "private enterprise" refers to privately funded economic entity which employs at least eight persons. (Art. 2). Private enterprise may be (1) sole investment enterprise; (2) partnership enterprise; or (3) limited liability company. (Art. 6). Sole investment enterprise is funded and managed by one person; said owner assumes unlimited liability for obligations of enterprise. (Art. 7). Partnership enterprise is jointly funded and managed by two or more persons who share its profits and losses, based on written agreement. Partners share unlimited liability for obligations of enterprise. (Art. 8). Limited liability company is one in which investor is only liable for company only up to amount of his investment; said company is liable only up to amount of its total assets. (Art. 9).

Following persons may apply to form a private enterprise: Villagers; persons awaiting employment in urban areas; operators of individual industrial and commercial ventures; persons who have resigned or were dismissed from previous posts; retired cadres, retired workers and other persons authorized under State laws, regulations and policies. (Art. 11).

Private enterprise may engage in production and business operations, as permitted by State laws, statutory regulations and policies, in fields such as industry, construction, transportation, commerce, catering, public service, repair and scientific and technological consultancy. Private enterprise may not engage in production and business operations related to war industry or finance and may not produce, market, or purchase products proscribed in China. (Art. 12).

Investors in private enterprise must hold legal title to its property and said property may be inherited according to law. (Art. 20). Private enterprise must open account with bank or other financial institution in compliance with State regulations and may apply for loan if it can prove its ability to repay said loan.

Registration.—Business operations of private enterprise may commence only after application for registration is approved by local Administration of Commerce and Industry and business license is procured. (Art. 15). Private enterprise which successfully registers as legal person must additionally register commencement of its operations and any amendments or cancellation of registration, according to Administrative Regulations governing Registration of Corporations. (Art. 19).

Personnel.—Recruitment of personnel by private enterprise will be based on written labor contracts which defines rights and obligations of both parties based on principles of equality, voluntary participation and unanimous acceptance via negotiation. Labor contract must be filed with local labor management bureau. (Art. 27). Employees of private enterprise will work eight hours per day (Art. 31) and may not be under 16 years of age (Art. 32).

Employees of private enterprise may organize trade union according to law and other legal rights and interests of said employees will be protected by state laws. (Art. 4). Private enterprise may establish private enterprise association. (Art. 5).

If private enterprise violates provisions of these regulations involving areas such as taxation, natural resources, industrial and commercial administration, prices, finances, standard measurements, quality, hygiene, or environmental protection laws, relevant bureau will enforce sanction according to law. (Art. 45).

Private enterprise income tax will be levied according to Regulations on Private Enterprise Income Tax which were passed on June 3, 1988, promulgated on June 25, 1988, and effective as of fiscal year 1988 (Art. 12) providing for income tax at basic 35% rate (Art. 3) and other relevant regulations (Art. 37). In addition, income received by private enterprise investor from wages and distribution of after-tax profit will be subject to individual income tax according to law. (Art. 39).

Sanctions for following violations will be administered by Administration of Commerce and Industry: (1) Withholding truth or lying on registration application or unlawfully commencing business operations prior to completion of registration procedures; (2) engaging in business activities beyond scope of business license or amending, re-registering or cancelling registration not in accordance with regulations; (3) forging, altering, leasing, transferring, selling or unlawfully reproducing business license. (Art. 41). Sanctions to be administered, depending on circumstances, include: Warning, fine, confiscation of illegal income, suspension of operations until case is resolved; or cancellation of business license or private enterprise.

PROCESS:

Return of service required in service of process in civil case. (Civ. Pro. Code). Person being served with process must record date of receipt and sign name, or affix his seal, on document. Date of service is date recipient signed return of service. Where court serves papers involving litigation, it should directly deliver them to party to be served, or if said party not present they should be delivered to adult member of said person's family who resides with such person, for signature and receipt. Where person to be served already appointed agent for service of process, then said agent should be served and should sign return of service. (Civ. Pro. Code).

If person to be served resists service of process, process server should request representative of relevant basic level organization or other person to come to place of service, explain circumstances and on return of service record reasons for refusal of service and date. Process server and witness should sign their names or affix their seals, and document to be served should be left at residence of person to be served. These acts regarded as service of process. (Civ. Pro. Code).

Where direct service of process encounters difficulties, other courts may be entrusted to represent trial court in serving process or process can be served by mail, which must be registered, return receipt. Date of receipt will be date of service. (Civ. Pro. Code). If whereabouts of person to be served unknown or use of other methods of service provided in this section will be of no effect, then service can be effected by formal government proclamation. Service will be completed within three months of date of said proclamation. Reasons for service by proclamation must be recorded in case file. (Civ. Pro. Code).

PROPERTY:

See topics Constitution and Government; Civil Code.

Ownership of property in China divided into three basic types, viz: (1) Socialist ownership by whole people, equivalent to ownership by state; (2) collective ownership, which is ownership by collective organization; and (3) private ownership by individuals or private entities. (Const. Art. 5; Revised Const. Arts. 7-10). Land, mineral resources, waters and forests are state owned (Const. Art. 5; Revised Const. Art. 8), except those forests, mountainous lands, grasslands, undeveloped lands and

PROPERTY . . . *continued*
beaches owned by collectives (Revised Const. Art. 8). Collective ownership, particularly in rural areas, has three levels, viz. that of commune, production brigade and production team. Latter is basic accounting unit. Land in cities deemed property of state. (Revised Const. Art. 10). Land in villages, towns and suburban areas is property of collective, except for portion belonging to state pursuant to law. Land used for private homes and farmed for private needs is property of collective. (Revised Const. Art. 10).

Private ownership by citizens of homes, personal property, work tools, vehicles, savings accounts, cash, small business, etc. protected by Constitution. (Art. 9). Revised Constitution protects right of citizens to own lawfully earned income, savings, houses and other lawful property. (Revised Const. Art. 14). Right of citizens to inherit private property is protected by Constitution. (Revised Const. Art. 15). State also protects lawful rights and interests of individual economy. (Revised Const. Art. 11). Private ownership of stock in joint venture corporations and assets of other business ventures by foreigners is protected by statute, e.g. Joint Venture Law, treaty, e.g. Trade Agreement between U.S. and China, and by contract and guarantees of government entities or Bank of China, e.g. compensation trade agreements guaranteed by Bank of China, and by Revised Constitution, Art. 12. Various localities in China are now selling foreign entities right to use land for specific periods e.g. 50 years.

In addition, long term interests in use of land, including perpetual interests in said use can be acquired by individuals for their homes and collective unit for collective purposes, as well as by urban organizations. In countryside farmers are protected in farming private plots of land for their own needs (Const., Art. 7; Revised Const. Art. 9); in keeping livestock in pastoral areas for their own need (Const. Art. 7; Revised Const. Art. 9); and in engaging in household sideline production (Const., Art. 7; Revised Const. Art. 9). Additionally, pursuant to central directive #75 issued on Sept. 29, 1980, on Progressively Strengthening and Improving Agricultural System of Responsibility, Chinese agriculture policy has devolved greater responsibilities on individuals and households for piece of land, which although owned by state or collective, nevertheless was contracted to farmer. Free market in agriculture is now quite extensive throughout China. In addition, commune has been deprived of its political functions, which have been granted to townships.

General Provisions of the Criminal Code (Art. 2) state that it protects rights of ownership of citizens to their lawful property. Art. 31 of Code states that those whose criminal acts cause economic loss to persons, aside from criminal punishment, will be required, according to circumstances, to make compensation for said loss.

REAL PROPERTY:

See topics Property; Civil Code; Trade Zones.

Land Administration.—

Land Administration Law was adopted at 16th Session of Standing Committee of the Sixth National People's Congress on June 25, 1986 and amended at Fifth Session of Standing Committee of the Seventh National People's Congress on 29 Dec., 1988. It provides that land in China is owned by socialist publicly, namely, ownership by all people and by collective organizations. (Art. 2).

No organization or individual may appropriate, buy, sell or otherwise engage in transfer of land by unlawful means.

State may, in public interest, requisition land owned by collectives under law.

Right of use of land owned by State and collectives may be transferred legally. State shall devise system for paid use of land owned by State. (Art. 2).

Land Administration Department under State Council is subject to Government for state-owned land. (Art. 5).

Land in urban district of cities is owned by State. Land in rural and suburban areas is owned by collectives, except for those belonging to State. House sites, privately farmed plots of cropland and hilly land are also owned by collectives. (Art. 6).

State-owned land may be used by State-owned units or collective-owned units. State-owned land and collective-owned land may be used by individuals. Units and individuals who use land have duties to protect, manage and reasonably use land. (Art. 7).

Ownership of land and right to use of land are protected by law, and organizations and individuals must not invade rights. (Art. 11).

Interim Regulations Governing the Assignment and Transfer of the Right to the Use of the State-Owned Land in Urban Areas were promulgated by State Council on May 19, 1990.

State, in accordance with principle of ownership rights being separated from right to use land, has implemented system in which right to use state-owned land in urban areas may be assigned and transferred with exclusion of underground resources, objects buried underground, and public works. (Art. 2).

Assignment of right to use land refers to act of State as owner of land to assign right to use land for certain number of years to users, who must in turn pay fees for assignment. (Art. 8).

Lease of right to use land refers to act of land user as lessor to lease right to use land together with aboveground buildings and other attached objects to lessee, who must in turn pay lease rentals to lessor. (Art. 28).

Land user has to pay all land utilization fees within 60 days of date when land use right granting contract was signed. If they are not paid within stated period, owner has right to terminate contract and is entitled to economic compensation for contract violations. (Art. 14).

Owner should, in accordance with contract stipulations, surrender land use right. If land use right is not surrendered, land user has right to terminate contract and claim compensation for contract violations. (Art. 15).

If land user wants to revise utilization purposes as stipulated in contract, user must obtain consent from owner, obtain approval from land and urban planning departments, sign new contract, pay readjusted utilization fees, and go through formalities of registration. (Art. 18).

Any company, enterprise, other organization or individual within or outside China may, unless otherwise provided by law, obtain right to use land and engage in land development, utilization, and management. (Art. 3). Land users which have obtained right to use land may, within term of land use, transfer, lease, or mortgage right to use land, or use it for other economic activities; their lawful rights and interests will be protected by laws. (Art. 4).

When land use right is rented out, lessor and lessee must sign contract for valuable consideration, and rent contract must not be contrary to state laws, regulations, or stipulations in contract granting land use right. (Art. 29). After land use right is rented out, lessor must continue to fulfill commitments as stipulated by land granting contract. (Art. 30). When land use right and buildings and auxiliary facilities on it are rented out, lessor must go through registration formalities. (Art. 31).

User which has obtained land use in form of transfer is entitled to use it for remainder of fixed term. (Art. 22). Owner or co-owners of buildings and auxiliary facilities on land enjoy land use right where buildings and auxiliary facilities are located. When ownership of buildings and auxiliary facilities on land is transferred, land use right transfers correspondingly, unless buildings and/or auxiliary facilities are transferred as movable property. (Art. 24). Transfer of land use rights and ownership of buildings and auxiliary facilities on it must go through transfer formalities.

When land use right and ownership of buildings and auxiliaries on ground are transferred in parts, it must be approved by land administration and house property management departments at city and county levels and go through transfer formalities as stipulated. (Art. 25). If transfer prices on land use rights fall below market prices, people's governments at city and county levels have priority to purchase them. When transfer prices on land use rights inflate irrationally, people's governments at city and county levels are entitled to take any measures necessary. (Art. 26). If utilization purposes of land, granted for valuable consideration, call for revision after land use right is transferred, it should be handled in accordance with Art. 18 of these regulations. (Art. 27).

Land use rights are mortgageable. (Art. 32). When land use right is mortgaged, buildings and auxiliary facilities on it are mortgaged correspondingly. When buildings and auxiliary facilities are mortgaged, land use right under them is mortgaged correspondingly. (Art. 33). When land use right is mortgaged, mortgagor and mortgagee must sign contract, for valuable consideration, which cannot be contrary to laws, regulations, or stipulations in land granting contract. (Art. 34). When use right of piece of land and buildings and auxiliary facilities on it are mortgaged, it is necessary to go through mortgage registration formalities. (Art. 35).

If mortgagor fails to pay debts at specific time or declares that it is disbanded or bankrupt during period when mortgage contract is effective, mortgagee has right to dispose of mortgaged property according to laws, regulations, and stipulations in mortgage contract. When land use right and ownership of mortgaged property are obtained as penalty, it is necessary to go through registration formalities for ownership transfer. (Art. 36). Mortgagees have priority to benefit from disposal of mortgaged property. (Art. 37). To have mortgage canceled for default or other reasons, it is necessary to go through registration formalities. (Art. 38).

Users of land must, in activities to develop, utilize and manage land, abide by laws and regulations, and may not jeopardize interests of society and public. (Art. 5). Land administration departments under people's government at or above county level must conduct supervision and inspection over assignment, transfer, lease, mortgage, and termination of right to use land. (Art. 6).

Registration of assignment, transfer, lease, mortgage and termination of right to use land and registration of aboveground buildings and other attached objects must be handled by local land administration departments and housing administration departments in accordance with land and pertinent regulations of State Council. Registration documents must be made available for public reference. (Art. 7).

Land administration departments under people's government at municipal and county level must, in conjunction with administration departments for urban planning and construction and housing administration departments, draw up plan concerning size and location, purposes, term and other conditions with respect to assignment of right to use land. Plan must be submitted for approval in accordance with limits of authority for approval as provided by State Council and must then be implemented by land administation departments. (Art. 10).

Contracts for assigning right to use land must be signed by land administration departments of people's government at municipal and county levels and land users in accordance with principle of equality, voluntariness and compensation for use. (Art. 11). Maximum term with respect to assigned right to use land must be determined in light of purposes listed below: (1) 70 years for residential purposes; (2) 50 years for industrial purposes; (3) 50 years for purposes of education, science, culture, public health, and physical education; (4) 40 years for commercial, tourism and entertaining purposes; and (5) 50 years for comprehensive utilization or other purposes. (Art. 12).

Assignment of right to use land may be carried out by negotiation, tender or auction. (Art. 13). After paying total amount of fees for assignment of right to use land, land user must go through registration to obtain certificate for land use and accordingly right to use land. (Art. 16). Transfer of right to use land refers to land user's act of reassigning right to use land, including sale, exchange, and donation. If land has not been developed and utilized in accordance with period of time specified in contract and conditions, right to use may not be transferred. (Art. 19). Transfer contract must be signed for transfer of right to use land. (Art. 20). With transfer of right to use land, rights and obligations specified in contract for assigning right to use land and in registration documents must be transferred accordingly. Ownership of aboveground building and other attached objects must also be transferred accordingly. (Arts. 21, 23).

Land use right is terminated at expiration of granting contract term, early withdrawal from use right, or loss of land. (Art. 39). State is not to recover land use rights from land users who have obtained them through legal procedures before terms of utilization expire. However, under special circumstances, State can recover land use rights before expiration date, in interest of public, pursuant to procedures as prescribed by law. When such recovery is made, compensation is to be offered according to years of utilization remaining and actual development of land by user. (Art. 42). When use of piece of land expires, State gratis recovers its use right and ownership of buildings and auxiliary facilities on it. Land user must return land use license and go through formalities to write off use right. (Art. 40).

When use of piece of land expires, user can apply to extend term of utilization. Extension is made by signing new contract in accordance with regulations hereof. User must pay for granting of land use right and go through registration formalities. (Art.

See Topical Index in front part of this volume.

REAL PROPERTY . . . *continued*

41). Free transfer of land use rights denotes that land users get land use rights gratuitously through various means as prescribed by law. (Art. 43). Land use rights obtained by individuals in accordance with these regulations are inheritable. (Art. 48).

The Interim Measures for the Administration of the Foreign-Invested Development and Management of Tracts of Land was promulgated by State Council on May 19, 1990 to attract foreign investment for development and management of tracts of land (hereinafter "tract development").

Term "tract development" as used in these measures means after obtaining right to use state-owned land, investor must carry out, as planned, comprehensive development of and construction on land, including levelling ground and land construction for such public works as water supply and drainage system, power and heat supply systems, roads, communication networks, and communication facilities, so that conditions may be adequate for land to be used for industrial or other construction purposes. Investors must then transfer right to use land for operating public utilities or proceed to construct such aboveground buildings as industrial structures with supporting facilities for production and basic services. It may also transfer or lease these aboveground buildings. (Art. 2).

With respect to projects to attract foreign investment for tract development, municipal or county people's governments must organize drawing up of tract development project proposals (or feasibility study reports). (Art. 3). Foreign investors who intend to invest in tract development must, in accordance with relevant laws, form Chinese-foreign equity joint ventures, Chinese-foreign contractual joint ventures, or wholly foreign-owned enterprises (hereinafter "development enterprise") to engage in development and management of land. Development enterprises should acquire state-owned land use rights over areas to be developed in accordance with Chinese laws.

Development enterprises must have right to act on their own in business operations and management in accordance with law, but they must have no administrative power in their development areas. Relationship between development enterprises and other enterprises is of commercial nature. (Art. 4). Development enterprises must draw up tract development plans or feasibility study reports which specify overall targets and respective targets for different stages of development, details and requirements in actual development, and plan to utilize developed land. Tract development plan or feasibility study report must, after examination and verification by municipal or county government, be submitted to people's government of province, autonomous region or municipality directly under Central Government for examination and approval. (Art. 7).

Transfer or mortgage of right to use state-owned land must be handled in accordance with laws and administrative rules and regulations on administration of land. (Art. 9). Development enterprises may attract investors to development areas to make investment, accept transferred right to use state-owned land, and launch enterprises. (Art. 10).

For tract development project which makes use of 1,000 mu or less of arable land or 2,000 mu or less of other land and whose amount of investment for comprehensive development falls within limits of power for examination and approval of government of province, autonomous region, or municipality directly under Central Government (including people's government or administrative committee of special economic zone), project proposal must be submitted to people's government of province, autonomous region or municipality directly under Central Government for examination and approval. With respect to tract development project which makes use of more than 1,000 mu of arable land or more than 2,000 mu of other land and whose amount of investment for comprehensive development falls within limits of power for examination and approval of government of province, autonomous region, or municipality directly under Central Government, project proposal must be submitted to State Planning Commission for examination, verification and overall balancing, and then to State Council for examination and approval. (Art. 3). When granting state-owned land use rights, for valuable consideration, to development enterprises, people's governments at municipal or county level in development areas, in accordance with laws and administrative regulations on state-owned land administration, should define area, purpose, and terms for granting, set forth land utilization fees and other conditions, sign contracts on grant of state-owned land use rights for valuable consideration, and submit them to relevant authorities for approval. (Art. 5).

After state-owned land use right is granted for valuable consideration, resources and buried objects found on or in state-owned land belong to State. If they need to be developed, relevant laws and administrative regulations should be observed. (Art. 6). These measures must be put into effect within limits of specific economic zones, open coastal cities and open coastal economic zones as of date of promulgation. (Art. 18).

Law of China concerning Administration of Urban Real Estate was adopted by National People's Congress on July 5, 1994, effective as of Jan. 1, 1995.

Granting of Land Use Rights.—State may grant rights to use state-owned land to land users for certain period, and land users must pay State fees for using land. (Art. 7). Regarding collectively owned land, it can be granted to land users provided it has been requisitioned and turned into state-owned land, (Art. 8). Granting of land use rights should comply with overall land use plan, urban plan and annual construction land use plan. (Art. 9).

Authority to grant land use rights is vested with government of county and city. (Art. 11). Granting of land use rights must adopt auction, bidding or discussions and negotiation between related parties. Rights to use land for purposes of commerce, tourism, recreational facilities or luxury housing must be granted through auction or bidding, if conditions permit. If conditions do not permit, they may be granted through mutual consultation and discussion. Prices for granting land use rights through consultation must not be lower than minimum prices set by State. (Art. 12). Maximum term of land use rights must be set by State. (Art. 13). Written contract must be executed upon granting land use rights by and between land users and land administrative authorities of cities or counties. (Art. 14).

Land users must pay prices for acquisition of land use rights according to contract. Land administrative authorities are entitled to rescind contract and claim damages for breach of contract. (Art. 15). When land users have paid prices as specified in contract, land administrative authorities must provide land to them in accordance with contract. Should they fail to provide land as required by contract, land users are entitled to rescind contract and claim restitution of prices they have paid to land administrative authorities. (Art. 16). Land users may also claim damages.

Purposes of land must not be changed unless otherwise approved by land administrative authorities. If approved, original contract must be modified or new contract must be executed to replace original one. (Art. 17). State must not take back land use rights properly and lawfully granted to land users before expiration of term, unless under special circumstances and for public interest, with payment of appropriate compensation to land users. (Art. 19). If land is extinct, land use rights must terminate. (Art. 20). If land users intend to extend term of land use rights after expiration, they must apply to land administrative authorities at least one year before expiration. If approved, new contract will be executed. (Art. 21).

Allocation of Land Use Rights.—Land users may obtain land use rights from State by allocation, and they pay only acquisition costs to State. (Art. 22). Land use rights obtained by allocation must not be subject to definite term unless otherwise provided by laws and regulations. Under following circumstances, State may allocate land use rights to land users: (1) land used by State organs or for military purposes; (2) land used for construction of urban infrastructures and public utilities; (3) land used for construction of state-supported key energy, transport and water conservancy projects; and (4) land used for other purposes as stipulated by laws and regulations. (Art. 23).

Real estate development must be undertaken in strict compliance with urban planning under principles of overall planning, rational layout, comprehensive development and balanced construction of all necessary coordinate facilities. (Art. 24). Those having obtained land use rights through granting must develop land in accordance with contract. Should they fail to start to develop land for one year after commencement date as specified in contract, idle land fee of less than 20% of prices of land use rights must be levied; should they still fail to start for two years after commencement date, land use rights must be taken back without any compensation, except delays are caused by force majeure or action of governments, or necessary preparatory work. (Art. 25). Design and construction of real estate project must comply with state standards and norms. No project may be transferred for use without inspection after completion. (Art. 26).

Real estate development enterprise refers to those that engage in development and operation of real estate for purpose of profit. To establish real estate enterprise, following requirements must be satisfied: (1) having its own name and organization; (2) having fixed site for business operations; (3) registered capital is in conformity with provisions of State; (4) possessing sufficient professionals and technical personnel; and (5) other requirements as may be provided by laws and regulations. (Art. 29).

Ratio between registered capital and total investment of real estate enterprise must be in conformity with relevant provisions of State. Should project be developed in stages, amount of investment for each stage must match scale of that stage, and such funds must be put into construction according to schedule specified in contract. (Art. 30).

Real Estate Conveyance.—Real estate assignment refers to right that holders sell, present or otherwise lawfully transfer their real estate to others. (Art. 36). Following real estates must not be assigned: (1) land use rights obtained through granting, which do not meet requirements for assignment as specified below; (2) rights restricted by rulings of judicial organs or administrative authorities; (3) land use rights which have been taken back lawfully; (4) common real estate where other owners disagree; (5) ownership and title at issue; (6) certificates of ownership have not been granted; and (7) other conditions as specified in laws and regulations. (Art. 37).

Land use rights obtained through granting may be assigned provided that: (1) prices of land use rights have been paid in full and certificates to use land have been issued; and (2) development of land has been in progress pursuant to transfer contract on land use right, and in case of housing construction, contribution to total investment has reached 25%, or in case of development of tracts of land, conditions for industrial use or other construction purposes have been met. (Art. 38).

Written contract must be executed for conveyance. (Art. 40). When real estate is transferred, all rights and obligations specified in land use rights granting contract must be transferred accordingly. (Art. 41). Regarding land use rights obtained by transfer, term of land use rights after conveyance must be remainder of original term less period used by original land user. (Art. 42).

Real Estate Mortgage.—Mortgage may be established on ownership of houses and their land use rights. Land use rights obtained through granting may be mortgaged. (Art. 47). Mortgage must be subject to written contract. (Art. 49). After execution of mortgage contract, new houses must not belong to mortgaged property. If it is necessary to sell mortgaged property, said new houses may be sold at same time, but proceeds of which do not belong to mortgaged property.

Property Leasing.—Lessor and lessee must enter into written contract which must specify term of lease, purpose, rental, responsibility for maintenance as well as other rights and obligations. Lease contract must be filed with real estate authorities for record. (Art. 53). Residential lease is subject to policies of State and cities at location of premises. Rental for commercial lease is subject to discussion between lessor and lessee. (Art. 54).

Real Estate Registration.—Land use rights and ownership of houses are subject to registration. Registration authorities are real estate departments of county government or above. (Art. 60). Real estate mortgages are also subject to registration with government departments designated by county government or above. (Art. 61).

SALES:

See topics Statistics, Standards and Quality Control; Contracts.

Generally, no particular form is required for purchase of personal property, but most of Chinese corporations engaged in international sales have standard form purchase and sales agreements that conform to standard international practice including provisions for price, quantity, method of payment, date of shipment, means of shipment, etc. Sales of buildings require notarial stamps and registration with local authorities, as well as payment of taxes.

State Council promulgated Provisional Regulations for the Administration of Commodity Prices (July 7, 1982), which provide regulations for administration for said prices under State Council policies and plans. State Council has authority additionally

See Topical Index in front part of this volume.

SALES . . . *continued*
to establish prices on important industrial and agricultural commodities, transportation, and on non-commodity fees. (Art. 4). Relatively important commodities and fees are under jurisdiction of local government bureau in charge of prices and other commodities and fees are to be established by industrial and commercial enterprises within ambit of national policy and regulations. (Art. 4).

Unless there are other regulations to contrary, administration of imported and exported commodities as well as those commodities of joint venture enterprises with foreign firms, enterprises with foreign investment, and whose sold to foreigners, overseas Chinese and Hong Kong and Macao compatriots are all governed by these regulations. (Art. 26).

Regulations combine principles of planned economy and those of market economy, taking into account market forces. (Art. 3). There are three forms of price determination, namely national, which is principal form and within scope of national regulations, prices established by rural markets and by enterprises. (Art. 3).

National Price Bureau proposes general price policy, as well as specific price policies, regulations and plans for approval by State Council. (Art. 9). Provincial level price departments carry out national plans and enforce regulations and formulate and enforce price standards within their jurisdiction. (Art. 10). Prices are differentiated on basis of wholesale, retail, region, standards, quality, season, purchase, sales, allocated goods, and supplies for principal commodities. (Art. 10[3]).

Industrial and commercial enterprises can establish prices on defective goods, within limits of regulations establishing gross profits on foodstuff enterprises, where said foodstuffs have no governmentally fixed unified price, establish prices for foodstuffs; according to type of commodity and range of fluctuation, establish basic prices for commodities whose prices fluctuate, pursuant to administrative procedures approved by State Council establish negotiated prices for agricultural products and byproducts purchased and sold on negotiated basis; based on restrictions in regulations of relevant commodity pricing organizations, establish trial sales prices for new products; establish pursuant to regulations, inter-enterprise prices on specialized products made by joint efforts; establish prices on products where there are no prices fixed by Government, as well as establish charges for non-commodity and handicraft items produced by joint efforts; and pursuant to regulations as to type and pricing principles, negotiate prices on small, light industrial, textile and handcrafted industrial products. (Art. 14).

Prices on heavy industrial products already established by government cannot be negotiated, but where necessary temporary prices can be fixed pursuant to regulations. (Art. 28).

In many cases prices of goods on both fixed commodity price market and free market fluctuate within certain price ranges.

Trial Provisions on Fixing Prices of Machinery Products According to Their Qualities and Grades, issued by State Economic Commission, Price Bureau and Ministry of Machinery Industry, effective Jan. 1984. These Trial Provisions permit state enterprises manufacturing general machinery products recognized as top quality by State Economic Commission to set prices for said products at 20% higher than state price lists. In general, quality products can be sold at prices from 8% to 12% higher than state list prices, and products with energy-saving attributes at prices 15% higher. Prices of products technically backward to be gradually lowered. This considered first step in modification of rigid price controls for state enterprises.

Advertising.—On Feb. 17, 1982 State Council promulgated Provisional Regulations Concerning Supervision of Advertising, consisting of 19 articles, effective May 1, 1982. On Oct. 26, 1987, these were replaced by new Regulations, consisting of 22 articles, effective Dec. 1, 1987.

Advertisements Law of China was adopted by National People's Congress on Oct. 27, 1994, effective as of Feb. 1, 1995. Advertisements must be true and lawful and comply with principle of spiritual civilization. Advertisements must not have any false information and not mislead or defraud consumers. Advertisers, advertising agents and advertisement publishers engaged in advertising activities must follow principles of fairness, honesty and good faith. (Art. 5). "Advertiser" refers to any legal person, other economic entity or individual that designs, produces and publishes advertisements by itself or acting through agents for purpose of selling commodities or services. "Advertising agent" means any legal person, other economic entity or individual acting as agent in designing and production of advertisement. "Advertisement publisher" refers to any legal person or other economic entity publishing advertisements on behalf of advertiser or advertising agent. (Art. 2).

Advertising Guidelines.—Contents of advertisement must be helpful for physical and mental health of people, promote improvement in quality of goods and services, protect lawful rights and interests of consumers, follow social and public morality and professional ethics, and safeguard dignity and interest of State. (Art. 7). Statements in advertisements of performance, origin of production, use, quality, price, producer and manufacturer, valid term and promise, and servicing of goods advertised must be clear and explicit. Advertisement, in which gifts are provided as incentives in promoting sales of goods or providing services, must state type and quantity of gifts to be given free. (Art. 9). Data, statistical information, investigation and survey information, digest and quotations used in advertisement must be true and accurate, and their sources must be cited. (Art. 10). Advertisement involving patented goods or patent methods must clearly indicate patent number and type of patent. Products which have not been patented must not be boasted as being patented. Use of unsuccessful patent applications or those which have been terminated, nullified or invalidated in advertisements is prohibited. (Art. 11). Advertisement shall be distinctive and make consumers identify it as advertisement. Mass media may not publish advertisements in form of news reports. Advertisement published through mass media must bear advertisement mark to distinguish it from news items so that consumers may not be misled. (Art. 13).

Advertisement must not belittle goods or services of other manufacturers or operators. (Art. 12).

Advertisements for Specific Products.—Advertisements relating to pharmaceuticals and medical apparatus and instruments must not contain following: (1) unscientific information, statements or promises on their efficacy; (2) rate of cure or efficacy; (3) comparing efficacy and safety with those of other medicines and medical apparatus and instruments; (4) name or image of medical research unit, academic organization, medical unit or expert, doctor or patient; and (5) any other information as may be prohibited by laws and administrative regulations. (Art. 14).

Contents of advertisements for pharmaceuticals must conform to standard instructions approved by public health authorities under State Council or public health authorities of provinces, autonomous regions and municipalities directly under Central Government. Advertisements for therapeutic pharmaceuticals which are to be used on physician's advice as directed by State must be marked "purchase and use subject to physician's prescription". (Art. 15). Special pharmaceuticals such as anaesthetic, narcotic, psychotropic, toxic and radioactive drugs must not be advertised. (Art. 16).

Advertisements for agricultural chemicals must not contain following: (1) claims of its safety such as nontoxicity or non-harmlessness; (2) unscientific affirmations or promises indicating its effectiveness; (3) characters, words or pictures that violate regulations on safe use of agricultural chemicals; and (4) such other matters as prohibited by law and administrative regulations. (Art. 17).

Publication of advertisements relating to tobacco or tobacco products through radio, cinematography films, television, newspapers, magazines or periodicals is prohibited. Erecting or placing advertisements for tobacco or tobacco products at public places such as waiting rooms, cinemas, theaters, conference halls and sports stadiums and gymnasiums is prohibited. Advertisements for tobacco or tobacco products must contain such warning: "Smoking is harmful to your health." (Art. 18). Contents of advertisements for foods, alcoholic drinks or cosmetics must comply with conditions in relevant hygiene license, and no medical jargons or words may be used so as to confuse them with pharmaceuticals. (Art. 19).

Advertising Activities.—Advertisers, advertising agents and advertisement publishers must, in their advertising activities, enter into written contracts, stipulating explicitly each party's rights and obligations. (Art. 20). No advertiser, advertising agent or advertisement publisher may resort to unfair competition of any form in their advertising activities. (Art. 21). Advertiser must, in commissioning design, production and publication of advertisements, appoint qualified and lawfully established advertising agent or advertisement publisher. (Art. 23).

Advertising charges must be reasonable and made known to public. Charge standards and measures must be registered with administrative departments in charge of price and industry and commerce authorities for record. Advertising agents and advertisement publishers must make public their charging standards and measures. (Art. 29). Advertising publishers must provide true information on media coverage, audience rate and circulation to advertisers and advertising agents. (Art. 30).

Examination of Advertisement.—Advertisements for such goods as pharmaceuticals, medical apparatus and instruments, agricultural chemicals or veterinary drugs which are published through radio, cinematography film, television, newspaper, magazine, periodical and other media, and other advertisements as provided by laws and administrative regulations, are subject to examination. Relevant competent administrative departments must examine and inspect, prior to their publication, contents of advertisements in accordance with relevant laws and administrative regulations; no advertisement can be published without such examination. (Art. 34).

Penalties.—Where false and misleading publicity on goods or services is made by using advertisement, advertising supervision authorities must order advertiser to stop publishing advertisement and to use amount equivalent to its advertising expenses to publish correction announcement to eliminate influence generated by such false and misleading advertisement; impose on advertiser fine of not less than amount of its advertising charges but not more than five times said charges; confiscate advertising charges of advertising agent and advertisement publisher responsible and impose on them fine of not less than amount of advertising charges but not exceeding five times amount of advertising charges; and in serious case, disqualify them, according to law, to carry on advertising businesses. Where act is serious enough to constitute crime, criminal liability must be pursued. (Art. 37).

Where publication of false and misleading advertisement affects consumers, thereby causing damages to their lawful rights and interests, advertiser must assume civil liabilities whilst advertising agent and advertising publisher, who have knowledge of or should have such knowledge of falsity of contents of advertisement, must be jointly liable according to law. Advertising agent or advertisement publisher, who fails to provide real name and address of advertiser, must bear full civil liabilities. Social organization or other organizations, which recommend goods or services to consumers in false and misleading advertisement and consequently cause damage to lawful rights and interests of consumers, shall also bear joint liabilities. (Art. 38).

Where publishing of advertisement violates prohibitive provisions as specified in advertising guidelines of this law, advertising supervision authorities must order advertiser, advertising agent and advertisement publisher responsible for advertisement, to stop publication of such advertisement and publish correction announcement, confiscate their advertising charges, and impose fine of not less than amount of advertising charges but not more than five times amount of advertising charges; and in serious case, disqualify them, according to law, to carry on any advertising businesses. Where act constitutes crime, criminal liability must be pursued. (Art. 39).

Where publishing of advertisement violates mandatory provisions of law, advertising supervision authorities must order advertiser, advertising agent and advertisement publisher, which are responsible for advertisement, to stop publication of such advertisement and publish correction announcement, and confiscate their advertising charges; and may impose fine of not less than amount of advertising charges but not more than five times amount of advertising charges. Where publishing of advertisement violates provisions of Art. 13 of this law, advertising supervision authorities must order advertisement publisher to publish correction announcement, and impose fine of not less than 1,000 yuan but not more than 10,000 yuan. (Art. 40).

Additional penalties and remedies for violations. (Art. 41-44).

International Sale of Goods.—China has ratified United Nations Convention on Contracts for the International Sale of Goods ("Sales Convention") which is now in force and effect as of 1 Jan. 1988. China had two reservations to "Sales Convention", namely Art. 1(b), which permits application of treaty beyond Contracting States via operation of law; and pursuant to Art. 96 have reserved provisions of Arts. 11, 29 or Part II that give effect to sales contracts other than in writing.

Sales Convention also ratified by U.S., applies to sale of goods between parties whose places of business are in different States, when States are Contracting States.

See Topical Index in front part of this volume.

SALES . . . *continued*
(Art. 11[a]). Convention does not apply to sales for personal, family or household use, auction, by authority of law, securities, negotiable instruments, ships, vessels or aircraft, or to electricity (Art. 2), nor to processing contracts (Art. 3). Parties to contract can exclude application of Sales Convention to contract or vary terms of any of its provisions by contract. (Art. 6).

Offer under Sales Convention is good if party making it intended to be bound, and if it indicates goods and makes provision for determining quantity and price or specifies them (Art. 14); it is effective when reaching offeree (Art. 14); acceptance is statement or conduct by offeree indicating acceptance, silence is not sufficient (Art. 18).

Sales Convention provides for specific performance, remedies for delivery of non-conforming goods (e.g. repair), if there is fundamental breach buyer can void contract, and of course sue for damages. (Arts. 4.5-5.2). Damages for breach of contract are measured as sum equal to foreseeable loss, including loss of profit suffered by party damaged as result of breach. (Art. 14). If contract has been voided, party claiming damages can claim difference between contract price and cost of substitute goods it purchased. (Art. 75). Party must attempt to mitigate its losses. (Art. 22).

SEALS:

Seals in China, having long history, are normal means of execution of contracts, though foreign trade contracts are at times not sealed, but signed by responsible parties.

In 1986 memorandum was issued by Supreme Court of China entitled "Regarding Concepts of Several Problems of Operation of Economic Contracts". While a discussion document, this memorandum has influenced practice in courts, and it in general requires that seal of organization be placed on economic contracts. In addition as noted below certain statutes specially provide that seal is required.

General Principles of Civil Law provide that, pursuant to law or articles of association of legal person, responsible individual who acts on behalf of said person is its legal representative. Only legal representatives can execute contracts. Clearly if not legal representative or not acting with authority on behalf of said representative, signature would normally not be effective to execute contract. Normally document appointing legal representative is in writing.

There are provincial regulations such as Regulations of Guangdong People's Government Regarding the Execution of Economic Contracts, which provide for certificate of legal representative which must contain organization's seal or certificate of entrustment of authority of legal person, latter of which also normally requires seal of organization. At time of signing economic contract these documents, in original, must be exchanged between parties, else prior to actual commencement of performance, contract is not enforceable. If contract has been partially performed, regulations do not specify what will occur if there is dispute and document has yet to be exchanged. Different judges appear to have different opinions, e.g. in San Shui County in county court, Guangdong province—judges during trial disagreed as to need for these documents after contract was partly performed and dispute arose.

Regulations of Contracts for Lending of Money, Art. 5 (promulgated by State Council and effective as of 1 Apr. 1985) provides loan contracts must be signed by legal representatives of both parties or by legal person who was entrusted to sign contract. Organization seal must be placed on contract.

Several other regulations provide for similar requirements such as early Trial Regulations on Industrial and Mining Product Contracts, 1981, which states that legal representative e.g. factory head, manager or important responsible production chief should sign contract, and if legal representative of organization must entrust signing of contract to another person, then said person should present other party with certificate of authority given to him.

Regulations for Contracts for Purchase of Industrial and Mine Products 1984, state that in execution of these contracts, legal representative must sign (by using his personal seal) and seal of organization must be placed on contract for it to have legal effect.

Regulations of Contracts for Construction, Survey and Design provides that responsible persons of parties must sign contract and official seal of organizations be placed on contract for it to be executed.

Similarly, Regulation of Contracts for Property Insurance provides for placing of seal by insurer for execution to be effective in certain contracts.

Thus in summary, placing of seal, and signature of organization's legal representative are required by several statutes and when not specified are frequently required by custom and practice, as legally effective means of executing contract. While certain contracts may be executed by signature of organization's legal representative or parties, this generally requires document entrusting this authority which itself will contain organization seal.

SECURITIES:

See topics Corporations; Joint Stock Companies.

History of Securities Development in P.R.C.—Securities market in China began with issuance of Government Bonds in 1981, at which point direct fund circulation between enterprises and individuals emerged. In 1984, Beijing Tianqiao Market and Shanghai Feile Acoustic Company issued shares to public while various companies of Guangdong province and Shandong province also issued shares and bonds to public. These capital raising activities are termed "Society Fund Collection" as opposed to bank loans. Shares issued at that time had specified fixed interest rates and dividends, and provided for subscribed money to be returned to investor within specified time. Thus, shareholders were exposed to no risk.

In Jan. 1985, The State Economic Reform Commission and People's Bank of China held "The Five Cities' Finance Reform Meeting" at Guangzhou, formally opening Chinese finance and securities market and permitting selected cities to issue business enterprise bonds to public. Banks also began to issue financial bonds.

In 1986, State Council promulgated Provisional Rule on Banking Administration, which named People's Bank of China as securities market's authority, and marked that securities issuance and trading markets were developing. That same year, stock trading business emerged through agents in Shanghai. In 1987, there were 44 cities in China which began over-the-counter securities transfers.

In 1988, trading of company bonds, stocks and financial bonds expanded. Transfer of bonds opened up as well. Most provinces or cities established securities companies with permission of People's Bank of China. These developments marked advent of securities industry in PRC.

In Nov. 1990, Shanghai Stock Exchange was founded, and in July 1991, Shenzhen Stock Exchange was established. Thus after ten years of experimentation, securities trading and issuance market was finally set up. Range of securities include: (1) government bonds; (2) financial bonds; (3) company bonds; (4) company shares and share options; (5) certificate for beneficiary investment trusts; and (6) other approved securities.

In 1993, State Council Securities Regulatory Commission ("CSRC") was established, and replaced People's Bank of China as securities market authority in China, thereby separating securities industry from banking industry.

In Oct. 1994, trading of bond futures began, but was suspended only seven months later in May 1995 because of its volatility and absence of sufficient government regulation.

Prominent characteristic of Chinese securities market development is that practice comes before legislation.

Securities Market of P.R.C.—Securities Market has developed rapidly in China. After initial testing stage, securities industry as a whole has entered into new stage of regulation.

Share Categories.—Currently there are in practice two types of shares issued by PRC joint stock limited companies: (1) Renminbi-denominated shares (A shares) and (2) Renminbi-denominated special shares (B shares). "A" shares may be further divided into State shares, State-owned legal entity shares and public shares. State shares are shares held by PRC state assets administration department or by another government agency authorised by such department. State-owned legal entity shares are shares held by PRC State-owned legal entities. Public shares are shares held by public in PRC.

B shares may be held by both foreign and local Chinese investors in Shenzhen but by foreign investors only in Shanghai. B shares are denominated in Renminbi, but are subscribed for and traded in foreign currencies (Hong Kong dollars on Shenzhen Stock Exchange and U.S. dollars on Shanghai Stock Exchange). With exception of restrictions on status of shareholder and type of currency in which shares are subscribed and traded, B shareholders have same rights and obligations as A shareholders.

In recent years, state owned companies have been encouraged to issue shares overseas. This attitude has led to creation of H & N Shares which are shares that may be held only by foreign investors and are listed on foreign stock exchanges (H shares are listed on Hong Kong Stock Exchange, and N shares are listed on New York Stock Exchange).

Issuance and Trading Volume of Securities.—By end of May 1996, total of 330 holding companies had been approved for listing on stock exchanges of Shenzhen and Shanghai. There are 80 B share listed companies and 20 H share listed companies. Total turn over value for 1994 for Shanghai and Shenzhen was 642.8 billion RMB, and 276.7 billion RMB, respectively.

Number of Investors and Agencies.—By end of May 1996, there were over 110 professional security companies and over 400 securities business institutions, with total of over 1,700 security trading branches. Number of A share investors is about 12 million.

By approval of China Securities Regulatory Commission ("CSRC"), there are 142 law firms, 74 accounting firms and 82 asset appraisal firms which are authorized to be involved in securities business in China. These agencies of securities industry provide necessary protection for regular operation of holding companies and issuance and trading of securities.

Securities Regulations.—

Laws and Rules Governing Holding Companies.—PRC Company Law ("Company Law"), which was promulgated by Standing Committee of the Eighth National People's Congress on Dec. 29, 1993 and effective as of July 1, 1994, contains regulatory framework for establishment, management and dissolution of joint stock limited companies and limited liability companies (collectively referred to in Company Law as "Companies"). See topic Corporations, subhead Company Law.

Company Law supersedes all previous laws, administrative regulations, local regulations and rules governing companies. Company Law expressly provides, however, that companies which were established prior to implementation of Company Law, pursuant to prior laws, administrative regulations, local regulations (including Shenzhen Provisional Regulations on Joint Stock Limited Companies; Shanghai Municipality Provisional Regulations on Joint Stock Limited Companies; Standard Opinion on Joint Stock Limited Companies; and Standard Opinion on Limited Liability Companies) shall continue to exist. However, these companies must comply with requirements of Company Law within prescribed period through implementation of detailed rules to be promulgated by State Council.

Special Provisions of the Council Concerning Share Offerings and Listings Outside the PRC by Joint Stock Limited Companies ("Special Provisions") were promulgated pursuant to Company Law and became effective on Aug. 4, 1994. Mandatory Provisions for the Articles of Association of Companies to be Listed Outside the PRC ("Mandatory Articles") were subsequently promulgated pursuant to Special Provisions by the State Council Securities Commission and State Economic Reform Commission on Oct. 4, 1994, and came into effect on same date.

Special Provisions and Mandatory Articles are technically applicable only to joint stock limited companies which offer and list their shares outside PRC. However, as Mandatory Articles provide comprehensive and standardised regulatory framework for management, organization and administration of PRC companies generally, company directors decided that it would be in company's interests to use Mandatory Articles as basis for drafting company's articles of incorporation. Accordingly, appropriate provisions of Mandatory Articles have been incorporated into most company's new articles of incorporation.

Rules and Regulations Governing Issuance and Trading of Securities.—There is as yet no comprehensive national securities law in PRC. National People's Congress is

SECURITIES . . . *continued*
currently deliberating on draft of national securities law. At present, rules and regulations governing issuance and trading of securities within PRC are Provisional Regulations for the Administration of the Issuance and Trading of Shares ("Securities Regulations") promulgated by State Council on May 3, 1993 and Detailed Implementing Rules for the Disclosure of Information by Joint Stock Limited Companies Issuing Shares to the Public ("Disclosure Rules") promulgated by China Securities Regulatory Commission ("CSRC") on June 10, 1993.

Prior to national regulation, various local regulations concerning stock issuance and trade were promulgated in Shanghai and Shenzhen. On Nov. 27, 1990, Shanghai municipality promulgated Rules of Shanghai Concerning the Administration of Securities Trading. On June 15, 1991, Shenzhen municipality promulgated Interim Rules of Shenzhen Concerning Administration of Stock Issuance and Trading.

Securities Regulations apply to any issuance and trading of securities and other related activities within PRC. Securities Regulations state that specific measures will be formulated separately for issuance and trading of securities by foreigners in PRC (i.e., B shares) and for issuance and trading of securities outside PRC (e.g., H shares issued by PRC companies which are listed and traded on Hong Kong Stock Exchange). Many provisions in Securities Regulations are applicable to all companies, as companies issuing shares to overseas investors would generally also issue, or have issued, shares to PRC investors, which shares are listed and traded on PRC stock exchange.

Regulatory Authorities.—Under Securities Regulations, Securities Commission of State Council ("Securities Commission") is authority in charge of securities markets within PRC, and it exercises complete supervision over securities markets in accordance with relevant PRC laws and regulations. CSRC is executive arm of Securities Commission, and it administers and supervises all activities relating to issuance and trading of securities. In 1993, district Securities Administration offices (i.e., Shanghai, Shenzhen Securities Administration offices) were established, and public issuance and trading of shares in these districts now requires approval of these offices.

Listing and Trading of Shares.—To have its shares listed on a PRC stock exchange, joint stock limited company must comply with following conditions prescribed by Securities Regulations and by Company Law: (a) issuance of shares to public with approval of Securities Commission; (b) minimum total after issue capitalization of RMB 50 million; (c) minimum of 1,000 shareholders with aggregate nominal value of at least RMB 1,000 and minimum aggregate nominal value held by individual shareholders of not less than RMB 10 million; (d) minimum of 25% of issued share capital of company in shares issued to public (15%, in case of company whose issued share capital exceeds RMB 400 million); (e) minimum three years profitable business operation (but where [1] company was established pursuant to reorganisation of former State-owned enterprise, or [2] if company was established only after implementation of Company Law and its main promoters are large or medium-sized State-owned enterprises, profitable business operation periods of company's predecessor or its promoters may be considered); (f) absence of any serious violation of law during preceding three years, including no false representations in its financial and accounting reports; (g) any other conditions prescribed by Securities Commission.

Directors, supervisors and managers of joint stock limited company are not permitted to keep profits if they sell their shares in company within six months after purchasing them, or buy shares of company within six months after selling their shares in company. In these situations such profits belong to company. This provision also applies to any legal entity shareholder holding more than 5% of voting shares of company, as well as its directors, supervisors and senior managers.

Repurchase by joint stock limited company of its issued and outstanding shares requires approval in accordance with relevant State regulations.

Shareholdings in and Takeovers of Listed Companies.—Shareholding of PRC individual may not exceed 0.5% of issued ordinary shares of any individual listed company. If individual's holdings exceed 0.5% then with prior consent of CSRC, company shall have right to acquire any excess portion at original purchase price or market price for shares, whichever is lower. However, if excess shareholding is due to reduction in total number of issued shares, company may not acquire excess portion until reasonable period of time has lapsed. Above limitation does not apply to holding of B shares by foreign investors who are individuals or to holding of shares issued outside PRC.

Where direct or indirect shareholding by any PRC legal entity reaches 5% of issued ordinary shares of listed company, such entity must submit written report to company, relevant stock exchange and CSRC, and make public announcement within three working days. However, if holding in excess of 5% is caused by reduction in total number of issued ordinary shares of company, such entity need not comply with above-mentioned reporting and public announcement requirements until reasonable period of time has lapsed.

Once PRC legal entity holds more than 5% of issued ordinary shares of listed company, it must submit within three working days written report to such company, relevant stock exchange and CSRC, and make public announcement each time its shareholding increases or decreases by 2% of issued ordinary shares. In both cases, legal entity may not directly or indirectly buy or sell such shares before expiration of two working days after submitting written report and making public announcement.

Where direct or indirect shareholding of any PRC legal entity other than promoter reaches 30% of issued ordinary shares of listed company, such entity must make takeover offer to all other shareholders of company within 45 working days. Offer must be cash offer and be made at higher of: (a) highest price paid by offeror for its shares within 12 months preceding takeover offer; or (b) average market price for such shares within period of 30 working days prior to takeover offer. Such entity may not purchase any more of shares of company until takeover offer.

Such takeover offer must remain open and may not be withdrawn for at least 30 working days from date of making of offer. All terms of takeover offer must be equally applicable to all shareholders holding same class of shares. During offer period and prior to expiration of 30 working days after end of offer period, offeror may not acquire shares of same class upon terms and conditions other than those contained in takeover offer.

If, upon expiration of offer period, offeror has not acquired 50% of total number of issued ordinary shares of listed company, takeover shall be deemed to have failed, but offeror may make new takeover offer. Aggregate amount of shares of that listed company which may be acquired by offeror in each subsequent year shall not exceed 5% of total issued ordinary shares of company. If, upon expiration of offer period, offeror has acquired more than 75% of total number of issued ordinary shares of listed company, trading of such company's shares on stock exchange shall cease. If upon expiration of offer period, offeror has acquired 90% of total number of issued shares of listed company, remaining shareholders have right to make compulsory sale of their shares to offeror upon same terms and conditions as those contained in takeover offer.

Disclosure Requirements.—Under Securities Regulations, listed company must prepare and submit following documents to CSRC and stock exchange on which shares of company are to be listed: (a) interim report within 60 days after end of first six months of each fiscal year; (b) annual report audited by registered accountant within 120 days after end of each fiscal year; and (c) Major Event Report.

Insider Trading and Other Securities Frauds.—The Interim Measures Against Fraudulent Activities Relating to Securities prohibit fraudulent activities relating to securities, which is defined to include insider trading, manipulating market, defrauding clients by brokers and false representations. Insider trading is defined to mean following: (a) trading in securities or advising others to trade in securities based upon privileged information; (b) revealing privileged information which may be used by traders; (c) obtaining privileged information through improper means, and subsequently trading in securities or advising others to trade in securities based upon such privileged information; (d) other insider trading activities.

Under above Provisional Measures, any person who has access to privileged information through lawful means may be insider. Insider information refers to any material information which is known, but has not been made public and which may influence price of securities in securities market. Material information is defined to include information relating to all major events as set out in section headed "Major Event Reports" referred to above. In addition, it also includes information on following: (a) changes in State policies that may have significant influence on securities market; (b) plans of securities issuer to distribute dividends and to increase capital and issue additional shares; (c) any decision of securities regulatory authorities to prohibit major controlling shareholder from transferring its shares; and (d) merger or acquisition of securities issuer.

Pre-offering Information Disclosure Obligation by Issuer.—Issuer must draft and make public prospectus, in addition to filing various documents with competent authority for approval and registration to meet mandatory requirements. (Int. Regs., Arts. 8-10, 13). Prospectus must be drafted in conformity with model form provided by State Securities Supervision Commission. All promoters or directors and chief distributor must sign prospectus, to assure there is no false or misleading statement or material omission in prospectus; they must assume liabilities therefrom. Prospectus must be made public two to five working days prior to underwriting period. Term of validity of prospectus is six months commencing from date when it has been signed by all responsible persons. Should prospectus expire, stock issuance must be stopped. Prospectus must bear following items: (1) name and domicile of SLC (company limited by shares); (2) brief introduction of promoters and issuers; (3) purpose of issue; (4) existing total shares, classes, total amount, face value of each share, offering price of each share for issuance, net asset value for each share before-and-after issuance, issuance fees and commissions; (5) subscription of promoters, structure of their shares, verification of capital; (6) name of underwriter, method of underwriting, amount of underwriting; (7) target offeree, time and place of issuance, methods of subscribing to shares and of making payment; (8) planned utilization of funds issued and forecast of interests and risks; (9) short-term development plan and profit forecast for next year which must be verified by chartered accountants; (10) major contracts of SLC; (11) major proceedings involving SLC; (12) names of directors, supervisors as well as their biographical notes; (13) basic information concerning business operations and relevant business development for preceding three years; (14) financial report for preceding three years audited by accounting firm, signed by two or more chartered accountants and with affixed seal of accounting firm; and (15) regarding recapitalization, utilization information concerning prior offerings. (Int. Regs., Art. 15).

Special Requirements for B-shares Issuance.—SLC intending to issue B-shares must satisfy requirements of A-shares issuance according to Shanghai Rules and Shenzhen Rules. Both rules address additional requirements that B-share issuer shall satisfy, particularly mandatory requirement that SLC must have stable and sufficient sources of foreign exchange income, to enable SLC to pay annual dividends of B-shares. Requirement is designed primarily to assure rights and interests of foreign investor. Issuance price of B-shares must not be less than A-shares of same issuance. Underwriter of B-shares must sell at same price during same underwriting period.

Listing Proclamation.—Besides various approval and registration procedures required of issuer prior to trading its stock on exchange, listed SLC must make public Listing Proclamation upon approval of Stock Exchange. In addition to main contents contained in prospectus, listing proclamation must include following items: (1) date and document number of Stock Exchange approval for listing stock of SLC; (2) information concerning stock issuance and stock structure, names and amount of shares held by top ten shareholders; (3) decision of shareholders' meeting in which SLC has authorized listing of its shares on Stock Exchange; (4) biographical data about directors, supervisors and senior officers and shares held by them; (5) SLC business operation and financial conditions for preceding three years, and profit forecast for subsequent year. (Int. Regs., Art. 34).

Post-offering Information Disclosure Obligation by Issuer.—After public listing of its stock, issuer must file various documents or report material events to Stock Exchange and State Securities Supervision Commission. All shareholders must have access to information disclosed by these documents. Information must be made public in nationally circulated newspapers. Issuer may also disclose information simultaneously in local publications designated by Stock Exchange.

Mid-term Report and Annual Report.—Listed SLC must file mid-term reports within 60 days after first six months of fiscal year and annual reports must be verified

See Topical Index in front part of this volume.

SECURITIES . . . *continued*
by chartered accountants within 120 days after fiscal year with State Securities Supervision Commission and Stock Exchange. Mid-term report and annual report must be formulated in conformity with mandatory requirements concerning accounting systems signed by authorized directors or managers and affixed with SLC's seal. Mid-term report must contain: (1) financial report; (2) analysis of financial situation and operating results by management; (3) major proceedings involving SLC; (4) changes in issued stock; (5) major issues subject to approval by shareholders with voting power. (Int. Regs., Art. 58).

Annual report shall include: (1) brief introduction to SLC; (2) brief introduction to major products or major services of SLC; (3) brief introduction to such property as plants, mines, real estate owned by SLC; (4) information concerning issued shares, including names of shareholders holding 5% or more of shares of SLC's common stock and top ten shareholders; (5) number of shareholders; (6) biographical information and shares held by them and remuneration of directors, supervisors, senior officers; (7) brief introduction to correlative persons of SLC; (8) abstract of financial information of preceding three years; (9) analysis concerning financial condition and management's operating results; (10) changes in issued bonds; (11) major proceedings involving SLC; (12) comparative financial report of preceding two years audited by chartered accountants. (Int. Regs., Art. 59).

Material Events Disclosure Obligation by Issuer.—Material events refer to those occurrences which may significantly affect price of stock of listed company of which shareholders lack any knowledge. Issuer must immediately upon occurrence of foregoing event, submit report to Stock Exchange and State Securities Supervision Commission to describe essence of foregoing events. Material events generally include following: (1) important contracts executed by issuer, which will obviously affect one or more elements of assets, obligations, rights, interests, business operating results; (2) significant changes in business operation policy or business scope; (3) major investments or purchase of long-term assets with relatively large expenditures in terms of value; (4) major liabilities; (5) breach of contract by issuers or failure to fulfil obligations when due; (6) major losses in business operations or otherwise; (7) major losses to assets; (8) significant changes in production and operations; (9) promulgation of new laws, statutes, policies and rules which may obviously affect operation of issuer; (10) change of chairman of board of directors, general manager, or 30% or more of directors; (11) shareholders holding 5% or more of aggregate common stock, their variation within 2% of aggregate common stock; (12) major proceedings involving issuer; and (13) liquidation or bankruptcy of issuer. (Int. Regs., Art. 60).

Disclosure Obligation by Insiders.—Where directors, supervisors, senior officers hold common stock of issuer, they must submit reports concerning their shares to State Securities Supervision Commission, Stock Exchange and issuer. Should any change occur in their share holdings, they must submit reports to foregoing authorities within ten days after occurrence of change. This obligation must survive their tenure in office. Proceeds of directors, supervisors, senior officer of SLC resulting from resale or repurchase of its shares within six months after purchase or sale of their stock must belong to SLC. (Int. Regs. Art. 38).

Obligations of Securities Dealers.—Art. 82 of Int. Regs. provides that rules concerning establishment and administration of securities dealers must be separately formulated. In Shanghai and Shenzhen, detailed rules concerning securities dealers were promulgated in 1990 and 1991 respectively. These local rules set forth in detail formation, business scope and discipline of securities dealers.

Domestic securities dealers intending to engage in B-shares business must be subject to special permits. Shenzhen Rules set forth additional requirement that B-shares dealers must (1) possess total funds of RMB 10,000,000 or above, among which foreign exchange must not be less than equivalent value of RMB 5,000,000; (2) have sufficient specialized personnel suitable for securities business involving foreign elements; (3) have necessary technical means, telecommunication facilities and settlement means required by securities business involving foreign elements; (4) other requirements mandated by competent authority. Foreign securities dealers may participate in B-shares underwriting and act as agents for domestic securities dealers by accepting clients abroad, provided they obtain approval from competent authorities of China and follow laws and regulations of China concerning B-shares.

Obligations of Securities Broker-Dealers.—Securities dealers must examine authenticity, accuracy and integrity of prospectus and other advertising materials. Should they find any false, misleading statements or major omissions, they must not put forward offer of shares. Should invitation to offer or offer have been put forward, marketing activities must cease and remedial measures shall be adopted. (Int. Regs. Art. 21). Securities dealers must submit annual business reports and balance sheets audited by chartered accountants to security authorities within 60 days after fiscal year (Shanghai Rules, Art. 48; Shenzhen Rules, Art. 48). Securities dealers must maintain customers' securities trading risk funds, so as to make up losses incurred in securities trading or other occurrences, or compensate clients for negligence of dealers (Shanghai Rules, Art. 49; Shenzhen Rules, Art. 48). Securities dealers and senior managerial personnel as well as other staff must not: (1) offer definitive advice to customers concerning rise and fall of securities prices; (2) warrant that they will fully or partially assume losses which may occur so as to attract customers to participate in securities trading; (3) unreasonably restrict business activities of specific customer by taking advantage of superior marketing power with attempt to eliminate their competitors; (4) engage in activities detrimental to fair trading or protection of shareholders interests; (5) disclose securities trading information of customers. Personnel engaged in securities business and securities administration must not hold, purchase or sell stocks directly or indirectly. (Int. Regs., Art. 39).

Fiduciary Obligations of Other Professionals.—Chartered accountants and their firms, assessors and working units, and attorneys and their law firms must check and verify authenticity, accuracy and integrity of documents issued by them in discharging their responsibilities in light of generally accepted codes of practice and morality. (Int. Regs., Arts. 18, 35). Professionals preparing audit reports, assets evaluation reports, and legal opinions for stock issuance of proposed issuer, may not purchase or hold stock of issuer during underwriting period and for six months after underwriting period. Professionals preparing auditing reports, assets evaluation reports and legal opinions for proposed listed SLC, may not purchase or hold stock of that listed SLC prior to publication of those documents, and may not purchase stock of such listed SLC within five working days from date these documents have been published.

Penalties.—State Securities Supervision Commission is responsible for administering laws and regulations concerning stock issuance and trading. Supervision Commission is empowered to undertake investigations into any entity or individual breaching foregoing laws and regulations. In significant cases, investigation must be carried out by State Securities Commission. Supervision Commmission may at its own discretion examine business activities of securities dealers.

To assure interests of shareholders, Stock Regulations impose severe penalties on offenders. SLC violating foregoing laws and regulations are subject to warning and/or compulsory return of illegally acquired funds, confiscation of illegal income and fines, depending on severity of offense. Should serious offense be committed, SLC will be disqualified from issuing shares to general public. Directors, supervisors and senior officers directly liable for foregoing offense will be subject to warning and/or fine of RMB 30,000-300,000. Where securities dealer violates foregoing enactment, it will be subject to warning and/or confiscation of illegally obtained shares and income, and/or fines, depending upon severity of offense. If it commits serious offense, securities dealer will be disqualified from engaging in security business. Leader and personnel directly liable for offense will be subject to warning and/or fine of RMB 30,000-300,000. Insiders divulging inside information, or purchasing and selling stocks by taking advantage of inside information or offering advice for others about stock trading, will be subject to confiscation of illegally obtained shares and income, and fine of RMB 50,000-500,000 depending upon severity of offense. Accounting firm, assets evaluation agency and law firm breaching fiduciary obligations, will be subject to warning, and/or confiscation of illegal income, and/or fines, depending on situation. Where serious offense is involved, foregoing agencies will be disqualified from rendering services in securities business. Accountants, assessors and attorneys directly liable for foregoing offense will be subject to warning, and/or fine of RMB 30,000-300,000. Where serious offense is involved, they should be disqualified from engaging in securities business. Where any other person suffers any damage from foregoing offenses, offenders will be liable for compensation. Where offenses are serious enough to constitute crime, criminal prosecution will be undertaken by State. (Int. Regs., Arts. 77, 78).

Legal Redress Available.—There are two options open to shareholders in disputes arising from stock listing and trading. They may submit their disputes to arbitral tribunals for mediation and/or arbitration provided that they have written agreements. (Int. Regs., Art. 79). They may commence legal action in court to settle disputes: Regarding B-shares, any dispute occurring in China concerning B-shares listing and B-shares trading will be governed by relevant Chinese laws and regulations and settled in territory of China. (Shanghai Rules, Art. 23; Shenzhen Rules, Art. 26).

Securities dealers and Stock Exchange, in disputes arising from stock issuance or stock trading, must submit their disputes to arbitral tribunals establishing or designated by State Securities Commission for mediation and/or arbitration. (Int. Regs., Art. 80). Securities dealers and Stock Exchange may not use court action to settle disputes among them.

Security Exchange.—As nonprofit making institution legal person whose creation and dissolution shall be subject to examination of Securities Commission of State Council and approval of State Council, is administered by municipal government where it is located, and supervised by Central Securities Supervision Commission. (Int. Prov., Arts. 3, 4, 6, 9). Security Exchange shall create public and fair market environment, provide convenient conditions facilitating smooth operation of securities trading. (Int. Prov., Art. 10). Functions of Security Exchange include: (1) provide spaces and facilities for securities trading; (2) formulate code of conduct of Security Exchange; (3) examine and approve listing application; (4) organize and spervise securities trading; (5) supervise listed SLC; (6) supervise securities trading activities of members of Security Exchange; (7) provide and administer information on security market; (8) other functions authorized by Central Securities Suprevision Commission. (Int. Prov., Art. 11).

Security Exchange is comprised of Members Meeting, Council and specialized committees. (Int. Prov., Art. 13). Members Meeting is supreme authority and held at least once per year. (Int. Prov., Arts. 14, 15). Functions of Members Meeting include: adopt articles of association; elect and dismiss directors; examine and approve work report of council and president; examine and approve financial budget and final accounts and other major issues. (Int. Prov., Art. 14). Council is policy-making body with tenure of three years and responsible to Members Meeting. (Int. Prov., Art. 16). Entry of members subject to approval of Council. (Int. Prov., Art. 17). Council has at least seven Directors, among which nonmember directors shall include at least $1/3$ of total directors. (Int. Prov., Art. 18). Quorum of Council meeting is $2/3$ of all Directors and decisions shall be adopted by $2/3$ consensus of all Directors present at meeting. (Int. Prov., Art. 18).

President with tenure of three years is legal representative of Security Exchange. President organizes daily management. (Int. Prov., Art. 20). In absence of President, Deputy President shall assme functions and powers of President. (Int. Prov., Art. 20). Security Exchange subordinates Listing Committee comprised of 13 members, Supervision Committee comprised of nine members. (Int. Prov., Arts. 22, 23, 26, 27). Directors of Council, President, Deputy Presidents and members of specialized committees are senior officers of Security Exchange. (Int. Prov., Art. 30).

Futures.—Chinese futures exchange began in 1992, with establishment of futures exchange for agricultural products in Zhenzhou. As of Aug. 1993, China has 12 national markets engaged in futures trading, with ten in eastern coastal areas. Key indexes for these national markets will be listed on world market. Nanjing Oil Exchange in Jiansu province has already released its quotation to world via Associated Press (AP) and Reuters. Shanghai Metals Exchange presents timely reporting of New York and London market quotations and members undertake international futures metal trading via Exchange. Preparation is underway to build 30 national futures markets primarily in coastal areas.

Futures Brokerage Companies.—

See Topical Index in front part of this volume.

SECURITIES . . . *continued*

Interim Rules Concerning Administration of Futures Brokerage Companies Registration were promulgated by State Industrial and Commercial Bureau on Apr. 28, 1993. Rules define "Future Brokerage Companies" as companies legally organized, which engage in futures transactions on behalf of their clients in their own name and in return charge commission. (Art. 2). Rules are also applicable to foreign investment companies legally organized in China, intending to engage in futures brokerage. (Art. 14).

Requirement of Registration.—Futures brokerage company must satisfy following principal requirements: (a) have name of company be in conformity with prescribed provisions; (b) have articles of association of company in conformity with prescription; (c) possess fixed premises and qualified telecommunication facilities; (d) have registered capital of RMB 10,000,000 or more; (e) have appropriate number of personnel compatible with scope of business, in which full-time futures brokers may not be less than 20; (f) legal representative and other senior officers must satisfy Art. 9 of Interim Provisions Concerning Administration of Approval Requirements and Registration of Legal Representative of Enterprise as Legal Person; (g) possess consummate organizations and sound financial and accounting system; and (h) other requirements provided for by laws and regulations. (Art. 3).

Registration authority for futures brokerage companies is State Industrial and Commercial Bureau. Those futures brokerage companies under jurisdiction of State Industrial and Commercial Bureau pursuant to Art. 5 of Regulation of China Concerning Administration of Enterprise as Legal Person Registration, must register with State Industrial and Commercial Bureau directly. Remaining futures brokerage companies will be transferred to State Industrial and Commercial Bureau for registration, after preliminary examination by local bureau of industry and commerce at provincial level, autonomous regions and municipalities directly under administration of central government. Procedures prescribed above shall govern establishment of branches of futures brokerage companies. (Art. 4). State Industrial and Commercial Bureau will decide whether to approve, or reject application for registration within 30 days from date when it has received application for starting business operation. (Art. 5). Regarding registration for starting operation of futures brokerage company, applicant must submit application and produce following documents and evidences: (a) documents and evidence required pursuant to Art. 15 of Regulation of China Concerning Administration of Enterprise as Legal Person Registration; (b) certificates in conformity with subparagraph 6, Art. 3 of these rules; (c) name list and their biographic notes of futures brokers; (d) certificates of self-owned or leased telecommunication facilities and specialized equipment; (e) where futures business involves special provisions of state, approval documents issued by relevant administrative authority must be submitted; (f) regarding international futures business, agreement and letter of intent must be submitted for futures brokerage business entered into with corresponding member company international in Futures Exchange; (g) where foreigners will be employed as senior officers in company, employment certificate and certificates must be submitted in conformity with subparagraph 6, Art. 3 of these rules and notarized by notary public in country or region where they are from; (h) where shareholding system is employed, relevant documents must be submitted pursuant to Prescriptive Opinions Concerning Companies Limited by Shares. (Art. 6).

Those futures brokerage companies having registered prior to promulgation of said rules, must apply for registration anew pursuant to Arts. 3-6 in said rules, within 90 days from promulgation of these rules. Where futures brokerage companies submit application for registration anew within prescribed time limits and fail to meet requirements set forth in said rules, State Industrial and Commercial Bureau must decide directly or advise their original registration authority to decide as to altering registration or cancelling registration within prescribed time. Where futures brokerage companies fail to submit application for registration anew, their original registration authority must revoke their business license. (Art. 12). Prior to promulgation of rules, where companies having been registered and concurrently engaged in futures brokerage satisfy provisions of these rules, they must alter registration in accordance with Regulations of China Concerning Administration of Enterprise as Legal Person Registration within 90 days after promulgation of rules; they must submit application to their original registration authority, which will transmit application to State Industrial and Commercial Bureau via their corresponding superior authority, if any, for separate approval on futures brokerage.

Prior to promulgation of rules, where companies registered and concurrently engaged in futures brokerage fail to satisfy provisions of rules, they must alter registration in accordance with Regulations Concerning Administration of Enterprise as Legal Person Registration within 90 days after promulgation of rules; they must submit application for altering registration to their original registration authority. Where companies fail to submit application within prescribed time, original registration authority is required to alter them. (Art. 13).

Rights and Obligations.—Futures brokerage companies must engage in business operations according to law, adhere to principles of fairness, openness and honesty and keeping one's word, and follow rules hereunder: (a) provide objective, accurate, prompt and efficient service; (b) open additional account for clients, deposits in financial institutions designated by registration authority, to be kept apart from their self-owned capitals; (c) record instructions of clients strictly according to facts and carry them out promptly; (d) keep complete daily transaction records, accounting vouchers and other major documents completely for five years or more; (e) maintain trade secrets for clients; (f) make open instructions and level asks to clients; and (g) pay business operation deposits to financial institution designated by registration authority within 60 days after registration process, which amount may not be less than 25% of their corresponding registered capitals. (Art. 7).

Futures brokerage companies are prohibited from any of following acts: (a) collude with each other privately and monopolize market; (b) offset each other privately; (c) fabricate and spread false or misleading information so as to mislead public; (d) falsify, alter or deal in various kinds of transaction vouchers and documents; (e) misappropriate clients' deposits; (f) arrange with clients to share profits or assume risks; (g) other acts that violate laws and regulations. (Art. 8).

Penalties.—State Industrial and Commercial Bureau and local bureau of industry and commerce at level of provinces, autonomous regions and municipalities directly under central government are entitled to exercise supervision and examination over futures brokerage companies in their respective jurisdiction. Futures brokerage companies must accept supervision and produce documents, account books, report forms and other relevant materials required for examination. (Art. 9). Where State Industrial and Commercial Bureau and local bureau at provincial level, autonomous regions and municipalities directly under central government find any act in violation of rules in their supervision in their respective jurisdiction, they may impose such penalties as warning, fines, confiscation of illegal earnings depending on severity of case. Such penalties as suspension of business for reconsideration, withholding or revoking business license may only be imposed by State Industrial and Commercial Bureau. Where act results in crime, authority of industry and commerce must promptly transmit case to judicial body. (Art. 10). Losses clients incur or disputes arising from acts where futures brokerage companies violate provisions of rules, must be dealt with in accordance with relevant laws of State. (Art. 11).

SEQUESTRATION:

Court, on its own initiative or on request of party, may take measures to assure availability of property of defendant to satisfy potential judgment.

SHIPPING:

Chinese ports are under general jurisdiction of China's Ministry of Communications. Harbor Superintendents and Port Affairs Bureaus at major ports are under jurisdiction of Ministry. China entered into agreement with U.S. on Maritime Transport with exchange of letters signed and effective as of Sept. 17, 1980. Regulations Governing Supervision and Control of Foreign Vessels were approved by State Council on Aug. 22, 1979. Harbor Superintendency Administration is to be notified a week prior to vessel's expected arrival at port, and shall receive report 24 hours in advance of arrival from vessel's port agent of estimated time of arrival and fore and aft drafts on arrival. (Art. 3). Vessel may not enter or leave port or navigate or shift berths in port without pilot appointed by Harbor Superintendency Administration. (Art. 4). Vessels must submit entry reports and ship's papers on arrival and departure report prior to leaving port. (Art. 5). Vessels navigating or berthing in Chinese port areas or coastal waters shall by day hoist national flag of country of registry, and on entering or leaving port or shifting betths shall additionally display signal-letters and relevant signals prescribed by Harbor Superintendency Administration. (Art. 23).

No vessel shall discharge oils, oily mixtures or other harmful pollutants or refuse within port areas and coastal waters of China. (Art. 35). Application must be made to Harbor Superintendency Administration to discharge ballast water, tank washings or bilge water. (Art. 36). Marine accidents must be reported in summarized form by telegram or radio-telephone as soon as possible, and if occurring outside port area, master, within 48 hours of vessel's arrival at first port of call, or within 24 hours if occurring in port, shall submit marine accident report to Harbor Superintendency Administration. (Art. 46). If accident occurs in port areas or coastal waters of China, and causes damage to property, death or personal injury, then master of vessel at fault shall render any possible assistance to ship and persons in distress, make timely report and be prepared for investigation and settlement. (Art. 47). There are special Regulations Governing Passage of Non-Military Vessels through Qiongzhou Straits and Bohai Straits.

China Ocean Shipping Company established in 1961 is subordinate unit of Ministry of Communications, and it owns general cargo ships, bulk ore and grain carriers, tankers, timber carriers, container ships, roll-on/roll-off ships and passenger ships. China Ocean Shipping Agency, established in 1953, also subordinate to Ministry of Communications, undertakes agency business for ships engaged in international civil transport and calling on Chinese ports. See Business Regulations of China Ocean Shipping Agency. Average adjustment in China is handled by Department for Average Adjustment established in 1969 within China Council for Promotion of International Trade. Department, at behest of hull insurers or shipowners, undertakes assessment of particular average for shipment to determine amount to be indemnified by insurers to shipowners in accordance with clauses of relevant marine insurance contract. In addition Department undertakes work of general average adjustment in order to determine compensation and contribution on basis of charter parties or bills of lading due as result of action properly taken for relieving ship or cargo from common dangers caused by natural calamities, accidents or other extraordinary circumstances. On Jan. 1, 1975 China Council for Promotion of International Trade issued Provisional Rules for General Average Adjustment. Art. 2 of said Rules provides in part that onus of proof is upon party applying for general average adjustment, and other parties to show their respective loss or damage and that expenses claimed are allowable as general average according to Rules. If claim submitted for adjustment as general average is due to fault of one of parties to contract of affreightment, for which it is not entitled to exemption from liability, no general average adjustment will proceed. (Art. 2).

See also topic Customs (Duty).

STATE ENTERPRISES:

See topic Bankruptcy.

State sector of economy is deemed leading force in national economy. (Const., Art. 7). Therefore, domestic economic organization in field of industry and commerce dealing in international area is almost entirely based on state enterprises. Naturally this does not include those enterprises to which foreign entities are co-venturers, sole owners or cooperative partners, nor compensation arrangements where foreign enterprises may own machinery or other goods of factory, etc. State corporations are organized as juristic persons, their powers are defined by their charters, liability can be limited, and they resemble commercial corporations, having neither cloak of sovereign immunity nor at times substantial assets of government behind them. Their assets are those they actually have been allocated or have earned. State is not responsible for their debts. These corporate entities can be sued and bring suit, enter into contracts, make compensation and demand compensation for contractual breaches. Such entities becoming increasingly significant in China, major corporate entities owned by state having substantial industrial responsibilities; e.g., The China State Shipbuilding Corp., China National Offshore Oil Corp., and The China Automotive Industry Corp. Commercial entities owned by state that at one time received all budgetary income from state, and in turn remitted all profit to state, are gradually being absorbed into tax

STATE ENTERPRISES . . . *continued*
system and must emphasize profitability. (Regarding Revised Methods of Subjecting Profits of State Enterprises to Tax [Trial Implementation] effective Jan. 1, 1983).

Audit Law of China was adopted at ninth session of Standing Committee of Eighth National People's Congress of China on Aug. 31, 1994 and entered into force on Jan. 1, 1995. According to this law, State practices system of supervision through auditing. State council and local people's government must establish audit institutions. (Art. 2). National Audit Office of State Council takes charge of audit work throughout country under leadership of Premier of State Council. (Art. 7). Audit institutions of local government must be in charge of audit work within their respective administrative areas. (Art. 8). Auditors are protected by law in performing their functions in accordance with law. No organization or individual may refuse or obstruct auditors from performing their functions, or retaliate against them. (Art. 15). Auditors must withdraw from performing audits if they have interest in auditees or audit items. (Art. 13). Auditors have obligations to keep State secrets and auditees' trade secrets in performing functions. (Art. 14).

National Audit Office must exercise supervision through auditing over implementation of budget of central government, and revenues and expenditures of central bank. (Arts. 17, 18). Audit institutions exercise supervision through auditing, including: (1) assets, liabilities, losses of state-owned monetary organizations and state-owned enterprises; (2) revenues and expenditures of state institutions; (3) budget implementation and final accounts of state construction projects; (4) revenues and expenditures of social security funds, public donations and other relevant funds and capital managed by governmental departments and public organization authorized by government; (5) revenues and expenditures of projects with aids or loans provided by international organizations or governments of other countries. (Arts. 18, 19, 20, 23, 24, 25). Audit institutions have authority to require auditees to submit their budgets or plans for financial revenues and expenditures; statements about budget implementation; final accounts and financial reports; audit reports produced by public audit firms; and other information relating to their revenues and expenditures. (Art. 31).

Auditors have authority to examine accounting documents, account books, accounting statements, and other information relating to revenues and expenditures of auditees. (Art. 32). When audit institutions conduct audits, auditees must not transfer, conceal, falsify or destroy their accounting documents, account books, accounting statements or other information relating to their revenues and expenditures. (Art. 34). Audit institutions may issue circulars about audit results to governmental departments and publish results to public. (Art. 36). While audit institutions form audit teams, they must serve audit notifications on auditees three days prior to execution of audit. (Art. 37). Audit teams must submit audit reports to audit institutions; however, prior to submission, they must solicit opinions of auditees. Auditees must, within ten days from date of receiving audit reports, send comments in writing to audit teams or audit institutions. (Art. 39). Audit institutions must, within 30 days from date of receiving audit reports, give appraisal of audit items and produce audit opinions and audit decisions. Audit decisions enter into effect from date when they are duly served. (Art. 40).

STATISTICS, STANDARDS AND QUALITY CONTROL:

See topic Sales.

Effective Jan. 1, 1984, law on statistics implemented whereby statistical departments to be set up at and above county level, and statistical officials to be employed at lower levels under State Statistical Bureau. All government organizations, mass organizations, enterprises, self-employed individuals, foreign firms in China and joint ventures must report designated statistics to departments concerned. Falsification, fabrication and misrepresentation not permitted.

Provisional Regulations for Total Quality Control in Industrial Enterprises promulgated by State Economic Commission on Mar. 18, 1980, which provided in principle that high prices to be paid for high quality, low prices for low quality (Art. 27), providing also rewards for quality (Art. 28) and cessation of enterprises whose products are consistently inferior, and reduction in salaries of leading cadres and suspension bonuses for workers producing inferior goods (Art. 30).

On July 31, 1979 State Council promulgated Regulations on Standardization Control, requiring that technical standards be established and implemented for all industrial goods in regular production, major farm products, engineering projects, environmental protection, safety, sanitation and other areas where technical requirements should be unified. (Art. 2). Internationally accepted standards and advanced foreign standards should be studied as far as possible. (Art. 7). Export products and engineering projects undertaken in foreign countries by Chinese organizations to have standards geared to needs of foreign markets. (Art. 8). Three standards provided: State, ministry and enterprise (Art. 11), lower standards not to contravene higher and ministry standards to be replaced by specialized standards (Art. 11). Standards to be drafted by departments in charge under State Council, e.g. State Administration of Standards (for industrial and agricultural products), State Capital Construction Commission (for engineering projects and environmental protection) and Ministry of Public Health. (Art. 13). Once standards endorsed and promulgated, they become technical decrees which must be strictly observed by all and are not to be altered without authorization. (Art. 18). Where violation causes serious accidents, economic sanctions and court action can be undertaken. (Art. 18). Award system provided and higher price allowed for better quality products. (Art. 29).

Several implementing regulations promulgated; e.g. State Bureau of Standardization and Metrology, on Nov. 16, 1981, promulgated Procedures for the Administration of Standardization of Industrial Enterprises (Provisional Implementation), and on Mar. 14, 1981 State Bureau of Standardization, State Economic Commission and State Commission of Machine Building promulgated Procedures for the Examination and Administration of Standardization of New Mechanical Electrical Products. On Mar. 17, 1982 Provisional Procedures for the Administration of the Adoption of International Standards promulgated, providing that "...vigorous adoption of international standards or advanced foreign standards is an important technical and economic policy" of China. (Art. 2). Reference made to standards of International Standard Organization (ISO) and International Electrotechnical Commission (IEC). (Art. 3). Guiding Rule three of ISO and Guiding Rule 21 of IEC should be conformed to in adopting standards. (Art. 13). Annotations of Provisional Procedures recognize various American standards such as those of American Society of Testing Material (ASTM), American Petroleum Institution (API), Electronics Industry Association (EIA), U.S. Military Standards (MIL), American Underwriters Laboratory Safety Standards (UL), as well as various European standards, e.g., Lloyd's Ship Classifications, British Standards (BS), standards provided by Comite Europeen de Normalization (CEN), etc.

STATUTES:

See topics Constitution and Government; Trade Zones.

Chinese law is predominantly written law. Law of custom is recognized in specific instances, e.g. in deciding some cases under Marriage Law, courts have considered customs of masses where not contrary to written law. National People's Congress and its Standing Committee are principal sources of national legislation. Congress has power to amend Constitution (Const., Art. 22[1]) and make laws (Const., Art. 22[2]). Standing Committee also has authority to enact decrees (Const., Art. 25[3]) as well as to interpret Constitution (Const., Art. 25[3]). State Council can formulate administrative measures, issue orders and decisions and propose legislation to National People's Congress or its Standing Committee. (Const., Art. 32[1], [2]).

Local legislative units have similar authority in areas under their jurisdiction (Const., Art. 36) as do so-called autonomous areas (Const., Art. 39) latter of which have to submit any laws that vary from national laws to Standing Committee of National People's Congress for approval (Const., Art. 39). Commission for Legal Affairs of Standing Committee of National People's Congress is organization that normally drafts legislation. Other national organizations contribute to drafting legislation, including State Planning Commission, Ministry of Civil Affairs, General Office of Standing Committee of National People's Congress, Supreme People's Procuratorate and Supreme People's Court. There are numerous orders, decrees and rules having force of law issued by various Ministries and Bureaus and other governmental entities. Concept of stare decisis is not recognized in China, but naturally decision by highest organs entitled to interpret law, such as Standing Committee of National People's Congress or Supreme Court, would affect in binding way decisions of lower courts and governmental entities.

TAXATION:

See topics Aircraft; Joint Stock Companies; Property; Trade Zones; Investment Incentives.

New Legislation.—As early as 1992, China took major step to unify its tax system adopting Law Concerning Tax Administration (hereinafter "Tax Law") on Sept. 4, 1992, effective as of Jan. 1, 1993; Regulations for Implementation of Tax Law (hereinafter "Tax Regs") were promulgated by State Council on Aug. 4, 1993, effective as of date of its promulgation. All taxes collected by tax authorities, including levying, cessation of levying, reduction, exemption, refund and payment of overdue taxes are governed by Tax Law and Tax Regs, with exception of customs duty, vessels tonnage and other taxes collected by customs. (Tax Admin Law, Arts. 2, 3, and 58; Tax Regs, Art. 2).

Income Tax (Individual and Enterprise).—Noteworthy changes were witnessed in income tax law. National People's Congress amended Law of China Concerning Individual Income Tax (hereinafter "Individual Tax Law") of Sept. 10, 1980, on Oct. 31, 1993, effective Jan. 1, 1994. In accordance with amendment, Individual Tax Law applies to both Chinese and foreign taxpayers. It supersedes Interim Regulations Concerning Individual Income Readjustment Tax promulgated by State Council on Sept. 25, 1986; and Interim Regulation Concerning Income Tax for Urban and Rural Individual Industrial and Commercial Households promulgated by State Council on Jan. 7, 1986, which applied solely to Chinese taxpayers. On Jan. 28, 1994, State Council promulgated Implementing Regulations of Individual Income Tax Law (hereinafter "Individual Tax Regs").

In addition, State Council promulgated Interim Regulations concerning Enterprise Income Tax (hereinafter "Enterprise Tax Regs 11") on Dec. 13, 1993, effective as of Jan. 1, 1994. Enterprise Tax Regs apply to all enterprises within territory of China regardless of their ownership, excluding foreign funded enterprises and foreign enterprises. It supersedes Regulations Concerning Income Tax on State Owned Enterprises (Draft), Rules Concerning Readjustment Tax for State Owned Enterprises promulgated by State Council on Sept. 18, 1984, Interim Regulations of China Concerning Tax on Collective Enterprises promulgated by State Council on Apr. 11, 1984, and Interim Regulations Concerning Income Tax on Private Enterprises promulgated by State Council on June 25, 1988.

Turnover Tax.—Radical changes were made in turnover tax. On Dec. 13, 1993, State Council promulgated package of turnover tax regulations, i.e., Interim Regulations of China Concerning Value-added Tax (hereinafter "Value-added Tax Regs"), Interim Regulations of China Concerning Land Value-added Tax (hereinafter "Land Tax Regs"), Interim Regulations of China Concerning Business Tax (hereinafter "Business Tax Regs") and Interim Regulations of China Concerning Consumption Tax (hereinafter "Consumption Tax Regs"), which were put into effect on Jan. 1, 1994. These regulations apply to all taxpayers. In addition, National People's Congress adopted Decision Concerning Application of such Interim Regulations Regarding Tax as Valuated Tax Regs, Consumption Tax Regs and Business Tax Regs to Foreign Funded Enterprises and Foreign Enterprises (hereinafter "NPC Decision") on Dec. 29, 1993, effective as of its promulgation. According to NPC decision, foreign taxpayers are governed by Regulations specified above; therefore Regulations Concerning Uniform Industrial and Commercial Constituted Tax (Draft) promulgated by State Council on Sept. 13, 1958, were repealed. Subsequent to promulgation of foregoing regulations, Ministry of Finance formulated and released detailed rules on Dec. 25, 1993, for implementation of these regulations i.e. Detailed Rules for the Implementation of Value-added Tax Regs (hereinafter "Value-added Tax Rules"), Detailed Rules for Implementation of Business Tax Regs (hereafter "Business Tax Rules") and Detailed Rules for Implementation of Consumption Tax Regs (hereinafter "Consumption Tax Rules"). State Tax Bureau issued Provisions Concerning Use of Special Invoices for Valuated Tax (for trial implementation), which was put into effect on Jan. 1, 1994.

Individual Income Tax.—

See Topical Index in front part of this volume.

TAXATION . . . *continued*

Taxpayers.—Like most countries, China employs rule of fiscal residence and source of income when determining tax jurisdiction. Any individual domiciled in China or having resided in China for one or more years, but not domiciled in China must pay taxes on his income sources inside and outside of China. (Individual Tax Law, Art. 1). Those individuals not domiciled and not residing in China or residing in China for less than one year in absence of domicile, must pay taxes only on income sourced inside China. (Individual Tax Law, Art. 1).

Taxable Income.—Incomes falling within any of following categories must be taxed (Individual Tax Law, Art. 2): (1) wages and salaries; (2) income from individual industrial and commercial households from production, business operations; (3) income from management contracts or management leases of enterprises, institutions; (4) remuneration for services; (5) copyright royalties; (6) other royalties; (7) income from interest, dividends; (8) income from leasing property; (9) income from property transfers; (10) unrealized income; (11) other income determined to be taxable by financial department of State Council. All income is calculated in RMB. If taxpayer obtains earnings in foreign currency, it will be converted into RMB according to exchange rate quoted by State Foreign Exchange Control Administration. (Individual Tax law, Art. 10). Exchange rate is rate of last day of preceding month when taxation certificate is filed. (Individual Tax Regs, Art. 41). For payment of overdue taxes, exchange rate is last day of preceding tax year beginning Jan. 1 and ending on Dec. 31 of that year. (Individual Tax Regs Arts. 41, 42).

Tax rate for individual income tax in China is divided into progressive tax rate and flat tax rate. (Individual Tax Law, Art. 3). Progressive tax rate of 5-45% is applied to wages and salaries, and progressive tax of 5-35% is applied to income of individual industrial and commercial households, and income from contract management or leasing management of enterprises or institutions. Flat tax rate of 20% is applied to copyright royalties and 30% deduction from taxable amount is permitted. With regard to service remuneration, flat tax rate of 20% is applied. Where specific amount of service remuneration is excessive, marginal tax may be levied and detailed rules must be formulated by State Council. Flat tax rate of 20% is applied to royalties, income from interest and dividends, income from property transfers, income from leasing property, unrealized income and any other income.

Tax Exemption.—There are ten categories of income which are exempt from tax (Individual Tax Law, Art. 4): (1) awards in science, education, technology, culture, health, physical sports, environmental protection granted by provincial government, ministries or commissions under State Council or above, and foreign organizations and international organizations; (2) interest on bank savings, interest on treasury bonds and financial bonds issued by State; (3) subsidies and allowances granted in accordance with uniform standards of State; (4) welfare money, survivor's pensions, relief payment; (5) insurance indemnities; (6) military severance pay, demobilization pay for soldiers of armed forces; (7) severance pay, retirement salaries, life subsidies for retired cadres and staff granted in accordance with uniform standard of State; (8) salaries of diplomatic officials, consular officials, other personnel of foreign embassies and consulate in China that should be free from tax under Chinese law; (9) income is exempt from tax as stipulated in international conventions acceded to by China and bilateral agreements concluded by China; (10) other income to be exempted from tax with approval of financial department under State Council.

Scope of Deductions.—Individual Tax Law specifies expenses and fees to be deducted from taxable income for each category of income. (Art. 6). With regard to wages and salaries, fixed monthly deduction of RMB 800 is permitted. Regarding income of individual industrial and commercial households, expenses, costs and losses may be deducted from their total annual income prior to taxation. As to income from contract management or leasing management of enterprises or institutions, reasonable fees may be deducted from total annual income. With respect to copyright royalties, remuneration for services, royalties and incomes from property leasing, if each individual payment is less than RMB 4,000, fixed amount of RMB 800 may be deducted; if each payment exceeds RMB 4,000, 20% may be deducted as expenses. As to income from property transfer, original value of property and reasonable expenses can be deducted. No deduction is allowed for income from interest and dividends, unexpected income and other income. Where individual donates his income to education and public welfare, donation may be deducted from taxable income in accordance with relevant provisions to be promulgated by State Council.

Where taxpayer having no domicile in China obtains wages and salaries in China, and where taxpayer having domicile in China obtains wages and salaries outside of China, additional expenses calculated in light of his average living standard, income standard and variation of exchange rate may be deducted from taxable income. Scope and standard of additional fees will be formulated by State Council.

Avoidance of International Double Taxation.—Method of tax credit: By end of 1991, China concluded bilateral tax agreements with 32 countries to facilitate its open door policy and to avoid international double taxation. China adopted method of limited tax credit to avoid double taxation on individuals. Where taxpayer obtains income outside of China, taxes paid outside of China on that part of income may offset taxes in China for such income. However maximum credit may not exceed taxable amount for that part of income sourced outside China, calculated in accordance with tax rate under Chinese tax law. (Individual Tax Law, Art. 7).

Enterprise Income Tax.—

Taxpayers.—All entepnises within territory of China, excluding foreign funded enterprises and foreign enterprises must pay tax on global income from production and business operation and on any other income. (Enterprises Tax Regs, Art. 1). Foreign-funded enterprises and foreign enterprises are governed by separate tax regime entitled Law of China Concerning Income Tax on Foreign Funded Enterprises and Foreign Enterprises (hereinafter "Foreign Enterprises Tax Law") adopted by National People's Congress on Apr. 9, 1991. Taxpayers subject to Enterprise Tax Regs enterprises or organizations include: (1) state owned enterprises; (2) collective enterprises; (3) private enterprises; (4) jointly-operated enterprises; (5) shareholding enterprises; (6) other entities obtaining income from production and business operations.

Taxable income refers to gross income less deductions. (Enterprise Tax Regulations, Art. 4). Gross income of taxpayers includes any of following categories (Enterprise Tax Regulations, Art. 5): (1) income from production and business operations; (2) income from property transfer; (3) income from interest; (4) income from royalties; (5) income from dividends; and (6) any other income.

Scope of Deductions.—Costs, expenses and losses related to income of taxpayers are deductible. (Enterprise Tax Regs, Art. 6). Deductible items include: (1) actual interest paid to financial entities by taxpayer during period of production and business operations. Where interest is paid to nonfinancial entity, deductible amount should not exceed that which financial entity would have charged for same type of loan during same period; (2) salaries paid to employees by taxpayer. Detailed standard for deductible salaries must be formulated by governments of provinces and autonomous regions and municipalities directly under central government, within limits prescribed by Ministry of Finance; (3) regarding trade union funds, employees, welfare funds and education funds paid by taxpayer, deductible amount will be 2%, 14% and 1.5% of deductible salaries respectively; (4) with respect to donations for public welfare and relief, deductible amount will be 3% or less of annual taxable income. In addition, other items may be deducted in accordance with laws, regulations and other tax provisions.

Tax Rate.—All taxpayers are subject to unified tax rate of 33% of their taxable income. (Enterprise Tax Regs, Art. 3). Foreign-funded enterprises are subject to tax rate of 30% plus 3% local income tax, except those in special economic zones, development zones and coastal port cities.

Avoidance of International Double Taxation-Method of Tax Credit.—Where taxpayer obtains income outside of China, taxes paid on that income abroad may be used to offset taxes in China for that part of income. However, maximum credit amount may not exceed taxable amount on that part of income sourced abroad, calculated in accordance with Chinese tax law. (Enterprise Tax Regs, Art. 12).

Value-added Tax.—

Taxpayers.—Any entity or individual selling goods or providing services for processing, repairing and supplying replacements on imported goods in China must pay value-added tax. (Value-added Tax Regs, Art. 1). Foreign funded enterprises and foreign enterprises engaging in activities specified above must pay value-added tax. (Value-added Tax Regs, Art. 27; NPC Decision, Art. 1).

Tax Rate.—Value-added tax rate is flat tax rate, falling into four types. (Value-added Tax Regs, Art. 2). For sale or import of most goods, tax rate is 17%. However, sale or import of following goods are subject to 13% tax rate: (1) cereals and edible vegetable oil; (2) tap water, central heating, air conditioning, hot water, gas, natural gas, liquefied petroleum gas, marsh gas and coal products for residents; (3) books, newspapers, magazines; (4) feed, chemical fertilizer, pesticide, farm machinery; (5) other goods to be decided by State Council.

Unless otherwise provided by State Council, there are no taxes on goods that are exported. For provision of services of repairing and supplying replacements, tax rate is 17%.

State Council may readjust tax rate specified above. (Value-added Tax Regs, Art. 2). Where taxpayer deals in two or more kinds of goods or taxable services which are subject to different tax rates, sales volume of goods or taxable services within different tax rate must be calculated separately, otherwise, higher tax rate will apply. For small scale taxpayers, standards of which will be separately formulated by Ministry of Finance, tax rate is 6% for sale of goods or taxable services. (Value-added Tax Regs, Arts. 11, 12). Tax rate may be readjusted by State Council. (Value-added Tax Regs, Art. 12).

Tax Calculation.—Taxes are calculated at each stage of commercial transaction. Sum of tax to be paid by taxpayer for sale of goods or taxable services is amount of tax remaining at sales level by offsetting tax at purchase level at that time. (Value-added Tax Regs, Art. 4). If amount of tax at sales level is not enough to offset tax at purchase level at that time, deficiency may be transferred to next stage for continual offset. (Value-added Tax Regs, Art. 4). Amount of tax at sales level is sum of sales volume multiplied by tax rate. (Value-added Tax Regs, Art. 5). Tax at purchase level refers to sum of value-added tax paid by or borne by taxpayer when it purchases goods or accepts taxable services. (Value-added Tax Regs, Art. 8). Amount of tax at purchase level deductible from tax at sales level, but is limited to sum of valued-added tax indicated in special invoice for value-added tax issued by seller or taxation certificate issued by customs. (Value-added Tax Regs, Art. 8). For agricultural products free of tax, deductible tax at purchase level is sum of purchase price multiplied by uniform deduction rate of 10%. (Value-added Tax Regs, Art. 8). Where taxpayer fails to obtain and maintain certificate of value-added tax deduction or certificate fails to indicate sum of value-added tax or other related items, tax at purchase level may not be deducted from tax at sales level. (Value-added Tax Regs, Art. 9). As to small scale taxpayers, amount of tax is sum of sales volume multiplied by tax rate, i.e. 6% (Value-added Tax Regs, Art. 13). Tax at purchase level may not be deducted. (Value-added Tax Regs, Art. 13).

With regard to imported goods of taxpayer, tax to be paid is sum of composite price multiplied by tax rate. (Value-added Tax Regs, Art. 15). Composite price is sum total of duty free price plus duty and consumption tax. (Value-added Tax Regs, Art. 15). Sales volume of taxpayer for sale of goods or taxable services must include total price plus fees paid by buyer. (Value-added Tax Regs, Art. 6). Tax on sales level must be excluded from sales volume. Sales volume is calculated in local currency, i.e. RMB. (Value-added Tax Regs, Art. 6). If sales volume of taxpayer is in foreign exchange, it will be converted into RMB according to exchange rate on foreign exchange market. (Value-added Tax Regs, Art. 6). If price taxpayer charges for selling goods or providing services is obviously low without justified reason, competent tax authority may readjust price. (Value-added Tax Regs, Art. 8).

Tax Exemption.—Where sales volume of taxpayer falls below minimum taxable sales volume set by Ministry of Finance, no value-added tax levied. (Value-added Regs, Art. 18). Some goods specified in Art. 16 of Value-added Tax Regs are exempted from value-added tax. These goods include: (1) agricultural products sold by producers; (2) contraceptives; (3) antiquated books; (4) imported devices and equipment for purpose of scientific research, experiment, education; (5) imported materials and equipment gratuitously given by foreign governments or international organizations; (6) imported equipment for compensation trade and business processing with overseas customers' materials and assembled with overseas customers' parts; (7)

See Topical Index in front part of this volume.

TAXATION . . . *continued*
articles imported directly by organizations for disabled and used specially for disabled; and (8) selling of one's own used articles.

In addition, only State Council can add new items to be exempt from Value-added Tax Regs and can reduce tax rate on certain goods. No department or local government may decide items for tax exemption and tax reduction. Where taxpayer deals in two or more items that are entitled to tax exemption or tax reduction, sales volume of each item must be separately calculated (Value-added Tax Regs, Art. 17), otherwise there will be no tax exemption or tax reduction.

Tax Authority.—Value-added tax will be levied by tax authority and value-added tax on imported goods will be levied by customs. Regular taxpayer must pay tax to competent tax authority in place where its organization is located. (Value-added Tax Regs, Art. 22.). Where head office and branch are located in different counties (cities), tax must be paid to competent tax authority where they are located. Upon approval of State Tax Bureau or its authorized authorities, organization may pay value-added tax for all of its branch offices to competent tax authorities in place where head office is located. Where regular taxpayer sells goods in other counties (cities), taxpayer must obtain certificate from appropriate tax administration for business activities in that place and must pay tax to competent tax authority in home country. If taxpayer fails to obtain certificate specified above, taxpayer pays tax to competent tax authority where goods are sold. Otherwise, overdue tax must be paid to competent tax authority located in home locality of taxpayer. Irregular taxpayer must pay tax to authority where goods are sold. (Value-added Tax Regs, Art. 22). As to imported goods, value-added tax must be paid by importer or agent to customs where goods are declared. (Value-added Tax Regs, Art. 22).

Land Value-added Tax.—

Taxpayers.—Any entity or individual who obtains income from assignment of right to use state-owned land, buildings and facilities must pay land value-added tax. (Land Tax Regs, Art. 2). If foreign-funded enterprises and foreign enterprises are engaged in activities specified above, they must pay land value-added tax. (NPC Decision, Art. 3). Where taxpayer fails to pay land valuated tax, land administration and housing administration will reject title transfer application of taxpayer. (Land Tax Regs, Art. 12).

Taxable Value-added Increments and Scope of Deductions.—Taxable income from sale of State-owned real estate refers to all income obtained in such transactions including income in cash, in kind and other revenues. (Land Tax Regs, Art. 5). According to Art. 6 of Land Tax Regs, following items are deductible: (1) payment for acquisition of land-use rights; (2) costs and expenses of land development; (3) costs and expenses of new buildings and their coordinate facilities, or appraisal price of used houses, buildings; (5) taxes, charges related to assignment of real estate; and (6) other deductible items prescribed by Ministry of Finance.

Where taxpayer conceals or falsifies prices of real estate transactions, provides false appraised items or sells real estate at prices lower than appraisal price without justified reason, it will be taxed according to appraisal price. (Land Tax Regs, Art. 9).

Tax Rate.—Progressive tax rate is employed. (Land Tax Regs, Art. 7). If taxable sum of value of real estate transaction does not exceed 50% of sum of deductible items, tax rate is 30%; where it is in excess of 50% but does not exceed 100% of sum of deductible items, tax rate is 40%; where it is in excess of 100% but does not exceed 200% of sum of deductible items, tax rate is 50%. For sum of value addition in excess of 200% of sum of deductible items, tax rate is 60%.

Tax Exemption.—If taxpayer builds residence of ordinary standard whose added value does not exceed 20% of sum of deductible items, transaction of such building is exempt from value added tax. Should real estate be taken or expropriated by State according to prescribed procedure, necessitated by national construction, it will be exempt from such value-added tax. (Land Tax Regs, Art. 8).

Business Tax.—

Taxpayers.—Any entity or individual providing certain category of services, selling certain intangible assets or selling immovable property, must pay business tax. (Business Tax Regs, Art. 1). Services which are subject to business tax include: communication, transportation, construction, banking, insurance, post, telecommunication, culture, sports, entertainment, and service trades including agency, hotels, catering, tourism, storage, leasing and advertising business. (Business Tax Regs, Art. 2, Business Tax Schedule). If foreign funded enterprises and foreign enterprise engage in activities specified above, they must pay business tax. (Business Tax Regs, Art. 15, NPC Decision, Art. 1).

Tax Rate.—Flat tax rate is employed by business tax but specific tax rate varies from trade to trade. (Business Tax Regs, Art. 2). For communication, transportation, construction, post and telecommunication, and culture, sports, tax rate is 3%. As to banking, insurance, service trades, sales of intangible assets and immovable property, tax rate is 5%. Tax rate ranges from 5% to 20% on entertainment. Business Tax Regulations empower governments in provinces, autonomous regions and municipalities directly under central government to formulate specific tax rates for various entertainment trades. (Business Tax Regs, Art. 2). Should taxpayer deal in two or more taxable items, business volume of different category of taxable items must be separately calculated. If business volume is not separately calculated, highest tax rate, of whichever item must be applied. (Business Tax Regs, Art. 3).

Tax Calculation.—Sum of business tax is taxable business volume multiplied by relevant tax rate. (Business Tax Regs, Art. 4). Taxable business volume is calculated in local currency, i.e. RMB. Should taxpayer conduct its business in foreign exchange, it must be converted into RMB according to exchange rate in foreign exchange market. (Business Tax Regs, Art. 4). Taxpayer is entitled to choose either exchange rate of day when business volume occurs or that of first day of same month. (Business Tax Rules, Art. 16). Whichever exchange rate is chosen must be used for one year. (Business Tax Rules, Art. 16). Taxable business volume of taxpayer shall include total sales costs and fees collected from providing taxable services, selling intangible assets and immovable property. (Business Tax Regs, Art. 5). In principle, no deductions are allowed for business volume, however, under following circumstances, deductions are allowed: (1) where transportation entity transports goods or passengers out of China and engages another entity in transporting those goods or passengers, taxable business volume will be total amount for entire transaction minus those fees paid to latter carrier; (2) where travel entity sends touring party out of China and employs other entities, taxable business will be remaining sum of total fees received after deducting those fees paid to latter travel entities; (3) where contractor subcontracts its project to others, taxable business amount will be remaining sum of total price of contract minus that paid to subcontractor; (4) for sub-loan business, taxable business volume will be remaining sum of interest on loan minus interest paid to prior lenders; (5) for buying and selling foreign exchange, securities, futures trading, taxable business will be sum remaining of selling price after deducting purchase price; (6) other circumstances provided by Ministry of Finance.

Tax Exemption.—Should taxable business volume of taxpayer fall below minimum taxable business volume, it will be exempt from business tax. (Business Tax Regs, Art. 8). Business Tax Regs specify six categories of services which will be exempt from tax (Business Tax Regs, Art. 6), namely: supporting services provided by kindergardens, organizations for disabled and aged, services provided by disabled, medical services by hospitals and clinics, educational services by schools, agricultural services and revenues from entrance tickets of public welfare organizations. Should taxpayer deal in two or more tax exempt or tax reduction items, taxable business volume of each item must be separately calculated, otherwise no tax exemption or tax reduction will be permitted. (Business Tax Regs, Art. 7).

Tax Authority.—Business tax will be collected by tax authority. (Business Tax Regs, Art. 10). Where taxpayer provides taxable services, it must pay tax to competent tax authority where services are rendered. (Business Tax Regs, Art. 12). If taxpayer engages in transportation, it must pay tax to competent tax authority where its organization is located. Where taxpayer sells land-use rights, it must pay tax to competent tax authority where land is located. Where taxpayer transfers other intangible assets, it must pay taxes to competent tax authority where its organization is located. Where taxpayer sells property, it must pay tax to competent tax authority where property is located. (Business Tax Regs, Art. 12).

Consumption Tax.—

Taxpayers.—Any entity or individual producing, manufacturing on commission basis or importing consumer goods prescribed by Consumption Tax Regulations (hereinafter "taxable consumer goods"), must pay consumption tax. (Consumption Tax Regs, Art. 1). Should foreign-funded enterprises or foreign enterprises engage in activities specified above, they must be subject to consumption tax. (Consumption Tax Regs, Art. 17; NPC Decision, Art. 1).

Taxable Consumer Goods and Tax Rate.—Taxable consumer goods are divided into 11 categories with approximately 30 products. (Consumption Tax Regs, Art. 2). Most consumer goods are subject to ad valorem tax and only four products are subject to specific tax. Specific tax is applied to millet wine, beer, gasoline, diesel oil. Tax rates are: RMB 240/ton of millet wine, RMB 220/ton of beer, RMB 0.2/liter of gasoline and RMB 0.1/liter of diesel oil. As to ad valorem tax, tax rate ranges from 3% to 45%. Regarding cigarettes, tax rates are respectively: 45%, for class A including all imported cigarettes, 40% for class B, 40% for cigars, 30% for cut tobacco. Other liquor and alcohol, tax rates are respectively: 25% for cereal spirits, 15% for potato spirits, 10% for other liquors, 5% for alcohol. Tax rate for cosmetics is 30%. Tax rate for skin, hair care products is 17%. For valuable jewelry, tax rate is 10%. For fire crackers, tax rate is 15%. Tax rate is 10% for auto, motorcycle tires. For cars, tax rate is 3-8% for sedans depending on their cylinder capacity, 3-5% for cross-country vehicles depending on their cylinder capacity and 3-5% for minibuses depending on their cylinder capacity.

Tax Calculation.—Consumption tax on taxable consumer goods will be levied when goods are sold. (Consumption Tax Regs, Art. 4). Should taxpayer use taxable consumer goods produced by itself for further manufacturing of taxable consumer goods, it will be exempted from taxes. Should taxpayer use them for any other purposes, it will pay tax when goods are transferred for use. (Consumption Tax Regs, Art. 4). For taxable consumer goods manufactured pursuant to commission order, agent must withhold tax when agent delivers goods to principal. (Consumption Tax Regs, Art. 4). For imported consumer goods, consumption tax will be levied when goods are declared at customs. (Consumption Tax Regs, Art. 4).

Sum of consumption tax is sum of taxable sales multiplied by tax rate. (Consumption Tax Regs, Art. 5). Sales include total sales price and fees that taxpayer obtains from selling taxable consumer goods. (Consumption Tax Regs, Art. 6). Sales are calculated in local currency, i.e. RMB. Should sales be conducted in foreign currency, it must be converted to RMB according to exchange rate on foreign exchange market. (Consumption Tax Regs, Art. 5). Taxpayer is entitled to choose either exchange rate of day when sales volume occurs or that of first day of same month. (Consumption Tax Regs, Art. 15). Whichever exchange rate is chosen must be used for one year. (Consumption Tax Regs, Art. 15).

Tax Authority.—Consumption tax will be levied by tax authority; but for imported goods it will be levied by customs. (Consumption Tax Regs, Art. 12). Unless otherwise provided by state, taxpayer must pay tax for taxable consumer goods produced by it to competent tax authority where its business accounting is carried out. (Consumption Tax Regs, Art. 13). For taxable consumer goods pursuant to commission order, it must be paid to competent tax authority where agent is located. For imported taxable consumer goods, importer or its agency must pay tax at customs where goods are declared. (Consumption Tax Regs, Art. 13).

Income Tax Law for Enterprise with Foreign Investment and Foreign Enterprises governing joint ventures between Chinese and foreign investment was adopted by Fifth National People's Congress on Sept. 10, 1980. Law provided that income tax rate on Joint Venture was 30%. In addition, a local surtax of 10% of assessed income tax was levied. Income Tax Law Governing Foreign Enterprise was adopted by Fifth National People's Congress on Dec. 13, 1981. It provided that income tax on foreign enterprises must be assessed at progressive rate for amount in excess of specific amount of taxable income. Tax rates ranged from 20% to 40%. In addition, local income tax of 10% of same taxable income was levied. Under these two tax laws, foreign investment enterprises paid income tax at range of tax rate of 30-50%. In order to make foreign investment in China more attractive and to bring China's taxation in line with other countries, Seventh National People's Congress adopted Income Tax Law of the People's Republic of China for Enterprises with Foreign Investment and Foreign Enterprises (herinafter "New Tax Law") on Apr. 9, 1991. New Tax Law, which introduces unified foreign investment tax regime, came into effect on July 1,

See Topical Index in front part of this volume.

TAXATION . . . *continued*

1991. The Detailed Implementing Rules Relating to the Income Law of the People's Republic of China for Enterprise with Foreign Investment and Foreign Enterprises (herinafter "Implementing Rules") were promulgated by State Council on June 31, 1991 and came into effect on same date as New Tax Law.

Application.—New Tax Law applies to all "foreign investment enterprises" in China and all "foreign enterprises", as defined under New Tax Law. "Foreign investment enterprises" include all equity and co-operative joint ventures as well as wholly foreign-owned enterprises established in China. "Foreign enterprises" is defined as all foreign companies and organizations which have establishments in China or whose income sources derived from overseas. Foreign enterprises shall pay income tax on income derived from sources in China. (New Tax Law Art. 3).

Tax Rate.—Income tax for enterprise with foreign investment, or foreign enterprise with establishment in China engaged in production and business operation shall be levied at rate of 30% on taxable income. Local income tax shall be levied on same taxable income at rate of 3%. (New Tax Law Art. 5). Taxable income shall be total income in tax year after deduction of costs, expenditures and losses in that year. (New Tax Law Art. 4).

Tax Preference.—Enterprises with foreign investment established in Special Economic Zones, or foreign enterprises with establishment in Special Economic Zones engaged in production and business operations, or enterprises with foreign investment established in economic and technological development zones engaged in production, are allowed to have reduced rate of 15% on their taxable income.

Enterprises with foreign investment engaged in production and established in economically open zones along sea coasts or in old city areas of cities in Special Economic Zones, or in economic and technological development zones, are allowed to have reduced tax rate of 24% on their taxable incomes.

Enterprises with foreign investment established in economically open zones along sea coast, in old city areas of cities in Special Economic Zones, in economic and technological development zones or in other areas designated by State Council, engaged in energy, communication, harbor, wharf or other projects encouraged by State may be allowed to have reduced tax rate of 15% on their taxable incomes. Specific measures related thereto shall be provided by State Council. (Art. 7).

"Special Economic Zones" in China refers to Special Economic Zones in Shenzhen, Zhuhai, Shantou, Xiamen and Hainan which are established in accordance with law or with approval of State Council. "Economic and technological development zones" refers to economic and technological development zones established in coastal port cities with approval of State Council. (Implementing Rules, Art. 69). "Coastal open development zones" refers to cities, counties and districts approved by the State Council to be coastal open development zones. (Implementation Art. 70).

"Enterprises with foreign investment engaged in production" refers to enterprises with foreign investment engaged in following lines: (1) machine-manufacturing and electronic industries; (2) energy industry (not including oil and natural gas exploitation); (3) metallurgical, chemical and building materials industries; (4) light, textile and package industries; (5) medical apparatus and pharmaceutical industries; (6) agriculture, forestry, animal husbandry, fishery and water conservancy; (7) construction industry; (8) communication and transportation industries (not including passenger transportation); (9) development of science and technology, geological survey and industrial information consultants which are directly at service of production and maintenance and repair services for production equipment and precision instruments; (10) other lines specified by competent department of taxation under State Council. (Implementing Rules Art. 72).

Reduced tax rate of 15% on taxable incomes applies to following: (1) production-oriented enterprises with foreign investment, estabished in old urban districts of cities where coastal open economic zones, Special Economic Zones and economic and technological development zones are located, and engaged in following: (i) technology-intensive or knowledge-intensive projects, (ii) projects with foreign investment of US$30 million and over, and with a long payback period, (iii) energy, transportation and port construction projects; (2) Chinese-foreign joint ventures engaged in port and dock construction; (3) foreign banks, banks with Chinese and foreign investment and other financial institutions established in Special Economic Zones and other areas approved by State Council, capital of which, however, must be provided by foreign investors or branches of which must have received working capital contributed by head office amounting to US$10 million or more, and which are scheduled for operation period of ten years or more; (4) production-oriented enterprises with foreign investment established in Shanghai Pudong New Area, and enterprises with foreign investment engaged in construction, energy and transportation projects such as airports, ports, railways, highways and power stations; (5) enterprises with foreign investment which are recognized to be high and new technology enterprises, and which are established in high and new technology industrial development zones approved by State Council; and enterprises with foreign investment which are recognized to be new technology enterprises established in Beijing New Technology Industrial Development Experimental Zone; (6) enterprises with foreign investment engaged in projects encouraged by State and established in other areas designated by State Council.

Enterprises with foreign investment engaged in projects listed in Item (1) in preceding paragraph shall, upon approval by State Administration for taxation of their applications, be levied on their taxable income at reduced rate of 15%. (Implementing Rules Art. 73).

Enterprise with foreign investment scheduled for operation for period of ten years or more in reduction shall be exempted from income tax in first and second profit-making years and allowed to have 50% reduction in income tax in third to fifth years, with exception of projects relating to petroleum, natural gas, rare metals, precious metals and such other exploitation projects for which separate provisions shall be provided by State Council. Enterprise with foreign investment shall pay back income tax that has been exempted or reduced if its actual operation period is under ten years.

If duration of preferential treatment in respect to exemptions and reductions of income tax granted to energy, communication, harbor, wharf and other major productive or nonproductive projects under regulations promulgated by State Council before execution of this law are longer than those provided in preceding paragraph, they shall continue their effect after implementation of this law.

Enterprise with foreign investment engaged in agriculture, forestry and animal husbandry or established in remote and economically undeveloped area may, upon approval by appropriate tax authorities of State Council of application filed by enterprise, be allowed reduced income tax rate of 15% to 30% on their taxable incomes for a period of ten years following expiration of term for exemption and reduction specified in preceding two paragraphs. (New Tax Law Art. 8).

"Regulations promulgated by the State Council before the execution of this Law" mentioned above refers to following regulations: (1) Chinese-foreign joint venture engaged in port and dock construction, operation period of which exceeds 15 years, may be allowed exemption from enterprise income tax from first to fifth profit-making years, and reduction of 50% from sixth to tenth years. (2) Enterprise with foreign investment established in Hainan Special Economic Zone and engaged in construction of infrastructure project such as airports, ports, docks, railways, highways, power stations, coal mines, water conservancy or in development and operation of agriculture, operation period of which exceeds 15 years, may be allowed exemption from enterprise income tax from first to fifth profit-making years, and reduction of 50% from sixth to tenth years. (3) Enterprises with foreign investment engaged in construction of energy and transportation projects such as airports, ports, railways, highways, power stations, operation period of which exceeds 15 years, may be allowed exemption from enterprise income tax from first to fifth profit-making years, and reduction of 50% from sixth to tenth years. (4) Enterprises with foreign investment established in Special Economic Zones and engaged in service industries with foreign investment exceeding US$5 million, with operation period for which is ten years or more, may be allowed exemption from enterprise income tax for first profit-making year and reduction of 50% for second and third years. (5) Foreign banks, banks with Chinese and foreign investment and other financial institutions established in SEZ or other areas approved by State Council, with capital from foreign investors or branches of which have received working capital contributed by head office amounting to US$10 million or more and which are scheduled for operation period of ten years or more, may be allowed exemption from enterprise income tax for first profit-making year and reduction of 50% for second and third years. (6) Chinese-foreign joint ventures which are recognized to be high and new technology enterprises and established in high and new technology industrial development zones of State approved by State Council, operation period of which is ten years or more, may be allowed exemption from enterprise income tax for first and second years. For enterprises with foreign investment established in SEZ and Economic and Technological Development Zones (ETDZ), preferential provisions of SEZ and ETDZ shall be applied. For enterprises with foreign investment established in Beijing New Technology Industrial Development Experimental Zone, preferential tax provisions of Beijing New Technology Industrial Development Experimental Zone shall be applied. (7) Export-oriented enterprises established with foreign investment may, upon expiration of period of exemption and reduction on enterprise income tax as provided in Tax Law, be allowed reduction of 50% on their enterprise income tax in accordance with tax rate stipulated Tax Law, if value of their export products for that year reaches 70% or more of total value of products for same year. However, export-oriented enterprises established in SEZ and ETDZ or other export-oriented enterprises which have paid their enterprise income tax at rate of 15%, shall be levied at rate of 10% if they meet above requirements. (8) Technologically advanced enterprises extablished with foreign investment may, upon expiration of period of exemption and reduction on enterprise income tax as provided in Tax Law, be allowed to pay their enterprise income tax at same rate as provided in Tax Law for further three and a half years if they continue to be technologically advanced enterprise. (9) Provisions relating to exemptions and reductions on enterprise income tax in other regulations promulgated or approved to be promulgated by State Council.

Foreign investor in enterprise with foreign investment who reinvests his shares of profit obtained from enterprise in enterprise to increase registered capital, or in other enterprises with foreign investment as capital contribution for scheduled period of not less than five years may, with approval of tax authorities of application filed by said investor, obtain refund of 40% of income tax paid on reinvested amount or enjoy other preferential treatment as stipulated by State Council. Investor who withdraws his reinvested funds in less than five years shall pay back taxed amount refunded. (New Tax Law Art. 10).

Tax Deduction.—Amount of income tax already paid outside China by enterprise with foreign investment for income derived from sources outside China may be deducted from total amount of tax payment on its taxable income in China. Amount of such reduction shall, however, not exceed amount of tax payable on taxable income derived from sources outside China as stipulated by this law.

Withholding Tax.—Twenty percent income tax shall be levied on income obtained from profits, interest, rentals, royalties and other sources in China by foreign enterprise which has no establishment in China, or by foreign enterprise which has establishments in China but which are not actually related to aforesaid incomes.

For payment of income tax in accordance with provisions in preceding paragraph, foreign enterprise which earns income shall be taxpayer, and paying unit shall be withholding agent. Taxes withheld on each payment by withholding agent shall, within five days, be turned over to State Treasury and income tax returns submitted to local tax authorities.

Following category of income shall be reduced or exempted from income tax: (1) Income tax on profits obtained by foreign investor from enterprise with foreign investment shall be exempted; (2) income tax on interest from loans granted to Chinese government and State Bank of China by international financial institutions shall be exempted; (3) income tax on interest on any loan granted to China's state bank at favorable lending rates by foreign banks is exempted; (4) royalties obtained from provision of proprietary technology for scientific research, energy development, development of communications, agriculture, forestry and animal husbandry or development of important technology may, with approval by appropriate authorities of State Council, be levied at reduced income tax rate of 10% and, where technology is advanced or conditions are preferential, may be exempted from payment of income tax. (New Tax Law Art. 19).

See Topical Index in front part of this volume.

TAXATION . . . *continued*

Payment of income tax under this Law shall be computed in Renminbi. All foreign currency income shall be assessed according to exchange rate quoted by State Administration of Foreign Exchange Control and shall be taxed in Renminbi. (New Tax Law Art. 21).

Tax Administration.—In case of failure to pay tax within prescribed time limit by any payer, or failure to turn over any withholding tax in prescribed time limit any withholding agent, tax authorities, in addition to setting new time limit for such payment, shall surcharge overdue time at 0.2% of overdue tax for every day in arrears, starting from first day of delay in payment. (New Tax Law Art. 22).

In case of disputes with tax authorities about tax payment, enterprise with foreign investment, foreign enterprise or withholding agent must pay tax in accordance with relevant regulations first before applying to higher tax authorities for reconsideration within 60 days after receipt of application for such reconsideration. If taxpayer or withholding agent does not accept decision made after such reconsideration, it can bring matter before local People's Court within 15 days after receipt of such decision on reconsideration.

If taxpayer does not accept penalty imposed by tax authorities, it may apply to higher tax authorities for reconsideration within 15 days after receipt of notice of such penalty. If taxpayer does not accept decision on such reconsideration, it may bring matter before People's Court within 15 days after receipt of decision on reconsideration. Taxpayer may also bring matter directly before People's Court within 15 days after receipt of notice of such penalty. If taxpayer neither applies for reconsideration nor brings matter before People's Court, but refuses to be penalized within time prescribed, authorities that decide penalty may apply to People's Court for enforcement. (New Tax Law Art. 26).

Non-retrospective Application.—For any enterprise with foreign investment already set up before promulgation of this law, relevant laws and provisions of State Council that were in force shall apply within approved term of venture in respect of its income tax rate which may be increased, or in respect of preferential treatment of tax exemptions or reductions it enjoys, which may be reduced, in accordance with this law. For any enterprise with foreign investment without fixed operational term, relevant laws and provisions of State Council that were in force before promulgation of this law shall apply within period stipulated by State Council. (New Tax Law Art. 27).

Other Tax Incentives.—Besides provisions governing incentives stated by Income Tax Law for enterprises with foreign investment and foreign investment and foreign enterprise, there are other provisions governing tax incentives according to relevant laws and regulations. See subheads on tax incentives infra.

Agreement for the Avoidance of Double Taxation and the Prevention of Tax Evasion with Respect to Taxes on Income ("Tax Agreement") signed on Mar. 21, 1984 between U.S. and China further strengthens this provision of law. This Tax Agreement specifically applies to income tax on joint ventures, income tax on foreign enterprises and local income tax. (Art. 2[i][a], [ii], [iii], [iv]).

Tax Agreement defines "permanent establishment" as fixed place of business through which business wholly or partly carried out, including branch, place of management, office, factory, workshop, mine, oil or gas well, quarry, building site or construction site, assembly or installation project, or supervision thereof if such project or activities continue for more than six months; installation drilling rig or ship used for exploration only if used for period of three months; furnishing of services, including consulting services, buty only for periods aggregating more than six months in any 12 month period. (Art. 5 [i], [2], and [3]). "Permanent establishment" does not include: Mere storage, display, or delivery facilities for goods belonging to enterprise or maintenance of goods for said purposes, or maintenance of goods solely for processing goods of another enterprise, or maintenance of fixed place of business for purpose of carrying on work of preparatory activity. (Art. 4). Acting through agent or broker of independent status, providing they are not acting wholly or almost wholly for said enterprise in non-arms-length transaction, should not be construed as having permanent establishment. (Art. 5[6]). Where person other than agent of independent status habitually exercises authority to conclude contracts in name of enterprise, that enterprise deemed to have permanent establishment. (Art. 5).

Profits of enterprise of U.S.A. taxable in China only if American enterprise conducts business in China through permanent establishment and only to the extent that said profits can be attributable to that permanent establishment. (Art. 7[i]). In determining profits of permanent establishment, deductions allowed for expenses incurred for that establishment, including executive and general administrative expenses so incurred, whether in China or elsewhere (Art. 7[3]), except those paid to head office for royalties (Art. 7[3]).

Dividends paid by company resident in China may be taxed in U.S. and China, but tax in China should not exceed 10% of gross amount of dividends (Art. 9[1], [2]), except if company paying dividends has permanent establishment in China, or performs independent professional services from fixed base and dividends paid are connected with such permanent establishment or fixed base (Art. 9[4]), then unless fixed base regularly available for period exceeding 183 days in calendar year (Art. 13[1]), there should be no taxes on said dividends in China and said dividends should only be taxed in China to extent to which attributable to that permanent base (Arts. 7[i] and 9[5]).

Interest paid to U.S. resident from entity in China may be taxed in China in amount not to exceed 10% (Art. 10[2]), except if due to government financed indebtedness which should be exempt from taxation (Art. 10[2]). However, if said business in which interest arises is conducted through permanent establishment in China or from fixed base for independent professional services and said debt is connected thereto, then provisions of Art. 13 or Art. 7 apply.

Royalties treated in fashion similar to dividends and interest. (Art. 11). Gains derived by U.S. resident from alienation in China of ships or aircraft operated in international traffic, and of movable personal property pertaining thereto, should only be taxed in U.S. (Art. 12[3]).

U.S. residents and citizens allowed credit against U.S. tax on income for income tax paid to China (Art. 22[2][a]) and where U.S. company owns at least 10% of voting rights in company resident in China from which U.S. company receives dividends, credit allowed for income tax paid to China by distributing company with respect to profits out of which dividends paid (Art. 22[2][b]).

There are "most favored nation" provisions in Tax Agreement. (Art. 23). Protocol to Tax Agreement permits U.S. to impose its social security tax, personal holding company tax and accumulated earnings tax notwithstanding any provision of Agreement. (Art. 3 of Prot.).

Tax Agreement.—On Mar. 21, 1984 U.S. and China initialed Agreement for the Avoidance of Double Taxation and the Prevention of Tax Evasion with Respect to Taxes on Income. This treaty was signed on Apr. 30, 1984 and on July 24, 1986 approved by Senate, together with protocol to prevent treaty shopping. Provisions effective as of Jan. 1, 1987. This Agreement also applies to individual income tax. (Art. 2). Income derived by individual resident in U.S. for professional services, if he has fixed base regularly available to him in China for purposes of performing his activities, or is present in China for period or periods exceeding in aggregate 183 days in calendar year concerned, may be taxed for income attributable to that fixed base or time period. (Art. 13[1]). Salaries, wages and similar remuneration derived from employment exercised in China by U.S. resident, insofar as derived from said employment, may be taxed in China (Art. 14[1], provided recipient present in China for period in excess of 183 days in calendar year (Art. 14[2][a]), and employer has permanent establishment or fixed base in China (Art. 14[2][c]) and employer also resident in China (Art. 14[2][b]). However, except for activities exercised in accordance with special programs for cultural exchange, income derived by American resident from personal activities in China by entertainer, musician or athlete is taxable in China. (Art. 16[1]). Teachers and research specialists at accredited educational or scientific institutions in China exempt from income tax for period not exceeding three years in aggregate for said work in China (Art. 19), as are students during their studies for reasonable period of time necessary to complete their education, for payments received from U.S. for maintenance and study, for grants and awards and for income for personal services performed in China in amount not in excess of US$5,000 (Art. 20). Tax Agreement also provides for elimination of double taxation, by providing credits for income tax paid in China by American resident or citizen. (Art. 22[2][a]). Diplomatic agents and consular officers retain their privileges. (Art. 26).

Property tax, paid on value of real property at time of construction, and covering factories, silos, buildings, residences, etc., is paid at annual rate of 1.2%. There are also land use fees that are under jurisdiction of Real Estate Administration Bureau that are paid per square meter of land use and depend on value or quality of land.

See also topic Trade Zones.

Tax Incentives for Interest on Loans.—(1) Interest income from loans to Chinese government or to China's state banks by international financing organizations shall be exempted from income tax. Interest income from loans provided at preferential interest rate by foreign banks to China's state bank shall also be exempted from income tax. (2) Interest income of foreign banks derived from deposits with China's state banks and from loans provided to China's state banks at normal interest rates shall be subject to income tax. However, reciprocal exemption from income tax shall be granted to those foreign banks from countries which exempt China's state banks from income tax on interest income from deposits and loans. (3) Income tax on interest derived from loans, advances and deferred payments under credit contracts or trade contracts before end of 1990 by foreign companies, enterprises and other economic organizations with China's companies or enterprises may, during effective period of contract, be taxed at reduced rate of 10%. (4) Following items of interest income may be exempted from income tax: (i) interest income from loans to China's state banks by foreign banks at international interbank offer rates. Stipulations in preceding clause may also be applied to trust and investment companies which are authorized by State Council to engage in foreign exchange business; (ii) interest income from loans to China National Offshore Oil Corporation by foreign banks at interest rates not higher than interbank offer rates; (iii) in case of seller's credit provided by foreign party's state bank for import of technology, equipment and commodities by China's companies, enterprises or institutions, interest on deferred payments paid by Chinese party to be received in turn by seller at interest rate not higher than that on Chinese party's buyer credit; (iv) interest received by foreign banks and individuals from deposit with China's state banks when interest rate on such deposits is lower than interest rate on deposits in home country of depositing bank or depositor; (v) cases where equipment and technology are provided to China's companies or enterprises or enterprises and in consideration, Chinese side uses such methods as buy-back or delivery of products to repay principal and interest, or uses processing fees or assembly fees to offset principal and interest.

Tax Incentives for Exploitation of Offshore Petroleum.—(1) If foreign enterprise engaged in cooperative exploitation of offshore petroleum resources holds two contract areas, loss incurred in one contract area, owing to termination of operation or other causes, shall be allowed to offset proceeds of other contract area. Taxable income shall be computed by combining results of two contract areas. (2) In order to encourage Chinese-foreign cooperative exploration of offshore petroleum, following imported goods for offshore operation shall be exempted from Industrial and Commercial Unified Tax (ICCT): (i) Machinery, equipment, spare parts and materials to be directly used in exploration; (ii) machinery, equipment, spare parts and materials to be directly used in development; (iii) parts, components, and materials that are required to be imported for manufacturing machinery and equipment in China for exploitation of offshore petroleum (including prospecting, well drilling, well cementing, well logging, oil extracting, work-over etc.). (3) Local surtax shall be exempted when ICCT is levied on crude oil income derived from Chinese-foreign cooperative exploitation of offshore petroleum. (4) Reasonable exploration expenses incurred by foreign enterprises in contract area, regardless of tangible or intangible costs, shall be capitalized and then amortized from revenues derived from any oil (or gas) field within same contract area that has gone into commercial production, but time limit of such amortization shall not be less than one year. Any subsequent exploration expenses incurred after commencement of commercial production shall be accumulated on yearly basis and amortized in chronological order against income of following year, but time limit of such amortization of annual exploration expenses shall not be less than one year. (5) For enterprises which are engaged in exploitation of offshore petroleum resources, all investments at development period shall be counted as capital expenditure with oil (or gas) field as unit, and depreciation shall be calculated from month when oil (or gas)

TAXATION . . . *continued*

field begins commercial production, but time limit of depreciation shall not be less than six years.

Tax Incentives for Know-how Fees.—Foreign companies, enterprises, and other economic organizations that do not have establishment in China shall pay income tax at reduced rate of 10% on know-how fees obtained from provision of following proprietary technology for use in China. Income tax may be exempted where technologies are advanced or terms are preferential. (1) Fees received from providing proprietary technology in development of agricultural, forestry, fishery and animal husbandry industries, including proprietary technology provided for improvement of soil or green pasture; development of barren hills and for full utilization of natural conditions; proprietary technology provided for new breeds of animals and plants and for production of highly effective, low toxication agricultural chemical; and proprietary technology provided in such areas as conduct of scientific management of agricultural, forestry, fishery and animal husbandry production, maintenance of ecological balance and enhancement of ability to defend against natural disasters; (2) know-how fees received from proprietary technology for conduct of scientific research or scientific experiments provided to China's academies of science, institutes of higher education and other scientific research units, or working in cooperation with China's scientific research units in conduct of scientific research; (3) know-how fees received from proprietary technology provided to China's key construction projects in development of energy and transportation; (4) know-how fees received from proprietary technology provided in areas of energy conservation, and prevention and control of environmental pollution; (5) know-how fees for following proprietary technology provided for development of China's important technological spheres: (i) Technology for production of major advanced mechanical and electrical equipment; (ii) nuclear energy technology; (iii) technology for production of large-scale integrated circuits; (iv) technology for production of optical integration, microwave semiconductors, and microwave integrated circuits as well as technology for manufacture of microwave electronic tubes; (v) technology for production of super speed computers and microprocessors; (vi) technology for photo conductive communication; (vii) technology for long-distance super-high pressure direct-current transmission; (viii) technology for liquification, gasification and comprehensive utilization of coal.

Tax Incentive in Economic and Technological Development Zones.—Fifteen percent preferential enterprise income tax shall be allowed for income derived from production, business operation and other sources from joint venture, cooperative enterprises or foreign enterprises of productive nature operating in economic and technological development zones of the 14 coastal port cities of Dalian, Qinhuangdao, Tianjin, Yantai, Qingdao, Lianyungang, Nantong, Shanghai, Ningbo, Wenzhou, Fuzhou, Guangzhou, Shanjian, and Beihai. Those with contract life of ten years or longer shall enjoy two-year holiday commencing from first profit-making year followed by 50% reduction in third to fifth year.

Foreign investors of joint venture in development zones are exempted from enterprise income tax when repatriating their share of profits from enterprise.

After expiration of reduction and exemption period of enterprise income tax in accordance with relevant provisions of export enterprise in development zone exporting 70% or more of their production; in terms of value, in any one year, may pay enterprise income tax at reduced rate of 10% for that year.

After expiration of reduction and exemption period of enterprise income tax in accordance with relevant provisions of state, technologically advanced enterprises in development zones may pay enterprise income tax at reduced rate of 10% for another three years.

Ten percent preferential income tax shall be levied on dividend, interest, rentals, royalties and other income sources in development zones by overseas investors who do not have establishments in China, except in cases where tax exemption is provided under law. Where terms and conditions for provision of funds or equipment are preferential or technology transferred in advance, it is necessary to grant additional tax reduction or exemption, matter shall be decided by people's government of municipalities where development zones are located.

Reduction and exemption of local income tax for development zones enterprises shall be decided by people's government of municipalities where development zones are located.

ICCT shall be exempted on building materials, production equipment, raw materials, spare parts and accessories, components, means of transport and office supplies imported by development zone enterprise for their own use.

ICCT shall be exempted for products manufactured and exported by development zone enterprise with exception of crude oil, processed oil and other goods for which state has separate provision.

Tax Incentives for Leasing.—Income tax on leasing fees, after deducting equipment price, obtained by foreign leasing companies from supply of equipment and related articles to China's companies or enterprises through leasing arrangements entered into before end of 1990 may, during effective period of contract, be paid at reduced tax rate of 10%.

Where interest is included in leasing fees, if loan agreement or contract and documents and vouchers for interest payment are sufficient to prove that interest rate conforms to seller's or buyer's credit interest rate, income tax shall be levied at rate of 10% on amount remaining after deduction of interest.

Leasing fees obtained by foreign leasing companies through such methods as buy-back or delivery of products may be exempt from income tax.

Tax Incentives for Export Enterprises and Technologically Advanced Enterprises.—After expiration of period allowed for reduction or exemption of enterprise income tax in accordance with provisions of State, export enterprise exporting 70% or more of their products, in terms of value, in any particular year may pay their enterprise income tax at half of existing tax rate for that year. If resultant tax rate after 50% reduction of enterprise income tax payable is below 10%, income tax shall be levied at rate of 10%.

After expiration of period allowed for reduction or exemption of enterprise income tax in accordance with provisions of State, technologically advanced enterprises may enjoy three-year tax reduction existing rate. Technologically advanced enterprises which do not qualify for such tax reduction or exemption may pay enterprise income tax at half of existing rate in first three profit-making years. If resultant tax rate after 50% reduction of enterprise income tax is below 10%, enterprise income tax shall be levied at rate of 10%.

Profits remitted abroad by foreign investors of export enterprises and technologically advanced enterprise with Chinese and foreign investment shall be exempted from income tax.

Foreign investors who reinvest profits distributed by enterprise to establish or expand export enterprise or technologically advanced enterprise for period of not less than five years shall receive full refund of enterprise income tax already paid on amount of reinvestment.

Tax Incentives in Old City Districts of the Fourteen Coastal Port Cities and Delta Regions.—Production enterprises with foreign investment which are established in old city district of the 14 coastal port cities, or in municipalities or towns are within three delta regions (hereinafter referred to as "the old city and open economic zone enterprise"). If enterprise is engaged in technology-intensive, or know-how intensive projects, or in projects in which foreign investor invests US$30 million or more and have long pay back period, or in energy, transportation, harbor construction projects, approved by Ministry of Finance, enterprise income tax shall be levied at reduced rate of 15%.

Subject to approval of ministry of finance, tax shall be paid at 80% of enterprise income tax as prescribed in tax law for those enterprises which are not entitled to tax reduction as prescribed in preceding paragraph but are engaged in following industry: (1) machine building, electronic industry; (2) metallurgy, chemicals, building materials; (3) light industry, textile and packaging; (4) medical apparatus, pharmaceutical; (5) agriculture, forestry, animal husbandry, agriculture and their related processing industries; (6) building and construction.

Reduction and exemption of local income tax of enterprise in old cities and open economic zone shall be decided by provincial or municipal people's government.

Ten percent preferential income tax shall be levied on dividends, interest, rentals, royalties and other income sources in old city districts and open economic zone by overseas investors who do not have establishment in China, except in case when tax exemption is provided under law. Where terms and conditions for provision of funds or equipment are preferential, or technology transferred is advanced, such that it is necessary to grant additional tax reduction or exemption, matter shall be decided by provincial or municipal people's government.

ICCT shall be exempted for products manufactured and exported by old city and open economic zone enterprise with exception of crude oil, processed oil and other goods for which state has separate provisions.

ICCT shall be exempted for production equipment, office or business equipment and building material imported as part of investment and additional investment of old city and open economic zone enterprise as well as for vehicles and office supplies imported for enterprise's own use.

ICCT shall be exempted for raw materials, spare parts, and accessories, components and packaging materials imported by old city and open economic zone enterprises for manufacturing of export products.

Tax Incentives for Permanent Representative Offices of Foreign Enterprises.—Permanent representative offices of foreign companies, enterprises and other economic organizations in China ("permanent representative offices") engaged in such activities as conducting market surveys, providing business information, business liaison, consultation and other services on behalf of their head offices, shall be exempt from Industrial and Commercial Unified Tax ("ICCT") and Enterprise Income Tax, provided they do not receive business or service income for their activities.

Permanent representative offices appointed by Chinese enterprises to act as their agents to promote their goods outside territory of China shall be exempt from ICCT and enterprises income tax on their commission income, rebates and handling fees, etc.

Commissions, rebates or handling fees received by permanent representative offices for acting as agents or intermediaries shall be subject to ICCT at reduced rate of 5%.

15% deemed profit rate which was originally assessed on permanent representative office which cannot substantiate its costs and expenses in order to calculate its actual taxable income shall be reduced to 10%. Income tax shall be payable on taxable income which shall be calculated on deemed basis based on representative office's business revenue.

Where China offices of foreign law firms or accounting firms charge their clients on time cost basis, out of pocket expenses incurred on behalf of clients may be excluded from taxable income in calculating ICCT.

Tax Incentives in Special Economic Zones.—Income tax shall be levied at reduced rate of 15% on income derived from production, business and other sources by joint ventures, cooperative ventures or enterprises with foreign investment (hereinafter referred to as "special zone enterprises") operating in Shenzhen, Zhuhai, Shantou and Xiamen.

For special zone enterprises engaged in industry, communications and transportation, agriculture, forestry and animal husbandry, which have contract period of ten years or longer, two-year tax holiday commencing from first profit-making year shall be allowed followed by 50% reduction in third to fifth year.

For special zone enterprises engaged in service industry, with overseas investment exceeding US$5 million and contract period of ten years or longer, income tax shall be exempt in first profit-making year followed by 50% reduction in second and third year.

Foreign investors in joint ventures in special economic zones shall be exempted from enterprise income tax when repatriating profits distributed from enterprise.

After expiration of reduction or exemption period of enterprise income tax in accordance with relevant provisions of state, export enterprises within special economic zones exporting 70% or more of their products, in value terms, in any one year, may pay enterprise income tax at reduced rate of 10% for such years.

After expiration of initial reduction or exemption period of enterprise income tax in accordance with relevant legal provisions, technologically advanced enterprises shall pay enterprise income tax at reduced rate of 10% for another three years.

Dividends, interest, rentals, royalties and other kinds of income sourced in special economic zones and derived by foreign investors which have no establishments in China are subject to income tax at reduced rate of 10% except cases where tax

See Topical Index in front part of this volume.

TAXATION . . . *continued*
exemption is provided under law. Where terms and conditions for provision of capital and equipment are preferential or technology transferred is advanced such that it is necessary to grant additional tax reductions or exemptions, matter shall be decided by government of special economic zones.

Reduction or exemption of local income tax for special zone enterprises shall be decided by government of special economic zones.

Export products of special zone enterprises shall be exempt from ICCT except for crude oil, processed oil or those for which state has separate provisions.

Special zone enterprises shall be exempt from ICCT for importation of machinery, equipment, raw materials, spare parts and accessories, means of transportation. For imported mineral oils, cigarettes, wines and other articles of daily use, ICCT shall be levied at half of tax rate prescribed in law.

Business income of branches of Hong Kong, Macau and foreign bank established in special economic zones shall be exempt from ICCT for certain specified period.

Interest income received by foreign, Hong Kong or Macau bank for loans made to branch office of foreign bank in special economic zones at inter-bank offer rates shall be exempt from withholding tax.

Interest income received by Hong Kong, Macau or overseas depositor from branch office of foreign bank in special economic zones shall be exempt from withholding tax or individual income tax.

Interest income received by branch office of foreign bank to its head office on working capital borrowed shall be exempt from withholding tax provided that interest rate is not higher than international inter-bank rates.

Tax Incentives in Hainan Island.—Enterprise income tax shall be levied at rate of 15% on income derived from production, business and other sources by enterprises established in Hainan Island (with exception of state banks and insurance companies). In addition, local income tax of 10% of assessed income tax shall be levied.

For enterprises engaged in development and operation of infrastructural facilities such as ports, harbours, airports, highways, railways, power states, coal minings, irrigation, etc., and enterprises engaged in agriculture, which have contract period of 15 years or more, shall be exempt from income tax in first to fifth profit-making years followed by 50% reduction in sixth to tenth years.

Enterprises engaged in industry, communications and transportation, which have contract period of ten years or more, two-year tax holiday commencing from first profit-making year shall be allowed followed by 50% reduction in enterprise income tax in third to fifth year. Where enterprise is confirmed by Government of Hainan Province as technologically advanced, income tax may be reduced by 50% during sixth to eighth years.

After expiration of reduction and exemption period of enterprise income tax in accordance with relevant provisions, enterprises engaged in industry or agriculture exporting 70% or more of their products in value terms in any one year may pay enterprise income tax at reduced rate of 10% for that year.

For enterprises engaged in service industry with total amount of investment exceeding US$5 million or RMBY20 million and contract life of ten years or more, shall be exempt from enterprise income tax in first profit-making year followed by 50% reduction in second and third years. Reduction or exemption from local income tax for enterprises in Hainan Island shall be decided by government of Hainan Province.

Dividends, interest, rental, royalties and other kinds of income sourced in Hainan Island and derived by foreign investors which have no establishment in Hainan Island shall be subject to income tax at rate of 10% except in cases where tax exemption is provided by law. Where necessary to grant tax reduction or exemption, matter shall be decided by government of Hainan Province.

Enterprises in Hainan Island importing machinery, equipment, raw materials, spare parts and accessories, means of communication and transportation, other goods and materials and office supplies are required for enterprises own construction and production purposes shall be exempt from customs duties, product tax or value-added tax.

Customs duties, product tax or value-added tax shall be reduced by 50% for goods imported by enterprises in Hainan Island for sale in Hainan market.

Products manufactured by enterprises in Hainan Island and sold in Hainan market shall be exempt from product tax or value-added tax, except for mineral oils, cigarettes, wines and few other products specified by government of Hainan Island which shall be subject to product tax or value-added tax at half of existing tax rates.

Foreign investors repatriating profits distributed from enterprise to overseas locations shall be exempt from income tax on amount of remittance.

Foreign investors or enterprises in Hainan Island which reinvest their shares of profits distributed from Hainan enterprises for period of not less than five years may obtain refund of 40% of income tax paid on amount of reinvestment. Where reinvestment is for construction of infrastructure in Hainan Island, or is used in agricultural enterprises, export-oriented enterprises or technologically advanced enterprises, total amount of income tax already paid on reinvested portion shall be refunded.

TORTS:

See topics Constitution and Government; Criminal Law; Damages; Libel; Civil Code.

It is clear that one can collect from courts for tortious injury. General Rules of Civil Law make provision for restraining orders and damages for tortious conduct. If said tortious act is result of criminal wrong, Criminal Code (e.g. Art. 137) provides for civil legal redress, viz., compensation. Those who damage or make off with private or public property must return it and make compensation.

TRADEMARKS:

Regulations Governing Trademarks (Trademark Regulations) were originally promulgated by State Council on Apr. 10, 1963 and Implementing Rules under Regulations Governing Trademarks were promulgated by Central Administration Bureau of Commerce and Industry on Apr. 25, 1963, which regulations effective until Mar. 1, 1983 and replaced by new regulations discussed below.

Under old regulations, China Council for Promotion of International Trade (CCPIT) had Trademark Registration Agency which handled trademark applications on behalf of foreign applicants. Trademark Department within General Administration of Commerce and Industry acted on all trademark applications and issued rejections and certificates of registration. Trademark registrations were valid for period of ten years from date of registration and could be renewed upon application, for ten year periods. Infringement actions could be brought by complaint to administration agencies or courts. Penalties included injunctive relief, monetary penalty, compensation for losses and confiscation of infringer's goods.

Under old regulations, right to exclusive use of trademark was acquired by registration, not mere usage. Foreigners could apply for trademark registration if applicant's country also accepts Chinese applications for trademarks, as does U.S., or if agreement on reciprocal registration of trademarks has been concluded, which U.S. and China have done, as have most western European countries, Thailand, Japan, Romania, Hungary, East Germany, Czechoslovakia and Argentina.

Local organizations of Administration of Commerce and Industry promulgated directives requiring publication of trademarks. For example, in Guangzhou trademark directive was issued by city Administration of Commerce and Industry requiring that all approved registered trademarks in Guangzhou be published, with registration number, in Guangzhou Daily.

On Aug. 23, 1982 new Trademark Law was promulgated by Standing Committee of People's Congress, which regulations took effect Mar. 1, 1983, superseding prior 1963 legislation. (Art. 43). Said Trademark Law was amended by National People's Congress Feb. 22, 1993, effective July 1, 1993, particularly to strengthen enforcement proceedings.

Trademarks approved for registration by Trademark Bureau are registered trademarks; registrant enjoys benefits of exclusive use and legal protection. (Art. 3). Trademark users responsible for quality of commodities bearing their trademarks, and relevant departments of Administration of Commerce and Industry must supervise quality of said commodities through trademark control, to prevent acts that deceive consumers. (Art. 6). Foreign persons must employ this Trademark Law pursuant to treaties between their nation and China, or international conventions of which both nations are signatories, or in accordance with principal of reciprocity. (Art. 9). Trademarks duly registered are valid for ten years from said approval. (Art. 23). Six months prior to termination of validity of said trademark, application must be made for extension of registration which, if approved, will be valid for ten years. If registrant fails to make such application within that period, extension of six months may be granted. (Art. 24).

Regulations provide that words and designs, or their form, must have manifest characteristics easy to distinguish. (Art. 7). Service marks enjoy same protection as trademarks. (Art. 4). Symbol of registration, or words "registered trademark" should accompany registered trademark. (Art. 7; Implementing Regs., Art. 26). Trademarks should not bear certain words or symbols, such as common symbol or name of commodity in question (Art. 8[5]); those that directly indicate quality, important raw material, functions, uses, weight, quantity or other characteristics of commodity (Art. 8[6]); those that contain exaggerated claims and are of deceptive nature (Art. 8[7]); those that are same as or similar to state names, flags, emblems, military flags or medals of China or other nations (Art. 8[1], [2]) or those same as or similar to banners, emblems or names of international organizations (Art. 8[3]), those same as or similar to symbol or name of Red Cross or Red Crescent (Art. 8[4]); those of discriminatory nature (Art. 8[7]), or those that harm socialist morality or have other bad influence (Art. 8[9]). Substantial enforcing authority granted to relevant administrative authority for industry and commerce regarding quality of goods under trademark (Implementing Regs. Arts. 19, 20, 21, 22, 23) and regarding infringement (Implementing Regs. 24, 26).

Promulgated on Mar. 10, 1983, State Council, pursuant to Trademark Law (Implementing Regs.), effective as of date of promulgation. Said implementing regs were replaced by new Implementing Regulations promulgated by State Administration of Industry and Commerce on Jan. 3, 1988, and it was revised by State Council on July 15, 1993. Foreign persons or foreign enterprises shall use Chinese language applications for registration of trademarks or other trademark related matters, and shall submit document of entrustment which is to include specific authority and nationality of entrustor. (Implementing Regs. Art. 14). Foreign persons or enterprises shall entrust all trademark application and other trademark matters to organizations specified by State Administration of Industry and Commerce. (Implementing Regs. Art. 3).

Interim Provision on Claims for Priority in Applying for Registration of Trademark.—After Chinese-US negotiations on protection of intellectual property was held in beginning of 1992, China revised its trademark law. Revisions cover following main point: (1) to extend protection of commodity trademark to that of service trademark, defense trademark, collective trademark, certificate trademark, brand trademark, (2) to shorten period from application to registration to within three months, (3) to establish trademark agency system, (4) to strengthen trademark protection and punish relentlessly trademark infringement.

Interim Provisions on Claims for Priority in Applying for Registration of Trademarks were approved by State Council. In accordance with Trademark Law of China and Paris Convention for the Protection of Industrial Property, Provisions on claims for priority in applying for registration of trademarks in China by nationals of state parties to Paris Convention are formulated:

From Mar. 19, 1985, Trademark Office of State Administration for Industry and Commerce shall entertain claims for priority made by nationals of state parties to Paris Convention in their application for registration of trademarks in China; from Mar. 19, 1985, nationals of state parties to Paris Convention, who after filing application for registration of trademark for same product in China, may claim priority within six months after first filing, in accordance with Paris Convention. (Arts. 1, 2).

Applicant who claims priority according to provisions of preceding paragraph shall, at time of filing application, submit written declaration, together with duplicate of first application for registration of trademark filed in another state party to Paris Convention. Duplicate shall be certified by department in charge of trademarks of that state, and application date and application number shall be clearly stated. Duplicate does not need to be authenticated, but other papers required to be submitted to Trademark Office shall be authenticated. When declaring claim for priority, applicant may, in case above-mentioned duplicate and related papers are not available, submit them within

See Topical Index in front part of this volume.

TRADEMARKS . . . *continued*
three months following date of second filing. If no written declaration is submitted or duplicate and related papers are not submitted at expiry of three months, applicant shall not be regarded as having claimed priority. (Art. 3).

When written declaration is approved, date of first application for registration of trademark filed in another state party to Paris Convention shall be regarded as application date in China. (Art. 4).

Rules for Appraisal of Trademarks.—Decree No. 37 of State Administration for Industry and Commerce of People's Republic of China.

Trademark Appraisal Commission of the State Administration for Industry and Commerce (hereinafter "Trademark Appraisal Commission") exercises power of final adjudication over decisions made by Trademark Office. (Art. 2). Where China is contracting party to international treaty related to trademark, and treaty has provided differently from Trademark Law and Implementing Regulations of the Trademark Law, provisions of international treaty prevail, with exception of those clauses to which China has declared reservations. (Art. 6). Trademark Appraisal Commission tries matters concerning trademark appraisal through review of written documents. (Art. 8). Any foreigner or foreign enterprise intending to apply for or participate in trademark appraisal in China, shall appoint any of such trademark agencies as designated by Trademark Appraisal Commission to act as its agent. (Art. 9). Trademark Appraisal Commission may accept and hear applications of following types: (1) to appeal Trademark Office decision on application for trademark registration; (2) to appeal objection decision of Trademark Office; (3) to appeal Trademark Office decision to deny application for assignment; (4) to appeal Trademark Office decision to deny application for renewal; (5) to appeal Trademark Office decision to cancel registered trademark; (6) disputation of registered trademark; (7) request for cancellation of trademarks whose registration is considered improper; (8) other trademark matters related to trademark appraisal as provided for by law or regulation. (Art. 10).

Application for appraisal of trademark should comply with following requirements: (1) Applicant must be legally qualified; (2) application must be made within time limit determined by law; (3) submission of required application and other related documents; (4) application for appraisal of trademark must be specific, stating relevant facts; (5) application must fall within scope of Trademark Appraisal Commission; and (6) payment of appraisal fee as specified by law. (Art. 16). Chinese language should be used by foreign persons or foreign enterprises intending to apply for or participate in trademark appraisal process in China. (Art. 17).

TRADE ZONES:

See topics Contracts; Corporations; Taxation.

Special geographical areas marked for economic reform and opening have been important in China, though in 1995 there was discussion of abolishing their preferential tax benefits. These areas fall into 12 categories: Special Economic Zones (SEZs), Coastal Open Cities, Economic and Technological Development Zones (ETDZs), Coastal Economic Open Areas, Border Open Cities, Border Economic Cooperation Zones, Inland Open Cities, High-technology and New Technology Development Zones (HTNTDZs), Taiwanese Investment Zones, Bonded Zones and Rural Reform Experiment Areas. Central departments in charge of coordination and administration of these special areas include: Special Zones Office of State Council, Taiwan Affairs Office under State Council, Touch-Plan Office of State Science Commission, General Administration of Customs and Rural Reform Experiment Office of Agricultural Ministry.

Special Economic Zones (SEZs).—SEZs are key enclaves for foreign investment with most liberal policies for tax incentives, foreign ownership and management autonomy. As of 1993, there are five SEZs: Shenzhen, Zhuhai and Shantou in Guangdong Province, Xiamen in Fujian Province and Hainan Province. SEZs, with mixed function of Free Trade Zones and Export Processing Zones, are designed to develop foreign oriented economy with industries as primary element, combining industries with trade and distribution functions of "windows" and "bases" in China's plan to open to outside investment. Shenzhen SEZ, founded in July, 1979, neighbors Hong Kong, has area of 327.5 km^2 and population of 1,200,000. Shenzhen SEZ includes three municipal districts. Shenzhen Municipal People's Congress and its standing committee and municipal government authorized to formulate local legislation in accordance with constitution and national laws and enforce in Shenzhen SEZ pursuant to decision of National People's Congress July 1, 1992. Zhuhai SEZ, founded in July 1, 1979, neighbors Macao, has area of 121 square kilometers and population of 200,000. Shantou SEZ, founded in July, 1979 and expanded to whole urban areas of Shantou, has area of 234 square kilometers and population of 856,400. Xiamen SEZ, founded in July, 1979, is on Taiwan strait and neighbors Taiwan, has area of 131 square kilometers and population of 380,000. Hainan SEZ covers whole Province. It was founded Apr. 13, 1988 and is largest SEZ in China. It includes three cities and 16 counties, has area of 34,000 square kilometers and population of 6,740,000.

Hainan Island.—Regulations of the State Council for the Encouragement of Investment and Development in Hainan Province were promulgated by State Council on May 4, 1988. These regulations provide that investors may make investment and undertake operation on Hainan Island in form of: (1) equity joint ventures using Chinese and foreign investment, contractual joint ventures using Chinese and foreign investment, wholly foreign-owned enterprises, as well as other varieties of enterprises permitted by law; (2) purchasing shares, bonds and other negotiable securities; (3) operating enterprises through holding shares, contracting or leasing; (4) investing and operating through investment modes introduced currently over the world. (Art. 5).

All state-owned lands on Hainan Island may be used with compensation. (Art. 6).

Mineral resources on Hainan Island may be exploited with compensation according to law. (Art. 7).

Exclusively foreign-invested banks, banks with Chinese and foreign investment or other financial institutions may be located on Hainan Island by approval of People's Bank of China. (Art. 9).

Enterprise income tax shall be levied at rate of 15% on income derived from production, operation and other sources by enterprises (except country's banks and insurance companies) established on Hainan Island. In addition, local surtax of 10% of assessed income tax shall be levied. (Art. 12).

Foreign-invested enterprises and enterprises with 25% of their shares held by foreign businessmen shall enjoy right to conduct import and export operations, import goods necessary for their production and operation, export their products. (Art. 14).

Machinery and equipment, raw materials, accessories and parts, means of transport and other materials and items as well as stationery and office equipment that production and operation of enterprise needs to import shall be exempt from customs duty, product tax, or value added tax. (Art. 15).

State protects investors' legitimate rights and interests according to law, and shall not nationalize or expropriate assets of investors. Under special circumstances, where public interest calls for action, state may exercise expropriation through legal procedures and appropriate compensation shall be made. (Art. 4).

Products manufactured by enterprises to be exported shall be exempt from export duties. (Art. 16).

Fujian Province has been granted special economic status, as has Xiamen city within province. Xiamen SEZ, under jurisdiction of Administrative Commission of Xiamen SEZ of Fujian Province, has designated 2.5 square kilometers in region of Huli for development of export processing zone. This zone, immediately adjacent to Dongdu wharf, contains factory buildings for investors to rent or purchase, as well as office buildings which are being developed. Subsequently entire city was made S.E.Z. Recently, Xiamen airport opened for traffic.

Standing Committee of 6th Fujian Provincial Congress on July 14, 1984 approved several statutes relating to Xiamen S.E.Z. which regulations were promulgated on Feb. 25, 1985 including:

Regulations on Registration of Enterprises in Xiamen Special Economic Zone.—Normal operations of foreign resident office requires registration (Art. 5) with Xiamen City Administration for Commerce and Industry (Art. 2). Prior to registration approval of foreign entities application must be received from Xiamen City Government or its authorized department. (Art. 3[1]). Foreign enterprises, resident offices and the like are considered to have been established only after their business license or registration certificate has been issued (Art. 6), only then can local bank account be opened (Art. 7). Resident certificates are renewable annually. (Art. 9).

Regulations on the Use of Land in Xiamen S.E.Z. promulgated on Feb. 24, 1985. Enterprise when in need of land must make application to Xiamen Urban and Rural Construction Commission (Art. 4), and within nine months of issuance of land use certificate enterprise must submit blueprints of overall design and construction plan, and within one year of said issuance commence construction (Art. 5) and complete construction on schedule, though extensions of time may be applied for (Art. 5).

Land use periods are determined by actual need; however longest periods are 40 years for industrial, communications and public utility projects, 20 years for commercial enterprises and service trades, 30 years for financial institutions and tourist projects, 50 years for property projects, 60 years for science, technology, education, culture and public health projects, 30 years for animal husbandry, crop farming, aquatic and poultry raising. (Art. 6). Extensions can be applied for before expiration of period. (Art. 6). Land use fees are to be charged; depend on location, use, how advanced technology; said fees may be adjusted at end of every three year period, and adjusted rate cannot be higher than 30% of original rate. During construction period 50% reduction in land use fee is permitted. (Art. 7). Preferential terms for lump sum advance payment for three year period are granted.

Land use rights but not land ownership is granted, though right to use land can be transferred. (Art. 9). Land can be reserved for development for up to two years but 50% of land use fee must be paid. (Art. 10).

For nonprofit making educational, scientific, technology, medical, public health and welfare projects, exemption may be granted from land use fees. (Art. 12). Also, special concessions may be granted for developing large tracts of land in S.E.Z. (Art. 13).

Regulations on Labor Administration in Xiamen S.E.Z. promulgated Feb. 24, 1985 permits enterprise to recruit its own workers and staff (Art. 3); probation period of three to six months is acceptable (Art. 3).

25% of total monthly wages of Chinese workers must be contributed each month by foreign enterprises to labor insurance fund for: Pensions, funeral costs of those who die of natural causes, disabled, deceased family, medical fees for retired, and unemployment allowance for those dismissed and without work. (Art. 8). In addition specified funds must be set aside by enterprise in S.E.Z. for welfare, including medical care assistance to those in difficulty, etc. (Art. 9). Finally enterprise must maintain insurance for those injured, disabled, killed or suffering occupational diseases. (Art. 10).

Work week is fixed at six days, 48 hours, overtime at least time and a half, holiday work double time. (Art. 11). Holidays are specified including one day per week plus seven days statutory holidays. (Art. 12). Wedding leave (three days), maternity leave (not less than 56 days), full sick leave pay for 13 days or less, then decreasing scale. (Art. 12).

2% of total wages of workers and staff to be allocated to trade union fees each month. (Art. 13). Dismissal of workers permitted pursuant to labor contract, must give one months notice, and must compensate worker if prior to term of contract pursuant to standard provided in Art. 14 of Regulations. Resignations also permitted and notification of one month required; if after training may be required to pay to enterprise portion of training expenses. (Art. 14).

Xiamen City Bureau of Labor arbitrates labor disputes; if not satisfied parties may appeal to court. (Art. 14).

Regulations on Economic Cooperation between Xiamen S.E.Z. and Domestic (Organs) promulgated Feb. 24, 1985, provide for 15% income tax rate for those domestic enterprises having foreign equity. (Art. 6). Products of such enterprises to be primarily for export. (Art. 7).

Beijing, Shanghai and Tianjin are also to be leaders in trade decentralization. Many provinces and localities have been given authority to independently approve commercial projects with foreign entities up to maximum amount of investment without need to obtain central government, or even provincial approval where locality is involved, of said projects. Recently, new regulations with particular regard to Shenzhen have been approved by central government to facilitate ease of entry and exit by foreign visitors, to simplify customs and to create almost open border with Hong Kong.

See Topical Index in front part of this volume.

TRADE ZONES . . . *continued*

Special Administrative Organization.—Guandong Provincial Administration of Special Economic Zones was established to exercise unified management over said zones. (Regulations on SEZ's of Guangdong, Art. 3). Guangdong Provincial Administration can issue registration licenses and land use permission for approved projects of foreign investors. (Regulations on SEZ's of Guangdong, Art. 7). Normally these areas are regarded as export oriented. (Regulations on SEZ's in Guangdong, Art. 9). Foreign investors are permitted to operate their enterprises independently in Special Economic Zones (Art. 10) and employ foreign personnel for technical and administrative work (Art. 10).

Tax Relief.—Means of production such as machinery, spare parts and raw materials, vehicles and other means of production which are imported from abroad are exempt from import duties. (Art. 13). Rate of income tax levied on enterprises in special zone is to be 15%. (Art. 14). Further preferential tax treatment is to be accorded enterprises established within two years of promulgation of these regulations with investment of US $5,000,000 or more and enterprises involving high technology or having relatively long cycle of capital turnover. (Art. 14).

Remittance of Profits.—After taxes, profits and salaries of foreigners and overseas Chinese of enterprises in zone can be remitted out of China. (Art. 15). Investors who reinvest profits in special zone for five years or longer can apply for exemption from income tax on such reinvestment. (Art. 16).

Preferential prices will be offered enterprises in special economic zone that use Chinese machinery, raw materials and other goods. (Art. 17).

Labor Service Companies are established in special economic zones and enterprises can test Chinese personnel before hiring them. (Art. 19). Said employees can be dismissed, pursuant to terms of labor contract, if necessary, since enterprises are to be managed according to their business requirements. (Art. 20).

Provisional Labor and Wage Regulations for Guangdong Special Economic Zones adopted Nov. 17, 1981 by Fifth Guangdong Provincial People's Congress, 13th Session. Regulations provide in part for hiring of staff and workers by foreign enterprises in China to be undertaken pursuant to labor contracts, which are subject to approval of Labor Bureau of special economic zone. (Art. 2). Labor contract is to include following: Labor discipline, protection, insurance and welfare, working hours and holidays, salary bonuses and fines, job specifications, terms of employment, dismissal and resignation. (Art. 2). Enterprises in special economic zone may hire workers through labor service company of Labor Bureau, or advertise for workers on their own with approval of Labor Bureau. (Art. 4). Labor remuneration is to be apportioned as follows: 70% directly to staff and workers as wages, 25% for use as social insurance for state, and 5% for other benefits for domestic Chinese employees of joint foreign-Chinese enterprise. (Art. 8).

Wages can be in form of piecework, hourly, daily, or monthly work, as enterprise sees fit. (Art. 9). Enterprise operated on six day work week, eight hours per day, with overtime provisions beyond that time. (Art. 10). Workers to receive special training for period of three months or more, may not tender their resignation until at least one year's service completed, but if insist on departing, must compensate enterprise for cost of their training. (Art. 15). Enterprise has right to lay off staff when employment becomes unnecessary in view of changes in production or technical conditions, or because of failure to meet requirements to reach specified standards after training period (if no suitable work to which employee could be reassigned). (Art. 16). Dismissed employees entitled to one month's wages for every year of service. (Art. 16). Employees can be dismissed for cause, but all cases of dismissal must be reported to Labor Bureau (Art. 17), to whom employee can appeal (Art. 18). Employer and employee have right to appeal decision of Labor Bureau to local People's Court. (Art. 18).

State Council approved establishment of Huli Special Economic Zone in May, 1980. Huli, which is within Xiamen municipality, has access to harbor facilities of Xiamen, including prospective container berth. It is anticipated that materials imported into Huli Special Economic Zone for construction and production will be exempt from duty. Three to five year tax holiday will be granted to enterprises located in zone. All utilities in Huli zone to factory door will be without cost. Foreign firms, in factories already constructed for them, will have full control of factories, subject only to Chinese law, which factories may be 100% owned, except for land and buildings which are to be leased, by foreign companies. Leases will be offered up to 30 years.

Land Regulations (Shenzhen).—Fifth Guangdong Provincial Congress, 13th Session, Nov. 7, 1981 adopted Provisional Land Regulations for Shenzhen Special Economic Zone. These regulations provide that authorized units and individuals have right to use land but do not have title to land. (Art. 5). Investors are issued certificate for land use (Art. 8), and are required to submit general blueprint, with construction and production plans, within six months after issuance of said certificate, and break ground on construction within nine months of its issuance, or certificate subject to forfeiture (Art. 9). Maximum length of land use varies according to type of enterprise as follows: Industrial use, 30 years; commercial use, including restaurants, 20 years; development of marketable housing, 50 years; tourism, 30 years; agricultural crops and animal husbandry, 20 years; medical, educational, scientific and technological development, 50 years. (Art. 15).

Land use certificate may be renewed upon expiry of terms set out in certificate. Charges for land use vary according to location and purposes for which land used, as follows: Renminbi/Yuan per sq. mtr. per annum: 60-100, tourism; 30-60, marketable housing; 70-200, commercial use; 10-30, industrial use. (Art. 16). Land use costs for raising of crops and animal husbandry is subject to negotiation and all land rates subject to readjustment once every three years, but said fluctuation must not exceed 30%. (Art. 16). Exceptionally advanced technological projects may be exempt from land use charges. (Art. 17). All residual substances, fumes and waste water accumulated in use of said land must be disposed of and treated in accordance with relevant Chinese laws. (Art. 22).

Land Regulations (Guangzhou).—Guangzhou Municipal People's Government promulgated Measures of Guangzhou Economic and Technological Development Zone on Compensatory Transfer and Assignment of Land on Mar. 9, 1988 with aim to effect appropriate use of land's resources, improve investment environment and facilitate testing system of compensatory assignment of land use rights within Guangzhou Economic and Technological Development Zone (hereinafter "Development Zone"). (Art. 1).

Guangzhou Municipal People's Government empowers Development Zone Administrative Commission to handle matters involving compensatory assignment of land use rights in Development Zone. Administrative Commission will be responsible for registering said rights, administering fee collection and issuing land use certificates on behalf of state. (Art. 2).

Land expropriated by Administrative Commission will, without exception, be subject to compensatory transfer; land may subsequently be assigned to another party. Subject of transfers and assignments will be restricted to land use rights. Land ownership and rights to various natural resources, minerals, hidden and buried objects found therein belong strictly to State and may not be assigned. (Art. 3). Duration of land use term will be determined by Administrative Commission in accordance with actual requirements of project, with maximum term of 50 years. (Art. 5).

Only Administrative Commission may be transferor of land use right in Development Zone. Transferee or assignor of land use rights may be domestic or foreign company, enterprise, other economic organization or individual. (Art. 4).

Transfer of land use rights refers to direct transfer of said rights to land user by Administrative Commission on behalf of Guangzhou Municipal People's Government. (Art. 7). Assignment of land use rights refers to re-transfer of land use rights to another party by transferee after it has acquired rights from Administrative Commission. Transferee of land use rights may, within duration of term of use and in accordance with various terms stipulated in transfer contract, assign all or part of its land use rights as gift or by lease, sale or exchange. (Art. 15).

Procedure.—Transfer of land use rights may occur as follows: (1) By agreement, whereby Administrative Commission consults and negotiates with perspective land user and, pursuant to mutual agreement, transfer contract will be signed, fee collected, registration procedures completed, and land use certificate issued; (2) by tender, whereby Administrative Commission extends invitations for tender to domestic and foreign organizations or individuals with proven capital credit and then selects successful tender in accordance with tender procedures; (3) by auction, whereby Administrative Commission organizes public auction of parcel of land for transfer, interested parties bid on said land and party with highest bid will win land use contract. (Art. 9). Price of land use rights will be determined through negotiations between two parties to transfer or assignment or through tender or at auction. (Art. 29). If Administrative Commission deems it necessary, however, said Commission may request that Guangzhou Municipal property evaluation department determine price of land use rights. (Art. 34).

Contract for assignment of land use rights which is signed within territory of China will be notarized by Guangzhou Notary Office. Contracts signed outside territory of China must be both notarized by public notary office in district where signed and certified by Chinese embassy, consulate or foreign affairs bureau in country (or region) of said district. (Art. 17).

Land use rights acquired by transfer or assignment may be used as mortgage on loan or other debts with Chinese or foreign bank or financial institution. (Art. 21).

If, at time of assignment of land use rights, amendments to original transfer contract are needed as regards planned usage of land, application must first be made to Administrative Commission land management department. Any amendments, changes, or supplements to original transfer contract must be verified and approved by said Commission prior to signing of assignment contract and registered title change of land. (Art. 20).

On expiration of term of use as stipulated in transfer contract, party with title to use rights must relinquish said rights and facilities on land to Administrative Commission at no charge and must cancel registration of said rights and land use certificate. Extention of term of use may be granted following application submitted to Administrative Commission at least six months prior to end of term; if said extention is granted, party must sign new transfer contract with Administrative Commission based on current price of use rights, undergo proper registration procedures, and obtain land use certificate. (Art. 36).

Chinese party to Sino-foreign equity joint enterprise or cooperative enterprise may only employ land rights as investment or as terms for cooperation if said rights were first acquired through transfer or assignment. (Art. 39).

According to State Council Regulations on Encouragement of Foreign Investment and implementation measures promulgated by Guangzhou Province, Guangzhou Municipality and Development Zone, technologically advanced enterprises and those involved with export in Development Zone may be favorably considered in land transfer cases. (Art. 41).

Administrative Commission will designate departments who will be responsible for providing consultation, arbitration and other services with regard to compensatory transfer and assignment of land in Development Zone. (Art. 42).

Infringements.—If any infringements of land ownership or use rights occur, Administrative Commission land management department may order end to infringement and claim compensation for losses or may file suit at People's Court. (Art. 49).

Use of Foreign Capital in Real Estate Transactions (Guangzhou).—On Sept. 1, 1989, new measures were enacted by Guangzhou Municipal Government to regulate use of foreign investment in real estate transactions such as house purchases, leases, trusts, and assignment of land use rights. Real estate here refers to private homes, industrial property, commercial or tourist facilities and public buildings. (Art. 2). These measures are applicable to wholly-owned foreign enterprises (including those of Hong Kong, Macau and Taiwan residents) joint-venture enterprises (JV's) and other enterprises having foreign investment (EFI's) which have valid business licenses and permission from state or local Guangzhou Administrative Bureau of Industry and Commerce to deal in real estate in Guangzhou. (Art. 3). Similarly, Chinese parties to JV's or EFI's must be properly commissioned and qualified to deal in real estate. (Art. 3).

Establishment.—Chinese parties wishing to deal in real estate must first apply to Guangzhou City and County Construction Committees for permit for technical qualification and EFI needs to obtain written approval from Guangzhou Foreign Trade and Economic Committee. Within 30 days after such approval, enterprise must apply for

See Topical Index in front part of this volume.

TRADE ZONES . . . *continued*
business license to Guangzhou Administrative Bureau of Industry and Commerce. (Art. 7[1][2][3]). Application will be rejected if registered capital of enterprise is less than RMB5 million (or foreign currency equivalent). (Art. 80).

Operations.—In real estate transactions, all Guangzhou laws governing land use rights must be adhered to by EFI. (Art. 9). Chinese party to JV or EFI who wishes to supply land in real estate transaction must first obtain permission from Guangzhou City Planning Bureau. Once this approval is obtained, Chinese party must sign contract with Guangzhou City Contracting Committee for land use rights. Within 90 days thereafter, land use rights, will be available.

Guangzhou Real Estate Administrative Bureau is responsible for registering transfer of land use rights when presented with duly signed contract between Chinese party and JV or EFI. (Art. 10). Buildings and land use rights of EFI's may be sold, exchanged or passed by inheritance in or outside of China at any price EFI chooses with contract signed by both parties. (Art. 15). EFI's may also mortgage land use rights, however mortgage contract must be notarized and registered with Guangzhou Real Estate Administration Bureau. (Art. 18). Foreign exchange needed by EFI's for real estate transactions must be obtained according to Regulations for Foreign Exchange Control. (Art. 22).

Taxation.—EFI's must register with tax authorities within 30 days of their establishment in China. (Art. 19). They are to pay taxes and land use fees according to relevant laws, but are also entitled to certain deductions and exemptions. (Art. 21).

Legal Liabilities.—Violations of any aspect of these new rules will result in penalties as ordered by relevant bureau. (Art. 24[7]). For example, failure to register for taxes will result in fines by tax authorities. Disputes which arise in real estate transactions of EFI's should preferably be resolved through consultation or mediation, failing this, in these disputes Chinese version of documents will always be binding document. (Art. 29).

Entry and Exit Regulations.—Provisional Entry and Exit Regulations of Guangdong SEZ's adopted at Fifth Guangdong Provincial Congress, 13th Session, Nov. 7, 1981. Foreigners, overseas Chinese, Hong Kong, Macao and Taiwan compatriots who enter SEZ's via country's open ports, or ports designated for SEZ, are subject to these regulations and subject to inspection on entering and leaving. (Art. 2). Those entering from Hong Kong or Macao who are foreign nationals or overseas Chinese should use their passports to obtain visas in Hong Kong or Macao before entering border checkpoints. Foreign nationals and overseas Chinese who need to travel regularly to and from SEZ, or who have set up factories there, work or live there, or purchased home there may apply for multiple exit-entry visas.

Economic Laws.—Shenzhen approved regulations on contracts, etc. relating to foreign matters.

Fourteen Coastal Cities, Hainan and Four SEZs.—Fourteen cities of Dalian, Qinghuangdao, Tianjin, Yantai, Qingdao, Lianyungang, Nantong, Shanghai, Ningbo, Wenzhou, Fuzhou, Guangzhou, Zhanjiang and Beihai, have been declared cities open to foreign trade with flexible economic policies similar to special economic zones.

Provisional Regulations on Reduction and Exemption of Enterprise Income Tax and Consolidated Industrial and Commercial tax for 14 Coastal Port Cities, Four S.E.Z.s and Hainan Island promulgated by State Council effective as of Dec. 1, 1984 for commercial industrial tax and 1984 tax year for income tax.

Fifteen percent enterprise income tax rate shall apply on income derived from business, production or other sources in four special economic zones and in economic and technological development zones within 14 coastal port cities. (c. I, Art. 1; c. II, Art. 1). In other parts of 14 coastal cities, and Shantou and Zhuhai areas outside special economic zone, 15% preferential enterprise income tax rate may be granted upon approval of Ministry of Finance if foreign investments exceed US$30,000,000, operations are technology or knowledge intensive, and require long lead time or belong to fields of energy, communications or port construction. (c. III, Art. 1).

In addition 20% reduction of enterprise income tax on standard rate, subject to approval of Ministry of Finance, is permitted on existing enterprises in 14 coastal cities, Shantou and Zhuhai areas outside S.E.Z. in six fields including: Building construction, medical and pharmaceutical, agriculture, animal husbandry, forestry, aquaculture, light industry, textiles, packaging, metallurgy, chemical, and building materials. (c. III, Art. 1).

Ten percent income tax on income from dividends, interest, rentals and royalties by those who do have establishments in China is provided in all above locations. (E.g. c. I, Art. IV).

Preferential enterprise income tax rate for Hainan Administrative Zone of Guangdong province is to be handled by reference to S.E.Z. tax regulations. (c. I, Art. 10).

There are various rules relating to commercial industrial tax: E.g. exemption in S.E.Z.'s for importation of machines, equipment, raw materials, spare parts and accessories, means of transportation and other means of production required for enterprise's own production purposes (c. I, Art. 5). Except for those on state restricted list exemption exists for commercial and industrial tax on products exported from S.E.Z. (c. I, Art. 6) and 50% reduction on said tax for products made by in S.E.Z. and sold in S.E.Z. For goods shipped inland from enterprises within S.E.Z., full consolidated commercial and industrial tax must be paid. (c. I, Art. 8). Similar rules apply in development zones.

All above rules apply to joint ventures, cooperative enterprises and wholly owned foreign subsidiaries (c. I, Art. 1) but are applicable to enterprise income tax and not individual income tax. In addition in both S.E.Z.s and development zones there is exemption from income tax on repatriation of profits by foreigners. (c. I, Art. 3; c. II, Art. 3).

Tax holidays in S.E.Z. and development zones of two years commencing from first profit making year, and 50% tax reduction for three following years can be received pursuant to application to special zone tax authorities by foreign enterprises engaged in projects in which contract is ten years or longer and enterprise is engaged in industry, communications, transportation, agriculture, forestry, or livestock breeding (c. I, Art. 1[1]; c. II Art. 1); enterprises in service industry with foreign investment in excess of U.S.$5,000,000 and contract of ten years or longer can apply for one year tax holiday followed by two years of 50% enterprise income tax reduction in S.E.Z.s (c. I, Art. 1).

Economic and Technological Development Zones (ETDZs).—As of Aug. 1993 there are 23 ETDZs approved by State Council, 16 of which are located in coastal port cities and seven newly approved on Apr. 4, 1993, are located in inland cities: Wuhan, Wuhu, Chongqing, Hangzhou, Shenyang, Changchun and Harbin. ETDZs differ from SEZs in four respects: SEZ is relatively independent administrative division, whereas ETDZ is Open Zone directly administered by municipality where ETDZ is located; SEZ develops comprehensive outside-oriented economy with industries as main force and combining industries with trade, while ETDZ engages industrial production and scientific research and depends on cities where it is located having tertiary industries; regarding preferential treatment for foreign investment enterprises, they may enjoy 15% preferential income tax rate in SEZs regardless of its production or nonproduction function, however, only FIEs having scientific and technological activities in ETDZs may enjoy said preference; consumption goods for livelihood and most means of productions imported in SEZs shall enjoy duty exemption or reduction, however in ETDZ only restaurant materials needed by tourism catering may enjoy duty exemption or reduction.

Legislation for Development Zones has been promulgated, first by Guangzhou city government on Apr. 9, 1985.

Interim Regulations on the Guangzhou Economic and Technological Development Zone provide development zone is comparatively independent, located in east Huangpu district, and is designed to establish productive enterprises, implement policy of introducing foreign investment together with domestic enterprises, introducing advanced scientific technology and the like. (Art. 2). Domestic Chinese entities outside zone are also encouraged to invest in zone. (Art. 4).

Administrative Committee of Guangzhou Economic and Technological Development Zone has been established to manage zone. (Art. 8). It has authority to formulate development plans, approve investment projects, approve income and consolidated industrial and commercial tax reductions, manage land in zones, supervise enterprises, coordinate with Guangzhou city government, protect legitimate rights and interests of workers, establish educational, cultural, health and public welfare functions, promulgate administrative management rules, and represent Guangzhou city government in foreign matters regarding zone. (Art. 9).

Special income tax treatment is specified for enterprises in zone at 15% pursuant to State Council rules. In addition 70% reduction in local income tax is provided by rules. (Arts. 12, 13). Registration is required of enterprises in zone. (Art. 23).

Interim Regulations of the Guangzhou Economic and Technical Zone concerning introduction of technology were promulgated on Apr. 9, 1985.

These rules require technology introduced by foreign entities to be advanced, applicable and having tangible economic efficiency. (Art. 5). Advanced is defined to be more advanced than same technology in China, being used or developed in industrially developed countries, or that it is of benefit domestically so as to raise domestic industry or product to world levels. (Art. 5). Technology is defined to include patented, patent pending, knowhow and software. (Art. 6).

There are in addition Tentative Procedures for Land Management in the Guangzhou Economic and Technological Zone, promulgated Apr. 9, 1985 that classify land by use and provide standard land use fees ranging from one yuan to 12 yuan per square meter per month. Land use fees for industrial use, or for communications and transportation industry is calculated at two yuan per square meter per year.

There are procedures for Implementation of Commercial and Industrial Taxes, that deal also with urban property taxes. Those owning buildings in development zones shall pay annual tax of 1.2% of construction costs or purchase price of building. (Art. 14). Tax of 18% of rental value of building must be paid on leased buildings. There is also five year property tax exemption on newly purchased or constructed buildings in zone. (Art. 16).

There are, in addition, annual vehicle license taxes which vary from 160 yuan for ordinary passenger car up to seven seats to 240 yuan for car with 11 or more seats. (Art. 19).

Interim Regulations on Certain Matters Relating to Domestic Associated Commercial or Service Enterprises; Tentative Procedures for the Registration and Administration of Enterprises; Tentative Procedures for Labor and Wage Management in Enterprise in the Zone were all promulgated on Apr. 9, 1985.

Special Administrative Zone.—Pursuant to treaty with Great Britain, Chinese government has agreed that commencing from 1997 when Crown Colony of Hong Kong will revert to full Chinese jurisdiction, Hong Kong will become special administrative zone, retaining most facets of its present legal and economic structure. Basic Law has been drafted for Hong Kong, which is equivalent of constitution, under Chinese constitution. There is presently negotiation over enactment of legislation to establish Supreme Court of Hong Kong to hear highest appeals from Hong Kong lower courts.

In establishing commission to consult on policy for new Hong Kong airport at Lantou Island, Hong Kong government has included representatives from China on commission and guaranteed to leave certain quantum of reserves in Hong Kong government coffers on turnover of Hong Kong to China in 1997.

Recently elections for small portion of seats in Hong Kong legislature gave overwhelming victory to party led by renowned barrister Martin Lee, trying to bring democracy to Hong Kong.

Shanghai's Pudong.—Special development zones in Shanghai, particularly in Pudong, have been given substantial authority and substantial infrastructure funds to develop this location for foreign investment. Central government has put great emphasis on increasing foreign investment in Shanghai. Regulations to Reduce or Eliminate Enterprise Income Tax and Industrial and Commercial Tax to Encourage Foreign Investment in Shanghai's New Pudong District were promulgated in 1990. Enterprise income tax of 15% was highest level subject to application accepted to eliminate said taxes on first two years of profit. (Art. 2). Companies with foreign investment exporting more than 70% of their productions or having been certified as having modern technology can reduce tax to 10% of profits. (Art. 3). There are numerous other regulations which encourage investment.

Regulations on land administration in Shanghai Pudong New Areas were promulgated by Shanghai Municipal People's Government on 10 Sept., 1990 and came into effect on same date.

See Topical Index in front part of this volume.

TRADE ZONES . . . *continued*

Under Pudong Land Regulations, system of using State-owned land in Pudong New Area with payment of consideration shall be adopted. By granting or transferring land-use rights or by charging land-use fees, those who need to use land may obtain land use rights. Granting of land-use rights shall be carried out by Municipal Land Administration Bureau, and contract on granting of land-use rights shall be concluded between Municipal Land Administration Bureau and land-user. (Art. 3).

Unless otherwise provided by law, corporations, enterprises, other organizations and individuals within or outside of China may obtain land-use rights in accordance with "Provisional Regulations of the People's Republic of China on Granting and Transferring of State-owned Urban Land Use Rights", "Provisional Procedures for Administration of Development and Operation of Tracts of Land by Foreign Investors" and "Measures of Shanghai Municipality on Paid Transfer of Land Use Rights". Enterprises invested by foreign investors in industry, agriculture, energy resources, transportation and infrastructure projects may also obtain land-use rights in accordance with "Measures of Shanghai Municipality for Administration of Land Used by Joint Ventures with Chinese and Foreign Investment". (Art. 4).

Land lots, land-use rights of which are granted can be either land with public facilities completed thereupon or tracts of land to be developed. (Art. 5).

Land users are allowed to lawfully transfer, lease, mortgage and inherit land-use rights, or to use such rights in other economic activities permitted by law within term specified after they have developed and constructed land plots in accordance with terms and conditions of contract on granting of land-use rights. Rights to use land which is to be developed and operated in tracts may be transferred in accordance with planning purpose after such land has been developed and constructed as provided in contract on granting of land-use rights. Land-use rights obtained in manner other than by granting or transferring shall not be transferred, mortgaged or leased. (Art. 6).

Maximum terms for granting of land-use rights are: (1) land used for commercial, tourism and recreational purposes - 40 years; (2) land used for industrial purposes - 50 years; (3) land used for educational, scientific research, cultural, public health and sports purposes - 50 years; (4) land used for residential purposes - 70 years. (Art. 7).

Granting of land-use rights shall be carried out through tendering, auction or negotiation. Generally, land used for purposes of commerce, tourism, recreation, finance, real estate development and other projects shall be granted through tendering and auction. When land-use rights are granted through negotiation, fees thus involved shall be determined by discussion between grantor and grantee in accordance with different land development costs, land beneficial results, grades of location, purpose, planning parameters, land-use terms and other conditions. (Art. 8).

Fees for granting of land-use rights shall be paid in currency, and in foreign currency by foreign enterprises. (Art. 9). Land-user may apply for renewal of terms of land-use rights upon its expiry in accordance with regulations. (Art. 10).

Chinese enterprises that have lawfully obtained land-use rights without consideration through administrative assignment are encouraged to use such rights in accordance with planning as conditions of investment and co-operation to establish joint ventures with foreign enterprises. Such rights to use State-owned land may be converted into shares as investment made by Government, part of which may be returned to original land user. Projects relating to industry, agriculture, energy resources, transportation and infrastructure established jointly with foreign businessmen shall pay land-use fees in accordance with "Measures of Shanghai Municipality for the Administration of Land Used by Joint Ventures with Chinese and Foreign Investment". (Art. 13).

In any cases of need required by State construction, municipal people's government may regain land-use rights without consideration which have been granted without consideration through administration assignment. Proper compensation shall be made for building and other attachment established therein in accordance with actual conditions. (Art. 15).

Users of State-owned land and owners and users of collectively-owned land shall report and register their ownership and land-use rights and reregister in case of any alteration thereof in accordance with relevant provisions. Granting of land-use rights and subsequent transfers, lease, exchange, inheritance, bestowal, mortgage and termination thereof, shall be registered at Shanghai Real Estate Registration Office. (Art. 17).

Chinese and foreign consultant and service agencies are allowed to be set up in Pudong New Area to provide service to real estate market. (Art. 19).

Hainan Province.—Hainan, new province, has been given very substantial authority and has promulgated numerous regulations to encourage foreign investment.

Yangpu Economic Development Zone approved by state council in Mar. 1992, is located at southern end of Yangpu Peninsula in Hainan SEZ. With area of 30 square kilometers, zone is segregated by facilities in order to implement closed administration. Land in Zone is granted to foreign investor for 70 years by means of one-time only assignment which is one of longest land-use right assignment periods leased to foreign investors. Relevant preferential policies of SEZs and Bonded Zones shall be implemented in said zone. Banks with foreign investment or other financial institutions may be created after approval of People's Bank of China. Functions and powers of administration and supervision shall be exercised uniformly by administrative authority in said zone.

Regulations of Yangpu Development Zone in Hainan Province adopted by Provincial People's Congress July 1, 1992, effective Apr. 2, 1993. Regulations provide that policies be more liberal than those implemented in other bonded zones and more flexible measures in funds, goods and individual's entry and exit shall be implemented. (Art. 2). High technology is largest sector, whole international trade, entrepôt trade, transit trade are also important sectors of trade. (Art. 3).

Coastal Economic Open Areas.—In Aug. 1993, 41 provincially directed cities and 218 counties (cities) were designated as Coastal Economic Open Areas in Chinese eastern coastal belt from South to North: namely Pearl River Delta Economic Open Area with 11 provincially directed cities and 42 counties (cities) located in southern coastal areas of Guangdong provincially directed cities and 80 counties (cities) located in middle of Chinese coastal eastern belt; Xiamen, Zhangzhou, Quanzhou and southern Fujian Economic Open Area with three provincially directed cities and 28 counties (cities) in southeast of Chinese eastern coastal belt, known as overseas Chinese bases; Shandong Peninsular Economic Open Area with four provincially directed cities and 26 counties (cities); Liaodong Peninsular Economic Open Area with seven cities and 16 counties (cities) in northern end of Chinese coastal belt: Hebei Coastal Economic Open Area with three cities and 12 counties neighboring Bohai Sea and Guangxi Coastal Economic Open Area with one city and five counties located in west of Chinese coastal line. FIEs with production, scientific and technological function enjoy 24% preferential income tax rate in said areas. Local income tax may be exempted or reduced at discretion of Province or provincially directed cities where said areas are located. FIEs engaged in power, communication, port, and technology-intensive or intelligence-intensive projects, or total foreign investment exceeding $30,000,000, may be granted 15% preferential income tax rate after approval of Ministry of Finance.

Border Open Cities.—As of Aug. 1993, 13 cities (counties, towns) were designated Border Open Cities: Heihe and Suifenhe in Heilonjiang Province, Huichun in Jilin Province, Manzhouli and Ernehot in Inner Mongolia Autonomous Region, Yining, Bole and Tacheng in Xinjiang Urgur Autonomous Region, Pingxiang and Dongxing in Guangxi Zhuang Autonomous Region, and Ruili, Wanding and Hekou in Yunnan Province. Provinces and Autonomous Regions may delegate powers and functions within own limit to government of said cities regarding administration of border trade and economic cooperation. Cities may examine and approve projects of border trade, processing and service cooperation within delegated limit at own discretion. Provinces and autonomous regions may delegate powers of foreign investment examination and approval within their own limit to cities. FIEs in cities may be granted 24% preferential income tax rate after approval of local tax authority. Investors from neighboring countries where said cities are located may contribute investment in means of production or other materials and equipment, which may be sold pursuant to provisions concerning border barter trade and be granted 50% reduction of duty and uniform consolidated industrial and commercial tax.

Border Economic Cooperation Zones (BECZs).—Certain Zones are divided from Border Open Cities and Dandong and Liaoning Province to form BECZs to encourage domestic investors to establish processing enterprises for exports to Commonwealth of Independent States (CIS) and corresponding tertiary industries. Machinery, equipment and other materials needed for infrastructure construction in Zones exempted from duties and product tax (Value Added Tax). Domestic jointly operated enterprises primarily manufacturing export products with required scale may be granted powers to handle import and export with neighboring countries and 24% preferential income tax rate. Incomes of domestic jointly operated enterprises and FIEs derived from barter trade with neighboring countries may be sold by themselves and granted 50% reduction of duties and Uniform Consolidated Industrial and Commercial Tax.

Inland Open Cities.—As of Aug. 1993, 23 cities were designated Inland Open Cities, including three inland border cities: Urmqi, Nanning and Kunming; 11 inland provincial capitals: Taiyuan, Hefei, Nanchang, Zhengzhou, Changsha, Chengdu, Guiyang, Xian, Lanzhou, Xining and Yinchuan; four coastal provincial capitals: Harbin, Changchun, Hohhot and Shijiazhuang; and five cities along Yangtze River: Chongqing, Wuhan, Yueyang, Jiujiang and Wuhu. Preferential policies afforded to coastal port cities granted to Inland Open Cities.

High-Techonology and New Technology Development Zones (HTNTDZs).—As of Aug. 1993, 27 HTNTDZs approved by State Council, which fall into three categories: 22 HTNTDZs located in intelligence-intensive large or medium-sized cities and open cities (areas): Beijing New Technology Development Experiment Zone, Wuhan Donghu New Technology Development Zone, Shenyang Nanhu Science and Technology Development Zone, Tianjin New Technology Industries Par, Nanjing, Xi'an, Chengdu, Changchun, Harbin, Changsha, Fuzhou, Guangzhou, Hefei, Chongqing, Hangzhou, Guilin, Zhengzhou, Lanzhou, Shijiazhuang, Jinan High Technology Industries Development Zone; two HTNTDZs are located in ETDZs: Shanghai Caohejing New Technology Development Zone, Dalian High Technology and New Technology Industries Park; three HTNTDZs located in SEZs: Shenzhen Science and Technology Industries Park, Xiamen Torch High Technology Industries Development Zone, Hainan International Science and Technology Industries Park.

Set of national regulations regarding HTNTDZs drafted by central departments promulgated early 1991. Requirements and Methods Regarding Confirmation of High Technology and New Technology Enterprises in State HTNTDZs (hereinafter "Requirements") and Interim Provisions Regarding Several Policies of State HTNTDZs (hereinafter "Interim Provisions") promulgated by State Science Commission on Mar. 6, 1991. Provisions Regarding Tax Policies In State Approved HTNTDZs (hereinafter "Provisions") promulgated by State Tax Bureau Mar. 6, 1991. Enterprises engaged in areas of High Technology and New Technology (HTNT), scheduled to operate no less than ten years should meet requirements to enjoy relevant preferences for high technology and new technology enterprises (HTNTE). Main requirements include: scientific and technical personnel having received college education comprise 30% of total staff in said enterprises and scientific and technical personnel engaged in research and development of HTNT products comprise 10% of total staff. (Requirements, Art. 5). Funds for HTNT and research and development shall comprise 3% of total income of said enterprise. (Requirements, Art. 5). Incomes derived from HTNT products and technological services should comprise 50% of total income of said enterprise. (Requirements, Art. 5). Preferences afforded to HTNTDZs substantially same as ETDZs.

HTNTDZs differ from SEZs and ETDZs in four respects: SEZs and most ETDZs located in coastal or border areas except seven new ETDZs approved on Apr. 4, 1993, whereas HTNTDZs located in cities where State Council deems necessary requirements satisfied; any enterprise located in SEZs may enjoy corresponding preferences, whereas only high technology and new technology enterprise confirmed by competent authority may enjoy preferences in HTNTDZs. HTNTDZs administrative system differs from SEZs, but is similar to ETDZs; secondary and tertiary industries main elements in SEZs and ETDZs, while high technology and new technology industries main forces in HTNTDZs.

Taiwanese Investment Zones.—Xiamen SEZ and Haichang and Xinlin areas under jurisdiction of Xiamen city and undeveloped parts of Fuzhou Mawei ETDZ were designated Taiwanese Investment Zones by State Council in May, 1989. These Zones are designed to attract Taiwanese investment to create export enterprises or introduce

See Topical Index in front part of this volume.

TRADE ZONES . . . *continued*
advanced technology from abroad to innovate existing enterprises. Special policies of SEZs should be implemented in Xinlin and Haichang Taiwanese Investment Zones. Preferences of ETDZs shall be implemented in Fuzhou Mawei Taiwanese Investment Zone. There are no Taiwanese Investment Zones in other provinces and centrally directed municipalities approved by State Council.

Bonded Zone.—As of Aug. 1993, there are six Bonded Zones approved by State Council; Shanghai Waigaoqiao Bonded Zone with area of ten square kilometers in Pudong New Area, Tianjin Port Bonded Zones with area of 1.2 square kilometers in Tianjin Port Shenzhen, Futian Bonded Zone with area of 1.35 square kilometers on North bank of Shenzhen River, Shenzhen Shatoujiao Bonded Zone with area of 0.2 square kilometers on North bank of Padeng Bay, Dalian ETDZ, and Guangzhou Bonded Zone with area of 1.4 square kilometers in Northeast of Guangzhou ETDZ. Bonded Zones segregated by facilities to implement closed administration. Cargo, vehicles and baggage of passengers entering and leaving the Zones shall be examined by customs. No persons live in zones except those security personnel. Goods imported by administrative authority and enterprises restricted to their own uses, where sold or assigned to areas outside of zones, are deemed imports. Goods entering zones from other areas shall be deemed exports, and relevant customs formalities apply. Machinery, equipment and other materials needed for infrastructure construction in Zones free from duties. Building materials, production and management equipment, fuel for production uses, reasonable amount of vehicles used in production and management, office articles and spare parts needed for repairing aforesaid machinery and equipment to be used by enterprises themselves exclusively free from duties. Raw materials, parts, components, packing materials imported for manufacturing export products shall be bonded from duties. Export products manufactured in Zones exempted from Export Duty and Uniform Consolidated Industrial and Commercial Tax (Product Tax or Value Added Tax). Products manufactured with imported materials or components must be fully exported. FIEs in said zones may enjoy 15% preferential income tax rate.

Rural Reform Experiment Areas.—In Sept., 1987, State Council created Rural Reform Experiment Areas. 21 Rural Reform Experiment Areas designated by State Council covering 150,000 square kilometers with population of 47,200,000 as of Aug., 1993. Contents of experiments fall into six categories: grain purchase and sale system reform in Xinxiang City in Henan Province of Yulin City in Guangxi Zhuang Autonomous Region; land system construction and scale operation experiment carried in Meitan County in Guizhou Province, Pingdu City in Shandong Province, Wu County, Wuxi County and Changshu City of Jiangsu Province, Nanhai City in Guangdong Province and Shunyi County in Beijing; construction of cooperative economic entities in Yutian Count in Hebei Province, Liquan County in Shanxi Province and Shangzhi City in Heilongjiang Province; rural banking system reform in Guanghan City in Sichuan Province; rural enterprise system in Buyang Prefecture in Anhui Province, Wenzhou City in Zhejiang Province and Zibo City in Shandong Province, and reforms in forestry, fishing, animal husbandry, state farms and poverty areas, in Sanming City in Fujian Province, Shanwei City in Guangdong Province, Huanghua City in Hubei Province, Bijie Prefecture in Guizhou Province and Huaihua Prefecture in Hunan Province. These are privileged areas to conduct new practices which are not expressly provided for by current laws and policies. These have accumulated valuable experience and contributed much to Chinese rural reform.

TREATIES:

See topics Consuls; Foreign Trade, Arbitration and Award.

TRUSTS:

See topic Securities.

Several trust companies have been established in recent years, with capital from government, to assist foreign trade development. For example, China International Trust and Investment Corporation (CITIC), enterprise established directly under State Council with substantial capital of 200,000,000 yuan exempt from taxation and turning over its profits to State, is expected to accumulate capital in total amount of 600,000,000 yuan in three to five years. CITIC has right to manage and use independently foreign exchange it borrows or earns and to engage in foreign exchange business, to set up financial companies or other forms of financial organizations in cooperation with other foreign monetary institutions.

VENUE:

Litigation by citizens in courts where defendant located have jurisdiction, however, if dwelling place of defendant and his domicile are different, jurisdiction then lies in courts situated where dependant usually resides. (Civ. Pro. Code, Art. 22). Regarding litigation by legal persons or other organizations, courts where defendant located have jurisdiction. (Civ. Pro. Code, Art. 22).

Where several defendants have different dwelling places and residences, thus being within jurisdiction of two or more courts, each court has authority to assume jurisdiction. (Civ. Pro. Code, Art. 22).

Venue in certain cases is where plaintiff has his dwelling place. If dwelling place differs from his domicile, then venue lies in residence where plaintiff usually resides; e.g. (a) where person not residing in Chinese territory brings suit concerning matters of personal status; (b) where person's whereabouts are unknown or person is declared missing in suit concerning matters of personal status; (c) where one brings suit against someone in process of being reeducated through labor (juvenile delinquent etc.); (d) where one brings suit against someone in prison. (Civ. Pro. Code Art. 23).

Where contractual disputes give rise to litigation, both court where defendant is located and where contract was drawn up have jurisdiction to hear case. (Civ. Pro. Code Art. 24).

Two parties to contract may specify in writing court having jurisdiction, including: where defendant resides, where contract was drafted, where contract was executed, where plaintiff resides, or where dispute arises. This specification must not infringe upon regulations governing sole or exclusive jurisdiction. (Civ. Pro. Code Art. 25).

Where insurance contract dispute gives rise to ligitation both court where defendant is located and where insurance matter is located have authority to assume jurisdiction. (Civ. Pro. Code Art. 26).

Where disputes over payment of bills give rise to litigation, both court where bills where to be paid and where defendant resides have authority to assume jurisdiction. (Civ. Pro. Code Art. 27).

Where litigation concerns acts which infringe or violate civil rights, court in area where alleged violation took place has jurisdiction. (Civ. Pro. Code Art. 29).

Litigation arising from demand for compensation for accidental damage caused by railway, road, water or air transport, court located in area where accident occurred has jurisdiction. Courts where ships collided, where vessel or ship arrived first, or where aircraft apparatus first landed or where defendant located have authority to assume jurisdiction. (Civ. Pro. Code Art. 30).

Where parties seek compensation for injuries resulting from ship collisions or other maritime accidents venue can be in courts located where accident occurred or where damaged ship originated or where ship causing damage was destined or where defendant lives. (Civ. Pro. Code Art. 31).

Those seeking fees for assistance to those endangered by perils of sea may utilize courts at location where assistance to those injured was undertaken. (Civ. Pro. Code Art. 32).

Where litigation arising from general average, court where ship first arrived or where general average adjustment takes place or where voyage ended has jurisdiction. (Civ. Pro. Code Art. 33).

Exclusive jurisdiction over following cases is provided pursuant to provisions of Art. 34 of Civ. Pro. Code: (a) cases arising from real property disputes are under jurisdiction of court where realty is located; (b) cases arising from port operations are under jurisdiction of courts at location of port; (c) cases involving inheritance of legacy are under jurisdiction of courts at location of heir's registered permanent residence prior to becoming heir or where principal part of legacy is located. (Civ. Pro. Code Art. 34).

Where two or more courts have jurisdiction over litigation, plaintiff can select one court in which to bring case; if plaintiff applies to two or more courts having jurisdiction to undertake litigation, first court to receive case must accept and hear matter. (Civ. Pro. Code Art. 35).

If court discovers that case it has accepted for trial is not within its jurisdiction, it shall transfer matter to court that does have jurisdiction. Court receiving transferred case may not of its own accord transfer this case once again, and if in doubt should report to higher level court and ask for determination as to jurisdiction. (Civ. Pro. Code Art. 36).

If court having jurisdiction cannot exercise its authority, then higher level court will determine jurisdiction. When dispute arises over jurisdiction, both parties should settle matter through consultation, but if consultation does not resolve dispute, disputant should report matter to higher level court which will determine jurisdiction. (Civ. Pro. Code Art. 37).

WILLS:

See topic Descent and Distribution.

COLOMBIA LAW DIGEST REVISER

Curtis, Mallet-Prevost, Colt & Mosle
101 Park Avenue
New York, New York 10178-0061
Telephone: 212-696-6141
Fax: 212-697-1559
Email: CMP-NY@mcimail.com

Reviser Profile

The Firm began in 1830 when two practicing lawyers started a long line of lawyers and law firms extending in an unbroken chain up to the present time. In 1897, the firm name became Curtis, Mallet-Prevost & Colt; in 1925 it was changed to Curtis, Mallet-Prevost, Colt & Mosle. The Firm is now made up of approximately 120 lawyers, including experts who have published extensively on such diverse subjects as international money management, transnational contracts, state contracts, litigation against foreign states, sovereign immunity and the act of state doctrine, and the International Court of Justice. Its principal offices are in New York City. There are branch offices in Paris, London, Frankfurt Am Main, Hong Kong, Washington, D.C., Houston, Texas, Newark, N.J., and Mexico City. The Firm has five departments: Corporate and International; Litigation; Real Estate; Tax; and Trusts and Estates. The corporate and international department acts as general counsel to various public and private corporations and individual entrepeneurs. Clients are in the banking, insurance, securities, manufacturing, real estate and oil and gas industries. In addition, the corporate and international department frequently acts as special counsel to domestic and foreign clients, providing assistance in financing, know-how licensing, the negotiation and drafting of all types of contracts and instruments, counselling on all aspects of corporate law, and establishing the vehicles necessary to enable clients to conduct their domestic and foreign business activities. The Firm's international work permeates all areas of its practice and involves questions of private international law, foreign law and an unusual amount of public and quasi-public international law. Traditionally, much of the Firm's international practice has been concerned with Latin America. The Firm maintains its excellence in that area, with its Mexican affiliate, and also through the expertise of Latin American lawyers based in the New York office. The Firm's international practice has undergone a major expansion beyond Latin America to Europe, Africa and the Near and Far East. The Firm's litigation practice includes commercial litigation and arbitration, and white-collar criminal defense. It has substantial experience in civil aviation matters; it also has represented foreign States in transnational litigation and international arbitration arising out of acts of nationalization and alleged breach of economic development or natural resource supply contracts. Among the Firm's clients in real estate matters are institutional lenders and investors, real estate developers, both individual and corporate, foreign and domestic investors and syndicators. The tax department has substantial experience in all aspects of domestic and international business tax matters and real estate taxation. The matters the tax department deals with on a regular basis include: Taxation of foreign investments; the structuring of corporate transactions, including mergers, acquisitions, liquidations and reorganization; federal and state tax litigation; and tax planning for U.S. and foreign individuals. The trusts and estates department engages in general domestic trusts and estates practice and in tax planning for foreign persons wishing to invest in U.S. assets through offshore trusts and corporations. It represents individuals, trust companies, and banks acting as fiduciaries. It works for various charitable organizations located both in the United States and abroad including private foundations, museums, universities and hospitals. A group of fiduciary accountants with vast experience in the field assists the lawyers of the trusts and estates department. Curtis, Mallet-Prevost, Colt & Mosle has served as a Reviser for most of Latin American Law Digests since 1930.

COLOMBIA LAW DIGEST

(The following is a list of all Topics, including cross-references, covered in this Digest.)

COLOMBIA LAW DIGEST

Revised for 1997 edition by

CURTIS, MALLET-PREVOST, COLT & MOSLE, of the New York Bar.

(Abbreviations used are: C. C. for Civil Code; C. Com. for Commercial Code; C. P. C. for Civil Procedure Code; F. C. for Fiscal Code. All Codes are cited by articles thereof.)

ACKNOWLEDGMENTS:

Private Documents may be acknowledged before a notary public or competent judge. (C. P. C. 252). See topics Notaries Public; Public Instruments.

Documents prepared in conformity with law of country where executed, are entitled to recognition in Colombian courts with same force as in country where executed, if they are duly authenticated; but when Colombian law requires a public instrument (q. v.) document must have force of such an instrument. Powers of attorney and other documents issued abroad to be used in Colombia must be authenticated by a consular or diplomatic agent of Colombia, whose signature must be certified by Ministry of Foreign Relations. (C. C. 21, 22; C. P. C. 188, 259-261).

ACTIONS:

Limitation of.—See topic Prescription, subhead Actions.

ADMINISTRATION:

See topic Executors and Administrators.

ADVERSE POSSESSION: See topic Prescription.

AGENCY: See topic Principal and Agent.

AIRCRAFT:

(C. Com. 1773-1909).

Commercial Code contains detailed provisions regarding subject. Government exercises general supervision over aviation and aircraft. Code guarantees freedom of aeronavigation over national territory provided specific regulations of law are strictly complied with. Code sets forth necessary requisites to register aircraft. Colombian enterprises must have at least 90% of Colombian workers; same provision is applicable to foreign companies having agent or branch in Colombia regarding personnel working in country.

Captain of aircraft is responsible for crew and passengers and is principal authority of same. Airports are divided into civil and military; former are public or private. All of them are subject to provisions of commercial code and regulations issued by aeronautical authority from time to time. In case of accident, injured person has right to receive indemnification and he must only prove that damages were caused by aircraft or by a person or thing related to it. Amount of damages varies, according to type and weight of aircraft and also to seriousness of injuries. Statute of limitations is two years, which runs from moment of accident. Aeronautical authority must regulate and classify services, routes, permits, and registration, of all aircraft in order to guarantee efficient and safe transportation. Code also regulates transportation by air of passengers as well as merchandise and luggage.

Aircraft registered in Colombia can be mortgaged. Those under construction can also be mortgaged if so stated in public instrument which must also contain characteristics of same. Other provisions contemplate attachment, sequestration and insurance of aircraft.

ALIENS:

(Const. Art. 100).

Aliens in general have the same civil rights and duties as citizens both with respect to persons and property. They are divided into transients and residents, the latter being subject to taxation. Aliens are exempt from military service. They lose the right to aliens' exemptions if they discharge elective or political offices or participate in seditious movements. Those taking part in politics may be expelled from the country. Aliens may hold real property, but foreign governments cannot hold real property except legation or consular buildings. (Law 22 of Nov. 22, 1946). All contracts made by the Government in Colombia with aliens must contain a clause stating that the alien subjects himself to the Colombian courts and laws and waives the right to make a diplomatic claim except in case of denial of justice, which denial shall not be considered as existing if the remedies allowed by Colombian law were available to the alien. (F. C. 42).

Not more than 10% of workmen nor more than 20% of certain employees, including management and those in positions of trust, may be aliens. Nationals have a right to salaries equal to the aliens for the same work. (Labor Code 74-75). Under the Petroleum Code at least 80% of personnel must be of Colombians and at least 75% of the salaries paid to them.

Decree 2268 of Dec. 22, 1995, regulates immigration issues. Aliens may enter Colombia with corresponding visa. Among others, most important are: Temporary, resident and business visas. Government keeps registry of aliens. Aliens cannot change residency without advising authorities accordingly. Permanent residency may be granted to foreigner residing in country continuously, said status is lost for absence from Colombia of more than two years. Decree establishes sanctions for aliens or national employers who do not comply with legal requirements and focuses on expulsion and deportation of foreigners from country.

ALIMONY: See topic Divorce.

ARBITRATION:

(Decree 2279 of Oct. 7, 1989 as am'd).

All matters on which compromise may be reached are allowed to be submitted to arbitration. Arbitration is also possible on disputes arising between parties related to commercial trusts (fideicomisos mercantiles). Arbitration agreement (pacto arbitral) may be in form of arbitral clause (cláusula compromisoria) concluded with regard to future disputes arising out of particular legal relationship, or in form of submission (compromiso), separate agreement to submit already existing dispute to arbitration. Decree recognizes enforceability of both and both have effect of waiver of right to assert cause of action before judges. Arbitration agreement can be evidenced by any kind of document, even by telex, fax or other means of communication which constitute record of agreement. Arbitrators may be empowered by parties to decide according to rules of law (en derecho), ex aequo et bono (en conciencia), based on technical principles (técnico) or to act as mediator (amicable compositeur).

Arbitrators must be Colombian citizens and in full enjoyment of their rights in instances where parties in conflict are Colombian and residents in Colombia and their dispute arose in Colombia. In any other case arbitrators may be foreigners. Number of arbitrators should be three unless parties have agreed on different uneven number.

Arbitrators have power to make provisional orders including interim measures of protection at request of either party, and to require any party to provide appropriate security in connection with such measures. Arbitrators have civil and commercial liabilities akin to liabilities of judges. They can also be disciplined. Grounds for disciplinary proceedings include fraud, abuse of authority, gross negligence and unjustified protraction or inaction in award. Deadline for arbitrators to issue award is six months counted as from first hearing unless parties have agreed on different term.

International arbitration is regulated by conventions ratified by Colombia. Colombia has ratified following multilateral conventions: On Recognition and Enforcement of Foreign Arbitral Awards, New York, 1958; on International Commercial Arbitration, Panama 1975 and on Extraterritorial Validity of Foreign Judgments and Arbitral Awards, Montevideo, 1979.

ASSIGNMENTS:

The assignment of a credit is not effective without the delivery of the document, if any, evidencing the right transferred. The assignment produces no effect against the debtor or third persons until the debtor has been notified by the assignee or has acknowledged the assignment. The assignment of a credit carries with it the securities or privileges thereof but not the personal defenses of the assignor. The assignor guarantees the existence of the credit but not the solvency of the debtor unless expressly stipulated. (C. C. 1959-1972).

ASSIGNMENTS FOR BENEFIT OF CREDITORS:

Assignment for benefit of creditors may be made by a debtor who in consequence of unavoidable accidents is unable to pay his debts. At request of any creditor he must prove that situation is not due to his fault. Assignment must cover all property except such as is not subject to attachment. Its effect is to extinguish debts to amount which can be obtained from property assigned; any balance remaining due must be satisfied from later acquired property. Assignment does not vest creditors with title to property but only with right to dispose of same or of its fruits until their credits are paid. Creditors may permit debtor to continue administering property and make agreements with him, with approval of a majority of creditors appearing. Merchant making an assignment for benefit of creditors is considered a bankrupt. (C. C. 1672-1683).

ASSOCIATIONS:

Associations are permitted if not against morals or public policy. Their organic documents are subject to approval by the President of Colombia. They constitute legal entities and their members are not liable for their debts, unless expressly so stipulated or the character of the association implies such liability. Unless otherwise provided in the by-laws a majority of members constitutes the deliberative body of the association and the vote of the majority is decisive. (Const., Art. 38; C. C. 633-652).

ATTACHMENT:

Attachment of property of the defendant may be requested if the plaintiff can present evidence of his claim and the debtor is in bad financial circumstances, or has disappeared or may elude payment. A bond is required before an order of attachment can issue. If a third person claims to be the owner of attached property, it is left with such person as depositary. Any attachment may be raised by giving bond.

Certain documents, such as judgments, public instruments and commercial documents, authorize immediate attachment. Interventions are decided in a brief summary proceeding. (C. P. C. 513-520, 579-580, 681-698).

BANKRUPTCY AND INSOLVENCY:

(Law 222 of Dec. 22, 1995 and C. Com. 1937-2010).

Law regulates reorganization process and mandatory liquidation proceeding before Superintendencia de Sociedades (Superintendencia) for juridical persons and before civil judge for individuals.

Reorganization process may be requested by debtor or creditor or by Superintendencia or civil judge without request of either party when any of following events occur: debtor's default of two or more debts, debtor is in very difficult economic situation, or when there exists reasonable suspicion debtor may be in either of above situations. Petition itself must comply with specific requirements of form and substance. Debtor may file petition provided no bankruptcy has been declared. Order opening reorganization process must appoint receiver who is responsible for analyzing debtor's business activity for previous three years, evaluate reorganization plan and prepare report for creditors' provisional meeting. Creditors' provisional meeting may accept or amend reorganization plan. Publication of notice to creditors and interested parties to appear is ordered. Debtor continues with administration of business under

See Topical Index in front part of this volume.

BANKRUPTCY AND INSOLVENCY . . . *continued*
supervision of Superintendencia, but its authorization is required for any act that may alter creditors' status. Creditors are grouped into different categories according to type of claims. Preliminary injunctions may be issued. Payment arrangements must be approved by Superintendencia as stipulated by law.

Mandatory liquidation proceeding may be declared at debtor's request or by Superintendencia when any of following events occurs: reorganization process ends by lack of agreement, absence of debtor or debtor abandons business or Superintendencia considers convenient to start proceeding after evaluation of reorganization petition. Debtor is removed from administration of assets which are liquidated by liquidator appointed by Superintendencia. Upon payment of debts liquidation proceeding ends and continuation of business can be declared. Administrators are jointly liable to shareholders and third parties if assets are insufficient for payment of debts because of their fault, and shareholders are liable if assets are insufficient when corporation was used to default creditor.

See also topic Fraudulent Sales and Conveyances.

BANKS AND BANKING:

(Law 45 of July 19, 1923, General Banking Law, Law 31 of Dec. 29, 1992, Decrees 239 of Feb. 3, 1993 and 663 of Apr. 1, 1993).

General Banking Law regulates commercial banks, development banks, savings banks, mortgage banks and rural banks. Government supervises through Superintendencia Bancaria that requires banks to comply with regulations set down by Law 45 of July 19, 1923. Banco de la República regulated by Law 31 of 1992 is in charge of: monetary policy and administration of monetary reserves, and it is issuing bank.

See also topic Exchange Control.

BILLS AND NOTES:

Bills of exchange (C. Com. 671-708) must contain following: Unconditional order to pay a specified amount of money, name of drawee, date of payment and indication if it is payable to bearer or to order. It can contain clauses related to interest and rates of exchange, if fixed at a proper amount. Bill of exchange can be drawn: at sight, at specified date or dates (if in installments), and at a certain date after date or sight. It can also be drawn to order of drawer, who in this case, has same obligations as an acceptor. If bill is payable at a certain time after sight, it must be presented for acceptance within one year of its date unless drawer extends such term or forbids its presentation before a certain time. Bill must be presented for acceptance in place and address designated on document. If such place is not indicated presentment must be made in drawee's residence; if bill mentions several places, holder can choose any of them.

Acceptance must be placed on document, using words "accept" or any other equivalent, and signature of drawee; his signature alone is enough to consider bill accepted. Acceptance must be unconditional, but he can pay a lesser amount than one indicated in bill. Any other indication introduced by drawee is equivalent to a refusal to accept.

Bill of exchange must be presented for payment when due or within eight following days. Presentation for payment of a bill of exchange drawn at sight must be made within a year of date of issuance. Holder cannot refuse partial payment, but he does not have to receive payment before maturity, unless otherwise agreed.

Protest is only necessary when drawer or any holder inserts clause "with protest" on document. Said act must be performed before a notary public in place indicated in document. Notary public must record in his books following: Literal reproduction of entire bill, fact that drawee or acceptor was requested to accept or pay it and reasons for refusal, and signatures of persons witnessing act.

Promissory notes (C. Com. 709-711) in general, are governed by all provisions regarding bills of exchange. However, in addition to requirements above specified they must contain name of payee, indication if it's payable to order or to bearer and date of payment. Maker has same rights and duties as acceptor of a bill of exchange.

Checks (C. Com. 712-751) can only be drawn in special forms issued and printed by banks; if drawn on other types of paper they are not negotiable instruments. Checks must contain following: Name of drawee bank and indication if it is payable to order or to bearer. Maker must have sufficient amount of funds in bank; reception of checks from drawee bank is prima facie evidence of funds. Checks are always payable at sight; any indication to contrary is considered void. In case of a post-dated check it is payable upon presentment. Checks must be presented for payment: Within 15 days after issuance if payable at same place; within one month if payable in same country of issuance, but at a different place; within three months if issued in a Latin-American country and payable in any other Latin-American country, and within four months if also issued in any Latin-American country and payable outside that area. Holder can refuse partial payment; however, if he accepts it, bank must insert on check amount paid and must return it to holder. Maker can revoke checks, and once bank has received a "stop payment order," it cannot pay them. Death or incapacity of maker does not exonerate bank of payment. In case of bankruptcy, judicial or administrative liquidation of maker's assets, drawee bank can refuse payment as of date of publication.

Banks must return to maker, together with proper balance statements, all checks drawn by him.

Other provisions in code regulate special checks such as "crossed checks" and travelers' checks. Either maker or holder can demand from drawee bank to certify existence of necessary funds in account; once check has been certified, maker and all endorsees are released from liability. However, certification cannot be partial and cannot be extended on bearer checks. Provisions regarding travelers' checks require that persons who pay or receive such checks must verify authenticity of signature of holder and must compare it to one signed before drawee-bank.

CHATTEL MORTGAGES:

There is no provision for chattel mortgages. See topic Pledges.

COLLATERAL SECURITY: See topic Pledges.

COMMERCIAL REGISTER:

(C. Com. 26-47, 1210; Decree 242 of Jan. 16, 1970, Res. 535 of Nov. 8, 1971, Decree 1788 of Sept. 26, 1972) must keep records of licenses granted to do business, commercial establishments, and their branches and subsidiaries, and it must also record all acts, books and documents when such formality is necessary. Registry is public, any person can examine books, files, and can take notes or copies of information recorded.

Chamber of Commerce is in charge of Registry, but Superintendency of Industry and Commerce exercises supervision and gives instructions on books, files, etc.

Following must be recorded in Commercial Registry: Merchants and agents such as commission merchants, agents representing national or foreign corporations; liquidations of community property when one of spouses is a merchant; attachments against merchants when prohibition to do business is necessary consequence, bankruptcy and composition agreements, name of trustee in bankruptcy; authorizations to minors to do business; corporate books and registries of shareholders, minute books of shareholders meetings; amendments or changes and liquidation of commercial companies and names of liquidators, agricultural and industrial pledges (Prenda agraria e industrial), etc.

Contracts and documents must be recorded in Chamber of Commerce with jurisdiction in place where they were granted and they must also be recorded in place of execution if different.

Registrar usually only records a summary of document unless interested parties demand otherwise. Chambers of Commerce can issue certificates establishing that documents are duly recorded. In case of public instrument regarding incorporation of commercial enterprises and subsequent amendments, following procedure is necessary: Certified copy of certificate of incorporation must be filed in Chamber of Commerce of principal domicile in a special book which must contain name, domicile number of public instrument, information of notary public before whom it was signed, etc. Same procedure must be followed in case of designation of legal representatives, liquidators and other persons in charge of liquidation. Commercial enterprises pay annual fee according to gross assets. Separate registration fees are collected from subsidiaries or affiliates conducting business in more than one jurisdiction of Chamber of Commerce.

Registration is subject to stamp tax. See topic Taxation, subhead Stamp Tax.

COMMISSIONS TO TAKE TESTIMONY:

See topic Depositions.

COMMUNITY PROPERTY:

See topic Husband and Wife.

CONDITIONAL SALES: See topic Sales (Realty and Personalty).

CONSTITUTION AND GOVERNMENT:

(Const. of July 18, 1991).

Colombia is democratic republic with representative form of government.

Legislative power is vested in a Congress composed of a Senate and House of Representatives. Number of senators and representatives is determined on basis of population and are elected by direct popular vote for four years. Executive power is vested in President. President is elected by direct popular vote for four years and can hold these offices for only one term. Deputy President is elected by popular vote at same time as President.

In administrative area, President is officially empowered to organize public credit, recognize national debt and arrange its service; regulate international exchange and foreign commerce and regulate customs duties, tariffs and charges. Exercise of these powers, however, is subordinate to laws passed by Congress.

Judicial power resides in Supreme Court of Justice and other Courts established by law, State Council and Constitutional Court. Supreme Court of Justice, State Council and Constitutional Court members are elected for eight years and cannot be reelected. Country is divided into departments, districts, municipalities and Indian territories.

CONTRACTS:

(C. C. 1494-1624, C. Com. 1-9, 20-25, 48, 74).

Nature, form, objects and obligations of contracts are governed generally by Civil Code. Nevertheless there is definite class of contracts known as commercial or mercantile contracts concerning which provisions of Civil Code are supplemented by Commercial Code. Civil Code, except as modified by Commercial Code, however, governs mercantile contracts.

To constitute contract there must be offer and acceptance express or implied. Offer is void if offeror dies or becomes incapacitated before acceptance is received. Offers may be retracted any time before acceptance if offeror has not renounced his rights to retract. Verbal offers must be accepted immediately. Modification of offer in acceptance constitutes new offer. Offeree may retract his acceptance any time before it reaches offeror. If offeree has accepted in ignorance of retraction by offeror or of his death or incapacity, he is entitled to reimbursement for all losses suffered by him and expenses incurred.

Only those persons having legal capacity may enter into contracts but only incapacitated person, his representative and third parties affected may have contract nullified because of incapacity. Ratification of contract made in one's name has same effect as previous authorization.

Objects of contract must be definite or subject to definite determination. Future inheritances and future hereditary rights cannot be object of contract.

Form of contract is determined by place where executed. If executed by various parties in different places, formalities are governed by law of place most favorable to its validity. According to Civil Code following contracts, except when executed at public auction, must be in form of public instruments (see topics Notaries Public and Public Instruments): Contracts regarding real property; extrajudicial partition of inheritances; contracts of incorporation or partnership and extensions of same or when part

CONTRACTS . . . *continued*

of capital is real property; contracts of marriage and dower; life annuities; transferring, repudiation or renunciation of hereditary rights; general and special powers of attorney for use in court, for administration of property or which concern public instrument or execution of one; adjustments with regard to real property; transfer of rights arising from transfer of public instruments; acts accessory to contracts which are in form of public instruments, and payments of obligations originating in public instruments, with exception of partial payments, interest and rent.

Contract which should be in form of public instrument but which is drawn up as private document, constitutes obligation to reduce same to public instrument. Same rule applies to verbal contracts. Penalty clauses in contracts are enforceable.

Contracts made in violation of laws of foreign country are void. Validity, nature and obligations of contracts to be carried out in Colombia are governed by Colombian laws, whether made in Colombia or in foreign country, but if they are to be carried out in foreign country they are governed by laws of that country. Contracts referring to real property in Colombia executed in foreign country are valid if in form of public instruments and properly legalized. If they are for purpose of transferring title to real property contracts must be protocolized by order of competent judge.

As stated above, civil law is supplemented by Commercial Code in respect to mercantile contracts. In general, law of contracts set forth above is generic and applies to all contracts whether mercantile or otherwise. Matters falling within scope of Commercial Code are those relating to transfer of personal property for purposes of obtaining profit from same whether in its form when transferred or after changing its form, operations of exchange, banking or brokerage, negotiations with regard to bills of exchange, checks or other endorsable paper, operations of factories, commercial agents, warehouses and transportation; suretyship and corporate transactions, freight, construction, purchase or sale of vessels, their equipment, provisioning and everything relative to maritime commerce, operations of factors, bookkeepers and other employees of merchants concerning their employers, agreements with regard to salaries of clerks and other employees of merchants; letters of credit, bonds, pledges etc. and other matters especially treated of in Code of Commerce. If contract is commercial as to one party, it is deemed commercial as to all parties. Commercial contracts may be evidenced by public instruments; by notations of mercantile agents and certificates of contents of their books; by private documents signed by parties or witness in contractor's name; by correspondence, telegrams, books of merchants, admission of parties, by witnesses and by presumptions. All blank spaces and amendments in mercantile contracts must be authenticated by signature of parties. Telegrams have same force as letters. Words are understood in their general sense. In case of ambiguity intention of parties must be sought and when found outweighs literal sense. Customs of business are taken into account in interpreting contract. In general, it may be said that contracts governed by Commercial Code are made with much less formality than those which depend solely on Civil Code and methods by which their existence and scope are proved are more numerous. Moreover, in many of classes of commercial contracts, such as bills of exchange, checks, partnership agreements, etc. special rules are provided in Commercial Code to govern their effect and operation. (See topics Bills and Notes; Corporations; Partnership.)

Public Contracts: Law 80 of Oct. 28, 1993 and Decree 2251 of Nov. 11, 1993 regulate contracts with Government and Public entities.

COPYRIGHT:

(Const. Art. 61).

Scientific, literary and artistic works as defined by law are protected. Law also protects performers in their rights. Copyrights include all kinds of intellectual (including software), scientific, literary and artistic creations reproduced by any means. Moreover, law protects as "independent copyright works", translations, adaptations, musical arrangements and other transformations on private intellectual works. To protect these copyright works written authorization from original owner of work is necessary. Law grants certain intellectual, moral and property rights to author, his successors or assignees. Right remains in force during life of author and for 80 years thereafter. When copyrights are owned by judicial persons period of protection is 50 years from publication. Rights of artists, performers, phonogram producers and radio transmission organizations are protected 50 years from first performance, publication of phonograms or transmission.

Only scientific works to be copyrighted may be registered in National Copyright Registry. Literary and artistic works, performances and other productions are protected by law without requiring registration. Assignments of copyright must be made in public instrument and likewise recorded. Registration of copyright must be effected within two months after publication; if not made in this period work is not protected until registered. Any act or contract related to copyright must be registered.

Letters are the property of the addressee, but they can be published only by the author except in case of litigation. Letters of a deceased person cannot be published for 80 years without the consent of the surviving spouse, or the children, the father or mother or other specified relatives of the author. National and foreign associations for the protection of authors' rights are recognized. Infringement of copyrights are subject to prison and fines, and illegal publications subject to seizure. (Law 23 of Jan. 28, 1982 as am'd by Law 44 of Feb. 5, 1993; Decree 3116 of Dec. 21, 1984 as am'd; Decree 1360 of June 23, 1989; Decision 351 of Dec. 17, 1993 of Cartagena Commission; Decree 460 of Mar. 16, 1995; Decree 162 of Jan. 2, 1996).

Certain provisions of Commercial Code regulate publishing contracts.

Colombia is a party to Convention on literary and artistic copyright, (Buenos Aires, 1910, revised Havana, 1928), to Inter-American convention on rights of author in literary, scientific and artistic works (Washington, 1946), to Convention for the Protection of Performers, Producers of Phonograms and Broadcasting Organization (Rome, 1961), to Convention of the Protection of Literary and Artistic Works (Berne, 1886) Revised 1971, to Universal Copyright Convention (Geneva, 1952) Revised 1971 and to Agreement on Trade-Related Aspects of Intellectual Property Rights, Marrakesh, Apr. 15, 1994.

CORPORATIONS:

Formation (C. Com. 98-121, 269, 373-376).—Articles of incorporation must state: (1) Name, nationality and domicile of shareholders, which cannot be less than five; (2) domicile of company; (3) business to be pursued and principal activities specifically stated; (4) capital, type and nominal value of shares and how and when they are to be paid up, which period cannot exceed one year; (5) when inventory and balance are to be prepared and dividends declared and proportion of profits withheld for reserve; (6) when and how shareholders' meetings are to be convoked and conducted; (7) method of administration, rights and powers of directors and stockholders; (8) duration; (9) manner of liquidation; (10) when and how differences must be submitted to arbitration; (11) name, domicile, rights and duties of managers or legal representatives of company; (12) powers and duties of fiscal auditor; and in general, any other lawful agreements. Name of corporation shall always be followed by words "sociedad anónima" or letters "S.A.".

Copy of articles of incorporation must be recorded in Mercantile Register of Chamber of Commerce of municipality of company's domicile and in any other municipality where company does business. (For registration fees and tax, see topics Commercial Register; Taxation, subhead Stamp Taxes.) Before corporation can start doing business, it must also obtain permission to function from Superintendent of Corporations. Request for permission must be accompanied by (1) Notarized copy of articles of incorporation and (2) certificate from a Colombian Bank stating that account has been opened in name of corporation and paid-in capital has been deposited.

Administrators are jointly and severally liable for damages caused by fraud or negligence to company, shareholders or third parties.

Stock and Stockholders (C. Com. 377-418).—Shares of stock may be registered. Shares are indivisible, so when one share is owned by several persons, they must designate one person to exercise rights of shareholders. Preferred shares are permitted if authorized by plural vote of shareholders representing no less than 75% of all subscribed shares, and if first offered to existing shareholders who may buy them proportionally to number of shares owned.

Each shareholder (which cannot be less than five) has right to: (1) Participate and vote in general meetings; (2) receive a proportional amount of profits; (3) freely transfer shares, unless other shareholders or company have preference to buy; (4) inspect books of corporation for 15 days prior to shareholders' meetings which examine company balance at end of fiscal year; and (5) receive a proportional amount of company assets at time of liquidation. Preferred shareholders, in addition to these rights, may have preference to be reimbursed up to nominal value of their shares at time of liquidation or any other exclusively economic prerogative. They may not have multiple votes or any rights that infringe on rights of common shareholders. There may be shares to compensate for services, work, technological contributions, etc. which merely carry a right to a proportional part of profits and, at time of liquidation, accumulated reserves.

Shares not subscribed for in articles of incorporation must be offered in accordance with rules of subscription. Except for preferred shares, and unless otherwise provided for in statutes or bylaws, board of directors shall approve rules of subscription. Rules of subscription must state: (1) Number of shares offered; (2) proportion and manner of acquisition; (3) duration of offer, which may last between 15 days up to three months; (4) price at which shares are being offered which cannot be less than nominal value; and (5) period allowed in which to pay for shares. When purchase of shares in installments is allowed, one-third of value of shares must be paid for upon subscription, and balance must be fully paid within one year. Shareholders have preference to buy new shares in proportion to shares they owned on date subscription was approved. Offer of shares without authorization by Superintendent of Corporations results in fines up to 50,000 pesos.

Companies cannot purchase their own shares except with consent of general shareholder's meeting by vote of at least 70% of shares; purchase must be made from profits and shares must be fully paid. Shares must be issued within one month after Superintendent of Corporations grants permit to corporation to do business. In case of loss or theft of shares, new certificates will be issued to owner upon his giving guarantee. Executives of corporation cannot buy or sell shares without authorization by two-thirds vote of board of directors or majority vote of shareholders.

Shareholders' Meetings (C. Com. 419-433).—They are necessary at least once a year, to examine condition of corporation, decide reserve levels beyond what is legally needed, appoint and remove directors and take other action required for corporation's interest. Meetings should take place at principal domicile of corporation, but may be convened at any place if all shares are represented, by any means of simultaneous or successive communication, or by written expression of shareholder's consent. Minutes of meeting must be kept and sent within 15 days after meeting to Superintendent of Corporations. Any action of meeting in contravention of law is void.

Directors (C. Com. 434-444).—Their powers and duties are expressed in bylaws. There must be at least three directors. They are appointed for stated periods and subject to removal. For each director, one substitute must be elected. There cannot be a majority of persons on board of directors that are related within third degree of consanguinity or second of affinity or by marriage. Unless otherwise provided for in bylaws, directors have power to do any act or execute any contract within social purpose of corporation. Directors must submit reports to shareholders' meetings with a statement of amounts and inventory for each fiscal period, reasonable information on financial position of company, and intended distribution of profits.

Balance and Dividends (C. Com. 445-456).—At end of every accounting period and at least once a year (Dec. 31) corporations must produce inventories and balance sheets of their business. Directors and legal representative must present to shareholder's meeting, balance of each accounting period, plus following documents: (1) Complete statement of gains and losses; (2) distribution of profits; (3) directors' financial report, with statement of salary expenses, fees to independent contractors, and advertising expenses, list of foreign assets and debts, and current investments in other companies; (4) recommendations on administration of corporation by legal representative; and (5) report of auditor. These documents, plus company books, must be made available to shareholders 15 days before shareholders' meeting.

See Topical Index in front part of this volume.

CORPORATIONS . . . *continued*

Corporations whose shares are traded on stock market must have their balance sheets audited by public accountant and published in newspaper wherever markets operate.

Dividends can be distributed only from net profits justified by inventories and balances, approved at shareholders' meetings. No dividends may be distributed until required reserve has been set aside and taxes paid. Corporations must have a "reserve fund" amounting to at least one-half of subscribed capital, formed with 10% of profits. Whenever reserve fund goes below 50%, corporation must again appropriate 10% of profits until reserve is at legal level. Dividends may be paid in money or, if 80% of shareholders represented at meeting approve, in shares repurchased by corporation.

Merger, Consolidation, and Spin-off.—Merger, consolidation or spin-off of same or different types of companies may be effected, and must be approved as provided for in amended bylaws of involved companies. Shareholders dissenting from decision approving merger, consolidation or spin-off of company have appraisal rights.

Dissolution and Liquidation (C. Com. 457-460).—Corporation must, among other grounds, be dissolved when period of its duration has expired; when its business purpose is no longer possible to be pursued; when losses occur which reduce its net worth to less than 50% of its subscribed capital; or when 95% of its shares are owned by one person. When net worth of corporation is reduced below 50% of subscribed capital, directors must immediately convoke a shareholders' meeting, which may take action within six months to reestablish net worth of company or may declare its dissolution. Once dissolution has been properly decided, liquidators must present to shareholders reasonable statements regarding its process, its balance sheet, and inventory. Following words must be added after corporate name: "in liquidation." Liquidators are personally liable in case of omission.

Government Supervision (C. Com. 266-293, Law 44 of May 6, 1981 and Decree 1827 of July 22, 1991).—It is exercised by Superintendent of Corporations to ascertain whether corporation is carrying out its corporate purposes, keeping necessary reserves, and books and records as provided by law, etc. Powers of Superintendent include general supervision of corporations, convoking shareholders' meetings, withdrawing shares from stock market, and suspending permission to conduct business.

Neither Superintendent nor his employees can own or acquire stock in companies being supervised.

Superintendent can suspend permission to do business when corporation (1) Is not fulfilling or is exceeding business purpose; (2) is not keeping its books and minutes in proper manner; (3) does not have legally-required reserves; (4) is unjustifiably distributing profits; and (5) is not fulfilling other legal obligations. Superintendent can order dissolution of corporation when it (1) Has not obtained permission to do business or to continue doing business; (2) has not corrected, in time allowed by Superintendent, irregularities which lead to suspension of permission to do business; (3) has a net worth below 50% of subscribed capital and has taken no steps to reestablish it; and (4) should be dissolved but shareholders cannot or do not dissolve it.

Foreign Corporations (C. Com. 469-497).—If they desire to do permanent business in Colombia they must (1) Register with a notary in place of its future domicile, copies of its articles of incorporation, bylaws, act or resolution which stipulates its establishment in Colombia, and documents that authorize existence of corporation and position and authority of its representatives; and (2) obtain permission from Superintendent of Corporations to do business in country. Act or resolution stipulating establishment of corporation should state: (1) Business to undertake; (2) amount of capital allotted to subsidiary and other sources of financing it; (3) place of future domicile; (4) duration of its business in Colombia and reasons for its termination; (5) designation of general agent, with one or more substitutes, to represent corporation in all business in Colombia and empowered to act in any way to further business goals; and (6) designation of auditor, who must be a permanent resident of Colombia.

Permanent business activities are following: (1) Opening commercial establishments or business offices, even if of only a technical or consulting business; (2) labor or service contracts; (3) any handling or investment of private funds; (4) any aspect of an extractive industry; (5) obtaining concession from Colombia or participating in any way in exploitation of same; and (6) functioning of shareholder meetings, board of directors, or management within Colombian territory.

To establish a subsidiary in Colombia, foreign corporation must vouch before Superintendency that capital allotted by principal corporation is covered. Foreign corporation doing permanent business in Colombia must maintain sufficient reserves and comply with all laws that govern national corporations.

Documents granted to corporation in foreign country will be authenticated by Colombian consul, or consul of friendly nation, in that country. Consul will show that corporation exists and conforms to laws of foreign country. Superintendent of Corporations can impose successive fines upon foreign persons who engage in activities violating law, as well as upon their representatives. Superintendent has same powers over foreign and domestic corporations. Corporations must register in chamber of commerce of its domicile (see topic Commercial Register) copy of amendments to its articles of incorporation, bylaws and acts designating or removing its representatives from country. Corporation may increase its capital in country without restriction but cannot reduce it except in accordance with law, and must keep, in books registered with chamber of commerce of its domicile, accounting of business done in Colombia. Corporations must file, at least at end of each year, balance sheet with Superintendency and chamber of commerce.

Financial accountants must inform Superintendency of irregularities which could cause suspension or revocation of corporation's permit to do business. When foreign corporation does not invest its allotted capital in activities within scope of its business purpose, Superintendency will impose successive fines on legal representative until capital is properly invested. When permit to do business is revoked, corporation must liquidate its business in Colombia. Profits obtained by subsidiary of foreign corporation must be liquidated in accordance with final balance sheet, approved by Superintendency. Consequently, subsidiary cannot make advances or turnover of capital to principal in part payment of future profits.

COURTS:

The judicial system consists of (a) ordinary courts having jurisdiction over civil, commercial and criminal cases; (b) administrative courts having jurisdiction over administrative matters; (c) labor courts with jurisdiction over labor disputes; and (d) minors' courts having jurisdiction over matters involving minors.

The ordinary courts comprise: (1) A Supreme Court, which decides appeals on errors of law and has original jurisdiction in certain proceedings against high functionaries, in certain admiralty matters, in controversies between departments and in controversies relating to government contracts; (2) superior district courts, which decide appeals from superior judges of judicial districts and circuit judges and have original jurisdiction in special matters in which the Government and the departments are parties; (3) superior judges of judicial districts, having jurisdiction in most felony cases; (4) circuit judges, who have jurisdiction in embezzlement and bankruptcy cases and in certain others concerning corporations; (5) civil, criminal and labor municipal judges, having jurisdiction in minor civil cases, misdemeanors and labor conflicts, respectively; (6) a Court of Conflicts, which settles controversies between jurisdictions. Annulment of religious marriages and divorce thereunder are under jurisdiction of ecclesiastical courts. (C. P. C. 7-43, 141-148).

The administrative courts comprise: (1) a Council of State, and (2) departmental administrative courts. In general, the Council has original jurisdiction over certain admiralty cases and river navigation matters; jurisdictional conflicts between the departments and the municipalities and between any of them and the national government; public lands concessions; cancellation of naturalization papers; appeals from certain decisions of the national government; etc. It also reviews appeals from departmental administrative courts and some national officials. The departmental courts hear cases regarding departmental ordinances, municipal resolutions, decisions of departmental and municipal executives; tax matters; etc. (Laws 167 of 1941 and 5 of 1958; Decrees 528 of Mar. 9, 1964, 1697 of June 24, 1965 and 1867 of July 16, 1965, as am'd by Law 16 of Mar. 28, 1968). There are lower courts and a Supreme Court of Custom Houses. (Decrees 700 of 1954, 2350 of 1955; Laws 73 and 188 of 1958).

Labor courts were created by Law 6 of 1945 and Decree 1745 of 1945 as amended. The procedure in these courts was approved by Decree 969 of March 27, 1946. These courts comprise a Supreme Labor Court, Sectional Labor Courts and lower labor courts.

Minors' Courts are regulated by Decree 2737 of Nov. 29, 1989. They hear cases of juvenile delinquency; abandonment or neglect, education and custody of children; paternity proceedings; child labor; etc.

Constitutional Court reviews for constitutional validity laws approved by legislative power and some decrees issued by executive power; and it is also responsible for decisions related to tutelar actions which protect rights of those accused of criminal offenses against abuses of public administration including judicial system.

CURRENCY:

Monetary unit is peso. Banco de la República is only bank authorized to issue notes, which are legal tender. (Law 31 of Dec. 29, 1992).

CURTESY:

There is no estate by curtesy.

CUSTOMS DUTIES:

See topics Exchange Control; Foreign Investments.

DEATH:

The presumption of death of a person may be judicially declared two years after his disappearance. The date of presumptive death is the last day of the second year from the date of disappearance. Two years after such judicial declaration, temporary possession of an absentee's property may be granted. Definitive possession may be granted when, at least two years after the presumptive death, 70 years have elapsed from the date of the absentee's birth or 15 years from the date of disappearance. (C. C. 96-109).

Deaths must be recorded in the Registry of Civil Status of the district where death occurs. Death certificates may be obtained from the Chief of the Registry of Civil Status. Fees, nominal in amount, are fixed by local regulations.

Actions for Death.—There is no specific provision of law creating these actions, but they may be supported under the general provisions (C. C. 2341 et seq.) to effect that any damage out of fault of one person to another is a tort. Some decisions have granted relief to relatives of deceased for damages by them suffered, when real and concrete and not speculative.

DECEDENTS' ESTATES:

See topics Descent and Distribution; Executors and Administrators; Wills.

DEEDS:

All transfers of title to real estate as well as all encumbrances must be done by public instrument (escritura pública). Such document has all characteristics of a deed and must contain accurate details regarding parties and real property involved.

Deeds must be prepared before a Notary Public who is a public official whose duties and responsibilities are more important than those under American Law. See topic Notaries Public.

Deeds must be written in Spanish; however, if parties do not know language sufficiently enough to understand transactions involved, they must be attested to by an interpreter who must also sign deed before Notary. Printed forms can be used, provided blanks are filled in carefully and without omissions; quantities must be expressed in numbers and in words; in case of doubt, words will prevail. Grantor and grantee must sign deed and both must be present at same time. If one is absent, an attorney in fact can represent him. Notaries will not authenticate a deed of transfer or encumbrances without proof that all taxes are paid. (Decree 960 of June 20, 1970 as am'd by Decree 2163 of 1970 and Law 29 of 1973, Decree 1250 of July 27, 1970; Decree 2148 of Aug. 1, 1983 as am'd by Decree 231 of Jan. 24, 1985).

DEPOSITIONS:

Testimony in civil cases is usually reduced to writing. Judges may commission other judges or officials to take such testimony. Letters rogatory to foreign countries are sent through the Ministry of Foreign Affairs. (C. P. C. 213-232, 298-299).

DESCENT AND DISTRIBUTION:

Estates of decedents pass either by will or by operation of law. The rights are transmitted from the moment of the decedent's death. The law designates various acts which render guilty parties incapable of inheriting, such as having committed a crime against the deceased, etc.

In default of testamentary provisions bulk of estate passes to following in order named: (1) Descendants; (2) adopted children; (3) ascendants; (4) adopting parents; (5) brothers and sisters; (6) children of brothers and sisters; (7) spouse; (8) Instituto Colombiano de Bienestar Social. Only part of decedent's estate may be disposed of freely by will; certain portion goes to heirs by operation of law.

"Asignaciones forzosas" or "forced legacies" are: (1) The support owed by the decedent to certain persons; (2) the conjugal portion pertaining to the surviving spouse who has insufficient means, which participation varies but never exceeds one-fourth of the estate; (3) the "legítimas" or legal portions pertaining to the obligatory heirs; and (4) the "mejoras" or betterments.

Obligatory heirs are the descendants and ascendants. One-half of the estate must be divided among them in accordance with the rules relating to intestate succession; this half makes up the legal portions. If there are no descendants testator may freely dispose of remaining half. If there are such descendants he must give one-fourth of his estate as betterments to one or more descendants and may freely dispose of only remaining fourth. Obligatory heirs may be disinherited for certain reasons, such has having committed crime against testator, etc.

In order to be entitled to the inheritance the heir must accept the same, and the acceptance may be unconditional or subject to the making of an inventory. If some heirs desire an inventory and others do not, all are obliged to accept subject to inventory. Acceptances may be express or implied. In the case of an unconditional acceptance the heir is liable for all the debts of the decedent, not only out of the estate which he accepts but also out of his own property. An acceptance with benefit of inventory or after making a formal inventory renders the heir responsible for the debts of the decedent only to the extent of the amount which he inherits and does not affect his own property. Partition of inheritance can be carried out by judge or by notary public.

The Colombian heirs of an alien dying intestate and leaving property in Colombia have the same rights in said property as they would have in the intestate estate of a Colombian. They may ask that their share in all the alien's property be adjudicated to them out of the property in Colombia. (Const. Art. 42, C. C. 250, 284, 1008-1054, 1226-1269, 1279-1410, Law 902 of May 10, 1988).

DESERTION: See topic Divorce.

DIVORCE:

Actions for nullity and separation in case of religious marriages are under exclusive jurisdiction of religious courts, in accordance with canon law, and judgments of these courts produce civil effects, but civil effects of religious marriages are ceased by divorce decree of family court. Ordinary courts hear actions for divorce and separation of persons married by civil ceremony, but in any case ordinary courts may adopt necessary preliminary measures, such as to designate where wife is to live during proceedings, determine who is to have provisional custody of children and award alimony and counsel fees to wife. Divorce dissolves marriage. Following are causes of divorce: (1) Extramarital sexual relations of either spouse; (2) habitual drunkenness; (3) absolute abandonment by either spouse of his or her respective duties; (4) insults, cruelty and physical abuse; (5) habitual use of drugs; (6) insanity or serious illness; (7) attempt to corrupt; (8) judicial or de facto separation for period over two years; and (9) mutual consent. (C. C. 152, 154-168; C. P. C. 427-446).

DOWER:

There is no provision for dower.

ENVIRONMENT:

(National Code of Renewable Natural Resources and Environmental Protection, Decree 2811 of Dec. 18, 1974 as am'd and its regulations, Law 99 of Dec. 22, 1993, Decree 1753 of Aug. 3, 1994, Decree 948 of June 5, 1995, Law Decree 2150 of Dec. 5, 1995).

National Code of Renewable Natural Resources and Environmental Protection grants to each person right to enjoy healthy environment and governs environmental regulatory process which includes environmental protection, natural resources conservation and sanctions. Environmental laws are considered of public interest and therefore claims are not subject to settlement. Law contains list of activities which are considered to potentially damage environment; creates Ministry of the Environment whose main function is environmental policy formulation. Law defines violations against environmental laws, establishes its sactions and preventive, punitive and corrective measures to repair damages caused. Within environmental protection are air, water, waste and noise pollution.

Air.—Stationary and mobile sources of emissions of pollutant elements must control emissions to maintain them within maximum permissible levels. Facilities with stationary source of emission must obtain operating license, which contains mandatory conditions.

Water.—Handling, treatment and disposal of waste water is regulated. Special permit is required to discharge pollutants to any body of water including municipal sewer system. Mandatory conditions include discharge limits.

Waste is considered hazardous when it is toxic or radioactive. Registration must be obtained before generating or handling waste. Generator is responsible for its disposal, including final treatment. There are requirements for locations and containers for storing waste and recycling. Importation of hazardous waste is prohibited.

Noise.—Stationary and mobile sources of noise must control production to maintain them within maximum permissible levels. Permissible levels vary within each zone. Facilities with stationary source of noise must comply with operating schedule for zone.

Environmental impact statements are required for activities such as oil, mining, chemical industry, nuclear energy generation, and infrastructure construction. Regulations which implement laws set forth requirements, procedures, conditions and limits that must be complied with. Administrative or criminal penalties are imposed for violations of laws. Sanctions include fines, temporary or permanent closure of facility, revocation of permits, depending on gravity of offense and prior violations.

ESCHEAT: See topic Descent and Distribution.

EVIDENCE: See topic Depositions.

EXCHANGE CONTROL:

(Const. Arts. 371 and 372, Law 9 of Jan. 17, 1991 as am'd, Decree 1746 of July 7, 1991, Resolutions of Junta Monetaria: 55 of June 20, 1991, 57 of June 26, 1991, as am'd and 21 of Sept. 2, 1993 as am'd).

Foreign exchange market is used for transactions related to importation and exportation of goods, foreign investment, Colombian investment abroad, private debts, avals and securities in foreign currency, among others. Personal services, sales and services to tourists and gifts or donations or any other amount under certain limits or regulated by law which can be negotiated freely. Foreign exchange transactions must be done by commercial bankers, finance firms and exchange houses. Exchange rate is determined by supply and demand. Export proceeds must be turned over to Banco de la Republica. Colombians can hold foreign exchange accounts abroad.

Exports.—(Decree 1144 of May 31, 1990). Exportation of national products is free, but it must be declared to Instituto de Comercio Exterior. However, Junta de Comercio Exterior may establish quality standards and degree of processing required for export goods, or may limit or prohibit exportation of certain products when demand of national market so requires.

Imports are subject to licence. All imports require registration with Instituto de Comercio Exterior and licence by same. Temporary admission of raw materials and parts for export goods is regulated by Decrees 2666 of Oct. 26, 1984 as am'd.

Import Tax.—Andean Group common external tariff is in force. Rates are 5%, 10%, 20% and up to maximum of 40%.

Foreign capital investments may be recognized as such if: (1) In machinery and equipment with non-refundable licence, contributed to capital; (2) consisting in foreign exchange sold to authorized institutions in order to make direct contribution to capital in national currency, or for acquisition of rights, shares or other securities; (3) national money with right of being sent abroad; (4) reinvestment of dividends attributable to recognized investment; (5) retained earnings with right of being sent abroad; and (6) intangible technological contributions, patents and marks.

Investments of foreign capital require registration with Banco de la República. Additional investments and remittance of profits must also be registered. Registration of investments gives right to: (a) Remit profits; (b) repatriate investment and reinvestments of profits therefrom which could have been sent abroad.

As a member of Andean Pact (Law 8 of Apr. 14, 1973) Colombia approved decision 291 of Cartagena Agreement Commission on "Common regime of treatment of foreign capital and of trademarks, patents, licenses and royalties."

EXECUTIONS:

Judgments for payment of money are carried into effect by attaching property of debtor. Property is advertised for sale and sale is held by judge. Bidders must deposit 20% of estimated value and lowest bid receivable at first auction is 70% of such value. If there are no bidders property is again advertised for sale; at such sale lowest admissible bid is 50%. If there is still no bidder a third day is designated for sale, at which bids of 40% may be received. If there are still no bidders property may again be advertised for sale and there may be new estimates of value, but no bid of less than 40% is accepted. There is no equity of redemption. (C. P. C. 523-539).

EXECUTORS AND ADMINISTRATORS:

(C. C. 1279-1442).

The office of executor cannot be exercised by blind, dumb, demented, incompetent, bankrupt or notoriously wicked persons, minors, illiterates except parents in certain cases, persons not domiciled in Colombia and persons who have been subject to certain legal penalties or guilty of certain moral lapses. The office is voluntary but an executor who declines or resigns without serious cause loses whatever legacy or bequest may have been made him except such as pertain to him as obligatory heir.

Although the testator may have entrusted the executor with the payment of debts, creditors may sue the heirs if the executor is tardy in making payment. With the consent of the heirs present an executor may sell personal property at a public sale and also real property if there is not sufficient ready money to pay the debts or legacies, but the heirs may prevent the sales by advancing the necessary money. The testator may provide that all or part of the estate be taken in custody by the executor. The heirs or legatees may ask that the executor be required to give bond.

The executor must conclude his labors within the time determined by the testator, or, if no time be determined, within one year, but the period may be extended by the judge. His compensation is such as may be determined by the testator, or, in default of such determination, by the judge. If for any reason there is no executor the heirs are charged with the execution of the testator's wishes and partition may be made by the heirs if all have capacity to dispose of their property; otherwise the judge appoints a partitioner who must effect partition within a year.

Upon the death of a decedent whether testate or intestate, any party in interest may ask that the personal property of the estate be taken into custody. If within fifteen days the estate or part of the same has not been accepted by the heirs and there is no executor designated to take over the estate, the judge may, upon the petition of an

EXECUTORS AND ADMINISTRATORS . . . *continued*
interested party, appoint a curator for the estate. The heirs obtain the administration of the estate as and when they accept the inheritance.

Claims.—Executors must publish notices to creditors and upon a partition of the estate set aside a sufficient amount to pay the known debts.

Creditors of decedents have the right to require payment of their claims, but the period to enforce the right and the extent of the right depend on whether there has been an unqualified acceptance of the estate by the heirs or an acceptance subject to the benefit of inventory. (See topic Descent and Distribution.)

In case of unqualified acceptance the creditor may present his claim at any time within the period of limitations. In this case the heir is obliged to pay all debts and charges on the property he inherited not only out of the accepted inheritance but also out of his own property; he is, however, liable only for his proportionate share of such debts and charges. In case of acceptance subject to inventory the heir is obliged to pay the debts of the decedent only up to the value of the property inherited.

Creditors may at any time demand the separation of the inherited property from the other property of the heir, so that their credits may have preference as against such inherited property over the other debts owing by the heir. Such separation can be demanded at any time within the period of limitations unless the creditor has already recognized the heir as debtor or the property inherited has been alienated by the heir or become confused with his other property.

EXEMPTIONS:

Among items exempted from attachment and execution are following: (1) Pensions, with some exceptions and limitations; (2) minimum wage plus 80% of excess thereof, but for amounts due to co-operative corporations or for family support and maintenance only, 50% is exempt; (3) life insurance policies and sums payable to beneficiaries other than insured; (4) payments to public works contractors while work progresses other than in actions for amounts owing workmen or purveyors; (5) certain properties such as railroads and waterworks on which service could not be interrupted without public inconvenience, but revenue therefrom can be attached; (6) beds and clothing of debtor and family; (7) machinery and instruments used for working; (8) uniforms and equipment of military men; (9) food and combustibles required by debtor and family for one month; (10) property held in fiduciary capacity; (11) rights entirely personal such as use and habitation; (12) articles used in religious rites. (C. C. 1677; C. P. C. 684).

FILING FEES: See topic Mortgages.

FORECLOSURE:

See topic Executions; Mortgages.

FOREIGN CORPORATIONS: See topic Corporations.

FOREIGN EXCHANGE:

See topic Exchange Control.

FOREIGN INVESTMENTS:

(Const. Arts. 100, 335; C.C. art. 1519; Law 9 of Jan. 17, 1991, Res. 51 CONPES of Oct. 22, 1991 as am'd).

Foreigners within Colombian territory enjoy same guarantees as are granted to nationals. Colombian Government policy toward foreign investment has been traditionally favorable.

Decision 291 of Commission of Cartagena Agreement on Common Regime for Treatment of Foreign Capital and of Trademarks, Patents, Licenses and Royalties is in force.

Direct foreign investment is authorized in all economic activities, except: National defense processing and disposal of toxic waste of foreign origin and real estate. Direct foreign investment on sea and air transport insurance; and on financial and banking entities has special regulations. Companies are classified as follows: (a) National company where more than 80% of its capital belongs to national investors; (b) mixed company where between 51% and 80% of its capital belongs to national investors; (c) foreign company where less than 51% of its capital belongs to national investors.

Direct foreign investment is authorized for establishment of branches by foreign companies. It is also authorized to participate in existing national or mixed companies to increase their capital. Foreign investors can acquire shares or equity held by national investors. Investment of individual foreign persons with legal residence in country may be considered national investment if they comply with special requirements, including declaration waiving their rights to repatriate capital and remit profits abroad. Direct foreign investment related to mining and to hydrocarbons requires authorization of Ministry of Mines and Energy. Foreign investors may invest in exploration and exploitation of hydrocarbons and in projects involving refining, transportation and distribution of hydrocarbons or in services inherent to hydrocarbons sector under special regulations. Foreign oil companies need not bring into country foreign currency earned in export of crude oil, except when required to pay their own expenses.

Foreign investors may acquire shares, quotas or bonds convertible in shares (bonos convertibles en acciones) of Colombian financial institutions (primarily banks, financial corporations, savings and housing corporations, leasing corporations, general deposit warehouses, insurance and reinsurance companies and trust companies). Any acquisition in one or more steps of 10% or more of subscribed shares of any financial institution requires prior approval of Superintendente Bancario.

Incorporation or organization of any financial institution by foreign investors also requires approval of Superintendencia Bancaria.

Foreign investors may invest through investment funds of foreign capital organized either in Colombia or abroad with subscriptions of either foreign individuals or entities for purpose of investing in stock market.

Investment Funds are authorized to invest in: (i) shares or bonds convertible into shares of Colombian companies, or of entities in which country or Fondo de Garantías de Instituciones Financieras participates; (ii) bonds issued by national companies, by country, its departments, municipalities, special districts and decentralized entities, paper issued by Fondo Nacional del Café, paper or securities issued or guaranteed by Colombian financial institutions which are subject to Superintendencia Bancaria, in latter case foreign investment is limited to 20% of total registered investment; and (iii) any other paper or securities authorized by Comisión Nacional de Valores. Investment funds may not invest in 10% or more of company's outstanding shares.

Repatriation of investments and of profits of investments in oil and financial sectors (except for foreign oil companies entitled to export crude) or through Investment Funds, is subject to rules applicable to foreign investment in general.

Foreign investors are entitled to re-export their invested capital plus any capital gains when they sell their shares, participations or rights to national investors or when company is liquidated. Sales of shares, participations or rights to another foreign investor must be registered at Banco de la República. Foreign investors must register their original investments, capitalizations and reinvestments with Banco de la República within three months from moment investment was made. Yearly profits may be remitted abroad in foreign currency.

Free Trade Zones.—(Law 109 of Dec. 12, 1985, Decree 2131 of Sept. 13, 1991 as am'd; Decrees 971 of May 31, 1993 and 2480 of Dec. 13, 1993; Law 9 of Jan. 17, 1991). Any national or foreign, natural or legal entity may operate in free zones privately administered by authorization of Ministry of Foreign Trade. There are three types of free industrial zones, for goods and services, for services and for technological services. All goods or raw materials entering free zone are exempt from any national, state or municipal tax, including consular duty. Foreign goods in transit may be reexported subject to Customs Code regulations. Merchandise previously brought into Colombian territory other than free zone whi ch has been manufactured or processed using national or imported materials from within or without free zone and which is then passed through free zone for exportation, must be covered by export license. Likewise, merchandise passed through free zone for importation into Colombia is subject to all importation requirements. Assembly of products for importation into Colombia is subject to special regulations whereas assembly of products for exportation, except those mentioned above, is unrestricted. Merchandise or products from Colombia which have been deposited in free zone and which have not been processed or transformed can be freely brought back into country. Profits of foreign investment in free zones can be remitted abroad without limitation, except when legislation is applied to free zones. Profits derived from operation within free zone are exempted from income taxes.

FOREIGN TRADE REGULATIONS:

See topic Exchange Control.

FRAUDS, STATUTE OF:

See topic Public Instruments.

FRAUDULENT SALES AND CONVEYANCES:

In cases of bankruptcy following acts and contracts of bankrupt may be annulled: (1) Acts relating to his property executed after declaration of bankruptcy; (2) acts executed within six months before cessation of payments to injury of creditors, if connivance between parties is proved; (3) following acts executed after cessation of payments; (a) gifts after such cessation or one year prior thereto, (b) payment of unmatured debts, (c) payment of matured debts otherwise than with money or commercial effects, (d) contracts with wife, partner, or relatives in second degree of affinity or fourth of consanguinity, (e) contracts of partnership, or fusion or alienation of mercantile establishments, (f) security bonds, (g) any acts of ownership or administration if other contracting party knew of cessation of payments. In general, contracts made in bad faith to prejudice of creditors may be set aside within one year. (C. Com. 1965-1972).

HOLIDAYS:

Jan. 1 (New Year's); Jan. 6 (Epiphany); Mar. 19 (St. Joseph); Maundy Thursday*; Good Friday*; May 1 (Labor Day); Ascension Day*; Corpus Christi*; Sacred Heart*; June 29 (SS. Peter and Paul); July 20 (Independence Day); Aug. 7 (Battle of Boyacá); Aug. 15 (Assumption); Oct. 12 (Columbus Day); Nov. 1 (All Saints); Nov. 11 (Independence of Cartagena); Dec. 8 (Immaculate Conception); Dec. 25 (Christmas).

* These are movable holidays.

HOMESTEADS:

A homestead may be constituted on unencumbered real estate not exceeding value fixed by law. It may be constituted in favor of (a) family composed of husband and wife with or without minor children, or (b) minor or two or more minors related in second degree of consanguinity. It is subject to attachment only by institutions financing its purchase; it cannot be mortgaged nor can it be sold with right of repurchase. (Law 70 of 1931; Law 91 of 1936; Law 9 of Jan. 11, 1989 as am'd).

HUSBAND AND WIFE:

(Const. Arts. 42 and 43; C. C. 176-212, 1771-1841).

Except for just cause, husband and wife are obliged to live together and mutually help each other.

Each spouse has the free administration and disposal of the property owned by such spouse when contracting the marriage and of all property acquired by such spouse during the marriage; but on dissolution of the marriage, or in any case in which according to the rules of the Civil Code a liquidation of community property is to be made, the spouses are considered as having been governed by the system of community property, and a liquidation is made accordingly.

Each spouse is liable for debts personally contracted, except debts made for the ordinary needs of the household or the support, education or establishment of the children, as to which the spouses are jointly liable to third persons and proportionately to each other.

Irrevocable gifts between the spouses are void, as well as contracts relating to real property, except the contract of general or special agency.

See Topical Index in front part of this volume.

HUSBAND AND WIFE . . . *continued*
Property acquired by common law spouses during time they live together as indicated by law is governed by community property system. (Law 54 of Dec. 28, 1990).

INCOME TAX: See topic Taxation.

INFANCY:

(C. C. Arts. 34, 250-268, 288-317, 339-345, 428-632, 1504, 1527, 1740-1741).

Age of majority is 18, but minor may be emancipated by his parents, or by marriage, and in certain cases by judicial decree. Contracts by males under 14 or females under 12 are void, and contracts by minors over those ages are voidable, except some by emancipated minors. Parental authority includes legal representation and administration and enjoyment of usufruct of infant's property, with some exceptions.

Law 75 of Dec. 30, 1968, has amended prior laws on filiation. Law is generally more favorable to infants as to presumptions of legitimacy, investigations of paternity, paternal recognition, support and rights of succession. Penal sanctions are provided to enforce child's right to proper care and support. Law 75 also created new public entity, Colombian Institute of Family Welfare (Instituto Colombiano de Bienestar Familiar), for protection of minors and promotion of stability and general welfare of Colombian families. Institute will administer all appropriations which are allocated to those purposes and has power to pass such resolutions as are necessary to carry out its programs.

Decree 2737 of Nov. 29, 1989 regulates adoption. Decree 2263 of Oct. 4, 1991 regulates authorization and operation of institutions for adoption. (See topic Descent and Distribution.)

INHERITANCE TAX: See topic Taxation.

INSOLVENCY:

See topic Bankruptcy and Insolvency.

INTEREST:

Legal rate is 6% but the parties may agree on any other rate. However, if the rate agreed upon exceeds by one-half the rate current at the time of the loan, the judge may reduce it to the current rate. Compound interest is prohibited. (C. C. 1617, 2231, 2235).

In commercial matters, parties may fix rate of interest for term of obligation, but rate cannot exceed current banking rate. This rate applies in absence of agreed rate. Interest on overdue amounts may not exceed twice the banking rate. This rate applies in absence of agreed rate. (C. Com. 884). Compound interest is prohibited except after one year of interest is overdue, and then only after an action is commenced, or by agreement of parties entered after maturity. (C. Com. 886).

INTESTACY:

See topic Descent and Distribution.

JUDGMENTS:

(C. P. C. 302-339, 693-697).

Final judgments rendered in a litigation are considered "res judicata," provided that new litigation is based upon same issue and cause of action as former, and that legal identity of parties is same in both litigations.

Foreign judgments have the force provided by treaty or, in the absence of treaty provisions, the force which in the foreign country is given to Colombian judgments. If the courts of the foreign country refuse to carry out Colombian judgments, the judgments of that country have no force in Colombia. If the judgment is comprised among those valid in Colombia according to the foregoing rule it will be enforced if: (1) It was rendered in a personal action; (2) it does not affect Colombian jurisdiction and is not contrary to public order or good customs; (3) it was duly rendered and is not subject to appeal in the country where it was rendered and its authenticity is proved by certificates of the Departments of Foreign Affairs of the foreign country and of Colombia.

LEGISLATURE:

The Colombian Congress meets annually on July 20. It may be called in special session by the Government. (Const., Art. 147).

See also topic Constitution and Government.

LIENS:

Credits are divided into five classes: (1) Those for judicial costs in matters favoring all creditors, necessary funeral expenses, expenses of last sickness to an amount under the control of the judge, salaries deriving from labor contracts, maintenance of the debtor and family for the last three months to an amount under the control of the judge, national and municipal taxes; (2) those of innkeepers, carriers and pledgees, which are liens on the property brought by the guest into the inn and the articles carried or pledged; (3) those of mortgage creditors, which are liens on the property mortgaged; (4) those of the Government against tax collectors and administrators, of municipalities and public charitable and educational institutions against collectors and administrators of their funds, of a married woman for her property administered by the husband as against his property, and of children and wards for their property administered by parents, guardians or curators as against the properties of such persons; and (5) those of common creditors.

The credits of the first, second and fourth class are considered preferred. Those of the second and third class constitute a lien on the specific properties to which they refer. In case of insolvency, however, those of the first class are preferred to all others if the other property of the debtor is not sufficient to pay them.

In commercial matters the consignee has a lien similar to that of the carrier against the articles received by him. Likewise in maritime matters the provisions of law relating to average designate the classes of credits which constitute a lien against the vessel. (C. C. 2488-2511; C. Com. 981-1035; 1555-1569).

Mechanics' Liens.—There are no special provisions corresponding to mechanics' liens in the United States of America.

LIMITATION OF ACTIONS:

See topic Prescription.

LIMITED LIABILITY COMPANIES:

See topic Partnership.

LIMITED PARTNERSHIP:

See topic Partnership, subhead Limited Partnership.

MARRIAGE:

(Const. Art. 42).

Marriage may be either by religious ceremony or by civil ceremony. Either party can be represented by special agent appointed by public deed before notary public. (Law 57 of Dec. 28, 1990). If by religious ceremony capacity of parties is determined by canon law. Religious marriages can be annulled only by religious courts whose judgments in such matters produce civil effects.

Males and females above 18 may marry by civil ceremony; if below that age they require consent of their parents or guardians. Ceremony is performed after an edict has been posted for 15 days.

Civil marriages are null in the following cases: (1) Error as to the person, but this can be alleged only by the party suffering the error and provided such party does not continue marital life after learning thereof; (2) age less than 14 in the male and 12 in the female; (3) lack of consent; (4) duress, to be alleged by the party suffering the same; (5) marriage between an adulteress and her accomplice if adultery was proved in court; (6) if one of the parties killed former spouse; (7) relationship by consanguinity in direct line or by affinity in first degree of direct line; (8) between brothers and sisters; (9) between adopter or wife and person adopted; (10) existing marriage; (11) if not performed before judge and witnesses. The nullity of religious marriages is determined by canon law.

Marriages between a guardian or his descendants and his ward are forbidden before the ward reaches 18 years unless the accounts of the guardianship have been approved and likewise marriages of a widower unless an inventory has been made of the property which his children inherited from their mother. (C. C. 110-151).

Aliens may be married by the diplomatic agent or consul of their country. (Law 266 of 1938).

MARRIED WOMEN:

See topics Executors and Administrators; Husband and Wife; Marriage.

MECHANICS' LIENS:

No special provision.

MINES AND MINERALS:

(Const. Arts. 332 and 360).

(Mining Code D. 2655 of Dec. 23, 1988 regulated by Decree 136 of Jan. 15, 1990, Decrees 01 of Jan. 4, 1993, 137 of Jan. 22, 1993 and 501 of Mar. 24, 1995).

Mining Code governs all mining related activities of nonrenewable natural resources located on surface or underneath, either inland or offshore except hydrocarbons.

All natural resources in surface or underneath belong to State which may undertake exploration and exploitation by itself or grant licenses or concession contracts related to such activities to private parties.

Mining activity is regarded as being of public interest. All individuals or juridical persons, domestic or foreign with legal capacity may obtain exploration or exploitation licenses or enter into concession contracts. However, foreign governments are by themselves excepted from abovesaid rule. Foreign governments may engage in mining activities through private companies in which they have an economic interest, provided such companies waive diplomatic protection. Foreign juridical persons must establish branch if they want to be permanently engaged in mining activities or appoint agent when activities are occasional. Exploration and exploitation rights may be transferred and encumbered to secure mining credits. Such rights are not inheritable but heirs enjoy preferential right to acquire same. Mining rights can be relinquished at any time and owners can withdraw from exploitation facilities all equipment, machinery and tools except when relinquishing is after 20 years of date of registration of title or in large mining ventures. Buildings and installations permanently adhered to land must be left in all instances, except when withdrawable without damaging facilities.

Preliminary surface exploration is free except to restricted areas. Law distinguishes mining ventures according to volume of minerals extracted during determined period of time as small, medium and large. Annual extraction volume allowable to small, medium and large mining ventures is geared to four different groups of minerals: Metals and precious stones, coal, construction materials and others.

Exploration and Exploitation Licenses.—Exploration license is granted for term that goes from one to five years, depending on size of area to be explored. Terms of one and two years may be extended one year. Area allocated for each license goes from 100 to 5,000 hectares. Small mining ventures licensees must file final report of activities and investments and working program. Medium and large mining ventures licensees must file report of activities performed once a year in addition to final report and investment and working program. Ministry should grant exploitation license for small mining activities or execute contract for medium and large mining activities upon expiration of exploration license and submission of final report and investment and working program.

Exploitation license is registered ten days after environmental license is issued. Exploitation license is granted for up to ten years from date of registration. Exploitation license may be extended once, extension is granted for same term as original one.

Mining Contracts.—Can be executed by Ministry of Mines and Energy or by decentralized agencies of said Ministry. Contracts executed by Ministry of Mines and Energy are concession contracts. All other contracts are executed by decentralized

MINES AND MINERALS . . . *continued*

agencies. Concession contracts grant concessionaire exclusive right to extract minerals specifically indicated in contract as well as minerals mixed therewith. Concession contract is registered ten days after environmental license is issued. Term of contract is 30 years from registration date. Concessionaires must establish pledge, bank or insurance guaranty in favor of government for 10% of estimated production for first two years.

Code establishes causes for cancellation of licenses and termination of concession contracts. Fines may also be imposed in certain cases.

Decentralized agencies may execute exploration and exploitation contracts with contractors either directly or by public bid. Prior authorization of Ministry of Mines and Energy is required for contracts involving large mining ventures. Decentralized agencies may also carry out exploration and exploitation activities through joint ventures with private parties.

Exploration and exploitation activities involving radioactive substances, coal, semi-precious and precious stones can only be carried out by decentralized agencies by themselves. Decentralized agencies may contract services of private parties to carry out such activities.

Exploration and exploitation activities in beaches and jurisdictional maritime areas can only be made by Ministry and decentralized agencies may contract services of private parties for such purpose.

Exploration and exploitation activities may be made through companies, corporations or "cooperativas" formed under Commercial Code or under rules of Mining Code. Holder of mining rights must prioritarily supply local market with exploited mining products; buy locally manufactured machinery, equipment and materials; and contract locally technical assistance. Colombian employees must share in at least 70% of total amount paid to specialized or qualified personnel and in at least 80% of total amount paid to blue collar personnel. Law indicates titles, licenses, contracts and liens related to mining activities which must be registered with Mining Registry.

State is entitled to receive from persons enjoying mining rights several economic benefits: (i) In large mining ventures exploration licensees must pay annually minimum daily wage for each hectare. Payment must be made in advance every year; (ii) exploitation of precious metals is subject to 3% of gross product, paid in kind or its equivalent in Colombian Pesos or in U.S. dollars, at election of Government. For non-precious metals royalty is 3% of sales price of raw mineral at pit or at market, provided year output is more than 100,000 tons; if less, no royalty applies. Exploitation of emeralds is governed by Arts. 1 to 7 of Decree 1244 of July 8, 1974 which levies 15% tax on gross value of production of private emerald mines. Exploitation of gold is subject to royalty of 3% on troy ounce price paid by Banco de la República. Exploitation of platinum is subject to royalty of 4% on price paid by abovesaid Banco; (iii) industrial and commercial companies of State are entitled to receive "participationes" (shares) deriving from exploration and exploitation contracts they execute; and (iv) other specific taxes assessed under special laws in connection with certain minerals.

Exemption of import duties on machinery, technical equipment, materials and spare parts imported by persons enjoying mining rights to be used in exploration, exploitation or transformation of minerals or for substitution of hydrocarbons by coal is granted. Likewise, exemption of import duties on capital goods to be used in exploitation of small gold mining ventures is granted.

Mining Code contains several provisions to protect workers involved in this activity.

Petroleum.—Under Decree 1056 of Apr. 20, 1953 (Petroleum Code) as am'd, and Law 20 of Dec. 22, 1969, regulated by Decree 1994 of Sept. 4, 1989, special concession contracts were made with Government for petroleum exploration and exploitation in lands where Government owns mineral deposits.

Decree 2310 of Oct. 28, 1974 ratified by Decree 896 of May 14, 1975 ended system of granting especial concession contracts to national or foreign individuals or corporations for exploration and exploitation of state-owned petroleum deposits. Any such contract still in force on Oct. 28, 1974 shall continue so until expiration, but from that date on, Empresa Colombiana de Petróleos shall carry on said explorations and exploitations by itself or through third parties under service, joint venture or other contracts under terms and conditions agreed.

Conservation.—To prevent waste of resources and environmental pollution, Decree 1895 of Sept. 15, 1973 established extensive technical safeguards of mandatory observance in exploration and exploitation of petroleum and gas. In respect to certain operations, concessionaires must obtain special permit and file frequent reports in official agencies. Heavy fines are imposed for infringement of these regulations.

Surface Tax.—During exploration and exploitation periods an annual surface tax is payable. During period of exploitation surface tax is same rate paid during last year of exploration by concessionaire. Surface tax is payable for whole extension of mine even though part of it belongs to private owner.

Royalties.—On production of petroleum or of natural gas in lands where Government owns minerals, royalties are payable in money or in kind.

Portions surrendered to Government at expiration of first year of exploitation, or lost by failure to pay royalties or taxes, or by renunciation or termination before 20 years of exploitation, are to be sold by Government to best bidder.

MONOPOLIES AND RESTRAINT OF TRADE:

(Const. Art. 336, Law 155 of Dec. 24, 1959 as am'd, Decree 3236 of 1962, Decree 1302 of June 1, 1964, Decree 2444 of Oct. 17, 1990, Decree 809 of Apr. 21, 1994, Decree 299 of Feb. 10, 1995, Law 256 of Jan. 15, 1996).

National Constitution provides that no monopoly may be established except as arbitrio rentistico (that is, one which produces revenue for State) and by virtue of law. No law which establishes monopoly shall be enforced until full conpensation has been paid to individuals who are thereby deprived of operation of lawful industry. Constitution also states that only privileges that may be granted are those relating to useful inventions and to means of communications.

Most important monopolies of State are postal service, telecommunications, and radio broadcasting.

Law 155 of Dec. 24, 1959 enacted certain provisions containing limitations and prohibitions against restrictive commercial practices. Art. 1 prohibits any agreement or convention which is directly or indirectly aimed at limiting production, supply, distribution, or consumption of domestic or foreign raw materials, products, commodities or services, and in general any practices, procedures, or systems tending to limit free competition, for purpose of fixing or maintaining inequitable prices to detriment of consumers and of producers of raw materials.

Government, however, may authorize signing of agreements or conventions which in spite of their limiting free competition are for purpose of protecting stability of basic sector of production of goods or services important to general economy.

Enterprises which produce, supply, distribute, or consume specific article or service and which have capacity to determine market prices due to quantity of respective article or service they control, shall be subject to supervision by State under provisions of this law. Government may intervene in fixing standards for weights and measures, quality, packing and classification of products, raw materials, and articles or commodities, with view to protecting interests of consumers and producers of raw materials.

Enterprises engaging in same producing, supplying, distributing or consuming activity in relation to given article, raw material, product, commodity, or service whose individual or joint assets amount to 20,000,000 pesos or more are required to report to Government operations they intend to carry out with respect to mergers, consolidation, or integration, regardless of form this shall take. Government, on recommendation of National Council on Economic Policy and Planning, shall oppose such operations if they would tend to produce undue restriction of free competition. If Government has not submitted its objection within 30 days after information was presented by enterprise concerned, operation may be undertaken.

Industrial enterprises which establish or which have already established direct distribution systems for their products or through independent or affiliated commercial enterprises may not sell their articles, goods, or products by procedures involving unfair competition against independent merchants selling same articles or products.

Commercial enterprises may not employ practices, procedures, or systems that tend to monopolize distribution, or engage in unfair competition to prejudice of other merchants.

Whenever industrial enterprise fixes sales prices to public, neither that enterprise, directly or through branches or distributors, nor independent merchants may sell at prices different from those fixed by producer, under penalty of incurring punishments prescribed for cases of unfair competition.

Law defines unfair competition as any act contrary to commercial good faith or honest and normal conduct of industrial, commercial, artisan, or agricultural activities.

Acts of unfair competition include any that are defined as such in international treaties and conventions, and particularly following: (a) Methods or systems designed to create confusion with competitor, his commercial establishment or his products or services; (b) methods or systems designed to discredit competitor, his commercial establishments, or his products or services; (c) methods or systems designed to disorganize competitive enterprise or to obtain its trade secrets; (d) methods or systems designed to drive away customers from competitor by acts other than normal and fair application of law of supply and demand; (e) methods or systems designed to create general disorganization of market; (f) false indications of origin or of quality and mention of false honors, prizes or medals; (g) engaging in activities of same kind as enterprise to which they belong, by partners, directors, and employees if such activities are detrimental to enterprise because they are contrary to good faith or to honest and normal conduct of business in market.

Any damages caused to third parties by practices, procedures, or systems prohibited by this law or by acts of unfair competition give right to legal action in regular courts.

Ministry of Development, directly or upon denouncement by any person, may ask Superintendency of Banks, Superintendency of Corporations, or Superintendency of Cooperatives to investigate violations of law. In event that enterprise is not subject to control of any of foregoing agencies, investigation will be conducted by Ministry of Development. Denouncement must be accepted by Ministry if reasons are duly presented, accompanied by summary evidence. Investigation shall be strictly confidential but may make use of reports on production, importations, use of domestic and foreign raw materials, and distribution and sales systems.

Investigated enterprise will be given period up to 30 days in which to answer charges, after which Ministry of Development will render its decision. With recommendation of Council on Economic Policy and Planning, penalties imposed may be withdrawal of shares from public securities market, or in event of repetition of offense, prohibition against operating. In addition, fine may be imposed, according to seriousness of offense. Appeal may be taken to Ministry itself, after which administrative channels are exhausted.

State may also adopt following measures: (a) Fix peremptory period by which prohibited practices, procedures or systems must cease; (b) subject enterprise whose practices are investigated to supervision by pertinent agency entrusted with control, for specified time, with respect to policies of production, costs, distribution and prices, and solely for purpose of ascertaining that enterprise does not continue restrictive commercial practices that brought about investigation.

All agreements, conventions or operations prohibited by Law No. 155 are absolutely void as having unlawful purpose.

Decree on unfair foreign trade practices protects local production from unfair practices of international trade imposing countervailing duties on import of foreign goods. Dumping and subvention are considered unfair practices. Dumping is defined as import of foreign goods at lower price than normal price in place of origin, and subvention as direct or indirect incentives, subsidies, premiums or assistance of any kind granted by foreign governments to producers, manufacturers, or exporters of goods. Decree on antidumping and compensatory duties contains regulations and administrative procedure in conformity with Agreement on Implementation of Article VI of General Agreement on Tariffs and Trade.

Protective measures on importation of products may be issued to protect local production of same or similar products, as indicated by law.

Consumer Protection Law.—Colombia also has law on Consumer Protection. (Law 73 of Dec. 3, 1981 and its regulations). In accordance with such law, Government has right to control production, distribution and sale of services and goods in defense of consumers.

See topic Foreign Investments.

MORTGAGES:

(C. C. 653, 662, 2432-2457; Law 52 of 1920; C. P. C. 554-560).

Mortgages must be executed before a notary in the form of public instrument (q.v.) and recorded in the mortgage registry. Their date and effect are counted only from the day of recording. They must describe the property in detail. Each party must be present before the notary. Mortgages made in foreign countries on property in Colombia are valid if recorded in the proper registry in Colombia. Mortgages made in Colombia must be recorded within 90 days; those made abroad within 180 days.

Only real property possessed under ownership or usufruct title and ships can be mortgaged. The mortgage covers movable property permanently attached or belonging to the soil such as machinery, implements and animals on farms.

Mortgages are foreclosed by summary action in the manner in which judgments are executed and pledges are foreclosed. See topics Executions; Pledges.

NEGOTIABLE INSTRUMENTS:

See topic Bills and Notes.

NOTARIES PUBLIC:

Notary must be attorney and have exercised profession for certain number of years depending upon notarial categories and responsibilities. In some districts it is necessary to have been working with Public Instruments Register Office for at least four years, or to have been law professor for six or practising attorney for ten years. Notaries are appointed for five years; however, they can be re-elected indefinitely, if compliance with provisions of law are always met; they are subject to supervision by Ministry of Justice. Office is incompatible with any other public office.

Instruments executed before notaries require certain formalities. Original instrument is written and signed in record book (protocolo) of notary which is retained by him as a permanent record; however, from time to time these records are sent for definitive filing in official office. Detailed system of indexes also has to be kept. Notaries must issue to parties formal certified copies (testimonios) which have effect of originals and may be presented in court. (Decrees 960 of June 20, 1970 as am'd by Decree 2163 of 1970 and Law 29 of 1973, 1250 of July 27, 1970, 1024 of Apr. 15, 1982, Decree 2148 of Aug. 1, 1983 as am'd by Decree 231 of Jan. 24, 1985, and Decree 3047 of Dec. 29, 1989).

PARTITION: See topic Real Property.

PARTNERSHIP:

Partnerships are considered legal entities. Before a mercantile partnership can do business partnership agreement must be drawn up in a public instrument executed before a notary. An extract therefrom, certified by notary, must be filed with Chamber of Commerce, recorded in local registry office and published in a newspaper in localities where partnership is to do business.

General Partnership ("Sociedad Colectiva," C. Com. 294-322).—Partners are jointly and unlimitedly liable for company's obligations; any agreement to contrary is void; however, partners are only liable to company's creditors after payment has been demanded from company and it has refused to pay.

Any type of companies and/or corporations, can be members of partnerships, if so decided with unanimous approval of members or in shareholders' meetings.

Any partner must request express authorization from his co-partners if he wishes to total or partially assign his interest in firm; to delegate to third party his rights to administer and/or to control company; to establish under his own name or by means of an agent, same type of business as partnership; and if he wishes to be a member or a shareholder in companies or corporations doing same type of business as partnership. Code contemplates specific sanctions in case of violation of obligations mentioned above.

Firm name can have name of one of partners followed by "and company," "brothers," "and sons" or any other similar expression to indicate that it is a partnership. If third person allows his name to be used in that manner, he is liable to creditors as if he were a partner. In case of death of a partner whose name has appeared in firm name, his heirs can continue using it, if after that, following words are included "and heirs."

All partners are allowed to administer company. However, they can delegate such function to other partners or even to third parties; in such case partners who have delegated such function cannot intervene in company's administration. Administration of company implies faculty to do all type of business in company's name if related to its purposes. Each partner is allowed to have one vote; therefore, assignment of parts of interest, administration, admission of new partners, as well as any other type of amendments to its rules shall be possible if unanimous consent of partners is given, unless otherwise provided in its statutes. Special causes for dissolution are: Death of one or more of partners (if company cannot continue with his heirs or with remaining partners), incapacity, bankruptcy, sale of interest, and resignation of partners, or if other partners do not wish to continue operations.

Limited Partnership ("Sociedad en Comandita," C. Com. 323-342).—In this partnership, one or more partners are subject to unlimited liability for partnership's obligations, and one or more partners are only responsible up to amount of capital subscribed, or contributed to company. Name of special or limited partner cannot appear in firm's name. Firm name is generally followed by words "sociedad en comandita" or its abbreviation "S. en C.". Special partners have no participation in management of company, although can attend meetings and express opinion.

Limited Partnership Issuing Shares ("Sociedad en Comandita por Acciones," C. Com. 343-352).—This type of company is unknown in American law. It has characteristics of general partnership regarding those partners who are jointly liable for company's obligations, and it is similar to corporations as to those special partners whose contributions are represented by shares. Company cannot do business with less than five shareholders. Capital of company must be represented by shares of equal value, and shares must be registered until they have been totally paid in. When company is formed, at least 50% of shares representing authorized capital must be paid in and at least one-third of value of each share must also be paid in. It is forbidden to state authorized capital without also announcing subscribed and paid-in capital. In many cases, in shareholders' meetings, rules established for corporations must be followed. However, decisions must be taken by unanimous vote of general partners and by majority of votes representing shares of special partners. A "reserve fund" must be created which shall be at least 50% of subscribed capital, and at least 10% of net profits of each fiscal year must be set aside in order to integrate it. Once 50% of said subscribed capital has been reached, company does not have to continue increasing it; if it diminishes, same procedure must be followed until reserve fund receives necessary amount. If 50% of subscribed capital is lost, company must be dissolved.

Limited Liability Company ("Sociedad de Responsabilidad Limitada," C. Com. 353-372).—Members are only liable up to amount of their contribution to company. However, in bylaws it can be stipulated that all or some members shall have greater liability or other type of consideration or additional guarantee, if nature, amount, duration, etc. are specified. Capital must be paid in toto when company is formed. It shall be divided into shares "of equal value" which can be assigned if conditions required in law or bylaws are fulfilled. Members are jointly liable if contributions are given in species. Members cannot exceed 25 in number; otherwise company is void. However, if during its existence number of members exceeds 25, within two months following that fact, it can be transformed into other type of company, or otherwise its members have to be reduced. Name of company must be followed by word "Limited," or "Ltda"; in absence of such requisite, members shall be jointly liable to third parties. Administration of company belongs to all and each one of its members who, aside from general rights and duties attributable to board of directors and/or shareholders' meetings, must undertake: To decide admission of new members as well as assignments of quotas; to decide exclusion of members; to demand from them additional consideration if necessary; to start proceedings against administrators or other officers of company, regarding nonfulfillment of their obligations towards it; and finally, to elect and to remove officers. In members meetings each member must have as many votes as quotas he holds in company. Decisions must be taken by plural number of members representing majority of quotas into which capital of company is divided. (By-laws can provide for greater majority.) Company must keep book of members, registered in Chambers of Commerce, in which shall be set forth names, nationality, domicile, identification documents and number of quotas that each member holds, as well as attachments, liens, and assignments of quotas. Members may assign their quotas; any stipulation to contrary is void.

Civil partnership ("sociedad civil", C.C. 2079-2141) is a partnership not formed for commercial purposes. A civil partnership may have form of an unlimited or limited partnership or of a corporation. Such partnerships are governed by rules of Civil Code and are distinguished from a commercial company by being regarded rather as an association of individuals; thus an obligation assumed by an unlimited civil partnership does not render partners jointly liable unless they have all subscribed to it in person or by attorney in fact.

PATENTS:

(Const. Arts. 150, §24, and 189, §27, C. Com. 539-582, Res. 0582 of Mar. 30, 1990; Decisions 344 and 345 of Oct 29, 1993 of Cartagena Commission, and Decrees 117 of Jan. 14, 1994, 533 of Mar. 8, 1994 and 2285 of Dec. 22, 1995).

Patents.—Any invention of products or proceedings in any technology field which are novel, represent inventive step and are susceptible of industrial application. Invention is novel when it is not within state of art.

Among others, discoveries, scientific theories and mathematical methods; scientific, literary and artistic works; therapeutic, surgical and diagnostic methods are not considered inventions. Inventions contrary to public policy, morals and against environment; on animal species and races and biological procedures to obtain them; inventions related to pharmaceutical products listed by World Health Organization as essential medicines; and related to substances composing human body are not patentable.

Petition must contain following: Personal information of petitioner; name of invention and complete description of it, accompanied by drawings and symbols or words, if that is the case, plus statement defining purpose and use of invention. Patent is granted to person that first petitions for it or to his heirs; if several persons have invented or discovered it, right is granted to all in common. In case petitioner is domiciled outside Colombia, petition must be accompanied by power of attorney. Patent owner must exploit it, directly or by granting license in any country member of Andean Pact. Industrial production or importation, distribution and commercialization of patented product, are considered exploitation of patent. Applications for foreign patents should be filed within one year after filing of application in first country. First patent application filed in any Andean Group Country gives priority right during one year in order to file in any other member country.

Patents are granted for 20 years from filing date.

Petitioner or owner of a patent can grant to third persons a license to exploit such invention by means of a written agreement called "contractual license." Compulsory licenses must also be granted in cases indicated by law. Either owner of patent, or licensee can start all necessary judicial proceedings for protection of rights granted by patent, including criminal proceedings in case of unauthorized use or usurpation by third parties.

Utility models for new forms of objects or mechanism, provided they have practical use, are registrable. Registration term is ten years from filing date.

Industrial designs are registrable if new. Registration confers right of exclusive use for eight years, nonrenewable. Applications are published and oppositions can be filed.

Decree 259 of Feb. 12, 1992 regulates trademark, patents and other transfer of technology contracts.

Trade Secrets.—Law also protects trade secrets and considers them as any confidential information that is valuable related to nature, characteristics or purposes of products, production methods or processes, distribution, commercialization of products or rendering of services that provides competitive or economic advantages to owner. Information considered trade secret must be expressed in tangible form such as documents, microfilm films, laser discs or any other similar means.

Vegetal species are protected when they are novel, homogeneous, distinguishable and stable and generic designation has been assigned to them. When registered certificate of holder is issued for 15 and 20 years, depending on type of vegetal variety.

See Topical Index in front part of this volume.

PATENTS . . . *continued*

See also topics Trademarks and Tradenames; Exchange Control, subhead Foreign Capital Investments.

PERPETUITIES:

Property cannot be prevented from vesting for a period exceeding 30 years, unless death of beneficiary be event which is to terminate period. (C. C. 800, 829, 1145).

PLEDGES:

(C. C. 2409-2431; C. P. C. 554-560).

A pledge requires delivery of pledged property to creditor.

Pledges are foreclosed by summary action in manner in which judgments are executed. If there is no sale, a new valuation is made and same procedure is followed; if no bid is received creditor may demand an award of a participation in property up to amount of his credit. See topic Executions.

Under C. Com. 1200-1220 all types of chattels can be object of commercial pledges which can be executed with or without delivery of them to creditor.

Pledge with delivery of chattels is considered concluded from agreement of parties, but creditor will have his lien on personal property when it is delivered to him or to a third person designated by parties. If not delivered to creditor, he can judicially request specific performance. Once chattel has been given in pledge, same cannot be object of a second one, until former has been totally paid. Debtor must reimburse creditor, or third party for all expenses that storage of goods demands. Statute of limitations is four years which runs from time obligation accrued.

Other type of pledge allows debtor to keep possession of chattels, when used in an economic exploitation and necessary for it. Document in which this pledge is recorded must contain at least following: Name and domicile of debtor and creditor, date, nature and value of obligation being guaranteed plus interest if any, date of maturity and information regarding chattels given in pledge, such as brands, models, numbers, quantity, in case of machinery; and quantity, sex, race, and weight in case of animals; and quality, quantity, etc. in case of seeds, fruits or crops; place in which goods are kept and indication and value of insurance contracts, if any. Contract must be recorded in commercial registry of place in which chattels are kept; pledges regarding motor vehicles are governed by special regulations. Debtor, who is allowed to keep goods has same obligations and responsibilities of a bailee. Statute of limitations is two years and runs from time obligation accrued.

PRESCRIPTION:

(C. C. 2512-2545; and several articles of C. Com.).

Acquisition of property or rights by virtue of possession and extinction of obligations by failure to require performance is called prescription. Prescription may be expressly or tacitly waived as far as it has run but no waiver can be made of future prescriptive periods.

In order to acquire by prescription, possession must be uninterrupted. Natural interruption exists: (1) When possession of property becomes impossible by a natural cause, as by inundation, in which case period of interruption is deducted; or (2) when a third person enters upon property, in which case entire previous prescriptive period is not counted unless possession is regained by legal proceedings. Civil interruption is produced by judicial demand.

Against a title recorded in registry of property prescriptive period does not run except by virtue of another recorded title. Ordinary prescriptive period as against persons living in Colombia is ten years for real property and three years for personal property; as against persons living in foreign countries these periods are doubled. Prescriptive period is suspended in favor of persons who are minors, demented, deaf and dumb, wards, and in favor of estates while there is no executor or known heir; it is always suspended between spouses.

Real property can be acquired by extraordinary prescription by possession for twenty years. In such case no title need be shown and there are no suspensions in behalf of incapacitated persons.

Actions.—Prescriptive periods in which right to enforce an obligation is lost vary according to nature of action. More important are: (1) Actions to recover an inheritance, 20 years; (2) ordinary suits on rights of action in which no special period is fixed, 20 years; (3) executory actions in which no special period is fixed, ten years; (4) actions based on marine loans, three years; (5) actions to annual or rescind contracts in which a legal requisite is lacking, actions to enforce a right to repurchase, actions to annul sales of real estate in certain cases of disproportion of price and value, actions to recover salaries or wages of workmen or compensation for labor accidents, four years; (6) actions to recover compensation due to attorneys, physicians, teachers and other professional men, three years; (7) actions for compensation to storekeepers, artisans, innkeepers and others paid occasionally or regularly, two years; (8) actions on warranties of real property, one to one and one-half years; (9) actions based on incorrect descriptions in sales of real property, actions for advances for construction or repair of vessels and payment of their crews, one year; (10) actions on warranty of personal property, actions to recover payments due for passage money, freight and general average, six months.

Most of above periods of prescription of actions are suspended in favor of incapacitated persons but after twenty years no suspension is taken into account.

Prescription of actions is interrupted by express or tacit recognition of debt by debtor and by judicial demand.

PRINCIPAL AND AGENT:

(C. C. 2142-2199; C. Com. Arts. 331-424).

An agency may be written or verbal, but for most purposes powers of attorney should appear in public instruments executed before a notary and should be detailed and explicit regarding powers conferred. Authority of person granting same must clearly appear.

A general power of attorney merely covers acts of administration. In order to buy, alienate or encumber real estate, make compromises or perform any other act outside ordinary course of administration, power to do so must be specifically granted. An agency is not perfected until accepted, but acceptance may be express or tacit. An agent must adhere strictly to instructions of principal. He may delegate his powers if not expressly prohibited from doing so, but is liable for acts of substitute if there was no authority to make delegation or if his appointee is notoriously incompetent.

Principal must reimburse agent for his expenses, pay him stipulated or customary compensation and indemnify him for losses suffered by reason of agency. Agent may retain goods of principal as a pledge for such payments.

Powers of attorney are terminated by: (1) Expiration of the term or business for which the power was granted; (2) revocation by principal; (3) resignation of agent; (4) death, bankruptcy, insolvency or loss of civil rights of principal or agent; (5) cessation of powers of principal if agency was constituted by virtue of such powers. In case of resignation agent must continue acting for a reasonable time until principal can make other arrangements.

Under C. Com. Arts. 331-424 similar provisions are contained regarding subject. Agent undertakes to execute gratuitously or for payment, one or more commercial activities in name of principal and to report about its performance. Once agency is expressly or tacitly accepted agent must execute or else is liable for damages. Agent is responsible for safekeeping and maintenance of merchandise unless damage or loss is due to force majeure or inherent defect or merchandise. He also must spread upon record, legally, damage or loss of merchandise and inform principal about it. Agent cannot pledge merchandise to fulfill his own obligations. He may act in his own name or in name of principal, in latter case only principal is obligated with respect to third persons and when he acts through another he is liable to principal if he wrongfully selected substitute.

Commercial Agency.—In Commercial Agency, agents are as follows: (1) Purchasing agents; (2) selling agents; (3) agents of transportation; (4) agents to execute banking operations. They have corresponding obligations regulated in Code.

PUBLIC INSTRUMENTS:

A public document or instrument is written by a notary in his own record book and signed by parties. Notary issues certified copies from book. Public records, certified copies thereof and other documents issued by public officials are authentic documents. Instruments executed by private individuals and not authenticated by a notary or judge are private writings. (See topic Acknowledgments.)

Public instruments constitute full proof of fact and date of their execution and, as between parties, of facts stated therein. As towards third persons a private instrument is considered as executed only from death of one of signers or from date on which it was recorded or inventoried by a competent official or on which it was presented in court or acknowledged before a notary, or since appearance of a new fact which allows judge to be certain of its existence.

Law designates numerous acts and contracts which must appear in a public instrument, among them being facts relating to alienation or encumbrance of real property, marriage settlements, acknowledgments of children and in general all contracts which limit property rights in real estate. (C. C. 1757, 1760, 1766; D. L. 960 of June 20, 1970; C. P. C. 251-293).

REAL PROPERTY:

Real property includes articles permanently attached to realty as well as articles permanently devoted to use and cultivation of realty, such as machinery, drain pipes, mining and agricultural utensils, fertilizer, animals placed on property for its cultivation or improvement, etc. Products of real estate are considered personalty for purpose of granting rights therein.

Property may be held in common in which event each co-owner is liable for his portion of expenses and entitled to his portion of benefits. Any co-owner may ask for partition of property, which partition will preferably be made in kind unless property be of such nature that it cannot conveniently be divided. (C. C. 656-661; 2322-2340).

Condominiums are regulated by Laws 182 of Dec. 28, 1948 and 16 of Jan. 16, 1985 regulated by Decree 1365 of Apr. 28, 1986.

RECORDS: See topic Registries.

REGISTRIES:

Registry of Public Instruments (Real Property Registry) (Decree 1250 of July 27, 1970 as am'd by Decrees 2156 of Nov. 9, 1970 and 1711 of July 6, 1984, 1380 of Aug. 12, 1972 and 2773 of Dec. 31, 1973).—Following must be registered: All documents and judicial or arbitral decisions pertaining to property rights on real estate and motor vehicles (except assignment of mortgages or pledges) and documents cancelling above registrations. Decree 208 of Feb. 13, 1975, as am'd by Decree 1265 of June 30, 1975, determines that powers of attorney (general and special) and open and closed wills must also be registered in this Registry.

Registrars are semi-judicial officers who, in most cases, do not transcribe entire document but only essential details. They refuse to record document if it is not in proper form.

Registry of Civil Status (Decrees 1260 of July 27, 1970, as am'd and supplemented) for records of births, marriages, deaths, acknowledgment of children and adoption.

See also topic Commercial Register.

REDEMPTION:

See topics Executions; Mortgages.

SALES (Realty and Personalty):

(C. C. 1547; 1849-1954).

A sale is perfected and binding when the vendor and vendee have agreed upon the thing sold and the price thereof though neither has been delivered; except that the sale of real property and rights and of an inheritance is not perfect until a public instrument is executed, but this exception does not apply to the sale of trees and pending fruits, building materials, etc. The determination of the price cannot be left to one of the parties.

SALES (Realty and Personalty) . . . *continued*

The expenses of execution of the instrument of sale are divisible between the vendor and the vendee unless otherwise stipulated. In the absence of an agreement to the contrary the vendor warrants the thing sold and the title thereto; and in any case he is liable for hidden defects in the thing sold if known to him and not called to the buyer's attention. If the buyer does not pay the price at the time stipulated the seller may institute suit for the price or ask for rescission of the contract. The parties may agree that in case of nonpayment of the price the contract shall be considered rescinded but such agreement cannot extend beyond four years.

Chattels may be sold under condition that title shall not pass until payment, but if buyer alienates unpaid-for chattel his seller is limited to an action in personam against him.

In private sales of real property rescission may be asked within four years by the vendor if it is found that the price received is less than half the just value of the property, and by the buyer if the value is less than half the price paid. If a sale of real property is made at a certain price for a unit of area the vendor must, if the area is found less than that stipulated, make up the difference or refund part of the price paid; if the area is found greater the buyer must pay more; but in either case if the difference exceeds 10% the sale may be annulled.

Commercial Code (C. Com. 905-967) contains similar provisions regarding subject. Price is essential element of this contract; if parties do not stipulate it or if it is impossible to determine it, sale is void; however, if buyer receives goods it is presumed that parties agree on price effective on date and place of delivery. If parties in order to determine price agree that it must be one quoted on markets, stock exchange, or similar establishments, it is understood prices quoted on date and place of signature of contract. Seller must deliver merchandise within term agreed upon. If nothing has been stipulated on subject, merchandise must be delivered within 24 hours after signature of contract unless nature of goods requires a longer period of time for delivery.

Normally, seller guarantees that goods have been sold without hidden defects, buyer must inform seller within 30 days after discovery of same, if malfunctioning occurs within period of time covered by guarantee. In any event in absence of any special period, statute of limitations is two years which runs from date of contract. Seller must prove that buyer knew or should have known hidden defects in merchandise sold at moment of contract.

Buyer must receive goods in place stipulated in contract and may demand from seller a receipt containing indication of merchandise sold, price, conditions of payment, etc. If no objections arise against contents of bill of sale, within three days after receipt, it is understood that its provisions were accepted.

SEALS:

Seals are not used in private matters. Public instruments executed before notaries have most of effects of sealed instruments in U.S.

SEQUESTRATION:

Persons claiming personal property which is in danger of alienation or dissipation may request sequestration of same. Bond is required before order of sequestration can issue.

SHIPPING:

(C. Com. 1426-1772).

Principal provisions with regard to shipping are found in Commercial Code, and several decrees and regulations, especially Decree 994 of Apr. 29, 1966, Decree-Law 48 of 1968 and its regulations, Decree 1208 of July 21, 1969 as am'd by Decree 2324 of Sept. 18, 1984 regulated by Decrees 1423 of June 30, 1989, and 586 of Mar. 16, 1990, Decree 2451 of July 31, 1986 as am'd and Decree 2327 of Oct. 25, 1991. In National enterprises participation of foreign capital cannot exceed 40% of total amount. All acts or contracts related to ownership or mortgages must be executed in public instrument. Code divides ships into two categories, those whose tonnage exceeds 25 tons and those under that figure. All ships registered in Colombia are considered of Colombian nationality and, therefore, must carry Colombian flag. Foreign ships in Colombian ports can only be subject to attachment for credit if same was granted in country. Auction of ships has to be held according to rules of Civil Procedure Code, but auction must also be announced with notices posted on ship and in Custom House of port where same is located. All foreign ships arriving at Colombian ports must have maritime agent authorized to represent them in country. Only Colombian citizens can be owners of commercial ships registered in Colombia; ships can belong to several owners under common or joint tenancy. If maritime agent is corporation, at least 60% of its corporate capital must belong to Colombian citizens, said agent must be registered in national maritime authority and, to do so must present information on ships, sureties, and certain affidavits concerning activities to be performed.

Captain is principal authority and crew and passengers must follow his instructions. Captain is also subject to certain obligations, such as to keep registration documents, patent of navigation, certificate of navigability, list of crew, passengers as well as bills of lading and insurance documents. Code sets forth in detail regulations regarding mortgages, transportation of passengers and cargo, "charter party contracts," sales, leases of ships and insurance contracts as well.

STATUTE OF FRAUDS:

See topic Public Instruments.

STATUTES:

Legislation of Colombia is codified but codes are subject to frequent amendments. Principal codifications are Civil Code which is based on Chilean Code; Commercial Code; Fiscal Code; Penal Code; Civil Procedure Code; Mining Code; Political and Municipal Code; Labor Code; and Customs Law.

TAXATION:

Real Estate Tax (Law 44 of Dec. 18, 1990).—Municipalities are authorized to create taxes of up to 16% of cadastral value of plots.

Income Tax.—(Decrees 624 of Mar. 30, 1989 as am'd, 868 of Apr. 26, 1989 and 2075 of Dec. 23, 1992).

I. Under "Income Tax" are included: (A) Basic income tax; (B) capital gains tax; (C) remittance tax. Taxes under (B) and (C) are called "complementary taxes."

II. Taxpayers.—(1) Individuals, national or foreign, Colombian residents for more than six continuous months within taxable year, or six continuous months ending within it, and nationals who reside abroad but have their families or principal place of business in Colombia, are subject to taxes (A) and (B) (I, supra) in respect to income and capital gains from Colombian or foreign sources. Foreign nationals residing in Colombia are exempt from tax on income and capital gains from non-Colombian sources during first five years of residency. Nonresident individuals are subject to above taxes only in respect to income and capital gains from Colombian sources and to assets situated in Colombia. (See also catchline VI, Remittance Tax.)

(2) Decedents' estates, when last domicile of decedent was in Colombia, are subject to same taxes levied on individuals (supra), from decedent's death to date of distribution, in respect to personal ("muebles") property, and to date of registration in respect to real property.

(3) Other taxpayers (juridic persons) are subject to taxes (A) and (C) (I, supra). Capital gains are taxed as regular income. (a) Corporations ("sociedades anónimas"), limited liability partnerships issuing shares of stock ("comanditarias por acciones") and irregular companies with similar features, respectively, to each of above, government enterprises industrial or commercial and national mixed capital companies are subject to basic income tax (A) (I, supra) on income from Colombian or foreign sources, without prejudice of their stockholders, subscribers, quota holders, etc. paying tax on dividends or profits. (See also catchline VI, Remittance Tax.) (b) Limited liability companies ("sociedades de responsabilidad limitada"), partnerships (sociedades colectivas"), limited liability partnerships not issuing shares ("comanditarias simples"), mining ventures known as "ordinary" mining companies, irregular companies with similar features to those above, "organized communities", corporations and associations for profit and private foundations, are subject to basic income tax (A) (I, supra) on income from Colombian or foreign sources, without prejudice of their partners, quota holders, etc. paying tax on profits. (c) Foreign corporations. Unless exempt under international treaties or Colombian laws, foreign corporations and other foreign entities of any kind, are subject to basic income tax (A) (I, supra) on income from Colombian sources. For purposes of this law, term "foreign" applies to juridic persons organized under laws of foreign country and having their principal domicile abroad. (See also catchline VI, Remittance Tax.) (d) Nonprofit corporations and associations and foundation of public or social interest are taxed under special regulations.

(4) Exemptions.—State and government dependencies, local governments, municipalities, and other denominations recognized by government, are exempt from basic income tax and complementary taxes (A)-(C) (I, supra). Also exempt are, for salary received, members of foreign diplomatic and consular services and their foreign office and domestic employees, and members of international organizations who, under agreements or treaties are entitled to this exemption. However, any of above receiving income from Colombian sources or who own property in Colombia are subject to tax in respect of such income and property.

As a way to facilitate filing of tax returns law authorizes presentation of exhibits thereto in magnetic tape. Individuals and decedent's estates do not need to file annual income tax return in cases indicated by law.

III. Basic Income Tax.—Gross receipts are total of ordinary and extraordinary income received. Gross receipts less refunds and discounts equal net receipts. Gross income is total net receipts less costs to produce income.

Rules on certain incomes. (A) Dividends and profits.

(1) Income of shareholders of corporations and assimilated entities (II, 3a, supra) arising from distributions of dividends or profits, in money or in kind of: (a) Preceding year or accumulated profits of several years, except when they are paid out of income that has been reported by distributing entity; (b) extraordinary distributions at transformation of corporation; and (c) extraordinary distributions at liquidation of corporation made to shareholders not individuals or decedents' estates in amount exceeding their investments. (2) Income of partners or quota holders ("socios, comuneros, asociados") of limited liability companies, and assimilated entities (II, 3b, supra): (a) From ordinary annual distributions of profits: their share, in proportion to their respective investment, in company's net income, after deducting income tax and legal reserve, except when they are paid out of income that has been reported by distributing entity. If company had losses, partner or quota holder must share them in same proportion. If portion of income comes from sale of fixed assets owned by company for more than two years, and partners or quota holders are individuals or decedents' estates, distribution is taxed as capital gains; (b) from distributions in money or in kind at liquidation of company: taxpayer's share in profits of last taxable year, plus his share in reserve and any excess over his investment (reimbursement of investment, plus his share in accumulated profits of years prior to that of liquidation are not taxable income). When partner or quota holder is individual or decedent's estate, any amount received in excess over his investment and profits is taxed as capital gains. Above rules apply, when not incompatible, to distributions at transformation of companies. Constructive dividends. Any payments made by corporations or any other juridic entities (II, 3a, b, supra) to individuals or decedents' estates which are "economically vinculated" to taxpayer (i.e. individual who himself or whose spouse or close relative owns 50% or more of company's capital) is presumed distribution of profits.

(B) Income from maritime, air or river transportation services received by foreign companies or by nonresident individuals is held as "mixed" income, and taxed on portion derived from services originating in Colombia, subject to special rules for its determination.

(C) Royalties of rentals from exploitation of motion picture received by nonresident individuals and foreign corporations are taxed on 60% of total received and those from exploitation of computer programs are taxed on 80% of total received.

TAXATION . . . *continued*

(D) Royalties for use of patents and trademarks or know-how, and services rendered in Colombia for technical assistance, are held as Colombian income and taxed accordingly. But salaries, commissions, fees, etc. paid for services abroad are not subject to tax.

(E) There are special rules for income of insurance companies, for income from trusts, etc.

Net income is gross income less authorized deductions, as follows: (A) Expenses necessary for production of income: (1) Repairs of real property up to 1% of capital valuation, or its cost, if higher, (2) interest, total amount if paid to entities under supervision of Superintendency of Banks; if to other entities, deduction is up to amount due at highest bank rate during taxable year. Interest on loans for payment of taxpayer's house, if lender is under supervision of Superintendency of Banks or loan is guaranteed by mortgage, (3) taxes on land, motor vehicles, registration and stamp, (4) personal services: salaries, workmen's social benefits, professional fees, commissions, etc. (5) social security, pensions, contributions to mutual funds for investment, etc. In case of salaries, fees, commissions, etc., which constitute income from work to recipient, and in payments of interests, royalties (See also "expenses abroad," B[5], below) or any other which constitute income from capital to recipient, deduction is not permitted unless taxpayer identifies recipient.

(B) Other deductions: (1) Amortization (within five years) of "necessary investments", meaning others than in land, such as in organization and installation of business, cost of acquisition or exploitation of mines and exploration and exploitation of petroleum, gas and other natural resources, depletion. Ministry of Mines shall determine term for amortization of investments under its jurisdiction; (2) depreciation; (3) bad debts written off; (4) losses of assets assigned to production, and business losses, which can be carried over five years; (5) expenses abroad up to 10% of taxpayer's net income, provided taxpayer substantiates same and identifies recipient at time of filing tax return and withholds tax when so required. Royalties for use of trademarks, patents and know-how are not deductible unless there is officially approved licensing agreement. No deduction is permitted for royalties paid by subsidiary to parent company abroad.

(C) Special exempt incomes: (1) Workers' benefits: indemnifications for accidents and sickness, maternity benefits, life insurance (sic), burial expenses (sic), unemployment, travel expenses, dividends when they are paid out of income reported by distributing entity, etc.; (2) interest from bonds and other government obligations issued prior to Sept. 30, 1974.

Presumptive net income for all taxpayers, is 7% of net capital worth ("patrimonio") as of last day of preceding taxable year.

Tax Rates.—(1) Individuals, national or foreign, Colombian residents, decedents' estates of Colombian nationals and of foreign nationals whose last domicile was in Colombia, and income derived from property donated or assigned for special purposes, are subject to progressive rate ranging from 0.11% to 35% on net incomes over 40,200,000 pesos. (2) Foreign nationals nonresidents. Income from Colombian sources is subject to fixed tax rate of 35%, if taxpayer has no agent ("apoderado") in Colombia. Same rate applies to their decedents' estates in Colombia. If foreign national has duly appointed agent in Colombia, progressive tax rate (above) applies. (3) Corporations and assimilated entities (II, 3a, supra) are subject to fixed rate of 35%. (4) Limited liability companies and assimilated entities (II, 3b, supra) are subject to fixed tax rate of 30%. (5) Foreign corporations (II, 3c, supra) are subject to fixed tax rate of 30%. Capital gains not reinvested are fully taxable subject to varying rates.

Withholding tax: On nonresidents: On payments of any income other than dividends, withholding tax fluctuates between 1% and 35% of gross payment. On dividend paid to foreign corporations, rate is 7%.

Withholding on Salaries.—Decree 2323 of Dec. 29, 1995 provides for rates for withholding purposes with respect to salaries.

Tax credits: (1) Individuals (II, 1, supra), national or foreign, Colombian residents, decedent's estates and companies have following deductions: percentage of tax refund certificates received for promotion of export of goods and services. (2) Branches of foreign companies forming part of consortium 30% of dividends received from consortium. (3) Donations: up to 30% of net income may be deducted. (4) Taxes paid abroad may be deducted up to amount of tax due in Colombia on same income.

IV. Capital gains tax is levied on net gains received by individuals and decedents' estates from: (1) Sale of fixed assets held for two years or more, gain being difference between sale price and cost of asset. Sale of assets held less than two years are taxed as income; (2) monetary corrections in construction-financing paper known as "UPAC"; (3) liquidation of corporations or of any other entities (II, 3, supra), in excess of invested capital, when such gain should not be distributed as dividends or profits; (4) amount actually received from inheritances, legacies, gifts, life insurance, lotteries and other prizes. If inheritance, legacy, or donation is other than in money, capital gains are value of such property shown in last income tax return of decedent or donor after deducting inheritance and gift taxes. If decedent or donor acquired said property within taxable year, its value cannot be less than that shown in last income tax return of former owner; (5) sale of fixed assets held for more than two years by limited liability companies and assimilated entities; (6) workmen compensations; (7) scientific, artistic and literary prizes.

Special Rules on Certain Capital Gains.—Gains from sale of fixed assets (IV, 1, supra). In sale of taxpayer's own house or apartment, 10% of gain per year of habitation since acquisition date is tax free. Gains from monetary corrections of paper "UPAC" (IV, 2, supra) are taxed on 60% of amount actually received on excess over 7% annually only. Gains from inheritances and legacies (IV, 4, supra) are taxed on 80% of amount actually received; 20% balance is exempt from income and capital gains taxes. Gains from lotteries and other prizes are taxed at 20%.

Net gains and Losses.—From above capital gains taxpayer shall deduct losses to determine net gains or losses.

Tax rate is same as for basic income tax table for individual taxpayers of basic income tax (supra).

Special Exemptions and Deductions.—Spouse and decedents with right to certain portion of inheritance ("legitimarios") are entitled to exemption of first 7,400,000 pesos from capital gains tax.

V. Remittance Tax applies to all remittances abroad of income and capital gains realized in Colombia regardless of who is beneficiary of income or recipient of draft. Rate is 8% on payments for motion picture services, and for royalties, interests, fees, and artistic and other services rendered in Colombia, and 1% in most other cases. However, rate is 5% for profits of foreign corporations obtained through their agencies or subsidiaries in Colombia. Reinvested profits are exempted of this tax.

Exemptions: Remittances for dividends, and interests derived from short-term credits relating to import and export of merchandise, capital assets or raw materials, if duly registered at Banco de la República.

VI. Procedural rules for claims relating to income and sales taxes are contained in Decree 624 of Mar. 30, 1989. Statute of limitations for claiming overdue taxes is five years, for imposing penalties and for correcting returns by Internal Revenue Office, is two years. Taxpayer's corrections must be done within two years from filing return.

VII. Integral Monetary Correction.—Taxpayers required by law to keep accounting books must adjust yearly monetary values of their financial statements in accordance with variable percentage registered by index of consumer prices as determined yearly by Departamento Administrativo Nacional de Estadística (Dane).

Stamp Tax.—Decree 624 of Mar. 30, 1989 as am'd.

Sales Tax.—(Decree 624 of Mar. 30, 1989 as am'd, regulated by Decree 45 of Jan. 8, 1991 and Decree 380 of Feb. 27, 1996). Levied on sale or importation of goods (movables) and services.

Exemptions.—Foodstuffs not specifically taxed, schoolbooks, drugs, insecticides, herbicides and like, seeds and fodders, fertilizers, heavy industrial machinery if not manufactured in Colombia, temporary importation of goods, repair of foreign ships, and export goods, among others, are exempt.

Tax basis is total value of sale including expenses such as financing and freight. In imported goods, value includes customs duties. If transfer is for free, or goods are for purchaser's own consumption, basis is commercial value of goods.

Rates.—General rate is 16%.

Taxpayers.—Manufacturers, importers, merchants and individuals or corporations who render services pay this tax. In exported goods (which are exempt) only exporter may obtain reimbursement of tax previously paid.

Surface Tax.—See topic Mines and Minerals, subhead Surface Tax.

TRADEMARKS AND TRADENAMES:

(Const. Art. 150, §24; C. Com. 583-618, Res. 0582 of Mar. 30, 1990, Decision 344 of Oct. 29, 1993 of Cartagena Commission; Decree 117 of Jan. 14, 1993; Decree 2285 of Dec. 22, 1995).

Trademarks and Slogans.—Those signs visible and sufficiently distinctive and susceptible of graphic representation can be registered as marks. Trademark is any sign used to distinguish products or services produced or commercialized by one person from same or similar products or services produced or commercialized by another person. Slogans are words, sentences or captions used as supplement to trademark. Any person or corporation may apply for registration of trade names or slogans employed or to be employed in relation to economic activities. Item registered may be sufficiently distinctive. Among non-registrable are: usual or necessary shapes of products or denominations and color thereof; shapes which provide functional or technical advantages to product or service concerned; signs or indication that may designate or describe quality, quantity, species, destination, value, place of origin, or any other characteristic data or information on goods or services on which they are to be used; marks contrary to law, those that are against public policy or that are intended to deceive consumers regarding nature, origin, type of manufacture, characteristics or aptitude to use products or services; those that reproduce or imitate coats of arms, emblems, phrases, of any State or of any international organization, without appropriate permit; title of literary, artistic or scientific works protected by copyright without permission of owner, denomination of protected vegetable varieties, those identical or similar to registered trade slogans and trade names, provided under circumstances public may be confused; those that are reproduction, imitation, translation, or total or partial transcription of distinctive signs, locally or internationally, well known, without taking into consideration classification of goods or services concerned; or because of similarity to well-known trademarks causes confusion to public independent of classification of goods and services for which registration is applied for.

Collective Marks.—Any sign that distinguishes origin or any other common characteristic of products or services of different enterprises which use marks under control of its owner.

Commercial Names.—Any person or corporation may deposit its commercial name for its protection with Superintendencia de Industria y Comercio, according to law.

Registration of trademark lasts ten years, but it may be renewed for ten year periods indefinitely if evidence is filed of use of mark in any Andean Group Country if applied for within last six months from date of expiration. Owner of trademark may grant license to use or exploit it.

Trademarks and commercial names can be cancelled for nonuse for consecutive three years by owner or licensee in any member country of Andean Pact.

Origin denominations may be declared at government's initiative or at petition of interested party. Authorization to use them may be granted for ten years, renewable.

Contracts for trademarks are registered according to Decree 259 of Feb. 12, 1992.

Law 14 of Mar. 5, 1979, forbids use of foreign words in names of products, services, companies and commercial establishments and in new trademarks registered after enactment of legislation.

Conventions.—Convention for the Protection of Industrial Property, Paris, Mar. 21, 1883, Stockholm Revision of July 14, 1967 as am'd on Sept. 28, 1979; General Inter-American Convention for Trademark and Commercial Protection, Washington, Feb. 20, 1929; Agreement on Trade-Related Aspects of Intellectual Property Rights, Marrakesh, Apr. 15, 1994.

See also topics Patents; Exchange Control, subhead Foreign Capital Investments.

TREATIES:

Colombia is a party, among others, to following:

See Topical Index in front part of this volume.

TREATIES . . . *continued*

Multilateral.—Convention on private international law (Bustamante Code), Havana, 1928; Montevideo treaty, 1980 (Latin American Integration Association); Cartagena Agreement, 1969 (Andean Common Market); Inter-American conventions: on proof of and information on foreign law and on execution of preventive measures, Montevideo, 1979; on international commercial arbitration, Panama, 1975; Multilateral Trade Negotiations, The Uruguay Round, Final Act, Marrakesh, Apr. 15, 1994 and Agreement Establishing the World Trade Organization, Marrakesh, Apr. 15, 1994; Convention establishing the Multilateral Investment Guarantee Agency (MIGA) with annexes and schedules. Seoul, Oct. 11, 1985.

United Nations Convention on Recognition and Enforcement of Foreign Arbitral Awards of 1958, approved by Law 39 of Nov. 20, 1990.

See also Selected International Conventions section.

TRUSTS:

(C. Com., 1226-1244, Res. 214 of Feb. 5, 1975).

Two types of trusts are allowed by law: inter vivos, which must be made in public instrument (i.e., notarial deed), and mortis-causa, which must be made in a will. Only credit institutions and trust societies (sociedades fiduciarias) duly authorized by Superintendency of Banks, can be trustees. Property in trust must be kept separate from other trustees' assets, and subject only to obligations derived from trust. Secret trusts are forbidden and also those on behalf of several persons in succession. Except for trusts for benefit of incapacitated persons or charitable institutions, duration is limited to 20 years.

VITAL STATISTICS: See topic Registries.

WILLS:

(C. C. 1055-1278).

Wills may be made by all persons except those under age of puberty, mentally incapacitated or unable to express their will clearly. Wills are opened and published in court of latest domicile of testator.

Testamentary Disposition.—Testator may dispose freely of his property only in so far as there are no heirs at law. (See topic Descent and Distribution). Legacies may be charged with conditions. Testamentary provisions are void if made in favor of notary or witnesses before whom will is signed, or in favor of their wives, ascendants, descendants, brothers or sisters, brothers-in-law or sisters-in-law or paid servants.

Forms.—With respect to form wills are either solemn or privileged. Solemn wills are: (1) Open, also called nuncupative or public; (2) closed or secret. Privileged wills are: (1) Oral; (2) military; (3) naval.

Open wills are executed before a notary and three witnesses or, where there is no notary, before five witnesses. They must express name, birthplace, age and residence of testator, and that he is of sound mind, names of persons whom he has married and of his children, stating whether they are living or dead, names and residences of witnesses, name of notary and place and date of execution of will. Will must be read aloud by notary or a witness to parties assembled and all must sign. Blind persons can execute only open wills.

See also topic Registries.

Closed wills are privately prepared and signed by testator and enclosed in a sealed envelope which testator must declare to contain his will, before a notary and five witnesses. A public instrument is then executed, setting forth details of act, and is signed by all persons assembled. Persons who cannot understand or be understood in conversation can make only closed wills. See also topic Registries.

Oral wills may be made in presence of three witnesses by a person in imminent danger of death. They are not valid if testator survives for over 30 days or if not reduced to writing by witnesses before a circuit judge within 30 days after testator's death.

Military wills may be made in time of war by military men, hostages and prisoners before certain army officers.

Naval wills may be made on the high seas before the commander or lieutenant commander of a Colombian man-of-war or before the captain, mate or pilot of a Colombian merchant vessel.

Witnesses.—Following cannot be witnesses to solemn wills executed in Colombia: minors below 18, persons mentally incapacitated or blind, or deaf or dumb or convicted of certain crimes, clerks of officiating notary, foreigners not domiciled in Colombia, persons not understanding testator's language, spouse, near relatives of testator or of notary, servants of testator or of such relatives or of any other witnesses or of an heir or legatee, father confessor of testator, or any person having an interest under will. At least two witnesses must be residents of place where will is made and one in three or two in five must know how to read and write.

In cases of privileged wills, any person of sound mind over 18 who sees, hears and understands the testator can be a witness, provided he has not been convicted of certain crimes and can read and write.

Revocation.—Wills validly executed are rendered invalid by revocation by testator. Revocation may be total or partial. A later will which does not expressly revoke a former will leaves in force all provisions of former will which are not in conflict with later one.

Foreign wills are valid in Colombia if executed in accordance with laws of country where made. Wills may be made abroad in form provided by Colombian law for solemn wills if: (1) Testator is a Colombian or a foreigner domiciled in Colombia; (2) witnesses are Colombians or domiciled in city of execution; (3) will is executed before a Colombian minister or secretary of legation or consul or minister of a friendly nation; (4) signature of chief of Colombian legation and seal of legation or consulate appears on will, if open, or on envelope if closed; (5) a copy of will or of minute on envelope is immediately sent to Minister of Foreign Affairs of Colombia.

COSTA RICA LAW DIGEST REVISER

Curtis Mallet-Prevost, Colt & Mosle
101 Park Avenue
New York, New York 10178-0061
Telephone: 212-696-6141
Fax: 212-697-1559
Email: CMP-NY@mcimail.com

Reviser Profile

The Firm roots began in 1830 when two practicing lawyers started a long line of lawyers and law firms extending in an unbroken chain up to the present time. In 1897, the firm name became Curtis, Mallet-Prevost & Colt; in 1925 it was changed to Curtis, Mallet-Prevost, Colt & Mosle. The Firm is now made up of approximately 120 lawyers, including experts who have published extensively on such diverse subjects as international money management, transnational contracts, state contracts, litigation against foreign states, sovereign immunity and the act of state doctrine, and the International Court of Justice. Its principal offices are in New York City. There are branch offices in Paris, London, Hong Kong, Frankfurt Am Main, Washington, D.C., Houston, Texas, Newark, N.J., and Mexico City. The Firm has five departments: Corporate and International; Litigation; Real Estate; Tax; and Trusts and Estates. The corporate and international department acts as general counsel to various public and private corporations and individual entrepreneurs. Clients are in the banking, insurance, securities, manufacturing, real estate and oil and gas industries. In addition, the corporate and international department frequently acts as special counsel to domestic and foreign clients, providing assistance in financing, know-how licensing, the negotiation and drafting of all types of contracts and instruments, counselling on all aspects of corporate law, and establishing the vehicles necessary to enable clients to conduct their domestic and foreign business activities. The Firm's international work permeates all areas of its practice and involves questions of private international law, foreign law and an unusual amount of public and quasi-public international law. Traditionally, much of the Firm's international practice has been concerned with Latin America. The Firm maintains its excellence in that area with its Mexican affiliate, and also through the expertise of Latin American lawyers based in the New York office. The Firm's international practice has undergone a major expansion beyond Latin America to Europe, Africa and the Near and Far East. The Firm's litigation practice includes commercial litigation and arbitration, and white-collar criminal defense. It has substantial experience in civil aviation matters; it also has represented foreign States in transnational litigation and international arbitration arising out of acts of nationalization and alleged breach of economic development or natural resource supply contracts. Among the Firm's clients in real estate matters are institutional lenders and investors, real estate developers, both individual and corporate, foreign and domestic investors and syndicators. The tax department has substantial experience in all aspects of domestic and international business tax matters and real estate taxation. The matters the tax department deals with on a regular basis include: Taxation of foreign investments; the structuring of corporate transactions, including mergers, acquisitions, liquidations and reorganization; federal and state tax litigation; and tax planning for U.S. and foreign individuals. The trusts and estates department engages in general domestic trusts and estates practice and in tax planning for foreign persons wishing to invest in U.S. assets through offshore trusts and corporations. It represents individuals, trust companies, and banks acting as fiduciaries. It works for various charitable organizations located both in the United States and abroad including private foundations, museums, universities and hospitals. A group of fiduciary accountants with vast experience in the field assists the lawyers of the trusts and estates department. Curtis, Mallet-Prevost, Colt & Mosle has served as a Reviser for most of Latin American Law Digests since 1930.

COSTA RICA LAW DIGEST

(The following is a list of all Topics, including cross-references, covered in this Digest.)

COSTA RICA LAW DIGEST

Revised for 1997 edition by

CURTIS, MALLET-PREVOST, COLT & MOSLE of the New York Bar.

(C. C. indicates Civil Code; C. Com. indicates Code of Commerce; C. C. P. indicates Code of Civil Procedure; C. Family indicates Code of Family. Numbers in code references indicate articles.)

ABSENTEES: See topic Death.

ACKNOWLEDGMENTS:

Documents requiring notarial authentication are executed as public instruments before notaries, who retain the original in their records and issue certified copies. However, any private document's signature may be acknowledged before a notary and then it substitutes for a public document unless this is specifically required. See topics Notaries Public; also Public Instruments.

Documents executed abroad for use in Costa Rica will be accepted if (a) they are executed in accordance with the laws of the place of their origin and (b) the signature of the official certifying the document is duly authenticated. (C. C. P. 374). Authentication may be obtained from Costa Rican consular or diplomatic officer. Such documents may also be executed before Costa Rican consular or diplomatic officers acting as notaries. (Art. 94, Law 39 of Jan. 5, 1943).

ACTIONS:

Actions for Death.—See topic Death.

Limitation of.—See topic Prescription, subhead Actions.

ADMINISTRATION:

See topic Executors and Administrators.

ADOPTION:

(C. Family 100-126).

Person over 25 years of age of good reputation and moral standing, with good economic and social standards, in full exercise of his civil rights may adopt minor or incapacitated minor or adult; in any case adopting party must be 15 years older than adopted party. There are special requirements for foreign adopting parties. Consent must be obtained from parents and court except when adopted person is adult. Husband or wife may also adopt provided consent of other spouse is given.

Adoption gives adopted person identical status with that of natural child, creating lines of kinship between adopted person and adoptive parents' family. Adoption extinguishes legal bonds between adopted person and his natural parents and family.

ADVERSE POSSESSION:

See topic Prescription.

AGENCY: See topic Principal and Agent.

ALIENS:

Aliens in general enjoy the same civil rights as citizens. Aliens remaining in the country over six months require a residence card. Tourists need a passport or a tourist card and must show a ticket for continuation of trip or return to country of origin. Vagrants, criminals, persons of bad conduct or about whom there be reports from abroad of being undesirable are not to be admitted, or may be expelled from the country. No tourist or transient is entitled to work except when his passport states he is a traveling agent or representative of commerce and holds commercial agent's visa. (Laws 13 of June 18, 1884; 1155 of Apr. 29, 1950 as am'd; Law 7033 of Aug. 4, 1986 and its regulations; Law 37 of June 7, 1940 as am'd; Law 8 of Apr. 21, 1941; Decree 4 of Apr. 26, 1942 as am'd; Decree 10686 of Oct. 19, 1979 as am'd. See topics Shipping; Immigration.

ALIMONY: See topic Divorce.

ASSIGNMENTS:

The assignment of a right is effected by delivery of the document evidencing the right. However, unless the document is payable to bearer or subject to transfer by endorsement, assignment has no legal effect as to debtor until he is notified thereof, by a notary or by registered letter or other authentic admissible manner, nor against third parties unless the assignment was made by public instrument or by private document if they had actual notice thereof or from: (a) Death of one of the signers, (b) presentation of the document to a public officer to form part of some proceeding or (c) presentation of the document to a notary for authentication of the date. The notified debtor must advise creditor within three days, about any defenses not appearing from the document losing them if he fails to do so. In the assignment of credit documents not subject to endorsement the assignor warrants only the legal existence of the credit and his own capacity to assign but not the solvency of the debtor unless otherwise stipulated. (C. C. 483, 1104-1116; C. Com. 490-494).

ASSIGNMENTS FOR BENEFIT OF CREDITORS:

There is no specific provision for such assignments. If the assets of a debtor are sufficient to cover his liabilities, he may make any assignment or other arrangement to which his creditors may agree; if the assets are insufficient to cover the liabilities he may be declared insolvent or bankrupt. (C. C. 884-888).

ATTACHMENT:

(C. C. P. 272-281, 438-447).

An attachment may be requested in order to prevent a debtor from evading a judgment by concealing or disposing of his assets. A bond must be given unless the creditor presents a document which under the law would authorize a summary action. In case of such attachment suit must be brought within one month, otherwise the plaintiff is liable for damages.

The following documents authorize a summary action of execution and an attachment without bond: (a) copies of public instruments duly certified by notary or other public officer, or certification from public registry that instrument is pending registration; (b) certifications from public registry; (c) private documents acknowledged before competent judge or declared acknowledged by default; (d) acknowledgments made in court or considered made by default; (e) any documents, as, for example, bills of exchange, on which law specifically authorizes summary action to be brought.

BANKRUPTCY AND INSOLVENCY:

(C. Com. arts. 851-967; C. C. 884-980; C. C. P. 30, 709-795).

Bankruptcy applies to merchants and corporations or commercial partnerships or associations. A debtor may petition to be adjudged bankrupt. Any creditor may also petition when he has one or more unpaid matured credits or the debtor has ceased in the payment of his obligations to others or debtor absconds or absents himself leaving no representative to make payments or without reason closes his place of business or assigns all his assets for the benefit of one or more creditors or it is established that he is engaged in ruinous, fraudulent or false schemes or when other facts prove that he is unable to pay. A decedent may be adjudged bankrupt if he died after having ceased payment of his obligations. A decedent's estate may also become bankrupt for failure to pay commercial obligations. Mortgagees and pledges may not petition for debtor's bankruptcy unless the in rem guarantee proves insufficient.

A bankruptcy declared abroad does not detract from rights of local creditors over assets in the country nor annul acts or contracts of the bankrupt, but branches of a foreign bankrupt are wound up if so requested by the foreign court. An insolvent branch of a foreign concern may be adjudged bankrupt even if its principal is not and then local creditors have priority over foreign creditors who had contracted with the branch.

Court may determine the date of cessation of payments up to three months back, but the appointed receiver may petition to extend its retroactivity to six months. Court notifies criminal court which then determines whether bankruptcy is excusable, culpable or fraudulent.

Receiver and alternate receiver ("curador") are appointed by court. Receivers must be lawyers, banks, corporations or commercial partnerships or associations. They have multiple duties, among them, collection of debts in favor of bankrupt and its legal representation in court; reporting to creditor's meeting on pending claims; taking possession of assets, selling them and proposing plan of distribution whenever amount of 25% of liabilities is available; appearing in criminal proceedings, etc.

Declaration of bankruptcy terminates obligation to pay interest, past or present, and renders all obligations of bankrupt due and payable. Credits are classified and paid in following order: with privilege on specific property, workers' credits, credits against the bankruptcy and common credits. Trustee may sell property given in mortgage or pledge guarantee even when debt guaranteed thereby is not due, but with proceeds he must pay principal, interest and expenses covered by the guarantee and withhold any balance. Unpaid balances of such debts become common credits.

Proceeds from realization of assets of bankrupt are distributed in payment of principal which is cancelled only pro tanto, the balances remaining due and payable immediately. However, if bankruptcy is not found to constitute a crime debtor is not to be sued for said balances during three years after distribution, statutes of limitations beginning to run at end of said period.

When the bankruptcy is not fraudulent it may cease by a composition. But no bankrupt who has not honored a prior composition may enter into another. If bankruptcy is due to fault, but not to fraud, the only composition acceptable to stop the bankruptcy is promise to pay all debts in full. No agreement with only one or some creditors is valid and, if made, those creditors lose their rights in the bankruptcy which then is adjudged as due to fault of bankrupt.

Bankrupt who was not adjudged culpable or fraudulent may be rehabilitated and the prohibitions and limitations against him vacated immediately after distribution of all his assets, but only after complying with the penalty imposed therefor and payment of all outstanding balances or fulfillment of the composition promises when adjudged culpable, and if fraudulent, only when three years have elapsed after complying with the penalty imposed and payment of all debts in full.

Bankruptcy of a partnership does not cause bankruptcy of its members but all their property is attached for payment of partnership's debts concurrently with members' separate creditors and if administrators are found guilty of tortious or fraudulent bankruptcy, any creditor may cause bankruptcy of its members. Bankruptcy of a corporation or other limited liability companies does not cause that of its members.

Administrators of corporations or partnerships or companies are liable as individual merchants but criminal penalties are applied only to those who intervened in wrongful acts to detriment of the creditors.

Insolvency proceedings are very similar to bankruptcies but apply to non-merchants. Any creditor may petition for declaration of insolvency which will be granted if court considers economic situation of debtor justifies such proceedings. Debtor may petition for composition with creditors provided he has not been declared insolvent within last five years and has kept accounts for one year, if required by law, and has not been found guilty of crimes against property or public trust. Composition may also be arrived at in insolvency proceedings. When proceedings terminate, insolvent shall be free of claim for unpaid balances during five years after declaration of insolvency,

See Topical Index in front part of this volume.

BANKRUPTCY AND INSOLVENCY . . . *continued*

except as otherwise agreed in composition. Thereafter creditors may claim said balances. However, if in criminal proceedings, insolvency is found to be fraudulent, creditors may disregard agreement and enforce their claims immediately on new property, provided allowance is made for insolvent and his family's maintenance.

BILLS AND NOTES:

(C. Com. 727-840).

Bill of exchange must state: (1) Title "bill of exchange" within its text; (2) unconditional order to pay a certain amount; (3) name of drawee who may also be drawer; (4) date of payment; or whether it is payable at sight or on a certain term after sight, in which cases interest may be agreed, otherwise interest clauses are invalid; if no rate is specified there can be no interest; interest runs from issuance date unless otherwise specified; if no maturity term is given it is payable at sight; (5) place of payment, otherwise it will be deemed payable at place mentioned near name of drawee which shall also be considered to be his domicile; bill may be made payable at domicile of a third person; (6) name of payee or to the order of whom payment must be made; (7) date and place of issue; if none appears it will be deemed issued at place mentioned near name of drawer; (8) name of drawer.

Drawer warrants acceptance and payment and may not contract away the latter warranty.

Bills of exchange even if not to order are endorsable in full, with no conditions. In case of blank endorsements holder may fill blank, reendorse bill or simply deliver it as bearer document. If not otherwise stated, any endorser warrants acceptance and payment; he may forbid new endorsement and then he is not liable to subsequent endorsees.

Defendant in an action on a bill cannot use personal defenses he may have against drawer or prior holders except when plaintiff acts knowingly to the prejudice of debtor. An endorsement after maturity is valid but if after protest for nonpayment or after lapse of the term for protest it only effects an assignment. Undated endorsements are presumed made in time, subject to rebuttal.

Acceptance may be required by the holder and it is necessary when bill is payable at a term after sight, and in this case it must be presented within one year of issuance unless the term is extended or limited by drawer or limited by endorsers. Drawee may request second presentation on the following day and holder then is not obliged to deliver the bill. Acceptance may be limited to a portion of the amount but any other qualifying statement amounts to refusal to accept, though such acceptance binds acceptor.

Failure to accept or pay a bill must be established by a notarial act of protest, made within presentation term and one extra day when presented on the last day if for nonacceptance or if for nonpayment in case of a sight bill and within eight days after maturity in other cases of nonpayment. Protests have detailed requisites. Duly protested bills give right to immediate attachment and sale of assets of the liable parties. Protest may be waived by words "return without expenses" or "without protest" or others similar, written and signed, but this does not dispense either presentation or the notices which must be given to holder's endorser and to drawer within four days after protest or after presentation if protest is waived. A notified endorser must notify his antecessor in line within two days.

Acceptor is liable for payment to the holder. Drawer, endorsers and guarantors of a bill are jointly liable to holder for principal and agreed interest and for 6% after maturity plus expenses, unless the bill is prejudiced for lack of presentation for acceptance when necessary or for payment or of the required protest. However, if failure to present or to protest is due to vis major of a general character, the terms are extended, but notice must be given to the proper parties and a note written on the bill. If the preventing force lasts more than 30 days the holder's action may be then exercised without those requisites.

An accommodation endorsement or guarantee in the same bill or on a supplementary paper constitutes the signer thereof as a jointly liable party for the drawer or for endorser for whom he gives it, even if the bill or the liability of said party is null for any cause which is not a defect of form. The words "for aval" and the signature are sufficient to constitute the joint guarantee.

Promissory notes must contain that title within the text and statement of maturity date and most of the requisites of bills of exchange, with no drawee. The rules applicable to bills of exchange apply to notes.

Checks must be written in forms supplied by drawee bank to drawer and must contain (1) Name of drawee; (2) place and date of issue; (3) name of person to whom or to whose order it is payable; (4) unconditional order to pay a certain amount spelled out and with figures or written with a protecting machine; (5) signature of issuer or agent. A bank may permit use of certain special protected forms. Checks are endorsable but if issued to bearer they are negotiable by delivery. Endorsements may be restrictive, such as for collection, to credit on a certain account or limit or amend drawer's liability or even state a specific purpose for use of the sum.

The transferor of a bearer check who does not endorse it warrants its legitimacy but not payment. Drawee bank must pay a valid check upon presentation regardless of date of issuance. Unpaid checks with a note of the cashier of the bank that it has not been wholly or partially paid gives a right to immediate attachment and execution against assets of the parties liable for amount due plus 25% for damages. Drawer and any payee who is an accessory to a fraud are subject to criminal liability. Payment may be stopped by drawer at his own risk by a written order in cases of theft, loss or duress and the check may be revalidated by a new statement on its reverse. A holder may also stop payment but only for four days. Crossed checks are legal. Checks may be certified and then are not subject to stop order unless returned to bank. No protest is required but a certificate of nonpayment must be obtained from the bank and notice given to endorsers within five days; otherwise the actions are lost against them.

Checks must be presented within one month if payable in the same place; three months if within Costa Rica and six months if issued abroad to be paid in Costa Rica. Neglect to present in time releases endorsers' liabilities.

Payments made by check are conditional to the check being honored upon presentation and otherwise the intended payment is null and void. "Traveler checks" may be issued by banks and must be paid by same bank, its branches and correspondents listed as such, within period of limitations. Refusal to pay gives immediate attachment rights and action for amount plus damages which never shall be less than 25%. "Traveler checks" of foreign banks sold in Costa Rica are subject to laws of place of issuance but seller is liable for their validity.

CHATTEL MORTGAGES:

(C. Com. arts. 530-581).

Personal property not exempt from attachment may be given in guarantee of any obligation. Ships are expressly included as personal property for this purpose. Aircraft may also be pledged under Civil Aviation Law 5150 of May 14, 1973 as am'd. Pledged articles may be delivered to creditor or to third person or remain in custody of debtor, but pledge or chattel mortgage must be constituted in public instrument or by private document acknowledged before notary or two witnesses and must be recorded in Registry of Pledges in order to be binding upon third parties if possession is retained by debtor.

Livestock products may be pledged for one year only; farm products harvested or not may be encumbered within the agricultural year of the contract; wood only if already cut; raw materials, elaborated or manufactured articles, at any stage, may also be pledged. Shares of stock, securities, mortgage cedulas and credits may be pledged but this, besides the recorded writing, requires delivery to creditor who acts as depositary, who cannot be authorized to appropriate and apply them to his credit althouth he may sell them through the court at public auction or through a broker when so authorized under certain procedural rules. Sale of other articles at public auction may be made through court or, when authority is granted, through a third person.

Basis for sales may be agreed upon.

Debtor who holds agricultural products may sell them when in season or ready for sale following certain procedure. If creditor makes opposition debtor may sell and deposit proceeds in court or with a bank under penalty of arrest until compliance.

Documents of pledge may be transferred by endorsement to a specified endorsee to whom endorser is jointly liable with debtor, unless words of limitation are inserted. Endorsement of a pledge document and any novation, extension or partial change must be in writing and has to be recorded, if the object remains in debtor's possession, and notice of the transfer given to him.

Pledge may be cancelled at any time by payment. If partial payment is accepted it must be noted in the document and recorded.

Foreclosure action is summary.

See also topic Mortgages.

COMMERCIAL REGISTER:

See topic Records.

COMMUNITY PROPERTY:

See topic Husband and Wife.

CONSTITUTION AND GOVERNMENT:

The legislative power is vested in a Congress having a single chamber. Congressmen are elected for four years. The President of the Republic is elected for four years and cannot be reelected for the following term.

The Republic is divided into provinces, these into cantons, and the cantons into districts. In each province there is a governor appointed by the President. The cantons are administered by municipal councils with limited local powers. (Constitution of Nov. 7, 1949 as am'd).

CONTRACTS:

(C. C. 1007-1044).

Their nature, formalities and capacity to enter into same, are generally governed by Civil Code. There are other legal rules applicable to contracts depending on whether contract falls within scope of commercial law, labor law, or administrative law.

To enter into a contract there must be an offer and acceptance. Offers may be retracted at any time before acceptance. Oral offers may be accepted immediately. A modification of offer in acceptance constitutes a new offer. Conditions necessary for validity of contracts are: capacity, object, "cause", consent and specific formalities when these are required by law.

Object of a contract must be definite or subject to definite determination. Formalities of contracts which will have effect in Costa Rica may be subject either to Costa Rican law or to law of place of execution. However, if Costa Rica law requires that a contract be executed in a public deed, a private document executed abroad shall have no legal effect in Costa Rica, regardless of whether such private document complied with laws of place of celebration. In civil contracts joint and several liability must be expressly stipulated by parties. However, such liability is presumed by law in case of commercial contracts, unless it is otherwise stipulated by parties. Commercial obligations are payable on day indicated in contract.

Civil Code permits to declare null and void specified clauses considered onerous to purchasers or to parties to sales contract, especially in latter case if contract is proforma or adhesion contract. In such case petition may be filed even by consumers protection organizations. Among specified clauses appear: Right to modify contract by seller; long period established by seller to accept; submission to foreign law in order to avoid local law; exclusion of right to sue in Costa Rican courts and many others relating to substance of contract.

Contracts with Government and with its agencies are regulated by Law 7494 of May 3, 1995 as am'd regulated by Decree 25038-H of Mar. 6, 1996.

COPYRIGHT:

(Law 6683 of Oct. 14, 1982 as am'd regulated by Decree 24611-J of Sept. 4, 1995, Decree 23485-MP of July 5, 1994 as am'd).

Author is entitled to: (1) Recognition of his quality as author, (2) delayed publication of his work even up to period of 50 years after his death, (3) right to oppose deformation, mutilation or modification of his work and any action detrimental to

COPYRIGHT . . . *continued*
same or to author's honor and reputation, (4) withdrawal from market of his work at any time, (5) right to use and exploit work.

Works Protected.—Protection is granted in respect to literary, scientific, didactic, musical, choreographical, pictorial, architectural, photographic and cinematographic works and any other works which, by analogy, can be regarded as artistic or intellectual productions and as long as they are expressed in form of writing, engraving, or in any other objective and durable form capable of reproduction or communication to public by any means; arrangements, compendiums, translations, versions, graphic characteristics, etc. authorized by their authors. Articles on current events may be reproduced unless prohibited by special or general reservation. In all cases, when reproduced, source must be given.

Duration.—Copyrights remain in force: (1) For life and 50 years after author's death. Then, or before if there are no heirs, they become public domain, (2) in case of posthumous works, term is 50 years from date of first publication, (3) if author remains anonymous for 50 years from first publication, right passes into public domain, (4) in case of joint authors, 50-year period begins upon death or last survivor, (5) in case of works owned by State, public entities and municipalities, duration is 50 years.

Registration.—Copyright Register, in which are recorded works submitted by authors, agreements or contracts which in any manner confer, modify etc. patrimonial rights of author, powers of attorney. Applicants must submit copies of work produced, published or reproduced. In case of moving pictures, copies of plot and shooting-script and photographs of principal scenes suffice or photocopies in case of pictures, sculptures, and similar works.

Foreigners in Costa Rica enjoy same rights of national authors.

Costa Rica has approved Pan-American Conventions regarding copyright, and Universal Copyright Convention. (L. D. 1680, Nov. 6, 1953 and D. 5682, May 5, 1975).

CORPORATIONS:

(C. Com. 102-219, 235, 245).

Corporation may be formed by public subscription or simultaneous organization but its articles of incorporation must always appear in a public instrument (see topic Public Instruments) which must be recorded in Mercantile Registry and must state: (1) Name preceded or followed by the expression "Sociedad Anónima" or "S.A." which may be registered in Office of Commercial Trademarks; (2) a minimum of two members; (3) 25% of each subscribed share must be paid in, but shares which are to be paid in kind have to be fully paid in; (4) number of shares of stock and par value of same in national currency denomination, classes if two or more; (5) other agreements regarding matters stated below.

Shares of Stock.—Establishment of corporations with bearer shares is prohibited, as well as corporations whose shares belong to corporation with bearer shares. Articles may require authorization of board of directors for transfer of registered shares and then notation must appear in share certificate. Non-par value shares are not permissible. Common shares have equal rights and one vote each.

Under one provision of law (art. 121) articles or amendments thereto may allow issuance of other classes of shares, with different denominations, preferences, privileges, restrictions and limitations as well as establishment of other terms and conditions regarding profits, corporate assets or specific business or any other corporate aspect. Under another provision (art. 145), voting rights of shares which are not common may be restricted or denied, but never for special meetings convened to modify corporate purpose, duration, transformation or merger or to change the domicile to a place out of Costa Rica. Any elimination of any preference of a class of stock must be approved by said class in special meeting.

A corporation may buy its own shares of stock under conditions specified by Code. While belonging to corporation, said shares cannot be represented at stockholders' meetings.

Shareholders' meetings must be held at least once a year for approval or rejection of the balance sheet after hearing the administrator's report; distribution of profits; appointment or dismissal of members of the council of administration, when necessary, and supervisors or auditors; and any other matters not reserved to special meeting, and proposed in the agenda. Special meetings convene for amendment to articles of incorporation or bylaws; issuance of other classes of shares not provided in by-laws and for other purposes when so required by law or document of incorporation. Shareholders representing 25% of capital may request that the meeting be called. Meetings may be held out of Costa Rica when so provided by articles. Quorum for ordinary meeting on first call shall be constituted by one-half of the shares with right to vote, and for special meetings by 75% unless higher number is required in articles of incorporation. Resolutions are formed by more than one-half of votes present at ordinary meetings and at special meetings by more than one-half of total number of shares with right to vote. On second calls any attendance constitutes quorum and more than one-half of votes present decides. Shareholders' meeting has all powers which law or articles of incorporation do not grant to another organ. Minority rights are protected.

Management.—Corporation is managed by a council of administration of no less than three members who need not be shareholders. Unless otherwise provided, council member first mentioned shall be president. He legally represents corporation, as well as other members specified in charter; they may delegate all or some of their powers to other members of council if charter permits, and appoint one or more managers. One-half of the number of council members is required for meetings and a majority of those present to form a resolution, the president having two votes in case of a tie. Meetings may be held at a place designated out of Costa Rica when articles of incorporation so provide.

Supervision.—Supervision of the corporation business shall be exercised as provided in articles of incorporation but when organized by public subscription one or more supervisors or auditors, shareholders or not, must be appointed, who have specific duties provided by law, among them, to request monthly balance sheets; report about yearly balance; call meetings of shareholders; be present at council and shareholders' meetings; receive complaints from shareholders and report on them to the council of administration.

Open Corporations are regulated by Law 7201 of Oct. 10, 1990 and by Code of Commerce. Corporations organized under Code of Commerce may become "open corporations" by complying with requirements of Law 7201 which considers: Open corporations as (1) those which have been authorized by Comisión Nacional de Valores to operate as such; (2) their stock is registered on Costa Rican stock exchange; (3) their capital is represented by nominative shares; (4) have at least 50 stockholders; (5) at least 10% of their capital shares is annually negotiated through stock exchange. Their designated name must be accompanied by words "Sociedad Anónima de Capital Abierto" or abbreviation "S.A. de C.A." No more than 10% of their capital can belong to single stockholder.

These corporations are subject to supervision of "Comisión Nacional de Valores".

Limited Liability Companies (C. Com. 19, 75-101), may be organized by a public instrument which must be rendered in Mercantile Registry, with a capital divided in "quotas" of 100 colones, or multiples thereof, having one vote each. Name must contain addition of expression "Sociedad de Responsabilidad Limitada" or "Limitada" or "S.R.L." or "Ltda." which must appear in invoices, documents, advertisements, etc. Liability of members is limited to contributions. Unanimous consent is required to permit transfer of quotas, but document of incorporation may reduce to minimum vote of 75%, and members have preference to take quotas offered, under same proposed transfer conditions and also company may purchase them, with profits, but said shares have no vote while in company's possession. One or more managers are administrators. Members must hold meeting per year to which they may appoint attorney in fact or proxy, even by letter. Legal reserve of 10% must be formed with 5% of profits. No distribution of dividends may be made unless out of profits.

Individual Limited Liability Concerns.—(C. Com. 9-16).

An individual may, by a public instrument (see topic Public Instruments) create an entity with juridical personality, with a name related to its object and not of a person, followed by the words "Empresa Individual de Responsabilidad Limitada" or "E.I. de R.L.," domicile, capital allocated to it and whether in cash, or in effects or property which must be transferred to the concern in the same act stating their value; object; period of duration; name of manager who may be owner, and period of his appointment if not permanent. Owner may withdraw only established profits and shall be liable with the property of the concern only. The concern may be sold. Winding up of the concern before lapse of its term is subject to special requisites for protection of creditors.

Foreign Branches of Corporations, Companies or Individual Concerns.—(C. Com. 226-233, 360-366).

A foreign organization, whether an individual concern, partnership, corporation, etc., which wants to have a branch or agency in Costa Rica must appoint and maintain an agent with the widest powers for the management of the business of the same. Document granting the power must state: (a) Purpose of branch and capital allotted thereto; (b) object of the principal, and capital, duration and names of representatives and administrators; (c) submission of agency or branch and its representatives to the laws and courts of Costa Rica regarding acts to be executed there including waiver of laws of the principal domicile; (g) proof of authority of the person appearing to grant the power. The standing of a partnership, corporation or company and the power of representation of their administrators may be proved by a certificate issued by Consul of Costa Rica or of a friendly nation, in his absence, that it is organized and authorized to act by laws of its principal domicile and that it is in good standing. Those documents and a document of the appointed agent accepting the power must be recorded in Mercantile Registry. Agents acting without those requisites being fulfilled are jointly liable with corporation for obligations contracted.

A foreign corporation which under its laws may transfer its principal offices to other countries may transfer it to Costa Rica filing the following, properly legalized, with Mercantile Registry: (a) Incorporation document and amendments; (b) consular certificate as mentioned above; (c) certificate of corporate resolution of transfer; (d) list of council members and legal representatives. Governing law continues to be law of incorporation except in what violates public policy. A later retransfer is permissible.

For one single act or business any foreign corporation or partnership or company may give a power of attorney, without need of registration of a branch or agency, stating authority of grantor and its representative to give it.

COURTS:

Justice is administered by: (a) Supreme Court of Justice formed by chambers which hears appeals on questions of law and fact in cases where judges acted as courts of original jurisdiction, action or proceedings for relief and habeas corpus; they also have certain administrative functions with respect to administration of justice; (b) Superior Courts; (c) Collegiate Courts (Tribunales Colegiados); (d) judges who have civil, criminal, labor or family jurisdiction in all except minor matters and hear appeals from minor judges (alcaldes); actuaries and arbitrators; (e) minor judges (alcades). (Judiciary Law 7333 of May 5, 1993).

CURRENCY:

(Monetary Laws 1367 of Oct. 19, 1951 as am'd; Law of Banco Central 1552, of Apr. 23, 1953 as am'd).

Monetary unit is colón, divided into 100 céntimos. That currency, in coins or represented by notes of Central Bank, constitutes legal tender for any kind of obligations payable in Costa Rica.

See also topic Exchange Control.

DEATH:

(C. C. 67-78).

An interested party may apply for a declaration of absence after two years from disappearance of absentee, unless absentee left attorney-in-fact in which case application may not be made until after ten years. These periods may be reduced by one-half if last report was that absentee was gravely ill or otherwise in danger of death.

DEATH . . . *continued*
Presumption of death may be declared when his absence continues 20 years after disappearance or ten years after declaration of absence or if 80 years have elapsed from birth of absentee.

Death records are kept by the Civil Registry. Death certificates may be obtained from the Chief of the Civil Registry of the district where the death occurred upon payment of a stamp tax and a nominal local fee.

Actions for Death.—Among the few provisions of Civil Code on torts, art. 1048, par. 6, provides that when a tort has been committed, if a decedent was under the legal duty to support a relative who loses his pension by reason of the death, said relative has a right of indemnization equivalent to lost pension. Court may, at its discretion, determine a lump sum instead.

DECEDENTS' ESTATES:

See topics Descent and Distribution; Executors and Administrators; Wills.

DEEDS:

Conveyances of real estate to be recorded must be by public instrument and contain a true statement of the consideration, since the state tax on transfers of title is based on the real consideration. Deeds must bear stamps depending on the amount involved and they must be recorded in the registry of property. Both grantor and grantee must sign the deed and must be present before the notary at the same time in person or by attorney in fact. An original deed executed in Costa Rica remains in the files of the notary, who gives to either party a certified copy which has the effect of an original in the courts of law. See topics Notaries Public; Public Instruments.

DESCENT AND DISTRIBUTION:

(C. C. 24, 520-576; C. Family arts. 229-233).

In absence of testamentary dispositions a decedent's estate passes to the following in order named: (1) children, parents and spouse but (a) spouse cause of a legal separation has no right to inherit and spouse separated de facto loses right to property acquired by other after separation; (b) spouse who receives community property inherits only amount required to complete the share due a spouse without community property; (c) common law spouses have right to inherit each other's property acquired during period of living together, if both are single and have been publicly living together for at least three years; (d) father inherits from his out of wedlock child, only when such child has been duly acknowledged or supported for at least two years; (2) grandparents and other ascendants; (3) brothers and sisters; (4) nieces and nephews; (5) parents; aunts and uncles; and (6) local boards of education with regard to decedent's local assets. Right of representation exists only in favor of descendants and nephews and nieces.

Certain persons are excluded from testate or intestate succession, as for example a person who committed a grave offense against the person or honor of the decedent, his parents, spouse or children, or who by fraud or violence induced the decedent to make a will or prevented him from making one.

Inheritances must be expressly accepted or may be refused. If they are accepted, the heir is liable for debts up to the value of the estate received by him. Acceptance may be unconditional or with benefit of inventory; in the former case the heir who is sued by a creditor of the estate is liable, unless he proves the assets are insufficient to pay the debt; in the latter case the creditor must prove that there are assets besides those inventoried.

Inheritance rights of common law spouses are regulated by law.

DIVORCE:

(C. Family 48-63).

Divorce dissolving marriage bond may be granted for: (1) Adultery of spouses; (2) attempt of either spouse against life of other; (3) attempt of one spouse to prostitute other one; (4) cruelty; (5) at request of either spouse when spouses have been judicially separated one year; (6) by mutual consent, but only after three years of marriage; (7) legal declaration of absence of either spouse; (8) separation in fact for at least three years.

The law specifies no particular period of residence in order to institute action for divorce but the initial pleading in every civil action must indicate a domicile within the jurisdiction. (C. C. P. 175).

The divorce action must be brought within one year after the cause came to the notice of the innocent party, and even if such party dies it may be continued by the heirs. When a divorce action is brought the judge may authorize the wife to leave the family home or order the husband to leave it. He may also allow the wife alimony if her income is insufficient, and decide as to the provisional custody of the children. In the judgment of divorce the judge may grant alimony to the innocent spouse sufficient to preserve the pecuniary position which such spouse had during the marriage. The children are awarded to the innocent spouse unless the judge orders otherwise, but children below five years are as a rule left with the mother. A guilty spouse loses any right to community property derived from the assets of the other spouse.

Separation may be granted for: (1) Any cause authorizing a divorce; (2) voluntary and malicious abandonment; (3) refusal of one spouse to support the other and children; (4) mutual consent; (5) insanity of either spouse for period over year, or other illness or serious changes in conduct of one spouse; (6) grave insults; (7) separation in fact for one year occurring after second year of marriage; (8) sentencing of one spouse to prison for three or more years for nonpolitical crime. Action may be brought only if person sentenced has remained prisoner for at least two consecutive years. Separation by mutual consent may be requested only after two years of marriage and parties must file written agreement relating to custody of children, responsibility for their support, alimony to be paid wife if her separate income is insufficient for her needs and disposal to be made of their property. If separation is asked on any other ground, same provisional measures are taken as in divorce. Reconciliation of spouses voids judgment, and in certain cases such reconciliation may be presumed.

DOWER:

No dower right. See topics Descent and Distribution; Husband and Wife.

ENVIRONMENT:

(Const. art. 50, Law 7554 of Oct. 4, 1995, Decrees 24715 of Oct. 6, 1995, 24867 of Dec. 12, 1995, and 25084 of Mar. 15, 1996).

Constitution establishes legal framework for environmental legislation granting to each person right to enjoy healthy and balanced environment. Law contains general rules for all productive sectors and considers environment and natural resources as national patrimony whose protection and conservation are public and social interest. Law contains such principles as prevention and control of environmental pollution, reparation of damages, environmental impact assessments and land use planning. Within environmental protection are air, noise, water, soil and waste. Entry of hazardous waste into country, whether actually or potentially dangerous, and of radioactive waste is prohibited. Administrative or criminal penalties are imposed for violation of law. Administrative sanctions include fines, partial or total, temporary or permanent closure of facility and cancelation of operating license. Criminal sanctions include fines and imprisonment as established by Criminal Code. Environmental liability is regulated by general principles of Civil Code which create obligation to indemnify for damages caused or to restore environment to previous state. Environmental Administrative Court is responsible for enforcing law.

EXCHANGE CONTROL:

Transactions with foreign exchange are subject to regulations to be issued from time to time by Central Bank of Costa Rica as provided by Law 1552 of Apr. 23, 1953 as am'd. Under Law 2202 of Apr. 14, 1958, mortgages and pledges in favor of nonresident foreigners and certain bonds may be agreed upon in foreign money.

Central Bank of Costa Rica publishes daily reference buying and selling exchange rate of foreign exchange for payment of foreign currency obligations which may be paid locally by delivery of national currency at this rate of exchange. Such rate is determined by prevailing rate for U.S. dollar according to supply and demand. Yearly remittances in dollars of interest and dividends are free.

EXECUTIONS:

When an order of execution has been issued and property attached, an appraisal is made of the property. A public auction under court auspices is then advertised. Bidders must deposit an amount equal to 15% of appraisal, unless relieved therefrom by party carrying on execution. If no bid is made, creditor may ask within one month for award of property at sale price or creditor may demand that new sale be held with reduction of 25% in appraised value and bidders must deposit 30% of appraisal value. If again there is no bidder, creditor may ask for award of property at one-half original appraisal or that third sale be held at which any bid is received, but if bid is less than one-half original appraisal, debtor is given short period to find another bidder. For third sale to be held bidders must deposit amount equal to 50% of appraisal value. After approval of sale, there is no right of redemption. (C. C. P. 647-659).

EXECUTORS AND ADMINISTRATORS:

(C. C. 541-567; C. C. P. 30, 876-927).

There can be but one executor or administrator, with a substitute in cases where he cannot act. If there is no executor appointed by will, the heirs and the surviving spouse by majority vote elect an administrator; in case of tie the judge decides. Until the executor or definitive administrator takes office the judge may appoint a temporary administrator, preferring the surviving spouse or a parent of the decedent.

The following cannot be executors or administrators: (1) Persons who cannot obligate themselves; (2) blind or deaf persons; (3) those under sentence for certain offenses; (4) those who have been guilty of fraud in the administration of the property of others. The incumbent may be removed at any time by interested parties, but if testamentary executor is removed without cause, he is entitled to his full commissions.

The estate vests in the heirs immediately on death of the decedent, but the executor or administrator has the administration thereof while the inventory is being prepared. Creditors may be paid as they appear, if privileged creditors are paid before expiration of six months, they must guarantee that they will return payment they may receive if creditor with priority right enforces his right within six months. As to liability of heirs for debts, see topic Descent and Distribution.

EXEMPTIONS:

(C. C. 981 and 984).

Following property of debtor is exempt from attachment: (1) Monthly salary portions exempted by Labor Code; (2) labor fringe benefits and alimentary pensions; (3) house furnishing and necessary clothing of debtor, his wife and children living with him; (4) books, machinery and tools of debtor, necessary for his work; (5) machinery and tools of craftsmen and farmers, necessary for individual workman and his children; (6) food for debtor's family for one month; (7) personal rights such as habitation of real property and property donated to debtor with prohibition of attachment by creditors, except improvements made by debtor. Items in (3), (4) and (5) may be attached by pledgee if pledge is registered, but those under (3) may be attached only for purchase price of same.

Labor Code, Art. 172, exempts minimum salaries. Salaries higher than minimum may be attached up to $^1/_8$ of excess up to three times minimum salary and $^1/_4$ for excess, but all salaries are attachable up to 50% for alimentary pensions.

FACTORS: See topic Principal and Agent.

FORECLOSURE: See topic Mortgages.

FOREIGN CORPORATIONS:

See topic Corporations.

FOREIGN TRADE REGULATIONS:

See topic Exchange Control.

FRAUDS, STATUTE OF:

See topics Contracts; Labor Relations; Public Instruments.

FRAUDULENT SALES AND CONVEYANCES:

(C. C. 900-911).

The following acts of the bankrupt or insolvent executed after the date as of which he is to be deemed insolvent are void: (1) Gratuitous contracts or those which should be considered such in view of insufficient consideration; (2) mortgages or privileges to secure earlier debts; (3) payment of unmatured debts; (4) payment of matured debts otherwise than in cash or commercial documents. Creditors may demand the annulment of other acts executed within the same period, such as the sale of real property, cancellation of mortgages, cancellation of unmatured credits and constitution of pledges, if the other party does not prove the actual payment of the consideration. The period is extended to two years before the insolvency declaration in the case of members of the family by consanguinity and affinity unless the other party proves payment and circumstances showing that he was unaware of the debtor's intention to defraud. Gratuitous acts or contracts executed within two years prior to the declaration of insolvency in favor of the spouse, ascendants, descendants, brothers and sisters, brothers- and sisters-in-law, sons- and daughters-in-law, fathers- and mothers-in-law, are void.

Creditors may demand annulment of simulated acts and contracts, of alienations when the grantee was aware of purpose to impair creditors' rights and of judgments obtained by connivance in order to defraud creditors.

HOLIDAYS:

Jan. 1 (New Year's); Mar. 19 (St. Joseph) Apr. 11; Maundy Thursday*; Good Friday*; May 1 (Labor Day); Corpus Christi*; July 25; Aug. 15; Sept. 15 (Independence Day); Oct. 12 (Columbus Day); Dec. 25 (Christmas).

*These are movable holidays.

HOMESTEADS:

(C. Family Arts. 42-47).

Homestead may be constituted for spouse or common law spouse, ascendants or minor descendants. Homestead cannot be alienated or encumbered without consent of both spouses or court authorization; and it is exempted from attachment except for debts or obligation contracted by both spouses.

HUSBAND AND WIFE:

(C. Family 33-47, 229-233; C. C. 595).

Spouses owe each other fidelity and assistance. Husband has responsibility to support family, but wife must contribute to it when she has her own assets.

The spouses may by duly recorded instrument make an antenuptial agreement as to property matters, which agreement may be modified after the marriage. If there is no such agreement, each spouse may freely dispose of property brought to the marriage by such spouse or acquired during the marriage and of the fruits of such property. Nevertheless property in possession of the spouses at the dissolution of the marriage is considered community property, to be distributed equally among the spouses, unless proved to have been brought to the marriage by one of the spouses or obtained by one of the spouses for a valuable consideration.

In the case of intestate succession, the surviving spouse is entitled to the same share as a child, but this share is diminished by the value of any community property. In the case of testate succession, the surviving spouse is entitled to such support as may be required; if the surviving spouse has sufficient property, there is no right to additional support.

Husband and wife may contract with each other and the wife requires no authorization from her husband to contract or appear in court.

Alimony rights of common law spouses are regulated by law.

IMMIGRATION:

(Law 1155 of Apr. 29, 1950 as am'd; Law 7033 of Aug. 4, 1986 and its regulations; Exec. Dec. 5 of June 1, 1941 as am'd; Law 13 of June 18, 1884 as am'd; Exec. Dec. 4 of Apr. 26, 1942; Law 37 of June 7, 1940 as am'd.

Prior authorization is required for entry into or departure from Costa Rica; such authorization is obtained from Department of Immigration. Applications for entry (except case of tourists or passengers in transit) must contain: name of applicant, date and place of birth, nationality, occupation, last place of residence, means of support possessed by applicant, purpose of entry. A foreign resident who leaves country must obtain a re-entry permit valid for one year.

Decree 21975 of Feb. 15, 1993 contained regulations to Law 7033 on two special categories of residents: "Pensioned Residents" and "Residents with an Income".

INFANCY:

(C. C. arts. 37-41, 835-836; C. Family 69-150; Laws 3260 of Dec. 21, 1963 and 3286 of June 20, 1964).

The age of majority is 18. Contracts by minors under 15 are void and if over 15 voidable, except when emancipated. Children under 18 are ordinarily subject to parental authority of both parents in case of conflict by Court decision at request of either parent; out of wedlock ones are subject to mother's. Parental authority includes custody, legal representation and administration, without obligation to account for income from minor's property, with certain exceptions. In absence or incapacity of parents guardian is appointed. Parents and guardians have restricted powers of disposition.

INSOLVENCY:

See topic Bankruptcy and Insolvency.

INTEREST:

(C. C. 1162-1166; C. Com. 497).

Legal interest is equal to interest paid by Banco Nacional de Costa Rica for six months' certificates of deposit. Contractual interest may be freely fixed by parties. Bank loans are subject to special rules. Central Bank of Costa Rica will determine maximum rate of interest for loans granted by official institutions.

INTESTACY:

See topic Descent and Distribution.

JUDGMENTS:

(C. C. P. 692-708).

Judgments are executed by means of a summary executory proceeding. A judgment does not constitute a lien on the property of the debtor, except with respect to property attached in the course of execution. A levy on real property must be recorded in a registry of properties.

Foreign judgments may be executed in Costa Rica if so ordered by the Supreme Court after giving the party against whom the judgment is directed a period of ten days to be heard. Execution of foreign judgment will not be approved if, from such judgment or from allegations and evidence of opposing party, it appears that: (1) Document is not duly authenticated; (2) judgment is not final judgment in country where rendered; (3) action was prosecuted without appearance of defendant, after being duly summoned; (4) judgment is contrary to public policy; (5) Costa Rican courts have exclusive jurisdiction; or (6) there is in Costa Rica pending case or final judgment rendered by local court on same matter.

LABOR RELATIONS:

(Const. art. 50-75, Labor Code).

National Constitution provides for right to work of individuals. Furthermore, Constitution guarantees workers equitable working conditions, a limited working day, paid days for rest and vacation, fair salaries and equal pay for equal service. Right of labor to organize trade unions and strike is also guaranteed by Constitution. Other Constitutional provisions protect (art. 50 to 75) welfare of family and its access to decent housing.

Labor relations are regulated by "Labor Code". Arts. 87 to 100 of Labor Code, contain special regulations for women and minors under 18 years. Private contracts may be oral only in following cases: agricultural labor and stock raising, domestic service, temporary work not exceeding 90 days, work for specific undertaking (por obra determinada) if amount involved is not over certain amount. Collective labor contracts must be always in writing.

If contract is for an indefinite period of time it is subject to termination by either party without an expression of cause, so long as prior written notice is given to other party. In certain cases a worker is entitled to an indemnification equal to one month's salary for every year of service. However, in general, termination of contracts by dismissal without due cause, subjects employer to payment of "severance assistance" (auxilio de cesantía) determined in accordance with years of service. Payments in lieu of advance notice and severance assistance are governed by Arts. 30 to 35. Arts. 203 to 261 of said law regulate occupational risks. Social security is compulsory and in some cases risk insurance is also compulsory.

LEGISLATURE:

Congress meets from May to July and from Sept. to Nov. in ordinary meetings, and in extraordinary meetings whenever it is called by Executive Power. (Const., art. 116).

LIENS:

Privileged credits in general comprise: (1) National and municipal taxes; (2) funeral expenses of debtor and members of his family; (3) medical services, medicines and food furnished during month preceding the insolvency; (4) salaries and wages for three months preceding insolvency. With respect to specific property, the following are liens in the order stated: (1) National and municipal taxes for one year prior to insolvency; (2) debts secured by mortgage or pledge; (3) rentals, which have a lien on the fruits of the property and on the furniture and other objects placed on the property by the lessee; (4) debts owing to creditors who have exercised the right of retaining the property for debts pertaining thereto. Creditors having such right of retention comprise: (a) Lessors, who as security for the payment of rental may retain the fruits of the property and the objects placed thereon by the lessee; (b) carriers, who as security for freight and expenses may retain the objects carried; (c) persons who have done work on objects of personal property, who may retain such objects until paid; and (d) commission merchants for fees and expenses. (C. C. 989-996, 1143, 1182, 1195; C. Com. 292, 336g).

LIMITATION OF ACTIONS:

See topic Prescription.

LIMITED LIABILITY COMPANIES:

See topic Corporations.

LIMITED PARTNERSHIP:

See topic Partnership.

MARRIAGE:

(C. Family 10-47; C.C. 27, 29).

The following marriages are legally impossible: (1) Of a person already married; (2) between ascendants and descendants; (3) between brothers and sisters; (4) between a person guilty, as principal or accomplice, of the death of one spouse, and the surviving spouse; (5) between adopted child and adopting parent and their children; (6) between persons of same sex. Following marriages may be annulled: (1) Those induced by error or duress; (2) of person mentally incapacitated; (3) of person less than 15 years

MARRIAGE... *continued*
old; (4) of impotent person, provided defect be perpetual, incurable and arising prior to marriage; (5) when performed before unauthorized official.

The following marriages are forbidden: (1) Of a person under 18 years without consent of parent or guardian; (2) of a woman before expiration of 300 days counting from dissolution or annulment of a previous marriage, unless a birth occurs in that period; (3) between a guardian or his descendants and ward, before accounts of guardianship are approved, unless deceased parents expressly authorized such marriage; (4) marriages without previous publications or dispensation of publications. Such forbidden marriages, if performed, are nevertheless valid, but delinquents are subject to punishment.

Marriages may be performed by Roman Catholic ceremony or by civil ceremony before official of civil registry or before notary public and two witnesses. Marriages by proxy are allowed.

Courts may of their own motion declare the nullity of legally impossible marriages and of marriages not performed by qualified functionaries or performed without the attendance of two qualified witnesses, and in the case of voidable marriages the annulment must be demanded by the party to whom said right is reserved. A marriage contracted with the legal solemnities and in good faith produces civil effects in favor of the spouse and children, even though later annulled.

MINES AND MINERALS:

(Const. art. 6, arts. 19, 145, 121, §14, art. 140, §19, L. 6797 of Oct. 4, 1982 and its Regulations, Decree 15442 of Apr. 26, 1984 as am'd, Decrees 14264 and 14265 of Feb. 4, 1983, Decree 19789 of June 6, 1990; Law 7399 of May 3, 1994 regulated by Decree 24735 of Sept. 29, 1995).

Mining in General.—State is owner of all geological resources within its territory and its exclusive economic zone. Mining activity is regarded as public interest. State may undertake exploration and utilization of mineral resources itself or it may grant such rights to individual, private entities, local or foreign, with exception of certain government officials and their relatives. Foreign states may participate in exploration and exploitation of mineral resources only as partners of Costa Rican Government.

State may reserve any zones for its exploration or exploitation. Petroleum and other hydrocarbons, and all energy resources are reserved to State, but special titles may be granted according to law and under conditions stated by Congress. Law establishes causes for expiration or cancellation of mining titles, when mining deposits become vacancies, available by direct request of any person. All mining activities and disputes are subject to Costa Rican law and jurisdiction. Foreign, natural or juridical persons not domiciled in Costa Rica must have agent and be recorded in Public Registry in order to apply for exploration permit or exploitation concession. Mining titles constitute jus ad rem, distinct from surface, although both may be possessed by same owner. They may not be alienated, encumbered or rented, except when special permission is granted. On termination of concession, all installations must be transferred to Government. Exploration permits are granted for maximum period of three years, which may be extended for two years. Area allocated for each permit varies in accordance with type of mineral, location and technical and economic capacity of applicant; but maximum allocated to any one individual or legal entity is 20 square kilometers.

Exploitation concessions are granted for maximum period of 25 years, which may be extended for period not to exceed ten years and in special cases may be extended with authorization of Congress. Area allocated to exploitation concession varies from one to ten square kilometers per applicant, depending on type of mineral and location.

Taxation.—Exploration permits and exploitation concessions are subject to annual surface royalty per square kilometer, which increase every two years. They are also subject to all taxes as indicated by Arts. 51, 52 and 54 of Law 6797 including income tax. Duty-free importation of capital goods and raw materials necessary for exploration, exploitation, manufacture, refining, transportation, or any other related activity are granted.

Petroleum.—State is owner of all petroleum deposits and any other hydrocarbon substances within its territory. Hydrocarbon activity is regarded as public interest enjoying preferential right to utilize surface with right to expropriation on payment of compensation. State may undertake exploration and exploitation of hydrocarbons itself or may enter into association, operation, service or concession contracts or any other kind of contracts with national or foreign individuals or companies through public bidding. Foreign companies domiciled abroad must open branch in order to execute contracts. All activities and disputes are subject to local law and jurisdiction. Contracting parties must post warranty to guarantee performance of contracts. Law establishes causes for termination of contracts. At termination of contract all equipment and installations must be turned over to State. Failure to perform may result in fines. Assignment of contracts requires prior authorization. Contracts for exploration or exploitation limited to maximum of 1.8 million hectares onshore and 1.2 million hectares offshore. Exploration may last three years renewable for three periods of one year each; exploitation may last up to 20 years, but when exploitation starts before end of exploration period, exploitation period is extended up to 26 years. Contractors may export whatever exportable surplus is left once local demand is satisfied. Contracting company must implement training programs. All contractors must file environmental protection program before starting operations, and contracts are subject to condition of approval of said program. Contracting companies pay income tax and are exempted from any other direct or indirect tax. Duty-free importation of capital goods and raw materials necessary for performance of contract, during exploration period and first ten years of exploitation period.

MONOPOLIES AND RESTRAINT OF TRADE:

Costa Rica Constitution (Art. 46) prohibits monopolies of a private nature and any act, even if grounded in law, which threatens or restricts freedom of commerce, agriculture or industry. Under Law 18 of June 9, 1915 ("Ley de Monopolio") any act which is intended to restrict or does in fact restrict or hinder free trade, commerce, industry or agriculture in country or in relation with foreign countries is prohibited. Violators are subject to penalties.

Law 3400 of Sept. 28, 1964 establishes that any person, enterprise, or association of persons which sells industrial products by themselves or through others, at prices equal to or less than cost of production or which effectively obtain same result through offer of premiums, gifts, payments, rebates or discounts, by means of bonds or coupons exchangeable for money, or by drawings to benefit of customers, shall be considered as monopolizing such business or industry and will be subject to same legal penalties established in Law 18 of 1915.

Central American Regulations on Unfair Trade Practices of Dec. 12, 1995 and Central American Regulations on Restrictive Covenants of May 22, 1996 implement principles established by Agreements of World Trade Organization.

Central American governments may issue restrictive covenants to protect temporarily local production from massive import of same or similar products that may cause pecuniary loss to local producers.

Law protects consumers' rights and promotes market freedom by preventing and prohibiting monopolies, monopolistic practices and other restrictive practices and regulations on economic activities. Any monopolistic practice, limitation, restriction or exclusivity in manufacturing and commercialization of goods and rendering of services is prohibited. Acts of monopoly include price fixing, limiting or controlling technical development of production of goods or services, limiting distribution, making exclusive rights agreements to tied-purchasing agreements and fixing resale price below or over cost. All agreements and collusive practices impeding, distorting or limiting competition are also prohibited, as well as abusive exploitation of dominant position in domestic market. There is "dominant position" when person for determined product is only one who offers or demands it in national market or where there is no competition. Law deals with consumers' rights to be informed; general representation and guaranties, products liability, credit operations, lack of performance, services, penalties for infringement of law and general regulations on subject. There are special regulations for advertisement of goods and services and for repression of unfair competition. Law is flexible policy instrument that Government can modulate according to needs of market. For this purpose Law has created public agency in charge of supervising enforcement of laws. (Law 7472 of Dec. 24, 1994 regulated by Decree 24533 of July 31, 1995).

MORTGAGES:

(C. C. 409-440, 471; C. C. P. 660-691).

Mortgages must be executed in form of public instruments and may refer only to real property. They cover fruits pending when compliance with obligation is demanded and all improvements and natural additions to property. However, under provisions of Code of Commerce (see topic Chattel Mortgages) machinery is not affected by mortgage of real property except when expressly included, and any duly recorded prior chattel mortgage on said machinery prevails over real property mortgage. In case of fruits chattel mortgage prevails even if recorded after land mortgage but before foreclosure action on latter is commenced.

Their lien includes three annuities of interest prior to foreclosure. If various parcels are mortgaged to secure same debt, amount for which each parcel is liable must be designated. Whenever debtor makes a payment he may demand reduction of mortgage.

Foreclosure follows the general rules of execution of judgments. The original debtor and the then owner of the property are summoned and notice is given to all mortgage creditors. In case of the foreclosure, property is sold free of liens and amount obtained is distributed among creditors according to their priority rights. In mortgage instrument parties may waive usual rules of execution, and in such case judicial sale is immediately held. After sale under foreclosure there is no right of redemption.

Re Vessels see topic Chattel Mortgages.

NOTARIES PUBLIC:

(Organic Notarial Law 39 of Jan. 5, 1943, as am'd).

Notaries are public officials authorized to act by Supreme Court. Notaries hold office indefinitely, but must give bond which must be renewed every year, and they remain under supervision of Supreme Court. They may act anywhere in Republic or outside country. In places where there is no notary, judge or alcalde acts as such.

Instruments executed before a notary must be prepared with certain formalities. They must be in Spanish and state the date, names of the parties, their age, profession, domicile, and whether married or single, also data as to witnesses. The notary must declare that he knows the parties or that they were identified by witnesses.

The notary retains the original document in a protocol and furnishes the parties with formal certified copies which have the effect of originals in court.

Notaries may issue certificates taken from Registry and public offices. Photocopies certified by notaries may be used.

PARTNERSHIP:

(C. C. 1196-1250; C. Com. 17-74; 243-245).

Commercial partnerships are considered legal entities. They are formed by public instrument executed before a notary and recorded in the mercantile registry; an extract from such instrument must be published in the official newspaper.

General partnership (sociedad en nombre colectivo) is a partnership in the usual form in which all partners have unlimited and joint liability among them but subsidiary to that of the partnership. Name must comprise the name of one or more of the partners, those omitted being covered by an additional reference. A person who tolerates inclusion of his name in name of a firm of which he is not a member becomes liable to third persons to same degree as the partners. A partner may not on his own account engage in same business as the partnership or have an interest in another company engaged in a similar business, unless authorized by his partners.

Limited partnership (sociedad en comandita) is a partnership in which there are one or more members with unlimited liability, who may but need not contribute capital, and limited liability partners who contribute capital and whose name must not appear in the partnership's name, which must be followed by the expression "y Compañía, Sociedad en Comandita" or "S. en C." Capital of limited members may be cash, property, invention patents, trade marks or scientific or artistic secrets, without personal work. Limited partner may not manage or administrate or act with power of

See Topical Index in front part of this volume.

PARTNERSHIP . . . *continued*
attorney, but in case of death of manager if there is no provision in articles of association, he may act on urgent matters with limited liability if no unlimited liability member is available.

Civil company (sociedad civil) is one which is not formed for commercial purposes. It is governed by the rules of the Civil Code and is distinguished from a mercantile company by being regarded rather as an association of individuals. The partners are not jointly or severally liable for debts of the company unless it is so stated in the obligation and the obligation was contracted by all the partners or under power of attorney from them.

Participating association (asociación en participación) is not strictly speaking a partnership and does not constitute a legal entity. It exists when merchants or companies grant others a participation in all or some of their business. It is similar to a joint venture. (C. Com. 663-666).

Foreign partnership may do business subject to some of the rules which apply to a foreign corporation. See topic Corporations.

PATENTS:

(Law 6867 of Apr. 5, 1983 and its Regulations, Decree 15222 of Dec. 12, 1983, as am'd by Decree 17602 of May 11, 1987, Law 6219 of Apr. 19, 1978 as am'd).

Patents may be obtained for products, machines, tools or manufacturing processes considered new and of industrial use. Novelty is destroyed by printed publication or public use of invention in any country, except when invention is revealed six months before application date at officially recognized exposition. Patents are granted for term of 12 years except in cases of patents on medicines, articles and substances for therapeutic use, beverages, foods, fertilizers, agrochemical products, herbicides and pesticides in which patent is granted for term of only one year. Foreign inventors may obtain patents for time during which their foreign patent is still to run, not exceeding 12 years. Patents must be exploited in country or in any Central American country with reciprocal treatment within four years from filing date or three years from granting date, otherwise any interested person may obtain license to exploit same with payment to inventor of compensation determined by Registry. Terms of license may be modified by parties or by Registry at any time.

Patents on pharmaceutical products for human use cannot be granted if products are not in use in country of origin.

Industrial designs and models may be registered if new and not known and exploited. Term of registration is five years.

Costa Rica is party to Convention for the Protection of Industrial Property, Paris, Mar. 21, 1883, Stockholm Revision of July 14, 1967 as am'd on Sept. 28, 1979.

PLEDGES:

Pledge contracts are governed by the chattel mortgage law. See topic Chattel Mortgages.

For vehicular pledges, see Traffic Law 7331 of Apr. 4, 1993 as am'd.

PRESCRIPTION:

(C. C. 26, 850-883; C. Com. 795, 968-986; Maritime Section of Code of Commerce of 1853 932-940).

The acquisition of property or rights by virtue of possession and the loss of rights by failure to enforce them is called prescription. Prescription may be waived, but only after it has run. Prescription is interrupted by recognition of the rights of the real owner or of the creditor, and by law suit, and it does not run against certain persons, as between parents and minor children, between guardians and their wards, and against soldiers in war time, or against domestic servants with respect to their wages, while they continue in the employment.

Ownership is acquired by positive prescription, the elements of which are: (1) A conveyance of the property, but in case of personal property, possessory rights and easements, mere possession raises a presumption of conveyance; (2) good faith; (3) continuous, public and quiet possession. Real property and rights are acquired by prescription in ten years from the time of recording. The right to possess is acquired in one year. Personal property is acquired in three years.

Actions.—Rights are lost by negative prescription. The prescriptive period in which the power to enforce rights is lost varies according to the nature of the right.

Period of limitation of actions not otherwise specified is ten years in general and four years for commercial transactions. Some of the specified periods follow: (1) Actions for materials supplied to construct or repair ships and for maritime insurance, five years; (2) actions arising from bills of exchange or promissory notes, four years; (3) actions to annul resolutions of a corporation or commercial company, for liability of administrators and directors of corporations or companies, for interest and rents resulting out of commercial transactions, salaries and professional fees payable in commerce, actions for price of commercial sales, one year, but interest, rent and pensions payable by semesters or more and for salaries and professional fees which are not out of commerce, are limited to three years; (4) tort actions, variable terms, depending on nature.

When there is a document in writing or a judicial decision recognizing the debt, the shorter term normally does not apply and the longer terms of ten years in general and four years for commercial transactions, begin to run.

PRINCIPAL AND AGENT:

(C. C. 1251-1300; C. Com. 235, 273-295, 314-322, 367-374).

An agency may be conferred by public or private instrument and orally, but can be proved only in accordance with legal rules of evidence. A general as well as an all-embracing power of attorney must appear in a public instrument (q. v.) and be recorded in the proper registry. A general power of attorney (poder general) covers acts of administration, including the right to lease for one year. An all-embracing power of attorney (poder generalísimo) covers all powers which the principal might exercise, including the power to alienate and encumber property, and excluding only acts which according to law must be performed by the owner in person or for which a special power of attorney is required.

The agent may delegate his powers if expressly authorized to do so, but is liable for the acts of his substitute if the latter is notoriously incompetent. The principal must reimburse the agent his reasonable expenses and for losses sustained through the agency if not due to the agent's fault and must pay him the stipulated or usual compensation. The agency terminates by: (a) Discharge of its object; (b) expiration of term; (c) revocation; (d) resignation of agent; (e) death, bankruptcy, insolvency or interdiction of principal or agent; (f) cessation of powers of principal if agency was conferred by virtue of such powers.

Commission merchant is a professional agent who normally acts for undisclosed principals and when he so acts becomes personally liable before other contracting parties who have no rights or duties toward principal. If he acts disclosing his principal's name the contract is between the latter and the other parties. He may be authorized orally or in writing. He may have a lien on certain assets for his fee and disbursements. Death of principal does not terminate the commission.

Factor is an attorney in fact of a merchant, holding very wide powers recorded in Mercantile Registry. Whenever he acts within ordinary course of business of establishment he binds owner as well as in any other case but with order of principal or his ratification, implied or apparent, and also even against orders or breach of trust, if within his power or in the ordinary course. Revocation of powers must be express or implied from the sale of the business and it is effective against third parties from recording in proper Registry.

An accountant is a keeper of the books and documents, correspondence and other papers, especially regarding accounts of a merchant. He may perform other acts of agency entrusted to him. His annotations in the accounts are binding on his principal.

A dependent is an employee acting within the establishment of a merchant. If he deals with public he represents the business in acts of which he is in charge and may receive the price paid in the act, unless public notices indicate to pay to the cashier. An employee authorized by circulars sent to correspondents by the principal to do certain acts binds the principal, but authority to draw against a current account must be in writing.

Representatives of foreign firms are specifically regulated by Code of Commerce Arts. 359-366, Law 6209 of Mar. 9, 1978 and Law 6333 of June 7, 1979, Decree 2937 of Apr. 10, 1973 as am'd, Decree 8599 of May 5, 1978 and Decree 13519-S of Apr. 19, 1982. All foreign firms may freely act in Costa Rica through representative of foreign firms duly established and may also act directly, occasionally, obtaining permit from proper authorities.

Law 6209 of Mar. 9, 1978 regulated by Decree 8599 of May 5, 1978 applies to rights and duties of local agents of foreign corporations, branches, and subsidiaries doing business in country. Agent can be any natural or juridical person, who continuously and independently prepares, and promotes sale of merchandise or services of foreign enterprises to local companies.

If principal chooses to terminate contract, without legal cause, he must indemnify agent with amount calculated on equivalent of four months of gross earnings for each year or practice during time of employment. However, value of indemnity cannot exceed total corresponding to amount calculated on more than nine years of employment time. Law defines concepts of agents, representatives, distributors and manufacturers of foreign firms. Causes for termination of representation or distributorship agreements, with liability for foreign corporation doing business in country are: offenses against property and goodwill of representative, distributor or manufacturer. Discontinuance of activities except if due to force majeure; unjustified restrictions on sales resulting in reduction in volume of transactions carried out by its representative, distributor or manufacturer; lack of due payment of commissions or fees; appointment of new representative, distributor or manufacturer, when affected party has exercised representation, distribution or manufacturing exclusively; any unilateral modification of contract and breach of contract. Causes for termination of representation, distribution or manufacturing contract, without liability for foreign corporation are: offenses against property and goodwill of foreign corporation by distributor or by manufacturer; judicially declared inability of or negligence by representative, distributor or manufacturer, as well as decrease or prolonged and substantial stagnation of sales, due to causes attributable to representative, distributor or manufacturer; infringement or violation by representative, distributor or manufacturer of trade secrets and confidentiality agreements by disclosing facts, know-how or techniques acquired during business relations; any other serious breach committed by representative, distributor or manufacturer with respect to its duties and contractual or legal obligations.

PUBLIC INSTRUMENTS:

Public instruments are documents executed with the legal formalities before a notary public (q. v.) or a public officer or issued by a public office. Other documents are private instruments. A public instrument constitutes proof of its execution and of the facts set forth therein with respect to the object of the agreement. The law requires numerous contracts to appear in public instruments, e.g., articles of incorporation or partnership, mortgages, etc., and no documents conveying or encumbering real estate can be recorded unless they are executed as public instruments. The date of a private writing is counted against third persons only from the death of the signer or from the time when the document was submitted to a public official or to a notary. A writing is required to prove an obligation of over 250 colones. Photo reproductions of official documents must bear certificate by official who authorizes them that they are true copies of originals, and official seal. (C. C. 28, 732-758).

REAL PROPERTY:

(Civil Code arts. Nos. 24, 264 to 519; Law 2755 of June 9, 1961 as am'd by Law 2779 of July 12, 1961).

Civil Code provides that laws of Costa Rica shall govern all matters concerning real property (inmuebles) located in Costa Rica even when they belong to foreigners. Real property includes objects permanently attached to realty as well as buildings and other structures. Everything which is attached to land, in a fixed, permanent manner, including buildings and structures, is real property by operation of law.

Law 3670 of Mar. 22, 1966 regulates condominiums.

RECORDS:

Law 5695 of May 28, 1975 as am'd is called "Law of the National Registry", regulated by Decree 24322 of May 12, 1995. Following documents must be registered: Real property titles, restrictions, attachments, leases and cooperative apartments and similar real property documents; organization of commercial companies, their amendments, dissolution, merger and similar documents; and documents related to Registry of Persons. Registrar shall determine whether documents fulfill legal requirements and harmonize with prior data of Registry.

There is Registry of Pledges of Moveable Property and one of Tradenames and Patents.

There is Civil Registry for births, marriages and deaths.

Vessels are registered under Law 12 of Oct. 22, 1941 and aircraft under Law 762 of Oct. 18, 1949, regulated by Decree 4440 of Jan. 3, 1975.

Vehicles and pledges of same are registered under Decree 16821 of Dec. 27, 1985. Transportation, in general is subject to Laws of Roads Administration 6324 of Apr. 30, 1979, as am'd, Law 7331 of Mar. 13, 1993.

REDEMPTION:

See topics Executions; Mortgages.

SALES (Realty and Personalty):

(C. C. 480-483; 1049-1123; C. Com. 438-489).

Between parties a sale is perfected and title passes when an agreement is reached on the thing to be sold and the price, independently of record in the registry or delivery. There are exceptions, as when fungible goods are sold by weight, count or measure, in which case title does not pass until the goods are weighed, counted or measured.

The seller is not obliged to deliver the thing sold until the price is paid, unless a term was granted for payment, nor even in this event if the buyer becomes insolvent. If real estate is sold by measure, any difference between the true area and that designated in the contract gives rise to a proportional increase or decrease of the price. If the property was sold as a whole, no change can be demanded in the price unless the difference in area exceeds one-tenth. If the area is found greater, the buyer may either pay the additional price or rescind the sale; if it is less, he may demand an additional area or a reduction in price, but he cannot rescind the sale unless the property, by reason of the smaller area, is found unserviceable for the purpose for which it is bought.

The right to repurchase cannot be reserved for longer than five years. A sale cannot be cancelled for hidden defects unless otherwise stipulated or unless they involve error annulling consent. The owner of stolen chattels may recover them within three years, unless the possessor purchased them at public sale or from a merchant selling similar articles; in such event the price paid must be reimbursed.

Commercial sales are defined and regulated by Code of Commerce. Some real property sales may be within its provisions. A bona fide purchase in a store of goods ordinarily dealt with in it cannot be object of replevin. If buyer examines his purchase he cannot claim later for defect of quality or quantity, but if he receives it as wrapped parcel or bale he may claim in writing in five days or in ten if the defects were hidden. Seller may demand immediate examination with no further claim. If express warranty of functioning is given, notice of failure must be given within 30 days of discovery of defect. There are provisions regarding sales subject to tasting or to testing, or by samples or known qualities.

Sales by instalments of identifiable property may be made with condition subsequent of termination for nonpayment and this condition binds third parties if contract is recorded in Registry of Personal Property. Seller must return price received but is entitled to indemnity for use and deterioration of the property.

Conditional sales (with reservation of ownership) are permitted for a period not exceeding three years, but buyer must keep seller informed of any change of address or of anything which might modify price of the purchased property; if buyer fails to inform, the obligation shall be due and payable.

Sales of establishments and bulk sales are subject to special rules for the protection of creditors, including publications, deposit of price, call of creditors' meeting and others, under penalty of nullity in favor of third parties.

SEALS:

Seals are not used in private matters. A document executed before a notary has most of the effects of a sealed instrument in the United States.

SHIPPING:

Costa Rican vessels may be owned by anyone who under the general laws of the Republic is authorized to acquire property. Costa Ricans are permitted to acquire and navigate foreign vessels as if such vessels had always been national vessels. An alien cannot be captain of a Costa Rican vessel unless he gives bond for an amount of at least one-half the value of the vessel. At least 75% of the crew of Costa Rican vessels must be Costa Rican citizens. Coastwise traffic is subject to concession by the Government. (Maritime Section of Code of Commerce of 1853, arts. 530-940; Laws 199 of Aug. 23, 1938 and 2220 of June 16, 1958; Decree 66 of Nov. 4, 1960).

Law 6267 of Aug. 29, 1978 regulates activities of foreign fishing vessels within 200 miles of seashore, requiring registration and fixing fees and applicable fines.

Costa Rican vessels in international trade need have only 10% of Costa Ricans in their crew and are subject to no taxes other than annual tonnage taxes. (Law 12 of Oct. 22, 1941 as am'd and Decree 1958 of Sept. 10, 1971).

STATUTES:

Most of the legal provisions are codified. The principal codifications are: Civil Code; Code of Family; Code of Commerce; Code of Civil Procedure; Penal Code; Code of Criminal Procedure; Organic Judiciary Law; Organic Notarial Law; Fiscal Code; Regulations of the Public Registry; Mining Code.

TAXATION:

Income Tax.—(Law 7092 of Apr. 21, 1988 as am'd and its regulations, Decree 18445 of Sept. 9, 1988 as am'd).

"Income Tax" includes: Tax on profits of companies, tax on salaries and pensions of individuals domiciled in Costa Rica and tax on remittance abroad.

Tax on profits is applicable to all juridical entities, including branches or permanent establishments, and individuals doing business or domiciled in country, undivided estates and trusts on all income obtained from Costa Rican sources.

Exemptions.—State, municipalities and government agencies, decentralized government entities, religious institutions, cooperatives, nonprofit organizations among others. Gross income is all revenues from activities as indicated by law. Net income is gross income minus deductions authorized by law. Unless proven otherwise loans evidenced in writing are deemed to yield interest at annual rate indicated by Central Bank or at average annual highest rates of banks of Sistema Bancario Nacional.

Deductions include: All necessary expenses to produce income, among them: salaries and bonuses; interest; bad debts; reasonable depreciation of machinery and other personal property of business; compensations to directors and members of other directive and advisory boards acting abroad; fees or compensations for technical-financial or similar advice from abroad, as well as royalties from patents, formulas, tradenames, franchises, etc. paid out of country; gifts to state and certain official agencies and charitable, scientific or educational organizations; travel expenses of owners, employees or technicians brought from abroad, necessary for production.

Professionals not keeping correct records or who do not normally issue receipts for their fees are presumed to have minimum annual net income as follows: (i) Physicians, dentists, architects, engineers, lawyers, notaries, public accountants, economists and real estate brokers, 1,335,000 colones. (ii) Land surveyors, experts, private accountants, technicians not indicated in (i) above, 890,000 colones. However, when professionals have been practicing less than five years above amounts are reduced by 50%.

Taxpayers owning living, recreation, summer or similar houses must include amount established by law as presumed income therefor.

Local branches, agencies and other permanent establishments of foreign companies or persons domiciled abroad are deemed to have following minimum annual net taxable income (unless proven otherwise): when engaged in transportation and communication, 15% of gross income; reinsurance, 10.5% of net value of reinsurance and of insurance provisions except life insurance; film production and distribution, 30% of gross income and international news, 30% of gross income. Juridical persons engaged in agricultural and cattle activities are deemed to have (unless proven otherwise) as minimum annual net taxable income amount equivalent to 5% of value of real estate utilized in such activities when such real estate is worth 4,000,000 colones or more.

Tax Rates.—For juridical persons rate is 30% of net taxable income, for small enterprises rate is either 10% or 20% of net taxable income, depending on annual gross income; non-active juridical persons are taxed at fixed amount. Individuals are exempt when annual net taxable income is less than 580,000 colones. Annual net taxable income in excess of 580,000 colones is taxed at rates ranging from 10% to 25%.

Tax Credit for Individuals.—Taxpayers may subtract annually from amount to be paid 2,400 colones for spouse; 1,800 colones for each child. Child must be either minor, totally supported by taxpayer; unable to work or student not over 25.

Dividends payable by stock corporations are subject to withholding tax of 15%. However, if stock corporation is registered with bolsa de comercio officially recognized and stockholder acquired stock through such bolsa de comercio withholding is only 5%.

Tax on Income from Work and Pensions.—Individuals who sell their services as employees or workers or receive pensions and who are locally domiciled are taxed monthly on income indicated by law. Income of workers, employees and retired persons is exempt when less than 131,000 colones per month. Income in excess of said amount is subject upon payment to withholding tax at rates of 10% or 15%.

Tax on Remittance Abroad.—Following payments to recipients domiciled abroad are subject to following withholding taxes only: (a) Interest paid to banks and financial institutions recognized by Central Bank is exempt. Interest paid to other parties domiciled abroad is subject to withholding tax of 15%; (b) income from production, distribution or other activities related to movie or television films or videotapes, 20%; radio novels and telenovels, 50%; salaries, 10%; commissions or any work compensation for services abroad to concerns in Costa Rica, 15%; for technical, financial, administrative or similar advice, 25%; reinsurance premiums, 15%; (c) income from news served by international agencies; production, distribution and activities related to phonograph records, short story tapes, photonovels and similar sound items, 20%; patents formulae, trademarks, franchises and royalties, 25%; (d) any kind of compensation paid to members of boards of directors, councils or similar organizations, 15%; (e) any other income remitted abroad different than above, 30%.

Dividends, profits, interests, commissions, royalties, remittances, premiums, and service compensations paid abroad (subject to 15%) may be wholly or partially exempted if proved that recipient gets no credit or deduction or these are for smaller amounts, against tax abroad. This does not apply when income is not taxed there.

In some communities, small municipal tax is payable each year, based on income, in addition to general income tax.

Special Treatment.—Law grants special benefits to exporters of nontraditional products to third markets. Tax incentives consist mainly in 100% exemption for 12 years as of 1984 of income tax on net profits originated in such exports; deduction of 50% of investment made in local export companies; and duty-free importation of capital goods and raw materials not produced locally and necessary to manufacture products to be exported.

Exporting companies may enter into contract for export and production for export with Government and receive following benefits: Reduced port fees, low interest on loans, accelerated depreciation, simplification of administrative procedures, technical assistance, tax credit certificates.

Temporary Imports.—Temporary duty free import of merchandise to be exported after repaired, reconditioned or assembled is allowed. Earned income is subject to income tax.

TAXATION . . . *continued*

Tax on Assets.—(Law 7543 of Sept. 14, 1995). Tax at annual rate of 1% of value of assets is assessed on all entities, individuals, undivided estates and trusts engaged in profitable activities according to law.

Real estate is subject to: (a) Tax on real property is payable to municipalities on assessed value of all real property of same taxpayer at rates from 0.30% to 1% (Law 7509 of May 9, 1995 regulated by Decree 24857 of Dec. 11, 1995); (b) property bordering or near new public works may be subject to Increase in Value Tax. There is also special annual tax on rural property for benefit of municipalities, called "Detalle de Camino" (Secondary Road Tax) determined for each taxpayer individually in relation with use he makes of secondary roads (Law 1851 of Feb. 28, 1955).

Tax on Constructions.—(Law 7088 of Nov. 30, 1987 as am'd and Decree 17878 of Dec. 1, 1987). Houses, apartments and condominiums and their fixtures with value over 5,000,000 colones are taxed at rate of 1% from 5,000,000 colones to 10,000,000 colones and 1.5% over 10,000,000 colones.

Transfer and Mortgage Tax.—(Law 2854 of Nov. 6, 1961). Tax of 2 per mil applies to transfers of vehicles and credits and to creation of mortgages and to mortgage certificates.

Tax on Transfer of Real Property.—(Law 6999 of Sept. 3, 1985 as am'd and its regulations Decree 21743 of Nov. 17, 1992). All transfers of real property are subject to this tax, except: (a) Transfers of house and land under colones 600,000, and any other transfer under colones 400,000; (b) inheritance distributions of real property, under same condition stated in (a); (c) transfers to individuals for public housing purposes; (d) transfers for less than colones 600,000 for family abode or rural property for supporting same; (e) several others of public interest. Tax rate is 3%.

Consumers Tax.—(Decree 14616 of June 10, 1983 as am'd and regulated by Decree 14617 of June 10, 1983). This tax applies to transfers of merchandise included in list prepared by executive power. Items must be of ultimate consumption and not raw materials or intermediate products and not essential or indispensable. They must also be nationally produced. Tax also applies to import of merchandise included in above mentioned list. Items exported by merchants are exempt. Rates are variable and are determined in above mentioned list.

Sales Tax.—(Law 6826 of Nov. 8, 1982 as am'd and regulated by Executive Decree 14082-H of Nov. 29, 1982 as am'd, Law 6849 of Feb. 18, 1983). This tax is levied on: (a) Sales effected in Costa Rica (except sales of real estate and of merchandise for exportation. Also exempted are among others most foodstuffs, medicines, veterinary drugs, fertilizers, and other items listed in art. 9 of law); (b) services rendered by hotels, restaurants, bars, night clubs, dry cleaning and automobile repair and paint shops; (c) imports, made by nonregistered persons; (d) television, telephone, telex and cable service; and (e) film development and photocopies. General rate is 13%.

Registry tax is payable for recording of real property conveyances and mortgages, powers of attorney, articles of incorporation and partnerships, etc. General rule is that rate is determined by amount involved, tax is 5 colones for each 1,000. There are special tables for cancellation of mortgages and for mortgages representing part of price of real estate. When there is no amount, or document comprises acts falling in both categories, there is a fixed tax or combination of both. (Law 4564 of Apr. 29, 1970 as am'd).

Stamped paper and revenue stamps are required for most documents used in courts or public offices and for many private transactions, such as deeds, mortgages, etc. Revenue stamps must likewise be affixed to many other documents. The amount depends on the nature of the document and the sum involved. In general all contracts and all shares of corporations require revenue stamps. Local checks require same amount of stamps whatever value. Any corporation and subsidiary of any foreign corporation are required to pay Education and Culture stamp tax for registration in Mercantile Register and annual tax on capital stock of corporation. (Law 26 of Nov. 21, 1914; Fiscal Code, arts. 238-248, 251, 252, 255-289; see also Law 2545 of Feb. 17, 1960, Law 2565 of May 23, 1960, Law 3245 of Dec. 3, 1963 and Law 5923 of Aug. 5, 1976 as am'd).

Tax on Premiums, Gifts or Compensations.—(Laws 34 of Dec. 21, 1940 and 3400 of Sept. 28, 1964). This tax is levied on premiums, gifts or compensations by means of bonds or coupons exchangeable for money or by drawings to benefit consumers. Tax is ten times value of premium, gift or compensation.

Free Zones (Law 7210 of Nov. 23, 1990 as am'd regulated by Decree 20355 of Apr. 2, 1991 as am'd). Promotion, administration and supervision of free zones regimes corresponds to "Corporación de la Zona Franca de Exportación, S.A.", mixed capital corporation. All types of industries, trading companies and services are allowed to operate there. They are exempt among others from import and export taxes, sales and consumers tax; tax on remittance abroad; ten years exemption from municipal taxes; real property tax; transfer of property tax; income tax exemption varies according to area or location of free zone. When established in free zones in less developed areas, companies may enjoy, for five years, bonus equal to certain percentage of amount paid in salaries during previous year. Dividends on profits paid or credited to nonresident individuals or juridical persons are not exempt in that they are taxed in their country of domicile and get credit for tax paid in Costa Rica. No restrictions exist for entering into and exiting from free zones of goods, negotiable instruments, local and foreign money.

TRADEMARKS AND TRADENAMES:

(Central American Convention for the Protection of Industrial Property Law 4543 of Mar. 18, 1970, Law 559 of June 24, 1946 am'd only on subjects not regulated by Convention.)

Trademarks comprise any sign, word, expression or any other graphic or material means which because of its special characteristics can clearly distinguish products, merchandise or services of person or corporation.

Trademarks are classified as industrial or manufacturers' marks, commercial marks and service marks.

Industrial or manufacturers' marks are those that distinguish goods produced or processed by specified manufacturing or industrial enterprise.

Commercial marks are those that distinguish goods commercial enterprise sells or distributes regardless of who produces them.

Service marks are those that distinguish activities of enterprises devoted to satisfaction of general needs by means other than manufacture, sale or distribution of goods.

Use of registration of following as trademarks is prohibited: (1) National flags or their colors, if latter appear in same order and positions as in former, coats-of-arms, insignia or distinguishing marks of Contracting States, their municipalities and other public bodies; (2) flags, coats-of-arms, insignia, devices or denominations of foreign nations unless authorization from respective government has been obtained; (3) flags, coats-of-arms, insignia, devices, denominations or acronyms of international agencies of which one or more Contracting States are members; (4) names, emblems and devices of Red Cross and of religious or charitable bodies legally recognized in any of Member States of this Convention; (5) designs of coins or notes that are legal tender in territory of any of Contracting Parties, reproductions of securities and other commercial documents or of seals, stamps, or revenue stamps, or revenue stamps in general; (6) signs, words or expressions that ridicule or tend to ridicule persons, ideas, religions or national symbols of third party states or international agencies; (7) signs, words or expressions, contrary to good morals, public order or good usage; (8) names, signatures, family names and portraits of persons other than person filing application without their consent or, if deceased, consent of their closest ascendants or descendants; (9) technical or common names of products, goods or services when they are intended to protect articles or services included in genus or species to which such names refer; (10) terms, signs or locutions that have passed into general use and which are used to indicate nature of products, goods or services, and qualifying and gentilitial adjectives. Trademarks that have become popular or widespread subsequent to their registration shall not be regarded as having passed into general use; (11) figures, denominations or phrases describing products, goods or services that are to be protected by trademarks or their ingredients, qualities, physical characteristics or use for which they are intended; (12) signs or indications that are used to designate type, quality, quantity, value or season of preparation of products or goods or of provision of services, unless they are followed by designs or phrases that particularize them; (13) usual and current form of products or goods; (14) plain colors considered separately, unless they are combined or accompanied by elements such as signs or denominations having particular or distinguishing character; (15) containers that are in public domain or have come into common use in any of Contracting States and, in general, those that are neither original nor novel; (16) mere indications of origin or denominations of origin, except as set forth in item (b) of Art. 35; (17) distinguishing marks already registered by other persons as trademarks for products, goods or services included in same class; (18) distinguishing marks that by reason of their graphic, phonetic or ideological similarity may mislead or result in confusion with other trademarks or with commercial names, publicity expressions or symbols already registered or in process of being registered, if it is intended to use them to distinguish products, goods or services included in same class; (19) distinguishing marks that may mislead by indicating false source, nature or quality; (20) maps. These may, however, be used as elements of trademarks if they represent country of origin or source of goods which they distinguish.

Registration is mandatory for chemical, pharmaceutical, veterinary and medicinal food products. Term of registration is ten years subject to renewals for equal periods. Licenses must be registered. International Mark Classification applies. Fees are: Registration of each mark or name $50, and of propaganda slogans or signs $25; renewal $50, transfer $10, any certificate or document $5.

Tradenames are also regulated by C. Com. 242-250.

Costa Rica is party to Convention for the Protection of Industrial Property, Paris, Mar. 21, 1883, Stockholm Revision of July 14, 1967 as am'd on Sept. 28, 1979.

TREATIES:

Legislative-Decree 4448 of Oct. 17, 1969 approves Agreement with U.S.A. regarding U.S. investments guaranties signed in City of San Jose on Nov. 22, 1968.

Pursuant to said Agreement, governments of Costa Rica and U.S. agree to consult each other and to exchange information regarding projects for investment in Costa Rica. U.S. Government shall not guarantee investment in Costa Rica unless Government of Costa Rica approves activities to which investment refers to. In case of controversy regarding interpretation or applicability of Agreement same shall be subject to negotiations by the two governments and, if possible shall be solved immediately. If within three months after starting negotiations both governments cannot reach a satisfactory agreement, controversy shall be sent to an arbitrator selected by mutual agreement of parties and his judgment shall be final and binding pursuant to applicable principles of international law. If arbitrator cannot be selected within three months after such request, then President of International Court of Justice shall appoint arbitrator. Extradition Agreement with U.S.A., ratified by Law 7146 of Apr. 30, 1990. Agreement on Exchange of Tax information with U.S.A., ratified by Law 7194 of Aug. 29, 1990.

Law 6165 of Dec. 2, 1977 approved Interamerican Conventions signed in Panama on Jan. 30, 1975 on: Conflict of Laws concerning bills of exchange, promissory notes and invoices; Conflict of Laws concerning checks; International Commercial Arbitration; Letters Rogatory; The Taking of Evidence Abroad and The Legal Regime of Powers of Attorney to be used abroad.

Central American Agreement on Tariff and Customs Regime and its Annex was ratified by Laws 6986 of May 3, 1985, 7005 of Sept. 27, 1985 and 7017 of Dec. 13, 1985. Establishes common regime that includes: Import tariff based on Brussels Nomenclature and ad valorem duties, law on customs value of merchandise and its regulations, uniform customs code and its regulations, regulations on tax exemptions.

Party to Multilateral Trade Negotiations, The Uruguay Round, Final Act, Marrakesh, Apr. 15, 1994 and Agreement Establishing the World Trade Organization, Marrakesh, Apr. 15, 1994.

TRUSTS:

(C. Com. 633-662; C. C. 292, 336, 582, 981 and 1396).

By a trust, which may be created by contract or by will, settlor dedicates certain property to specific purposes, delegating the realization of said purposes to a trustee

See Topical Index in front part of this volume.

TRUSTS . . . *continued*
(administrator) who may be a natural or juridical person. Document of creation must contain description of corpus, rules of administration, unless left to discretion of trustee, indication of person or persons who are the beneficiaries, after administration expenses and trustee's fees are paid. Trustee must give guarantee if so requested in document of creation. It may also determine to whom must pass the remainder after termination of trust, otherwise it reverts to settlor or his estate. No limitations or encumbrances may be placed by trustee on the trust property.

Following are forbidden: (a) Secret trusts; (b) trust for benefit of successive beneficiaries if substitution is to take place upon death of one of them; (c) trusts for more than 30 years in favor of juridical persons, unless beneficiary is a state or charitable institution; (d) trusts assigning to trustee a benefit, commission or economical advantage in excess of the fee granted. If no fee is fixed it will be determined by judge. Trust ends by realization of its purpose or its becoming impossible; by the happening of a subsequent condition; by express agreement between settlor and trustee; and by revocation by settlor.

Under general provisions of law, a usufruct (similar to an estate for life or years) may not be established in favor of two or more persons to enjoy alternatively or successively; a grant by last will and testament may not be left to be enjoyed by a beneficiary in substitution for another grantee, except in the case when the latter cannot or refuses to accept it. In general, and except as a valid trust, gifts cannot be made subject to reversion or remainder rights, but a donor may provide for some limitations to free disposition for up to ten years or until donee reaches age of 25 and that corpus be exempt from attachment for same period. (Law 2112 of Apr. 5, 1957).

VITAL STATISTICS: See topic Records.

WILLS:

(C. C. 28, 45, 577-595, 734).

Wills may be made by all except persons mentally incapacitated or under 15 years of age. The witnesses must have the qualifications required for witnesses to documents executed before notaries. (See topic Notaries Public.) Wills are either open or closed.

Open wills may be made: (a) Before a notary and three witnesses, but if the will is written by the testator himself, only the notary and two witnesses are required; or (b) before four witnesses, without a notary, if the will is written by the testator himself or before six witnesses if it is not written by the testator. The will must state the place, date and hour where signed; be read before the witnesses by the testator or by a person he may designate, or by the notary; and be signed by the testator, notary and witnesses. If the testator cannot sign, the will must so declare. If the will is in a foreign language, two interpreters are required if it is made before a notary, or all the witnesses must know the foreign language if it is made only before witnesses.

Privileged open wills may be made by soldiers in time of war, before an officer and two witnesses, or by persons at sea before the captain and two witnesses, but if the testator writes the will himself, only the two witnesses are required. Such a will is valid only if the testator dies in the situation in which he made it or within thirty days thereafter.

Closed will need not be written by the testator but must be signed by him. The will, enclosed in a sealed envelope, must be presented to a notary who makes a note on the envelope stating: (a) That it was presented to him by the testator; (b) declarations of the testator as to the number of pages in his will, as to whether it was written and signed by him and whether it contains any erasures or corrections. This note must be signed by the notary, testator and three witnesses. The envelope with the will is then returned to the testator. Blind and illiterate persons cannot make closed wills.

Testamentary Dispositions.—Testator may freely dispose of his estate but he must set aside sufficient to support his children until their maturity or during their lives if they are invalids; also his parents and also his wife; but if such persons have sufficient property he need leave nothing for their support. Not over 10% can be left to religious institutions, and following persons and their near relatives are excluded from taking by will: (1) Guardian of unemancipated minor testator, unless he has rendered his accounts or is testator's ascendant or brother; (2) teachers or custodians of minor testator; (3) physician or confessor who attended testator in his last illness; (4) accomplice of adulterous spouse; (5) notary or clerk who acted in making of will; nevertheless in cases (2) and (3) remunerative legacies are valid, as well as provisions in favor of persons who would be legal heirs of testator.

Foreign wills are given effect if valid according to the laws of the country-where made, or if made in accordance with the Costa Rican laws.

See Topical Index in front part of this volume.

CZECH REPUBLIC LAW DIGEST

(The following is a list of all Topics, including cross-references, covered in this Digest.)

CZECH REPUBLIC LAW DIGEST

Revised for the 1997 edition by

ZEINER GOLAN NIR & PARTNERS, Prague in co-operation with PROFESSOR JUDr. ZDENEK KUCERA, DrSc. of the Faculty of Law of the Charles University, Prague, Czech Republic.

Abbreviations used are: OSR, obcansky soudni rad (code of civil procedure) (Act no. 99/1963 Sb., full wording, no. 240/1993 Sb., amended by no. 117/1994 Sb.); ObchZ, obchodni zakonik (commercial code) (Act no. 513/1991 Sb., amended by Acts no. 264/1992 Sb., no. 591/1992 Sb., no. 600/1992 Sb., no. 286/1993 Sb., no. 156/1994 Sb., no. 84/1995 Sb., and no. 142/1996 Sb.); OZ, obcansky zakonik (civil code) (Act no. 40/1964 Sb., full wording Act no. 47/1992 Sb., as amended by Act no. 264/1992 Sb.); Sb., Sbirka zakonu (collection of laws); ZP., Zakonik prace (Labour Code) (Act no. 65/1965 Sb., full wording no. 126/1994 Sb.).

PRELIMINARY NOTE:

Czech Republic (CR), which was part of Czech and Slovak Federative Republic (CSFR) until Dec. 31, 1992, is sovereign independent state as result of Jan. 1, 1993 division of Federation into two separate states. By virtue of Constitutional Act No. 4/ 1993 Sb., legal acts of former CSFR remain in force in territory of Czech Republic. Furthermore, also by virtue of same act, Czech Republic has succeeded to all rights and duties of former CSFR arising out of international law, with exception of duties connected with territory that is not under sovereignty of Czech Republic.

Czech Republic is member of Council of Europe and has signed association agreement with EC, presently undergoing process of ratification.

ABSENTEES:

During absence abroad, person may generally delegate authority to any person, subject to provisions of law regarding power of attorney; see topic Principal and Agent.

For purposes of legal proceedings, court may appoint curator for person who is absent from his place of domicile or if place of domicile is unknown. (OSR, §29 and OZ, §29). Curator appointed in course of court proceeding represents absentee and protects his/her interests. (OSR, §29). Any documents delivered to curator are considered to be delivered to absentee. Curator may act in name of absentee only in cases concerning respective matters heard by court and may not enter into any legal transactions exceeding framework of case heard by court.

Court may appoint curator for absentee in proceedings concerning declaration of death. (OSR, §195/2).

Czech court may appoint curator for foreigner in case that service of process on his known address in foreign country was unsuccessful. (OSR, §29).

ACKNOWLEDGEMENTS:

Document Prepared Abroad.—Public documents issued by courts or authorities abroad must be acknowledged (legalized) by Czech consular officer, which may legalise document only in case document certified by Ministry of Foreign Affairs of respective country. CR is not party to Hague Convention of Oct. 5, 1961 on abolishing requirement of legalization for foreign public documents and "apostille" made pursuant to this convention is insufficient for purposes of Czech law. CR has concluded bilateral agreements on regarding legal services, including recognition of acknowledgments, with Bulgaria, Hungary, Poland, Romania, Belgium, France, Cyprus, Greece, Spain, Switzerland, Italy, Austria, Tunisia and Finland.

Document Prepared in CR for Use Abroad.—Acknowledgment of document copies and signatures may be done by municipal authorities and by district authorities. (Act No. 41/1993 Sb.). Public notaries perform verification and acknowledgment of original documents. (Act No. 358/1992 Sb.). In event notary or authorized person does not understand language in which document is written, it must be first translated and verified by translator. Document must be legalized by Ministry of Justice, unless bilateral or international agreement applies.

See topic Notaries Public.

ACTIONS:

Commencement of Proceedings.—Rights and duties resulting from proceedings are regulated by OSR. Legal and physical persons commence proceedings by written submission to court of first instance, normally district courts. In commercial matters regional courts operate as courts of first instance. (OSR, §9). Proceedings may be commenced orally, recorded by any court and then transferred to proper court, in order to keep effect of submission as of date record was made. Actions may be submitted via cable, but it is necessary to make written record of such submission no later than three days after sending cable.

Appropriate Forum.—Regulated by OSR, §§84-89a. Generally for venue, court with subject matter jurisdiction located at place of legal seat of defendant. In case where district court has subject matter jurisdiction, court seated in district where citizen is domiciled, where entity has its seat or where event on which claim is based occurred, should state be defendant. For subject matter jurisdiction, see topic Courts.

OSR, §87 stipulates competence of court which plaintiff may select instead of local forum. OSR, §88 regulates competence of courts other than local forum which must be selected by plaintiff in order to submit action.

Action against foreign entity is submitted to court with subject matter jurisdiction seated in district of CR in which defendant has representative or other body authorised to manage its affairs. Participants of proceedings concerning business matters may make written agreement stipulating competence of court other than usual first instance, unless law stipulates exclusive competence. (OSR, §89a).

Parties.—Pursuant to proposal of participant, court may allow other parties to take part in proceedings. Consent is required if party will act as co-plaintiff. Substitution of parties is allowed upon agreement of parties. (OSR, §92). Individual who has legal interest in result of action may take part either on side of plaintiff or defendant in position of by-participant, except in action involving divorce or marital status. (OSR, §93).

Evidence.—From investigation of matter, particularly examination of witnesses, expert opinions, records, documents and examination of participants may serve as proof. If method of providing proof is not prescribed, it is decided by court. (OSR, §125). Evidence has to be presented in manner that preserves state, economic, commercial and official secrets. (OSR, §124). Legal regulations published or announced in Collection of Laws of CR do not require any proof. If according to conflict of law rules, choice of law agreed by parties to contract included, law of foreign state is to be applied, court is obliged to take all necessary measures to ascertain foreign law. Should it be necessary, court can request opinion of Ministry of Justice or expert opinion. (§53, Act no. 97/1963 Sb., amended by Acts no. 158/1969 Sb., no. 234/1992 Sb. and no. 264/1992 Sb.). In such cases, court must apply foreign law ex officio.

Costs.—Court awards remuneration of costs to winning party. In case of partial success, costs are divided proportionally or court may decide none of participants are entitled to costs. Costs include court fee, lost earnings of participants, cost of proof, interpretation and lawyers fees. (OSR, §137). Remuneration of lawyers fees is limited to amounts stipulated by Decree no. 270/1990 Sb., amended by no. 573/1992 Sb. Plaintiff pays court fee when submitting action. Amount is stipulated by Act no. 36/1995 Sb. Generally, fee is 4% of requested damages, or not less than 500 Kc, up to maximum of 500,000 Kc in civil cases or 1,000,000 Kc in commercial cases. If subject of action does not involve action for damage, fee is 1,000 Kc, in commercial case 5,000 Kc.

ADOPTION:

Basic provisions on adoptions are contained in Family Code. (Act no. 94/1963 Sb., in full wording Act no. 66/1983 Sb. §§63-77). CR is member of Convention on the Rights of Children. (no. 104/1991 Sb.).

Relationship established by adoption has same legal effects as between natural parents and children. Upon adoption, rights and duties between natural parents and adoptee are terminated and adoptee receives family name of adopter along with rights and duties arising from family relations. Person may adopt minor if: (1) He has legal capacity to act; (2) he will provide way of life which guarantees benefit for adoptee and society; (3) appropriate difference of age between adopter and adoptee exists; (4) consent of husband or wife of adopter, if applicable; (5) consent of natural parents, legal representatives or court appointed guardian under certain circumstances (§§67, 68); (6) consent of minor if able to comprehend consequences of adoption, unless purpose of adoption would be frustrated.

District court in district of adoptee's address is competent to hear adoption action. Adoptee has to be under care of adopter at least three months before court's decision. In addition to above mentioned requirements, court considers if state of health of adopter and adoptee is convenient for purpose of adoption.

Setting Aside Adoption.—May occur if adopter or adoptee bring court action. Important reasons are required. Legal relationship between natural parents and adoptee is reestablished. (§73).

Inviolable Adoption.—Adoption where adopter is entered in "Register of Birth" instead of true parents. Adoptee must be minor person over one year. Other conditions required. (§§74-77).

AFFIDAVITS:

Affidavits are not permitted as substitute evidence in court proceedings. Exception to general rule involves administrative proceedings according to Administrative Proceedings Act. (Act no. 71/1967 Sb., am'd by Act no. 159/1973 Sb.), which provides conditions for use of "Declaration of Honour" instead of evidence, unless: (1) Special provision stipulates otherwise; (2) equity of participants is breached; (3) public interest is breached.

Exception in court proceedings involves affidavits by request of foreign court or administrative office. (§57, Act no. 97/1963 Sb.).

See topics Acknowledgments; Depositions.

AGENCY:

See topic Principal and Agent.

ALIENS:

Though several definitions of "alien" exist under Czech law, usual meaning is person without CR citizenship.

In field of personal and property rights, aliens generally hold same rights as Czech citizens. (§32, Act no. 97/1963 Sb., am'd by Acts no. 158/1969 Sb., no. 234/1992 Sb. and no. 264/1992 Sb.). They can engage in entrepreneurial activity on same conditions and in same scope as citizens of CR, unless specifically provided otherwise by law. (ObchZ, §21).

Aliens generally do not have voting rights; they are not subject to military conscription; they generally need residential and working permits; they may only own real estate in accordance with exchange control laws.

Individual having citizenship of two or more states, one of which is CR, is treated as Czech citizen.

See also topics Foreign Exchange; Corporations; Taxation; Labour Relations; Immigration.

Corporations Controlled or Owned by Aliens.—See topics Foreign Investment; Corporations.

See Topical Index in front part of this volume.

ALIMONY:

See topics Divorce; Infants.

ARBITRATION AND AWARD:

Commercial disputes arising out of foreign and domestic trade relations may be referred by parties to arbitration on territory of CR as well as outside CR. (Act no. 216/1994 Sb.).

Arbitration court established in 1949 by Czechoslovak Chamber of Commerce and Industry continues to operate in CR, rules for which were issued by former Federal Ministry of Foreign Trade. (Regulation no. 14/1988 Sb., novelised by Reg. no. 136/1990 Sb. and Reg. no. 391/1992 Sb.).

Every arbitration agreement must be in writing or by mutual exchange of letters, telexes, telegrams or other writings. Procedure, including selection and involving of arbitrators or arbitration court, as well as other aspects connected with awards is described in Act on Arbitration. (Act no. 216/1994 Sb.).

Foreigner may be appointed as arbitrator if having full legal capacity.

Parties, experts and witnesses can be heard only if they appear of their own free will. Only individuals presented by one of parties are considered as evidentiary. Arbitrators cannot render preliminary measures, but parties may apply for such measures before appropriate State court. If arbitrators apply, court can take emergency compulsory measures which arbitrators are not allowed to take.

Entering arbitration action has same legal consequence as bringing action before normal court. Arbitral awards are final and enforceable. Action for annulment of award can be brought at competent court in specific cases itemised in law. Execution is made by court in accordance with stipulations of OSR.

Foreign Arbitral Awards.—CR is party to following international arbitration conventions: New York Convention on Recognition and Enforcement of Foreign Arbitral Awards, dated June 10, 1958 (see Part VII of this volume); Geneva Convention on Enforcement of Foreign Arbitral Awards, dated Sept. 26, 1927; Geneva European Convention on International Commercial Arbitration, dated Apr. 21, 1961; Convention on the Settlement of Investment Disputes between States and Nationals of other States, Mar. 18, 1965. CR is also bound by provisions of Geneva Protocol on Arbitration Clauses dated Sept. 24, 1923 and by number of bilateral treaties.

See topic Exchanges.

ASSIGNMENT FOR BENEFIT OF CREDITORS:

See topics Assignments and Bankruptcy.

ASSIGNMENTS:

Assignment of Claim.—Creditors may transfer claims and all rights and obligations connected therewith to third parties without consent of debtors, however debtor must be notified. Written form is required for assignment. Claims which cease to exist on death of creditor, claims whose contents would change with change of creditor and claims which are not subject to execution cannot be assigned. It is not possible to assign claim, if in contradiction with agreement with debtor. Debtor retains objections against claim. (OZ, §§524-530).

Assignment of Debt.—Third persons may, upon agreement with debtor, assume obligation of debtor, if creditor consents, thereby releasing original debtor. Creditor may provide consent to original debtor or to person assuming debt. Person assuming debt by agreement with creditor without agreement of debtor will become co-debtor. Agreement on assignment of debt must be written. Objections or defences which debtor has against creditor may also be asserted by person taking over debt or by co-debtor. Contents of obligation do not change with assignment, but guarantee of debt provided for by third persons continues only if guarantor consents to change in person of debtor. (OZ, §§531, 532). In case of sale of enterprise, debts pass to buyer without consent of creditor, but seller has position of surety as to debts passing to buyer. Buyer is obliged to notify creditors of assignment of debts and seller is obliged to notify debtors of assignment of claims. (ObchZ, §477).

Assignment of Property, Real or Personal.—See topic Sales.

ASSOCIATIONS:

Associations of Citizens.—Citizens have right to freely associate for legal purposes without any permission by state authority. On basis of law of associations, citizens may found societies, unions, movements, clubs and trade union organisations. (Act no. 83/1990 Sb., am'd by Acts no. 300/1990 Sb., no. 513/1991 Sb. and no. 68/1993 Sb.). Legal persons may be members of associations. State authorities may interfere with position and activity of associations only within framework of law.

Associations are not allowed if objective is to deny or restrict personal, political or other rights; they seek to achieve objectives by means in contradiction with constitution and law; or they are armed or have armed components (other than those possessing or using fire arms for sport purposes or for legal hunting).

Associations are legal persons, founded by registration. Preparatory committee of at least three people submits request for registration, one of which has to be older than 18 years. Articles of association must be annexed to request for registration and must indicate: (1) Name of association; (2) legal seat; (3) objectives of its activity; (4) bodies of association, methods of their establishment and officials entitled to act on their behalf; (5) provisions concerning organisation units, if established; (6) principles of economic management.

Request for registration is submitted to Ministry of Interior. If request is complete, it will register within ten days from day of submission. No formal decision on registration of association is issued, it will be only taken as notice and ratified copy returned to applicant. Association ceases to exist by voluntary dissolution, merger with other association or by decision of ministry on dissolution.

Associations may conclude between themselves written agreements on cooperation. (Act no. 83/1990 Sb.).

Organisations with International Element.—Conditions for activities of organisations with international element are governed by Act no. 116/1985 Sb., in wording of Act no. 157/1989 Sb. Organisation with international element is defined as international nongovernmental organisation, organisation of foreign citizens or special organisation to represent Czech interests in international organisation. These organisations can be established, carry out activities and have seat in CR only on basis of permission issued in conformity with above mentioned law.

Contract of Association According to OZ.—In conformity with OZ, §829, several persons may associate in form of oral or written agreement to jointly share efforts in achieving agreed objective. Such associations do not possess rights and obligations, as they are not legal persons. Agreement may require participant to develop activity for achievement of agreed objective and refrain from activity which would render achievement of objective more difficult or impossible. (OZ, §830). Additionally, participants may be obliged to provide money or other things for purposes of association. (OZ, §831).

Participants' contributions or items acquired through execution of joint activity become co-property of all participants, in equal shares, unless agreement does not stipulate otherwise. Participants are obliged jointly with respect to obligations to third persons. (OZ, §§834, 835). Unless agreement stipulated otherwise, participants make decisions concerning common affairs unanimously. (OZ, §836). Participant has right to obtain information of economic situation of association. Any agreement provisions in contradiction with this right are invalid. (OZ, §837). Participant may withdraw from association, but not at time which would result in detriment to other participants. Participants may be expelled from association for serious reasons, upon unanimous decision of other participants, unless agreement stipulates otherwise. (OZ, §838).

See also topic Corporations.

ATTACHMENT:

In Czech law, there is no equivalent for attachment as conceived in American Law. It is possible in form of interlocutory injunction only. Interlocutory injunction is permissible in case it is necessary to temporarily regulate relations of parties or if there is concern that execution of judgment would be endangered. Specific circumstances where interlocutory injunctions may be issued are: (1) Payment of alimony; (2) child custody; (3) to provide partial remuneration for work, if case involves labour relations and plaintiff does not work for serious reasons; (4) deposit of money or property to custody of notary; (5) to prevent disposal or use of property or rights; (6) to order act, refrain act. (OSR, §76).

BANKRUPTCY:

Czech law defines bankruptcy as situation in which debtor is overburdened with debts. (Act on Bankruptcy and Settlements no. 328/1991 Sb., am'd by Acts nos. 471/1992 Sb., 122/1993 Sb., 42/1994 Sb., 74/1994 Sb., 117/1994 Sb., 156/1994 Sb., 224/1994 Sb., 84/1995 Sb. and 94/1996 Sb.; subsidiary application: OSR).

Debtor, creditors or company liquidator may propose bankruptcy proceedings. Proceedings can also be proposed only to verify if debtor is overburdened with debts. Bankruptcy court is regional or municipal court, within whose jurisdiction debtor's seat or residence is located. Debtor's property must minimally cover cost of court proceedings, with debtor responsible for payment of at least 10,000 Kc upon order of court. Petition made by creditor must be supplemented with documentation supporting claim, as well as evidence demonstrating that debtor is bankrupt. Within 15 days of delivery of petition, some debtors (those having at least 50 employees) may request three month protection period, which may be extended additional three months. (Act no. 94/1996 Sb.).

If court accepts petition, it issues decision on declaration of bankruptcy. This decision includes invitation of creditors to file their claims and appointment of administrator. Term for filing claims is 30 days from day on which bankruptcy was declared. Declaration becomes effective on day decision is displayed on court's notice board.

Effects of Declaring Bankruptcy.—Management of estate is taken over by administrator; legal actions concerning bankrupt's property taken by him are null and void in relation to his creditors (see topic Fraudulent Sales and Conveyances); pending claims and liabilities related to bankrupt's assets become mature; action on claims may be filed only against administrator; bankrupt's proxies, unaccepted offers for contracts are terminated; bankrupt's shared matrimonial property rights become invalid. (§14, Act no. 328/1991 Sb.). Company may continue activities after issuance of bankruptcy declaration, subject to control of creditors.

Reviewing of Claims.—Subject of review hearing is list of debtor's assets and liabilities, as well as list of bankrupt's estate compiled by administrator; bankrupt and creditors may dispute validity and amount of all submitted claims. Claim is considered identified if approved by administrator and not contested by any creditors. Bankrupt's contest is irrelevant as to identification of claim.

Creditors, whose claims are contested, may bring action against opposing creditors and administrator. Claim is then argued before court or appropriate administrative body, depending on nature of claim. If administrator contests claim submitted by creditor, creditor must file action on claim within 30 days or claim will be barred.

Special claims may be satisfied during bankruptcy proceedings: i.e., claims seeking to exclude item from assets; claims related to administration of bankrupt's assets; claims seeking separate satisfaction (secured by lien, pledges or mortgages); employee claims. Other claims may be satisfied only after court decision on distribution of assets according to distribution schedule.

After satisfaction of such special claims, other claims are satisfied in following order: (1) Claims of bankrupt's employees arising from labour relations payable for three years before declaration of bankruptcy and claims for alimony; (2) taxes, fees, duties, social security contributions arising within three years before declaration of bankruptcy; (3) other claims. If impossible to satisfy all claims in same class, they will be satisfied in proportionate manner.

Involuntary Composition.—Bankrupt may propose to conclude bankruptcy proceedings by compulsory settlements only before issuing of distribution schedule. Court considers following in deciding on acceptance of settlement: (1) Honesty of bankrupt (§35); (2) full satisfaction of secured claims, subsistence allowance, claims related to administration of bankrupt's assets, employees' claims and claims mentioned above as (1) and (2).

BANKRUPTCY . . . *continued*

Main condition for court confirmation is approval of settlement by majority of creditors whose total votes represent more than three quarters of all filed claims. Creditors, whose rights are not limited by compulsory settlements and creditors related to bankrupt do not have voting rights. Court may reject proposal, even if creditors have approved, provided that one creditor has special advantages, settlement is inappropriate to financial situation of debtor or creditors receive less than one third of claims.

Voluntary Composition.—Debtor may propose voluntary settlement to court if his situation corresponds to conditions for declaring bankruptcy, provided that bankruptcy order has not yet been declared. For conditions see subhead Involuntary Composition, supra, except of satisfaction of non-preferred claimants, who must be offered payment of at least 45% of claims within two years.

Bankruptcy proceedings are applicable to bankrupt's moveable property abroad (unless otherwise stipulated by international treaty [§69]).

In case of bankruptcy proceedings abroad, bankrupt's moveable property on territory of CR will be surrendered to foreign court upon its request provided that State of such court observes reciprocity and such property is not subject of bankruptcy declared by Czech court. Property can be delivered only after Czech court considers right to exclude property item from assets or right to separate satisfaction, acquired before receiving request of foreign court.

Special provisions apply to insolvent state enterprises, and to state enterprise, if at least 50% of stock of such debtor has been subject to voucher privatisation (§67); other special provisions apply to private farmers and primary agricultural production (§67).

See topic Fraudulent Sales and Conveyances.

BILLS AND NOTES:

Though CR has never ratified either Geneva Convention on Bill of Exchange signed on June 7, 1930 or Geneva Convention on Checks signed on Mar. 19, 1931, both Conventions were in fact incorporated into legal system by Act no. 191/1950 Sb.

There are two types of bills—"drawn bill of exchange" (cizi smenka) corresponding to Anglo-American bill of exchange and "own bill of exchange" (vlastni smenka) corresponding to Anglo-American promissory note. Latter is treated as kind of former.

Essential requirement given by law, i.e., statement to effect that instrument is bill of exchange, must be respected, otherwise instrument will be invalid. Bill may be drawn on issuer or on account of third party. Bill may come due at sight, at certain time after sight, at certain time after day of issuance or on specified date.

Issuer of bill is liable for its acceptance and payment, although his liability for acceptance can be limited. Default of acceptance or of payment must be evidenced by protest levied by certain authorities.

Bill is transferable by unconditional endorsement unless it expressly states "not to order".

Checks.—To fulfil requirements given by law, must contain statement indicating that instrument is check. Acceptance written on check has no legal effect. Check is payable at sight and may be drawn on indicated person with provision "to order", on indicated person with provision "not to order", or to bearer. Checks drawn "to order of the issuer" are allowed. Check with no indication is considered check to bearer. Check drawn on indicated person may be transferred by endorsement, even if not having provision "to order".

Check drawn and payable in same country must be presented for payment within eight days after issuance. Check drawn in country different than place of payment must be presented for payment within 20 days, if drawing and payment places are on same continent, otherwise in 70 days.

Action against person whose liability is based on bill/check can be made in simplified process (OSR, §175), result of which is decision called "Bill of Exchange/check payment order".

Conflict of laws rules are included in Act no. 191/1950 Sb., on bills of exchange and on checks. Capacity of person to incur liabilities under bill or check is determined by law of his nationality, unless such law declares another law to be applicable. Liability incurred by person is, however, binding if incurred in country, according to law of which liability would be valid. As to form of obligations, lex loci is applicable; but obligations of Czech nationals towards other Czech nationals incurred abroad, need only comply with requirements of Czech law. Substantive law applicable to obligations of issuer of "own bill of exchange" and of acceptor of "drawn bill of exchange" is law of place of performance. Other obligations under bill and obligations under check are ruled by law of place where signatures were affixed. Law of place of performance also rules as to whether bill may be accepted only in part and whether holder must accept partial payment, and for measures which must be taken in case of loss or theft of bill. Law of place where bill was issued determines time within which recourse must be taken, whereas form and limitation of action for protestation are ruled by law of country in which protest is taken.

Checks may be drawn on person on whom checks may be drawn according to law of place of performance.

CHATTEL MORTGAGES: See topics Liens, Pledges.

COMMERCIAL REGISTER:

Commercial register ("obchodni rejstrik") is public list kept by each of Register Courts ("rejstrikovy soud") containing data regarding entrepreneurs and enterprises as stipulated by ObchZ. Data to be found in register includes: Business name and seat; identification number ("identifikacni cislo" abbr. ICO); scope of business activities; legal form; name of statutory bodies; amount of registered capital; and other facts required by law, together with all changes of previously registered facts. (ObchZ, §28). Legal persons begin their existence only upon their entry into commercial register.

Following persons are incorporated into commercial register: (1) Business companies (also organisation units of foreign persons); (2) cooperatives and other legal persons, if so stipulated by law; (3) foreign persons according to ObchZ, §21 (foreign person, legal as well as physical, is authorized to carry on enterprise on territory of CR on basis of registration into commercial register); (4) physical person, who lives on territory of CR and is entrepreneur under ObchZ (this person shall be incorporated upon own request or if stipulated by special act). (ObchZ, §3).

Procedure.—Application for registration, with officially verified signature of authorized person, is filed together with following documents: Memorandum of association (or notarial deed); certification of contribution of basic capital; signature specimen of those authorized to act on behalf of entity; power of attorney if applicable; trade authorisation; other documents confirming facts to be registered; if foreign natural person will be registered as person authorized to act on behalf of enterprise, residence permit in CR.

As long as any factual data are not recorded in commercial register, they are not effective notice to third parties relying in good faith on facts appearing in register. (ObchZ, §27). Disqualification to do business is possible from failure to register or to inform register of change.

CONSTITUTION AND GOVERNMENT:

Czech Republic came into existence on Jan. 1, 1993, after division of former Czech and Slovak Federative Republic into Czech Republic and Slovak Republic, respectively.

Constitution (Constitutional Act no. 1/1993 Sb.) states that CR is sovereign, united, and democratic State respecting rule of law and based on respect of rights and freedoms of man and citizen. Part and parcel of Constitutional order ("ustavniho poradku") is List of Fundamental Rights and Freedoms inspired by International Covenant on Civil and Political Rights and by International Covenant on Economic, Social and Cultural Rights.

Parliament is composed of two chambers: House of Representatives (Poslanecka snemovna) and Senate (Senat). House of Representatives has 200 deputies elected for four years terms. Senate has 81 senators elected for six years terms, one third of whom are elected every two years. (*Note:* Senate has yet to be established.) Head of state is president, elected for five years at common session of both chambers of Parliament.

Art. 99 of Constitution stipulates that CR is composed of municipalities which are basic territorial self-governing entities. Higher territorial self-governing entities are zeme (lands) or kraje (regions). (*Note:* These higher territorial entities have yet to be established.)

Constitutional Act no. 4/1993 Sb. stipulates that constitutional Acts, Acts and other legal prescriptions of Czech and Slovak Federative Republic remain in force on territory of CR. (Art. 1/1). According to this constitutional act, CR has taken over rights and duties of Czech and Slovak Federative Republic, arising out of international law, with exception of duties connected with territory which is not under sovereignty of CR. (Art. 5/2). By virtue of this provision, CR is now contracting state of international treaties mentioned in this digest by which Czech and Slovak Federative Republic was bound.

Political parties are entitled to receive public subsidies, if they have acquired, in view of results of last election, seats in parliament. Right to compensation includes electoral expenses, up to level stated by law. (Act no. 424/1991 Sb., am'd by Acts no. 468/1991 Sb., 68/1993 Sb., 189/1993 Sb. and 117/1994 Sb.).

CONTRACTS:

OZ, §§43-51 sets forth fundamental and special provisions on contracts, however, these provisions apply to commercial matters only in cases when ObchZ does not regulate individual type of contract. ObchZ, §§409-755 provides provisions of law regulating contracts concluded between commercial parties.

Contract is concluded at moment offer to conclude contract is accepted. Silence or inactivity by themselves do not manifest acceptance. (OZ, §44/1). Contract may be concluded by writing, orally or in silence with manifestation of intent. Written contract signed by parties is necessary if explicitly required by law, particularly if contract relates to property transfer. (OZ, §46). In event law stipulates contract has to be accompanied by decision of certain authority, contract becomes effective only as result of such decision. (OZ, §47/1). ObchZ, §§269-288 provides special conditions for contracts between commercial parties, including public offers and tenders.

Repudiation.—Contract may be repudiated only in instances stipulated by law or upon agreement of contracting parties. Repudiation renders agreement void from inception, unless legal regulations or parties stipulate otherwise. (OZ, §48). One-sided repudiation is possible in case party has concluded contract under duress or under extremely disadvantageous conditions. Legal act does not have force if made in error arising from fact decisive for realisation of legal act and person to whom act is addressed has either caused its provocation or must have known about it. Act is also invalid if error was intentionally provoked by said person. Act remains valid in case of error in motive. (OZ, §49a). In cases of fundamental breach of contract between commercial parties, party may repudiate if he informs other party without undue delay. In case of non-fundamental breach, additional reasonable period must be provided before repudiation. (ObchZ, §§345, 346).

Agreement to Conclude Future Contract.—Concluded by parties in form of writing committing to enter into contract within specified time, provided that essential provisions of contract have been agreed upon. Obligation to conclude future contract extinguishes if circumstances which parties took into account when establishing obligation changed to such extent that obliged party cannot be reasonably required to conclude future contract. Should contract not be concluded within agreed period, expression of intention of party may be replaced by decision of court, if requested within period of one year. (OZ, §50a). Similar provisions apply to commercial contacts. (ObchZ, §§289-292).

Excuses for Nonperformance.—Person who fails to perform duty arising out of obligation in commercial relations is liable to compensate for losses of injured party, unless failure to perform is due to circumstances precluding liability. (ObchZ, §373). Obstacles which occur independently, beyond will and control of party and which prevent performance of duty, are considered as circumstances precluding liability unless it cannot be reasonably assumed that party would prevent or overcome obstacle or its consequences and that party would foresee obstacle at time of establishment of

CONTRACTS . . . *continued*
obligation. Liability will not be precluded by obstacle which occurred when party was already in default or which is due to economic situation of party. Effects precluding liability are limited only to time of duration of obstacle with which effects are connected. (ObchZ, §374). In commercial relations arising from international trade, lack of official licence necessary for performance of duties of party is not considered as circumstance precluding liability. (ObchZ, §736).

Applicable Law.—Conflict of law rules are contained in Act no. 97/1963 Sb., amended by Acts no. 158/1969 Sb., no. 234/1992 Sb. and no. 264/1992 Sb. According to §9 of this act, parties can make choice of applicable law for their relations. Choice can also be decided from conduct of parties (per facta concludentia) but there must not be doubt about expression of will of parties. Conflict rules of selected law are not regarded, unless otherwise stipulated by parties. In case applicable law has not been selected by parties, §10 of act provides that relations of parties are regulated by law which corresponds to reasonable settlement of applicable contractual relation. Act no. 97/1963 Sb., as amended, provides following guides, as a rule: (1) Contracts of sale and contracts of work are governed by law of place of seat (residence) of seller or of provider of work at time of conclusion of contract; (2) contracts concerning immovable,—by law of place where immovable is situated; (3) contracts concerning transport,—by law of place of seat or residence of carrier or of forwarding agent at time of conclusion of contract; (4) contracts of insurance,—by law of place of seat of insurer at time of conclusion of contract; (5) contracts of commission and similar contracts,—by law of place of seat of person executing commission at time of conclusion of contract; (6) commercial representative contracts and brokerage contracts,—by law of place of seat of person for whom commercial representative or broker executes activity at time of conclusion of contract; (7) contracts concerning multilateral barter transactions,—by law application of which corresponds best to settlement of relations in their entirety.

Contracts not enumerated above are regulated, as a rule, by law of state in which both parties have their seat. If parties do not have seat in same state, contract is regulated by law of place where contract was concluded. If contract was concluded between absent parties, it is governed by law of place of seat of acceptor.

Provision of international treaties binding CR are not affected. CR is contracting state of Vienna UN Convention on Contracts for the International Sale of Goods, of Apr. 11, 1980 (with reservation according to Art. 95, that CR is not bound by subparagraph [1] [b] of Art. 1 of this Convention) and of number of international treaties concerning international transport. (See topic Treaties.)

CONVEYANCES:

See topic Deeds.

COPYRIGHT:

Copyright is regulated by Act no. 35/1965 Sb. on literary, scientific and artistic works, am'd by Acts nos. 89/1990 Sb., 247/1990 Sb., 318/1993 Sb., 237/1995 Sb., 86/1996 Sb. and by Act no. 468/1991 Sb. on radio and television broadcasting, am'd by Acts nos. 597/1992 Sb., 36/1993 Sb., 253/1994 Sb., 40/1995 Sb., 237/1995 Sb. and 301/1995 Sb.

CR is bound by following conventions and treaties: Bern Convention on Protection of Literary and Artistic Works of Sept. 9, 1886 (amended version signed in Paris July 24, 1971); Universal Convention on Copyright of Sept. 8, 1952 signed in Geneva (amended version signed in Paris July 24, 1971); International Convention for Protection of Performers, Producers of Phonograms and Broadcasting Organisations signed in Rome Oct. 26, 1961; Convention for Protection of Producers of Phonograms against Unauthorised Duplication of their Phonograms signed in Geneva Oct. 29, 1971; Convention on International Entry of Audio-visual Works signed in Geneva Apr. 18, 1989; Convention on Establishment of World Organisation for Intellectual Property signed in Rome July 14, 1967 (amended version signed in Paris July 24, 1971). CR also concluded bilateral treaty with former USSR on Mutual Protection of Copyright of Mar. 18, 1975.

Literary, scientific and artistic works are protected if result of creative activity of author. Translations, treatment of works, collected and combined works as well as film works and works of co-authors are protected. Computer programs are subject to copyright.

Right to work originates at moment when such is expressed in words, in writing, by drawing, sketch or in any or perceptible form. Copyright relates both to work as whole and to its individual parts. No registration is needed.

Author is entitled: (1) To protection of authorship, in particular to inviolability of work and, if work is used by another person, to have work used in manner which does not detract from its value; (2) to dispose of work, in particular to decide on publication and to authorise use; (3) to be remunerated for use of creative work.

Right to protection of authorship is not transferable. Work may only be used with author's permission, unless authorisation is provided directly under law. Authors grant their permission to use works by contract, including contracts on lending and renting copies of original work.

Copyright is not violated by using theme to create new, original work. Author's permission is not required nor is remuneration required in limited instances given by Copyright Act, i.e., reproduction or imitation of work which has been published for personal need, if marked "copy" or "imitation"; in case of quoting excerpts from published works, if listing author and title of work; or if used by organisation in reporting timely event by photography, film, radio or television, if work performed or displayed during such event is used to justified extent.

Legitimate owner of copy of computer programs is not required to demand permission and to pay remuneration to make reproduction or adaptation for purpose of operation of computer itself, for archive purpose, for replacement of legitimately acquired copy that was lost, destroyed or otherwise impaired.

Broadcast and television organisations may broadcast works made already public, without author's permission, if they list author and title of work and pay remuneration for each broadcast.

If author of work being created within scope of employment, for employer whose activities include publishing or other publication, refuses to give consent without serious reason, employer may seek court ordered consent.

Ministry of Culture may substitute by its decision author's permission to translate works of foreign nationals into Czech, provided that international treaties allow and under conditions specified therein.

Copyright generally lasts throughout author's lifetime and 50 years after death. In case of works of co-authors and of combined works, 50 years after death of co-author who survived other. Duration of copyright to work which forms part of estate and which was published for first time within last ten years of term set above is extended to ten years beginning from publication of work. Special duration applies for following: Anonymous works and works created under pseudonym, where identity of author is unknown, 50 years after publication; film works, 50 years after made public; annuals and periodicals published by organisations (legal entities), ten years after publication; photographic works, throughout author's lifetime and ten years after death. Copyright passes to heirs. If one co-author has no heirs, share accrues to other co-authors.

Acquisition of original is not automatically connected to right to dispose of work. Author who transferred original against payment may demand reasonable settlement from any acquirer who has obtained unjustified material benefit from further transfer of ownership to work. It is impossible to waive this claim in advance.

Author whose copyright was violated may demand: (1) That violation of his right will be prohibited; (2) that consequences of violation be removed; (3) appropriate satisfaction; (4) compensation for damage. Violation of copyright is punishable under §32 of Act no. 200/1990 Sb., am'd by Acts no. 124/1993 Sb., no. 290/1993 Sb., no. 234/1994 Sb., no. 82/1995 Sb. and no. 279/1995 Sb. on offences, and under §152 of Criminal Code, Act no. 140/1961 Sb., am'd by Acts no. 65/1994 Sb. and no. 91/1994 Sb.

CORPORATIONS:

Introductory Note.—For better understanding, please note following difference in Czech legal terminology. Under ObchZ, §56, corporation (business company) is juristic person founded for purpose of undertaking business activities. Czech law recognises following "business companies" (obchodní spolecnosti): General commercial partnership (verejná obchodní spolecnost); limited partnership (komanditní spolecnost); limited liability company (spolecnost s rucením omezenym); joint stock company (akciova spolecnost). In this regard, it should be noted that American notion of corporation would not cover general commercial partnership and limited partnership as they exist under Czech law.

Verejna Obchodní Spolecnost (General Commercial Partnership).—(ObchZ, §§76-92). Entity in which at least two persons (juristic or natural) carry on business activities under common business name (including designation "v.o.s.") and bear joint and several liability for obligations of company with all their property. Partners' rights and duties are governed by partnership contract which must include: Business name and seat of general commercial partnership; details of partners (business name and seat of juristic person and name and address of natural person); scope of business activities; provisions governing rights and duties of partners.

Partners' monetary and capital investments become property of partnership. Profits or losses are divided equally, unless partnership contract specifies differently. Distribution of profits or losses is based upon annual financial statement, with profit payable within three months from day of approval of annual financial statement, unless agreed otherwise in partnership contract.

Partners are subject to ban on competitive conduct unless other partners consent. Each partner is considered statutory body, unless partnership contract stipulates that partners act jointly. Partner may withdraw provided at least two partners remain, but shall remain liable for obligations arising before his withdrawal. Death of partner is ground for dissolution, unless partnership contract states otherwise. In this event, heirs may succeed deceased partner or claim proportionate settlement share of partnership property.

Komanditní Spolecnost (Limited Partnership).—(ObchZ, §§93-104). Entity in which one or several limited partners bear limited liability for firm's obligations up to amount of unpaid parts of registered investments (limited partners—"komanditisté") and one or several general partners bear unlimited liability (general partners—"komplementári").

Partnership contract includes, at minimum, following: Business name (including designation "k.s.") and seat of partnership; designation of partners including business name plus seat of legal entity, and name plus residence of individual; scope of activities; designation of which partners are general and limited partners; amount of each limited partner's investment; provisions governing rights and duties of partners. In event name of partnership includes name of limited partner, this partner will bear liability for partnership obligations as general partner.

Only general partners are entitled to manage partnership, other matters are decided jointly by general partners and limited partners according to simple majority, unless partnership contract stipulates otherwise. General partners form statutory body of partnership. Each general partner is entitled to act on behalf of firm, unless partnership contract provides otherwise. Consent of all partners is required to amend partnership contract. Limited partners are entitled to check accounting documents and to receive annual financial statement. Limited partners are not subject to ban on competitive conduct, unless partnership contract stipulates otherwise.

Profits are divided into two portions—one payable to general partners, other payable to limited partners; these portions are equal, unless partnership contract stipulates otherwise. General partners divide their parts equally and limited partners in proportionate shares according to paid in investment, unless partnership contract shares otherwise.

Death of limited partner, limitation of his legal rights, or declaration of bankruptcy concerning his property are not reasons for dissolution of limited partnership. If participation of all limited partners is terminated, general partners may agree to transform their limited partnership into general commercial partnership without liquidation. In event limited partnership is dissolved and dissolution is connected with its liquidation, all partners shall be entitled to proportionate parts of their paid investment,

See Topical Index in front part of this volume.

CORPORATIONS . . . *continued*
with limited partners having preference. Any surplus liquidation balance is distributed in same ratio as profits.

Spolecnost S Rucením Omezenym (Limited Liability Company).—(ObchZ, §§105-153). Entity whose registered capital is made up of members' investments, agreed in advance. Company is liable for breach of its obligations with its entire property, with member's liability limited to any unpaid amount of his pledged investment. Limited liability company may be founded by one person, with maximum number of members being 50. Minimum amount of registered capital is 100,000 Kc, with minimum amount of members investment at 20,000 Kc.

Memorandum of association must contain; Business name (including designation "s.r.o" or "spol. s r.o.") and seat of company; information about members, i.e., business name plus seat of legal entity and name and residence of individual; scope of business activities; amount of registered capital and amount of each member's initial investment; name of first executives and manner in which they will represent company; names and residences of members of first supervisory board, if established; provisions governing rights and duties of members.

No less than 30% of every pledged investment must be paid up prior to submission of petition asking for incorporation into commercial register. Any balance of pledged investment must be paid under conditions and within period set by memorandum of association or articles of association, but always within five years following incorporation into commercial register.

Ownership interest represents rights and duties of member and corresponding participation in company. Members are entitled to part of profits proportionate to paid-up investments, unless memorandum of association states otherwise. Upon its incorporation, it is obligatory for company to establish reserve fund at level and according to procedures stipulated in memorandum of association and law. (ObchZ, §124).

Company bodies are general meeting, executives, and supervisory board (optional). Unless agreed otherwise or stipulated by law, amendment to memorandum of association normally requires consent of all members. Amount of registered capital and amount of each member's investment may never be reduced below minimum legal levels. Executives are obliged to publicise reduction of registered capital within 15 days of resolution and again within 30 days from first notice.

Each member is entitled to only one ownership interest. Member may transfer interest to another member or third party on basis of written contract, subject to approval of general meeting, unless memorandum of association provides otherwise. Member may propose that court cancel his participation if he cannot be justly required to remain in company any longer. Member can be expelled from company if he substantially neglects duties. Members may ask court to wind up company for any reasons and under any conditions stipulated in memorandum of association or allowable under law. (ObchZ, §§151, 152).

Akciová Spolecnost (Joint Stock Companies).—(ObchZ, §§154-220). Entity requiring minimum capital of 1,000,000 Kc divided among certain number of shares of certain nominal value. Shares may either be registered in name of shareholder, or bearer shares. Transfer of registered share becomes effective upon entry of transfer into shareholders list. Employee shares, total nominal value of which must not exceed 5% of capital stock, may be issued. Shares with preference rights concerning dividends may be issued, but total nominal value must not exceed 50% of capital stock. Debentures up to 50% of capital stock may be issued, subject to special regulations.

Company is not allowed to subscribe for shares of its own capital stock and may redeem issued shares only under limited circumstances.

Joint stock company may be founded by one party, if juristic person (entity); otherwise by two or more. Register court incorporates joint stock company into commercial register upon submission of founding agreement and articles of association including: Business name (with designation "a.s."), seat of company and business activities; proposed amount of capital stock; number of shares and nominal value; subscribed investments of individual founders (if founded on basis of call to subscribe, specific additional details must be included); provisions governing internal matters. Furthermore, company must comply with following requirements prior to registration: Proper constituent General Meeting has been held, in event that such meeting is required by statutes of company; subscribers have subscribed capital stock in full and have paid up no less than 30% of capital stock in form of monetary investments (except employee share); company's articles of association have been approved; members of company bodies have been elected. Company is obliged to create and contribute to reserve fund.

Government permission is required for formation of joint stock company in some instances, i.e., if company will engage in banking, investment or insurance business.

Corporation is managed by board of directors, consisting of no fewer than three members, elected for maximum of five years by general meeting. Articles of association may stipulate that members of board of directors will be elected and recalled by supervisory board. Supervisory board consists of no fewer than three members elected for maximum of five years, two thirds of whom are elected by general meeting, and one third by employees of company, provided there are more than 50 full-time employees at time of election.

Cooperatives.—(ObchZ, §§221-260). Organisation of unspecified number of members, founded either to undertake business activities, or to satisfy economic, social or other requirements of its members. Cooperative is juristic person liable for breach of its obligations with all of its property. Members, numbering at least five, unless two or more are legal entities, do not bear liability for obligations of cooperative. Registered basic capital cannot be less than 50,000 Kc, with no minimum investment of members specified by law. It is formed upon holding of first members meeting, at which amount of basic capital and individual capital contributions are determined, statutes are approved and election of officers is held. Notarial deed, copy of statutes, and verification of payment of at least one half of capital are submitted for incorporation into commercial register.

Upon its incorporation, cooperative is bound to create indivisible fund, amount of which will be not less than 10% of registered basic capital. Cooperative has following bodies: Members assembly (highest body of cooperative); board (charged with managing cooperative); auditing commission (entitled to check all activities of cooperative); other bodies established under statutes.

Foreign Corporations.—Foreign person's authorisation to conduct business activities on territory of CR is established on day person, or person's organisational unit, is incorporated into commercial register. (ObchZ, §21). Foreign person (physical or juristic), via his enterprise or organisational unit on territory of CR, is authorized to conduct scope of business activities as specified in entry in commercial register. Trade licence must be issued for such business activities (see topic Licenses). Same conditions apply to relocation of foreign entity registered office to CR, however such relocation of registered office must be allowed by laws of country where company has its seat and country of foundation of company. (ObchZ, §26).

See topic Aliens.

COURTS:

In conformity with Art. 81 of Czech Constitution, judicial power is executed by independent courts on behalf of Republic.

Constitutional Court, composed of 15 judges appointed for ten years by President of Republic with consent of Senate, decides issues specified by Art. 87 of Constitution. Decision of Constitutional Court is executable as soon as it has been promulgated as specified by law, unless court specifies otherwise. Executable decisions of this court are binding on all authorities and persons.

System of courts in CR is set forth in Art. 90 of Constitution, along with Act no. 335/1991 Sb., amended by Act no. 264/1992 Sb., no. 17/1993 Sb. and no. 292/1993 Sb. System is formed by Supreme Court (Nejvyssí soud), Supreme Administrative Court (Nejvyssí správní soud), Superior Courts (Vrchní soudy), Regional Courts (Krajské soudy) and District Courts (Okresní soudy).

Supreme Court is highest judicial authority in affairs falling within competence of courts, with exception of matters decided on by Constitutional Court or Supreme Administrative Court. Supreme Court decides on appeals on decisions made by Superior Courts acting as courts of appeal and decides on recognition and enforceability of foreign judgments. Superior Court is competent to review decisions made by central authorities of CR, with exception of decisions involving pension and health insurance, or material security of applicants for employment in conformity with prescriptions on employment. (OSR, §246). Court also decides disputes concerning competence between courts and authorities of State administration. Superior Courts decide on appeals on decisions made by Regional Courts as courts of first instance and as court of appeal for decisions made by Regional Courts acting as courts of appeal.

Regional Courts are composed of president, vice-presidents, and further judges and assessors. Decisions are made by tribunals. Regional Courts are competent to decide matters in first instance as defined in OSR, §9. They decide on appeals of decisions made by District Courts.

District Courts are competent to hear all proceedings in first instance, unless Regional Court has competence according to OSR, §9. Within sphere of administrative justice, courts review legality of decisions made by public administrative authorities on basis of claims or appeals. Regional Courts are competent to revise such decisions, if law does not stipulate otherwise.

Supreme Administrative Court decides in last instance on administrative decisions.

CURRENCY:

Legal currency is Czech Crown (Kc), divided into 100 hellers or "halere". Czech National Bank has exclusive right to issue bank notes and to mint coins.

Powers and duties of Czech National Bank are detailed in Act no. 6/1993 Sb., am'd by Act no. 60/1993 Sb. Czech National Bank is central authority within scope of foreign exchange laws.

See also topic Foreign Exchange.

CUSTOMS:

Czech customs duties consist of import duty, export duty and antidumping duty. (Act no. 13/1993 Sb., am'd by Act no. 35/1993 Sb.).

Dumping is understood as case when foreign goods are imported to CR for lower price than usual price of competing goods in CR and possibility exists of detrimental effect to Czech production or its development. (Act no. 13/1993 Sb., am'd by Act no. 35/1993 Sb.).

All imported goods are subject to duty, with exception of goods mentioned in customs tariffs as duty free. Additionally, goods mentioned in international agreement as duty free are not subject to payment of customs duty. At present, no export duties are effective.

Customs duty is fixed by tariff, which contains general rates, contract rates, preference rates contained in international agreements and preference rates applicable bilaterally. (Regulation no. 525/1991 Sb., am'd by Reg. no. 603/1992 Sb., Reg. no. 618/1992 Sb. and Reg. no. 13/1993 Sb.). Rates of tariff are determined and issued by government (Acts nos. 335/1993 Sb. and 265/1994 Sb.). CR uses single customs tariff system in conformity with GATT principles.

Basis for levy of duty is customs value, which for imported goods is transfer value. Payment does not have to be in form of transfer of currency, it can be realised by credit or security, either directly or indirectly.

Customs authorities are General Directorate of Customs, regional customs authorities and local customs authorities. Customs authorities collect value added and consumption tax on imported goods, fees connected with export and import and road tax levied on foreign transport vehicles.

Customs declaration can be filed in written form, oral form, or by data transfer. Declarant must be Czech person, except cases of releasing goods to transit, cases of limited use or when customs authority gives approval. Sanctions for customs offences range from warning, to penalties (2,000 to 2 million Kc) and forfeiture of goods.

Customs free zones and customs free warehousing premises are established by government decree.

CR is member of General Agreement on Tariffs and Trade (GATT).

DEATH (PRESUMPTION OF AND ACTIONS FOR):

Legal capacity of physical person to have rights and duties originates with moment of birth and terminates upon death. Court declares physical person dead, in case death is not possible to show by prescribed manner and court establishes death by other

DEATH (PRESUMPTION OF AND ACTIONS FOR) . . . *continued*
manner. Court also declares death in case of missing physical person, if it is possible with regard to all circumstances to reach conclusion that person is no longer alive. (OZ, §7). Death is evidenced by death certificate or by declaration of death.

Application for declaration of death may be filed by anyone possessing legal interest in declaration of death. (OSR, §195). Declaration of death of Czech citizen can be issued only by Czech court. Declaration of death with regard to alien can be issued by Czech court with legal effects for persons with permanent residence in CR and for property situated in CR. (§43, Act no. 97/1963 Sb., on Private International Law and International Procedure, am'd by Acts no. 158/1969 Sb., no. 234/1992 Sb. and no. 264/1992 Sb.).

See topic Descent and Distribution.

DEEDS:

Deeds, in common law form, do not exist in CR. To transfer ownership of real property, duly executed contract of sale or transfer or decision of court is recorded in real estate register.

See also topics Mortgages, Husband and Wife.

DEPOSITIONS:

CR is party to Hague Convention on the Taking of Evidence Abroad in Civil or Commercial Matters of Mar. 18, 1970. (No. 129/1976 Sb.). Normal procedure for obtaining evidence under convention is to send necessary information, including exact questions, if desired, to Ministry of Justice (designated as Central Authority according to convention), which then transmits Letters of Request to competent local Czech court. See Part VII of this volume for Convention and forms.

In cases not covered by Hague Convention, Letter of Request will be sent, as case may be, on basis of Hague Convention on Civil Procedure of Mar. 1, 1954 (No. 72/1966 Sb.), or of Hague Convention on Civil Procedure of July 17, 1905 (No. 3/1927 Sb and No. 84/1930 Sb.), or of bilateral treaty binding on CR; otherwise Letter of Request will be executed on condition of reciprocity and must be submitted through diplomatic channel. It cannot be sent directly, unless international treaty provides otherwise.

If court which is to execute letter is not known, it need not be specified. It is advisable, even if court is designated, to add words "or other appropriate authority" in order to avoid delays.

Counsel may appear at examination of witness. Letter of Request will be executed according to Czech law of procedure. Nevertheless, if requested by foreign authority and if not contrary to Czech public order, Letter of Request can be executed according to foreign law of procedure (e.g., in form of deposition taken upon oath). (§57, Act no. 97/1963 Sb., on Private International Law and Law of International Procedure, am'd by Acts no. 158/1969 Sb., no. 234/1992 Sb. and no. 264/1992 Sb.).

Evidence in a Foreign Country.—Can be taken upon request of Czech court made under respective international treaty or, if no such treaty, through appropriate diplomatic channel. Evidence is effective if it satisfies requirements of Czech law, even if not in accordance with foreign law. Evidence abroad can be taken also by Czech diplomatic or consular office authorized by Ministry of Foreign Affairs, if not contrary to law of respective foreign state.

DESCENT AND DISTRIBUTION:

Inheritance is acquired upon death. (OZ, §460). In case of intestate death, heirs under law are entitled to inherit. Same applies if testament concerns only part of estate. (OZ, §461). Inheritance not acquired by heir devolves to state. (OZ, §462).

Intestate succession is divided into following order: First—Decedent's children and spouse, each of them acquiring equal share. If any of children shall not inherit, their share is acquired by their descendants per stirpes (OZ, §473); Second—should decedent's descendants not inherit, then spouse, parents of decedent and those who lived with decedent at least one year before his death in common household and, who, for that reason took care of common household or were dependent on decedent for their subsistence. Heirs of second order inherit equal shares, however spouse always inherits at least one half of estate (OZ, §474); Third—should neither decedent's spouse, nor his parents inherit, then siblings of decedent and those who lived with decedent at least one year before his death in common household and, who, for that reason took care of common household or were dependent on decedent for their subsistence. Should one of decedent's siblings not inherit, his/her share is acquired by his/her children per stirpes (OZ, §475); Fourth—should none of heirs of third order inherit, then grandparents of decedent inherit in equal parts. Should one of decedent's grandparents not inherit, his/her share is divided among his/her children per stirpes. (OZ, §475a).

Probate.—Some rights are not transferable to heirs, these are terminated with death, i.e., individual purely personal rights, some rights flowing from Family Code, etc. Transfer of rights and duties upon death is regulated by inheritance law. Right to property transfers from deceased to heirs at moment of death. Conditions of transfer to heir are: (1) death of physical person; (2) legal right of inheritance;(3) capacity of heir to inherit; (4) will of heir to accept inheritance.

Heir can refuse inheritance by oral declaration in court or by written declaration sent to court. Refusal can be made within one month from day when heir was informed about inheritance. (OZ, §§463-468).

Probate proceedings are commenced by court of last domicile of decedent. Court appoints notary seated in district of court to execute each act on testate proceedings. Notary prepares all documents necessary for issuance of court decision. Court confirms: (1) Inheritance by single heir; (2) that estate not acquired by heirs devolves to state; (3) approval of agreement on settlement between heirs; (4) inheritance pursuant to intestate shares, should there be no agreement among heirs. (OZ, §§481-484).

Should general interest require, court may appoint administrator for all or part of estate for duration of court proceedings.

Legitimate Shares and Disinheritance.—See topic Wills.

Applicable Law.—Legal relations of inheritance are governed by law of state which decedent was citizen at time of death. Ability to institute and cancel testament is governed by law of state which person was citizen at time of expression of will. Testament form is governed by law of state which person was citizen at time when testament was made, but form prescribed by law of place where testament was made is sufficient. (§§17, 18, Act no. 97/1963 Sb., am'd by Acts no. 158/1969 Sb., no. 234/1992 Sb. and no. 264/1992 Sb.).

Jurisdiction.—In case of real estate on territory of CR left by deceased alien, court proceedings as to this real estate must be taken at competent Czech court. Regarding movable property on territory of CR left by deceased alien, court proceedings must be taken at competent Czech court if: State of alien's nationality does not reciprocate with CR in inheritance of Czech citizen in such state; if foreign state refuses to dispose of movable property of deceased or does not answer; or in cases when deceased alien had his residence in CR and heir with residence in CR applies. In other cases, Czech court takes only necessary measures to safeguard property which will be passed to competent authority in native state of deceased. (§45, Act no. 97/1963 Sb., am'd by Acts no. 158/1969 Sb., no. 234/1992 Sb. and no. 264/1992 Sb.). Dispositions of international agreements are not affected.

DISPUTE RESOLUTION:

See topic Arbitration and Award.

DIVORCE:

Divorce is regulated by Act no. 94/1963 Sb. Marriage is dissolved solely upon court decision. Act does not specify reasons leading to divorce, but leaves court to decide whether to grant divorce, provided relations between spouses are irretrievably broken and marriage does not fulfil its social purposes. Court must take into consideration interests of minor children. (§24). Court considers reasons leading to breakdown of marriage, but does not include specific reasons in decision.

District court seated in place of last common domicile of spouses has jurisdiction. Action for divorce includes action on rights and duties as to minor children born in marriage. As such, divorce decree includes decision on custody and support of minor children.

Divorced spouse unable to support him/herself (in judicial practice, in case of illness or in case support of minor children) is entitled to claim support. Court considers circumstances of parties and reasons causing divorce. Claim for support ceases to exist if spouse concludes new marriage, otherwise claim shall be without period of limitation.

Joint property division may be decided by court only on basis of separate proposal submitted after divorce comes into force.

Aliens.—If neither spouse is Czech citizen, jurisdiction of Czech court is applied if at least one spouse has residence in CR and decision of court would be recognised in states both spouses are citizens of, or if at least one spouse has residence in CR for period over 180 days. (§38, Act no. 97/1963 Sb., am'd by Acts no. 158/1969 Sb., no. 234/1992 Sb. and no. 264/1992 Sb.). Divorce is governed by law of state spouses are citizens of at moment of filing action. Czech law applies only in cases when foreign law which normally should have applied would not allow divorce or would allow it under extremely difficult circumstances, provided at least one spouse resides in CR for extended period. (§22, Act no. 97/1963 Sb., am'd by Acts no. 158/1969 Sb., no. 234/1992 Sb. and no. 264/1992 Sb.).

Foreign court decision on divorce regarding Czech citizen may be recognised by Supreme Court in special procedure. If both spouses were citizens of state which decision arises from at time of court decision, or if decision of foreign court is recognised by both states spouses are citizens of, decision is recognised by CR without further procedure. (§§67-68, Act no. 92/1963 Sb.). International agreement provisions obligatory for CR are not affected.

In addition to number of bilateral international agreements (see topic Treaties) Hague Convention on the Recognition of Divorces and Legal Separation of June 1, 1970 (Act no. 131/1976 Sb.) is binding for CR.

See also topic Husband and Wife.

ENVIRONMENT:

Act no. 17/1992 Sb. defines basic terms and principles in field of environmental protection, basic duties in regard to environmental protection, as well as basic provisions for environmental impact assessment. Principals and provisions of this act are further developed in implementing legislation, as follows:

Act no. 238/1991 Sb., as am'd by Act no. 300/1995 Sb. defines waste, special waste, dangerous waste, producers of waste, handling waste and its neutralisation, together with stipulating rights and duties of authorized bodies of State administration and duties of producers and transports of waste. Powers and responsibilities of authorized bodies are detailed in Act no. 311/1991 Sb., as amended by Acts no. 349/1992 Sb. and no. 466/1992 Sb.

State administration is executed by Ministry of Environment, Czech Inspection of Environment and district authorities.

Based on Decree no. 521/1991 Sb., every legal or physical entity authorized to do business in CR which produces waste is obliged to keep records of waste as specified in this Decree. Furthermore, Decree no. 401/1991 Sb. requires that producers of over 100 tons of waste per year or 50 kilograms of dangerous waste per year are required to develop programmes on waste handling.

Duties of waste producer are: (1) To make program for waste handling in accordance with Decree no. 401/1991 Sb.; (2) to keep different waste separately; (3) to keep dangerous waste separately; (4) to report character, quantity, as well as ways of using and neutralisation of special waste to authorized authority; (5) to use produced waste as resource, secondary raw material or energy source; (6) to assure neutralisation of waste, in case it is not possible to reuse; (7) to keep records on kinds and quantity of produced waste, as well as ways of storing, usage or neutralisation; (8) to state in shipping list, product packaging or in use instructions, information on possibilities of recycling unconsumed parts of product or methods of neutralisation. Penalties ranging from 10,000 to 10,000,000 Kc are levied for breaching duties.

Act no. 138/1973 Sb. stipulates basic duties in use and regulation of waters; cases when approval of relevant authorities are necessary to deal with waters; duties to protect water; and conditions on release of waters into municipal sewage. Act no. 458/

ENVIRONMENT . . . *continued*
1992 Sb. defines responsibilities of relevant State administrative authorities as regards supply, administration, processing and usage of water.

Act no. 124/1993 Sb., am'd by Acts no. 390/1993 Sb. and no. 134/1994 Sb. defines and regulates offenses in area of environmental protection of forests, agricultural and water resources.

EXCHANGE CONTROL:

See topics Foreign Exchange; Aliens.

EXCHANGES:

Stock Exchange.—Must be formed as joint stock company, governed by provisions of ObchZ applied with variations stipulated in Act no. 214/1992 Sb., am'd by Acts nos. 216/1994 Sb., 61/1996 Sb. and 152/1996 Sb. Licence granted by Ministry of Finance is required. Foreign entities or persons and legal entities with foreign capital participation higher than 50% of basic capital, having seats in CR, may acquire stock exchange shares, total nominal value of which may not exceed one third of basic capital of exchange.

Foreign securities can be traded if accepted by exchange chamber and if issued according to laws of country of origin.

Disputes arising out of on-exchange trading may be resolved by arbitration court of respective stock exchange according written agreement of parties, otherwise by normal courts. No general norm applicable to arbitration procedure has been established to date.

Commodity Exchange.—Legal entity sui generis, governed otherwise by provision on limited liability company of ObchZ, if Act no. 229/1992 Sb., am'd by Acts nos. 216/1994 Sb. and 105/1995 Sb. or regulations do not have other provisions (see topic Corporations). License granted by Ministry of Economy and/or by Ministry of Agriculture is required. Founders must be registered in commercial register. Further members accepted by exchange chamber must be licensed for production, processing, trading or granting services regarding commodities traded on exchange. There is no additional limitation for aliens. Disputes arising out of on-exchange trading may be resolved by arbitration court of exchange according written agreement of parties, otherwise by normal courts. Under Commodity Exchange Act (no. 229/1992 Sb.) procedure of Arbitration Act (no. 216/1994 Sb.) (see topic Arbitration and Award) shall apply.

EXECUTIONS:

District Courts are competent for ordering and realisation of execution through methods specified in OSR. Executions can be ordered upon judgment, court settlements, certain enforceable documents set up before Public Notary, decisions of administrative authorities and arbitral awards.

Execution of decision imposing payment of pecuniary amount can be realised by wage deductions, assignment of claim, sale of movable assets or sale of real estate.

Execution of decision imposing obligation other than payment of pecuniary amount conforms to nature of obligation imposed and can be realised by evacuation, removal of thing, division of joint thing and execution of work and operations.

Executions can only be ordered upon motion of entitled person. It is necessary to annex copy of decision marked with writ of execution to motion. Writ of execution is indicated on decision by first instance court.

With respect to execution of decision concerning support of minors, president of tribunal makes written request to debtor to comply with decision or court settlement. If this is unsuccessful, president of tribunal gradually imposes fines on obliged person; individual fines must not exceed 2,000 Kc.

Exceptions.—Executions cannot be enforced upon movable assets and real estate whose sale is prohibited by special prescription or which are not subject to execution in conformity with special prescriptions. Executions cannot be enforced upon items which are in propriety of debtor, if debtor needs these items for satisfaction of his personal material needs, needs of his family, for fulfilment of his labour or enterprise tasks, as well as items whose sale would be in contradiction with morality.

Execution of Foreign Judgments.—Foreign judgment has effect in CR if it is final and has been recognised by Czech courts. (Act no. 97/1963 Sb., on Private International Law and Law of International Procedure, in wording of Acts no. 158/1969 Sb., no. 234/1992 Sb. and no. 264/1992 Sb. [§§63-66]). Foreign judgment can be neither recognised nor enforced if: (1) Matter lies within exclusive jurisdiction of Czech courts, or if Czech legal provisions on competence of Czech courts applied to foreign country would not admit case to be heard by courts or authorities of given foreign state; (2) Czech authority has already issued final decision on same matter or foreign decision from third country has been already recognised in CR; (3) participant of proceedings against whom foreign judgment is to be recognised, was denied possibility of defending his rights and to take part in proceedings, especially if respective order to appear before court or motion to open proceedings was not served properly; (4) foreign judgment is contrary to public order; (5) reciprocity is not granted (reciprocity is not required if foreign decision is not directed against Czech citizen or Czech legal person). Execution of foreign judgment must be ordered by decision of Czech court. Examination of foreign judgment as to substance in merits of matter is not admitted.

See topic Judgments.

EXECUTORS AND ADMINISTRATORS:

Function of executor is not provided for by Czech law. Process of administering estate is done by court and notary public, with possibility of delegation of some simple tasks to court officers under supervision of court. Court may appoint administrators under special circumstances, see topic Descent and Distribution.

FOREIGN EXCHANGE:

Foreign exchange laws in CR impose obligations primarily on residents. (Act no. 528/1990 Sb., am'd by Act no. 228/1992 Sb., full wording Act no. 457/1992 Sb., am'd by Act no. 219/1995 Sb.). Foreign exchange authorities are Czech National Bank and Ministry of Finance. Breach of foreign exchange regulations can result in penalties ranging from fines to forfeiture. Major offences may also result in criminal liability.

Resident Legal Entity or Individual.—(1) Have duty to report to authorities receivables and debts towards nonresidents, on real estate, bank account and property interests abroad, holdings of foreign securities or import/export of currency in excess of 200,000 Kc or foreign currency equivalent; (2) is obliged to bring or transfer any settlements of claims paid abroad and foreign exchange resources held abroad to CR (exemptions are available); (3) is entitled to open foreign exchange account with approved bank and use funds freely, except for circumstances set forth by law; (4) may invest directly abroad (foundation of wholly owned company, participation in new or existing company of at least 10% of assets, shareholder loan of minimum five year term or reinvestment of profits). Approved bank must provide foreign exchange resources to pay obligations and to cover expenses arising in foreign currency. Exchange permits required to open bank account abroad (some exceptions apply), to accept loan from nonresident or to make investments abroad other than direct investment.

Nonresident Individual or Entity.—(1) Entitled to open accounts in foreign or local currency with approved bank and have free disposal of such accounts for all transactions (except of trading foreign exchange resources); (2) is free to export or transfer abroad foreign exchange resources if not acquired in CR illegally; (3) may acquire ownership rights to real estate in CR only if law expressly allows (see topic Real Property); (4) is under no duty to offer any foreign exchange resources for exchange; (5) is obliged to apply for certification on imported gold. Golden coins can be exported if non-resident proves legal purchase.

FOREIGN INVESTMENT:

Basic legal regulation governing direct business activity of foreign persons in CR is contained in Commercial Code. (ObchZ, §§21-26).

Foreign persons may develop business activity in territory of CR under same conditions and to same extent as Czech persons, if law does not stipulate otherwise. "Foreign Person" means physical or legal person having domicile or seat outside territory of CR. (ObchZ, §21). Carrying on business activity in territory of CR means engagement of person in business activity, if it has enterprise or organisational unit located in territory of CR. Authorisation of foreign person to engage in business activity in territory of CR becomes effective from day of registration of this person, or its organisational unit, into commercial register, within extent of its scope of activities entered into commercial register. (ObchZ, §21). Apart from registration in commercial register, foreign person developing business activity in CR through organisational unit must also comply with conditions defined by Trade Act. (Zivnostenský zákon, Act no. 455/1991 Sb., am'd by Acts no. 231/1992 Sb., no. 591/1992 Sb., no. 273/1993 Sb., no. 303/1993 Sb., no. 38/1994 Sb., no. 42/1994 Sb., no. 136/1994 Sb., no. 200/1994 Sb., no. 235/1995 Sb., no. 286/1995 Sb. and no. 94/1996 Sb.).

Foreign person may, for purpose of developing business activity, take part in establishment of Czech legal entity or take part in existing Czech legal entity as member or partner. Foreign person may also found Czech legal entity or become only associate of Czech legal entity, if allowed by law. (ObchZ, §24).

Property of foreign person connected with business activity in CR and property of legal entity with foreign capital participation can be expropriated or ownership rights restricted only on basis of law and in public interest which cannot be otherwise satisfied. Appeal against such decision may be submitted to court. In taking such measures, compensation corresponding to full value of property affected must be provided without delay. Such compensation is freely transferable abroad in foreign currency. (ObchZ, §25). Provisions of international treaties are not affected.

Legal entity founded under law of foreign state for purpose of developing business activity and having its seat abroad, can relocate its seat to territory of CR, provided that this is permitted by law of state in which such legal entity has its seat, and if legal entity has been founded under law of another state, also by this law. Such relocation becomes effective from day of registration of respective legal entity in commercial register. (ObchZ, §26).

CR is bound by Washington Convention on resolving disputes arising from investment between states and citizens of other states concluded on Mar. 18, 1965 and by Washington Convention on multilateral agency for investment guarantees concluded on Oct. 11, 1985. Number of bilateral agreements on investment protection exist between CR and: France, Austria, Switzerland, Finland, Sweden, Canada, Norway, Australia, Slovenia, Romania, The Netherlands, Belgium and Luxembourg, Denmark, Great Britain and Northern Ireland, China, U.S.A., Greece, Philippines, Singapore, Ukraine, South Korea, Thailand, Lithuania, Albania, Peru, Hungary, Estonia and Latvia.

See topics Aliens; Corporations; Licenses; Taxation.

FOREIGN TRADE REGULATIONS:

Organisation can engage in foreign trade in conformity with scope of business activity registered in commercial register.

State interventions are addressed by Act no. 42/1980 Sb., am'd by Acts no. 113/1990 Sb., no. 513/1991 Sb., no. 228/1992 Sb. and no. 223/1994 Sb. on trade relations with foreign countries as amended by ObchZ and are regulated in terms of specific detail by Decree no. 560/1991 Sb., on import and export licenses, amended Decree no. 130/1993 Sb. Latter decree stipulates that goods and services indicated in annexes to this decree may only be imported to or exported from CR by authorised persons on basis, to extent, and under conditions determined in license. Licenses are granted by Ministry of Commerce and Industry.

As to import of goods indicated in annex A, part III., of Decree no. 560/1991 Sb., am'd by Acts no. 130/1993, Sb. no. 300/1993 Sb., no. 088/1994 Sb., no. 175/1994 Sb., no. 192/1995 Sb. and no. 156/1996 Sb., license is granted automatically to each applicant, for import of certain goods in fixed quantity and within fixed time period. Such licenses serve for registration.

Regarding import or export of goods indicated in other annexes to above decree, licenses are awarded for import or export of certain goods in fixed quantity or value in fixed time period so that total of exported or imported goods or value would not exceed yearly limits established with respective central authorities.

Export of objects of historical, artistic or cultural value requires export certificate.

See Topical Index in front part of this volume.

FOREIGN TRADE REGULATIONS . . . *continued*

Indirect regulation of foreign trade is realised by customs prescriptions, as well as by foreign exchange prescriptions.

See topic Foreign Exchange.

FRAUDS, STATUTE OF:

CR has no statute of frauds, but see generally topic Contracts.

FRAUDULENT SALES AND CONVEYANCES:

Acts performed by debtor, which defraud creditor's valid claims are voidable in relation to creditor if debtor has undertaken such acts in previous three years with intention to defraud creditor (animus fraudandi), provided intent was known to other party (creditor has burden of proof); as well as acts in previous three years, which defraud creditor, between debtor and person close to debtor (generally defined as family member, see OZ, §116) or performed by debtor for benefit of same persons; in this case creditor's intent and knowledge of close persons are assumed, with exception of case that other party, despite exercising all due care, could not have recognised debtor's intention to defraud creditor. (Act no. 40/1964 Sb., in latest wording Act no. 47/1992 Sb., am'd by Acts no. 264/1992 Sb. and no. 267/1994 Sb.).

Action for avoiding fraudulent act is to be brought against person who benefited from debtor's act. Effect of successful action is that defrauding act is ineffective against creditor, i.e., creditor may seek satisfaction of his claim from what was removed from debtor's assets by debtor's act. If this is not possible, creditor is entitled to compensation from person who benefited from defrauding act.

In case of bankruptcy, right to bring action belongs to creditors and administrator. (Act no. 328/1991 Sb., as am'd by Acts no. 471/1992 Sb., no. 122/1993 Sb., no. 42/1994 Sb., no. 74/1994 Sb., no. 117/1994 Sb., no. 152/1994 Sb., no. 224/1994 Sb., no. 84/1995 Sb. and no. 94/1996 Sb.).

See also topic Bankruptcy.

GARNISHMENT:

Used in two methods of execution: Deduction of wages and assignment of claim, i.e., in procedure of execution of enforceable decision of court and as interlocutory injunction. Regarding deduction of wages, it is not possible to garnish so called "basic amount" as defined by Decree no. 185/1993 Sb. Pursuant to this decree, sum of 1,500 Kc per month must remain for debtor, with additional exemption of 600 Kc for each person whom debtor supports. For husband/wife of debtor, sum of 600 Kc is exempted, even if he/she has independent income. In case deduction of wage is executed against both husband and wife, exempted sum of 600 Kc is applied jointly for their dependants. Above amount of 3,000 Kc, deduction of wage may be made without limitation.

See topic Executions.

HOLIDAYS:

Act no. 93/1951 Sb. on State Holidays, Days of Labour Calm, Memorial and Significant Days, amended by Acts no. 218/1991 Sb. and no. 74/1994 Sb.

Legal Holidays are: Jan. 1 (New Year's Day); Easter Monday; May 1 (Labour Day); May 9 (Liberation Day); July 5 (Day of Slavic Creed Messengers—Cyril and Methodej); July 6 (Memory of Jan Hus); Oct. 28 (Independence Day); Dec. 24, 25, 26 (Christmas Days).

HOMESTEADS:

Czech legal system does not recognise homestead.

HUSBAND AND WIFE:

Spouses are entitled to represent each other in common matters. Act of one spouse regarding common matters binds both jointly and severally. Other matters require consent of both spouses, otherwise legal act is not valid. (OZ, §145).

Property owned by one spouse before marriage remains separate property during and after marriage. All property acquired by one spouse during marriage is jointly owned, with exception of inherited property, gifts and things for personal needs or necessary for occupation of one of spouses. (OZ, §143). Notarized agreement signed by both spouses may alter extent of ownership of joint property stipulated by law or may postpone commencement of joint property relationship until date of end of marriage. (OZ, §143a).

Joint property of married couple dissolves upon end of marriage or during marriage for important reasons upon decision of court. (OZ, §148).

Parties may agree upon settlement on division of joint property. Settlement proceeds on principle that shares of both spouses are equal. (OZ, §§149, 150). Needs of minor children are of primary importance. Judicial practice prefers material division of joint property, financial settlement is in case full material settlement is not possible.

Conflict of Laws.—Personal and property relations of spouses in marriage with foreigner and among foreigners are governed by law of state in which spouses are citizens. Should they be citizens of different states, above relations are governed by Czech law. Agreement on matrimonial property rights is considered pursuant to rights decisive for property relations of spouses at time agreement was effected. (§21, Act no. 97/1963 Sb., am'd by Acts no. 158/1969 Sb., no. 234/1992 Sb and no. 264/1992 Sb.).

See also topic Divorce.

IMMIGRATION:

Aliens require visa for entering CR. There are bilateral treaties excepting citizens of most European states and U.S. from this obligation for 30 to 90 day periods.

Aliens may obtain short term residence permit valid for maximum 180 days. Permit for long term stay is granted for period necessary to reach applicants aim, maximum of one year; this may be renewed upon request. (§§4, 5, Act no. 123/1992 Sb., am'd by Act no. 190/1994 Sb. and no. 150/1996 Sb.). Permanent residence permit is granted under stipulations of Act no. 123/1992 Sb., am'd by Act no. 190/1994 Sb., especially because of humanitarian reasons.

Acquiring Czech citizenship is governed by Act no. 40/1993 Sb., am'd by Acts no. 272/1993 Sb., no. 337/1993 Sb. and no. 139/1996 Sb. Generally, citizenship can be acquired by birth, if one parent is Czech citizen, or if at least one parent, who is stateless person, has permanent residence in CR and child was born in territory of CR; by recognition or determination of paternity if father is Czech citizen; by discovery of child under 15 years of age in territory of CR; and by naturalisation.

Upon request alien can be awarded Czech citizenship provided that: (1) He has permanently resided in CR for at least five years; (2) he can prove surrender or loss of any other citizenship; (3) he was not sentenced for intentional criminal offence in past five years and (4) he proves knowledge of Czech language.

Aliens classified as refugees under Act no. 498/1990 Sb., am'd by Act no. 317/1993 Sb., have same status as citizens with exceptions enumerated in Act. Alien, entering or staying on territory of CR illegally, may be expelled or deported. (§16, Act no. 123/1992 Sb.).

For working permits see topic Labour Relations.

See also topic Aliens.

INDUSTRIAL PROPERTY RIGHTS:

Industrial property covers patents on inventions and industrial designs (see topic Patents), rights to marking (see topic Trademarks and Trade Names), utility designs, appellations of origin, topographies of microelectronic semiconductor products, new varieties of plants and breeds of animals.

Utility Designs.—Technical solutions, which are new, beyond mere specialist's skill and which are susceptible of industrial application. (Act no. 478/1992 Sb.). Act stipulates further conditions as to what may be subject to utility design protection. First-to-file system similar to patents is used. Compulsory license may by granted by Industrial Property Office under circumstances given by law. Utility design is valid for four years beginning day of filing prior invention/patent application regarding same subject. Duration may be extended twice, each time for three years. Special register for utility designs within Patent Office. Violation results in civil liability and criminal liability under §151 of Criminal Code no. 140/1961 Sb., am'd by Acts no. 65/1994 Sb. and no. 91/1994 Sb.

Topographies of Microelectronic Semiconductor Products.—Product of creative activity of author and which are unusual in semiconductor industry, are protected by Act no. 529/1991 Sb. Under this Act, parts of topography, which may be used independently, as well as portrayal used for manufacturing of topographies are protected. Protection starts upon first public use of topography, provided that application for registration is filed within two years thereafter with Industrial Property Office or on day of filing with Office, if topography has not been used in public earlier. Protection expires ten years from end of calendar year when protection was established. If not filed with Office, or if not publicly used, right to protection expires 15 years after topography created. Other rules, including registration with Office and compulsory license generally correspond with provisions on patents. Violation can result in civil liability or criminal liability under §151 of Criminal Code no. 140/1961 Sb., am'd by Acts no. 65/1994 Sb. and no. 91/1994 Sb.

New Varieties of Plants and Breeds of Animals.—Governed by Act no. 132/1989 Sb. and no. 93/1996 Sb., which applies to economically important varieties and genera of plants and animals, listed in Decree no. 134/1989 Sb., amended by Decree no. 515/1991 Sb. Ministry of Agriculture registers and grants breeders' and cultivators' certificates, which confirm: (1) Cultivation of variety/breeding of breed; (2) name with designation of kind/genus; (3) authorship; (4) right of owner of certificate to commercial use of variety/breed; (5) duration of protection of rights towards variety/breed. Authorship originates in moment of creation of variety/breed, and cannot be transferred to another person. Name of author must be designated in application. If meeting legal conditions, Ministry of Agriculture may grant compulsory license. Certificate is valid from day of filing with Ministry and its duration is: (1) For breeds—as long as breed exists; (2) for variations of hop, wine grapes, fruit, decorative and forest woods—25 years; (3) other variations—20 years. Violation of rules set by law is regarded as offence and is, along with civil liability, punishable by fine up to 5,000 Kc.

See topics Patents; Trademarks and Trade Names.

INFANTS:

Age of majority is 18 years. Minors are represented by guardians, normally parents. Minor may reach majority by concluding marriage (see topic Marriage). If both parents of infant are dead, have been deprived of parental rights or have no competence to make legal acts, court appoints curator for infant. Physical person, preferably relative of infant, or state body may be appointed curator. Curator is subordinated to court supervision. Should guardian manage property of infant, approval of court is necessary for disposal provided it does not concern common matter. In case of conflict of interest between guardian or curator on one side and infant on other side, court appoints special curator.

Persons under 15 years have no criminal liability, from 15 years through 18 years are treated preferentially under criminal law and labour laws.

Parents are obliged to support their children. Normally duty ceases to exist at end of 18 years, sooner if child is able to support him/herself, later in cases of illness or continuous education. Children who are able to support themselves are obliged to provide their parents sufficient sustenance if parents require. Law does not make distinction between children born in or out of marriage.

Concerning care of infant, competent court is district court in district in which infant is domiciled.

Conflict of Laws.—Relations between parents and children are regulated by law of state of which child is citizen. If child is living in CR, Czech law can be applied if this application is in interest of child. Maintenance claims of parents towards children are regulated by law of state of which respective parent is citizen. (§24, Act no. 97/1963 Sb., am'd by Acts no. 158/1969 Sb., no. 234/1992 Sb. and no. 264/1992 Sb.). Provisions of international treaties binding CR are not affected.

CR is member of following international agreements concerning infants and minors: Hague Convention on the Recognition and Enforcement of Decision Relating to

INFANTS . . . *continued*
Maintenance Obligations in Respect of Children of Apr. 15, 1958 (no. 14/1974 Sb.) and Hague Convention on the Recognition and Enforcement of Decisions Relating to Maintenance Obligations of Oct. 2, 1973 (no. 132/1976 Sb.).

INSOLVENCY:

Main characteristic of insolvency is included in Act on Bankruptcy and Settlements no. 328/1991 Sb., amended by Acts no. 471/1992 Sb., no. 122/1993 Sb., no. 42/1994 Sb., no. 74/1994 Sb., no. 117/1994 Sb., no. 156/1994 Sb., no. 224/1994 Sb., no. 84/1995 Sb. and no. 94/1996 Sb.

Insolvency is defined as position of debtor, who is unable to meet payments overdue to number of creditors for protracted period of time. In addition, physical person (if entrepreneur) or legal entity is considered to be insolvent if overburdened with debts, i.e., liabilities exceed assets.

See topic Bankruptcy.

JOINT STOCK COMPANIES:

See topic Corporations.

JUDGMENTS:

Judgments of Czech courts against which no further appeal lies are enforceable by way of execution.

Recognition and execution of foreign judgments is regulated by Act no. 97/1963 Sb., am'd by Acts no. 158/1969 Sb., no. 234/1992 Sb. and no. 264/1992 Sb. on international private law and law of international procedure. For recognition of foreign judgments, two basic conditions must be met: Judgment must be definitive (final) judgment having force of law and it must be recognisable by Czech authorities.

Main groups of foreign judgments regulated by law are foreign decisions in property matters and foreign decisions in matters of civil status. For latter, if Czech citizen is concerned, conditions of recognition are more severe and form of recognition is prescribed by law.

Recognition of Foreign Judgments.—Foreign judgments in marital matters and matters of determination of paternity, in case at least one participant in proceedings was Czech citizen, are governed by special requirement that foreign decision be recognised by decision of Supreme Court after hearing of general prosecutor. If all participants were aliens and nationals of state in which decision was issued or foreign decision is recognised in home state of all participants, foreign decision will be recognised without further proceedings.

Foreign judgments can be neither recognised nor enforced, if: (1) Czech legal provision on competence of Czech courts applied to foreign countries would not admit case to be heard by courts or authorities of foreign state, or if matter lies within exclusive jurisdiction of Czech courts; (2) Czech authority has already issued final decision on same legal action or foreign decision has been previously recognised; (3) participant of proceedings against whom foreign judgment is to be recognised was denied possibility of defending his rights and to take part in proceedings, especially if respective order to appear before court or motion to open proceedings was not served properly; (4) foreign judgment is in contradiction to public order; (5) it is proved that similar decisions by Czech authorities are not recognised in respective foreign state if foreign judgment is directed against Czech physical or legal person.

Execution of Foreign Judgments.—Distinction between recognition and execution of foreign judgment in property matter must be made. Recognition will be realised without special decision, i.e., Czech authority takes regard of foreign judgment as in case of Czech judgment in same matter. Execution of foreign judgment in property matter must be ordered by decision of Czech court. (decision exequatur).

It is always necessary to justify ordering of execution, but examination of foreign judgment as to substance in merits of matter is not allowed. Otherwise, execution of foreign judgment according to general prescriptions is realised in same manner as execution of domestic judgments with respect to property rights.

CR is party to number of multilateral and bilateral treaties dealing with this subject. Multilateral treaties include The Hague Convention of Apr. 15, 1958 on Recognition and Enforcement of Decisions Relating to Maintenance Obligation in Respect of Children; The Hague Convention of Oct. 2, 1973 on Recognition and Enforcement of Decision Relating to Maintenance Obligations; The Geneva Convention of Sept. 26, 1927 on Enforcement of Foreign Arbitral Awards; New York Convention of June 10, 1958 on Recognition and Enforcement of Foreign Arbitral Awards.

For bilateral treaties, see topic Treaties.

See also topic Executions.

LABOUR RELATIONS:

Labour relations are ruled generally by Labour Code (Zakonik prace [abbr. ZP], Act no. 65/1965 Sb., full wording no. 126/1994 Sb., as am'd by Acts no. 118/1995 Sb. and no. 287/1995 Sb.), but also by other acts and collective labour agreements. Social security and trade union activities, both regulated by law, constitute important part of labour relations.

Discharge.—Written notice delivered to other party required to terminate employment. Organisation can only give notice to employee for reasons expressly indicated in ZP, §46. General notice period of two months is same for organisation and employee; however in case of notice given by organisation for reasons of its winding up, transfer to another organisation or redundancy of worker period is three months.

Organisation must not give notice to employee during so called "protection period" (ZP, §48) i.e.: When employee is recognised to be temporarily disabled; in time of service in military forces; when worker is on long-term leave of absence for execution of public service; when employee is pregnant or when female employee or single parent is permanently taking care of at least one child under three years of age.

Immediate termination is only possible exceptionally and in case: Employee has been finally sentenced for intentional criminal offence with imprisonment for over one year, or for at least six months, if intentional criminal offence was committed during fulfilment of labour obligations; or if employee is guilty of gross breach of labour discipline. (ZP, §53).

Hours of Work.—Fixed at maximum 43 hours per week. Workers younger than 16 years have maximum of 33 hours per week. Reduction of hours of work, overtime work and scheduling of working hours are responsibility of management within guidelines of ZP, §§84-99.

Wages.—(Act no. 1/1992 Sb., as am'd by Acts no. 590/1992 Sb., no. 10/1993 Sb., no. 37/1993 Sb., no. 74/1994 Sb. and no. 118/1995 Sb.). Minimum wage for one hour worked by employee is 13.6 Kc or 2,500 Kc month. (Decree no. 303/1996 Sb.). In case of employee with partial disability pension or minor worker older than 16 years 1,900 Kc. Wage compensation is paid after monthly period worked unless labour contract or collective agreement stipulates otherwise.

Child Labour.—Labour competency starts when citizen reaches 15 years of age. However, organisation may not negotiate labour contract in which day of starting work would be prior to finishing of obligatory school attendance by citizen.

Female Workers.—(ZP, §§150-158). Organisations are obliged to establish, maintain and improve hygienic and other premises for women. Women must not be employed in underground extraction of minerals or in excavations of tunnels, with exception of managing functions or nonmanual work, health care and social services, practice during studies and nonmanual work connected with supervisory, control or study activities. Only women older than 18 years may work at night. Ministry of Health determines workplaces in which women or pregnant women are prohibited from working. Pregnant women doing prohibited work or work which endangers pregnancy must be temporarily transferred by organisation to more suitable work without loss of earnings. Pregnant women and women taking care of children under one year may not be sent to work outside municipality of their work place or domicile. Organisations are required to consider needs of women caring for children when allocation workers for shifts. Maternity leave of between 28 weeks to three years is allowed.

Annual Leave.—(ZP, §§101-106). Employees who have worked for uninterrupted period of 60 days during calendar year for same employer are entitled to annual leave or proportionate part if employment has been less than one calendar year. Generally leave will be three weeks, however employees who have been part of labour force for 15 years after their 18th birthday are entitled to four weeks. Higher amounts of leave may be agreed upon in collective agreements.

Discrimination.—ZP stipulates that citizens have right to work and free choice of work, to just and satisfactory labour conditions and to protection against unemployment. They have these rights without limitation and without discrimination whatsoever on basis of race, colour, language, sex, social origin, age, religion, political or other opinions, political membership, trade union activity, adherence to national or ethnic group or other position.

Labour Unions.—In case legal prescriptions in existence prior to 1990 gave rise to authorisation for trade union movements, such authorisations now relate to trade union organisations created on basis of free trade union association. (Act no. 120/1990 Sb., am'd by Act no. 3/1991 Sb.). If in employer's organisation multiple trade union organisations exist, employer must, in cases involving all employees, and when generally binding acts require negotiations with or consent of trade unions, fulfil these obligations with respect to all trade unions involved, if not mutually agreed otherwise. If all trade union organisations involved do not agree within 15 days of being requested as to whether they consent, then opinion of trade union having highest number of members in employer's organisation becomes decisive. Above mentioned rule is used as well for collective bargaining, on understanding that respective trade unions operating in employer's organisation may act on behalf of collective of workers with legal effects for all workers only upon common and mutual agreement, if they will not otherwise agree among themselves and with employer's organisation.

Labour Disputes.—In conformity with Act no. 2/1991 Sb., amended by Act no. 519/1991 Sb., no. 29/1993 Sb., no. 118/1995 Sb. and no. 155/1995 Sb. labour disputes are disputes concerning conclusion of collective agreements and disputes concerning respect of obligations set forth by collective agreements, which do not give rise to rights of individual employees. In case of dispute, parties may agree on selection of mediator. In absence of agreement, Ministry of Labour designates mediator on motion by either contracting party. In case of dispute concerning conclusion of collective agreement, such motion can be submitted only after lapse of 60 days from presentation of written proposal for conclusion of such agreement. Proceedings before mediator are considered unsuccessful if dispute is not resolved within 30 days from day mediator has been informed of substance of dispute. If proceedings before mediator are unsuccessful, contracting parties may demand arbitrator to decide dispute. In case collective agreement is not concluded after proceedings before mediator and contracting parties do not request arbitrator, strike may be declared as last resort in dispute concerning conclusion of collective agreement.

Workers Compensation.—If worker suffers injury or dies while fulfilling labour tasks or in direct connection therewith, organisation with whom worker had labour relation at time of accident is held responsible for damages so caused. Organisation is obliged, within extent to which it is responsible for loss, to provide compensation for wage loss (maximum 3,000 Kc monthly), pain (maximum 18,000 Kc), diminished social usefulness (maximum 42,000 Kc), reasonable expenditures connected with medical treatment and material damage. If worker died as consequence of accident at work or occupational disease, organisation is obliged to provide, within extent of its responsibility, compensation of reasonable expenditures connected with treatment, appropriate expenditures connected with funeral, expenditures connected with support of survivors, lump-sum compensation of survivors 8,000 Kc to child, 5,000 Kc to spouse and material damage.

Unemployment Compensation.—In conformity with Employment Act no. 1/1991 Sb., full wording no. 450/1992 Sb., amended by Act no. 307/1993 Sb., no. 39/1994 Sb., no. 118/1995 Sb. and no. 160/1995 Sb. citizens have right to appropriate employment corresponding to health condition, age, qualification and skills, duration of previous employment and lodging possibilities. If within seven calendar days from submission of application, appropriate employment or retraining possibility for new employment is not secured, he is provided with material assistance. Material assistance is provided to applicant who worked at least 12 months in last three years before

LABOUR RELATIONS . . . *continued*
submitting application, if regulation does not determine shorter period. Material assistance is provided to applicant for maximum one year. After this time, social security prescriptions apply. Level of material assistance is 60% of average net wage earned by applicant in his last employment, paid for period of first six months, and at least 50% of this wage thereafter, if regulation does not fix other rate.

Foreign Workers.—Foreigners who are employed in CR are subject to laws of CR; however, they can only be employed if they hold residency permission in CR, as well as permission for employment. Permission for employment is not required for employment in following cases: (1) Individual with recognised refugee status, if he/she has been in territory of CR for three years or has concluded marriage with Czech citizen or has at least one child with Czech citizenship; (2) individual was awarded permission for permanent residence in territory of CR; (3) individual is family member of member of diplomatic corps, consular office or family member of employee of international governmental organisation with headquarters in territory of CR, if mutuality is guaranteed by international treaty.

With regard to Czech legal regulations, ZP, §6 stipulates following: (1) Labour relations between workers and foreign organisations in territory of CR, as well as labour relations between foreigners working in territory of CR and domestic organisations are subject to ZP, if international private law does not stipulate otherwise; (2) labour relations of workers of international organisation with headquarters in territory of CR established by international treaties, are subject to ZP, if these treaties or other international conventions do not stipulate otherwise; (3) labour relations of employees of enterprises with foreign capital participation and organisations with international element with headquarters in territory of CR are subject to ZP, unless law under prescriptions of international private law holds otherwise; (4) Government of CR may, by decree, determine regulation different from ZP for labour relations of organisations under (2) above and those organisations with foreign capital participation.

LAW REPORTS, CODES, ETC.:

Official reports of decisions are issued approximately quarterly by Supreme Court, considered as important source of law, but no decision is binding for future cases.

Publishing of Commercial Bulletin is based on Decree No. 63/1992 Sb. Commercial Bulletin includes all information which is to be published according to ObchZ, together with court decisions in commercial cases provided that court approves publishing.

Ministry of Finance periodically publishes among its decrees list of maximum prices for items such as medicines, optical goods and energy.

Laws of CR are codified, appearing in Sbirka zakonu (collection of laws) as they are enacted.

LEGISLATURE:

See topic Constitution and Government.

LICENSES:

Trading licenses are required for any business involving practice of trade. (Act no. 455/1991 Sb., am'd by Acts nos. 231/1992 Sb., 591/1992 Sb., 273/1993 Sb., 303/1993 Sb., 38/1994 Sb., 42/1994 Sb., 136/1994 Sb., 200/1994 Sb., 237/1995 Sb., 286/1995 Sb. and 94/1996 Sb.). "Trade" is defined as systematic independently managed activity, conducted by natural or legal person in his own name and at his own liability for purpose of making profit under conditions stipulated by law. License is required for each activity. Acquisition of single trade license for conducting of all sub-activities involved in manufacture of particular product or provision of certain service is possible.

For obtaining license or concession certain qualifications must be proved (specialised education and experience of certain duration according to kind of activity, etc.). Only in cases of so-called "free trades" registration suffices without proof of education and experience. General conditions are age over 18 years, capacity to make legal acts and integrity (lack of criminal record or bankruptcy). Individual must offer proof of his/her lack of criminal record by submission of relevant documents from state of which person is citizen, as well as states in which individual has had long term residency (over three months without interruption) for three years prior to making application. If nominee is not citizen of CR, he must be able to prove ability to communicate in Czech language.

Legal persons must nominate responsible representative with residence in CR who must fulfil conditions required for respective trade. If entrepreneur does not fulfil specific conditions for exercising trade or does not have residence in CR, he must nominate responsible representative who fulfils conditions required and has residence in CR. Foreign entrepreneur, physical as well as legal person, may start exercising trade after entry into commercial register.

Relevant trade licensing office may propose fines for practice of trades without license or failure to comply with provisions of Act.

Special permits are required for certain business activities, e.g., in fields of banking and insurance.

See topics Aliens; Commercial Register.

LIENS:

OZ, §§551-558, provides that parties may agree to secure claim by written agreement for deduction of wages or income, contract creating lien, assignment of debt or transfer of right.

Contractual Penalty Under OZ.—If parties agree on contractual penalty, party who breaches obligation is bound to pay penalty, even if entitled party has not sustained any damage due to breach. Contractual penalty must be concluded in writing with specification of amount of penalty or manner of determination. Debtor is obligated to fulfil secured obligation after paying penalty, unless agreement holds otherwise. Debtor is not obliged to pay contractual penalty if he did not cause breach of obligation, unless agreement determines otherwise. (OZ, §§544, 545).

Guarantee Under OZ.—Established on basis of written declaration. Creditor is obliged to inform guarantor of amount of claim. Guarantor may refuse to render performance if debtor was not able to satisfy obligation due to creditor's fault. In case guarantor satisfies claim, he may raise against creditor all defences which debtor would have against creditor. Acknowledgment of obligation by debtor is effective against guarantor only if he consented in acknowledgment. Guarantor has right of indemnification from debtor after satisfying obligation. (OZ, §§546-550).

Other liens under OZ are acknowledgments, garnishment, pledges and mortgages, all of which are addressed in individual topics of this digest.

ObchZ presents special provisions on liens applicable to contractual relations arising from commercial matters. (ObchZ, §§297-323).

Contractual Penalty Under ObchZ.—Court is authorized to reduce disproportionately high penalty to amount of actual damage, taking account of value and matter of secured claim. Withdrawal from or repudiation of contract has no effect on claim of payment penalty. (ObchZ, §§300-302).

Guarantee Under ObchZ.—May be applicable to future or conditional obligation. Creditor is entitled to seek satisfaction from guarantor only if debtor has not fulfilled due obligation after creditor made written request to debtor to do so, unless request is impossible or futile. If several guarantors exist, each is liable for entire debt. Guarantor has position of co-debtor in relation to his co-guarantors. Guarantor, who has performed his obligation assumes rights of creditor against debtor. Guarantee terminates with extinguishment of secured obligation, but not if due to debtor's incapacity to perform obligation for reason of dissolution of legal person being debtor. (ObchZ, §§303-312).

Bank Guarantee Under ObchZ.—Established by written undertaking of bank in letter of guarantee, stating that bank will pay creditor if third party fails to fulfil obligation and if other conditions stipulated in letter are met. If bank guarantee is confirmed by another bank, creditor may seek satisfaction from any of banks. Bank which confirmed and fulfilled obligation has right to claim performance from bank which requested confirmation. In contrast to ordinary guarantee, creditor is not obliged to ask debtor to fulfil obligation first, bank may be requested in writing directly, unless letter of guarantee stipulates otherwise. Bank may seek satisfaction from debtor. Legal relationship between bank and debtor is regulated according to mandate contract. (ObchZ, §§313-322).

See also topics Mortgages; Pledges.

LIMITATION OF ACTIONS:

Provided right has been statute-barred by expiration of terms of prescription mentioned below, debtor is entitled to plead prescription. If debtor raises prescription, court is prevented from according statute-barred right to creditor. Court regards prescription only if debtor raises issue, which debtor may do at any time within course of proceedings. (OZ, §100). Right of prescription may not be disclaimed.

Term of prescription commences on date it was possible to assert right for first time. All rights are subject to prescription with exception of right of ownership. General term of prescription is three years. (OZ, §101). Rights concerning deposits on bank accounts may not be statute-barred as long as deposit relations still exist. (OZ, §100).

Special provisions control following rights: (1) Term concerning right to compensation for damage is two years and commences on day when injured party learned of damage and discovered who was responsible, but at latest three years, unless damage was caused intentionally, in which case ten year term applies from day when damage occurred (OZ, §106); (2) term concerning right to demand return of unjust enrichment is two years and commences on date when injured party learned of unjust enrichment and discovered party liable for act, but at latest three years, or in case of intentional unjust enrichment, ten years latest from day when intentional act occurred (OZ, §107); (3) claims against carrier and forwarding agent are barred after one year with exception of compensation for damage from transport of persons (OZ, §108); (4) rights corresponding to easement become barred unless they are executed within period of ten years (OZ, §109); (5) right adjudicated by final decision of court or other administrative body is barred ten years after day performance should have been made on basis of decision (OZ, §110); (6) right acknowledged by debtor in writing as to its grounds and amount is barred ten years after day acknowledgment was made, unless term of performance was indicated in acknowledgment, in which case right is barred ten years from expiration of indicated term (OZ, §110); (7) ten year term applies to separate instalments arising on basis of decision or acknowledgment, with term for individual instalment beginning on day it becomes payable (OZ, §110); (8) interest and recurrent performances are barred after three years, except in case of rights adjudged by final court decision or written acknowledgment, in which case this term applies only to interest or recurring performance arising after decision or acknowledgment. (OZ, §110).

Change in person of debtor or creditor has no effect on running of term of prescription. Term of prescription does not run during period debtor is asserting right before court or other appropriate body. (OZ, §112). Term does not begin nor run with regard to rights among spouses, minors or persons required to have statutory representative on one hand, and statutory representative on other hand, unless concerning interest or recurrent performance. Term related to persons who are obliged have statutory representative commences after representative is appointed. (OZ, §§113, 114).

Regarding matters exclusively governed by ObchZ.

General term is four years. (ObchZ, §397). Regulation of periods of prescription in ObchZ is for most part parallel with Convention on Limitation Periods in International Sale of Goods, New York, June 14, 1974, to which CR is contracting state.

See topic Actions.

MARRIAGE:

Marriage is governed by Act no. 94/1963 Sb. Furthermore, CR is contracting party to New York Convention on Consent to Marriage, Minimum Age for Marriage and Registration of Marriage of Dec. 10, 1962.

Marriage is concluded by declaration of consent of man and woman before state authority in presence of two witnesses or by declaration of consent before dignitary of state recognised church. Should citizen of foreign state conclude marriage in CR, submission of certificate of legal capacity to conclude marriage issued by respective authority of foreign state is required. No limitation exists on conclusion of marriage

See Topical Index in front part of this volume.

MARRIAGE . . . *continued*
between foreigner and citizen of CR. Marriage ceases to exist upon decision of divorce, on death of spouse or after certification of death of spouse.

Both spouses are obliged to satisfy needs of family pursuant to their means and abilities. Spouses decide family matters mutually, are considered equal and have same rights and duties.

Capacity to enter into marriage and conditions of validity of marriage are governed by law of state person is citizen of. Form of marriage is governed by law of place marriage was concluded. (§§19, 20, Act no. 97/1963 Sb, am'd by Acts no. 158/1969 Sb, no. 234/1992 Sb. and no. 264/1992 Sb.).

Prohibited Marriages.—Prohibitions include: Marriage between married man and married woman; among relative of direct lineage; between siblings; between relatives by adoption provided adoption is still valid; marriage between minors, i. e, persons under 18 years, however court may allow marriage with minor older than 16 years for important reason.

See also topics Divorce; Husband and Wife; Infants.

MONOPOLIES AND RESTRAINT OF TRADE:

Abuse of economic competition is either unfair competitive behaviour (unfair competition) or unpermitted restriction of economic competition. Former is generally regulated by ObchZ (§§41-55), latter is governed by Act no. 63/1991 Sb., in wording of Acts no. 495/1992 Sb. and no. 286/1993 Sb., on protection of economic competition.

Unfair Competition.—Conduct within economic competition that is contrary to good practise of competition and is qualified as causing detriment to other competitors or consumers is prohibited.

Following are regarded as unfair competition: (1) False advertising; (2) deceitful description of goods and services; (3) contributing toward mistaken identity; (4) exploitation of competitor's reputation; (5) bribery; (6) discrediting; (7) unauthorised disclosure of business secrets; (8) endangering consumers' health or environment. Persons whose rights were violated or endangered by unfair competition may demand: That perpetrator abstain from his infringing acts and remove offending situation; appropriate satisfaction; compensation for damage and forfeiture of unjustified gains. (ObchZ, §§44-52).

Final judgment on such claim, rendered even to only one plaintiff, is applicable towards other entitled persons. Court may entitle winning plaintiff to publicise decision at cost of guilty party.

Trade Restraints.—Act no. 63/1991 Sb., in wording of Acts no. 495/1992 Sb. and no. 286/1993 Sb. applies to all doing business in CR, having enterprise or permanent residence in its territory, and also to acts outside country if they effect domestic market. Acts effecting foreign markets are governed by this act only if stipulated so by international treaties binding CR.

Cartels.—Defined as agreed or other acts of mutual understanding, in whatever form (concerted practices included), resulting in or capable of exclusion or restriction of competition. Such agreements are illegal and void unless receiving exemption from competition office. No distinction between horizontal and vertical cartels is made.

Following are primarily indicative of illegal cartel acts: Direct or indirect price fixing; commitments to limit or control production, sale, technological development or investment; market or supply source sharing; commitment of at least one party to conclude tied sales; commitments to discriminate against customers; commitments to limit market access of those not party to agreement; exclusion or restriction of right to withdraw from agreement.

Prohibition does not apply to following types of agreements, which however, require approval from competition office to be valid: Use of uniform trading, supply or payment conditions, with exception of price agreements which are always prohibited; rationalisation agreements, if not resulting in considerable restriction of competition; rebate agreements, if rebate represents real appreciation and does not result in discrimination of other customers and market share of less than 5% of Republic wide market or less than 30% of local market supplied regularly by parties to agreement.

Application for exemption may be requested for certain cartel agreements containing prohibited acts and must prove that exemption is in public interest, considering if cartel contributes to production of goods or technological and economic development. Exemption is granted for specific period and may be conditional. Cartel agreement containing following types of provisions does not qualify for exemption: Commitment to exclusive selling of goods which are subject of agreement; commitment to price or volume fixing of similar goods or commitment to exclude certain entrepreneurs meeting objective selection criteria from activities covered by agreement; breaching of rules or practise of competition; substantial restriction of licensee or owner of intellectual properties.

Mergers.—Fall under respective authority's control if resulting or having capacity to result in restriction of competition in relevant market. Mergers include legal or actual opportunity to control whole or part of another entrepreneur's enterprise. Market share of involved parties exceeding 30% of total turnover in relevant market is found as endangering competition. Merger agreements require approval of respective authority in order to be valid. Approval is to be granted if economic advantages of merger outweighs potential restriction of competition. Approval may be granted for specified period and may be conditional.

Monopolistic and Dominant Positions.—Monopolistic position is gained if entrepreneur alone or under agreement with other entrepreneurs has no competition in relevant market. Dominant position exists if entrepreneur supplies at least 30% of relevant market with identical, comparable or interchangeable products in one calendar year. Such positions have to be immediately announced to authorities and must not be abused. Following, among others, are considered indication of abuse of position: Direct or indirect enforcement of disproportionate trading terms; tied obligations; discrimination toward other market participants; restriction on production, sale or technological development in order to gain unjustified benefit at purchasers expense.

Office for Economic Competition of CR is authority which grants exemption and approvals, prohibits mergers and abuse of monopolistic and dominant positions, and imposes penalties for breach of laws in this sphere. Penalties may be up to 5% of preceding years turnover. If party gained benefit in kind, penalty may include amount equal to value of benefit gained. Penalties may be repeatedly imposed.

Proceedings before competition office result in final decision only reversible by court examination applied for within 30 days after delivery of decision. Person, legal or natural, whose rights were infringed by restriction of competition may demand: That perpetrator abstain from infringing conduct; that perpetrator removes wrongful situation; appropriate satisfaction; compensation for damage and; forfeiture of unjustified gains.

Final judgment is also applicable for any other entitled persons. Court may entitle winning plaintiff to publicise decision at cost of guilty party.

MORTGAGES:

General provisions on mortgages are included in OZ, §§151a-151v. Under these provisions, mortgage is derivative of lien used to secure debt and its accessories. In case of nonperformance, secured creditor is entitled to seek satisfaction of claim from pledged immovable. Contract under which immovable is pledged must be written and entered into real estate register in order to be effective. (Acts no. 265/1992 Sb., no. 344/1992 Sb., no. 210/1993 Sb., no. 89/1996 Sb. and no. 90/1996 Sb.). In case of multiple mortgages, time of creation is decisive as to priority.

Mortgage may be established on basis of debenture, issued according to special regulations, if it is noted in debenture that claims are secured by mortgage of certain real estate (mortgage bond). (ObchZ, §§297-299). Claims secured by mortgage bonds must be registered in real estate register. Person entitled to claim rights from registered mortgage bond has status of mortgagee.

Judicial mortgage is established by order of execution and must be registered in real estate register. (OSR, §§338a, 338b). Execution of judicial mortgages may be ordered if it is proved that immovable is owned by debtor. Claims covered by judicial mortgages are executable by sale of immovable.

See topic Liens.

MOTOR VEHICLES:

License is necessary for driving of motor vehicles in CR. Condition for issuing of driving license is minimum age 18 years and passing of driving exams. License is valid for lifetime and must be produced to police on demand. Vehicles driven on motorways must bear sticker indicating payment of user fee of between 400 Kc and 2,000 Kc, depending on weight of vehicle. (Act no. 134/1994 Sb.).

Alien may drive motor vehicle in CR on basis of international driving license (valid one year from entry into CR or in certain cases on basis of valid home country license). Drivers in CR use right hand side of road.

Motor vehicles driven in CR must be insured for liability. Decree of Ministry of Finance no. 492/1991 Sb., am'd by Acts no. 582/1992 Sb., no. 327/1993 Sb., no. 246/1994 Sb. and no. 307/1995 Sb. on Insurance is related to responsibility for damage of owner and driver of motor vehicle, which is in register of motor vehicles of CR or which is registered abroad, if motor vehicle comes in territory of CR and damage is caused in territory of CR.

Unless driver has international card of motor vehicle insurance, valid in territory of CR and for subject motor vehicle, duty to have Czech insurance starts from day of entry of motor vehicle in territory of CR. Insurance must be paid for whole period of residency of alien, at minimum for one month.

Motor vehicles used for entrepreneurial activity or for other activity in direct connection with enterprising are subject to road tax. (Act no. 16/1993 Sb., am'd by Acts no. 302/1993 Sb. and no. 243/1994 Sb.). Tax is paid on motor vehicles with Czech or foreign registration.

NOTARIES PUBLIC:

Regulated by Act no. 358/1992 Sb. Notaries are appointed by Minister of Justice pursuant to recommendation of Chamber of Notaries. Notaries must be citizens of CR, have university degree in law, complete apprentice period and notarial examination. Notary is appointed for one of district courts, but is entitled to execute activity anywhere in territory of CR.

Activity of notaries is governed by Chamber of Notaries under supervision of Ministry of Justice.

Notaries are entitled to offer following legal assistance: (1) Provide legal advice; (2) represent physical or legal person in proceedings with state or other authorities, except for adoptions and marriage; (3) issue documents; (4) perform property administration; (5) perform function of administrator in bankruptcy and settlement proceedings.

Notaries perform following functions in capacity of judicial commissioner: (1) Settlement of inheritance; (2) deposit of testaments, securities and other documents; (3) verification of authenticity of signatures and authenticity between copy and original of document; (4) certification of minutes of meetings; (5) certification of declarations of persons made in his presence; (6) issuance of bill protests and other documents.

On basis of notarial authorisation, some activities may be executed by notarial candidate or other notarial employee.

Notarial records and documents on certification are public documents.

See also topic Descent and Distribution.

PARTNERSHIP:

See topic Corporations.

PATENTS:

Patents are regulated by Act no. 527/1990 Sb., am'd by Act no. 519/1991 Sb., on Inventions, Industrial Designs and Rationalisation Proposals and by following conventions, to which CR is party: Paris Convention of Mar. 20, 1883 for Protection of Industrial Property; Strasbourg Agreement on Int'l Patent Classification of Mar. 24, 1971; Patent Co-operation Treaty signed in Washington, D.C. June 17, 1970; Budapest Treaty of Apr. 28, 1977 on Int'l Recognition of Deposit of Micro-organisms for Purpose of Patent Procedure.

Patents are granted and other registrations are done by Industrial Property Office in accordance with Act no. 14/1993 Sb.

PATENTS . . . *continued*

Only inventions which are new, which involve inventive step and which are susceptible of industrial application are subject to protection. Following are not considered as inventions: (1) Discoveries, scientific theories and mathematical methods; (2) mere appearance of products; (3) schemes, rules and methods for performing mental acts; (4) programs for computers (see topic Copyright) and (5) mere presentations of information. Patents are not granted for: (1) Inventions contrary to public interest, particularly principles of humanity and morality; (2) methods of prevention, diagnosis and treatment of diseases of human or animal body and (3) plan or animal varieties and biological processes for production and improvement of plants and animals (with exception of industrial microorganisms serving for production and biotechnological process and products thereof) which are patentable).

Right to patent belongs to inventor or his successor in title. Inventor is person who created invention by means of his own creative work. Coinventors are entitled to patent in proportion in which they participated in creation of invention. Where inventor created invention within employment relationship, right to patent passes to employer, unless otherwise agreed in contract. Inventor is entitled to appropriate remuneration for invention.

Owner of patent has exclusive right to: (1) Use invention; (2) grant consent for use by other persons; (3) pass patent to others; (4) appropriate remuneration from any person who uses subject of patent application after it has been published, and, in case of international application, after translation into Czech language has been published.

Duration is 20 years beginning day of application. Patent protection lapses: (1) On expiration of its term; (2) if corresponding administrative fees were not paid in time by owner of patent; (3) on relinquishment by owner, in such case patent shall terminate as from date on which office receives written declaration by owner.

Office annuls patent if it ascertains, after granting, that conditions for granting laid down by law were not met. If grounds for annulment concern only part of patent, it will be annulled in part. Annulment has retroactive effect to date of its validity. Request for annulment may be filed even after lapse of patent, if person making demand proves his legal interest.

Patent owner may offer licenses to use patent, if offer is registered with Office. In such case administrative fees payable by owner to maintain patent are reduced to one half. Compulsory license can be granted by Office where no agreement is reached in conclusion of license contract in case owner of patent does not use his patent at all, or uses it insufficiently and cannot give legitimate reasons for his failure to act or where important public interest is endangered by nonuse. Compulsory license may not be granted prior to expiration of four years as from filing date of patent application or three years as from date of grant of patent, whichever period expires last. Compulsory license is not exclusive license and it does not effect patent owner's right to compensation in respect of value of license.

Priority right begins with filing application. Priority right under international treaties must be claimed in application and further proved, otherwise will not be taken into consideration. Application is published by Office 18 months after it has been filed. Afterwards, any person may submit objections to patentabillity of invention. Further application for "full examination" must be filed within 36 months from filing date and may not be withdrawn. Office has to carry out full examination immediately after request has been filed. Office may also carry out full examination ex officio. Applicant is entitled to answer examiner's objections and amend patent application. Grants of patents are published in Patent Bulletin.

Industrial Design.—Appearance of product that is new and susceptible of industrial application may be registered. Law indicates in particular what is not considered as industrial design. Office will register if not contrary to public interest, particularly principles of humanity and morality. Rules applicable to industrial designs are more or less same as those that apply to patents. Validity of industrial design is five years from filing. Validity may be extended by office for maximum of three five year periods.

Rationalisation Proposals.—Technical improvements of manufacturing or operational nature and any solution to problem of safety, protection of health at work or protection of environment, if no patent or industrial design already exists. Applicant must offer proposal to his employer if it concerns scope of employer's activities. Right to freely dispose of rationalisation proposal if employer does not conclude agreement for acceptance of offer and for corresponding remuneration within two months from receipt of offer.

In case of violation of all above rights, inventors, authors of industrial designs and rationalisation proposal creators are entitled to: (1) Prohibition of infringement; (2) removal of consequences; (3) compensation for damages and (4) appropriate satisfaction. Violation of these rights results to liability under §151 of Criminal Code no. 140/1961 Sb. as amended by Acts no. 65/1994 Sb. and no. 91/1994 Sb.

PLEDGES:

Under provisions of OZ, pledge is security claim on real estate, moveables and claims created on basis of written contract or approved testament or by law. In case of nonperformance of secured claim, creditor is entitled to seek satisfaction of claim from pledge. (OZ, §§151a-151m).

In case of moveables, contract comes into effect by delivery of thing to creditor or by indication of establishment of pledge in document which affirms debtor's ownership which is necessary for disposition of object. Contract must also specify object which is encumbered and that debt is secured. Pledge may be established for purpose of securing obligation to arise in future. (OZ, §151b). Time of establishment is decisive for determining priority of satisfaction. (OZ, §151c).

Pledge is also effective against person who acquired encumbered property, if at time of conclusion of contract person knew or should have known about pledge; acquirer is thus liable up to value of acquired property. (OZ, §151d).

Creditor must take due care of encumbered property and protect it from damage, loss or destruction. Use is possible only with consent of debtor. Debtor is obliged not to do anything which impairs value of property. If value of encumbered property is depreciated to extent that security for debt becomes insufficient, creditor has right to ask debtor to supplement security. In case debtor does not do so, portion of debt not secured immediately matures. (OZ, §151e).

Creditor is authorized to seek satisfaction from encumbered property if secured claim is not satisfied duly and in time, even if secured claim has become statute-barred. (OZ, §151f).

ObchZ provides that pledge may be established for commercial claims arising in future provided fixed time and maximum amount of claim are agreed. (ObchZ, §299).

Pledge of Claim.—Claim may be pledged if object of its performance is thing, right or something of economic value. Such pledge is established by written contract and includes interest on claim and other accessories. Pledge of claim is effective against sub-debtor only if debtor notifies in writing or if establishment of pledge is proven to him by creditor. Creditor is obliged to notify debtor about sub-debtor's performance of his obligation. (OZ, §§151h-151j).

Sub-lien.—Established if claim secured by lien is encumbered by pledge. Consent of owner of property is not required, but sub-pledge may be asserted against owner only if he has been notified of its establishment. If pledged claim is not satisfied to holder of sub-pledge on maturity, he may seek satisfaction from property secured by sub-lien, having same status and rights as creditor. (OZ, §§151k-151m).

For pledges and mortgages in relation to commercial parties regulated by ObchZ, see topic Mortgages.

PRESCRIPTION:

See topic Limitation of Actions.

PRINCIPAL AND AGENT:

Representation by agent is permitted in CR (except some cases i.e. concerning family law). (OZ, §§22-33). Representation by agent establishes rights and duties directly in name of principal. Person who does not have legal capacity for specific matter, or person whose interests conflict with those of principal cannot be agent. Representation comes into being on basis of law, by decision of state authority (statutory representation), or on basis of power of attorney. Agent must act on behalf of principal personally or can appoint other agent if allowed by law or participants agree. Power of attorney must be in writing if it includes more than specific juridical act, or if act to be performed must be in writing.

Principal generally appoints agent on basis of power of attorney, which must contain extent of agent's authorisation. In case of legal person, right to act on behalf of principal arises form power of attorney given from statutory body. Power of attorney terminates upon: (1) Realisation of object of power; (2) revocation by principle; (3) revocation by agent; (4) death of agent; (5) dissolution of legal person.

If entrepreneur is physical person, he acts personally or by means of agent. Legal person acts by means of its statutory body or agent who is registered at commercial register.

Procura.—ObchZ recognises various types of powers of attorney, one of which is "Procura". (ObchZ, §§14-16). Entrepreneur can appoint procurist to carry out all legal acts for which special power of attorney is necessary. Procura allows authorisation to sell or burden real estate, only in case specifically mentioned. Restrictions on powers of procurist made by means of internal instructions have no legal effect on third parties. Procura is effective from entry into commercial register. It must contain name and residency of procurist with sample signature. If more than one procurist is authorized, ability to act independently or jointly must be detailed.

PRIVATISATION:

Purpose of privatisation in CR is transformation of ownership of state property with maximum participation of population. Privatisation consists of two parts:

Small Scale Privatisation.—Intended as method of privatisation of small business units (shops, small factories, etc.). (Act no. 427/1990 Sb. in wording of Acts no. 54/1990 Sb., no. 528/1990 Sb. and no. 541/1990 Sb.). Relates primarily to lease of small enterprise units for periods of two to five years, with prices realised by sale at auction. Only for Czech citizens, direct foreign capital participation is not allowed, with exception of cases of repeated auction.

Large Scale Privatisation.—Intended as method of privatisation of large economic units (factories, business organisations). (Act no. 92/1991 Sb., in wording of Acts nos. 92/1992 Sb., 264/1992 Sb., 541/1992 Sb., 544/1992 Sb., 210/1993 Sb., 306/1993 Sb. and 224/1994 Sb.). Enterprises or investors created privatisation projects which were then reviewed and approved by Ministry of Privatisation. Privatisation project includes details of economic, technical and physical transformation of enterprise, along with details of investors and any proposal for participation in voucher system. Voucher system is designed as method to allow participation of citizens in economic transformation of industry. For payment of 1,000 Kc, each citizen was eligible to claim voucher book of 1,000 points to be used for bidding for shares in privatised companies. First wave of large privatisation involving major part of offered property was completed in 1992. Value of shares was determined according to supply and demand. Citizens could use their voucher points to invest directly into enterprises or assign points to privatisation funds to invest on their behalf.

Issuing of shares to citizens was delayed due to division of CSFR, but was completed in first half of 1993. Remaining enterprises will be disposed of in second wave of privatisation, begun in spring 1994.

REAL PROPERTY:

Within framework of laws on personal ownership of apartments (Act no. 72/1994 Sb., am'd by Act no. 273/1994 Sb.), apartments and non-dwelling spaces are considered to be independent real estate. Buildings are not part of land. However, trees and other plants are integral part of land, if special prescriptions do not stipulate otherwise.

Ownership and other rights concerning real estate must be registered with real estate register. (Acts no. 265/1992 Sb., no. 344/1992 Sb., no. 210/1993 Sb. and no. 90/1996 Sb.). Entry into real estate register is necessary for acquisition and transfer of rights on real estate.

In conformity with Art. 14 of Charter of Fundamental Rights and Freedoms, foreigners and foreign legal entities can acquire ownership and other property rights

See Topical Index in front part of this volume.

REAL PROPERTY . . . *continued*
under conditions determined by law. State guarantees them equal protection of ownership and other property rights, in compliance with stipulations of Charter of Fundamental Rights and Freedoms.

Acquisition of domestic real estate by foreigners in CR depends on their legal position under Foreign-Exchange Act no. 219/1995 Sb. and Act no. 229/1991 Sb., am'd by Acts no. 42/1992 Sb., no. 93/1992 Sb., no. 39/1993 Sb., no. 183/1993 Sb., no. 131/1994 Sb., no. 166/1995 Sb., no. 29/1996 Sb. and no. 30/1996 Sb. These laws provide that land cannot be transferred to ownership of foreign-exchange nonresidents (see topic Foreign Exchange). These individuals and legal persons may only acquire land under very limited circumstances, primarily inheritance, or if special law stipulates so. Provisions of OZ set forth no stipulation which would limit rights of foreigners to inherit real estate in CR, regardless of fact whether deceased was resident or nonresident. Special laws which enable foreign-exchange nonresidents to acquire ownership of real estate are: Act no. 403/1990 Sb., am'd by Acts no. 458/1990 Sb., no. 528/1990 Sb., no. 137/1991 Sb., no. 264/1992 Sb. and no. 115/1994 Sb., which enables foreign-exchange non-residents to acquire real estate by restitution, provided compensation for such real estate has not been covered by international treaties; Act no. 427/1990 Sb. on so-called small-scale privatisation, which enables, in limited cases, individuals who are Czech citizens or were Czech citizens after Feb. 25, 1948, or legal entities composed exclusively of such physical persons, to acquire certain real estate by means of auction and in case of repeated auction also foreign person; Act no. 92/1991 Sb. on so-called large-scale privatisation entitles foreign citizens and foreign legal entities to acquire ownership to privatised property under same conditions as Czech citizens and Czech legal entities.

RECORDS:

See topic Law Reports, Codes, Etc.

SALES:

ObchZ (§§409-470) contains principal provisions on sale of goods. Purchase contract must contain individual description of goods or at least kind, purchase price or at least method of determining price later, unless parties manifest their will to conclude contract without determining price. (ObchZ, §§409). In event parties manifest will to conclude contract without price, seller may demand payment of purchase price for which such goods, or comparable goods, were, as rule, sold at time when contract was concluded under terms similar to those of contract. (ObchZ, §448).

Seller is obliged to deliver goods to buyer, to pass over documentation related to goods, and to enable buyer to take title to goods in accordance with contract and law. (ObchZ, §411).

Transfer of Title.—Buyer acquires title to goods as soon as delivered goods are passed to buyer. (ObchZ, §443/1). Parties may agree in writing that buyer takes title later. (ObchZ, §445). Unless contract, as regards transfer of title, implies otherwise, it is presumed that buyer takes title when purchase price has been fully paid. (ObchZ, §445). Should parties agree in writing, buyer may acquire title before delivery, provided that contract concerns goods determined individually or determined according to kind, and that at time of transfer of title, such goods are sufficiently marked so as to be differentiated from other goods. (ObchZ, §444). Buyer acquires ownership rights even in event that seller is not owner of sold goods, unless at time when buyer was to acquire title, buyer knew that seller was neither owner, nor authorised to sell goods. (ObchZ, §446).

Seller undertakes to deliver goods in quantity, quality and presentation stipulated in contract and must arrange for goods to be packed and made ready for forwarding in manner stipulated in contract. (ObchZ, §420). Should contract quantity be only approximated, seller is entitled to determine exact quantity of goods to be delivered, deviation may not exceed 5% of quantity stipulated in contract. (ObchZ, §421).

Defects.—Seller is liable for defects in goods until moment when risk of damage passes to buyer, even when such defect becomes apparent only afterwards. (ObchZ, §425/1). Buyer is obliged to inspect goods as soon as possible upon transfer of risk of damage and is obliged to notify buyer of defects without delay, immediately after buyer has detected or should have detected such defects. (ObchZ, §427).

In event contract is fundamentally breached by delivery of defective goods, buyer may demand: (1) Removal of defects either by substitution for defective goods, providing missing goods or by removing legal defects; (2) removal of defects in goods by repair, if repairable; (3) adequate discount from purchase price; (4) repudiation of contract. (ObchZ, §436/1). Buyer has choice of demands, provided that he notifies seller of choice without undue delay. Once buyer has asserted certain claim, this claim cannot be changed without seller's consent. In addition to remedies stipulated in §436/1, buyer is entitled to compensation for damage or to contractual penalty, if agreed.

In event that delivery of defective goods constitutes non-fundamental breach, buyer may demand either delivery of missing goods and removal of remaining defects of goods, or discount of purchase price. (ObchZ, §437/1). If buyer demands removal of defects, additional reasonable period must be provided to seller. During this additional period, buyer cannot exercise rights flowing from defects in goods, except for claim for damage and contractual penalty. (ObchZ, §437/3). If seller fails to remove defects in goods within reasonable period, buyer may claim discount from purchase price or repudiate contract, provided that he informs seller of intention when determining additional reasonable period or within reasonable time prior to repudiation of contract. (ObchZ, §437/5).

Risk of Damage.—Risk of damage to goods passes to buyer upon delivery, or, if failing to do so in time, at time when seller enables buyer to dispose of goods and buyer breaches contract by not taking delivery of goods. (ObchZ, §455).

If, under contract, seller is to hand over goods to certain carrier at fixed place for forwarding to buyer, risk of damage passes upon handing over goods to carrier at that place. Damage to goods which occurred after passing of risk to buyer has no effect on buyer's obligation to pay purchase price, unless damage occurred due to breach of obligation by seller. (ObchZ, §461/1).

Warranties.—By issuing warranty for quality of goods in writing, seller undertakes obligation to deliver goods which will be fit to be used for agreed or customary purpose for fixed period or which will retain agreed or customary properties for fixed period. Obligation for warranty can be contained in contract or in declaration of seller, especially in form of letter of guaranty. (ObchZ, §§429-432).

International Sale of Goods.—CR is contracting state of UN Convention on Contracts for the International Sale of Goods of Apr. 11, 1980, and of Convention on the Limitation Period in International Sale of Goods, New York, June 14, 1974.

See topic Contracts.

SEQUESTRATION:

Court may order, only as interlocutory injunction, property placed in custody of Public Notary. (OSR, §76).

See topic Executions.

STATUTES:

See topic Law Reports, Codes, Etc.

TAXATION:

System of taxes in CR consists of income tax, value added tax, real property taxes, road tax, inheritance, gift and real property transfer taxes, consumption tax and environment protection tax.

All Czech tax residents, both local and foreign, are subject to these taxes. Where there is double tax treaty, tax relief will apply (see topic Treaties).

Income Tax.—Physical person pays tax on income arising from dependant activity, entrepreneurial activity, capital property or leasing less allowable expenses and deductions. (Act no. 586/1992 Sb., am'd by Acts nos. 35/1993 Sb., 96/1993 Sb., 157/1993 Sb., 196/1993 Sb., 323/1993 Sb., 42/1994 Sb., 114/1994 Sb., 259/1994 Sb., 85/1994 Sb. full wording, 299/1994 Sb., 32/1995 Sb., 83/1995 Sb., 87/1995 Sb., 118/1995 Sb., 147/1995 Sb., 149/1995 Sb., 248/1995 Sb. and 28/1996 Sb. full wording). Insurance proceeds, credits, inheritance and prizes are not treated as income. Employee benefits such as company car used for private purposes are taxable as income. Foreign individuals present in CR more than 183 days in calendar year are subject to tax on worldwide income, unless qualified as "expert with specialized knowledge", in which case only CR source income is taxable. Rates vary from 15 to 40%.

All legal persons, with exception of general commercial partnership, are subject to corporate income tax. Tax period is calendar year. Legal persons with permanent place of business in CR are taxed on both local and foreign income. Legal persons without permanent place of business in CR are taxed only on their income derived from sources in CR. Net profit is taxed at rate of 39%. Special tax rates apply for income from management fees, licensing fees, interest, leasing and dividends arising from source in CR paid to legal and natural persons without permanent seat in CR. (See topic Treaties.) Tax is to be withheld at source in preceding instances.

Value Added Tax.—Obligation to register and to collect this tax comes into effect if individual has quarterly turnover in excess of 750,000 Kc. (Act no. 588/1992 Sb., am'd by Acts nos. 196/1993 Sb., 321/1993 Sb., 42/1994 Sb., 136/1994 Sb., 258/1994 Sb., 133/1995 Sb., 27/1996 Sb. full wording and 95/1996 Sb.). If desired, voluntary registration is possible if these amounts are not met. VAT tax rates are: 22% on goods (with some exceptions at 5%, i.e., most foods, energy, heating); 5% on services (with some exceptions at 22%, i.e., hotel, accommodation and boarding services, leasing, repairs, truck transport); 5% on transfer of ownership of structures and buildings; 5% on transfer and use of rights. Basic VAT tax period is one month. If turnover achieved in previous calendar year was lower than ten million Kc, tax period is quarterly.

Road Tax.—Road motor vehicles, wheel-tractors and trailers and semi-trailers if having registration number plate and used for business purposes are subject to this tax. (Act no. 16/1993 Sb., am'd by Acts nos. 302/1993 Sb., 243/1994 Sb. and 339/1992 Sb.). Road tax must be paid by owner of vehicle as stated in vehicle registration document. Fiscal period is calendar year. In case of vehicles used in international transport, fiscal period is period during which vehicle was within CR territory.

Real Property Tax.—Companies and individuals who own real property are subject to separate taxes on real property and improvements on real property. (Act no. 338/1992 Sb., am'd by Acts nos. 315/1993 Sb., 242/1994 Sb., 174/1995 Sb. and 248/1995 Sb.). Basis for calculation of taxes is area of land or buildings, with rates varying depending on district in which property is located.

Excise Tax.—Paid on production or import of tobacco products, wine, beer, benzene. (Act no. 587/1992 Sb., am'd by Acts nos. 199/1993 Sb., 325/1993 Sb., 136/1994 Sb., 260/1994 Sb., 148/1995 Sb., 25/1996 sb. and 95/1996 Sb.). All tobacco products sold in CR must bear tax stamps.

Indirect Taxation.—Contributions to system of national health insurance and social security fund are required for all individuals employed in CR and their employers. Level of insurance premiums is 13.5% of monthly gross wages, of which 4.5% is paid by employees and 9% by employers. Contributions payable to Social Security Fund (comprising old-age/retirement fund and unemployment fund) are at rate of 26.25% of gross wage for employer and 8.75% for employee.

TRADEMARKS AND TRADE NAMES:

Trade Names.—Deemed as designation under which entrepreneur (enterprise) enters into legal relations when conducting business activities. (ObchZ, §§8-12). They must be distinguishable from other trade names. To distinguish between two similar trade names of legal entities, provision of name with different geographic location is sufficient unless these entities conduct activities in same line of business, or in such lines of business which may be confused in course of economic competition. To distinguish between two corresponding trade names of natural persons, statement in respect of different location of business activity is sufficient.

Trade name of natural person is created by his/her name and surname, and may include distinguishing addendum specifying further person of entrepreneur or his/her line of business. Trade names of legal persons include addendum specifying legal form, and are registered, along with further information on legal entity, with commercial register (see topic Commercial Register). Where legal entity is not registered with commercial register, its trade name is name under which it was established.

TRADEMARKS AND TRADE NAMES . . . *continued*

Transfer of trade name without simultaneous transfer of enterprise is not allowed. Should only part of enterprise be transferred to new owner, transfer of trade name is allowed if remaining part of original enterprise conducts its business activities under another trade name, or if it is liquidated.

If right to trade name is infringed, holder is entitled to demand: (1) Prohibition of further infringement; (2) removal of consequences; (3) appropriate satisfaction; (4) compensation for damages; (5) that decision be published at cost of guilty party. Criminal liability is regulated by §150 of Criminal code no. 140/1961 Sb., am'd by Acts no. 65/1994 Sb. and no. 91/1994 Sb.

Trademarks.—Trademark is sign, which may be verbal, figurative, three-dimensional or combined, capable of affording distinctive nature to goods or services of various manufacturers or suppliers and which is registered in Trademark Register. (Act no. 137/1995 Sb.). Following may not constitute trademark: (1) Simple name, simple image or other simple sign denoting nature of goods or services; (2) simple geographical denomination that is official or generally known; (3) misleading or false denomination; (4) denomination that is identical with well-known mark (§18) registered in name of another legal or natural person; (5) denomination identical with trademark registered in name of another legal or natural person for goods and services of same kind; (6) denomination identical with that of protected plant or animal variety; (7) denomination whose use would be contrary to interests of society; (8) denomination whose use would be contrary to obligations of CR under international treaties on protection of marking of goods and services to which it is party or deriving from its membership in organisation.

Following may not be generally registered: (1) Denominations having no distinctive nature or consisting essentially of descriptive elements; (2) denominations containing official names of states or administrative units, signs of state sovereignty or emblems, armorial bearings, flags, names and abbreviated names of intergovernmental international organisations enjoying protection on territory of CR or imitation thereof; (3) denominations containing official signs of control or warranty, hallmarks or traffic signs, names and abbreviated names of units of measure and monetary units or any imitation thereof; (4) denomination comprising trade name, forename, surname or likeness of person other than applicant, unless legal or natural person filing application for registration or person to whom application has been assigned is able to submit written authorisation from person entitled to assert right to protection of trade name, forename, surname or likeness of person concerned; (5) denominations comprising wordings identical with those of registered appellation of origin or denominations misleadingly similar to such appellation, unless application for trademark is filed by registered user of such appellation of origin and denomination described in application also contains additional wording enabling it to be distinguished from registered appellation of origin.

Denomination identical with registered trademark, registration of which has expired, is excluded from registration for period of two years for goods or services of same kind, unless registration of such denominations is applied for by legal entity or natural person in whose name trademark was registered when it expired.

Two types of trademarks: Individual and collective. Former serves to mark goods or services of entity/person in whose name trademark is registered; latter serves to mark goods or services of entities/persons associated in exercise of economic activity. Written agreement on filing and utilisation must be attached to application for registration of collective mark. Collective mark may only be used in conjunction with individual mark, or failing such mark, in conjunction with name of legal person or with forename and surname of natural person in such way that origin of goods or services thus marked shall be clear.

During application procedure, applicant may transfer by written application for registration for all or some of goods or services stated in application to another entity/person who fulfils conditions laid down in law, i.e., conducting authorized economic activity to which trademark relates and upon approval of Office. Applicant may divide application which contains several products or services until time of entry in Register, retaining priority from original application. Trademark may be provided as security.

Rights to trademark begin on day trademark is registered with Register of Trademarks, held by Industrial Property Office (úrad prumyslového vlastnictví) in Prague. Entities or persons having their legal seat in CR may file for registration abroad only after they file in CR.

Priority begins with filing of application. Priority based on international treaties must be claimed in application for registration and proof of right must be furnished within period of three months as from filing; failing that, Office will not take application into account.

Applicant has right to answer objections of Office and to amend and clarify his application. If application meets formal requirements of Act, it is announced in Bulletin of the Industrial Property Office, following which eligible parties have three month period in which to file objections to registration of announced mark.

Term of protection is ten years as from filing date of application for registration. At request of owner term may be extended for ten years periods.

Trademarks can be both transferred and licensed with approval of the Industrial Property Office.

In case of violation of rights, owner may require: (1) Prohibition of infringement of rights; (2) suppression of consequences; (3) compensation for damage. At request of owner, customs authorities will not clear goods which infringe owner's right afforded in accordance with law. Violation also results is criminal liability under §150 of Criminal Code no. 140/1961 Sb., am'd by Acts no. 65/1994 Sb. and no. 91/1994 Sb.

Designation of Origin of Goods.—Geographical designation of country, region or location, which is commonly known as information on where product originates, quality or distinction of which is specially given by geographical environment, including natural or human consideration. Industrial, handicraft, agricultural and natural products are regarded as eligible products. (Act no. 159/1973 Sb.).

Protection starts by registration with Register of Designation of Origin, held by Industrial Property Office, and is unlimited in time. Registered designation may be used by registered person only, licences are not permitted and designation must not be used as designation of sort of goods. If meeting conditions of previously registered designation, further user may apply for registration regarding its products.

In case of violation of rights registered user may request following: (1) Prohibition of infringement; (2) suppression of consequences; (3) compensation for damage. Criminal liability by §150 of Criminal Code no. 140/1961 Sb., am'd by Acts no. 65/1994 Sb. and no. 91/1994 Sb.

CR is party to Paris Convention of Mar. 20, 1883 for Protection of Industrial Property; Stockholm Convention of July 14, 1967 establishing World Intellectual Property Organisation; Madrid Convention on International Registration of Trademarks, Apr. 14, 1891, Stockholm wording of July 14, 1967; and Lisbon Convention of Nov. 31, 1958 on Protection of Appellations of Origin.

TREATIES:

On Jan. 1, 1993, Czech Republic succeeded Czech and Slovak Federative Republic in all international obligations into which latter entered. Consequently, CR is party to, inter alia, following international Conventions:

General.—International Monetary Fund and International Bank for Reconstruction and Development—IMF (Bretton Woods, July 22, 1944); Charter of the United Nations and Statutes of the International Court of Justice (June 26, 1945/Dec. 20, 1965); Constitution of the Food and Agriculture Organisation of the UN.—F.A.O. (Oct. 16, 1945); Constitution of the U.N. Educational, Scientific and Cultural Organisation—UNESCO (Nov. 16, 1945); Constitution of the World Health Organisation—WHO (July 22, 1946); Constitution of the International Labour Organisation ILO (Oct. 10, 1946); General Agreement on Tariffs and Trade—GATT (Oct. 30, 1947); Articles of Agreement of the International Finance Corporation (Nov. 3, 1955); Statutes of the International Atomic Energy Agency (Oct. 25, 1956); Articles of Agreement of the International Development Association—IDA (Jan. 26, 1960); Constitution de l'Union Postale Universelle—UPC (Oct. 9, 1874); Convention on the Establishment of the International Civil Aviation Organisation (Dec. 12. 1944); Convention on the Establishment of the World Meteorology Organisation (Oct. 11, 1947); Convention on the Establishment of the World Tourism Organisation (Sept. 27, 1970); International Covenant on Civil and Political Rights (Dec. 19, 1966); International Covenant on Economic, Social and Cultural Rights (Dec. 19, 1966); Convention on the Law of Treaties (May 23, 1969); Convention Internationale Des Telecommunications (Oct. 2, 1947); Convention Establishing the World Intellectual Property Organisation (July 14, 1967); Convention on the International Maritime Consultation Organisation—IMCO (Mar. 6, 1948); Vienna Convention on Diplomatic Relations (Apr. 18, 1961); Vienna Convention on the Law of Treaties between States and International Organisations or between International Organisations (Mar. 21, 1986); Convention on the establishment of International Organisation for Legal Metrology (Paris, May 28, 1958); Convention on the Exchange of official publications and governmental documents between States; Convention on International Exchange of Publications; Agreement on the Establishment of the Organisation for Co-operation in Iron Metallurgy—INTERMETAL (Moscow, July 15, 1964); Agreement on the Establishment of Organisation for Co-operation in the Industry of Rolling Bearings (Moscow, Apr. 25, 1964); Convention on the Establishment of Council for Customs Co-operation (Brusel, Dec. 15, 1950); Convention on Privileges and Immunities of International specialised agencies; Convention on Privileges and Immunities of IAEA (Vienna, July 1, 1954); Convention on Establishment of the Secretarial of the Conference on Security and Co-operation in Europe and on Privileges and Immunities of this Secretarial and further institutions of the CSCE (Paris, Dec. 11, 1991); European Agreement on Work Vehicles' Teams in International Road Transport (Geneva, June 1, 1970); Convention on Patent Co-operation (Washington, June 17, 1970); ILO Conventions Nos. 142, 77, 78, 124, 136, 159, 160, 161, 95, 148, 164, 102, Association agreement with European Union (Oct. 4, 1993), Constitution of the World Trade Organisation (WTO) (Apr. 15, 1994), Accession to Statutes of Council of Europe (June 30, 1993).

Conventions on Diplomatic and Consular Relations.—Vienna Convention on Diplomatic Relations (Apr. 18, 1961); Vienna Convention on Consular Relations (Apr. 24, 1963).

Multilateral International Conventions on Legal Assistance and Enforcement of Judgments.—Hague Convention related to court Procedure in Civil Matters (July 17, 1905); Hague Convention related to Procedure in Civil Matters (Mar. 1, 1954); New York Convention on the Recovery Abroad of Maintenance (June 20, 1956); Hague Convention on the Recognition and Enforcement of Decisions Relating to Maintenance Obligations in Respect of Children (Apr. 15, 1958); Hague Convention on the Service Abroad of Judicial and Extrajudicial Documents in Civil or Commercial Matters (Nov. 15, 1965); Hague Convention on the Taking of Evidence Abroad in Civil or Commercial Matters (Mar. 18, 1970); Hague Convention on Recognition of Divorces and Legal Separations (June 1, 1970); Hague Convention on the Recognition and Enforcement of Decisions Relating to Maintenance Obligations (Oct. 2, 1973).

Conventions Unifying Choice of Law Rules.—Hague Convention on the Law Applicable to Traffic Accidents (May 4, 1971); Hague Convention concerning International Administration of the Estates of Deceased Persons (Oct. 2, 1973).

Conventions Relating to Arbitration.—Geneva Protocol on Arbitral Clauses in Commercial Matters (Sept. 24, 1923); Geneva Convention on the Enforcement of Foreign Arbitral Awards (Sept. 26, 1927); New York Convention on the Recognition and Enforcement of Foreign Arbitral Awards (June 10, 1958); European Convention on International Commercial Arbitration (Geneva, Apr. 21, 1961).

Convention in Field of International Transport.—Convention on International Transport by Railway—COTIF (May 9, 1980); Convention on International Transport by Railroad of Merchandise (SMGS); Convention on International Direct Associated Transport Railroad—Water (Sofia, Dec. 14, 1959); Convention on International Transport of Persons (SMPS); Convention on the Unification of Some Rules Concerning International Aviation Transport (Warsaw, Oct. 12, 1929); Protocol amending the Convention on the Unification of Some Rules Concerning International Aviation Transport (1955); Convention on Unification of Some Rules on International Air transportation executed by person other than contract transporter, amending the Warsaw Convention (Guadalajara, Sept. 18, 1961); Convention on Transport Contract in International Road Cargo Transport (CMR) (Geneva, May 19, 1956); Convention on general conditions of International transportation of persons by buses (Berlin, Dec. 5,

See Topical Index in front part of this volume.

TREATIES . . . *continued*
1970), Convention on International Maritime Organisation (IMO) (Geneva, Mar. 6, 1948).

Convention in Field of Protection of Copyright and Industrial Rights.—Paris Convention of Mar. 20, 1983, for the Protection of Industrial Property Rights; Strasbourg Agreement on International Patent Classification of Mar. 24, 1971; Patent Cooperation Treaty signed in Washington, DC., on June 17, 1970; Budapest Treaty on International Recognition of Deposit of Micro-organisms for Purpose of Patent Procedure (Apr. 28, 1977).

Conventions in Field of Penal Law.—Convention on criminal offences and some other offences committed on board plane, of July 24, 1984; European Convention on Extradition (Dec. 13, 1957); European Convention on Mutual Assistance in Penal Matters (Apr. 20, 1959); European Convention on Transfer of Penal Proceedings (May 15, 1972); European Convention on Suppression of Terrorism (Jan. 27, 1977); European Convention on Transfer of Condemned Persons (Mar. 21, 1983).

Conventions on Protection of Investment.—Agreements on Protection of Investments have been concluded with following countries: Canada, Norway, Netherlands, Slovenia, Australia, Federal Republic of Germany, Economic Belgium—Luxembourg Union, Denmark, Great Britain and Northern Ireland, Spain, China, Greece, U.S., Austria, Egypt, France, Finland, Sweden, Switzerland, Philippines, Singapore, Ukraine, South Korea, Thailand, Albania, Peru, Hungary, Lithuania, Latvia, Estonia. Czech Republic is also party to Convention on the Solution of Disputes Arising from Investments between States and Citizens of Other States (Mar. 18, 1965).

Convention on Avoidance of Double Taxation.—Most of these treaties follow model drafted by OECD. Conventions have been concluded with following countries: Belgium, Brazil, China, Denmark, Finland, France, India, Italy, Japan, SFRJ, Cyprus, Nigeria, Netherlands, Norway, Austria, Greece, Sweden, Great Britain, Canada, Federal Republic of Germany, Spain, Sri Lanka, Luxembourg, Poland, Slovakia, Tunesia, U.S., Romania, Israel, Hungary, Australia, Ireland, Indonesia, Thailand, Lithuania, Egypt, South Korea, Latvia, Estonia.

Conventions Regulating Only International Legal Assistance.—Convention on Legal Assistance in Civil Matters concluded with the United Kingdom of Great Britain and Northern Ireland of Nov. 11, 1924 with additional amendments (contracts); Agreement on Mutual Legal Assistance in Civil and Commercial Matters concluded with Swiss Confederation of Dec. 21, 1926; Agreement on Mutual Legal Assistance in Commercial Matters concluded with Portugal, of Nov. 23, 1927; Agreement on Mutual Relations in Court of Civil and Commercial Matters concluded with Turkey, of Aug. 22, 1930; Agreement on Mutual Legal Relations, Documents and Legal Information with Final Protocol concluded with Austria of Nov. 10, 1961; Contract on Legal Assistance in Civil, Family and Commercial Matters concluded with Belgium of Oct. 15, 1984.

Conventions Regulating Only Recognition and Enforcement of Judgments.—Convention on Recognition and Enforcement of Judgement concluded with Swiss Confederation of Dec. 21, 1926; Convention on Recognition and Enforcement of Judgement concluded with Portugal of Nov. 23, 1927.

Conventions Regulating International Legal Assistance Including Recognition and Enforcement of Judgments.—Convention on Legal Assistance in Civil and Commercial Matters recognition and enforcement of judgments and extradition concluded with Tunisia, of Apr. 12, 1979; Convention on Legal Assistance in Civil and Penal Matters concluded with Afghanistan of June 24, 1981; Convention on Legal Assistance in Civil and Penal Matters concluded with Cyprus, of Apr. 23, 1982; Convention on Legal Assistance in Civil and Penal Matters concluded with Greece, of Oct. 22, 1980; Convention on Legal Assistance in Civil, Family and Penal Matters concluded with Algeria, of Dec. 9, 1983; Convention on Legal Assistance, Recognition and Enforcement of Judgments in Civil Matters concluded with Spain, of May 4, 1987; Convention on Legal Assistance and Regulation of Legal Relation in Civil, Family, Labour and Penal Matters concluded with Poland, of Apr. 3, 1989; Convention on Mutual Legal Assistance in Civil, Family and Penal Matters concluded with People's Democratic Republic of Korea, of July 17, 1989; Convention on Legal Assistance and Regulation of Legal Relations in Civil, Family and Penal Matters concluded with the People's Republic of Hungary, of Mar. 28, 1989; Convention on Legal Assistance in Civil and Penal Matters concluded with People's Democratic Republic of Yemen, of Jan. 19, 1989; Convention on Legal Assistance in Civil and Penal Matters concluded with Italy, of Dec. 6, 1985; Convention on Legal Assistance, Recognition and Enforcement of JUDGMENTS in Civil, Family and Commercial Matters concluded with France, of May 10, 1984; Convention on Legal Assistance in Civil, Family and Penal Matters, concluded with Syria, of Apr. 18, 1984; Convention on Legal Assistance in Civil, Family and Penal Matters, concluded with Romania, of Oct. 25, 1958; Convention on Legal Assistance and Legal Relations in Civil, Family and Penal Matters, concluded with the former Soviet Union, of Aug. 12, 1982; Convention on Legal Assistance and Legal Relations in Civil, Family and Penal Matters, concluded with Bulgaria, of Nov. 25, 1976; Convention on Legal Assistance in Civil, Family and Penal Matters, concluded with Yugoslavia, of Jan. 20, 1964; Convention on Legal Assistance in Civil, Family and Penal Matters, concluded with Albania, of Jan. 16, 1959; Convention on Legal Assistance in Civil Matters concluded with Romania of July 11, 1994.

TRUSTS:

Trusts within meaning of equity are not known to Czech Law.

WILLS:

Testament must be made by one testator only, indicating day, month and year and be signed by testator, otherwise it is not valid.

Testament Forms.—(1) Written and signed in own hand (OZ, §476a); (2) signed in presence of two witnesses, with express declaration in presence of two witnesses that document is last will and testament (OZ, §476b); (3) testator who cannot read or write, expresses testament in presence of three witnesses. Document is prepared and read and signed by attendant witnesses. Other specific formalities apply (OZ, §476c); (4) in form of notarial record (OZ, §476d).

Only legally competent persons may act as witnesses. Testamentary or statutory heirs or persons close to them, may not act as witnesses, writers, readers or interpreters for purpose of execution of testament. (OZ, §§476d, 476f).

Testator designates heirs in testament and may specify their shares or assets and rights which will accrue to them. Unless testament stipulates otherwise, all shares are understood to be equal. (OZ, §477). Testator may establish foundation in testament, provided testament contains founding statutes of said foundation. (OZ, §477). Conditions attached to testament shall be of no legal consequences. (OZ, §478).

Legitimate Share.—Minors are entitled to minimum share corresponding to their intestate share. Adults are entitled to minimum share representing one half of their intestate share. Should testament contradict legitimate shares, applicable provisions will be invalid. (OZ, §479). Same is not valid in case of disinheritance of said heirs.

Disinheritance.—Testator may disinherit successor if: (1) Successor did not provide testator with necessary aid in illness, old age and other important cases; (2) successor does not show permanent and real concern about testator; (3) successor has been sentenced for intentional criminal offence resulting in imprisonment for at least one year; (4) successor continuously leads improper life-style. (OZ, §469a).

Testator must explicitly indicate grounds for disinheritance in document on disinheritance, which must fulfil same formalities as testament and must indicate if disinheritance shall concern disinherited person's successors. (OZ, §469a).

Cancellation and Amendment of Testament.—Later testament cancels former to extent it is inconsistent with former. Testator may revoke his testament, which revocation has to be written in same form as testament. (OZ, §480).

Applicable Law.—Ability to make and cancel testament, as well as consequences of defects in testament and its expression are governed by law of state testator was citizen of at time of manifestation of will. Same applies for identification of other kinds of dispositions done in case of death. Form of testament is governed by law of state testator was citizen of at time of making testament, however it is sufficient if testament corresponds to law of state in whose territory testament was made. Same applies for form of cancellation of testament. (§18, Act no. 97/1963 Sb., am'd by Acts no. 158/1969 Sb. and no. 234/1992 Sb.).

See Topical Index in front part of this volume.

Convention in Field of Protection of Copyright and [illegible] [illegible]

[illegible]

Conventions in [illegible] Postal [illegible] [illegible]

[illegible]

Convention on [illegible] [illegible]

DENMARK LAW DIGEST

(The following is a list of all Topics, including cross-references, covered in this Digest.)

DENMARK LAW DIGEST

Revised for 1997 edition by

FALBE-HANSEN, BRUUN & BRUUN, Barristers and Solicitors of the Copenhagen Bar.

Denmark is member of EU. See also European Union Law Digest.

ABSENTEES: See topic Death.

ACKNOWLEDGMENTS:

The great majority of documents can legally be signed in the presence of two witnesses. Only documents of the greatest importance (especially wills) ought to be signed before a notary public.

When documents are signed abroad for use in Denmark it is recommended that the signature be legalized by a Danish diplomatic or consular officer or notary public. However, failure to use notary public will not render document illegal or invalid.

ACTIONS:

Right to sue is not restricted to cases covered by certain "actions" like in English or Roman law. Generally any human interest fit for legal protection can be maintained by a lawsuit.

Foreign claimants may be asked to deposit security for costs unless international treaties to contrary exist.

Limitation of.—See topic Limitation of Actions.

ADMINISTRATION:

See topic Executors and Administrators.

AFFIDAVITS:

See topic Depositions.

Sworn statements of facts made out of court, e.g., before a notary public, are unknown in Danish law, and are inadmissible as evidence against protest of opponent.

Expert witnesses must be appointed by court and parties in unison lest their report be rejected as evidence.

AGENTS:

See topic Principal and Agent.

ALIENS:

According to Alien Act No. 562 of June 30, 1995 citizens from Finland, Iceland, Norway and Sweden are free to enter and stay in Denmark.

Citizens from other EU countries are free to enter for nonprofessional stay not exceeding three months or six months if in search of employment.

In principle visa is required for all other entries—however, this requirement is dispensed with through various treaties.

Special rules apply for refugees. Denmark has ratified EEC-convention on asylum.

The legal position of aliens is, in general, the same as that of Danish citizens. According to statute No. 566, 8/28 1986 title to real property by persons not domiciled in Denmark or not having been so at an earlier time for at least five years can only be acquired on approval of Minister of Justice. In case of acquisition by way of inheritance and matrimony approval of Minister of Justice is not required. Approval is not required for corporations and citizens of EU-countries when purpose is to establish branches or agencies in Denmark or to take employment in Denmark.

Corporations Owned or Controlled by Aliens.—Rule as to acquisition of real property does also apply to corporations not having their domicile in Denmark; in this respect it may be decisive if corporation be registered here. See topic Joint Stock Companies.

ARBITRATION AND AWARD:

There is no general statutory provision for arbitration.

All present and future differences may be submitted to arbitration by an agreement. Arbitration clauses are frequently inserted in agreements for sale of coal, timber, grain, etc., requiring all disputes to be submitted to arbitration.

Danish awards and foreign awards under New York Convention on the Recognition and Enforcement of Foreign Arbitral Awards are directly enforceable. Other awards must be approved by Danish court before being enforced.

ASSIGNMENTS:

Property and proprietary rights of any kind can, in principle, be assigned.

If a claim is transferred by assignment notice must be given to the debtor; otherwise the transfer is not valid against the creditors of the assignor. Information to the debtor is also necessary to prevent him from paying to the assignor. Notice is not necessary regarding negotiable documents.

The assignor is responsible only for the claim being "verum," and he is, generally, not responsible for the claim being "bonum."

Assignment or transfer of IOUs, mortgages and other instruments of debt triggers stamp duty for payment of which both parties are liable.

ASSIGNMENTS FOR BENEFIT OF CREDITORS:

A voluntary assignment of this kind is permitted but must be for the benefit of all creditors who must actively vote in favor of settlement scheme.

Claims for salaries to employees and claims secured by mortgage will, as far as possible, be fully paid, but otherwise no preferences may be made, and all creditors must be paid pro rata.

The assignee, who can be an ordinary private person (in most cases the debtor's own lawyer), publishes notice of the assignment and mails notice to all creditors whose names and addresses are indicated in the debtor's files.

ASSOCIATIONS:

An association may be formed for any legal purpose without the intervention of public authorities and is recognized as an artificial person; it may, however, have its name and badge registered and thereby protected. Basic fee for registration DKK 1,000 plus additional fee DKK 1,500 for registration of special logo.

ATTACHMENT:

By application to the court a creditor may obtain authority to attach ("arrest") the property of or debts owing to his debtor. Bailiff will only act against full indemnity. Legal proceeding to justify "arrest" must be initiated within seven days.

Attachment ("arrest") of person is very seldom used, and can only be employed to force debtor to reveal nature and whereabouts of his assets. Maximum six months imprisonment.

See also topic Executions.

ATTORNEYS:

In Denmark there is no distinction between barristers and solicitors. All attorneys at law are admitted to bar and are authorized to act as solicitors/attorneys/counselors.

All attorneys must be accepted and appointed by Danish Ministry of Justice. All activities of attorneys are regulated by Danish Administration of Justice Act. Attorneys must be solvent, of age and good character in order to be appointed. Also applicant must possess law degree (Candidatus Juris) from Danish university followed by satisfactory apprenticeship of not less than three years with attorney admitted to appeal courts.

All attorneys must be members of Danish Bar Association and are as such bound by its Articles of Association. Appointment as attorney does not require Danish citizenship. All attorneys operating in Denmark must be covered by professional indemnity insurance with minimum coverage currently adjusted by Bar Association.

If deemed feasible considering nature of case attorneys from another Scandinavian country may be allowed to appear in Danish courts. According to EEC Directive of Mar. 22, 1977, attorneys admitted to bar in another EU state are entitled to market their services in Denmark and are allowed to appear in Danish courts if seconded by Danish attorney admitted to court in question.

All foreign attorneys must keep in mind that all court hearings whatsoever are indispensably conducted in Danish language. Courts—or Bar Association under appeal to courts—can disbar attorney in case of violation of regulations on how to treat entrusted funds, criminal offences, professional misconduct or conduct unbecoming member, or if attorney has substantial unsettled debt to public.

Danish Bar Association does not undertake to establish direct contact with specific lawyers within jurisdiction.

AUTOMOBILES: See topic Motor Vehicles.

BANKRUPTCY:

Bankruptcy Act No. 588 of 9/1 1986 is applicable to all persons, estates of deceased persons, corporations, joint stock companies, etc.

A debtor who cannot meet his obligations may be declared bankrupt on his own petition or on the application of a creditor. On being declared bankrupt an inventory of all the property and books of the debtor is taken. The creditors must give notice of their claims and submit them for examination by the bankruptcy court. Creditors are paid in a specific order of preference in accordance with existing legal rules.

Bankruptcy court or receiver appointed by court at recommendation of creditors (normally one or more lawyers) will send notice by letter to all creditors whose names and addresses are found in debtor's files.

Bankruptcy proceedings are rather slow and costly. Creditors generally prefer a sort of private liquidation by one or two persons, "liquidators" (mostly solicitors) elected by the creditors, which arrangement is cheaper and quicker.

Debtor according to Statutory provisions may declare suspension of payments and register this decision with Probate Court. Purpose of such suspension often is to avoid bankruptcy and in most cases supervisor of debtor's business or estate is appointed by Probate Court. Material dispositions require approval of appointed supervisor. Suspension of payments is not publicized but Probate Court will give information on it at request of creditor. Suspension of payments may last up to three months but Probate Court may prolong term for up to total of 12 months, however, not for more than three months at a time. In event of subsequent bankruptcy assets and debts as at date of registration of suspension of payments will be decisive.

Debtor who proves to Probate Court that he is not able to nor has he any prospect of being able to meet his financial obligations may obtain court's decision to effect that debt is eliminated or reduced. Such decisions can be obtained only by physical persons.

See also topic Fraudulent Sales and Conveyances.

BILLS AND NOTES:

Essential rules are similar to rules in other European countries. (Law No. 559 of Aug. 25, 1986).

Bills ("Veksler") must be stamped as follows: Bills issued for a short time (eight days after presentation or 14 days from the date of issue) are exempted of stamp duty. All other bills are to be stamped with 1 Krone for each 1,000 Kroner or part of 1,000 Kroner. Nonaffixation of stamps does not affect validity or negotiability of bill.

See Topical Index in front part of this volume.

BILLS AND NOTES . . . *continued*

Bonds secured on real property, bonds secured on a registered ship or aircraft, bonds issued to bearer and bonds made out in creditor's name and provided with an endorsement to effect that they may be transferred to other persons are negotiable, which means that they may validly be transferred to other persons without informing debtor. Bonds, which are made out in creditor's name and which bear no endorsement to effect that they may be transferred to other persons, may be validly transferred only against transferrer's creditors provided debtor is informed of transfer. (Law No. 669 of Sept. 23, 1986).

Cheques can be issued without a stamp.

A cheque issued and payable in Denmark must be presented for payment within 20 days from day of issue. A cheque issued in some other European country, or in a country bounded by Mediterranean, must likewise be presented within 20 days from day of issue. A cheque issued in another continent must be presented within 70 days from day of issue. (Law No. 558, 8/25 1986).

CHATTEL MORTGAGES:

Chattels may be mortgaged in a similar way as real property by way of a registered document. See topic Pledges.

COLLATERAL SECURITY: See topic Pledges.

COLLECTIONS:

Collections are handled by most lawyers. Collection fees are as follows:

Basic fee	Dkk. 300	plus following:
Up to	Dkk. 1,500	20%
Following	Dkk. 1,500	15%
Following	Dkk. 3,000	10%
Following	Dkk. 6,000	5%
Following	Dkk. 12,000	2%

For any part of claim over kr. 24,000 fee is 1.5%.

If claim is secured, fee is lower.

Above fees are about to be disallowed by Competition Counsel. Fees will then be calculated on time spent.

COMMERCIAL REGISTER:

See topics Joint Stock Companies and Partnership.

A general commercial register does not exist.

CONDITIONAL SALES: See topic Sales.

CONSTITUTION AND GOVERNMENT:

Denmark is a hereditary democratic Kingdom. The Danish Constitution is based on Montesquieu's principle of partition of power. Under the Constitution in force, amended on June 5, 1953, "Parliamentarism" was established by statute (the ministers dependence of Parliament).

The executive power is vested in King (Queen). On death of a King throne will pass to his son or daughter, however, males take priority over females and in case of several children of same sex, eldest will have priority.

Judiciary.—The judges are appointed by the King for lifetime, yet they are to retire when 70 years of age. They are independent of administration and Parliament. It is within the province of the courts to decide whether a law passed by Parliament is in conflict with the Constitution.

CONSUMER PROTECTION:

The Danish Marketing Act imposes rather harsh obligations on sellers mainly for protection of consumers. Bans on for instance distribution of gifts conditional on purchase and random distribution of prizes are upheld in newest revision of act.

Also any marketing entity must be very careful when granting various bonus schemes.

Ban on unsolicited personal, written or oral applications to consumers in their private homes. Within seven days consumer can unilaterally cancel any agreement or contract brought about by or in such applications.

CONTRACTS:

Contracts are equally binding whether they are made orally or in writing. (Law Book of 1683, book 5, c. 1, §2).

Excuses for Nonperformance.—Same as in other modern European law.

Applicable Law.—If not expressly agreed upon by parties, proper law of contract will be considered to be place where debtor has his residence or place of business or place of performance.

Denmark is contracting State to EEC Convention on Civil Jurisdiction and Judgments.

Government contracts are in principle dealt with according to same rules as other contracts.

Distributorships, Dealerships and Franchises.—No specific legislation deals with these types of business arrangements, but comprehensive case law exists. Termination notices towards dealers etc. have been granted sometimes up to six months or more, and possibility of compensation exists. Possible restrictions may be found in Marketing Act and Competition Act.

See also topic Principal and Agent subhead Trade Agents.

CONVEYANCES: See topic Deeds.

COPYRIGHT:

(Law No. 395 of June 14, 1995).

An author has the sole right to publish his works in writing, in mechanical or chemical reproductions, on the stage (including cinema), through the medium of instruments, by recitations, etc. The protection includes ballets, pantomimes, musical compositions and mathematical, geographical or topographical productions, etc.

An artist, architect or photographer has the sole right to publish his works.

Protection period prolonged to 70 years.

Designs and utility models may be protected for professional use through registration. (Law Nos. 251 of Apr. 17, 1989/130 of Feb. 26, 1992).

CORPORATIONS:

See topic Joint Stock Companies.

COUNSELORS:

See topic Attorneys.

COURTS:

The judicial system of Denmark consists of: (a) city courts in practically all towns; (b) two appeal courts, one in Copenhagen for East of Denmark, and another in Viborg for West of Denmark; (c) Supreme Court in Copenhagen is Appeal court before which cases from whole country can be handled.

As rule case can only be tried at two levels. Appeal of minor cases restricted.

CURRENCY:

The Danish National Bank holds a monopoly on the issuing of paper money. (Law No. 116 of Apr. 7, 1936). To cover the notes issued by the National Bank it must have gold to the value of at least 25% of the total sum of notes issued; for the remainder the Bank must have easily negotiable, good and safe assets; but from this decision dispensation was obtained at the breaking out of the war in Sept. 1939.

In year 1931 Denmark joined Great Britain in leaving gold standard.

Foreign currency may only be bought and sold through banks and brokers authorized by Danish authorities and may only be bought with permission of National Bank. (Law No. 522 of Aug. 31, 1988). All transactions exceeding Dkk. 60,000 or equivalent in foreign currency must be reported to National Bank specifying purpose of transaction.

As a rule the National Bank will give permission to export money out of Denmark, provided the money is to be applied to the payment of interest on bonds and dividends on shares abroad. Shares and bonds may only be exported from Denmark by permission of the National Bank.

Monies abroad due to creditors living in Denmark must be collected at the earliest possible moment; when foreign monies have reached Denmark, there is an obligation to realize them to the National Bank.

Foreign individuals or corporations operating in Denmark through branch offices are considered Danish residents towards Foreign Exchange Act.

See also topics Foreign Investments; Foreign Trade Regulations; and Exchange Control.

CURTESY:

In Denmark there exists a certain form of "curtesy," giving the surviving husband or wife the right to continue in the possession of the joint property as long as he or she does not marry again. This right cannot be exercised against protest of children of deceased who are not also children of survivor.

CUSTOMS:

Main rules in force are to be found in Law No. 1116 of Dec. 22, 1993. Denmark is member of EU.

See also topic Foreign Trade Regulations.

DEATH:

Person absent and unheard from for ten years raises presumption of death. Absence unheard from for one year may in special cases raise presumption of death if, for instance, ship or aircraft by which missing person travelled has disappeared. Presumption of death must be established by court proceedings. (Law No. 587 of Jan. 9, 1986).

Spouse, children or heirs may petition for judgment declaring missing person dead. Court fee is minimum Dkk. 500. Court appoints lawyer to represent missing person.

To obtain official death certificate, foreign lawyer should write to probate court ("Skifteretten") in town or district where person died. Fee is about $16.

Actions for Death.—Any person who intentionally or negligently causes the death of another is held liable in damages to those who have thereby lost a breadwinner for the loss suffered, including disturbance or wrecking of position, affairs or health, but not for purely mental suffering; also funeral expenses may be claimed to a reasonable extent. Law is also applicable to foreigners.

DECEDENTS' ESTATES:

See topics Descent and Distribution; Executors and Administrators; Wills.

DEEDS:

Deeds ("Skoeder") are only used for transferring of title to real estate, ships and aircraft. Deeds must be recorded in public registry in order to be valid transfers as against creditors and bona fide acquirers. Stamps for deeds amount to basic fee of Dkk. 700 plus 0.6% or 1.2% of purchase price or public evaluation.

DEPOSITIONS:

Application regarding examination of witnesses in Denmark must be made through diplomatic channels to the Danish Ministry of Justice, who will send the case to the proper Danish court, where the case will be treated. By Law No. 149 of Apr. 21, 1965 oaths have been abolished.

Depositions may also be taken in Denmark without assistance from courts. However, there are no possibilities of swearing in witnesses—not even in court.

DESCENT AND DISTRIBUTION:

After payment of debts, succession duty, taxes and other duties, estate of deceased or, if there be surviving spouse, excess over share of such spouse, is distributed as follows, each class of which member is living taking to exclusion of subsequent classes: (1) Children and descendants of deceased children; (2) parents and descendants of deceased parents; (3) grandparents and their children. (Law No. 215 of May 31, 1963).

Surviving spouse takes one-third if descendants are left, and in other cases whole estate as single heir; according to Law No. 396 of 1990, surviving spouse is entitled to whole estate if this, in connection with his or her own means, does not exceed 150,000 Kroner.

Illegitimate children inherit from their mother as though legitimate and, if born after Jan. 1, 1938, inherit from their father also in same way.

Obligatory Heirs.—See topic Wills, subhead Testamentary Disposition.

Liability of Heirs.—Main rule is that heirs are not liable for debts of deceased unless they make a declaration to this effect, in which case they become jointly liable for whole debts of deceased and not merely to extent of assets.

Escheat.—In case none of aforementioned persons survive deceased, and no will having been made, state inherits estate.

DIVORCE:

(Law No. 148 of Mar. 8, 1991).

Divorce may be had after a separation of one year or six months if both parties agree. Divorce may also be obtained on usual reasons: Adultery, desertion, confinement for infamous crime punishable by imprisonment for two years or more, bigamy, insanity, etc.

Separation as to bed and board may be had by mutual consent and on the usual reasons: Cruelty, lack of support, adultery, and so forth.

Remarriage.—See topic Marriage.

DOWER:

Nothing exactly corresponding to dower exists in Denmark.

EXCHANGE CONTROL:

See topics Currency; Foreign Investments. Cash amounting to Dkk. 60,000 or equivalent in foreign currency may be imported or exported freely. Import or export of amounts in excess of Dkk. 60,000 or equivalent in foreign currency call for notification to the Danish National Bank.

EXECUTIONS:

Upon final judgment of a court or upon an agreement an attachment can be issued against the property—movable or land—of the debtor.

EXECUTORS AND ADMINISTRATORS:

Executors are appointed by will of deceased, but the appointment must be approved by the authorities. Executors must be Danish residents.

The executor must, by an insurance policy or in some other satisfactory manner, give security to the authorities in an amount equal to the value of the estate, and acts under a rather severe control from the public authorities. From Jan. 1st, 1997, executors or "estate administrators" must have special license from Ministry of Justice.

An executor is entitled to possession and control of all property and to receive rents, interest and other profits thereof.

When no executor is appointed the probate court ("Skifteretten") or the heirs jointly have jurisdiction of the administration of the estate.

If deceased did not appoint executor heirs may settle and distribute estate among themselves provided that all heirs are of age and are present either personally or by proxy and agree to private settlement. In case heirs are unable to agree upon settlement estate is handled by probate court ("Skifteretten").

EXEMPTIONS:

Debtor is entitled to exemption from execution of all assets necessary to maintaining modest home and modest standard of living for himself and his family. Exemption, however, does not apply to real estate. Also debtor is entitled to exemption from execution of all assets up to value of 3,000 Dkk. when assets are necessary for his or his family's business, earnings or education. Unearned wages of laborers or servants etc. are exempt from execution and earned wages are exempt for seven days after period in which earned. Normally assets tied up in pension schemes or pension funds are exempted from execution.

FOREIGN EXCHANGE: See topic Currency.

FOREIGN INVESTMENTS:

Right of foreigners to invest capital in Denmark is in principle unlimited. However, restrictions exist in areas of real estate, banking and insurance.

Returns on capital invested in Denmark by foreigners may without difficulty be remitted to foreign countries. See topic Currency.

FOREIGN TRADE REGULATIONS:

Denmark is a member of EU from Jan. 1, 1973 and foreign trade regulations follow those of EU, however, certain exceptions in transition period.

FRANCHISES:

See topic Contracts, subhead Distributorships, Dealerships and Franchises.

FRAUDS, STATUTE OF:

Denmark has no statute of frauds; a verbal contract is just as binding as a written. In most cases, however, it is desirable to have a transaction in writing, and if a transaction must be registered (e.g., deeds or mortgages), it must, of course, be in writing and witnessed by two ordinary witnesses or an advocate or a notary public.

FRAUDULENT SALES AND CONVEYANCES:

Transactions giving undue preference to any creditor can be declared null and void if made in a certain period before bankruptcy.

GARNISHMENT:

In a civil case, plaintiff may apply to court for permission to cite any third person as a codefendant, provided it is not due to negligence of plaintiff that this was not done from very beginning.

HOLIDAYS:

The legal holidays are: Sundays, New Years Day, Easter holidays (4), Whitsun holidays (2), Christmas day, Boxing Day, and some other special holidays. Saturday has for some years in fact been a half holiday for shops, banks and offices and is now full holiday for banks etc. See Law No. 102 of Mar. 3, 1993. All employees have statutory right of five weeks holiday per year and holiday allowance of 12.5% of gross salary.

HOMESTEADS:

Legislation protecting small holdings, etc. against creditors does not exist in Denmark. See topic Exemptions.

HUSBAND AND WIFE:

An alien woman who marries a Dane does not acquire his nationality (Regulation No. 409 of Dec. 17, 1968); her conjugal right will be determined by Danish law, if he, at the time of marriage, be domiciled in Denmark.

All that the parties own at the moment of the marriage or later on acquire will be a part of their community property unless a special arrangement is established.

Each party has the right, inter vivos, to dispose of what each has brought into the community with exception of the house in which they are living and the furniture in the house, which cannot be sold or mortgaged without the consent of both.

Marriage settlement may reserve ownership to and right to dispose of and administer real or personal property for each of the parties to the marriage.

After marriage general rule of joint estates cannot be altered by one party unilaterally. Separate estates—wholly or partly—by wish of one party call for prenuptial agreement to be registered before marriage.

IMMIGRATION:

(Law No. 462 of June 26, 1987).

Consent of Ministry of Justice must be obtained for settling down for more than three months or for taking up any occupation, salaried or not.

INCOME TAX: See topic Taxation.

INFANTS:

(Law No. 387 of June 14, 1995).

Persons under age of 18 are infants. Contracts entered into with infant cannot be enforced against him, even after he has reached his 18th year. After his 18th birthday he may ratify contracts entered into prior to his reaching that age, in which case such contracts will be fully binding on him.

INHERITANCE TAX: See topic Taxation.

INSOLVENCY: See topic Bankruptcy.

INTEREST:

In commercial transactions, legal interest is 5% over discount of National Bank of Denmark. Parties may agree to any rate which is not unreasonable.

If no specific agreement exists, debtor's obligation to pay interest is triggered by certain demand or by legal action.

For certain tax purposes legal minimum interest rate is fixed by fiscal authorities semiannually. Use of lower rate between closely related entities may trigger various taxes.

JOINT STOCK COMPANIES:

Three persons or more may as organizers form a corporation "Aktieselskab," short: "A/S" (societé anonyme). Before starting, company must be registered in a special register under "Erhvervs-og Selskabsstyrelsen". Minimum share capital is DKK 500,000. Minimum of two of organizers must be domiciled in Denmark unless dispensation is granted. Shareholders who have fully paid for their shares have no further liability for obligations of company.

Majority of members of board must be domiciled in Denmark or another EU-country, but dispensation can be obtained.

An "aktieselskab" is a practical basis for business activities in Denmark and is much used by foreign firms.

A corporation cannot, as a normal rule, acquire agricultural areas.

Fees for registering joint stock company are: DKK 3,000 plus annual fee DKK 620.

Private Companies (Anpartsselskaber).—These companies can be organized by one or more founders with minimum capital of DKK 125,000. Normally, at least one founder must be Danish citizen. Partners of these companies have no personal liability.

Fees for registering private company are: DKK 2,300 plus annual fee DKK 490.

See Topical Index in front part of this volume.

JOINT STOCK COMPANIES . . . *continued*

NOTE: Foreign companies wishing to operate or do business in Denmark must—as a rule—establish branch office or form subsidiary—either to be registered in Danish Company Register.

JUDGMENTS:

A foreign judgment can be rendered executory only after examination and approval of Danish court.

However, judgments covered by EEC Convention on Civil Jurisdiction and Judgments are—as rule—directly enforceable.

LABOR RELATIONS:

Rules as to protection of workmen and other employees are given in Law No. 184 of Mar. 22, 1995 and these persons are insured against accidents according to Law No. 73 of Feb. 1st, 1995 premiums being paid by employers. Provisions for protection of work environment are laid down in Law No. 184 of Mar. 1995; and great number of specific promulgations for specific areas. Relations between master and servants (domestic and agricultural), between master and apprentices and between employer and staff are regulated by statutes, viz., Law No. 115 of Mar. 19, 1980, Law No. 480 of June 22, 1990, and Law No. 516 of July 23, 1987. As to workmen and employers, relations including wages, working hours, etc. are regulated by general agreements periodically entered into by central organizations, this state of affairs being legally recognized since 1920's.

LAW REPORTS, CODES, ETC.:

See topics Reports; Statutes.

LEGISLATURE:

The King (Queen), in connection with Danish "Folketing" (Parliament) consisting of one chamber, has legislative powers. (Constitution of June 5, 1953).

LICENSES:

See topic Patents.

He who holds a patent may, within limits of his own right, grant license to others on conditions agreed upon.

LIENS:

The right to retain goods belonging to another exists in respect of goods given to a man for transport, repairing, storing, etc., until payment for the transport, repair or for storing has taken place. Attorney has right to retain his client's papers, and hotel-keeper has right to retain guest's effects, until amount due is paid.

LIMITATION OF ACTIONS:

Various laws provide for specific periods of limitation. The principal periods are:

Twenty years for claims on the basis of written documents (judgment and IOU's).

Five years for claims regarding payment for goods sold, for transport of goods, for wages, for damages in torts, etc.

MARRIAGE:

(Law No. 148 of Mar. 8, 1991).

Marriageable age is 18 years. Exemption may be given, particularly if bride be pregnant.

Before marriage both parties have to inform authority granting licence as well as other party, whether party has or expects children with another man or woman.

MARRIED WOMEN:

See topics Husband and Wife; Marriage.

MONOPOLIES AND RESTRAINT OF TRADE:

Combinations of capital are not prohibited and actually exist. Some restraints exist regarding pharmacies and manufacturers of spirits and beer.

Arrangements or stipulations, which are made by one or more individual concerns or associations with regard to price conditions, conditions of production, selling possibilities or transport conditions, which prevent or essentially restrict the unshackled development of prices or freedom of trade, must generally be registered with a special controlling committee. Such arrangements or stipulations are prohibited in case they involve or are believed to involve unreasonable prices or other unreasonable restraint of trade. (Law No. 114 of Mar. 10, 1993).

MORTGAGES:

A special form and signature before witnesses is required by law for mortgages on real and movable property. Mortgages must be published and recorded in an official register.

MOTOR VEHICLES:

Motor vehicles are subjected to some special and rather severe provisions regarding speed, license of driving, yearly tax, compulsory insurance, etc.

As rule residents may only use vehicles carrying Danish license plates.

NEGOTIABLE INSTRUMENTS:

See topic Bills and Notes.

NOTARIES PUBLIC:

The duties of a notary public are not carried out by authorized private persons, e.g., solicitors. In Copenhagen there is a special official acting as a notary public; outside Copenhagen these duties are carried out by the local judge.

PARTNERSHIP:

Partnership may be formed by two or more persons. If carrying on trade, craftmanship or industry it must be registered in a special register under Danish Company Register. In all cases a written and signed agreement is recommended. All partners are jointly and personally liable for all obligations of partnership. "Sleeping partner" is liable for partnership's debt only to extent to which he has contributed to capital.

In many cases a joint stock company is preferred to a partnership

As to "private companies", see topic Joint Stock Companies.

PATENTS:

(Law No. 587 of July 2, 1993 and No. 900 of Nov. 29, 1995).

Any person, whether Dane or foreigner, has the right to obtain patent protection.

Patents are granted for 20 years. During period of patent holder may "use" his patents; if he does not, he runs risk of losing protection. Order No. 547 of Oct. 25, 1978 deals with "secret patents" concerning military inventions.

Fees for applying for Danish patent are basic fee of DKK 3,000 plus additional fee of DKK 300 for each patent claim above ten. Fee for international patent application is DKK 3,000. Fee for filing complaint over decision from Patent Authorities is DKK 2,000. There are number of other special fees for various applications.

Within 20 year period, annual fee ranging from DKK 500 up to DKK 4,800 is to be paid. Fees for entire period total DKK 47,750.

PLEDGES:

The pledging of chattels can be arranged through delivery of the chattels to the creditor or to a third person who promises to keep the chattels for the benefit of the creditor.

The pledging of chattels can also be arranged so that the debtor keeps the chattels but signs and delivers to the creditor a "pledging document" containing a list of the chattels. This document must be registered.

PRESCRIPTION:

See topic Limitation of Actions.

PRINCIPAL AND AGENT:

Representation by an agent is permitted.

A person who acts as an agent need not be of age.

A special form of representation in commercial matters is the so-called "prokura" which transfers to the representative (the "prokurist") all the same rights of disposal as the principal has, except the right to sell or mortgage real estate.

Power of attorney can be issued in any language. When signed abroad it is recommended that the signature be legalized by a Danish diplomatic or consular officer.

Trade Agents.—Business relationship is established by agreement. Certain protections of agent are statutory (Law No. 272 of May 2, 1990) and cannot be dispensed with by agreement. Termination calls for notice of one month per year or fraction of year of relationship up to maximum of six months. Possibility of compensation to agent upon termination up to maximum of one year's commission.

REAL PROPERTY:

From Jan. 1st, 1996, buyers of real estate meant entirely for private residence have been granted period of six business days from signing of contract in which to "regret" and cancel contract against payment of "penalty" 1% of purchase price to seller.

See also topics Aliens; Deeds.

RECORDS:

Deeds, mortgages, etc., must be recorded.

There are also commercial registers, maritime registers, aircraft registers, association registers and registers for births, marriages, deeds, etc.

REPLEVIN:

No statutes covering replevin.

Any person having a right to the possession of certain goods may claim the delivery by aid of the public authorities.

It is strictly forbidden to take back the goods by one's own means.

REPORTS:

Official printed reports of all decisions do not exist; but the most important decisions of the courts are reported in "Ugeskrift for Retsvaesen."

RESTRAINT OF TRADE:

See topic Monopolies and Restraint of Trade.

SALES:

A codification of Apr. 6, 1906, and common law rules apply.

Conditional sales are permitted and are much used for the sale of great number of consumer goods.

Filing in an official register is not necessary.

When selling on credit to consumers rules in Law No. 398 of June 13, 1990 must be strictly followed. Retention of title towards consumers conditional upon cash down payment of 20% of purchase price.

Notices Required.—In case of nonconforming delivery buyer must give notice immediately and at all events within a year after delivery. Buyer has burden of proof as to notice being given, but any particular form, such as writing is not prescribed.

Applicable Law.—According to Law No. 118 of May 9, 1984, parties to contract may decide competent law by their express agreement. In other cases proper law will as basic rule be law of place of performance for seller or law of state with closest relation to contract.

See Topical Index in front part of this volume.

SALES . . . *continued*

See topic Consumer Protection in relation to protection of consumers.

New Product Liability Act passed and phrased according to EEC-Directive of July 25, 1985 entered into force on June 10th, 1989.

New Competition Act entered into force on Jan. 1st, 1990.

International Sale of Goods.—United Nations Convention on Contracts for the International Sale of Goods, in force on Mar. 1, 1990, and applies to contracts entered into after this date. However, Convention does not apply to settlement of conflicts between parties residing in Denmark, Finland, Iceland, Norway and Sweden. See topic Treaties and Part VII, Selected International Conventions.

SEALS:

Seals are used by public authorities, but it is not necessary for the validity of a document for a seal to be affixed.

Company seals are not used in Denmark.

SEQUESTRATION:

A sort of "sequestration" of real property may be obtained.

SHIPPING:

Laws concerning shipping are essentially codified in Law No. 653 of Oct. 13, 1989.

To be deemed a Danish ship at least two-thirds of the ship must belong to persons who are Danes. If the ship belongs to a Danish joint stock company two thirds of the directors of the board must be Danes residing in Denmark. All shareholders can be foreigners.

Every ship must be measured, examined and filed in a special shipping register; vessels can be mortgaged by registering in this register. (Law No. 588 of Sept. 29, 1988).

Vessels which are owned by foreign nationals might under certain conditions be registered in Danish International Ships' Register. Such registration will restrict Danish collective wage and work agreements to persons domiciled in Denmark.

STATUTE OF FRAUDS:

See topic Frauds, Statute of.

STATUTES:

No complete codification of the judicial rules exists in Denmark. Special codifications govern penal, maritime, commercial and procedure laws and some other laws.

TAXATION:

It is impossible in a few lines to explain the contents of the Danish tax laws, which are very complicated and must be carefully studied.

Income tax is levied on all residents and estates on all personal income and income from capital irrespective of source or origin of income or location of assets. Personal income is taxed progressively by 50, 56 or 68%, income from capital is taxed by 50-56%. Corporations and certain foundations and other legal entities pay 38% on all kinds of taxable income. Corporate tax may be reduced to 34%, if tax is paid on account.

Expatriates working in Denmark for period of more than six months but not exceeding three years are granted partial tax relief normally to flat rate of 25%.

Property tax ("fortune tax") is to be paid by the same persons who pay income tax and by all estates of deceased persons. Danish joint stock companies do not pay property tax.

Inheritance tax has been substituted by estate tax. If heirs are offspring flat rate of 15% is levied on inheritance exceeding DKK 180,000. In case of other heirs additional tax of 25% is levied if inheritance exceeds DKK 180,000.

Stamp Duty.—Execution of many kinds of documents—such as deeds, mortgages, rent and loan agreements and many others triggers stamp duty ranging from 0.3% and up to 4% of values involved.

Non-defrayment of stamp duty does not affect validity of document, but all signing parties are liable for payment of stamp duty. (Law No. 805 of Jan. 12, 1986).

Gasoline Tax.—Act No. 543 of Jan. 22, 1994 imposes tax of DKK 3.70 (about 70¢) per liter of gasoline.

Other Taxes.—There are other taxes, especially personal taxes. Danish tax system is so complicated—with exception of law of 1969 regarding taxation of corporations (digested above under subhead Income Tax) that it is impossible to give a short, intelligible explanation of them. Denmark uses a progressive system. From Jan. 1, 1970 distinction has to be made between (a) income, tax being deducted by employer immediately by payment, and (b) income.

Dividend Tax.—From Jan. 1, 1970 a tax on dividends paid by Danish companies was introduced. (See now Law No. 728 of Aug. 5, 1994, §§65-67.) It amounts to 30% and is retained by company.

Transfer of Goods and Services.—Value Added Tax (General Purchase Tax) of 25% is applicable to transfer of goods and services.

Energy Taxes.—Special taxes on consumption of gas, oil and electricity have been introduced for purpose of curbing consumption.

TRADEMARKS AND TRADENAMES:

(Law No. 341 of June 6, 1991).

Danes, as well as foreigners, may obtain protection through registering. As to registration by associations, see topic Associations.

Characteristic marks may be registered as trademarks for all sorts of goods.

Tradenames can be registered only for goods specified in connection with the registration. A High-court judgment has widened the limits concerning tradename registrations, and the difference between trademarks and tradenames is therefore now of little importance.

Fees.—Costs for registration of trademarks and tradenames amount to DKK 1,550 plus DKK 300 for each class for first ten years, and same for following ten years. See Notification of May 29, 1987.

Foreigners wishing to register trademark in Denmark must appoint local representative—for instance Danish lawyer. As a rule it is of no consequence whether or not trademark has been registered in country of owner.

Danish Patent Office operates with international classification of goods and services. Nonuse of trademark through period of five years creates risk that trademark may be attacked or lost.

TREATIES:

Denmark is member of EEC. In order to avoid double taxation, great number of treaties have been entered into.

Denmark is a party to: (a) Convention on Service Abroad of Judicial and Extrajudicial Documents in Civil or Commercial Matters (Ratified July 21st, 1969 and in force as of Oct. 1st, 1969); (b) Convention on Taking Evidence Abroad in Civil or Commercial Matters (Ratified May 25th, 1972 and in force as of Oct. 7th, 1972); (c) United Nations Convention on Recognition and Enforcement of Foreign Arbitral Awards (Ratified Nov. 24th, 1972 and in force as of Mar. 21, 1973); (d) Convention between the Government of the United States of America and the Government of the Kingdom of Denmark for the Avoidance of Double Taxation and the Prevention of Fiscal Evasion with Respect to Taxes on Estates, Inheritances, Gifts and certain other Transfers (Ratified by Denmark, Nov. 8, 1984).

Denmark is not party to Convention Abolishing the Requirement of Legalisation for Foreign Public Documents.

International Sale of Goods.—United Nations Convention on Contracts for the International Sale of Goods, in force on Mar. 1, 1990, and applies to contracts entered into after this date. However, Convention does not apply to settlement of conflicts between parties residing in Denmark, Finland, Iceland, Norway and Sweden. See topic Sales and Part VII, Selected International Conventions.

TRUSTS:

Danish law does not know trusts of the sort used in America.

Appointment of a person as "trustee" can be arranged, but is very seldom done in Denmark.

WILLS:

Will cannot be made by one who has not attained age of 18 years, or is not mentally competent.

Testamentary Disposition.—Person may dispose of such part of his property by will as law does not obligate him to leave to his heirs.

Obligatory heirs are husband and wife, children and descendants. One-half of estate may nevertheless be disposed of. (Law No. 215 of May 31, 1963).

Execution.—A will can be signed in the presence of two witnesses, whose signatures must be written beneath the signature of the testator, but it is recommended, if possible, to sign a will in the presence of a notary public.

Foreign Wills.—A will made in a foreign country is, as a rule, valid in Denmark if executed in accordance with the formalities required in the country where executed.

DOMINICAN REPUBLIC LAW DIGEST REVISER

Curtis Mallet-Prevost, Colt & Mosle
101 Park Avenue
New York, New York 10178-0061
Telephone: 212-696-6141
Fax: 212-697-1559
Email: CMP-NY@mcimail.com

Reviser Profile

The Firm began in 1830 when two practicing lawyers started a long line of lawyers and law firms extending in an unbroken chain up to the present time. In 1897, the firm name became Curtis, Mallet-Prevost & Colt; in 1925 it was changed to Curtis, Mallet-Prevost, Colt & Mosle. The Firm is now made up of approximately 120 lawyers, including experts who have published extensively on such diverse subjects as international money management, transnational contracts, state contracts, litigation against foreign states, sovereign immunity and the act of state doctrine, and the International Court of Justice. Its principal offices are in New York City. There are branch offices in Paris, London, Frankfurt Am Main, Hong Kong, Washington, D.C., Houston, Texas, Newark, N.J., and Mexico City. The Firm has five departments: Corporate and International; Litigation; Real Estate; Tax and Trusts and Estates. The corporate and international department acts as general counsel to various public and private corporations and individual entrepreneurs. Clients are in the banking, insurance, securities, manufacturing, real estate and oil and gas industries. In addition, the corporate and international department frequently acts as special counsel to domestic and foreign clients, providing assistance in financing, know-how licensing, the negotiation and drafting of all types of contracts and instruments, counselling on all aspects of corporate law, and establishing the vehicles necessary to enable clients to conduct their domestic and foreign business activities. The Firm's international work permeates all areas of its practice and involves questions of private international law, foreign law and an unusual amount of public and quasi-public international law. Traditionally, much of the Firm's international practice has been concerned with Latin America. The Firm maintains its excellence in that area, with its Mexican affiliate, and also through the expertise of Latin American lawyers based in the New York office. The Firm's international practice has undergone a major expansion beyond Latin America to Europe, Africa and the Near and Far East. The Firm's litigation practice includes commercial litigation and arbitration, and white-collar criminal defense. It has substantial experience in civil aviation matters; it also has represented foreign States in transnational litigation and international arbitration arising out of acts of nationalization and alleged breach of economic development or natural resource supply contracts. Among the Firm's clients in real estate matters are institutional lenders and investors, real estate developers, both individual and corporate, foreign and domestic investors and syndicators. The tax department has substantial experience in all aspects of domestic and international business tax matters and real estate taxation. The matters the tax department deals with on a regular basis include: Taxation of foreign investments; the structuring of corporate transactions, including mergers, acquisitions, liquidations and reorganization; federal and state tax litigation; and tax planning for U.S. and foreign individuals. The trusts and estates department engages in general domestic trusts and estates practice and in tax planning for foreign persons wishing to invest in U.S. assets through offshore trusts and corporations. It represents individuals, trust companies, and banks acting as fiduciaries. It works for various charitable organizations located both in the United States and abroad including private foundations, museums, universities and hospitals. A group of fiduciary accountants with vast experience in the field assists the lawyers of the trusts and estates department. Curtis, Mallet-Prevost, Colt & Mosle has served as a Reviser for most of Latin American Law Digests since 1930.

DOMINICAN REPUBLIC LAW DIGEST

(The following is a list of all Topics, including cross-references, covered in this Digest.)

DOMINICAN REPUBLIC LAW DIGEST

Revised for 1997 edition by

CURTIS, MALLET-PREVOST, COLT & MOSLE of the New York Bar.

(C. C. indicates Civil Code; M. C. indicates Minor Code; C. Com. indicates Code of Commerce; C. C. P. indicates Code of Civil Procedure; E. O. indicates Executive Order. Numbers in Code references indicate articles.)

ACKNOWLEDGMENTS:

Certificates of acknowledgment in the form customary in the United States are unknown in the laws of the Republic. Documents which in the United States would ordinarily require a certificate of acknowledgment are executed before a notary public who certifies in the instrument itself to the facts which are usually contained in a certificate of acknowledgment. The original executed instrument is kept by the notary and forms part of his record. (See topic Notaries Public.) However, instruments executed in accordance with land registry law may merely be acknowledged before notary public or judge.

Documents executed in the United States for use in the Republic may be acknowledged in the usual manner; the notary's signature should be authenticated by a competent official; and the latter's signature should be legalized by a Dominican consular or diplomatic officer. In general it is better to execute such documents in the Spanish language and Dominican form or in the English language but following the Dominican form. (Law 716 of 1944).

ACTIONS:

Actions for Death.—See topic Death.

Limitation of.—See topic Prescription, subhead Actions.

ADMINISTRATION:

See topic Executors and Administrators.

ADOPTION:

(M.C. arts. 27-96).

Person over 25 years of age, in full exercise of his civil rights and of good reputation may adopt minor under 15 years; in any case adopting party must be 15 years older than adopted party.

There are two types of adoption: Full adoption (adopción privilegiada) and partial adoption (adopción simple). Full adoption gives adopted person identical status with that of natural child, creating lines of kinship between adopted person and adoptive parent's family. Full adoption extinguishes legal bonds between adopted person and his natural parents and family. Partial adoption creates same juridical ties between adopted and adopting parties as exist between parents and children; but does not create any legal relationship between adopted party and family of adopting party, nor between latter and family of adopted party. Partial adoption does not extinguish legal bonds between adopted person and his natural parents and family. Partial adoption may be revoked. Adoption where parties are subject to different jurisdictions and domicile is governed by law of domicile of adopted party in matters related to his capacity, legal age, consent by parents or legal representatives, authorization to leave country and law of domicile of adopting parents in matters of their legal capacity, consent and other requirements. Change of nationality is not produced by adoption.

ADVERSE POSSESSION: See topic Prescription.

AGENCY: See topic Principal and Agent.

AIRCRAFT:

Law 505 of Oct. 23, 1969, supersedes all former laws and applies to both foreign and domestic private airplanes and common carriers, their crews, passengers and cargo. Its application covers flights over territorial jurisdiction of Dominican Republic as well as planes landing thereon. Law specifies that all pilots must be aware of navigational laws of country and all planes, crews, and passengers will be governed by Dominican Law while in flight within territorial jurisdiction or while on Dominican soil. Several provisions govern registration and identification, documentation, commercial permits for foreign and domestic airlines, flight patterns and prohibition against photography from airplanes within Republic.

Dominican Republic is a party to Convention on Commercial Aviation signed at Havana, Feb. 15, 1938 and Conventions on International Aviation signed at Chicago, Dec. 7, 1944. (Resolution 964 of Aug. 11, 1945).

ALIENS:

An alien has the same civil rights as are granted to Dominicans by the treaties of the country to which he owes allegiance. After obtaining the government's permission to establish his residence in the Republic and during such residence he enjoys all civil rights. Except in mercantile matters a transient alien plaintiff must give bond for costs and damages, unless he possesses sufficient real property in the Republic. (C. C. 11-16).

As to acquisition by aliens of real property, Decree 2543 of Mar. 22, 1945 as am'd by Decree 860 of Mar. 8, 1983, requires prior authorization from executive power; exempted from that requirement associations comprised of at least 51% ownership by citizens of Dominican Republic. Decree 3768 of June 7, 1969 requires prior authorization from executive power for aliens to acquire real property for purpose of constructing family housing, conducting commercial or industrial activities, developing urban areas or constructing buildings to promote tourist industry.

Aliens require governmental permission to enter the country, which permission is freely granted to temporary visitors and certain others. Person admitted as immigrant must obtain residence permit and annually renew same, paying corresponding fees. (Law 95 of 1939 as am'd, Immigration Regulations of 1939).

In any business at least 80% of employees must be Dominicans and at least 80% of payroll must go to Dominicans. Executive and managerial positions must preferably be filled by Dominicans. (Labor Code, Law 16-92 of May 29, 1992).

See also topic Descent and Distribution.

ALIMONY: See topic Divorce.

ASSIGNMENTS:

The assignment of a credit, right or action is perfect as between the parties from the moment there is agreement as to the thing assigned and the price, even before there is tradition. Tradition is effected, as between assignor and assignee, by delivering the document evidencing the debt or right. As regards third persons the assignee will not be protected until the debtor is notified of the assignment or accepts it. The assignment of a credit carries with it the accessories thereof such as securities. The assignor of a credit or other incorporeal right guarantees its existence even though no guaranty be expressed, but he does not warrant the solvency of the debtor unless expressly stipulated and only up to the amount of the price received. (C. C. 1583, 1689-1694).

ASSIGNMENTS FOR BENEFIT OF CREDITORS:

A debtor who is unable to pay his debts may assign all his assets to his creditors. Such assignment may be made by agreement with the creditors or under judicial order. When the assignment is by agreement the terms thereof govern; when under judicial order the creditors may sell the assets and apply the proceeds to the payment of their claims. Should the proceeds be insufficient to meet all claims the debtor remains liable for the unpaid balance. (C. C. 1265-1270).

ASSOCIATIONS:

(Law 520 of July 26, 1920 as am'd by Law 1143 of 1946 and Law 660 of July 19, 1982).

Two or more natural or juridical persons may incorporate association not for pecuniary profit with power to sue and be sued, to make contracts and hold real and personal property, to make loans and issue bonds, to issue stock, etc. Charter and by-laws must be submitted to Executive Power for approval which may be refused: (a) When association is formed for illegal purpose; (b) for failure to designate period of duration or (c) for failure to designate agent to receive service of process, etc. On approval extract giving name, purposes, officers, duration, etc., of association must be published in local newspaper. Members are liable only to extent of their contributions. Association may be dissolved on resolution of majority of members provided such majority also represents majority of stock or assets of association, by applying to court, which appoints one or three liquidators. Foreign associations not for pecuniary purposes may be registered. Associations and federations other than foregoing, labor unions and employers' groups, also require governmental authorization. (Law 267 of 1940).

ATTACHMENT:

Attachment may issue on behalf of creditors holding written evidences of indebtedness, but unless the action is prosecuted promptly the attachment will be dismissed. Even without written evidence of indebtedness a creditor may, with the permission of the court, attach property: (1) of a transient debtor which is found in the commune where the creditor resides, and (2) in urgent situations where the collection of an apparently good credit is imperiled. Attachment in an action similar to replevin may be ordered only by courts of first instance. (C. C. P. 557-651, 822-831).

BANKRUPTCY:

(C. Com. 437-614).

A merchant who suspends payments is considered in a state of bankruptcy. Bankruptcy may be of three kinds: (1) Inability in the ordinary course of business, to meet obligations; (2) caused by imprudent or dissipated conduct of the bankrupt; (3) involving fraudulent acts of the bankrupt. In the last two cases the bankrupt may be punished under the Penal Code. A deceased merchant may be declared bankrupt within one year after his death. Bankruptcy may be declared by the court on the petition of the bankrupt or of one or more creditors or on its own motion. On the declaration of bankruptcy by the court the bankrupt loses the administration of all his property, his debts fall due and his unsecured debts cease to bear interest. One or more temporary receivers are appointed and a meeting of creditors is called; permanent receivers are then appointed. Receivers may sell perishable goods and continue the business on order of the court. The bankrupt may be placed under arrest in certain cases or required to give a bond conditioned on his appearance whenever called.

Creditors who have failed to file their claims at the time of the appointment of permanent receivers are notified by publication in the newspapers and by letters mailed by the clerk of the court, to file such claims within 20 days from the date of publication. Creditors residing outside of the Republic have a longer period; claims of persons residing in the United States must be filed within two months from such publication. On expiration of these periods the credits are verified, and thereupon a meeting of creditors is called to consider composition offers. A composition requires the vote of a majority of the creditors who at the same time represent three-fourths of the total of claims allowed and verified and claims allowed conditionally. Objections to the composition may be filed by creditors as well as by the receivers and are determined by the court. A fraudulent bankrupt cannot make a composition with his creditors. No distribution of assets may be made among creditors residing in the Republic without first setting aside funds for the payment of a corresponding portion of the dividend to

See Topical Index in front part of this volume.

BANKRUPTCY . . . *continued*
creditors residing abroad. A bankrupt may be discharged from bankruptcy on petition to the Supreme Court of Justice if all sums owing by him have been paid in full with interest together with all expenses. A bankrupt who has acted fraudulently cannot be discharged.

No bankruptcy proceeding may be brought in court without a previous attempt at an amicable settlement, upon petition by a creditor or the debtor, made to the Department of Industry, Commerce and Banking through the Chamber of Commerce of the debtor's domicile. (Laws 4582 of Nov. 3, 1956 and 5260 of Nov. 30, 1959).

See also topic Fraudulent Sales and Conveyances.

BILLS AND NOTES:

(C. Com. 110-189).

Bill of exchange must be dated and must state: (1) Amount payable; (2) name of drawee; (3) date when and place where payable; (4) value received in money, in merchandise, on account, or otherwise. It must be drawn to the order of a third person or the order of the drawer and must state whether it is first, second, third, etc., of exchange. When fictitious names or places are mentioned it is considered only as a contractual promise.

The drawer and endorsers are jointly liable for its acceptance and payment. On notice of protest for nonacceptance the drawer and endorsers must give bond to guarantee payment. Acceptance may not be conditional but may be limited to a certain amount. If so limited the bearer must protest the bill as to the difference. A bill must be accepted within 24 hours from presentation and if it is not returned within that time either accepted or not, whoever retained it is liable for damages to the bearer.

In case of protest for nonacceptance the bill may be accepted by a third person acting for the drawer or any endorser. Such third person must without delay notify the person for whom he acted. The bearer, however, retains all his rights against drawer and endorsers.

A bill of exchange may be drawn: (1) At sight; (2) at one or more days, months, or "usos" (periods of 30 days) after sight; (3) at one or more days, months or "usos" from date; (4) at a certain day after date, etc. A bill at sight is payable on presentation. The maturity of a bill payable at a certain period after sight is determined by the date of acceptance or of the protest for nonacceptance. A bill payable on a holiday must be paid the day before. There are no days of grace.

The ownership of a bill is transferred by endorsement which must be dated and set forth value received and the name of the endorsee; without such data the endorsement is a mere power of attorney.

Drawers, acceptors and endorsers of a bill are jointly liable to the bearer.

The "aval" is a guarantee by one who is not a party to the bill. It may be made on the bill or by a separate document.

In the absence of special agreements, the bearer of a bill drawn abroad and payable in the Republic at sight or a certain time after sight, must demand payment or acceptance within the following periods: three months from its date if drawn in the United States or the Antilles; four months if drawn on the American continent from the Rio Grande to the Orinoco; five months if drawn elsewhere in South America; six months if in Europe or elsewhere. Bills drawn in the Republic for payment abroad must be presented in the same respective periods.

In case of nonpayment of a bill it must be protested on the day after maturity, or if that be a holiday on the following day. Protest is required although there was a protest for nonacceptance and although the drawee has died or become bankrupt. Protest is made through two notaries, or a notary and two witnesses, or a bailiff and two witnesses. In the event of failure to protest, the bearer loses his rights against the endorsers, and also against the drawer if he made provision of funds. In case of protest of drafts drawn in the Republic and payable abroad, actions against drawers and endorsers residing in the Republic must be brought within the same respective periods mentioned above for presentation of drafts drawn abroad and payable in the Republic.

Notes to order must be dated and state: (1) Amount; (2) payer; (3) maturity; (4) value received in money, merchandise, on account, or otherwise. They are in general governed by the same rules as bills of exchange, except as to the need of acceptance.

Checks must state (a) the word "check" in the text of the document, (b) order to pay a specific sum expressed in words and figures, or only in figures if printed with perforating machine, (c) name of drawee, necessarily a bank, and place of payment, but if place not expressed it is presumed to be the place shown next to name of drawee, (d) date and place where drawn, but if place not shown it is presumed to be placed next to name of drawer. Most provisions elsewhere applicable to checks are in force. Checks may not bear interest. Endorsements guarantee payment unless otherwise stated, but endorsements after protest or expiration of time for presentation are mere assignments of a credit. Checks are payable at sight; if issued payable in the Republic they must be presented for payment within two months after date, if issued abroad, within four months, otherwise the holder loses his special rights. In case of nonpayment the holder must protest and notify his endorser. Crossed checks are allowed. (Check Law No. 2859 of 1951).

CHATTEL MORTGAGES:

Chattel mortgages may be given and must be registered under the name of pledges without delivery or "universal pledges," described under topic Pledges.

COLLATERAL SECURITY: See topic Pledges.

COMMERCIAL REGISTER: See topic Corporations.

COMMUNITY PROPERTY:

See topic Husband and Wife.

CONSTITUTION AND GOVERNMENT:

A constitution was promulgated on Nov. 28, 1966. Dominican Republic is a representative democracy. Its form of government is centralized. Republic is politically divided into a National District and provinces, each of these being subdivided into municipalities.

Power is divided among executive, legislative and judicial branches. Congress is composed of two houses. Members of Congress and President are elected by direct vote for term of four years. Judicial power is vested in Supreme Court and in other courts forming judicial system. President appoints governors of provinces.

COPYRIGHT:

(Law 32-86 of July 4, 1986 regulated by Decrees 82-93, 84-93 and 85-93 of Mar. 28, 1993).

Law protects rights of authors with respect to all intellectual work of creative nature, whether literary, scientific or artistic in character, whatever their kind, form of expression, merit or destination, including literary works, musical compositions, paintings, sculptures, cinematographic works, photographs, works for broadcasting and television. Copyright in works produced in collaboration belong to co-authors in common. Unless agreed otherwise, copyright in works produced for individual or juridical person under service contract belong to such individual or juridical person. Author or co-authors are entitled to their agreed fee only. Translations, adaptations, transformations, or arrangements of other works with authorization of author of original work, constitute personal creations and are deemed to be intellectual works distinct from original works. Law also protects performers and entertainers. Author of intellectual work, by sole fact of its creation, possesses right with respect to work which includes moral and property rights protected by law without need of deposit, registry or other formality. Moral rights are unassignable and unlimited in time, they include right to make work known publicly, to use name or pen name, to assert paternity of work or keep it in anonymity, to oppose plagiarism, defamation or mutilation, and to withdraw work from circulation or suspend any manner of utilization thereof, after payment of damages, if any. Property rights entitle author to enjoyment of pecuniary benefits from use of his works. They include rights of reproduction, translation, adaptation or modification, performance and broadcasting, sale and any other manner, known or unknown, for disposition, utilization or exploitation thereof. Property rights are assignable and transferable upon death.

As general rule, property rights are protected under Law during life of author plus 50 years after his death or death of last surviving co-author, at which time, or before if there are no heirs, work becomes of public domain. However, nonresident foreign authors are protected for above period of time or for period of time afforded by country where work has been first published or protected, whichever is shorter. Producer of motion picture is protected for 30 years from first projection; photographs are covered for ten years from first publication or public exhibition; works published anonymously are protected for 50 years from first publication unless author is revealed, where general rule applies. State may decree, by reason of public utility or social interest, that work becomes of public domain at any time prior to expiration of above periods. In these instances author is entitled to fair compensation. Law applies only to nationals and to persons domiciled in countries which are parties of copyright conventions and treaties where Dominican Republic is party. Law also contains detailed provisions regarding transfer of rights, reproduction of works, publishing contracts, representation contracts and author's associations. Violation of author rights constitutes felony punished by prison and fines. All acts related to copyrights must be registered at National Registry of Copyright.

Dominican Republic is a party to Inter-American Convention on rights of author in literary, scientific and artistic works (Washington, 1946) and to Universal Convention on rights of author revised in Paris on July 24, 1971.

CORPORATIONS:

(C. Com. 31-46, 56-63; Laws 1041 of 1935, 3567 of 1953, 5260 of Nov. 30, 1959 and 5546 of June 13, 1961).

Corporations may be constituted by seven or more persons and do not require governmental authorization. Their name must begin or end with the words "Compañía por Acciones", "Socidad Anónima" or "Compañia Anónima" or the letters "C. por A.", "S. A." or "C. A." and mention the object of the activities or the name of a member thereof. They must be constituted by written agreement. Within one month a duplicate or notarial copy of the articles of incorporation must be filed in the court of the places where the corporation is established, together with a list of the subscribers to the stock of the company, and an extract from the articles of incorporation must be published in the newspapers, which publications must state the authorized and paid-up capital. Upon organization, stock companies must pay tax based on percentage of capital. Before commencing operations companies must obtain special authorization from Dept. of Industry and Commerce. Within two months corporation must be registered in Mercantile Registry of place where it is established. Also any changes in corporate structure must be so recorded. At least one-tenth of authorized capital must be subscribed and all subscriptions paid up before corporation can be constituted. If company's activity is to be manufacturing, it must also obtain certificate of industrial registration from Dept. of Industry and Commerce. Both mercantile registrations and industrial registrations carry fixed fee, according to authorized capital.

Shares may be to bearer or registered. Preferred shares are permitted. Shareholders are not liable beyond the value of their shares.

Directors need not be shareholders unless the by-laws so provide. The by-laws may require directors to give bond. When the by-laws require directors to be owners of a certain number of shares, such shares are inalienable during their term of office and must be registered and deposited in the treasury of the company as a guarantee. Directors may delegate their powers if the by-laws permit but are liable to the company for the acts of the persons to whom they delegate. They are regarded as attorneys-in-fact of the shareholders and are liable only as such.

Shareholders' meetings must be held annually. The by-laws designate the number of shares necessary in order to participate in the meetings and the number of votes to which shareholders are entitled, but at the first meeting any shareholder may participate, with a maximum of ten votes. Ordinarily shareholders representing one-fourth the capital constitute a quorum, and if no quorum is obtained, another meeting may be called to be held with any number appearing; but at the first meetings and at all

CORPORATIONS . . . *continued*
meetings to change the by-laws or extend or curtail the term of the company, the quorum consists of shareholders representing one-half the capital. The shareholders appoint one or more financial inspectors to report at the next annual meeting.

Reserve.—At least one-twentieth of the annual profits must be set aside as a reserve until such reserve amounts to one-tenth of the capital.

After establishing the reserves specified in the law or the by-laws further sums may be set aside as reserves if a dividend of 8% has been declared. (art. 57).

Dissolution.—If three-fourths of the capital is lost the directors must call a shareholders' meeting to decide whether the company should be dissolved and such decision must be published. One year after the number of shareholders is reduced to less than seven, the corporation may be dissolved on the petition of any interested party.

Government Authorization.—All persons and companies desiring to engage in commercial or industrial activities must obtain an authorization from the Department of Labor and Industry. For that purpose an application must be filed giving data as to the partners or stockholders and a governmental certificate must be obtained. (Law 5260 of 1959).

Foreign corporations require the authorization of the government to establish themselves in the country. (C. C. 13). For that purpose they must file a copy of their articles of incorporation and by-laws and the power of attorney of their representative empowered to request the authorization. Commercial and industrial enterprises must also set forth, on forms obtained from the Department of Industry and Commerce, information relating to nationality and residence of partners, managers, directors and shareholders; later changes in officials and shareholders must likewise be reported. Foreign corporations have in practice been required to give only the names, nationality and addresses of their directors and principal shareholders, as appearing in the Company's books. Registration in the Mercantile Registry of the place where the corporation will operate must be made within two months. (Law 5260 of 1959). See also topic Principal and Agent.

Remittances Abroad.—See topic Exchange Control.

Corporate Fees.—The costs payable in connection with the incorporation of a company comprise notarial fees depending on the amount involved, registration fees, publication costs, and a proportional tax on the authorized capital. Petitions for authorizations of foreign corporations require revenue stamps. (Law 3567 of 1953).

COURTS:

Justice is administered by: (1) A Supreme Court which hears appeals for errors of law, appeals for unconstitutionality, and ordinary appeals in matters arising in the courts of appeals, has original jurisdiction in accusations against certain high officials and in questions between the state and municipalities, and exercises a general supervision over the courts; (2) nine courts of appeals which hear appeals from lower courts and have original jurisdiction in accusations against certain functionaries; (3) superior administrative court having jurisdiction over complaints against governmental administrative acts; (4) land courts; (5) courts of first instance having civil and criminal jurisdiction; (6) judges of instruction who have functions of committing magistrates; (7) justices of peace; (8) juvenile courts; (9) labor courts. (Const., arts. 63-77; Law 821 of Nov. 21, 1927, as am'd; Labor Code Law 16-92 of May 29, 1992).

CURRENCY:

Monetary unit is the gold peso, divided in 100 cents. Only Central Bank may issue bank notes, which are legal tender. (Law 1528 of Oct. 7, 1947 as am'd by Law 764 of Apr. 6, 1978).

See also topic Exchange Control.

DEATH:

When a person has disappeared for four years, interested parties may apply to court to have him declared an absentee. Such declaration may not be made until one year after the decree ordering the investigation. If the absentee left an attorney-in-fact, he may not be declared an absentee until ten years after his disappearance. Thereupon, provisional possession of his estate may be granted to his heirs and 30 years thereafter, or 80 years after the date of his birth, any security given for the administration of his estate may be canceled by court order. (C. C. 112-143).

Death certificates may be obtained from the official of the Registry of the Civil Status, a nominal fee being charged.

Actions for Death.—There is no wrongful death statute specifically providing for actions of this kind. However, said actions may be supported under the general language of the few provisions of Civil Code on torts (C. C., art. 1382 et seq.). Dominican Republic recognizes as a source of authority French jurisprudence under which damages have been granted to a decedent's close relatives, especially when they were found to have a right to support.

DECEDENTS' ESTATES:

See topics Descent and Distribution, Executors and Administrators, Wills.

DEEDS:

Conveyance of real property in order to be recorded at Land Registry may be in public instrument or private document which must contain true statement of consideration, since tax on transfers of title is based on real consideration. In public instrument both grantor and grantee must sign and be present before notary at same time in person or by attorney-in-fact. Notary retains original document and delivers to interested parties certified copy which has effect of original in courts of law. Private document very simple form, which must be acknowledged before notary or judge and recorded. Transfer tax and recording fees are reasonable. (Law 1542 of Oct. 11, 1947 as am'd; Land Registry Law). See also topic Notaries Public.

DESCENT AND DISTRIBUTION:

(C. C. 718-892; C. C. P. 907-1002; Law 357 of 1940).

In the absence of testamentary dispositions, a decedent's estate passes to the following, in the order named: (a) Descendants; (b) parents and brothers and sisters; (c) ascendants; (d) collaterals to the twelfth degree; (e) surviving spouse; (f) the state. When the estate goes to ascendants and collaterals, it is divided into two parts, of which one goes to the relatives on the father's side, and the other to the relatives on the mother's side.

Aliens have the same inheritance rights as Dominicans. In case of a division of an estate between alien and Dominican co-heirs, the latter are entitled to receive from the property in the Republic a part equal to the value of property located abroad from which they are excluded for any reason.

Even though there be a will, a part of the estate goes to certain heirs by operation of law. (See topic Wills, subhead Testamentary Disposition).

The following are excluded from testate or intestate succession: (a) Persons who murdered or attempted to murder the author of the inheritance; (b) persons who made slanderous accusations against him; (c) an heir who being of age and hearing of the decedent's death by violence, does not lay the matter before the courts.

An inheritance may be accepted expressly or impliedly or it may be refused. Acceptance may be unconditional or with benefit of inventory. In the latter case, an inventory of the inheritance is made and the heir is liable to creditors only up to the amount shown in such inventory. If acceptance is unconditional, the heir is liable for the debts of the decedent in the proportion of his shares of the estate. Creditors may demand that property of the deceased be kept separate from that of the heir.

If the heirs are all present and of age, they may make the partition in the manner they consider advisable; otherwise the partition is made under judicial auspices. The court decides controversies and may appoint a partitioner.

DIVORCE:

(Laws 1306-B of 1937, as am'd).

Divorce dissolving the marriage bond may be demanded in the courts of the Republic only by persons married by civil ceremony, or by Catholic ceremony prior to Aug. 6, 1954. It may be granted for: (1) Mutual consent; (2) incompatibility of character, but only after five years of marriage and provided there are no children; (3) formal declaration of absence, after an absence of four years; (4) adultery; (5) sentence for crime, except for political offenses; (6) cruel treatment or grave insults; (7) abandonment of the home for two years; (8) habitual drunkenness or immoderate use of narcotics.

The competent court is that of the domicile of the defendant if resident of the Republic, otherwise the domicile of the plaintiff. Domicile is considered to be bona fide residence in the Republic. In case address of wife is unknown, filing of divorce suit must be announced in advance in a daily newspaper. Public prosecutor must be heard in all divorce actions. Judgments of divorce must be recorded in civil registry within two months after expiration of time for appeal, otherwise they become inoperative; in case of divorce by mutual consent, judgment must be recorded within eight days after its date.

The court may assign alimony pendente lite to the wife and determines where she is to live during the proceedings. The judgment determines who is to have custody of the children, the following rules being observed: (1) Children are distributed as agreed by the parties; (2) if there be no agreement (a) children under four years remain in the custody of the mother unless the divorce was granted for causes (4), (5), (6) or (8) above mentioned (b) children over four years old go to the spouse obtaining the divorce unless the court orders otherwise. In any case both parents preserve the right to look after the maintenance and education of the children and are obliged to contribute thereto in proportion to their resources.

Divorce by mutual consent is not allowable before the expiration of two years after the marriage nor after 30 years of married life, nor when the husband is 60 years old or over and the wife 50 years old or over. Before applying to the court the parties must make an inventory of their property, agree on the custody of the children and determine where the wife is to live during the proceedings and her alimony pendente lite. The parties appear before the judge who designates a date not less than 30 nor more than 60 days later for a hearing, and gives judgment eight days after the hearing.

A divorced wife cannot marry again for ten months after the divorce unless it be the same husband. The spouse guilty of any of the causes (4) to (8) above mentioned loses all advantages derived from the other spouse through the marriage.

The dissolution or annulment of Catholic marriages since Aug. 6, 1954, is reserved to ecclesiastical courts of the Catholic Church. Their judgments are registered in the civil registry.

Law 142 of May 18, 1971, amends previous laws on subject and allows foreigners, even if not residents of country, to obtain divorce by mutual consent provided one spouse is physically present before court and other one is represented by a special attorney. In this case, court, after a short period of time, and previous approval of public ministry, must grant divorce. Judgment is recorded in civil registry and a summary of same is published in a local newspaper.

Separation, not dissolving the marriage bond, may be demanded by persons married by Catholic ceremony since Aug. 6, 1954. It is granted for: (1) adultery; (2) sentence for crime, except for political offenses; (3) cruel treatment or grave insults; (4) abandonment of the home for one year; (5) habitual drunkenness; (6) formal declaration of absence. Procedure follows that provided for divorce. Separation involves separation of property and returns to wife the free disposal of her property. Children are awarded to innocent spouse or to the Catholic spouse if they are not of the same faith, unless the judge decides otherwise taking into consideration the welfare of the child and its Catholic education. The spouses may by mutual consent request annulment of the separation decree.

DOWER:

No dower right. See topics Descent and Distribution, also Husband and Wife.

EXCHANGE CONTROL:

(Monetary Law 1528 of Oct. 9, 1947 as am'd; Law of Banco Central 6142 of Dec. 29, 1962 as am'd; Exchange Control Law 251 of May 11, 1964, as am'd).

EXCHANGE CONTROL . . . *continued*

Bank deposits in foreign money may be kept only with authorization of Central Bank which is entitled to order conversion at any time. Under Monetary Law, clauses of payment in the country in foreign currency are null and void except when interpreted as promise to pay equivalent in local currency, at rate of contract or payment date, whichever more favorable to debtor. For payments of interest and principal of obligations to be sent abroad, advance approval of loan or contract is required. Exchange control policy is determined by Monetary Board and administered by Central Bank. Foreign exchange for imports must be authorized by Central Bank. Exporters must surrender to Central Bank foreign exchange proceeds from export.

See also topics Foreign Investment; Taxation.

EXECUTIONS:

By virtue of a judgment, property may be attached. The form of attachment and manner and time of sale depend on the kind of property involved. In the case of personal property, the period between the attachment and sale may be brief, and such property is sold to the highest bidder, but silver cannot be sold below its real value and jewelry not below the amount of appraisal by experts. In the case of real property, the attachment is recorded in the public registry, extensive notifications must be given to the owner of the property and other interested persons, and publications must be made in the newspapers. The creditor may stipulate that bidders must make a deposit. The property is sold to the highest bidder, or if there are no bids, it is awarded to the creditor for the amount designated by him beforehand. Within eight days after the sale other persons may make a new bid at least 20% higher than the amount for which the property was awarded and in consequence of such new bid another sale is held. Once the property is definitely adjudged, the debtor has no right of redemption. (C. C. P. 545-748).

EXECUTORS AND ADMINISTRATORS:

(C. C. 870-882, 1025-1034; C. C. P. 907-1002).

A testator may appoint one or more executors and empower them to take possession of all or part of the personal property, but this right cannot extend beyond one year and one day. If the testator has not granted such right it cannot be exercised and in any case the heir may obtain the property by paying the executor the amount necessary for the bequests. Executors have the duty of seeing to the preparation of an inventory of the estate, and execution of the will, and must render accounts within one year. The following cannot be executors: (a) Persons incompetent to obligate themselves; (b) minors.

When a person dies, his property passes immediately to his heirs. As to liability of heirs for debts, see topic Descent and Distribution.

EXEMPTIONS:

The beds of the debtor and children living with him and their clothing cannot be attached for any kind of credits. The following are also exempt from attachment: (a) Articles which have become real property by destination, but they may be attached as part of such real property; (b) professional books to the value of 300 pesos; (c) machinery and apparatus for teaching and for the practice of science and arts, to the value of 300 pesos; (d) equipment of soldiers; (e) workmen's utensils; (f) foodstuffs for the maintenance of the debtor and his family for one month; (g) one cow, three sheep or two goats, with their sustenance for one month. The foregoing may, however, be attached in certain actions such as actions on vendor's liens, leases of lands where the objects were used, etc.

There can be no garnishment of salaries or wages paid by a municipality, nor, with certain exceptions, of advances for aliments or of legacies or gifts designated by the grantor as not subject to attachment. (C. C. P. 580-582, 592). Salaries, wages and pensions of a private employee may not be garnished beyond one-third of their amount. (Law 2453 of 1950). No garnishment may be levied on salaries, wages or pensions owing by the State or government agencies or on obligatory savings accounts. (Law 4577 of 1956).

Law 1024 of Oct. 24, 1928 am'd by Law 5610 of Aug. 25, 1961 creates the family homestead not subject to attachment or execution. Under Law 472 of Nov. 2, 1964, property allotted by National Housing Institute is considered as family homestead.

FOREIGN CORPORATIONS: See topic Corporations.

FOREIGN EXCHANGE:

See topic Exchange Control.

FOREIGN INVESTMENT:

(Law 16-95 of Dec. 8, 1995).

Foreign investors have same rights and duties as national investors, except as expressly indicated in this law and in special laws.

Direct foreign investment is authorized in all economic activities, except: Public health, environment, disposal of toxic waste of foreign origin; and national security and defense which require prior authorization of competent authority.

Foreign investment is defined as foreign source contribution made by individuals or juridical persons. Direct foreign investment may be effected in form of freely convertible foreign currency, assets, capitalization of profits, investment of profits entitled to repatriation, equity contributions of intangibles or in intangible technological contributions, such as marks, industrial models, technical assistance. Direct foreign investment is authorized for establishment of new companies and to participate in existing companies; acquisitions of real estate and financial assets, subject to special rules.

In general, no prior authorization is required for foreign investment. However, foreign investment must be registered with Central Bank within 90 days from date of investment in order to get Certificate of Registration of Foreign Investment. Such registration allows investors to repatriate capital and profits abroad. See also topics Exchange Control; Taxation.

FOREIGN TRADE REGULATIONS:

See topic Exchange Control.

FRAUDS, STATUTE OF:

A private or notarial document is required for all obligations involving over 30 pesos. Authentic documents are those executed before notaries or other qualified public officers; they are proof of their contents as between the parties and their successors. Private writings, when acknowledged, have the same force between the parties as authentic documents, but as to third persons their date is counted only from the date of their registration or from the death of one of the signers or from the day on which they are listed in a document prepared by a public official. Private documents containing mutual agreements are not valid unless executed in as many originals as there are interested parties, but a single original is sufficient if all parties have the same interest. If they carry an obligation to pay a sum of money, they must be in the handwriting of the obligor or he must add to his signature a statement, in his handwriting, of the amount due; except when such documents are issued by merchants, artisans, workmen or servants. (C. C. 1317-1348).

FRAUDULENT SALES AND CONVEYANCES:

The following acts or payments after the date determined by the court as the date of cessation of payments or within ten days before such date, are void: Gratuitous transfers of property; payment of unmatured debts; payments of matured debts otherwise than in money or merchandise; mortgages for debts previously contracted. Other payments made or acts done after cessation of payments may be annulled if the other contracting party had notice of such cessation. The registration of mortgages effected after a date ten days before the cessation of payments may be annulled if over 15 days elapsed between the date of the mortgage and the date of registration, these periods being subject to extension if the place of registration is distant from that of the execution of the mortgage. Creditors may attack any act executed by the debtor to defraud them. (C. Com. 446-449; C. C. 1167).

GARNISHMENT: See topic Exemptions.

HOLIDAYS:

Jan. 1 (New Year's); Jan. 6 (Epiphany) unofficial; Jan. 9 (National Census Day); Jan. 21 (Day of La Altagracia); Jan. 26 (Duarte Day); Feb. 27 (Independence Day); Good Friday*; May 16 (Election Day); Corpus Christi*; Sept. 24 (Our Lady of Mercy); Dec. 25 (Christmas).

* These are movable holidays.

HOMESTEADS: See topic Exemptions.

HUSBAND AND WIFE:

(Const., art. 19; C. C. 203-226, 1387-1581; C. Com. 7; Laws 390 of Dec. 14, 1940 and 2125 of 1949).

Spouses have the joint obligation of supporting and educating their children. The husband may choose the family residence but the wife may appeal to court if he abuses this right. The husband must support the wife, but if she has property of her own she must contribute to the household expenses. A married woman has the same civil rights as a single woman. She may freely engage in any business or profession, but the husband may object and appeal to court if the interests of the home would suffer.

Unless there is a premarital contract providing otherwise, a marital community is deemed to exist with respect to the property of the spouses. The community property comprises: (a) All personal property owned by the spouses when contracting the marriage and everything which they receive during the marriage as a gift or bequest, unless the grantor provided otherwise; (b) all income and revenue received by the spouses during the marriage; (c) all real property acquired during the marriage. The marital community is dissolved by death, divorce, separation, and separation of property by judicial decree. The husband is the administrator of the community property and may alienate and mortgage it without the wife's consent, but may dispose by will only of his share therein.

INFANCY:

(C. C. arts. 371-488, 1123-1125, 1304-1314; Law 985 of Aug. 31, 1945).

The age of majority is 18. Contracts by minors are voidable. Minors are subject to parental authority of legitimate father or natural father who has acknowledged infant within three months after birth, and upon his death or absence, of the mother. Parental authority carries with it enjoyment of the usufruct of the minor's real and personal property, with certain exceptions, until emancipation or until the minor reaches 18 years of age. The father or upon his death or absence mother is legal guardian of minor, and as such has powers of custody legal representation and administration. In the absence of parents a guardian is appointed. Parents and guardians have limited powers of disposition.

INSOLVENCY: See topic Bankruptcy.

INTEREST:

Legal interest is 12%. No higher rate can be stipulated except that pawn establishments may charge as high as 4% a month. If over 12% is collected the excess is applied first to interest then due, balance to principal; if the debt has been cancelled the creditor may be required to restore such excess collections with legal interest. Habitual usury is punishable by fine and imprisonment. (Law 312 of July 1, 1919).

INTESTACY: See topic Descent and Distribution.

JUDGMENTS:

(C. C. 2123, 2134; C. C. P. 116-165, 545-556).

A judgment constitutes a judicial mortgage in favor of the creditor, which is, however, not effective against third persons until recorded in the public registry.

JUDGMENTS . . . *continued*

Foreign judgments can be executed only if their execution has been ordered by a court of the Republic, unless otherwise determined by treaty.

LABOR RELATIONS:

(Const. art. 8, §11, Labor Code of May 29, 1992; Decree 258-93 of Oct. 1, 1993). National Constitution provides for right to work of individuals and guarantees workers limited working day, minimum wages, paid days for rest and vacations, social security, right of labor to organize trade unions, right to strike and profit sharing.

Labor relations are regulated by Labor Code which presumes that in all personal labor relations, labor contract exists unless there is provision to contrary. Labor contracts may be oral or written; in case of written contracts all amendments must be in writing. Labor contracts can be for indefinite period, for certain period for specific service or work. In any company or establishment at least 80% of workers must be Dominicans who earn at least 80% of total payroll. Positions of administrators, managers, directors and any other executive position shall be filled preferably by Dominicans. Eight hour working day is in effect with maximum of 44 hours per week with resting period of 36 hours per week. Certain exceptions are allowed. Overtime is limited by law. Workers are allowed vacation of 14 days when they have been working for at least one year up to five years and of 18 days after five years.

Employers must participate with 10% net annual profits to all employees under contract for indefinite period of time. Employers must also pay employees Christmas bonus.

Workmen's compensation is payable in case of labor accidents and occupational diseases as indicated by law. To protect employees, employers must secure from insurance company bond to guarantee up to four months of payroll payments in event of insolvency.

Contract for indefinite period of time is subject to termination by mutual consent, or by either party, as long as prior written notice is given to other party. When employer exercises right of termination, employer must pay employment compensation to employee. In case notice is not given, employer must also pay severance. Labor Code indicates causes of dismissal without any responsibility to employer. If employer cannot prove legal cause for dismissal, employer must pay unemployment compensation, severance and amount equal to salaries which employee could have earned during pending case for court decision, limited to six months.

Labor Code contains special regulations for minors under 16 years and for women. Pregnant women cannot be dismissed during pregnancy and up to three months after delivery; dismissal between three and six months after delivery must be authorized by Labor Department. In case of legal dismissal of pregnant women employer must pay damages equal to five months regular wages, plus other benefit payments she is entitled to.

LEGISLATURE:

Congress meets in regular session twice a year, in February and August. (Const., art. 34).

See also topic Constitution and Government.

LIENS:

(C. C. 2092-2113; C. Com. 546-548).

The following are privileged credits with respect to all personal property: (a) Judicial costs; (f) funeral expenses; (c) expenses of last illness; (d) wages of servants for the past and current year; (e) debts for maintenance of debtor and his family incurred in last six months when owing to retail merchants and incurred during last year when owing to wholesale merchants and boarding house keepers.

The following credits enjoy a privilege with respect to specific chattels: (a) Rentals, with respect to the fruits and crops of the property and its furnishings; (b) pledge credits, with respect to the article pledged; (c) expense of preserving property, with respect to such property; (d) unpaid purchase price, with respect to the article or while it remains in possession of the buyer, except in case of bankruptcy; (e) debts owing to innkeepers, with respect to guests' effects; (f) transportation costs, with respect to articles transported.

The following credits enjoy a privilege on specific real property: (a) Unpaid purchase price; (b) amounts advanced for purchase; (c) rights of co-heirs to secure their share in the partition; (d) sums due to architects, masons, workmen, etc.; (e) amounts advanced to satisfy claims of workmen. Such privilege on real property must be recorded in the public registry.

LIMITATION OF ACTIONS: See topic Prescription.

LIMITED PARTNERSHIP: See topic Partnership.

MARRIAGE:

(C. C. 63-76; Laws 1044 of Oct. 24, 1928, 659 of 1934; Laws 3931 of 1954, 4624 of 1957, 4999 of Sept. 24, 1958; Law 14 of Apr. 22, 1994).

Marriages are of two kinds: (1) by Catholic ceremony, which are governed by rules of the Catholic Church and should be recorded in the civil registry within five days; (2) by civil ceremony. Civil marriages are performed by the officials having charge of the civil registry, or, if they are not available, by a local justice of the peace. Ministers of religion other than Catholic are forbidden to perform a marriage ceremony unless the civil ceremony has been performed.

Males below 16 years of age and females below 15 cannot marry without a dispensation from the judge of first instance. Persons below 18 require the consent of parents, grandparents or the family council.

Marriages are prohibited: (a) Between ascendants and descendants, legitimate or natural, by consanguinity or affinity; (b) between an adopter and the person adopted or the surviving spouse of the person adopted; (c) between persons convicted as authors or accomplices of the death of the spouse of either; (d) between legitimate or natural brothers and sisters; (e) when either party is demented; (f) between persons already married by a still subsisting civil or Catholic marriage.

A marriage performed in a foreign country between Dominicans, or between a Dominican and an alien, is valid if performed in accordance with the law of that country, if the provisions of the Dominican law have not been violated.

MARRIED WOMEN:

See topics Husband and Wife; Marriage.

MINES AND MINERALS:

The State is the owner of all mineral and fossil substances, whoever may be the owner of the surface, but private persons may obtain concessions to work them in accordance with the mining laws. (Const., art. 100).

Under Mining Law 146 of May 12, 1971, which applies to all natural mineral substances except mineral water, hydrocarbons, gravel and sand, and radioactive minerals, mining matters are under jurisdiction of General Department of Mining. Law suspended all previous mining legislation.

Exploration.—Surface surveys may freely be made throughout the Republic except in areas covered by exploration permits or mining concessions. Permission must first be obtained from private property owners to explore their land. If such permission is denied, appeal may be made to General Director of Mining. Mining claims may be filed with General Department of Mining as a result of discoveries made during these surveys. Three year permits, renewable for up to two additional years, may also be obtained for more extensive exploration in specific areas from Office of Secretary of Department of Commerce and Industry. Holder of an exploration permit has exclusive option of obtaining exploitation permits within area covered by exploration permit. No one person or entity may obtain permits covering areas totalling more than 30,000 mining hectares. One mining hectare is defined as an area 100 meters square and of unlimited depth. If no work has been accomplished in area within three months after permit is issued, Department may declare permit forfeited. Other causes of forfeiture include suspension of work for periods in excess of six months.

Above provisions have not been repealed. However, by Decree 3528 of June 4, 1973, except for exploration works already underway, all exploration concessions and/or their transfer have been suspended. State only shall conduct explorations, and if results thereof prove satisfactory, exploitation concessions shall be granted, through competitive bidding to individuals or juridical persons. Provisions of this decree do not apply to petroleum deposits and related products.

Mining concessions may be obtained from Office of Secretary of Department of Industry and Commerce, with a favorable report from General Department of Mining, by any foreign or domestic persons or entities, but foreign governments may not own any concessions or hold rights therein. Foreign companies who desire to obtain exploitation or treatment concessions must incorporate locally. Local registration is sufficient to obtain exploitation permits. Concessionaires shall have right to exploit, process and dispose of all mineral substances extracted from within perimeter of its concession for a period of 75 years, but every 25 years concessionaires shall be subjected to tax laws in force at that time. One person or entity may not hold concessions covering more than a total of 20,000 mining hectares.

It is not necessary to hold exploitation concession to obtain treatment concession and build a processing plant for mineral substances if such substances are to be acquired from third parties, but in such case prior authorization must be obtained from above-mentioned department.

Exploitation and treatment concessionaires may obtain expropriation of such land as is required for mining purposes. Easements for easier extraction of minerals may also be obtained. They may also construct such facilities as may be necessary for transportation, pumping, power and other related purposes. Exploitation and processing plant concessionaires must begin operations within one year of grant of concession. Failure to do so may result in loss of concession, as may suspension of work for periods in excess of two years.

Concessions and other mining rights may be transferred (see suspension of certain transfers, under subhead Exploration, supra), pledged or otherwise encumbered to third parties who could have been granted concession initially. Such transferences must be registered in Public Registry of Mining Rights in order to be effective against third parties.

General Department of Mining maintains a public registry of corporate charters of concessionaires, permits and concessions, transfers or leases thereof, easement contracts and expropriation proceedings resulting from mining activities. Residues from exploitations and treatment shall be deposited in proper places and liquid and gaseous discharges shall be free of contaminating substances which may endanger animal or vegetable life. Concessionaires may be liable for damages caused by pollution.

Exploitation and exploration concessionaires must pay annual license fees per mining hectare, depending on total area held by concessionaire.

Failure to comply with Mining Law 146 may result in fines and confiscation of all installations and extracted minerals.

Sand, gravel and rock concessions are governed by special regulations. (Law 123 of Mar. 2, 1971).

Petroleum.—Under Petroleum Law 4532 of 1956 as am'd by Law 4833 of 1957, deposits of petroleum, asphalt, naphtha and other hydrocarbons may be explored, exploited and beneficiated only under contracts with Executive subject to such conditions as may be approved. Exploitation rights are granted for unlimited time and on such area as may be agreed upon. Such contracts are submitted to Congress and after approval may not be modified without consent of both parties. They may be granted only to Dominican individuals or companies, or to foreign individuals or companies submitting themselves to Dominican laws. Foreign governments may not have any participation in petroleum concessions nor hold shares of companies owning such concessions. Concessionaires are entitled to such tax exemptions as may be specified in their contracts. If not prohibited by contract, they may assign it to others and encumber it for financial purposes. Government must be notified of transfers or encumbrances before contracts are definitely made. Concessions may be cancelled for violations of law or concession, cancellation likewise affecting transfers and encumbrances.

See Topical Index in front part of this volume.

MORTGAGES:

(C. C. 1244, 2114-2203; Land Registry Law 1542 of Oct. 11, 1947).

Mortgages are of three kinds: (1) By act of law, such as those of minors on the property of their guardians and those of the state on the property of officials administering its revenues; (2) judicial, resulting from court judgments; (3) conventional, established by agreement of parties. They can be imposed only on real property and its accessories and usufruct.

Conventional mortgages must be constituted before two notaries or before one notary and two witnesses. They cannot be constituted by an instrument executed abroad unless so provided by treaty or special law. The property must be described and the amount of the mortgage must be specified. Mortgages have preferences as against other creditors only from the date of their record except as to certain mortgages by act of law, but in these cases the mortgage debtor is obliged to record the mortgage at once and is subject to criminal liability if he imposes another lien without announcing the existence of the mortgage. The courts may in their discretion grant the debtor additional time for the payment of the debt. Mortgage records under the Land Registry Law are effective indefinitely; other mortgage records are effective for ten years and may be renewed. Mortgages are foreclosed according to the procedure provided for executions levied on real property. See topic Executions.

MOTOR VEHICLES:

Law 241 of Dec. 28, 1967 as am'd, which contains complete regulations governing motor vehicles and public ways, revokes all previous laws except Law 16 of Oct. 16, 1963 and Law 502 of Nov. 24, 1964.

Director of Internal Income must keep a registry of all motor vehicles authorized to use public ways, and in which detailed information on vehicles and owners thereof is to be filed.

Minors between 16 and 18 years of age are permitted to operate motor vehicles in special circumstances: if they are emancipated by marriage or if their parents present affidavit in which they accept responsibility for fines said minors may incur and for damages which they may cause.

In case of traffic accidents, code provides for fines or imprisonment or both depending upon seriousness of injuries inflicted upon persons involved.

License plates are required for all motor vehicles, and drivers must obtain license which must be renewed annually.

Tourist may, upon filing an application, bring his motor car into country free of custom duties for maximum period of 90 days provided said vehicle will be used solely for personal and not commercial purposes. After 90 day period has elapsed, owner must pay custom duties required to import motor vehicles into country.

NEGOTIABLE INSTRUMENTS:

See topic Bills and Notes.

NOTARIES PUBLIC:

Notaries are appointed by Supreme Court for life, one or more for each commune according to population. Appointee must have degree as lawyer or notary. Certain documents executed before notary must have two witnesses, residents in commune. Notary cannot act in documents in which relatives of notary by consanguinity or affinity in direct line or to fourth degree in collateral line are parties; neither can his employees be witnesses to wills executed before him. (C.C. 975). Notary retains original document as part of his notarial record and delivers to interested parties certified copies which have force of originals. (Law 301 of June 18, 1964).

PARTNERSHIP:

(C. Com. 18-55; C. C. 1832-1873).

Partnerships may be formed by notarial instruments or private instruments. A notarial copy, if the partnership was formed before a notary, or a duplicate, if formed by private instrument, must be filed in the court of the places where the partnership is established and an extract must be published in the newspapers. If the capital of a limited partnership is represented by shares, additional data must be filed regarding the subscription of the capital.

General partnership (compaõnía en nombre colectivo) is one in which the partners have unlimited liability for the engagements of the partnership.

Limited partnership (compaĩnía en comandita) is one in which there are partners not liable beyond their contribution to partnership. Special partner can have no part in management even under power of attorney. Capital of limited partnerships may be represented by shares, in which case limited partnership is called "compaĩnía en comandita por acciones." Face value of such shares cannot be less than DR$5 per share. (art. 51)

Government Authorization.—All persons and companies desiring to engage in commercial or industrial activities must obtain an authorization from the Department of Labor and Industry. For that purpose an application must be filed giving data as to the partners or stockholders and a governmental certificate must be obtained (Law 5260 of 1959).

Civil partnership (sociedad civil) is one constituted for other than mercantile purposes and is governed by the rules of the Civil Code. One partner cannot obligate the others without a power of attorney and in dealing with third persons the contracting partners are liable for equal amounts, unless otherwise stipulated.

PATENTS:

(Laws 4994 of Apr. 26, 1911 as am'd and 5613 of Aug. 25, 1961).

Patents may be granted for any new discovery or invention comprising: (a) New methods of manufacturing industrial products; (b) new apparatus for manufacturing such products; (c) discovery of a new industrial product and application of perfected methods in order to obtain better results than those known; or (d) pharmaceutical compositions if approved by the medical board of the Republic. No patents are granted for credit or financial plans or combinations. The duration of patents may be five, ten or 15 years. Patents of five or ten years may be extended to 15 years on paying difference in fees. Rights to patent are lost if discovery or invention is not exploited in Republic in five years or if exploitation ceases for three consecutive years, or if owner of patent imports articles manufactured abroad similar to those patented.

The author of an invention patented abroad may obtain a patent in the Republic, but its duration cannot extend beyond that of the foreign patent. Patents are void if the discovery, invention or application is not new, or conflicts with public order, security, morals or the laws.

Dominican Republic is a party to Convention on inventions, patents, designs and industrial models (Buenos Aires, 1910), and to Paris Convention for protection of industrial property of Mar. 20, 1883 (Law 912 of May 4, 1928).

PLEDGES:

(C. C. 2071-2084; C. Com. 91-93, 109; Law 249 of Apr. 8, 1943 and Law 6186 of Feb. 12, 1963).

Pledge normally requires delivery of pledged object to the creditor or to a third person and a written document duly recorded, and if the pledge is placed on a nonnegotiable credit, it requires also notice to debtor. Creditor may not dispose of pledged property nor appropriate it even if authorized by the contract, but he may request appraisal made by two experts appointed by court and have it sold there at public auction or given to him for payment pro tanto.

Pledge given to secure a commercial transaction may be constituted and proved by any evidentiary means, including a written document, correspondence, entries in books of accounts and even witnesses, if court rules them admissible. Pledge of a negotiable instrument may be constituted by an endorsement in guarantee; if of a registered share of stock, by transfer in guarantee recorded in books of the corporation; if a nonnegotiable credit as stated above for noncommercial transactions. Delivery of the pledged article or document is a requisite. In case of default and after eight days notice given to pledgor, sale of the pledged property may be made at public auction through exchange agents or brokers or by other officers if designated by the court.

"Pledge without delivery" may be established under Law 6186 upon agricultural products, harvested or not, livestock and products therefrom and on equipment and machinery in general, the guarantee being limited to 70% of the objects pledged. This pledge requires a document before Justice of the Peace, in duplicate and must be recorded with Justice of the Peace of domicile of the debtor. These contracts are negotiable and may be transferred by endorsement. Debtor acts as depositary and must place the objects at disposal of the court for sale upon requirement unless he pays immediately.

Merchandise deposited in warehouses, under authority of the same Law 6186, may not be transferred or pledged but warrants or certificates issued by the warehouse may be so affected by endorsement.

Banks and agricultural associations may grant credits to groups of farmers, with certain limitations as to amounts, with a "universal pledge" regulated by the same Law 6186.

PRESCRIPTION:

(C. C. 1304, 2219-2279; C. Com. 189, 430-434).

The acquisition of property or rights by virtue of possession and the extinction of obligations by failure to require performance is called prescription. Prescription may be waived as far as it has run, but it cannot be waived in advance. Prescription must be specifically pleaded and may be alleged at any time unless circumstances show that it has been waived. Prescription may run against the state, public establishments and municipalities.

In general, in order to acquire by prescription it is necessary to possess continually, uninterruptedly, quietly, publicly, unmistakably and as owner. Possession originating in violence is not deemed to begin for prescriptive purposes until the violence ceases. Natural interruption occurs when the possessor is deprived of the enjoyment of the property for over a year by the former owner or by a third person; civil interruption occurs in case of the institution of a suit at law. Ownership of real property is acquired by possession with title and in good faith in five years if the real owner is a resident of the judicial district where the property is located and in ten years if he lives outside of the district; and it may be acquired in 20 years without title or good faith. Possession of personal property is equivalent to title but the real owner may recover it in three years.

Actions.—The prescriptive periods in which rights of action are lost vary according to the nature of the action. Some of the more important are: (1) All real and personal actions for which no other period is designated, 20 years; (2) actions to annul or rescind contracts, actions of wards against guardians, actions relating to bills of exchange or acts of commerce, five years; (3) actions of lawyers for fees, two years; (4) actions of physicians, druggists, bailiffs, merchants (for goods sold to nonmerchants), teachers, and servants under yearly contract, actions for maritime freight, sailors' wages, supplies and materials advanced for ships, and work done on ships, and actions for delivery of merchandise carried, one year; (5) actions of teachers for monthly lessons, by innkeepers and workmen, tort actions, and actions on unpaid checks, six months.

PRINCIPAL AND AGENT:

A power of attorney may be given by notarial document or by private writing and may be oral in matters of 30 pesos or less. A general power of attorney grants only powers of administration. Power to alienate, mortgage, or perform other acts of ownership must be specifically conferred. An agent appointing a substitute is liable for the acts of the latter if he was not empowered to appoint the substitute or if the substitute was notoriously incompetent. An agency terminates by (a) revocation, (b) resignation of the agent or (c) death, incompetency or insolvency of principal or agent. The appointment of a new agent for the same matter implies a revocation as to the previous agent from the time the latter was notified thereof. Commission merchants have a lien for their expenses on the merchandise consigned to them. (C. C. 1984-2010; C. Com. 94, 95).

Relationship between local agents or distributors of foreign firms and their principals is regulated by Law 173 of Apr. 6, 1966, as am'd; and Law 622 of Dec. 23, 1973. Agency contract cannot be terminated at will by principal without payment of due

PRINCIPAL AND AGENT . . . *continued*
compensation, unless for "just cause" as defined in this law. Compensation includes actual value of all investments and expenses agent incurred in establishing and operating business, value of inventory, value of agents' lost profits; principal may also be required to pay amount equivalent to five years gross earnings; if contract is less than five years, additional compensation is equal to five times average annual profit during actual number of years.

Establishment of foreign companies in Dominican Republic is subject to special requirements if activity concerns importation and/or distribution of foreign merchandise.

RECORDS:

The Torrens System of land registration is in force. (Land Registry Law 1542 of Oct. 11, 1947 as am'd, Law 4479 of 1956). Titles which have not yet been passed on by land court may be transferred, encumbered and recorded according to legislation previously existing, but are often in confused condition.

Vital Statistics.—There is a "registry of the civil status" for recording births, marriages and deaths. (Laws 659 of July 17, 1944 as am'd).

SALES (Realty and Personalty):

A sale is perfected when the parties have agreed on the object and the price, although neither has been delivered. The seller guarantees the title and warrants against hidden defects unless otherwise stipulated. The right to repurchase cannot be reserved for over five years; if a longer period is designated it is reduced to five years. (C. C. 1582-1701; C. Com. 109). See also topic Assignments.

Conditional sales of personalty possible of identification, under condition that title shall remain in vendor until payment of price or fulfilment of some other condition, must be recorded by vendor in special registry within 30 days. Such record creates lien but it may be cancelled by owner at any time or by purchaser if he proves he has acquired ownership of property sold. If condition is not fulfilled, vendor may cancel sale and seize object. In such cases parties, by mutual agreement or through experts, must liquidate accounts, taking into consideration condition of object, amount payable for its use, sums paid on account and other factors. Vendors must obtain special permit to engage in business. Each transaction subject to 1/2% tax on price. (Law 483 of Nov. 9, 1964, as am'd).

Conditional sales of realty must specify the proportion of the consideration to be returned by the vendor if the sale is canceled, which proportion cannot be less than 60% of the amounts paid. In case of cancellation, the vendor may acquire improvements erected on the property by the vendee, at a discount of 20% from their value at time of cancellation. (Law 596 of Oct. 31, 1941).

Administration with Promise of Sale.—Realty and personalty may be delivered for administration with an option to purchase. The contract need not be recorded, but the signatures require notarial certification. (Law 4969 of Aug. 7, 1958)

SEALS:

Seals are not used in private contracts. Notarial instruments have most of the effects of sealed instruments in the United States.

SHIPPING:

National vessels are: Those matriculated as such in port captaincies and those seized in war or by court action. Dominican vessels navigating between foreign ports must visit a Dominican port at least every six months. Coastwise trade is restricted to national vessels. Dominican persons or companies owning Dominican vessels may sell them or change the flag on payment of 1% of their value. They may purchase foreign vessels abroad and obtain a certificate from Dominican consul authorizing vessel to proceed to a Dominican port and be examined and registered. Nationals and foreigners, in order to serve in the merchant marine, must be registered in the port captaincy. (Coast Guard Law No. 3003 of 1951). Maritime contracts and liens, the rights and duties of captains and crews and other admiralty matters are regulated in the Code of Commerce (arts. 190-436), the provisions of which are similar to those of the French law. The Republic has adopted the international conventions relating to Maritime Collisions and Assistance, approved in London in 1948 and in Brussels in 1910 and 1921.

STATUTES:

Codes of Dominican Republic are Civil Code; Code of Civil Procedure; Code of Commerce; Penal Code; Code of Criminal Procedure; Tax Code and Labor Code. Current laws are published in government paper, "Gaceta Oficial."

TAXATION:

(Tax Code, Law 11-92 of May 15, 1992 and regulations of Oct. 6 and 26, 1993 and Nov. 18, 1993).

Tax Code includes general provisions, proceedings and sanctions; income tax; tax on transfer of manufactured products and services; and consumers tax.

Income Tax.—Subject to tax are: individuals, juridical persons resident or domiciled in Dominican Republic, and undivided estates of decedents whose last domicile was in Dominican Republic, all income from local sources and foreign income from investment and financial profits. Nonresidents or non-domiciled individuals and juridical persons are taxed on income from Dominican Republic sources. Law distinguishes among income from local sources: income from capital investment property or rights, situated or economically used in country; from commercial, industrial, mining, and similar activities; from personal services; from exploitation of industrial property or know-how; from technical assistance; from lease; from loans; income from export and import as determined by law.

Presumed Income.—In case of foreign transportation companies operating in country to other countries presumed income is 10% of gross amount of fares and freight; for insurance companies domiciled or not, presumed income is 10% of gross premium received; producer, for distributors or agents of foreign films presumed income is 15% of price paid; for communication companies, presumed income is 15% of gross income; forestry, agricultural and cattle activities, presumed income is 10% of real estate value as determined by law.

Exempt Income.—Among income exempted from tax is: income received by State and its subdivisions, by chambers of commerce and production, by religious and charitable institutions, by sport associations; workers compensation, severance, unemployment, life insurance proceeds, alimony, inheritance and donations; stock dividends paid by corporation; amounts received by companies for increases of capital; interest received by individuals from financial institutions established in country.

Gross Income includes: salaries, fees, commissions, gains from transfer of goods, pensions, interests, rents, royalties.

Among deductions permitted: expenses necessary to produce income, interest, taxes and fees, risk insurance premiums, casualty losses due to Acts of God or force majeure, bad debts; donations to charity institutions, funds for research, losses; contributions to pension and retirement plans; depreciation calculated according to law.

No deduction is allowed for personal expenses of owner, partner or manager, profits used to increase capital, income tax, losses caused by illegal activities; general expenses unless of trustworthy documents or vouchers; payment of profits or salary or any remuneration or compensation to owner, partner, shareholder or to his spouse or relative in excess of normal payments for services rendered, and without effective proof of performance of duty.

Capital gains from transfer of personal property as well as gains derived from transfer of real property are subject to tax as provided by law.

Rates.—Individuals and undivided estates up to three years from deceased's death are taxed at rates of 15%, 20% and 25%. Juridical persons and undivided estates after three years of deceased's death are taxed at 25% rate. Permanent establishment of foreign companies are taxed at 25%.

Withholding Tax.—Payments to nonresident or non-domiciled persons are subject to withholding tax of 25% with certain exceptions, including interest at 15%. Payments to resident individuals and undivided estates are subject to withholding tax of 20% for rents, 10% for fees for personal service; 15% for National Lottery prizes; 2% for transfer of real and personal property; 10% for any other payments except dividends. Payments of dividends to individuals or juridical persons, residents or not, domiciled or not are subject to withholding tax of 25%.

Tax Credits.—Taxpayers may deduct on their returns income tax paid abroad, withholdings, advance payments of tax. Employers are taxed at 25% on value of additional compensation paid to employees, such as education, life and health insurance premiums, rent, car, salaries of domestic personnel, discounts.

Tax on Transfer of Manufactured Products and Services.—Tax is levied on transfer and importation of manufactured products and services. Among exempted products are foodstuffs, books, newspapers, medicines, petroleum, fertilizers, insecticides. Taxed services are telecommunications, lodging, restaurant, night clubs, leasing, among others. Rate is 8%.

Consumer Tax.—Tax is levied on transfer of some locally produced goods at manufacturer's level, and import of some goods, and services. Transfers made for consideration, or disposal of merchandise by owners for any purpose are taxed. Exempted are products for personal use, samples, temporary imports. Alcoholic beverages and tobaccos locally produced are taxed at 10% ad valorem. Imported wines, tobacco, toiletries, rugs, carpets, precious stones, jewelry, domestic appliances, motor vehicles among others are taxed at rates ranging from 5% to 80%. Services are taxed: national and international telecommunications and insurance at 10%, air transportation at 20%, hotel services at 5%.

Tax Incentives.—All tax exemptions for reinvestment of dividends on industrial projects were abolished. Tax exemption granted to industries under repealed incentives laws remain in force for three years.

Real Estate Transfer Tax (Law 32 of Oct. 14, 1974).—All transfers, including conditional sales and expropriations, of real estate are subjected to 2% on value of transaction.

Tax on Luxury Houses and Urban Vacant Lots.—(Law 18 of Feb. 5, 1988 as am'd and regulations of Oct. 6, 1993). Tax is levied on luxury houses worth DR$500,000 or more and all urban vacant lots. Tax rate is 0.50%, except for luxury houses occupied by owners or transferred to ascendants or descendants, in which case, tax rate is 0.25%.

Inheritance and gift taxes depend on degree of relationship and amount involved. They range from 1% on amounts of from DR$500 to DR$2,000 in favor of relatives in the direct line, to 32% on amounts of over DR$500,000 in favor of collaterals beyond the third degree and unrelated persons. If beneficiary resides abroad the tax is paid with 50% surcharge. (Laws 2569 of Dec. 4, 1950, as am'd). Archives, libraries and certain book collections owned by private individuals, when dedicated to promotion of culture on non-lucrative basis, are exempt from this tax. (Law 473 of Nov. 2, 1964).

Stamp Tax.—(Law 2254 of Feb. 14, 1950 as am'd). Most contracts and transactions are subject to this tax. Amounts depend on nature of documents and sum involved, general rate for most contracts is 0.2% of contracted value, but special rates apply to numerous other documents.

Licenses.—Every physical or juridical person carrying on any occupation, business or profession must annually obtain a license, called patente, paying the fee designated in law. (Law 213 of May 8, 1984 as am'd).

Free Zones.—(Law 8-90 of Jan. 15, 1990 as am'd). National or foreign individual or legal entity may establish and manage free zones, and operate in free zones by special authorization. Free zones are created for manufacture of goods and services for export. All types of industries, trading centers and services are allowed to operate there, with few exceptions. They are exempted from income tax, import and export taxes and duties, consumers tax and tax on transfer of manufactured products and services, for 20 years when located in border area and for 15 years when located in any other part of country. Companies are allowed to sell in domestic market up to 20% of their production, and unlimited amount of goods if they contain at least 25% of local imputs, subject to payment of import duties. They are also allowed to buy from

See Topical Index in front part of this volume.

TAXATION . . . *continued*
local suppliers raw materials and semi-elaborated goods and services, exempted from import duties, with some exceptions. Law has special provisions for termination of operations in free zones. Infringement of law can carry cancelation of authorization to operate or to export, or imposition of fine.

Law 69 of Nov. 16, 1979 as am'd and its regulations, Decree 1609 of Mar. 13, 1980 as am'd by Decree 1460 of Oct. 5, 1983 establish tax incentives for export of some nontraditional products and also regulate temporary duty-free import.

Law 532 of Dec. 12, 1969 as am'd, was enacted to promote investment in agriculture and ranching. Tax exemption is given for importing agricultural and fishing machinery and equipment, fencing wire, automatic milking machines and similar equipment, for imports of cattle, fertile eggs, veterinary medicines and concentrated feed products. Regulations provide for extension of roads, electrical networks, new schools, insurance and availability of financing from government. Such financing is not obtainable by aliens or foreign corporations.

Tourism.—Organic Law of Tourism is contained in Law 541 of Dec. 31, 1969. Its purposes are to promote foreign and national tourism within Republic. Foreign tourist agencies must obtain authorization from Department of National Tourism ("Dirección Nacional de Turismo") to maintain offices or engage in activities within country. Jurisdiction of Department comprises hotels, restaurants, tourist guides, chauffeurs, souvenir stores and entertainment enterprises.

Law 542 of Dec. 31, 1969, created Hotel and Tourist Incentive Corporation ("Corporación de Fomento de la Industria Hotelera y Desarrollo del Turismo"). Its purposes are to promote acquisition, construction and conservation of hotel and tourist services. Loans are obtainable from Corporation to finance projects if specified prerequisites are complied with. Maximum period of 20 years for repayment is exacted, except for unusual circumstances. Loan itself may not exceed 40% of value of property pledged as collateral.

See also topic Mines and Minerals.

TRADEMARKS AND TRADENAMES:

Trademark may consist of any distinctive mark on the articles involved or their containers, but cannot comprise: (a) Arms or public insignia, national or foreign; (b) a name which the petitioner may not legally use; (c) the indication of a locality which is not the origin of the article; (d) words or designs offensive to individuals or public decorum, or referring to some person without his express consent; (e) the reproduction or imitation of a mark already registered for an article of the same kind. Likewise the following cannot be registered as trademarks: (a) the form or color of the product or container; (b) terms in general use; (c) designations used to distinguish the kind of products; (d) geographic names standing alone. A trademark must be registered in the Department of the Treasury and Commerce and may be designated to continue for five, ten, 15, or 20 years, at the end of which period it may be renewed. It is lost if not used within one year. (Law 1450 of Dec. 30, 1937 as am'd).

Dominican Republic is a party to Convention for protection of commercial, industrial and agricultural trademarks and commercial names (Santiago de Chile, 1923), and to Paris convention for protection of industrial property, of Mar. 20, 1883 (Law 912 of May 4, 1928).

See also Part VII of this volume.

TREATIES:

Dominican Republic is a party, among others, to following:

Multilateral.—Convention on private international law, Havana, 1928 (Bustamante Code); Inter-American Convention of Conflict of Laws concerning bills of exchange. Signed in Panama on Jan. 30, 1975; Inter-American Convention on legal regime of powers of attorney to be used abroad. Signed in Panama on Jan. 30, 1975; Multilateral Trade Negotiations, The Uruguay Round, Final Act, Marrakesh, Apr. 15, 1994 and Agreement Establishing the World Trade Organization, Marrakesh, Apr. 15, 1995.

Bilateral.—With U.S.A.: Agreement of May 2, 1962, on investment guaranties (13 UST 440, TIAS 5005). See also topics Copyright; Patents; Trademarks and Tradenames. With Canada: Convention of Aug. 6, 1976 for avoidance of double taxation and prevention of fiscal evasion with respect to taxes on income and on capital.

Dominican Republic is not a party to following: (1) Convention on Service Abroad of Judicial and Extrajudicial Documents in Civil or Commercial Matters; (2) Convention on Taking of Evidence Abroad in Civil or Commercial Matters; (3) United Nations Convention on Recognition and Enforcement of Foreign Arbitral Awards.

See also Part VII of this volume.

TRUSTS:

Trusts as developed in the common law are unknown. Testamentary trusts are prohibited, but property may be given or left to children or to brothers or sisters with the provision that it shall pass to their children, or given or left to a third person until the testator's children reach majority. (C. C. 896-898, 1048-1058; Law 356 of 1940)

USURY: See topic Interest.

VITAL STATISTICS: See topic Records.

WILLS:

(C. C. 893-930, 967-1074).

All persons of sound mind may make wills. Minors under 16 are subject to restrictions, and those over 16 may dispose of only half of the property of which an adult might dispose. Wills are (1) holographic, (2) by public act or (3) secret. Witnesses must be of age, Dominican citizens and in possession of their civil rights.

Holographic will is one entirely in the handwriting of the testator.

Will by public act is made before one or two notaries and two witnesses. It is written out by one of notaries, read to testator in presence of witnesses and signed by those present, but in country districts only one witness need sign if there are two notaries, or two witnesses if there is one notary. Legatees cannot be witnesses, nor their relatives to fourth degree, nor clerks of notary.

Secret will is written by the testator himself or by another for him and signed by him and enclosed in a sealed paper. In the presence of six witnesses the testator presents it to the notary, who writes a minute on the envelope which all sign.

Special wills may be made by soldiers, or on board vessels, or in case of epidemics.

Foreign Wills.—Dominican abroad may make holographic will or will in form which is legal in foreign locality. Wills made abroad cannot affect property in Republic until they are registered at testator's last known residence in Republic. If they contain provisions relating to real estate in Republic they must also be recorded in locality where such real estate is situated.

Testamentary Dispositions.—The testator may dispose freely of only such part of his estate as is not by law reserved to his heirs. The part of which he may so dispose is one-half if he leaves one legitimate child or descendants thereof, or both paternal and maternal ascendants; one-third if two children; one-fourth if three or more children; three-fourths if ascendants in only single line. Reserved part goes to children or ascendants. If he leaves neither descendants nor ascendants, he may dispose freely of entire estate.

ECUADOR LAW DIGEST REVISER

Curtis, Mallet-Prevost, Colt & Mosle
101 Park Avenue
New York, New York 10178-0061
Telephone: 212-696-6141
Fax: 212-697-1559
Email: CMP-NY@mcimail.com

Reviser Profile

The Firm began in 1830 when two practicing lawyers started a long line of lawyers and law firms extending in an unbroken chain up to the present time. In 1897, the firm name became Curtis, Mallet-Prevost & Colt; in 1925 it was changed to Curtis, Mallet-Prevost, Colt & Mosle. The Firm is now made up of approximately 120 lawyers, including experts who have published extensively on such diverse subjects as international money management, transnational contracts, state contracts, litigation against foreign states, sovereign immunity and the act of state doctrine, and the International Court of Justice. Its principal offices are in New York City. There are branch offices in Paris, London, Frankfurt Am Main, Hong Kong, Washington, D.C., Houston, Texas, Newark, N.J., and Mexico City. The Firm has five departments: Corporate and International; Litigation; Real Estate; Tax; and Trusts and Estates. The corporate and international department acts as general counsel to various public and private corporations and individual entrepreneurs. Clients are in the banking, insurance, securities, manufacturing, real estate and oil and gas industries. In addition, the corporate and international department frequently acts as special counsel to domestic and foreign clients, providing assistance in financing, know-how licensing, the negotiation and drafting of all types of contracts and instruments, counselling on all aspects of corporate law, and establishing the vehicles necessary to enable clients to conduct their domestic and foreign business activities. The Firm's international work permeates all areas of its practice and involves questions of private international law, foreign law and an unusual amount of public and quasi-public international law. Traditionally, much of the Firm's international practice has been concerned with Latin America. The Firm maintains its excellence in that area, with its Mexican affiliate, and also through the expertise of Latin America lawyers based in the New York office. The Firm's international practice has undergone a major expansion beyond Latin America to Europe, Africa and the Near and Far East. The Firm's litigation practice includes commercial litigation and arbitration, and white-collar criminal defense. It has substantial experience in civil aviation matters; it also has represented foreign States in transnational litigation and international arbitration arising out of acts of nationalization and alleged breach of economic development or natural resource supply contracts. Among the Firm's clients in real estate matters are institutional lenders and investors, real estate developers, both individual and corporate, foreign and domestic investors and syndicators. The tax department has substantial experience in all aspects of domestic and international business tax matters and real estate taxation. The matters the tax department deals with on a regular basis include: Taxation of foreign investments; the structuring of corporate transactions, including mergers, acquisitions, liquidations and reorganization; federal and state tax litigation; and tax planning for U.S. and foreign individuals. The trusts and estates department engages in general domestic trusts and estates practice and in tax planning for foreign persons wishing to invest in U.S. assets through offshore trusts and corporations. It represents individuals, trust companies, and banks acting as fiduciaries. It works for various charitable organizations located both in the United States and abroad including private foundations, museums, universities and hospitals. A group of fiduciary accountants with vast experience in the field assists the lawyers of the trusts and estates departments. Curtis, Mallet-Prevost, Colt & Mosle has served as a Reviser for most of Latin American Law Digests since 1930.

ECUADOR LAW DIGEST

(The following is a list of all Topics, including cross-references, covered in this Digest.)

ECUADOR LAW DIGEST

Revised for 1997 edition by

CURTIS, MALLET-PREVOST, COLT & MOSLE, of the New York Bar.

(Abbreviations used are: C. C., Civil Code; C.M., Code of Minors; C. Com., Code of Commerce; C. C. P., Code of Civil Procedure. Numbers refer to articles of these codes.)

ABSENTEES: See topic Death.

ACKNOWLEDGMENTS:

Formal documents are executed before a notary public who retains original and issues certified copies. In addition, signatures on private documents may be acknowledged before notary public. Form of instruments is determined by law of place where they are executed, but where Ecuador laws require a public instrument, no private writings will be accepted. Instruments executed abroad require authentication by Ecuadorean diplomatic or consular officers. (C. C. 16, 17; C. C. P. 194 and Decree 1404 of Oct. 26, 1966 as am'd. See also topics Notaries Public; Public and Private Instruments.

ACTIONS:

Actions for Death.—See topic Death.

Limitation of.—See topic Prescription.

ADMINISTRATION:

See topic Executors and Administrators.

ADOPTION:

(C. C. 332-348; C.M. 103-129).

Adoption is institution by virtue of which a person called adopting party acquires rights and duties of a parent towards a minor called adopted party.

Any person over 25 may adopt minor under 21 years, provided he is at least 14 years older than such minor and obtains consent of parents and court. Widowers, single or divorced persons may adopt only minors of same sex of adopting party, unless adopting party is 30 years older than adopted party. Married people can adopt minors of any sex provided consent of both spouses is given.

Rights and obligations of adopted children are generally same as those of legitimate children; however they have no rights of inheritance from relatives of adoptive parent nor does adoptive parent inherit property of adopted child, or of his relatives. Adoptive child does not lose any of his rights towards his natural parents or relatives.

Adoption can be revoked: (a) When both parties agree to do so, if adopted is 18 years of age, and (b) in case of ingratitude of adopted.

ADVERSE POSSESSION: See topic Prescription.

AGENCY: See topic Principal and Agent.

ALIENS:

Aliens in general enjoy the same civil rights as citizens. Entry of paupers, criminals, etc., is prohibited and government may expel aliens who take part in Ecuador politics or are guilty of crime or whose presence is considered menace to morals or public order. All aliens must register with Registry of Aliens within 30 days of their arrival. Immigrant aliens must prove minimum income per month or provide certain other guaranties and must obtain identity card. Nonimmigrant aliens may be granted up to three month renewable visa. (Const., art. 18; Decrees 1897 and 1900, Dec. 27, 1971 as am'd, Decree 1991 of June 30, 1986 as am'd). Latin Americans and Spaniards by birth domiciled in Ecuador may apply for Ecuadorean citizenship without loss of their own, under certain conditions. (Const., art. 9).

See also topics Corporations; Descent and Distribution; Mines and Minerals.

ALIMONY: See topic Divorce.

ASSIGNMENTS:

Title to personal property and rights may be transferred by public or private instruments. (See topics Deeds; Public and Private Instruments; Sales [Realty and Personalty].) The assignment of a credit is not effective with respect to the debtor or third persons until the debtor has been notified or has acknowledged the assignment. (C. C. 1868-1876; C. C. P. 99).

ASSIGNMENTS FOR BENEFIT OF CREDITORS:

Assignment of all his property for benefit of creditors may be made by non-merchant debtor who as result of inevitable accident is unable to meet his liabilities. Assignment procedure shall be administered by court. Creditors must accept it unless debtor has been guilty of culpable actions. Effect of assignment is to relieve debtor from attachments and to extinguish his debts as far as they can be paid from assigned property, but he continues liable for balance. Assignment does not transfer title to creditors but authorizes them to dispose of property or administer it. Merchants cannot assign for benefit of creditors; any request to do so causes them to be considered bankrupts. (C. C. 1657-1667; C. C. P. 514-525). See topic Bankruptcy and Insolvency.

ATTACHMENT:

Attachments may issue in summary actions on obligations clearly appearing from certain instruments having executory force such as confessions under oath before a judicial authority, judgments, first copies of public instruments, private documents acknowledged in court, bills of exchange, wills, etc. Third persons may intervene if their rights would be directly impaired. If the intervenor claims the ownership of the property attached the proceedings are stayed until the question is decided; if the intervention is based on other grounds, the proceedings continue, but the proceeds of sale may be impounded if the intervenor's rights are based on an instrument having executory force.

Sequestration or retention of the property which is the subject of the litigation or guarantees the credit may be ordered if (1) the credit is proved by documentary evidence and (2) it is proved that the debtor's property is insufficient to cover the debt or is in danger of disappearing or being hidden or alienated. Likewise, in certain cases the debtor may be restrained from alienating his real property. (C. C. P. 423-428, 912-938).

BANKRUPTCY AND INSOLVENCY:

(C. C. P. 518-613; C. Com. 1012-1024).

Bankruptcy (quiebra) is the name given to insolvency proceedings of merchants. A merchant is considered bankrupt when he makes assignment of all his assets for the benefit of his creditors or when he is insolvent, fails to comply with an order of payment, or to pay his obligations to three or more persons, or to designate property on which an attachment might be levied. There are three kinds of bankruptcy: (1) Fortuitous, when due to fortuitous circumstances; (2) culpable, when caused by imprudent or dissipated conduct; (3) fraudulent, when involving fraudulent acts of the debtor. On declaration of bankruptcy the property of the bankrupt is judicially seized and delivered to a receiver. As a result of the bankruptcy the bankrupt becomes incompetent to administer his property; except family property and one-half of any property acquired later shall be brought to the bankruptcy and the other half left to him for his and family expenses; he may be imprisoned in case of fraud, in any event he may not leave the locality without giving bond. The receiver sells the perishable property and may sell all the assets if the debtor agrees. Meetings of creditors determine whether the receiver should continue the business, resolve as to the classification of credits, and decide on agreements with the bankrupt; these agreements require the vote of two-thirds of the creditors present holding three-fourths of the credits represented at the meeting, or three-fourths of the creditors present holding two-thirds of the credits represented. If there is no agreement, the assets are liquidated and distributed by the receiver. A bankrupt who pays up his debts entirely, or to the extent agreed on, is rehabilitated, but culpable bankrupts can be rehabilitated only after suffering their punishment, and fraudulent bankrupts not until five years after the punishment.

Suspension of payments may be declared in favor of a merchant who, having assets sufficient to cover his liabilities, foresees the possibility of not being able to do so at their maturity. If assets are less than 90% of liabilities or if there were debts due before the petition, bankruptcy must be declared.

Insolvency proceedings (concurso de acreedores) relate to non-merchants. They are instituted when the debtor makes an assignment for the benefit of creditors or when he is deemed insolvent because he fails to pay a judgment or to designate sufficient assets on which an attachment may be levied. Same procedure as with bankruptcy applies.

See also topic Fraudulent Sales and Conveyances.

BANKS AND BANKING:

(General Law of Institutions of Financial System of May 12, 1994, Law on the Monetary Regime and Bank of State, Decree-Law 02 of May 7, 1992 as am'd).

Components of financial system are Central Bank, public and private financial institutions and other institutions controlled by Superintendency of Banks. Monetary Board regulates entire banking and credit system, including Central Bank, and it is highest policy making body within financial system. Board is composed of six members from public and private sector. Superintendency of Banks supervises operation of banks, companies or personal activities, and their compliance with all laws and regulations. Central Bank, under direction of Monetary Board, administers nation's monetary and foreign exchange policies. It also supervises private banks in conjunction with Superintendency of Banks. Central Bank supervises monetary policy through reserve requirements, credit ceilings on commercial bank lending and interest rate ceilings for loans and deposits. Foreign banks may establish branches in Ecuador with prior authorization of Superintendency of Banks.

BILLS AND NOTES:

(Code of Comm., Arts. 410-489).

Bills of exchange must state: (1) The words "bill of exchange" or that it is to order; (2) specific amount; (3) drawee; (4) maturity; (5) place of payment; (6) payee; (7) date and place where drawn; (8) signature of drawer. If no maturity date is expressed the bill is considered a sight draft. A draft may be drawn to the order of the drawer or against the drawer or for account of a third person.

Endorsements must be unconditional and cannot be partial. However, they may be made for collection or in other forms indicating agency. An endorsement specifically made to bearer is void.

Endorsements may be in blank, in which case legal holder is regarded as endorsee; same applies when endorsement is to bearer. They may also be to a specific person.

A draft drawn at a certain period after sight must be presented for acceptance within six months after date unless a different time is determined by drawer or the time is shortened by an endorser. Drawee may ask that draft payable at his domicile be presented to him again for acceptance at another address in same city. Draft may be drawn for payment: (a) At sight; (b) a certain period after sight; (c) a certain period after date; (d) on a specific date. Maturity of a draft payable a specific time after sight is determined by date of presentation. Other kind of maturity or successive maturities render draft null and void. Interest may be promised in drafts payable at sight or term after sight. In others, interest clauses are deemed "not written."

See Topical Index in front part of this volume.

BILLS AND NOTES . . . *continued*

Drafts must be presented for payment on due date or on one of the subsequent three working days. Bearer cannot refuse partial payment but must keep draft until fully paid. Bearer may enforce his rights even before maturity: (a) in case acceptance is refused or of partial acceptance; (b) in case of bankruptcy of drawee or of acceptor. And after maturity for lack of payment. Failure to accept or pay must be proved by a protest in due form. Protest for failure to accept must be made within the three working days following presentation but always before maturity. Protest for failure to pay must be made on one of the three working days after maturity. Sight drafts are only protested for lack of payment and protest should be made day of maturity or within following three working days. After protest for failure to accept it is unnecessary to present draft for payment or to protest for failure to pay. In case of failure to accept or pay judge, notary or broker having intervened in the protest must notify same to other interested persons next day. Drawer may relieve holder from making protest by inscribing on draft words "without protest" or equivalent words.

Promissory notes must state: (1) The words "promissory note" or that it is to order; (2) promise to pay a specific sum; (3) maturity; (4) place of payment; (5) payee; (6) date and place where issued; (7) signature of maker. If no maturity date is expressed the note is considered payable at sight. Most of the provisions regarding bills of exchange are applicable to promissory notes.

Checks.—(Codification in Law of Sept. 20, 1975; Res. SB-95-0076 of Dec. 28, 1995). Checks may be issued only against banks authorized to receive deposits. Drawer must have provision of funds or credit granted. Following requisites are necessary: (a) Word "Check" in language used; (b) unconditional order to pay certain sum of money; (c) name of drawee; (d) place of payment, but if not stated place written beside drawer's names applies and if several, the first; (e) place and date of issue; (f) signature of drawer. Check may be payable to specified person, with or without addition of words "to the order" or "not to the order" or may be to bearer. It may be issued in favor of same drawer. Interest is not includable. If signature of minor or incompetent person appears, check is valid as against other signers. Issuer warrants payment. Unless clause "not to the order" is inserted, check to specified payee is endorsable. Endorsements may not be partial nor may be granted by drawee. Endorsement to bearer is equivalent to blank endorsement. If not made without recourse or similar reservation endorser warrants payment. Except if made "for collection" or other clause showing agency, endorsement transfers all rights, but endorsement after period for presentation on after protest is only assignment. Check is payable always at sight. Checks issued and payable in Ecuador must be presented within 20 days; if issued abroad and payable in Ecuador term is 90 days and if vice versa term follows law of country of issue. Presentation to clearing house is effective. Stop order may be given in writing by drawer to drawee giving reason therefor, at his own risk. If holder has lost check drawer must stop payment. There are provisions on crossed and certified checks. Latter are irrevocable. Check protested within term for presentation gives right to executive action, with immediate attachment and sale for payment. Drawer and endorsers and guarantors are jointly liable, but if check is not presented timely only drawer remains liable, unless he had funds in drawee's hands and these are lost after presentation period, when he becomes discharged. Notice of dishonor must be given by holder to drawer and his endorser within four days of protest.

CHATTEL MORTGAGES:

The law recognizes pledge of chattels, without delivery, with registration, and agricultural and industrial pledges. The former is called "Special Commerce Pledge" and may be granted only to a registered merchant on goods sold by him on credit. It must be executed in duplicate writing with details of persons and goods involved and recorded in a special registry, otherwise it is not binding on third parties. Creditor is entitled to have the thing pledged shown at any time. Failure to comply with his request for 48 hours renders debt due and payable. Proceedings for sale of pledged object are summary. Sale is made by an auctioneer designated by a court, after expert appraisal. Failure to produce object pledged or deliver it for sale, its destruction, transfer or change of place, where it must be kept under the contract, are punishable under Penal Code. Counterpart of the document held by pledgee is negotiable by endorsement and annotation on the margin of the recording entry. Partial payments must be annotated on the same. Debtor may advance payment before due date by tendering principal and interest to date of payment only. Installment with pledge may be made in printed forms and then creditor's counterpart may have detachable coupons exchangeable against the corresponding payment without annotation on the document. Separate bills or notes may be issued for installments. (Law 548-E of Sept. 24, 1963).

Agricultural pledges may be constituted on (a) animals and their increase, (b) fruit pending or gathered, (c) products of forests and agricultural industries and (d) agricultural machinery and utensils. Industrial pledges may be constituted on industrial machinery, installations, tools, utensils and other elements of industrial labor, animals destined for the service of an industry and products industrially transformed. If the pledge relates to pending fruits or objects regarded as real property the consent of mortgage creditors must be obtained. The pledge contract must appear in writing and be recorded in a special registry. In case of default the property is sold by judicial sale. (C. Com. 576-600).

Any person or corporation who habitually deals in contracts permitting repurchases, or loans with pledge, is subject to the supervision of Superintendent of Banks and must give a guarantee bond to obtain a license to operate, being subject to assessment for support of the office of Superintendent, ranging from 15% to 20% of interest or profits obtained, excepting certain institutions and banks. (Law 967 of Nov. 14, 1963).

CLAIMS: See topic Executors and Administrators.

COLLATERAL SECURITY: See topic Pledges.

COMMERCIAL REGISTER:

See topic Records.

COMMUNITY PROPERTY:

See topic Husband and Wife.

CONSTITUTION AND GOVERNMENT:

Codification of May 30, 1996 of Constitution issued by Government on Jan. 15, 1978 as am'd. Republic of Ecuador, form of State in which Ecuadorian Nation is constituted, is unitary, sovereign, independent, and democratic; its government is of the people, representative, elective, responsible and alternating. Official language is Spanish but other native languages are recognized as part of national culture. Capital of Republic is city of Quito. Regarding citizenship, Constitution provides that every Ecuadorian man or woman over 18 years of age is citizen.

Legislative function is exercised by National Congress which is composed of representatives elected by national balloting. National Congress appoints four legislative committees, each one of them having five representatives. Members of National Congress hold office for four years and can be reelected.

Executive power is exercised by President of Republic who represents all States, shall hold office for four years and can be reelected for consecutive period. President is elected by absolute majority of suffrage in direct, universal and secret balloting. Constitution grants special powers and duties to President, among others, to execute and enforce Constitution, laws, decrees and international agreements; to authorize, promulgate or veto laws passed by National Congress and plenary of legislative committees; to maintain internal order; to appoint and freely remove ministers of state, governors of provinces and other administrative officials; to contract and authorize loans; to be chief of police forces; to declare state of emergency and then exercise extraordinary powers, such as ordering collection of taxes and other revenues in advance, closing and establishing ports temporarily, establishing prior censorship for mass media, suspending constitutional guaranties with some exceptions.

Constitution also contains special sections regarding Vice President, Ministers of State and judicial functions.

Civil Rights.—Foreigners have same rights as nationals with limitations established by law and Constitution, but they do not have political rights. Government guarantees its inhabitants following rights, among others: Inviolability of life; personal integrity and right to its total development; right to express thought and opinions freely, provided civil and criminal responsibility are shown. Capital punishment is not allowed, also forbidden is any discrimination for reasons of race, color of skin, language, religion or political opinions; there is equal protection before law, inviolability of home and correspondence, freedom of labor, commerce and industry and freedom to meet and associate together for pacific purposes; freedom to travel in territory of Republic, to change domicile, to leave and return to country; right to keep political and religious convictions secret; personal freedom and safety. Government protects family as fundamental unit of society. Government promotes culture, artistic creativity and scientific research. Education is duty of Government.

CONTRACTS:

Civil Code (arts. 1603-2390) governs civil contracts and applies as second source as well to commercial and labor contracts.

In general, a civil contract may be: unilateral or bilateral; gratuitous or for monetary consideration; commutative; aleatory; principal or accessory; real; formal or consensual.

Object of a contract must be definite or subject to definite determination. Future inheritances and future hereditary rights cannot be object of a contract.

Civil contracts involving more than 2,000 Sucres must be in writing and cannot be proved by parol evidence.

Form of contract is determined by place where executed.

Indemnity for damages includes monetary damages and loss of expected profits.

See topic Principal and Agent.

Public Contracts.—(Const., art. 16, Law 95 of Aug. 14, 1990 as am'd and Decree 2392 of Apr. 26, 1991 as am'd). Contracts executed with government, state agencies and state enterprises are subject to special rules.

CONVEYANCES:

See topics Deeds; Notaries Public; Public and Private Instruments.

COPYRIGHT:

(Decree 610 of July 30, 1976; Decision 351 of Dec. 17, 1993 of Cartagena Commission; Decree 1282-A of Dec. 1, 1993).

Law grants certain intellectual, moral and property rights to author, his successors or assignees, regarding scientific, literary and artistic works. Copyrights include all kinds of intellectual (including software), scientific, literary and artistic creations reproduced by any means. Law also protects translations, adaptations, musical arrangements and other transformation of private intellectual works; to protect these copyright works written authorization from original owner of work is necessary. Performers' rights are also protected. Literary and artistic works, performances and other productions are protected by law without requiring registration. Protection runs for life and 50 years in favor of successors.

Ecuador has ratified the Interamerican Convention of June 22, 1946 (Decree Feb. 1, 1947), Universal Copyright Convention (Decree 476, Dec. 31, 1956).

CORPORATIONS:

(Codification in Law of June 28, 1977 as am'd).

Organization and Authorization.—Corporation may be formed by public subscription, subject to detailed rules, specially as to appraisal of property contributed and approval of same and to first meeting of subscribers and document of organization and it must also comply with the requisites of a simultaneous corporate organization. Corporation may also be formed by simultaneous organization, in a public document containing articles of incorporation, which then must be submitted to Superintendencia de Compaõnías who approves them and orders document to be recorded in Registry of Commerce. Same procedure is required for any amendment, extension or dissolution before end of term. Document containing articles of incorporation must state: (1) Place and date of execution; (2) nationality and domicile of incorporators, who must be five

See Topical Index in front part of this volume.

CORPORATIONS . . . *continued*
or more; (3) corporate object specifically stated; (4) name, which must refer to principal object and to which words "Compañía Anónima" or "Sociedad Anónima," or initials "C.A." or "S.A." respectively, must be added and term of duration which must be for a limited period of time; (5) corporate capital; number of shares of stock and par value of each share; classes, if several; (6) subscription of capital; amounts paid in cash or in property and value attributed to latter; (7) domicile of corporation (corporations and other companies constituted in Ecuador must have their principal domicile in Ecuador); (8) form of administration and power of administrator; (9) time and form for calls to stockholders' meetings; (10) form to elect administrators and statement as to who will be officer having legal representation; (11) rules for distribution of profits; (12) cases in which corporation may be dissolved before its term lapses; and (13) how liquidators will be elected. Articles of incorporation must also be published. Corporations are under supervision of Superintendency of Corporations. Authorization granted to corporation may be revoked by violation of law or by-laws. Upon revocation corporation is dissolved and liquidated.

A corporation may be transformed into a company of mixed public and private ownership (compañía de economia mixta).

Mixed public and private companies (compañías de economia mixta) may be exonerated from payment of taxes and stamps.

Foreign and domestic companies, supervised by Superintendencia de Compañías must pay annual contribution to offset that institution's expenses. That amount is determined by value of company's assets. In case of foreign companies, only assets within Ecuador are considered. Contribution will not exceed .1% of value of assets per year. Mixed public-private enterprises and public utility companies pay 50% of normal contribution. Penalty interest is levied on delayed payments.

Each year, a company must supply to Superintendency the following: (a) annual general balance; (b) statement of profits and losses; (c) annual report; (d) names of administrators and legal representatives; (e) names of stockholders, recorded in stock book; (f) financial movements of goods and services; (g) other specified data. Superintendency may furnish government officials final report on information submitted by companies doing business with government or its agencies. (L. 122 of Mar. 3, 1983).

Companies which do not supply necessary information, and thereby call into question their legal status, may be divested of all legal rights. Superintendency may initiate liquidation proceedings and designate a stockholder's meeting for naming of liquidators. Five years from date of dissolution, Superintendent will notify Registrar of Commerce (Registrador Mercantil) of termination of company's existence.

Management.—Corporation is managed by administrators who need not be shareholders. They are subject to removal and their services may be remunerated. They are regarded as agents. Office of administrator cannot be held by company's bankers, constructors, lessees or purveyors of material. Administrators cannot perform for corporation any transaction falling outside its purpose; they cannot transact any business with company for their personal account and, unless authorized, they cannot delegate their administrative duties, but may appoint attorneys in fact for special matters. They are severally liable for truth of original stock subscriptions and payments, existence of dividends declared, existence and accuracy of corporation's books, compliance with stockholders meeting's resolutions and duties required by law or corporate documents, and any damage suffered through their fault.

Dividends can be paid only out of collected earnings. At least 10% of annual net profits must be set aside for a legal reserve fund until same amounts to at least 50% of capital. 50% of annual net profits must also be set aside for payment of dividends to shareholders, unless unanimous resolution to contrary taken in a general shareholders meeting.

Shareholders' meetings must be held at least once a year. Quorum for different purposes is determined by by-laws, but at least one half of paid-in capital must be represented at first call; if a smaller amount appears, a second call is issued, whereupon any amount of capital constitutes a quorum. Shareholders may be represented by addressing letter to administrator, or power of attorney, unless otherwise provided by articles of incorporation. Administrators cannot represent shareholders. Shareholders appoint auditors to examine books and operations of corporation. Minority of 25% of shareholders may appeal to courts against decisions of majority.

If capital diminishes by one half or more, corporation must be liquidated unless shareholders prefer to make up difference or reduce capital to the actual figure, provided it is enough to attain corporation's objectives and not less than minimum.

Stock.—To constitute a corporation it is necessary that the entire capital be subscribed by at least five stockholders and that at least one fourth of capital be paid in. Shares may be divided in classes with preferences and must be registered; shares may be paid in cash or in property, provided latter is suitable for purposes of corporation and if it consists in credits transferor must warrant its existence and legality and solvency of debtor. Shareholders are liable only for unpaid portion of their stock. Until fully paid in, subscribers of shares are liable for amount subscribed even though they assign shares. Shares are registered, but while not fully paid no definitive certificate may be issued.

Foreign companies require authorization to do business in Ecuador: corporations and limited partnerships issuing shares of stock must secure approval of Superintendencia de Compañías, others of local judge. To obtain such approval they must file a copy of their corporate documents and a certificate of Ecuadorean consul that company is duly constituted and authorized to act in country of its domicile and that it is empowered to do business abroad, and certificate of bank deposit in capital integration account for total amount appointed for activities in country which would never be less than legal minimum. Said fund can only be reduced by same rules governing reductions of capital. All companies, both national and foreign must have a fully authorized representative in Ecuador registered with Registry of Commerce to carry out all business and especially to answer claims and fulfill all obligations. If representative is a foreigner he must be a resident of country. Power of attorney of said representative must also be recorded. Company which contracts obligations to be fulfilled in Ecuador and has no representative there may be regarded as an absconding debtor and curator may be appointed for it. All foreign companies in order to contract with government must be domiciled in country.

Financial corporations must be incorporated as Sociedades Anónimas (S. A.), with domicile in Ecuador. Industrial development of country either with national or foreign capital must be their principal objective. Government will guarantee long term foreign loans for economic development, made to private or mixed national industries. Nondistributed dividends of these corporations will be exempt from income tax for period of three years, starting from date of incorporation and beginning of their activities. (Codification in Law of Jan. 27, 1987 and its regulations).

Insurance companies (Codification of Feb. 28, 1967 as am'd) are subject to strict regulations and supervision. Among principal requirements, insurance business must be carried out only by duly organized corporation or cooperative; sole purpose of such organization must be to carry on insurance business; required reserve fund must be no less than 50% of its paid-in capital, which is to be formed with no less than 10% of each year's profit until completion of such amount. Also insurance companies are required to invest in certain bonds and securities. Foreign companies authorized to do business in Ecuador must deposit certificates of such investments in Banco Central or other banks established in Ecuador. Lives of persons residing in Ecuador, property located in Ecuador and ships and aircraft under Ecuadorean registration cannot be insured by companies not authorized to do business in country, except when authorized companies cannot provide such insurance.

To do business in Ecuador foreign companies must file application with Superintendente de Bancos, supplying among other data and documents name of a duly empowered agent in Ecuador and a certified statement of competent authority in its country of origin to effect that applicant has been in business for no less than five years and that it is authorized to carry on operations in foreign countries.

See also topic Foreign Investments.

Corporate Fees and Taxes.—Articles of incorporation and their amendments require payment of registry fee that is paid when documents are recorded in Commercial Registry.

See topic Taxation.

COURTS:

Justice is administered by: (1) Supreme Court of Justice, which hears certain appeals, has original jurisdiction in certain cases such as those relating to contracts made by executive, accusations against high functionaries, etc., and exercises general supervision over courts; (2) superior courts which hear appeals from lower courts and have certain additional functions; (3) criminal judges in each province, having jurisdiction in criminal matters; (4) local judges in provinces and cantons, who have jurisdiction in civil matters. (Organic Judiciary Law, as codified by Decree 891 of Sept. 11, 1974 as am'd).

CURRENCY:

Monetary unit is the Sucre, divided in 100 cents. Obligations in foreign money payable in Ecuador are paid in national currency at exchange rate prevailing at time of payment. (Law on Monetary Regime and Bank of State, Decree—Law 02 of May 7, 1992 as am'd, arts. 3 and 4).

CURTESY:

There is no estate by curtesy. As to rights of surviving husband, see topics Descent and Distribution; Husband and Wife.

DEATH:

Presumption of death of an absentee may be judicially declared after two years have elapsed since disappearance; thereupon three years after absence provisional possession of his property may be granted to his heirs. Definitive possession of property is granted after ten years or after six months when disappearance occurred in war, shipwreck, or any other similar danger. Definitive possession dissolves marriage of absentee. (C.C. 66-80).

Deaths are recorded in the Civil Registry of the jurisdiction where death occurred. Death certificates may be obtained by application to the Civil Registrar of the district. Nominal stamp taxes and fees are set by local regulations.

Actions for Death.—There is specific statute creating action for wrongful death in Civil Code under which anyone who causes damage to another is liable. Statute of limitations of tort action is four years from tort's date. (C. C. 2241-2261).

DECEDENTS' ESTATES:

See topics Descent and Distribution; Executors and Administrators; Wills.

DEEDS:

(C.C.P. 168-194).

Conveyances of real estate must be by public instrument (q.v.) and contain a true statement of the consideration since the state tax on transfers of title is based on the real consideration. Deeds must likewise bear stamps depending on the amount involved and be recorded in the Registry of Properties. Both grantor and grantee must sign the deed and both must be present before the notary at the same time. If one is absent he must be represented by an attorney in fact. The original deed, if executed in Ecuador, remains in the files of the Ecuadorean notary who gives to either party a certified copy which has the effect of an original in the courts of law.

Wife has no dower right.

DESCENT AND DISTRIBUTION:

In the absence of testamentary dispositions a decedent's estate passes to the following, in the order named: (1) Descendants; (2) ascendants and spouse; (3) brothers and sisters; (4) State. Descendants of deceased heirs succeed them by right of representation.

In accordance with Law 115 of Dec. 22, 1982, spouse and common-law wife have same hereditary rights.

Aliens have the same inheritance rights as an Ecuadorean. The Ecuadorean heirs of an alien have the same rights in his estate as they would have in the estate of an

DESCENT AND DISTRIBUTION . . . *continued*

Ecuadorean and may demand that their claims be satisfied out of the alien's property in Ecuador.

Even though there be a will, a part of the estate goes to certain heirs by operation of law. (See topic Wills, subhead Testamentary Disposition). Certain persons are excluded from testate or intestate succession, as for example, persons who were guilty of crime against the decedent or his spouse or legitimate ascendants or descendants.

Inheritances may be accepted expressly or impliedly or may be refused. If accepted the acceptance may be with benefit of inventory, in which case an inventory of the property is prepared and the heir is liable to creditors only up to the amount shown in such inventory, or it may be unconditional, in which case the heir is liable for all debts of the decedent in the proportion of his share of the estate. If there is no one appointed by the testator to make the partition the heirs make the partition themselves, minors and incompetents being represented by their guardians, with judicial approval. In case of controversy the judge appoints the partitioner. (C. C. 1015-1058; 1267-1314; 1360-1428).

DIVORCE:

(C. C. 104-129).

Divorce dissolves marriage bond and may be obtained by mutual consent or granted for: (1) Adultery; (2) cruelty; (3) grave insults or hostile attitude showing habitual lack of harmony; (4) frequent threats against life of spouse; (5) attempt against life of spouse; (6) wife giving birth to child conceived before marriage if proved illegitimate; (7) acts intended to corrupt spouse or children; (8) incurable and contagious disease; (9) habitual drunkenness or drug addiction; (10) sentence for imprisonment for felonies; (11) absence of sexual relations with separation for one year, upon complaint of deserted party only, or with separation for three years at request of either party. Court must take into account educational background, social position and any other reasonable considerations.

No particular length of residence is specified, but bona fide domicile is required. False attribution of residence of defendant annuls the judgment if action is filed within one year. During this period no new marriage may be contracted.

The action must be brought within one year from the time when the cause came to the knowledge of the offended party in cases (1), (5) and (7) and from the time when it accrued in most other cases. For divorce by mutual consent the parties submit a petition to the judge who after two months holds a hearing and attempts their reconciliation; if not successful he grants the divorce.

The parties must agree as to custody and support of the children; this agreement may at any time be modified by the judge for good cause shown. In general the mother is entitled to the daughters and to the sons under age of puberty; the other sons may choose the parent they prefer; but this rule is modified when the mother was guilty of adultery or there are other good reasons why she should not have the custody of the children. Children in custody of spouse who remarries may be demanded by the other spouse.

Alimony in amount determined by the court, may be allowed to a wife or to husband. Innocent spouse who has insufficient property is entitled to one-fifth of property of other spouse or amount which added to his/her property will be equivalent to such fifth. Upon judgment of divorce marriage community property is divided.

A judgment of divorce is not effective until recorded in the Civil Registry. A marriage contracted in Ecuador, when either spouse is Ecuadorean, may be annulled, or dissolved by divorce, only by Ecuadorean judges.

DOWER:

No dower right. As to rights of widow, see topics Descent and Distribution; Husband and Wife.

EXCHANGE CONTROL:

(Decree-Law 02 of May 7, 1992).

Monetary Board established exchange system with three exchange markets: Official and intervention markets, administered by Central Bank, and free market, which prevailing rate of exchange is determined by supply and demand. Monetary Council authorized private banks to deal in foreign exchange. Violators of exchange control regulations are subject to fines and in some cases to suspension of right to obtain import and export permits and to closing of their place of business. In order to import and export special permit must be issued. Export proceeds must be surrendered to authorized private banks and financial companies in return of local currency at intervention market rate. Import payments are made at intervention market rate.

EXECUTIONS:

When an order of execution has been issued and property attached, an appraisal is made of the property. The court then designates a day for receiving public bids, which call is advertised. The creditor may be a bidder. Written bids are filed and cannot be for less than two-thirds of the appraised value. If no bidders offer this amount, new bids are called for on the basis of a valuation of one-half the original appraisal, and likewise the creditor may demand a levy on additional property. After the sale there is no equity of redemption. (C. C. P. 423-498).

EXECUTORS AND ADMINISTRATORS:

If there is no executor appointed by the testator the heirs are charged with carrying out the testator's wishes. The law designates a number of classes of persons who cannot be executors, among them being persons whom the law considers physically, mentally or morally unfit; also persons not living in Ecuador, clerics, soldiers and married women, except with the consent of their husband or the judge. An executor must conclude his work within the time designated by the testator or within one year, but this period may be extended by the court for another year.

When a person dies his property passes immediately to his heirs and may be held by them unless the testator has provided otherwise. An heir who accepts the inheritance unconditionally is liable for all the debts of the decedent according to his proportion of the inheritance; if he accepts with benefit of inventory he is liable only for the value of the property received by him. The executor must publish a notice to creditors, and must pay the debts if the testator charged him with this duty; but in any case he must see that a sufficient amount be set aside for debts in the division of the estate and if he is tardy in paying debts the creditors may bring suit against the heirs. Creditors may demand that the property of the deceased be kept separate from that of the heir. (C. C. 1315-1359; 1397-1420).

EXEMPTIONS:

The following property of the debtor is exempt from attachment: (1) Bed and clothing of debtor, his wife and children; (2) professional books up to 20,000 sucres in value; (3) machinery and instruments for teaching or practicing science or art up to 20,000 sucres in value; (4) soldiers' uniforms and equipment; (5) utensils of artisan or farm worker; (6) food and combustibles for family use for one month; (7) objects possessed as trustee; (8) rights whose use is personal to debtor, such as right of habitation; (9) property given to debtor with declaration that it is not subject to attachment, provided value was at time judicially appraised, but increments may be attached; (10) salaries of public employees, except for aliments; (11) salaries and pensions up to 300 sucres per month, and one-half thereof over that sum, except in suits for support; (12) homestead. (C. C. 1661; C. C. P. 451; Laws Aug. 3, 1938, Nov. 1, 1940).

FORECLOSURE:

See topics Chattel Mortgages; Mortgages.

FOREIGN CORPORATIONS: See topic Corporations.

FOREIGN EXCHANGE:

See topic Exchange Control.

FOREIGN INVESTMENTS:

(Decree 415 of Jan. 8, 1993).

The Common Regime for Treatment of Foreign Capital and of Trademarks, Patents, Licenses and Royalties (Decision 291 of Commission of Cartagena Agreement) is in force. No prior authorization is required for foreign investment to participate in national, mixed or foreign companies (as such companies are defined below). However, foreign investment must be registered with Banco Central del Ecuador after registration with Mercantile Registry.

For foreign investment purposes, companies are classified as follows: (a) Foreign Company: one whose capital, in hands of national investors, amounts to less than 51% or, if that percentage is higher, is not properly reflected in opinion of Central Bank in technical, financial, administrative and commercial management; (b) National Company: one in which more than 80% of capital belongs to national investors, provided that in opinion of competent authority, that proportion is reflected in technical, financial, administrative and commercial management of company; (c) Mixed Company: one whose capital belongs to national investors in a proportion which may fluctuate between 51% and 80%.

Individual foreign persons are allowed to invest in newly created or already existing enterprises and to participate as shareholders in closely held or stock corporations with previous notice to Ministry of Industries, Commerce, Integration and Fishing (MICIF), provided that investor has to be legal resident.

Foreign investors are entitled to re-export their obtained capital when they sell their shares, participations or rights to national investors or when company is liquidated.

Foreign investors are allowed to transfer abroad annual profits of registered investment after payment of income tax.

License agreements on transfer of technology and use and exploitation of foreign patents and trademarks do not require prior authorization. All transfer of technology agreements must be registered with MICIF.

Controversies arising from application of Regime for Treatment of Foreign Capital and of Trademarks, Patents, Licenses and Royalties may be subject to arbitration.

For tax in foreign loans see topic Taxation.

FOREIGN TRADE REGULATIONS:

See topic Exchange Control.

FRAUDS, STATUTE OF:

See topic Public and Private Instruments.

FRAUDULENT SALES AND CONVEYANCES:

The following are void: Any agreement made by a creditor with the bankrupt or other person stipulating advantages in consideration of his vote, and any agreement made by a creditor after the cessation of payments stipulating advantages for himself with respect to the assets of the bankruptcy. Alienations or mortgages of the property of a decedent by his heirs within six months after the estate vests may be annulled unless made with the object of paying creditors of the estate. (C. C. P. 571; C. C. 1437).

HOLIDAYS:

Jan. 1 (New Year's); Good Friday*; May 1 (Labor Day); May 24 (Battle of Pichincha); Aug. 10 (Independence Day); Oct. 9 (Guayaquil Independence); Nov. 2 (All Souls); Nov. 3 (Cuenca Independence); Dec. 25 (Christmas). (Labor Code art. 64).

* This is movable holiday.

HUSBAND AND WIFE:

The spouses owe each other fidelity and protection and they have equal rights and duties.

Before contracting marriage or after by mutual consent parties may agree on marriage articles regarding property matters. In absence of such agreement parties are presumed to enter into marriage community comprising following property: (1) Salaries and emoluments earned by each spouse during marriage; (2) fruits and revenues of

See Topical Index in front part of this volume.

HUSBAND AND WIFE . . . *continued*
both separate and community property; (3) money and personalty brought by parties into marriage, such money and value of personalty to be restored by community; (4) property acquired by either spouse during marriage for valuable consideration. Either spouse may administer property of community, but in order to alienate or encumber community real property acquired during marriage, consent of other spouse is required.

In absence or inability of spouse administrator, other spouse is given by court administration of community and property of former.

A legally separated spouse has inheritance rights and conjugal portion in estate of deceased spouse.

Upon dissolution of the community each spouse or his or her estate is entitled to one-half of the property.

Upon the death of a spouse the surviving spouse is entitled to a marital portion amounting to one-fourth of the estate or equivalent to the obligatory share of legitimate child only if surviving spouse cannot sustain him- or herself. (See topic Wills.) If surviving spouse has property marital portion is diminished by value of such property. All amounts received by surviving spouse from estate of deceased, including share in community property, are credited to marital portion. (C. C. 134-239; 1218-1225; C. Com. 12-18; Law 73 of Aug. 14, 1981).

Common law marriage is regulated by Law 115 of Dec. 22, 1982.

INCOME TAX: See topics Corporations; Taxation.

INFANCY:

(C. C. 279-331).

Paternal authority (Patria Potestad) comprises rights and duties that legitimate parents have upon their children. Father or mother is legal administrator of his children's estate; but may lose this right in case of gross and habitual negligence in such administration.

Age of majority is 18 years, but a minor may previously be emancipated; this puts and end to paternal authority. Emancipation can be voluntary, legal, or judicial.

Voluntary emancipation is granted by parents and has to be done by public instrument acknowledged by a Notary Public and with judicial approval. Legal emancipation occurs when: (a) Parents are dead; (b) by marriage; (c) by judgment granting possession of parents' estate if they have disappeared; and (d) when infant reaches age of 18 years. Judicial emancipation occurs by judgment of courts in case of severe mistreatment that endangers mental and physical health of infants or when parents have been sentenced to four or more years in jail.

Emancipation, once granted, is irrevocable.

Code of Minors (Código de Menores) and Law 170 of Aug. 4, 1992 created National Board of Minors (Consejo Nacional de Menores) to protect and educate minors. Code also covers certain provisions regarding alimony for infants in case of divorce or insolvency of parents and child abuse. Severe penalties are imposed in case of violation of provisions of law.

Parental authority can be suspended by Judge of Minors in case there is strong evidence that either parent suffers from mental incapacity, alcoholism or any kind of drug addiction, neglect or lack of interest in education of minor.

Other provisions of law contemplate prevention of minors' antisocial behavior and correction of it with adequate treatment.

INHERITANCE TAX: See topic Taxation.

INSOLVENCY: See topic Bankruptcy and Insolvency.

INTEREST:

Legal and maximum permissible rate is 23% for private civil and commercial transactions except for external credit, where limit is 2% over libor or prime. Bank's operations have fixed rates according to type and duration of operation. If rate higher than legally permitted one is stipulated, creditor loses 20% of his credit in addition to other penalties. Interest on interest is prohibited. Usurious rates presumed when creditor gives receipt of interest payment without concretely indicating sum or value received. (C. C. 2135-2142; C. Com. 560).

INTESTACY: See topic Descent and Distribution.

JUDGMENTS:

Judgments may be executed by means of a summary executory action within five years after they are rendered. A judgment does not constitute a lien on the property of the debtor except with respect to property attached in the course of execution. A levy on real property must be recorded in the registry of properties.

Foreign judgments may be executed in Ecuador if: (1) They infringe no Ecuadorean law; (2) it is so provided by treaty; (3) in the absence of a treaty, it appears from the letters rogatory requesting the execution that (a) the judgment is a final unappealable judgment according to the laws of the country where rendered and (b) was rendered in a personal action. (C. C. P. 273-306, 423-428).

LABOR RELATIONS:

Provisions of Labor Code (Law of Aug. 16, 1978 as am'd) govern relations between employers and employees.

Labor contracts may be: individual or collective; express or implied; oral or written. Contracts shall have a minimum duration of one year with exception of those involving domestic services, trainees, apprentices and others specified by law. Most labor contracts must be in writing. They could be in private or public document and must be registered at Labor Inspector's Office or at Labor Court of place of employment. If employer dismisses employee, he must pay severance equal to three months' salary to employees with up to three years of employment and for more than three years' employment amount equal to one monthly salary for each year of employment up to maximum of 25 monthly salaries. If employer or employee gives notice of termination of labor contract to other party employer must pay employee equivalent of 25% of last salary for each year of employment. If employee abandons his job without giving prior notice to employer, employee must pay employer amount equal to 15 days' salary. Under Law of July 14, 1942 as am'd, all private employers and employees must be covered by compulsory social security. Benefits provided by social security include following: sickness and maternity insurance; disability and old age; widowhood and orphan's; insurance against occupational accidents. Employers must distribute among their employees at least 15% of net profits obtained at end of each fiscal year.

Existence of employee associations or unions is guaranteed by Constitution and by Labor Code under art. 409 et seq.

Regulations on health and safety were approved by Decree 2393 of Nov. 13, 1986.

Workers compensation governed by regulations of Sept. 18, 1990.

LEGISLATURE:

Congress meets annually on August 10. Special sessions may be called.

LIENS:

Privileged credits in general are as follows in the order stated: (1) Judicial expenses; (2) funeral expenses; (3) expenses of last illness; (4) salaries, wages and pensions of laborers, which have preference even above mortgages; (5) debts for maintenance of debtor and family for last three months; (6) state and municipal taxes. These credits do not affect mortgaged properties unless they cannot be covered from all the other properties of the debtor.

There are various liens on specific properties, such as: (a) Debts to innkeepers as to objects brought into the inn; (b) debts to carriers as to objects carried; (c) debts secured by pledge as to articles pledged (See topic Pledges); (d) debts for premiums to the insurer on objects insured; (e) debts for construction and repair, while the object remains in possession of the person for whose account the debt was incurred; (f) sellers in possession, for price; (g) and others by special laws. After the foregoing credits and the mortgages have been satisfied, the following have preference as to the balance remaining: (1) Credits of the treasury against collectors or administrators of government property; (2) credits of public charitable and educational institutions and of municipalities and churches against collectors and administrators of their funds; (3) credits of a married woman for her property administered by her husband, against his property; (4) credits of children for their property administered by their parents, against the parents' property; (5) credits of persons under guardianship against the guardians and in certain cases against the husband of a female guardian. (C. C. 2391-2415; C. Com. 196, 247; C. C. P. 554).

LIMITATION OF ACTIONS:

See topic Prescription.

LIMITED PARTNERSHIP: See topic Partnership.

MARRIAGE:

(C. C. 81-103).

Marriages must be performed before a civil functionary and two witnesses. A marriage by religious rite must be preceded by a civil ceremony. Marriages by proxy are allowed. A void marriage legally performed produces civil effects with respect to the spouse who acted in good faith and the children.

In order to marry, a person must have attained the age of 18 years, but persons under that age may marry with consent of parents or guardian. The following are grounds for annulment: relationship by consanguinity in direct line or to second degree in collateral line, or by affinity in first degree; insanity; impotence; existing marriage; marriage of male under 14 or female under 12 years old; marriage of surviving spouse and principal or accomplice of death of one's spouse; error as to person, duress, mental illness, kidnapping. Statute of limitation of action for annulment is two years as of date of marriage or when innocent party has knowledge of ground, except in case of previous marriage and relationship by consanguinity in direct line. Widow may not remarry within 300 days after her husband's death unless she files proof of non-pregnancy; guardian or his descendants and ward may not marry until accounts of guardianship are liquidated.

Ecuadorian diplomatic agents and consuls general may celebrate marriages between Ecuadorians outside Ecuador and between aliens domiciled in Ecuador.

MARRIED WOMEN:

See topics Dower; Executors and Administrators; Husband and Wife; Marriage; Wills.

MINES AND MINERALS:

Law 126 of May 28, 1991 regulated by Decree 2831 of Oct. 22, 1991 as am'd provides that mines are property of State, which conducts all mining activities, either directly or by granting mining rights with third parties. State may reserve any zone for its exploitation or exploration. There remain certain areas not regulated by this law but which come instead within special laws governing hydrocarbons, radioactive substances and mineral water.

Mines in General.—Mining activity, including smelting, refining and commercialization, is public utility. Mining concessions are considered real property distinct from surface, may be alienated, rented, encumbered or transferred by inheritance, but ownership is not considered as transferred nor is mortgage effective for third persons until recorded in Mining Registry. Mining policy is executed by Corporación de Desarrollo e Investigación Geológico- Minero- Metalúrgica which may create mixed economy companies with national or foreign companies or individuals. Law establishes causes for expiration or cancellation of contracts. All mining activities and disputes are subject to Ecuadorian law and jurisdiction. All individuals or juridical persons, domestic or foreign with legal capacity may obtain exploration or exploitation concessions. Prospecting is free. Exploration concessions are granted for two years which may be extended twice for periods of two years. Area allocated for exploration is up to 5,000 "héctareas mineras", as stipulated by law. Exploration concessions guarantee owners

See Topical Index in front part of this volume.

MINES AND MINERALS . . . *continued*
right to exploitation concessions. Exploitation concessions are granted up to 20 years, renewable; area allocated is up to 3,000 "hectáreas mineras".

Taxes.—Exploration and exploitation are subject to annual surface rights which are adjusted every year as stipulated by law. All mining activity is subject to income tax on taxable income which represents difference between gross income and authorized deductions from gross income. There is royalty of 3% on value of gross production of all minerals. Importation of capital goods and raw materials necessary for all mining activity pays duties at lowest rate.

Petroleum.—(Decree 2967 of Nov. 6, 1978, as am'd, codifies Hydrocarbons Law). Hydrocarbon industry, including production, refining, transport and commercialization, is public utility. Expropriation of property may be conducted for development of industry. Primary goal is refining within Ecuador. Hydrocarbon policy is dictated by Ministries of National Defense and of Energy and Mines. In accordance with Decree 1491 of Jan. 31, 1983 as am'd, and Law 45 of Sept. 18, 1989 regulated by Decree 935 of Sept. 26, 1989, Empresa Estatal Petróleos del Ecuador (PETROECUADOR) or its subsidiaries may execute contracts for exploration and exploitation of hydrocarbons with private developers under various stipulated arrangements by bid or individual evaluation or creating mixed economy companies with national or foreign companies duly established in country and having signed agreement renouncing all diplomatic recourse. (Decree 1286 of Nov. 7, 1985). Professional services that need to be performed by PETROECUADOR may be performed by itself or by others through professional services agreements. Each contract of exploration or exploitation is limited to maximum of 200,000 hectares onshore and 400,000 offshore. Companies must also commit themselves to minimum annual investment of US$120 per hectare onshore and US$181 per hectare offshore during first three years of exploitation period. Exploration may last four years renewable for two more years. If oil is found company can enter into 20-year exploitation agreement, renewable according to public interest. If commercial find is made PETROECUADOR will reimburse either in cash or in crude, at latest PETROECUADOR negotiated spot price investment and cost incurred during exploration phase. Both can be done simultaneously in areas partially explored. Contracting parties must post guaranty of 20% of projected investment. At termination of contract all equipment and installation must be turned over to PETROECUADOR. Contracting company must employ Ecuadorian nationals for at least 95% of its blue collar positions, 90% of its administrative employees and 75% of its technical personnel, during first five years; contracting company must also implement program of technical and administrative instructions, and after first five years of exploration period, all blue collar positions and administrative employees must be Ecuadorian nationals and at least 90% of its technical personnel.

Educational surcharge is levied on production. Minimum of 10% of net profits must be reinvested within five years in national petroleum industry or in government bonds and notes. Measures necessary for environmental protection are required.

Government authorizes exploitation of petroleum or natural gas in accordance with agreements provided by law. Contractors have option to buy whatever exportable surplus is left once local demand is satisfied, provided their purchases do not exceed 50% of output from their units. No export tax is levied on purchase of crude. State requires guaranty right of compensation for itself from production and marketing in cash or petroleum. Compensation in cash royalties is measured by monthly gross production and ranges from 12½% to 18%. Partial payment may be required at beginning of each year. All oil and gas pipe lines must be authorized by Government. Royalties, income tax, State participation, reasonable rate of return on capital and world prices control price set for petroleum, which is uniform for all products, both raw and refined. Contract may be cancelled under stipulated conditions. Such cancellation results in immediate reversion of area of contract to State and loss of installations and equipment and depository guaranty. Fines may also be imposed in certain cases. Foreign investments and foreign loans made in or to petroleum industry must be registered with Central Bank of Ecuador.

Assignment of contracts is regulated by Decree 809 of May 27, 1985 as am'd.

Taxes.—Contracting companies pay income tax at rate of 44.4% and at rate of 25% on amounts of income reinvested in same activities. (Law 56 of Dec. 20, 1989 as am'd).

MONOPOLIES AND RESTRAINT OF TRADE:

(Const. 1978, art. 194).

State guarantees freedom of commerce and industry. Monopolies are prohibited. However, Government may establish monopolies by law because of special national needs or interests. These public monopolies are not transferable to private individuals.

Anti-dumping Regulations (Decision 283 of Commission of Cartagena Agreement of Mar. 21, 1991 and Decree 2722-A of Sept. 13, 1991). Law protects local production from unfair practices of international trade, imposing countervailing duties on import of foreign goods. Dumping and subvention are considered unfair practices. Dumping is defined as import of foreign goods at lower price than normal price in place of origin, and subvention as direct or indirect incentives, subsidies, premiums or assistance of any kind, including preferential exchange rate granted by foreign governments to producers, manufacturers, transporters or exporters of goods in order to make them more competitive on international market.

Consumer Protection Law.—(Law 107 of Aug. 7, 1990 and its regulations Decree 2201-A of Feb. 2, 1991). Law deals with: Consumers' right to be informed; general representations and warranties, services, publicity and general regulations on subject.

MORTGAGES:

Mortgages must be executed in the form of a public instrument (q.v.) or at a purchase under execution of an attachment. They may be made in a foreign country with respect to property in Ecuador. They are effective only from the date of their record in the registry. A mortgage can be given only on real property and on vessels. Mortgages are foreclosed by a summary executory suit. After foreclosure there is no right of redemption. (C. C. 2333-2360).

NEGOTIABLE INSTRUMENTS:

See topic Bills and Notes.

NOTARIES PUBLIC:

Notaries are public officials, appointed by a superior court. They must be citizens, over 30 years of age, and must pass a competitive examination. They hold office for four years and are under supervision of courts of their district.

Instruments executed before a notary must be prepared with certain formalities. They must be in Spanish and state the date, the names of the parties, their age, domicile and whether married or single; also data as to the witnesses. The notary must declare that he knows the parties or that they were identified by two witnesses. Notarial instruments must have three witnesses. Employees and relatives of the notary to the fourth civil degree of consanguinity and second of affinity cannot be witnesses and certain other classes of persons are also excluded as witnesses. The notary retains the original document in a protocol and furnishes the parties with formal certified copies which have the effect of originals in court. (Decrees 1404 of Oct. 26, 1966, as am'd, Law 35 of July 2, 1986, and Law 97 of July 6, 1988, 1366 of Oct. 20, 1966 as am'd by Law 18 of Jan. 1, 1986, and Judiciary Law, arts. 153-163; C. C. P. 168-194).

PARTNERSHIP:

(C. Com. 262-293; 298-367; C. C. 1984-2046; Codification in Law of June 28, 1977, am'd by Decree 1848-D of Sept. 19, 1977, Decree 3135-A of Jan. 4, 1979).

Commercial partnerships are considered as legal entities. They are formed by a public instrument (q.v.) executed before a notary; an extract therefrom must be recorded in the registry of commerce and published in the newspapers.

General partnership (compañía en nombre colectivo) is partnership formed by two or more individuals to undertake business under firm name. Firm name must comprise names of partners or name of one or more of them followed by words "y Compañía" unless partnership is successor of former partnership, in which case former name may be retained but it must be followed by word "sucesores". Partners must pay their subscribed contribution, participate in company's losses, and compensate company for damages due to their actions in case of exclusion and they cannot on their own account engage in same business as partnership, and unless allowed by other partners, they cannot have interest in another company formed for same kind of business. Their rights are: to participate in profits, in discussions, to vote on resolutions and appointment of administrators, control the administration and appeal to court for removal of administrators for incompetence or fraud.

Limited partnership (compañía en comandita) is a partnership in which one or more partners are not liable beyond amount of capital they have subscribed. Name of a special partner cannot be included in firm name which must always be followed by words "Compañía en comandita", or its abbreviated form "C. en C." Nor can special partners perform any act of management, even as attorney in fact of general partners. Capital of a limited partnership may be divided into registered or bearer shares, all of equal par value and at least one tenth of capital must be contributed by general partners. Many provisions relating to corporations are applicable, including requirement of judicial approval.

Limited Liability Companies (Compañía de Responsabilidad Limitada).—These companies are formed by at least three or not more than 25 members who are liable only up to their individual contributions and carry out commercial activities under firm name which must always be followed by words "Compañía Limitada" or its abbreviated form "C. Ltda." Its capital cannot be represented by negotiable certificates and is divided into cumulative and undivided participations of 1,000 sucres, or multiples thereof, each. Local juridical persons, with exception of banks, insurance, savings and investment companies, may be members of limited liability companies. Foreign corporations of any kind cannot be members. Capital must be entirely subscribed and at least 50% of each participation paid in. Unanimity is necessary for transfer of participations and for admission of new members. Said agreement requires public instrument which must specify rights of members as to company's administration and must be recorded in Mercantile Registry. But each member has right to participate in adoption of resolutions, with one vote for each participation, and to participate in profits. No member may be compelled to increase his contribution and in case of capital increase or transfer of any member's participations the others have preemptive rights. In certain cases one or more members has right to request General Meeting for removal of managers or administrators. General Meeting is company's highest authority and convenes at least once a year. Its resolutions are adopted by majority vote representing more than 50% of members present. It appoints and removes managers and administrators; approves balance sheet; decides distribution of profits; approves transfer of participations; decides increase or reduction of capital and extension of company's term or dissolution of company before its term expires.

Civil company (sociedad civil) is one which is not formed for commercial purposes. It is governed by the rules of the Civil Code and is distinguished from a mercantile company by being regarded rather as an association of individuals; thus, unless otherwise expressed in the company instrument, the partners are not jointly and severally liable for debts of the company, but each is liable for his proportionate part and for part of the liability of an insolvent partner. A civil company may have the form of a general partnership in which all partners are managing partners or jointly select an attorney in fact to act for them; or of a limited partnership, in which one or more partners are liable only for the amount they contribute; or of a corporation, in which case the rules governing mercantile corporations apply.

PATENTS:

(Decisions 344 and 345 of Oct. 29, 1993 regulated by Decrees 1344-A of Dec. 21, 1993 as am'd and 3708 of Apr. 10, 1996; Patent Law concerning Exclusive Exploitation Rights of Invention, codification in Law of Oct. 5, 1976 only on subjects not regulated by Decision).

Any invention of products or proceedings in any technology field which are novel, represent inventive step and are susceptible of industrial application. Invention is novel when it is not within state of art in Ecuador. Among others discoveries, scientific theories and mathematical methods; scientific, literary and artistic works; therapeutic,

PATENTS . . . *continued*
surgical and diagnostic methods are not considered inventions. Inventions contrary to public policy, morals and against life or health of people or animals and environment; on animal species and races and biological procedures to obtain them; inventions related to nuclear substances, to pharmaceutical products listed by World Health Organization as essential medicines; and related to substances composing human body are not patentable.

Patents are granted for 20 years from filing date. Patent owner must exploit it, directly or by granting license in any country member of Andean Pact. Industrial production or importation, distribution and commercialization of patented product, are considered exploitation of patent. Compulsory licenses may be granted in case of declared emergency or national security reasons, and to guarantee free competition and avoid abuse of dominant position in market. Utility models for new forms of objects or mechanism, provided they have practical use are registrable. Registration term is ten years from filing date. Industrial designs are registrable if new. Registration confers right of exclusive use for eight years, nonrenewable. Applications are published and opposition can be filed. Law also protects trade secrets and considers them as any confidential information that is valuable and provides competitive or economic advantages to owner. Information considered trade secret must be expressed in tangible form such as documents, microfilm films, laser discs or any other similar means.

Vegetal species are protected when they are novel, homogeneous, distinguishable and stable and generic designations have been assigned to them. Registered certificate of holder is issued for 20 or 25 years, depending on type of vegetal variety.

PLEDGES:

Pledge contracts are not effective unless the pledged object is delivered to the creditor. In case of default the creditor may demand that the pledge be sold at public sale or, if no admissible bid is received, that it be appraised by experts and delivered to him at the appraised value; any stipulation to the contrary is void. Commercial pledges must be in duplicate writing to be effective against third parties and then they become negotiable by endorsement before maturity. Pledge of a credit requires notice to debtor but if of a document to the order it is endorsed in guarantee; registered shares need recording of transfer in guarantee in the company's books and bearer shares or documents require delivery only. (C. C. 2310-2332; C. Com. 569-575). "Special commercial pledge" can only be constituted by registered merchants on articles sold by them.

As to commercial pledge without delivery and agricultural and industrial pledges, see topic Chattel Mortgages.

PRESCRIPTION:

(C. C. 2416-2448; C. Com. 723; 1002-1011).

Acquisition of property and rights by virtue of adverse possession and extinction of obligations by failure to require performance within statute of limitations is called prescription. Prescription may be waived but only after it has run.

Adverse Possession.—In order to create prescriptive title, possession must be uninterrupted. Personal property is acquired by ordinary prescription in three years and real property in five years, but as against persons living outside of country period is doubled. Ordinary prescription requires good faith and is subject to suspension in favor of minors and certain other incompetents. Any property may be acquired by extraordinary prescription in 15 years even without good faith and such prescription is not subject to suspension.

Statute of Limitations.—Prescriptive period in which right to enforce obligation is lost varies according to nature of obligation. More important are: (1) Ordinary actions not otherwise limited, ten years; (2) summary executory actions, five years; (3) actions to rescind contracts for duress, error, fraud or legal incapacity, four years; (4) actions for fees of lawyers, physicians, teachers and others exercising liberal arts, three years; (5) actions of merchants and artisans for goods sold, of employees and servants for salaries, and actions for amounts due to innkeepers, transportation agents and others whose services are only occasionally used, two years. These prescriptive periods are suspended in favor of minors and certain other incompetents, but in no case can period of prescription exceed 15 years. Prescription of actions is interrupted by express or tacit recognition of the debt on part of debtor and by judicial demand.

Actions in commercial matters follow the rules of ordinary civil actions when the Code of Commerce does not provide otherwise. In connection with bills of exchange the following periods of prescription apply: (a) Against acceptor, three years; (b) of bearer against endorsers and drawer, one year; (c) of endorsers against each other and drawer, six months. In certain maritime matters the following prescriptive periods apply: (a) Actions derived from maritime insurance, five years; (b) actions for supplies to vessels, for salaries in constructing and repairing vessels and for wages of crew, one year; (c) actions for collection of passage money and contributions to general average, six months.

PRINCIPAL AND AGENT:

An agency may be conferred by public or private instrument or orally. Acceptance may be express or implied. A general power of attorney covers only acts of administration; in order to alienate, encumber, etc., the power must be specifically granted. The agent may delegate his powers if not forbidden to do so, but if he was not expressly authorized he is liable for the acts of his substitute. The principal must reimburse the agent for his expenses and for any loss he may suffer by reason of the agency if not due to the agent's fault. The agency terminates by: (1) Discharge of the business of the agency; (2) expiration of term; (3) revocation; (4) renunciation; (5) death of principal or agent, bankruptcy or insolvency or judical interdiction of either; (6) marriage of a woman agent; (7) cessation of the powers of the principal if the agency was given by virtue of such powers.

Commercial factors and employees must state that they act in the name of their principals. If they fail to do so they are personally liable. They are understood to have acted for their principals if: (1) The contract was of a kind made in the ordinary course of business; (2) they contracted by order of the principal although the operation was not in the ordinary course of business; (3) the principal ratified the contract; (4) the result of the agent's action is beneficial to the principal. In all such cases third parties may proceed either against the principal or the agent. Factors and commercial employees cannot delegate their powers without notice to or consent of the principal.

A commission merchant is an agent of an undisclosed principal, assuming the liability of his contracts. The other parties have no claim or duty with respect to principal. If he acts disclosing his character and name of principal then the rights and liabilities are between principal and contracting parties. He has lien for his fees and expenses on property in his possession. (C. C. 2047-2103; C. Com. 117-139; 374-409).

Decree 1038-A of Dec. 23, 1976, regulates and defines distributorship agreements establishing grounds for termination of contract, elements which comprise indemnification and legal proceedings to recover same. Causes for termination of commercial agency contracts, without liability to foreign principal are: serious breach of contract or legal obligations by representative, agent or distributor; acts or omissions of representative, agent or distributor that prejudice principal's interests; bankruptcy or insolvency and termination or liquidation of activities of representative, agent or distributor. Otherwise foreign principal must indemnify distributor, agent or representative.

PUBLIC AND PRIVATE INSTRUMENTS:

Public instruments are documents executed with the legal formalities before a notary public (q.v.) or other competent public officer. Other documents are private instruments. A public instrument constitutes full proof of its date and fact of its execution but it constitutes proof of declarations it contains only with respect to parties to instrument. Law requires numerous contracts to appear in public instrument, e.g., articles of incorporation or partnership, deeds of real estate, mortgages, etc. Date of private writing is counted against third parties only as of date of death of one of signers or date when it was entered in public registry or presented in court or inventoried by competent official. Writing is required to prove any obligation of over 2,000 sucres. (C. C. 1742-1758; C. C. P. 168-210).

RECORDS:

There is a registry in each canton for the recording of documents relating to the conveyance and encumbrance of real property. Registrars do not transcribe the entire document but only the essential parts and they may refuse to record a document with serious defects. There are also commercial registries where certain data relating to merchants and corporations must be recorded, and civil registries for recording births, marriages and deaths. (C. C. 721-733; C. Com. 29-36; Civil Registry Law recodified by Decree 402 of Feb. 10, 1966, Regulations in Decree 670 of Mar. 25, 1965; and Law of Registrations and Recordings as codified by Decree 1405 of Oct. 26, 1966).

REDEMPTION: See topics Executions; Mortgages.

SALES (Realty and Personalty):

A sale of personal property generally is perfected and risk of loss passes when the vendor and vendee have agreed on the thing sold and on the price, but title passes on delivery. A sale of real property, easements, annuities or inheritances is not perfect until proper instrument of conveyance has been executed or delivery has taken place. Costs of instrument of sale and other accessories are for account of vendor in absence of special stipulations.

The vendor warrants the thing sold and the title thereto. Even if the title warranty be waived he is liable for the price unless the buyer knew the danger or bought at his risk. The vendor is not liable for defects which are visible or could easily have been ascertained by the buyer. Even though he stipulates that he will not be liable for hidden defects, he is liable for those which he knew and did not declare.

If the price is not paid, the vendor may ask that the sale be cancelled. A stipulation that nonpayment of the price rescinds the sale cannot be made for a longer period than four years. The right to repurchase cannot be reserved for longer than four years and cannot be assigned.

Rescission may be asked within four years from date of execution of contract by vendor if it is found that price received is less than one-half value of property, and by vendee if it is found that property is worth less than one-half price paid.

In commercial sales the vendor is liable for hidden defects for six months if the goods were delivered in Ecuador and for one year if they were dispatched abroad. If the buyer refuses without just cause to receive the goods purchased, the seller may demand the rescission of the sale with indemnity for damages or he may deposit the goods in court and sue the buyer for the price and interest. (C. C. 1759-1863; C. Com. 169-202).

Bulk sales and sales of whole concerns are subject to special rules and recordings.

Conditional sales are governed by Law 548-E of Sept. 24, 1963, under which seller of personal property may reserve title until payment of price is made. Only identifiable items may be subject to conditional sale. Three counterparts of the contract are required with the necessary details of parties, objects and conditions and place where object will be kept; whether bills, notes or other instruments of payment are issued and whether commercial pledge has been given also. Contract must be recorded in Registry of Property. Upon default property must be returned to seller who, if so agreed, may keep the installments already paid but not in excess of one-third of the full price, excess over which must be refunded. Buyer may repossess goods by paying arrears within 15 days after default. Seller has option to petition a court for sale of the property for payment. If buyer becomes bankrupt seller may repossess and trustees in bankruptcy substitute for the buyer. If an insured object is destroyed creditor is entitled to recover from the insurance proceeds.

International Sale of Goods.—United Nations Convention on Contracts for the International Sale of Goods, in force on Feb. 1, 1993. See topic Treaties and Part VII, Selected International Conventions.

SEALS:

Seals are not used in private matters. A document executed before a notary has most of the effects of a sealed instrument in the United States.

See Topical Index in front part of this volume.

SEQUESTRATION: See topic Attachment.

SHIPPING:

Captains and officers of vessels of Ecuadorean registry must be Ecuadorean citizens except when no professional title is required. Only Ecuadorean citizens and alien residents in Ecuador can be owners of a national vessel. Traffic between the principal ports is open to all vessels, national and foreign; traffic between smaller ports is restricted to national vessels. Vessels may be mortgaged. (Customs Law; Port Regulations; C. C. 2343; Decrees 116 of Jan. 25, 1951 and 333 of Mar. 6, 1957). Many provisions of admiralty law are found in the Code of Commerce. (arts. 724-1011).

Law 178 of Feb. 12, 1974, regulated by Decree 1143 of Sept. 20, 1985, of Promotion of Fishing Activities and art. 633 of Civil Code extends national sovereignty up to distance of 200 marine miles, measured from low tide marks.

Law 147 of Mar. 23, 1992 establishes that cargo coming in or going out of Ecuador can be transported in local or foreign vessels based on principle of reciprocity and international conventions. Temporary restrictions may be imposed on foreign vessels if country of origin imposes any restrictions on Ecuadorian cargo vessels. All maritime transport companies importing or exporting cargo must register their rates with Dirección General de la Marina Mercante y del Litoral.

Law 3409 of Apr. 19, 1979 regulated by Decree 1048 of July 22, 1982 grants tax incentives to national or mixed maritime transport companies, and companies in charge of constructing and repairing vessels.

STATUTE OF FRAUDS:

See topic Public and Private Instruments.

STATUTES:

Most of the legal provisions are codified. The principal codifications are: Civil Code, Code of Commerce, Organic Law of Judiciary, Code of Civil Procedure, Penal Code, Code of Criminal Procedure, Labor Code, Military Code, Municipal Law, Customs Law, Port Regulations.

TAXATION:

There is a Fiscal Code which refers to taxes in general, interpretation of tax laws, collection of taxes and certain procedural matters. (Fiscal Code, Decree 1016-A of Dec. 23, 1975 as am'd).

Industrial Development Benefits.—Decree 1414, Sept. 22, 1971 as am'd and its regulations, Decree 427 of Jan. 11, 1985 as am'd to promote industrial development grants tax and import duties reductions and exemptions, some for terms of five years and longer.

Law applies to intermediate and finished products industries both foreign and domestic, and other "special" industries, designated by Ministries of Industry and Finance. Benefits of Law include: (1) Potential exclusion of competing foreign goods from country; (2) exoneration from certain transactional taxes and stamps; (3) exoneration from stock transfer tax; (4) exoneration from tax on transactional capital; (5) exoneration from import and export taxes; (6) 30% reduction in import duties on machines, etc.

Specific benefits may include exoneration from state and local taxes and 80% reduction of customs duties and sales taxes for five years. After five years, 100% exemption from duties on machine imports and 70% on spare parts is granted. Certain other benefits are allowable depending on nature and classification of industry.

To obtain benefits, following categories of applications must be made: (1) Exoneration; (2) inscription; (3) classification; (4) reclassification; (5) customs duties modification; (6) deductions for investment and reinvestment. Business will then be classified on basis of technical and economic data evaluation. Central Bank will control importation of machines, spare parts and raw materials. Benefits may be extended to importers of used machines and used spare parts.

Violation of law is subject to fines, payment of all taxes, etc., and suspension or revocation of benefits. Verifications of compliance are made. Businesses are required to: (1) Comply with all laws and regulations; (2) maintain proper accounting; (3) provide income tax and other declarations; (4) cooperate with authorities; (5) employ Ecuadorean nationals, except if skills required cannot be obtained; (6) publish annual general balance publicly. Businesses must buy national products as first preference. Businesses may solicit protective measures against "dumping" practices; also, provisions will be made to avoid ruinous competitive practices domestically.

If a company is engaged in various types of production, it will be classified according to its predominant activity, usually that which accounts for greater than 50% of total sales. Changes in sales, name of firm, purpose, merger, division or other modifications must be approved by Interministerial Committee (Comité Interministerial). Companies will contribute 5% of benefits of concessions for purposes of administration and developmental training and investment. Business may solicit reclassification of its category of benefits, if its operations change.

Law 90 of Aug. 2, 1990 regulates draw-back activity.

Income Tax.—(Law 56 of Dec. 20, 1989 as am'd and its regulations; Decree 2411 of Dec. 30, 1994 as am'd and Decree 2959 of Dec. 31, 1991). Income earned from Ecuadorian sources by individuals, undistributed estates, and national or foreign companies and income earned abroad by locally domiciled Ecuadorian individuals and national companies are taxed under this Law.

Law considers income from Ecuadorian sources income earned by national or foreign individuals from any kind of property or activities or labor, income earned abroad by national and foreign individuals from individuals or national or foreign companies domiciled in Ecuador, or from Ecuadorian public entities, capital gains from transfer of personal or real property, royalties from patents, trademarks, copyright and transfer of technology, profits paid by local companies, interests, inheritances, legacies and donations of assets located in Ecuador, lottery, raffle, game or similar awards or gains.

Deductions, among others, are: Insurance premiums, losses due to acts of God or force majeure, traveling expenses, depreciation and amortization according to law, wages and salaries paid, indemnification, social security contributions, bad debts, exchange differences, investment amortization; payments abroad according to law; payments to parent companies under 5% of net income.

Tax rates for undistributed estates and individuals domiciled in Ecuador range from 10% to 25%. Heirs, legatees and donees are taxed at 10% on amounts over 36,013,000 sucres. Nonresident foreign individuals are taxed at 25% rate on total income when services are not performed on regular basis.

Corporations organized in Ecuador, branches of foreign corporations domiciled in country and permanent establishments of non-domiciled foreign corporations are subject to tax at 25% rate. Profits and dividends credited or paid to nonresidents are taxed at 25% rate and subject to withholding; except when dividends are paid out of profits already subject to 25% corporate rate and qualified for tax credit. Other income or gains remitted, paid or credited abroad is subject to withholding tax at 33% rate. Interest, any other financial earnings and capital gains from sale of securities are not considered as global income and are subject to single tax at 8% rate, without any deductions with some exceptions.

Salaries and taxable payments are subject to system of withholding at source as provided by Law.

Monetary Adjustments.—Taxpayers required by law to keep books, must adjust yearly monetary values of their financial statements in accordance with variable percentage registered by National Index of Consumer's Prices as determined yearly by Instituto Nacional de Estadística y Censos.

Credits.—Withheld tax constitutes a credit against tax to be paid. If distributed dividends proceed from foreign incomes foreign tax may be credited in accordance with tax applied in country of origin to income from Ecuadorean sources subject to former's tax laws, but credit is limited to amount of tax to be applied.

When an individual receives salary compensation abroad which is considered taxable as from Ecuadorean sources, tax paid on same in foreign country is credited as per regulations.

Value Added Tax.—(Law 56 of Dec. 20, 1989 as am'd by Law 72 of May 16, 1990 and its Regulations Decree 2411 of Dec. 30, 1994 as am'd). Tax is levied on transfer and importation of goods, in all stages of commercialization, and on rendering specific services at rate of 10%. Transfer and importation of some goods are exempted from this tax, such as medicines, books, seeds, chemical products used in agriculture, raising of animals, hunting and fishing. Taxable services include laundry, dry cleaning; telecommunications, except radio and T.V.; leasing; services rendered by restaurants, night clubs, coffee shops, bars, and similar establishments; hotels, motels, boarding houses and similar establishments.

Excise tax (Law 56 of Dec. 20, 1989 as am'd and its Regulations, Decree 2411 of Dec. 30, 1994 as am'd).—Tax is levied on specified products at importer or producer level only. Tax rates vary from 5% to 260%. Products taxed include cigarettes, beer, soft drinks, alcohol and alcoholic beverages. Excise tax is included in taxable base of value added tax.

Transfer and registry taxes are collected on conveyances of property, inscriptions of merchants and numerous other acts. (See topic Records.)

Tax on Motor Vehicles.—(Law 04 of Dec. 8, 1988, regulated by Decree 423 of Feb. 13, 1989 as am'd).

Tax is levied on all passenger and freight motor vehicles used for public or private transportation. Tax is calculated on motor vehicle's value fixed by government according to make, year, model, etc., at rates ranging from 0.5% to 4%.

Tax on Loans.—Decree 317 of Mar. 25, 1974 as am'd by Law 139 of July 8, 1983 and Law 06 of Dec. 22, 1988 taxes all credit transactions in local currency by private institutions at rate of 1%.

Under Decree 506 of July 6, 1976 authorized and registered external loans must pay to Central Bank, at time of registration tax in accordance with following rates: on part payable within six months, 2%; on part payable within 12 months, 1.5% on part payable within 18 months, 1%; on part payable within 24 months, 0.5%; part payable over 24 months does not pay tax.

Double Taxation.—Ecuador has approved agreement to avoid a double taxation between member countries of Andean Common Market and Standard Agreement on double taxation between member countries and other nonmember countries. (Cartagena Agreement).

Free Zones.—(Law 01 of Feb. 18, 1991 as am'd regulated by Decree 2710 of Sept. 10, 1991). Free zones can be publicly or privately operated under supervision of "Consejo Nacional de Zonas Francas" (CONAZOFRA). All types of industries, trading and service companies are allowed to function there. Importation and exportation of raw materials, goods, equipment are duty free. Companies are exempted from all taxes for period of 20 years from installation date, renewable, up to CONAZOFRA and they are not subject to exchange control regulations and foreign investment regime; therefore, there are no restrictions for repatriation of capital and remittance of profits abroad.

TRADEMARKS:

Those signs visible and sufficiently distinctive and susceptible of graphic representation can be registered as marks. Trademark is any sign used to distinguish products or services produced or commercialized by one person from same or similar products or services produced or commercialized by another person. Slogans are words, sentences or captions used as supplement to trademark.

Following cannot be used as trademarks: Letters, words, arms and emblems used by the nation or municipalities or by foreign states or cities or by international organizations; name or picture of person without consent of such person, or descendant if person is dead; generic terms; local common names used to describe products; form and color of products; title of literary, artistic or scientific works protected by copyright without permission of owner, marks contrary to law, those against public policy, denomination of protected vegetal varieties, those identical or similar to registered trade slogans and trade names provided under circumstances public may be confused; those that are reproduction, imitation, translation or total or partial transcription of distinctive signs, locally or internationally, well known, without taking into consideration classification of goods or services concerned; or because of similarity to well-

TRADEMARKS . . . *continued*
known trademarks causes confusion to public independent of classification of goods and services for which registration is applied for. Term of registration is ten years subject to renewals for periods of ten years indefinitely if evidence is filed of use of trademark in any country member of Andean Pact. Renewal application can be filed during six months after expiration ten-year period. Trademarks can be cancelled for nonuse for consecutive three years by owner or licensee in any member country of Andean Pact. (Codification of Trademarks, Law of Sept. 24, 1976, Decision 344 of Oct. 29, 1993 of Commission of Cartagena Agreement regulated by Decree 1344-A of Dec. 21, 1993).

TREATIES:

Ecuador is party to the following: Convention on Private International Law (Bustamante Code), Havana 1928; Andean Pact, Cartagena 1969; Latin American Integration Association, Montevideo 1980; Latin American Economic System, Panama 1975; United Nations Convention on Recognition and Enforcement of Foreign Arbitral Awards 1958; Interamerican Convention on Copyrights June 22, 1946; Universal Convention on Copyrights Dec. 31, 1956; Andean Pact double taxation agreement; Interamerican Treaties on Patents of Invention, Industrial Drawings and Models and Trademarks, Mexico, Jan. 27, 1902, Rio de Janeiro, Aug. 23, 1906. Buenos Aires, Aug. 20, 1910; Interamerican Conventions on Trademarks, Buenos Aires, Aug. 20, 1910; Agreement on Patents and Privileges of Invention (Bolivarian Congress), Caracas, 1911; Interamerican Treaty of Arbitration for Pecuniary Claims, Mexico, Jan. 20, 1902; Interamerican Convention on Literary and Artistic Copyrights, Mexico, Jan. 27, 1902; Interamerican Convention on Exchange of Official, Scientific, Literary and Industrial Publications, Mexico, Jan. 27, 1902; Interamerican Conventions on Pecuniary Claims, Rio de Janeiro, Aug. 13, 1906, Buenos Aires, Aug. 11, 1910; Interamerican Convention on International Law, Rio de Janeiro, Aug. 23, 1906; Interamerican Convention on Uniformity of Nomenclature for Classification of Merchandise, Santiago, May 3, 1923; Interamerican Convention on Status of Aliens, Havana, Feb. 20, 1928; Interamerican Convention on Commercial Aviation, Havana, Feb. 20, 1928; Charter of the Organization of American States, Bogota, Apr. 30, 1948, Buenos Aires, Feb. 27, 1967; Interamerican Convention for promotion of Interamerican Cultural Relations, Caracas, Mar. 28, 1954; Panamerican Sanitary Code, Havana, Nov. 14, 1924; General Treaty on Interamerican Arbitration, Washington, Jan. 5, 1929; Interamerican Convention on Transit of Airplanes, Buenos Aires, June 19, 1935; Agreement establishing Interamerican Development Bank, Washington, Apr. 8, 1959; Agreement on Literary and Artistic Property (Bolivarian Congress), Caracas, July 17, 1911; Agreement on Extradition (Bolivarian Congress), Caracas, July 18, 1911; Agreement on Judicial Acts of Aliens (Bolivarian Congress), Caracas, July 18, 1911; Treaty for Prohibition of Nuclear Weapons in Latin America, Tlaltelolco, Feb. 14, 1967; Agreement establishing Latin American Energy Organization (OLADE), Lima, Nov. 2, 1975; Inter-American Convention on Conflict of Laws concerning Bills of Exchange, Promissory Notes and Invoices. Signed in Panama on Jan. 30, 1975; Inter-American Convention on Conflict of Laws concerning Checks. Signed in Panama on Jan. 30, 1975; Inter-American Convention on Letters Rogatory. Signed in Panama on Jan. 30, 1975; Inter-American Convention on Taking of Evidence Abroad. Signed in Panama on Jan. 30, 1975; Inter-American Convention on Legal Regime of Powers of Attorney to Be Used Abroad. Signed in Panama on Jan. 30, 1975; Inter-American Conventions: On Conflicts of Law concerning Checks, on General rules of private international law, on execution of preventive measures, on extraterritorial validity of foreign judgments and arbitral awards, additional protocol to Inter-American convention on letters rogatory and on domicile of natural persons in private international law. Signed at Montevideo on May 8, 1979. Multilateral Trade Negotiations, The Uruguay Round, Final Act, Marrakesh, Apr. 15, 1994 and Agreement Establishing the World Trade Organization, Marrakesh, Apr. 15, 1994.

International Sale of Goods.—United Nations Convention on Contracts for the International Sale of Goods, in force on Feb. 1, 1993. See topic Sales (Realty and Personalty) and Part VI, Selected International Conventions.

TRUSTS:

Chapter V of Law 1192 of Dec. 12, 1963 on Credit Operations contains several provisions on trusts. However, they do not amend but clarify those contained in the Civil Code on this matter. (C. C. Arts. 766-795). Law expressly authorizes assignment or devise of property on condition that it shall later pass to another, provided it has not been constituted in fraud of third parties. Trust can be created by will or by contract. Secret trusts are prohibited as well as those in favor of two or more successive beneficiaries. Period of trust cannot exceed 30 years unless beneficiary is public or charitable institution or nonprofit making museum of art or science.

USURY: See topic Interest.

VITAL STATISTICS: See topic Records.

WILLS:

(C. C. 1059-1266).

Wills may be made by all persons except those who: (1) Are civilly dead; (2) are below the age of puberty; (3) have been adjudged incompetent on account of insanity; (4) are not in their sound senses; (5) cannot clearly express their will orally or in writing.

Wills are either: (1) Solemn; or (2) less solemn or privileged. Solemn wills are always in writing and are of two classes: (a) Open, nuncupative or public; or (b) closed or secret. The following cannot be witnesses to a solemn will: (a) Minors below 18 years; (b) persons of unsound mind; (c) blind, deaf or dumb persons; (d) persons convicted of certain crimes; (e) clerks of the officiating notary; (f) undomiciled aliens; (g) those who cannot understand the language of the testator.

Open wills are made either before a notary or judge and three witnesses; or before five witnesses. They must state the name of the testator; his birth place; his nationality; his residence if he lives in Ecuador; his age; the fact that he is of sound mind; the names of the persons he married; the names of his children, legitimate and illegitimate; the names of the witnesses; the date; and the name of the notary or judge. The will must be read aloud in the presence of the testator and the witnesses by the notary or judge, if any, or by one of the witnesses. The testator, the witnesses and the notary or judge sign the document. If the will was made before a notary or judge no further probate is necessary; if it was made before witnesses only it must be probated in court. Blind persons can make only open wills, before a notary or judge, and the same must be read aloud twice by different persons.

Closed wills require a notary and five witnesses. A judge cannot act in place of a notary. The will having been written by the testator, or by another and signed by him, it is enclosed in an envelope which is sealed and handed by the testator to the notary in the presence of the witnesses with the statement that it contains his last will. On the envelope the notary writes a minute of the presentation stating that the testator is of sound mind; the name and domicile of the testator and each witness; and the date; and the same is signed by all present. The envelope containing a closed will cannot be opened until the signatures thereon have been proved in court.

Privileged wills are of two kinds: (a) military; (b) maritime. Military wills may be made by soldiers in time of war, in writing, before an officer, chaplain or surgeon and three witnesses. A maritime will may be made on Ecuadorean vessels before the captain or mate.

Testamentary Disposition.—In making a will the testator must necessarily observe the following requirements: (a) He must provide for the marital portion which the law allows the surviving spouse (see topic Husband and Wife); (b) one-half the balance of the estate must be distributed accordingly to the rules of intestate succession among certain heirs designated by the law as obligatory heirs, namely, descendants, legitimate ascendants and illegitimate parents, and the other half may be freely disposed of by the testator; (c) if there are descendants a further fourth of the estate must go to them, distributed as the testator may desire, and he may freely dispose of only the remaining fourth.

Foreign wills are valid in Ecuador if executed in accordance with the laws of the country where they were made. Ecuadoreans and aliens domiciled in Ecuador are allowed to make wills abroad before an Ecuadorean diplomatic officer or consul, accordingly to the rules covering Ecuadorean solemn wills; the witnesses must be either Ecuadoreans or aliens domiciled in the city where the will is made.

EL SALVADOR LAW DIGEST REVISER

Curtis, Mallet-Prevost, Colt & Mosle
101 Park Avenue
New York, New York 10178-0061
Telephone: 212-696-6141
Fax: 212-697-1559
Email: CMP-NY@mcimail.com

Reviser Profile

The Firm began in 1830 when two practicing lawyers started a long line of lawyers and law firms extending in an unbroken chain up to the present time. In 1897, the firm name became Curtis, Mallet-Prevost & Colt; in 1925 it was changed to Curtis, Mallet-Prevost, Colt & Mosle. The Firm is now made up of approximately 120 lawyers, including experts who have published extensively on such diverse subjects as international money management, transnational contracts, state contracts, litigation against foreign states, sovereign immunity and the act of state doctrine, and the International Court of Justice. Its principal offices are in New York City. There are branch offices in Paris, London, Frankfurt Am Main, Hong Kong, Washington, D.C., Houston, Texas, Newark, N.J., and Mexico City. The Firm has five departments: Corporate and International; Litigation; Real Estate; Tax; and Trusts and Estates. The corporate and international department acts as general counsel to various public and private corporations and individual entrepreneurs. Clients are in the banking, insurance, securities, manufacturing, real estate and oil and gas industries. In addition, the corporate and international department frequently acts as special counsel to domestic and foreign clients, providing assistance in financing, know-how licensing, the negotiation and drafting of all types of contracts and instruments, counselling on all aspects of corporate law, and establishing the vehicles necessary to enable clients to conduct their domestic and foreign business activities. The Firm's international work permeates all areas of its practice and involves questions of private international law, foreign law and an unusual amount of public and quasi-public international law. Traditionally, much of the Firm's international practice has been concerned with Latin America. The Firm maintains its excellence in that area, with its Mexican affiliate, and also through the expertise of Latin American lawyers based in the New York office. The Firm's international practice has undergone a major expansion beyond Latin America to Europe, Africa and the Near and Far East. The Firm's litigation practice includes commercial litigation and arbitration, and white-collar criminal defense. It has substantial experience in civil aviation matters; it also has represented foreign States in transnational litigation and international arbitration arising out of acts of nationalization and alleged breach of economic development or natural resource supply contracts. Among the Firm's clients in real estate matters are institutional lenders and investors, real estate developers, both individual and corporate, foreign and domestic investors and syndicators. The tax department has substantial experience in all aspects of domestic and international business tax matters and real estate taxation. The matters the tax department deals with on a regular basis include: Taxation of foreign investments; the structuring of corporate transactions, including mergers, acquisitions, liquidations and reorganization; federal and state tax litigation; and tax planning for U.S. and foreign individuals. The trusts and estates department engages in general domestic trusts and estates practice and in tax planning for foreign persons wishing to invest in U.S. assets through offshore trusts and corporations. It represents individuals, trust companies, and banks acting as fiduciaries. It works for various charitable organizations located both in the United States and abroad including private foundations, museums, universities and hospitals. A group of fiduciary accountants with vast experience in the field assists the lawyers of the trusts and estates department. Curtis, Mallet-Prevost, Colt & Mosle has served as a Reviser for most of Latin American Law Digests since 1930.

EL SALVADOR LAW DIGEST

(The following is a list of all Topics, including cross-references, covered in this Digest.)

EL SALVADOR LAW DIGEST

Revised for 1997 edition by

CURTIS, MALLET-PREVOST, COLT & MOSLE, of the New York Bar.

(Abbreviations used are: C. C.—Civil Code; C. Fam.—Code of Family; C. Com.—Code of Commerce; C. C. P.—Code of Civil Procedure; L. D.—Legislative Decree. Numbers in code references indicate articles.)

ABSENTEES: See topic Death.

ACKNOWLEDGMENTS:

Acknowledgments may be made before a notary, and must state the age, business and domicile of the person making the acknowledgment. Documents so acknowledged are regarded as authentic, and of date certain as to third persons from date of acknowledgment. Important documents are executed as public instruments before notaries, who retain the original in their records and issue certified copies. See topics Notaries Public; Public Instruments.

Documents executed abroad for use in El Salvador will be accepted if executed in accordance with the laws of the respective country and authenticated by a diplomatic or consular officer of El Salvador or by the Minister of Foreign Affairs of the foreign country and the Minister of Foreign Affairs of El Salvador. In cases where the Salvadorean laws require a public instrument as evidence, no private writing will be accepted. (C. C. 17, 18; C. C. P. 261; Notarial Law 218 of Dec. 6, 1962 as am'd).

ACTIONS:

Actions for Death.—See topic Death.

Limitation of.—See topic Prescription, subhead Limitation of Actions.

ADMINISTRATION:

See topic Executors and Administrators.

ADOPTION:

(C. Fam. arts. 165-185).

Adoption is irrevocable and extinguishes legal bonds between adopted party and natural family, must be authorized by Attorney General of El Salvador and by Salvadorian Institute for Protection of Minor and approved by judge. Adopting party must be of good reputation, under 45 years of age and at least 15 years older than adopted party. Consent is required from spouse of adopting party, from adopted party who is over 12 years old, from parents, if adopted party is under their "patria potestad" and from Attorney General when adopted party is under tutorship, abandoned or orphan. Adoption where parties are subject to different jurisdictions besides complying with same requirements as local parties, adopting party must have been married for at least five years, comply with all requirements for adoption in its own jurisdiction and prove existence of public institution dedicated to protection of minors or family in their domicile which will take care of interest of adopted party.

ADVERSE POSSESSION:

See topic Prescription.

AGENCY: See topic Principal and Agent.

ALIENS:

In general, aliens enjoy same civil rights as citizens, but small industry and commerce is limited to native born citizens of Central American countries. A special license (patent) must be obtained by any alien wishing to engage in commercial or industrial activities. Aliens or corporations controlled by aliens whose countries deny to Salvadoreans right to own real property, cannot acquire rural realty in El Salvador except for industrial purposes. Aliens must register in central immigration office. All employers must limit number of foreign employees to no more than 10% with no more than 15% of sum of salaries. (Const. arts. 47, 96-100; Alien Law approved by Decree 299 of Feb. 20, 1986; Immigration Law 2772 of Dec. 19, 1958, am'd by Decree 595 of May 28, 1964, and Decree 1022 of Mar. 10, 1982; Regulations by Decree 33 of Mar. 9, 1959, and Decree 1020 of Mar. 10, 1982; Law 552 of Dec. 21, 1967; Labor Code, Law 15 of July 4, 1972 and Law of Regulation of Commerce and Industry 279 of Mar. 4, 1969 as am'd, regulated by Decree 9 of Jan. 27, 1970).

See also topic Immigration.

ALIMONY: See topic Divorce.

ASSIGNMENTS:

The assignment of a personal right is made by delivery of the instrument evidencing the same, with a written statement signed by the assignor and giving the date of the assignment and the name of the assignee. It does not bind the debtor nor third parties unless the debtor has been notified thereof or has accepted it. In the assignment of a credit document the assignor warrants the existence of the credit, but does not warrant the solvency of the debtor unless otherwise stipulated, and then only up to the amount of the price he received. Bills of exchange and documents to order or bearer are subject to the special rules of the Code of Commerce. (C. C. 1691-1702).

ASSIGNMENT FOR BENEFIT OF CREDITORS:

An assignment for the benefit of creditors is the voluntary abandonment by the debtor of all his assets when in consequence of unavoidable accident he cannot pay his debts. The creditors must accept the assignment unless the debtor was guilty of fraud or has dissipated his property or has received reductions or extensions from the creditors. The assignment does not transfer title to the property but only the right to dispose thereof. The debtor may be left in charge of the administration. The debts are extinguished only up to the amount obtained from the property assigned. (C. C. 1484-1494. See also topic Bankruptcy and Insolvency).

ATTACHMENT:

Attachment may be obtained before or during a suit when: (1) The object sued for is in danger of being lost or deteriorated; (2) the debtor intends to dispose of his property; (3) the debtor is an alien not domiciled in the country; (4) a debt is owing by a third party for plaintiff's property acquired by such party. The plaintiff must give bond, and the defendant may raise the attachment by giving bond. The following authorize a summary action and an attachment without bond: (1) Public instruments, i.e., instruments executed before a notary; (2) authentic instruments, i.e., those issued by public officials, including tax notices; (3) acknowledged instruments, including private documents acknowledged before a judge or notary, and drafts and promissory notes if duly protested and their signatures are acknowledged; (4) judgments. Suits relating to real estate may be registered as a lien on the property. (C. C. P. 142-156, 586-632; C. C. 719-730).

BANKRUPTCY AND INSOLVENCY:

(C. C. P. 659-777; C. Com. 498-552).

Insolvency proceedings may be voluntary or necessary. The proceeding is voluntary when the debtor makes an assignment for the benefit of creditors. It is necessary when demanded by one or more creditors and it is shown that two or more executions have been issued against the debtor and there is not sufficient property to satisfy them. In declaring the insolvency the judge orders the attachment of the debtor's property, appoints a temporary depositary and may order the arrest of the debtor unless he gives bond. A meeting of creditors is called, unrepresented foreign creditors being notified through their consul. The meeting elects a depositary and a receiver who administers and liquidates the estate and distributes the proceeds, reports being made to the creditors.

At any time after the creditors' claims have been examined and approved an agreement between the insolvent and his creditors may be proposed. The agreement is considered at a creditors' meeting and requires for its approval the vote of two-thirds of creditors present representing at least three-fifths of all liabilities. In order to be reinstated a debtor must show that his debts have been paid in full, and culpable or fraudulent insolvents must have served their punishment.

Bankruptcy relates to merchants and must be declared by commercial judge in special proceeding. Bankruptcy may be declared under certain conditions, such as: Nonpayment of liquid and mature obligations; lack of assets on which to levy for execution; absconding for more than 15 days without leaving an agent in charge of legal obligations of enterprise; voluntarily closing enterprise for 15 days or more if there are pending obligations; transfer of assets to prejudice of creditors; fraudulent, prejudicial or fictitious activities to avoid compliance with obligations; petition by merchant himself; default in obligations resulting from composition with creditors; and, in general, similar situations.

Bankruptcy of a company also causes bankruptcy of members with unlimited liability but bankruptcy of members does not produce bankruptcy of company. De facto companies and companies in process of liquidation may also be adjudged bankrupt.

Petition may be filed by public attorney, bankrupt himself or any creditors and, in case of companies, by any member whenever stockholders' meeting or administrators refuse to file petition.

Bankruptcy can be fortuitous, culpable or fraudulent. Bankrupt is not allowed to administer his business and cannot be appointed officer of any commercial concern, but he may administer: Business strictly related to his person or to his civil and political status; earnings from personal work, obtained after declaration of bankruptcy, which may be reduced by court; and assets exempt from attachment under law.

Foreign declarations of bankruptcy produce effects in El Salvador whenever enforceable under provisions of Civil Procedure Code, but creditors domiciled in country will have preference over creditors domiciled abroad.

Law sets forth in detail provisions regarding effects of bankruptcy upon obligations and acts of bankrupt. All fraudulent acts, regardless of date of execution, are invalid but if for consideration, bad faith of third party is necessary. Acts executed after date to which judgment decree is retroactive are irrebutably presumed fraudulent, if made without or for inadequate consideration, or when consisting of payment of obligations not yet due. Acts made after such effective date are presumed invalid unless otherwise established, if consisting of payments made in kind which were not object of promise, or consisting in creation of in rem rights to secure obligations prior to such effective date of bankruptcy, if there was no promise to give guaranty or if obligation resulted from receipt of money or assets delivery of which was not attested by a notary when required.

Any payment act or transfer by bankrupt is also presumed fraudulent even if there was consideration, if made after effective date of bankruptcy and third party knew of merchant's situation.

See also topic Fraudulent Sales and Conveyances.

BILLS AND NOTES:

Bills of exchange (C. Com. 702-787) must contain following: Words "bill of exchange" written on document; place, day, month and year in which it is drawn, unconditional order to drawee to pay a sum of money; name of drawee; place and date of payment; name of payee; signature of drawer or of person that signs it upon

BILLS AND NOTES . . . *continued*
drawer's request. Bill of Exchange can be drawn: at sight; at specified time after sight; at specified time after date; at certain date.

If date of payment is not indicated in text, bill must be considered payable at sight. Bill can be drawn to order of same drawer, in such case drawer is considered acceptor. Drawer can designate as place of payment domicile of third party wherever that place may be. Drawer can also designate his domicile or residence for payment of bill.

Acceptance.—Bill must be presented for acceptance either by a holder in due course or by a holder at place and address indicated in document. If for any reason such address or place is not indicated, presentment for acceptance must be made at residence of drawee. If bill indicates several places for acceptance, holder can present it at any of them. Bill payable at certain time after sight must be presented for acceptance within year after its date. Any of holders can reduce term if it is so allowed on bill. Acceptance must appear on document and words "I accept," or words of other equivalent meaning must appear on bill, followed by signature of drawee. However, only drawee's signature is enough to operate as full acceptance. Acceptance must be unconditional, but it can be done for an amount less than sum indicated on bill. Any other change introduced by drawee/acceptor is equivalent to a refusal. If drawee after acceptance cancels same, before returning bill, such act is also a refusal. Acceptance of bill means that drawee must pay it when due. If drawer pays accepted bill drawer has action against drawee. Drawee does not have any action against drawer nor any other persons whose signatures appear on bill.

Aval guarantees in full or in part payment of bill. Such guarantee can be given by any person that has negotiated bill or by any other person stranger to it. Aval shall be written in document with expression "by Aval" or any other equivalent words, and must bear signature of guarantor. If Aval cannot be written on document, it can be stated in another paper, provided it is firmly attached to first one. Aval guarantees total amount of bill and must indicate person guaranteed. Guarantor is jointly liable with person whose signature has been guaranteed and his obligation is valid even though principal obligation might be void. Aval is void only when there are formal defects in document.

Payment must be made at place and address indicated in document. If for any reason document does not mention such address it can be presented for payment at commercial address or domicile of drawer or drawee. Presentment for payment must be made when due or next working day; when payable at sight it must be presented for payment within one year after issuance. Payment must be made upon presentment and delivery of document. Holder can refuse partial payment, but if it is so received he can withhold document until total amount is paid. Holder is not bound to receive payment before bill is due.

Protest can be made in case of failure to accept or failure to pay. Protest must be performed before a notary public with requirements indicated in law. However, when bill of exchange is presented either for acceptance or payment to a bank, statement of same refusing to accept or pay shall have same effects as protest before a notary public.

Promissory note (C. Com. 788-792) must contain following: Words "promissory note" written on document; unconditional promise to pay a determined amount of money; name of payee; date and place of payment; date and place where document is issued and signature of maker.

If promissory note does not mention when it is due, it shall be considered payable at sight and if place of payment is not mentioned it must be understood to be domicile of maker; promissory note when drawn at a specified time after sight must be presented for payment within a year of its date. In general, all articles and regulations applicable to bills of exchange also regulate promissory notes.

Checks (C. Com. 793-838) must contain following: Number and series; word "check" written on document; name and domicile of drawee bank; unconditional order to pay a determined amount of money indicating such amount in letters and numbers (any contrary clause in check shall be considered void and as if it were not written); name of payee or to his order, or indication that it is a bearer check; place and date of issue; signature of maker.

Instrument shall only be a check if drawn on a duly authorized bank; if document has been corrected, erased, or altered it is void.

Checks can be drawn: (1) to name of a person who can be maker or a third person, in both cases it shall be understood that it is "or to the order" of them; (2) in favor of a person with clause "not to the order," "non-negotiable," or any other equivalent, in such instance, check is not negotiable; (3) to bearer.

Checks are always payable at sight; any other indication to contrary is void. It must be presented for payment to drawee bank or to any of its agencies in country.

Checks must be presented for payment: Within 15 days after issuance if payable at same place, within a month if issued in national territory and payable at different place than place of issuance, within three months if issued abroad and payable in national territory, within three months if issued in national territory to be paid abroad, provided foreign laws do not conflict.

Commercial Code also provides for other types of checks such as: Check for payment in certain accounts, certified check, travelers check, check with guaranteed amount or limited check, circular check and cashier's check.

Maker has right to request bank to certify check; such certification cannot be partial or to a lesser amount. Certified check is not negotiable. When check has been certified, only person liable for payment is bank. If bank writes following words on face of check "accepted," "good" or any other equivalent, or sole signature of any of its agents this can be deemed a certification.

Only banks and financial institutions can issue cashiers' checks, which must be in favor of a specified person.

CHATTEL MORTGAGES:

There is no provision for chattel mortgages. See topic Pledges.

COLLATERAL SECURITY: See topic Pledges.

COMMERCIAL REGISTRY:

(Legislative Decree 271 of Feb. 15, 1973 as am'd by Dec. 504 of Dec. 13, 1973, regulated by Dec. 33 of May 7, 1973).

Registry is made up of a division and three departments: (a) Registry of Merchants and Commerce and Industry, licenses classified in three sections: (i) individual merchants, (ii) corporate merchants, and (iii) mercantile concern; (b) Registry of Mercantile Documents divided in four sections: documents of incorporation, powers of attorney, appointments of agents and credentials, contracts of personal property sale by installments and others subject to recording; (c) Registry of Patents, Trademarks and Industry; copyrights and names and distinguishing commercial signs.

Both natural and juridical persons must be registered, except individual merchants whose assets do not exceed 10,000 colones and mercantile concerns with less than 20,000 colones in assets. No concern may operate without being registered. Documents involving mercantile acts and contracts are subject to registration and if not registered do not have any effect against third parties.

COMMUNITY PROPERTY:

See topic Husband and Wife.

CONSTITUTION AND GOVERNMENT:

(Constitution promulgated on Dec. 15, 1983 as am'd). Government is republican, democratic and representative and is composed of three branches: Legislative, Executive, and Judicial power. Territory of Republic, aside from its present boundary, includes adjacent sea with distance of 200 marine miles measured from line of lowest tide, and also comprises air space above, subsoil, and continental shelf. Freedom of navigation and aero-navigation are not affected by provisions described above, if performed in accordance with principles of international law.

Following are Salvadorians by birth: those born in territory of country; those born in foreign country, but of Salvadorian father or mother and also other natives of Central America who being domiciled in El Salvador declare to authorities their desire to become citizens. Other provisions also state who can be citizens by naturalization. Juridical persons if constituted in accordance with laws of country and having legal domicile there, are also Salvadorians.

Legislative power is vested in a legislative assembly of deputies having a single chamber and elected for three year period.

Republic is divided into departments and these into municipalities; at head of each department there is a governor appointed by president. Municipalities are administered by municipal councils with limited local powers. Constitution sets forth in detail powers and duties of legislative assembly which, among others are: To make rules for its internal government, to enact, interpret, amend and repeal statutory laws, to create judicial districts and establish offices as indicated by Supreme Court, to levy taxes on all classes of property and income, and in event of war to declare compulsory loans if normal public revenues are insufficient, to establish and regulate national currency and to determine administration and circulation of foreign currency, etc.

President of Republic is elected for five years and cannot be re-elected until another term has elapsed.

Judicial power is vested in Supreme Court of Justice whose judges are designated by Legislative power, and one of whom is its president.

Constitution in subsequent articles provides for public wealth, economic regime, individual and social rights, etc.

CONTRACTS:

Civil Code (Arts. 1308 to 2064) contains general principles. These apply supplementarily to commercial contracts and also to labor contracts.

A contract is an agreement by virtue of which one or more persons bind themselves toward one or more other persons, or reciprocally among themselves to give, to do, or not do something. Civil contracts involving more than 200 colones must be in writing and cannot be proved by witnesses unless there is a writing which gives credibility to parol evidence. Future inheritances and future hereditary rights cannot be object of a contract.

CONVEYANCES: See topic Deeds.

COPYRIGHT:

(L.D. 604 of July 15, 1993 regulated by Decree 35 of Sept. 28, 1994).

Law grants moral and pecuniary rights to author, his successors or assignees regarding scientific, literary and artistic works. Copyrights include all kinds of intellectual (including software), scientific, literary and artistic creations reproduced by any means. Law also protects translations, adaptations, arrangements and other transformation of intellectual works. Performers' rights are also protected. Works are protected by law without requiring registration.

"Moral rights" are unassignable and unlimited in time of enjoyment, including right to make work known publicly, use of name or pen name, assert paternity of work, oppose plagiarism or deformation, mutilation, change or abridgment of work or title. Any violation of moral rights gives action for damages.

Pecuniary rights are granted for enjoyment of pecuniary benefits from use of author's works, including all kinds of reproduction, performance and broadcasting with some exceptions. These rights are assignable by inter vivos acts or transfered upon death. Protection is for life of author plus 50 years after death of author or last surviving co-author. If author appears to be corporation or collective entity protection lasts 50 years from Jan. 1 of year following year of first publication.

El Salvador has ratified Berne Convention for protection of literary and artistic works.

CORPORATIONS:

(C. Com. 191-295 and Dec. 448 of Oct. 9, 1973).

See Topical Index in front part of this volume.

CORPORATIONS . . . *continued*

Corporations can be organized provided name is followed by words "Sociedad Anónima" or its abbreviation "S.A.". Omission of this requisite means that shareholders and directors shall be jointly and severally liable without limitation. In order to incorporate, following requirements must be met: Capital of corporation cannot be less than 20,000 colones and must be entirely subscribed; 25% of value of each share must be paid-in in cash; value of each share must be totally paid-in when payment is made in goods rather than in money. In any case, one-fourth of total capital of corporation must be paid-in.

Certificate of Incorporation must contain following information: Name, age, profession, nationality and domicile of natural persons, and name, nationality and domicile of juridical persons that integrate company, type purpose, corporate name, duration or express declaration that it is constituted for indefinite time; amount of capital stock, or at least minimum capital stock required by law; shareholders' contribution either in cash or in goods and value attributable to latter; management of corporation stating names, powers and obligations of respective officers; distribution of profits and losses among shareholders; constitution of reserves; and, finally, requisities to dissolve and wind up its business and rights and duties of persons to do so. Aside from requisites above mentioned (which are common to all types of companies) corporations required, in addition to, to include in certificate of incorporation following data: Subscription of shares indicating amount of paid-in capital; conditions in which difference shall be paid in, number of, par value and type of shares in to which capital is divided; determination of rights, duties and limitations in case of preferred stock; indication of all other types of stock; powers to shareholders to subscribe or to increase capital of corporation; manner in which board of directors and auditors shall be elected, time and conditions in which they shall hold office and how to fill in vacancies; provisions to call for general and/or special meetings of shareholders and also how to call for extraordinary meetings.

In addition, under Law of Regulation of Commerce and Industry (Law 279 of Mar. 4, 1969 as am'd, regulated by Decree 9 of Jan. 27, 1970) corporations having foreign shareholders or administrators, directors, managers or general attorneys in fact must have a minimum capital of 200,000 colones if dedicated to commerce, or 100,000 colones if dedicated to industry. (See also topic Aliens.)

Shares.—(C. Com. 126-172; 207-219). In general shares must have nominal value of ten colones or its multiples. Each share is indivisible, but several persons can own shares if represented by one of them. Co-owners are jointly liable to corporation. Shareholders must pay total amount of shares subscribed for, according to terms agreed upon; liability shall only extend to amount of shares owned. Corporations are not allowed to issue shares at less than par value. They are also forbidden to issue shares if no valuable consideration has been paid or will be paid in future. Shares must be registered until fully paid. Later on, they may be converted into bearer shares if so allowed by certificate of incorporation. Before delivery of shares, corporations can issue provisional certificates.

Other articles of Commercial Code contain regulations as to manner and time of share issuance, sales of stock and payments as well. Corporations are not allowed to acquire their own shares except at auction or by judicial decision.

Stock certificates must also contain certain information such as: Name, domicile and duration of corporation; all details regarding certificate of incorporation; name of shareholder (if registered shares); amount of capital stock and total amount of shares (number and series); indication as to whether or not shares have been fully paid and signature of administrators that pursuant to certificate of incorporation must sign them. If corporations issue registered shares they must also keep a record of shareholders, and transactions regarding same.

Certificate of incorporation may allow division of capital stock into different classes of shares; otherwise there is only one class of shares.

Each share gives right to one vote, although preferred stock can be issued with limited voting power. Such shares cannot vote in general shareholders' meetings, only in extraordinary ones. Preferred shares are entitled to dividends, which cannot be less than 6% of nominal value; certificate of incorporation can authorize payment of higher dividends. When corporation is liquidated these shares have preference to common ones. If no dividends are paid for more than three fiscal years to preferred shares, they shall be converted, automatically, into common shares, and, therefore, they will have full voting rights.

Corporations must pay dividends in cash.

Any agreement restricting voting rights of shareholders is void, except in case of shares that have not been totally paid.

Shareholders' meeting (C. Com. 220-253) when properly called is highest authority of company. Meetings are divided into ordinary and extraordinary. Ordinary meetings shall be convened at least once a year within five months after closing of fiscal year and must decide, among other matters included in agenda, following: To approve actions taken by board of directors; annual report and balance sheet and information of auditor regarding profits and losses; to designate and to remove directors and auditors; to determine their salaries if they have not been fixed in certificate of incorporation; and to distribute profits.

Extraordinary meetings may be called in order to discuss following matters: Modification of certificate of incorporation, new issuance of debentures or bonds, redemption of shares with funds of corporation and any other matters that in accordance with law and/or by-laws must be considered in extraordinary meetings.

A call for a meeting must be sent 15 days before date of meeting, unless certificate of incorporation indicates a longer period. If shares are registered, notice must be also sent to such shareholders. Notice must contain: Name of corporation, type of meeting which is called for, indication of necessary quorum, place, date and hour of meeting, matters to be considered, and name and office of person calling it.

Shareholders representing at least 5% of capital can make request in writing, at any time, to board of directors to call for a general meeting of shareholders in order to decide business indicated in such petition; if board of directors refuse to do so, call must be made by Court (commercial judge) of domicile of corporation upon request of interested shareholders. General shareholders' meeting to be valid must be represented by a quorum of shares entitled to vote, and resolutions are valid when passed by a majority of votes present.

Management.—(C. Com. 254-281). Corporations must be administered by one or more directors who do not need to be shareholders. Directors are elected by general shareholders' meetings, unless certificate of incorporation provides otherwise, that is to say, directors can be elected by special meetings representing different categories of shares. Directors shall hold office for five years unless certificate of incorporation determines a shorter period of time. Directors can be re-elected; board of directors is necessary, even if there are only two directors in which case one shall be president with power to decide in case of a tie. Third persons cannot represent directors in their functions, since such duty is strictly a personal one.

Board of directors passes resolutions if majority of members are present and if taken by majority of votes. Certificate of incorporation can specify that in certain cases directors are required to give bond, to guarantee fulfillment of their obligations. Other articles of code determine rights and duties of managers; said office is also personal and cannot be exercised by agents.

Administrators of corporations, either directors or managers are not allowed: To use capital of corporation for their particular business; to do business in name of corporation if different from purposes specifically indicated in certificate of incorporation; to enter into commercial or industrial contracts similar to those of corporation, or to do business directly or indirectly with corporation, unless they are expressly authorized, in each case, by shareholders. Directors are jointly liable for administration of corporation. Shareholders representing at least 25% of capital stock can sue administrators if certain requisites of law are complied with.

Balance Sheets and Annual Reports.—(C. Com. 282-294). Corporations must present every year a balance containing detailed information of profits and losses, which must be concluded within three months after closing of fiscal year. Administrator or board of directors in its case, must deliver it to auditor who within 30 days after reception of same must give opinion about it.

Balance sheets and annual report must be discussed and approved in general stockholder's meeting and if approved, must be published in Official Gazette within 15 days after meeting.

In order to be auditor it is necessary to fulfill certain requisites, among others: To be Salvadorian; to be a certified public accountant duly registered in auditors' professional registry. Among his obligations, he must determine incorporation and existence of same, and of its inventories and balances; he must inspect at least once a month corporate books, etc. General shareholders' meetings can remove auditors at any time.

Reserves.—(C. Com. 295). Corporations must set aside, every year, in order to form what is known as "reserve fund," 7% of net profits; minimum legal limit of said fund must be one-fifth of total capital stock. Two-thirds of amount of fund must be invested in stock of other Salvadorian or Central American enterprises; remaining one-third can be invested according to purposes of corporation.

Limited Partnership Companies Issuing Shares.—(C. Com. 296-305). This type of corporation is unknown in American law. Its main features are that some partners are jointly and severally liable for corporate obligations (as in a general partnership), but limited partners are only liable up to amounts of shares owned in such concern. This type of company must have one or more partners and several limited shareholders. Capital stock must be divided into shares, partners must subscribe for at least one share. Shares issued to shareholders must be registered and cannot be transferred unless unanimous consent of other shareholders and partners.

Partners must administer company, although other provisions also contemplate possibility of shareholders' meetings.

This type of company is regulated by rules of limited partnership companies regarding rights and duties of partners; as to shareholders, general principles of corporations are applicable.

See also topic Partnership.

Corporations with Variable Amount of Capital.—(C. Com. 306-314). Any type of company can adopt system of "variable capital" which means that same can be increased (or decreased by new quotas or by admission of new shareholders. Shares must always be registered.

Merger and Consolidation of Corporations.—(C. Com. 315-325). This is possible when two or more corporations integrate a new one, or when one of them absorbs the other. New corporation acquires all rights and duties of old ones. Agreement to merge must be taken by shareholders of each corporation according to their own rules and must be registered in commercial register of domicile of each of corporations merged. After registration, agreement and last balance sheet of corporation must be published; 90 days after said publication, merger is final. Shareholders that do not agree with said merger are allowed to resign.

Liquidation of Corporations.—(C. Com. 326-342). Once corporation has been dissolved it must be liquidated; therefore, after corporate name there must be included following words: "in liquidation." Liquidators (who are designated by shareholders) must be administrators and agents of corporation and are personally liable for their acts, if exceeding their duties. If certificate of incorporation does not contain rules as to how corporation must be liquidated it must be performed under directions given by all shareholders entitled to amend certificate of incorporation. Among other obligations, liquidators must do following; wind up its business, sell assets, prepare final balance sheet (which must be filed in commercial registry) and give to each shareholder his quota in remaining assets, if any. While corporation is in process of liquidation, shareholders can receive partial payments if circumstances so allow.

This chapter of Commercial Code also applies to other types of corporations, as well, as all types of partnerships.

Foreign Corporations.—(C. Com. 358-361 and arts. 15 to 25 of Decree 448 of Oct. 9, 1973). Foreign corporation if incorporated according to foreign laws can do business in country provided: It can show that it has been legally incorporated according to laws of incorporating country; shows that pursuant to said law and to its own statutes it can establish branches and agencies according to provisions of Salvadorian Commercial Code and also that resolution to do business in country has been legally adopted, or that it has legal capacity to move its domicile to new place of business; it must permanently have at least one agent in country with broad powers to sign all acts and transactions to be performed in Republic; it has sufficient assets in order to develop its activities; shows that its purposes are legal pursuant to national laws and

See Topical Index in front part of this volume.

CORPORATIONS . . . *continued*
that they are not against public policy; and accepts and agrees to obey laws and codes of country.

Documents mentioned above must be sent to Superintendence of Companies (Superintendencia de Compañías), and if requisites of law are complied with, it shall grant authorization to do business in country. To that effect, it shall fix a certain period of time in order to allow corporation to start operations, and at same time it shall order registration of same in commercial register of place where corporation shall have its principal office.

Foreign corporations that have been incorporated in accordance with foreign laws and which are authorized to do business in country shall be considered domiciled in place where principal office is located.

Furthermore, commercial code provides that foreign corporations having branches and agencies in country dedicated to banking, insurance and, in general, all financial corporations, must invest in country certain amounts of mathematical reserves required by law. Government authorities must determine, from time to time, whether such deposits have been properly made.

Corporate documents require stamp paper, amount depending on capital involved.

COURTS:

The judicial power is exercised by: (1) A supreme court which has administrative functions regarding courts and lawyers and judicial functions in certain cases; (2) chambers of second instance which hear appeals from judges of first instance and have original jurisdiction in certain cases; (3) judges of first instance having original jurisdiction in most civil, commercial and criminal matters; (4) justices of peace. (Judiciary Law, Decree 123 of June 12, 1984 as am'd; Const. arts. 172-190).

CURRENCY:

(L. D. 746 of Apr. 22, 1991).

Monetary unit is colón, and is divided in 100 cents. Only Banco Central de Reserva de El Salvador may issue bank notes and these are legal tender. Obligations are paid in El Salvador in national currency but international obligations payable abroad or in El Salvador, foreign money securities issued by Government or Banco Central and some others may be payable in agreed currency.

See also topic Exchange Control.

DEATH:

The presumption of death of an absentee may be judicially declared and the provisional possession of his property may be granted to his heirs, after four years have elapsed since his disappearance. Thereafter definitive possession of the property is granted when eighty years have elapsed since his birth, or 20 years since his disappearance, or 15 years since the declaration of the presumption of death. However, definitive possession is granted after four years when the disappearance occurred in war or shipwreck or similar danger. (C. C. 79-93).

Death certificates may be obtained from the Registry of the Civil Status, the fees consisting of a stamp tax and a municipal tax, both nominal in amount.

Actions for Death.—There is no specific statute creating this action, but it may be supported by the general provisions on torts contained in Civil Code. (Arts. 2065-2085). In practice separate civil action for wrongful death is not exercised. Under Criminal Code, any damage resulting out of crime must be liquidated in the criminal action and under Criminal Procedure Code no civil action lies while the criminal action is pending.

Law 420 of Sept. 11, 1967 establishes special rules and procedures for criminal and civil damage actions resulting from motor vehicle accidents.

DECEDENTS' ESTATES:

See topics Descent and Distribution; Executors and Administrators; Wills.

DEEDS:

Conveyances of real estate, and of easements and inheritances, must appear in a public instrument, unless the value is less than 200 colones, in which case a private document before two witnesses is sufficient. (C. C. 1605). If the consideration expressed appears inadequate an appraisal of the value of the property is made, since the state tax on the transfer is based on the real value, and for the purposes of such appraisal the deed must declare the amount of the rental, if the property has been rented and the kind of crops and value of the annual production, in the case of rural property. (Law Aug. 11, 1928). Both grantor and grantee must sign the deed and must therefore be present before the notary at the same time in person or by attorney-in-fact. An original deed executed in El Salvador remains in the files of the notary, who gives to either party a certified copy which has the effect of an original in the courts of law. See topics Notaries Public, Public Instruments.

DESCENT AND DISTRIBUTION:

(C. C. 952-995, 1146-1191, 1235).

In the absence of testamentary dispositions a decedent's estate passes to the following classes of persons in the order named, the persons in each of the respective classes sharing equally: (1) children, parents, surviving spouse, common law spouse; (2) grandparents and other ascendants, grandchildren, natural father who voluntarily acknowledged children; (3) brothers and sisters; (4) nieces and nephews; (5) aunts and uncles; (6) cousins; (7) University of El Salvador and hospitals.

Deceased children are represented by their descendants but in collateral line representation extends only to grandnephews and grandnieces.

Certain persons are excluded from testate and intestate succession, as for example, persons convicted of a crime against the life, honor or property of the decedent, his spouse or his ascendants or descendants, or who by force or violence induced the decedent to make a will or prevented him from making one.

The acceptance of an inheritance must be expressly declared. Acceptance may be unconditional or with benefit of inventory; in the former case the heir is liable for the debts of the decedent in proportion to his share in the estate; in the latter case he is liable only up to the amount actually inherited by him.

DIVORCE:

(C. Fam. 104-117; C. C. P. 576-585).

Divorce dissolving the marriage bond may be granted for: (1) mutual consent; (2) separation for one or more consecutive years; (3) any cause that makes living together impossible. In third case only innocent party may ask for divorce.

The court of first instance of the conjugal domicile is the court competent to take cognizance of divorce actions. (C.C.P. 576). No particular length of residence is required.

The court determines the amount payable for alimony and for support of children.

A divorce by mutual consent must be requested by the parties in person or by attorney expressly appointed for that purpose. With their petition parties must file agreement regarding division of their property and custody of their children.

Upon judgment of divorce there is a liquidation of community property. Children are awarded to either or both spouses after hearing Public Attorney.

DOWER:

No dower right. See topics Descent and Distribution; Husband and Wife.

EXCHANGE CONTROL:

(L. D. 746 of Apr. 22, 1991).

Currency transactions are made only through Banco Central de Reserva de El Salvador or for its account. Commercial banks and exchange houses are free to purchase and sell foreign exchange for authorized transactions at rate determined by supply and demand. Banco Central de Reserva de El Salvador fixes weekly exchange rate applicable to transactions between Banco Central and public sector, to foreign exchange surrendered by exporters and to calculation of tax payments. Foreign currency bank accounts are authorized. Export registration certificate from Banco Central is required for all exports exceeding certain amount and export proceeds must be surrendered to Banco Central. Import licenses are required for some items.

EXECUTIONS:

When an order of execution is issued, announcements are posted and published. An appraisal of the property is made unless the parties have agreed on a value. The date of sale is then posted and the sale is held under the auspices of the court. No bid is received for less than two-thirds the appraised value. If there are no bidders the plaintiff may ask that the property be adjudicated to him for two-thirds of the appraised value, or that the real estate be delivered to him so that he may apply its revenues to his credit. Otherwise the property remains on deposit or under administration and its revenues are delivered to the creditor until a bidder appears or the debt is paid. After the sale there is no right of redemption. (C. C. P. 633-645).

EXECUTORS AND ADMINISTRATORS:

The heirs or their legal representatives are the administrators of the estate and have the duty of carrying out the testator's directions. No executor may be appointed by will. The estate vests in the heirs immediately on the death of the testator and suits for or against the estate are carried on by them. If any of the heirs be incompetent and lacks a legal representative, the court appoints a guardian to represent him. If some of the heirs delay in accepting the inheritance, those first appearing act as administrators, but the court may require them to give bond. In case of disagreement among the heirs regarding the administration the court decides. For the partition of property the court appoints a partitioner who must be a lawyer, but the decedent may by will appoint a partitioner without this qualification (C. C. 1162-1168, 1192-1257. See also topic Descent and Distribution).

EXEMPTIONS:

The following property is exempt from attachment: (1) Pensions for support; 80% of other pensions; salaries of 100 colones or less but if in excess thereof only from 5% to 20% may be garnished; (2) bed and necessary clothing of the debtor and his wife and children; (3) professional instruments, furniture and books; (4) implements to teach a science or art; (5) soldiers' uniforms and equipment; (6) tools of artisans or farmers and ungathered field crops; (7) food and combustibles of the debtor's family for one month; (8) personal rights, such as habitation; (9) real property given or devised as not subject to attachment, up to value appearing in appraisement made at time of delivery and judicially approved; (10) savings of public employees in cooperative societies under government supervision; (11) homesteads, recorded as such; (12) life annuities to extent decided by court to be necessary for support of debtor and dependents. (C. C. 1488 as am'd; C. C. P. 619; Labor Code, art. 133; and Law 267 of Feb. 22, 1963).

FORECLOSURE: See topic Mortgages.

FOREIGN CORPORATIONS:

See topic Corporations.

FOREIGN EXCHANGE:

See topics Currency and Exchange Control.

FOREIGN INVESTMENT:

(L. Decree 960 of Apr. 24, 1988, as am'd, regulated by Decree 1 of Jan. 9, 1990).

Foreign investment is defined as foreign source contributions made by foreign individuals or juridical persons in freely convertible currency; in tangible property such as machinery, equipment, parts, raw materials; in intangible property such as marks, commercial names, patents, copyright, leasing; reinvestment in local currency originating from profits, capital gains, sale of shares, as well as foreign currency loans made to individuals or juridical persons locally domiciled. Foreign investment is allowed in all economic areas. All foreign investment must be registered at Ministerio de Economía. Registered foreign investors have no limitation to remit profits abroad,

FOREIGN INVESTMENT . . . *continued*
except when profits are from investments in commercial activities and services, remittance of net profits each year is then limited to 50% of registered investment; registered foreign investors are entitled to repatriate their original investment plus any capital gains and they are also exempted from withholding tax on dividends.

FOREIGN TRADE REGULATIONS:

See topic Exchange Control.

FRAUDS, STATUTE OF:

See topic Public Instruments.

FRAUDULENT SALES AND CONVEYANCES:

Payments, alienations and other acts by a debtor in fraud of creditors may be annulled. See topics Bankruptcy and Insolvency; Sales (Realty and Personalty).

HOLIDAYS:

Jan. 1 (New Year's); Maundy Thursday*; Good Friday*; May 1 (Labor Day); Corpus Christi* (half day holiday); Feasts of San Salvador*; Sept. 15 (Independence Day); Oct. 12 (Columbus Day); Nov. 2 (All Souls'); Nov. 5 (First Call to Independence) half day holiday; Dec. 25 (Christmas).

* These are movable holidays.

HUSBAND AND WIFE:

(C. Fam. arts. 36-89, 118-126).

Husband and wife have equal rights and duties, should live together and owe each other fidelity and mutual assistance.

Before contracting marriage the parties may make an agreement regarding ownership and administration of their property. Such agreement must be recorded; it may be modified after the marriage but the modification must be recorded. Parties may agree on either of three systems: separation of assets, participation of profits or community property. If there is no premarital agreement, parties are subject to community property. Agreement ceases by agreement of parties or by judicial declaration of invalidity or dissolution.

Parties' consent is required for mortgage or sale of real estate used as family dwelling.

IMMIGRATION:

(Constitution arts. 96-110; Law on Immigration 2772 of Dec. 19, 1958 as am'd regulated by Decree 33 of Mar. 9, 1959 and Law 58 of Sept. 2, 1964).

Law classifies foreigners entering country into: (a) tourists; (b) temporary residents and (c) permanent residents.

(a) Tourists must present a tourist card or passport visaed by a Salvadorian Consul and are allowed to stay 90 days. This period may be renewed once.

(b) Temporary residents may remain in country one year for following reasons: (i) to engage in some scientific, cultural or sport activity; (ii) to work as a technician or a skilled worker; (iii) to engage in any other temporary, lawful activity. Technicians must apply for advance authorization of Ministry of Interior submitting a copy of respective contract. Other residents may not work in remunerative activities except with special authorization.

(c) Permanent residents: passport and a visa is required. Permanent residency will not be granted if work applicant intends to do may cause displacement of or competition with Salvadorians. Permanent residents may engage themselves in remunerative or lucrative activities.

A special category of "Resident with an Income" not allowed to work is established by Dec. 476 of Nov. 8, 1973 as am'd.

INFANCY:

(C. C. arts. 26, 41, 1316-1318, 1552-1554, C. Fam. arts. 202-246).

Age of majority is 18. Contracts by males under 14 females under 12 are void and, if over those ages, voidable, except by emancipated minors in some cases. Infants are subject to parental authority of father and mother or one of them. Parental authority includes custody, administration and legal representation. In absence of parents guardian is appointed. Parents and guardians have limited powers of disposition.

INSOLVENCY:

See topic Bankruptcy and Insolvency.

INTEREST:

Legal interest is 6% per annum but parties may stipulate any other rate. Compound interest is prohibited. (C. C. 1963-1967; L. D. 276 of Aug. 30, 1992).

INTESTACY:

See topic Descent and Distribution.

JUDGMENTS:

(C. C. P. 441-453).

Judgments are executed in a summary proceeding. A judgment does not constitute a lien on the property of the debtor except with respect to property attached. A levy on real property must be recorded in the public registry.

Foreign judgments have the effect designated in the treaties with the respective country. If there is no treaty on the subject with the foreign country, the foreign judgment is effective in El Salvador if the following requisites exist: (1) That it was rendered in a personal action; (2) that it was not rendered by default; (3) that the obligation on which it is based is legal in El Salvador; (4) that it is duly authenticated. For the execution of a foreign judgment the approval of the Supreme Court is required after hearing the opposite party.

LABOR RELATIONS:

Labor is a social function and has protection of State. Art. 37 of Constitution guarantees minimum wage which must be sufficient to satisfy normal family needs of worker. Right to strike is recognized in Art. 48.

Social Security is compulsory. Employers, workers and State shall contribute to payment of insurance premiums.

Labor relations are regulated by provisions of Labor Code. (Dec. 15 of June 30, 1972 as am'd). Work week may not exceed 44 hours, shifts of 39 hours for night work. Every worker is entitled to a day rest with pay for each working week and paid vacation after a year of continuous work. 90% of personnel of any concern must be Salvadorians except in special circumstances qualified by Minister of Labor. There are special regulations for minors and women's work.

Except for agricultural work, domestic service, labor agreements should appear in writing, but lack of formalities may not be prejudicial to laborer if he can prove terms of his contract.

Employees and laborers are protected against unjust termination of contract. Disability resulting from labor accident and certain other occupational risks are specifically covered. (Art. 316, etc.).

Social Security Law No. 1263 of Dec. 3, 1953 created Salvadorean Social Security Institute. Basic regulations were issued in Dec. 37 of May 10, 1954 and Dec. 11 of Sept. 25, 1968; as am'd by Law 100, Dec. 14, 1978 and Decree 54 of July 21, 1986.

LEGISLATURE:

Legislative Assembly meets in regular session on May 1 of each year. It shall also meet in extraordinary sessions whenever necessary. (Const. 1983, art. 122).

LIENS:

There are three classes of privileged credits: (1) Those affecting all property of the debtor, namely, judicial costs in the general interest of the creditors, funeral expenses, and 80% of sums payable for support; (2) those affecting specific property, such as the liens of (a) innkeepers on debtor's effects brought to the inn, (b) carriers on articles carried, for cost of transportation and damages, and (c) pledgees on the article pledged; (3) mortgage credits. The law recognizes certain other liens, such as maritime liens and miners' liens. (C. C. 2212-2230).

LIMITATION OF ACTIONS:

See topic Prescription.

LIMITED PARTNERSHIP:

See topic Partnership.

MARRIAGE:

(C. Fam. arts. 11-35, 90-117).

Marriage ceremony is performed by Attorney General, mayor or departmental governor or notary public, but foreigners with less than five years of residence may not marry before notary and advance publication is required. Marriages by proxy are allowed. No religious marriages may be performed unless there has been previous civil ceremony.

Marriages of following persons are prohibited: (1) Minors under 18 years old; (2) persons mentally incapacitated; (3) persons already married. Marriages between following persons are also prohibited: (1) Relatives by consanguinity or adoption in direct line; brothers and sisters; (2) surviving spouse and person implicated in death of deceased spouse. Minors below age of 18 require consent of parents, guardian, or Attorney General.

Marriages are considered invalid and may be annulled for following causes: (a) causes for absolute nullity of marriage are: (1) not contracted before proper authority, (2) lack of consent by any party, (3) parties are of same sex, (4) prohibited marriages above mentioned, except case of minors; (b) causes of relative nullity of marriages are: (1) error in person, (2) duress, (3) not contracted in presence of witnesses, (4) minority of either party. Marriages where consent was given under error or duress, but such marriages are validated if parties live together three months after error was known or duress ceased.

A marriage contracted abroad by a Salvadorean according to the laws of a foreign country or the Salvadorean laws is valid in El Salvador.

Law regulates common law marriage.

MINES AND MINERALS:

(L.D. 544 of Dec. 14, 1995 and Decree 68 of Aug. 7, 1996).

State is owner of all mineral deposits within its territory and its continental shelf. State may grant rights of exploration, exploitation, processing and commercialization to individuals, private entities, whether local or foreign, with exception of certain government officials and their relatives. All mining activities and disputes are subject to Salvadorian law and jurisdiction. Mining titles constitute jus ad rem, distinct from surface. Prior permission is required to alienate, encumber or inherit. Exploration licenses are granted for maximum period of three years, which may be extended for two years; maximum allocated area is 50 square kilometers. Exploitation concessions are granted for maximum period of 30 years, which may be extended. Rights to process and commercialize minerals are included in exploitation concession. Environmental impact assessment is mandatory. On termination of concessions area to which concession was granted must be immediately reverted to State and installations must be transferred to State without compensation. Exploration licenses and exploitation concessions are subject to all taxes. Royalty equal to 3% of value of exploited metal mineral must be payed to State and 1% to municipality where mine is located for exploitation of metal and nonmetal minerals.

Petroleum Law, Decree 626 of Mar. 17, 1981, regulates promotion, development and control of exploration and exploitation of hydrocarbons, as well as their transportation. Hydrocarbons are property of State. Executive Power is authority in charge of Law's application. Executive Commission of Rio Lempa (C.E.L.) has exclusivity for exploration and exploitation of mineral substances and may execute contracts with

MINES AND MINERALS . . . *continued*
other parties aimed to achieve said activity. Types of contracts are: (a) Operation contracts, in which contracting party bears risk for mining operation being compensated with percentage of total production obtained; (b) contracts for rendering of services, in which contracting party agrees on behalf and at risk of C.E.L., to perform specific petroleum activities, furnishing all technology, capital, and machinery necessary to carry out contracted work for certain amount of cash, or its equivalent in petroleum or gas. Arts. 30, 31, 32, and 33 of Law establish obligations of natural or juridical persons that enter into any of above-mentioned agreements with C.E.L. Foreign corporations will be subject to regulations established in C. XIII, Tit. II of Commercial Code in order to enter into these license agreements with exception of "prestation of services" in which case Ministry of Economy may authorize it.

Payments made to contractor for exploitation of petroleum and gas are taxed by so-called "Specific Direct Tax", which must be paid in accordance with Arts. 62 and 65 of Law. C.E.L. shall be withholding agent for payment of said tax. Transportation service for hydrocarbons will be furnished by C.E.L. or through third contracting parties. Any controversy arising out of license agreements shall be resolved by arbitration. Registry for activities related to hydrocarbons will be kept by C.E.L., organization and functioning of which shall be governed by further regulations.

MONOPOLIES AND RESTRAINT OF TRADE:

Art. 110 of Salvadorian Constitution of 1983 proscribes all types of monopolies in hands of private, natural or juridical persons.

Art. 14 of Decree 279 of Mar. 12, 1969 forbids any practices or financial transactions on production, commercial and pricing practices aimed at elimination of free competition or creation of monopolies.

Central American Regulations on Unfair Trade Practices of Dec. 12, 1995 implemented principles established by Agreements of World Trade Organization protect Central American products from unfair practices of international trade imposing countervailing duties on import of goods out of area.

Central American governments may issue restrictive covenants to protect temporarily their local production from massive import of same or similar products that may cause pecuniary loss to local producers.

Consumer Protection Law.—(L. D. 267 of Aug. 31, 1992). In accordance with this law, Government has right to control production, distribution and sale of services and goods in defense of consumers. Law deals with monopoly, publicity of goods and services, professional ethics, and fines and penalties for its infringement. Law establishes, Dirección General de Protección al Consumidor, government agency to research marketing of products and apply law.

MORTGAGES:

(C. C. 2157-2180; L. D. 2011 of 1955).

Mortgages must be executed in the form of public instruments and are not valid unless recorded in the mortgage registry. Mortgages made abroad on property in El Salvador are valid if duly recorded. Only realty, some aircraft and ships can be mortgaged. The mortgage covers the increases and improvements of the property as well as sums due for rentals and insurance, but a mortgage of mines or quarries does not cover substances separated from the soil. A property already mortgaged may be mortgaged again notwithstanding any stipulation to the contrary.

When property encumbered by mortgage is sold at a public sale under execution, it is sold free of the encumbrance if the mortgage creditor was duly summoned; in such case the proceeds of the sale are devoted to the payment of liens in their order of preference. Mortgage foreclosures follow the general rules of summary actions and execution of judgments. After the sale there is no right or redemption.

NOTARIES PUBLIC:

(Notarial Law, D. 218 of Dec. 6, 1962 as am'd and 593 of May 28, 1964; C. C. 1007-1015. See also Law 516 of May 4, 1978 on photostatic copies, Law 48 of Sept. 14, 1978 on notaries acting abroad, and Decree 1073 of Apr. 13, 1982 as am'd by Decree Law 772 of Apr. 25, 1991 on voluntary jurisdiction).

Notaries require the authorization of the Supreme Court. The following may be notaries: (1) Lawyers who obtained their law diplomas in El Salvador; (2) native Salvadoreans who obtained their law diplomas abroad; (3) naturalized Salvadoreans and Central Americans who obtained their diplomas abroad, and have resided in the country two years immediately before becoming notaries. In certain cases judges of first instance and justice of the peace act as notaries, and likewise Salvadorean diplomatic and consular agents sometimes have notarial functions.

Instruments executed before a notary must be prepared with certain formalities. They must be in Spanish. The notary must declare that he knows the parties or that they were identified. The notary retains the original document in a protocol and furnishes the parties with certified copies which have the effect of originals in court.

See topic Acknowledgments.

PARTNERSHIP:

(C. Com. 44-125).

General Partnership.—(Sociedad Colectiva: C. Com. 73-92). In general partnership, partners can use as company name, name of one or more partners accompanied by "and company" or other similar words, e.g., "and brothers." Partners are jointly liable for debts of company; any agreement exempting partners of such responsibility is null and void towards third parties; partners among themselves can stipulate that responsibility of one or more is limited to certain amount. Any person that allows his name to appear in any or all documents of company shall be considered a partner, also subject to unlimited responsibility. It is formed by public instrument recorded in Commercial Registry, and must state all personal data of partners, domicile, purpose, duration, etc. Company must be administered by one or more managers who can be partners or third persons. In general, unless contrary intention is shown, all decisions must be taken by majority of votes, e.g., removal of administrators. In general rules, governing corporations are also applicable to companies, such as responsibility of partners, managers, reserve fund, dissolution, liquidation, etc.

Limited Partnership.—(Sociedad en Comandita: C. Com. 93-100). In this company one or more partners are special partners liable only for amount of their contribution. In this case name of company must have following words "and company" or "S. en C."; if requisite is omitted, it shall be treated as a general partnership. If special partner allows his name to appear in firm name or engages in management of same, he is jointly liable with general partners.

Limited Liability Company.—(Sociedad de Responsibilidad Limitada: C. Com. 101-125). Limited liability company, as its name indicates, is a company where all partners are only liable up to amount contributed to it. Its name must be followed by words "Limitada" or "Ltda."; omission of this requisite means that all partners are personally and unlimitedly liable for obligations of company. Capital of company cannot be less than 10,000 colones; industrial contributions or other type of consideration rather than cash is not allowed. Any person alien to company that tolerates inclusion of his name in firm name is liable to third parties doing business with company. This type of company cannot have more than 25 partners; otherwise, it shall be null and void. It must have special book called "registry of partners," which shall be kept by one of administrators and in which must be recorded names and contributions of all partners. Other provisions of Code regarding general partnership and/or corporations are also applicable to these companies such as administration, reserve fund, dissolution, liquidation, etc.

Individual Limited Liability Company.—(Empresa de Responsibilidad Limitada Individual: C. Com. 600-622). This type of company is authorized to operate if name of individual owner is followed by words "Empresa de Responsibilidad Limitada Individual," or its abbreviation "E. de R. L.". In order to form it, it is necessary to prepare an inventory regarding all assets that shall integrate its patrimony. Several articles of Code regulate manner to integrate such corporate capital, if assets consist of shares or other valuable goods. In general, public instrument, constitutive of company must contain name and personal data of owner, name of company, purposes, domicile, capital and all information regarding reserves, etc. Its capital can be subject to increase or decrease, but it requires previous approval by Supervisor of Commercial Companies. Other provisions also regulate situations regarding dissolution and liquidation.

Minimum Capital.—Any entity with foreign members or administrators, directors, managers or general attorneys in fact must have minimum capitals required for corporations dedicated to commerce or industry under Law of Regulation of Commerce and Industry 279 of Mar. 4, 1969. (See topic Corporations; also topic Aliens).

See also topic Corporations.

PATENTS:

(L.D. 604 of July 15, 1993 regulated by Decree 35 of Sept. 28, 1994).

Invention Patents.—Any invention of products or proceedings which are novel, represent inventive step and are susceptible of industrial application. Invention is novel when it is not within state of art. Any individual or juridical person who invents or discovers or improves something of industrial application may obtain patent. Discoveries, scientific theories and mathematical methods; economic or business plans, principles or methods; surgical, therapeutic or diagnostic treatment methods, inventions contrary to public policy and morals, are not patentable. Patents are granted for 20 years from filing date, except for medicines that are granted for 15 years from filing date. Patent gives exclusive right of exploitation but compulsory license may be granted in case of declared emergency or national security reasons. Patent rights are transferable.

Utility Models.—Any new model which may be applied to industrial object may be registered as ownership of author. Utility models are new forms of objects or mechanism, which, provided they have practical use, are registrable. Registration term is ten years from filing date. Provisions regarding patents are applicable to models.

Industrial Designs.—Any new design which may be applied to industrial object may be registered as ownership of author if no publicity thereof has been made in any form. Registration is five years, renewable for additional five years.

Trade Secrets.—Law also protects trade secrets and considers them as any confidential information that is valuable and provides competitive or economic advantages to owner. Information considered trade secret is protected even if it is not expressed in tangible form.

Treaties.—El Salvador has ratified Paris Convention on Industrial Property.

PLEDGES:

A pledged object must necessarily be delivered to creditor. In case of non-payment of debt, creditor may demand sale of pledge at public sale and if there is no admissible bid, he may demand that pledge be adjudged to him for its appraised value. If appraised value be less than 200 colones, pledge may be awarded to creditor at such value without need of public sale. Parties may stipulate that creditor keep or dispose of pledge at a designated value without need of a sale. (C. C. 2134-2156).

Commercial Code (1525-1538) also contains provisions regarding subject. Credits or goods can be subject of this contract. It can be executed by debtor himself, or by a third party, even without approval of debtor. Usually object of pledge must be delivered to creditor or can be given to a third party in order to be kept by him.

PRESCRIPTION:

(C. C. 1658, 1668, 2231-2263; C. Com. 995-998 among other provisions).

The acquisition of property or rights by virtue of possession and the loss of rights by failure to enforce them is called prescription. Prescription may be waived expressly or tacitly as far as it has run. The rules of prescription apply also to the State and to municipalities. Prescription is interrupted: (a) Temporarily when natural causes require a temporary relinquishment of possession; (b) permanently when another person takes possession and is not ousted; (c) when another claimant brings suit against the possessor, but in this case the interruption can be alleged only by such other claimant and only if the suit is properly prosecuted and not dismissed.

Ownership is acquired by ordinary or extraordinary prescription. By ordinary prescription real property is acquired in ten years and personal property in three years, but as against persons residing abroad and unrepresented in the Republic the periods are

PRESCRIPTION . . . *continued*
extended, every two days being counted as one. Property is acquired by extraordinary prescription in 30 years of open, uninterrupted possession, without need of showing any title.

Limitation of Actions.—Prescriptive period in which power to enforce rights is lost varies according to nature of action. More important are: (a) Ordinary actions not otherwise limited, 20 years; (b) summary actions, ten years; (c) actions between partners, two years; (d) title warranty actions, four years; (e) actions for fees of professional men, three years; (f) actions of employees for salaries and wages, two years; (g) actions of commercial clerks for cost of repairing or provisioning vessels, one year; (h) actions for rescission of personal property sales, six months in civil contracts.

In the acquisition of property by ordinary prescription and in the extinguishment of the actions designated under (a) and (b) above, the prescriptive period is suspended with respect to minors, demented persons, deaf and dumb persons, persons under guardianship, and claimants of an inheritance. However, after thirty years such suspension is no longer considered.

Commercial Code (995-998) also sets forth certain rules regarding subject, for example: (1) Actions for rectifications in checking account balances, six months; (2) actions to declare void agreements taken in shareholders' meetings, checks, bills of exchange, actions for hidden defects in merchandise, actions concerning transportation contracts and actions regarding liability of administrators, auditors and interventors of companies, one year; (3) actions derived from contracts such as partnerships, sales, deposits, commissions, banking credits, etc., two years. Notwithstanding above, in general, mercantile rights shall prescribe in five years. Parties are not allowed to modify terms of prescription by mutual agreement.

PRINCIPAL AND AGENT:

(C. C. 1875-1931).

An agency may be conferred in writing or orally, or tacitly, but in court it can be proved by witnesses only in accordance with general rules of evidence, and a private document will not be accepted where a public instrument is required. A general power of attorney covers only acts of administration; a special power is required for other acts, such as to sell, mortgage, compromise, etc. Principal must reimburse agent for expenses and for damages caused by agency and pay stipulated or usual compensation.

An agency is terminated by: (a) Termination of business or expiration of time for which given; (b) revocation by principal; (c) resignation of agent; (d) death, bankruptcy or insolvency, or declaration of incapacity, of principal or agent; (e) cessation of principal in capacity in which he conferred agency.

Commercial Code (1083-1097) also regulates this matter. Agent undertakes commercial transactions in name of his principal. Salary must be stipulated by mutual agreement, but in absence of it, commercial practice of place when it is executed must be taken into account. In case agent refuses to continue with contract, he must communicate such refusal to principal within eight days, but nevertheless, he must take necessary steps to protect merchandise remitted to him or kept under his control. Agent must keep merchandise in good condition and is responsible for any damage, unless some unforeseeable event or hidden defect in merchandise releases him from liability. Agent must enter into insurance contracts to protect merchandise under custody, but he is free of any responsibility if he has received orders from his principal to contrary. Agent must fulfill his duties according to instructions received and if such instructions are not clear enough he must proceed according to local practice in force in that particular market. Agent also has lien on goods sent to him for amount of his advances, expenses, credits, etc.

Other provisions of Commercial Code (1066-1082) regulate commission merchant; he acts on his own account as undisclosed agent of a principal before third parties.

Agents Representing Corporations.—(C. Com. 392-410, 1066-1097). Natural juridical persons can be agents. In case of absence of agreement regarding salaries, agent is allowed to receive a commission proportionate to amount of business involved according to practice in such place. If, due to principal's fault, business is not completely successful, nevertheless, agent has right to receive total amount of compensation as agreed upon. In case of unilateral termination of contract, either one is allowed to receive payment for damages or expenses incurred, which Commercial Code sets forth in detail.

PUBLIC INSTRUMENTS:

A public instrument is a document executed by or before a notary public or other competent official. It is full proof of the fact of its execution, and the declarations made therein are proof against the parties or their successors. The law requires numerous contracts to be executed as public instruments, e.g., mortgages, articles of incorporation, etc. Other documents are private documents. With respect to third persons, a private document is effective only from the death of one of its signers, or the date on which it was presented in court or was registered or inventoried by a public officer or acknowledged before a notary. A writing is required to prove as obligation of over 200 colones. (C.C.1569-1585. See also topic Notaries Public).

REAL PROPERTY:

Arts. 102 and 105 of Salvadorian Constitution guarantees every person free disposition of his property except owners of rural real property over 245 hectares. Expropriation is possible only by reasons of public or social interest, when authorized by law and subject to just compensation. (Art. 106, Const.).

Rural real property may not be acquired by foreigners in whose countries of origin Salvadorians do not have this right, except in case of land for industrial establishments.

Lands and buildings or improvements of any kind attached thereto are real property as well plants and trees and, in general, anything united to land in a fixed and permanent manner. Arts. 587, etc., of Civil Code list different ways to acquire real property; occupation, accession, adverse possession and conveyance. For a transfer to be binding on third parties it must be recorded in Registry of Real Property. (Arts. 673, etc., Civil Code.).

Law 157 of Mar. 22, 1979 regulates lease of rural farms or portions thereof.

Dec. 4 of Jan. 17, 1978 regulates parcelization for commercial purposes of agricultural or forest lands.

Decree 153 of Mar. 5, 1980 as am'd regulates agrarian reform.

Decree 31 of Feb. 21, 1961 as am'd regulates condominiums.

RECORDS:

There is a public registry of real property, mortgages and judgments. Registrars may refuse to record a defective instrument or one as to which their books show an inconsistent entry, and from such decisions an appeal may be taken to the courts. There is also a registry of the civil status, for the recording of births, marriages, divorces, etc., and a mercantile registry for the recording of articles of incorporation and partnership, powers of attorney, etc. (C. C. 303-337, 673-744; C. Com. 456-487; Law of May 14, 1897 as am'd, L.D. 292 of Feb. 19, 1986 and its regulations Decree 24 of Apr. 29, 1986; Law 271 of Feb. 15, 1973 as am'd, regulated by Decree 33 of May 7, 1973 as am'd).

REDEMPTION:

See topics Executions; Mortgages.

SALES (Realty and Personalty):

(C. C. 651-672, 1597-1686).

A sale is perfected when an agreement is reached as to thing sold and price, but title does not pass until delivery of personalty or transfer of realty by deed. (See also topic Deeds.) Even if payment be made for promise of a contract, either party may withdraw, with loss of sum paid by him who paid it or loss of double such sum by him who received it; however, if no time limit is specified, there may be no withdrawal after two months; and if payment was expressly made as part of purchase price, or as a token of agreement, sale is perfected. Taxes and costs of deed and of delivery are for account of seller.

If seller delays delivery, buyer may either insist on contract or cancel it, with damages in either case; but if buyer has failed to pay or in case of a sale on installments, if his financial position suffers, seller may demand payment or security. Right to repurchase cannot be reserved for over four years and cannot be assigned. Seller warrants against serious hidden defects. If real estate sold on basis of its area is found to have a different area from that declared, an adjustment of price is made; but if difference exceeds 10%, purchaser has option of rescinding contract.

Commercial sales (C. Com. 1013-1050) involve those executed within normal exploitation of commercial enterprise, and those involving commercial things. Following sales are not considered commercial: Those performed by farmers regarding animals and crops and artisans of objects manufactured by them. In absence of price, it shall be understood to be fixed, if it is one rated at stock exchange or market, national or foreign at a certain date, if indicated. If a bona fide purchaser buys goods or merchandise from a store and later on he finds out that owner of store was not authorized to sell them, nevertheless, sale is considered valid. If buyer is allowed to examine goods at time of purchase, he cannot have action against seller in case of defects. However, if purchaser received merchandise wrapped up or packed, and if he could not reasonably inspect such goods, he has action against seller if exercised within eight days after reception of goods. In case of hidden defects of merchandise buyer has 15 days after discovery of them to denounce such fact before a notary public. Seller guarantees for a determined period of time that goods were sold in good condition and, unless contrary agreement, buyer must denounce any defect regarding functioning of goods or machinery within 30 days after discovery. Statute of limitations, in this case, is six months after date of such report. In absence of any specific period, it shall be understood that guarantees are given for a three year period.

Provisions of Code regulate in detail sales "documents against acceptance," "documents against payment" and sales "cost, insurance, freight" (CIF), "free on board" (FOB), and "cost and freight" (CF).

In case of sales of goods in installments, it is agreed that buyer acquires ownership of them when total amount or at least certain amount of price has been paid for. In this instance contract must be registered in Registry of Commerce, if value is above 1,000 colones. Other articles of code regulate necessary procedure to follow in case of nonpayment or nonfulfillment of conditions indicated in contract. In general, taxes and insurance, if any, must be paid by buyer, and all risks and damages to goods must be borne by him too.

SEALS:

Seals are not used in private matters. A document executed before a notary has most of the effects of a sealed instrument in the United States.

SHIPPING:

Vessels constructed in El Salvador or owned by Salvadoreans are entitled to Salvadorean registry; other vessels may also be so registered by authorization of the Executive. Coastwise trade is restricted to Salvadoreans. (Navigation Law 236 of 1933). Most of the admiralty provisions are found in Arts. 476-769 of old Code of Commerce. However, certain provisions of new C. Com. also regulate matter, such as bills of lading.

STATUTES:

Most of legal provisions are codified. Principal codifications are Civil Code; Code of Civil Procedure; Penal Code; Code of Criminal Procedure; Code of Commerce. Laws are published in government paper entitled "Diario Oficial."

TAXATION:

Real estate transfer tax is exempted up to 250,000 colones, and 3% on excess of 250,000 of value of property transferred. (L. D. 552 of Dec. 18, 1986 as am'd).

Income Tax (L. D. 134 of Dec. 18, 1991 as am'd and its regulations, Decree 101 of Dec. 21, 1992 as am'd).—Individuals and trusts domiciled in El Salvador, and estates

TAXATION . . . *continued*
of decedents whose last domicile was in El Salvador, until inheritance is accepted, are subject to taxation on incomes received from sources in or out of country.

Other individuals, estates and trusts and any corporation or juridical person whether national or foreign, domiciled or not, are subject to tax on income from Salvadorian sources only.

Among others, the following items are exempt: insurance proceeds; gifts and inheritances; rent from house occupied by owner; interest received by credit institutions domiciled abroad; workers compensation; severance; pensions.

Among items which are deductible are necessary expenses to produce income, salaries, social security payments, interests, depreciation, investment for welfare of workers, gifts to charitable institutions, insurance premiums, bad debts under certain circumstances, traveling expenses, rent paid for personal or real property use in production of taxable receipts.

Individuals with income other than salary may also deduct up to 5,000 colones, for each of following expenses: hospital and medical, educational. Individuals with income from salary only up to 50,000 colones have single deduction of 12,000 colones.

Rates.—

Individuals, estates and trusts domiciled in El Salvador are exempted on first 22,000 colones and their income is subject to tax rates of 10%, 20% or 30%. Tax cannot exceed 25% of net income. Individuals, estates and trusts not domiciled in El Salvador are taxed at rate of 25% on net income. Juridical persons domiciled or not are exempted on first 75,000 colones and their net income is taxed at rate of 25%.

Withholding Tax.—Payments to resident individuals are subject to withholding tax calculated according to special procedure. Payments to nonresident individuals and non-domiciled juridical persons, trust and estates are subject to withholding tax, at 20% rate with certain exceptions, such as cultural, artistic and sports activities which are subject to 5% rate on gross income. Lottery awards to same individuals are subject to 25% rate. Resident individuals are subject to 10% withholding tax on interest and fees paid for services.

Tax on Dividends and Capitalizations from Profits.—Under income tax law, dividends are generally exempt from withholding taxes, but stockholders must declare them in their own return, excepting stock dividends. However, when distributee is a corporation not domiciled in country or individual residing abroad 20% must be withheld.

Interest payments by financial institutions are subject to withholding tax at 10%.

Salaries and other permanent service compensations are subject to system of withholding at source as provided by Regulations.

Lottery, raffle, game or similar awards or gains in excess of 1,000 colones are subject to 2% withholding tax if recipient is domiciled in the country, and 25% if otherwise, and then on entire amount. These taxes do not apply to national lotteries or other exempt awards.

Any withholding tax on payments in kind must be made in cash in proportion to market value of assets.

Capital gains from sale, exchange or negotiation of personal or real property assets, realized by a taxpayer not habitually dedicated to that kind of activities are to be recognized according to a special formula, dividing the gain by the number of years of holding of the property and adding the quotient to the ordinary taxable income. This sum is subject to the corresponding ordinary tax. The over-all rate thus applied, i.e., the rate resulting from dividing the tax for said sum of taxable income, is divided by 2 and the resulting one-half is the rate to be applied to rest of gain not included as ordinary income. When there are several gains from assets held for different numbers of years a similar formula applies, adding up all the quotients of the several gains and subtracting the quotients of the losses and the result, if positive, is added to ordinary income. Tax rate on this is divided by 2 and the result is rate applicable to rest of gain not included as ordinary income.

If a sale has been subject to gift, tax, as presumed gift under the special law, the capital gain of the seller is not taxable.

Gift tax ranges from 2% on gifts between 10,000 and 15,000 colones to descendants and ascendants, to 56% on amounts over 1,000,000 colones to unrelated persons. If heirs are aliens not domiciled in republic, tax ranges from 30% payable by ascendants, descendants and spouse, to 60% payable by unrelated persons, whatever amount of gift.

Sales between spouses or close relatives are presumed to be taxable gifts. (L. D. 123 of Nov. 8, 1974 as am'd).

Sales Tax.—(L. D. 296 of July 24, 1992 as am'd regulated by Decree 83 of Sept. 22, 1992 as am'd). Tax is levied on transfer, import, export and sales of most goods and rendering services at rate of 13%.

Export Incentives Law.—(L. Decree 460 of Mar. 15, 1990 as am'd regulated by Decree 68 of Nov. 27, 1990). Law grants special benefits to industries dedicated to export services and nontraditional products outside Central American region. Tax incentives consist mainly in reimbursement of import taxes and other indirect taxes paid by export activity equal to 8% of FOB value of exported goods, for export service reimbursement is 8% of bill value, and 100% exemption from stamp tax. Companies exporting 100% of their production are also exempted from 100% of tax on patrimony.

Free Zones Law.—(L. Decree 461 of Mar. 27, 1990 as am'd regulated by Decree 56 of Sept. 20, 1990). National or foreign individual or legal entity may establish and manage free zones, and operate in free zones by authorization of Ministry of Finance. Owners and managers of free zones are exempted from income tax for 15 years from start of operation, from tax on business net capital and from stamp tax and other indirect taxes on rents received in free zones. Companies operating in free zones engaged exclusively in export and companies in bonded areas exporting their entire production or engaged in international markets of goods are exempted from income tax and from tax on business net capital for ten years from start of operation, which can be extended to 20 years. Raw materials, equipment machinery, parts, components and everything necessary for establishment, management and operation in free zones may be imported duty free. Infringement of law can carry suspension of cancellation of authorization, or imposition of fine.

TRADEMARKS:

(Central American Convention for the Protection of Industrial Property L.D.85 of Sept. 29, 1988; Laws of July 20, 1921 as am'd govern only on subjects not regulated by Convention).

Trademarks comprise any sign, word, expression or any other graphic or material means which because of its special characteristics can clearly distinguish products, merchandise or services of person or corporation.

Trademarks are classified as industrial or manufacturers' marks, commercial marks and service marks.

Industrial or manufacturers' marks are those that distinguish goods produced or processed by specified manufacturing or industrial enterprise.

Commercial marks are those that distinguish goods commercial enterprise sells or distributes regardless of who produces them.

Service marks are those that distinguish activities of enterprises devoted to satisfaction of general needs by means other than manufacture, sale or distribution of goods.

Use of registration of following as trademarks is prohibited: (1) National flags or their colors, if latter appear in same order and positions as in former, coats-of-arms, insignia or distinguishing marks of Contracting States, their municipalities and other public bodies; (2) flags, coats-of-arms, insignia, devices or denominations of foreign nations unless authorization from respective government has been obtained; (3) flags, coats-of-arms, insignia, devices, denominations or acronyms of international agencies of which one or more Contracting States are members; (4) names, emblems and devices of Red Cross and of religious or charitable bodies legally recognized in any of Member States of this Convention; (5) designs of coins or notes that are legal tender in territory of any of Contracting Parties, reproductions of securities and other commercial documents or of seals, stamps, or revenue stamps, or revenue stamps in general; (6) signs, words or expressions that ridicule or tend to ridicule persons, ideas, religions or national symbols of third party states or international agencies; (7) signs, words or expressions, contrary to good morals, public order or good usage; (8) names, signatures, family names and portraits of persons other than person filing application without their consent or, if deceased, consent of their closest ascendants or descendants; (9) technical or common names of products, goods or services when they are intended to protect articles or services included in genus or species to which such names refer; (10) terms, signs or locutions that have passed into general use and which are used to indicate nature of products, goods or services, and qualifying and gentilitial adjectives. Trademarks that have become popular or widespread subsequent to their registration shall not be regarded as having passed into general use; (11) figures, denominations or phrases describing products, goods or services that are to be protected by trademarks or their ingredients, qualities, physical characteristics or use for which they are intended; (12) signs or indications that are used to designate type, quality, quantity, value or season or preparation of products or goods or of provision of services, unless they are followed by designs or phrases that particularize them; (13) usual and current form of products or goods; (14) plain colors considered separately, unless they are combined or accompanied by elements such as signs or denominations having particular or distinguishing character; (15) containers that are in public domain or have come into common use in any of Contracting States and, in general, those that are neither original nor novel; (16) mere indications of origin or denominations of origin, except as set forth in item (b) of Art. 35; (17) distinguishing marks already registered by other persons as trademarks for products, goods or services included in same class; (18) distinguishing marks that by reason of their graphic, phonetic or ideological similarity may mislead or result in confusion with other trademarks or with commercial names, publicity expressions or symbols already registered or in process of being registered, if it is intended to use them to distinguish products, goods or services included in same class; (19) distinguishing marks that may mislead by indicating false source, nature or quality; (20) maps. These may, however, be used as elements of trademarks if they represent country of origin or source of goods which they distinguish.

Registration is mandatory for chemical, pharmaceutical, veterinary and medicinal food products. Term of registration is ten years subject to renewals for equal periods. Licenses must be registered. International Mark Classification applies. Fees are: Registration of each mark or name $50, and of propaganda slogans or signs $25; renewal $50, transfer $10, any certificate or document $5.

Certain provisions of C. Com. also regulate matter.

Convention for the Protection of Industrial Property (Paris, 1883) Revised 1967 as am'd 1979.

TREATIES:

El Salvador is a party, among others, to following:

Multilateral: Convention on private international law (Bustamante Code, Havana, 1928); General Treaty of Central America Economic Integration signed in Nicaragua, 1960 and its Protocol; Inter-American Convention of Laws Concerning Bills of Exchange, Promissory Notes and Invoices. Signed in Panama on Jan. 30, 1975; Inter-American Convention on International Commercial Arbitration. Signed in Panama on Jan. 30, 1975; Inter-American Convention on Letters Rogatory. Signed in Panama on Jan. 30, 1975; Inter-American Convention on the Taking of Evidence Abroad. Signed in Panama on Jan. 30, 1975; Inter-American Convention on the Legal Regime of Powers of Attorney to be used abroad. Signed in Panama on Jan. 30, 1975. Central American Agreement on Tariff and Customs Regime. Signed in Guatemala on Dec. 27, 1984, ratified by D. L. 293 of Jan. 4, 1985.

TRUSTS:

Commercial Code (1233-1262) allows three types of trusts: Inter vivos, mortis-causa (in which case a will is required) and those of mixed nature, that is to say, that trust starts when settlor is still alive, but continues running after his death. Trustee must perform his duties according to trust contract and in absence of particular details, it is understood that trustee cannot be beneficiary of it, and presence of third party beneficiary is indispensable requisite. Beneficiary is allowed to sue trustee, if he has exceeded powers granted. In any case all goods and assets given in trust must return to settlor or vest definitively in beneficiary after maximum term of 25 years. However, trusts in favor of Government, municipalities or charitable institutions can be settled in

See Topical Index in front part of this volume.

TRUSTS . . . *continued*
perpetuity. Settlor can set up a trust for his own benefit. Documents must be registered in Registry of Commerce and/or Registry of Real Estate, as case may be. Trust cannot be gratuitous; in case no compensation has been fixed to trustee, he is allowed to receive 5% of net income produced by goods object of trust.

Other rules of Code determines causes for substitution of trustee and for termination of trust, as well.

WILLS:

(C. C. 996-1145 and Notarial Law Art. 40).

Wills may be made by all except: (1) Persons below age of puberty; (2) demented persons; (3) persons temporarily not of sound mind by reason of intoxication or otherwise; (4) those who cannot clearly express their will orally or in writing. Wills are formal or privileged.

Formal wills are (1) open, also known as nuncupative or public, or (2) closed. The following cannot be witnesses to a formal will executed in El Salvador: (a) Minors below 18 years old; (b) persons temporarily or permanently not of sound mind; (c) blind persons, deaf persons, dumb persons; (d) persons convicted of crimes against property or forgery; (e) persons of notoriously vicious conduct; (f) fraudulent debtors; (g) heirs, their relatives within fourth degree of consanguinity and second of affinity, and legatees; (h) relatives within same degrees of notary before whom will is made; (i) aliens not domiciled in El Salvador; (j) persons who do not understand language of testator.

Open wills are made as public instruments before a notary or judge with the presence of three witnesses. The will must state name and domicile of testator, notary and each witness; place and date of execution; whether testator is of sound mind; age, place of birth, nationality and domicile of testator; names of persons whom the testator married and children, stating whether living or deceased. The will must be read aloud in the presence of the witnesses, and signed by the testator, witnesses and notary. There are special rules for deaf and blind testators.

Closed wills must be signed by the testator and presented by him in a closed envelope to a notary or judge in the presence of seven witnesses, with a statement that the envelope contains his will. A minute of such statement is written on the envelope by the notary, setting forth that the testator is of sound mind, the names of the testator and each witness, and the date, and is signed by the testator, witnesses and notary.

Privileged wills may be made by soldiers in time of war and by persons on board Salvadorean vessels. They are made before certain officers and require fewer formalities than formal wills.

Foreign wills may be made by Salvadoreans in accordance with the laws of the country where they are; or before a Salvadorean diplomatic or consular officer by Salvadoreans or by foreigners domiciled in El Salvador.

Testamentary Dispositions.—The testator must set aside an amount sufficient for the support of the persons to whom he owes support, namely, his spouse, descendants, ascendants and brothers or sisters, if their means of substance are inadequate, but such persons may be deprived of support in certain cases when they have proved themselves unworthy, as by committing a grave offense against the testator or his spouse, ascendants or descendants. If the amount assigned for support is insufficient, the judge may designate an amount or assign a lump sum not exceeding one-third of the net estate. No testamentary provision may be made in favor of the notary or other official before whom the will is executed, nor their wife, ascendants, descendants, brothers or sisters, brothers-in-law or sisters-in-law or servants, and the same rule applies with respect to witnesses of closed wills.

See Topical Index in front part of this volume.

ENGLAND LAW DIGEST REVISER

Crockers
10 Gough Square
London, EC4A 3NJ, England
Telephone: 011 44 171 353 0311
Fax: 011 44 171 583 1417

Reviser Profile

History: The firm was founded by Sir William Charles Crocker before the First World War. The foundation of the practice was built on the handling of compensation claims on behalf of Insurance Companies and Lloyd's Underwriting Syndicates. During the two decades between the wars, Sir William expanded the firm's field of operation into company and commercial work, conveyancing and probate.

Areas of Emphasis and Growth: Crockers provides a service in all branches of the law, including Company and Commercial Work, Domestic and Commercial Conveyancing, Tax Planning, Wills and Probate and Litigation; Commercial Litigation still forms a major part of the firm's business, in particular Libel, Copyright, Personal Injury and Commercial Disputes.

The firm has seven partners, one associate and twelve other fee earners. Mr. Richard Hudson is the senior partner.

Client Base: The firm's clients include leading Lloyd's brokers and underwriting agents, property developers, builders, Insurance Companies, charities and a broad range of public and private companies. Litigation work for the major insurers is principally, but by no means limited to, libel and copyright actions and personal injury claims. The firm also has a substantial private client base on whose behalf all varieties of work are undertaken.

Firm Activities: The firm encourages its partners and fee earners to take active roles both inside and outside the profession; positions held by members of the firm include leading roles in charitable concerns, directorships and honorary positions with commercial and other organisations.

Management: Each department is headed by a partner or partners who are responsible for and supervise the work of that department. Policy decisions affecting the firm as a whole are made by all the partners collectively.

Significant Distinctions: Sir William Charles Crocker was President of The Law Society in 1954, and an Honorary Member of the American Bar Association. Patrick Hodgson, an associate of the firm for many years, was legal adviser to The Secretary of State for the U.S. Navy during the Second World War.

James Crocker, who was Senior Partner and later a Consultant of the firm, was President of the Vintage Sports Car Club for many years and Chairman of a Parliamentary Action Committee dealing with varied aspects of road traffic legislation.

Rupert Grey serves as Trustee for the Born Free Foundation, Drive for Youth and The Liverpool Institute for Performing Arts.

As professional partnerships expand into substantial commercial organisations to serve the major corporate clients in the U.K., there are many clients, both private and commercial, who prefer to be treated as and by individuals, and Crockers continues to carve out a niche amongst such clients in the increasingly competitive world in the City.

ENGLAND LAW DIGEST

(The following is a list of all Topics, including cross-references, covered in this Digest.)

ENGLAND LAW DIGEST

Revised for 1997 edition by

CROCKERS, Solicitors of the Supreme Court of Judicature, London, EC4A.

See topics Law Reports; Statutes.

England is member of EU. See also European Union Law Digest.

ABSENTEES:

In absence abroad person may generally delegate authority to any person of full capacity. Usual to give power of attorney. Under Powers of Attorney Act 1971 it is no longer necessary to file powers of attorney at Central Office of High Court. Special rules relating to trustees abroad contained in Trustee Act 1925. Power may be given to sue or accept service of proceedings but strictly construed.

Power is revoked upon donor becoming mentally incapable. Under enduring Powers of Attorney Act 1985 person may delegate authority to attorney which will endure after donor has become mentally incapable. Attorney shall, as soon as practicable, make application to court for registration of instrument creating power. Power may be limited or unlimited as donor wishes.

ACKNOWLEDGMENTS:

For form see topic Affidavits and Statutory Declarations, subhead Form, Jurat.

ACTIONS:

Generally any person may sue or be sued in English courts subject to rules of procedure framed by courts. Questions relating to evidence such as competence of witness and methods and sufficiency of proof are matters of procedure governed by rules of English courts. Thus, no action is maintainable in England on contract abroad and enforceable by foreign law if proof required by English law is wanting. With certain exceptions English courts cannot take judicial notice of foreign law, which is presumed to be the same. Onus is on one who asserts difference to prove it. May be proved by properly qualified witness or by reference to code.

Plaintiffs resident abroad may be ordered to pay court sum to ensure defendants legal costs will be met by plaintiffs if plaintiffs fail in action. Sum is refunded if plaintiffs succeed.

Limitation of.—See topic Limitation of Actions.

ADMINISTRATION:

See topic Executors and Administrators.

ADOPTION:

Legal adoption in England and Wales regulated by The Adoption Act, 1976, as amended by Children Act, 1989 part 7, schedule 10. Court may, subject to certain provisions in Act, on being satisfied with respect to certain matters, authorise applicant to adopt infant (person under 18) who has never been married. Applicants and joint applicants must be at least 21.

Application can be made by two spouses jointly; otherwise no order can be made authorising more than one person to adopt an infant nor upon the application of one spouse without consent of the other, unless court waives such consent, being satisfied that the spouses have separated permanently or that the other spouse cannot be found or is incapable of giving such consent.

An order cannot be made where the sole applicant is a male and the infant is a female unless the court is satisfied that there are special circumstances.

Conditions Precedent.—Applicant, or at least one of them where application is by married couple, must be domiciled in part of U.K. or in Channel Islands or Isle of Man if full adoption order is required. Infants' parents (or mother if illegitimate) must give consent which may only be dispensed with by court if parent cannot be found or adoption is in child's best interest and consent was being withheld unreasonably or parent has neglected or persistently ill-treated child.

The court may impose, in an adoption order, such terms and conditions as it thinks fit. Court may, for example, order payment to mother. Imposition of conditions in adoption orders should be vary rare course.

Subject to stringent exceptions, neither adopter nor parent or guardian of infant may make or receive or agree to make or receive any payment or other reward in consideration of adoption: Payments have been authorised by court in surrogacy cases but commercial surrogacy is illegal.

Order cannot be made unless: (a) Where applicant not relative or child not placed through adoption agency or court, child is at least year old and has lived with at least one applicant for past 12 months and (b) sufficient opportunities have been afforded to appropriate authority to see child and applicant in home environment. Where more appropriate, custodianship, under Children Act 1975, may be ordered.

Effect of Adoption.—Upon an order being made, all parental responsibility, obligations and liabilities of parent or guardian are extinguished and vest in, and are exercisable by and enforceable against, adopter. Where adopters are married couple, adopted child is treated in law as if born as child of marriage. In case of unmarried couple, adoption order can be granted to one partner with joint residence order in favour of both partners. Child adopted by one person is to be treated by law as if he had been born to adopter in wedlock.

When, after making of an adoption order, adopter or adopted person or any other person dies intestate in respect of any real or personal property (other than property entailed before date of order) that property devolves as if adopted person were child of adopter born in wedlock and not of any other person. In any disposition of real or personal property made by gift intervivos or by will, after date of an adoption order: (1) any reference (express or implied) to child or children of adopter includes, unless contrary intention appears, a reference to adopted person; (2) any reference (express or implied) to child or children of adopted person's natural parents or either of them, unless contrary intention appears, excludes adopted person; and (3) any reference (express or implied) to a person related to adopted person, unless contrary intention appears, is construed as a reference to person who would be related to him if adopted person were child of adopter born in wedlock and not child of any other person. Will or codicil made after Apr. 1, 1959 is to be treated as made on day of testator's death. These provisions do not affect devolution of any property on intestacy of a person who died before Jan. 1, 1950, or any disposition made before that date.

Foreign Adoption.—The Adoption Act 1968 gives effect to Convention on Adoption enabling adoptions authorised in other countries to be effectual in U.K. Act also covers certain adoptions taking place in non-Convention countries.

Provisional Adoption.—A person not domiciled in England, Wales or Scotland may apply for such an order authorising him to take a child out of the country for the purpose of adopting it under the law of applicant's domicile.

A register called the "Adopted Children Register" is kept. Searches of it can be made and certified copies of any entry obtained.

Adoption Services.—Local authorities are required to establish adoption services to provide inter alia, counseling; arrangements for assessing children and prospective adopters and placing children; temporary board and lodging where needed. Independent adoption agencies must be approved by Secretary of State.

AFFIDAVITS AND STATUTORY DECLARATIONS:

Affidavits.—Affidavit is written statement of facts sworn by deponent before person authorised to administer oath. In U.S. affidavit for use in England should be sworn before notary or British consul. They are usually used in judicial proceedings.

An affirmation instead of an oath may be made where it is not reasonably practicable without inconvenience or delay to administer an oath in manner appropriate to person's religious belief. (Oaths Act, 1978).

For use in the High Court affidavits are required to be written, typewritten or printed in black ink, on metric size A4 paper, bookwise, with margin on left side.

Form.—An affidavit is commenced with the title of the action, e.g.:

Forms

In the High Court of Justice 19. . (Initial of plaintiff). No. (in Court index).
Queen's Bench Division (or Chancery Division)
(In Chancery, add "In the Matter of the Estate of . . . ., deceased," or as the case may be)

Between James Brown Plaintiff
—and—
John Smith Defendant

Full christian and surnames and true place of abode of deponent, and his description, must then be stated. For U.S. a proper form is as follows:

I, (full names), of No. . . . . Street . . . Town . . . ., County in the State of . . . . United States of America (description) . . . . make oath and say

Then set out the facts deposed to in the first person in paragraphs numbered consecutively and, as nearly as may be, confined to a distinct portion of the subject in chronological order. An affidavit must be confined to facts within deponent's own knowledge, except in interlocutory proceedings, and certain other defined exceptions where statements as to his belief, with sources and grounds thereof, may be admitted.

Every quotation must be placed between inverted commas, and dates, sums and numbers expressed in figures not words. Alterations or interlineations should be avoided, but if made must be authenticated by initials of officer before whom affidavit is sworn; and, in case of erasure, words and figures appearing at time of swearing affidavit to be written on erasure must be rewritten and signed or initialled in margin by such officer.

Jurat.—An affidavit is formally concluded by the jurat, a memorandum of the place, time and person before whom it is sworn.

Full address sufficient for identification must be given and jurat should follow immediately after end of text. It must not be written on page upon which no part of statements in affidavit appears.

The deponent must sign his usual signature or make his mark at the right of the jurat, not beneath it, and the signature and full official character and description of the person before whom the affidavit is sworn, his official seal of office attached, must follow immediately after the jurat, in the form as follows:

Forms

Sworn by the deponent . . . . (Name) . . . . at . . . . in the County of . . . . State of . . . . United States of America on the . . . . day of . . . . 19 . ., Before me, ... } (Signature of Deponent)
(Signature of Officer)
(Seal) . . . . (Title of Officer)

Sworn at . . . . this . . . . . day of. . . . .
Before me, (Signature of Deponent)
(Signature of Solicitor/Commissioner for Oaths) Solicitor/Commissioner for Oaths

If the deponent is blind, or illiterate, the jurat

See Topical Index in front part of this volume.

AFFIDAVITS AND STATUTORY DECLARATIONS . . . *continued*
is as follows:

Sworn by the deponent . . . . (name) at (place and date as above) . . . . . . I having first truly distinctly and audibly read over the contents of the above affidavit to the said deponent who seemed to perfectly understand the same and made his mark thereto in my presence. Before me, (etc., as above).	The mark of X (Deponent's name)

On front page of affidavit and on backsheet one must state: (i) Party on whose behalf it is filed, (ii) initials and surname of deponent, (iii) number of affidavit in relation to deponent and (iv) date when sworn e.g. Defendant: J Smith: 1st: 6.6.1986.

For use in county courts affidavits are, for most purposes, prepared on specially printed forms provided free by each court. They must, however, be sworn in same manner as those for use in High Court.

If deponent is atheist affidavit may be affirmed rather than sworn and jurat is altered by replacing word "sworn" by "affirmed".

Exhibits.—Any document may be referred to in the body of an affidavit, as an exhibit, thus: "the said letter is now produced and shown to me and marked 'A.B.'" (the deponent's initials are generally used).

Where there is more than one exhibit best course is to use as exhibit marks deponent's initials followed by consecutive numbers, as thus "A.B.1." "A.B.2." etc. By this means exhibits to affidavits of several witnesses are readily identified.

Every exhibit referred to in an affidavit must be marked with the short title of the cause or matter, as hereinbefore set out for an affidavit, and bear a certificate signed by the officer before whom the affidavit is sworn, as follows:

Form

A. B. v. C. D. (title of action)

This is the Exhibit marked "A.B." (or "A.B.1.") referred to in the Affidavit of X.Y. sworn in this action (if Chancery, "Matter" not "Action") this . . . . day of . . . ., 19. .."

Before me,
(Name and Title of Officer.)

Statutory Declarations.—Solemn verification of facts, usually used in cases other than judicial proceedings, e.g. conveyancing, tax, company matters.

Form.—They must start with:

"I A.B. of (Address) do solemnly and sincerely declare as follows . . . . . ."

Last paragraph should read:

"AND I make this solemn declaration believing the same to be true and by virtue of the provisions of the Statutory Declarations Act 1835."

Remaining requirements are as for Affidavits.

Jurat.—

Declared before me at (address) on Signature of Declarant
(date)
signature and qualification of person taking declaration

AGENCY: See topic Principal and Agent.

ALIENS:

Nationality covered by British Nationality Act 1981. Alien is person who is neither Commonwealth citizen nor British protected person nor citizen of Republic of Ireland.

Alien cannot hold any office and not qualified for any municipal, parliamentary or other franchise. Except in wartime, alien may sue or be sued and is triable in criminal matters. See topic Actions.

Visitors.—Only British citizens, citizens of Republic of Ireland and "patrials" have right of abode in U.K. Others must obtain leave to land here. Aliens must, in most cases, register with police after staying three months. E.E.C. nationals not subject to entry restrictions. See topic Immigration.

With effect from Oct. 21, 1991 visitors who have been admitted to U.K. for stay of six months (other than for purposes of receiving private medical treatment) will not be permitted to extend duration of their stay.

British Citizenship.—

On 1 Jan. 1983 British citizenship automatically acquired, except certain formerly stateless persons, by all persons who till then citizens of U.K. and colonies who have right of abode in U.K. Certain persons registered under transitional provisions of British Nationality Act 1948 become British citizens if ancestral connection with U.K.

After 1 Jan. 1983 following become British citizens: (a) Children born in U.K. at least one of whose parents is British citizen or is settled in U.K.; (b) foundlings; (c) persons born in U.K. one of whose parents subsequently becomes: (i) settled here or (ii) British citizen if that person has lived in U.K. for ten years from birth; (d) children adopted by order of court of U.K.; (e) children born overseas to British citizen if one of his parents: (i) British citizen otherwise than by descent or (ii) British citizen in crown service etc.; and (f) persons registered by Secretary of State as British citizens. Secretary of State may register as British citizens children born abroad if one of parents British citizen by descent and certain requirements of residence in U.K. satisfied. British dependent territory citizens, British overseas citizens, British subjects or British protected persons to be registered as British citizens if living in U.K. lawfully for five years and without restriction for 12 months preceding application or special circumstances. Gibraltarians to be British citizens. Persons may be naturalised as British citizens if resident in U.K. for five years (and not absent from U.K. for more than specified periods), of good character, having sufficient knowledge of English, Welsh or Scottish Gaelic and intending to remain in U.K. or enter crown service. Where fact leading to naturalisation is subsequently found to be incorrect, this does not automatically nullify naturalisation. Those married to British citizens required only to reside in U.K. for three years preceding application (with certain restrictions on periods spent out of U.K.). After 1st Dec. 1990 British Nationality (Hong Kong) (Registration of Citizens) Regulations 1990 and British Nationality (Hong Kong) Act 1990 makes provision in relation to registration of up to 50,000 persons. British Nationality (Hong Kong) (Selection Scheme) Order 1990 gives effect to scheme whereby Governor of Hong Kong may make recommendations in respect of persons falling within four classes within quota prescribed by scheme.

Special transitional provisions enabling those already in process of acquiring rights to citizenship under previous enactments to acquire British citizenship.

Renunciation and Resumption.—Persons may renounce British citizenship if have another nationality or citizenship or except to acquire such. Persons who have renounced British citizenship entitled once only to resume British citizenship again. Otherwise resumption of British citizenship at discretion of Secretary of State.

British Citizenship by Descent.—Persons born outside U.K. with certain family connections with U.K. are British citizens by descent.

British Overseas Citizenship.—Persons who before 1 Jan. 1983 citizens of U.K. and colonies and who do not become British citizens or British dependent territories citizens become British overseas citizens.

British Subject.—Only British subjects without citizenship on 1 Jan. 1983 remain British subjects.

Commonwealth Citizenship.—Persons who not British citizens, British dependent territories citizens, British overseas citizens or British subjects but who citizens of certain countries formerly part of British Empire are Commonwealth citizens, e.g., South Africa, Canada, Australia, New Zealand, India, Sri Lanka, Ghana, Malaysia, Jamaica etc.

Property.—For all practical purposes property of every description may be taken, acquired, held and disposed of by alien in same manner in all respects as by British citizen except he may not own British ship or even share in one but may own shares in English company which owns such ship.

Corporation Owned or Controlled by Alien.—See topic Corporations, subhead Overseas Companies.

See also topic Immigration; and European Union Digest, topic Internal Market, subheads Free Movement of Workers and Freedom to Provide Services.

ASSIGNMENTS:

Assignments of legal choses in action are governed by Law of Property Act, 1925. Any absolute assignment by writing under the hand of the assignor (not purporting to be by way of charge only) of any debt or other legal thing in action of which express notice in writing has been given to the debtor, trustee or other person from whom assignor would have been entitled to claim such debt or thing in action, is effectual in law (subject to equities having priority over right of assignee) to pass and transfer from date of such notice: (a) The legal right to such debt or thing in action; (b) all legal and other remedies for the same and (c) power to give a good discharge for the same without concurrence of assignor. Provided that if debtor, trustee or other person liable in respect of such debt or thing in action has notice (a) that assignment is disputed by assignor or any person claiming under him or (b) of any other opposing or conflicting claims to such debt, or thing in action, he may either call on persons making claim thereto to interplead concerning the same or pay the debt or other thing in action into court. (§136). Furthermore, this section enables legal assignments of legal things in action to be made so that assignee can sue in his own name without joining assignor as party. Assignments of this kind need not be for valuable consideration but must be of whole debt and not of part thereof and written notice to debtor or trustee of fund is essential. Assignment is subject to prior equities.

Assignments of life assurance must be by deed in accordance with the Policies of Assurance Act, 1867.

Equitable assignments both of legal and equitable things in action are recognized as valid. In such assignments the formalities of the statute need not be complied with, but must be complete so that the assignee can demand payment from the debtor. The equitable assignee cannot sue in his own name but must use assignor's name. Notice in writing to debtor is essential, as priority of assignee's rights depends on date of such notice and he is entitled to be paid out of the fund in the order in which he gives notice to the debtor or other person by whom the fund is distributable.

ASSIGNMENTS FOR BENEFIT OF CREDITORS:

By the Deeds of Arrangement Act, 1914, under which any instrument whether, under seal or not, made by, for or in respect of the affairs of a debtor (a) for the benefit of his creditors generally or (b) where debtor was insolvent at date of execution of instrument, for benefit of any three or more of his creditors, otherwise than in pursuance of the law relating to bankruptcy, is deemed to be a deed of arrangement and subject to the provisions of the Act. The following classes of instruments in particular are included: (a) Assignments of property; (b) deeds of, or agreements for, composition and in cases where creditors of debtor obtain control over his property or business; (c) a deed of inspectorship for purpose of carrying on or winding up business; (d) letter of license authorising debtor or any other person to manage, carry on, realise or dispose of business with view to payment of debts and (e) any agreement entered into for purpose of carrying on or winding up debtor's business or authorising debtor or any other person to manage, carry on, realise, or dispose of debtor's business, with view to payment of his debts.

A deed of arrangement is void unless it bears ad valorem duty stamp and is registered with Registrar of Bills of Sale within seven clear days after its execution, if executed in England, or if executed abroad, within seven clear days after time at which it would in ordinary course of post, arrive in England if posted within one week after execution thereof.

A deed for benefit of creditors generally is void unless before or within 21 days of registration it receives the assent in writing of a majority in number and value of creditors. A trustee under a deed must file a statutory declaration that the requisite majority of creditors have assented at time of registration or if deed is assented to after registration within 28 days thereof. He must also give security unless a majority of creditors dispense with it.

ASSIGNMENTS FOR BENEFIT OF CREDITORS . . . *continued*

A debtor is at liberty to make a private arrangement with his creditors upon any terms to which he can get them to agree, but no creditor is bound to join in such a deed unless he thinks proper.

See topic Bankruptcy and Insolvency for additional arrangements available under Insolvency Act 1986.

ASSOCIATIONS:

See topic Partnerships.

ATTACHMENT:

Attachment of debts may be either by:

Garnishee proceedings (which see); or by

Charging order making land, stocks and shares or fund in court available to satisfy judgment for ascertained sum of money, but it will not be made against executor of judgment debtor, in respect of property of infant, or against property of defaulter on Stock Exchange. Proceeds from property sale can also be available. On order being made judgment creditor has same (but no greater) powers as though debtor made valid and effective charge in his favour; or by

Stop order, which may be obtained against fund in court, gives notice to court of creditor's claim and prevents fund being dealt with without his knowledge; or by

Stop notice, i.e., anyone claiming to be interested in any stock registered in its books may serve notice on company to prevent company dealing with shares without first giving him an opportunity of asserting his claim. Claimant must make affidavit in prescribed form and file it with notice at Chancery Chambers or District Registry, from which he will obtain office copies of documents to serve on company. Before dealing with shares company will notify claimant, who within 14 days after notice was sent must apply for injunction against company.

Attachment of Earnings Act 1971 gives court power to enforce maintenance orders and judgment debts against debtors by attaching their earnings.

ATTORNEYS AND COUNSELORS:

These terms are not used in UK—legal profession consists of barristers and solicitors. One cannot be both a barrister and a solicitor at same time. Barrister's main function is to act as advocate in court, but he may also give advice and opinions to his instructing solicitors. Solicitor gives legal advice to his clients and conducts legal proceedings. Solicitors have full rights of audience in lower courts and limited rights in higher courts.

Admission.—To be admitted as solicitor, one must: (1) enrol with Law Society whilst still student; (2) successfully complete necessary examinations (including Legal Practice Course); and (3) serve two years' Articles of Clerkship, usually within law firm. To practice as solicitor, one must: (1) have been admitted as solicitor; (2) hold current Practising Certificate; and (3) be listed on Roll of Solicitors.

To be admitted as barrister, one must: (1) be admitted to one of four Inns of Court (Inner Temple, Middle Temple, Gray's Inn and Lincoln's Inn); (2) successfully complete necessary examinations (including Bar Examination); and (3) normally serve one year's pupillage. There are various bars to admission, including being adjudged bankrupt, being convicted of certain criminal offences, and being solicitor. Before, during or after pupillage, pupil will be "called to the Bar".

Continuing Legal Education.—There is mandatory system of continuing legal education for solicitors.

Discipline.—The Solicitors' Disciplinary Tribunal has power to strike name of solicitor off Roll or require him to answer allegations contained in affidavit, where there are certain grounds which are specified by statute present or solicitor has been found guilty of conduct unbefitting to solicitor (such as conviction for certain criminal offences). For barristers, each of four Inns of Court has disciplinary jurisdiction over its members. Complaints are investigated by Professional Conduct Committee of General Bar Council, who may refer matter to disciplinary tribunal. If charge is proved, tribunal can make order for disbarment, suspension, repayment of fees, or order that Treasurer of barrister's Inn reprimand him. It is the Inn which carries any sentence into effect.

Professional Bodies.—Professional body for solicitors is Law Society, 113 Chancery Lane, London, WC2A 1PL, England (Tel: 0171 242 1222), which exists both to further interests of solicitors and to discharge statutory functions in relation to their admission, conduct and discipline. General Council of the Bar, 3 Bedford Row, London, WC1R, England (Tel: 0171 242 0082) is equivalent organisation which exists to further interests of barristers.

Privileges and Immunities.—Both barristers and solicitors are ineligible for jury service, and enjoy absolute privilege that no defamation action will lie against them for statements made in course of judicial proceedings.

Contingency fees for solicitors are banned in UK, so that, win or lose, client is ultimately responsible to his solicitor for his fees (although frequently, losing client will be ordered to pay both his and his opponent's costs).

Licenses.—Solicitor may not practice without practising certificate, issued annually by Law Society on payment of fee.

Lien.—Solicitor has two liens: (1) right to retain property in his possession until his costs have been paid; and (2) right to ask court for order that property which is recovered as result of solicitor's efforts, be held as security for costs he has incurred in obtaining such recovery. In theory, there is no reason why barrister should not exercise lien over documents in his possession, until his fee has been paid.

AUTOMOBILES: See topic Motor Vehicles.

BANKRUPTCY AND INSOLVENCY:

Corporate Insolvency.—

Company Voluntary Arrangements (Insolvency Act 1986).—Scheme is available whereby company may conclude effective arrangement with its creditors which will be subject to supervision of qualified insolvency practitioner (infra).

Administration Orders (Insolvency Act 1986).—Court can make Administration Order to place management of company in hands of Administrator. Court will do so if satisfied that, inter alia, order would bring about continued survival of company or, failing that, efficient realisation of company's assets. Application is by petition to court presented by either company, its creditors or directors or all or any of those parties acting together or separately. On his appointment statement of company's affairs in prescribed form and verified by affidavit must be submitted to Administrator. Administrator is required within specified period to send statement of his proposals to Registrar of Companies, all creditors and send copies to members of company. Administrator has all necessary management powers including authority to call meetings and to appoint and remove directors.

Administrative Receiver (Insolvency Act 1986).—Administrative receiver is receiver or manager of company's property appointed by debenture holders. 1986 Act codifies Rules relating to receivers. Receiver will have power conferred upon him by instrument under which he was appointed and in addition statutory powers. On his appointment receiver must send company and its creditors notice of his appointment. Within three months of his appointment administrative receiver must send report to Registrar of Companies and to company's creditors containing information about company's financial situation.

Winding Up.—Insolvency Act 1986 modifies Companies Act 1985. Winding up of companies may be voluntarily by either creditors or members or compulsorily by order of court or by resolution of members.

Bankruptcy; Individual Insolvency.—Individuals can also propose composition or scheme of arrangement with their creditors.

Bankruptcy Proceedings (Insolvency Act 1986).—Creditor serves statutory demand upon debtor requiring payment. If debtor fails to comply with demand within three weeks nor has it been satisfied by Court, creditor may petition court for bankruptcy order. Amount of debt concerned must equal or exceed bankruptcy level, currently £750. Debt is for liquidated sum payable to petitioning creditors, either immediately or at some future date and is unsecured. Court will not make bankruptcy order unless it is satisfied that debt has not been paid nor secured nor has debtor any reasonable prospect of being able to pay it when it falls due. Court may dismiss petition if it is satisfied that debtor has made offer to secure or compound for debt in respect of which petition is presented. To be valid debtor must be domiciled or physically present in England and Wales when petition is presented.

Right of debtor to petition for his own adjudication as bankrupt is preserved by §272 of 1986 Act. Debtor must petition on grounds that he is unable to pay his debts, and his petition must be accompanied by statement of his financial affairs. Court may appoint insolvency practitioner who will report to court on debtor's state of affairs and will consider whether proposal for voluntary arrangement is suitable. Court may make bankruptcy order, appointing official receiver of bankrupt's estate pending appointment of trustee in bankruptcy. Where bankruptcy order has been made otherwise on debtor's petition bankrupt must submit statement of his affairs to official receiver within 21 days of his bankruptcy. Trustee in bankruptcy will carry out administration of bankrupt's estate. Bankruptcy will continue until discharged. Under 1986 Act most bankrupts will be automatically discharged after period of three years.

Criminal Offences.—1986 Act revises offences contained in Bankruptcy Act of 1914.

Insolvency Practitioners.—1986 Act introduces system of licensing of insolvency practitioners who have to be authorised by recognised professional body or by relevant authority appointed by Secretary of State.

See also topic Assignments for Benefit of Creditors.

BARRISTERS AND SOLICITORS:

See topic Attorneys and Counselors.

BILLS AND NOTES:

Bills of exchange (including cheques) and promissory notes are regulated by Bills of Exchange Act, 1882, and Cheques Act 1957.

A bill is not invalid because it (a) is not dated, (b) does not specify the value given or that any value has been given therefor or (c) does not specify place where drawn or where payable.

Inland and Foreign Bills.—An Inland bill is one which is or on its face purports to be (a) both drawn and payable within the British Isles or (b) drawn within the British Isles on some person resident therein. Any other bill is a foreign bill. There is no longer any stamp duty on bills. Foreign bills must be protested on dishonour; inland bills need not be.

Cheques.—Bill of exchange drawn on a banker and payable on demand. However (a) cheques are not accepted and therefore holder cannot sue banker on whom a cheque is drawn and (b) drawer is not discharged by holder's failure to present in due time unless he suffers damage and (c) under Acts a banker is protected in certain cases where wrong payment is made or an endorsement is unauthorised or forged and (d) drawer is under a duty of reasonable care towards banker in drawing cheque and (e) rules as to crossing only apply to cheques.

Days of Grace.—Three days of grace no longer added to time of payment where bill not payable on demand (matter now governed by Banking and Financial Dealings Act 1971). Bill is due and payable on last day of time for payment, as fixed by bill unless it is a nonbusiness day when it is then due on succeeding business day. Nonbusiness day is (a) Sun., Sat., Good Friday, Christmas Day; (b) Bank holiday under Act; (c) day proclaimed by Crown as a public fast or thanksgiving; and (d) any day declared by order under Act as a nonbusiness day.

Holder in Due Course.—A person who takes a bill complete and regular on its face before it was overdue, without notice of previous dishonour, in good faith and for value and without notice of defect in title of person who negotiated it, is a holder in due course and holds the bill free of defects of title of prior parties and may enforce payment against all parties liable on the bill. One who derives title from a holder in

See Topical Index in front part of this volume.

BILLS AND NOTES . . . *continued*
due course and is not himself a party to any fraud or illegality affecting the bill has all the rights of holder in due course, although he may have notice of the prior defect. This does not apply to cheques marked "not negotiable," to which the holder cannot give better title than the person from whom he took it had. Every party to a bill is deemed to have become a party thereto for value and each holder is prima facie deemed to be a holder in due course.

Presentment for acceptance is necessary where bill (1) is payable after sight, (2) expressly stipulates it shall be presented for acceptance or (3) is payable elsewhere than at residence or place of business of drawee. If on presentment for acceptance it is not accepted within customary time (stated to be 24 hours) the presentor must treat it as dishonoured by nonacceptance. These provisions do not apply to cheques and notes.

Presentment for payment must be made in case of bill not payable on demand on day it falls due and in case of bill payable on demand within reasonable time after issue or indorsement. Where bill is dishonoured by nonacceptance, presentment for payment is not necessary.

Notice of dishonour must be given, in case of dishonour by nonacceptance or nonpayment, to the drawer and each indorser. Any drawer or indorser to whom notice is not given is discharged unless notice is waived or otherwise dispensed with in accordance with the Act. Dishonoured foreign bills must be noted and protested. There is no need to note and protest a foreign note as distinguished from a foreign bill.

Conflict of Laws.—Where a bill drawn in one country is negotiated, accepted or payable in another, the rights, duties and liabilities of the parties are determined as follows: (1) Validity of the bill as regards requisites of form is determined by the law of the place of issue; validity of a supervening contract (e.g., acceptance, indorsement, etc.) is determined by the law of the place where such contract was made. (2) Interpretation of the drawing, indorsement or acceptance is determined by the law where the contract was made, provided that where an inland bill is indorsed in a foreign country the indorsement must, as regards the payer, be interpreted according to the law of the United Kingdom.

BILLS OF SALE:

See topic Chattel Mortgages; also topic Sales.

CERTIORARI:

Order of certiorari is recognised means of procuring through medium of Queens Bench Division inspection of proceedings of courts of inferior jurisdiction in order that they may be reviewed and rectified.

Grounds of Issue.—When there is some defect or informality apparent on face of proceedings, where there is want of jurisdiction, where it is clear and manifest that adjudication has been obtained by fraud, or where there has been a denial of natural justice.

Procedure.—Leave must be obtained within prescribed time limits (normally three months although there is power to extend time limit inherent in jurisdiction of court) and application is made ex parte to judge, and must be accompanied by statement setting out name and description of applicant, relief sought, grounds, and by affidavits verifying facts relied on. If leave is granted application for certiorari is in criminal case to Divisional Court and in civil case, to judge in open court by way of originating motion. Affidavit must be filed subsequently. Grant of order is discretionary and Court has no power to amend proceedings but proceedings may be quashed and retrial ordered or direction to convict or acquit may be made. This order may be applied for by prosecution by way of appeal from acquittal in lower court.

CHATTEL MORTGAGES:

All mortgages of chattels, except those executed by limited companies, which require registration under the Companies Act (see topic Corporations) and mortgages of aircraft (which are governed by Mortgaging of Aircraft Order 1972), and mortgages of ships come under Bills of Sale Acts, 1878 to 1891. They must be for sum of not less than £30, be duly attested and registered within seven clear days, or if executed out of England within seven clear days after time at which it would in ordinary course of post arrive in England if posted immediately after execution, and be according to form specified in Bills of Sale Acts; otherwise such chattel mortgages are void, even against grantor. Copies have to be filed and are open to public inspection. Registration must be renewed every five years.

CLAIMS:

See topic Executors and Administrators.

COLLATERAL SECURITY: See topic Pledges.

COMMERCIAL REGISTER:

See topics Corporations; Trademarks and Tradenames, subhead Tradenames.

COMMISSIONS TO TAKE TESTIMONY:

See topic Depositions and Discovery.

CONSTITUTION AND GOVERNMENT:

Legislature.—The British Constitution is unwritten in the sense that there is no document or statute laying down the law of the constitution and therefore all the laws can be altered by the Sovereign legislative body, i.e., the Crown in Parliament, composed of the House of Commons, the House of Lords and the Crown. Membership of E.E.C. by Treaty restricts Parliament's legislative powers to those not in conflict with Treaty.

Each House is presided over by a Speaker. The Queen has a right to appoint a Speaker to the House of Lords and in default of special appointment, the Lords may elect their own Speaker, but in practice the Speaker of the House of Lords is the Lord Chancellor. The Speaker of the House of Commons is a member of the House elected by the House, subject to the Queen's approval.

Bills are divided into two classes: (1) Public Bills, subdivided into (a) money bills and (b) bills other than money bills; and (2) Private Bills.

A public bill, other than a money bill, will become law without the consent of the Lords if it is passed in the Commons, and sent up to the Lords in two successive sessions. But one year must elapse between the date of the second reading in the Commons in the first session and the date when it is passed by them in the second session. By the Parliament Act, 1911, if a money bill is not passed unamended by the House of Lords within a month of its being sent up it becomes law on the Royal assent being signified.

Executive.—The executive consists of the Queen in Council, the work being carried on by the Cabinet, a body which has no official corporate existence but which is composed of the ministers at the head of the Government departments, who hold their office during the Queen's pleasure. The ministers are severally responsible to Parliament for their actions and the Cabinet as a whole is responsible to Parliament for its joint and several administration.

Judiciary.—All judges are appointed by the Queen on recommendation of Lord Chancellor and derive authority from her. But once appointed they hold office during good behaviour and if appointed after 1993 Judicial Pensions & Retirement Act must retire at age of 70, otherwise at age of 75.

See also European Union Digest, topic Legislature.

CONTRACTS:

Gratuitous promise even though made in writing is not enforceable unless it is made in deed under seal. Otherwise there must be agreement between parties intending to create legal relationship based upon offer and acceptance with consideration moving from promisee to promisor. Adequacy of consideration immaterial but there must be some benefit accruing to promisor.

Privity.—Person not a party to contract cannot sue upon it even if it is for his benefit unless it is insurance policy of vendor of property and he is purchaser, or he is a principal suing on contract made for him by agent or contract constitutes a trust and person seeking to sue is beneficiary thereunder.

No action may be brought in following cases, unless agreement or promise, or some note or memorandum thereof, be in writing and signed by party to be charged or someone by him lawfully authorised: (1) Whereby to charge a defendant on any special promise to answer for debt, default or miscarriage of another; (2) or on any contract for sale of lands or of any interest therein or concerning them or for any lease thereof for more than three years. (Statute of Frauds, 1677, §4; Law of Property [miscellaneous provisions] Act 1989).

Excuses for Nonperformance.—A contract which is not capable of performance when made is in general void. Doctrine of frustration operates to excuse further performance where (i) it appears from nature of contract and surrounding circumstances that parties have contracted on the basis that some fundamental thing or state of things will continue to exist or that some particular person will continue to be available or that some future event which forms the foundation of the contract will take place, and (ii) before breach performance becomes impossible or only possible in a very different way to that contemplated without default of either party or owing to a fundamental change of circumstances beyond control and original contemplation of parties. To excuse nonperformance impossibility must be in nature of a physical or legal one and not merely a relative impossibility, i.e., referable solely to the ability or circumstances of the promiser.

Act of God or Queen's enemies may also excuse performance. Act of God is generally an extraordinary occurrence or circumstance which could not have been foreseen or which could not have been guarded against.

A statute may also render performance impossible, which is sufficient excuse.

Rescission.—Contract may be rescinded at instance of party induced to enter it by a misrepresentation of facts made by other party. This is so, even if contract performed. Damages may be ordered by court in lieu of rescission and are also available in addition to rescission (or damages in lieu) where this representation is negligent or fraudulent.

Unfair Terms.—Liability for death or personal injury through negligence cannot be restricted by contract. Liability for other damage through negligence can only be restricted by contract if reasonable. Consumer protected against unreasonable exclusion of liability clauses in written standard terms of business; consumer also protected against unreasonable indemnity clauses. Unfair terms provisions do not apply to international supply contracts unless one party consumer resident in England and essential steps necessary for contract were taken in England. Special provisions apply to international passengers. (Unfair Contract Terms Act 1977).

Applicable Law.—Interpretation and effect and rights and obligations of parties are governed (with certain exceptions) by law which parties agree or intend shall govern it or which they are presumed to have intended, known as the proper law of the contract. Law expressly stipulated will be proper law of contract provided selection is bona fide and there is no objection on grounds of public policy even where law has no real connection with contract. Where parties make no stipulation courts decide by considering contract as a whole and are guided by certain presumptions.

Government Contracts.—As result of Crown Proceedings Act 1947, proceedings by or against Crown in contract are, for most part, governed by same rules of procedure as proceedings between subjects.

See also topics Deeds; Sales.

CONVEYANCES: See topic Deeds.

COPYRIGHT:

Law relating to copyright has now been consolidated in Copyright, Designs and Patents Act 1988.

Nature of Copyright.—Copyright is property and consists of the exclusive right to do or authorise others to do the acts in relation to the original work in question which is set out in the Act. Any other person who does such acts infringes the copyright.

COPYRIGHT . . . *continued*

Copyright in literary, dramatic or musical works extends to the act of reproducing the work in any material form, publishing or performing it in public, or making any adaptation of the work. Adaptation includes transforming work to or from a dramatic form, translating it, or turning a literary or dramatic work into a series composed wholly or mainly of pictures for production in a book or newspaper. Copyright in artistic works which are paintings, sculptures, drawings, engravings and photographs, works of architecture and models or other works of artistic craftsmanship extends to the act of reproducing or publishing the work or televising it.

Copyright in musical, dramatic, literary or artistic works lasts for 70 years after death of the author, if his true name is published, or 70 years after first publication, whichever is longer. For joint authorship, copyright runs from death of the survivor.

The author of work is entitled to the copyright therein, except where work is done in course of employment when employer is entitled to copyright. Employee usually does not get any moral rights either. In case of photographs and films commissioned for private and domestic use, copyright belongs to photographer, but commissioner has certain moral rights which are designed to prevent invasion of privacy.

Ownership of design right in commissioned design belongs to commissioner and not designer which can create conflict as design itself is artistic work, copyright in which belongs to designer.

No registration of copyright is necessary.

Copyright in sound recording extends to the act of making a record or broadcasting such a record of the original recording. The copyright is owned by the person who owns the original record embodying the recording.

Copyright in a film extends to the acts of making a copy of it, broadcasting it, or causing it to be seen or heard in public. Soundtract of film is "sound recording" and gives rise to separate copyright than that in film itself.

Copyright in a sound or television broadcast extends to the acts of making a copy or film of such broadcast or rebroadcasting such broadcasts. Broadcast includes all transmissions by wireless, telegraphy, including satellite transmissions. There are separate provisions for cable transmissions.

Copyright in a sound recording, or broadcast lasts for 50 years from first publication.

Copyright may subsist in character or appearance of published form of a literary, dramatic or musical work whether or not copyright subsists in the work itself. However, protection may only last 25 years.

Computer programmes are treated as enforceable copyright works and are included in definition of "literary works". Additional rights apply so that "copying" includes storing work in any medium by electronic means or making copies which are transient or incidental to some other use of work. Adaptation includes translation which includes conversion into or out of computer code or language. Moral rights relating to right to be identified as author of work or right to object to derogatory treatment of work do not apply to computer programs.

Moral Rights.—

Right of Paternity.—Author of copyright literary, dramatic or artistic work and director of copyright film has the right to be identified as author or director of work. This does not apply when musical work is performed in public. Owner of right must "assert" his right before there can be any infringement of it.

Right of Integrity.—Authors of works and film directors may object to certain types of "treatment" of work, e.g. addition to, deletion from, alteration or adaption to work if it is derogatory, i.e. distorts or multilates work or is prejudicial to honour or reputation of author. It does not prevent destruction of work.

There are number of exceptions where rights of paternity or integrity are not granted.

False Attribution of Work.—Person can complain against untrue assertion that he is author of work.

Right to Privacy.—In relation to photographs and films commissioned for domestic or private use, commissioner has rights not to have copies of work issued, exhibited, shown or broadcast to public.

Infringement.—The owner of a right, or the exclusive licensee may sue on an infringement and provision is made for the taking of accounts, recovery of damages and their amount in certain cases, and the granting of injunctions. There is no longer any action in conversion. In any action, copyright is assumed to exist and the author named assumed to be the true author. Owner of copyright in literary, dramatic or musical work may give notice of work to Customs authorities and prohibit import of any copies for period up to five years. Use of any literary, dramatic or musical work in which copyright exists for purposes of private study, research, literary criticism or reporting of current events is only allowed subject to stringent restrictions. Use in judicial proceedings is also excluded as is use in schools or the giving of a recitation in public by one person of a literary or dramatic work. Certain libraries are excluded from being liable for breach of copyright for doing certain acts. It is permitted to use any work which is incidentally included in any artistic work, sound recording, film broadcast or cable programme. However, any work deliberately included is in infringement of copyright.

Performance Rights.—Performance of dramatic or musical work or variety act or recitation of literary work gives rights to performer which are infringed (if certain qualifying circumstances apply) by making recording, transmitting live, exploiting recording by showing or playing it in public or dealing, possessing or importing illicit recording unless, of course, it is done with performer's consent.

Recording Rights.—Performers can confer exclusive right on someone to record performances. Live broadcast does not infringe recording rights, nor does any recording made with consent of performer (despite fact that owner of recording right has not consented). Broadcast of recording of performance is in infringement of rights of owner of recording rights.

Copyright Tribunal.—This replaces Performing Rights Tribunal and has jurisdiction over licensing schemes and licences granted by licensing bodies. Schemes would include system operated by Performing Rights Society whereby licenses are granted to users of music in certain public places which may otherwise have been in breach of performer's rights. Licensing schemes can cover literary, dramatic, musical works, films, sound recordings and computer programmes.

There is right of appeal from Tribunal on point of law to High Court.

Extent of Operation of Act.—Act applies to England, Wales, Scotland and Northern Ireland. Work qualifies for protection by reference to "(a) author or (b) country where work was first published or in case of broadcast or cable programme, whether broadcast was made or cable programme sent". "Authors" qualify for protection if they are British citizens, nationals, citizens of British dependent territories or domiciled or resident in UK at time when work was made or domiciled or resident in any other state work in party in Berne Convention or Universal Copyright Convention.

If there is no qualified author, protection will be given to works "first published" in UK or any Convention county.

Act may apply to British colonies and dependancies, if so ordered, and in that case may be limited by local laws. Order in Council may further extend Act to other countries giving rights under it to persons living there or works published there. Similar provisions may be made for international organisations. Copyright may be denied to nationals of countries which do not give adequate protection to British works.

Reciprocal Arrangements.—Great Britain has ratified the Berne Convention with certain reservations; and in order to give effect to this, Act provides that, by means of Orders in Council, the protection of the Act may be extended. Such Orders now extend to television and sound broadcasting, but no such Order in Council is to be made in favour of a foreign country unless that country has granted or undertaken to grant reciprocal copyright protection to works which are entitled to British copyright. Orders in Council have already been made in favour of countries which are parties to the Berne Convention and Universal Copyright Convention.

Assignment.—Copyright is transmissible by assignment, testamentary disposition or by operation of law as personal moveable property. An assignment may be of the whole copyright or part of it and can be subject to limitation. It must be in writing signed by or on behalf of the assignor. Where an unpublished work is disposed of by will, it is inferred that the copyright passes with the work, unless the contrary is expressed in the will.

Certain moral rights can be assigned or disposed of by will.

Registered Designs and Design Rights.—Where design of article comprises simply work of art, e.g. painting of vase, such works are protected by copyright for 70 years and even prevents three dimensional reproductions of it. If design is inventive, product may be patentable and therefore protected for 20 years.

Under Registered Designs Act 1949, as amended by Copyright, Designs and Patents Act 1988, new design may be registered affording 25 years protection (extended from 15 years). Design means "the features of shape, configuration, pattern or ornament applied to an article by any industrial process, being features which in the finished article appeal to and are judged by the eye, but does not include a method or principle of construction or features of shape or configuration of an article which are dictated solely by function which the article has to perform or are dependent upon the appearance of another article of which the article is intended by the author of the design to form an integral part." Design is not registerable if appearance of article is not material to whether or not someone buys it. There are special provisions where applications have been lodged for existing designs which would have been registerable before 1988 Act, but are no longer so as they are now under definition of unregistered design right.

Under above methods, protection was therefore not given to designs of purely functional nonartistic works. New design right introduced by Act now subsists in original (not common place) design of "any aspect of the shape or configuration (internal or external) of the whole or part of an article". As there is no reference to eye appeal, right applies to functional and aesthetic designs. Design right does not subsist in method of principle of construction (which may be patentable), features of shape or configuration of article which enable article to be connected to or placed in, around or against another article so that either article may perform its function or are dependent upon appearance of another article of which article is intended by designer to form integral part or surface decoration. However, design rights may subsist in such articles if they include special original design features.

Designer is first owner of design rights unless it is created by employee in course of his employment or commissioned, in which case right belongs respectively to employer or commissioner.

Design rights expire 15 years from year in which design was first recorded in design document or article was first made from design, whichever is first. However, if article is exploited commercially in first five years of that period, duration is ten years from first commercial exploitation.

Owner has exclusive right to reproduce design for commercial purposes. Owner's rights are infringed if someone copies designs or article, or knowingly deals with designs or articles which are in infringement.

Licences of right are to be available to anyone to manufacture protected article during final five years of term.

Design right and copyright may subsist concurrently but if copyright protection is available, this method of protection must be used first. Design rights can subsist concurrently with registered design.

Design rights only apply to designs recorded or articles made after 1st Aug. 1988.

See also European Union Digest, topic Copyright.

CORPORATIONS:

Companies with limited liability are regulated by Companies Act 1985 (as amended by Companies Act 1989) and are divided into public and private companies. There is no limitation on amount of capital but public company must have authorised minimum share capital of at least £50,000.

Single person may form limited company. Public company is defined by 1985 Act as company limited by shares or guarantee: (a) Whose memorandum states that it is public company and (b) which has complied with provisions of Companies Acts for registration as public company. Private Company is company which is not public company. Public company usually invites public to subscribe by issue of prospectus.

CORPORATIONS . . . *continued*
Name of public company must end with words "public limited company" or its abbreviation P.L.C. and word "limited" may not precede that phrase. Name of private company must end with "limited" or its abbreviation Ltd.

Companies must register memorandum of association setting out name, address, registered office, objects, statement that liability of its members is limited and also showing amount of company's nominal capital and number and value of shares into which such capital is divided.

Objects of the company are set out in memorandum which is company's charter and acts which do not come within scope of "objects clauses" are ultra vires. Under Companies Act 1989, however, validity of act done by company can no longer be called into question by virtue of anything in Company's Memorandum, i.e. fact that act done by company is ultra vires its Memorandum will not prejudice third parites. Companies almost invariably file Articles of Association which are rules governing internal regulation of company, duties of directors, rights of voting etc. If Articles of Association not filed statutory rules known as "Table A" govern internal management. Application for registration of companies is made to Registrar of Companies, to whom proposed memorandum and articles are submitted.

Fees.—There is fixed registration fee of £20. If company wishes to change its name it must register new name for which there is fee of £20. On filing annual return and balance sheet there is fee of £16.

Prospectus.—Company issuing a prospectus must set out therein certain particulars as prescribed by rules made by Secretary of State specified in Acts and must comply with Stock Exchange requirements. Public companies which do not issue prospectus are required before first allotment of shares or debentures to file statement in lieu of prospectus containing similar particulars to those required to be set out in prospectus.

A copy of every prospectus issued by or on behalf of a company or in relation to an intended company, signed by every person who is named therein as a director or proposed director of the company and have endorsed on or attached to it any consent to its issue required from any experts must be delivered to Registrar of Companies on or before date of publication, and no prospectus may be issued until this is done.

Reports.—Every company must file every year a statement in form of a balance sheet and containing summary of its capital, liabilities, and its assets.

Under Companies Act 1985 disclosure is required in company's accounts of numerous items, e.g., statement of company's shareholding in subsidiaries, statements in subsidiary's accounts of its holding company, directors' remuneration in "steps" of £5,000 and same for higher paid employees. Under 1985 Act experts reports are required when shares are allotted for noncash consideration or for noncash assets acquired from subscribers etc.

All companies must file at Companies Registry every year return (Annual Return) containing specified information such as names of members, details of directors, etc. If company has share capital, return must give particulars of its share capital including extent to which it is paid up. Return must be in statutory form and be signed by director or secretary.

Under Companies Act 1985 directors are personally responsible for filing of accounts within time limits specified; failure to do so will result in fines. Act also regulates appointment, removal and resignation of auditors and augments auditors' powers to require information in respect of subsidiaries. Any officer of company who knowingly or recklessly misleads or deceives auditors is guilty of offence.

Registration of Mortgages.—Every mortgage or charge falling within categories specified in Companies Act 1985 (as amended by 1989 Act), subject to certain exceptions, must be registered at Companies Registry. Categories are: (1) charges on land or any interest in land, (2) charges on goods or any interest in goods, (3) charges on goodwill, intellectual property, book debts or uncalled share capital or calls made but not paid, (4) charges for securing issues of debentures or (5) floating charges on all or part of company's property.

Company creating such charge or acquiring property subject to such charge must file particulars of charge within 21 days after date of charge's creation or date of acquisition of property subject to charge.

If particulars are not filed company and its officers are liable to fine.

Charge is created by company and if particulars are not filed within 21 day period charge may be void against administrator/liquidator of company and against any person who acquires interest for value in property subject to charge.

Every company must keep at its registered office copy of any charges over its property and register of charges. Copies and register are open to inspection by creditors or members of Company without fee and to inspection of any other person on payment of such fee as may be prescribed.

Control of company is vested in directors who may be appointed by signatories to memorandum or by articles or by shareholders. Acts contain provisions as to liability of directors. Directors of public companies must retire at 70 years.

Companies Acts make provision to protect minority shareholders, employees and persons dealing with company. Provisions include protection against oppression of minority shareholders, maintenance of capital, restrictions on distribution of profits and assets and restrictions upon transfer of shares by person having inside knowledge of company.

Overseas Companies.—Every company incorporated outside the U.K., establishing place of business within it, is required under heavy penalty to file: certified copy of its charter, statute, or other instrument constituting or defining its constitution and form 691, particulars contained therein include list of its directors; and name and address of some person resident in U.K. authorised to accept service of process or any notices required to be served on company, name of company and its country of incorporation and address of its place of business in Great Britain.

Insurance Corporations.—Companies Act provides considerable restrictions on insurance business in conjunction with Insurance Companies Act 1982 which consolidates Insurance Companies Acts 1974, 1980 and 1981.

Inspection.—Act contains certain provisions for inspection of corporation's affairs by Board of Trade Inspectors on application of a certain minimum number of members. Act contains further extensive powers which allow Board of Trade itself to carry out "informal" investigation of books and papers of corporation. No request for appointment of inspectors has to be made, and Board does not have to state any formal reasons for wishing to make any inspection.

Taxation.—See that topic.

Winding Up.—Company may be wound up either voluntarily or compulsorily, in both cases usual reason being insolvency. See topic Bankruptcy and Insolvency.

The Criminal Justice Act 1993, Part V, amends and restates law on insider dealing.

The Insolvency Acts of 1986 and 1994 governs law of corporate insolvency, disqualification of directors, wrongful trading, receivership, and winding up of companies. See topic Bankruptcy and Insolvency.

Financial Services Act 1986.—See topic Securities and Investments.

COURTS:

Magistrates Courts.—Minor criminal matters, preliminary investigation of indictable offences, as well as some civil or quasi-civil matters (e.g., affiliation proceedings) are dealt with by Magistrates Court presided over by unpaid justices of peace or by paid stipendiary magistrates. Minor criminal offences are tried summarily, but in case of indictable offences prisoner will be committed to Crown Court to be tried on indictment.

Crown Court.—Established by Courts Act 1971. Crown Court able to sit anywhere in England and Wales. All trials on indictment take place before Crown Court which also exercises appellate jurisdiction from Magistrates Courts. Judges of Crown Court are High Court judges and Circuit judges and Recorders. They sit with justices of peace in case of appeals and committals for sentence.

Magistrates Courts fix place at which person is to be tried on indictment, and defendant or prosecutor, if dissatisfied with place fixed by Magistrates Court may apply to Crown Court for direction varying place of trial.

Circuit Bench.—Circuit judges appointed either from barristers or solicitors of at least ten years' standing, or from recorders who have held office for at least five years. Recorders are appointed from solicitors or barristers of ten years' standing.

Circuit judges are able to sit in Crown Court and county courts and also, if so requested by Lord Chancellor, available to assist High Court judges in trial of civil actions. Recorders able to sit as part-time judges of Crown Court.

Juries.—Lord Chancellor responsible for summoning of jurors for all courts except coroners' courts. Majority verdicts may be given in civil and criminal matters. There is no right to examine jury for prejudice or to have all black or all white jury, and judge no longer has power to order all male or all female jury.

County Courts.—England and Wales is for these purposes divided into districts by Lord Chancellor who may alter number and boundaries of districts. In each district county court sits at one or more places in it to decide civil matters. The Courts and Legal Services Act 1990 contained changes to allocation of business between, and transfer of business between, High Court and County Courts. Accordingly, since 1st July 1991, actions in respect of personal injuries must normally be commenced in County Court unless claim is worth £50,000 or more; action worth less than £25,000 must normally be tried in County Court, and those worth £50,000 or more must normally be tried in High Court; with those in middle going either way depending on whether they meet certain criteria. Special provisions apply to claims of less than £1,000 for personal injury damage and less than £3,000 for property damage.

Ecclesiastical courts have jurisdiction in certain Church matters.

Supreme Court of Judicature, which sits continuously in London, is divided into two parts: (1) The High Court of Justice, divided (for convenience of administration only) into Queen's Bench Division (including Admiralty and Commercial Court), Chancery Division (including Probate, Companies, Patents and Bankruptcy Courts), and Family Division; (2) Court of Appeal.

High Court of Justice exercises original jurisdiction and appellate jurisdiction from inferior courts in civil matters. Queen's Bench Division has a limited criminal jurisdiction which is rarely exercised.

Court of Appeal is composed of Lord Chancellor and any ex-Lord Chancellor, Lord Chief Justice, Master of the Rolls, President of Family Division, Vice-Chancellor and not more than 32 Lord Justices. It hears appeals from High Court or from order of county court judge on point of law, and appeals from court martial.

Central Criminal Court (the Old Bailey) sits every month in London to try any indictable offence committed in London and its environs or on the high seas.

Court of Appeal (Criminal Division) sits in London to hear appeals in criminal matters from Crown Courts, including Central Criminal Court.

House of Lords is composed of Lords of Appeal who must have held high judicial office for two years or have been for 15 years practising barristers or solicitors in England or Northern Ireland or practising advocates in Scotland. They are appointed by letters patent and are entitled to sit and vote as Lords of Parliament. All lay peers have theoretically the right to sit and vote, but right has fallen into disuse. An appeal lies to House of Lords from Court of Appeal and in limited circumstances from Court of Appeal (Criminal Division). Court has original jurisdiction in cases of claims to peerages and decides questions as to disputed elections. In criminal matters it has both original and appellate jurisdiction. It is court of final appeal.

Judicial Committee of the Privy Council consists of the Lord Chancellor, the Lords of Appeal, if Privy Councillors, and other members of the Privy Council who have held high judicial office in the United Kingdom or the colonies. It is the court of final appeal from the Ecclesiastical Courts and from the Courts of the Colonies, the Channel Islands and the Isle of Man.

See also topic Estates in Chancery, and European Union Digest, topic Courts.

CURRENCY:

Bank of England has exclusive right to issue paper money in England and Wales. Notes issued by Bank are legal tender in England, Northern Ireland, Scotland and Wales. Part of notes issued is covered by gold coin and gold bullion. Remainder,

CURRENCY . . . *continued*
known as "fiduciary note issue" must be covered by securities. Great Britain left gold standard in 1931. One pound notes are no longer issued.

Unit of currency is pound sterling which is divided into 100 pence.

See also topic Exchange Control.

CURTESY:

Abolished by Administration of Estates Act, 1925 in the case of a wife dying after Dec. 31, 1925.

CUSTOMS:

Customs duties are levied on many imports. Different rates apply to the various categories of goods and in many cases vary according to the country of origin. Commissioners of Customs and Excise responsible for collection and management of duties of customs and exise. They perform their functions subject to direction and control of H. M. Treasury. H. M. Customs & Excise also and enforce V.A.T. system. (See topic Taxation.) They may also stop importation of certain prohibited articles.

U.K. is member of EEC and enjoys special relationship with other member states for these purposes.

See also topic Taxation, and European Union Digest, topic Customs Duties.

DEATH:

Presumption of Death.—Application by a personal representative must be made to the court where it is not certain that death has occurred. The law presumes a man to be dead if he has not reasonably been heard of for seven years and all appropriate enquiries have been made, but each case is considered as question of fact, and period can be less than seven years. There is no legal presumption as to time of death. Since 1925, if two or more persons apparently die simultaneously, legal presumption is that younger died later than older. (§184, Law of Property Act 1925). Presumption does not apply between husband and wife where elder dies wholly or partially intestate. However, §1(1) Law Reform (Succession) Act 1995 provides that if intestate's spouse does not survive for 28 days then he/she is not deemed to have survived his/her spouse. See also topic Marriage, subhead Dissolution.

Registration.—All deaths must be registered locally. See topic Records, subhead Births, Deaths and Marriages.

Actions for Causing Death.—By Fatal Accidents Act 1976, personal representatives may on behalf of relatives of decedent sue within three years if death was caused by some wrongful act, neglect or default. Measure of damages is loss of support suffered. By Law Reform Act 1934 all causes of action subsisting against or vested in decedent shall survive against, or, as case may be, for benefit of his estate. No contract can exclude action for causing death. (Unfair Contracts Terms Act 1977).

DECEDENTS' ESTATES:

See topics Descent and Distribution; Executors and Administrators; Records; Wills.

DEEDS:

Note: §1 Law of Property (Miscellaneous Provisions) Act 1989 requires presence of attesting witness to signature of person executing deed and that deed makes it clear on face of itself that it is intended to be deed. It is no longer necessary for deeds executed by individuals to be sealed.

A corporation or company executes a deed in the manner provided by its articles of association, but a deed executed by a corporation aggregate in favour of a purchaser is sufficiently executed if its seal is affixed thereto in the presence of its clerk, secretary or other permanent officer or his deputy and a member of the governing body of the corporation. (Law of Property Act §74). §36A(3) Companies Act 1989 also provides that company need not have common seal; subsection (4) states that document signed by director and secretary or two directors of company and expressed to be executed by company has same effect as if executed under common seal of company.

A person authorised by a power of attorney or any other power to convey an interest in property on behalf of a corporation sole or aggregate, may execute the conveyance by signing the name of the corporation in the presence of a witness and in the case of a deed, fixing his own seal.

A deed does usually require registration. (§74). But see topic Records.

Land in England is of either freehold or leasehold tenure.

It is an offence for an unqualified person to draw a deed for reward.

Stamp Duty on Purchase Deeds.—Stocks and shares 1/2%. Freehold property up to £60,000 nil, above £60,000, 1%. To obtain reduced rates as above appropriate certificate of value must be inserted. There is separate scale of charges for leasehold property and is calculated by reference to premium paid, annual rent and length of term.

DEPOSITIONS AND DISCOVERY:

By Rules of the Supreme Court O. 38 evidence may be given by affidavit: (a) By order of court if in circumstances of case it thinks it reasonable to do so; (b) on any motion, petition or summons including interlocutory applications; (c) in default actions in rem and in references in admiralty actions. Court will not order affidavit evidence where such evidence will be strongly contested and its credibility depends on court's view of witness.

The court or a judge may make any order for the examination on oath before the court or judge or any officer of the court, or any other person, and at any place, of any witness or person, and may empower any party to any such cause or matter to give such deposition in evidence therein on such terms as the court or judge may direct.

Under Civil Evidence Act 1968, in civil proceedings oral or written statements of witness admissible if witness not called. Appropriate notice of intention to use statement must be given to opponent within 21 days of setting case down for trial (or as ordered by court). Police and Criminal Evidence Act 1984 governs admissability of hearsay evidence in criminal cases.

Obtaining Evidence Out of the Jurisdiction.—Any party desiring to cross-examine a deponent to an affidavit may serve upon the party filing it a notice in writing requiring the deponent to attend for cross-examination at the trial. Unless deponent attends accordingly, affidavit may not be used as evidence except on special leave of the court.

Evidence out of the jurisdiction may be obtained: (a) By appointment of a special examiner, or in the case of a country with which a convention has been made, by examination of witnesses before the British consular authority in that country; (b) by letters of request, available for all countries, but not employed in U.S., which prefers method (a); or (c) court may order that evidence may be given by witness in foreign jurisdiction by means of live television link-up with court.

The examination takes place in the presence of the parties, their counsel and their solicitors or agents, and the witnesses are subject to cross-examination and re-examination.

Depositions taken before an officer of the court, or before any other person appointed to take the examination, are taken down in writing by or in the presence of the examiner, not ordinarily by question and answer, but so as to represent as nearly as may be the statement of the witness, and when completed must be read over to the witness and signed by him in the presence of the parties, or such of them as may think fit to attend. If the witness refuses to sign the depositions, the examiner may do so.

When the examination of any witnesses is concluded, the original depositions, authenticated by the signature of the examiner, must be transmitted by him to the central office of the Supreme Court and there filed.

The person taking the examination under these rules may, and if need be must, make a special report to the court touching such examination and the conduct or absence of any witness or other person thereon, and the court or a judge may direct such proceedings and make such order as, on the report, they or he may think just.

Except where otherwise provided or directed by the court or a judge, no deposition may be given in evidence at the hearing or trial without consent of the party against whom it is offered, unless the court or judge is satisfied that deponent is dead, beyond the jurisdiction of the court or unable from sickness or other infirmity to attend the hearing or trial, in any of which cases the deposition certified as above is admissible in evidence, saving all just exceptions, without proof of the signature to such certificate.

Statements admissible under Civil Evidence Act 1968 may be made out of jurisdiction.

Perpetuating Testimony.—Any person who would under the circumstances alleged by him to exist become entitled, on the happening of any future event, to any honour, title, dignity or office, or to any estate or interest in any property, real or personal, the right or claim to which cannot by him be brought to trial before the happening of such event, may commence an action to perpetuate any testimony which may be material for establishing such right or claim.

Witnesses may not be examined to perpetuate testimony unless an action has been commenced for the purpose.

Obtaining Evidence for Foreign Tribunals.—Under Evidence (Proceedings in Other Jurisdictions) Act 1975, application may be made to High Court for Order for evidence to be obtained in England. High Court must be satisfied that application is made in pursuance of request issued by court or tribunal ("requesting court") exercising jurisdiction and that evidence to which application relates is to be obtained for purposes of civil proceedings which have been instituted or which are to be instituted before requesting court.

High Court may make such order for obtaining evidence as may appear appropriate for giving effect to request. Order may require specified person to take appropriate steps. In particular, Court may make provision for: (a) Examination of witnesses orally or in writing; (b) for production of documents; (c) for inspection, photographing, preservation, custody or detention of any property; (d) taking of samples of any property; (e) medical examination of any person including taking and testing of samples of blood. Order shall not require any particular steps to be taken unless steps can be required for obtaining evidence for purposes of civil proceedings in High Court. Order requiring person to give evidence not on oath may be made if this is asked for by requesting court. No order may be made requiring person to state what documents relevant to proceedings have been or are in his possession, custody or power or requiring any person to produce any documents other than particular documents specified in order as being documents appearing to High Court to be or likely to be in his possession, custody or power.

Discovery.—In civil cases after pleadings have closed, each side must send other List of Documents stating in Schedule 1, Part I relevant documents which are in their custody, possession or power, in Part II documents which they refuse to produce described generally and in Schedule 2, documents which party once had but now no longer has.

If one party refuses to give discovery of particular documents, other can apply to Court.

Certain matters can be dealt with by interrogatories.

Court can order parties to exchange experts reports before trial. At pretrial review Court must direct every party to serve on other parties within ten weeks (or such other period as Court may specify) and on such terms as Court may specify, written statements of oral evidance which party intends to adduce on any issues of fact to be decided at trail. Where party fails to comply it is not entitled to adduce evidence without lease of Court. (County Court Rules 1981 Order 20 rule 12A[10]).

Usually one does not know how many or who either side is going to call as witnesses. Court may, however, if it thinks fit for disposing fairly and expeditiously of any matter and saving costs, direct that parties serve written statements of oral evidence of witnesses as to fact.

In criminal cases, if either party wants to, full committal hearing can be requested, in which case summary of evidence is heard and witnesses can be called.

DESCENT AND DISTRIBUTION:

Following are rules generally applied on intestacy once letters of administration have been granted. (Testate succession governed by properly executed will of testator.)

Surviving spouse takes whole of estate absolutely if deceased leaves no issue and no parent or brother or sister of whole blood or issue of such brother or sister. If deceased leaves issue, surviving spouse takes all personal chattels (very wide term), £125,000 free of tax with interest at 6% and life interest in half residue, issue taking balance and

See Topical Index in front part of this volume.

DESCENT AND DISTRIBUTION . . . *continued*
other half residue after death of surviving spouse. If no issue, but parent or brother or sister of whole blood or issue of such brother or sister, surviving spouse takes all personal chattels, £200,000 free of tax with interest at 6% and half residue absolutely; if parent or parents survive, half residue passes to such parent or parents absolutely but if no parent survives half-residue passes to brothers and sisters of whole blood.

Where the matrimonial home forms part of the deceased's residuary estate, surviving spouse can generally require the interest in the house to be appropriated towards any absolute interest of his or hers.

When there is no surviving spouse the surviving issue take the whole estate in equal shares upon statutory trusts. If there is no issue but parent(s), he or she takes and if both parents survive, they take in equal shares. If there is neither issue nor parent(s), relatives take as follows: (1) brothers and sisters of the whole blood and their issue; (2) brothers and sisters of the half blood and their issue; (3) grandparent(s) in equal shares; (4) uncles and aunts being brothers and sisters of the whole blood of a parent and their issue; (5) uncles and aunts being brothers and sisters of the half blood of a parent and their issue; (6) the Crown, Duchy of Lancaster or Duke of Cornwall.

Illegitimate Children.—Under Family Law Reform Act, 1987, illegitimate child (or issue) and both his parents shall have same rights to succeed (on intestacy on or after Jan. 1, 1970) as if child were legitimate. Rebuttable presumption is to be made that illegitimate child's father has predeceased him. Existing rights of legitimated or adopted children are preserved where that would be advantageous.

As to allowance for maintenance of dependants not properly provided for by will, see Wills.

DISPUTE RESOLUTION:

Disputes can be resolved by means of negotiation, alternate dispute resolution methods (ADR), arbitration or litigation. Only arbitration and litigation have binding and enforceable effect on parties.

Mandatory Dispute Resolution.—

Arbitration.—Many statutes provide for settlement of disputes or differences by means of arbitration. Reference to arbitration may be compulsory but in other cases is optional with one or both parties electing arbitration (see subhead Voluntary Dispute Resolution, catchline Arbitration, infra). Arbitration is mandatory for instance under County Court Rules 1981 Order 19 rule 3 for any proceedings in which sum claimed or amount involved does not exceed £3,000 (or £1,000 in personal injury cases) unless judge orders case to be heard by trial if appropriate. Statutory arbitration and voluntary arbitration are governed by Arbitration Acts of 1950 and 1979 unless excluded by arbitration agreement. Whether reference is made to arbitration by statute or voluntarily procedure is same.

Voluntary Dispute Resolution.—

ADR.—All ADR methods are voluntary by parties and decisions are normally nonbinding. ADR is appropriate where parties wish to maintain ongoing business relationship but is not appropriate if either party needs injunction to preserve or protect rights or where legal precedent is needed. Many organisations offer ADR services. ADR methods include:

Mediation (or conciliation) is main method of ADR. Parties meet before neutral mediator in private who assists in reaching settlement. Talks held on a without prejudice basis and settlement may later be recorded in contract or consent order and therefore binding on parties.

Minitrial - panel consisting of neutral mediator and one senior executive from each party hear presentations of both parties and in complex cases evidence of witnesses. No formal court rules apply. Formalised type of mediation. Any judgment is nonbinding.

Judicial appraisal - written or oral presentations made to senior legal figure (such as retired judge) who appraises merits of case. Parties can contract beforehand on whether appraisal is open or on a without prejudice basis and whether it will be adapted into binding decision afterwards.

Early neutral evaluation is same as judicial appraisal but held in front of nonlegal expert such as technical expert.

Adjudication (or ombudsmen) - written or oral presentations made to adjudicator who acts as valuer or is expert. Decisions are binding without right of appeal unless parties contract otherwise.

Dispute Review Board/Dispute Advisor - formalised mediation with panel of experts or single advisor to advise or adjudicate between parties at outset of complex contracts. Decisions are nonbinding on parties.

Arbitration.—Parties may volunteer to go to arbitration. Many commercial contracts have arbitration clause whereby parties agree to use arbitration if dispute arises. Under statute parties may have option to use arbitration before proceeding with litigation. For instance arbitration may be used for settling divorce terms and cases which are referred to any judge of Commercial Court or Official Referee such as most shipping and construction cases can be heard by way of arbitration under Courts and Legal Services Act 1990 and Supreme Court Act 1981.

Arbitration tribunal is heard in private by one, or sometimes several, arbitrators nominated in arbitration agreement or otherwise appointed by court. Arbitration tribunals are normally heard orally with usual court rules applying unless parties elect for document-only arbitration. Arbitrator decides all questions of law and fact unless arbitrator is nonlegal expert when all points of law must be referred to court. Decision known as award is binding and enforceable with limited rights of appeal.

DIVORCE:

Grounds for divorce and judicial separation contained mainly in Matrimonial Causes Act 1973. See also Matrimonial and Family Proceedings Act 1984 which provides, inter alia, absolute bar on petitions for divorce within one year of marriage.

Grounds for Divorce.—§1 MCA 1973 provides that sole ground for divorce is that marriage has broken down irretrievably. §1(1) provides that proof of such breakdown is only afforded if one or more of following conditions are fulfilled: (a) that respondent has committed adultery and that petitioner finds it intolerable to live with him; (b) that respondent has behaved in such a way that petitioner cannot reasonably be expected to live with him (Note: There is no requirement that behaviour complained of must be cause of irretrievable breakdown); (c) that respondent has deserted petitioner for continuous period of at least two years immediately preceding presentation of petition; (d) that parties have lived apart for continuous period of at least two years immediately preceding presentation of petition and respondent consents to decree; (e) that parties have lived apart for continuous period of at least five years immediately preceding presentation of petition. Providing that at least one of these conditions is fulfilled, court must pronounce decree unless either it is satisfied that marriage has not in fact broken down irretrievably or, where sole evidence of breakdown is five years separation, it is of opinion that decree should be refused because it would result in grave financial or other hardship to respondent and in all circumstances it would be wrong to dissolve marriage (§5).

Petitioner's solicitors are to certify whether question of reconciliation has been discussed and court is given power to adjourn proceedings if there appears to be a reasonable possibility of reconciliation. §2 set out provisons as to fact raising presumption of breakdown. It encourages resumption of cohabitation for total period, not exceeding six months wihtout prejudicing right to petition.

§10 provides that where only evidence of breakdown is separation and respondent consents to divorce, decree nisi may be rescinded if petitioner has misled respondent about any matter she took into account in deciding to give her consent. By §5, where a decree nisi is pronounced solely on basis of five years' separation, respondent may apply to court to consider her financial position and court is not to make decree absolute unless it is satisfied either that petitioner should not be required to make financial provision for respondent or that provision has been made which is reasonable or fair or best that can be made in circumstances. Further, decree may be made absolute even though such provision has not been made if it is desirable that it should be made absolute without delay and a satisfactory undertaking has been given by petitioner. §7 provides for rules to be made to enable agreements or arrangements between parties to be referred to court for its opinion and directions.

§17 abolishes former grounds of judicial separation and provides instead that grounds shall be those mentioned in §1. In a suit for judicial separation, court shall not be concerned with question whether marriage has irretrievably broken down.

Financial provisions on divorce or judicial separation are governed by, inter alia, Matrimonial Proceedings and Property Act 1970, Matrimonial Causes Act 1973, Matrimonial Homes and Property Act 1981 and Matrimonial and Family Proceedings Act 1984 and Family Proceedings Rules 1994.

Jurisdiction.—In order that English Courts may have jurisdiction to grant decree of divorce either party to marriage must be domiciled in England-Wales on date when proceedings are brought or either party must have been habitually resident in England-Wales for period of one year ending with date proceedings are commenced.

Foreign divorce decrees are recognized under Recognition of Divorces and Legal Separations Act 1971 if: (1) Either spouse habitually resident in jurisdiction of foreign court; (2) either spouse was a national of country granting decree; (3) either spouse domiciled in country granting decree within that country's meaning of domicile where country in question accepts doctrine of domicile; (4) decree is recognised in country of both parties domicile. Act also provides for mutual recognition of divorces and judicial separations granted in any part of British Isles.

Decree.—At the hearing of the petition for a decree of dissolution or nullity (i.e., trial), decree nisi only is granted, but at end of six weeks (on application by petitioner) this decree will be made absolute on application of petitioner unless in meantime Queen's Proctor (court official) is able to show cause why it should not be. Until decree nisi is made absolute parties are unable to marry again but thereafter there is no restriction on remarriage.

A decree nisi may be made absolute on application of respondent if petitioner does not apply for decree absolute within three months after time when such application could have been made.

Judicial Separation.—For grounds, see subhead Grounds for Divorce, supra.

In suits for judicial separation and restitution, residence of both parties in England at the beginning of the proceedings, even if domiciled abroad, is sufficient, and in a restitution suit if the domicile of the petitioner is originally English, residence of the petitioner is sufficient.

Annulment of Marriage.—See topic Marriage.

Dissolution of Marriage on Presumption of Death.—See topic Marriage.

DOMICILE:

Nobody can have more than one domicile. It connotes "permanent home," country where a person is when he is not travelling and is generally domicile of origin or domicile of choice. By virtue of Domicile and Matrimonial Proceedings Act 1973 it is now possible for wife to acquire separate domicile to that of her husband. Infant (under 16) is deemed to have domicile of his father unless parents are living apart in which case infant has domicile of parent with whom he has his home.

ENVIRONMENT:

Until recently common laws of nuisance and negligence were major forms of protecting environment from pollution. This meant that actions were brought either by individuals or Attorney General and therefore generally dealt with private property. Law grew due to litigation but was piecemeal, it is now supplemented by various statutes, main one being Environmental Protection Act 1990 which seeks to integrate pollution control. By 1996 it is hoped that many industries will have to have permit to be able to operate. Her Majesty's Inspectorate of Pollution is main agency for enforcement of antipollution legislation.

Atmospheric Pollution.—Environmental Protection Act 1990 makes it statutory nuisance to release trade dust into atmosphere which is prejudicial to health. The Clean Air Act provides for regulations on new chimneys such as height and filters. The Control of Pollution Act 1974 allows regulations to be made regarding content and composition of fuel used in motor vehicles.

Pollution on Land.—This is partly controlled by statutes such as Environmental Protection Act 1990 and Town and Country Planning Act 1990.

See Topical Index in front part of this volume.

ENVIRONMENT . . . *continued*

Noise Pollution.—Various acts cover noise emitted from airports and motor vehicles.

Inland Water Pollution.—This is covered by Public Health Act 1936 and Water Resources Act 1991. Trade effluents which are taken by inland waterways to the sea are covered by Water Industries Act 1991.

Pollution of Sea.—This is partly covered by Water Resources Act 1991 and Food and Environmental Protection Act 1985. These mainly incorporate international rules and conventions.

General Supervision.—

Refuse Collection.—Each local council is responsible for this in their area. There is right to have household rubbish collected.

Litter.—Crown Bodies have responsibility to keep their land free from litter, as do councils. Councils can ensure that landowners have same responsibility. Maximum fine for littering is now £2,500.

Dogs.—It is responsibility of local councils to clear dog mess, byelaws can be passed providing for dogs to be kept on a lead and poop scoops to be used.

Recycling.—Department of the Environment has overall responsibility for recycling, but local councils should provide recycling points in their area.

Nuisance.—Again it is responsibility of each local council to deal with complaints such as noise, smells, fumes and dust. Police only have powers with regard to noise pollution when breach of peace is likely to occur.

ESTATES IN CHANCERY:

Information respecting any fund is obtainable only on request giving correct title of suit or matter to which fund is placed, signed by applicant. Information is not given to applicant, other than solicitor, unless he satisfies paymaster of court that request may properly be complied with. Mere coincidence of surname of original owner of property with surname of party to suit is not sufficient evidence of genuine ground of claim. When request for information is made through solicitor, he must state name and address of person whom he represents and that he is of opinion that such person is beneficially interested in fund. Therefore persons instructing solicitors to put forward claims should send full particulars of grounds on which their claims are based. Funds in court can be dealt with only by order of court.

EVIDENCE: See topic Depositions and Discovery.

EXCHANGE CONTROL:

There are no restrictions on transfer of funds into or out of U.K.

EXECUTIONS:

Attachment or execution may issue to enforce a judgment. If the amount of judgment, including debt and costs is £750 or over, bankruptcy proceedings may be instituted against judgment debtor. If debt is £750 or over and undisputed, company debtor can be wound up after appropriate notice in writing requiring payment in 21 days.

Where a debtor does not obey an order to pay money proceedings may be taken to enforce payment by way of execution either by writ of fieri facias, by attachment of debts due to the debtor (see topic Garnishee Proceedings) or by equitable execution by way of appointing receiver and in certain circumstances by sequestration (q.v.).

The commonest method of levying execution is by means of the writ of fieri facias in High Court, which is order of court directed to sheriff of county in which judgment debtor resides directing him to take possession of debtor's goods and chattels of sufficient value to cover judgment debt and costs and costs of enforcement. On receipt of writ sheriff, through his officer, seizes debtor's goods and proceeds to sell them by public auction, accounting to creditor for the proceeds.

Equivalent form of enforcement in County Court is warrant of execution and is executed by Bailiff of court for district in which it is to be executed.

The writ of elegit has now been abolished.

Equitable Execution.—Where the property of the judgment debtor cannot be reached by any other means, execution by way of appointment of a receiver by the court may be ordered.

Exemptions.—(1) Tools, books, vehicles, equipment necessary for debtor's personal use in his employment, business or vocation may not be seized. (2) Clothing, bedding, furniture, household equipment and provisions necessary for satisfying basic domestic needs of debtor and his family may not be seized. (3) Money in hands of third person, property of lunatic under control of Court protection, partners share in partnership, property held in fiduciary capacity, goods of debtor deposited with another person as security for debt, and goods on hire may not be seized. *Note:* (a) Money, banknotes, bills of exchange, promissory notes, bonds, specialities or securities for money may be seized. (b) Costs of earlier attempts at enforcement are recoverable when taking current enforcement steps unless unreasonably incurred. (§15 Courts and Legal Services Act 1990).

EXECUTORS AND ADMINISTRATORS:

Upon death of a person whole of his property, both real and personal, devolves upon his personal representatives, who in cases where he has left a will are his executors, and in cases where he has died intestate, his administrator and to whom probate of will or letters of administration, as case may be, is granted by Principal Registry of Family Division or District Probate Registry of probate court. If no executor appointed, estate vests in President of Family Division until letters of administration are taken out. Such grant is made at any time after seven days from death have elapsed in case of executors and 14 days after death in case of administrators. Executor is not required to furnish any security. In case of administrator guarantee by sureties may be required in certain cases.

The powers of an executor appointed under a will valid by English law or by the law of the domicile are accepted here as being the same as those of an English executor similarly appointed. No evidence of the extent or duration of his powers is required.

Inheritance tax (see topic Taxation) may be payable before probate can be granted or letters of administration issued.

An executor or administrator who has advertised for claims against the deceased's estate, and given public notice of his intention to divide up the estate after a specified date (being not less than two months away), is not liable after he has divided up estate amongst beneficiaries in respect of claims of which he has not received notice (except for claims under Inheritance [Provision for Family and Dependants] Act 1975 and claims by beneficiaries of will rectified by Court under §20 Administration of Justice Act 1982, where estate has been distributed within six months of grant of representation).

Except for very small estates, if person (whatever his nationality or domicile at time of his or her death) dies leaving property (even if only debt) in this country grant of either probate of will or administration of estate must be obtained here before his or her executor or administrator respectively may deal with such property.

As to allowance for maintenance of dependents not properly provided for by will, see topic Wills.

EXEMPTIONS: See topic Executions.

FIDUCIARIES:

See topics Executors and Administrators; Trusts.

FINANCIAL SERVICES:

See topic Securities and Investments, subhead The Financial Services Act 1986.

FOREIGN EXCHANGE: See topic Exchange Control.

FOREIGN INVESTMENT:

There are no exchange controls and capital may be moved in and out of U.K.

FOREIGN TRADE REGULATIONS:

Many complicated provisions apply. Law consolidated in Alcoholic Liquor Duties Act 1979, Customs and Excise Duties (General Reliefs) Act 1979, Customs and Excise Management Act 1979, Excise Duties (Surcharge or Rebates) Act 1979, Hydrocarbon Oil Duties Act 1979, Matches and Mechanical Lighters Duties Act 1979 and Tobacco Products Duty Act 1979.

Generally speaking, goods imported subject to customs duty or value added tax at various rates. Importation of forged coins, indecent matter, goods bearing false trademarks or falsely described and certain drugs prohibited. Importation of agricultural products, food, animals, explosives and certain drugs subject to controls. Export of certain antiques prohibited and export of certain metal wastes subject to EEC quotas.

U.K. is member of European Economic Community, hence certain preferences for member states. No exchange control restrictions.

See also topic Exchange Control, and European Union Digest, topics Foreign Trade Regulations; Internal Market, subheads Free Movement of Goods, Free Movement of Workers and Freedom to Provide Services.

FRAUDS, STATUTE OF: See topic Contracts.

FRAUDULENT SALES AND CONVEYANCES:

A conveyance of property, to any other person other than a bona fide purchaser for value without notice of the fraudulent intent, made with intent to defraud creditors, is voidable at the instance of any person prejudiced thereby. (Law of Property Act, 1925, §172)

A voluntary disposition of land, made with intent to defraud a subsequent purchaser, is voidable at the instance of such purchaser. (Law of Property Act, 1925, §173).

Voluntary settlements, although not fraudulent, are voidable under certain circumstances. (Insolvency Act 1986).

GARNISHEE PROCEEDINGS:

A creditor who has obtained a judgment in the High Court for any sum of money may apply to the court ex parte on affidavit by himself or his solicitor stating that judgment has been obtained and is unsatisfied and for what amount and that a third person owes money to the debtor and is within the jurisdiction of the court. The court will order such third person (garnishee) to appear before its proper officer to show cause why he should not pay such sum to the judgment creditor so far as necessary to satisfy the debt and costs. If the garnishee admits his liability an order is made; if he disputes it an issue is directed. Payment by the garnishee under the order is a valid discharge to the garnishee. The process may be used to attach to earnings or money held by debtor's bankers.

HOLIDAYS:

New Year's Day, Good Friday, Easter Monday, May Day, (1st Mon. in May) Spring Holiday (last Mon. in May), late Summer Holiday (last Mon. in Aug.) Christmas Day and Boxing Day are Bank Holidays in England and Wales and no business of any kind is transacted, all banks and Stock Exchange being closed.

If Boxing Day, Christmas Day or New Year's Day fall on Sat. or Sun., then extra days are taken as holiday in lieu.

No bank transacts business after closing for day, i.e., 3:00 p.m. in City, 5:00 p.m. for main branches, 4:30 p.m. for other minor branches. Main branches also have extra opening hours on Sat. mornings for financial advice.

HUSBAND AND WIFE:

The position of husband and wife in law was much modified by Law Reform (Married Women and Tortfeasors) Act, 1935.

By §1 married women were placed on a footing similar to single women for all purposes connected with holding of property, entering into contracts, torts, judgments

HUSBAND AND WIFE . . . *continued*
and bankruptcy. By Law Reform (Husband and Wife) Act 1962 both parties to marriage have right of action in tort against each other subject to court's discretion in certain circumstances.

§3 of 1935 Act releases husband from liability for his wife's torts and for her antenuptial debts. He still remains liable for post-nuptial contracts made as his agent.

Married Woman's Property Act, 1983 provides that money and property derived from housekeeping allowance shall in absence of agreement to contrary be treated as belonging to husband and wife in equal shares.

Matrimonial Homes Act 1983 amends law relating to rights of husband and wife to occupy a dwelling house which has been matrimonial home. It protects against eviction a spouse not entitled by virtue of beneficial estate or interest to occupy it and provides for such statutory right of occupation to be registered as charge against house.

See also topic Domicile.

IMMIGRATION:

Regulated by Immigration Act 1971 as amended by British Nationality Act 1981 and Statement of Changes in Immigration Rules. (HC 395 [1994]).

Right of abode under 1971 Act is given to British citizens as defined by 1981 Act and those defined Commonwealth citizens who retain their present right of abode for their lifetimes.

British citizenship is acquired by birth in UK, adoption by British citizen, registration, naturalization or descent. Broadly, descent gives British citizenship to person born outside UK whose father or mother is British citizen, by registration if one parent is British citizen, by marriage if woman to British citizen, or if person born in dependant territory. Further any person born outside UK after 1st Jan. 1983 is British citizen if either parent was British citizen otherwise than by descent or was serving outside UK under EU institution, Crown or other designated service, recruitment for which took place in UK, as in case of EU institution in member state.

Those who are not included in above categories must obtain leave to enter U.K. from Immigration Officer. Secretary of State may make regulations concerning landing and embarking and conditions to be imposed upon them. Immigration Officer's decision may be appealed in all cases except where Home Secretary personally certifies that refusal to grant entry is for public good, e.g., national security.

E.U. nationals may enter and work in U.K. without restriction. Recent Order under §§3(3)(a), 4(1) of Immigration Act 1971 imposing certain reporting requirements on Iraqi nationals who are not either British citizens or persons exercising enforceable community rights. Also see Statement of Changes (as above).

See also topic Aliens, and European Union Digest, topic Internal Market, subheads Free Movement of Workers and Freedom to Provide Services.

INCOME TAX: See topic Taxation.

INDUSTRIAL PROPERTY RIGHTS:

See topics Copyright; Trademarks and Tradenames; Patents.

INFANTS:

Age of majority, 18 for both sexes. An infant can, by Act of Parliament, be declared of full age before he is 18 but his status of infancy cannot be changed in any other way.

Disabilities.—

Contracts.—Infants contracts are generally voidable at instance of infant, though binding on other party. Exceptions to this rule are contracts for necessaries (e.g. food, clothing, medicine) and certain others (e.g. service and apprenticeships). Even a contract which from its nature would be binding on an infant may be incapable of being enforced against him on account of its particular terms being prejudicial to his interests or onerous upon him. Contracts obviously prejudicial to infant are wholly void, e.g. a loan or penal bond.

Property.—A legal estate in land cannot be held by an infant, but by way of beneficial title under trust for sale or settlement.

Illegitimacy.—See topic Descent and Distribution.

General.—An infant is under a general incapacity to exercise rights of citizenship or perform civil duties, e.g. voting in parliamentary or local government elections.

Ratification of Contracts.—A voidable contract can be repudiated by infant either during infancy or within a reasonable time after he attains full age. However, no action can be brought to charge a person upon a promise made after attaining full age to pay debt contracted during infancy or upon ratification made after full age of promise or contract made during infancy. This does not apply so as to relieve infant of obligation arising out of contract affecting property of permanent nature.

Actions.—Civil proceedings on behalf of an infant must be brought by some person called his next friend; proceedings against an infant are defended by a guardian ad litem. Any person within jurisdiction and not himself incapable of instituting proceedings can fill above offices, preference being given to a parent or guardian. Court gives preference to parent to act in those capacities and will only substitute another person if parent has acted improperly and against child's interests.

Adoption.—See topic Adoption.

INHERITANCE TAX: See topic Taxation.

INSOLVENCY: See topic Bankruptcy and Insolvency.

INTEREST:

Interest is payable either: (1) When allowed by a particular statute as on a bill of exchange or solicitor's bill of costs; or (2) by express or implied agreement between the parties. In the absence of statute or contract, no interest can be charged.

There is no law against usury and lender and borrower may make any agreement they wish as to rate of interest, except that Consumer Credit Agreements are governed by Consumer Credit Act 1974. Credit bargain can be reopened if it is extortionate under §§137 to 140. There is no statutory definition of extortionate.

Court also has power to award interest in any debt or damages case. Interest on property damage is generally awarded at rate of 8% from date of loss. Personal injury damages (pain and suffering) carry interest at rate of 2% from date of service of writ or summons. Period and rate of interest however remains at Court's discretion. Interest is also payable on judgments in High Court and in County Court on judgments of £500 or more.

INTESTACY: See topic Descent and Distribution.

JUDGMENTS:

Any actionable wrong can be rectified by a judgment, decree or order of the court.

In cases of liquidated demands (e.g., bills, cheques, accounts for goods sold, etc.), sued for in High Court, summary judgment may be obtained where it is clear there is no prima facie defence. Judgment in default can be entered where defendant does not acknowledge writ, does not file defence, or fails to heed court order.

Foreign judgments for fixed amounts can be enforced by action in the English courts and cannot normally be reopened provided the defendant was present in the jurisdiction of the foreign court when the proceedings were begun or submitted to it, e.g., by defending the foreign proceedings.

Judgment for multiple damages, judgment based on provision or rule of law specified or described in order and judgment or claim for contribution in respect of damages awarded by either of aforementioned judgments may not be registered and no UK Court may entertain proceedings at common law for recovery of any sum payable under such judgment.

Under the Administration of Justice Act, 1920, judgments obtained in many parts of the British Commonwealth can be registered in the High Court if the Court thinks it just and convenient and provided application is made within 12 months. Under the Foreign Judgments (Reciprocal Enforcement) Act, 1933 as extended, a judgment for a fixed amount obtained in Belgium, Burma, France, India and certain other countries can be registered in the High Court as of right within six years. On registration a foreign judgment may be enforced in the same manner as judgments of the High Court of England. Certain formalities regarding application for registration and notice to the debtor must be observed and power is given to the Court to cancel registration on certain grounds.

Maintenance Orders (Reciprocal Enforcement) Act 1972 makes provision for reciprocal enforcement of maintenance acts between U. K. and other countries to be designated by Order in Council.

There are reciprocal arrangements for enforcing judgments of EU member states. See European Union Digest, topic Judgments.

LABOUR RELATIONS:

Individual rights principally governed by Employment Protection Act (Consolidation) Act 1978, Employment Act 1980, Employment Act 1982, Employment Act 1989 and Employment Act 1990. (§§11, 12, 14, 15 and 17 of which came into force on 1st Nov. 1990). Trade unions and collective labour relations governed mainly by Trade Union and Labour Relations (consolidation) Act 1992 and Trade Union Reform and Employment Rights Act 1993, Employment Protection Act 1975, Employment Act 1980 and Employment Act 1982.

Code of Practice.—Secretary of State to prepare code containing practical guidance on industrial relations. No liability under Act for breach of code but admissible as evidence in proceedings.

Workers Rights.—Acts protect workers employed for continuous period of two years against unfair dismissal. Worker gains rights to redundancy payment after continuous employment of two years and maternity rights without any qualifying period of employment. Disputes referred to Industrial Tribunal who can award compensation or reinstatement where practical if negotiations with conciliation service (ACAS) provided for under Act have broken down.

Trade Disputes.—Acts provide union and employers associations with limited immunity from actions in tort in respect of certain acts done in connection with trade disputes as defined by Act, and grant limited rights of peaceful picketing in connection with trade disputes.

List of Union and Employers Associations.—Certification officer (ACAS employee appointed by Secretary of State) keeps list of these bodies. Can refuse to enter name of body if its rules do not comply with requirements of Act. Bodies entered on list entitled to tax benefits.

Accounts.—Unions and Employers Associations under duty to keep audited accounts and make annual returns to certification officer, and to make their annual returns and rules available for inspection by any person.

Employer's Liability (Compulsory Insurance) Act 1969 requires employers to insure against their liability for personal injury to their employees. Certain employers are exempted from this duty namely: Nationalized industries and Town, County and Borough Councils.

Sex Discrimination Act 1975 and Equal Pay Act 1970 prevent discrimination on grounds of sex or marital status in employment field except where sex is genuine occupational qualification.

Race Relations Act 1976 prohibits discrimination in employment on ground of race.

Wages Act 1986 makes provision for payment of wages, and alters certain redundancy arrangements. Trade Union Reform and Employment Rights Act 1993 abolished Wages Councils; this means that there is now no statutory wage fixing or minimum wage legislation.

See also European Union Digest, topic Labor Law.

LAW REPORTS:

There is no official reporting of English Law cases except on the criminal side, but there are a number of unofficial reports such as All England Law Reports published by Butterworth & Co. (Publishers) Ltd., 35 Chancery Lane, London, WC2A 1EL. Such reports are accepted as authentic in practice and other reports made by barristers are accepted by the courts. In case of dispute reference can be demanded to papers filed at Record Office.

See, as to statutes, topic Statutes, and European Union Digest, topic Reports.

LEGISLATURE:

See topic Constitution and Government, and European Union Digest, topic Legislature.

LICENSES:

These are required for many activities including following: To conduct a betting office or gaming club or hold lottery, fly aircraft, be in possession of firearms, sell intoxicating liquors, hold market or fair or conduct street trading, drive motor vehicle on public road, conduct business as money lender or pawnbroker, fish, kill game or marry or use television receiver. Term is also used to describe certain contractual arrangements e.g., relating to copyright patents and occupation of land.

Licensing (Amendment) Act 1985 amends Licensing Act 1964 in relation to orders for extended hours.

See also topic Foreign Trade Regulations.

LIENS:

A lien is a right in one person to retain in his possession goods belonging to another until certain demands of his against the owner have been satisfied.

It is a personal right and exists only in respect of goods received rightfully, and cannot be transferred. The right may be excluded by express agreement or the course of dealing between the parties. It is a right merely to retain possession and no charges in respect of warehousing may be made, and except in the absence of statute, e.g., innkeepers, it confers no right of sale, without legal process against the debtor. It must be distinguished from equitable and maritime liens, i.e., rights given to creditors to have certain specific property applied in satisfaction of their demands.

The right of lien is given by law in two classes of cases: (1) to persons who are under a common law duty to render services, as e.g., carriers, on the goods carried, for the price of the carriage, and innkeepers, on the baggage of their customers, for the amount of the customer's account; (2) to persons rendering services, spending money, skill or labour, on the property of another person employing them for that purpose, as, e.g., all agents and artificers.

A lien may be either: (1) general, for a general balance owing to a creditor by the debtor, e.g., the right of a solicitor to retain his client's papers for a general balance due to him; or (2) particular, a right over goods until certain demands are satisfied, e.g., the ordinary right of a seller to retain particular goods until payment of their price.

An hotel keeper has a right, if his account remains unpaid, to sell by public auction any personal effects, goods, or livestock of the guest left or deposited with him or in his hotel. But no such sale may be made until he has had the goods for six weeks, nor until one month after he has advertised the intended sale in one London newspaper and one local newspaper circulating in the district in which the goods were left.

A bankers' lien is the right of a banker to retain securities belonging to his customer for money due on a general balance.

A trustee has an equitable lien for expenses lawfully incurred in connection with the trust premises; a limited liability company may create a lien upon its own shares.

Lien may arise through right of subrogation, as where third party to contract for sale uses its money to pay purchase price at purchaser's request.

The right of lien is lost: (1) by discharge of the debt; (2) by tender of the debt; (3) by taking security for the debt under circumstances inconsistent with its continued existence.

It is suspended by taking a negotiable instrument as payment, but unless it is taken as absolute satisfaction the debt will revive on its dishonour, even though it is in the hands of assignees for value.

LIMITATION OF ACTIONS:

Governed by Limitation Act 1980 which consolidates previous Acts. Actions must be commenced within following periods. This list contains more common types of proceedings only; there are many others for which special time limits are laid down.

Twelve years: On speciality; to recover land or money charged on land, claim on deceased estate (but not interest on entitlement).

Six years: All actions in tort (including infringement of copyright), other than those for damages which consist of or include damages for personal injuries or death, or libel or slander, on simple contracts to recover arrears of rent or damages in respect thereof, to recover mortgage interest or damages in respect thereof, to recover loans, to recover award under seal, sums recoverable by statute, for contributions between joint tortfeasers, for interest on legacy, to enforce judgment and interest thereon.

Latent Damage Act 1986 alters Limitation Act 1980 in cases of actions for negligence in respect of latent damage not involving personal injury. Limitation period is now either six years from date cause of action accrued, or three years from date plaintiff first had enough knowledge to bring action.

Three years: All actions for tort and simple contract for damages for negligence, nuisance or breach of duty where such damages include damages for personal injury or death, or libel or slander. Time runs when right of action accrued or claimant should have known of right of action. Provisions as to when plaintiff presumed to have known. Court has discretion to extend time if fair to do so in circumstances. Guidelines in Act.

Maritime Actions.—Time limits for maritime collisions are laid down by Maritime Conventions Act 1911.

The Crown.—Subject to certain exceptions, the Acts bind the Crown.

Persons under Disability (i.e., an infant or of unsound mind).—Period of limitation does not begin to run until disability ends or person dies. The period is then six years except for actions for contribution (two years) or death (three years) or personal injury (three years).

Fraud or Mistake.—Where action based on fraud of defendant, his agent or any person through whom he claims or his agent; or is concealed by any such person as aforesaid; or is for relief from consequences of mistake, time runs from when plaintiff discovered fraud or mistake or could with reasonable diligence have discovered it.

MARRIAGE:

(The Marriage Acts, 1948 to 1983).

Age of consent, for both males and females, is 16 years. Consent of parents or guardians is needed if either party is under 18 years.

Marriage must be celebrated in one of the following ways: (1) by special licence; (2) by common licence; (3) by publication of banns; (4) by certificate of the Superintendent Registrar, either (a) with or (b) without licence.

Medical examinations and blood tests not required.

If either party to a marriage has been previously divorced, a certified copy of the decree absolute must be produced at the ceremony.

Prohibited Marriages and Annulment.—Matrimonial Causes Act 1973 sets out grounds on which a marriage is null and void ab initio, namely, (1) not a valid marriage under Marriage Acts 1949-70, (2) parties within prohibited degrees (infra), (3) either party under 16, (4) certain formal requirements relating to marriage were not complied with, (5) either party already lawfully married, (6) parties not respectively male and female at birth, (7) polygamous marriage celebrated abroad and either party domiciled at time of marriage in England or Wales. In such cases decree of nullity is not legally necessary but it may be granted and resort to Court for that purpose is usual and proper. These provisions apply to marriages celebrated after 31st July 1971. Statutory law as to marriages celebrated before 1st Aug. 1971 is preserved in Matrimonial Causes Act 1973 Sched. 1.

There is only one canonical disability and that is inability of either spouse to have marital intercourse. It must exist at time of marriage and be of an immovable nature. In this case marriage is good until it is declared null and void and so before parties are able to remarry court's decree is required. An agreement between parties not to institute a suit for nullity is complete defence.

In nullity proceedings it would now seem that mere residence in England at commencement of proceedings is not sufficient to found jurisdiction. Statutory exceptions conferring divorce jurisdiction also apply here. See topic Divorce.

Prohibited Degrees of Relationship.—Marriages are void between a man and persons in the first column or between a woman and persons in the second column hereunder:

Mother	Father
Adoptive mother or former adoptive mother	Adoptive father or former adoptive father
Daughter	Son
Adoptive daughter or former adoptive daughter	Adoptive son or former adoptive son
Father's mother	Father's father
Mother's mother	Mother's father
Son's daughter	Son's son
Daughter's daughter	Daughter's son
Sister	Brother
*Wife's mother	*Husband's father
*Wife's daughter	*Husband's son
*Father's wife	*Mother's husband
*Son's wife	*Daughter's husband
*Father's father's wife	*Father's mother's husband
*Mother's father's wife	*Mother's mother's husband
Wife's father's mother	Husband's father's father
Wife's mother's mother	Husband's mother's father
*Wife's son's daughter	*Husband's son's son
*Wife's daughter's daughter	*Husband's daughter's son
Son's son's wife	Son's daughter's husband
Daughter's son's wife	Daughter's daughter's husband
Father's sister	Father's brother
Mother's sister	Mother's brother
Brother's daughter	Brother's son
Sister's daughter	Sister's son

However marriage after 1986 between persons in categories above starred will by Marriage (Prohibited Degrees of Relationship) Act 1986 not be void provided parties are over 21 at date of marriage and that neither were treated as child of family of other while under 18 or certain members of family have died. Conditions to be fulfilled depend on category parties fall within.

Jurisdiction for annulment exists as follows: (1) If either party is domiciled in England-Wales when proceedings commenced or (2) either party resident in England-Wales for one year ending with date proceedings commenced or (3) if either party died before proceedings commenced and either was at death domiciled in England-Wales or had been habitually resident in England-Wales for one year ending with date proceedings commenced.

Matrimonial Causes Act 1973 provides that marriage celebrated after 31st July 1971 is voidable on any of following grounds: (a) non-consummation due to incapacity of either party; (b) wilful refusal to consummate; (c) either party did not consent due to duress, mistake, unsoundness of mind, or otherwise; (d) either party suffering from mental disorder at time of marriage so as to be unfit for marriage; (e) respondent suffering from having venereal disease in communicable form at time of marriage; (f) respondent pregnant per alium at time of marriage. In cases (c) to (f) proceedings must be brought within three years of marriage and in cases of (e) and (f) petitioner must have been ignorant of grounds at time of marriage. Marriage will not be avoided where

MARRIAGE . . . *continued*
(a) unjust to respondent, or (b) petitioner led respondent reasonably to believe that he would not petition on discovery of grounds. Decree of nullity no longer retrospective and collusion no longer a bar. Where marriage annulled on any of grounds (supra), children of that marriage are legitimate if they would have been legitimate if marriage had been dissolved instead of annulled.

Dissolution.—A married person who alleges that reasonable grounds exist for believing his or her spouse to be dead may present a petition to have death presumed and the marriage dissolved.

MARRIED WOMEN:

See topics Husband and Wife; Marriage.

MONOPOLIES AND RESTRAINT OF TRADE:

Subject to the following, is governed by common law rules.

Fair Trading Act 1973 empowers Director General of Fair Trading to control undesirable trade practices and individual traders who flout legal obligations. Monopolies and Mergers Commission empowered by this Act to investigate and report on possible existence of: (a) Monopoly situation, (b) transfer of newspaper assets, or (c) possible creation of merger situation which qualifies for investigation, i.e. situation where at least one of enterprises under control of body corporate in U.K. and merged enterprise has (to greater extent) one quarter of market, or value of assets taken over exceeds £5,000,000.

Companies Act 1989 introduces new provisions to supplement 1973 Act and to simplify merger control: (1) Notice of proposed merger can be given to Director General to obtain advance clearance, (2) Secretary of State may take undertakings from parties involved in merger rather than referring matter to Commission.

Competition Act 1980 empowers Director General of Fair Trading to investigate activities which may amount to anti-competitive practice. Reports submitted to Secretary of State for laying before Parliament for publication. Undertaking not to take part in anti-competitive practice may be required. Failing undertaking, order prohibiting practice may be made. U.K. is member of EU and EU anti-competition laws apply.

The Restrictive Trade Practices Acts 1976 and 1977 provide for control of commercial agreements which are contrary to public interest. Acts make compulsory registration of agreements between two or more manufacturers or suppliers carrying on busi-ness in U.K. which impose restrictions on two or more parties to agreement as to prices, conditions of sale, quantity of goods supplied, process of manufacture, or persons or areas to or from which supplies are to be made. For this purpose trade association is treated as aggregate of its members. Agreements for price rebates over certain amount of goods supplied are also included. Certain agreements, such as those authorised by statute, licence agreements for patents, registered designs or trademarks, supply of goods for export, production of goods outside U.K., or agreements for exchange of know-how, are excluded from registration.

After registration the agreements are called up before Restrictive Practices Court and an agreement will be declared to be void as being contrary to public interest, unless the Court is satisfied that the restrictions are reasonably necessary, beneficial to the public, necessary for trade reasons, their absence would cause unemployment or injure the export trade, or they are necessary to fit in with another agreement found legal by the Court. The Act further prohibits the enforcement by means of collective measures of resale price conditions attached to goods, and enables individual suppliers imposing such conditions to enforce them by legal proceedings against traders acquiring goods with notice of such conditions. The Deregulation and Contracting Out Act 1994 allows ministers to repeal any provision in any enactment which requires imposition of any burden on any person in carrying on of trade, business or profession, makes provision regarding enforcement procedures and appeals and allows Secretary of State to accept undertakings in lieu of Director of Fair Trading making monopoly reference to commission.

See topic Sales, subhead Resale Price Maintenance, and European Union Digest, topic Monopolies and Restraint of Trade.

MORTGAGES:

The Law of Property Act, 1925, provides that a mortgage of an estate in fee simple can be effected in law by a demise for a term of years subject to a proviso for cessation on redemption, or a charge by deed expressed to be by way of legal mortgage. A mortgage of a term of years absolute may be effected only by subdemise or charge by deed expressed to be by way of legal mortgage.

Where a mortgage is made by deed expressed to be by way of legal mortgage, the mortgagee has the same protection, powers and remedies as if: (1) In case of a mortgage of a fee simple he had a mortgage term of three thousand years, or (2) in case of a mortgage of a term of years absolute he had a sub-term less by one day than the term vested in the mortgagor.

The mortgagee has the following powers: (1) To sell the mortgaged estate provided that the mortgage money has become due and either (a) notice has been served requiring payment and there has been default in whole or part thereof for three months, or (b) interest under the mortgage is two months in arrear or (c) there has been a breach of some other covenant in the mortgage; (2) to insure the mortgaged property against loss or damage by fire; (3) to appoint a receiver, which power is exercisable in the same circumstances as the power of sale; (4) when in possession, to cut and sell timber or to contract for any such cutting and sale; (5) when in possession, to make leases or accept surrenders of the leases for certain limited purposes and periods.

Priority of mortgages of registered land take effect in order of entry on Register (subject to any contrary entries). Priority of mortgages of unregistered land made after 1925 (not being mortgages protected by deposit of documents relating to legal estate) is governed by date of registration of mortgage as land charge. (Law of Property Act. 1925, §97). Registration as land charge is deemed to be actual notice to subsequent mortgagee or purchaser of land, except that in case of prior mortgagee who is seeking to make further advances to rank in priority to subsequent mortgages where prior mortgage was made expressly for securing current account or further account, registration is not deemed to be actual notice to him of subsequent mortgage if mortgage was not registered when his original mortgage was created or when last search was made by him or on his behalf whichever event last happened. Prior mortgagee may make further advances to rank in priority to subsequent mortgagees, legal or equitable, only if: (1) Such arrangement has been made with subsequent mortgagees; (2) he made his further advance with no notice of intervening mortgages; or (3) his original mortgage imposes obligation on him to make such further advances.

See topic Real Property for distinction between registered and unregistered land.

Discharge or Satisfaction.—A receipt indorsed on or written at the foot of or annexed to a mortgage in respect of all moneys thereby secured operates in the case of a mortgage by demise or sub-demise to determine the term or merge it in the reversion and, in any other case, as a reconveyance of the mortgage to the person who immediately before the execution of the receipt was entitled to the equity of redemption, and in either case as a discharge of the mortgaged property.

The receipt must state the name of the payer and be executed by the chargee by way of legal mortgage or person in whom the property is vested and who is entitled to give a receipt. If the payer is not the person entitled to the immediate equity of redemption, the receipt operates as if the benefit of the mortgage had by deed been transferred to him unless (1) it is otherwise expressly provided or (2) the mortgage is paid out of capital money or other money in the hands of a trustee and properly applicable for the discharge of the mortgage and it is not expressly provided that the receipt is to operate as a transfer.

By §116 of the Act, a mortgage term becomes a satisfied term and ceases when the money secured has been discharged but without prejudice to the right of a person having only a limited interest in the equity of redemption to require the mortgage to be kept alive by transfer or otherwise. See also topic Chattel Mortgages.

MOTOR VEHICLES:

Vehicle licence is required to be taken out by person keeping vehicle. Number plates must be displayed front and rear and must be of requisite size. Receipt for motor tax (see subhead Motor Tax, infra) must be exhibited on front windscreen.

Operator's licence is required under §60 Transport Act 1982 from Traffic Commissioner for use on road of goods vehicle for carriage of goods (a) for hire or reward or (b) for or in connection with any trade or business carried on by applicant. No badge necessary, except on public service vehicles and must be fixed and exhibited on vehicle as prescribed by Public Service Vehicles (Operators Licence) Regs. 1986, but licence must be produced to police on demand. Licence may be suspended in case of violations regarding motor vehicles.

Transfers.—Registration document is provided by Driver Vehicle Licensing Centre for each new or transferred vehicle and DVLC must be notified in proper form of each transfer by transferor and transferee.

Operation Prohibited.—Person under 16 years of age may not operate any motor vehicle. Person over 16 may operate moped, over 17 motor car or motorcycle. Person under 21 may not drive heavy or light locomotive (vehicles weighing over 7¼ tons) or motor tractor, except agricultural tractor used on farm. Person under influence of liquor or drug may not operate.

A visitor from U.S. may drive in Britain provided that he is in possession of a licence valid in U.S. and has not been in Britain for more than 12 months.

Parking.—No vehicles at any time may park on part of a street which is marked with double yellow line. When there is a single yellow line this restriction applies during normal business hours although reference should be made to notices in street stating times of restrictions. In certain areas vehicles may only park at meters during normal business hours. Local authorities have power to remove from roads cars which have broken down and appear to be abandoned and cars towed away may be sold if not claimed after six weeks. Certain local authority may clamp cars which are illegally parked.

Tests.—Road Traffic Act 1988. Vehicles may be stopped on a road and tested as to the condition of certain parts. Annual testing of vehicles registered for three years or more is compulsory before vehicle licence issued (MOT [Ministry of Transport]). Certain vehicles, e.g., of visiting forces, exempted.

Accidents.—In case of accident causing damage or injury to any person, vehicle or animal (except cats, rabbits, fowls, geese, etc.) driver must stop, give any particulars required and report the accident to the police station or to constable as soon as reasonably practicable and in any case within 24 hours and produce insurance certificate to police either when reporting accident or within seven days at police station selected.

Insurance.—Anyone using, or permitting another to use, a motor vehicle on a road must be insured against liability for personal injury to third persons and passengers and damage to property or goods and must be in possession of certificate of insurance in statutory form. (Road Traffic Act, 1988). American visitors, if their policies cover accidents in England, can obtain certificate of foreign insurance from Royal Automobile Club or Automobile Association.

The Third Parties (Rights against Insurers) Act, 1930, gives the third party a right of action direct against the insurer if insured is bankrupt or in liquidation.

Road Traffic Act 1988 obliges insurers to satisfy any judgment not satisfied by insured provided that insurer receives notice of commencement of proceedings from third party prior to or within seven days of their commencement.

Motor Insurance Bureau has agreed with Minister of Transport to satisfy any judgment obtained against driver of motor vehicle which is not satisfied within seven days for any reason (e.g., no policy, risk not covered, policy voidable), provided: (a) notice of proceedings given to Motor Insurance Bureau before or within 7 days after their commencement, (b) liability is one required to be covered by statute. Motor Insurance Bureau has also agreed to compensate hit and run victims in certain cases.

Motor Tax.—Annual tax for motor cars is £140. Tax may be paid annually or in six monthly periods. Receipt containing material particulars is given and this must always be fitted into circular disc attached to front of car so that it is open to police inspection.

See Topical Index in front part of this volume.

MOTOR VEHICLES . . . *continued*

It is offence to drive car in respect to which tax has not been paid. Motorcycles are taxed according to cylinder capacity of engine.

Visitors should produce their International Insurance Certificate ("Green Card") and vehicle registration certificate at port of entry and will obtain exemption for period of 12 months.

Car Tax.—Abolished by Car Tax (Abolition) Act 1992.

NEGOTIABLE INSTRUMENTS:

See topic Bills and Notes.

NOTARIES PUBLIC:

Applications for appointment as notary public for this country must be made at the Court of Faculties: The Sanctuary, Westminster. Notarial Faculties for London are granted after: (1) service by the applicant with a London notary for five years; (2) admission to the freedom of the Scriveners' Company.

Faculties for any other place in England or Wales are granted: (1) After service with a notary for five years; (2) to solicitors, where the applicant can show, by memorial to the Master of the Faculties, the need for the appointment.

The cost of a faculty for this country (including the stamp duty) is about £20.

PARTNERSHIPS:

These are either ordinary partnerships (Partnership Act, 1890) or limited ones (Limited Partnership Act, 1907). In an ordinary partnership each partner impliedly confers upon his copartners apparent authority to incur debts on behalf of the partnership to bind all partners. Limited partnerships are very rare; the limited partner's liability is restricted to the amount of his capital. He is not to take part in management of partnership business and shall not have power to bind firm. If he takes part in management, he shall become general partner and be liable for all debts and obligations of firm.

A partnership exists between persons carrying on a business in common with a view to profit. Neither common ownership of property nor sharing of gross returns by itself creates a partnership but an unqualified agreement to share profit and loss is very strong evidence of partnership.

A partnership firm has no legal personality distinct from the members composing it but partners can sue and are liable to be sued in their firm name. A receiving order in bankruptcy may be made against the firm and it operates as if it were made against each of the persons who at its date are partners in the firm.

Under Companies Act, permitted number of partners is 20 and is without restriction for lawyers', accountants' and stockbrokers' partnerships.

Under Income and Corporation Taxes Act 1988 income tax assessment on individual partners is treated as part of that partners own individual taxation liability.

As to firm name, see topic Trademarks and Tradenames, subhead Tradenames.

PATENTS:

Note: Copyright, Designs and Patents Act came into force on 1st Aug. 1989 and amends Patent Act 1977 to minor extent. There are special provisions now for patents of pharmaceutical products.

Law of patents was considerably changed by Patents Act, 1977. It establishes new system of domestic law, gave effect to EEC Patents Convention and Patents Court.

Transitional Provisions.—Patents granted and applications for patents made before June 1, 1978 remain governed by Patents Act, 1949 but subject to certain amendments of which most important relate to duration. Patents granted before June 1, 1967 still run for 16 years with limited right to extension. Patents granted between June 1, 1967 and June 1, 1978 will now run for 20 years but without any right to extension. Unless contrary appears all further references under this topic are to law established by Patents Act, 1977.

Patentability is elaborately defined. Invention is not patentable unless it is new, involves inventive step and is capable of industrial application. Some inventions are never patentable, particularly scientific theories, aesthetic creations, computer programmes and biological processes except for those involving microbiology.

Application for patent may be made by any person whether British citizen or not. Patents are granted primarily to inventor or joint inventors but may also be granted to any person entitled to legal interest in invention in U.K. at time of invention. They may also be granted to successors in title of either class of persons.

Mode of Application.—System of provisional protection under 1949 Act has been replaced for new applications by system of priority dates. Generally, priority date is date of filing of application at Patent Office. Priority may be gained if documents filed contain indication that patent is being applied for, applicant is identified, invention is described and filing fee paid, even though documents do not fully comply with Act and Patent Rules 1978. But such application will be treated as withdrawn unless within overall period of (generally) three and one-half years requirements as to claims and abstracts are complied with and preliminary examination and search and substantive examination are both requested. Thus although priority may sometimes be gained without full compliance with Act and Rules, it will almost always be necessary to file prescribed proper documents later. Formal application must be in prescribed form, containing request for grant of patent, specification describing invention, abstract giving technical information and claim or claims. Claim or claims serve to delimit precise nature and extent of invention being patented. If patent is granted in respect of any claim or claims, it is their wording which forms basis of subsequent infringement proceedings. Consequently they must be carefully and precisely drafted. Official searches made on application are now divided into two stages of preliminary examination and search and substantive examination. Two fees are payable.

Objections and Grant.—In contrast to 1949 Act objections are not receivable except by third parties as to whether they are entitled to patent invention in question. However any person may lodge written observations as to whether invention is patentable at all. If Patent Office decides that application complies with Act and Rules patent is granted upon payment of fee. It takes effect from date of publication in Official Journal and runs 20 years from date of filing of application. Renewal fees must be paid at end of fourth year from filing and every year thereafter or else patent ceases.

Revocation.—Third party may apply to court or comptroller of Patent Office to revoke patent on any of following grounds, but no other: (A) Invention was not patentable. (B) Patent was not granted to person entitled to make application. Ground (B) can only be invoked by person who has obtained prior finding of court or comptroller that he was person truly entitled to patent invention. Further, except in cases of fraud, ground (B) cannot be invoked unless proceedings which produced that finding were commenced within two years of grant of patent. (C) Specification of patent does not disclose invention clearly and completely enough for skilled person to perform it. (D) Matter disclosed in specification of patent extends beyond that disclosed in application for patent as filed. (E) Protection conferred by patent has been extended by amendment which should not have been allowed.

Infringement.—Right to sue for infringement does not arise until patent is published and only in respect of acts after publication. Broadly, infringement may be defined as commercial use of or dealing with patented product or process without consent of proprietor of patent. In case of process there is no infringement unless user or dealer knew or ought to have known that his acts constituted infringement. Defendant to infringement action can rely on any ground of defence common to all actions but he may only attack validity of patent on grounds available upon application to revoke. Usual relief granted to successful plaintiff is injunction coupled with damages or account of profits. Damages or account will not be ordered against defendant honestly and reasonably ignorant of patent. Failure to register transaction passing property in patent, license or sub-license within six months or if six months was too short as soon as practicable, also bars right of transferee to damages or account. Although secret prior user is no longer ground for revocation, bona fide prior use may be continued without constituting infringement.

Registration.—System of registration has been extended by 1977 Act. Grants, assignments, mortgages, vesting assents and court orders in relation to patent applications, patents, licenses and sub-licenses are all registrables. Priority of claims in respect of such property depends upon order of registration unless earlier unregistered transaction was known to person claiming under later registered transaction.

Licenses.—To use or deal with patent can of course be negotiated with proprietor in ordinary way. There is also system of compulsory and semi-compulsory licensing. Under latter, proprietor who is perfectly willing to grant licenses on such terms as comptroller may decide are reasonable can at any time apply to have entry in register to effect that licenses under patent are available as of right. If applicant for license as of right cannot agree on terms with proprietor they will be settled by comptroller. Under former, any person may at any time after three years from grant apply to comptroller for compulsory license upon such terms as are reasonable. Possible grounds for application are that: (A) Invention can be worked commercially in U.K. but is not being worked at all or to fullest practical extent; (B) U.K. demand for patented product is not being met on reasonable terms or is being met to substantial extent by imports; (C) commercial working of patent in U.K. is being prevented or hindered by imports of patented products or products produced by patented process; (D) injury to commerce and trade of U.K. by reason of refusal of licenses on reasonable terms; (E) injury to commerce and trade of U.K. by reason of imposition of conditions by proprietor. Finally Crown has certain right to use patented inventions compulsorily upon such terms as may be agreed or as may be ordered by court.

Invalidity of Certain Contracts.—Under both 1977 and 1949 Acts certain restrictive convenants in connection with patented material are rendered void. More important are new provisions protecting rights of employees to their inventions as against their employers. These apply to persons mainly employed in U.K. and to persons attached to place of business in U.K. who are not mainly employed anywhere or whose place of employment cannot be determined. Employee's invention is his own unless made in course of usual or special duties in circumstances where he might reasonably be expected to make invention or unless invention was made in course of his duties and these duties and his responsibilities were such that he had special obligation to further his employer's interests. In those cases invention is his employers but he is entitled to compensation to be assessed by court or comptroller. Any contract diminishing those various rights is to that extent unenforceable.

International Element.—One of major purposes of 1977 Act was to bring U.K. law into line with EEC Patent Convention. Broadly, any EEC patent is to be treated as patent under 1977 Act. Patent Co-operation Treaty is older system applying to many countries including U.S. Applications to patents offices of countries adhering to treaty establish earlier priority date for U.K. purposes provided that application to U.K. Patent Office is filed within 12 months of filing of foreign application and declaration is made specifying earlier application.

Court.—1977 Act abolished Patents Appeal Tribunal and replaces it by Patents Court which is part of Chancery Division of High Court of Justice.

Patent Agents.—Applications to and proceedings before Patent Office are generally made and conducted by patent agents. They are not lawyers in strict sense but are highly skilled in relevant law and practice. They are governed by Chartered Institute of Patent Agents, Staple Inn Buildings, London WC1.

See also European Union Digest, topic Patents.

PERPETUITIES:

Property may not be settled for a period longer than that of a life or lives in being plus 21 years, unless settlor or testator specifies a period of years not exceeding 80 years as perpetuity period.

By the Law of Property Act, 1925, §163, where in any instrument coming into operation after 1925 the date of absolute vesting of capital or income or the ascertainment of a beneficiary or class of beneficiaries depends on the attainment by the beneficiary or members of the class of an age exceeding 21 years, and there is a gift over in the event of a total or partial failure of the original gift, the age of 21 years is substituted for the age specified if, but for this section, the gift would be void for remoteness.

PERPETUITIES . . . *continued*

Under Perpetuities and Accumulations Act 1964 instead of substituting age of 21 years there is substituted in instruments taking effect after July 16, 1964 the age nearest the specified age, consistent with gift being valid.

Accumulations.—By §164 of Law of Property Act 1925, as am'd by Perpetuities and Accumulations Act 1964, property may not be settled by instrument or otherwise in such manner that income thereof shall be wholly or partially accumulated for any longer period than: (a) Life of grantor or settlor; (b) 21 years from death of grantor, settlor or testator; (c) duration of minority or respective minorities of any person or persons living or en ventre sa mere at death of grantor, settlor, or testator; (d) duration of minority or respective minorities only of any person or persons who under limitations of instrument directing the accumulations would, for time being if of full age, be entitled to the income directed to be accumulated; (e) 21 years from date of settlement on; or (f) minority or minorities of any persons in being. Section does not apply to any provision: (1) For payment of debts of grantor, settlor, testator or other person; (2) for raising portions for any child or remoter issue of testator, grantor, settlor or person taking an interest under any settlement directing the accumulation or to whom any interest is thereby limited; or (3) respecting accumulation of produce of timber or wood.

PLEDGES:

A pledge of personal chattels is the transfer by delivery of immediate possession thereof by way of security for an advance, whether past or present, the pledger remaining the owner of the chattel but the pledgee acquiring a right to sell (but not to foreclose) if the advance be not repaid on the due date.

PRESCRIPTION:

See topic Limitation of Actions.

PRINCIPAL AND AGENT:

Common law rules apply. In general the principal is responsible for the acts of his duly authorised agent. An agent acting for an undisclosed principal is personally liable. An agent acting outside his authority is liable on an action for breach of warranty of authority.

Power of Attorney.—Any competent person may grant power of attorney to another person to enable attorney to act as agent of donor with, inter alia, power to execute deeds on donor's behalf. In general power continues until revoked by donor although in some circumstances consent of attorney is required. (Powers of Attorney Act 1971).

Under Enduring Powers of Attorney Act 1985 "enduring" power of attorney may be granted. This will be granted in special form which will include explaining note that power endures despite subsequent mental incapacity of donor, subject to registration in Court of Protection.

See also topic Absentees.

PROCESS:

Service of Process.—In criminal and County Court matters service is usually made by the appropriate court official because the case is conducted through the court. In County Court where service is to be effected otherwise than by court official copy of summons must be filed at Court instead of request. In any High Court or other proceedings there are few restrictions on who may serve any writ or notice, although this is usually done by or on behalf of firm of solicitors. Proceedings may be served personally or by post although choice will affect time for entering of appearance to action. Divorce proceedings may be served by Court, or petitioner's solicitors although personal service may not be effected by petitioner himself, on behalf of petitioner's solicitors. Service is also effected by leaving document at document exchange (where solicitors address for service includes numbered box) or at document exchange which transmits documents daily to it.

REAL PROPERTY:

In general, by the Law of Property Act, 1925, §1, the only estates in land capable of subsisting or of being conveyed or created at law are (a) an estate in fee simple absolute in possession and (b) a term of years absolute; and the interests in land which may be so dealt with at law are: (a) An easement, right or privilege in or over land for an interest equivalent to a fee simple absolute in possession, or a term of years absolute; (b) a rent charge in possession on land, either perpetual or for a term of years absolute; (c) a charge by way of legal mortgage; (d) land tax, tithe, rent-charge and any other similar charge on land not created by an instrument; (e) rights of entry over or in respect of a legal term of years absolute or annexed for any purpose to a legal rent-charge.

Land held by two or more persons must be held by them as joint tenants in law but in equity they can be joint tenants (survivorship applies) or tenants in common (no survivorship). Land cannot be held in law by more than four persons but if more, four legal owners will be trustees for all.

Land Registration.—There are two systems of conveyancing:

(I) Unregistered.—Where evidence of title lies in title deeds. Certain interests can be protected by registration as land charges under Land Charges Act 1972.

(II) Registered.—Where title to property is registered at H.M. Land Registry. Register becomes conclusive evidence of title. Most of England and Wales is now designated as area of compulsory registration of title but title is not registrable until property is transferred on sale or let on long lease for term of more than 21 years.

See also topic Aliens, subhead Property.

RECEIVERS:

See topics Executions, subhead Equitable Execution; Mortgages.

RECORDS:

As to various instruments which must be registered or recorded, see topics Assignments for Benefit of Creditors; Chattel Mortgages; Corporations; Sales.

Land Registration.—Title to property may be registered at H.M. Land Registry and is open to public inspection.

See topic Real Property, subhead Land Registration.

Births, deaths and marriages are registered in the first instance with the local registrar, who forwards the necessary particulars to the Registrar-General of Births, Deaths and Marriages, St. Catherine's House, London W. C. 2. Copy of certificates may be obtained from General Register Offices, Smedley Hydro, Southport, Merseyside PR8 2HH, for fee of £15 for postal application. Alternatively, expedition fee of £27.50 is payable guaranteeing return of certificate within 48 hours. Copies may be obtained personally from Saint Catherine's House, 10 Kingsway, London W.C.2. for fee of £6 or expedition fee of £22 ensuring return within 24 hours of application.

Probate.—Copy of probate with will can be inspected at Somerset House, Strand London, WC2.

Companies.—Records of company accounts, annual returns, shareholdings, special resolutions are kept in Companies House, Maindy Way, Cardiff, Wales.

REPLEVIN:

Governed by common law rules. This is process of restoration or recovery of detained goods on security given for submission to trial and judgement. County court has jurisdiction up to any amount, but in certain cases action may be removed to High Court.

REPORTS: See topic Law Reports.

SALES:

Sales are regulated by Sale of Goods Act 1979 as amended by Sale of Goods (Amendment) Act 1994, Sale and Supply of Goods Act 1982 and by reference to Misrepresentation Act 1967 and Unfair Contract Terms Act 1977 and other related statutes.

It is defined that a seller is an unpaid seller when: (a) The whole of the price has not been paid; or (b) a negotiable instrument has been received as conditional payment and has not been duly met.

Irrespective of the rights of an unpaid seller by action he has also the right, if the title in the goods has not passed, to withhold delivery. If the title in the goods has passed to the buyer the seller has: (a) A lien on the goods for the price while he is in possession of them; (b) in case of the insolvency of the buyer a right of stopping the goods in transit after he has parted with possession; (c) right of resale as limited by Sale of Goods Act.

Applicable Law.—See topic Contracts, subhead Applicable Law.

Consumer Protection Act 1987 enables regulations to be made imposing safety requirements as to composition, contents, design, packing, etc., of all goods and as to instructions or warnings to be marked on them or issued with them and give powers for enforcement of regulations. Trading Stamps Act 1964 makes provision for regulating issue, use and redemption of trading stamps.

Resale Price Maintenance.—Resale Prices Act 1964 abolishes resale price maintenance in U.K. except where shown to be in public interest. Except in case of exempted goods, any term in a contract relating to a sale of goods which provides for minimum prices to be charged on resale of those goods in U.K. shall be void. Procedure for registration of goods for exemption, within time limits. See also European Union Digest, topic Internal Market, subhead Free Movement of Goods.

Bills of Sale.—An absolute bill of sale must be registered with the Registrar of the County Court of the district in which the grantor lives within seven days after the making or giving hereof. (Bill of Sale Act, 1878). For security bills of sale see topic Chattel Mortgages.

Stoppage in Transitu.—The law on this subject is chiefly governed by the Sale of Goods Act. By that act goods are deemed to be in course of transit from the time when they are delivered to a carrier by land or water or other bailee for the purpose of transmission to the buyer until the buyer or his agent in that behalf takes delivery from such carrier or other bailee.

The unpaid seller may exercise his right of stoppage in transitu, either (1) by taking actual possession of the goods or (2) by giving notice of his claim to the carrier or other bailee in whose possession the goods are. Such notice may be given either to the person in actual possession of the goods or to a principal of an agent so in possession. The notice to be effectual must be given in sufficient time to enable the principal to communicate it to his servant or agent in time to prevent delivery. Where notice is given to a ship-owner it is his duty to transmit it with reasonable diligence to the master of the ship.

Where a document of title to the goods has been lawfully transferred to any person as buyer or owner of the goods, and that person transfers the document to a person who takes it in good faith, without notice and for valuable consideration, then, that transfer was by way of sale, the unpaid seller's right of lien or stoppage in transitu is defeated, and if the transfer was by way of pledge or other disposition for value, the unpaid seller's right of lien or stoppage in transitu can only be exercised subject to the rights of the transferee.

Credit sales are governed by Consumer Credit Act 1974. Consumer credit agreement is defined as credit agreement for no more than £15,000. Act requires such agreement to be in writing and to contain certain information. Copy agreement to be sent to consumer within seven days. Opportunity, in some circumstances, for consumer to withdraw from agreement within five days of receiving copy agreement.

Act provides for transfer of title by hirer in certain cases in which a purchaser buys without notice of hire purchase agreement.

At present there are restrictions on the disposal and possession of certain goods under Hire-Purchase or Credit Sale Agreements and Hiring Agreements, particularly vehicles.

SALES . . . *continued*

See also subhead Warranties, infra.

The Trade Descriptions Acts 1968 and 1972 provide criminal sanctions for persons knowingly or recklessly making false statements with regard to goods for sale or provision of services or accommodation.

Misrepresentation Act 1967 provides for rescission of any contract entered into as a result of a misrepresentation even when misrepresentation has become a term of contract and even when contract has been executed. When misrepresentation is innocent, court may award damages in lieu of rescission at its discretion; when it is negligent, court may award damages for negligence as well as rescission or again damages only, in lieu of rescission, at its discretion.

Warranties.—The Sale and Supply of Goods Act 1994 implies following terms in contracts for sale of goods: (1) Seller has right to sell goods and that goods are free from any charge or encumbrance not disclosed; (2) when sale is by description as defined in Act that goods correspond to that description; (3) where goods sold in ordinary course of business that goods supplied are of satisfactory quality except in relation to defects brought to buyer's attention before contract or where buyer examines goods all defects which that examination ought to reveal; (4) where goods sold in ordinary course of business that goods are fit for purpose for which they are required provided that buyer impliedly or expressly makes known to seller purpose for which goods are required except where circumstances show that buyer did not rely, or it would be unreasonable for him to rely, on sellers skill or judgment; (5) where sale is by sample that bulk corresponds with sample in description and quality and that buyer should have reasonable chance of comparing the two.

Above conditions cannot be excluded by parties to contract in case of "consumer sales" (as defined) or in any other case where such an exclusion would be unfair or unreasonable in accordance with guidelines laid down by Act. Seller can never exclude warranty of good title. Neither can seller exclude terms of satisfactory quality, fitness for purpose and conformity to description where sale is consumer sale. Consumer sale is sale in ordinary course of business of goods of type ordinarily bought for private use to person who does not buy them in ordinary course of business. Implied warranties may be excluded in all other sales where it is fair and reasonable to do so within guidelines laid down by Act. Similar provisions apply to hire purchase contracts.

The Supply of Goods and Services Act 1982.—§1 defines term "contract for transfer of goods". Contracts for sale of goods, hire-purchase agreements, transactions under Trading Stamps Act 1964, transfers by deed and agreements for mortgage are excluded. Contracts not precluded from being contract for transfer of goods if service also provided or because consideration involves something other than money. §§2-5 make provisions for terms implied in such contracts relating to title etc., transfer by description, quality or fitness and transfer by sample similar to those made in relation to contracts for sale of goods by Sale of Goods Act 1979. (See subhead Warranties, supra.)

§§6-10 relate to contracts for hire of goods. §6 defines term "contract for hire of goods". Hire-purchase agreements and transactions under Trading Stamps Act 1964 excluded. Contracts not precluded from being contract for hire of goods if service is also provided or consideration involves something other than money. §§7-10 make provision for terms to be implied in such contracts relating to title etc., hire by description, quality or fitness and hire by sample similar to those in relation to contract for sale of goods by Sale of Goods Act 1979. (See subhead Warranties, supra.)

The Sale of Goods Act (Implied Terms) Act 1973 implies in §§8 to 10 same conditions into contracts of hire purchase that Sale of Goods Act 1979 implies into contracts for sale.

Unfair Contract Terms Act 1977.—In contracts for supply of goods liability for death or injury resulting from negligence cannot be excluded. Liability for loss or damage cannot be restricted or excluded in guarantees of goods and can only otherwise be excluded if reasonable in circumstances of contract. Unfair Terms in Consumer Contracts Regulations 1994 provides that, with certain exceptions, any term which has not been individually negotiated in contracts concluded between consumer and seller or supplier must not be unfair.

Consumer Protection Act 1987 provides for strict liability of manufacturers and suppliers of defective products which cause damage to individuals subject to certain defences. Act also governs giving of price indications.

International Sale of Goods.—Uniform Laws on International Sales Act 1967, gives effect in U.K. to Uniform Law on International Sale of Goods and Uniform Law on Formation of Contracts for such sales.

SEALS:

See topic Deeds.

SECURITIES AND INVESTMENTS:

The Financial Services Act 1986.—This Act has established new system for regulation of U.K. securities and investment industry. Broadly, Act requires anyone carrying on investment business, term which it defines very widely, to obtain authorisation from Securities and Investments Board, to whom powers are delegated by Secretary of State for Trade and Industry. Persons subject to Act have to comply with extensive set of rules governing conduct of investment business.

See also European Union Digest, topic Corporations.

SEQUESTRATION:

This rare mode of execution is available against one who has disobeyed an order of the court. It empowers the sequestrators to enter on the lands of defendant and receive the rents and profits and to take possession of his personal property until he complies with the order. With court's leave they may sell the personal property and pay the proceeds into court. This is only available in High Court.

SHIPPING:

Courts.—Admiralty division of High Court and, for smaller matters, County Court in its Admiralty jurisdiction deal with shipping litigation.

Ships.—Ownership, mortgages, registration, construction, safety equipment etc. are covered by Merchant Shipping Acts 1894 to 1994. There are over 30 Acts so named, many of which are repealed. Main Acts: Merchant Shipping Act 1894, Merchant Shipping Act 1970, Merchant Shipping Act 1974, Merchant Shipping Act 1979, Merchant Shipping Act 1981, Merchant Shipping Act 1983, Merchant Shipping Act 1984, and Merchant Shipping Act 1988, Aviation & Maritime Security Act 1990, Carriage of Goods by Sea Act 1992 and Merchant Shipping (Registration etc.) Act 1993. Many enactments relating to Merchant Shipping (along with certain other enactments) have been consolidated in Merchant Shipping Act 1995 and Shipping & Trading Interests (Protection) Act 1995. Under Interpretation Act 1978, §17(2)(b) regulations made under repealed legislation are continued in force unless otherwise selected. By virtue of Merchant Shipping Act 1995, §314, Sch. 14, para. 2 any references in any other Act (not amended by 1995 Act, Sch. 13), or in any instrument made under any other Act to registration of ship or fishing vehicle under certain earlier enactments is construed, unless context requires otherwise as, or as including, reference to registration under 1995 Act Part II (§§8-23).

Crew.—Merchant Shipping Acts provide for manning of ships, certification, authority, liability and welfare of masters, officers, and crew. The Merchant Shipping Act 1988 makes further provision for giving of financial assistance in connection with training of seamen and crew relief costs, and for establishment of Merchant Navy Reserve (see subhead Ships, supra for effect of consolidation).

Safety.—Dangerous Vessels Act 1985 enables harbour masters to prohibit vessels from entering jurisdiction of harbour authority, or to require their removal therefrom in certain circumstances. The Safety at Sea Act 1986 deals with safety of equipment and crew. The Merchant Shipping Act 1984 part I makes further provision with respect to safety of shipping. Provision has been made for suppression of unlawful acts against Safety of Ships by Aviation & Maritime Section Act 1990.

Carriage of Goods by Sea.—Covered by charterparty, bill of lading and various common law rules. Carriage of Goods by Sea Act 1971 amended by Merchant Shipping Act 1981 overrides contrary common law rules. This Act gives effect to "Hague Visby rules" in International Convention for the Unification of Certain Rules of Law relating to Bills of Lading (see subhead Ships, supra for effect of consolidation).

Carriage of Passengers.—Subject to numerous statutory regulations. Main Act is Merchant Shipping Act 1894. Responsibilities of owner and master, see Merchant Shipping (Passenger Ship Construction Survey) Regulations 1984.

Pilotage and Towage.—Pilotage regulated by Pilotage Act 1987. Towage is matter of contract between parties (see subhead Ships, supra for effect of consolidation).

Collisions.—Collision Regulations 1972 (as amended) made under Merchant Shipping Acts provide rules for all British vessels upon high seas subject to any local rules. Under Merchant Shipping (Distress Signals and Prevention of Collisions) Regulations 1987 and Merchant Shipping Act 1984, person whose negligence causes ship to collide liable. Owner vicariously liable. Master liable for own negligence or breach of contract. Owners of injured ship, owners of cargo or other property and persons suffering personal injuries or death have right to damages. Damages, subject to certain limitations, generally follow principle of full compensation (see subhead Ships, supra for effect of consolidation).

Liens.—Maritime liens recognised by English Law are for bottomry and respondentia bonds, salvage of property, seamen's wages and damage. Statutory lien attaches when property is arrested in action in rem in English court. Wharfinger, harbour and dock authorities, and repairer have various liens (see subhead Ships, supra for effect of consolidation).

Lighthouses.—Corporation of the Trinity House controls lighthouses, buoys and beacons for England and Wales and Commissioners for Irish Lights control same in Northern Ireland (see subhead Ships, supra for effect of consolidation).

Pollution.—Oil pollution covered by Prevention of Oil Pollution Act 1971, giving effect to International Convention for Prevention of Pollution of Sea by Oil 1954. Offence to discharge oil into sea. Emission of black smoke by ship in territorial waters offence under Clean Air Act 1956. Licence required to dump substance: (a) In U.K. waters, or (b) in any waters by British ship, under Dumping at Sea Act 1974. The Merchant Shipping Act 1988 makes further provision with respect to liability and compensation for oil pollution and Merchant Shipping (Oil Pollution) Act 1971.

Hovercraft governed by Hovercraft Act 1968.

Limitation and Exclusion of Liability.—Law regarding rights of shipowners and others to limit or exclude liability largely contained in Merchant Shipping Acts 1894 to 1981.

Registration.—Merchant Shipping (Registration etc.) Act 1993 (not yet in force)—establishes central register of ships in UK under control of Registrar General of Shipping and Seamen.

STATUTE OF FRAUDS: See topic Contracts.

STATUTES:

Official Statutes are published by H. M. Stationery Office, High Holborn, London, W.C.2. A comprehensive volume of statutes is printed in Halsbury Statutes published by Butterworth & Co. (Publishers) Ltd. Halsbury House, 35 Chancery Lane, London WC2A 1EL.

As to law reports, see topic Law Reports.

TAXATION:

All taxation is imposed by Parliament and is collected either by deduction at source of taxable payment or from taxpayer by Inland Revenue direct or by Customs and Excise Officials at ports and airports.

See Topical Index in front part of this volume.

TAXATION . . . *continued*

There is no taxation with respect to the ownership of property except as hereinafter stated.

Income Tax is imposed on annual income or profits accruing to any person residing in U.K. from any property, trade, profession or vocation whether in U.K. or elsewhere, and on income or profits of persons residing outside U.K. from any property, trade, profession or vocation within U.K. (Income and Corporation Taxes Act 1988).

From June 4, 1990 income (and capital gains) of husband and wife are separately taxed. Each spouse has separate basic rate band and there is no aggregation of income. Personal allowance is given to each spouse and in addition husband receives married couple's allowance, unless couple elect otherwise.

For tax purposes, fiscal year is from Apr. 6 in one year to Apr. 5 in following year.

Income above personal allowances for financial year 1996-1997 will be charged as follows:

	Rate
£3,900	20%
£21,600	24%
over £25,500	40%

Investment income surcharge has been abolished.

(1) Personal allowance for single person £3,765; for married couple—allowance of £1,790 (monthly reduction in year of marriage £149.17).

(2) Personal allowance single person (over 65, under 75) £4,910 or over £5,000. Married couple's allowance (elder spouse under 75) £3,115. Married couple's allowance (elder spouse 75 or over) £3,155.

(3) Widow's bereavement allowance £1,790.

(4) Additional relief for children £1,790.

(5) Blind persons allowance £1,250.

British subjects residing abroad are entitled to the same allowances as though residing in the United Kingdom since 1988. Same allowances are made to residents of Channel Islands and Isle of Man, Commonwealth Citizens, Republic of Ireland citizens, persons in service of territory under Crown protection and to certain persons resident abroad for health and those who are or have been in service of Crown or widows of same or are employed by missionary society.

Allowances are made as against ascertained tax for premium payable on certain insurance policies. Allowance on premiums for life assurance policies has been abolished for policies taken out after 13th Mar. 1984. Maximum allowance allowable for premiums on retirement annuity policies is set out in table below. Mortgage interest relief is available on first £30,000 loan for purchase of principal private residence at rate of 15%.

Retirement annuities: limits for qualifying premiums

Age in years at beginning of year of assessment	Maximum Percentage
50 and below	17½%
51 to 55	30%
56 to 60	35%
61 or more	40%

Self assessment is being brought in for tax year 1996-7 in case of employees regulations provide for collection of tax by weekly deductions from their salaries. Tax on interest arising on public loans, etc., is deducted at source.

Nonresidents can obtain repayment of the whole tax deducted from income from sources outside of the United Kingdom.

Visitors.—Briefly visitors from abroad are liable to tax:

(1) *On income arising in this country,* but income from certain Government securities is exempt.

(2) *When They Are Resident in United Kingdom on Income Arising Abroad.*—The basis of liability is amount received in or remitted to United Kingdom.

The terms "resident" and "ordinarily resident" have technical meanings and each case is dealt with on its own facts. For example, a visitor is regarded as a "resident" if he maintains a place of abode in United Kingdom (he then pays tax for any year in which he visits United Kingdom); or if he makes regular visits for substantial periods (e.g., average three months a year for five consecutive years); or if he remains in U.K. for six months in income tax year (6th Apr.-5th Apr.). It is emphasized that provisions affecting visitors are intricate and above is only intended as guide. Inland Revenue is prepared to give assistance to visitors on these questions.

Corporation Tax.—Income and Corporation Taxes Act 1988, provides for all companies resident in U.K. to be chargeable to corporation tax on all income and on all capital gains. Companies with profits over £1,500,000 pay tax at 33%. Companies with profits below £300,000 pay tax at 24%. Gradually increasing rate of taxation for companies with profits between £300,000 and £1,500,000. In addition, such companies have to deduct income tax at standard rate from all dividends paid by them and to pay tax so deducted to Revenue. It follows that profits which company retains are subject to corporation tax only. "Close company," that is in main company controlled by not more than five persons, is subject to different tax rules. Likewise, close investment holding company, defined by long statutory test, is also subject to different tax rules.

National Insurance.—In addition to income tax, employers pay National Insurance Contributions as follows:

Class 1 Contributions

Standard Rate Earnings per week (£'s)	Employers
61—109.99	3%
110.00—154.99	5%
155.00—209.99	7%
210.00—455.00	10.2%
Over 455.00	10.2%

Individuals earning below £61 per week or £3,172 per year continue to have no liability. Those earning above this level have liability calculated at 2% rate on earnings up to lower limit and at flat 10% rate for contracted-in employees (8.2% for contracted out) on amounts between limit and upper earnings limit (£455 per week or £23,660 per year).

Stock Dividend Options.—Where a corporation gives a shareholder an alternative, however expressed, enabling him to receive additional shares instead of a cash dividend, any shares (other than redeemable shares) which it so issues are treated as a distribution for Corporation Tax purposes and subject to income tax as if alternative cash dividend paid.

Capital Gains.—Capital Gains Tax Act 1979 imposes tax on total amount of chargeable gains accruing to individual or corporation chargeable in year of assessment (e.g. 6th Apr. 1996 to 5th Apr. 1997) after deducting allowable losses. Base value of assets held on Mar. 31, 1982 will be rebased to that date so that only gains or losses since that date will be brought into account. However, new base shall not apply if higher gain or higher loss would be created than under regime existing before Finance Act 1988. For individuals rates of tax apply as if chargeable gains were top slice of income (i.e. 24% or 40%). Tax arises on "disposal" of "assets" which are widely defined to include options, debts, incorporeal property, and currency other than sterling. There is no tax on cumulative gains of less than £6,300 and there are arrangements for double taxation relief and disposals involving foreign element. (§§10-19). Capital losses in current year may be set against gains in that year or future year. Government nonmarketable securities and savings certificates are exempt.

Double Taxation.—In certain circumstances unilateral relief is given from income tax and profits tax in respect of tax payable under the law of any territory outside the United Kingdom by allowing the last mentioned tax as a credit against income tax or the profits tax.

U.K. Party to many double taxation agreements with other countries. International agreement comes into force in U.K. by Statutory Instrument after considerable delay. Hence agreements usually come into force retrospectively.

Following are agreements between U.K. and U.S.A.: Convention of 31 Dec. 1975, Exchange of Notes on 13 Apr. 1976, Amending Protocol of 26 Aug. 1976, Amending Protocol of 31 Mar. 1977, Amending Protocol of 15 Mar. 1979 (all of which came into force under Statutory Instrument No. 568 of 1980), Dividend Regulations of 2 Aug. 1946 (No. 1331 of 1946), Amending Dividend Regulations of 31 Mar. 1955 (No. 499 of 1955), Amending Dividend Regulations of 25 May 1961 (No. 985 of 1961) and Amending Dividend Regulations of 22 May 1980 (No. 779 of 1980), Double Taxation Relief (Taxes on Income) Order 1980 and Amending Dividend Regulations 1994 (No. 1418 of 1994).

Following are agreements between U.K. and Canada: Convention of 8 Sept. 1978 (Statutory Instrument No. 790 of 1980), Amending Protocol of 15 Apr. 1980 (No. 1528 of 1980), Dividend and Interest Regulations of 4 June 1980 (No. 780 of 1980) and Amending Dividend and Interest Regulations of 27 Nov. 1987.

Inheritance.—On death tax is charged on property passing on death and on cumulative basis takes account of gifts within seven years of death. There is no charge on lifetime gifts between individuals or on gifts into accumulation and maintenance trusts, trusts for disabled and interest in possession trusts. There is charge for lifetime gifts into and out of discretionary trusts and gifts involving companies. Periodic charges on discretionary trusts are on ten yearly basis. When donor dies within seven years of making gift gift will be taxable with cumulation of chargeable transfers in previous seven years. Gift will be taxed on its value at date of death at rate of 40% for transfers made after 15th Mar. 1988.

Tax is borne primarily by donor. Nil rate threshold is £200,000.

Inter vivos gifts made more than three years before death attract lower rate than on death.

Gifts between spouses inter vivos and on death are exempt. Other main exemptions are gifts up to £3,000 in any tax year.

Gifts to charities and political parties are exempt, £100,000 limit on exemption for gifts to political parties having been abolished for transfers from 15th Mar. 1988.

Value Added Tax (V.A.T.).—Introduced by Finance Act, 1972, V.A.T. is payable on supply of all goods or services, unless specifically exempted, in U.K. by registered person in course of his business, and on import of goods into U.K. by any person. Any person whose turnover exceeds £47,000 per annum unless turnover for next year will not exceed £45,000 (no provision for quarter turnovers any more) must register under Act. Special provisions are made for companies with turnover of less than £300,000 per annum.

Registered person can reclaim tax (input tax) on goods or services supplied to him except where his business makes exempt supplies.

Where a supply is zero rated, no tax shall be chargeable on supply but it shall be treated in all other respects as a taxable supply and therefore any input tax may be reclaimed.

V.A.T. is chargeable at basic rate of 17½% with effect from 1 Apr. 1991 except for reduced rate of 8% for supplies of fuel and power for domestic, residential or nonbusiness charity use.

Council Tax.—From 1st Apr. 1993, Community Charge is replaced by Council Tax. (Local Government Finance Act 1992). Level is fixed locally by each billing authority depending on its financing needs, and is subject to Secretary of State for Environment's power to cap level chosen by authority. Whilst amount due it linked to saleable value of property on 1 Apr. 1991 (properties are allocated to one of eight bands), discounts are available for single occupants and for certain adults such as students, care workers etc.

Stamp Duty.—There is a stamp on all agreements for sale of a business or any interest therein, dispositions of land or of any interest in land, letters or powers of attorney, transfers of stocks and shares, creation of loan or share capital of a company, any bond or covenant and policies of life insurance. Documents from abroad must be stamped within 30 days after being received in this country or heavy penalty by way of additional stamp duty is imposed. Failure to stamp within prescribed time entails heavy penalties, but generally speaking, does not invalidate document.

Motor Tax.—See topic Motor Vehicles.

Customs Duties.—See topic Customs.

TRADEMARKS AND TRADENAMES:

Trade Marks Act 1994 which came into force on 31st Oct. 1994 and amends domestic law and implements international obligations.

New regime replaces that created by Trade Marks Act 1988, although those marks registered under old regime remain effective and applications made prior to date 1994 Act came into effect will be decided by applying provisions of 1938 Act.

Under new regime right to exclusive use of trademark is obtained by registration—such registration is now for ten years, but may be renewed for periods of ten years.

What Can Be Registered.—Registration may now be obtained for sign capable of being represented graphically which is capable of distinguishing goods or services of one undertaking from those of another. It may consist of words, including personal names, designs, letters, numerals or shape of goods or their packaging. Registration will be refused if sign is devoid of any distinctive character or which consists exclusively of sign which may serve to designate kind, quality, quantity, intended purposes, value, geographical origin, time of production of goods or of rendering of services or signs or indications which have become customary in current language or in bona fide and established practices of trade. Same cannot be trademark if it consists exclusively of shape which results from nature of goods themselves, which is necessary to obtain technical result or give substantial value to goods. Trademark shall not be registered if it is contrary to public policy or to accepted principles of morality or is of such nature as to deceive public.

Registration is responsibility of Comptroller General of Patent, Designs and Trade Marks—Registrar—who will cause appropriate investigation to be completed before registering any trademarks.

Applications for registration should contain request for registration, name and address of applicant, statement of goods or services to which trademark is to apply and representation of trademark, together with appropriate fee and statement that trademark is being used by applicant or with his consent in relation to those goods or services in which he intends that it should be used.

Infringement of registered trademark occurs if sign is used in course of trade which is identical to or similar to trademark and used in relation to goods or services similar to those for which trademark is registered or identical or similar sign is used in relation to similar goods or services where trademark has reputation in U.K. and its use is detrimental to distinctive character of trademark.

Remedies for infringement are damages or account profits, and injunction to prevent further infringement and order for delivery up if sought.

Tradenames (Business Names Act 1985).—Firms, individuals and corporations carrying on trade in name other than true name not required to register tradename. Tradenames indicating connection with government and words specified in regulations not to be used without approval of Secretary of State. If tradename consists of surnames and/or corporate names of all partners (with or without permitted additions), no special legal requirements. Permitted additions to names are addition of forename or its initial, "s" at end of surname, or addition merely indicating business carried on in succession to former owner of business. If tradename not of type already described, all business letters, written orders for goods or services, invoices and receipts and written demands must state names of proprietors of business and for each proprietor address within Great Britain at which service of any document relating to business will be effective. All premises where business carried on and to which customers have access must display in prominent position so as to be easily read notice containing such names and addresses. If more than 20 partners, and no partners names on document, sufficient compliance for firm to keep at place of business list of names and addresses of all partners. Trade documents must then state that such list open to inspection at that place.

Penalties for Breach of Act.—Firm in breach of provisions unable to sue (unless court considers it equitable), if defendant shows he has claim against firm arising out of contract and he unable to pursue by reason of firm's breach of Act or that he has suffered financial loss in connection with contract by reason of firm's breach of Act.

Registered Designs.—See topic Copyright, subhead Registered Designs and Design Rights.

TREATIES:

U.K. has many commercial treaties, agreements and exchange of notes, too numerous to list, some of which have been running for several hundred years. A list of all treaties is published annually called Index to Treaty Series published by H.M. Stationery Office. Every three or four years a general index is compiled. U.K. is a member of EU. (Vienna Convention of law of Treaties of 1969 entered into in force Jan. 1980).

U.K. is party to: (1) Convention on Service Abroad of Judicial and Extrajudicial Documents in Civil or Commercial Matters, (2) Convention on Taking of Evidence Abroad in Civil or Commercial Matters, (3) United Nations Convention on Recognition and Enforcement of Foreign Arbitral Awards, (4) Convention Abolishing the Requirement of Legalisation for Foreign Public Documents. Draft treaty between USA and U.K. for reciprocal enforcement of judgments has been initialled but is thought unlikely to be ratified and brought into force in its present form.

See topic Taxation, subhead Double Taxation.

See also Selected International Conventions section.

TRUSTS:

A strict settlement of a legal estate inter vivos is made by means of a vesting deed and a trust instrument. (Settled Land Act, 1925). The vesting deed conveys the land to the tenant for life, contains a description of the land, sets forth any additional powers conferred on tenant for life and name of person entitled to appoint new trustees and bears a stamp duty. The trust instrument declares the trusts, appoints trustees and contains power to appoint new trustees.

It is possible also to create an immediate binding trust for sale of land in which case the trustees are joint tenants with all powers of tenants for life and trustees under the Settled Land Act. An express trust of land or any interest therein must be evidenced in writing. (Law of Property Act, 1925, §53).

A trust is irrevocable unless the settlor reserves a right of revocation, but it may be set aside in certain circumstances. See topic Fraudulent Sales and Conveyances.

Duties of Trustee.—These are numerous and include: (1) To follow settlor's directions and to secure trust property by reducing it to possession; (2) to invest trust funds in any of investments specified in Trustee Investments Act 1961 (see subhead Trustee Investments Act 1961, infra) or in any other investments expressly authorised by trust instruments; (3) to keep accounts and to produce them to any beneficiary when required and to give him all reasonable information as to trust estate.

Powers of Trustee.—These include powers expressly given by trust instruments and (subject to any contrary intention expressed by trust instrument) powers given to trustees by Trustee Act 1925, including: (1) Trustee for sale has power to sell or concur in selling all or any part of property and in every trust for sale, unless contrary intention appears, power to postpone sale is implied. (2) Where trust instrument authorises trustees to apply capital money for any purpose they may raise money by sale, conversion, calling in or mortgage of all or any part of trust property for time being in possession. This does not apply to settled land act trustees or trustees of charity. (3) Trustees can give receipt which is good discharge. Sole trustee other than trust corporation cannot give good receipt for proceeds of sale or other capital money arising under trust for sale or for capital money arising under Settled Land Act, 1925. There must be two trustees or trust corporation. (4) Trustees are empowered to insure trust property against loss or damage by fire up to 3/4 of value of property, except where trust instrument forbids it or where they are bound forthwith to convey property absolutely to any beneficiary on his request. They also may compromise actions, pay trust money into court and so obtain discharge in cases of difficulty, maintain infants, and make advances of capital in certain circumstances.

Liability of Trustee.—A trustee is liable only for a breach of trust committed by himself. (Trustee Act, 1925, §30). There is, as a rule, a right of contribution between trustees who are liable for breach of trust but this does not apply if they have all been guilty of fraud. One trustee must, however, indemnify the others (a) where he has received the trust money or is otherwise alone morally guilty, (b) where he acted as a solicitor to the trust and the breach of trust was committed on his advice and (c) where he is a beneficiary.

Some protection is afforded to a trustee who has been guilty of a breach of trust by Trustee Act, 1925, §61, under which the court may relieve him if he has acted honestly and reasonably and ought fairly be excused, and he is also protected where a beneficiary who is sui juris and fully informed of facts concurs in breach, confirms breach or releases trustee.

Variation of Trusts.—By the Variation of Trusts Act, 1958, the High Court has a discretionary power to vary trusts for the benefit of children or other persons whose interests may be uncertain. Though Trustee Investments Act 1961 retains court's discretion to extend investment powers under this Act beyond limits set by 1961 Act such discretion exercised only in special circumstances.

Trustee Investments Act 1961 extends powers of investment for trustees. Act provides for division of trust fund into two halves, one half to be invested in gilt-edged securities and other half to be invested in "equities." Trustees protected in exercise of these extra powers subject to certain conditions.

WILLS:

Any adult, male or female, of sound mind, may make a will. Infant cannot make a will, unless a soldier in actual military service or a mariner or seaman at sea. Person of unsound mind cannot make a valid will, except during a lucid interval. Alien has same testamentary capacity as British subject. It would appear that a felon may dispose of his property by will.

Will must be in writing and signed by testator or by some other person in his presence and by his direction, and it must appear that testator intended by his signature to give effect to will (§9 Wills Act 1837 am'd by Administration of Justice Act 1982), and such signature shall be made or acknowledged by testator in presence of two or more witnesses present at same time, and such witnesses shall attest and sign will or acknowledge their earlier signature in presence of testator but not necessarily in presence of each other. Will should not be witnessed by beneficiary or spouse of beneficiary named in will. Wills Act 1968 ensures that will is still valid if containing disposition to one of witnesses provided that there are two further witnesses neither of whom benefits under will. Upon death of testator, where there is no opposition, probate of will may be granted to executors by probate court at expiration of seven days after death of deceased.

Probate of Foreigner's Will.—Wills Act 1963 provides generally that a will will be held to be validly executed as regards form if it satisfies requirements of internal law of any of the following: (a) Territory where it was executed; (b) territory where testator was domiciled, either at time of execution or at death; (c) territory where testator had habitual residence either at time of execution or at death; (d) in state of which, either at time of execution or at death, he was national; (e) so far as it disposes of immoveable property, territory where property situated. In practice, upon production of sealed and certified copy of probate granted by proper court of foreign country where testator was domiciled at his death, court will follow such grant in granting probate here upon application here by executor.

Will disposing of land situate in England must comply with English form.

Allowance for Maintenance of Dependents.—Under Inheritance (Provision for Family and Dependents) Act 1975 certain persons may make application to court for payment out of deceased's estate. Court may make order for reasonable financial provision for spouse, whether or not that provision is needed for his or her maintenance or reasonable financial provision for his or her maintenance in case of other applicants, for applicant if court considers reasonable financial provision has not been made.

Persons for whom provision may be made are: (a) Spouse, (b) former spouse who has not remarried, (c) child, (d) person (not child of deceased) who, in case of marriage to which deceased at any time party, was treated by deceased as child of family in relation to that marriage, (e) any person immediately before death of deceased being maintained partly or wholly by deceased. Illegitimate children treated as legitimate children. (Family Law Reform Act 1969).

Application for provision must, except with permission of court, be made within six months from date on which representation in deceased's estate first taken out. In construing application, court must have regard to: (a) Present or likely future financial

WILLS . . . *continued*
resources and needs of applicant, (b) present or future likely financial resources and needs of any other applicant, (c) present or future likely financial resources and needs of any beneficiary of estate, (d) obligations and responsibilities of deceased to any applicant or beneficiary of estate, (e) size and nature of estate, (f) any physical or mental disabilities of any applicant or beneficiary, and (g) any other matter including conduct of applicant or any other persons as court considers relevant.

Where surviving spouse or former spouse who has not remarried applies, court must also have regard to: (a) Applicant's age and duration of marriage, (b) applicant's contribution to welfare of family and (c) provision applicant might reasonably expect on divorce.

See Topical Index in front part of this volume.

EUROPEAN UNION LAW DIGEST REVISER

De Bandt, van Hecke & Lagae
Rue Brederode 13
B-1000 Brussels, Belgium
Telephone: 32 2 517 94 11
Fax: 32 2 513 97 13; 513 52 48

Reviser Profile

History: The firm was founded in Brussels in 1969 and has offices in Brussels, Antwerp, London and New York. The firm is member of "Alliance of European Lawyers" (EEIG).

Areas of Emphasis and Growth: The firm engages exclusively in a business oriented practice and operates as a full service firm with departmental specialization, including Business and Finance, Corporate, European Community Law, International Taxation, Labour and Litigation. The firm consists of 26 partners, 1 counsel and 100 associates, with a support staff of 80 persons including paralegals.

Client Base: Clients of the firm are predominantly international corporations, a large number of which are operating in Europe from a Belgian base.

Firm Activities: All lawyers of the firm are members of the Brussels or Antwerp, Belgium Bar and three of its partners are also qualified to practice before the Supreme Court of Belgium. Two other partners are members of the New York Bar.

Management: The firm is managed by a committee of partners of varying seniority. The Management Committee monitors performance, client relationship, economic and technological development as well as firm growth and reports to the full Partners Meeting.

EUROPEAN UNION LAW DIGEST

(The following is a list of all Topics, including cross-references, covered in this Digest.)

EUROPEAN UNION LAW DIGEST

Revised for 1997 edition by
DE BANDT, VAN HECKE & LAGAE, Brussels

(Abbreviations used are: Art. [Article]; Dec. [Decision]; Dir. [Directive]; EAEC [European Atomic Energy Community]; ECSC [European Coal and Steel Community]; EEC [European Economic Community]; EU [European Union]; EC [European Community]; Reg. [Regulation]).

INTRODUCTION:

In 1952 ECSC was set up by Paris Treaty; in 1958 EEC and EAEC (known as Euratom) were set up by Rome Treaties. Three European Communities have same original Member States: Belgium, France, Federal Republic of Germany, Italy, Luxembourg and Netherlands. In 1973 Denmark, Ireland and United Kingdom became Member States of European Communities, followed in 1981 by Greece, in 1986 by Portugal and Spain, and in 1995 by Austria, Finland and Sweden. Since adoption of EU Treaty signed in Maastricht on 7 Feb. 1992, three Communities created by Paris and Rome Treaties have been embodied within EU. Pursuant to Art. A of EU Treaty, EU is founded on EC supplemented by policies and forms of cooperation established by EU Treaty. This is reflected in Art. B of EU Treaty which identifies three pillars upon which EU rests. First pillar of EU, which was already object of EC, lies in creation of area without frontiers, through strengthening of economic and social cohesion and establishment of Economic and Monetary Union, ultimately including single currency. Second pillar of EU is implementation of Common Foreign and Security Policy including framing of common defence policy. Third pillar of EU relates to development of Cooperation on Justice and Home Affairs.

COMMON FOREIGN AND SECURITY POLICY:

Common Foreign and Security Policy (CFSP) constitutes second pillar on which EU is based. Arts. J to 1.11 EU Treaty provide for framework within which systematic cooperation between Member States will take place where they have essential interest in common.

In matters covered by CFSP, EU is represented by its Presidency. General principles and guidelines for joint action are defined by European Council which brings together Heads of State or Government of Member States and President of Commission. Council of Ministers will, by unanimous decisions, carry out implementing tasks. In case of imperative need, unilateral measures may still be taken as matter of urgency by Member States but only in accordance with objectives of joint action and after notification to Council. EC Commission will be fully associated and European Parliament regularly informed of decisions adopted in this field.

COMPETITION RULES:

See topics Monopolies and Restraint of Trade and State Aid.

CONSTITUTION AND GOVERNMENT:

Constitution consists of treaties establishing European Communities: ECSC Treaty covering production and distribution of coal and steel, EEC Treaty (called EC Treaty since Maastricht Treaty on European Union) relating to economic activity generally and EAEC Treaty dealing with peaceful use of atomic energy. Constitution also includes Convention on Common Institutions, making as of 1958 European Parliament and Court of Justice common to three European Communities and "Merger Treaty" setting up as of 1967 one Council and one Commission of European Communities. In addition, European "Single Act" entered into force in July 1987, strengthening institutions and powers of EC. EU Treaty should mark new stage in European integration. Objective is to promote Economic and Monetary Union, implement Common Foreign and Security Policy, introduce Citizenship of EU, develop Cooperation on Justice and Home Affairs and maintain in full "acquis communautaire". EU Treaty entered into force on Nov. 1, 1993, last instrument of ratification having been deposited on Oct. 13, 1993. *Note:* Intergovernmental Conference ("IGC") opened in Mar. 1996 and will discuss amendments to EU Treaty, i.a. on decision-making and functioning of institutions.

Treaty on the European Economic Area (EEA) was signed between European Communities, its Member States on one hand and Member States of EFTA, on other hand, in May 1992. EEA-Treaty entered into force on Jan. 1, 1994. As a result, "four freedoms" contained in EC-Treaty as well as competition rules will apply throughout EEA.

Institutions in General.—Council, Commission, European Parliament and Court of Justice are institutions common to ECSC, EC and EAEC. Council consists of one cabinet-level representative of government of each Member State; votes are taken unanimously or by qualified majority depending on subject-matter dealt with; Council has its Secretariat in Brussels, but meets also in Luxembourg. Commission, based in Brussels, consists of 21 members appointed for five years by agreement among Member States; members of Commission are independent from Member States during tenure; Commission can be censured by special vote of European Parliament; Commission has administrative staff of about 12,000. European Parliament consists of directly elected representatives (since 1979); Secretariat is based in Luxembourg, plenary sessions are held in Strasbourg and extraordinary sessions and Committee meetings in Brussels. Court of Justice, based in Luxembourg, consists of 17 judges appointed for six years by agreement among Member States; eight Advocates-General, appointed on same terms, share responsibility to issue individual nonbinding opinions on cases submitted to Court. By Council Decision of Oct. 24, 1988, Court of First Instance was established which has been attached to Court of Justice of European Communities.

Founded on EC, EU is governed by EC institutions with exception of European Council, which is institution of EU and not of EC. European Council brings together Heads of State and Government of Member States and President of Commission. It is entrusted with task of providing EU with necessary impetus for its development and must define general political guidelines thereof. Certain competences of EU are outside EC legal order and thus expressly excluded from jurisdiction of Court of Justice. Justice and Home Affairs are reserved for cooperation among Member States and Common Foreign and Security Policy are matters left to Member States and EU. They remain subject to intergovernmental relations of Member States.

Legislative Power.—See topic Legislature.

Executive Power.—Legislation of European Communities is executed by Member States under supervision of Commission. (Arts. 5 and 155 EC Treaty). In some cases, Commission itself executes Treaty provisions or Community legislation, e.g. competition law (powers to order termination of infringements and to impose fines), anti-dumping and anti-subsidy law (regulatory powers). Art. 10 of "Single Act" confers on Council also power to execute Community legislation (modification of Art. 145 EC Treaty).

Judicial Power.—See topic Courts.

Supremacy of Community Law.—In case of conflict with Member State law, Community law prevails and provisions which are directly applicable can be invoked as such by interested parties in national courts. Provision of Community law has direct effect when it is clear, unconditional and sufficiently precise to confer rights on individuals.

Supremacy of Community law implies that Member States are obliged to make good loss and damage caused to individuals by breaches of Community law for which they can be held responsible. Actions taken by individuals for damages must be brought before national courts, subject to national procedural rules. However, procedural rules which are discriminatory or render virtually impossible or excessively difficult such action must be set aside by national courts. As to substance, it results from case law of Court of Justice that individuals may claim compensation for consequences of loss and damage caused, provided (i) EC provision concerned entails granting of rights to individuals, (ii) it is possible to identify those rights on basis of said provisions and (iii) there is causal link between breach of State's obligation and loss and damage suffered by injured parties. Further, liability of State cannot be conditioned upon existence of fault by State and compensation may be claimed for period prior to judgment confirming infringement when breach is sufficiently clear. It is, in principle, for national courts to verify whether those conditions are fulfilled.

COPYRIGHT:

Law of Member States governs copyright. Nevertheless, Council directive 93/98 harmonises terms of protection of copyright and certain related rights. Obstacles to free movement of copyrighted goods within EC have been tempered through doctrine of "Community-wide exhaustion", adopted by Court of Justice: once copyright owner or licensee puts goods on market in one Member State, he is estopped from relying on copyright to prevent imports of same goods in other Member States. Whether doctrine applies to copyrighted goods imported from third countries is matter for national law to decide.

Furthermore, doctrine of "Community-wide exhaustion" only applies to copyrighted goods. Nonmaterial aspects of copyright still can be assigned by contract for one or some Member States only, e.g. right to exhibit motion pictures by cable television.

CORPORATIONS:

Corporations formed in accordance with law of Member State and having registered office, central administration or principal place of business within EC enjoy right of free establishment in all Member States on same conditions as citizens of Member States. (Art. 58 EC Treaty).

Law of Member States governs corporations. However, pursuant to Art. 54 (3) (g) EC Treaty (now, Art. 54[3][f]), EC has harmonized by Directives some topics, such as safeguards required of corporations for protection of members and others (First Directive 1968), formation, maintenance and alteration of corporation capital (Second Directive 1976), annual accounts (Fourth Directive 1978), annual accounts and consolidated accounts of banks and other financial institutions (Dir. 8/12/1986, O.J. 1986, L372/1), mergers of limited liability corporations (Third Directive 1978), division of limited liability corporations (Sixth Directive 1982), consolidated accounts (Seventh Directive 1983), approval of persons responsible for carrying out statutory audits of accounting documents (Eighth Directive), information which should be provided by foreign branches (Eleventh Directive) and single-member private limited liability companies (Twelfth Directive).

Proper EC corporation law also develops through Reg. 2137/85 on European Economic Interest Grouping (EEIG), promoting cooperation in one entity between corporations from different Member States.

COURTS:

Judicial power in European Communities is exercised by Court of Justice and Court of First Instance. Court has jurisdiction to pronounce on actions for annulment or for failure to act brought by Council or Commission against each other, or by Member State against Council or Commission. Private persons and corporations can bring these actions, when act or failure to act is of individual scope. They also can bring action for damages against European Communities. Court of First Instance deals with staff cases, all direct actions by "natural or legal" persons against Community institutions (including competition, agriculture, fisheries, European Funds—regional or social, transport, state aids and, from Mar. 15, 1994, anti-dumping cases) and cases arising from application of ECSC Treaty. Decision of Court of First Instance is subject to right of appeal to Court of Justice on points of law only.

COURTS . . . *continued*

Member State courts enforce Community law on behalf of interested parties. In case of doubt about interpretation or challenge of validity of acts made by Community institutions, request for preliminary ruling may be lodged with Court of Justice. (Arts. 177 EC Treaty and 150 EAEC Treaty; as to validity of acts only, Art. 41 ECSC Treaty). Member State courts of last resort are bound to refer to Court of Justice interpretation or validity questions arising before them. Preliminary rulings of Court of Justice are binding for Member State courts applying them to facts of case.

ECSC, EC and EAEC Protocols on Court of Justice, annexed to Treaties, and Rules of Procedure, decided by Court of Justice and Court of First Instance and approved by Council, govern direct actions (e.g. time-limits, language used, interventions, incidents) and preliminary rulings. President of Court of Justice and of Court of First Instance may order interim-relief on special request.

CURRENCY:

Member States have different currencies. ECU (European Currency Unit) is uniform accounting unit based on basket of national currencies. Rates of conversion are published on daily basis in Official Journal of European Communities ("C" series, standing for "Communications"). Special conversion rates into national currencies exist for ECU used in connection with common agricultural policy (so-called "green" rates). One of objectives of Maastricht Treaty is creation, by 1998, of common currency.

See topic Economic and Monetary Union.

CUSTOMS DUTIES:

Intra-EU Trade.—Among Member States, import and export duties or charges having equivalent effect are prohibited. Rule applies whether goods originate in Member State or in third country but are in free circulation in at least one Member State (that levied customs duties applicable on import into EU from third countries).

Trade with Third Countries.—Goods imported into EU from third countries are subject to Common Customs Tariff (known as CCT), enforced by Member States on behalf of Community. Duties are levied according to CCT schedules based on Harmonized System nomenclature. In case of litigation, Member State courts pronounce on classification of goods into CCT schedules. CCT schedules are part of EC law. Court of Justice can give interpretation through preliminary rulings procedure. Taxable base is actual price of transaction determined at arm's length. If there is none, substitutes are: (1) Normal transaction value of identical or similar goods sold to be imported into EU; (2) deductive value obtained by some deductions from price at which identical or similar imported goods are sold in EU between nonrelated parties; (3) computed value obtained by sum of manufacturing cost, profit usually inherent in sale price of identical or similar goods exported from third country and finally, transportation and insurance cost from third country to outside border of EU.

Special regimes of customs duties cover imports from third countries in EC for processing, or result from trade agreements with some third countries. Besides, EC applies General System of Preferences (GSP).

ECONOMIC AND MONETARY UNION:

First pillar of EU is Economic and Monetary Union ("EMU"). Pursuant to Art. 109J EU Treaty, EMU must be achieved following three stage timetable.

First stage took place under existing Rome Treaties. It aimed at completion of internal market (see infra, topic Internal Market) and creation of single financial area in framework of European Monetary System ("EMS"). EMS provides that each national currency has ECU-related central rate around which fluctuation margins have been established. When certain thresholds have been reached, central banks intervene to correct situation. Second stage began on Jan. 1994 with establishment of Economic and Monetary Institute ("EMI"). Its main task is to strengthen coordination of monetary policies, prepare for institution of single currency, monitor EMS and facilitate use of ECU. By 31 Dec. 1996, European Council will decide whether majority of Member States meet four convergence criteria, i.e. (i) price stability (rate of inflation of no more than 1.5% above average of three best performing countries); (ii) government deficit not exceeding 3% of GDP and public debt not exceeding 60% of GDP, (iii) stable exchange rates within EMS, and (iv) interest rates no more than 2% above three best performing countries over previous 12 months. On that basis, European Council will decide whether it is appropriate to enter third stage and, if so, will set up date for beginning of third stage. If no date has been fixed by end of 1997, European System of Central Bank ("ESCB") consisting of European Central Bank ("ECB") and national central banks must be established by July 1998 and stage three will irrevocably start on Jan. 1999. Participating Member States will agree on conversion rates at which currencies will be irrevocably fixed. EURO will then become single currency. ESCB will define and implement monetary policy of Community, conduct foreign exchange operations, hold and manage official foreign reserves of Member States and promote smooth operation of payment systems. ECB will have exclusive right to authorise issuance of EURO bank note in Community by ECB and national central banks.

ENVIRONMENT:

Legislation.—In 1987, Single European Act gave Treaty basis to Community environmental policy. Arts. 130R, 130S and 130T, as recently amended by Maastricht Treaty, concisely define principles and objectives of Community environmental policy as developed through Action Programmes adopted by Member States since 1973. At present, Fifth Action Programme is being implemented, covering years 1992-2000. These articles also give indication of respective competences of Community and of Member States and contain provision on relations with third countries and international organisations. Legislative procedure is spelt out and possibility of introducing safeguard clauses is foreseen. On the other hand, Art. 100A offers alternative procedure for adopting environmental measures which have impact on establishment and functioning of internal market. Safeguard measures based on protection of environment may be adopted by Member States under Art. 100A(4). On basis of those provisions, EC has enacted more than 300 legislative measures, most of them being directives harmonising national laws. Besides horizontal measures protecting environment in general, as for example Directive on assessment of effects of certain public and private projects on environment, EC has adopted vertical measures applicable to specific types of pollution. In particular, there exists EC legislation on waste management, water protection, prevention of noise pollution, nuclear safety, monitoring of atmospheric pollution, chemicals, industrial risk and biotechnology, efficient use of space, conservation of wild fauna and flora and international cooperation.

General Supervision.—Commission ensures full application of EC legislation, generally directives, by Member States. Directives must be transposed into national laws which will be enforced by national bodies subject to supervision by national courts. Since Nov. 1993, European Environment Agency, which is located in Copenhagen, cooperates with Commission. Its function is to ensure supply of objective, reliable and comparable information at EC level on state of environment by processing information on environmental data which has been collected through national networks.

FOREIGN TRADE REGULATIONS:

Art. 113 EC Treaty empowers Community to regulate trade with third countries. Using this power, Council enacted EC Reg. 2423/88 and ECSC Dec. 2424/88 on anti-dumping and countervailing duties. Following Uruguay Round, EC Reg. 2423/88 was replaced by EC Reg. 3283/94. These duties aim at avoiding injury to EU industry caused by import from third countries at dumped or subsidized prices. According to Reg. 2423/88, duties should also be collected on products introduced into commerce of EU after having been assembled in EU, if assembly is carried out by related or associated party, started or substantially increased after opening of anti-dumping investigation or if value of parts, originating in country of exportation of product subject to anti-dumping duty, exceeds value of all other parts by at least 50%. Commission leads investigation as to existence of dumping practice, state subsidies and injury to EU industry resulting therefrom. Commission may impose provisional duties, Council imposes definitive duties. As to anti-dumping duties, system is based on 1979 GATT Anti-Dumping Code as modified on Apr. 15, 1994 by agreements concluded during Uruguay Round.

In addition, quantitative restrictions (referred to as "safeguard measures") can be put to imports from third countries, causing injury to EU industry. For agricultural imports from third countries, special system of upward price adjustment must prevent disturbance of common agricultural policy within EU.

EU export to third countries as well as domestic market protected by Reg. 2641/84 against illicit commercial practices of third countries that cause injury to EU industry. Reg. 2641/84 is known as "new commercial policy instrument". It has been recently modified by Reg. 522/94 (Mar. 7, 1994). EU agricultural exports may be subsidized.

Court of Justice considers GATT rules not to be self-executing within EU.

INTERNAL MARKET:

EC Treaty, by establishing common market and progressively approximating economic policies of Member States, seeks to unite national markets into single market having characteristics of domestic market. (Case 270/80, Court Reports 1982, 348, no. 16).

Free Movement of Goods.—For abolition of customs duties among Member States, see topic Customs Duties. Quantitative restrictions to imports, exports and transit, as well as measures having equivalent effect, are prohibited (Arts. 30-34 EC Treaty), unless they can be justified on one of grounds stated in Art. 36 EC Treaty. For Court of Justice, all trading rules enacted by Member States which are capable of hindering, directly or indirectly, actually or potentially, intra-EU trade are to be considered as measures having effect equivalent to quantitative restrictions. (Case 8/74, Court Reports 1974, 852, no. 5). Nevertheless, application to products of other Member States of national provisions restricting or prohibiting selling arrangements does not constitute measure having equivalent effect to quantitative restrictions. (joint cases C-267 and C-298/91, Court Reports 1993, 6097).

Free Movement of Workers.—Member States must refrain from limiting access of citizens of other Member States to national labor market. Freedom to cross Member State borders with view of taking up employment, or just seeking employment, is guaranteed. Nonetheless, Member States can remove from national territory migrant worker, citizen of other Member State, for reasons of public policy relating to individual behavior of worker. (Arts. 48-51 EC Treaty). During period of employment and thereafter, no discrimination on grounds of citizenship is allowed.

Freedom of Establishment.—Citizen or corporation of one Member State may establish independent business in other Member State on same conditions as nationals of latter Member State can. (Arts. 52-58).

Freedom to Provide Services.—Citizen or corporation of one Member State may provide services in another without being established, on condition to respect rules governing providing of services on basis excluding discrimination between citizens and citizens of other Member States, or between established and non-established business. (Arts. 59-66 EC Treaty).

Free Movement of Capital.—This principle has no direct effect. Council Directive 88/361/EEC (1988 O.J. L 178/5) provides for complete liberalization of capital movements by July 1, 1990 for eight Member States and by Dec. 31, 1992 for Greece, Ireland, Spain and Portugal. For Portugal and Greece, deadline may be further delayed by Council on proposition of Commission for maximum three years. Accordingly, Greece was authorized to temporarily continue to apply restrictions until June 30, 1994. (1992 O.J. L 409/33).

JUDGMENTS:

Recognition and enforcement of other Member States' judgments is governed by Brussels Convention of 27 Sept. 1968, binding on Belgium, Federal Republic of Germany, France, Italy, Luxembourg, Netherlands, Denmark, Ireland, United Kingdom (in three latter countries by virtue of Oct. 9, 1978 Adaptation Convention), Greece (by virtue of Oct. 25, 1982 Adaptation Convention), Spain and Portugal (by virtue of May 26, 1989 Adaptation Convention). All Member States, save Belgium and Denmark, ratified new Convention. New Member States, i.e. Austria, Finland and

See Topical Index in front part of this volume.

JUDGMENTS . . . *continued*
Sweden are not parties to Brussels Convention, but are signatories to Lugano Convention of Sept. 16, 1988 which was concluded between EFTA Countries and Member States of EC. Lugano Convention provides for regime similar to Brussels Convention.

Convention deals with civil and commercial matters, except for family law, bankruptcy and insolvency procedures. Court of Justice may interpret Convention through preliminary rulings requested by some Member State courts.

Convention contains uniform system on jurisdiction in international cases. When system is observed and decision on merits conforms to public policy of other States, full faith and credit in courts of all Member States bound, is guaranteed.

JUSTICE AND HOME AFFAIRS:

Justice and Home Affairs is third pillar of EU. (Art. K. to K.9 of Maastricht Treaty). It covers matters which affect public order, law enforcement and immigration from third countries and which therefore are of common interest to Member States.

In those areas, Member States inform and consult one another within Council of Ministers with the view of coordination of their actions and, if necessary, adoption of joint positions. It may also adopt joint action according to principle of subsidiarity if objectives of EU are better achieved in this way than by individual Member States acting on their own or drawing up conventions. Finally, Council may decide that matters covered should be dealt with by means of harmonising legislation under Art. 100C of EC Treaty. In its task, Council is assisted by Co-ordination Committee consisting of senior national officials.

LABOR LAW:

Labor law remains different from one Member State to another. EC Treaty contains one basic rule to be directly enforced by Member States courts: Men and women should receive equal pay for equal work. (Art. 119).

Besides, EC directives harmonizing aspects of labor law led to uniformity of national laws as to equality between men and women for general employment conditions, mass dismissals and employees' rights in case of bankruptcy of employer, transfer or merger of business, and setting up of European Works Council in multinational companies.

LEGISLATURE:

Legislative power has different structure in ECSC and EC/EAEC. In ECSC Commission has power to adopt legislative measures on own initiative, on advice, as case may be, of Council, European Parliament and Consultative Committee representing interested business and workers in fields of coal and steel. Exceptionally, assent of Council is needed, e.g. to declare period of manifest crisis in production of coal or steel. (Art. 58 ECSC Treaty).

In EAEC, in nearly all cases, Council acts on proposal from Commission, and depending on subject matter dealt with, after advice of European Parliament and/or Economic and Social Committee representing business and workers. Unanimity is required for act constituting amendment to that proposal. (Art. 119 EAEC Treaty).

In EC, Council has power to adopt legislative measures on proposal from Commission, and depending on subject matter dealt with, after advice, in cooperation or with co-decision of European Parliament. Under consultative procedure, Commission transmits its proposal to Council which consults European Parliament and/or Economic and Social Committee. Council can amend proposal only with unanimity. Following cooperation procedure (Art. 189C EC Treaty), Council acting by qualified majority adopts common position on proposal from Commission and after advice of European Parliament. If European Parliament by absolute majority amends or rejects it, Commission reexamines proposal and transmits it to Council. Where European Parliament rejected initial proposal, Council must act by unanimity. Finally, under co-decision procedure (Art. 189B EC Treaty), where European Parliament indicates by absolute majority that it intends to reject common position, conciliation procedure takes place under aegis of Conciliation Committee which comprises representatives of Council and European Parliament. Where Committee does not adopt joint text, Council may adopt its common position unless European Parliament rejects text by absolute majority.

MONOPOLIES AND RESTRAINT OF TRADE:

Prohibition of Restrictive Practices.—Art. 85 (1) EC Treaty prohibits all agreements between undertakings, decisions by associations of undertakings and concerted practices which may affect trade between Member States and which have as their object or effect prevention, restriction or distortion of competition within common market. Art. 65 (1) ECSC Treaty prohibits all agreement between undertakings, decisions by associations of undertakings and concerted practices tending directly or indirectly to prevent, restrict or distort normal competition within common market.

Art. 85 (3) EC Treaty allows for exemption of restrictive practices from prohibition stated in Art. 85 (1). Commission decides on individual exemptions requested on special form. On delegation of Council, Commission has granted block exemption for exclusive distribution agreements (Commission Reg. No. 1983/83); exclusive purchasing agreements (Commission Reg. No. 1984/83); franchise agreements (Commission Reg. No. 4087/88); technology licensing agreements (Commission Reg. No. 240/96), which covers patent and know-how licensing agreements; motor vehicle distribution and servicing agreements (Commission Reg. No. 1475/95); specialization agreements (Commission Reg. No. 417/85); research and development agreements (Commission Reg. No. 418/85); and certain agreements in insurance sector (Commission Reg. No. 3932/92). Several block exemptions also exist in air transport field, in maritime transport and in insurance sector. Generally, conditions for exemption, stated in Art. 85 (3), are: (1) Restrictive practice contributes to improving production or distribution of goods or to promoting technical or economic progress; (2) it allows consumers fair share of resulting benefit; (3) it is indispensable to attainment of said objectives; (4) it does not eliminate all possibility of competition. Art. 65 (2) ECSC Treaty provides for possible authorization by Commission of specialization agreements or joint-buying or joint-selling agreements that meet certain conditions.

Prohibition of Abuse of Dominant Position.—Art. 86 EC Treaty prohibits any abuse by one or more undertakings of dominant position within common market or in substantial part of it, insofar as it may affect trade between Member States. Art. 66 ECSC Treaty subjects concentration of undertakings to prior control of Commission, whether it is effected by merger, acquisition of shares or parts of undertaking or assets, loan, contract or any other means of control.

No exemptions of Art. 86 EC Treaty can be given.

Monopolies or oligopolies are not prohibited as such under Art. 86 EC Treaty. Only abuse of dominant position is prohibited, e.g. directly or indirectly imposing unfair purchase or selling prices or other unfair trading conditions; limiting production, markets or technical development to prejudice of consumers; applying dissimilar conditions to equivalent transactions with other trading parties, thereby placing them at competitive disadvantage; making conclusion of contracts subject to acceptance by other parties of supplementary obligations which, by their nature or according to commercial usage, have no connection with subject of such contracts ("tying"). Enforcement and investigation are parallel to Art. 85 EC Treaty.

Case-Law.—Restrictive practices involving pricing (horizontal or vertical price fixing, discriminatory pricing) are per se contrary to Art. 85 (1) EC Treaty. Discriminatory or predatory pricing by undertaking with dominant position on relevant market violates Art. 86 EC Treaty. Restrictive practices involving distribution may fall under Art. 85 (1), but Commission is willing to grant exemptions under Art. 85 (3), e.g. block exemptions of Reg. 1983/83 and Reg. 1984/83 (exclusive distribution and exclusive purchasing agreements), when choice of customers by distributor (also in other Member States) as well as parallel import from other Member States into territory of distributor remain free. Besides exclusive distribution agreements, selective distribution agreements may be exempted on individual basis depending on effect on competition of their conditions. Restrictive practices involving cooperative joint ventures or cooperation between undertaking may also fall under Art. 85 (1), but here again Commission is willing to grant individual exemptions under Art. 85 (3) if conditions of this provision are met (see Commission guidelines on joint ventures, basis of Commission assessment in view of application of Art. 85 [3] to joint ventures). Restrictive practices contained in licensing or franchising agreements are prohibited under Art. 85 (1), that Commission Reg. No. 240/96 and Reg. No. 4087/88 list clauses exempted under Art. 85(3).

Enforcement of EC/ECSC competition law rests with Commission. Commission leads investigation into restrictive practices, has exclusive power to decide on requested exemption, to order termination of infringement and to impose fines when restrictive practice has not been notified to Commission nor was exempt from such notification. (See EEC Reg. no. 17 of 1962.) As to investigation, Commission can require information by decision and proceed to in-house searches. Cooperation with investigation is compulsory. If necessary, Commission may obtain it through imposition of fines. Commission is currently contemplating granting immunity from imposition of fines to undertakings informing Commission of illegal cartel in which they have participated.

Court of First Instance takes cognizance of all annulment actions brought by interested undertakings against Commission decisions.

Interim-measures may be ordered as to payment of fines or compliance with investigative decision or termination order of Commission. Court recognizes legal privilege for communications between independent lawyer entitled to practice in at least one Member State and his client to extent communications relate to client's defense in competition case.

Member State courts also enforce EC competition law by prohibiting practices caught by Art. 85(1) or Art. 86 and by declaring restrictive practices void under Art. 85(2). If need be, they request preliminary ruling from Court of Justice.

Merger Control—In Dec. 1989, Council of Ministers adopted Regulation 4064/89 requiring enterprises to notify concentrations with Community dimension to EC Commission with view of determining whether such concentrations create or strengthen dominant position as result of which effective competition would be significantly impeded in Common Market. Regulation entered into force on Sept. 21, 1990. (O.J. 1989, L395/1). Concentrations with community dimension are reviewed by Commission. Commission has maximum of one month to decide if concentration raises serious doubts as to its compatibility with common market. If serious doubts are raised, Commission opens proceedings and has to decide as to compatibility or not of concentration within additional period of four months. So far, Commission has opposed five notified concentrations.

PATENTS:

Law of Member States governs patents. In 1973, European Patent Convention was signed by number of European countries (outside EC framework), entered into force in 1977: European Patent Office, based in Munich, administers unified procedure for grant of patent in countries concerned.

From viewpoint of EC law, patents are subject to doctrine of "Community-wide exhaustion" (see topic Copyright).

PRODUCT LIABILITY:

Law of Member States governs product liability. In 1985 EC Directive on product liability was adopted, creating supplementary possibility for consumers to obtain damages from manufacturer or importer in EC. Directive does not however revoke more favorable national law.

REPORTS:

European Court Reports (ECR) contain in chronological order all judgments of Court and opinions of Advocates-General, published by Office for Official Publications of European Communities (Luxembourg), under responsibility of Court itself. There also exist unofficial (and most often incomplete) reports, e.g. Common Market Law Reports (London).

See Topical Index in front part of this volume.

STATE AID:

Arts. 92-94 EC Treaty restrict power of Member States to grant state aid which distorts or threatens to distort competition by favouring certain undertakings or production of certain goods. State aid includes any aid granted by State or through State resources such as investments, grants, writing-off of debts, provision of capital or deferment of payment taxes. Existing aids, i.e. aids in existence at time of entry into force of EC Treaty, are kept under constant review by Commission. Planned new aid or modification of existing aid must be notified by Member State to Commission. Member State may not put proposed measures into effect until procedure has resulted in final decision. Procedure follows two-stage approach. During first stage, Commission examines whether there are serious doubts as to compatibility of aid. If not, it will close procedure and authorize aid. In case of serious doubts, it must open second phase of procedure and give notice to parties concerned to submit their comments. If Commission decides that aid is incompatible, Member State concerned must abolish or alter such aid within specified period of time. Commission now requires that States recover unduly paid state aid from undertaking concerned. If State does not comply with its decision, Commission may directly bring action for infringement before Court of Justice. Individuals have rights of action before national courts, and courts are competent to take measures in respect of State aids which were not notified to Commission or to prevent implementation before authorization by Commission.

STATUTES:

Legislative power is exercised through specific instruments. (Art. 14 ECSC Treaty; Art. 189 EC Treaty; Art. 161 EAEC Treaty). In ECSC, decisions with general scope of application operate as statutes; decisions with individual scope of application contain directly binding implementation rules; recommendations are binding as to goals to be reached, but leave those to whom they are addressed, freedom as to choice of means. In EC and EAEC, regulations operate as statutes; directives are binding as to the goals to be reached, but leave to Member States freedom as to choice of means; decisions contain implementation rules directly binding on those to whom they are addressed.

ECSC decisions and recommendations with general scope of application and EC/EAEC regulations and directives are published in Official Journal of European Communities ("L" series, standing for "Legislation"). Sometimes ECSC decisions and recommendations with individual scope of application and EC/EAEC Decisions are also published in Official Journal of European Communities (L series).

Court of Justice held that directives, although not directly applicable as regulations are (see Art. 189 EC Treaty), may produce direct effect, so that private person or corporation is allowed to invoke directive against Member State which failed to implement it. Inconsistent national law then must be discarded by Member State Courts.

TAXATION:

No-Discrimination in Internal Taxation.—No Member State shall impose, directly or indirectly, on products of other Member States any internal taxation (as opposed to customs duties) of any kind in excess of that imposed directly or indirectly on similar domestic products, i.e. products competing on same relevant market such as e.g. different brands of wine. No Member State shall impose either on products of other Member States any internal taxation of such nature as to afford indirect protection to other products, i.e. products relating to each other as substitutes, e.g. beer producing Member State without wine industry levies consumption tax on wines only. Discrimination is prohibited as to taxable base, rates, facilities of payment of tax. See generally Art. 95 EC Treaty.

VAT Harmonization.—Pursuant to Arts. 99 and 100 EC Treaty, Council Directive 77/378, as last modified by Directive 95/7, harmonised value added taxes (VAT) throughout Community, as to operation of VAT and basis of assessment. EC obtains 1.4% of VAT levied in Member States as own budgetary resources.

In 1993, new transitory regime for VAT provided by Directive 94/76 entered into force in context of enlargement of EU to Austria, Finland and Sweden. Cross border formalities are abolished for operations between taxable persons, while purchase by individuals are only subject to VAT of originating country. Directive 92/77/EEC provides for suppression of increased rates, single "normal rate" with minimum of 15% and possibility for Member States to apply, for certain goods and services, one or two reduced rates which may not be less than 5%.

TRADEMARKS:

Law of Member States governs trademarks. Since different trade mark laws of Member States contain disparities which impede free movement of goods and freedom to provide services within EU, Council has in its Directive 89/104/EEC (1989 O.J. L 40/1) provided for approximation of trade mark laws. Harmonization will be limited to those national provisions of law which most directly affect functioning of internal market. Directive has to be implemented by Member States by Dec. 28, 1991. For Belgium, Netherlands and Luxembourg uniform Benelux trademark law entered into force. Benelux Court can interpret this law through preliminary rulings procedure copied on Art. 177 EC Treaty.

Commission has undertaken great efforts to create Community trademark. Council Regulation No. 40/94 (1994 O.J. L 11/1) on Community trademark is based on Art. 235 EC Treaty. It entered into force in Mar. 1994. It was amended for implementation of agreements concluded in framework of Uruguay Round. (1994 O.J. L349/83). From Jan. 1996, Community trademark can be obtained by registration at Office for Harmonisation in Internal Market, which is based in Alicante, Spain. Applicable procedural provisions are laid down in Commission Regulations No. 2868/95 and No. 2869/95 (1995 O.J. L303/1 and 33), and Regulation No. 216/96 (1996 O.J. L28/11).

From viewpoint of present EC law, trademarks are subject to doctrine of "Community-wide exhaustion" (see topic Copyright).

TREATIES:

Several provisions of EC Treaty provide for power to conclude agreements with third countries. Thus Art. 113 (trade agreements necessary to common commercial policy) and Art. 238 (association agreements). Examples are free trade agreements with EFTA (European Free Trade Association) countries and association agreement with ACP countries (Lomé Convention with African, Caribbean and Pacific countries). More generally, Court of Justice accepts that EC has treaty-making power in every field of internal competence without prior adoption of internal legislation, when conclusion of international agreement is necessary to achieve EC Treaty objectives that cannot be attained by adoption of autonomous rules. (Opinion 1/76). Power is then to be exercised pursuant to Art. 228 EC Treaty. When not the case, Court considers that external competence becomes exclusive only insofar as common rules have effectively been established at internal Community level. Therefore, with regard to General Agreement on Trade in Service ("GATS") and Agreement on Trade-Related Aspects of Intellectual Property Rights ("TRIPS") negotiated by Commission within framework of GATT, and with regard to Third Revised Decision of OECD on national treatment, Court concluded that, since harmonization achieved at EC level was only partial, EC and Member States have joint competence. (Opinions 1/94 and 2/92). Conversely, in respect of human rights, Court observed that EC has no internal competence and thus cannot adhere to European Convention on Human Rights. (Opinion 2/94).

COUNCIL OF THE BARS AND LAW SOCIETIES OF THE EUROPEAN COMMUNITY

CONTENTS

1 PREAMBLE

1.1 The Function of the Lawyer in Society

In a society founded on respect for the rule of law the lawyer fulfils a special role. His duties do not begin and end with the faithful performance of what he is instructed to do so far as the law permits. A lawyer must serve the interests of justice as well as those whose rights and liberties he is trusted to assert and defend and it is his duty not only to plead his client's cause but to be his adviser.

A lawyer's function therefore lays on him a variety of legal and moral obligations (sometimes appearing to be in conflict with each other) towards:—

—the client;

—the courts and other authorities before whom the lawyer pleads his client's cause or acts on his behalf;

—the legal profession in general and each fellow member of it in particular; and the public for whom the existence of a free and independent profession, bound together by respect for rules made by the profession itself, is an essential means of safeguarding human rights in face of the power of the state and other interests in society.

1.2 The Nature of Rules of Professional Conduct

1.2.1 Rules of professional conduct are designed through their willing acceptance by those to whom they apply to ensure the proper performance by the lawyer of a function which is recognised as essential in all civilised societies. The failure of the lawyer to observe these rules must in the last resort result in a disciplinary sanction.

1.2.2 The particular rules of each Bar or Law Society arise from its own traditions. They are adapted to the organisation and sphere of activity of the profession in the Member State concerned and to its judicial and administrative procedures and to its national legislation. It is neither possible nor desirable that they should be taken out of their context nor that an attempt should be made to give general application to rules which are inherently incapable of such application.

The particular rules of each Bar and Law Society nevertheless are based on the same values and in most cases demonstrate a common foundation.

1.3 The Purpose of the Code

1.3.1 The continued integration of the European Community and the increasing frequency of the cross-border activities of lawyers within the Community have made necessary in the public interest the statement of common rules which apply to all lawyers from the Community whatever Bar or Law Society they belong to in relation to their cross-border practice. A particular purpose of the statement of those rules is to mitigate the difficulties which result from the application of "double deontology" as set out in Article 4 of the E.C. Directive 77/249 of 22nd March 1977.

1.3.2 The organisations representing the legal profession through the CCBE propose that the rules codified in the following articles:—

—be recognised at the present time as the expression of a consensus of all the Bars and Law Societies of the European Community;

—be adopted as enforceable rules as soon as possible in accordance with national or Community procedures in relation to the cross-border activities of the lawyer in the European Community;

—be taken into account in all revisions of national rules of deontology or professional practice with a view to their progressive harmonisation.

They further express the wish that the national rules of deontology or professional practice be interpreted and applied whenever possible in a way consistent with the rules in this Code.

After the rules in this Code have been adopted as enforceable rules in relation to his cross-border activities the lawyer will remain bound to observe the rules of the Bar or Law Society to which he belongs to the extent that they are consistent with the rules in this Code.

1.4 Field of Application Ratione Personae

The following rules shall apply to lawyers of the European Community as they are defined by the Directive 77/249 of 22nd March 1977.

1.5 Field of Application Ratione Materiae

Without prejudice to the pursuit of a progressive harmonisation of rules of deontology or professional practice which apply only internally within a Member State, the following rules shall apply to the cross-border activities of the lawyer within the European Community. Cross-border activities shall mean:—

(a) all professional contacts with lawyers of Member States other than his own; and

(b) the professional activities of the lawyer in a Member State other than his own, whether or not the lawyer is physically present in that Member State.

1.6 Definitions

In these rules:—

"Home Member State" means the Member State of the Bar or Law Society to which the lawyer belongs.

"Host Member State" means any other Member State where the lawyer carries on cross-border activities.

"Competent authority" means the professional organisation (s) or authority (ies) of the Member State concerned responsible for the laying down of rules of professional conduct and the administration of discipline of lawyers.

2 GENERAL PRINCIPLES

2.1 Independence

2.1.1 The many duties to which a lawyer is subject require his absolute independence, free from all other influence, especially such as may arise from his personal interests or external pressure. Such independence is as necessary to trust in the process of justice as the impartiality of the judge. A lawyer must therefore avoid any impairment of his independence and be careful not to compromise his professional standards in order to please his client, the court or third parties.

2.1.2 This independence is necessary in non-contentious matters as well as in litigation. Advice given by a lawyer to his client has no value if it is given only to ingratiate himself, to serve his personal interests or in response to outside pressure.

2.2 Trust and Personal Integrity

Relationships of trust can only exist if a lawyer's personal honour, honesty and integrity are beyond doubt. For the lawyer these traditional virtues are professional obligations.

2.3 Confidentiality

2.3.1 It is of the essence of a lawyer's function that he should be told by his client things which the client would not tell to others, and that he should be the recipient of other information on a basis of confidence. Without the certainty of confidentiality there cannot be trust. Confidentiality is therefore a primary and fundamental right and duty of the lawyer.

2.3.2 A lawyer shall accordingly respect the confidentiality of all information given to him by his client, or received by him about his client or others in the course of rendering services to his client.

2.3.3 The obligation of confidentiality is not limited in time.

2.3.4 A lawyer shall require his associates and staff and anyone engaged by him in the course of providing professional services to observe the same obligation of confidentiality.

2.4 Respect for the Rules of Other Bars and Law Societies

Under Community Law (in particular under the Directive 77/249 of 22nd March 1977) a lawyer from another Member State may be bound to comply with the rules of the Bar or Law Society of the host Member State. Lawyers have a duty to inform themselves as to the rules which will affect them in the performance of any particular activity.

2.5 Incompatible Occupations

See Topical Index in front part of this volume.

2.5.1 In order to perform his functions with due independence and in a manner which is consistent with his duty to participate in the administration of justice a lawyer is excluded from some occupations.
2.5.2 A lawyer who acts in the representation or the defence of a client in legal proceedings or before any public authorities in a host Member State shall there observe the rules regarding incompatible occupations as they are applied to lawyers of the host Member State.
2.5.3 A lawyer established in a host Member State in which he wishes to participate directly in commercial or other activities not connected with the practice of the law shall respect the rules regarding forbidden or incompatible occupations as they are applied to lawyers of that Member State.

2.6 Personal Publicity
2.6.1 A lawyer should not advertise or seek personal publicity where this is not permitted.
In other cases a lawyer should only advertise or seek personal publicity to the extent and in the manner permitted by the rules to which he is subject.
2.6.2 Advertising and personal publicity shall be regarded as taking place where it is permitted, if the lawyer concerned shows that it was placed for the purpose of reaching clients or potential clients located where such advertising or personal publicity is permitted and its communication elsewhere is incidental.

2.7 The Client's Interests
Subject to due observance of all rules of law and professional conduct, a lawyer must always act in the best interests of his client and must put those interests before his own interests or those of fellow members of the legal profession.

3 RELATIONS WITH CLIENTS

3.1 Acceptance and Termination of Instructions
3.1.1 A lawyer shall not handle a case for a party except on his instructions. He may, however, act in a case in which he has been instructed by another lawyer who himself acts for the party or where the case has been assigned to him by a competent body.
3.1.2 A lawyer shall advise and represent his client promptly conscientiously and diligently. He shall undertake personal responsibility for the discharge of the instructions given to him. He shall keep his client informed as to the progress of the matter entrusted to him.
3.1.3 A lawyer shall not handle a matter which he knows or ought to know he is not competent to handle, without co-operating with a lawyer who is competent to handle it.
A lawyer shall not accept instructions unless he can discharge those instructions promptly having regard to the pressure of other work.
3.1.4 A lawyer shall not be entitled to exercise his right to withdraw from a case in such a way or in such circumstances that the client may be unable to find other legal assistance in time to prevent prejudice being suffered by the client.

3.2 Conflict of Interest
3.2.1 A lawyer may not advise, represent or act on behalf of two or more clients in the same matter if there is a conflict, or a significant risk of a conflict, between the interests of those clients.
3.2.2 A lawyer must cease to act for both clients when a conflict of interests arises between those clients and also whenever there is a risk of a breach of confidence or where his independence may be imparied.
3.2.3 A lawyer must also refrain from acting for a new client if there is a risk of a breach of confidences entrusted to the lawyer by a former client or if the knowledge which the lawyer possesses of the affairs of the former client would give an undue advantage to the new client.
3.2.4 Where lawyers are practising in association, paragraphs 3.2.1 to 3.2.3 above shall apply to the association and all its members.

3.3 Pactum de Quota Litis
3.3.1 A lawyer shall not be entitled to make a pactum de quota litis.
3.3.2 By "pactum de quota litis" is meant an agreement between a lawyer and his client entered into prior to the final conclusion of a matter to which the client is a party, by virtue of which the client undertakes to pay the lawyer a share of the result regardless of whether this is represented by a sum of money or by any other benefit achieved by the client upon the conclusion of the matter.
3.3.3 The pactum de quota litis does not include an agreement that fees be charged in proportion to the value of a matter handled by the lawyer if this is in accordance with an officially approved fee scale or under the control of competent authority having jurisdiction over the lawyer.

3.4 Regulation of Fees
3.4.1 A fee charged by a lawyer shall be fully disclosed to his client and shall be fair and reasonable.
3.4.2 Subject to any proper agreement to the contrary between a lawyer and his client fees charged by a lawyer shall be subject to regulation in accordance with the rules applied to members of the Bar or Law Society to which he belongs. If he belongs to more than one Bar or Law Society the rules applied shall be those with the closest connection to the contract between the lawyer and his client.

3.5 Payment on Account
If a lawyer requires a payment on account of his fees and/or disbursements such payment should not exceed a reasonable estimate of the fees and probable disbursements involved.
Failing such payment, a lawyer may withdraw from the case or refuse to handle it, but subject always to paragraph 3.1.4 above.

3.6 Fee Sharing with Non-Lawyers
3.6.1 Subject as after-mentioned a lawyer may not share his fees with a person who is not a lawyer.
3.6.2 The provisions of 6.1 above shall not preclude a lawyer from paying a fee, commission or other compensation to a deceased lawyer's heirs or to a retired lawyer in respect of taking over the deceased or retired lawyer's practice.

3.7 Legal Aid
A lawyer shall inform his client of the availability of legal aid where applicable.

3.8 Clients Funds
3.8.1 When lawyers at any time in the course of their practice come into possession of funds on behalf of their clients or third parties (hereinafter called "client's funds") it shall be obligatory:
3.8.1.1 That client's funds shall always be held in an account in a bank of similar institution subject to supervision of Public Authority and that all clients' funds received by a lawyer should be paid into such an account unless the client explicitly or by implication agrees that the funds should be dealt with otherwise.
3.8.1.2 That any account in which the client's funds are held in the name of the lawyer should indicate in the title or designation that the funds are held on behalf of the client or client's of the lawyer.
3.8.1.3 That any account or accounts in which client's funds are held in the name of the lawyer should at all times contain a sum which is not less than the total of the client's funds held by the lawyer.
3.8.1.4 That all client's funds should be available for payment to clients on demand or upon such conditions as the client may authorise.
3.8.1.5 That payments made from client's funds on behalf of a client to any other person including
a)payments made to or for one client from funds held for another client and
b)payment of the lawyer's fees,
be prohibited except to the extent that they are permitted by law or have the express or implied authority of the client for whom the payment is being made.
3.8.1.6 That the lawyer shall maintain full and accurate records, available to each client on request, showing all his dealings with his client's funds and distinguishing client's funds from other funds held by him.
3.8.1.7 That the competent authorities in all Member States should have powers to allow them to examine and investigate on a confidential basis the financial records of lawyer's client's funds to ascertain whether or not the rules which they make are being complied with and to impose sanctions upon lawyers who fail to comply with those rules.
3.8.2 Subject as aftermentioned, and without prejudice to the rules set out in 3.8.1 above, a lawyer who holds clients funds in the course of carrying on practice in any Member State must comply with the rules relating to holding and accounting for client's funds which are applied by the competent authorities of the Home Member State.
3.8.3 A lawyer who carries on practice or provides services in a Host Member States may with the agreement of the competent authorities of the Home and Host Member State concerned comply with the requirements of the Host Member State to the exclusion of the requirements of the Home Member State. In that event he shall take reasonable steps to inform his clients that he complies with the requirements in force in the Host Member State.

3.9 Professional Indemnity Insurance
3.9.1 Lawyers shall be insured at all times against claims based on professional negligence to an extent which is reasonable having regard to the nature and extent of the risks which lawyers incur in practice.
3.9.2.1 Subject as aftermentioned, a lawyer who provides services or carries on practice in a Member State must comply with any Rules relating to his obligation to insure against his professional liability as a lawyer which are in force in his Home Member State.
3.9.2.2 A lawyer who is obliged so to insure in his Home Member State and who provides services or carries on practice in any Host Member State shall use his best endeavours to obtain insurance cover on the basis required in his home Member State extended to services which he provides or practice which he carries on in a Host Member State.
3.9.2.3 A lawyer who fails to obtain the extended insurance cover referred to in paragraph 3.9.2.2 above or who is not obliged so to insure in his Home Member State and who provides services or carries on practice in a Host Member State shall in so far as possible obtain insurance cover against his professional liability as a lawyer whilst acting for clients in that Host Member State on at least an equivalent basis to that required of lawyers in the Host Member State.
3.9.2.4 To the extent that a lawyer is unable to obtain the insurance cover required by the foregoing rules, he shall take reasonable steps to draw that fact to the attention of such of his clients as might be affected in the event of a claim against him.
3.9.2.5 A lawyer who carries on practice or provides services in a Host Member State may with the agreement of the competent authorities of the Home and Host Member States concerned comply with such insurance requirements as are in force in the Host Member State to the exclusion of the insurance requirements of the Home Member State. In this event he shall take reasonable steps to inform his clients that he is insured according to the requirements in force in the Host Member State.

4. RELATIONS WITH THE COURTS

4.1 Applicable Rules of Conduct in Court
A lawyer who appears, or takes part in a case, before a court or tribunal in a Member State must comply with the rules of conduct applied before that court or tribunal.

4.2 Fair Conduct of Proceedings
A lawyer must always have due regard for the fair conduct of proceedings. He must not, for example, make contact with the judge without first informing the lawyer acting for the opposing party or submit exhibits, notes or documents to the judge without communicating them in good time to the lawyer on the other side unless such steps are permitted under the relevant rules of procedure.

4.3 Demeanour in Court
A lawyer shall while maintaining due respect and courtesy towards the court defend the interests of his client honourably and in a way which he considers will be to the client's best advantage within the limits of the law.

4.4 False or Misleading Information
A lawyer shall never knowingly give false or misleading information to the court.

4.5 Extension to Arbitrators Etc.

See Topical Index in front part of this volume.

The rules governing a lawyer's relations with the courts apply also to his relations with arbitrators and any other persons exercising judicial or quasi-judicial functions, even on an occasional basis.

5. RELATIONS BETWEEN LAWYERS

5.1 Corporate Spirit of the Profession

5.1.1 The corporate spirit of the profession requires a relationship of trust and co-operation between lawyers for the benefit of their clients and in order to avoid unnecessary litigation. It can never justify setting the interests of the profession against those of justice or of those who seek it.

5.1.2 A lawyer should recognize all other lawyers of Member States as professional colleagues and act fairly and courteously towards them.

5.2 Co-operation Among Lawyers of Different Member States

5.2.1 It is the duty of a lawyer who is approached by a colleague from another Member State not to accept instructions in a matter which he is not competent to undertake. He should be prepared to help his colleague to obtain the information necessary to enable him to instruct a lawyer who is capable of providing the service asked for.

5.2.2 Where a lawyer of a Member State co-operates with a lawyer from another Member State, both have a general duty to take into account the differences which may exist between their respective legal systems and the professional organisations competences and obligations of lawyers in the Member States concerned.

5.3 Correspondence Between Lawyers

5.3.1 If a lawyer sending a communication to a lawyer in another Member State wishes to remain confidential or without prejudice he should clearly express this intention when communicating the document.

5.3.2. If the recipient of the communication is unable to ensure is status as confidential or without prejudice he should return it to the sender without revealing the contents to others.

5.4 Referral Fees

5.4.1 A lawyer may not demand or accept from another lawyer or any other person a fee, commission or any other compensation for referring or recommending a client.

5.4.2 A lawyer may not pay anyone a fee, commission or any other compensation as a consideration for referring a client to himself.

5.5 Communication with Opposing Parties

A lawyer shall not communicate about a particular case or matter directly with any person whom he knows to be represented or advised in the case or matter by another lawyer, without the consent of that other lawyer (and shall keep the other lawyer informed of any such communications).

5.6 Change of Lawyer

5.6.1 A lawyer who is instructed to represent a client in substitution for another lawyer in relation to a particular matter should inform that other lawyer and, subject to 5.6.2 below, should not begin to act until he has ascertained that arrangements have been made for the settlement of the other lawyer's fees and disbursements. This duty does not, however, make the new lawyer personally responsible for the former lawyer's fees and disbursements.

5.6.2 If urgent steps have to be taken in the interests of the client before the conditions in 5.6.1 above can be complied with, the lawyer may take such steps provided he informs the other lawyer immediately.

5.7 Responsibility for Fees

In professional relations between members of Bars of different Member States, where a lawyer does not confine himself to recommending another lawyer or introducing him to the client but himself entrusts a correspondent with a particular matter or seeks his advice, he is personally bound, even if the client is insolvent, to pay the fees, costs and outlays which are due to the foreign correspondent. The lawyers concerned may, however, at the outset of the relationship between them make special arrangements on this matter. Further, the instructing lawyer may at any time limit his personal responsibility to the amount of the fees, costs and outlays incurred before intimation to the foreign lawyer of his disclaimer of responsibility for the future.

5.8 Training Young Lawyers

In order to improve trust and co-operation amongst lawyers of different Member States for the clients' benefit there is a need to encourage a better knowledge of the laws and procedures in different Member States. Therefore, when considering the need for the profession to give good training to young lawyers, lawyers should take into account the need to give training to young lawyers from other Member States.

5.9 Disputes Amongst Lawyers in Different Member States

5.9.1 If a lawyer considers that a colleague in another Member State has acted in breach of a rule of professional conduct he shall draw the matter to the attention of his colleague.

5.9.2 If any personal dispute of a professional nature arises amongst lawyers in different Member States they should if possible first try to settle it in a friendly way.

5.9.3 A lawyer shall not commence any form of proceedings against a colleague in another Member State on matters referred to in 5.9.1 or 5.9.2 above without first informing the Bars or Law Societies to which they both belong for the purpose of allowing both Bars or Law Societies concerned an opportunity to assist in reaching a settlement.

See Topical Index in front part of this volume.

FINLAND LAW DIGEST REVISER

Castrén & Snellman
Erottajankatu 5A
Post Office Box 233
00131 Helsinki, Finland
Telephone: 358 9 228 581
Fax: 358 9 655 919
Email: info@castren.fi
URL: http://www. castren.fi

Reviser Profile

History: The firm was founded in Helsinki the 1st of June 1888 by Kaarlo Castrén and Frans Emil Snellman. In November 1896 the law office was entered into the trade register as the first law firm in Finland. Today Castrén & Snellman is one of the largest law firms in Finland.

Castrén & Snellman has seven partners, Messrs. Bertel Åkermarck, Eero Relas, Pekka Sirviö, Jouko Huhtala, Mikael Aspelin, Pekka Jaatinen and Jan Kuhlefelt and nineteen associates. The total staff is 60 persons.

Area of Emphasis: Castrén & Snellman is a full service firm in general legal practice, however, with accentuation on Corporate and Business law, International Legal Transactions, Mergers and Acquisitions, Commercial Litigation and Arbitration, Tax Law, Real Estate, Intellectual Property, Trademark Law and Patent Litigation and Insolvency Law.

Clients are served in Finnish, Swedish, English, Estonian, Italian, German, French and Russian.

Client Base: A majority of the clients represented by Castrén & Snellman are foreign owned subsidiary companies and local medium to large corporations engaged in activities in Finland and abroad.

The clients are a.o. found in the chemical and oil business, in the electronic, building construction and textile industry and in the field of air transportation and advertising.

Firm Activities: All partners are members of the Finnish Bar Association and of local professional associations.

The partners of the firm are engaged in international activities such as International Bar Association and the Young Lawyers International Association (AIJA).

The firm has worldwide professional contacts and works in especially close cooperation with law firms in other Nordic countries. Castrén & Snellman has also developed good working relations with lawyers in Estonia and the firm is able to serve clients in all Baltic countries.

Branch: Since 1994 Castrén & Snellman has maintained a branch office in St. Petersburg, Russia.

Internet: For more information about the firm please see our homepage at http://www.castren.fi or send an email to info@castren.fi.

FINLAND LAW DIGEST

(The following is a list of all Topics, including cross-references, covered in this Digest.)

FINLAND LAW DIGEST

Revised for 1997 edition by

CASTRÉN & SNELLMAN, of the Helsinki Bar.

See topics Law Reports; Statutes.

Finland is member of EU. See also European Union Law Digest.

ABSENTEES:

Interest of an absentee in matters concerning his property and with regard to his rights as an heir, a legatee or a beneficiary are attended to by a trustee appointed by court. This applies also to cases where heirs to a decedent are unknown or uncertain. See also topic Death.

ACKNOWLEDGMENTS:

Documents acknowledged before a notary public abroad and intended for use in Finland should have the signature of the notary public certified by a Finnish consular officer or if possible by a county clerk whose signature in turn should be certified by a Finnish consular officer.

ACTIONS:

Limitation of.—See topic Limitation of Actions.

AFFIDAVITS:

Use of affidavit is confined to certain cases where oath is administered by court only.

ALIENS:

Sojourn of an alien in Finland is governed by permit on passport or permit secured in Finland for a specified time. According to general rule, alien is without political rights and ineligible to hold public office. Property rights of alien and right to engage in business and occupations are also supervised in some particulars.

On Jan. 1, 1993 new law came into force which supervises and, in some cases restricts, acquisition of real estate in Finland. Permission from Provincial Environment Agency is required for acquisitions when estate is situated within border zone or when estate apparently is meant to be used for free-time living or recreation.

Without authorities' permission in each individual case, alien or foreign company may not stake claim to mineral discovery in Finland, nor acquire or exploit discovery already claimed.

Alien may not: (a) Own a share in a Finnish vessel, nor, with one exception carry on cabotage; (b) engage professionally in foreign exchange trading; (c) carry on business in materials intended for development of atomic energy nor build, own or use a plant destined for production of materials intended for development of such, nor build, own or use an atomic reactor.

Corporations Owned or Controlled by Aliens.—On Jan. 1, 1993 new law came into force which supervises and, when national advantage requires, restricts aliens' and foreign corporations' gaining of power in improtant companies. National advantage is defined as: (a) securing of national defence; (b) prevention of serious economic, public or environmental difficulties; and (c) public order and safety and health of citizens. Subject to supervision and restrictions are only companies of substantial size. If company is reckoned to be important company and exceeds limits of size set out in law, permission for acquisition from Ministry of Commerce and Industry.

As to the right of inheritance, see topic Descent and Distribution.

See also topics Death, subhead Actions for Death; Commercial Register; Joint Stock Companies.

ARBITRATION AND AWARD:

Since Dec. 1, 1992 there has been new Arbitration Act in force in Finland. New law has been drafted with aim of conformity with international developments in arbitration and it follows main principles of UNCITRAL model law. Provisions regarding arbitration in foreign states are based on principles of New York Convention.

Arbitral award is original nullity: (1) To extent arbitrators have decided on subject matter of dispute in which no settlement by arbitration is allowed under Finnish law; (2) to extent award is in conflict with basis of Finnish legal system; (3) if award is so vague or incomplete that it cannot be determined how dispute has been settled; (4) if award has not been made in writing or if it has not been signed by arbitrators.

Validity of award may be contested by action in court of jurisdiction, normally within three months after it has been awarded, if: (1) Arbitrators have exceeded their competence; (2) arbitrator has not been appointed in appropriate way; (3) arbitrator should have been disqualified and party has not forfeited his right of referring to grounds for disqualification; (4) parties have not been given sufficient opportunity to present their case.

It is up to arbitrator to decide whether they have jurisdiction or not and, after lapse of three months after award has been granted, there is no legal redress in this respect.

ASSIGNMENTS:

A creditor may assign and transfer his claim to another. Unless a negotiable instrument is in question, an instrument of indebtedness may not be assigned and transferred to the damage of the debtor. The debtor may avail himself of all defenses against the assignee and transferee, which were available to him against the original creditor. If a negotiable instrument is transferred, the debtor does not have this advantage.

The transfer of a nonnegotiable instrument presupposes an agreement between the transferor and transferee. There is no prescribed form for this agreement. On the other hand, a transfer must be indorsed on the instrument when it is a negotiable instrument. This indorsement can be confined to a mere blank indorsement, where by law it has been specially provided (for instance as to bills of exchange). A bearer instrument may be negotiated by transfer of possession to transferee.

ASSIGNMENTS FOR BENEFIT OF CREDITORS: See topic Bankruptcy.

ASSOCIATIONS:

The furthering of an enterprise having for its purpose the assisting of its members in carrying on business, or otherwise alleviating their living condition, is made possible by the organization of co-operative associations. The liability of the members depends on whether the association agreement contains any liability for additional payment.

In general, the business of a co-operative association may be in any field of economic endeavor, but it may not enter the insurance business. The co-operative association may be either a production co-operative or a consumer co-operative.

The co-operative association is organized by a written agreement. The smallest number of members is five persons. A notice of the co-operative association must be made for the commercial register. The name of the co-operative association must contain the word co-operative association ("osuuskunta") or the word "osuus".

The affairs of a co-operative association are determined by its members, or their representatives at the annual meeting, at which is also elected the board of directors of the co-operative association. The board of directors also represents the co-operative association against third persons. If the membership decreases below five members, the board of directors must proceed to have the co-operative association dissolved.

In the meetings of members, each member has one vote. In changing the by-laws, in so far as that is permitted, a majority of qualified voters is required.

Co-operative associations engaged in loaning money and their central funds are permitted under specified conditions to accept deposits. (Co-Operative Associations Law, 28/5-1954).

See also topics Aliens; Commercial Register; Joint Stock Companies; Partnership.

ATTACHMENT:

By attachment is meant action which is determined by proper court of first instance upon petition, by which specified real or personal property is taken into custody to secure debt or other right. If execution officer, when executing precautionary measure, finds that risk for waste of property probably is small or circumstances otherwise give reason to it or applicant gives his consent, injunction against dispersion of property can be rendered instead of attachment.

After attachment had been granted by court of first instance proper bailiff executes it upon petition. Grounds for granting petition are that there is danger that debtor conceal or destroy property. Debt must be due or about to become due. Existence of debt must be established by credible facts.

After the attachment or injunction against dispersion of property has been granted, petitioner must, within specified time, commence action for debt. If this is neglected, attachment or writ to prevent waste is void. Plaintiff must furnish attachment bond required by official. (Code of Procedure, 22/7 1991).

ATTORNEYS AND COUNSELORS:

It is not compulsory to use advocate in Finland, nor does advocate have sole right to appear in court: party to case has legal right to represent him- or herself in court of law. Only advocate or otherwise honest, suitable and able person who has full legal capacity is qualified to function as attorney or as trial counselor.

Finnish Bar Association: Address: Simonkatu 12 B, 00100 HELSINKI; Telephone: 90-6942 744; Telefax: 90-6948 237.

Qualifications of Advocate.—Only those members of Finnish Bar Association who have been registered in list of attorneys are entitled to call themselves advocates. Advocate is to be citizen of Finland or of some other European Economic Area Member State who has reached age of 25 years and obtained law degree. He or she is also to have full legal capacity and be known to be honest and otherwise suitable to work of advocate. He or she is also required to pass examination in advocacy law given by Finnish Bar Association, and must also have worked within field of judicature for minimum of four years. After coming into force of EEA agreement, person who is qualified to function as advocate in other EEA Member State can also be accepted as advocate. Such person is required to participate in examination given by Finnish Bar Association and thus indicate that he or she is sufficiently familiar with Finnish legislation and advocacy.

Advocates' Duties and Their Supervision.—Advocate is to fulfill duties bestowed upon him or her with integrity and concienciousness and to observe code of professional ethics in all activities. Outlines of these universal rules are included in 1958 Advocates Act and in rules of Finnish Bar Association. It is obligation of board of directors of Finnish Bar Association to supervise advocates to assure that they fulfull their duties. All members of disciplinary board of Association function with responsibility of judge.

See also topic Principal and Agent.

BANKRUPTCY:

The court of first instance administers the bankruptcy law.

A petition in bankruptcy may be presented to the court upon specified grounds by either the creditor or debtor; by the creditor, for instance, when the debtor has disappeared or execution has been levied on property of the debtor for the benefit of

BANKRUPTCY . . . *continued*
some other creditor and it is feared that for this reason the creditor cannot be paid, or if an execution upon his property has been unsatisfied and no funds were available for its payments or if the debtor conceals his property to the damage of his creditors. The provisions as to merchants are more severe.

Petition in bankruptcy must be in writing, and as all other papers in bankruptcy proceedings, must be presented to court in duplicate. In bankruptcy proceeding court of first instance conducts examination of debtor, hearings of creditors, and gives order and decree in bankruptcy. According to appreciable changes in Bankruptcy Rule trustees conduct examination of claims and call of creditors. At creditors' hearing debtor must under oath give statement of his assets and liabilities and court appoints trustees, one or more, to take bankrupt estate into their custody until examination of claims and to administer same. Appointing of trustees is generally governed by wishes of creditors representing majority of total claims.

At the examination of claims, each creditor must generally present his claim in writing or by electrical transmission; at same time he must state what preference he claims from assets of debtor. To claim must be appended certified copies of documents upon which claim is based. Also claims in foreign language must be accepted and claims must be translated in Finnish or Swedish by trustees. Proofs of claim may also be sent to court by mail within stated time, i.e., before examination of claims.

At examination of claims creditors select committeemen, one or more, to undertake final liquidation, paying of dividends, etc.

A creditor who fails to make proof of claim loses the right to receive payment out of the bankruptcy fund.

Before a bankruptcy decree is ordered the parties may dispose of the matter by composition. The composition with creditors must be in writing and filed in court. If it is found to be subscribed by the debtor and all bankruptcy creditors, the court will confirm same, and will order that the bankruptcy is thus brought to a conclusion.

In the decree of bankruptcy, all uncontested claims are ordered paid. If an objection has been made to a claim necessitating the examination of other persons or witnesses, the creditor or trustee is directed to establish his claim by separate action within specified time.

The supervision and liquidation of the property of a debtor adjudged bankrupt is determined by the creditors at their meeting and the trustees must act accordingly within the provisions of the law. After completing their duties trustee must give their final account. Party may file objections to this final account in court. (Bankruptcy Rule, 9/11-1868). According to Act of Dec. 13, 1985 debtor who in grave manner has acted against his creditors' interests may be forbidden to do business for at most five years on demand of district attorney.

Rescheduling.—On Feb. 8, 1993 Corporate Rescheduling Act entered into force. Aim of law is to rehabilitate viable business activities of debtor in difficulties and to ensure necessary prerequisites for this and to reschedule debts. Process of enforced debt restructuring or rescheduling closely resembles American Chapter 11 of Bankruptcy Act. There are, though, some major differences, e.g. that Finnish law provides that one or more administrators always are appointed.

Application for rescheduling, which is made to proper court of first instance, can be made either by: (a) Debtor; (b) creditor or several creditors jointly, except creditor whose claim is contested; or (c) so called probable creditor. Conditions for initiating procedure are that either: (a) Debtor together wth at least two creditors, whose claims represent at least 20% of known debts, make application jointly; (b) there is danger of insolvency for debtor; or (c) debtor is insolvent.

Administrator is appointed by court of first instance upon proposal made by Committee Creditors. In order to fulfill purpose of process and to attend to creditors' interest, administrator's most important duties are to: (1) Prepare report on company and its finances; (2) supervise activities of company during proceedings; and (3) draft proposal for rescheduling program.

Committee of Creditors may be appointed as joint representation for creditors if court finds it necessary. Committee's assignment is to assist administrator as advisory organ.

After proceedings have been initiated several legal consequences follow: (1) debtor is neither allowed to pay nor give security for debts that result from time before proceedings, except under certain circumstances; (2) no collection measures may be taken regarding debts that result from time before proceedings and initiated measures cannot be finished. Some exceptions exist; (3) no levy of execution can be carried out; (4) although debtor's authority over his property and actions remain in general, he may not without consent of administrator, e.g.: (a) Draw new credit; (b) assign fixed, current or liquid assets of company; (c) terminate agreements; or (d) surrender company's property into bankruptcy.

Rescheduling program shall, apart from report on assets and liabilities of company, include proposals for restructuring financing and operations such that company might be rendered healthy one once again. Furthermore proposal for rescheduling debts shall be included. Debts can either be changed by: (1) Changing time schedule for repay; (2) directing payments at interest in first hand and at capital in second; (3) reducing credit costs; or (4) reducing amount of remaining debt.

If application of surrendering company's assets into bankruptcy has been made, but court has not yet declared company bankrupt, before application of rescheduling is filed, latter shall be decided upon first. Same applies to bankruptcy application that is filed during consideration of rescheduling application in court.

Individuals.—On Feb. 8, 1993 a Rescheduling of Debts and Liabilities of Individuals Act came into force. This law follows, wherever applicable, same principles as Corporate Rescheduling Act.

BILLS AND NOTES:

Bills of Exchange.—A bill of exchange is a negotiable instrument, the form of which is strictly prescribed by law and in which consideration is conclusively presumed. A special feature of the obligation under a bill of exchange is its severity toward the debtor and the possibility of securing a judgment and execution thereon in a shorter time and in a more simplified manner. In a bill of exchange each indorser in general is liable to subsequent indorsers.

The parties to a bill of exchange, according to the general rule, are the drawer, the drawee (who after the acceptance of the bill is known as the acceptor) and the payee. A bill of exchange may be made payable to or by the drawer himself.

A bill of exchange must bear the words "bill of exchange" ("vekseli"), the place and time of issue, the amount of money payable, the name of the payee and drawee, the address of the drawee, the time when the bill is payable and the signature of the drawer. The name of the acceptor is written on the face of the instrument and the indorsements on the back. The transfer may be either by full indorsement or by blank indorsement.

If the obligation to pay based on the bill of exchange is not fulfilled, a protest must be made to an official at the latest on the second day, the result of which is that the maker of the protest preserves his bill of exchange rights against all parties liable on the instrument. After these rights under the bill of exchange are lost the bill of exchange is considered to be an ordinary promissory note to which do not attach the advantages as to proof and collection inherent in a bill of exchange. However, in order to preserve the rights under the bill of exchange, an action on the same must be commenced within a specified time, for instance against the acceptor within three years from the due date. Actions against the indorser and drawer must be commenced within one year.

The procedure to be followed by a holder of a bill of exchange in order to preserve his rights where it is payable outside of Finland, is governed by the law of that place or the accepted custom and usage. (Bills of Exchange Law, 14/7-1932).

Checks.—A check must contain on its face the word "check" ("shekki"), place and time of drawing, an order to pay a specified sum of money, the name of the bank who shall pay the check and the signature of the drawer.

A check is payable at sight, even though it contains a different time of payment or if the time of payment is not mentioned. A check may be made payable to a designated person or to bearer.

A check may be transferred the same as a bill of exchange. In order to preserve the retroactive cause of action, a check must be presented for payment at latest on 20th day after date of issue, excepting checks issued outside Europe which are subjected to payment on 70th day after date of issue. Check payable abroad is governed by law of place of payment. There are separate provisions on this point concerning checks issued abroad.

In order to preserve the retroactive cause of action where a check presented for payment is not paid, a protest for nonpayment or equivalent proof is necessary. (Check Law 19/9-1932).

CHATTEL MORTGAGES:

See topic Pledges.

CLAIMS:

The relationship between two parties, whereby one is entitled to demand a payment from the other for his own benefit is called the right of debt.

A claim may arise by agreement. An agreement may be made either orally or in writing. Even for a written agreement of indebtedness, generally no special form has been provided by law.

A specified person may be designated as the debtor or, in case of a negotiable instrument, a specified person or order, or the bearer of the instrument of indebtedness.

A claim may become due at a specified time, on demand or after notice. If no mention is made of this in the instrument of indebtedness, payment must be made on demand.

A claim may be against several parties, who in that case are jointly liable. Joint liability may be either per capita liability, in which case each is liable pro rata for his share, or it may be joint liability where each is liable for his own share and that of the others. If the creditor releases one who is jointly liable, he can demand from the remainder only the amount remaining when the pro rata share of the one released has been deducted from the amount due. A joint liability is changed by thus releasing one party to a pro rata liability.

A claim may also be based on liability for damages for personal injury. In the law of Finland the main rule is that the injury, in order to give rise to a liability for damages, must be caused by carelessness or negligence.

A claim is discharged by payment, by substituted performance, renewal of the debt, by release, by confusion, by cancellation, by the preclusion. Payment assumes here that there has been a mutual claim, in the same amount and that both sums are due.

The failure to file a claim, for instance, in cases where notices to creditors are published in manner provided by law, the so-called annual summons, results in preclusion of the claim.

COMMERCIAL REGISTER:

(Act of Feb. 2, 1979).

Those desiring to carry on trade, manufacturing, handicraft or other business are obliged prior to starting business activities to file notification with commercial register (base report).

Commercial register is kept by Patent and Registration Office in Helsinki. Entries to commercial register and documents filed are open to public and entries are generally published in Official Gazette.

Notification (base report) to commercial register must contain, inter alia, name (firm) of merchant, partnership, commandite company, joint stock company, etc., objects of business and address.

As to joint stock companies, notification must contain following: Firm, date of acceptance of articles of association, field of activity, domicile, share capital number and nominal value of shares, maximum and minimum share capital if stated in articles of association, paid amount of share capital, provisions in articles of association regarding shares of different classes (e.g., different voting rights), full name, domicile and citizenship of members of board of directors and managing director and who is entitled to sign for company.

Changes in registered conditions and dissolution of business must also be reported to register.

COMMERCIAL REGISTER . . . *continued*

If no notification has been made to commercial register within ten years, company may, after procedure prescribed by law, be removed from register.

In case of failure to register, fine must be paid, sentence passed by court of first instance.

CONSTITUTION AND GOVERNMENT:

According to the Constitution of July 17, 1919, Finland is a republic with a parliamentary form of government. Legislative power rests with the Parliament and the President of the Republic. The highest executive power rests with the President of the Republic together with the Ministers. The judicial power rests with the independent courts. The President of the Republic is elected for six years.

CONTRACTS:

According to Contracts Act of June 13, 1929 (result of co-Nordic legislation) contracts ensue from acceptance of offer. This is not applicable to contracts fixed in form by law and certain other contracts as pledge of personal property that require conveyance of object. In case of oral offer, acceptor must accept immediately unless time of grace is granted. Other offers must be accepted within stated or reasonable time. Promisor and acceptor are respectively bound by offer and acceptance which cannot be withdrawn or revoked unilaterally subsequent to other party taking part. Contracts are valid regardless of form, except, inter alia, sale of real property and some others. Force majeure is a generally accepted excuse for nonperformance. Invalidity of contract can be alleged in cases enumerated in Act and including duress, fraudulent persuasion, exercise of undue influence and incapability or mental disorder of contracting party. Good faith of a third party is protected in most instances. Contracts Act of June 13, 1929 has been am'd by Act of Dec. 17, 1982. By virtue of this amendment rules on general adjustment of exorbitant stipulations were inserted. According to these, conditions which are exorbitant may be adjusted or ignored. Other conditions may be modified or entire contract may be set aside if unreasonable condition is of such importance that it cannot reasonably be demanded that contract shall be valid.

Applicable Law.—There are no statutory rules concerning conflict of laws in contracts except as regards bills of exchange and checks.

Government Contracts.—There are no special rules for government contracts.

See also topic Sales.

CONVEYANCES: See topics Deeds; Sales.

COPYRIGHT:

The author of an intellectual product has within specified limits the sole right to place the same within reach of the public. By intellectual product is meant literary, artistic, and scientific products, among others, writings, oral presentation, musical compositions, paintings, works of art, works on dancing and motion picture art, city plan drawings, drawings of scientific and technical nature, and also translations and adaptations of these works.

The author may assign his rights to another in part or entirely. The author's rights after his death pass to the distributees of the estate according to law. The author's right is in force during the lifetime of the author and for 50 years from the end of the year in which the author died. (Copyright Law, 8/7-1961).

CORPORATIONS:

See topics Associations; Joint Stock Companies.

COURTS:

The courts of general jurisdiction in the first instance are city courts. Next higher courts are courts of appeal, and highest court is the Supreme Court. In administrative and executive field there are governors of provinces and magistrate courts, and highest tribunal is Supreme Administrative court.

Special tribunals are the Court of the Realm, the Military Court, the Bishops Council (in ecclesiastical affairs), General Court of Revision (in matters of Government Accounts), the Land Division Court, Insurance Council, Supreme Court for Officials and Marketing Court.

CURRENCY:

The legal currency is the Finnmark (markka), which is divided in 100 pennies (penni).

Bank of Finland (Suomen Pankki) holds a monopoly on issue of paper money. As security for the value of the notes issued are, exceeding the value of the gold reserve, easily negotiable assets.

In Oct. 1931 Finland left the gold standard.

CURTESY:

Does not exist in Finland.

CUSTOMS DUTIES:

Finland is member of EU and custom regulations of EU therefore apply in Finland.

Finland is a member of Customs Co-operation Council and customs tariffs are based on Brussels nomenclature.

Finland has made Finefta agreement with Efta countries in 1961. As a result industrial goods from Efta countries (and Russia) enter Finland free of duty.

See also topic Treaties.

DEATH:

If a person dies and the death appears unnatural a post-mortem examination must be held and if the result of this examination still is unsatisfactory an inquest must be held to ascertain the cause of death.

A petition to have a person declared legally dead may be presented ten years after the close of the calendar year during which the person was last known to have been alive; or if the person would be more than 75 years of age, when five years have passed; or if the person is known to have disappeared in combat, shipwreck or the like, from which it might be inferred that he or she is actually or in all probability dead, then the petition may be presented when three years have passed since the end of the year in question.

The petition must be filed with the court which would be the proper forum if the person were alive. If such a forum cannot be established the petition may be presented to the applicant's own forum.

The court summons the absentee and any person who might know about the former must give notice to the court before a certain day, fixed at least six months after summons has been published in official gazette. If court at fixed day has no information that absentee may be alive, court will declare that person be considered dead. Day of death will be fixed to earliest possible time, when person in question according to time limits, as stated above, could have been declared legally dead. (Law, 23/4-1901).

See topic Records.

Actions for Death.—In case of death caused by criminal action, widow or child is entitled to plead in court for damages or necessary allowance, and other relatives for damages. There is no maximum or minimum rate of allowance prescribed by law but this depends inter alia on the criminal's solvency and the deceased's own share of guilt.

Action must generally be taken within ten years, but if crime is prescribed later, action can take place within that time.

Special stipulations concern damages caused by motor vehicles, aeroplanes, trains, etc., in which cases liability for payment of damages might occur even if no crime is at hand.

The above-said concerns also foreigners.

DEEDS:

Generally, juridical acts may be performed either orally or in writing. But the written form is necessary for legal effect in transfers of real property, ante-nuptial agreements, partnership or joint stock company agreements, etc. See topics Husband and Wife, subhead Conveyance of Property; also Sales.

DEPOSITIONS:

A court of first instance in Finland must give its official aid to foreign judicial officers, if they are requested to take an oath, conduct an examination, inspect a document or to inspect any other object which can be brought into court without difficulty. A court of Finland may also permit testimony to be taken in a controverted matter or in a criminal proceeding or in a proceeding by petition before a foreign official.

DESCENT AND DISTRIBUTION:

Finnish Law of Succession has been renewed by Code of Succession (CoS) of 5/2/1965, which was partially prepared in cooperation with Swedish authorities. As a result it is closely related to corresponding Swedish Code.

Range of relatives entitled to succeed to property of intestate has hitherto been unlimited. But in CoS, it has been restricted so that cousins and more distant relatives no longer have right of inheritance from intestate. If no one takes by virtue of succession, estate belongs to State.

Spouse will inherit if deceased leaves no issue. Upon death of surviving spouse, whole estate with few exceptions will be divided in half between heirs-at-law of each of spouses, but not to those heirs of predeceased who are more remote than nephews or nieces.

As regards right of succession of children, two exceptions should be noted: (a) If deceased during his life has made his child an advancement, this shall be deducted from his share of estate unless donor's intention was to contrary; (b) if deceased has left infant child dependant on additional means for its upbringing and education, addition to share of estate may be granted in lump sum from undivided estate.

Illegitimate child has right of succession after his mother and her relatives, as well as after his own descendants. If paternity of illegitimate child has been confirmed in accordance with Paternity Act (Law 5/9-1975), child will also take after his father and his paternal relatives. Adopted child takes, after his adoptive parents, as child of marriage.

Condition of right to claim share upon intestacy is that heir has not forfeited his right of succession.

Right of succession may become barred by time, i.e., if heir does not within ten years take any measures with view to receiving his share of estate. Anyone who by wilful criminal act has caused death of another is precluded from deriving any benefit either from intestacy or under will of deceased.

Administration of estate may be handled by representatives themselves, or they may leave this to administrator appointed by court upon application by one of representatives. If will appoints executor, he will take possession of estate to exclusion of heirs of blood, but not of surviving spouse.

Apportionment or distribution may be in form agreed by personal representatives. If representatives cannot agree on apportionment, they may apply to court for appointment of special distributor or apportioner. Distribution must always be effected by apportioner when one of representatives makes such a demand, or one of representatives is a minor or a ward of court, or if share of one of representatives has been seized. Administrator or executor may on request of representatives and without special appointment act as apportioner.

DISPUTE RESOLUTION:

Mandatory Dispute Resolution.—In Finnish legislation mandatory dispute resolution exists in form of factfinding (panel of laymen). Factfinding organs are established especially in field of social security. Factfindings can be submitted to Appellate Board for Accident Insurance, Appellate Board for Pension, Labour Council, Unemployment

DISPUTE RESOLUTION . . . *continued*
Benefit Appellate Board, Data Protection Board, Equality Board, Competition Council, Board of Correction and Average Adjuster.

Voluntary dispute resolution can be divided into two subcategories: Arbitration (see topic Arbitration and Award) and factfindings which are only recommended decisions. Party may choose whether to institute proceedings in court of first instance or in factfinding. Voluntary factfindings may be submitted to Employment Invention Board, Copyright Council, Treatment Injury Board, Board of Agriculture, Traffic Damage Board and Consumer Complaint Board.

DIVORCE:

Grounds for Separation and Divorce.—Court can terminate cohabitation on demand of both spouses or either spouse and rule that other spouse must leave common home. Such decision is in force not more than two years.

Spouses have right to divorce after consideration period of not less than six months and not more than one year.

Divorce is possible without consideration period when spouses have lived separately last two years. (Law 16/4-1987).

A marriage is dissolved by a lawful court, which at the same time decrees regarding the care and education of the children and the duty to support. (Marriage Law, 13/6-1929).

Proceedings for divorce can be taken in Finland if husband and wife both are Finnish citizens or if plaintiff is Finnish citizen and is or previously was domiciled in Finland. This is also applicable under such circumstances that plaintiff has been domiciled in Finland for the last two years or defendant is domiciled in Finland. Finnish law is applied.

If none of parties is Finnish citizen there must be ground for divorce according to law of country of husband or wife. If one or other has been domiciled in Finland for last two years, only Finnish law is applied. (Law 5/12-1929).

DOWER: See topic Husband and Wife.

ENVIRONMENT:

Finnish environmental legislation is sector-based. Finland does not have comprehensive code of environmental protection. Finnish legislation concerning pollution control is, for example, regulated separately from viewpoints of air and water pollution control, noise abatement, waste management and so on.

Environmental regulation is based on decisions of authorities, including approval of land use plans and granting environmental permits. Authority makes its decision case-by-case, based on general provisions and administrative guidelines.

Because of Finland's membership in EU environmental EU directives shall be implemented in Finland.

Air.—Air Pollution Control Act is main rule concerning protection of air. Most essential means of air pollution control are general regulations issued by Council of State. Regulations set limitation for concentration of substance in emission. General regulations are directly binding on plant operators, importers of fuel, etc.

Public Health Act also controls air pollution caused by stationary plants.

Water.—Rules on water pollution control are included in comprehensive Water Act. Water Court grants permits for water pollution. If permits needed are not granted, polluter may be fined. Water Act does not define precisely what kind of activity needs permit. Permit is needed if activity has banned effect on environment. Banned effects are defined in Water Act.

Waste.—Waste Act regulates generally waste collecting, transport and treatment of waste. Principles of Act apply to recycling and revise of waste and avoiding harm to environment from wastes.

Compensation for Environmental Damage.—Act on Compensation for Environmental Damage has been passed. (Act 737/1994). Act makes it easier to get compensation for damages. Operator, or assignee, is strictly liable for his activities.

EQUALITY:

Law on equality between men and women is in force from Jan. 1st, 1987. (Law 8/8-1986).

Law concerns especially working life but not religious or private life.

Law contains general prohibition against discrimination in working life: Less qualified person of one sex must not be employed instead of better qualified person of opposite sex.

If employer acts against discrimination prohibition compensation of FIM 10,000-30,000 can be awarded discriminated person.

It is also prohibited to announce job for only men or women without acceptable grounds.

As supervising authority acts as equality ombudsman.

EXCHANGE CONTROL:

See topic Foreign Exchange Regulations.

EXECUTIONS:

The highest executive authority is court of first instance. Whether execution can be issued, is determined by proper court of first instance, and in special cases provided by law, by subordinate officer having charge of executions against property.

If one has a final judgment against his adversary in a controverted matter, it can be enforced by execution without delay. However, where a judgment has been secured in a lower court, even though the judgment has not become final, a levy may be made, but the property cannot be sold. Personal property must be levied on before real property, unless attached to the realty. A levy gives right to a certain type of pledge, which in bankruptcy gives a preference to the property levied on. Real property cannot be sold until the judgment is final. Property levied on is sold at execution sale, at which care must be taken not to prejudice the rights of those having better claim to the property than the debt for which the levy was made. (Execution Law, 3/12-1895).

EXECUTORS AND ADMINISTRATION:

See topic Descent and Distribution.

EXEMPTIONS:

All the personal property of a debtor cannot be levied on, and for instance his clothing, bedding, beds, necessary furniture and household utensils, necessary working tools, etc., are exempted. Amount of exempt property is fixed yearly by Ministry of Justice.

Creditor cannot levy on more than one-third of wages of his debtor.

FOREIGN EXCHANGE REGULATIONS:

Summary of Prevailing Exchange Control Regulations.—Prevailing foreign exchange regulations are based on law of Dec. 13, 1985. This law gives right to exchange control in exceptional circumstances, otherwise rules are not applied in practice.

Most foreign exchange transactions allowed without Bank of Finland approval. However, certain financial institutions need approval for specified foreign exchange transactions.

From Oct. 1, 1991 restrictions concerning foreign currency loans taken by private persons or partnerships have been abolished.

Certain banks as authorized "Foreign Exchange Banks" are entitled by Bank of Finland to deal in foreign exchange, e.g., to buy and sell foreign means of payment, assets, etc., to arrange payments between Finland and abroad and to hold in safe custody and deal with foreign assets and property in Finland.

Import of Goods.—Liberation of import has proceeded and import has to a great extent been made free, with the exception of countries which have closed bilateral trade agreements with Finland. Import licenses are granted by the Licensing Authorities and given for that period which corresponds to the terms of delivery according to the contract. Thus the goods shall be imported into the country and the payment effected within the period the license is valid. Upon request the Licensing Authorities can grant an extension to the validity of the license.

Export of Goods.—Export licensing was discontinued in 1962, except for metal scrap, certain food products and ships. Exporters of other products need only submit an export declaration, which is automatically approved except when (a) there are reasons to believe that goods will be re-exported to a third country or that exchange controls are being circumvented; (b) exportation could be in conflict with conditions contained in bilateral agreements.

FOREIGN INVESTMENTS: See topic Aliens.

FOREIGN TRADE REGULATIONS:

See topic Foreign Exchange Regulations.

FRAUDS, STATUTE OF:

Concept unknown in Finland. See topics Claims, Contracts, Deeds, Real Property, Sales.

GARNISHMENT:

See topics Attachment, Executions, Exemptions.

GUARANTY:

By an undertaking of guaranty is meant a contract, by which one person becomes obligated to a second person on the liability of a third person. As to the form of an undertaking of guaranty, the law contains no provisions. It can, therefore, be oral or in writing. A guaranty may be personal, in which case the guarantor guarantees the debtor. Generally, however, a guaranty means a property guaranty, by which the guarantor undertakes in a specified event to pay a certain sum of money. The law of Finland makes a distinction as to personal debt guaranty and the simple ("legal") guaranty. In the first mentioned case, the guarantor undertakes to become bound jointly with the debtor, and in the latter case, the guarantor undertakes to pay any deficiency remaining after execution or bankruptcy of the debtor. In the personal debt guaranty, the guarantor is released unless within 12 months after due date a demand for payment of the debt is made.

If there are several guarantors for the same debt, the guaranty may be joint and several, when each guarantor is liable for himself and for the others, so that the debt may be collected from any one of them; or the guaranty may be per capita, when each guarantor is liable only for his share (pro rata parte). The undertaking is joint and several if the guarantors have not divided the liability among themselves by an express provision.

A guarantor, who has paid the debt, is subrogated to the rights of the creditor as against the debtor and the other guarantors.

HOLIDAYS:

Legal holidays are New Year's Day; Epiphany, Jan. 6th; Good Friday; Easter and second day of Easter; Ascension Day; May 1st; second day of Whitsuntide (or Pentecost); Midsummer's Day, in June; All Saints' Day in Nov.; Christmas Day and second Christmas Day; a legal festival day is Finland's Independence Day, Dec. 6th.

HUSBAND AND WIFE:

Both spouses, after marriage, secure their own surnames or either of spouses may secure surname of other spouse. Spouses are mutually possessed of equal legal rights as right of representation by husband has been abolished. Each spouse has right to make contracts with third persons and in his or her own behalf to sue and defend in courts. Spouses may make contracts between themselves; as of 1992 they may make gifts to each other if gifts are notified to court of first instance.

Marriages contracted prior to Jan. 1, 1930, were governed by the principle of joint ownership. The property of spouses in general belonged to them both. However, by law and by ante-nuptial agreement certain property or certain type of property might

HUSBAND AND WIFE . . . *continued*
belong personally to one or other of spouses. (Law 15/4-1889). In marriages contracted after Jan. 1, 1930, principle of separate property governs. Property which belongs to spouse upon entering marriage, continues to belong to that spouse, and same is true as to property obtained during marriage. Spouses, upon certain conditions, are entitled to control their own property. Rule is that each spouse is solely liable for debts contracted by such spouse.

The spouses have a dower right in the property of each other. A surviving spouse on distribution of the estate receives one-half of the surplus. No dower right exists to property concerning which such provision is made in an ante-nuptial agreement, deed of gift or last will and testament. A spouse may lose the dower right by a criminal act or by conduct injurious to the other spouse. The dower right may be excluded upon demand of one spouse when the other has become bankrupt.

Conveyance of Property.—Spouse may not without written consent from other spouse convey or let real property which is used entirely or mainly as home of spouses.

Neither may spouse without written consent from other spouse convey common home of spouses or chattels intended for mutual use of spouses or work equipment used by other spouse or chattels intended for personal use of other spouse or children.

If such property as defined above is sold without consent buyer must return property without compensation under certain conditions. If common home is rented equal rules apply on conveyance of rental right.

If consent is denied by other spouse without acceptable reason court may rule otherwise. (Law 16/4-1987).

Persons intending to enter matrimony and persons married under the law in force Jan. 1, 1930, may by agreement change the property arrangement which would otherwise exist between them according to the provisions of law. Under the earlier law, such agreement could relate to the share of the spouses or so-called dower right, to their joint estate, and partly concerning the control of property. Under the present law, it may be provided in such agreement that no dower right shall exist to certain property. Such agreement must be in writing and filed with the court for safekeeping.

Under the main rule according to the marriage law in force Jan. 1, 1930, each spouse is solely liable for the debts such spouse has contracted during the marriage or prior thereto. Exceptions are such debts as have been contracted jointly, or debts contracted by either spouse for the support of the family. (Marriage Law, 13/6-1929).

IMMIGRATION:

Residence permit is required for a non-Scandinavian wishing to stay in Finland longer time than agreed in contract for repealing visa system between his home country and Finland (as a rule, three months). Application is filed with local police.

Work permit is required for a non-EEC national wishing to work in Finland. Permit must have been obtained prior to entry to Finland. See also topic Aliens.

INFANCY:

According to Finnish law age of majority is 18. Agreements entered into by minor are invalid until above age is reached. There are some exceptions as regards marriage pact, means earned with own work and contract of employment. Parents or, in their absence, appointed person, act as guardian. Court of first instance can under certain conditions lengthen deficiency in authority up to age 22. Minors below age of 15 cannot be punished for criminal offences and have only subsidiary responsibility for damages. Up to age of 18 there is reduced penalty. Minors below age of 15 can give evidence at court only with consent of latter. See also topic Marriage.

INTEREST:

(Interest Act of Aug. 20, 1982).

Interest Act is applied on money debts with some exceptions. There is no liability to pay interest on debts before due date. If definite date of payment is agreed in advance and payment is not made in due time debtor is liable to pay interest from due date. If no due date is agreed interest is payable when one month has elapsed from day when creditor claimed payment and stated that default of payment includes liability to pay interest.

Rate of interest concerning goods credit reference is interest rate established by Bank of Finland plus 7% per annum, and concerning bank credits agreed rate of interest plus 4%, however, no higher than reference interest rate plus 10%. Regarding other debts it's still possible to agree upon rate of interest.

In case of damages interest is payable one month from day when payee claimed damages and presented statement of facts which reasonably enables payor to consider claim.

In case of wilful damage interest is payable from day when damage occurred. Irrespective of one month period interest is payable from date of lawsuit.

Criminal code prohibits usury.

JOINT STOCK COMPANIES:

Note: Finland is in process of revising its current companies act. Most important anticipated changes are described at end of this topic.

(Company Act of Sept. 29, 1978).

Introductory Provisions.—Finnish joint stock company is corporation carrying on activities with capital contributed shareholders and divided into specific numbers of shares without personal liability of shareholders for obligations of company.

Share capital must not be less than 15,000 Fmk. Share capital may be fixed in articles of association at minimum and maximum. Minimum may not be less than one-fourth of maximum.

Shares shall be issued at equal par value. There must be at least three shares.

Formation.—Company is formed by one or several founders to be Finnish, Icelander, Norwegian, Danish or Swedish citizens resident in Finland or Finnish corporation or foundation. Not more than half of founders may be resident in other Scandinavian countries. Partnership and commandite company may be founder provided partners with personal liability for partnership's or commandite company's obligations are Finnish citizens or citizens of other Scandinavian countries resident in Finland.

Ministry of Trade and Industry may grant other founders, e.g. aliens, permission to subscribe shares.

Founders shall draw up, date and sign deed of formation including articles of association and subscription list. At constituent meeting decision to form company is reached and board of directors and auditors are elected. Company shall apply to Patent and Registration Office for registration not later than six months after decision to form company was made. Total par value of shares subscribed for will be registered as companies share capital. At registration share capital must not be below minimum share capital and half of share capital must be paid.

Prior to registration, company can neither acquire rights nor enter into obligation, nor can it sue, complain or defend in court or before any other authority. Persons acting in company's name before it is registered are personally liable for such action. At registration liability passes to company provided that obligation results from deed of formation or has arisen subsequent to formation of company.

Articles of association shall specify: (a) Name of company, (b) municipality in Finland where company is to be located, (c) objects of company, (d) share capital or minimum and maximum share capital, (e) par value of shares, (f) number, or minimum and maximum numbers, of board members and auditors as well as deputy board members, if any, and for how long period they are elected, (g) manners for convening general meetings of shareholders, (h) matters to be dealt with at annual general meeting of shareholders, and (i) fiscal year.

Articles of association may provide that shareholders or others shall have right to redemption where share has passed to new owner.

Shares—Share certificates shall be signed by board of directors. Signatures may be printed. Certificate shall state name of company, serial number of shares, par value and date of issue. Share certificates may not be issued before full payment and registration.

Share certificate represents title to share. Bona fide holder of share certificate, who can prove his title by unbroken chain of transfers or endorsements in writing from duly registered shareholder to specific person or in blank, is protected as legitimate shareholder and is entitled to be registered as shareholder.

Board of directors shall keep share register in which all shares and shareholders shall be registered. This register, which is open to public, is basis for checking shareholders and their votes at general meeting of shareholders. Shares must be fully paid not later than 12 months after registration of company.

Book-Entry Securities System.—Finnish listed companies, whose shares are quoted on Helsinki Stock Exchange, are required to transfer their shares to book-entry securities system. Requirement does not apply to foreign companies quoted on Helsinki Stock Exchange. Transfer of other companies, including companies quoted on OTC list and Brokers' list is voluntary and requires approval of Central Share Register.

Instruments other than equity-ranked instruments may be transferred to book-entry system at request of registrar representing issuer.

Increase of Share Capital.—Share capital may be increased by subscription of new shares against payment (new issue) or by issue of shares or by increase of par value of existing shares without payment (bonus issue). Resolution to increase share capital shall be adopted at general meeting of shareholders. Act gives detailed provisions as to contents of resolution.

Increase of share capital by bonus issue may be effected by transfer to share capital of: (a) Such amounts as may be distributed as dividends. (b) amounts from revaluation reserve and statutory reserve, or (c) amounts originating from revaluation of value of fixed assets.

Convertible Debt Instruments.—Company may for consideration issue convertible debt instruments or debt instruments with right of option to subscribe to new shares.

Reduction of Share Capital.—Share capital may be reduced for: (a) Transfer to statutory reserve or immediate coverage of loss, (b) repayment to shareholders, or (c) transfer to reserve for purposes to be decided by general meeting of shareholders.

Share capital may be reduced by: (a) Redemption or consolidation of shares, (b) withdrawal of shares without repayment, or (c) reduction in par value of shares with or without repayment.

Acquisition of Own Shares.—Company may not, except in very special cases, acquire its own shares or accept such shares as security. Agreement which violates this prohibition is invalid.

Management of Company.—Management is handled by board of directors and managing director.

Board of directors shall consist of at least three members. If share capital or maximum share capital is less than 1,000,000 Fmk, board may consist of one or two members, provided that at least one deputy is appointed. Board of directors is elected by general meeting of shareholders. Articles of association may stipulate that one or more directors, however less than half of total number of directors, are elected by other procedures.

In company where share capital or maximum share capital amounts to at least 1,000,000 Fmk, board of directors shall appoint managing director. In other companies board of directors may appoint managing director. Managing director does not have to be member of board. Vice managing director may also be appointed. Managing director and at least two-thirds of total number of directors must be Finnish citizens resident in Finland unless Ministry of Trade and Industry permits otherwise.

Board of directors shall represent and sign for company. Board of directors represents company in dealing with third parties, as well as before court and other authorities. Board of directors may authorize director, managing director or any other person to represent and sign for company unless such delegation of authority is prohibited by articles of association. Managing director may always represent and sign for company with regard to measures which are within his duties.

General Meeting of Shareholders.—Shareholders' right to take decisions in company affairs is exercised at general meetings of shareholders. Shareholder may exercise his rights at general meeting of shareholders personally or by proxy. Unless otherwise prescribed in articles of association shareholder has as many votes as he has shares.

See Topical Index in front part of this volume.

JOINT STOCK COMPANIES . . . *continued*

Resolution of general meeting of shareholders shall be adopted by simple majority. In case of tie, chairman has casting vote except that election of directors and auditors shall be decided through drawing of lots. For certain important resolutions qualified majority is required. Annual general meeting of shareholders shall be held within six months from end of each fiscal year. At this general meeting resolutions shall be passed in respect to: (a) Adoption of income statement and balance sheet, (b) approbation of company's profit or loss according to balance sheet, (c) directors' and managing director's discharge from liability, (d) election of directors and auditors, and (e) other matters which according to Companies Act or articles of association shall be dealt with at this meeting.

Extraordinary general meeting of shareholders shall be held whenever board of directors may find it appropriate or when auditor or owners of one-tenth of all shares request this for special purpose.

Auditing.—General meeting of shareholders shall elect one or more auditors. Auditor may be individual or accounting firm. At least one auditor must be Finnish citizen resident in Finland or accounting firm approved by chamber of commerce. In certain cases one auditor has to be auditor approved by chamber of commerce.

Auditor shall render report to general meeting of shareholders for every fiscal year. Auditor's report shall contain, inter alia, statement on directors' and managing director's discharge from liability, statement on adoption of balance sheet, income statement and proposed allocation of company's profit or loss as made in directors' report.

Dividends.—Resolution to distribute dividend shall be adopted at general meeting of shareholders. Dividends may not exceed total amount of profits shown in balance sheet for last fiscal year and other disposable capital less loss shown in balance sheet and amounts to be transferred to statutory reserves.

General meeting of shareholders may not distribute dividends which are higher than proposed or approved by board of directors. However, shareholders representing not less than 10% of share capital may, in certain circumstances, call for distribution of higher dividend according to stipulations in Companies Act, however by no means more than 5% of company's own capital.

Liquidation.—General meeting of shareholders may resolve that company shall be liquidated.

Where board of directors discovers that company's equity capital is less than one-third of share capital, board shall refer as soon as possible to general meeting of shareholders question of liquidating company. Unless balance sheet adopted at annual general meeting during next fiscal year shows that equity capital amounts to half of share capital, board of directors shall, if general meeting does not resolve to liquidate company, apply to court to order liquidation of company.

General meeting of shareholders which resolves or court which orders that company shall be liquidated shall at same time appoint one or more liquidators. Liquidators shall replace board of directors and managing director and shall be responsible for carrying out liquidation.

Auditor's appointment does not terminate by fact that company enters into liquidation.

Act gives detailed provisions for administration of liquidation.

Name of Company.—Name of company shall contain word "osakeyhtiö" or "aktiebolag" or their abbreviation (Oy—Ab) and shall be clearly distinguishable from other names previously entered into Commercial Register. Where name of company is to be registered in two or several languages, each version shall be mentioned in articles of association.

Name of division or other business units may be registered in addition to name of company.

Miscellaneous.—Act contains detailed provisions regarding merger, compulsory transfer of minority shares in subsidiary, damages, penalties and registration.

See also topic Aliens.

Reforms in Companies Act.—Finland is in process of amending its Companies Act to correspond with EC legislation. Finnish government has, after several years of preparation, submitted proposal to Parliament for extensive revision of current Companies Act. Following text describes most important changes in proposal compared to current legislation.

1. Distinction between Public and Private Company.—One of most significant changes is introduction of two different types of limited liability companies. Private limited liability company has minimum share capital of 50,000 marks (approximately 10,000 USD). Public limited liability company has minimum share capital of 500,000 marks (approximately 100,000 USD). Only securities of public company may be offered to public and be publicly traded on stock markets. Development of securities' market and new demands on protection of investors are main reasons behind this division.

As general rule all existing limited liability companies are considered private companies when changes come into force, with exception of companies whose issued securities are currently publicly traded.

2. Payment of Share Capital.—Rules concerning payment and registration of share capital will be changed. Under current system only half of share capital has to be paid when company is registered with Trade Register. Under new rules all of share capital that is to be registered has to be paid at time of registration. If property, other than cash, is given as payment of shares statement from certified public accountant must be obtained.

3. Group Aspects.—According to proposal definition of group is to be changed. Decisive factor for formation of group is to be actual authority. In addition, corporations under parent company's authority other than limited liability companies also belong to group. This is significant expansion of group definition compared to current legislation.

4. New Financial Instruments.—Proposal includes rules whereby certain commonly used financial instruments are defined. Reforms are proposed in order to meet national and international demands of corporate finance, and after reforms mezzanine financing especially will become easier.

4.1. Preference Share.—Introduction of preference share is proposed. Preference share would give right to vote only in matters defined either in law or in Articles of Association. According to proposal preference share would give right to vote only when company's general meeting would vote on changing Articles of Association, if proposed change would change preference share's right compared to other shares.

Preference share has better right to company's profit than normal shares. It may be prescribed in Articles of Association of company that dividend may be paid retroactively. In liquidation, however, only nominal value of preference share is returned, unless otherwise prescribed in Articles of Association.

4.2. Preferred Capital Loan.—Proposal includes rules governing preferred capital loan. Loan is defined as liability but can be marked as equity item in balance sheet of company.

Loan can be repaid only under certain preconditions. During company's activities loan equity can be returned only if full coverage for company's restricted equity capital and other undistributive capital can be secured. Further, loan has lowest priority not including share capital of company in liquidation or bankruptcy. No security can be issued for preferred capital loan.

Preferred capital loan is expected to be widely used tool in Finnish corporate finance.

4.3. Options.—According to proposal, options can be issued without any loan, possibility not allowed under current legislation.

4.4. Acquiring Own Shares.—According to proposal, company may acquire its own shares with its equity. However, public company cannot normally own more than 5% of its shares or votes. In addition, public company can only acquire or sell its own shares in stock markets one week after having issued official announcement thereof.

5. Changing of Company Form.—Rules governing merger compensation are to be amended. According to proposal in cases when merger compensation consists of other than shares in receiving company merging company's shareholders have right to get part of compensation in cash.

5.1. Mergers.—Further, merger agreement is to be replaced with merger plan, in which economic situation of parties and merger compensation are to be defined.

5.2. Divisions.—Division of companies is to be eased through new rules allowing company to divide its businesses into several companies without liquidation, as current legislation demands. According to proposal division can be carried out either by forming two or more new companies or by forming one or more companies of part of old company.

5.3. Redemption of Shares.—Right and duty to redemption of shares will apply to anyone owning directly or through group, controlling while dividing company is liquidated over 90% of company's shares and its total number of votes. However, shares that do not give right to attend company's general meeting are not taken into consideration.

6. Changing of Articles of Association.—Procedure to change rights of share class in relation to other share class is to be simplified. Current rule of approval of nine-tenths of share class at company's general meeting is proposed to be lowered to two-thirds. However, approval also has to be obtained from owners representing more than 50% of share class.

Certain company restructurings including mergers, divisions and purchase of company's own shares require qualified voting majority in each class of shares.

7. Obligation to Disclose.—When new law is enacted, each company is obliged each year to file its financial statements with Trade Register. In addition, public companies are required to prepare semiannual financial statements. Detail worth mentioning is that all companies are obliged to mention registered business name, domicile, address and trade register number in letters and blank forms that company uses. Furthermore, if company is in liquidation company must mention that as well.

8. Coming into Force of Changes.—As EC treaty of accession does not stipulate any transfer time for implementation of company law directives changes are proposed to come into force as soon as possible, although at earliest in 1997.

JUDGMENTS:

With reference to enforcing a judgment of a foreign court, the President of the Republic may, in accordance with a treaty entered into with a foreign country or upon the principle of reciprocity, direct that a judgment of a foreign court by which a plaintiff or intervening party has been ordered to pay court costs, must be enforced in Finland. The enforcement of such a judgment should be requested of the officer having charge of executions either through diplomatic channels or the party may present a petition, and the request must be accompanied by the document, the enforcement of which is requested. At the same time there must be presented a certificate from an official of the foreign country stating that the judgment is final, and a certificate that the first mentioned certificate has been issued by the proper official. See also topic Treaties.

LABOR RELATIONS:

Main rules concerning protection of workmen and other employees as follows: Employment contracts concluded individually between employers and employees are regulated by Employment Contracts Act of Apr. 30, 1970. Provisions of this Act are applicable unless agreed otherwise, but this Act also contains a number of mandatory provisions. Stipulation under which either party consents to refrain from membership of an association is void according to Act, which thus guarantees freedom of association. As to collective agreements there is Collective Agreements Act of June 7, 1946. Disputes concerning collective agreements are settled by Labor Court. (Labor Court Act of June 7, 1946). Working time is legally fixed in General Hour of Works Act of Aug. 2, 1946 to be eight hours daily and at maximum of forty hours weekly. A number of statutes contain provisions regarding working time under special circumstances and in certain occupations. Working hours in agriculture and forestry are not regulated by legislation. Annual overtime up to 200 hours is allowed with increased wages for overtime and Sunday work. There are special provisions concerning child labor and female labor. Child and female labor is prohibited in certain occupations. According to Employee's Annual Holiday Act of Mar. 3, 1973 every employee is entitled to two days' (after one year's employment $2^1/_2$ days') paid annual vacation for each month during which he has worked for more than 14 days. Most important item of legislation in field of employee protection is Protection of Labor Act of June 28, 1958. Employee

LABOR RELATIONS . . . *continued*

protection is enforced by industrial inspectors. Labor Council grants exceptions from provisions concerning employee protection.

See also law on equality, topic Equality.

Act of Feb. 3, 1984 regulates procedure for termination of employment contract. Act contains, inter alia, stipulations regarding compulsory negotiations between parties if employee considers termination unlawful as well as rules concerning compensation for unlawful terminations.

Compulsory pension insurance for employees was adopted by Acts of July 8, 1961 and Feb. 9, 1962, premiums to be paid by employers.

See also law on equality, topic Equality.

LAW REPORTS:

The judgments of the Supreme Court are published in its yearbook. The judgments of the Supreme Administrative Court are likewise published in its yearbook. Complete records of the decisions of lower courts are not published.

LEGISLATURE:

The legislative power in Finland is administered by Parliament together with the President of the Republic. The initiative to a new law may be taken by the President, the Council of State or by an individual member of the Parliament. After being passed in Parliament a law must be ratified by the President but if he refuses ratification the law becomes valid if it is passed by the Parliament again after new general elections.

The President of the Republic and the Council of State can also issue decrees in less important matters without the assistance of Parliament.

LICENSES:

See topics Aliens; Foreign Exchange Regulations.

LIENS:

A landlord has the right to retain goods which the tenant has upon leased land or in a building until the payment of rent. A similar right of retention belongs to a house owner and the keeper of an inn to the goods of a tenant found in the house or inn, and an artisan to chattels on which he has made repairs. An attorney at law may retain the papers of his client until the expenses and fee have been paid.

LIMITATION OF ACTIONS:

A claim becomes outlawed according to the general rule in ten years. The fact that the time prescribed for payment is longer than ten years, does not prevent the claim from becoming outlawed. The running of the statute of limitations may be prevented even by the creditor reminding the debtor of his claim.

Criminal action must be taken either one, two, five, ten or 25 years after the crime has been committed, depending on prescribed punishment of the crime in question.

Compensation claim due to crime should generally be made within ten years, but if crime is prescribed later, action can be taken within that time.

MARRIAGE:

Persons must have reached age of 18 to be married, unless Ministry of Justice for special reasons has allowed exception from age limit.

A marriage may be solemnized by a church or civil wedding. Prior to marriage, population register authorities must determine that no impediments to marriage exist.

The freedom of marriage is restricted by impediments such as consanguinity or affinity, relationship of adoption, mental disorder and defectiveness and former subsisting marriage.

MINES AND MINERALS:

(Mining Act of Sept. 17, 1965).

Natural mineral resources are conceded to the claimers, i.e., to the finders of the mineral resources. The legislation is thus built on a claiming-system and not on a concession-system as in several other countries. A prospector must announce his claim to the local bailiff and after this file it within one year with the Ministry of Trade and Industry. The concession will be granted to him if the formal conditions are fulfilled.

Aliens may only be granted concessions on special application with the consent of the Council of State.

MONOPOLIES AND RESTRAINT OF TRADE:

On Sept. 1, 1992 new law on Limitation of Competition came into force. With new law Finland has mainly introduced principle of prohibiting collusions between undertakings or any other arrangements which have as their object or effect prevention, restriction or distortion of competition. Therefore all sorts of cartels, including fixing of purchase or selling prices, limiting of production and sharing of markets, are prohibited.

Upon application Competition Office can make exceptions to prohibition. Exception is possible if limitation of competition contributes to improving of production or distribution of goods or to promoting technical or economic progress, while allowing consumers fair share of resulting benefit.

Prohibited also is abuse of dominant position on specific market.

On request undertakings or associations of undertakings are obliged to give Competition Office all information and documentation necessary to investigate case of limitation of competition. If undertaking or association of undertakings break rules set out in law, fines up to 10% of each undertaking's involved annual turnover can be imposed.

Competition Office can oblige undertaking in dominant position on market to inform Office of Business Acquisitions which may have effect on competition.

In preparing law, competition laws and practice of EC have been observed. Competition Office pays attention to practice of EC competition authorities when deciding whether Finnish Competition Law has been infringed in specific case. Unfair trade practices are regulated by Incompatible conduct in business Act of Dec. 22, 1978.

From beginning of year 1995 Finland is member of EU. EU competition rules are applicable.

See also topic Treaties.

MORTGAGES:

A mortgage is an act by an official by which the creditor is given the right of pledge to the real property of a debtor for the security of a debt, or by which are strengthened certain insecure chattel rights in such manner that they are not defeated upon change of ownership to the real property.

A mortgage as security for debt may be secured even without the consent of the debtor by one having due from the owner of real property a certain sum of money or goods or by one who has the right to secure from such owner a certain income or pension. A mortgage is lawful on any freehold estate in the rural sections, on a building and building lot in the cities and, to a fractional part of the property and under certain conditions, on a building or other establishment situated on the land of another. A mortgage may also be given on a leasehold estate and on buildings erected thereunder, if the leasehold is assignable without the consent of the lessor. See also topic Husband and Wife, subhead Conveyance of Property.

A mortgage is petitioned from court of first instance. Mortgage does not have to be renewed. It gives preference from date mortgage application proceeding is commenced. Mortgage may also be discharged either in part or entirely. Foregoing applies to mortgage as security for right of use as well as mortgage as security for debt. (Mortgage Law, 9/11-1868).

A bus or a truck that has been registered according to Motor Vehicle Law may be mortgaged for a debt. Such a mortgage is obtained from authority with which vehicle is registered. (Car Mortgage Law, 12/12-1972).

A mortgage may also be granted on a vessel, on a private railroad or on real property as security for right to cut timber, and as security for right to partition a specified area. Under certain conditions, it is possible to obtain ratification of a mortgage covering a growing forest, without subjecting the realty as such to liability for the mortgage.

MOTOR VEHICLES:

A motor vehicle, before its use, must be approved at the proper inspection, registered within a specified time and provided with an identifying license plate. The general rule is that the owner of the motor vehicle is liable for any damage to persons or property arising from such vehicle even though he is not the cause of said damage. The owner of a registered motor vehicle, as security for the payment of the damages which he or his driver may be called upon to pay, must take out and keep in force insurance in an insurance institution approved by the state. (Motor Vehicle Law 4/10-1957 and Traffic Insurance Law 26/6-1959).

NEGOTIABLE INSTRUMENTS:

See topic Bills and Notes.

NOTARIES PUBLIC:

The duties are exercised in the cities by the magistrates and by the bailiffs in the rural districts. (Law Aug. 6, 1960).

PARTNERSHIP:

So-called open company or mercantile (general partnership) has to have minimum of two partners who carry on trade together on basis of written partnership agreement and who are personally liable for obligations of partnership. Partner cannot assign his partnership interest without consent of all other partners. Consent of all partners is also required for accepting new partner into partnership.

Limited partnership (commandite company) must have minimum of two partners, general partner and limited (silent) partner. General partner is personally liable for obligations of partnership, but silent partner's obligations are limited to amount of his investment in partnership.

Firm name of partnership must clearly differ from any other firm name already recorded in commercial register.

Act on so-called open companies and commandite companies came into force on Jan. 1, 1989. Act brought no major changes to previous law, but it is codification of previous customary law and prescribes especially procedure regarding dissolution of such company.

See topics Commercial Register; Aliens, subhead Corporations Owned or Controlled by Aliens.

PATENTS:

Patents can be granted for new inventions that can be used in industry. Before invention can be considered as new, it is required that it differs from what is known prior to date application for new patent was filed. Patent may be granted to inventor or his assignees. If inventor resides abroad, law requires representative resident in Finland. Written application for patent is filed with patent authority. Application must contain explanation of invention (with necessary drawings); name and address of inventor; detailed claim for patent protection in Finnish or Swedish; and finally, application fee. Foreign inventor must appoint patent representative in which case power of attorney has to be filed. When application has been accepted in preliminary manner for public notice of same, exposition fee must be paid by applicant. Result of public notice of application statements against same must be filed in writing within three months to patent authority. When final decision has been given, granted patent is registered and public notice given.

Patent is valid for period of 20 years from day application was filed. Yearly patent fee must be paid. If patent is not exercised to considerable extent within three years from date it was granted or four years from date application was filed, court may upon application by any other party grant a forced licence for applicant to use patent on terms and conditions determined by court. As a rule in matters concerning patent right, City Court of Helsinki is proper authority. Patent Law of Dec. 15, 1967 has been am'd by Law of June 6, 1980. By virtue of this amendment rules on international patent applications were inserted. (Patent Cooperation Treaty of June 19, 1970). In order to complete international application as far as Finland is concerned, applicant must

See Topical Index in front part of this volume.

PATENTS . . . *continued*
within 20 months from filing date of international application or, if priority is claimed, from date of required priority, file with patent authority translation in Finnish or Swedish of international application and pay stipulated fee.

PLEDGES:

The right of pledge is such a right to a chattel as entitles the creditor to use the sale price of the chattel pledged in order to obtain a certain sum of money. Changes in title to pledged chattels have in general no effect on rights of pledgee. Right of pledge survives even though the debt secured by pledged chattel is outlawed. Both real and personal property may be pledged. To preserve right of pledge to real property against new owners of realty, mortgage is necessary. (See topic Mortgages.) Pledging of chattel requires delivery of chattel to creditor, except in cases where enterprise mortgage is permissible. (See topic Chattel Mortgages.) Use of pledge chattel for payment of debt is accomplished by converting chattel to cash. Sale of chattel by auction is usually stipulated in agreement made at time of pledging. Real property is sold at judicial sale.

Enterprise Mortgage Law, 24/8-1984 came into force on Jan. 1, 1986. Personal property of all enterprises and other business of which notification is filed with commercial register may be mortgaged for payment of debt. Mortgage comprises chattels, immaterial rights, rights to use specified chattel and claims belonging to enterprise.

Enterprise mortgage gives preference in event property is sold at judicial sale or in case of debtor's bankruptcy. Enterprise mortgage is secured by application to Patent and Register Office in Helsinki. Application is made on form fixed by registration authorities and it must include note and debtor's consent to mortgage. Enterprise mortgage is valid until it is discharged.

PRESCRIPTION:

See topic Limitation of Actions.

PRINCIPAL AND AGENT:

There is no mandatory representation by attorney-at-law in legal proceedings in Finland. Both parties to controversy, plaintiff as well as defendant, have right to use attorney. Attorney or agent who conducts litigation must be authorized by his principal. Written authorization is required. This does not concern advocates. See topic Attorneys and Counselors. Authorization is given in form of power of attorney.

Form of general power of attorney is open power of attorney. It is not necessary to specify purpose of which power of attorney is issued, and therefore, it is sufficient to use wording: "open power of attorney."

A procuration (prokura) is an oral or written authorization which a mercantile company enrolled in the commercial register has given to a specified person and has expressly declared to be a procuration. A person authorized under procuration (prokurist) has the authority to act for his principal in all things appertaining to the conduct of the principal's business. Unless expressly authorized, prokurist cannot sell, mortgage or pledge his principal's real property. In signing name of principal, prokurist must add thereto, to indicate procuration, letters "p. p." or words "per procuram". Entry of procuration in commercial register is not essential, but if it is reported, entry of alteration or revocation of such procuration becomes mandatory. It is inherent in procuration that mentioning it as such notifies third person of content of authorization.

Commercial Representatives.—(Act of May 8, 1992). As stated in Act, commercial representative is one who as agent for principal has undertaken to promote, for principal's account, sales of goods by obtaining purchase offers for principal or by concluding sales agreements in principal's name. Commercial representative is either agent with permanent place of business or salesman.

General.—Act is applied only if nothing contrary follows from contract or from custom of trade.

Agency agreement shall be made in writing if one of parties so requests.

If application of any provision in agency agreement would obviously be repugnant to sound business practice or otherwise unreasonable, provision may be modified or set aside.

Both agent and principal are obliged to inform each other of circumstances which might be of importance regarding sales work.

Commission.—Agent has right to commission while agency agreement is in force for all sales agreements which he has concluded or which otherwise can be attributed to his cooperation. Even after termination of agency agreement agent has equal right if buyer's offer has reached principal before termination of agency agreement. If sales agreement has been concluded after termination of agency agreement, but it is based on work performed by agent while agency agreement was in force, agent is entitled to so-called after commission. Amount of after commission is, provided that agency agreement has been in force for more than a year, considered to be three months average commission of previous year if no other evidence is produced and if period of notice of termination is less than six months.

Agent, who has exclusive rights to operate within specified territory, is entitled to receive commission for all sales agreements concluded without his cooperation with customers from that territory or of that clientele.

If no rate of commission has been agreed upon, commission shall be fixed according to what is commonly paid for similar or equivalent services at agent's place of business.

Termination.—Agency agreement concluded for fixed period of time expires if period agreed upon has elapsed. If agency agreement is concluded for indefinite period of time, it can be terminated after three months from end of calendar month during which notice was delivered. If agency agreement has been in force for less than a year, period of notice is, correspondingly, one month. On certain important grounds, a few of which are listed in Act, agency agreement may be rescinded forthwith. Even though there is no ground for rescission, contracting party may still make agency agreement expire prematurely, but he has to compensate other party for damages thus caused.

If rescission of agency agreement is result of party's wilful or negligent act or agreement has lapsed because of bankruptcy of party, other party is entitled to compensation.

If agent, on basis of agreement made with principal or in mutual understanding with him has invested money in buildings, stocks, machinery etc. in order to fulfil agency agreement, agent, if he, because of expiry of agency agreement cannot have these investment costs covered, has right to receive special reasonable compensation for loss thus caused to him. If agreement is rescinded by principal owing to wilful or negligent behaviour of agent, agent does not have this right.

Act further states in detail rights and duties arising from agency contract, time and method of calculation and payment of commission and about apparent authority of agent and principal's relationship to third parties.

Act took effect on 1st of Nov. 1992 and is not applied, unless otherwise agreed and with exception of a few provisions, to agency contracts which were in force on that day.

Membership in EU brought EU rules on agency in force in Finland.

REAL PROPERTY:

The law of Finland draws a sharp distinction between real property and personal property. This distinction is important, for instance, in inheritance, matrimonial and tax law matters, in questions concerning property under mortgage, the form of a sale, etc. As real property are considered land and farms in the rural districts, the appurtenances and buildings of a farm in the rural districts, the buildings and lots in cities, the land and buildings within the city limits, which are on the so-called city conditional land. As real property is also included growing timber and all chattels in buildings which are attached to walls, ceilings, floors, etc., in such manner that they cannot be removed without injury to the realty.

RECORDS:

There is new computer-based real property register. Information in database is valid as evidence and presumed to be correct. All juridical acts pertaining to real property must be recorded in database.

In addition there are kept an association register, a ship register, a patent register, a register of matrimonial or ante-nuptial agreements, a motor vehicle register, etc.

See topic Commercial Register.

Births, deaths and marriages are, until Finland establishes a National Registry of Persons, still registered with the local parish priest, who for a nominal fee will issue certificates as to birth, death and marital status of any member of this parish. The registration regarding persons not belonging to the church is kept by County Registrars. These certificates are accepted as legal evidence by the Finnish courts.

REPORTS: See topic Law Reports.

SALES:

General.—Subject matter of sale may be either real or personal property.

A sale of real property requires a prescribed form. It must be in writing and there must be two witnesses (one official) to the sale. Usually, there is prepared in connection with the sale, in addition to the deed, a written contract of sale. When the sale has been thus completed, the buyer secures for the sale a proclamation, which means notice of the sale by means of having the sale proclaimed by a court. Title passes, however, immediately when the sale is made.

Sales of personal property are not restricted to any set form. The sale may be made either in writing or orally. A sale of personal property may be either the sale of individual property or a brokerage sale, in which one party agrees to procure for the other party either a specified quantity of described goods or a specified quantity from a certain stock of goods. In the sale of personal property, unless it is a brokerage sale, title passes to the buyer at the moment the sale is completed.

If a part of the purchase price of real property is unpaid, the real property becomes pledged for its payment with a preference for a period of time prescribed by law.

Sales of Goods (Act of Mar. 27, 1987).—Act applies to sale and exchange of chattel unless otherwise agreed or usage or trading practice prevails. Act is applied only if nothing to contrary follows from Consumer Protection Act.

Delivery is to be made at seller's place of business or residence. If goods are to be transported delivery takes place when handed over to buyer or to carrier. If no time is agreed performance must be made within reasonable time from date of purchase. Either party may withhold performance until performance by other party is tendered. Risk of loss passes on delivery unless otherwise agreed or implied. Goods shall be suitable for same purpose as goods of same kind normally are used. In case goods are sold "in existent shape" (as they are) delivery is deemed defective if goods are in considerably worse condition than buyer had reason to expect considering price and other circumstances. If no price is fixed buyer must pay what is reasonable considering nature and quality of goods, market price and other circumstances.

Delay in performance may entitle buyer to claim fulfillment or cancel contract and claim damages. Right to cancel on account of delay arises only if breach of contract is of essential importance to buyer and seller must have realized this.

Seller is not obliged to perform delayed delivery if there are insurmountable obstacles to delivery or delivery would cause unreasonable sacrifice. Buyer must claim fulfillment of delayed delivery within reasonable time. Unless buyer, when asked if willing to accept delayed delivery, answers without unreasonable delay, right of delivery is forfeited. If delivery already made is found to have been delayed, buyer's right to cancel contract or claim damages is forfeited unless intention to do so is declared within reasonable time after buyer received information of delivery.

If defective goods are delivered and this is not dependent on buyer or circumstances on his part, buyer may claim rectification, re-delivery, price reduction or cancel contract. Besides he may claim damages. Buyer is liable to examine as soon as possible after delivery of goods. Shall goods be transported from place of delivery, buyer may examine goods after arrival. Notification of defects must be given within reasonable time after buyer has noticed or should have noticed defect. Notwithstanding

SALES . . . *continued*
buyer's above mentioned obligation to examine goods and complain, right of action remains if seller is guilty of gross negligence or has acted against faith and honour.

Buyer may claim rectification if this does not cause seller unreasonable costs or inconvenience. Right to claim re-delivery on account of defect does not arise if breach of contract is of minor importance for buyer and seller has realized or should have realized this. If seller does not rectify, buyer is entitled to compensation for having goods rectified. Although buyer does not claim rectification or re-delivery seller is entitled to take respective measures if this does not cause buyer unreasonable inconvenience and buyer is reimbursed for his costs.

If stipulations re rectification or re-delivery do not apply or seller fails to take either measure within reasonable time after buyer's notification, buyer is entitled to reduction of price. Right to cancel arises only if breach of contract is of essential importance to buyer and seller realized or should have realized this. Right to cancel is contingent upon notice within reasonable time after buyer became or should have become aware of defect.

If buyer fails to pay in time seller may claim performance or cancel contract and claim damages. He is also entitled to interest and, under certain circumstances, to keep goods.

Seller may cancel contract for late payment if buyer's breach of contract is essential. If goods are in buyer's possession seller may cancel contract only if seller reserved such right or buyer refused to take delivery of goods.

Right to cancel contract for late payment or buyer's failure to take delivery is forfeited unless intention to do so is declared before buyer has executed his duties.

If party's actions or economic circumstances after sale have become such that there are reasonable reasons to presume that party will not fulfill essential part of his duties, other party has right to cancel his performance, if opposite party does not give acceptable guarantee for his fulfillment of contract. Similar rules apply if there are reasons to presume that breach of contract will occur, and other party would have right to cancel contract on basis of breach.

If party has gone bankrupt and has not yet fulfilled its duties notice shall be received from bankrupt's estate whether estate will fulfill. If estate within reasonable time gives notice that it will fulfill and gives acceptable guaranty for its fulfillment, sale may not be cancelled. If goods are delivered to buyer or his estate after bankruptcy, seller can claim goods be returned unless payment is made immediately.

Compensation for breach of contract includes compensation for costs, price-difference, lost profit and other direct or indirect loss. Indirect loss is among others loss caused by reduction of production or turnover, loss caused by fact that goods cannot be used as intended, lost profit because of nonfulfillment of contract with third party, loss caused by damage to other goods or similar unexpected loss.

Party suffering damage shall try to minimize its loss. If buyer does not fetch goods in time seller shall take care of goods on buyer's account. Same rule applies to buyer if he wishes to refuse acceptance of goods he already has received. In both cases seller and buyer have right to compensation for costs. If it is not possible to take care of goods or to continue taking care of them, goods may be sold. Surplus shall be paid to other party.

This law is in force from Jan. 1st, 1988. On contracts made before that day former law shall apply.

Consumer Protection (Act of Jan. 20, 1978).—Consumer Protection Act concerns supply, sale and marketing of commodities to consumers for private use. Act prohibits marketing practices which are incompatible with good marketing standards or otherwise unfair to consumers, for example untrue or misleading information, offers combined with gifts or casual benefits which imply that buyer buys several goods or makes effort to buy something else as well. Consumer Ombudsman and Market Court supervise that Act is observed. Market Court may fine seller who does not observe Act. Consumer cannot be deprived of these rights by contract. Seller's liability for damages is judged according to normal liability principles and implies seller's negligence.

Product Liability (Act of Sept. 1, 1991).—Entrepreneur (importer, manufacturer and in some cases seller of products) is obliged to compensate any and all damages caused by product which they have imported, manufactured or sold irrespective of negligence. Law is in conformity with EC-regulations except that there is no self risk in Finland for damages caused to objects.

Warranties.—See topic Guaranty.

International Sale of Goods.—United Nations Convention on Contracts for the International Sale of Goods, in force on Dec. 15, 1987. See topic Treaties and Part VII, Selected International Conventions.

SEALS:

Although many courts and departments use their own seals on official documents they have really no effect on the legality of documents as Finnish law contains no provisions concerning seals.

SEQUESTRATION: See Attachment.

SHIPPING:

Governed principally by Maritime Law of July 15, 1995.

This law applies also to coastal and domestic traffic. Ships are considered Finnish if Finn or Finnish corporation owns more than 6/10 of ship.

A central register is maintained of all Finnish ships of at least 15 meters long. This register contains information regarding ownership, etc.

As a rule the shipowner is personally liable for all debts he or the master incurs for the shipping company. In many cases, however, the shipowner's responsibility is restricted to the ship and freight, this applying to debts incurred by the captain in that capacity without the shipowner's power of attorney. The same applies to damage which the captain or the crew have caused through mistakes or neglect in their duties, as well as loans which the captain in cases of need obtain to continue the journey, protect the cargo, or carry it further. The master of a ship has, while away from the home port, a wide legal power of attorney to act on behalf of the shipowner and even to incur indebtedness.

Based on regulations in the law, there arise pledge rights in ship and freight or in loaded cargo as security for certain claims. Under this class come the claims, mentioned in the foregoing paragraph, as well as claims for salvage and master's and crew's claims for wages.

STATUTES:

The law of Finland is based in a large measure upon the codification of the law of Sweden from the year 1734, which has, however, been greatly changed and amplified by newer legislation since Finland was separated from Sweden in 1809.

TAXATION:

Direct Taxes.—

Major changes in tax reform effective from 1995, including division of tax rates 28% for private individuals concerning earned income and investment income. Latter has fixed tax rate of 28%.

National income tax is the most important of direct taxes. It is proportional for corporations and progressive for individuals. Income tax rate for corporations is flat tax rate 28%. All taxes told (including local income tax and church tax), effective tax burden for individuals may amount to 65%.

Corporate income taxation is governed by Law on Taxation of Income from Economic Activity of 1968 (revised from Jan. 1, 1993). This law contains broad notion of income. In principle, all realized capital gains are taxable in net corporate result, according to fixed 28% tax rate. Partnerships are totally transparent legal entities taxed on partners. All costs and losses are deductible if related to procurement of income. Personal living expenses, taxes and hidden profit distribution are not deductible. Losses are carried forward within ten years. Starting from Jan. 1, 1995 income from practically all tax haven companies is taxed in Finland.

Finland has full imputation system (avoir fiscal). Principal of system is that company profit distributed as dividend is taxed at corporate tax rate. This tax is credited against resident shareholders tax liability, resulting in extra tax or tax refund depending on receiver's tax percentage.

Taxable income of individual is determined in accordance with person's net income. However, individuals are entitled to some special deductions. Married persons are taxed separately. Gain on sale of real estate and personal estate are taxed as investment income (28% tax rate). Gains of selling one's own house are tax exempt under certain conditions.

Real estate tax is from beginning of 1993 levied upon owning real estate, with express exceptions mentioned in law. Real estate is defined as any independent registration unit land owning. Law also applies on buildings situated on real estate. Tax percentage is decided by and the tax is paid to municipality where real estate is situated. Percentages normally vary between 0.20 and 0.80% of tax value of real estate (lower percentage limits, 0.10-0.40%, for housing).

Net wealth tax is assessed on all assets of monetary value belonging to individuals and partnerships. Taxpayer may deduct his liabilities; nonresident, however, may deduct only liabilities connected with assets in Finland.

Local income tax is a proportional tax collected from every natural person or person pursuing business from a permanent establishment in municipality. Rate varies from 15 to 20% depending on municipality.

Church tax is imposed on basis of taxable profit for local taxation. Tax rate is about 1% payable by individual members of church. All persons between 16 and 63 years of age must pay national pensions premiums and health insurance premiums.

Among direct taxes payable to State is inheritance and gift tax which is progressive and depending on consanguinity between parties concerned.

State income and wealth tax, local income tax, church tax and national pensions and health insurance premiums are collected during tax year through a prepayment system. Employer is obliged to withhold these taxes from all wages paid to his employees. In connection with these withholdings, employer must pay to State an employer's social security premium.

Direct taxation is carried out by municipal tax bureaus. Appeals against their decisions and proceedings can be made to higher authorities and finally to Supreme Administrative Court which handles tax cases as highest instance.

Indirect Taxes.—

New Value Added Tax Act.—Act came into force June 1, 1994. Main difference from old Turnover Tax Act is that practically all services are taxable.

Excise Duties.—Main excise duties are those on liquid fuels and tobacco. In addition, excise tax is payable on sweets, some confectionery products, malt beverages, spirits, wine made of berries and mineral beverages.

Miscellaneous Taxes.—There are furthermore a great number of different miscellaneous taxes and duties such a stamp duties, registration fees, fees of governmental offices and officials, motorcar taxes, credit tax etc. (Income and Net Wealth Tax Law 29/12/1988; Municipal Laws 8/12-1873 and 15/6-1898; Law on the Taxation of Income from Economic Activity 24/6-68; Inheritance and Gift Tax Law 12/7-40; Turnover Tax Act 22/3-91 and Taxation Law 12/12-58). 15% withholding tax is levied on interest payment paid to residents. See also topic Treaties.

TRADEMARKS:

(Law, 10.1.1964).

Trademarks, which may be either pictorial or wordmarks, are registered in black and white or color for period of ten years, and renewed for ten years at a time. Foreign applicants must have agent residing in Finland. Application is filed with Trademark Office in Helsinki. City Court of Helsinki handles all matters which concern trademark disputes involving foreign owners of trademarks. On filing, registration fee of 1.100 FIM plus fee of 400 FIM for each class, must be deposited. So called home certificate is, however, needed for certain countries. Renewal application must be followed by fee of 1.250 FIM and fee of 600 FIM for each additional class.

TREATIES:

Finland has acceded to following treaties concerning legal assistance: Convention Relating to Civil Procedure (1 Mar. 1954, Hague), Convention on Service Abroad of

See Topical Index in front part of this volume.

TREATIES . . . *continued*
Judicial and Extrajudicial Documents in Civil or Commercial Matters (15 Nov. 1965, Hague), Convention on Civil Procedure (17 July 1905, Hague) and Protocol concerning accession thereto (4 July 1924, Hague), Convention on Settlement of Investment Disputes between States and Nationals of other States (18 Mar. 1965, Washington).

Finland is party to following treaties concerning recognition and enforcement of foreign decisions: Inter-Nordic Treaty on Recognition and Enforcement of Court Decisions of Another Member Country (Copenhagen 16 Mar. 1932), Convention on Recovery Abroad of Maintenance (20 June 1956, New York), Inter-Nordic Treaty on Recovery of Maintenance (Oslo 23 Mar. 1962), Convention concerning Recognition and Enforcement of Decisions relating to Maintenance Obligations toward Children (15 Apr. 1958, Hague), Convention on jurisdiction and enforcement of judgments in civil and commercial matters (Lugano Sept. 16, 1988).

Finland is also a party to Convention on Recognition and Enforcement of Foreign Arbitral Awards (10 June 1958, New York).

Finland has ratified agreement on European Economic Area. Agreement has come into force Jan. 1, 1994.

Since Jan. 1, 1995 Finland has been member of European Union and therefore EU conventions apply in Finland.

See also Selected International Conventions section.

Tax Conventions.—Tax conventions for avoidance of double taxation exist between Finland and following countries: Australia, Austria, Barbados, Belgium, Brazil, Bulgaria, Canada, China, Czech Republic, Denmark, Egypt, Estonia, the Faroe Islands, Federal Republic of Germany, France, Great Britain, Greece, Hungary, Iceland, India, Indonesia, Ireland, Israel, Italy, Japan, Korea, Latvia, Lithuania, Luxembourg, Malaysia, Malta, Morocco, The Netherlands, New Zealand, Norway, Philippines, Poland, Portugal, Romania, Russia, Singapore, South Africa, Spain, Sri Lanka, Sweden, Switzerland, Tanzania, Thailand, Turkey, Ukraine, USA, Yugoslavia, Zambia.

Agreements covering only income derived from sea and air transport have been made with Argentina.

There are also agreements on death duties and gift taxes with several countries.

In 1955, Finland's application for membership in United Nations was accepted. Finland joined in 1950 General Agreement of Tariffs and Trade (GATT) and in 1961 became associated member of European Free Trade Association (EFTA). In 1969 Finland joined the OECD.

See also Selected International Conventions section.

International Sale of Goods.—United Nations Convention on Contracts for the International Sale of Goods, in force on Dec. 15, 1987. See topic Sales and Part VII, Selected International Conventions.

TRUSTS:

Finnish law does not know trusts of the sorts used in U. S. A.

WILLS:

Right to dispose by will belongs to: (1) Person who has attained age of 18 years; (2) person who is or has been married even though he or she is younger than 18 years; (3) person who has attained age of 15 years regarding such property that has accumulated through his or her own earnings.

A will must be made in writing with two witnesses simultaneously present. The witnesses must sign the will after testator has signed it or acknowledged his signature. The witnesses must know that they have witnessed a will, but they need not know its contents. If a will in case of emergency cannot be executed in such form, a "will of emergency" may be made orally in the presence of two witnesses, or even without witnesses, by testator's own hand. The will of emergency becomes illegal, if testator does not within three months after the state of emergency ceased make a will in the manner above. All these regulations also apply to alterations and codicils.

If a person leaving descendants (children, adopted children or their descendants) gives away by will so much of his or her estate that the descendant's share will be less than one-half of what it would be if deceased had died intestate, the descendants can bring an action to invalidate the will in this respect.

The legatees or an executor of a will must take care that the will acquires legal force. This is done by serving will on legal heirs.

See Topical Index in front part of this volume.

FRANCE LAW DIGEST REVISER

Coudert Frères,
52, Avenue des Champs-Elysées
75008 Paris, France
Telephone: 011 33 1 53836000
Fax: 011 33 1 5383 6060
Email: info@paris.coudert.com
New York Office: Coudert Brothers, The Grace Building, 1114 6th Avenue, New York, NY 10036-7703. Telephone: 212-626-4400.

Reviser Profile

History and General Description: Coudert Brothers was founded in 1854 in New York by three brothers whose father had emigrated from France in 1825. Coudert Frères was opened in Paris in 1879 and was the first European office of an American law firm.

Coudert Brothers has over 350 lawyers worldwide practicing in eighteen cities including New York, Washington, San Francisco, Los Angeles, San Jose, London, Brussels, Paris, Hong Kong, Singapore, Tokyo, Beijing, Shanghai, Sydney, Sao Paulo, Bangkok, Jakarta and Moscow. The firm specializes in transnational legal transactions and its clients are for the most part companies, banks, governments and individuals exercising an activity on an international scale.

As French avocats, Coudert Frères is fully qualified to give advice and opinions on French law and to appear before French courts. Of the approximately sixty attorneys at Coudert Frères, over two-thirds are French nationals, while the others originate from, or are admitted to practice in, the United States, Canada, Australia, United Kingdom and Luxembourg. Two of the members of the firm have been decorated with the French "Legion d'Honneur" and several partners are respected figures in the field of international arbitration.

Legal work is conducted regularly in both French and English. Coudert Frères maintains close operating relations with the other offices of Coudert Brothers in order to handle international transactions.

Description of Practice Areas: The essential part of the practice of the firm in Paris is focused on the activities of multinational corporations in France, Europe and the former Soviet Union ("CIS"), as well as on the activities of French companies in France and elsewhere in Europe, the former Soviet Union ("CIS"), North America (and particularly in the United States), South America, Africa and Asia.

General Commercial Law: The lawyers involved in this practice provide services in connection with the full range of investment and other activities of foreign companies in France as well as on behalf of French corporate clients. This practice includes drafting and negotiating all types of commercial contracts and providing advice on questions of French law, the laws of the United States, the laws of the various states in which attorneys of the office are admitted to practice and (in conjunction with attorneys admitted to practice in the local country in question) the laws of other jurisdictions.

Corporate Law and Mergers and Acquisitions: This practice area includes both the direct handling of French corporate reorganizations, mergers, acquisitions, takeovers of public companies and insolvencies and the supervision and coordination of acquisitions, divestitures and reorganizations occurring in other countries, either as single or related transactions. This activity frequently involves contacts with governmental authorities. Principal clients include French and foreign public and privately held companies and, in particular, major United States, Japanese and European companies.

Real Estate: The firm's real estate department frequently represents foreign companies and individuals in major real estate development and construction projects in France. The firm also works in association with notaries in Paris and throughout France in connection with aspects of real estate transactions which require notarial participation. Major clients of the firm include U.S., U.K., French, Japanese and other international developers, investors, construction companies and financial institutions involved in real estate transactions in France and elsewhere in Europe.

Labor Law: Specialists in this field handle a range of employment matters including the negotiation and drafting of individual and collective labor agreements, the negotiation and documentation of individual and collective dismissals and negotiations with labor authorities and trade unions. The labor law department also handles applications for residence and work permits for employees of corporate clients.

Taxation: Coudert Frères has a team of qualified tax lawyers providing advice for multinational corporations on the interpretation and application of American, French and European tax legislation and international tax treaties. The firm's tax specialists are also called upon to advise on the tax planning aspects of acquisitions, divestitures, reorganizations and liquidations handled by the firm.

CIS (former Soviet Union) Practice: The firm's CIS Practice Group is comprised of approximately twenty-five attorneys in six Coudert offices around the world, several of whom are permanently resident in Moscow. Lawyers in the Group advise clients on a wide variety of projects, including joint ventures, technology licenses, turnkey projects, oil concessions and other mineral resources projects, compensation trade arrangements, tax matters, export licensing, and establishing representative offices in the Russian Federation, Ukraine and the other republics of the former Soviet Union. In advising clients, Paris office CIS specialists work closely with the firm's Moscow office as well as other lawyers within the Group.

East European Practice: Lawyers practicing in this area provide advice and services to clients in connection with investment and trade projects in Eastern Europe, including joint ventures, investments in local corporate entities, real estate and privatization projects, primarily in Hungary, Czechoslovakia, Poland and Yugoslavia, as well as Bulgaria, Rumania and Albania.

International Arbitration and Litigation: For many years the firm has had a close involvement with international litigation and arbitration. The firm has acted frequently in major arbitrations under the rules of the International Chamber of Commerce and under the auspices of the arbitration arm of the World Bank (ICSID) as well as in other significant cases such as arbitrations against the governments of Libya and Iran.

Arbitration clients include large French public companies, American and other multinational corporations and foreign governments. Since the merger of the French legal professions on January 1, 1992, a number of senior litigation specialists ("avocats" or barristers) have joined the firm and assist clients involved in litigation before courts in France and other jurisdictions.

EEC and Competition Law: Lawyers practicing in this area concentrate on providing advice on EEC and French competition law and on defending companies which are the targets of antitrust and anti-dumping investigations. Paris office lawyers work closely with lawyers in the firm's Brussels office. Clients include some of the largest American, French and Japanese multinationals.

International Banking, Financial and Insurance Law: The firm is involved in many types of international financial transactions including transnational leasing operations, project finance, sovereign debt restructuring, export credits and Eurodollar financings in the United States, Europe and Asia. Clients include French, American, European, Korean and Japanese banks. The firm also advises clients on French insurance law matters.

African Practice: The firm provides advice to clients on all aspects of foreign investment and commercial transactions in Africa including agreements relating to petroleum and other mineral projects, joint venture contracts, incorporation of companies and the negotiation of various matters with government authorities in Africa. The firm also acts for African governments in connection with World Bank and other projects.

Asian Practice: Given its extensive presence in the Far East, the firm often provides advice to clients in matters relating to investments and commercial dealings in Asia.

Admiralty Law and Practice: The firm has several specialists working in the area of maritime law, handling complex maritime contracts and claims relating to admiralty matters.

Media and Entertainment Law: Lawyers practicing in this area provide advice on a variety of matters pertaining to the entertainment field, including feature film productions, licensing for television and cable operators and related intellectual property matters.

Private Companies and High Net Worth Individuals: Lawyers specialized in this area provide advice to privately-held corporate clients and to individuals on the legal and tax aspects of their international investments as well as on estate planning and estate administration matters.

FRANCE LAW DIGEST

(The following is a list of all Topics, including cross-references, covered in this Digest.)

FRANCE LAW DIGEST

Revised for 1997 edition by

COUDERT BROTHERS, New York City, and COUDERT FRÈRES, Paris.

(C. C. indicates Civil Code; C. Com.—Code of Commerce; C. C. P.—Code of Civil Procedure; C. G. I.—General Code of Taxes; C. P. I.—Code of Intellectual Property; C. T.—Labor Code; N.C.C.P.—New Code of Civil Procedure.)

France is a member of EU. See also European Union Law Digest.

ABSENTEES:

New law of Dec. 28, 1977 (J.O. Dec, 29, 1977), applicable as of Mar. 31, 1978, has modified Civil Code provisions on absentees.

When there exists doubt as to continued life of any person who has disappeared from his last domicile and of whom there is no evidence of further existence, interested parties or public authority ("Ministère Public") may apply to court ("Juge des Tutelles") of his last domicile for judgment of "presumption of absence". (C. C. 112). Court may designate relatives or any other person to represent absentee and administer his property. Powers of representative, and in particular power to dispose of absentee's property, are subject to restrictions similar to those applying to guardians of minors. (C. C. 113). (See topic Guardian and Ward.) Court may fix amount of representative's remuneration and may replace representative. If absentee reappears, he takes property in its state at time of reappearance. (C. C. 118-119).

Ten years after judgment of "presumption of absence", court may, upon request of interested parties or of public authority ("Ministère Public") declare absence conclusive. (C. C. 122). Specified public notice requirements must be met. Judgment is rendered one year after public notices (C. C. 125) and has same effect as death (C. C. 128). If absentee reappears, he takes property, including property which he should have received during absence, in its state at time of reappearance. (C. C. 130). Marriage remains dissolved even though judgment of absence may have been annulled. (C. C. 132).

If above procedure of judgment of "presumption of absence" followed by judgment of absence is not followed, interested parties or public authority may apply for judgment of absence after 20 years from absentee's disappearance. (C. C. 122).

As of Apr. 1, 1979, judgments of absence rendered under old law which were published before Apr. 1, 1969 in accordance with old provisions shall have same effect as judgment of absence under new law. All bonds given under old judgments shall then be discharged and heirs may request distribution of absentee's estate. (Art. 10, Law 77-1447 of Dec. 28, 1977).

Estate to which there is no claim becomes property of State. (C. C. 768).

See also topic Death.

ACKNOWLEDGMENTS:

Documents acknowledged before notary public in U.S.A. which are intended for use in France should have signature of notary public certified by county clerk and signature of county clerk certified by a French consular or diplomatic officer in place where documents were executed. (Decree of Oct. 23, 1946 Art. 3). If documents are to be produced outside of French diplomatic and consular posts signature of consul must be legalized by French Ministry of Foreign Affairs. (Decree 65-283 of Apr. 12, 1965).

France is signatory to Convention of Oct. 5, 1961 (J.O. Jan. 28, 1965) and to European Convention of June 7, 1968 (J.O. Nov. 2, 1970) eliminating requirement of legalization of consular or diplomatic certification between France and signatory countries. However, documents acknowledged before notary in France which are intended for use in foreign countries should be sealed as well as signed by notary. (Circulaire 78-19 of Nov. 30, 1978).

ACTIONS:

Civil actions are brought before local Tribunal d'Instance or Tribunal de Grande Instance depending on amount at stake and subject matter. (See topic Courts). Civil actions include all actions relating to contracts, torts and other obligations, property, succession, and domestic relations. Commercial actions must be brought before local Tribunal de Commerce. These actions include: disputes concerning contracts between merchants and banks; all internal disputes in corporations, companies or partnerships of a commercial nature; all disputes relating to maritime acts, commercial acts or contracts (see topic Contracts) among any persons whatsoever; all matters of insolvency or bankruptcy involving commercial entities; operations of agents in connection with purchase or sale of real estate. (C. Com. 631, 634). All actions are commenced by service of process (assignation), both before civil and commercial courts. There exist accelerated forms of procedure in case of urgency. Although concept of equity, as such, does not exist, certain types of equitable relief are available, e.g., injunctions in tort action for unfair competition.

Special actions and special courts exist for administrative affairs, labor relations, agricultural matters and social security affairs.

Parties may agree to submit dispute to arbitrator instead of proceeding to litigation. (See topic Arbitration and Award.)

Foreign law may be proved in any judicial proceeding by attestation by legal officer or lawyer of country involved (Certificat de coutume). These attestations, duly certified, are then submitted to court under same conditions as any other evidence, i.e., their weight is entirely at discretion of court.

Limitation of.—See topic Limitation of Actions.

ADMINISTRATION:

See topic Executors and Administrators.

AFFIDAVITS:

There is no general instrument upon oath analogous to affidavit. However, declaration upon honor ("declaration sur l'honneur"), which is not notarized, may be used in legal proceedings. Proof of specific facts, as family relationships, may be made by declaration ("acte de notoriété") before notary or judge of "Tribunal d'instance".

See also topic Notaries Public.

AGENCY: See topic Principal and Agent.

ALIENS:

Aliens remaining in France more than three months must obtain residence permit ("carte de séjour"). (Ordonnance No. 45-3853 of Nov. 2, 1945 as modified by Law No. 93-1027 of Aug. 24, 1993).

Prior to their arrival, aliens who wish to be employed in France must obtain long term visa ("visa de long séjour") from French consular officials of area in which they reside. Prospective employer must submit application for long term visa to local office of National Agency for Employment ("Agence Nationale pour l'Emploi"), which submits it to Labor Ministry for approval; file is then sent to Immigration Office ("Office des Migrations Internationales") and thereafter forwarded to French Consulate of place of residence of applicant. Ministry of Interior may also review application. Before issuance of visa, French Consulate will require applicant to undergo medical examination. Local police authorities then issue one year temporary residence and work permit.

Aliens must obtain trader's card ("carte de commerçant") if they plan to set up business in France or to work as: (a) President or general manager of French corporation; (b) manager ("gérant") of any other French company; (c) manager ("gérant") of French commercial partnership; or (d) manager of French branch of any foreign business concern. Local police authorities issue trader's card, as well as temporary resident permit, only after applicant obtains permanent visa ("visa d'établissement"). French Consulate delivers visa after approval of application by: (1) Consulate, (2) Foreign Affairs Ministry, (3) Police Department, and (4) Chamber of Commerce for alien's place of business. (Circular of Oct. 26, 1985).

More generally, Law of July 17, 1984 protects aliens rightfully residing in France by establishing new residence permit ("carte de résident") that is valid for ten years and automatically renewable. This permit is ordinarily obtained after three years of residency in France, though exceptions exist. It allows holder to exercise professional activity of his choice.

To work in France, EEC nationals with employment contract need obtain only residence permit, which is generally valid for five years.

An alien enjoys in France same civil rights as are conceded to French citizens by his own nation under treaties with France. There are no restrictions on right of aliens to own real property, but such property is governed by French law. (C. C. 3). Alien may dispose of his property by acts inter vivos or by will on same basis as French national. However, investments in France by nonresidents are regulated by Ministry of Finance. (See topic Exchange Control).

Judicial jurisdiction is asserted over nonresident alien with regard to any obligation entered into in France, or anywhere else, to which French national is party. (C. C. 14, 15). French party may waive jurisdiction of French courts. Courts allow suit by aliens in most cases.

Under the Franco-American Establishment Treaty of 1959 U.S. citizens enjoy national treatment in France in the fields of: press freedom (Art. II); legal aid (Art. III); patent rights, trade marks, registered trade names and labels of guaranty (Art. VIII) and commercial activity (Art. V). In other fields Treaty provides that obligations imposed on U.S. nationals in France shall be no heavier than those imposed on aliens of other nationalities, and in field of taxation, U.S. nationals are not to be taxed more stringently than French nationals under similar circumstances (Art. IX). Treaty also grants American nationals free access to courts.

Marriage.—Upon marriage to French man, foreign woman no longer acquires French nationality automatically (Art. 37 French Nationality Code), but foreign spouse of any French national may acquire French nationality by filing declaration under following conditions: (i) declaration must be filed two years after date of marriage, and (ii) at date of filing declaration, community of life between spouses must have been continuous for two years, and (iii) French spouse must still have French nationality at time of filing (Art. 37-1, as modified by Law No. 93993 of July 22, 1993), which, during year after filing has been officially received, French government may oppose (Art. 39). Making such declaration may cause loss of U.S. citizenship by Americans. (8 U.S.C. §1481[a][1]).

French citizen marrying alien may make written declaration to give up French nationality so long as he has acquired citizenship of spouse and both normally reside abroad, except French men aged less than 35 may exercise this right only after fulfilling military obligations. (Art. 94).

Corporations Owned or Controlled by Aliens.—There is no general disqualification from alien ownership or control of business entities in France. However, investment regulations must be observed and corporation with substantial alien ownership or control may be disqualified or subject to special authorizations with respect to their right to participate in certain activities or economic sectors (e.g., communications, transportation, banking, mining and mineral exploitation, electricity).

See Topical Index in front part of this volume.

ALIENS . . . *continued*

See also topics Associations; Copyright; Corporations; Descent and Distribution; Exchange Control; Foreign Investment; Foreign Trade Regulations; Immigration; Industrial Property Rights; Judicial Recovery and Liquidation; Limited Companies; Shipping; Taxation.

ALIMONY: See topic Divorce.

APPEAL AND ERROR: See topic Courts.

ARBITRATION AND AWARD:

Arbitration is method of dispute resolution which is frequently resorted to in France.

Parties' freedom to refer their dispute to arbitration is restricted. (arts. 2060-2061 of Civil Code). See topic Dispute Resolution.

Parties to domestic contract deemed commercial for each of them, may decide that any dispute arising out of their contract will be submitted to arbitration. (Art. 631 of Commercial Code). In domestic commercial contracts, parties may waive their right of appeal against arbitral awards on merits of case. (art. 1482 of New Code of Civil Procedure, hereafter "N.C.C.P."; Decree No. 81-500 of May 12, 1981). However, award remains subject to annulment by court in following cases: (i) if arbitral tribunal rules when there was no arbitration agreement or basis was void or expired agreement; (ii) if arbitral tribunal was formed irregularly or sole arbitrator irregularly appointed; (iii) if arbitral tribunal ruled without complying with terms of reference which were conferred upon it; (iv) when right of each party to present its case has not been respected; (v) in all cases of nullity provided for in art. 1480 of N.C.C.P.; (vi) if arbitral tribunal violated rule of public policy.

French International Arbitration Law is contained in arts. 1492-1507 of N.C.C.P. and offers liberal system of international arbitration. Under French law, international arbitration is arbitration which involves international commercial interests. Arbitrator decides dispute according to rules of law chosen by parties; in absence of such choice, according to those he deems appropriate. In all cases, he takes into account trade usages.

Recognition and enforcement rules are applicable to arbitral awards rendered abroad (either on domestic or international arbitration) or rendered in France in international arbitration. Under art. 1498 N.C.C.P., arbitral awards are recognized in France if their existence has been established and if such recognition is not clearly contrary to international public policy ("ordre public international"). Appeal from decision granting recognition or execution lies only in specific cases (see art. 1502 N.C.C.P.). International arbitral awards can be challenged by action to annul on basis of grounds provided for in art. 1502 N.C.C.P., provided award was rendered in France.

ASSIGNMENTS:

Basic rules for assignments are set out in Code Civil. These are executed by delivering instrument of assignment to assignee (C. C. 1689) but assignment is not effective against third parties (including obligor) until assignee gives formal notice to obligor by sheriff ("huissier") (C. C. 1690). Payment by obligor before receipt of such notice is valid discharge. (C. C. 1691). No seals are required in France. Depending on type of assignment, special rules may apply which may or may not figure in Civil Code. For example:

Obligor can get release from litigated claim that has been assigned by paying assignee actual amount paid for assignment. (C. C. 1699). This does not apply, however, to assignment to co-heir or joint owner or to creditor in satisfaction of debt. (C. C. 1701).

Under Code du Travail R.145-1 (as modified by Decree No. 87-857 of Oct. 22, 1987) only portion of salaries can be assigned.

For assignments involving bills and notes, see topic Bills and Notes.

Art. 61 of Law of Jan. 24, 1984 has facilitated assignment of accounts receivable in relation with professional activity to obtain credit from financial institutions.

ASSOCIATIONS:

Associations are nonprofit organizations governed by law of July 1, 1901 as modified. Right of association is freely recognized without any special formality, but only associations registered with Préfecture possess legal personality.

Registered associations have normally only limited legal capacity. They can receive contributions from their members, government subsidies, unregistered gifts from all sources and gifts from public interest establishments. They may purchase personal property but are only entitled to acquire real property strictly necessary for their objects. They may sue or be sued in their own name.

Associations terminate at time set in their bylaws or by prior unanimous decision of their members, or by decision of general meeting of members if bylaws so permit. Estate must be assigned and cannot be shared between members.

Registered association may, after three years of existence, be "recognized as of public interest" by Decree of Ministry of Interior on recommendation of Conseil d'Etat. 1966). Three year probationary period is not required if resources of association are sufficient to assure its financial equilibrium. (Art. 10 of Law of July 1, 1901). Recognized associations or associations dealing with family, research, religion or charity matters, may receive gifts and legacies upon administrative authorization by decision of Préfer with jurisdiction over association's registered office. (Decree of June 13, 1966 as modified).

Gifts and legacies to recognized associations having charitable purposes or whose resources are used exclusively for scientific, cultural or artistic purposes are exempt from gift and inheritance taxes. (C. G. I. 795; see topic Trusts, subhead Foundations). Arts. 200 and 238 bis of C.G.I. authorize individuals and business enterprises to deduct gifts to associations from their taxable income or profits. Such gifts are only deductible by individuals at rate of 40% of amount given either up to 1.25% of taxable income when association is of general interest or up to 5% of taxable income for associations recognized to be of public interest. Business enterprises may deduct from taxable profit up to 0.2% of turnover for gifts to associations recognized to be of general interest and up to 0.3% of turnover for those of public interest.

Law No. 85-698 of July 11, 1985 authorizes associations that have had business activity for at least two years to issue bonds and debentures. Such associations must be registered at registry of commerce and include in by-laws provisions regarding management and supervision by corporate entity. Provisions of Law No. 66-537 of July 24, 1966 regarding board of directors, directorate ("directoire") and management of companies as well as liability with regard to management are applicable to such associations.

In connection with any such bond or debenture issuance, associations must report certain information regarding issuance. Bonds may be offered for public subscription, subject to authorization pursuant to Art. 82 of Law No. 46-2914 of Dec. 23, 1946, and to supervision by Commission for stock exchange operations ("Commission des opérations de Bourse").

Members meeting must be held within six months following end of each commercial year to approve annual accounts. Members meeting must also be held if associations' assets suffer critical decrease, in order to decide upon continuation or dissolution. Law No. 84-148 of Mar. 1, 1984 on prevention and amicable settlement of companies' financial difficulties is applicable to such associations.

Associations may join companies or other associations in economic groups ("groupements d'intérêt économique") pursuant to Ordinance No. 67-821 of Sept. 23, 1967 on such groups. If said group is formed only by associations, Law of July 11, 1985 is applicable.

Only associations which have economic activity are subject to accounting regulation. Such associations must establish annual accounts and appoint statutory auditor if, at closing of fiscal year, they satisfy two of following criteria: 50 salaried employees; turnover of more than 20,000,000 francs before taxes; balance sheet indicating assets in excess of 10,000,000 francs.

ATTACHMENT:

Law No. 91-650 of July 9, 1991 replaced Law of Nov. 12, 1955 which created general remedy of prejudgment attachment by permission of judge where creditor shows urgency and well-founded claim. (Arts. 67 et seq. of Law of 1991). This law was completed by Decree No. 92-755 of July 31, 1992.

In addition, particular form of prejudgment attachment is available in specific situation. Creditor may have property to which he claims rights, attached and delivered to third party or indeed retained under judicial supervision by debtor himself, until court has passed on rights of all parties concerned. ("Saisie-revendication", Arts. 155 et seq. of Decree of July 31, 1992). This action is available even when property is originally in possession of third person.

See topic Executions.

ATTORNEYS AND COUNSELORS:

Effective Jan. 1st, 1992, and pursuant to Law No. 90-1259 of Dec. 31, 1990, legal profession was reorganized and prior distinction between "avocats" (litigators) and "conseils juridiques" (counselors) no longer exists. New profession consists only of "avocats" who may give legal advice and appear in court. Transitional measures are applicable for ex-"conseils juridiques". Attorneys admitted to practice in foreign countries may become "avocats" under certain conditions.

Admission.—Applicants must hold "Maîtrise en droit" i.e. law degree obtained after four years of study in law school. Decree of Dec. 26, 1991 lists other degrees, which are considered as equivalent to "Maîtrise en droit" for purpose of admission. List includes foreign degrees necessary in order to practice regulated legal profession in foreign country. In addition, European Directive 89/48/CEE of Dec. 21, 1988 regarding mutual recognition of diplomas must be taken into account.

Applicants must then pass examination for admission to "Centre Régional de Formation Professionnelle" (CRFP) where they follow one year training course, including classes and internships in law firms and/or legal departments of companies and/or courts. At end of this one year period, applicants are required to pass examination and receive "Certificat d'Aptitude à la Profession d'Avocat" (CAPA) entitling them to admission to bar.

Admission of Foreign Attorneys.—Attorneys from EU countries may be admitted upon passing special exam. Attorneys from non-EU countries may be admitted on basis of "de facto" reciprocity. These attorneys are required to pass professional exam.

Registration of Attorneys.—Attorneys admitted to practice are registered with Bar ("Barreau") in locality of their professional practice.

French avocats are only allowed to appear alone before courts of civil jurisdiction (Tribunal de Grande Instance) of Bar to which they are admitted. In order to appear before such courts in other jurisdictions, they must engage "correspondant", who is registered with bar of that jurisdiction. French avocats may appear before any commercial court. Foreign lawyers from non-EU countries may not appear in French courts, even accompanied by French avocat.

Status of Attorneys.—Traditionally, "avocats" have practiced law as independent professionals. Under this status, "avocats" are allowed to have their own clients, even if they are associates in law firm. Above mentioned Law of Dec. 31, 1990, now allows "avocats" to be salaried employees. Salaried "avocats" are subject to different social security regime than independent "avocats" and may not have their own clients. Whether working as independent advisors or as salaried employees, all "avocats" are subject to same ethical rules.

Code of Ethics.—Attorney-client privilege: correspondence and exchanges of any kind between "avocat" and his client are absolutely confidential.

Correspondence and contacts between "avocats" are confidential and in principle may not be used in court.

French procedure is adversarial and "avocat" for each party must communicate to "avocat" for other party written pleadings and supporting evidence. Any correspondence addressed to court must be communicated to "avocat" of other party.

"Avocats" are subject to obligations regarding legal assistance to indigents.

Specialization.—CRFP may grant to "avocat" certificate of specialization. Criteria used to grant such certificate are degrees and practice experience in area of specialization. Specialization of "avocat" may be mentioned by words "Conseil en   " or

See Topical Index in front part of this volume.

ATTORNEYS AND COUNSELORS . . . *continued*
"Spécialiste en ", or "Titulaire du certificate " followed by name of specialization. C.N.B. has proposed list of 14 areas of specialization.

Professional Associations include: The Conseil National des Barreaux (CNB) which represents profession before administration and monitors harmonization of rules of profession. CNB also determines categories of persons who may benefit from European Directive 89/48/CEE of Dec. 21, 1988 regarding mutual recognition of diplomas. Its members are elected from each "Barreau" (local Bar Association).

Address and phone: 161 boulevard Pereire, 75017 PARIS, tel. 44.01.01.80, fax. 44.01.01.81.

Local Bar Association: there is one Barreau for each Appellate Court jurisdiction ("Cour d'Appel"). Each "Barreau" has Conseil de l'Ordre.

Addresses and phone numbers may be obtained from local "Cour d'Appel".

AUTOMOBILES: See topic Motor Vehicles.

BANKRUPTCY AND JUDICIAL SETTLEMENT:

See topic Judicial Recovery and Liquidation.

BILLS AND NOTES:

France is signatory to Geneva Agreements of June 7, 1930 on promissory notes and bills of exchange. Legislation has been enacted for internal application of provisions of said Agreements. (C. Com. 110-189).

A bill of exchange ("lettre de change" or "traite") which fulfills all requirements brings parties within trading law ("acte de commerce"), regardless of whether they are traders or nontraders (see topic Commercial Law), and whether or not bill was given in respect of a purely civil transaction. Consequently, suits in respect thereof are brought before commercial courts.

Formal requirements are similar to those of Anglo-American law, except that words "Bill of Exchange" must appear on document. No statement of consideration is necessary. "Provision" must be made by drawer. This is considered to have been done if drawee at time of maturity is indebted to drawer in a sum at least equal to amount of bill. Acceptance presupposes "provision" and is proof of such in respect to indorsers. In case of dispute, drawer has burden of proving that drawee had, at maturity of bill, adequate "provision". (C. Com. 116). Drawee cannot refuse to accept bill created for payment for merchandise sold.

Bills may be drawn at sight. In that case they must be presented for payment within one year. (C. Com. 132). Drawer may shorten or lengthen this period. There are no days of grace. Bills falling due on Sun. or holiday are payable on succeeding business day.

Bill may be endorsed before or after maturity. Mere signature of indorser is sufficient to constitute indorsement. Antedating indorsement is forgery. All those whose signatures appear on bill of exchange are jointly liable to bearer. (C. Com. 151). Persons sued on bill of exchange may not set up against holder in good faith defenses based entirely on their relationship with drawer or with previous holders. Holder in bad faith is one who assented to bill being indorsed to his benefit, knowing that drawee would not be able to set up against drawer or previous holder defense based on its relationship with latter. (C. Com. 121). Bearer must notify indorser of nonpayment within four days of presentation, and each successive indorsee must notify his indorser within two days of receipt of notification. Negligence may give rise to damages which cannot in any case exceed amount stated in bill. (C. Com. 149). Defenses cannot be opposed to discounting bank, unless it is proved that at time draft was discounted, bank knew that (i) "provision" would not be present at term, or (ii) that situation of preceding holder was doomed. Bank is deemed to have cognizance, at time of discount, that it was preventing accepting drawee from arguing of lack of provision.

If holder does not protest by notarized deed, drawer's failure to pay within two days of maturity, he loses his right against endorser (C. Com. 148-A); if there was provision at time of maturity, he also loses his right against drawer (C. Com. 156).

In order to be paid, holder may draw new bill of exchange ("retraite") on one of his guarantors and payable on sight for amount of principal, expenses and cost of exchange. Amount of expenses includes protest fees, brokerage, interest and stamp duties. (C. Com. 163-165).

If bill of exchange is modified by any party during course of its circulation, drawer and all indorsers prior to change are held to original obligation, while all subsequent indorsers are bound by terms of new obligation. (C. Com. 178). Forgery of signature of drawer does not bind him in any way, but indorsers are bound under forged instrument. (C. Com. 114).

Omission of words "bill of exchange" or of names of drawer and drawee, of date and place of issuance and of payment, of order to pay, or of sum to pay, may result in nullity of bill of exchange. (C. Com. 110).

"Facture protestable" created by Ordonnance no. 67-838 of Sept. 28, 1967, implemented by Decree No. 67-1243 of Dec. 22, 1967, was abolished by Law No. 81-1 of Jan. 2, 1981, implemented by Decree No. 81-862 of Sept. 9, 1981. New law creates another form of commercial paper, aimed at simplifying transfer (or pledge) of claims in favor of credit institutions only, and applies to claims arising solely out of business activity ("créances professionnelles") as opposed to financial claims. Transfer (or pledge) of claim is made effective by simple remittance of "bordereau" bearing reference "acte de cession (ou de nantissement) de créances professionnelles", which is statement evidencing transfer (or pledge) of one or several claims. In order to be valid, bordereau must bear some specific references as set forth by law, and credit institution must date it with indelible means. Latter can prevent debtor from paying transferor by sending him notice bearing specific references as provided for in Decree No. 81-862 of Sept. 9, 1981. Such bordereau can then be endorsed by other credit institutions only, and circulate like bill of lading.

Promissory notes ("billets à ordre") are subject to rules relating to bills of exchange in so far as these concern maturity, indorsement, joint and several liability, payment, protest, rights and duties of holder. Promissory note must be dated and must set forth name of payee, as well as time and place of payment; it must also contain undertaking by drawer to pay determined amount. It must contain words "Promissory Note." (C. Com. 183). Omission of above may result in nullity as would omission of debtor's signature.

In all debtor-creditor relationships, payment through promissory notes allowed to debtor only if specifically envisaged by parties and mentioned in invoice. If promissory note not received by creditor within 30 days of sending of invoice, creditor may issue bill of exchange which debtor must accept pursuant to conditions provided by law. (C. Com. 189 bis A).

In respect of bills of exchange and promissory notes all actions against acceptor are barred by limitation after three years from maturity. Actions of bearer against drawer or indorsers are barred after one year from protest. Actions of indorsers against other indorsers or drawer are barred after six months from repayment of bill or note by indorser or from date of action against indorser. (C. Com. 179).

In case of judicial proceedings, the period of limitation is calculated from last formality accomplished. (C. Com. 179). Defendant setting up statute of limitations under this section may be required to affirm under oath that nothing further is due, and if action is against heirs or representatives they may be required in similar manner to affirm under oath that to best of their belief nothing is due.

Finally, for both forms of bills, lack of stamp entails impossibility of proceeding against signers in case of failure of payment. (C.G.I. 1840 T bis). As long as bill is not stamped, no person or company or public establishment may cash it, and notaries or huissiers may object to it.

Checks must be payable at sight. Place and date of drawing must be stated. Check can be drawn only on banker, stockbroker, or other authorized financial institution, and it must contain word "check". It may be drawn in favor of specified person or to his order, or to bearer. (Law of Oct. 30, 1935, modified by Law No. 72-10 of Jan. 3, 1972, Law No. 75-4 of Jan. 3, 1975 and Law No. 91-1382 of Dec. 30, 1991).

"Provision" must exist at time of issue of check, i.e. drawer must have claim free from all liability and payable on demand against drawee.

Drawee is obliged to pay all checks presented of 100 francs or less during one month from date of issuance. If drawee pays check he is then subrogated to rights of beneficiary. Stop-payment orders are possible only if check is lost or stolen or payee is bankrupt. (Art. 32 of Decree).

Anyone who negligently or wilfully draws check without provision or who withdraws provision after he has drawn check, or who instructs bank not to pay, can be prosecuted under criminal law of Jan. 3, 1975, Decree No. 75-903 of Oct. 3, 1975 and Law No. 91-1382 of Dec. 30, 1991 with respect to security of checks and payment cards. Pursuant to Art. 65 of above-cited 1991 Law, person drawing non-provisioned check may not draw another check for ten years, unless he pays amount of check as well as penalty in proportion to amount of non-provisioned check. No penalty is assessed, however, if amount for which check was drawn is paid within one month of date of drawing ("regularization") and if this was only regularization during previous 12 months. Penalty doubles upon fourth regularization in any 12 month period. Any non-provisioned check drawn in excess of 10,000 francs must be made public (Decree of May 26, 1992). Banque de France centralizes all information from drawee about payment of checks drawn. Such information is published by Banque de France for all banks and financial institutions. Individuals may consult Banque de France regarding checks in their possession for small fee. Beneficiary must return non-provisioned check to drawer.

Rules governing liability of endorsers and drawers are same as those which govern bills of exchange. Check must be presented for payment within eight days if issued and payable in France, and within 20 days or 70 days if issued outside of France but payable in France, depending on whether issued in Europe or outside Europe. Computation starts from date of issuance. (Art. 29 of Decree). Protest must be made before time for presentation expires.

Actions brought against drawer or endorser are barred after six months and against drawee after one year from expiration of presentation period. (Art. 52 of Decree).

Checks delivered by banks to customers are normally "barred" (imprinted with parallel lines, usually oblique) and are not endorsable, except to bank or other authorized financial institution. They may be presented to drawee for payment only through bank. Unbarred checks are available if requested but are subject to small stamp duty.

CHATTEL MORTGAGES:

Chattel mortgages exist in limited cases provided by law. Most important is general mortgage (nantissement) on entire business as going concern (fonds de commerce), which includes firm equipment, tradename, patents and trademarks, good will, lease rights, but not inventory of merchandise or accounts receivable and accounting books. This general mortgage must be filed within 15 days of creation with Registrar (Greffe) of Tribunal of Commerce. Mortgage is null and void if not registered; registry provides protection against bona fide purchasers. (Law of Mar. 17, 1909).

By Law of Jan. 18, 1951, chattel mortgage may be placed on all types of industrial and professional equipment. Recordation requirements are essentially same as for general mortgage. Chattel mortgages also exist for automobiles, ships and airplanes, each under special procedure, e.g., for automobiles, registry at Préfecture within three months of registry of new car on pain of nullity. (Decree of Sept. 30, 1953). As rule, failure to register within various periods prescribed renders mortgage null and void. Except for automobiles, no consumer goods may be subject to chattel mortgages.

Note that default in payment by mortgagor never gives mortgagee right to possession, but only right to compel forced sale by public auction at which he can be bidder. (C. Com. 93).

See also topic Records.

COLLATERAL SECURITY: See topic Pledges.

COMMERCIAL LAW:

French Law distinguishes between traders and nontraders. Traders (commercants) are persons who are engaged in trading transactions as their regular occupation. They must register with Register of Commerce. (Decree of Mar. 23, 1967, art. 1 and May 30, 1984, art. 7). Traders are subject to special commercial tribunals, and they may be declared bankrupt. They must keep daily or monthly business records which may be received in evidence in commercial litigation. They must also have prepared annual

COMMERCIAL LAW . . . *continued*
balance sheets and profit and loss statements. All such books, documents and business correspondence must be kept for ten years.

Included as trading transactions are all purchases of goods for purposes of resale or hire, contracts of carriage, contracts for supply of goods, or relating to agencies, business offices, auction galleries, contracts of exchange, banking and brokerage, transactions involving public banks, obligations between merchants, traders, and bankers, bills of exchange (regardless of persons contracting), and contracts in respect of ships, marine insurance and wages and hire of crew. (C. Com. 632, 633). Transactions between traders are brought before commercial courts; parties to commercial contract may provide for arbitration. (C. Com. 631). All forms of evidence may be used in actions against trader. (C. Com. 109).

See topics Actions, Aliens, Bills and Notes, Contracts, and Courts.

COMMERCIAL REGISTER: See topic Records.

COMMISSIONS TO TAKE TESTIMONY:

See topic Depositions.

COMMUNITY PROPERTY:

See topic Husband and Wife.

COMPANIES:

See topics Corporations; and Partnership.

CONDITIONAL SALES: See topic Sales.

CONSTITUTION AND GOVERNMENT:

The "Fifth Republic."—Present constitution of France was approved by referendum held on Sept. 28, 1958, and promulgated on Oct. 4, 1958. Institutions created form what is called "Fifth Republic." Constitution was amended by constitutional law of June 4, 1960 in order that Member States of Community could, by agreement, become fully independent, while still remaining in Community. Subsequent to this law all former Autonomous Republics became independent but remained connected with France through Cooperation Agreements.

Territory.—French Republic now comprises: (a) Metropolitan France including Corsica (b) Overseas Departments (Guyane, Guadeloupe, Martinique, Réunion, St. Pierre et Miquelon) (c) Overseas Territories (Polynésie Française, Nouvelle Calédonie et dépendances, Terres Australes et Antarctiques Françaises, Wallis et Futuna). Mayotte Island has special status of territorial collectivity ("collectivité territoriale").

Cooperation agreements varying in scope and content have been concluded with following countries: Burundi, Cameroun, Central African Republic, Congo, Zaire, Ivory Coast, Benin, Gabon, Guinea, Burkina-Faso, Mali, Mauritania, Niger, Ruanda, Senegal, Chad, Togo, Malagasy Republic. Other cooperation agreements have been entered into with newly independent countries such as Ukraine and Ouzbekistan.

Fundamental Rights of the People.—Unlike that of 1946, Constitution of 1958 does not list fundamental civic and economic rights of the People. In short Preamble, it reaffirms Human Rights and principles of National Sovereignty by way of general reference to Declaration of Rights of 1789 and to Preamble of Constitution of 1946.

Basic Principles.—France is indivisible, secular, democratic and social Republic. Its principle is: Government of the people, for the people, and by the people. (Art. 2). National sovereignty belongs to French people and is exercised by votes of representatives of people and by referendum. (Art. 3). All French citizens of both sexes who have reached 18 years of age enjoy civil and political rights and qualify for electoral franchise, under conditions determined by the law. Subject to reciprocity, citizens of European Union residing in France qualify for electoral franchise and eligibility in local (town) elections under conditions provided by EU Treaty. Such citizens cannot be elected as mayor or deputy mayor and cannot participate in election of senators. (Constitutional Law of 25 June 1992). Naturalized citizens acquire electoral franchise and eligibility from date of their naturalization, under same conditions of majority as other citizens.

President of Republic is elected for seven years by universal direct suffrage. Pursuant to law of Mar. 11, 1988, candidates must forward statement of their financial situation to Constitutional Council; if elected, similar statement must be published at end of their term. Electoral expenses are limited to FRF 90 million for candidates in first ballot and FRF 120 million for candidates in second ballot. (Organic Law of 19 Jan. 1995). Legal entities, except political parties or groups, cannot contribute to financing of campaign of presidential candidate. (Same rules apply to Parliamentary and local elections.) In case of vacancy of presidency or disability of President, his functions are temporarily exercised by President of Senate with exception of powers under Arts. 11 and 12 of Constitution. If President of Senate is impeded from exercising functions of President, these are exercised by government. New President of Republic is elected not less than 20 nor more than 30 days after expiration of mandate of previous President or not less than 20 nor more than 35 days in case of vacancy. In case of death or disability of candidate, Constitutional Council may decide to postpone elections or reorganize them depending upon when death or disability occurs. (Art. 7). President of Republic appoints Prime Minister and, upon proposition of Prime Minister, other members of government. (Art. 8). He presides over Council of Ministers (Art. 9), Superior Council of Judiciary (Art. 65) and Superior Councils and Committees of National Defense (Art. 15). He is chief of Armed Forces. (Art. 15). He can exercise right of pardon. (Art. 17). He negotiates and ratifies international treaties, some classes of which require prior legislative approval. (Arts. 52 and 53). He promulgates laws adopted by Parliament (Art. 10) and signs ordinances and decrees adopted by Council of Ministers (Art. 13).

After having taken the advice of Prime Minister and of Presidents of both Houses of Parliament, President of Republic may dissolve National Assembly. General elections must take place not less than 20 nor more than 40 days after dissolution. Second dissolution cannot take place within one year from general election. (Art. 12).

Upon proposition of government or of both Houses of Parliament, President may submit to approval by referendum laws concerning organization of public authorities, modification of Nation's economic and social policy along with public services concerned, approval of agreements with Member States of Community or ratification of treaties. (Art. 11).

In case of serious and immediate threats to institutions of Republic, to independence of nation, to integrity of its territory or to fulfillment of its international commitments, President of the Republic may assume emergency powers. (Art. 16).

The government consists of Prime Minister and Ministers. Members of government cannot be, at same time, members of Parliament or national representatives of business or professional organizations. They cannot hold other public office and cannot engage in business or professional activities. (Art. 23). Newly appointed ministers must provide statement of their patrimonial situation. (Law of 8 Feb. 1995). Members of government have access to both Chambers of Parliament and must be heard when they request it. (Art. 31).

The Prime Minister directs activity of government. He is responsible for National Defense, ensures execution of laws and appoints all civil and military officials. (Art. 21).

The National Assembly may pass motion of censure on government. Such motion can be moved only if endorsed by at least one-tenth of membership of Assembly and can be adopted only by vote of majority of membership. If motion is rejected, its signatories cannot renew it in course of same session, except for case referred to in following paragraph. (Art. 49).

Prime Minister, after consultation with Council of Ministers, can request vote of confidence from National Assembly on program of government or on statement of general policy or on passing of law. In latter case, law is deemed to have been adopted if motion of censure is not moved within 24 hours and adopted, as indicated in foregoing paragraph. (Art. 49).

Parliament is composed of two Houses: the National Assembly and the Senate. (Art. 24). Pursuant to reform dated Aug. 4, 1995, parliament meets for nine-month session, beginning on first working day of Oct. and ending on last working day of June. There are maximum of 120 working days, although supplementary days may be added. It is called "session unique".

The National Assembly is elected on territorial basis, by universal and direct suffrage. (Art. 24). If no candidate in constituency has absolute majority in first round, second round is held one week later and candidate with greatest number of votes is elected. All elected representatives ("députés") must provide "Commission for financial transparence of political life" with affidavit regarding their financial situation and patrimony. (Organic Law of 19 Jan. 1995). Decree dated Mar. 4, 1996, pursuant to law of Mar. 11, 1988, sets at FRF 526,500,000 total amount of public financial support granted to various parties regarding elections to National Assembly.

The Senate consists of senators, elected by indirect suffrage, for term of nine years, one-third of its membership being renewed every three years. Senate has no veto power since Assembly can always overrule it on second hearing.

Parliament meets every year in two ordinary sessions. First session lasts from first Tues. of Oct. until third Fri. of Dec. Second session opens on last Tues. of Apr. and its duration cannot exceed three months. (Art. 28).

Extraordinary sessions may be summoned at request of Prime Minister or of majority of members of National Assembly. In latter case, duration of session cannot exceed 12 days. (Art. 29).

Parliament exercises legislative power. Following matters are within its competence: Fundamental rights and liberties of citizens; duties imposed on person and property of citizens in interest of national defense; nationality, status and competence of persons, matrimonial status, estates and gifts; major criminal offenses; criminal procedure; amnesty; creation of new Courts of Justice; rights and duties of judges; taxation; issue of money, electoral law for parliamentary and local elections; creation of classes of public establishments; fundamental guarantees granted to civil and military officials; nationalization of enterprises and transfer of enterprises from public to private ownership. Parliament also determines basic principles governing following matters: general organization of national defense; self-administration of local collectivities, powers and financial resources of same; education; laws of property and of civil and commercial obligations; labour law, and social security. (Art. 34). All other matters belong to Executive Branch and are determined by governmental decrees. (Art 37).

The Judiciary.—Constitution provides for Superior Council of Judiciary (Art. 64) and establishes principle that judges shall not be removable. This autonomy has been reinforced under new art. 65 of Constitution. Organization and operation of courts is left to ordinary legislation. Justice is administered by two separate and independent systems of courts: judicial and administrative. Highest judicial court is Cour de Cassation; supreme administrative court is Council of State (Conseil d'Etat). Conflicts in jurisdiction between administrative and judiciary courts are arbitrated by High Court called Court of Conflicts (Tribunal des Conflits). High Court of Justice has jurisdiction over cases of high treason involving President of the Republic. Its powers expire on first Tues. of fifth year following its election. Court of Justice has jurisdiction over matters involving Government ministers. (Constitutional Law, July 27, 1995). Constitutional Law dated Apr. 4, 1995, modified criminal liability of ministers. From now on, they fall within jurisdiction of Court of Justice of Republic (Cour de Justice de la République) as regards crimes and offenses committed during their term of office. Anyone suffering from such misconduct can file claim. Commission renders decision over admissibility of claim. Then, Court of Justice of Republic rules. Appeal is possible. See also topic Courts.

Local Administration.—French Constitution recognizes existence of local administrative bodies, which are Communes (municipalities), Departments and Overseas Territories. (Art. 72).

Law of Mar. 2, 1986 created new local administrative bodies, called Regions, administered by council elected by universal and direct suffrage. Regions are granted substantial independent economic power to foster economic growth within their jurisdiction. Law of Jan. 3, 1983 transfers new powers from State to local bodies.

Constitutionality of Laws.—Courts have no power to determine constitutional validity of laws. Constitutional Council is established (Art. 56) consisting of nine

CONSTITUTION AND GOVERNMENT . . . *continued*
members, of which three are appointed by President of Republic, three by President of National Assembly and three by President of Senate. Members of Constitutional Council are appointed for term of nine years, one-third of membership being renewed every three years. President of Republic, Prime Minister and Presidents of both Houses of Parliament may submit any law to Constitutional Council before promulgation for advice on its conformity with Constitution. Such submission may also be made by resolution signed by 60 Deputies or 60 Senators. For certain laws deemed of fundamental importance by Constitution ("lois organiques"), submission to Constitutional Council is mandatory. (Art. 61). Laws declared unconstitutional by Council cannot be promulgated nor applied. (Art. 62). Constitutional Council supervises legal regularity of elections of President of Republic and of members of Parliament as well as proper conduct of referendums. (Arts. 58, 59, 60).

CONSUMER PROTECTION:

In French law, consumption is recognized as legal act which permits consumer to obtain good or service in view of satisfying personal or familial need. Law protects consumer in use of disposable and durable goods, such as food and housing, as well as in receipt of services, both material (repair, insurance, credit) and intellectual (medical, legal), which are destined to satisfy personal or familial need. Utilization of public services, such as postal, telephone, and hospital services, is also characterized as act of consumption for purpose of French law.

Consumer, in legal sense, is individual who accomplishes act of consumption referred to in above definition. Nonetheless, French law of consumer protection is concerned with particular category of acts rather than particular class of persons.

Private and Public Enforcement.—Enforcement of consumer rights is assured by representative organizations of both private and public law. Among private organizations, Associations of Consumers are most important.

Department for Detection of Consumer Fraud and Quality Control and National Consumer Committee are under control of Ministry for Consumer Affairs which also coordinates actions by public bodies in sphere of consumer protection. Other governmental units which participate in protection of consumer affairs are: Service of Instruments of Measure (Ministry of Industry); Customs Bureau (Ministry of Finance); Veterinary Service of Dietary Hygiene (Ministry of Agriculture); and Inspection Service of Pharmacy and Health (Ministry of Health). In addition, law of Dec. 22, 1966, created National Institute of Consumer Affairs, public institution which has subsequently developed expertise in several areas: Analysis and documentation of information provided by press and of legal, economic and new technological developments. Institute, managed by majority of consumers, both informs and counsels consumers on recent developments in consumer affairs. Decree of July 12, 1983 creates National Council for Consumer Affairs. Presided over by Minister for Consumer Affairs, Council allows for confrontation, concertation and negotiation between consumers and professionals.

Interdisciplinary.—French law of consumer protection is interdisciplinary. Areas of law important to consumer protection are civil law, criminal law, civil and criminal procedure, administrative law and tax law.

EEC law also applies to extent that French consumer protection law must respect provisions of EEC Treaty of Rome.

Principal Sources of Law.—The Consumer Code ("Code de la consommation") created by Law No. 93-949 of July 26, 1993 has codified numerous laws relating to consumer protection, principal of which are listed below. Decrees, Arrêtés have not yet been codified.

The Civil Code, which in Arts. 1641 to 1649 holds seller responsible for all hidden defects in merchandise sold. (Arts. L. 211-1 of Consumer Code). (See topic Sales, subhead Warranties.)

Law of Aug. 1, 1905 provides criminal treatment for fraud or falsity in sale of goods or services no matter how perpetrated and whether in respect to nature, origin, essential qualities or composition, or by delivery of quantity or kind of goods or services other than that specified in contract, or concerning use, inherent risks, controls effectuated or safety instructions. (Arts. L. 213-1 to L. 216-1 of Consumer Code). Numerous decrees and arrêtés have been promulgated with respect to individual products. Decree of Dec. 7, 1984 provides specific rules regarding labelling and presentation of foodstuffs.

Law of July 21, 1983 establishes general obligation of safety. Products and services which fail to meet it are prohibited or regulated. (Arts. L. 221-1 to L. 225-1 of Consumer Code). Law also modifies some provisions of Law of Aug. 1, 1905.

Arrêtés of Sept. 16, 1971 and Sept. 2, 1977 obligate professionals to clearly and correctly announce price of their products and services.

Art. 44 of Law of Dec. 23, 1973 forbids all false and misleading advertising practices, whether so considered because they are patently false or merely tend to mislead. (Arts. L. 121-1 to L. 121-7 of Consumer Code). Law of Dec. 27, 1973, known by name Loi Royer, forbids false and misleading advertising practices and permits recognized private associations to initiate civil actions in interest of consumers. Law of Dec. 31, 1975, aimed at protecting French consumers (in broad sense) from misunderstanding, requires use of French language in transactions concerning goods and services. Law does not cover relations between foreign exporter and French importer; however, labelling for goods sold at retail level must be in French.

Law No. 78-23 of Jan. 10, 1978 protects consumers with respect to health and safety of goods and services and contains further measures, against fraudulent sales practices. (Arts. L. 115-27 to L. 115-33, L. 561-1 and L. 561-2, L. 132-1 to L. 132-5 of Consumer Code). Law No. 95-96 of Feb. 1, 1995 which implements EC Directive of Apr. 5, 1993 prohibits abusive clauses in consumer sales contracts. (Art. L. 132-1 of Consumer Code). Attached to Law is non-limitative list of 17 clauses which may be deemed abusive (relating to effective knowledge by consumers of contractual provisions, possibility to cancel sale, determination of price, warranty limitations, indemnification and termination clauses, unilateral changes by seller). In addition to this list special commission has established list of abusive clauses which are prohibited. (Law No. 78-23 of Jan. 10, 1978) particularly provisions concerning terms of payment, jurisdiction and limitation of seller's warranty. Such clauses are null and void, and may result in nullity of entire contract as well as in criminal penalties.

Law No. 78-22 of Jan. 10, 1978 on credit sales transactions provides that advertisement of credit sales must indicate name of lender, purpose and duration of loan, total cost, effective interest rate and other transaction charges, and contains other rules governing consumer credit sales. (Arts. L. 311-1 to L. 315-15 of Consumer Code). Law No. 84-66 of Jan. 24, 1984 adds some provisions to law of Jan. 10, 1978 which regulate credit sales whose cost are totally or partially supported by seller himself. For door-to-door sales, Law No. 72-1137 of Dec. 22, 1972 provides that buyer may renounce contract within seven-day period regardless of date of delivery of goods or services. (Arts. L. 121-21 to L. 121-32 of Consumer Code). Decree of Oct. 12, 1972 requires labelling of all prepacked food products. Law No. 92-60 of Jan. 18, 1992 provides additional measures to protect consumers by expanding type of activity which is prohibited by professionals selling door-to-door and further regulating comparative advertising and labelling. (Arts. L. 111-1 to L. 111-4, L. 114-1, L. 211-2, L. 121-18 and L. 121-19, L. 121-8 to L. 121-11, L. 122-3 to L. 122-5 of Consumer Code).

Prior municipal authorization is required for sale of unused goods in liquidations, forced sales and "sales". (Law of Dec. 30, 1906). Sale of goods involving rebates is regulated by Arrêté 77-65/P of Sept. 2, 1977. "Snowball" sales tactics, whereby consumer obtains goods or services free or at reduced prices in exchange for procuring sales to or subscriptions by third parties, are forbidden by Law of Nov. 5, 1953. (Arts. L. 122-6 and L. 122-7 of Consumer Code). Ordinance of Dec. 1, 1986 (no. 86-1243), prohibits sales, offers to sell goods, and rendering of services which give right to premium or bonus; unless premium or bonus consists in giving more of same good. This rule does not apply to inexpensive goods or to rendering of minor services or to gifts. Law of May 21, 1836 prohibits sales accompanied by lottery.

See also topics Interest; Sales.

CONTRACTS:

French law of contracts varies, to some extent, according to whether contract is deemed to be commercial or civil. Contract is deemed commercial when entered into by trader for purposes of commerce. Contracts between trader and non-trader may be deemed commercial as to trader, and civil as to non-trader.

Civil contracts may be either oral or in writing. Oral contracts are valid without any special formality. Contracts of value equal to or exceeding FRF 5,000 must be in writing and their validity may not be proven by witnesses. Parol evidence is not allowed to alter or challenge contents of any written contract (C. C. 1341) except where there is element of written proof ("commencement de preuve par écrit") in support of alteration or challenge. However, element of written proof must come from party against which alteration or challenge is alleged. (C. C. 1347).

Written contracts may be made either privately, as simple contracts, or by formal instrument before notary ("acte authentique"). (C. C. 1317-1322). For certain types of agreements such as gifts, prenuptial agreements and mortgages, notarial deeds are mandatory.

Private contracts must be made in as many originals as there are parties to agreement with differing interests and number of originals must be expressly indicated in document. No witnesses are required for validity of such contracts.

Commercial Contracts.—Parol evidence is permissible to establish existence or contents of most commercial contracts, regardless of amount of money involved. Nevertheless, contract made by trader for trader's personal purpose must be proven according to civil rules. Contracts between corporations, contracts on maritime rights, and contracts for sale of fonds de commerce (entire going business concern, including goodwill), as well as credit paper (bills of exchange, promissory notes) can only be proven by written evidence.

Exchange of correspondence may establish written contract.

Extensive body of law pertaining to "leasing" contracts has been developed, principal applicable text being Ordinance of Sept. 28, 1967.

Commercial contracts are not required to be registered, but may be registered voluntarily. In contract concluded between trader and consumer, any clause that aims at or whose consequence is to unbalance parties' obligations in favor of trader is disregarded. (List of sample clauses which might be regarded as aiming at or resulting in imbalance between parties obligations is attached to French Consumer Code—some may be fixed by decree.) This concerns every type opf contract, whether freely negotiated or not. Such contract may survive if its structure is not altered, should invalid clause be essential one for trader. These provisions (set forth by art. L. 132-1 of Consumer Code) are part of public policy and are applicable whenever consumer lives in member state of EU, or whenever contract has been proposed, concluded or performed within EU.

Formation of Contracts.—Four elements are essential to validity of contract: Consent of parties (which may result from intent letter); legal capacity to contract of both parties; specific object not contrary to public policy; and "cause," analogous to consideration. Valid contracts have force of law between contracting parties. (C. C. 1134). Contract may not be reformed or modified by courts for reasons of equity or otherwise. (Cass. Com. Dec. 18, 1979). Laws considered as relating to public policy and morals ("ordre public") may not be derogated from by contract.

Secret contracts concluded in addition to a publicly made contract in order to annul or modify this public contract are not necessarily void. Such secret contracts, however, concluded in order to conceal from tax authorities part of principal in sale of real estate, or of "fonds de commerce" (entire going business concern including goodwill), or of lease are void. Unilateral promise to lease or sell real estate or fonds de commerce is invalid unless evidenced by notarial instrument or private contract placed on record within ten days of promissee's acceptance. (C. G. I. art. 1840A).

Many types of contracts are subject to compulsory registration with fiscal authorities within one month from day of signature, notably: Contracts concerning conveyances of movable or immovable property; leases; prenuptial agreements; and contracts concerning formation, modification and winding up of partnerships and corporations. Registration of contracts requires payment of registration taxes, rate of which varies in accordance with value and specific nature of contract. An oral offer must be accepted at once. Written offer may be accepted during time specified, if any, or within reasonable time according to circumstances. Current case law permits revocation of

CONTRACTS . . . *continued*
offer until moment when offeree dispatches acceptance. Offer must be accepted unequivocally; any modification of offer by acceptance is deemed refusal. Silence is deemed acceptance if offer has been made for personal interest of offeree.

Contract is formed at moment of acceptance. Disputes over construction of contract are generally governed by law and in courts of place of acceptance, absent contrary stipulation by parties.

Nonperformance.—Disputes as to performance of contract are governed by law parties have chosen, unless this law would violate French public policy. (See subhead Applicable Law, infra.)

For nonperformance or defective performance aggrieved party may seek rescission and/or damages plus interest, but only after making formal request for good performance (mise en demeure). (C. C. 1138, 1139, 1146, 1184). Specific performance is not generally available. Contract may stipulate liquidated damages in event of nonperformance or defective performance (clause pénale, C. C. 1152) and courts customarily enforce such clauses without more. Court can, even ex officio, reduce or increase stated amount of liquidated damages if manifestly unfair. Court can also reduce such stated amount in proportion to benefit conferred by any partial performance. Any contrary stipulation is ineffective.

Nonperformance or defective performance may be excused by "force majeure"; this concept covers all events which are exterior to party in breach, and which are unforeseeable and irresistible; such events include acts of State, acts of God, and some acts by third party. (C. C. 1148). War or strike may constitute force majeure in some circumstances, but insolvency or change of economic position will not.

France has ratified United Nations Convention on Contracts for the International Sale of Goods (J.O. Dec. 27, 1987) applicable to transactions between parties established in different countries, which modifies French rules concerning liability arising from such contracts.

Applicable Law.—1980 Convention on the Law Applicable to Contractual Obligations referred to as Rome Convention, came into force on Apr. 1, 1991 and applies to contracts made after that date.

Rome Convention supersedes French conflict of laws rules which applied to obligations now in scope of Convention.

Rome Convention applies to any civil or commercial contracts whether or not entered into between nationals of EU member states (i.e. is worldwide in effect).

Some matters are excluded from scope of Convention of which most significant are arbitration agreement and choice of forum clauses, insurance relating to risks within EU (Convention however applies to contract of reinsurance), questions governed by law of companies, and obligations under negotiable instruments to extent they arise out of their negotiable character.

General choice of law rules to be found in Art. 3 and 4 of Convention provide that parties are free to choose governing law to their contract. In absence of choice, contract is to be governed by law of country which is most closely connected. Convention then provides for presumptions to determine country which is most closely connected with contract.

Convention also provides for specific rules to be applied to certain consumer contracts or individual employment contracts.

Government Contracts.—Government as rule enters into contracts for economic purpose only on basis of acceptance of bids, with specifically negotiated contracts being exception. Conditions and specifications of bids are set forth in general publication to all bidders and thereafter constitute part of contract. Contractor may receive funds on account of work done or advances on future work. Contractor must furnish bond of 3 to 10% of contract price and may also have part of funds on account withheld to insure good performance. These bonds may be replaced by personal guaranty or bank guaranty in some cases.

French Language.—Under Law No. 94-665 of 4 Aug. 1994 all contracts to which public entity or private entity performing mission of public service is party, whatever purpose and form of such contracts, must be drafted in French. Foregoing rule does not apply to contracts entered into by public entity operating industrial and commercial activities when such contract is to be fully performed outside of France. When such contracts are entered into with one or several foreign parties, French version may be accompanied by one or several versions in another language which may be equally binding.

COPYRIGHT:

Law No. 92-597 of July 1, 1992 has gathered several existing laws into new code, "Code de la propriété intellectuelle" ("C.P.I."). This new code groups existing provisions governing both copyrights and related rights and industrial property rights. Other than codifying different laws promulgated on different dates, new code does not provide any modifications to state of law.

Law No. 92-1336 of Dec. 16, 1992 regarding entry into force of new criminal code provides possibility that legal entities may be found criminally liable. Accordingly, this law added Art. L. 335-8 to C.P.I. which provides criminal liability for legal entities and defines applicable penalties.

Law of July 3, 1985, effective as of Jan. 1, 1986 applying to rights of authors, performing artists, record and video producers, and audiovisual broadcasting companies, provides extensive revision of law of Mar. 11, 1957 on literary and artistic property. New law also provides for creation of payment for private copy, for video and audio works, establishment of royalty collection and distribution companies, protection of software programs, and for special protections and sanctions.

Creation of artistic or intellectual work vests in author or artist absolute ownership of work and sole right of exploitation. Foreigners generally have equal right to protection of law.

Law expressly protects all books and other literary, artistic and scientific writings (including lectures), choreographic and musical works, audiovisual works (including cinematographic works and other works composed of animated sequences with or without sound), photographic works, drawings and printings, architectural, sculptural and graphic works (including plans) as well as software programs, garment designs or housing decoration. (Art. L. 112-2 C.P.I.). Case law requires protected work to be original ("expression of the artist's personality"). Such works are protected regardless of their format, merit or destination (Art. L. 112-1 C.P.I.) from moment of creation, even incomplete (Art. L. 111-2 C.P.I.).

Rights of Author ("droit d'auteur").—Sole author has right to divulge and exploit his work. This right remains in force during his lifetime and accrues to benefit of his heirs for 50 years after his death (Art. L. 123-1 C.P.I.) or death of last living author for collaboration works. (Art. L. 123-2 C.P.I.) Musical compositions with or without words are now protected for 70 years after death of author. (Art. L. 123-1 C.P.I.). Collective works are protected for 50 years after publication. (Art. L. 123-3 C.P.I.). After publication of work, author cannot forbid private and free presentations or copies and must accept, in certain circumstances, citation of his work and press reviews, provided his name is indicated.

Author or artist also enjoys perpetual and nonassignable moral right ("droit moral") giving him and his heirs recourse against others, including his assignee, for any distortion, modification or reproduction of his work which tends to discredit his name, his reputation or original spirit of work. Contract assigning rights in all future works of author is void.

Author may assign jointly or separately right to reproduce and right to perform ("droit de représentation") his work. (Art. L. 122-7 C.P.I.). New law gives general definition of performance so as to encompass communication by any means. (Art. L. 122-2 C.P.I.). This includes television broadcasting and transmission via satellite.

Law also contains specific provisions governing representation, publishing and audiovisual production contracts. Absent contrary proof, following individuals are presumed co-authors of audiovisual work: Screenwriter, adaptor, scriptwriter, composer of original musical score, director and author of original work. (Art. L. 113-7 C.P.I. as modified). However, producer deemed assignee of right to exploit audiovisual work unless production contract provides otherwise. (Art. L. 132-24 C.P.I.). Moral right of authors of audiovisual work vests as soon as work is in its final version (Art. L. 121-5 C.P.I.), which must be established by mutual consent between film maker (or co-authors) and producer. Final version may not be modified without authorization of director (or co-authors) and producer. Transfer of work from audiovisual to other medium for purpose of further exploitation requires prior consent of director. Adaption of written work to audiovisual medium requires specific written contract separate from contract governing publication. (Art. L. 123-1 and L. 123-2 C.P.I.).

Related Rights.—(Tit. II of Law of July 3, 1985). Related rights ("droits voisins") are newly created rights which protect artist, performing artists, record and video producers, and audiovisual communications companies. "Performing artist" is one who represents, sings, recites, plays or executes in any other manner literary or artistic work, show, circus or puppet act. (Art. L. 212-1 C.P.I.). Such artist has identical nonassignable right ("droit moral") in performance. (Art. L. 212-2 C.P.I.). Related rights are perpetual and may be transmitted to heirs. Only artist may authorize attachment, reproduction and public communication of his performance. (Art. L. 212-3 C.P.I.).

According to new law, prior to commercial release, record and video producers have right to forbid any reproduction of their records or videos, including any public sale, exchange or rental, as well as any public communication thereof. (Arts. L. 213-1 and 215-1 C.P.I.).

Audiovisual works may not be divided so as to assign video rights separately from soundtrack. Prior to commercial release audiovisual communication companies also have right to forbid reproduction, public disposal, televised broadcasting and paid public communication of their programs. (Art. L. 216-1 C.P.I.).

Remuneration for Private Copies of Records and Videos.—Manufacturers or importers of recording information and tapes must pay royalties for private copies to collecting companies which distribute said royalties among authors, artists and producers responsible for work. Distribution occurs only if record or video is originally made in France, except as otherwise provided by treaties. (Arts. L. 311-1 to 311-8).

Royalties Collecting and Distribution Companies.—(Arts. L. 321-1 to 321-12). These civil companies are composed of associates who must be authors, artists, producers or their entitled parties. They have certain obligations with regard to by-laws, financing, accounting, and certain of their acts are under control of Ministry of Culture. Associations which formerly collected and distributed royalties transferred all or part of their property to these newly created companies.

Software Programs.—Pursuant to Law No. 94-361 of May 10, 1994, software programs are now protected for same length as rights of authors, i.e. 50 years after death of author. (Art. L. 123-1 of Intellectual Property Code). Any reproduction and unauthorized copy (except safeguarding copy) is copyright infringement which may lead to attachment of software. Software programs created by employee under labor agreement belong to employer.

Protection and Sanctions.—Cinematographic works and videos must be registered, and contracts must be published in special register.

Videos designed for private use are controlled by "Centre National de la Cinématographie", administrative agency, and persons involved must keep documents for proof of origin and destination of videos. (Art. 52 of Law of July 3, 1985 [not codified in C.P.I.]).

If representatives of deceased author manifestly abuse use or even nonuse of right of divulgation and exploitation of works they have been granted at death of author, civil courts are empowered to order all necessary measures. (Art. L. 121-3 C.P.I.). Courts may also forbid creation or continuation of activities of collecting company.

Infringement of law is criminal offense which may be punished by imprisonment and fine (Art. L. 335-2 C.P.I.) and authorized attachment of illegal records, videos and software as well as all equipment fixed for this purpose (Art. L. 332-4 and L. 335-1 C.P.I.). In addition, copyright infringement may be sanctioned by closure of establishment, attachment of profits, and bill-posting or publication of conviction order. Author can request prosecution by public prosecutor in order to obtain civil damages. Suit may also be brought before civil courts only without criminal charges.

France and U.S. have subscribed to Berne Convention for the Protection of Literary and Artistic Works (U.S. adhesion effective Mar. 1, 1989). France and U.S. also signatories to Universal Copyright Convention, which provides reciprocal protections if certain formalities respected. Law of July 8, 1964 has introduced principle of reciprocity. If foreign country does not adequately and sufficiently protect works

See Topical Index in front part of this volume.

COPYRIGHT . . . *continued*
published elsewhere, works published in said foreign country will not benefit in France from protection afforded by French law.

Intellectual and artistic property rights may be freely licensed or assigned without being submitted to any government agency for approval. In certain cases licenses and assignments must be declared to Ministry of Industry. (Decree of May 26, 1970). See also topic Exchange Control.

CORPORATIONS:

Corporations in General.—French equivalents of corporation are either "société anonyme" ("S.A."), "société par actions simplifiée" ("S.A.S.") or "société à responsabilité limitée" ("S.A.R.L."). Liability of shareholders of these companies is limited to their investment. Law governing S.A. and S.A.R.L. is French Company Law of July 24, 1966 which also governs following commercial entities: "Société en nom collectif" (see topic Partnership, subhead General Partnership ["société en nom collectif"]), and "société en commandite" (see topic Partnership, subhead Special Partnership ["société en commandite simple"]).

Law No. 66-537 of July 24, 1966 as modified substantially revised and codified French Company Law. Law became effective Apr. 1, 1967 and all corporations formed after that date are governed by its dispositions. Corporations in existence prior to Apr. 1, 1967 are also governed by Law as of Oct. 1, 1968. Law No. 66-537 of July 24, 1966 has been modified by Law 81-1162 of Dec. 30, 1981, designed to harmonize French company law with Second Directive adopted by Commission of the European Community on Dec. 13, 1976. Law of Dec. 30, 1981 applies to companies formed on or after Jan. 2, 1982. Companies formed before that date will be covered by new law as of July 1, 1982, and must harmonize their articles of incorporation and by-laws with new law before July 1, 1985. Further modifications have, in particular, been made by Law No. 83-1 of Jan. 3, 1983, Law No. 83-353 of Apr. 30, 1983, Law No. 84-148 of Mar. 1, 1984, Law No. 85-1321 of Dec. 14, 1985, Law No. 88-15 of Jan. 5, 1988, and Law No. 94-126 of Feb. 11, 1994. Dispositions of Law No. 94-126 are meant to provide greater flexibility to corporations.

Corporations in Form of Sociétés Anonymes.—S.A. is stock company whose capital is divided into shares.

Purposes.—Any lawful and specific purpose.

Term of Corporate Existence.—Any duration up to 99 years. (Art. 2).

Firm name must contain phrase "société anonyme" or "S.A."

Incorporators.—S.A. must be formed by minimum of seven shareholders, either individual or corporate, and this minimum must continue to exist during life of corporation. If during life of S.A., number of shareholders falls below seven for one-year period, Tribunal of Commerce may, upon request of any interested party, order dissolution of S.A. However, Tribunal may at its discretion grant S.A. maximum period of six months to increase number of shareholders to that required by law. Tribunal cannot decide on dissolution, if on day it is ruling on merits of case, this regularization has taken place.

Capital.—Minimum capital is FRF 1,500,000 for S.A. seeking investment from public and FRF 250,000 for other S.A.s. S.A. will be considered to seek investment from public if it is listed on stock exchange or if its shares are placed with banks, investment houses or stockbrokers or if it makes use of publicity for sale of shares. In addition, Commission des Opérations de Bourse considers that S.A. seeks investment from public when it has more than 300 shareholders.

Articles of Incorporation and By-laws.—Articles and by-laws ("statuts") state corporate name, purpose and term of existence, corporate seat or office, amount of capital, par value and type of shares issued, and number of qualification shares for directors. Where contributions in kind are made for stock, judicially appointed auditor ("commissaire aux apports") makes report on value of property, which report is annexed to articles of incorporation and by-laws before their signature. For S.A. not seeking public investment no shareholders' meeting is held prior to formation and therefore articles of incorporation and by-laws name first board of directors and legally required auditors ("commissaires aux comptes").

Filing of Draft Articles.—S.A. seeking investment from public must file draft copy of articles of incorporation signed by person or persons acting as founder with Registrar of Tribunal of Commerce in locale of future corporate seat. Only after such filing can capital be subscribed. This requirement does not exist for S.A. not seeking investment from public.

Head Office.—Law No. 84-1149 of Dec. 21, 1984, provides that any corporation may have its head office in premises occupied by other corporations or, in case of small corporations, where manager lives. However, in latter case, term of domiciliation of corporation may not exceed two years as from date of registration of such corporation at Commercial Register. (Decree No. 85-1280 of Dec. 5, 1985).

Incorporation.—Formalities for formation of S.A. not seeking investment from public are greatly simplified under Law of July 24, 1966 am'd by Law of Jan. 3, 1983. S.A. is formed by: (1) Drafting articles of incorporation and by-laws; (2) subscription in full of stated capital; (3) payments of at least one-half of such capital; (4) deposit of funds as prescribed by regulations; (5) certificate drawn up by depositary of funds (bank) recording subscriptions and payments; (6) signature of articles of incorporation and by-laws by shareholders themselves or by proxy.

As between parties, S.A. is formed from date of signature of articles of incorporation and by-laws. However, S.A. does not become legal entity until it has been duly inscribed upon Register of Commerce, after having fulfilled procedural requirements set forth in regulations. Until such inscription, actions taken on behalf of S.A. are responsibility of those who act in its name and their personal liability is extinguished only if S.A. ratifies their acts. (Art. 5).

S.A. seeking investment from public must follow more complicated procedure. Articles of incorporation must have been duly filed and certain legal information published. Subscription to shares issued for cash is made by signing subscription bulletin. All subscription bulletins, together with at least 50% of nominal value of each share subscribed for cash, must be deposited with notaire or in specially designated bank account. Subscriptions and payments are recorded in certificate issued by depositary (bank) upon presentation of subscription bulletins. Immediately thereafter founder can issue call to all subscribers for organization meeting. This meeting is held subject to formal requirements and delays established by regulations.

Organization meeting is required only for S.A. seeking investment from public, and consists of general meeting of shareholders that precedes formation of company. Each stockholder has as many votes as shares of stock he holds or represents by proxy. Organization meeting ascertains regularity of subscription and payment recorded in certificate of depositary (bank), approves articles of incorporation and by-laws, names first board of directors and special auditors ("commissaires aux comptes"), if applicable, approves report of judicially appointed auditors ("commissaires aux apports") as to value of contributions in kind, and, upon acceptance of their functions by board of directors and special auditors, declares S.A. duly organized.

Filing of Articles and Other Formalities.—After organization of S.A., there must be filed with Tribunal of Commerce: Two originals of articles (or two copies certified by notaires); two copies of certificate of depositary of funds with list of subscribers and statement of payments appended thereto; two certified copies of minutes of organization meeting; and one copy of lease for head office. Documents so filed are open to public inspection and copies may be secured upon payment of small fee. Also, notice of formation must be published in legal notice newspaper and must include summary of essential features of articles. S.A. must be inscribed upon Commercial Register, which will assign to it registry number and SIRENE number (Instruction of Ministry of Justice, Dec. 24, 1975) which must appear with indication of corporate name, registered capital and corporate seat on all letterheads. Finally, S.A. must file with tax registration office, with local fiscal authorities and social security authorities.

Registration tax of 1% is no longer due at formation of S.A. on par value of shares and at each increase in capital on capital increment pursuant to Art. 6 of Law No. 85-695 of July 11, 1985. Under certain circumstances rate is higher for shares issued for contributions in kind of real estate or of intangibles such as good will. Until Dec. 31, 1987, capitalization of loans from controlling shareholder outstanding for 12 months or more is taxed at flat FRF 1,050 rather than at 1% rate. (Finance Law No. 83-1179, Dec. 29, 1983).

Paid in Capital Requirements.—Regulations require all subscriptions for contributions in kind and 50% of liquid capital subscriptions be paid up at time of incorporation. Balance must be paid up within period of five years.

Amendment of Articles.—Only extraordinary shareholders' meeting ("assemblée générale extraordinaire") has power to amend articles of incorporation and by-laws, including changing corporate purpose, duration, corporate name and registered office, or effecting merger, increase or decrease of authorized capital and premature dissolution. Amendment of articles must be approved by two-thirds majority. Change of registered office to new address within same or adjacent department may be effected by board of directors but decision must be ratified by general shareholders' meeting ("assemblée générale").

Increase or Decrease of Authorized Capital.—Except in cases of stock dividend payments and capitalization of reserves, extraordinary shareholders' meeting is competent to decide upon increase or decrease in capital. S.A.'s capital is increased either by issuance of new shares, or by increase in value of existing shares. Increase in value of existing shares must be by unanimous vote, except for increase in value of existing shares by capitalization of reserves. Shareholders have preferential right to subscribe to new shares issued for cash. Each shareholder may waive his preferential right. Shareholders' meeting which decides on increase in capital may eliminate preferential right of subscription in favor of one or more persons. (Art. 186 of Law of July 24, 1966 am'd). Where S.A. grants stock options to its employees, preferential right as to stock covered by said options is relinquished by existing shareholders in favor of such employees. (Law No. 70-1322 of Dec. 31, 1970 and implementing Decree No. 71-418 of June 7, 1971). In case of capital reduction, special auditors ("commissaires aux comptes") must be advised of project at least 45 days beforehand and make report to extraordinary shareholders' meeting before reduction can be voted. Reduction of capital to amount less than legal minimum can only be decided upon subject to condition precedent of increase in capital bringing amount of capital up to legal minimum unless S.A. is changed into another commercial entity. S.A. whose shares are listed on stock exchange have right under certain conditions in connection with profit-sharing plans and with stock option plans, to buy their own shares. (Ordinance of Sept. 28, 1967, Law No. 70-1322 of Dec. 31, 1970 and implementing Decree No. 71-418 of June 7, 1971, Arts. 217-1 and 217-2 of Law No. 66-537 of July 24, 1966, am'd by Law No. 81-1162 of Dec. 30, 1981). See also topic Labor Relations.

By-laws.—See catchline Articles of Incorporation and By-laws, supra.

Stock.—Shares must have minimum par value fixed by by-laws. (Law No. 88-15 of Jan. 5, 1988). Basically, shares may be issued in either bearer or nominative form at option of shareholder, but articles of incorporation and by-laws may require all shares to be in nominative form. As of Oct. 1, 1982, shares must be nominative, although bearer shares may still be issued by most publicly held corporations. All corporations traded on French principal and secondary stock exchange ["code officielle" and "second marché"] may issue bearer shares. Corporations traded on so-called "Hors côte" may only issue bearer shares if volume of transactions in such shares is significant. By Ordinance of Sept. 28, 1967, all insiders of S.A. whose shares are listed on stock exchange must have their shares and those of their minor children in both S.A. and its subsidiaries in registered form. Shares issued for cash must remain registered shares as long as they are not fully paid up.

Preferred shares may be issued with special rights to dividends or on dissolution; these rights may be cumulative. Non-voting shares are permitted subject to special conditions (Law No. 78-741 of July 13, 1978), and shares with multiple votes only in extremely limited circumstances (e.g., double votes for fully paid in shares).

Except in few cases, S.A. may not hold its own shares as treasury stock.

Pursuant to Law 81-1160 of Dec. 30, 1981, effective Nov. 3, 1984, French company shares have been dematerialized, i.e. they are no longer represented by certificates. Nominative or bearer share certificates are now cancelled and replaced by simple entry in account in name of shareholders maintained by issuing S.A. or financial institution approved by Ministry of Finance.

As noted above, except for one other limited exception, only S.A. whose stock is listed on a French exchange and S.A. whose stock is actively traded "over-the-

See Topical Index in front part of this volume.

CORPORATIONS . . . *continued*
counter" can still issue what are called "bearer" shares (accounts in name of shareholder for such "bearer" shares can only be maintained by financial institution approved by Ministry of Finance). All other S.A.s must have nominative shares. Distinction between "bearer" and nominative shares is now mostly artificial: Only difference is that "bearer" shares accounts are held by such financial institution and not by issuing S.A.

Transfer of Stock.—Law No. 66-537 permits articles of incorporation and by-laws to restrict alienability of shares to third parties; such restriction cannot prohibit transfers by way of inheritance, liquidation of community property or transfers to spouse or direct relation except if S.A. reserves shares for its employees, in which case articles of incorporation may provide that these shares may neither be inherited by, nor transferred to non-employees. (Art. 274). Restriction of alienability is not absolute, and if board of directors or management committee refuses permission for transfer, it must arrange for purchase of shares by shareholder or third party or, with consent of seller, by S.A. itself. (Art. 275).

Transfers of nominative shares are entered in stock accounts upon presentation of transfer instrument. (Ordre de Mouvement).

No shares may be transferred by shareholder until S.A. is inscribed on Register of Commerce. In case of increase in capital, shares are negotiable as of date of realization of said increase in capital (i.e., in case of cash increase, date of certificate of deposit of funds; or, in case of increase in capital by incorporation of receivables and reserves, date of extraordinary general shareholders' meeting).

Bonds and Debentures.—S.A. having been in existence for at least two years may issue bonds and debentures provided shareholders have approved annual balance sheets of S.A. for last two years and provided that capital has been fully paid in. These restrictions are not applicable if bonds are issued in favor of salaried employees under profit-sharing plan. (Art. 285). Issues of FRF 1,000,000,000 or more per year require prior declaration to bank.

Convertible debentures may be issued but are subject to restrictions provided by law. Ordinance of Sept. 28, 1967 provides that in case of merger, reimbursement of bondholders will only be required upon court determination rendered at request of bondholders after their "assemblée générale."

Law No. 83-1 of Jan. 3, 1983 created new class of debentures, "Debentures with rights of subscription", which may be issued by extraordinary shareholders' decision. (Art. 194-1—194-11 of Law of July 24, 1966).

Law 81-1160 of Dec. 30, 1981 (see supra, catchline Stock), effective Nov. 3, 1984, also applies to bonds and debentures.

Certificates of Investment.—By Law of Jan. 3, 1983, extraordinary shareholders' meeting may decide, by increasing capital or dividing existing shares, upon creation of certificates of investment which represent financial rights and voting certificates which represent other rights. Certificates of investment cannot represent more than 25% of capital. (Arts. 283-1 to 283-5, Law of July 24, 1966). In Oct. 1986 Commission des Opérations de Bourse indicated that certificates of investment may not carry double voting right.

Bonds with Detachable Warrants.—Law No. 1321 of Dec. 14, 1985 permits issuance of bonds with detachable warrants. Issuance of such bonds is decided upon by extraordinary shareholders meeting, which is free to determine period of validity of attributed rights, and is not subject to prior time period imposed by administration before capital increases are implemented.

Independent Warrants.—Law No. 85-1321 of Dec. 14, 1985 also permits issuance of independent warrants which are not tied to other securities, and which give right to subscribe to capital increase of issuing company. Such warrants must be approved by extraordinary shareholders meeting.

Reporting Requirements ("Auto Control").—Art. 356 of Law No. 66-537 provides that any individual or corporate entity at any time holding more than one-twentieth, one-tenth, one-fifth, one-third or one-half of outstanding shares in French corporation must inform said corporation of total number of shares held within two weeks after relevant threshold is reached. In companies which are officially quoted, Art. 356-1 and following Arts. of Law No. 66-537 provide that any individual or corporate entity at any time holding more than one-twentieth, one-tenth, one-fifth, one third, one half or two-thirds of outstanding shares or voting rights in French corporation must inform said corporation of total number of shares held within two weeks after relevant threshold is reached. Company's articles of incorporation and by-laws may provide for additional obligation to furnish information relating to holding of less than one-twentieth of capital, but not less than 0.5% of capital. In companies which are officially quoted, shares exceeding fraction which should have been declared are deprived of right to vote at any shareholders' meeting which takes place within two years after date notification should have occurred. If such corporation is listed on stock exchange, said individual or corporate entity must inform French stock exchange ("Conseil des bourses de valeurs") of number of shares held within five trading days after relevant threshold is reached. Shares held by such individual or corporate entity include all shares that said individual or corporate entity controls or has right or option to control directly or indirectly.

In addition, corporations directly or indirectly controlled by another corporation must report to such corporation as well as to each controlling corporation amount of shares said controlled corporations directly or indirectly hold in each of controlling corporations' stock. Such notification must be made whenever shareholdings have changed as result of acquisition or transfer of shares within preceding month.

Stockholders' Rights and Liabilities.—Liability of each stockholder is strictly limited to amount of his investment determined by his subscription. Rights of shareholders include right to vote, to contest resolutions of general meetings, to receive dividends and to share in distribution of assets in case of liquidation.

Law No. 66-537 provides obligations of all S.A.s to furnish to shareholders, upon request at any time, pertinent financial information, including latest income statement, balance sheet and report of special auditors as well as list of the ten (limited to five when personnel does not exceed 200) most highly paid employees or agents of S.A. (Art. 168). Regulations set forth conditions and terms for obtaining such information. In addition, shareholders have right to communication of same information for prior three years as well as reports and attendance records of prior shareholders' meetings.

Before issuance of any shares on stock exchange can be effected, S.A. must submit documentation, which will be available for public inspection, to Commission for Stock Exchange Operations. From first fiscal year starting after Dec. 31, 1984 and only until end of first fiscal year starting after Dec. 31, 1986, when corporation controls directly or indirectly one or more companies which in turn hold shares in corporation, votes cast by controlled companies at corporation's shareholders' meeting may not represent more than 15% of all votes cast by present or represented shareholders. Starting from first fiscal year beginning after Dec. 31, 1986, this percentage was reduced to 10%.

Stockholders' Meeting ("Assemblée Générale").—General shareholders' meeting ("assemblée générale") is highest authority of S.A. Regular meeting must be held annually within six months of end of fiscal year (Art. 157) for purpose of approving balance sheet and income statement, voting allocation of profits and electing and dismissing directors and special auditors. Quorum for regular shareholders' meeting is one-fourth of registered shareholders on first call with no specified minimum on second call (Art. 155). Decisions are taken by majority of votes of shareholders present or represented. Shareholder may be represented at meeting by another shareholder or by spouse but not by third persons. Shareholders may vote by mail. (Art. 161-1, Law of July 24, 1966).

Decree of Mar. 14, 1986 describes specific terms and conditions pursuant to which shareholders may vote by mail.

Votes by mail must comply with certain requirements as to form. In addition, votes must be received by company at least three days before meeting, unless shorter period of time allowed by by-laws.

If vote called on question raised during shareholders' meeting, shares of shareholders who voted by mail are not taken into account for calculation of quorum or vote on such question, unless intent or effect of question is to amend or to render inoperative, in whole or in part, resolution set forth on agenda for meeting, in which case shares of shareholders who voted by mail taken into account for calculation of quorum and treated as having voted against relevant question.

Extraordinary shareholders' meeting ("assemblée générale extraordinaire") is only corporate body competent to fulfil several important functions. See catchlines Amendment of Articles, Increase or Decrease of Authorized Capital, supra; and Dissolution, infra. Quorum for extraordinary shareholders' meeting is one-third of registered shareholders on first call and one-fourth on second call. (Art. 153). Decisions are taken by two-thirds of votes of shareholders present or represented. Shareholders may vote by mail. (Art. 161-1, Law of July 24, 1966).

Bylaws may not provide for quorum and/or majority disposition which are not in conformity with law.

Alien Stockholders.—See topic Exchange Control.

Voting Trusts.—Proxy votes by other shareholders are permitted, but voting trusts and other agreements in respect to voting are void.

Management.—Law No. 66-537 provides that S.A.s may be managed, as provided for in articles of incorporation and by-laws, either by traditional board of directors ("conseil d'administration") or by management committee ("directoire") functioning under supervision of shareholders council ("conseil de surveillance"). Adoption of latter must be made either in articles or by vote of extraordinary shareholders' meeting. Otherwise, former is deemed to be management regime. Ordinance No. 86-1135 of Oct. 21, 1986 provides that employees of company may designate employee as director subject to special provision of articles and bylaws.

Management by Board of Directors.—S.A.s may be managed by board of directors ("conseil d'administration") whose number, specified in articles of incorporation, may be anywhere from minimum of three to maximum of 24, subject to certain exceptions (see Law No. 66-537, Art. 89). Maximum term of office is six years for directors elected at general shareholders' meeting and three years for directors named in articles of incorporation and by-laws. Shorter term of office may be provided for in articles of incorporation and by-laws.

As of Oct. 1, 1972, articles of incorporation and by-laws of every S.A. are supposed to set age limit for all directors or percentage thereof; unless articles of incorporation and by-laws provide otherwise, not more than one-third of directors serving on board may be over 70.

Directors are eligible for re-election. Director who dies or resigns during his term of office may be replaced by decision of board of directors provided that number of remaining directors is no less than three, and such action must be presented to next general shareholders' meeting for ratification. Directors may be removed from office at any time, without indemnity, by vote of shareholders at ordinary general shareholders' meeting. If corporate entity is elected as director, as is permitted by law, it must designate physical person as its permanent representative on board of directors, and such person is, together with corporate entity, subject to civil and penal sanctions for breach of director's duties. Person cannot serve at same time and on same board both as director and permanent representative.

Director must own number of shares stipulated in S.A.'s articles of incorporation and by-laws which must at least be equal to number of shares providing access to shareholders' meeting. No person may serve simultaneously on more than eight boards of directors and shareholders' councils of French S.A.s and not more than one-third of members of board may have employment contracts with S.A. In no event may employee having employment contract be elected to board unless his employment contract corresponds to bona fide employment. At least half of board must be physically present for meetings to be valid and decisions are taken by majority of those present or represented. Articles of incorporation and by-laws can provide for higher majority if unanimously accepted, but quorum cannot be changed. Any action undertaken with unlawful quorum is null and void.

Board of directors is given widest powers of management consistent with corporate purposes stated in articles of incorporation and by-laws. Powers of board of directors include following: (1) Calling meetings of shareholders and establishing agenda; (2) drawing up income statement and balance sheet; (3) authorizing contracts between S.A. and one of its directors or between S.A. and another company in which director has interest; (4) authorizing any financial guarantees or endorsements of obligations of other persons or companies; and (5) electing president and, upon nomination by president, electing his principal assistant, general manager ("directeur général").

Directors may receive fee for attendance at board meeting ("jetons de présence") but may not normally receive other remuneration in their capacity as directors. They

CORPORATIONS . . . *continued*

may not, as a rule, enter into contracts with S.A. without prior board approval, and, subsequent report must be made to shareholders' meeting, which is to ratify agreement.

President of S.A. must be director. No company may be president, and no person may be president of more than two boards of directors. President has responsibility for general management of S.A. which he represents in its dealings with third parties. He has appropriate powers limited only by corporate purpose and reservation by law of certain powers to board of directors and to shareholders. Third parties may rely upon these statutory powers and are not bound by additional limitations on powers of president which may be provided for in articles of incorporation and by-laws. In case of incapacity, president may provisionally delegate his functions to one of directors. As of Oct. 1, 1972, articles of incorporation and by-laws are supposed to set maximum age limit for president of board. Unless articles of incorporation and by-laws provide otherwise, president of board cannot be more than 65 years old. (Law No. 506-537 of July 24, 1966, Law No. 70-1284 of Dec. 31, 1970).

Powers of general manager ("directeur général") are defined by board of which he is an agent but not necessarily a member. However, in dealing with third parties, general manager is deemed to have powers similar to those of a president. In S.A. having capital of at least FRF 500,000, there may be two general managers. In S.A. having capital of at least FRF 10,000,000, there may be five general managers, on condition that at least three of them are directors. As of Oct. 1, 1972, articles of incorporation and by-laws are supposed to set age limit for general managers. Unless articles of incorporation and by-laws provide otherwise, general manager cannot be over 65.

No director other than president or such director receiving special delegation or director designated as deputy general manager may exercise any managerial function.

Alien Managers.—Before alien, other than Common Market national, can act as president or as general manager ("directeur général"), he must obtain special "trader's card" ("carte de commercant") from Préfecture de Police or departmental préfecture. Alien deputy general manager must have worker's card ("carte de travail") just as any alien employee.

Management by Management Committee and Shareholders' Council.—Provisions of law No. 66-537 of July 24, 1966 authorizes management of S.A. by management committee ("directoire") functioning under control of shareholders' council ("conseil de surveillance"). Shareholders' council has many resemblances to board of directors of traditional S.A. Shareholders' council is composed of minimum of three and maximum of 24 members. As of Oct. 1, 1972, articles of incorporation and by-laws are supposed to set age limit for members of shareholders' council applicable to all or percentage of those members. Unless articles or by-laws provide otherwise, no more than one-third of members of shareholders' council may be over 70.

Maximum term of office of council is six years for members elected at general shareholders' meeting and three years for members named in articles of incorporation and by-laws. Shorter term of office may be provided in articles of incorporation and by-laws. No person may be member of more than eight shareholders' councils and boards of directors. Members of council may be removed from office by vote of shareholders at ordinary shareholders' meeting at any time.

Corporate entity may be elected member of council but it must designate person as its permanent representative on council, and such person is, together with corporate entity, subject to civil and penal sanctions for breach of duties as member of council. Employees having employment contracts may be elected as members of council. Person may not serve at same time and on same council both as member and permanent representative. Member must own number of shares stipulated in S.A.'s articles of incorporation and by-laws. Member of shareholders' council may not be member of management committee ("directoire"). Shareholders' council elects president and vice-president whose duty is to call meetings of council and to direct meeting. At least half of members of council must be present for meetings to be valid, and decisions are taken by majority of those present or represented. (Art. 139). Quorum cannot be changed, but articles of incorporation can provide for higher majority.

Shareholders' council, like board of directors in traditional S.A., represents interest of shareholders. Unlike board of directors, however, council has no management powers. Its function, rather, is to supervise actions of management committee, which must deliver to it a report at least every three months as well as a financial report (balance sheet and income statement) annually. (Art. 128). In addition, council: (1) May require additional reports from management committee at any time; (2) delivers report at annual shareholders' meeting regarding management of S.A.; (3) authorizes contracts between S.A. and one of members of management committee or shareholders' council (or between S.A. and another company in which member of either body has interest); (4) authorizes any financial guarantee or endorsements by S.A. of obligations of other persons or companies; (5) authorizes transfer of real property or total or partial transfer of participations; (6) has power to call meeting of shareholders.

Pursuant to Law No. 85-1321 of Dec. 14, 1985, Conseil de Surveillance may grant remuneration to their President and Vice President.

S.A. is managed by management committee ("directoire") which is composed of from two to five members, except for S.A. with stated capital of less than FRF 1,000,000 in which case "directoire" may consist of single member called single general manager ("directeur général unique").

Corporate entity may not be member of management committee. Management committee, as well as its president, or "directeur général unique," is elected by shareholders' council. Articles of incorporation and by-laws should provide for term for these offices lasting from two to six years. If not expressly provided by articles, term is fixed at four years. Members need not be shareholders and may be members of more than two management committees. No person may be member of more than two management committees. Members of management committee may be removed from office by vote at general shareholders' meeting, but such removal, without just cause, may give rise to action for damages.

Management committee is given widest powers of management consistent with corporate purpose as stated in articles of incorporation and by-laws except for certain specified powers reserved by law to shareholders' council and shareholders. Articles of incorporation and by-laws determine manner in which management committee shall meet and make decisions. President of management committee or single manager represents S.A. in its dealings with third parties. Articles of incorporation and by-laws may require that certain decisions of management committee be submitted to shareholders' council for approval, but third parties are not bound by such restrictions.

Dividends can be declared only by general shareholders' meeting from reserves at its disposition. Payment must be made available by S.A. for payment to stockholders within nine months of closing of fiscal year, although stockholders may choose to be paid after this period.

However, dividends on account may be distributed before close of fiscal year, if audited partial balance sheet drawn up during fiscal year indicates that S.A. has during this period realized profits (after allowances for depreciation, prior losses, and legal and statutory reserves), sufficient to cover such dividends. Board of directors or management committee may decide whether to distribute such dividends on account, and fixes amount and date of distribution. (Decree of Dec. 24, 1969, Art. 8; Law of Jan. 6, 1969, Art. 15; Law No. 81-1162 of Dec. 30, 1981). Shareholders' meeting approving accounts of fiscal year may give shareholders choice of receiving their dividends in cash or in shares issued by S.A. if expressly provided by articles of incorporation and by-laws. (Law of Jan. 5, 1988).

Accounts.—Supervision of corporate accounts must be entrusted to special auditors ("commissaires aux comptes") first named at time of incorporation in articles of incorporation and by-laws of S.A. not seeking investment by public and by organization meeting of shareholders in other S.A.s. Term of office is six years. Subsequent to incorporation, special auditors are named by general shareholders' meetings.

Law No. 66-537 requires that special auditors be named from list established by government. Prerequisites for listing are established by regulations intended to strengthen professional and technical qualifications. Mission of special auditors has been expanded so as to include duty to certify regularity and good faith of financial reports as well as their accuracy, and also to ensure equality among shareholders. (Art. 228). Under Law of Apr. 30, 1983, they have to certify that annual accounts exactly reflect financial situation of S.A. Special auditors have right of inspection of all accounts and business papers of S.A.s, including inspection of accounts of parent and subsidiary. They inform board of directors (or management committee) of results of their investigations and deliver report to annual shareholders' meeting. They have right to call shareholders' meeting.

Manner of presenting accounts has been harmonized with 4th E.E.C. Directive by Law of Apr. 30, 1983 and Decree of Nov. 29, 1983.

Corporation must file following documents with Tribunal of Commerce: Two copies of annual accounts, board of directors of shareholders' council report, special auditor's report, and proposal for allocation of financial results. (Law of 30 Apr. 1983 and Decree of 29 Nov. 1983).

Dissolution occurs upon expiration of time stated in articles of incorporation, decision of special meeting of shareholders, or by court order in cases provided for by law. In particular, in event S.A. assets fall below one-half of registered capital, shareholders' meeting must be called within four months following approval of accounts showing such loss for purpose of deciding whether to dissolve S.A., within two years after end of fiscal year during which such loss of capital occurred, S.A. must reduce its capital by at least amount of loss or restore its net assets to at least one-half, of registered capital. (Law of Jan. 6, 1969). Liquidator, appointed by general meeting of shareholders, or by court decree, attends to liquidation of S.A. Dissolution and name of liquidator must be registered with Register of Commerce. When liquidation is accomplished, entry of S.A. on Register of Commerce is cancelled.

Corporations in Form of Sociétés à Responsabilité Limitée.—Law No. 66-537 of July 24, 1966 remains applicable to limited liability companies ("sociétés responsabilité limitée" or "S.A.R.L."), which companies resemble in large measure small, closely held American corporations. Liability of members ("associés") of S.A.R.L.'s is limited to their contribution in capital. Law No. 85-697 of July 11, 1985 has instituted new forms of S.A.R.L.: "Entreprises unipersonnelles à responsabilité limitée" or "E.U.R.L.", one-person limited liability corporations, and "exploitations agricoles à responsabilité limitée" or "E.A.R.L.", limited liability agricultural enterprises.

As result, article 1832 of Civil Code now provides that corporation is instituted through contract between two or more persons, or may be created by single person's voluntary act. When corporation formed by single person, such person called single member ("associé unique").

Formation.—One or more persons may create "S.A.R.L." for maximum duration of 99 years. (Art. 2 of 1966 Law as am'd). Membership may not exceed 50 in S.A.R.L., with exception of E.U.R.L. Companies may be members; however, single member of E.U.R.L. may not be another one-man corporation. Individual may be single member of several E.U.R.L.'s. (Art. 36-2 of 1966 Law as am'd). If above two prohibitions violated, any interested party may request dissolution of corporation in accordance with paragraph two of Art. 36-2 of 1966 Law as am'd. Minimum capital of S.A.R.L. created on or after Mar. 1, 1985 is FRF 50,000. All participations must be fully subscribed and paid up. There is registration tax of FRF 500 on capital paid in cash.

Investment by nonresident in S.A.R.L. is subject to regulations of Ministry of Finance. See topic Exchange Control.

S.A.R.L. is formed by all members or by single member signing articles of incorporation and by-laws which must indicate duration of S.A.R.L., its name, its purposes and amount of stated capital, as well as division of participations among members, if applicable. Articles and by-laws need not be notarized. Articles and by-laws must indicate value of any contributions in kind in standard S.A.R.L. Evaluation of contributions in kind must be fixed by special auditor ("commissaire aux apports") who is appointed either by unanimous decision of future members of S.A.R.L. or by judicial decision upon request of one of future members. 1985 Law provides that such auditor may be appointed by single member in E.U.R.L. If no contribution in kind exceeds FRF 50,000 or if total value of such contributions does not exceed half of stock capital, such appointment is not required in one-man corporation.

As between parties S.A.R.L. is formed from date of signature of articles of incorporation and by-laws. However, S.A.R.L. does not become legal entity until it has been duly inscribed upon Register of Commerce after having fulfilled procedural requirements established by regulation. Registration number must appear on all S.A.R.L. stationery together with indication of S.A.R.L. capital, form, and head office. Until

See Topical Index in front part of this volume.

CORPORATIONS . . . *continued*
inscription on Register of Commerce, actions taken on behalf of S.A.R.L. are responsibility of those who act in its name and their personal liability is extinguished only if company ratifies their acts. (art. 5).

There must be publication of formation of S.A.R.L. in legal notice periodicals, stating: (1) Existence of limited responsibility; (2) name of S.A.R.L. and designation of principal office; (3) purpose of S.A.R.L.; (4) person or persons authorized to manage and sign for S.A.R.L.; (5) amount of capital; (6) date of formation and period of existence of S.A.R.L.; and (7) dates of filing.

Management.—S.A.R.L. is managed by one or more managing directors ("gérants") named by member(s) but who need not be members themselves. As opposed to prior law, S.A.R.L. may not be managing director. Managing director may be removed from office by vote by members without cause. However, if such removal is unjustified it may give rise to damage action. (art. 55).

Unless limited by articles of incorporation and by-laws, managing director or directors may take any action consistent with S.A.R.L.'s purposes, and such action vis-à-vis third parties is binding on S.A.R.L.

Third parties are not bound by special limitations on powers of managing directors which may be provided in articles of incorporation and by-laws. Where there is more than one managing director, third parties may in principle rely upon acts of any one of them.

Any agreement between S.A.R.L. and one of its members or managing director must be made object of special report by managing director or special auditor which, in turn, must be approved by members. However, if there is no special auditor, agreements between S.A.R.L. and managing director are subject to prior approval by member(s). (Art. 6 of 1985 Law). If approval is refused, any harmful consequences of agreement are charged to contracting managing director or member. Such supervision procedure excluded when agreements between S.A.R.L. and managing director or member concern common operations and are concluded in normal terms.

Alien, other than Common Market national, acting as managing director must obtain a "trader's card" ("carte de commerçant") from Préfecture de Police or departmental prefecture. No registration on Register of Commerce is possible without such card.

Dividends.—See subhead Corporations in Form of Sociétés Anonymes, supra.

Accounts.—Members may name special auditors ("commissaires aux comptes") to supervise accounting and financial reports of S.A.R.L. Decree of Mar. 1, 1985 (Art. 6) implementing Law of Mar. 1, 1984 on prevention and amicable settlement of company difficulties, requires company to appoint Statutory Auditor and Replacement Statutory Auditor for six year term when any two of following three criteria have been met during two preceding fiscal years: (i) Total assets on balance sheet exceed FRF 10,000,000; (ii) turnover (excluding V.A.T.) exceeds FRF 20,000,000; (iii) average number of salaried workers exceeds 50. For fuller description of functions of special auditors, see subhead Corporations in Form of Sociétés Anonymes, supra.

S.A.R.L.s must file following documents with Tribunal of Commerce within month following approval of accounts: Annual Accounts, Management Report, Special Auditor's Report, and proposal for allocation of financial results. (Decree of Nov. 29, 1983).

Participations may not be offered for public subscription. They are not represented by certificates and transfers can only be made by transfer document served upon S.A.R.L. Participations may be transferred only with consent of majority of associates representing three-fourths of capital. (art. 45). If consent refused, S.A.R.L. must within three months from such refusal acquire or cause to be acquired participations so offered at price fixed under usual provisions of Civil Code. S.A.R.L. may also, with consent of member proposing transfer, within same three months repurchase and cancel participations involved to reduce its capital by their face value. If neither solution reached after three months, member proposing transfer may proceed as originally proposed, provided he had held his participation for at least two years; otherwise participation cannot be transferred.

Transfers between members are not restricted by law, but articles of incorporation and by-laws may provide restrictions of equal, but not greater, severity than those provided by law for third party transfers.

In case of contributions and acquisitions effected by means of community property, spouse of person who has decided to make acquisition must be informed in advance in order to allow new spouse to assert right to one half of shares. Furthermore, this must be notified in act, failure to do so making it null and void.

Transfers by way of inheritance or liquidation of community property, or to spouse or direct relation are not restricted by law but some restrictions may be in articles and by-laws.

Members' Rights and Duties.—Annual meeting of members must be held within six months of close of fiscal year of S.A.R.L. Prior to such meetings management must make available to members pertinent financial information, including latest income statement and balance sheet. (art. 56 and Art. 60-1 of 1966 Law as modified by 1985 Law). In one-man corporations management submits such documentation to single member who must approve within six months. Members may also obtain similar information for prior three years pursuant to conditions established by regulation. Members have right to submit written questions which must be answered by managing director at meeting.

Members' meeting approves accounts for fiscal year; vests increased authority in managing directors if necessary; and generally decides upon all questions not requiring extraordinary collective decision ("décision collective extraordinaire") by absolute majority on first call and by majority of votes cast on second call. Extraordinary collective decisions can be made only with consent of majority of members representing at least three-fourths of capital and are required to alter articles of incorporation or by-laws, increase or reduce capital, or dissolve S.A.R.L. Change of nationality or transformation of S.A.R.L. to partnership or other forms of corporation normally requires unanimous approval. In one-man corporations, single member has same powers as members meeting in other S.A.R.L.s. S.A.R.L. can be transformed into S.A. by simple majority if net assets exceed FRF 5,000,000.

If S.A.R.L. becomes S.A., one or more special auditors must be appointed by Judge of Tribunal of Commerce to determine current value of assets.

Dissolution.—In case company's net assets fall below one half of registered capital as of July 1, 1982, managing director or special auditor must, within four months after approval of accounts showing such loss, consult members about possibility of dissolution. If members decide not to dissolve S.A.R.L., capital must, within two years, be reduced by amount of loss or S.A.R.L.'s net assets must be restored to at least one-half of registered capital as of July 1, 1982. (Law No. 69-12 of Jan. 6, 1969 as am'd by Law No. 81-1162 of Dec. 30, 1981). In any case, decision must be published according to rules established by decree. Cause for dissolution also arises when S.A.R.L. retains more than 50 members or when capital falls below legal minimum. Other causes of dissolution are those common to all forms of Commercial societies. See subhead Corporations in Form of Sociétés Anonymes, supra.

From moment of its dissolution, S.A.R.L. is in liquidation being realization of assets and payment of creditors in order to proceed with distribution between members of remaining assets.

However, dissolution of one-man corporation does not give way to liquidation, but instead transfer of universality of E.U.R.L. property to sole member with right of opposition given to creditors.

Corporations in Form of Société par Actions Simplifiée-S.A.S.—Law No. 94-1 of Jan. 3, 1994 instituted simplified company form called Simplified Shares Company ("Société par Actions Simplifiée" or "SAS"). Originally SAS was meant as vehicle for joint ventures between other companies and to answer concerns of businesses who complained about rigidity of existing French corporate structures.

In practice, SAS may also be used to set up subsidiaries 99% owned by foreign corporation.

Only corporations may be shareholders in SAS. Individuals, GIEs and associations may not be shareholders in SAS.

Corporations' shareholders in SAS must have minimum paid-up capital of FF 1.5 million (or equivalent in foreign currency).

SAS must have minimum of two shareholders. Minimum capital is FF 250,000 and must be entirely paid-up upon subscription. SAS may not solicit funds from public.

Management structure is freely set-up in by-laws. Only minimum requirement concerns office of President. President represents SAS with third parties and limitation of President's powers are not binding on third parties.

President may be corporation or individual and may be appointed for determined or undetermined duration.

When President (or member of collective supervisory body set by by-laws) is corporation, directors of that corporation are subject to same conditions and liabilities as if they were themselves President (or member of collective supervisory body).

By-laws may also provide for collective management based, for example, on SA model of management (i.e. Board of Directors and President, or Supervisory Board ["Conseil de Surveillance"] and "Directoire").

By-laws may freely set rules according to which shareholders made decisions. Resolutions may be adopted by holding actual meeting, by correspondence, by fax or by circulating written consent for signature.

However, following decisions can only be made by extraordinary shareholders' meeting: increases and decreases in capital; decision to merge, split-up or contribute SAS to capital of another company; nomination of statutory auditors; decisions regarding review of yearly accounts and distribution of dividends.

Unanimity is also required to modify certain provisions of by-laws such as those regarding: nontransferability of shares; shareholders' agreements concerning share transfers; expulsion of shareholder; and suspension of shareholder's voting right when control of that shareholder has changed.

Foreign Corporations.—Such corporations desiring to do business in France through branch must comply with exchange control regulation (see topic Exchange Control). Foreign corporation must file with Registrar of Tribunal of Commerce two certified copies of its charter and by-laws, legalized by French Consul, as well as various supporting papers, all accompanied by French translations. Branch must have office address, evidenced by commercial lease.

Foreign corporation must also be inscribed on Register of Commerce, filing special forms specifying, among other things, representative entitled to sign for and administer French office of corporation. If said representative, or director, is alien other than Common Market national, he must obtain "trader's card" ("carte de commercant") from Préfecture de Police or departmental préfecture. If said representative is of French nationality, no trader's card is required.

Foreign corporation complying with these legal formalities has same legal position as French corporation. Foreign corporations doing business in France are subject to same taxation as French corporations for their profits made in France, but with special provisions with regard to dividends.

Corporate Taxes.—See topic Taxation.

COURTS:

French court system is basically divided into two separate orders: judicial courts and administrative courts. Conflicts between the two orders as to their jurisdiction are settled by special court called "Tribunal des Conflits" which is composed of judges of both orders.

Judicial Courts.—Judicial system consists of two levels: courts of first instance and courts of appeal which may examine or reexamine both questions of fact and law. There is also Supreme court, called "Cour de cassation", which is not third level insofar as "Cour de Cassation" reexamines eclusively questions of law. Rules relating to French judicial system are to be found in New Code of Civil Procedure ("Nouveau Code de Procédure Civile - NCPC"). First level includes: (1) "Tribunal de grande instance" which is composed of three judges and has jurisdiction over all matters except those coming within jurisdiction of special court by reason of subject matter of case or of amount involved when it exceeds FRF 30,000; this Tribunal has civil and criminal chambers. Latter deal with misdemeanors ("délits") which are punishable by imprisonment or fine in amount of at least FRF 25,000 (see art. 381 of Penal Code). (2) Special courts are subject to special procedural rules, e.g. assistance of lawyer is not compulsory and proceedings are oral. Following are regarded as courts with special jurisdiction: "Tribunal d'instance" which is composed of single judge and has jurisdiction over certain actions depending on subject matter of case and involving no more than FRF 30,000 (see art. R 321-1 of NCPC); "Tribunal de Commerce" is

COURTS . . . *continued*
composed of lay judges elected by tradesmen and has jurisdiction over commercial matters (see art. 631-634 of Code de Commerce); "tribunal de police" deals with petty offenses ("contraventions") with fines in amount of no more than FRF 20,000 (Criminal Code, art. 521); "Conseil de Prud'hommes" has jurisdiction over labor matters (see art. R 421-1 of NCPC); other special courts exist which have jurisdiction over claims relating to Social Security and agricultural leases.

Second level is: "Cour d'Appel". There are 34 Courts of Appeal with territorial jurisdiction over one to six departments each. Each Cour d'Appel has jurisdiction over appeals from Tribunal de Grande Instance and appeals from Tribunal d'Instance. Each chamber of "Cour d'Appel" is composed of at least three magistrates and may reverse decision of lower court on both points of fact and points of law. If "Cour d'Appel" modifies or reverses decision, it issues final judgment and matter is not returned to lower court. Judge of "Cour d'Appel" acts as President of Assize Court and is appointed for each session together with two or more associate judges who may be members of either "Cour d'Appel" or "Tribunal de Grande Instance." These judges, together with nine jurors, form Assize Court ("Cour d'Assises") which has jurisdiction over felonies. Assize sessions are held in each department.

"Cour de Cassation" is located in Paris. It is composed of three civil chambers, commercial chamber, social chamber and criminal chamber. "Cour de Cassation" reviews points of law only from final decisions, whether they be from "Tribunal d'Instance," "Tribunal de Grande Instance" or "Cour d'Appel." If "Cour de Cassation" does not reject appeal it sends decision back to another lower court of same echelon as court which issued judgment under review. If new court does not comply with decision of "Cour de Cassation," party may again petition for review on same point of law and case is then heard by court composed of magistrates of all chambers of "Cour de Cassation" ("assemblée plenière"). If "assemblée plenière" does not reject petition, decision of lower court is quashed and case may be handed to third lower court of same echelon which must comply with decision of Assemblée plenière unless assemblée renders final decision.

Law No. 91-491 of May 15, 1991 instituted new proceeding whereby judicial courts can seek interpretation and advice of "Cour de Cassation" in connection with any new issue of law which appears to be problematic in numerous disputes brought before such courts. Equivalent procedure already exists before "Conseil d'Etat", in matters of administrative law, pursuant to Law No. 87-1127 of Dec. 31, 1987. It should be noted, however, that referral to "Cour de Cassation" so instituted by 1991 Law is not available in criminal matters.

Lower court must suspend all proceedings until "Cour de Cassation" renders its opinion on issue submitted to it, which it must do within three months from date of referral. Measures required by emergency and measures of merely preventive nature may still be ordered by lower court, however. Pursuant to Decree No. 92-228 of Mar. 12, 1992, lower court using this new proceeding to refer legal issue to "Cour de Cassation" must advise parties in dispute of their right to submit written pleadings with respect to such issue, if they have not yet done so.

It must be noted that opinion of "Cour de Cassation" has no binding authority on lower court who referred matter to it. It is, however, communicated to parties in dispute.

Administrative courts hear cases involving government contracts and torts of government departments, certain tax cases and appeals against administrative decisions. Administrative courts are divided into three echelons. Lowest echelon consists of administrative tribunals or "Tribunaux Administratifs", of which there are 31 with territorial jurisdiction over one to six departments each. Second echelon, created by Law of Dec. 31, 1987, is "Cour Administrative d'Appel", of which there are five with territorial jurisdiction over five to nine "Tribunaux Administratifs" each. This echelon has been in effect since Jan. 1989, and has jurisdiction over appeals from lowest echelon. Highest echelon, "Conseil d'Etat", located in Paris, hears some appeals against decisions of administrative tribunals, appeals against decisions of second echelon, and also has jurisdiction for appeals against ministerial decisions based on breach or rule of law or ultra vires.

CURRENCY:

Fundamental unit of currency is franc, divided into 100 centimes. New franc equals 100 old francs, official currency before 1959 revaluation.

CURTESY:

This common law institution does not exist in France. See topic Husband and Wife.

CUSTOMS DUTIES:

Customs regulations are contained in Code des Douanes.

Responsibilities and Powers of Customs Authorities.—Responsibilities are multifold, encompassing collection of customs duties and other taxes, enforcement of foreign exchange regulations, sanitary inspections ("police sanitaire"), inspections of imported regulated products, inspections of works of art for exportation, and customs control of persons.

Power of customs authorities extends to entire territory of France. Customs agents have power to conduct extensive investigations. They may demand and seize any documents of special interest to customs services and may inspect and search houses.

Procedures for Clearance of Goods.—All imported merchandise, regardless of how it is transported, must be submitted to customs for clearance and declared in detail at nearest customs office. There are now simplified procedures, provided for by contract between customs authorities and enterprises, for clearing goods on business premises.

Customs Duties.—Today, almost all French customs duties are established by GATT or by bilateral agreements. Merchandise imported from non-EU countries is subject to common foreign tariff ("tarif extérieur commun") levied by all EU countries. (French customs authorities publish each year up-dated Customs Tariff.) Since July 1, 1968, EU has prohibited customs duties among member states except on certain agricultural products. In addition, customs duties on exports no longer exist.

Other tariffs and taxes, e.g., VAT on imported goods, stamp duties, and taxes on tropical goods and oil products, are paid to customs authorities at French border.

Exemptions of Customs Duties.—Exemptions from customs duties may apply to merchandise that merely passes through France, that stays in France only temporarily, that is imported in order to be reexported later after modification in France, or that is reimported after having been exported. Applicants must declare merchandise for which exemption is sought; this declaration must be accompanied by guarantee made by solvent third party.

Prohibitions.—Importation of narcotics and certain pharmaceutical products is prohibited. Subject to EEC rules, customs agencies enforce quotas on certain imports and restrict "dumping" of imports at artificially low prices.

Disputes and Sanctions.—Customs litigation, except for questions involving liability of customs agencies, is handled by civil and criminal courts. Procedural rules are stricter in customs cases than in most other cases.

Anyone who participates in or benefits from customs fraud is liable to criminal sanctions, which range from fines (which may be substantial) to confiscation of merchandise or imprisonment. Administrative sanctions, such as revocation of temporary exemptions, may also apply.

Finally, customs authorities have power to settle disputes relating to customs violations by ordering accused to pay flat sum. Such settlement precludes further legal action.

See also topics Taxation; Exchange Control.

DAMAGES:

See topics Death; Industrial Property Rights; Torts.

DEATH:

Certificate of death is established by registrar ("officier de l'état civil") of place of death upon proof of death. However, special legislation permits court declaration of death without specific proof in case of disappearance during war or under circumstances of accident. (C. C. 78-90).

Presumption of Absence.—When person disappears from his last domicile and there is no evidence of his further existence, interested parties or public authority ("Ministère Public") may apply to court ("Tribunal de Grande Instance") of his last domicile for judgment of presumption of absence. (C. C. 112). Court may designate heirs or any other person to represent absentee and administer his property. (C. C. 113). Ten years after judgment of presumption of absence, court may, upon request of any interested party or public authority, declare absence conclusive. Judgment produces same effect as death. If above procedure has not been followed, court may declare absence if absentee has disappeared from his domicile without any news for 20 years. (C. C. 122). (Law of Dec. 28, 1977, J. O. Dec. 29, 1977). See topic Absentees.

Actions for Death.—There are no special statutory provisions for actions for wrongful death. Such actions may be brought by persons toward whom deceased had obligation of support on legal theory of direct harm to plaintiff by reason of death. Damages may include pecuniary loss to plaintiff as well as "moral" harm representing grief.

French courts now show distinct tendency to receive actions brought by persons not related to deceased by blood or marriage, such as fiancé favorably. (Cassation Chambre mixte, Feb. 27, 1970).

In addition to civil action for damages, it is possible to request damages by joining as civil party in criminal prosecution for voluntary or involuntary homicide.

Presumption as to Survivorship.—Presumption only applies where several persons respectively entitled to inheritance perish in same event and when it is impossible to determine who died first. If those who perished together were under 15 years old, eldest will be presumed to have survived. If they were all older than 60 years, youngest will be presumed to have survived. If some were younger than 15 years old and others older than 60, former will be presumed to have survived.

If those who perished together were older than 15 but younger than 60, male is always presumed to have survived when there is equality of age or when difference in age is no greater than one year. If those who perished were of same sex, youngest is presumed to have survived. (C. C. Art. 720-721 and 722).

According to case law, presumptions of fact, however, must prevail over presumptions of law.

DECEDENTS' ESTATES:

See topics Descent and Distribution; Executors and Administrators; Forced Heirship; Wills.

DEEDS:

All instruments for transfer of real property interest must be by notarial act or contract. Notary keeps original deed in his files. Extracts from deed are entered upon Register of Real Estate Mortgages. (Decree of Jan. 4, 1955). Failure to register leaves instrument valid as between parties, but enables bona fide purchaser to obtain good title to property. Under registration statute, first person to register among several claiming under deeds from last registered owner acquires good title.

Notary must verify that seller is owner of real property. (Trib. Civ. Seine Jan. 15, 1889). Also he must verify status of liens and mortgages registered on property before sale and at moment of publication of sale. (Cour de Cassation Jan. 4, 1966).

See topics Notaries Public; Real Property; Records.

See also topic Husband and Wife, subhead Alienation of Property.

DEPOSITIONS:

(Arts. 733-748 of new Code of Civil Procedure).

Rules relating to internal depositions are to be found in Arts. 730-732 of NCCP. By contrast, those relating to international depositions are contained in Arts. 733-748 of NCCP whereby French judge may request diplomatic authority to obtain evidence or to perform some other judicial act in another State within limits determined by other State. France has thus signed Hague Convention on the Taking of Evidence Abroad in

DEPOSITIONS . . . *continued*

Civil and Commercial Matters dated Mar. 18, 1970 (French Decree dated Apr. 9, 1975 and Jan. 24, 1989) which improves methods for obtaining of evidence between Contracting States (notably U.S.).

Pursuant to Hague Convention, courts may request taking of evidence by competent authority of another Contracting State, either by means of Letter of Request ("commission rogatoire") or by intervention of diplomatic officer or consular agent of France. This agent is granted power to take his own nationals' or even other nationals' evidence subject to certain conditions. Request is made via French "Ministère de la Justice (Service civil de l'entraide judiciare internationale)", 13 Place Vendôme, 750001 Paris, in accordance with French provisions. (Arts. 733-748 of NCCP). Evidence should be taken exclusively within premises of Embassies or Consultates, on premises which are accessible to public. Person whose evidence is sought may have assistance of lawyer etc.

Letters rogatory issued by courts of countries non-signatory to Convention are transmitted through ordinary diplomatic channels and must be translated into French. Documents will be transmitted by French Ministry of Foreign Affairs to Minister of Justice, which will in turn transmit them to State's Attorney ("Procureur de la République") of tribunal to which they are addressed. Judge is designated to carry out requests.

Law 80-538 of July 16, 1980 shields French corporations from having to give information to foreign anti-trust and other foreign public authorities and prevents taking of depositions in France other than depositions specifically authorized by Hague Evidence Treaty of 1970 (depositions before Consular Office at U.S. Embassy after specific authorization of French Ministry of Justice, or Letters Rogatory). Sanctions are two to six months in jail and/or FRF 10,000 to FRF 20,000 fines.

Depositions obtained abroad according to local procedure may be used in France provided manner in which they are obtained does not violate French public policy. They are given same value as domestic testimony, but appraisal of all testimony is strictly matter of court discretion. (J. O. Apr. 17, 1975).

DESCENT AND DISTRIBUTION:

Rules of succession to real property and personal property are same. There is no doctrine of primogeniture. Certain persons (e.g., person sentenced for murder or attempted murder of deceased) are excluded from succession. (C.C. 727).

Order of intestate inheritance is as follows:

(1) Legitimate and illegitimate lawfully acknowledged children and descendants thereof take entire estate per stirpes by representation, subject to right of usufruct of surviving spouse. (C. C. 731, 757, and 767).

(2) Surviving spouse has right of usufruct of: One-fourth of estate, if decedent left one or more legitimate or lawfully acknowledged illegitimate children; one-half if decedent left brothers or sisters, descendants of brothers or sisters, forebears, or illegitimate children conceived during marriage. (C. C. 767). Such right of usufruct may not be invoked if surviving spouse has received intervivos gifts or testamentary bequests from decedent equal to or exceeding amount of usufruct.

(3) If there are no children or descendants thereof, estate goes to parents and brothers and sisters or their descendants, one-fourth to each parent and one-half to be divided among brothers and sisters. (C. C. 748). If only one parent is alive, three-fourths is divided among brothers and sisters. (C. C. 751). If there are no parents brothers and sisters or their descendants take whole. (C. C. 750). Share of brothers and sisters and their descendants is divided equally, per stirpes, if all are of same marriage; if they are of different marriages, equally between paternal and maternal lines of decedent with those of full blood taking in both lines and of half blood in one line only. (C. C. 752).

(4) If there are no children or descendants thereof, and no brothers and sisters or their descendants, the estate goes to ascendants. (C. C. 746), being divided into two equal parts, one for paternal line and one for maternal line (C. C. 733). The ascendant in nearest degree takes one-half in his line to exclusion of more remote. (C. C. 746). If there are no ascendants in one line, whole estate goes to ascendants of other line (C. C. 753) except where there is also surviving spouse who, in such case, has right of usufruct to one-half of estate (C. C. 767).

(5) If there is no one closely enough related to inherit, or if there are only collateral heirs other than brothers or sisters or their descendants, estate goes entirely to surviving spouse. (C. C. 765). If there is no surviving spouse, estate is divided into two equal parts and distributed among collateral relatives in each line up to sixth degree. But collaterals up to twelfth degree may take if decedent was incapable of making a will but had not been declared insane. (C. C. 755). If there is no surviving spouse and no relatives of degree entitled to take in one line, that one-half then goes to collaterals of other line. (C. C. 755).

(6) If there are no descendants or ascendants and no collaterals capable of taking and no surviving spouse, the estate escheats to the state. (C. C. 723, 768).

Relationship is determined by degrees. In direct line each generation is degree, in collateral line number of generations is counted up to common ancestor and from such common ancestor to person whose relationship is to be determined, but not counting common ancestor. Thus grandson is related to his grandfather in second degree; two brothers are related in second degree; first cousins in fourth degree. (C. C. 735-738). Representation takes place ad infinitum in direct descending line. In each of two ascending lines nearer ascendant excludes more remote. In collateral line representation is allowed only as regards descendants of brothers and sisters of deceased. Where representation is allowed division takes place per stirpes. (C. C. 739-743).

Children and their descendants in right of representation inherit without distinction, even if they are issue of different marriages. (C. C. 745). Illegitimate children, duly acknowledged, have in general, same rights as legitimate children in estate of their parents, of other forebears, in estate of brothers, sisters, and other collateral heirs. (C. C. 757). Reciprocally, parents and other forebears of duly acknowledged, illegitimate child, as well as brothers, sisters, and other collateral heirs, have right of succession as if child were legitimate. (C. C. 758). Illegitimate children, whose mother or father was at time of conception married to another person, do not exclude this other person from right of succession to deceased spouse where this other person would otherwise have right to succession. In such case, illegitimate children and nonparent spouse will each receive half of what nonparent spouse would have received in absence of illegitimate children. (C. C. 759). Illegitimate children, whose mother or father was married at time of their conception and had legitimate children from such marriage, share in estate of such parent along with legitimate children, except each will receive only half of what he would receive if all of children, including himself, were legitimate. (C. C. 760).

If the estate goes to ascendants or collaterals it is divided into two equal parts, one for the maternal line and one for the paternal line. The relatives of the half-blood take in one line only, but relatives of the full blood take in both lines, except in case of division among brothers and sisters of deceased which is expressly provided for by Art. 752 C. C. (C. C. 733).

The state is an irregular heir and must get courts to put it in possession (envoi en possession) whereas other heirs and surviving spouse succeed directly without need of intervention of court. (C. C. 724).

Usufruct of surviving spouse is calculated on fictitious sum that includes all property decedent disposed of inter vivos or by will to relatives entitled to inherit, as well as property in estate at decedent's death. But surviving spouse can only enforce this right of usufruct against property that is actually found in estate and cannot prejudice rights of children. (C. C. 767). (See topic Forced Heirship.) Heirs on posting bond can compel surviving spouse to accept annuity of equivalent amount instead of usufruct. If surviving spouse is divorced or judicially separated from decedent he or she gets no rights in estate.

French law governs all real property situated in France regardless of nationality or of place of death of decedent.

As to personal property of such inheritance, French courts usually consider that inheritance status is determined by law of last domicile.

Both principles are subject to special exceptions through international treaties and agreements.

On other hand, aliens inherit property in same way and upon same basis as French citizens. However, in case of an estate partly in France and partly abroad, French heir in competition with foreigner has full rights, notwithstanding French rules about equal distribution, to take previously out of part of estate in France, same value as he would be deprived of in part situated abroad on behalf of aforesaid heir. (Law July 14, 1819, art. 2).

See also topics Wills; Forced Heirship.

Death Duties.—See topic Taxation.

DESIGNS AND MODELS:

See topic Industrial Property Rights.

DISPUTE RESOLUTION:

In France most disputes in civil and commercial matters are resolved by courts as expense of judicial proceedings in civil matters remains relatively low and so-called alternative dispute process (contractually agreed measures such as conciliation, mediation and minitrials) has not achieved popularity noted in some common law jurisdictions (notably U.S.).

Contractually agreed arbitration of commercial disputes is recognized exception and is frequently resorted to, particularly in international matters (see topic Arbitration and Award). Some matters may not be submitted to arbitration. Art. 2060 of Civil Code prohibits any reference to arbitration of questions of status and capacity of individuals, divorce or separation, disputes involving local authorities or public bodies, public work contracts or contracts having object which is contrary to public order. Where parties have legally agreed to arbitrate dispute, court to which dispute is referred must, at instance of party requiring arbitration, decline jurisdiction and refer parties to arbitration. (Art. 1458, Civil Code).

Within framework of judicial proceedings variety of dispute resolution techniques may be resorted to, some having mandatory character.

Mandatory Dispute Resolution Measures.—

Mandatory Conciliation/Mediation.—In following instances, attempt at conciliation is required by law either prior to issuing formal proceedings or prior to case being submitted for judgment.

(i) Employment Matters.—As rule, employment matters come within jurisdiction of Industrial Tribunal ("Conseil des Prud'hommes").

In relation to individual proceedings before Conseil des Prud'hommes: Conseil's jurisdiction is invoked either by request to office of court's clerk ("greffe") or by parties appearing voluntarily before conciliation bureau ("bureau de conciliation"). (art. R 516-8 of Labor Code). Parties are summoned in any event to appear before bureau de conciliation. (art. R 516-11 of Labor Code). Bureau de conciliation attempts to conciliate parties. (art. R 516-13 of Labor Code). Failure by plaintiff to appear before bureau de conciliation results in case being dismissed. Plaintiff is then only entitled to renew action once. "Conseillers-rapporteurs" may be appointed in order to prepare case for judgment and to report to court. Conceillers may attempt to conciliate parties and draw up minutes of any settlement agreement reached by parties before them.

However, disputes concerning increases in remuneration may be submitted to "juge d'instance". Art. R 145-9 of Labor Code provides for compulsory attempt at conciliation as part of such procedure.

(ii) Divorce.—Attempt at conciliation is compulsory before judicial proceedings are commenced unless divorce is agreed upon by parties. Further attempts at conciliation may be made during course of proceedings, regardless of ground of divorce relied upon (see art. 251 of Civil Code). "Juge aux affaires familiales" (judge in charge of family matters) has duty to attempt to conciliate spouses before and in course of proceedings (art. 1074 NCCP) and must summon spouses to conciliation hearing (art. 1108 NCCP). In event of conciliation, this must be recorded in minutes. In event of non-conciliation, spouses may be given leave to bring action for divorce. (art. 1111 NCCP).

(iii) "Tribunal Paritaire des Baux Ruraux" (Commission for Agricultural leases). (NCCP arts. 882, 887, 888).

Parties are always summoned to conciliation hearing. In event of non-conciliation, minutes must specify terms of settlement offer made and rejected.

See Topical Index in front part of this volume.

DISPUTE RESOLUTION . . . *continued*

(iv) Agricultural Undertakings in Financial Difficulty.—Law No. 88-1202 of 30 Dec. 1988, art. 29, provides for compulsory attempt at conciliation with creditors before receivership or bankruptcy proceedings can be commenced.

Mandatory Fact-Finding Processes.—Most fact-finding processes are initiated by judge and can therefore be qualified as mandatory. French judge may order special investigative measures ("mesures d'instruction") with view to preparing case for hearing and determination as regards factual issues in dispute. He may order one or more "mesures d'instruction". (arts. 143 and 232 NCCP). First level of such measures include findings ("constatations") and opinion ("consultation"). For findings see arts. 249-255 NCCP; for consultation see arts. 256-262. "Expertise judiciaire" is more formal mesure d'instruction, which is only ordered when findings or an opinion would not suffice. (see arts. 263-284-1 NCCP). It is worth noting that technicians cannot conduct conciliation between parties. (art. 240-1 NCCP). "Juge aux affaire familiales" may also order qualified third-party to carry out social inquiry ("enquête sociale") if he feels that further information is required before deciding issues relating to children (visiting rights, parental authority etc.). (art. 287-2 of Civil Code and arts. 1079-1080 NCCP). In relation to employment disputes, fact-finding process may be delegated to "conseillers-rapporteurs". (art. R 516-21 Labor Code).

Voluntary Dispute Resolution.—

Conciliation/Mediation.—In context of voluntary dispute resolution, distinction may be drawn between judicial conciliation and extrajudicial conciliation.

Judicial Conciliation and Mediation.—In France, most mediation and conciliation takes place within judicial system, upon judge's initative and/or control. As rule, it is part of judge's duty to conciliate parties. (art. 21 NCCP). Mediation has been held by Supreme Court ("Cour de Cassation") to be nothing but application of art. 21 NCCP.

Title VI NCCP contains general provisions on conciliation. (art. 127-131). They specify that there can be conciliation between parties either of their own initiative or at judge's initiative and that this may take place at any time in course of proceedings. (art. 127 NCCP). Even if it results from judge's initative, conciliation nevertheless requires parties' agreement. Any agreement reached by parties, even partial, must be recorded in minutes. (art. 130). These may be submitted to judge, so as to become enforceable as judgment ("force exécutoire"). (art. 129). Legislator has confirmed general principle contained in art. 21 in relation to specific tribunals. See art. 768 in relation to Tribunal de Grande Instance, arts. 830-835 and 840, 841, 847 in relation to Tribunal d'Instance, art. 863 in relation to Tribunal de Commerce, art. R 516 of Labor Code in relation to Conseil des Prud'hommes, arts. 910 and 941 NCCP in relation to Cour d'appel, arts. 1074, 1108, 1111 in relation to divorce proceedings. In addition, Law No. 95-125 of 8 Feb. 1995, which concerns civil proceedings only, for first time contains specific provisions in relation to mediation and conciliation conducted by third party rather than by judge. Decree is yet to be issued to deal with outstanding questions, such as qualifications required to act as mediator/conciliator, form of referral, etc. Main provisions of law may be summarized as follows: subject to parties' agreement, judge may appoint third party to conduct preliminary conciliation whenever required by law see subhead Mandatory Dispute Resolution Measures, supra save as regards separation and divorce proceedings; third party to act as mediator at any stage of proceedings; statements of parties not to be disclosed to judge unless agreed upon by parties; third-party to inform judge of outcome of conciliation/mediation. It is possible to submit any agreement reached to judge to give it force exécutoire.

It is worth noting that, before Tribunal d'instance, parties may issue summons "for the purpose of a preliminary attempt at conciliation". Request may be made by simple letter addressed to office of court's clerk. (art. 830 NCCP). In addition, although collective labor disputes are not subject to compulsory requirement of prior attempt at conciliation, option of submitting same to conciliation is preserved. (arts. R 523-1 and R 513-2 Labor Code). In addition, once election to do so has been made, parties are obliged to attend conciliation hearing and to facilitate process. (arts. R 523-3 and 523-4 Labor Code). Finally, collective bargaining agreements may provide for conciliation mechanism.

Although conciliation and/or mediation are not provided for in any penal legislation, there exists spontaneous recourse to mediation in criminal proceedings, in particular when victim and accused know each other or in relation to minor acts of delinquency.

Extrajudicial Conciliation.—Conciliation may take place in relation to private law disputes but also in context of public law matters.

(i) Private Law.—Parties are free to appoint any third party to act as conciliator. However, there exists body of "auxiliaries of justice" ("auxiliaires de justice") known as conciliators, which was formed pursuant to Decree 78-381 of 20 Mar. 1978, as amended by Decree 81-583 of 18 May 1981 and explained in "circular" of 27 Feb. 1987. Number of such conciliators has decreased significantly over last ten years. They act as volunteers, and are mainly selected amongst retired magistrates and lawyers. Their task is to "facilitate independently of any judicial proceedings the amicable resolution of disputes bearing upon the rights of which the parties are free to dispose of". Their jurisdiction is invoked informally. They have no power to determine dispute.

Conciliation is also provided for in relation to specific issues: commercial undertakings in financial difficulty (Law No. 84-148 of 1 Mar. 1984, as am'd by Law No. 94-475 of 10 June 1994), local conciliation commission for leases (Law No. 89-462 of 6 July 1989); Commission for personal over-indebtedness (Law No. 89-1010 of 31 Dec. 1989 and Law No. 91-650 of 9 July 1991).

(ii) Public Law.—Conciliation and mediation are two techniques of wide application in public law. Function of "Mediateur de la République" was created by Law of 3 Jan. 1973. Art. 13 of Law of 13 Jan. 1989 characterizes him as of "independent authority". Jurisdiction is invoked informally by natural or legal persons, via member of Parliament (député) or senator, or upon latter's initative. He must determine whether administration concerned by complaint has acted in conformity with its duties as public service and offer solutions to dispute. He enjoys wide investigative powers.

Other public law conciliation mechanisms exist in relation to specific industries and functions: cinema, book publishing, environmental issues, taxes.

Fact-Finding Processes.—Party contemplating action may, prior to issuing proceedings, request judge under summary procedure, ex parte or inter partes, to order "mesure d'instruction" whereby judge or third party ("technicien") will seek to gather and protect evidence which may be decisive in any future proceedings. (art. 145 NCCP).

Parties may also request investigative measures as part of existing proceedings. (art. 143 NCCP).

Amiable Composition.—Parties may, after dispute has arisen, confer upon judge power to rule as amiable compositeur (ex aequo et bono), which allows judge to depart from strict legal principles and to adjudicate dispute in accordance with notions of fairness and equity. Parties' freedom may, however, only be exercised in relation to rights of which they have free disposition. (arts. 12 and 58 NCCP; see also art. 2060 of Civil Code). Parties may also confer powers of amiable composition to arbitrator. (arts. 1474 and 1497 NCCP).

Settlement.—Arts. 2044-2058 set out legal framework for settlements. Art. 2044 recognizes parties' freedom to enter into settlement agreement for purpose of bringing dispute to end or of avoiding future litigation, subject to their having necessary capacity in relation to subject-matter of proposed settlement. (art. 2045 NCCP). Settlement agreement must be made in writing, although absence of writing will not invalidate agreement. There is no settlement unless parties make mutual concessions to each other. As between parties, issues covered by settlement agreement are res judicata. (art. 2052 NCCP). For possibilities of rescinding agreement, see arts. 2053-2054. For circumstances when agreement is null and void, see arts. 2055-2056 NCCP.

Arbitration.—Freedom to enter into arbitration agreement is embodied in art. 2059 of Civil Code. Law relating to arbitration is contained in Part IV of NCCP. (arts. 1442-1507). Specific rules apply in relation to international arbitration; they are set out in arts. 1492-1507 NCCP. For further details as to validity of arbitration clauses in domestic and international arbitration, see topic Arbitration and Award.

DIVORCE:

In France, issue of divorce is governed by Law No. 75-617 of July 11, 1975 as amended by Laws No. 85-1372 of Dec. 23, 1985, No. 87-570 of July 22, 1987 and No. 93-22 of Jan. 8, 1993. French law provides for divorce in three instances: (1) Divorce by mutual consent of both parties after six months of marriage on mutual petition and submission of proposed settlement agreement, which need not indicate reasons for divorce, to "juge aux affaires familiales" (judge in charge of family matters whose office is attached to Tribunal de Grande Instance). Petition is examined by judge in presence of parties, and if they persist, he instructs them to renew petition after three months. Failure to renew nullifies proceedings. Judge may disapprove proposed settlement agreement and divorce if he finds it does not sufficiently protect children or one of parties. Otherwise he approves agreement and grants divorce. Costs are equally supported by both parties (C. C. 230-236); (2) in event of separation of six years or more or severe mental illness of spouse, other spouse can petition for divorce, specifying how obligations towards other party and children will be met. Judge may refuse divorce on showing by other party that divorce would result in grave material or mental suffering. Here, divorce is always pronounced against spouse who petitioned for divorce regardless of any wrongdoing on his part. (C. C. 237-241); (3) divorce still granted upon grounds of acts constituting serious and repeated violations of marital duties rendering marital state intolerable, including adultery, violence, gross insults, cruelty or conviction for infamous crime punishable pursuant to provisions of Art. 131-1 of Penal Code. Reprehensible conduct of party petitioning for divorce may be taken into account by court. Even in absence of counterclaim, divorce may be granted on grounds of common wrong-doing. (C. C. 242-246).

Conflict of Laws.—Divorce and separation are governed by French law when both parties are French citizens, or when both parties are domiciled in France, or when there is no assumption of jurisdiction under foreign law and French courts are competent. (C. C. 310). Husband and wife may have separate domicile. (C. C. 108).

Proceedings.—"Juge aux affaires familiales" renders divorce judgment and determines parental authority, alimony questions, what possible third party will be entrusted with care of children (C. C. 247 and 256) and alimony obligations of parent who was not awarded parental authority, or with whom children do not reside habitually. Proceedings are not public. In case of mutual consent or of facts admitted by both parties indicating marital state intolerable, divorce judgment is rendered by judge. In event of six years separation or mental illness, and in case of facts indicating marital state no longer tolerable, reconciliation meeting must be held in front of judge. If it fails, case is brought before Tribunal. Judge may order any temporary measure he deems necessary before final judgment. (C. C. 247 to 259-3).

Remarriage.—Without special permission from civil court divorced woman, regardless of nationality, is prohibited from remarrying within 300 days from date of order authorizing separation pendente lite, or lacking such order, from date when divorce becomes effective, unless in meantime she gives birth to a child or produces medical certificate stating that she is not pregnant. (C. C. 228, 261).

Name.—Any woman who is divorced reacquires surname which she had before marriage which is dissolved by judgment but in certain cases she may keep surname of her former husband. (C. C. 266).

Alimony.—In any instance of divorce, one of parties may be awarded monthly or capital sum to compensate for change created by divorce in living conditions. (C. C. 270 to 280-1). In divorce granted on grounds of unilateral fault or desertion, party at fault may have to indemnify other party for any material damage or mental suffering caused by divorce. (C. C. 265-269). Nature and amount of compensation are determined by judge.

Children.—As regards parental authority, Law of Jan. 8, 1993 (arts. 36 to 41) has established right for child to be raised, insofar as possible, by both parents even if they are divorced, following notice and approval by judge in charge of family matters. In case of divorce, parental authority over children is awarded to one or both parties in best interest of children. Each parent, however, continues to have same rights as before divorce in regard to superintending, maintenance and education of children and must therefore be informed of important changes affecting life of children and each must contribute to maintenance in proportion to own resources and resources of other parent. Property rights given to children by law or acquired by marriage settlements are not affected by divorce of their parents. (C. C. 286-295). Judge decides in interest

DIVORCE . . . *continued*

of children whether parental authority is exercised jointly or not; if jointly, he designates parent with whom children reside habitually. Children may, on exceptional basis, be entrusted to third party who is not member of family, or if one cannot be found, to educational institution, according to interest of children. Law of Jan. 8, 1993 which came into force on Feb. 1, 1994 has recognized right for children to be heard by judge in any proceedings which concern them (until 1994, only children over 12 were granted this right). (C. C. 388-1). In some cases, minor children have even been allowed to become parties in their parents' divorce based on Art. 12 of Convention on the Rights of the Child ratified by France. (Law No. 90-548 of July 2, 1990 and Decree No. 90-917 of Oct. 8, 1990).

Separation may be granted by court on same grounds for which divorce may be granted. After judgment of separation has been entered for three years, if there has been no reconciliation either party is entitled to apply to court, and have entered judgment of divorce thereon. (C. C. 296-309).

Judgment of separation carries with it separation of property. In case of reconciliation, separation of property continues but cannot be set up against third parties unless special deed is signed before notary and duly published. (C. C. 305).

DOWER:

This common law institution does not exist in France. Under community property regime, wife automatically enjoys half interest in assets purchased by spouses during marriage with their own income or savings, and in gifts to spouses, unless donor expresses contrary intention. See topic Husband and Wife.

ENVIRONMENTAL LAW:

In French law protection of environment is dealt with in two ways through application of: (1) General rules of law to particular nuisance, (2) specific legislation in designated areas such as town planning, public health, waste, and air and water pollution.

Most important in field of environmental protection is Law No. 76-663 of July 19, 1976 which came into effect Jan. 1, 1977. In addition, Law No. 61-842 of Aug. 2, 1961 deals with air pollution, Law No. 64-1245 of Dec. 16, 1964, as amended by Law No. 92-3 of Jan. 3, 1992, deals with water pollution, Law No. 75-633 of July 15, 1975 deals with waste of urban and industrial origin, Law No. 76-599 of July 7, 1976 with marine pollution, Law No. 76-629 of July 10, 1976 with protection of nature and Law No. 95-101 of Feb. 2, 1995 with reinforcement of protection of envirnoment. Other legislation exists (e.g., in field of chemical products mandatory remedial measures in buildings containing asbestos), or may be enacted by either national or local authorities. More general rules contained in Civil Code, Code of Expropriation for Public Purposes, Forestry Act, Rural Law, Code of Town Planning, Penal Code, and Code of Public Health, may be applicable in particular cases.

Thus, legal entities can be found guilty of environmental offenses and fined. Nevertheless, this does not prevent managers of such entities from being held personally liable if they are at fault.

Classified Installations.—Aim of Law No. 76-663 of 19 July 1976 and implementing Decree 77-1133 of 21 Sept. 1977, modified by Decree No. 93-245 of 25 Feb. 1993 is to protect environment, public health, public security and salubrity as well as nature, agriculture, sites and monuments against all forms of dangers or adverse effects which are likely to arise from operation of factories, and generally all publicly or privately owned or operated installations. This law provides extensive and detailed list known as "nomenclature of classified installations" of industrial activities which may not be operated without prior approval by, or prior declaration to, competent administrative authority depending on gravity of nuisance inherent to their operation. First category installations may be opened only with specific authorization of local representative of French state ("Préfet"). After procedure which includes various consultations and public inquiry, authorization (or refusal) is granted in form of "arrêté" which sets forth technical and environmental standards with which establishment must comply. Defaut of reply within time limits does not amount to acceptance and investments must be postponed until administration has issued decision. Second category installations may normally be opened only by prior written declaration to "Préfet" and are only subject to general "arrêtés" issued on industry-by-industry basis in department concerned. Both types of establishment normally are exempt if duly created prior to publication of Law No. 76-663 or of any decree adding applicable industry to "nomenclature of classified establishments", and if in compliance with certain registration requirements.

Classified establishments are subject to special tax when authorization is granted. Supplemental tax may be levied if industry presents special environmental risks.

Failure to comply with standards set forth in authorization of "Préfet" or in general "arrêtés" is punishable by fines and, in certain cases, imprisonment of responsible individuals or closing down facility. All establishments subject to inspection by administrative authority. When operator of classified installation changes, new operator must notify "Préfet" of such change within one-month period following actual take over of installation.

When operator of classified installation decides to close it down, it must so notify "Préfet" and is bound to take all necessary measures to prevent any subsequent danger or adverse effect to environmental interests.

Air Pollution.—Law of Aug. 2, 1961, provides that buildings, industrial and commercial establishments, and vehicles or other personal property must be constructed, exploited or used so as to avoid pollution and odors endangering health and public safety. Particular implementing decrees, e.g., Decree No. 74-415 of May 13, 1974, determine cases and conditions in which regulation of building construction, vehicular equipment, use of inflammables and motor fuel, heating equipment and apparatus installed in industrial, commercial and professional establishments, and emission of smoke, dust, gas, etc. into atmosphere, is carried out with various administrative measures related thereto. Special protection zones where polluting elements may not exceed standards fixed by ministerial "arrêtés" may be created (see e.g., "Arrêtés" of Jan. 27, 1993, related to use of solidified mineral fuels in units of combustion; "Arrêté" of Mar. 9, 1993, concerning gaseous emissions of cement ovens in order to limit nuisances caused by pollution). Various tax incentives provided for establishments which comply with dispositions of law. (See e.g., Decree No. 75-975 of Oct. 23, 1975.) Decree No. 93-299 of Mar. 4, 1993, exempting from professional tax for limited period units of sulfurization of diesel and heavy fuel. By Law 80-513 of July 7, 1980 Agency For Air Quality "l'Agence pour la qualite de l'air" has been created. Said Agency should allow grants and loans within framework of its activity. Enterprises which erect buildings are, in certain cases, allowed exceptional depreciation if such premises comply with environmental regulations. (C. G. I. Art. 39 quinquies D, E, F). *Note:* Proposed law on air quality should be soon adopted. It focuses on air pollution caused by transportation vehicles and monitoring of air quality in major cities.

Water Pollution.—Law of 1964, as amended by Law No. 92-3 of Jan. 3, 1992 and related decrees (see e.g., Decrees 73-218 and 73-219 of Feb. 23, 1973; Decree 75-177 of Mar. 12, 1975; Decree No. 93-742 of Mar. 29, 1993 relating to authorizations and declarations); Decree No. 93-1038 of Aug. 27, 1993 relating to prevention of water pollution by agricultural nitrates, subject to administrative control pumping and discharge of water by industrial sites subject to 1976 Law on Classified Installations, regardless of nature of water (ground and underground, continental and seawater) within limits of territorial waters.

Table called "nomenclature", enacted by decree, will list thresholds beyond which pumping or discharge of water will be subject to declaration or authorization. Operating permit, which includes permit to discharge used water or to take underground and groundwater will be granted by "Préfet" after consultations. Nomenclature will also list installations, works (public works, road works, private works . . .) and activities which, in one way or another, affect water plan or water quality, whether or not such installations, works and activities are polluting.

Law provides for various fines and imprisonment penalties for damaging fish life, health or waterlife and for operating or carrying out work without authorization or with withdrawn or suspended authorization. Environmental associations of at least five years of age are acknowledged right to claim damages in criminal proceedings for both direct and indirect damages to environment.

Law of 1964 created national and local agencies dealing with water pollution problems, namely, on national level, National Committee for water and, on local level, basin committee and financing agency for each water basin. Local water basin committees are consulted on all local issues relating to water pollution. Local financing agencies facilitate implementation of initiatives of general interest with respect to basin (for example providing funds for work project). Similar procedure is organized by Law of 1992 at smaller units' level; local water commission is responsible for drafting, reviewing and controlling implementation of programs. Law provides for inventories of all surface waters with respect of pollution.

Waste.—Law of July 15, 1975 modified by Law No. 92-646 of July 13, 1993 provides that any person producing domestic or industrial waste is responsible for its elimination, including final treatment. Elimination must be carried out in such manner as to avoid harmful effects on environment. Specific national and local regulations apply to use and treatment of special types of waste (e.g., PCBs, PCTs, used oils, used solvents, cyanide and chromium compounds, laboratory and hospital waste and nuclear waste). These regulations usually require procedures such as maintenance of waste disposal records ("système de bordereaux"), and disposal of waste only through licensed companies. Decree No. 92-377 of Apr. 1, 1992 organizes disposal of consumer goods packagings. As of Jan. 1, 1993, producers of such packagings have to contribute to final disposal thereof, either by organizing disposal and elimination of above wastes through returnable packagings or special locations where packagings may be disposed of, or by entering into contract with specially licensed waste disposer. Under Decree No. 94-609 of 13 July 1994, only authorized means of eliminating industrial packaging waste is reuse, recycling or other methods aimed at obtaining reusable materials, including incineration which leads to energy recovery. Simple incineration is no longer allowed. Specific regulations regarding disposal of waste are also often contained in "arrêtés" adding industries to "nomenclature of classified establishment". Decree dated Sept. 18, 1995, provides for new tax levied on all operators of istallations for elimination of special industrial waste (definition in decree), under certain circumstances. This tax may be passed on to waste producers.

Law No. 91-1381 of Dec. 30, 1991 amending 1976 Law on Classified Installations provides that disposal of nuclear wastes shall be subject to temporary administrative authorization unless otherwise provided in further laws.

Noise.—Law No. 92-144 of 31 Dec. 1992 provides protection against "noise pollution" which may be harmful to health or environment. Decree No. 95-79 of 23 Jan. 1995 sets forth standards to be met with respect to noise emissions. This Decree provides that manufacture, import, sale, transfer or use of any item whose noise emissions exceed certain limits is prohibited. Manufacturers or sellers must ensure that items comply with regulatory limits through homologation, certification or declaration, depending on extent of risk. Two decrees dated Apr. 18, 1995 facilitate process for establishing existence of domestic noise, insofar as it abolishes notion of fault and suppresses acoustic control.

Labels.—Labelling obligations may be imposed by law or regulation, e.g. under Decree No. 94-566 of 7 July 1994, and certain dometic appliances must have labels setting out information concerning energy consumption and noise production of product.

Authority.—All national governmental authority relating to environmental policy is exercised by Ministry of Environment.

Law of 2 Feb. 1995 sets up National Communion of Public Debate which may be seized by ministers, 20 representatives ("députés") or senators or by regional council to debate of any major operation of development of national interest.

In field of environment, important legislation ("Directives") has developed on EEC level, including Seveso Directive of June 24, 1982 governing prevention of industrial accidents and Directive of June 28, 1984 regulating industrial air pollution, amended by Directive of Nov. 24, 1988 concerning manufacture of aerosols.

Pursuant to its ratification on Jan. 7, 1991, France is also signatory to Basel Convention on "Cross-Border Control of Hazardous Wastes and their Disposal" (signed May 22, 1989 and effective May 6, 1992).

See Topical Index in front part of this volume.

ESCHEAT: See topic Descent and Distribution.

EVIDENCE: See topic Depositions.

EXCHANGE CONTROL:

French Exchange Control Regulations are set forth in Decree No. 89-938 of Dec. 29, 1989 (as modified by Decrees No. 92-134 of Feb. 11, 1992, No. 94-658 of July 27, 1994 and No. 96-117 of Feb. 14, 1996) and, as regards direct investments, Order of Feb. 14, 1996.

Direct Investments.—Decree of Dec. 29, 1989 defines direct investments as: (1) acquisition, creation or extension of any business, branch or individual undertaking; (2) any other operations which, alone or with others, concurrently or consecutively, have effect of permitting one or several persons to acquire or increase de facto control over company carrying out industrial, agricultural, commercial, financial or real estate activity, or to assure expansion of such company already under their control.

Direct Foreign Investments in France.—Direct investments (as defined above) made in France by nonresidents, by companies directly or indirectly under foreign control, or by French establishments of foreign companies as well as sales between nonresidents of shares of resident company are deemed to be direct foreign investment in France by Decree of Dec. 29, 1989. However, shareholdings in French listed companies are specifically not considered as direct investments provided they do not exceed 20% of share capital and/or voting rights in target company. (Art. 1 of Decree of Dec. 29, 1989, as modified). Order further states that (i) French nonlisted company is deemed to be under foreign control when nonresidents, or French companies controlled by nonresidents, hold more than 33.33% of its share capital or voting rights and (ii) French listed company is deemed to be under foreign control when nonresident or French company controlled by nonresidents (or group of investors) holds directly or indirectly more than 20% of its capital or voting rights. It is however specified that French Ministry of Economy may use other thresholds and other criteria (such as financing, commercial agreements, call agreements) to determine whether there exists de facto control even if above thresholds were not reached.

Decree No. 92-134 of Feb. 11, 1992 permits free direct foreign investment in France of less than 50,000,000 FF in existing companies whose turnover (including subsidiaries) is no greater than 500,000,000 FF.

Direct foreign investments in France are generally subject to prior declaration to and prior authorization by Ministry of Economy. Such authorization is deemed granted when Ministry has not objected to proposed investment one month after receiving above declaration.

Direct investments in France are exempted from prior authorization and/or prior declaration. Investor must, however, file declaration at time of its investment, provided they do not concern certain "sensitive" sectors (such as activities relating to public authority, public health and safety, production and sale of weapons and war material) which remain subject to prior authorization by Ministry of Economy. Such authorization is deemed granted when Ministry has not objected to proposed investment one month after receiving above request.

However, following direct investments in France are exempted from prior declaration and authorization: (1) creation of branch or new enterprise; (2) expansion of activity of existing enterprises; (3) increase in percentage ownership in French company under foreign control when such increase is made by investor already holding more than 66.66% of share capital or voting rights; (4) subscription to capital increase of French company under foreign control by investor, provided such investor will not increase its percentage ownership at that time; (5) direct investment transactions between companies which are part of same group; (6) loans, advances, guarantees, consolidation or writing-off of debts, subsidies or contributions to branches, granted to French enterprise under foreign control by controlling investors; (7) taking share ownership in French enterprises having real estate activity other than construction of buildings for sale or lease; (8) direct investments not exceeding FRF 10 million in hotel enterprises, craft industry enterprises, retail business enterprises, retail enterprises, miscellaneous merchant services and quarry or gravel businesses; (9) acquisition of agricultural land.

Implementation and liquidation of foreign investments in France as well as creation of branch or new enterprise with investment exceeding FRF 10 million and acquistion of land used for purposes of wine production require filing of report.

French direct investments abroad are not subject to controls but require filing of report within 20 days from date of their implementation if they exceed FRF 5 million.

Current Operations and Operations on Securities.—Transfers of cash between France and abroad must be made through intermediary credit or financial institutions licensed pursuant to Banking Law No. 84-46 of Jan. 24, 1984.

Statistical declarations must be made annually to Bank of France for (i) transfers of funds between France and abroad or within France between residents and nonresidents, and direct financial operations abroad (in particular, payments made from or received into foreign bank accounts or made by set-off) and (ii) currency or interest swaps. Residents whose cumulative monthly payments abroad or with nonresidents not made through intermediary credit or financial institutions do not exceed FRF 100,000 are exempt from requirement to declare. French residents of foreign nationality are similarly exempt for payments made exclusively abroad.

Bank of France may set terms and conditions of declaration by which resident reports its direct operations abroad or in France with nonresidents, either directly or through intermediary credit or financial institution.

Enterprises or groups of enterprises whose payments for goods and services abroad exceed FRF 1,000,000,000 during one calendar year must declare directly to Bank of France total of such operations with foreign entity or in France with nonresidents. Enterprises or groups of enterprises which exceed this threshold during year 1990 must reach agreement as to terms and conditions of declaration of total of their operations with foreign entity or within France with nonresidents with Bank of France, before Jan. 1, 1992, for balance of payments purposes. Enterprises which exceed this amount in future periods have maximum time limit of one year calculated from close of corresponding fiscal year in which to set terms of application of this provision with Bank of France.

Residents must provide Bank of France with annual statement concerning loans made directly abroad and repayments relating thereto, as well as foreign currency loans entered into with credit or financial institutions and repayments relating thereto, if total amount payable exceeds FRF 500,000,000.

Bank of France may obtain from residents whose total assets or total liabilities abroad exceed FRF 10,000,000, any information necessary to keep statistics on France's international economic position.

Decree No. 89-938 of Dec. 29, 1989 provides new rules governing issuance and marketing of foreign securities in France.

Admission of stocks for trading in regulated market, issuance of securities whether or not public offering ("appel public à l'épargne"), and placement or sale of securities are subject to prior authorization except in following cases: (1) Securities issued by OECD nationals, except for shares of mutual funds issued by non-EU or non-EEA nationals; (2) securities issued by EU institutions and other international organizations of which France is member or issued under EEA Agreement; (3) loans guaranteed by Republic of France; (4) shares connected with securities already listed in France or whose issuance or offering in France has previously been authorized; (5) securities whose issuance in France has been previously authorized.

Stocks and securities that are issued by State, State institutions, foreign companies or international institutions and that are marketed in France are subject to prior authorization.

EXECUTIONS:

New regime of execution by attachment of debtor's personal property came into effect on Aug. 1, 1992. (Law No. 91-650 of July 9, 1991 [J.O. July 14, 1991]). To attach or seize property, unsecured creditors must obtain enforceable title ("titre exécutoire"); however, where merely preventive measures are sought, no such title is required.

Special judge ("juge de l'exécution") is instituted to deal with disputes and authorize preventive measures. Execution measures relating to monetary claims are called "saisies-attribution" and effect immediate transfer of attached debt to creditor. Special procedures exist for attachment of funds held by banks ("saisie-attribution bancaire") and of payments due from employer ("saisie-attribution des rémunérations").

Execution measures relating to claims other than monetary are called "saisies-vente" and give creditors right to attach and sell any of debtor's tangible movable property. (Other special execution procedures exist with respect to vehicles, intangible movable property and real property.)

Preventive measures ("mesures conservatoires") may be granted by court order to any creditor having well-founded claim collection of which is compromised by certain events. Preventive measures can take form of either attachment ("saisie-conservatoire"), which affects debtor's ability to dispose of its personal property, or security interest ("sûreté judiciaire") on real estate, business or securities granting creditor preferential right and "droit de suite", i.e., right with respect to secured property that cannot be defeated even by change in ownership.

Sale of real property subject to attachment must be made by auction. Some types of property, for example homesteads, are immune from execution. Attachment of ships and airplanes is subject to special procedures.

Treaties, such as Brussels Convention of Sept. 27, 1968 (applicable to EU members) and Treaty for Unification of Certain Rules Applicable to Conservatory Attachment of Sea Ships of May 10, 1952, contain special rules on execution procedures in France.

See also topics Attachment; Exemptions; Garnishment.

EXECUTORS AND ADMINISTRATORS:

There is no procedure exactly corresponding to probate or grant of administration. Estate vests directly in heirs (héritier—French word—includes next of kin), who continue "personality" of deceased. No one is bound to accept succession, and acceptance may be unconditional or subject to inventory. (C. C. 774, 775). Heirs must accept or refuse succession within 30 years of date of death. (C. C. 789). Within such 30-year period heir may accept succession notwithstanding his previous refusal, unless already accepted by other heirs. (C. C. 790). Refusal to accept succession must be made in writing and registered with clerk of court of domicile at time of death. (C. C. 776, 784). Heirs may accept with "benefit of inventory", in which case special proceeding is followed with result that heirs are not charged with debts of estate greater than their distributive share. Unless they accept "with benefit of inventory" heirs are deemed to have accepted succession unconditionally, in which case they bear estate liabilities indefinitely and estate creditors may move against their own assets. (C.C. 802).

Administration is in hands of heirs, but if none are known to exist provisional administrator and ultimately curator is appointed by court ("Tribunal de Grande Instance") of district in which estate procedure was opened. Specific legatees are not responsible for debts. No legal requirement as to advertising for creditors. In general, rules governing ordinary collections apply.

Testator may appoint executor. (C.C. 1025). Purpose of appointing executor is to bring about prompt payment of legacies. Testator may specifically grant seizin ("saisine") to executor over all or part of movables and personal property. Seizin thus granted executor may not exceed period of one year and one day after death. (C. C. 1026). Executor has no power over immovables, or real property, as devisee can protect his own interests by having his rights registered. However, case law validates specific authorization by testator to executor to sell real assets, receive and distribute price thereof, if there are no surviving reserved heirs. Minor and, according to case law, incompetent adult cannot act as executor but nonresident alien may.

If testator does not specifically grant seizin ("saisine") to executor, he becomes essentially agent, without significant functions, of heir or universal legatee. With seizin, he may take possession of movables, place property under seal to protect interests of minors and absent persons, and make a notarized inventory. (C C., art. 1031). He is obligated to pay all legacies from movables and may accordingly sell movables at auction. He may act on his own authority against heir or universal legatee if they refuse to comply with terms of will and accordingly may be represented in legal proceedings. Executor's powers and functions are personal and do not pass to his heirs on his death. (C. C. 1032).

See Topical Index in front part of this volume.

EXECUTORS AND ADMINISTRATORS . . . *continued*

Whenever there are heirs with right to a reserve (see topic Forced Heirship), certain proceedings are necessary to vest universal legatee with property.

See also topics Descent and Distribution; Wills.

EXEMPTIONS:

General principle to be found in Art. 2092 of French Civil Code is that whoever has contracted personal debt is bound to have recourse to all his property, real and personal, present and future in order to meet his obligation.

However, following items are exempted from seizure (see Law dated July 9, 1991 and Decree No. 92-755 dated July 31, 1992): (1) property which law declares exempted from seizure; (2) provisions, sums and pensions of alimentary nature (except those which have been already paid; (3) disposable portion of property declared to be exempted from seizure by testor or grantor except for proportion which may be authorized by court in favor of creditors after date of gift or of opening of legacy; (4) personal property necessary to life and work of debtor and his family except for payment of its purchase price within limits determined by NCCP; however personal property remains seizable if not located at domicile or place of work of debtor; (5) necessary items for handicapped individuals or necessary for health of sick persons.

Only a part of salaries of workmen and servants can be seized whatever total salary. Same applies to employees and civil clerks.

FIDUCIARIES:

See topics Executors and Administrators; Trusts.

FORCED HEIRSHIP:

Certain portions of a person's property cannot be given away by him, either by transfer inter vivos or by will. This reserve portion (réserve) amounts to one-half of his property if he leaves one child; if he leaves two children he can only give away a third; if he leaves three or more, only one-fourth of his property; without any distinction being made between legitimate and illegitimate children duly acknowledged except case of C. C. 915 (see infra). (C. C. 913). Under head of "children" are included more remote descendants, who, however, take per stirpes. (C. C. 913-1).

If a person has no children, and leaves one or more ascendants in both the paternal and maternal lines, he can dispose only of half of his property by gift or will. If he leaves ascendants in only one line, he may dispose of only three-fourths. (C. C. 914). But this share reserved to ascendant or ascendants may be cut down to usufruct in case decedent gives title ("nue-propriété") to said share to his surviving spouse. (C. C. 1094).

When an illegitimate child, whose mother or father was married at time of conception, has right of succession to his parent along with legitimate children born of marriage, his part in estate is half of what it would be if all children, including himself, were legitimate according to forced heirship rules. (C. C. 915). If he alone, or together with other children not born of marriage, has right to succession, disposable portion of estate in favor of any other person besides protected spouse is as indicated in abovementioned C. C. 913. (C. C. 915-1).

If there are no ascendants or descendants, there is no reserve. (C. C. 916).

The husband or wife may, either by the marriage contract or during the marriage, in case he or she leaves no children or descendants, convey by will or deed to the other spouse the fee in all the property which he or she could convey to a stranger and in addition the remainder interest of that portion reserved to the ascendants for life. (C. C. 1094).

In case where spouse leaves children or descendants, whether born of marriage or not, and whether legitimate or illegitimate, spouse may give to other spouse either that amount of property which he could give to stranger, or quarter of his property and usufruct in remaining three-quarters, or usufruct in all his property. (C. C. 1094.1).

In case where spouse leaves only illegitimate children conceived during marriage, spouse may give to other spouse either three quarters of his property, or half of his property and usufruct in remaining half or usufruct in all of his property. (C. C. 1097).

Dispositions of property made in contravention of these rules are valid, but reducible down to legal amount. (C. C. 920-930). In order to determine disposable part, all property conveyed inter vivos is fictitiously included in estate and given value as of time of decedent's death (C. C. 922) except for goods transferred in "donation-partage", which are valued as of date of gift on conditions stated in C. C. 1078. Only heirs benefiting from forced heirship may demand reduction of conveyances inter vivos (C. C. 921) and then only after all legacies are exhausted (C. C. 923, 925). Legacies are reduced pro rata (C. C. 926) except where testator requests priority of legacies (C. C. 927).

Disposable part may be given in whole or part to any heir or heirs, by will or gift, in which case it is not required to be brought back into estate at donor's death, if, in case of gifts, it is stipulated in deed or later, that this is in addition to that heir's part. (C. C. 919). If such stipulation was not expressly made by decedent, value as of time of donor's death of all gifts made inter vivos to any of decedent's heirs is added to estate and used in computing reserve and disposable portion thereof.

As real property situated in France is governed by the lex rei sitae a disposition of the same by a nonresident alien must take into account the provisions above set forth relating to the réserve.

FOREIGN CORPORATIONS:

See topic Corporations.

FOREIGN EXCHANGE:

See topic Exchange Control.

FOREIGN INVESTMENT:

All investments by nonresidents in France are subject to currency exchange and other regulation. See generally topic Exchange Control. In addition, certain economic sectors are state-owned, such as communications and electricity, and others are withdrawn altogether from foreign investment, or require specific authorization, such as marine, air and land transportation, petroleum extraction, banking and insurance.

Treaty of Establishment of Nov. 25, 1959 between France and U.S. governs rights of American nationals and enterprises to enter and invest in France. After covering rights of entry and sojourn, free access to courts and tribunals and other personal rights, treaty guarantees to American nationals and enterprises treatment as French nationals with respect to engaging in commercial, industrial, financial and other remunerative activities. (art. V). Accordingly, American nationals and enterprises may establish branches, organize companies, acquire majority interests in existing companies, and control and manage enterprises engaged in communications, air or water transport, banking, exploitation of natural resources, and production of electricity. (art. V[2]).

American nationals or enterprises may acquire any interest in real or personal property of any kind (except ships), including patents, trademarks, and other industrial property, and are entirely free to dispose of such property interests. (arts. VII, VIII). Expropriation of such property may only be for public purpose and upon payment of just compensation. (art. IV[3]).

Taxation of American nationals or enterprises, with or without permanent establishment in France, shall not be more burdensome than that of nationals or enterprises of France. (art. IX[1]). French enterprises owned or controlled in whole or in part by American nationals or enterprises shall not be subject to any form of taxation or obligation relating thereto which is more burdensome than that upon like French owned or controlled enterprises. (art. IX[3]). Fees relating to police or other formalities shall be no heavier than those imposed on aliens of any other nation. (art. IX[7]).

Free flow of investment capital is set as goal of treaty, and therefore treaty states principle that exchange control restrictions are to be at minimum level necessary to protect currency reserves, with repatriation of investment earnings or proceeds on liquidation to be in general unhindered. (art. X). Finally, express reservations permit limitation of above rights by measures designed to check monopolies or restraints of competition (art. XI) or by measures for regulation of fissionable materials, arms and munitions or measures necessary to protect essential security interests (art. XII).

See also topic Taxation.

FOREIGN TRADE REGULATIONS:

Imports.—According to their nature and country of origin, imports are either free or subject to quota restrictions. Latter must be covered by import licenses. Procedure for obtaining such licenses is laid down in Arrêté and Avis of Jan. 30, 1967 (Journal Officiel, Jan. 31, 1967, p. 1127) and subsequent amendments published in Journal Officiel.

Exports.—As a general rule, exports are free, subject to prohibitions published from time to time in Journal Officiel. Merchandise covered by prohibitions requires export licenses, but exporters can obtain long-term commitments from Government to issue such licenses. For procedure, see J. O. Jan. 31, 1967, p. 1129, and subsequent Avis published in Journal Officiel.

Export Control.—Certain goods and technologies expressly mentioned on document called "List" are subject to strict control with respect to final destination or country of origin. Applicable regulation and "List" are codified in "Avis" from Ministry of Economy, Finance and Budget. (J.O. Nov. 29, 1990, as modified by J.O. Dec. 21, 1990). Law No. 92-1477 further restricts movement of certain goods such as weapons and art works.

Intermédiaire Agréé.—Decree 68-1021 of Nov. 24, 1968 and circulars of Nov. 25 and Nov. 27, 1968, as implemented by subsequent decrees and circulars, have imposed requirement on importers and exporters to effect all exchange transactions, movements of capital and payments relating to their export-import transactions through "intermédiaire agréé" (banks, Treasury Public, Bank of France, financial departments of Post Offices, "Caisse des Dépôts et Consignations"). Such authorized agents are listed in Arrêté of Aug. 26, 1969, and subsequent arrêtés published from time to time in Journal Officiel.

See topic Exchange Control.

FRAUDS, STATUTE OF:

In civil contracts oral testimony is not sufficient to prove claim amounting to 5,000 francs or more. (C. C. 1341). This rule does not apply to commercial transactions, where such testimony is theoretically admissible, regardless of amount involved. (C. Com. 109).

When one party alone agrees to pay sum of money or deliver specific thing, this should be stated in document signed by obligor who should write in full sum or quantity while also writing numerals. (C. C. 1326).

FRAUDULENT SALES AND CONVEYANCES:

Creditor may act to exercise rights on behalf of and institute legal action against his debtor in order ultimately to protect his own credit interest in event debtor, by negligence or through outright refusal, does not act himself. However, creditor cannot exercise certain rights of predominantly personal nature, such as debtor's rights to alimony payments. Subject to that limitation creditor can exercise right belonging to his debtor and faces every defense his debtors could have faced. (Action oblique, C. C. 1166). Creditor may also attack contracts or instruments of transfer made by his debtor in fraud of his own rights. (Action Paulienne, C. C. 1167). There are special procedures to challenge fraudulent transfers between spouses, or by decedent to devisees or legatees, or by insolvent. (Art. 107, Law No. 85-98 of Jan. 25, 1985 on judicial recovery and liquidation).

GARNISHMENT:

Law No. 91-650 of July 9, 1991 (ratified by Decree No. 92-755 of July 31, 1992) has modified existing garnishment law.

Garnisher must have document acknowledging liquidity and exigibility of debt (Art. 55) and must serve process to garnishee indicating identity of debtor, sums owed, nature of debt and unavailability of such sums (Art. 56). Within eight-day period,

GARNISHMENT . . . *continued*
garnishment process is notified to debtor and indicates relevant court where debtor may challenge garnishment within one month. (Art. 58). If no protest is made within one month, garnisher will have right to receive immediate payment from garnishee. (Art. 61). If garnishment is challenged by debtor, competent judge ("juge de l'exécution") of place where debtor is domiciled settles matter. (Art. 65).

Law of July 11, 1972 allows Treasury to use simplified administrative procedure to recover sums owed to State (such as taxes and fines) by individuals or corporations, directly from depository banks or employers.

In principle, family allowances not assignable and not attachable, except in cases of undue payment provoked by fraud or false declaration and of payments related to family alimony, child maintenance and education and unpaid rents or nonrepayment of debt contracted for acquisition of property. (Art. 12 of Law of Jan. 4, 1985; and Decree of Aug. 2, 1985, codified at Art. L552 of Social Security Code). Specific rules apply to garnishment of remuneration owed by employer to employee. Share of remuneration which may be attached ranges from 5% for tranche of remuneration below FRF 17,400 to 100% for tranche beyond FRF 104,100. (Art. R 145-2 of French Labor Code—Decree 20 Sept. 1994).

GIFTS:

Deed of gift of real property must be by notarial act (C. C. 931) and expressly accepted by donee before donor becomes bound (C. C. 932). Gift of personal property is valid where there is actual delivery. Actual delivery may occur by simple transfer of funds from one bank account to another. Acceptance by minors and incapacitated persons must be by their legally appointed guardians. (C. C. 935). Gift can never include future property (C. C. 943), but it is possible to transfer remainder interest as gift, usufruct being kept by donor.

Gifts are as a rule irrevocable with revocation possible only in following cases: Express stipulation by donor that gift be returned if donee predeceases donor with or without surviving descendants (C. C. 951); nonperformance of express conditions of gift (C. C. 953); proof of base ingratitude, as refusal to provide basic necessities to donor in need (C. C. 953); subsequent birth of children (C. C. 953); gifts between spouses made during marriage (C. C. 1096). Further, extent to which donor may make valid gift is limited by legal reserve requirements as is any disposition of property by will (see topic Forced Heirship) and donee is liable for same tax as on property passing by succession (see topic Taxation). In case of divorce rendered on grounds of exclusive fault of one of spouses, guilty party automatically loses benefit of gifts received from other spouse. (C. C. 267).

All donees may ask judge to revise conditions and charges of deeds or gifts received, if after change of circumstances, performance and compliance are rendered difficult or seriously damaging for donees. (Law of July 4, 1984 as codified in C. C. 900-2 to 900-8).

See also topics Forced Heirship and Notaries Public.

GUARDIAN AND WARD:

Guardianship (C. C. arts. 389-475) includes four essential legal institutions:

(1) Conseil de Famille.—(C. C. arts. 407-416). This family council plays major role in guidance of minor as well as in management of his property. Family council authorization is required for all important transactions. Council is composed of four to six members designated by juge des tutelles (judge of guardianship) who presides over council. (C. C. arts. 407 and 415). Council is created either ex officio by judge or when requested by any personconcerned such as relatives, creditors or government. It meets at request of judge, relatives, creditors, government attorney, or ex officio. (C. C. art. 405).

(2) Guardian.—(C. C. arts. 397-406). Guardian is designated as follows: (a) Either by testament or declaration before notary of father or mother last deceased ("tutelle testamentaire"); (b) by law in favor of closest ascendant ("tutelle légale"); or (c) by family council at request of juge des tutelles ("tutelle dative"). Guardian is supervised by family council and deputy guardian ("subrogé tuteur").

(3) Deputy Guardian (Subrogé Tuteur).—(C. C. arts. 420-426). His main duty is to supervise management of minor's property. Law of Dec. 14, 1964 which modified Civil Code has attributed greater importance to this guardian. He represents minor when minor's interests are in conflict with those of guardian.

(4) Juge des Tutelles.—(C. C. arts. 393-396). This judge of guardianship has general supervisory capacity and in exceptional cases may be substituted in place of family council.

Law of June 6, 1984 (Code de la Famille et de l'Aide Sociale) created special guardianship to assist and represent orphaned or abandoned children ("pupilles de l'Etat"), but with only two legal institutions ("conseil de famille" and guardian) represented by state officials.

Adoption formalities have been modified and require parents desiring to adopt child to receive prior approval ("agrément") from relevant administration ("Aide sociale á l'enfance") of place of residence of future parents. (Decree of Aug. 23, 1985; J.O. Sept. 5, 1985).

Government attorney must be notified of most legal proceedings involving guardians and wards. (Decree of Dec. 27, 1985; J.O. Dec. 29, 1985).

HOLIDAYS:

Suns. and following days are legal holidays: Jan. 1, Easter Monday, Ascension Thursday, May 1, May 8, Pentecost Monday, July 14, Aug. 15, Nov. 1, Nov. 11, and Christmas. No process may be served on Sun. or legal holiday without court permission.
(C. C. P. 664).

HOMESTEADS:

Law of July 12, 1909 created institution of homestead ("bien de famille"), house or divisible portion thereof or house and land adjoining or in neighbor-hood which is occupied and worked by family, or house with shops or workshops (along with materials and tools) occupied and worked by family of workmen and provided that institution of homestead be governed by Civil Code. Value of whole at time of creation may not exceed FRF 50,000. (Law of Mar. 12, 1953). Foreigners may benefit from homestead law only if they are domiciled in France. Homestead cannot be mortgaged or attached or seized for debt, even in event of owner's bankruptcy. Deed to homestead must be in form of notarial act, with fulfillment of legal notice requirements to permit third parties to challenge title or proper valuation of homestead, followed by registration with local civil court of general jurisdiction. (Decree of Mar. 26, 1910).

HUSBAND AND WIFE:

Regulation of marital relations, provided for in C. C. arts. 214 to 226 and 1387 to 1581, was revised by law of July 13, 1965 (J. O., July 14, 1965), which entered into effect Feb. 1, 1966, modified by Law of Dec. 23, 1985 (J.O. Dec. 26, 1985) effective July 1, 1986 which substantially amends or replaces above cited provisions of Civil Code. New law enlarges, under all marital regimes, rights of married woman. Married woman may now have her own bank account, and may establish a business without prior consent of her husband as well as retain any income therefrom after fulfillment of matrimonial obligations, and may choose to exercise her profession under maiden name with option of adding husband's name. Wife may act alone in ordinary transactions without being considered agent of husband, and either spouse may enter into contracts binding other spouse for upkeep of family or education of children. New provisions (C. C. arts. 214 to 226), generally providing for rights and obligations of spouses, apply to marriages contracted under old law as well as to marriages taking place after Feb. 1, 1966.

Matrimonial Regimes.—Marital property regime is fixed either by law, if spouses are married without contract, or by contract. Contract must be drawn up by notary before marriage. Minor has capacity to bind himself in marriage contract, provided that parent or guardian consenting to marriage assents to contract. (C. C. arts. 1387-1399).

Marriages which occurred before Feb. 1, 1966 without contract are governed by community property regime of former law, but administration of property (including right of each spouse to arrange and enjoy income from his separate property) is governed by provisions of new law. Spouses could until Dec. 31, 1967, by declaration before notary, elect to be governed by substantive provisions of new community property law.

Marriages which took place prior to Feb. 1, 1966 pursuant to contract continue to be governed by terms of contract and, with certain exceptions, property is still administered under provisions of prior law. However, spouses could, until Dec. 31, 1967, by declaration before notary, elect to be governed under provisions of new law relating to their particular contractual regime.

Dotal system was abrogated by law of July 13, 1965. Persons married under this system continue to be governed by terms of their marriage contracts, but they were able to decide to change over to community or separate property regime before Feb. 1, 1968.

Spouses married either before or after enactment of new law may, upon showing of good cause and fulfillment of certain formalities, modify their marital regime, either in whole or in part, by notarized act approved by civil court. (C. C. art. 1397). Both legal and contractual regimes may be modified, but, modification is only possible after two years under one regime have elapsed.

Community Property.—Subject of community property regime is quite complex, and only brief summary can be given here. For rules, see C. C. arts. 1400 to 1581 as modified.

If no marriage contract is made, system of community property prevails. Under old law, community assets consisted of: Personal property possessed by spouses at time of marriage or acquired during marriage, either by inheritance or by inter vivos gift, unless donor expressed contrary intention; income received during marriage from property of any nature owned at time of marriage or acquired thereafter; and all real property purchased during marriage. Immovables (real property) were presumed to have been purchased until contrary was shown. Immovables belonging to either spouse at time of marriage or afterwards inherited or received as a gift did not become community property.

As of Feb. 1, 1966 this legal regime was modified and now assets acquired by one spouse prior to marriage, or during marriage through succession, bequest, or gift where donor does not specifically intend that gift enter community, are not community assets. In general, however, any movable or immovable property is presumed to be acquired by community unless it is demonstrated that it belongs to one of spouses. (C. C. arts. 1401 to 1405).

Community is liable only for following debts: necessary expenses for family and for children's education and extra contractual commitments (C. C. arts. 1409 to 1420). If one spouse refuses to contribute to common expenses, other spouse may request court to seize part of his salary or income.

Community can be dissolved by death, divorce, separation or decree of court and by change of matrimonial regime. (C. C. art. 1441). Special rules govern accounting.

Community system may be modified by contract. Since Feb. 1, 1966 it has been possible to adopt by contract previous legal regime. It has also been possible to exclude personalty, either wholly or in part; to provide for separate responsibility for debt; to grant wife right to reassert sole ownership over property she brought to community, either at time of marriage or afterwards; to give survivor right to withdraw a certain sum or specific thing from assets before any division takes place; to give parties unequal shares; or finally, to provide for community in all property or subject to whatever conditions the parties will. (C. C. arts. 1497-1527).

Parties may agree that each spouse shall retain separate ownership of separate property, and, in such case, each spouse retains entire management of his property and full enjoyment of income therefrom. (C. C. arts. 1536-1541).

Alienation of Property.—New law provides that both husband and wife have power individually to manage community assets. Spouse cannot, without prior consent of other, give away any asset of community, nor can he sell, mortgage or transfer rights in real property or in business belonging to community. Further, spouse may not alienate property rights whose transfer must be published according to law. Finally, granting of commercial or agricultural leases is forbidden. (C. C. 1425). Spouse can dispose by will only of his share in community. (C. C. Arts. 1421–1424).

HUSBAND AND WIFE . . . *continued*

Capital is inalienable except under special circumstances. Wife's property not made part of her dowry constitutes her paraphernalia, over which she has right of management and enjoyment. (C. C. arts. 1540-1581). Upon dissolution of marriage, dowry is part of wife's estate.

Married woman may be public trader. She may bind herself and her property in respect of transactions relating to her business. If matrimonial property regime existing between spouses is that of community, married woman trader may, under new law, have sole power to manage and dispose of assets necessary for her profession, but each spouse liable for acts executed by other without fraud. (C. C. 1421). In case of bankruptcy, spouse of debtor establishes inventory of personal property according to matrimonial regime adopted. Liquidator may join all property acquired during marriage to assets of creditors. Spouse of debtor or creditors may not challenge advantages given by one spouse or other in marriage contract or during marriage. (Law of Jan. 1, 1985, Arts. 111 to 114). Married woman may, in most cases, charge, mortgage or sell realty, but not stipulated dowry, if married under dotal system.

IMMIGRATION:

Visas.—Pursuant to Law No. 93-1027 of Aug. 24, 1993, persons entering France except EEC nationals must obtain either tourist visa (for stay of three months or less) or long-term visa ("visa de long séjour") for stay exceeding three months, from local French Consulate of area in which they reside. To do so, evidence of sufficent means to remain in France must be shown. (See topic Aliens.) Such persons may also be required, subject to international agreements, to furnish guarantees of repatriation, and entry into France may be refused to aliens for reasons of public order ("Ordre Public"). (Law No. 80-9 of Jan. 10, 1980).

Pursuant to Decree No. 70-29 of Jan. 5, 1970, completed by Decree No. 77-957 of Aug. 19, 1977, nationals of European Union countries are entitled to residence permits, indefinitely renewable as of right, under conditions set forth therein.

Citizenship.—Aliens who have been residents of France for five years, and have duly held residence permit during that time, may apply for French nationality. (French Nationality Code, art. 62). This duration is reduced to two years where applicant holds French university degree or can or has rendered "important" services to France. (art. 63). Alien may be exempt from any length of stay altogether if, for example, he has rendered "exceptional" services to France, served in combat unit of French Army, is spouse or child of person acquiring French nationality or belongs to cultural and linguistic French Entry. (art. 64).

Application for French citizenship should be submitted to Préfet of Department where applicant has established his residence, who, upon due enquiry, transmits application to Ministry of Social Affairs. Minister's decision is published in Journal Officiel in form of decree.

INDUSTRIAL PROPERTY RIGHTS:

General Note.—Both France and U.S. are members of Convention of International Union for protection of industrial property of Mar. 20, 1883 (short: Paris Convention) applying to patents, trademarks and designs and models. Both countries have ratified Lisbon revision of Oct. 31, 1958, effective since Jan. 4, 1962, and Stockholm revision of July 14, 1967, which came into force in France on Aug. 12, 1975. France has also ratified Washington Treaty of June 19, 1970 on International Patent Cooperation (see Law 77-682 of June 30, 1977) which came into force for France on Feb. 25, 1978, Munich Convention of Oct. 5, 1973 on European Patents (see Law 77-683 of June 30, 1977) which has been in force since Oct. 7, 1977, and Luxembourg Convention of Dec. 15, 1975 on EEC patents (see Law 77-684 of June 30, 1977) which is not yet in force. Decree 78-1011 of Oct. 10, 1978 (J.O. of Oct. 15, 1978), issued to implement Law 77-683, establishes fees for filing of European patents. Treaty of Budapest of Apr. 8, 1977 on international recognition of patent registration of microorganisms came into force in France in Nov. 1980. (Decree no. 80-954 of Nov. 25, 1980). Law of Nov. 26, 1990 adapts existing industrial property legislation in order to streamline registration procedures and to encourage French industry to seek protection of such rights.

Law No. 92-597 of July 1, 1992 has gathered several existing laws into new code, "code de la propriété intellectuelle." This new code groups existing provisions governing both copyrights and related rights and industrial property rights. Other than codifying different laws promulgated on different dates new code does not provide any modifications to state of law.

Decree No. 95-385 of Apr. 10, 1995 (J.O. of Apr. 13, 1995) has collected all intellectual property decrees into C.P.I. Other than codifying different decrees promulgated on different dates, new decree does not provide any modification to present state of Law.

Patents.—(C.P.I., art. L. 611-1 to L. 615-22).

Patents under C.P.I. contain claims defining scope of patent, as in U.S. There is a patent office opinion based on novelty and priority. Applicant may contest opinion and revise his claim. Official opinion is published with patent, which also contains reference to international classification established by European Cultural Convention of Dec. 19, 1954.

Any natural person or legal entity, whether or not citizen or resident of France, who has invention of new industrial product or new process, or new application of known process for obtaining an industrial result or product, may, individually or jointly with others, apply for French patent by filing application in French with "Institut National de la Propriété Industrielle," submitting at same time duplicate copies of full description of invention and of drawings illustrative thereof. Application must contain claims which define scope of protection applied for (unlike previous law which required no formulation of claims). Initial claims contained in application may be modified until final opinion is published by Institute of Industrial Property. Protection granted is limited to what may validly be claimed by description and drawings. Court of Appeal of Paris has immediate and exclusive jurisdiction to hear any complaints formed as a result of a rejected application.

Following are unpatentable: Purely scientific or theoretical principles without industrial application, creations which are exclusively decorative, financial schemes, rules for games and, in particular, programs or instructions for operation of computers.

Medicines can henceforth be protected by patent, but not by certificate of utility. New therapeutical use of medical product is not patentable.

Two protective rights are available under C.P.I.: (a) Patent ("brevet"); (b) Certificate of Utility ("Certificat d'Utilité"). Patent covers all inventions including medicinal products. Certificate of Utility, protected right introduced by C.P.I., is intended for protection of inventions of minor importance and concerns any type of invention, including chemical products or manufacturing processes. It must comply with same rules as those required for patents. However, it does not have to undergo an examination for novelty and may not be issued for protection of medicinal products. Certificate of Utility is not covered by Paris Convention (and it is uncertain whether such protective right may serve as basis of priority).

Life of a patent is 20 years from date of application; life of Certificate of Utility is six years from date of application.

Patent and "Certificat d'Utilité" are subject to payment of annual fees, amount of which is specified in Arrêté of Dec. 28, 1992. Nonpayment of any one annual fee within six months of its due date results in irrevocable extinction of patent. It should be noted that Certificate of Addition ("Certificat d'addition") used to be granted to holder of principal Certificate of Utility or of principal patent for inventions relating to at least one claim of principal patent. Such titles are no longer issued. (Law of Nov. 26, 1990). However, those Certificates of Addition which were already delivered at date 1990 law entered into force, remain valid as long as does principal Certificate of Utility or patent to which it is accessory.

Inventions of employee made pursuant to employment contract including inventive activity or pursuant to researches and studies of which employee is in charge belong to employer who may directly apply for patent in his own name without any assignment from employee. His rights to compensation are governed by contract and by various industry-wide collective labor conventions. These conventions usually cover not only laborers but also engineers and administrators ("cadres"). Under French case law, rights of employees provided for in these conventions may not be validly abridged or waived by individual contract.

Any other inventions belong to employee, unless made in area of his firm activities or on basis of knowledge or use of means and technics specific to firm or data provided by firm. In this case, employer is entitled to obtain part or whole of ownership or use of rights attached to patent obtained by employee. Employee has to obtain fair compensation fixed by agreement between him and his employer or by specific body in case of failure to reach such agreement.

Foreigners who are domiciled or established in countries not signatories of Paris Convention are protected by French Law, provided French domiciliaries enjoy reciprocal protection in said countries.

Under Paris Convention and Washington Treaty, international priority may be claimed by applicant who files his patent in France within 12 months of his first filing in another member country.

Notification of License Agreements and Assignments.—Under Arts. R 624-1 to R 624-7 of C.P.I., licenses and assignments of industrial property rights are subject to administrative formalities. All agreements involving assignments or licenses to or by French resident of any industrial property rights, including technical, scientific, and engineering assistance and other forms of knowhow, must be submitted to Ministry of Industry within a month of their execution. Ministry furnishes registration number which must be utilized by licensed banks (intermédiaires agrées) in clearing fees for transmission abroad. Decree no longer provides for Ministry to issue "opinion" on agreement, but it is expected that Ministry will transmit information concerning agreements to fiscal authorities and Bank of France. Arrêté of May 26, 1970 sets forth procedure to be followed in making notification to Ministry. License agreements presently in force need not be submitted to Ministry unless modified.

Prior authorization of exchange control authorities no longer required for transfer of royalties or other payments by French entities to non-French entities under agreements assigning or licensing patents, trademarks, know-how and other industrial property rights. (Law No. 66-1008 of Dec. 28, 1966). See topic Exchange Control.

Notice of patent licenses may have to be given to EU Commission, unless license agreement falls within group exemption under EU Commission Regulation No. 2349/84 of July 23, 1984 which applies to agreements in force on 31 Mar. 1996, or under EU Commission Regulation No. 240/96 of 31 Jan. 1996, which applies to agreements effective as of 1st Apr. 1996.

Recording.—Assignments and licenses to be enforceable against third parties must be recorded on Special Register at Institut National de la Propriété Industrielle.

Compulsory Licenses.—C.P.I. defines two general types of compulsory licenses: "License obligatoire" (mandatory licenses) and "license d'office" (license granted ex-officio to Government).

Licenses Obligatoires.—Any natural or legal person may, three years after issuance of patent or four years after filing of application therefor and after having unsuccessfully demanded a license from patentee, obtain from Tribunal de Grande Instance, a "license obligatoire," if at time of such request patentee, without valid excuse, has for more than three consecutive years either totally abandoned exploitation of his patent or failed to exploit it sufficiently enough to satisfy French market needs. "License obligatoire" is nonexclusive and nonassignable without court approval; court determines scope, duration and reasonable royalties. Applicant for "license obligatoire" must prove he is able to exploit patent in serious and effective manner.

Holder of patent relating to improvement over invention already patented by a third party ("brevet de perfectionnement") cannot exploit his patent without authorization from owner of earlier patent; similarly, owner of earlier patent cannot exploit patent of improvement without authorization from owner of patent of improvement. Failing such authorization, holder of patent of improvement may after the three or four year period referred to in paragraph immediately above obtain license to exploit patent which forms basis of improvement and, in turn, holder of earlier patent may obtain license to exploit patent of improvement.

License d'Office.—(a) Public Health: In case of medical patents, Minister of Public Health may ask Minister of Industrial Property to declare such patents open to compulsory government licensing if medicines are made available to public in insufficient quantity or quality, or at unreasonable prices; (b) National Economy: Minister of Industrial Property may require holders of patents other than medicines to exploit their patents so as to satisfy needs of national economy. If after one year such a request has

INDUSTRIAL PROPERTY RIGHTS . . . *continued*
not been complied with and if absence of exploitation or insufficiency of quality or quantity is seriously prejudicial to national economic expansion or public interest, patent may be subjected to compulsory government licensing and any qualified person, as of date of issuance of decree declaring patent open to compulsory government licensing, may apply to Minister of Industrial Property for granting of "license d'office"; (c) National Defense: State may, for purposes of national defense, obtain "license d'office" at any time for itself or for third party.

Licenses for exploitation obtained for patents affecting public health, national defense or national economy are nonexclusive and may not be assigned or transferred. They are granted by decision of Minister of Industrial Property which decision sets terms and conditions and duration of licenses; royalties, however, absent agreement of parties, are fixed by Tribunal de Grande Instance.

Infringement.—In case of infringement, an order from Tribunal de Grande Instance may be obtained authorizing real or symbolic seizure ("saisie contrefaçon") of infringing articles by a "huissier" (process server). Main purpose of this procedure is to discover and determine existence and extent of suspected infringement. Patent infringement is generally civil offense, but all prejudice knowingly caused is penal offense punishable by fine and/or imprisonment. However, criminal court has jurisdiction only after civil court has acknowledged infringement. Both civil and criminal action must be brought within three years of occurrence of alleged wrong. Additional remedy may be confiscation of all infringment products or, in case of process patent, even of special tools or machines which are designed to produce infringing article.

Know-how.—Although not defined by legislative text, know-how is recognized by case law as form of property which may be transferred and protected by agreement. Notice of transfers of know-how may have to be given to EU Commission, unless transfer falls within group exemption under EU Commission Regulation No. 556/89 of Nov. 30, 1988 which applies to agreements in force on 31 Mar. 1996, or under EU Commission Regulation No. 240/96 of 31 Jan. 1996, which applies to agreements effective as of 1st Apr. 1996.

Designs and Models.—(C.P.I., art. L. 511-1 to L. 521-7).

Any object which is not patentable, may be protected as model or design if it has unique shape or form or surface design (including color scheme) which distinguishes it from other similar products and which appeals to the esthetic sense. Such esthetic shape or surface design must be original. Exclusive proprietary right to such creation is acquired by its author through mere act of creating it; registration as design and model is mere prima facie evidence of ownership. (Author may also acquire rights in object based on C. P. I. provisions relating to authors' and artists' rights. See topic Copyright.)

Procedures for registration of designs and models is as follows: Applicant must deposit with "Institut National de la Propriété Industrielle" (if domiciled in Paris or outside France) or otherwise with Clerk of Commercial Court of applicant's domicile, reproduction of design or model, which will be accepted if it is properly described and if its publication would not be contrary to public policy. Protection is valid for 25 years, renewable upon applicant's request for second 25-year period.

Infringement suit in the case of models and designs is similar to that in the case of patents or of trademarks, and, similarly, it can be initiated by preliminary seizure proceeding ("saisie-contrefaçon"). Infringement proceedings, however, are available only to owner of registered design and model, and suit may be started only after publication of such registration. Bad faith is always presumed when there is infringement (cf. Trib. Corr. of Belfort, Apr. 25, 1980. G.P. 12-13 Sept., 1980 P. 8). Damages for infringing acts committed by defendant after registration of design and model but before its publication will be awarded only if knowledge and bad faith on part of defendant are proved.

Owner of unregistered design or model may proceed against infringers either under the special C. P. I. provisions protecting authors' and artists' rights (see topic Copyright), or he may sue them for unfair competition under general tort provisions of Civil Code.

In order to be enforceable against third parties, contracts affecting rights to design or model must be registered with National Register of Designs and Models.

Under Paris Convention, international priority may be claimed by applicant who files his French design and model registration within six months of his first filing in another member country.

Decree No. 92-792 and Arrêté of Aug. 13, 1992 provide detailed rules for registration of designs and models.

Semi-conductor Chips.—(C.P.I., art. L. 622-1 to L. 622-7). Legislation is similar to U.S. Chip Law. Law provides protection for "final or intermediary topographies" of semiconductors if they (1) "demonstrate an intellectual effort of the inventor" and (2) are not commonly used in semiconductor field. Protection is acquired by registration with National Institute of Industrial Property (Institut national de la propriété industrielle) for period of ten years. Protection may be lost if chip is not commercially used. Reproduction of registered chip is prohibited except for purposes of evaluation, analysis or education. Marketing or importing of unlawfully reproduced chips is also prohibited. Reverse engineering is permitted if it leads to development of another chip design which can be protected under Law. Law refers to relevant provisions of patent law concerning transfer and acquisition of rights conferred by registration, sanctions and dispute resolution.

Foreigners are protected if either (1) they are domiciled or resident or established in EU; or (2) they market, pursuant to exclusive license for entire EU, chip not previously protected by Law; or (3) they are domiciliaries or established in countries in which French domiciliaries enjoy reciprocal protection.

Trademarks.—(C.P.I., art. L. 711-1 to L. 716-16).

Trademarks may be registered to cover goods as well as services. Registrable as trademarks are any names, including proper names, fictitious names, geographical names, or any arbitrary or imaginary words, signs or symbols, characteristic forms or shapes of products or their containers or presentation, labels, wrappers, emblems, stamps, seals, combinations or dispositions of colors, designs, reliefs, letters, numerals, and, in general, any and all material signs serving to identify and distinguish products or services from similar products or services. (Registration of proper name will not prevent natural person from using in good faith his own name in his business activities, but court may prohibit or regulate manner of using such unregistered proper name so as to avoid confusion of public with identical or similar name registered as trademark.) Under new law, sound effects and music may be registered as trademarks.

Not registrable are trademarks: (1) Containing elements contrary to public order or morals, (2) containing elements prohibited by Art. 6 ter of Paris Convention (national and international emblems), (3) consisting exclusively of necessary or generic designation of product or service or containing deceptive or misleading indications, or (4) consisting exclusively of indications or descriptions of essential quality or composition of product or service. It seems, however, that generic or usual designation may become registrable when it has been in use for long period of time. (cf. Cass. com. May 7, 1980. Société Verrerie de Biot. G.P. Oct. 12-14, 1980).

Under old law, there was no official examination of originality or priority before registration (such questions were examined by court in infringement action), nor opposition proceedings, but application could be rejected for material irregularity, nonpayment of fees, or if trademark fell into one of excluded categories enumerated above. Under present law, registration may be refused for lack of originality or based on opposition proceeding. Registration may be challenged by existing trademark holder or its licensee within six months of request for registration. Rights in trademark acquired by registration may only be challenged within three years of registration request unless bad faith of registrant is shown. Registration requests filed before effective date of new law will be processed and examined according to law being replaced. Court of Appeals of Paris has exclusive jurisdiction to hear any complaints resulting from rejected application. (C.P.I. contains provisions necessary for implementation of law and for implementation of opposition proceeding. New proceeding allows individuals with anterior rights to oppose registration of trademark.)

Applications for registration may be filed by any natural person or legal entity either directly with National Institute of Industrial Property (Institut National de la Propriété Industrielle) or through clerk of commercial court of applicant's domicile or permanent business establishment. Trademark registration is subject to payment of fees set forth in Arrêté of Dec. 28, 1992. Foreigners with no domicile or permanent business establishment in France may register trademarks and enjoy full protection of law even without first filing in home country, provided that applicant is domiciliary or established in member country to Paris Convention or of country granting reciprocal privileges to French domiciliaries. Such foreigners must file trademark application directly with National Institute of Industrial Property and elect domicile in France for that purpose.

Benefit of priority date of foreign registration, if any, may be obtained under Paris Convention if French application is filed within six months of foreign application, but such priority must be claimed in writing at time of filing French application, or, upon payment of late fee, within six months thereof.

All applications are classified, entered on National Trademark Register, and published in Bulletin Officiel by National Institute of Industrial Property. France uses International Trademark Classification comprising 34 classes of goods and eight classes of services.

Duration of registration is ten years from date of filing application; it may be renewed for indefinite number of additional ten year periods. Formalities of renewal are same as of registration. Renewal registration should be effected before expiration of preceding term (in which case new period starts with date of renewal application), but it may also be undertaken any time within six months of expiration of preceding term upon payment of late fee (in which case new period starts with date of expiration of preceding term).

Property right in trademark is created only by registration; mere use of unregistered trademark does not provide basis for legal protection. As between two registrants in good faith, one with earlier filing date, or earlier Convention priority date, has precedence and may apply to court for radiation or assignment of later registrations. Exception is made for "well-known trademarks" covered by Art. 6 bis of Paris Convention, whose owners, even without registration in France, may demand cancellation of confusingly similar registered trademarks. If such conflicting trademark has been registered in good faith, action for cancellation under this provision is limited to five years from its registration date.

French trademark registration may be obtained without showing previous use of trademark by applicant or existence of established business. However, all rights in trademark are forfeited if trademark is not publicly and unequivocally exploited, without valid excuse, for five years preceding challenge in court. Exploitation in only one class of trademark registered in several classes of goods and/or services, may be sufficient to save that trademark from forfeiture with respect to other, unexploited classes, but only if such partial forfeiture would create confusion of public detrimental to remaining exploited portion of registered trademark. Issue of forfeiture can be raised either as defense in infringement suit or in separate court action by any interested party. Burden of proving sufficient exploitation or valid excuse is upon owner of trademark. Under new law, statute of limitation for infringement action is three years. Infringement action may be brought by trademark holder, or by its licensee if trademark holder takes no action after receiving notice from licensee. Absolute bar to infringment action exists after five years from registration, except where registration was procured in bad faith.

Manufacturers' syndicates, trade associations, regional organizations, etc., may register "collective trademarks" to be used by their members to indicate origin, quality, or composition of their goods or services. Use of "collective marks" is strictly regulated and penalties are provided for misuse or abuse. Law permits applicant for registration of trademark to commence infringement action against third party, after notice to such third party of application, for acts of infringement occurring after such notification. Applicant may obtain seizure ("saisie contrefaçon") subject to verification of application and notification, and court will suspend judgment pending actual registration and publication.

Trademark infringement covers unlawful copying (contrefaçon), affixing or using (apposition frauduleuse), imitating (imitation frauduleuse) of someone else's registered trademark in connection with same or similar goods or services so as to create confusion in minds of customers or clients, or knowingly holding, handling, selling, or offering for sale, goods or services under infringing mark. Action for trademark infringement is similar to patent infringement (see subhead Patents, supra). Suit may

INDUSTRIAL PROPERTY RIGHTS . . . *continued*
be commenced by real or descriptive seizure of articles bearing infringing mark, as well as of books and records showing extent of infringement; it may be prosecuted either in criminal or civil action, and criminal penalties are provided for in addition to civil damages (they may include confiscation of all articles bearing infringing trademark).

Trademark assignments, licenses and pledges can be made independently of any transfer of going business (good will); they must be evidenced by writing, and, in order to be enforceable against third parties, they must be recorded on National Trademark Register at National Institute of Industrial Property. Agreements involving foreigners are subject to conditions set forth above under subhead Patents. Licenses, but not assignments or pledges, may be granted for limited territory within France. Collective trademarks may not be assigned or pledged.

Under terms of special Franco-Italian treaty of Oct. 21, 1959, in effect since Jan. 31, 1961, any applicant for French trademark may have his registration extended to Italy with same effect as if he had filed it directly in Italy.

France is signatory to Madrid Convention (Nice Revision of June 15, 1957), but foreigners may take advantage of international trademark registration provided thereunder only if they have citizenship, domicile, or permanent business establishment in one of member countries (U.S. and U.K. are not members).

Plant Variety Rights.—Arts. L. 623-1 to L. 623-35 of C.P.I. organize protection of plant variety rights. Plant varieties are protected (art. L. 623-1) when they are uniform, distinct, stable and new. Each plant variety may benefit from "Certificate of Plant Variety" ("Certificat d'Obtention Végétale") which gives its owner exclusive right to produce, sell or offer to sell all or part of plant in France. (art. L. 623-4). Such certificate is granted for period of 20 years or 25 years if plant variety production requires long period. (art. L. 623-13). Any infringement to rights resulting from certificate is criminal offense punished by penalty.

European Council Regulation of July 27, 1994 (No. 2100/94) established system of community plant variety rights as sole and exclusive form of community industrial property rights for plant varieties. Such protection will be without prejudice to rights of Member States to grant national property rights for plant varieties. However, varieties which are subject matter of community plant variety rights cannot be subject matter of any other form of national plant variety rights or patents.

See also topics Copyright and Unfair Competition.

INFANTS:

Age of majority is 18 for both sexes. (C. C. arts. 388 and 488 as modified by Law of July 5, 1974). Infant may be emancipated at 16 by declaration of mother or father and hearing of other parent if possible received by judge of Guardianship Court. (C. C. art. 477 as modified by Law of June 5, 1974 and Law of Jan. 8, 1993). Infant is automatically emancipated by marriage (C. C. 476) or after completion of service in armed forces. Emancipated minor must still obtain authorizations and consents to marry (see topic Marriage) or to be adopted. (C. C. 481). Emancipated minor may not engage in commerce as major. (C. C. art. 487).

Law of Dec. 23, 1985 (J.O. Dec. 26, 1985) effective July 1, 1986, modifies rules concerning administration of assets of minor children. (C. C. 383, 389, 389-1, 389-2). Legal administration now attributed either to parent(s) exercising parental authority (jointly to father and mother or one parent only in certain circumstances), or to judge of guardianship ("juge des tutelles") if one parent dead and surviving parent barred from parental authority.

Children may now add name of other parent to official surname, as usage name only, without condition, if they have reached age of majority, or with approval of person exercising parental authority in case of minors. (Art. 43, Law of Dec. 23, 1985).

France has ratified International Convention on voluntary recognition of children born to unmarried parents. (Law of Jan. 1, 1985).

France has ratified Convention on the Rights of the Child. (Law No. 90-548 of July 2, 1990 and Decree No. 90-917 of Oct. 8, 1990). Law No. 93-22 of 8 Jan. 1993 has considerably modified procedure concerning recognition of child (art. 5) and their civil status, in particular when they are born abroad and they acquire or regain French nationality (art. 12).

It has also modified regime with regard to legitimate and illegitimate descent, as well as adoption. (c. II of Law). In particular, it has established principle of joint parental authority by recognizing right for child to be raised by both parents. For this purpose, it has appointed judge in charge of matrimonial matters (Juge aux affaires matrimoniales "JAM") having special jurisdiction to deal with these types of disputes.

New Law No. 94-629 dated July 25, 1994, regarding "famiily policy" provides certain number of provisions allowing government financial allocation in case of adoption.

See also topic Divorce, subhead Children.

INSOLVENCY:

See topic Judicial Recovery and Liquidation.

INTEREST:

Art. 1153-1 of French Civil Code provides that monetary judgments bear interest at legal rate which, unless otherwise provided by law, starts to run as of date of judgment or such other date as judge may determine. Legal rate of interest is fixed in France by decree each calendar year. For instance, rates fixed for last three years are as follows: 8.40% (1994), 5.82% (1995) and 6.65% (1996).

For all matters, legal interest rate is fixed for each civil year by Decree. For each year it is calculated as average of previous 12 monthly averages of rates of return on 13-week fixed rate Treasury bonds.

Contractual interest rate must be in writing. It can exceed legal rate, as long as rate stipulated is not prohibited by law.

Usury is defined as interest exceeding ordinary rate applied by banks during preceding quarter for similar operations by more than 33.33%. Usury thresholds are published quarterly in French Official Journal. Usury is also criminal offence. (Law of Dec. 28, 1966, see C. C. art. 1907 and Decree of Mar. 21, 1967).

INTESTACY:

See topic Descent and Distribution.

JUDGMENTS:

Bilateral treaties for enforcement of foreign judgments exist with Algeria, Austria, Belgium, Benin, Bulgaria, Cameroon, Chad, Congo, Egypt, Great Britain, Hungary, Ivory Coast, Madagascar, Mauritania, Morocco, Quebec, Rumania, Senegal, Spain, Switzerland and Togo. Less formal bilateral arrangements (some applicable only to specified subject matter) exist with Brazil, China, Czechoslovakia, Dahomey, Djibouti, Germany, Tunisia and U.S. France is party to EEC Convention on Jurisdiction and Enforcement of Judgments in Civil and Commercial Matters of Sept. 27, 1968 (ratified by Decree No. 73-63 of Jan. 13, 1973), to subsequent Protocol of 1971 providing for interpretation of Convention by European Court of Justice (entered into force for France by Decree No. 76-298 of Mar. 31, 1976) and to 1973 Hague Convention on Recognition and Enforcement of Judgments relating to Maintenance Obligations (entered into force for France on Oct. 1, 1977 by Decree No. 77120 of Sept. 22, 1977). France has also signed but not ratified Lugano Convention on Jurisdiction and Enforcement of Judgments in Civil and Commercial Matters of Sept. 16, 1988. In absence of treaty, foreign judgments are normally enforceable by order ("exequatur") delivered by Tribunal de Grande Instance after proceedings. Foreign judgments concerning personal status or creating rights ("jugements constitutifs") are enforceable without exequatur, except where enforcement with respect to property or where coercive action against persons is required. Under French law, recognition and enforcement in France of foreign judgments are subject to specific conditions established by decision dated Jan. 7, 1964 (see in Gaz. Pal. 1964, p. 372) of French Supreme Court ("Cour de cassation"). These conditions are as follows: (1) foreign court must have had jurisdiction to settle matter according to French international private law (see decision of French Supreme Court dated Feb. 6, 1985, in Dalloz 1985, p. 469); (2) foreign judgment must not be contrary to French international public policy and to rules of natural justice (see decision of Supreme Court dated Oct. 4, 1967, Dalloz 1968, p. 95); (3) law applied by foreign court must have been law applicable according to French conflict of laws rules; (4) foreign proceedings must have been in due process and (5) foreign judgment must not have been obtained by fraud ("fraude à la loi"). In addition, foreign judgment must be final and conclusive in country in which it was delivered. In no case will facts be reexamined. Plaintiff has burden of proof as to these by use of documents and expert testimony, normally in form of certificate of law.

If enforcement (exequatur) is granted, foreign judgment becomes in legal effect a French judgment. No mortgage ordered by foreign court is possible until exequatur is granted. (C. C. 2123 and N.C.C.P. 509).

France is also party to bilateral and multilateral treaties on recognition and enforcement of foreign arbitral awards including New York Convention of June 10, 1958 (ratified by France on June 26, 1959) and Geneva Convention of Sept. 26, 1927 (ratified by France on May 12, 1931). France is also party to EEC Convention of Apr. 21, 1961 (ratified by France on Dec. 16, 1966) and Washington Convention on Settlement of Investment Disputes between States and Nationals of other States of Oct. 14, 1966 (ratified by France on Aug. 21, 1967).

Fines for Delay in Civil Cases.—To ensure execution of court decisions, Law of July 9, 1991 gives courts power to levy fines for delay. Fines may be definitive or provisional; judges may reduce or revoke provisional fines, even when nonexecution of court order has been proved.

JUDICIAL RECOVERY AND LIQUIDATION:

Judicial recovery and liquidation of enterprises ("redressement et liquidation judiciaires des entreprises") are governed by (Law No. 85–98 of Jan. 25, 1985 and Decrees Nos. 85–1387 and 85–1388 of Dec. 27, 1985) effective Jan. 1, 1986. They provide single procedure for both restructuration and possible eventual liquidation of insolvent enterprises, including all non-state-owned corporate entities and sole proprietorships. Subsidiaries of foreign entities carrying on business in France are subject to procedure on same basis as French entities. Law No. 88-15 of Jan. 5, 1988, Decree No. 88-430 of Apr. 21, 1988 and Law No. 94-475 of 10 June, 1994 further amend 1985 Law. Decree No. 89-339 of May 29, 1989 (effective June 1, 1989) and Decree No. 94-910 of Oct. 21, 1994 (effective Oct. 22, 1994) further modify Decree No. 85-1388 of Dec. 27, 1985.

Law No. 88-1202 of Dec. 30, 1988 extends application of above procedure for judicial recovery and liquidation to farmers, subject to minor modifications such as provision for mandatory conciliation procedure.

Judicial liquidation is no longer mandatory prerequisite to dissolution. (C. C. 1844-5, as am'd by Art. 2 of Law No. 88-15). Pursuant to Law No. 94-475, preliminary "alert" procedure can be initiated by auditors and President of "Tribunal de commerce".

Procedure starts with either voluntary declaration or determination by court on demand of creditor or public prosecutor of date of cessation of payments. Jurisdiction over proceeding lies with court of enterprise's registered office at time petition filed unless registered office transferred within preceding six months, in which case court of former location has jurisdiction. (Art. 1 of Decree No. 85-1388, as am'd by Art. 12 of Decree No. 89-339 and Art. 4 Law No. 85-98 of Jan. 25, 1985). Creditor-requested liquidation of agricultural holding is preceded by mandatory conciliation procedure. (Art. 7 of Decree No. 85-1388, as am'd by Art. 14 of Decree No. 89-339). Procedure may also start in event of debtor's nonperformance of financial commitments undertaken pursuant to amicable settlement with creditors (under Law No. 84–148 of Mar. 1, 1984 on prevention and amicable settlement of enterprises' difficulties and Art. 5 Law No. 85-98).

Recovery procedure, which may either be "simplified" or "standard" depending upon size of enterprise, authorizes court to order "observation period", which lasts six months renewable once and which can be exceptionally prolonged for additional

See Topical Index in front part of this volume.

JUDICIAL RECOVERY AND LIQUIDATION . . . *continued*
period of eight months at request of public prosecutor (total of 20 months). (Law No. 88-15 and Decree No. 94-910), or prolonged up to maximum of two years if management lease ("location-gérance") agreement with third party is involved. (Arts. 42 and 94 et seq.). However, observation period may be avoided in cases when enterprise is to be directly liquidated, i.e. when enterprise has stopped any activity or its recovery is considered as impossible. During this period, activities of enterprise may continue and debtor normally remains in charge. (Arts. 35 and 32). Debtor may be assisted by court-appointed "administrator" which may take over management of debtor (former receiver or "syndic" no longer exists). "Judicial commissioner" appointed by court supervises procedure.

Claims must be declared by creditors within two months (or four months for foreign creditors) after publication of court decision opening procedure. (Art. 66 of Decree No. 85-1388, as am'd by Art. 6 of Decree No. 88-430). Creditors are kept informed of main steps of procedure. Liquidation proceedings are effective from date of court decision opening procedure, not date of its publication. (Art. 2 of Decree No. 88-430). 1985 Law no longer provides for general body ("masse") or meeting of creditors, but all creditors (secured and unsecured, privileged or not) are now represented by one representative appointed by court. (Art. 46). Judicial commissioner may also appoint controllers upon creditors' request.

Following actions performed after date of cessation of payments are null and void: transferring assets for no consideration, entering into grossly unbalanced agreements, paying debts before their due dates, paying debts other than through normal payment procedures, or granting any security interest over company's assets for existing debts, etc. (Art. 107).

Payment of all claims incurred prior to court decision opening procedure is forbidden during observation period. (Art. 33). Litigation concerning such claims, including privileged claims, is postponed until creditor has declared his claim. Procedures are then resumed but only aim at establishing and valuing claims. (Art. 48 L. No. 85-98). Other legal actions are maintained during "observation period", including actions brought before "prud'homme" Court. Claims not due at date of opening decision are not accelerated on account of decision; all provisions to contrary are deemed null and void. (Art. 56).

Administrator may require performance of existing contracts which are not terminated nor rescinded by insolvency, notwithstanding any legal or contractual provision to contrary. (Art. 37).

At end of observation period, court either orders continuation of enterprise and/or partial or total transfer of its assets or else liquidation of enterprise. Claims not yet due become payable only if either transfer of all assets or liquidation takes place. (Arts. 91 and 160). Order of liquidation or total transfer of assets is grounds for dissolution of enterprise. (C. C. 1844-7, as am'd by Art. 3 of Law No. 88-15). Effect of orders may be suspended pending appeal. (Art. 155[2] of Decree No. 85-1388).

Order of preference among creditors has been changed. Claims incurred after decision opening procedure are paid as they mature and upon liquidation or transfer of all assets in preference before all other claims, including certain privileged or secured claims, but excepting certain privileged labor claims. (Art. 40). Substitution of security presenting "equivalent advantages" may be ordered by court if necessary in absence of agreement by creditors. (Art. 78).

Law no longer presumes mismanagement of debtor, but if there is proof of mismanagement contributing to insufficiency of debtor's assets, managers (including de facto managers) may be held liable for debts. (Art. 180).

In addition, if manager has abused corporate assets for personal ends or committed fraudulent act, court may impose personal bankruptcy, or prohibit him from managing, operating, controlling, directly or indirectly any commercial, artisanal or agricultural business entity. These prohibitions are imposed for at least five years. (Art. 185 et seq.). Court may require sanctions to be published. (Art. 15 of Decree No. 88-430). Court may order such prohibitions against manager unable to pay debts for which he was made liable. (Art. 190).

In case of fraudulent bankruptcy ("banqueroute"), court may order penal sanctions. (Art. 196 et seq.)

See also topic Sales.

LABOR RELATIONS:

Prior to employment, declaration of employment must be made by employers to Social Security bodies. All prospective employees must undergo medical examinations, with supplementary examinations required annually for adults and quarterly for minors. Employee's name and basic information about him must be made available to local labor inspector. Salary records must also be kept and detailed pay slips given to all employees. (C.T.R. 143-2). Foreign employees must obtain permit for work and residence before starting employment. (C.T.R. 341-1). Nationals of EEC countries are not subject to above requirements. Clandestine work is prohibited and punished with criminal sanctions as of first violation. (C.T.L. 362-3).

According to EC Directive of Oct. 14, 1991, employment contracts for indefinite period of time concluded as of July 1, 1993 must be in written form and contain certain mandatory information. Moreover, employment contracts must be in French language, and translation may be supplied to employee, if so requested. (C.T.L. 121-1).

Pursuant to C.T.L. 321-1-2, when employer contemplates modifying employment contract substantially for economic reasons, employee must be formally notified thereof, and has one month upon receipt of such notification to make known his refusal.

Termination by employer of employment contracts concluded for indefinite period of time are subject to special procedures, details of which vary according to reasons for dismissal, size of firm, number of employees dismissed if dismissal is based on economic reasons.

If dismissal of employee is based on reasons other than economic reasons, employer must call employee to meeting to state reason for dismissal and listen to his explanations (employee has right to assistance from another employee of firm during this meeting and/or to special outside counsel in firms where there are no personnel representatives); and one full day after date of such dismissal meeting employee is notified by registered mail with acknowledgment of receipt with mention of reasons for dismissal if made for fault committed by employee.

If dismissal is based on economic reasons, employer must: (1) Call employee to meeting as mentioned above; (2) meet and discuss terms of economic layoff (if it concerns more than one person) with Labor Management Committee ("Comité d'Entreprise") or Personnel Representatives ("Délégués du Personnel"), depending on size of firm; (3) inform local labor authorities of dismissal (contents of information given to local labor authorities and control of this authority on application of procedure are broader if dismissal concerns collective layoff of more than ten employees); (4) notify employee of dismissal by registered mail with acknowledgment of receipt mentioning reasons for dismissal. (Date at which dismissal can be notified is subject to delays which depend in particular upon professional category of person dismissed, and number of employees dismissed.)

Economic collective layoffs are accompanied by social measures proposed by employer in favor of dismissed employees such as training courses, financial aid for elderly employees and priority in rehiring. Firms are required to propose special training courses ("congé de conversion") to dismissed employees which are financed partly by employer and partly by governmental bodies. Firms employing more than 50 employees planning to dismiss ten people or more are required to propose social measures for dismissed employees in form of report called "Plan Social" to labor management committee for discussion.

Violations of dismissal procedures may be sanctioned by fines and damages to employees. Improper termination of employee's contract gives employee right to damages. Procedures for economic dismissal may be nullified by court if firm fails to comply with requirements of Plan Social. (Law of Jan. 27, 1993). From Aug. 1, 1992, dismissal of employees over age 50 requires payment of additional contribution by employer (from one to six months salary).

For termination of contracts of indefinite duration, except in case of dismissal for serious offence, all employees having worked more than six months must receive time notice which varies from one month (for employment duration of six months to two years) to two months (employment duration of over two years). (C.T.L. 122-6). Time notice for executives is usually three months. C.T. Arts. L. 122-5 & 6 extend benefit of time notice provisions to some employees who have worked less than six months with same employer.

Personnel representatives benefit from special protection and prior authorisation of competent labor authority must be requested to dismiss all types of personnel representatives.

Employment contracts may be terminated any time during trial period, in principle without formal procedure; short notice period may be required by labor agreement or collective bargaining agreement.

Employer must, when any labor contract is terminated, provide employee with work certificate whatever reasons for termination of contract. Voucher showing all sums paid employee upon termination of labor contract ("reçu pour solde de tout compte") may be contested by employee in writing within two months of date of signature by employee.

Law of July 25, 1985 as modified by Law of Dec. 1993 creates new management system of personnel, so-called "groupement d'employeurs", which is association composed of individuals or companies (employing up to 300 employees). New system permits exchange of employees among members when labor needed is insufficient to hire full-time employee. (C.T.L. 127, paragraphs 1 to 7).

Contracts may be concluded with temporary work agencies under conditions defined by law including requirements with respect to when employer may hire temporary employee, duration of work assignment and renewal terms thereof. (C.T.L. 124-2, 124-2-1; 124-2-2; 124-2-4).

Employment can be made for definite period of time; such employment is subject to specific rules provided by Law of July 12, 1990. Cases where this type of contract can be used are in principle limited to execution of punctual and specific task and is not supposed to cover on durable basis permanent job existing in company. (C.T.L. 122-1). Those contracts must be in writing. In cases where this type of contract can be used, term must be specified in contract; it can be renewed once; renewal term cannot exceed initial term; total duration of contract (renewal included) cannot exceed depending on particular case, nine, 18, and 24 months. In some other cases, such as replacement of employee on sick leave, term of contract need not be specified. Employment contract of fixed duration cannot be terminated except for serious breach ("faute grave") or force majeure. Subject to specific cases and specific rules, if terms of contract continue to be honored after expiration, it becomes contract of indefinite duration. (C.T.L. 122-3-10). Such contracts are governed by specific provisions and may give rise to reduction of employer's social contributions. (Law of Dec. 20, 1992).

Any employer deciding to take action against employee because of fault committed by employee must inform employee in writing stating reasons for action. For any action other than of minor importance, employer must call employee to preliminary meeting during which employee can be assisted by another employee.

Principle of nondiscrimination for normal and legitimate use by employee of constitutional right to strike is specifically recognized. (C.T.L. 521-1). Except for serious fault committed by employee, dismissal or any sanction or measure taken by employer against employee because of participation in strike is automatically void. Employee may ask not only for damages but also for reappointment to job. (July 1985 law codified in C.T.L. 122-45, paragraph 1 and 521-1).

Work week is limited to 39 hours and daily work to ten hours (C. T. L. 212-1); stationary work is limited to 35 hours per week as of Dec. 31, 1983. For certain activities with slack hours, amount of time spent in business can exceed 39 hours (e.g., retail stores, hotels). Prior authorization of labor inspector must be requested for overtime exceeding statutory or conventional limit. In any case, total work hours cannot exceed 48 hours in a week. Hourly rate is automatically increased by at least 25% for first eight hours of overtime and 50% for overtime above eight hours. (C. T. L. 212-5, 6-7). In firms of more than ten employees, employee is allowed compensatory rest period equal to 50% (reduced to 20% in case of emergency work) of overtime hours worked in excess of 42 total hours during week but in limit of 130 overtime hours per year or statutory limits. Compensatory rest is equal to 50% each overtime hour in firms of less than 11 employees and to 100% in firms employing at least 11 persons worked over limit of 130th overtime hour. (C.T.L. 212-5-1, modified by Law

LABOR RELATIONS . . . *continued*
of Jan. 2, 1990). Above limitation on duration of working hours and distribution of number of hours per week over year may be amended by collective bargaining agreement.

Annual paid vacation is required by law at rate of two and a half days per month of work or total of 30 work days for year. (C. T. L 223-2, modified by Ordinance of Jan. 16, 1982).

Employees can, under special conditions in each case, take leaves of absence for certain family events, maternity, (including necessary medical exams before and after birth [Law of Jan. 27, 1993]), adoption, training or education of young children, creation of business or in case of sabbatical leave.

In event of transfer of business new employer must take over all existing labor agreements. (C. T. L 122-12).

Wages are negotiated by each concern with employees or labor unions subject to minimum wage agreed upon in collective labor agreement (convention collective) for each employment category. Guaranteed minimum hourly rate (S.M.I.C.), is currently FRF 37.72 throughout France as of May 1, 1996.

As of Sept. 16, 1985 payrolls may be declared by employer in simplified form on computerized program subject to conformity with Law of Jan. 6, 1978 on "Informatique et libertés". Salaries exceeding FRF 10,000 per month must be paid by check. (Decree Oct. 7, 1985).

Minors under 16 cannot be employed by business concerns. Minors under 18 are forbidden to work at certain dangerous jobs and night work. They are entitled to more liberal paid vacations. Their wages may be lower than adults' wages: (20% less from age 16 to 17; 10% less from 17 to 18) except if paid by piece or by output, or if they have six months' experience. Minors benefit from special labour contracts during their apprenticeship which bind employer to "pay wages required by the law and provide for practical training ("formation professionnelle")" within firm and outside in special centers for training.

Internal statute ("règlement intérieur") must be drawn up in firms employing 20 persons or more. Statute provides for hygiene and safety rules as well as disciplinary ones. (Law of Aug. 4, 1982).

Payroll Tax and Social Benefits.—Employer contributions for payroll taxes and social benefits amount to cost over base salary of approximately 44%. Most important mandatory contributions are following:

Social Security Contributions.—Based upon portion of employees' monthly salary between FRF 1 and FRF 13,540, contributions for retirement pensions is 14.75% (8.20% paid by employer, 6.55% paid by employee).

Based on total salary, contributions are as follows: (a) For sickness and death, 19.60% (employer pays 12.80% and employee pays 6.80%); (b) for widows insurance, 0.10% paid by employee; (c) for family allowance: 5.40% (all paid by employer); (d) for retirement pension, 1.60% (all paid by employer).

Employer Social Security Contributions may be reduced for certain types of employment agreements.

Unemployment Insurance.—On basis of gross salary up to FRF 13,540 per month: 6.60% (4.18% paid by employer and 2.42% paid by employee) and on basis of gross salary from FRF 13,540 to FRF 54,160 (as of July 1, 1996): 7.15% (4.18% paid by employer and 2.97% paid by employee) plus special contribution of 0.35% paid by employer on portion of monthly salary up to FRF 54,160; executive contributions to unemployment fund (APEC) are 0.06% on portion of salary between FRF 13,540 and FRF 54,160 (0.036% paid by employer and 0.024% paid by employee) and additional annual contributions of FRF 56.16 paid by employer and FRF 37.44 paid by employee.

Contributions to ASF (Association for the Financial Structure) is 1.96% (1.16% paid by employer and 0.80% paid by employee) on portion of monthly salary between FRF 1 and FRF 13,540 and 2.18% (1.29% paid by employer and 0.89% paid by employee) on portion of monthly salary between FRF 13,540 and FRF 54,160.

Complementary Retirement Pension and Social Benefits.—Executive ("cadres"): Complementary retirement pension on portion of monthly salary between FRF 1 and FRF 13,540: 5.625% (3.375% + 3.375% paid by employer and 2.25% paid by employee). On portion of monthly salary between FRF 13,540 and FRF 54,160: (a) 16.25% (for companies created as of Jan. 1, 1981): 10.625% paid by employer and 5.625% paid by employee, (b) 12.1% (for companies created as of Jan. 1, 1981): 8.47% paid by employer and 3.63% paid by employee. On portion of monthly salary between FRF 54,160 and FRF 108,320 (as of July 1, 1995): 16.25% (no statutory distribution of contribution between employer and employee).

Nonexecutive: Complementary retirement pension between FRF 1 and FRF 40,620, 5.625% (employer pays 3.375% and employee pays 2.25%).

General Social Tax ("Contribution sociale généralisée").—All compensation subject to Social Security taxes, as well as other types of income, is subject to new 2.4% social tax paid entirely by employee. As of Feb. 2, 1996, new social tax ("Remboursement de la Dette Sociale, Ros") to be paid on all compensation and amounting to 0.5%.

Taxes Based on Salaries.—Payroll tax 4.25% on portion of annual salary below or equal to FRF 40,010, 8.50% on portion above FRF 79,970 and below or equal to FRF 79,970, 13.60% on that portion exceeding FRF 79,970. This payroll tax is only imposed upon employers who are not subject to value added tax (TVA). Apprenticeship tax (on most commercial and industrial companies): 0.5% on total salary of previous year. Additional contribution of 0.1% of salary of previous year plus, all paid by employer. Tax for permanent education of personnel: 1.5% of total salaries of current year (paid by employers of more than nine persons) and 0.15% of total salaries of current year (paid by employers of less than ten persons). Construction tax: 0.45% of total salary (paid by employer). Rent subsidy tax: 0.10% on portion of salary limited to FRF 13,540 (paid by all employers) and 0.40% on total salary paid by employers of more than nine persons. Solidarity tax: applicable to companies (with some exceptions) turnover of which is at least FRF 5,000,000 (taxes excluded) per year, 0.13% of turnover (taxes excluded) (paid by employer). Transport tax (applicable in major cities): rates vary with city (2.20% in Paris area) (paid by employer) plus reimbursement to employee of 50% of cost of public transport. (Law of Jan. 23, 1990).

Certain employment and pension contributions are not assessed to employees over 60 years of age.

Number of above-mentioned contributions are assessed on basis of Social Security ceiling or multiple of such; Social Security ceiling is set at FRF 13,540 from July 1, 1996.

Normal retirement age is 60 as from Apr. 1, 1983, with respect to liquidation at full rate of social security retirement pension. In principle, right to receive retirement pension is subordinate to definitive ceasing of previous professional activity.

Mandatory Profit-Sharing. ("Participation aux fruits de l'expansion de l'entreprise").—

(a) Profit Sharing Plans ("Accords").—Ordinance of Oct. 21, 1986 as codified by Law of July 25, 1994 under Art. L. 442-1 and following Arts., provides for different formulas to favor participation of employees in results or capital of their employing company which are accompanied by tax advantages and social exonerations for employees and company if conditions provided by said regulations are met. Minimum profit sharing plan remains mandatory in firms employing 50 or more employees.

(b) Company Savings Plans.—Ordinance dated Oct. 21, 1986 as codified under Art. L. 443-1 and subsequent Arts. and implementing decree of July 17, 1987 as codified by Decree of Apr. 11, 1995 under Art. R.441-1 and following Arts. provide for voluntary company savings plans enjoying tax and social advantages. They consist of purchase of stocks and debentures by means of employees' and company's voluntary payments. Stocks and debentures so purchased are to be held by employees for minimum five-year period.

(c) Stock Option Plans ("Actionnariat").—Company Law of July 24, 1966 has been am'd by Law No. 70-1322 of Dec. 31, 1970 and implementing Decree No. 71-748 of June 7, 1971 to allow S.A.s and special partnerships by shares to implement stock option plans in certain circumstances. Extraordinary general shareholders' meeting, upon proposal of board of directors ("conseil d'administration") or of management committee ("directoire"), as appropriate, and on recommendation of special auditors ("commissaires aux comptes"), may authorize either board or management committee to grant to all or part of salaried employees of S.A. and special partnership by shares or of its subsidiaries, options exercisable within maximum five-year period to purchase such companies' stock. Maximum amount of stock available to one employee, total percentage of such companies' stock which can be covered by such options, and other terms and conditions for application of such law are set forth in Decree of June 7, 1971. Slightly different system has been created to apply to all S.A.s and special partnerships by shares listed on Stock Exchange by Law 73-1196 of Dec. 27, 1973 and Decree No. 74-319 of Apr. 23, 1974.

Labor-Management Relations.—

Personnel representatives ("délégués du personnel") are required by C. T. art. L 420-1, in every enterprise with usually more than ten employees. They are elected by all employees divided in classes according to their functions, e.g., laborers, technicians, engineers, office employees, etc., with classes determined by most important labor unions among employees. (L 420-7). Since Law 93-13.13 of Dec. 20, 1993 these representatives serve for two years and are eligible for reelection. Their function is to present to management all grievances, both individual and group, relating to salaries, work safety, hygiene, social benefits, etc. (L 420-5). However, any employee has right to present his own grievances to management. Personnel representatives must be received by management at least once a month.

Labor-Management Committee ("Comité d'Entreprise").—Labor-Management Committee exists by law in every enterprise employing 50 employees or more. (L 431-1). This includes foreign-owned companies having their business in France even if their "sièege social" is located abroad. (Conseil d'Etat June 29, 1973). In enterprises having one or several centers of activities employing 50 or more persons, labor management committees called "comité d'etablissement" for each such centers are created. (Art. L 435-1). These "comités d'etablissements" are represented by some of their members at "comité central" of firm which holds meeting at least once every six months at head office of firm. "comité d'entreprise" or "comité d'etablissement" holds meeting which is called by general manager or his representatives. Since Law No. 93-13.13 of Dec. 20, 1993, periodicity of meetings depends on size: less than 150 employees, meetings are held every two months except if members of Labor Management Committee serve also as personnel representative. Committee members are elected by all employees divided in classes according to their functions, with classes determined by major labor unions among employees. (L 433-2). General manager or plant manager is member ex-officio and chairman of labor-management committee. Elections are conducted by management in collaboration with principal labor unions, with members elected for two year term and eligible for relection. (L 433-12). Committee is not intended to be organ for transmitting grievances but rather one for labor-management cooperation. List of duties is set forth by C. T. art. L 432-1 et seq. as modified by Law of Oct. 28, 1982. Committee must be informed and consulted on all questions related to organization, management and general affairs of company, introducing in firm of new technologies. Quarterly or half-yearly, depending on size of staff, employer informs Committee in particular on evolution of sales, financial situation of firm, methods of production, employment situation.

At least once a year management must give committee a general report on activity of business stating profits, turnover, investments, productivity, structure and amount of wages and plans for following year (L 432-4), and committee can make recommendations based thereon. In every commercial company, committee is entitled to same documents as shareholders and has right to representation at all meetings of board of directors by two members with right to speak but no vote. (L 432-4). In addition, every enterprise employing more than 300 employees must submit to committee report giving general figures of enterprise to permit evaluation of performance of enterprise in social and labor-management field ("Bilan social"). (C.T.L. 438-1.2.9).

In case of bankruptcy, labor-management committee (or personnel representatives or employees) may now be invited by court to elect employee representative to participate in bankruptcy procedure and control all credits due to employees for employment contract. (Bankruptcy Law of Jan. 25, 1985 as modified).

When there is group of companies constituted by ruling company, its subsidiaries and companies controlled by ruling company, Group Committee must be created. This rule concerns only companies with head office in France. Purpose of creation of Group

See Topical Index in front part of this volume.

LABOR RELATIONS . . . *continued*

Committee is to collect financial and labor information concerning each company of Group for transmission to all companies of Group. This Committee must meet at least once a year. (Law of Oct. 28, 1982).

European Directive of Sept. 22, 1994 created European Labor Management Committee for companies employing at least 1,000 employees in countries of European Union (except U.K.) and employing at least 150 employees in two or more member States.

In firms employing 50 persons or more Safety and Hygiene Committee must be created, purpose of which is to contribute to protection of health and security of employees, improvement of their working conditions. (Law of Dec. 23, 1982). Law of Aug. 4, 1982 complemented by Law of Jan. 3, 1986 gives direct and collective right to all employees to express themselves on work conditions. Practical means of exercise of this right defined by agreement between employer and either labor unions or labor representatives.

Labor Unions.—Labor Union Unit may be created in any firm whatever number of employees. Nomination of Union representatives benefiting from statutory rights is limited to firms of 50 employees or more. (Law of Oct. 28, 1982).

In enterprises where one or more labor-union representatives ("délégués syndicaux") exist, employer must meet annually with labor representatives to negotiate questions relating to wages and hours.

Accidents at Work.—Employer must notify Caisse Primaire of Social Security within 48 hours of learning of employee accident at work or on way to or from work except for minor accidents which may be filed on special register replacing infirmary register. (Law of Jan. 3, 1985 at art. 71 effective Jan. 1, 1986; Decree Oct. 22, 1985). Upon declaration of employer, Social Security pays indemnity to victim which includes compensation during temporary incapacity, reimbursement for medical and surgical costs, drugs and accessories including artificial limbs, transportation expenses, costs of treatment and retraining, a pension in case of permanent incapacity, and, in case of death, a pension to beneficiary. Costs are borne partly by employer with annual rate of contribution calculated for each risk category according to number of employees, size and activity of firm, and total wages of personnel, in liaison with Comités Techniques connected with Regional Social Security Offices. Rate is reviewed annually.

Separation Indemnities.—In case of labor contracts of undefined duration, each employee who has been employed by same employer for more than two years must, upon discharge, receive legal minimum separation indemnity. However, employees who have been discharged for serious offense ("fautes graves") are not entitled to this benefit. (C. T. art. L 122-9). Separation payment cannot be less than sum equal to either 20 hours of pay (for employees paid by hour) or 1/10 of month's salary (for employees paid monthly) multiplied by number of years of employment plus 1/15th of month's salary multiplied by number of years of employment over ten years of seniority. Salary base is three or 12 month average prior to discharge. Law of Jan. 7, 1981 provides for special separation indemnities in case of discharge following accident at work, other than accident occurred on home return, or professional decease.

Collective Bargaining Agreements and Labor Union Agreements.—Collective bargaining agreements are negotiated in practically all fields of activity; number of them are automatically applicable to firms having activity falling into field of application of particular collective bargaining agreement; these agreements contain provisions regarding status of employee during execution of employment agreement or upon termination of same, which are equal to or more favorable than those provided by law and which prevail over labor code conditions when more favorable; certain firms are subject to application of labor union agreements negotiated outside firm which may concern, for example, procedure to apply in case of collective economic layoff.

Unemployment Allowances.—Employees who are unemployed after having been dismissed, or after expiration of term of their contract, or after having given their resignation for reasons recognized as well founded by ASSEDIC, can get unemployment allowances if certain conditions are fulfilled.

Periods during which unemployment allowances are granted vary according to age of employee and length of contribution to unemployment regime. After four months of contribution, employee can get basic allowance equal to FRF 56.95 per day plus 40.4% of average of last 12 months' salary preceding unemployment. At expiration of period of validity of basic allowance, employee can obtain final allowance called "allocation de fin de droit", amounting to FRF 88.66 minimum per day (or FRF 122.90 in some cases), within global limit for unemployment allowances which vary according to age of employee and length of employment. Maximum amount of allowances is maintained at 75% of reference salary and minimum amount guaranteed is 57.4% of reference salary. (Monthly reference salary is taken into consideration with limit of FRF 54,160 for second semester of 1996.) Duration of allowance depends upon age of employee and time during which employee has contributed to unemployment regime. Maximum duration of allowances taken globally is 45 months for employee aged from 50 to 55, and 60 months for employee over 55 years old provided he has contributed to regime at least 27 months during last 36 months of employment.

In case of dismissal not justified by serious and valid reasons, employer must by court injunction reimburse all or part of unemployment allowances to institutions making payments (ASSEDIC).

Special allowances are granted to employees suffering from partial employment due to reduction of their working hours by their employers. Allowances are also given to following: Unemployed workers following training and persons retired early in certain circumstances; and persons who are excluded from unemployment regime due to insufficient contributions or following expiry of their rights.

(Terms of unemployment regime have been modified by agreement dated July 18, 1992.)

See also topic Holidays.

LANDLORD AND TENANT:

Commercial Leases.—Leases of premises utilized for business, industry or trade, are generally described as commercial leases and governed by decree of Sept. 30, 1953, which has been substantially amended by a number of subsequent laws and decrees. Under present law, duration of commercial lease must be at least nine years with right of termination by tenant at end of each three-year period; however, on original entry into premises, parties can agree to term of two years or less ("bail précaire") but tenant then has no right of renewal and rent increases are free. If tenant remains after two years or if lease renewed, it automatically becomes nine-year lease by operation of law.

Principal significance of commercial lease is tenant's right either to renew lease upon expiration or, if landlord refuses renewal, to receive substantial indemnity for loss of leasehold right. This right arises if tenant has operated business, industry or trade for more than three consecutive years in premises. Leasehold right, with right to renewal or compensation in lieu thereof, is referred to as "droit au bail" or "propriété commerciale." Right can be defeated by landlord only for legitimate cause such as serious breach by lessee. Ceiling applies to rent on renewal. (Decree of July 3, 1972 and Law of Dec. 26, 1975).

Every three years, either party may request change in rent. Change may not exceed variation of official index of construction costs unless leasehold value has increased by over 10% due to change of commercial nature of locale. If parties are unable to agree on new rent, it will be determined by court action.

Subleases of commercial premises are forbidden without consent of landlord unless lease provides to contrary. If rent in sublease is higher than in principal lease, landlord has right to corresponding increase in rent. Subtenant has right of renewal against sublessor to extent of latter's right against landlord. On expiration of principal lease, authorized subtenant generally has right of renewal against landlord.

Commercial lessee may assign leasehold right to successor in business, without consent of landlord. Otherwise, consent is necessary unless assignment permitted by lease.

Under Law No. 71-585 of July 16, 1971, tenant may engage in additional activities related to principal business, provided landlord is informed thereof. Tenant may also request permission from landlord to engage in new and unrelated activities; landlord can refuse only for serious cause but can be authorized by court to increase rent.

Residential and Professional Leases.—Leases are governed by three different laws, Law of Sept. 1, 1948, Law of June 22, 1982 and Law of Dec. 23, 1986, which apply according to date of signature or renewal of lease.

New Law of July 6, 1989 replaces certain provisions of Law of Dec. 2, 1986, granting stronger protections for tenants and reinstating certain aspects of law of June 22, 1982. Most significant changes are as follows: Landlord may now refuse to renew lease only if he intends to sell property, occupy premises, or has just cause (i.e. tenant has failed to fulfill his obligations); initial rents for old premises which have not been improved in previous six months are set by reference to standard rents for comparable premises; and on renewal, rent increase may exceed standard rent increase only if rent is obviously subnormal.

Law of Dec. 23, 1986, known as Loi Méhaignerie, applies to all leases signed after Dec. 23, 1986 and is destined to replace other two entirely. This law provides that lease must be in writing. Lease must be concluded for minimum of three years; however, if lessor can justify at time of conclusion of lease forthcoming professional or family occurrence necessitating that he take back premises, lease may be for less than three years, within one year minimum. Lessor may not terminate lease for occupancy by himself or member of his family, contrary to previous law. Tenant may terminate lease at any time with three months notice. Contrary to previous law, tenant has no right to renewal of lease; lessor must, six months before end of lease, notify tenant of either termination or terms of renewal; failing acceptance by tenant of lessor's terms within three months, lease is terminated; in case of acceptance, lease is renewed for three years; if lessor fails to notify tenant either way six months before end of lease, lease is automatically renewed for three years. Rent can be fixed freely by parties at conclusion and at each renewal of lease; increases in rent during term of lease can only occur yearly and must not exceed increase of cost of construction index. Subleasing must be authorized in writing by lessor, as under previous law.

Law of Sept. 1, 1948, which, until Law of Dec. 23, 1986, still applied in most cities to leases in buildings constructed before Sept. 1, 1948, is destined to disappear progressively under new law. Only premises which do not satisfy certain requirements of comfort and fitness for habitation remain fully governed by Law of Sept. 1, 1948, where lease may be oral or written; tenant has right to remain in premises upon expiration of term of lease and rent ceiling is imposed. However, to incite lessors to improve premises, law provides that rent may be set freely if premises are in conformity with given requirements of comfort and fitness for habitation and are rented for six years at least. At end of such term, Law of Dec. 23, 1986 shall apply. Vacant premises having remained subject to Law of Sept. 1, 1948 must now be governed by Law of Dec. 26, 1986 when rented out for residential use and by French Civil Code if for professional use. Lessors of premises currently rented under Law of Sept. 1, 1948 can offer tenant new lease governed by Law of Dec. 23, 1986 or by French Civil Code if premises for professional use; tenant or occupant has two months to accept or refuse; in case of refusal, either party can seize commission or tenant can refer matter to court; failing referral to court within six months of lessor's proposal, tenant is deemed to have refused offer and must evacuate premises within six months. If agreement is reached, new lease must be concluded for eight years and at its term shall be entirely subject to Law of Dec. 23, 1986.

Agricultural Leases.—These are governed by special legislation, codified in Agricultural Code under Decree of Apr. 16, 1955.

LAW REPORTS AND LEGAL MATERIALS:

Law of France is codified system, principally based on five original or Napoleonic codes: Code Civil, Code de Procédure Civile, Code de Commerce, Code Pénal and Code de Procédure Penale. Code Civil contains the basic legal framework of society, including civil status, contracts and torts, family law, property and succession. Nouveau Code de Procédure Civile (revised 1975) and Code de Procédure Civile (1806 ed., as subsequently modified) govern organization, jurisdiction and procedure of civil courts. Code de Commerce regulates commercial transactions, bills and notes, maritime law, bankruptcy, commercial procedure, and jurisdiction of commercial courts. Code Pénal (revised 1992 "Nouveau Code Pénal") and Code de Procédure Pénale (revised 1992 and 1993) contain respectively criminal law and criminal procedure.

LAW REPORTS AND LEGAL MATERIALS . . . *continued*
Important new compilations are Code Général des Impôts, or general tax code, Code du Travail or labor code, Code de la Propriété Intellectuelle (1992) or intellectual property Code ("C.P.I."), and Code de la Consommation or consumers code. These codes are those edited by Dalloz and Litec; they are issued annually, and contain all significant supplementary laws and annotations to leading decisions.

Current constitution, that of Fifth Republic, is of Oct. 4, 1958. Statutes and decrees are published in Journal Officiel de la République Française (cited as J. O.), which appears daily. There are yearly cumulative indexes. There is also unofficial but widely used Bulletin Legislatif Dalloz.

Other than Bulletins des Arrêts de la Cour de Cassation and Recueil des Arrêts du Conseil d'Etat, there are no official reports of judicial decisions. There are four general compilations which are unofficial. Recueil Sirey (cited: S), begun in 1801, consist of monthly issues containing annotated decisions of Cour de Cassation, decisions (often annotated) of appellate and significant trial courts, administrative decisions, and legislation. This recueil was merged with Recueil Dalloz on Jan. 1, 1965. Recueil Dalloz (cited: D), begun in 1808, consists today of weekly publications containing articles, annotated reports of courts of all levels, summaries of additional decisions, and legislation. La Gazette du Palais (cited: Gaz. Pal. or G. P.), began publication in 1881 and consists today of biweekly issues of briefly annotated case law and legislation together with doctrinal articles. La Semaine Juridique (cited: J. C. P.) is weekly publication for practitioner begun in 1927 and containing doctrinal articles, annotated case reports and legislative texts.

Only significant legal dictionary is Dalloz, Dictionnaire de Droit. Most significant encyclopedias are Répertoire Dalloz and loose leaf service of Juris-Classeur for corporate, civil, commercial, labor, administrative and tax matters. Doctrinal presentations by leading commentators are regarded as very significant authority, on a plane with court decisions. Some of most significant treatises in basic areas are: Planiol, Traité Pratique de Droit Civil (current ed. Ripert & Boulanger); Colin and Capitant, Cours Elémentaire de Droit Civil Français (current ed. Julliot de la Morandière); Marty and Raynaud, Droit Civil; Mazeaud, Leçons de Droit Civil; Hamel and Lagarde, Traité de Droit Commercial; Ripert, Traité Elémentaire de Droit Commercial; Hemard, Sociétés Commerciales; Bouzat, Traité de Droit Pénal; Hémard, Les Contrats Commerciaux; Batiffol and Lagarde, Droit International Privé; Laubadère, Traité Elémentaire de Droit Administratif; tax practitioners rely on Lefèbvre, Feuillets de Documentation Pratique (Impôts Directs, Impôts Indirects, and Enregistrement) while most commonly used corporate forms are found in Joly, Dictionnaire du Droit des Sociétés Anonymes and Dictionnaire du Droit des Sociétés à Responsabilité Limitée.

LEGISLATURE:

See topic Constitution and Government.

LICENSES:

See topic Industrial Property Rights.

LIENS:

Liens may be created expressly by contract as in the case of pledges (C. C. 2073; see topic Pledges) and antichreses (C. C. 2085; see topic Mortgages). They may also arise by operation of law, for example in following cases: (1) In cash sales seller has lien until price is paid (C. C. 1612) or, in sales on credit, if buyer becomes bankrupt or unable to pay (C. C. 1613); (2) in sales where seller has right of repurchase, buyer may retain property until not only purchase price is refunded but also value of repairs or improvements. (C. C. 1673); (3) in deposits (C. C. 1948); (4) where property is condemned by state for public purpose (C. C. 545); (5) in transporting merchandise by ship, carrier has lien for freight charges (Art. 2, Law No. 66-420 of June 18, 1966); (6) hotel keepers and carriers have liens for their charges (C. C. 2102); (7) workman has mechanic's lien (C. C. 570); (8) co-heir has lien for improvements made on any real estate he must return to decedent's estate (C. C. 867); (9) person who buys stolen goods at market or fair has lien thereon until he has received price he paid (C. C. 2280); (10) tenant evicted by third person who buys premises can retain premises until he is indemnified by his prior landlord (C. C. 1749).

There are other liens which have been established by case law such as in case of persons performing meritorious services officiously, agents, architects and orchestra conductors.

LIMITATION OF ACTIONS:

Rules in relation to limitation of actions are to be found in Arts. 2219-2281 of Civil Code.

Periods of Limitation.—General period of limitation is to be found in Art. 2262 of Civil Code whereby all actions, both in rem and in personam, are barred at end of period of 30 years, without any necessity for party who alleges this limitation period to show title, and without opponent being able to rely upon any defense based on bad faith.

Periods of limitation in relation to other matters are set out under following articles. For instance, with respect to tort liability, period of limitation of actions is of ten years as of knowledge of damage or its aggravation (see Art. 2270-1 of C. C.).

In addition, French law provides for special limitations of actions in Arts. 2271-2281 of C. C., varying from six months to five years. For instance, limitation of two years applies to actions brought by doctors, surgeons, dentists and chemists for professional services and medicines supplied by them and to actions brought by traders against non-traders for payment of goods sold by them. Period of five years applies to salaries, arrears of perpetual rent charges or annuities, alimony, rent of town houses or of agricultural property, interest on money lent, and in general in respect of every sum payable yearly or at shorter intervals. For defendant-debtor to interpose successfully defense of limitation for periods of six months to five years, he must, if required by plaintiff-creditor, affirm under oath that debt has in fact been paid. If debtor is dead his widow or heirs may be required to make declaration under oath that they are unaware that debt is due. Taking of such oath cannot be required as regards annuities, alimony, maintenance, interest, rent or salary.

Even if the creditor has continued to furnish supplies, services and work, etc., during the period, the statute will continue to run unless he has rendered an account stated or a schedule of obligation or had a summons issued. (C. C. 2274).

Actions between traders ("commerçants") relating to their business affairs must be brought within ten years after cause of action arises, unless shorter period is specially prescribed by law. See also topic Sales. (C. Com. Art. 189 bis). Limitation of three years after maturity applies to bills of exchange, promissory notes and to actions against bank for payment of check.

A limitation of five years after guardianship ceases applies to claims of ward against his guardian. (C. C. 475).

Actions on ordinary insurance policies must be brought within two years from date of damage; actions on marine insurance policies must be brought within two years from date of contract. (Insurance Code, art. L 114-1 and L 172-31). Period of one year applies for actions in case of loss of goods or luggage and period of two years for action in case of collisions. (Laws of June 18, 1966, July 7, 1967). See topic Bills and Notes for limitations relating to same when given by traders. In addition, limitation of ten years for structural defects or of two years for minor repairs, applies to architects and contractors (see arts. 1792, 2270 of C. C.).

A court cannot on its own motion set up a plea of limitation (C. C. 2223), but it may be set up by the creditors of an interested party (C. C. 2225).

Causes Which Interrupt or Suspend Period of Limitation.—As general rule, these periods of limitation may be interrupted or suspended by variety of causes provided for in French law.

Period of limitation may be interrupted by writ (including by summary proceeding as "référé-provision"), by order to pay or by attachment (see art. 2244 of C. C.). In addition, period of limitation may be interrupted by acknowledgment of debt by debtor. (art. 2248 of C. C.).

Limitation period runs against all persons, unless they come within exception provided for in law (see art. 2251 of C. C.). For instance, limitation does not run between spouses (see art. 2253 of C. C.) nor does it not run against minors who are not emancipated nor against adults who are under guardianship except for what is stated in art. 2278 (see art. 2252 of C. C. and also exception provided for in arts. 2257, 2258).

It runs against estate having neither claimant nor heir even though no administrator has been appointed. (C. C. 2258). Limitation of ten years for structural defects, or two years for minor repairs, applies to architects and contractors. (C. C. 1792, 2270).

LIMITED COMPANIES:

See topic Corporations.

MARRIAGE:

Marriage takes place before civil official at domicile of one of parties in presence of at least two but not more than four witnesses. Domicile may be acquired for this purpose by prior 30 days residence in arrondissement or district. Publication by notice ("bans") posted at door of city hall of arrondissement for ten days preceding marriage. Medical certificate required. (C. C. 63, 165). These may be dispensed with in very rare cases by local district attorney. (C. C. 169). Marriage abroad between French citizens or between French citizen and foreigner is valid if in accordance with law of place where celebrated, or if celebrated by certain specified consular agents. Publication required in both cases. (C. C. 170).

American citizen to marry in France French citizen or another foreigner must produce in addition to medical certificate various documents establishing identity, date and place of birth, and nationality. Alien to marry in France must also produce identity card delivered by French authorities, valid for three years, or obtain special authorization. Before bans can be posted at city hall, medical certificate must in all cases be provided and authorities may require other documents depending on circumstances.

Man must have completed his 18th year, and woman her 15th year. (C. C. 144). Under these ages, authorization from Procureur de la République (Attorney General) is necessary. (C. C. 145). Minor must also have consent of one parent or if both parents are dead or incompetent, of grandparents or, if none, of family council. (C. C. 148-155). No consent necessary for remarriages. Unless specially authorized by President of Civil Court, woman cannot remarry until 300 days after dissolution of her preceding marriage. (C. C. 228).

Prohibited Marriages.—Marriage is prohibited in direct line between all legitimate or illegitimate ascendants, and descendants and connections by marriage in same line (C. C. 161); in collateral line between legitimate or illegitimate brother and sister (C. C. 162); and, between uncle and niece or aunt and nephew (C. C. 163). But President of République may allow marriages between brother-in-law and sister-in-law, uncle and niece or aunt and nephew. (C. C. 164).

See also topic Notaries Public.

MARRIED WOMEN:

See topics Aliens; Dower; Executors and Administrators; Husband and Wife; Marriage.

MINES AND MINERALS:

Mining Code, which governs exploration and exploitation of mines and minerals, including liquid or gaseous hydrocarbons, has been substantially modified by Law No. 94-588 of July 15, 1994 and its implementating Decrees: No. 95-427 of Apr. 19, 1995, relating to procedure for granting mining titles, No. 95-696 of May 9, 1995, relating to authorization procedure for commencing mining works, and application of mine policing (control of mining work consequences on water and environment). Ministerial order (arielé) dated July 28, 1995 was signed by Minister of Industry to supplement Decree No. 95-427 of Apr. 19, 1995, and to set out filing places for applying for mining titles.

Although theoretically surface landlord is legal owner of sub-surface as well (C.C. art. 552), any drilling or digging deeper than ten meters below surface must be declared to government supervisor of mines ("Ingénieur en Chef des Mines")(art. 131, Mining Code), and any activity involving exploration or exploitation is subject to prior government approval.

See Topical Index in front part of this volume.

MINES AND MINERALS . . . *continued*

One of goals of new Law of July 15, 1994 is simplification of various existing mining rights. As result, new code only contains two mining titles: exploration permit, which grants right of exploration, and concession, which grants right of exploitation of minerals (former "Exploitation Permit" no longer exists).

Right to explore for minerals may be obtained as follows: (a) by surface owner or by person with owner's consent after declaration to local Prefet; (b) by authorization from Minister in charge of mines (for renewable two year period) (if owner of surface has not consented); or (c) by virtue of exploration permit granted by government decree. Only exploration permit grants exclusive right of exploration for certain substances within defined perimeter. There are two types of exclusive exploration permit (c above): H permit for liquid and gaseous hydrocarbons, and M permit for other mineral substances. Both H and M permits are granted for maximum period of five years, and are renewable twice for same period of time. Holder of exclusive exploration permit is entitled to conversion thereof into concession, if results are favorable.

Concession allows its holder exclusive right to exploit minerals for maximum period of 50 years, and is renewable twice for 25 years. Concession is non-assignable right in rem (art. 36, Mining Code), entirely separate from surface ownership, and cannot be mortgaged.

Procedures for application for exploration permits and concessions are set forth in Decree No. 95-427 of Apr. 19, 1995. Main change in new law is that no public inquiry is required before exploration permit is granted: upon filing application for permit, notice ("avis") is published in Official Journal ("Journal Officiel") of both France and European Union (EU), which is followed by 90-day period for submission and evaluation of competing applications. After application period, Administration of Mines chooses best (financially and technically) proposal, and transmits it to "Conseil Général des Mines", for avis, before transmittal to Minister in charge of Mines, who will grant permit by ministerial decree ("arrêté"). Concessions, however, are still subject to public inquiry during 30 days after publication of avis in Journal Officiel. Upon evaluation of application, it is transmitted to Minister of Mines and then to Conseil d'Etat which then grants concession by decree.

Decree No. 95-696 of May 9, 1995 sets forth authorization procedure for commencement of mining works and environmental regulations applicable to such works.

Provisions of Law on water resources, dated Jan. 3, 1992, are integrated in provisions of this Decree.

Open cast mining and quarries regime has been modified by Law No. 94-588 of July 15, 1994, to take into consideration law No. 93-3 of Jan. 4, 1993 which subjects quarries to legislation concerning protected sites and their regulated access.

Right to exploit quarries is subject to exclusive quarries permit. (arts. 109-119, Mining Code).

MODELS AND DESIGNS:

See topic Industrial Property Rights.

MONOPOLIES AND RESTRAINT OF TRADE:

Monopolies and restrictive trade practices are presently governed by two sets of legal rules in France: (a) Art. 85 et seq. of Treaty of Rome of 1957 instituting European Economic Community, and Regulations issued thereunder, most important of which is Council Regulation No. 17 of 6 Feb. 1962 (O.J. 1962 No. L13/204/62); and (b) Ordinance No. 86-1243 of Dec. 1, 1986 as implemented by Decree No. 86-1309 of Dec. 29, 1986 on freedom of prices and competition; violation of prohibitions set forth in Rome Treaty and Ordinance of 1986 entail civil sanctions (nullification of agreement) and administrative fines; certain limited violations of French ordinance of 1986 constitute criminal offense.

EEC Competition Law.—Art. 85.1, Treaty of Rome prohibits any "agreements between undertakings, decisions by associations of undertakings, and concerted practices which may affect trade between Member States and which have as their object or effect the prevention, restriction or distortion of competition within the common market". Under Art. 85.2, such restrictive agreements and practices are automatically void. However, under Art. 85.3, restrictive agreements and practices may be individually exempted from prohibition of Art. 85.1 if EC Commission is satisfied that these agreements and practices contribute "to improving the production or distribution of goods or to promoting technical or economic progress, while allowing consumers a fair share of the resulting benefit, and [do] not: (a) impose on the undertakings concerned restrictions which are not indispensable to the attainment of these objectives; (b) afford such undertakings the possibility of eliminating competition in respect of a substantial part of the products in question".

Art. 85.1 applies to agreements between and practices of undertakings. EC institutions entrusted with power to apply Art. 85 to concrete cases, namely EC Commission and Court of Justice of European Communities, have given "undertaking" extensive interpretation, covering any economic or professional activity, exercised independently and yielding profits. Although extremely broad, such definition excludes from scope of Art. 85, inter alia, relationships between parent companies and their subsidiaries where parent company and its subsidiary "form an economic unit within which the subsidiary has no real economic freedom to determine its course of action on the market and if the agreements or practices are concerned merely with the internal allocation of tasks between the undertakings". (Centrafarm B.V. v. Sterling Drug Inc. [1974]).

Art. 85.1 applies to agreements (oral or written, whether legally binding or not), to decisions adopted by associations of undertakings and binding upon members of association concerned, and to concerted practices. Commission and Court of Justice define concerted practice as form of cooperation between undertakings intended to lessen risks of competition; existence of such cooperation is generally inferred from parallel conduct (such as simultaneous price increases) and from proof of contracts between undertakings (Ici et al. v. Commission [1972], re Suiker Unie et al. v. Commission [1975], re Wood Pulp [1985]).

Art. 85.1 prohibits agreements and practices which have restriction of competition as object or effect. It does not matter whether competition is effectively restricted, provided it appears from clauses of agreement, considered in its economic and legal context, that agreement is aimed at restricting competition. (Société Technique Minière v. Maschinenbau Ulm [1966], L'Oréal v. De Nieuwe AMCK [1980]). Restrictive agreements or practices will however fall outside Art. 85.1 if they do not restrict competition to appreciable extent. (Völk v. Vervaecke [1969]). Guidance on meaning of "appreciable" provided by Commission in "Notice concerning agreements of minor importance" (Sept. 3, 1986, O.J. C231/2 of Sept. 12, 1986). However, quantitative criteria defined in Notice (market share, aggregate turnover of undertakings concerned) should not be relied upon heavily: Notice is not binding on Commission or Court of Justice. (re Industrieverband Sohnhofener Natursteinplatten [1980]).

Finally, Art. 85 applies only to restrictive agreements and practices which restrict trade between Member States. (Similarly, Art. 86 applies to abuses of dominant position only insofar as they affect trade between Member States.) This test is standard of jurisdiction for application of EEC anti-trust rules. For test to be met, "it must be possible to foresee with a sufficient degree of probability on the basis of objective factors of law or fact that agreement in question may have an influence, direct or indirect, actual or potential, on the pattern of trade between Member States". (Société Technique Minière v. Mashinenbau Ulm [1966]). As for restriction of competition, alteration of flow of trade between Member States must be perceivable for restrictive agreement or practice to fall within Art. 85.1. Where test is met, EEC anti-trust rules take precedence over anti-trust laws of Member States. This does not preclude application of national laws to restrictive practices falling within Art. 85.1; however, application of national laws must be compatible with administration of Community law. (Walt Wilhelm v. Bundeskartellamt [1969]).

Art. 85.1 applies to vertical as well as horizontal agreements which restrain competition either between parties to agreement or between one of them and third parties. Such agreements include: Price fixing, limitation or control of production, technical development or investment, market sharing or sharing of sources of supply, discriminatory practices and tied-in sales.

Agreements prohibited by Art. 85.1 and which are not exempted from this prohibition are void. This applies only to clauses of agreement which are prohibited. It is for national courts, applying their own law, to decide whether other parts of agreements are severable and enforceable. (Société de Vente de Climents et Bétons de l'Est S.A. v. Kerpen & Kerpen GmbH & Co. KG [1983]).

Some of agreements cited above can never be exempted: such as agreements which have as their object or effect compartmentalization of EEC market (See: re Deere and Co., John Deere Export et al.; National Farmers Union v. Cofabel NV [1985]), or prevention of price competition (re Wood Pulp [1985]). However, most agreements submitted to Commission may benefit from exemption provided for in Art. 85.3, depending on whether agreements fulfill conditions set forth in this provision. These conditions include selective distribution systems (Metro-SB-Grossmärkte GmbH & Co., KG v. Commission [1977], re Saba [No. 2], O.J. 1983 No. L376/41), franchising agreements (Pronuptia, Court of Justice, Jan. 28, 1986), joint ventures (Carbon Gas Technologie GmbH, O.J. 1983 No. L376/17), exclusive purchasing agreements, exclusive distribution agreements, research and development agreements, specialization agreements (re Agreements between Imperial Chemical Industries Plc and BP Chemicals Limited, O.J. 1984 No. L212/1), patent and know-how licensing agreements, trademark licensing agreements, etc. However, agreements can only be exempted from prohibition of Art. 85.1 if they are notified to EC Commission (infra). In order to avoid notification of inumerable agreements, EC Commission has issued so-called "block exemption" Regulations. These Regulations specify which restrictions on competition may be included in specific kinds of agreements, these restrictions being deemed indispensable to attainment of objectives set forth in Art. 85.3. To ensure that competition will not be eliminated "in respect of a substantial part of the products in question", block exemption Regulations provide for quantitative limits with respect to market share and turnover of undertakings which participate in agreement. EC Commission has adopted block exemption Regulations for exclusive distribution agreements (Commission Regulation No. 1983/83 of 22 June 1983, O.J. 1983 No. L173/1), exclusive purchasing agreements (Commission Regulation No. 1984/83 of 22 June 1983, O.J. 1983 No. L173/5), patent licensing agreements (Commission Regulation No. 2349/84 of 23 July 1984, O.J. 1984 No. L219), motor vehicles distribution and servicing agreements (Commission Regulation No. 123/85 of 12 Dec. 1984, O.J. 1985 No. L15), research and development agreements (Commission Regulation No. 418/85 of 19 Dec. 1984, O.J. 1985 No. L53), specialization agreements (Commission Regulation No. 417/85 of 19 Dec. 1984, O.J. 1985 No. L53), franchise agreements (Commission Regulation No. 4087/88 of 30 Nov. 1988, O.J. 1988 No. L359) and know-how licensing agreements (Commission Regulation No. 556/89 of Nov. 30, 1988, O.J. 1989 No. L61).

Agreements which clearly fall within these Regulations need not be notified to Commission; they are automatically exempted from prohibition of Art. 85.1. In case of doubt, it is always advisable to notify agreement to Commission in order to obtain individual exemption pursuant to Art. 85.3. Agreements which fall outside Regulation may still benefit from individual exemption where additional restrictions which they place on competition can be justified by particular circumstances of case.

Art. 86, Treaty of Rome prohibits "any abuse by one or more undertakings of a dominant position within the common market or in a substantial part of it . . . insofar as it may affect trade between Member States."

Court of Justice has defined dominant position as "a position of economic strength enjoyed by an undertaking which enables it to hinder the maintenance of effective competition on the relevant market by allowing it to behave to an appreciable extent independently of its competitors and customers and ultimately of consumers". (United Brands Co. v. E.C. Commission [1978]). Determination of existence of dominant position held by undertaking requires precise analysis of relevant market, including analysis of its structure, of behavior of undertaking concerned in market, and of results of this behavior. (Hoffman-La Roche & Co. AG v. E.C. Commission [1979]).

Abuse of dominant position consists of any practice which may directly prejudice consumers. However, it also covers practices which prejudice them indirectly by further reducing competition still existing. (Europemballage Corp. and Continental Can Co. Inc. v. E.C. Commission [1973]). Abuses of dominant position thus include, inter alia, mergers (id.), refusal to supply (Institute Chemioterapico Italiano Spa and Commercial Solvents Corporation v. E.C. Commission [1974]), exclusive supply agreements (Hoffman-La Roche & Co. AG v. E.C. Commission [1979]), and unfair prices (United Brands Co. [Chiquita] [1976]).

MONOPOLIES AND RESTRAINT OF TRADE . . . *continued*

Abuse of dominant position within EEC falls within Art. 86 only if it affects trade between Member States, as discussed above. (Art. 85.1).

Arts. 85 and 86 apply to undertakings whether or not established in Community. Application of EEC anti-trust rules to undertakings established outside Community is based either on "effect theory" or on "economic unit theory". According to effect theory, Art. 85 applicable to undertakings outside EEC if "the results of the agreements, decisions or concerted practices extend to the territory of the common market". (Commission notice relating to imports of Japanese products in Community, 21 Oct. 1972, O.J. 1972 No. C111/13). Same principle applies with respect to Art. 86. According to economic unit theory, where conduct of subsidiary within EEC may be imputed to its parent company outside Community because subsidiary has no real economic autonomy (so that parent company and subsidiary act together as "economic unit"), EC Commission and Court of Justice have power to issue orders against or to impose fines upon parent company. (Instituto Chemioterapico Italiano Spa and Commercial Solvents Corporation v. E.C. Commission [1974]).

Undertakings may always request opinion of Commission as to applicability of Art. 85 or 86 to agreements they conclude or practices they adopt. Such request may take form of application for negative clearance or of notification. Under negative clearance procedure, undertaking asks Commission to certify that, on basis of facts known to it, there are no grounds for action on its part under either Art. 85.1 or 86. On other hand, notification is procedure necessary in order to obtain individual exemption under Art. 85.3. Form of application for negative clearance same as that of notification, form A/B. (Commission Regulation No. 27 of 3 May 1962, O.J. 1962 No. L35/1118/62, as am'd by Commission Regulation No. 2526/85 of 5 Aug. 1985, O.J. 1985 No. L240/1).

If EC Commission considers agreements to fall within Art. 85.1 and not capable of exemption, notification will provide participating undertakings with protection against fines which EC Commission might otherwise impose. (Council Regulation No. 17 of 6 Feb. 1962 Art. 15, para. 5, O.J. 1962 No. L13/204/62). Such protection is not available if undertaking applies for negative clearance only or relies on block exemption Regulation not applicable to agreement in which it participates. Fines may amount to 10% of turnover of each of undertakings participating in infringement of Art. 85 or 86. (Council Regulation No. 17, Art. 15, para. 2).

Anti-trust procedures may also be initiated by filing of complaint by third party with EC Commission. Finally, EC Commission may institute proceedings on its own initiative. Its investigating powers are defined in Council Regulation No. 17.

Anti-trust procedures are generally settled by adoption of formal decision: Negative clearance, exemption or prohibition and order to terminate infringement. However, cases may also be settled informally by voluntary elimination of restrictive practice or issue, by Commission, of so-called "comfort letter", by which Commission informs undertaking involved that there is no reason for it to intervene under EEC anti-trust rules and that EC Commission's file is henceforth closed. Unlike negative clearance or exemption decisions, comfort letters are merely administrative documents in which EC Commission expresses opinion on agreement or practice involved. (France v. Giry, S.A. Guerlain et al. [1980]; Anne Marty S.A. v. Estée Lauder S.A. [1980]; Lancômoe and Cosparfrance Nederland v. Etos and A. Heyn Supermarkt [1980]; L'Oréal v. De Nieuwe AMCK [1980]). Rulings of EC Commission can be challenged before Court of Justice if conditions laid down in Art. 173 of Treaty of Rome are fulfilled.

Limitation periods have been introduced in community law, with respect to imposition of fines and penalties for infringement of EEC anti-trust rules. For most violations, limitation period is five years from termination of infringement. (Council Regulation No. 2988/74 of 26 Nov. 1974, O.J. 1974 No. L319/1).

French Competition Law.—Provisions of French Ordinance of Dec. 1, 1986 are similar but not identical to those of Rome Treaty. French Ordinance prohibits: (1) Written or tacit agreements and concerted practices which have as their object or may have as their results to restrict free play of competition; (2) abuse of dominant position; and (3) abusive exploitation by enterprise or group of enterprises of dependent economic state of client or supplier enterprises. Above agreements or concerted practices and abuses of dominant position or economic dependency are not prohibited, however, if their effect is to promote development of economic progress, from profits of which users derive equitable part and provided they are indispensible to achieve this objective of economic progress. In this regard, exemptions may be granted by ministerial decree to certain categories of agreements but, contrary to European Community law, no procedure has been established for individual notification and exemption of agreements.

Certain practices may be considered per se offenses under French Ordinance of Dec. 1, 1986 even if they do not qualify as anticompetitive agreement, abuse of dominant position or exploitation of situation of economic dependence. Some specific per se offenses may give rise to criminal sanctions. Main per se offenses are: (1) minimum price fixing (maximum pricing is not prohibited) (Art. 34); (2) discriminatory practices (Art. 36); (3) refusal to supply (Art. 30); (4) sales at loss (Art. 32); (5) tying arrangements (Arts. 30 and 36); (6) failure to communicate tariffs and conditions of sale (Art. 33); and (7) selling goods to consumers with bonuses. Direct or indirect minimum price fixing (including imposition of minimum margin) is criminal offense. Fines up to 100,000 FF may be imposed for price fixing, selling at loss and failing to communicate tariffs and conditions of sale. Minimum price fixing, refusing to supply to consumers, sales at loss, tying arrangements imposed on consumers and professionals failing to communicate tariffs and conditions of sale are criminal offenses. Discriminatory practices, refusing to supply to professional (manufacturer, wholesaler or retailer) and tying arrangements imposed on professionals give rise to per se actions in tort.

Infringements of Ordinance of Dec. 1, 1986 are brought before Competition Council, administrative agency created by Ordinance. It is composed of 16 members appointed for six-year terms by Government upon recommendation of Minister of Economy. Council has authority to impose injunctions on enterprises in order to reestablish competition and also has authority to impose administrative fines of up to 5% of before-tax turnover realized in France during previous year. If offender is not enterprise maximum fine is 10,000,000 FF.

French law recognizes certain exemptions to competition rules: (1) Art. 10(1) of Ordinance of Dec. 1, 1986 provides that Arts. 7 and 8 will not apply when prohibited agreement or practice results from application of legal or regulatory provisions; (2) Art. 10 of Ordinance authorizes Minister of Economy to grant "block exemptions" by decree upon recommendation of Competition Council; and (3) Art. 10(2) of Ordinance provides that Arts. 7 and 8 do not apply if Competition Council grants "case-by-case" exemption.

Merger Control.—At the EEC level, Council Regulation No. 4064/89 on merger control, to become effective on Sept. 21, 1990, was adopted on Dec. 21, 1989. EEC Regulation No. 4064/89 provides that all "concentrations having Community dimension" must be notified to Commission prior to concentration. In principle, concentrations of Community dimension are reviewed exclusively by Commission and others exclusively by Member States. But where "distinct" domestic markets are involved, Member States may be allowed to re-examine mergers above threshold for national law application.

Pursuant to EEC Regulation No. 4064/89, Community dimension criterion is met when two thresholds are attained: (a) aggregate worldwide turnover of parties concerned of over ECU 5 billion; and (b) aggregate EEC turnover of at least two of parties concerned of over ECU 250 million. There is no Community dimension if each of groups achieves more than two-thirds of its aggregate EEC turnover within one and same country. (Art. 1).

Notification to EEC Commission is obligatory within one week of execution of agreement, announcement of public takeover or exchange bid, or acquisition of controlling interest, whichever occurs first. (Art. 4).

Implementation of concentration may not take place before three weeks after notification.

Concentration which creates or strengthens dominant position such that competition in Common Market or significant part thereof is significantly impeded is incompatible with Regulation 4064/89. (Art. 2[3]).

EEC Commission has one month from date of receipt of notification (Art. 10) to decide that concentration is not of Community dimension, to declare concentration is compatible, or to initiate proceedings (which allows four months to reach decision).

At the French level, Law of July 19, 1977 as am'd by Ordinance of Dec. 1, 1986 established control over concentration. Any market concentration affecting sufficiently competitive market of substitutable products may be subject to control if enterprises concerned hold more than 25% of sales or purchases of said market, or realize together turnover exceeding 7,000,000,000 francs while two parties to operation realize each turnover of at least 2,000,000,000 francs. If such market concentration does not contribute to economic and social progress sufficiently to compensate for harm to competition by other economic or social factors, it may be prohibited by Minister of Economy and Finance.

Operations of concentration may be notified to Minister of Economy and Finance in which case Minister has six months to oppose transaction or to subject same to specific conditions. Failing notification, there is no time limit to action by Minister.

See also topic Unfair Competition.

MORTGAGES:

Mortgages ("hypothèques") are of three classes: (1) Legal such as that belonging by law to minor on property of his guardian. (C. C. 2121); (2) judicial, arising from judgment against debtor (C. C. 2123); and (3) contractual, which can be created only by instrument formally executed before notary (C. C. 2127). Contract executed abroad cannot create mortgage on property in France, absent international agreements to contrary. (C. C. 2128). Property subjected to mortgage and amount due must be specifically described and stated in instrument. (C. C. 2129).

Mortgages have priority according to date of registration with Registrar of Real Estate Mortgages. For mortgage debts to be paid within fixed period, registration of mortgage will be effective for period not exceeding two years beyond this fixed period for repayment, or total of 35 years, whichever is shorter. Registration must be renewed prior to its expiration date to retain priority of mortgage. (C. C. 2154). Personal obligation of mortgagor remains if mortgage is not duly registered, but mortgagee loses all protection against bona fide purchasers. (C. C. 2134). Mortgage can only be cancelled by formal release, either by notarial act or by judgment. (C. C. 2157).

If mortgagor defaults in payment while still owning property, mortgagee may cause property to be attached and sold at auction to satisfy mortgage debt. (See topic Attachment). If proceeds of sale are not sufficient to pay debt, creditor may proceed against debtor on his personal obligation.

Purchaser from mortgagor has right to "purge" property of mortgage by payment at time of purchase to mortgagee either of full debt if it is inferior to purchase price, or of purchase price if it is inferior to debt. (C. C. 2184). In latter case, property is free of mortgage but mortgagee may proceed against principal debtor on his personal obligation for unpaid balance. If mortgagee finds purchase price too low, he may compel sale at auction, provided he agrees to commence bidding at a price 10% above purchase price. (C. C. 2185). If there is no purgation at time of sale, and if principal debtor later defaults, owner may still offer to "purge" by paying mortgagee amount of debt up to purchase price of property, then assuming pro tanto mortgagee's rights against debtor on latter's personal obligation. If owner declines to purge, mortgagee may cause property to be attached and sold at auction, retaining his rights against principal debtor for unpaid balance. (C. C. 2169).

Privileges.—Certain liens have by law priority over all mortgages (C. C. 2095), most important being that of Treasury (Trésor public) (C. C. 2098), that of Social Security (C. C. 2101), that of seller of real estate for unpaid purchase price, or that of architect or contractor for expense of construction or repairs (C. C. 2103). They must be registered in Register of Real Estate Mortgages with priority based on date of registration. (C. C. 2106; see topic Records). However, seller has two months in which to register, without loss of priority in that time. (C. C. 2108).

Antichresis is device in French law whereby creditor acquires right to collect revenue of real estate and apply it against interest and principal of debt. (C. C. 2085). Unless otherwise agreed, creditor must pay taxes and maintain property in good repair. (C. C. 2086). This does not prejudice other existing mortgages or preferences. (C. C. 2091).

See also topic Notaries Public.

MOTOR VEHICLES:

Bona fide foreign tourists whose habitual residence is outside France who buy automobiles of French manufacture in France are entitled to form of registration of vehicle called "TT" ("transit temporaire") if following conditions are met: (i) their habitual place of residence is outside customs territory of European Community or DOM (Département d'Outre-Mer); (ii) their stay in European Community is temporary; and (iii) they engage in no lucrative activity during their temporary stay in France.

This registration is valid for six months and, in certain cases, may be extended for six months more. Automobile may be sold only to another foreign tourist. Buyer entitled to new "TT" registration, valid for six months. Import duties and value added tax are not required to be paid on purchase price of automobiles which are to receive "TT" license plates. Letters in licence plate range from "TAA" to "TZZ" (Decree of Dec. 12, 1993). Automobiles of foreign manufacture delivered in France to foreign tourists whose habitual residence is outside France are also entitled to "TT" registration provided that vehicle had no prior registration in its country of origin. At expiration of "TT" registration period, vehicle must either be physically removed from France or regular French registration must be obtained. In case of vehicles of French manufacture this requires payment of value added tax based on current fair value. In case of vehicles of foreign manufacture it requires payment of these taxes and also import duties.

Members of the diplomatic corps, employees of international organizations and foreign students studying in France are entitled to special registration valid as long as owner retains status originally entitling him to.

At expiration of such registration or loss of status same conditions apply as in case of "TT" registration (see above).

Tourist arriving in France no longer presents at frontier customs documents such as "tryptique" or "carnet de passage." However, motor vehicle insurance is now compulsory in France and tourists must either present international motor insurance card valid for France or subscribe to nonrenewable insurance policy issued at frontier valid for two, seven or 21 days.

Before regular French registration, vehicles of foreign manufacture must be made to conform with French safety regulations. Vehicles (except motorcycles) under regular French registration are subject to an annual tax ("vignette") based on horsepower and age. Vignette is now collected by départements. (Arts. 24 and 26 of Budget Law for 1984 of Dec. 29, 1983).

See topic Torts.

NEGOTIABLE INSTRUMENTS:

See topic Bills and Notes.

NOTARIES PUBLIC:

Position of notary (Notaire) is of high importance. He is "Officier Ministériel" appointed by Minister of Justice, must have passed qualifying examinations and had required minimum professional experience. Notaries have exclusivity with respect to preparation of deeds of sale, mortgages, and other instruments affecting real property interests, as well as deeds of gift and marriage contracts. Such instruments prepared by notary are called notarial acts. Number of notaries is strictly limited. Decree No. 67-868 of Oct. 2, 1967 defined manner notaries may join together to form professional associations (sociétés civiles professionnelles) created by Law No. 66-879 of Nov. 29, 1966 and modified by Law No. 72-1151 of Dec. 23, 1972 and by Decree 75-979 of Oct. 24, 1975. Notary's right to practice is subject to no territorial limitations. (Decree 86-728 of Apr. 29, 1986).

Notary's function is to verify and keep on file or to make record of certain instruments which by law must be in authentic form or which parties desire in such form. Notary is not allowed unless authorized by President of Tribunal de Grande Instance to reveal such instruments to persons other than parties thereto, their heirs and assigns. For deeds of sale, notary must verify that seller owns real property. (Trib. Civ. Seine Jan. 15, 1889). In addition, he must verify status of liens and mortgages registered on property before sale and at moment of publication of sale. (Cour Cassation Jan. 4, 1966). Notary also drafts wills according to instructions of testator. He may also certify existence of basic facts upon declaration of witnesses before him (certificat de notoriété), e.g. family relationships. These certificates are then accepted as prima facie evidence in legal proceedings, as in settlement of decedents' estates.

If notary drafts instrument, he retains original permanently on file. Certified copies are provided to all parties having separate interest. Notarial instrument is absolute proof of any agreement between parties and their heirs and legal representatives. (C. C. 1319). Notary will issue certified copies for use in legal proceedings. In such case, he is personally liable both for accuracy of copies and legal validity of original act, if he prepared it.

Notary will also provide certified copies of private acts or contracts presented to him, retaining one such copy in his files. In such case, he is personally responsible only for accuracy of copy and not legal validity of original instrument. Notary may be liable for damages arising from unsound advice given by him based on matters and knowledge within his competence. (J.C.P. 1975 II, 18164; Cass. Civ. ler Oct. 2, 1979, Nov. 14, 1979, Feb. 12, 1980).

Fees charged by notary for acts within notary's sphere of exclusivity are determined based on rates fixed by decree. (Decree No. 78-261 of Mar. 8, 1978 and Decree No. 86-358 of Mar. 11, 1986). Fees charged by notary for acts outside notary's sphere of exclusivity are not subject to fixed rates.

PARTNERSHIP:

1966 revision of French company law (Law No. 66-537 of July 24, 1966) deals extensively with commercial partnerships and represents codification and modification of previous law. For effective dates of company law, see topic Corporations.

Partnerships may be either general partnerships ("sociétés en nom collectif"), special partnerships ("sociétés en commandite simple"), or special partnerships by shares ("sociétés en commandite par actions"). There is also form of association analogous to joint venture ("société en participation"). Under law, all forms of partnerships except société en participation are henceforth considered to be commercial; and, so under jurisdiction of commercial, not civil, tribunals and subject to bankruptcy proceedings. See topic Commercial Law. Formation of partnerships is subject to regulations regarding publication and inscription at Register of Commerce as provided in Decree No. 67-236 of Mar. 23, 1967 (J. O. Mar. 24, 1967), Decree No. 67-237 (J. O. Mar. 24, 1967 and Arrêté of Aug. 31, 1978).

Investment or participation by nonresident in partnership subject to regulations of Ministry of Finance. See topic Exchange Control.

General partnership ("société en nom collectif") may be given name which is invented or which includes name of one or more persons associated with partnership. (Law of July 11, 1985). Name must be preceded or followed by words "société en nom collectif" or "SNC". (Decree No. 86-9009 of July 30, 1986). Partners' liability is unlimited. Each partner represents firm, unless articles provide to contrary. Each foreigner, except EU citizens, who become partner, or manager ("gérant"), must obtain special "trader's card" ("carte de commerçant") from Préfecture de Police or departmental préfecture. Acts relating to alienation or mortgaging of real property require assent of all partners. Partnership assets constitute primary fund for satisfaction of partnership creditors. Partnership creditors may also bring suit against individual partner, but must first establish their status as partnership creditors either by judgment against partnership or by recognition of claim by partnership and proof of inadequacy of partnership assets.

New law increases protection of members by providing that unanimous agreement of partners is necessary for transfer of partnership interest and that annual meeting must be held to approve accounts for that fiscal year.

Decree of Mar. 1, 1985 (Art. 6) implementing Law of Mar. 1, 1984 on prevention and amicable settlement of company difficulties, requires partnership to appoint Statutory Auditor and Replacement Statutory Auditor for six year term when any two of following three criteria have been met during two preceding fiscal years: (i) Total assets on balance sheet exceed FRF 10,000,000; (ii) turnover (excluding V.A.T.) exceeds FRF 20,000,000; (iii) average number of salaried workers exceeds 50.

Special partnership ("société en commandite simple") may be given name which is invented or which includes name of one or more persons associated with partnership, either general partners (commandités) or special partners (commanditaires). General partners are basically subject to same regulations as general partnership's partners (see subhead General Partnership ["société en nom collectif"], supra). Special partners are liable for partnership debts only to amount that they have agreed to contribute. They cannot participate in management, but may act in advisory capacity.

Unless otherwise provided in articles, unanimous consent of partners is necessary for transfer of special partner's interest. Annual meeting is necessary to approve accounts for that fiscal year. (Concerning auditors, see last paragraph of subhead General Partnership ["société en nom collectif"], supra.)

Special partnership by shares ("société en commandite par actions") lies between special partnership and corporation ("société anonyme"). Minimum capital is FRF 1,500,000 for société seeking investments for public, FRF 250,000 for others. Rules for constitution of société en commandite par actions are similar to those for société anonyme. See topic Corporations. Special partner's liability is limited to unpaid part of subscription. Business is carried on by general partner or partners, known as managers ("gérants"), whose management is supervised by a committee of inspection ("conseil de surveillance"), composed of not less than three shareholders appointed by general meeting of shareholders. Members of committee incur no personal liability for their manner of supervision, but are liable for own faults in carrying out duties. They submit annual report to shareholders. Profits distributed in form of dividends.

As of Oct. 1, 1972, articles of incorporation and by-laws supposedly set age limit for managing directors which shall not exceed 65 unless articles of incorporation and by-laws expressly provide otherwise. Also, as of same date age limit must be set for members of committee of inspection applicable to all or percentage of those members; unless articles or by-laws provide otherwise, no more than one-third of active members of committee may be older than 70. (Law 70-1284 of Dec. 31, 1970).

Law requires that special auditors ("commissaires aux comptes") be appointed to control financial reports and accounts of partnership. For description of functions and qualifications of special auditors, see topic Corporations.

Special partnership by shares may now be transformed into corporation or limited liability company by decision of shareholders at extraordinary meeting with approval of majority of partners.

Société en Participation.—Law of Jan. 4, 1978, which came into force in mid-1978 and, in some cases mid-1980, has modified provisions of Civil Code relating to "Société en participation" in some areas, including disclosures of interest to third parties and termination of "société". Société en participation, which can be either civil or commercial depending on particularity of agreeable members, is analogous to joint venture. It is formed by written or even verbal contract, which need not be notarized for commercial purposes. Unless different organization is provided for in statutes, applicable rules concerning organization are those which affect "société" as entity, though "société en participation" is not legal entity. Each partner contracts in his own name and is personally liable to third party, unless société is sold to third party, in which case partner is jointly and severally liable. If "société" is of predetermined duration, each partner can, in principle, terminate its existence at any time.

PATENTS: See topic Industrial Property Rights.

PERPETUITIES: See topic Trusts.

PLEDGES:

A pledge (gage) is civil or commercial, depending on the debt guaranteed.

Civil pledge can be established by registered instrument only. In event of default in payment creditor who holds pledge cannot dispose of it. He must obtain court order allowing him to sell property pledged or order giving him right to take property in payment of debt. Should value of pledge exceed amount of debt, amount payable to creditor is determined by expert appointed by court. (C. C. 2073 et seq.).

PLEDGES . . . *continued*

The commercial pledge can be established without special formalities and can be proved by any legal means, such as the correspondence exchanged, or books of parties. Creditor can foreclose pledge by selling it at public auction eight days after demand has been served on debtor by sheriff ("huissier") if debtor has not paid within time specified. (C. Com. 91 et seq.).

With respect to both kinds of pledge, the property must actually be in the possession of the creditor, or deposited with a third party. Certain pledges can be established without actually divesting owner of possession, as in case of pledges on "fonds de commerce" (entire going business concern, including goodwill) and liens on automobiles.

If merchandise is in warehouse pledge is made by endorsement of warehouse certificate to creditor and by transcription of this endorsement on books of warehouse.

If a debt due by a third party is given in pledge, an instrument duly registered on paper with fiscal stamps affixed must be served on debtor by means of sheriff ("huissier"). (C. C. 2075). Pledge of "professional" debt can be granted to credit institution in simplified form ("bordereau") as provided by Law No. 81-1 of Jan. 2, 1981. See topic Bills and Notes.

Registered securities may be pledged, but this fact must be noted in books of corporation issuing securities. In addition, if corporation is of noncommercial type (société civile), any pledge of its shares is subject to specific registration with registrar (greffe) of Commercial Court.

See also topic Chattel Mortgages.

PRESCRIPTION:

See topic Limitation of Actions.

PRICES:

Prices in France have been subject to many successive regulations by Ministry of Finance.

Former regulation, resulting from Ordinance No. 45-1483 of June 30, 1945, applying to price controls by industrial production prices, resale prices or imported goods and goods for distribution, prices of services and indexation clauses, has been removed by Ordinance No. 86-1243 of Dec. 1, 1986 and Decree No. 86-1309 of Dec. 29, 1986.

Ordinance No. 86-1243 of Dec. 1, 1986 and Decree No. 86-1309 of Dec. 29, 1986 affirmed principles whereby prices of goods, products and services are freely determined by market forces and free competition.

Administration retains right to intervene in fields or zones which are characterized by structural absence of competition due to monopoly (e.g. gas, electricity) or various regulations (e.g. chemicals, books). Also, control can be reestablished in case of exceptional increase in price.

Ordinance No. 86-1243 of Dec. 1, 1986 and arts. L. 113-1 to L. 113-3 of Consumer Code impose on professionals obligation of information of their prices to consumers and to professional customers. Arrêté of Dec. 3, 1987 requires any information on products or services to show total sum (including taxes) effectively due by consumers. Manufacturers, services providers, distributors or importers have to provide to any professional upon request their price lists and general terms and conditions. These documents must compulsorily provide specific information (rebates if any, terms of payment, penalties for late payment etc.).

Ordinance No. 86-1243 of Dec. 1, 1986 does not apply to prices resulting from special regulations applicable to certain fields (e.g. banks, insurance, agricultural, coal and steel products), services (e.g. road or rail carriage of goods, air transportation, urban public transportation, taxis), or professions, which are still in effect.

Law No. 87-588 of July 30, 1987 makes exception to Ordinance No. 86-1243 of Dec. 1, 1986 by authorizing Ministry of Economy or Ministry of Public Health to fix prices and profit margins of products and services which are reimbursed by social security.

See also topic Unfair Competition.

PRINCIPAL AND AGENT:

There is no required form of authorization of an agent, which may be by notarial act, private agreement, letter or even telegram. (C. C. 1985). However, agency relation must be confirmed by notarial act in certain cases, e.g., for inter vivos gift, gifts between spouses, revocation of gift or testament, recognition of illegitimate child, entering into contract of marriage, execution of bill of sale of real property, or creation or release of mortgage. General agency gives authority to transact all business of principal. However, in general it authorizes only management or administration and not disposition of principal's property. General agent therefore cannot alienate, mortgage, pledge or otherwise transfer principal's property unless he is given express authorization clearly defining sort of transaction empowered. (C. C. 1988).

Special agency exists when agent is limited to performance of specific acts. (C. C. 1987).

Agency authorization may be in a language other than French, but it must be accompanied by a legal translation before use in any legal procedure. Practice is that authorization, regardless of its language, must conclude with words, immediately before signature of principal, "bon pour pouvoir" (good for authority), written in hand of principal. It is advisable to have foreign agency authorization or power of attorney notarized and then legalized by French consulate.

Agent is bound to his principal to execute his agency according to instructions given him by such principal. (C. C. 1991). However, case law has developed doctrine of apparent authority, obligating principal in any contractual obligation when third party has relied in good faith on agent's appearance of power to act. (C. C. 1998). An agent does not ordinarily bind principal by any non-contractual tort, but he may if circumstances indicate principal's specific power to control or command details of his actions. An employee in a master-servant relation will bind his employer for all injuries to third parties, virtually without any scope of employment limitation. (C. C. 1384, see topic Torts).

Agency relation ends: (1) By revocation by principal, which may be at will, except that principal must indemnify agent for injury sustained if agent has an interest in continuation of agency (C. C. 2004); (2) by renunciation by agent, at will, provided principal is indemnified for any loss sustained thereby (C. C. 2007); (3) by death of either, except that heirs of principal are bound by acts of agent when latter does not know of principal's death (C. C. 2003, 2008).

Commercial Agents.—Decree of Dec. 23, 1958 and Law 91.593 of June 25, 1991 defined status of commercial agents ("agents commerciaux") professionally engaged in buying and selling for account of another and prescribed special register kept at Tribunal de Commerce upon which their names must be inscribed. Arrêté of Jan. 8, 1993 requires all commercial agents (physical and legal persons) to register with Office of Registrar of Tribunal of Commerce once every five years. (See topic Records.) For alien commercial agents formality of registration requires possession of valid trader's card. (See topic Aliens.) Commercial agency relationship should be evidenced by written instrument executed in as many originals as there are contracting parties. Commercial agent is obligated to execute precisely charge with which he has been entrusted. He must regularly inform principal of acts done on his behalf. He is liable to principal for all faults committed in course of execution of terms of agency contract (C. C. 1992) and faults of his sub-agents (C. C. 1994).

Commercial agent is independent and free to act on behalf of any other firm, but he must obtain consent of principal before he may represent competitors. Contract may contain noncompetition clause, forbidding agent to engage in same line of business or to represent competitors after termination of contract, provided that noncompetition clause is reasonably limited in time and geographic scope. Noncompetition clause is valid for two years after termination of contract. Commercial agent agreement can only be requalified as employment agreement if it is proven that agent has permanent and subordinate legal relationship with principal. (Law of Feb. 11, 1994).

Commercial agency may be revoked by principal in case of substantial deficiency of performance by agent. Otherwise revocation gives agent right to indemnity for injury sustained.

Courts generally have not distinguished between commercial agents and other agents with regard to award of indemnity for improper revocation of agency.

Decree of Dec. 23, 1958 is applicable to contracts entered into before June 1991. Contracts concluded after June 28, 1991 are submitted to law of June 25, 1991, which does not require any special registration or written instrument as condition of applicability. However, each party may, upon request, receive from other written document evidencing commercial agency relationship. (Art. 2 of 1991 Law). Under 1991 Law, contract may contain noncompetition clause barring agent from representing competitors after termination of contract, provided noncompetition clause is limited in time (two years after termination of contract) and is expressly set forth in contract. Commercial agency may be revoked by each party in case of material breach by other party, "force majeure", termination of agency due to agent or assignment of agency by agent. Otherwise, revocation gives agent right to indemnity for injury sustained. (Art. 12, paragraph 1 of 1991 Law).

Decree of June 10, 1992 has imposed certain obligations on principals such as communicating all relevant information to agents and transmitting quarterly commission statement to agents. This decree is applicable to contracts submitted to law of June 25, 1991 and to all contracts after 1994. As from Jan. 1, 1994, Law of June 25, 1991, Decree of June 10, 1992 and Arrêté of Jan. 8, 1993 are applicable to all commercial agency contracts currently in force, including those signed prior to June 28, 1991.

REAL PROPERTY:

A basic distinction in French law is made between immovables, roughly equivalent to real property, and movables, roughly equivalent to personal property. Real property consists of: (1) Property immovable by nature, as land and buildings or structures thereon; (2) immovables which include fixtures, animals required for cultivation, and machines or installations indispensable for factories or commercial premises; (3) types of interests traditionally classified as immovables, as usufruct, servitude, mortgage, and certain privileges (liens).

Real property may be acquired by accession, succession, prescription, or contract: *Accession* is increase of existing land by act of nature, e.g., alluvial lands. (C. C. 551)

Succession involves passage of title by direct descent to heirs, or by universal legacy or specific devise. Change of title by intestate as well as testate succession must be registered upon Register of Real Estate Mortgages (Bureau de la Conservation des Hypothèques—see topic Records).

Prescription is acquisition of title, by adverse possession, which must be continuous, public, unequivocal, and peaceful. (C. C. 2229). Normal statute of limitations is 30 years (C. C. 2262), but it is reduced to term of 10 to 20 years, depending on location of property, provided adverse possessor acts in good faith and under color of title (C. C. 2265). Successive periods of adverse possession may be cumulative. (C. C. 2235). Period of prescription is interrupted by failure to exercise possessory acts for more than one year (C. C. 2243), by challenge of possession made by true owner (C. C. 2249), or by recognition by adverse possessor of title of true owner (C. C. 2248). True owner may protect his title by action before local civil tribunal (action pétitoire); adverse possessor may protect his possession against third parties by possessory action before same tribunal (see subhead Possessory Actions, infra).

Acquisition by Contract.—Every creation or transfer of real property interest by contract must be by notarial act registered upon Register of Real Estate Mortgages. (See topic Records.) This includes deeds of sale, deeds of gift, contracts creating rights of usufruct or servitudes, long term leases, attachment liens, contracts creating or dissolving tenancy in common and condominium. (Law of Mar. 23, 1855, supplemented by Decree Law of Oct. 30, 1935 and Decree of Jan. 4, 1955). Failure to register enables acquisition of property by bona fide purchaser or loss of priority to subsequent transferee who first registers.

Usufruct.—Analogous to a life estate (C. C. 578), usufruct gives right to one person to use and enjoy property while another remains vested with bare title. Usufruct may be created by operation of law, e.g., rights of surviving spouse (see topic Descent and Distribution), or rights of parents over property of infants; or from contract of gift or sale. (C. C. 579). Though most often given for life, usufruct may also be for fixed term. (C. C. 617). Usufructuary enjoys personal use of property, receiving all income and exercising full administration, but may not alienate or mortgage property. (C. C.

See Topical Index in front part of this volume.

REAL PROPERTY . . . *continued*
582-599). Inventory is made at outset of usufruct. Usufructary must not waste and may usually be compelled to post bond for this purpose. (C. C. 600, 601).

Servitudes.—Servitudes may be created by operation of law, sometimes in public interest (passage of electric power lines), sometimes for private interest (right of way to wholly enclosed tract); by contract; or by prescription during period of 30 years under same conditions as adverse possession of other interests. Servitudes created by contract must be by notarial act, registered upon Register of Real Estate Mortgages. (C. C. 637-710).

Tenancy in Common.—Tenancy in common (indivision) exists when several persons jointly are owners of specific tract, usually derived simultaneously by succession or gift. Any juridical act concerning whole property requires unanimous consent. Joint tenant can use tenancy in common (C. C. 815–9) (against consideration when for his private use) when he does so for normal purposes. Gains and losses of tenancy in common are shared in proportion to share held of tenancy in common. Law 76-1286 of Dec. 31, 1976 institutes new rules applicable to joint tenancies existing as of July 1, 1977. However, joint tenancy agreements entered into prior to July 1, 1977 continue to be governed by old rules unless parties agree to apply new rules. Under old rules, each co-tenant may freely dispose of individual interest without consent of others. Under new rules, each co-tenant may dispose of his individual interest provided terms of sale and identity of buyer are notified to other co-tenants who may generally exercise preemptive right (transfer to usufructuary who is not joint owner is still subject to preemptive rights). (C. C. 815-14). Except in few cases provided by law or by contract, any co-tenant at any time may compel partition. (C. C. 815). If property is by nature indivisible, any co-tenant may demand its sale at auction, or demand to have his interests purchased by others. Co-tenants may by contract exclude partition for period of five years, which term may be renewed. (C. C. 1873-3). Concept of joint tenancy is not recognized by French law.

Condominium companies, called "sociétés constituées en vue de l'attribution d'immeubles aux associés par fractions divises," were created by Law of June 28, 1938 and are currently governed by Title II, Law of July 16, 1971 as modified by Law No. 71-1054 of Dec. 24, 1971, with additional modification of Tit. 2 by Law No. 72-649 of July 11, 1972 and Decree No. 78-704 of July 3, 1978. Ownership of condominium shares gives right to use, and upon dissolution, to ownership of a predetermined part of company's real estate holding.

Company objectives may be construction, purchase, management or maintenance of real estate; companies may be run according to civil or commercial regulations.

Possessory Actions.—There are three types of possessory actions analogous to replevin designed to enable an aggrieved party to recover possession or to defend quiet possession of interest in real property. Plaintiff must prove quiet possession within at least a year preceding the action; however, it is possible to take action against author of violent dispossession, even when plaintiff has not possessed property for full year. (New Civil Procedure Code arts. 1264-1267 following Decree No. 81-500 of May 12, 1981, effective as of Jan. 1, 1982). These possessory actions are intended to protect possession when: (a) Complainant's quiet possession is being disturbed in fact or in law; (b) complainant fears disturbance in his quiet possession through construction in course of adjacent building; (c) complainant has been dispossessed in fact. If there exists contract between disputing parties relating to that possession, court will not allow use of possessory actions but allow only litigation based on that contract.

Action must be brought before local court of general jurisdiction within one year from time of disturbance; decision of court will only be given as to possession and not to title. (New Civil Procedure Code arts. 1264-1267 following Decree No. 81-500 of May 12, 1981 effective as of Jan. 1, 1982). Judgment normally orders any action necessary to put real property in condition it was in before disturbance to possession began.

With respect to movable properties, possession implies title. However, person who has lost or from whom movable property has been stolen may bring claim to recover property against person in whose hands lost or stolen property is found within period of three years from date of loss or robbery. (C. C. art. 2279). If person in whose hands property is found has purchased it from merchant, person who has lost property cannot recover it until he reimburses other for purchase price. (C. C. art. 2280).

See also topic Notaries Public.

RECORDS:

There are a number of public registers created by special laws either to make certain basic information relating to a person or to an enterprise a matter of public record, or to confer a priority or presumption of title in some property interests in favor of party making the registration.

Principal registers are:

(1) Civil Status Register.—This register is kept in every commune and arrondissement. All vital statistics (birth, marriage, divorce and death certificates) relating to citizen are entered on register of place where born, regardless of subsequent domicile.

(2) Office of Registrar (Greffe) of Tribunal of Commerce.—Here must be deposited copies of articles of incorporation or association and related documents of every stock corporation formed in France, every foreign corporation having office in France, every limited liability company, commercial partnership, and special partnership by shares as well as registration records of commercial agents. Any substantial modification of articles of incorporation or association must be filed in same office.

General mortgage of a going business (nantissement de fonds de commerce) and chattel mortgage on industrial and professional equipment must also be registered here within 15 days after creation or mortgage is null and void.

(3) Register of Commerce.—Ordinance 58-1352 of Dec. 27, 1958 and various later Decrees including Decree of May 30, 1984 and Arrêté of Feb. 9, 1988 set forth regulations and various technical details concerning Register of Commerce. This public Register exists in each department in France and all persons or companies, domestic or foreign, which are engaged in commercial activity in France, either directly, or through intermediary of branch or agent, or in any other manner, must apply to clerk of Tribunal of Commerce for registration of their principal office in Register of Commerce. In order to be treated as legal entities, companies carrying on noncommercial activity must also apply. Traders must apply for registration within two weeks after commencement of activity. No specific time period is provided for companies. However, companies must apply for registration as soon as possible after completion of incorporation formalities including publication formalities.

If trader or company has several offices within Tribunal's territory, then it must apply for registration of each additional office. If it has offices within territory of several Tribunals of Commerce, it must apply for "secondary" registration for each one. If office is transferred to territory of another Tribunal, new registration must be sought within one month of transfer. Termination of activity must also be declared within one month.

Application must be made by trader ("commerçant") or legal representative of company.

All individuals applying for registration must present, among other elements, following information: Name and personal domicile; date and place of birth; nationality; documents which enable commerçant, if foreigner, to live and work in French territory (carte de commerçant); date and place of marriage, matrimonial regime, and clauses of marriage contract and its amendments (Art. 16 of Law of Feb. 11, 1994) which might affect free disposition of goods of spouses; activities engaged in; operating name; persons empowered to act in his name; address of domestic and foreign offices; date of commencement of operations. (Art. 8 of Decree of May 30, 1984).

All companies must supply certain information including: Articles of incorporation ("statuts"); acts naming persons to positions of management, direction and control of company; declaration required by Art. 6 of Law of July 24, 1966 of procedures complied with to organize company. Declaration that procedures to organize company were complied with is no longer necessary, whether for formation or for amendment of articles of incorporation. (Art. 18 of Law of Feb. 11, 1994). Registrar verifies compliance. However, declaration is still required in case of merger. S.A.R.L. must file report of special auditors ("commissaires aux apports") evaluating contributions in kind. S.A.s must file declaration of capital subscription with list of subscribers, number of shares subscribed to and sums paid in by each subscriber. If S.A. seeks public investment, minutes of organization meeting and report of special auditors ("commissaires aux apports") evaluating contributions in kind and granting special advantages must be presented. In addition, all companies must indicate: Purpose and form; particular legal status; capital; activity; date of fiscal year end; address of head office of company with indication of principal office, and, if applicable, address of other foreign or domestic offices; term of existence; references of members personally responsible for corporate debts; references of members and third persons having power to engage company; and documents which permit trader, if foreign, to live and work in France (carte de commerçant).

Upon registry, registration number which must appear on all commercial documents as well as on stationery is assigned to person or entity.

Modifications must be made within one month in Register of Commerce if situation of person or company changes (Art. 22 of Decree of May 30, 1984), in order to be demurrable to third parties.

In addition, certain documents relating to judicial settlement, liquidation, orders forbidding exercise of commercial activities, and withdrawal of trader's card are filed at Register of Commerce.

Registration in Register of Commerce raises presumption that inscribed is commerçant. Individuals may not avail themselves of their status as commerçants unless they are registered in Register of Commerce, but they may not invoke their failure to register to avoid responsibilities and obligations that this status entails. Persons who must be registered in Register of Commerce may not in dealing with third parties make use of facts whose publication is mandatory but has been neglected, while third parties may avail themselves of such facts if they so wish. Presumption as to commercial status cannot be asserted against third parties or Administration if they prove contrary. (Art 64 of Decree of May 30, 1984).

Traders and directors of commercial operations are liable to certain penal sanctions if they refuse, after judicial decree, to register themselves in Register of Commerce or if, in bad faith, they give inexact or incomplete information concerning their field and method of operation. (Ordinance of Dec. 27, 1958). Order of Sept. 24, 1984 relative to registration of public companies has been replaced by Order of Feb. 9, 1988, simplifying rules and procedures of registration.

(4) Register of Trade.—All local artisans must be entered in register maintained by local guild chambers.

(5) Register of Associations and Foundations.—This is located in Préfecture of Police of Paris and in Préfectures of every department. It is registry of nonprofit associations and foundations and contains extracts from their articles of association. Association is legal entity only upon registration. Declaration to registry contains name and purpose of association, offices, names, occupations, domiciles and citizenship of managers of association. Changes in management of association must also be declared. (Actually, there is no "register" as such. Law of 1901 merely provides that anybody has access to declaration and articles of association at préfecture.)

(6) Register of Real Estate Mortgages ("Bureau de la Conservation des Hypothèques").—There are about 350 "bureaux des hypothèques" throughout France, where register is held. This register records all events affecting title to real property in district covered by register, e.g., deeds of sale, mortgages, transfers by testate or intestate succession, tenancies in common, long term leases and contractual servitudes. Bureau also keeps separate dossier for each tract in every commune ("fichier immobilier"). Fichier immobilier itself is divided in two subdossiers, "fiche personnelle" and "fiche réelle", which allow doing research either from names of owners or from description of real property.

Priority of deeds, mortgages or other instruments is determined by date of registration and not date of transaction. Mortgages must be renewed every ten years, if installment or last installment is not determined or if it is prior to or simultaneous with registration, and two years if principal of debt must be paid on one or more determined dates, to preserve priority. Failure to register mortgage means that right to possession is lost as against bona fide purchasers, but personal liability of mortgagor remains. However, seller has two months to register his lien for unpaid purchase price and only thereafter does it become subordinate to mortgages previously registered. Failure to

RECORDS . . . *continued*
register deed of sale means that title may be lost to bona fide purchaser. First among several claimants to register acquires good title regardless of date of contract of sale.

(7) Register of Automobile Mortgages ("Gages").—This is located at Préfecture in each department. Recordation must be made within three months of initial registration of new vehicle or it is null and void.

(8) Fiscal Register ("**Bureau d'Enregistrement Fiscal**").—This local register records actual date of all legal transactions on application by interested party.

(9) National Institute of Industrial Property.—This register, located in Paris, includes all patents, trademarks, tradenames, trade symbols and models or designs, etc. In general, registration creates presumption of title which may be rebutted by proof of prior art or usage by another. See topic Industrial Property Rights.

(10) Public Register of Cinematography.—This register, also located in Paris, contains under film title record of all production and employment contracts, credit agreements and mortgages, and sale or distribution agreements concerning film. Similarly, all court decisions regarding film must be registered. Failure to register causes loss of priority, but does not invalidate contract or mortgage.

(11) Public Register of Computer Files.—Before being put into operation, each nominative computer file must be declared to (and in certain cases authorized by) National Commission on Data Processing and Freedom (created by Law No. 78-17 of Jan. 6, 1978). Failure to do so can subject offender to penalties.

(12) Forward Agents Register.—Decree of Mar. 5, 1990 creates Forwarding Agents Register ("Registre des Commissionnaires de Transport"); registration certificate ("Certificat d'inscription") with Register entitles forwarding agent to exercise his activity throughout French territory (excluding overseas departments and territories). Certificate is personal and granted for unlimited period of time and is not assignable. Each region of France has own Forwarding Agents Register. Change in forwarding agent's status must be filed with Register. Registration application requirements are contained in Arrêté of Sept. 25, 1990. Registration is subject to conditions relating to professional aptitude, respectability and financial capacity. Forwarding agent may be removed from Register in following cases: (1) Failure to continue to meet conditions for registration; (2) abandonment of this activity for one year or longer; (3) violation of transport regulations; or (4) delays in payments owed to carriers. Non-EC forwarding agents may be registered in France provided their country of origin allows French nationals to become forwarding agents under same conditions.

See also topics Associations, Chattel Mortgages, Corporations, Deeds, Industrial Property Rights, Limited Companies, Mortgages, Partnership, Principal and Agent, Real Property, Trusts.

REPLEVIN: See topic Real Property.

SALES:

Contract of sale may be made by notarial deed or in form of a private agreement. All sales contracts may be proved by these documents. Commercial contracts can also be proved by note or order of broker duly signed by parties or by accepted invoice, by correspondence, by books of parties, or in proper commercial cases, by oral testimony. (C. C. 1582; C. Com. 109). See topic Frauds, Statute of. In principle, contracts of sale between spouses are prohibited.

Sale is complete between parties, and, subject to contractual provisions reserving title in seller until purchase price is paid in full, ownership passes to buyer moment there is agreement as to object and price, even though no delivery has taken place, nor price paid. (C.C. 1583). Sales price must be reasonably related to value of object of sale and not merely symbolic and must be specifically set forth or clearly determinable in contract, or contract is void. When goods are sold by weight, number, or measure, risk of loss does not pass to buyer until goods have been weighed, counted or measured. Rule is otherwise if sale is by lot. In case of wine, oil and other things which it is usual to inspect before purchasing, sale is not complete until buyer has inspected and accepted goods. (C. C. 1585-1587). In distribution contracts, reference to seller's standard prices may be deemed sufficient, under certain circumstances, to render price clearly determinable.

Principal obligations of seller are to deliver goods and to give certain warranties. Expenses incurred in delivery of goods are borne by seller unless contract provides otherwise. (C. C. 1602-1609). If earnest money has been paid ("arrhes"), either party may still withdraw, buyer by forfeiting money and seller by returning twice the amount. (C. C. 1590). Buyer has risk of loss from time object should have been made available, unless a formal demand on seller to deliver it has been made. (C. C. 1138). Interest runs on purchase price if seller has caused a legal demand delivered by a "huissier" to be issued against buyer. (C. C. 1652).

Promise to sell real estate, real rights, or business goodwill is void if not contained in notarized or private act registered at tax registry office within ten days after acceptance by buyer. (C.G.I., art. 1840-A).

In the case of sales of real property which have to be executed by notarial deed, the seller is entitled to rescind a sale if consideration received by him is less than five-twelfths of real value. In this case buyer has choice of either returning property on receiving back price paid, or of keeping it upon payment of balance of fair value subject to reduction of one-tenth of total value. Buyer has no right of rescission on ground of inadequacy of consideration. (C. C. 1674-1685). Action must be brought within two years of date of sale. Value to be considered is value at time of sale.

Buyer has remedy of rescission if object of sale is altered between its condition at moment of sale and time of delivery, provided he has first without success requested seller to remedy deficiencies. (C. C. 1184, 1614).

In case of sales of personal property, rule that possession is regarded as equivalent to title is important. Suit may be brought for recovery of lost or stolen property within three years of date of loss or theft. Person in actual possession of stolen or lost property bought at fair or market, or at public sale, or from merchant selling similar articles, cannot be forced to return article to original owner, unless latter reimburses to person in possession price he paid for it. Sale on credit of consumer goods having ready market, of automobiles, and of tools and equipment is subjected to special regulations. (C. C. 2279, 2280).

See also topics Consumer Protection; Notaries Public.

Warranties.—Unless parties have agreed differently, seller warrants buyer against dispossession and latent defects, entitling buyer to either return defective goods, rescind contract, and collect damages in circumstances below, or retain goods but reduce purchase price by amount set by appraiser. Action by buyer should be brought as quickly as possible after discovery of defect but time limit for bringing same depends on nature of defect and practice of trade as determined by court. However, in case of contract for construction of building, action for hidden defects must be brought within ten years of delivery of completed structure, that for apparent defects, within one month of delivery of completed structure. (C. C. 1625, 1641-1646).

Warranty against hidden defects includes those rendering thing unfit for use intended, or reducing its value for that purpose to such extent that buyer would not have taken it or would have paid less for it if he had known of defects. Liability for hidden defects arises even if seller was unaware of them, unless he stipulated to contrary. If seller was aware of defects in things sold, he is liable for return of price and for damages directly caused by defects and foreseeable at time of contract's conclusion. If he was ignorant of defect, he is only liable for return of price and repayment of expenses occasioned by sale. Case law presumes that professional seller (including producer of good) knows of hidden defect, even if buyer is also professional. Presumption is deemed irrebuttable. If contract contains liquidated damage clause, court is held to that award provided faulty performance was not intentional. (C. C. 1150). However, court may lower or increase damages if such clause is manifestly excessive or inadequate. (C. C. 1152). See also topic Contracts.

Applicable Law.—Disputes over sales of real property are governed by law of situs. For personal property, governing law is usually that of place of delivery, absent contrary stipulation, but courts will apply other governing law if it seems more in accord with will of parties (l'autonomie de la volonté) gathered from conditions and circumstances of sale.

Conditional sales agreements ("clauses de réserve de propriéte"), reserving title and right to repossession in seller, are now valid against third parties by virtue of Law No. 80-335 of May 12, 1980. In judicial settlements and bankruptcies, right must be exercised within four months of publication of judgment (see topic Judicial Recovery and Liquidation). Another security device, limited to certain types of goods, is purchase price chattel mortgage, as for new automobiles. See topic Chattel Mortgages.

See also topic Notaries Public.

International Sale of Goods.—United Nations Convention on Contracts for the International Sale of Goods, in force on Jan. 1, 1988. See topic Treaties and Part VI, Selected International Conventions.

SEALS:

The seal does not exist in France.

SEQUESTRATION:

Sequestration by agreement ("séquestre conventionnel") is deposit by one or more parties of object (whether real or personal property) whose ownership is contested into hands of third party, who is obligated to deliver it at end of dispute to person deemed entitled to it. (C. C. 1956). Delivery of object by person holding it in deposit can only be made by consent of all parties involved, except that holder must return it to person from whom obtained if legally sufficient reason (as grave illness) compels him no longer to retain it.

In general, sequestration may only be ordered by courts ("judicial sequestration") when: (1) Title or possession of real or personal property is disputed among several persons; (2) personal property of debtor is attached to satisfy debt; (3) debtor voluntarily delivers property to sequestration to satisfy obligations arising from outstanding debt. (C.C. 1961). In fact, however, courts have not hesitated to order sequestration of property whenever such measure appeared necessary or useful for preservation of parties' rights.

Person who is custodian of the property has normal powers of administration, but not of disposition. Custodian has lien for payment of expenses incurred for preservation of sequestered object. (Cass. Civ. June 29, 1875). For liability of custodian, see decision of Cass. Comm. of Dec. 19, 1977.

SHIPPING:

French maritime law is mainly to be found in Code of Commerce which contains rules relating to legal position of ships, charter party and bill of lading, salvage and general average, shipowners and maritime sales. It should be noted that, in most cases, French law refers to treaties concluded by France for purpose of unifying international maritime law.

With respect to conflict of laws, general rule is that State may exercise its jurisdiction over ships which fly its flag. In order to be granted right to fly French flag, which is basis for intervention and protection under French law, it is necessary to comply with conditions under which France will grant its nationality to a ship.

These conditions are contained in Law No. 67-5 dated Jan. 3, 1967 (entered into force on Feb. 5, 1968 and modified by Law No. 96-151 dated Feb. 26, 1996), whereby ships shall be owned: (1) either by nationals of Contracting State of the European Community or, as regards merchant vessels or pleasure boats, by nationals of Contracting State of the European Economic Area (EEA) or, (2) entirely by companies having their head office in France or in another Contracting State of the European Community or, as regards merchant vessels or pleasure boats, in Contracting State of the EEA provided, in two latter cases, that ships remain under control of permanent establishment located in France. (Law of Feb. 26, 1996). However, head office of company may also be located in foreign country if treaty so provides. Another condition required by French law is delivery of registration certificate as French ship (acte de francisation) which must be kept on board. This certificate is also considered as evidence of shipowner's identity.

Ownership may be acquired by shipbuilding contract, sales contract, etc. Although designated as personal property, ships are subject to specific rules which are similar to rules relating to real property. In this respect, any transaction in relation to title of ownership must be in writing. In addition, ships may be mortgaged. Each mortgage

SHIPPING . . . *continued*

must be in writing and registered in public register. It is valid for period of ten years. Mortgage duly effected abroad may be recognized in France if ship becomes French. Each coowner is entitled to mortgage his own share. Under French law, following may be mortgaged: ship and its accessories or, if ship is lost, payment of indemnities relating to insurance, salvage, contribution to general average and loss and/or damage of ship. However, mortgages do not extend to freight. Mortgages rank immediately after maritime liens.

In accordance with International Convention for the Unification of Certain Rules relating to Maritime Liens and Mortgages to which French Law dated Jan. 3, 1967 refers, following may give rise to maritime liens on ship, on freight and on accessories of ship: (1) legal costs incurred in order to procure its sale and distribution of proceeds of sale, (2) tonnage dues, other public taxes etc., (3) claims arising out of employment contracts for master, crew and others, (4) remuneration for assistance and salvage and contribution of vessel in general average, (5) indemnities for collisions or other navigation accidents, (6) claims resulting from contracts entered into or acts done by master. Maritime liens are valid for period of one year except liens which are connected with ship's preservation or continuation of voyage which are extinguished at end of period of six months.

Rules relating to arrest of ships are to be found in Law of Jan. 3, 1967 (Arts. 70-74) and Decree No. 67-967 of Oct. 27, 1967 (Arts. 26-56) whereby ships may be arrested in France by creditors either for sale at public auction ("saisie-exécution") or as conservatory measure in order to prevent ship from leaving port ("saisie-conservatoire"). With respect to latter, ships may be arrested on basis that claim appears to be valid in principle. (Art. 29 of Decree dated Oct. 27, 1967 modified by Decree dated Feb. 24, 1971). It should be noted however that France is signatory to International Convention for the Unification of Certain Rules relating to the Arrest of Sea-Going Ships dated May 10, 1952. It follows that international rules must prevail over provisions of law of 1967 and be applied to arrest in France of any ship flying flag of Contracting State. As general rule, Convention states that ship may be arrested in respect of any maritime claim listed in Art. 1 but in respect of no other claim. Ship arrested may be released provided that sufficient bail or other security is furnished by person in possession of ship. As far as ship flying non-Contracting State flag is concerned, claimant has option: he may request arrest of ship on basis of 1952 Convention or rules provided for under Law of 1967.

Rules relating to charter party and bill of lading are to be found in Law No. 66-420 dated June 18, 1966, modified by Law No. 86-1292 dated Dec. 23, 1986. Former are complementary whereas latter, referring to rules provided for in International Convention for the Unification of Certain Rules of law relating to Bills of Lading (1924 Brussels Convention modified), are imperative. Under French law, bill of lading (B/L) has various functions: (1) it is evidence of contract of carriage concluded by shipper and carrier. Bill of lading must be at least in duplicate and signed by carrier; (2) it is prima facie evidence of receipt by carrier of goods; (3) it is equivalent to goods therein described. It follows that transfer of B/L means transfer of goods.

STATUTE OF FRAUDS:

See topic Frauds, Statute of.

STATUTES:

A law is voted by Parliament, promulgated by President within 15 days, unless he decides to refer it to Constitutional Court or to Parliament for further reading, and published in Journal Officiel, collection of Laws and Decrees. Publication in Journal Officiel of decree of promulgation and of text of law is formal requisite of legality. Law, inserted in Journal Officiel, is deemed known by all and becomes effective in Paris following day and elsewhere shortly thereafter unless otherwise stipulated.

Following are also published in Journal Officiel with force of law: Decrees from President, or from Prime Minister, and made for execution or application of laws (Const. of Oct. 4, 1958, art. 34); regulatory decrees of President or Prime Minister made in all non-legislative matters (Const., art. 37); ministerial or interministerial regulatory orders signed by one or more ministers which determine details of application of laws; ordinances from Government having force of law (Const., art. 38).

Orders issued by Republic Commissioners in their departments or by Communes are not published in Journal Officiel, but are contained in special publications.

See also topics Constitution and Government; Law Reports and Legal Materials.

TAXATION:

Taxation of Individuals.—Nonresident individual of France is taxed on his individual French source income or, if he disposes of residence in France, on three times rental value if higher than his French source income. However, residents of countries which have tax treaties with France are not subject to French income tax based on rental value of any such residence.

Foreigner who maintains his habitual residence in France or transfers his center of interest to France or either is salaried or independently employed in France is considered domiciled in France and is not subject to tax based on rental value of his residence. French citizens and foreigners having no residence in France are subject to taxation on income from French sources, but this rule is mitigated to some extent by tax treaties with various countries. For example, salaries received by U.S. employees for work accomplished in France are exempt from French tax: (i) If they spend less than 183 days there during year, (ii) if salary is paid by employer not resident of France, and (iii) if employee's salary is not deducted from French taxable income of French branch of American employer.

Individual income tax is assessed per household, i.e. on total income earned by taxpayer, taxpayer's spouse and dependent children. Family situation of a taxpayer, if he is a French citizen or a foreigner residing in France, is taken into consideration for computation of tax. Depending on his family status, taxpayer is assigned a certain number of "parts" (single, one part; married, two parts; each child, one-half part unless child is crippled or a dependent of solitary parent or starting with third child and thereafter, in which cases child is one part). With number of "parts" and amount of total net income, it is possible to determine amount of tax. (C.G.I. art. 194).

Rates vary from 0% to maximum of 56.8% for 1996 on 1995 taxable income (gross income less applicable deductions).

The following income tax, after reduction, is due from taxpayers with net taxable income of FRF 250,000: (a) if unmarried, FRF 81,605; (b) if married with no children, FRF 51,815; and (c) if married with one child, FRF 42,894.

If income tax does not exceed certain thresholds, taxpayers are entitled to some tax reduction.

Expenses incurred in earning income are generally deductible; employees are generally entitled to standard deduction of 10% for business expenses (or actual expenses, at their option), and additional deduction of 20%; thus, such persons are taxed on 72% of net salary. For 1995 salaries, amount of 10% deduction is limited to FRF 74,590 and amount of 20% deduction applies only to part of net salary not in excess of FRF 680,000 after first 10% deduction. (Art. 158 C.G.I.). Salaried persons holding more than 35% of capital of company, majority managers and partners in partnerships subject to corporate income tax are entitled to deduction of 20% on portion of their salary between FRF 1 and FRF 478,000 and 10% on portion between FRF 478,000 and FRF 680,000. Members of certain qualified tax associations ("associations agréées") carrying out independent activity are entitled to deduction of 20% on portion of income between FRF 1 and FRF 469,000 and 10% on portion of income between FRF 478,000 and FRF 680,000.

Itemized deductions are permitted for certain items (i.e. interests, gifts, life insurance, investment in new rental housing, equity contributions). Within certain limits deductions or tax credits are allowed for interest paid on purchase or construction of main residence, for life insurance premiums, for donations, for pensions paid to parents and for investment in new rental housing. For gross income from most real property, there is automatic 13% deduction (15% for certain rural real property) after which further deduction is made for interest on loan relating to property and/or its maintenance. This deduction is 25% for new rental housing. Losses pertaining to real estate may be offset against overall income if not exceeding FRF 70,000. Losses in excess of FRF 70,000 may be carried over for five years. Other systems of deductions apply to other types of income. Individual shareholder takes into income amount of dividend received grossed by 50% tax credit. He therefore has tax credit of 50% of dividend. E.g., for dividend of FRF 100 received by shareholder, his taxable income therefrom will be FRF 150 and he will have tax credit of FRF 50.

See also subhead Other Principal Taxes, infra.

Individual Annual Wealth Tax.—All individuals who are tax-domiciliaries of France are subject to wealth tax if their worldwide taxable assets, as of Jan. 1, 1996 are valued in excess of FRF 4,610,000. Wealth tax is also imposed on all individuals who, although not otherwise subject to taxation in France, have taxable assets located in France valued in excess of FRF 4,610,000 unless tax treaty stating otherwise applies. Professional assets, objects of art, collectors' items, industrial or literary, or artistic property rights are not subject to wealth tax. Investments in French securities by non-French residents are also exempt. Liabilities and other charges are deductible from gross value of taxable assets. Net taxable assets exceeding FRF 6,610,000 but less than FRF 7,500,000 are subject to 0.5% tax; net taxable assets exceeding FRF 7,500,000 but less than FRF 14,880,000 are subject to 0.7% tax; net taxable assets exceeding FRF 14,880,000 but less than FRF 23,100,000 are subject to 0.9% tax; net taxable assets exceeding FRF 23,100,000 but less than FRF 44,730,000 are subject to 1.2% tax; net taxable assets exceeding FRF 44,730,000 are subject to 1.5% tax. As from 1995, amount of wealth tax is increased by surtax of 10%. If amount of wealth tax and income tax exceeds 85% of net taxable income of individuals who are tax domiciliaries of France, wealth tax is capped. According to draft finance law for 1995, these rates could be increased by 10%.

Estate and Gift Taxes.—Rates of estate tax ("droits de succession") range from 5% to maximum of 60% of net estate depending on value of estate, and marital status of decedent, relationship between decedent and heirs or legatees, and nature of assets transfered.

When beneficiary is spouse or child, estate and gift tax rates range from 5% to 40%.

Against portion of the estate which is bequeathed to or inherited by the surviving spouse, there is tax exemption of FRF 330,000. For direct descendants (living or represented) or for ascendants, there is tax exemption of FRF 300,000. Such exemption may apply once every ten years.

Abatement of FRF 300,000 is granted for property passing to heir, legatee or donee whose ability to earn his livelihood is diminished as result of permanent physical handicap. Abatements are cumulative as of Jan. 1, 1992. Tax exemption of FRF 100,000 covers portion of estate inherited by each brother or sister who is single, divorced or separated and who fulfills age and other conditions.

Gift tax ("droit de donation") is, generally speaking, levied at same rate as estate tax except that tax on certain gifts to descendants (donation-partage) is reduced by 35% when donor is less than 65 years of age and by 25% when donor is 65 years of age or more but less than 75 years of age and gift is made prior to 12/31/1977. Other gifts made prior to such date may also benefit from reduced rate of taxation.

Income Tax on Companies.—Corporations ("Sociétés Anonymes" or "Sociétés par Actions Simplifiées"), Limited Liability Companies ("Sociétés à Responsabilité Limitée"), and "Sociétés en Commandite par Actions" are subject to corporate income tax. Partnerships as well as joint ventures ("Sociétés en Participation") are taxed as passed through entities unless they elect to be subject to corporate income tax. Other entities ("Sociétés en Commandite Simple", "Entreprises Unipersonnelles à Responsabilité Limitée") may be subject to either corporate tax or individual income tax depending upon their shareholders, their activity, etc. Companies created in specific areas benefit from certain favorable tax treatments.

Corporate income tax is applied at rate of 36.66% for financial years ending on or after Jan. 1, 1995.

Consolidated Return Groups.—Group may elect to file consolidated return if it meets following conditions: (i) Parent company must not be 95% controlled by another corporation subject to French income tax; and (ii) parent company must directly or indirectly hold at least 95% of stock of electing subsidiaries.

If these conditions are met, consolidated taxable income of group is determined by combining taxable incomes and deficits of members of group. This total is subject to adjustments designed to avoid double taxation or double deductions and to neutralize

TAXATION . . . *continued*
certain operations within group. Group's net taxable income is then subject to corporate income tax.

Withholding Taxes.—Dividends paid by French companies to French residents and companies are not subject to withholding tax. Dividends paid to nonresidents are subject to withholding tax of 25%. With respect to dividends paid to American residents by French company, withholding tax is imposed, under tax treaty, at reduced rate of 15%. Treaty further reduces this withholding tax to 5% when dividends are paid by French company to American company (entitled to Treaty benefits) holding at least 10% of capital of company. This 25% withholding tax rate is reduced by other tax treaties entered into by France. It is not levied, subject to certain conditions, if beneficiary of dividends is EU corporation.

C.G.I., Art. 242 quater provides that residents of States having concluded tax treaties with France may benefit from tax credit attached to dividends paid to French residents. U.S. residents may, subject to certain conditions, receive such tax credit.

Foreign corporations are subject to 36.66% tax on income realized through permanent establishment in France or if it engages in complete commercial cycle in France (e.g., buying and selling merchandise in France) or has agent in France with authority to bind company. Most tax treaties (including U.S. treaty) limit liability of foreign corporations to such tax to those having permanent establishment or agent in France.

In addition, under Art. 115 "quinquies" of C.G.I., profits derived from French sources by foreign companies are deemed distributed annually to shareholders not having their domicile or head office in France. 25% withholding tax is thus imposed on after corporate tax profits of French branch. Such withholding may be reduced by international tax treaties and is subject to later adjustment or refund if (i) amount subject to withholding tax exceeds total income distributed by foreign company or (ii) foreign company can demonstrate that amounts were distributed to French residents. This 25% tax is generally reduced or eliminated by most tax treaties.

For American companies having permanent establishments in France, such branch profit withholding tax is, pursuant to Franco-American Tax Treaty, imposed at rate of 5% of after corporate tax profits of permanent establishment.

"Précompte" is special tax of 50% of amounts distributed by company to residents or to nonresidents which applies when company distributes income which was not previously taxed at full standard rate (36.66% in 1996) or which was earned more than five years before year of distribution. It is paid by company. Residents of countries which have tax treaties with France are granted either credit equal to 50% of dividend received or receive repayment of sum equal to "précompte" paid by French firm. This sum is treated as dividend and as such is subject to withholding tax.

Deductibility of interest payments made by French company to shareholders is permitted for tax purposes if company's capital is entirely paid up. (Ordinance of Sept. 28, 1967). Also, if lending shareholder or shareholders are (i) subject to corporate tax and (ii) considered as controlling or managing company or more than 50% of voting rights or capital of company, interest deduction will not be allowed where amounts loaned exceed 150% of capital of borrowing company, except if loan is from French parent company to subsidiary as well as in case of certain tax treaties. Deductible interest paid to controlling shareholder(s) limited to average rate on private bonds (7.72 in 1995).

Withholding on Interest Payments.—Interest payments to foreign residents are generally exempt. Some exceptions apply (e.g., certain shareholders' loans) in which case, interest payments are subject to withholding tax at rates of 15% to 50% depending upon nature and term of debt as well as applicable tax treaty (if any).

Withholding Tax on Other Income.—Other income received by non-French residents may be subject to withholding tax. Royalties and remuneration of services are subject to withholding tax at 33.33% unless rate is reduced by applicable treaties.

International Tax Evasion.—Following provisions are intended to defeat international tax evasion: (1) C.G.I. art. 57 reintegrates into income taxable in France profits indirectly transferred to an enterprise located outside France by a French company controlling it or controlled by it or without any control situation if foreign enterprise is located in tax haven country; (2) sums received by foreign company for services rendered by one or more individuals or companies may be taxable to latter if: (a) latter controls foreign company, (b) latter cannot show foreign company has industrial or commercial activity other than rendering of taxable service, or (c) if foreign company is established in tax haven (C.G.I., art. 155A); (3) payments made by French domiciliaries to foreign domiciliaries having favored tax situation are deductible by French domiciliaries only if it can be proved payments are for real goods or services at normal prices (C.G.I. art. 238A); (4) companies owning French real property may be subject to annual tax equal to 3% of market value of those properties. Numerous exceptions apply, notably to French or foreign companies resident of countries having tax treaties with France, provided they disclose certain information to French tax administration (C.G.I. art. 990 D to 990 H); (5) French corporation owning directly or indirectly 10% or more of tax haven company or branch is subject to 36.66% corporate tax on its pro rata share of such company's profits unless proof is provided that operation of subsidiary in tax haven country does not have effect of localizing income in tax favored country. (C.G.I. art. 209 B).

Other Principal Taxes.—

Payroll Tax and Social Benefits.—See topic Labor Relations, subhead Payroll Tax and Social Benefits.

Personal Property Tax ("taxe d'habitation").—Charged annually against every individual or company having at his disposal on Jan. 1 of each year a dwelling and is based on assumed unfurnished rental value of property. Rate varies from one commune to another. Assets subject to taxe professionnelle are exempt from taxe d'habitation. (C.G.I. arts. 1407 et seq.).

License Tax ("Taxe Professionnelle").—Law No. 75-678 of July 29, 1975 replaced former "Patente" with "Taxe Professionnelle," affecting most persons engaged in commercial or professional activities. Base for "Taxe Professionnelle" is rental value of tangible fixed assets and 18% of all salaries paid previous year (1/10 of gross collections for professionals and certain middlemen employing less than five salaried workers). License tax can be limited to 3.5% to 4% of value-added depending upon turnover of taxpayer. Value-added is difference between: (i) Turnover plus ancillary income, plus grants and subsidies, plus rebates obtained, plus inventories at year end; (ii) purchase of commodities, plus purchase of services, plus rebates on sales granted by company to clients, plus miscellaneous management expenses (telephone, other facilities, etc.) plus transport expenses, plus inventories at beginning of year. Special exemptions apply with respect to newly formed companies, new branches and environmental protection.

Stamp Duty.—Deeds made before notary or other public official, agreements deposited in files of notary or attached to deed, agreements mandatorily or voluntarily subject to Registration Duty (see that catchline below), subscription blanks, proxies for stockholders' meetings and certain other limited categories of documents listed in art. 34 ff. of Law of Mar. 15, 1963, are subject to stamp duty. Amount of duty is on a per page basis, varying with size of page. (C.G. I.905 et 907). Minimum duty is FRF 34 for both sides of 21 x 29.7 cm page but documents containing several pages written on one side only with other side indelibly cancelled need only pay half duty. (Law of Dec. 29, 1978).

Value Added Tax ("Taxe sur la Valeur Ajoutée").—Value added tax is noncumulative tax levied at every taxable stage of production, distribution, on delivery of goods or services. Burden of tax is generally borne by final consumer.

Normal TVA rate is 20.6% and super low rate of 5.5% is applicable.

Deliveries of goods are subject to TVA if goods are located in France. By way of exception, supply and acquisition of goods between EEC member states are subject to special regime under which supply of good is generally exempt in country of departure and taxable in country of destination. Exports to non-EEC states from France are exempt from TVA. Real estate transactions and related services are, subject to certain conditions, subject to TVA if real property is located in France. Rentals are subject to TVA if property is furnished or exploited in France. Specific types of services including engineering, accounting, insurance and advertising services, as well as licensing of patents, trademarks, copyrights and other similar rights are subject to TVA when: (a) Parties providing and benefitting from such services are residents of France; (b) party providing services is resident of France and beneficiary is resident of Common Market country where TVA is not applicable to services rendered; or (c) party providing services is established outside of France and beneficiary is resident of France and subject to TVA in France. Services rendered by qualified member of legal profession are subject to TVA.

Registration Duty (Droits d'Enregistrement).—This tax is paid on transactions evidenced by written documents and, in some cases, on transfers, even when not so evidenced. According to their nature some documents are taxed at a fixed rate (e.g., FRF 500 for commercial agreements) and there is no compulsory time limit for their registration. Other transactions (e.g. sale of going concern transfer of clientele, agreements having effect of enabling one contracting party to conduct activity previously conducted by other contracting party) are taxed at proportional rate and must be registered within prescribed time limit (usually one month). This tax does not apply to documents signed outside of France except for transfers which would be taxable even in absence of document.

Capital Gains Tax.—Pursuant to Law No. 76-660 of July 19, 1976 individuals are taxed on certain capital gains by inclusion of such capital gains, determined according to nature of asset and length of time held, in overall income. Sale of professional practice with gross revenues of less than FRF 350,000 and sale of business with gross revenues of less than FRF 1,000,000, or FRF 300,000 if business consists in performance of services, are exempt from capital gains tax if practice or business concerned has been principal activity for at least five years prior to sale. Otherwise sale of assets by professionals (corporations or individuals) are generally taxed as follows: capital gains from sale of fixed assets are classified according to long term (assets held two years or more) or short term (assets held less than two years). Amount which was deducted from taxes on basis of depreciation of any asset is short term gain, even if assets are held more than two years. Net short term gain (difference between short term gain and short term loss) during same fiscal year is taxed as ordinary income. Net short term loss is deductible from ordinary income and is subject to ordinary rules of carry-forward of losses. Net long term capital gain (difference between long term gain and long term loss) is taxed at special rate of 19% for corporate activities, 16% (plus social taxes of 3.9%) for commercial and noncommercial activities. Net long term capital loss can be used only to offset net long term capital gains for fiscal year and ten succeeding years.

Capital gains taxable to individuals include following:

(1) Real Property. Under art. 150C of General Tax Code, sale of principal residence is generally exempt from capital gains tax. Otherwise determination is made based on nature of property and time it is held. Capital gains from sale of buildings and land (other than farmland or property on which purchaser intends to effect construction) are included in gross income if occurring within two years after purchase. For sales made after two years of purchase, capital gain, if any, is calculated as follows for persons whose activity is not trading in real estate. First, purchase price, including related expenses, is increased by official inflation rate during holding period. Second, gross fiscal capital gain so determined is reduced by 5% for each year of ownership beginning with third year. Therefore, sales of properties held for more than 22 years are exempt from capital gains tax. Remark: Following capital gains are also exempt from tax: Capital gains realized by resident or nonresident individual who was French tax resident for at least one year, upon sale of his main residence or of other building if individual does not own his main residence (this last exemption may only apply once); those realized on sale of inexpensive agricultural land, and those realized on sale of property when total real estate value does not exceed FRF 400,000. If exemptions do not apply nonresident individuals are generally taxed at 33 1/3%.

Profits from Construction: For resident individuals, profits from construction are generally taxed at capital gains rates. Nonresident individuals are taxed at flat rate of 33 1/3%, save for case of nonresident who actually oversees or manages construction of building in France to whom 50% rate applies.

(2) Gains realized upon sale of shares, by individuals, are generally taxed at 16% (plus social charges of 3.9%). If, however, shareholder owns less than 25% interest in company during five years preceding sale, and total transaction does not exceed FRF 200,000 in 1996 per calendar year, capital gain is exempt. Capital gains realized by nonresident are exempt.

(3) Precious metal (gold, silver and platinum) is taxed at rate of 7.5% calculated on sales price.

See Topical Index in front part of this volume.

TAXATION . . . *continued*

(4) Antiques more than 100 years old, (objects, collectors' items and jewellery) are also taxed at rate of 7% of sales price in private sale and rate of 4.5% sales price in public sale.

General Social Tax. ("Contribution sociale généralisée").—All individuals domiciled in France are subject to 2.9% tax based on (1) income derived from activity, or from substitute to such activity, and (2) income or gains derived from property.

Tax Treaties.—See Topic Treaties.

TORTS:

Liability in tort (responsabilité civile) is based on Civil Code (arts. 1382-1386) and has been further developed by case law. Basic principle is that any person by whose fault ("faute") damage is caused to another is obligated to repair damage. (C. C. 1382). Plaintiff must prove his injury, defendant's acts or omissions constituting fault, and the causation. Fault in this context includes both intentional wrongs and negligence. (C. C. 1383). Misuse of legal right is deemed to be covered by Art. 1382. Such misuse includes use of legal right with malevolence or other improper purpose. Person liable for damages must fully compensate injured party no matter what degree of fault. Party at fault may, partly or totally, be exonerated from liability if he proves that damage results from force majeure, fault of victim or act of third party.

Virtual absolute liability is, however, created under arts. 1384 and 1385 when damage is caused by act of a person under supervision of defendant (employer-employee, master-servant, parent-child, teacher-student relations) or by a thing under control ("garde") of defendant (e.g. automobile), or by animal which is or should be under control of defendant. Liability in these cases can be avoided as in those of fault. Special provision makes owner of real property liable to any person for injuries caused through defect in construction or maintenance of property. (C. C. 1386).

Economic torts and product liability have been widely developed by application of the principle of art. 1382. See topic Unfair Competition. With respect to product liability, EEC Directive dated July 25, 1985 relating to Approximation of the Laws, Regulations and Administrative Provisions of the Member-States Concerning Liability for Defective Products deals with this matter. Words "Product Liability" refers to liability imposed on manufacturer, distributor or seller of defective product for injuries or damages to property caused by product. As general rule, Directive imposes system based upon non-fault liability which means that, in order to recover damages, person who suffered damage merely has to prove the existence of product defect, damage and causal connection between damage and defect. Although France has already been condemned by European Court of Justice, France has not yet implemented this Directive in French law.

In addition to general rules of liability, special systems of liability exist. For instance, operators of aircraft bear strict liability pursuant to Art. L322.3 of Decree of Mar. 30, 1967 and by Warsaw Convention. Damages for passengers are limited to higher of FRF 750,000 or any figure set through revision of Warsaw Convention. (Law no. 76-529 of June 18, 1976).

France has ratified United Nations Convention on Contracts for the International Sale of Goods (J.O. Dec. 27, 1987) applicable to transactions between parties established in different countries, which modifies French rules concerning liability arising out of such contracts.

With respect to motor vehicle liability, Law No. 85-677 dated July 5, 1985 provides not only for special rules of liability but also for specific system of compensation in favor of victims (see Insurance Code). The Guarantee Fund ("Fonds de Garantie") provides compensation to victims (or their heirs or successors in interest) for personal injuries suffered in accidents including where vehicle involved is unidentified or uninsured or when insurer of vehicle is insolvent. (Art. L-420-1 of Insurance Code).

TRADEMARKS AND TRADENAMES:

See topic Industrial Property Rights.

TREATIES:

Among other treaties, France is signatory of: Treaty of Rome (European Economic Community); Treaty of Paris (European Coal and Steel Community); European Atomic Energy Treaty (Euratom); European Bank for Recovery and Development (BERD); General Agreement on Tariffs and Trade (G.A.T.T.); North Atlantic Treaty. The Maastricht Treaty on European Union signed Feb. 7, 1992 in force since Nov. 1, 1993 amends the three European Treaties (Rome, Paris and EURATOM). Those three Communities are not changed into a Union but unity of States is created which is legally separate from the Communities and is juxtaposed to them, yet entwined with them in many ways. Cooperation Agreements exist with most former French Colonies. See topic Constitution and Government.

For Treaty of Establishment with U.S., see topic Foreign Investment. A Consular Convention with U.S., replacing and terminating Consular Convention of 1853, was signed on July 18, 1966 and entered into force on Jan. 7, 1968.

France also ratified many treaties including:

In relation to International Contracts.—

Uniform Law Conventions.—The United Nations Convention on Contracts for International Sale of Goods dated Apr. 11, 1980 (The Vienna Convention); The Geneva Convention on Agency in the International Sale of Goods dated Feb. 17, 1983.

Conflict Rules Conventions.—The Convention on the Law Applicable to International Sales of Goods dated June 15, 1955; The Rome Convention on the Law Applicable to Contractual Obligations dated June 19, 1980; The Hague Convention on the Law Applicable to Agency dated Mar. 14, 1978; The Hague Convention on the Law Applicable to Products Liability dated Oct. 2, 1973.

In relation to International Disputes.—

Arbitration Conventions.—The New York Convention on the Recognition and Enforcement of Foreign Arbitral Awards dated June 10, 1958; The Geneva European Convention on International Commercial Arbitration dated Apr. 21, 1960.

Litigations Conventions.—The Hague Convention on the Service Abroad of Judicial and Extrajudicial Documents in Civil or Commercial Matters dated Nov. 15, 1965; The Hague Convention on the Taking of Evidence Abroad in Civil or Commercial Matters dated Mar. 18, 1970; The Brussels Convention on Jurisdiction and the Enforcement of Judgments in Civil and Commercial Matters dated Sept. 27, 1968.

In relation to Tax Treaties.—France has entered into double taxation treaties in respect of income and/or capital with following countries: Algeria, Argentina, Australia, Austria, Bahrein, Bangladesh, Belgium, Benin, Brazil, Bulgaria, Burkina Faso, Cameroon, China (People's Republic of), Canada, Central African Republic, Commores and Mayotte, Congo, Czech Republic and Slovak Republic, Cyprus, Denmark, Ecuador, Egypt, Finland, Gabon, Germany, Ghana, Greece, Hungary, Iceland, India, Indonesia, Iran, Ireland, Israel, Italy, Ivory Coast, Japan, Jordan, Kuwait, Lebanon, Luxembourg, Madagascar, Malawi, Malaysia, Mali, Malta, Mauritania, Mauritius, Mexico, Monaco, Morocco, Netherlands, New Caledonia, New Zealand, Niger, Nigeria, Norway, Oman, Pakistan, Philippines, Poland, Polynesia (French), Portugal, Quatar, Republic of Russia, Rumania, Saint Pierre et Miquelon, Saudi Arabia, Senegal, Singapore, South Africa, South Korea, Spain, Sri-Lanka, Sweden, Switzerland, Thailand, Togo, Tunisia, Turkey, United Arab Emirates, U.K., Venezuela, Yugoslavia (France is honoring Yugoslavia Treaty with respect to Bosnia-Herzegovina, Croatia, Macedonia and Slovania) and Zambia.

Double Taxation Treaties Recently Entered into Force.—Convention with Japan for avoidance of double taxation and prevention of fiscal evasion with respect to taxes on income: this convention, signed on Mar. 3, 1995, entered into force on Mar. 24, 1996 and replaced 1964 tax treaty as amended. (Décret May 13, 1996 in J.O. May 16, 1996). This convention will apply from Jan. 1st, 1997; Convention with U.S. for avoidance of double taxation and prevention of fiscal evasion with respect to taxes on income and capital: this convention, signed on Aug. 31, 1994, entered into force on Dec. 30, 1995 and replaced 1967 tax treaty as amended. (Décret Mar. 15, 1996 in J.O. Mar. 22, 1996); Convention with South Africa for avoidance of double taxation and prevention of fiscal evasion with respect to taxes on income: this convention signed on Nov. 9, 1993 entered into force on Nov. 1st, 1995; Convention with Sweden for avoidance of double taxation and prevention of fiscal evasion with respect to taxes on inheritance and settlement: this convention, signed on June 8, 1994, entered into force on Feb. 1st, 1996 and replaced 1936 tax treaty as amended. (Décret Mar. 11, 1996 in J.O. Mar. 16, 1996).

Double Taxation Treaties Recently Signed But Not Yet Entered into Force.—Convention with Bolivia for avoidance of double taxation and prevention of fiscal evasion with respect to taxes on income and capital: signed on Dec. 15, 1994; Convention with Ghana for avoidance of double taxation and prevention of fiscal evasion with respect to taxes on income: signed on Apr. 5, 1993; Convention with Israel for avoidance of double taxation and prevention of fiscal evasion with respect to taxes on income and capital: signed on July 31, 1995 and will replace 1963 tax treaty; Convention with Pakistan for avoidance of double taxation and prevention of fiscal evasion with respect to taxes on income and capital: signed on June 15, 1994 and will replace 1966 tax treaty; Convention with Zimbabwe for avoidance of double taxation and prevention of fiscal evasion with respect to taxes on income and capital: signed on Dec. 15, 1993.

Pending Protocols Not Yet Entered Into Force.—Amendment to 1976 Convention with Cameroon: Mar. 31, 1994; Amendment to Convention with Norway: Apr. 7, 1995; Amendment to 1977 Convention with Malta: July 8, 1994.

Other More Limited Tax Agreement Exist With Following Countries.—French Polynesia, Monaco, Panama, Quebec, Syria, Zaïre.

See also topic Judgments.

TRUSTS:

Concept of "trust" does not exist under French law. Dispositions of property whereby the donee or the heir or legatee under the will is required to keep property intact and transfer it to a third person are void both as to the beneficiary and the trustee. (C. C. 896). Parents may provide that the whole or a part of their property not belonging to "réserve" (see topic Forced Heirship) shall vest in child for life, with remainder over to child or children of such child. But no further entailing is permitted. Person having no children may create life estate in disposable part of his property in favor of his brothers and sisters with remainder to children of life tenant. Remainder must in all cases be to children indiscriminately; it may not be to certain of them. Guardian may be appointed to carry out trust. (C. C. 1048-1074).

Note, however, that a legacy "de residuo" is valid. This type of legacy passes to second legatee upon death of first legatee. However, first legatee is not obliged to keep principal of legacy intact.

Foreign trusts are generally recognized by French courts unless incompatible with French public international order. Trustee in such case is permitted to exercise certain property rights under French law. His powers and duties are governed by terms of trust and by rules of equity. (J.C.P. 1975 II, 18168). Foreign trusts involving French real estate are deemed valid only as to disposable portion (see topic Forced Heirship). With respect to succession, French case law normally treats trust as transparent entity for tax purposes, as trustee is not deemed owner of corpus.

Foundations.—In essence, foundations consist of res administered for cultural, social, scientific or charitable purpose by board of directors in legal form analogous to an association. (See topic Associations.) Model by-laws for foundations have been prepared by administrative court, Conseil d'Etat, and regularly updated by such court. Request must be made through Prefecture for letter of approval issued by Conseil d'Etat. This letter of authorization establishes foundation as legal entity capable of receiving gifts or legacies. Gifts and legacies to scientific, cultural or artistic foundations are exempt from gift or estate taxes, provided Ministry of Finance certifies foundation as truly disinterested. (C. G. I. 795). There is special register for associations and foundations. (See topic Records.)

Testator cannot create foundation by will, but he can give universal legacy to named person, upon condition that latter establish foundation. Such instructions, however, are merely precatory and named person is free to disregard wishes of testator, remaining nonetheless universal legatee.

New type of foundation, "foundation d'enterprise," was created by Law No. 90-559 of July 4, 1990 in order to encourage activities of foundations. This law allows such

TRUSTS . . . *continued*
foundations to be created for limited periods and simplifies necessary administrative authorizations.

UNFAIR COMPETITION:

Unfair competition ("concurrence déloyale") is tort, developed by case law from basic fault concept of C. C. 1382, that any person whose fault in act or omission causes damage to another is obligated to repair damage. Torts of this special type include: Denigration of competitors; creation of confusion by using tradenames, symbols, wrappings or containers imitating those of competitors; claiming falsely to be purveyor to government or particular persons or to be holder of prizes or medals; copying of advertisements or catalogues of another in manner calculated to deceive public; manipulative use of famous trademarks or products to attract clients and sell competing items to them; bribing or inducing employees of another to leave their employer or to reveal trade secrets or otherwise injure their employer. Fraud need not be shown, negligence or fault is sufficient.

Objective and scientifically based criticism of product for purpose of informing public and not of denigrating product not deemed unfair competition.

Advertising by comparison of resale prices for identical products was long deemed to be unfair competition but has recently been allowed by statute. (Law of Jan. 18, 1992, J.O. Feb. 1, 1992, p. 53).

See also topic Monopolies and Restraint of Trade.

WILLS:

Mutual wills or wills executed in one instrument by two or more persons in favor of a third are invalid. (C. C. 968). A will may be: (1) Holographic; (2) notarial; (3) mystic. (C. C. 969).

The only essentials as to the form of a holographic will are that it must be entirely handwritten, dated (date must be clearly indicated) and signed by testator. (C. C. 970). Recent case law has admitted that, if will is not dated, proof of date can be settled by internal elements or external elements, if latter find their principles and roots in some internal elements they confirm.

A notarial will is one executed in the presence of two notaries or of one notary and two witnesses. Testator dictates his will to notary who writes it down word for word in continuous and simultaneous presence either of two witnesses or of second notary. Once dictation is completed, will is re-read and signed by testator who confirms that it expresses his desires and countersigned by notary, witnesses and, if such be the case, second notary. (C. C. 971-974).

A mystic will is drawn up by the testator or some third person and the document is then signed by him and sealed up. The document so sealed is handed to the notary in the presence of at least two witnesses in whose presence the notary encloses the sealed document in another covering which is also sealed. The testator must make a declaration to the effect that the paper contains his will and that it is written by himself or by a third person and signed by him. A protocol of such declaration is drawn up by the notary on the outer covering, and this protocol is signed by the notary, the testator and the witnesses. These acts must be uninterrupted by any other business. (C. C. 976).

Witnesses must be French citizens and of age. No legatee and no relative (up to and including fourth degree) of legatee, and no clerk of notary can be witness to notarial will. Husband and wife cannot both be witnesses to same will. (C. C. 975, 980). Special rules govern wills made by persons in armed services. (C. C. 981-984).

French citizens while abroad may make holographic wills or wills in accordance with form prescribed by law of place where will is made. (C. C. 999). Wills made by alien in France may be made in accordance with French law or with national law of alien. While real property situated in France is subject to French law (C. C. 3), alien residing abroad may dispose of same by will made in accordance with form prescribed by law of place where drawn. Will must be registered in France at place where property is situated and, as is generally required for wills drawn up outside of France for their execution as to both real and personal property situated in France, at place where decedent had last or last known domicile in France. (C. C. 1000). Wills which do not respect above mentioned rules are invalid. (C. C. 1001).

A minor who has attained the age of 16 can dispose, by will, of his property to the extent of one-half the amount that he would be permitted by law to dispose of were he a major. (C. C. 904).

Legacies.—There are residuary or universal legacies ("legs universels"), general legacies ("legs èa titre universel") and specific legacies ("legs particuliers"). (C. C. 1003, 1010, 1014). Residuary or universal legatee has to get delivery of property from heirs who are entitled to reserve (C. C. 1004; see topic Forced Heirship), but if there are none he is seized as matter of right (C. C. 1006). Nevertheless, he must obtain possession by order of President of Court if will is holographic or mystic. General legatee must get delivery of his legacy from heirs entitled to reserve or, if none, from universal or residuary legatee. (C. C. 1011). Both universal or residuary legatee and general legatee are liable for payment of debts and charges of succession and of specific legacies according to proportion of their legacies to entire succession. (C. C. 1009, 1012).

A general legacy gives to the legatee a right to goods bequeathed as of date of death. Legatee may enforce his rights against heirs, except for amount of legal reserve, and costs are borne by estate. But specific legatee cannot take possession or claim income or interest until he has brought his action for delivery (C. C. 1014) except in case of annuity or pension for nourishment or where testator has provided to contrary (C. C. 1015).

Wills can be revoked in whole or in part only by subsequent will or by specific act of revocation executed before notary. Case law does not permit proof of contents of lost or destroyed will. Subsequent will which does not contain express revocation clause cancels in prior will only such provisions as are incompatible with these contained in subsequent will. (C. C. 1036).

Estate tax treaty between France and U.S. entered into effect Oct. 17, 1949. New estate and gift tax treaty between France and U.S. entered into effect on Oct. 1, 1980. France ratified, on Dec. 24, 1967, Hague Convention on Conflicts of Law relating to Form of Testamentary Dispositions to which U.S. is not signatory.

Recently, Art. 1 of Decree dated June 13, 1966 has been replaced by Art. 1 of Decree No. 94-119, dated Dec. 20, 1994 which states that acceptation of legacies by public companies, religious associations and all others covered by Art. 6 of law of 1901 must be authorized by "Préfet" having jurisdiction where association is located.

See also topics Forced Heirship; Notaries Public.

See Topical Index in front part of this volume.

GERMANY LAW DIGEST REVISER

Boesebeck, Barz & Partner
Darmstadter Landstrasse 125
D-60598 Frankfurt, am Main, Germany
Telephone: (49)(69) 96236-0
Fax: (49)(69) 96236-100
Berlin, Germany office: Schlueterstrasse 37, 10629 Berlin. Telephone: (49)(30) 88 57 45-0. Fax: (49)(30) 88 57 45-99.
Dresden, Germany office: Heideparkstrasse 4, 01099 Dresden. Telephone: (49)(351) 82961-0. Fax: (49)(351) 82961-99.

Reviser Profile

Members of Firm (Partners):

Albrecht Stockburger
Dr. Georg Hohner
Eckart Wilcke
Dr. Günter Paul
Dr. Richard H. Sterzinger
Dr. Harald Seisler
Nikolaus Ley
Werner Michael Waldeck
Dr. Claudius Dechamps
Dr. Hinrich Thieme
Klaus Racky
Dr. Rainer Bommert
Dr. Volkmar Jesch
Dr. Thomas Lindemann
Ingo Winterstein
Dr. Alexander von Negenborn
Joachim Hilla
Dr. Hartwig Graf von Westerholt
Ursula Holler
Bernhard Kuhn
Oliver Felsenstein

of Counsel:

Dr. Rolf Berninger
Klaus H. Roquette

In addition, Boesebeck, Barz & Partner have a substantial number of associate lawyers on their staff.

History and General Description: The firm was founded in 1919 and has been based in Frankfurt since. The firm opened additional offices in Berlin and Dresden in 1990. The Warsaw office was opened in 1991 and the Zagreb office in 1994.

Boesebeck, Barz & Partner provides a broad range of legal service to the national and international corporate, industrial, trade and financial communities and numbers among its domestic and foreign clients major banks, service companies, retail chains and national and multi-national corporations active in practically all sectors of business.

Several of the partners are notaries (civil law notaries); several partners hold degrees from foreign law schools; several partners hold positions in corporate, public and professional bodies, and several partners are respected figures in the field of national and international arbitration.

Legal work is conducted regularly in German, English, French and Polish. Boesebeck, Barz & Partner maintains operating relations with law firms in virtually each of the countries of Europe and in the major business centers in order to handle international transactions.

Description of Practice Areas: The firm's major areas of practice are general corporate, mergers and acquisitions, finance, banking, litigation and arbitration, international trade and transactions, joint ventures, environment, utilities, real estate, anti-trust, tax, labor and employment, zoning and building, general representation.

The firm's general corporate practice encompasses all aspects of business law, including advice on doing business in Germany and establishment or incorporation of subsidiary companies for foreign parties. The firm has been involved in major mergers and acquisition transactions, representing participating corporations, or banks, investment banks or similar institutions.

The finance practice includes the entire range of financing vehicles, from public offerings to private placements of debt and equity securities, banking law, including establishment of banking institutions and all aspects of exchange law. The international trade and transactions practice provides advice, counselling and representation to domestic and foreign clients with respect to international trade regulations, export financing and licensing, foreign investments in Germany and German investments abroad, international sales and distributorships.

The anti-trust practice includes advice in the area of mergers and acquisitions, the national and international aspects of trade regulation, distributor-dealer relations, etc.

The full range of environmental matters includes representation in judicial and administrative proceedings, pertaining mainly to the chemical industry, retail chains, public utilities and the field of energy.

In real estate matters the firm represents investors, investment banks, developers, builders, contractors, both domestic and foreign, on new construction or purchase or sale of residential and commercial buildings and properties, leasing, on condominium conversion and sophisticated financings, including notarial conveyancing.

Tax advice is available in connection with the full range of transactions and other matters on which the firm advises its clients.

The practice in intellectual property handles matters involving trademarks, copyrights, patents, advertising, unfair competition and the like. Moreover, the firm practises in the field of computer law including software development, licensing and maintenance contracts.

The firm handles EEC related judicial and administrative proceedings.

In labor and employment law the firm handles a range of employment matters including the negotiating and drafting of labor agreements, the negotiation and documentation of individual and collective dismissals, etc.

For many years the firm has had an involvement with international litigation and arbitration. The firm has acted frequently in major arbitrations under various rules.

GERMANY: LAW DIGEST OF THE FEDERAL REPUBLIC OF GERMANY

(The following is a list of all Topics, including cross-references, covered in this Digest.)

GERMANY: LAW DIGEST OF THE FEDERAL REPUBLIC OF GERMANY

Revised for 1997 edition by

BOESEBECK, BARZ & PARTNER, of the Frankfurt/Main Bar, the Berlin Bar and the Dresden Bar

(Abbreviations used are: BGB, Bürgerliches Gesetzbuch, Civil Code of FRG; FRG, Federal Republic of Germany; GDR, German Democratic Republic; HGB, Handelsgesetzbuch, Commercial Code; KO, Konkursordnung, Bankruptcy Law; WG, Wechselgesetz, Act of Bills and Notes; ZGB, Zivilgesetzbuch, Civil Code of GDR; ZPO, Zivilprozessordnung, Code of Civil Procedure; RGBl., Reichsgesetzblatt, former Official Gazette; BGBl., Bundesgesetzblatt, Federal Statutes Gazette; GewO, Gewerbeordnugn, Industrial Code. On occasion, the above abbreviations for laws of the FRG are used for laws of the GDR bearing the same name; in such cases, the abbreviation is followed by a "/" and the specification FRG or GDR. Example: ZPO/FRG and ZPO/GDR.)

Germany is member of EU. See also European Union Law Digest.

PRELIMINARY NOTE:

Division of Germany.—With unconditional surrender after World War II responsibility for Government was assumed by four occupying powers, U.S., Great Britain, France and Soviet Union. Each power occupied specific zone of Germany; Berlin, although situated in Soviet Zone, was occupied by all four powers and was to be governed by inter-allied Authority. At Potsdam Conference it was agreed that, although program of decentralization should be carried out, Germany must be treated as single economic unit. Allies' plans for common policy in Germany proved abortive because of their own divergent interests, and increasing deadlock characterized meetings of Allied Control Council. In Mar. 1948, Soviet Union left Allied Control Council, thus initiating division of Germany into Western state, Federal Republic of Germany (Bundesrepublik Deutschland) and into Eastern state, German Democratic Republic (Deutsche Demokratische Republik).

In Western zones much administrative responsibility was handed over to Germans during 1946/1947, and State (Länder) Governments were set up, and state parliaments (Landtage) elected. In 1948 German Economic Council adopted plan providing for Federal German Government for three western zones and summoning of constituent assembly, without cooperation of Soviet Union and consequently without integration of zone occupied by Soviet Union. Parliamentary Council, elected by Landtage of Länder of three Western zones met at Bonn on Sept. 1st, 1948 to draft constitution. Basic Law (FRG) was passed by Parliamentary Council on May 8, 1949, four days later approved by Western Allied military governors, proclaimed on May 23, 1949 and put into effect next day.

GDR formed in 1949 in zone occupied by Soviet Union as response to creation of FRG. Constitutions drafted by "National Council", resolved by "National Congress" on May 5, 1949 and approved by Soviet Military Administration. New "National Council" constituted on Oct. 7, 1949 as provisional "People's Chamber" (Parliament) put constitution into force. By law of July 23, 1952 five states (Länder) of GDR were dissolved and replaced by 14 districts.

Reunification of Germany.—Through so-called Peaceful Revolution, which was promoted primarily by grass-roots movements in GDR and in eastern part of Berlin, political, social and legal structures in this area underwent complete change as of Fall of 1989. This transformation culminated in transacted reunification of both parts of Germany. Since GDR and East Berlin joined FRG in accordance with Art. 23 of "Basic Law" (Grundgesetz) as effective until Aug. 31, 1990, these two parts once again form political, economic and legal unit. Resolution to join FRG was passed by GDR parliament (Volkskammer) on Aug. 23, 1990. It became effective on Oct. 3, 1990. On this day reunification of Germany was accomplished.

This development was preceded by initial "State Treaty on the Creation of a Monetary, Economic and Social Union" (Staatsvertrag über die Schaffung einer Währungs-, Wirtschafts- und Sozialunion), which became effective already on July 1, 1990. Objectives of contract were, among others, to prepare national unity and to install social market economy also in GDR. With this contract, Deutsch Mark became only legal currency of GDR. Contract further provided that significant parts of Federal German economic law (esp. commercial and corporate law, bank law, and laws governing insurance and competition) as well as labour and social legislation be adopted by GDR.

Act of GDR joining FRG in accordance with Art. 23 of "Basic Law" did not, in fact, require any special legal act on part of FRG, since resolution to join became effective simply as result of its declaration. Nevertheless, governments of both German states agreed to stipulated terms of union in second comprehensive State treaty, so-called "Unification Treaty" (Einigungsvertrag).

Furthermore, external aspects of reunification were to be settled in cooperation with the four occupying powers. Occupied status of Germany still prevailed. In particular, question of alliance had to be settled, whereby pressure exerted primarily by USA to ensure that unified Germany belong to NATO (and only to NATO) posed a certain problem. However, this point of view also met with general approval in both parts of Germany. These issues were negotiated with the four occupying powers in so-called 2-plus-4 talks. Break-through came on July 16, 1990, when Soviet leadership finally declared its willingness to refrain from insisting—even temporarily—that new Germany also be member of Warsaw Pact and to withdraw Soviet troops from Germany within four-year transition period.

2-plus-4 talks were concluded on Sept. 12, 1990 in Moscow, when the four occupying powers and two German states came to agreement of sovereignty, granting reunified Germany full national sovereignty. Until this agreement became effective, the four powers temporarily refrained from exercising their rights of dominion, so that as of Oct. 3, 1990, Germany has essentially become, albeit only provisionally, sovereign once again. In meantime, parliaments and responsible organs of the four allied powers have either ratified or accepted this agreement (treaty between the two Germanys and the four allied powers on Final Arrangement for Germany). Agreement became effective Mar. 15, 1991. By that date unrestricted sovereignty of reunified Germany has been definitively reestablished.

Second State treaty—Unification Treaty—comprises two appendices with approximately 250 pages of legislation governing application of Federal German law to area of now former GDR, as well as perpetuation of GDR law with, in some respects, highly complex transitional stipulations. Basically, however, simple process whereby GDR joins FRG in accordance with Art. 23 of "Basic Law" as effective until Aug. 31, 1990 and accompanying dissolution of GDR automatically imply that Federal German law is now effective in all of Germany.

Following sections will indicate principal points of Unification Treaty with special regard to transitional stipulations for area of former GDR. Owing to multitude of such regulations, subject cannot be dealt with in its entirety.

Unification Treaty also contains provisions for reprivatisation and restitution of confiscated property in realm of former GDR. Seperate topic (Reprivatisation and Restitution) is devoted to this point in following remarks. Major source of controversy and constitutional reservations is fact that Unification Treaty favors acceptance of property confiscations which occurred between end of Second World War and foundation of GDR. Meanwhile, Federal Constitutional Court has decided that these confiscations are upheld. (See topic Reprivatisation and Restitution.)

ABSENTEES:

In absence abroad person may generally delegate authority to any person of full capacity. It is usual to give power of attorney. Power may be given to sue or accept service of proceedings, but strictly construed. Foreigner conducting business in Germany must appoint resident representative responsible to authorities; see topic Aliens, subhead Status.

If absentee's whereabouts unknown and his property interests are at stake, upon request of interested party "curator absentis" may be appointed, who acts for absentee at his risk and at his charge—also in actions—until absentee reappears or appoints attorney. (BGB, §§1911, 1921). For purposes of commencing suit against absentee whose whereabouts are unknown, no "curator absentis" is necessary because Code of Civil Procedure provides for service by publication—constructive notice. See also topic Death.

ACKNOWLEDGMENTS:

Ordinarily form of acknowledgment utilized in country where acknowledgment is taken may be employed. In all cases it is advisable to have acknowledgments to be used in Germany certified by German consular or diplomatic officer. Acknowledgments to be used in U.S.A. may be taken before American consular officials in Germany. If acknowledgment is taken before German notary or other public official, his signature may directly be certified by American official in Germany without intervening certification by his respective superior authority and of diplomatic official (Minister, Chancellor). See law of Aug. 28, 1969 (BGBl. I, p. 1513) concerning notarial documents.

Germany is party to Hague Convention of Oct. 5, 1961 providing that foreign public documents (of courts, administrative agencies, notarial and official certification on private documents, etc.) are exempt from requirement of legalization by diplomatic and consular representatives of country in which document is submitted, provided documents carry simple uniform acknowledgment ("Apostille") serving as proof of signature or seal. Agreement remains in force for five years with successive five year automatic renewals and became law in Germany on June 22, 1965.

See also topic Notaries Public.

ACTIONS:

Generally any person or legal entity may sue or be sued in German courts subject to rules of procedure. As to claims against German government see topic Constitution and Government, subhead Sovereign Immunity; as to claims against foreign states see topic Courts, subhead Jurisdiction over Foreign States.

Rules governing procedure in civil actions are set forth in Code of Civil Procedure. There is only one form of civil action. All actions are commenced by filing statement of claim with court. Service of process on defendants is accomplished ex officio by court. Except before municipal courts (Amtsgericht) parties must be represented by attorney-at-law who is admitted before respective court.

There are no special modes of proof of foreign claims. See topic Treaties and Conventions. For proof of foreign law, see topic Foreign Law.

Limitation of.—See topic Limitation of Actions.

Appropriate Forum.—On jurisdiction as to subject matter, see topic Courts. Appropriate venue generally is place of residence of defendant. Appropriate venue also may be: place of performance of contract; place of tort; situs of real property; situs of assets; place of company's branch if litigation involves such branch's business.

Security for Costs.—Aliens, resident or nonresident, commencing civil action before German court must, upon demand by defendant, post security for costs which defendant may incur in such action, unless reciprocity exists with country of which

See Topical Index in front part of this volume.

ACTIONS . . . *continued*
plaintiff is citizen. Reciprocity is considered to exist with signatories of Hague Convention on Civil Procedure as well as with some other countries (as e.g., Chile, Ecuador, Greece, Iran, Lebanon, Libya, New Zealand, Turkey, U.K.). As to nationals of U.S., German-American Treaty of Friendship, Commerce and Navigation of Oct. 29, 1954 (implemented by Law of May 7, 1956) provides for exemption from obligation for posting security if U.S. plaintiff (individual or company) has his permanent residence or subsidiary (branch) or real property sufficient to meet costs, in district of court before which suit is pending in Germany or if otherwise reciprocity exists with plaintiff's home state in U.S. (No reciprocity with: Hawaii, Mississippi, New Mexico, Vermont, Canal Zone. Reciprocity only if U.S. plaintiff has been granted legal aid: Louisiana, North Carolina, Oklahoma, Tennessee, Texas, Wisconsin. Reciprocity with Alaska and Michigan, if plaintiff has his permanent residence or branch in Germany in district of court hearing case. With respect to other states reciprocity exists if plaintiff has permanent residence or branch in Germany.)

Costs.—Court costs and attorney's fees are, with respect to domestic litigation, fixed by statute and rates are in proportion to litigated sum. Needy persons may apply to court for legal aid. (ZPO, §114 et seq.). Losing party has to bear all costs, including lawyers' fees and reasonable expenses of winning party. Fees for witnesses (and expert witnesses) are part of court costs which must be advanced by parties. Contingency fees are considered unethical. Citizens and legal entities of former GDR are granted 20% discount on court fees. This also applies to fees due to notaries in former GDR. Lawyers' fees are reduced by 20% for lawyers with offices in former GDR as well as in cases where lawyers represent citizens or legal entities residing or located in former GDR before courts of former GDR outside of East Berlin.

ADMINISTRATION:

See Executors and Administrators.

AFFIDAVITS:

Affidavit is written statement of facts sworn by deponent before person authorized to administer oath. Such affidavit is unknown in Germany. However, written statement "in lieu of an oath" (eidesstattliche Versicherung) may be executed, and person executing false statement "in lieu of an oath" is subject to criminal charges. Abroad, written statement of facts in lieu of oath for use in Germany should be sworn before notary or German consul. When sworn before notary certificate as to his authority must also be attached.

Formal affidavit, in German or foreign language, to be executed in Germany for use abroad may be sworn before notary or respective consul in Germany, depending upon requirements under respective foreign law. When sworn before German notary certificate as to notary's capacity (legalization) can be attached to affidavit; see topics Acknowledgments; Depositions.

AGENCY: See Principal and Agent.

ALIENS:

Generally, aliens entering Germany must hold valid passport and visa, either tourist or long term visa. Nationals of many countries including U.S. are exempted from tourist visa requirement. Nationals of EC countries may enter Germany with identification card only. As matter of right they are, under certain conditions set forth in EC doc. 70-29 of Jan. 5, 1970, entitled to residence permit which is prerequisite for alien remaining in Germany for three months or more. Travel, residence and even practice of profession have been substantially liberalized among EC countries.

See also topic Immigration and European Communities Law Digest.

Status.—Aliens have substantially similar rights and duties as German nationals. Basic civil rights guaranteed by Constitution protect aliens in like manner as German nationals. However, this does not apply to items such as right to vote or privilege of unrestricted choice of occupation. Persons violating German laws may be deprived of privilege to remain in country by not renewing residence permit or by revocation of such permit and, unless privileged to political asylum, such person may then be deported.

Germany's attitude towards foreign investment and trade is considered very liberal. But like any German investor, foreigner must observe commercial laws and regulations concerning foreign trade, cartel law, and business in general.

Germany has numerous controls designed to safeguard health and to restrict activities of unqualified persons (i.e., food, pharmaceutical and medical products, transport, banks, insurance companies, handcrafts, restaurants and hotels) also applying to aliens but not revoking basic principle that any foreign enterprise may establish itself in Germany either as branch or through subsidiary company. There is no discrimination against foreign investment. Foreigner may conduct his business without German participation in either ownership or management (but see topic Corporations, subhead Codetermination), he may take over or invest in existing business; or he may participate in joint venture. There are no special rules to be followed by foreign enterprise, nor are there any restrictions on foreign ownership of land or buildings or any other property. Foreigner need not become resident in Germany to conduct his business, although when not in country he must appoint resident representative responsible to authorities. Certain investment incentives are available to foreigners in same manner as to domestic investors.

Constitution contains safeguards against expropriation without differentiation between nationals and non-nationals. Although not prohibited entirely, expropriation may take place only upon explicit act incorporating adequate compensation due upon expropriation and only for reasons of public interest.

For all practical purposes property of every description may be taken, acquired, held and disposed of by alien in essentially same manner as German subject. See also topic Real Property.

Nonresident aliens are subject to tax on their income from German sources. Resident individuals, i.e. persons having customary place of abode in Germany, are subject to tax on their worldwide income. Tax credits and exemptions are available. Numerous Double Taxation Treaties provide for additional relief. German tax law does not require special tax clearance for individual leaving country. Tax authorities may, however, make claims on property of taxpayer in Germany to satisfy any outstanding tax debt.

Upon marriage to German spouse alien does not automatically acquire German citizenship or even right to remain in Germany without compliance with immigration requirements; however, immigration or residency requirements in such case are even more liberalized and application for residence permit or naturalization may not be denied unless there are specific reasons. See topic Immigration.

ALIMONY:

Relatives in direct line are, by statute, obliged to provide maintenance to each other if one is needy and other is able to provide such maintenance without endangering his own adequate subsistence. Welfare paid to needy person by governmental welfare department may be recovered from person obliged to provide maintenance.

Spouses have mutual obligation to support each other; as to alimony after divorce, see topic Divorce.

Germany is party to New York Convention on Recovery Abroad of Maintenance of June 20, 1956. (BGB1. II, 1959, 149).

See also topic Infants.

ANTI-TRUST LAWS:

See Monopolies and Restraint of Trade.

ARBITRATION AND AWARD:

Parties may agree to submit dispute to arbitration except such matters of which parties have no right to dispose. Contracts to arbitrate future disputes must refer to specific legal relations. Arbitration agreements must be made in writing, and they may not contain any clause which does not refer to arbitration agreement, unless agreement is included in contract among merchants concerning matter of their business. Awards may be enforced after they have been declared executory by court; Germany is party to U.N. Convention on Recognition and Enforcement of Foreign Arbitral Awards of June 10, 1958. (BGBl. II, 1961, 121). See also topic Judgments.

ASSIGNMENTS:

The assignment of personal property is effected by agreement about the transfer of title and by the transfer of possession to the assignee.

Assignment of debts is, except where claims are transferred by virtue of law or by judicial act, effected by agreement between assignor and assignee. Notice to debtor is not required, but is advisable to prevent bona fide debtor from discharging his debt by payment to assignor. (See BGB, §398 et seq.).

ASSIGNMENTS FOR BENEFIT OF CREDITORS:

Property of insolvent person can be assigned to trustee chosen by creditors by voluntary agreement as well as by judicial settlement under law of Feb. 26, 1935, as am'd, concerning settlements to avoid bankruptcy (Vergleichsordnung). See topic Bankruptcy. Vergleichsordnung will be replaced by new insolvency law with effect of Jan. 1, 1999.

ASSOCIATIONS:

Association (Verein) is nonprofit organization. Civil status is ruled by BGB, §21 et seq., public law of associations is ruled by law of Aug. 5, 1964 (BGBl. I, 593) as am'd. Right of association is freely recognized without any special formality. Only association registered with associations-register constitutes legal entity. Association is legally represented by directorate (Vorstand) who may act for association. Commitments by directorate vis-à-vis third parties are binding on association, even if these commitments exceed association's purpose (no ultra vires concept), unless third party has knowledge that directorate contravened internal restrictions of authority. See also topics Corporations; Partnership.

ATTACHMENT:

Where it is shown to satisfaction of court that without attachment execution of future judgment on money claim might be frustrated or rendered difficult, attachment will be granted prior to judgment. Such is presumed where judgment would have to be executed in foreign country. (ZPO, §916 et seq.). This attachment is called "Arrest."

AUTOMOBILES: See Motor Vehicles.

BANKRUPTCY:

Bankruptcy proceedings may be commenced in case of insolvency of a debtor, and such insolvency is presumed if debtor has suspended payments. In case of corporations, excess of liabilities over assets establishes ground for bankruptcy. Bankruptcy petition regarding decedent's estate can be based only on this latter ground. To voluntary petition of bankrupt complete schedule of assets and liabilities must be annexed. Creditor's petition must establish insolvency and offer proof in support of claim. Creditor petitioning for bankruptcy must give security for court costs. If bankruptcy proceedings are started abroad, creditors are not barred from executing on assets located in Germany.

Bankruptcy proceedings in Germany also include property of bankrupt in foreign countries. However, foreign law determines whether or not bankruptcy proceedings in Germany are recognized in foreign country. Though Germany recognizes bankruptcy proceedings in foreign countries, recognition does not prevent creditors from executing on assets located in Germany on other grounds. However, foreign law decides whether restitution may be claimed. If bankrupt has no residence in Germany but operates business through branch establishment, bankruptcy proceedings only concern assets located in Germany. After bankruptcy proceedings have been instituted, court appoints trustee (receiver) and provisional committee of creditors. Assets of bankrupt comprise only such property as belonged to him at time of institution of bankruptcy proceedings and was at that moment subject to execution. Trustee may attack as void

See Topical Index in front part of this volume.

BANKRUPTCY . . . *continued*

transactions entered into by debtor after he has suspended payment or after presentation of bankruptcy petition against him, provided such transactions are prejudicial to creditors and that other party at time of such transaction had knowledge that debtor had suspended payment or was insolvent or that bankruptcy petition had been presented against him. Same applies to transactions by which satisfaction or security is given to creditor who is aware of facts. In certain cases transactions made within ten days before suspension of payments or presentation of bankruptcy petition can also be voided. Transactions entered into with intention of prejudicing creditors, if such intention was known to other party and certain gifts made within one year (in some cases within two years) prior to commencement of bankruptcy proceedings may also be contested. Prejudice is presumed with contracts made with spouse or other relatives within one year before institution of bankruptcy proceedings. Rescission other than in bankruptcy is also provided for in law of July 21, 1879 (RGBl., p. 277) prohibiting fraudulent transfers (Anfechtungsgesetz).

Creditors must give notice of their claims and submit them for examination. Time allowed for filing varies from two weeks to three months. Claim must clearly state cause of action, amount of claim, and also set forth any rights of priority claimed. Notice of claim may be filed by agent or attorney acting under power of attorney. Creditors failing to present their claims within specified time must pay costs of special examination. If claim is rejected, it may be established by litigation. Preliminary distribution is ordinarily made after examination, subject, however, to consent of committee of creditors. Proceedings end with final distribution, which requires consent of court.

Receiver's notes are not known in German law. Expenses for managing estate (Massekosten) and funds required for fulfillment of contracts entered into by trustee (Masseschulden) take precedence over claims of creditors. Creditors who have lien on, or similar right to property which forms part of assets can demand separate satisfaction out of such property and participate in bankruptcy proceedings only to extent of any deficiency. Certain tax liabilities, wages, etc., receive preferred treatment on distribution of assets. Persons owning assets which are in possession of bankrupt may withdraw such assets. See topic Chattel Mortgages. If bankrupt has disposed of such assets before commencement of proceeding, owner can claim full countervalue owed by purchaser to bankrupt and not paid to him before opening of proceeding. Pledge, mortgage or similar title gives priority to holder of these rights.

Settlement may be effected between debtor and ordinary creditors provided it is consented to by majority present at meeting of creditors and representing at least three-fourths of total amount of claims of creditors who are not excluded from voting in case of composition (i.e., consenting spouse), and is approved by court. Such composition must grant equal rights to all ordinary creditors and must yield at least 35% of their claims. It is binding on creditors who have been outvoted.

Domestic and foreign creditors are on an equal footing.

The bankruptcy law (Law of Feb. 10, 1877, RGBl., p. 351, as am'd) is applicable to all persons, estates of decedents, and corporations or other legal entities.

Under the law of Feb. 26, 1935, regarding composition to avert bankruptcy, a person who has become insolvent may, in order to avert bankruptcy, apply for institution of judicial composition proceedings. Composition accepted in course of such proceedings by duly qualified majority of creditors and confirmed by court is binding on all creditors. See also topic Assignments for Benefit of Creditors.

Bankruptcy law is not effective on territory of former GDR. Here, old GDR bankruptcy law ("Gesamtvollstreckungsordnung"), which was revised by GDR parliament in 1990 and in 1991 by FRG Parliament retains much of its validity. Especially noteworthy are additional regulations on possible interruption of bankruptcy proceedings so as to enable debtor to rehabilitate himself along lines of US Bankruptcy Code.

New laws on bankruptcy and composition (Insolvenzordnung) and rescission of fraudulent transfers (Anfechtungsgesetz) have been resolved by German lawmakers and will become effective Jan. 1, 1999 replacing also GDR bankruptcy law.

BILLS AND NOTES:

German law distinguishes sharply between bills of exchange (Wechsel) and checks (Scheck). This distinction is so pronounced that such matters are covered by two different codes, one dealing with bills of exchange (Wechselgesetz of June 21, 1933, RGBl. I, p. 399), other dealing with checks (Scheckgesetz of Aug. 14, 1933, RGBl. I, p. 597). Main difference is that bill of exchange is based upon personal credit of parties to bill while check drawn on bank or banker is means of payment only.

Germany is party to Treaty of Geneva of June 30, 1930, concerning Uniform Law of Bills and Notes. (BGB1. II, 1953, 148; BGB1. II, 1960, 2315).

The law of bills of exchange deals with two types of such instruments, one is the "drawn bill of exchange" (gezogener Wechsel), corresponding with American bill of exchange. The other is "own bill of exchange" (eigener Wechsel), corresponding with American promissory note.

The "drawn bill of exchange" must contain: (1) express designation as a bill of exchange in any language in which bill is drawn, (2) unconditional order to pay a definite amount of money, (3) name of drawee, (4) time of payment, (5) designation of a place where payment shall be made, (6) name of payee, (7) day and place of making, (8) signature of maker. If one of above mentioned requisites is absent, document is not considered bill of exchange. There are, however, certain exceptions to this rule; most important being that bill of exchange where time of maturity is absent is considered payable on sight.

The bill may be drawn on the maker or his order; it may be drawn on the account of a third party. If the amount is expressed in figures and words, the words prevail in case of discrepancy. Invalidity of one signature (e.g., minority, forgery, etc.) has no effect upon validity of genuine signatures on instrument. Bill of exchange must not be drawn to bearer. Bills may fall due at sight, at certain time after sight, at certain time after day of issuance, or on certain date.

The drawer of a bill is liable for its acceptance and payment; his liability for acceptance can, however, be eliminated. Unless it is eliminated he has to pay to holder in case of nonacceptance sum stated in bill with discount owing to payment before maturity. If bill has been issued or endorsed without being filled in completely and later on has been filled in contrary to agreement made with drawer or endorser, nonobservation of such agreement may not be asserted against third holder unless he acquired bill in bad faith or with gross negligence.

There are no days of grace, but any bill may be presented for payment within two business days following the day on which the bill is payable, and unless protest is waived, must be protested for purpose of having recourse against drawer and endorsers. Holder of protested bill is entitled to amount of bill plus cost of protest and other expenses, interest at 6% (or as fixed by Federal Bank, see topic Interest) from date of maturity, and commission of not over 1/3%. Endorser who cashes bill is entitled to be reimbursed for what he paid to previous holder plus his own expenses, plus 6% interest from date of payment and not over 1/3% commission. Holder and endorser are entitled to issue new bills for amounts due to them. This right of recourse is barred after one year for holders and after six months for endorsers. Period of limitation for suit against acceptor is three years, beginning with stated time of payment.

The capacity of an alien to incur liabilities under a bill is determined by the law of his nationality unless such law declares another law to be applicable. A liability incurred by an alien is, however, binding if incurred in a country according to the law of which the liability would be valid. As to the form of obligations the lex loci is applicable; but obligations of German nationals need only comply with the requirements of German law. The substantive law applicable to the obligations of acceptors is the law of the place of performance. Other obligations under a bill are ruled by the law of the place where the signatures were affixed. The law of the place of performance also rules as to whether a bill may be accepted only in part and whether the holder must accept a partial payment, and for the measures which must be taken in case of loss or theft of a bill. The law of the place where the bill was issued determines the time within which recourse must be taken, whereas form and limitation of action for protestation are ruled by the law of the country in which the protest is taken.

The "own bill of exchange" (similar in function to promissory note) has to contain: (1) Designation as "bill of exchange" as above, (2) unconditional promise to pay certain amount of money, (3) time of payment, (4) place of payment, (5) name of payee, (6) date and place of making, (7) signature of maker (promisor). Lack of date of maturity renders note due on sight. Other rules about drawn bills of exchange are applicable by analogy.

Check should be drawn on a bank or bankers or certain public corporations, but is considered valid if drawn on some other party. It must be unconditional and payable at sight. It must contain order to drawee to pay certain amount of money. It must state place and date of drawing and must be signed by drawer and contain either word "Scheck," or, if drawn in foreign language, corresponding designation in that language. Validity of check drawn abroad is governed by similar principles as validity of bill. It is sufficient if requirements of place of payment as to form are observed. Certified checks are permissible under certain conditions, although, on principle, check is not subject to acceptance.

Domestic checks are ordinarily made payable to bearer, and banks generally require all checks to be drawn in this manner. The drawer or holder of a check may write across its face the words, "Nur zur Verrechnung." This affords some measure of protection as a check crossed in this manner can only be credited to the bank account of the holder and not paid out in cash (similar to: "For deposit only"). Law also provided for generally and specially crossed checks.

Checks drawn in Germany and payable there should be presented within eight days after they are drawn as otherwise any right of holder by way of recourse against drawer and indorsers is lost. After expiration of eight days drawer may revoke it. If there has been no revocation, right of drawee to pay after expiration of eight days is not affected. If drawn in country different from place of payment, time for presentation varies between 20 and 70 days, latter time being applicable for checks drawn in U.S. and payable in Germany.

Checks payable in a foreign country may be drawn on persons on whom checks may be drawn according to laws of such country.

Endorser is liable to holder for payment of check also in cases of bearer checks. Payer has similar rights of recourse against previous endorsers as in case of bills of exchange, such rights being barred after six months. Instead of formal protest drawee bank or clearing office may certify nonpayment on check presented to it. Check may be presented for payment even before date of issuance noted thereon.

Tax.—Bill of exchange or checks are not subject to any tax or stamp duty. Former tax on bills of exchange has been abrogated by law on Feb. 22, 1990 with effect of Jan. 1, 1992.

See also topic Negotiable Instruments.

CARTEL LAW:

See topic Monopolies and Restraint of Trade.

CHATTEL MORTGAGES:

There is no exact equivalent for a chattel mortgage in Germany, but there may be a conditional sale. See topic Sales.

In Germany, transfer of title for security has become customary law. To some extent, chattel mortgage resembles transfer for security. Transfer of movables is made by informal agreement between creditor and debtor on transfer of title whereby concrete property conveyance conditions are agreed upon. Security agreement, not identical with legal transaction, serves as basis. To be effective, registration of transfer for security in public register is not necessary. Security transactions as provided for in Uniform Commercial Code are unknown in German law. Debtor retains possession and possible use whereas title passes to creditor. Transfer for security grants secret lien and is externally not recognizable. Debtor continues to be considered financially sound. This fact implies certain danger for all creditors. However, debtor must separate transferred items from his property, e.g., by separate storing, by marking or registration in special books or lists. Specified items or impersonal entity (warehouse), even reversionary right may be transferred. Agreement may be reached by resolutory condition, i.e., conditioned by full performance of secured claim. In this case, title to secured goods is automatically reconveyed to debtor upon fulfillment of condition.

In case of bankruptcy of debtor, creditor has right of sequestration (KO, §48) or right of separation (KO, §43). In case of nonpayment, rights of creditor resemble those

See Topical Index in front part of this volume.

CHATTEL MORTGAGES . . . *continued*
of governing pledgee. Provisions are set forth in security agreement. Unsecured creditors may refer to law prohibiting fraudulent transfers or prove that owner of security has taken over full property of debtor and is therefore responsible according to BGB, §419 or that transfer for security is void according to BGB, §138.

Cession for security means that debtor transfers to creditor for security purposes claim or other title which debtor has against third party. Institution equals transfer for security. Also in this case, entry in register for effectiveness of cession is not necessary. Tax authorities regard only debtor as liable for taxes as creditor has but nominal right of ownership, real title having remained with debtor.

COMMERCIAL LAW:

Commercial Code (HGB) governs legal relationships of merchants. Merchants are all persons engaged in business specified in HGB, §1 et seq. For this purpose partnerships and corporations are considered merchants. Commercial Code contains, e.g., rules concerning principal and agent, general and limited partnerships, contracts concluded by merchants, and accounting rules for all kinds of merchants, including companies. See also topic Corporations, subhead Accounting. To large extent HGB (Commercial Code) was already introduced in the then GDR by initial "State Treaty on the Creation of a Monetary, Economic and Social Union" (cf. Preliminary Note, subhead Reunification of Germany). As of Oct. 3, 1990, it is also effective in former GDR, with certain negligible qualifications.

COMMERCIAL REGISTER:

Commercial Register is maintained at municipal court (Amtsgericht called Registergericht for that purpose) and records registration of commercial enterprises and merchants. Registration constitutes constructive notice to public and, in certain cases, is legal prerequisite, i.e., corporation has no legal existence without such entry. All forms of mercantile and industrial enterprises such as individual merchants (term being word of art in German law, "merchant" having special legal status enabling him to engage in business transactions under provisions of Commercial Code [HGB] and other business laws), general and limited partnerships, stock corporations and companies with limited liability have to be registered in Commercial Register. Also legal representatives of firm, in particular members of management as well as members of supervisory board, have to be listed in Commercial Register. Any amendment has to be filed for registration by legal representative(s) of enterprise. Commercial Register is open to public and any person may ask for official certificate of entries and for certified copies of any document filed with Register.

See also topic Patents for Patent Register maintained by Patent Office for patents, designs and trademarks as well as topic Monopolies and Restraint of Trade for Cartel Register which is kept at Federal Cartel Authority, for all licensed cartels.

CONSTITUTION AND GOVERNMENT:

Structure and authority of Germany's government is derived from Basic Law (Grundgesetz) of May 23, 1949 (see Preliminary Note at beginning of this Law Digest). Word "constitution" was avoided in 1949 in order to be left for future new constitution of united Germany. When unification took place, Basic Law was only amended and no new constitution was set into force.

FRG consists of 16 Länder. Before reunification these were Bayern (Bavaria), Baden-Württemberg, Rheinland-Pfalz, Hessen (Hess), Saarland, Nordrhein-Westfalen, Niedersachsen, Bremen, Hamburg, Schleswig-Holstein and West Berlin. With reunification of Germany the five Länder which had been formed in GDR (Brandenburg, Mecklenburg-Vorpommern, Sachsen [Saxony], Sachsen-Anhalt and Thüringen [Thuringia]-so called "Neue Bundesländer") joined FRG on Oct. 3, 1990, thus becoming federal states of FRG. Berlin, with its western and eastern parts, now forms state of Berlin. Parliaments, governments and ministries were established in all five new federal states. As in old states, governments are headed by prime ministers.

New Länder have put into force new constitutions of their own. In meantime new Länder had adopted transitional set of regulations passed by parliament of GDR before its dissolution. This introductory state law, which was uniform for all new states, regulated basic questions of constitutional and administrative jurisdiction, etc. In most respects, this law was superceded by Unification Treaty (cf. Preliminary Note, subhead Reunification of Germany). However, new states are in process of enacting their own laws in accordance with their legislative sovereignty as established by Basic Law of FRG (see below), with varying degrees of progress. In other respects, old law of GDR remained effective in new states after unification treaty, insofar as it proved compatible with fundamental constitutional principles of FRG and insofar as object of such legislation did, in fact, fall under jurisdiction of federal states by Basic Law. In limited number of cases, former GDR legislation can become legislation of FRG. Otherwise, unification treaty provides detailed regulations for perpetuation of many GDR laws and often stipulates modifications ("Massgaben") for their continued application. Same applies for law of FRG. Here, basic ruling is that FRG state law does not extend its effectiveness to former GDR. Federal legislation, on other hand, does fundamentally apply in former GDR, unless unification treaty qualifies applicability of certain laws in former GDR (likewise with modifications) or exempts former GDR from their application.

Certain functions are specifically province of Länder notably education and law enforcement; yet even here attempt is made to maintain degree of uniformity among Länder through joint consultative bodies. Governments of Länder are generally parallel in structure to that of Bund but need not be. In 13 of Länder, head of government has his own cabinet and ministers; each has its own parliamentary body, but in city states of Hamburg, Bremen, and Berlin, mayor is simultaneously head of government of Land. Municipal senates serve also as provincial parliaments, and municipal offices assume nature of provincial ministries.

Administrative subdivisions of Länder are known as Regierungsbezirke (departments) that are divided into Kreise (counties). Kreise themselves are further subdivided into Gemeinden, roughly "boroughs" or "municipalities" which through long German tradition have considerable local autonomy and responsibility in administration of schools, hospitals, housing and construction, social welfare, public services and utilities, and cultural activities.

Unification Treaty establishes that Berlin is capital city of reunified Germany. Seat of parliament and government were to be decided upon at later date. After much heated public and parliamentarian debate Bundestag (federal parliament) decided that following prolonged transitional period of ten to 12 years, Berlin shall be seat of federal parliament and government. A few government agencies are, however, to remain in Bonn.

Fundamental Rights of People.—Basic Law exhibits features similar to Constitution of U.S.: its formal declaration of principles of human rights and of bases for government of man.

Basic Principles.—Federal Republic of Germany is democratic and social federation. All governmental authority is derived from people, such authority exercised by people in voting as well as by representatives of people through legislative, executive, and judicial power. Legislature is bound by Constitution; executive and judicial power is bound by law. All German citizens of both sexes who have reached 18 years of age enjoy civil and political rights and qualify for voting.

Federal Legislative Power is exercised by two chambers, Bundestag and Bundesrat:

Bundestag is cornerstone of German political system. It consists of 656 members (subject to slight variation caused by system of election) which are elected in general, direct, popular elections held every four years.

Bundesrat (Federal Council) consists of delegates of Länder. In Bundesrat, Länder themselves exercise authority to protect their rights and prerogatives. Its members are appointed by governments of Länder, each Land sending certain number of members, depending on size of population. Delegations are bound by instructions of their governments.

Federal legislative power is exercised by two chambers, Bundestag and Bundesrat. All legislation originates in Bundestag, and Bundesrat's consent is necessary only on certain matters directly affecting interests of Länder, especially in area of finance and administration, and for legislation in which questions affecting constitution are involved. Bundesrat may exercise restraint on Bundestag by rejecting certain routine-legislation passed by lower chamber, but unless bills fall within certain categories, its vote may be overridden by simple majority in Bundestag. Should President of Federal Republic be absent for long periods or withdraw from office, speaker of Bundesrat deputizes for him. Legislative competence is partly with federation, partly with Länder. Powers of federal legislature are kept in careful balance with those of Länder. Certain matters such as foreign affairs, defense, matters affecting citizenship, currency and minting, customs and international trade, post and telecommunications are in exclusive competence of federal legislative bodies. Some other fields are subject to concurrent legislation; i.e. Bundestag may set out certain guidelines for legislation; each individual Landtag may pass appropriate legislation in conformity with guidelines set by Bundestag. In principle, Bundestag initiates or approves legislation in matters in which uniformity is essential, but Länder otherwise are free to act in areas in which legislative authority is not expressly resolved to federal bodies.

Executive Power.—

President of Federal Republic of Germany is formal chief of state. Intended to be elder person of stature, he is chosen for term of five years by assembly specially convened which consists of members of Bundestag and equal number of members elected by popular representative bodies of Länder according to principles of proportional representation. Apart from representing Germany among other nations and signing all federal legislation and treaties, President nominates Federal Chancellor. Among President's important functions are those of appointing federal judges and certain other officials and right of pardon and reprieve. In case of absence he will be substituted for by speaker of Bundesrat.

Chancellor is head of federal government. He is elected by majority vote of Bundestag and then appointed by President. Chancellor is vested with considerable independent powers and initiates government policy. His cabinet and its ministries also enjoy extensive autonomy and powers of initiative. Chancellor can be deposed by absolute majority of Bundestag by electing his successor. Government may not be dismissed by President. President may not even in a crisis call upon political leader at his discretion to form new government.

Judicial Power.—Basic Law emphasizes strongly independent position of courts, especially in right of Federal Constitutional Court (Bundesverfassungsgericht) to declare law unconstitutional and void.

Independent position of judiciary is secured by grant of independency to individual judges who are bound solely by constitution and law and are not subject to any order or other oppression or removal from office. Judges for state courts and for federal courts are elected by special committees.

Basic Law provides for, besides Constitutional Court, federal supreme courts in fields of regular, administrative, finance, labor and social law. Courts of lower instances in these fields are state courts; thus, no parallelism of state courts and federal courts exists. Organisation and operation of courts is regulated by ordinary laws. See topic Courts.

Law.—German law is based on two ancient systems: German law, derived from Germanic tribal conventions of antiquity, and Roman law. Laws are codified.

International Law.—Common rules of international law are considered to be part of law governing in Federal Republic of Germany; moreover, in cases of conflict they have supremacy over national law, and create direct rights and duties for residents of Germany. (Art. 25 of Basic Law).

Law Enforcement.—Law enforcement is reserved to Länder; except Federal Border Police no nationwide police force exists. Each Land maintains its own force which is charged with all phases of enforcement throughout each Land except where their function is assumed by municipal police force. However, federal offices may investigate certain actions, notably those incident to internal and external security of Federal Republic, and criminal actions that transcend confines of Länder. In state of national emergency Länder forces may be put under command of federal authority.

Sovereign Immunity.—Defense of sovereign immunity is not available to German government in German courts if plaintiff can comply with one of statutory provisions admitting his claim. Access to courts is guaranteed by Art. 19 of Federal Constitution (Basic Law) to everyone whose rights have been violated by authoritative power.

CONSTITUTION AND GOVERNMENT . . . *continued*

Moreover, BGB, §839 explicitly creates civil liability of officer for compensation for damages caused by violation of his official duties owed to third parties. By virtue of Art. 34 of Federal Constitution, Federal Republic in principle assumes such liability. However, German government being sued in foreign court is likely to raise, in compliance with rules of international law, defense of sovereign immunity. See also topic Courts, subhead Jurisdiction over Foreign States.

CONTRACTS:

While several principal aspects of German contract law are in accordance with principles prevailing in U.S. (e.g., offer and acceptance, mutual consent, etc.), there are several fields where German contract law differs widely from American. Main provisions are set forth in Civil Code (BGB). Special provisions are to be found in Commercial Code (concerning merchants), and in Laws on Bills of Exchange and on Checks, in various corporation laws and in other special laws. Apart from general provisions of Codes, certain categories of contracts (e.g., sale, gift, lease, etc.) are dealt with in the Codes at some length.

An offer made during a personal negotiation between parties must be accepted at once; same applies to an offer made by telephone. An offer made to an absent person (by mail, by telegraph) can be validly accepted only so long as offeror may expect to obtain answer under ordinary circumstances. However, American theory that offer is accepted at time of mailing or cabling, by using same media (post, telegraph) as offeror, is unknown; rather acceptance only becomes effective upon receipt by offeror. If offeror dies before receiving duly forwarded acceptance, contract is nevertheless valid. If offeror fixes time for acceptance, acceptance must be in his hands before such time elapses.

Oral contracts are generally valid and may be proved by any means of evidence, unless the law provides otherwise. Certain contracts must be in writing, especially: The establishment of a foundation inter vivos; assuming a mortgage upon a purchased property; a lease for more than one year; promise of an annuity; guaranty and suretyship, but if the assumption thereof is a commercial transaction on part of guarantor, no writing is needed (HGB, §§350, 351); abstract obligation, which means promise to pay without reference to other contractual duties; acknowledgment of debt; assignment of mortgage, and others. Notarial or judicial document is required for: Assignment of one's entire property or fraction thereof; transfer of real estate and encumbrance thereof, and other special cases; including especially promise of gift. See also topic Corporations.

Consideration is not a requisite for the validity of a contract; hence gift contracts are valid. Also other contracts are valid without consideration, except when nature of contract requires it, e.g., sale or lease.

Contracts for benefit of third parties are valid, and generally third party acquires a direct right of enforcement of contract against obligor.

Principal claim of obligee is performance (specific performance in American terminology). In contrast to American law, claim for damages is only subsidiary claim. In order to be entitled to damages, obligee must send notice to obligor, informing him that he has fixed time for performance and that after lapse of this time, performance will not be accepted but damages will be claimed. Also in this respect German law differs widely from American principles.

In order to avoid social hardships, tenancy and labor legislation of FRG is only partially effective in former GDR. Protection from unwarranted termination of tenancies is more extensive than protection afforded in FRG. In realm of tenancy legislation, object was to prevent mass notices of termination and eviction actions on part of owners who could have brought legal claims—e.g. to establish higher rent—on basis of restitutions (cf. topic Reprivatisation and Restitution). Raising of rents is subject to strict limitations, and even commercial rents must remain within range of the then so-called regional norm.

Consumer Protection.—Most important are: Law Concerning General Terms and Conditions (Gesetz zur Regelung des Rechts der Allgemeinen Geschëaftsbedingungen) of Dec. 9, 1976 (BGB1. I, p. 3317), applicable to most of standardized contracts, even between merchants; Consumer Credit Act (Verbraucherkreditgesetz) of Dec. 17, 1990. (BGB1. I, p. 2840) See topic Sales, subhead Sale with Payment by Instalments); Law Concerning the Withdrawal from Door-to-Door Contracts and Similar Contracts (Gesetz über den Widerruf von Haustëurgeschëaften und ähnlichen Geschäften) of Jan. 16, 1986 (BGB1. I, p. 122); Law Concerning Producers' Liability (Produkthaftungsgesetz) of Dec. 15, 1989 (BGB1. I, p. 198).

Excuses for Nonperformance.—No liability for nonperformance arises if performance becomes impossible by reason beyond power of obligor, such as destruction by accident, Act of God, or default by obligee. (BGB, §323).

If obligee is liable for impossibility (BGB, §§276-278), obligor keeps his claim for equivalent and must only be debited with what he saved due to exemption from his performance (BGB, §324).

If obligor is liable for impossibility, obligee may choose whether he wants to claim damages for nonperformance, withdraw from contract or claim rights as set forth in §323 if applicable (BGB, §325).

Should obligor be in default (BGB, §284), obligee is entitled to withdraw from contract after having given grace period and refuse performance or claim damages for nonperformance.

If obligor infringes further rules of conduct resulting from obligation (called positive infringement of claim) he must also pay damages to obligee (case law).

Theory of nonexistence or unforeseeable change of base of contract (Fehlen oder Wegfall der Geschëaftsgrundlage) applied by courts provides for extraordinary remedy. Contract may be reformed or even rescinded in order to comply with fundamentally changed situations.

Since Oct. 3, 1990, principles set forth under this subtitle also apply on territory of former GDR, since they are established in Civil Code/FRG, which, in this respect, has also become effective in former GDR, where it has replaced provisions of Civil Code/GDR.

Applicable Law.—Form of contract is ruled by law which governs legal situation to which contract refers. Form of law of place where contract is concluded is, however, sufficient. This is not true for contracts by which there is any actual disposal of things, transfer of property or creation of title. Principles of conflict of law are laid down in Introductory Law to German Civil Code (EGBGB), Art. 27 et seq. Parties' autonomy is recognized. If there is no express or implied choice, law to which contract has its closest connection is applicable. Art. 28 EGBGB establishes appropriate legal presumption based on criteria such as place of performance, etc.

Uniform Law on the International Sale of Goods and Uniform Law on Formation of Contracts for International Sale of Goods of July 17, 1973 (BGBl. I, pp. 856 and 868) as of Jan. 1, 1991 have been replaced by United Nations Convention on Contracts for International Sale of Goods (see topic Sales).

EGBGB also applies in former GDR. However, for legal proceedings concluded before Oct, 3, 1990, former GDR law remains effective, especially its legislation on application of laws, provisions of which closely resemble those of EGBGB.

COPYRIGHT:

Significant development is enactment of German Copyright Law (Gesetz über Urheberrecht und verwandte Schutzrechte) of Sept. 9, 1965 (BGBl. I, p. 1273, as am'd).

Period of copyright for literary, musical and other original and creative works, i.e., architectural, photographic, motion pictures, computer programs, etc. ends with expiration of 70th year after author's death, except that period of ten years from publication is applicable to works published more than 60 but less than 70 years after author's death. Work is published ("erschienen") if it is accessible to public with consent of copyright owner. Varied terms of copyright protection are applied to co-authorship, anonymous works, editions of works in public domain, etc., mostly based upon term of ten years upon publication or 70 year term if author becomes known. Photographic works are protected for 25 years after publication; same period (after first performance, manufacture, etc.) also protects performing artist, manufacturer of mechanical devices, film producer, broadcasting station for performance or material in film or broadcast. Models and designs are protected for period not exceeding 20 years for designs and ten for models according to Registered Design Act respectively Law on Utility Models. See topic Patents, subhead Design Patent.

Law contains many important features such as compulsory license provision to manufacturers of sound recording devices, personality rights of authors and others. Even though copyright for title of book or magazine is in effect, publishing in certain publications is common.

No copyright registration is necessary except in case of models and designs. (See also topic Patents.) Among remedies available to owner of copyright for infringement are restraining order, request for accounting or destruction of infringing article and damages where infringement is wilful or negligent. Copyright can be bequeathed or assigned, with certain limitations.

Law protects works of German citizens regardless of whether and where published, and foreign works first published in Germany, provided 30 days have not elapsed since publication of such work elsewhere; otherwise protection of foreign works is governed almost exclusively by two international Conventions:

Germany is member of Berne Convention of Sept. 9, 1886, granting extensive minimum protection to musical and literary works of member countries. With exception of U.S. and Soviet Union, most important countries in world adhere to Berne Convention.

In 1955, U.S., Germany, and some other countries ratified Universal Copyright Convention of Sept. 6, 1952 (Welturheberrechtsabkommen). Protection under Convention, while not as sweeping as under Berne Convention, is extensive and almost uniform.

Germany is also a party to other international conventions (see topic Treaties and Conventions) and to bilateral agreements with many countries, but those agreements are important only in case of very few countries that are not parties to Berne Convention or Universal Copyright Convention.

Interesting features of law are extension of liability for royalty payments to manufacturers, distributors and users of tape recorders, even if use is entirely private, and a thorough coverage of rights and obligations of performing right societies in the territory and other persons or agencies administering similar rights concerning, among others, distribution of profits among members, establishment of balance sheets, arbitration, etc., under jurisdiction of German Patent Office.

Copyright protection in former GDR: As of Sept. 13, 1965, GDR enacted its copyright law. (Gesetz über das Urheberrecht, GB1. I. S. 209). Provisions do not differ substantially from West German law, but protection for creative work ends already 50 years after author's death. For West German copyright holders, Statute grants protection only in accordance with Bern Convention, which GDR joined in 1971. Since Convention refers back to GDR law, all copyright infringements before reunification on Oct. 3, 1990, must be judged under this Statute.

CORPORATIONS:

German law recognizes two main types of corporations which may be formed for all lawful (not necessarily business) purposes: (1) "Aktiengesellschaft" (corporation limited by shares), which corresponds to American stock corporation; and (2) "Gesellschaft mit beschränkter Haftung" (company with limited liability), which has no equivalent in American law. Less popular are "Kommanditgesellschaft auf Aktien" (KGaA, stock corporation with elements of limited partnership) and "bergrechtliche Gewerkschaft" (see subhead Special Corporations). GmbH & Co. KG, basically limited partnership whose sole general partner is GmbH, was for time of great practical importance because it combined limited liability with tax advantages of partnership. Less attractive now due to new law diminishing impact of double taxation at corporate and shareholders' level.

Basic difference between Anglo-American and German law is that in Germany concept of "ultra vires" acts is unknown. German corporation is not confined to objects which articles of incorporation enumerate. Its legal capacity to act is unlimited.

"Aktiengesellschaft (AG)."—Corporation Law (Aktiengesetz) of Sept. 6, 1965 (BGBl. I, p. 1089), as am'd by laws of Aug. 14 and 15, 1969 (BGBl. I, pp. 1146, 1171 and 1189), Law of Oct. 25, 1982 to implement 3 Directive of the European Community (BGB1. I, p. 1425), Law of Dec. 19, 1985 to implement 4, 7, and 8 Directives of European Community (BGB1, I, p. 2355), Law of Nov. 11, 1990 to implement

See Topical Index in front part of this volume.

CORPORATIONS . . . *continued*
Directive of EC on Financial Statements of Banks, 2nd Law to Promote the Financial Market of July 26, 1994 (BGBI. I, p. 1749) and Law of Aug. 2, 1994 to implement "small Corporation" (BGBI. I, p. 1961).

Corporation may be formed by one or more (natural or corporate) persons, all of whom may be foreigners or nonresidents (§2), as separate legal entity with liability limited to corporation's capital (§1). Articles of incorporation which require notarial or court record must contain corporate name (as a rule derived from objects of undertaking, adding "Aktiengesellschaft") (§4), domicile, subscribers, objects, amount of share capital, whether in cash or kind, par value and classes (if any) of shares, and form of corporation's public announcements (§23). Minimum capital is DM. 100,000. (§7). Shares without par value are unknown. Shares must have par value of at least DM. 5.— and they may not be split. Higher par value shares (Aktiennennbeträge) must have par value divisible by DM. 5.—. (§8). There may be common or preferred stock. (§11). Cumulative voting rights are prohibited unless Minister of Economics of State (Land) where corporation is domiciled, permits exception. (§12). Cumulative preferred shares may be issued as nonvoting stock (§139), but par value of shares may not exceed that of other shares. Articles of incorporation determine whether shares must be issued to bearer (Inhaberaktien) or to registered holder (Namensaktien), but shares must be "Namensaktien" if issued prior to full payment of minimum face value, and in that case part payment made must be indicated on share certificate. Articles of incorporation may provide for conversion of bearer share into shareholder's certificate and vice-versa. (§§10, 24). Entitlement to share certificate can be excluded or restricted in Articles of Association.

Stock capital is raised in cash and/or kind but, if latter, articles of incorporation must specify object of transfer, person from whom it is acquired, par value of shares issued or compensation paid therefor. (§27). Assets have to be transferred in full and 25% of minimum par value plus difference (in case of "Aktiennennbeträge") has to be paid prior to registration. (§§36, 36a). In case corporation is formed by one shareholder only sole shareholder has to provide security for outstanding part of contribution.

Corporation comes into existence by registration in Commercial Register of its domicile (see topic Commercial Register) on application of all incorporators, managers and supervisors. (§36). Court must register corporation, provided it finds, upon proper examination that articles of incorporation comply with minimum requirements and after managers and supervisors confirm to court that they have checked incorporation proceedings and rendered incorporation report ("Gründungsbericht" §32), or in case of shares issued against assets other than cash, examiners appointed by court upon nomination by local Chamber of Industry and Commerce give same assurance upon auditing of incorporation (Gründungsprüfung §33) and all shares have been subscribed to. Registration must also be accompanied by articles of incorporation, all contracts, documentation of appointment of managers, supervisors and facsimile signatures of managers. (§37).

Commercial register is to be notified immediately, if all shares are held by one shareholder.

Board of Management (Vorstand) must consist of at least one manager (or two if corporation's stated capital is more than 3,000,000 DM, unless articles of incorporation provide explicitly for one manager only); it may consist of several managers. Managers conduct business of corporation jointly unless otherwise stipulated by articles of incorporation; articles may, however, not provide that quorum can be constituted by minority of managers. They are representatives of corporation. Their power to act on behalf of corporation may be restricted internally but not with effect towards third persons. Acts of management exceeding such internal restrictions are nevertheless valid. Managers are, however, responsible to corporation for any such excess and, moreover, they occupy fiduciary relationship to corporation and are obliged to exercise same care as ordinarily prudent and diligent manager in like position would. Each individual manager may be held liable by corporation, or, under additional requirements, by shareholder (derivative suit). Members of board of management are appointed by supervisory board for single period not exceeding five years at a time; appointment may be renewed, but not earlier than one year before expiration. In cases of emergency, court may temporarily appoint managers.

Supervisory Board (Aufsichtsrat) consists of at least three members. Articles of incorporation may provide for additional board members but not more than nine for corporations with stated capital of up to 3,000,000 DM, and not more than 15 for corporations with stated capital of up to 20,000,000 DM and not more than 21 for corporations with higher stated capital. Number of supervisors must be divisible by three. If corporation is subject to co-determination laws, number of members of supervisory board is substantially different (see subhead Co-determination). Shareholders meeting (Hauptversammlung) elect all members of supervisory board unless employees are, by co-determination law, granted right to elect certain number of supervisors. Member of supervisory board may not be person who is already member of supervisory board of ten (under certain conditions 15) other corporations which are required by law to have supervisory board. No person who is member of board of management of "dependent" corporation (abhängiges Unternehmen) may be supervisor of dominant corporation. Person who is member of board of management of corporation may not be supervisor in second corporation whose board of management includes manager who is supervisor of corporation in which proposed member is manager. Articles of incorporation may require personal qualifications for persons to be supervisors, but only for supervisors to be elected by shareholders. Articles of incorporation may grant preferred right to appoint supervisor to certain stockholder or to holders of certain class of shares, number of supervisors thus to be appointed not exceeding one-third of total number of supervisors to be elected by shareholders. Term of office of supervisors may not exceed date of shareholders' meeting discharging managers and supervisors for fourth business year. Substitute for supervisor may be elected or appointed for same term to take office in case of removal or resignation of supervisor before expiration of term. Supervisor may not simultaneously be member of board of managers or permanent substitute for such member, and may not be representative (Prokurist, Handlungsbevollmächtigter) of corporation; but supervisor may represent manager or other agent of corporation for specified period not exceeding one year. Supervisors must elect chairman and at least one vice-chairman, whose names are recorded in Commercial Register; minutes of meetings are signed by chairman and must include date of meeting, quorum, agenda. Supervisors in general act as board by resolution at properly called meeting. Absent special statute or provision by articles of incorporation, majority of authorized number of supervisors constitutes quorum, minimum being three supervisors being present at meeting. Any action required or permitted to be taken by supervisory board may be taken without meeting by resolution in writing, by telex, or by phone, if no supervisor dissents from such kind of proceeding. Supervisory board may appoint committees of its own members to act for board, but essential functions of board need to be exercised by entire board.

Designated function of board in general is to supervise and control conduct of business of board of management. Supervisors are not authorized to conduct business, neither individually nor as board. Supervisory board and board of management are distinctly separate bodies. Supervisory board in particular has authority to inspect in person or by experts. If it is necessary for benefit of corporation, supervisory board may call for shareholders' meeting. Moreover, articles of incorporation or supervisory board itself may provide that certain kinds of corporate business may be conducted only upon approval by supervisory board.

Supervisors and managers may be foreigners without German domicile or residence and need not be shareholders.

Corporate stationery must contain indication of legal form of corporation, its place of business, registration number of Commercial Register, names of all managers and of chairman of supervisory board.

Annual balance sheet, profit and loss statement, annex and report of management are, as rule, not approved by general meeting of shareholders but submitted to supervisory board after audition. (§170). Supervisory board accordingly reports to general meeting. (§171). If managers and supervisors agree, balance sheet is final unless they wish to put it before general meeting for approval. (§173). In this case, or if supervisors and managers dissent, balance sheet is submitted for approval to general meeting (§175), which decides by simple majority of votes represented.

Ordinary shareholders' general meeting which takes place once a year within first eight months of business year (§120) as a rule passes on appointment of supervisors and public accountants, distribution of profits, if any (dividends to be paid, profits carried forward, reserves, etc.); reports of managers and supervisors; change in articles of incorporation, means of raising capital and reduction thereof; dissolution of company and discharges of managers and supervisors (§§119, 120).

General meeting of shareholders is called by managers' resolution by majority vote (§121) with at least one month advance notice (§123) but, if circumstances warrant, must be called at request of shareholders' minority representing stock capital of 5% or less, if articles of incorporation permit. Publication of calling not required and registered letter sufficient, if all shareholders are known. Articles of incorporation may condition right to participate in meeting upon deposit of stock at least ten days prior to meeting. (§123). If all shareholders are present in meeting and consent resolution can be made without observance of statutory requirements for calling. All resolutions passed at general meetings must be laid down in notarial protocol and submitted to Commercial Register together with list of persons present at meeting. (§130). However, unless shares are admitted to stock exchange trade and no resolutions are passed requiring three-quarter majority, simple minutes signed by chairman of supervisory board is sufficient recording. Voting is by majority. Each share carries one vote. Articles of Association may fix maximum number of votes in case shareholder owns several shares. Vote is suspended on shares owned by corporation or subsidiaries. (§§133, 134).

Articles of incorporation can be amended only by three-quarter vote of shareholders present at ordinary or extraordinary general meeting. Articles of incorporation may prescribe another majority which, if corporation's purposes are to be changed, may be higher. (§179).

Any increase of nominal capital against issue of new shares requires majority vote of at least three-fourths of stock capital represented at meeting. Articles of incorporation may provide for higher majority in case of issuance of preferred non-voting shares.

New shares are subscribed by written declaration (Zeichnungsschein) in duplicate and must recite date of resolution to increase capital, nominal value and kind of shares, date at which optional shares become invalid unless capital has in fact been raised prior to stated deadline, etc., and failure to include all necessary statements invalidates new shares and excludes liability on part of corporation. (§185). Articles of incorporation may authorize capital increase within five years after incorporation or after amendment of articles of incorporation authorizing increase. Generally, shareholders have preemptive right to acquire new shares in proportion to previous holdings. (§186). Capital can also be increased out of corporation's own funds or legal reserves if latter exceed one-tenth of corporation's capital (§208), on basis of last balance sheet. Resolution to increase capital must be entered in Commercial Register.

Corporation may also issue bonds, profit-sharing or convertible. Issue requires three-fourths majority of shareholders' meeting unless articles of incorporation provide otherwise. (§221).

Corporation is dissolved by resolution of at least three-quarters of shareholders, by bankruptcy and on expiration of period provided for in articles of incorporation. (§262). Combination of all shares in one hand does not dissolve corporation. On dissolution it is liquidated by liquidators except if bankruptcy proceedings are opened and receiver is appointed. (§265). Assets may be distributed not earlier than one year after third public announcement to creditors requesting them to notify liquidators of their claims. (§272). Dissolution and corporation's final liquidation are registered by court. (§263).

Corporations may be merged or consolidated with other corporations, general or limited partnerships, registered cooperatives or mutual insurance associations. Merger or consolidation is governed by new Transformation Act (Unwandlungsgesetz) of Oct. 28, 1994 (BGB1. I, p. 3210), which has come into force with effect of Jan. 1, 1995.

See also topic Securities.

"Gesellschaft mit beschränkter Haftung (GmbH)."—This is another form of corporation. (Law of Apr. 20, 1892, repeatedly amended). Due to its simpler organization, corporation with limited liability is more convenient than an Aktiengesellschaft in cases where capital is small or number of shareholders is limited. As all shares of a

See Topical Index in front part of this volume.

CORPORATIONS . . . *continued*
Gesellschaft mit beschränkter Haftung may be combined in one hand it is often appropriate form for subsidiary companies.

The main differences between an Aktiengesellschaft and a Gesellschaft mit beschränkter Haftung are that in case of the latter:

The shares are transferable only by a notarial (or court) protocol (§15) in order to prohibit stock exchange transactions. As a rule no share certificates are issued; if issued, their transfer is not sufficient to transfer the shares. Articles of incorporation may (and as rule do) provide for special restrictions on transfer of shares, e.g., consent of shareholders' meeting or of managers. (§15).

There need be only one incorporator (natural or corporate person, German or alien). Articles of incorporation (as well as subsequent amendments , §53) must be in notarial form (§2). Shareholders may hold business interests (shares) which may be of different denominations (minimum par value of business interest: 500 DM). Aggregate business interests constitute stated capital which must be at least 50,000 DM. Upon incorporation, at least 25% of each business interest must be paid in, either in cash or in kind. Upon incorporation, at least 25% of cash capital contributions must be paid in, amounting to at least 25,000 DM. Noncash capital contributions must be made in full.

There must be at least one manager (§6), natural person, German or alien, who is appointed by shareholders (§46). Supervisory board is optional, not obligatory (§52); but see also subhead Co-determination. Shareholders may vote orally, in writing or at meetings. No notarial protocol is required unless articles of incorporation are amended.

The corporate name must contain the words "mit beschränkter Haftung" (with limited liability) or abbreviation. (§4).

The corporation comes into existence by registration in the commercial register on application of managers. (§11). Business interests may be issued against cash or assets (§5), no official examination of incorporation proceedings takes place in either case. Court registers corporation on managers' assurance that 25% of capital in cash and/or all assets (if any), at least 25,000 DM, are at their free disposal. (§8).

The liability of the shareholders is as a rule limited to the unpaid part of their shares. They are, however, ratably liable if another shareholder fails to pay up his share in full. (§24). Articles of incorporation may provide for additional liability of shareholders in certain cases. (§26). Under certain circumstances, shareholders' loans to GmbH will be treated as capital to effect that reimbursement cannot be requested. (§32a).

Unless articles of incorporation specifically provide differently, many provisions of Corporation Law (Aktiengesetz) of Sept. 6, 1965 are now applicable to optional or mandatory supervisory board of GmbH, as for instance to their number, personal requirements, remuneration, etc. (see subhead Aktiengesellschaft [AG], supra) to GmbHs being part of holding group.

Last GmbH law which was effective in GDR derived, like its corporation law, from times of German empire, i.e. from year 1892. On basis of law passed on June 21, 1990, Federal German GmbH law became effective as of July 1, 1990. Since former law of GDR stipulated minimum capital of only GDR-Mark 20,000, adjustment provisions had to be made for increase to DM 50,000. Basically, to avoid compulsory deletion from commercial register (cf. Commerical Register), corporations must raise their capital to this level by July 1, 1995 GmbHs which applied for registration in commercial register in former GDR between July 1, 1990 and Oct. 3, 1990 had to increase their capital before July 1, 1992.

Accounting.—Corporate (AG; GmbH; KGaA) accounting is ruled by Commercial Code (HGB), §§238-335, as am'd by law of Dec. 19, 1985 to implement 4, 7 and 8 Directives of the European Community (Bilanzrichtliniengesetz, BGB1. I, p. 2355), together with some additional rules regarding "Aktiengesellschaften" contained in "Aktiengesetz". See also subhead Aktiengesellschaft (AG), supra. Distinction is made between "small", "intermediate", and "large" corporations. "Large" are corporations admitted to quotation on stock exchange and corporations meeting at least two of following requirements: Balance sheet total over 15.5 million DM; turnover over 32,000,000 DM; labor force over 250. "Intermediate" are corporations meeting at least two of following requirements: Balance sheet total over 3.9 million DM; turnover over 8,000,000 DM; labor force over 50.

Management has to draft annual accounts (balance sheet, profit and loss statement, annex) and report within first three months of new business year. In case of "small" corporations period may extend to six months. (HGB, §264). "Small" and "intermediate" corporations' accounting procedures are simplified in many ways in comparison with "large" corporations' accounting. Accounts and report are audited by sworn public accountants, except in case of "small" corporations. (HGB, §§316-324). After submission to shareholders' meeting, accounts and report of managers and supervisors (if any) are kept on file with register court and are open to inspection for everybody and also published. (HGB, §§325-329). But that applies to "small" corporations only in respect of balance sheet and annex.

Annex must explain balance sheet and profit and loss statement and contain, in addition to information on managers' and supervisors' remuneration (including profit-sharing, commissions, and any other benefits) information about contingent liabilities not shown in balance sheet, relations to affiliated and associated enterprises, etc. (HGB, §§284-288).

Report must describe major events, if any, of current year up to meeting, corporation's foreseeable future development, and corporation's technical developments and research and development activities. (HGB, §289).

From 1990 onwards consolidated annual accounts (balance sheet, profit and loss statement, annex, report) are mandatory for corporation holding group of companies meeting at least two of following requirements: Aggregate balance sheets worldwide total over 46.8 million DM (unconsolidated) or 39,000,000 DM (consolidated); aggregate worldwide turnover over 96 (cons.) or 90 (uncons.) million DM; worldwide labor force 500 or more. For credit institutions and insurance companies there are special parameters. (HGB, §§290-315). Consolidated annual account is audited by sworn accountants, kept on file with register court and open to inspection for everybody, and also published. (HGB, §§316-329). Before 1990, consolidated account pursuant to new rules may be chosen voluntarily. If so, new rules apply in their entirety.

Co-determination.—German business enterprises, under certain conditions, are co-determined by representatives of labor force and unions by virtue of four different statutory frameworks.

Co-determination in Enterprises of Mining and Steel Industry is regulated by law of May 21, 1951 (BGBl. I, p. 347, Montanmitbestimmungsgesetz), as am'd, and by law of Aug. 7, 1956 (BGBl. I, p. 707 Mitbestimmungsergänzungsgesetz), as am'd.

Enterprises of mining and steel industry carried on in legal form of Aktiengesellschaft (AG) or Gesellschaft mit beschränkter Haftung (GmbH) or bergrechtliche Gewerkschaft (see subhead Special Corporations, infra) and either employing more than 1,000 employees or being so-called "Einheitsgesellschaften" (companies divested under Law No. 27 of Allied High Commission of May 16, 1950) must have supervisory board, depending upon amount of stated capital, of 11 (5 + 5 + 1) or 15 (7 + 7 + 1) or 21 (10 + 10 + 1) members; half of members to be elected by shareholders, and other half to be elected by employees, and "neutral man" upon nomination by all other members of supervisory board to be elected by shareholders. Director of personnel (Arbeitsdirektor) is appointed as member of board of management by majority of supervisory board including majority of workmen's members. Likewise, Arbeitsdirektor cannot be removed from board of management against majority of workmen's members of supervisory board.

Co-determination Law of May 4, 1976 (BGBl. I, p. 1153, Mitbestimmungsgesetz) provides for equal workmen's representation in supervisory boards of all business associations (except those which are subject to co-determination for mining and steel industry) carried on in legal form of AG, Kommanditgesellschaft auf Aktien (KGaA), GmbH, incorporated bergrechtliche Gewerkschaft or Erwerbs- und Wirtschaftsgenossenschaft (for-profit co-operative association), and having regularly more than 2,000 employees. Exempt are associations directly serving political, religious, charitable, educational or scientific purposes or arts, and media associations as press, editors, broadcasters. Number of employees of affiliate association in one of legal forms subject to co-determination, is to be added to number of employees of parent association for purposes of co-determination, if parent company "dominates" affiliate (Aktiengesetz, §§15-18). Thus, holding company may very well be subject to co-determination although having itself only few employees. Moreover, company in legal form being subject to co-determination, which is general partner in limited partnership (KG) has to add number of employees of partnership to number of its own employees if majority of limited partners also constitutes majority (by capital or by voting power) in company which is general partner.

Foreign companies, i.e. companies incorporated or established under foreign law and doing business in Germany, are not subject to co-determination; however, subsidiaries incorporated under German law in one of legal forms shown above, although shares may be held partially or entirely by foreigners, have to comply with co-determination law.

Substance of co-determination is that all companies being subject to it must have supervisory board, half of whose members are to be elected by shareholders and other half by employees. Representatives of labor force on board consist partially of employees of company and partially of representatives of labor unions. Supervisory board has 12 members (six shareholders' representatives, four employees, two union representatives) in companies with not more than 10,000 employees, 16 members (8 + 6 + 2) in companies with not more than 20,000 employees, and 20 members (10 + 7 + 3) in companies with more than 20,000 employees. Labor force members of board are to be elected directly by employees if not more than 8,000 employees are entitled to vote; otherwise employees elect electors who then elect members of board. One member of each different group of employees, blue-collar workers, white-collar employees and management employees (Arbeiter, Angestellte, leitende Angestellte) must be elected to board; groups shall be represented proportionally.

Supervisory board shall, by two-thirds majority, elect one of its members as chairman and one as vice-chairman. If required majority is not reached, shareholders' representatives elect chairman and labor force representatives elect vice-chairman.

Supervisory board, by two-thirds majority, appoints members of board of management. If required majority is not reached, supervisory board votes by one-half majority requirement on proposal made by committee of supervisory board, previously having been set up exclusively for purposes of this voting procedure. If majority requirement is not met, third election procedure shall take place in which chairman has two votes.

Enterprises, not being co-determined under foregoing, are subject to co-determination according to §§76, 77 of Works Council Act of Oct. 10, 1952 (BGBl. I, p. 681) and to §129 of Works Council Act of Jan. 15, 1972 (BGBl. I, p. 13), if they are carried on in legal form of AG or KGaA without regard to number of employees, or, having legal form of GmbH or bergrechtliche Gewerkschaft, if they have more than 500 employees. Such companies must have supervisory board. One-third of its members are to be elected by employees. Right to appoint managers of GmbH is reserved for shareholders.

Every enterprise, without regard to its legal form, no matter if single proprietorship or association and no matter whether or not it is co-determined under rules shown supra, is subject to entire Works Council Act of 1972 (Betriebsverfassungsgesetz), if it has five or more employees. Employees may elect works council (Betriebsrat) whose main function is, unlike previously described co-determination which provides for participation of labor force in decision-making upon conduct of business, to care for working condition of employees. Thus, works council has certain specified rights to be informed, to be heard and to participate in decision-making of management concerning personnel matters; for example, termination of employment contract may be invalid without works council being heard before. See topic Labor Relations.

Special Corporations.—There are several kinds of co-operative associations (Genossenschaften) regulated by special laws. They have no capital stock, but are simply combinations of persons. They have rights of corporation if formed in compliance with law and are numerous and used for various lawful trade purposes, especially for smaller and medium sized handicraft and agricultural purposes. Minimum number of members is seven and their liability, whether limited or unlimited, depends upon form of association.

Laws regulating co-operative associations in FRG now also apply in former GDR, where co-operative association played major role particularly in agriculture in form of

See Topical Index in front part of this volume.

CORPORATIONS . . . *continued*
"Landwirtschaftliche Produktionsgenossenschaft" (LPG). LPGs had to be transformed into co-operative associations in accordance with law of FRG as of Dec. 31, 1991.

Similar to American membership corporation are the "Vereine," associations which obtain legal capacity through entry into register. See also topic Associations.

Investment Funds.—Most important statutory provisions are: Capital Investment Companies Acts of: (i) Apr. 16, 1957 as am'd on Jan. 14, 1970 (Gesetz über Kapitalanlagegesellschaften, BGB1. I, p. 127 and by law of Feb. 22, 1990 to implement EC-Directive of Dec. 20, 1985 BGB1. I, p. 266) concerning investment in securities, silent partnerships, real property and hereditary building rights, and (ii) Dec. 17, 1986 (Gesetz über Unternehmensbeteiligungsgesellschaften, BGBl. I, p. 2488) concerning establishment of companies for purpose of investing in business interests of domestic companies and one-man enterprises (silent partner interest; see also topic Partnership, subhead Silent Partnership) not admitted to official or semiofficial listing (see topic Securities); Law on the sale of Foreign Investment Fund Shares (Gesetz über den Vertrieb ausländischer Investmentanteile) of July 28, 1969 (BGBl. I, p. 986, as am'd).

Change of Corporate Form.—Corporation may change its corporate form into another form of corporation as well as into general or limited partnership, noncommercial partnership or registered cooperative. Transformation also is possible by assigning corporation's property to one shareholder. Shareholder's resolution to this effect requires a majority of three-quarters or 90% or even consent of all shareholders respectively. Recording in Commercial Register is legal prerequisite for validity of transaction. For details see new Transformation Act (Unwandlungsgesetz) of Oct. 28, 1994 (BGB1. I, p. 3210), which has come into force with effect of Jan. 1, 1995. Tax benefits are granted in cases of merger or transformation by Tax Law of Sept. 6, 1976. (BGBl. I, p. 2641).

Special restrictions apply to certain kinds of corporations. Insurance companies (with certain exceptions, e.g., reinsurers) are controlled by a Federal Supervisory Office with its seat in Berlin, and similar control is exercised by state over banking corporations.

Foreign Corporations.—Foreign corporations may do business in Federal Republic of Germany with or without maintaining a branch. Establishing a branch requires a special permit of minister of economy of respective state (Land). If business of a respective German enterprise needs a special permit (e.g., Banks) such is also required for branches of foreign corporations. Branch must be registered into commercial register of court in district where branch is located. Various formalities are to be fulfilled, e.g., to application shall be attached an officially certified copy of articles of incorporation. See topic Real Property.

See also topic Foreign Trade and Foreign Investment.

Income Tax on Corporations.—See Taxation.

Publication.—All the publications provided for in the above laws must be published in the "Bundesanzeiger" (Federal Gazette).

Former GDR.—Corporate forms listed above also existed in former GDR up until its final day, even if they served no practical purpose, since all economic activities were channeled through publicly owned enterprises called "Volkseigene Betriebe" (VEB). By law of June 17, 1990, ("Treuhandgesetz"—trust law), "Treuhandanstalt" (National Trust Agency), renamed Bundesanstalt für vereinigungsbedingte Sonderaufgaben—BVS—as of Jan. 1, 1995, became sole shareholder of all these enterprises, which were simultaneously, by same law, transformed into "Aktiengesellschaften" or "Gesellschaften mit beschränkter Haftung" GmbH.

See also topic Monopolies and Restraint of Trade.

COURTS:

System.—As distinguished from U.S., with its parallelism of state and federal courts, Germany has single court system. It is divided into several orders, scope of jurisdiction depending upon subject matter to be decided upon: General matters (civil and criminal), labor relations, administration, taxes, social security, constitution.

Courts for General Matters (regular courts) have jurisdiction over civil matters which are not assigned to special courts (e.g. labor matters), and over criminal matters.

Lowest regular court is Amtsgericht (Municipal or Lower Court). Its civil jurisdiction extends to litigation where amount in controversy does not exceed DM 10,000 and to noncontentious jurisdiction including probate and guardianship activities, bankruptcy and settlement procedures, execution of judgments and other decrees, maintenance of registers such as registers for land, commercial associations, noncommercial associations, marital property status. In Amtsgericht all civil cases, contentious and noncontentious, are heard before single judge. Venue of Amtsgericht usually covers city or county. See also topic Actions, subhead Appropriate Forum.

Courts of next resort are Landgerichte (District Courts). Venue of Landgericht usually covers several Amtsgericht districts. Appeals from judgment or decree of Amtsgericht may be taken, for reasons of fact or of law, to Landgericht. Landgericht, as court of first instance, has jurisdiction over all civil litigation where amount in controversy exceeds DM 10,000. Chambers are composed of three professional judges, but cases may be assigned to single judge unless general importance or factual or legal difficulty requires mandatory hearing by all three judges. Litigation on commercial matters involving registered merchants (including corporations and commercial associations) on both sides may be assigned to "commercial chamber" (Kammer für Handelssachen) bench of which being composed of presiding professional judge and two merchants as associate lay-judges.

While before Amtsgericht parties to litigation may argue their case personally, before Landgericht (and before courts of higher instances) party needs to be represented by attorney admitted to practice before that specific Landgericht.

Appeals, for reasons of fact or of law, from judgment or decree of Landgericht may be taken to Oberlandesgericht (Court of Appeals), except from Landgericht's decision rendered as appellate decision.

Highest civil (and criminal) court is Bundesgerichtshof (Federal Supreme Court) located at Karlsruhe. It decides on appeals for reasons of law, not of facts, taken from decisions of Oberlandesgericht.

Labor Courts (Arbeitsgerichte) are vested with jurisdiction over disputes between employers and employees arising out of labor relations, over questions of collective bargaining and also over questions of co-determination (see topic Corporations) insofar as labor relations are at stake.

Structure is that of three instances, District Labor Court being lowest one. Bench in all instances includes two lay-judges, one being nominated by employers' union, other by labor union.

Administrative Courts (Verwaltungsgerichte) are vested with jurisdiction over matters of administrative law, such as zoning, immigration, state licenses including licenses under foreign trade regulations. Governmental (federal, state, municipalities) acts. e.g., denial of license applied for, generally become final unless suit is brought before Verwaltungsgericht by addressee of such decree, within certain period of time after rendition of such decree. Administrative court system consists of three instances.

Tax Courts (Finanzgerichte), consisting of two instances, have jurisdiction over tax matters including customs duties and other taxes on international and foreign trade.

Social Courts (Sozialgerichte), consisting of three instances, have jurisdiction in matters governed by social legislation, such as social security and public mandatory health insurance.

Federal Constitutional Court (Bundesverfassungsgericht) and State Constitutional Courts have competence to control constitutionality of all private individual and public legislative or governmental acts with binding force erga omnes.

Courts in Former GDR.—Former courts of GDR no longer exist. All five new Länder meanwhile have established system of courts as it is existing in other parts of Germany and which is organized as described above.

Jurisdiction over Foreign States.—Situation concerning jurisdiction of German courts over foreign states is governed by decision of Federal Constitutional Court of Apr. 30, 1963, holding with force of law that rule of international law granting foreign States general immunity from jurisdiction of domestic courts can no longer be established, thus abandoning rule of absolute immunity and adhering to rule distinguishing between acts jure imperii (sovereign acts) and acts jure gestionis (acts in legal transactions of private law). Distinction between sovereign and non-sovereign state activities is not to be based on motive or purpose of activity of state or on connection of activity with sovereign function of state. Nor is it considered to be relevant whether state activity is commercial as there is no intrinsic difference between commercial activity of state and other non-sovereign activity of state. Distinction is based on nature of act of state or of resulting legal relation. Relevant is whether foreign state acted in exercise of its sovereign power, thus within sphere of public law, or acted like private person, thus within sphere of private law. Qualification of state activity is, in principle, made pursuant to national law, subject to rules of international law. In international law generally recognized sphere of sovereign (public) activity includes activity of foreign and military power, legislation, exercise of police power, and administration of justice. In exceptional cases, international law may render it necessary to qualify activity of foreign state as jure imperii because it falls within intrinsic sphere of public power although domestic law qualifies it as activity of private law.

Federal Republic of Germany is signatory to European Convention on State Immunity of May 16, 1972.

Enforcement of Judgment against Foreign State.—Federal Constitutional Court with decision of Dec. 13, 1977 held with force of law that there is no generally accepted rule in international law which would a priori prevent forum state from execution of judgment against foreign state; execution of judgment on non-sovereign activity of foreign state may be made against assets of foreign state located in forum state unless these assets serve official sovereign function of that foreign state. Waiver of immunity as to assets is recognized and given effect.

See also topic Constitution and Government, subhead Sovereign Immunity.

CURRENCY:

Legal currency is Deutsche Mark (DM). By law of July 26, 1957, Federal Reserve Bank (Deutsche Bundesbank) has been established with exclusive right to issue currency notes.

Deutsch Mark is also currency and only legal tender of former GDR, namely since conclusion of first State Treaty on July 1, 1990 (cf. Preliminary Note, subhead Reunification of Germany). Bank deposits and current liabilities and claims were exchanged from Mark/GDR to DM at specific rates (3:1, 2:1 and 1:1, depending on amount involved and on whether natural persons or trading companies, GDR citizens or others were involved). Mortgages entered into land register in currency of German Reich (Reichsmark, Goldmark) and never adapted in former GDR are to be recalculated into DM at rate of 2:1.

Foreign Exchange.—Foreign trade and payments are regulated by law of Apr. 28, 1961, BGBl. I, p. 481 as am'd (Aussenwirtschaftsgesetz-AWG) and regulation in version of Aug. 31, 1973, BGBl. I, p. 1069 as am'd (Aussenwirtschaftsverordnung-AWV) which liberalize foreign exchange as matter of principle subject only to special restrictions as specified. Persons entering Federal Republic of Germany may import any foreign or German currency in unrestricted amounts. In same way, they may export any currency when leaving territory. Credit Cards and Traveler's Checks may be used.

See also Foreign Trade and Foreign Investments.

CURTESY:

Curtesy does not exist in Germany.

CUSTOMS:

Germany is integrated member of European Community (EC) where customs duties have been abolished before Jan. 1, 1993. (Uniform European Charta of Feb. 2, 1986). Provisions and orders of Council or Commission of EC (mostly concerning control over food supplies and other commodities, general flow of merchandise or uniform prices) of common concern to all members, become legally binding upon member countries and part of their national law immediately upon publication thereof in Official Gazette of European Communities (German Edition: Amtsblatt der Europäischen Gemeinschaften).

CUSTOMS . . . *continued*

Principal special statutes are Customs Law of June 14, 1961 (BGBl. I, p. 737) as am'd by law of May 18, 1970 (BGBl. I, p. 530). General Customs Regulations of Nov. 29, 1961 (BGBl. I, p. 1937) and Customs Tariff Law of Dec. 23, 1960 (BGBl. II, p. 2425). Entry of Federal Republic of Germany into EC has exposed these laws to permanent amendments.

Local or regional customs authorities decide upon classification of imported goods in general customs tariff rate and also determine their value for customs purposes. Decisions of customs authorities are appealable to tax courts.

Foreign nationals or foreign residents are subject to same extent and in same manner to German customs as are German nationals or residents.

Federal Republic of Germany has joined General Agreement on Tariffs and Trade (GATT).

DEATH:

Missing persons may be declared dead. (Law of July 4, 1939, RGBl. I, p. 1186 as am'd by law of Jan. 15, 1951, BGBl. I, p. 63 and law of July 26, 1957, BGBl. I, p. 861).

In order to be declared dead, a person must be missing. A person is missing when his or her whereabouts are unknown for a long period of time and no news has arrived during that period showing whether such person was living or not, so that reasonable doubts arise whether he or she is still alive. A person is not missing whose death is established. The latter case is, of course, the ordinary case. When a person dies within Germany, a public physician establishes the death and notifies the proper authorities; but a person might have died under unusual circumstances, e.g., on the battlefield, but the death was witnessed by other persons; in such event death can be proved. Both categories of decedents are, however, not "missing persons." The following provisions concerning declaration of death cover only persons designated as "missing" within the meaning of the definition set forth supra.

A missing person may be declared dead through certain proceedings, including a public proclamation, if the following conditions are met: (a) If since the end of year within which missing person was still alive pursuant to information obtained, ten years have elapsed; in case, however, missing person would be 80 years of age at time of declaration of death, said period is reduced to five years. No declaration of death, however, may be issued before end of year in which missing person would have achieved age of 25. (b) If person belonging to armed forces participated in war or in war-like undertaking, was missed within zone of danger and has been missing since, he may be declared dead after lapse of one year since conclusion of peace, or since time when war or war-like undertaking was in fact ended. If circumstances show great probability of death, year may be counted from moment person was missed. (c) If person was missing during journey at sea, especially in case of ship-wreck, he may be declared dead when six months have elapsed after wreck or any other event causing his disappearance. (d) Lapse of time of three months is sufficient for declaration of death of person who disappeared during flight, especially in case plane was wrecked. Three months must be counted from day of wreck of plane or from any other event which caused person to be missing. (e) If person was exposed to great risk of life under other circumstances than enumerated in (b) to (d) and has been missing since, he can be declared dead, provided that one year has elapsed since moment such danger has ended or its end can be assumed, depending on circumstances of case. This latter provision is especially applicable to the inmates of concentration camps whose whereabouts could not be ascertained and who are missing.

The declaration of death creates the presumption that the missing person is dead. Details of the moment when death should be presumed are set forth in §9 of the law.

As long as a missing person is not declared dead by decree of the court, such person is presumed to be alive. For lack of proof that out of several persons, who died or were declared dead, one survived the others, a presumption is created that they died simultaneously.

Generally, the proceedings for declaration of death can be brought before a German court—generally the court of the last domicile—only if deceased was a German citizen or had his or her permanent domicile in Germany while still alive, or in cases where there is legitimate interest that death be declared by German Court.

The petition for the declaration of death must be filed with municipal court (Amtsgericht) in non-contentious proceedings. Interested parties entitled to file petition are: (1) District Attorney; (2) legal representative of missing person (e.g., father of minor, guardian, etc.); (3) spouse, legitimate issue or such issue which has right of legitimate issue; (4) parents; (5) any person having legal interest therein (e.g., creditor, legatee, etc.).

The petitioner must show that his allegations are credible; thereupon the court will publish a proclamation by which the missing person is summoned to appear before the court within a certain period of time (not less than six weeks and no more than one year) or else he will be declared dead. This publication must be made in certain newspapers and in court. After the lapse of time provided for in the publication, the court will issue an order of declaration of death, which must also be published in the same manner as the proclamation.

After declaration of death, estate proceedings may start. Estate will be distributed according to the results of these proceedings. By declaration of death, marriage of person declared dead is dissolved, and surviving spouse may remarry.

If a person declared dead was not dead and reappears, such person may apply for nullity of the declaration of death. His marriage, however, remains dissolved. While he, or she, has no right to demand the dissolution of the new marriage of his, or her, former spouse, each spouse of the new marriage has the right to apply for the dissolution of the new marriage. (For details see Marital Law, §§38 and 39). But a person wrongly declared dead may claim the restitution of his property from the heirs and legatees to whom such property was distributed. (BGB, §2031).

By law of July 7, 1955, BGBl. I, p. 401, it was established that law of 1951 (see supra) was not in any way changed by International Convention of Apr. 6, 1950, Concerning Declaration of Death of Missing Persons.

Petitioners, however, have choice to proceed either on basis of above law or of Convention. For latter proceedings Amtsgericht Schïoneberg-Berlin has exclusive jurisdiction (Publication of Ministry of Justice dated July 4, 1956, Off. Publ. No. 127).

Damages for Wrongful Death.—BGB, §844 provides that person who wrongfully caused death of another is obligated for primary obligations of deceased. If at time of injury deceased was or might have been under a legal obligation for maintenance of another, he who had caused death can be held to same obligation as deceased would have had during his probable lifetime. If deceased was bound by law to perform service for third party in his household or business, he who caused death is obligated to compensate third party by payment of annuity. (BGB, §845). Law does not make exceptions with regard to foreigners.

DEEDS:

Deeds, in the common law sense, are unknown in Germany. The transfer of real property is effected by a declaration of both parties before the recording judge or notary (Auflassung) and by entry of the transfer of title in the real estate register (Grundbuch). There was no "Auflassung" in GDR. Alteration of Grundbuch, which was likewise prerequisite for transfer of real property, occurred solely on basis of document of contract of purchase. Federal German law is effective as of Oct. 3, 1990. See also Husband and Wife, subhead Common Property; also Records; also Sales.

DEPOSITIONS:

Germany is party to Hague Convention on Taking of Evidence Abroad in Civil or Commercial Matters of Mar. 18, 1970. (BGB1. II, 1977, 1452, 1472).

Normal procedure for obtaining evidence under Convention is to send necessary information, including exact questions if desired, to proper German Authority (one Central Authority has been designated for each Land) which then transmits this information to proper local German court.

See Part VII of this volume for Convention and proper forms.

If testimony of German citizen is needed for use in foreign court, depositions of voluntary witness may be taken by commission before foreign diplomatic or consular officials.

Letters rogatory will be executed by German courts. They must be submitted through appropriate foreign channel and through German Minister for Foreign Affairs and Minister of Justice to appropriate German court authorities. They cannot be sent directly. Owing to indirect method of transmission considerable delay may occur and it is advisable to employ counsel in Germany to expedite transmission through various ministries. Counsel may appear at examination of witnesses. German courts act by virtue of their own judicial authority and it is preferable to send open commission. If court which is to execute letters is not known, it need not be specified. It is advisable, even if court is designated, to add words "or other appropriate authority" in order to avoid delays.

Depositions in a Foreign Country.—Can be had upon request of the German Court before which the action is pending, by means of Questionnaires or Letters Rogatory, either to the German Consul or to a competent authority of the country concerned, or, if applicable, under Hague Convention referred to above.

If circumstances warrant, taking of depositions can also be entrusted to the parties. In that event, the respective party is obligated to produce a public instrument covering the deposition. (ZPO, §§363, 364).

DESCENT AND DISTRIBUTION:

The rules governing descent and distribution apply both to movable and immovable property. The law groups the lines of descent according to orders. The first order includes the descendants of the deceased, the second order the parents of the deceased and their descendants, the third order the grandparents of the deceased and their descendants, the fourth order the great-grandparents of the deceased and their descendants, the fifth and further orders include more remote ancestors of deceased and their descendants. In first three orders distribution is per stirpes; in fourth and further orders, per capita. Presence of relatives in previous order excludes rights of relatives in more distant orders. Children inherit in equal parts. In second order, in case both parents survive, they inherit alone in equal parts. In case either is deceased and has left descendants, these descendants receive share of deceased. In case no descendants survive, surviving parent inherits whole. In third order, in case all four grandparents survive, they inherit alone in equal parts. Upon death of grandparent on either side, same rule is followed as in second order. If both grandparents on one side are deceased and leave no descendants, other grandparents or their descendants inherit in whole.

In the fourth order or following order the surviving great-grandparents, or more remote ancestors, inherit per capita. In case no great-grandparents or ancestors survive, the descendant of them who is nearest in relationship to the intestate inherits alone, or if there are several equally near, they inherit per capita.

Surviving spouse receives, along with the first order of relatives, mentioned above (i.e. the issue), one fourth of the estate; along with relatives of the second order (the parents and their issue) and with the grandparents, one-half of the estate, whereby the shares of the relatives aforementioned are reduced accordingly. If no relatives of the first or the second order nor grandparents are left, but a spouse survives, the latter inherits the entire estate to the exclusion of more remote relatives.

If surviving spouse inherits along with relatives of second order or with grandparents, he or she inherits also, in advance, objects belonging to matrimonial household and wedding gifts. Rights of intestate inheritance are excluded if decedent had applied for divorce or if he had agreed to application for divorce brought by surviving spouse, or, before application was made, if he was entitled to apply for divorce. Surviving spouse may, however, have claim for alimony against estate. (BGB, §1933; see also topic Divorce).

See also topic Husband and Wife for distribution in case of spouses married under legal marital régime of "community of increases."

If spouses are married under régime of separate property, surviving spouse and one or two children of decedent inherit equal parts. (BGB, §1931).

Illegitimate children of deceased have an inheritance compensation claim against the heirs. (BGB, §1934a et seq., as established by law of Aug. 19, 1969, BGBl. I, p. 1243).

In cases of inheritance in former GDR before Oct. 3, 1990, order of succession is governed by former GDR law, which closely resembles FRG inheritance legislation.

DESCENT AND DISTRIBUTION . . . *continued*
Spouses always inherited same proportion as children, however, no less than one-quarter of inheritance. If deceased person had no offspring, surviving spouse was sole heir. Illegitimate children born since Oct. 3, 1990 come into inheritance as described above (BGB, §1934a ff.); if they were born before Oct. 3, 1990, inheritance law treats them as equals to legitimate children of deceased.

Certificate of Inheritance.—Provision is made for the issuance, by the probate court, of a certificate of inheritance, which proves the right of succession. (BGB, §§2353-2370).

Legitimate Portions.—See topic Wills.

Distributorships, Dealerships and Franchises.—Distributorships and dealerships, which are practically same under German law, have been "developed by case law on basis of individual contracts" and are subject to general provisions of sales (BGB §433 et seq. and HGB §373 et seq.), commercial agency (HGB §84 et seq.), service contracts (BGB §611 et seq.) and management of business (BGB §675). Distributor or dealer ("Vertragshändler or Eigenhändler") is someone who consistently distributes merchandise from certain manufacturer or supplier in its own name and on its own account.

Franchisee is special kind of dealer who, against franchise fee, has been authorised by franchisor to distribute certain merchandise or services using name, trademark, as well as commercial and technical know-how, and complying with organizational and advertising methods developed by franchisor. Franchisor shall grant technical and sales assistance and is entitled to exercise control of franchisee's business operations. (BAG BB 1979, p. 325).

If specific period is not agreed, reasonable notice is required to terminate distributor or franchise agreement. Rules relating to termination of commercial agency(§§89 et seq. HGB) may apply if position of distributor or dealer is sufficiently analogous to that of commercial agent.

DIVORCE:

Divorce is regulated by BGB. New regulations became effective July 1, 1977. However, previous law concerning alimony between divorced partners remains valid in cases of divorce prior to July 1, 1977.

Divorce may be granted by court (and only by court). Sole ground is disruption of conjugal relationship if it is not expected that spouses would restore matrimonial relationship. Law irrefutably presumes that conjugal relations are disrupted if spouses have been separated for three years. If both spouses agree to divorce, irrefutable presumption is valid after one year of separation. In case of separation of less than one year divorce may be granted only if continuation of marriage would be undemandable hardship for applicant because of reasons arising from person of other spouse. Factors such as adultery, serious violation of marital duties, immoral conduct, mental derangement, contagious and repulsive diseases, are likely to be considered by court as causing undemandable hardship. Unless spouses have been separated for more than five years, divorce may be denied, although conjugal relations are disrupted, if court finds that overwhelming interests of minor children from marriage or very specific exceptional situation of respondent who opposes application for divorce, necessitate maintenance of marriage. (BGB, §§1565-1568).

Divorced wife may resume her maiden name, or, if couple had previously chosen wife's maiden name as family name, husband may resume his previous name. (BGB, §1355; see also topic Marriage).

If, after divorce, spouse cannot support himself, he may claim alimony from other, if his inability to support himself rests upon one of following grounds: Self-support cannot be expected because of education of and care for child born of divorced marriage, or because of advanced age or sickness; spouse does after divorce not immediately find adequate job; spouse, in expectancy of marriage, had ceased or not begun education or continued education and, immediately after divorce, starts education which, after completion, will enable him to be self-supporting; dominating reasons in equity demand alimony. Alimony is not to be granted if grant would be heavily unreasonable. (BGB, §§1569-1580). Upon death of spouse his estate is liable for alimony to surviving spouse. (BGB, §1586 b). If retirement benefits have accumulated to either spouse during marriage, such benefits will be allocated to both spouses equally. (BGB, §§1587-1587 p). These provisions are now also effective in former GDR. Accumulated retirement benefits earned in former GDR have been taken over into FRG social security system by transformation law of July 25, 1991. (BGBl. I, p. 1606).

For support of spouse divorced before Oct. 3, 1990, old GDR law applies, whereby spouse is less favorably endowed (temporary limitation of extent of support). In divorce cases occurring after Oct. 3, Federal German law also applies to former GDR. Since Oct. 3, 1990, support claims of children are, in all cases, governed by Federal German law.

Annulment of Marriage.—Governed by law of Feb. 20, 1946, as am'd (Ehegesetz). Both parties may apply to court for declaration of nullity of marriage. Nullity may be based upon lack of form, lack of legal capacity, in cases of bigamy, in cases where marriage is null and void because of consanguinity. Except in latter two cases, nullity is deemed waived if couple continues marriage for certain time. Child born from void marriage is legitimate to extent to which it would have been legitimate if marriage had been valid. Support is regulated as in case of divorce.

Moreover, a party may sue at the court for dissolution of marriage in certain cases, especially in case of error in ceremony, in case of wilful deceit, which does, however, not include misstatement about financial circumstances, and in case of threat, unless such marriage is later ratified by couple. Right to such action expires within one year from knowledge. Financial consequences are same as in case of divorce.

As to missing spouse, see topic Death.

Aliens.—German courts assume personal jurisdiction if one of spouses is German, or if wife at time of marriage was German or, in case both spouses are aliens, if at least one of them is residing in Germany and German divorce decree will be recognized by laws governing husband.

Applicable law depends on nationality of spouses. If both spouses are aliens of same nationality, law of nationality applies. In case of aliens of different nationalities, law of last common domicile is applicable. If spouse seeking divorce is, or, at time of marriage was, German national, divorce can also be granted under German law.

Foreign divorce decree may be recognized in Germany if rendered under that law which is applicable under rules of German international private law; decree will not be recognized if considered rendered under violation of German public policy or if foreign court under German rules is considered not having jurisdiction.

DOWER:

Dower does not exist in Germany.

ENVIRONMENT:

Environmental protection is one of main principles of German policy. Hence, there have been number of legislative activities during last decades. In 1994 "preservation of the natural basis of existence" was even constitutionally protected by amendment of basic law. (Art. 20 a Grundgesetz as am'd on Oct. 27, 1994, BGBl. I, 1994, 3146).

Federal system divides legislative and executive powers in environmental issues between federal and state authorities. Most basic regulations to preserve soil, water, air, and individual or public health were enacted by federal powers. In some fields, e.g. water resources management, protection of nature, and care of landscape, federal legislation has only constitutional competence to enact framework laws. (Rahmenvorschriften, Art. 45 Grundgesetz). State laws fill them out by supplementing with more detailed rules. Besides, there exist additional local by-laws, especially on field of planning law and nature conservation.

Execution of environmental acts, even of federal origin, is mainly incumbent on state authorities. This may sometimes result in varying administrative practices in different states. Uniform administrative rules prevent a too wide-spread variety in execution of federal acts.

Administrative acts of environmental authorities are generally submitted to the control of the administrative courts.

Protection of Clean Air.—Federal Pollution Control Act (Bundesimmissionsschutzgesetz—BlmSchG), first enacted on Mar. 15, 1974 (BGBl. I, 1974, 721) and extensively amended in following decades is heart piece of German environmental legislation "to protect before harmful environmental impacts" (§1 BlmSchG). This act differs between two types of installations. Those installations listed in "Ordinance Concerning Installations Requiring A Permit" (Verordnung über genehmigungsbedürftige Anlagen / 4. BlmschV of July 24, 1985, BGBl. 1, 1586), amended subsequently require permit procedure because of their probability to generate hazardous emissions (e.g. steel mills, chemical plants). Other installations require no special permit but they are nevertheless subject to operating requirements given by Federal Pollution Control Act.

Federal Pollution Control Act is meanwhile complemented by 22 federal ordinances. One of them is "Technical Instructions Air" (TA Luft) of Feb. 27, 1986. (GMBl. 1986, 95). This ordinance contains, inter alia, detailed requirements for prevention and minimization of emissions and regulations about quantities of emissions allowable.

Further, there exist numerous federal and state acts and ordinances to regulate environmental dangers in particular scopes (e.g. safety of nuclear installations, protection before air traffic noise).

Water Resources Management.—Any usage of water requires authorisation by competent water authority. Legal foundation therefor is Federal Water Management Act (Wasserhaushaltsgesetz) of Sept. 23, 1986 (BGBl. I, 1986, 1664, am'd subsequently) as framework law. It is completed by state water acts. These acts codify conditions and obligations for permits and licenses to use water.

Waste Water Act (Abwasserabgabengesetz) of Sept. 13, 1976 (BGBl. I, 1976, 2721, am'd subsequently) intends to minimize water pollutions by levying charges from generators of waste water.

Waste Management.—Recycled Use and Waste Disposal Act (Kreislaufwirtschafts- und Abfallgesetz) of Sept. 27, 1994 (BGBl. I, 1994, 2705) is codified approach to give waste avoidance and recycling priority over dumping of waste. This act is supplemented by several ordinances concerning particular types of waste, e.g. Ordinance of Old Oil (Altölverordnung) of Oct. 27, 1987 (BGBl. I, 1987, 2335), or special treatments, e.g. Ordinance on the Cross Border Transportation of Waste (Verordnung über die grenzüberschreitende Verbringung von Abfällen) of Nov. 18, 1988 (BGBl. I, 1988, 2126).

Packaging Ordinance (Verpackungsverordnung) of June 12, 1991 (BGBl. I, 1991, 1234) is regarded as important step to avoid waste, as it requires manufacturer and distributor of products to take used packagings back and to provide for their reuse or recycling.

EXCHANGE CONTROL: See Currency.

EXECUTIONS:

Execution is granted in respect to judgments, arbitration awards, as well as for settlements made and recorded in court; also in respect to special payment orders of court (Vollstreckungsbescheide) and in respect to so-called executory documents drawn at will of both parties by notary public or in German court.

In order to execute a judgment or other enforceable instrument the plaintiff in general must obtain an official copy with certification of enforceability. (vollstreckbare Ausfertigung).

Movable property of debtor is seized by bailiff (Gerichtsvollzieher), his outstanding debts and other valuable rights are attached by decree of court. See Garnishment.

Execution on immovable property is effected either by registration of a judicial mortgage (Zwangshypothek) on application of the plaintiff in real estate register, or by sequestration (Zwangsverwaltung) or by public sale (Zwangsversteigerung, see Law of Mar. 24, 1897, RGBl., p. 97, as am'd) of real property by decree of court. Also these measures are to be entered into estate register. See also topic Sequestration. (ZPO, §§704-945).

Judgments and awards against Federal Republic, State thereof, or government agency, are executionable. Execution of money awards requires special notice to

EXECUTIONS . . . *continued*
public officials, execution is not to commence prior to end of period of four weeks after proper notice. Certain assets of public interest and importance are exempt from attachment. (ZPO, §882 a). As to recognition and enforcement of foreign judgments, see topic Judgments.

EXECUTORS AND ADMINISTRATORS:

There is no requirement under German law that testator appoint executor for his estate.

If no executor is appointed or in case of intestacy, testamentary or intestate heir or heirs are vested with possession and management of estate and also authorized to dispose of it.

An executor may be named in a will or his appointment left to the court, but he is not an executor in the American sense of the term and is not vested with property. If the executor accepts the office he takes possession of the estate and deprives the heir of the right of administration and of disposing of the estate. Functions of executor may extend to entire administration of estate or be confined to performance of certain acts. Where executor has been appointed suits must be brought by or against him, and in certain cases right of action also exists against heir. (BGB, §2197 et seq.).

Where suit is brought by person asserting right of compulsory shares (see topic Wills) it must be brought against heirs to establish right thereto, and against executor for purpose of enforcing its execution in estate under his administration.

Administrators in the sense of that term in American law are not known in German law, all the powers and authorities of an American administrator being vested in the heir or heirs respectively. The appointment of a German estate manager (Nachlassverwalter), whose rights and duties pertain both to real and pesonal property, and who may be appointed either on motion of an heir or of a creditor, is a legal means for settling the liabilities of an estate. In the case of such an appointment upon motion of the heir it restricts liability for debts of the deceased to the estate and excludes personal liability of the heir. A motion for the appointment of an administrator made by a creditor must be filed within two years after the heir has accepted the estate, and be based on an allegation that the payment of the lawful debts of the deceased is endangered in the absence of such an appointment. When an administrator is appointed he takes possession of the estate and assumes all rights of management and disposition, and claims must then be enforced by a suit against the administrator. (BGB, §1975).

Claims cannot be enforced against estates until three months after the heir has accepted the inheritance, or in case he has during the first year thereafter applied for the issue of a public citation to creditors, until after the termination of the proceedings commenced by such public citation. The creditors may be required by public citation to present their claims within a specified period, and any creditor who, without belonging to one of the excepted privileged classes (such as, for example, certain secured creditors), does not present his claim within such period, is excluded from the division of the estate, with the result that the heirs, in so far as they have not forfeited their privilege of limited liability, may meet an action on the part of such creditor with the defense that the estate is exhausted. If anything is left of the estate the heir must surrender it to the creditor for his satisfaction by way of execution. Unsecured creditors who do not present their claims within five years from the death of the deceased are in general subject to the same defense.

FOREIGN CORPORATIONS:

See topics Corporations; Real Property.

FOREIGN EXCHANGE: See Currency.

FOREIGN INVESTMENT:

See topic Foreign Trade and Foreign Investments.

FOREIGN LAW:

Proof of Foreign Law: Applicable foreign law is ascertained by courts ex officio. Parties are to assist court in its inquiries. Application of foreign law being considered a matter of fact, it cannot be appealed to Federal Supreme Court. See topic Courts.

FOREIGN TRADE AND FOREIGN INVESTMENTS:

Foreign Trade Law of Apr. 28, 1961, BGBl. I, p. 481 (Aussenwirtschaftsgesetz-AWG) and regulation of Aug. 31, 1973, BGBl. I, p. 1069, as am'd (Aussenwirtschaftsverordnung-AWV) liberalize foreign trade and investment as a matter of principle, in particular merchandizing and capital transactions. See topic Currency.

Government may impose restrictions on business; those restrictions, however, being only permissible for certain purposes, e.g., for meeting obligations under international treaties and for protecting German economy.

Export of goods is free of license; some exceptions, however, exist. Goods permitted to be imported are listed in regulation, which enumerates goods that may be imported from countries without license. But regulations of European Community's institutions take precedence over German regulations also with respect to extent of liberalization. Thus, most of foreign trade is liberalized. Also money and security transactions between residents and nonresidents are liberalized. See topic Currency. Within Common Market countries any discrimination against citizens or corporations of other member states is prohibited. Even in case of liberalized trade, most transactions must be reported to governmental authorities.

Foreign Investment Shares.—Law concerning Distribution of Foreign Investment Shares and Taxation of Revenues from Foreign Investment Shares of July 28, 1969 (BGBl. I, p. 986) provides minimum regulations for activity of foreign investment companies selling securities in Germany (foreign mutual fund). Provisions apply to distribution by public offering, by public advertising or by similar manner; they do not apply to foreign investment shares listed for official trading on German stock exchange.

Distribution of foreign investment shares is permissible, if foreign investment company designates as representative a domestic credit institution, if fund assets are held by custodian bank, if domestic credit institution is designated as transmittal agent for payments made by or destined for shareholders, if terms of contract meet certain conditions, etc. Person who acquires shares shall be provided with terms of contract, sales prospectus of foreign investment company and copy of application to conclude contract. Sales prospectus must contain all data of material significance for judging shares.

Foreign investment company shall publish in Federal Gazette a financial report at end of each business year and currently the offering and redemption price. For publications, advertising material and all documents, German wording is binding. Notice of intent to distribute foreign investment shares within German territory must be given to Federal Control Office for Credit Matters in Berlin.

Whereas public offering of shares in foreign mutual fund may only take place if fund complies with Foreign Investment Law of 1969 (supra), and whereas private offerings of shares in such fund are allowed but are distinct tax disadvantage to investors if requirements of above law are not met, public offering and sale of securities issued outside country by foreign companies requires prior notification to Federal Authority for Supervision of Banks, which may interdict activities under certain circumstances. Offering as agent is subject to special license. (GewO, §34c). Soliciting of investors by telephone is prohibited. See also topic Securities.

FOREIGN TRADE REGULATIONS:

See topic Foreign Trade and Foreign Investments.

FRAUDS, STATUTE OF:

Germany has no statute of frauds; but see topic Contracts, supra.

In certain cases the law demands a notary's deed or court deed (authentic act). Principal cases are: Assignment of assignor's property in its entirety or in proportional share; contracts concerning interest in real property; waiver of certain inheritance rights; and marriage settlements (see topic Husband and Wife).

FRAUDULENT SALES AND CONVEYANCES:

Pursuant to a law of July 21, 1879, as am'd (Anfechtungsgesetz), aside from bankruptcy proceedings, transactions can be attacked by a creditor as void as against him, if entered into by debtor with intention of prejudicing his creditors provided that other party was aware of such intention; also contracts for value entered into with spouse or other relations within one year before attack is made, if prejudicing creditors, and also dispositions entered into by debtor without valuable consideration during last year, or, if made in favor of spouse, during two last years before contest. See also topics Bankruptcy; Sales.

GARNISHMENT:

Attachment of outstanding debts and of assets of debtor is done by decree of court pursuant to which debt is assigned to judgment creditor up to amount of his claim. This decree (Pfändungs-und Überweisungsbeschluss), together with garnishee order stating that debtor is forbidden to pay to his creditor, must be served on debtor and his creditor. (ZPO, §§828-863).

HOLIDAYS:

Legal holidays are New Year's Day, Good Friday, Easter Monday, Labor Day (May 1), Ascension Day, Whit-Monday, Reunification Day (Oct. 3), Repentance Day (on 2d last Wed. in Nov., but only in Saxony), Christmas Day and Dec. 26. In addition, Reformation Day (Oct. 31) is holiday in Protestant districts and Epiphany (Jan. 6), Corpus Christi, All Saints' Day (Nov. 1) in Roman Catholic districts.

Time periods expire on next working day, if last day of period would fall on holiday, Sun. or Sat.

HOMESTEADS:

Law of May 10, 1920, as am'd (Heimstättengesetz) providing for creation of "homesteads" (for residential or economical purposes) has been abrogated by law of June 17, 1993 with effect of Oct. 1, 1993.

HUSBAND AND WIFE:

Conflict of Laws.—Common national law of spouses applies to personal relations. If spouses neither have nor have had common nationality, national laws of common domicile or, if there is no common domicile, national law of state to which closest common links exist, apply.

Marital Régimes.—There are three marital régimes.

"Statutory marital régime of community of increase" (BGB, §§1363-1390) determines spouses' property rights if they do not stipulate otherwise. It provides separation of husband's and wife's property, including separate management thereof. Only one common item survived: "The community of increases" (Zugewinngemeinschaft), subjecting surplus (if any), that is difference between amount of property of each spouse at time of marriage and at time of dissolution of régime (by divorce, by death, but also by contractual termination of statutory régime) to common interest and to specific treatment, which is different in case of dissolution of marriage by death and otherwise.

In the event of death, the adjustment of the interests is achieved by the increase of the intestate share of the surviving spouse by one-fourth of estate, without regard to fact that no increase at all may have actually taken place. If, in case of testate succession, surviving spouse receives no bequest, he has right to claim share which would accrue to him in case marriage is dissolved otherwise than by death.

In the latter case, the following provisions govern: The increases of the respective properties are compared; if the increase of one spouse's property exceeds the increase of the property of the other spouse, the later is entitled to claim one-half of such balance.

In spite of the separate management of the respective properties of the spouses, there are certain restrictions with respect to the right of disposal thereof. No spouse may alienate his or her property as a whole without the consent of the other spouse. Such consent may be supplemented by the court upon motion for good cause shown. Lack of consent renders such a transaction ineffective. Objects belonging to the

HUSBAND AND WIFE . . . *continued*
common household cannot be disposed of by one spouse without the consent of the other spouse.

Spouse may adopt by notarial contract—before or after marriage—another system of marital régime, but only one régime provided for in Code; reference to foreign system is not permitted and not valid. Reference may, however, be made to foreign system of country of which one spouse is national or where one of spouses has his residence when marriage takes place or when contract is concluded, if it is concluded after marriage.

One system is (full) separation of property. A contract, which provides that rules regarding community of increase shall not apply, has same effect.

Common Property.—System of common property (Gütergemeinschaft) is optional régime and has consequence that in case of dissolution thereof (by mutual consent, by death or divorce) each spouse, or his or her heirs, become owners of one-half of such common property. Notarial contract is required. It must also contain provisions as to which spouse shall manage common property. If no such provision is set forth, both spouses must manage property together. Certain objects, so-called "reserved property" (Vorbehaltsgut), are excluded from community. Apart from "legal reserved property" (gifts or bequests made to one of spouses), spouses may also include in their contract other assets which shall be considered "reserved property." "Reserved property" is managed and disposed of independently by its owner. No spouse has right to dispose of assets belonging to common property without consent of other spouse; no spouse has right of demanding division of common property.

Separate Property.—System of separate property is optional régime and provides complete separation of husband's and wife's property.

As statutory régime of matrimonial property, GDR acknowledged state of common property, whereby all wealth accumulated on regular basis during marriage belongs jointly to both spouses. Property brought into marriage remains in possession of spouse in question; same applies for objects which he or she inherits or receives as gifts during marriage, as well as for smaller personal belongings. As of Oct. 3, 1990, this system of marital property is automatically transformed into Federal German marital régime of community of increase (cf. above), unless one of spouses had declared before Amtsgericht by Oct. 1992 that former GDR legal system of marital property is to remain effective for his/her marriage. This does not apply if spouses have previously made contract in favor of another marital régime.

Personal Relations.—They are ruled by principle of equality of rights. There is no disability of married woman. Spouses are mutually obliged to support. Spouse doing household work normally fulfills this obligation. There are no restrictions on contracts made by married woman or between spouses. When living in legal marital régime of community of increases, disposal of entire assets of one spouse or things belonging to household is only valid with consent of other spouse. Spouses may, upon marriage, declare to registrar whether to use husband's or wife's name as family name. Absent such declaration wife acquires husband's name. Spouse losing original name may add it to family name after declaration to registrar. According to latest jurisdiction of Federal Constitutional Court each spouse may use original family name.

German nationality of spouse remains unchanged by marriage to foreigner, but is lost when acquiring foreign nationality upon application. Foreigner married to German may obtain German nationality, if he is losing or abandoning his own nationality and if he shows that he will adopt German way of life.

See also topics Death; Divorce.

IMMIGRATION:

Visitors.—Visitors for business or for pleasure may freely land in Germany, with valid passport or in case of nationals of EC-countries with identification card only. For some countries there still is visa requirement. Alien allowed to enter must register with Aliens Authority (Ausländerbehörde) if he intends to remain in Germany for three months or longer.

Gainful Occupation.—Foreigner taking job, except temporary work for foreign employer, or otherwise gainfully employed must have: (1) Proof of identity (passport, identification card); (2) residence permit (Aufenthaltserlaubnis), to be obtained from Aliens Authority (through German Consulate). This permit is usually valid for one year but may be renewed annually. After five years of residence, permanent permit may be granted. These permits are, for good cause at any time, revocable; (3) work permit (Arbeitserlaubnis). Nationals from EC countries are exempted from requirement of work permits. Upon application of prospective employer to labor exchange, preliminary work permit may be issued to enable prospective employee to obtain entry visa. Final work permit will be issued after residence permit has been issued. Work permit may be issued for specific jobs only; it generally is subject to time limitations of one or two years, but it is renewable.

Only employees need work permit; directors, managers, legal representatives of foreign companies as well as assembly and repair technicians following import of equipment for short term work, but no trainees or apprentices, are excluded from work permit requirement.

So are self-employed persons, however, these have to report to local supervisory agency for business and trade (Gewerbeaufsichtsamt) before starting proposed business in Germany and, in absence of objections to enterprise (personal, commercial, environmental or other reasons) may be granted certificate of registration (Gewerbeanmeldeschein).

Immigration requirements do not, or under substantial modification, apply to consular persons, members of international organizations, crewmen and persons in transit.

Naturalization.—Certificate of naturalization may be granted to alien of good standing who is likely to integrate into German people and who has residence in this country and who is able to support himself and his dependents.

INFANTS:

Minority lasts until person reaches age 18.

Contracts.—Infants under seven years and incompetent persons cannot make any legal binding declaration and must be represented by legal representative. For any declaration of minor, between seven and 18 years, consent of his legal representative (parents, guardian) is necessary, unless minor acquires only advantage thereby. Minor can only enter into contract if his legal representative consents thereto. In certain cases even additional consent of guardianship court is required.

If, however, a minor enters into contract whereby he fulfills his obligations out of means given to him by his parents or by third person, for purpose of contract or free disposition of minor, no consent is needed.

If the legal representative, upon consent of the guardianship court, authorizes a minor to start a business of his own, the minor becomes unconditionally (i.e., without any consent) "sui juris" with respect to the ordinary transactions of such business. If minor, upon consent of his legal representative, takes an employment, he becomes "sui juris" with respect to transactions connected with this employment.

Support of Minor.—Child support unto age of 18 or until child's education (including university) has reasonably come to end, is mandatory for parents regardless of neediness or parents' financial situation. However, free education system (no tuition) practically limits parents' obligation to payments for livelihood which, in case of needy parents, may be substituted by variety of government scholarships and loans to qualifying pupils or students.

Germany is party to Hague Conventions on Law Applicable to Support Obligations toward Children of Oct. 24, 1956 (BGB1. II, 1961, 1012; BGB1. II, 1972, 589), on Competence of Authorities and Law Applicable in Field of Protection of Minors of Oct. 5, 1961 (BGB1. II, 1971, 217) on Recognition and Enforcement of Judgments on Support Obligations of Oct. 2, 1973 (BGB1. II, 1986, 825), on Civil Right Aspects of International Kidnapping of Minors of Oct. 25, 1980 and on Recognition and Enforcement of Custody Decisions for Minors and Restitution of Custody of May 5, 1980 (BGBl. II, 1990, p. 206).

INSIDER DEALING:

See topic Securities.

INTEREST:

If interest is to be paid on any money debts by law (as in case of default, BGB, §288), or by agreement, 4% (5% if parties are merchants) interest may be demanded, unless another rate has been provided for by agreement (BGB, §246). In case of agreements concluded before Jan. 1, 1987, debtor can, if rate exceeds 6%, pay debt before maturity except in case of bonds payable to bearer. (BGB, former §247). In case of agreements concluded on or after Jan. 1, 1987, borrower may, after ten years from whichever is later of complete draw down of principal or signing of new agreement on date of repayment or interest rate, prematurely terminate agreement by giving six months notice, irrespective of interest rate provided for in agreement; floating rate loans may be terminated at any time upon three months notice. (BGB, §609a). Merchants may demand, in case of transactions of a commercial character on side of both parties, an interest rate of 5% from due date. (HGB, §§352, 353).

Interest rate on right of recourse if a bill of exchange or a check is dishonoured, is 2% higher than discount rate from time to time fixed by Federal Reserve Bank; at least, however, 6%. (Law of July 3, 1925).

INTESTACY: See Descent and Distribution.

INVESTMENTS IN FORMER GDR:

In connection with reunification, German legislature basically decided to reverse instances of property confiscation effected by government authorities on territory of GDR between 1949 and 1990 (cf. Preliminary Note, subhead Reunification of Germany, and topics: Real Property, subhead Real Property in Former GDR and Reprivatisation and Restitution). To this end, Unification Treaty established between two German states on occasion of their reunification included so-called Property Law (Vermögensgesetz), regulating details of restitutions.

Particularly fact that former (dispossessed) owners must agree to sales and long-term lease contracts involving such property has seriously hampered investment activities in territory of former GDR. However, considering sad state of economy and housing situation in former GDR, such activities should be given priority. Thus, unification treaty includes law on special investments (Investment Law—Investitionsgesetz), whereby property subject to claims for restitution may nevertheless be sold to investors, provided this measure creates or preserves jobs, serves housing requirements of population or contributes towards providing necessary infrastructure.

However, it soon became apparent that this law alone was not sufficient. For one thing, it only applied to real property; for another, former owners could block sale to investors through court measures. Finally, after reunification, it was often unclear who was actually authorized to dispose of property in question (community, city, district or county, state, Federal Republic of Germany, "Treuhandanstalt"—national trust agency which was founded prior to reunification, or even new, private owner, whose ownership of or right to purchase confiscated property had been acknowledged).

Due to discontent with existing law, considered hindrance to quick investment in former GDR, second law revising Property Law and other laws was passed on July 14, 1992. (BGB1. I, p. 1257). It replaced Investment Law ("Investitionsgesetz") and famous §3a of Property Law by new Law on the Priority of Investment over Pending Restitution Claims ("Investitionsvorranggesetz"). Companies and real property may be sold to investor by present owner in larger number of cases than before. Thus restitution claim pending can be neglected and claimant only gets compensation at fair market value. Certain safeguards apply in order to avoid misuse. Present owner may also submit investment plan of his own bringing him into same position as buying investor. Once investment plan is submitted by investor or present owner, claimant is given two weeks by relevant authority to offer investment of his own. Within total of six weeks after notification, restitution claimant may outline his counter-plan of investment. Claimant will be given priority over other investors if his plan matches or exceeds other investors' plans (in terms of jobs or housing created or secured, infrastructure improved). For first time this new law provides opportunity for restitution claimants, who want to invest in their former property and are not willing to wait for authorities' restitution decision, to force present owner to sell property in question to restitution claimant. Upon final positive restitution decision claimant may claim back

See Topical Index in front part of this volume.

INVESTMENTS IN FORMER GDR . . . *continued*

purchase price paid, otherwise claimant has to pay fair market value (even if agreed purchase price was lower) (see topic Real Property).

"Treuhandanstalt" is, by law, sole shareholder of former "Volkseigene Betriebe" VEB (publicly owned enterprises) (cf. topic Corporations, subhead Former GDR). Its task to privatize or liquidate enterprises has basically been completed by end of 1994, with only few enterprises left for sale or liquidation.

JUDGMENTS:

Judgments of foreign courts are enforceable in Germany, if courts of respective foreign country also enforce judgments of German courts (Reciprocity). Not enforceable are foreign judgments in cases in which, under German law, court rendering judgment would not have jurisdiction, or defendant was a German citizen and was not served within jurisdiction or through German authorities, or where enforcement would be contrary to public policy (ordre public), and in certain other cases.

Reciprocity can be assumed between German and U.S. Federal Courts. As to U.S. state courts reciprocity differs. Reciprocity can be assumed for US-states which enacted Uniform Foreign Money-Judgments Recognition Act of 1962; they are Alaska, Colorado, California, Massachusetts, Michigan, Minnesota, Missouri, New York, Ohio, Oklahoma, Oregon, Texas and Washington.

European Community Convention on Jurisdiction and Enforcement of Judgments in Civil and Commercial Matters of Sept. 27, 1968 (BGBl. II, 1972, p. 775) provides for special rules applying to enforcement of judgments of courts of member states.

Foreign Arbitration Awards.—Their enforcement or vacatur is regulated by ZPO, §1044 and U.N. Convention on Recognition and Enforcement of Foreign Arbitral Awards of June 10, 1958. (BGBl. II, 1961, 121).

Awards are generally recognized and enforced in Germany unless they are not binding under law in country where rendered or are contrary to public policy of Germany, or if party against whom awards were made was not sufficiently notified or for some other reason was unable to defend case.

LABOR RELATIONS:

Labor relations are ruled by labor law, i.e., not only acts and prescriptive law but also collective labor agreements between management and labor. Fundamental labor regulations are to be found in Civil and Commercial Code. Important legislation for protection of labor are acts to protect employees (Law of Aug. 25, 1969, BGBl. I, p. 1317, as am'd) and especially pregnant employees and nursing mothers (Law of Jan. 24, 1952, as am'd on Apr. 18, 1968, BGBl. I, p. 315) against arbitrary dismissal, acts to protect juveniles and invalids and regulation of working hours of Apr. 30, 1938 (RGBl. I, p. 447). There are exact statutory notice periods, and discharging without notice is not possible except for cause. Extensive rights of co-determination have been affirmed in favor of employees' council by Works Council Act of Jan. 15, 1972. (BGBl. I, p. 13). See topic Corporations, subhead Co-determination.

Contracts between Employers' Associations and Trade Unions (Tarifverträge) are binding, in principle, upon the members of the contracting parties only; yet, the State Governments may declare them as generally binding and thereby they also become the source of law for labor relations between unorganized employers and employees.

Unfair labor practices are reviewed by Labor Courts which may also adjudge damages therefor. Courts have no authority to prevent strikes in advance.

See also topic Courts.

Former GDR.—Small number of labor provisions in GDR still remain in force for territory of former GDR. Subject is too extensive for detailed elaboration here. Provisions serve to ensure greater protection of employees (GDR employees can, in principle, be given two-weeks' notice), but also involve other areas, such as continued wage payments in case of illness, vacations, maternity leave, liability of employees and damage claims against employer. In meantime, all five new Länder have established labour courts. If proceedings have been commenced before Dec. 31, 1992, arbitration board law must be observed: generally, company's arbitration board must be heard in advance. Contracts between employers' associations and trade unions ("Tarifverträge", cf. above) remain effective in territory of former GDR till replaced by new contracts under FRG law. Right of employees to organize in trade unions, as provided for in Grundgesetz of FRG, was already established on July 1, 1990.

LAW REPORTS, CODES, ETC.:

Germany is a country of codified law, which means that only the provisions set forth in the different codes are considered the law; no decisional or judiciary law, i.e., law by precedent, exists, and doctrine of *stare decisis* is unknown. Decision of higher court is only law of particular case, and, if matter is remanded, lower court is bound thereby. In all other respects, lower courts are independent and not bound by any precedents. However, decisions of higher courts are frequently cited and quoted and also followed by lower courts, not as "the law," but because of their reasoning and persuasive force. Authority is also accorded opinions of scholars, set forth in textbooks, commentaries and monographs or pamphlets.

Official publication of a (written) law appears in Bundesgesetzblatt (BGBl.) formerly Reichsgesetzblatt (RGBl.), or, as far as Länder (States) are concerned, in their "Landesgesetzblatt." Generally in use, however, by courts as well as by attorneys, are annotated editions of codes.

There are official collections of decisions of several Federal Courts (see topic Courts); also legal periodicals contain many decisions.

LEGISLATURE:

See Constitution and Government.

LICENSES:

Before any new enterprise can be started (without distinction as to foreigners or nationals owning business) certain formalities need to be observed which, primarily, are matter of registration only. Thus, reports and registration may have to be made with agency for business and trade (Gewerbeaufsichtsamt), local tax office (Finanzamt), commercial register (Handelsregister), local social security office (Versicherungsanstalt), local chamber of commerce (Industrie-und Handelskammer). New enterprise may be subject to reporting duty with central bank of state (Landeszentralbank) concerned in case of acquisition by nonresident if investment exceeds certain amount of money.

Special permits are required for certain business activities, e.g., in fields of banking, insurance, brokers, investment consulting and so forth. To obtain such permit necessary qualifications or financial ability to conduct such business generally must be proven. EU subjects are granted specific relief. If business concerns handcrafts there are requirements as to owner being licensed in that handcraft or employing someone so licensed.

Nonresidents generally are subject to same or similar licensing requirements. Individual's foreign license may be recognized by virtue of bilateral treaties. Residents of EC countries have, in principle, same status as Germans.

Imports and exports are usually free of licensing requirements, except for certain obligations under international agreements (as, e.g., agricultural products subject to EC rules) and except specific licensing requirements concerning trade in certain products listed in Import and Export List (for example armaments and other strategic or technical products). Especially under EU rules, quota arrangements have to be observed.

See also topics Aliens, Corporations, Foreign Trade and Foreign Investments, Immigration, Monopolies and Restraint of Trade.

LIENS:

Lien is right in one person to retain in his possession goods belonging to another until certain demands of his against owner (or contracting party) have been satisfied. It is personal right and exists only in respect of goods received rightfully. Right may be excluded by express agreement or course of dealing between parties. It is right primarily to retain possession. However, after at least one month's notice to debtor, goods may be sold. See also topic Pledges.

Commission merchants, forwarders, warehousemen, carriers, building-contractors and landlords are protected by statutory liens on processed articles for their charges. (HGB, §§383-451; BGB, §§559, 647).

LIMITATION OF ACTIONS:

German statute of limitations prevents claimant from enforcing a right but does not extinguish obligation itself. Thus, a party performing his obligation after period of limitation has expired cannot claim restitution thereof. Claimant who is prevented from directly enforcing his claim by statute of limitation, may nevertheless obtain satisfaction of his claim from security.

Regular period of limitations of action in civil law is 30 years. Two year period applies to many transactions of every-day life. Four year period is provided for certain business claims. Limitation period for tort claims for damages is three years. Several shorter periods (12 and six months) are applicable to particular claims, down to six weeks for claims against seller of animals based on statutory guaranty. Even though period of limitation for particular action may have been less, 30 year period governs after judgment has been rendered.

Peculiar to two and four years period of limitation is beginning of period, which is computed from end of calendar year in which claim arose and which ends correspondingly with close of year two or four years later respectively. Three year period in respect of tort claims for damages runs from learning of damages and identity of tortfeasor. (BGB, §852).

Various other laws, particularly as regards taxes and duties, provide for specific periods of limitation, the period regarding taxes and duties not exceeding ten years.

The German law distinguishes between suspension (Hemmung) and interruption (Unterbrechung) of the period. In the former case, the period continues to run after the fact causing the suspension has ceased to operate; in the latter case, the whole period starts running again after the time of the interruption has ended. Cases of suspension are extensions of time for performance, suspension of the administration of justice (justitium) and acts of God or other causes of force majeure. Cases of interruption are the institution of a suit or taking of measures tantamount to it at law as well as any admission of the debt in any manner whatsoever, and acts of execution upon a judgment rendered. Simple demand does not cause interruption.

Due to war and post-war time, various laws, regulations and ordinances have been issued to extend limitation by suspension.

Different from limitation of action is case where law or private agreement provides for certain period of time within which such action may only take place (Präklusivfrist). While limitation must be pleaded to have court take it into consideration and leaves natural obligation even after judgment, limited period of time (Präklusivfrist) for action must be given recognition by court ex officio.

Former GDR.—As of Oct. 3, 1990, valid claims within former GDR fall under BGB/FRG statute of limitations. However, former GDR provisions continue to apply for suspension and interruption of period of limitation. If period of limitation defined by BGB/FRG is shorter than under GDR law, then this shorter period begins on Oct. 3, 1990 provided that BGB/FRG statute of limitation period had already expired. In no case, however, shall period of limitation expire before date upon which it would have expired according to former GDR law.

MARRIAGE:

Marriage is regulated by law of Feb. 20, 1946, as am'd (Ehegesetz).

A valid marriage ceremony can take place only before sworn registrar. Two witnesses must be present. Parties are at liberty to have a religious ceremony also but latter is of no legal effect.

Required marriage age is 18 years. However, marriage age may be reduced by court to 16 years on application, if future spouse is not minor. A minor needs consent of his legal representative or competent guardian. See also topic Infants.

Prohibited Marriages.—Important prohibitions are: There can be no marriage between relatives in a direct line; between full or half brothers and sisters; between relatives by marriage in direct line. No marriage can be entered into until former

MARRIAGE . . . *continued*
marriage has been declared void or dissolved by court. If woman wishes to enter second marriage, she must wait ten months after dissolution of first marriage, but exceptions may be granted upon application.

Foreign.—Marriage is considered valid under rules of German private international law if each of spouses has entered into marriage validly under laws of country of which he or she is citizen. Marriages to be concluded in Germany before German official have to be in compliance with form as provided for by German laws. Marriages concluded in foreign country by Germans, aliens, or aliens to Germans are, as to form, considered valid if form was in compliance with rules in force in that foreign country. Alien desiring to enter into marriage in Germany must procure special certificate issued by appropriate authority of his home country (Ehefähigkeitszeugnis). This requirement may be waived only for good cause.

Marriage within Germany between parties neither of whom is German citizen, may be concluded before person duly empowered by government of country of which either party is national, according to form prescribed by law of that country. Certified copy of entry of that marriage is to be filed with German registrar.

Germany is signatory to Hague Convention on Conclusion of Marriage of June 12, 1902 (RGBl. 1904, 221) and to Paris Convention on Conclusion and Recognition of Validity of Marriages of Sept. 10, 1964 (BGBl. II, 1969, 445).

MONOPOLIES AND RESTRAINT OF TRADE:

Law against Restraint of Competition (Gesetz gg. Wettbewerbsbeschränkungen) of July 27, 1957, in new version of Feb. 20, 1990. (BGBl. I, p. 235). This law applies to all restraints of competition which have effects within territory of Federal Republic of Germany, even if they are caused outside this territory. While in general cartels are prohibited, certain exceptions are allowed. "Condition cartels", setting forth principal conditions of contracts for purchase or sale of goods binding upon members, and "discount cartels", binding members to grant certain discount in case of transactions exceeding certain volume, may be allowed in discretion of Cartel Authority. Contracts are valid only if authority does not object within three months. This regulation does not affect contracts or resolutions concerning uniform business principles, delivery and payment conditions or foreign business. Cartel Authority may also allow agreement to reduce overproduction by members to actual demand if adjustment is made in consideration of overall economy and public policy. Cartels for rationalization, distributing certain fields of activities to certain members, and cartels for specialization may also be allowed, however, without any price fixing. For members of cartels consisting of small and medium-sized firms all agreements concerning restraint of competiton may be allowed upon special application. Export cartels, restricted, however, only to foreign markets, are generally allowed, but must be reported to Cartel Authority. Import cartels may be admissible if agreement concerns only import and German purchaser faces no or only insubstantial competition by supplier. Moreover, Federal Minister of Economics may permit any creation of cartel if limitation of free competition becomes necessary for general welfare. There are detailed rules for proceedings. With exception of pure export cartels, any licensed cartel must be registered in Cartel Register; cartels not registered are null and void and even punishable.

Fixing of resale prices is not allowed with exception of publication materials and tobacco products. However, resale prices of brand-name goods may be recommended under certain circumstances. Recommendation of resale price need not be filed with Cartel Office but may be declared null and void in cases of abuse. Restrictions on acquirer or licensee of patents, registered designs or brands which are not within scope of protected privilege are per se null and void. Agreements concerning transfer or exploitation of know-how are or become null and void if know-how does not or does no longer promote in doubtless manner technology or if know-how is not or is no longer secret.

Enterprises dominating market (monopolies and oligopolies) are submitted to control of Cartel Authorities to determine whether or not they misuse their market position. Mergers must be reported without undue delay, e.g., if participating enterprises collectively at any time during business year preceding merger had turnover proceeds of at least 500,000,000 DM. If by merger market-dominating position will be created or reinforced, Federal Cartel Office may prohibit such merger unless it also improves competition, and this improvement outweighs disadvantages of market-domination. Consent to be given by Cartel Authorities for mergers may be made subject to certain conditions to be fulfilled by merging enterprise. Concerted practices now are illegal as they are according to European cartel law. Under certain circumstances (in particular because of misuse of market power), Cartel Authorities have right to investigate prices, having been set by virtue of dominant marketing positions.

Under certain circumstances pre-merger notification to Cartel Authorities is required. Notice of merger plan must be given before consummation of merger if consolidated sales of one or more of participating enterprises during last preceding fiscal year amounted to 2,000,000,000 DM or if consolidated sales of two or more participating enterprises during such period amounted to 1,000,000,000 DM. For certain branches (trade, banking, insurance business, press) special rules exist for determination of turnover proceeds in regard to reporting duties to Cartel Authorities. Cartel Authority notifies parties in writing whether merger plan will be prohibited. As to substance, restrictions on mergers involving large scale enterprises were severed.

Disregard of provisions of law may be considered to be an offence and be punished with a fine and up to threefold amount of excess profit obtained by offence. In addition, Cartel Authority may order forfeit of excess profits to Authority.

Also of great importance are antitrust provisions in Treaty of Rome, founding European Economic Community, of Mar. 25, of 1957 (Arts. 85, 86 EEC-Treaty), and in so-called Montan-Union-Treaty, i.e. Treaty concerning Foundation of the European Community regarding Coal and Steel, of Apr. 18, 1951 (Arts. 65-67 ECCS-Treaty) which provisions partially supplement national antitrust provisions of EC-Members. On Sept. 21, 1990 Merger Control Rules of EEC became effective, now partially shifting authority for pre-merger control to EEC commission. See topic Monopolies and Restraint of Trade in European Communities Law Digest (in this volume).

Unfair Competition.—Law against unfair competition of June 7, 1909 (RGBl., p. 499, as am'd) has had with regard to its importance broad interpretation in jurisdiction and literature. Only some main aspects can be mentioned.

Most important provision of this law allows claim for omission or damages against anybody acting in commerce for purposes of competition contra bonos mores. It is not necessary that these motives are sole or even main ones. Furthermore, it is not necessary that defendant has acted on his own behalf; in consequence of this principle, law provides claim of omission against entrepreneur in whose favor employee or third person, considered to be charged in largest sense of notion, has acted.

Broad and important is jurisdiction concerning comparative advertising. In principle this kind of competition is not allowed; Federal Supreme Court, however, has developed a number of exceptions which become more and more important. It is furthermore prohibited to attract customers with unfair methods, i.e., methods which normally do not influence a buyer's decision for buying. A businessman may not discredit his competitor or his goods, nor use good name of a competitor for his own business purposes. Infringements of laws in connection with distribution of goods are also considered unfair trade practices, entitling not only public authorities but also competitor to take action. §§3 and 4 of law forbid making false or misleading statements concerning distributed products or their origin. Leading principle in interpretation of advertising or other sales promotion methods is that it matters only how a normal, not particularly careful consumer would interpret method; if only part of consumers misunderstand message, this sales method is illegal. Normal procedure for stopping unfair competition is by way of injunction (einstweilige Verfügung).

MORTGAGES:

Real estate may be subject to a mortgage securing a debt (Hypothek) and where no such debt is expressly mentioned, on behalf of a certain amount of money to be paid out of land only (Grundschuld), or from annuity (Rentenschuld). Entries are made under recording acts. See topic Records. (BGB, §1113 et seq.). According to Civil Code mortgages must be registered in terms of German currency.

In former GDR, there was only possibility of debts; moreover, in case of personal ownership (not ownership by enterprise or people), such debts could only be related to claims based on real estate property and directed against owner thereof. To back credits for building, credit institutions could file construction mortgages ("Aufbauhypotheken") which had priority over all other mortgages. First State Treaty between FRG and GDR ended this system.

Since then, mortgage rights as defined by FRG law can be cited to back all claims, not just claims related to property in question. Construction mortgages no longer exist (although those already in existence continue).

MOTOR VEHICLES:

Operator's license is required. Minimum age is 18 years. After trial period of two years following driving test, license becomes valid for lifetime of licensee and must be produced to police on demand. Nevertheless, license may be suspended in case of violations regarding motor vehicles. Aliens may drive within Germany for up to one year after first entry on basis of international operator's license or, in certain cases, of their valid home country's license. German operator's license may be granted to alien after theoretical and practical driving-test, in certain cases on basis of international or home country's license without taking test.

Vehicle Registration.—Every vehicle driven in Germany must be registered; registration-plate must be displayed in front and rear and must be of requisite size. Registration tax is to be paid for and during time of registration. Registration-card is issued by local authorities upon registration of vehicle and must be produced to police on demand; registration-card has to be surrendered upon deregistration. All vehicles registered in Germany are subject to periodic technical inspections.

Transfers.—Registration-book comes with vehicle. Upon registration of vehicle this book is issued by local registration authority, showing name of registered owner; and on transfer of vehicle such book must be sent to authority for registration. Upon transfer, new registration-card is issued by local authority.

Liability.—Registered owner of car is liable for all injury or damage caused by operation of car whether by negligence or not, if vehicle is used with his permission. Owner's strict liability is limited to certain amounts. Owner is not liable if he can prove that accident causing injury or damage was caused solely by other person's negligence.

Insurance is compulsory on motor-vehicle against liability for injury or damages caused by operation of vehicle to third persons. Plaintiff is entitled to action directly against insurer. Upon border crossing into Germany with motor-vehicle registered in foreign country operator must present international insurance-card, with certain exceptions.

NEGOTIABLE INSTRUMENTS:

Bills of exchange, promissory notes and checks are negotiable instruments by operation of law (see topic Bills and Notes). Certain other instruments may be made negotiable by statement to that effect. Through their endorsement or possession they confer upon holder in due course rights evidenced by and incorporated in such instruments.

Bill of Lading (Konnossement).—Bill of lading is document whereby carrier certifies that he has received specified quantity of merchandise which he promises to deliver to lawful holder of document. Instrument may be sold, deposited, mortgaged, pledged, etc., in same way as merchandise itself, and may be negotiated by endorsement.

Warehouse Receipt (Lagerschein).—Warehouse receipt is closely related to bill of lading. It states that warehouseman has received merchandise specified in it. Warehouse receipt is usually made out to one party only and is not negotiable, but it may be made negotiable by endorsement if issued by certain specially licensed and governmentally supervised warehouses.

Merchant's Trade Acceptance (Kaufmännische Anweisung).—Merchant's trade acceptance is document similar to bill of exchange or check. It is unconditional order to merchant to take certain action. It is used mainly to transfer goods. If it is made out

NEGOTIABLE INSTRUMENTS . . . *continued*

to transfer money, regulations on bills of exchange and checks are applicable. Merchant's trade acceptance may be made negotiable by endorsement by statement. Merchant who is instructed to perform action may accept it in same way as drawee accepts bill of exchange.

Merchant's Unconditional Promise (Kaufmännischer Verpflichtungsschein).—Merchant's unconditional promise is similar to promissory note. Merchant promises thereby that he will effect certain action for benefit of lawful holder of instrument. This promise must be unconditional and without reference to obligation on which it is based. It may be made negotiable by statement to this effect.

Marine Insurance Policy (Transportversicherungspolice).—This is only insurance policy which may be made negotiable under German law.

Private Debenture Payable to Bearer (Inhaberschuldverschreibung).—Private debenture payable to bearer is instrument in which maker promises to perform certain act on demand of bearer of instrument. It is regulated by Civil Code. Unlike promissory note, this promise need not be abstract. Defenses against bearer of instrument are limited. Title to document is transferred by delivery. Actions on instrument are barred only after 30 years from date of issue or maturity. Anyone may issue private debenture payable to bearer. Government license is no longer required.

Mortgage Payable to Bearer (Inhaberhypothek, Inhabergrundschuld).—Mortgage on real estate may be given in such manner as to entitle any holder of mortgage deed to demand payment from mortgagor. This instrument is rarely used. It is similar to private debenture payable to bearer. It is transferred by conveyance of title and delivery.

Bearer Shares (Inhaberaktien).—Share certificates payable to bearer, used by stock corporations, are also negotiable.

NOTARIES PUBLIC:

They must be German citizens and with few exceptions have same professional qualifications as judges and must be in full possession of civil rights. In some parts of FRG notaries are, for time being, lawyers functioning also as attorneys and notaries at same time.

Law of Feb. 24, 1961 (BGBl. I, p. 98) as am'd, regulates status of notaries public. Their activities consist chiefly in drawing up certain formal papers and declarations, contracts of sale, mortgage instruments, wills, establishing of corporations, transfer of shares of companies with limited liability, protests of bills of exchange and checks, certification of signatures and copies. They are also competent for administration of oaths if an oath is necessary to execute a right in foreign countries. They also may take statements in lieu of an oath. Notary may also issue certificates for use in foreign countries concerning existence or seat of a legal entity or partnership, changes in firm name, merger or other circumstances which are registered in a trade register. See topic Affidavits.

The fees of notaries are regulated by law and are on a graduated scale according to the amount involved in the transaction.

In territory of former GDR, there are only notaries who act exclusively as such. In Berlin (both parts), all notaries must, at same time, be attorneys. With regard to notary costs for citizens and legal entites in former GDR, cf. topic Actions, subhead Costs.

PARTNERSHIP:

The commercial partnerships of German law do not correspond exactly with what is meant by "partnership" in American law. While the German law comprises under this term commercial enterprises only, or enterprises which are conducted in the way of commercial enterprises, the American term comprises some features which pertain in German law to the associations (Gesellschaften) of the civil law under the Civil Code, but the last named associations differ in nearly all essential points from what is called a partnership in American law.

Partnership of German law (Offene Handelsgesellschaft) provided for in HGB, §§105-160, is reserved to commercial enterprises. It is not a legal entity but has some features in common with a juristic person. It is entitled to carry on business and acquire rights in name of firm; it may sue and be sued under such name. Name of firm is registered in commercial register, kept by municipal court (Amtsgericht) and all entries demanded by law concerning partnership are registered under such name of firm. Partnership may even sell business with name of partnership to single person, and such person will then be permitted to use partnership's firm name provided that succession is indicated, for business conducted by him alone. Firm name, on foundation of partnership, must contain either name of all of partners or, if less, words indicating partnership (& Co., & Cie.). Partnership may have distinct partnership property.

Every partner is obliged and entitled to participate in the management of the business unless other provisions are made in the partnership agreement. Thereby some partners may be entirely excluded from the management, or several partners may attend to it collectively only. Profits and losses may be divided according to the agreement.

Different from the management is the representation to third parties. Here the same rules as to management apply and each partner may bind the firm and the other partners. Restrictions of a partner are only allowed to a certain extent and, in order to become operative as against third persons, must be recorded in the commercial register. In dealing with a partnership, it is advisable to ascertain whether the partner purporting to act for the firm is placed under any restriction which fact is ascertainable from an inspection of the commercial register.

The partners are liable for all debts and liabilities of firm, jointly and severally, and directly also. Any new partner, in joining partnership (which does not require dissolution of old partnership and forming of new one), becomes liable for all debts of partnership. Any creditor may, instead of firm, sue any single partner, if he so desires, or firm and all or any of partners. On other hand, firm keeps its property, which is property common to partners, separate from private property of each partner. Private creditor of single partner may not levy against any of assets of firm, but is confined to his right to have partnership dissolved at end of financial year with six months notice and levy against capital portion of his debtor due to him upon liquidation of firm.

Creditors in a bankruptcy proceeding against the partnership may follow it up by bankruptcy proceedings against each partner. Bankruptcy proceedings against a single partner merely dissolve the partnership. Other reasons of dissolution are agreement to dissolve, or death of a partner unless the partnership agreement, in such a case, allows continuing the partnership with the heirs of the deceased partner or among remaining partners. After dissolution liquidation takes place. Partners themselves are liquidators by operation of law unless court, upon application for good reasons, appoints another liquidator.

Limited partnership (Kommanditgesellschaft) is composed of at least one partner whose liability is unlimited, and one or more other partners whose liability is limited to amounts they have agreed to bring into business as their share of capital as registered in commercial register. Limited partner, who has not fully paid in amount he has agreed to put up, is liable to creditors of partnership up to that amount. Limited partner is not entitled to participate in management and cannot represent company in dealings with third person unless he receives special power of attorney for such purpose. Name of limited partner may not figure in name of firm. (HGB, §§161-177a).

Partner whose liability is unlimited may be "Gesellschaft mit beschränkter Haftung," see topic Corporations, and its shares may be held by limited partners.

Silent partnership (stille Gesellschaft) is a partnership only between parties, partly subject to provisions of Civil Code as to civil associations, and does not operate as a partnership against third persons; it has no firm name, and no entry is made in commercial register. For debts and liabilities of business only owner, not silent partner, is liable to any creditor. (HGB, §§230-237).

Civil partnership (Gesellschaft des bürgerlichen Rechts) is general form of partnership of which purpose may be any business not considered as commercial matter by HGB. It is ruled by BGB, §705 et seq.

Partnership of Professionals (Partnerschaftsgesellschaften Angehöriger Freier Berufe).—By Law of July 25, 1994 new form of partnership for professional persons—lawyers, auditors, tax consultants, physicians, etc.—has been introduced. Character similar to commercial partnership (Offene Handelsgesellschaft—see above). Rules for Commercial Partnership apply to large extent, in particular as far as participation in management, representation to third parties and joint and several liability for debts and liabilities of firm is concerned. Yet, professional liability can be restricted to acting partner. Firm name of partnership must contain words "und Partner" or "Partnerschaft" plus reference to partners' professions.

European Partnership according to Law of Apr. 14, 1988 (BGBI. I, 1988, p. 514) may be established by contractors or unemployed persons. Provisions are quite similar to German partnership law. Partners of at least two EC member states are necessary.

PATENTS:

Governed by Patent Law of May 5, 1936, in new version of Dec. 16, 1980 (BGBl. I, 1981, 1), as am'd by Act for Improvement of Protection of Intellectual Property Rights and Fighting of Product-Piratery (PrPG, BGB1. I, p. 422) on Mar. 7, 1990. By virtue of this law Convention of Nov. 27, 1963 on Unification of Certain Points of Substantive Law on Patents for Invention, Patent Cooperation Treaty of June 19, 1970 and Convention on The Grant of European Patents (European Patent Convention) of Oct. 5, 1973 are also applicable in Germany. Therefore, there exists possibility of making use of European patent in Germany. Patents are granted by German Patent Office for new inventions which are susceptible of industrial use. Now, inventions of products obtained by chemical processes are patentable as well as inventions of food, luxuries and drugs. If inventor has already publicly described or used invention, patent protection may still be applied for within six months. If inventor is not identical with applicant he must be named in application, in publication, in patent qualification and in register, except upon inventor's request.

Examination Department (Prüfungsstelle) has to examine application to determine if it obviously does not comply with prescribed requirements. If it states such deficiencies, Examination Department shall request applicant to eliminate them within a specified time.

Patent Office now only upon request examines application to determine whether it conforms to prescribed requirements and whether subject is patentable. Such request can be made by patent applicant as well as by any other party within period of seven years from filing patent application. If not, patent application is considered to be withdrawn. Patent Office only states if invention is obviously patentable.

Request can be limited so that Patent Office shall only determine which printed material is relevant with regard to patentability of invention applied for.

18 months from date of filing application, Patent Office grants upon request to anyone inspection of application as well as models and samples belonging to files; if a priority date is claimed, this 18 month period will commence at such priority date. Patent Office publishes periodically in Patent Journal announcements of possibility of inspecting files of not yet published patent applications. From this announcement on, applicant may demand adequate damages from person who has used subject of application although he knew or should have known that invention used by him was subject of this application; applicant, however, has not yet the claims which will be given to him by publication of application.

If application conforms to prescribed requirements and if Patent Office considers that grant of a patent is not precluded, it shall order application to be published. From date of publication, applicant enjoys legal effects of a patent, either until grant of patent applied for, or until refusal of application.

Effect of patent is, that patentee alone is entitled to produce subject matter of invention industrially, to bring it on market, to offer it or to use it. If patent protects a process, its effect is extended to products directly obtained by that process.

If these exclusive rights are violated, patentee (or applicant of published application) may require that violation cease and in case of intentional or negligent violation, may claim for damages. If infringer is charged only with slight negligence, damage may be reduced between damage of injured party and advantage of infringer.

Federal Patent Court (Bundespatentgericht) decides appeals from decisions of Examination Department and Patent Divisions of Patent Office and proceedings for declaration of nullity or revocation of patents and for grant of compulsory licenses. Appeal on point of law from decisions of Board of Appeal of Patent Court, whereby

See Topical Index in front part of this volume.

PATENTS . . . *continued*
appeal from decisions of Examination Department and Patent Divisions has been decided, lies to Federal Supreme Court (Bundesgerichtshof), if Board of Appeal has given leave in its decision to appeal on point of law. Further appeal from decisions of Nullity Boards of Patent Court lies to Federal Supreme Court.

The patent protection lasts for 20 years from the date of the application. New patents are published by the Patent Office and entered into the patent register. A patent may be revoked two years after a compulsory license (see infra) has been granted, if the invention is exclusively or mainly manufactured outside of Germany.

Person's without domicile or business establishment in Germany must appoint an attorney or a patent attorney as their representative if they wish to deal with the Patent Office or exercise the rights under a patent.

Patent Bar.—To be admitted to examination for admission to German Patent Bar held at Patent Office, applicants must hold degree in natural sciences or technology and show proof of minimum of three years special legal education and six months practical experience in patent attorney's office according to Patent Attorneys' Code (Patentanwaltsordnung) of Sept. 7, 1966. Code also sets strict standards of professional ethics, defines rights and obligations of patent attorneys (Patentanwälte) and creates Patent Bar Association with executive committee of seven. Also transitory provisions for compliance with certain aspects by patent attorneys previously admitted to practice.

Inventions of employees are regulated by a law of July 25, 1957. (BGBl., p. 756). Law distinguishes between "free inventions" of employee and "inventions in service" or "bound inventions." Latter are inventions of employee based upon activities of latter in trade or service of employer or upon experience gained by employee in such trade or service. All other inventions of employee are "free inventions."

Bound inventions must be reported to the employer in detail, and the employer has the right to lay claim to the same by written notice to employee within four months. If the employer does so, he has to register the invention in the patent register and has to pay to the employee a reasonable compensation. If the parties cannot agree thereon, they must first resort to an arbitration board, appointed by the President of the Patent Office, and this board must try to reach a settlement; if no settlement is accepted the parties may resort to the courts.

Free inventions must also be reported to the employer who may, within three months, inform the employee that the invention is not a free invention in his opinion. In case no agreement comes about, the parties may resort to the arbitration board and, finally, to the courts. Before the employee may use a free invention otherwise, he must offer it to the employer who may accept it within three months. If the employer accepts the offer, but the parties cannot agree on the compensation, they may resort to the courts.

These legal provisions cannot be impaired by contract to the employee's disadvantage.

Licenses.—Patentee may grant licenses, and an exclusive license may be entered in patent register on application. Patent Office may give a compulsory license and fix terms and royalty after publication or grant of patent, if public interest so requires and patentee refuses to grant a license on reasonable terms.

In case the registered patentee declares irrevocably his general willingness to grant a license to every interested party against a reasonable royalty, his patent fees are reduced to one half.

Models.—In addition, inventions which concern tools or other practical implements may be protected by a kind of "little patent" called Gebrauchsmuster (design, utility, petty) according to provisions of Law on Utility Models of May 5, 1936, as am'd on Aug. 28, 1986 (BGBl. I, p. 1455); and am'd on Mar. 7, 1990 (BGB1. I, p. 422). They are registered by Patent Office on application and are protected by such registration. They are designated as D. B. G. M. (Deutsches Bundes-Gebrauchsmuster). Protection is granted to new models and devices designed for use or work to extent that new means have been designed to accomplish object such as in arrangement of parts or in design of model, and also to extent that known designs are applied to new work or objects. Accordingly models complying with requirements of patent law as to novelty and usefulness may be patented, but in cases where they do not come within patent law, protection may still be secured by registration as Gebrauchsmuster. With application for registration, there must be filed in patent office a full description of model, with all necessary drawings. Inspection of register and of files of registered designs including files of cancellation procedures is open to anyone; and besides this, Federal Patent Office upon request grants inspection of files to anyone if and insofar as a justifiable interest is substantiated. Period of protection is three years, subject to renewal for each two years up to period not exceeding ten years. Foreigners must be represented in same manner as under Patent Law.

§36 of German Patent Law contains detailed standards and requirements that must be met when filing applications for registration of patents or models (Gebrauchsmuster).

Design Patent.—Registered Design Act (Geschmacksmustergesetz) of Jan. 11, 1876 (RGBl., p. 11) as am'd on Mar. 7, 1990 (BGB1. I, p. 422) protects industrial property like patent law; matter of protection, however, being aesthetic design, it is part of copyright law. Effect of design patent is, that copy or imitation of model or design for professional use is reserved to patentee. Registration provided, protection is granted for one to three years, on special application and additional for up to 20 years. Design patent, however, offers only very limited protection.

Conventions.—Germany is one of parties to International Convention of Paris, 1883, version of June 15, 1970 (BGB1. II, 1970, 293, 391), and of Berne Convention of July 30, 1920. There are various other treaties dealing with patents, made between Germany and various foreign countries separately. See also topic Treaties and Conventions.

Former GDR.—Patents and copyrights pending or registered in former GDR enjoy same protections as patents and copyrights pending or registered at German Patent Office. German Patent Office processes all applications. Objections to applications and registrations may be made as in case of all other patents and copyrights. According to Act on Extension of Industrial Property Rights ("Erstreckungsgesetz" of Apr. 23, 1992 BGB1 I, p. 938) protection of patents, models, design patents and trademarks effective either in territory of former FRG or territory of former GDR is extended to respective other territory.

PERPETUITIES:

As to conveyances of properties to trustees upon trust perpetuities are forbidden by law under the rule, that reversionary heirs, etc., must become invested with their share within 30 years from the testator's death, with certain exceptions. (See BGB, §§2109, 2162, 2163, 2210).

PLEDGES:

Movable objects and assignable claims may be the subject of pledge (Pfand), the creditor obtaining possession of the object or an assignment of the claim. (BGB, §1204 et seq.).

In order to allow for pledging of movables without transfer of possession, there has been introduced in practice transfer of title for security (Sicherungsübereignung). See topic Chattel Mortgages.

PRESCRIPTION:

See topic Limitation of Actions.

PRINCIPAL AND AGENT:

In general, representation by an agent is permitted. Only in exceptional cases, mostly concerning family law, agency is not permitted. (BGB, §164 et seq.).

In German law, the decisive point whether the principal or the agent shall be bound by the agency is the intention of the agent expressed to the third party. If agent has not disclosed principal, normally relationship of principal and agent is matter only between such parties, and does not operate as to third person, and neither undisclosed principal nor third person with whom agent dealt acquires any rights against or assumes any obligation to the other.

To prove the powers of the agent, a written power of attorney may be issued to him. Relative to third parties, such power of representation may be established either by exhibiting such power of attorney or by a declaration to that effect by the principal directed to the third party. Revocation of the power takes place in the same way as the power has been conferred, i.e., by written revocation or oral declaration to the third party. The authority to revoke such power depends upon the legal relationship underlying the granting of the power. The power may be made irrevocable by contract. Death of the principal does not necessarily terminate agency. Whether or not power is terminated depends on underlying contract.

Commercial law recognizes various classes of powers of attorney, most extensive of which is procura which is not known in American law. Procura confers upon agent, called "Prokurist," all powers connected with conduct of a business, except sale of business itself and disposal of real estate. It cannot be restricted by principal except so as to bind the "Prokurist" to act collectively only with another "Prokurist" or principal or a director of a corporation or with restriction to one of several branch offices, and it virtually confers powers upon "Prokurist" tantamount to powers of principal himself. It must be recorded in commercial register, and may be revoked at any time by principal; also revocation has to be registered in commercial register in order to bind third persons.

Commercial agent (Handelsvertreter) is defined as an independent contractor—not an employee—whose business consists of finding customers and negotiating contracts for his principals.

Powers of attorney which are requested in connection with applications for entries in the land register or commercial register must be notarized.

REAL PROPERTY:

Ownership of land and buildings and existence of mortgages or charges thereon, are evidenced by entries in real estate title register or land register (Grundbuch) for each area, kept at municipal court (Amtsgericht; see topics Courts, Records, Deeds). Transfers of title, and creation and settlement of charges, require attestation by notary and only become legal upon registration in land register. Vendee, not vendor, usually (subject to negotiation) pays fees (notary, court, property agent) on real estate transaction. In many cases, municipalities by statute, or third persons by agreement, have preemption right.

Building permits are required for practically all kinds of construction including building of houses; stringent zoning laws regulate where and how building may be erected. Environmental laws may require special construction devices for protection of environment. Variety of laws regulate use of privately owned real property (maintenance of buildings for housing; preserving landmarks) and also prevent municipalities from selling property of public interest or use to private owners. Agricultural property may be sold only with governmental approval.

Leasing of real property by paying capital sum at outset of fixed term, instead of rent, is not recognized. Investment in housing complexes may be influenced by laws practically establishing system of rent control.

Capital gains on real estate transactions which are not part of investor's business, are taxable only if "speculative" (see topic Taxation). Real property is subject to real property tax levied in way of millage upon special value (Einheitswert). Moreover, value of real property is to be entered into financial statement being basis for capital tax levied on taxpayer's total assets.

Real Property in Former GDR.—In former GDR, real property did not have same meaning as it has within Federal German legal and economic system. Personal ownership of real property was only supposed to be possible to extent that personal use was actually involved. Beyond such property, there was co-operative property ("genossenschaftliches Eigentum"), people's property ("Volkseigentum") and so-called property of citizens' social organizations ("Eigentum gesellschaftlicher Organisationen)—as well as property of (socialist or "bloc") parties and its affiliated enterprises, all together also termed socialist property ("sozialistisches Eigentum"). Factories and enterprises belonging to people as well as state institutions were permitted to use people's real property for purpose of fulfilling their designated tasks. This was called

See Topical Index in front part of this volume.

REAL PROPERTY . . . *continued*
"Rechtsträgerschaft". People's property could not be sold (exception: special statute passed in Mar., 1990); such property may not be encumbered by mortgages.

Confiscated property, property for which ownership was renounced, or property where state exercised its so-called right of pre-emption (which it enjoyed in every proffered sale and which was practically speaking form of confiscation, since only symbolic compensation was paid) all became people's property. As of unification date people's property no longer exists. Ownership of real property by law was assigned to former "Rechtsträger", Federal State, Länder, counties, municipalities or transformed corporation. For cases in doubt Law on the Assignment of property formerly owned by people ("Vermögenszuordnungsgesetz", BGB1. I, 1991, p. 766, 784) provides for binding assignments by order of relevant authority. Parties' property came under fiduciary control of independent commission for investigating property of mass organizations according to GDR parties law (GB1. I, §66) amended as of May 31, 1990 ("Parteiengesetz"). After reunification, control was shifted over to Treuhandanstalt (renamed Bundesanstalt für vereinigungsbedingte Sonderufgaben–BVS–as of Jan. 1, 1995), which is now in charge of all restitution claims concerning parties' property.

Buildings erected by agricultural production cooperatives, by publicly owned enterprises on private land or by private person (for housing purposes) on people's property became property separate from land (which is not possible according to FRG law, where ownership of real property and buildings on it is inseparably linked). Solution of legal problems resulting from frictions between property owner (mostly West German) and building owner or user with formal position close to ownership (mostly East German) is subject to property revision law ("Sachenrechtsbereinigungsgesetz") of Sept. 21, 1994. (BGB1. I, p. 2457). Under law building owner/user may choose between transforming his right into (temporal) building lease and purchasing property for 50% of its market value. In order to facilitate agreements and to prepare for court proceedings, compulsory mediation procedure before public notary is installed.

Legal relations between present users of confiscated real estate—rent or usufructurary lease—and owners of estate after restitution are subject to law of Sept. 21, 1994 (Schuldrechtsänderungsgesetz) (BGB1. I, p. 2538) inter alia regulating compensation for usage and restricting possibility to terminate right to use up until 2015.

Until those laws came into force, present situation was freezed by so-called "Moratorium", Art. 233, §2a of Introductionary Statute of the German Civil Law Code ("Einführungsgesetz zum Bürgerlichen Gesetzbuch"). Building owner cannot be deprived of property's possession, if possession is based upon using certificate issued by State authorities in former GDR.

Transitional ruling which became effective with reunification (cf. Preliminary Note, subhead Reunification of Germany) provides that separate ownership of buildings will continue to exist in future.

Regarding restitution of or compensation for former people's property acquired through confiscation, cf. topics Reprivatisation and Restitution and Investments in former GDR.

RECORDS:

Land titles and all encumbrances on land, as mortgages, etc., are recorded in registers kept according and relating to parcels of land, all transactions affecting a parcel being entered in appropriate columns by the registry officials. These records (Grundbuch) are public in a restricted sense; anybody who has a well founded interest (mortgagees, heirs, prospective creditors, etc.) may inspect the records, relating to the particular parcel of land. Their legal meaning is far-reaching because of the legal system of public credence accorded to them and embodied in Civil Code and anything similar to what is known in American law as search of title is obviated thereby.

Other registers are the commercial register, maritime register for ships, register for airplanes, association register, and marriage property register, for their respective purposes. All these registers are managed by competent municipal court (Amtsgericht).

The "public credence" aforementioned means that any entry in the records is notice to the world. Nobody can be excused for ignoring the contents of the entry. On the other hand, every person acting in reliance upon such entries in good faith will get the full protection of the law.

There are no public officials charged with the general official registration of contracts or other instruments. Public credence to the texts of contracts and other private declarations is secured by judicial or notarial authentication.

REPORTS: See topic Law Reports, Codes, Etc.

REPRIVATISATION AND RESTITUTION:

Property belonging to people in territory of former GDR was, generally speaking, acquired through confiscation, with inadequate or no compensation (cf. topic Real Property subhead Real Property in the Former GDR). Same is true for corporations, GmbH's and partnerships (cf. related sections above). These are called people's enterprises ("volkseigene Betriebe"). Confiscated property could be given to people's enterprises for their use; on occasion, it was also given to private persons. Latter case was especially frequent in period between end of Second World War and founding of GDR in year 1949. Private persons were, for most part, small farmers or refugees from lost Eastern parts of Germany. Most so acquired agricultural land had to be incorporated into agricultural production co-operative ("Landwirtschaftliche Produktionsgenossenschaften [LPG]"), which were founded in 1950's. These confiscations of agricultural (and also woodland) property, which were carried out in time from 1945 to 1949, were given name Land Reform ("Bodenreform"). Land Reform property in former GDR could be acquired without proper registration in land register by inheritance or Act of State on basis of change of possession regulation ("Besitzwechselverordnung"). All changes of possession with regard to Acts of State are currently executed before land is subjected to restitution claims. This so-called "subsequent subscription solution" is applied because changes in ownership were not strictly registered throughout GDR due to fact that actual permission to use land was not based upon registered ownership but upon agricultural production cooperatives (LPG) authority as laid down in LPG-Statute.

Unification treaty between FRG and GDR provides that, essentially, unfair confiscations—with exception of confiscation between 1945 and 1949—are to be reversed upon demand of damaged person(s). These principles, like those described in following, are found in Property Law (Vermögensgesetz), which became legally effective as part of Unification Treaty. (cf. Preliminary Note, subhead Reunification of Germany). Claims for restitution or compensation had to be made before Oct. 13, 1990 or, following unification, by Mar. 31, 1991. Where such applications were made on time, they prevented sale of property or conclusion of long-term contracts binding possessions involved. Also where claims were filed too late, such contracts were forbidden, provided they had not yet been concluded. Final deadline for filing restitution claims has been introduced into Property Law by amendment of July 14, 1992. Deadline was Dec. 31, 1992 for companies and real property, June 30, 1993 for movable property. Special rules for confiscations resulting from criminal court rulings and similar acts do apply. Legal questions involved will take years, if not decades, to resolve.

Property confiscated under National Socialist régime is to be restituted insofar as possible, much as occurred in FRG after Second World War.

According to so-called Compensation Law (Entschädigungsgesetz) of Sept. 27, 1994 (BGB1. I, p.2624) where restitution is impossible (due to: change in use of property, or use in interest of general public, with considerable construction expenses involved; use in apartment or settlement complex; commercial use, where restitution would significantly impair firm's operation; etc.) or where property should not be restituted (land is needed for new commercial complex), basically only compensation shall be paid. Compensation is granted by means of negotiable bonds issued by Federal Special Fund, so-called Compensation Fund, which is established for that purpose. Bonds bear 6% p.a. interest as of Jan. 1, 2004 and are due to repayment in four annual tranches starting 2005. Compensation is calculated according to complicated regulations of Compensation Law. Basis of calculation of estate is last unit tax value assessed before confiscation multiplied by a factor of 3 to 20 depending on status of property. Compensation for enterprises is its last unit tax value multiplied by factor of 1.5. Monetary assets are assessed by their nominal amount. Amounts stated as Reichsmark (RM) are converted to Deutsch Mark (DM) at rate of 2 for 1. From calculated amounts—so-called equalisation of war burdens levy—paid by West German government in years of 1950 to 1970—and, if resulting compensation exceeds DM 10,000.—, deduction according sliding scale of 30% (for compensations of DM 10,000,— to DM 20,000,—) to 95% (compensation exceeding DM 3,000,000.—)is made. Compensation Fund is fed from several sources. Law does not provide for contributions by restitution claimants to Compensation Fund. Some claimants consider value gap between restitution and compensation unfair and unconstitutional.

Basically, restitution of enterprises is to be effected in such way as to reestablish former ownership and participation relations (were applicable, among heirs). In order to process these cases—estimated in thousands—offices to resolve property questions have been created at county, municipal and state levels. Moreover, federal bureau for entire former GDR has been established.

In days before Oct. 13, 1990, but also in subsequent weeks and months, these offices received over 1,000,000 claims for restitution, mainly involving real estate, but also other forms of property (enterprises, moveable objects, bank assets, etc.). It will take years, maybe even decades, to settle all these cases.

This amounted to serious impediment in way of urgently required investments in former GDR (cf. topic Investments in Former GDR), since, as described above, such cases prohibited sales or even simply conclusion of long-term contracts. Moreover, because mortgages and hypothecs could not be issued for such property, necessary investments could not be financed by banks. Thus, legislature enacted laws to eliminate deterrents in way of privatisation of enterprises and to promote investments (cf. topic Investments in Former GDR).

In public opinion, there was much criticism of fact that confiscations between 1945 and 1949 are to be excepted from restitution policy. While Federal German Supreme Court, in decision anticipated with great suspense throughout nation, declared that it is constitutional to uphold such confiscation, nevertheless, German parliament resolved so-callled Adjustment Performance Law (Ausgleichsleistungsgesetz) of Sept. 27, 1994 (BGB1. I, p. 2628), regulating form of settlement and providing for compensation payments. It covers cases of confiscation between 1945 and 1949 based on occupation law or jurisdiction of occupying power. Compensation payments are calculated and settled according to rules of "Entschädigungsgesetz" (see above), i.e. by means of negotiable bonds. Yet, monetary assets and securities stated as Reichsmark (RM) bear compensation of 50% of first RM 100.—, 10% of exceeding amounts up to RM 1,000.—. and 5% of amounts exceeding RM 1,000.—. Amounts stated as Deutsche Mark of Deutsche Notenbank are compensated by 50%. Total of such compensations for monetary assets and securities is limited to DM 10,000.—.

Moreover, "Ausgleichsleistungsgesetz" provides for possibility of enterprises employing agricultural areas since before Oct. 3, 1990 or former proprietors of confiscated agriculturally used areas or woodlands being natural persons to purchase real estate to favourite terms. Price for land is calculated as treble of unit tax values in year 1935, plus surcharge for buildings and immediately exploitable woodlands. Restitution claims of public bodies (states, cities, communities etc.) are dealt with seperately under Arts. 21, 22 Unification Treaty and Law on the Assignment of Property formerly owned by people (Vermügensznordnungsgesetz).

SALES:

Provisions regarding sales (BGB, §433 et seq.) relate to sale of goods and of real property. They are correspondingly applied to choses in action. Bargain and sale, in German law, is not real contract, but strict obligatory contract, executory on part of each party, and is to be distinguished from conveyance or transfer of title which does not pass through agreement itself. By agreement which, unless it relates to real property, does not require any form, seller is obligated to transfer thing sold to purchaser and to confer ownership upon him. In case of real property, transfer of title is effected by agreement of both parties before recording judge or notary to effect that title shall pass to purchaser (Auflassung) and respective record in land register (Grundbuch). Purchaser, by agreement, is obligated to pay purchase-money agreed upon and to accept realty sold. In case of movables, title passes to purchaser only when actual corporeal transfer of goods sold has been effected, but corporeal transfer

SALES . . . *continued*
may be avoided by contract whereby seller retains possession with understanding that he is bound to surrender to purchaser on notice or at specified time. Moment of transfer is determining factor for settling question as to when fruits (income and profits) belong to purchaser and liabilities are to be assumed by him, as well as risk of deterioration or loss. If at purchaser's request seller transmits things sold to place other than place of performance, risk passes to purchaser as soon as seller has delivered thing to forwarder, freighter or other person or institution designated to handle shipment. Agreement is, relative to performance, governed by general rules applying to contracts, and there may be, in case of nonperformance, action for performance or damages respectively.

Warranties.—In case of sale of corporeal things, particular rights are granted to purchaser in event of deficiencies destroying or diminishing ordinary use or such use of object sold as was contemplated by agreement. Then, at his election, purchaser may withdraw from agreement, or demand reduction in purchase price, or request performance through delivery of goods in perfect state in case of sale of generic goods. He has action for damages in event of absence of qualities warranted or if deficiencies were concealed maliciously. Limitation of six months after delivery of goods, or one year after transfer of real property applies to actions for withdrawal, reduction and damages; of 30 years, if malice of seller intervenes. First mentioned limitation of action may be extended by agreement, contrary to rule, otherwise obtaining, that such period may be shortened, but not extended, by agreement. Detailed rules obtain in event of statutory deficiencies in sale of animals. If sale is made to merchant, special supplementary rules of Commercial Code (HGB, §373 et seq.), e.g. duty to inspect goods, apply.

Product liability is subject to different legal frameworks.

Arts. 823 et seq. of Civil Code provide for tort claims in case of negligence. Frequently shift of burden of proof applies. Limitation of claims occurs three years upon either perception of damage and identification of tort feaser, in any case 30 years after tort action (e.g. delivery).

In addition, Product Liability Act of Dec. 1989 (BGB1. I, 1989, p. 2198 as am'd) provides for strict liability of producers of certain goods and electricity. Liability covers damages exceeding DM 1,125, up to ceiling amount of DM 160 million. Producer is liable if product is less safe than consumer could have reasonably expected. Limitation of claims takes effect three years after date upon which damage, defect and producer have been identified if claim is also brought to court within ten years after particular type of product has been first marketed.

Conditional Sales.—This legal institution is in keeping with German law. (Partially ruled by BGB, §455).

Seller retains title to goods sold and supplied to buyer, transfer of title to buyer being effected only on full payment of purchase price and/or performance of any other conditions for transfer of property agreed upon; up to that time buyer has real equitable right to acquire such property, and seller's retained title is restricted due to its purpose as security.

Should buyer be in default, seller is entitled to withdraw goods supplied under conditional sale and to satisfy himself out of secured claim; for a possible deficiency, buyer remains obligated. Registration in a public register is not necessary.

Notices Required.—If the party who is not in default, insists upon performance, he must notify the other party accordingly, allowing him adequate time to comply with the terms of the contract. (BGB, §326). See topic Contracts. No written notice is required. If time of performance is specified or if performance must take place within a certain period of time, or time is otherwise of essence (Fixgeschäft), no such additional period of time is necessary in order to apply consequences of nonperformance. (HGB, §376). No giving of additional time is required if seller clearly indicates that he is not willing to perform.

Notice of rescission must be express, but no special form is required.

Sale with Payment by Instalments.—Unless buyer is registered in Commercial Register as a merchant, buyer who pays purchase price by instalments is protected by Consumer Credit Act (Verbraucherkreditgesetz) of Dec. 17, 1990. (BGB1. I, p. 2840).

International Sale of Goods.—On Jan. 1, 1991 United Nations Convention on Contracts for the International Sale of Goods (BGBl. II, 1989, pgs. 586, 588) came into operation. States signatory to this Convention are e.g.: France, Italy, Austria, Scandinavian States, USA and Peoples' Republic of China. Convention replaces relevant statutory provisions of domestic laws and Convention Relating to Uniform Law on the International Sale of Goods/Convention Relating to Uniform Law on Formation of Contracts for the International Sale of Goods.

Applicable Law.—See topic Foreign Law.

Stoppage in Transitu.—There are provisions for stoppage in transitu in certain cases, whether the goods are being carried on land or on board ship. To exercise the right the duplicate bill of lading (Frachtbrief) must be produced if it has been receipted by the carrier.

Bankruptcy of Buyer.—Goods which have reached a bankrupt buyer only after the opening of the bankruptcy proceedings may be claimed by the seller if not fully paid for. The provisions appear in different laws, especially BGB and HGB.

Restriction of Sales or Other Conveyances.—Works of art and other cultural goods whose removal from Germany would result in an essential loss of German cultural goods will be entered in a list of such goods. A license is required to transfer such objects abroad, whether by sale or otherwise. This license is to be applied for to, and is granted or denied by, the Federal Minister of the Interior. (Law of Aug. 6, 1955, BGBl. I, p. 501).

SEALS:

Only public authorities, including notaries public, and public corporations carry a seal and are supposed to affix it to their signatures. The use of a seal by a private person or corporation has no meaning in a legal sense. The signature of corporations or other commercial companies is binding when in conformity with the signature registered in the commercial register.

SECURITIES:

Admission to Stock Exchange.—Bremen, Düsseldorf, Frankfurt am Main, Hamburg, Hannover, Munich, Stuttgart and Berlin have their own stock exchanges, with largest ones at Frankfurt and Düsseldorf. Sales of fixed interest securities are major activity, most significant being mortgage bank bonds and government bonds.

Securities may either be listed to stock exchange trading with official quotation (amtliche Notiz) as top segment of market or admitted to stock exchange trading with nonofficial quotation (geregelter Markt). "Geregelter Markt" enables companies of intermediate size to more easily enter capital market, while providing necessary investor protection. Listing to official trade or admission to geregelter Markt comes only after approval by competent stock exchange authority: "Admission Committee" (Zulassungstelle/ZulassungsansschuB). Moreover, securities may be traded on floor of stock exchange (Freiverkehr) without official listing or admission but by means of acceptance of association of Stock Dealers only. Prospectus is required for securities offered publicly according to Securities Prospectus Act of Dec. 13, 1990 (BGB1. I, p. 2749), providing language for several exceptions, and Regulations on Securities Prospectus of Dec. 17, 1990 (BGB1. I, p. 2869). In case of securities listed for official trade provisions of Exchange Act of May 27, 1908 apply to contents of prospectus which must include: History of company and its objects; description of business, its present and anticipated course; latest financial statements with explanation of all major items appearing on balance sheet; appropriation of profits and payment of dividends for past three years.

Prospectus must be prepared in cooperation with sponsoring bank represented on stock exchange. Sponsoring bank and issuer file application for listing, enclosing prospectus, copies of annual reports of company for past three years, and certain other documents including proof of validity of issue of securities to be admitted. After approval by Listing Committee, prospectus is published by issuer and "initial listing" (Einführung), official quoting of securities, takes place.

In case of admission of securities to regulated market (geregelter Markt) or trading of securities in free market (Freiverkehr) provisions of Securities Prospectus Act and Regulations on Securities Prospectus apply.

If information in prospectus is incorrect, misleading or incomplete those who issued prospectus, as well as those who initiated its issue are jointly and severally liable to any holder of respective securities for damages. Claim comes under statute of limitations five years from admission of securities in case of admission of securities to official trade or after publication of prospectus in other cases.

Trading in securities is done by banks that buy and sell on exchange for their customers through official brokers (Kursmakler).

Public offering and sale of negotiable straight debt securities requires approval of Federal Minister of Commerce (Bundesminister für Wirtschaft). However, approval is not required for issue of equity securities, nor are such issues subject to any other regulations. Informal regulations do exist for offering of straight debt securities, controlled by unofficial "Central Capital Market Committee" (Zentraler KapitalmarktausschuB) set up by leading banks.

Usually, group of underwriters arranges issue of securities. It is normal for underwriters to take over issue of securities and carry sole risk of its success or failure. Banks serve as underwriters and usually give issue prestige. See also topic Foreign Trade and Foreign Investments.

Change of Stock Exchange Act of July 11, 1989 (BGB1. I, 1989, p. 1412) extends range of permissible futures operations.

Securities transactions executed at stock exchange or over-the-counter are subject to new Securities Trading Act (Wertpapierhandelsgesetz) of July 26, 1994. (BGB1. I, p. 1749). This law introduced Federal Securities Trading Supervisory Authority (Bundesaufsichtsamt für den Wertpapierhandel). Function of this authority is to supervise trade in securities, options, futures, derivatives and similar financial instruments.

Forward Transactions.—Under Exchange Act (Börsengesetz), financial forward transactions as well as commmodity futures transactions (collectively called Börsentermingeschäfte) are valid only if both parties to transaction have special power of concluding such transactions. Only traders registered in Commercial Register and few public law enterprises not registered are automatically empowered to enter into forward transactions. Same applies to foreign traders who, if they were domestic, would be empowered per se. Traders not registered, such as individuals, acquire such power only if risks inherent in forward transactions are properly explained in writing to them by someone who per se has such power. Legal requirement of those written explanations must be distinguished from advice required under law of consultancy contracts.

Insider Dealing.—Having come into force with effect of Aug. 1, 1994, statutory insider regulations are provided by new Securities Trading Act (Wertpapierhandelsgesetz), which was introduced as part of Second Financial Market Development Act of July 26, 1994. (BGB1. I, p. 1749). Insider regulations apply to financial instruments such as securities, options, futures and derivatives provided that they are listed on stock exchange trading with official quotation (amtliche Notiz), admitted to stock exchange trading with nonofficial quotation (Geregelter Markt) or traded in free market on floor of stock exchange (Freiverkehr).

According to these rules it is prohibited for insiders to acquire or sell instruments on own account or on account of third party or for third party utilising knowledge of insider facts or to inform third parties unauthorised on insider facts or to make such information accessible to third parties. Moreover, insiders are not intended to recommend on basis of knowledge of insider facts third parties to acquire or sell insider instruments. Third parties having knowledge of insider facts (secondary insiders) are prohibited to acquire or sell insider instruments on own account or on account of third parties or for party utilising knowledge of insider facts.

Insider facts are all those facts not known to public related to one or more issuers of insider instruments or related to insider instruments, which if becoming known to public are likely to significantly affect market price for insider instruments. Insider instruments are securities, options, futures, derivatives and similar negotiable rights admitted to trade at German exchange or exchange in EU member state or being traded at free market.

Insiders are individuals, who have knowledge of insider facts as member of management board or supervisory body or as general partner of issuer or enterprise associated with issuer, or due to their share in capital of issuer or enterprise associated with issuer

See Topical Index in front part of this volume.

SECURITIES . . . *continued*
or according to their determination by virtue of their profession, employment or office. Secondary insider is any person having information of insider facts.

Compliance with inisider legislation is supervised by Federal Securities Trading Supervisory Authority. Insider dealing offences are subject to criminal penalties.

Essential part of new law to prevent insider dealing is strict obligation (§15) of companies listed at domestic stock exchange to immediately publish facts likely to influence stock exchange price of listed instruments (so-called ad hoc information). Same applies to issuer of bonds with regard to facts impairing ability of issuer to comply with its obligations. Before publishing facts issuer must notify Board of Stock Exchange with which instruments are listed and Federal Securities Trading Supervisory Authority. Ad hoc information must be published either in supra-regional newspaper appointed by exchanges or via electronic news service received by substantial number of banks, stock exchange traders and insurances.

Investment Counselling.—Legal relationships between investors in securitites market and counsellors are governed by law of consultancy contracts as partly regulated in new Securities Trading Act (Wertpapierhandelgesetz), which insofar has come into force with effect of Jan. 1, 1995. Usually, such contract is already implied when counsellor offers advice to investor, i.e., irrespective of whether consideration is given or not. Basically, counsellor is under duty to give true and complete advice as to both investor's individual circumstances and to character of potential investment itself. Normally it is sufficient for counsellor to advise verbally, but in case of some forward transactions which are deemed to carry significant risk written advice must be given. In case of negligent breach of this duty, normally it is presumed as matter of fact that investor would have acted according to hypothetical advice counsellor should have given. As consequence counsellor may become liable for damages to investor.

Apart from counsellor's liability under law of consultancy contract, also third parties such as directors of corporate counsellors may become liable in tort for wilfully inflicting damages upon investor contrary to public policy.

Netting in Case of Bankruptcy.—New Introductory Code to the Insolvency Act of Oct. 5, 1994 as well as art. 15 of Second Financial Market Development Act of July 25, 1994 provide same statutory regulations governing netting by close-out of pending financial forward transactions in event of one party to transaction becoming bankrupt. Regulation, which has come into force with effect of Oct. 6, 1994, excludes official receiver's optional choice under general insolvency law, i.e. his option either to unilaterally require performance of pending contract or to have performance replaced by ordinary department in bankruptcy. Rather, where more than one financial forward transaction is pending between bankrupt and counterparty, new statute provides that all outstanding contracts are liquidated and replaced by single liquidation claim. Single liquidation claim results from netting of positive and negative market values of various contracts if these contracts are combined in master agreement providing that contracts can only be terminated as whole. Thus so-called cherry-picking is rendered impossible for official receiver.

SEQUESTRATION:

Execution on real property of defendant can be effected by way of sequestration (forced administration, Zwangsverwaltung). On motion of creditor, who has an enforceable claim, real estate of debtor is attached by decree of court of execution and placed in hands of administrator in trust, who has to manage real estate and receives rents and profits, out of which creditor's claims are paid.

Sequestration must be entered into land register (Grundbuch).

SHIPPING:

All German vessels employed for the transportation of goods or passengers on the sea constitute the German merchant marine.

Vessels which are in exclusive ownership of German nationals are considered as German and as such entitled to show national flag of German merchant marine. When operated by commercial companies, all partners must be Germans; when operated by corporations or other corporate bodies vested with rights of a juristic person, seat of administration must be within Federal Republic of Germany, irrespective of whether capital is owned by Germans or foreigners.

Every vessel must be examined and measured as to its tonnage while under construction and on completion a certificate of admeasurement is issued by the competent authority. Such certificate is one of the so-called ship's papers. Another is the certificate of the vessel, which is issued by the court of her home port and testifies as to registration of the vessel in the ship register.

Owner of a vessel may be an individual, a partnership or a corporation. There is also a form of partnership peculiar to the shipping business, called Reederei. This is distinct from the partnership of the commercial law in many respects and governed by the particular rules of the maritime law. The rights, duties and liabilities of such part owners in relation to each other are placed on flexible basis.

In maritime law, the liability of the owner of a vessel, in many instances, is restricted to the vessel and what belongs to it (appurtenances, freight), while in other cases his personal liability is provided in addition to the liability of the vessel. But even in the case of the restricted liability, there is no such procedure as the suit in rem in American admiralty law, directed against the vessel itself, since in every case the suit can be directed against owner or master, even though no personal liability be asserted.

There are liens peculiar to maritime law, not requiring actual possession of the vessel, the particular liens being enumerated in the maritime code (for claims for wages of master and crew, salvage-money, average, etc.). They have an order of their own. There is also a special kind of mortgage on ships, registered in the ships' register.

A special law has been enacted in regard to vessels engaged in navigation on German inland waters. Its principles are very similar to those of the maritime code, though there are many deviations as to particulars.

STATUTE OF FRAUDS: See Frauds, Statute of.

STATUTES: See Law Reports, Codes, etc.

SUPPORT:

See topics Alimony; Divorce; Infants.

TAXATION:

There are taxes of Federal Republic, taxes levied by states (Länder) and those levied by communities. Foreigners are subject to taxation only if they are either domiciled in Germany or actually living there longer than merely temporarily, which is considered to be the case if they stay longer than six months within territory. Otherwise foreigners are subject only to a tax on certain income from German sources and on certain property located in Germany, rate of which amounts at least to 25% of income. Persons subject to such limited tax liability are not entitled to deduct expenditures specially allowed for unlimited taxpayers, personal allowances, nor deductions for exceptional burdens. Double Taxation Treaty exists between Federal Republic of Germany and U.S. with respect to German income tax, corporation tax, trade tax and capital tax. For details see this treaty in its 1966 version. (BGB1. II, 1965, 1611).

The most important taxes are:

(1) Income Tax on Individuals (Einkommensteuer).—It is based upon Income Tax Law. Taxable is income from business and profession, from agriculture and forestry, from employment, investment, rentals and annuities. Any other income is tax free, in particular capital gains, if not connected with business and speculation, lottery prizes, alimony, etc. From net income, special deductions are provided for under special circumstances. Also deductible are expenses connected with earning of income (business expenses), certain taxes (but not income tax), insurance premiums, contributions, etc. Spouses may file joint returns if they elect to do so; in that event, income is split as in U.S.

Income tax rate is on a progressive scale up to 53% which is reached at income of approximately 120,000 DM. Extraordinary income, e.g., from sale of unincorporated business is taxed at preferred rates.

Capital gain is considered "speculative" in case of resale of real property before two years, of securities and shares before six months have elapsed since acquisition thereof. Foreign tax credits are allowed. In general, taxable period is calendar year. Business enterprises keeping books may choose another tax year. Change from calendar year to another tax year requires consent of Tax Authority. Losses have to be carried back for two years with amount, however, not exceeding 10,000,000 DM. Further losses may be carried forward for five years.

Certain items of income are taxed by deduction at source (withholding tax). Most important items are investment income such as dividends and interest, salaries and wages. Withholding tax is credited against tax finally to be assessed. Deduction at source is also applied to other items of income, e.g., royalties payable to foreign creditors. In case of persons subject only to limited tax liability, deduction at source is applied to further items of income such as income derived from activity as artist or performer, writer, journalist or photographic reporter, including activity of these kinds exercised on behalf of a radio or television service, income derived from utilization of activities as defined just above and income arising from payments for use of or right to use copyrights and industrial patents as well as know-how. In these cases, tax liability is deemed to have been discharged by withholding tax, provided, however, that this income is not part of a business located in Germany.

(2) Corporation Tax (Körperschaftssteuer).—This is income tax corporations are subject to. Corporate taxation system allows full credit at shareholder level for income taxes paid by corporation. Tax rate is split as to profit distributed as dividend (30%) and profit not distributed (45%). For 30% imposed on distributed profit, relief is granted at shareholder level. Thus shareholder who receives dividend of 60 increases his income by credit of 30 against his individual income tax liability (imputation credit). Such credit is given only to German tax residents, but not to persons subject only to limited tax liability. Tax rate for foreign companies doing business in Germany through branch is 42%, determination of profits being limited to branch operation. For rest, rules of individual income tax apply in principle.

(3) Trade Tax (Gewerbesteuer).—This tax is levied by municipalities. It applies to most industrial and commercial enterprises. Tax is composed of three parts: tax on income, on capital, and in some cases on wages paid. Computation of profit is nearly same as for corporation tax with certain special additions and deductions. Calculation of tax rate is rather complicated. In practice, 12 to 18% of taxable income can be assumed. Amount of trade tax is deductible for purpose of determination of income and corporation tax.

(4) Capital Tax (Vermögenssteuer).—This tax is levied on property of individuals and corporations. Tax rate is for individuals 0.5%, as of 1995 1% (0.5% agriculture and forestry assets) and for corporations 0.6% annually of total assets. Certain parts of property are exempt from this tax. For evaluation of operating assets, taxpayer has to draw up a financial statement as per Jan. 1. Real property is to be entered at its special value as determined for tax purposes (Einheitswert). Certain free allowances are conceded.

Persons subject to limited tax liability, in particular foreigners, are subject to capital tax only on certain German assets, mainly operating assets, agricultural and forest property, real property, patent rights and trade marks which are used in business, and other intellectual property, assets leased to a German enterprise, mortgage loans and other claims if secured on German real property.

(5) Turnover Tax (Umsatzsteuer).—Turnover tax in form of value added tax, is assessed on basis of proceeds received by entrepreneur for deliveries effected or services rendered within Germany. Entrepreneur, however, is allowed to deduct value added tax charged to him by his suppliers (Vorsteuer=pre-tax) from amount of tax to be paid by him to tax authorities. In sale or service invoices, value added tax is to be included as separate item. Under this system, net amount of tax payable by entrepreneur depends upon amount of pre-tax (Vorsteuer) paid to his suppliers and allowable as tax credit.

TAXATION . . . *continued*

Standard tax rate is 15% as of Jan. 1, 1993. Reduced rate of 7% is applicable to certain turnovers, such as foodstuffs, agricultural products, printed matter, certain professional services and traffic.

Certain deliveries and services are tax exempt such as export, capital and money circulation, lease of real estate, medical services and all services to non-German tax residents listed in §3a Turnover Tax Act, such as legal, economical and technical advice, granting of licences, data processing, transfer of know-how, etc. Imports are subject to equalization tax at same rate.

(6) Inheritance and Gift Tax.—Inheritance tax is a tax on individual inheritance, not on estate; it is imposed upon heir; gift tax (gifts inter vivos) is imposed jointly upon donor and donee. Estate is jointly liable for these taxes.

If decedent or donor are nonresidents, only share devolving upon German beneficiaries is taxable. If neither testator or donor, nor beneficiary, are German residents, only real estate or certain business property located in Germany is taxable. Mortgages, which must be registered in land register (Grundbuch), are considered realty.

Applicable tax rate depends upon size of share received and degree of kinship of beneficiary to decedent or donor and varies from 3 to 35% for a (surviving) spouse or child, and from 20 to 70% for unrelated beneficiaries. Highest tax rate of 70% is applicable to persons without relationship to decedent or donor receiving more than 100,000,000 DM.

Incidence of double taxation with estates of U.S. citizens in Germany is largely avoided following U.S.-German Convention for the Avoidance of Double Taxation with Respect to Taxes on Estates, Inheritance, and Gifts of Sept. 22, 1982 (in force in Germany since June 27, 1986).

There are several other taxes, federal taxes as well as local ones, which cannot be dealt with due to lack of space. Tax for transfer of realty is in general 2%, plus additional local taxes imposed by municipalities where real estate involved is located.

Stamp Tax.—See Bills and Notes.

Former GDR.—Unification treaty (cf. Preliminary Note, subhead Reunification of Germany) provides that whole of Germany be considered one tax territory as of Jan. 1, 1991. These is, however, special tax legislation with referennce to territory of former GDR, providing taxation advantages especially for commercial investments. Investment tax incentives in form of capital investment grants have already been resolved (Capital Investment Grants Law of June 24, 1991 [BGB1. I, p. 1322]): for investments up until June 30, 1992, 12%; for investments between July 1, 1992 and Jan. 1, 1995, 8%. However, investment must have been initiated before Jan. 1, 1993.

Former GDR investment law covered period until Dec. 31, 1991. According to this legislation, disclosure of latent assets in process of transfering commerical goods to former GDR corporation, usually subsidiary, could temporarily be avoided by creating reserve which, after ten years have elapsed, must be liquidated at profit within period of another ten years. Particular advantage to transfering enterprise is that benefitted former GDR corporation can, in turn claim all depreciations, not on book value of transfering enterprise, but rather on so-called partial value ("Teilwert"), which is much higher and more closely approximates real value. Moreover, losses of former GDR corporation can be effectively claimed for tax purposes by parent corporation by creating reserve for them which is reckoned up against future profits of subsidiary firm. After five years at latest, this reserve of parent corporation must be liquidated at profit, unless parent firm has already sold its participation in subsidiary firm. Finally, losses on part of former GDR operation of FRG firm can be fully claimed for tax purposes.

Aside from tax-free capital investment grants, there are taxable investment subsidies. (Law on the Common Task of Improving Regional Economic Structures of Oct. 6, 1969, am'd July 3, 1991). For equipment of new factories (machines) and for constructing or extending buildings, subsidy can be up to 23%; for expanding enterprise, up to 20%, whereby at least 15% more job opportunities or additional 50 jobs must be created. Subsidies for investments to raise efficiency can be up to 15%. Investments, which must always be related in time to construction, acquisition, expansion or thorough rationalization of enterprises, must be concluded within time span of three years. Program is limited for five years, annually funded by federal government and Länder with 3 billion DM. EC regional development fund is contributing additional 1 billion DM annually in 1991-1993.

Adjustment of balances of former GDR enterprises to FRG system is regulated by so-called DM balance law ("DM-Bilanzgesetz"). This law also contains number of regulations for drawing up balance sheets and annual reports, since business enterprises in former GDR never produced any balance sheets or annual reports which were actually meant to convey realistic picture of their economic state. As of July 1, 1990, all enterprises in GDR had to be newly evaluated in terms of their property value (DM opening balance), after which their capital had to be newly assessed.

Furthermore, law (Fördergebietsgesetz—Regional Promotion Law) has been enacted for territory of former GDR and West Berlin, whereby investors can write off considerable amounts as well as benefit from extensive tax privileges. EC Commission is presently proceeding in accordance with Art. 93, par. 2 Treaty of Rome to determine whether provisions for forming tax free capital reserves and provisions on investment grants are to be considered state aids in violation of Art. 92 Treaty of Rome.

TRADEMARKS:

Trademark Law of May 5, 1936 in version of Jan. 2, 1968 is replaced by new law (Markengesetz) of Oct. 25, 1994 (BGB1. I, p. 3082) with effect of Jan. 1, 1995.

Any person who intends to use a trademark in his business in order to distinguish his goods or services from those of others may apply for mark to be registered in register of trademarks which is kept with Federal Patent Office. "Any person" means merchants, commercial partnerships and corporations of any kind. Trademark may consist of words, or pictures and designs, or both. Moreover as of Jan. 1, 1995 letters, numbers, acoustic marks, three-dimensional forms including shape of goods or its packing can be protected. Marks can be assigned and licensed. Trademarks or service marks no longer are distinguished. According to jurisdiction there are certain limitations as to what marks may be employed. Marks which are in general use in certain trade or industry, such for example as figure of Chinese in tea trade, may not be registered, nor may any marks which consist merely of numbers or single letters be registered. Same rule applies to words which contain statements exclusively relating to manner, time or place of manufacture of goods in question, or quality, purpose, price and quantity relations of goods, coats-of-arms of foreign states and inland cities, indecent, scandalous or deceiving marks, marks which encroach on personal business name of another. New law (Markengesetz) might result in modifications of recent jurisdiction.

Objections against registration of a new trademark can be filed by one who has previously made use of mark for identical or similar merchandise. Third party may request cancellation of trademark registered for at least five years if it has not been used within last five years before request of cancellation.

Appeals can be taken to the Patent Court from decisions of the Examining Division of the Patent Office. Last resort is the Federal Supreme Court (Bundesgerichtshof).

The right to the exclusive use of the trademark expires ten years from the date of registration, but it may be renewed for successive periods of ten years without limitation of time upon payment of new general fee. Trademark must have been used within five years after registration otherwise anyone may claim for deregistration.

An enterprise having no business establishment in Germany may demand trademark protection in Germany. It must appoint a lawyer or patent attorney as its representative. His powers pertain to maintaining all the rights of the owner of the trademark under the law. It must furthermore prove that the trademark is protected in the country where the business is located.

Germany is a member of Paris Convention as modified in Washington and The Hague, and of Madrid Conventions as likewise modified, and Trademark Convention of Vienna of June 1973. With a few countries, not including U.S., it has special treaties on subject. There is, however, reciprocity with U.S.

TREATIES AND CONVENTIONS:

Federal Republic of Germany is party to, inter alia, following multilateral agreements:

General: International Monetary Fund and International Bank for Reconstruction and Development—IMF (Bretton Woods, 22.7.44); Charter of the United Nations and Statute of the International Court of Justice (26.6.45/20.12.65); Constitution of the Food and Agriculture Organization of the U.N.—FAO (16.10.45); Constitution of the U.N. Educational, Scientific and Cultural Organization—UNESCO (16.11.45); Constitution of the World Health Organization—WHO (22.7.46); Constitution of the International Labour Organization—ILO (9.10.46/25.6.53); General Agreement on Tariffs and Trade—GATT (30.10.47); Convention Establishing a Customs Co-operation Council (15.12.50); Articles of Agreement of the International Finance Corporation (25.5.55); Convention Establishing the Multilateral Investment Guarantee Agency—MIGA (11.10.85); Statute of the International Atomic Energy Agency (26.10.56); Agreement Establishing the Inter-American Development Bank (8.4.59); Articles of Agreement of the International Development Association—IDA (26.1.60); Convention on the Organization for Economic Co-operation and Development—OECD (14.12.60); Constitution de l'Union postale universelle—UPC (10.7.64/14.11.69/5.7.75); Convention Internationale Des Telecommunications (12.11.65/25.10.73); Agreement Establishing the Asian Development Bank (4.12.65); Convention establishing the World Intellectual Property Organization (Stockholm 14.7.67); Agreement Establishing the International Funds for Agricultural Development (13.6.76); Convention on the International Maritime Satellite Organization—INMARSAT (3.9.76); Convention for the Protection of Human Rights and Fundamental Freedoms (4.11.50); Convention on the Prevention and Punishment of the Crime of Genocide (9.12.48); Statute of the Council of Europe (5.5.49); Treaty Establishing the European Economic Community—EEC—and the European Atomic Energy Community—EURATOM—(Rome 25.3.57); Treaty on the European Union (Maastrich Treaty—7.2.1992); Treaty Establishing the European Coal and Steel Community (18.4.51); Uniform European Charta EEA (28.2.1986); European Convention on Establishment (13.12.55); Convention on Securing Aviation "EUROCONTROL" (13.12.1960); Convention for the Establishing of a European Space Agency (30.5.75); Convention for the Establishing of an European Telecommunication Satellite Organisation EUTELSAT (15.7.1982); European Charta of Regional Self Administration (15.10.1985); European Social Charter (18.10.61); North Atlantic Treaty Organization—NATO (4.4.49/17.10.51); Hague Convention for the Peaceful Settlement of Disputes (29.7.1899/18.10.07); European Convention for the Peaceful Settlement of Disputes (29.4.57); Vienna Convention on Diplomatic Relations (18.4.61); Vienna Convention on Consular Relations (24.4.63); Agreement among Government of United States, Governments of Member States of the European Space Agency, the Government of Japan and the Government of Canada on Cooperation in the Detailed Design, Development, Operation and Utilization of the Permanently Manned Civil Space Station (28.09.88); Vienna Convention on the Law of Treaties between States and International Organization or between International Organizations (21.03.86).

International Cooperation in Legal Matters.—

Procedure: Statute of the Hague Conference on International Private Law (31.10.51); International Convention Relating to the Arrest of Seagoing Ships (10.5.52); International Convention on Certain Rules Concerning Civil Jurisdiction in Matters of Collision (10.5.52); Hague Convention relating to Procedure in Civil Matters (1.3.54); Convention on the Recovery Abroad of Maintenance (20.6.56); Convention on the Law Applicable to Alimony Obligations to Infants (24.10.56); *Conventions on the Service Abroad of Judicial and Extrajudicial Documents in Civil or Commercial Matters (15.11.65); *Convention Abolishing the Requirement of Legalisation for Foreign Public Documents (The Hague, 5.10.61); European Convention on the Abolition of Legalization of Documents Executed by Diplomatic Agents or Consular Officers (7.6.68); European Convention on Information on Foreign Law (7.6.68); *Convention on the Taking of Evidence Abroad in Civil or Commercial Matters (18.3.70); Convention on Serving of Documents in Administrative Matters (24.11.1977).

Recognition and Enforcement: *United Nations Convention on the Recognition and Enforcement of Foreign Arbitral Awards (New York 10.6.58); Protocol on Arbitral Clauses in Commercial Matters (24.9.23); Convention on the Enforcement of Foreign Arbitral Awards (26.9.27); European Convention on International Commercial Arbitration (Geneva 21.4.61/Paris 17.12.62); Convention on the Settlement of Investment

See Topical Index in front part of this volume.

TREATIES AND CONVENTIONS . . . *continued*
Disputes between States and Nationals of Other States (18.3.65); Convention on Jurisdiction and the Enforcement of Judgments in Civil and Commercial Matters (27.9.68—Protocol 3.6.71).

*For text see Selected International Conventions section.

Trade: International Convention Concerning the Transport by Railroad of Merchandise—CIM—and of Persons and Baggage—CIV (7.2.70); Convention on the Contract for the International Carriage of Goods by Road—CMR (19.5.56); Convention Providing a Uniform Law for Bills of Exchange and Promissory Notes (7.6.30)—for Cheques (19.3.31); United Nations Convention on Contracts for the International Sale of Goods (01.01.91).

Family: Conventions on Marriage, Divorce and Guardianship (23.6.02); The Hague Convention on Effects of Matrimony (The Hague 17.7.05), ineffective with respect to Germany as of Aug. 23, 1987; Convention on the Political Rights of Women (New York 31.3.53); Convention on the Nationality of Married Women (New York 20.2.57); Convention on Law Applicable to Child Support Obligations (The Hague 24.10.56); Convention on Recognition and Enforcement of Judgments Concerning Child Support (The Hague 15.4.58); Convention on Jurisdiction and the Law applicable to Protection of Minors (The Hague 5.10.61); Convention on the Conflicts of Laws relating to the Form of Testamentary Dispositions (The Hague 5.10.61); Convention on Abolishing the Discrimination of Women (18.12.1979); Hague Convention on Civil Rights Aspects of International Kidnapping of Minors (Oct. 25, 1980); Convention on Recognition and Enforcement of Custody Decisions on Minors and Restitution of Custody (May 29, 1980); UN-Convention on the Rights of the Child (20.11.89).

Intellectual and Industrial Property Rights: Paris Convention for the Protection of Industrial Property Rights (20.3.1883) with Madrid-Protocol (15.4.1891) and Brussels-Amendment (14.12.1900) as revised at Stockholm (14.7.67); Berne Convention for the Protection of Literary and Artistic Works (9.9.1886); Montevideo Convention for the Protection of Literary and Artistic Works (11.1.1889); Madrid Convention on International Registration of Marks (14.4.91) as revised at Stockholm (14.7.67); Madrid Convention on Suppression of False or Misleading Indications of Origin on Goods (14.4.1891) as amended at Stockholm (14.7.67); Hague Convention on International Deposition of Industrial Designs and Models (6.11.25) as amended at Stockholm (14.7.67); Universal Copyright Convention (6.9.52) as amended at Paris (24.7.71); Nice Convention on International Classification of Products and Services (15.6.57) as subsequently revised in Geneva, May 13, 1977 (BGBl. II, 1981, 358); Stockholm Convention Establishing the World Intellectual Property Organization (14.7.67); Patent Co-operation Treaty (19.6.70); Strasbourg Agreement Concerning the International Patent Classification (24.3.71); European Patent Convention (5.10.73).

International Sale of Goods.—United Nations Convention on Contracts for the International Sale of Goods, in force on Jan. 1, 1991. See topic Sales and Part VII, Selected International Conventions.

Tax Treaties.—

Avoidance of Double Taxation on Income and Property.—Most treaties for avoidance of double taxation on income and property taxes negotiated by Germany follow draft model published by OECD in 1963. They therefore tend to be similar in broad outline although frequently differing in detail. Agreements have been concluded with: Argentina, Australia, Austria, Belgium, Brazil, Bulgaria, Canada, Chile, China (People's Republic of), Colombia, Cyprus, Czechoslovakia, Denmark, Ecuador, Egypt, Finland, France, Greece, Hungary, Iceland, India, Indonesia, Iran, Ireland, Israel, Italy, Ivory Coast, Jamaica, Japan, Jugoslavia, Kenya, Korea (Rep. of), Kuwait, Liberia, Luxembourg, Malaysia, Malta, Mauritius, Morocco, Netherlands, New Zealand, Norway, Pakistan, Paraguay, Philippine Islands, Poland, Portugal, Romania, Sambia, San Marino, Singapore, South Africa, Spain, Sri Lanka, Sweden, Switzerland, Thailand, Trinidad/Tobago, Tunisia, Turkey, U.K., Uruguay, U.S.A., U.S.S.R., Venezuela, Zambia; Zimbabwe.

Inheritance Tax.—Austria, Greece, Israel, Sweden, Switzerland, U.S.A.

Special Relief Concerning Income from Shipping and/or Air Transportation.—Afghanistan, Brazil, Chile, China, Colombia, Ethiopia, Iraq, Italy, Jordan, Kuwait, Lebanon, Paraguay, South Africa, Syria, Uruguay, USSR, Venezuela, Yugoslavia, Zaire.

Former GDR.—German Democratic Republic—Arts. 11 and 12 of Unification Treaty (cf. Preliminary Note, subhead Reunification Treaty) provides that former national treaties of FRG retain their validity, while former national treaties of GDR be analysed together with respective parties to treaties, allowing for maintenance of confidence and weighing various interests involved according to principles of free and democratic system, so as to establish or achieve their continuation, amendment or annulment, as case may be.

TRUSTS:

Trusts within the meaning of law of equity for purposes of reaching equitable aims are not known in German law, since there is no distinct system of equity jurisprudence, and all such aims are reached by provisions of the civil law, mainly through certain legal institutions such as guardians, administrators, receivers and executors. In the law of succession and descent and distribution there is no division of title, as between the trustee and the holder of the equitable right, since the right of title is not subject to a division at all.

WILLS:

Wills and contracts of inheritance are governed by Civil Code.

A last will and testament may be made only by the testator personally and never through an agent. A minor may make a valid will if he is 16 years old or more. An adult, declared incompetent, cannot make a valid will.

Last will and testament can be executed in two manners:

(a) Holograph will: A will, written in longhand by testator and signed by him; no witnesses are needed for validity of such will. Law advises testators to add exact date (day, month and year) and place where will was executed, but omission of these items does not render will invalid. Minors and persons who cannot read, are excluded from right of making a holograph will.

(b) Will before a notary.

Testator may explain his will to notary who thereupon drafts will; testator may also submit to notary written will, in which case writing may have been done by third person, or will may be typewritten. Notary must read will and ascertain that will is valid, except where will has been submitted in sealed envelope. These proceedings must be taken to minutes, which must be signed by testator and notary. Documents must be deposited with district court. Minors or persons unable to read can only make will before notary.

Contract of inheritance may be executed before a notary. Such a contract is binding upon parties and may be altered or modified only upon mutual consent.

Emergency Wills.—If it is to be feared that a person will die before notary can be called he may execute will before a mayor in presence of two witnesses.

In case of emergency (war, high seas, etc.) will may be declared orally before three witnesses.

The "emergency wills" set forth in the foregoing two paragraphs become invalid, if the testator is still alive after three months from the execution of such will.

Mutual wills may be executed only by spouses.

Revocation of a will may be effected by express declaration of revocation in form of a will, by destroying will, by erasing same or of parts of it, in which latter case only these parts are deemed revoked, or by execution of new will. If, however, such new will does not contain express revocation of former will, former will remains valid as to provisions which are not inconsistent with new will.

Legitimate Portions (Compulsory Shares).—The spouse and the children (or in their place their issue) of the deceased, and where there are none, parents have statutory claim in estate amounting to one-half of their intestate shares (see topic Descent and Distribution). If they are not accordingly provided for in will, they have right of action against heir for payment in cash of proportionate amount of estate. In exceptional cases testator may deprive them of their legal portions, but ground of deprivation must be named in will. Right of deprivation is available against any of testator's descendants who are guilty of certain crimes or actions against testator, against parent or spouse who is guilty of certain serious offenses.

Foreign Wills.—Form of wills is ruled by Convention on Conflicts of Laws relating to Form of Testamentary Disposition of Oct. 5, 1961. (BGBl. II, 1965, 1144). Testamentary disposition is valid if its form complies with internal law of place where testator made it, or of nationality of testator, or of place of domicile of testator, or of place in which testator had his habitual residence, and, for immovables, of place where they are situated.

GIBRALTAR LAW DIGEST REVISER

Messrs. Marrache & Co
Post Office Box 85
5 Cannon Lane
Gibraltar
Telephone: 350 79918
Fax: 350 73315
Email: marrache@gibnet.gi

Reviser Profile

History: Marrache & Co. have enjoyed sustained growth over the years and now ranks as one of the largest law firms in Gibraltar.

The firm pioneered in Gibraltar the concept of integrating in-house Spanish and Danish lawyers. At present the vast majority of work undertaken by the firm is of an international nature.

Marrache & Co is a full service firm in general legal practice. The areas of expertise for which the firm is renowned are Company and Commercial, Banking, Tax, Insolvency and Trade Mark and Copyright.

The firm also has a recognised specialisation in Financial Services, Insurance, Shipping (Financing and Registration), Trusts and Probate and Labour Law.

Members of the firm are members of the Bar of England and Wales, Republic of Ireland, Denmark, and Spain, and are also members of several associations, including the International Tax Planning Association and the International Bar Association.

Significant Distinction: F. Ashe Lincoln QC (Consultant) is a Master Bencher of The Honourable Society of the Inner Temple.

GIBRALTAR LAW DIGEST

(The following is a list of all Topics, including cross-references, covered in this Digest.)

GIBRALTAR LAW DIGEST

Revised for 1997 edition by

MESSRS. MARRACHE & CO, of the Gibraltar bar.

(Dependent territory of EU under Article 227[4] of Treaty of Rome)

PRELIMINARY NOTE:

Gibraltar has been crown colony of U.K. since 1713; in 1973 Gibraltar entered European Community as dependent territory under Art. 227(4) of Treaty of Rome following accession to Community of the United Kingdom. Gibraltar enjoys political stability and its sovereignty is safeguarded by Gibraltar constitution in which the British Government has undertaken never to disregard the freely and democratically expressed wishes of Gibraltarians. Gibraltar is self-governing, it enacts its own laws (termed Ordinances) independently of U.K. and its legal system is based on common law and statute law of England.

ABSENTEES:

In absence of person abroad, person may generally delegate authority to any person of full capacity. It is usual for power of attorney to be granted. As in England, Powers of Attorney Act 1971 applies to and is enshrined in Gibraltar Powers of Attorney Ordinance. Pursuant to this Ordinance it is no longer necessary to file Powers of Attorney in Supreme Court of Gibraltar. Provisions of Powers of Attorney Ordinance are enacted without prejudice to those of §18 of Gibraltar Trustees Ordinance that relate to power to authorise receipts of money by banker or solicitor.

ACTIONS:

It is general rule that any person and or entity may sue or be sued in Courts of Gibraltar, subject to rules of procedure relating to courts. Questions relating to evidence such as competence and compellability of witnesses and methods and sufficiency of proof are matters of procedure governed by rules of evidence that apply in same manner in English courts. As in English courts, courts in Gibraltar cannot take judicial notice of foreign law, onus is on one who asserts difference to prove it. May be proved by expert qualified witness or by reference to code.

Plaintiff resident abroad is normally ordered to pay court in Gibraltar sum that ensures defendant's legal costs will be met by plaintiff if plaintiff fails in action. If plaintiff succeeds as in English courts, Gibraltar courts will refund sum originally paid into court.

ADMIRALTY:

See topic Shipping.

ADOPTION:

Legal adoption in Gibraltar regulated by The Adoption Ordinance, Court may, subject to certain provisions in Act on being satisfied with respect to certain matters, authorise applicant to adopt infant (person under 18) who has never been married. Applicants and joint applicants must be at least 21.

Application can be made by two spouses jointly; otherwise no order can be made authorising more than one person to adopt infant nor upon application of one spouse without consent of other, unless court waives such consent, being satisfied that spouses have separated permanently or that other spouse cannot be found or is incapable of giving such consent.

Order cannot be made where sole applicant is male and infant is female unless court is satisfied that there are special circumstances.

Conditions Precedent.—Applicant must be domiciled in Gibraltar. Infants' parents (or mother if illegitimate) must give consent which may only be dispensed with by court if parent cannot be found or adoption is in child's best interest and consent was being withheld unreasonably or parent has consistently neglected child.

Court may impose, in adoption order, such terms and conditions as it thinks fit.

Effect of Adoption.—Upon order being made, all rights, duties, obligations and liabilities of parent or guardian are extinguished and vest in, and are exercisable by and enforceable against, adoptor.

AFFIDAVITS AND STATUTORY DECLARATIONS:

Affidavits.—Affidavit is written statement of facts sworn by deponent before person authorised to administer oath. They are usually used in judicial proceedings.

Affirmation instead of oath may also be made in manner appropriate to person's religious belief.

For use in Supreme Court affidavits are required to be written, typewritten or printed in black ink, on metric size A4 paper, bookwise, with margin on left side.

Form.—Affidavit is commenced with title of action, e.g.,

Forms

In the Supreme Court of Gibraltar

(initial of plaintiff) No. (in Court index)

(In Chancery, add "In the Matter of the Estate of . . . . . . deceased" or as the case may be)

B E T W E E N:

Mr X — Plaintiff

and

Mr Y — Defendant

Full christian and surnames and true place of residence of deponent, and his occupation, must then be stated.

Every affidavit should set out facts deposed to in first person in paragraphs numbered consecutively and as far as possible be, confined to distinct portion of subject in chronological order.

Dates, sums and numbers must be expressed in figures not words. Alterations or interlineations must be authenticated by initials of officer before whom affidavit is sworn and, in case of erasure, must be rewritten and signed or initialled in margin by such officer.

Jurat.—Affidavit is formally concluded by jurat, memorandum of place, time and person before whom it is sworn.

Full address sufficient for identification must be given and jurat should follow immediately after end of text. It must not be written on page upon which no part of statements in affidavit appears.

Deponent must sign his usual signature or make his mark at right of jurat, not beneath it, and signature and full official character and description of person before whom affidavit is sworn must follow immediately after jurat, in form as follows:

Forms

Sworn by the deponent . . (Name) . . .)
at) (Signature of Deponent)
)
on the day of)

Before me
(Signature of Solicitor/Commissioner for Oaths)
Solicitor/Commissioner for Oaths

On final page of affidavit one must state (i) Party on whose behalf it is filed; (ii) date when filed.

For use in other courts affidavits are sworn in same manner as those for use in Supreme Court.

Exhibits.—Any document may be referred to in body of affidavit as exhibit, thus: "the said letter is now produced and shown to me marked 'AB' " (deponent's initials are generally used).

Where there is more than one exhibit best course is to use as exhibit marks deponent's initials followed by consecutive numbers as thus "AB 1" "AB 2" etc. By this means exhibits to affidavits of several witnesses are readily identified.

Every exhibit referred to in affidavit must be marked with short title of cause or matter, as hereinbefore set out for affidavit and bear certificate signed by officer before whom affidavit is sworn, as follows:

Form

This is the Exhibit marked "AB 2" (or "AB 1") referred to in the Affidavit of XY sworn in this action (if Chancery, "Matter" not "Action") this . . . . . . day of 19

Before me
(Name and Title of Officer)

Statutory Declarations.—Solemn verification of facts, usually used in cases other than judicial proceedings e.g., conveyancing, tax, company matters.

Form.—They must start with:

"I, AB of (Address) do solemnly and sincerely declare as follows . . . . . ."

Last paragraph should read:

"AND I make this solemn declaration believing the same to be true and by virtue of the provisions of the Statutory Declarations Act 1835".

Remaining requirements are as for Affidavits.

Jurat—

Declared before me at (address) on, Signature of Declarant (date)

Signature and qualification of person taking declaration.

ALIENS:

If one is registered as Gibraltarian under Gibraltarian Status Ordinance then there is automatic right to reside in Gibraltar. Persons entitled to be registered accordingly are any British subject who: (a) was born in Gibraltar on or before 30 June 1925; or (b) is legitimate child of male person entitled to be registered under paragraph (a) above; or (c) is descendant by legitimate male descent of male person entitled to be registered under paragraph (a) or (b) above and whose father or paternal grandfather was born in Gibraltar; or (d) is wife or widow of person entitled to be registered under paragraph (a), (b) or (c) above; or (e) is legitimate child of male person who has been registered by viture of order made by Governor; or (f) is descendent by legitimate male descent of male person who has been registered by virtue of order made by Governor and his father or paternal grandfather was born in Gibraltar; or (g) is wife or widow of person who has been registered by virtue of order made by Governor or who is entitled to be registered under paragraph (e) or (f) above; or (h) is born in Gibraltar and is legitimate child of male person who is registered in Register; or (i) is wife or widow of person entitled to be registered under paragraph (h) above. (§4, subsection 1).

Governor may, in his absolute discretion, order registration of any person who satisfies Governor that: (a) Gibraltar or Great Britain is his country of origin; (b) he is British subject; (c) he is of good character; (d) he has sufficient knowledge of English language; (e) he has his permanent home in Gibraltar; (f) he has been resident in Gibraltar for period amounting to not less than 25 years in aggregate including whole of period of ten years immediately preceding date of application; (g) he intends to make his permanent home in Gibraltar.

See Topical Index in front part of this volume.

ALIENS . . . *continued*

It is offence to attempt to employ as worker any person who is not resident of Gibraltar without first notifying manager of central employment exchange of particulars of vacancy to be filled. It is also offence to employ any worker who is not resident of Gibraltar without permit so to do in prescribed form which Director of Labour and Social Security is empowered to grant. Director of Labour and Social Security shall not issue permit for employment of worker who is not resident of Gibraltar unless he is satisfied as to numerous requirements which include following: (a) that there is no resident of Gibraltar registered under §15 of Employment Ordinance (which deals with register of persons seeking employment) who is in opinion of Director capable of undertaking and suitable for particular employment in respect of which employment is sought; (b) that terms and conditions of employment are not less favourable than those prescribed by law or generally observed by good employers; (c) that prospective employer has made adequate efforts to find resident of Gibraltar who is capable of undertaking and suitable for employment where these have been unsuccessful so no suitable worker is in opinion of Director capable of undertaking and suitable for employment who is registered under §15; (d) that prospective employer genuinely intends to employ worker in employment; (e) that valid written contract of employment is duly entered into by prospective employer and worker has been produced to and approved by Director; (f) that worker is in possession of valid passport and that this passport would continue to be valid for period of not less than duration of contract.

Director issues certificate of employment which is to be inserted in identity carnet of worker. Director may in his discretion refuse to grant permit, for example in case of employment of worker where in his opinion that decision is warranted by situation in labour market. (§§20 and 21 of Employment Ordinance).

There is also civilian register for issue of identity carnets and this is dealt with in Civilians Registration Ordinance. This is register of all civilians who are in or who may at any future time enter Gibraltar. Card containing prescribed particulars (referred to as Identity Carnet) is issued in respect of every registered person in accordance with regulations under this Ordinance.

There are obviously exceptions to this Ordinance, for example visitors who come to Gibraltar for single period not exceeding 24 hours or who are temporarily in Gibraltar for sole purpose of travelling to some other place.

Matters of immigration are regulated by Immigration Control Ordinance. No non-Gibraltarian can enter or remain in Gibraltar unless he is in possession of: (a) valid entry permit; (b) valid permit of residence; or (c) valid certificate.

When satisfied that any person who would but for his inability to comply with requirements of paragraph 5, subsection 2(c) or 7(c) of Schedule 1 to British Nationality Act 1981 be otherwise eligible to apply for naturalisation as British Dependent Territories Citizen under provisions of §18 of British Nationality Act 1981 Governor may, in his absolute discretion, by order exempt any such person from compliance with abovementioned requirements. (§12). However nothing in this Ordinance requires any Gibraltarian or British Dependent Territories Citizen having connection with Gibraltar to obtain or hold any permit or certificate which may be issued under this Ordinance.

There is right of residence of men married to Gibraltarian women although Principal Immigration Officer may refuse permit of residence in certain circumstances such as on grounds of public policy or public security. There is also right of residence for children of Gibraltarian women.

Principal Immigration Officer is responsible for issue to non-Gibraltarians of permits of residence. However, Governor may also order Principal Immigration Officer to issue permit of residence in certain circumstances such as to any person who in his opinion is of good character where it would be in interests of Gibraltar that he be issued with such permit.

There is no appeal to any Court from any decision of Principal Immigration Officer or from any decision of Governor under this Ordinance. Granting of certificate to person shall not confer upon that person any right to have his name entered in Register of Gibraltarians established under Gibraltarian Status Ordinance nor shall it confer upon him any rights or privileges conferred by law upon Gibraltarians.

There are special provisions relating to community nationals. Community national may enter Gibraltar on production by such national of valid identity card or valid passport. Community national who has entered Gibraltar may at any time apply to Principal Immigration Officer for residence permit. In interests of public policy, public security or public health Principal Immigration Officer may refuse to allow community national to enter Gibraltar or may refuse him residence permit or may cancel residence permit.

Law has recently been changed by Immigration Control Ordinance Rules of 1993 insofar as Community Nationals (and particularly British citizens) are concerned, which appear to restrict rights of residence of U.K. nationals not resident in Gibraltar prior to 1st July 1993.

ARBITRATION AND AWARD:

See topic Dispute Resolution.

ASSIGNMENTS FOR BENEFIT OF CREDITORS:

By Deeds of Arrangement Ordinance 1914, under which any instrument whether under seal or not, made by, for or in respect of affairs of debtor (a) for benefit of his creditors generally or (b) where debtor was insolvent at date of execution of instrument, for benefit of any three or more of his creditors, otherwise than pursuant to Law relating to bankruptcy is deemed to be Deed of Arrangement and subject to provisions of Ordinance. Following classes of instruments particularly included: (a) Assignment of property; (b) deeds of, or agreements for composition; (c) in cases where creditors of debtor obtain control over his property or business, Deed of Inspectorship for purpose of carrying on or winding-up business; (d) letter of licence authorising debtor or any other person to manage, carry on, realise or dispose of business with view to payment of debts and (e) any agreement entered into for purpose of carrying on or winding-up debtor's business or authorising debtor or any other person to manage, carry on, realise, dispose or debtor's business, with view to payment of his debts.

Deed of Arrangement is void unless it is registered with Registrar of Deeds of Arrangement within seven clear days after its execution in Gibraltar, or if executed abroad, within seven clear days after time at which it would in ordinary course of post, arrive in Gibraltar if posted within one week after execution thereof.

Deed for benefit of creditors generally is void unless before or within 21 days of registration it receives assent in writing of majority in number and value of creditors. Trustee under deed must file statutory declaration that requirements, that majority of creditors have assented at time of registration or, if deed is assented to, registration within 28 days thereof. He must also give security unless majority of creditors dispense with it.

Debtor is at liberty to make private arrangement with his creditors upon terms to which he can get them to agree, but no creditor is bound to join in such deed unless he thinks proper.

ATTACHMENT AND EXECUTION:

Attachment and enforcement of debts may be by several methods:

(1) Garnishment by attaching monies owing from third party to judgment debtor and obtaining payment of such monies directly from third party to judgment creditor.

(2) Charging Order in court making stocks and shares or fund available to satisfy judgment for ascertained sum of money. On order being made judgment creditor has same powers as though debtor made valid and effective charge in favour.

(3) Stop Order may be obtained in court against fund which gives notice to court of creditor's claim and prevents fund being dealt with without its knowledge.

(4) Stop Notice.—Anyone claiming to be interested in any stock registered in its books may serve notice on company to prevent company dealing with shares without first giving opportunity at asserting claim.

(5) Writ of Fieri Facias.—Writ filed at Court Registry by judgment creditor enabling court bailiff to seize goods of debtor in satisfaction of debt.

(6) Transfer to Court of First Instance.—Supreme Court money judgment may also be transferred to court of first instance for enforcement. Debtor is summoned and examined as to his means and court makes order as to payment.

(7) Bankruptcy.—Such proceedings may also be available (see topic Bankruptcy and Insolvency).

(8) Winding-Up/Receivership.—Corporate debts may also be enforced in this manner (see topic Bankruptcy and Insolvency).

ATTORNEYS AND COUNSELORS:

In Gibraltar, unlike U.K. or Republic of Ireland, Supreme Court (Amendment) Ordinance, 1986 allows "every person holding the office of Attorney General, Law Draftsman, Senior Crown Counsel or Crown Counsel shall, so long as he continues to hold such office, have and enjoy all the rights and privileges of a barrister entitled to practice in Gibraltar." (§28[3]). Furthermore, "every person duly approved, admitted and enroled as a solicitor of the Supreme Court of Gibraltar shall be at liberty to act also as a barrister." (§30[2]).

Jurisdiction over Admissions.—Admissions are regulated by Supreme Court Ordinance, which includes Supreme Court (Amendment) Ordinance 1986.

Eligibility.—So as to be eligible applicant must satisfy educational requirements listed below.

Registration As Law Student.—There is no statutory requirement.

Educational Requirements.—All barristers and solicitors obtain their legal education outside Gibraltar.

For any person to become fully qualified barrister or solicitor in Gibraltar, that person must begin his legal education by becoming law graduate at University or Polytechnic, in U.K. or Republic of Ireland; or, become non-law graduate in University or Polytechnic in U.K. or Republic of Ireland, after which one year Common Professional Examination conversion course must be obtained, at one of the approved institutions.

Before Chief Justice approves, admits and enrolls barrister to Supreme Court of Gibraltar (regulated by §28 of Supreme Court [Amendment] Ordinance, 1986), that person must satisfy following requirements: (a) he has been called to Bar in England and Northern Ireland or Republic of Ireland, or has been admitted as advocate in Court of Session in Scotland; (b) he is not at time of application for admission disbarred, or removed from role of advocates in Scotland, or suspended from practice as such barrister or advocate; (c) since his admission in U.K. or Republic of Ireland, he has completed period of at least six months' pupillage with practising barrister of at least five years professional standing in England, Northern Ireland, Republic of Ireland or Gibraltar, or practising advocate of at least five years professional standing in Scotland, or has completed practical training course approved by Council of Legal Education in England or by equivalent body in Northern Ireland, Republic of Ireland or Scotland; and (d) he intends on admission to practice in Gibraltar either alone or in partnership with another barrister or solicitor.

Before Chief Justice approves, admits and enrolls solicitor to Supreme Court of Gibraltar (under §30 of Supreme Court [Amendment] Ordinance, 1986), that person must satisfy following requirements: (a) he has been admitted as solicitor of Supreme Court of England, or in any court of record in Northern Ireland or Republic of Ireland, or as solicitor admitted to practice in Scotland; (b) he is not at time of his application for admission struck off rolls or suspended from practice as solicitor; and (c) he intends on admission to practice in Gibraltar either alone or in partnership with another barrister or solicitor.

Petition for Admission.—Petitions for admission to Bar are regulated by Supreme Court Ordinance, Barristers and Solicitors Rules, Part II, §§4-6.

Application to be admitted and enroled as barrister or as solicitor, shall be made by petition in form contained in schedule (to Supreme Court Ordinance). It must be verified by oath or by statutory declaration and shall be filed in Registry, with two recent testimonials to good character of applicant.

That person must also deliver to Registry notice intimating that he has so applied, which notice shall (unless Chief Justice shall otherwise allow) be posted and continue to be posted in Supreme Court for 21 days before any order is made on petition.

ATTORNEYS AND COUNSELORS . . . *continued*

Examination.—Rules as to examinations are contained in Supreme Court Ordinance, Barristers and Solicitors Rules, Part II, §5.

It is at Chief Justice's discretion as to whether applicant, to be admitted as barrister or solicitor, appears before Admissions and Disciplinary Committee, before hearing of his petition.

It is also discretion of Chief Justice as to whether applicant is admitted to local Gibraltar Bar.

Clerkship.—No statutory provision.

Admission Pro Hac Vice.—Barristers and solicitors who satisfy Educational Requirements, listed above, are normally accepted for admission to Gibraltar Bar, on pro hac vice basis, by Disciplinary and Admissions Committee. Majority of such lawyers are usually Queen's Counsellors who come to Gibraltar from U.K. or Republic of Ireland.

Compensation.—In Gibraltar there is no compensation fund, however, every practitioner must be fully insured.

Disbarment or Suspension.—Disciplinary powers are regulated by §34 of Supreme Court Ordinance. This legislation empowers Chief Justice to act with reasonable cause.

Mandatory Continuing Legal Education.—None.

Speciality Certification Requirements.—None.

Professional Association.—General Council of the Bar in Gibraltar is constituted by its own Constitution and it is governing body of Bar.

Its objectives are to maintain standards, honour independence of Bar, and to promote, preserve and improve services and functions of Bar.

It makes special provisions arising out of peculiar nature of Bar as fused profession and to regulate professional business normally conducted by solicitors and to exercise functions similar to those of Law Society, insofar as they are applicable to Gibraltar.

It represents and acts for Bar generally as well as in its relations with others and also in matters affecting administration of justice.

BANKRUPTCY AND INSOLVENCY:

Corporate Insolvency.—Companies Ordinance 1930.

Winding-up of company may be either (a) by court, (b) voluntary, or (c) subject to supervision of court.

(a) Winding-Up by Court.—Company may be wound up by court if: (i) company has by special resolution resolved that company be wound-up by court; (ii) if default is made in delivering statutory report to Registrar or in holding statutory meeting; (iii) company does not commence its business within a year from its incorporation, or suspends its business for a whole year; (iv) number of its members is reduced, in case of private company, below one, or in case of any other company, below seven; (v) company is unable to pay its debts; (vi) court is of opinion that it is just and equitable that company should be wound up.

(b) Winding-Up Voluntarily.—Company may be wound up voluntarily either by "members voluntary winding-up" or "creditors voluntary winding-up". In case of former, directors of company must file statutory declaration to effect that company will be able to pay its debts within period not exceeding 12 months from commencement of winding-up.

(c) Winding-Up Subject to Supervision of court.—When company has passed resolution for voluntary winding-up, court may make order that voluntary winding-up shall continue, but subject to such supervision of court, and with such liberty for creditors, contributories or others to apply to court, and generally on such terms and conditions as court thinks just.

Personal Insolvency.—Bankruptcy Ordinance 1934.

Debtor commits act of bankruptcy in Gibraltar in each of following cases: (a) if in Gibraltar or elsewhere he makes conveyance or assignment of his property to trustee or trustees for benefit of his creditors generally; (b) if in Gibraltar or elsewhere he makes fraudulent conveyance, gift, delivery or transfer of his property, or of any part thereof; (c) if in Gibraltar or elsewhere he makes any conveyance or transfer of his property or any part thereof, or creates any charge thereon, which would under Ordinance or any other enactment be void as fraudulent preference if he were adjudged bankrupt; (d) if with intent to defeat or delay his creditors he does any of following things, namely, departs out of Gibraltar, or being out of Gibraltar remains out of Gibraltar, or departs from his dwelling-house, or otherwise absents himself, or begins to keep house; (e) if execution against him has been levied by seizure of his goods under process in action in any court, or in any civil proceedings in Supreme Court, and goods have either been sold or held by marshal for 21 days; (f) if he files in court declaration of his inability to pay his debts or presents bankruptcy petition against himself; (g) if creditor has obtained final judgment or final order against him for any amount, and, execution thereon not being stayed has served on him Bankruptcy Notice and he does not within seven days comply with requirements of notice or satisfy court that he has counterclaim, set off or cross demand which equals or exceeds amount of judgment debt or sum ordered to be paid, and which he could not set up in action in which judgment was obtained, or proceedings in which order was obtained; (h) if debtor gives notice to any of his creditors that he has suspended, or that he is about to suspend, payment of his debts.

Creditor is not entitled to present bankruptcy petition unless: (a) debt owing is for £500 or more; (b) debt is liquidated sum; and (c) act of bankruptcy has occurred within three months before presentation of petition.

BANKS AND BANKING:

Banking business in Gibraltar is regulated by Banking Ordinance 1992 which incorporates second Banking Directive of European Community. Major implication of this new Ordinance for Gibraltar is that branches of European Community banks may set-up in Gibraltar without need for further authorisation procedures, and thus Gibraltar licensed banks (whether originally from EEC or not) may branch out into Europe with only need for notification between banking supervisory authorities to be effective.

Minimum capital required for new banking licence is 5 million ECU. This requirement is minimum EEC capital required throughout EEC.

Returns.—Annual accounts and auditor's reports of existing licensees are verified and closer collaboration between auditors of banks and Banking Supervisor is encouraged. Ordinance also gives auditors limited indemnity regarding disclosure.

Confidentiality.—Under new Ordinance banking confidentiality is now insured under both common law (that existed before Ordinance) and now under Part XI of Ordinance. Thus §82(9) of Ordinance makes it criminal offence for person to disclose information subject of course to usual exceptions.

BARRISTERS AND SOLICITORS:

See topic Attorneys and Counselors.

BILLS AND NOTES:

Bills of exchange (including cheques) and promissory notes are regulated by Bills of Exchange Ordinance.

Bill of exchange is unconditional order in writing, addressed by one person to another, signed by person giving it, requiring person to whom it is addressed to pay on demand or at fixed or determinable future time sum certain in money to or to order of specified person, or to bearer.

Inland and Foreign Bills.—Inland bill is one which is or on its face purports to be (a) both drawn and payable in Gibraltar or (b) drawn in Gibraltar upon some person resident therein. Any other bill is foreign bill.

Cheques.—Cheque is bill of exchange drawn on banker payable on demand.

Promissory Notes.—Promissory note is unconditional promise in writing made by one person to another signed by maker, engaging to pay, on demand or at fixed or determinable future time sum certain in money, to, or to order of, specified person or to bearer.

CERTIORARI:

Order of Certiorari is recognised means of procuring through medium of Supreme Court in Gibraltar in order to obtain inspection of proceeding of courts of inferior jurisdiction in order that they may be reviewed and rectified.

Grounds of Issue.—Invoked when there is some defect or informality apparent on face of proceedings, where there is want of jurisdiction, where it is clear and manifest that adjudication has been obtained by fraud, or where there has been denial of natural justice.

Procedure.—Leave must be obtained, application made ex parte to judge and must be accompanied by statement setting out name and description of applicant, relief sought, grounds, and by affidavit verifying facts relied on.

CHATTEL MORTGAGES:

All mortgages of chattels, except inter alia those executed by limited companies which require registration under Companies Act (see topic Corporations) and mortgages come under Bills of Sale Ordinance. They must be for sum of not less than £30; be registered within seven days, or, if executed out of Gibraltar, within seven clear days after time at which it would in ordinary course of post arrive in Gibraltar if posted immediately after execution and be according to form specified in Ordinance; otherwise such chattel mortgages are void, even against grantor. Copies have to be filed and are open to public inspection. Registration must be renewed every five years.

COMMERCIAL REGISTER:

See topics Corporations and Trademarks and Tradenames.

CONSTITUTION AND GOVERNMENT:

General.—As result of constitutional conference held in late 1960s Gibraltar was granted constitution in 1969. Such constitution outlines fundamental rights and freedoms of individual, offices of Governor and Deputy Governor and among other matters incorporates functions of legislature, executive and judicature into statute.

Legislature consists of Governor and Assembly. Latter consists of Speaker, Attorney General, Financial and Development Secretary and 15 elected members.

Executive.—Executive authority of Government of Gibraltar vests in Governor on behalf of Her Majesty Queen Elizabeth II. Constitution regulates composition of Gibraltar Council and Council of Ministers.

Judiciary.—Chief Justice, Additional Judge, President of Court of Appeal and Justices of Appeal are appointed by Governor on advice from British Government.

CONTRACTS:

Gratuitous promise even though made in writing is not enforceable unless it is made in deed under seal. Otherwise there must be agreement between parties intending to create legal relationship based upon offer and acceptance with consideration moving from promisee to promisor. Adequacy of consideration immaterial but there must be some benefit accruing to promisor.

Privity.—Person not party to contract cannot sue upon it even if it is for his benefit unless it is insurance policy of vendor of property and he is purchaser, or he is principal suing on contract made for him by agent or contract constitutes trust and person seeking to sue is beneficiary thereunder.

Excuses for Nonperformance.—Contract which is not capable of performance when made is in general void. Doctrine of frustration operates to excuse further performance where (i) it appears from nature of contract and surrounding circumstances that parties have contracted on basis that some fundamental thing or state of things will continue to exist or that some particular person will continue to be available or that some future event which forms foundation of contract will take place; and (ii) before breach performance becomes impossible or only possible in very different way to that contemplated without default of either party or owing to fundamental change or circumstances beyond control and original contemplation of parties. To

CONTRACTS . . . *continued*
excuse nonperformance impossibility must be in nature of physical or legal one and not merely relative impossibility, i.e. referable solely to ability or circumstances of promiser.

Act of God or Queen's enemies may also excuse performance. Act of God is generally extraordinary occurrence or circumstances which could not have been foreseen or which could not have been guarded against.

Statute may also render performance impossible, which is sufficient excuse.

Rescission.—Contract may be rescinded at instance of party induced to enter it by misrepresentation of facts made by other party. This is so, even if contract performed. Damages may be ordered by court in lieu of or in addition to rescission where this representation is negligent or fraudulent.

Unfair Terms.—Liability for death or personal injury through negligence cannot be restricted by contract if reasonable. Consumer protected against unreasonable exclusion of liability clauses in written standard terms of business; consumer also protected against unreasonable indemnity clauses.

Applicable Law.—Interpretation and effect and rights and obligations of parties are governed (with certain exceptions) by law which parties agree or intend shall govern it or which they are presumed to have intended, known as proper law of contract. Law expressly stipulated will be proper law of contract provided selection is bona fide and there is no objection on grounds of public policy even where law has no real connection with contract. Where parties make no stipulation courts decide by considering contract as a whole and are guided by certain presumptions.

Government Contracts.—As result of Crown Proceedings Ordinance or against Crown in contract are, for most part, governed by same rules of procedure as proceedings between subjects.

See also topic Deeds.

CONVEYANCES:

See topic Deeds.

COPYRIGHT:

The United Kingdom Copyright Act, 1956 (as amended) was extended to Gibraltar by Copyright (Gibraltar) Order of 1960 with certain exceptions and modifications. The Copyright (International Organisations) Order 1957 was also extended to Gibraltar subject to certain modifications. Also extended to Gibraltar have been The Copyright (Taiwan) Order 1985 and The Copyright (Computer Software) Order of 1987 subject to certain exceptions and modifications.

These Orders provide for copyright in original, literary, dramatic, artistic and musical works and in sound recordings, cinematograph films, broadcast and published editions of such works.

CORPORATIONS:

General.—The Gibraltar Companies Ordinance is based almost exclusively on United Kingdom Companies Act of 1929. The Companies Ordinance has been amended throughout the years in accordance with prerequisites that have arisen from time to time. Thus mode of incorporating company in Gibraltar is similar to that of U.K.

There are four separate and distinct categories of companies available in Gibraltar; (i) resident controlled company, (ii) nonresident controlled company; (iii) exempt company and (iv) qualifying company.

(i) Resident Controlled Companies.—These companies are chargeable for taxes on their worldwide income after deduction of all expenses which are wholly and exclusively incurred on production of that income. Rate of tax on adjusted company profits is currently 35%. Apart from normal business expenses, allowable expenses include: (a) Depreciation of business assets, fixtures and fittings, plant and machinery, 15% per annum on reducing balance. Commercial vehicles and company cars (subject to business use) computers, videos, etc., 25% per annum on reducing balance. (b) Employers' contributions to be approved provident or pension funds. (c) Interest payments on capital employed in acquiring income.

Losses can be carried forward indefinitely to be offset against future profits, but cannot be carried back and offset against prior year profit.

Dividends must have tax deducted at standard rate of 35%. If tax so deducted exceeds tax chargeable on company's profits, excess must be paid over to Commissioner of Income Tax in Gibraltar. If it is less than tax on profits, difference can be carried forward and set off against first excess that arises on future occasion. Interest on loans must also have tax deducted at standard rate of recipient (35% company and 30% individuals).

(ii) Nonresident Controlled Companies.—Nonresident owned and controlled companies incorporated in Gibraltar which do not trade, earn or remit income to Gibraltar are not liable to company tax. Annual accounts must be submitted to Gibraltar Tax Authorities, together with letter of confirmation of foregoing.

Nonresident company is however taxable on income accruing in, derived from, or received in Gibraltar, as well as on income arising directly or indirectly through their agents, except that nonresidents are not taxable in Gibraltar on: (a) income from ownership, chartering or operating of any ship (whether registered at Port of Gibraltar or not) and; (b) income from certain Government loans, as specifically exempted by Governor.

Assessments for nonresident companies are made in their own name or in name of their agents in Gibraltar.

(iii) Exempt Companies.—Exempt company is one which is incorporated in Gibraltar and registered under Companies (Taxation and Concessions) Ordinance. Provided following conditions are complied with, such registration entitles company and/or beneficial owner to be exempt from all income tax and estate duty in Gibraltar: (a) No Gibraltar resident is beneficially interested in shares of company. (b) Paid up share capital is minimum of £100 or equivalent in any foreign currency. (c) Company does not, without consent of legal authorities, transact any trade or business in Gibraltar except with other exempt companies or qualifying companies. (d) No changes in beneficial ownership or objects for which company was formed are made without approval of authorities. (e) Register of members must be kept in Gibraltar. (f) Annual tax is paid by due dates of 31 Mar. and 30 Sept.

Annual tax payable by company is either £225 (if it is ordinarily resident in Gibraltar) or £200 (if it is not ordinarily resident).

Registered branch of overseas incorporated company can also obtain exemption status under C(TC)O provided it conforms to above conditions and is liable to annual tax at rate of £300.

There are no restrictions on appointment of directors or officers of exempt company and meetings may be held inside or outside Gibraltar thus allowing companies to be managed and controlled from Gibraltar. In addition, exempt company can maintain and administer office premises in Gibraltar to transact business with nonresidents or similar companies. Captive or general insurance companies carrying on business under Assurance Companies Ordinance would fall into this category.

No stamp duty is payable by any person on any document relating to issue, allotment, renunciation, transfer, assignment or disposition of shares in exempt company.

There is secrecy provision in Ordinance that prevents disclosure of details concerning beneficial owners of exempt and qualifying companies.

(iv) Qualifying Companies.—Qualifying company is one which is incorporated in Gibraltar or is registered branch of overseas incorporated company and is registered under Income Tax (Qualifying Companies) Rules 1983. Following conditions are applicable: (a) No Gibraltar resident is benefically interested in shares of company. (b) Paid up share capital is minimum of £1,000 or equivalent in any foreign currency. (c) Company does not transact any trade or business in Gibraltar except with other qualifying companies or exempt companies. (d) Register of shares must be kept in Gibraltar and, in case of registered branch, certified true copy thereof. (e) Company has deposited sum of £1,000 with Government of Gibraltar as security for future taxes. (f) Company has paid fee of £250 for qualifying certificate.

Taxation shall be charged on profits of company at specific rate, depending on arrangements agreed with Financial and Development Secretary.

As with exempt companies, there are no restrictions on appointment of directors, holding of meetings or servicing of office premises. Neither is stamp duty payable on transactions involving shares in qualifying company.

Insurance Companies.—The Insurance Companies Ordinance of 1987 regulates granting of licenses in order to conduct insurance business. Insurance company is required to maintain minimum guarantee fund in amount which differs depending on particular circumstances of each case and type of business to be written.

When dealing with company writing general business, minimum guarantee fund will fluctuate between approximately £287,000 and £574,000.

Taxation.—See topic Taxation.

COURTS:

Magistrates Court.—Criminal matters of less serious nature; commital of more serious cases to Supreme Court and certain civil matters (e.g. matrimonial jurisdiction). Magistrates Courts are presided over by two or three lay Justices or one Stipendiary Magistrate.

Court of First Instance.—Jurisdiction in several civil matters of more minor nature; for example, monetary claims are limited to £1,000. Jurisdiction extends to wide range of civil matters (e.g. personal injury, possession of land) and is based on certain ceilings of jurisdiction.

Supreme Court.—It is composed of several jurisdictions. It is presided over by Chief Justice and by additional Judges appointed pursuant to 1969 Constitution: (1) Chancery Jurisdiction—deals with general civil and company matters. (2) Criminal Jurisdiction—hears criminal cases to be tried on indictment and appeals from Magistrates Court. (3) Admiralty Jurisdiction—for maritime matters. (4) Divorce & Matrimonial Jurisdiction. (5) The Supreme Court in its ordinary jurisdiction also hears other general civil matters such as claims in contract, tort, equity, for personal injuries etc.

Court of Appeal hears appeals in its civil and criminal jurisdiction from all matters determined in Supreme Court. It is composed of President and two Justices of Appeal and ordinarily sits twice a year in Feb./Mar. and Sept./Oct. Chief Justice is ex officio Court of Appeal Judge and has jurisdiction in certain matters.

Judicial Committee of Privy Council consists of Lord Chancellor, Lords of Appeal, Privy Counsellors and other members of Privy Council who have held judicial office in U.K. or certain other dependent territories in Commonwealth. It is court of final appeal from Court of Appeal of Gibraltar.

CURRENCY:

Unit of currency in Gibraltar is pound sterling although there is local note and coinage issue which is at par with sterling. Gibraltar was first European Territory to issue ECU based coinage which is legal tender.

CUSTOMS:

Gibraltar is not subject to value added tax nor to sales tax. Customs duties are levied on most imported goods with certain exceptions and these are generally liable to import duty of 12%.

Gibraltar is dependent territory of European Community under Art. 227(4) of The Treaty of Rome.

DEATH:

Presumption of Death.—Application by personal representative must be made to court where it is not certain that death has occurred. Law presumes person to be dead if not reasonably been heard of for seven years but each case is considered as question of fact and period can be less than seven years. There is no legal presumption as to time of death.

Registration.—All deaths must be registered locally.

Actions for Causing Death.—Relatives of decedent may sue within three years if death was caused by some wrongful act, neglect or default. Measure of damages is loss of support suffered. Causes of action subsisting against or vested in decedent shall survive against or as case may be for benefit of his estate.

See Topical Index in front part of this volume.

DEEDS:

Deeds executed by individuals are to be sealed and witnessed.

Corporation or company executes deed in manner provided by its articles of association but deed executed by corporation aggregate in favour of purchase is sufficiently executed if its seal is affixed thereto in presence of its clerk, secretary or other permanent officer or his deputy and member of governing body of corporation.

Person authorised by power of attorney or any other power to convey interest in property on behalf of corporation sole or aggregate, may execute conveyance by signing name of corporation in presence of witness and in case of deed fixing his own seal.

Deed does usually require registration.

Land in Gibraltar is of either freehold or leasehold tenure.

Stamp Duty on Purchase Deeds.—Real Property at 1.26%.

DEPOSITIONS AND DISCOVERY:

Local provisions are substantially similar to English law. Application to take evidence by deposition in Supreme Court by application under Order 39 of Rules of the Supreme Court 1985, including examination of person outside jurisdiction by special examiner. There are provisions in Evidence Ordinance of Gibraltar for taking of evidence required for proceedings in other jurisdictions.

By Rules of the Supreme Court Order 38 evidence may be given by affidavit: (a) By order of court if in circumstances of case it thinks it reasonable to do so; (b) on any motion, petition or summons including interlocutory applications: (c) in default actions in rem and in references in admiralty actions. Court will not order affidavit evidence where such evidence will be strongly contested and its credibility depends on Court's view of witness.

Court or judge may make any order for examination on oath before court or judge or any officer of court, or any other person, and at any place, of any witness or person and may empower any party to any such cause or matter to give such deposition in evidence therein on such terms as court or judge may direct.

Under Civil Evidence Act 1968, in civil proceedings oral or written statements of witness admissible if witness not called. Appropriate notice of intention to use statement must be given to opponent within 21 days of setting case down for trial (or as ordered by court). However, it should be noted that Police and Criminal Evidence Act 1984 is not applicable in Gibraltar. More reliance on common law principles most of which are now enacted in Criminal Proceedings Ordinance.

Discovery.—In civil cases after pleadings have closed, each side must send other List of Documents stating in Schedule 1, Part I relevant documents which are in their custody, possession or power, in Part II documents which they refuse to produce described generally and in Schedule 2, documents which party once had but now no longer has.

If one party refuses to give discovery of particular documents, other can apply to court.

Certain matters can be dealt with by interrogatories.

Court can order parties to exchange experts reports before trial.

Usually one does not know how many or who either side is going to call as witnesses. Court may, however, if it thinks fit for disposing fairly and expeditiously of any matter and saving costs, direct that parties serve written statements of oral evidence of witnesses as to fact.

In criminal cases, full committal hearing can be requested in which case summary of evidence is heard and witnesses can be called.

DISPUTE RESOLUTION:

Dispute resolution in Gibraltar is regulated by Arbitration Ordinance.

Mandatory Dispute Resolution.—Subject to certain provisos disputes may be referred to special referee or arbitrator under Order of Court in any cause or matter (other than criminal proceedings by Crown). Special referee or arbitrator appointed is deemed to be officer of Court and to have authority prescribed by rules of Court or Court direction. Report or award made by special referee or arbitrator on any such reference shall, if adopted by Court, be equivalent to verdict of jury.

Voluntary Dispute Resolution.—Parties may enter into written agreement to submit present or future differences to arbitration whether arbitrator is named therein or not. Such agreement is irrevocable except by leave of Court and shall have same effect in all respects as if it had been made by Court Order.

DIVORCE:

Matrimonial Causes Ordinance governs grounds for divorce and judicial separation provides, inter alia, bar on petitions for divorce within five years of marriage.

Grounds for Divorce.—Provides that sole ground for divorce shall be that marriage has broken down irretrievably. Provides that proof of such breakdown is only afforded if one or more of following conditions are fulfilled: (a) that respondent has committed adultery and that petitioner finds it intolerable to live with him; (b) that respondent has behaved in such way that petitioner cannot reasonably be expected to live with him; (c) that respondent has deserted petitioner for continuous period of at least three years immediately preceding presentation of petition; (d) that parties have lived apart for continuous period of at least three years immediately preceding presentation of petition and respondent consents to decree; (e) that parties have lived apart for continuous period of at least five years immediately preceding presentation of petition.

Jurisdiction. In order that Gibraltar may have jurisdiction to grant decree of divorce either party to marriage must be domiciled in Gibraltar on date when proceedings are brought or either party must have been habitually resident in Gibraltar for period of one year ending with date proceedings are commenced.

Decree.—At hearing of petition for decree of dissolution or nullity (i.e., trial), decree nisi only is granted. At end of six weeks on application by petitioner, this decree will be made absolute unless in meantime respondent shows why it should not be. Until decree nisi is made absolute, parties are unable to marry again but thereafter there is no restriction on remarriage.

Decree nisi may be made absolute on application of respondent if petitioner does not apply for decree absolute within three months after time when such application could have been made.

ENVIRONMENT:

General.—Gibralter enactment governing environmental control is Public Health Ordinance. Main provisions deal with disposal of sewage, buildings and sanitation, refuse removal, nuisances, offensive trades, noise and supply of water, to name but a few. With regard to recycling of waste, there are no specific provisions in Gibralter law at this time due to fact that as result of its size, there are no facilities in Gibralter to process waste and possibility of exporting simply for purpose of recycling is likely to be uneconomic venture.

Ordinance is supplemented by numerous subsidiary regulations and these relate to procedure and enforcement of main body of legislation. Scope of legislation can be illustrated by reference to particular examples.

General Nuisances.—Reference is made to statutory nuisances, which include inter alia, accumulation of dust, inadequate ventilation, maintenance of refuse bins and condition of wells and reservoirs concerned with storage of water used for human consumption. Such nuisances are first dealt with through service of abatement notice. If such notice is disregarded, person on whom it was served can be summoned to appear before magistrates' court. There are various courses of action open to court in deciding how to deal with offender, ranging from fine to order that offender execute any works necessary for abatement of nuisance. Should offender still fail to comply with court order, larger fine can be imposed together with daily fine for each day that nuisance continues.

Other forms of statutory nuisance are that of smoke and noise, which can also be controlled in same manner as in preceding paragraph.

Water.—In case of water, Gibralter law has been brought into line with current EEC directives, dealing with analysis and maintenance of water supply, protection of groundwater, pollution of aquatic environment and quality of bathing water. With regard to water analysis, schedule provides necessary criteria to be applied on analysis. Powers are given to relevant national authority to seek enforcement of these criteria. In any case, water is only supplied by Gibralter government at this time and therefore there are no independent suppliers to regulate.

General Supervision.—Monitoring of relevant provisions of Public Health Ordinance is carried out through various departments of Ministry of Environment, which itself is located at following address: Environmental Health Department, Ministry for the Environment, 37 Town Range, Gibralter, Tel: (350)70620, Fax: (350)74119.

EXCHANGE CONTROL:

There are no exchange controls and thus capital may be moved in and out of Gibraltar. As result of suspension of exchange controls in U.K. in 1979, Gibraltar also removed all exchange controls. Thus Gibraltar companies, individuals and other entities may hold and operate bank accounts in any currency anywhere in world and may convert funds into other currencies in Gibraltar.

FINANCIAL SERVICES:

See topic Securities and Investment.

FOREIGN EXCHANGE:

See topic Exchange Control.

FOREIGN INVESTMENT:

There are no exchange controls and capital may be moved in and out of Gibraltar.

FOREIGN TRADE REGULATIONS:

See topics Corporations; Currency; Exchange Control and Aliens.

FRAUDS, STATUTE OF:

Asset Protection Trust legislation was recently enacted in Gibraltar. Amendments were introduced to Bankruptcy Ordinance providing that if disposition is made into settlement and settlor at time of disposition is not insolvent and does not become insolvent, disposition is not voidable at instance or upon application by any creditor of settlor.

Legislation specifically excludes application to such trusts as are registered thereunder of Fraudulent Conveyances Act 1571 and of §42 of Bankruptcy Ordinance which is identical provision to §42 of Bankruptcy Act of U.K. Gibraltar's asset protection trust legislation is therefore unique, as it falls within provisions of bankruptcy law, rather than failing within ambit of fraudulent conveyancing laws.

FRAUDULENT SALES AND CONVEYANCES:

Conveyance of property, to any other person other than bona fide purchaser for value without notice of fraudulent intent, made with intent to defraud creditors, is voidable at instance of any person prejudiced thereby.

Voluntary disposition of land, made with intent to defraud subsequent purchaser, is voidable at instance of such purchaser.

See also topic Bankruptcy and Insolvency.

GARNISHMENT:

Local provisions are substantially similar to English law.

See also topic Attachment and Execution.

HOLIDAYS:

New Year's Day, Good Friday, Easter Monday, May Day (1st Mon. in May), late Summer Holiday (last Mon. in Aug.), Christmas Day and Boxing Day are Bank Holidays in Gibraltar and no business of any kind is transacted, all banks being closed.

If Boxing Day or Christmas Day or both fall on Sat. or Sun., then extra days are taken as holiday in lieu.

HOLIDAYS . . . *continued*

No bank transacts business after closing for day i.e. 3:30 p.m.

HUSBAND AND WIFE:

Position of husband and wife in law was much modified by Law Reform (Married Women and Tortfeasors) Act 1935.

By §1 married women were placed on footing similar to single women for all purposes connected with holding of property, entering into contracts, torts, judgments and bankruptcy. By Law Reform (Husband and Wife) Act 1962 both parties to marriage have right of action in tort against each other subject to court's discretion in certain circumstances.

§3 of 1935 Act releases husband from liability for his wife's torts and for her antenuptial debts. He still remains liable for postnuptial contracts made as agent.

All these matters are subsumed now into Married Women Ordinance in Gibraltar.

IMMIGRATION:

See topic Aliens.

INFANTS:

Age of majority, 18 for both sexes.

Disabilities:—

Contracts.—Infants contracts are generally voidable at instance of infant, though binding on other party. Exceptions to this rule are contracts for necessaries (e.g., food, clothing, medicine) and certain others (e.g., service and apprenticeships). Even contract which from its nature would be binding on infant may be incapable of being enforced against him on account of its particular terms being prejudicial to his interests or onerous upon him. Contracts obviously prejudicial to infant are wholly void e.g., loan.

Property.—Legal estate in land cannot be held by infant.

General.—Infant is under general incapacity to exercise rights of citizenship or perform civil duties, e.g., voting in parliamentary or local government elections.

Ratification of Contracts.—Voidable contract can be repudiated by infant either during infancy or within reasonable time after he attains full age. However, no action can be brought to charge person upon promise made after attaining full age to pay debt contracted during infancy or upon ratification made after full age of promise or contract made during infancy. This does not apply so as to relieve infant of obligation arising out of contract affecting property of permanent nature.

Actions.—Civil proceedings on behalf of infant must be brought by some person called his next friend: proceedings against infant are defended by guardian ad litem. Any person within jurisdiction and not himself incapable of instituting proceedings can fill above offices, preference being given to parent or guardian.

INHERITANCE TAX:

The Estate Duties Ordinance of Gibraltar makes provision for payment of estate duty in Gibraltar. Residents of Gibraltar are liable to estate duty on all their personal and real property situated in Gibraltar with proviso that value of their property situated outside Gibraltar is aggregated with former to arrive at relevant rate to be used. With respect to property situated outside Gibraltar, only personal property (not real property) is subject to estate duty.

Nonresidents of Gibraltar are liable to estate duty only on their real and personal property situated in Gibraltar.

There are number of reliefs available from estate duty; most noteworthy in respect of shares in, and assets held by, exempt and qualifying companies, banks or building society accounts of nonresidents.

INSOLVENCY:

See topic Bankruptcy and Insolvency.

INTEREST:

Interest is payable either: (1) pursuant to statute, or (2) by express or implied agreement between parties.

Claim for interest must be specifically pleaded and in absence of statute or contract no interest can be charged.

There are laws against usury in Moneylenders Ordinance and credit bargains may be re-opened if they are extortionate.

JUDGMENTS:

Procedure of Gibraltar Supreme Court on its civil jurisdiction is very largely based on English Supreme Court Practice (or "White Book"). Procedure in Court of First Instance is similar to English County Court procedure but increasingly, with advent of changes in law in both England and Gibraltar, becomes more different.

Gibraltar courts may award judgment in default if defendant fails to acknowledge service, fails to deliver defence or ignores Court Order. Summary judgment may be obtained where there is no defence Judgments may be enforced by several methods (for examples see topic Attachment and Execution).

Judgments for fixed amounts obtained in many parts of British Commonwealth and in High Court of England can be registered in Supreme Court and enforced as judgments of Supreme Court. Certain formalities regarding application for registration must be observed and court retains power to cancel registration on certain grounds.

LABOUR RELATIONS:

See topic Aliens.

LAW REPORTS, CODES, ETC:

Considered judgments of Supreme Court and Court of Appeal of Gibraltar are collected in Registry. Reports of Gibraltar cases in Supreme Court and Court of Appeal are reported in commonwealth law reports and number of Privy Council decisions have been reported in several British law reports.

LEGISLATURE:

See topic Constitution and Government.

LICENCES:

The Trade Licensing Ordinance of Gibraltar provides for licenses to be required for carrying on trade or businesss in Gibraltar. Licenses are advertised in official publication The Gibraltar Gazette and in newspapers. Objections are heard before Trade License Committee which will grant or reject license.

LIENS:

Lien is right in one person to retain in his possession goods belonging to another until certain demands of his against owner have been satisfied.

It is personal right and exists only in respect of goods received rightfully, and cannot be transferred. Right may be excluded by express agreement or course of dealing between parties. It is right merely to retain possession and no charges in respect of warehousing may be made, and except in absence of statute (e.g., innkeepers), it confers no right of sale, without legal process against debtor. It must be distinguished from equitable and maritime liens, i.e., rights given to creditors to have certain specific property applied in satisfaction of their demands.

Right of lien is given by law in two classes of cases; (1) to persons who are under common law duty to render services, as e.g., carriers, on goods carried, for price of carriage, and innkeepers, on baggage of their customers, for amount of customer's account; (2) to persons rendering services, spending money, skill or labour, on property of another person employing them for that purpose, as, e.g., all agents and artificers.

Lien may be either; (1) general, for general balance owing to creditor by debtor, e.g. right of solicitor to retain his client's papers for general balance due to him; or (2) particular, right over goods until certain demands are satisfied, e.g., ordinary right of seller to retain particular goods until payment of their price.

Hotel keeper has right, if his account remains unpaid, to sell by public auction any personal effects, goods, or livestock of guest left or deposited with him or in his hotel. But no such sale may be made until he has had goods for six weeks, nor until one month after he has advertised intended sale in one London newspaper and one local newspaper circulating in district in which goods were left.

Banker's lien is right of banker to retain securities belonging to his customer for money due on general balance.

Trustee has equitable lien for expenses lawfully incurred in connection with trust premises; limited liability company may create lien upon its own shares.

Lien may arise through right of subrogation, as where third party to contract for sale uses its money to pay purchase price at purchaser's request.

Right of lien is lost: (1) by discharge of debt; (2) by tender of debt; (3) by taking security for debt under circumstances inconsistent with its continued existence.

It is suspended by taking negotiable instrument as payment. Unless it is taken as absolute satisfaction debt will revive on its dishonour, even though it is in hands of assignees for value.

LIMITATION OF ACTIONS:

Governed by Limitation Act 1939, Law Reform (Limitation of Actions etc.) Act 1954, Limitation Act 1963 and Law Reform (MP) Act 1971 that are relied on by Limitation Ordinance of Gibraltar.

Actions must be commenced within following periods:

Twelve Years: No action to be brought by any person recover any land after expiration of 12 years from date on which right of action accrued to him; or if it first accrued to some person through whom he claims.

Six Years: None of following actions shall be brought after expiration of six years from date on which cause of action accrued: (a) actions founded on simple contract or tort: (b) actions to enforce recognisance; (c) actions to enforce award, where submission is not by instrument under seal; (d) actions to recover any sum recoverable by virture of any enactment, other than penalty or forfeiture or sum by way of penalty or forfeiture.

There are many other special time limits laid down apart from abovementioned ones.

MARITIME:

See topic Shipping.

MARRIAGE:

This matter is regulated by Marriage Ordinance.

Marriage may be solemnized or contracted: (a) in place of worship (i) after due publication of banns, or exhibition of notice at place or two places or worship, or (ii) under delivery of Bishop's Licence, or (iii) under delivery of Governor's Licence, or (iv) under delivery of Registrar's Certificate; (b) in Registrar's Office (i) after due notice, or (ii) after issue of Registrar's Certificate, or (iii) under delivery of Governor's Licence; (c) at any place under delivery of Governor's Licence.

In every case of marriage intended to be contracted under authority of Registrar's Certificate, one of parties, both having resided in Gibraltar for period of not less than seven days then next preceding, shall give notice of intended marriage in prescribed form making such declaration as may be prescribed to Registrar. On receipt of notice of intended marriage and upon payment of prescribed fee, Registrar shall forthwith enter particulars set forth in such notice, and also date of receipt of such notice, in book they call Marriage Notice Book, and shall post copy of such notice in conspicuous place in office for period of not less than 21 days from time of reciept thereof.

Notwithstanding above at any time after expiration of one clear day next after date of entry of notice, upon payment of prescribed fee, Registrar can issue special certificate. No such special certificate shall be issued unless one of parties to intended marriage shall appear personally before Registrar and shall produce Affidavit or Statutory Declaration made by each of parties, each such Affidavit or Statutory Declaration to contain certain prescribed particulars.

See Topical Index in front part of this volume.

MARRIAGE . . . *continued*

Age of consent for both males and females is 16 years. Consent of parents or guardians is needed if either party is under 18 years.

Prohibited degrees of relationship is same as for U.K.

Jurisdiction for annulment exists as follows: (1) If either party is domiciled in Gibraltar when proceedings commence; or (2) either party resident in Gibraltar for one year ending with date proceedings commenced; or (3) if either party died before proceedings commenced and either was domiciled in Gibraltar or had been habitually resident in Gibraltar for one year ending with date proceedings commenced; or (4) marriage was celebrated in Gibraltar.

Court also has jurisdiction to entertain proceedings for death to be presumed and marriage to be dissolved if and only if petitioner: (a) is domiciled in Gibraltar on date when proceedings have begun; or (b) was officially resident in Gibraltar for period of oen year ending with that date.

Following are grounds on which decree of nullity may be made: (a) that either party was permanently impotent or incapable of consummating marriage at time of marriage, or (b) parties are within prohibited degrees of consanguinity or affinity as provided in Marriage Ordinance, or (c) that former husband or wife of either party was living at time of marriage and marriage with such previous husband or wife was still in force, or (d) that consent of either party to marriage was obtained by force of fraud in any case in which marriage might be annulled on this ground by England, or (e) that marriage has not been consummated owing to wilful refusal of respondent to consummate marriage, or (f) that either party to marriage was at time of marriage of unsound mind or was then suffering from mental disorder of such kind or to such extent as to be unfit for marriage and procreation of children or subject to recurrent attacks of mental disorder.

MONOPOLIES AND RESTRAINT OF TRADE:

There is no statutory regulation of monopolies, but common law rules apply. It is monopoly and against policy of law for any person or group of persons to secure sole exercise of any known trade throughout Gibraltar. Permitted monopolies may come into being by Crown Grant or statute; i.e. Post Office. Therefore agreement may be void as being monopoly or otherwise as being in restraint of trade at common law. Agreement may be illegal at common law if by causing control over trade or industry to pass into hands of individual or group of individuals it creates monopoly calculated to enhance prices to unreasonable extent. Such agreement is merely unenforceable; it is not illegal in any criminal sense, nor does it give any cause of action to third person. Agreements in restraint of trade are illegal to extent that they are unreasonable.

MORTGAGES:

Law in this area in substantially similar to that of England. Main enactment that is still law in Gibraltar is Conveyancing and Law of Property Act 1881 as amended.

NEGOTIABLE INSTRUMENTS:

See topic Bills and Notes.

NOTARIES PUBLIC:

Notaries Public of Gibraltar are appointed by England and almost same procedure for appointment exists as with Notaries in England.

PARTNERSHIPS:

Partnerships may be either (1) Ordinary partnerships, which are governed by Partnership Ordinance (based on Partnership Act 1890); or (2) limited partnerships which are governed by Limited Partnership Ordinance (which is based on Limited Partnership Act 1907).

In ordinary partnership each partner impliedly confers upon his co-partners apparent authority to incur debts on behalf of partnership to bind all partners. Limited partnerships are rare; limited partner's liability is restricted to amount of his capital.

PATENTS:

Governed by Patent's Ordinance of Gibraltar, Ordinance provides for registration of patents that have already been registered in U.K. to be registerable in Gibraltar within three years from date of issue of patent.

Once necessary documentation is received by Registrar of Patents in Gibraltar certificate of registration is issued.

PERPETUITIES:

This area is governed by Perpetuities and Accumulation Ordinance of 1986.

Under this Ordinance, trust may continue for 100 years, if non-charitable and not dealing for valuable consideration in certain options in real property. And under Trusts (Recognition) Ordinance 1990, requirements of forced heirship and/or other civil law restrictions on freedom of dispositions of assets by settlor, will be unenforceable in Gibraltar against trutees.

PLEDGES:

As in U.K., pledge of personal chattels is transfer by delivery of immediate possession thereof by way of security for advance, whether past or present, pledger remaining owner of chattel but pledgee acquiring right to sell (but not to foreclose) if advance is not repaid on due date.

PRESCRIPTION:

See topic Limitation of Actions.

PRINCIPAL AND AGENT:

Common Law Rules apply. In general principal is responsible for acts of his duly authorised agent. Competent person may grant Power of Attorney to another person to act as agent, power continues until revoked.

REAL PROPERTY:

Area substantially same as in England.

See topic Deeds.

RECEIVERS:

Receivers may be appointed by debenture holders and receiver will have powers conferred upon him by instrument under which he was appointed.

SECURITIES AND INVESTMENT:

The Financial Services Ordinance and The Financial Services Commission Ordinance provide for regulation of investment and certain other services and provide regulatory and licensing framework.

The Financial Services Ordinance came into force on 17 Jan. 1991 with its objective defined as regulating (a) carrying out of investment business and certain controlled activities in Gibraltar, (b) promotion, establishment and operation of collective investment schemes and (c) establishment of investment exchanges and clearing houses.

Thus any investment business or controlled activity may only be carried on in Gibraltar pursuant to license being issued by Financial Services Commission of Gibraltar. Thus it is necessary prerequisite in Gibraltar to obtain licence from Financial Services Commission in amongst other categories following; (a) Investment dealer/broker; (b) investment manager; (c) investment adviser; (d) insurance broker; (e) professional trustee and (f) company manager.

SHIPPING:

Jurisdiction and practice of admiralty law in Gibraltar is very similar to that which applies in England and Wales and is generally governed by Supreme Court Act 1981 and Merchant Shipping Ordinance and Port Ordinance. Courts have discretion to decide on any dispute or claim irrespective of where claim arises or nationality of parties. Most common maritime claims dealt with are in respect of: ownership, possession, mortgages, damages to or caused by ship, carriage of goods, salvage, charterparties, bills of lading, crews wages and other claims, possessory liens, maritime liens, and pollution. Court of Gibraltar may defer to contract or to consent of parties, in exercising jurisdiction of choice for resolution of any dispute.

TAXATION:

There is no value added tax legislation in Gibraltar and thus Gibraltar is not subject to any value added tax whatsoever. There is also no capital gains tax in Gibraltar and capital gains are therefore not subject to taxation. Tax year in Gibraltar runs from 1 July to 30 June. Tax legislation in Gibraltar follows to large extent income tax legislation of U.K. Taxation of nonresident individuals and of resident individuals differs substantially.

Nonresident and Qualifying Individuals.—Individuals who are not ordinarily resident or domiciled in Gibraltar and have no income derived in Gibraltar (except income from exempt and qualifying companies) may apply for Qualifying Certificate. Qualifying Individual will be charged to tax on his worldwide income at rate of not less than 2% as may be specified on Certificate, but total amount so charged cannot exceed £20,000.

Nonresidents of Gibraltar are not subject to Gibraltar tax on bank and building society interest received in Gibraltar.

High Net Worth Individuals:—Legislation dealing with these individuals has been enacted to encourage acquisition of property in Gibraltar. Worldwide income of individual who meets qualifying requirements is assessed in normal way by Gibraltar tax authorities but tax is levied only on first £45,000 of assessable income, thus maximum tax liability for full year of assessment at current rates would be of £19,750 for full year of assessment. Minimum annual tax payable would be of £10,000.

Prerequisites to qualify as high net worth individual in Gibraltar are (i) individual must have approved residential accommodation in Gibraltar, (ii) said accommodation to be available for exclusive use of individual for period of not less than seven months per year, (iii) individual to reside in property for minimum of 30 days in each year and (iv) accommodation may be purchased or rented.

Relocated Executives.—Individual employed in Gibraltar who has been designated as relocated executive possessing specialist skills will be taxed in amount of £10,000 per annum. This amount is payable by 12 equal monthly instalments irrespective of actual remuneration that executive receives and also irrespective of whatever benefits from employment executive receives.

Prerequisites to qualify are that executive must (i) possess skills essential to operation of his/her employer, (ii) not have been employed in or from within Gibraltar in previous two years and (iii) have residential accommodation available in Gibraltar purchased or rented.

Resident Individuals.—Individuals who are ordinary resident in Gibraltar are generally assessed on their worldwide income. Rates of personal taxation in Gibraltar range from 20% to 50% of taxable income.

See also topic Corporations.

TRADEMARKS AND TRADENAMES:

Trademarks are regulated under Trade Marks Ordinance of Gibraltar that is based on Trademarks Act 1938, Trademarks (Amendment) Act 1984 and Patents, Designs & Marks Act 1986.

Ordinance provides that any person who is registered proprietor of trademark in U.K. may apply to have trademark registered in Gibraltar.

Apart from prerequisite of registration in U.K. before registering in Gibraltar, law in this area is substantially similar to law in U.K.

Tradenames and/or business names are registered in Gibraltar under Business Names Registration Ordinance that is based on Registration of Business Names Act 1916.

TREATIES:

Gibraltar has no double tax agreements with any country.

See Topical Index in front part of this volume.

TREATIES . . . *continued*

Under Art. 227(4) of Treaty of Rome Gibraltar entered European Economic Community in 1973 following accession to Community of the United Kingdom as dependent territory.

By Art. 28 of Accession Treaty acts of Community institutions relating to common agricultural policy and value added tax do not apply to Gibraltar. Gibraltar is also by this Treaty excluded from Customs Union and thus Common Customs Tariff does not apply to Gibraltar.

TRUSTS:

Law in this area is significantly similar to that of U.K. Virtually all trusts recognised by English rules of equity may be created and enforced. Trustee Ordinance of Gibraltar is based on Trustee Act 1933. Trustee Ordinance the Variation of Trusts Act 1958 now applies to Gibraltar under Application of English Law Ordinance. Perpetuity and accumulation periods have been fixed at 100 years pursuant to 1986 Perpetuities and Accumulations Ordinance.

Trusts are created in Gibraltar in same way as in England. Formal trust deed is drawn up in Gibraltar and most common forms of trust are discretionary trust and life interest trust.

Gibraltar trust is completely confidential arrangement and is not recorded in any register. It has no minimum capital requirements, no annual filing fees and there are no provisions for requirements of annual accounts or audits.

Taxation of Trusts.—Income received by any trust or beneficiary under trust is exempt from taxation provided that (a) it is created by or on behalf of nonresident of Gibraltar; (b) residents of Gibraltar are expressly excluded as beneficiaries either specifically or under discretionary power of trustees and (c) income is derived from outside Gibraltar, with exception of income from bank deposit accounts, exempt or qualifying companies.

If trust complies with above conditions it is exempt from Gibraltar tax even if trustees are residents of Gibraltar.

Trusts of public nature are completely exempt from income tax provided that profits are applied solely for purpose of trust.

See also topic Frauds, Statute of re Asset Protection Trusts.

WILLS:

Any adult, male or female, of sound mind, may make will. Infant cannot make will, unless soldier in actual military service or mariner or seaman at sea. Person of unsound mind cannot make valid will, except during lucid interval. Alien has same testamentary capacity as British subject.

Will must be in writing and signed by testator or by some other person in his presence and by his direction and it must appear that testator intended by his signature to give effect to will and such signature shall be made or acknowledged by testator in presence of two or more witnesses present at same time and such witnesses shall attest and shall subscribe will in presence of testator and in presence of each other. Will should not be witnessed by beneficiary or spouse of beneficiary named in will. Upon death of testator where there is no opposition, probate of will may be granted to executors by probate court.

Probate of Foreigner's Will.—Wills Ordinance provides generally that will to be held as validly executed as regards form if it satisfies requirements of internal law of any of following: (a) Territory where it was executed; (b) territory where testator was domiciled, either at time of execution or at death; (c) territory where testator had habitual residence either at time of execution or at death; (d) in state of which, either at time of execution or at death, he was national.

Allowance for Maintenance Dependents.—Under Inheritance (Provision for Family and Dependents) Ordinance certain persons may make application to court for payment out of deceased's estate. Court may make order for reasonable financial provision for applicant if court considers reasonable financial provision has not been made.

Applicant for provisions must, except with permission of court, be made within six months from date on which representation in deceased's estate first taken out.

See Topical Index in front part of this volume.

GREECE LAW DIGEST

(The following is a list of all Topics, including cross-references, covered in this Digest.)

GREECE LAW DIGEST

Revised for 1997 edition by

DR. TRYFON J. KOUTALIDIS, of the Athens Bar.

See topics Law Reports, Codes, Etc., and Statutes.

Greece is member of EU. See also European Union Law Digest.

Greece became 10th full member of EEC by virtue of Treaty of Athens dated 28 May 1979. Treaty was ratified by Law 945 of 7/27 July 1979. Treaty provides for transitional period for Greece in certain matters.

ABSENTEES:

If a person of full age is absent and of unknown domicile or of known domicile but unable to administer his property, and further if such property is in need of administration, the court may appoint a guardian (administrator) of such property. See also topic Death.

ACKNOWLEDGMENTS:

Documents acknowledged before a notary public or other authority in a foreign country cannot be used in Greece (in absence of treaty provisions to contrary) unless signature of notary or such other authority has been certified by proper Greek consular officer whose signature, usually, must be authenticated by Ministry of Foreign Affairs.

ACTIONS:

There is no distinction in Greece between law and equity. Code of Civil Procedure, an enactment (Compulsory Law 44/1967) which entered into force on Sept. 16, 1968 forms basis of procedural law. Code has been considerably amended by Law Decrees 657/1971, 958/1971, 490/1974, Law 1478/1984, Law 1562/1985, Law 1649/86, Law 1682/87, Law 1738/87, P.D. 278/87, Law 1816/88, Law 1858/89, Law 1867/89, Law 1868/89, Law 1941/91 and Law 2145/93.

Commencement.—As a rule, an action is commenced by filing with appropriate court and subsequently by serving same on defendant.

Parties.—Every action must be prosecuted in name of the real or interested party except that guardians and certain other persons authorized by law may sue or be sued in their own name.

Intervention.—Any third party having a lawful interest may intervene in any suit without previously obtaining permission of court.

Limitation of.—See topic Limitation of Actions.

Proof of Foreign Law.—Foreign law may be taken cognizance of by courts ex officio but usually proof of what such law consists of must be submitted. Institute for International and Foreign Law of Athens renders opinions on foreign law which courts accept.

Appeal.—As a rule, an appeal against a judgment of a court of first instance lies as of right and no permission of court which issued judgment is required for the exercise of an appeal.

ADOPTION:

Adoption is now governed by Ch. 13 of Civil Code and by Law Decree 610 of 17/21 Aug. 1970 as am'd by L. D. 193/1973 and Law 1329/1983. Latter concerns adoption of persons up to age of 18. Adoption is accomplished by court judgment. Adoption must be in interest of adopted person. Adopting parent must have completed his 30th, and in certain cases, his 50th year of age. Adopting person must not have any natural descendant, unless natural descendant suffers of incurable disease or important reasons justify adoption. Court may in special cases allow person below age of 30 to adopt. Between adopting parents and adopted child there must be difference in age of 18 years or in case of adoption by one of spouses of other's child, 15 years.

On principle, only one adoption may be effected by same person. However, two or more persons may be adopted by same act and, in special cases, court may allow an adoption even if there has been a previous adoption. If adopter is an alien and person to be adopted a Greek national, adoption must be effected with assistance of certain social service organisations.

Consent of person being adopted is required; if such person is a minor, consent of his parents, guardian or curator is required. Court may, in certain cases, provide such consent if said persons are unable or unwilling to do so; if person to be adopted is married, consent of spouse of such person is required. If adopting person is married, then consent of his spouse is required. Court can decide exception in certain cases.

Proceedings.—The adoption is effected by an order of the court. If the adopter is married, in addition to his own consent that of his spouse is also necessary. Consent is granted either before court or notary public or, if adopter is abroad, before Greek Consul.

Name.—Adopted person takes surname of adopting parent but he may add his own surname.

Effects of Adoption.—After adoption has been completed, legal liens between adopted person and his natural family remain, unless otherwise provided. Parental care is exercised exclusively by adoptive parents and never returns to natural parents. Adopted person and his descendants, provided latter have been born after adoption, inherit from adopting parents but not from relatives of adopting parents. Adopter does not inherit from adopted person, nor latter's relatives. Adoption may be dissolved by decree of court on certain grounds. Alien under age of 18, on adoption by Greek national, acquires Greek nationality. On being adopted by alien, Greek minor may be divested of his Greek nationality if by adoption he acquires nationality of his adopter and permission of Minister of Interior is obtained.

Illegitimate child may now be adopted by his illegitimate parent.

AFFIDAVITS:

Affidavits are not strict evidence. They should preferably be sworn before a Greek consular officer. If sworn before a commissioner of oaths, notary public or other authority in a foreign country, signature of such officer must be certified by proper Greek consular officer. Law Decree 105/1969 as supplemented by law 1599/1986, provides simplified form for sworn statement.

ALIENS:

Disabilities.—Aliens may not be employed or carry on any profession in Greece without special permission of State nor may they attest as witnesses to notarial contracts or be appointed arbitrators or guardians or minors of Greek nationality. They are also subject to a number of other disabilities. After Greece's adhesion to EEC, number of such disabilities have been removed for EEC nationals. EEC residents are not considered as aliens.

Alien workmen, as a rule, are assimilated to Greek nationals with respect to social insurance and compensation for injuries.

Property.—Aliens may acquire immovable property by purchase or lease in all parts of Greece with exception of certain provinces including number of Greek islands. Legislation has been introduced exempting European Community nationals from these restrictions. Mining rights may, however, be acquired by aliens in such provinces by special permission.

Corporations Owned or Controlled by Aliens.—On principle, Greek corporations may be formed, owned or controlled by aliens. However, foreign-owned corporations, including those formed and established in Greece, may not own land or lease it on long-term leases in frontier areas.

Cross-references.—See also topics Companies; Husband and Wife; Immigration; Shipping.

APPEAL AND ERROR: See topic Courts.

ARBITRATION:

Arbitration is governed by arts. 867-903 of Code of Civil Procedure, as amended recently by Law 2331/1995.

Private disputes can be resolved by arbitration (except from labour disputes).

Conditions of arbitration are that parties consent in writing (either before or after dispute arises) and that they are free to dispose object of dispute. State can consent to arbitration only after legal opinion by State Legal Council is given and joint decision by Minister of Economy and competent Minister is taken.

Arbitrators can be appointed persons of full capacity to contract and with political rights. Judge can be appointed as only arbitrator or as umpire. Remuneration of arbitrators is determined by law to percentage of dispute's award.

Arbitration procedure is determined by arbitrators. However principle of equality of parties and principle of audi alteram partem must be respected.

Arbitral decision is not subject to appeal but recourse to another arbitral court can be agreed upon. Decision produces precedent and constitutes enforceable title. Annulment of decision for reasons enumerated in law can be asked before Court of Appeal.

Institutional Arbitration.—By Presidential Decrees permanent arbitrations can be constituted in stock and commodities exchanges, in chambers and in professional unions of public law.

International arbitration concerns resolution of disputes with foreign elements and is governed by more flexible rules.

Obligatory Arbitration.—See topic Dispute Resolution.

Recognition and Execution of Foreign Arbitral Decisions.—See topic Foreign Judgments.

ASSIGNMENTS:

An assignment may be affected by agreement, by operation of law or by judgment of court. Assignment of claim is not binding upon debtor until he receives notice of assignment. As a rule, assignor is responsible for validity of claim assigned but is not responsible for solvency of debtor.

Special rules apply to assignment of negotiable instruments. Claims which cannot be garnished (see topic Garnishment) are not assignable.

ASSIGNMENTS FOR BENEFIT OF CREDITORS:

See topic Bankruptcy.

ASSOCIATIONS:

Associations are nonprofit organizations governed by Arts. 78-106 of Civil Code. Right to associate is freely admitted but in order to obtain legal personality, association must be recognized by Court and its statutes must be filed with it.

See Topical Index in front part of this volume.

ATTACHMENT:

A creditor may obtain attachment of his debtor's property by virtue of an executory title. Following are considered executory titles: (a) Final judgments of Greek courts or judgments of Greek courts which have been declared immediately executable, (b) arbitration awards, (c) certain official records of courts, (d) notarial documents, (e) certain special orders of courts, (f) foreign judgments which have been declared executable by Greek courts, and (g) certain other titles recognised as executable by law. Certain assets may not be attached.

ATTORNEYS AND COUNSELORS:

In Greece only one profession of legal representative exists, lawyer, whose legal status is governed by Code of Lawyers. (Law Decree 3026/1954).

Capacity of lawyer is acquired by registration with Bar Association, after having taken oath and been appointed as lawyer by Presidential Decree.

Conditions to become lawyer are Greek or member-state of E.U. nationality. Interested person must be graduate of law school and succeed in practical tests, after having completed 18-month stage. Maximum age is 35 years.

Competences.—Lawyer represents and defends his client in courts, committees, disciplinary councils. He gives legal advice and opinions, he takes legal care of customs, tax and administrative cases, and attends signature of notarial contracts. Lawyer can exercise his profession only before courts of his local Bar, while in other courts he must be assisted by local lawyer. Appearance before court of appeal or Supreme Court presupposes completion of certain years of practice.

Duties.—Lawyer has duty of confidentiality towards information about his client acquired through exercise of his profession. He is subject to disciplinary power of his Bar.

Incompatibilities.—Lawyer must not, under penalty of being disqualified, undertake salaried civil service or another activity incompatible with profession.

Fees.—Lawyer receives fees which correspond to percentage of value of case's object and cannot be lower than sum prescribed by law. Payment can depend on result of trial. Lawyer can also receive fixed remuneration, if he offers his services permanently to client.

Law Companies.—(art. 1, §2, Law 1649/1986—Presidential Decree 518/1989). Lawyers can establish civil law companies with legal personality. Contributions can be in work or in kind. Latter do not influence company share. Partners can be only lawyers. Administration is exercised by administrator. Before third parties company and lawyer who handles cases are fully responsible.

Freedom of Supply of Legal Services from Lawyers of EU Member-States.—(Presidential Decree 258/1987—Directive of the European Council 77/249). Lawyers, citizens of member-state of European Union, can appear before Greek court with Greek lawyer in order to support specific case.

Free Establishment of Lawyers of EU Member-States.—(Presidential Decree 52/1992—Directive of the European Council 89/48). Citizens of EU member-states can be appointed as lawyers in Greece. That presupposes graduation from three-year law school and success in test of Greek law. After appointment they become equal to their Greek colleagues.

BANKRUPTCY:

Only traders, which term includes also trading corporations (limited partnerships, unlimited partnerships, limited companies, companies of limited liability and co-operative societies) may be declared bankrupt. A trader who suspends payment of his debts, or who makes a statement to secretary of proper court that he suspends such payment is in a state of bankruptcy and may be declared bankrupt by court of its own motion, or upon application of such trader or of any of latter's creditors.

A deceased trader may be declared bankrupt within one year from his death if he had suspended the payment of his debts prior to his death. The bankruptcy of a limited or unlimited partnership involves also the bankruptcy of the partners whose liability is unlimited.

Bankruptcy may be fortuitous, culpable or fraudulent. In the two latter cases the bankrupt is liable to prosecution under the penal law, and special provisions apply.

Procedure.—Bankruptcy judgment appoints a rapporteur judge and also a provisional receiver (provisional syndic) pending appointment of definitive receiver (syndic) decrees that bankrupt's property be sealed, fixes date and place of first meeting of creditors for purpose of electing definitive syndic and for declaration of claims, and orders publication of notices relating to bankruptcy. Same judgment may also fix date on which payment of bankrupt's debts is deemed to have been suspended but this date may not be earlier than two years prior to judgment. Court likewise may decree arrest of bankrupt.

Effects of Bankruptcy.—From date of bankruptcy: (1) Bankrupt is divested of administration of his property, which is entrusted to syndic; (2) all proceedings against bankrupt other than such as are instituted by syndic are suspended, with exception of proceedings taken against bankrupt by creditors whose claims have become due and are secured by hypothec, pledge or lien; (3) all claims against bankrupt become due; (4) interest ceases to accrue against bankrupt, except interest due on claims which are secured by hypothec, pledge or lien; (5) all transactions concerning estate subject to bankruptcy effected by bankrupt after bankruptcy judgment are void, as far as creditors are concerned.

Transactions Prior to Bankruptcy Judgment.—Certain transactions effected prior to judgment during a period commencing ten days prior to date on which bankrupt is deemed to have suspended payment of his debts, and ending on date of judgment, are void. Thus, following are void: Transactions without any consideration whereby movable or immovable assets of bankrupt are reduced; all payments whether in cash or by assignment, sale, set off, or otherwise made in respect of debts prior to their maturity, as well as all payments in satisfaction of matured debts other than by cash or by bills of exchange or promissory notes; all hypothecs (whether effected on strength of an agreement or of judgment of court), provisional hypothecs and all pledges constituted on property of debtor which have been obtained for purpose of securing a debt contracted prior to constitution thereof. If however such hypothecs and pledges have been constituted in favour of a bank or certain credit institutions after Oct. 31, 1959 they are not affected by bankruptcy. Other transactions effected during same period may be declared void by court.

Claims must be submitted for verification to secretary of court or syndic within certain time limits.

If any claims are submitted after expiration of said time limits and are duly verified, they are entitled only to such dividends as are distributed after their submission. All claims have to be confirmed by a sworn statement of claimant. Creditors residing abroad may be exempted by order of rapporteur judge from obligation to make such sworn statement, such order being subject to appeal on part of other creditors concerned.

Termination of Bankruptcy Proceedings.—Bankruptcy proceedings, unless a composition is effected, are terminated either by liquidation of bankrupt estate or by an order of court terminating bankruptcy if no funds are available for continuation of same.

Revocation of Judgment.—Bankruptcy judgment may be revoked by same court which pronounced bankruptcy, on application of bankrupt debtor if all creditors who have filed with court give their consent thereto.

Compositions.—A composition is binding upon creditors only if it is agreed by a majority of creditors. Such majority must represent three-fourths of the definitely approved claims if dividend offered by debtor is equal to at least 60% of amount of claims. If dividend offered is less than 60%, but more than 25%, it is required that such majority should represent four-fifths of claims. If dividend offered is less than 25%, a majority of two-thirds of creditors, representing three-fourths of said claims, is required.

Claims of wife of debtor and certain of his relations, as well as claims secured by a hypothec, pledge or a lien are not computed in the voting, but a secured claimant may take part in voting, if he renounces to such security as to at least one-third of amount of secured claims.

A composition may also be effected if bankrupt assigns to his creditors the whole of his property. For such composition, a usual majority, as mentioned above, is required.

No composition is binding unless certain formalities have been complied with, and it has been confirmed by the court. In the latter case, it is binding on creditors who did not take part in the creditors' meetings. If the bankrupt be convicted for fraudulent bankruptcy, either prior or after the composition, the latter becomes void. The composition may likewise be set aside by the court, if the bankrupt fails to execute the terms of the composition concluded.

A composition may also be effected out of court, but in such case consent of all creditors is required.

Rehabilitation.—A bankrupt is rehabilitated on expiration of ten years after bankruptcy judgment, if latter is followed by a judicial composition, or prior to that date if bankrupt has paid to creditors in full both principal and interest or obtains a complete release from them. Rehabilitation may also be granted by court if bankrupt has fulfilled all terms of composition agreements and in some other special cases. Assets acquired by bankrupt after his rehabilitation cannot be attacked by bankruptcy creditors. Rehabilitated bankrupt cannot be declared bankrupt in respect of debts contracted prior to bankruptcy in respect of which he has been rehabilitated. Rehabilitation cannot be obtained if bankrupt has been convicted of fraudulent bankruptcy.

See also topic Commercial Law.

BILLS AND NOTES:

In respect of all bills and notes issued in Greece on or after Apr. 15, 1932, the Convention of Geneva dated June 7, 1930, regarding the uniformity of laws in respect of bills and notes applies. Bills and notes are governed by Law 5325/1932.

Bills of Exchange.—A bill of exchange must contain words "bill of exchange," bear a date, place of issue and payment, a simple and clear mandate to pay a certain sum, name of party which is to pay same and name of party to whose order it is payable, date of maturity and signature of drawer; bills may be drawn at sight. Mere signature of an endorser is sufficient to constitute an endorsement. All those whose signature appears on a bill of exchange are jointly liable to bearer. Bearer must notify endorser within four days of presentation and each successive endorser must notify his endorser within two days from receipt of notification. Payment may be made two days from maturity. Protest must be made within two working days of maturity.

Promissory Notes.—These are subject to rules relating to bills of exchange insofar as these concern maturity, endorsement, joint and several liability, payment, protest and rights and duties of holder. A promissory note must be dated and set forth sum to be paid, must contain name of party to whose order it is payable and date of payment. It must also contain a promise to pay and words "Promissory Note."

In respect of bills of exchange and promissory notes, all actions against acceptor or signatory are barred by limitation after three years from maturity. Actions against endorsers are barred one year from protest.

Bills and notes, if not properly stamped when issued or accepted in Greece, are invalid as such. See also topic Courts.

Checks.—In respect of all checks issued in Greece on or after Jan. 1, 1934, the three Conventions signed in Geneva on Mar. 19, 1931, regarding (a) the uniform law in connection with checks, (b) the settlement of certain conflicts on certain checks and (c) in respect of stamps, apply with certain exceptions. Checks are governed by law 5360/1933.

A check must be payable at sight. It must contain word "check," a simple and clear order of payment of a certain sum, name of person who is to pay check and who must be a banker, place of payment, date and place of issue and signature of drawer. It may be drawn in favour of a specified person or to his order or to bearer.

Provision must exist at time of issue of check, i.e., drawer must have a claim free from all liability and payable on demand against drawee. Any person who draws a check without a provision may be sentenced on conviction to imprisonment.

Rules governing liability of endorsers and drawers are same as those governing bills of exchange. A check must be presented for payment within eight days, if issued and

BILLS AND NOTES . . . *continued*

payable in Greece, 20 days if issued in same continent in which it is payable and 70 days if issued in a different continent. Checks issued in Mediterranean countries are deemed to be issued in same continent.

All actions of bearer against endorsers and drawer are barred by limitation six months from date on which time for presentation expires. Protest must be made before date on which time for presentation expires.

A check on which two parallel lines, usually drawn obliquely, have been drawn, must be presented for payment only through a banker.

CHATTEL MORTGAGES:

These do not exist in Greece. See topic Pledges.

COLLATERAL SECURITY:

See topic Pledges.

COMMERCIAL LAW:

Greek law distinguishes between traders and nontraders. Traders are persons engaged in trading transactions as their regular occupation or certain legal or natural persons designated as traders by statute. Traders must keep certain books which, if regularly kept, may be received as evidence in suits between traders relating to commercial matters. Traders are liable to personal detention for the enforcement of a judgment entered against them for their commercial debts. Only traders may be declared bankrupt. Oral evidence may be used as proof in commercial suits.

COMMERCIAL REGISTER:

There is no commercial register. However, under Law 1746/88 as amended "concerning the constitution of Commercial and Industrial Chambers" merchants must file certain data with appropriate Chamber.

COMPANIES:

The form of company which corresponds more or less to the stock corporation in the United States is the Anonymos Etairia which will be referred to as "Limited Company."

Both domestic and foreign limited companies are subject to supervision of Ministry of Trade.

Formation of Companies.—For the purpose of forming a limited company, it is first necessary for a notarial act to be drawn embodying the statutes of the company, that is to say, both the memorandum of the company and the articles of association.

This document must be approved by Ministry of Trade and published in appropriate section of Government Gazette. Statutes of a company must provide for certain matters required by law. If any part of capital of company does not consist of cash, it must be assessed by a special committee appointed by Ministry of Trade. One-fourth, at least, of company's capital must be paid up within three months from date of constitution of company, balance within ten years. Capital of a limited company may not be less than ten million drachmae. (Law 2065/1992). In case of banking company, minimum capital is four billion drachmae.

Under Law 2081/92, statutes of company must be controlled by Chamber of Commerce, as far as name of company is concerned.

Head office of a Greek limited company must be situated in Greece.

Under Presidential Decree No. 409/12-28/11/1986 Greek legislation concerning limited companies is brought into line with EU Law.

Directors' Meetings.—In order to form a quorum, one-half of total number of directors must be represented at all meetings of board of directors, and at least three directors must be personally present. Same director cannot represent at any meeting more than one director, in addition to himself.

Meeting of board of directors cannot take place abroad unless this is provided for in statutes and a special permission is obtained from Ministry of Trade.

Alien Directors.—With the exception of certain companies governed by special laws, there is no limitation as to the number of aliens who may be directors in a Greek limited company.

General meetings of shareholders must take place at place where company's head office is situated.

In order to have a quorum for a general meeting, there must be present a number of shareholders, representing one-fifth of the company's capital, except in special cases where a number of shareholders representing two-thirds of such capital is required. No resolution can be passed unless an absolute majority is obtained. There are special cases where a majority of three-fifths is required. If a quorum is not obtained at a first meeting, any number of shareholders is sufficient for a quorum, but in certain cases a certain minimum number of shareholders is always required for a quorum.

Reserve.—At least 5% of the company's annual net profits must be set aside as a regular reserve fund until the reserve fund reaches one-third of the company's capital.

Dividends.—Out of company's net profits there must be deducted first amount required as above for reserve fund, then a first dividend of at least 6% and balance may be distributed as provided in statutes.

Suspension of Payments.—A limited company having suspended its payments instead of being declared bankrupt may be placed either under administration and management of company's creditors or alternatively under compulsory liquidation in accordance with a special procedure which has been prescribed by Law Decree 3562, Oct. 8, 1956.

Nominal Shares.—By virtue of law 2328/95 (para. 1, art. 15) and Presidential Decree 82/1996, Greek limited by shares companies, which wish to undertake public works or supplies, have to modify their articles of association in order to convert their bearer shares into nominal shares and to invite shareholders to name themselves. Greek companies limited by shares, shareholders of such companies which are legal persons, shareholders of latter which are legal persons and so forth, must convert their shares into registered shares until ultimate shareholder (natural person) can be identified. Above obligation does not apply to non-Greek legal entities which are shareholders of above Greek companies limited by shares. Shareholder, who does not respond to invitation of company and does not name himself, is deprived of any rights emanating from shares and cannot participate in General Assembly of company.

Foreign Limited Companies.—A foreign limited company may not carry on business in Greece unless permission is obtained from Ministry of Trade, which is published in Government Gazette. To obtain such permission, it is necessary to submit an application to Ministry of Trade, stating date on which company was incorporated abroad, and to appoint an attorney duly authorized to accept service in Greece on behalf of company of all legal process and other documents and an agent in this country to represent company generally.

It is also necessary to submit a power of attorney under which such agent has been appointed, and a list of names and surnames of persons qualified to represent company in company's country.

The accounts of all foreign limited companies must be kept in the Greek language.

Foreign insurance companies establishing themselves in Greece must deposit 5,000,000 drs. as security.

Foreign Companies.—Under Compulsory Enactment 89 of 1/1.8.1968 "Concerning the establishment in Greece of foreign industrial/commercial Companies" considerable privileges and advantages are granted to foreign companies establishing themselves in Greece. This enactment has been amended and extended to maritime companies as well as under Compulsory Enactment 378 of 17/17.4.1968.

Companies of Limited Liability.—A company of limited liability may be formed under Law 3190 of Apr. 27, 1955. Such company is similar to "Gesellschaft mit beschränkter Haftung" of German law. A company of limited liability may be constituted only by notarial contract, copy of which is filed with respective district court. Summary of contract is published in Bulletin of Limited Companies of Government Gazette. Capital of such a company may not be less than three million drachmae. (Law 2065/92).

By virtue of art. 43a of law 3190/1955, as added by art. 2 of Presidential Decree 279/93, it is possible that only one person constitutes one member company of limited liability.

Maritime Companies.—Under Law 791 of July 5/6, 1978, foreign maritime companies establishing themselves in Greece are governed by law of place of their incorporation.

Under Law 959 of 21/24.8.1979, "Concerning a Maritime Company", special provisions are made for maritime companies whose sole object must be maritime trade. Minimum amount of capital is drs. 300,000. Agreement for formation of company must be in writing and company must be registered in Special Registries of Maritime Companies.

E.E.C. Law.—Presidential Decree 409 of 12/28 Nov. 1986 provides for adaptation of Greek company legislation to EEC rules.

Taxation.—See topic Taxation.

CONSTITUTION AND GOVERNMENT:

Following a plebiscite held on Dec. 8, 1974, Greece became a republic. A new constitution entered into force on June 9, 1975. There is a unicameral legislature which elects President of Republic and government must have confidence of Legislature. Constitution has been recently amended, powers of President being curtailed. (Mar. 6, 1986).

Executive power is entrusted to both President and Government. However, country's general policy is determined by Government alone. Organization and function of Greek Government is ruled by Law 1557/85 as amended. Government consists of Prime Minister and Ministers, each of whom is in charge of particular Ministry.

CONTRACTS:

Principles governing Greek law of contracts differ in many respects from principles prevailing in U.S. Three elements are essential to validity of a contract: (a) consent of the parties; (b) legal capacity to contract of both parties; and (c) an object not contrary to law or public morals. In certain cases, "cause," the equivalent of consideration, is also required.

Contracts for benefit of third parties are valid and generally the third party acquires a direct right of enforcement against debtor.

The principal claim of the creditor is performance (specific performance in American terminology). A claim for damages is a subsidiary claim.

Contracts may be either oral or in writing. Oral contracts are valid without any formality but oral testimony is not sufficient to prove a claim exceeding Drs. 30,000 unless it is a commercial transaction. Further, oral contracts may not be concluding concerning a considerable number of transactions such as sale of land, etc. Written contracts may be made either privately as simple contracts or by formal instrument before a notary public. Contracts concerning a considerable number of transactions such as sale of land, disposal of estates, etc., must be notarial contracts.

Excuse for Nonperformance.—Nonperformance of a valid contract may be excused, mainly (a) if performance of the contract has become impossible due to a cause for which debtor is not responsible, (b) if debtor has retained right to withdraw from the contract, and (c) if the other party is obliged to perform first his prestation and has not done so. Also, nonperformance may be excused in certain circumstances if performance may cause undue hardship to debtor (Art. 388 C.C.) and if to demand performance may be considered as an abuse of a right (Art. 281 C.C.)

Applicable Law.—Under Art. 25 C.C., law applicable to the contract is the law to which parties submitted themselves; failing such submission, contract is governed by "the law appropriate to the contract in view of the specific circumstances," which seems equivalent to English "proper law" doctrine. Greece has ratified International Convention of Rome of 19.06.1980 which determines applicable law in contractual obligations between contracting parties within Member-States of European Union.

Government Contracts.—In certain cases, Government contracts must be ratified by law and usually performance bond is required. Greek law acknowledges Government contracts as special category of contracts, and allocates disputes arising from them to Administrative Courts. (Law 1406/1983). To qualify as such, contract must be "contract with the central or local government" as party. Public constructions are

See Topical Index in front part of this volume.

CONTRACTS . . . *continued*
ruled by Law 1418/84 and Presidential Decree 609/85 as amended. See also topic Foreign Investment.

Filing with Tax Authorities.—Under Law 4085/1960 as amended by Law 1828/1989, private lease agreements concerning immovable property over certain amount and in certain areas, must be filed with taxation authorities within 30 days, otherwise are unvalid.

Under para. 16 of art. 8 of Law 1988/1990 any contract concluded between parties one of which is engaged in commerce or profession, must be filed within ten days with proper tax authorities, otherwise is invalid.

COPYRIGHT:

Authors, composers, painters, designers, sculptors, turners and engravers have the exclusive right of publishing and reproducing their works during their lifetime and of assigning their rights to third persons. They have also moral protection right of their personal link with their creation (moral right). (Law 2121/1993).

Such protection extends till end of their life and expires 70 years after their death, counting from end of year of death.

The above protection applies to works in writing or artistic works produced in this country, and may be extended to similar works produced abroad under a special decree on condition of reciprocity. Such protection has been extended to works in writing and artistic works produced in the United States by a decree which came into force on Mar. 1, 1932. Greece is also a signatory of the Convention of Berne dated Sept. 9, 1886, as amended by the Conventions of Berlin, Rome and Brussels dated Nov. 13, 1908, June 2, 1928 and June 26, 1948, respectively and a recent enactment, Law Decree No. 4254 of 11/17 Oct. 1962, has ratified the International Convention signed in Geneva on Sept. 6, 1952 and annexed Protocol Nos. 1, 2, and 3. Greece has also ratified by Law 100/1975 revision of Berne Convention made in Paris in July 1971.

CORPORATIONS: See topic Companies.

COURTS:

Judicial power is exercised by Courts of Law. Judicial independence is basis for judicial review of constitutionality of laws and of constitutionality and legality of statutory instruments.

There are in Greece, administrative, civil and criminal courts of law. Council of State is administrative court of first and last instance with jurisdiction over applications for review of administrative acts. It is also Supreme Court which decides final appeals against judgments of lower administrative courts. These courts are of first and of second instance.

Civil courts adjudicate all "private disputes" as well as cases of non-contentious proceeding.

As a rule, final judgment of tribunal of first instance is subject to appeal before proper court of appeal having jurisdiction on matter. Against judgment of court of appeal, a further appeal is allowed before Supreme Court (Arios Pagos) of Athens on points of law only. If judgment of court of appeal is reversed by Supreme Court, case is again referred to another court which is, as a rule, a court of appeal other than one which pronounced judgment reversed.

There are no special commercial courts. Petty cases are tried by lower courts called courts of peace.

An action on a bill, a promissory note or check is tried by single member of court of first instance or by a justice of Court of Peace under a summary procedure.

Under Art. 623 of Code of Civil Procedure, an order of payment may be obtained for monetary claims if such claims are based on a public or private document.

Administrative and taxation matters are dealt with by special administrative courts, highest of which is Council of State.

CURRENCY:

The legal currency is the drachma. A new drachma has been established as from May 1, 1954, one drachma being equal to 1,000 old drachmae. The drachmae mentioned in this law digest are new drachmae.

Gold Bullion, Gold Coins and Foreign Exchange.—The following restrictions are in force:

(1) The stipulation in Greece of undertakings in gold bullion or coins is prohibited. Likewise the stipulation in Greece of an undertaking in foreign currency is prohibited but there are exceptions, such as in the case of international transactions and certain loans. Further a deposit in foreign currency is permissible with certain banks if made by a physical person residing permanently outside Greece or by a juristic person having its seat outside Greece; also by any person in Greece possessing free exchange.

(2) The sale and purchase of foreign exchange and foreign bank-notes may be transacted only by Bank of Greece and duly authorized other banks. Such sale is allowed only for: (a) payment of such imports as have been duly authorized; (b) requirements of persons residing or travelling abroad; (c) payment of such debts in foreign exchange due by local residents to foreign creditors as arise from commercial transactions.

(3) All exporters of commodities from Greece to foreign countries have to sell to one of the aforesaid banks all proceeds in foreign exchange arising from such exportations.

(4) The importation from abroad of certain commodities is subject to permission of the proper authorities.

(5) Exportation of both foreign and Greek securities, dividends, coupons, etc., without a special permission of the Bank of Greece is prohibited.

(6) Exportation and importation of any amount of drachmae exceeding 40,000 is prohibited.

(7) Loans in drachmae against a security in bullion, foreign currency, foreign exchange, or foreign securities are prohibited.

(8) All claims of creditors residing in foreign countries and payable in Greece are blocked and the debtor must pay the debt directly into a blocked account in the name of the creditor, with the Bank of Greece or one of the other authorized banks. Such blocked accounts cannot be deblocked without special permission of the Bank of Greece.

(9) Arts. 49–53 of Treaty whereby Greece adhered to EEC provide for free movement of capital between member states and deblocking of blocked accounts held in Greece by nationals of member states.

This has as yet not been fully implemented. However, by Executive Orders 1931–1934/3.5.1991, Bank of Greece has now authorised Greek residents to purchase bonds, shares and immovable property in EEC countries. By Executive Order 2093/11-6-92, Bank of Greece has also authorised Greek residents to purchase bonds, shares, etc. even in non-EEC countries.

(10) Now, in certain cases it is permitted to Greek residents to have locally account in foreign exchange.

CUSTOMS DUTIES:

Greece entered into EEC on Jan. 1, 1981 and after expiration of five-year transitory period it has become full member effective Jan. 1, 1986. Goods imported from other EEC countries are basically duty and tax free subject to minor exceptions. Imported goods from outside EEC are subject to Common Customs Tariff (CCT) and classified as per Brussels Standard International Trade Classification of Commodities.

Import of products duty-free for manufacturing and reexport is allowed.

Tariff law was revised by Law decree 4088/1960. It comprizes 99 chapters covering 9806 classes of articles and consists of 322 pages in quarto. Rates are fixed either ad valorem or at fixed rates per weight. Classification of imports into above classes is effected in accord with certain rules fixed by above law. For visitors of Greece residing abroad a franchise is granted as regards unused personal effects of a value not exceeding $150.

DEATH:

Presumption of death may be established by an order of court and at application of any person whose rights are dependent on such death. Such presumption is admitted by court if person in respect of which presumption has been applied for has disappeared whilst being in danger of his life or if no information has been received from him for a considerable time. Application cannot be submitted to court prior to lapse of at least one year from date of danger or at least five years from last information. If court considers evidence produced satisfactory, it pronounces party concerned to be presumed to be dead and at same time fixes date as from which such presumption starts operating. Should party presumed to be dead reappear, any person who has received any assets out of estate of presumed decedent is liable to refund same. See also topic Absentees.

Actions for Death.—A party who under law is responsible for decedent's death is liable to pay medical, nursing and funeral expenses to persons who under law have to bear such expenses. He is also liable to pay a compensation to any person who under law was entitled to receive alimony from deceased or to receive certain services from him (for instance those rendered by a wife to her husband by keeping house for him).

Party responsible for deceased's death has further to pay an indemnity to decedent's family. The law is not settled as to what members of such family are entitled to an indemnity, but in accord with a good authority such right is accorded to all members who were closely connected with decedent. The latter is a question of fact which has to be established by the court, but it is generally admitted that parents, spouse, issue, brothers and sisters have such right. These laws apply also to aliens. There is no statutory limit as to amount of indemnity. See also topic Limitation of Actions, subhead Torts.

Death certificate may be obtained by application to the proper civil registry.

DEEDS:

A conveyance of real property and a constitution of real rights generally, including hypothecs, is not valid unless effected by notarial act which has to be registered in the proper registry of land property. Also any agreement embodying a promise to conclude a contract regarding any of above matters is not valid unless embodied in a notarial contract.

DEPOSITIONS:

Depositions may be made under oath either before a notary public or before a Justice of the Peace. It is possible also for a deposition to be made before a U.S. consular officer in Greece for use in the U.S. Greek courts may request American courts and vice versa to take testimony under a "commission rogatoire." Depositions abroad may be taken before Greek consular officers. See also topic Affidavits.

DESCENT AND DISTRIBUTION:

Movable and immovable property of a person dying intestate passes to his heirs in following order, subject, as a rule, to rights of surviving spouse, if any there be, each class of which a member is living taking to exclusion of subsequent classes.

(1) Descendants, which term includes legitimate issue, adopted children and their descendants, also certain classes of illegitimate issue. Descendants of first degree take in equal shares, with certain exceptions. Descendants of second and following degrees succeed per stirpes, i.e., they step into share of their predeceased parent.

(2) Parents, brothers, sisters and the children and grandchildren of brothers and sisters. The parents, brothers and sisters succeed in equal shares. The children and grandchildren of predeceased brothers and sisters succeed per stirpes. Brothers and sisters of the half blood and their children and grandchildren, if they coinherit with parents or brothers and sisters of the whole blood or with children and grandchildren of such heirs, receive one half of the share of an heir of the whole blood of an equal degree.

(3) Grandfathers and grandmothers of the deceased and their children and grandchildren in the following order. (a) If the grandfather and grandmother of both lines are all alive they succeed in equal shares. (b) If the grandfather or grandmother of the paternal or maternal line are not alive, then the share of such deceased grandparent passes to his children and grandchildren. (c) If there is no surviving child or grandchild, then his share passes to the surviving grandparent of the same line and if such

DESCENT AND DISTRIBUTION . . . *continued*

grandparent is not alive, to his children and grandchildren. (d) If there is no surviving grandparent of either the paternal or maternal line and there are no surviving children or grandchildren from such predeceased grandparents of same line then estate passes to surviving grandparents of other line or to children and grandchildren from same. In all above cases children succeed in equal shares and grandchildren per stirpes.

(4) Great grandfathers and great grandmothers of the deceased. These inherit in equal shares, irrespective whether they belong to the same or a different line.

Surviving spouse receives one fourth of estate if deceased leaves descendants; one half and certain personal chattels, if deceased, not leaving descendants, leaves other heirs; and whole of estate if deceased leaves neither issue nor other heirs.

Determination of Heirship.—A certificate of heirship termed "Klironomitirion" is granted by proper district court following a special procedure and at application of heir or heirs.

Advancements during decedent's life are taken into account only in the case of forced heirs. See topic Wills.

Liability of Heirs.—Heirs are liable for debts of deceased in proportion to their respective share, but if they have accepted inheritance with "benefit of inventory" their liability is limited to extent of value of estate. An heir may however refuse to accept an undesirable inheritance. Renunciation of such inheritance must be made within certain period and before secretary of proper court.

Escheat.—If intestate left neither surviving spouse nor heirs, estate passes to state.

DESERTION: See topic Divorce.

DISPUTE RESOLUTION:

Disputes of private law are usually resolved by court judgment after action has been brought before court. Alternate dispute resolution is achieved as follows:

Voluntary Resolution.—

Compromise is concluded by persons who consent to resolve dispute by mutual concessions. There are two kinds of compromise: judicial compromise is effected by statement before court or notary public, while trial is pending. If statement is made by attorney who represents litigant, special power of attorney is required. After statement of compromise has been made trial is waived and records of trial whereby compromise was recorded constitute enforceable title. (art. 904 of Greek Code of Civil Procedure); extrajudicial compromise is contract which does not waive judicial proceedings but can provoke dismissal of action, if it is invoked as objection.

Mediation is exercised ex officio by judge of court of peace (see topic Courts) before commencement of proceedings. (art. 208 C. Civ. Pr.). Mediation can be also asked before trial by person who intends to bring action. If mediation succeeds, judicial compromise is drawn up. Otherwise judicial proceedings continue or action is finally brought before court.

Arbitration.—See topic Arbitration.

Mandatory Resolution.—

Effort to Compromise.—(art. 214A of Code of Civil Procedure, as added by art. 15, §1 Law 2298/1995). When action is brought for private dispute which can be subject of compromise and falls within competence of court of first instance, claimant has to invite defendant to try amicable resolution of dispute. If this condition is not fulfilled, action is dismissed. If meeting of litigants turns into compromise, record is ratified by competent judge and constitutes enforceable title. Otherwise judicial proceedings continue. Effect of this procedure is suspended by art. 18 of Law 2335/95 until 16.09.1996.

Obligatory Arbitration.—Disputes which arise between Greek State and investors of foreign capital under application of laws for protection of foreign investments (Laws 2687/51, 4171/61, 849/78, 1116/80, 1962/82, 1892/90) must be obligatorily resolved by arbitration. See topic Foreign Investment.

DIVORCE:

Very considerable changes have been introduced in Divorce Law by Law 1329 of 15/18 Feb. 1983. Now divorce is granted if: (a) Marital relationship has been so strongly disturbed that continuation of marriage is intolerable for petitioner; this is presumed in case of adultery, bigamy, desertion or if attempt on life of spouse has been made; (b) spouses have lived apart for four years; (c) spouse has been declared by court to have disappeared and (d) both parties consent to divorce, provided marriage has lasted for at least one year.

Jurisdiction.—On principle, action for divorce is brought before tribunal of first instance of defendant's domicile; however, Greek courts are always considered competent to pronounce divorce when one of parties to marriage was Greek irrespective of domicile; further, Greek courts are considered competent to dissolve marriage if parties were resident within their jurisdiction.

Greek courts have no jurisdiction to pronounce divorce of aliens if according to law of nationality of both spouses such jurisdiction is not recognized.

Alimony.—Court may compel party to pay alimony if other party is unable to support him- or herself. Extent of such alimony is determined according to means of party liable to pay same and may be altered from time to time by court.

Custody of children is determined by court. Parties may agree on terms of custody. Both parents retain right to communicate with child.

Support of Children.—Both parents are responsible for maintenance and care of children.

Foreign Divorces.—Law is not yet quite settled whether foreign judgments pronouncing divorce of Greek subjects are valid in Greece. According to one opinion, such divorces should be declared executable in Greece by Greek courts.

DOWRY: See topic Husband and Wife.

ENVIRONMENT:

Protection of environment is provided by art. 24 of Constitution as mandate of State. Alteration of use of public forests is particularly forbidden, while at same time all forests which are destroyed, have to be obligatorily reafforested.

Centerpiece of Greek environmental law is Law 1650 of 15/16.10.1986, as completed by administrative statutes issued under its authorisation. Activities and works which may affect negatively environment, cannot be permitted unless environmental assessment study is filed with administrative authority and is approved by it.

Air and sound pollution is monitored and combatted. Measures are taken for protection of waters, of land, for management of solid and hazardous wastes, radioactivity etc.

Territories of natural beauty and originality can be put in special status of protection.

Rare specimens are protected. Downgraded areas are assisted.

Sanctions are inflicted against violators of provisions of law (imprisonment, fines and indemnity).

EXCHANGE CONTROL:

See topics Currency; Foreign Investment; Foreign Trade Regulations.

EXECUTIONS:

Enforcement of pecuniary judgments may be obtained by seizure of debtor's immovable and movable property and sale of same under forced auction, and in certain cases by his personal arrest. Judgment in respect of pecuniary debts may also be enforced by means of forced administration of debtor's land property or business by a receiver appointed by court.

As a rule execution of a judgment of court of first instance is stayed pending decision of court of appeal.

Execution proceedings may be stayed by court.

EXECUTORS AND ADMINISTRATORS:

See topic Descent and Distribution.

EXEMPTIONS:

Art. 953, §§3 and 4 of Code of Civil Procedure provide for articles exempted from seizure. Further, art. 982 of said Code provides that inter alios, shares of participation in a partnership, wages, pensions, alimony and social insurance dues may not be attached, with certain exceptions when one fourth of same may be seized. See also topic Garnishment.

FORCED HEIRS: See topic Wills.

FOREIGN EXCHANGE:

See topics Currency; Foreign Investment; Foreign Trade Regulations.

FOREIGN INVESTMENT:

For purpose of encouraging investment in Greece of capital imported from abroad, special facilities and guarantees are provided by Law Decree 2687 of 1953, as implemented by Law Decree 2928 of 1954 and Compulsory Law 916/1971. Term "Foreign Capital" includes not only foreign exchange, but also machinery and material, vessels exceeding 1,500 tons registered under Greek flag, inventions, technical methods and trademarks, provided that they are invested in productive enterprises. Art. 107, para. 1 of Constitution provides for protection of certain foreign investments in Greece.

More important of such facilities and guarantees are the following: (a) Bank of Greece has to provide necessary exchange for repatriation of capital and remittance abroad of interest and profits. Amount however of capital allowed to be repatriated cannot exceed for every year 10% of invested capital. Likewise amount remitted for interest cannot exceed 10% and for profits 12% of said capital. (b) Such enterprises established by investment of foreign capital may employ aliens for the higher posts of their technical and administrative personnel. (c) Certain facilities in respect of taxation, custom duties and municipal and other rates are provided. Also reduction of fees in respect of registration of hypothecs (mortgages), constitution of pledges, and of notarial duties. Following are inter alios also provided: (d) Freedom to export goods produced by such enterprises; (e) exemption from retrospective taxation; (f) right of these enterprises to keep their accounts in foreign currency imported to Greece; (g) equality of treatment with local similar enterprises; (h) exemption from compulsive expropriation; (i) exemption from all kinds of requisitions unless when Greece is in a state of war and then only in consideration of an equitable compensation to be established by agreement between Greek Government and respective investor.

All such facilities and guarantees are established every time by agreement between investor concerned and Greek Government which agreement is confirmed by decree or ministerial order. Such decree or order may not be amended without agreement of such investor.

Special taxation and other facilities have been extended by Law 4171/1961 to important productive investments of a value not less than 90 million drachmae. Recently promulgated Law 1892 of 31/31.7.1990 provides various incentives and advantages for investors.

See also topics Currency; Foreign Trade Regulations.

FOREIGN JUDGMENTS:

Code of Civil Procedure provides in Art. 905 for enforcement of foreign judgments in Greece.

Under said Art. 905, a civil judgment issued by a foreign court may be enforced in Greece if it has been previously declared executable by a decision of proper Greek court. Such Greek court is single member court of first instance of domicile, or failing domicile, of residence of judgment debtor or, in absence of either domicile or residence, single member court of first instance of Athens.

See Topical Index in front part of this volume.

FOREIGN JUDGMENTS . . . *continued*

Courts will declare a foreign judgment enforceable in Greece if: (a) It is enforceable according to law of state whose courts issued it; (b) it is not contrary to good morals or public policy in Greece; (c) court which issued it was, under Greek law competent to deal with matter; (d) party which lost case was not denied right to defend itself and, generally, to appear before courts, unless such denial was made pursuant to a provision which applies also to nationals of state whose courts issued judgment; and (e) it is not contrary to a previous decision of a Greek court, pronounced in same case and constituting res judicata for litigants between whom judgment was issued. Greece has ratified International Convention of Brussells of 27.09.1968, which determines international jurisdiction of courts of member-states and simplifies recognition and execution of foreign judgments.

Art. 906 of Code of Civil Procedure provides that foreign arbitration awards may be enforced in Greece if provisions of Art. 903 of said Code are met.

Enforcement of Foreign Arbitration Awards.—Greece is party to Geneva Protocol of 1923 and Convention signed in Geneva on Sept. 26, 1927 concerning enforcement of foreign arbitration awards. Greece has also signed and ratified by Law Decree 4220 of 19/19 Sept. 1961 International Convention on the Recognition and Enforcement of Foreign Arbital Awards, signed in New York on June 10, 1958 and annexed Protocols 1, 2 and 3. Greece applies this convention on basis of reciprocity. Greece has ratified International Convention of Washington of 16.03.1966 for regulation of disputes related to investments between states and foreign citizens.

Subject to provisions of international treaties, under Art. 903 of Code of Civil Procedure, foreign arbitration award is considered as res judicata in Greece provided: (a) Submission to arbitration was validly made, and, according to Greek law, matter may be dealt with by arbitration, (b) award is final and no recourse against its validity is pending, (c) party which lost had not been denied right to defend itself, and (d) award does not conflict with decision of Greek Court on same matter constituting res judicata between parties or with public policy and good morals.

FOREIGN TRADE REGULATIONS:

Exports.—As a rule a permission of Bank of Greece is required which is granted subject to certain conditions and formalities. The foreign exchange resulting from such exports must be transferred to Bank of Greece. Only persons duly registered with the proper Chambers of Commerce or Chambers of Industry may conduct export trade.

Imports.—Previously existing restrictions as to quantity and quality of imports and qualifications of importer, have been repealed since July 1953 by virtue of a resolution of Board of Foreign Trade No. 45700 of 7th July 1953, as am'd by resolution of same Board numbered 6550/55 and 6560/55 respectively. All imports are now free with exception of certain goods for which a proper permission is required, but all imports are subject to various formalities.

See also topics Currency; Foreign Investment.

FRAUDS, STATUTE OF:

Greece has no statute of frauds. See also topic Contracts.

FRAUDULENT SALES AND CONVEYANCES:

Apart from bankruptcy proceedings (which can be addressed only against traders) an alienation of property can be attacked by a creditor as void against him, if contracted by debtor with intention of prejudicing his creditors, provided that other party in favour of whom alienation was made, was aware of such intention of debtor and provided that debtor's property is not sufficient to satisfy creditor's claims. Knowledge by said third party of creditor's fraudulent intention is presumed if such alienation by creditor is made to a spouse or to certain of creditor's relations. This presumption applies if alienation was made during last year before attack.

GARNISHMENT:

A garnishment is effected by serving on garnishee of document containing exact description of title and claim under and for which garnishment is effected, amount or object for which garnishment is effected, an order to garnishee not to deliver to debtor and appointment of an address attorney. Garnishee must within eight days declare before justice of peace whether in fact he is in possession of sum or object garnished. Failure to do so within stipulated period is considered as a negative declaration. Garnishee is liable for any damages suffered by garnisher from his negative or incorrect reply.

Property Which May Not Be Garnished.—Salaries, wages, pensions and social insurance payments cannot be garnished unless in respect of certain claims for alimony and then only up to a certain proportion of amount of such salaries or wages.

There are also a number of other debts which cannot be garnished, including salaries with certain exceptions and amounts due to contractors.

HOLIDAYS:

Following are legal holidays: Suns.; Jan. 1st; Epiphany; first Mon. of Lent; Mar. 25th; Good Fri.; Easter Mon.; Apr. 23rd; May 1st; June 11th; Aug. 15th; Oct. 28th; Dec. 25th and 26th.

On legal holidays, bills of exchange and promissory notes cannot be protested, nor summons served. If a bill of exchange falls due on a holiday, it is extended until the following day when it can be protested. All time limits provided for in the civil procedure which fall due on a holiday are similarly extended.

HOMESTEADS:

Do not exist in Greek law.

HUSBAND AND WIFE:

Under recent enactment, Law 1329 of 16/18 Feb. 1983, there is now complete equality between spouses in marriage. Matters affecting marital life are determined jointly and, in case of disagreement, by court. Wife maintains her maiden surname but for social occasions may use her husband's surname or add it to her own. Each spouse contributes to marital expenses according to his or her means and ability.

Nationality of Wife.—An alien woman marrying a Greek now does not acquire automatically Greek nationality. Following Law 1438/1984 alien woman marrying Greek national who wishes to acquire such nationality must apply for and obtain it.

A Greek woman marrying an alien loses her Greek nationality if under her husband's national law she acquires the latter's nationality unless she makes a proper declaration that she wishes to retain her Greek nationality. If such marriage of a Greek woman is dissolved, she may recover the Greek nationality subject to certain formalities.

Property Relations.—Dowry has been abolished by Law 1329/1983.

On principle, on marriage, each spouse retains his or her property, there being as yet no community of property between them. However, on dissolution of marriage personal chattels used in household may be divided amongst spouses and court may award use of marital home to either party, irrespective of ownership of same. Further, there is presumption that $^1/_3$ of property acquired during marriage (except through inheritance) has been acquired by party not owning it and may be claimed by latter.

Maintenance.—Both spouses must contribute to marriage expenses according to their means. If cohabitation is interrupted for proper cause, maintenance expenses are paid to spouse by other if former is unable to maintain him- or herself. Greece has signed and ratified by Law Decree 4421 of 7/11 Nov. 1964 International Convention signed in New York on June 20, 1956 concerning recovery abroad of maintenance.

IMMIGRATION:

There is no legislation in Greece concerning immigration similar to such American legislation. As a rule, an alien's right to enter, reside and work in Greece is subject to permission of Ministries of the Interior and Labor. Geneva's Convention of 1951 has been ratified by Legislative Decree 3989/1959 and is applicable in Greece. New Law 1975/1991 rules right to enter, reside, work and be deported. This law reflects EEC rules and in particular those enacted in Convention of Schengen. See also topic Aliens.

Nationality.—Code of Nationality (as now in force) governs acquisition etc. of Greek nationality. On principle, Greece accepts jus sanguinis. Greek law does not recognize dual nationality if one of nationalities is Greek, i.e., in eyes of Greek law, person with dual nationality, one of which is Greek, is only Greek national. Greek national may not divest himself of his nationality without permission of state. Now also see Law 1438/1984 and Law 2130/1993. Greek woman who marries alien may retain her nationality provided certain formalities are observed.

Greece has signed and ratified by Law 536/3/8.2.1977 International Convention signed in Paris on Sept. 10, 1964 concerning exchange of information on matters regarding acquisition of citizenship.

INFANTS:

Majority begins with completion of 18th year of age. Minor of 15 may, with general consent of his parents or guardian conclude labor contract.

Actions.—Infant is represented in court by his parents or guardian. Parents may not proceed to certain actions particularly alienation of infant's property, without consent of court.

INSOLVENCY:

See topic Bankruptcy.

INTEREST:

Legal interest, as well as interest which is due in case of default of payment, is at present 28%. Rate of agreed interest cannot exceed 26%.

When no interest has been agreed on, it is not due, as a rule, before proper notice of payment is given to debtor, but there are certain exceptions. Thus interest is due automatically when certain date has been stipulated for payment.

The rate of interest on monies due by the State is 6%, unless otherwise agreed by special contract or an act of Parliament.

Under Geneva Convention, rate of interest on foreign drafts is 6% p.a. Clause contained in draft for payment of interest is invalid under said Convention.

Usury.—An agreement for payment of an usurious rate of interest is invalid as to excess over lawful rate. Usurious interest paid may be recovered.

JOINT STOCK COMPANIES:

See topic Companies.

JUDGMENTS: See topic Foreign Judgments.

LABOR RELATIONS:

Minister of Labor supervises enforcement of labor legislation. Labor relations are dealt with both under the Civil Code (Art. 648-680) and under a considerable number of special enactments.

Wages and salaries and conditions of work are subject of written or oral contracts between employers and employees but pay rates cannot be less favorable than the ones provided by the respective Collective Labor Agreements and hygienic and safety conditions must be observed. Collective Labor Agreements are negotiated from time to time between Trade Unions and the respective Employers' Organizations and must be properly registered.

Employees as a rule must be engaged through Government employment agencies.

Minors under age of 14 may not be employed. Minors between ages of 14 and 16 may be employed after medical examination as to their fitness to work and only in certain kinds of work. Women may not be employed in night work or in certain hazardous or heavy occupations.

Normal working hours are eight hours per day for six days of the week; in many cases however, shorter working hours are provided for and five day working week has now been established for state, banking and other employees. Persons working at

LABOR RELATIONS . . . *continued*
night, overtime, and on Sundays are entitled to additional remuneration. After completing one year's employment, employees are entitled to annual paid holiday. Employees are entitled to pay even if absent from work due to sickness for period of one to six months depending on time of their employment.

Employees engaged for a specific period may not be dismissed before expiration of such period unless for proper cause. Employees engaged for indetermined period may be dismissed without cause if they have been employed for over two months provided compensation fixed by law is paid to them; failure to pay such compensation renders dismissal void.

All persons in private employment must be insured with Social Insurance Organization (I.K.A.) and with Unemployment Insurance Fund.

Labor disputes are tried in first instance by special labor tribunals.

As a rule, strikes are permitted and, on principle, right to strike is protected by Constitution. (Art. 23 para. 2). Lock-outs, on principle are not permitted.

Trade unions are based on the right of association which is protected by Constitution and are governed by special legislation and the international conventions of which Greece is a party. Employers have their own organizations in the form of associations and federations which are organized either on a regional basis or by related industries.

Disputes are usually settled either by direct negotiations between employers' organizations and trade unions or by arbitration tribunals.

LANDLORD AND TENANT:

Rent Controls.—Under Law 1703 of 25/27 May 1987 as amended by Law 2041/92 leases of industrial, commercial and professional premises are subject to various restrictions.

Certain leases of residential premises are subject to rent control and some restrictions. (Law 1898/90 as am'd by Law 1953/1991).

LAW REPORTS, CODES, ETC.:

Greece is a country of codified law, i.e., only provisions set forth in enactments are considered as law; no decisional or judicial law, i.e., law by precedent, exists and doctrine of stare decisis is unknown except now under a recent amendment of law in certain cases of judgments of Supreme Court (Arios Pagos). Lower courts are independent and are not bound by precedent except in above-mentioned case. However, decisions of higher courts are frequently cited and followed by lower courts not as law but on account of their reasoning and persuasive force.

Official publication of all law is made in Government Gazette. There are no official publications of reports or decisions of the courts (except in case of decisions of Conseil d'Etat) but many collections of such decisions exist as well as a considerable number of law journals which publish same.

At present there are various codes in force including a Civil Code, Commercial Code, Criminal Code, etc., and various other codes are being prepared.

LEGISLATURE:

Under Greek Constitution, legislative power is exercised by Parliament and President of Republic. In normal cases powers of President are confined to promulgating and publishing acts of Parliament. Within limits of Constitution (especially those drawn by provisions on human rights) Parliament is subject to no restraint regarding what and how to legislate.

Delegation is allowed except where Constitution requires "formal Law" that is, act of Parliament, instead of simply a "law", which may also be any statutory instrument.

As a rule, such "formal laws" are needed for imposition of taxes, but also in many important areas, including "exercise and protection of individual rights".

See topic Constitution and Government.

LICENSES:

Exercise of most professions and trades as well as the operation of factories etc., are subject to licenses. See also topic Patents.

LIENS:

Liens may be created either by contract (see topic Pledges) or by provision of law. There is a considerable number of latter, including in favor of hotelkeeper on effects belonging to guests brought into hotel (Art. 838-839 Civ. Code); on certain agricultural products, including tobacco; for loans granted by banks; on articles brought into leased premises, for the lease (Art. 604-607 Civ. Code); on car which has caused damages for same under Law 3769/1929; on ships in certain cases; etc.

LIMITATION OF ACTIONS:

As a rule the period for limitation of actions in civil and commercial proceedings is 20 years but there are many exceptions. The most important are the following:

Five years limitation applies to claims of tradesmen; industrials and artisans, in respect of goods delivered and work performed; to claims of people who engage professionally in agriculture, breeding of livestock, fishery and forestry for goods supplied; to claims of carriers for goods carried; to claims of hotel keepers and restaurateurs in respect of accommodation and food supplied to their customers; to claims of servants and workers for their salaries and wages; to claims of teachers for their fees; to claims of physicians, midwives, notaries public and attorneys for their fees and costs; to claims for dividends and arrears of interest or rent, etc.

Three years limitation applies to the claim of the bearer against the acceptor of a bill of exchange or the maker of a promissory note, to insurance claims, and to claims arising from the workmen compensation laws, unlawful competition and patents.

One year limitation applies to claims for pensions and subsidies due by the state and to claims of the bearer against the drawer and endorsers of a bill of exchange and the endorsers of a promissory note; also to salvage claims.

Six months limitation applies to claims of endorsers against drawer and other endorsers of a bill of exchange and to claims for resiliation of a sale or reduction of sale price on account of defects of goods sold or absence of qualifications stipulated by vendor.

Commencement of Period.—Period of limitation, as a rule, starts with accrual of claim, but in certain cases, such as insurance claims and salvage, from expiration of year in which claim accrued.

Torts.—Period of limitation for claim arising out of tort is five years commencing from date on which injured party became informed both of damage and of the tort-feaser, but period of limitation cannot exceed 20 years from date of commission of tort. If tort constituted punishable offence which under penal law is subject to longer period of limitation such period applies also to any claim of damages which may accrue as result of such offence.

Limitation is interrupted by commencing an action, by an acknowledgment of the debt, by the registration of a hypothec and by the service of a writ of payment.

MARRIAGE:

Parties to marriage must be 18 years old; court may allow persons less than 18 years old to marry if there are strong reasons militating for this.

Consent required of parent or guardian or tutor for persons under 18 years of age. If they refuse, consent may be granted by court if necessary in interest of infant.

License of bishop is required in order to perform Christian orthodox ceremony and is granted at application of proposed spouses and after previous publication of banns. Latter may be omitted if important reasons exist.

Ceremony.—Under Law 1250 of 3/7 Apr. 1982, marriage may be solemnized either by religious service or by civil ceremony. Civil marriages contracted between Greeks abroad prior to Law 1250/1982 are now recognized as valid unless new valid marriage has been contracted.

Annulment of marriage may be decreed by court on various grounds enumerated in Arts. 1350-1352, 1354, 1356-1357, 1359-1360 and 1362 of Civil Code. (art. 1 of Law 1250/1982).

Children born out of an annulled marriage are legitimate, but children born out of a prohibited marriage between certain blood relations are assimilated to illegitimate children who have been voluntarily recognised by their fathers.

MARRIED WOMEN:

See topics Descent and Distribution; Husband and Wife; Marriage; Wills.

Under new constitution there is on principle complete equality between sexes. This has now been legislated by Law 1329 of 16/18 Feb. 1983.

MINES AND MINERALS:

Mining is governed by Mining Code. Mining rights are separate from right in land. Mining rights can be granted only by state. Special law is required for granting of mining rights concerning precious and certain other metals, and oil.

MONOPOLIES AND RESTRAINT OF TRADE:

Monopolies.—Law 703 of 26.09.1977, as amended and completed by laws 1934/1991, 2000/1991 and 2296/1995, is governing control of monopolies and oligopolies and protection of free competition.

Committee for Protection of Competition is established, as independent administrative authority, which controls application of law and whose decisions are subject to appeal before administrative courts.

Abuse of dominant position in national market or of relation of economic dependence shall be prohibited.

Concentration of enterprises (i.e. merger, acquisition of control) is not prohibited as such. However, concentrations have to be notified to Competition Committee within 30 days from realization (if they concern 10% of market shares or 10 million ECU turnover) or within ten days (if 25% of market share is concerned or 50 million ECU turnover). Latter concentrations can be prohibited by Competition Committee, in case they restrict competition in national market significantly. Exception can be ordered by Ministers of Commerce and National Economy, if particular reasons exist.

Penalties are inflicted upon those violating provisions of that act.

Concentrations of wide community dimension are subject to control by Committee of European Union.

MORTGAGES (HYPOTHECS):

In civil law a debt may be secured by a hypothec on alienable immovable property or on a usufruct. The hypothecee's right is accessory to a principal obligation.

For the constitution of a hypothec both a valid title (right) to a hypothec and the registration of such title with the office of the Registrar of Hypothecs are required. Such a title to a hypothec may exist either as a result of a notarial contract between the owner of the hypothecated property (hypothecator) and the hypothecee or on the strength of the law, as in favour of a minor on the immovables of a guardian for any claim arising out of the administration of the minor's property by the guardian or in favour of the state for taxes due. Likewise a judgment of the court or an arbitration award are a proper title to register a hypothec for the sum adjudged.

A provisional hypothec called "prenotation" may also be acquired by a decision of court as security for a claim pending obtaining of a final judgment confirming such claim and effects of prenotation are conditional upon such confirmation. Prenotation is invalidated if, within 90 days from confirmation by court of claim for security of which is was granted, it is not converted into a mortgage.

The hypothec first registered secures a priority over all subsequent hypothecs. A hypothec can be registered only for a specified amount of money.

Under Law 4112/1929 as am'd by Law Decree 4001/1959, banks may obtain mortgage on industrial machinery or plants. Such mortgage extends on machinery or plants installed even if ownership of same has been retained by seller thereof.

In shipping law a debt may be secured either by a hypothec on vessel or by mortgage.

See Topical Index in front part of this volume.

MORTGAGES (HYPOTHECS) . . . *continued*

Under Law Decree No. 3899 (1958) a new form of a hypothec on a vessel has been established called "preferred hypothec" under which inter alios creditor may acquire management of the vessel and upon the debtor failing to pay his debt may sell vessel without necessity of resorting to a sale by public auction, as prescribed in the ordinary hypothec.

See also topic Attachment.

MOTOR VEHICLES:

Vehicle License.—No motor vehicle may be driven without a vehicle license; number plates must be displayed both front and rear and altering plates is an offense. Foreign motor vehicles may circulate with foreign license numbers for three months which may be extended for another nine months.

Driver's License.—No person may drive without a license. Minimum age for obtaining license is 18. Aliens may drive in Greece if they possess an international driving license.

Accidents.—In case of accident, driver must stop, assist injured person, give any information required and report to police; failure to do so is punishable with up to three years imprisonment.

Liability of Vehicle Owner.—Owner is liable for any damages caused by his vehicle even if such damages were not caused by him personally. His liability is limited to value of vehicle.

Lien.—An injured person has a lien on vehicle which caused the injury.

Traffic Regulations.—Traffic is regulated by Traffic Code. Greece is signatory of international convention signed in Paris on Apr. 24, 1926.

NATIONALITY: See topic Immigration.

NOTARIES PUBLIC:

A notary public is appointed for life by the Minister of Justice and must be at least 25 years old and an advocate at the time of his appointment. The number of notaries in each town is limited and the powers of a notary are territorially limited.

Special duties of notaries include, inter alios, the engrossment of certain contracts (sale contracts, etc.) and of all the instruments which parties desire to make in authentic form, to preserve same on file as a record and to issue certified copies. He may accept sworn statements and may examine witnesses on commission in certain civil cases.

PARTNERSHIP:

There are two forms of commercial partnerships, viz., partnerships in which liability of all partners is unlimited, and those in which, in addition to partners of unlimited liability, there is also at least one partner whose liability is limited to a certain amount. Either form of partnership constitutes a separate corporate entity which is independent from that of partners and may sue or be sued as such.

Formation.—Partnership agreement must be in writing and agreement must be registered with court of first instance within whose jurisdiction head office of partnership is established. If partnership has one or more branch offices, such registration must be repeated in respective court where each branch is situated. A partnership may be formed either under a notarial act or under a private indenture. In either case, ad valorem stamp duties are payable.

Name.—If name of deceased partner is included in tradename after his death it cannot be used without consent of the heirs of deceased.

Rights and Liabilities of Partners Inter Se.—They are determined by the partnership agreement and by certain rules which in some cases supersede the partnership agreement.

Rights and Liabilities of Partners as to Third Persons.—In both forms of partnerships, partners whose liability is unlimited are jointly and severally liable for liabilities of partnership. A limited partner who commits an act of administration of partnership business becomes jointly liable with unlimited partners for all obligations of partnership.

Dissolution.—In case of a partner's death partnership may continue between surviving partners. Partners may agree that in event of death of any partner partnership will continue with heirs of deceased partner.

Administration of partnership property is conducted by liquidator or liquidators. If no liquidator has been appointed all partners act jointly as liquidators.

Administration of the Partnership Property.—The administration is conducted by such of the unlimited partner or partners as have been appointed administrators. If no administration has been appointed then all unlimited partners act as administrators.

PATENTS:

Under Law 1733 of 18/22 Sept. 1987 patents are now granted by Industrial Property Organization. Patent is granted for new invention capable of industrial application; invention may refer to product, method or industrial application. Yearly annuity is due for maintaining patent in force.

All documents must be submitted in Greek.

All transfers and permissions for use, or generally for exploitation of a patent, must be registered in Registries of Patents and published in Government Gazette.

Foreign Patents.—In case of application for a patent for an invention already patented abroad, applicant must produce a certificate of foreign authority from which patent was obtained showing that application for patent was submitted to such authority or that a patent has already been granted. Where appropriate, treaty priority may be claimed. This is case for U.S. patent applications.

Duration of protection is 20 years, commencing on the day following the date on which the application for patent was filed. Rights of patentee devolve to his heirs and are transferable by will or by act inter vivos.

Annulment.—Patents may be declared void by a judgment of Court if: (a) Owner of patent is not inventor or latter's assignee, (b) invention is not capable of being patented in accordance with art. 5 of law, (c) description is not sufficient for invention to be applied by expert, and (d) object of patent granted extends beyond protection demanded. Nullity may be partial.

Licenses.—Patentee may grant to third persons a license to use and exploit invention. Under certain conditions licence to use patent may be granted without owner's permission but compensation must be paid.

International Convention.—Greece is member of International Convention of Nov. 19, 1920, regarding Central Office of Patents as well as Convention of Paris concerning Protection of Industrial Property as now in force after its amendment in Stockholm in 1967. Such amendment was ratified by Law 213/15/20.11.1975. Greece has signed and ratified by Law 1607/1986 Convention on the Granting of European Patents signed in Munich on Oct. 5, 1973.

Transfer of technology, including patents for same under European Convention of 5 Oct. 1973 is now governed by Law 1733 of 18/22 Sept. 1987.

PLEDGES:

All pledges must be constituted under a notarial document or a private indenture, and in the latter case the date of such a document must be placed on record in accordance with special rules provided by the law.

No pledge is valid unless property pledged is placed in custody of creditor, or of a third person appointed by agreement between pledgor and pledgee.

In event of nonpayment, creditor may sell property pledged if pledge is confirmed by an executory title, failing which he may apply to court for an order for sale of property. Sale can be effected only by public auction, with exception of stock exchange securities which may be sold in stock exchange. If proceeds of sale are not sufficient to cover debt and costs of sale creditor may proceed against debtor for balance. Any agreement entitling creditor to retain property pledged or to sell same without above formalities is void if contracted before debt becomes payable. Same applies to any agreement whereby debtor is exempted in toto or partly from formalities prescribed by law.

An assignable claim may be pledged under a document date of which must be placed on record in manner provided by law and notice of such pledge must be given to debtor.

Special facilities apply to pledges made in favor of certain banks in Greece, and also, subject to the obtention of a special licence from the Government, to pledges made in favor of Greek limited companies whose capital exceeds a fixed minimum, of certain limited or unlimited partnerships under certain conditions and of foreign limited companies.

Special rules apply to commercial pledges and other special pledges, such as "agricultural pledges," "pledges on tobacco" and "pledges in connection with goods which have been warehoused with the general warehouses." Also by art. 6 of Law Decree 4203 (1961) in conjunction with Royal Decree 188 (1962), a pledge, called special cinematographic pledge, has been established on motion picture films and certain other motion picture material as well as on claims concerning exploitation of motion picture films.

PRESCRIPTION: See topic Limitation of Actions.

PRINCIPAL AND AGENT:

Powers of attorney executed in this country must, as a rule, be drawn by a notary public. The original document is filed with a notary public and authenticated copies of same are supplied upon application.

Powers of attorney executed abroad on matters requiring notarial power of attorney in Greece are not valid in Greece unless they have been drawn or attested by local notary public. In both cases, they must be authenticated by nearest Greek consular authority.

A power of attorney is cancelled by death of the constituent or by revocation, but it is advisable to limit such power to a fixed period. Powers of attorney to be used in litigation are valid for five years.

PROCESS:

If service of a writ or any other document is required to be effected in Greece in accordance with the Greek law, it has to be done through a proper process server who is an officer of the court. The process server after the service has been effected issues a certificate of service in which the document served is adequately described. If the process server cannot find at the address of the party to be served any person to whom the document to be served can be duly delivered, the document is affixed at the said address in the presence of two witnesses.

Both the document to be served and the certificate of the process server have to be in Greek. If a document in a foreign language is desired to be served in accordance with the Greek law by a process server it will have to be translated into Greek.

If service in Greece of a writ or other document before a U.S. court is required and it is sufficient in eyes of that court that document be served in accordance with laws in U.S., practise in Greece is for service to be effected by delivery of document to person to be served therewith and for person effecting service to sign an affidavit before U.S. Consulate. If document to be served cannot be adequately described in affidavit, it must be annexed to same. It is therefore advisable to send to person who will undertake service at least two copies of document to be served.

REAL PROPERTY:

In certain provinces including a number of islands, real property cannot be transferred without permission of authorities.

See also topics Aliens; Deeds.

RECORDS:

See topics Deeds; Partnership; Pledges; Sales; Trademarks.

See Topical Index in front part of this volume.

REPORTS:

See topic Law Reports, Codes, Etc.

SALES:

Sale contract is valid if parties are in agreement as to property sold and sale price. For sale of real property, vessels and motor vehicles a notarial act is required. A sale does not effect transmission of ownership of personal property sold unless latter has been delivered. In case of real property or other real rights ownership passes upon registration of respective contract with proper registry of real property.

Warranties.—Vendor warrants buyer against dispossession. Vendor is responsible if property sold has defects affecting its value or its use or if it does not possess warranted qualifications; but is not responsible for defects known to buyer at time of sale or for absence of warranted qualifications if such absence was known to the buyer.

In all cases where vendor is so responsible, buyer may claim return or reduction of price. Buyer may also claim damages for absence of warranted qualities or for defects which were known to vendor.

Conditional Sales.—A sale may be made on condition that the title remains vested in the vendor until the purchase price has been fully paid.

Sales by payment in instalments have been restricted by Law-Decree 3338 (1958).

Notices Required.—As a rule, notice of a sale is required only in the case of sale by forced auction.

Applicable Law.—See topic Contracts.

SEALS:

Seals are not used in private contracts. Only public authorities or officials, including notaries public have a seal. Use of seal by private person or corporation has no legal significance. Notarial instruments have most of effects of sealed instruments in U. S. A.

SEQUESTRATION:

Court may order property in dispute, or debtor's property which has been attached, placed in custody of third party or even in custody of one of parties as trustee.

SHIPPING:

Code of private shipping law became operative on Aug. 28, 1958, and has been embodied in Statute 3816 of 26/28 Feb. 1958. It consists of 297 articles and is too extensive to allow a summary in this digest.

The sale of a vessel is not valid unless effected in writing and registered in proper shipping registry.

The sale or hypothecation (the latter subject to certain exceptions) of the whole or of a portion of a Greek passenger ship of over 500 tons to an alien, without permission of the Greek Government is invalid.

The sale or hypothecation to an alien of cargo boats and tankers with the exception of Liberty ships is free, but permission of the Ministry of Mercantile Marine is required in respect of certain countries which do not include the United States of America, the members of the British Commonwealth, those of Western Europe and Latin America.

See also topics Companies; Taxation.

STATUTES:

The Civil Law in Greece was, until recently, the old Roman Law, as amended by the Byzantine Law, but many matters, such as divorce, wills, intestate succession, acknowledgment of illegitimate children, guardianship of minors, insane persons and prodigals, hypothecs, pledges, interest, etc., had been settled by special laws.

A new Civil Code came into force on Feb. 23, 1946. For a brief period in 1946 (Feb. 23 to May 10) another Civil Code was in force but was abrogated retroactively on May 10, 1946. Also, a new Penal Code and a new Code of Criminal Procedure have come in force as from Jan. 1, 1951.

There also is a Commercial Code, a Shipping Code, and a Code of Civil Procedure.

Where a statutory citation has two dates, first is date of signature, second is day of publication of enactment in Government Gazette.

See also topic Law Reports, Codes, Etc.

STAY OF EXECUTION: See topic Executions.

TAXATION:

Income Tax.—On principle all natural persons who are domiciled in Greece or are residing in this country for six months during each year and have taxable income of over 1 million drachmae p.a. are liable to income tax which includes supertax and ranges up to 50%.

There are certain supplementary impositions on income tax. Dividends from equity may be taxed separately at up to 47%.

Under Law 2065/92, there is presumption that possession of motor car, yacht, airplane and/or purchase of certain assets including real estate entails certain amount of income as specified by law. Law 2214/94 expanded system of presumptions to other cases also.

Income of wife is declared by husband but is taxed separately. Income of minor child is for taxation purposes added as rule to that of mother or father.

Greek Limited Companies.—After Law 2065/92 all profits of corporations operating in Greece (Greek and foreign companies operating in Greece through permanent establishment) shall be subject to taxation of rate of 35%. This tax covers also taxation obligation for dividends distributed to shareholders. Art. 23 of Law 2214/94 ruled that in case company enters Athens Stock Exchange, this company is subject to taxation of rate of 40%.

Foreign Enterprises.—Foreign companies, partnerships of similar associations and organisations are subject to income tax at same rates as Greek limited companies on such part of their profits as is derived from Greece. If such foreign enterprise is nonprofit concern it is subject to 20% tax on any income derived from rents or dividends in Greece.

Special tax of 10% to 15% of income tax is levied in favour of Agricultural Insurance Organisation.

Profits derived from income from sale of tobacco leaves are subject to special provisions.

Inheritance tax is graded according to relationship of heir or beneficiary to deceased and according to taxable amount. Certain amount of estate is exempted from tax. After Law 2065/92 four grades of heirs are created and tax payable ranges from 5%-65%.

If estate is not declared to taxation authorities within period prescribed by law, fine of up to 25% of tax is imposed.

Other Taxes.—There are also other taxes including turnover tax, stamp duty, tax on donations and tax on transfer of real rights on land as well as capital gains tax on sale of real property. Under Law 2065/92 tax on land property is imposed with deductions for agricultural land and first residence. By Law 1477/1984 Greek indirect taxes are being brought into line with European Community tax law. Value Added Tax of 6%, 18% or 36% has been imposed as from Jan. 1, 1987 by Law 1676/1986. By Law 1921/1991 10% withholding tax has been imposed on interest on bank deposits.

Penal Provisions.—It is now criminal offence punishable with imprisonment not to make income tax return, to make false declaration of income, not to declare assets of estate, and not to pay certain taxes imposed. According to Art. 20 of Law 1914/1990 Minister of Finance may provide information concerning taxation matters to EEC member states. He may also request such information from such states.

Administrative Courts are competent to decide over disputes between revenue authorities and tax bearer on matters of taxation. (Law 1406/1983).

Treaties.—There are special provisions for avoidance of double taxation and there are also treaties with certain countries including U.S. and Great Britain on this matter. With U.S.A. there is (a) Convention for the Avoidance of Double Taxation and the Prevention of Fiscal Evasion with Respect to Taxes on Income signed Feb. 10, 1950 and ratified in Greece by Law Decree No. 2548 of the 16/27 Aug. 1953; (b) Convention for the Avoidance of Double Taxation and the Prevention of Fiscal Evasion with Respect to Taxes on the Estate of Deceased Persons, signed Feb. 20, 1953 and ratified in Greece by Law Decree No. 2734 of 31 Oct./12 Nov. 1953.

TRADEMARKS:

Trademarks are governed by Law 2239 of 16 Sept. 1994.

Acquisition of right on trademark presupposes application to administrative committee of trademarks, accompanied by ten impresses of trademark (and ten coloured impresses, if trademark is coloured), treasury voucher for government fees, notarial power of attorney and appointment of attorney in fact. Application must also determine categories of products (from total of 34) or of services (from total of eight), by which trademark is categorized.

Right on trademark is acquired from moment that decision of administrative committee of trademarks which accepts it is registered to special registrar, provided that trademark in question disposes distinctive character and does not constitute counterfeit or imitation of duly preregistered and not deleted trademark, which is used for same or similar product.

Beneficiary is entitled to use exclusively trademark in order to distinguish his products or services, and to exclude third parties from its use. Protection of trademark lasts for period of ten years and can be renewed indefinitely by filing, during last year of protection, petition for renewal and upon payment of government fees.

Unlawful use of trademark is punished by at least three years of imprisonment and/or fine.

Courts may grant injunction measures prohibiting unlawful use of trademark.

Right on trademark is transferable by succession, by contract or in case of forced execution, even without transfer of business itself. Beneficiary can also give to third party his written consent, so that another trademark which is identical or similar to preregistered trademark can be registered. Use of trademark can be assigned to third party by written agreement which is registered to special registrar after decision of administrative committee, unless that creates confusion or is opposed to morality and public order.

Right on trademark expires if beneficiary resigns from it or after deletion which is decided by administrative authority in case (inter alios) that beneficiary fails to market products or services within five years from its registration, or has ceased for five years to do so, or if beneficiary's business has ceased to operate for five years.

Right expires automatically if it is not renewed within prescribed time.

Beneficiary of right on trademark can be also cooperative or professional association (collective trademark). This trademark is used by members of association, but its protection can be invoked only by association or cooperative.

Foreign Trademarks.—For registration of a foreign trademark in addition to requirements prescribed for registration of a local one, it is necessary to produce a proper power of attorney and a certificate showing that the foreign trademark has been duly registered in the country of origin accompanied by a Greek translation. Such certificate is not required if country of origin relieves applicants for registration of a Greek trademark from such certificate. A foreign trademark duly registered in Greece becomes independent from the trademark of the country of origin.

Change of seat or address must be duly registered.

International Convention.—Greece has adhered to International Convention of Paris-Brussels-Washington-Hague-London of 1934 for Protection of Industrial Property as am'd in Stockholm on July 14, 1967. (Law 213/1975).

Priority.—When priority is claimed under the International Convention, the certificate of foreign registration must be submitted within six months of such registration.

TREATIES:

See topics Bills and Notes; Copyright; Foreign Judgments; Husband and Wife; Patents; Taxation; Trademarks.

TREATIES . . . *continued*

Pursuant to art. 28.1 of Greek Constitution "The generally acknowledged rules of international law as well as International Conventions, as of the time they are sanctioned by law and become operative according to the conditions therein shall be an integral part of domestic Greek law and shall prevail over any contrary provision of the law".

Since Jan. 1, 1981, Greece became tenth member of European Economic Community by virtue of Treaty of Athens of 28 May 1979. Treaty was ratified by Law 945 of 7/27 July 1979. Treaty provides for transitional period for Greece in certain matters. With Law 2077/92 European Convention of Maastricht has been also ratified.

Greece has adhered and ratified by Law 844 of Dec. 21, 1978 European Convention for Abolishing the Legalization of Documents executed by Diplomatic and Consular Agents, signed in London on June 7, 1968.

See also Selected International Conventions section.

TRUSTS:

Trusts, exploitation, meaning of American law, are unknown in Greece.

There is only one Greek law referring to Trust: LD 118/73 "on Inheritance Taxation, Donation Taxation, etc. which in art. 175 provides that on assets situated abroad, however acquired and taxed in Greece as long as by last will and testament of the deceased same have been placed under the management of a 'Trust' of the Anglosaxon law, the beneficiaries of the sums received from time to time are taxed for such sums, unless they are relieved under another law provision, and the parties to which the estate will finally devolve are taxed for the full ownership acquired by them at the time of such acquisition".

WILLS:

Persons mentally incapacitated and minors cannot make will.

Testamentary Disposition.—No limitations except those provided in favour of forced heirs. (See subhead Forced Heirs, infra.)

Form and Execution.—There are three principal forms of wills.

Holographic will must be written entirely by hand of deceased and signed by latter, no attestation being required.

Notarial will must be drawn by a notary public and signed by the testator in the presence of the same notary and three witnesses or one witness and another notary public.

Secret will as a rule must be signed by the testator but may be written by any other person or typed or printed and must be delivered by the testator to a notary public in a sealed envelope, such delivery being duly attested by the notary public in a special document which is signed by the testator, the notary public and the witnesses.

Special rules apply to military wills, to wills drawn on a Greek ship in the course of her journey or in a foreign port and to wills drawn during an epidemic or other extraordinary circumstances.

Probate.—There is no probate in American sense, but a will is published by court.

Witnesses.—A spouse, ascendants or descendants and collateral relations up to the third degree of the testator or a person taking a benefit under a will cannot act as a witness to such will when attesting is required.

Revocation.—A will is revoked by a special act of revocation which is drawn by a notary public in the presence of three witnesses. A holographic will may be also revoked if it is destroyed by the testator in person with the intention of revoking it. A secret will may be also revoked if the testator withdraws such will from the notary with whom it was deposited. Marriage does not affect a will made before marriage or in contemplation of marriage, except in so far as regards rights of spouse as a "forced heir." (See subhead Forced Heirs, infra.)

Revival.—The revocation of a will whereby a previous will has been revoked effects the revival of such previous will.

Legacies.—Unless testator has provided otherwise a legacy is, as a rule, payable upon death of testator.

Lapse.—Legacy lapses if legatee predeceases testator.

Forced Heirs.—Certain heirs of testator are entitled to receive a portion of estate even against his will. These heirs are called "forced heirs" and their portion "statutory share." Statutory share is equal to one-half of share which such heirs would have received if testator had died intestate. Such forced heirs are: descendants of testator (including adopted children and such of latter's descendants as were born after adoption, legitimized children and their descendants and certain classes of illegitimate children), and parents and spouse of testator, if such parties would have inherited from deceased if he had died intestate.

The forced heirs succeed to the testator in the same way as the heirs appointed in the will.

Forced heirs may be excluded from the testator's estate if they are properly disinherited by the testator on special grounds prescribed by the law. Under art. 21 of Law 1738/1987, restrictions concerning forced heirs do not apply to Greeks resident abroad for 25 years.

See Topical Index in front part of this volume.

GUATEMALA LAW DIGEST REVISER

Curtis, Mallet-Prevost, Colt & Mosle
101 Park Avenue
New York, New York 10178-0061
Telephone: 212-696-6141
Fax: 212-697-1559
Email: CMP-NY@mcimail.com

Reviser Profile

The Firm began in 1830 when two practicing lawyers started a long line of lawyers and law firms extending in an unbroken chain up to the present time. In 1897, the firm name became Curtis, Mallet-Prevost & Colt; in 1925 it was changed to Curtis, Mallet-Prevost, Colt & Mosle. The Firm is now made up of approximately 120 lawyers, including experts who have published extensively on such diverse subjects as international money management, transnational contracts, state contracts, litigation against foreign states, sovereign immunity and the act of state doctrine, and the International Court of Justice. Its principal offices are in New York City. There are branch offices in Paris, London, Frankfurt Am Main, Hong Kong, Washington, D.C., Houston, Texas, Newark, N.J., and Mexico City. The Firm has five departments: Corporate and International; Litigation; Real Estate; Tax; and Trusts and Estates. The corporate and international department acts as general counsel to various public and private corporations and individual entrepreneurs. Clients are in the banking, insurance, securities, manufacturing, real estate and oil and gas industries. In addition, the corporate and international department frequently acts as special counsel to domestic and foreign clients, providing assistance in financing, know-how licensing, the negotiation and drafting of all types of contracts and instruments, counselling on all aspects of corporate law, and establishing the vehicles necessary to enable clients to conduct their domestic and foreign business activities. The Firm's international work permeates all areas of its practice and involves questions of private international law, foreign law and an unusual amount of public and quasi-public international law. Traditionally, much of the Firm's international practice has been concerned with Latin America. The Firm maintains its excellence in that area, with its Mexican affiliate, and also through the expertise of Latin American lawyers based in the New York office. The Firm's international practice has undergone a major expansion beyond Latin America to Europe, Africa and the Near and Far East. The Firm's litigation practice includes commercial litigation and arbitration, and white-collar criminal defense. It has substantial experience in civil aviation matters; it also has represented foreign States in transnational litigation and international arbitration arising out of acts of nationalization and alleged breach of economic development or natural resource supply contracts. Among the Firm's clients in real estate matters are institutional lenders and investors, real estate developers, both individual and corporate, foreign and domestic investors and syndicators. The tax department has substantial experience in all aspects of domestic and international business tax matters and real estate taxation. The matters the tax department deals with on a regular basis include: Taxation of foreign investments; the structuring of corporate transactions, including mergers, acquisitions, liquidations and reorganization; federal and state tax litigation; and tax planning for U.S. and foreign individuals. The trusts and estates department engages in general domestic trusts and estates practice and in tax planning for foreign persons wishing to invest in U.S. assets through offshore trusts and corporations. It represents individuals, trust companies, and banks acting as fiduciaries. It works for various charitable organizations located both in the United States and abroad including private foundations, museums, universities and hospitals. A group of fiduciary accountants with vast experience in the field assists the lawyers of the trusts and estates department. Curtis, Mallet-Prevost, Colt & Mosle has served as a Reviser for most of Latin American Law Digests since 1930.

GUATEMALA LAW DIGEST

(The following is a list of all Topics, including cross-references, covered in this Digest.)

GUATEMALA LAW DIGEST

Revised for 1997 edition by

CURTIS, MALLET-PREVOST, COLT & MOSLE, of the New York Bar.

(Abbreviations used are: C. C.—Civil Code; C. Com.—Code of Commerce; C. C. P.—Code of Civil Procedure; J. L.—Judiciary Law; D.—Decree; L. D.—Legislative Decree. Numbers in code references indicate articles.)

ABSENTEES: See topic Death.

ACKNOWLEDGMENTS:

Acknowledgment may be made before a notary, whose certificate must also be signed by the signer and witnesses of the instrument acknowledged, and who must make a note of the matter in his record. (L. D. 314 of 1946). Usually documents requiring notarial authentication are executed as public instruments before notaries, who retain the original in their records and issue certified copies. See topics Notaries Public; Public Instruments.

Documents executed abroad for use in Guatemala will be accepted if they are executed either in accordance with the laws of the place where executed or in accordance with Guatemalan laws. Authentications must be obtained from a Guatemalan consular or diplomatic officer. (J. L. Decree 2 of Jan. 2, 1989 as am'd; C. C. P. 190).

ACTIONS:

See topic Death, subhead Actions for Death.

Limitation of.—See topic Prescription, subhead Actions.

ADMINISTRATION:

See topic Executors and Administrators.

ADVERSE POSSESSION:

See topic Prescription.

AGENCY: See topic Principal and Agent.

ALIENS:

In general, aliens enjoy same civil rights as citizens. They may engage in industry and commerce and own real property and are not obliged to become citizens or to pay special taxes. Constitution of 1985, arts. 122 and 123 reserves right to establish limitations to foreign ownership of land in zone of 15 kilometers along borders and three kilometers along seashores, but Art. 635 of Civil Code establishes limitations in 15 kilometer zone along both, borders and seashores.

Nonresident aliens may be summoned before a Guatemalan court in case of: (a) Actions in rem relating to property in Guatemala, (b) illegal acts committed by alien in Guatemala, (c) obligations contracted abroad stipulating that Guatemalan courts shall have jurisdiction. (J.L. XXV).

Foreigners with tourist cards may remain in country for a period of six months, extendable for an equal period. (D. 861, Dec. 12, 1951). Immigrants require specific approval of Ministry of Foreign Relations.

In every business and industry 90% of employees must be Guatemalans. Foreigners need special permit to work within country. (Labor Code art. 13, Resolutions of Mar. 27, 1961, Dec. 24, 1965 and Apr. 8, 1967).

See also topics Corporations, subhead Foreign Corporations; Mines and Minerals; Immigration.

ALIMONY: See topic Divorce.

ASSIGNMENTS:

Choses in action are assignable except when otherwise agreed or when nature of the right does not permit it. If referred to real property or other rights requiring recording in Registry of Property assignment must be made in a public document. When a credit is assigned for a smaller amount debtor may be discharged by paying assignee said smaller amount plus expenses. Assignments do not bind obligor unless judicial or notarial notice or other agreed notice is given to him or when he signifies knowledge. Debtor may oppose to assignee personal defenses he had against assignor before assignment. Assignor warrants existence and validity of the credit at time of the assignment and not solvency of the debtor except if so agreed. In case of document transferable by mere endorsement or delivery these rules do not apply. Assignment of commercial credits respecting assigned enterprise is valid against third persons, although debtor is not notified or has not accepted such assignment, provided assignment is recorded in Commercial Registry. However, bona fide debtor shall be released if he pays debts to assignor. (C. C. 1443-1452; C. Com. 659).

ASSIGNMENTS FOR BENEFIT OF CREDITORS:

An assignment for benefit of creditors is voluntary abandonment by debtor of all his assets, when in consequence of inevitable accident he cannot pay his creditors. Assignment may be judicial or extrajudicial and it does not transfer title to the property but only right to dispose thereof. When a judicial assignment has been approved, debtor is deprived of administration of his property and if he is an individual, debts are discharged by the payments made even if not covering whole amount, but if debtor is a company, liability of its members continues according to the contract or type of corporate organization. (C.C. 1416-1422; C.C.P. 347-370). See also topic Bankruptcy and Insolvency.

ATTACHMENT:

Notice of a suit affecting real property may be recorded as a lien in the registry of property, but the plaintiff may be required to give bond to secure payment of damages should he fail in his action. Attachments may also be requested when there is danger that the property in dispute may be lost or damaged or that the debtor may hide or dispose of his assets; in such cases a bond must be given as determined by the judge. The following authorize a summary action of execution and an attachment without bond: (1) Final judgments; (2) arbitrator's decision not subject to appeal; (3) mortgage credits; (4) mortgage bonds or certificates; (5) pledge credits; (6) formal compromise; (7) agreement arrived at during suit. (C.C.P. 294-326, 523-537; C.C. 1149-1166).

See also topic Liens.

BANKRUPTCY AND INSOLVENCY:

(C.C.P. 347-400; C.C. 1416-1422).

Provisions of Civil Procedure and Civil Codes govern insolvency and bankruptcy, both of merchants and non-merchants. Traditionally, substantive matters related to bankruptcy have been dealt with in Commerce Code and provisions on insolvency have been left to Civil Code and Civil Procedure Code.

Code of Commerce has omitted chapter on bankruptcy and therefore this matter must be governed by general provisions of law.

Insolvency.—Voluntary submission to creditors takes place when an offer is submitted to them by natural or artificial persons, whether merchants or not, who have suspended payments or are about to do so, or who have been declared in bankruptcy, if the same is not fraudulent or culpable. Such offer may comprise: (1) assignment of property; (2) administration of property; (3) extensions and discounts. It may be extrajudicial, in which case the offer requires acceptance by all creditors and must be done in a public instrument. It may also be proposed in court, in which case judge appoints an examining committee consisting of two creditors and a third person, as well as a depositary to intervene in the debtor's administration. If the committee reports falsehood or fraud the debtor is declared in bankruptcy. Otherwise, a meeting of creditors is called; notice for foreign creditors being served on their representative or consul. At the meeting decisions may be taken by a majority of votes representing three-fifths of the credits, but larger majorities are required if the proposed discount exceeds 50%. Secured creditors need not participate; if they do, they must abide by the decision but do not lose their security. If the debtor's offer is not accepted he is declared insolvent or bankrupt.

Forced submission to creditors or insolvency occurs: (1) When the debtor's offer is rejected by the creditors or disapproved by court; (2) when three or more executions are issued against the debtor and not enough property is found to satisfy them. The judge appoints an investigating committee as in the case of voluntary submission, also a depositary to take over the insolvent estate, and calls a meeting of creditors. All debts of the debtor mature and interest ceases thereon. If no agreement is reached between the debtor and creditors the judge declares the debtor bankrupt and orders his arrest unless the examining committee reports that the insolvency was not culpable.

See also topic Fraudulent Sales and Conveyances.

BILLS AND NOTES:

(C. Com. 441-489).

Bills of exchange must state: (1) Words "bill of exchange" in text of instrument; (2) date and place of issue; (3) rights created by document; (4) place and date of execution or exercise of said rights; (5) signature of drawer. In successive documents signatures can be stamped by any controlled system provided at least one signature is hand written. (Art. 386). It must also state: (1) Unconditional order to pay a determined amount of money; (2) name of drawee; (3) type of maturity.

If no maturity date is expressed, bill is payable at sight (Art. 443); if place of issue is not stated, it is deemed to be domicile of drawer; if place of payment is not stated, it is also deemed to be domicile of drawer. If drawer has several domiciles, or if bill mentions several places of execution, holder of bill may choose among them one most convenient to his interests. (Art. 386).

Bills may be to order of drawer and may be drawn against drawer or for account of a third person and may be payable at domicile of third person. Drawer guarantees acceptance and payment. Bills payable at sight or at days after sight may bear interest; in such case if rate is not expressed, it is 6%. Bills may be drawn payable: (a) On a certain date; (b) a certain period after date; (c) at sight; (d) specified days after sight. They are payable on their maturity date. There are no days of grace.

Endorsements may be in blank, by simple signing of endorser; if blank, holder may transfer document without endorsement. Endorsements are allowed for collection or as pledge. Endorsement after maturity is valid, but if after protest or time for protest, it has effect of a mere assignment of rights.

Bills may be presented for acceptance at any time before maturity. If drawn at days after sight, they must be presented for acceptance within one year, but drawer may vary this period and endorser may shorten time designated. Acceptance may be limited to part of amount. If acceptance be refused, holder must make protest and give notice within two labor days to his assignor or other person obliged to pay. If bill is protested for nonpayment, he must give notice within two labor days to his assignor. If drawer or endorser has waived protest, bill must nevertheless be presented and notice of failure to honor it must be given. Protest for failure to accept exempts from requirement of presentation for payment and protest for nonpayment.

Protests are made before Notary Public; however, if payment is made before end of following day, protest is cancelled.

Protest must include: (1) Literal reproduction of bill and endorsements; (2) demand made on drawer to accept or to pay bill with indication as to whether drawee was present or not; (3) drawee's reasons for denying acceptance or payment; (4) signature of person on whom protest is made, or statement that he could not or would not sign;

BILLS AND NOTES . . . *continued*
(5) place, date, hour and signature of authorizing officer and (6) notary public must record officially (protocolizar) such protest.

If bill is presented to a bank, bank's statement regarding denial of acceptance or payment shall have same valid effect as a protest before a notary public.

However, protest shall be necessary only when drawer of bill inserts on bill's reverse side the clause: "with protest." If such clause is written by a person other than drawer, it shall be considered invalid. If, notwithstanding fact that protest is not necessary any more, holder of bill protests it, expenses and fees shall be paid by him.

Promissory notes (C. Com. 490-493) are governed in general by rules relating to bills of exchange. Conventional interests can be stipulated on note. Payment can also be made through successive amortizations. Maker is obligated in same manner as acceptor of a bill of exchange.

Checks must show: (1) Word "check" in text; (2) unconditional order to pay a specified sum; (3) name of drawer; (4) place of payment; (5) date and place where drawn; (6) signature of drawer. If place of payment is not specified it is deemed to be place of domicile of maker. Checks may be drawn payable to a specified person or to order or to bearer. All checks except those to bearer may be transferred by endorsement but endorsements to bearer are not permitted. Checks must be presented for payment within 15 days. Presentation and nonpayment may be proved by: (1) Protest; (2) statement of drawee written on check showing date of presentation; (3) statement of bank.

There are special provisions regarding "crossed checks," "checks to be credited on account of holder," "certified checks," "guaranty checks," "cashier's checks," "traveler's checks," "checks with receipt stub," and "checks stating consideration therein." Checks are also governed in general by rules relating to bills of exchange. (C. Com. 494-543).

CHATTEL MORTGAGES:

(C.C. 904-916).

There is no provision for chattel mortgages in general, but mortgages may be constituted on many kinds of personal property in the form of agrarian, cattle and industrial pledges, the pledged property remaining in possession of debtor. Following may be so pledged: (1) Machinery, tools and instruments used in agriculture or in any kind of industry; (2) movables used in operation of an industrial establishment or a farm; (3) animals of any kind and their fruits and products; (4) fruits, whether pending, cut or future; (5) any kind of raw material and products of factories or industries, whether finished or unfinished; (6) products of mines and quarries; (7) products of plants and plants that can only be utilized when cut. Only pending crop can be pledged but if it does not cover the entire credit balance will be paid from following crop and the credit fully discharged thereby even if said crop is insufficient. In case of cattle or industrial pledges any balance will be paid from proceeds of the two following years, and it will be fully discharged even if proceeds of the third year prove insufficient.

Vehicles and other identifiable objects may be pledged without delivery in guarantee of a commercial transaction. Pledge contract must appear in a public instrument (see topic Public Instruments) and be recorded in real property registry.

COLLATERAL SECURITY: See topic Pledges.

COMMERCIAL REGISTER: See topic Records.

COMMUNITY PROPERTY:

See topic Husband and Wife.

CONSTITUTION AND GOVERNMENT:

Constitution promulgated on May 31, 1985 as am'd. Legislative power is vested in Congress having single chamber. Congressmen are elected for four years and can be reelected. President of Republic is elected for four years and cannot be reelected.

For administrative purposes, national territory is divided into departments, and these into municipalities. Departments are administered by Governor. Municipalities are autonomous and exercise their powers by Mayor.

CONTRACTS:

Articles 1517 through 1604 of Civil Code govern civil contracts and are supplementarily applied to commercial contracts.

Civil contracts involving more than 300 quetzales must be in written form. All contracts, which must be registered or recorded in public registries, have to be executed in public deeds whatever their amount may be.

Contracts among merchants and contracts involving commercial matters are governed by articles 669 through 1039 of commercial code. It may be generally said that commercial contracts are much less formally executed than civil contracts. Clauses concerning arbitration are valid even when contracts are not executed in public instruments.

Public Contracts.—(L.D. 57-92 of Oct. 21, 1992 and Accord 1056-92 of Dec. 22, 1992). Contracts executed with government, state agencies and state enterprises are subject to special rules.

COPYRIGHT:

(Const. art. 42; Decree 1037 of Feb. 11, 1954).

Copyright is granted on literary, scientific and artistic works, published or not. The right comes into existence by the mere creation of the work without need of deposit, registry or other formality, but the work may not be utilized publicly or for profit without authorization of the Guatemalan Association of Authors and Composers and payment of fees to this Association. The right terminates 50 years after the death of the author, or 50 years after publication if the author is a juridical entity. The law applies only to nationals and domiciled aliens; the protection of other aliens is governed by the international treaties and conventions ratified by Guatemala. Guatemala has approved the Inter-American Copyright Convention of June, 1946 (Decree 844 of Nov. 7, 1951), and has also ratified Universal Copyright Convention, on July 28, 1964. See also topic Treaties.

C. Com. 824-851 regulates steps prior to publishing literary, scientific and artistic works. Publishing contract is one entered into by owner of work and publisher who assumes obligation to print it and to distribute it.

If contract fails to stipulate number of editions to be published, it shall be understood only one edition will be printed and if number of issues is omitted, it shall be considered that number cannot be less than 500, nor more than 1,000. Editor has right to stipulate sale price; however, it cannot be so high that it might limit circulation of work. Unless otherwise agreed, it shall be understood that author shall receive 25% of sale price to public. Author shall reserve right to correct or make any change in his work if he deems it necessary up to moment work is sent to printer. After that author still can correct his work, provided he does not damage interests and/or increase editor's responsibilities. Edition shall be considered sold out when less than 20% of original edition remains unsold.

CORPORATIONS:

(C. C. 15-31-C. Com. 10-58; 86-194).

Foundations, associations and charitable institutions (churches, schools, hospitals, etc.) are governed by principles of civil law found in above-mentioned articles of Civil Code.

Commercial Code applies to corporations and to any type of company seeking to realize profits. Such corporations must be registered in Commercial Registry in order to be an entity different from partners and/or shareholders.

Commercial companies must be governed by their respective charters provided agreement is not in conflict with Commercial Code. Partners and/or shareholders are not allowed to enter into secret agreements or reserve rights not expressly mentioned in charter or by-laws; if so, said secret agreements shall be void.

Articles of incorporation and all amendments of any kind thereto must appear in a public instrument which must be duly recorded in Commercial Registry within a month after said instrument's authorization. Recording act must state: (1) Type of company; (2) name or commercial name, if any; (3) domicile and also domicile of its branches; (4) object; (5) duration; (6) capital; (7) name of notary public that authorizes public instrument of incorporation, place and date; (8) administrative councils, powers of administrators and (9) officers' councils if any. (Art. 337).

Corporation ("Sociedad Anónima," abbreviated "S.A.") is a company that has capital divided into and represented by shares. Responsibility of each shareholder is limited to payment of subscribed shares. Authorized capital is maximum amount that corporation can issue in shares, which can be totally or partially subscribed at moment of incorporation and must be expressed in charter of same.

Initial paid-in capital must be at least Q. 5,000. Term begins to run from date of incorporation of company when recorded in Commercial Registry. Commercial companies can be formed for indefinite periods of time. (Art. 24).

Shares (C. Com. 99-131), either registered or to bearer, must be par value shares. All shareholders must have right to vote in proportion to capital represented by their shares, except when articles of incorporation create a special class of shares with limited vote, in which case such shares must have preference upon liquidation and a minimum 6% dividend. Until shares are fully paid up, temporary certificates are issued stating amount paid on account.

All shares must contain following information: (1) Name, domicile and duration of corporation; (2) date of incorporation act, place of execution, name of notary public that authorized it and date of recording in Commercial Registry; (3) name of owner of share, if nominative; (4) amount of authorized capital and way such capital shall be distributed; (5) nominal value; its type and registration number; (6) specific rights and duties inherent in type of shares and also a statement of rights and duties pertaining to other type of shares, if so provided; and (7) signature of administrators that according to by-laws must sign them.

Shareholders' meetings (C. Com. 132-161) must be held at least once every year. Calls are published in official newspaper, called "Diario de Centro América", and in another paper. Dividends may be declared only by shareholders and only from net earnings as shown by accounts and none can be declared until annual reserve payments required by by-laws have been covered.

Management.—(C. Com. 162-183). Directors need not be stockholders. Their powers and liability are governed by provisions of corporate documents, law and general rules of agency. They must render accounts to shareholders.

Limited liability companies (C. Com. 78-85) of not over 20 members may be formed, in which liability of each member is limited to capital contributed by him or such additional amount as may be stipulated. Name of company must be similar to that of a partnership, adding word "Limitada," which can be abbreviated "Ltda." or "Cía. Ltda.," without which company is regarded as a general partnership. Capital must be fully paid before company may be organized, and foreign limited liability companies may not act in Guatemala without proof of such payment. These companies are in general governed by rules relating to partnerships. See topic Partnership.

Foreign corporations (C. Com. 213-221) that have been constituted abroad and that have their seat of administration or principal object of enterprise in territory of Guatemala shall be governed, including validity of requirements of incorporation act, by Guatemala Commercial Code. Form of incorporation act shall be governed by laws of country of origin.

Corporations legally incorporated abroad that wish to establish or operate in any way in Guatemala or wish to have one or more branches must comply with provisions of Commercial Code and must have at least one agent permanently in country. Requirements to operate in Guatemala: (1) Foreign corporations must prove that they have been constituted in accordance with laws of country of incorporation; (2) certified copy of their articles of incorporation and by-laws, if any, as well as any amendments thereto; (3) proof that corporation has passed a resolution through its competent body for this purpose; (4) appoint in Guatemala a representative agent with broad powers to do all kinds of business and to legally represent corporation before courts. If these powers and duties are not granted, he nevertheless will be able to perform them by operation of law; (5) set aside capital assigned for its operations in Guatemala with

CORPORATIONS . . . *continued*

a clause that corporation will respond for its obligations with its property both in Guatemala and abroad; (6) declaration that corporation will be subject to laws of Guatemala for all acts and transactions executed in country and also a declaration that its representatives or employees shall not invoke foreign laws; (7) declaration that before leaving Guatemala, it shall also comply with legal requirements; and (8) certified copy of latest general annual balance together with a statement of profits and losses.

Insurance corporations must be Guatemalan. No foreign corporations or branches may operate in country. Certain risks must be insured in Guatemala, but if local companies cannot cover risk, Superintendency may permit taking insurance abroad. (Decree-Law 473 of May 4, 1966).

COURTS:

Justice is administered by: (1) A supreme court of justice which hears appeals on questions of law, and also on questions of fact in cases where the court of appeals acted as a court of original jurisdiction; (2) a court of appeals with chambers in different parts of the country, which hears appeals from the courts of first instance and has original jurisdiction in proceedings against certain officials; (3) a contentious-administrative court which decides appeals from administrative officials and questions relating to Government contracts; its decisions may be appealed to the supreme court; (4) judges of first instances who have civil and criminal jurisdiction in all except minor matters and hear appeals from the minor judges; (5) minor judges, comprising justices of peace. Higher courts also have certain administrative functions with respect to judicial matters. (Const. arts. 203-222; J. L. Decree 2-89 of Jan. 10, 1989 as am'd).

See also topic Infancy.

CURRENCY:

(Const. art. 132; Decree 203 of Nov. 29, 1945 as am'd and Law 215 of Dec. 20, 1945 and Decree 16 of Mar. 7, 1973).

The monetary unit is the quetzal, divided into one hundred cents. Only the Banco de Guatemala may issue bank notes and coin money which are legal tender for all obligations payable in the country. Any contractual clause in foreign currency is void, except payments to be made abroad from Guatemala and viceversa, securities issued by the government or by the Banco de Guatemala in foreign money and deposits in foreign currency with banks pursuant to Regulations. (See topic Exchange Control.)

CUSTOMS:

Customs are regulated by Central American Customs Code of Dec. 28, 1984 and D.L. 146 and 147 of Dec. 12, 1985. Decree 22-73 of Apr. 5, 1973 created free trade and industry zone named Santo Tomás de Castilla.

DEATH:

If a person's whereabouts be unknown, a guardian may be appointed for his property. Administration may be granted to the absentee's relatives. Three years after administration has been granted to relatives, or five years after date of disappearance, absentee may be declared presumptively dead and his heirs may obtain definitive possession of his estate. This declaration may also be issued after one year of disappearance of a person in case of war or ship wreck or aircraft accident or immediately if he disappeared on occasion of explosion, fire, earthquake, flood, etc. (C. C. 42-77).

Guatemala has adhered to Convention on Declaration of Death of Missing Persons sponsored by United Nations.

Death certificates may be obtained from official in charge of Civil Registry of district where death occurred; a nominal fee is charged.

Actions for Death.—Within provisions of Civil Code on torts, art. 1655 provides that in case of personal injuries victim is entitled to expenses for health recovery and damages resulting from total or partial disability to work estimated in view of duties of victim to support his family and circumstances of victim and capacity of payment of defendant and that in case of death victim's heirs or persons having right to be supported by decedent, may claim indemnity under above rules. Such actions are limited to one year. (art. 1673).

DECEDENTS' ESTATES:

See topics Descent and Distribution; Executors and Administrators; Wills.

DEEDS:

(Notarial Code arts. 29-76, L.D. 37-92 of June 22, 1992 regulated by Accord 737-92 of Aug. 27, 1992).

Conveyances of real estate to be recorded must be by public instrument and contain a true statement of the consideration, since the state tax on transfer of title is based on the real consideration. Deeds must bear stamps depending on the amount involved and they must be recorded in the registry of property. Both grantor and grantee must sign the deed and must therefore be present before the notary at the same time in person or by attorney-in-fact. An original deed executed in Guatemala remains in the files of the notary, who gives to either party a certified copy which has the effect of an original in the courts of law. See also topics Notaries Public; Public Instruments.

DESCENT AND DISTRIBUTION:

(C.C. 917-1123).

In absence of testamentary disposition decedent's estate passes, without prejudice to rights of support which other relatives may have, to the following in order named: (1) Legitimate, illegitimate and adopted children and spouse, not having community property rights or having such rights representing less than intestate share, for the deficiency; (2) nearest ascendants and spouse; (3) brothers and sisters, legitimate or illegitimate; (4) collaterals to fourth degree, nearer relatives excluding those more remote; (5) State and Guatemalan universities in equal parts.

Certain persons are excluded from testate or intestate succession, as for example a person who committed or attempted to commit homicide as against the decedent or his spouse, ascendants or descendants, or who by fraud or violence induced the decedent to make a will or prevented him from making one.

Inheritances may be expressly refused or expressly or tacitly accepted. If accepted, heir becomes owner of estate as of time of decedent's death. He is liable for debts and other charges only up to amount of estate.

DIVORCE:

(Const. art. 55, C.C. 153-172, C.C.P. 426-434).

Divorce dissolving marriage bond may be granted at request of innocent party filed within six months of knowledge of the facts, on grounds of: (1) Infidelity; (2) cruelty or grave insults; (3) attempt of one spouse against life of other or of the children; (4) abandonment or unjustified absence for over one year; (5) wife giving birth to a child conceived before marriage and of which husband had no knowledge; (6) incitation of spouse to prostitution or of children to corruption; (7) refusal to perform legal duty to support and assist spouse and children; (8) dissipation of family resources; (9) habits of gambling, intoxication or use of narcotics, when they jeopardize family or cause domestic discord; (10) slanderous accusation or report of a crime by other spouse; (11) sentence to over five years imprisonment for crime; (12) incurable disease prejudicial to spouse or descendants; (13) impotence, permanent and incurable; (14) incurable mental illness; (15) separation judicially declared.

The court determines the alimony to be paid by the guilty party to the innocent party. The wife is entitled to alimony while she observes good conduct and does not remarry; the husband only if he is incapacitated for work and does not remarry. During the divorce action sons over ten years remain in custody of father, other children in custody of mother, unless court decides otherwise.

On a judgment of divorce there is a liquidation of the community property. The spouses may make agreements as to the property and the custody of the children, but cannot abridge the rights of the children to support and education.

A divorce by mutual consent cannot be requested before a year has elapsed from the marriage. With the petition for such divorce the spouses must file an agreement as to alimony and the custody and support of the children. The court calls a hearing at which the parties must be personally present if in Guatemala.

Separation may be granted for any cause which is a ground for divorce. A separation which has lasted for six months may be converted into divorce on petition of either party, a hearing being granted to the other.

Annulment of marriage, see topic Marriage.

DOWER:

No dower right. See topics Descent and Distribution; Husband and Wife.

ENVIRONMENT:

(Decree 68-86 of Dec. 5, 1986 as am'd).

Law establishes general rules for conservation, protection and improvement of environment to benefit quality of life. Within environmental protection are air, water, hazardous waste and noise pollution. Environmental impact statements are mandatory for any activity that may damage environment. Entry of hazardous waste into country, whether actually or potentially dangerous, and of radioactive waste is prohibited. Administrative or criminal penalties are imposed for violation of law. Administrative sanctions include warnings, fines, temporary or permanent closure of facilities or immediate suspension of activity causing damage, depending on gravity of offense and prior violations. Criminal sanctions include fines and imprisonment as established by Criminal Code. Environmental National Commission is responsible for enforcing law.

EXCHANGE CONTROL:

Guatemalan currency law (Decree 203 of Nov. 29, 1945 as am'd) establishes that exchange control may be imposed as emergency measure when Government considers that economic situation of country is instable.

Exchange control is regulated per frequent resolutions issued by Junta Monetaria of Banco de Guatemala. There are two foreign exchange rates: reference rate used for valuing goods for customs purposes and banking rate for all transactions. Foreign exchange is negotiated freely in commercial banks and exchange houses.

EXECUTIONS:

Execution proceedings are held when petition therefor is based on a final judgment or arbitration award, mortgage or pledge credits, bond or certificate or coupons thereof, compromise settlement in public document or stipulation in court. An "executive summary action" lies when based on an "executive title" such as a public document or a private one acknowledged before a notary or in court, commercial documents such as bills and notes protested when necessary, or not protested if otherwise; entries on account books certified by a notary; insurance, savings and similar policies issued by authorized entities. In all cases the documents must show duty to pay an amount of money which is determined or determinable by simple arithmetical calculations and past due. In promises to deliver specific property court orders immediate delivery or sequestration if it fails or attachment of other assets to cover damages. In promises to do or perform an act court orders performance within a discretionary term and upon failure orders attachment of property for estimated damages or for payment to a third party chosen by plaintiff to perform for the other. If performance consists in granting a right by a writing judge acts as attorney-in-fact for defendant and executes document. If promise is to forebear court orders reestablishment of things to former state if possible, estimating damages if otherwise or for noncompliance and then ordering attachment and sale of assets to pay such damages or payment for compliance by a third person.

In cases of "execution proceedings" no term to file defenses or evidence is granted. In "executive action" five days are granted to file defenses and ten days to prove them. On decision, if against defendant, sale of assets and payment to plaintiff takes place. However, rights of the parties may be disputed again in ordinary action.

In both cases an appraisal is made of the attached property unless parties have agreed on a value; in case of real property amount of debt or of tax assessment may be taken as a basis. A public auction under court auspices is then advertised. Bidders

See Topical Index in front part of this volume.

EXECUTIONS . . . *continued*
must deposit 10% of their bids unless relieved from this obligation by plaintiff. Highest bid is accepted, but the property may be taken at same price by co-owners, mortgage creditors and plaintiff. No bid is received of less than 70% of appraised value of property; if no such bid is made, another auction is held at which lowest bid may be 60% of appraised value; if there is still no admissible bid, there is another auction at which lowest admissible bid is again reduced 10%; and successive auctions are thus held, rate being reduced each time by 10%. After judicial approval of the sale, there is no right of redemption. (C. C. P. 294-339).

EXECUTORS AND ADMINISTRATORS:

(C. C. 1041-1067; C. C. P. 503-511).

An executor or administrator must be over 18 years of age, capacitated to administer property, not incapacitated to acquire property by inheritance, and not holding the office of judge or prosecuting attorney, except for estates of relatives. He ceases in office one year after death of testator unless will provides otherwise. An administrator is appointed only if executor appointed by will cannot act and heirs request the appointment. If will appointed no executor, heirs are charged with carrying out testator's wishes.

The estate vests in the heirs immediately on death of the decedent, but the executor or administrator pays the debts and legacies and has the administration of the property until the heirs take it over. The executor or administrator represents estate in court except if otherwise provided by the will.

EXEMPTIONS:

(C.C.P. 306-307 and Law 1421 of Jan. 20, 1961).

Following property is exempt from attachment: (1) Municipal commons and property granted by government, if the concession prohibits attachment; (2) sums owed to public works contractors, except as to claims of workmen or suppliers of materials, but sums owed after conclusion of the work may be attached; (3) salaries, wages and fees in their entirety, except such percentages as authorized by special laws; (4) present and future amounts payable for support and maintenance; (5) necessary furniture and clothing of debtor and his family and provisions for one month; (6) books, tools and necessary instruments for debtor's profession, art or craft; (7) rights of use and usufruct and other strictly personal rights; (8) state pensions less than Q. 100 per month and pensions to invalids; (9) redemption and proceeds rights from life and accident insurance policies; (10) tombs; (11) property excepted by special laws.

FACTORS: See topic Principal and Agent.

FORECLOSURE: See topic Mortgages.

FOREIGN CORPORATIONS:

See topic Corporations.

FOREIGN EXCHANGE:

See topics Exchange Control; Currency.

FOREIGN INVESTMENTS:

See topics Exchange Control; Corporations.

FRAUDS, STATUTE OF:

See topics Contracts; Labor Relations; Public Instruments.

FRAUDULENT SALES AND CONVEYANCES:

(C. C. 1794, 1795, 1807).

Sale of goods that belong to another is void; seller must return price if he has collected it and must pay damages if he has acted in bad faith.

Representatives of minors, incapacitated persons, or absentees and bailees, administrators, interventors ("interventores"), or liquidators cannot sell goods under their care without complying, in each particular case, with formalities prescribed by law.

If same chattel has been sold to different persons, bona fide buyer in possession of same shall be deemed legitimate owner; if none of them is in possession of it, first sale in time shall be valid.

If thing sold is real property, sale first recorded in Registry shall be valid; if sale is not recorded, then first sale in time shall be valid.

HOLIDAYS:

Jan. 1 (New Year's); Maundy Thursday*; Good Friday*; Holy Saturday*; May 1 (Labor Day); June 30 (Army Day); Sept. 15 (Independence Day); Oct. 20 (Revolution Day); Nov. 1 (All Saints); Dec. 24 (Christmas Eve, half holiday); Dec. 25 (Christmas); Dec. 31 (New Year's Eve, half holiday).

*These are movable holidays.

HUSBAND AND WIFE:

(C. C. 108-143, 278-292).

The spouses owe each other support proportionate to their personal and financial circumstances. The wife has the right and duty to direct the work in the home and to care for her husband's interests in domestic affairs.

An agreement as to property matters is required before all marriages in which (a) either party owns property valued at 2,000 quetzales or owns or exercises a trade or profession producing over 200 quetzales a month, (b) either party administers property of a minor or person under guardianship or (c) the wife is Guatemalan and the husband a foreigner or naturalized citizen. The agreement must be recorded and is subject to modification at any time after marriage. It must state: (a) Assets and liabilities of each spouse, (b) whether they adopt system of marriage community property or that of separation of property and (c) rules under which their property is to be administered.

If no pre-nuptial agreement was made, each spouse may freely dispose of property held before marriage and property acquired with the proceeds therefrom or gratuitously, and the marriage community system applies to (1) the products of their separate property, (2) purchases made from such products, (3) the products of their labor and industry and (4) property remaining on dissolution of the marriage if it does not clearly appear to which spouse the same belonged. The husband is the administrator of such marriage community property and either party may at any time demand its termination. Each spouse can freely dispose of property registered under his name, but in case of disposition of community property, he has to account to other spouse for such disposition.

Under the system of separate property each spouse has ownership and administration of property belonging to him or her and exclusive ownership of products therefrom, as well as of salaries, wages or fees from personal services or exercise of commercial or industrial activities.

In any case furnishings of home belong to wife, except articles of husband's personal use. Community property is to be used for payment of purchases made by either spouse for use of family and, if insufficient, separate property of spouses must be used. Debts contracted prior to marriage are a charge only on the separate property of the spouse who made them; expenses of illness or funeral of either spouse are a charge on the community and on the separate property.

In marriages of aliens of the same nationality, in default of any agreement, the administration of their property is governed by their national law at the time of marriage; if they are of different nationalities, by the law of the first matrimonial domicile. A change of nationality of either or both spouses does not affect the administration of their property.

IMMIGRATION:

(D.L. 22-86 of Jan. 10, 1986 regulated by Accord 59-86 of Jan. 10, 1986; Dec. 421 of Sept. 30, 1965; Decree-Law 1266 of Dec. 18, 1958; Law 58 of July 30, 1973 as am'd regulated by Acuerdo of Feb. 15, 1974).

Foreigners are classified into: Transients, tourists, immigrants, residents, refugees and persons without country.

Applications to hire foreign employees or workmen shall be filed before Ministry of Labor enclosing following: (a) Documentary evidence of technical abilities of such workmen; (b) lack of criminal record (c) a certificate issued by a public accountant stating number of foreign and national workmen working for same employer. All documentary evidence still has to be filed in Spanish language and duly translated and legalized if issued abroad.

All permits shall be granted for one year and subject to further renewals. This applies to professionals and technicians.

INFANCY:

(Const. art. 50; C. C. arts. 8, 252-277, 293-351, 835, 1251, 1303, 1312, 1976, 2152, 2163).

The age of majority is 18. Ordinarily, contracts by minors are void, but nullity must be claimed within two years after entering into the contract. Minors are subject to parental authority of the father and mother. Parental authority includes custody, legal representation and administration of the real and personal property of the minor, with certain exceptions. In the absence of parents a guardian is appointed. Parents and guardians have restricted powers of disposition.

Legislative Decree 78-79 of Nov. 28, 1979 approves Code of Minors (Código de Menores) and creates National Council for Minors (Consejo Nacional de Menores) to protect and educate minors. Juvenile Courts (Tribunales de Menores) are also created to prevent antisocial behavior and to correct it with adequate treatment. Other provisions contemplate corresponding proceedings and final methods to resolve it.

INSOLVENCY:

See topic Bankruptcy and Insolvency.

INTEREST:

The legal rate of interest is 6% but other rates may be agreed upon freely except on loans by insurance companies and other enterprises subject to special laws or regulations. On loans of money or debts for supply of foodstuffs or consumer goods, given to laborers by any person or company (except credit companies), the maximum rate is 8%.

Extortion and the detention of contractual benefits notoriously prejudicial to another who granted them out of necessity or inexperience or ignorance are crimes and give action for restitution with damages. (D. 1755 of Nov. 9, 1935, ratified by D. L. 2092 of Mar. 10, 1936. D. 307 of June 7, 1955 and Law 1421 of Jan. 20, 1961 and C. C. art. 1542).

INTESTACY:

See topic Descent and Distribution.

JUDGMENTS:

(J. L. Decree 2 of Jan. 2, 1989 as am'd; C. C. P. 340-346; L. D. 2121 of Mar. 23, 1936).

Judgments are executed by means of a summary executory proceeding. A judgment does not constitute a lien on the property of the debtor except with respect to property attached in the course of execution. A levy on real property must be recorded in the public registry.

Foreign judgments, in the absence of a specific treaty, are given the same effect as is given in the foreign country to Guatemalan judgments. If the foreign country does not execute Guatemalan judgments, the foreign judgment will not be executed in Guatemala. In any event, the following requisites must concur with respect to the foreign judgment: (1) That it was rendered in a personal action, civil or mercantile; (2) that it was not rendered by default or against a reputed absent person who resides in Guatemala; (3) that the obligation on which it is based is legal in Guatemala; (4) that it

JUDGMENTS . . . *continued*

is a final judgment; (5) that it was not based on a political crime or a common crime connected therewith; (6) that it is duly authenticated.

LABOR RELATIONS:

(Const. arts. 101-106; Labor Code, arts. 18-87).

Individual contracts may be oral only in following cases: (a) agricultural labor; (b) domestic services; (c) temporary work not exceeding two months; (d) trabajo por obra determinada.

Labor contracts must be in written form and executed with three copies.

If employer terminates contract without "just cause" employee is entitled to: (a) indemnification for termination of contract whose amount shall depend upon time employee has worked for such employer; and to (b) damages, for an amount equivalent to salaries not received by employee during period included from date of dismissal to date of payment of compensation up to 12 months of salaries and legal expenses.

Besides regular salaries employers must pay workers, according to their performance, annual bonus equivalent to monthly salary.

LIENS:

(C. C. P. 379-397).

Credits other than mortgage and pledge credits are classified in following order: (1) Credits for support and maintenance and for personal services already due, and, regarding merchants, salaries of managers and employees for one year before state of bankruptcy plus time up to its adjudication; (2) credits for expenses of debtor's last illness, will, inventory, funeral and inheritance proceeding; (3) credits recorded on public instruments, in order of their dates of execution; and (4) common credits comprising all other credits not included in above. Cost of judicial and bankruptcy proceedings have first priority.

Mortgage and pledge credits are payable separately from encumbered property and any remaining balance after payment is to be applied for benefit of other creditors.

In cases of exclusion of a partner, company may withhold his share of capital and profits until termination of pending balances up to moment of such exclusion. Term of withholding cannot be longer than three years.

Creditor, when debt is due, may withhold debtor's movable or immovable property that is under creditor's custody or of those goods represented by negotiable instruments of credit.

In case thing withheld is attached, person in possession of it shall have following rights: (1) To keep thing as judicial bailee and to take necessary steps if goods might suffer considerable loss of value; (2) to have preferential right to be paid prior to others if goods withheld were under his custody by means of same contract that created such credit; (3) to be paid prior to creditor that attached property if second credit is originated after withholding.

Innkeepers may also withhold guests' property if after 30 days of termination of lodging contract, hotel bills are not paid; creditor may sell property in public auction. (C. Com. 233; 682; 872).

LIMITATION OF ACTIONS:

See topic Prescription.

LIMITED PARTNERSHIP:

See topic Partnership.

MARRIAGE:

(Const. art. 49; C. C. 78-107; 144-152; 173-189).

The marriage ceremony is performed by a mayor, the councilman taking his place, a notary public or a priest or minister duly registered. Marriages by proxy are allowed.

The following marriages are void: (a) Those of persons already married; (b) between ascendants and descendants by consanguinity or affinity; (c) between brothers and sisters of whole or half blood.

The following marriages are prohibited: (1) When the male is less than 16 years of age or the female less than 14, unless the female conceived before the said age and consent is given to the marriage by the person having authority therefor; (2) when either party is less than 18 years of age, unless previous consent is obtained from the person authorized to give the same; (3) where 300 days have not elapsed since the legal dissolution or annulment of a previous marriage of the female, unless she gave birth within that period or unless the spouses were separated before that time; (4) marriages of guardians or their descendants with the person under guardianship until after approval of the guardianship accounts; (5) marriages of persons having children under their parental authority, without a judicial inventory of the children's property; (6) marriage of adoptive parent with adopted person while adoption is still valid. Such marriages, if performed, are considered valid, but violators are liable according to law.

A marriage may be annulled: (1) When either spouse consented under error, fraud or duress; (2) in case of incurable impotence before marriage; (3) when either party was mentally incapacitated; (4) when one of spouses is guilty of murder of other spouse's spouse.

Consensual unions of persons who have lived together for over three years may be registered and give parties rights and obligations similar to those of husband and wife.

MINES AND MINERALS:

(Const. arts. 121 and 125).

The state is considered owner of all mines. Mines of metals may be obtained under the mining law, and petroleum concessions under the petroleum law. Mines, including petroleum deposits, consitute a property separate from that of the surface.

Mines in General.—(Decree-Law 69 of July 3, 1985 as am'd by D.L. 125 of Dec. 10, 1985). Rights relating to minerals are classified in prospecting, exploration concessions and exploitation contracts. Neither foreign states, nor Guatemalan government officials in charge of matters concerning mining rights, can directly or indirectly hold any such rights. Any individual or juridical person, national or foreign, can be granted mining rights.

Prospecting is defined as search or investigation limited to surface of terrain. If prospector extends his activity beyond this limit, concession may be cancelled. This concession is granted without exclusivity and for one year with two one-year renewal periods; it is nontransferable and it does not entail priority rights. When prospecting is carried on upon privately cultivated land, owner's permission is necessary.

Exploration concession refers to search and investigations conducted underground. It entails exclusive right to the mineral under the concession. Concession is granted for period of one to three years, which can be extended to five years. Shape of concesssion is that of polygon with area 500 square kilometers. Concessionaire is required to make minimum investment and to render comprehensive annual report of his operations.

Exploitation contract entails exclusivity, and can be extended to other minerals which may appear mixed with that extracted under contract. Rights to this contract can be transferred with authorization of Ministry of Energy and Mines. Term of this contract is granted for 25 years with an extension from ten to 25 more years. Shape of contracted area is rectangle oriented from north to south and east to west with maximum area of 50 square kilometers. No individual or juridical entity may hold exploitation contracts consisting of more than 200 square kilometers. Contractors have to render annual report on operation and furnish government with technical and financial information concerning enterprise.

Taxation.—Prospecting is free. Exploration and exploitation are subject to (1) Fixed tax: exploration, five quetzales per square kilometer, and five quetzales for renewals; exploitation, 100 quetzales per square kilometer and 150 quetzales for transfers or renewals; (2) area tax per square kilometer, applicable only to exploitation contracts, of 100 quetzales for first ten years, 200 quetzales for succeeding years; (3) "regalia," or royalty on output, 5%; and (4) income tax in accordance with Decree-Law 26-92 of May 6, 1992.

Exploitation contracts become void when transferred to persons precluded by law to hold ownership over mining operations. In such cases all permanent installations pass on to state without compensation. Contractors must employ Guatemalan technicians when available, and Guatemalan workers up to 80% of total labor employed, accounting for at least 85% of total payroll.

Petroleum.—(Decree-Law 109-83 of Sept. 15, 1983 as am'd and its regulations, A. 1034-83 of Dec. 15, 1983 as am'd by A. 753-92 of Sept. 7, 1992). Hydrocarbon industry, including production, refining, transport and commercialization, is public utility. Expropriation of property may be conducted for development of industry. Primary goal is refining within Guatemala. Hydrocarbon policy is dictated by Ministry of Energy and Mines and by National Petroleum Commission. Ministry of Energy and Mines may execute oil operation contracts for exploration and exploitation of hydrocarbons with private developers under various stipulated arrangements by individual evaluation or creating mixed economy companies with national or foreign companies duly established in country and having signed agreement renouncing all diplomatic recourse. Professional services that need to be performed by Ministry may be performed by itself or by others through oil service agreements. Each contract of exploration is limited to maximum 300,000 hectares onshore and 480,000 hectares offshore and of exploitation is limited to 150,000 hectares offshore and onshore. Companies must also commit themselves to drill at least one well in their first three years, followed by two wells each in fourth, fifth and sixth years of operation, to get to total of seven wells in six years. Reduction of one well each of last three years of operation can be authorized in special circumstances. Companies are permitted to recover all exploration, development and production costs in given contract area before government receives production share of 30% plus royalty payment; all production passes to government after 25 years.

In government participation is included corresponding income tax to be paid by private party and in general any other tax imposed on capital and profits from oil operations of exploitation and production.

State makes express reservation of rights to receive its corresponding participation in kind or in money. In case of monetary participation total amount shall be computed taking as basis price of reference in international market. This price shall be fixed by Executive Branch.

Term of oil operations agreement shall not exceed 25 years. In case private party does not strike hydrocarbons commercially exploitable, before end of sixth year of existence of contract, said contract shall be considered automatically terminated.

It is provided also that private party shall relinquish gradually portions of said area so that at end of fifth year 50% of that area has in fact been relinquished.

Contracts will be made only with private parties which possess sufficient technical and financial capacity and proven experience and which are duly created according to laws of country or authorized to do business in Republic if they are foreigners.

It shall be stipulated in agreements that upon termination of them for any reason, all buildings, permanent installations, machinery, equipment and any other property connected with oil operations shall be transferred in full ownership to State free of any cost or encumbrance.

Private party contracting with government shall be bound to sell to State amounts of hydrocarbons that State may require, in addition to participation above cited and therefore such private party shall only be free to dispose for export of portions exceeding those requirements.

Minimum amount of investment shall be established in each agreement.

Foreign concerns carrying out oil operations pursuant to this law must give option to Guatemalan nationals to participate in those operations with capital contributions of at least 5% of total capital to be invested during first three years of contract. (Accord 09-86 of Jan. 7, 1986). It is possible for private parties to import duty free all machinery and equipment required for oil operations provided that they are not satisfactorily made in country.

Taxes.—Contracting companies pay income tax, as stipulated by law and Accord 412-84 of May 28, 1984 as am'd by Accord 534-85 of July 2, 1985. They are also subject to stamp tax and fees established by arts. 35 and 45 of law. Remittances abroad are exempted of any tax.

Quarries.—Legislative-Decree 47-69 of Sept. 11, 1969 (Law of Quarries, "Ley de Canteras") regulates exploration and exploitation of quarries, which are defined as those deposits of natural rocks to be used in construction and ornamentation of buildings; granites, basalt, sand, marble, plaster and the like. Semiprecious stones are

MINES AND MINERALS . . . *continued*
also included. However, precious stones, phosphate, nitrate and salt are still regulated by Code of Mines.

License from Ministry of Economy is required to explore and exploit quarries over 10,000 cubic meters. No physical or juridical person is allowed to exploit quarries over 50 square kilometers. Licenses shall be preferably granted to guatemaltecos or to corporations in which 50% or more of capital belongs to nationals. Exploration licenses shall be given for one year and exploitation ones for a term not exceeding 40 years. Law also regulates rights and duties of miners and mining companies providing sanctions for non-fulfillment with its provisions.

MONOPOLIES AND RESTRAINT OF TRADE:

(Const. art. 130; C. Com. 361; 362; 663).

Any kind of monopolies is prohibited. All enterprises must contract with anybody requesting their products or services, observing equal treatment among diverse categories of consumers. Any act contrary to bona fide commerce or to normal and honest development of mercantile activities, shall be considered unfair competition and consequently unjust and prohibited. Following acts, among others, shall be deemed unfair competition: (1) To deceive or to confuse public through false statements regarding origin or quality of products or services or false indication of honors, or prizes obtained by same; (2) to release false news to influence buyer to purchase; (3) to damage another company, through imitation of its products, brands, tradenames, or impeding access of customers to its premises.

Seller of an enterprise must abstain during next five years from date of sale, from opening a new enterprise that due to its object, location and any other circumstance, might divert customers from sold enterprise, thereby constituting unfair competition.

Central American Regulations on Unfair Trade Practices of Dec. 12, 1995 implement principles established by Agreements of World Trade Organization. Central American governments may issue restrictive covenants to temporarily protect their local production from massive import of same or similar products that may cause pecuniary loss to local producers.

MORTGAGES:

(C. C. 822-879; C. C. P. 297-306).

Mortgages must be executed in the form of public instruments and may refer only to real property. They affect only the property on which they are constituted and the mortgagor cannot be made personally liable for the debt even by express stipulation. They cover the natural accessions, unpledged crops and rents not collected at their maturity and two annuities of interest prior to foreclosure. Constitution and acceptance of a mortgage must be express. If the mortgaged property diminishes in value the creditor may consider the mortgage matured unless the debtor increases his security.

Foreclosures follow the general rules of execution of judgments, except that no appraisal is made of the property, but the value agreed by the parties or the amount of the mortgage is taken as the value. The debtor has the right of redemption only up to time judicial sale is consummated. No deficiency judgment is allowed.

NOTARIES PUBLIC:

(Notarial Code, L. D. 314 of Nov. 30, 1946 as am'd).

The title of notary is obtained by following prescribed educational courses similar to those required for the title of lawyer. A notary must possess such a title, registers his diploma in the Supreme Court, not be a cleric, be over 21 years of age, native-born Guatemalan, and of known integrity. He holds office indefinitely but remains under the supervision of the courts.

Instruments executed before a notary must be prepared with certain formalities. They must state the date, names of the parties, their age, domicile, profession and whether married or single. The notary must declare that he knows the parties or that they were identified by witnesses.

Witnesses are required for wills executed before a notary and gifts causa mortis, and are optional in other instruments; witnesses must be over 21 years old, know how to read and write, know Spanish, have no manifest interest in the matter, not be deaf, dumb or blind, nor relatives of the notary, nor relatives of the parties except in certain cases. The notary retains the original document in a protocol and furnishes the parties with copies which have the effect of originals in court. Upon the death of a notary his records are deposited in a general archive of protocols.

PARTNERSHIP:

(C. Com. 14-67).

Commercial Code applies to partnerships and to any type of company seeking to realize profits. Such company must be registered in Commercial Registry in order to be an entity different from partners, and must be governed by incorporation agreement provided same is not in conflict with Commercial Code. Partners are not allowed to enter into secret agreements or reserve rights not expressly mentioned in articles of document; if so, said secret agreements shall be void.

Articles of incorporation and all amendments of any kind thereto must appear in a public instrument which must be duly recorded in Commercial Registry within a month after said instrument's authorization.

Collective Company is entity that exists under a firm name (razón social) and in which all partners are jointly and unlimitedly liable for company's debts.

Firm name must have name of one or more of partners adding words "and Co." (y Compaõnía) or letters "S.C." (Sociedad Colectiva meaning General Partnership).

If a person, that is not a partner, allows his name to appear in firm name, he shall be subject to same obligations and liabilities as partners. Name of a partner who no longer belongs to partnership must be eliminated unless firm name be retained followed by word "Sucesores" which can be abbreviated "Sucs." (meaning "heirs"). Partners may not on their own account engage in same business as partnership. Partnership can be liquidated where losses are over 60% of capital.

Recording act must state: (1) Type of company; (2) firm name; (3) domicile and domicile of its branches; (4) object; (5) duration; (6) capital; (7) name of notary public that authorizes public instrument of incorporation, place and date; (8) administrative councils; and (9) officer's councils if any. (Art. 337).

Limited partnership or "Sociedad en Comandita Simple" (C. Comm. 68-77), consists of one or more partners who are jointly and unlimitedly liable and one or more partners with limited liability to amount of capital contributed by them.

Firm name can be formed with name of one or two of unlimited partners followed by obligatory inclusion of words "y Compañía, Sociedad en Comandita" which can be abbreviated "y Cía. S. en C." meaning "and Company, Limited Partnership."

Limited partner who permits inclusion of his name in firm name becomes as much liable as if he were a general partner.

Participation of limited partners may be represented by shares, in which case, company shall be automatically called "Sociedad en Comandita por acciones" meaning "Limited Partnership issuing shares." In this event, requirements applicable to corporations shall also apply to this kind of company. (C. Comm. 195-212 as am'd).

PATENTS:

(Const. art. 42, D.L. 153-85 of Dec. 30, 1985).

Any invention considered as new, which results from inventive activity and is susceptible of industrial application is patentable in accordance with terms of law. Inventions may be of products or of methods. Patents cannot be granted for discoveries which are product of nature without any human intervention, plants, animals, commercial and financial systems or plans; methods for therapeutic and surgical treatment; beverages and food products, except methods to produce them; inventions contrary to law or good customs. As to chemicals only methods for processing them are patentable.

Unless there is express agreement to contrary, inventions by workers or agents specifically hired for matter, belong to principal. If person was not hired to work on invention projects, and invention results from his work by using data or means available by reason of his work, invention belongs to worker. Employers, however, have preferential rights in case of assignment or granting of license. Patents are granted for 15 years from filing date, except in cases of patents on methods to process chemical compounds in which patent is granted for term of ten years. When inventor fails to exploit patent in country in effective manner or patent has not been locally exploited within four years from granting date, license to exploit patent can be granted by Registro de la Propiedad Industrial in favor of third parties upon request therefor.

Patents are void: (a) When granted in violation of law; (b) when invention patented does not fulfill requirements; (c) when drawings or descriptions necessary to comprehend or execute invention are omitted; (d) when applicant of patent is not owner of invention. Patents expire: (a) On termination of period for which they were granted; (b) for failure to pay annuities; (c) if invention is not locally used within six years after granted; or (d) if its industrial exploitation is interrupted for more than two consecutive years.

Utility models for new forms of objects, may also be patented, provided they are susceptible of industrial application. Registration confers right of exclusive use for ten years. Industrial designs and drawings may likewise be patented if new and may be applied to industry and no publicity or commercialization thereof has been made before filing of application. Registration grants exclusive rights for five years, renewable for five more if design or drawing is used in country.

Infringement of patent is punishable crime. Owner of patents may also file civil proceedings and recover damages.

PLEDGES:

Pledge contract must be in writing and pledged object must normally be delivered to creditor or a third person designated by parties, except in case of agrarian, cattle and industrial pledges. (See topic Chattel Mortgages). However, in other cases, creditor may authorize debtor to keep pledged article. Any stipulation that creditor may assume ownership of pledged article in payment is null and void. (C. C. 880-916).

PRESCRIPTION:

(C. C. 620-654; 1501-1516, 1585; C. C. P. 296; C. Com. 513, 626-628, 916, 1308-1313).

The acquisition of property or rights by virtue of possession and the loss of rights by failure to enforce them is called prescription. Prescription may be waived as far as it has run, but waiver of future prescription is not allowed. Prescription is interrupted: (a) If possessor is deprived of possession or enjoyment for one year; (b) by law suit unless same is withdrawn or dismissed; (c) by express or implied recognition. It does not run: (1) against minors or incompetents while they have no legal representative; (2) between parents and children under parental authority; (3) between guardians and wards; (4) between husband and wife; (5) between co-owners.

Ownership is acquired by positive prescription, elements of which are (a) Public, peaceful and continued possession, (b) a conveyance and (c) good faith when acquiring, which is presumed unless contrary is shown. Real property is acquired by prescription in ten years, personal property in two years.

Actions.—Rights are lost by negative prescription. The prescriptive period in which the power to enforce rights is lost varies according to the nature of the right. The more important are: (a) Actions not otherwise limited, and mortgage actions, ten years; (b) summary actions, accounting actions, actions on maritime loans or insurance, two years; (c) actions for an accounting or against acceptors of bills of exchange, three years; (d) actions for fees, salaries and wages, actions of merchants for sales price, actions of innkeepers for meals, actions to recover pensions and rentals, two years; (e) actions for rescission of contracts, for damages, actions of holders of bills of exchange against drawers and endorsers, actions on advances to vessels or for wages of crew, one year; (f) actions of holders of checks against drawer, actions of endorsers of bills of exchange and checks against each other and against drawer, actions for maritime freight and particular average, six months.

PRINCIPAL AND AGENT:

(C. C. 1686-1727; C. Com. 263-291; 303-331).

See Topical Index in front part of this volume.

PRINCIPAL AND AGENT . . . *continued*

An agency must be conferred by a public instrument unless amount involved is less than Q. 1,000. Authority to alienate, mortgage, guaranty or compromise must be specifically granted by public instrument. Agent may delegate his powers if expressly authorized to do so, but he is liable if substitute of his own choosing is notoriously incompetent or insolvent. Principal must reimburse agent for his expenses and for damages caused him by agency. Agent is entitled to a compensation if he does not expressly state that his services are gratuitously rendered.

An agency is terminated by: (1) Conclusion of period established for its duration, (2) termination of business for which it was conferred, (3) revocation by principal, (4) resignation of agent, (5) death or interdiction of principal or agent, (6) bankruptcy or principal, and (7) dissolution of entity having conferred agency.

Contracts for exclusive representation or distribution of products may be terminated only by mutual consent; termination of agreed period; just cause, as defined; will of representative with three months notice to principal; will of principal at any time, being subject in this case to pay damages to representative, measured as provided in Law 78-71 of Sept. 20, 1971.

Factors are those persons that although not merchants, have management of an enterprise or establishment. To be a factor it is necessary to have legal capacity in order to be able to represent another person according to civil laws. Factors must act under agency contract with representation granted by merchant or by written contract of labor. Said contracts must be registered in Commercial Registry to be valid. However, limitations on factors's powers, although recorded in Commercial Registry, shall have no effect against bona fide third parties.

Factors must have special powers to sell or encumber real property, to obtain loans, to represent principal in court and to do all those acts that in general do not pertain to scope of authority granted. Factors must act in name of their principal, otherwise they are personally liable, unless contract refers to objects comprised in an establishment known to belong to another or unless principal ratifies factor's performance. Factors's powers are not terminated by death of principal, but by sale or dissolution of establishment. Neither factors, nor clerks may delegate their powers without principal's consent.

Commercial agents are those persons who act permanently with one or more principals, promoting commercial contracts or executing them in their principal's name. Commission merchant can be: (1) Dependent: if act under principal's instructions, belong to his enterprise and is bound to him by a labor contract; (2) Independent: If act through own enterprise and if bound to principal by a commercial contract or agency contract.

Commission merchants do not require a formal power of attorney; any written document is sufficient, or a verbal power ratified in writing before transaction is concluded. They may act in their own name, they are not required to give name of their undisclosed principal, but in such case, are liable as though business were their own.

PUBLIC INSTRUMENTS:

Documents executed with the legal formalities before a notary public (q.v.) are called public instruments. Authentic documents are most documents issued by public officers. Other documents are private documents. Public and authentic documents are received in court as full proof without further verification. The law requires numerous contracts to appear in public instruments, e.g., articles of incorporation or partnership, mortgages, etc. A document to be recorded must be public document. Commercial contracts for more than Q. 1,000 or other contracts for more than Q. 300 must appear in writing. (C. C. 1574-1578; C. C. P. 177-193; Notarial Law 314 of Nov. 30, 1946 as am'd).

RECORDS:

(C. C. 369-441, 1124-1250).

There is public registry comprising registries of: (a) Real property, (b) agrarian pledges, (c) wills and estate proceedings (created by Decree 73 of Oct. 15, 1975, regulated by Res. 49 of May 31, 1976) and (d) special works such as railroads, wharves, etc. Registrars do not transcribe entire document but only essential parts and may refuse to record defective documents: appeal may be taken to court from their decision.

There is also a mercantile registry for certain documents relating to merchants and companies, as well as a civil registry for recording births, marriages, deaths, divorces, acknowledgments of children, guardianship, citizenship and aliens.

REDEMPTION:

See topics Executions; Mortgages.

SALES (Realty and Personalty):

(C. C. 1543-1573, 1680, 1790-1851; C. Com. 695-713).

Between parties, sale is perfected and title passes when an agreement is reached as to thing sold and price, though neither has been delivered. If goods were sold specifying their kind and quality, buyer has right to cancel contract if goods are not of kind and quality agreed upon. Sale of real property produces no effect against third parties unless recorded.

In absence of an agreement, price must be paid at time and place of delivery. Buyer may retain price until delivery of thing sold, and in case he is disturbed in his possession or has reason to fear disturbance he may, unless otherwise stipulated, retain as much as necessary of price. In case there is no agreement between parties as to price or manner of determining it, there is no sale. Sales by installments with reservation of ownership until buyer pays entire price, are valid. Such contracts may be cancelled under specific conditions for lack of payment of four or more installments. Buyer is not allowed to impose any encumbrances on property or to alienate his right without seller's written authorization.

Seller warrants against hidden defects which render thing sold useless or diminish its value to such extent that buyer would not have bought it. He must also make good defects which he knew and did not communicate to buyer, but is not liable for visible defects. In case real property is sold by area, any difference between true area and that designated in contract gives rise to proportionate increase or decrease in price; if difference is over 10% buyer has option to rescind contract.

Repurchase clauses in sales contracts are not valid. Promises to sell in future are valid under certain circumstances and may be granted up to two years if relating to real property and up to one year if otherwise. If so stipulated, sale may be rescinded at request of seller if someone makes a better offer within a fixed period of time of not more than six months for real property or three for personal property.

Commercial Sales.—In sales against documents, seller fulfills his obligation when he delivers to buyer documents representing goods sold and any other documents indicated in contract or required by law. Unless otherwise agreed, payment of purchase price must be made when documents are delivered; buyer cannot refuse payment because of defects related to quality of goods, unless he has proof of such defects.

Other provisions of C. Com. relate to sales F.O.B.; F.A.S.; and C.I.F. In sales of mercantile goods parties are free to agree on options to purchase without time limitations.

SEALS:

Seals are not used in private matters. A document executed before a notary has most of the effects of a sealed instrument in the United States.

SHIPPING:

Vessels constructed in or out of Guatemala may obtain Guatemalan registry in the ports designated for that purpose. The applicant must present a certificate of residence if an individual and a certificate of the mercantile registry if a company. Guatemalan vessels must touch at Guatemalan ports at least once or twice a year. They are divided into five classes: (1) Ocean vessels; (2) vessels for coastwise trade along Guatemala or Central America; (3) fishing boats; (4) boats for port use; (5) vessels under construction. (D. 1329 and 1355 of 1932). The more important admiralty provisions are found in old Code of Commerce, Arts. 827-1319 with exception of Arts. 1214-1307 that were repealed by C. Com.

STATUTES:

Most of the legal provisions are codified. The principal codifications are the Civil Code, relating to persons, domestic relations, property rights, successions, obligations and contracts; Code of Commerce; Code of Civil Procedure; Penal Code; Code of Criminal Procedure; Judiciary Law; Fiscal Code; Customhouse Code. The laws are published in a governmental paper entitled "Diario de Centro América".

TAXATION:

Stamped paper and revenue stamps are required for most contracts and transactions. Amount depends on nature of document and sum involved, general rate being 3%, but special rates apply to numerous other documents. Penalties are provided for failure to comply with provisions of law. (Decree 37-92 of June 22, 1992 and its regulations Accord 737-92 of Aug. 27, 1992).

Real Estate Transfer Tax.—On transfer of real estate there is tax of 1% of contract or catastral value of real estate transferred. (L. D. 1153 of May 20, 1921, as am'd).

Real Property Tax.—(Decree 62-87 of Oct. 6, 1987 as am'd and its regulations Accord 451-88 of June 28, 1988). Real property, whether urban or rural, is subject to real estate tax on value assessed by taxpayer himself or by tax administration. Value includes constructions, fixtures and permanent cultivations. Tax is calculated on aggregate catastral value of all real property belonging to same taxpayer. Rates are: for properties over Q.2,000 up to Q.20,000, 0.2%; from Q20,001 to Q.70,000, 0.6%; and for properties over Q.70,000, 0.9%. There is tax on large uncultivated estates. (L. D. 1551 of Oct. 17, 1962, regulated by Resolution of Feb. 9, 1963).

Inheritance Tax.—The tax on inheritances depends on amount involved and degree of relationship, ranging from 1% in the case of transfers of 50,000 quetzales or less to children and spouse, to 25% in case of transfers of over 500,000 quetzales to unrelated persons. Money in local banks is exempt. Money in banks abroad is subject to tax and to surtax of 3%. (L. D. 431 of Nov. 18, 1947, as am'd by D. 202 of Jan. 12, 1955 and 366 of Aug. 6, 1955 and 1276 of Mar. 12, 1959; Regulations by Res. of Feb. 24, 1964).

Income Tax.—(Decree 26-92 of May 7, 1992 as am'd and its regulations Accord 624-92 of July 24, 1992 as am'd; Accord 913-90 of Sept. 21, 1990). Tax is applicable to all individuals and juridical entities for income locally obtained. Branches, permanent or temporary establishments of foreign companies or persons, estates, irregular companies and trusts in country are subject to tax.

Exemptions.—State, Municipalities and government agencies, decentralized government entities, religious institutions, universities, Indian communities, cooperatives and nonprofit organizations among others.

Gross income is all revenues from activities as indicated by law. Excluded are, among others, interest from bonds or titles of the Government and its agencies, including municipalities; dividends, including stock dividends, and participations or benefits which had been already taxed in another form during the same period; and are paid to taxpayers locally domiciled.

Net income is gross income minus deductions authorized by law. Deductions include expenses necessary for production of income and cost of same and of the objects sold and of services rendered, including freight, commisssions, salaries, for actual services; labor indemnifications and social security benefits; depreciation of assets; interest and finance charges; rents; taxes; all amounts reinvested in housing for laborers and in land for farmers' laborers; medical assistance to laborers; contributions to pensions; losses; bad debts; some charitable gifts; expenses in technical research and royalties up to 5% of gross income.

Following personal expenses are annually deductible: up to Q.24,000, not subject to proof for taxpayer; social security contributions; life insurance premiums, if policies are issued by locally authorized companies; alimony payments.

There are guides to estimate net income of export and import trades if returns are not satisfactory. It is irrefutable presumption that net income from international transportation business of foreign companies is 8% of corresponding gross, as indicated by

TAXATION . . . *continued*
law; that net income of foreign companies from foreign movie production, distribution or intermediation is no less than 60% of gross obtained in Guatemala; that net income from foreign reinsurance or resuretyship, is 10% of premiums.

Rates.—Natural person's taxable income is subject to employment income at tax rate ranging from 15% on first Q. 20,000 to 30% on amounts over Q. 65,000 annually and other income at 30% rate. Juridical person's taxable income is subject to 30% rate annually.

Following payments to recipients domiciled abroad are subject to withholding taxes: Dividends, 12.5%; interests, and technical services 20%; royalties, 30%; any other payment, 30%.

Registry.—Any person or corporation must be registered in Taxpayer Registry.

Tax on Assets.—(Decree 35-95 of Apr. 28, 1995). Tax at annual rate of 1.5% of value of assets is assessed on all legal entities and individuals engaged in commercial and agricultural and cattle activities according to law.

Tax on Interests.—(Decree 26-95 of Apr. 25, 1995). Tax at monthly rate of 10% on all interests credited or paid to individuals and legal entities locally domiciled.

Value Added Tax (D.L. 27-92 of May 7, 1992 as am'd and its regulations; Accord 508 of June 24, 1992 as am'd).—Tax is applied to: Transfer, sale and importation of goods into country, leasing, nonpersonal services rendered within country with exceptions established by law. Tax is levied on net price obtained by deducting normal price discounts or other reductions made according to commercial usage. General rate is 10%.

Miscellaneous.—There are various miscellaneous taxes, such as a slaughter-house tax, poll-tax for roads, vehicles tax (D. 80 of Sept. 10, 1974 as am'd), alcohol, wine, cider, beer, etc. will pay tax, rate of which varies with each particular item (D.L. 74-83 of July 6, 1983); tobacco tax (D. 61 of Dec. 23, 1977).

Mines.—See topic Mines and Minerals, subhead Mines in General.

Special Treatment.—Law Decree 29-89 of June 13, 1989 and its regulations (Export Promotion and Drawback Law) establishes parameters for drawback and export production operations. Detailed investment proposal must be presented for evaluation. During evaluation period, companies may begin importing duty-free capital goods and raw materials for operation, if bond for same amount of deferred taxes is deposited in guaranty to be forfeited if investment proposal is denied. Tax incentives include duty-free importation of capital goods and raw materials necessary for export product, and ten-year tax holiday for those companies whose country of origin does not permit tax credit against foreign taxes paid.

Imported goods must be reexported. Penalties are provided for failure to comply with provisions of agreement; if any imported goods are sold within country fine of double import duties is imposed. Companies that import more goods than necessary for export production must pay full amount of deferred taxes on all unused raw materials or surrender goods to customs for public auction.

TRADEMARKS:

(Central American Convention for the Protection of Industrial Property Law 26 of Mar. 28, 1973, L.D. 882 of Dec. 31, 1924 and 2079 of Apr. 27, 1935 as am'd only on subjects not regulated by Convention).

Trademarks comprise any sign, word, expressions or any other graphic or material means which because of its special characteristics can clearly distinguish products, merchandise or services of person or corporation.

Trademarks are classified as industrial or manufacturers' marks, commercial marks and service marks.

Industrial or manufacturers' marks are those that distinguish goods produced or processed by specified manufacturing or industrial enterprise.

Commercial marks are those that distinguish goods commercial enterprise sells or distributes regardless of who produces them.

Service marks are those that distinguish activities of enterprises devoted to satisfaction of general needs by means other than manufacture, sale or distribution of goods.

Use or registration of following as trademarks is prohibited: (1) National flags or their colors, if latter appear in same order and positions as in former, coats-of-arms, insignia or distinguishing marks of contracting states, their municipalities and other public bodies; (2) flags, coats-of-arms, insignia, devices or denominations of foreign nations unless authorization from respective government has been obtained; (3) flags, coats-of-arms, insignia, devices, denominations or acronyms of international agencies of which one or more contracting states are members; (4) names, emblems and devices of Red Cross and of religious or charitable bodies legally recognized in any of member states of this convention; (5) designs of coins or notes that are legal tender in territory of any of contracting parties, reproductions of securities and other commercial documents or of seals, stamps, or revenue stamps, or revenue stamps in general; (6) signs, words or expressions that ridicule or tend to ridicule persons, ideas, religions or national symbols of third party states or international agencies; (7) signs, words or expressions, contrary to good morals, public order or good usage; (8) names, signatures, family names and portraits of persons other than person filing application without their consent or, if deceased, consent of their closest ascendants or descendants; (9) technical or common names of products, goods or services when they are intended to protect articles or services included in genus or species to which such names refer; (10) terms, signs or locutions that have passed into general use and which are used to indicate nature of products, goods or services, and qualifying and gentilitial adjectives. Trademarks that have become popular or widespread subsequent to their registration shall not be regarded as having passed into general use; (11) figures, denominations or phrases describing products, goods or services that are to be protected by trademarks or their ingredients, qualities, physical characteristics or use for which they are intended; (12) signs or indications that are used to designate type, quality, quantity, value or season of preparation of products or goods or of provision of services, unless they are followed by designs or phrases that particularize them; (13) usual and current form of products or goods; (14) plain colors considered separately, unless they are combined or accompanied by elements such as signs or denominations having particular or distinguishing character; (15) containers that are in public domain or have come into common use in any of contracting states and, in general, those that are neither original nor novel; (16) mere indications of origin or denominations of origin, except as set forth in item (b) of Art. 35; (17) distinguishing marks already registered by other persons as trademarks for products, goods or services included in same class; (18) distinguishing marks that by reason of their graphic, phonetic or ideological similarity may mislead or result in confusion with other trademarks or with commercial names, publicity expressions or symbols already registered or in process of being registered, if it is intended to use them to distinguish products, goods or services included in same class; (19) distinguishing marks that may mislead by indicating false source, nature or quality; (20) maps. These may, however, be used as elements of trademarks if they represent country of origin or source of goods which they distinguish.

Registration is mandatory for chemical, pharmaceutical, veterinary and medicinal food products. Term of registration is ten years subject to renewals for equal periods. Licenses must be registered. International Mark Classification applies. Fees are: Registration of each mark or name $50, and of propaganda slogans or signs $25; renewal $50, transfer $10, any certificate or document $5.

TREATIES:

Multilateral.—Bustamante Code of Private International Law (Havana, Feb. 20, 1928. Latin American Economic System (SELA) Panama 1975); Convention on the Practice of Learned Professions. Mexico City, Jan. 28, 1902; Convention on the Status of Aliens, Havana, Feb. 20, 1928; Interamerican Convention on International Commercial Arbitration, Panama, Jan. 30, 1975.

Guatemala maintains copyright relations with other American states and with France and Spain on basis of following agreements: (a) Rio de Janeiro Copyright Convention, 1906; (b) Buenos Aires Copyright Convention, 1910; (c) Havana Copyright Convention, 1928; (d) Washington Copyright Convention, 1946; (e) Copyright Treaty with Spain, 1893; (f) Copyright Treaty with France, 1895. Guatemala ratified Universal Copyright Convention by Decree-Law 251.

Central American Treaties.—Agreement on system of Central American integrated industries. Signed June 10, 1958, Tegucigalpa; Protocol. Signed Jan. 29, 1963, San Salvador; Central American agreement on uniform road signs. Signed June 10, 1958, at Tegucigalpa. (With Costa Rica, Honduras and Nicaragua); General Treaty on Central American economic integration. Signed Dec. 13, 1960, at Managua and its Protocol; Agreement establishing Central American Bank for Economic Integration. Signed Dec. 13, 1960, Managua; Charter of Organization of Central American States. Signed Dec. 12, 1962, Panama City; Central American Convention for the Protection of Industrial Property, San José, 1968.

TRUSTS:

(C. Com. 766-793).

Trusts may be established by contract or will. Settlor transfers certain goods or rights to trustee for certain preestablished purposes. Trustee receives them with specific limitation to do only those acts required to fulfill trust's purposes.

Settlor must have legal capacity to administer his patrimony; in case of minors, incapacitated persons, or absentees, a trust can be created by their legal representatives. Beneficiaries must also have legal capacity to receive benefits of trust. Only duly authorized banks established in Guatemala can be trustees. Credit institutions can also act as trustees after having been specially authorized to do so by Monetary Board. Trust established by contract must be prepared before a notary public; it must contain trustee's acceptance and it must also state estimated value of goods given in trust. Maximum duration is 25 years unless beneficiary is an incapacitated person, or suffers an incurable illness, or it is a charitable institution. Trusts may also be extinguished: (1) If purpose of its creation has been fulfilled; (2) if its fulfillment is impossible; (3) if resolutory condition has been complied with; (4) by express agreement between settlor and beneficiary; (5) by settlor's revocation if such right had been expressly reserved in constitutive agreement; (6) by trustee's resignation, nonacceptance, or his removal if he cannot be replaced by another trustee; and (7) by judicial judgment.

Secret trusts and those in favor of several beneficiaries succeeding previous one upon his death are void unless said beneficiaries were alive or conceived at time of settlor's death. Several other provisions govern rights and duties of parties among themselves, and with third persons as well as taxes and fees.

USURY: See topic Interest.

VITAL STATISTICS: See topic Records.

WILLS:

(C. C. 924-976; C. C. P. 460-477; Notarial Code 42, 52, 53).

Any person having full civil capacity may dispose of his property by will. Following are incapacitated: (a) Persons declared under interdiction, (b) deaf-mutes and those unable to speak who cannot express themselves in writing and (c) those not under interdiction but not having their mental capacity or full power of volition at time of execution of will. Following cannot be witnesses: (1) Minors below 16 years of age; (2) illiterate persons or those not knowing Spanish; (3) persons evidently interested in will; (4) deaf and dumb or blind persons; (5) notary's relatives.

Wills are common or special. Common wills comprise the open and the closed will.

Open wills are made as public instruments before a notary. They require two witnesses, but if the testator cannot sign or is blind an additional witness is needed, and if he does not know Spanish two interpreters must translate his wishes. The will must state the place, date and hour of signing; it must be read aloud at one sitting before the witnesses by the testator himself or a person designated by him; and be signed by the testator, notary, witnesses, and interpreters, if any.

Closed wills may be written by the testator or another person, and must be signed by the testator or another at his request. Will is enclosed in an envelope which is sealed by testator in presence of notary and two witnesses with statement that it contains his will; if testator cannot sign a further witness is required, and if he does not know Spanish two interpreters must be present. On envelope notary writes a minute of the act, and same is signed by testator, notary, witnesses, and interpreters, if any.

See Topical Index in front part of this volume.

WILLS . . . *continued*

Special wills are open wills made by soldiers in time of war, or open or closed wills made on merchant or war vessels. They are made before certain officers and require presence of two witnesses.

Foreign wills may be made by Guatemalans in accordance with the laws of the country where they are; or on foreign vessels in accordance with the laws of the vessel's nationality; except that Guatemalans cannot make joint wills.

Testamentary Dispositions.—The testator may freely dispose of his estate but he must set aside sufficient to support those to whose support he is obligated by law, namely, his minor children, parents, spouse and in certain cases his brothers and sisters. The following are excluded from taking by will: (1) Those excluded from descent benefits (See topic Descent and Distribution); (2) ministers of any religion, unless relatives of testator; (3) physicians who assisted testator in his last illness, unless relatives; (4) notary before whom will was made and his relatives; (5) guardian and his relatives if the guardianship accounts are unapproved, unless relatives of testator; (6) foreign institutions of any kind.

See Topical Index in front part of this volume.

HONDURAS LAW DIGEST REVISER

Curtis, Mallet-Prevost, Colt & Mosle
101 Park Avenue
New York, New York 10178-0061
Telephone: 212-696-6141
Fax: 212-697-1559
Email: CMP-NY@mcimail.com

Reviser Profile

The Firm began in 1830 when two practicing lawyers started a long line of lawyers and law firms extending in an unbroken chain up to the present time. In 1897, the firm name became Curtis, Mallet-Prevost & Colt; in 1925 it was changed to Curtis, Mallet-Prevost, Colt & Mosle. The Firm is now made up of approximately 120 lawyers, including experts who have published extensively on such diverse subjects as international money management, transnational contracts, state contracts, litigation against foreign states, sovereign immunity and the act of state doctrine, and the International Court of Justice. Its principal offices are in New York City. There are branch offices in Paris, London, Frankfurt Am Main, Hong Kong, Washington, D.C., Houston, Texas, Newark, N.J., and Mexico City. The firm has five departments: Corporate and International; Litigation; Real Estate; Tax; and Trusts and Estates. The corporate and international department acts as general counsel to various public and private corporations and individual entrepreneurs. Clients are in the banking, insurance, securities, manufacturing, real estate and oil and gas industries. In addition, the corporate and international department frequently acts as special counsel to domestic and foreign clients, providing assistance in financing, know-how licensing, the negotiation and drafting of all types of contracts and instruments, counselling on all aspects of corporate law, and establishing the vehicles necessary to enable clients to conduct their domestic and foreign business activities. The Firm's international work permeates all areas of its practice and involves questions of private international law, foreign law and an unusual amount of public and quasi-public international law. Traditionally, much of the Firm's international practice has been concerned with Latin America. The Firm maintains its excellence in that area, with its Mexican affiliate, and also through the expertise of Latin American lawyers based in the New York office. The Firm's international practice has undergone a major expansion beyond Latin America to Europe, Africa and the Near and Far East. The Firm's litigation practice includes commercial litigation and arbitration, and white-collar criminal defense. It has substantial experience in civil aviation matters; it also has represented foreign States in transnational litigation and international arbitration arising out of acts of nationalization and alleged breach of economic development or natural resource supply contracts. Among the Firm's clients in real estate matters are institutional lenders and investors, real estate developers, both individual and corporate, foreign and domestic investors and syndicators. The tax department has substantial experience in all aspects of domestic and international business tax matters and real estate taxation. The matters the tax department deals with on a regular basis include: Taxation of foreign investments; the structuring of corporate transactions, including mergers, acquisitions, liquidations and reorganization; federal and state tax litigation; and tax planning for U.S. and foreign individuals. The trusts and estates department engages in general domestic trusts and estates practice and in tax planning for foreign persons wishing to invest in U.S. assets through offshore trusts and corporations. It represents individuals, trust companies, and banks acting as fiduciaries. It works for various charitable organizations located both in the United States and abroad including private foundations, museums, universities and hospitals. A group of fiduciary accountants with vast experience in the field assists the lawyers of the trusts and estates department. Curtis, Mallet-Prevost, Colt & Mosle has served as a Reviser for most of Latin American Law Digests since 1930.

HONDURAS LAW DIGEST

(The following is a list of all Topics, including cross-references, covered in this Digest.)

HONDURAS LAW DIGEST

Revised for 1997 edition by

CURTIS, MALLET-PREVOST, COLT & MOSLE, of the New York Bar.

(Abbreviations used are: C. C., Civil Code; C. Family, Code of Family; C. C. P., Code of Civil Procedure; C. Com., Code of Commerce. The numbers refer to the articles of these Codes.)

ABSENTEES: See topic Death.

ACKNOWLEDGMENTS:

Documents are not acknowledged as in the United States, but the legal effect of an acknowledgment is obtained by executing the document before a notary as a public instrument (see topic Public Instruments). Foreign instruments are considered valid if executed according to the law of the respective country, but if the Honduras law requires a public instrument no private instrument is admissible. Foreign instruments must be authenticated by a consular or diplomatic officer of Honduras or, if none, of a friendly nation, or by a diplomatic representative of the respective country in Honduras. (C. C. 15, 16; C. C. P. 325).

ACTIONS:

Actions for Death.—See topic Death, subhead Actions for Death.

Limitation of.—See topic Prescription, subhead Actions.

ADMINISTRATION:

See topic Executors and Administrators.

ADOPTION:

(C. Family 120-184).

Person over 25 and under 51 years of age, in full exercise of his civil rights and of good reputation may adopt minor under 18 years; in any case adopting party must be 15 years older than adopted party. Consent must be obtained from adopted party when it is over 21 years old, tutor, parents and court. Husband or wife may also adopt provided consent of other spouse is given.

There are two types of adoption: Full adoption (adopción plena) and partial adoption (adopción simple). Full adoption gives adopted person identical status with that of natural child, creating lines of kinship between adopted person and adoptive parent's family. Full adoption extinguishes legal bonds between adopted person and his natural parents and family. Only couples married over three years may full adopt. Partial adoption creates same juridical ties between adopted and adopting parties as exist between parents and children; but does not create any legal relationship between adopted party and family of adopting party, nor between latter and family of adopted party. Partial adoption does not extinguish legal bonds between adopted person and his natural parents and family. Partial adoption may be ended or revoked. There are special requirements for foreign adopting parties.

ADVERSE POSSESSION: See topic Prescription.

AGENCY: See topic Principal and Agent.

ALIENS:

Aliens in general have same civil rights as citizens. They may acquire property and engage in business in accordance with general laws; however they may not own rural real property in a 40 kilometer zone along border and seashore. (Constitution arts. 30-35, 61, 101, 107).

Decree 34 of Oct. 1, 1970 regulates status of aliens as well as nationals in Honduras (Ley de Población y Política Migratoria). Permanent foreign residents are required to register with General Direction of Population; detailed provisions of law have to be complied with in order to obtain permanent visas. This decree also provides grounds for deportation of foreigners which, among others, are: to imperil national security, political or social order; to enter country fraudulently; to be engaged in illegal business; etc. Foreigners already living in Honduras are also subject to this decree. Foreign technicians can enter country if they already have a contract to work there and if employer shows lack of national technicians in that particular field; such foreign technician must teach and train at least three nationals, working for same employer, the secrets and skills of his profession.

Immigrants may lose their status as permanent residents if they leave country for 18 consecutive months or for 90 consecutive days during first two years of permanence in Honduras.

Employers may not have more than 10% of foreign employees or pay them more than 15% of total payroll. (Labor Code, Law 189 of May 19, 1959; Constitution art. 137).

See also topics Descent and Distribution; Immigration; Marriage; Real Property; Wills.

ALIMONY: See topic Divorce.

ASSIGNMENTS:

The assignment of a right of action is made by delivery of the instrument evidencing it with a signed statement fulfilling certain requisites. The debtor must be notified of the assignment. Bills of exchange and notes to order or bearer are subject to special provisions of Code of Commerce. (C. C. 716, 1666-1676; C. Com. 449-643). See topics Bills and Notes; Deeds; Public Instruments; Sales (Realty and Personalty).

ATTACHMENT:

To secure the result of an action one or more of the following measures may be requested if sufficient reasons are proved: (1) Sequestration of the object of the suit; (2) appointment of a supervisor; (3) attachment of specific property; (4) prohibition to do certain things. An attachment may be issued without bond in summary actions, which may be based on certain documents designated in the law, such as: (1) Public instruments; (2) private instruments judicially acknowledged; (3) commercial drafts not attacked as false, etc. Third persons may intervene, but if the intervention relates to real property it must be based on a written instrument. (C. C. P. 270-285, 447-508).

BANKRUPTCY AND INSOLVENCY:

(C. Com. 1318-1683; C. C. P. 524-654; C. C. 1440-1453).

Bankruptcy (quiebra) relates only to merchants. A merchant who fails to pay his current obligations is considered bankrupt and may be so declared on his own petition or that of any creditor or of the public prosecutor. He thereupon becomes incompetent to manage his affairs, and his debts mature and with certain exceptions cease to bear interest. Bankruptcies are of three kinds: Fortuitous, culpable and fraudulent. Culpable and fraudulent bankrupts are subject to imprisonment. The court appoints a receiver and presides over meetings of creditors called to discuss the approval of claims or offers of settlement. The debtor may at any time make offers of settlement; unless an agreement is reached the estate is liquidated.

Agreements may be made by a majority of the creditors present representing three-fifths of the liabilities. Fortuitous bankrupts are discharged on promising to pay, when able, their debts not extinguished by law; culpable bankrupts, when they have served their imprisonment, if they have paid their creditors, and in case payment was not made in full, then within three years after their imprisonment; fraudulent bankrupts only upon fully paying their debts and after three years have elapsed from their imprisonment.

Decree 13 of Mar. 22, 1982 am'd art. 111 of Banking Law and establishes that credits of bank which are registered at Central Bank have preference in payment over same type of unregistered credits in case of bankruptcy.

Suspension of payments may be requested by a merchant before bankruptcy, with a call for a meeting of creditors for the consideration of an agreement to prevent bankruptcy. Creditors' meetings and deliberations are subject to the same rules as applied in cases of bankruptcy.

Insolvency proceedings are voluntary when requested by the debtor, and necessary when demanded by a creditor or in cases where there are three or more overdue obligations or two or more executions pending against the debtor and he fails to make provision therefor or when such proceedings are demanded by a creditor or declared by the court in case the debtor has absconded. In consequence of the proceedings all the assets and liabilities are considered together, a provisional receiver is appointed by the court, a meeting of creditors is called and a definitive receiver is appointed. Unless an agreement is reached with the creditors the estate is liquidated.

See also topic Fraudulent Sales and Conveyances.

BILLS AND NOTES:

(C. Com. 449-643).

Instruments drawn in favor of a specific person are presumed drawn to order and are negotiable even though not drawn to order, unless the document or an endorsement contains the words "not to order" or "not negotiable."

Bills of exchange, if payable after sight, must be presented for acceptance within six months after date, but this period may be reduced by any person obligated or the drawer may amplify the period or forbid the presentation of the bill before a specific date. The presentation for acceptance of bills payable on a certain date or a specific period after date is optional, unless the drawer makes it obligatory. Endorsements must state: (1) endorsee, but endorsement may be in blank and name inserted by holder; (2) kind of endorsement, whether in ownership, for collection or as guaranty; lack of statement on this point establishes presumption that title passes; (3) place and date, but if not stated bill is presumed made at domicile of endorsee and on day he acquired the document, unless there is proof to contrary; (4) signature of endorser.

In case of failure to accept or pay there must be a notarial protest; if for failure to accept, within two days after presentation but before maturity; for failure to pay, within two days after maturity. After protest for failure to accept, it is unnecessary to present bill for payment or to protest for failure to pay. Protest in proper form authorizes a summary action at law.

Promissory notes are generally governed by the rules relating to bills of exchange, except that there is no acceptance, and the maker is generally regarded as acceptor.

Checks may be drawn only on a banking institution duly authorized by the Executive. They may be to order or to bearer. They must be presented within 15 days if payable in the locality where drawn, within one month if drawn elsewhere in the national territory, within three months if drawn abroad, or if drawn in Honduras and payable abroad and if foreign law does not designate a different period; but although a check is not presented or protested in time, the drawee must pay it if there are sufficient funds. The death of the drawer does not excuse the drawee from paying, but notice of drawer's bankruptcy or suspension of payments requires drawee to refuse payment. A holder may not reject a partial payment. A check presented in due time and not paid must be protested within two days. Crossed checks are allowed and checks may be issued solely for credit to account.

CHATTEL MORTGAGES:

Chattel mortgages are permitted for various commercial transactions as well as mortgages on mercantile establishments, vessels and aircraft. Such mortgages must be recorded in the proper registries. Lien contracts for industrial and agricultural purposes

See Topical Index in front part of this volume.

CHATTEL MORTGAGES . . . *continued*
must be recorded both in the Commercial and Real Property Registries. (C. Com. 916-928, 1313-1317; Civil Aeronautics Law 146 of Sept. 3, 1957, as am'd). See topics Pledges; Sales (Realty and Personalty).

COLLATERAL SECURITY: See topics Pledges; Sales (Realty and Personalty).

COMMERCIAL REGISTER: See topic Records.

CONSTITUTION AND GOVERNMENT:

(Decree 131 of National Constitutional Assembly of Jan. 11, 1982 as am'd). Honduras is centralized republic. Legislative power is vested in Congress; it consists of one Chamber, whose members are elected for four years. Members of Congress are elected on basis of population. President is also elected for four years, no reelection allowed. For administration purposes, country is divided into departments, which are divided into towns administered by municipal councils.

CONTRACTS:

Obligations derived from contracts have force of law between parties and must be fulfilled according to terms of agreement.

Civil contracts involving over 200 lempiras must be in writing. Under Arts. 1573 to 1575, following require a public instrument: (a) contracts for creation, transfer, modification or extinction of rights in rem, (b) leases of real property for more than three years, (c) prenuptial agreements.

Commercial contracts are governed by Comm. Code and supplementarily by Civil Code. Special Commercial contracts are: agency; brokerage; certain deposits; trusts; transportation; insurance; commercial surety; copyrights and others.

CONVEYANCES:

See topics Deeds, Notaries Public, Public Instruments.

COPYRIGHT:

(D. 141-93 of Aug. 30, 1993).

Law grants moral and property rights to author, his successors or assignees regarding literary and artistic works. Copyrights include all kinds of intellectual (including software) literary and artistic creations reproduced by any means. Law also protects translations, adaptations, arrangements and other transformation of intellectual works. Phonogram producers and performers' rights are also protected. "Moral rights" are unassignable, nontransferable and unlimited in time of enjoyment, including right to make work known publicly, use of name or pen name, assert paternity of works, oppose plagiarism, or deformation, mutilation, change or abridgment of work or title. Violation of moral rights gives action for damages. "Property rights" for enjoyment of pecuniary benefits from use of his work, including reproduction, performance and broadcasting, with some exceptions. These rights assignable by inter vivos acts or transferred upon death, or law disposition. Protection is for life of author plus 50 years after his death or last surviving co-author; if author appears to be collective entity or company or in case of audiovisual works protection lasts 50 years from first publication. Photographic works and applied art rights last 25 years from time taken or done. Copyright already registered in foreign country may be registered in Honduras only for time during which original copyright is still to run. Fine and imprisonment may be imposed on violators.

Honduras signed the Inter-American Convention on Copyright and Literary Property in Washington, June 22, 1946. Ratification was promulgated by Resolution 1561 of Jan. 15, 1947. Convention for protection of phonogram producers against nonauthorized reproduction signed in Geneva on Oct. 29, 1971 was approved by Decree 144-89 of Sept. 21, 1989.

CORPORATIONS:

(Constitution art. 334; C. Com. 13-37, 90-354).

A corporation may be formed by notarial instrument or by public subscription. The articles of incorporation must state: (1) place and date; (2) name, nationality and domicile of founders; (3) kind of company; (4) object; (5) name, which must refer to principal activity of company and be followed by words "Sociedad Anónima" or abbreviation "S. A."; if an individual permits his name to appear in the corporate name, he becomes subject to corporate liabilities; (6) duration or statement that it is indefinite; (7) capital, or minimum capital if amount is variable; (8) contribution of each member or value of assets contributed if not in money; (9) domicile; (10) form of administration and powers of administrators; (11) appointment of administrators; (12) manner of distributing profits and losses; (13) reserves; (14) reasons for dissolution; (15) rules for liquidation; (16) manner of electing liquidators; (17) capital paid in, and capital authorized and subscribed; (18) number, face value and nature of shares; (19) manner of paying unpaid portion of shares. If the corporation is formed by public subscription, the authorization of the Ministry of Financing must be obtained.

A company must have at least five founders, each subscribing at least one share. The capital must be at least 25,000 lempiras fully subscribed; at least 25% of the value of each share payable in money must be paid in and the full value of each share payable in property other than money. At least 25,000 lempiras must be initially paid in.

The instrument of organization must be recorded in the Public Registry of Commerce. For this purpose, a petition is made to the civil judge who submits the matter to the government attorney and after a hearing gives his decision.

Capital is represented by shares of a face value of ten lempiras or multiples thereof. Shares may not be issued for less than face value; until fully paid up, they must be registered shares, when paid up they may be exchanged for bearer shares. Shareholders are liable only for unpaid price of shares. Corporations may not acquire their own shares except by judicial order in payment of company credits, nor may they make loans on their shares. There may be special classes of shares. Shareholders have preferential right to subscribe for issues of additional shares. If there are shares with limited voting rights they are entitled to a 7% dividend before a dividend is paid on common shares. There may be founders' participations giving merely the right to a part of the profits for a specified time. New share issues cannot be made until all previous issues are paid in.

Bond issues may be registered, to order or to bearer, in denominations of ten lempiras or multiples thereof. They may be redeemed by lot or above par only if the interest is over 5%. Their amount may not exceed the net assets of the corporation, except for acquisition of property, in which case the limit may be exceeded up to three-fourths the value of such property. Bondholders may designate a common representative, individual or a bank. Meetings of bondholders are subject to rules similar to those governing meetings of shareholders.

Shareholders' meetings must be held at least once a year. Shareholders representing at least 25% of the capital may demand the calling of special meetings. In regular meetings one-half the shares with right to vote must be represented and a majority rules; in special meetings at least three-fourths of the shares must be represented and a majority of one-half the shares rules; but if a second call is necessary, any number of shareholders attending suffices for a quorum.

Administration may be by an administrator or by directors, who need not be shareholders. Their office may not be discharged by proxy and they must give a bond designated in the articles of incorporation. One-half the number of directors form a quorum and resolutions are adopted by vote of a majority of those present. If there are more than three directors, a minority of 25% of the capital may elect one-third of the directors. The shareholders also elect one or more supervisors (comisarios) to supervise the operations of the company.

Foreign corporations in order to do business, must (1) prove that they are legally constituted according to the laws of their country, (2) prove that according to such laws and their by-laws they have the right to establish branches and that the pertinent resolution was validly adopted, (3) keep a permanent representative in Honduras, (4) assign a fund for their activities in Honduras, which may be reduced only with the authorization of the Department of Finance, (5) show that their objects are legal, and (6) agree to submit to the courts and laws of Honduras. A petition must be made to the Department of Finance which may authorize the foreign company to do business in Honduras if the Department considers such action advisable in the general interest. In this case it designates the term within which the company must begin operations in Honduras.

Companies of variable capital are companies whose capital may be increased by later contributions of the shareholders or the entry of new shareholders or decreased by the withdrawal of contributions. Their name must be followed by the words "de capital variable" or the abbreviation "de C. V." They must have a minimum capital and their shares must always be registered shares.

Fees.—All companies formed under the Code of Commerce pay an incorporation tax of 2/10 of 1% of the authorized capital and the same for every increase of capital and extension of the period of the company. There are also moderate fees for recording in Mercantile Registry, and native corporations require stamped paper and stamps, depending on their capitalization, for their corporate instruments.

COURTS:

Justice is administered by: (1) A Supreme Court which hears appeals from the courts of appeals, exercises general supervision over the judiciary and has jurisdiction in certain other matters; (2) courts of appeals which hear appeals from judges of letters; (3) judges of letters having original jurisdiction in most civil, family and criminal matters; (4) justices of peace. (Law of Organization and Powers of Courts, of 1906 as am'd, Decree 71-87 of June 22, 1987). There are Labor Courts of Appeals at Tegucigalpa and S. Pedro Sula.

CURRENCY:

(Monetary Law 51 of Feb. 21, 1950, as am'd).

Monetary unit is the lempira which is divided in 100 cents. Obligations in foreign money payable in Honduras are dischargeable by delivering the equivalent amount of lempiras, but obligations in foreign exchange incurred through financial system and stock market and international transactions are excepted. Only Banco Central is authorized to issue bank notes which have value as legal tender.

CURTESY:

No estate by curtesy.

DEATH:

Where there is no knowledge of a person's whereabouts he is deemed a mere absentee. Five years after disappearance if absentee is 60 years old by end of five year period, two years if disappearance occurs when taking part in act of war, and one year if disappearance arises under circumstances indicating danger of death, absentee may be declared presumptively dead. Date of presumptive death is last day of second year from date of disappearance. (C. C. 83-89).

A record of deaths is kept by the Civil Register of each district. Death certificates may be obtained from the Chief of the Civil Registry. Nominal fees are fixed by local regulations.

Actions for Death.—There is no statute recognizing the action for wrongful death. However, this action could be supported by the general provisions on torts contained in Civil Code (arts. 2236 et seq.) under which any act or omission causing damages to a person by fault or negligence of another gives right to compensation.

DECEDENTS' ESTATES:

See topics Descent and Distribution; Executors and Administrators; Husband and Wife; Wills.

DEEDS:

Deeds must be executed as public instruments before a notary public. They must contain a statement as to encumbrances on the property. They are subject to stamp and

DEEDS . . . *continued*
transfer taxes depending on the actual consideration. See topics Notaries Public; Public Instruments. See also topic Taxation.

DESCENT AND DISTRIBUTION:

(C. Family 336, C. C. 958-978).

In the case of intestacy the property passes to the following in the order named, the amount of the several shares varying according to which ones of the relatives mentioned under the several numbers survive the decedent: (1) Descendants; (2) ascendants and spouse; (3) brothers and sisters and spouse; (4) collaterals to sixth degree; (5) municipality. Honduran heir of alien has same rights in alien's estate as he would have according to Honduran law in estate of citizen of Honduras. See also topic Husband and Wife.

DESERTION: See topic Divorce.

DIVORCE:

(C. Family 232-356; C. C. P. 743-752).

A divorce causes the dissolution of the marriage bond. The following are grounds for divorce: (1) Adultery of spouse; (2) attempt of either spouse against life of other or their children; (3) serious and frequent cruelty by one spouse against other or against children; (4) refusal of one spouse to support other and children; (5) habitual use of narcotics; (6) separation in fact for two years; (7) attempt to corrupt other spouse or their children; (8) abandonment by one of spouses for over two years.

The Code does not prescribe any particular length of residence in order to bring action for divorce; but bona fide domicile in Honduras is a prerequisite.

The court may make the necessary provisional orders, including orders for alimony. In the final judgment the children are awarded to the innocent party. Innocent wife is entitled to alimony.

A divorce by mutual consent may be agreed upon if the parties are of age and two years have elapsed from the date of marriage. For such purpose they must personally appear before the judge, who attempts to reconcile them and if not successful summons them for another appearance in 60 days, at which time the matter is finally decided.

A separation in fact of spouses without dissolution of marriage may be decreed after one year of marriage by mutual consent or by request of either party.

DOWER:

No dower right.

EXCHANGE CONTROL:

(Decree 53 of Feb. 3, 1950 as am'd; Decree 16-92 of Feb. 24, 1992).

All negotiations of foreign exchange must be made through Banco Central de Honduras or for its account. Private parties may maintain assets in foreign exchange. Central Bank may regulate acquisition and negotiation of foreign exchange. There are two foreign exchange markets: inter-bank, used for foreign trade, income remittances and capital repatriation, exchange rate is determined by supply and demand; and free market for any transaction. Remittances of dividends and profits, royalties, interest and principal of loans or repatriation of capital are free.

See also topic Foreign Trade Regulations.

EXECUTORS AND ADMINISTRATORS:

(C. C. 1169-1295; C. C. P. 1019-1045).

The heirs or other legal representatives are the executors and administrators of an estate, and the appointment of an executor is expressly prohibited. If the heirs cannot agree they may appoint an administrator and if there is no accord he is appointed by the judge.

An inheritance may be accepted with or without benefit of inventory. If accepted with benefit of inventory the effect is to make the heir liable only up to the amount shown by the inventory. If accepted freely he is liable generally for the debts of the decedent, in the proportion of his participation in the estate. The creditors may have the right to intervene in the making of the inventory and the heirs may abandon the estate to the creditors.

EXEMPTIONS:

The following are not subject to attachment: (1) Minimum wage; (2) bed and necessary clothing of the debtor and his children; (3) professional books up to 200 lempiras in value; (4) machinery and instruments used for teaching a science or art, up to 200 lempiras in value; (5) uniforms and equipment of soldiers; (6) utensils of a debtor who is an artisan or farmer; (7) food and combustibles for the debtor and his family for one month; (8) purely personal rights such as that of habitation; (9) municipal buildings and school houses; (10) railroads and their equipment. Workmen's minimum salary, vacation salary and first 100 lempiras of salary and 75% of excess are also exempt. (C. C. 1444; C. C. P. 462; Const. 1982).

FIDUCIARIES: See topic Trusts.

FOREIGN CORPORATIONS: See topic Corporations.

FOREIGN EXCHANGE:

See topics Exchange Control and Currency.

FOREIGN INVESTMENTS:

(Constitution, art. 336; Decree 80-92 of May 29, 1992 regulated by Accord 345-92 of Sept. 10, 1992).

Law promotes national and foreign investment and joint ventures. All investments must be registered at Secretaría de Economía y Comercio which issues "Certificado de Inversión" which grants investors right to enjoy all guaranties of investments' law. Law guarantees, among others, availability of foreign currency and authorization to open bank accounts in foreign currency, nondiscrimination rights, access to local financing, freedom of production and commercialization of goods and services, no limitations on ownership of property, registration, use and exploitation of trademarks, patents and other industrial property rights. Trademarks will be cancelled if they are not used within 18 months from registration date. All investments are subject to tax system in force and must comply with labor and social security laws. Investments in health, national security, and environment preservation areas require prior authorization of Secretaría de Economía y Comercio. See also topic Immigration.

FOREIGN TRADE REGULATIONS:

(Decree 97 of Dec. 31, 1970; Decree 151-87 of Oct. 2, 1987; Decrees 212-87 and 213-87 of Dec. 14, 1987 as am'd; and Decree 108-90 of Sept. 26, 1990 as am'd regulated by Accord 1866 of Oct. 22, 1990 as am'd; Accord 136-92 of Mar. 16, 1992).

Imports must be registered at Central Bank. Request to open sight letters of credit for import payment requires up to 100% guarantee deposit. Importers are subject to ad valorem import duties, unless expressly exempted therefrom.

Export requires export declaration filed at Central Bank. Foreign exchange proceeds must be surrendered to Central Bank.

Physical or juridical persons dedicated to commerce, intending to import or export goods must register and obtain identification card.

FRAUDS, STATUTE OF:

See topic Public Instruments.

FRAUDULENT SALES AND CONVEYANCES:

Acts of a debtor in fraud of creditors before the declaration of bankruptcy are void if the third party knew of the fraud, and in any case if there was no valuable consideration. Fraud is presumed if the debtor after the date as of which the bankruptcy is declared to have existed alienates property for less than its value or pays unmatured debts, or if after such date and in the absence of good faith of the third party he pays matured debts in a manner not customary or imposes guaranty liens on his property. (C. Com. 1463-1468).

HOLIDAYS:

Jan. 1 (New Year's); Holy Week*; Apr. 14 (Panamerican Day); May 1 (Labor Day); Sept. 15 (Independence Day); Oct. 3 (Morazán); Oct. 12 (Columbus Day); Oct. 21 (Armed Forces Day); Dec. 25 (Christmas).

* These are movable holidays.

HOMESTEADS:

(C. Family 82-98).

Homestead exempt from attachment and execution may comprise dwelling house, cultivated property, and industrial and commercial establishments. Maximum value of homestead exemption is 100,000 lempiras.

HUSBAND AND WIFE:

(C. Family 41-44, 64-81).

Husband and wife must live together; these provisions do not apply when their observance might cause serious injury to either spouse or their children. Spouses may before marriage, make agreements by notarial instrument as to their property and may modify such agreements. If there is no agreement, each spouse is owner of and may dispose of any property such spouse owned at time of marriage or acquired during marriage. Property possessed by spouses on dissolution of marriage is presumed common property and is equally distributed among them, unless there is proof that it was brought to marriage or acquired by one of spouses.

Spouses must mutually assist each other. They may contract with each other and the wife requires no authorization of her husband or of the judge, to contract or appear in court. They must support their children in proportion to their respective property. A surviving spouse who is in need is entitled to one-fourth, called the marital fourth, in the estate of the deceased spouse. This right cannot be claimed by a spouse who has abandoned the other or who was the guilty party in a separation suit.

IMMIGRATION:

(National Constitution arts. 30 to 35; Civil Code; Leg. Dec. 34 of Oct. 1, 1970; Accord 8 of Aug. 19, 1988; Leg. Dec. 93-91 of July 30, 1991 and its regulations of July 28, 1993).

Tourists are allowed to stay up to 90 days. Foreigners entering country as technicians must apply for a permit from Ministry of Foreign Affairs. Those who wish to work in Honduras must obtain an identification card issued for this purpose by Ministry of Labor (this is not necessary for employers). Special visas are granted to foreign investors and foreign merchants. Status of "residentes pensionados" and "residentes rentistas" is granted to individuals with income from foreign sources. They are exempted from payment of income tax, and are allowed to import duty free motor vehicle every five years; duty free importation of personal effects is granted once. They must spend at least four months per year in Honduras.

Under Dec. 39 of Oct. 15, 1965, small industry and trade are reserved to Honduras citizens.

INFANCY:

(C. Family 16, 17, 99-101, 185-198).

The age of majority is 21. Contracts by males under 14 and females under 12 are void and, if over those ages, voidable except some by emancipated minors. Infants are subject to parental authority. Parental authority includes custody, legal representation and administration and enjoyment of usufruct of minor's real and personal property, with certain exceptions. In absence of parents guardian is appointed. Parents and guardians have restricted powers of disposition.

See Topical Index in front part of this volume.

INSOLVENCY: See topic Bankruptcy and Insolvency.

INTEREST:

The legal rate for civil transactions is 6%. (C. C. 1367). Legal interest in mercantile transactions is determined by the Department of Finance. Compound interest is allowed among merchants. (C. Com. 707, 710).

INTESTACY: See topic Descent and Distribution.

JUDGMENTS:

(C. C. P. 223-241).

Judgments do not constitute a lien except upon property on which execution has been levied and after registration in public registry.

Foreign judgments have the effect provided by treaty; if there is no treaty they have the same effect as is given to Honduran judgments in the foreign country; if the foreign country does not execute Honduran judgments, the foreign judgment cannot be executed in Honduras. If none of these rules apply, the foreign judgment will be executed in Honduras provided: (1) It was rendered in a personal action; (2) it was not obtained by default; (3) the obligation on which it is based is legal in Honduras; (4) the certified copy of the judgment contains the requisites necessary in the foreign country so that it may be considered authentic, and those required in Honduras for its authenticity.

LABOR RELATIONS:

Rights of employees and laborers are regulated by Constitution of 1982 (arts. 127-144); Labor Code (Decree 189 of May 19, 1959 as am'd, Decree 112 of Oct. 29, 1982, Decree 135-94 of Oct. 12, 1994 and Accord 02-95 of Feb. 6, 1995). Labor regulations are public law and are binding on all employers and employees. Any acts or stipulations which imply renunciation, diminution, or distortion of rights conferred on workers by Constitution, Labor Code, social or welfare laws, are null and void ipso jure even if they are included in labor contract or in any other agreement. Labor contracts may be made between employer or association of employers and workman or union or federation of unions. Employers are prohibited from employing less than 90% of Honduran workers or paying less than 85% of total wages to Hondurans, in their respective enterprises. Both percentages may be changed in certain cases.

Regular working day has as many hours as is whatever is agreed upon by parties, or in default of agreement, legal maximum. Regular working hours for day's work may not exceed eight hours a day or 44 hours a week, equivalent to 48 hours of wages. Regular working hours for night work may not exceed six hours a day or 36 hours a week. Maximum duration of mixed day of work is seven hours per day or 42 hours a week. There are certain exceptions. Amount of wages may be stipulated freely but may not be lower than legal minimum. Wages must be paid in legal tender. Minimum wage is fixed periodically by Government. Fixing of minimum wage automatically modifies all labor contracts that stipulate lower amount, by raising this to minimum without affecting any other stipulations. Minimum wage cannot be attached. Worker may share in earnings or profits of his employer but never assume his risks or losses. Worker is entitled to: (1) One day of rest, preferably Sun., for every six days of work; (2) to receive pay on holidays or national days fixed by law; (3) to annual paid vacation; and (4) permanent workers to receive two months' pay in June and in Dec. Length and time of vacation is governed by labor law. Minors under 16 are prohibited from working. Minors under 17 are prohibited from performing night work or overtime. Working hours for them may not exceed six hours a day or 30 hours a week. Every pregnant woman worker is entitled to compulsory leave, to be paid at same rate as work, for period preceding childbirth and she retains her employment and all rights under labor contract.

LEGISLATURE:

See topic Constitution and Government.

LIENS:

(C. C. 2244-2262; C. Com. 704, 1520-1532).

Certain credits have preference over others with respect to specific property.

As regards specific personal property the following are preferred: (a) Credits for construction, repair and purchase price; (b) pledge credits; (c) credits for transportation, on object transported until thirty days after delivery; (d) credits for lodging, on the property of the debtor in the inn; (e) farming credits, on the crops; (f) rent, on the crops of the estate and on the debtor's property thereon. If the personal property has been taken away the creditor may within thirty days claim it from the person in whose possession it is.

With respect to specific real property the following are preferred: (a) State taxes for one year; (b) insurance premiums for two years; (c) mortgages and farming credits duly recorded; (d) judicial attachments duly recorded; (e) unrecorded farming credits.

In general the preferences on property are: (a) Municipal taxes for one year; (b) credits for judicial expenses, funeral expenses, expenses of last illness during one year, salaries and wages during one year, advances for maintenance for one year; (c) credits appearing in public instruments and in judgments.

In bankruptcies there are a few variations of these rules.

LIMITATION OF ACTIONS: See topic Prescription.

LIMITED PARTNERSHIP: See topic Partnership.

MARRIAGE:

(C. Family 11-63).

Only civil marriages are recognized and persons performing a religious marriage without the previous performance of a civil marriage are liable to punishment. The civil ceremony is performed by the mayor or by notary public after publication of notice.

The following cannot marry: (a) Males below 18 and females below 16 years of age; (b) persons of unsound mind; (c) impotent persons; (d) minors who have not obtained consent of their parents or guardians; (e) widow or divorced woman within 300 days after termination of previous marriage unless child is born before. Marriages between following are prohibited: (a) Ascendants and descendants; (b) brothers and sisters; (c) collaterals by consanguinity to fourth degree; (d) convicted adulterers; (e) convicted principals or accessories of death of spouse of either contracting party; (f) guardians and wards. Judge may grant dispensations in number of foregoing cases.

Marriages validly performed in a foreign country are valid in Honduras. Aliens wishing to marry in Honduras must give evidence that they are not married and that under their national law they are not incapacitated for marrying.

No action lies for breach of promise of marriage.

Code regulates common-law marriages.

MARRIED WOMEN:

See topics Husband and Wife; Marriage.

MINES AND MINERALS:

Mining Code, Decree 143 of Dec. 26, 1968 as am'd by Decree 1968-87 of Oct. 27, 1987 and Decree 37-89 of Apr. 5, 1989; and Regulations by Res. 159 of Aug. 30, 1971; Decree 56-91 of May 22, 1991. State is owner of all mines and exercises direct control over them; however, State may grant permits for exploration and/or exploitation according to terms of Code.

Mines constitute real property distinct from that of soil.

Quarries are considered part of soil where located; however, their exploitation by public interest must also be governed by provisions of Code.

Mineral substances, except hydrocarbons and their derivates, which are governed by their special law, are divided for purposes of law into quarries and mines. "Quarries" are defined as those deposits of natural rocks to be used in construction and ornamentation of buildings; and ceramics' industry, granites, basalt, sand, marble, plaster and the like. Natural deposits of fertilizers for soils are also considered quarries, except sulphur phosphate, nitrate and salts of similar nature. All deposits of mineral substances, different from quarries, including precious stones and gems, are considered "mines."

State reserves right to determine specific regulations for exploitation, transportation and sale of special mineral substances when it deems it in national interest.

Code contemplates three phases for profitable use of mineral resources: prospecting (cateo), exploration, and exploitation. Prospecting consists of a general examination of soil, and its object is to discover evidence of mineral substances. Exploration comprises whole amount of superficial and underground work, necessary to establish continuity and strong evidence of mineral substances in order to decide whether or not there exists an important mineral deposit. Finally, exploitation comprises all operations destined for extraction and preparation of mineral substances to be able to obtain industrial and commercial benefits.

Prospecting is free all over territory of Republic, except in lands covered by a valid permit of exploration, or by a valid concession of exploitation, or in zones prohibited or reserved by State for public welfare. In all cases, exploration and exploitation cannot be made without a previous permit or concession.

Any natural or juridical person, national or foreigner, complying with requisites of Honduran laws may obtain permits mentioned above provided there is previous fulfillment of dispositions and provisions established by present Code.

Natural or juridical persons, either national or foreign, in order to have exploration permits and concessions of exploitation must be previously registered in public registries of mines and of commerce. Foreign corporations must be authorized for exercise of commerce and register and have domicile in capital, Tegucigalpa. However, if corporation is interested in concession related to mines in national reserve zones, obtainable only in public bidding, it may file its bid and, if successful, it must register and get necessary authorization to exercise commerce within 120 days. (Dec. 457 of May 11, 1977).

Following persons cannot obtain permits: (1) Foreign governments, corporations or companies that directly or indirectly are connected with them, and foreigners employed by foreign governments; (2) those that owe some duty to State derived from payments or services from mining rights or related to such, unless they give bond, surety, pledge, mortgage or encumbrances in amounts sufficient to guarantee State's rights; (3) public officers that directly pass resolutions regarding mining affairs.

Exploration.—General permit of exploration confers to owner within limits of his perimeter and at any depth therein, exclusive right to prospect for and explore all mineral substances with deposits that are considered "mines," except limitations by rights acquired by third persons or by declaration that said zones are prohibited or reserved.

Exploration permits give following rights: (1) To extend permit, if permittee proves he has complied with all obligations during such period; (2) to obtain one or several concessions of exploitation for one or more mineral substances if so found in area; and (3) to freely dispose for purposes of complementary investigation of all minerals obtained during exploration works in amounts that shall be determined by mining authorities by means of a previous declaration.

Exploration permit cannot be divided into smaller ones; and it cannot have encumbrances of any kind. It can be assigned or sold only in its totality with previous authorization of "General Direction of Mines and Hydrocarbons." Assignees must assume all assignor's obligations.

Exploration permit shall be granted to natural or juridical person if application is presented to "General Direction of Mines and Hydrocarbons." After application is received, petitioner shall have six months to prepare for mining authorities a program in which he indicates technical and financial means that he proposes to use and annual minimum investments he intends to make.

Once program is accepted, exploration permit shall be issued through a contract concluded between Secretary of Natural Resources and petitioner.

Exploration permit can cover an area between a minimum of 400 hectares and a maximum of 50,000 hectares according to petitioner's technical and financial means.

MINES AND MINERALS . . . *continued*

Exploration permittees cannot have permits that together exceed 200,000 hectares. Exploration permit shall be granted for no less than two years nor more than four years according to mining authorities' decision. Such permit may be extended one or more times provided its total duration including extensions, does not exceed six years.

Application for exploration permit must express: (1) Name, nationality and domicile of petitioner or his agent. In case of a company, it must include: type of company, its name, domicile and nationality of legal representative or agent; (2) place and date; (3) perimeter and measurements of area requested; (4) name of area and number of years during which exploration shall take place. Map of national territory where area is located must also accompany application.

Exploitation concession comprises only one mining lot of a minimum extension of 100 hectares up to 400 hectares. Exploitation concession constitutes real property which can be mortgaged during its term.

No natural or juridical person can exploit nor be owner of exploitation mining lots that together exceed 20,000 hectares; although Code provides certain exceptions.

Exploitation concession can be divided or grouped together with others of same kind; it can also be assigned, leased or encumbered, with previous governmental authorization. Concession shall be granted for 40 years which can be extended 20 years more. Extension can be requested after one half of original period has elapsed or at least three years before expiration of total term.

In each particular concession certain general bases can be set forth that, without conflicting with provisions of Code, can contemplate: (1) Special conditions for exploitation; (2) conditions regarding use of exchange (divisas) and transfer of capital; (3) conditions to satisfy necessities of country, for natural or manufactured products; (4) conditions to satisfy hydraulic resources, electricity and general utilities; (5) any other clause that parties estimate convenient, such as scholarships for specialization and practice of students.

Application to obtain an exploitation concession must be presented to Secretary of Natural Resources through "General Direction of Mines and Hydrocarbons." Such application must contain: (1) Name of petitioner; (2) name and location of mining lot indicating its municipal and departmental jurisdiction; (3) surface of lot; (4) mineral substances to exploit; (5) description of measurements of lot; (6) description of perimeter and description of neighboring lots; (7) owner of lands where requested lot is located; and (8) name of legal agent of petitioner. Application must also be accompanied by maps, technical analysis, estimation of mineral reserves, etc. Within three days "General Direction of Mines and Hydrocarbons" shall accept or reject application, and if accepted political governmental department pertaining to lot shall also receive copy of same, so in a period no longer than 30 days latter must inform about accuracy of petition's contents.

Summary of application must be published in official gazette ("La Gaceta") and in any other newspaper of respective department, three times within a period of ten days. Cost of publication shall be borne by petitioner.

Code also contains requirements to measure mining lots. (Provisions too technical and detailed to be summarized here.)

Once all requisites are complied with, Secretary of Natural Resources must finally rule on said petition. If verdict is affirmative, such concession shall be registered.

Exploration or exploitation concessions in national reserve zones may be acquired by public bidding only. General basis thereof will be fixed by executive resolution, including price for obtaining information, amount of bond required and minimum royalty to be paid. This resolution must be published in local newspapers and Official Gazette as well as in Europe and U.S. specialized publications, inviting bids to be submitted in 90 days. Concessionaire cannot transfer his rights or enter into subcontracts except after five years and after exploration, as promised, is completed. However, two or more companies may file joint bids. (Dec. 457 of May 11, 1977).

Public Registry of Mines is a division of "General Direction of Mines and Hydrocarbons." All concessions must be registered as well as encumbrances, acts and contracts related to them. Following data must be recorded: (1) Incorporation, modification and dissolution of mining enterprises; (2) natural persons in order to be able to receive exploration permits or exploitation concessions; (3) acts, contracts, etc. in connection with mining industry; (4) contracts concluded with public entities regarding prohibited or national reserve zones; (5) contracts whose specific object is exploitation of mines; (6) easements and expropriations; (7) any other act expressly connected with Code or Regulations.

Recording of documents is obligatory and any person can examine its books and request certified copies of records.

Following books shall be available: (1) Mining concessions; (2) expropriations and easements and (3) mining enterprises, private miners and contracts.

General Provisions.—Permissioners and concessioners have to comply strictly with following obligations: (1) To prepare security regulations that must be known by all employees and must also be approved by "General Direction of Mines and Hydrocarbons;" (2) to provide to workers total medical assistance absolutely free up to first six months of illness; one doctor and one surgeon both of Honduranian nationality, must be on location, for each 200 workers or fraction of not less than 50; (3) to have security personnel to guaranty development of normal activities; (4) to establish and to support grammar school for benefits of workers' children provided its number is over 20 minors. Teachers and students shall be governed by same laws as regular public schools; and (5) any other regulations established by Labor Code, Sanitary Code and laws of country.

"General Direction of Mines and Hydrocarbons" shall dictate security regulations necessary for transportation, storage and use of explosives required by permittees and concessioner.

Permittees and concessioners must keep up to date following data: (1) Map with all technical, topographic, geologic and geophysical information related to mine; (2) map describing superficial works; (3) map describing underground works and its corresponding superficial area; (4) diary of works performed, specially including accidents and injuries if any; (5) registry of employees and workers and (6) in case of concessions registry of production, sale, storage and exportation of mineral substances removed.

Special mineral substances are following: (1) Gold, platinum and silver; (2) precious stones and gems; (3) radioactive substances and those used in generation of atomic energy; and (4) substances that due to necessities of economic development or temporary strategic interests are so declared by Decree of Executive Power. Said special mineral substances shall be governed by specific regulations.

Quarries.—Exploration of same in federal property is free, but its exploitation as well as in case of private quarries is subject to special permit.

Provisions of Code regarding quarries are very similar to those applicable to mines; therefore are not summarized here.

Taxation of Mines and Quarries.—All natural and juridical persons must pay a tax applicable to all exploration permits.

Following taxes are created for exploitation concessions, payable by natural or juridical persons: (1) Fixed tax for concession and its extension if any; (2) surface tax; and (3) production tax.

I. Owners of special exploitation permit of quarry located in federal property shall pay a tax which rate shall be 10% or 5% according to classification made by Executive Power taking into account cost of exploitation, value of quarry and any other pertinent factor.

(a) To obtain exploration permit rates are: Up to 400 hectares, Lempiras 200; from 400 to 10,000 hectares, Lempiras 1,000; from 10,000 to 50,000 hectares, Lempiras 4,000.

For extensions, rates are: Up to 400 hectares, Lempiras 400; from 400 to 10,000 hectares, Lempiras 2,000; from 10,000 to 50,000 hectares, Lempiras 8,000.

(b) To obtain exploitation concession, rates are: Up to 100 hectares, Lempiras 400; from 100 to 400 hectares, Lempiras 1,000.

For extensions rates are: Up to 100 hectares, Lempiras 800; from 100 to 400 hectares, Lempiras 2,000.

II. Surface tax shall only apply to exploitation concessioners, which must pay annually following percentage for each mining lot: First and second year, L. 1 per ha.; third and fourth year, L. 2 per ha.; fifth and sixth year, L. 3 per ha.; seventh and eighth year, L. 4 per ha.; ninth and tenth year, L. 4.50 per ha.; from tenth year on L. 5 per ha.

III. Production taxes are paid quarterly on percentage basis according to annual sales. New mines are exempted from production tax up to five years from date of initial exploitation. In case of corporations total amount of income tax, production tax and export tax to be paid should not exceed 55% of net income, for any amount in excess concessioners get credit of tax applicable to production tax to be paid. Credit of tax applicable to production tax is also granted when corporation operates with losses.

Deduction from income tax of 15% off net annual taxable income reinvested on fixed assets for mining purpose for ten year period from date of concession.

See topic Taxation, subhead Income Tax.

Sanctions.—Fine from 5,000 Lempiras to 10,000 Lempiras, aside from civil and criminal actions, shall be applicable to following infractors: (1) Exploitation concessioners of mines and quarries that do not comply with security regulations established by decree; (2) to one who destroys or removes fortification installations of mines; (3) illicit removal of mineral substances as well as exploration and exploitation works undertaken without permit; (4) falsification of concession documents; and (5) to concessioner who pollutes with poisoning substances rivers, or lakes, if such substances can seriously injure third parties.

Code also includes sanctions for minor infractions which in no case shall exceed 5,000 Lempiras.

Finally, rights and duties acquired or contracted before enactment of present Code shall continue in force under provisions of new one.

Petroleum.—(Decree 194 of Oct. 31, 1984 and its regulations, Accord 1276 of June 24, 1985).

State is owner of all petroleum, hydrocarbon and gas deposits within its territory, its exclusive economic zone and continental shelf. Investigation, exploration, exploitation, refining, storage, transportation and commercialization of oil are regarded of public interest. Expropriation of property may be conducted for development of industry. State may carry out this activity by itself or may enter into operation contracts with national or foreign individuals or companies through public bidding or private contracting. In order to execute operation contracts companies must be registered in Registry of Commerce. Foreign companies must additionally designate agent. In its performance of obligations under operation contracts contractor may subcontract some operations keeping control and overall responsibility. Law establishes causes for termination of contracts. All activities and controversies are subject to local law and jurisdiction. Contracting parties must post guaranty to guarantee performance of operation contracts. In most instances at termination of operation contract all equipment and installations must be turned over to State. Investigation permits are granted for up to 18 months. Operation contracts for exploration or exploitation are limited to maximum of 100,000 hectares onshore and 200,000 hectares offshore. Exploration may last four years renewable for two more years. If oil is found contractor company can enter into 20-year exploitation contract renewable for five more years. If commercial exploitation is made State will compensate contractor with crude of up to 85% of net production at price calculated in accordance with art. 56 of Law, until investment and costs incurred during exploration phase are recovered. After total amortization of investment above percentage will be up to 50% of net production. State may request contractor to sell up to 50% of production received by contractor as compensation in order to satisfy local demand.

Operation contracts may be assigned. Operation contracts may be cancelled under conditions indicated by law. Such cancellation results in immediate reversion of area of contract to State and loss of installations and equipment. Guaranty is then enforced. Failure to perform may result in fines.

Taxes.—Exploitation is subject to annual surface rights of ten lempiras per hectare and if contract is renewed 20 lempiras. All activity is subject to income tax and to other general taxes depending on case.

MONOPOLIES AND RESTRAINT OF TRADE:

Art. 339 of Honduran Constitution, forbids monopolies in favor of private, natural or juridical persons.

MONOPOLIES AND RESTRAINT OF TRADE . . . *continued*

Art. 423 of Commercial Code sanctions agreements which restrict commercial activities of a businessman with respect to one place or region and a given type of commerce so long as duration of such agreements does not exceed ten years.

Consumer Protection Law.—(D.L. 41-89 of Apr. 19, 1989 as am'd). Law deals with: Consumers right to be informed; general representation and warranties; credit operations; services; lack of performance; sanctions and fines, and general regulations on subject. Direccion General de Comercio Interior is in charge of enforcement of law.

MORTGAGES:

Mortgages must be constituted by a notarial instrument and recorded in the public registry. The property mortgaged must be definite and the amount must be stated. If the amount is uncertain an estimate must be given. If the mortgaged property diminishes in value the creditor may demand that further security be furnished or that the debt be paid. As against third persons the mortgage covers the interest of the current year and of two preceding years. A mortgage expires ten years after registration, but for mortgages of mortgage banks the period is 30 years. (C. C. 2098-2196; C. Com. 1317).

NEGOTIABLE INSTRUMENTS:

See topic Bills and Notes.

NOTARIES PUBLIC:

(Notarial Law 162 of Mar. 29, 1930 as am'd; C. C. 1497-1512).

In order to be a notary it is necessary to be a lawyer or to have obtained a notary's diploma. Notaries keep a registry containing the original of all documents executed before them and issue certified copies of such documents, which copies have the force of originals. Once a year they send to the Supreme Court a duplicate copy of documents authenticated by them during the year.

Instruments executed by notaries must be in Spanish, written clearly in long-hand and in ink without abbreviations or blank spaces. They require two witnesses of either sex who may not be employees of the notary nor relatives within the fourth degree of consanguinity or second of affinity of the notary or of any of the parties. A notary cannot act in instruments containing provisions in his favor or in favor of a relative within the said degrees of relationship. He must know the parties or they must be identified.

Notaries can execute instruments abroad when parties are from Honduras or instruments executed are for use in Honduras.

PARTNERSHIP:

A commercial partnership is a legal entity, but the rights and obligations of the partners are similar to those of partners in the United States.

General partnership (sociedad colectiva) is one in the usual form in which all partners have unlimited liability. It is administered in the manner designated in the partnership articles. The instrument of organization must be recorded in the Public Registry of Commerce; for this purpose a petition is made to the civil judge who submits the matter to the government attorney and after a hearing gives his decision. Any modification must likewise be recorded. (C. Com. 13-57).

Limited partnership is one in which certain partners are liable only for the amount which they have contributed. The special partners can have no part in the management nor can their names appear in the firm name. The firm name must be followed by the words "Sociedad en Comandita" or the abbreviation "S. en C." (C. Com. 58-65).

Limited partnership with shares is similar to the limited partnership except that its capital is divided into shares at least one-tenth of which must be subscribed by the special partners who may not alienate them without the consent of the other special partners and the majority of the general partners. (C. Com. 271-277).

Cooperative companies may not have more than twenty members. Their capital is divided into legal participations of not less than 25 lempiras. Their name must indicate the purpose of the company and be followed by the words "Sociedad Cooperativa Limitada" or "Sociedad Cooperativa Suplementada" or the abbreviations "S. C. L." or "S. C. S." Many rules relating to corporations also apply to cooperatives. (C. Com. 278-298).

Limited Liability Companies occupy a position between a corporation and a partnership. The name must be followed by the words "Sociedad de Responsabilidad Limitada" or the abbreviation "S. de R. L." Such a company may not have more than twenty-five members; the capital may not be less than 5000 lempiras and the participations must be in amounts of 100 lempiras or multiples thereof. The members are liable only for the amount of their participations. The participations are not represented by documents and may not be transferred without the consent of the other members, who have a preferential right to acquire them, or a majority of the other members if the company articles so provide. The names of the members and transfer of participations must be recorded in the Public Registry. Meetings of members necessarily must be held at least once a year. (C. Com. 66-89).

Civil partnership (sociedad civil) is one constituted for other than mercantile purposes and is governed by the rules of the Civil Code. Unless expressly agreed otherwise the partners are liable for the partnership debts only in the proportion of their interest in the partnership. (C. C. 1782-1887).

PATENTS:

(L.D. 142-93 of Sept. 7, 1993).

Invention Patents.—Any invention of products or proceedings which are novel, represent inventive step and are susceptible of industrial application. Invention is novel when it is not within state of art. Discoveries, scientific theories, business plans, principles or methods; software, surgical, therapeutic or diagnostic treatment methods, vegetable or animal species, literary or artistic works among others, are not patentable. Patents are granted for 20 years from filing date, except for pharmachemical or pharmaceutical products and processes to obtain them that are granted for 17 years from filing date. Patent gives exclusive right of exploitation but compulsory license may be granted in case of declared emergency or national security reasons and when patent has not been exploited during first three years. Patent rights are transferable.

Utility Models.—Any new model which may be applied to industrial object may be registered as ownership of author. Utility models are new forms of objects or mechanism, which, provided they have practical use, are registrable. Registration term is 15 years from filing date. Provisions regarding patents are applicable to models.

Industrial Designs.—Any new design which may be applied to industrial object may be registered as ownership of author if no publicity thereof has been made in any form. Registration is five years, renewable for two additional five year periods.

Trade Secrets.—Law also protects trade secrets and considers them as any confidential information that is valuable and provides competitive or economic advantages to owner. Information considered trade secret must be expressed in any tangible form.

Conventions.—Convention for the Protection of Industrial Property, Paris, Mar. 21, 1883, Stockholm Revision of July 14, 1967 as am'd on Sept. 28, 1979; Agreement on Trade-Related Aspects of Intellectual Property Rights, Marrakesh, Apr. 15, 1994.

PLEDGES:

The article pledged must be delivered to the creditor or to his representative. As between the parties the contract is effective from the time of such delivery; but in order to affect third persons it must appear in a notarial instrument. In case of default the pledge may be sold judicially or, if the parties have so agreed, by a third person at public sale; any agreement allowing the creditor to appropriate the pledge is void.

Mercantile pledges must likewise be delivered to the creditor or a third person actually or symbolically, but may remain in possession of the debtor when the pledge is given on articles necessary for the operation of the industry. Bills of exchange may be pledged by endorsement in guaranty of pledge. (C. C. 2056-2097; C. Com. 916-928, 1289-1307).

See also topics Chattel Mortgages; Sales (Realty and Personalty).

PRESCRIPTION:

(C. C. 2263-2303; C. Com. 579, 580, 772, 775, 1317, 1684-1708).

The acquisition of property or rights by virtue of possession and the extinction of obligations by failure to require performance is called prescription. Prescription may be waived as far as it has run, but the waiver of future prescription is void.

In general in order to acquire by prescription it is necessary to possess in good faith, with a legal title, as owner, publicly, quietly and uninterruptedly. Natural interruption occurs when for any reason possession ceases for over a year, and civil interruption in case of the institution of a suit at law. Ownership of personal property is acquired by possession for three years in good faith or six years without other conditions; but ownership of stolen articles cannot be acquired by the guilty person until the right to institute the penal action has been lost by prescription. Real property is acquired by possession for ten years with good faith and a legal title, or for 20 years without these conditions. Prescription does not run against a recorded title except by virtue of another recorded instrument.

Actions.—The prescriptive period in which rights of action are lost varies according to the nature of the action. Some of the more important periods are: (a) thirty years, mortgage action by mortgage banks; (b) ten years, actions to recover real property and personal actions not otherwise limited; (c) six years, actions to recover personal property; (d) five years, actions on mercantile contracts not otherwise provided for; (e) three years, summary actions on negotiable instruments; (f) two years, actions to recover rents or other periodical payments, actions founded on most commercial contracts such as articles of incorporation and partnership, sales, commercial deposits, banking and credit operations, insurance, guaranty, etc.; (g) one year, actions by lawyers, notaries, druggists, servants, innkeepers, storekeepers, for services rendered or merchandise sold, action for annulment of stockholders' resolutions and for enforcement of liability of corporation directors and supervisors, actions on travelers checks and transportation contracts and for hidden defects in goods purchased; (h) six months, summary actions against endorsers of negotiable instruments; actions on checks and for rectification of current accounts, actions for defects of goods guaranteed for a definite time. The prescription of actions is interrupted by judicial or extrajudicial demand or by acknowledgment of the debt.

See specific topics for special limitations.

PRINCIPAL AND AGENT:

A general power of attorney grants only powers of administration. Power to compromise, sell, mortgage, or perform other acts of ownership must be specifically conferred. An agent appointing a substitute is liable for the acts of the latter if he was not empowered to appoint a substitute or if the substitute is notoriously incompetent. An agency terminates by: (a) Revocation; (b) resignation of the agent; (c) death, incompetency, bankruptcy or insolvency of the principal or agent. Commission agents have a lien for their expenses on articles consigned to them. (C. C. 1888-1918; C. Com. 355-379, 731-738, 804-841).

Relationship between local agents or distributors of foreign firms and their principals is regulated by Decree 549 of Nov. 24, 1977 am'd by Decree 804 of Sept. 10, 1979. Only Honduran persons or corporations may be agents. Those representing persons dealing with vehicles, electric or electronic equipment or objects or other durable items, must keep spare parts or accessories and service of maintenance and repair, with severe penalties for failure. Agency contract cannot be terminated at will by principal without payment of due compensation based upon specified criteria, unless for "just cause". Law establishes as "just cause" breach of contract, fraud, continued decrease in sale or distribution of merchandise or services due to negligence of distributor, infringement of trade secrets and confidentiality agreements, bankruptcy of distributor, failure to render account and information as agreed, any act of distributor that prejudices introduction of merchandise on market or sale or services thereof. Statute of limitations is three years. Civil and Commercial Codes must apply in cases not specifically contemplated by law.

PUBLIC INSTRUMENTS:

(C. C. 1497-1512, 1526-1531; C. C. P. 320-337).

Public instruments are instruments authenticated by a notary or competent public official. They are proof of their object and date, and as between the parties they are proof of the statements made therein. The law designates numerous contracts which must appear in public instruments, such as sales of real estate, mortgages, articles of incorporation, partnerships, etc. Other public documents are documents in the public archives, judicial orders and others.

Private documents, when acknowledged before a judge, have the force of public instruments as between the parties and their successors. The date of a private document is not effective as to third persons except from the death of any of the signers or the date of registration of the document or the date when it was delivered to some public officer. Contracts involving over 200 lempiras must be in writing.

REAL PROPERTY:

Civil Code, arts. 599 to 927 and some special laws, such as Dec. 45 of Oct. 23, 1965, Law of Condominiums, govern all matters referring to property and property rights.

National Constitution guarantees property rights and establishes that expropriation may be imposed only on grounds of public benefit and after a fair compensation.

RECORDS:

There is a public registry of property for the recording of deeds, mortgages, judgments, attachments, etc. Only public or authentic instruments can be recorded Registrars are semi-judicial officers who may refuse to record a deed if it is not in legal form or if the rights of the grantor do not appear from the registry. An appeal lies from their decisions to the courts. Besides the property registry there are commercial registries for recording corporate and partnership documents, powers of attorney, etc. There is also a civil registry for recording vital statistics. (C. C. 296-387, 2304-2368; C. Com. 384-421).

SALES (Realty and Personalty):

(C. C. 1605-1676; C. Com. 691-711, 763-792).

A sale is perfected when the parties have agreed on the object and the price, although neither has been delivered. The seller guarantees the title and warrants against hidden defects, unless otherwise stipulated; if he knew of the defects he is liable in any case.

Conditional sales are allowed as well as sales with reservation of title until price is paid. If the objects sold can be identified such contracts are binding on third persons if recorded in the Public Registry.

SEALS:

Seals are not used in private contracts. Public documents (q.v.) have most of the effects of sealed instruments in the United States.

SHIPPING:

The Code of Commerce contains provisions regarding the rights and duties of captains and crews and rules relating to admiralty matters. (C. Com. of 1940, 733-1038; C. Com. of 1950, 1314). Honduran flag may be used by merchant vessels holding permanent or temporary registry. Temporary registry is granted up to nine months, while waiting permanent registry. Applicant may be national or foreign, individual or juridical person, locally domiciled or non-domiciled. Registered vessels are not required to travel to local ports. Vessels are registered at Vessel Registry, but all acts related to ownership and encumbrance of registered vessels must be recorded at Registry of Merchant and Real Property. Coastwise trade is reserved to national vessels which are those registered according to law. (Organic Law of National Merchant Marine Decree 167-94 of Nov. 15, 1994).

STATUTES:

The more important legal provisions are codified, the principal codifications being: Civil Code; Code of Civil Procedure; Code of Family; Code of Commerce; Penal Code; Law of Criminal Procedure; Law of Organization and Powers of the Courts; Mining Code; Code of Public Instruction; Notarial Law. Copies of other laws are often difficult to obtain. Current laws appear in official newspaper called "La Gaceta."

TAXATION:

Income Tax.—(Law 25 of Dec. 20, 1963 as am'd, regulated by "Acuerdo" 799 of Nov. 19, 1969 as am'd). Tax is imposed on incomes of any individual or corporation, whether national or foreign, having domicile in Honduras, from any kind of property or activities or labor, whether source of income is within or without country or wherever payment of income is made. Nonresident persons and corporations domiciled in Honduras are subject to tax on income from Honduras sources only.

Among exempt items appear the following: insurance proceeds paid by Honduras insurance companies; income from governmental subdivisions; gifts, inheritances and legacies; National Lottery awards. Deductible items include, among others, ordinary and necessary expenses for production of income; certain insurance premiums; interest on loans which, in opinion of Director of Internal Revenue, were obtained for production of income, but interest paid on corporate capital or on loans granted by the owners or close relatives or by members or shareholders of a corporation or legal entity is not deductible; taxes, except income tax; losses from damages to assets; amortization of bad debts; 10% of investment in free housing for laborers and 20% of other constructions for the general welfare of same; salaries; bonuses within limitations; depletion of certain property, within limitations established by Director of Internal Revenue; charitable gifts; certain social security contributions.

Personal exemption of Lempiras 10,000 for medical, dental and laboratory services rendered to individual taxpayer or to his dependents except when reimbursed by health insurance. Individual taxpayer may also deduct expenses incurred in practice of profession, art or craft or in shop or in production and upkeep of farms, as well as interest on loans for agricultural or cattle production; depreciation of agricultural equipment, machinery and buildings, gifts and legacies donated to State up to amount not exceeding 10% of net taxable income.

Rates.—Individuals residing or domiciled in Honduras are subject to income tax rates ranging from 10% on income from L.50,001 to L.100,000 to 30% on income over L.1,000,000. First L.50,000 are exempted. Juridical persons domiciled in Honduras are subject to following rates: 15% rate up to L. 100,000 and 35% rate on amounts over L. 100,000 of net income and to surcharge of 10% of tax on incomes over L. 500,000, and for incomes over L. 1,000,000 surchage is 10% of tax on second L. 500,000 and 15% on tax on amounts in excess of L. 1,000,000. When several concerns or corporations having similar or complementary commercial activities belong in more than 40% of capital of each to same owners or members or their spouses, they must file consolidated return. Income in nature of dividends is subject to proportional tax rate of 10%. Interest on securities, on savings accounts and on securities related to nonbanking private sector sold on stock exchange paid to individual or juridical persons, in local or foreign currency, is subject to 10% fixed rate and is excluded from normal taxable income.

Individuals and corporations not residents or domiciled in Honduras are subject to tax to be withheld when possible on incomes from local sources, payable when the income is sent abroad, as follows: 30% on income from real or personal property, 15% on dividends and participations in profits, 5% on interest from commercial transactions, bonds and other securities, 10% on interest on securities related to nonbanking private sector sold on stock exchange, on interest on savings accounts with banks, savings and credit associations and other financial institutions, 10% on profits or proceeds from aircraft, vessels or land motor vehicles, 5% on income from communications concerns; 10% on royalties from mines or other natural resources; 25% for use of patents, designs, procedures, marks, etc.; 35% on salaries and compensation for services; 15% on income or profits earned by foreign enterprises from their branches or subsidiaries; 15% on insurance premiums and bonds of any kind; 30% on public spectacles, film and video tapes 10%, others 20%. Ministry of Finance may grant total or partial exemption of tax on interest of capitals invested in projects of economic importance for country.

Capital gains earned by individuals or juridical persons domiciled and non-domicile in country are taxable at rate of 10%. Agricultural and cattle concerns, mining, tourism and manufacturing concerns may request that certain capital losses be accepted as deductible and carried over for up to three years. Capitalization of reserves or profits is exempted from taxes.

Tax on Assets.—(Decreè 137-94 of Oct. 12, 1994). Tax at annual rate of 1% of value of assets is assessed on all legal entities and individuals engaged in commercial activities according to law.

Inheritance and Gift Tax.—(Decree 67 of Feb. 15, 1938, as am'd by Decree-Law 187 of Dec. 29, 1955, reinstated by Decree 236 of Dec. 30, 1964 regulated by Accord 574 of 1955). Taxpayers are classified in six groups. Group I, formed by children of decedent or donor pay 1%. Group II, parents, 2%. Group III, other ascendants and legitimate collaterals, 3% Group IV, other collaterals, 5%. Group V, relatives by affinity, 8%; and Group VI, strangers or legal entities, 10%. Foreigners not domiciled in Honduras pay 20%. Estates of less than 10,000 lempiras are exempt. Decree 4 of Aug. 9, 1965 grants term of three years for payment of this tax, from date when such tax is assessed by Tax Office.

Sales Tax.—(Decree-Law 24 of Dec. 20, 1963, as am'd; Regulations by Accord 1478 of Aug. 11, 1983). General 7% sales tax rate on net price of merchandise and certain services must be paid by importers and industrial concerns. Tax rate is 10% on beer, liquors, cigarettes and tobacco products. This tax is levied only once. Excluded are some items already subjected to special taxes. Sales of services by natural or juridical persons are exempt if not rendered in restaurants, cabarets, night clubs, social clubs, hotels and boarding houses, telecommunications and advertising. Other exemptions include pharmaceutical products for human and veterinary use, agricultural and dairy products, fresh meat, fish, vegetables and fruit (not canned), coffee, spices, fibers, raw minerals, vaccines, salt, medicines, textbooks, periodicals and other school materials, imported raw materials, machinery, industrial equipment, accessories and spare parts to be used in production of exempted articles or goods, and imported agricultural equipment, machinery, accessories and spare parts.

Other taxes include: (a) Customs and port duties (Decrees 151-87 of Oct. 2, 1987, 212-87 of Dec. 14, 1987 as am'd by Decree 134-89 of Sept. 14, 1989, and Decree 213-87 of Dec. 14, 1987 as am'd); (b) alcohol and alcoholic beverages (Decree 20 of Nov. 30, 1956 as am'd); (c) stamp tax and stamped paper (Decree 75 of Apr. 24, 1911 as am'd); (d) real property tax (Decree Law 5 of Feb. 20, 1958 as am'd); (e) real property transfer tax ranging from 2% to 4% (with some exceptions such as acquisition of real estate by Government for public interest or sale of real estate of minors or disabled to provide for their needs) of consideration (Law 76 of Apr. 9, 1957, am'd by Decree 873 of Dec. 26, 1979 and Law 166 of Oct. 10, 1957; Decree 54 of Aug. 25, 1966). Deeds, mortgages and most documents used in ordinary course of business are subject to stamp tax generally depending on amount involved.

Free Zones.—(Decree 37-87 of Apr. 7, 1987 as am'd by Decree 84-92 of June 12, 1992 as am'd regulated by Accord 684 of July 13, 1987). Law establishes requirements to be complied with by private companies in order to own and manage free zones authorized by Ministry of Economy and Commerce. Companies' owners and managers of free zones are exempted from income tax payment for 20 years, municipal taxes for ten years, and duty free import of equipment, machinery parts, construction materials necessary for construction and operation of free zones which are not produced in country. There are two types of free zones: export processing zones for manufactured goods to be exported and touristic free zones, created for promotion and development of tourism. National or foreign individuals and juridical persons may operate in free zones by entering into contract with administrating company, and their profits are exempted from income tax except for foreign individuals and juridical person who are allowed to credit, in their country, income tax paid in Honduras. Entry of goods to free zones is exempted from all taxes, sales and production in free zones and real property is exempted from state and municipal taxes. Goods and merchandise exported or imported in and from free zones are exempted from all taxes.

See Topical Index in front part of this volume.

TRADEMARKS AND TRADENAMES:

(Decree 142-93 of Sept. 7, 1993).

Trademarks and Slogans.—Trademark is any sign visible and distinctive used to distinguish products or services produced or commercialized by one enterprise from same or similar products or services produced or commercialized by another enterprise. Among those non-registrable are: usual or necessary shapes of products or denominations and color thereof; shapes which provide functional or technical advantages to product or service concerned; signs or indications that may designate or describe any characteristic of products or services concerned; those against morals or public policy or that are intended to deceive consumers regarding nature, origin, type of manufacture characteristic or aptitude to use products or services; those identical or similar to slogans or trade names used by another person provided under circumstances public may be confused; those that are reproduction, imitation, translation, or total or partial transcription of distinctive signs, locally well known, causes confusion to public independent of classification of goods and services for which registration is applied for. Those which may be confused with marks already registered; merely generic or geographic names or names of persons or things. Registration is for ten years, renewable. Marks may be canceled for nonuse in one year. Licenses must be registered but registry may be denied if it does not provide for control of quality or if it limits exportation or sale prices or if it restricts use of raw materials, equipment, etc., unless necessity of restriction is proved, or for excessive royalties or for obligation to employ certain personnel permanently or for submission to foreign courts. Classification of NIZA 1957 applies.

Collective Marks.—Any sign that distinguishes origin or any other common characteristic of products or services of different enterprises which use marks under control of their owner.

Commercial names of enterprises or industrial, commercial or service establishments are protected by law without requiring registration. Proof of existence of enterprises must be filed every five years in order to keep commercial name protected. Origin denominations may be registered for indefinite period of time. Law prohibits unfair competition and penalizes violators.

Conventions.—Convention for the Protection of Industrial Property, Paris, Mar. 21, 1883, Stockholm Revision of July 14, 1967 as am'd on Sept. 28, 1979; Agreement on Trade-Related Aspects of Intellectual Property Rights, Marrakesh, Apr. 15, 1994.

TREATIES:

Multilateral.—Havana Convention on Private International Law (Bustamante Code) Havana 1928; Panama Convention on Latin American Economic System (SELA) Panama 1975; Interamerican Convention on Copyright and Literary Property, Washington June 22, 1946; Central American Economic Integration, with Costa Rica, El Salvador, Guatemala and Nicaragua; Multilateral treaty of free trade and Central American economic integration. Signed June 10, 1958, Tegucigalpa; General treaty on Central American economic integration. Signed Dec. 13, 1960, Managua; Agreement establishing the Central American Bank for Economic Integration. Signed Dec. 13, 1960, Managua. Multilateral Trade Negotiations, The Uruguay Round, Final Act (Marrakesh, Apr. 15, 1994) and Agreement Establishing the World Trade Organization (Marrakesh, Apr. 15, 1994).

Bilateral with U.S.—Treaty of friendship, commerce, and consular rights. Signed Dec. 7, 1927, Tegucigalpa; Trade agreement. Signed Dec. 18, 1935, Tegucigalpa. Entered into force Mar. 2, 1936. Partly terminated Feb. 28, 1961; General agreement for economic and technical cooperation. Signed Apr. 12, 1961, Tegucigalpa.

TRUSTS:

Banks authorized to act as trustees may accept trusts to realize certain acts with respect to certain property. Such trusts may not have a longer term than 30 years, unless the beneficiary be a public or a charitable institution. The benefits may not pass to various persons in succession unless such persons be alive or conceived at the time of the death of the person establishing the trust. Trusts as they exist in the common law are unknown in Honduras. A testator may leave secret instructions to testamentary trustee, who can not be obliged to reveal them or to render accounts. (C. Com. 1033-1062; C. C. 1220-1224).

VITAL STATISTICS: See topic Records.

WILLS:

(C. C. 979-1167).

All persons may make wills except: (a) Those below the age of puberty; (2) those of unsound mind; (3) those temporarily not in possession of their faculties by reason of intoxication or otherwise; (4) those who cannot clearly express their will orally or in writing. Wills are: (1) Solemn; or (2) privileged. Solemn wills are subdivided into: (1) Open, nuncupative or public wills; and (2) closed or secret wills. The law contains a lengthy list of persons who cannot be witnesses of solemn wills, among them being: (a) Persons below 18 years of age; (b) those of unsound mind; (c) blind, deaf or dumb persons; (d) vicious persons; (e) undomiciled aliens; (f) servants and relatives within the third degree of the testator; (g) persons having an interest in the will; (h) the father confessor.

Open will is made before a notary and three witnesses; it is read aloud and signed by all present. Besides the place and date it must state where the testator was born, his nationality, his domicile, age, the names of the persons whom he has married and the names of his children.

Closed will is a will signed by the testator and enclosed in an envelope which the testator declares before a notary and five witnesses to contain his will. The notary writes a memorandum of such declaration on the envelope and all sign the same.

Privileged wills are: (1) Those made without the intervention of a notary in the case of epidemics or imminent danger of death, but they become void sixty days after the termination of the epidemic or danger of death, or if not proved by the witnesses before a judge within 90 days after the death of the testator; (2) military wills made by soldiers in a campaign; (3) naval wills made on Honduran vessels at sea.

Testamentary Dispositions.—The testator may freely dispose of his property, the only obligatory provisions which he must make being: (a) Provisions for the support of his needy children, parents and others whose support devolves upon him; (b) the marital fourth pertaining to the necessitous surviving spouse (see topic Husband and Wife).

Foreign wills are accepted as valid if made in the form required by the foreign country and if the authenticity of the instrument is duly proved. A Honduran or an alien domiciled in Honduras may also make a will before a diplomat or consular official of Honduras; in such event an open will requires three witnesses and a closed will seven witnesses, all the witnesses being Hondurans, residents in the locality.

HONG KONG LAW DIGEST

Robert W. H. Wang & Co.
Solicitors and Notaries
8th & 18th Floors
Nine Queen's Road Central
Hong Kong
Telephone: 852 2 843 7333
Fax: 852-2 845 5566
Email: msimonx@counsel.com

Reviser Profile

The firm was established in 1980. It has 11 partners and 120 fee earners and staff. Is is one of the larger and more progressive firms in Hong Kong. The firm is managed by a committee of senior partners under the Senior Partner who has overall responsibility for management and administration. The Senior Partner works with the Administration Department and the Heads of Departments.

Anna Wu, the Senior Partner, has recently stepped down from the Hong Kong Legislative Council but remains involved with a variety of governmental and professional organizations. She is the vice-chairman of the Consumer Council and is a former President of the Asian Patent Attorneys Association (Hong Kong).

A number of the partners and senior personnel are actively involved with various governmental and professional organizations including the Law Society, Chambers of Commerce and Professional Associations.

The practice is broadly based and covers most areas of international and domestic business law. There are 4 principal departments, being Conveyancing; Corporate Finance, Commercial and Banking; Intellectual Property and Litigation in addition to others such as those dealing primarily with China, Singapore and European matters and those covering Immigration, Probate and Shipping.

Languages: business can be conducted in English, Cantonese, Mandarin, Shanghainese, German, French and Spanish.

Conveyancing: the firm advises on real estate matters generally including acquisitions and sales ranging from large scale commercial, hotel and residential developments to individual domestic and business premises. All relevant matters such as tenancies, mortgages, licences and government conditions are covered. Suitable arrangements are made for overseas developments and properties such as those in China and other locations in the region.

Corporate Finance, Commercial and Banking: transactions such as acquisitions and disposals, joint ventures, syndicated loans as well as banking transactions and documentation generally and securities matters both for listed and unlisted corporations. Corporate secretarial services for overseas and domestic corporations. The firm has strong European connections and is a recommended firm for a number of consulates and trade commissions. Native German speakers serve the many German speaking clients.

Intellectual Property: dealing with registration of trade and service marks, patents and designs and copyright matters for a wide variety of products and businesses. Protection of intellectual property rights generally. The firm can make suitable arrangements for worldwide registrations and is active in arranging suitable registrations and enforcements in China.

Litigation: all areas of civil litigation and arbitration for domestic and foreign clients including international trade, insurance, banking, insolvency, employment, personal injury, family and divorce.

General: client base is diverse and covers local and international businesses, including major banks, multinationals, property developers, manufacturers and distributors. The firm has a strong network of clients and associates and seeks, where appropriate, to be proactive rather than reactive.

There is a very close association with the firm of Robert W.H. Wang & Woo in Singapore and the firm actively promotes interchange and business activity between Singapore and Hong Kong. The firm also has a strong network with other associates in Europe, North America and throughout the world.

The firm was the inaugural compiler of the Martindale-Hubbell Digest for Hong Kong and has since acted as Reviser.

HONG KONG LAW DIGEST

(The following is a list of all Topics, including cross-references, covered in this Digest.)

HONG KONG LAW DIGEST

Revised for 1997 edition by

MESSRS. ROBERT W. H. WANG & CO., Solicitors and Notaries, Hong Kong.

References to "Cap." mean the Chapter of the Laws of Hong Kong.

Note: Legislative changes will occur (for example, in Industrial Property law) in connection with change of sovereignty from United Kingdom to the People's Republic of China in mid-1997. Number of changes are in process of being considered. Some are noted in the Digest. It will be important to check the up-to-date position on specific areas with Hong Kong counsel.

ABSENTEES:

In absence abroad, person may generally delegate authority to any person of full capacity, usually by power of attorney. It is not necessary to file powers of attorney with any governmental or judicial authority. Power may be limited or unlimited as donor wishes.

As long as permitted by and in accordance with company's constitution, its directors may empower any person either generally or in respect of specified matters as company's attorney to execute deeds on its behalf outside Hong Kong. Deed executed by such attorney binds company as if under its seal.

ACTIONS:

Generally, any person may sue or be sued in Hong Kong courts subject to applicable procedural rules.

All causes of action with some exceptions, such as defamation, vested in or against individual survive death of that person for benefit of or against estate.

Action on foreign contract or course of dealings can be brought in Hong Kong if any party to action is in Hong Kong, if contract was made or was to be performed in Hong Kong, if there is sufficient connection with Hong Kong or if Court is of view that Hong Kong is appropriate jurisdiction for case to be tried more suitably in interests of parties and for end of justice.

Unsuccessful party to action will pay costs of successful party. Plaintiff not resident in jurisdiction may be required to lodge in Court or otherwise give security for amount equivalent to defendant's costs. In practice usually only proportion of costs will be recoverable.

Judicial Review.—

Certiorari.—Order made on judicial review by High Court of decision of inferior court or tribunal or public authority if High Court concludes that decision should be set aside.

Mandamus.—Order requiring inferior court or tribunal or person or body of persons charged with public duty to carry out its judicial and other public duties. No order lies against Crown but can lie against officer of Crown who is obliged by statute to do some ministerial or administrative act which affects rights or interest of applicant.

Prohibition.—Order restraining inferior court or tribunal or public authority from acting outside its jurisdiction.

Application for judicial review can only be made with leave of Court and must be made within three months from date when grounds for application first arose unless Court is satisfied there are grounds for extending time.

Limitation.—See topic Limitation of Actions.

Service of foreign process can be effected in accordance with rules applicable to service of Hong Kong process, for example, by postal or personal service.

Alternatively, service of process issued in country which is party to civil procedure convention, including Hague Convention, can be effected by written request from Consulate or other authority from that country to Chief Secretary of Hong Kong requesting that service be effected through Supreme Court.

Proof of Foreign Law.—Where foreign law is pleaded in any action, particulars must be given.

There is presumption that foreign law is same as Hong Kong law unless contrary is proved by party who asserts it is different. Foreign law can be proved by expert giving oral evidence at trial. Finding or decision on question of foreign law can be adduced in evidence on appropriate notice.

See also topic Executions.

ADMINISTRATION:

See topic Executors and Administrators.

ADOPTION:

Child can be adopted by any parent or relative over 21 or any other person over 25. There are restrictions on single males adopting female children. Persons who are medically unfit or over 45 will not be permitted to adopt. Joint applications to adopt infant cannot be made by persons in de facto relationships. Applicant(s) and child must reside in Hong Kong.

Consent of natural mother or guardian is required unless she has abandoned or otherwise neglected child. Consent of natural father is not required if he was not married to mother at time of birth, nor named in child's birth certificate and has not subsequently had contact with or maintained child. Consent is revocable at any time prior to Order being made. Court can dispense with consent.

Child must reside with prospective adoptive parents for six months after giving notice to Court and Social Services Department of intention to adopt, before application can be made, or 13 weeks in case of application by natural parent. Social Services Department reports to Court on fitness of applicants and whether application is in best interests of child.

It is offence to give or receive any remuneration in respect of adoption. It is also offence to publish without consent of Director of Social Welfare that child is available for adoption.

Upon Order being made, natural parents give up all parental rights and child becomes child of adopters. Birth certificate is re-issued in name of adopters. Access by natural parents to child is unlikely to be permitted. If infant is adopted outside of Hong Kong and adoption is legally valid according to law of country in which adoption was granted, adoption shall have same effect as if made in accordance with Hong Kong law.

Adoption Ordinance (Cap. 290) does not effect status or rights of any person adopted in Hong Kong under Chinese Law and Custom before Dec. 31, 1972.

AFFIDAVITS AND STATUTORY DECLARATIONS:

Affidavits must be expressed in first person and unless directed otherwise by Court state deponent's place of residence, occupation and description. If deponent is employee of party to cause or matter in which affidavit is sworn, he must state that fact. If deponent is deposing as professional or in business or other occupational capacity, he may state his address as being his place of work, identifying position held and name of his firm or employer, if any.

Every affidavit must be signed by deponent and jurat completed and signed by person before whom it is sworn. Affidavits must be sworn by deponent personally attending before Hong Kong solicitor, notary public or other officer duly authorised to administer oaths.

Affidavits may be sworn in any part of Commonwealth outside Hong Kong before judge, officer or other person duly authorised, or any commissioner authorised by Court. In any other foreign country, affidavit may be sworn before judge or magistrate, being authenticated by his relevant official seal, or before notary public or British Consular Officer.

Deponent can affirm his statement in alternative to swearing oath. (Oaths and Declarations Ordinance [Cap. 11]).

Form, content and jurat of affidavits and affirmations similar to that included for England Law Digest.

Statutory declarations may be taken and received by justice, notary, commissioner or other person authorised by law to administer oaths. Declaration shall be made in following format:

Declaration

I, A.B., of , solemnly and sincerely declare [Insert facts]

And I make this solemn declaration conscientiously believing the same to be true and by virtue of the Oaths and Declarations Ordinance.

(Sgd.) A.B.

Declared at
this day of 19

Before me

[Signature and designation]

Affidavit, affirmation or declaration of person who is unfamiliar with English language should contain declaration or oath by interpreter to effect that contents of statement have been interpreted to deponent.

AGENCY:

See topic Principal and Agent.

ALIENS:

See topic Immigration.

APPLICABLE LAW:

See topic Constitution and Government.

ASSIGNMENTS:

Assignments of debts and other legal things in action and equitable assignments of both legal and equitable things in action, similar to law of England.

See England Law Digest.

ASSOCIATIONS:

See topic Partnerships.

ATTACHMENT:

Any sum standing to credit of person in deposit account with recognised financial institution can be attached.

No attachment of wages of judgment debtor except in favour of Crown in respect of civil debt due to it.

See topic Executions.

See Topical Index in front part of this volume.

ATTORNEYS AND COUNSELORS:

Divided into solicitors and barristers. Profession is governed by Legal Practitioners Ordinance. (Cap. 159).

Solicitor is person whom client consults for legal advice and assistance generally. Solicitors advise on wide range of personal and business matters and appear as advocates in lower courts.

Generally, Hong Kong solicitors hold LL.B degree from University of Hong Kong or City University of Hong Kong or equivalent (or other undergraduate degree plus requisite Common Professional Examination ("CPE") and have completed Postgraduate Certificate in Laws ("PCLL"). Following PCLL, two-year trainee solicitorship with solicitors' firm, or suitable in-house lawyer, is required.

For admission as solicitor in Hong Kong, foreign lawyers must show that they are "fit and proper persons", have "good standing" in their own jurisdiction and (i) have resided in Hong Kong for minimum of three months before admission; or (ii) intend to reside in Hong Kong for minimum of three months post-admission; or (iii) are ordinarily resident in Hong Kong for at least seven years; or (iv) have been present in Hong Kong for minimum of 180 days of each of seven or more years. In addition: (i) lawyers from common law jurisdictions must pass The Law Society's Overseas Lawyers Qualification Examination and complete minimum of two years' trainee or post-admission experience; and (ii) lawyers from non-common law jurisdictions with minimum of five years' post-admission experience must pass written and oral examinations to qualify, or otherwise, they must have minimum three years' trainee or post-admission experience and complete requisite CPE or equivalent, plus PCLL.

Solicitors are regulated by Law Society of Hong Kong: Room 1403 Swire House, 11 Chater Road, Central, Hong Kong. Tel.: (852) 28460500; fax: (852)28450387.

Barristers primarily represent client in court and argue case. Clients may not approach barristers directly but must do so via solicitor or other permitted professional.

There are ostensibly three main routes to become barrister. Hong Kong route requires Bachelor of Laws of University of Hong Kong or City Polytechnic University of Hong Kong and PCLL. U.K. route involves qualification as barrister in England or Northern Ireland or admission as advocate in Scotland. Commonwealth route is used by law graduates from recognised Commonwealth universities, who must obtain PCLL.

Solicitors and barristers may transfer from one branch of profession to other upon satisfying relevant requirements of The Law Society and Bar Association, as case may be.

Following PCLL, one-year period of pupillage in barristers' chambers is required. Applicant must also be permanent Hong Kong resident within meaning of Immigration Ordinance (Cap. 115) or Commonwealth citizen or citizen of Ireland who has been ordinarily resident in Hong Kong for at least seven years.

Barristers are regulated by Hong Kong Bar Association: Floor LG2, The Supreme Court, 38 Queensway, Hong Kong. Tel.: (852) 28690210; fax: (852) 28690189.

Foreign lawyers and law firms wishing to practise foreign law in Hong Kong must be approved and registered by The Law Society.

Foreign lawyers must provide documentary evidence of policy of indemnity insurance comparable to that required of solicitors in Hong Kong. They may be employed by registered foreign or local firms.

Foreign firms must prove substantial reputation overseas, as well as substantial reputation of one partner intending to practise in Hong Kong, during preceding five years.

Associations between foreign and local law firms in Hong Kong must be registered. Member firms of registered associations may share fees, profits, premises, management and staff.

There are no current proposals by Bar Association for relaxing existing restrictions on foreign lawyers wishing to practise as barristers in Hong Kong.

AUTOMOBILES:

See topic Motor Vehicles.

BANKING AND CURRENCY:

There is no Central Bank in Hong Kong. Three banks, Hongkong and Shanghai Banking Corporation, Standard Chartered Bank and Bank of China operate as note-issuers. Note-issuing, clearing and Government banking are carried out by commercial banks, but control of liquidity, stabilization of exchange rate and lender of last resort are responsibility of Monetary Authority. New Coinage Ordinance empowers Governer in Council to declare, mint, issue and demonetize coins in Hong Kong.

Monetary Authority has also assumed functions of former Commissioner of Banking under Banking Ordinance. (Cap. 155). These include maintaining general stability and effective working of banking system and supervising licensing and registration of authorised institutions, being banks, local representative offices, deposit-taking companies and restricted licence banks.

Monetary unit is Hong Kong dollar which is pegged to US dollar at rate of HK$7.8 to US$1.

See topic Exchange Control.

BANKRUPTCY:

Law is contained in Bankruptcy Ordinance. (Cap. 6).

Debtor commits act of bankruptcy if (a) in Hong Kong or elsewhere he makes conveyance or assignment of his property to trustee for benefit of his creditors generally, (b) in Hong Kong or elsewhere he makes fraudulent conveyance, gift, delivery or transfer of his property, (c) in Hong Kong or elsewhere he makes conveyance or transfer of any part of his property or creates any charge which would be void as fraudulent preference if he were adjudged bankrupt (fraudulent preference is made when debtor is insolvent and he transfers or mortgages property to creditor with intention of preferring that creditor over others if adjudged bankrupt on petition presented within six months of transfer—it is not necessary to demonstrate fraud), (d) with intention to defeat or delay his creditors he departs from Hong Kong or departs from his dwelling-house or usual place of business or removes his property or any part of his property out of jurisdiction of Hong Kong courts, (e) there has been execution against him and goods have been either sold or held by bailiff for more than 21 days, (f) he files in Court declaration of his inability to pay his debts or presents bankruptcy petition against himself, (g) creditor files and serves bankruptcy notice and debtor has not complied with notice within prescribed time or is unable to resist notice (bankruptcy notice may be issued by Court to judgment creditor who has obtained final order; notice must be in prescribed form and will state that debtor should pay judgment debt or amount due or secure or compound it to satisfaction of Court), (h) he gives notice to any of his creditors that he has suspended or that he is about to suspend payment of his debts.

Hong Kong courts have jurisdiction in bankruptcy proceedings if at time of act of bankruptcy debtor (a) was present in Hong Kong, (b) was ordinarily resident in Hong Kong or had place of residence in Hong Kong, (c) was carrying on business in Hong Kong personally or by means of agent or manager or (d) was member of firm or partnership which carried on business in Hong Kong. This nexus must be demonstrated when petition is presented.

Creditor shall not be entitled to present bankruptcy petition against debtor unless (a) debt owed by debtor to petitioning creditor or to two or more petitioning creditors is in aggregate at least HK$5,000, (b) debt is liquidated sum payable immediately or at some certain time in future, (c) act of bankruptcy relied on must have occurred within three months before presentation of petition, (d) debtor has requisite nexus with Hong Kong.

On Court making receiving order, Official Receiver is constituted receiver of assets of debtor and will take control of them. Assets do not vest until adjudication. Official Receiver may appoint special manager if satisfied that nature of debtor's business requires such appointment. General meeting of creditors must be held for purpose of considering whether proposal for composition and scheme of arrangement is to be accepted, to adjudicate debtor bankrupt, to appoint trustee and decide whether there should be committee of inspection. Trustee's function is to realise bankrupt's assets. Official Receiver or any other person may be appointed trustee.

Bankruptcy relates back to time of act of bankruptcy on which receiving order is based. All property will be available for distribution to creditors except (a) property held by bankrupt on trust for another person and (b) tools of trade of bankrupt, necessary clothing and bedding and that of his family not exceeding HK$3,000.

As general rule bankruptcy does not affect rights of secured creditors.

Claims are paid in following order of priority (a) preferential creditors (including employees claiming under Protection of Wages on Insolvency Fund and Crown), (b) ordinary creditors (dealt with pari passu), (c) creditors who have claims for interest (paid at 8% per annum from date of receiving order), (d) deferred claims (where married woman has been adjudicated bankrupt, her husband will not be entitled to any dividend until claims of other creditors have been met).

Bankrupt may at any time apply to Court for discharge from bankruptcy. Application cannot be heard until after public examination. Trustee may make application for discharge. Trustee will make report on bankrupt's affairs and conduct.

Official Receiver is permanent official appointed by Government with powers and duties defined by Ordinance.

Note: Legislative amendments have been proposed in this area but it is not known when and to what extent they may be enacted.

See also topic Insolvency.

BARRISTERS AND SOLICITORS:

See topic Attorneys and Counselors.

BILLS AND NOTES:

Bills of Exchange Ordinance (Cap. 19) is substantially reproduction of English Bills of Exchange Act 1882 and Cheques Act 1957. As in England, rules of common law, save insofar as inconsistent with express provisions of Ordinance, continue to apply to bills of exchange, promissory notes and cheques. Conflict of law rules substantially same as English rules.

BILLS OF SALE:

Bills of Sale Ordinance (Cap. 20) is substantially reproduction of English Bills of Sale Acts, 1878 to 1891. Bill of sale must be for sum of not less than HK$150, be duly attested and registered within seven days or, if executed out of Hong Kong, within seven days after time at which it would in course of post arrive in Hong Kong. Further, bill of sale will be void unless made in accordance with form specified in Ordinance. Registration must be renewed at least once every five years.

See topic Chattel Mortgages.

CHATTEL MORTGAGES:

Mortgages of personal chattels (as defined), except those executed by companies which require registration under Companies Ordinance (see topic Corporations), fall within Bills of Sale Ordinance. See topic Bills of Sale.

COLLATERAL SECURITY:

See topic Pledges.

COMMERCIAL REGISTER:

There is requirement to register businesses and overseas corporations with place of business in Hong Kong.

See also topics Corporations; Patents; Trademarks.

CONSTITUTION AND GOVERNMENT:

Hong Kong remains British colony until 30th June 1997. In recent years use of "colony" has been discouraged in favour of "territory".

Hong Kong's present framework of government follows traditional pattern for British colonies. Governor represents British Crown and has powers to veto legislation. Letters Patent & Royal Instructions form basis of Hong Kong's present governance.

CONSTITUTION AND GOVERNMENT . . . *continued*

Until June 30, 1997 Governor is to follow direction of Secretary of State for Foreign and Commonwealth Affairs (responsible British government minister), although in practice Hong Kong has enjoyed wide autonomy in its internal affairs. As from July 1, 1997 Governor will be replaced by China-appointed "Chief Executive" (see Basic Law infra).

Other arms of government are Executive Council and Legislative Council. Executive Council is in effect cabinet and comprises senior civil servants and official appointees. Legislative Council is territory's legislature. Since Sept. 1995 elections, Council consists of: 20 members directly elected by geographical constituencies; 30, directly elected by functional constituencies (elected representatives of specified professions, business and labour); and ten, indirectly elected by electoral college chosen at district level.

Common law and rules of equity are in force so far as applicable to Hong Kong circumstances, subject to modification as those circumstances require and to any amendment by Order in Council, or applicable legislation.

Under 1984 Joint Declaration by U.K. and China, Hong Kong will become Special Administrative Region of China on 1st July 1997. Upon resumption of sovereignty by China, Hong Kong will be subject to Basic Law which shall be Hong Kong's mini constitution for period 1st July 1997 to 30th June 2047.

China enacted Basic Law in 1990. It includes provision for appointment of local Chief Executive (who will be Chinese and Hong Kong resident); individual rights and duties; political and judicial structures; civil servants; and relationship between Hong Kong Special Administrative Region and China.

Joint Declaration and Basic Law provide that capitalist system and way of life of Hong Kong will be unchanged for 50 years after resumption of Chinese sovereignty and Hong Kong will have high degree of autonomy in its internal affairs.

Basic Law (Art. 8) provides that laws previously in force in Hong Kong, that is common law, rules of equity, ordinances, subordinate legislation and customary law shall be maintained, except for any that contravene Basic Law and subject to any amendment by legislature of Hong Kong Special Administrative Region.

Hong Kong's Bill of Rights Ordinance (Cap. 383) was enacted in 1991 and provides for application of relevant provisions of International Covenant on Civil and Political Rights. Existing law which is in conflict with Bill of Rights is repealed and no longer the law. Bill binds only Government and public authorities and those acting on their behalf and does not apply to inter-citizen rights.

CONTRACTS:

Hong Kong law of contract essentially follows that of England and in many respects English common law and equity apply.

See also topic Sales.

Applicable Law.—Same as under English law.

Excuses for Nonperformance.—Same as under English law.

Exemption Clauses.—See subhead Unfair Terms, infra; topic Sales, subhead Consumer Protecton.

Under Motor Vehicle Insurance (Third Party Risks) Ordinance (Cap. 272) and Employees Compensation Ordinance (Cap. 282) any condition in policy of insurance providing that liability shall be denied by reference to act or omission happening after event giving rise to claim shall be of no effect upon that claim.

Government Contracts.—Proceedings can be taken and enforced against Crown. Such proceedings are governed by Crown Proceedings Ordinance. (Cap. 300).

Infants Contracts.—Infancy is defence in respect to debts, damages or demand where jurisdiction for such claims falls within High Court or Small Claims Tribunal (jurisdiction in respect to claims not exceeding HK$15,000) save and except for (a) necessary goods and services for which infant must pay reasonable price (Sale of Goods Ordinance); (b) benefits of permanent nature other than for necessary goods and services unless avoided upon reaching majority or within reasonable time thereafter.

However, in District Court there is no exemption for infant from liability in respect to action for any debt, damages or demand for claim up to HK$120,000.

See also topic Infancy.

Privity.—Same as under English law. See also topic Assignments.

Rescission.—Essentially same as under English law. See England Law Digest.

Unfair Terms.—Pursuant to Control of Exemption Clauses Ordinance 1989 (Cap. 71), similar to English law except that limits and reasonableness of unfair terms provisions do not apply to international supply contracts. Also, such provisions do not apply if Hong Kong law is law of contract only by choice of parties but will apply if contract term applies or purports to apply law of another territory in order to evade operation of Ordinance or if one party to contract dealt as consumer and was then habitually resident, and contract was essentially made, in Hong Kong.

Unconscionable Contract Terms Ordinance (Cap. 458) empowers Court to refuse to enforce any terms adjudged "unconscionable" as against consumer (having regard to relative bargaining positions, conduct and understanding of parties, duress or unreasonable conditions, and consideration paid).

Misrepresentation Ordinance (Cap. 284) deals with misrepresentations, whether fraudulent or innocent.

Distributorships, Dealerships and Franchises.—There is no specific legislation on these areas. Position is governed by general contract law and by trade mark law to lesser extent.

See also topic Trademarks and Passing Off.

COPYRIGHT AND REGISTERED DESIGNS:

Statute.—Copyright Act 1956 ("1956 Act") as amended by Design Copyright Act 1968 extends to H.K. by Copyright (Hong Kong) Orders 1972 and 1979.

Treaties.—Through U.K., Berne Convention and Universal Copyright Convention extend to H.K., hence convention countries enjoy copyright protection in H.K.

Protection.— Law protects not idea per se but material form in which it is expressed, namely, as in artistic, dramatic, musical and literary works, sound recordings, cinematograph films, television and sound broadcasts and published editions of works. No registration is required.

Copyright can subsist in work if it is original and created with skill and labour of author who is either qualified person (i.e. being resident and domiciled in U.K. or H.K. or is national of convention countries to which 1956 Act applies) or work is first published in U.K. or H.K. or in convention country.

For artistic, dramatic, musical and literary works, copyright extends to reproducing, publishing, performing, broadcasting, retransmitting or adapting work. Monopoly shall subsist for 50 years from death of author or 50 years after first publication. Exception: for artistic works for design which is registrable as registered design and has been industrially applied by manufacture of three-dimensional products in accordance therewith, term of copyright protection shall be for 15 years only from first publication or marketing.

For films, copyright extends to copying, broadcasting or showing in public. Soundtrack associated with film is sound recording which is entitled to separate protection. Monopoly shall subsist for 50 years from first publication.

For television or sound broadcasts, copyright extends to copying or rebroadcasting. Monopoly shall subsist for 50 years from first publication. Copyright (Amendment) Ordinance 1994 provides for copyright protection of cable television and programs similar to U.K. Cable and Broadcasting Act 1984.

By 1987 Order in Council, U.K. Copyright (Computer Software) Amendment Act 1985 (merged into U.K. Copyright, Designs and Patents Act 1988) was extended to H.K. Under this Act, computer programmes are protected as literary works.

Ownership.—Author who first puts idea in material form is legal owner, save for works created in course of employment where, in general, copyright is vested in employer and save for commissioned works where, in general, person commissioning is beneficial owner and can call upon author to assign to him copyright in works created pursuant to commission.

Assignment must be in writing signed by or on behalf of assignor.

Licence granted by owner of copyright shall be binding upon every successor in title to his interest in copyright, except purchaser in good faith for valuable consideration and without notice (actual or constructive) of licence or person deriving title from such purchaser.

Infringement.—It is infringement to reproduce copyright work in substantial manner or deal in course of trade with such infringing works. Question of substantial reproduction is to be determined by reference to quality not quantity. Court will determine whether there are objective similarities between copyright work and infringing copy and whether there is causal connection between the two.

In taking action for enforcement, affidavit purporting to have been made by copyright owner before notary public and stating that (i) at time specified therein copyright subsisted in work or other subject matter; (ii) person named therein is owner of copyright in work or other subject matter; and (iii) copy of work or other subject matter exhibited to affidavit is true copy of work or other subject matter, shall be admitted without further proof in any proceedings under Ordinance.

Civil remedies including injunctions, delivery up of goods, recovery of damages (including, where appropriate, damages on conversion basis), taking of accounts and discovery are available.

Criminal remedies are available under Copyright Ordinance by which any person who possesses, for purposes of trade or business, infringing copy of work or other subject matter in which copyright subsists is guilty of offence.

Enforcement of provisions under Copyright Ordinance is through Customs and Excise Department. Penalties shall be by way of fine as well as imprisonment.

Registered Designs.—

Statute.—United Kingdom Designs (Protection) Ordinance 1964.

Treaties.—Paris Convention.

Procedure.—No independent registration in H.K. is necessary as Ordinance extends like privileges and rights as though certificate of registration in U.K. had been issued with extension to H.K. However, consideration is being given to having independent registration of designs in H.K.

Protection lasts for as long as U.K. registered design is in force. i.e. 15 years from grant. Design is registrable if it is novel, has eye-appeal and is not solely dictated by function.

Registered proprietor of design shall not be entitled to recover any damages in respect of any infringement of copyright in design from defendant who proves that at date of infringement he was not aware, nor had any reasonable means of making him aware, of existence of registration of design.

For design which has been industrially applied by manufacture of three-dimensional products in accordance therewith, term of copyright protection shall be for 15 years only from first publication or marketing.

Infringement.—In determining question of infringement, only shapes and configuration will be considered and not functions. Matter must be judged by eyes of inexpert customers. Not only may articles be put side-by-side for comparison but test of imperfect recollection also applies.

Civil remedies such as injunction, delivery up of goods, damages and discovery are available.

Layout-design (Topography) of Integrated Circuits.—

Statute.—Layout-design of Integrated Circuits Ordinance. (Cap. 445).

Protection.—Law protects ownership in layout-design (topography) of integrated circuits. Layout-design (topography) means three-dimensional disposition of elements of integrated circuit and of interconnections of integrated circuit or such three-dimensional disposition prepared for integrated circuit intended for manufacture. Law does not protect layout-design created before operation of Ordinance. No registration is required.

Ownership.—Must be original and recorded in documentary form or incorporated into integrated circuit.

Rights of Owner.—Infringement of owner's rights if any person reproduces part or whole or exploits protected design.

Duration.—Ten years from end of year first commercially exploited anywhere in world. If not exploited, 15 years from end of year of creation.

See Topical Index in front part of this volume.

COPYRIGHT AND REGISTERED DESIGNS . . . *continued*

Assignment must be in writing and signed by or on behalf of assignor.

Licence granted by owner binds each successor-in-title except purchaser in good faith for value without notice and person deriving title from such purchaser.

Remedies.—Civil remedies, including injunction, seizure of goods, recovery of damages, taking of accounts and discovery.

CORPORATIONS:

Companies Ordinance (Cap. 32) which regulates corporations is substantially based on U.K. Companies Act of 1948.

Any two or more persons (including bodies corporate) may form limited company. Apart from issuance of at least two shares, there is no prescribed minimum amount for issued or authorised share capital.

Private company means company which by its Articles of Association restricts right to transfer its shares, limits number of shareholders to 50 and prohibits any invitation to public to subscribe for its shares or debentures. Company which does not impose such restrictions is public company. Public company may invite public to subscribe for its shares, usually by issue of prospectus. Name of limited company must end with word "limited" or its abbreviation "ltd.".

Companies may be formed as limited company (liability of members limited by shares or guarantee) or unlimited company (liability of members unlimited). Unlimited company can be reregistered as limited company, but not vice versa.

Public company may choose to become listed company, defined in Companies Ordinance as company which has any shares listed on Hong Kong Stock Exchange. Stricter requirements are imposed on listed companies or companies which are members of groups of which listed company is member.

Listed company is also regulated by Listing Rules of Stock Exchange and by legislation such as Securities (Stock Exchange Listing) Rules and Securities (Disclosure of Interests) Ordinance. (Cap. 396). See subhead Registers, infra.

Securities (Insider Dealing) Ordinance (Cap. 395) prohibits insider dealing in listed companies' securities and their derivatives (including contracts for differences, rights, options and interests), although it is not criminal offence.

Pursuant to Memorandum of Understanding between Securities and Futures Commission ("SFC") and The Stock Exchange of Hong Kong Limited ("SEHK"), SEHK is solely responsible for day-to-day administration of all listing related matters while SFC has statutory duty to oversee SEHK to ensure effective and impartial discharge of functions by SEHK. However, certain functions known as "SFC Listing Related Functions" continue to be discharged by SFC. Example is administration of Hong Kong Code on Takeovers and Mergers.

Significant number of listed companies have, in recent years, re-domiciled in offshore jurisdictions. Additionally a number of sizeable China corporations have listed in Hong Kong under arrangements between SFC and SEHK and relevant Chinese authorities. Listing Rules apply with modifications to overseas issuers as they do to Hong Kong issuers.

Companies must register Memorandum of Association setting out name, address, registered office, objects, statement of liability of members and amount of company's authorised share capital with number and value of shares into which such capital is divided.

Objects of company are set out in Memorandum which is company's charter. Acts which do not come within scope of "objects clause" (or ancillary powers) are ultra vires. Powers of company formed on or after 31st Aug. 1984 shall include, unless excluded or modified, those set forth in Ordinance.

Companies almost invariably file Articles of Association which are rules governing internal regulation, duties of directors, rights of voting, etc. If Articles not filed, statutory regulations known as "Table A" govern internal management. Applications for registrations of companies are made to Registrar of Companies, to whom proposed Memorandum and Articles are submitted.

Note: If enacted, Companies (Amendment) Bill 1996 will provide for abolition of doctrine of ultra vires. It will confer on company same powers as natural person, in addition to what it can do by virtue of its corporate status. Act of company outside its stated objects will not be invalid. Doctrine of constructive notice (as result of Registrar of Companies keeping copy of Memorandum or Articles) will also be abolished.

Prospectus.—Public company issuing prospectus (or if applicable, statement in lieu of prospectus) must set out particulars specified in Ordinance and if applicable must comply with SEHK and SFC requirements. Copy of every such prospectus (or statement) signed by every named director or proposed director or by his agent authorised in writing must be duly delivered to Registrar as required by Ordinance. No prospectus may be issued (or shares or debentures allotted) until this has been done. Every prospectus must be in English language and contain Chinese translation. Registrar takes no responsibility as to contents of prospectus.

Reports.—Every year companies must file with Registrar annual return in requisite form signed by director and company secretary containing specified information such as names of members, details of directors, etc. If company has share capital, return must give particulars of its share capital including extent to which it is paid up. Public companies are required to file accounts. Overseas corporations which have place of business in Hong Kong need to deliver to Registrar for registration return of any alteration in prescribed particulars and, for public company equivalent corporations, accounts.

In addition to foregoing, company is required to register with Registrar changes in share capital, special resolutions, changes in directors, secretary, registered office etc.

Directors.—Bodies corporate can act as directors of another company provided latter is private company which is not member of group which includes listed company.

Secretary of company must, if individual, ordinarily reside in Hong Kong or, if body corporate, have registered office or place of business in Hong Kong.

Registers.—Company must maintain various registers (available for inspection) including registers of members, directors, debenture holders and charges.

Under Securities (Disclosure of Interests) Ordinance (Cap. 396) listed company must maintain register of substantial shareholders' interests in its shares (where interest including related parties exceeds 10% of share capital carrying voting rights) and of directors' interests including related parties in its shares and debentures and in those of associated companies. Such information is also to be supplied to Stock Exchange.

Registration of Mortgages.—Mortgages and charges falling within categories specified in Companies Ordinance shall, so far as any security is conferred thereby, be void against liquidator and any creditor of company unless prescribed particulars and relevant instrument are delivered to Registrar within five weeks after date of creation. Time is slightly extended for charges created out of Hong Kong comprising property situate outside Hong Kong.

Categories include charges to secure any issue of debentures; charges on land or any interest therein; charges on book debts; floating charges on company's undertaking or property; charges on ship or any share in ship; and charges on goodwill, on patent, or licence under patent, on trademark or on copyright or licence under copyright.

Control of company is generally vested in its directors. Ordinance contains provisions on liability of directors. Companies (Amendment) Ordinance 1994, based on U.K. Company Directors (Disqualification) Act 1986, makes it easier for directors to be disqualified.

Companies Ordinance and, where applicable, Listing Rules make provision for protection of minority shareholders including protection against oppression of minority shareholders, maintenance of capital, restriction on distribution of profits and assets and disclosure of notifiable transactions.

Winding Up.—See topic Insolvency.

Foreign corporations establishing place of business in Hong Kong are required to register under Ordinance.

Companies (Amendment) Ordinance 1991 introduced major changes based on 1985 U.K. Act regarding financial assistance by company for acquisition of its own shares and purchase of such shares and also restrictions on distributions. Listing Rules are relevant for listed companies.

See also topics Fraudulent Preference; Fraudulent Trading.

COURTS:

Supreme Court consists of High Court of Justice and Court of Appeal.

High Court consists of Chief Justice, Judges appointed by Governor, Deputy Judges appointed by Chief Justice and Masters.

High Court is superior court of record, original and appellate jurisdiction. Civil jurisdiction is unlimited save as specifically provided for in any other legislation and includes Admiralty, Probate and Family Court jurisdictions.

Court of Appeal consists of Chief Justice and Justices of Appeal appointed by Governor.

Court of Appeal is superior court of record. Civil jurisdiction consists of appeals from most judgments and orders of High Court and such appeals as lie from District Court direct to Court of Appeal.

Criminal jurisdiction consists of appeals from High Court and District Court including applications and references by Attorney General for review of sentence or on questions of law.

Court of Appeal has authority and jurisdiction of court or tribunal from which appeal was brought to hear and determine any appeal and in relation to amendment, execution and enforcement of any judgment or order made on appeal. Appeals may lie as matter of right to Court of Appeal or may only be brought with leave of court or tribunal in question.

Privy Council.—Until June 30, 1997, appeals to Judicial Committee of U.K. Privy Council from Hong Kong Court of Appeal lie as of right where disputed matter amounts to minimum of HK$500,000 or at discretion of Court if, in its opinion, subject of appeal is of great general or public importance.

Court of Final Appeal will be established prior to July 1, 1997 and will assume and replace function of Privy Council on July 1, 1997. Court of Final Appeal will hear Civil Appeals as of right if at least HK$1,000,000 is involved or at discretion of Court if, in its opinion, subject of appeal is of great general or public importance. There will be statutory right of Criminal Appeal if there is point of law involved or risk of substantial and grave injustice. Rules for Court of Final Appeal are presently being drafted.

District Court.—Civil jurisdiction to hear and determine: (1) any action, counterclaim or set off in contract or tort for amount in excess of HK$15,000 and not more than HK$120,000; (2) action for recovery of land where annual rent, rateable value or annual value of land, whichever is least, does not exceed HK$100,000; (3) proceedings in respect of administration of estates not over HK$120,000; (4) foreclosure and redemption of any mortgage not exceeding HK$120,000; (5) divorce and family proceedings.

Action in which counterclaim exceeds Court's jurisdiction can be transferred to High Court.

District Court has power to grant injunctions in matters affecting moveable property of value not exceeding HK$120,000 and in respect of any contractual claim for amount not exceeding HK$120,000. Court has similar powers of enforcement to High Court.

Criminal jurisdiction consists of criminal actions transferred from Magistrates Courts in respect of which maximum sentence of imprisonment on any one charge or aggregate of two or more consecutive terms does not exceed seven years or one year in case of default of payment of fine and certain offences under Labour Tribunal Ordinance. (Cap. 25).

Lands Tribunal.—Division of District Court with jurisdiction to determine applications for new tenancies and possession of leased properties under Landlord & Tenant (Consolidation) Ordinance. (Cap. 7). Lands Tribunal has same jurisdiction as District Court to grant legal and equitable remedies and relief and is also empowered to transfer proceedings to High Court or District Court.

See Topical Index in front part of this volume.

COURTS . . . *continued*

Magistrates Courts.—Presided over by Magistrates. Deal with minor criminal offences punishable on summary conviction where penalty imposed upon conviction for offence does not exceed fine of HK$10,000 and/or imprisonment for six months, preliminary investigations of indictable offence prior to transfer to High Court or District Court and some civil or quasi-civil matters, for example, affiliation proceedings and money lenders licensing.

Small Claims Tribunal.—Civil jurisdiction to hear any monetary claim founded in contract, quasi-contract or tort for amount not exceeding HK$15,000.

Tribunal can on its own motion or application of any party transfer proceedings to District Court or High Court, including where any counterclaim and/or set off exceeds Tribunal's jurisdiction. Any party, or officer or servant of corporation, has right of audience. Legally qualified persons are prohibited from appearing for any party before Tribunal.

Labour Tribunal.—Exclusive jurisdiction for all claims for breach of term, express or implied, of contract of employment including claims for severance payments brought within one year of termination of employment. Tribunal can of its own volition decline jurisdiction and transfer claim to High Court or District Court. Party or officer or servant of incorporated or unincorporated entity has right of audience. Legally qualified persons do not have right of audience on behalf of claimant or defendant.

CURRENCY:

See topic Banking and Currency.

CUSTOMS:

Hong Kong is generally perceived as free port although customs duties are levied on some imports. Rates applicable to relevant categories of goods are governed by Dutiable Commodities Ordinance. (Cap. 109).

DATA PROTECTION:

New Personal Data (Privacy) Ordinance (No. 81 of 1995) is expected to come into effect towards end of 1996. It protects privacy of living individuals in relation to their personal data.

DECEDENTS' ESTATES:

See topic Descent and Distribution.

DEEDS:

In case of individuals, every deed must be signed, sealed and delivered by party to be bound or by his attorney and attested by at least one witness who must add to his signature his address and occupation or description. In case of companies, common seal must be used and attestation must be in accordance with company's Articles of Association.

Conveyancing and Property Ordinance (Cap. 219) states that any deed signed by individual shall be presumed to be sealed as such provided that document describes itself as deed or states that it has been sealed or bears any mark, impression or addition intended to be or to represent seal or position of seal. Further, where deed is executed by corporation in favour of person dealing with it, it will be deemed to have been duly executed if it purports to bear company seal affixed in presence of and attested by its secretary or other permanent officer of company and member of its board of directors or by two members of that board.

Person authorised by power of attorney to execute deed on behalf of corporation may execute deed by signing his own name or name of corporation and affixing his seal.

DEPOSITIONS AND DISCOVERY:

Court may, in any cause or order or if it appears necessary for purposes of justice, make order for examination on oath of any person before judge, officer or examiner of Court or some other person.

If person to be examined is out of jurisdiction, application may be made for order of issue of letter of request to judicial authorities of country concerned to take or cause to be taken evidence of any person in that country. Evidence will be taken on deposition by examiner or shorthand writer. Examination shall be conducted as if at trial and person examined may be cross-examined and reexamined. Validity of any objection to answer question will be decided by Court.

Deposition taken in above manner shall be received in evidence at trial.

Hong Kong court may, on request being made by foreign court in connection with pending or contemplated proceedings, order witness resident in Hong Kong to be examined by any official, proper person nominated by person applying for Order or any other qualified person as Court sees fit. Evidence of person to be examined shall be taken on deposition if Court is satisfied it has jurisdiction to make Order to give effect to request and in exercise of its discretion, it should make such Order.

Discovery.—After close of pleadings, each party to action will disclose all documents which are or have been in its possession, custody or power relating to matters in question in action. Documents privileged from production are (1) documents protected by legal professional privilege, (2) documents tending to incriminate or expose to forfeiture party who would produce them, (3) documents privileged on grounds of public policy.

(1) Legal professional privilege: (a) Letters and other communications between party and its legal adviser if document came into existence for purpose of getting and giving legal advice and assistance to client irrespective of whether litigation is contemplated or pending. (b) Documents coming into existence in connection with or for purpose of contemplated or pending litigation. (c) Documents coming into existence for purpose other than to seek advice or to instruct lawyer or expert may not be privileged notwithstanding that litigation may have been contemplated or commenced. (d) Privilege may be waived either voluntarily or by disclosure of privileged document or part on discovery or during course of proceedings.

(2) Documents tending to incriminate or expose party to proceedings or penalty under statute may be privileged.

(3) Documents may be privileged on grounds that production would be injurious to public interest, i.e. that withholding document is necessary for proper functioning of public service.

Other documents protected from disclosure include "without prejudice" communication, namely, any communications between parties for purpose of resolving dispute whether or not marked "without prejudice".

Further or specific discovery can be ordered by Court.

Witness Statements.—Court may, if it thinks fit for disposing fairly or expeditiously of any action or for saving costs, order exchange of written statements of oral evidence relating to issues of fact to be adduced at trial by each party's witnesses. Such statements are to stand as evidence-in-chief. Amendments and supplemental statements can only be served with leave of Court.

Evidence in Affidavits or Statements.—Computer or other records made in other legal proceedings or if person is not to be called or who cannot be called as witness may be adduced in evidence with leave of Court.

DESCENT AND DISTRIBUTION:

Distribution of intestates' estates is governed by Intestates' Estates Ordinance which came into effect on 7th Oct. 1971. Following are rules generally applied on intestacy once Letters of Administration have been granted.

Surviving spouse takes whole of estate absolutely if deceased leaves no issue and no parent or brother or sister or issue of such brother or sister. If deceased leaves surviving issue, surviving spouse takes sum of HK$500,000 free of death duties and costs with interest at 5% and half residue, issue taking other half residue. If no issue but parent or brother or sister or issue of such brother and sister, surviving spouse takes HK$1,000,000 free of death duties and costs with interest at 5% and half residue absolutely; if parent or parents survive, half residue passes to such parent or parents absolutely but if no parent survives half residue passes to brothers and sisters.

Where there is no surviving spouse surviving issue take whole estate in equal shares. If there is no issue but parent, parent takes. If both parents survive, they take in equal shares. If there is neither issue nor parent(s), relatives take as follows: (1) brothers and sisters of intestate and their issue; (2) grandparent(s) of intestate in equal shares if more than one; (3) uncles and aunts of intestate being brothers and sisters of parent of intestate; (4) Crown as bona vacantia.

Illegitimate Children.—Where death occurs after 19th June 1993, illegitimate person is now entitled to succeed on intestacy under Parent and Child Ordinance 1993 (Cap. 429) as would legitimate person. Entitlement under intestacy also extends to legitimate and illegitimate children of illegitimate persons. Similar rules apply to brothers and sisters, nephews and nieces, uncles and aunts and cousins.

See also topics Infancy and Wills.

DISCRIMINATION:

New Sex Discrimination Ordinance (No. 67 of 1995) renders unlawful certain kinds of sex discrimination, sexual harassment and discrimination on grounds of marital status or pregnancy. New Disability Discrimination Ordinance (No. 86 of 1995) renders unlawful discrimination against mental or physical disability or disease.

DISPUTE RESOLUTION:

Mandatory Dispute Resolution.—If party to arbitration agreement commences legal proceedings such proceedings may, in case of domestic arbitrations, be stayed under §6 of Arbitration Ordinance (Cap. 341), ("AO"), and must, in case of international arbitrations, be stayed under Art. 8 of UNCITRAL Model Law, so that arbitration can proceed. Certain other conditions need to be satisfied before stay is given. Factors affecting whether arbitration agreement is international are (1) parties place of business; (2) place of substantial part of obligations of commercial relationship; (3) place with which subject matter of dispute is most closely connected; (4) place of business which has closest relationship to arbitration agreement; or (5) habitual residence.

Alternative Dispute Resolution.—In addition to litigation and arbitration, there are number of methods of alternative dispute resolution which are becoming increasingly used in Hong Kong. These include mediation, conciliation and adjudication.

Mediation.—In Jan. 1994 mediation group was set up by Hong Kong International Arbitration Centre. Where there is mediator, parties cannot be forced to reach agreement. However, if there is arbitration agreement, and agreement is reached through mediation and parties enter into written agreement, then §2C of AO provides that settlement agreement may be enforced as arbitration award. No further legal proceedings would have to be commenced for settlement to be enforced save for application to Court for leave to enforce award.

Conciliation.—As per §2A of AO, where arbitration agreement provides for appointment of conciliator and further provides that person so appointed shall act as arbitrator if conciliation fails, no objection shall be taken to conciliator becoming arbitrator.

Adjudication.—Features in Hong Kong Government's Airport Core Project ("ACP") conditions of contract and Provisional Airport Authority conditions of contract for new Hong Kong Chek Lap Kok Airport. The Government ACP Adjudication Rules provide that "both parties agree to be bound by an Order of the Adjudicator and any liability of one party to make payment to the other party pursuant to such an order shall be deemed a debt due."

Hong Kong International Arbitration Centre: The Secretary-General, 38th Floor, Two Exchange Square, 8 Connaught Place, Hong Kong. Tel: (852) 2525 2381; Fax: (852) 2524 2171.

DIVORCE:

Matrimonial Causes Ordinances (Cap. 179) applies. *Note:* New amendments which came into force June 24, 1996, substantially alter rules in matrimonial proceedings. See subhead Amendments, infra. Presently, Hong Kong Court has jurisdiction in proceedings for divorce if: (a) if either party was domiciled in Hong Kong at date of

DIVORCE . . . *continued*
presentation of petition; (b) in proceedings by wife, (i) she has been resident in Hong Kong for three years; (ii) if deserted, husband was immediately before desertion domiciled in Hong Kong; (c) either party has substantial connection with Hong Kong.

Jurisdiction for proceedings for judical separation as for divorce if both parties are resident in Hong Kong at date of petition.

Proceedings for divorce cannot be brought within first year of marriage except in cases of exceptional hardship to petitioner or exceptional depravity on part of respondent.

Sole ground for divorce is irretrievable breakdown of marriage on one of following facts: (a) adultery on part of respondent and petitioner finds it intolerable to live with him/her; (b) respondent has behaved in such way that petitioner cannot reasonably be expected to live with him/her; (c) respondent has deserted petitioner for continuous period of at least one year immediately preceding presentation of petition; (d) parties have lived apart for continuous period of at least one year immediately preceding presentation of petition and respondent consents to decree; (e) parties have lived apart for continuous period of at least two years immediately preceding presentation of petition where no consent is forthcoming.

Petitioner cannot rely on adultery of respondent if parties continue living together for six or more months after date on which petitioner became aware of adultery. For purposes of determining whether parties have been separated for continuous period of one or two years, they must be living separate and apart. No account will be taken of any resumption of living together for period not exceeding six months. Where adultery is alleged, party alleging shall make person alleged to have committed adultery with other party to marriage party to proceedings unless excused by Court on special grounds for doing so.

Respondent to petition on grounds of five years separation may oppose grant of decree nisi on grounds that dissolution of marriage will result in great financial hardship and it would be wrong in all circumstances to dissolve marriage. Court will not grant decree absolute until satisfied that petitioner is not required to make financial provision for respondent or financial provision is fair and reasonable or best that can be made in circumstances.

On hearing of petition, Court will, if satisfied with facts alleged by petitioner that marriage has irretrievably broken down, grant decree nisi which can be made absolute on expiration of six weeks from date of grant subject to power of Court to rescind decree nisi.

Upon decree of judicial separation being granted, petitioner is no longer required to cohabit with respondent. Person shall not be prevented from applying for divorce on same facts as proved in support of grant of decree of judicial separation.

Court can make decree of presumption of death and dissolution of marriage if other party to marriage has been continuously absent from petitioner and petitioner has no evidence to believe other party is alive for period of seven years or more.

Either party to proceedings for divorce or judicial separation may make claim against other for financial provision including maintenance pending suit, periodical payments, secured periodical payments, lump sum, settlement of property, transfer of property or variation of settlement.

On application for Order relating to custody of or access to child, Court may make such Order as it considers fair and which is in best interests of child.

Former spouse, who has not remarried, of person who dies domiciled in Hong Kong may make claim against deceased's estate for financial provision or further financial provision within six months from date of death. Court will take into account what would be reasonable for financial provision for survivor and that person's conduct in relation to deceased and any other matter which appears relevant or material. Similarly wife who has not remarried, infant son or unmarried daughter, or son or daughter who is not capable of maintaining himself or herself because of mental or physical disability may make claim for periodical payments or financial provision from deceased's estate.

Foreign decrees of divorce will be recognised if decree of divorce was obtained in country in which either spouse was habitually resident or national. Decree of divorce or legal separation obtained outside Hong Kong may not be deemed valid if obtained by one spouse without notice to other or if other spouse was not given opportunity to take part in proceedings or if it would be manifestly contrary to public policy to recognise decree.

As of June 24, 1996, no action shall lie for damages for adultery or criminal conversation. There is also new joint application for divorce and in such case, Court shall not hold that marriage has broken down irretrievably unless it is satisfied of either one or both of following facts: (1) parties have lived apart for continuous period of one year; and (2) not less than one year prior to making of application notice signed by each party was given to Court and notice was not subsequently withdrawn.

DOMICILE:

For estate duty (see topic Taxation, subhead Estate Duty), factors such as domicile, residence and nationality of deceased are generally irrelevant.

Conceptually, though, approach on domicile is similar to that expressed in England Law Digest.

ENVIRONMENT:

Existing legislation covers air, water, noise and waste disposal. Failure to comply can attract prison sentences and/or substantial fines.

Air Pollution Control Ordinance (APCO) (Cap. 311) controls pollution from stationary sources by establishment of ten air control zones and licensing system. Premises operating "specified process" must be licensed or, if established pre-1983, exempted. Most such premises are, in fact, exempted. Additionally, Town Planning Ordinance (Cap. 131) requires environment to be factor in approval of building plans.

Various regulations limit emission of smoke, sulphur dioxide, nitrogen oxide and particulates from industrial plants.

APCO also requires petrol retailers to take all reasonable steps to stock and sell unleaded petrol. Stringent emission design standards are imposed on post-1992 vehicles.

By 1997, Hong Kong government intends to license all major air polluting industrial processes through Environmental Protection Department (EPD).

Ozone Layer Protection Ordinance (Cap. 403) brings into force Vienna Convention for the Protection of the Ozone Layer 1985 and Montreal Protocol on Substances that Deplete the Ozone Layer 1987 by prohibiting manufacture of CFCs and three halons.

Water Pollution Control Ordinance (Cap. 358) prohibits discharge of poisonous or noxious matter into Hong Kong waters, establishes ten water control zones with individual water-quality objectives, and licenses discharges of pollutants in water control zones only. Those established pre-1981 are exempt from licensing. EPD is empowered to require owner of wastewater treatment facility in water control zone to repair or modify operations.

Building Ordinance (Cap. 123) empowers Building Authority to require construction and maintenance of waste treatment facilities, sewage works and related systems.

Merchant Shipping (Prevention and Control of Pollution) Ordinance (Cap. 413) and its regulations control dangerous and large amounts of oil and other toxic substances carried by tankers in accordance with International Convention for the Protection of Pollution from Ships 1973.

Noise Control Ordinance (Cap. 400) regulates industrial noise to levels according to area, time of day and impact of other noise sources through permit system.

Civil Aviation (Aircraft Noise) Ordinance (Cap. 312) and subsidiary regulations ensure that subsonic jets are certified in accordance with International Convention on Civil Aviation.

Various regulations limit motor vehicle and railway noise pollution.

Waste Disposal Ordinance (Cap. 354) provides for licensing of waste collection, disposal services (including waste treatment and recycling), land use for waste disposal (excluding landfills operated by Civil Engineering Department), waste importation and control of livestock waste. Chemical waste producers and transporters must register with EPD and provide adequate storage. Waste must be conveyed by licensed collector to licensed site. EPD "trip tickets" monitor waste movement. However, definition of chemical waste is not unequivocal; many textile processing effluents may be said to fall outside definition in Ordinance.

New Dumping at Sea Ordinance controls disposal of waste at sea and reproduces UK Dumping at Sea Act.

Implementation of Basel Convention on transboundary movement of chemical waste is planned.

Environment Impact Assessment.—Hong Kong government intends to make statutory requirement for environmental impact assessments and detailed public consultations for major development projects. Environmental Impact Assessment Bill 1996 proposes that Environmental Impact Assessment ("EIA") will be necessary if project falls within extensive Schedule of Designated Projects. Applicant must prepare EIA report based on study brief and technical memorandum supplied by Hong Kong Government. Designated projects may not be constructed or operated without compliance with Environmental Permit (and conditions).

General Supervision.—Environmental Protection Department, 24th-28th Floors, Southorn Centre, 130 Hennessy Road, Wan Chai, Hong Kong. Tel.: (852) 2835 1018, fax: (852) 2838 2155.

EVIDENCE:

See topic Depositions and Discovery.

EXCHANGE CONTROL:

There are no exchange control restrictions on transfer of funds into or out of Hong Kong.

EXECUTIONS:

Judgment or order of Court, including judgments or awards of foreign courts or arbitrators enforceable in Hong Kong, may be enforced as follows:

1. Writs of Execution: (i) Writ of fieri facias—order to Court appointed officers to take possession of judgment debtor's goods and chattels of value to satisfy judgment and sell such goods at public auction and pay proceeds after deduction of costs of execution to judgment creditor. Property of company liable to seizure includes debentures; (ii) writ of possession—to enforce judgment or order giving possession of land; (iii) writ of delivery—to enforce judgment or order giving delivery of any goods; (iv) writ of sequestration—rarely used process of contempt in cases of disobedience of order or judgment by judgment debtor permitting property to be seized until judgment debtor has purged his contempt and complied with original order.

Execution can be issued to enforce payment of any money or costs by Crown, any government department or officer of Crown.

2. Garnishment.—Judgment creditor who has obtained judgment or order for at least HK$1,000 against judgment debtor who is owed any debt or some other sum by third party (garnishee) may seek order that such sum be paid directly to creditor in full or partial satisfaction of judgment or order.

Application is made ex parte by affidavit. Garnishee is required to attend before Court to show cause why such sum should not be paid to judgment creditor. If garnishee does not dispute debt, Court will make order absolute which can be enforced in same manner as any other order for payment of money. If liability is disputed, Court will determine issue summarily or order that any question necessary for determining liability of garnishee be tried.

See topic Attachment.

3. Examination of Judgment Debtor.—Court may on application of judgment creditor order judgment debtor to attend before Court and be orally examined on oath as to (1) what debts he may have owing to him, (2) what means he has of satisfying judgment or order.

If judgment debtor is body corporate, director or other officer can be ordered to attend and be asked same questions.

Court may order judgment debtor to produce any relevant books or documents.

EXECUTIONS . . . *continued*

Failure to comply with order to attend court, refusal to make full disclosure or wilful disposal of assets to avoid satisfying judgment amount is contempt punishable by committal to prison or prohibition from leaving Hong Kong until debt is satisfied.

4. Charging Order.—Judgment creditor may apply ex parte on notice for order imposing charge over any property of judgment debtor or property in respect of which judgment debtor has interest to secure payment.

Interest includes interest held by debtor beneficially or under trust.

Property includes: (1) land; (2) securities including (a) government stock, (b) stock of any body incorporated in Hong Kong or outside Hong Kong being stock registered in register kept in Hong Kong, (c) units of any unit trust in respect of which register of unit holders is kept in Hong Kong; (3) funds in Court.

Charge may be extended to cover dividends, interest, other distributions or bonus issues.

Court will take into account personal circumstances of debtor and whether any other creditor of debtor will be unduly prejudiced by such order.

Court will, if satisfied that sums are owed to judgment creditor, make order to show cause why charging order should not be granted. On further consideration of matter, Court will either make order absolute, with or without modification, or discharge it.

Court has power to order enforcement of charging order by sale of property charged.

5. Stop Notice.—Order obtainable by person claiming to be beneficially entitled to interest in any securities in respect of which Charging Order can be obtained may seek order prohibiting judgment debtor from disposing of or dealing with securities without notice to judgment creditor of proposed transfer or payment. Similarly Court may make order prohibiting transfer of or dealing with securities or payment out of funds in Court.

6. Appointment of Receiver.—Court has power to appoint receiver by way of equitable execution which shall operate in relation to all legal estates and interests in land of judgment debtor.

7. Injunctions.—High Court may grant interlocutory or final injunction during course of proceedings or following judgment to restrain party to proceedings whether or not domiciled, resident or present in jurisdiction, from removing from jurisdiction of High Court or otherwise prohibiting removal of assets within jurisdiction.

Party seeking injunction may be required to give undertaking in damages to defendant and undertake to bank or innocent third party to pay any expenses reasonably incurred by them.

Court is also empowered to grant injunction to prevent any threatened or apprehended waste or trespass.

Court has power to order delivery up of goods and restrain disposal of goods, property and assets of debtor or judgment debtor. Court has further power to permit applicant to enter premises and search for and remove articles relating to infringement of applicant's rights.

8. Committal.—Court has power to punish contempt by committal to imprisonment.

9. Bankruptcy; Winding-up of Company.—See topic Insolvency.

10. Prohibition Order.—Court, if satisfied that person owing money or subject to monetary judgment or order will leave Hong Kong thereby obstructing or delaying satisfaction of judgment, may make order prohibiting that person from leaving Hong Kong. Order renewable after one month for total of three months. Order is served on Director of Immigration and Commissioner for Police. Judgment debtor is liable to arrest and to be brought before Court in event he seeks to leave Hong Kong. Court can, on application, discharge order or impose such terms as it considers fit including ordering debtor to pay amount into Court.

11. Exemptions from Execution.—Tools and equipment necessary for debtor's employment, clothing, bedding, furniture and household equipment necessary for basic needs of debtor and his family may not be seized.

Chattels in which judgment debtor has equitable interest cannot be seized. Property owned by co-owners cannot be seized on behalf of third party unless two persons have separate and different interests in chattel in which case judgment debtor's interest only can be sold. Property on hire cannot be seized.

Person who claims ownership or interest in property seized on execution can intervene and apply to Court to determine any question relating to ownership.

EXECUTORS AND ADMINISTRATORS:

Probate and Administration Ordinance (Cap. 10) together with Non-Contentious Probate Rules set out law relating to probate and letters of administration and to administration of estates of deceased persons. Rules of English law governing rights and duties of executors and administrators generally apply. See England Law Digest.

Where deceased left will, person or persons entitled to grant of probate or administration with will annexed shall be determined in accordance with following order of priority, namely: executor; any residuary legatee or devisee holding in trust for any other person; any residuary legatee or devisee for life; ultimate residuary legatee or devisee; any specific legatee or devisee or any creditor; any legatee or devisee on happening of any contingency.

Where person dies wholly intestate, persons having beneficial interest in estate shall be entitled to grant of administration in following order of priority, namely: surviving spouse; children of deceased or issue of any such child who predeceased deceased; parent of deceased; brothers and sisters of deceased or issue of any predeceased brother or sister of deceased; Official Administrator.

Where deceased died domiciled outside Hong Kong, Court may order that grant issue to (a) persons entrusted with administration of estate by court having jurisdiction at place where deceased died domiciled; (b) person entitled to administer estate by law of place where deceased died domiciled; (c) such person as Registrar may direct in absence of (a) and (b). In all cases, Court will require affidavit as to foreign law to be sworn by attorney-at-law at place where deceased died domiciled. Without such court order, grant may be issued to executor or any person named in will whose duties constitute him/her executor; or in accordance with Hong Kong laws as if deceased died domiciled in Hong Kong, where whole of estate in Hong Kong consists of immovable property.

Grants to Estate of Commonwealth Residents.—Hong Kong Probate Registry shall have jurisdiction to reseal grants of probate or letters of administration (or exemplification) made by court of probate in any part of British Commonwealth or by British Court.

Estate duty (see topic Taxation) must be settled before probate can be granted or letters of administration issued.

FOREIGN CORPORATIONS:

See topic Corporations.

FOREIGN EXCHANGE:

No restrictions on foreign exchange. Local dollar is pegged to U.S. dollar. See topic Banking and Currency.

FOREIGN INVESTMENT:

Generally no restrictions on foreign investment.

FRAUDS, STATUTE OF:

In Hong Kong all that remains of U.K. Statute of Frauds Act is provision relating to formalities for contracts for sale of land. This provision is found in §3 of Conveyancing and Property Ordinance. (Cap. 219).

Conveyance of property to any person other than bona fide purchaser for value without notice made with intent to defraud creditors is voidable at instance of any person thereby prejudiced.

Voluntary disposition of land made with intent to defraud subsequent purchaser is voidable at instance of such purchaser.

Voluntary settlements, although not fraudulent, are voidable under certain circumstances. (Bankruptcy Ordinance Cap. 6).

FRAUDULENT PREFERENCE:

See topic Bankruptcy for individual.

By Companies Ordinance any conveyance, mortgage, delivery of goods, payment, execution or other act relating to property made or done by company within six months before commencement of its winding up which for individual would be fraudulent preference shall, if company is wound up, be deemed fraudulent preference of its creditors and be invalid accordingly. Any conveyance or assignment by company of all its property to trustees for benefit of all its creditors shall be void. Where anything made or done is void as fraudulent preference of person interested in property mortgaged or charged to secure company's debt, person so preferred shall be subject to same liabilities, and have same rights, as if he had undertaken to be personally liable as surety for debt to extent of charge in property or value of his interest, whichever is less.

FRAUDULENT TRADING:

Companies Ordinance provides that if in course of winding up company it appears that any business of company has been carried on with intent to defraud creditors or for any fraudulent purpose, Court may declare that any person knowingly party shall be personally responsible without limitation of liability for all debts or other liabilities of company as Court may direct.

GARNISHMENT:

See topic Executions.

HUSBAND AND WIFE:

Married woman is capable of acquiring, holding and disposing of property, rendering herself and being rendered liable in respect of any tort, contract debt or obligation. Married woman is capable of suing or being sued in tort or contract and is subject to law relating to bankruptcy and enforcement of judgments.

All property belonging to or acquired by woman before or after marriage shall belong to her as if she were unmarried.

Parties to marriage have right of action in tort against each other. However, Court may stay action brought during subsistence of marriage if of view that no substantial benefit will accrue to either party.

Court can consider any question between husband and wife as to title and property.

Husband is not, by reason only of being husband of woman, liable for any tort committed by her or any contractual liability or debt incurred by her.

IMMIGRATION:

Law relating to immigration and deportation is set out in Immigration Ordinance. (Cap. 115). Hong Kong permanent resident enjoys right of abode in Hong Kong, that is to say he has right (a) to land in Hong Kong; (b) not to have condition of stay imposed upon him; (c) not to have deportation order made against him; (d) not to have removal order made against him.

Immigrant is person not Hong Kong permanent resident. Hong Kong permanent resident is: (1) Any person wholly or partly of Chinese race who has at any time been ordinarily resident in Hong Kong for continuous period of not less than seven years. (2)(A) Any person who is British Dependent Territories citizen and who has connection with Hong Kong (there are detailed provisions on whether person has connection with Hong Kong); (B) any person who is British Dependent Territories citizen who has at any time been married to person specified in subparagraph (A). (3) Any person who is Commonwealth citizen and who immediately before 1st Jan. 1983 had right to land in Hong Kong by virtue of §8(1)(a) of Ordinance as then in force.

Resident British Citizen—British citizen who has at any time been ordinarily resident in Hong Kong for continuous period of not less than seven years.

Resident U.K. belonger—U.K. belonger who was at any time before 1st Jan. 1983 ordinarily resident in Hong Kong for continuous period of not less than seven years.

IMMIGRATION . . . *continued*

Rights enjoyed by Resident British Citizen and Resident U.K. belonger are similar to those enjoyed by permanent resident except that deportation orders may be imposed against them.

Under visa regulations introduced in mid-Sept. 1992, persons from many parts of world are allowed to visit Hong Kong for up to three months without visa.

Persons having right of abode or right to land in Hong Kong do not require visa to work in Hong Kong. Similarly, British citizens do not require such visa. Persons having no right of abode or right to land in Hong Kong and who are not British citizens must obtain visa to come to Hong Kong for employment or investment.

Note: With change of sovereignty for Hong Kong, there will be substantial changes for criteria for Hong Kong permanent residents and for those seeking residence in Hong Kong. Details will be available closer to July 1997.

INCOME TAX:

See topic Taxation.

INDUSTRIAL PROPERTY RIGHTS:

See topics Copyright and Registered Designs; Patents; Trade Descriptions; Trademarks and Passing Off.

INFANCY:

Age of majority is 18 years.

Infant can only bring claim in High Court through his next friend or guardian ad litem but may sue or defend action within jurisdiction of District Court unless Court is of view that infant cannot properly present his case or defend action in which case Court can order representation of infant through his next friend or guardian ad litem.

Contracts entered into with minor are generally unenforceable except for necessaries, i.e. objects necessary for infant having regard to his station in life, and registered contracts of apprenticeship. See topic Contracts.

Will made by infant is not valid except for privileged wills i.e. made under provisions applicable to making of wills by members of armed forces or seamen.

No child under age seven can be guilty of offence. Minor cannot be imprisoned for failing to pay fine. Minor over 16 shall not be imprisoned unless Court is of opinion that there is no other method of dealing with that person.

Both father and mother are guardians of infant and have same rights in respect of child. If parents are unmarried, mother is sole guardian; father will only have such rights in respect of child as may have been ordered by Court on application brought by father. On death of parent, surviving parent shall be guardian of infant either solely or with any guardian appointed by deceased or, where appropriate, Court appointed guardian.

District Court has jurisdiction to hear matters relating to custody, guardianship, wardship and maintenance of child. Court may appoint guardian(s) of child with or to exclusion of parent and give directions in relation to disputes between joint guardians of child.

Illegitimate child is legitimated on marriage of its parents. Also Parent and Child Ordinance has reduced legal disabilities associated with illegitimacy.

See also topics Descent and Distribution and Wills.

INHERITANCE TAX:

See topic Taxation.

INSOLVENCY:

Insolvency law is contained in Companies Ordinance, Companies (Winding Up) Rules and Bankruptcy Ordinance. Companies Ordinance provides for application of bankruptcy law in winding up companies. Companies incorporated in Hong Kong can be placed in either voluntary liquidation or compulsory liquidation by order of Court. Voluntary liquidation can be either members voluntary liquidation or creditors voluntary liquidation.

Voluntary liquidation may be commenced by resolution of directors supported by statutory declaration that company cannot by reason of its liabilities continue its business.

Basis on which company can be placed in voluntary liquidation is same for both members voluntary and creditors voluntary winding up. Company may be placed in voluntary liquidation if (a) Memorandum and Articles of Association provide for company to exist for specified duration and that has expired, (b) shareholders resolve by special resolution (75% of those who attend personally or by proxy) to wind up company, (c) shareholders resolve by special resolution that company cannot by reason of its liabilities continue its business and it is advisable to wind it up.

In members voluntary liquidation declaration of solvency must be made and special resolution is required. Liquidator must be appointed at same time as special resolution is passed.

Liquidator will realize assets of company and complete administration and pay dividend. Assets do not vest in liquidator; they remain assets of company. Liquidator acts as agent of company and is in fiduciary position to company and in compulsory liquidation is officer of Court.

Compulsory liquidation is commenced when petition is filed. Court will hear petition and make winding up order if appropriate. Official Receiver will be appointed as Provisional Liquidator and convene first meeting of creditors and contributories (contributory has been held to be member holding partially or fully paid shares). First meeting of creditors and contributories will vote on appointment of liquidator and whether or not to appoint committee of inspection.

Company may be placed into compulsory liquidation if (a) shareholders resolve by special resolution to wind company up, (b) company suspends its business within one year of incorporation or suspends its business for one year, (c) number of shareholders is reduced below two, (d) company is unable to pay its debts, (e) Memorandum and Articles of Association of company provide that company be wound up on certain event occurring and that event occurs, (f) it is just and equitable for company to be wound up. Registrar of Companies may petition for winding up if (a) company is being carried on for unlawful purpose or for any lawful purpose but which it cannot carry out, (b) in last six months company has not had two directors or secretary, (c) company has persistently failed to pay statutory fees or been in breach of Companies Ordinance.

At any time after petition has been presented, Court may make order staying legal proceedings commenced against company.

After winding up order is made Official Receiver as Provisional Liquidator takes possession and control of company's property. After winding up order has been made, statement of affairs must be made by director of company. Statement of affairs will include (a) particulars of assets and liabilities, (b) list of secured and nonsecured creditors, (c) particulars of securities.

Any transfer or mortgage of property to creditor made within six months prior to commencement of winding up which if done by individual would be fraudulent preference will be invalid as fraudulent preference. See topic Fraudulent Preference.

If in course of liquidation it appears that any business of company has been carried on with intent to defraud creditors of company or creditors of any other person or for any fraudulent purpose, persons who were knowingly parties can be held responsible for all or any of company's debts without limitation. See topic Fraudulent Trading.

Where company is being wound up, floating charge on undertaking or property of company created within 12 months of commencement of winding up shall, unless proved that company was solvent immediately after charge created, be invalid except to cash amount paid to company at or after creation of and in consideration for charge together with prescribed interest.

Preferential claims of unsecured creditors are paid before ordinary creditors. Preferential claims include certain employees' claims and Crown claims which have become due and payable within 12 months before commencement of winding up. Ordinary creditors' claims are dealt with pari passu. See topic Bankruptcy.

If debt did not specifically provide for rate of interest, interest may be recovered at rate of 8% per annum from time debt was repayable up to date of winding up order.

Company incorporated outside Hong Kong whether or not registered as foreign corporation and whether or not carrying on business in Hong Kong may be wound up in Hong Kong if (a) company has been dissolved or ceased to carry on business, (b) it is unable to pay its debts, (c) it is just and equitable that it be wound up.

Most provisions relating to winding up of companies in Hong Kong apply to foreign companies wound up in Hong Kong.

See also topic Bankruptcy.

INTEREST:

Interest can be charged only if agreed between parties.

Claim for interest can be made in any action at such rate and for such period as may have been agreed. In absence of any contractual entitlement for interest, interest is recoverable generally from date of issue of proceedings at rates fixed by Court from time to time.

It is offence to lend or offer to lend money at effective rate of interest which exceeds 60% per annum. No agreement for repayment of loan or interest where rate exceeds 60% per annum is enforceable. Court may reopen loan transactions if interest is extortionate. Loan transaction is presumed to be extortionate if effective rate of interest exceeds 48%.

INTESTACY:

See topic Descent and Distribution.

JUDGMENTS:

Monetary judgments, awards and orders of Court can be enforced in prescribed manner—see topic Executions.

Judgment can be entered if defendant fails to acknowledge service, file defence or comply with Court Order.

Summary judgment may be granted if Court is satisfied upon hearing affidavit evidence that there is no defence or no issue which should be tried at trial with oral evidence.

Enforcement of Foreign Judgments.—Judgments of some reciprocating Commonwealth and foreign countries can be registered and enforced in Hong Kong as if judgments of Hong Kong Courts if: (1) judgment is final and conclusive and not interlocutory or default judgment and no appeal lies against it or is still pending; (2) judgment is for sum of money not being sum payable in respect of taxes or like charges or fine or penalty; (3) bringing of proceedings in overseas court was not contrary to agreement under which any dispute would be settled otherwise than by proceedings in that foreign court; (4) party against whom judgment was given, brought or agreed to bringing of proceedings in overseas court and counterclaimed or otherwise submitted to jurisdiction of overseas court.

Party will not be regarded as having submitted to jurisdiction of overseas court if he appeared only to (1) contest jurisdiction of court; (2) seek dismissal or stay of proceedings on grounds that dispute should be submitted to arbitration or determination of courts in another country; (3) protect or obtain release of property seized or threatened to be seized in proceedings.

No proceedings may be brought by party in Hong Kong on cause of action in respect of which judgment has been given in his favour in proceedings between same parties in court of overseas country unless that judgment is not enforceable or entitled to recognition in Hong Kong.

Application to register judgment is made ex parte on affidavit within six years of date of judgment or, if appeal, last judgment. Judgment, if registered, is enforceable in same manner as judgment of Hong Kong Court.

Registration of judgment may be set aside if Court is satisfied (1) judgment is not judgment to which provisions apply, (2) courts of country of original court had no jurisdiction, (3) judgment debtor did not receive notice of proceedings in sufficient time to enable him to defend action and did not appear, (4) judgment was obtained by fraud, (5) enforcement of judgment is contrary to public policy in Hong Kong, (6) rights of judgment are not vested in person by whom application for registration is made, (7) subject matter of proceedings was immoveable property outside country of original court, (8) judgment debtor was person entitled to immunity in country of original court and did not submit to jurisdiction of that court.

See Topical Index in front part of this volume.

JUDGMENTS . . . *continued*

Provisions in relation to enforcement of foreign judgments will be subject to ratification by China for post-July 1, 1997 period.

Reciprocal Enforcement of Maintenance Orders.—Maintenance Orders made in some reciprocating Commonwealth countries may be registered in Hong Kong if it appears that person to make payment under Order was residing in Hong Kong; Order may be enforced as judgment made in District Court of Hong Kong subject to Court's entitlement to refuse to confirm Order if payer establishes any defence he may have raised in proceedings in which Order was made, or confirm Order or make such alterations as it thinks reasonable.

Registered Order is enforceable as civil debt. Court has power to vary registered Order.

Judgments of nonreciprocating jurisdictions cannot be registered but if final can be sued upon and may be relied upon in such proceedings.

JUDICIARY:

See topic Courts.

LABOUR RELATIONS:

Individual rights principally governed by Employment Ordinance (Cap. 57), which applies to all employees, but there are limits on amounts payable. Any term in contract of employment purporting to reduce employee's benefit under Ordinance is void.

Minor Employment Claims Adjudication Board deals with claims for up to five claimants for maximum amount per claimant of HK$5,000.

Labour Tribunal deals with all other employment disputes. See topic Courts, subhead Labour Tribunal.

In absence of contractual provision, contract of employment is deemed to be contract for one month renewable from month to month determinable on one month's notice or payment of money in lieu.

Employer entitled to dismiss summarily if employee wilfully disobeys lawful or reasonable order; misconducts himself, such conduct being inconsistent with due and faithful discharge of his duty; guilty of fraud or dishonesty; or habitually neglectful of duties; or for any other common law ground entitling determination without notice.

Damages for wrongful termination of contract of such sum as is equal to amount of wages that would have accrued during period of notice.

Employee may terminate without notice on grounds including fear of physical danger by violence or disease not contemplated by employment; being permanently unfit; subjected to ill-treatment by employer.

Female employees employed for 26 weeks are entitled to maternity leave of four weeks before and six weeks after confinement and if employed for more than 40 weeks, paid maternity leave. Employer is not permitted to pay money in lieu of maternity leave.

Employment of pregnant woman employed for period of 12 weeks or more cannot be terminated unless she fails to give requisite notice of pregnancy.

Employee is entitled to be member of union. Employers are prohibited from preventing exercise of union activities, discriminating against union member when offering employment and terminating employment because of union membership.

Wages are to be paid directly to employee in legal tender. However, with consent of employee, wages may be paid: (a) by cheque, money order or postal order; (b) into account in his name with any bank licensed under Banking Ordinance; or (c) to his duly appointed agent.

Employees employed under continuous contract of employment are entitled to: (1) end of year payment equal to one month's salary or proportionate to period of year worked, if such payment is term of contract of employment; (2) sickness allowance, if employed for one month or more, accruing at rate of two days for each completed month of employment in first 12 months and thereafter four paid days each month to cumulative total of 120 days; (3) paid leave for public holidays, at least one rest day per week and not less than seven days holidays.

Subject as provided, there is entitlement to severance pay if employee employed for continuous period of not less than 24 months, if laid off or dismissed by reason of redundancy, i.e. employer has ceased to carry on business for which employee was employed or requirement of business for employees to carry out work of particular kind has ceased or diminished. Long service payment provisions may be applicable if no liability for severance payment.

Employer is liable to pay compensation for: (a) personal injury by accident or contraction of occupational disease resulting in total or partial incapacity or (b) death arising out of or in course of employment or arising while travelling to or from place of employment or on travelling arranged by employer.

Employer not entitled to employ employee unless there is in force in relation to such employee policy of insurance issued by insurer for full amount of liability of employer for any injury to such employee by accident arising out of or in course of his employment.

Employment (Amendment) (No. 1) Bill 1996 proposes extended protection and increased flexibility in benefits available to pregnant women.

Employment (Amendment) (No. 2) Bill 1996 proposes to (1) amend definition of wages; (2) deem contract of employment terminated by employer if he fails to pay wages for more than one month; (3) provide for presumption that annual payment or annual bonus is not gratuitous payable only at discretion of employer; (4) reduce qualifying service for pro rata payment from 26 weeks to three months; (5) provide payment of interest on outstanding wages; and (6) remove percentage reduction in long service payments.

Recently enacted Occupational Retirement Schemes Ordinance (Cap. 426) ("ORSO") does not require employers to establish retirement scheme, but its implications are significant for employers currently operating scheme or intending to establish one in future. Object of Ordinance is to set up compulsory registration system for retirement schemes operated by private sector to ensure that these schemes are properly funded, operated and monitored. New Mandatory Provident Fund Schemes Ordinance (No. 80 of 1995) ("MPFO") provides for establishment, registration and management of nongovernmental mandatory provident fund schemes. MPFO is distinct from ORSO. MPFO obliges all employers and employees to participate in retirement schemes; ORSO regulates operation of voluntary retirement schemes. There will be some degree of overlap as MPFO will recognise some voluntary schemes registered under ORSO. Although existing employees in ORSO may be exempted, new employees will have to join MPF scheme.

See topic Discrimination.

LANDLORD AND TENANT:

Leases are generally governed by principles of contract but increase of rent and termination or renewal of tenancies of certain premises are subject to Landlord and Tenant (Consolidation) Ordinance. (Cap. 7).

LAW REPORTS:

Law Reports published by Hong Kong Government include Hong Kong Law Reports, Hong Kong Tax cases and Inland Revenue Department Board of Review Decisions. *Note:* Comprehensive set of law reports has been published by commercial publishing house and commercial publication of Hong Kong law commentaries is in progress.

LEGISLATURE:

See topic Constitution and Government.

LIENS:

Lien is legal right entitling person in possession of chattels to retain them until all claims and accounts of person in possession against owner of chattels for services rendered or monies spent or work carried out on property of other have been satisfied.

Lien can be (1) general, i.e. common law right arising from general usage or by express agreement entitling person in possession to retain goods until all claims and accounts of person in possession against owner are satisfied (e.g. solicitor's entitlement to retain client's papers until discharge of all sums due); (2) particular, i.e. right at common law to retain goods in respect of which charges have been incurred until those charges are paid (e.g. carrier's right to retain goods in respect of which freight remains unpaid).

Lien is unassignable personal right which lasts for as long as possession of goods persists. It is defence not right of action. There is no entitlement of sale unless provided for by statute.

Lien is lost by (1) tender of payment, (2) abandonment, (3) taking alternative security, (4) loss of possession and (5) in cases of liquidation, receivership and bankruptcy where lien had not fully taken effect at relevant time.

Express entitlement in Sale of Goods Ordinance (Cap. 26) for unpaid seller, i.e. one to whom full price has not been paid or tendered, including seller's agent to whom bill of lading has been endorsed, to exercise lien until payment notwithstanding that title may have passed to buyer. There is limited right of resale where property has not passed from unpaid seller. See topic Sales.

Lien is terminated when (a) unpaid seller delivers goods to carrier or other bailee for purpose of transmission to buyer without reserving right of disposal, (b) buyer or agent lawfully obtains possession of goods, (c) by waiver.

LIMITATION OF ACTIONS:

Governed by Limitation Ordinance. (Cap. 347).

Actions in contract or tort or to enforce award must be brought within six years from date on which cause of action accrued.

Claims for damages for personal injuries or arising from death must be commenced within three years from date of event from which injuries arose or from death. In limited circumstances, Court has power to extend period.

Claims for or in respect of land including claims to secure land or money secured by mortgage must be brought within 12 years. Crown is entitled to bring any action in respect of land at any time prior to expiration of 60 years from date on which right of action accrued.

Claims based on fraud or relief from mistake or in circumstances of concealment by defendant of any fact relevant to plaintiff's right of action must be brought within six years of discovery of fraud, mistake or concealment or time when such fraud, mistake or concealment could with reasonable diligence have been discovered. However, no action can be brought to recover property or set aside any transaction where innocent third party has acquired property for valuable consideration since fraud, concealment or transaction took place.

Limitation period in respect of right of action accruing to person under disability is extended to six years from date when person ceased to be under disability or died whichever event first occurred.

LIMITED PARTNERSHIPS:

See topic Partnerships.

MARRIAGE:

Parties to marriage must be at least 16 years old. If either party is under 18 years of age and not widow or widower, consent of party's father is required; alternatively mother's consent if father is dead or incapable of giving consent or Court if neither parent's consent is available.

Notice of intended marriage must be given by at least one party appearing before Registrar of Marriages personally and swearing formal affidavit confirming there is no impediment to marriage and if either party was previously divorced, producing decree absolute or certified copy.

Marriage must be celebrated in Office of Registrar or licensed place of worship unless special licence is obtained.

Person not permanent resident of Hong Kong whose previous marriage has been dissolved may not be granted certificate to marry in Hong Kong if dissolution of previous marriage is not recognized in country in which that person is domiciled.

Grounds for marriage being null and void include (a) parties being within prohibited degrees of kindred or affinity (for prohibited degrees of relationships, see England Law Digest); (b) either party under age of 16; (c) marriage was not celebrated in

MARRIAGE . . . *continued*
accordance with Marriage Ordinance (Cap. 181); (d) at time of marriage either party was already married.

Grounds for marriage taking place after 30th June 1972 being voidable include (a) not consummated because of incapacity or wilful refusal; (b) either party not validly consenting because of duress, mistake or unsoundness of mind; (c) either party suffering from mental disorder so as to be unfit for marriage.

Decree of nullity will not be granted if respondent satisfies Court that petitioner knowing that marriage could be avoided led respondent to believe he or she would not do so, or if it would be unjust to respondent to grant decree.

Voidable marriage shall be treated as if it existed up to time of annulment.

Jurisdiction for nullity proceedings is same as for divorce.

Chinese customary marriages and Chinese modern marriages celebrated in accordance with established rites before 7th Oct. 1971 can be recognised as valid marriages.

See topic Husband and Wife.

MORTGAGE:

Conveyancing and Property Ordinance (Cap. 219) provides that mortgage of legal estate can be effected in law by charge by deed expressed to be by way of legal mortgage only.

Mortgagee has following powers: (1) to sell mortgaged property provided that mortgage money has become due and either (a) notice has been served requiring payment and there has been default in whole or part for one month, or (b) interest under mortgage is one month in arrears, or (c) there has been breach of some other covenant in mortgage; (2) to insure mortgaged property against loss or damage by fire; (3) to appoint receiver, which power is exercisable in same circumstances as power of sale; (4) when in possession, to lease or accept surrender of lease of mortgaged property.

Priority of mortgages takes effect in order of date of creation if registered within 30 days (Land Registration Ordinance Cap. 128) (subject to any contrary entries). Registration is deemed to be actual notice to subsequent mortgagee or purchaser of land. Prior mortgagee may make further advances to rank in priority to subsequent mortgagees, legal or equitable, only if (1) such arrangement has been made with consent of subsequent mortgagees; (2) his further advance does not exceed, with any other outstanding advance, maximum amount secured; or (3) where prior mortgagee is authorised institution (as defined in Banking Ordinance Cap. 155) and original mortgage is expressed to secure all moneys which may, from time to time, be owing.

Discharge or Satisfaction.—Receipt written on or annexed to mortgage in respect of all moneys thereby secured operates in case of mortgage by assignment as reconveyance of mortgaged property to person who immediately before execution of receipt was entitled to equity of redemption and in other cases as discharge of mortgage. Receipt must be executed by mortgagee by way of legal mortgage or person in whom mortgage is vested and who is entitled to give receipt.

MOTOR VEHICLES:

Governed by Road Traffic Ordinance (Cap. 374) and related legislation.

Every motor vehicle must be registered and annually licensed. Owners of private cars manufactured six years or more before date from which car is to be licensed must obtain certificate of roadworthiness. Similarly, owners of light goods vehicles manufactured one year or more before date from which light goods vehicle is to be licensed must obtain certificate of roadworthiness. Owner must renew certificate yearly thereafter.

Every driver must have passed requisite test (or hold valid and current foreign driving licence) and have Hong Kong licence to drive (renewable yearly or every third year). Visiting drivers from abroad holding valid foreign driving licences may drive for period of 12 months from last date of entry into Hong Kong. Driving licences will not be issued to persons under 18.

Any person using or permitting another to use motor vehicle must be insured against third party risks. Rights against insurers of third party risks are conferred on third parties in event of insured becoming insolvent.

Tax is charged on first registration of motor vehicles. Dealers must publish retail price list of their vehicles, including standard and optional accessories but excluding first registration tax. Importers and distributors of motor vehicles must register with Commissioner for Transport within 30 days of commencement of business. Importers must file returns on importation of motor vehicles. Electric vehicles exempt from first registration tax for period of three years.

NATIONALITY:

See topic Immigration.

NEGOTIABLE INSTRUMENTS:

See topic Bills and Notes.

NOTARIES PUBLIC:

Notaries exercise functions in Hong Kong and are governed by Legal Practitioners Ordinance (Cap. 159) which has same regulations as under English law.

PARTNERSHIPS:

There are either ordinary partnerships (Partnership Ordinance—Cap. 38) or limited ones (Limited Partnerships Ordinance—Cap. 37). Partnership Ordinance is based on U.K. Partnership Act of 1890 and Limited Partnerships Ordinance is based on U.K. Limited Partnership Act of 1907. Law is almost identical to English law.

In ordinary partnership each partner impliedly confers upon his co-partners authority to incur debts on behalf of partnership to bind all partners. Limited partnerships are very rare; limited partner's liability is restricted to amount of his capital.

Partnership firm has no legal personality distinct from members composing it but partners can sue and are liable to be sued in their firm name.

Under Companies Ordinance, permitted number of partners shall not be more than 20 but with no restriction for solicitors, accountants and stockbrokers partnerships.

PATENTS:

Statute.—Registration of United Kingdom Patents Ordinance 1979.

Treaties.—Paris Convention (International Union) 1883-1967 (effective for Hong Kong as from 16th Nov., 1977), Patent Cooperation Treaty 1970 (effective for Hong Kong as from 15th Apr., 1981).

Procedure.—There is no independent patent granting system in Hong Kong. However, consideration is being given to independent granting and registration of patents in H.K. To acquire protection under Registration of Patents Ordinance, once British patent or European patent designating U.K. has been obtained, grantee must apply for reregistration in H.K. within five years of grant. Application must be accompanied by (1) certificate from British Comptroller-General of Patents, Designs and Trade Marks giving full particulars of grant, (2) certified copy of specification together with drawings (if any) relating to patent, (3) statutory declaration setting out interest and title of applicant, (4) Authorisation of Agent, (5) in case of patent specification not in English, certified copy of English translation.

Upon payment of prescribed fees and after application is advertised in Hong Kong Government Gazette, Certificate of Registration will be granted.

Protection.—Reregistration in H.K. conveys same protection as enjoyed by patentee in U.K. under its U.K. or European patent designating U.K. and remains in force for so long as patent is maintained.

Assignment/licence of patent or patent application should be recorded in order to be effective against third parties.

Infringement.—Patent is infringed if anyone without consent of proprietor makes, disposes of, offers to dispose of, uses or imports any items including items embodying patent process and keeps any such items whether for disposal or otherwise as well as uses invention process. Action can only be brought upon issue of Certificate of Registration in H.K.

Usual remedies available are injunction, damages, delivery up of goods and discovery.

PERPETUITIES:

See topic Trusts.

PLEDGES:

Same as under England Law Digest.

POWER OF ATTORNEY:

See topic Absentees.

PRINCIPAL AND AGENT:

Common law rules apply. In general principal is responsible for acts of his duly authorised agent. Agent acting for undisclosed principal is personally liable. Agent acting outside his authority is liable on action for breach of warrant of authority.

REAL PROPERTY:

In general, apart from system of registration, applicable law is substantially pre-1925 English law of real property as modified by Conveyancing and Property Ordinance (Cap. 219) (which enacted some of provisions of English Law of Property Act 1925) but in New Territories (as defined in Interpretation and General Clauses Ordinance [Cap. 1]) Chinese customary law is still relevant. All titles are leasehold derived from British Crown.

Situation after 1997 is now governed by Joint Declaration of British and Chinese Governments and by Basic Law of Hong Kong Special Administrative Region of China. See topic Constitution and Government.

Conveyance of legal estate must be by deed only.

Land Registration.—Current system of registration is that of deeds and not of title. Except bona fide leases at rack rent for term not exceeding three years, all unregistered deeds and instruments shall be absolutely null and void against subsequent bona fide purchaser for valuable consideration. (Land Registration Ordinance, Cap. 128). Instruments shall have priority according to instrument date if registered within 30 days after execution. In other cases, priority follows date of registration but charging order only day after registration. Registration is deemed to be actual notice to subsequent mortgagee or purchaser. It is expected that system of registration will be changed to that of title registration and, to this extent, Land Titles Bill has been introduced for consideration by Legislative Council.

RECEIVERS:

See topics Executions; Bankruptcy; Insolvency.

SALES:

Sale of Goods Ordinance (Cap. 26) substantially reproduces U.K. 1979 Act. Ordinance is codification of law on subject and deals with formalities of contract, ascertainment of price, implied undertakings, sale by sample, rights of unpaid sellers, actions for breach of contract and so on.

Contract of sale may be made in writing or by word of mouth, or partly in writing and partly by word of mouth, or may be implied from conduct of parties. Contract for sale of goods is defined as contract whereby seller transfers or agrees to transfer property in goods to buyer for money consideration called price. Contract may be absolute or conditional.

Unless expressly stipulated, time of payment is not deemed to be of essence. Whether any other stipulation as to time is of essence or not depends on terms of contract.

Implied terms include: (1) seller has right to sell goods, (2) in sales by description, goods will correspond with description, (3) for goods sold in course of business, goods are of merchantable quality but not for defects specifically drawn to buyer's attention or if buyer examines goods prior to making contract, as regards defects inspection ought to have revealed, (4) if buyer makes known purpose for which goods bought,

SALES . . . *continued*
goods are reasonably fit for that purpose except where buyer does not or it is unreasonable for him to rely on seller's skill and judgment, (5) in sale by sample, bulk will correspond with sample in quality; buyer shall have reasonable opportunity to compare bulk with sample and goods are free from defects rendering them unmerchantable which would not be apparent on reasonable examination of sample, (6) goods are free from any charge or encumbrance not disclosed or known to buyer before contract made and buyer will have quiet enjoyment subject to any charge which seller has disclosed.

Unpaid seller entitled to withhold delivery and exercise lien if property has not passed to buyer. See topic Liens.

Remedies.—If title has passed and buyer has not paid, seller entitled to bring action for price.

If buyer does not accept and pay for goods, seller can claim estimated loss directly resulting from refusal to accept. Measure of damages is usually difference between contract price and market or current price at time goods ought to have been accepted or if no time for acceptance stipulated, at time of neglect or refusal to accept.

Buyer entitled to bring action for damages for nondelivery. Measure of damages is difference between contract and market or current price at time of delivery.

Court can order specific performance of contract.

Seller may be liable for rescission and/or damages in event of misrepresentation. See topic Contracts, subhead Misrepresentation Ordinance.

New Supply of Services (Implied Terms) Ordinance (Cap. 457) substantially reproduces U.K. supply of Goods and Services Act 1982. Terms implied into contract for services include reasonable care and skill, time for performance and price. Exclusion of implied terms as against consumer is outlawed.

Consumer Protection.—Provisions seeking to exclude liability for breach of contract or negligence not prohibited by statute or contained in international supply contract will only be upheld to extent that they are reasonable. (Control of Exemption Clauses Ordinance [Cap. 71]). New Consumer Goods Safety Ordinance (Cap. 456) imposes safety standards and regulations for range of consumer goods and their packaging.

New Unconscionable Contracts Ordinance (Cap. 458) increases consumer protection in Hong Kong.

See also topics Contracts, subhead Unfair Terms; Trade Descriptions.

SHIPPING:

Admiralty jurisdiction is exercised by High Court.

Treaties.—New Merchant Shipping (Liner Conferences) Ordinance (No. 59 of 1995) implements Convention on a Code of Conduct for Liner Conferences signed at Geneva on Apr. 6, 1974.

Navigation.—Main statutes governing shipping and navigation are Merchant Shipping Ordinance and Merchant Shipping (Safety) Ordinance and subsidiary legislation. Regulations made under Merchant Shipping (Safety) Ordinance implement International Convention for Safety of Life at Sea 1974 and International Convention on Load Lines 1966. These Ordinances deal with seaworthiness, safety, lifesaving appliances, fire appliances and protection, signals of distress and prevention of collision, load lines, certification, discipline and welfare of master, officer and crew, accidents, marine courts, tonnage measurement, construction, survey and safety certificates, etc.

Registration.—By Merchant Shipping (Registration) Ordinance (Cap. 415), independent Hong Kong Shipping Registry was established in 1990. Ordinance makes provision for registration of ships and mortgages in Hong Kong. Previously ship and mortgage registrations in Hong Kong were governed by English Merchant Shipping Acts as applied to Hong Kong. Under and subject to provisions of Merchant Shipping (Registration) Ordinance, ship is registrable if (i) majority interest is owned by one or more qualified person or persons, or (ii) it is operated under demise charter by body corporate being qualified person. "Qualified person" means any of (i) Hong Kong resident, (ii) Hong Kong incorporated company, and (iii) overseas company registered under Part XI of Companies Ordinance. Demise charter registration has been introduced. When survey cannot be carried out in time, provisional certificate of registry can be obtained pending completion of survey and issuance of certificate of registry. With provisional registration, ship can commence trading immediately and mortgages can be registered. Ships on Hong Kong register will be British ships and can continue to enjoy those rights and privileges until 30th June 1997.

Crew.—Previous nationality restrictions for ranks of master, chief mate and chief engineer have been removed. There are no nationality or residence requirements for master and crew serving on Hong Kong registered foreign-going ships. Merchant Shipping (Seafarers) Ordinance came into effect on Sept. 2, 1996. This Ordinance and subsidiary legislation consolidate and amend law relating to seafarers, in particular in relation to registration, employment, discharge, repatriation, conduct and disciplining of seafarers. This Ordinance and subsidiary legislation also stipulate provisions for examination and certification of officers and other seafarers for employment on Hong Kong ships, manning scale and standards, health, safety, crew accommodation and welfare of seafarers. This Ordinance also provides for establishment of (inter alia): (1) Seafarer's Authority (to replace Seaman's Recruiting Authority); (2) Mercantile Marine Office (to replace Seaman's Recruiting Office); (3) Seafarer's Advisory Board (to replace Seaman's Recruiting Advisory Board).

Pilotage.—Pilotage Ordinance stipulates compulsory pilotage by licenced pilots except for certain exempted ships, e.g. government ships, vessels engaging in salvage operation, passenger ferries between Hong Kong, Macau and China within river trade limits and other vessels exempted by Pilotage Authority.

Port Control.—Control of vessels, port facilities, dues and clearance, etc. are governed by Shipping and Port Control Ordinance.

Pollution.—Merchant Shipping (Prevention and Control of Pollution) Ordinance and subsidiary legislation provide for prevention and control of pollution from ships. Regulations made under Ordinance implement International Convention for the Prevention of Pollution from Ships and protocol relating thereto. Under Shipping and Port Control Ordinance, it is offence for vessel to discharge oil or mixture containing oil in Hong Kong waters unless falling within defence under Ordinance (i) securing safety of vessel, (ii) preventing damage to vessel or its cargo, or (iii) saving life. Emission of smoke in such quantity as to be nuisance by vessels in Hong Kong waters is offence.

Dumping at Sea Ordinance reproduces U.K. Dumping at Sea Act 1974 in Hong Kong, regulating dumping of waste materials at sea. See also topic Environment.

Carriage of Goods by Sea.—Carriage of Goods by Sea Ordinance 1994 implements Hague-Visby Rules.

Liens.—Maritime liens recognised under English law are applicable in Hong Kong.

STATUTE OF FRAUDS:

See topic Frauds, Statute of.

STATUTORY DECLARATIONS:

See topic Affidavits and Statutory Declarations.

TAXATION:

There is no total income tax in Hong Kong. Hong Kong's major taxes are Profits Tax; Property Tax and Salaries Tax. Individuals normally resident in Hong Kong may be able to reduce their tax liability under these three tax sources by electing Personal Assessment (see subhead Personal Assessment, infra).

Profits Tax.—Persons, including corporations, partnerships, trustees and bodies of persons carrying on any trade, profession or business in Hong Kong are chargeable to tax on all profits arising in or derived from Hong Kong. There is no distinction between residents and nonresidents. Resident may receive profits from abroad without suffering tax; conversely, nonresident may suffer tax on profits arising in Hong Kong, either directly or in name of his agent who is required to retain sufficient money to pay tax.

Where true profits of nonresident cannot be readily determined, Commissioner of Inland Revenue may compute same on fair percentage of turnover in Hong Kong or where applicable by apportioning overall profits in ratio of turnover of various branches outside Hong Kong.

Persons effecting payment to nonresident sportsmen, entertainers and similar persons who perform in Hong Kong for commercial occasion or event must withhold tax from such payment.

Nonresidents are charged at same rate as residents, but resident consignees are required to provide details of gross proceeds from local sales on behalf of nonresident consignors and pay tax at 1% of gross proceeds or such lesser sums as are agreed. This tax is recoverable from consignor.

Royalties received by nonresidents from exhibition or use in Hong Kong of films, tapes or recordings or for use in Hong Kong of patent, design, trademark or copyright are taxed on gross receipts at effective rate of 1.65% (company) or 1.5% (other). However, as from 4th Mar. 1993, where royalties are paid to associates, effective rates are 16.5% (company) and 15% (other).

Profits tax is currently chargeable at 15% for unincorporated businesses and at 16.5% for corporations. Exemptions are made in case of charitable institutions and trusts of public character.

Capital Gains.—Not taxable.

Dividends.—Not taxable on receipt; no withholding taxes on payment.

Property tax charged on net assessable value of any land or building in Hong Kong at rate of 15%, i.e. on assessable value less Government rates paid by owner and statutory allowance for repairs and outgoings of 20% of assessable value after deduction of rates. Corporate lessors of land are not subject to Property Tax but are subject to Profits Tax.

Salaries Tax.—Chargeable on all income arising in or derived from Hong Kong offices and employments. Separate taxation applies to income of husband and wife but if overall tax liability of any married couple is greater than it would otherwise be under aggregation, they may elect to be jointly assessed. In Hong Kong year of assessment is 1st Apr. to 31st Mar. There is no pay-as-you-earn system.

Salaries tax is charged at progressive rates rising to 25% but amount of tax charged will not exceed 15% of net assessable income less charitable donations.

Personal Allowances.—There are basic allowances and allowances for children, dependent parents and single parents.

Business registration fee for 1996/1997 HK$2,000 plus levy of HK$250.

Personal Assessment.—Income from profits tax, property tax and salaries tax is aggregated and from total following may be deducted: (1) business losses incurred in year of assessment; (2) losses brought forward from previous years under Personal Assessment; (3) approved charitable donations; (4) interest payments on money borrowed for purpose of producing property income; and (5) personal allowances. Tax at marginal rates (as per salaries tax) will be imposed on balance. Credit is given for tax already paid and refund may be made.

Stamp duty is levied on sales or purchases of Hong Kong stock and requires contract note to be stamped within prescribed period and ad valorem duty of HK$3 per HK$1,000 or part thereof to be payable (usually equally by buyer and seller). Relevant transfer is to be endorsed in relation thereto.

Stamp duty is also payable on documentation relating to land (including sales, assignments and agreements for sale) at rates of up to 2.75% (latter for properties valued above HK$3.5 million).

There are reliefs from stamp duty for transfers of shares and of property between associated companies.

Estate duty is imposed by Estate Duty Ordinance (Cap. 111) on value of all property situated in Hong Kong which passes on person's death including gifts made by person within three years prior to death.

Where death occurs on or after 1 April 1995, estates valued at HK$6 million or less are exempt from duty. Duty is charged on sliding scale on principal value of estate. Estate duty is not payable in respect of assets situate outside Hong Kong.

Among allowances are quick succession relief, matrimonial home, funeral expenses and debts and mortgages incurred for valuable consideration due by deceased to persons or institutions in Hong Kong.

TAXATION . . . *continued*

Principal Value of Estate HK$	*Estate Duty on Total Value*
6.5m or below	Exempt
over 6.5m to 8m	6%
over 8m to 9.5m	12%
over 9.5m and above	18%

General.—There is no generally applicable value added or sales tax in Hong Kong. Duty is payable on certain products such as alcohol, tobacco and petroleum products under Dutiable Commodities Ordinance. (Cap. 109). Hotel Accommodation Tax is levied on accommodation charges (at rate of 5%). Airport Departure Tax is HK$100 for persons 12 and over.

Hong Kong has no general tax conventions with either U.K. or any other territory; however, Inland Revenue Ordinance provides credit relief when profits chargeable to tax in Hong Kong have borne tax in another Commonwealth territory (which, in this context, does not include U.K.). There are no special tax incentives for overseas investors.

TRADE DESCRIPTIONS:

Trade Descriptions Ordinance (Cap. 362) prohibits false trade descriptions, false marks and misstatements in respect of goods provided in course of trade; confers power to require information or instructions relating to goods to be marked on or to accompany goods or to be included in advertisements; restates law relating to forgery of trademarks.

Enforcement of provisions under Ordinance is through Customs and Excise Department.

Remedy shall be by way of criminal prosecution by Crown. Complainants may institute separate civil proceedings.

TRADEMARKS AND PASSING OFF:

Statutes.—Trade Marks Ordinance (Cap. 43) and Rules follow U.K. counterparts closely. Enactment of Trade Marks (Amendment) Ordinance 1991, which came into operation in Mar. 1992, expanded existing system of registration to provide for registration of trademarks for services in addition to those for goods.

Treaties.—Hong Kong, through U.K., has acceded to Paris Convention. Convention priority may be claimed for applications filed within six months from first convention application.

Trademark is mark used or proposed to be used in relation to goods or services for purpose of indicating, or so as to indicate, connection in course of trade between goods or services and some person having right either as proprietor or as registered user to use mark, whether with or without indication of identity of that person. Trademark may be device, name, signature, word, letter, numeral or any combination thereof.

As in U.K., register is divided into two parts, viz. A and B. Trademark can only be registered if it is adapted to distinguish or is capable of distinguishing goods or services of owner from those of other traders.

To be registrable in Part A, mark must contain or consist of at least one of following particulars (1) name of company, individual or firm represented in special or particular manner; (2) signature (except in Chinese characters) of applicant; (3) invented word or words; (4) word or words not descriptive of goods or services for which mark is used and not geographical name or common surname; (5) any other distinctive mark.

In some cases mark which does not appear, on face of it, to be inherently distinctive can nevertheless be registered in Part B. In determining whether trademark is capable of distinguishing goods or services as aforesaid, Registrar may have regard to extent to which (a) trademark is inherently capable of distinguishing goods or services and/or (b) by reason of use of trademark or of any other circumstances, it is in fact capable of distinguishing as aforesaid.

Trademark may be registered in Part B notwithstanding any registration in Part A or vice versa (subject of course to compliance with respective registrability requirements as stated above) in name of same proprietor of same trade mark or any part or parts thereof.

Procedure.—Application is made on prescribed form in respect of relevant class(es) of goods/services desired in accordance with Nice International Classification. Examination as to prior conflict and registrability will take place within 12 months and acceptances are published in Government Gazette for opposition for two months. Thereafter, certificate will issue.

Protection.—Trademark when registered is initially valid for seven years and can thereafter be renewed indefinitely for successive periods of 14 years each. Registered mark must be put to use within five years of grant of registration or it will be vulnerable to cancellation for nonuse.

License.—Should be in writing but recordal with Trade Marks Registry is not mandatory, unless proprietor does not itself use mark and requires to rely on licensee's use, in which case, licensee should be recorded as registered user. Agreement must contain provisions as to control by proprietor over licensee's use.

Assignment of trademark may be with or without goodwill of business concerned in goods in respect of which mark was registered. In case of assignment without goodwill, it must be recorded with Trade Marks Registry within six months from date of assignment and where mark being so assigned was in use at time of assignment, assignment must be advertised to give notice to public of change of proprietorship.

Associated marks must always be assigned as whole and not separately.

Under new Trade Marks Rules, assignee of pending application is to be treated as applicant for registration where assignor also assigns other registered mark or marks, one or more of which relates to (i) same goods or (ii) same description of goods, or (iii) services or description of services associated with goods or goods of that description.

Infringement.—Civil remedies of damages, injunction, delivery up of goods and discovery apply. As regards action in respect of marks registered under: (1) Part A of register: plaintiff has only to prove (a) his mark is registered and (b) defendant uses mark identical or so nearly resembling it as to be likely to deceive or cause confusion that mark is registered trademark of defendant as rightful proprietor or that use thereof imports reference to defendant or its goods being connected in course of trade to rightful proprietor. (2) Part B of register: no injunction or other relief shall be granted to plaintiff if defendant establishes that use of which plaintiff complains is not likely to deceive or cause confusion.

Passing-off.—Common law tortious action of passing-off is available if trademark owner (whether registered or not) can prove (1) trade reputation; (2) infringer has used substantially confusing similar mark; (3) confusion and/or deception has been or is likely to be caused as result of such use and (4) damage is likely or has occurred. Action is not restricted to registered or unregistered trademarks but can be invoked in respect of "any badge of recognition" by which proprietor has become well known, such as packaging, advertising character, shape of product, etc.

TREATIES:

Being dependent territory of U.K., Hong Kong lacks full international personality to enter into treaties. Normally international treaty is entered into by government of U.K. and, if desired, extended to Hong Kong. Examples of treaties extended to Hong Kong include International Covenant on Civil and Political Rights, Berne Convention on Copyright, Universal Copyright Convention and Geneva Convention on the Execution of Foreign Arbitral Awards.

As far as external commercial relations are concerned, Governor has been formally entrusted with executive authority to conclude and implement trade agreements with states, regions and international organizations. By way of example, Hong Kong is separate contracting party to World Trade Organisation (WTO) and to Multi-Fibre Arrangement (MFA).

As from 1st July 1997, Hong Kong Special Administrative Region is empowered by Basic Law and using name "Hong Kong, China" to maintain and develop relations and conclude and implement agreements with foreign states and regions and relevant international organizations in areas such as economic, trade, financial and monetary, sports and communications fields. See topic Constitution and Government.

See also topic Taxation.

TRUSTS:

Trustee Ordinance (Cap. 29) substantially follows UK Trustee Act 1925. See England Law Digest.

WILLS:

Hong Kong law of wills substantially follows general principles of English law of wills. English legislation consolidated and amended in 1970 in Wills Ordinance (Cap. 30) (as am'd by Wills [Amendment] Ordinance [No. 56 of 1995]) consists of Wills Act 1837, Wills Act Amendment Act 1852, Wills (Soldiers and Sailors) Act 1918, Wills Act 1963 and Wills Act 1968. Parent and Child Ordinance, which came into operation on 19th June 1993, makes provision for inclusion of illegitimate persons in testamentary gifts. Entitlement of illegitimate persons applies not only to persons born illegitimate but also to persons who trace their relationships through illegitimate person.

See England Law Digest.

Allowance for Maintenance of Dependants.—Deceased's Family Maintenance Ordinance (Cap. 129) has been repealed by new Inheritance (Provision For Family and Dependants) Ordinance (No. 58 of 1995) which provides that such person who was wholly or substantially maintained by deceased person including former spouse of deceased, or partner by union of concubinage, may apply for provision of maintenance out of estate of deceased.

HUNGARY LAW DIGEST REVISER

Nagy és Trócs ányi
Pálya Utca 9,
H-1012, Budapest, Hungary
Telephone: (36)1-212-0444
Fax: (36)1-212-0443
Email: NTBP@MAIL.DATANET.HU
New York Office: Nagy & Trócsányi, 1114 Avenue of the Americas, New York, NY.
Telephone: 212-626-4206. Fax: (36)1-212-0443. Email: NTNY@IX.NETCOM.COM
Switzerland Office: Nagy und Trócsányi GmbH. Birsigstrasse 2, CH-4054 Basel.
Telephone: (41) 61-225-4311. Fax: (41) 61-225-4323.
Sweden Office: Nagy & Trócsányi Affarsjurist AB. Birger Jarlsgatan 12 2TR., S-11434 Stockholm.
Telephone: (46) 08-679-8585. Fax: (46) 08-679-8586.

Reviser Profile

History: Nagy és Trócsányi was the first law firm founded in Hungary following the legal reforms of 1991 which permitted the creation of private law offices. The law firm's founders have drawn together an outstanding group of lawyers with experience in the fields of, inter alia, corporate law, trade, banking, finance, securities, taxation, real estate, telecommunications, media and litigation. The diverse areas of expertise of Nagy és Trócsányi's attorneys provide clients conducting business in Hungary a comprehensive range of domestic and international legal services.

Due to the synthesis of well trained and highly experienced lawyers and the high quality of legal services provided to its clients, Nagy és Trócsányi is the largest and fastest growing law firm in Hungary.

Nagy és Trócsányi is the first, and as yet the only Hungarian law firm to have opened affiliated offices abroad. The Basel, Switzerland office was opened in early 1993. In addition to providing general services to clients involved in Swiss-Hungarian business relations, the Basel office is substantially engaged in transnational taxation, banking and finance. Nagy és Trócsányi's New York office opened in late 1993. The New York office is primarily engaged in Hungarian and American business, in assisting Hungarian companies with their legal matters and litigation in the United States and providing legal services to American businesses operating in Hungary. In October 1996 Nagy és Trócsányi established a Stockholm office to provide similar services to those engaged in Hungarian-Swedish commerce.

Areas of Practice:

Securities, Banking and Financial Practice: Complex transactions require broad experience in corporate finance when dealing with investment and commercial bankers, with securities and with planning business strategies. The firm's experience encompasses dealing with corporate securities of all kinds as well as negotiating and preparing all kinds of business instruments.

Joint Ventures and Acquisitions: The firm has experience negotiating joint venture arrangements, preparing documents for such transactions, as well as representing foreign clients in acquiring domestic companies. Such transactions required the application of foreign regulations and international tax planning.

Privatization: The firm's attorneys have participated in the privatization of major Hungarian enterprises. Not only do they have experience in privatizing an enterprise, but also they have cooperated and worked closely with the leaders and lawyers of the Hungarian privatization agencies and maintain good working relationships with them.

Taxation: The firm's practice encompasses a wide range of tax matters, including corporate and business tax planning and consultation, structuring business organizations and reorganizations in light of tax considerations, negotiating and preparing tax-related corporate documents such as stock option plans, shareholders agreements, merger and joint venture agreements, buyouts and stock and asset acquisitions.

Telecommunications: The firm is heavily involved in the privatization and related matters of the Hungarian telecommunications sector advising Hungarian governmental agencies, private parties and foreign strategic and financial investors.

Media: The firm's practice in the media sector involves newspapers, radio, television and cable TV businesses and transactions.

Trade: The firm has advised a number of corporate clients on domestic and international trade relations, negotiated trade deals and prepared all kinds of contracts related to national and transnational trade.

Project Financing: The firm's attorneys represented clients and were involved in finding and negotiating financing arrangements for corporate clients.

Bankruptcy: The firm's attorneys have an active bankruptcy practice involving liquidations, restructuring of debts with investment banks and other financial institutions, collecting debts, advising and protecting clients against possible future bankruptcy, dealing with corporate matters, and negotiating settlements and litigating such matters at the courts.

General Litigation, Arbitration: The firm's attorneys are trained and prepared to handle corporate matters and litigation. The firm's litigation practice is foremost related to diverse corporate and finance practice encompassing breach of contract, real estate, securities, corporate takeovers, business torts and tax matters. The practice includes working with lawyers of government authorities while negotiating settlements in these disputes, as well as handling cases before arbitral tribunals.

Technology, Trademark and Intellectual Property: The firm has represented a number of companies in the licensing of copyrights, trademarks, patents and know-hows. Through our international clients, we have an active practice with international intellectual property rights.

Government Agencies: The firm's attorneys have been asked on several occasions to review draft legislation and advise government agencies on how to incorporate practical consideration into legislation.

HUNGARY LAW DIGEST

(The following is a list of all Topics, including cross-references, covered in this Digest.)

HUNGARY LAW DIGEST

Revised for 1997 edition by

NAGY & TRÓCSÁNYI, of the Budapest and New York Bars

("C.C." refers to "Civil Code"; "C.P.C." refers to "Civil Procedure Code"; "I.P.L.C." refers to "International Private Law Code".)

ABSENTEES:

Person who is absent, removed, or away from domicile or usual place of residence, may generally delegate authority to any person of full legal capacity. Exceptions apply in cases of citizenship or family status. Before court, absentee may in most cases be represented only by attorney at law, guardian, close relative, or by someone who is joint party with absentee in procedure. (§§474-487 C.C.; §§66-74 C.P.C.).

If absentee's whereabouts are unknown or absentee is otherwise impeded in managing her own affairs, upon request of any party, local municipality will appoint temporary or permanent curator to oversee interests of absentee. Curator's authority towards property is substantially same as that of guardian's. (§224 C.C.).

ACKNOWLEDGMENT:

Acknowledgments are to be taken before Hungarian notary public. If document is to be used abroad, signature shall be certified by Ministry of Justice and further by Ministry of Foreign Affairs. Acknowledgments may be taken abroad before Hungarian consular or diplomatic officials, whose signature will suffice without further certification.

Unless otherwise required by international agreement, foreign acknowledgments intended for use in Hungary are to be certified in usual diplomatic way, and finally by Hungarian official authority.

Both U.S. and Hungary are parties to Hague Convention of 1961 on abolishing the requirements of legalization for foreign public documents. Acknowledgments for U.S. use may be taken before U.S. consular officer in Budapest. For countries not parties to 1961 convention, Hague Conventions of 1905 and 1954 apply. "Apostille" for foreign use is executed in Hungary by Ministry of Justice (Igazsagügyi Minisztérium), Budapest.

ACTIONS:

Every legal person, whether individual, including fetus, or any legal entity may sue and be sued. "Quasi entities" of Hungarian law, like partnerships, as far as they may be directly subjects of rights and duties, may also sue and be sued solely in their name or jointly with their partners or members. Hungarian Government and its agencies do not enjoy either civil law or procedural immunity within Hungary, unlike foreign states or governments. (Those, their diplomats and other officials of same status are immune from Hungarian jurisdiction.) Rules governing civil procedure are set forth in Code of Civil Procedure, Act 1952:III., as amended several times.

There is only one form of civil action. All actions are commenced by filing statement of claim with court. Service of process on defendants is accomplished ex officio by court. Parties do not have to be represented by attorney at law before courts, except for party appealing to Supreme Court and for party registering or amending articles of incorporation for corporations. Incapable persons are represented by guardian who exercises their powers. Unless otherwise regulated by law, claims against Hungarian State are to be brought against Minister of Finance.

Security for Costs.—Foreign plaintiffs, unless privileged by international agreement or reciprocal practice of law, upon request of defendant, may be required to deposit costs of defendant in advance. (§§89-92 C.P.C.). Hungarian citizens, even if domiciled and citizen of another country are not considered foreigners with regard to security. (See topic Treaties and Conventions, subhead General of Private Law Nature.)

Appropriate Forum.—On subject matter jurisdiction, see topic Courts. Appropriate venue is generally domicile of defendant individual and seat of defendant entity. Lack of domicile or seat results in venue based on residence, or, if unknown, last known residence. Alternative appropriate venues may be place of work, study, service, performance of contract, damage, real estate, situs of assets against defendants lacking even temporary residence or place of company's branch. According to regulations of I.P.L.C., foreign laws are generally applied if foreign elements in claim are stronger than Hungarian ones. (See topic Foreign Law.)

Costs.—Court filing fee is generally 6% of value of claim, but minimum HUF 2,000 and maximum HUF 750,000. (Act 1993: LXXV). Filing fee is to be paid by plaintiff when filing claim with Court, unless allowances based generally on plaintiff's needy circumstances or on law are applicable. (1991, Act 1990:XCIII, formerly Act 1986:I, as am'd several times.) Losing party has to bear all costs, including filing fee, lawyers' fees and reasonable costs of winning party. Lawyer's fees, which generally are not limited by law, are capped in first instance civil procedure at 5% of adjusted claim. Fees for witnesses and expert witnesses are considered court costs, and are to be deposited in advance by parties upon order of judge.

Limitation of.—See topic Limitation of Actions.

Lack of Jurisdiction.—See topic Courts.

AFFIDAVITS:

Formal affidavit, confirmed by oath or affirmation of party, taken before person having authority to administer it, is unknown in domestic Hungarian law. Nevertheless, like any written or printed declaration or statement of facts made voluntarily, affidavit taken abroad may be used as evidence before Hungarian court, and will be subject of deliberation by judge.

Affidavit for foreign use, depending on requirements of respective foreign law, with or without being sworn, may be executed before notary public, in Hungarian or in other languages spoken by notary public (usually available languages are those of neighboring nations, English and French).

AGENCY:

Hungarian law lacks exact equivalent to common law theory of agency. Agency-like relations are regulated by law of contracts. For principal's liability see topic Damages.

ALIENS:

Substantive status of aliens in Hungary is that of Hungarian nationals as to basic human rights. Nevertheless this does not apply to citizen rights and some social rights, such as right to vote and free social security. Aliens with permanent residence may vote in local elections.

For entering country, permanent residence, for-profit occupation; see topics Immigration; Foreign Investment.

APPEAL AND ERROR:

Judiciary.—Practically all final judgments and orders of trial courts (first instance courts) are subject to appeal, for reason of fact or law. Appeal in civil cases may be taken within 15 days (in drafts or bills of exchange cases within three days) after service of copy of judgment or order. Cross-appeal may be taken within eight days after service of notice of appeal. Upon appeal execution of first instance decision will be stayed, except e.g. for child alimony. There is one stage of appeal. Appellate decision is binding. No appeal may be taken from decision of appellate court. However, within 60 days of binding judgment or decision of appellate court, party or person affected by decision or prosecutor may petition for further review under supervision procedure, which will be adjudged in most cases by three judge panel of Supreme Court. Appellate court or Supreme Court may remand case back for further consideration or may modify decision. (§§233-275 C.P.C.).

Administrative Decisions.—Resolutions of central or local administrative bodies are subject to administrative appeal, in which case higher level administrative organ will decide. Administrative appeals may generally be taken within 30 days of initial decision. Judicial complaints may usually be filed within 30 days of final administrative decision, and will be adjudged in two stage civil procedure. (§50[2] Constitution, §§324-341 C.P.C., as am'd by Acts 1991:XXVI and 1992:LXVIII).

ARBITRATION AND AWARD:

Parties may voluntarily agree to submit disputes to arbitration, in advance or at later time, if at least one party is engaged in business. However, parties may not agree to submit their disputes to arbitration if they may not freely alienate, encumber or otherwise dispose of disputed property or dispute is regulated by special procedure of CPC. Arbitration agreement or arbitration clause must be in writing. Agreement is considered to be in writing if made in letter, telefax, telegram or similar means. Similarly, it is written agreement if one of parties declares it to be in petition to court and other party does not object. Requirement of written agreement satisfied if written agreement between parties refers to other enforceable document containing arbitration clause and such written agreement states that latter forms part of it.

Parties may appoint sole arbitrator or panel of arbitrators according to their agreement or may turn to permanent court of arbitration. Panel shall decide by majority vote. If agreement does not provide applicable procedural rules, arbitrator(s) may establish own rules of procedure or may refer to rules of procedure of any permanent court of arbitration. Unless parties otherwise agree, language of procedure is Hungarian. Panel may ask assistance of local court and authorities in enforcement, taking evidence, etc.

If referral of dispute to arbitration is duly made, courts have no jurisdiction to decide matter. Awards need no special recognition procedure and are to be enforced by ordinary county courts. Exceptional judicial review of awards is available only if award exceeds arbitration agreement or is violative of public order. (§62 I.P.L.C.). For procedural rules and competencies of arbitration panel, see Act 1994:LXXI.

Court of Arbitration attached to Hungarian Chamber of Commerce and Industry (Magyar Kereskedelmi és Iparkamara) has jurisdiction for resolution of disputes arising from domestic or international commercial matters of individuals or entities under agreement of parties made in writing or if stipulated by international convention. Chamber has concluded agreements with U.S., Korean, Italian, Austrian and Swiss Chambers of Commerce on arbitration. (See optional arbitration clause suggested by American Arbitration Association and Hungarian Chamber of Commerce in Memorandum of Agreement of Sept. 7, 1984 for U.S.-Hungarian joint ventures.) Rules of procedure for Court of Arbitration are available upon request from Chamber, which rules correspond to rules of other internationally accepted arbitration fora. Progressive fee rate applies to value of claim as indicated in following chart.

Court of Arbitration's fee in USD:

Registration fee		**300.00**
Value of Claim		**Administration costs**
up to 50,000	2.4%	but not less than 240
–100,000	1,200 + 1.6%	on exceeding 50,000
–200,000	2,000 + 1.2%	on exceeding 100,000
–500,000	3,200 + 0.8%	on exceeding 200,000
–1,000,000	5,600 + 0.4%	on exceeding 500,000
–5,000,000	7,600 + 0.2%	on exceeding 1,000,000
over 5,000,000	15,600 + 0.12%	on exceeding 5,000,000
Value of Claim		**Arbitrators fee per capita**
up to 50,000	1.2%	but not less than 120
–100,000	600 + 0.8%	on exceeding 50,000
–200,000	1,000 + 0.6%	on exceeding 100,000
–500,000	1,600 + 0.4%	on exceeding 200,000

See Topical Index in front part of this volume.

ARBITRATION AND AWARD . . . *continued*

–1,000,000	2,800 + 0.2%	on exceeding 500,000
–5,000,000	3,800 + 0.1%	on exceeding 1,000,000
over 5,000,000	7,800 + 0.06%	on exceeding 5,000,000

State revenue to be paid is 1% of value of subject matter but minimum HUF 1,000 and maximum HUF 100,000. (Act 1993: LXXV).

Both U.S. and Hungary are parties to U.N. Convention on Recognition and Enforcement of Foreign Arbitral Awards of 1958.

ASSIGNMENTS:

Assignment as separate document is not required by law. Transfer of any property, real or personal, is affected by contract of parties, unless otherwise required by contract itself. Nevertheless, if wording of contract requires separate assignment, transfer of property cannot be performed without it.

For assignment of rights and delegation of duties see topic Contracts, subhead Contractual Rights.

ASSOCIATIONS:

Association (Egyesület) is not-for-profit organization (differentiated from "business association"; see topic Corporations). As legal entity, it is separate from its members, who are not liable for debts of association. Main rules applying to its civil status are set forth in Civil Code (§§61-65), administrative rules are given by Act 1989:II on Associations, as amended by Act 1989:XXXIII and Act 1993:XCII on political parties. Although they are not-for-profit organizations, associations may perform additional for-profit activities, and profit therefrom will be free from taxation, if devoted to not-for-profit purposes and does not exceed 10% of total income or HUF 10 million in tax year. For-profit and not-for-profit income must be kept separately. Associations may not be of discriminatory nature. Association may be founded by its charter to be adopted by founding members, declaring some special not-for-profit purpose. Upon this charter association is to be registered with associations' register of County Courts. Association has to form its own governing body, which represents it. No preliminary or additional permit or license is required. Separate form of association is public association.

Political parties do not fall under legal notion of associations, mainly because of their political purposes; nevertheless, organizational rules applicable to them are analogous to those of associations. (Act 1989:XXXIII, as am'd by Acts 1990:LXII, 1991:XLIV, 1992:LXXXI and 1993:CX). From Jan. 1, 1995, Act 1994:XVI on Chambers of Industry and Commerce provides special rules on such professional self-governing bodies.

ATTACHMENT:

For purpose of securing execution of future judgment on money claim or in order to secure claim in real estate, attachment may be granted by court prior to judgment.

ATTORNEYS AND COUNSELORS:

Lawyers practicing law in Hungary are either attorneys at law or in-house legal counselors. (1983:4.tvr, as am'd by Act 1991:XXIII and by Act 1995:I). As of Oct. 1, 1991 attorneys at law either may undertake solo practice or be partners or associates of law firms, which are to be organized in form of professional companies (Ügyvédi Iroda). Attorneys at law are fully licensed, i.e. they are authorized to perform both civil and criminal functions for clients, including drafting and countersigning legal documents, giving legal advice and representing clients before courts, administrative authorities, etc. Performing regular practice in foreign trade or patent law requires post-graduate degree or equivalent in this field.

Qualifications.—Practicing lawyer has to be holder of Hungarian doctor's degree in law, and has to have passed Bar Examination. Applicant is allowed to sit for examination after not less than two years of Hungarian legal practice. To practice as attorney at law, one has to be resident citizen of Hungary and be admitted to a county bar. Membership is open for all qualified lawyers satisfying above requirements.

Attorney-client privilege and duty means that attorney has right to and is obliged to protect confidential communications with clients.

Some foreign lawyers or law firms have established commercial representative offices, and through these are active in advising clients and drafting legal documents in other countries.

AUTOMOBILES:

See topic Motor Vehicles.

BANKRUPTCY:

Bankruptcy is regulated by Act 1991:IL as am'd by Act 1993:LXXXI and 1993:CIII. This Act is similar to U.S. Bankruptcy Law and contains provisions as to bankruptcy, liquidation and final settlement.

Bankruptcy proceedings provided by this Act do not apply to banks, however, liquidation proceedings do, with some exceptions. Bankruptcy, liquidation and final settlement proceedings include all assets of companies. During bankruptcy or liquidation proceedings, within 15 days of receiving request debtor and liquidator or trustee of assets should inform creditors about finances and assets of economic organization and inform employees about issues concerning them. These two proceedings fall into debtor's County Court's jurisdiction.

Bankruptcy Proceedings.—Debtor may declare bankruptcy with prior approval of General Meeting or other main governing body of debtor. Court at expense of creditor(s) appoints trustee of assets. Trustee manages and supplies information on assets and finances of organization. Debtor gets 90 day grace period from payment of debts during which time debtor must propose suitable program to restore its solvency, propose plan of agreement and call for negotiations with creditors. Final agreement is reached if more than 1/2 of creditors whose credit became due before date of declaring bankruptcy and 1/4 of those creditors whose credit did not yet become due on said date agree to granting grace period. If agreement is made, Court declares procedure finished. If not, liquidation procedure may commence. Under agreement creditors or third parties may assume debt, obtain assets from debtor or guarantee its obligations. Agreement must contain program approved by creditors, mode of procedure and control; possible rescheduling of payment deadlines, canceling or assuming creditors' claims, and anything parties think important to restore debtor's solvency. Creditors may charge trustee to supervise compliance with agreement. If no agreement is concluded, Court starts liquidation proceedings within 15 days.

Liquidation proceedings start at debtor's, creditor's or liquidator's request or upon order of Corporation Court. In case of simultaneous liquidation and bankruptcy proceedings, latter is considered valid, unless debtor intends to start immediately with liquidation procedure without exercising its right to 90 day grace period. If creditor requests liquidation, reasons must be stated. Debtor may accept or deny request. When debtor denies request, Court examines case and announces solvency or insolvency. In latter case Court may grant grace period for not more than 30 days. When resolution of insolvency goes into effect, Court orders corporation's liquidation, orders announcement thereof, appoints liquidator and notifies Corporation's Court and various authorities, such as competent tax authority, labor office and bank where debtor's accounts are held. Director of corporation must prepare inventory, annual or simplified report or balance sheet and submit it to liquidator and tax authority and further must prepare report on remaining or hidden environmental damages. Director may be fined sum not exceeding 50% of his income received from corporation in year preceding liquidation if he fails to comply. At beginning of liquidation proceedings all debts become due. Agreement between creditor(s) and debtor may be concluded during liquidation proceedings. On debtor's request Court can call negotiations with liquidator participating. During negotiations Court determines, on liquidator's proposal, assets concerning agreement; debtor and creditors may agree on order of satisfaction, modes, proportion and modification of deadlines, or anything parties think important to restore debtor's solvency. Agreement needs approval of at least 50% of creditors in each group (groups [b], [d], [e], [f] and [g], see table below), if their claims amount to at least two-thirds of claims of parties entitled to agree. Liquidator assesses finances of and claims against corporation, informs debtor and creditors, may terminate all contracts (excluding lease-contracts, contracts for educational support, labor contracts, collective bargaining contracts or loan agreements entered into in ordinary course of business with private persons), collects claims due debtor and sells its assets at highest possible price taking into consideration creditors' right of preemption. Liquidator exercises employer's rights. When money is sufficient to pay creditors, liquidator can make interim liquidation balance, and such balance shall be approved or disapproved by Court. In latter event, procedure must continue. Reserves must be created to satisfy liquidation costs and disputed claims of creditors. At end of liquidation proceedings, but not later than two years from beginning thereof, final balance, account, report and tax return must be prepared by liquidator and filed with Court and tax authority. If creditor does not agree with final balance or report, Court hearing is scheduled with participation of debtor, creditors and liquidator. If no objection is raised Court decides on costs, satisfaction of creditors' claims (see table below), bank accounts and other duties of liquidator, closing liquidation proceedings and liquidation of debtor and its affiliated companies, if any.

Order of satisfaction of Claims is: (a) costs of liquidation (including wages and salaries, severance payments); (b) claims secured over six months from beginning of proceedings by pledge or lien; (c) allowances, damage- and life-annuity; (d) private claims from noneconomic activity (i.e. damages, guarantees); (e) social insurance debts, taxes, public debts; (f) other claims; (g) default interests as mentioned above and effective from liquidation.

If assets are not sufficient to satisfy all claims, those qualified under (a) and (b) must be fully satisfied, then those under (c) and (d) proportionally.

If assets are not sufficient to satisfy all claims under (e), (f) and (g), satisfaction of these creditors' claims should be performed proportionally.

If assets are not sufficient to satisfy all claims under (e), social insurance debts should be fully satisfied, others proportionally.

Simplified liquidation proceedings must start at liquidator's request when assets do not cover even costs of liquidation or when realization of proceedings is technically not possible because of deficiency in bookkeeping or recording.

Final settlement is performed when economic organization is dissolved without legal successor, other than in liquidation proceeding. Decision on final settlement should be filed with Court by director of corporation and also with Land Office, tax and Social Security Authority, labor and environmental office and affected banks. Creditors must present their claims within 30 days after announcement of final settlement. Settlor's duty during proceedings is similar to liquidator's.

BANKS AND BANKING:

As of Jan. 1, 1987 Hungarian National Bank, Inc. (Magyar Nemzeti Bank Rt.) is regulated as Western-style central banks are. (Act 1991:LX). Pursuant to successive reforms, commercial domestic banks, banks with foreign participation and banks with unanimous foreign ownership have been established. (Foreign banks involved in joint ventures or having subsidiary in Hungary are, inter alia, ABN Amro Bank, Banco di Sicilia, Bank Leumi, Banque Nationale de Paris, Banque Paribas, Citibank, Creditanstalt Bankverein, Credit Lyonnais, Commerzbank, Daiwa Securities, Deutsche Bank, Dresdner Bank, Fransabank, International Finance Corporation, Lubljanska Banka, Nomura Securities, Österreichische Volksbanken Porsche Bank AG, Westdeutsche Landesbank.) Privatization of banking is of primary importance for Government. Government Commissioner responsible for privatization of banking sector was appointed in 1994 by Gov. Decree 1095/1994 (X. 28). Banks are to be formed as corporations limited by shares (részvénytársaság), and are subject to requirements concerning stated capital, equipment, and expertise. Foreign owned banks may be opened upon consent of Government. Banks may be fully-licensed or specialized in any field of banking.

As of Dec. 1, 1991 new Act 1991:LXIX as am'd several times on financial institutions and financial institutional activities came into force.

Financial institutions in Hungary are (i) Hungarian National Bank, (ii) fully-licensed commercial banks, (iii) specialized financial institutions, (iv) investment banks and (v) savings banks. Permissible financial institutional activities are enumerated by law.

See Topical Index in front part of this volume.

BANKS AND BANKING . . . *continued*

Banks may not manage investment funds, and as of May 26, 1994, banks may not engage in insurance activities and other activities not closely related to activities of financial institutions. (§4). Some limitations apply depending on form of bank. Carrying on banking activity in foreign currency needs approval of State Bank Supervisory Board and consent of Hungarian National Bank.

Foreign participation over 10% of stated capital of bank must be licensed by Government. License is to be conditioned by factors like foreigner's equity and stated capital, its business reputation, its results for past five years, whether it has Hungarian speaking CEOs, its undertaking obligation with regard to training of bank's personnel, reciprocity in foreigner's home country, and anticipated effects on economic competition in banking sector.

Minimum stated capital is HUF one billion in case of commercial bank, HUF 500 million for specialized financial institutions and investment banks, and HUF 100 million for savings banks. (§10). At formation, cash contributions must reach above specified amounts and must be paid up before commencing activity. Financial institutions operating in form of company limited by shares, may only have registered shares. Since Jan. 1, 1993 financial institutions must reach and continuously maintain 8% weighted asset risk reserve ratio calculated according to provisions of banking supervision. (§23). Assets of bank must be classified, with risk reserve equal to 20% of substandard, 50% of doubtful and 100% of bad debts. (§28). By adopting Gov't. Decree 1078/1993 government introduced Bank Consolidation Program to assist ten major Hungarian banks in eliminating their so-called "dubious" assets. At these banks, capital restructuring was carried out by capital increases and for this particular reason, State bonds were issued. By doing so, these ten banks were able to eliminate "dubious" assets and create necessary reserves. Banks engaged in deposit taking must be members of National Deposit Insurance Fund. Banks may also voluntarily raise deposit insurance funds.

Control of banking is under State Bank Supervisory Board (Állami Bankfelügyelet). Bank supervision is regulated in c. VII. Besides control exercised by State Bank Supervisory Board, banks operating in form of company limited by shares must maintain internal control unit led by Supervisory Board of bank. Such unit controls lawful operation of bank. Banks must also have internal regulations maintaining safety and soundness of system.

Special rules apply to owners, managers and employees, secrets, advertisements, inhouse regulations, accounting, auditing, capital decrease and insolvency. Act 1994:XLII established Hungarian Export-Import Bank Co. Ltd., main purpose of which is to provide banking services to companies engaged in trade or business or rendering services of Hungarian origin. This financial institution is wholly owned by Hungarian State. Hungarian financial legislation recently introduced regulation on money laundering. (Act 1994:XXIV).

BILLS AND NOTES:

See topic Commercial Paper.

BONDS:

See topic Securities.

BROKERS:

Security brokerage activity (forgalmazás) is broken down into three categories. These are: (1) "issue brokering" (értékpapír-forgalombahozatal), i.e. preparing prospectus in interest of new issue sale, offerings for sale, managing subscription and sale, and taking obligation to purchase or subscribe securities that failed to be sold or subscribed; (2) "Stockjobbing" (értékpapír-kereskedelem) i.e. trade with securities on one's own account; (3) "Stockbroking" (értékpapír-bizomány) i.e. trade with securities in one's own name and for benefit of others. Corporations wishing to engage in brokerage have to apply for each applicable license from National Securities and Exchange Commission (Állami Értékpapir és Tózsde Felügyelet), which license must be granted according to conditions enumerated in Securities Act 1990:VI.

(1) Issue broker licence is available to limited liability companies and companies limited by shares with registered stock incorporated in Hungary, regardless of nationality of owners, if (a) companies have HUF 50,000,000 or more paid in stated capital, (b) issue brokerage and additional activities are their sole incorporated purpose, (c) they are adequately equipped, (d) qualified officers are hired, and (e) their regulation of business is approved by National Securities and Exchange Commission.

(2) Stockjobber licenses are issued under same conditions, as at point (1).

(3) Stockbroker licenses require same conditions as under point (1), except that paid-in stated capital of companies with limited liability (Kft) must be 5,000,000 or more and of Corporations Limited by Shares (Rt) 10,000,000 or more.

Brokers' officers qualified for Budapest Stock Exchange must have passed Commission's examination and have appropriate work experience of not less than two years.

CHATTEL MORTGAGE:

Chattel mortgage has no equivalent in Hungarian law. Security interest may be secured in some other contractual way.

See topics Contracts; Liens.

COMMERCIAL LAW:

Commercial law is not incorporated in one code. Act 1875:XXXVII on Commercial Code is in force only with respect to promissory notes and warehousing. For-profit corporations are regulated by Act 1988:VI. Private entrepreneurs are governed by Act 1990:V. These acts seem to be stable, governing commercial matters liberally.

Foreign trade is regulated by Act 1974:III and several executive type orders, as amended fundamentally several times in recent years. Domestic trade is governed by Act 1978:8I on domestic trade, as amended several times.

See also topics Foreign Trade; Corporations; Monopolies and Trade Restraints; Treaties and Conventions.

COMMERCIAL PAPER:

Commercial papers are drafts or bills of exchange (váltó), checks (csekk), several forms of certificates of deposit (letéti jegy, kincstárjegy) and several "promissory" notes (takarékbetétfajták, szövetkezeti részjegy, célrészjegy), regulated separately by types.

Both sight and time drafts are commonly used. Bank drafts (bank checks) and cashier's checks are used primarily in international transactions. Certificates of deposit and notes vary concerning negotiability and interests.

To compare see also topics Banks and Banking; Securities.

COMMERCIAL REGISTER:

All business entities, including business partnerships, must be, and even private entrepreneurs may be, registered in one of Firms Registers (Cégjegyzék) held and maintained by Corporation Courts (Cégbíróság), which are organized within County Courts. Registration is not only of declarative, but with some exceptions, of constitutive nature, i.e. corporations or other business entities come into being by decision of Court ordering their incorporation (registration), retroactively to date of founding document, after having carefully checked corporate documents. For this reason registration generally takes several weeks but, meanwhile corporations may be de facto active.

Apart from identification data, main business information must be registered, including names and addresses of agents.

On request Corporation Court furnishes certificate of existence (similar to that of U.S. MBCA §1.28; "cégkivonat"), which is public document containing most important data concerning firm.

For patent and trademark registering see topics Patents; Trademarks.

Documents Required for Registering Company.—For forms of companies, see topic Corporations.

I. General Requirements (Regardless of Form of Company).—(1) Completed registration request form (available at Court) which varies depending upon form of company, signed by required representative of company—one original. (2) Articles of Incorporation (contract of association) of company—one original and two authenticated copies. (3) Original specimen signatures authenticated according to Hungarian legal procedures. (4) Any licenses that are necessary to form or to operate company. (5) If company has foreign corporate shareholders or equity holders, official "extract of registration" of foreign shareholder (or authenticated copy) with authenticated Hungarian translation or certificate of good standing with authenticated Hungarian translation showing that shareholder or equity holder exists according to law of its country. (6) Receipt showing payment of publication fee. (7) In case of merger, preliminary license of Economic Competition Office is needed or statement of corporation that such license is not needed. (8) Minutes of Meeting of Shareholders or Board or Directors electing Board of Directors or Managing Director and Supervisory Board and Auditor, as case may be. (9) If power to represent company has been delegated by Managing Director or Board of Directors, certificate to this effect. (10) Statement of acceptance of Directors and members of Supervisory Board and Auditors. (11) Legal entity equity owners or stockholders of company, if any, must deliver their extract of negotiation. (12) Statement of membership in chamber of industry or commerce, if any. (13) Land registry extract if real estate forms part of share capital.

II. Special Requirements for Rt's.—(1) (a) Founders' statement (contents prescribed by law), (b) subscription list, (c) certificate of publication of notice of founding shareholders' meeting, (d) minutes and list of participants of founding shareholders' meeting. In case of private placement Articles of Incorporation are to be presented instead of (a)-(d). (2) Certificate of bank or other financial institution where company has its accounts to effect that portion of capital payable at foundation is paid in. (3) Opinion of accounting firm on value of any in kind contributions.

III. Special Requirements for Kft's.—(1) List of equity holders. (2) Certificate of bank or other financial institution in which Kft. has its accounts to effect that cash contributions have been paid in. (3) Statement by Managing Director(s) that all in kind contribution(s) are available to company. (4) Statement of acceptance of appointment by members of Supervisory Board and statutory auditors.

COMMODITIES:

Commodities may be (1) negotiable articles with economic value; (2) natural resources that can be utilized in same way as goods; (3) exchange value; (4) negotiable rights with economic value; (5) or index formed out of groups of above. However, securities may not be considered commodities. (Commodities Exchange Act 1994: XXXIX; §1[1]).

Commodities Exchange.—Commodity exchange is private legal entity established by at least 50 Founding Members by subscribing minimum capital of HUF 150,000,000. Formation must be approved by Government, upon proposal of Minister of Finance. Commodity Exchange is governed by its General Meeting and important role is given to Commodity Exchange Council, Supervisory Board, professional Commodities, Secretariat and Stock Exchange Clearing House.

Membership may be granted to corporations that are legal entities, State Owned Enterprises (SOEs) and cooperatives if those have: (1) bylaws approved by National Securities and Exchange Commodity Commission; (2) sufficient reserve funds to carry out such activity; (3) paid membership fee; (4) certified its registration with Firms Register and other competent registers. Furthermore, applicant must state that it shall fulfill requirements imposed on it by Charter of the Commodity Exchange.

Application for membership may only be denied if: (1) there are no vacant memberships; or (2) applicant cannot fulfill one or more requirements listed above. Memberships may be purchased and sold only in manner specified in Charter of the Exchange.

Commodity Exchange is supervised by Securities and Exchange Commission.

CONCESSION:

Operation of state or local government owned properties or exercise of state or local government owned activities may be granted to private entity through contract of concession or through founding economic organization with state or local government majority ownership. Permissible concessions are as follows: operation of countrywide

See Topical Index in front part of this volume.

CONCESSION . . . *continued*
public roads, railways, canals, ports and piers, civil airports, regional public utilities, telecommunications background networks and frequencies, local government owned public roads and utilities, mining research and exploitation, pipeline transport and storage, production and turnover of fissile materials and narcotics, organization and performance of games of chance, postal and telecommunications services excluding "cable televisions", railway passenger and goods transport and bus transportation.

For special industries Ministries' rules (ágazati törvény) may allow performance of certain actions of above mentioned activities without contract of concession (liberalized actions). Examples of such special rules are Act 1993:XLVIII on Mining and Act 1994:XLVIII on Electric Power.

Contract of concession should be awarded by competition invited by state or local government. Winner's articles of incorporation should contain activities stated in contract of concession. Party of contract of concession may be Hungarian or foreign natural persons or corporate bodies, or company thereof without legal personality. Contract is valid for fixed time but not more than 35 years. Property rights concerning state or local government properties do not change, but Ministries' rules concerning exploited natural resources may provide differently. Legal disputes should be regulated by Hungarian courts, but in case of foreign party, international court of arbitration may also act.

Competitive process awarding concession is public unless national defence or security interests require exclusivity. Call for competition must be announced in two national newspapers and in local papers at least 30 days before opening day of competition.

Corporation which receives concession should be formed by parties within 90 days after having signed contract of concession, to perform actions permitted by concession. If it also needs authority's permit, corporation's activity may only be performed after having received permits, but in case of withdrawal thereof contract of concession will not be considered invalid for six months. Corporation's purposes are limited to activities needing concession or closely related to them. Corporation is entitled to possess and use certain state or local government owned properties or make profit thereof, but cannot alienate utilization right or assign right to other corporation without state or local government permission. (Act 1991:XVI).

CONSTITUTION AND GOVERNMENT:

Republic of Hungary.—(Magyar Köztársaság). After common law style constitutional development of basic laws during more than ten centuries, first "written" constitution of country was adopted in 1949, by Act 1949:XX. It has been modified several times, basically in 1972, and fundamentally in 1989 and 1990. Changes since 1989 have resulted in essentially new constitutional structure. Hungary is unitarian, non-federative country; its territory is divided into 19 counties and capital city, Budapest, has county status. Constitution, as amended in 1989, is based on doctrine of separation of powers, where legislature is to make laws, executive is to carry them out and judiciary is to interpret them and to adjudicate disputes under law.

Parliament.—Legislative power is vested in Parliament (Országgyűlés), consisting of one house. Members of Parliament are elected for four years by all Hungarian citizens of full legal capacity.

President of Republic (köztársasági elnök) is elected by two-thirds majority of Parliament for five years. President represents unity of nation and is safeguard of rule of law.

National Auditing Commission (Állami Számvevöszék) of Parliament controls national budget and state property. Its president and deputy presidents are elected by two-thirds majority of Parliament.

Independent Officials.—Attorney General (Legföbb Ugyész), upon proposal of President of Republic, is elected by Parliament and is head of state prosecutors offices. Ombudsmen are elected by Parliament for independent control of rule of law, and one ombudsman is for ethnic minorities. For rights and duties of ombudsman for independent control of rule, see newly adopted Act 1993:LIX and 1993:LXXVII.

Prime Minister is, on proposal of President of Republic, elected by Parliament. As head of executive branch, Prime Minister represents state and is chairman of Government, which consists of 17 ministers with or without portfolio. Ministers are appointed by President of Republic, upon recommendation of Prime Minister. Foreign trade and investment falls under authority of Minister of International Economic Relations (formerly named Minister of Commerce). Government controls ministers, and some other authorities and bodies, of importance among them is State Privatization and Property Holding Company (Állami Privatizációs és Vagyonkezelo Rt.). See also topic Corporations, subhead State Owned Enterprise.

Judiciary.—*Constitutional Court* is separated from ordinary judiciary. It has right to annul acts of Parliament and other laws if in contravention of constitution.

Supreme Court (Legfelsóbb Bíróság) is highest regular court of justice in country, whose President, on proposal of President of Republic, is elected by Parliament. Vice presidents of Court, proposed by President of Court, are appointed by President of Republic. Judges of country, according to constitution, are independent, governed only by law and are appointed by President of Republic. See also topic Courts.

Bill of Rights.—Constitution incorporates rights adopted in UN Universal Declaration of Human Rights and further supplements them with social and economic rights of citizens. Freedom of competition and enterprise are constitutional rights, which can only be limited by special act, adopted in way otherwise necessary to amend Constitution.

Local Government.—Municipalities are governed by local self-government (helyi önkormányzat). Powers of local government are vested in representative body (helyi önkormányzat) elected by citizens and resident aliens, who are residents thereof. Representative body, headed by mayor (polgármester) who is elected by body itself, instructs and overviews local administration. Police, water and environmental protection administration is centralized under ministries. County governments are of similar structure, where representatives are elected by local representative bodies. For capital city and some other bigger cities special rules apply. (Act 1990:LXV as am'd by Act 1992:LV and Act 1994:LXIII).

Jurisdiction of local governments with regard to traffic and water administration, agriculture, cultural activities, public welfare, building administration, environmental protection, zoning, industry and trade, etc. are regulated by Act 1991:XX and Orders of Government 18-26/1992 (I.28) Korm.

CONTRACTS:

Definitions and Basic Concept.—General rules of "law of obligations" are set forth in §§198-338 of Civil Code. Essentially, contract is agreement between two or more persons creating obligations to do or not to do particular things. Unless otherwise required by law (e.g. in case of real estate, corporation, business partnership, foreign trade) contracts may be concluded either in writing or orally. Contract implied in fact is true contract, evidenced by conduct of parties. Contract is made by any proper expression of mutual consent (consensual contract), i.e. offer and its acceptance. Consideration is not required. Contract itself affects transfer of ownership, except in case of real estate, ownership to which will be transferred by its registration in Land Register. There are no special requirements of law for contracting party when contracting with Government or municipalities; i.e. authorities themselves are responsible for their legal capacity.

Categories classified by Civil Code (like contracts for sale, lease, enterprise, mandate, insurance, gift, foundation, etc.) are not obligatory types. Parties may create any obligation that is legally enforceable expressing their consent at least with regard to essential or qualified as essential questions. Pre-contract creates legal obligation to enter into contract at later time. Contracts might be, inter alia, blanket (covering number of items), certain (depending on will of someone), hazardous (depending on uncertain event), commutative or independent, conditional, open ended, etc. Unlawful contracts are void, and as such, unenforceable by either parties to contract, and if performed or executed, restoration of status quo may be asked (in integrum restitutio), without time limit. Voidable contract may be voided by party by reason of defense such as duress, undue influence, fraud, infancy, mistake in facts; generally within five years from performance. It is worth noting, that referring to changes of essential circumstances (clausula rebus sic standibus) may be proper defense against and before performance.

Legal Capacity to Enter into Contract.—Persons 18 years of age and over have full capacity. Minors over 14 and persons judicially declared to be of limited competence may enter into contracts with consent of their guardian. Consent is not required if contract is of lesser importance or does not impose duty on them. Minors under 14 and persons who are judicially declared incompetent or are incompetent as matter of fact may not enter into contracts, and if nevertheless such contract is made it will be void. Entities are fully capable (no ultra vires liability), except in relations which are obviously characteristic of human beings.

Some contracts, e.g. those between spouses, those forming partnership and company (articles of incorporation are of contractual nature) and real property purchase contracts need to be countersigned by attorney at law or legal counselor.

As far as legal capacity of foreigners is concerned, their domestic laws are to be applied in order to determine legal capacity, unless they are contrary to Hungarian public order. (Act-Order 1979:13, §64). See also topic Foreign Law.

Contractual Rights.—If two or more persons together constitute one party to contract, these two or more persons jointly promise to perform contract's obligation. If obligation is divisible into separate items, each contractor is obliged to be liable for her part. If contract is not divisible, each contractor is liable for full performance. Unless otherwise expressed in contract, divisibility is to be tested according to joint or several nature of contract.

Third party beneficiary for whose benefit promise was made, will be directly entitled only if so stipulated in contract itself, i.e. unless otherwise declared, beneficiary may not maintain action against promisor. Stipulated beneficiary will be entitled, when she learns about contract, but if she disapproves it, all rights, privileges and defenses go to promisee.

Assignment of rights, except if contract involves personal element or if prohibited by statute, may be performed between assignor and assignee, without consent of obligor, who needs only to be given notice. Once notice has been given, obligor is to carry out obligation only towards assignee. Contract of assignment may be made without consideration.

Party may perform duties through delegate, unless otherwise stipulated or other party has substantial interest in having original promisor perform. Party delegating remains liable under original contract. Delegation of duties discharging delegator needs consent of obligee. Novation by three-party agreement may have same effect, i.e. discharging delegator and substituting third party delegatee.

Discharge and Remedies for Breach of Contract.—Normally contract is terminated by performance of terms of agreement. Discharge by rescission places each party in original position by returning any property or money that has been delivered or paid (in integrum restitutio). Waiver, relinquishing rights for future, leaves parties in position where they are at that time. Confusion of parties, and in certain contracts death, results in discharge. Any kind of alteration or modification may discharge contract or some duties thereof. Repudiation may be legal way of discharging and also breach of contract, depending on nature of contract. Party suffering damages by breach of contract is entitled to bring action for damages or if it is minor breach, i.e. promisee received substantial benefit, may sue for cure or price adjustment, if still interested in performance.

Applicable Law.—In international transactions parties have free choice as to applicable law. If such stipulation is lacking, law to which contract has its closest connection is applicable. Thus, unless otherwise chosen by parties, according to Hungarian international private law, in contractual disputes generally law of vendor, donor, testator, entrepreneur, etc. is to be applied, i.e. more generally, law of party whose performance is specific in contract. Lex loci is to be applied in real estate cases, and lex fori if conflict cannot otherwise be solved or in public law interest case. See topic Foreign Law.

Definitions of International Chamber of Commerce (INCOTERMS), as revised in 1990, are customarily used in trade. See topic Foreign Trade.

COOPERATIVES:

Cooperatives were re-regulated by Act 1992:II, as amended by 1992:VI, 1993:XIX and 1994:XLIV. Members of cooperative may be individuals (minimum age 18, or 14 with consent of guardian, §42) and also legal entities. Number of legal entity members cannot exceed that of individuals. For foreigners' membership, Company Act #1988:VI, §§4, 7(2) and 9 apply. Minimum number of promoting members is five; in case of school or credit cooperatives minimum 15. (§7).

Establishment.—Founding General Meeting has to decide upon founding cooperative and shall adopt Charter (Alapszabály) thereof. Charter shall be public deed or countersigned by attorney at law or in-house legal counsel. (§6). Charter and other documents of procedural nature shall be filed with Firms' Register within 30 days of founding for registration and publication. (§7). Registration of cooperatives is, however, not only of declarative but also of constitutive nature, i.e. cooperative comes into being legally by decision of Court ordering incorporation (registration), after having carefully checked each foundation document. Upon Court's resolution registering cooperative into Firms' Register, level of "de jure" existence is achieved retroactively to time of adopting Charter, unless later date was fixed therein. In absence of Court's resolution, which constitutes legal personality for cooperative, contractors' liability for contracts concluded in name of cooperative will remain unlimited. Having adopted Charter, legal capacity to operate on behalf of "de facto" cooperative actually exists, nevertheless liability of contractors will be similar to that defined in U.S. Model Business Corporation Act §2.04. (§8).

Representation.—Chairman of Board of Directors, Managing Chairman, Managing Director or another member of Board may each individually represent cooperative.

General Meeting.—Power of General Meeting is regulated by §20, which meeting consists of members of cooperative. General Meeting is to be called by Board of Directors 15 days before meeting and together with agenda, at least once a year. General Meeting shall be called if 10% of members or Board of Supervisors proposes meeting, indicating agenda.

Delegates' Meeting, Divided General Meeting.—If Charter stipulates, instead of General Meeting, either Delegates' Meeting (küldöttgyûlés) or Divided Meetings (részközgyûlés) exercise power thereof. Local governing bodies (helyi önkormányzati egység) may be elected by place of work, organizational structure, place of living or based on some joint interest.

Board of Directors (igazgatóság) of at least three directors and Chairman thereof is to be elected by members by General Meeting. One Managing Chairman is to be elected if cooperative has less than 50 members. Board (or Managing Chairman) is managing organ of cooperative, which exercises all power not vested in other bodies of cooperative.

Board of Supervisors (Felügyelôbizottság) of at least three supervisors and Chairman thereof is to be elected by General Meeting. If less than 50 members, auditor or one supervisor is to be elected.

Committee of Reconciliation (egyeztetô bizottság) of at least three members may be elected by General Meeting for balancing interests and resolving debates.

"Cooperative Bond".—Cooperative Bond (részjegy) represents interest of member in cooperative. Each bond must have same face value. When establishing or joining cooperative, each member has to subscribe to Cooperative Bond, payment of which is to be made according to provisions of Charter. Cooperative Bond is non-negotiable instrument, and it cannot be transferred. It entitles holder to interest from taxed profit.

"Cooperative Share" (szövetkezeti üzletrész).—Capital surplus originating from taxed profit of cooperatives, if not distributed among members, shall be devoted to creation or increase of cooperative share capital. This cooperative share capital shall be broken down into Cooperative Shares which are to be distributed proportionally among existing holders of such shares and among those not yet holding such shares. This Share is entitled to dividends. It can be transferred, nevertheless cooperative and its members have preemptive rights therefor. Holder of this Share, even if not member, may appear in General Meeting without right to vote.

Transformation of previously existing Cooperatives is regulated by Act 1992:II on entry into force of Act 1992:I on cooperatives and on interim rules thereto. Simplified appraisal of cooperatives' assets is governed by Order of Government 34/1992 (II.19) Korm.

COPYRIGHT:

Copyrights are regulated by Civil Code (§§86-87) and by Act 1969:III as am'd by Act 1994:VII and executive orders accordingly.

Copyright covers authorship of literary, musical, dramatic, choreographic, graphic, sculptural, audiovisual works, sound recordings, and works of same original, creative nature, fixed in any media of expression. Also computer software is protected under copyright. Generally term of copyright protection expires 70 years from death of author. Dealings in copyright do not effect author's moral rights, e.g. right to be recognized as author, and as such, these moral rights are not subject to expiration. As of Feb. 23, 1994, actor's performances, radio and TV broadcasting organizations and sound recorders are more widely protected by copyright. (Act 1994:VII).

To be subject of copyright, work has to be perfected to certain level, i.e. ideas, procedures, concepts, principles, discoveries may not be protected by copyright. Nevertheless, these works may be protected under Civil Code.

Author Copyright Office (Szerzöi Jogvédö Hivatal) is agency dealing with registration and protection of copyrights, and also provides services to authors.

See also topic Treaties and Conventions.

CORPORATIONS:

Corporate rules of Commercial Code (Acts 1875:XXXVII & 1930:V; amended several times) have been replaced by new Business Corporation Act (Törvény a Gazdasági Társaságokról) of predominantly German model. (Act 1988:VI, as am'd several times). This act did not effect existence of previously formed corporations.

Hungarian legal notion of "business" (or translated literally: economic) corporations, as collective term, similar to German "Handelsgesellschaft", covers two groups of business entities. One substantially corresponds to American for-profit corporations, other to for-profit partnerships. Corporation-like "business corporations" are (as delineated in numbered subheads, infra): (1) Corporation Limited by Shares, (2) Company with Limited Liability, (3) Joint Enterprise, (4) Business Association. Partnership-like "business corporations" are: (5) General Partnership and (6) Limited Partnership.

Although cooperatives and state-owned enterprises are incorporated legal entities with liability limited to their capital, they are not enumerated under legal notion of "business corporations". Nevertheless, these kinds of business entities are corporations-in-fact, with some special rules concerning shareholders' rights.

Investors, domestic or foreign, private, corporate or public, may, in general, equally form and participate in corporations. As of Jan. 1, 1991, acquisition of foreign majority or unanimous foreign ownership in corporation is not subject of any approval, permission or license, not even that of exchange control. There are no differences between public and private corporations.

Foreign individuals are not exempt from withholding tax on dividends, unlike foreign corporations. (See topic Taxation.) Foreign arbitration and, theoretically, foreign law clauses may be covenanted for in articles of incorporation.

Corporation may be formed for any lawful business purpose or purposes. Purposes, i.e. scope of activity, for which corporation is formed, must appear in articles of incorporation. Regardless of what is contained in articles of incorporation, legal capacity of corporation is unlimited (no ultra vires liability) i.e., contract beyond scope of stated corporate activity will not necessarily be invalid. Corporation has to be registered with Corporation Court within whose jurisdiction its seat is established; and also branch offices are to be separately registered, if located in some other county.

(1) Corporation Limited by Shares (Részvénytársaság; hereinafter referred to as "Rt") is corporation corresponding to U.S. M.B.C.A.'s notion of private, domestic, for-profit corporations, to German "Aktiengesellschaft" or to French "Societé Anonyme". Fundamental characteristic of Rt is, that it is separate legal entity, having existence separate from its shareholders, acting through its agents. Liability of Rt is limited to its own capital, i.e. its shareholders are not liable therefor, except that they are to contribute its shares' nominal, or if higher, issue value.

Rt may be promoted by one or more natural or legal persons, who are supposed to act as incorporators, and usually are shareholders. Their number may not be less than two. Stated capital cannot be less than HUF 10,000,000, at least 30% thereof, but not less than HUF 5,000,000, must be contributed in cash, while rest may be in other than cash, i.e. in kind. Upon promotion, shares are open for subscription, when 10% of par value has been paid in. Oversubscription may be refused by promoters according to promotion or at first (Forming) Shareholders' Meeting. Within 60 days from successful subscription, first (Forming) Shareholders' Meeting is to be called. Before opening this Meeting subscribers must pay-in up to 30% of par value. Rest is due not later than one year from incorporation. Forming Shareholders' Meeting will adopt articles of incorporation, which, by contrast to those of other forms of corporations, necessarily has to follow wording of Act unless otherwise permitted by Act itself. Articles of incorporation are to be countersigned by attorney at law or legal counselor, i.e. notarial or court deed or record is not required.

If promoters agree to subscribe to all shares, there is no need for Forming Shareholders' Meeting, and rights thereof shall be vested in promoters. Instead of articles of incorporation, Deed of Foundation must be prepared. Promoters must pay in 30% of sum stated in Deed of Foundation. Government-budget entity or bank may form Rt alone, i.e. it may be sole shareholder. Otherwise sole shareholder Rt may be developed by acquiring all shares by one entity. In case of bankruptcy, sole shareholder will be personally liable for debts of corporation, thus piercing corporate veil.)

Articles of incorporation (alapszabály) must contain name and seat, address of corporation; scope of activity; duration of existence (which may be perpetual); statement about stated capital; classes, number and par value of shares (no shares without par value: subscribing with contribution in kind is to be based on appraisal, which is to be accepted by Forming Shareholders' Meeting, and shares against contribution in kind will be issued otherwise in regular way); conditions of paying-in unpaid portion of subscription; way of signing for Rt; procedural rules according to Shareholders' Meeting, Board of Directors, Supervisory Board and Auditor; rules applying to distributing profit; and way of announcement of corporate notices. Articles of incorporation must state whether shares were issued against other than cash, and if advantages were warranted for promoters; procedural rules to be applied to different classes of shares and bonds, if any; procedure of redemption of shares. Business provisions may be incorporated into articles of incorporation or settled in bylaws, if adopted. Bylaws constitute contract either between Rt and its shareholders or among shareholders themselves. No special form is required for validity of bylaws or any contracts of that kind, unless it is part of articles of incorporation.

Articles of incorporation together with other required documents of procedural nature shall be delivered to Corporation Court (Cégbíróság) for filing within 30 days from adoption. Registration cost for Rt (like for Kft and other business entities with legal personality) is 2% of stated capital with minimum of HUF 10,000 but not more than HUF 300,000. (Act 1993:LXXV). Upon coming into force of Court's resolution registering corporation into Firms' Register, level of "de jure" existence is achieved retroactively to time of adopting articles of incorporation, unless later date is fixed therein. In absence of Court's resolution, which constitutes legal personality for corporation, contractors' liability for contracts concluded in name of Rt is unlimited. Having adopted articles of incorporation, legal capacity to operate on behalf of "de facto" corporation actually exists, nevertheless liability of contractors will be similar to that defined in U.S. M.B.C.A. §2.04.

Shares created and issued by Rt may be of one or more classes, which classes may differ from each other as to right to vote, sharing profit, etc. Shares may be either "payable to bearer" or "registered by name" by nature. Bearer share obtained by foreigner must be converted into registered share within three months, otherwise foreigner may not exercise shareholder's right. Regular share certificates, which are negotiable instruments, may be issued if stated capital is fully paid in.

Preferred shares not exceeding 50% of regular stock capital, may be entitled to preference on dividends, and may represent limited voting rights, at same time.

Special registered shares may be issued with designation that these shares will be passed from original shareholder to public interest foundation or association, after

See Topical Index in front part of this volume.

CORPORATIONS . . . *continued*

period of time defined in articles of incorporation ("trust shares"). This public interest foundation or association usually serves interest of employees. Nevertheless, surplus from difference between par value and market price of trust shares at moment of transfer of them to public interest foundation or association will be allocated to original shareholder. If this foundation or association is formed for benefit of more than 50 employees, dividend or any part of it might also be distributed to foundation or association, even before passing shares themselves.

If capital surplus, i.e. excess of net assets over stated capital, is converted to stated capital, 10% thereof may be issued as "employee shares". Transfer of employee shares is restricted.

Fixed interest rate shares may also be issued up to 10% of stated capital. For these shares, besides or instead of dividend, prefixed rate of interest is to be paid.

Bonds (profit-sharing, or not) may be issued with right to be converted into shares, whenever bondholder requests so (convertible bonds), or with option to buy shares when issued in future (optional bonds).

Not exceeding one-third of stated capital, Rt may purchase its own shares, nevertheless these shares must be either sold or redeemed and canceled within three years.

In general, increase of stated capital may occur in three ways: by converting surplus to stated capital, by converting convertible bonds to shares, or (if Rt is in existence already for one year) by issuing new shares. It is worth noting that initial capital cannot be increased by issuing new shares in first year of operation. In each case Shareholders' Meeting is to decide, but Board of Directors if authorized in Articles of Incorporation also has right to increase stated capital by converting surplus to stated capital or by issuing new shares. All shares must be fully paid before issuing new ones, except if issuance is for contribution in kind. Shareholders' Meeting may reduce stated capital by redemption of shares owned by Rt itself, if any; or by determining reduced par value (exchange, overprinting or fusioning of shares); or by redemption and cancellation of shares (with obligation to refund). Public notice of intention to adopt resolution reducing stated capital must be given twice. After that, within 90 days from publishing second notice, creditors may present claims against Rt to meet its obligations even if not yet due, or may demand guaranties. Before filing reduction in stated capital, Court will require Rt to perform settlements with creditors, who presented claims.

Shareholders' Meeting is basic forum for shareholders to exercise their property rights. Unless shorter period is required by articles of incorporation, Shareholders' Meeting is to be called at least annually, upon published notice and agenda, which are to be served not later than 30 days before Meeting. Upon request of shareholders representing not less than 10% of stated capital, Meeting must be called within 30 days. Shareholders may vote in classes, in person or by proxy. Majority constitutes quorum, unless Act, articles of incorporation or bylaws require more. According to Act three-fourths quorum is required to amend articles of incorporation, to raise or reduce stated capital, to decide on privileges and limitations of classes, for merger, consolidation or voluntary dissolution or any variety thereof and to decide on transformation of types of shares by overprinting thereof. These three-fourths quorum items, and voting for directors, members of Supervisory Board, auditor, voting for balance sheet (which includes profit and loss statement), distributing profit, and voting for issuing preferred bonds are subject to decision of Shareholders' Meeting. When limiting any rights of classes of shares, three-fourths majority of all classes directly concerned is required. Decisions of Shareholders' Meeting are to be delivered to Corporation Court within 30 days. Each shareholder, director or member of Supervisory Board may bring action against Rt, demanding Corporation Court supervise any unlawful decision of Shareholders' Meeting.

Board of Directors, consisting of not less than three and not more than 11 directors, is to be elected by Shareholders' Meeting for not more than five years. Directors may be reelected at any time. Board or any director may be removed by Shareholders' Meeting with or without cause at any time. Unless otherwise stated in articles of incorporation, directors jointly, i.e. Board of Directors as body, manage business and act on behalf of corporation. There is no citizenship or residence requirement for directors, but articles of incorporation or bylaws may prescribe such requirements or establish other qualifications. Decision making process and operational procedure of Board of Directors must be laid down in charter of Board and is adopted by Board itself. Board appoints its chairman or president, and may remove her without cause.

Supervisory Board is required for all Rt's. It consists of not less than three members (supervisors), who must be elected by Shareholders' Meeting, for not longer than five year period, which is renewable. Each member of Board may be removed with or without cause at any time. If annual average number of full-time employees exceeds 200, one-third of supervisors are to be elected by employees. Supervisor shall not be director or auditor of Rt. There is no citizenship or residency requirement for supervisors, but articles of incorporation or bylaws may prescribe such requirements or establish other qualifications. Supervisory Board elects its chairman, and with consent of Board of Directors sets forth its procedural charter. Supervisory Board, as body or through its members, supervises management and operation of business, and if it finds it necessary, may employ experts. Supervisory Board prepares reports to Shareholders' Meeting, and if deemed necessary, Supervisory Board may call Shareholders' Meeting.

Auditor.—At least one auditor is to be elected by Shareholders' Meeting from among individuals or companies qualified and licensed as auditors in Hungary. Auditor may not be director or employee of Rt. Apart from this qualification, same rules apply to election of auditor, as apply to directors. Auditor has to control accounting and corporate finance, and is to consolidate annual balance sheet, as condition for its adoption.

Consolidation, merger, split-up (with dissolving parent-corporation), transformation from one "business corporation" form to another, or voluntary dissolution of Rt may be decided with three-fourths quorum of Shareholders' Meetings, and generally rules of capital reduction are applied, if corporation would be less capitalized after. If Rt holds three-quarters of shares of another Rt (controlled Rt), first (parent) Rt will be liable for controlled (subsidiary) Rt's debts, although first Rt will have administrative privileges in control. Acquiring significant part (greater than 25%) in another Rt requires public notice. These rules and additional rules concerning Rts apply only to Rts, i.e. not to other forms of corporation, such as company with limited liability (Kft).

To be dissolved, corporation has to be liquidated by person or persons, possibly other than directors, appointed by Shareholders' Meeting or, if not, by Court. Liquidator is not entitled to conduct new business, being rather trustee for purpose of winding up affairs and discharging Rt debts. Remaining assets may be distributed six months after third notice is published giving notice of liquidation to creditors. Unless otherwise prescribed in articles of incorporation, remaining assets are to be distributed among shareholders in proportion to their shares and according to classes.

Investment funds, stock exchange agent corporations, or any other special function firms may be created in form of corporation limited by shares or as limited liability companies and may be required to meet special conditions according to amount of stated capital and personal qualifications. Banks may only be formed as companies limited by shares. See also topics Brokers; Securities.

(2) Company with Limited Liability (Korlátolt Felelosségu Társaság, hereinafter referred to as Kft) is another form of business corporation, corresponding to company under Limited Liability Company Act of 1992 of Delaware (c. 18), German "Gesellschaft mit beschränkter Haftung", or French "Societé à Responsabilité Limitée". Although Kft has no precise equivalent in American law, it can be characterized as simpler form of for-profit corporation. Liability of Kft is limited to its stated capital, i.e. liability of members corresponds to that of shareholders in Rt. In other words, and only for purpose of explanation, Kft can be described as limited partnership of only limited partners, without general partner.

Even one member is enough to form Kft (member or partner is "shareholder" of Kft, corresponding to German "Gesellschafter" or French "associé"). Stated (authorized) capital cannot be less than HUF 1,000,000, at least 30% thereof, but not less than HUF 500,000, must be paid-in in cash at time of incorporation; remainder, or after having been incorporated, whole stated capital may be in kind. Before registration with Court, 50% of each cash contribution to stated capital but not less than HUF 500,000, must be contributed to company, rest is due not later than one year. In case of sole member Kft, whole stated capital is due immediately. Contributions in kind must be available before registration with Court.

Ownership rights of each member towards company are embodied in "business parts" (corresponding to "limited liability company interest" under Delaware law, or to German "Geschäftsanteil"), which may differ in value from one another, but each must be of par value not less than HUF 100,000. (Nevertheless, business parts may be owned jointly, and in this case each owner has authority to represent other owners towards company.) Business parts, as such, are subject to transfer, unless prescribed otherwise in articles of incorporation. Members have preemptive rights over business part for sale to others. Multi-member Kft, authorized by vote of three-fourths quorum of Members' Meeting, may purchase its own business parts, not exceeding one-third of its stated capital. While owned by Kft, these business parts represent no right to vote and must be sold or redeemed in one year. Business part is not kind of security, i.e. no shares may be issued on stated capital or to represent owners' rights, and if issued, will be invalid.

To form Kft, members conclude articles of incorporation corresponding to certificate of formation under Delaware law (társasági szerzödés) or instead, sole member issues charter of company, which is to be countersigned by attorney at law or legal counselor, i.e. neither notarial nor court deed or record is needed. Articles of incorporation, together with other documents of procedural nature, must be delivered to Corporation Court for filing, within 30 days from their adoption. Effect of incorporation is same as with Rt. Articles of incorporation must contain name, seat, and address of Kft, name and address of members, scope of activity, stated capital and business parts, conditions of pay-in of unpaid portion of business parts, voting rights at Members' Meeting (which do not necessarily correspond to proportion of business parts), procedure to resort to in case of tie votes, name or names of first managing director or directors, way of signing for company, and if otherwise obligatory, names of first supervisors and auditor. If members agree on following dispositions, they are also to be settled in articles of incorporation: contribution in kind and its value; additional services provided by members besides stated capital; authorization of Members' Meeting to prescribe additional payments; permitting redemption of business shares; authorization of all members for management and representation; limiting managing director's capacity to represent company; establishment of Supervisory Board and appointment of auditor, if not otherwise obligatory.

Members' Meeting is governing body of Kft and forum for members to exercise their property rights. Unless otherwise required in articles of incorporation, it is to be called annually, similar to Rt's Shareholders' Meeting, with exception that notice and agenda need not be published. Unless otherwise required by law or by articles of incorporation, majority constitutes quorum. Decision on some subjects belongs to discretion of Meeting as of right, most notably decision on balance sheet, increasing and reducing stated capital, distribution of profit, spin-off and redemption of business parts, expelling member, voting for directors, supervisors and auditor, and removing them; confirmation of contracts exceeding one-quarter of stated capital or generally contracts with members or directors or contracts concluded before incorporation; claims against promoting members, directors and supervisors; (three-quarters quorum) voting for amending articles of incorporation, dissolution, transformation to another corporation form, consolidation, merger and spin-off decisions on establishing other corporations. Members, if there is no dissent among them, may in writing decide these matters without formal Members' Meeting. Member, managing director or supervisor may sue concerning any unlawful decision of Meeting.

Managing director or directors are to be elected by Members' Meeting for period of not more than five years, and may be reelected. As in case of Rt, there are no citizenship or qualification requirements for directors. With three-quarters quorum, Meeting can remove directors, with or without cause, at any time. Managing director and directors, unless otherwise required in articles of incorporation, jointly manage business and act on behalf of company.

Supervisory Board.—If annual average number of full-time employees exceeds 200, if multi-member Kft's stated capital exceeds HUF 20,000,000, or if there are more than 25 members, Supervisory Board must be elected.

Auditor must be elected at sole-member Kft, and if stated capital exceeds HUF 50,000,000.

See Topical Index in front part of this volume.

CORPORATIONS . . . *continued*

Rules to be applied to Supervisory Board and auditor are similar to those of Rt. Rules to protect creditors' interests, similar to those described for Rt, apply to procedures of dissolution, reduction of stated capital or any restructuring with same effect.

(3) "Business association" (Egyesülés) is not-for-profit, non-limited (full and joint) liability corporation of entities for lobbying, organizing and coordinating joint activities in furtherance of their business. Although legal entity, its financing and liability rules are similar to those of general partnership. As form of business corporation it is of less importance.

(4) "Joint enterprise" (Közös Vállalat) is for-profit, non-limited liability corporation of entities, being separate legal entity. Its members are liable for its debts in proportion to their contributions. Although still existing in relatively great numbers, as surviving corporate form, it is of declining importance.

(5) General partnership (Közkereseti Társaság, hereinafter referred to as Kkt) is in Hungarian law qualified as business corporation, nevertheless, it widely corresponds to American notion of general partnership, as defined by U.S. U.P.A. §6; modelled after German "Offene Handelsgesellschaft" and functionally similar to French commercially active "Societé an Participation". As far as same basic rules apply to all forms of business corporations, these rules apply to General and Limited Partnerships (e.g. to capitalization, regulated procedure for increase and reduction of stated capital, arbitration, necessity of countersigned articles of incorporation, duration, court registration and supervision, balance sheet, appraisal, taxation, tax allowances, liquidation, etc.).

In general, partnership is association of two or more individuals or entities to carry on business for profit as co-owners. (Individuals may be unlimited liability [general] partners or members only in one business corporation.) Although not separate legal entity, nevertheless, in contractual relations partnership may be party to contracts, and in its name it may be entitled and obliged, own property, and sue or be sued (possibly together with its partners). Partners are jointly and severally liable for debts not covered by assets of partnership. Incoming partner, who joins established partnership, will be liable for obligations already existing only to extent of her supplied capital. Retiring partner will not be liable for debts incurred after retirement. If license is required (e.g. driving license for truck driving) for conduct of business, one of partners or employees must have it. Personal activity of each partner is presumed; in transactions they all are agents for partnership unless otherwise prescribed in articles of partnership.

Articles of Partnership.—Partnership is to be created by articles of partnership (társasági szerződés; i.e. partnership agreement or contract). For its formalities see catchline Articles of Incorporation in subhead Company with Limited Liability, supra. Same basic rules apply as with Kft. Partnership must be capitalized as much as necessary, i.e. there is no legal requirement for minimum amount of stated capital or for procedures for its distribution. Partners decide transactions and matters of partnership, generally by vote of majority of quorum. Law requires unanimous quorum for amending articles, and for transactions beyond scope of usual activity, and two-thirds quorum is required to remove capacity of partner to represent and be agent for partnership or to expel partner. Removal or withdrawal of any partner does not affect dissolution of partnership.

(6) Limited partnership (Betéti Társaság, hereinafter referred to as Bt) differs from general partnership in that it has one or more limited partners, whose liability to creditors of partnership is limited to amount invested or payable as stated capital by her in partnership. Bt corresponds to American notion of limited partnership, as defined by U.S. U.L.P.A. §1, German "Kommanditgesellschaft" or French "Societé en Commandite Simple". Apart from limited partners' liability and fact that limited partners have no right to represent or manage Bt, rules applying to Bt are those of Kkt. It is worth noting, that if Bt has in its firm's name name of limited partner, her personal liability will be unlimited.

State Owned Enterprise.—For practical reasons state owned enterprises (hereinafter referred to as SOE) may be defined as specially formed and operated for-profit corporations owned by state. (Act 1977:VI on State Enterprises, as am'd several times). There are two basic forms of SOEs: enterprises under direct administrative control (over 30% of SOEs) and those that are not directly controlled (over 50%). Modifications of Act on SOEs in 1984-1985 abolished direct state control over majority of SOEs. In short, state is legal owner of both kinds of enterprises, but in case of direct control SOEs state exercises ownership rights, while in case of nondirect control SOEs special management body of enterprise itself exercises these rights.

Direct Controlled SOEs.—There are two types of direct controlled SOEs: public enterprises (utilities), and other enterprises. Decisions over transforming separate departments (shops) within enterprise into legally separate entities, dissolution of enterprise, and merger with other enterprises are made by founder (appropriate ministry).

Nondirect Control SOEs.— There are two types of nondirect control SOE: enterprises led by enterprise council (of employees, managers and one member appointed by founder), and enterprises led by employees' representative body (characteristic of smaller enterprises). Decisions over transformation are within authority of enterprise council or representative body.

Following its creation State Privatization and Property Holding Company, Ltd. (Állami Privalizációs és Vagyonkezelo Rt., hereinafter referred to as ÁPV Rt.) may retain rights of founder. (Acts 1995:XXXIX; see also topic Foreign Investment).

Change of corporate form within and among business corporations is possible, if special requirements of corporation to be formed by transformation are fulfilled. In interest of creditors, transformation has to be duly published and according to nature of transformation, change in capitalization rules of capital reduction apply. (Act 1992:LV). This law applies also to transformation of cooperatives and state owned enterprises, when changing into corporate forms.

Common rules applying to all SOEs and corporations are: project for transformation and audit of assets must be prepared and value of assets may not exceed value determined by licensed auditor. Plan of transformation must contain, among other things, information on objectives to be achieved by transformation, letter of intent of new parties (shareholders, members) and draft of articles of incorporation. Decision on transformation is to be published in official gazette Cégközlöny. Entity formed after transformation is legal successor of former enterprise. In case of transformation rules of Corporation Act are to be applied, with some exceptions.

Publications.—Official and necessary publications of firms are to appear in Cégközlöny, which is official gazette of Corporation Courts published by Ministry of Justice.

Foreign Corporations.—See preamble to this topic; see also topics Foreign Investment, Investment Protection, Currency, Taxation. See also topic Cooperatives.

COSTS:

See topic Actions.

COURTS:

System.—Being unitarian, non-federal state, Hungary has unified court system, wherein only Constitutional Court is separate from system of Courts. First level of regular courts is that of local courts, second is 20 County Courts and third is Supreme Court. Labor courts are organized beside County Courts. (§§32/A, 45-50 Const., 10-47 C.P.C., Act 1989:I).

Constitutional Court.—(Alkotmánybíróság). It was established by Act 1989:XX-XII. on amendment of Constitution. Fifteen judges of Court are elected by Parliament by two-thirds majority for nine years. Court's competence includes review of acts and orders, and it has right to annul them (cassation).

Local Courts (or named Municipal Court in towns; Helyi Bíróság or Városi Bíróság) exercise first instance civil (up to HUF 10,000,000) and criminal (misdemeanors and minor felonies) jurisdiction.

County Courts (named in Budapest Capital City Court; Megyei Bíróság and Fővárosi Bíróság) act as appellate court in appeals from local courts and labor courts, exercise first instance jurisdiction in business, civil (over HUF 10,000,000) and criminal (more serious felonies) matters and perform administrative judicial review. At County Courts, as appointed by Parliament, separate Military panels are set up.

Labor Courts (Munkaügyi Bíróság) are first instance courts. Labor Court decisions are reviewed by County Court.

Supreme Court (Legfelsöbb Bíróság) never exercises first instance jurisdiction, but is second instance from County Court and military court decisions. In exceptional cases it acts as third instance court reviewing binding judgments and final orders on objections of President of Supreme Court and that of Attorney General.

Judges.—President of Supreme Court is elected by Parliament, other judges are appointed by President of Republic. Judges are to be professionals with law degree, legal experience and qualifications. Except for minor cases, first instance courts decide in "council", which regularly consists of one professional judge and two laymen (Ülnök). Professional judge and laymen have same rights concerning final judgments and orders, i.e. majority decides. Second instance courts regularly consist of three professional judges, and majority decision controls.

Enforcement.—Binding judgments and orders of established courts of justice and awards of arbitrations are to be enforced by County Courts' Office of Enforcement (Vegrehajtoi Iroda). Enforcement of foreign judgments is to be performed in same way. (See topics Arbitration and Award; Judgments.)

Exclusive Jurisdiction.—Hungarian courts have exclusive jurisdiction over personal status of Hungarian citizens (except if foreign judgment has already been awarded, it is to be recognized); real estate in territory of Hungary; estate of Hungarian citizen testator in Hungary; claims against Hungarian state, government or its agencies; claims against Hungarian diplomats and other immune persons; domestic securities; and Hungarian industrial property rights. (§55 I.P.L.C.).

Lack of Jurisdiction.—Hungarian courts have no jurisdiction over foreign states, diplomats, and other immune persons, and in cases of foreign industrial property rights. (§56 I.P.L.C.). See also topic Foreign Law.

CURRENCY:

Legal currency of Republic of Hungary is Forint (HUF or Ft), which was introduced in 1946. One Ft is divided into 100 fillérs (f). Right to issue currency notes is vested in Hungarian National Bank, Inc. (Magyar Nemzeti Bank, hereinafter referred to as MNB), whose shares are owned by Hungarian State.

Foreign exchange is monopoly of MNB, which in fact has delegated this power to commercial banks. MNB issues official exchange rate of Ft with respect to other currencies from time to time, which rate is calculated with respect to basket of cross rates of 50% in USD and 50% in DEM. This exchange rate is obligatory for commercial banks. MNB has power to alter Ft-rate to this basket up to 5% annually. Revaluation of Ft exceeding this percentage is privilege of Government.

See also topics Banks and Banking; Foreign Exchange; Foreign Investment; Foreign Trade.

CURTESY:

Does not exist in Hungarian law. See topic Wills.

CUSTOMS:

Act 1995:C on Customs of Dec. 1, 1995, repealed old laws on this topic and set new regulations. According to Act, customs duty is based on value of goods, which is primarily calculated by market value of goods. Market value is generally price actually paid or what would be paid for goods when being exported to Hungary. Act puts forth other rules for calculating market value if this is not possible.

Importer must declare value of goods and prepare customs clearance requests with Customs Authority. In some circumstances, origin of goods must be verified by Certificate of Origin. Importer is responsible for payment of customs duties, handling fees and statistical charges.

Importer pledges goods as security for Customs Authority until customs duty has been fully paid. Goods may be sold by Customs Authority in case of failure of payment in order to collect duties, but only pursuant to judgment of court. However, security deposit may be requested instead of goods. Deposit may be in form of cash,

CUSTOMS . . . *continued*
bank guarantee, Customs Authority-approved agreement between payor and domestic entity undertaking joint and several liability for payment of duty, or warehouse receipt.

Act stipulates circumstances where goods may be free of customs duties, such as when goods are sent to foundations, churches or charitable organizations. Medical instruments and medicine sent to hospitals are also duty-free as long as hospital refrains from selling, leasing or lending goods for three years from date of customs handling of goods.

Customs Authority stipulates duties owed in HUF and states amount in writing. Customs duties should be paid within five business days of receipt of invoice, but postponement or installment payment can be requested during that time.

DAMAGES:

Like other "civil law" or "continental law" systems, Hungarian civil law sets apart damage caused in connection with contract or contractual relation (breach of contract) from damage out of contract (tort). For breach of contract see topic Contracts.

Torts.—Intentional torts (like assault, battery, false imprisonment, infliction of emotional distress, or trespass to land or to chattels, conversion of chattels) and also unintentional torts (like negligence and those of special duties) are listed under legal notion of damage-out-of-contract (§339 and supra, C.C.). According to theory of damage-out-of-contract, anyone who causes damage to anyone else unlawfully, has to compensate for it. It is to be understood that there is only one cause of action. Damages are always compensatory and never punitive. Elements of cause of action are: (i) Act or omission by defendant, (ii) unlawful intent or negligence of defendant, (iii) damage to plaintiff, both actual loss (damnum emergens) and lost profit (lucrum cessans), (iv) causation between i-iii. General defense is that defendant exercised reasonable diligence. Degree of diligence required for defendant depends on identity of defendant and all circumstances, as deliberated by Court. Injured party must act reasonably to minimize damage and where damages are unnecessarily aggravated or increased through failure to do so, additional damages are not recoverable.

Strict liability applies to (i) abnormally dangerous activities, (ii) activities carried out by ward under care of guardian, (iii) activities carried out by employee, member of cooperative, representative or agent, (iv) falling objects from buildings. (§§345-353 C.C.).

(i) One who carries out abnormally dangerous activity, or in practice, maintains abnormally dangerous condition (e.g. has car) will be liable for harm it causes to person or property of others, unless she can prove cause of harm was out of scope of her activity. If both plaintiff and defendant were carrying out some dangerous activity, strict liability rule does not apply. Limitation of action is three years.

(ii) Guardian will be liable for harm caused by ward under her care, unless she proves behavior was reasonably diligent.

(iii) Employer, cooperative, or individual will be jointly and severally liable for harm caused by agent.

This rule applies to harm caused by employee of government, its agencies, and other authorities as well. Defense of government bodies can be that plaintiff had not exhausted regular remedies available within administrative or judicial process. Limitation of action is one year.

(iv) Owner of building or condominium will be liable for harm caused by objects falling from building, unless she proves reasonable diligence. For damage caused by object hung on building, liability falls on person in whose interest object had been hung.

Keeping wild animals carries strict liability.

DEATH:

Missing person may be declared dead by Court. Procedure may start after five years have elapsed from disappearance. It is up to Court to fix day of death. Declaring someone's death has same effect as death itself. (§§22-25 C.C.).

DISSOLUTION OF MARRIAGE:

See topic Divorce.

DIVORCE:

According to Family Law Code (Act-Order 1972:26, am'd several times), marriage may be dissolved either by annulment or by divorce. No grounds for divorce are needed after certain time living separately. Declarations of annulment and divorce may be issued only by Court. There is no legal status comparable to separation.

As far as domestic relations law is concerned, Hungary is not title theory jurisdiction. Consequently, title theory of alimony between spouses does not exist. However, equitable distribution of marital property is warranted unless otherwise stipulated in prenuptial or separation agreement of spouses.

When child custody is to be provided for, both spouses theoretically enjoy equal rights and legal practice tends to keep siblings together. In any matrimonial action or in independent action for child support, Court shall order either parent to pay temporary child support or child support without requiring showing of immediate or emergency need. Court shall not consider misconduct of either party but shall make its award for child support after consideration of all relevant factors. See also topic Marriage.

ENVIRONMENT:

Act 1976:II on Protection of Human Environment declares main principles on protection of environment, including protection of land, water, air and nature. There are separate laws on protection of land, forests, fishing, building construction, water management, air pollution, waste management, etc., establishing quality standards and detailed rules of protection.

As far as protection of water is concerned, Act 1964:IV as am'd contains rules protecting clean and healthy water. Supplementing legislation is Order of Council of Ministers 27/1978 on Canalization and Water Supply, Act-Order 1979:28 on Streams and Lakes of International Importance and 18/1992 (VII.14) KHVM on Public Water Utilities. There are separate rules on protection of Hungarian lakes such as lakes Balaton and Velencei and rivers such as Danube and Tisza. Regarding latter, Hungary is party to international agreement on protection of river Tisza.

Trees and forests are protected by Act 1961:VII and 21/1970 (VI.21) Korm. on protection of trees. Detailed rules on use of wood and government plans regarding maintenance and development of forests are found in 120/1991 (IX.15) Korm., 126/1993 (IX.22) Korm., 4/1983 (III.16) BM-MÉM, 12/1994 (III.31) FM, etc. There are territories declared part of Hungarian national heritage or otherwise of distinguished importance; separate decrees of Ministry of Environmental Protection and Community Development are devoted to protect those areas.

As to protection of clean air, Order of Council of Ministers 21/1986 (VI.2) declares behavioral rules, and 4/1986 (VIII.10) EÜM and 5/1990 (XII.6) NM contains list of materials likely to cause air pollution, on countrywide system of measuring air pollution, etc. There are cities and economic areas endangered by air pollution; decree of Ministry of Environmental Protection and Community Development 3/1988 (VI.10) KVM and Government Plan 1079/1993 (XII.23) Korm. Hat. institutes measures thereon. Hungary is party to 1979 Geneva Convention on Prevention of Transborder Air Pollution. Prevention of air pollution caused by nuclear plants is regulated by 1/1980 (II.6) OKTH.

Safe utilization of nuclear energy is regulated by Act 1980:I on Nuclear Energy. Health and safety concerning nuclear plants is regulated by 4/1979 (V.29) EÜM and 3/1982 (V.6) BM. Zoning and housing rules in neighborhood of nuclear plants are found in 4/1983 (III.30) IpM. Hungary is party to European Nuclear Research Institute and International Nuclear Energy Agency.

As far as solid waste is concerned, main rules thereon are found in 1/1986 (II.21) ÉVM-EÜM. Storage and disposal of liquid waste is regulated by 2/1985 (II.16) ÉVM-EÜM and disposal of nuclear waste by 1/1985 HM. As far as dangerous waste is concerned, 56/1981 (XI.18) contains rules on control of such materials.

In general, anyone violating rules on protection of environment, may be subject to fine, civil damages and criminal sanctions. Furthermore, person causing such harm is obliged to reorganize activities in order to avoid such harm in future.

Environmental protection is coordinated by Ministry of Environmental Protection and Community Development. Minister of Environmental Protection and Community Development is responsible for establishing long run projects for preservation and development of human environment and issues orders therefor. Ministry is supported by Environmental Protection Superintendence responsible for establishing standards, issuing licenses, and imposing sanctions on violators. Some authority of minister is delegated to municipalities which, in frame of such authority, may issue municipal orders regulating protection of regional environment.

Order of Council of Ministers 55/1987 (X.30) contains rules on importing certain dangerous materials from abroad. Import of such materials requires license of Environmental Protection Superintendence.

EVIDENCE:

System of evidence before courts is regulated by Civil Procedure Code (Act 1952:III, as am'd several times; §§163-211). There is no limitation on what courts may consider as evidence in civil procedure, i.e. witnesses, expert witnesses, documents and papers, etc. In criminal procedure tainted evidence may not be considered. As far as presentation of evidence is concerned, Courts' role is more determinative than it is under U.S. rules of evidence.

FOREIGN EXCHANGE:

Act 1995:XLV on Foreign Currency effective Jan. 1, 1996 regulates foreign exchange control which is overseen by Hungarian National Bank (HNB). Foreigners' cash or in kind contributions in newly established or existing business organizations and repatriation of profit need not be registered with or approved by HNB. Foreign currency loans extended by foreign shareholders need approval by HNB if loans expire within a year. For loan duration exceeding one year, HNB requires notice within six days after granting of loan if loan amount does not exceed 50 million USD; otherwise, 60 days notice prior to granting loan is required. In latter case, HNB has right to intervene in transaction and postpone for maximum of three months, but his is seldom exercised.

Act contains detailed provisions for establishing enterprises abroad by Hungarian individuals or entities for which no approval by Foreign Exchange Authority need be given if following conditions exist: (i) Hungarian individual or entity's share of capital in foreign venture exceeds 10% while acquiring interest in venture; (ii) laws of foreign country ensure that Hungarian individuals or entities can transfer their income to Hungary in convertible foreign exchange; (iii) Hungarian individual or entity is not liable for more than value of his/its shares in foreign venture; (iv) foreign country is member of OECD or has in-force investment protection agreement with Hungary; (v) Hungarian individual or entity has paid all allowances, social security, health care and other debts connected with customs, taxes, etc.; (vi) there were no bankruptcy or liquidation proceedings pending against Hungarian individual or entity during year of establishing foreign venture, and no such proceeding existed during two preceding calendar years; (vii) Foreign Exchange Authority did not previously deny approval of foreign venture based on facts existing under (vi); (viii) Hungarian entity's chief officer was not chief officer of any entity during time period mentioned in (vi) which failed to fulfill its obligations imposed by Act.

Most securities transactions involving foreign citizens in Hungary and Hungarian citizens in foreign countries need prior approval. There are additional provisions regarding transactions carried out through foreign exchange accounts of Hungarian individuals or entities located in Hungarian banks.

FOREIGN INVESTMENT:

Foreign Investment Act 1988:XXIV (as am'd by Act 1990:XCVIII and 1991:LXV) comprises basic rules with regard to investment of foreigners in Hungary. For foreign corporations see topic Corporations; for tax allowances see topic Taxation; see also topics Investment Protection; Aliens; Customs.

Among several international programs encouraging foreign investments in Hungary (see also topic Investment Protection) "PHARE" program of Group-24 (EEC, EFTA members, and U.S., Australia, Canada, Japan, New Zealand) dedicates US $11 billion

FOREIGN INVESTMENT . . . *continued*
for Hungarian and Polish investments among other priorities. Apart from regular foreign investments following mostly EEC standards which are governed by general rules of several branches of law, privatization of state owned property continues to offer attractive investment possibilities in coming couple of years.

Privatization of State Owned Property.—Privatization of state owned property is conducted by State Privatization and Property Holding Company (hereinafter referred to as "ÁPV Rt"), successor of former two state-owned companies, State Property Agency and State Property Holding Company. ÁPV Rt is corporation wholly owned by Hungarian State and operating in form of Rt. ÁPV Rt is managed by Board of Directors consisting of 11 members appointed by Hungarian Government. Operation of ÁPV Rt is controlled by Supervisory Board also consisting of 11 members.

Main task of ÁPV Rt is to privatize state owned assets that government intends to sell. Techniques encouraged by ÁPV Rt are, inter alia, public tender for sale, closed tender with invitation, public auction, public offering, private placement, and sale of shares on securities exchange. Act contains detailed rules on tender process (both public and closed), contents of tender offer, evaluation of offers, etc. According to Act, closed tender offer may be made only in exceptional case. In case of public tender offer, publication of offer and most important data on corporation to be privatized in two major Hungarian newspapers and in official gazette of ÁPV Rt shall be made.

If stated capital of corporation to be privatized is below HUF 600 million and number of full-time employees thereof is less than 500 in annual average, then simplified privatization procedure may be initiated by ÁPV Rt. ÁPV Rt shall publish list of enterprises subject to such simplified privatization indicating lowest sale price thereof and offerors may announce cash offers within 90 days thereof.

There are separate privatization techniques employed by ÁPV Rt like installment purchase, privatization leasing, management buyout, employee share programs, etc.

Certain state property, such as public utilities, state assets identified as of strategic economic importance, or property serving national defense or other special purposes of state may not be sold as whole but state must retain stake in it. When state retains stake, such stake shall be at least 25%+1 vote and may be up to 100%, but right of management of such shares may be assigned to third parties. Such third parties may be retained through (i) leasing of state property in consideration for participating in profit earned; (ii) contracting for management of state property (alienation or encumbering of property rights is not allowed) in consideration for keeping value of assets at agreed level; (iii) contracting for portfolio management (alienation or encumbering of property rights is allowed) in consideration for increasing asset value.

U.S. Investors.—U.S. SEED Act from Nov. 1989 entitled Private Overseas Investment Corporation (OPIC), U.S. government agency, to participate in Eastern European Growth Fund, and provided for creation of Hungarian-American Enterprise Fund of $60,000,000. This Act authorized U.S. Agency for International Development (AID) to permit expansion of Trade and Development Program (TDP) into Hungary. AID also develops and implements training and expert program for Hungary. U.S. Department of Commerce opened information center in 1990 to provide information to companies seeking to do business in Hungary. §§303 and 304 of SEED Act authorized Export-Import Bank of U.S. to include Hungary fully in Eximbank programs, providing direct loans to U.S. exporters and Hungarian purchasers of U.S. products, guaranties to U.S. banks financing U.S. exports, and insurance against nonpayment.

FOREIGN LAW:

In international conflicts of law, in substantive questions, laws of foreign countries may be applied in Hungary, as regulated by Act-Order 1979:13. on International Private Law, usually referred to as International Private Law Code. Applicable procedure is lex forum.

Disputes on ownership, possession, mortgage, or in general "in rem" claims are to be decided under lex loci, i.e. law of place where subject of claim is located. (§21).

In law of contracts or obligations, system of choice of law is following: (i) Parties are free to stipulate law to be applied to their dispute (§24) and (ii) absent stipulation by parties, in dispute on sale, personal law of vendor applies; on lease, law of lessor; on copyright and industrial property rights, law of purchaser; on deposit, law of bailee; on mandate, law of mandator; on commission, law of commissioner; on agency, law of agent; on transportation, law of transporter; on banking, financing and credit, law of lender or creditor; on insurance, law of insurer; and on gift, law of donor (§25). In case of real estate contracts lex loci applies; of entrepreneurship, securities, and alimony, law of place of performance (lex loci contractus) applies. (§§26, 28). Disputes on stock exchange, bid, and corporations shall be decided according to lex loci. (§27). Shares and bonds are to be adjudged by law of issuer (§28). If rules cited here under (i) and (ii) do not apply to contract, applicable law is that of residence or seat of party who is obliged. If this additional rule is inapplicable, law to which transaction of contract has its closest connection is to be applied. (§29).

For recognition of foreign judgments see also topic Judgments. For exclusive jurisdiction of Hungarian courts and for lack of Hungarian jurisdiction see also topic Courts.

FOREIGN TRADE:

Foreign trade is regulated by Act 1974:III on Foreign Trade, Act-Order 1987:8 on Application of Civil Code in Foreign Trade, Order of Government 112/1990, Order of Minister of International Economic Relations 6/1990 as am'd by 10/1991 and 11/1992 NGKM. Foreign trade authority rests with Ministry of International Economic Relations (formerly Ministry of Commerce).

Foreign Trade Activity.—Developments in recent years, since 1987, resulted in liberalized foreign trade. All for-profit or not-for-profit entities and private entrepreneurs may engage in foreign trade, i.e. in export and import of products, services, and rights. For foreign trade activity since Jan. 1, 1988 no permission, and from Jan. 1, 1991 no registration is needed. Non-business individuals may engage in foreign trade concerning their own patents, artistic or agricultural products.

Licensing.—Import or export license is required only in exceptional cases for products enumerated by law. (Gvt. Order 112/1990). In fact, in 1990 import of commodities against hard currencies was already about 90% free of license. Export of some products needs to be licensed to avoid violence to quotas in other countries. Import of some consumer products (mainly textiles, foods, motor vehicles, certain articles made of precious metal) is limited by quota, as enumerated by law. (49/1994 IKM).

Representative Offices.—For purpose of trade, foreigners may establish direct commercial representation and/or information, promotion and service offices, which are not considered separate legal entities, but nevertheless are to be entered into Firms' Register with Corporation Courts. (Order of Minister of Commerce 3/1989). Foreign law firms' branches are also preferably set up as representations of their home offices. Although representative offices are allowed to engage in all "representation-like" commercial activities, this activity may fall under taxation. (See topic Taxation, subhead Corporation Tax.)

Trade barriers are regulated by Order of Government 61/1990 (X.1) Korm, as amended several times; by authorization of GATT Art. XXI, Act 1974:III on foreign trade §29(1), Act-Order 1966:2 tvr on custom duty law §§16, 18.

See also topics Foreign Investment; Treaties and Conventions.

FOUNDATIONS:

Foundations (Alapítvány) (§§74/A-74/G C.C.) are civil law entities.

Foundation may be formed for any public interest, charitable, or religious purpose by charter of foundation, executed by founder or founders, which is subject to court registration. Purpose of foundation is to be set forth in its charter, and unless governing body of foundation (usually curatorium) is established in charter, court will appoint one. In case of dissolution, assets of foundation are to be distributed for purpose established in charter, or if there is none, to another purpose which is similar to that of foundation.

Donations to incorporated foundations or for public interest purposes can be deducted only if foundation is registered by tax authority as receiver of tax deductible donations, i.e. they serve following purposes: curing/prevention of disease, scientific research, environmental protection, protection of monuments, culture, education, student or popular sport, religion, protection of public order or security, or above mentioned purposes on behalf of old or disadvantaged people, national and ethnic minorities in Hungary, ethnic Hungarian groups abroad, or asylum-seekers. Donations serving acquisition or promoting predetermined financial advantages are excluded.

HOLIDAYS:

Legal holidays are Jan. 1 (New Year's Day), Mar. 15 (Anniversary of Independence War of 1848), Whit Monday, Easter Monday, May 1 (Labor Day), Aug. 20 (St. Stephen's Day), Oct. 23 (Anniversary of Revolution of 1956), Dec. 25-26 (Christmas Days).

HUSBAND AND WIFE:

See topics Divorce and Marriage.

IMMIGRATION:

Visitors for business or pleasure may enter Hungary with valid passport and visa, as tourists or for long term. Visas are available at Hungarian embassies and consulates in person or by mail, or when entering country by land or by air. There is no visa requirement for U.S. nationals and nationals of Austria, Argentina, Benelux states, Canada, China, Costa Rica, former CMEA countries, Denmark, Ecuador, Estonia, Finland, France, Germany, Greece, Iceland, Ireland, Italy, Korean Republic, Latvia, Lithuania, Malta, Norway, Portugal, San Marino, Seychelles, Singapore, Slovakia, Slovenia, Sweden, Switzerland, U.K., and Uruguay. Visa requirements toward some other countries are currently being negotiated.

Gainful Activities.—Performing some jobs requires work card, work permit (available at local Labor Centers in Hungary) and visa or residency permit for work. Employment based on civil law contract between foreigner and Hungarian employer is also considered labor relation. No work permit will be issued for job when suitable quantity of qualified manpower is available in Hungary or activity falls into list made by Minister of Labor containing jobs that no foreigner is allowed to perform due to unemployment in Hungary. There is no need for work permit for board members of Hungarian corporations with foreign participation. Request for work permit must be filed by employer with foreigner's health and qualification certificate in Hungarian attached. Work permit is valid for not more than a year, but can be extended. If civil law contract based on competitive bidding is basis for foreigner's employment, employer may apply for group-frame-permit ("csoportos keretengedély") listing number, qualification of foreigners and their future activity. This permit is valid until termination of civil law contract. Work permits based on frame-permit are also available at Labor Centers.

For self-employment no work permit is required, nevertheless, for obtaining residence permit, registration or application thereof, as self-entrepreneur or that of company, is usually required.

Permanent residency if not for gainful occupation, is available for persons who are able to support themselves and their dependents, as well as persons receiving asylum, where standards of international agreements are to be applied.

Naturalization.—Act 1993:LV governs acquisition of Hungarian nationality. Certification of naturalization may be granted to alien who has been resident of Hungary for eight years, who has clean record, who is able to support himself and his dependents, whose naturalization does not interfere with interest of state and who successfully completes basic course on constitutional law. Course and exam are in Hungarian. This duration can be reduced to three years if, for example, alien is spouse or child of Hungarian citizen, or recognized as refugee by Hungarian authorities. Alien may be exempt from length of stay requirement if important interest of Hungarian Republic is involved. Decision on granting certificate of naturalization to alien is made by President of Republic of Hungary upon presentation by Minister of Home Affairs.

INFANTS:

For legal capacity of minors see topic Contracts. For child support see topic Divorce.

INSURANCE:

Insurance is regulated in Hungarian law by Civil Code provisions concerning contracts. Parties determine exact conditions in insurance contract (insurance policy). Insurable events include (a) damaging event defined in contract; (b) death or reaching certain age; or (c) accident causing injury, disability or death. Insurance contract can only be created in writing. Insurance policy also comes into existence if insurer does not respond to offer within 15 days. Filling out insurance policy (certificate, insurance stamp) replaces written agreement or declaration of acceptance of insurer. Insurer and insured are necessarily parties to insurance contract. Insured person need not necessarily be identical with person obliged to pay insurance premium. In life or accident insurance, beneficiary may be appointed. First insurance premium is due on conclusion of contract, all other premiums are due on first day of each period covered by premium.

Property damage insurance may be concluded only by legal person who is interested in protection of property or who concludes contract to benefit interested person. Sum of insurance shall not exceed real value of insured property. Insured is obliged to mitigate damages. Insurer is exempt from payment if it proves that damages have been caused illegally by (a) insured and/or contracting party; (b) relative living in their household; or (c) employees and/or agents of insured who hold positions listed in regulations; or if damages have been caused deliberately or by gross negligence by members or organs of insured, listed in regulations.

In case of liability insurance, insurer shall not be exempt from payment to injured or damaged person even if injury or damage is caused by deliberate or grossly negligent conduct of insured. Settlement agreement between insured and injured or damaged person shall bind insurer if insurer acknowledges it.

In life insurance contracts, beneficiary may be (a) person named in contract; (b) holder of insurance policy; or (c) heir of insured.

Concerning accident insurance, rules of life insurance and property insurance shall be applied.

INTEREST:

In contractual relations interest is to be paid, except in private relations among individuals unless otherwise stipulated. Interest on interest is prohibited among individuals. Unless lower rate is stipulated, interest among individuals is 20% per annum, according to C.C. If higher rate is stipulated, it will be void in excess of Code's rate (§232 C.C.), unless one party is bank or some other financial institution, where different rules apply.

See also topic Banks and Banking.

INVESTMENT PROTECTION:

Foreign investments are protected by domestic law, international treaties and encouraged by administrative measures, corporation, trade, tax, customs laws. From point of view of privileges and advantages, all public or corporate entities are considered foreign if their seat is abroad; and all individuals, even Hungarian emigrants, are considered foreigners if they are permanent foreign residents.

Domestic Guaranties.—Act 1988:XXIV on Investments of Foreigners, as amended several times, declares, that "investments of foreigners enjoy full protection and security". This act offers guaranties against nationalization and expropriation. This act insures that withholding of capital and profit cannot be limited and must be perfected in currency of investment. State itself is responsible for all these provisions.

International Guaranties.—Hungary has concluded investment guaranties agreements with U.S., most EEC and all former CMEA countries, Australia, Canada, China, Cyprus, Israel, Kuwait, Morocco, Norway, South Korea, Switzerland, Thailand and Uruguay. All these agreements offer guaranties against nationalization and for withdrawing invested capital and profit. As of Apr. 21, 1988, World Bank's Multilateral Investment Guarantee Agency (MIGA) offers investment guaranties for foreign investments in Hungary. See also topic Treaties and Conventions.

Investors from U.S.—§302 of U.S. "Support for East European Democracy Act" (SEED Act), which was signed into law Nov. 28, 1989, made Hungary eligible for Overseas Private Investment Corporation (OPIC) programs and provided that OPIC shall support projects in Hungary. OPIC, U.S. public corporation, provides for two types of assistance to U.S. investors: financing enterprising through direct loans, loan guaranties and equity investments, and insurance of investments against political risks. OPIC agreement was ratified by Hungary as of Dec. 27, 1989, through Order of Council of Ministers 74/1990 (IV.25).

JUDGMENTS:

According to International Private Law Code of Hungary (Act-Order 1979:13), except if Hungarian courts have exclusive jurisdiction (see topic Courts), judgments of foreign courts are to be recognized and enforced without procedure of recognition, and reciprocity is not considered.

Foreign judgments even within exclusive Hungarian jurisdiction, are recognized in cases like divorce, guardianship and adoption, if one of parties is foreign resident.

Foreign judgments may not be recognized, if they contradict Hungarian public order, if foreign court according to its domestic rules did not have jurisdiction, if Hungarian resident involved was not represented before court, if judgment violates res judicata, and if same procedure had started in Hungary before foreign one resulting in recognizable judgment.

Foreign Arbitration Awards.—See topics Arbitration and Award; Treaties and Conventions.

LABOR RELATIONS:

New labor law (Act 1992:XXII as am'd by Act 1993:XIII) was enacted in 1992 to create new labor relationships appropriate to changed conditions. New Labor Act is specifically oriented to accommodate free market conditions in labor market. In general, Act covers labor relationship when work is performed in Hungary, or if abroad in Hungarian company's employ. Act does not cover labor relationship when work is performed in Hungary by employee employed by foreigner.

Act prescribes, in detail, rules of operation and powers of trade unions in workplace. Collective bargaining agreements, that are mandatory to observe for nonmembers of trade unions, are entered into at workplaces. Workers' Councils (Üzemi Tanács) must be elected at workplaces with over 50 employees. Councils have approval rights in matters affecting welfare monies and assets as set forth in collective bargaining agreements and in issuing workers' protection rules. Councils have rights to express opinions on matters of, inter alia, reorganization, restructuring, privatization, modernization, training, rehabilitation of workers, annual vacation plan, internal rules affecting important interests of workers, etc.

Act also prescribes rules for entering into labor relation between employer and employee, contents of labor contract, modes of performing work, full and part time work, modification of labor contract, etc.

Labor relationship terminates upon (a) employee's death, (b) dissolution of employer without successor and (c) conclusion of definite period of labor relationship. Labor relationship can be terminated by (a) mutual agreement, (b) normal termination, (c) special termination and (d) without notice during tryout period. Fixed time labor relationship can only be terminated by mutual agreement or normal termination. Normal termination can be made by either employer or employee. In normal termination, employer must give cause regarding capacity or behavior of employee or cause concerning operation of employer. Normal termination by employer is not possible during illness, unpaid leave to tend to ill child, pregnancy plus six months, or army service. Very special cause need be given for termination during five years before retirement. Notice for termination is minimum 30 days and maximum one year. Notice period is determined by number of years of employment. During half of notice period, employee need not actually work. Normal termination warrants severance payment. Special termination is possible by either employer or employee if other willfully or out of gross negligence substantially breaches important obligation or otherwise behaves in way that makes employment impossible. Special termination is possible within three months from obtaining knowledge of such breach or behavior but maximum within six months of occurrence of such breach or behavior.

Apart from national holidays, employees are entitled to 20-30 work days as holidays annually, depending upon their age. Extra holidays must be given for special circumstances (e.g. minors, parents, disabled persons, etc.). Special paid and unpaid holidays must be given during and after pregnancy. Liability of employer or employee for damage caused in relation to employment is also regulated. Special rules apply to employees in managerial or executive positions.

Social Security is governed by Act 1975:II., as amended several times.

Free medical care is citizen's right in Hungary, financed by Social Security Fund, which obligations are state guaranteed. Fund covers pensions, sick-list payments (generally 75% of wages), family allowances (payment to families for minors, HUF 2,370-3,400 per child monthly, Act 1990:XXV, as am'd several times), child-welfare subsidies (sick-list payment for mother or father, if one of them is not working in order to be able to care for their child of less than three years of age), and other social security subsidies of less importance.

Main incomes of Fund are employers' pay-in (44% after wages) and employees' pension and health insurance pay-in (10% of wages). Self-employed pays these two payments, alone after her income. For covering unemployment payments, employers are to pay 7% of salaries paid and employees 2% from their salaries; as regulated by §64 of Act 1991:IV, as am'd by 1992:LXXX.

Insurance companies offer additional domestic and foreign services. Act 1995:XII introduces several cutbacks in social security services.

Dismissal Indemnity.—Indemnities are payable in event of dismissal of employees, based on Labor Code (Act 1992:XXII) which stipulates conditions under which indemnities are required to be paid. Indemnities must be paid if employment relationship is terminated by employer or if employer ceases to exist and there is no successor. Notwithstanding above requirement, no indemnities are required if (a) employment relationship is terminated by employer because employee "deliberately or out of gross negligence breached in substantial way some essential obligation required by and related to employment relationship" or employee's behavior or conduct makes it impossible to continue employment relationship, or (b) employee is eligible for retirement or employment relationship concerned is not employee's primary employment relationship (i.e. it is second job and other job is more important).

Further condition of eligibility for indemnities is that employment relationship must have been in existence for specific period of time as indicated in following table.

Amount to be paid as indemnity is defined by reference to employee's "average" salary:

Duration of Employment	Indemnity
At least 3 years	1 months salary
At least 5 years	2 months salary
At least 10 years	3 months salary
At least 15 years	4 months salary
At least 20 years	5 months salary
At least 25 years	6 months salary

The "average" salary used when calculating indemnity may not exceed five times minimum wage (in May 1995, HUF 12,200). Amount of indemnity must be increased by three months average salary if employment relationship is terminated within five years preceding age for retirement.

LAW REPORTS, CODES:

In Hungary, as civil law country, law is codified, and only provisions set forth in acts and orders are considered to be law. Nevertheless Constitutional Court is entitled by constitution to exercise judicial review of acts and orders and to annul them. Judgments are not of stare decisis nature by law, nevertheless, opinions of higher courts serve as measure for practice. Supreme Court occasionally issues guiding

LAW REPORTS, CODES . . . *continued*
principles and measures (irányelv, elvi döntés), which are of obligatory nature. Supreme Court in its periodical publishes number of its decisions (and sometimes those of other courts) supposed to be "leading cases".

No act or order may be in force without being officially published. Official publication of acts, Parliament resolutions, orders of Government, Ministers and other government agencies, decisions of Constitutional Court and guiding principles and measures of Supreme Court appear in "Magyar Közlöny", official gazette of Republic of Hungary.

Each ministry has its own official gazette. Supreme Court publishes monthly "Bírósági Határozatok". Annual official collection of all acts and orders of previous year is published by Ministry of Justice and Government Office, under title "Törvények és Rendeletek Hivatalos Gyújteménye". Ministry of Justice publishes sixeight volume collection of acts and orders in force and in use under title "Hatalyos Jogszabályok Gy jteménye".

There are other collections and periodicals, e.g. Hungarian-English-German language monthly "Hatályos Magyar Jogszabályok", which republishes acts and orders thought to be of interest to foreigners.

LEGISLATION:

See topic Constitution and Government.

LIENS:

New Lien Law Act 1996:XXVI has unified previously inconsistent laws on this topic. Subject of lien can be anything that can be possessed, assignable right or accounts receivable. Lien cannot be based on portion of item. If real property is pledged as security, whole parcel of land as described in land registry must be pledged.

Types of lien are: (i) pledge on real property; (ii) pledge on personalty; and (iii) pledge on assignable right or accounts receivable. Lien on such items can be created by contract, law, or court judgment. If mortgage on real property is pledged as security, security agreement must be in writing and recorded in land registry. If mortgage on personalty or personal wealth is pledged as security, security agreement must be in form of public legal document and must be entered into registry of National Chamber of Notary Publics. If personalty is pledged as security, transfer of possession to pledgee is necessary to create valid lien. Security agreements may only be enforced pursuant to judgment of court.

LIMITATION OF ACTIONS:

Statute of limitations is defence which prevents claimant only from enforcing right but does not extinguish obligation itself, and court cannot recognize "limitation of action" ex officio. Thus, party performing in spite of statute of limitations may not reclaim. Further, claim barred by statute of limitations may be asserted against claim of debtor arising from similar or same relation; or claimant may obtain satisfaction from security of debtor, if there was any.

Regular period of statute of limitations is five years. Period shorter than one year may be extended to one year in writing. Any act of claimant to force debtor to perform interrupts time period, which is to start again from beginning. Expiration of period will be suspended for not more than one year, if claimant, for acceptable reasons, cannot enforce claim. (§§324-327 C.C.).

MARRIAGE:

Age of marriage, for both males and females, is 18. Marriage is to be solemnized before local municipality, after waiting period of three months from registration. Religious marriage is of no legal effect unless solemnized in other country where that form of marriage is recognized (lex loci actus). Medical examinations or blood tests are not required; nevertheless before first marriage under age of 35 it is mandatory to obtain health advice. One who has previously divorced has to produce certified health advice. If in doubt, foreigners may be required to prove their legal capacity. Marriage by proxy is not possible; presence of parties is required.

Marriage is prohibited between close relatives and where there is existing prior marriage of either party. Prohibition of being under age of consent may be cured.

Prenuptial agreement, before or after marriage ceremony, may cover questions of marital property, children's and wife's family name, or other matters considered necessary.

Husband and wife have equal rights within marriage; they are to decide together on parental powers, property matters, domicile, etc.

For dissolution of marriage see topic Divorce.

MONOPOLIES AND TRADE RESTRAINTS:

Antitrust rules applicable to corporations limited by shares were set up by Corporation Act §§321-330.

Prohibition of insider trading of securities is laid down by Act 1990:VI §§75-80 on Securities and Stock Exchange and §229/A of Penal Code. See also topic Securities.

Antidumping regulations were set up by Government Order 69/1994 (V.4) Korm, implementing and giving procedural rules for GATT Anti-dumping Code of 1979. Anti-dumping procedure falls under jurisdiction of Minister of International Economic Relations. Antidumping procedure is initiated by written complaint of any representative of domestic industry. Within nine months from filing application, Ministry of International Economic Relations shall make decision and publish it in official gazette, "Magyar Közlöny". During its procedure, Ministry may require additional information from parties regarding circumstances of case, may issue temporary restraining order if allegations are likely to be proven, and may levy antidumping duty, amount of which may not exceed amount of subsidy or difference between dumping and market price.

To protect market, if domestic production would be endangered by greater quantity of imports, under procedure similar to that of antidumping, import contingents for no longer period than one year may be applied by Minister of International Economic Relations. (Government Order 113/1990 [XII.23] Korm, as am'd by 68/1992 [IV.14] Korm).

Consumer Protection.—In public interest, National Consumer Protection Council is entitled to bring suit against business entities, attacking adhesion contracts or any clause in such contracts (actio popularis). If this standardized contract form or any part of it gives unilateral advantages, it may be nullified and voided by court's judgment. Nevertheless, judgments do not affect contracts already performed. (§209 C.C.). For authority of Consumer Protection Supervisory (Fogyasztóvédelmi Fôfelügyelôség) see 95/1991 (VII.23) Korm, as am'd several times, recently by 82/1995 (VII.6.) Korm. See also topic Product Liability, and Act 1990: LXXXVI on Unfair Market Conduct.

MOTOR VEHICLES:

Vehicle registration is required. Before and after registration periodical inspection is prescribed for all vehicles. Upon inspection and registration, vehicle licence is to be issued by police. Licence plates on front and rear are necessary.

Operator's licence is required. Licence is available upon examination and driving test for persons 17 or over. Health conditions effecting driving abilities must be checked every five years. International licence is valid in Hungary. In case of suspension of driver's license or series of violations of Highway Code, driver must attend courses with programs regarding nature of violation (deficiency in traffic qualification or behavior, drunk-driving etc.).

Insurance covering strict liability of owner, i.e. all damages to other persons, is required for operation of vehicle, including foreign ones. All domestically owned or operated vehicles are necessarily insured against damage to others. (Government Order 58/1991 as am'd by 84/1992). Foreigners may be asked to prove their insurance at border when entering country, unless required otherwise by international agreement.

Liability of owner covers all injuries and damage to other persons caused by operation of car. This strict liability permits very few defenses.

Environmental checking should be performed first during period 1 May 1992-30 Apr. 1993 in month when vehicle license document expires and afterward in every third year for catalytic engines and annually for other engines.

NOTARIES PUBLIC:

As of Jan. 1, 1992 notaries' activities are regulated by Act 1991:XLI, Orders of Minister of Justice 13, 14, 15/1991. Notary Public is no longer officer of local court of justice but private entrepreneur, who must be qualified lawyer. Notary may attest and certify legal documents, make wills and notarize legal documents, exercise first stage probate jurisdiction and perform certain official acts. Notary may also administer oath or statement "en lieu" of oath, if required for foreign use.

PARTNERSHIP:

Commercial partnerships, i.e. General and Limited Partnerships, are discussed under topic Corporations. (There is no for-profit "silent or secret partnership", like "Stille Gesellschaft" in German law.)

Not-for-profit partnership (corresponds to German "Bürgerliche Gesellschaft", or French noncommercial "Societé en Participation") is regulated by §§568-578 of Civil Code. It is voluntary association of persons, not considered separate legal entity, and may be organized by agreement written or oral, for purposes other than for profit. All partners are classified as general partners, having unlimited liability. For construction association and common law marriage, partnership rules are to be applied.

PATENTS:

Patents are granted by National Patent Office (Országos Találmányi Hivatal), for technical inventions and processes, except for chemical products and drugs. For effect of patent see Paris Union. In short, by patent granted to inventor, exclusive rights to make, use and sell invention are secured. Patent protection lasts for 20 years. (§§86-87 C.C.; Act 1995:XXXIII).

Patent protection process starts with application, which is required to contain accurate description of patent. In patent process party may be represented by patent attorney or attorney at law. Upon request Patent Office examines application before publishing it in periodical Patent Journal (Szabadalmi Közlöny). Publication without search results in provisional protection. Patent may be issued by and upon search of Patent Office and is to be published and entered into Patent Register kept by Patent Office. Permanent licenses and rights (e.g. royalty, term of licence, limitations) may be entered in Patent Register. Licenses may be granted prior to issuance of patent.

In case of inventions of employees, labor contract determines who owns patent, employer or employee, and rights to patent.

Design patent on models and designs are regulated by Act-Order 1978:28, as amended.

For patent suits, County Courts have jurisdiction. For tax treatment of patents see topic Taxation, subhead Personal Income Tax. See also topic Treaties and Conventions.

PRODUCT LIABILITY:

Act 1993:X on product liability, effective Jan. 1, 1994, is in compliance with European Community Directive issued in 1985 on same subject. Product means all movables and electric power. Manufacturer is producer of end product, interim product and raw material, as well as any person indicating himself as being manufacturer of product by labelling same with his name, trademark or other distinctive marking. In case of imported products, obligations of manufacturer shall be applied to importer. Distributor is also qualified as manufacturer when actual manufacturer and/or importer of product is untraceable or until distributor informs injured person of person, manufacturer or distributor from whom product had been acquired.

Damage covers non-pecuniary loss or damage, if, and to extent that it exceeds HUF 10,000.

Based upon above, damage is qualified as follows: pecuniary and non-pecuniary loss or damage caused by death, bodily injury or illness; and loss or damage exceeding HUF 10,000 to other property caused by defective product, provided other property in question is designated as subject of personal use or consumption, and has been used by injured for such purposes.

PRODUCT LIABILITY . . . *continued*

Product is defective when it does not provide safety generally expected with special regard to purpose of product, reasonably expected use of product, information related to product, date of marketing of product, as well as state of art and technology. Fact that another product with higher safety is subsequently marketed, does not make product defective.

Manufacturer of product has strict liability for loss or damage caused by deficiency of product. Injured is required only to prove loss or damage, deficiency of product and causation.

Contractual limitation or exclusion of liability towards injured is null and void. Manufacturer is discharged from liability if it proves that: product was not marketed by it, product was not manufactured for commercial marketing and/or was not manufactured or marketed in its field of business, product was not defective at time of marketing and became defective later, deficiency of product at time of marketing by manufacturer was beyond recognition given state of art and technology, or deficiency of product was caused by law or compulsory regulation.

Statute of limitations is ten or three years starting when injured person learns of deficiency of product or cause of deficiency and identity of manufacturer.

Act does not impair contractual or extra-contractual rights for compensation of injured person, or any other remedial possibilities provided by separate legislation.

Act came into force on Jan. 1, 1994, and applies only to products marketed after this date. Rules of general liability apply to products marketed prior to this date.

Consumer Protection Supervisory Board is independent authority with general competence having power of public authority. In order to protect consumers' interest and quality protection, Supervisory Board exercises control over compliance with rules and regulations related to commercial activities and consumers' services, as well as enforcing quality standards, and informs consumers of its findings—especially of results of product comparison examinations—as well as fosters enforcement of consumer rights and imposes penalties defined by separate legislation.

For instance, Supervisory Board is authorized to prohibit or impose certain conditions on marketing of products falling under quality objections, to prohibit marketing of products without compulsory preliminary quality control, to order closing of store in case of circumstances threatening life and health of consumers, etc.

Similar authority is given to Commercial Quality Control Institute (KERMI) which is entitled to prohibit marketing of products not subjected to compulsory preliminary quality control.

PUBLIC PROCUREMENT:

Act 1995:XL on Public Procurement requires central government, local municipalities, public bodies, public foundations and all other institutions included in central government's or local municipality's budget to request bids on purchases if such purchases are directly related to public activity and exceed certain limit. Limit is stipulated in separate statute each year. For 1996 following limits apply: (i) for purchase of goods—HUF 10 million; (ii) for construction—HUF 20 million; (iii) for technical construction plans—HUF 5 million; (iv) for services—HUF 5 million. Terms such as "purchase of goods" and "service" are defined in Act.

Value of purchases determined by highest average price calculated without V.A.T. Act declares that dividing of purchase into separate parts so as to avoid tender is prohibited. According to Act, public acquisitions must be made through open or invitation based tenders. Each Hungarian company subject to Act must publish in official gazette "News of Public Acquisitions" that it intends to purchase goods or services or to make investments falling within scope of Act.

In certain circumstances, domestic companies or companies using domestic workforce have advantage in bidding.

Disputes arising out of public acquisitions settled either by Public Acquisitions Council or by Arbitration Committee of Public Acquisitions, consisting of three public acquisition officers.

REAL PROPERTY:

Real estate is accurately registered at counties' Land Office (Földhivatal). Ownership of and any rights to real estate, including mortgages, are to be entered in real estate register (ingatlannyilvántartás), therefore these rights are evidenced by register. Thus title search is relatively easy job, and title insurance is not customary. (Order of Minister of Agriculture 1/1990).

Zoning rules are to be adopted by published administrative orders. Local municipality has authority to issue building licences, which are required for practically all work not in-house. (Act 1964:III., as am'd several times).

Land Act.—New Act on Land was enacted in 1994 (Act 1994:V) that limits acquisition of farmland by both domestic and foreign individuals and entities.

Under Act, Hungarian individuals may acquire maximum of 300 hectares of farmland or farmland valued at 6,000 Golden Crown (Golden Crown is old measure showing value of land). Hungarian legal entities or corporations which are not legal entities may not acquire farmland. However, this rule does not apply to state, municipalities or public foundations.

Foreign individuals or legal entities may not acquire farmland except when they exchange their already acquired farmland for other farmland, and farmland received in exchange may not be greater than farmland formerly owned. Purchase of farmland with compensation coupons for actual expropriation is also possible.

These rules do not affect acquisition and ownership of land acquired before this Act entered into force. New Act did not apply to pending sales.

Farmland may be leased for long term (maximum of ten years) by Hungarian and foreign individuals, legal entities or corporations without legal entity. Hungarians, foreign individuals and legal entities may acquire up to 300 hectares or 6,000 Golden Crown. Cooperatives, however, may acquire maximum of 2,500 hectare or 50,000 Golden Crown.

Other rights connected to farmland, i.e. easements, riparian rights etc. are regulated by Civil Code.

Ownership by Foreigners.—Acquisition by foreigners of real property not designated as agricultural land or protected nature area is permitted by Act LV of 1994 on Arable Land and 7/1996 (I.18) Gov. Decree. This decree introduces more liberal rules than earlier laws. Except concerning property that is inherited, any foreign individual or legal entity may acquire ownership of real property not designated as agricultural land or protected nature area after receiving permission of head officer of city and county administrative office where property is located. Mayor's permission shall be granted if foreign ownership does not interfere with interests of municipality or other public interests and: (i) foreigner has permanent residence permit, or (ii) real property of foreigner has been acquired pursuant to Law Decree 24 of 1976 on Dispossession as amended several times, or (iii) foreigner exchanges domestic real estate for other domestic real estate, or (iv) acquisition terminates prior co-ownership, or (v) foreigner acquires real property as gift from close relative, or (vi) foreigner has been legitimately living in Hungary for at least five years for working purposes.

Mayor's permission may be withheld if foreigner's state does not afford same rights to Hungarian citizens or legal entities as it affords its own residents on basis of reciprocity or international treaty. After mayor has declared that ownership by foreigner does not interfere with interests of municipality, application for permission is filed with head officer of local administrative office. Following documents shall be attached to application: (i) documentation certifying citizenship of foreigner; (ii) copy of contract of sale for real property; (iii) copy of pertinent entry of land registry, not more than three months old; (iv) tax and value certification, not more than three months old; (v) certification issued by Hungarian financial institution or place of exchange certifying currency conversion of security deposit, purchase price or, in case of property exchange, difference of value between properties; (vi) declaration of mayor's approval; and (vii) certification of degree of relationship in case of gift.

Regulations concerning payments set out in Act XCV of 1995 on Foreign Exchange apply. Acquisition of real property by diplomatic or consular representative or international organization is regulated by Ministry of Foreign Affairs, which grants permission on basis of reciprocity or international treaty.

SEALS:

Only public seal, used by public authorities, is legally recognized in Hungary. Although use of "private" seal of corporation or person has no legal effect, it is widely used and commonly belongs to signatures of firms.

SECURITIES:

Securities are either evidence of obligations to pay money (e.g. bonds) or of rights to participate in earnings and distribution of corporate and other property (e.g. shares). (Securities Act 1990:VI. §3). Other negotiable instruments such as commercial papers (in UCC's term) are not considered securities. (See topic Commercial Papers.) Securities Act applies to all securities issued and sold through public offerings. (Regarding private offerings of exempt securities, see also topic Corporations, subhead (1) Corporation Limited by Shares.)

Budapest Stock Exchange (Budapesti Értékpapírtőzsde) reopened in 1990. Exchange is private legal entity, formed by not less than 15 corporations, and of not less than HUF 150,000,000 stated capital, approved upon proposal of Minister of Finance by Council of Ministers. Articles of association and statutes of Stock Exchange are to be approved by National Securities and Exchange Commission (Állami Értékpapír és Tózsde Felügyelet). Stock Exchange government is headed by General Meeting (Közgyúlés) of all members, which elects and removes members of Stock Exchange Council. Stock Exchange Council (Tözsdetanács) consisting of 5-13 individuals and is executive body of Stock Exchange. Supervisory Board of not less than five individuals is to be elected by General Meeting. Ethical Committee is and professional committees may be established by General Meeting. Secretariat, headed by Managing Director, is in charge of direction and management of business. General Meeting establishes arbitration for deciding exchange disputes.

Public Issue and Sale.—Except for treasury or government securities, issuer of shares (if for increasing stated capital) and bonds must have been in business for not less than 12 months. Prospectus must be published, which prospectus is subject to preliminary approval of Securities and Exchange Commission. Bonds may be sold by hiring issue broker. Act prescribes contents of prospectus, and how it is to be made available to public with public offerings. If subscription is obligatory or desired, conditions and period open for subscription must be duly published. Period may be extended only once for 60 days with approval of Securities and Exchange Commission. Unless prospectus made it possible in advance, period cannot be closed earlier than published.

Reporting.—Until securities are on market, issuer must publish its basic business data annually, including balance sheet, and profit and loss statement (Regular Report). In cases enumerated by law, Extraordinary Report is to be published and sent to Securities Exchange Commission in two days, if corporation's business is affected by significant changes.

Security Certificates.—Printing, administration and physical nullification of securities are governed by Gov. Decree No. 98/1995 (VIII.24). Decree applies to securities issued in series in Hungary, as well as securities issued abroad but put into circulation in Hungary.

Only printer that is in possession of valid license is entitled to print securities. License is granted by Securities and Exchange Commission with consent of Expert Institution of the National Security Office (Nemzetbiztonsági Hivatal Szakértői Intézete). License can be granted only to printer registered in Hungary whose conditions are in compliance with those required by law. License is granted for indefinite period of time.

Securities can only be stamped during modification of type or nominal value of securities, subject to previous written authorization of issuer, while maintaining recognizability of securities. Securities cannot be physically nullified within one year after termination of rights and obligations embodied in securities. Physical nullification of securities can occur by burning, shredding or any equivalent method in presence of Commissioner. Nullification procedure shall be certified by notary. Legality of procedure is supervised by Securities and Exchange Commission and, if securities were issued by financial institution, State Bank Supervisor (Állami Bankfelűgyelet).

SECURITIES . . . *continued*

Securities printed abroad can only be put into circulation in Hungary if issuer undertakes to comply with regulations set forth by Securities and Exchange Commission regarding printing of securities.

See also topic Brokers.

SOCIAL SECURITY:

See topic Labor Relations.

TAXATION:

Developments during last seven years have resulted in tax structure that is highly comparable to that of EEC. Also, improvements in systemizing accounting and auditing regulations, as well as appraisal methods, have enabled foreign auditor firms to maintain network of accounting and auditing. Hungarian state revenues are theoretically structured on basis of three basic taxes as enumerated in subheads below: (1) personal income tax, (2) corporation tax, and (3) turnover tax. There are no taxes like capital tax, capital stock tax, stock transfer tax, sales or trade tax (other than value added turnover tax), excess profit tax, license tax, stamp tax, special franchise tax and most importantly there is no capital gains tax.

Other state revenues that are of less economic importance are following: (i) item differentiated consumption tax, (ii) estate transfer fee, and (iii) inheritance and gift tax. Tax administration and procedures are separated from regular local administration. All tax administration decisions are subject to regular judicial review. Hungary has tax treaties or conventions of OECD Model Treaty type for avoidance of double taxation of income with great number of countries, including U.S. and most EEC members, which treaties overrule regular tax rules if more favorable to taxpayer.

(1) Personal income tax (Személyi Jövedelemadó) regulated by Act 1995:CXVII. It is direct tax levied on income of individuals who are or considered to be Hungarian residents (generally after stay of 183 days in a year in Hungary). All income is taxable, theoretically no matter what origin or source is, including but not limited to employment, business or profession, investment, rents and annuities, transfer of estates, etc., unless exempted by law. Generally, exempt incomes are state provided family allowances, child-welfare subsidy, social security allowances, scholarships, fellowships, alimony or child support. Donations to incorporated foundations or for public interest purposes are partially deductible if receipient is registered by tax authority as tax deductible donation receiver. Tax on dividends and on capital gains is 10%. However, interest income on savings accounts (both foreign currency and foreign accounts), on debentures (including capital gain on sale of publicly traded debt instruments) and capital gain on investments made by individuals through their "capital accounts" as defined by Act, are taxed at 0%.

Progressive tax rate applies to tax base incomes, i.e. to personal income reduced by exemptions and deductions, as follows in HUF:

Tax base	Figures
HUF 0-150,000	20%
HUF 150,001-220,000	HUF 30,000 plus 25% in excess of 150,000
HUF 220,001-380,000	HUF 47,500 plus 35% in excess of 220,000
HUF 380,001-550,000	HUF 103,500 plus 40% in excess of 380,000
HUF 550,001-900,000	HUF 171,500 plus 44% in excess of 550,000
HUF 900,001-	HUF 325,500 plus 48% in excess of 900,000

There is no special or excess profit rate for extraordinary incomes.

Certain kinds of real estate mortgage interest payments, pension contributions or life insurance fees are tax deductible and special deduction applies to handicapped individuals.

Income from savings, dividends, bonds and securities is separated from general income and is taxed at special rate of 10%.

Net income originating from real estate transfer within ten years of purchase after Jan. 1, 1982, or from noncommercial transfer of other estates (tangibles), is considered part of and is to be added to regular income falling under progressive taxation.

Some types of income (wages or wage-like income, interest, etc.) are, at least partially, taxed at and by sources of income. Tax already deducted this way is to be credited against tax payable when filing tax return.

Hungary has concluded agreements on avoidance of double taxation with a number of countries. E.g. according to U.S.-Hungarian treaty income received by individuals resident in U.S. for services performed as independent contractor in Hungary during tax year is exempt from income tax upon: (i) not staying in Hungary more than 183 days, and (ii) not having fixed base, permanent establishment in Hungary. Income for labor or dependent personal services is exempt upon: (i) not staying in Hungary more than 183 days, (ii) paid by or on behalf of nonresident employer, and (iii) not borne by fixed base or permanent establishment in Hungary. Special rules apply to professors, teachers, researchers and students.

(2) Corporation Tax (Társasági adó) regulated by Acts 1991:LXXXVI, as am'd several times, in 1995 by Acts 1995:XLVIII and 1995:CVI.—It is direct tax levied on profit of corporations, or more generally, on profit of any for-profit activity, i.e. production or service. All enterprises, whether private, municipal, or state owned, any form of corporation, not-for-profit organizations in respect of their for-profit activities with some exceptions, and partnerships, are equally subject to this tax. Foreign entities, even without permanent establishment in Hungary, are also subject to corporation tax with regard to income from their for-profit activities carried out in Hungary. Not-for-profit organizations, churches, and foundations are not subject to corporation tax if profit of their for-profit activities does not exceed 10% of total income or HUF 10,000,000 in tax year.

As of Jan. 1, 1993 important new rule is that interest is not deductible from tax base if paid on loans to parent company, if such loan exceeds four times stated capital of subsidiary. Special transfer pricing rules apply if connected enterprises (25% respective ownership, sister companies or substantial influence on management) do not deal at arms length.

Tax base is profit resulting from difference between gross income and costs and expenditures, depreciation of assets, and some special deductions. Dividend income of corporation is exempt from tax base. Carry-forward of net operating losses is permitted by law, generally for five years. Losses of first two fiscal years of newly established entities may be forwarded for unlimited period. As from 1992, carry-back net operating losses of agricultural branch is possible, generally for two years. General rate of corporation tax is 33.3% of tax base, if dividend distribution is made. If not, corporation tax is 18% of tax base.

Tax allowances (maximum amounting to sum of calculated tax) are received regularly in form of direct tax deduction. First group of titles (§13) promotes export activities (where calculated tax is to be reduced by 6-30% of interest paid after loans utilized therein). Second and most important group of titles emerges with regard to foreign participation in Hungarian corporations. (§12). These allowances combine aspects of foreign participation itself and preference for important activities enumerated by law. This second sort of allowance (without ones mentioned previously, although they might be combined up to total of calculated tax) are summarized in following chart:

Qualifications (A) and (B)	Tax Allowances in %
(A) If (a) stated capital of corporation is minimum HUF 50 million, and (b) foreign participation therein is minimum 30%, and (c) 50% of income originates from product manufacturing or (self-built) hotel operation	
—in first five years of operation	60%
—after five years up to end of tenth year	40%
(B) If corporation is qualified as above (A)(a) and (A)(b), and performs activities enumerated by law as highly important	
—in first five years of operation	100%
—after five years up to end of tenth year	60%

Qualifications for tax allowances under above chart are available only for companies which were set up and qualified for above requirements before Dec. 31, 1990.

If foreign shareholder, partner or owner of corporation reinvests dividends to increase stated capital of such corporation, corporation itself will be entitled to tax return to extent of sum of this increase in stated capital. (§12). This rule applied for last time to dividends distributed from profit made in 1993.

Special rules apply to permanent establishments of foreign entities. (Annex 6.).

Council of Ministers' Order 64/1990, as amended under number 35/1990 insures special corporation tax and V.A.T. allowances available for firms doing business in defined area of municipalities considered disadvantageous territories.

Offshore.—Act 1991:LXXXVI on Corporate Tax grants tax release of 85% of income tax to corporations meeting following requirements: (i) corporation is limited liability company or company limited by shares organized under Hungarian law and registered in Hungary with corporate domicile in Hungary; (ii) it has 100% (direct or indirect) foreign ownership; (iii) it has obtained authorization from Ministry of Finance granting quasi-extraterritoriality; (iv) it is engaged exclusively in trade or business with third countries or renders services exclusively in relation to third countries provided that such services do not include financial services; (v) it keeps its funds necessary for operation of company in Hungary; (vi) it retains Hungarian attorneys in its domestic administrative and court procedures; (vii) more than 50% of its officers, directors and supervisory board members as well as their employees must be citizens and residents in Hungary and auditor of company must be registered in Hungary; (viii) furthermore, neither company itself nor its owners may have any interest in Hungarian partnership, limited liability company, company limited by shares or cooperation.

Application for offshore status must be filed with Ministry of Finance. Once status is obtained, company may do accounting in foreign currency, may maintain its accounts with foreign banks abroad (except for part of its capital necessary to do business in Hungary), furthermore it may take and extend credit from and to non-Hungarians, both individuals and corporations, do business with such parties in foreign currency and keep funds gained in foreign currency.

(3) Turnover tax (Általános Forgalmi Adó; hereinafter referred to as V.A.T.) newly regulated by Act 1992:LXXIV, as amended several times. Since 1988 it is EEC modelled value added tax, payable regularly on distribution or supply (including import) of all goods and services, on base and in percentage of and together with price or fee by customer. Therefrom grantor of service will be allowed deduction for tax paid by and charged by suppliers. Export of goods and services is taxed at zero rate. (§29). Basis of V.A.T. in case of import is distributor's or supplier's price including transportation, customs, and customs duty together. (§27). Customs free import generally is free from V.A.T. with some exceptions. (§31). Rate of V.A.T. applicable is 12% or 25% depending on items. (§§28-29 and Annex #1.). 25% rate might be taken as standard, nevertheless, there are preferred rates and exemptions to be applied to certain goods and services, as well as certain tax free services, enumerated by law.

V.A.T. may be refunded and therefore is to be returned to foreign travellers (Order of Government 4/1993 [I.13] Korm. am'd by 2/1994 [I.11] Korm.), foreign corporations (2/1993 [I.13] Korm.), diplomatic and consular bodies (Order of Government 3/1993 [I.13] Korm., as am'd recently by 27/1994 [III.2] Korm.), and if paid in connection with building or renovating of condominiums or homes.

Enumerated by law, number of services (e.g. financing, social security, research and development, copyright, social and cultural services), and with some exceptions, import, if being custom-free, are free from V.A.T.

(4) Following are other tax provisions, which occasionally are of importance: Business entities are to pay Technical Training Contribution (Szakképzési hozzájárulás), which is in general 1.5% of annual gross wages and salaries paid by company. (Act 1988:XXIII, as am'd recently by Act 1995:CXXIV).

As of Feb. 1, 1992, conditioned by international reciprocity, diplomatic and consular staff upon invoice may ask for refund of consumption tax levied on fuel up to HUF 30,000 per capita yearly. (Order of Minister of Finance #1/1992 (I.20) PM, by authorization of Act 1991:LXXVIII on Consumption Tax).

TAXATION . . . *continued*

As of July 1, 1993, Act LVIII as recently am'd by Act 1995:LXVIII regulates production, storing, import, export, wholesale trade and retail of fuel, tobacco, alcoholic beverages and coffee in Hungary. This new law imposes stronger regulations as to control, licensing and administration of V.A.T. and Consumption Tax connected to above products.

Purchaser of real estate has to pay real estate transfer tax (Act 1990:XCIII, as recently am'd by Act 1995:LXVIII), which is 10% of contracted price (in case of home and condominium 2% on portion of purchase price below HUF 4,000,000 and 6% on part exceeding HUF 4,000,000). Contribution of real estate to company as stated capital or withdrawal if splitting off is tax free. (§26). Inheritance and gift tax (Act 1990:XCIII, as effective from Jan. 1, 1994) is 11% in relation to immediate relatives, 15% among wider circle of relatives and 21% for others, irrespective of value of subject. Tax on condominiums and homes is one half of stated value. Citizenship or residency of parties does not affect rates to be applied.

Local taxes are to be regulated by Act 1990:C as am'd by 1991:XXIV, 1992:LXXVI and 1993:LXVI and are levied by local governments or municipalities. Nature of these taxes may be either communal, property tax or entrepreneurship tax. Communal (public utilities) tax of companies cannot exceed HUF 2,000 per employee a year. Property tax on buildings cannot be more than HUF 900 per square meter or 3% of value per year, on land HUF 200 per square meter or 1% of value per year. Entrepreneurship tax cannot exceed 1.2% of companies' annual net income.

TRADEMARKS:

Any distinctive word, name, symbol, or device or combination thereof, through which product or commodity of particular manufacturer or merchant may be distinguished from those of others, can be registered as trademark in Hungary. There are certain restrictions as to marks which cannot be used as trademark; in general, those lacking distinctive nature. (Act 1969:IX as am'd by Act 1994:VII).

According to Act 1969:IX on trademarks, registration starts with application of holder of right to product or commodity to National Patent Office. Application must include at least name and address of petitioner, name, symbol, etc. to be registered and list (specification) of goods. Patent attorney's or lawyer's assistance is required for administrative procedure.

Hungarian Patent Office issues certificate of trademark. Period of protection is ten years with possibility of renewal. Holder has exclusive right to use trademark in connection with all goods included in goods list and can license usage.

Trademark protection terminates if protection period is not renewed, if holder gives up protection, if trademark is not used for five years in Hungary, or if protection is canceled.

See also topic Treaties and Conventions.

TREATIES AND CONVENTIONS:

Hungarian Republic is party to, inter alia, following multilateral agreements:

General of Public Law Nature: Charter of U.N. and those of its specialized organizations, FAO, ILO, UNESCO, WHO, and Statute of the International Court of Justice, Convention for the Protection of Human Rights and Fundamental Freedoms, Convention on the Prevention and Punishment of the Crime of Genocide; General Agreement on Tariffs and Trade—GATT, including Customs Valuation Code, Free Trade Agreement with EFTA, Association Agreement with EU as of Jan. 1, 1994, OECD; Anti-dumping Code, Agreement on Technical Barriers to Trade, that on Import Licensing Procedures, that Regarding Bovine Meat; International Bank for Reconstruction and Development—Worldbank, including International Monetary Fund—IMF, Articles of Agreement of the International Finance Corporation—IFC, Convention Establishing the Multilateral Investment Guarantee Agency—MIGA, Articles of Agreement of the International Development Association—IDA; Statute of International Atomic Energy Agency; Council for Mutual Economic Assistance; Constitution de l'Union postale universelle—UPC; Convention Internationale des Telecommunications; Convention Establishing the World Intellectual Property Organization; Hague Convention for the Peaceful Settlements of Disputes; Vienna Convention on Diplomatic Relations; Vienna Convention on Consular Relations; Geneva Convention relating to status of refugees (with geographical limitation), New York Convention on Racism, European Convention on Extradition and Strasbourg Convention on Prevention of Torture.

General of Private Law Nature: Hague Conventions relating to Procedure in Civil Matters, 1905, 1954; Hague Convention Abolishing the Requirement of Legalisation for Foreign Public Documents 1961; Convention on the Recognition and Enforcement of Foreign Arbitral Awards 1958; UN Convention on Contracts for the International Sale of Goods 1980.

Family Law: Convention on the Political Rights of Women 1953; International Convention on Enforcement of Judgments Concerning Child Support 1956; Convention on the Nationality of Married Women 1957; Convention on Recognition and Enforcement of Judgments Concerning Child Support 1956; Convention on the Civil Aspects of International Child Abduction 1980.

Investment Protection.—Agreements on protection of investments have been concluded with following countries: Australia, Austria, Belgium, Canada, China, Cyprus, Czech Republic, Denmark, France, Germany, Great Britain, Greece, Indonesia, Israel, Italy, Kuwait, Luxembourg, Malaysia, Mongolia, Morocco, Netherlands, Norway, Republic of Kasakhstan, Republic of Moldova, Romania, Russian Federation, South Korea, Spain, Sweden, Switzerland, Thailand, Turkey, Uruguay, and U.S.A.; agreements also with OPIC and MIGA.

Intellectual and Industrial Property: Paris Convention for the Protection of Industrial Property Rights; Berne Convention for the Protection of Literary and Artistic Works; Madrid Convention on International Registration of Marks.

Taxation.—Most treaties and conventions on avoidance of double taxation on income and property tax follow model drafted by OECD. Agreements have been concluded with following countries: Australia, Austria, Belgium, Brazil, Canada, China, former CMEA Countries, Cyprus, Denmark, Germany, Egypt, Finland, France, Great Britain, Greece, India, Israel, Italy, Japan, S. Korea, Luxembourg, Malaysia, Malta, Netherlands, Norway, Pakistan, Republic of Kasakhstan, Republic of Moldova, Russia, Slovakia, South Africa, Spain, Sweden, Switzerland, Thailand, Ukraine, and U.S.A., former Yugoslavia.

Trade.—Convention Relating to a Uniform Law on the Formation of Contracts for the International Sale of Goods; International Convention Concerning the Transport by Railroad of Merchandise (CIM) and of Persons and Baggage (CIV); Convention on the Contract for the International Carriage of Goods by Road (CMR). The most important bilateral trade agreements have been concluded with the EEC, Fed. Rep. Germany, and South Korea.

International Sale of Goods.—United Nations Convention on Contracts for the International Sale of Goods, in force on July 19, 1987. See Part VII, Selected International Conventions.

TRUSTS:

Trust, as legal institution and title to property right, held by one party for benefit of another, is unknown in Hungarian law. Since it is not prohibited by law, property relations of trust nature may nevertheless be created by contract.

WILLS:

Wills and contracts of inheritance are governed by §§623-672 of Civil Code. Although interpretation of will by Court follows principle of favor testamenti, lack of any of formalities makes will invalid. Last will and testament may be public or private; private may be holograph or autograph, or in emergency, declared orally. Minor age 14-18 or person with otherwise limited capability may only make public will to which consent of guardian or of any authority is not required. One who is blind, illiterate or in condition of incapability to read or to sign cannot make either holograph or autograph will. Although will is lost or destroyed, if not intentionally destroyed by testator, will stays in force.

Public will may be executed before notary public or local court in official way of public records, and is deposited with notary public or Court, although fact of deposit with notary or Court has no legal effect. Testator may deposit unwitnessed private autograph or holograph will with notary public, however, this deposition does not affect private nature of will. Revocation of will may be effected by express declaration of revocation in form of will, by destroying or by execution of new will. Taking back will from notarial deposit will not effect revocation.

Private holograph will must be named as such, handwritten, dated (month, day, year and place) and subscribed entirely by testator with her own hand, and need not be witnessed or notarized.

Private autograph will, apart from same formalities of holograph will (except for requirement of handwriting), has to be witnessed by two uninterested persons of full legal capacity, i.e. will has to be subscribed or acknowledged as such in joint and continuous presence of witnesses, who have to subscribe it.

Oral, private will may be done in life-threatening emergency, if written will is impossible or virtually impossible to make. Oral will has to be performed and directly named as such in joint and continuous presence of two witnesses, who are not beneficiaries, in language they understand. If after three months testator is still alive and will is not repeated in another form, will is no longer in force.

Joint or mutual will is entirely invalid. Disposition about change of heir to estate, conditioned by certain event or date is also invalid. Nevertheless, conditional legacy or bequest is valid. Invalid disposition does not effect validity of will, as a whole. Only someone who is interested in will may claim invalidity of will or any disposition thereof.

Contract of inheritance must satisfy formal requirements of will. Spouses, as testators, may be jointly one party to contract. Revocation or modification of contract needs consent of both parties.

Compulsory portion is statutory claim in estate of descendents or, if there is no descendent, of parents, for half of estate, which in absence of will would be inherited by them. Compulsory portion of spouse is life long usufruct of estate, limited to her/his personal needs. In exceptional cases, based on some significant cause, testator may deprive compulsory heirs of inheritance.

As for validity of foreigners' will, testator's personal law, or in the lack of such, lex loci actus are to be applied.

Inheritance Tax.—See topic Taxation.

WITNESSES:

Witness in civil or criminal or any other official procedure is to be called by and questioned before Court or some other authority. Declarations, whether under oath or not, given in advance will be considered by Court and will have same value as any written evidence, without being preferred in any sense.

See also topics Contracts, Evidence, and Wills.

INDIA LAW DIGEST REVISER

Mulla & Mulla & Craigie Blunt & Caroe
Jehangir Wadia Building
51 Mahatma Gandhi Road
Bombay 400 001, India
Telephone: 9122-2044960; 9122-2875121
Fax: 9122-2040246; 9122-2044717
Email: Internet:mulla•mulla@axcess•net.in
Other Office: 209, Regency Enclave, 4 Magrath Road, Bangalore 560025. Telephone: 9180-5550370. Fax: 9180-5598549. Email: Internet: banlore.mulla@axcess.net.in

Reviser Profile

The firm is India's largest law firm. Our origin dates back to the end of the last century when Sir Dinshaw Mulla and his brother, Rustom Mulla established the firm in 1895. Sir Dinshaw Mulla was a Privy Counsellor and author of several legal works including Contract, Partnership, Sale of Goods, Insolvency, Civil Procedure Code etc., and which even today are leading authorities. They merged in 1952 with Messrs. Craigie Blunt & Caroe, that firm being solicitors in the East India Company. Since then the firm has grown to its current strength of over 150 inclusive of lawyers, fee earners and administrative staff. Individual partners concentrate on different areas of the firm's practice enabling the providing of specialist legal, commercial and technical services to clients. The firm has built up very close working relationships with lawyers throughout the world. Many of the firm's lawyers are qualified Solicitors of the Supreme Courts of England and Hong Kong. Most of the firm's partners travel widely in the course of their work which enables them to make invaluable international contacts. Many of our partners have presented papers at International and Domestic Law Conferences. One of the firm's Senior Partners was the past President of the Solicitors' Law Society and past President of the Indian Merchants Chamber (being the first and the only Solicitor to occupy this position in the Chamber). Another Senior Partner of the firm is the Chairman, Indian Council of Arbitration (Western Region) was also Chairman, Law Committee of the Indian Merchants Chamber and was also on the Government of India's N.R.I. (Nonresident Indians), Consultative Committee, a Senator of the university of Bombay and on its Board of studies for law. The firm is the Reviser of India Law Digest for Martindale-Hubbell International Law Directory and the Indian correspondents for Euromoney Publications plc, the India correspondents for Shawcross & Beaumont-Air Law, Aviation Reports and the India correspondents for Lloyd's Maritime and Commercial Law Quarterly.

Areas of Practice: Corporate, Mergers and Acquisitions, Foreign Investments, Joint Ventures, Antitrusts Law, Banking and Securities Law, Air Law, Aircraft Finance, Maritime and Transport Law, Ship Finance, Marine & General Insurance Law, Product Liability, Litigation, Taxation, Trade and Customs Law, Environmental Law, Oil and Gas, Real Estate, Commodities, Labour, Arbitration, Bankruptcy, Intellectual Property and General Entertainment Law.

INDIA LAW DIGEST

(The following is a list of all Topics, including cross-references, covered in this Digest.)

INDIA LAW DIGEST

Revised for 1997 edition by

MULLA & MULLA & CRAIGIE BLUNT & CAROE, Solicitors, Bombay.

See topics Law Reports, Codes, Etc.; Statutes.

ACTIONS:

See also topic Admiralty Jurisdiction.

Civil Actions are governed by Code of Civil Procedure V of 1908 as am'd. Code applies to High Courts of every State within India, District Courts subordinate to High Courts, and Inferior Courts within Districts; also partly to Revenue Courts, Provincial Small Cause Courts and Presidency Small Cause Courts in Bombay, Madras and Calcutta. Actions in Supreme Court of India are governed by Supreme Court Rules and Code of Civil Procedure. Constitution of India also confers upon Supreme Court, as well as High Courts, powers to entertain petitions by way of writ. These writs may be in nature of habeas corpus, mandamus, prohibition, quo warranto and certiorari.

Jurisdiction and Res Judicata.—Courts have jurisdiction to try all suits of civil nature including those regarding rights to property, office, including religious office, caste property, temple property, rights of worship, burial, religious processions; but not revenue matters, matters within ambit of Criminal Procedure Code 1898, and landlord and tenant suits, or some other matters such as industrial relations etc. for which special courts are provided by special statutes. Criminal defamation comes under Indian Penal Code. Courts cannot proceed with trial of any suit in which matter in issue is directly and substantially same as in previously instituted suit between same parties which is pending in any other court; but pendency of suit in foreign court does not preclude Indian Courts from trying suit founded on same cause of action. (§§9, 10). Courts cannot try any suit in which matter in issue is directly and substantially same as in former suit between same parties which has been heard and finally decided. (§11).

Foreign judgments are conclusive regarding any matter directly adjudicated upon between same parties except in following cases: (1) Where judgment has not been pronounced by Court of competent jurisdiction; (2) where it has not been given on merits of case; (3) where it appears on face of proceedings to be founded on incorrect view of International Law or refusal to recognise law of India where applicable in any such case; (4) where proceedings were contrary to natural justice; (5) where judgment was obtained by fraud; (6) where it sustains claim founded on breach of any law in force in India. (§13).

Enforcement.—Foreign judgments may be enforced by proceedings in execution in certain specified cases only (where reciprocity exists between India and foreign country; see subhead Reciprocity, infra); or by suit in India upon judgment. Limitation period for such suit is three years from date of judgment. (Limitation Act 1963, Sch. 1, Art. 101). Pendency of appeal in foreign country will not bar suit in India on foreign judgment. But where foreign court applying lex fori holds suit is not barred by its own law of limitation, it cannot be said to have refused to recognise law of India simply because suit was barred here.

Suits on Foreign Awards.—Arbitration awards in foreign countries are not subject to above six grounds of attack. (§13). Foreign awards recognised pursuant to Convention on Recognition & Enforcement of Foreign Awards done at New York, 1958 or Protocol on Arbitration clauses signed at Geneva in 1923 and convention on the Execution of Foreign Arbitral Awards may be enforced by proceedings under Arbitration and Conciliation Act, 1996. These enforcement proceedings are summary in nature. Foreign awards may also be enforced by instituting action on awards in India. (See topic Arbitration and Conciliation, subhead Arbitration, catchline Foreign Awards.)

Presumption.—Indian Courts presume upon production of any document purporting to be certified copy of foreign judgment that such judgment was pronounced by court of competent jurisdiction unless contrary appears on record. Presumption can be disproved by facts. (§14).

Place of Suing.—Every suit must be instituted in court of lowest grade competent to try it by pecuniary value of suit. (§15). Subject to pecuniary or other legal limitation, suits regarding immovable properties must be instituted where such property is situate. (§16). Suits for compensation for torts or actionable wrongs done to person or movable property may be instituted, at option of plaintiff, either in court within whose local limits wrong occurred or court within whose jurisdiction defendant resides, or carries on business, or works personally for gain. (§19). Subject to above, other suits must be instituted in court within whose jurisdiction either defendant resides or carries on business or cause of action arises. (§20). Corporation is deemed to carry on business at its sole or principal office in India. Objection to jurisdiction must be lodged at earliest possible opportunity in court of first instance and will not be entertained later. (§21). Suits may be transferred to more appropriate courts. (§§22, 23, 24, 25).

Institution of Suits.—Every suit must be instituted by presentation of plaint or other manner prescribed. (§26). Once suit is duly instituted, summons must be issued to defendant to appear and answer claim. Summons may be served in manner prescribed. (§27 and Order 5).

Service of Foreign Summonses.—Summons and other process issued by (1) Any civil or revenue court in India to which Code does not extend; (2) any civil or revenue court established or continued by Central Government authority outside India; or (3) any civil or revenue court outside India to which Code applies by Central Government notification, may be sent to courts in territories to which Code extends and may be served as if they were summons issued by such courts. (§29).

Courts have power to order discovery and inspection of documents, and issue summons to persons to attend to give evidence or order any facts to be proved on affidavit. (§30). Court has power to compel attendance. (§32).

Judgment and Decree.—After hearing case, court must pronounce judgment and decree. (§33). Where decree is for payment of money court may order interest on principal sum payable not exceeding 6% per annum. Where liability in relation to sum adjudged arises out of commercial transaction (i.e. transaction connected with industry, trade or business of party incurring liability) court may award interest at rate exceeding 6% but not exceeding contractual rate of interest, if any, or rate at which moneys are lent or advanced by nationalised banks in relation to commercial transactions. (§34).

Costs.—See topic Costs.

Limitation of Actions.—Limitation Act XXXVI of 1963 prescribes period of limitation for various actions and applications. Period of limitation in majority of cases for filing civil suit is three years from date when cause of action arises. Government however can (except in suit before Supreme Court in exercise of its original jurisdiction) file suit within 30 years from time when cause of action arose.

Execution.—Decree may be executed either by court which passed it, or by court to which it is sent for execution. (§38). Court which passed decree may send it to another court for execution if person against whom decree is passed: (1) Actually and voluntarily resides or carries on business or works within local limits of jurisdiction of such other court; (2) has property within jurisdiction of such other court; (3) has immovable property within such jurisdiction and order is regarding sale or delivery of such property; or (4) for any other reason recorded by court in writing. (§39). Other court must be in India, and it must certify fact of execution of such decree. (§41). All questions arising out of execution are determined by court executing decree. (§47).

Reciprocity.—Where certified copy of decree of any superior court of any reciprocating territory has been filed in a District Court, decree may be executed in India as if it had been passed by District Court. Together with certified copy must be filed certificate from superior court stating extent if any to which decree has been satisfied or adjusted and such certificate is conclusive proof of such facts. Reciprocating territory means any country or territory outside India which Central Government may by notification in Official Gazette declare to be a reciprocating territory, and superior courts may be specified in notification. Decree means any judgment under which sum of money is payable but not in respect of taxes, fines or other penalty. At present U.K. is one of countries so notified as reciprocating territory and House of Lords, Court of Appeal, High Court in England, Court of Session in Scotland, High Court in Northern Ireland, Court of Chancery of the County Palatine of Lancaster and Court of Chancery of the County Palatine of Durham are declared as Superior Courts.

Fiji, Singapore, Aden, New Zealand, Malaysia, Trinidad & Tobago and Cook Islands and Western Samoa have also been notified as reciprocating territories. (§44A).

Limitation Period for Execution.—Twelve years from date of decree sought to be executed or date of default in making payment or delivery under decree. Court may waive limitation in cases of fraud or force. Limitation Act applies. (§48).

Transferees and Legal Representatives.—Holder of decree is subject to equities against legal representatives of judgment debtor but only to extent of properties held by representative. (§§49, 50).

Means of Execution.—Court has large powers to enforce execution of decree by attachment and sale of property, arrest and detention in prison (power of arrest and detention is very rarely exercised e.g. fraudulent disposal of assets to evade execution), appointment of receiver, etc. (§51). Where any property has been attached, any private alienation of it is void (§64) as against all claims enforceable under attachment. There are large number of safeguards for execution of decrees, especially against immovable properties, including prevention of benami purchases at court sales.

Court has power to distribute assets among all decree-holders. (§73).

Suits Against Foreign Rulers, Ambassadors and Envoys.—No ruler of foreign state may be sued in any court in India without written consent of Central Government, and subject to several other conditions. No ruler can be arrested under code, or any decree be executed against property of such ruler. It applies to ambassadors, envoys, High Commissioners, and members of staff or retinue of rulers. (§86). Foreign ruler may sue and be sued in name of his State. (§86).

Special provisions exist for procedure, including statutory notice, in bringing suits against (1) government; (2) government officers. (§§79, 80).

Charities.—Special provisions are made regarding suits concerning public charitable trusts. (§92).

Appeals.—Provision is made regarding appeal from original decree to court exercising appellate jurisdiction and for appeals from appellate decrees. (§§100-103). Appeal lies to Supreme Court from any judgment, decree or final order framed by High Court in exercise of its appellate or original jurisdiction or any such judgment which is certified to be fit for appeal to Supreme Court (§109); High Court has also powers of review, reference and revision (§§113-115).

Parties.—Women in Purdah are not compelled to appear in person before court. (§132). President, Vice-President of India, Speaker of Lower House of Parliament, Ministers of Central Cabinet, Judges of Supreme Court, Governors of States, administrators of Union Territories, Speakers of State Legislative Assemblies, Chairman of same, Ministers of States, Judges of High Court and certain other persons are privileged to claim exemption from personal appearance. Members of Legislative Assemblies are exempt from civil arrest during continuance of Legislative Assembly sessions and in days before and after Assemblies are in sessions.

Persons under disability (i.e., minors, lunatics) may be served by next friend or guardian ad litem. (§147). All persons may be joined in one suit as plaintiffs in whom any right to relief in respect of or arising out of same transaction or series of actions or transactions is alleged to exist whether jointly, severally or in alternative where if such persons brought separate suits, any common question of law or fact would arise (Order 1, Rule 1) and all persons may be joined as defendants against whom any right etc.

ACTIONS . . . *continued*
exists where if separate suits were brought any common question of law or fact would arise (Order 1, Rule 3).

Suit must be framed to include whole claim (Order 2, Rule 1-3) but joinder of claims is only allowed in certain cases if property is immovable.

Summons must be served on defendant and defendant must appear at date and place fixed by summons. (Order 5). Where defendant resides out of India and has no agent in India, summons must be addressed to defendant at place of his residence and sent by post (if postal communication exists). (Order 5). Service in foreign territory is otherwise through court of area where defendant resides or through political agent if Central Government has appointed such person in such territory under powers vested in it. Where defendant is member of armed forces service is to commanding office, copy retained by defendant. (Order 5). Civil Procedure Code follows generally principles of English Rules of Supreme Court. (See England Law Digest.)

Proof of Foreign Law.—India follows principles of English law of evidence. (See England Law Digest.) All questions of foreign law are treated as questions of fact and must be so proved. As regards foreign claims, principles of Private International Law as followed in England generally apply.

See also topic Death.

ADMIRALTY JURISDICTION:

High courts have jurisdiction to arrest foreign vessels in Indian waters, whether or not defendant resides or carries on business in India or cause of action arose within local limits of Court's jurisdiction.

Till Bombay High Court ruling in M.V.NICOS and Supreme Court ruling in M.V.ELIZABETH Admiralty jurisdiction was as existed under Admiralty Courts Act, 1840 extended by Admiralty Courts Act, 1861 enforceable in India by Colonial Courts Act, 1890. Prior to M.V.ELIZABETH Admiralty Jurisdiction confined to: (1) Repairing, building, equipping vessel, if at commencement of action vessel or its sales proceeds are under arrest; (2) necessaries supplied; (3) physical damage to goods carried into Indian port by vessel; (4) damage caused by vessel; (5) ownership, possession, employment and earning of Indian vessel; (6) seaman's wages earned on vessel; (7) mortgage claim if vessel or its sales proceeds under arrest.

Post M.V.ELIZABETH Admiralty Jurisdiction is extended with progress of legislation in England; High Court can exercise powers in same manner and extent as English High Court; Admiralty Jurisdiction invocable against sister vessel if beneficial ownership in sister vessel is same as in vessel causing claim. However, Bombay High Court in matter of M.T. "LEONTAS" decided in Dec. 1993 took contrary view that sister vessel cannot be arrested. Hence, law is presently ambiguous particularly since Bombay High Court has in June 1994 relating to M.V. "ELIZABETH" taken view that even charterer can arrest vessel for claim for despatch.

"Maritime Claim" not defined by statute. In M.V.ELIZABETH held that English Supreme Court Act, 1981 (which catalogues maritime claims with reference to Unified Rules under Brussels Convention, 1952 on Arrest of Seagoing Ships) can be regarded as International Common Law and can be adopted by Indian Courts to fill lacunas in relevant Indian legislation.
(See also topic Shipping.)

ADOPTION:

There is no statutory enactment in India providing for adoption of child by persons other than Hindus. Adoption among Hindus is governed by Hindu Adoptions and Maintenance Act (LXV VIII of 1956). However, other persons like Indian Muslims, Christians, Parsees, Jews and foreign nationals can resort to provisions of Guardian and Wards Act, 1890 for purpose of facilitating such adoption by being declared guardians of child sought to be adopted. At present inter-country adoption or adoption by foreigners can only be processed under Guardian and Wards Act, 1890.

Hindu Adoption and Maintenance Act LXV VIII of 1956.—A Hindu family must have male heir, inter alia, for performing funeral rites. When married Hindu has no son, grandson (sons's son) or great grandson (sons's son's son) born to him or her, he or she may adopt son. When married Hindu has no daughter or granddaughter (sons's daughter) born to him or her, he or she may adopt daughter. Act overrides customary law. Person giving in adoption and adopter must have capacity. Adoption must comply with requirements of Act.

Guardian and Wards Act, 1890.—Act enacted for providing for appointment of guardian of person or property of minor. When court is satisfied that it is for welfare of minor that order should be made appointing guardian of his person or property or both or declaring person to be such guardian, then it may so order. (§7[1]). Applications with regard to guardianship of person of minor are to be made to District Court having jurisdiction in place where minor ordinarily resides. (§9[1]). On application (by petition), court, if satisfied that there is ground for entertaining, will fix date for hearing and cause notice of application and of date fixed for hearing to be served on parents of minors if residing in any State to which Act extends, persons, if any, named in application as having custody or possession of person of minor, person proposed in application to be appointed guardian and any other person to whom special notice in opinion of court should be given. (§17). In appointing guardian of minor, court will be guided by what appears to, in circumstances, be for welfare of minor, having regard to age, sex, religion of minor, character and capacity of proposed guardian, wishes of any deceased parent, any existing or previous relations of proposed guardian with minor or his property. (§26). Guardian of person of minor appointed by court shall not, without leave of court by which he was appointed, remove ward from limits of its jurisdiction except for such purposes as may be prescribed.

Inter-Country Adoption.—

Procedure.—Provisions of Guardian and Wards Act, 1890 Act VII of 1890 as noted above are to be followed for purpose of carrying through inter-country adoption as there is no law of adoption. Intending foreign adopter makes application to court for being appointed guardian of person of destitute and abandoned child whom he/she wishes to adopt and for leave of court to take child to country of adopter on being appointed such guardian.

Under Bombay High Court (Original Side) Rules, when foreigner applies for being appointed guardian of Indian child applicant or his advocate must furnish copy of application to Secretary, Indian Council of Social Welfare, Bombay and inform Secretary of date of hearing requesting that any representation that Council may make be submitted in duplicate to Prothonotary & Senior Master of High Court at least four days before hearing. Court may, while disposing of application, direct applicant to pay costs of Council and in such event Prothonotary shall not issue certified copy of order on application until applicant produces Council's receipt for payment of costs. When foreign national is declared guardian of Indian children with permission to remove such children out of India, copy of such order shall be endorsed to Government of India, Ministry of Education & Social Welfare (Department of Social Welfare).

Requirement of Foreign Adopter: (1) Application from intending foreign adopter desiring to adopt must be sponsored by social or child welfare agency recognised or licensed by government of country in which foreign applicant is resident; (2) social or child welfare agency which sponsors application must get home study report prepared by professional worker indicating basis why application is sponsored and whether foreigner wishing to adopt is fit and suitable and has capacity to adopt; (3) application must be accompanied by: (a) recent photograph of family, (b) marriage certificate of foreigner and his or her spouse, (c) declaration concerning their health with certificate of medical fitness duly certified by medical doctor, (d) declaration of financial status with employer certificate, if applicable, income tax assessment orders, bank references and particulars of property owned, (e) declaration stating their willingness to be appointed guardian and undertaking to adopt child according to law of their country within period of two years from date of arrival of child in their country, and to give intimation of adoption to court appointing them guardian and also to social or child welfare agency in India, further that they would maintain child and provide education according to their status and send reports of progress of child with photographs quarterly during first two years and thereafter half yearly for three years, (f) power of attorney of foreigner wishing to adopt in favour of officer of social or child welfare agency in India processing case authorising attorney to handle case on behalf of foreigner in case he/she is not in position to come to India; (4) social or child welfare agency sponsoring application must certify that foreigner seeking to adopt is permitted to do so according to law of his country; (5) all certificates, declaration and documents accompanying application of foreigner to be notarised by notary public whose signature should be attested by officer of Ministry of External Affairs or Justice or Social Welfare of country of foreigner or by officer of Indian Embassy or High Commission or Consulate; (6) social or child welfare agency sponsoring application must undertake when forwarding application to social or child welfare agency in India that it will ensure adoption of child by foreigner according to law of adopter's country within two years and will send two certified copies of adoption order to social or child welfare agency in India through which application for guardianship is processed so that one copy is filed in court and other remains with agency; (7) social or child welfare agency sponsoring application must agree to send to social or child welfare agency concerned progress reports of child, quarterly during first year and half yearly for subsequent year or years until adoption is effected; (8) social or child welfare agency sponsoring application of foreigner must undertake that in case of disruption of family of foreigner before adoption it will care for child and find suitable alternative placement with approval of concerned social or child welfare agency in India and report such alternative placement to court handling guardianship proceedings so that court and concerned social and child welfare agency in India can pass information to Secretary of Ministry of Social Welfare, Government of India.

Practice.—Recognised social and child welfare agency must consider which child would be suitable for being given to foreign applicant and would fit with his family and environment and send photograph and child study report of such child to foreign applicant for his approval. There must be specific approval for specific child. After receipt of such approval application for appointment of foreigner as guardian of child can proceed. Guardianship order shall make provision for deposit of sum of money or bond to enable child to be repatriated should it become necessary. Guardianship order may permit social or child welfare agency which has taken care of child pending selection for adoption to receive such amount as court thinks fit from foreigner appointed as guardian of such child. Guardianship order to have photograph of child countersigned by officer of court. Proceedings are as far as possible to be disposed of within two months from filing application. Proceedings are held in camera. Register of names and particulars of children where order for appointment of guardians has been made together with addresses and particulars of adoptive parents is to be maintained by Ministry of Social Welfare, Government of India. Government of India will send to Indian Embassy or High Commission in country of prospective adopter names, addresses and particulars of prospective adoptive parents together with particulars of children taken so that there is watch over welfare and progress of children adopted.

AFFIDAVITS: See topic Notaries Public.

AGENCY: See topic Principal and Agent.

AIRCRAFT:

India is a signatory to Warsaw Convention of 1929, and to protocol to said convention signed at Hague in 1955, an international convention for unification of certain rules relating to international carriage by air. Convention governs, and in most cases limits, liability of carriers for death or personal injury and in respect of loss or damage to baggage as well as cargo. Rules embodied in Convention and protocol thereto have been given statutory recognition in India by Carriage by Air Act, 1972. Though Act applies to international carriage by air, it has been made statutorily applicable to domestic carriage as well, subject to certain modifications. Liability of air carrier in respect of death of passenger undertaking domestic carriage is now fixed, subject to certain exceptions, at Rs. 500,000.

Anti-Hijacking Act, 1982.—In recent years, there has been increase in offences by way of unlawful seizure of aircraft or hijacking. Convention for Suppression of Unlawful Seizure of Aircraft was drawn up at diplomatic conference held at The Hague in Dec., 1970 for adoption of States, by representatives of 77 Governments. For

See Topical Index in front part of this volume.

AIRCRAFT . . . *continued*
dealing more effectively with offences involving unlawful seizure of aircraft or hijacking, India has ratified this Convention and passed Anti-Hijacking Act, 1982.

Suppression of Unlawful Acts against Safety of Civil Aviation Act, 1982.—India is signatory to Convention drawn up at diplomatic conference held at The Hague in Dec. 1970 for dealing with hijacking and Convention adopted at diplomatic conference held at Montreal in 1971 for Suppression of Unlawful Acts against the Safety of Civil Aviation. Rules embodied in Convention have been given statutory recognition and effect in India by Suppression of Unlawful Acts against Safety of Civil Aviation Act, 1982.

ALIENS:

Position of aliens in India is governed by Foreigners Act XXXI of 1946. Act describes "foreigner" as person who is not a citizen of India. India however recognises a quasi-dual citizenship. Persons who are citizens of Commonwealth Countries are also thereby "Commonwealth Citizens of India." See topic Constitution and Government, subhead Citizenship.

Central Government has power to make orders regulating entry of foreigners into and deportation from India. (§3).

Property.—Permission of Reserve Bank of India is required in case of transfer of monies and other property by and to aliens.

However, Reserve Bank of India has recently granted general permission to foreign citizens of Indian origin, whether resident in India or abroad, to purchase immoveable property in India for their bonafide residential purpose. Consideration for such purchasers should be met either out of inward remittances in foreign exchange through normal banking channels or out of funds from amounts known as N R I, F C N R Accounts maintained by such persons with banks in India.

Such properties can also be disposed of and repatriation of original investments in respect of property purchased, on or after 26th May, 1993, is permitted up to amount of consideration originally remitted from abroad, provided property is sold after period of three years from date of final purchase deed or from date of payment of final instalments of consideration amount, whichever is later.

Applications for repatriation are required to be made within 90 days of sale in prescribed form. See topic Exchange Control.

Corporations Owned or Controlled by Aliens.—See topics Corporations or Companies, subheads Foreign Corporations, and Subsidiaries; Exchange Control; Foreign Investment.

ARBITRATION AND CONCILIATION:

Arbitration.—Law of arbitration prior to passing of Arbitration and Conciliation Act, 1996 ("Act") was Arbitration Act, 1940. For quite some time need was felt for modelling arbitration law on international standard and for introduction of arbitration law of international standards, and government felt need for introduction of mechanism of conciliation as effective alternative mode of dispute resolution mechanism. Accordingly government enacted 1996 Act.

Arbitration law in India is now based on UNCITRAL Model Law on International Commercial Arbitration, 1985, and UNCITRAL Conciliation Rules of 1980. New Act covers both domestic, as well as international commercial arbitration. Provisions of Act apply in case arbitration agreement is established. Arbitration agreement is established if there is document signed by both parties or on exchange of letters, telex, telegrams or any other ways of telecommunication or if it is exchange of statement of claim and defence in which existence of agreement is alleged by one and not denied by other party in writing.

Act gives arbitration precedence over juridical proceeding. All awards made under Act shall be construed to be domestic award for purposes of enforcement. Interim relief in nature of resolution, custody or sale of goods, securing amount in dispute, detentions, preservation or inspection of property, interim injunction, appointment of receiver or other interim measures or protection as may be appropriate can be obtained from appropriate court, either before, during or any time after award becomes decree for enforcement.

Constitution of Arbitral Tribunal and procedure for appointment of member of tribunal are matters to be chosen by parties under arbitration agreement. If parties fail to reach consensus on constituting of arbitral tribunal, they may apply to Chief Justice of appropriate Court or any person or institution designated by such Chief Justice may constitute arbitral tribunal. In appointing arbitral tribunal Chief Justice shall take into consideration various special conditions which may have been prescribed under arbitration agreement between parties who refer matter for arbitration. Composition of arbitration tribunal can be challenged on certain grounds, e.g. that there are sufficient justifiable doubts as to independence or impartiality of arbitrator. Appointment of arbitrator by parties can also be challenged on grounds which may arise after appointment has been made. Arbitral tribunal has wide powers including power to adjudicate on jurisdiction, and to grant interim reliefs during pendency of arbitration proceedings.

Procedure to be adopted in arbitration proceeding can be chosen by parties and rules prescribed under Code of Civil Procedure 1908, or Indian Evidence Act, 1872 are not mandatory. Place of arbitration and language for arbitration is left to choice of parties. Manner of oral or written pleadings in arbitration proceedings can be agreed upon by parties and is subject to tribunal's discretion. Arbitral award can be passed ex parte in certain cases. Examination of witness, recording of evidence, expert evidence and issue of process during proceedings with assistance of appropriate court is also permitted.

Law Applicable in Arbitration Proceeding.—In case of domestic arbitration, arbitration is to be held in accordance with substantive law of India. In international commercial arbitration law applicable shall be one chosen by parties and failing this law which arbitral tribunal considers as appropriate. Arbitral award can be passed with consent of parties. Such arbitral award shall be on same status as arbitral award passed in matter adjudicated upon by arbitral tribunal. Manner in which arbitration award can be implemented or enforced is also prescribed by Act. Upon passing of award, or arbitral tribunal being unable to act in proceeding or upon agreement between parties, arbitral proceeding stands terminated.

Parties can seek clarification, correction, amendment or addition to arbitral award within specified period or time and such clarification amendment, addition or correction shall be granted by tribunal within specified period of time in order to enable parties to successfully give effect to arbitral award.

Arbitral award passed by arbitral tribunal can be challenged before court of appropriate jurisdiction upon application on ground that party was incapacitated, arbitral tribunal was in excess of jurisdiction, that procedure was abrogated, that subject matter of dispute was not capable of settlement under law in force and award is in conflict with public policy of India. Arbitral award is considered as decree passed by civil court under Code of Civil Procedure, 1908 and shall be final and binding on parties if not challenged on appeal. Provisions of execution of decree apply to enforcement of award. Interim applications before arbitral tribunal or appropriate Court for interim reliefs and award passed by arbitral tribunal can be appealed upon by either of parties before appropriate Court which has jurisdiction to hear such appeal.

Foreign Awards.—Certain foreign awards are recognised and enforcible if they are passed in any of countries which are signatories to New York Convention of 1961 or Geneva Convention of 1923 and if Central Government has notified in Official Gazette that any of these conventions applies to such countries. These enforcement proceedings are summary in nature. Other foreign awards may also be enforced by instituting action on awards in India (see subhead Foreign Judgments, topic Actions.

Foreign awards if valid are treated on par with decree passed by Indian civil court and same are enforceable by court having jurisdiction as if decree has been passed by such court.

Enforcement of foreign awards could be rejected by appropriate court on ground mentioned in §44A of Indian Code of Civil Procedure, 1908.

There are powers vested in High Courts of various states to frame rules regarding procedure before such court. Central Government may by notification prescribe rules with regard to arbitration and conciliation.

Conciliation.—Arbitration and Conciliation Act, 1996 (Act) also provides for important alternate dispute resolution mechanism viz. Conciliation. Act enables parties in defined legal relationship to refer particular dispute for conciliation. Such conciliation could be with assistance of one or more conciliators. Conciliator(s) could be appointed by agreement between parties. It is stipulated that conciliator(s) shall assist parties to reach amicable settlement of their dispute and while doing so conciliator is to follow principles of objectivity for justice while giving consideration to rights and obligations of parties under their contract and is required to take into consideration commercial practices and circumstances surrounding disputes. As regards procedure to be followed in conciliation proceedings there are no strict rules prescribed. However maintenance or confidentiality of information disclosed during conciliation is mandatory. Settlement arrived upon in conciliation proceedings shall have same effect as arbitral award and accordingly it shall be treated as decree passed by Court.

ASSIGNMENTS:

Transfers of rights, debts and choses in action or actionable claims are governed by Transfer of Property Act IV of 1882, §§130 et seq.

Procedure.—Transfer of actionable claim whether with or without consideration is effected only by execution of instrument in writing signed by transferor or his duly authorised agent and is complete and effectual upon the execution of such instrument. Thereupon all rights and remedies of transferor, by way of damages or otherwise, vest in transferee whether notice is given or not; provided that every dealing with the debt or other actionable claim by debtor or other person from or against whom transferor would but for such instrument of transfer as aforesaid have been entitled to recover or enforce such debt or other actionable claim is (save where debtor or such other person has received express notice of the transfer) valid as against such transfer.

Transferee of an actionable claim may upon execution of such instrument of transfer as aforesaid sue or institute proceedings for same in his own name without obtaining transferor's consent. Section does not apply to transfer of marine or fire policy of insurance.

Notice.—Every notice of transfer of an actionable claim shall be in writing signed by transferor or his agent duly authorised or in case transferor refuses to sign by transferee or his agent, and must state name and address of transferee.

Transferee's Liability.—Transferee of actionable claim takes subject to all liabilities and equities to which transferor was subject in respect thereof at date of transfer. Where transferor of a debt warrants solvency of debtor, the warranty, in absence of contract to contrary, applies only to his solvency at time of transfer and is limited, where transfer is made for consideration, to amount or value of such consideration. Where debt is transferred for purpose of securing existing or future debt, debt so transferred if received by transferor or recovered by tranferee is applicable first in payment of cost of such recovery, secondly in or towards satisfaction of amount for time being secured by transfer and residue if any belongs to transferor or other person entitled to receive same.

Above provisions do not apply to stocks, shares, debentures or negotiable instruments.

ASSOCIATIONS:

Registration of associations is not compulsory but is desirable under Indian Law which provides for registration of two types of associations: (1) Labour Trade Unions; and (2) Societies.

Under Societies Registration Act XXI of 1860 any society formed for promotion of literature, science, fine arts, diffusion of useful knowledge or political education or for charitable purposes may be registered as society under Act. Minimum number of persons required to form a society is seven. Memorandum of association in which names of founder-members and objects of society are stated may be filed with Registrar. Copy of rules of society, as amended from time to time, must also be filed. Payment of fee is required upon registration, and annual list of members must also be filed.

Advantages of registration as a society are as follows: (a) Members of association may sue or be sued as a society in name of president, chairman, trustees or such other persons as are appointed for purpose; (b) judgment may be passed by or against

ASSOCIATIONS . . . *continued*
society and not against representative person in his private capacity nor against his personal property; (c) society has power to sue any member; (d) society has power to alter, extend or abridge its objects; (e) it is exempt from payment of certain taxes under Indian Income Tax Act 1961.

Dissolution.—Three-fifths of total membership of society must vote for society to be validly dissolved. In certain cases, government consent is required. No member may receive any profit from society's assets, which latter cannot be distributed among members; but assets may be given to some other society. Society may also be wound up as "unregistered association" under §582 of Companies Act, 1956.

For Trade Unions refer to topic Industrial and Labour Laws.

ATTACHMENT:

Code of Civil Procedure V of 1908, Order 21, Rules 41-57 provide for attachment of property.

Where decree is for payment of money, decree holder may apply to court for an order that: (a) Judgment debtor or (b) any officer of corporation, or (c) any other person be orally examined as to whether any or what debts are owing to judgment debtor and whether judgment debtor has any and what other property or means of satisfying decree; and court may make an order for attendance and examination of such judgment debtor, or officer or other person and for production of any books or documents.

Where decree for payment of money has remained unsatisfied for period of 30 days, Court may, on application of decree-holder and without prejudice to its power under sub-rule (1), by order requiring judgment-debtor or, where judgment-debtor is corporation, any officer thereof, to make affidavit stating particulars of assets of judgment-debtor.

In case of disobedience of any order made under sub-rule (2), Court making order, or any Court to which proceeding is transferred, may direct that person disobeying order be detained in civil prison for term not exceeding three months unless before expiry of such term Court directs his release. (Rule 41).

Where decree directs an enquiry as to rent or mesne profits or any other matter, property of judgment debtor may, before amount due from him has been ascertained, be attached as in case of an ordinary decree for payment of money. (Rule 42).

Where property to be attached is movable property other than agricultural produce in possession of judgment debtor, attachment shall be made by actual seizure and attaching officer shall keep property in his own custody or in custody of one of his subordinates and shall be responsible for due custody thereof, provided that when property seized is subject to speedy and natural decay or when expense of keeping it in custody is likely to exceed its value, attaching officer may sell it at once. (Rule 43).

Where property to be attached is agricultural produce, attachment shall be made by affixing copy of warrant of attachment (a) Where such produce is a growing crop, on land on which such crop is sown or (b) where such produce has been cut or gathered on threshing floor or place for trading out grain or like or fodder stack on or in which it is deposited; and another copy on outer door or on some conspicuous part of house in which he carries on business or personally works for gain or in which he is known to have last resided or carried on business or personally worked for gain; and produce shall thereupon be deemed to have passed into possession of court. (Rule 44).

Where agricultural produce is attached, court shall make such arrangements for custody thereof as it may deem sufficient and for purpose of enabling court to make such arrangement, every application for attachment of a growing crop shall specify time at which it is likely to be fit to be cut or gathered. (Rule 45).

Subject to such conditions as may be imposed by court in this behalf either in order of attachment or in any subsequent order, judgment debtor may tend, cut, gather and store produce and do any other act necessary for maturing or preserving it; and if judgment debtor fails to do all or any of such acts, decree holder may with permission of court and subject to like conditions do all or any of them either by himself or by any person appointed by him in this behalf and costs incurred by decree holder shall be recoverable from judgment debtor as if they were included in or formed part of decree.

Agricultural produce attached as a growing crop shall not be deemed to have ceased to be under attachment or to require re-attachment merely because it has been severed from soil.

Where an order for attachment of growing crop has been made at a considerabe time before crop is likely to be fit to be cut or gathered, court may suspend execution of order for such time as it thinks fit and may in its discretion make a further order prohibiting removal of crop pending execution of order of attachment.

Growing crop which from its nature does not admit of being stored shall not be attached under this rule at any time less than 20 days before time at which it is likely to be fit to be cut or gathered. (Rule 45).

In case of (a) Debt not secured by negotiable instrument or (b) share in capital of corporation or (c) other movable properties not in possession of judgment debtor except property deposited in or in custody of any court, attachment shall be made by written order prohibiting (1) In case of debt, creditor from recovering debt and debtor from making payment thereof until further order of court; (2) in case of shares, person in whose name share may be standing from transferring same or receiving any dividend thereon; (3) in case of other movable property except as aforesaid, person in possession of same from giving it over to judgment debtor. (Rule 46).

Copy of such order shall be affixed on some conspicuous part of courthouse and another copy be sent, in case of debt, to debtor; in case of share, to proper officer of corporation; in case of other movable property (except as aforesaid), to person in possession of same.

Debtor prohibited under (1) above may pay amount of debt into court and such payment shall discharge him as effectually as payment to parties entitled to receive same.

Where property to be attached consists of share or interest of judgment debtor in movable property belonging to him and another as co-owners, attachment shall be made by notice to judgment debtor prohibiting him from transferring share or interest or charging it in any way. (Rule 47).

Where property to be attached is salary or allowance of a servant of (1) Government or (2) railway company or (3) local authority, court, whether or not judgment debtor or disbursing officer is within local limits of court's jurisdiction, may order that amount shall, subject to provisions of §60 be withheld from such salary or allowance either in one payment or by monthly instalments as court may direct; and upon notice of order to such officer as appropriate Government may by notification in Official Gazette appoint in this behalf.

Where such salary or allowance is to be disbursed within local limits to which Code extends, officer or other person whose duty it is to disburse same shall withhold and remit to court amount due under order or by monthly instalments. Where such salary or allowance is to be disbursed beyond limits of Code, officer or other person within limits whose duty it is to instruct disbursing authority regarding amount of salary or allowance to be disbursed, shall remit to court amount due under order, or monthly instalment, and shall direct disbursing authority to reduce aggregate of amounts from time to time to be disbursed by aggregate of amounts from time to time remitted to court. (Rule 48, sub-rule 1).

Where attachable proportion of such salary or allowance is already being withheld and remitted to court in pursuance of previous and unsatisfied order of attachment, officer appointed by Government in this behalf shall forthwith return subsequent order to court issuing it with full statement of all particulars of existing judgment. (Rule 48, sub-rule 2).

Every order made under this rule unless it is returned in accordance with provisions of sub-rule 2 shall without further notice or other process bind appropriate Government, or railway company or local authority while judgment debtor is within Code limits, and while he is beyond Code limits if he is in receipt of any salary or allowances payable out of revenues of Central or a State Government, or funds of railway company doing business in India, or local authority in India; and appropriate Government or railway company or local authority shall be liable for any sum paid in contravention of this Rule. (Rule 48, sub-rule 3).

Save as otherwise provided by this rule, property belonging to partnership shall not be attached or sold in execution of decree other than decree against firm, or against partners in firm as such. (Rule 49, sub-rule 1).

Court may, on an application of holder of decree against partner, make order charging interest of such partner in partnership property and profits with payment of amount due under decree and may, by same or subsequent order, appoint a receiver of share of such partner in profits (whether declared or accruing) and of any other money which may be coming to such partner in respect of partnership, and direct accounts and enquiries and make an order for sale of such interest or other orders as may have been directed or made if a charge had been made in favour of decree holder by such partner, or as circumstances of case may require. (Rule 49, sub-rule 2).

Remaining partners are at liberty to redeem interest charged, or in case of sale being directed, to purchase same. (Rule 49, sub-rule 3).

Every application for order under sub-rule 2 shall be served on judgment debtor and on his partners or such of them as are within India. (Rule 49, sub-rule 4).

Every application made by any partner of judgment debtor under sub-rule 3 shall be served on decree holder and on judgment debtor and on such of other partners as do not join in application and as are within India. (Rule 49, sub-rule 5).

Service under sub-rule 4, or 5, shall be deemed to be service on all partners and all orders made on such applications shall be similarly observed. (Rule 49, sub-rule 6).

Where a decree has been passed against a firm, execution may be granted (a) Against any property of partnership; (b) against any person who has appeared in his own name under Rule 6 or 7 of Order 30, or who has admitted on pleadings that he is, or who has been adjudged to be, a partner; (c) against any person who has been individually served as a partner with a summons and has failed to appear, provided that nothing in this sub-rule affects or limits provision of Sec. 247, Indian Contract Act. (Rule 50, sub-rule 1).

Where decree holder claims to be entitled to cause decree to be executed against any person other than such a person as is referred to in sub-rule 1 clauses (b) and (c) as being a partner in firm, he may apply to court which passed decree for leave and where liability is not disputed such court may grant such leave or where liability is disputed may order liability of such person to be tried and determined. (Rule 50, sub-rule 2).

Where liability of any person has been tried and determined under sub-rule 2, order made thereon has same force and is subject to same conditions as to appeal or otherwise as if it were a decree. (Rule 50, sub-rule 3).

Save as against any property of partnership, decree against a firm shall not release, render liable or otherwise affect any partnership therein unless he has been served with a summons to appear and answer. (Rule 50, sub-rule 4).

Where property is a negotiable instrument, not deposited in court, nor in custody of public officer, attachment shall be made by actual seizure and instrument shall be brought into court and held subject to further orders of court. (Rule 51).

Where property to be attached is in custody of any court or public officer, attachment shall be made by a notice to such court or officer requesting that such property and any interest or dividend becoming payable thereon may be held subject to further orders of court from which notice is issued. Provided that where such property is in custody of court, any question of title or priority arising between decree holder and any other person, not being judgment debtor, claiming to be interested in such property by virtue of any assignment, attachment or otherwise, shall be determined by such court. (Rule 52).

Where property to be attached is a decree, either for payment of money or for sale in enforcement of a mortgage or charge, attachment shall be made: (a) If decrees were passed by same court, then by order of such court; and (b) if decree sought to be attached was passed by another court, then by issue to such other court of notice by court which passed decree sought to be executed, requesting such other court to stay execution of its decree unless and until: (1) court which passed decree sought to be executed cancels notice; or (2) holder of decree sought to be executed or his judgment debtor applies to court receiving such notice to execute its own decree. (Rule 53, sub-rule 1).

Where court makes an order under clause a of sub-rule 1 or receives an application under subhead 2 of clause b of said sub-rule, it shall on application of creditor who has attached decree or his judgment debtor, proceed to execute attached decree and apply net proceeds in satisfaction of decree sought to be executed. (Rule 53, sub-rule 2).

Holder of a decree sought to be executed by attachment of another decree of nature specified in sub-rule 1 shall be deemed to be representative of holder of attached

See Topical Index in front part of this volume.

ATTACHMENT . . . *continued*

decree and to be entitled to execute such attached decree in any manner lawful for holder thereof. (Rule 53, sub-rule 3).

Where property to be attached in execution of decree is a decree other than a decree of nature referred to in sub-rule 1, attachment shall be made by notice by court which passed decree sought to be executed to holder of decree sought to be attached prohibiting him from transferring or charging same in any way; and where such decree has been passed by any other court also by sending to such other court a notice to abstain from executing decree sought to be attached until such notice is cancelled by court from which it was sent. (Rule 53, sub-rule 4).

Holder of decree attached under this rule shall give court executing decree such information and aid as may reasonably be required. (Rule 53, sub-rule 5).

On application of holder of decree sought to be excuted by attachment of another decree, court making an order of attachment under this rule shall give notice of such order to judgment debtor bound by decree attached and no payment or adjustment of attached decree made by judgment debtor in contravention of such order after receipt of notice thereof, either through court or otherwise, shall be recognised by any court so long as attachment remains in force. (Rule 53, sub-rule 6).

Attachment of immovable property: (1) Where property is immovable, attachment shall be made by order prohibiting judgment-debtor from transferring or charging property in any way, and all persons from taking any benefit from such transfer or charge, such order shall take effect, where there is no consideration for such transfer or charge, from date of such order, and where there is consideration for such transfer or charge, from date when such order came to knowledge of person to whom or in whose favour property was transferred or charged.

Order shall also require judgment-debtor to attend Court on specified date to take notice of date to be fixed for settling terms of proclamation of sale.

Copies of order shall also be forwarded to Collector with request that appropriate entries showing attachment levied on property may be caused to be made in revenue records, city survey records or village panchayat records as may be required in particular case.

Order shall be proclaimed at some place on or adjacent to such property by beat of drum or other customary mode, and copy of order shall be affixed on conspicuous part of property and then upon conspicuous part of court-house, and also, where property is land paying revenue to Government, in office of Collector of the District in which land is situated, and also, where property is situated within Cantonment limits, in office of Local Cantonment Board and Military Estates Officer concerned, and, where property is land situated in village, also in office of Gram Panchayat, if any, having jurisdiction over that village. (Rule 54).

Where (a) Amount decreed with costs and all charges and expenses resulting from attachment of any property are paid into court; or (b) satisfaction of decree is otherwise made through court or certified to court; or (c) decree is set aside or reversed, attachment shall be deemed to be withdrawn and in case of immovable property, withdrawal shall, if judgment debtor so desires, be proclaimed at his expense and copy of proclamation shall be affixed in manner prescribed by last preceding rule. (Rule 55).

Where property attached is current coin or currency notes, court may at any time during continuance of attachment direct that such coin or notes or a part thereof sufficient to satisfy decree be paid over to party entitled under decree to receive same. (Rule 56).

Where any property has been attached in execution of a decree but, by reason of decree holder's default, court is unable to proceed further with application for execution, it shall either dismiss application or for any sufficient reason adjourn proceedings to a future date. Upon dismissal of such application, attachment shall cease. (Rule 57).

ATTORNEYS AND ADVOCATES:

The High Courts at Bombay, Calcutta and Madras exercise Original Civil Jurisdiction. Original Civil Jurisdiction of the High Court at Bombay extends to Greater Bombay. Exercise of Original Civil Jurisdiction comprises all civil suits amount in which exceeds Rs. 50,000, and applications, petitions and Writs and also comprises Admiralty and Vice-Admiralty suits and proceedings, Insolvency and Company winding-up business, Testamentary and Intestate matters, Land Acquisition References, References and applications under Income Tax Act, Wealth Tax Act, Gift Tax Act, Sales Tax Act, Customs Act, Central Excise and Salt Act, Gold Control Act, etc.

Attorneys.—Solicitors, also referred to as attorneys, are advocates who further qualify through Solicitors' Examination (now only conducted by The Bombay Incorporated Law Society under aegis of Bombay High Court). Solicitors mainly are in Bombay and Calcutta (Madras having abolished "dual system"). Broadly stated attorneys are well versed in non-litigious commercial law practice such as corporate law, international funding and financial transactions, foreign investment, intellectual property rights, environmental laws, taxation acts, shipping law, etc. Solicitors of Bombay High Court have right to practice in High Court as Advocates on Record and also as Advocates on Record in Supreme Court of India on their completing five years as Advocates. Each High Court has own procedure to admit Advocates on Record to practice. Further information about solicitors enrolled in Bombay and Calcutta respectively may be obtained from Bombay Incorporated Law Society, High Court Annexe, Bombay 400 001 and The Law Society, High Court, Calcutta 700 001.

Advocates.—Advocates Act XXV of 1961 governs all matters regarding Advocates in all States of India. Dual system of Solicitors and Advocates prevailing, on original side of Bombay & Calcutta High Courts has been abolished since 1976.

General.—Act envisages a single class of practitioners at Bar of all States of India, namely advocates. It also envisages Common Roll of Advocates for whole of India (§20) whereby advocate registered on Roll of Bar Council of one State would be entitled to practice in every State in India. High Courts of various states have framed rules for purposes of advocates "acting" in causes. As general rule advocate registered with Bar Council of one state cannot "act" in cause in another state but he can appear in any cause if he is instructed by advocate registered in such other state.

Persons Who May be Advocates.—Barristers who have been called to Bar of England or of Scotland before Dec. 31, 1967 may be enrolled as advocates of any State Bar Council on payment of necessary fees. Members of foreign bars may also be allowed to appear with permission of Chief Justice in particular cases. To qualify as advocate in India today, candidates must obtain law degree of Indian University (§§24 and 28) and thereafter, upon payment of necessary fees and obtaining Sanad (Registration Certificate) will be enrolled as advocates of State High Court and would then be entitled to practice in any of High Courts or subordinate courts of that State.

Citizenship and Other Requirements.—It is not necessary to be citizen of India to be enrolled as advocate. Citizen of any country which permits duly qualified Indian citizen to practice in its courts is entitled to be enrolled as advocate. (§24). Advocates must be not only majors (i.e., over 18 years of age) but also have completed 21 years. (§24).

As to Advocates on record of Supreme Court, they must make application to Supreme Court to be enrolled as Advocates and to "act" in Supreme Court and admission is governed by Rules made by Supreme Court. Any advocate enrolled in any of High Courts is entitled as of right to appear in Supreme Court without making any special application.

The tendency in the country now is to have a uniform or integrated Bar for the whole of India. As stated above, the High Courts of Maharashtra and Calcutta are the only Courts in India which exercise Original Civil Jurisdiction and are thus the only Courts where the dual system, viz., an Advocate being instructed by an Attorney, still prevails in practice. Frequently, advocate, instead of being instructed by attorney, is instructed by advocate on record. All other High Courts exercising Appellate Jurisdiction, that is, hearing of appeals and revision applications from all Courts subordinate to High Court in State have what is known as unitary system where Advocate can appear by himself without being instructed by anyone else. As matter of practice, however, in every important appeal there is always senior and junior Advocate and costs of two Advocates are generally allowed to successful litigant against his opponent. Details of admission requirements may be obtained from Bar Councils of relevant States (for Maharashtra and Goa—The Bar Council, High Court Annexe, Bombay 400 001).

BILLS AND NOTES:

Law relating to issue and negotiation of bills and notes, i.e., promissory notes, bills of exchange and cheques has been codified by Negotiable Instrument Act 1881. This Act like other Indian statutes relating to mercantile transactions is based on English Common Law. Promissory note is required to be in writing, containing unconditional undertaking of maker who signs it, to pay certain sum of money only, to certain person or his order, or to bearer of note. (§4). Section 31 of Reserve Bank of India Act 1934 places restriction on issue of bills and notes payable to bearer on demand; though cheques, drafts, and hundis which are payable to bearer on demand may be drawn on person's account with banker, shroff or agent. Section further prohibits issue of bearer promissory note except by Bank or Central Government. Bill of exchange differs from promissory note in that it contains unconditional order directing certain person to pay certain sum of money only. Cheque is a bill of exchange payable on demand and is drawn on a bank. (§6). All indigenous negotiable instruments in vernacular languages are termed as "hundi." Hundi is subject to local usages and is unaffected by provisions of Act. Bill of exchange is accepted by drawee by signing his assent hereon and delivering it or giving notice of his assent, and thereupon his liability accrues on bill. Bills and notes must be supported by consideration (for consideration see topic Contracts). Bill of exchange must be presented for acceptance when it is payable, after sight. Promissory note payable at certain period after sight must be presented to maker for acceptance. In no other cases is presentment for acceptance necessary. Cheques, being payable on demand, no presentment for acceptance is necessary. Bills and notes payable to bearer are negotiable by delivery while those payable to order are negotiable by endorsement and delivery. Such bills and notes may be further negotiated unless right of negotiation is restricted or excluded. They cannot be negotiated only for part of sum appearing due thereon. Indorser of bills and notes becomes liable thereon unless he expressly excludes his liability. Promissory notes and bills of exchange (not cheques) should be stamped in accordance with Indian Stamp Act. An unstamped instrument is not admissible in evidence.

Days of Grace.—Bills and notes not payable on demand, at sight or on presentment, are at maturity on third day after day on which they are expressed to be payable. Provisions relating to maturity and days of grace are contained in §§22 to 25. If day on which instrument matures is public holiday as defined it shall be deemed to be due on next preceding business day.

Special Requirements (re Consideration).—Bills and notes must be supported by consideration (see topic Contracts). If there is no consideration or if it subsequently fails, no obligation of payment is created between parties to transaction. But if such party has transferred instrument to holder for consideration such holder and every subsequent holder may recover amount due on instrument; §§44 and 45 provide for proportionate reduction of liability under instrument in case of part failure of consideration which consists of cash or kind. It is presumed, until contrary is proved that instrument was made, drawn, accepted, indorsed, negotiated or transferred for consideration.

Compensation.—§117 lays down rules for payment of compensation to holder or indorser in case of dishonour of bills or notes. Holder is entitled inter alia to expenses properly incurred in presenting, noting and protesting it while indorser is inter alia entitled to expenses caused by dishonour and nonpayment.

Summary of Main Provisions of Act.—Person capable of contracting may bind himself by being party to instrument but minor may bind all parties except himself. Corporation cannot be party to instrument unless it is so empowered under law. (§26). Person may bind himself by duly authorised agent. Agent who indicates clearly that he signs as an agent does not render himself personally liable. Legal representative of deceased person who signs, is personally liable unless he restricts his liability to extent of assets received by him. §§30 to 38 deal with liability of parties to instrument, e.g., drawer, drawee, maker and acceptor. §58 deals with rights of possessor or indorsee of lost instrument or one obtained by offence or fraud or unlawful consideration.

Chapter IX lays down manner in which dishonoured bills and notes may be noted and protested. Noting and protest of dishonoured instrument is not necessary under Act, but there are certain advantages in noting and protest. Foreign bills of exchange

BILLS AND NOTES . . . *continued*
must be protested for dishonour if such protest is required by laws of place where drawn. (§104).

Chapter XVI deals with foreign instruments. In absence of contract to contrary, liability of maker or drawer of instrument is determined by law of place where it is made or drawn, and liability of acceptor or indorser by law of place where instrument is payable. Law of place where instrument is payable determines what is dishonour and whether such notice is necessary. §104 deals with protest of foreign bills of exchange. If foreign instrument is made, drawn, accepted or indorsed outside India but in accordance with Indian law, then any subsequent acceptance or indorsement made in India would not be invalidated by fact that agreement evidenced by such instrument is invalid according to law of foreign country concerned.

This is in nature of exception to general principle that person cannot give better title than what he has. Thus, person who finds lost instrument gets no title to it. So is case where person obtains instrument by theft or fraud, for unlawful consideration, or forges instrument. However, except in case of forgery, possessor or indorsee who is holder in due course or claims through any person who is holder in due course is entitled to receive amount due under instrument.

Where cheque payable to order purports to be endorsed by payee, bank is discharged by payment in due course even though signature of payee may have been forged. (§85). Section however gives no protection to banker when drawer's signature on cheque is forged and if any payment is made pursuant to such cheque, banker cannot debit customer's account.

Prosecution For Dishonour.—(§§138-142). Person who draws cheque on bank account maintained by him is deemed to have committed offence and shall be punished by imprisonment for term extending to one year and/or fine extending to twice amount of cheque, if such cheque is dishonoured: (i) For insufficiency of funds, or (ii) exceeding arrangements with bank, (iii) cheque presented for payment within six months from date on which it was drawn or within period of validity of cheque, whichever is earlier, (iv) payee or holder of cheque, within 15 days of dishonour, makes written demand on drawer of cheque and (v) drawer of cheque fails to make payment within 15 days of receipt of notice. If cheque is drawn by company every person in charge of and responsible for conduct of business of company is deemed guilty unless such person proves that offence of dishonour was committed without his knowledge or he had exercised all due diligence to prevent commission of offence. *Note:* (i) company includes a firm, (ii) prosecution must be commenced within one month by written complaint to competent Magistrate, (iii) in such prosecution it is not open to drawer to set up defence that at time of issuing cheque he had no reason to believe that cheque would be dishonoured.

Conflict of Laws.—See topic Contracts.

CHATTEL MORTGAGES:

See topics Contracts; Corporations or Companies.

Transfer of Property Act referes to mortgages of immovable property and Indian Contract Act refers to pledges of moveable property. Neither Act deals with mortgages of moveable property. It has been held that under Indian Law there can be valid mortgage of moveables (in India). Such mortgage when not accompanied by delivery of possession is still operative save and except against bona fide purchasers without notice. Mortgagee of movable property is entitled to decree for sale just as much as mortgagee of immovable property. Mortgagee of movable property in possession has right to sell property without intervention of Court, if after proper notice mortgagee fails to pay mortgage money.

CODES:

See topics Law Reports, Codes, Etc.; Statutes.

COLLISIONS: See topic Shipping.

COMMERCIAL REGISTER:

Companies Act 1956 provides for registration of companies (see topic Corporations or Companies) and Partnership Act for registration of partnership firms (see topic Partnership). There is no statutory requirement in India for businessmen to be registered on a commercial register.

CONSTITUTION AND GOVERNMENT:

India is Sovereign Socialist Secular Democratic Republic within Commonwealth of Nations formerly known as British Commonwealth.

The Constitution of India is a written one, abopted and enacted by an elected Constituent Assembly with the declared object of securing to all its citizens justice, social, economic and political; liberty of thought, expression, belief, faith and worship, equality of status and opportunity, and fraternity assuring dignity of individual and unity and integrity of nation. It came into force on 26th Jan. 1950. It is elaborate and comprehensive document containing 415 articles divided into 24 parts and 10 Schedules.

Indian Union is Union of 25 States and seven Centrally administered Union Territories.

Main Features of the Constitution.—The Constitution has both federal and unitary features. It provides for autonomy of the Constituent States and division of powers and responsibilities between the Union and the States. Though there is such a division of powers there are provisions for control by the Union both over the administration and legislation of the States. The Constitution even empowers the Union to entrust its executive functions to a State by its consent (Art. 258) and a State to entrust its executive functions to the Union (Art. 258A).

During normal times the federal features of the Constitution prevail but in emergencies the Constitution enables the Government at the centre to assume powers and to exercise controls which only a unitary system of Government can do. In normal times the Union Executive is entitled to give directions to the State Governments in regard to specified matters only (Art. 257) but when a proclamation of emergency is made by President, power of Union Executive to give directions extends to all matters. Constitution takes care to provide for unity in basic matters which are essential to maintain unity of country namely (a) a single judiciary, (b) uniformity in fundamental civil and criminal laws and (c) common all-India Services.

Part I of the Constitution declares that India shall be Union of States and that Indian Parliament may by law add or form new States and alter areas, boundaries or names of existing States.

Citizenship.—The subject of citizenship is dealt with in Part II. There is only one citizenship for the whole of India—the Indian Citizenship. There is no State Citizenship. Every person who at commencement of Constitution had his domicile in India and who was born in India, or either of whose parents was born in India, or who had been ordinarily resident in India for not less than five years immediately preceding such commencement, would be citizen of India. (Art. 5). Art. 8 provides for citizenship by registration of persons of Indian origin residing outside India.

Article 11 gives power to Parliament to make provision regarding all matters relating to citizenship. Accordingly Parliament has passed an Act called the "Citizenship Act, 1955" which supplements the provisions of the Constitution. It provides that Citizenship may be acquired by (a) birth, (b) descent, (c) registration, (d) naturalisation and (e) integration of territory, and may be lost by (a) renunciation. (b) voluntary acquisition by an Indian citizen of citizenship of another Sovereign State and (c) deprivation by order of the Central Government. The Act makes special provision for Commonwealth citizenship and provides that every person who is a citizen of any of the Commonwealth Countries, would by virture of that citizenship have the status of Commonwealth Citizenship in India.

Fundamental Rights.—Part III of Constitution is an important Part and deals with fundamental rights. Article 13 as it originally stood declared all laws inconsistent with or in derogation of the fundamental rights, void. By 24th Amendment Act, Art. 13 has been amended, by which this Article will not apply to any amendment made in Constitution under Art. 368, which deals with procedure for Amendment of Constitution.

The fundamental rights conferred by the Constitution are:

(1) Right to equality (Arts. 14 to 18);
(2) Right to freedom (Arts. 19 to 22);
(3) Right against exploitation (Arts. 23 and 24);
(4) Right to freedom of religion (Arts. 25 to 28);
(5) Cultural and educational rights (Arts. 29 and 30);
(6) Certain rights in relation to property (Arts. 31A and 31B). Right to hold property which was formerly available under Arts. 19(1)(f) and 31 has ceased to be fundamental right by Constitution 44th Amendment Act, 1978 and same is now, under Art. 300A, one of constitutional rights;
(7) Right to constitutional remedies (Arts 32 to 35).

Some of the fundamental rights are available only to Citizens, viz.: (1) protection against discrimination on grounds only of religion, race, caste, sex or place of birth (Art. 15); (2) equality of opportunity in matters of public employment (Art. 16); (3) freedom of speech, assembly, association, movement, residence, property and profession (Art. 19); (4) cultural and educational rights of minorities (Arts. 29, 30).

Other fundamental rights can be claimed by all persons, citizens or foreigners.

In order to secure social equality conferment of titles by States has been abolished. (Art. 18).

Property.—Right to property is not fundamental right and property may be acquired by competent authorities in exercise of powers statutorily conferred. Quantum of moneys awarded on such acquisition is not justiciable except on grounds specified if acquisition is under Land Acquisition Act.

Limitations on Fundamental Rights.—It may be mentioned that the fundamental rights are not absolute. They are subject to limitations if (a) the Security of the State, (b) public order, (c) decency and morality, (d) friendly relations with foreign States so require. Thus there can even be preventive detention in the interest of the security of the State both in normal times as well as in times of emergency.

In order to adequately protect fundamental rights and make them effective, Constitution has conferred on Supreme Court of India which is apex court in hierachy of Indian judiciary, concurrently with High Courts of States, power to grant effective remedies in shape of issue of Writs of Habeas Corpus, Mandamus, Prohibition, Quo Warranto and Certiorari whenever such rights are violated. Hence person whose fundamental right is violated or interfered with can apply either to Supreme Court under Art. 32 or to High Court under Art. 226 for issue of appropriate writ without filing suit.

Preventive detention is permissible under special statutes. Strict compliance by authorities with terms of such special statutes is mandatory. Where detention is irregular, courts will interfere by issue of high prerogative writs under constitution.

The Fundamental Rights can be suspended in an emergency declared by the President.

Directive Principles of State Policy.—The Constitution lays down certain principles, which Art. 37 declares to be fundamental in the governance of the country and which it shall be the duty of the State (i.e., the Government and Parliament of India and the Government and the legislature of each State) to apply in making laws. These directive principles, unlike fundamental rights, are not justiciable. They embody the aims and aspirations of the State. Most of these directive principles are intended to help in establishing economic and social democracy and guide the State, which aims at being a "Welfare State," to secure and protect "a social order in which justice, social, economic and political shall inform all the institutions of the national life" (Art. 38). Part IV of the Constitution accordingly requires the State to direct its policy towards securing:

(a) adequate means of livelihood for citizens (Art. 39[a]);
(b) control and distribution of material resources of the community so as best to subserve the common good (Art. 39[b]);
(c) that the operation of the economic system does not result in concentration of wealth and means of production to the common detriment (Art. 39[c]);
(d) equal pay for equal work (Art. 39[d]);
(e) living wage for workers (Art. 43);

See Topical Index in front part of this volume.

CONSTITUTION AND GOVERNMENT . . . *continued*

(f) right to work and to education (Art. 41);
(g) protection of child and youth against exploitation and against moral and material abandonment (Art. 39[f]);
(h) just and humane conditions of work and maternity relief (Art. 42);
(i) free and compulsory education for children up to 14 years (Art. 45);
(j) raising of the level of nutrition and the standard of living and improvement of public health (Art. 47);
(k) public assistance in case of unemployment, old age, sickness and disablement and in other case of undeserved want (Art. 41);
(l) conditions of work ensuring a decent standard of life and full enjoyment of leisure and of social and cultural opportunities (Art. 43);
(m) free legal aid (Art. 39A);
(n) participation of workers in management of industries (Art. 43A);
(o) protection and improvement of environment and safeguarding of forests and wildlife (Art. 48A).

Other important objectives laid down are:

(1) Establishment of uniform Civil Code for all citizens (Art. 44); (2) Organisation of village Panchayats (Committees) as units of self government (Art. 40); (3) Separation of the judiciary from the Executive (Art. 50); (4) Prohibition of the consumption of intoxicating drinks and drugs except for medicinal purposes (Art. 47); (5) Organisation of agricultural and animal husbandry and prohibition of slaughter of useful cattle (Art. 48); (6) Promotion of international peace and security, maintenance of just and honourable relations between nations; fostering respect for international law and treaty obligations; encouraging settlement of international disputes by arbitration (Art. 51[a] to [d]).

Although these principles are not legally enforceable in any Court, they have been recognised as guiding principles in matters of judicial interpretation. By Constitution (25th Amendment) Act 1971, new Article 31C was inserted, which provided, inter alia, that no law giving effect to provisions of Part IV of Constitution would be void on ground that it was inconsistent with fundamental rights relating to equality, freedom and property. It was further provided that if such law contained declaration that it was for giving effect to said provisions, it could not be called in question on ground that it did not do so. This Amendment Act has been upheld in substance by Supreme Court in case of His Holiness Keshavnanda Bharti v. The State of Kerala and another. However, Court struck down provision which prohibited Court from going into question whether law was in fact enacted to give effect to said provisions.

Fundamental Duties.—New chapter (Part IVA) on subject of Fundamental Duties was added in year 1977, which consists of ten duties.

The Union Executive.—

The President is the Executive head of the Indian Union. He is elected by an electoral college consisting of the elected members of both Houses of Parliament (i.e., Council of States and House of People), and elected members of Legislative Assemblies of States. (Art. 54). Executive powers of Union are vested in President. He has to exercise them in accordance with Constitution (Art. 53[1]) with aid and advice of Council of Ministers (Art. 74[1]). He is also Supreme Commander of defence forces. (Art. 53[2]).

He holds office for a term of five years and is eligible for re-election only once.

The Vice President is elected by the members of both Houses of Parliament assembled at a joint meeting. (Art. 66). He also holds office for a term of five years. (Art. 67). He has to act as the Ex-Officio Chairman of the Council of States. The Vice President acts as President and discharges the functions of the President during casual vacancy in the office of the President.

Powers of the President.—The President has, under the Constitution, the following powers:

(1) *Administrative Powers.*—These include the power to appoint and remove the Prime Minister and other Ministers of the Union, the Governor of a State, etc., and also to appoint the Judges of the Supreme Court and various High Courts after consulting prescribed constitutional functionaries as he may deem necessary (Arts. 124[2], 217[i]) and remove them on address of Parliament. All executive action of Union must be taken in name of President and all contracts and transfers of property made on behalf of Central Government must be expressed to be made by President.

(2) *Legislative Powers.*—All bills passed by the Parliament require the assent of the President before they become effective and he can withhold his assent to all bills other than money bills. He can issue ordinances which would have the same effect as Acts of Parliament when the Parliament is not sitting. He has the power of summoning and prorogation of the Houses of Parliament and to dissolve the House of the People. (Art. 85).

(3) *Emergency powers arising out of war or internal disturbance or failure of the Constitution:* The President may issue a proclamation of emergency for two months. This period can be extended by the Houses of Parliament. The proclamation would turn the federal constitution into a unitary one and the Parliament can then make laws for the whole of India and even in respect of matters which are within the exclusive jurisdiction of the States, and if a State Government cannot be carried on in accordance with the Constitution, the President may issue a proclamation and assume to himself all functions of the State and declare that the Powers of the State Legislature shall be exercised by or under the authority of Parliament. (Art. 356[1][a] and [b]). Such a proclamation will have to be approved by the Parliament. (Art. 356[3]).

(4) *Power of Pardon.*—The President can grant pardons, reprieves, respites or remissions of punishment to persons convicted by courts. (Art. 72).

(5) *Miscellaneous Powers.*—As the head of the Executive, the President has been vested by the Constitution with certain miscellaneous powers. For instance:

(a) Power to make rules and regulations relating to various matters;

(b) Power to give instructions to a Governor of a State to promulgate an ordinance, if it requires the previous sanction of the President (Art. 213[1]);

(c) He can refer any question of public importance for the opinion of the Supreme Court (Art. 143);

(d) He can appoint commissions to report on specific matters.

Council of Ministers.—Though all executive powers are vested in the President, the Constitution requires him to act as the constitutional head of the Executive and exercise his powers in accordance with the aid and advice of the Council of Ministers, with the Prime Minister as its head. The Prime Minister is appointed by the President; the other Ministers on the advice of the Prime Minister. The Council of Ministers is collectively responsible to the House of the People and all ministers must within six months of their appointment be members of either House of Parliament. See subhead The Union Legislature, infra.

The Attorney General.—The Constitution provides for an Attorney General of India to offer legal advice to the Union Government. He is appointed by the President and can be dismissed by the President alone.

Comptroller and Auditor-General of India.—There shall be Comptroller and Auditor-General of India to be appointed by President under Art. 148(1) and may be removed by impeachment. His duty is to be guardian of purse and to see that no part of it is spent without authority of Parliament.

The Union Legislature.—The Indian Parliament consists of the President and the two Chambers, viz., the Lower House known as the Lok Sabha (i.e., the House of the People) which represents the people of the entire country, and the Upper House known as the Rajya Sabha or the Council of States which represents the constitutent units. The Lok Sabha, or the House of the People, consists of not more than 525 members directly elected by the voters in the States (Art. 81[1][a]) and 20 to represent Union territories.

The Council of States consists of not more than 250 members, of whom 12 are nominated by the President from persons having special knowledge or practical experience in Literature, Science, Art and Social Service (Art. 80[1] and [3]); remainder representatives of States and Union territories. Representatives of States are elected by elected members of Legislative Assembly and representatives of Union territories are chosen in such manner as Parliament may by law prescribe (Art. 80).

The House of the People chooses two members of the House to be respectively Speaker and Deputy Speaker. The Vice President is the ex-officio Chairman of the Council of States. (Art. 89).

Bill, other than money or financial bill, may be introduced in either of Houses of Parliament (Art. 107[1]) and requires passage in both houses before it can be presented for President's assent. When a bill is passed in one House it is sent to other House. Latter may reject bill altogether in which case provisions regarding joint sitting of Houses may be applied by President. (Art. 108). When bill is passed by both Houses of Parliament either singly or at joint meeting it is presented to President for his assent. If he withholds his assent there is an end to bill. If he gives his assent bill becomes Act from date of his assent. President may return bill for reconsideration of Houses. If Houses pass bill with or without amendments it is presented to President for his assent after such reconsideration, in which case he has no power to withhold his assent. (Art. 111).

A money bill can be introduced only in House of People and not in Council of States. (Art. 109[1]). Council of States cannot reject money bill nor amend it. It must, within 14 days from date of its receipt, return bill to House of People with its recommendations. That House may either accept or reject all or any of recommendations.

Legislative Lists.—The Constitution contains three Legislative Lists in the Seventh Schedule. The first is called the "Union List" which enumerates under 97 heads, the subjects over which the Union Parliament has exclusive control. In this list are included such important matters as defense, external affairs, preventive detention, war and peace, citizenship, post and telegraphs, currency and banking, foreign loans, insurance, etc.

The second is called the "State List" and enumerates under 66 heads, the subjects over which the State Legislatures have exclusive control.

The third list, called the "Concurrent List," enumerates under 47 heads the subjects upon which both Union and State Legislatures can make laws.

In a conflict between Union and State laws on concurrent subjects, the Union Law prevails. (Arts. 251, 254).

In order to ensure harmony between Union and State, Constitution lays down that executive power of every State shall be so exercised as to ensure compliance with laws made by Parliament and is not to impede or prejudice executive power of Union. (Art. 256).

Inter-State Council.—President has power to appoint Inter-State Council for purpose of achieving inter-state co-ordination. Such Council would have power: (a) To inquire into and advise upon disputes between States; (b) to investigate and discuss subjects of common interest to Union and States; and (c) to make representations for better coordination of policy or action on any subject. (Art. 263).

State Executive.—Executive power of a State is vested in "Governor" and all executive actions in each State are taken in his name. Governors of States are appointed by President. Governors appoint Ministers, Advocate General of State and members of Public Service Commission of State. He has to assent to bills and has power to promulgate ordinances, but in practice all his powers are exercised by Ministers. Union Government represented by President consults State Government before choosing a Governor and Governor is usually chosen from outside State of which he is appointed Governor.

Council of Ministers.—Every State has a Council of Ministers led by the Chief Minister to advise the Governor in the exercise of his function except in regard to his discretionary powers. The Governor must choose as the Chief Minister the person who leads the majority party in the State Legislature, or to select the person who can in his opinion command a workable majority in the State Legislature. The other Ministers are appointed by the Governor on the advice of the Chief Minister. The State Chief Minister has a position somewhat equal to that of a Prime Minister inside his own State. He is the leader of the party in power and chooses the ministers.

Advocate General of the State.—The Constitution provides for the appointment of the Advocate General of a State. He is appointed by the Governor. (Art. 165[1]), [3]). He can attend legislative sessions and take part in discussions on matters in which

See Topical Index in front part of this volume.

CONSTITUTION AND GOVERNMENT . . . *continued*
expert legal knowledge is required. (Art. 177). His duty is to advise Government on legal matters pertaining to his State. (Art. 165[2]).

State Legislatures.—

Legislative Council.—In some of the States the legislature consists of two Houses, called the Legislative Assembly and the Legislative Council. In the rest, there is only one house, viz., the Legislative Assembly. (Art. 168). The Constitution provides for a simple procedure by which a State may abolish the Legislative Council or create one by a resolution of the Legislative Assembly of the State concerned, passed by a two-thirds majority of members present and voting, followed by an Act of Parliament. The membership of the Council is not to exceed one-third of the total number of members in the Legislative Assembly provided the total number shall in no case be less than 40. (Art 171). The members of the Legislative Council of a State are partly nominated and partly elected, $^{5}/_{6}$th of the total number being elected and $^{1}/_{6}$th nominated by the Governor: (1) One-third are to be elected by electorates consisting of members of Municipalities, District Boards and other local authorities in the State; (2) $^{1}/_{12}$th by the University Graduates and persons possessing equivalent qualifications; (3) $^{1}/_{12}$th by teachers in educational institutions within the State; (4) One-third by members of the Legislative Assembly from amongst persons who are not members of the Assembly; (5) The remainder are to be nominated by the Governor on the basis of their special knowledge and practical experience in respect of such matters as literature, science, art, co-operative movement and social service.

Legislative Assemblies.—The Legislative Assembly of each State is mainly composed of members chosen by direct election on the basis of adult suffrage from territorial constituencies. The Governor however has power to nominate such number of members of the Anglo-Indian Community as he deems fit, for the first 40 years from commencement of Constitution if they are inadequately represented in Assembly. (Art 333).

The duration of the Legislative Assembly is five years, but it may be dissolved sooner by the Governor and the term of five years may be extended in case of proclamation of emergency by the President of the Union.

The Legislative Assembly has its Speaker and Deputy Speaker and the Legislative Council its Chairman and Deputy Chairman. The Legislative procedure in a State Legislature having two chambers is broadly similar to that in Parliament except in certain respects.

So far as money bill is concerned Legislative Council has no power apart from making recommendations to Assembly for amendments or withholding bill for period of 14 days. Assembly may accept or reject such recommendations. (Art. 198). As regards other bills Council can only interpose some delay in passage of such bills for period not exceeding three months. If Council does not consent to bill Assembly sends it back to Council, but ultimately view of Assembly prevails. (Art. 197).

The position of the Legislative Council is weaker than the Council of States at the Centre. In case of disagreement between two Houses of the Union Parliament it is resolved by a joint sitting. There is no such provision for solving differences between the two houses of the State Legislature but the view of the Assembly prevails. After a bill is passed by the Houses of the Legislature it must go before the Governor who may give his assent to the bill in which case it becomes law at once. He may, in the case of a bill other than a money bill, return the bill for reconsideration to the House with his recommendation, but if the bill is again passed by the Legislature it would be incumbent upon the Governor to give his assent to the bill which will thereupon become law. The Governor may even reserve the bill for the consideration of the President. The Governor would be bound to do so where the law would derogate from the powers of the High Court of the State under the Constitution. (Art. 200).

Courts.—

Supreme Court of India which is highest legal tribunal of land consists of Chief Justice of India and not more than 25 other judges who are appointed by President. (Art. 124).

Supreme Court has: (a) Original jurisdiction (Arts. 32, 131, 143, 363); (b) appellate jurisdiction, (1) in constitutional matters (Arts. 132, 133), (2) civil matters (Art. 133), (3) criminal matters (Arts. 134, 136); (c) advisory jurisdiction (Arts. 143, 145).

High Courts in States.—There is a High Court for each State (Art. 214) consisting of Chief Justice and other judges as President may from time to time appoint. (Art. 216).

High Court has power: (a) To issue writs (Art. 226); (b) have superintendence over all courts and tribunals under it (Art. 227); (c) to withdraw cases to itself (Art. 228); (d) to appoint officers and servants of High Court (Art. 229); (e) to control subordinate courts (Art. 235).

Election Commission.—Part XV of Constitution deals with election. Election Commission consists of Chief Election Commissioner and other Election Commissioners all of whom shall be appointed by President. Chief Election Commissioner acts as Chairman of Election Commission. (Art. 324[2]).

Functions of Election Commission are: (a) Superintendence, direction and control of preparation of electoral rolls; (b) conduct of all elections to Parliament and to Legislature of every state; (c) of elections to offices of President and Vice President. (Art. 324[1]).

Election petitions are to be filed in High Court and an appeal to lie to Supreme Court.

Amendment of the Constitution.—The Constitution allows amendments to be made therein without much difficulty.

Alterations of certain provisions of the Constitution are declared by the Constitution itself as not to be deemed to be amendment of the Constitution. These provisions can be altered by the Union Parliament in the ordinary course by passing legislation by a simple majority. Apart from the provisions which relate to the federal scheme, hereinafter referred to, the other provisions of the Constitution may be amended by the Union Parliament without ratification of the amendment by State Legislatures, only by adopting the procedure prescribed by Art. 368.

Amendment.—From procedure laid down in Constitution for its amendment it could be said that Indian Constitution is partly flexible and partly rigid. Constitution provides for three methods of amendments of its provisions: (1) Certain provisions of Constitution can be amended by bare majority which is required for passing of any ordinary law. Amendments contemplated in Arts. 4, 169 and 240 fall within this method and they are specially excluded from purview of Art. 368 and procedure laid down in Art. 368 is not applicable to them; (2) all constitutional amendments other than those referred to in (1) above may be initiated by introduction of bill in either House of Parliament. When bill is passed in each House by majority of total membership of that house and by majority of not less than two-thirds of members of that House present and voting, it is presented to President for his assent. Upon receiving President's assent to bill, Constitution stands amended in accordance with terms of bill (Art. 368); (3) if Constitutional amendments mentioned in (2) above seek to make any changes in vital provision of Constitution regarding (a) manner of election of President (Arts. 54 and 55), (b) extent of executive power of Union (Arts. 73 and 162), (c) High Courts for Union Territories (Art. 241), (d) Union Judiciary (Ch. IV of Part V), (e) High Courts in State (Ch. V of Part VI), (f) legislative relation (Ch. I of Part XI), (g) any of list in Seventh Schedule, (h) representation of States in Parliament, or (i) provisions of Art. 368, amending bill shall also require to be ratified by Legislatures of not less than one-half of States by resolution to that effect passed by those Legislatures before Bill is presented to President for his assent (Art. 368).

Constitution has since its commencement been amended 59 times.

CONTRACTS:

Introduction.—Law of contract has been codified and is to be found in Indian Contract Act IX of 1872. Indian Contract Act is based on English common law on subject. Sale of Goods and Partnership are governed by separate statutes. See topics Sale of Goods; Partnership.

General Considerations.—Concepts of proposal, promise, consideration, voidable contract and void agreements, free consent, undue influence, fraud, misrepresentation and other similar concepts in Act are similar to those in English law. Unlike English common law, consideration may proceed from promisee or any other person. (§2[1][d]). Section 63 of Act which provides that promisee may dispense with or remit wholly or in part, performance of promise made to him, makes wide departure from English common law. Contract with minor is void under Indian law, and not voidable, as in England.

Agreements made by free consent of parties competent to contract, for lawful consideration with lawful object and not expressly declared to be void are valid contracts. (§10). Agreement, consent to which has been obtained by coercion, fraud, misrepresentation or undue influence, is voidable at option of party whose consent was so caused. Coercion may include unfair bargaining position or economic duress, particularly in contracts of employment. Under §23 of Act, consideration or object of an agreement is lawful unless it is forbidden by law or is of such a nature that if permitted, it would defeat provisions of any law or is fraudulent or involves or implies injury to person or property of another or court regards it as immoral or opposed to public policy. Inadequacy of consideration does not by itself avoid an agreement if consent was freely given by promisor but the inadequacy of consideration is taken into account by court in determining question whether consent was freely given. See, however, subhead When Writing Required, infra.

An agreement in restraint of the marriage of any person other than a minor is void. Similarly under §27 every agreement by which one is restrained wholly or partially, from exercising a lawful profession, trade or business of any kind is to that extent void. But one who sells the goodwill of a business may agree with the buyer to refrain from carrying on a similar business, within specified local limits provided such limits appear to the court reasonable, regard being had to the nature of the business. This section invalidates many agreements which may be held good under English common law.

Likewise an agreement in restraint of legal proceedings, is void. Wagering agreements are also void and no suit can be brought for recovering anything alleged to be won on any wager.

Where both parties (and not merely one party) are under mistake of fact essential to agreement, agreement is void. Mistake as to an Indian law will not make contract voidable. Mistake as to foreign law has same effect as mistake of fact.

Liability under joint contracts has been made joint and several and where two or more persons have made joint promise, release of one of such persons does not discharge other joint promisor. These sections are variation of rules of English law on subject.

Chapter V of Act deals with certain relations resembling those created by contract. For example, §70 in this chapter provides that where a person does anything for another not intending to do so gratuitously and such other person enjoys benefit thereof, latter is bound to make compensation to former. This section is considered to go far beyond English common law.

Breach.—Chapter VI of Act deals with consequences of breach of contract. On breach of contract, party in default is liable for loss or damage which naturally arose in usual course from breach or which parties knew likely to result from breach. Party entitled to compensation for breach is obliged to minimise or diminish loss or damage arising from breach, by means available to him, and he is entitled to receive reasonable compensation but not exceeding sum if any mentioned in contract as payable on breach. Measure of damages generally is difference between contract price and market price of goods at date of breach.

Excuses for Nonperformance.—Sections 51 to 58 deal with and set down circumstances in which party to contract may not perform his part of contract. Section 56 provides that agreement to do an impossible act is void. If act becomes impossible or unlawful subsequently, contract becomes void. But if party knew or could have known with reasonable diligence that obligation to be performed by him was impossible or unlawful, he must compensate other party for loss caused through nonperformance. Further, party who is himself responsible for frustrating event cannot take advantage of §56. War condition and strike of workers may, depending on special circumstances and nature of contract discharge parties to contract. Commercial impossibility, e.g., exorbitant rise in price of goods contracted to be supplied, will not determine contract. If time is of essence of contract, and party fails to do it within time, contract is voidable at instance of other party.

See Topical Index in front part of this volume.

CONTRACTS . . . *continued*

Sureties, Etc.—Chapter VIII of Act deals with subject of indemnity and guarantee, surety, principal debtor and creditor, surety's liability, continuing guarantee, discharge of surety, the law being substantially same as in England. Consideration is necessary to support a guarantee; anything done or any promise made for benefit of principal debtor is sufficient consideration for giving guarantee. Liability of surety is coextensive with that of principal debtor. Surety would be discharged by any variance (except variation to surety's benefit) in contract between principal debtor and creditor, without consent of surety, or by act or omission on part of creditor which would affect remedy of surety or if principal debtor is discharged or if creditor released security to extent or value thereof. Surety upon payment or performance of all that he is liable is vested with all rights of creditor and is entitled to benefit of security available to creditor. Guarantee obtained by misrepresentation or concealment of material circumstances renders guarantee invalid.

Bailments and Pledges.—Chapter IX of Act deals with bailments and pledges. Bailment is delivery of goods for some purpose on condition that goods would be returned when purpose is accomplished. Pledge is bailment of goods as security for payment of debt or performance of promise.

Bailor bound to disclose defects in goods otherwise he would be liable for damages. (§150). Bailee bound to take care of goods as ordinary man of prudence. (§151). Bailee making unauthorised use of goods is liable for damage to goods. (§152). Sections 155 to 157 deal with effect of mixture of goods by bailee with his goods. Increase or profit accruing from goods must be returned to bailor. Section 170 deals with liens of bailee who has rendered service involving exercise of labour and skill in respect of goods bailed. Under §171 of Act, bankers, factors, wharfingers, attorneys of High Court and policy brokers have right to retain as security for general balance of account, any goods bailed to them in absence of contract to contrary. Goods pledged cannot be retained for purpose other than for which they are pledged. (§174). If pledgor makes default in payment of debt or performance of promise, pledgee may either file suit or sell goods after giving notice and if sale proceeds are not sufficient, recover balance from pledgor. (§176).

Bonafide Purchasers.—The rights of persons acting in good faith with mercantile agents who are with the consent of owner in possession of goods or documents of title to goods have been protected under §178 of Act. This is exception to common law principle that no person can give better title than he himself has.

See topic Principal and Agent.

When Writing Required.—An agreement is not necessarily required to be in writing but if agreement is made without consideration and is made on account of natural love and affection between parties standing in near relation to each other then Act requires that it should be in writing and also registered under Indian Registration Act. Similarly agreement without consideration is valid if it is promise to compensate wholly or in part person who has already voluntarily done something for promisor or something which promisor was legally compellable to do. If it is promise to pay wholly or in part debt which would otherwise have been time-barred, and is made without consideration, it is required to be in writing and signed by promisor. (§25).

Interest in Immovables.—Under the Indian Registration Act, all instruments of gifts of immovable property and all non-testamentary instruments purporting or operating to create, declare, assign, limit or extinguish, whether in present or in future, any right title and interest of the value of Rs. 100/—or more to or in immovable property must be registered with the Sub-Registrar of Assurances.

Applicable Law.—Principles of private International Law as practised in England are applied in India.

General rule is proper law of contract governs all matters of essential and formal validity, interpretation, construction, implementation and effect, but not capacity to contract. Proper law is law of country which parties intended contract to be governed by, provided intention was bonafide and legal; if no intention existed or could be implied from terms of contract, proper law is objectively determined as law of country with which contract has closest connection in fact. (see Dicey: Conflict of Laws).

Distributorships, Dealerships and Franchises.—See topic Principal and Agent.

See also topic Partnership.

COPYRIGHTS:

International Copyright.—India is signatory member of Berne Copyright Convention, and of Universal Copyright Convention (Geneva) which became effective here in Jan. 1958. (§§40-43, Indian Copyright Act, 1957).

Copyright in India was governed by Copyright Act 1914 which implemented English Copyright Act 1913 in British India, and is now goverened by Copyright Act XIV of 1957 which largely follows English Copyright Act 1956. (See England Law Digest.) Act provides for copyright office and appointment of Registrar and Deputy Registrar of Copyrights (at Education Ministry North Block, Secretariat, New Delhi) and Copyright Board. Registration is not compulsory (§45) but author in India may ask for registration by application in prescribed form and Registrar, after making due enquiries, enters particulars in Register (§45). Register is open to inspection (§47) and is prima facie evidence of particulars entered therein (§48). Copyright Board has certain powers similar to those of civil courts when trying a suit for infringement of copyright (§§74, 75); civil courts also have jurisdiction to grant all remedies such as injunction, damages, accounts etc. Registrar has powers to prevent importation of works constituting infringement of copyright in India. (§53).

Following Acts Constitute Breach of Copyright.—Any act which (1) infringes exclusive rights of owner; (2) permits public performance of copyrighted work constituting breach; (3) makes for sale, hire, or sells, or lets for hire or by way of trade displays or offers for sale or hire, or distributes either for purpose of trade or to such an extent as is prejudicial to owners of copyright, or exhibits in public by way of trade, or imports otherwise than for private and domestic use, any copies infringing copyrighted work. (§51). Certain acts do not constitute infringement. (§52). Copyright also exists in translations, performance rights and broadcasts.

To control audio and video piracy stringent provisions exist including displaying on record/cassette and container name and address of person making record/cassette, declaration that maker has obtained necessary licence or consent of owner of copyright etc. (§52A) and prescribing penalty by way of imprisonment up to term of three years and fine for contravening these provisions (§68A). Police officers are empowered to seize without warrant all copies of infringing work and plates used for making infringing copies.

CORPORATIONS OR COMPANIES:

(Companies Act, 1956 as am'd from time to time). *Note:* Substantial amendments are under consideration.

Government Supervision.—Government Officers who exercise supervision over corporations and companies, are Registrar of Companies and Regional Director of the Government of India, in each state, Department of Revenue and Company Law Board, Ministry of Finance. Companies Act, 1956 provides for various returns to be filed with and notices to be given to Registrar of Companies, such as return of allotment of shares, annual returns, notice regarding consolidation or division or increase of share capital etc. Registrar in each state acts in consultation with Regional Director of that state.

Act contains several sections which provide for obtaining of sanction or approval of Central Government, such as approval to increase number of directors of public company in cases where increase in number makes total number of directors more than 12, amendment of any provision relating to appointment or reappointment of managing or wholetime director. Such applications for approval or sanction must be made in certain matters to Registrar of Companies or Regional Director of State concerned and in other matters to Secretary, Company Law Board, Ministry of Finance, Department of Revenue and Company Law Board, New Delhi. Act also contains several provisions by which powers are conferred upon Company Law Board in respect of following, among other, matters: (a) Rectification of Register of Members, (b) restraining fraudulent persons from managing companies, (c) production of documents and evidence before inspector appointed under act, (d) granting of relief in cases of oppression and mismanagement, (e) conducting enquiry referred to it by government where there are circumstances suggesting (i) that any person concerned in conduct and management of affairs of company is or has been in connection therewith guilty of fraud, misfeasanse, persistent negligence or default in carrying out his obligations and functions under law or breach of trust; or (ii) that business of company is not or has not been conducted and managed by such person in accordance with sound business principles or prudent commercial practice; or (iii) that company is or has been conducted and managed by such person in manner which is likely to cause or has caused serious injury to interest of trade, industry or business to which such company pertains; or (iv) that business of company is or has been conducted or managed by such person with intent to defraud its creditors, members or any other persons or otherwise with fraudulent or unlawful purpose or in manner prejudicial to public interest. Powers are conferred on Company Law Board and also on Government in appropriate cases to remove from office any director or any other person concerned in conduct or management of affairs of company who is in breach of duties and in suitable cases, to appoint such number of persons as directors as it may think fit and necessary to effectively safeguard interests of company or its shareholders or public interest, in order to prevent oppression to any members of company or mismanagement thereof. Government may in fit case direct company to amend its articles of association to provide for adopting principle of proportional representation for appointment of directors to extent of at least two-thirds of total number of its directors, appointment to be made once in every three years and on such appointment being made, no change in board of directors shall be made by members or directors of company, unless change be confirmed by Government.

Central Government is also empowered to appoint person as public trustee to discharge functions and exercise rights and powers conferred on him by or under Act. Where any shares or debentures in company are held in trust by any person, trustee has to make declaration to public trustee and file copy thereof with company. Thereupon rights and powers exercisable, at any meeting of company or at any meeting of any class of members of company, by trustee as member of company shall cease to be exercisable by trustee as such member and shall become exercisable by public trustee. In order to enable public trustee to exercise rights and powers aforesaid he shall be entitled to receive and inspect all books and papers under Act, which member is entitled to receive and inspect. These provisions, however, are not applicable where trust is not created by any instrument in writing or even if it is by instrument in wiriting, trust money invested in shares or debentures does not exceed Rs. 100,000 or if it exceeds Rs. 100,000 does not exceed either Rs. 500,000 or 25% of paid up share capital of company, whichever is lower.

Company Supervision.—Is in board of directors. Subject to superintendence, control and direction of board of directors, a company can appoint a Managing or wholetime Director or a Manager to manage its business and affairs. Every public company with paid-up share capital of Rs. 1,00,00,000 or private company which is subsidiary of public company must have managing or whole-time director or manager.

See also subheads Directors, Officers, Subsidiaries, infra.

Purposes.—All commercial, trading and industrial purposes to extent authorised by Memorandum of Association. Any activities undertaken by company beyond objects set out in its Memorandum will be considered ultra vires and illegal. No change in memorandum of association can be made with respect to its purposes or objects, unless special resolution is passed by its members by three-fourths majority voting at general meetings of company in person or by proxy and unless such change or alteration is confirmed by Company Law Board, on petition duly made to it.

Name.—Every company must use the word "Limited" at the end of its name, except as next stated. As to an "Unlimited Company," see Stockholders' Liabilities, infra, item (a).

Kinds.—A Company having 50 members or less and, prohibiting issue of its shares to the public and restricting transfer of its shares is called a "Private" Company. All other companies are "Public" Companies, including those which now commonly known as "Section 43A Companies" (see subhead Subsidiaries, infra). "Private" Company must use words "Private Limited" at end of its name. No Company can be registered by name which Government considers undesirable or which is identical with or too nearly resembles existing Company. Company may change its name with

CORPORATIONS OR COMPANIES . . . *continued*
approval of Government and by Special Resolution passed by its members, which requires to be passed by three-fourth majority of votes, by show of hands or proxy, at General Meeting of Company.

See also subhead Subsidiaries, infra.

Term of Corporate Existence.—Perpetual.

Incorporators.—At least two persons in case of Private Company and seven in case of Public Company.

Prospectus.—Every company which intends to offer shares or debentures to public for subscription by issue of prospectus must compulsorily make application to one or more recognised Stock Exchanges for permission that shares and debentures be dealt with on Stock Exchange. See subhead Stockholders' Liabilities, item (c), infra.

Certificate or Articles of Incorporation.—Every Company must file a Memorandum of Association with the Registrar of Companies. It must be stamped and signed by the minimum number of members required to form it and must state:

(a) its name;

(b) the State (within India) in which its Registered Office is to be situate;

(c) the objects or purpose of the Company;

(d) that in case of a Company limited by shares, that the liability of its members is limited;

(e) the amount of its share capital and the division thereof into shares of a fixed amount.

There are Regulations prescribed by Act for management of public Company and are contained in Table "A" thereto. Company can, however, have its own "Regulations" which should conform to provisions of Act, and generally for sake of convenience most public Companies have their own Regulations which are embodied in their Articles of Association which must be registered with Registrar of Companies. Articles of Company must be stamped and signed by subscribers to its Memorandum and can be altered by Special Resolution of its members. Only one stamped copy of Memorandum and Articles of Association of Company need be filed and on registration thereof. Registrar issues Certificate that Company is incorporated.

Filing of Certificate or Articles.—The Certificate is not filed with the Registrar but is issued by him to the Company which has to preserve it forever. The Memorandum and Articles have to be filed with the Registrar as above.

Incorporation Tax or Fee.—Fee of about Rs. 9,000 is payable to Registrar for registration of company having share capital of Rs. 1,000,000. Fees increase on graduated scale up to maximum fee of Rs. 800,000. *Note:* Under relevant state laws stamp duty on Memorandum and Articles of Association (generally in proportion to authorised capital) is also payable.

Filing Fees.—Nominal fee not exceeding Rs. 120/—in any case has to be paid to Registrar for filing some formal papers.

Licence to Do Business.—A public Company cannot commence business or exercise any borrowing powers, unless:

(a) shares to be subscribed for in cash have been allotted to an amount not less in the whole than the minimum subscription. Minimum subscription means the amount stated in the Prospectus of a Company as the minimum amount which, in the opinion of the Directors, must be raised by the issue of share capital in order to provide for: (i) the purchase price of any property purchased or to be purchased by the Company, (ii) any preliminary expenses payable by the Company and commission for subscribing for shares, (iii) the repayment of any monies borrowed by the Company in respect of any of the foregoing matters, (iv) working capital, and (v) any other expenditure required for the purposes of the Company;

(b) every Director has paid for his shares in cash;

(c) no money is liable to be repaid to applicants for any shares offered for public subscription by reason of any failure to apply for, or to obtain, permission for the shares to be dealt in on any recognised Stock Exchange; and

(d) there has been filed with the Registrar of Companies a Declaration signed by one of directors or secretary that above clauses (a), (b) and (c) have been complied with. Before commencing business, Company must either file Prospectus or Statement in Lieu of Prospectus with Registrar of Companies.

For few industrial concerns, mentioned in Schedule to the Industries Development & Regulations Act (see topic Industries [Development and Regulation] Act) sanctions and licences have to be obtained from Central Government under that Act.

Organization.—Every public company must hold a statutory meeting within six months from date on which Certificate is issued to it by Registrar for commencing business, and a Statutory Report must be presented thereat setting out particulars as to shares allotted, share subscriptions and other amounts received by company, particulars of preliminary expenses incurred by it, particulars of its directors and secretary and certain other particulars. Every company must hold an annual general meeting in every financial year within 15 months of date of last annual general meeting (first annual general meeting being required to be held within 18 months from date of incorporation), for passing its balance-sheet and profit and loss account, declaring a dividend (if any), appointing directors in place of those retiring by rotation and appointing auditors and fixing their remuneration. Balance sheet and profit and loss account should relate to period beginning with day immediately after period for which account was last submitted and ending with day which shall not precede day of meeting by more than six months or where extension has been granted by Registrar by more than six months from extension so granted. An extraordinary general meeting of company may be held for transacting any extraordinary business. There are various statutory provisions as to length of notice for same, place of holding meeting, quorum thereat, voting by show of hands and proxies, and taking of a poll. A body corporate (whether an Indian or a foreign company) may, by a resolution of its board of directors, authorise any person as it thinks fit to act as its representative at any such meeting. In certain matters, Act requires a special resolution to be passed by members of company. Such a resolution is required to be passed by a three-fourths majority of votes in person or by proxy, of persons present and entitled to vote at that meeting. All other resolutions are called ordinary resolutions and may be passed by a bare majority.

Paid-in Capital Requirements.—See subhead Licence to Do Business, supra.

Amendment of Certificate or Articles.—A Certificate of Incorporation is never required to be amended except when the name of a Company is changed. Every alteration in the Memorandum or Articles of Association of a Company is required to be registered with the Registrar of Companies and copies of the amendments are to be incorporated in each copy of the Memorandum and Articles issued after the date of the relevant amendment. For listing purposes Articles must comply with relevant listing requirements.

Increase or Decrease of Authorised Capital Stock.—Company may increase its capital, if so expressly authorized by its Articles, by passing ordinary resolution (see subhead Organization, supra). If out of authorised capital, new shares are to be issued from time to time, then no such resolution is necessary, but such shares must be issued to existing members in proportion to their existing holdings, unless company in general meeting gives any directions to contrary by means of special resolution. This latter provision does not apply to preference shares. On any proposed increase of capital of company, whether by issue of rights shares or bonus shares or otherwise, none of them can be issued or allotted to foreign individual or corporation, whether already member of company or not, without permission of Reserve Bank of India, under Foreign Exchange Regulation Act, but foreign equity participation up to 51% is now permissible and provisions have been introduced to permit capital increase to bring foreign collaborators' holding to 51%. Issue of shares to promoters/collaborators should be, broadly stated, at market related prices. Capital of Company can be decreased or reduced by passing Special Resolution and by obtaining Order of competent court confirming reduction. Company cannot buy its own shares.

By-Laws.—The Articles of Association of a Company are its By-Laws or Regulations. See subhead Certificate or Articles of Incorporation, supra.

Stock.—Only two kinds of shares can be issued by a public Company, namely, Preference Shares and Equity Shares. Nonvoting shares are prohibited. A private Company (see subhead Name, supra) may issue any other kind of shares also, such as founder's shares or deferred shares.

Generally, companies in India do not issue stock, but only shares. See also subhead Stockholders—(General Rights), infra.

Preference shares can be issued only if so authorised by Articles. They are entitled to preference over equity shares in respect of payment of a fixed dividend which may be cumulative or noncumulative and of return of capital in case of a winding-up. Preference shares are generally given a voting right only on resolutions which directly affect rights attached to them, for example, if dividend thereon remains in arrears for at least two years or on a resolution for winding-up of company or for re-payment or reduction of its share capital. No company limited by shares can after 15 June 1988 issue any preference shares which are irredeemable or are redeemable after expiry of period of ten years from date of issue. Irredeemable preference shares issued prior to 15 June 1988 must be redeemed by Company within five years from commencement of Amendment Act, 1988. Similarly, preference shares issued prior to 15 June 1988 which, by terms of issue, are not redeemable within ten years from date of issue and which have not been redeemed before commencement of Amendment Act, 1988 must be redeemed on date on which such shares are due for redemption or within ten years from commencement of Amendment Act, whichever is earlier. Where Company not in position to redeem such shares within above period, with consent by Company Law Board Company may issue further redeemable preference shares and on issue thereof unredeemed shares shall be deemed to have been redeemed. Failure of compliance entails penalty up to Rs. 1,000 for each day of default and imprisonment up to three years for officer in default.

Global & American Deposit Receipts etc.—Government, by administrative guidelines, has permitted Indian companies meeting prescribed norms to issue Global/American Deposit Receipts (GDR/ADR); debt instruments, Euro Bonds (EB) and convertible bonds (CB) which are all designated in U.S. Dollar terms. In contrast, underlying equity (for GDR/ADR) is designated in Indian currency. For such issue, requisite resolutions of shareholders (and amendments to Articles of Association, where necessary) have to be passed/made, increasing capital (where necessary), permitting creation of GDR/ADR; EB; CB, authorising directors to make requisite arrangements, including accepting conditions as may be imposed by authorities and in principle approval obtained from Ministry of Finance, Government of India, New Delhi. After in principle approval, arrangements with Lead Managers, issue structure, coupon rate etc. are made, final approval from Finance Ministry is required. If foreign equity after DR issue exceeds 51% or if issuer company implements projects beyond Annexture III of 1991 Industrial Policy (see topic Industries [Development and Regulation] Act) approval of Foreign Investment Promotion Board (FIPB) is essential. Reserve Banks' approval under Foreign Exchange (Regulation) Act, 1973 is necessary, but generally would follow on government's approval. Issue and filing prospectus with Securities & Exchange Board of India (SEBI), Registrar of Companies is also necessary. GDR/ADR/EB/CB (which are quoted on international exchange, generally Luxembourg) are freely transferable to nonresidents outside India, Indian residents cannot acquire such securities. GDR/AR holders may redeem DRs to underlying equity at any time (company may prefer initial lock-in period, usually 45 days) through overseas depository which will, on redemption of DR obtain equity from local custodian. Pending redemption, depository is registered holder of shares on company's records. To protect controlling interest company may require depository to have voting agreement. Bonds issues may also have put or call options attached. Holders of GDR/ADR may transfer underlying equity only through stock exchange in India, with requisite Reserve Bank approval. Pending redemption issuing company remits dividend/interest to depository which, in turn, pays out holders of GDR/ADR/EB/CB. Withholding tax on dividend and interest on bonds is 10%. Long term capital gains on transfers in India are also 10%. No Indian capital gains arise on transfers outside India.

Stock Certificates.—A certificate issued under the Common Seal of the Company specifying any shares held by a member are prima facie evidence of his title to such shares. A certificate must be issued within three months after the allotment of any shares, and within two months after the application for registration of the transfer of any shares in the books of the Company. Shares in a public Company cannot be allotted for the first time unless a Prospectus or a Statement in Lieu of Prospectus is filed with the Registrar of Companies. Several matters must be stated and Reports set

See Topical Index in front part of this volume.

CORPORATIONS OR COMPANIES . . . *continued*

out in the Prospectus or in the Statement in Lieu of Prospectus, as per various details set out in the long schedules annexed as Schedules II and III respectively to Act. Return as to allotments must be made and filed with Registrar within one month after allotment. In case of shares allotted for consideration other than cash, contract in writing constituting title of allottee to allotment with certain other relevant documents must be filed with Registrar.

Issuance of Stock.—Shares may be issued for cash or in consideration of property or machinery, etc., sold to company or for services rendered or for technical assistance or know-how made available to company or in lieu of royalty for trademark or patent rights or other noncash, considerations. In case of subsequent allotments, unless contrary direction is given by company in General Meeting, all new shares must first be offered to holders of equity shares in proportion to their holdings at date of each offer. See also subheads Capital Issues, infra; and Increase or Decrease of Authorised Capital Stock, supra.

Transfer of Stock.—A transfer cannot be registered except on production of the relevant share certificate with proper instrument of transfer (in prescribed form) duly stamped and executed by transferor and transferee or on production of probate or other legal representation or decree of court, etc., showing transmission of share by operation of law. Board of directors are entitled, if so authorised by articles, to refuse to register transfer or transmission, but in case of public company or private company which is subsidiary of public company, appeal may be made to Company Law Board against any such refusal, and after duly hearing parties, Board may direct either that transfer or transmission be registered and award damages or that it need not be registered by company. However, in case of companies whose securities are listed on recognized stock exchange, company may refuse to register tender of any of its securities only on any one or more of following grounds: (1) That instrument of transfer is not proper or has not been duly stamped and executed or that certificate relating to security has not been delivered to company or that any other requirement under law relating to registration or such transfer has not been complied with; (2) that transfer of security is in contravention of any law; (3) that transfer of security is likely to result in change of composition of board of directors as would be prejudicial to interests of company or to public interest; (4) that transfer of security is prohibited by any order of any court, tribunal or other authority under any law for time being in force. Directors earlier had wide powers to refuse registration of transfer so long as directors acted bona fide. These powers are now substantially curtailed particularly for companies with shares listed on stock exchange.

Moreover, certain restrictions exist on any individual firm, group (as defined in Act) constituent of group, body corporate or bodies corporate under same management (as defined in Act) acquiring equity shares in public company, or private company which is subsidiary of public company exceeding 25% of paid up equity share capital of such company. In such cases, shares of company in question cannot be acquired without previous approval of Central Government. There are similar restrictions on transfers by body corporate or bodies corporate under same management holding 10% or more of subscribed equity share capital of any other company without previous approval of Central Government as also transfers by body corporate or bodies corporate under same management holding 10% or more of equity share capital of foreign company having established place of business in India to any Indian citizen or any body corporate of India without previous approval of Central Government. Aforesaid restrictions, however, come into play only in cases of acquisition or transfer of shares by or to person who or which is registered under provisions of Monopolies and Restrictive Trade Practices Act, 1969 or would be as result of acquisition or transfer of shares, undertaking registrable under that Act. See topic Monopolies and Restrictive Trade Practices.

Stock Transfer Tax.—Stamp duty on market value of share is levied on each transfer under relevant state stamp laws, but none on transmission by operation of law. Company may, after giving at least seven days advertisement in newspaper close its Register of Members for period or periods not exceeding 45 days in each year, but not exceeding 30 days at any one time.

Stockholders—(General Rights).—

(a) Preference Shares must carry a preferential right to be paid a fixed amount of dividend, subject to income-tax, and also carry, on a winding-up, or repayment of capital, a preferential right to be repaid the capital paid up thereon. It is optional for any Company to give any further or additional rights to preference shareholders, both as regards dividends and as regards return of capital.

(b) A member holding an Equity Share can vote on every resolution placed before the Company, in proportion to his share of its paid-up capital. A member holding a Preference Share has, however, only a restricted right to vote in the cases mentioned above. No Company can issue shares (not being Preference Shares) which carry voting rights or rights as to dividend, capital or otherwise which are disproportionate to the rights attaching to the holders of other shares (not being Preference Shares).

(c) Where different classes of shares are issued by a Company, the rights attached to any class of shares may, if so authorised by its Memorandum or Articles, be varied with the consent of the holders of at least three-fourths of the issued shares of that class or by a special resolution passed at a separate meeting of the holders of those shares. Any dissenting shareholders holding in the aggregate at least 10% of the issued shares of that class may, however, apply to the court to have the variation cancelled, and the decision of the court on any such application shall be final.

(d) Every member is entitled to inspection of the Minutes of every General Meeting and to be furnished with a copy thereof on payment of a nominal fee. This right, however, does not extend to the Minutes of the meetings of Directors.

(e) Every member is entitled to be furnished with every balance-sheet and profit and loss account, Auditors' Report and Directors' Report of a Company but company whose shares listed on stock exchange makes available these documents for inspection at its registered office for 21 days preceding meeting and forwards to all members salient features of such documents, company then need not furnish these documents to members except those who specifically request.

Stockholders' Liabilities.—

(a) A Company not having the liability of its members limited by the Memorandum to an amount, if any, unpaid on its shares, is termed an "unlimited Company" and the liability of the members to contribute towards the debts and liabilities of the Company is unlimited, but such Companies are rarely formed in India.

(b) If in case of a public Company, the number of members falls below seven, or in case of a private Company, below two, and if the Company carries on business for more than six months while the number is so reduced, every member who is cognisant of this fact, shall after such six months be personally liable for the payment of the whole debts of the Company contracted thereafter.

(c) Every promoter or director of company who authorises issue of prospectus inviting persons to subscribe for shares in or debentures of company, shall be liable to pay compensation to every subscriber of its shares or debentures for any loss or damage sustained by such subscriber who subscribes on faith of such prospectus by reason of any untrue statement included therein.

(d) Any person who, either by knowingly or recklessly making any statement, promise or forecast, which is false, deceptive or misleading or by any dishonest concealment of material facts, induces or attempts to induce another person to subscribe for or underwrite shares or debentures, is punishable with an imprisonment of five years or with a fine up to Rs. 10,000/—or both.

Stockholders' Meetings.—See supra under subhead Organization. As to proxies, every member of Company, is entitled to appoint proxy, but proxy cannot speak at meeting. Every Resolution, unless poll is demanded, must be decided on show of hands. Proxy is entitled to vote only on poll being demanded. Proxy must be deposited with Company at least 48 hours before meeting. Proxy must be in writing and signed by appointer, and in case of body corporate, it must be under its seal or be signed by officer or attorney duly authorised by it. In case of public company, before or on declaration of result of voting, poll may be ordered to be taken by chairman of meeting on his own motion and must compulsorily be ordered to be taken by him on demand made: (a) By any member or members present by proxy and holding shares in company (i) which confer power to vote on resolution not being less than one-tenth of total voting power or (ii) on which aggregate sum of not less than Rs. 50,000 has been paid up. However in case of private company such poll could be demanded by one member if not more than seven such members are personally present and two such members present if more than seven such members are personally present. In case of private company, poll may be demanded by one member present in person, if seven such members are personally present, and by two such members, if more than seven such members are personally present. Member in arrears in respect of calls made on shares is not entitled to vote in respect thereof. On poll, member is entitled to as many votes as shares held and member entitled to more than one vote, may use or cast all his votes in same way or in different ways in respect of different shares held by him.

Directors.—A public Company or a private Company which is a subsidiary of a public Company, must have at least three Directors. A private Company must have at least two directors. The maximum number of directors of a Company is fixed by the Articles. There is no restriction in the Act as to citizenship or residence of directors. Directors need not be stockholders or shareholders. However, a Company has the option to prescribe by its Articles that a director must hold certain qualification shares not exceeding in all 5,000 rupees in value. In default of and subject to any regulations in the Articles, the subscribers of its Memorandum of Association shall be deemed to be the directors of the Company, until the directors are duly appointed as hereinafter mentioned. Not less than two-thirds of the total number of directors of a public Company, or of a private Company which is a subsidiary of a public Company, shall (a) be persons whose period of office is liable to determination by retirement of directors by rotation, and (b) be appointed by the Company in General Meeting. The remaining directors in the case of any such Company, and the directors generally in the case of a private Company which is not a subsidiary of a public Company, shall, in default of and subject to any regulations in the Articles, also be appointed by the Company in General Meeting. At the first Annual General Meeting of a public Company or a private Company which is a subsidiary of a public Company, held next after the date of the General Meeting at which the first directors are appointed by the Company as aforesaid and at every subsequent annual General Meeting, one-third of such of the directors for the time being as are liable to retire by rotation, or the number nearest to one-third, shall retire from office. A retiring director is eligible for re-election. Maximum of 12 can be appointed by public company without necessity of obtaining prior government consent. Consent is required for appointments exceeding 12. Board can also fill in any casual vacancies. Additional director appointed by board can hold office only until next annual general meeting of company, and director appointed by them to fill in casual vacancy can hold office only up to date up to which director in whose place he is appointed would have held office. Appointment of any director must be voted on individually. Articles may provide for appointment of not less than two-thirds of total number of directors of public company or of private company which is subsidiary of public company, according to principle of proportional representation, whether by single transferable vote or by system of cumulative voting or otherwise, appointments being made once every three years and interim casual vacancies being filled in accordance with provisions, mutatis mutandis, of Act, with regard to filling in of other casual vacancies by board. There is no age limit for retirement or appointment of directors.

See also subhead Subsidiaries, infra.

Directors' Meetings.—A meeting of board of directors must be held at least once in every three calendar months and at least four such meetings must be held in every year. It may be held anywhere. Notice of every meeting of board should be given in writing to every director for time being in India, and at his usual address in India to every other director. Quorum for a meeting of board is one-third of its total strength (any fraction contained in that one-third being rounded off as one) or two directors whichever is higher. For this purpose, "total strength" means total strength of board, after deducting therefrom number of directors, if any, whose places may be vacant at time. Where at any time number of interested directors (that is, directors whose

CORPORATIONS OR COMPANIES . . . *continued*
presence cannot be counted for purpose of forming quorum at meeting of board, by reason of their being interested in any contract or transaction discussed or voted upon thereat) exceeds or is equal to two-thirds of total strength, number of directors who are not interested, shall be quorum during such time. Resolutions can be passed by circular (that is, without board meeting) by circulating draft of resolution, together with necessary papers, to all directors then in India (not being less in number than quorum fixed for meeting of board) and to all other directors at their usual address in India, and such resolution must be approved by such of directors as are then in India, or by majority of such of them, as are entitled to vote on resolution.

Powers and Duties of Directors.—The Board of Directors are entitled to exercise all such powers and to do all such acts and things as the Company is authorised to exercise and do except to the extent to which such powers are to be exercised and acts and things are to be done by the Company in General Meeting according to the relevant provisions of the Act in that behalf.

The following powers can be exercised only at a meeting of the Board and not by circular Resolution: (a) power to make calls on shareholders for monies unpaid on shares; (b) power to issue debentures; (c) power to borrow monies otherwise than on debentures; (d) power to invest the funds of the Company; and (e) power to make loans.

The powers specified in sub-clauses (c), (d) and (e) may be delegated to the extent authorised by the Board in a certain manner.

Certain powers of the Directors must be exercised only at Board meetings duly assembled, but other powers may be exercised even by circular Resolution. The following powers cannot be exercised by the Board of Directors of a public Company or of a private Company which is a subsidiary of a public Company, without the consent of such Company in General Meeting, namely: (a) power to sell, lease or otherwise dispose of substantially the whole of the undertaking of a Company; (b) power to remit or give time for repayment of any debt due by a Director except in case of renewal or continuance of an advance made by a banking company to its directors in ordinary course of business; (c) power to invest, otherwise than in trust securities, the sale proceeds resulting from the acquisition of any undertaking of the Company; (d) power to borrow monies (apart from temporary loans obtained from the Company's bankers in the ordinary course of business) in excess of the paid-up capital of the Company and its free reserves; and (e) power to contribute to charitable and other funds not directly relating to the business of the Company or the welfare of its employees, any amounts in excess of Rs. 50,000/—or 5% of its average net profits during three immediately preceding financial years, whichever is greater. Contributions to political parties or purposes are permissible within same limit, but disclosure must be made in company's accounts. Government companies or companies not in existence for three financial years cannot make such contributions.

Director must not vote at a board meeting on any contract or arrangement to be entered into on behalf of company if he is directly or indirectly concerned or interested therein, but he may do so at a shareholders' meeting, and he should disclose his interest therein before same is entered into. Director cannot hold any office or place of profit under company or its subsidiary other than that of a managing director, manager or legal or technical adviser, without previous consent of company accorded by a special resolution. For purposes of Act, a company is deemed to be a subsidiary of another, if (a) that other controls composition of its board of directors, or (b) that other holds more than half in nominal value of its equity share capital.

See also subhead Subsidiaries, infra.

Liabilities of Directors.—Each director must disclose to company particulars of office held by him in any other body corporate as a director, managing director, manager or secretary of any other body corporate. He must also disclose particulars of his shares or debentures in company. He cannot assign his office as director of company. He cannot appoint an alternate director during his absence from India for meetings of board which are ordinarily held during that period, but board may appoint alternate director during his absence. Generally, such alternate director is appointed with consent of absent director. Person can be managing director or manager of only two companies. Central government may however permit any person to be appointed as managing director of more than two companies if central government is satisfied that it is necessary that companies should for their proper working function as single unit and have common managing director. No compensation can be paid to director for loss of office as such, except to managing or whole-time director, and that too subject to various restrictions. Director is bound to comply with various detailed provisions relating to disclosures and statements to be made in prospectus or statement in lieu of prospectus to be filed by a public company, otherwise he can be exposed to civil and criminal proceedings for suppression of material facts from or misrepresentations therein. Every director will be liable to punishment if to his knowledge dividend declared by company is not paid within 42 days from date of declaration, to its shareholders. Directors are responsible for proper books of account being kept by company, and for proper balance-sheets and profit and loss accounts of company being made out for each financial year of company and for same being laid before every annual general meeting of company. They are bound to lay before every such general meeting their report as to state of company's affairs, and other particulars laid down in Act. Penalities are prescribed for contraventions of such provisions of Act. If affairs of any company are mismanaged by directors, central government or competent court has power to hold investigation in respect of same and take proceedings against delinquent directors, and such proceedings can be taken even at instance of certain minimum prescribed minority of shareholders. Suitable orders for setting right affairs of company can be made by government or court, without company being wound up.

Remuneration of Directors.—Remuneration of directors can be determined either by articles or by a resolution of company in general meeting, subject to following restrictions: (a) Remuneration of a managing or whole-time director must not exceed 5% of net profits of company, or where there is more than one such director, 10% for all of them together; (b) remuneration of any other director shall not exceed 1% of the net profits of company, if there be a managing or whole-time director or manager of company, and it must not exceed 3% of net profits of company, if there be no managing or whole-time director or manager of company; (c) if there be managing director or manager, remuneration of all of them and of other directors of company must not exceed 11% of net profits of company. There are detailed provisions in Act for determining mode in which net profits of a company are to be arrived at. Approval of Government for appointment and remuneration of managing director/manager/whole-time director is not required except where guidelines under Schedule XIII to Act are not followed.

See also subhead Subsidiaries, infra.

Officers.—Directors, managing directors, managers, secretary or any person in accordance with whose directions or instructions Board of Directors or one or more directors are accustomed to act are officers. Managing Director is director entrusted with substantial power of management, subject to superintendence control and direction of Board. Manager has management of whole or substantially whole of affairs of company. Director may also be appointed manager. Only individuals can be director, managing director, manager, secretary.

A company cannot appoint at same time more than one of following categories of managerial personnel viz., (a) managing director and (b) manager.

(b) Secretary and Other Officers.—Secretary must have prescribed qualifications and is appointed to perform certain duties as specified in Act or any other ministerial or administrative duties. No tax free remuneration can be paid to any secretary or other officer. Secretary or other officer may be entrusted with keeping of books of account and other registers and records of company and with work of making and filing Returns and other prescribed particulars with Registrar of Companies, and for otherwise complying with various provisions prescribed by Act. Contraventions thereof may expose them to penalties laid down in Act, and proceedings may also be taken by Government or competent court for their acts of omission and commission. Every company having paid-up share capital of at least Rs. 2,500,000 shall have whole-time secretary.

See also subhead Subsidiaries, infra.

Principal Office.—It is the Registered Office of the Company of which notice is registered with the Registrar of Companies. It cannot be removed outside local limits of any city, town or village where it is situated without a special resolution passed by the company. If the registered office of the company is to be transferred from one state to another in India, special resolution and confirmation of Company Law Board is necessary.

General Powers of Corporations.—These are laid down in the Memorandum of Association of a Company and cannot be exceeded. See also subhead Purposes, supra.

Dividends.—No dividend shall be declared except out of profits of company and except to registered shareholders, or their authorised agents. A dividend must be paid within 42 days of its declaration. No higher dividend can be declared by a company in general meeting than that recommended by directors. Directors may declare an interim dividend before end of any financial year. No dividend shall be declared by company except after transferring to its reserves such percentage of its profits up to 10% thereof as may be prescribed by Government.

Sale or Transfer of Corporate Assets.—Board of directors of a public company or its subsidiary in general meeting cannot, except with consent of company in general meeting, sell, lease or otherwise dispose of whole, or substantially whole, of undertaking of company.

Books and Records.—Every Company should keep the following Books and Records:—

(a) Minutes of General Meetings,
(b) Minutes of Board Meetings,
(c) Register of Members,
(d) Transfer Register,
(e) Register of Debenture-holders,
(f) Register of Mortgages and Charges,
(g) Register of Directors, Manager and Secretary,
(h) Register of Directors' Shareholdings,
(i) Register of Investments,
(j) Register of Contracts or arrangements in which Directors are interested or concerned, and
(k) the usual Books of Account.

The above Registers and Books should be kept at the Registered Office of the Company.

Any member of the Company can inspect any of the above registers and books, except the Minute Books of the Directors and the Books of Account. Some of these registers and books may be inspected by creditors of the Company and some by other persons also.

Reports.—The Directors of a Company must make their Report every year as to the state of the Company's affairs and attach the same to every Balance-Sheet laid before the Company in General Meeting. Report of Directors must contain: (a) State of Company's affairs; (b) amounts, if any, proposed to be carried to any reserves; (c) amount, if any, which it recommends should be paid by way of dividends; (d) material changes if any, affecting financial position of Company which have occurred between end of financial year to which balance-sheet relates and date of report; (e) conservation of energy, technology absorption, foreign exchange earnings and outgo. The Report of the Auditors of Company on its accounts and on every balance sheet and profit and loss account should be attached thereto. Auditor's Report should state: (a) Whether he has obtained all information and explanations necessary for purpose of his audit; (b) whether proper Books of Account have been kept by Company, as required by law, and (c) whether Company's balance sheet and profit and loss account dealt with by report are in agreement with books of account of Company.

Copies of the Directors' Report and of the Auditor's Report must be sent to every member of the Company (subject to exception—see subhead Stockholders—[General Rights], supra) and must be filed with Registrar of Companies.

Corporate Bonds or Mortgages.—Company may create a charge or mortgage on any of its properties and assets, including its book debts, uncalled share capital, goodwill, trade mark, patent or other intangible assets. It can also create a charge for purpose of securing any issue of debentures. All such charges and mortgages must be registered with Registrar of Companies within 30 days after creation thereof.

See Topical Index in front part of this volume.

CORPORATIONS OR COMPANIES . . . *continued*

Merger and Consolidation.—If the Memorandum of Association of any Company empowers it to amalgamate with another Company, it can be amalgamated or consolidated with or merged into another Company. This can be done by taking proceedings in the competent court for the purpose, and certain formalities must be gone through before the court makes an order for such amalgamation. A domestic Corporation cannot be amalgamated with a foreign Corporation, except that a domestic Corporation may be allowed to subsist as a subsidiary of a foreign Corporation. There is no prescribed percentage vote of stock-holders or shareholders required for approving an amalgamation Scheme, but generally a substantial majority vote is accepted by the court before it exercises its discretion in favour of accepting the scheme. There are no taxes payable on an amalgamation of two Companies.

Dissolution.—A Company can be wound up either by the court or voluntarily by its members. There are detailed provisions in the Act setting out the circumstances under which a Company may be wound-up, and what steps and proceedings should be taken before it can be finally dissolved.

Court's Supervision.—High Court of state in which Registered Office of Company is located has jurisdiction to entertain legal proceedings instituted under Act against Company. Broadly, such jurisdiction is now confined to liquidation and amalgamation, other powers of High Court now exercisable by Company Law Board.

Insolvency and Receivers.—Liquidation of insolvent companies is also governed by Act. Receiver of Company or of its assets is not generally appointed by court, but instead Liquidator is appointed to wind up Company and its affairs. There are various detailed provisions laid down in Act about manner in which affairs of insolvent Company are to be wound up by its liquidators.

Foreign Corporations.—There is no prohibition in the Companies Act against foreign corporations doing business in India. Permission under Foreign Exchange Regulation Act, 1973 is essential. Employment of foreign nationals is no longer restricted by Foreign Exchange Regulation Act. However, residence of foreign nationals is regulated by Home Ministry by granting visas. Foreign Corporation can establish its branches in India, but it must file with Registrar of Companies, within one month of establishment of its place of business within India: (a) certified copy of Charter defining its constitution; (b) full address of its principal office; (c) list of its Directors and Secretary; (d) name and address of any person resident in India, authorised to accept on its behalf any notice or other documents required to be served on it, and (e) full address of its principal place of business in India. It must inform Registrar from time to time of any changes which may occur in any of above particulars to be filed with him. It must also file with Registrar copies of its balance sheet and profit and loss account in prescribed form and should comply with certain other formalities laid down in Act, which are not of very important nature. Certain amount of stamp duty and fees have to be paid on registration of Corporation in India, but amount thereof is comparatively nominal. If any foreign corporation fails to comply with these provisions, it and each of its officers or agents, who is in default, shall be punishable with fine up to Rs. 1,000/—and in case of continuing offence, with additional fine of Rs. 100/—per day during which default continues. If any foreign corporation ceases to have place of business in India, it should forthwith give notice of fact to Registrar. Except as aforesaid, none of provisions of Companies Act apply to any foreign corporation. There are, however, restrictions under Foreign Exchange Regulation Act, 1973 which require prior approval for foreign body corporate establishing branch in India.

See also subhead Subsidiaries, infra.

Subsidiaries.—Broadly speaking, a Company is deemed to be a subsidiary of another if, but only if, that other controls the composition of its Board of Directors or that other exercises or controls more than half of the total voting power of such Company, or holds more than half in nominal value of its equity share capital. Composition of Board of Directors deemed to be controlled by another company if that company has power, exercisable at its discretion without consent or concurrence of any other person, to appoint or remove all or majority of directors. Further, if one Company is subsidiary of another, then Company which is subsidiary of subsidiary, is also subsidiary of said other Company.

§43A is innovation by which private company is deemed to become public company under following circumstances: (a) Where not less than 25% of paid up share capital of private company is held by one or more bodies corporate; (b) where average annual turnover of private company is not less than such amount as may be prescribed. At present amount prescribed is Rs. 50 million; (c) where not less than 25% of paid up share capital of public company is held by private company; (d) where private company accepts, after invitation is made by advertisements, deposits from public (other than its members, directors or their relatives). Such companies may, however, continue to have restrictive provisions as to transfer of shares and number of members may at any time be below seven.

See also topic Exchange Control.

Capital Issues.—Effective Feb. 1992, Securities Exchange Board of India ("SEBI") statutorily constituted. Broadly, SEBI's functions are to protect investor interests in securities; to promote development of securities market and to regulate securities market including: (a) regulating business in stock exchanges or other securities markets, (b) registering and regulating business of stockbrokers, merchant bankers, underwriters, portfolio managers, bankers to issue and other intermediaries in any manner associated with securities market, (c) regulating and registering mutual funds, (d) promoting and regulating self-regulatory organisations, (e) prohibiting fraudulent and unfair trade practices relating to securities market, (f) investors' education and training of intermediaries in securities market, (g) prohibiting inside trading, (h) regulating substantial acquisition of shares and takeovers, (i) inspecting and auditing of stock exchanges and other self-regulating bodies, (j) performing functions and exercising powers as delegated by Government Securities Control (Regulation) Act.

SEBI guidelines for issue provide: (1) Companies listed on exchange which have made at least one issue in past and have paid dividend continuously can determine price of new issue. (2) New companies making issue for first time, must issue at par. (3) Existing unlisted companies issuing shares may offer at premium, if company has three years track record of profitability. (4) Companies issuing shares to increase promoters' holding, including nonresident participation to 51% (or inviting nonresident participation) (see topic Foreign Investment) may issue shares at price determined by shareholders by special resolution, such price not being lower than price calculated per prescribed formulae i.e. 10% over average price prevailing over preceding six months.

Guidelines for underwriting, reserved quota, listing on exchanges must be complied with.

COSTS:

Under the Code of Civil Procedure applicable in India, the costs of all suits and applications are in the discretion of the court and the courts have full power to determine by whom or out of what property and to what extent such costs should be paid. Generally however the costs of an action are allowed to a successful party and where the court directs that any costs shall not follow the event (i.e., the result of the suit), the court must state its reasons in writing. Costs are only allowed in civil matters, never in any criminal matter. Except in the High Courts at Bombay and in Calcutta which exercise original civil jurisdiction, (see topic Attorneys and Advocates) costs in all other courts are quantified and costs payable to both parties are generally specified in decree of court. This does not, however, prevent Advocates from claiming from their own clients whatever fees, special or otherwise, may have been agreed to be paid by client to Advocate. In suits or applications filed on Original Side of High Courts at Bombay and Calcutta (see topic Attorneys and Advocates), costs awarded to successful party include both attorneys and counsel's costs which are taxed by Officer specially appointed by High Court for purpose and known as Taxing Master. Attorneys of Bombay and Calcutta High Court, with court's order, may have costs taxed against client even in non-contentious matters. Provisions for taxation of costs are hardly ever resorted to. Costs allowed by courts are very low. Successful litigant to whom costs are awarded therefore does not recover his actual costs. Lawyers, as rule, attend on basis of fees agreed with clients (contingent fees are prohibited) and not taxed costs or costs awarded by courts.

Security for Costs.—Security for costs may be ordered by a court (at any stage for reasons to be recorded) in favour of defendant. Order for security shall be made where plaintiff or plaintiffs are residing out of India and do not possess any immoveable property. If order for security is not complied with, court makes order dismissing suit but suit may be restored, after notice to defendant, if plaintiff shows sufficient cause for noncompliance.

COURTS:

See topic Constitution and Government.

DEATH:

Presumption.—Under Indian Evidence Act, when person is not heard of for seven years by persons who would have naturally heard of him, burden of proof that he is alive is on person who affirms that he is alive.

Corollary of this proposition by Indian Evidence Act §114 is that person not heard of for seven years by persons mentioned in proposition is presumed to be dead in proceedings where such presumption is required (and justified by circumstances), e.g., in application for representation to his estate, proceedings in respect of marriage or divorce in which he was involved, etc.

Registration.—Death of person has to be registered with prescribed authority. When required, such authority issues extract relating to relevant entry in deaths register on payment of small fee.

Actions.—When person dies, representation to or administration of his estate may have to be obtained. If deceased was party to a suit and cause of action survives in law, his heirs or legal representatives will have to be brought on record of suit.

When person dies as result of accident arising out of and in course of his employment as workman defined in Workmen's Compensation Act, his dependants are entitled to apply for payment of compensation by his employer to Commissioner for Workmen's Compensation within two years from date of death or further time granted by Commissioner on sufficient cause for delay being shown. When person dies of accident arising due to wrongful act, neglect or default of another person, his representatives are entitled to sue such other person for benefit of wife, husband, parent and child of deceased, for damages in competent court of law under Fatal Accidents Act. When death arises by reason of accident involving motor vehicles, claim for compensation should be made to Motor Accidents Tribunal within six months. Tribunal has power, for sufficient cause to condone delay. In practice Tribunal liberally exercises its powers to condone delay in filing claim application.

Tax.—See topic Taxation, subhead Estate Duty.

DESCENT AND DISTRIBUTION:

How property of person devolves after his death depends on religion professed by deceased. Therefore different sets of rules apply according to whether deceased was Hindu, Moslimedan, Parsi, Christian, etc.

Hindus.—Until 1956, Hindus were governed by traditional Hindu Law derived from original texts given by sages of antiquity, custom and usage and as interpreted by various courts.

Hindu Succession Act, 1956 codified law to very large extent.

Basic concept of Hindu law that Hindu was joint in his estate with other members of his family and so on death of male member of joint and undivided Hindu family his interest in property devolved by survivorship on continuing male members has been altered to permit Hindu to bequeath his share of joint family property, share being ascertained as if on death there was notional partition. Female heirs are put on par with male heirs; widow's limited interest (right of enjoyment with limited power of disposal) is abolished; classes of heirs (on intestacy) are prescribed, proximate class excluding remoter class. Recent amendment in Maharashtra alters basic concept of Hindu Law so that daughters are on par with sons and property devolves by survivorship on daughter also.

DESCENT AND DISTRIBUTION . . . *continued*

Parsis.—In matter of succession and inheritance Parsis are governed by Indian Succession Act, 1925, in same way as Christians, Jews and even in some respects Hindus and Mohammedans.

However there are certain special rules which exclusively govern Parsis in matter of intestate succession specifically dealt with in §§50 to 56 of Indian Succession Act, 1925.

Devolution of property on intestacy depends on whether deceased was male or female.

In case of males: (a) Where he dies leaving widow and children, property is so divided that share of each son and widow is double share of each daughter; (b) where he dies leaving children, but no widow, then distribution is such that share of each son is double share of each daughter. After 1991, share of daughter is equal to that of son and distinction between male and female is removed.

However in either of above cases, where male Parsi dies also leaving one or both parents in addition to widow and children, then father gets share equal to half share of son, and mother gets share equal to half share of daughter.

In case of female: (a) If she dies leaving widower and children, then property is distributed so that widower and each child (whether son or daughter) will receive equal share; (b) if she dies leaving only children and no widower, then property is divided among children in equal shares.

Where Parsi dies leaving any lineal descendant, or if Parsi dies without leaving any lineal descendant but leaving widow or widower, then Indian Succession Act makes elaborate and exhaustive provisions for distribution of estate of Parsi who dies intestate.

In case Parsi dies without lineal descendants or widow or widower then his property devolves on next-of-kin according to elaborate rules made in Act. These rules are framed on basis of "degree of propinquity", that is nearness of blood. Scheme of distribution is that first paternal relatives are to be exhausted up to paternal great grandfather and paternal great grandmother and their lineal descendants, then relatives from maternal side are to be exhausted.

Moslems are governed by traditional Mohammedan law.

Except as above, succession and testamentary disposition is under Indian Succession Act, which prescribes how wills made, revoked; rules governing legacies and intestate devolution; rights, responsibilities and disability of executors/administrators; when legal representation to deceased's estate mandatory etc.

DIVORCE:

Marriage and divorce go together in most statutory enactments on personal law in India. See topic Marriage for relevant Acts.

Note: Family Courts Act has been enacted (generally lawyers are not permitted to represent parties) to bring about amicable resolution between parties. This legislation is new. Following principles still apply.

Hindu Divorce.—Any Hindu marriage may be dissolved by petition presented by either spouse on any of following grounds: other party (1) has had voluntary sexual intercourse with any person other than spouse; (2) has ceased to be Hindu by conversion to another religion; (3) has been incurably of unsound mind or has been suffering continuously or intermittently from mental disorder (including mental illness, arrested or incomplete development of mind, psychopathic disorder or disability including schizophrenia) to such extent that spouse cannot be reasonably expected to live with other; (4) is suffering from virulent and incurable form of leprosy; (5) is suffering from veneral disease in communicable form; (6) has renounced world by entering any religious order; (7) has not been heard of as being alive for seven or more years by persons who would have naturally heard from party concerned; (8) has treated spouse with cruelty; (9) has deserted spouse for two years immediately prior to petition. Either spouse may petition for divorce on ground that there has been no resumption of cohabitation for one year or more after decree for judicial separation or decree for restitution of conjugal rights. Petitioning wife has additional grounds for divorce viz. (1) where marriage was solemnized prior to Act, husband had second wife by second marriage contracted prior to commencement of Act provided other wife is alive at date of presenting petition, (2) husband has been guilty of rape, sodomy or bestiality after marriage, (3) order for maintenance of wife has been passed against husband under §18 of Hindu Adoption & Maintenance Act or under §125 of Code of Criminal Procedure and since such order, cohabitation between parties has not been resumed for one year or more, (4) her marriage (whether consummated or not) was solemnized before she attained age of 15 years and she has repudiated marriage after attaining age of 15 years but before attaining age of 18 years.

Divorce may also be obtained by mutual consent of both spouses on ground that: (1) They have been living separately for period of one year or more, (2) they have not been able to live together, (3) they have mutually agreed that marriage should be dissolved.

Procedure.—Petition cannot be presented within one year of marriage (§14) with exception in cases of exceptional hardship or depravity (§14). Divorced persons may re-marry after period of appeal has expired. (§15). Divorce is by petition to District Court within whose jurisdiction marriage was solemnised or parties last resided together. (§19). Petition must state ground of divorce and also that no collusion exists between parties. (§20). Petition must be verified by petitioner. (§20). Divorce proceedings are governed by Civil Procedure Code 1908. (§21). Court must consider following before granting decree: (1) Petitioner is not taking advantage of his or her own wrong or disability; (2) has not connived at or condoned acts complained of; where ground is cruelty, that such cruelty has not been condoned; (3) there is no collusion between parties; (4) no unnecessary or improper delay in presenting petition; (5) there is no legal ground why relief should not be granted. (§23). Court must endeavour to reconcile parties before granting divorce. Court may order respondent to pay maintenance for either husband or wife pendente lite (§24) or subsequently permanent alimony and maintenance (§25). Court may make any order regarding custody, maintenance and education of minor children consistently with their wishes. (§26). Court may make orders regarding disposal of joint marriage properties. (§27). Appeals lie from decision of District or High Court in ordinary way on all points except costs of parties. (§28).

Restitution of Conjugal Rights and Judicial Separation.—When either spouse has without reasonable cause withdrawn from society of other, aggrieved party may apply by way of petition to District Court for restitution of conjugal rights; court may grant decree on being satisfied of truth of statements in petition, and on there being no legal ground why petition should not be granted. (§9). Either spouse may petition court for decree of judicial separation on any of following grounds available for divorce listed at (1) to (9) supra. Wife may also petition for judicial separation on three additional grounds for divorce available only to petitioning wives (supra). (§10). Court has power to rescind decree of judicial separation if it considers it just and reasonable to do so, upon petition by either party. (§10).

Muslim Divorce.—Divorce among Muslims is governed by Muslim customary law. As with marriage there are slight differences between the various communities but following principles are applicable to all Muslims. In addition there is Dissolution of Muslim Marriages Act VIII of 1939 which enables divorce by wife.

The "Nikha" or contract of marriage may be dissolved in any one of following ways: (1) By husband at his will without intervention of court, known as Talak; (2) by mutual consent of spouses without intervention of court, known as Khula; (3) by wife without husband's consent according to terms of contract made before marriage known as Mubara'at; (4) by judicial decree under Act, at suit of either spouse.

Talak.—Any Muslim of sound mind who has attained puberty may divorce his wife whenever he desires, without assigning any cause. Talak may be effected either orally by spoken words or by written document called Talaknama. No particular form of words is required for oral talak; if words are express, or clear, no proof of intention to divorce is required; but proof of intention is required where words are ambiguous. It is not necessary that talak be pronounced in presence of wife, or even addressed to her; but wife should know of it for purposes of dower and her alimony may continue until she is informed although divorce is valid even without her knowledge. Talak in writing is effected by Talaknama which may be deed by which divorce is effected or may only be record of fact of an oral talak. Deed may be executed in presence of Kazi (priest) or wife's father or other witnesses. Deed may be in customary form, i.e., properly superscribed and addressed so as to show name of writer or person addressed, called "manifest" if it can be easily read and understood. Intention of divorce is then presumed and no proof required. But if deed is not in customary form or not manifest then intention must be proved; if deed is manifest and in customary form it takes effect immediately even if wife is not informed. But for purposes of dower, wife must be informed. Talak may be effected in following ways: (1) Talak ahsan, consisting of single pronouncement of divorce made during a "tuhr" (period between menstruations) followed by abstinence from sexual intercourse for period of "iddat," (2) Talak hasan, consisting of three pronouncements made during successive "tuhrs," no intercourse taking place during any of the three "tuhrs"; (3) Talak-ul-bidat or talaki-badai, consisting of three pronouncements made during a single tuhr either in one sentence (e.g. I divorce thee thrice) or in separate sentences, e.g., (I divorce you; I divorce you; I divorce you) or of a single pronouncement made during a "tuhr" clearly indicating an intention irrevocably to dissolve marriage, e.g., "I divorce thee irrevocably." Talak in ahsan form becomes irrevocable and complete on expiration of iddat period. Talak in hasan form becomes irrevocable on third pronouncement irrespective of iddat period. Talak in badai form becomes irrevocable immediately upon pronouncement irrespective of iddat. Until talak becomes irrevocable, husband has option to revoke it, either expressly or impliedly as by resuming intercourse. Talak in writing becomes irrevocable and takes effect immediately on its execution, provided there are no words showing a different intention. Husband has power to divorce, but may delegate this power to wife or third person absolutely or conditionally, and for a particular period or permanently. Delegate may then pronounce divorce accordingly. Temporary delegation of power is irrevocable; permanent delegation may be revoked. However, wife may by agreement either before or after marriage stipulate for liberty to divorce herself in specified contingencies provided these are reasonable and not opposed to policy of Muslim law. This power is irrevocable and may be exercised at any time.

Ila is a species of constructive divorce whereby husband abstains from intercourse for minimum period of four months pursuant to vow. Fulfilment of vow does not per se operate as divorce but gives wife right to demand judicial divorce.

Zihar is a form of inchoate divorce; when husband compares his wife to his mother or any female within prohibited degrees, wife can refuse intercourse with him until he performs penance. In default of penance, wife can apply for judicial divorce.

Khula is a divorce by consent and at instance of wife. Wife gives or agrees to give consideration to husband for her release from marriage tie; terms of bargain are matters of arrangement between spouses and wife may release her dower and other rights for benefit of husband as consideration. Failure to pay consideration does not invalidate divorce; though husband may sue wife for recovery of consideration. Form is commercial: offer by wife to compensate husband if he releases her from marital ties and acceptance of offer by husband. Acceptance completes contract and operates as divorce. Execution of deed (Khula-nama) is customary. Khula divorce is by consent, but aversion is on wife's side and she desires divorce.

Mubara'at.—When aversion is mutual and both sides want divorce, it is called mubara'at. Either side may offer divorce, but once accepted it is complete. No need for written document; however, wife is obliged to observe "iddat."

In both Khula and Mubara'at divorces, wife relinquishes her dower, usually, but husband is obliged to maintain her during iddat, and also maintain any children by her.

Judicial Divorce at Suit of Wife.—Under Disolution of Muslim Marriages Act VIII of 1939; wife can sue for divorce on following grounds: (1) Whereabouts of husband unknown for period of four years; (2) failure by husband to provide maintenance for wife for two years; (3) sentence or imprisonment on husband for seven years or more; (4) failure without reasonable cause to perform marital obligations; (5) impotence of husband; (6) insanity of husband; (7) repudiation of marriage by wife; (8) cruelty of husband; (9) husband suffered from leprosy or virulent venereal disease; (10) any other ground recognised by Muslim law, e.g., she was married by father before 15 years and repudiated marriage before 18 years of age. (§2). Incompatibility of temperament is not a ground for divorce under (10) but cruelty and desertion are.

On valid divorce being effected, wife may marry another husband on completion of "Iddat" period if marriage was consummated; if unconsummated she may marry immediately. Husband may re-marry up to four wives immediately. Wife becomes

See Topical Index in front part of this volume.

DIVORCE . . . *continued*
entitled to payment of dower immediately if marriage was consummated. If unconsummated and dower was fixed, she is entitled to half fixed amount, but Act does not affect customary law rights to dower. (§5). Divorced Muslim woman can claim iddat during iddat period. (Muslim Woman Protection of Rights on Divorce Act, 1986). As soon as divorce becomes irrevocable, mutual rights of inheritance cease and cohabitation and intercourse are unlawful. If intercourse does occur, offspring is illegitimate, but parties may re-marry by observing certain customs.

Parsee Divorce.—Parsees may be divorced only under Parsi Marriage and Divorce Act III of 1936 (except where Special Marriage Act applies i.e. marriage is not registered under Parsi Marriage & Divorce Act but under Special Marriage Act). If either spouse is continually absent from other for seven years without any person who would naturally hear from parties concerned having done so, marriage may be dissolved at instance of either party. (§31). Either spouse can sue for divorce on any of following grounds: (1) That marriage has not been consummated within one year of solemnisation owing to wilful refusal of defendant; (2) defendant has been of unsound mind at date of marriage and has been habitually so until commencement of suit; but plaintiff must be ignorant of this fact at date of marriage and suit must be filed within three years of marriage; (3) defendant has been incurably of unsound mind for period of at least two years prior to commencement of proceedings or has been suffering continuously or intermittently from such mental disorder so that plaintiff cannot reasonably be expected to live with defendant; (4) defendant was pregnant by some man other than plaintiff at time of marriage; but plaintiff must be ignorant of fact at time of marriage; intercourse must not have taken place after he came to know; suit must be filed within two years of date of marriage; (5) defendant has committed adultery, fornication, bigamy, rape or an unnatural offence after marriage; suit must be filed within two years of plaintiff coming to know of fact; (6) defendant since solemnization of marriage has treated plaintiff with cruelty or has behaved in such way as to render it improper to compel plaintiff to live with defendant; (7) defendant has voluntarily caused grievious hurt, after marriage, to plaintiff or infected plaintiff with venereal disease, or caused (wife) plaintiff to submit to prostitution; suit must be filed within two years of each offence; (8) defendant is undergoing imprisonment of seven or more years for offence under Indian Penal Code; defendant must have served one year's sentence prior to suit being filed; (9) defendant has deserted plaintiff for at least two years; (10) decree or order has been passed against defendant by magistrate awarding separate maintenance to plaintiff, and parties have not had marital intercourse for minimum one year since date of decree or order; (11) defendant has ceased to be Parsee by conversion to another religion. Either spouse may sue for divorce: (1) On ground that there has been no resumption of cohabitation for at least one year after decree for judicial separation or (2) that there has been no restitution of conjugal rights for at least one year after decree for restitution of conjugal rights. Provided however, that no decree for divorce on ground mentioned in (1) if plaintiff has not complied with order of maintenance passed against him either under §40 of Act or under §125 of Code of Criminal Procedure.

Divorce by mutual consent may also be obtained if spouses have been living separately for at least one year; they have not been able to live together and they have mutually agreed that marriage should be dissolved. No suit for divorce by mutual consent would lie until at least one year has expired from date of marriage.

Procedure.—Where ground for divorce is adultery, plaintiff must make person with whom adultery is alleged to have been committed co-defendant; where petitioner is husband, court may order such co-defendant to pay costs of proceedings. (§33). Court may grant decree after being satisfied of following points: (1) Act or omission complained of has not been condoned; (2) spouses are not colluding together; (3) plaintiff has not connived at or been accessory to act or omission; (4) there has been no unnecessary or improper delay in instituting suit; (5) there is no legal ground why relief should not be granted. (§35). Defendant may counterclaim for any relief under Act. (§37). Court has power to grant alimony pendente lite to wife or husband and permanent alimony subsequently. Court may dispose of joint matrimonial property as deemed just and proper. (§42). Proceedings shall be "in camera." (§43). Trial must in presence of five Parsee delegates in Parsi Chief Matrimonial Court or District Court; Civil Procedure Code 1908 governs Procedure. (§44). All questions of law and procedure shall be determined by judge, but decision on facts must be that of majority of delegates before whom case is tried; where delegates are evenly divided judge has casting vote. (§46). Appeal lies to High Court on certain grounds only. (§47). When time for appeal has expired parties are free to marry again. (§48). Court has power to make orders regarding custody, maintenance and education of children under 16 years of age. (§49). If divorce is on ground of wife's adultery, court has power to order settlement of wife's property for benefit of children. (§50).

Restitution of Conjugal Rights and Judicial Separation.—Where either spouse has deserted or without lawful excuse ceased to co-habit with other spouse, offended party may sue for restitution of his or her conjugal rights. Court may grant decree if satisfied of truth of allegations in plant and if there is no just ground why relief should not be granted. (§36). Any married person may sue for judicial separation on same grounds as for divorce or on ground that defendant has been guilty of such cruelty towards plaintiff or their children, or used such personal violence, or has behaved in such a way as to render it improper in judgment of court to compel plaintiff to continue to live with defendant. (§34).

Divorce Under Special Marriage Act XLIII of 1954.—This Act applies to dissolution of marriage contracted under Act. Petition for divorce may be presented by either spouse to District Court on any of following grounds: that respondent (1) has after solemnization of marriage, had voluntary sexual intercourse with any person other than spouse; (2) has deserted petitioner without cause for period of two years minimum immediately prior to presentation of petition; (3) is undergoing prison sentence of seven or more years for offence under Indian Penal Code, but petition must be presented after three years term has been served; (4) has treated petitioner with cruelty since solemnisation of marriage; (5) has been incurably of unsound mind or has been suffering continuously or intermittently from mental disorder (including mental illness, arrested or incomplete development of mind, psychopathic disorder or disability including schizophrenia) to such extent that spouse cannot be reasonably expected to live with other for minimum three years prior to petition; (6) has been suffering from venereal disease in communicable form; (7) has been suffering from leprosy (not contracted from petitioner); (8) has not been heard of as alive for seven years by person who would be likely to hear from party. Either spouse may petition for divorce on ground that there has been no resumption of cohabitation for one year or more after decree for individual separation or there has been no restitution of conjugal rights for one year or more after decree for restitution of conjugal rights. Further ground for wife petitioner: (1) that husband has since solemnisation of marriage been guilty of rape, sodomy or bestiality; (2) order for maintenance of wife has been passed under §18 of Hindu Adoption Maintenance Act or under §125 of Code of Criminal Procedure and since such order cohabitation between parties has not been resumed for one year or more. (§27).

Divorce may also be obtained by mutual consent of both parties on ground that: (1) They have been living separately for period of one year or more; (2) they have not been able to live together; (3) they have mutually agreed that marriage should be dissolved.

Procedure.—Petition may not be filed within one year of marriage with certain exceptions. (§29). Petition must be to District Court within whose jurisdiction marriage was solemnised or spouses last resided together. (§31). Petition must state ground for divorce and also that no collusion exists between spouses. (§32). Statement must be verified. (§32). Proceedings shall be "in camera." (§33). Court must ascertain following points before granting decree: (1) Ground for relief exists; (2) where ground is adultery, petitioner has not in any manner been accessory to or connived at or condoned adultery; (3) where ground is cruelty, petitioner has not condoned it in any manner; (4) when divorce is by mutual consent, such consent has not been obtained by force, fraud or undue influence; (5) petition is not presented or prosecuted in collusion with respondent; (6) there was no unnecessary or improper delay in instituting proceeding; (7) there is no legal ground why relief may not be granted. (§34). Court must endeavour to reconcile parties before granting decree. (§34).

Where respondent opposes divorce on ground of petitioner's adultery, desertion or cruelty, court may grant respondent same relief as if he or she had presented petition. (§35). Court has power to order husband to pay alimony pendente lite (§36) and permanent alimony and maintenance subsequently (§37). Such orders may be varied subsequently. (§37). Court has power to make orders for custody, maintenance and education of children in accordance with their wishes; such order may be subsequently revoked, varied or suspended. (§28). Appeals lie to High Court; procedure is governed by Civil Procedure Code. (§§39, 40). High Court has power to make rules regulating procedure. (§41).

Restitution of Conjugal Rights and Judicial Separation.—When either spouse has, without reasonable excuse, withdrawn from society of other, aggrieved party may apply by way of petition to District Court for restitution of conjugal rights. Court may order decree if it is satisfied of truth of statements in petition and if there are no legal grounds why application should not be granted. (§22).

Petition for judicial separation may be presented to District Court by either spouse on same grounds as for divorce above; and further on ground of failure to comply with decree of restitution of conjugal rights. On decree being granted, it will no longer be obligatory for petitioner to co-habit with respondent; but court may on application by either spouse rescind decree if it thinks it just and reasonable to do so. (§23).

Divorce Act IV of 1869.—Christian marriages may be dissolved under this Act, and marriages of persons domiciled in India at time of petitioning for divorce; decrees of nullity may be obtained where marriage was solemnised in India and petitioner is resident here at time of petition; any other decree, e.g., restitution of conjugal rights of judicial separation, alimony, settlements or custody of children, can only be granted if petitioner resides in India at date of petition. (§2).

High Courts and District Courts have jurisdiction (§§4, 5) and such courts act on same principle as English Divorce Court (§7).

Grounds.—Husband may petition for divorce on ground of wife's adultery after marriage. Wife may petition on following grounds: (1) After her marriage her husband has changed his religion and gone through form of marriage ceremony with another woman; (2) is guilty of incestuous adultery; (3) or bigamy with adultery; (4) or marriage with another woman with adultery; (5) or rape, sodomy or bestiality; (6) or adultery coupled with cruelty which would otherwise entitle her to divorce a mensa et thoro; (7) or adultery coupled with desertion without reasonable excuse for two years or more. (§10).

Procedure.—Petition must state ground of dissolution. (§10). Where husband petitions he must make alleged adulterer a co-respondent except in following cases with court's consent (1) Respondent leads prostitute's life and petitioner does not know of any single person with whom adultery was committed; (2) name of alleged adulterer is unknown despite efforts to discover; (3) alleged adulterer is dead. (§11). Court must be satisfied of facts stated on petition and also be satisfied petitioner was not accessory to or connived at second form of marriage, or adultery, or has not condoned same. Court must also enquire into any counter-charges against petitioner. (§12). If court is not satisfied by requirements it can dismiss petition. (§13). If court is satisfied on evidence that petitioner's case is proved and there was no connivance or condonation it can pronounce divorce decree provided that petitioner has not committed adultery during marriage or been guilty of unreasonable delay in presenting or prosecuting petition or guilty of cruelty towards spouse, or has deserted or wilfully separated from spouse without reasonable excuse or acted in any way conducive to adultery complained of. (§14). If respondent opposes petition on certain grounds court may award respondent some relief as is prayed against him or her. (§15). Court must first pronounce a decree nisi which may be made absolute after minimum period of six months, during which it may be set aside by proof of collusion. (§16). Decree granted by District Court judge must be confirmed by High Court. (§17).

Restitution of Conjugal Rights and Judicial Separation.—When either spouse has without reasonable excuse withdrawn from society of other, offended spouse may apply by petition to District or High Court for restitution of conjugal rights. Court, on being satisfied of truth of statements in petition and that there are no legal grounds why application should not be granted may grant decree. (§32). Any ground for divorce or nullity may be pleaded in answer to petition. (§33).

In lieu of a decree a mensa et thoro (which is no longer available) either spouse may obtain decree of judicial separation on ground of adultery, cruelty, or desertion for

See Topical Index in front part of this volume.

DIVORCE . . . *continued*
more than two years. (§22). Application is by way of petition to District or High Court. (§23).

Effect.—Separated wife is considered as unmarried regarding any property acquired by or devolving upon her; and she may dispose of such property as if she were unmarried, even if she subsequently co-habits with her husband. She has same rights of action as unmarried woman (see topic Husband and Wife) but is entitled to alimony. (§§24, 25). Decree of judicial separation may be reversed by application to court which granted decree on ground it was obtained in petitioner's absence or there was reasonable ground of desertion. (§26).

Nullity.—Any spouse may petition district or High Court to declare marriage null and void (§18) on following grounds: (1) Respondent impotent at dates of marriage and institution of suit; (2) parties are within prohibited degrees of consanguinity or affinity; (3) either party was lunatic or idiot at time of marriage; (4) either party was already validly married to third person at date of so-called marriage; (5) that marriage was obtained by force or fraud. (§19). Every nullity decree obtained in District Court must be confirmed by High Court. (§20). When marriage is pronounced nullity on grounds (3) or (4) above, children of marriage are deemed legitimate and can succeed to estate of parent competent to contract marriage. See also topic Marriage, subhead Christian Marriages, infra.

Alimony, Costs, Damages, and Settlements.—Where husband petitions for divorce or judicial separation, he may join alleged adulterer as co-respondent and is entitled to claim damages from him. (§34). Court has further power to order co-respondent to pay costs. (§35). Court has power to order alimony pendente lite to be paid to wife (§36) and subsequently permanent alimony (§37) on monthly or weekly basis, directly or to a trustee (§38). Court has power to order settlement for benefit of children out of any property held by wife if it deems fit to do so (§39) and make enquiries into any ante or post nuptial settlements (§40).

Custody of Children.—Court has power to make orders regarding custody, maintenance and education of minor children during and on making decree in a suit for judicial separation (§41) and may also make such orders after decree on petition, on behalf of children (§42). Court has similar powers to make orders in respect of divorce and nullity decrees, and may further, if it deems fit, place children under protection of court. (§§43, 44).

ENVIRONMENT:

Following Acts deal with Environmental Protection:

The Air (Prevention and Control of Pollution) Act of 1981.—Under Air Act, all industries operating within designated air pollution control areas must obtain "consent" (permit) from state boards. States are required to prescribe emission standards for industry and automobiles after consulting Central Board and noting its ambient air quality standards.

Prior to its amendment in 1987, Air Act was enforced through mild court-administered penalties on violators. 1987 Amendment strengthened enforcement machinery and introduced stiffer penalties. Now, boards may close down defaulting industrial plant or may stop its supply of electricity or water. Board may also apply to court to restrain emissions that exceed prescribed standards. Notably, 1987 Amendment introduced citizens' suit provision into Air Act and extended Act to include noise pollution.

The Water (Prevention and Control of Pollution) Act of 1974.—Act vests regulatory authority in state boards and empowers these boards to establish and enforce effluent standards for factories discharging pollutants into bodies of water. Central Board performs same functions for union territories and coordinates activities among states.

Boards control sewage and industrial effluent discharges by approving, rejecting or conditioning applications for consent to discharge. State boards also minimise water pollution by advising state governments on appropriate sites for new industry.

Prior to its amendment in 1988, enforcement under Water Act was achieved through criminal prosecutions initiated by boards, and through applications to magistrates for injunctions to restrain polluters. 1988 Amendment strengthened Act's implementation provisions. Now, board may close defaulting industrial plant or withdraw its supply of power or water by administrative order; penalties are more stringent; and citizens' suit provision bolsters enforcement machinery.

The Water (Prevention and Control of Pollution) Cess Act of 1977.—The Water Cess Act was passed to help meet expenses of Central and state water boards. Act creates economic incentives for pollution control and requires local authorities and certain designated industries to pay cess (tax) for water consumption. These revenues are used to implement Water Act.

The Wild Life (Protection) Act of 1972.—The Wild Life Act provides for state wildlife advisory boards, regulations for hunting wild animals and birds, establishment of sanctuaries and national parks, regulations for trade in wild animals, animal products and trophies, and judicially imposed penalties for violating Act. Harming endangered species listed in Schedule I of Act is prohibited throughout India. Hunting other species, like those requiring special protection (Schedule II), big game (Schedule III), and small game (Schedule IV) is regulated through licensing. Few species classified as vermin (Schedule V) may be hunted without restrictions. Act is administered by wildlife wardens and their staff.

Amendment to Act in 1982, introduced provisions permitting capture and transportation of wild animals for scientific management of animal populations.

The Indian Forest Act of 1927.—Act deals with four categories of forests, namely, reserved forests, village forests, protected forests, and nongovernment (private) forests. State may declare forest lands or waste lands as reserved forests, and may sell produce from these forests. Any unauthorised felling of trees, quarrying, grazing and hunting in reserved forests is punishable with fine or imprisonment, or both. Reserved forests assigned to village community are called village forests. State governments are empowered to designate protected forests and may prohibit felling of trees, quarrying and removal of forest produce from these forests. Preservation of protected forests is enforced through rules, licenses and criminal prosecutons.

The Forest Act is administered by forest officers who are authorised to compel attendance of witnesses and production of documents, to issue search warrants and to take evidence in inquiry into forest offences. Such evidence is admissible in magistrate's court.

Forest (Conservation) Act of 1980.—Central Government enacted Forest (Conservation) Act in 1980. As amended in 1988, Act requires approval of Central Government before state "dereserves" reserved forest, uses forest land for non-forest purposes, assigns forest land to private person or corporation, or clears forest land for purpose of reforestation. Advisory Committee constituted under Act advises Centre on these approvals.

The Insecticides Act of 1968.—Act established Central Insecticides Board to advise Centre and states on technical aspects of Act. Committee of this Board registers insecticides after examining their formulas and verifying claims regarding their safety and efficacy.

Manufacture and distribution of insecticides is regulated through licensing. Violation of Act's registration and licensing provisions can lead to prosecution and penalties. Central and state governments are vested with emergency powers to prohibit sale, distribution and use of dangerous insecticides.

The Atomic Energy Act of 1962.—Regulation of nuclear energy and radioactive substances in India is governed by Atomic Energy Act of 1962, and Radiation Protection Rules of 1971. Under Act, Central Government is required to prevent radiation hazards, guarantee public safety and safety of workers handling radioactive substances, and ensure disposal of radioactive wastes. Nuclear research, manufacture and transport of radioactive substances, and production and supply of atomic energy and nuclear-generated electricity also fall within Centre's authority.

The Factories Act of 1948.—1987 Amendment to Factories Act introduced special provisions on hazardous industrial activities.

1987 Amendment inter alia empowers states to appoint site appraisal committees to advise on initial location of factories using hazardous processes.

Occupier (of factory) is required to maintain workers' medical records and must employ operations and maintenance personnel who are experienced in handling hazardous substances. Permissible limits of exposure to toxic substances are prescribed in Second Schedule to Act. Safety committees consisting of workers and managers are required periodically to review factory's safety measures.

The Environment (Protection) Act of 1986.—Act is "umbrella" legislation designed to provide framework for Central Government coordination of activities of various central and state authorities established under previous laws, such as Water Act and Air Act.

EXCHANGE CONTROL:

(See also topic Foreign Trade Regulations.)

Exchange control was first introduced in 1939 by rules framed under Defence of India Act, 1939 and was continued by enactment of Foreign Exchange Regulation Act, 1947 since repealed by Foreign Exchange Regulation Act 1973 which came into effect from 1st Jan. 1974 but substantially relaxed. Since Feb. 1993 Rupee is freely convertible on trade account and foreign exchange may be freely purchased for import of goods and services. Remittances for other purposes require Reserve Bank permission.

Residents of India as defined in Act cannot, without permission (general or special) from Central Government and/or Reserve Bank of India: (a) Sell, buy, lend, borrow, exchange or otherwise acquire foreign exchange except foreign exchange obtained from authorised dealer; (b) make any payment to or to credit or account of nonresident; (c) take any loan, overdraft or other credit facilities from nonresident; (d) export any goods on lease or hire; (e) transfer any security, such as shares or debentures to nonresident; (f) issue any security to nonresident; (g) acquire, hold or dispose of any foreign security; (h) settle or gift any property, so as to create an interest in favour of person who, at time of settlement, is resident outside India; (i) refrain from or defer collecting any debt due from nonresident; (j) export currency; (k) export securities; (l) acquire, hold, transfer or dispose of in any manner, immovable property situate outside India; (m) nonresident or alien resident or company (other than banking company) not established under Indian law cannot carry on in India or establish in India office or place of business for any trading commercial or industrial activities nor acquire whole or part of an undertaking in India carrying on such activities; (n) nonbanking company with more than 40% nonresident interest cannot carry on any activity relating to agriculture or plantation nor acquire whole or part of undertaking in India of any person or company carrying on any activity relating to agriculture or plantation or purchase shares in such company; (o) act or accept appointment as agent in India of any person or company in trading or commercial transactions of such person/company. Furthermore they may be required by notifications to: (1) Surrender to authorised dealer existing holdings of foreign currency; (2) deposit with authorised depositories any foreign securities; (3) sell foreign securities and repatriate proceeds to India; (4) make return to Indian authorities of all holdings of foreign currency and securities; (5) use any powers they possess to make foreign companies declare dividends, surrender currency and to do any of other acts that Indian residents may be called upon to do. To promote investments in India several facilities have been offered to nonresidents of Indian origin to set up industries/commercial undertakings in India and also to invest moneys in approved securities or even in shares of companies listed on Indian stock exchanges.

Indian companies are permitted to raise finance by issue of equity or debt instruments abroad (see topic Corporations or Companies, subhead Global & American Deposit Receipts etc.). Foreign Institutional Investors (FII) are also permitted to subscribe for shares in Indian companies, so long as holding of individual FII is within 5% of company's equity and aggregate of FII investment is within 15% of company's equity.

§18A introduced to permit forfaiting-trade finance involving discounting of medium term export receivables, presently through Export Import Bank of India (Exim Bank). On completion of export negotiation, Indian exporter obtains through Exim Bank forfaiting quote from overseas forfaiting agency; if quote acceptable exporter concludes export contract, providing for overseas buyer issuing avalised (guaranteed by bank) without recourse promissory notes or for exporter to draw on overseas buyer avalised (guaranteed by bank) bills of exchange. Notes/bills of exchange and shipping documents forwarded to Exim Bank through bank of exporter/overseas buyer. Exim

See Topical Index in front part of this volume.

EXCHANGE CONTROL . . . *continued*
Bank collects discounted proceeds and pays into nostro account of exporter's bank, from which proceeds remitted to exporter in India. Forfaiting charges, fees etc. must be spelt out in export contract.

Appointment of Authorised Dealers.—Act authorises Reserve Bank of India on application to authorise any person to deal in foreign exchange. Such authorisations empower authorised dealers to deal either in all foreign currencies or to deal in specified foreign currencies only. Such authorised dealers are divided into two classes. Several banks have been given licences to deal in foreign exchange. Apart from such banks, there is a group of licensed dealers known as "Authorised Money Changers" who are engaged in business of buying and selling foreign currency notes and coins.

Under §8 of Act unless previous general or special permission of Reserve Bank of India has been obtained, there is a prohibition (a) for any person, other than authorised dealer, to buy or otherwise acquire or borrow from, or sell or otherwise transfer or lend to, or exchange with, any person not being authorised dealer, any foreign exchange; (b) for any person resident in India, other than authorised dealer, to buy or borrow from or sell or lend to, or exchange with, any person not being an authorised dealer, any foreign exchange from utilizing foreign exchange obtained for given purpose for any other purpose.

No person is permitted under §9 to make payments directly or indirectly to or for credit of or by order or on behalf of person resident outside India except with general or special permission of Reserve Bank of India. Similarly, drawing, issuing or negotiating of bills or notes or acknowledgment of any debt which creates right to receive payment by person resident outside India requires general or special permission of Reserve Bank of India. §9 also prohibits receipt otherwise through authorised dealer of any payment by order or on behalf of any person residing outside India.

Under §16 of Act, no person, who has right to receive any foreign exchange or payment in Rupees from person resident outside India, shall, except with permission of Reserve Bank, do any act or refrain from doing an act which may delay or cancel receipt of such foreign exchange or payment. §13 prohibits import and export currency notes or bank notes or coins whether Indian or foreign without permission of Reserve Bank. Export of gold, silver and precious stones is permissible subject to regulations under Import & Export Trade policy. Currency even in transit through India is prohibited unless it is distinctly manifested as such.

Under §14 of Act and notifications issued thereunder, every person in or resident in India who owns or holds or who may hereafter own or hold any foreign exchange whether held in India or abroad, expressed in currencies specified in territories appended to notification, is required, before expiration of one month from date of order, or in case of person who after Act comes into operation becomes owner within one month from date of his owning or holding, to offer same or cause it to be offered for sale to an authorised dealer. Central Government may also direct any such person who is entitled to assign any right to receive foreign exchange which has been specified as aforesaid to transfer that right to Reserve Bank. Order applies, practically to all currencies other than currency of Nepal and Bhutan. Order, however, does not apply inter alia to foreign exchange held by authorised dealers and maintenance of and operation of any accounts in foreign currency maintained outside India by persons in or resident in India but not domiciled therein.

§18 provides for control over repatriation of sale proceeds of exported goods.

§19 prohibits, without prior approval of Reserve Bank, sending of securities outside India; transferring any security or creating or transferring any interest in security to or in favour of nonresident; and requires Reserve Bank confirmation to transfer of shares, bonds or debentures of company registered in India by nonresident or alien to another person resident in India.

§26 prohibits resident guaranteeing debt or other obligation or liability of nonresident or of resident due or owing to nonresident unless general or special permission of Reserve Bank is obtained.

§27 prohibiting Indian participation in business outside India is deleted.

§28 prohibits: (a) A person resident outside India; (b) a person resident in India who is not a citizen of India; (c) a company other than a banking company which is not incorporated in India, or any branch of such company, from acting or accepting appointment as agent in India of any person or company in trading or commercial transactions of such person or company.

Under §30 a foreign national cannot practice any profession or carry on any occupation, trade or business in India where such national desires to acquire any foreign exchange for remittance outside India out of any monies received by him in India by reason of such profession, occupation, trade or business. Restrictions on foreign nationals taking employment in India are removed but visa, residence permits etc. continue.

§31 prohibits noncitizens from holding, acquiring, transferring (by sale, mortgage, lease, gift or settlement) immovable property situated in India. These restrictions have been relaxed by general exemption issued by Reserve Bank subject to certain conditions viz. property may be purchased for bona fide residence; such property should not be let except where it is not immediately required for residential purposes; rental income or sales proceeds (including income arising from investment of sales proceeds) shall not be repatriated outside India. Foreign companies which operate in India under §28 or 29 may acquire property for carrying on their activities in India and also create security on such property for borrowings.

§47 of Act prohibits any person from entering into contracts or agreements which would either directly or indirectly evade or avoid any of provisions of Act or rules or directions made thereunder.

Enforcement of Exchange Control Laws.—For purpose of gathering facts, power is conferred upon government and Reserve Bank of India to issue directives. If Central Government or Reserve Bank of India or any officer of enforcement authorised in that behalf considers it necessary or expedient to obtain and examine any information, book or other document either in possession of person, or in opinion of Central Government or Reserve Bank or such officer possible for such person to obtain and furnish. Central Government or Reserve Bank of India or such officer may by an order, in writing, require such person to furnish, or obtain and furnish, to Central Government or to Reserve Bank of any person specified in order, such information, book or other document. Person upon whom valid order or direction under §33(2) is issued is obliged to comply with same and on his failure to comply, he will be liable to be prosecuted and punished under §56 of Act, punishment being imprisonment for three years or unlimited fine or both.

Penalties for Offences.—Where any person contravenes provisions of Act, or any rule, direction or order made thereunder, except §§13, 18(1)(a) and 18A Director or other officer of Enforcement authorised in that behalf, may impose a penalty not exceeding five times amount or value involved in such contravention or Rs.5,000/- whichever is more.

In addition to penalty which may be imposed, he is liable, in case of offences where amount or value involved exceeds Rs100,000/-, to imprisonment which shall not be less than six months but which may extend to seven years and with unlimited fine. In any other case, term of imprisonment may extend to three years with or without fine. For a second offence and for every subsequent offence, such person is punishable with imprisonment which shall not be less than six months but which may extend to seven years and with fine. In case of a second or subsequent offence, court may, in addition to such sentence as aforesaid, direct that such person shall not carry on such business as court may specify for a period not exceeding three years being a business which is likely to facilitate commission of such offence.

If any person on whom a penalty has been imposed by adjudicating officer fails to comply with any of its directions then upon a conviction by court, he is punishable with imprisonment for a term which may extend to two years or with fine or with both.

§58 of 1973 Act provides for punishment for vexatious search, detention, arrest etc. by an officer of enforcement. Such officer upon a conviction by a court is punishable with fine which may extend to Rs.2,000/-.

Under Act, Enforcement Directorate may either proceed with Departmental adjudication or refer matter to competent court or both proceedings may be taken simultaneously.

Enforcement Officers.—Powers conferred upon Enforcement Officer under Foreign Exchange Regulation Act are: (a) Power to call for information; (b) power to search suspected persons (§34); (c) power to arrest person and power to release on bail or otherwise subject to same power as officer-in-charge of police station under Code of Criminal Procedure (§35); (d) power to stop and search conveyances (§36); (e) power to search premises (§37); (f) power to seize documents (§38); (g) power to examine persons (§39); (h) power to summon persons to give evidence and produce documents.

Preventive Detention.—See topic Constitution and Government, subhead Limitations on Fundamental Rights.

Investments in India by Nonresident Indians.—

Nonresident Indians are those who come under any of following categories: (a) Indian citizens who stay abroad for employment or for carrying on business or vocation or any other purpose in circumstances indicating indefinite period of stay outside India; (b) Government servants deputed abroad on assignments with foreign Governments or regional/international agencies like World Bank (IBRD), IMF, World Health Organisation (WHO), and Economic and Social Commission for Asia and the Pacific (ESCAP); (c) officials of State governments and public sector undertakings deputed abroad on temporary assignments or posted to their branches or offices abroad.

Nonresident Indians become residents of India only when they come back to country for employment or for carrying on in India any business or vocation or for any other purpose indicating indefinite period of stay in India. They are not regarded as persons resident in India during their short visits to India, say, for holidays, business visits, etc. Indian citizens who take up jobs on completion of their higher studies abroad are regarded as nonresidents only from time they take up jobs abroad.

Persons of Indian Origin.—Person is deemed to be of Indian origin if he at any time held Indian passport or he or either of his parents or grandparents was Indian and permanent resident in undivided India at any time. Wife of citizen of India or of person of Indian origin is also deemed to be of Indian origin even though she may be of non-Indian origin.

Bank Accounts.—Indian nationals and persons of Indian origin resident abroad can open bank accounts in India freely out of funds remitted from abroad or foreign exchange brought in from abroad or out of funds legitimately due to them in India. Reserve Bank has granted general permission to banks in India which are authorised to deal in foreign exchange ("Authorised Dealers") to open such accounts freely.

Investment in India.—Liberal facilities are available for nonresidents of Indian nationality or origin for investment in India. Their funds brought in through normal banking channels as well as amounts lying in their nonresident accounts can be invested in Government securities, units of UTI, proprietory and partnership concerns and in shares of public and private limited companies. Most of facilities available to nonresident Indians are also available to overseas companies, partnerships, societies and bodies corporate which are directly or indirectly owned to extent of at least 60% by nonresident Indian or trusts in which beneficial interest to extent of at least 60% is irrevocably held by nonresident Indians. Various investment schemes are described below:

(i) Investment without Repatriation Facilities.—(a) Investment in proprietory/partnership firms: Nonresidents of Indian nationality or origin are permitted to invest in proprietory/partnership firms provided they undertake not to seek at any time repatriation of their capital investment and income earned thereon. Investment can be made without any restriction on nature of activity proposed to be conducted by firm. Such investments are allowed up to 100% of issued capital of investee firm without any obligation on part of nonresident investors to associate any resident investors as partners. No prior permission of Reserve Bank will be necessary.

(b) Investment in shares of companies through stock exchange: Investments in shares and debentures of companies through recognised stock exchange in India by nonresidents of Indian nationality/origin are permitted freely without any limit on quantum or value of investment, provided nonresident investor furnishes undertaking not to seek repatriation of capital invested and income earned thereon. Payment for such investments can be made either by remittances from abroad or from investor's nonresident (external) rupee account/FCNR account or nonresident ordinary rupee account. Such investments are, however, subject to ceiling of 5% of total paid up equity capital of company concerned or 5% of total paid up value of each series of

See Topical Index in front part of this volume.

EXCHANGE CONTROL . . . *continued*

convertible debentures by all eligible nonresident investors taken together. If, however, company concerned so resolves, aforesaid ceiling of 5% may be raised to 24%. These ceilings apply to purchases of equity shares and convertible debentures through stock exchange on both non-repatriation and repatriation basis. In order to avoid references for specific approval for each transaction, Reserve Bank grants general permission to investor's bank in India which he may authorise to undertake purchase and sale of shares/debentures on this behalf.

(c) Direct investment in new issues of Indian companies: Nonresidents of Indian nationality or origin who undertake not to seek at any time repatriation facilities are permitted to subscribe freely to new issues of shares of any public or private limited company engaged in any business activity except real estate business i.e. dealing in land and immovable property for commercial purposes with view to making profits or deriving income therefrom and agricultural/plantation activities. Such investments are allowed up to 100% of issued capital of investee company without any obligation on part of nonresident investors to associate any resident Indian in equity capital of company at any time.

Investment can be made either by remittances from abroad or from investor's nonresident (external) rupee account/FCNR account or ordinary nonresident rupee account. In such cases Indian companies proposing to issue shares to nonresidents of Indian nationality or origin may apply in prescribed form ISD (Appendix VII) to office of Reserve Bank under whose jurisdiction Head/Registered Office of company is situate, together with non-repatriation undertaking (Appendix VIII) obtained from each nonresident investors. It is not necessary for nonresident investors to seek separate permission from Reserve Bank to purchase shares of company.

(ii) Investment on Repatriation Basis.—(a) Investment in Units of UTI, Government securities: Nonresidents of Indian nationality or origin may freely purchase units of UTI, Central and State Government Securities and National Plan/Saving Certificates by effecting remittances from abroad or by withdrawing from their nonresident (external) rupee accounts or FCNR accounts. Dividend/interest income from investment as well as sale proceeds/maturity proceeds of securities purchased by remittances from abroad can be remitted outside India or may be credited to investors' nonresident (external) rupee accounts with prior approval of Reserve Bank which is granted freely. Where such investments are made by withdrawing funds from nonresident (external) rupee accounts, dividend/interest/sale proceeds/maturity proceeds may be freely credited to those accounts. Nonresidents of Indian nationality or origin may also invest in India development Bonds. Interest on these Bonds will be computed in dollars/pounds, as case may be and repayment of bonds on maturity will also be at the then dollar/pound rate.

Entire income from UTI units purchased by remittances from abroad or out of funds held in nonresident (external) rupee accounts or FCNR accounts is exempt from Indian income tax.

Investments in National Savings Certificates and India Development Bonds are free from Indian income tax, wealth tax and gift tax.

(b) Portfolio investment in shares and debentures: Nonresidents of Indian nationality/origin can make portfolio investment in shares (both equity and preference) and convertible debentures quoted on stock exchanges in India with full benefits of repatriation of capital invested and income earned thereon, provided: (A) Shares/convertible debentures are purchased through stock exchange; (B) purchase of shares/convertible debentures in any one company by each nonresident investor does not exceed 1% of paid up value of equity capital/convertible debentures of company with proviso that investor can purchase debentures up to 1% of total value of each debenture series, if company has issued convertible debentures in different series; and (C) payment for such investments is made either by fresh remittances from abroad or out of funds held in investor's nonresident (external) rupee account/FCNR account with bank in India.

If nonresident investor has already acquired shares in particular company with repatriation benefits under any of schemes outlined above to full extent of permissible limit mentioned at (B) above, he will not be eligible to acquire any further shares of that company through stock exchange with repatriation benefit. He can, however, acquire additional shares on non-repatriation basis.

Portfolio investment in non-convertible debentures through stock exchange as well as direct investment in new issues of such debentures will be allowed with full benefits of repatriation of capital and income earned thereon without any monetary limit on investment.

Under general permission granted by Reserve Bank, designated banks of investors can now purchase equity shares/convertible debentures without specific approval of Bank for each transaction, subject to overall ceiling of: (i) 5% of total paid-up equity capital of company concerned and (ii) 5% of total paid-up value of each series of convertible debentures, as case may be. Overall ceiling of 5% will apply to purchases of equity shares and convertible debentures through stock exchange on both repatriation and non-repatriation basis and will cover such purchases by all categories of eligible nonresident investors, viz., individuals of Indian nationality/origin and overseas companies, partnership firms, societies and other overseas corporate bodies owned by such persons to extent of at least 60%. If issuing company so resolves, nonresident investors can acquire shares/debentures through stock exchange under portfolio investment scheme. Such investment limited to 24% of issued capital or 24% of total paid-up value of each series of convertible debentures issued by company, subject to same conditions as above.

(iii) Investment in New Issues of Indian companies under 40% Scheme.—Under this scheme, nonresidents of Indian nationality or origin are permitted to make investment up to 40% in new issues of shares or convertible debentures of any new or existing company (other than FERA company, i.e. company in which more than 40% interest is held by nonresidents) raising capital through public issue with prospectus. Investment can be made only in companies raising capital for setting up new industrial/manufacturing projects or for expansion/diversification of existing industrial/manufacturing activities. Additionally, investment under this scheme can also be made in new or existing companies engaged in: (a) Hospitals, (b) hotels with 3, 4 or 5 star rating, (c) shipping, (d) development of computer software and (e) oil-exploration services. Investment under 40% scheme would enjoy full repatriation benefits in respect of capital and income earned thereon, provided it is made either by fresh remittance of foreign exchange from abroad or out of balance held in nonresident investors' (external) rupee accounts or FCNR accounts. They are also allowed to invest with full repatriation benefits in capital raised by public limited and private limited companies other than through issue of prospectus, up to 40% of new capital issue of company subject to quantitative ceiling of Rs. 40 lakhs.

(iv) 100% Investment.—To give incentives for making investments in Indian companies, nonresident investors are permitted to invest with full repatriation benefits up to 100% in issue of equity capital or convertible debentures of private/public limited company engaged in or proposing to engage in high priority industries (see topic Foreign Investment, subhead High Priority Industries) without requiring any prior approval of Government of India. Approvals for such investments will be granted by Reserve Bank provided (i) contributions towards investment in equity shares/convertible debentures are received by remittance from abroad or from investors' nonresident (external) rupee accounts or FCNR accounts and cover foreign exchange requirement for import of capital goods, if any; (ii) in case of industries in consumer goods sector, outflow on account of dividend payments is balanced by export earnings over period of seven years from commencement of commercial production; (iii) proposed project is not located within 25 kilometres from periphery of standard urban area limits of city having population of more than 1,000,000 according to 1991 census. 100% investment with full repatriation facilities is also permitted in industries requiring compulsory licensing, items reserved for small scale sector (subject to satisfying export obligation in this regard) as well as other industries except those reserved for public sector. Nonresident Indians may also participate in revival of sick industrial units in India by making bulk investment on private placement basis upto 100% of equity capital of such company. Repatriation of capital brought into India for revival of sick company will be permitted after minimum period of five years, on merits of individual cases, after taking into account future payment liabilities of investee company.

(v) Nonresidents of Indian nationality or origin and overseas corporate bodies (i.e. in which 60% capital is held by such nonresidents) are now permitted to invest up to 51% in unlisted companies operating in all industries except in high priority industries (see topic Foreign Investment, subhead High Priority Industries). Such investment will be permitted on repatriable basis.

(vi) Deposits with Public Limited Companies with Repatriation Benefits.—Nonresidents of Indian nationality or origin will be permitted to place funds with public limited companies in India including Government undertakings with limited liability with full repatriation benefits, provided: (a) Deposits are made in conformity with prevailing rules and within limits prescribed for acceptance of deposits by such companies, and (b) funds are made available by depositors either by remittance from abroad or by payment from their nonresident (external) FCNR accounts. This facility will also be extended to overseas bodies owned by nonresidents of Indian nationality/origin to extent of at least 60%. This facility is available only for three-year deposits.

(vii) Investment in Immovable Property.—Reserve Bank by general exemption has permitted foreign citizens of Indian origin (whether or not resident in India) to (i) purchase/sell commercial real estate and (ii) gift to/receive gift from relative up to two residential houses if gift tax is paid. Exemptions not applicable to farm houses, plantations, agricultural land. Foreign citizens of Indian origin (whether or not resident in India) are similarly permitted to acquire property for bona fide residential purpose if purchased from foreign exchange remitted through bank, or purchaser's nonresident external rupee account or foreign currency nonresident/special deposit accounts maintained with banks in India. Rent or sales proceeds of such property are not repatriable. General exemption also granted for Indian citizens resident abroad or foreign citizens of Indian origin to rent out Indian residential property but rental income and investments from such income is not repatriable and must be deposited in nonresident (ordinary) rupee account maintained with bank in India.

See also topic Foreign Investment.

EXECUTIONS: See topic Actions.

EXECUTORS AND ADMINISTRATORS:

Indian Succession Act, 1925 (XXXIX of 1925) makes statutory provision for law relating to executors and administrators.

Executor is person to whom execution of last will of deceased person is, by testator's appointment, confided (§2[c]) and administrator is person appointed by competent authority to administer estate of deceased person when there is no executor (§2[a]).

Powers of Executor or Administrator.—Executor or administrator has same power to sue in respect of all causes of action that survive deceased and may exercise same power for recovery of debts as deceased had when living. (§305). All demands whatsoever and all rights to prosecute or defend any action or special proceedings existing in favour of or against person at time of his death, survive to and against his executors or administrators except (1) Causes of action of defamation and assault as defined in Indian Penal Code; (2) or other personal injuries not causing death of the party; and (3) where after death of party, relief sought could not be enjoyed or granting it would be negatory. (§306).

Executor or administrator has power to dispose of property of deceased in such manner as he thinks fit. (§307).

Executor or administrator may incur expenditure (1) On any acts necessary for proper care and management of estate; and (2) with sanction of High Court on such religious, charitable and other objects and on improvements of property as may be reasonable and proper. (§308).

When there are several executors or administrators, powers of all may, in absence of direction to contrary, be exercised by any one of them who has proved will or taken out administration. (§311).

Upon death of one or more of several executors or administrators, in absence of any direction to contrary in will or grant of letters of administration, all powers of office become vested in survivors or survivor. (§312).

Administrator of properties unadministered has, with respect to such properties, same powers as original executors or administrators. (§313).

Administrator during minority has all powers of ordinary administrator. (§314).

See Topical Index in front part of this volume.

EXECUTORS AND ADMINISTRATORS . . . *continued*

When grant of probate or letters of administration is made to married woman, she has all powers of ordinary executor or administrator. (§315).

Duties of Executor or Administrator.—(1) To provide funds for performance of necessary funeral ceremonies of deceased in manner suitable to his condition, if property sufficient was left for purpose (§316); (2) must (a) within six months from grant of probate or letters of administration, exhibit in court inventory containing full and true account of all property in possession and all credits and also all debts owing by any person to which executor or administrator is entitled in that character; and (b) within one year from grant exhibit account of estate showing assets which have come to his hands and manner in which they have been applied or disposed of. Intentional omission of exhibiting inventory ordered by court or intentional exhibition of false inventory are offences under §§176 and 193 respectively of Indian Penal Code (§317); (3) must collect with reasonable diligence, property of deceased and debts that were due to him at time of his death (§319) and pay thereout, in following order: (a) reasonable funeral expenses, according to status of deceased; death-bed charges, including fees for medical attendance; boarding and lodging charges incurred one month prior to his death (§320); (b) expenses of obtaining probate or letters of administration and costs incurred in those proceedings (§321); (c) wages for services rendered to deceased within three months prior to his death by any labourer, artizan or domestic servant (§322); and (d) debts of creditors of deceased equally and ratably as far as assets of deceased will extend (§323); (4) may pay off legacies only after payment of all debts of deceased (§325).

Disabilities.—Executor or administrator cannot receive commission or agency charges at scale higher than that fixed in respect of Administrator General by or under Administrator General Act 1963 (§309); nor directly or indirectly purchase property of deceased. If he does so, transaction becomes voidable at instance of any other person interested in property sold. (§310).

Executor of His Own Wrong (Executor de son tort).—Person who intermeddles with estate of deceased, or does any other act which belongs to office of executor, while there is no rightful executor or administrator in existence, thereby makes himself an executor "of his own wrong." But intermeddling for purpose of: (1) preserving goods of deceased; (2) providing for his funeral; (3) providing for immediate necessities of his family or properties; or (4) dealing in ordinary course of business with goods of deceased received from another; does not make executor "de son tort." (§303).

Executor de son tort is liable to (1) rightful executor or administrator; (2) any creditor of deceased; (3) any legatee under will to extent of assets which may be coming to his hands after deducting: (a) payment made to rightful executors and administrators; (b) payments made in due course of administration. (§304).

Liability for Devastation.—When executor or administrator misapplies estate of deceased or subjects it to loss or damage he is liable to make good loss or damage so occasioned. This sort of conduct on part of executor or administrator is technically called "devastavit," i.e., wasting of estate, and such executor or administrator is called "devastant." (§368). When he occasions loss to estate by neglecting to get in any part of property of deceased, he is liable to make good the amount. (§369).

Miscellaneous Provisions.—Assent of executor or administrator is necessary to complete legatee's title to his legacy. (§332). Executor or administrator is not bound to pay or deliver any legacies until expiration of one year from testator's death, even if testator desires that it should be paid earlier. This is known as executor's year. (§337).

FOREIGN EXCHANGE:

See topics Exchange Control and Foreign Trade Regulations.

FOREIGN INVESTMENT:

The Industrial Policy 1991 welcomes foreign investment and technology collaboration to obtain high technology to increase exports and expand production base.

Equity Participation.—Automatic approval will be given for direct foreign investment up to 51% foreign equity in high priority industries. (See subhead High Priority Industries, infra.)

These approvals will be available if foreign equity covers foreign exchange requirement for import of capital goods. In case of industries in consumer goods sector payment of dividends will be monitored through Reserve Bank of India to ensure that outflows of dividend balanced by export earnings over period of time. Other foreign equity proposals including proposals involving 51% equity but which do not meet any or all of above criteria will continue to need prior clearance from Government under general procedures in force. Foreign equity proposals need not necessarily be accompanied by foreign technology agreements. To provide access to international markets, majority foreign equity holding up to 51% equity will be allowed for trading companies primarily engaged in export activities.

Technical Collaboration.—Automatic permission will be given for foreign technology agreements in high priority industries (see subhead High Priority Industries, infra) up to lump sum payment of Rs. 10,000,000, 5% royalty for domestic sales and 8% for exports, subject to total payments of 8% of sales over ten year period from date of agreement or seven years from commencement of production. Prescribed royalty rates are net of taxes and calculated according to standard procedures.

For foreign technology agreements in hotel industry (which is within category of high priority industries) automatic permission available subject to fulfillment of following: (a) Technical and consultancy services: lump sum fee not exceeding U.S. $200,000; (b) franchising and marketing public support: up to 3% of gross room sales; (c) management fees: up to 10% of foreign exchange earnings provided foreign party puts in 25% of equity. This will also cover payments for marketing and public support.

In respect of industries other than specified high priority industries, automatic permission will be given subject to same guidelines as above if no free foreign exchange is required for any payments. All other proposals will need special approval under general procedures in force.

No permission is necessary for hiring of foreign technicians, foreign testing of indigenously developed technologies.

High Priority Industries.—Broadly, following categories of industries are included in list of High Priority Industries, viz.: (1) Metallurgical industries; (2) boilers and steam generating plants; (3) prime movers; (4) electrical equipment; (5) transportation; (6) industrial machinery; (7) machine tools and industrial robots and their controls and exercises; (8) agricultural machinery; (9) earth moving machinery; (10) industrial instrument; (11) scientific and electromedical instruments and laboratory equipment; (12) nitrogenous and phosphatic fertilisers; (13) chemicals (other than fertilisers); (14) drugs and pharmaceuticals; (15) paper and pulp including paper products; (16) automobile tires and tubes; (17) plate glass; (18) ceramics; (19) cement products; (20) high technology reproduction and multiplication equipment; (21) carbon and carbon products; (22) pretensioned high pressure RCC pipes; (23) rubber machinery; (24) printing machinery; (25) welding electrodes other than those for welding mild steel; (26) industrial synthetic diamonds; (27) synthetic diamonds, industrial, unworked or simply sawn or roughly shaped; synthetic diamonds industrial, worked; (28) extraction and upgrading of mineral oils; (29) prefabricated building material; (30) soya products; (31) certified high yielding hybrid seeds and synthetic seeds; (32) all food processing industries other than milk food, malted food flour but excluding items reserved for small scale sector; (33) all items of packaging for food processing industries excluding items reserved for small scale sector; and (34) hotels and tourism related industry.

Note: List is illustrative and not exhaustive. Clarification of details within broad headings is responsibility of administrative Ministries.

See also topics Corporations or Companies; Exchange Control; Industries (Development and Regulation) Act.

FOREIGN TRADE REGULATIONS:

Imports and Exports are governed by Imports and Exports Policy of Government generally valid for five years at a time. Government has power to ban import/export of any commodity at any time, such ban operates prospectively not affecting commitments made (e.g. letter of credit established) prior to date of ban. Imports are under licenses. Open General Licences i.e. without restrictions as to user or individual licences which may be reserved for specific commodities, value of import and specific user. As incentive to exports, import licences are available to persons who have affected exports. Remission/refund of excise duty may also for available on exported Goods.

Under §18 of Foreign Exchange Regulation Act, 1973 Government has power to prohibit exports unless exporter furnishes declaration of full export value and undertakes to repatriate such value. Export, without permission of Reserve Bank, is precluded from doing or refraining to do anything whereby payment is delayed beyond prescribed period or made otherwise than in prescribed manner or sale proceeds do not represent full export value. Under §18A without prior permission of Reserve Bank goods cannot be sent out of India on lease, hire or any arrangement other than sale.

FRAUDS, STATUTE OF: See topic Contracts.

GARNISHMENT:

See topic Actions. Civil Procedure Code 1908 Order 21, Rule 46, deals with garnishee orders. Rule provides special procedure for payment where garnishee resides outside jurisdiction and debt is also payable outside jurisdiction. Indian courts are not competent under this rule to issue a prohibitory order upon a person resident outside limits of its jurisdiction in respect of property which is also beyond such limits.

Where garnishee denies debt it is not business of court to enquire whether debt is really due; decree-holder may have it sold or he may have a receiver appointed under §51 with power to him to sue garnishee to recover debt from him.

Where garnishee admits debt, court would order payment of debt or so much of it as is admitted to be due into court. Court cannot make an order on garnishee before debt has become payable.

See topic Attachment.

Garnishee Order Regarding Company in Liquidation.—Where judgment is recovered against a company which is in voluntary liquidation, invariable practice of courts is to stay execution of judgment unless there are very exceptional reasons for exercising its discretion otherwise.

GUARDIAN AND WARD:

This is governed by Guardians and Wards Act VIII of 1890.

Jurisdiction.—Court of Wards, High Courts and District Courts have jurisdiction. (§§3, 4A).

Selection and Appointment of Guardian.—Act does not interfere with personal law governing power to appoint guardians of person and property of minors. (§6). Court may appoint guardian, where it is in interest of minor's welfare to do so, of his person or property or both. (§7). Any person who desires to be, or claims to be, guardian of minor, or any friend, or relative, or District Collector of area where minor ordinarily resides or has property, or Collector having authority over class of persons to whom minor belongs may apply to court to have order issued appointing him guardian. Where application is for guardianship of minor's person, District Court where minor ordinarily resides has jurisdiction; where for guardianship of property, District Court where minor ordinarily resides or place where he has property; any other court approached may return application to proper District Court. (§§7, 8, 9).

Form of Application.—Where applicant is not Collector, it is by petition signed and verified in same way as a plaint under Civil Procedure Code 1908. (§10). Number of details such as name, age, sex, description of property and others must be stated in petition. (§10). Court must be satisfied that there is ground for application; it fixes date for hearing and serves notice to all parties concerned. (§11). Court may make interim order for protection of minor and interim protection of person and property pending hearing (§12) and after hearing evidence may make order of appointment (§13). Separate guardians may be appointed for person and property of minor. If minor has several properties, Court may appoint separate guardians for any one or more properties. (§15). Court must take into consideration whether appointment of particular guardian is in interest of minor, e.g., age, sex, religion, character, capacity, relationship with and wishes of minor's deceased parents, minor's choice if minor is old

GUARDIAN AND WARD . . . *continued*
enough to form intelligent preference etc. (§17). Guardian cannot be appointed in following cases: (1) Where minor's property is under superintendance of a Court of Wards; (2) where minor is married female whose husband is not unfit to be guardian of her person; (3) where minor's father is alive and is not unfit to be guardian of minor's person. (§19).

Powers and Duties.—Guardian stands in fiduciary relation towards ward and save as provided by will or other instrument appointing him, must not make any profit out of his office. This relationship extends to purchases by guardian of property of ward and by ward of property of guardian immediately upon or soon after ward ceases to be minor, and to all transactions between them while influence of guardian still lasts or is recent. (§20). Minor is incompetent to act as guardian except of his own wife or child. (§21). Guardian is entitled to such remuneration as the court thinks fit. (§22).

Duties of Guardian of Person.—(1) Look to ward's support, health and education and such other matters as personal law of ward requires (§24); (2) if ward leaves or is removed from guardian's custody, court may make order for his return if it deems fit to do so (§25). Guardian may not remove ward to place outside appointing court's jurisdiction (§26) except with court's leave.

Duties of Guardian of Property.—(1) Guardian is bound to deal with ward's property as carefully as man of ordinary prudence would deal with his own; (2) he may do all acts which are reasonable and proper for realisation, protection or benefit of property. (§27). In case of testamentary guardian, his power to mortgage, charge, transfer by sale, gift, exchange or otherwise, immovable property belonging to ward is subject to restrictions imposed by will unless he has been declared guardian under Act and court permits otherwise by specific order. (§28). In case of guardian other than Collector or testamentary guardian, court's permission is required before doing following: Mortgage or charge, or transfer by sale, gift, exchange or otherwise, any part of ward's immovable property, or lease such property for terms exceeding five years, or exceeding more than one year after date on which ward ceases to be minor. (§29). Transfers made contrary to §§28 and 29 above are voidable at instance of any other person affected thereby. (§30). Court will not grant permission unless transfer is in ward's interest and certain requirements are complied with (§31); court may vary powers of such guardian (other than Collector) from time to time (§32). Guardian has right to apply by way of petition to court for opinion, advice or direction on management or administration of ward's property. (§33).

Qualification.—Such guardian of property may be required to give bond, before being appointed, to duly account for ward's property or make statements at fixed periods regarding administration of such property (§34) or exhibit his accounts to court, or pay balance of moneys into court, as court directs, or apply for maintenance, education and advancement etc. of ward or such persons as are dependant on ward (§34).

Liabilities of Guardian.—Where guardian has given administration bond to court, any person may petition court that bond is not properly observed. Court may, if it thinks fit, transfer bond to some proper person who may sue on it directly in his own name and is entitled to recover on it as trustee for ward for any breach of bond. (§35). Where no bond was given any person may as next friend of ward during ward's minority, with leave of court, sue guardian or his representative for account of ward's property and may recover as trustee of ward, such amount as is payable by guardian. (§36). Guardian is also generally liable to ward. (§37).

Termination of Guardianship.—Where there are two or more joint guardians, guardianship continues to survivors until fresh appointment by court. (§38). Court may remove guardian on application of any person interested or on its own accord for any of following causes: (1) Abuse of trust; (2) continued failure to perform trust duties; (3) incapacity to perform trust duties; (4) ill-treatment or neglect of ward; (5) contumacious disregard of provisions of Act or any order of court; (6) conviction of offence which court thinks renders him unfit to continue as guardian; (7) for having interests adverse to faithful performance of his duties; (8) for ceasing to reside within limits of its jurisdiction; (9) in case of guardian of property only, for bankruptcy or insolvency; (10) by reason of guardianship ceasing under personal law to which ward is subject; but (7) and (8) do not apply to guardians appointed by will except under certain conditions. (§39). Guardian may apply to court to be discharged. (§40).

Cessation of Guardianship.—Powers of guardian of person cease (1) By his death, removal or discharge; (2) by Court of Wards assuming superintendance over minor; (3) by ward ceasing to be minor; (4) in case of female ward by marriage to person not unfit to be her guardian; (5) where ward's father was previously unfit to be guardian but subsequently becomes fit.

Powers of guardian of property cease on same grounds as (1), (2) and (3) above, but court may require him to deliver possession of property or render accounts of property held in past, belonging to ward. (§41). Court may appoint fresh guardian as successor to guardian who is dead, discharged or removed. (§42).

Hindu Minority and Guardianship Act XXXII of 1956.—This Act made special provisions for guardianship of Hindu children and prevailed over Hindu customary law. Natural guardians of Hindu minor in respect of his person and property are: (1) Father, then mother, where minor is boy or unmarried girl provided that custody of minor who has not completed age of five years shall ordinarily be with mother; (2) mother and then father in case of illegitimate boy or unmarried girl; (3) husband in case of married girl. (§6). But guardian must be Hindu who has not completely and finally renounced the world. (§6). Natural guardianship of adopted son lies in adoptive father and after him adoptive mother. (§7).

Powers of Guardian.—To do all acts which are necessary, reasonable or proper for benefit of minor or for realisation, protection or benefit of minor's estate. (§8). Guardian cannot bind minor by personal covenant. (§8). Natural guardian must have prior permission from court to do following: (1) Mortgage, charge, transfer by sale, gift, exchange or otherwise part with any immovable property of minor; (2) lease such property for more than five years or for term extending more than one year beyond date on which minor will attain majority. (§8).

Minor cannot act as guardian of property of another minor. (§10). De facto guardian cannot deal with minor's property. (§11).

HUSBAND AND WIFE:

Married woman's capacity to hold property is governed by Married Women's Property Act III of 1874 as am'd, but Act does not apply to women or their husbands who professed Hindu, Muslim, Buddhist, Sikh or Jain religions at time of marriage. (§2).

Disabilities of Married Women.—Cannot acquire separate domicil of choice different from that of husband. Disabilities are governed by personal law to which a married woman is subject.

Separate Property.—Wages or earnings of any married woman in any employment, occupation or trade carried on by her and not by her husband are her separate property. (§4). So too any money or separate property acquired by her through exercise of literary, artistic or scientific skill; also all savings from and investments of such wages, earnings and property. Married women can effect separate insurance policies independently of husband (§5); this enures as separate property. Contract is valid. Insurance policy taken out by husband on his own life for benefit of wife is deemed to be trust for her benefit and does not form part of his estate. Provisions of this section apply even when policy of insurance is effected by male Hindu, Muslim, Buddhist, Sikh or Jain. Various requirements and limitations exist, differing from State to State. (§6).

Hindu Married Women.—By Hindu Adoptions and Maintenance Act LXXVIII of 1956. Hindu wife is entitled to be maintained by her husband during her lifetime. (§18). She is so entitled even if living separately from husband if (1) He is guilty of desertion, or abandons her without reasonable cause, and without her consent or against her wish or wilfully neglects her: (2) he has treated her cruelly or she reasonably fears to live with him; (3) he is suffering from a virulent form of leprosy; (4) he has another wife living; (5) he keeps a woman in loco uxoris in same house in which wife habitually resides, or lives with such concubine elsewhere; (6) he has been converted to another religion; (7) there is any other cause justifying her living separately. (§18). But Hindu wife is not entitled to maintenance if she is unchaste or ceases to be a Hindu by conversion to another religion. (§18).

Hindu wife is entitled to maintenance after her husband's death by her father-in-law, provided she is unable to maintain herself out of her own property or earnings or from her husband's, own mother's or own father's estate or from her son or daughter or their estates, and if father-in-law is able to maintain her. (§19).

Hindu man or woman is bound to maintain his or her legitimate or illegitimate children and his or her aged or infirm parents (§20) until children become majors, and so long as parents are unable to maintain themselves (§20). Heirs of deceased Hindu (See topic Descent and Distribution, subhead Succession Amongst Hindus) are bound to maintain dependants of deceased out of estate inherited from deceased. (§22).

Muslim Women.—By Muslim Personal Law Shariat Application Act XXVI of 1937 all questions regarding special properties of women including personal property inherited or obtained under contract, by way of gift, marriage, dissolution of marriage including talaki, ila, zihar, lian khula and imbara'at (see topic Divorce, subhead Muslim Divorce) maintenance, dower, guardianship, gifts, trusts, trust properties, and wakfs are governed by Muslim Personal law. (§2).

Desertion and Nonsupport.—Christian deserted wives (under Divorce Act IV of 1869, see topic Divorce) may apply to court for protection of any properties acquired after marriage and after being deserted. Court may, if satisfied desertion was without excuse and that wife is maintaining herself by her own industry or property, order protection of her earnings against husband and his creditors. (§28). But order may be subsequently varied or terminated at behest of husband if court thinks fit to do so. (§29). If husband seizes or uses wife's property after order is made, wife can sue him for return or delivery of specific property or its pecuniary value. (§30). Wife is in same position as if she were unmarried in all other respects. (§31).

Contracts.—Capacity to contract (see topic Contracts) depends partly upon personal law of person concerned. See subheads Hindu Married Women; Muslim Women; Desertion and Nonsupport, supra.

Maintenance.—Husband having sufficient means, is bound to maintain his wife who is unable to maintain herself. (§125 CRPC). Amount of maintenance under this section not to exceed Rs.500/-. Wife includes woman who has been divorced and has not remarried.

Actions.—Married women may bring action for such property as is her separate property under Indian Succession Act 1865 or of M. W. Property Act, 1874, in her own name against all persons for protection and security of such property. She is liable for suits, processes and orders regarding such property as if she were unmarried. (§7 M. W. Property Act). Married women also liable on contracts regarding separate property. (§8). Husband is not liable for wife's ante nuptial debts (§9) nor for breach by wife of any trustee, executrix or administratrix position unless he has intermeddled (§10).

By Civil Procedure Code 1908 (Order 31, R. 3) husband is not necessary party to suit by or against married woman in her capability as executrix, administratrix or trustee.

Marriage of female plaintiff or defendant does not cause suit to abate and decree against female defendant may be executed against her alone.

Husband also may with permission of Court, be held liable for judgment decree against wife only in those cases where he would be liable for her debts. Decree in favour of wife may, with permission of Court, be executed on application of husband, where husband is by law entitled to subject matter of decree. (Order 22, R.7).

Agency.—By Indian Contract Act IX of 1872 §187, liability of husband for a wife's debts depends upon principles of agency and husband is only liable when it is shown that he expressly or impliedly sanctioned what wife has done. This is a question of fact in each case.

IMMIGRATION:

See topic Aliens.

INDUSTRIAL AND LABOUR LAWS:

Preferatory Remarks.—Industrial expansion after independence resulted in considerable and increasing industrial regulation and labour legislation. Legislation has sought to regulate employer-employee relationship in its various aspects (including welfare of workers); machinery for settlement of disputes; and for formation and activities of trade unions. Statutes do not cover entire field, and reference to case law is essential.

Detailed summary of numerous Acts is impossible. Nevertheless in order to give general view of industrial and labour laws reference may be made in broad outlines to some of important subjects such as: (1) Fixation of wage scales, (2) "dearness allowance" paid to workmen to compensate for rise in cost of living, (3) "bonus" which has come to be regarded as employees right to participate in surplus profits to earning of which they have contributed by reference to statute and case law.

Central and State Legislation.—Under Constitution of India, both Central Government and State Governments have powers to legislate on matters relating to labour. Parliament legislates on subjects which are of All India character and require uniformity throughout country, but in most of its Acts, States are given powers to prescribe rules, so that each State can frame rules to meet its own particular requirements. However rules framed under State Act should not, of course, be derogatory of or inconsistent with provisions of Parliament Act.

The Central Government Acts.—It would be impossible to deal with all Acts passed by States. Reference is made here to only some of most important Central Acts which have all India operation. These Acts are:

(1) Industrial Disputes Act, 1947.
(2) The Factories Act, 1948.
(3) Industrial Employment (Standing Orders) Act, 1946.
(4) Workmen's Compensation Act.
(5) Payment of Wages Act.
(6) Indian Trade Unions Act, 1926, as amended by Act of 1947.
(7) Employees' State and Insurance Act, 1948.
(8) Payment of Bonus Act, 1965.
(9) Administrative Tribunals Act, 1985.

Industrial Disputes Act, 1947.—This Act makes provisions for investigation into and settlement of industrial disputes and also provides for setting up Works Committees of representatives of employers and employees and prohibition of strikes and lockouts closure of industry; retrenchment of surplus labour and other ancilliary matters. Act is in operation in whole of India except State of Jammu and Kashmir.

Industry to Which the Act Applies.—What is "industry" to which the Act applies often gives rise to nice questions of law. Industry means any systematic activity carried out by cooperation between employer and his workmen (including agency and contract employment) for production, supply or distribution of goods or services with view to satisfy human wants or wishes whether or not any capital has been invested for purpose of carrying on such activity or such activity is carried on with motive to make any gain or profit and definition now also includes dock workers and any activity relating to production of sales or business or both carried out by establishment. Agricultural operations; educational, scientific and research institutions; noncommercial institutions owned/managed by charitable/social/philanthropic organizations; government activity of sovereign nature; domestic service; and cooperative activities (subject to exceptions) are not "industry". (§2[j]).

Works Committee.—In any industrial establishment in which 100 or more workmen are employed, the Government has a right to pass an order requiring the employer to constitute a Works Committee consisting of an equal number of representatives of employers and workmen engaged in the establishment. The duty of the Works Committee is to promote measures for securing and preserving amity and good relations between the employers and the workmen and to that end to comment upon matters of their common interest and endeavour to compose any material difference of opinion in respect of such matters. (§3).

Machinery for Settlement of Disputes.—

Grievance Settlement Authority.—Any industrial establishment in which more than 50 workmen are employed shall provide for grievance settlement authority for settlement of industrial disputes of workmen employed. (§9C).

Conciliation.—Whenever demands are made by labour or industrial disputes arise or are apprehended, the matter is taken up by an officer appointed by the Government who is designated as the Conciliation Officer. He may act on his own initiative, or on being approached by any party. He is charged with the duty of mediating in and promoting the settlement of industrial disputes. He is, however, not invested with power to direct the parties to settle their disputes in any particular manner. The Conciliation Officer may call for and inspect any document which he has ground for considering to be relevant to the industrial dispute. (§11). Strike or lock-out during pendency of conciliation proceedings is illegal except in specified circumstances.

If a settlement of the dispute is arrived at in the course of conciliation proceedings, the officer sends a report to the Government together with a Memorandum of Settlement signed by the parties. If no such settlement is arrived at, the Conciliation Officer sends to the Government a full report setting forth the steps taken by him for ascertaining the facts relating to the disputes and for bringing about an amicable settlement and the reasons why a settlement could not be reached. If on a consideration of the report the Government is satisifed that there is a case for reference to the Tribunal then it makes such a reference.

Industrial Tribunals.—The Government has constituted several Industrial Tribunals for adjudication of industrial disputes. The right to constitute a Tribunal is in the State Governments and disputes usually referred to them are of industries located in a particular state. The Central Government has also a right to constitute a National Tribunal for adjudication of industrial disputes involving questions of national importance or of such nature that industrial establishments situate in more than one state are likely to be interested in or affected by such disputes. Reference of industrial disputes may be made by Government or parties to dispute may agree voluntarily to refer disputes to Tribunal by written agreement. (§10A).

Procedure & Powers of Tribunals.—The tribunal has same powers as a Civil Court (a) for enforcing attendance of any person and examining him on oath; (b) compelling production of documents; (c) issuing commission for examination of witnesses outside its jurisdiction. The tribunal is also empowered to appoint one or more persons having expert knowledge to advise it in the matter.

Procedure.—On a matter being referred to a Tribunal, either by the Government or by agreement of parties, it issues notices to the contestants, who are required to file their respective statements, after which parties are heard and they are at liberty to adduce such evidence oral or documentary as may be thought necessary. On conclusion of the proceedings, the Tribunal proceeds to give an Award. Any Award or decision given by the Tribunal is subject to an appeal to the Supreme Court of India but unless a substantial question of law is involved the Court is generally not inclined to entertain appeals. The award is published in the Government Gazette and the parties are supplied with copies thereof.

Award.—

The award becomes enforceable on the expiry of 30 days from the date of its publication. However, the Government may on public grounds affecting national economy or social justice declare that the whole or any part of the award shall not become enforceable on the expiry of 30 days.

Period of Operation of the Award.—The award generally remains in operation for a period of one year after it becomes enforceable. The Government may before the expiry of the period extend the operation by any period not exceeding one year at a time but so that the total period does not exceed three years. Notwithstanding the expiry of the period of operation, the award continues to be binding on the parties until the period of two months elapses from the date on which the Notice is given by any party to the other intimating its intention to terminate the award. (§19).

Strikes and Lock-Outs.—The right to strike is a legitimate weapon in the hands of the workmen to serve their legitimate demands and ventilate their grievances. The expression "strike" is defined to mean a cessation of work by a body of persons employed in the industry acting in combination or a concerted refusal to work of any number of persons employed in the industry. (§2 [q]). The expression "lock-out" is defined to mean closing of a place of employment or suspension of work by employer.

Prohibition of Strikes and Lock-outs.—No workman who is employed in any industrial establishment can go on strike in breach of contract, and no employer of any such workmen can declare a lock-out: (a) during the pendency of proceedings before the Tribunal and two months after conclusion of such proceedings, or (b) during any period in which a settlement or Award is in operation in respect of any of the matters covered by such settlement or Award. (§23). During period of strike wages may be deducted.

A strike or a lock-out which contravenes the above provisions is illegal. However, a lock-out declared in consequence of an illegal strike, or a strike declared in consequence of an illegal lock-out, is not to be considered as "illegal." (§24). No person can expend or apply any money in direct furtherance or support of any illegal strike or lock-out (§25).

Notice of Change.—No employer can affect any change in the conditions of service of workmen in respect of any of the matters specified in the next paragraph (a) without giving to the workmen a notice in the prescribed manner of the nature of the change proposed, or (b) within 21 days of giving such notice. However, no notice is required when the change is effected in pursuance of any settlement or award. The matters requiring the notice of change are:

(a) Wages; (b) contribution to Provident Fund either by the workmen or by the employers; (c) compensatory and other allowances; (d) hours of work and rest intervals; (e) leave with wages and holidays; (f) starting, alterations or discontinuance of shifts; (g) classification of employees by grades; (h) withdrawal of any customary concession or privilege or change in usage; (i) introduction of or alterations in rules of discipline; (j) rationalisation or standardisation or employment of plant or technique likely to lead to retrenchment; (k) any increase or reduction (other than casual) in the number of persons employed in any occupation or process or department or shift not due to forced matters. (§9A).

Layoff and Retrenchment.—"Lay Off" is defined to mean the failure, refusal or inability of an employer on account of shortage of coal, power or raw materials or accumulation of stocks or breakdown of machinery or for any other reason to give employment to workmen.

Compensation for Lay Off:—Whenever a workman who has completed not less than one year's continuous service is laid off, he is to be paid for all days during which he is laid off, compensation equal to 50% of his wages and dearness allowance provided that compensation during any period of 12 months shall not be for more than 45 days. (§25C).

No compensation is payable to a workman who has been laid off: (a) If he refuses to accept an alternative employment in the same establishment or any other establishment belonging to the same employer situate in the same town or village or within a radius of five miles from the establishment; (b) if he does not present himself for work at the appointed time once a day and (c) if such laying off is due to a strike or slowing down of production in another part of the establishment (§25E).

The provisions relating to lay-off compensation do not apply to: (a) Industrial establishment in which less than 50 workmen at an average per working day are employed in the preceding calendar month or (b) industrial establishments which are of seasonal character or in which the work is performed only intermittently.

Retrenchment.—"Retrenchment" is defined to mean the termination by an employer of the services of a workman for any reason whatsoever otherwise than as a punishment by way of disciplinary action. This expression does not include (a) voluntary retirement, (b) retirement of the workmen on reaching the age of superannuation if the contract of employment contains a stipulation in that behalf or (c) termination of services of a workmen on the ground of continued ill health.

Conditions of Retrenchment and Compensation.—No workman in any industry who has been in continuous service for not less than one year can be re-trenched until: (a) the workman is given one month's notice indicating the reasons for retrenchment or workmen is paid in lieu of such notice wages for the period of the notice, (b) the workman is paid at the time of retrenchment, compensation equivalent to 15 days

See Topical Index in front part of this volume.

INDUSTRIAL AND LABOUR LAWS . . . *continued*
average pay for every completed year of service or any part thereof in excess of six months and (c) notice in the prescribed manner is served on the Government.

Procedure for Retrenchment.—In the absence of any agreement, the employer has ordinarily to retrench the workman who was the last person to be employed in the category in which retrenchment takes place unless for reasons to be recorded the employer retrenches any other workmen. In other words the principle, in cases of retrenchment, is "First come last go and last come first go." Where retrenchment takes place and later the employer proposes to take into employ any person, he must give an opportunity to the retrenched workmen to offer themselves for re-employment who will have preference over other persons.

Retrenchment Compensation in Case of Transfer of Undertakings.—Even where the ownership or management of an undertaking is transferred from one employer to another, every workman in continuous service for not less than one year becomes entitled to notice and compensation in accordance with the rules discussed above. However, no such notice or compensation would be necessary in cases of transfer if the following conditions are fulfilled: (a) the service of the workman is not interrupted by such transfer; (b) the terms and conditions of such service after such transfer are not in any way less favourable to the workmen than those applicable to them immediately before the transfer; (c) the new employer is under the terms of such transfer legally liable to pay to the workmen in the event of their retrenchment at a future date, compensation on the basis that their services have been continuous and are not interrupted by the transfer. (§25FF).

Retrenchment Compensation On Closure.—Where an undertaking is closed down for any reason, every workman becomes entitled to notice and compensation in accordance with the provisions indicated above, provided that if the undertaking is closed down on account of unavoidable circumstances beyond the control of the employer, the compensation is not to exceed the workman's average pay for three months. (§25FF).

Conditions of Service of Workmen to Remain Unchanged under Certain Circumstances.—During the pendency of proceedings before a Conciliation Officer or a Tribunal in respect of an Industrial Dispute no employer can, in regard to any matter connected with the dispute, alter to the prejudice of workmen the conditions of services applicable to them. Similarly, during the pendency of such proceedings, no workmen connected in such dispute can be discharged or punished for misconduct connected with the dispute except with the express permission in writing of the authority before which such proceedings are pending.

However, during the pendency of such proceedings an employer may in accordance with the standing orders: (a) alter in regard to any matter not connected with the dispute the conditions of service applicable to that workman or (b) for any misconduct not connected with the dispute discharge or punish the workman provided that such workman is paid wages for one month and an application is made by the employer to the authority before whom the proceedings are pending for approval of the action taken by the employer. (§33).

Before any disciplinary action is taken against any workman resulting in dismissal or discharge or other penalty, it is necessary to observe the rules of natural justice, but as this topic is covered by case law, discussion on the subject will be found under a suitable heading.

Representation of Parties.—A workman who is a party to a dispute, may be represented by: (a) An officer of a Registered Trade Union of which such workman is a member or (b), an officer of a Federation of a Trade Union to which the Trade Union concerned is affiliated or (c), where the workman is not a member of any Trade Union, by an officer of any Trade Union connected with the industry in which the workman is employed or by any such workman employed in such industry.

Any employer may be represented in any such proceedings by: (a) an officer of an Association of employers of which he is a member or, (b) an officer of a Federation of Association of employers to which such Association is affiliated, and (c) where an employer is not a member of any such association of employers, by an officer of any Association connected with the industry concerned.

No party is entitled to be represented by a legal practitioner in any conciliation proceedings. In any proceedings before a Tribunal a party may be represented by a legal practitioner with the consent of the other parties to the proceedings and with the leave of the Tribunal. (§36).

Unfair labour practices have been specified in Fifth Schedule.

The Indian Factories Act, 1948.— Act is enacted to provide for the welfare of labour in factories and makes provisions for hours of work, holidays, lighting and ventilation, meal time and over-time, regulations as to health and safety devices for protection of workmen employed in the factories.

The object which the Act seeks to achieve is implementation of as many provisions of the International Labour Organization Code of Industrial Hygiene as are applicable under Indian conditions. The provisions relating to the periodical medical examinations of young persons and the submissions of plans for factory buildings to the authorities have also been taken from the International Labour Conventions.

A "Factory" is defined to mean any premises (1) whereon ten or more workers are working or were working on any day of the preceding 12 months and in any part of which a manufacturing process is being carried on with the aid of power, and where a manufacturing process is carried on without the aid of power the number of workers should be 20 or more. The person charged with the duty of carrying out the provisions of the Act is referred to as "occupier" in the Act. "Occupier" is defined to mean a person who has ultimate control over the affairs of the factory.

Approval, Licensing and Registration of Factories.—Pursuant to the powers given by this Central Act, various State governments have made rules requiring (a) the previous permission in writing of the State government for the site on which the factory is to be situated, (b) the submissions of plans and specifications of the proposed factory and (c) the registration and licencing of factories and fees payable for the same and for the renewal of licences. (§6).

Implementation of the Act.—In order to implement the provisions of the Act, the States are authorised to appoint Inspectors who have wide powers such as (a) to enter any place which is used as a factory, (b) to make examination of the premises, the plant and machinery and require the production of documents relating to the factory, and (c) to exercise such powers as may be prescribed by the Government for carrying out the purposes of the Act. (§§8, 9).

Health.—Every factory must be kept clean and free from effluvia arising from any drain or other nuisance. (§11). Effective and suitable provisions must be made for adequate ventilation by circulation of fresh air and keeping up a certain temperature in the factory premises according to the prescribed rules. (§13). Rules have also been made in respect of factories in which humidity of the air is artificially increased. No part of any factory may be overcrowded to an extent injurious to the health of the workers. Every factory must also provide and maintain sufficient and suitable lighting (natural or artificial or both). (§§11-20).

Safety.—In every factory the machinery, handling of which may cause injury, must be securely fenced by safeguards of substantial construction in accordance with the rules framed. No young person (i.e. one who has not completed his eighteenth year of age) can work on any machine unless he is fully instructed as to the dangers arising in connection with the machine and only after receiving sufficient training. In every factory all floors, steps, stairs, passages, etc., must be of sound construction and properly maintained and provision must be made for safe means of access to every space at which a person is required to work. Every factory must also provide suitable means of escape in case of fire and there must also be effective and clearly audible means of giving warning in case of a fire. (§§21-41).

Welfare of Workers.—Every factory must provide adequate and suitable facilities for washing and for keeping clothing not worn during working hours. It is also obligatory to provide and maintain first-aid boxes or cupboards equipped with the prescribed contents. Rules are also made requiring certain factories employing more than 250 workers to run a canteen for their use. A factory employing more than 150 workers must provide adequate and suitable shelters or rest rooms and a suitable lunch room for the workers. (§§42-50).

Working Hours For Adults.—An "Adult" is defined in the Act to mean a person who has completed his 18th year of age. (§2A). No adult worker can be required or allowed to work in the factory for more than 48 hours in any week. Subject to this over all limit no adult worker can be required or allowed to work for more than nine hours a day. This bar is an absolute one and mere payment of overtime wages cannot get over the bar. (§§51, 54).

The periods of work each day must be so fixed that no period shall exceed five hours at a time. The effect of this is that hours of work during the day should be suitably spaced so as to allow adequate rest to worker. No worker should be made to work for more than five hours before he has an interval of rest of at least half an hour. (§55).

Weekly Holidays.—Every worker working in a factory must be given one day's rest in seven. The day of rest need not necessarily be a Sunday. The day of rest may also not necessarily be the same day in each week. One day may be substituted for the other for rest provided that such substitution should not result in any worker working more than ten days continuously without a holiday for a whole day. (§52).

Overtime Payment.—Where a worker works in excess of the hours prescribed, he is entitled to wages at the rate of twice his ordinary rate of wages. (§59). The State government may make rules and provide for exemption from the above restrictions in case of persons holding position of supervision or management or those employed in a confidential position. (§64).

Employment of Young Persons.—A child under the age of 14 years cannot work in any factory. However, a child above the age of 14 years is permitted to work in any factory but he cannot work: (a) for more than four and one-half hours a day or (b) during the night.

Leave.—Every worker who has worked for a period of 240 days or more in a factory during a calendar year must be allowed during the subsequent year leave with wages as follows: (a) If an adult, one day for every 20 days of work performed; (b) if a child, one day for every 15 days of work performed. (§79).

A worker who has been allowed leave for not less than four days, in the case of an adult, and five days in case of a child, can claim payment of wages in advance for the leave period. (§81).

Penalties and Procedure.—Different kinds of penalties are prescribed for contravention of the provisions of the Factories Act, and in many cases criminal prosecution may also be launched and if certain facts are established, the result may be either imposition of fine or imprisonment of the person found guilty of the offence.

Industrial Employment (Standing Orders) Act, 1946.— Expression "Standing Orders" means a set of rules governing the conditions of recruitment, discharge, disciplinary action, holidays, leave, etc. The Act applies to industrial establishments employing 100 or more workmen and to such other industrial establishments as Government may specify.

The employers and the employees are normally bound by the terms of the contract of service. However, the agreement stands modified by the Standing Orders.

The employer must submit, within six months from the date on which the Act becomes applicable, to an officer appointed in that behalf, the draft of the Standing Orders on various matters set out in the Schedule appended to the Act.

Some of the important items in the Schedule are: (a) Classification of workmen, e.g., permanent, temporary, etc.; (b) hours of work, holidays, pay days and wage rates; (c) termination of employment and the notice to be given for the purpose by either party; (d) suspension or dismissal for misconduct; (e) means of redress of workmen against unfair treatment.

When the draft of Standing Orders is submitted to the officer concerned, he forwards a copy to the Trade Union, if there be any, or if there is no Trade Union to the workmen in a certain prescribed manner. (§5). Thereafter he proceeds to call a meeting of the parties and after hearing them the draft of the Standing Orders is settled and certified. Any person aggrieved by the order of the officer certifying the draft can prefer an appeal to the appellate authority constituted under the Act.

Date of Operation.—The Standing Orders come into operation on the expiry of 30 days from the date they are certified, and where there is an appeal, on the expiry of seven days from the date of the Order passed in appeal.

Posting of Standing Orders.—The text of the Standing Orders must be prominently posted by the employer in English and in the language understood by the majority of the workmen in the establishment on special boards at or near the entrance. (§9).

See Topical Index in front part of this volume.

INDUSTRIAL AND LABOUR LAWS . . . *continued*

Duration of Standing Orders.—The Standing Orders cannot, except by an agreement, be modified until the expiry of six months from the date on which they become operative. (§10). The Government has powers to exempt any industrial establishment from all or any of the provisions of the Act if it is satisfied that in the interest of the industry or for any cogent reasons it should be so done.

Workmens' Compensation Act, 1923.—Employers have absolute liability to compensate workman for injuries sustained by him in course of employment and rules governing payment of such compensation are to be found in this Act.

When a claim is made it is not open to an employer to contend that there was contributory negligence on the part of the employee or that the employee alone was negligent or that injury was due to negligence of fellow-employee nor is it open to employer to say that when employee entered employment he assumed risk or ought to have known of risk and therefore nothing should be paid to him.

The general principle is that compensation should ordinarily be given to workmen who sustain personal injuries by accident arising out of and in course of their employment. Compensation is also given in certain cases when a workman contracts certain kinds of occupational disease peculiar to his employment.

The rates of compensation payable are set out in one of the Schedules appended to the Act. Injury sustained by a workman may result either in partial disablement or total disablement. "Partial disablement" is where it is of a temporary nature and reduces the earning capacity of a workman in any employment in which he was engaged at the time of the accident, and where the disablement is of a permanent nature, it reduces his earning capacity in every employment which he was capable of undertaking at that time. "Total disablement" means such disablement, whether of a temporary nature or a permanent nature, as incapacitates a workmen for all work which he was capable of performing at the time of the accident. The rates of compensation for different kinds of disablements discussed above vary materially from each other.

Employers Liability.—If personal injury is caused to a workman by accident arising out of and in the course of his employment his employer is liable to pay compensation in accordance with the provisions hereafter discussed, provided that the employer is not liable: (a) In respect of injuries not resulting in total or partial disablement of a workman for a period exceeding three days; (b) in respect of any injury caused by an accident which is directly attributable to (1) the workmen having been at the time under influence of drinks or drugs, (2) wilful disobedience of the workman to an order expressly given, or a rule expressly framed, for the purpose of securing the safety of the workmen or (3) wilful removal or disregard by the workman of any safety guard or other device which he knew to have been provided for the purpose of securing safety of workman. (§3).

Amount of Compensation.—The amount of compensation payable to a workman is made to depend on two factors. The first factor is where the accident causes death or where it results in injury. If injury results then the question arises whether such injury produces partial disablement or total disablement. The amount of compensation also depends on whether the workman injured is an adult or a minor; the second factor on which compensation depends is the monthly wages drawn by the workman injured. The distinction is also made between an adult and a minor. An adult workman is entitled to higher compensation than the workman who is a minor.

Different kinds of injuries for which compensation becomes payable have also been set out at length in one of the schedules to the Act, such as (a) loss of right arm above or at the elbow, (b) loss of leg at or above the knee, (c) loss of one eye, (d) loss of thumb, (e) loss of one phalanx of thumb, (f) loss of any finger, etc. In this Schedule, each injury set out also indicates the percentage of loss of earning capacity for the purpose of determining the extent to which the disablement is partial because the amount of compensation also depends on the extent of disablement caused by the injury.

The amount of compensation payable to workmen for death or disablement also depends on monthly wages earned by the workman concerned.

Occupational Diseases.—Some of the occupational diseases for which compensation is payable are: (a) poisoning by nitrous fumes, (b) chrome, ulceration or its sequelae, (c) pathalogical manifestations, due to radium and other radioactive substances, (d) X-rays, (e) primary epitheliomatous cancer of the skin and (f) asbestosis.

The compensation for any occupational disease is payable only if any particular disease is contracted in the course of a specified employment. (§4). If a worker were to contract any occupational disease while not in the specified employment, he can recover no compensation from his employer.

Payment & Distribution of Compensation.—Compensation payable in respect of a workman whose injury has resulted in death or compensation payable to a woman or a person under a legal disability (e.g., a minor) has to be deposited with the Commissioner for Workmens Compensation and no such payment can be made directly and even if made is deemed to be no payment at all. The compensation deposited in respect of a deceased workman is apportioned among his dependants in such proportion as the Commissioner may think fit. In other cases the compensation deposited is paid to the workman entitled thereto in such manner as the Commissioner may direct. (§8).

Notice and Claim.—No claim for compensation can be entertained by the Commissioner unless notice of the accident is given as soon as practicable after the happening thereof and unless the claim is preferred before the Commissioner within two years of the occurence of the accident or in case of death within two years from the date of death. (§10).

Powers of the Commissioner.—The provisions of the Act are administered by an officer appointed by the Government designated as the Commissioner for Workmens Compensation.

Some of the powers with which the Commissioner is invested are: (a) when he receives information that a workman has died as a result of an accident, he may require the employer to submit a statement giving the circumstances attending the death of the workman and (b) all the powers of a civil Court for taking evidence on oath and compelling production of documents and material objects.

Medical Examination.—Where a workman gives notice of an accident, he is bound to submit himself to medical examination if the employer desires to have him examined at his own cost by a qualified medical practitioner. The Commissioner has also powers to direct medical examination of an injured employee. If the employee refuses to submit himself to such examination or in any way obstructs the same, his right to compensation is suspended during the continuance of such refusal or obstruction. (§11).

Remedies of Employer Against Strangers.—Where a workmen recovers compensation from his employer and the circumstances are such as to give rise to a legal liability of some third party, then the employer after making payment, can claim to be indemnified by the person so liable and may recover from such party the amount of compensation which the employer has already paid. (§13).

Contracting Out.—Any contract or agreement, whereby the workman relinquishes his right of compensation from the employer for personal injury is null and void in so far as it purports to remove or reduce the liability to pay compensation under the Act.

Appeal.—Any party dissatisfied with a decision given by the Commissioner, may file an appeal to the High Court of the State, but only certain specified orders are appealable. (§30).

Payment of Wages Act, 1936.—This Act is passed for regulating payment of wages to certain classes of workmen employed in industries. Object of passing Act was to avoid delays which occur in payment of wages to employees and to regularise practice of imposing fines on them.

Responsibility for Payment of Wages.—Every employer is responsible for payment to persons employed by him of all wages required to be paid under the Act. (§3). The person responsible for payment of wages must fix periods (referred to in the Act as Wage Periods) in respect of which wages are payable. No wage period can exceed one month. (§4).

Time of Payment of Wages.—The wages of every person employed in a factory or industrial establishment in which less than 1,000 persons are employed must be paid before the expiry of the seventh day after the last date of the wage period. In any other establishment wages must be paid before the expiry of the tenth day after the last date of the wage period.

When the employment of any person is terminated the wages earned by him must be paid before the expiry of the second working day from the date on which such employment is terminated. (§5).

All wages must be paid only in current coin or currency notes or in both.

Permissible Deductions.—The general rule is that the wages of an employee must be paid to him without any deductions of any kind. However, certain deductions are authorised such as: (a) Fines (imposed and realised in the manner hereinafter stated); (b) for absence from duty to the extent and in the manner prescribed by §9 of the Act; (c) for damage to or loss of goods entrusted to the employee or for loss of money for which he is accountable in the manner prescribed by §10 of the Act; (d) for housing accommodation supplied; (e) for such amenities and services supplied by the employer as may be authorised by the Government in the manner prescribed by §11; (f) for recovery of advances or for adjustments of over-payments, as prescribed by §12; (g) for income tax payable by an employee; (h) deductions required to be made by an order of a court; (i) for subscriptions to any Provident Fund to which the Provident Act of 1925 applies, or any other Provident Fund approved by the State Government; (j) for payment to co-operative Societies approved by the State Government in the manner prescribed by §13 of the Act; (k) deductions made with the written authorisation of the employee for payment of any premium on his Life Insurance Policy. (§7).

Fines.—An employer must exhibit on the premises of his factory a notice specifying such acts and omissions on the part of the employees rendering them liable for payment of fines. Previous approval of the State Governments or of the prescribed authority must be taken before specifying such acts and omissions.

Fine can only be imposed on an employee in respect of acts and omissions specified in notice set out above and no other. No fine can be imposed on employee until he has been given opportunity of showing cause against imposition of fine.

The total of fine in any wage period may not exceed an amount equal to 3% of wages payable in respect of that wage period. No fine can be imposed on employee who is under age of 15 years, nor can fine be recovered by instalments or after expiry of 60 days from date on which it was imposed.

All fines and realisations thereof must be recorded in a special register and all realisations must be applied only to such purpose beneficial of the persons employed in the factory or establishments as are approved by the prescribed Authority.

Remedies for Aggrieved Employee.—Any employee whose wages have been illegally deducted or the payment of whose wages have been delayed may file a claim with the Authority constituted under §15 of the Act. Such claim must be presented within 12 months from the date on which the deduction is made or from the date on which the payment of the wages had become due. The authority has been empowered to condone the delay for a sufficient cause.

On receiving a claim the Authority proceeds to give notice to the employer concerned, and after hearing the parties passes Orders according to law.

Powers of Authority.—The Authority appointed to investigate claims has all the powers of a civil Court for the purpose of taking evidence, and of enforcing the attendance of witnesses and to compel production of documents.

Appeal.—Any party aggrieved by the Order of Authority may prefer an appeal to a civil court specified in §17.

Bar of Suits.—No civil Court may entertain any suit for the recovery of wages or for any deductions from wages in so far as the sum so claimed: (a) forms the subject of an application under the Act and which is pending before the Authority, or (b) could have been recovered by an application under the Act.

Contracting Out.—Any contract or agreement whereby an employee relinquishes any right conferred by the Act is null and void in so far as it purports to deprive him of his such right.

The Indian Trade Unions Act, 1926.—This Act provides for registration of Trade Unions and in certain respects defines the law relating to registered Trade Unions.

A *"Trade Union"* within the meaning of the Act means any combination whether temporary or permanent formed primarily for the purpose of regulating the relations between workmen and employers or between workmen and workmen or between employers and employers or for imposing restrictive conditions on the conduct of any trade or business and includes any federation of two or more Trade Unions. (§2[h]).

See Topical Index in front part of this volume.

INDUSTRIAL AND LABOUR LAWS . . . *continued*

Registration of Trade Unions.—Any seven or more persons by subscribing their names to the rules of the Trade Union and otherwise complying with the provisions of the Act can apply for registration of a Trade Union. (§4).

The application for registration is made to the Registrar appointed under the Act and this application must comply with certain requirements of the Act and must contain particulars prescribed in that behalf, such as names and occupations of the members, name of the Trade Union, etc. (§5).

The Registrar, on being satisfied that the Trade Union has complied with all the requirements of the Act registers it by entering in a register the particulars relating to it and issues a certificate of registration. (§§8, 9).

Cancellation of Registration.—A certificate of registration may be withdrawn or cancelled on the application of the Trade Union, or if the registrar is satisfied that the certificate of registration has been obtained by fraud or mistake, or that the Trade Union has ceased to exist or that it has wilfully contravened any of the provisions of the Act. (§10).

Body Corporate.—Every registered Trade Union becomes a body corporate by the name under which it is registered and has perpetual succession and a Common Seal with power to acquire and hold properties and to enter into contracts.

Rights and Liabilities of Registered Trade Unions.—The general funds of a Registered Trade Union can be spent only on specified objects, the main being the conduct of trade disputes on behalf of the Union or any member thereof and payment of compensation to members for loss arising out of trade disputes. (§15). However, it is open to a Trade Union to constitute a separate fund from contributions from members for the promotion of the civic and political purposes. (§16).

Immunity from Legal Proceedings.—No suit or legal proceedings may be maintained in any civil court against any Registered Trade Union or any officer or members thereof in respect of any act done in contemplation or furtherence of a trade dispute on the ground only that such act induces some other persons to break a contract of employment or that it is an intereference with trade, business or employment of some other person. A Registered Trade Union cannot be made liable in any suit or other legal proceedings in any civil court in respect of any tortious act done in contemplation or furtherence of a trade dispute by an agent of the Union if it is proved that such person acted without the knowledge of or contrary to expressed instructions given by the representatives of the Union.

Annual Returns.—A Trade Union must send every year to the Registrar a general statement audited in the prescribed manner of all receipts and expenditure together with a statement showing all changes of officers of the Union during the year.

Rights of Recognised Trade Unions.—The executives of a Recognised Trade Union are entitled to negotiate with the employers in respect of matters connected with a trade dispute and to carry on correspondence with the employers. The executives of a Recognised Trade Union are entitled to display notices of a Trade Union in any premises in which its members are employed and the employers must afford reasonable facilities for that purpose. (§28 F).

Employees State Insurance Act, 1948.—This Act provides for certain benefits to employees in case of sickness, maternity and employment-injury. Under the Act, a Statutory Corporation has been set up called "Employees State Insurance Corporation" (hereinafter referred to as "the Corporation") which administers the Scheme propounded in the Act. (§3). The Scheme is one of the compulsory State Insurance providing for the benefits conferred by the Act on the employees and enumerated herein below. In pursuance of the Scheme as envisaged in the Act, all employees in the factories or establishments to which the Act applies are insured.

Contributions.—The employees and employers both must make contributions and all contributions go to the Corporation and are paid in to a fund called "Employees State Insurance Fund." (§26). The moneys in the Fund are to be principally applied for payment of the monetary benefits and for providing medical treatment and attendances to the insured persons and where medical benefit is extended to the families by the Act for giving such medical facilities to the families.

The rates at which the employers and the employees have to make contributions are specified in the first Schedule appended to the Act.

A week is a unit in respect of which all contributions are payable under the Act and such contributions fall due on the last day of the week. (§39).

No employee whose average daily wages are below Rs. 1½ has to make any contribution but even in such a case the employer is required to make a contribution according to the rules prescribed. (§42). In case of employees drawing average wages of more than Rs. 1½ rates of contribution, both by employees and employers vary depending on the amount of wages. No employer can by reason of his liability to make contribution, reduce directly or indirectly the wages of his employees.

Benefits.—Benefits given to the insured persons under the Act are governed by certain rules found in the Act and are of different kinds, the chief of them being the following: (a) periodical payment in case of sickness certified by a duly appointed medical practitioner; (b) periodical payments in case of confinement to an insured woman certified to be eligible for payment by the authorities concerned; (c) periodical payments to a person suffering from disablement as a result of employment injury duly certified; (d) periodical payments to dependants of an employee who dies as a result of employment injury; (e) medical treatment for attendance on employees.

The rates at which these monetary benefits are given have been set out in the Second Schedule appended to the Act.

A right to receive payment of such benefit is not transferable or assignable nor can any such benefit be attached or sold in execution of an order of the Court.

No employee may claim sickness benefit or maternity or disablement benefit in respect of any day on which he works and receives wages.

A recipient of sickness or disablement benefit must observe certain conditions, namely: (a) remain under medical treatment at a hospital or clinic provided under the Act and carry out the instructions given by the medical officer; (b) do nothing which might retard or prejudice his chance of recovery; (c) cannot leave the area in which medical treatment is given without the permission of the medical officer; (d) submit to examination by duly appointed medical officer.

Corporation's Right to Recover Damages.—Where an employment injury is sustained by an insured person, by reason of negligence of the employer to observe any of the safety rules or by reason of any wrongful act of the employer, the Corporation becomes entitled to be reimbursed by such employer in such amount as the Corporation is liable to pay to the employee under the Act.

Adjudication of Disputes.—Under the Act a court has been set up called "Employees Insurance Court" which decides claims and questions of liability arising between the Corporation, employees and employers.

Exemption.—The Government has been given a right to exempt any factory or establishment from the provisions of the Act in proper cases.

Payment of Bonus Act, 1965.—See subhead Case Law, catchline Bonus, infra.

Administrative Tribunals Act, 1985.—This Act makes provision for adjudication or trial of disputes and complaints with respect to recruitment and conditions of service of persons appointed to public service and posts in connection with affairs of Union or of any State or any local or other authority within territory of India or of any corporation owned or controlled by Government notified for purpose and for matters connected therewith.

§29 has made specific provision for transfer of pending cases. It lays down that every suit or other proceeding pending before any court or other authority immediately before date of establishment of Tribunal under this Act, being suit or proceeding, cause of action whereon it is based is such that it would have been if it had arisen after such establishment within jurisdiction of such tribunal, shall stand transferred on that date to such Tribunal provided that nothing in section shall apply to any appeal pending before a High Court or Supreme Court. Act does not apply to: (a) Any member of naval, military or air forces or any other armed forces of Union; (b) any person governed by provisions of Industrial Disputes Act 1947 in regard to such matters in respect of which he is governed; (c) any officer or servant of Supreme Court or of any High Court; (d) any person appointed to Secretarial staff of either House of Parliament or to Secretarial staff of any State Legislature or House thereof or in case of Union territory having Legislature, of that Legislature.

From any order or decision of Administrative Tribunal any appeal will lie only to Supreme Court under Art. 136 of Constitution of India.

Case Law.—Some of more important aspects of Labour and Industrial Laws have been evolved by Tribunals and Courts and Case Law covers very vast field. Some important subjects are: (a) Fixation of Wage Scales; (b) Dearness Allowance; (c) Bonus; (d) disciplinary action against employees for misconduct.

Fixation of Wage Scales.—The Wage fixation is governed by the following principles:

(1) In the fixation of rates of wages which include within its compass the fixation of scales of wages also, the capacity of the industry to pay is one of the essential circumstances to be taken into consideration except in cases of bare subsistence or minimum wage where the employer is bound to pay the same irrespective of such capacity;

(2) The capacity of the industry to pay is to be considered on an industry-cum-region basis after taking a fair cross-section of the industry, and

(3) The proper measure of gauging the capacity of the industry to pay should take into account the elasticity of demand for the product, the possibility of tightening up the organization so that the industry could pay higher wages without difficulty and the possibility of increase in the efficiency of the lowest paid workers resulting in increase in production considered in conjunction with the elasticity of the demand for the product, no doubt against the ultimate background that the burden of the increased rate should not be such as to drive the employer out of business.

Dearness Allowance.—"Dearness allowance" is intended to provide for an increase over the basic pay in order to meet a rise in the cost of living where it is expected that it will be only of a temporary character. Instead of having revisions of wage scale to meet such contingencies, practice has been to fix basic wage at level below which prices will not go down so far as can reasonably be foreseen. Increase over and above this point due to rise in cost of living is provided for by grant of dearness allowance.

Soon after the commencement of the World War II in 1939, the system of dearness allowance came into existence due to a steep rise in cost of living.

In India there are two principal methods providing for dearness allowance. The first method is to fix flat rates or definite percentages of basic salary as dearness allowance varying, if need be, with the scale of salaries and with slabs. The second method is to link dearness allowance with rise or fall of cost of living index figures.

For various towns and centres index figures are published in the Indian Labour Gazettes. Various other Commercial Bodies such as Bombay Mill Owners Association also publish such figures from time to time. Apart from this, the Government also publishes All India Cost of Living Index Figures.

Bonus.—Term "bonus" is applied to cash payment made in addition to wages and is governed by Payment of Bonus Act 1965.

By this Act every employer in private sector (with few statutory exceptions) and certain employers in public cum private sector must pay bonus to every employee. (§10).

Bonus must be paid to every employee earning salary up to maximum ceiling of Rs. 2,500-per month. Minimum rate of bonus is 8.33% of employees' earned salary or RS. 100-per year, whichever is higher. Maximum bonus payable under Act is 20% of employee's wages.

Bonus is paid out of available surplus of gross profit of every accounting year. Available surplus is gross profit for that accounting year after deduction of certain sums specified in §6 of Act. Where available surplus exceeds minimum bonus fixed under Act, it must be utilised in payment of higher rate of bonus up to maximum of 20% of earned basic salary.

Before bonus becomes payable employee must have worked for at least 30 working days minimum in that accounting year. Working days include those on which employee was on leave under Industrial Employment Act 1946 or Industrial Disputes Act 1947 or on leave with salary, or absent due to temporary disablement caused by accident in course of employment or on maternity leave with salary. Bonus must be paid within eight months of close of accounting year.

Establishment which is newly set up need not pay bonus until accounting year in which employer derives profit from establishment or from sixth year following that accounting year in which employer first sells goods produced by him, whichever is earlier.

See Topical Index in front part of this volume.

INDUSTRIAL AND LABOUR LAWS . . . *continued*

Disciplinary Action.—If an employee is found guilty of any misconduct, he may be dismissed, discharged, censured or be subjected to a proper penalty.

However, before taking any action against an employee for misconduct, it is necessary that the employer observe principles of natural justice and this is done by adopting the following procedure: (a) An employee against whom disciplinary action is to be taken should be given a charge sheet setting forth the circumstances appearing against him; (b) a date should be fixed for enquiry giving sufficient time to the employee to prepare his explanation and to produce any evidence which he wishes to tender in his defence; (c) he be permitted to appear before the officer conducting the enquiry to cross examine any witnesses on whose evidence the charge rests and to examine witnesses and produce other evidence in his defence.

On the conclusion of such enquiry if the management comes to the conclusion that the employee concerned is guilty of the charge, then steps may be taken for disciplinary action. Employee must be given opportunity to show cause against punishment proposed to be imposed.

If the rules indicated above are not complied with then the order of dismissal may be attacked by the employee as bad in law giving rise to a claim for reinstatement and back wages.

It may also be stated that even if the procedure indicated above is adopted and yet it is found that an employer in taking disciplinary action has not acted bona fide and his motives in taking the action were to victimize the employee, say for example, for his Trade Union activities then the Industrial Tribunal has powers to enquire into the matter and in proper case set aside the order passed by the management and direct reinstatement of the employee with such compensation as may be thought proper.

INDUSTRIES (DEVELOPMENT AND REGULATION) ACT:

Provisions have been greatly relaxed (see, infra, subhead Relaxation).

The Government of India has passed the Industries (Development and Regulation) Act, 65 of 1951 to provide for the development and regulation of certain industries. The Act extends to whole of India. Industries which are covered by Act are mentioned in First Schedule to Act. Broadly, following categories of industries are included in First Schedule viz: (1) Metallurgical industries (ferrous and non-ferrous); (2) fuels; (3) boilers and steam generating plants; (4) prime movers; (5) electrical equipment; (6) tele-communications; (7) transportation; (8) industrial machinery; (9) machine tools; (10) agricultural machinery; (11) earth-moving machinery; (12) miscellaneous mechanical and engineering industries; (13) commercial office and household equipment; (14) medical and surgical appliances; (15) industrial instruments; (16) scientific instruments; (17) mathematical, surveying and drawing instruments; (18) fertilizers; (19) chemicals (other than fertilizers); (20) photographic raw film and paper; (21) dye stuffs; (22) drugs and pharmaceuticals; (23) textiles (including those dyed printed or otherwise processed); (24) paper and pulp including paper products; (25) sugar; (26) fermentation industries; (27) food process industries; (28) vegetable oils and vanaspati; (29) soaps, cosmetics and toilet preparations; (30) rubber goods; (31) leather, leather goods and pickers; (32) glue and gelatin; (33) glass; (34) ceramics; (35) cement and gypsum products; (36) timber products; (37) defence industries; (38) cigarettes.

The above-mentioned industries are hereinafter referred to as the Scheduled industries.

Central Advisory Council.—Chapter II of the Act provides for establishment of Central Advisory Council for the purpose of advising the Central Government on matters concerning the development and regulation of Scheduled industries and Development Council consisting of representatives of owners of industrial undertakings and of employees employed therein and of consumers to perform such functions as may be assigned to it for increasing the efficiency or productivity in the Scheduled industries for which it is established.

Registration, etc.—Chapter III of the Act provides for registration of existing industrial undertakings, not belonging to the Central Government, appertaining to Scheduled industries and issuing of certificates of registration; licensing of such new industrial undertakings and laying down of conditions of its operations and locations; issue of license for producing or manufacturing new articles; revocation and amendment of licences in certain cases; issue of licence for effecting substantial expansion or changing the location of an industrial undertaking which has been registered; procedure for the grant of licence or permission; power to the Central Government to cause investigation to be made into scheduled industries or industrial undertakings where there has been or is likely to be a substantial fall in the volume of production or marked deterioration in the quality of production or a rise in the price of any article or class of articles relatable to that industry or there is necessity to take action to conserve any resources of national importance. On completion of investigation the Central Government, if satisfied, may issue directions for regulating the production or stimulating the industry or prohibiting any practice which might reduce an undertaking's production capacity or economic value or controlling prices and regulating the distribution of any article or class of articles.

Control.—Chapter IIIA contains provisions regarding direct management or control of industrial undertakings pertaining to Scheduled industries by the Central Government in certain cases, namely where such industrial undertaking has failed to comply with its directions or where an industrial undertaking in respect of which an investigation has been made is being managed in a manner highly detrimental to the scheduled industry or public interest. An order issued in this behalf shall have effect for such period not exceeding five years normally as may be specified but Central Government may direct that the order may be extended even after five years if it is in public interest to do so. On the issue of such order all persons in charge of the management shall be deemed to have vacated their offices as such and any contract of management between the undertaking and any managing agent or director shall be deemed to have terminated without compensation for loss of office or premature termination.

Chapter III AA has been introduced to provide for management or control of industrial undertakings owned by companies in liquidation. Under new Chapter III AB power is given to Central Government to provide that in cases of such undertakings, all or any of following Acts, viz. Industrial Employment (Standing Orders) Act, Industrial Disputes Act and Minimum Wages Act, shall not apply or shall apply with specified modifications, additions or omissions. In such cases, Central Government may also declare that operation of all or any contracts, assurances, agreements, settlements, awards, standing orders or other instruments shall remain suspended as specified by its order. New Chapter III AC deals with liquidation and reconstruction of companies.

The Central Government is authorised under Chapter IIIB of the Act, so far as it appears to it to be necessary or expedient for securing the equitable distribution and availability at fair price of any article or class of articles relatable to any scheduled industry, to make an order providing for regulating the supply and distribution (including control over the price) of all such articles and of trade and commerce therein.

For the purpose of ascertaining the position or working of any "Industrial Undertaking" to which the Act applies the Central Government may authorise any person to enter and inspect any premises or to order the production of any book, document, register or record or to examine any person having the control of or employed in connection with any "Industrial Undertaking."

Section 29C of the Act provides that no suit or prosecution or other legal proceeding shall lie against any person for anything which is done in good faith or against the Government for any damage caused or likely to be caused by anything done in good faith in pursuance of the Act.

If any person contravenes or attempts to contravene or abets the contravention of certain provisions of the Act he would be punishable with imprisonment which may extend to six months or with fine which may extend to Rs. 5,000/— or with both and in the case of a continuing contravention with an additional fine which may extend to Rs. 500/— for every day during which such contravention continues after conviction for the first such contravention.

Relaxation.—By Notification No. 477(E) dated July 25, 1991, Government has abolished licensing for all industrial undertakings and necessity for obtaining consequent approvals of Government for substantial expansion of existing industrial undertakings and for manufacture of new articles, subject to fulfillment of certain conditions. Notification has three Schedules; Schedule I lists industries reserved for public sector; Schedule II gives list of industries which are reserved for compulsory licencing; Schedule III is list of industries reserved for small scale ancillary sector.

Industries Reserved for Public Sector.—Following categories of industries are reserved for public sector: (1) Arms and ammunition and allied items of defence equipment, defence aircraft and warships; (2) atomic energy; (3) coal and lignite; (4) mineral oils; (5) mining of iron ores, manganese ore, crome ore, gypsum, sulphur, gold and diamond; (6) mining of copper, lead, zinc, tin, molybdemum and wolfram; (7) minerals specified in Schedule to the Atomic Energy (Control of Production and Use) Order, 1953; and (8) railway transport.

Industries in Respect of Which Industrial Licencing is Compulsory.—In respect of following broad categories of industries, industrial licencing is compulsory, viz.: (1) Coal and lignite; (2) petroleum (other than crude) and its distillation products; (3) distillation and brewing of alcoholic drinks; (4) sugar; (5) animal fats and oils; (6) cigars and cigarettes of tobacco and manufactured tobacco or tobacco substitutes; (7) asbestos and asbestos based products; (8) plywood, decorative veneer and other wood based products; (9) raw hides and skins and leather; (10) tanned or dressed fur skins; (11) motorcars; (12) paper and newsprint; (13) electronic aerospace and defence equipment; (14) industrial explosives; (15) hazardous chemicals; (16) drugs and pharmaceuticals (according to drug policy); (17) entertainment electronics; (18) white goods (domestic refrigerators, dish washing machines, washing machines, microwave ovens, air conditioners).

Items Reserved for Exclusive Manufacture in Small Scale Sector.—Broadly, following categories reserved for manufacture in small scale sector: (1) Food and allied industries; (2) textile products including hosiery; (3) wood and wood products; (4) paper products; (5) leather and leather products, including footwear; (6) rubber products; (7) plastic products; (8) injection moulding Thermo plastic products; (9) chemicals and chemical products; laboratory chemicals and reagents; (10) dyestuff; (11) natural essential oils; (12) glass and ceramics; (13) mechanical engineering excluding transport equipment; (14) electrical machinery appliances and apparatus including electronics; (15) electronic equipments and components; (16) transport equipment boats and truck body buildings; (17) auto parts components and ancillaries and garage equipment; (18) bicycle parts, tricycles and perambulators; (19) miscellaneous mathematical and heavy instruments; (20) sports goods; (21) stationery items; (22) clocks and watches.

INFANTS:

Age of Majority.—By Indian Majority Act IX of 1875 as am'd every person domiciled in India attains majority on completing 18 years of age. (§3). But minor who has guardian appointed of his person or property by court of justice or court of wards attains majority on completion of 21 years of age. (§3). Notwithstanding above, act does not have any effect regarding capacity of any person to act in following matters: (1) Marriage; (2) dower; (3) divorce; (4) adoption; (5) religion or religious rites and usage of any class of citizens; (6) capacity of any person who has attained majority under law applicable to him before this Act came into force. (§2). Requisite ages of capacity for above differ and are prescribed by relevant governing statutes or customs.

Actions.—Governed by Order 32 of Civil Procedure Code 1908. Every suit by minor is instituted in his name by person called next friend. If this is not done, defendant may apply to have suit struck off with costs payable by filing attorney. Minor may defend suit by guardian ad litem appointed by court for purposes of suit. Appointment may be made on application in name or on behalf of minor or by plaintiff. Such application must be supported by affidavit stating guardian has no interest in suit adverse to minor and is fit person to be so appointed. Notice of application to appoint guardian ad litem must be served on minor, and minor's guardian, or father or other natural guardian. Any person who is major and of sound mind and has no interest adverse to minor may be appointed guardian ad-litem. No person shall, without his consent in writing, be appointed guardian for suit.

Adoption.—See topic Adoption.

INFANTS . . . *continued*

Limitations.—Minor's contract in India is absolutely void ab initio (not voidable). See topic Contracts. But minor may hold shares in company through guardian on his behalf. See topic Corporations or Companies.

Child Labour (Prohibition and Regulation) Act, 1986.—It is prohibited to employ children under 14 years of age to work in certain occupations such as transport of passengers, goods or mails by railway or with port authority within port limits, etc. Children under 14 years of age cannot be employed in workshops, wherein certain processes, such as carpet weaving, manufacture of explosives, fireworks, etc. are carried on.

Factories Act.—No person who has not completed his 14th year, shall be allowed to work in factory. Person between ages of 14 and 18 shall not be permitted to work in factory unless he is certified to work in factory after examination by certifying surgeon. No child (i.e. person below 15 years) shall be permitted to work in factory at night or for more than four and a half hours in a day.

See also topic Contracts.

JUDGMENTS:

See topic Actions, subhead Foreign Judgments.

LABOUR RELATIONS:

See topic Industrial and Labour Laws.

LAW REPORTS, CODES, ETC.:

Decisions of Supreme Court are reported in All India Reports and Supreme Court Reports. Supreme Court Cases & Judgements Today. Supreme Court Reports are officially recognised reports. Its decisions are binding upon all High Courts and subsidiary courts of every State in India. Decisions of High Courts of each State are separately reported in Law Reporter for that State, e.g., Maharashtra Law Journal, Bombay Cases Reporter and Bombay Law Reporter for Bombay High Court decisions, Madras Law Journal for Madras High Court decisions etc., and in All Indian Reports. These decisions are binding on High Court and subsidiary courts of particular State, but have only persuasive value in High Courts of other States. Following is list of chief law reports: All India Reports (AIR); Supreme Court Reports (SCR); Bombay Law Reporter (BLR); Bombay Cases Reports (B.C.R.); Maharashtra Law Journal (Mah.L.J.); Madras Law Journal (MLJ); Calcutta Weekly Notes (Cal.WN); Company Cases (Co.Cas); Indian Law Reports (ILR); Gujrat Law Reporter (GLR); Labour Law Journal (LLJ); Income Tax Reports (ITR); Sales Tax Cases (STC); Sales Tax Reports (STR); Excise Law Times (ELT); Criminal Procedure Code (CRPC).

Codes are reported officially in Government Official Gazettes (Government of India Gazette and Gazette of each State) and can also be found in Civil Court Manual; All India Reporter Civil Manual; Criminal Court Manual and AIR Criminal Manual.

See also topic Statutes.

LEGISLATURE:

See topic Constitution and Government.

LICENSES:

See topic Industries (Development and Regulation) Act.

LIENS:

Indian Contract Act, 1872 contains main provisions. Bankers, factors, wharfingers, attorneys-at-law and policy brokers are entitled to retain, as security for general balance of account, any goods bailed (see subhead Bailments and Pledges under topic Contracts) to them. (§171). Bailee of goods who has rendered service involving exercise of labour or skill in respect of goods bailed, has, in absence of contract to contrary, right to retain such goods until he receives due remuneration for service rendered in respect of such goods. (§170). Finder of goods has lien over goods until owner gives compensation for trouble and expense voluntarily incurred by finder to preserve goods and to find owner (though finder has no right to sue for such compensation). (§168). Pawnee is entitled to retain goods pledged for payment of debt (or performance of promise) for interest on debt and all necessary expenses incurred by him in respect of possession or preservation of goods pledged. (§173). In absence of contract to contrary, agent is entitled to retain goods, papers and other moveable and immoveable property of principal received by him until amount due to himself for commission, disbursements and services in respect of same has been paid or accounted for. (§221).

Sale of Goods Act, 1930, empowers unpaid seller of goods, who is in possession of them, to retain possession until payment or tender of price in three cases, viz., (a) where goods are sold without stipulation as to credit, (b) where goods are sold on credit, but term of credit has expired, and (c) where buyer becomes insolvent. (§47).

Companies may, by virtue of their articles of association (or under Regulation 9 of Table A of Companies Act, 1956) have a first and paramount lien (a) on every share (not being a fully-paid share) for all moneys called or payable at a fixed time in respect of that share, and (b) all shares (not being fully-paid shares) standing registered in name of a single person for all money presently payable by him or his estate to company.

LIMITATION OF ACTIONS: See topic Actions.

MARRIAGE:

Personal law in India depends to large extent upon customary law of community to which person belongs. Laws relating to marriage are to be found partly in statutes, Indian Special Marriage Act XLIII of 1954, Hindu Marriage Act XXV of 1955, Christian Marriage Act XV of 1872, Parsee Marriage and Divorce Act III of 1936 and partly in customary law of Muslims, Hindus, Buddhists, Jains, Sikhs, Parsees, Christians, Jews etc.

Hindu Marriages.—Hindu may get married either under customs of his tribe or caste or under provisions of Hindu Marriage Act XXV of 1955, but Act prevails where customary law conflicts with its provisions.

Capacity.—Marriage can be validly solemnised between two Hindus if: (1) Neither party has legal spouse living at time of marriage; (2) parties are not lunatics or idiots; (3) husband has completed 21 years and bride 18 years of age; and (4) parties are not within prohibited degrees of relationship (§5); severe penalties may be inflicted if these requirements are not observed (§18).

Ceremonies.—Eight types of marriage, are recognised by customs; where customs of two parties differ, marriage may be solemnised in accordance with customs of either party.

Registration.—Section 8 provides for registration of Hindu marriages in Hindu Marriage Registers kept in each state of India. Exact requirements differ according to each State's legislative provisions; but in any case, validity of Hindu marriage is in no way affected by omission to make entry in register.

Void and Voidable Marriages.—Marriage is void if either party has spouse living at time of marriage (i.e. union must be monogamous); and if parties marry within prohibited degrees.

It is voidable on following grounds: (1) Respondent was impotent at time of marriage and continued to be so until institution of suit; (2) either party was an idiot or lunatic at time of marriage; (3) where consent is required, it was obtained by fraud or force; (4) respondent was pregnant by some other man at time of marriage. Section 12 provides procedural safeguards to render a voidable marriage a nullity by decree of court.

Polygamy and Polyandry.—Hindu marriages after commencement of Act are strictly monogamous. Bigamy is severely punishable. (§17).

Effect of Void and Voidable Marriages.—Children of such marriages are legitimate but they forego any rights in property of their parents which they might otherwise have been entitled to. (§16).

Muslim marriages are governed entirely by Mohammedan customary law. Variations in ceremonies and formalities exist among various Muslim communities, such as Bohras, Khojas (followers of H.H. The Aga Khan), Ithnasheris etc., but basic principles set out below apply to all communities:

Marriage is contract performed by way of Nikah ceremony which has for its object the procreation and legalization of children.

Capacity.—Every Muslim of sound mind who has attained puberty may enter into Nikah or contract of marriage. Lunatics and minors who have not attained puberty may be validly contracted in marriage by the guardians. Marriage of Muslim who is of sound mind and has attained puberty is void if it is brought about without his consent, i.e., consent of majors is required, but not that of minors, as parties to marriage. However, after Restraint of Child Marriages Act it is doubtful whether "child marriages" can be validly performed even among Muslims.

Essentials.—It is essential for valid Muslim marriage that proposal is made by or on behalf of one of parties to marriage (usually husband's side) and acceptance of proposal is given by or on behalf of other party (usually wife's side) in presence and hearing of two males or one male and two female witnesses who are adult Muslims. Usually, father of would-be husband approaches father of would-be bride and makes offer ceremonially or formally; and father of would-be bride accepts offer. Marriage is contract between familes of two parties as much as between parties themselves. Proposal and acceptance must both be expressed at one meeting. Proposal made at one meeting and acceptance made at another meeting do not constitute valid marriage. Writing is not essential, nor is any religious ceremony essential. But it is customary that consent or on behalf of parties be recorded before Kazi (Priest) and consenting parties appear before him. Usually three Nikha forms are signed by or on behalf of each of parties to marriage; one is kept by husband or party on his behalf; one by wife or party on her behalf and one by Kazi or recording officer.

No other marriage except a marriage by way of Nikha is recognised in Muslim law.

Dower.—In Nikah contract, sum is specified by way of "mahr" (roughly dowry) which is sum of money or other property which wife is entitled to receive from husband in consideration of marriage. It is not necessary for husband to pay this immediately; payment may be made in installments during course of their married life. Amount specified may be increased after marriage. But if husband wishes to dissolve marriage he must pay wife full amount specified in Nikah contract before he does so. Widow has right to retain possession of her husband's estate in lieu of dower. Dower becomes confirmed upon consummation of marriage, or by valid retirement or by death of either spouse.

Prohibited Degrees.—Person may not marry his or her father, mother, sister, brother, aunt, uncle, niece, nephew, grandfather, grandmother, grandson or granddaughter. Man may not marry his wife's mother or grandmother, his wife's daughter or granddaughter, wife of his father or paternal grandfather, wife of his son, or his son's son or his daughter's son.

Polygamy and Polyandry.—Muslim male may not have more than four wives at same time; if he marries a fifth when he already has four the marriage is not void, merely irregular.

Muslim woman may not have more than one husband at any time.

Valid, Irregular and Void Marriages.—Muslim marriage which complies with all essentials is valid. Other marriages may be irregular or void. "Irregular marriage" is one which is not unlawful in itself but unlawful for something else, i.e., where irregularity arises from external circumstances, e.g., lack of witnesses. "Void marriage" is one which is unlawful in itself, prohibition being absolute and perpetual.

Following are irregular: (1) Marriage contracted without required number of, or without any, or not in presence of witnesses; (2) marriage to fifth wife when four are already validly married and existing; (3) marriage with woman undergoing "iddat" (iddat is compulsory period of seclusion for woman whose marriage has been dissolved by either divorce or death); (4) marriage of Muslim man with "Kitabia," i.e., a Jewess or Christian or another Muslim woman is valid, but that with a non-Kitabia (i.e., Zorastrian) is irregular; (5) man may not have at same time two wives who are so related to each other by consanguinity, affinity, or fosterage that if either of them were a male, they could not have lawfully intermarried, but if a man does so marry two wives, marriage is irregular, not void.

See Topical Index in front part of this volume.

MARRIAGE . . . *continued*

Following marriages are void: (1) Marriage of Muslim of sound mind who has attained puberty, to which he or she has not consented; (2) marriage to woman whose husband is alive and not validly divorced; (3) marriage to person within forbidden degrees of relationship.

Effect of Irregular and Void Marriages.—Void marriage is no marriage at all; it creates no civil rights or obligations between parties; offspring are illegitimate. Irregular marriage is terminable at will by either party before or after consummation by words showing intention to separate, e.g., "I have relinquished you." Marriage has no legal effect before consummation; after consummation wife is entitled to dower; must observe iddat; and issue are legitimate. But no mutual rights of inheritance between spouses are created by such marriage.

Parsi marriages are governed by Parsee Marriage and Divorce Act III of 1936. Act codifies Parsee customs, and is applicable to all Parsees throughout world.

Capacity.—Both parties to marriage must be born Parsees (Zoroastrians). Parties must not be related to each other in any of degrees of consanguinity or affinity which are prohibited. Parsi male must have completed 21 years of age and Parsi female must have completed 18 years of age. (§3). Schedule lists 66 prohibited degrees of relationship.

Essential Validity.—Marriage must be solemnised according to Parsi form of ceremony called "Ashirvad" by Parsee priest in presence of two other Parsee witnesses. This is not merely a matter of formal validity. Marriage is invalid if this essential is not observed. (§3).

Prohibition of Bigamy.—Parsee marriages are strictly monogamous. Bigamy is a criminal offence and severely punishable. (§§4, 5). Officiating priest is also penalised (§11) for participating in such a marriage.

Other Prohibitions.—Parsee may not contract marriage during lifetime of his or her wife or husband until such marriage has lawfully been declared null and void, or has been dissolved by divorce, declaration or dissolution under 1936 Parsee Marriage and Divorce Act.

Void Marriages.—Suit for declaration of nullity of marriage may be brought if consummation of marriage is through natural causes impossible.

Christian Marriages.—Marriages between persons professing Christian faith in India are governed by Indian Christian Marriage Act XV of 1872. Certain sections, however, do not apply to persons professing Roman Catholic faith, although they be Christians for purpose of Act.

Capacity.—It is only necessary for one of parties to profess Christian faith in order to get married under Act. (§4).

Consent.—Parental consent is not required where parties are majors. Consent of any of following persons is required if either party is a minor (i.e., under 18 years): father if living; or guardian; if no guardian, then mother; if no such person exists in India, consent is not required. (§19).

Persons Who May Solemnise Marriages.—Every marriage under this Act must be solemnised by one of following persons, or marriage is void: (1) Any minister who has received episcopal ordination, so long as marriage is according to rules, rites, ceremonies and customs of his church; (2) any clergyman of Church of Scotland provided marriage is to be solemnised according to rules, etc. of that church; (3) any minister of religion licensed under Act to solemnise marriages; (4) by or in presence of marriage registrar appointed under this Act; (5) any person licensed to grant certificates of marriage between Indian Christians. (§§4, 5).

Special Marriage Act XLIII of 1954.—This act facilitates marriage between persons not belonging to same communities, or having different religions or nationalities. Scope of Act extends to whole of territory of India as well as to intending spouses who are both Indian citizens domiciled abroad.

Capacity.—Man must have completed 21 years and woman 18 years of age. Neither party should be lunatic or idiot, or have legal spouse living at time of marriage. Neither party should be within prohibited degrees of relationship mentioned in First Schedule of Act.

Notice.—Parties to marriage must give notice of their intention to solemnise marriage under this Act in specified form to marriage officer of district in which at least one of parties has resided for period of not less than 30 days immediately preceding date upon which such notice is given. (§5). Notice is entered into Marriages Notice Book which is open to inspection on payment of small fee; if one party does not permanently reside within district, notice is sent to respective district office and displayed there. (§6). Any person may, before expiry of 30 days from date on which notice has been published, object to marriage but only on grounds that parties lack capacity.

Marriage may be solemnised on expiry of 30 days from date of notice.

Procedure.—Marriage officer cannot solemnise marriage if objection has been lodged until he has enquired into objection and is satisfied that it ought not to prevent solemnisation of marriage. Inquiry must be completed within 30 days from date when objection was lodged. If objection is unheld, parties can appeal to District Court. Marriage officers have all powers vested in a civil court under Code of Civil Procedure 1908 in carrying out enquiry. (§9).

Foreign Procedure.—Where objection is lodged before marriage officer outside India, in respect of marriage outside India, he cannot solemnise marriage but must transmit all records together with his own statement to Central Government, Delhi; decision of Central Government is final. (§10).

Procedural Formalities.—Before marriage is solemnised, parties and three witnesses must in presence of marriage officer sign declaration in form specified and declaration must be countersigned by marriage officer. (§11). Marriage must be solemnised at office of marriage officer or at such other place within reasonable distance therefrom as parties may desire, and upon such condition and payment of such additional fees as may be prescribed. Marriage may be solemnised in any form which parties choose to adopt. But it will not be complete and binding on parties unless and until parties say to each other in presence of marriage officer, three witnesses and in any language understood by parties. "I (A) take you (B) to be my lawful (wife or husband). (§12).

Marriage Certificate.—After marriage is solemnised, marriage officer must enter certificate thereof in form specified in book called Marriage Certificate Book. Certificate must be signed by parties and three witnesses. Once certificate is entered into book by officer, certificate is deemed to be conclusive evidence of fact that marriage under this Act has been solemnised and that all formalities respecting signature of witnesses have been complied with. (§13).

Default.—Whenever marriage is not solemnised within three months from date on which notice of it was given to marriage officer, or where appeal has been filed to District Court, then within three months from date of decision of District Court, or where records were sent to Central Government, within three months from date of Government's decision, notice and all other proceedings shall be deemed to have lapsed; marriage officer cannot solemnise marriage until fresh notice has been given and other procedure followed. (§14).

Effect.—Marriage under this Act severs parties from being members of undivided (joint) Hindu, Buddhist, Sikh or Jain family. (§19).

Persons do not acquire any special rights of succession by virtue of Act which they would not otherwise have had vested in them. (§20).

Nullity (Void and Voidable Marriages).—Marriages are void on following grounds under this Act: (1) Respondent was impotent at time of marriage and at time of institution of suit; (2) either party had spouse living at time of marriage; (3) either party was lunatic or idiot; (4) man was under 21 years and woman under 18 years at time of marriage; (5) parties were within prohibited degrees of relationship. (§24).

Following marriages are voidable: (1) Unconsummated marriage due to wilful refusal of respondent; (2) if respondent was pregnant by some person other than petitioner at time of marriage; (3) consent of either party was obtained by coercion or fraud. Act provides procedural safeguards for bringing suit for nullity in appropriate district court. (§25).

Effect of Such Marriages.—Any child of marriage begotten before decree of nullity is made who would have been legitimate otherwise, shall be deemed to be legitimate notwithstanding nullity decree. But such children cannot acquire rights in property of any persons other than their parents which they could have acquired only by reason of being legitimate children of their parents. (§26).

Scope of Act.—This act is not of mandatory nature. Persons may elect to make use of facilities provided by it in order to get married, but they do not necessarily have to observe it. Marriage not celebrated in accordance with this Act is not thereby rendered invalid. (§42). Act prohibits bigamy. (§§43, 44).

Registration.—Any marriage in India may be registered under Special Marriage Act. (§15). Certain requirements must be fulfilled. Parties must apply to marriage officer by form jointly signed by both, to have their marriage registered. Officer must give public notice of this, and after 30 days must, if satisfied that all requirements are fulfilled, enter certificate of marriage in Marriage Certificate Book. This Certificate must be signed by spouses and three witnesses. (§16). If officer refuses to register, aggrieved person may within 30 days from date of refusal appeal to district court whose decision is final. (§17). Effect of such registration is that marriage shall be deemed to be solemnised as under Special Marriage Act; all children born of marriage shall be deemed to be legitimate children. But children are not entitled thereby to property of any person other than their parents to which they would otherwise have not been entitled. (§18).

By Indian Matrimonial Causes (War Marriages) Act XL of 1948 where marriages were solemnised during war period between husband who at time of marriage was domiciled out of India and wife who was domiciled in India, Indian High Courts have jurisdiction to hear divorce, nullity cases as if parties were domiciled in India. See topic Divorce.

MONOPOLIES AND RESTRICTIVE TRADE PRACTICES:

Monopolies and Restrictive Trade Practices Act, 1969 (in nature of anti-trust legislation) enacted to ensure that operation of economic system does not result in concentration of economic power to common detriment, for control of monopolies, for prohibition of monopolistic, restrictive and unfair trade practices and for matters incidental thereto. Commission has been appointed under Act, with powers of civil court, to conduct inquiries and hearings and to advise Government under Act. Provisions relating to Registration of Undertakings; prior approval for substantial expansion; setting up of new undertakings; mergers, amalgamations have been deleted. Central Government and Commission are given power to pass any orders to remedy or prevent mischief resulting from monopolistic trade practices. All agreements relating to restrictive trade practices falling within categories specified in Act are to be registered with Registrar of Restrictive Trade Practices. Commission has powers to inquire into restrictive trade practices and pass orders if it is of opinion that practice is prejudicial to public interest. Commission also has similar powers in respect of trade practices which amount to unfair trade practices under Act. Commission also has power to grant temporary injunction in certain cases and award compensation.

MOTOR VEHICLES:

This is governed by Motor Vehicles Act of 1989 (amended in 1994 effective 14th Nov. 1994).

Driver's Licence.—No person can drive motor vehicle in India unless he has effective licence issued to him in person. Persons under 18 years of age may not drive in public places; and persons under 20 years may not drive transport vehicles in public places, subject to exceptions.

Duration.—Driver's licence is valid for maximum five years before renewal is necessary.

Tests.—Appropriate state licensing authority may specify tests before issuing licence. If applicant holds licence issued by competent authority of any country outside India, no test is required.

Insurance.—Every vehicle must be insured at least against third-party claims. Driving vehicle without such insurance is offence.

Silence Zones and Parking.—Certain Indian cities have silence zones where motor vehicle horns may not be sounded. Entry into such areas is marked by road sign of

See Topical Index in front part of this volume.

MOTOR VEHICLES . . . *continued*
black horn with large white cross running diagonally across it. Parking in demarcated areas may be prohibited or otherwise restricted.

Vehicle Registration.—Every vehicle driven in India must be registered, and have its registration plate suspended easily visible from vehicle. Registration is in state where vehicle is normally kept.

Renewal of Registration.—Vehicles over 15 years old must undergo prescribed test for road-worthiness.

Diplomatic Corps Vehicles.—Special rules issued by Central Government from time to time govern registration, import, sale, transfer and export of vehicles belonging to diplomatic or consular officers. (§24A).

Temporary Registration.—Persons may apply for vehicles to be temporarily registered for period not exceeding one month (not extensible). (§25).

Effective Registration.—Vehicle effectively registered in one place in India need not be registered anywhere else in India. (§28).

Transfer of Ownership.—Transferor must report to registration authority within 14 days of transfer and send copy to transferee. Transferee must report with copy to registration authority within whose jurisdiction he resides, and obtain fresh registration. (§31).

Compensation for Accidents.—Motor accidents Claims Tribunals are established under Act to adjudicate upon and award compensation for loss of life/limb arising out of motor accidents. Quantum of compensation would depend upon earning capacity of victim, disability suffered etc. Whether victim had contributed to accident is also relevant factor to be considered while awarding compensation, subject to exception of "no fault" liability.

Act has also introduced concept of "no fault liability". Where fatality results, heirs of victim are entitled to compensation of Rs. 50,000 (earlier Rs. 25,000) in first instance irrespective of whether or not victim was guilty of negligence. Similarly for injury resulting in permanent disability, compensation of Rs. 25,000 (earlier Rs. 12,000) is awarded to victim whether or not owner of vehicle or any other person was guilty of negligence. No fault liability compensation is payment in first instance and will be adjusted against any further compensation awarded to victim/his heirs against owner/insurer of vehicles. (§140).

Claim for compensation must be filed with Tribunal within six months. Tribunal has powers, for sufficient cause shown, to condone delay in filing claim. In practice Tribunal is quite liberal whilst considering applications for condonation of delay.

Note: Statutory obligation on driver of vehicle involved in accident to arrange medical help for injured and to report accident at earliest to nearest police station.

Amended Act has introduced new provision for speedy disposal of cases under §163A (which is alternative to §140) under which compensation is to be paid in full as per structured formula on principle of no fault liability.

Tourist Information.—Central Government has power to make rules regarding import, export and transfer of vehicles into or out of India. These rules are subject to frequent change; and copy of latest rules and information should be obtained from Ministry of Transport or External Affairs Ministry Secretariat, New Delhi or from nearest High Commission or Embassy by persons intending to bring a car into India. It is advisable to write at least six months in advance of importing car into India. Vehicles in India are driven on left hand side of road.

NOTARIES PUBLIC:

Profession of notaries is regulated in India by Notaries Act LIII of 1952 which came into effect on 14/2/53. Power to appoint notaries is vested in Central Government which may appoint notaries for whole or any part of India; and in State Government which may appoint for whole or any part of State. (§3).

Persons Who May be Appointed.—Legal practitioners or other persons who possess such qualifications as may be prescribed. (§3).

Registration.—Central and State Government maintain registers of notaries appointed under Act. Every register includes following particulars: (1) Notary's full name, date of birth, residential and professional address; (2) date on which his name is entered in register; (3) his qualifications; (4) any other prescribed particulars. (§4).

Requirements.—Every notary who intends to practise as such is entitled, on payment of necessary fees, to have his name entered in register and to certificate authorising him to practise for period of three years from date of issue of certificate. This certificate is renewable for further period of three years at its expiry by application to appropriate Government and payment of necessary fees. (§5). Different rules exist in various States regarding details. (§5A). Annual list of notaries is published by each State and Central Governments in official gazette. (§6).

Seal.—Every notary must use a seal of prescribed form and design. Every exercise of any undermentioned power must be under his official seal and power. (§§7, 8).

Powers and Duties.—Notary has power to do following acts: (1) Verify, authenticate, certify, attest to execution of any instrument; (2) present any promissory note, hundi or bill of exchange for acceptance or payment or demand better security; (3) note or protest dishonour by nonacceptance or nonpayment of any promissory note, hundi or bill of exchange or protest for better security or prepare acts of honour under Negotiable Instrument Act 1881 (XXVI of 1881) or serve notice of such note or protest; (4) note and draw up ship's or boat's protest or protest re demurrage and other commercial matters; (5) administer oath to, or take affidavit from any person; (6) prepare bottomry and respondentia bonds, charter parties and other mercantile documents; (7) prepare, attest or authenticate any instrument intended to take effect in any country or place outside India in such form and language as may conform to law of place where such deed is intended to operate; (8) translate and verify translation of any document from one language to another; (9) any other act which may be prescribed. (§8). None of foregoing shall be deemed to be Notarial Act except when done by Notary under his signature and Official Seal.

Authentication.—Before 1952, see England Law Digest. After 1952, notary may authenticate, certify or attest execution of any instrument. No separate forms of endorsement in this respect have been prescribed.

Limitations on Practice.—No person may practice as a notary or do any act under an official notarial seal unless he has a certificate as mentioned above. (§9). Exceptions exist under Act.

Expiration of Commission.—Government appointing notary may remove his name from register on following grounds; (1) If so requested by notary; (2) if he has not paid prescribed fee; (3) if he is an undischarged insolvent; (4) if he has been found guilty of professional or other misconduct.

Persons who falsely represent themselves as notaries or do any notarial act are punishable by three months imprisonment and/or fine. (§§10, 12).

Recognition of Acts Done by Foreign Notaries.—Where Central Government is satisfied that any country outside India whether by its law or practice, recognises notarial acts done by notaries within India, Central Government has power to declare by notification in official gazette that notarial acts done lawfully by notaries within such a country shall be recognised in India. At present such recognition is extended to U. K., Isle of Man and Channel Islands; and Hungary (§14).

PARTNERSHIP:

Law of partnership formerly contained in Contract Act, is now codified by Indian Partnership Act 1932. English Act on this subject has been taken as model. Partnership is result of contract between two or more persons agreeing to share profits of business carried on by one or more acting for all. Minors cannot contract and therefore cannot be partners but may be admitted to benefits of partnership but incur no personal liability. Partners are principals as well as agents of each other for purpose of business. Chapter III deals with relations of partners inter se but is subject to contract to contrary.

Chapter IV deals with relations of partners with third parties. Section 19 vests in partners authority to carry on business and enumerates certain acts which do not fall within authority implied by section. Chapter V deals with admission, retirement, expulsion and insolvency of partners etc.; liability of estate of deceased partner; rights of outgoing partner; and revocation of continuing guarantee by change in firm.

Registration.—Under Code of Civil Procedure a partnership firm can sue or be sued in firm name but it has been provided in Indian Partnership Act that in order to entitle a firm to sue it must have been registered as a firm with Registrar of Firms appointed by Government for purpose. It is therefore advisable for every partnership firm in India to get itself registered with Registrar of Firms and any changes in constitution of firm should similarly be notified to Registrar and entered in his Register. Registration under Partnership Act is now mandatory in some states. Any statement, intimation or notice recorded in Register of Firms shall, as against any person by whom or on whose behalf such statement, intimation or notice was signed, be conclusive proof of any fact therein stated. Certified copy of entry relating to firm in books of Registrar of Firms may be produced in proof of fact of registration of firm and of contents of any statement, intimation or notice recorded therein.

Note.—Income Tax Act earlier contained separate provisions for registration of firms under that Act for income tax purposes. Registration under Partnership Act is distinct from income tax registration.

Dissolution.—Chapter VI deals with dissolution, i.e., breaking up of firm. Firm may be dissolved: By agreement of all partners (§40); (2) by adjudication of all or all but one partner as insolvent; (3) by business becoming unlawful (§41); (4) subject to contract between partners by efflux of time; (5) completion of its purpose; (6) death of partner or adjudication of partner as insolvent (§42); (7) by notice in case of partnership at will; (8) and by intervention of court on grounds set out in §44. Insolvent partner ceases to be partner on date on which adjudication order is made whether firm is thereby dissolved or not. Where under a contract between partners, firm is not dissolved by adjudication of partner as insolvent, estate of partner so adjudicated is not liable for any act of firm nor is firm liable for any act of insolvent after date of order of adjudication.

In order that public may have notice it is required under §72 of Act that notice relating to retirement or expulsion of partner or dissolution of registered firm should be given to Registrar of Firms and should also be published in local Official Gazette and in at least one vernacular newspaper circulating in district where firm has its principal place of business.

PATENTS:

Statute presently in force is Patents Act, 1970, which came into force on Apr. 20, 1972. Previous statute was Patents and Designs Act, 1911, which provided for registration not only of patents but also of designs. Provisions of 1911 Act, so far as they related to patents, have been replaced by Patents Act, 1970; remaining provisions of Patents and Designs Act, 1911, continue to be in force and that Act is now known as Designs Act, 1911. Main changes effected by new legislation are to shorten period of registration of patents and to provide for easier machinery for compulsory licencing of patients.

PLEDGES:

Indian Contract Act §172 et seq. (see topic Contracts) defines pledge as bailment of goods as security for payment of a debt or performance of a promise. Pawnee may retain goods pledged not only for payment of debt or performance of promise but for interest on debt and all necessary expenses incurred by him in respect of possession or for preservation of goods pledged. Pawnee may not retain pledge for debt or promise other than that for which goods are pledged. Defaulting pawnor may redeem goods even after time stipulated for payment of debt or performance of promise has passed, before actual sale of goods, but he must in addition, pay any expenses which have arisen from his default. Act confers general rights on pawnee in event of pawnor's default.

PRINCIPAL AND AGENT:

Law of Principal and Agent is found in §§182 to 238 of Indian Contract Act. Law is substantially same as in England. (See England Law Digest.) Consideration is not necessary to create agency. Any person can become agent except minor and person of unsound mind who will not be responsible to principal in accordance with provisions

PRINCIPAL AND AGENT . . . *continued*

of Act. Agent's authority may be express or implied. Agent's authority includes every lawful thing necessary to execute it. In an emergency agent has authority to do all such acts for purpose of protecting his principal from loss as would be done by a person of ordinary prudence in his own case under similar circumstances. Sections 190-195 deal with appointment of sub-agent, principal's responsibility for sub-agent's acts and relation between principal and sub-agent. When sub-agent is properly appointed, principal is responsible for sub-agent's acts as regards third party, though agent is responsible to principal for sub-agent's acts. Principal may ratify act done by another without his authority and if he ratifies act, same effects follow as if act had been performed by his authority. Knowledge, however, is requisite for valid ratification. Sections 201-210 deal with termination and revocation of agent's authority. If agent disregards instructions of his principal and a loss be sustained, he must make good loss to principal. Amount of skill and diligence required for an agent is amount of skill and diligence possessed by persons engaged in similar business. Agent dealing on his own account in business of agency, without consent of principal, must make good to principal benefit resulting therefrom. In absence of contract to contrary, agent has lien on property and papers of principal received by agent, for remuneration due to him. A principal is bound to indemnify agent against consequences of lawful acts performed by agent. In absence of any contract to that effect, agent cannot personally enforce contracts nor be bound by contracts on behalf of principal. Such contract as mentioned would be presumed where contract is made by agent for sale or purchase of goods for merchant resident abroad or where agent does not disclose name of his principal or where principal though disclosed, cannot be sued. Person falsely contracting as agent is not entitled to performance of contract but is liable for damage which other side incurs by such dealings. If principal induces belief in third persons that agent's unauthorised acts were authorised, principal would be liable to third persons as if acts and obligations were within scope of agent's authority.

Distributorship, Dealership and Franchises governed by contractual terms and under Contract Act. No special features/restrictions exist. Special considerations apply under Foreign Exchange Regulation Act, 1947 (see topic Exchange Control). Public limited company cannot appoint sole selling agent for term exceeding five years and with approval of company in General Meeting. Central Government has power to call for information of terms of appointment of sole selling agent, and if Government of opinion that such terms are prejudicial to company's interest, it has power to vary terms. Government also has power to prohibit, by gazette notification, appointment of sole selling agents where Government believes demand of any goods is in excess of supply. In certain cases, sole selling agents of companies are precluded from claiming compensation for loss of office.

PROCESS: See topic Actions.

REAL PROPERTY:

In India words, immovable property, include, inter alia, all that is meant by real property in English law. Transfer of Property Act does not give any definition of immovable property beyond excluding standing timber, growing crops and grass.

In Act, transfer of property means an act by which a living person conveys property to one or more other living persons, and words, living person, include a company or association or body of individuals, whether incorporated or not.

Sales and Exchanges.—A transfer by way of sale or exchange in case of tangible immovable property (i.e., corporeal hereditament of English law) of value of Rs. 100 and upwards, or in case of a reversion or other intangible thing (i.e., incorporeal hereditament of English law) can be made only by registered instrument. Other such transfers may be made by delivery. A contract that sale of immovable property shall take place on terms settled between parties does not, of itself, create any interest in or charge on such property.

Mortgages and Charges.—Legal mortgages in statutory modes in which immovable property is transferred for securing loan, debt or pecuniary liability of Rs. 100 or upwards can be effected only by a registered instrument signed by mortgagor and attested by two witnesses. Other such mortgages may be made by delivery. But equitable mortgages are recognised and where a person in towns of Calcutta, Madras and Bombay and any other Government notified town delivers to creditor or his agent documents of title to immovable property, with intent to create a security thereon, transaction is called a mortgage by deposit of title-deeds. Legal charge is created where immovable property of one person is by act of parties or operation of law made security for payment of money to another, and transaction does not amount to a mortgage.

Leases.—Under Act, a lease of immovable property from year to year or for any term exceeding one year, or reserving a yearly rent, can be made only by a registered instrument executed by both lessor and lessee. Other leases may be made by oral agreement accompanied by delivery of possession.

Note.—Under Income Tax Act sale, lease or other disposition (except gift) of immovable property for consideration mentioned in document exceeding Rs. 1 million in certain specified metropolitan areas requires prior permission of tax authorities. Different areas have different ceilings specified. These authorities have power to acquire property on payment of consideration mentioned in document and on such acquisition property vests in Government free from encumbrances.

Gifts.—For making a gift of immovable property, transfer must be effected by registered instrument signed by or on behalf of donor and attested by at least two witnesses, but a gift of movable property may be made by delivery.

Tenancy in Common and Joint Tenancy.—Both tenancy in common and joint tenancy of immovable property are recognised in India. However, contrary to English law, presumption is in favour of tenancy in common.

Registration.—Registration of documents of transfer is to be with Registrar of Assurances under Indian Registration Act. Under Income-Tax Act, 1961, where any document required to be registered under Indian Registration Act, purports to transfer, assign, limit or extinguish right, title or interest of any person to or in any property (other than agricultural land) valued at more than Rs. 200,000 no registering officer is to register any such document unless the Income-Tax Officer certifies that such person has either paid or made satisfactory provision for payment of all existing liabilities under Income-Tax Act, 1961, Excess Profits Tax Act, Business Profits Tax Act, Indian Income-Tax Act, 1922, Wealth Tax Act, and Gift Tax Act or that registration of document will not prejudicially affect recovery of any existing liability under any of aforesaid Acts.

Sanctions.—Under Acts pertaining to public trusts, it is necessary to obtain prior sanction of Charity Commissioner in respect of transfer of immovable property by public charitable trusts. Under Acts pertaining to agricultural lands, it is necessary to obtain prior sanction of Collector in respect of transfer of land used for agricultural purposes to person who is not an agriculturist. *Note:* Recently in Maharashtra, requirement for obtaining Collector's sanction prior to sale of agricultural lands, has been dispensed with, when land is being purchased for industrial use, provided certain conditions are complied with. For sale of property belonging to minors or Hindu undivided family, court's sanction is taken to show that proposed sale is beneficial to minor/members of Hindu undivided family.

Ceiling Area.—Under Acts pertaining to agricultural lands, there is a prescribed maximum limit or ceiling on holding of agricultural land to provide for more equitable distribution amongst peasantry.

Under Urban Land Ceiling and Regulation Act, 1976, no person entitled to hold any vacant land in excess of ceiling limit prescribed under Act, subject to certain exceptions. Ceiling limit varies between 500 square metres and 2,000 square metres depending upon area where land is situated. Land on which buildings constructed are not covered by Act except when transfer of lands and buildings, whether by way of sale, gift or otherwise, is proposed (as to which see below). Land appurtenent to building is not taken into account for determining ceiling to extent of that portion thereof required under building regulations to be kept open and, in addition, in case of any building constructed before commencement of Act, further 500 square metres of land.

Where person holds vacant land in excess of ceiling limit he must file return with competent authority within prescribed time. Thereafter, Government may delcare that excess vacant land shall be deemed to have been acquired for which compensation at rate of Rs. 10 per square metre, subject to maximum of rupees two lakhs will be paid.

Act not to apply to land held by: (1) Government, (2) armed forces, (3) government banks, (4) public charitable or religious trusts, (5) cooperative societies, (6) educational, cultural, technical institute or club as may be approved by Government, (7) foreign state for purposes of its diplomatic consular mission, (8) United Nations, and (9) any international organisation for any official purpose or for residence of members of staff of such organisation, provided that there is agreement between Government of India and such international organisation that such land should be exempted. Government has also got power to exempt application of Act in cases of undue hardship in special cases.

No person holding urban or urbanisable land with building may transfer same whether by way of sale, gift or otherwise without permission of competent authority. Competent authority may, on receipt of application seeking permission for sale, grant permission and take over land and building at market value plus 30%. If no reply to application seeking permission received within 60 days then competent authority shall be deemed to have granted permission.

SALE OF GOODS:

The sale of goods is regulated by the Indian Sale of Goods Act III of 1930. The Sections now enacted by the Indian Sale of Goods Act originally formed part of the Indian Contract Act Chapter VII. (See topic Contracts.) Contract of sale may be oral or in writing.

The Act makes a distinction between conditions and warranties, a condition being a stipulation essential to the main purpose of the contract, the breach of which gives the right to repudiate the contract, whereas a warranty is a stipulation collateral to the main purpose of the contract, the breach of which gives rise to a claim for damages, but not to the right to reject the goods or repudiate the contract. The Act lays down specific rules as to when the property in the goods passes from the seller to the buyer. It also deals with the right of an unpaid seller against the goods and gives him a lien to retain possession of the goods until payment, if the goods are in his possession, and if the goods are not in his possession there is also a right in an unpaid seller to stop the goods in transit. In cases of breach the party in default may be sued for the price of the goods or for damages and in case of failure to deliver specific or ascertained goods the court may decree specific performance of the contract if the contract is such as should be specifically enforced.

Warranties.—In a contract for sale of goods, there is no implied warranty or condition as to quality or fitness for any particular purpose (§16 of Sale of Goods Act) unless: (1) Buyer has, relying on seller's skill or judgment, made known to him particular purpose for which goods are required and seller ordinarily deals in such goods; or (2) sale is by description from seller who deals in goods of that description; or (3) such implied warranty is annexed by usage of trade.

See also topics Principal and Agent, and Partnership.

Applicable Law.—See topic Contracts.

Sales Tax.—See topic Taxation.

SALES:

See topic Sale of Goods.

SECURITIES:

See topic Corporations or Companies, subhead Capital Issues.

SHIPPING:

Carriage of goods by sea governed by (i) Merchant Shipping Act, 1958, (ii) Indian Carriage of Goods by Sea Act, 1925 and (iii) Indian Bill of Lading Act, 1856 and also general statutes like Marine Insurance Act, 1963, Indian Ports Act, 1908, Major Port Trusts Act, 1963, Customs Act, 1962 etc.

SHIPPING . . . *continued*

Merchant Shipping Act, 1958.—Act deals with registration of Indian ships, transfer and mortgages of ships or shares, national character and flag, employment of seamen, provisions regarding ship's survey, granting of certificates, maintenance of records on board, safety at sea, fire fighting appliances, construction of ships including nuclear ships, rules regarding loadline (in conformity with International Loadlines Conventions, 1966), radio requirements according to International Radio regulations, collisions, accidents at sea, liability, wreck, salvage, limitation of shipowner's liability, navigation, prevention of pollution, investigation and enquiries. Changes have been made in this Act to confer more protection on mortgagee of ship and sole mortgagee could foreclose and institute legal proceedings without Court action.

Act has various provisions to enforce territorial jurisdiction. Only Indian ships can ply in coastal waters; all accidents and loss of Indian ships must be reported to Central Government; and rules as to division of loss, damages for personal injuries and right of contribution.

Prior to Multimodal Transportation of Goods Act 1993 shipowner's liability was limited up to aggregate amount not exceeding amount equivalent to (a) 1,000 francs for each ton of vessel's tonnage where there are property claims only; (b) 3,100 francs per ton where there are personal claims only; (c) 3,100 francs per ton where there are both personal and property claims, first portion equivalent to 2,100 francs for each ton exclusively appropriated towards payment of personal claims and second portion equivalent to 1,000 francs for each ton shall be appropriated towards payment of property claims, provided where first portion is insufficient to pay personal claims unpaid balance shall rank rateably against second portion relating to property claims. By this Act Carriage of Goods by Sea Act has been amended with result that Art. IV has been amended as follows: (1) for words and figures "amount exceeding 1001 per package or unit", words and figures "amount exceeding 666.67 Special Drawing Rights per package or unit or two Special Drawing Rights per kilogram of gross weight of the goods lost or damaged, whichever is higher" shall be substituted.

By virtue of this shipowners' liability which was originally as per Hague Rules has now been brought to level as prescribed by Hague Visby Rules.

Indian Carriage of Goods by Sea Act, 1925.—Act governs carriage of goods by sea, follows English Carriage of Goods by Sea Act 1924 and contains Hague Rules regulating rights/obligations of parties to Contract of Carriage.

Indian Bills of Lading Act, 1856.—Act prevents Master or other person signing from questioning Bill of Lading in hands of bona fide holder for value on ground that goods have not been laden. Rights under Bills of Lading to vest in consignee or endorsee and does not affect right of stoppage to transit or claim for freight and renders Bill of Lading in hands of consignee etc. conclusive evidence of shipment against Master etc.

International Conventions.—India has ratified International Convention for Prevention of Pollution of Sea by Oil, 1954 as amended from time to time.

India is not party to (i) International Convention for the Unification of Certain Rules of Law relating to Bills of Lading, Brussels 1924; (ii) Brussels Protocol of 1968 (adopting Hague-Visby Rules); (iii) United Nations Convention on the Carriage of Goods by Sea Act, 1978 (adopting Hamburg Rules); (iv) International Convention relating to the Arrest of Sea-going Ships, Brussels, 1952; (v) Brussels Conventions of 1952 on civil and penal jurisdiction in matters of collision; (vi) Brussels Convention of 1926 and 1967 relating to maritime liens and mortgages. However, Supreme Court in M.V. ELIZABETH decided in Feb. 1992 held that principles incorporated in these conventions are themselves derived from common law of nations as embodying felt necessities of international trade and are as such part of common law of India and applicable for enforcement of maritime claims.

(See also topics Taxation; Admiralty Jurisdiction.)

STATUTES:

Acts of Parliament relating to matters falling within Central Government list and concurrent list are enacted by Parliament (both Upper and Lower Houses) passing bill which receives President's sanction. Central Government Statutes are published in Official Gazette, bearing serial number, name and date of enactment. Each State within India also has law-making power for matters falling within State Governments' and concurrent lists. Legislation is passed by Legislative Assembly of each State. Enactments are officially published in State Official Gazette in similar manner.

Civil Court Manual and All India Reporter (AIR) Manual contain comprehensive collection of all Central Government legislative enactments on civil matters. Criminal Court Manual contains similar collection of criminal law enactments.

See also topic Constitution and Government.

SUCCESSION AND INHERITANCE:

See topic Descent and Distribution.

TAXATION:

Estate Duty.—Estate Duty Act, 1953, came into force in India on Oct. 15, 1953. It was based on U.K. Finance Acts relating to levy of death duties. Estate Duty was abolished in India with respect to deaths occurring on and after Mar. 16, 1985.

Gift Tax.—This tax was introduced by Gift Tax Act, 1958 which came into force on Apr. 1, 1958. Tax is payable in respect of any gifts made by person during previous accounting year. Word "person" includes Hindu undivided family, company or association or body of individuals or persons whether incorporated or not.

Gifts include: (a) Where property is transferred otherwise than for adequate consideration, difference between market value of property on date of transfer and value of declared consideration. However, this clause will not apply where property transferred to Government or value or consideration for transfer is determined or approved by Central Government or Reserve Bank of India; (b) where property is transferred for consideration which, having regard to circumstances of case, has not passed or is not intended to pass, amount of consideration which has not passed or is not intended to pass; (c) where there is release, discharge, surrender, forfeiture or abandonment of any debt, contract or other actionable claim or of any interest in property, value of release, discharge, surrender, etc. However, bona fide releases, discharges, etc., will not be covered; (d) where person causes property to be transferred to joint names of himself and another jointly without adequate consideration and such other person makes appropriation from or out of property, amount of appropriation; (e) where person having interest in property (being either limited interest or life interest or remainderman's interest), surrenders or relinquishes his interest or otherwise allows interest to be terminated without consideration or for consideration which is not adequate, value of interest so surrendered, relinquished or allowed to be terminated or amount by which such value exceeds consideration received; (f) where member of Hindu undivided family converts his separate or individual property into property belonging to family by throwing it into common stock of family, value of so much of converted property as members of Hindu undivided family other than such individual would be entitled to, had partition taken place at date of transfer.

No gift tax is payable in respect inter alia of following gifts: (1) Gift of immovable property situated outside India; (2) gift of movable property situated outside India unless donor being individual is citizen of India and is ordinarily resident in India or not being individual is resident in India during previous year in which gift is made. Individual shall be deemed to be resident if he is regarded as resident under provisions of Income Tax Act. Company is deemed to be resident in India if it is company registered under Companies Act, 1956 or earlier Indian Acts relating to companies or if during previous year control and management of company was situated wholly in India; (3) by nonresident of amounts standing to credit of his nonresident (external) account with any Indian Bank; (4) by Indian citizen or nonresident of Indian origin of any convertible foreign exchange remitted from outside India to his relative. Person would be of Indian origin, if he or either of his parents or any of his grandparents were born in India; (5) by citizen of India or nonresident of Indian origin to any relative in form of any foreign exchange asset purchased from amounts remitted to India in convertible foreign exchange; (6) of property in form of Savings Certificates, Special Bearer Bonds, Capital Investment Bonds (latter subject to maximum of Rs.10,00,000 in any one or more years); (6A) of property in form of relief bonds subject to maximum of Rs. 5,000,000/- in one or more years; (7) to institution or fund established for charitable purposes to which provisions of §80 G of Income-Tax Act, apply; (8) to places of religious worship like temples, churches, mosques, etc.; (9) to dependent relative on account of his/her marriage up to or maximum of Rs.10,000 for each such relative; (10) under will; (11) gifts made in contemplation of death; (12) for education of donor's children to reasonable extent; (13) to employee by way of bonus, gratuity or pension to extent amount is proved to be reasonable and is made solely in recognition of services rendered by employee.

Value of any property gifted is normally estimated on open market basis. If gift is not revocable for stated period, value of property gifted is capitalised value of income from property gifted during period for which gift remains irrevocable.

As per present provisions of law, gift tax is payable by donor, but if it is not recoverable from donor, it can be recovered from donee. It is proposed to amend law by providing that gift tax will be payable by donee and not donor. This change is proposed to be brought in as antitax evasion measure. Gift tax payable in respect of any gift comprising any immovable property shall be first charge on that property but bona fide purchaser for valuable consideration without notice will be protected.

Act does not apply to gifts made by: (a) Government company or corporation established under Central, State or Provincial Act; (b) company other than private company as defined under Companies Act, provided affairs of company or more than 50% of total voting powers were at no time controlled or held by less than six persons; (c) company which is subsidiary and in which more than 1/2 of nominal value of equity share capital is held by company referred to in clause (b); (d) any company to Indian company in scheme of amalgamation; and (e) any public religious or charitable institution or fund whose income is exempt from payment of income tax.

Rates of Gift Tax.—Gift tax is chargeable at flat rate of 30% on value of all taxable gifts after basic exemption of Rs.30,000/-.

Wealth Tax.—This tax was introduced by Wealth Tax Act, 1957. It came into force on Apr. 1, 1957. It is chargeable for every financial year in respect of the net wealth on the corresponding valuation date of every individual or Hindu undivided family.

Valuation date in relation to any year for which assessment is to be made means last date of previous year as defined in Income-tax Act. Previous year under Income-tax Act is 31st of Mar. for all assessees. Therefore valuation date for all assessees will be 31st of Mar.

Wealth tax is payable at flat rate of 1% on value of following assets in excess of Rs.15 lakhs: (1) Any guest house or residential house and/or farm house situated within 25 kms from local limits of any municipality or cantonment board but excluding: (a) residential house alloted by company to employee or officer or director in whole time employment having gross annual salary of less than Rs.2 lakhs, (b) residential house forming part of stock-in-trade; (2) motor cars other than those used in assessee's business of hiring motor cars or used as stock-in-trade; (3) jewellery, bullion and furniture, utensils or other articles made wholly or partly of gold, silver, platinum or other previous metal other than those used as stock-in-trade; (4) yachts, boats and aircraft other than used by assessee for commercial purposes; (5) urban land, i.e. land within jurisdictionof municipality or cantonment board and within 8 kilomteters from local limits of such municipality or cantonment board as may be notified but excluding (i) land on which construction is not permissible, (ii) land on which building is constructed with approval of appropriate authority, (ii) unused land held by assessee for industrial purposes for period of two years from date of acquisition; (6) cash in hand in excess of Rs. 50,000/- of individuals and HUF and in cases of other assessees any amount not recorded in books of accounts.

These assets are alone chargeable to wealth tax. In computing net wealth, debts owed by assessee on valuation date, if incurred in relation to such assets, shall be deducted.

Further, wealth of minor child is added to that of parent who has greater net wealth; or where marriage of parents does not subsist, with that of parent who maintains minor. Assets acquired by minor child from self earned income and held on valuation date will not be added.

Schedule to Wealth-tax Act lays down rules for determining values of certain assets. Immoveable property is normally valued at 12.5 times net maintainable rent (i.e. municipal rateable value of property less deductions on account of municipal taxes and

TAXATION . . . *continued*

further deduction of amount equivalent to 15% of such rateable value on account of repairs, insurances, expenses on collection of rent, etc.). If property is let out and rent actually received is more than rateable value, then rent actually received is to be considered for determining net maintainable rent for purposes of valuation. If any property is purchased or acquired after 1st Apr. 1974 and its cost of acquisition is more than value arrived at on basis of capitalised value of net rental income, then value of property will be cost of acquisition. This provision however does not apply to self occupied residential house, where cost of acquisition is less than Rs.50 lacs if house is situated at Bombay, Delhi, Calcutta, Madras and Rs.25 lacs if house is situated in any other place.

Shares of companies which are not quoted on Stock Exchange are valued at 80% of break up value i.e. value arrived at by deducting value of all liabilities from value of all assets shown in Balance Sheet of company. Shares of company quoted on stock exchange are valued at stock exchange quotation on valuation date. Assessee has however option of adopting average value on valuation date and nine preceding valuation dates.

Expenditure Tax.—Repealed.

Sales Tax.—In the interest of the national economy certain amendments were made in the Constitution by the Constitution (Sixth Amendment) Act, 1956, whereby (a) taxes on sales or purchases of goods in the course of inter-State trade or commerce were brought expressly within the purview of the legislative jurisdiction of the Indian Parliament and (b) restrictions could be imposed on the powers of State legislatures with respect to the levy of taxes on the sale or purchase of goods within the State where the goods are of special importance in inter-State trade or commerce.

The amendments at the same time authorised Parliament to formulate principles for determining when a sale or purchase takes place in the course of inter-State trade or commerce or in the course of export or import or outside a State in order that the legislative spheres of Parliament and the State Legislatures become clearly demarcated.

Accordingly the Central Sales-Tax Act, 1956 (hereinafter called "the Act") was passed by Parliament. It formulates principles for determining when a sale or purchase of goods (a) takes place in the course of inter-State trade or commerce or (b) outside a State or (c) in the course of import into or export from India. It provides for the levy, collection and distribution of taxes on sales of goods in the course of inter-State trade or commerce which, under the constitution, are beyond the powers of the State governments to tax; and declares certain goods to be of special importance in inter-State trade or commerce and specifies the restrictions and conditions to which State laws imposing taxes on the sale or purchase of such goods of special importance, shall be subject.

Inter-State Sales.—Section 3 of the Act provides that a sale or purchase of goods shall be deemed to take place in the course of inter-State trade or commerce if the sale or purchase (a) occasions the movement of goods from one State to another, or (b) is effected by a transfer of documents of title to the goods during their movement from one State to another. A sale "occasions the movement" of goods, if movement is result of covenant or incident of contract. (1960, 11 STC, 655).

The tax payable by any dealer on sales of goods effected by him in the course of inter-State trade or commerce, whether such sales fall within sub-clause (a) or (b) of the above-mentioned Section is levied, collected and retained by State from which movements of goods commence.

Intra-State Sales.—Section 4(1) provides that subject to the provisions contained in Sect. 3, when a sale or purchase of goods is determined in accordance with Sub-section (2) thereof to take place inside a State, such sale or purchase shall be deemed to have taken place outside all other States.

Sub-section (2) of §4 provides that a sale or purchase of goods shall be deemed to take place inside a state if the goods are within the State (a) in the case of specific or ascertained goods, at the time the contract of sale is made; and (b) in the case of unascertained or future goods, at the time of their appropriation to the contract of sale by the seller or by the buyer, whether assent of the other party is prior or subsequent to such appropriation.

Sales in Course of Export or Import.—Section 5 of the Act provides that a sale or purchase of goods shall be deemed to take place in the course of the export of the goods out of or import of the goods into the territory of India only if the sale or purchase either occasions such export or import or is effected by a transfer of documents of title to the goods after the goods have crossed the customs frontiers of India, in case of export and before the goods have crossed the customs frontiers of India in case of import.

The Central Sales-Tax Act, broadly speaking, authorises the imposition of tax on sales in the course of inter-State trade or commerce at the rate of 2% of the turn over, 3% after 1st July 1966 in case of sales to Government, of any goods and sales to a registered dealer other than Government of goods specified in his registration certificate. Goods declared to be of importance in inter-State trade are charged at rate applicable inside State, while other goods are charged at rate of 10% or at State rate, whichever is higher. Goods exempted from tax under State law or subject to tax at rate less than 2% (3% after 1st July 1966) are exempt or, as case may be, charged at lower State rate.

Goods mentioned in §14 of the Act such as coal, cotton, cotton-fabrics, cotton-yarn, hides and skins, iron and steel, jute, rayon, oil, seeds, sugar, tobacco, woollen fabrics, and silk are declared to be of special importance in inter-State trade or commerce and accordingly it is provided that every sales-tax law of a State shall, in so far as it imposes or authorises imposition of a tax on sale or purchase or such goods, be subject to following restrictions, viz.: that rate of tax shall not exceed 2% of sale or purchase price and it shall not be levied at more than one stage. Above ceiling rate is raised to 3% with effect from 1st July 1966.

State Sales Tax.—Sales or purchases of goods taking place inside a State are within the powers of that particular State to tax. Sales outside State, or in course of import or export, or in course of inter-State trade are outside State's power of taxation.

Almost every State within the Union of India has enacted a Sales Tax Act imposing sales and purchase taxes at specified rates on dealers within the State having specified yearly turnovers, in respect of intra-State sales and purchases, that is sales and purchases which would be deemed to take place inside that State according to the principles formulated by the Central Sales Tax Act. Hire purchase and leasing of goods and equipment is now very prevalent, particularly for commercial/industrial users in view of income tax benefits. Lease as opposed to sale entails no passing of property and obviates sales tax liability. Most Indian states have now enacted special sales tax laws levying sales tax even on hire purchase/leasing transactions.

Stamp duties are regulated by the Indian Stamp Act, 1899. Each State has power under Entry No. 63 of List II in the Seventh Schedule of the Constitution of India to make laws with respect to a stamp duty payable in that State on every instrument, excepting bills of exchange, cheques, promissory notes, bills of lading, letters of credit, policies of insurance, transfer of shares, debentures, proxies and receipts. Under Entry No. 91 of List I in the Seventh Schedule of the Constitution rates of Stamp Duties on these last mentioned instruments can be prescribed only by the Union Government.

Several States have enacted laws with respect to Stamp Duty payable in respect of instruments other than bills of exchange, cheques etc., as mentioned above.

All instruments chargeable with duty must be stamped before or at the time of the execution. Any instrument whether executed or not and whether previously stamped or not may be sent to the Stamp Office for adjudication, and in case of documents already executed within one month from the date of execution. Any instrument which bears the certificate of the Stamp Office that the full duty with which it is chargeable has been paid or that no duty is chargeable will be deemed to be duly stamped or not chargeable to duty as the case may be and such certificate will be conclusive. Instruments executed abroad must be stamped within three months after being received in India.

If an instrument chargeable with a duty of one anna, or half an anna only, or a bill of exchange or promissory note is not stamped or not properly stamped, it cannot be admitted in evidence. Any other instrument not properly stamped may be admitted in evidence on payment of the duty with which the same is chargeable and the penalty which may be imposed thereon. The penalty may amount to ten times the amount of the proper duty or deficient portion thereof. If any instrument chargeable with duty and not duly stamped by accident, mistake or urgent necessity, not being an instrument chargeable with duty of one anna, or half an anna only, or a bill of exchange or promissory note, is produced by any person of his own motion before the Stamp Office within one year from the date of the execution thereof, the Stamp Office may, on payment of the duty with which it is chargeable and the penalty, if any, levied thereon, certify by endorsement that the proper duty and penalty have been paid.

Income tax is normally payable for an "assessment year" at rates fixed by annual Finance Acts and is based upon total income of "previous year." Assessment year is Indian financial year, Apr. 1-Mar. 31. Previous year is period of 12 months from 1st Apr. to 31st Mar. In case of newly set up business previous year will be period from date of setting up of business and would end on 31st Mar.

Tax is on income of previous year and not on income of assessment year. Though tax is assessed in succeeding year upon results of year before, tax is actually paid on most incomes before assessment year begins by withholding at source or by way of advance payment.

Rates of tax are not provided for by Act, but are enacted every year by annual Finance Act. Tax system is "slab system," so that successive slabs of income are charged at progressively higher rates of tax. Surcharges are also levied on amount of income tax.

Indian income tax is annual tax both in its imposition and structure, each previous year being a separate unit. Income and losses in prior years are irrelevant, unless they come under special provisions concerning the carry forward of business losses, capital losses or similar provisions.

Imposition of Tax.—Tax is on every person, which includes individual, company, firm, association of persons or body of individuals (whether incorporated or not); local authority and every artificial juridical person not falling within any of preceding categories.

"Company" means: (1) Any Indian company; or (2) any body corporate incorporated by or under laws of country outside India; or (3) any institution, association or body which is or was assessable or was assessed as company for any assessment year under Indian Income Tax Act, 1922 (11 of 1922), or which is or was assessable or was assessed under 1961 Act as company for any assessment year commencing on or before first day of Apr., 1971; or (4) any institution, association or body whether incorporated or not and whether Indian or non-Indian, which is declared by general or special order of Board to be company; provided that such institution, association or body shall be deemed to be company only for such assessment year or assessment years (whether commencing before first day of Apr., 1971 or on or after that date) as may be specified in declaration. Foreign companies other than those mentioned above do not fall within definition of "company," but they can apply to Central Board of Direct Taxes to be so declared. Though such declaration cannot be obtained as of right, normally there is no difficulty in case of foreign public limited companies. Foreign companies not obtaining such declaration are liable to pay as association of persons.

Total Income.—Tax is on total income of entity, which includes capital gains. However, distinction between capital receipt and income receipt is relevant for determining rate of tax, capital gains normally being taxed at lower rate.

Tax depends upon, and is determined by, whether taxpayer is resident in India. Individual is resident in India if he: (a) Is in India in previous year for period or periods amounting in all to 182 days or more; (b) having within four years preceding previous year been in India for period or periods amounting to 365 days or more, is in India for period or periods amounting in all to 60 days or more in previous year. However, citizen of India who leaves India for purpose of taking up employment outside India or who is member of crew of Indian ship would be treated as resident in India, if he is in India for 180 days or more or citizen of India who leaves India for purpose of taking up employment outside India, will be treated as resident in India if he is in India for 182 days or more. It is further provided that citizen of India or person of Indian origin who is outside India and comes on visit to India, shall be treated as resident if he is in India for more than 150 days. Company is resident if: (a) It is

See Topical Index in front part of this volume.

TAXATION . . . *continued*
Indian company or (b) if control and management of its affairs are situated wholly in India in previous year.

Resident pays tax on his entire income regardless of place of receipt or accrual. Nonresidents pay tax on income which is received or is deemed to be received in India or which accrues or arises or is deemed to accrue or arise in India.

There is a third category of assessees, viz., person who is resident, but not ordinarily resident in India. Persons who are resident but not ordinarily resident are assessed in exactly same manner as persons who are resident and ordinarily resident, but subject to one special exemption. Residents who are not ordinarily resident are exempt from tax in respect of income accruing outside India, unless it is derived from business controlled in or profession or vocation set up in India or is received or deemed to be received in India. Individual is said to be not ordinarily resident in any previous year if he has not been resident in India in nine out of ten previous years preceding that year or has not during the seven previous years preceding that year been in India for period or periods amounting in all to 730 days or more.

Receipt of Income.—Income received in India is subject to tax even if income accrued outside India. Receipt may be by taxpayer or his agent and can be in cash or kind. If income is received in India, entire amount is taxable, there being no provision for apportionment as there is in cases where income accrues in India.

Receipt as a basis of liability refers to first occasion when recipient gets money under his control. Once amount is received as income, any remittance or transmission of amount to another place does not result in "receipt" at other place. Therefore, if nonresident receives income outside India, he would not be subject to Indian tax when he remits or transmits it to India.

Accrual of Income.—Under Indian Act, receipt is not sole test of taxability. Taxpayer may be taxed on income which has accrued. Income accrues when taxpayer acquires right to receive it. Income once taxed on accrual cannot be taxed again when it is received. No general test can be laid down to determine place where income accrues. Question is to be decided on facts of each case. In case of a business of buying and selling goods, profits accrue as general rule at place where contract is entered into and sale made. Where contract is made in one place and sale is effected in another place, profits should be apportioned between the two locations. In business of manufacturing and selling goods, profits must be apportioned between place of manufacture and place of sale. Salaries and pensions accrue in India if they are earned there. Dividends paid by Indian company accrue in India even though they be declared and paid outside India.

§9 enumerates certain categories of income which are deemed to accrue or arise in India as follows: (1) Income falling under head "Salaries" if it is earned in India; (2) salary income paid by Government to Indian citizens for rendering services outside India; (3) dividend paid by Indian company outside India; (4) interest payable on money lent and brought into India—however force of this provision is considerably relaxed by various exemptions in respect of foreign borrowings; (5) royalty payable by Government or by resident to nonresident—basically royalty income consists of consideration for right to exploit product know-how; (6) income by way of fees for technical services payable by Government or by resident to nonresident. Fee for technical services has been defined as meaning consideration for rendering of managerial, technical or consultancy services including provision of services of technical or other personnel; (7) income accruing or arising directly or indirectly from or through any property in India or source of income in India or through transfer of capital asset situated in India; (8) income accruing or arising from or through as "business connection" in India. Term "business connection" has not been defined in Act. Dealing with this term, Supreme Court of India observed that "business connection" involves relation between business carried on by nonresident which yields profits or gains and some activity in taxable territories (India) which contributes directly or indirectly to earning of those profits or gains. Its prerequisite is element of continuity between business of nonresident and activity in taxable territories, stray or isolated transaction not being normally regarded as business connection. Expression "business connection" postulates real and intimate relation between trading activity carried on outside taxable territories and trading activity within territories, relation between two contributing to earning of income by nonresident in his trading activity. Examples of business connection are: (1) Maintaining branch office; (2) appointing agent in India for systematic and regular purchase or sale of goods or for other business purpose. In case of nonresident, however, no income is deemed to accrue in India from operations confined to purchase of goods in India for export. Mere canvassing of offers by resident taxpayer and communication thereof to nonresident for acceptance and execution has been held not to constitute business connection; (3) forming local subsidiary company to sell products of foreign parent company; (4) close financial association between Indian and foreign concern; and (5) grant of continuing licence to Indian concern to exploit for profit asset belonging to foreign concern, e.g. licence for use of patent. In case of business connection where some of operations are carried out within and some outside India, profits of business should be apportioned and only that portion of profits attributable to operations carried out in India are taxable in India.

Royalty income and income from fees for technical services which are received by nonresident are taxed at uniform rate of 30% of gross royalty or gross amount of fees for technical services. No deduction in respect of any expenditure is allowed while computing royalty income and income from fees for technical services. However, if different rates are prescribed in Double Taxation Avoidance Agreements (DTA) entered into between India and various foreign countries, then rates prescribed in DTA will prevail.

Certain concessional rates of tax are prescribed for nonresidents, foreign institutional investors etc. in order to attract foreign investment.

Dividend income received from Indian company by nonresident is taxed at rate of 25% of gross dividend income. Here again if different rates are prescribed in DTA, then rates prescribed in DTA will prevail.

Dividend income received on units of specified mutual funds or units of Unit Trust of India which are purchased by Overseas Financial Organisation in foreign currency and long-term capital gain arising from transfer of such units purchased in foreign currency, shall be taxed at rate of 10%. No deduction shall be allowed in computing dividend income or long-term capital gain. "Overseas Financial Organisation" has been defined as meaning any fund, institution, association, or body incorporated outside India which has entered into arrangement for investment in India with public sector bank or public financial institution or specified mutual fund.

Where nonresident purchases bonds or shares in Indian companies in foreign currency, dividend or interest income shall be taxed at 10% and long-term capital gain arising from transfer of such bonds or shares shall also be taxed at 10%. No deductions shall be allowed in computing dividend income or long-term capital gain.

Where total income of foreign institutional investor includes dividend income on shares or securities listed on recognized Stock Exchange or short term and long term capital gain arising from transfer thereof, then interest or dividend income of such shares or securities will be taxed at rate of 20%; short term capital gain arising on their transfer will be taxed at 30% and long-term capital gain at 10%. Expression "Foreign Institutional Investor" has been defined as meaning such investor as may be specified by Central Government by Notification in Official Gazzette.

Tax will be deducted at source from dividend income payable to nonresidents and to foreign institutional investors and from capital gains arising to nonresident.

Exemptions.—Several exemptions are offered by Act, apart from special tax reliefs, rebates and incentives to new industrial undertakings hereinafter mentioned. Chief of these exemptions are in respect of: (a) Income derived from property held under trust wholly for public charitable purposes. Exemption is subject to following main conditions: (i) Income is applied to such charitable purposes in India, (ii) charitable trust is registered with Commissioner of income-tax, (iii) charitable trust does not undertake any business activity, (iv) trust funds are invested in specified Government securities, (v) no portion of income was property of trust enures for benefit of settlors/trustees, their relations etc., (vi) trust is non-communal in nature; (b) income derived from property held under trust which is applied wholly for religious purposes in India provided that other conditions laid down in (i) to (v) above are satisfied; (c) agricultural income; (d) receipts of casual and nonrecurring nature (other than winnings from lotteries and capital gains which are taxed at concessional rates) to maximum limit of Rs.5,000 in any year; (e) in case of nonresident income from specified Central Government securities or bonds which may be specified in Official Gazette as also interest income on amount standing to credit of nonresident external account of nonresident individual; (f) value of any Leave Travel Concession or Assistance received from employer subject to such conditions as may be prescribed including conditions regarding number of journeys and maximum amount that may be exempted; f(i) death-cum-retirement gratuity subject to such limits as may be specified by Central Government (present limit is Rs. 100,000/-); (g) payments in commutation of pension; (h) payment received as cash equivalent of leave salary at time of retirement, superannuation etc. not exceeding six months salary subject to maximum of Rs.30,000; (i) retrenchment compensation subject to maximum of Rs.50,000/-; (k) payments from provident funds to which Provident Fund Act applies and payment from other recognised provident funds; (1) payments from approved superannuation funds; (m) house rent allowance subject following limits, viz, 50% of salary, if accommodation is in Bombay, Calcutta, Delhi or Madras and 40% of salary if accommodation is at any other place or amount by which rent actually paid exceeds 10% of salary or actual house rent allowance received by employee whichever is least; (n) scholarships for meeting cost of education; (o) income of university or other nonprofit educational institutions; (p) income of hospital existing solely for philanthropic purposes and not for purposes of profit; (q) enrolment fees, subscription and other income of professional institutions or associations; (r) income of associations or institutions for promotion of sports and games; (s) income of authorities, administrating places of public religious worship like temples, churches etc.; (t) income of trade union; (u) income of Trustees of Provident Fund, superannuation fund, gratuity fund etc.; (v) interest income on certain specified Government securities, National Defence gold bonds, special bearer bonds, capital investment bonds, National Savings certificate etc.; (w) interest received by nonresident Indian citizens or persons of Indian origin on specified savings certificates issued by Central Government; (x) any payment received in pursuance of awards given by Government for literary, scientific or artistic work or for proficiency in sports and games; (y) any gallantry award approved by Central Government; (z) annual value of one palace owned by former ruler; (z1) income of any housing board or town planning authority; (z2) income of Scientific Research Association; (z3) amount of subsidy received for scheme of replantation or replacement of rubber, coffee, cardomn plants; (z4) income of industrial undertaking which is established in free trade zone (entire production of such undertaking has to be exported); and (z5) any profits and gains derived from 100% export oriented undertaking i.e. industrial undertaking approved by Central Government and which exports its entire production. Income is exempt for period of five years.

Nonresidents, foreign citizens and foreign companies are given further exemptions. Following income of nonresident is exempt from tax: (a) Interest income on specified Central Government securities; (b) interest or premium on redemption of bonds issued by Central Government under loan agreement with International Bank For Reconstruction and Development or Development Loan Fund of U.S.A.; (c) interest on bonds issued by industrial undertaking or financial corporation in India under loan agreement with above Bank or fund which is guaranteed by Central Government; (d) interest on moneys standing to credit of nonresident (external) account in any bank in India in accordance with foreign exchange regulations; (e) interest on specified savings certificates issued by Central Government; (f) interest payable by Government or local authority on moneys borrowed outside India; (g) interest payable by industrial undertaking on loans taken from financial institution in foreign countries provided approval of Central Government is obtained; (h) interest payable by industrial undertaking on moneys borrowed or debt incurred outside India for purchase of raw materials or capital equipment provided approval of Central Government is obtained; (i) interest payable by certain specified financial institutions in India on moneys borrowed outside India provided agreement approved by Central Government, etc.; (j) profit derived from 100% export oriented undertaking which produces or exports computer programmes and computer software.

In case of foreign citizens, further exemptions are given in respect of: (a) (i) Passage monies received from employer for employee, wife and children in connection with his proceeding on leave out of India, (ii) passage monies received by employee for his children studying outside India and travelling to India during vacations, (iii) passage monies received from employer or former employer for himself, his wife and children in connection with proceeding to his country after retiring from or termination of

See Topical Index in front part of this volume.

TAXATION . . . *continued*

services in India, in all cases subject to such conditions as Government may prescribe; (b) remuneration received by ambassador, high commissioner, envoy, minister, chargé d'affaires, commissioner consular, or secretary, advisor or attaché of embassy, high commission, legation or commission of a foreign state; (c) remuneration received as consul de carriere; (d) remuneration received by trade commissioner or other official representative of foreign government, provided reciprocal arrangement for exemption exists between the two countries; (e) income of members of staff of officials referred to in items (b), (c) and (d) above if member is subject of country represented and is not engaged in any business, profession, vocation or employment in India and in case of staff of trade commissioner or other official representative, provided reciprocal arrangement for exemption exists between the two countries; (f) remuneration received by employee of foreign enterprise for services rendered in India provided foreign enterprise is not engaged in any trade in India, his stay does not exceed 90 days and such remuneration is not deductible from income chargeable to tax in India; (g) in case of technician who is employed after 31st Mar., 1993 by Government, local authority, Scientific Research Institute or business carried on in India and who was not resident in the four financial years preceding year in which he arrived in India and tax on his remuneration is paid by employer then tax so paid by employer for period not exceeding 48 months from date of his arrival in India would be exempt from tax. Earlier provisions exempting remuneration up to Rs.4,000/- per month have been deleted from 1st Apr., 1993; (h) salaries received by nonresident in connection with his employment on foreign ship where his stay in India does not exceed 90 days in previous year; (i) salaries received for services rendered as professor or other teacher in university or other educational institution for period of 36 months from date of arrival, provided such individual is not resident in India in any of four financial years preceding year of arrival and his contract of service is approved by Central Government; (j) remuneration received for undertaking any research work in India for period of 24 months, provided research work is in connection with scheme approved by Central Government and payment is made directly or indirectly by foreign government or body; (k) remuneration received by individual, who is nonresident and noncitizen of India, but comes to India in connection with shooting of cinema film and for rendering services in connection with such shooting.

Heads of Charge.—Income is charged under heads salaries, income from house property, profits and gains of business or profession, capital gains and income from sources other than those specified above. Each head of income has its own separate rules of computation of income and deductions allowable while computing income. These are briefly discussed below:

Salary Income.—Salary due from employer or advance salary paid by employer (though not due) and arrears of salary paid (if not charged to tax for earlier previous year) would be chargeable to tax. Salary income is charged to tax if it is earned in India, that is services are rendered in India, irrespective of whether salary is paid or payable in India or outside India. Monetary value of certain perquisites like rent-free accommodation, accommodation provided at concessional rent, value of any benefit or amenity provided free of cost is taxable as salary income. Income Tax Rules provide for computation of monetary value of such perquisites. Value of any benefit or amenity granted free of cost or at concessional rate will not be treated as perquisite if income of employee under head salary does not exceed Rs.24,000/-. In computing salary income deduction of sum equal to 33$^{1}/_{3}$% of salary subject to maximum of Rs.15,000/- is allowed. However, where employer provides motor car or other vehicle for personal use (i.e. other than official use and for travelling to and from place of work) deduction is limited to Rs.1,000/-. Employees drawing salary up to Rs.40,000/- per annum are not required to submit voluntary return of income. All other individual taxpayers whose income exceeds Rs.40,000/- per annum are required to file such return of income.

Income from House Property.—Annual value of house property that is any buildings or lands appurtenant thereto is chargeable under this head. Annual value has been defined as sum for which property might reasonably be expected to let from year to year. In case actual rent received is in excess of annual value, rent actually received would be assessable. In places where rent control or rent restriction laws are in force annual value cannot exceed standard rent which landlord can recover from tenant. Income from self-occupied property is no longer taxable as was case prior to 31st Mar. 1986. In computing income under this head, expenditure on reparis and collection charges (20% of annual value), insurance premium, annual charge, ground rent and interest on moneys borrowed for acquisition or construction of property are deductible.

Profits and Gains from Business or Profession.—Profits and gains of any business or profession which is carried on at any time during previous year is taxable under this head. In computing business income, all revenue expenditure (not being personal expenditure) laid out or expended wholly and exclusively for purpose of business or profession would be allowed as deduction. However, certain categories of expenditure are statutorily disallowed either wholly or partially. Important among these are: (a) Entertainment expenditure which is allowed up to limited extent; (b) expenditure on travelling and local expenditure incurred on employees in excess of specified limits; (c) expenditure on maintenance of guest house; (d) any expenditure incurred in excess of Rs.10,000/- in respect of which payment is made otherwise than by way of crossed cheque drawn on bank or bank draft; (e) expenditure incurred or payment made to persons related to or connected with assessee where income tax officer is of opinion that expenditure is excessive or unreasonable having regard to fair market value of goods or services; (f) entertainment expenditure is allowed only up to certain limits, viz., Rs.10,000/— plus 50% of excess. Balance is disallowed.

In computing business income, depreciation on building, plant, machinery etc. is allowed. Normal rates of depreciation are as follows:

(i)	buildings mainly used for residential purposes	5%
(ii)	buildings not mainly for residential purposes such as office and factory buildings etc.	10%
(iii)	hotel buildings	20%
(iv)	furniture and fittings	10%
(v)	furniture and fittings used in hotels, restaurants, boarding houses, educational institutions, meeting halls, cinema house, theaters etc.	15%
(vi)	plant and machinery (general rate)	25%
(vii)	motor cars	20%
(viii)	ships and ocean going vessels	20%

Higher rates of depreciation have been prescribed for certain specific items of plant and machinery like aircraft, air and water pollution control equipment, energy saving devices, etc.

Depreciation is computed on basis of written down value of block of assets. Sale proceeds of any assets sold during year is deducted from value of block of assets and similarily cost of assets purchased is added to value of block of assets for computing depreciation. If sale proceeds exceed written down value of block of assets, then difference is taxed as short term capital gain.

Certain special provisions have been made for computing business income of nonresident companies. Important among these are: (a) Limited allowances for Head Office expenditure; (b) royalty income; (c) income from shipping business; (d) income from oil exploration business; and (e) income from operation of aircraft.

Deduction claimed by nonresident companies for head office expenditure is limited to 5% of adjusted total income or average head office expenditure or head office expenditure attributable to business of nonresident company in India whichever is least. Head office expenditure includes executive and general administrative expenditure incurred outside India including expenditure on rent, rates, taxes, repairs, insurance of premises outside India, salaries, wages, travelling expenses of employees outside India etc.

Where nonresident is engaged in business of operation of ships, sum equal to 7$^{1}/_{2}$% of freight paid or payable to him or to any person on his behalf on account of carriage of passengers, livestock, mail or goods shipped at any port in India shall be deemed to be income and chargeable to tax in summary manner. However, assessee has option to claim that assessment shall be made on his total income and tax payable on such basis shall be determined in accordance with provisions of Income Tax Act and if such claim is made, then payment made on basis of 7$^{1}/_{2}$% of receipts shall be treated as payment in advance of tax leviable and difference between sum so paid and amount of tax payable shall be paid by assessee or refunded to him as case may be.

Before departure of any ship from any Indian port, master of ship shall prepare and furnish to Income Tax Officer return of amount of freight paid or payable to owner on account of carriage of passengers, livestock, mail or goods shipped at that port. Tax on 7$^{1}/_{2}$% of such freight is payable by master of ship. Port clearance is not granted till Customs Officer is satisfied that income tax payable has been duly paid or that satisfactory arrangements have been made for payment of tax. In practice, agents or regular steamship companies give indemnity or guaranty for payment of tax.

Where assessee is engaged in business of providing services or facilities in connection with or supplying plant and machinery on hire to be used in prospecting extraction and production of mineral oil in India then 10% of aggregate of amounts paid or payable to (whether in or out of India) or received or deemed to be received by assessee on account of provision of services and facilities in connection with supplying plant or machinery to be used for prospecting, extraction and production of mineral oil would be taxable as business income.

Where nonresident is engaged in business of operation of aircraft sum equal to 5% of aggregate of amounts paid or payable (whether in or out of India) on account of carriage of passengers, livestock, mail or goods from any place in India or amounts received in India on account of carriage of passengers, livestock, mail or goods from any place outside India shall be deemed to be profit of business.

Where foreign company is engaged in business of civil construction or erection of plant and machinery or testing or commissioning thereof in connection with turn-key power project approved by Central Government, then 10% of consideration paid or payable shall be deemed to be profits and gains of business and foreign company shall be taxed accordingly.

No income shall be deemed to accrue or arise to nonresident, who is engaged in running news agency or publishing newspapers, magazines or journals or conducting activities for collection of information in India for transmission thereof outside India. Income of news agency set up in India solely for collection and distribution of news as may be notified by Government is exempt from tax. Exemption is subject to condition that news agency applies its income and accumulates its income for application solely for collection and distribution of news and does not distribute its income among its members.

Further no income shall be deemed to accrue or arise to nonresident from operations which are concerned with shooting of any cinema film in India.

Income received by sportsmen who are not citizens of India and are nonresidents for participation in games or sports or for advertisement or contribution of articles relating to game or sport in magazines, newspapers, journals are taxed at rate of 10%. However, no deduction in respect of expenditure or allowances is given.

Capital Gains.—Any profits or gains arising from transfer of capital assets are chargeable to tax under this head. Capital gains are computed by deducting from consideration received for transfer of assets: (a) All expenditures incurred wholly and exclusively in connection with transfer, and (b) cost of acquisition and cost of improvements to capital asset.

Capital assets are either short term capital assets or long term capital assets. Long term capital assets are assets held by assessee for period of three years prior to date of transfer. However where capital asset is share in company then period of holding is reduced to one year. Short term capital assets are those held for less than three years (one year in case asset is share in company) or units of Unit Trust of India or other approved mutual funds prior to date of transfer. Gains arising from transfer of long term capital assets are taxed at concessional rates, viz., 20% for individuals and HUFs, 20% for companies and 30% for other assessees like firms, associations of persons, body of individuals, etc. In computing capital gain cost of acquisition or cost of improvement, as case may be, is increased by certain percentage for every year for which capital asset is held (cost inflation index) which is notified by Government.

In cases of assets acquired prior to 1st Apr. 1981, assessee can substitute fair market value of assets on 1st Apr. 1981 for cost of acquisition and improvement.

Capital gains are not charged to tax in certain cases, principal among these are where: (a) Entire net sale proceeds of residential house owned for more than three years are utilised for purchase or construction of another residential house within stipulated time; (b) entire net sale proceeds of agricultural lands are utilised for purchase of other agricultural lands within stipulated time; (c) entire net sale proceeds of capital assets other than residential house held for more than three years which are

See Topical Index in front part of this volume.

TAXATION . . . *continued*
invested in purchase of residential house provided assessee does not own any other residential house; (d) sale proceeds of land, building, machinery, etc. owned by industrial undertaking situated in urban area are utilised within period of one year from date of transfer for purpose of acquiring land, constructing buildings, purchasing land and machinery etc. resulting from shifting of business undertaking from such urban area.

Conversion of capital assets into stock in trade of business will also be taxable under head "capital gains".

Income from Other Sources.—Income from sources other than those specified above, like dividend income, interests on securities, if securities are not held as assets of business, board meeting fees, income from letting out machinery, plant etc. are chargeable to tax under this head.

Other Peoples Income.—Following income of other persons is included in income of taxpayer: (a) Income arising by virtue of revocable transfer; (b) income arising to person by virtue of transfer where there is no transfer of assets from which income arises; (c) all income accruing or arising to minor child will be added to income of that parent whose total income is greater; or where marriage does not subsist, with income of parent who maintains minor child. However, child's income accruing or arising on account of personal exertion or exercise of skill or specialised knowledge will not be added; (d) income arising to spouse of taxpayer from assets transferred directly or indirectly to spouse otherwise than for adequate consideration or in connection with agreement to live apart.

Some Special Tax Reliefs, Rebates, Incentives Etc.—(a) New industrial undertaking started or new hotels set up in any backward area after 31st Dec. 1970, are allowed deduction of 20% of profits of such undertaking or hotel in computing their income; (b) profit derived from newly established industrial undertaking set up in backward State or undertaking set up in any part of India for generation or generation and distribution of power; (c) resident Indian assessees and resident Indian companies deriving income from execution of foreign project (which includes contract for construction project and installation of plant and machinery entered into with foreign government, foreign statutory or public authority or foreign enterprise) are allowed deduction of 25% of profits arising from execution of such foreign project provided consideration is received in convertible foreign exchange; (d) deduction of expenditure incurred for undertaking programmes for conservation of natural resources, re-forestation, etc.; (e) entire profits derived by Indian company or resident assessee from export of goods or merchandise are exempt from tax provided sale proceeds are received in convertible foreign exchange during accounting year or within six months from end of accounting year. If assessee's turnover includes export turnover and other turnover proportionate profits exempted; (f) deduction of one-sixth of amount paid by assessee for acquiring any know-how for purpose of his business. Know-how has been defined as any industrial information or technique likely to assist in manufacture or processing of goods etc.; (g) new industrial undertakings manufacturing articles other than those specified in Eleventh Schedule or ships and hotels are allowed deduction of 20% (25% where assessee is company) of profits and gains derived from such new industrial undertaking, ship or hotel provided that production commences, or ship is used or hotel starts functioning between 1st Apr. 1981 and 31st Mar. 1991. (h) With effect from assessment year 1991-92 inter-corporate dividend income will be entirely exempt provided such dividend income is utilised by recipient company to pay dividend to its shareholders. In case dividend income is from units of Unit Trust of India amount of deduction shall be limited to 4/5th of such income for A.Y.94-95 and 2/5th of such income for A.Y.95-96 and thereafter no deduction shall be allowed; (i) resident Indian companies engaged in business of hotel or tour operators or travel agents will be allowed deduction of 50% of profits derived from services to foreign tourists, provided receipts are brought into India in convertible foreign exchange within six months. (Profits derived by resident Indian companies from export outside India of computer software and from providing technical services outside India in connection with development or production of computer software are exempt from tax.) (j) resident Indian companies receiving income by way of royalty, commission, fees etc. from foreign Government or foreign enterprise for transferring know-how are allowed deduction of 50% of fees provided: fees are brought in convertible foreign exchange; (k) income of industrial undertaking which manufactures and produces articles or things after Apr. 1, 1981 in free trade zone is exempt from tax for period of five years from and inclusive of year in which production commences; (l) other reliefs and rebates also allowed, prominent among these are: (1) rebate from tax of 20% of amounts contributed towards Employees' Provident Fund, Public Provident Fund, premium on life insurance policies, subscription to Savings Certificates, investments made for purchase of house, repayment of loan borrowed for purchase of house, etc.; (2) rebate of 50% of amounts donated to certain charitable funds and institutions, (3) deduction of amount not exceeding Rs.25,000/- towards repayment of loan taken from financial or charitable institutions for purpose of higher education or payment of interest on such loan, (4) relief in respect of amounts paid to scientific research institutions or rural development funds set up by Government, (5) rebate of expenditure incurred on payment of rent up to maximum of Rs. 400 per month, (6) deduction in respect of income from dividends from Indian companies, interest on Government securities, units of unit trust and other specified investments subject to certain ceiling limits; (7) deduction up to Rs.3,000 for medical insurance premium paid for self, wife or dependant children.

Procedure for Assessment.—Every assessee if his total income exceeds maximum amount chargeable to tax has obligation to file return of income in prescribed form on or before specified dates which are as follows: (a) Companies—30th Nov.; (b) assessees having income from business or profession, whose accounts have to be audited under Income-tax Act or under any other law—31st Oct.; (c) assessees having income from business or profession whose accounts do not have to be audited—31st Aug.; (d) all other assessees—30th June. For delayed filing of return—interest at 2% per month or part thereof is chargeable. Before filing return, all taxes, interests etc. due on basis of returned income must be paid.

Prior to assessment year 1989-90 assessment had to be made by Income-tax Officer before expiry of two years from end of assessment year for which income was assessible. Under revised procedure in more than 90% of cases returns filed will be accepted and intimation sent to assessee. In remaining cases, Income-tax Officer has to serve notice within six months from time return is furnished calling upon assessee to produce evidence and materials in support of return. Such assessments should be completed within two years from end of assessment year in which return was filed.

Appeals.—First appeal against any assessment order lies to Appellate Assistant Commissioner of Income Tax/Commissioner of Income Tax (Appeals). Such appeal to be filed within 30 days of receipt of assessment order. Second appeal can be filed with Income Tax Appellate Tribunal either by assessee or Income Tax Officer from order of first appellate authority within 60 days of receipt of appellate order. Decision of tribunal on disputed questions of fact is final. Reference can be made by assessee or Income Tax Officer to High Court on questions of law arising out of tribunal's order. Appeal can be filed to Supreme Court against any decision of High Court on reference if High Court certifies case as fit one to appeal to Supreme Court.

Authority for Advance Rulings has been set up. Such authority shall consist of eminent persons and chaired by retired Judge of Supreme Court. Nonresident applicant who is desirous of obtaining advance ruling (which has been defined as determination by authority of question of law or fact specified in application in relation to transaction which has been undertaken or is proposed to be undertaken by applicant) should make application in prescribed form and accompanied by fee of Rs.2,500/-. Such application cannot be made in case question raised is pending before any Income Tax Authority, Appellate Tribunal or Court or involves determination of fair market value of property or relates to transaction which is designed for avoidance of income tax.

Authority after examining application and further material and hearing applicant shall pronounce its advance ruling on question specified in application within six months from date of receipt of application. Such advance ruling shall be binding not only on applicant but also on Income Tax Department.

Rates of Tax.—Rates are annually prescribed by Finance Acts. For assessment year 1996-97 i.e. year ended 31st Mar. 1996, rates are as follows:

(A) In cases of individuals:

1.	Where total income does not exceed Rs.40,000/-	Nil
2.	Where total income exceeds Rs.40,000/- but does not exceed Rs.60,000/-	15% of amount by which total income exceeds Rs.40,000/-
3.	Where total income exceeds Rs.60,000/- but does not exceed Rs.1,200,000/-	Rs.5,000/- + 30% of amount by which total income exceeds Rs.60,000;
4.	Where total income exceeds Rs.1,200,000	Rs.23,000/- + 40% of amount by which total income exceeds Rs.1,200,000.

In case of companies: (1) For domestic company—40%; (2) for company other than domestic company—55%.

In case of firm 40%. Share of partner in profits of firm will not be assessed to tax in his hand. Besides, salary and interest paid to partner is allowable as deduction in computing firm's income up to certain limits.

Special rates have been laid down for royalty income, fees for technical services, dividend income etc. receivable by foreign company as set out earlier.

Deduction of Tax at Source.—Provision is made for deduction of tax at source in respect of various kinds of income such as salary income, interest on securities, dividend income etc., at differing rates. Tax deducted at source is subsequently taken into account and adjusted at time of final assessment.

Surcharge on Corporation Tax.—Surcharge of 75% on corporation is also levied.

Surtax on Companies.—By The Companies (Profits) Surtax Act 1964, additional tax has been imposed on companies (other than those which have no share capital) on excess or super profits. Surtax is levied at percentage of chargeable profits as exceed statutory deduction which is 15% of capital of company as computed under provisions of Act or Rs. 2,00,000 whichever is greater. This Act is now repealed.

TRADEMARKS:

Under Trade and Merchandise Marks Act, 1958, (herein called said Act) replacing Indian Merchandise Marks Act, 1889 and Trade Marks Act, 1940, a person claiming to be proprietor of trade mark used or proposed to be used by him, may apply (§18) to Registrar of Trade Marks for its registration which would give him exclusive right to its use in relation to goods in respect of which it is registered (§28).

Register of Trade Marks is divided into two parts, Part A and Part B. Section 9 of said Act provides that a trade mark cannot be registered in Part A unless it contains or consists of at least one of following particulars: (a) Name of company, individual, or firm represented in special or particular manner; (b) signature of applicant or his predecessor in business; (c) one or more invented words; (d) one or more words having no direct reference to character or quality of goods and not being a geographical name, or a surname, or personal name or any common abbreviation thereof, or name of a sect, caste or tribe in India; (e) any other distinctive mark. Any other name, signature or word cannot be registered in Part A except upon evidence of its distinctiveness. Distinctive means "adapted to distinguish" goods with which proprietor of trade mark is or may be connected in course of trade from goods not so connected.

Trademark to be registrable in Part B of Register must, if not distinctive, be "capable of distinguishing" such goods with which proprietor of trademark is or may be connected in course of trade, from goods not so connected. Distinctiveness required for registration in Part B is less stringent than that required for registration in Part A. Mark may not be "adapted to distinguish" yet may be "capable of distinguishing." Registrar may give preliminary advice about a mark's distinctiveness. (§103).

Said Act prohibits registration of a mark: (a) use of which is likely to deceive or cause confusion; (b) use of which would be contrary to any law in force; (c) which contains scandalous or obscene matter; (d) which is likely to hurt religious susceptibilities of any class or section of citizens of India; (e) which would be disentitled to protection in court; (f) which is identical or deceptively similar to another already registered in respect of same goods or description of goods (except in case of honest concurrent use or of other special circumstances); (g) which consists of word which is commonly used and accepted name of a single chemical element or compound; (h) which falsely suggests a connection with any living or recently dead person (except with consent of such person or his legal representative).

See Topical Index in front part of this volume.

TRADEMARKS . . . *continued*

Mere fact that trade mark has been registered in foreign country does not entitle it to be registered in India, nor does rejection of mark by foreign country debar its registration in India.

Any person claiming to be proprietor of trademark used or proposed to be used by him may apply to Registrar for registration in Part A or Part B of Register. (§18). Such person may be manufacturer or importer or trader dealing in any goods selected by him.

Every application for registration, which fulfils requirements of the Act, is advertised in Trade Marks Journal. Any person interested may oppose registration of mark by giving notice in writing in prescribed time and in prescribed manner to Registrar of opposition to registration. Registrar serves a copy of notice of opposition on applicant for registration who must file his counter-statement within prescribed time and copy thereof is served upon person giving notice of opposition. Both applicant for registration and opponent may submit in prescribed manner evidence on which they rely and they are heard by Registrar, if they so desire, before Registrar decides whether and subject to what conditions and limitations, if any, registration is to be permitted. (§21).

Trademark may be limited wholly or in part to specified colours. Trademark registered without limitation of colour shall be deemed to be registered for all colours. (§10).

When application for registration has been accepted, Registrar may register trademark in Part A or Part B of Register and trademark shall be registered as of date of making of application for registration. (§23).

Registration holds for seven years and is renewable every seven years on application within prescribed time before expiration of last registration. (§25).

Registration of trademark gives registered proprietor exclusive right to use of trademark in relation to goods in respect of which trademark is registered and to obtain relief in respect of infringement of trademark. (§28).

Nonuse of trademark for period of five years or more (except in case of special circumstances in trade which prevent use of mark) makes a mark liable to be removed from Register or to have limitations imposed on its registration. (§46).

Where trademark consisting of invented word has become so well known as respects any of goods for which it is registered and used that its use by any person in relation to other goods would be likely to indicate a connection in course of trade between those other goods and proprietor of mark, defensive registration of such mark in relation to such other goods (on which it has not been used) may be obtained by proprietor of mark. (§47). Such defensive registration is not liable to be cancelled merely on ground of nonuse.

Mark which is adapted in relation to any goods to distinguish in course of trade, goods certified by any person in respect of origin, material, mode of manufacture, quality, accuracy or other characteristic, from goods not so certified, may be registered as certification trademark (§62) on requirements of the Act being fulfilled.

Any person aggrieved by any contravention or failure to observe condition relating to entry, or by absence or omission from Register of Trade Marks of any entry or by any entry made in Register without sufficient cause or wrongly remaining on it, or by any error or defect on any entry, may apply to Registrar or to High Court in prescribed manner and Tribunal may make appropriate order for making, expunging or varying the entry as it thinks fit. (§56).

Assignment.—Subject to certain restrictions and exceptions (§§36-43), a registered trademark is assignable and transmissible with or without goodwill of business as to all or some only of goods for which it is registered (§37) while unregistered trade mark cannot be assigned otherwise than with goodwill of business concerned except that it may be transferred without goodwill of business in cases where it is used in same business as registered trade mark and both marks are transferred to same person and at same time and both marks are related to same goods. Assignment without goodwill will not take effect unless assignee applies to Registrar within six months and carries out Registrar's directions as to advertisement. (§41).

Person other than registered proprietor, may be registered as registered user of trademark under certain conditions. (§§48, 49). However, Registered user does not have right of assignment or transmission. (§53).

Infringement is use by person who is not registered proprietor or registered user of mark identical with or deceptively similar to registered trademark in relation to any goods in respect of which trademark is registered and in such manner as to render use of mark likely to be taken as being used as trademark. (§29).

No person shall be entitled to institute any proceeding to prevent or recover damages for infringement of unregistered mark. But nothing in Act shall be deemed to affect rights of action against any person for passing off goods as goods of another person or remedies in respect thereof. (§27).

In a suit to restrain infringement or passing off, court may grant injunction and, at option of plaintiff, either damages or account of profits together with or without order for delivery up of infringing labels and marks for destruction or erasure. (§106).

Use of a trademark for purpose of reasonably indicating that goods are adapted for use in particular manner does not constitute infringement (§30), nor does use by person of his own name or that of his place of business or of name or name of place of business of any of his predecessors or use of any bona fide description of character or quality of goods amount to infringement or passing off (§33). Where person has used his mark before date of registration of trademark and also before date of first use of such latter mark, use of prior mark cannot be restrained. (§33).

Penal provisions are included in Act (§78 et seq.) for use of mark deceptively similar to another's mark which may amount in specified cases to falsifying or applying false trademark or for selling goods to which false trademark is applied, etc.

Implied Warranty.—On sale or in contract for sale of any goods to which trademark or mark or trade description is applied, seller shall be deemed to warrant that mark is genuine mark and not falsely applied or that trade description is not false trade description, unless contrary is expressed in writing and signed by or on behalf of seller and accepted by or on behalf of buyer. (§96).

Reciprocity.—Where person has made application for registration of trademark in country which affords to Indian citizens similar privileges as granted to its own citizens, and that person or his legal representative or assignee makes application for registration of trademark in India within six months after date on which application was made in other country, trademark shall, if registered under this Act, be registered as of date on which application was made in other country. Where any country specified by Central Government does not accord to citizens of India same rights in respect of registration and protection of trademark as it accords to its own nationals, no national of such country shall be entitled to be registered as proprietor of trademark in Part A or B of register or as assignee or registered user of trademark in India. (§132).

All indexes maintained by Registrar of Trade Marks, notices of opposition, counter-statements and similar documents are open to public inspection. (§125).

Related Acts.—Some cognate Acts are Patents Act, 1970 and Designs Act, 1911, Emblems and Names (Prevention of Improper Use) Act, 1950, Indian Standards Institution (Certification Marks) Act, 1952 and Indian Copyright Act, 1957.

The Trade and Merchandise Act, 1958, has been sought to be replaced by new Act, for which purpose Trademarks Bill, 1993, was introduced in Parliament. Bill has been passed by Lower House of Indian Parliament and is awaiting clearance by Upper House.

WILLS:

The statutory law relating to Wills is embodied in the Indian Succession Act, being Act No. XXXIX of 1925. The formal requirement of wills follows the English pattern.

Capacity.—Every person, male or female, of sound mind, not being a minor, may dispose of his or her property by will. A married woman may dispose by will any property which she could alienate by her own act during her life. Deaf or dumb or blind persons are not incapacitated for making a will if they are able to know the implication of it. A person who is ordinarily insane may make a will during a lucid interval but no person can make a will while he is in such a state of mind whether arising from intoxication or from illness or from any other cause, that he does not know what he is doing. (§59).

No person having nephew or niece or any near relative has power to bequeath any property to religious or charitable uses except by will executed not less than 12 months before his death and deposited within six months of its execution in place provided by law, namely, office of Sub-Registrar of Assurances of district for safe custody of wills of living persons. (§118 of Indian Succession Act). This is now of limited application. It does not apply to Hindus, Buddhists, Sikhs, Jains, Mohammedans and Parsis.

Aliens, whether friends or enemies, if not disqualified by mental incapacity or minority, may dispose of property by will.

Hindus.—By virtue of the Hindu Succession Act, 1956, being Act No. XXX of 1956, any Hindu can, by will, dispose of any property in accordance with the provisions of the Indian Succession Act, 1925, including his interest in joint family property, subject to the right of maintenance of minor sons and unmarried daughters, the widow, the parents and the widowed daughter-in-law. (§30 of the Hindu Succession Act).

Mohammedans.—The Indian Succession Act does not apply to Mohammedans. They are governed by their own personal law. Every Mohammedan of sound mind and not a minor can dispose of his property by will which may be either verbal or in writing. A Mohammedan cannot by his will dispose of more than one-third of the surplus of his estate after payment of funeral expenses and debts. Bequest by a Mohammedan in excess of the legal third cannot take effect unless all the heirs consent thereto after the death of the testator. Also, a Mohammedan cannot bequeath anything to an heir and the bequest to an heir will be invalid unless the other heirs consent after the testator's death. A Mohammedan Will is not required to be probated.

Execution.—An unprivileged will (see catchline A Holograph Will, infra) must be in writing and every testator must sign or affix his mark to the will or it must be signed by some other person in his presence and by his direction. The signature or mark of the testator or the signature of the person signing for him must be so placed that it shall appear that it was intended thereby to give effect to the writing as a will. The will must be attested by two or more witnesses each of whom has seen the testator sign or affix his mark to the will or has seen some other person sign the will in the presence of and by the direction of the testator or has received from the testator a personal acknowledgment of his signature or mark, or of the signature of such other person; and each of the witnesses must sign the will in the presence of the testator, but it is not necessary that more than one witness be present at the same time and no particular form of attestation is necessary. (§63 of the Indian Succession Act).

A holograph will, that is, one written and signed by the testator himself, is included in the definition of an unprivileged will. It must be attested by two witnesses. Persons governed by the Indian Succession Act are not competent to make a nuncupative or oral will, though Mohammedans may make an oral will as stated above.

Revocation.—A will may be revoked or altered by the maker of it at any time when he is competent to dispose of his property by will. An unprivileged will is revoked by the marriage of the maker or by another will or codicil declaring an intention to revoke the same and executed in the same manner in which an unprivileged will is required to be executed or by burning, tearing or by destroying the same by the testator or by some person in his presence and by his direction with the intention of revoking the same. (§70 of the Indian Succession Act).

In Military Service, etc.—Any soldier or airman employed in an expedition or engaged in actual warfare or any mariner at sea may, if he has completed the age of 18 years, make a privileged will. (§65 of the Indian Succession Act). A privileged will may be in writing or by word of mouth. If it is verbal, it must be declared before two witnesses, present at the same time. A verbal will shall be null and void at the expiration of one month after the testator shall have ceased to be entitled to make a privileged will. If it is a written will and it is written wholly by the testator, neither the signature of the testator nor attestation is necessary. If it is written by some other person wholly or in part, the signature of the testator is necessary but attestation is not. A privileged will may be revoked by an unprivileged will or by an act expressing an intention to revoke accompanied by such formality as would be sufficient to give validity to a privileged will and by other ways as prescribed for revoking an unprivileged will. (§66 of the Indian Succession Act).

See Topical Index in front part of this volume.

WILLS . . . *continued*

If a beneficiary named in the will witnesses the will, its validity is not affected, but the benefiting witness and the respective husband or wife of the witness loses all interest under the will. (§67 of the Indian Succession Act).

A will relating to immovable property in India must comply with the provisions of the Indian Succession Act as mentioned above. The validity of a will relating to movable property in India will depend upon the general law of the domicile of the deceased at the date of his death.

Foreign Wills.—Wills made by persons who are not domiciled in India so far as same relate to immovable property situate within India must be in accordance with law relating to execution of wills in India. (See subhead Execution, supra.) Will made by person who is not domiciled in India, so far as it relates to movable property of such person whether in India or elsewhere, must be executed in accordance with law of his domicile at time of his death wherever will may be executed, and courts in India will deal with instrument exactly as court of testator's domicile would deal with it. If foreign will has been proved and is deposited in court of competent jurisdiction outside India and properly authenticated copy of will is produced, letters of administration may be granted with copy of such copy of will annexed. No further proof is required as to due execution of will. "Authenticated copy" does not mean that copy of will should be under seal of foreign court, notarially certified copy would do. If foreign will is not so proved, courts in India on receipt of authenticated copy will take evidence as to due execution of will according to law of country in which testator was domiciled, and in case of movable property court will satisfy itself as to law relating to execution of wills in force in such country.

No probate can be granted in India in the case of a will executed in India by a foreigner, which only disposes of property outside India.

If a foreigner has left property in India, letters of administration must be obtained from a competent Indian court in respect of such property although deceased may have had his domicile in a country in which law relating to succession differs from law in India. Grant of administration by a foreign court or even by a court in British Dominions outside India is not sufficient.

See also topic Descent and Distribution.

See Topical Index in front part of this volume.

IRELAND LAW DIGEST REVISER

Gerrard, Scallan & O'Brien
Hainault House
69/71 St. Stephen's Green
Dublin 2, Ireland
Telephone: 353-1-478-0699
Fax: 353-1-478-0324

Reviser Profile

History: The firm was founded in 1968 as a result of a merger of two other firms, Ryan Scallan & O'Brien and Thomas Gerrard & Co. Ryan Scallan & O'Brien was itself the result of a merger in 1966 between John L. Scallan & Co. and Ryan and O'Brien. The three original constituent elements of the firm can trace their history back to the early 19th century and John L. Scallan & Co. was the third earliest law firm in Dublin.

Areas of Business: The firm provides a full service to personal and commercial clients in all areas other than criminal law. Its main emphasis is on commercial law. Departmental specialisation has been developed and there are departments dealing with Conveyancing Environmental and Property Law, Trusts and Probate, Litigation and Commercial/Company Law. The firm has recognised specialisation in Banking and Financial Services, Mergers and Acquisitions, Stock Exchange and Capital Markets, Competition, Insolvency, Insurance, Shipping, Aircraft, Commercial Litigation and Labour Law.

Members of the firm have developed an expertise in intellectual property rights, sophisticated financing techniques, labour law, mining and natural resources law and European Union law and have taken cases to the Supreme Court in Ireland on numerous occasions and have also taken cases to the Court of First Instance and the European Court of Justice.

Client Base: The firm acts as solicitor for many of the banks, financial service companies and insurance companies operating in Ireland as well as a number of the major industrial and commercial companies both Irish owned and multinational and has a wide base of clients in manufacturing, service industry and high technology companies.

Structure: The firm comprises nine partners, five associates, one consultant and a number of assistant solicitors. It is managed by a management committee headed by the managing partner, John Glackin, who reports to monthly partners meetings and who consults from time to time with various sub-committees on different aspects of the practice such as technology development, finance and staff relations.

General: The partners and associates regularly attend and have addressed conferences organised by the International Bar Association, Association Internationale des Jeunes Avocats and INSOL and are encouraged to attend and lecture to Continuing Legal Education courses organised by the Incorporated Law Society of Ireland and the Society of Young Solicitors.

IRELAND LAW DIGEST

(The following is a list of all Topics, including cross-references, covered in this Digest.)

IRELAND LAW DIGEST

Revised for 1997 edition by

GERRARD, SCALLAN & O'BRIEN, Solicitors of Courts of Justice, Ireland.

(Statutes are cited by reference to their short titles [if any] and the calendar years in which they were passed, or by their latest collective citations [where applicable].)

Ireland is member of E.U. See also European Union Law Digest.

Note: Revisions reflect the law as at 31 July 1996.

ABSENTEES:

Presumption of Death.—See topic Death.

See also topics Limitation of Actions; Foreign Exchange, Investments and Trade.

ACKNOWLEDGMENTS: See topic Deeds.

ACTIONS:

See topics Courts; Death; Judgments.

Limitation of.—See topic Limitation of Actions.

ADMINISTRATION:

See topic Executors and Administrators.

ADOPTION:

Adoption is legalized by Adoption Acts, 1952 to 1991 which established Board empowered, under certain conditions, to make adoption order in case of child not less than six months or more than seven years old who is legitimate, illegitimate, legitimated or orphan or abandoned child in certain circumstances (whether legitimate or illegitimate). Welfare of child is first and paramount consideration in any matter relating to arrangements for or making of adoption orders by Board or court. Applicant, morally and financially suitable, must be married couple living together both of whom are not less than 21 years old or if any one of them is mother or father or relative of child, one of whom is not less than 21 years old, or subject to exception mother or father or relative, not less than 21 years old. Consent of child's mother, father (in case of legitimated child), guardian or custodian required unless dispensed with by Board.

Adoption order is not made unless applicants are ordinarily resident in Ireland and have been so resident during preceding year and applicant, if married, has consent of his or her spouse unless couple are legally separated or spouse has deserted or applicant, with just cause, left spouse. Adoption order vests in adopter parental rights and duties and releases child's mother or guardian therefrom. Property rights between child and adopter same as lawful child and parent. Adoption Child Register is kept. Adopter, parents or guardian must not receive payment or other reward for adoption. Adoptions effected outside Ireland in place where either or both of adopters were domiciled, habitually resident or ordinarily resident may be recognised as valid adoption and recorded in Register of Foreign Adoptions. Child subject of foreign adoption may be under 18 years old or, if adoption effected prior to 1991, under 21 years old.

Under 1991 Act adoption made in foreign jurisdiction will be recognised under Irish law if adoption has essentially same legal effect in ending and creating parental rights and duties to child in foreign country as if it were Irish adoption order.

A child under seven years of age who is an Irish citizen cannot be removed out of Ireland. This restriction does not apply to removal of (1) illegitimate child under one year old by or with approval of mother or if mother dead, of a relative for purpose of residing with mother or a relative outside Ireland; (2) any child under seven years old by or with approval of a parent, guardian or relative of child. Guardian must be appointed by deed, will, or court order.

The Adoptive Leave Act, 1995 provides for minimum period of adoptive leave for employed adoptive mother and, in certain circumstances, for employed adoptive father. Social Welfare Act, 1995 introduces adoptive leave benefit, payable in same way as maternity benefit. Redundancy Payment Act, 1967 and Minimum Notice and Terms of Employment Act, 1973 have been extended to such employees. (Adoptive Leave Act 1995). Protection afforded by Unfair Dismissals Act, 1977.

ADVERSE POSSESSION:

See topic Limitation of Actions.

AFFIDAVITS:

Sworn before a Commissioner for Oaths.

Under Solicitor's (Amendment) Act, 1994 every solicitor who holds Practising Certificate is authorised to have documents sworn before him provided he has no interest in proceedings.

See topic Notaries Public.

ALIENS:

An alien may hold real and personal property (except shares in an Irish ship or aircraft in case of alien of nonreciprocating State) in same manner as Irish citizen. (Aliens Act 1935, §3). See, however, topic Real Property, subhead Purchases of Land. All aliens require permit, or in exceptional circumstances passport with proper visa to enter country. Aliens spending more than three months within Ireland must register with police department and notify of any subsequent change of address. Alien must obtain permit from Minister for Enterprise and Employment before entering into any contract for employment. Irish Nationality and Citizenship Act, 1986 tightened rules on citizenship on descent. 1994 Act has cured administrative defects in 1986 Act.

Naturalization is provided for by the Irish Nationality and Citizenship Acts 1956 and 1994. Citizen of another member state of E.U. is not alien and can travel freely throughout E.U. merely on production of valid identity card or passport. No visa is necessary.

Corporations Owned or Controlled by Aliens.—It is government policy to encourage such corporations and in practice it can be said no disqualifications apply. To obtain benefits such as grants, it is necessary to register company in Ireland. Shares in it can be held by parent corporation.

See also topic Corporations, subhead Foreign Corporations.

ALIMONY: See topic Divorce.

APPEAL AND ERROR: See topic Courts.

ARBITRATION AND AWARD:

Regulated under Arbitration Acts 1954 to 1980 which include enforcement of certain foreign awards under New York and Washington Conventions. See topic Dispute Resolution.

ASSIGNMENTS:

Leasehold estates and personal property may be transferred by assignment (may be absolute or by way of security).

ASSIGNMENTS FOR BENEFIT OF CREDITORS:

A debtor may enter into a deed of arrangement with his creditors, but no creditor is bound to join. Such a deed must be registered under the Bills of Sale Acts, 1879 and 1883, within seven days of its execution, or, if executed out of Ireland, within seven days of its receipt in Ireland, if posted immediately after its execution.

An actual conveyance or assignment for benefit of creditors, when executed, constitutes an act of bankruptcy and any creditor or creditors for over £50 not being a party or parties to the deed may avail thereof. A declaration of trust would not, however, appear to be within this category. Such an assignment is an act of bankruptcy.

See topic Bankruptcy.

ASSOCIATIONS:

Unincorporated associations can be formed, such as clubs and partnerships. Usually such associations have rules. Many professional bodies such as The Law Society of Ireland and Institute of Chartered Accountants have statutory charters. Any association with more than 20 members whose object is gain must be incorporated under Companies Acts in order to be legally recognised as existing. Exceptions are partnerships of accountants or solicitors.

Constitution Art. 40 safeguards right to join or not join.

Acts, including Trade Union Acts 1871-1975, regulate Unions.

See topics Partnership and Labor Relations.

ATTACHMENT:

See topics Executions; Garnishment; Judgments.

ATTORNEYS AND COUNSELORS:

Irish legal profession is divided into solicitors and barristers. Solicitors act as legal advisers to clients and conduct legal proceedings on their behalf, instructing barrister when necessary. They have right of audience before all courts but rarely use it in higher courts. Most cases before District Court are conducted by solicitors as advocates.

Intending solicitors must obtain university degree or other educational requirements, work for minimum of two years as trainee in offices of established solicitor, and take further examinations, including one of competence in Irish language, before being admitted as solicitor.

Self-regulating body of solicitors profession is Law Society of Ireland (ILSI). Solicitors are required to obtain yearly practising certificate issued by ILSI and are regulated under Solicitors Acts 1957 and 1994.

Barristers are sole practitioners and act both as advocates with right of audience in all courts and as legal consultants. They usually accept instructions directly from Irish solicitors although in matters which are not subject of litigation in Ireland they may be instructed by lawyers qualified to practice in other EU states.

After obtaining degree at university, or other educational requirements and becoming member of Honourable Society of King's Inns, intending barristers must undergo course of studies provided by King's Inns and must pass further examinations, including test of proficiency in Irish language. They may then be called to Bar by Chief Justice. If they intend to practice, they must serve one year period of apprenticeship (called devilling) with established barrister before being permitted to practice alone.

Discipline over Bar is exercised by Benchers of King's Inns and interests of profession are catered for by General Council of the Bar, elected representative body of Bar.

See note at head of Digest as to 1996 legislation covered.

See Topical Index in front part of this volume.

ATTORNEYS AND COUNSELORS . . . *continued*

Foreign lawyer is free to act as legal consultant provided that he does not represent himself to be solicitor or barrister advising on Irish law. Certain activities e.g. conveyancing and administration of estates of deceased persons, are reserved by statute to solicitors. EU lawyers may appear and plead in Irish courts provided they do so with assistance of Irish qualified lawyer. When they appear in court they must be instructed by Irish solicitor.

Bar association that assists foreign lawyers seeking local counsel: Law Society of Ireland, Blackhall Place, Dublin 7.

BANKRUPTCY:

The law as to bankruptcy is codified by Bankruptcy Act 1988, and special provisions relating to companies are contained in Companies Acts, 1963-1990. See topic Corporations, subheads Winding Up, Receiverships, Court Protection.

A debtor can be adjudicated a bankrupt on his own petition by filing a declaration of insolvency, but for the purpose of doing so he must prove that he is possessed of assets worth £1,500.

Creditors can make a debtor bankrupt in several ways. The most usual way is where a creditor to whom the debtor is indebted in a sum of at least £1,500, obtains "bankruptcy summons," which issues from court of bankruptcy. This summons is served on debtor, who, if trader, has to satisfy claims within 14 days. Failure to pay amount claimed by bankruptcy summons (unless debt is disputed) constitutes "act of bankruptcy" and creditor may then present and file in court petition for adjudication of debtor as bankrupt.

The following are acts of bankruptcy: (a) Failure to answer bankruptcy summons within prescribed time; (b) that debtor has in Ireland or elsewhere made conveyance of his property to trustees for benefit of his creditors generally; (c) that debtor has, with intent to defeat and delay his creditors, departed from Ireland, or being out of Ireland has remained out of Ireland, has departed from his dwelling house or otherwise absented himself; (d) that execution issued against debtor on any legal process for purpose of obtaining payment of not less than £1,500 has been levied by seizure and sale of his goods or return of "no goods" has been made by sheriff; and (e) if debtor makes fraudulent conveyance of any part of his property.

Irish law (in addition to the steps taken to obtain a full bankruptcy) provides for a condition of insolvency short of bankruptcy in only two ways. (1) The first of these is one which is entirely outside the jurisdiction of the bankruptcy court and is controlled by the creditors of a debtor themselves, viz., a creditors' trust deed. This deed must be registered as a bill of sale (see topic Assignments for Benefit of Creditors) and constitutes an act of bankruptcy, of which any creditor for over £50, not a party to the deed, may avail himself. (2) The second method is by the filing of a petition in the court of bankruptcy for an arrangement with creditors. This is the method generally resorted to by debtors in embarrassed circumstances who are anxious to avoid the stigma of bankruptcy.

Either in full bankruptcy or in an arrangement with creditors under the court official assignee/trustee adjudicates on claims of creditors. Creditor whose claim is rejected at instance of official assignee has right of appeal to judge. Secured debts are protected as to the security, and certain other debts have priority and include as follows: (1) One year's local rates or taxes; (2) one year's income tax; (3) four months' salary of clerk or servant not exceeding £2,500, and (4) four months' wages of laborer or workman not exceeding £2,500. In case of winding up of company, preferential payments include: (1) One year's local rates; (2) one years assessment of all assessed taxes, including income tax and corporation profits tax; and (3) four months' salary or wages of clerk, servant, workman or labourer not exceeding £2,500, together with all accrued holiday money.

The first sitting before the court in all arrangement matters is invariably preceded by a meeting of creditors when the debtor attends and is examined and submits an offer of composition for consideration of his creditors, the latter having before them a condensed balance sheet. In addition to this balance sheet, the debtor is bound to file in court a full statement of his affairs verified by oath.

Whether the creditors at the preliminary meeting agree to or dissent from the debtor's offer the whole matter must come before the court at the "private sitting" and then proposal of debtor is fully discussed before judge by counsel. If three-fifths in number and value of creditors vote in favour of accepting offer sitting is passed; but if voting by number and value is hostile to debtor's offer, judge may turn proceedings at once into full bankruptcy or may adjourn matter for further consideration on the debtor's request to improve on offer submitted.

In a full bankruptcy the proceedings are public and "public sittings" are held.

The expression "private" conveys that the proceedings, though held in open court, are technically regarded as confidential and it is contempt of court for any newspaper to report them. This reporting veto does not apply to proceedings in bankruptcy and notice of sittings and proceedings are actually published in Iris Oifiguil and newspapers.

The debtor in an arrangement matter may apply to the court, on a report from the registrar that he has carried out the terms of the resolution and that his creditors have been satisfied in accordance with the tenor thereof, for a certificate of conformity.

In a full bankruptcy the debtor will as rule obtain discharge if: (a) He has paid all fees, expense and preferential creditors and has obtained consent of all his creditors; (b) when debtor's estate has been fully wound up and (i) his creditors have received 50% dividend or (ii) 12 years have elapsed since bankruptcy commenced.

Fraudulent Preferences.—Every conveyance or transfer of property or charge thereon made, every payment made, every obligation incurred and every judicial proceeding taken or suffered by any person unable to pay his debts, in favour of any creditor or any person in trust for any creditor, with a view to giving such creditor or any surety or guarantor a preference over the other creditors, shall, if the person making, taking, paying or suffering the same is adjudged bankrupt on a petition presented within six months, be deemed fraudulent and void against his assignees or trustees. And any conveyance, mortgage, delivery of goods, payment, execution or other act relating to property made or done by or against a company within six months before the commencement of its winding up which, had it been made or done by or against an individual within six months before the presentation of a bankruptcy petition on which he is adjudged a bankrupt, would be deemed in his bankruptcy a fraudulent preference, shall in the event of the company being wound up be deemed a fraudulent preference of its creditors and be invalid. And any conveyance or assignment by a company of all its property to trustees for the benefit of all its creditors is void. If any of above transactions apply to connected person within two years of winding up shall be deemed to be fraudulent preference unless contrary is shown. Floating charge created within 12 months before commencement of winding up is invalid except to amount of any cash paid to company at time of or subsequently to creation of charge, unless it is proved that immediately after creation of charge company was solvent. Where floating charge is created in favour of connected person and is created within two years before winding up, it shall be invalid.

BANKS AND BANKING:

Regulated by Central Bank Acts 1942, 1971 and 1989 and Statutory Instrument 395 of 1992. Provide for licensing and supervision of banks including restriction on carrying on of banking business to bankers holding licence and maintaining deposit in Central Bank. Central Bank administers deposit protection account which compensates depositors in part in event of insolvency of licence holder. Approval of Central Bank is necessary requirement for acquisition of shareholdings in banks above specified percentage. Regulatory role of Central Bank extends to number of other financial activities other than banks, including building societies and Statutory Instrument 395 of those establishing in International Financial Services Centre Futures and Options Exchange and Moneybrokers. Credit institution established and licensed in one Member State of E.U. may carry on any activity listed in Second Banking Coordination Directive of E.U. in another Member State without obtaining license. Other activities outside scope of Directive will require license.

Part IV of Criminal Justice Act, 1994 which came into effect on 1 May 1995 imposes duties on banks, other financial institutions and designated persons to prevent money laundering. They must establish identity of their account holders, maintain adequate records and inform authorities of suspicious transactions. Handling of property with knowledge or in belief that it is proceeds of criminal activity is offence.

Investment Limited Partnerships Act 1994 allows fund managers in Ireland to provide investment opportunities to foreign investors in more attractive and convenient forms. Act overcomes problems affecting limited partnerships under 1907 Act, as it related to mutual funds.

Consumer Credit Act, 1995 revises and extends law relating to consumer credit, hire purchase and hiring. It sets out requirements for advertising of credit and for form and content of credit agreements. Consumers are given right to withdraw from credit agreement within ten day "cooling-off" period. Persons engaging in business of money lending must hold licence granted by Director of Consumer Affairs.

Investment Intermediaries Act 1995 provides for authorisation and supervision of investment business firms and investment product intermediaries by Central Bank and Minister for Enterprise and Employment.

See topics Building Societies; Currency; Bills and Notes.

BARRISTERS AND SOLICITORS:

See topic Attorneys and Counselors.

BILLS AND NOTES:

Law as to bills of exchange, promissory notes and cheques is codified by Bills of Exchange Act 1882 extended by Cheques Act 1959. Bills of Exchange Act 1882 is same statute as English Bills of Exchange Act 1882. As in England, rules of common law, save in so far as they are inconsistent with express provisions of Act, continue to apply to bills of exchange, promissory notes and cheques. Conflict of law rules are same as English rules. See England Law Digest.

Cheques Act 1959 protects bankers from liability for paying cheques on which there is an irregular or no endorsement (§1), and protects bankers who collect payment of instruments for their customers who have no title to instrument.

See also topic Taxation, subhead Stamp Tax.

BILLS OF SALE: See topic Chattel Mortgages.

BONDS:

Common law prevails. §27 of Insurance Act, 1989 now permits licensed banks to issue bonds in course of their banking business. Where bank issues bond at request of customer it will obtain counter-indemnity from customer authorising bank to debit customer's account with such payment.

BUILDING SOCIETIES:

Building Societies Act 1989 consolidates and reforms law on Building Societies enabling them to provide much wider range of activities such as insurance, hire purchase and foreign exchange.

Act imposes new supervisory regime entrusting Central Bank as Societies' shareholders' guardian. Act extends winding up mechanism of Companies Acts to Societies.

CHARGES:

Company may create fixed or floating charges over its assets. In case of floating charge, company is free to deal with charged assets in ordinary course of its business.

Where person holds fixed charge over book debts of company and company fails to pay any Pay As You Earn Tax or Value Added Tax to Revenue Commissioners i.e. Super-Preferential for which it is liable, then said person shall, on being notified accordingly in writing by Revenue Commissioners, become liable to pay such outstanding amounts on due demand. (Finance Act 1986). Fixed charge holder's liability is limited to amount received by him from company after he has been notified. If fixed charge holder notifies Revenue Commissioners within 21 days of creation of charge

CHARGES . . . *continued*
his liability is further confined to amount which company fails to pay after he has been notified by Revenue Commissioners. (Finance Act 1995).

CHATTEL MORTGAGES:

Chattel mortgages are more usually referred to as bills of sale. All such mortgages of chattels, if reduced to writing, must be in form prescribed by Bills of Sale Acts, 1879 and 1883, and for sum of not less than £30; they must be registered in Central Office of the High Court within seven days of execution and copies are on file open to public inspection. Noncompliance with any of these particulars renders the deed void even as against the grantor. In case of company, charge should be registered in Companies Office. Under Agricultural Credit Act, 1978 where chattel mortgage relates to livestock and machinery used in relation to agricultural and fish produce, it must be registered within one month from its date in Circuit Court Office serving area in which land of mortgagor is situate. Bill of Sale of this stock is void and incapable of registration.

COMMERCIAL REGISTER:

Under Registration of Business Names legislation any person carrying on business under name other than his own must register. Simple form can be obtained from Business Names Registry, Dublin Castle. If carrying on business under its corporate name without any addition, company registered under Companies Act, 1963 need not register. See also topic Partnership.

CONDITIONAL SALES: See topic Sales.

CONSIGNMENTS: See topic Sales.

CONSTITUTION AND GOVERNMENT:

The Constitution of Ireland is written and contained in Constitution of Ireland Act, 1937, as amended by subsequent referenda.

The name of the state is Eire, or, in the English language, Ireland. It is declared by the Republic of Ireland Act, 1948, that the description, as opposed to name, of state shall be Republic of Ireland.

The sole and exclusive power of making laws, known as Statutes or Acts, is vested in the legislature, known as the Oireachtas, which consists of the President and two houses, the House of Representatives, otherwise called "Dail Eireann," and the Senate, otherwise called "Seanad Eireann." The Oireachtas sits in Dublin.

All citizens who have attained age of 18 years and otherwise complied with electoral laws, have right to vote for members of Dail Eireann and to take part in referenda.

Seanad Eireann consists of 11 members nominated by the Prime Minister, six members elected by certain University graduates, and 43 members chosen by limited electorate from five specially constituted panels.

The executive power of the state is exercised by the Government, which consists of not less than seven nor more than 15 members (Ministers), who are appointed by President on nomination of Prime Minister. Government is responsible to Dail Eireann. Head of Government is Prime Minister, otherwise called "The Taoiseach". Government meets and acts as collective authority, and is collectively responsible for Departments of State administered by members of Government who are empowered to make statutory rules, orders and regulations.

For purposes of local government, country is divided into 29 county council areas and ten corporation areas and local government is carried on by bodies known as county councils, corporations, urban district councils and town commissioners which have power to strike rates and generally to provide for local conditions, upkeep, repair of roads, etc.

CONTRACTS:

The law of Contracts is mostly derived from Common Law and the provisions of the Statute of Frauds and Sale of Goods Act 1893 (as amended by Sale of Goods and Supply of Services' Act, 1980) apply in Ireland. See also topics Frauds, Statute of; Infancy; Sales.

Excuses for Nonperformance.—Breach of contract by other party, force majeure.

Applicable Law.—Governed by Contractual Obligations (Applicable Law) Act 1991. This gives effect to Rome Convention on contractual obligations. Basic principle is that contract shall be governed by law chosen by parties. In absence of choice contract shall be governed by law of country with which it is most closely associated. Consumer contracts and employment contracts are amongst important exceptions to this principle.

Government Contracts.—No special requirements or conditions for contracts with Government.

Unfair Terms.—EC (Unfair Terms in Consumer Contracts) Regulations 1995 apply to consumer contracts entered into after 31.12.94 which have not been individually negotiated, for example, preprinted standard form documents. Term "unfair" is defined. Use of plain, intelligible language is required. Provision is made for severance of unfair term. Director of Consumer Affairs is empowered to apply to court for order prohibiting use of unfair term.

CONVEYANCES: See topic Deeds.

COPYRIGHT:

Law is contained in Copyright Acts, 1963 and 1987 and certain statutory instruments made under Acts. Copyright matters are dealt with by Controller of Industrial and Commercial Property, 45 Merrion Sq. Dublin 2. Copyright means exclusive right to do, and to authorise other persons to do, following acts (inter alia): (a) To reproduce, publish, perform in public, broadcast, cause to be transmitted to subscribers to diffusion service, or adapt any original literary, dramatic or musical work to which Acts apply; (b) to reproduce, publish, include in television broadcast, or cause to be transmitted to subscribers to diffusion service, any artistic work to which Acts apply; (c) to make record embodying sound recording, to cause published sound recording or any reproduction thereof to be heard in public or broadcast or transmitted to subscribers to diffusion service without payment, to cause unpublished sound recording or any reproduction thereof to be heard in public, broadcast or transmitted to subscribers to diffusion service; (d) to make copy of cinematograph film, cause it to be seen or heard in public, broadcast it or cause it to be transmitted to subscribers to diffusion service; (e) to film or photograph television broadcast made by Radio Telefis Eireann from Ireland, or part of it, otherwise than for private purposes, to record it, or to cause it to be seen or heard in public by paying audience, or to re-broadcast it; (f) to record sound broadcast made by Radio Telefis Eireann from Ireland, or cause it to be heard in public by paying audience, or re-broadcast it; (g) to make, by any photographic or similar process, reproduction of typographical arrangement of any published edition of literary, dramatic or musical work to which Acts apply.

Copyright subsists: (a) In a literary, dramatic, musical or artistic work, for lifetime of author and 70 years after his death (see infra); (b) in a sound recording, for 50 years after sound recording is made (see infra); (c) in cinematograph film 70 years after death of last of following persons to survive, namely: (i) principal director, (ii) author of screenplay, (iii) author of dialogue, (iv) composer of music specifically created for use in cinematograph film; (d) in television or sound broadcast, for 50 years after first transmission is made; (e) in published edition of literary, dramatic or musical work, for 25 years from end of year in which edition was first published.

Term of Protection of Copyright Directive (93/8EEC) was transposed into Irish law in 1995 and extends duration of copyright in published literary, dramatic, musical and artistic works from period of life of author plus 50 years from end of year in which author died, to life of author plus "seventy years after his death, irrespective of the date when the work is lawfully made available to the public". Directive also extended period of protection in films from 50 to 70 years, and period is to commence not on publication but on death of last of four measuring lives referred to above. Directive provides that copyright in sound recording will expire 50 years after making of records. Furthermore, if sound recording is lawfully published or communicated to public during this period, rights will expire 50 years from date of first publication or first communication, whichever is earlier. Under 1963 Act works that were unpublished would not attract commencement of copyright until publication. Under Directive, death of author triggers copyright term, regardless of publication. If protection expires prior to publication, then person who first lawfully makes work available to public, will be entitled to copyright protection over work for 25 years from date on which work, recording, broadcast or film was first lawfully published or communicated to public. Directive provides that if work is protected by copyright in any one of Member States on 1st July 1995, it shall be entitled to increased term of protection under Directive in all Member States, even though copyright under national laws of other Member States had expired. Therefore, works which fell into public domain on expiration of old copyright term will be brought back into copyright protection still subsisted under laws of another Member State.

There is no registration of copyright, author of work being first owner of copyright therein. Maker of a sound recording or cinematograph film, or person by whom it was commissioned and paid for, is owner of copyright therein; Radio Telefis Eireann is owner of copyright in a television or sound broadcast made by it; and publisher of an edition of a literary, dramatic or musical work is owner of copyright therein. Computer Programme Directive (91/250/EEC) which has been transposed into Irish law identifies computer programmes as being protected by copyright law. Copyright is transmissible by assignment (in writing signed by or on behalf of the assignor), by testamentary disposition, or by operation of law as personal or moveable property. Application of an assignment may be limited to one or more of the restricted acts, one or more countries, or part of work. Owner of a copyright may grant a license in respect thereof, binding on his successors in title.

Owner or exclusive licensee of copyright which has been infringed can obtain relief by way of damages, injunction, accounts or otherwise.

Copyright shall not apply to designs capable of being registered as registered design under Industrial and Commercial Property (Protection) Act 1927. Copyright shall last for five years from date of registration in case of design which is registered and period may be extended by application to Controller and on payment of requisite renewal fee, for further two periods of five years up to maximum of 15 years from date of registration. Copyright will not apply to reproduction of articles which are purely functional where object is one of number in excess of 50, of identical objects which have been manufactured and made commercially available by owner of copyright or by person authorised by him.

Copyright protection afforded by Copyright Act 1963 is extended on reciprocal basis to works first published in, and to citizens and residents of foreign countries which are parties to International Union for the Protection of Literary and Artistic Works (Berne Convention) or to Universal Copyright Convention.

Text of new copyright Bill updating copyright law is currently being prepared under auspices of Department of Enterprise and Employment and it is expected that necessary amendments arising from Rental and Lending Directive (93/8EEC), Cable Satellite Directive (92/100/EEC) and Data Based Directive will be included in new Bill.

CORPORATIONS:

In Ireland, the term "corporation" is usually applied to municipal bodies.

Law as to companies is contained in Companies Acts, 1963 to 1990. In case of private company, last word of name of company incorporated under Acts with limited liability must be word "limited"; which is sometimes contracted to "Ltd." In case of public company, last word of name of company incorporated under Acts with limited liability must be words "public limited company"; which is sometimes contracted to "p.l.c.". Incorporated company can be known and described by its name in Irish language in which case last word of name is "Teoranta" or "Teo." in abbreviation in case of private company, and "cuideachta phoibli theoranta" or "c.p.t." in abbreviation in case of public company.

See note at head of Digest as to 1996 legislation covered.

See Topical Index in front part of this volume.

CORPORATIONS . . . *continued*

Taxation.—See topic Taxation, subhead Tax Relief.

Formation of Companies.—Private company is one which by its articles: (a) Restricts right to transfer its shares; (b) limits number of its members (exclusive of present or past employees) to 50; and (c) prohibits any invitation to public to subscribe for shares or debentures. Since 1st Oct., 1994, under European Communities, (Single Member Private Limited Companies) Regulations 1994, private limited company may have only one member. Company must have at least two directors.

Public limited company requires seven or more persons for purposes of incorporation. Public companies must have minimum issued share capital of £30,000 and at least one-quarter of nominal value of such shares and all of share premium (if any) must be paid up.

Both classes of companies must have two or more directors and company secretary and must register memorandum of association stating: (1) Name of company; (2) objects and powers of company; (3) how liability is limited; and (4) amount of nominal capital and number and value of shares into which same is divided. Printed copy of articles of association or by-laws (if any) must be lodged in Companies Registration Office. If there are none, then form of articles set out in first schedule to 1963 Act and known as "Table A" applies and becomes articles of company.

Registration Fees.—Fee or duty payable to State: (a) On formation of a company as to paid up capital; (b) conversion into capital company of a company which is not a capital company; (c) increase in capital of a company by contribution of assets of any kind other than through capitalisation of profits or of reserves but including conversion of loan stock into share capital; (d) increase in assets of a company by contribution of assets of any kind in consideration not of shares in company's capital but of rights of same kind as those of members of company such as voting rights; (e) transfer from third country to State of effective centre of management of a company whose registered office is in third country; (f) transfer from third country to State of registered office of company whose effective centre of management is in third country; (g) transfer from Member State of E.U. to State of effective centre of management of company not considered to be capital company in other Member State; (h) transfer from Member State of E.U. to State of registered office of company whose effective centre of management is in third country and not considered to be capital company in Member State of E.U. from which registered office is transferred; is chargeable at rate of 1% on amount of actual value at date of transaction of assets of any kind contributed or to be contributed in connection with transaction after deduction of liabilities attaching to such assets and of expenses incurred in connection with such contribution or of amount of actual value at date of transaction of assets of any kind of company concerned after deduction of liabilities and of expenses incurred in connection with transaction.

No fee or duty is payable in certain cases on reconstruction or amalgamation of companies.

Prospectus.—A public company issuing a prospectus must set out therein matters specified in Part 1 of Third Schedule to 1963 Act and set out reports specified in Part 2 of said Third Schedule.

Annual Return.—Every company having a share capital must make an annual return to Registrar containing following particulars (inter alia): (1) Address of registered office; (2) situation of registers of members and debenture holders; (3) summary of share capital and debentures, distinguishing between shares issued for cash and shares issued as fully or partly paid up otherwise than in cash; (4) particulars of indebtedness in respect of mortgages and charges; (5) list of past and present members; (6) particulars of directors and secretaries. There must be annexed to annual return certified copies of balance sheet and of auditor's report on, and directors' report accompanying, such balance sheet. Companies (Amendment) Act, 1986 requires balance sheet and profit and loss accounts to be detailed and in form prescribed by statute, with lesser requirements for small/medium sized companies.

The European Communities (Branch) Disclosures Regulations, 1993 and European Communities (Accounts) Regulations, 1993 require filing of financial statements by external companies with Irish branches and certain unlimited companies and partnerships where liability of members or ultimate members is limited. They continue harmonisation of reporting requirements under Companies Acts and by European Communities (Companies: Group Account) Regulations, 1992 and European Communities (Credit Institution Accounts) Regulations, 1992.

Borrowing.—A company cannot borrow beyond powers (if any) set out in its memorandum and articles of association and any such attempted borrowing is void. Money borrowed by company may be secured by: (1) Legal mortgage of specific parts of its property; (2) equitable mortgage by deposit of title deeds with lender; (3) mortgage of chattels; (4) bonds; (5) promissory notes and bills; (6) floating charge evidenced by debentures; (7) debenture stock. Such mortgages or charges must be registered in Companies Registration Office within 21 days of their creation, to preserve priorities against third parties.

Directors/Officers.—Companies Act 1990 introduces greater element of transparency in dealings between companies and their directors, preventing insider dealing and imposing duty of disclosure on directors of their interest in contracts, shares and debentures of company. Act also imposes personal liability on officers of company for reckless or fraudulent trading. Professional indemnity insurance is often obtained.

Stock transfer tax is 1% in case of all stocks at purchase price or amount of market value. See topic Taxation, subhead Stamp Tax.

Winding Up.—A company cannot be made bankrupt, but it may be wound up in three ways: (1) Compulsorily by the court; (2) voluntarily, by the company as either (a) a members voluntary winding up or (b) a creditors' voluntary winding up. Court may order related companies to be wound up as if they were one company. Certain debts are given priority (similar to those in bankruptcy) and after they are paid, all unsecured creditors are on equal footing and must be paid equally.

Fraudulent Preference.—Basic concept is same as in bankruptcy. Burden of proof is on liquidator although in case of connected person, onus is on creditor.

Fraudulent Transfer of Assets.—1990 Act empowers Court, where just and equitable to do so, to order person to return property of company being wound up which was disposed of to perpetrate fraud on company, its members or creditors.

Reckless/Fraudulent Trading.—Receiver, creditor, contributory or liquidator may apply to Court for order that directors or other knowing parties are guilty of fraudulent or reckless trading and should be held responsible for some or all of company's debts and liabilities. Fraudulent and reckless trading also constitute criminal offence.

Receiverships.—Receiver may be appointed to company under debenture or on application by debenture holder to Court. Receiver appointed by Court is officer of Court whereas receiver appointed under debenture is agent of company. Receiver's function is to receive and get in all assets of company and dispose of them to pay principal sum and interest due to debenture holder. Receiver may also be appointed manager of company's affairs.

Court Protection.—Companies (Amendment) Act, 1990, was introduced in order to facilitate survival of company in financial difficulties by placing it under protection of High Court. Examiner may be appointed where it appears to Court that company is or is unlikely to be able to pay its debts. This appointment will prevent company being wound up or its assets being seized by creditors. Examiner must report to Court and present proposals and scheme of arrangement if he thinks company has viable future. Court will decide whether it is to be implemented or not.

Manufacturing Companies.—It is policy of Irish Government to encourage foreign investment in industry. See topic Taxation.

Foreign Corporations.—Every company incorporated outside Republic of Ireland establishing a place of business within Republic of Ireland is required, within one month, to file with Registrar of Companies: (1) Certified copy of its charter or memorandum and articles or by-laws written in English; (2) list of the directors and secretary; (3) name of person resident in Ireland on whom process against company may be served and company's principal place of business in Ireland; and (4) balance sheet and profit and loss accounts and, if company is a holding company, group accounts. All alterations in above particulars must be notified and filed at once. A statement or balance sheet must be filed every year. Noncompliance with above requirements subjects company and its officers and agents to heavy penalties.

See topic Bankruptcy.

See also topic Building Societies.

COURTS:

Courts of Justice in Ireland are established by Courts (Establishment and Constitution) Act 1961 and further regulated by Courts (Supplemental Provisions) Acts 1961 to 1988 and Courts Act 1991.

In cases of contract or tort: (1) District Court has jurisdiction up to £5,000 and there is right of appeal to Circuit Court; (2) Circuit Court has jurisdiction in such cases up to £30,000 or unlimited jurisdiction by consent of all parties and there is right of appeal to High Court; (3) High Court has unlimited jurisdiction and appeal lies to Supreme Court.

Courts and Court Officers' Act, 1995 establishes Judicial Appointment's Advisory Board to facilitate judicial training and to extend powers of Masters of the Courts.

In equity suits Circuit Court has jurisdiction where annual value of lands (Poor Law Valuation) does not exceed £200 or amount of personalty involved does not exceed £30,000. High Court has unlimited jurisdiction in equity and Circuit Court may exercise unlimited jurisdiction if parties consent.

Procedure for processing small claims under £500 in District Court other than through civil process was introduced by District Court (Small Claims Procedure) Rule, 1991. Certain cases are excluded from procedure. It empowers clerk to attempt to reach compromise between parties. In event of continued dispute, matter can be referred to judge of District Court for resolution.

See also topic Judicial Review.

Admiralty jurisdiction exercised by High Court.

CRIMINAL LAW:

Bail.—A right under common law. (State v. O'Callaghan, 1966 I. R. 504). Criminal Justice Act, 1964 introduced new changes to criminal law and procedure including giving of notice of alibi evidence, agreeing evidence, majority verdicts in court trials and provisions concerning offences committed on bail.

Legal aid regulated by Criminal Justice Act, 1962. Rudimentary state aid in criminal cases obtainable. Rudimentary non-statutory state aid available in certain civil cases depending on parties means, although proposals are under consideration for more extensive civil legal aid.

Juries are governed by Juries Act, 1976. All persons over 18 years of age are liable for service unless disqualified or excused.

CURRENCY:

Central Bank of Ireland has monopoly of note issue in form of legal tender notes. Currency is Irish Pound divided into 100 pennies. Value of Irish Pound is maintained with certain intervention limits with currencies of other E.U. Member States participating in European Monetary System.

Decimal Currency.—Change-over to decimal currency based on 100 New Pennies to £ from Feb. 1971.

See also topic Foreign Exchange, Investments and Trade.

CURTESY:

Tenancies by curtesy were abolished by Succession Act, 1965, effective Jan. 1, 1967. See, however, topic Descent and Distribution.

CUSTOMS:

Customs duties are levied on many imports. Different rates apply to the various categories of goods and in many cases vary according to the country of origin. As

CUSTOMS . . . *continued*
there are so many categories and also frequent changes in the rates, it is desirable to check the position on any individual commodity which it is sought to import. In many cases licences can be obtained for the free importation of goods. Customs duties do not generally apply within E.U.

Generally speaking tourists can bring in all their personal belongings intended for their own use.

See also topic Foreign Exchange, Investments and Trade.

DAMAGES:

Common law prevails. Civil Liability Act 1961 allows court to apportion damages. Damages may be awarded by court in respect of pecuniary loss, non-pecuniary loss and property damage. They may also be determined by arbitrator appointed under provisions of contract agreed between parties to dispute. See topic Death.

Criminal Injury.—Limited code awarding compensation from ratepayers of locality to applicant on proof of injury to property being malicious. Notice within seven days of injury required. Regulated by Malicious Injuries Acts 1981 and 1986. Covers only damage in excess of £100 caused by riot or acts of terrorism. Under Criminal Damage Act, 1991, persons who intentionally and recklessly damage property belonging to another may be ordered to pay compensation in addition to or instead of fine or imprisonment. Compensation to be assessed on basis of damages recoverable in civil action.

DATA PROTECTION:

Data Protection Act 1988 gives effect to Council of Europe Data Protection Convention, and is designed to protect privacy of individuals with regard to automated personal data. Act entitles "individuals" to establish existence of automated personal data kept in relation to them, to have access to data (with some exceptions) and to have inaccurate data rectified or erased. It imposes various obligations on persons who keep automated personal data, e.g. data must be accurate, kept for lawful purposes, not be disclosed in any manner incompatible with those purposes, and be protected by adequate security measures. Generally, persons keeping data owe duty of care to data subjects to extent that Law of Torts does not already so provide. Act provides for appointment of Data Protection Commissioner with power to investigate complaints, to supervise operation of legislation, and where necessary, to require compliance with its provisions. Commissioner's Office is located at Block 4, Irish Life Centre, Talbot Street, Dublin 1. Certain categories of persons and bodies keeping personal data are required to register with Commission, e.g. public sector, financial institutions, insurance companies, direct marketing, credit reference, debt collecting, data processing agencies and those who keep particularly sensitive data (political opinions, health, criminal convictions etc.).

New EC Directive (95/46/EC) was adopted in this area by Council of European Communities on 24 July 1995. In general, only slight modifications to existing Irish legislation will be required to implement it. However it introduces one very significant change in that it extends to all information, including manual information and "paper files". 1988 Act is limited in application to computerised information. While period of three years is allowed for general implementation of Directive and further nine year period is allowed in respect of provisions relating to "paper files". Directive also introduces limited exceptions for data used for literary, journalistic or artistic purposes but effect of these exceptions is still unclear.

DEATH:

If it is established that no news of a person has been received for a period of seven years by those who would ordinarily hear of him, if he were living, and that enquiries, suitable to circumstances have been made, there arises rebuttable legal presumption that such person is dead. There is, however, no legal presumption that such person died on any particular date during such period of seven years, or that he was alive at its commencement.

Survivorship.—Succession Act, 1965, effective Jan. 1, 1967, provides that where persons died in circumstances rendering it uncertain which of them survived, for purpose of distribution of their estates, they are deemed to have died simultaneously.

Actions for Death.—The Civil Liability Act, 1961, provides that where the death of a person is caused by the wrongful act (including a crime) of another such as would have entitled the party injured, but for his death, to maintain an action and recover damages in respect thereof, the person who would have been so liable is liable to an action for damages for the benefit of the dependants of the deceased. Any member of the family of the deceased who suffers injury or mental distress is a dependant for this purpose. Only one action for damages may be brought against the same person in respect of the death. It must be commenced within three years from the death, and must be brought for the benefit of all the dependants. It may be brought by the personal representative of the deceased or, if at the expiration of six months from the death there is no personal representative or no action has been brought by the personal representative, by all or any of the dependants. Damages will be amount which judge considers proportionate to injury resulting from death to each of dependants, respectively, for whom or on whose behalf the action is brought. There is no statutory limitation on amount which may be awarded (except in case of damages awarded for mental distress, where these are recoverable). In assessing damages, no account is taken of any sum payable on death of deceased under any contract of insurance, or of any pension, gratuity or other like benefit payable in consequence of death. In addition, damages may be awarded in respect of funeral and other expenses actually incurred by deceased, his dependants or personal representative by reason of wrongful act. These provisions apply to actions brought in Ireland in respect of death in Ireland of person from another country.

Death Certificates.—See topic Records.

DEEDS:

Deeds executed by individuals must be signed, sealed and delivered and should be executed in presence of two credible witnesses, who, in addition to signing their names, should subscribe their addresses and descriptions, businesses or occupations. Deeds executed by companies under common seal, countersigned usually by two directors or one director and company secretary. Date should be inserted at time of execution, in words and not in figures. If any alteration, interlineation or erasure appears on face of deed it should be noted in attestation subscribed by witnesses and also that same was made previous to execution.

Certain statutes require the execution to be verified by affidavit attached to and made part of the document.

In practice it is advisable to have all deeds for execution outside Ireland and U.K. executed in presence of: (1) Irish consul, vice-consul, pro-consul or consular agent; or (2) notary public, in which case certificate of secretary of roll of notaries or clerk of court or other responsible officer certifying appointment and identifying signature of such notary public should be attached to deed; also, signature of secretary of roll of notaries or clerk of court or other responsible officer should be duly authenticated by Ireland consul. Deed may be executed in presence of two witnesses, one of whom should make appropriate affidavit of subscribing witness before Ireland consul.

Stamp duties are payable on deeds once deed falls within First Schedule of the Stamps' Act, 1891 as amended. See topic Taxation.

DEPOSITIONS:

Where it appears to national court that any tribunal of competent jurisdiction in foreign country before which any civil or commercial matter or any criminal matter not of political character is pending, requires testimony of any witness within jurisdiction of national court, court will on application of person duly authorized by foreign tribunal make such order as is necessary for obtaining of evidence of witness.

The application is made under the Foreign Tribunal Evidence Act, 1856, and may be obtained ex parte from the master in civil matters and from the judge at chambers in criminal matters. The general practice of the court is to appoint one of its own examiners to take the evidence of witnesses. Evidence taken in pursuance of the act need not be limited to what is admissible by Irish law. Witnesses may be subpoenaed.

Court may, where necessary, order examination on oath before court, or any officer of court, or any other person, and at any place, of any witness, and may allow deposition of such witness to be adduced in evidence on such terms as court may direct. In general, no deposition may be given in evidence without consent of opposite party unless deponent is dead, beyond jurisdiction, or unable from sickness or other infirmity to attend.

DESCENT AND DISTRIBUTION:

Regulated by Succession Act, 1965 which became effective Jan. 1, 1967. It should be noted that old law will affect estates of persons who died before Succession Act came into effect.

Under Succession Act all estate whether real or personal of deceased person devolves and becomes vested in personal representative of a deceased, notwithstanding any testamentary disposition.

If deceased died intestate leaving (1) spouse and no issue, spouse takes whole estate; (2) spouse and issue, spouse takes two-thirds of estate and remainder goes to issue equally, unless all issue are not in equal degree of relationship to deceased, in which event distribution is per stirpes; (3) issue and no spouse, entire estate is distributed among issue as above; (4) neither spouse nor issue, estate is distributed between his parents in equal shares if both survive intestate but if only one survives that parent takes entire estate; (5) neither spouse, nor issue, nor parent, his estate is distributed between his brothers and sisters in equal shares and if any brother or sister does not survive intestate, surviving children of deceased brother or sister shall, where any other brother or sister of deceased survives him, take in equal shares, share that their parent would have taken if he or she had survived intestate; (6) neither spouse, nor issue, nor parent, nor brother, nor sister, his estate shall be distributed in equal shares among children of his brothers and sisters; (7) neither spouse, nor issue, nor parent, nor brother, nor sister, nor children of any deceased brother or sister, his estate shall be distributed in equal shares among his next of kin who are the persons who at date of death stood nearest in blood relationship to deceased; relatives of half blood shall be treated as, and shall succeed equally with, relatives of whole blood in same degree.

Rights Where There is a Will.—Succession Act provides that even when deceased has made a will, surviving spouse is entitled to one-half of estate if deceased leaves no children and to one-third of estate if deceased leaves spouse and children. If testator has failed in his moral duty to make provision for child, such child can apply to court for an order that provision be made for him or her out of estate. Spouse can give up his or her right during lifetime of deceased by signing written document.

Special Right of Spouse to Dwellinghouse.—Surviving spouse may require the personal representative to appropriate dwellinghouse and any household chattels of deceased in or towards satisfaction of his or her share. This right must be exercised within six months from receipt by spouse of written notification of right from personal representatives (which they are bound to give) or one year from taking out of grant of representation.

Unworthiness to Succeed.—Rights of surviving spouse and children to share in estate as legal right or on intestacy or (in case of children) to have provision made by court may be lost e.g., where spouse has been guilty of desertion continuing up to death for two years or more or a spouse or child has been guilty of serious offence against deceased or any spouse or child of deceased.

DISPUTE RESOLUTION:

Mandatory Dispute Resolution.—Certain disputes are required to be subject of specific dispute resolution or arbitration procedures to which Arbitration Acts, 1954 to

DISPUTE RESOLUTION . . . *continued*
1980 will not apply, for example, disputes on certain terms and conditions of employment and under specific legislation including Acquisition of Land (Assessment of Compensation) Act, 1919; Minerals Development Acts, 1940 to 1979; §260 of Companies Act, 1963 in combination with Companies Clauses Consolidation Act, 1845; Industrial Relations Acts, 1946 to 1959. In addition, tribunals and commissions provide similar mediation opportunities for taxation, valuation and labour disputes. In family law for marriage dissolution mediation recommendation is prerequisite.

Voluntary Dispute Resolution.—Mediation and alternative dispute resolution techniques are used occasionally in complex and specialist disputes e.g. commercial, maritime. Small civil claims can be processed by small claims process. See topic Arbitration and Award.

DIVORCE:

Jurisdiction in matrimonial matters is exercised by High Court and by Circuit Court. Law is regulated by Matrimonial Causes and Marriage Law Amendment Act, 1870-1871 and by Courts Act, 1981.

Further to referendum in 1995 constitutional ban on divorce has been lifted and Family Law (Divorce) Bill, 1996 is under legislative review to amend existing law.

Judicial separation can now be obtained under Judicial Separation and Family Law Reform Act 1989. Prior to this Act action for Decree of Divorce A Mensa et Thoro was most appropriate remedy. This action has now been abolished. Application for Decree of Judicial Separation may be made to Circuit Family Court or to High Court on certain grounds which include adultery, continuous desertion, and marital breakdown. As counterbalance Act provides stringent reconciliation attempts prior to issuing of Decree. Court may also make order as regards custody of children, property adjustment orders, periodical payments, and lump sum orders, as well as miscellaneous ancilliary orders. Neither party may lawfully remarry while other is living.

Maintenance Act 1994 gives effect to EU Convention on simplification of procedures for recovery of maintenance payments.

DOMICILE:

Common law prevails but there is no domicile of dependence in case of married women, who can acquire their own domicile.

DOWER:

Dower was abolished by Succession Act 1965, effective Jan. 1, 1967. See, however, topic Descent and Distribution.

ENVIRONMENT:

Waste.—The Waste Management Act, 1996 consolidates and updates existing waste law in Ireland. It is framework piece of legislation implementing and facilitating future implementation of both national and international legislation. It, inter alia, reorganises public authorities functions in regard to waste, introduces system of licensing collection, disposal and recovery of hazardous and non-hazardous waste, imposes obligations on producers, distributors, retailers and consumers of waste and promotes recycling, reuse of waste and waste minimisation in general.

Mining waste is governed by Minerals Development Act, 1940 and Petroleum and other Minerals Development Acts, 1960-1979. The Foreshore Acts 1933 and 1922 govern deposit of waste on foreshore.

Water.—Principal statutes controlling water pollution are Local Government (Water Pollution) Acts, 1977 and 1990 which mainly concern inland water pollution. Fisheries (Consolidation) Act, 1959 and Dumping at Sea Act, 1981 concern, inter alia, pollution of inland and coastal waters. Foreshore Acts, 1933 and 1992 contain provisions protecting seashore and foreshore. Oil Pollution of the Sea (Civil Liability and Compensation) Act, 1988 and Sea Pollution Act, 1991 deal with prevention and control of pollution of sea by oil, noxious and harmful substances, sewage or garbage. Various domestic regulations and EU legislation apply.

Legislation listed above creates series of offences, penalties and duties. System of licences in respect of discharges to waters and discharges to sewers is in existence. Local and sanitary authorities are granted certain powers, such as power to require steps be taken to prevent or abate water pollution, power to take action to prevent or abate water pollution, certain powers of entry and inspection and power to recover costs incurred in taking proceedings for offences under legislation. Local authorities may, and in certain circumstances must, make water quality management plans. Application may be made to High Court to order termination, mitigation or remedy of effects of entry or discharge into waters together with recovery of certain costs. Provision also exists under legislation for obtaining water pollution injunction. In certain circumstances civil liability for pollution is imposed.

Air pollution is governed principally by Air Pollution Act, 1987. System of control is similar to that set up by legislation governing water pollution. Local authorities have power to declare area to be special control area and can, and must in certain circumstances, prepare air quality management plan. Minister for the Environment has power to specify air quality standards and emission limit values.

Noise.—Regulation of noise pollution is governed by Environmental Protection Agency Act, 1992. Under Environmental Protection Agency Act, 1992 (Noise) Regulations, 1994, Minister for the Environment has power to make various regulations to prevent or limit noise pollution. Environmental Protection Agency ("EPA") (see subhead Environmental Protection Agency, infra) and local authorities are given power to require steps to be taken to prevent or limit noise pollution.

Complaints procedure by means of application to District Court is available in certain circumstances.

Common Law.—In addition to statutory control of environmental pollution both at domestic and EU level, law of tort provides source of legal environmental control in Ireland. Main areas of claim are in areas of nuisance, negligence, trespass and under rule in Rylands v. Fletcher (rule providing for strict liability in certain circumstances where property owner allows something which he has introduced or allowed to remain on his property, to escape causing damage to other property).

Integrated Pollution Control.—System of integrated pollution control was introduced by Environmental Protection Agency Act, 1992 which system abandons old approach requiring separate licences for discharges to separate media. Any activity of class specified in this Act (apart from established activities) must not be carried out after date prescribed by regulation without valid integrated pollution control licence ("IPC Licence"). Activities not so specified continue to be subject to existing licensing requirements unless Minister for Environment otherwise directs by order. Established activities within meaning of Environmental Protection Agency Act, even if specified, will not require IPC Licence unless Minister specifies by order that IPC Licence is required. IPC Licence will not be granted unless activity complies with BATNEEC (best available technology not entailing excessive costs) specifications established by EPA.

Environmental Protection Agency.—EPA was established by Environmental Protection Agency Act, 1992. It is independent supervisory body. Its functions include, inter alia, licensing, regulation and control of activities for environmental protection, monitoring quality of environment, establishment and maintenance of data bases of informaton, making arrangements for dissemination and availability of such information to public, provision of support and advisory services for purposes of environmental protection to local and other authorities, promotion and coordination of environmental research and liaison with European Environmental Agency. EPA prepares various reports, codes of practice, quality standards, emission limit values and guidelines. It has power to supervise local authorities in performance of their statutory functions in respect of environmental protection and has powers in respect of preparation of hydrometric programmes and environmental monitoring programmes.

Number of powers of public authorities to control air and water pollution have been extended to EPA in respect of IPC licensed activities. These powers include power to apply to court for order requiring prohibition, termination or reduction of emission or discharge, prosecution of offences in respect of air and water pollution, power to require steps be taken to prevent or abate pollution and certain powers of entry and inspection and recovery of costs incurred in taking proceedings.

Penalties.—Environmental Protection Agency Act, 1992 introduced more stringent penalties and fines in respect of pollution offences. Penalties for offences under Act itself range from maximum fine of £1,000 and/or imprisonment for one year on summary conviction to maximum fine of £10,000,000 and/or imprisonment for ten years on conviction on indictment.

Environmental Impact Statements.—Pursuant to Environmental Impact Assessment Regulations, 1989-1994, any planning application for specified developments within meaning of regulations must be accompanied by environmental impact statement ("EIS"). In addition, local authorities have discretion, in certain circumstances, to call for EIS. Where project requires not only EIS but also application for IPC Licence, planning authorities are prohibited from considering any matters relating to risk of environmental pollutions from activity which matters are solely within ambit of EPA.

Access to Information.—Access to Information on the Environment Regualtions, 1993 set up procedures for public access to environmental information. Greater public access to documents relating to applications to EPA for IPC Licences has been provided by subsequent regulations.

EU Ecomanagement and Audit Scheme.—has been introduced in Ireland which is part of EU-wide voluntary scheme for recognition of environmental management systems at management sites.

EUROPEAN UNION:

See topic Treaties; also European Union Law Digest.

EVIDENCE: See topic Depositions.

EXCHANGE CONTROL:

See topics Currency; Foreign Exchange, Investments and Trade.

EXECUTIONS:

The term "writ of execution" includes writs of fieri facias, elegit, sequestration and attachment. Writ of execution remains in force for 12 months, but may be renewed by order for further period of 12 months and so on.

When a plaintiff obtains a money judgment, the debtor's goods may be seized under a writ of fieri facias, which directs the sheriff to cause the amount of the debt to be realized by a sale of the debtor's effects.

Supplementary Proceedings.—If the sheriff reports that the debtor has no goods the plaintiff may apply to the court for an order to have the defendant brought up and orally examined as to his means and also as to what debts (if any) are due to him.

The debtor may also be ordered under §6 of Debtors Act, 1872, to pay judgment by such installments as court may direct; on failure to pay installment which debtor is shown to have had means to pay, he may be imprisoned for six weeks. If debtor is not legal owner of, but merely has equitable interest in goods, plaintiff may apply to court to have himself or some other person appointed receiver by way of equitable execution.

EXECUTORS AND ADMINISTRATORS:

On the death of a person, intestate, all his estate, real and personal, vests in his personal representative. In the case of an executor estate vests on date of decedent's death, but powers of administrator commence only from date of his appointment, property meanwhile being vested in President of High Court.

A personal representative may insert proper advertisements for creditors and so obtain protection against personal liability for any debts of which there may be no notice.

EXECUTORS AND ADMINISTRATORS . . . *continued*

It is the duty of an executor and an administrator to collect all debts due to, and discharge all liabilities due by the deceased and generally to do everything necessary to reduce the personal assets to cash with a view to winding up the estate as quickly as possible. He is allowed a year from the date of the death within which to do this, and a legatee or next of kin cannot demand payment of or sue for his legacy or distributive share, until after the expiration of this period, unless will provides to contrary.

Personal representatives are not allowed any statutory fees for their services, nor are they entitled to charge for same. They cannot delegate the discretionary part of their duties, but they may delegate the more formal part thereof and employ lawyers, auctioneers, bankers, etc., who are paid by the estate.

An administrator with or without the will must, prior to appointment, enter into a bond to the President of the High Court in double the amount or value of the personal estate and produce two sureties (or one surety if arranged through an insurance company) for the due and lawful administration of the estate. An executor need not enter into such a bond or produce sureties.

In the ordinary administration the proceedings are outside the court. The personal representative lodges in the proper department of the Inland Revenue a verified inventory of the assets and liabilities as at the date of decedent's death; this is more generally referred to as a schedule of assets or inland revenue affidavit. The estate duty (see topic Taxation) is then assessed and, having paid duty, representative completes necessary papers and files them in probate court with his application for grant of probate or letters of administration. If everything is in order grant issues and then personal representative administers estate which is under his sole control or under joint control if there are two or more acting executors or administrators.

If there is unusual difficulty in the administration or if the personal representative anticipates such, he may apply to the court for an order to have the administration carried out under the control of the court; or a creditor or beneficiary may take this step. The court, if satisfied as to the necessity for its intervention, will make an order accordingly and at the same time direct such inquiries and accounts to be made and taken in chambers as may appear to be necessary. In this event the creditors' claims are carefully scrutinized by the examiner attached to the court and every step in the administration is carried out under the supervision of the court.

An executor may retain a debt due by the deceased to himself out of the assets. Even where the estate is insolvent he may retain the debt in full out of assets actually passing through his hands, as against a creditor in equal degree.

See topic Descent and Distribution.

FACTORIES:

Regulated by Safety in Industry Act, 1955 and Safety, Health and Welfare At Work Act, 1989.

The Health and Welfare at Work (General Application) Regulations, 1993 remove rules as to maximum weights which may be lifted by employees and impose duty on employers to take appropriate measures to reduce risk of back injury.

FAMILY:

See topics Adoption, Alimony, Divorce, Husband and Wife, Infancy and Marriages.

FISHERIES:

The law relating to fisheries has been codified by the Fisheries Acts 1959 to 1983.

FOREIGN EXCHANGE, INVESTMENTS AND TRADE:

There are no controls exercised by State over foreign exchange dealings. However, UN sanctions apply to Serbia, Montenegro, Haiti, Iraq and Libya.

Currency limitations in respect of travellers and persons coming to live should be checked in each case with Central Bank of Ireland, Dame Street, Dublin 2. State sanction is required for import of certain classes of goods. Some goods require import licenses from Departments of Enterprise and Employment or Agriculture and Food. Certain tax free concessions are permitted to nonresidents investing capital in mineral developments.

See also topic Currency.

FOREIGN INVESTMENT:

See topic Foreign Exchange, Investments and Trade.

FOREIGN TRADE REGULATIONS:

See topics Currency; Customs; Foreign Exchange, Investments and Trade.

FRAUDS, STATUTE OF:

§2 of the Irish Statute of Frauds, 1695 requires that three classes of contracts must be supported by written evidence namely: (a) contracts of guarantee; (b) contracts for sale of lands or interest therein; (c) contracts not to be performed within one year.

See also topic Sales.

GARNISHMENT:

A plaintiff who has obtained an ordinary money judgment may execute it as against debts due to defendant by other parties within jurisdiction of court. Procedure is by way of garnishment or attachment of debt.

HOLIDAYS:

There are nine public holidays in Ireland. Jan. 1, Mar. 17 (St. Patrick's Day), Easter Mon., 1st Mon. in May, 1st Mon. in June, 1st Mon. in Aug., last Mon. in Oct., Christmas Day and Dec. 26. See topic Labor Relations.

HOTELS:

Under common law, Innkeepers Acts and Hotel Proprietors' Act, 1963. Information on registration and licensing requirements are available from Board Failte, Baggot Street Bridge, Dublin 2.

HUSBAND AND WIFE:

Married Women's Status Act 1957 enacted that a married woman can acquire property, contract, sue and be sued in contract and in tort and be made a bankrupt as if she were unmarried; these rights and liabilities apply between her and her husband, inter se. This Act (S.11) abolished a husband's liability for his wife's torts or contracts committed or entered into before or after marriage. A husband is made liable if he is in default in payment of alimony under a court order in which case he becomes liable for necessaries supplied to his wife. The Family Home Protection Act, 1976, restricts right of either spouse to convey any interest in family home without consent in writing of other spouse.

See topic Divorce.

IMMIGRATION:

See topics Aliens; Foreign Exchange, Investments and Trade.

INCOME TAX: See topic Taxation.

INFANCY:

Person under seven years is called infant and there is irrebuttable presumption that infants are incapable of committing crimes. Person under 18 years is called minor and minor between seven and 14 years is presumed to be incapable of committing crime, but this presumption is rebuttable by evidence of mischevious discretion. Generally minors cannot make contracts enforceable against themselves unless contract is shown to be for advantage of minor. Minor cannot be party to civil action on his own; he sues by his "next friend" and defends by his "guardian ad litem." Guardianship of Infants Act 1964 makes welfare of child paramount consideration in any proceedings.

INHERITANCE TAX: See topic Taxation.

INJUNCTIONS:

Under Common Law, courts make interim, interlocutory, perpetual and mandatory injunctions.

INSOLVENCY: See topic Bankruptcy.

INSURANCE:

Insurance in Ireland is governed by national regulations implementing E.U. Directives. These Directives ensure that nationals of one Member State of E.U. can establish insurance undertaking or branch of undertaking in any other Member State.

Member State is obliged to permit undertaking duly authorised in one Member State and complying with specific requirements, to operate in its territory in providing direct nonlife insurance and direct life assurance where initiative is taken by policy holder. In all other cases of insurances, Member State where service is to be provided is permitted to require undertaking to obtain authorisation.

Life Assurance and Non-Life Insurance Regulations 1994 give effect to European Directives which provide for single authorisation systems of supervision of insurance undertakings operating throughout EU. Key requirements of Regulation are filing of annual return, annual actuarial investigation in case of life assurance and introduction of mandatory 15 day "cooling off" period for most life assurance policy holders.

Under Insurance Act, 1964 as amended, Insurance Compensation Fund was established to protect nonlife policy holders. Compulsory contributions must be made by solvent nonlife insurers.

Regulation of insurance intermediaries is governed by Insurance Act, 1989 where they are required to be bonded once their turnover exceeds £25,000 in respect of nonlife insurance and £25,000 or 25% of turnover, whichever is greater in respect of life insurance.

Health Insurance Act, 1994 provides for establishment of Health Insurance Authority.

INTEREST:

Legal rate of interest in absence of any contract is 8%. Rate of interest may be varied by Government Order at two year intervals. Judgments for money carry interest at legal rate of interest from their date.

The highest rate which may be charged by licensed money lenders is 39% per annum, but even though this rate is not exceeded the court may, if it deems the rate charged excessive, treat the transaction as harsh and unconscionable and reduce the amount of the claim and interest to a reasonable sum. (Moneylenders Acts, 1900, 1933).

JOINT STOCK COMPANIES:

See topic Corporations.

JUDGMENTS:

Where a judgment or order directs a person to pay any money or deliver up or transfer any property, real or personal to another, he is bound to obey such judgment or order on being duly served with same, without demand.

Enforcement.—An ordinary money judgment may be enforced by fieri facias (see topic Executions) on being registered as mortgage against lands under Judgment Mortgage (Ireland) Act, 1850 and Judgment Mortgage (Ireland) Act, 1858. Judgment for recovery or delivery of possession of land may be enforced by writ of possession. Mandatory order or injunction may be enforced by writ of sequestration or order for attachment for contempt of court.

JUDGMENTS . . . *continued*

Foreign Judgments.—Judgment of foreign court is entitled to no precedence over a simple contract debt, but it may be sued on in same manner as a debt. Exemplified and duly authenticated copy of judgment or certificate thereof can be used to ground action. Defendant must have expressly or impliedly submitted to jurisdiction of foreign court. Note I.A.C. v. L.C. Ltd. 1965 I.R. 264.

The European Convention on jurisdiction and enforcement of judgments in civil and commercial matters is effective in Ireland from 1st June 1988 and judgments obtained in contracting States can be enforced by ex-parte application for enforcement order.

JUDICIAL REVIEW:

Rules of Court allow application to High Court for judicial review seeking certiorari, mandamus, prohibition or quo warranto. Court has power to grant declarations or injunctions on judicial review and can also award damages. Procedure is by way of application in first instance ex parte to seek leave to apply for judicial review on stated grounds. If leave granted, matter proceeds to full hearing, initially on affidavit.

LABOR RELATIONS:

Industrial Relations Acts 1946 to 1990, set up machinery for regulating rates of pay and conditions of employment and established tribunal, Labour Court, to which trade disputes can be referred, but there is no compulsion to use machinery thus set up or to refer disputes to Labour Court, and this is only done by mutual consent of employers and workers in each case. Decision of Labour Court is not binding on either party.

Agricultural Workers.—Detailed legislation exists regarding minimum wages and holidays of agricultural workers.

Holidays.—Regulated by Holidays (Employees) Act 1973 under which employers are bound to give their employees at least three weeks paid annual leave, in addition to public holidays.

Occupational Injuries Insurance.—In substitution for former Workmen's Compensation Code, State Social Insurance has been extended since May 1, 1967, to include compensation for disablement or loss of life following occupational injury, and benefits are now paid by State to workman (except one employed otherwise than in manual labour and earning more than £1,200 per annum) who is incapacitated, or to dependants of such workman who is killed as result of accident in course of his work. Fund for this purpose is provided by monies collected on insurance stamps paid for by employer. Employer may still be liable to workman in common law and normally insurance is taken out against this risk.

Redundancy.—Redundancy Payments Acts, 1967 to 1979, set up scheme entitling certain workers who become redundant to payments from fund financed jointly by employers and workers.

Unfair Dismissals Act, 1977 protects and provides redress for employees unfairly dismissed. The Unfair Dismissals (Amendment) Act, 1993 extends protection to employees hired under series of fixed term contracts. Where employees are hired through employment agency, hirer will be deemed for purposes of legislation to be employer. Financial loss need no longer exist in seeking redress. Employees who are parties to illegal contract are not prevented from recovering compensation.

Protection of Employment Act, 1977 protects workers threatened by redundancy.

Insolvency of Employer.—Certain debts to employees payable by State on insolvency of employer under Protection of Employees (Employers Insolvency) Act, 1984.

Unemployment Compensation.—Regulated by Social Welfare Acts, 1933 to 1980. See topic Associations.

Minimum Notice.—Under Minimum Notice and Terms of Employment Act, 1973, as amended by Terms of Employment (Information) Act, 1994, employers are required to give minimum notice to employees depending on their length of service. Terms of Employment (Information) Act, 1994 requires employers to give their employees written terms of their employment and to notify them of any changes in this regard; also provides for employee redress if Act is breached.

Part-time Employees.—Under Worker Protection (Regular Part-time Employees) Act, 1991, regular part-time employees enjoy same protection under redundancy, minimum notice, unfair dismissal, maternity, employers' insolvency and holidays legislation as full time workers. Threshold requirement is eight hours work per week.

Women.—Under Anti-discrimination (Pay) Act, 1974 it is implied term of contracts of employment that women be paid same rate as men for similar work.

Employment Equality Act, 1977 makes unlawful kinds of discrimination on grounds of sex or marital status, and sets up Employment Equality Agency.

Maternity Protection of Employees Act, 1981 gives entitlement to 14 weeks paid maternity leave with option of four further weeks unpaid. Maternity Protection Act 1994 introduced measures to improve safety and health of pregnant worker now allows for male employee leave where mother of child dies. Act further extends employee protection against unfair dismissal.

Adoption Leave.—See topic Adoption.

Safety, Health and Welfare at Work.—The Safety, Health and Welfare at Work Act of 1989 establishes national authority for occupational safety and health to supervise safety in workplace. Act sets down general duties of employers and employees and also covers designers and constructors of workplaces. Act provides for criminal prosecution for failure to comply.

Trade Disputes are defined in §8 of Industrial Relations' Act, 1990 and §10 sets out legality of acts committed in contemplation or furtherance of trade dispute. Act also provides for necessity of secret ballot before strike action. Requirement comes into effect in 1992.

Payment of Wages.—Payment of Wages' Act, 1991, prescribes various modes by which wages must be paid by employer. Deductions from wages may only be made in manner and circumstances provided for under Act.

Pensions.—Pensions Act, 1990, introduced protection of pension entitlements of people changing jobs so that they will not lose rights they have accrued. Act also provides that there shall be no discrimination on basis of sex in respect of any matter relating to occupational benefit scheme.

Transfer Of Undertakings.—European Communities (Safeguarding of Employees Rights on the Transfer of Undertakings) Regulations, 1980 was introduced to protect employees' statutory and contractual rights in event of change of employer in context of business transfer.

LANDLORD AND TENANT:

Regulated by Landlord and Tenant Acts, 1860, and 1967 to 1994. Rent Restrictions Acts, 1960 and 1967, Housing (Private Rented Dwellings) Acts, 1982 and 1983 and Common Law. Landlord and Tenant Act 1994 extended continuous occupancy requirement of commercial tenancy from three years to five years before right to renew lease to maximum of 20 years passes to tenant.

Fee Farm Grant.—Peculiar to Ireland; grant of a fee simple subject to a rent.

Kinds of Tenancy.—Lease for term of years under seal. Tenancies from year to year, month to month or week to week may be made by oral agreement.

See topic Real Property.

LAW REPORTS, CODES, ETC.:

Official Irish Law Reports are published by the Incorporated Council of Law Reporting for Ireland (address: Four Courts, Dublin).

See topic Statutes.

LEGISLATURE:

See topic Constitution and Government.

LICENCES:

Professions and certain types of business are licensed and controlled under separate statutes; types of businesses which require licenses include moneylenders, pawnbrokers, bookmakers and betting shops, chemist shops, sale of intoxicating liquors.

New Manufacture Licence.—See topic Corporations, subhead Manufacturing Companies.

Motor Vehicles and Driving Licences.—See topic Motor Vehicles.

LIENS:

A lien gives a mere right of retainer; there is no right of sale. It is either particular or general. A particular lien is the right to retain the goods in respect of which the debt arises; a general lien is the right to retain goods in respect of a general balance on account. An attorney's lien is of two kinds: (a) A general lien on title deeds and documents to ensure payment of his fees and costs; (b) a particular lien on funds recovered for his client for payment of costs of suit.

LIMITATION OF ACTIONS:

Statute of Limitations 1957 as amended by Act of 1991 provides that no action can be brought for breach of contract or in tort after six years have elapsed since accrual of right of action: limitation is three years where claim arises for personal injuries or defamation. Relevant date in personal injuries' actions is three years from date of accrual or date of knowledge (as defined by 1991 Act) of person injured.

Actions for recovery of possession of land are barred and title to land is extinguished after 12 years have elapsed since right of action accrued under doctrine of Adverse Possession. Period is 30 years where State Authority is suing to recover land.

Where the person entitled is under a disability (i.e., lunacy or infancy) these limitation periods are extended. But mere overseas absence does not give rise to any extension of these periods.

Claim to estate of a deceased person must be brought within six years of accrual of right. Actions against deceased persons must be brought against estate within two years of death.

MARRIAGES:

All marriages in Ireland are registered in the Customs House, Dublin. New rules on age and procedure for marriage were introduced by Family Law Act, 1995 which also enables Courts to make declarations on marital status. Divorce is being introduced in Ireland. (See topic Divorce.) Complications can arise in cases of persons married, divorced absolutely and remarried in foreign countries. Courts will in limited circumstances grant decrees of nullity thereby allowing remarriage at law. (See topic Divorce.)

MASTER AND SERVANT:

Common law prevails. See topic Labor Relations.

MINES AND MINERALS:

Regulated by Acts including Minerals Development Acts, 1940 to 1995, and Continental Shelf Act 1968. See also topics Factories; Labor Relations.

MONOPOLIES AND RESTRAINT OF TRADE:

Under Competition Act, 1991, Minister for Enterprise and Employment may request Competition Authority to investigate possible abuse of dominant position and may having considered Authority's report, order adjustment of dominant position by sale of assets or otherwise. Under Mergers, Monopolies and Takeovers (Control) Act, 1978 as amended by 1991 Act. Minister for Industry, Commerce and Energy may, having considered Commission's report, actually break up monopoly or make its continued existence subject to conditions. Also, under 1978 Act Minister must be notified of proposed mergers or takeovers where gross assets of enterprises not less than £10,000,000 or annual turnover not less than £20,000,000. He may then prohibit proposed merger or takeover completely or allow it subject to certain conditions. §4 of 1991 Act renders void agreements between undertakings, decisions of associations of

MONOPOLIES AND RESTRAINT OF TRADE . . . *continued*
undertakings and concerted practices which have as their object or effect prevention, restriction or distortion of competition in trade of goods or provision of services in Ireland or substantial part of Ireland. §5 of 1991 Act prohibits abuse of dominant position. §2 of 1996 Act makes breach of §§4 and 5 of 1991 Act criminal offence and imposes fines up to £3,000,000 or 10% turnover and/or up to two years imprisonment on company and senior managers. New broad enforcement powers conferred on Competition Authority to restrict anticompetitive behaviour and abuses of dominant position.

Competition Authority may grant licence in respect of these agreements in certain circumstances. Authority may also issue certificate to certify that particular agreement does not offend provisions of 1991 Act.

MORTGAGES:

See topic Chattel Mortgages.

Mortgages of land may be effected by a legal mortgage by deed or by an equitable mortgage whereby the documents of title are deposited with mortgagee. Unpaid mortgagee brings action for receiver to be appointed over lands or for lands to be sold.

The mortgagor has an equity of redemption which entitles him to redeem the mortgage on payment of sum due for principal and interest and any agreement which limits this right is void.

Judgments may be enforced as mortgage by registration of amounts of judgment debt and costs over debtor's lands under provisions of Judgment Mortgage (Ireland) Act, 1850 as amended.

MOTOR VEHICLES:

Motor vehicles must be licensed and annual road tax paid at following rates: Up to and including 1,000 cubic centimeters (cc's) £92; from 1,001 cc's to 2,500 cc's rates vary from £138 to £488, from 2,501 cc's upwards rates vary from £572 to £800 (maximum). Goods vehicles are taxed at progressive rates. Vehicles over 30 years pay reduced tax of £25. Imported motor vehicles must also be registered with Revenue Commissioners and vehicle registration tax paid. Registration tax is paid on percentage of open market value of vehicle. Rates of vehicle registration tax for vehicles under 2,500 cc's is 23.2% and for vehicles over 2,500 cc's is 29.25%.

Fee for driving license is £12 for three years or £20 for ten years and there is test.

Owners of motor vehicles must insure against third party risks including injuries to passengers. Road Tax and Insurance discs must be displayed on vehicles.

Foreign Vehicles.—Visitors bringing motor vehicles into Ireland from abroad are free from road tax for 160 days which may, under certain circumstances, be extended to six months. If they carry policies covering accidents in Ireland they may obtain certificates of insurance from Automobile Association, Dublin, or Royal Irish Automobile Club. Normally, display of registration plates of country of origin is sufficient but in each case position should be checked with Automobile Association or Royal Irish Automobile Club. Irish residents driving foreign registered vehicles are liable to have vehicle confiscated by Customs Authorities.

Generally speaking, if a driver has a full driver's license in his own country, he need not obtain an Irish driving license. Road Traffic Act 1994 increased severity of penalties and powers to curb drunk driving and other driving offences.

NEGOTIABLE INSTRUMENTS:

See topic Bills and Notes.

NOTARIES PUBLIC:

Are officers of the Supreme Court of Justice before whom are sworn affidavits intended to be used in foreign courts of law.

PARTNERSHIP:

Is an Association of two or more persons for the purpose of business. The liability of each partner extends to his entire assets and each partner is entitled to act as agent for and bind the others in their common business.

Except for partnerships of solicitors and accountants, partnership for purpose of gain may not have more than 20 partners. Any greater number must incorporate as company. See topic Associations.

Partners often use a business name and an index of such business names is kept in Dublin Castle pursuant to Registration of Business Names Act, 1963.

It is possible to form partnership which extends to one or more of partners privilege of limited liability under Limited Partnerships Act, 1907. However, there are severe restrictions. In addition to partners whose liability is limited, there must be one or more "general partners" whose liability is unlimited. Limited partner cannot take part in management of business without losing his immunity from liability. In practice, very few such partnerships are formed in Ireland. Investment limited partnerships see topic Banks and Banking.

PATENTS:

Register of Patents kept at Patent Office, 45 Merrion Square, Dublin 2. Law is regulated by Industrial and Commercial Property (Protection) Acts 1927 to 1958 and Patents Act 1992.

Application for patent must be in writing in form prescribed by rules and accompanied by: (a) two copies of specification containing clear and complete description of invention, (b) two copies of drawings, (c) two copies of claim or claims, (d) two copies of abstract containing summary of subject matter contained in specification and (e) appropriate fee. Provision for late filing of drawings and claims. Invention must be new, susceptible of industrial application and involve inventive step. Invention shall be considered new if it does not form part of state of the art as of date of filing of application. Where previous application has been filed in State or any Foreign State, applicant may obtain priority by having date of prior application deemed to be date of subsequent application, provided subsequent application made within period of 12 months from prior application. Priority is relevant in determining whether invention forms part of state of the art, and which of two or more inventors is entitled to grant of patent. Applicant must file declaration of priority and copy of previous application certified or otherwise verified to satisfaction of Controller of Patents by authority which received previous application.

Patent application must be published by Controller of Patents as soon as practicable after expiry of 18 months from date of filing of application. Applicant may on payment of fee request Controller to cause search to be undertaken in relation to invention and patent application may be amended in light of search report. If Controller decides to grant patent he must publish notice to that effect. Patent takes effect from date of notice and remains in force for period of 20 years from date of filing of application. Patent renewal fees are due annually commencing in third year from date of filing of application. In event of nonpayment of renewal fee patent will lapse. Patent provisionally comes into force on date of publication of application. Application may also be made for short-term patent of ten years duration. Same procedure applies in relation to application for and grant of patent. Sufficient if invention subject of application is new and susceptible of industrial applications provided not clearly lacking inventive step.

Owner of patent may obtain injunction, declaration, order for delivery of product covered by patent, award of damages or account of profits. Validity of patent may be challenged in course of such proceedings and Court, if it finds that patent is only partially valid, may protect it accordingly. Rights conferred by patent do not extend e.g. to acts done privately for noncommercial purposes or acts done for experimental purposes relating to subject matter of relevant patented invention. It is defence in action for damages or account of profits if defendant was not aware and had no reasonable grounds for believing that patent existed. Owner of patent may sue for infringement occuring between date of publication of application and date of publication of notice of grant of patent. Court may make declaration that particular activity does not constitute infringement of patent.

Patent may, at request of patentee, be endorsed with words Licences of Right. Effect of this is to give any person right to licence under patent on such terms as, in default of agreement, may be settled by Controller, subject to conditions specified in Act. Any person may after expiry of three years from grant of patent apply to Controller seeking entry on register that licences be available as of right. Application may be granted on grounds that subject of patent is not being commercially worked or that demand for product in state is not being met, among others.

Fees.—Following are fees payable to state in respect of patents.

	£
1. Application	
Twenty year patent	117
Ten year patent	55
2. Patent renewal fees	
Before expiration of third year from date of filing of application	54
Before end of each succeeding year fee payable is greater than fee for preceding year; fee in respect of twentieth year.	369

PEDIGREE:

Information from Genealogical Office, Dublin Castle.

PERPETUITIES:

Common law applies.

PLEDGES:

Pledges of goods as distinct from mortgages or liens are governed by the Pawnbrokers Acts, 1964 and 1965.

PRESCRIPTION:

See topic Limitation of Actions.

PRINCIPAL AND AGENT:

Common Law principles apply to this relationship. Generally, an agent for a known principal, whether his identity be disclosed or not, is not personally liable for his acts as agent and the principal is always liable.

The European Communities (Commercial Agents) Regulations, 1993 governs rights and duties of commercial agents, termination of agency contracts, provision of compensation, right to commission and to minimum notice period of termination.

PRODUCTS' LIABILITY:

E.C. Directive on products' liability was incorporated into Irish Law by virtue of Liability for Defective Products' Act, 1991. Act introduced strict liability for defective products which will operate simultaneously with principles of common law, negligence in relation to manufacture and supply of defective products.

At common law, liability attaches for negligent manufacture, sale or repair of goods which would be dangerous to reasonably forseeable user and if there was lack of reasonable care in work.

Act provides that producer (as defined by Act) shall be liable in damages in tort for damage caused wholly or partly by defect in his product. Right of action under Act is extinguished after ten years from date product is put into circulation. Producer cannot exclude or limit his liability by any term of contract, notice or in any other manner.

REAL PROPERTY:

See also topics Descent and Distribution; Landlord and Tenant; and Sales, subhead Sales of Land.

An owner in fee simple of real property may alienate it during his lifetime by writing or by his will, subject to Succession Act, 1965. See topic Descent and Distribution.

REAL PROPERTY . . . *continued*

Letting or subdivision of agricultural land is restricted and in general can only be effected with consent of Land Commission.

Purchases of Land.—Land Act, 1965, provides that no interest in land not situate in county borough, borough, urban district or town shall become vested in person who is not "qualified person" except with written consent of Land Commission. "Qualified person" includes (inter alia): (1) Irish citizen or national of member state of E.C.; (2) person continuously resident in Ireland during preceding seven years; (3) person acquiring land exclusively for purpose of industry other than agriculture; or (4) for private residential purposes where land does not exceed five acres.

Right to Purchase Fee Simple.—Landlord & Tenant Act, 1967 to 1984 give lessees holding under certain types of long leases and some yearly tenants right to purchase fee simple. Tenant serves notice on landlord and pays compensation. Landlord and Tenant (Ground Rents) Act, 1978 prevents creation of new leases reserving ground rents on dwellings.

Registration of Title.—At present registration of title to land is compulsory only in certain limited cases, but since Jan. 1, 1966, legislation has been in force designed ultimately to make compulsory the registration of all titles to land in a central Land Registry.

RECORDS:

Registry of Deeds, Henrietta Street, Dublin 1.

Land Registry and Public Records Office, Chancery Street, The Setanta Centre, Nassau Street and The Irish Life Centre, Lower Abbey Street, Dublin.

Certificates of birth, marriage and death from Registrar, 31 Molesworth Street, and 8/9 Lombard Street, Dublin. Fee, £5.50 (full) or £3.50 (short).

Stillbirths Registration Act, 1994 provides for registration of stillborn children.

REPORTS:

See topic Law Reports, Codes, etc.

SALES:

Sales of goods are regulated by the Sale of Goods Acts, 1893 to 1980.

No contract for sale of any goods of the value of £10 or upwards is enforceable by action unless the buyer accepts part of the goods so sold and actually receives same or gives something in earnest to bind the contract or in part payment, or unless some note or memorandum in writing is made and signed by the party to be charged or an agent on his behalf.

A contract of sale may be either absolute or conditional. If the property in the goods is at once transferred from the seller to the buyer the sale is absolute, but if such transfer is to take place at a future time or subject to some condition (to be fulfilled thereafter) the contract is merely an agreement of sale or conditional sale.

The seller may by the terms of a contract for sale of goods reserve the right of disposal of the goods until certain conditions are fulfilled, in which case (notwithstanding delivery to a carrier or ship for the purpose of transmission to the buyer) the property in the goods does not pass to the buyer until the conditions imposed are fulfilled. When goods are shipped and by the bill of lading the goods are deliverable to the order of the seller or his agent the seller is prima facie deemed to reserve the right of disposal. Where the seller draws on the buyer for the price and transmits the bill of exchange and bill of lading to the buyer (together) to secure acceptances or payment of the bill of exchange, the buyer is bound to return the bill of lading if he does not honor the bill of exchange and if he wrongfully retains the bill of lading without honoring the bill of exchange the property in the goods does not pass to him.

Unless otherwise agreed, the goods remain at the seller's risk until the property therein is transferred to the buyer, but when such property is so transferred the goods are at the buyer's risk whether or not delivery has been made. This latter rule is subject to the proviso that if delivery has been delayed through the fault of either buyer or seller the goods are at the risk of the party in fault as regards any loss which might not have occurred but for such fault.

Where the seller is authorized to send the goods to the buyer, delivery to a carrier or shipper for transmission to the buyer is prima facie deemed to be a delivery to the buyer; but although the carrier is ordinarily the agent of the buyer to receive the goods he is not his agent to accept. The goods are liable to be stopped in transit.

Goods may by arrangement be accepted conditionally and acceptance may in such case be withdrawn on failure of condition. Resale by buyer is strong evidence of acceptance. Where goods which he has not previously examined are delivered to buyer he is not deemed to have accepted them unless and until he has had a reasonable opportunity of examining them, and (unless otherwise agreed) when seller tenders delivery to buyer seller is bound, on request, to afford buyer a reasonable opportunity of examining goods.

Where the seller is bound to send goods to the buyer but no time for sending them is fixed, the seller is bound to send them within a reasonable time, which is a question of fact.

Delivery of goods and payment of price (unless otherwise agreed) are concurrent conditions.

Breach by seller of condition of contract for sale of goods entitles buyer to reject goods and treat contract as repudiated, unless he has "accepted" goods, when he can only treat breach of condition as a breach of warranty entitling him to damages.

Buyer is deemed to have accepted goods when he so intimates to seller or when goods have been delivered to him and he does any act in relation to them which is inconsistent with ownership of seller, or when after lapse of a reasonable time he retains goods without intimating to seller that he has rejected them.

Applicable Law.—See topic Contracts.

Notices Required.—Buyer is not generally required to give written notice of nonconforming delivery in order to enforce his rights against seller. But where goods are delivered to buyer, which he retains in his possession but does not accept, he should intimate (not necessarily in writing) to seller that he has rejected them, in which case he will not be bound to return them, nor will he be deemed to have accepted them.

Warranties.—Regulated by Sale of Goods Acts, 1893 to 1980, (S.G.A.). Merchandise Marks Acts, 1887 to 1978 and common law. S.G.A. 1893 implies conditions as to vendor's title and warranties of buyer's quiet possession and freedom from undeclared charges; if sale is by description, condition is implied that goods correspond with description. Warranties of quality and fitness are implied: (a) Where buyer makes known to seller purpose for which goods are required, so as to show that buyer relies on seller's skill and judgment, and goods are of description which it is in course of seller's business to supply; (b) where goods are bought by description from seller who deals in goods of that description (provided that if buyer has examined goods, there shall be no implied condition as regards defects which such examination ought to have revealed); (c) by usage of trade.

Express warranty or condition does not negative a warranty or condition implied by S.G.A. unless inconsistent therewith.

When sale is by sample there are implied conditions (1) That bulk shall correspond with sample in quality; (2) that buyer shall have a reasonable opportunity of comparing bulk with sample; (3) that goods shall be free from any defect rendering them unmerchantable which would not be apparent on reasonable examination of sample.

Merchandise Marks Act, 1887 §17 provides inter alia that on sale of goods to which trade description has been applied, vendor shall be deemed to warrant that trade description is not false trade description within meaning of this Act.

The Consumer Credit Act 1995 provides implied warranties that hirer shall enjoy quiet possession and that goods are free from charges, and implied conditions as to vendor's title and that goods are of merchantable quality. Where hirer makes known particular purpose for which goods are required, there shall be implied condition that goods shall be reasonably fit for such purpose.

Consumer Information Act, 1978 established office of Director of Consumer Affairs to keep eye on consumer affairs generally.

Pyramid Sales Act, 1980 prohibits inducing of persons to participate in pyramid selling schemes.

Sales of Land.—Subject to the Conditions of Sale which are generally restrictive a purchaser is entitled to be given 40 years title by the vendor.

Special provisions apply in the case of registered land as the folio is conclusive proof of the vendor's ownership but there may be unregistered rights dating from the time before the holding was put on the register which rights are protected by a note as to equities and unless this note is cancelled, a purchaser must investigate the preregistered title.

SEQUESTRATION:

See topic Judgments, subhead Enforcement.

SHIPPING:

Mercantile Marine regulated by Mercantile Marine Act, 1955 and Merchant Shipping Acts, 1894 to 1992 which affect safety at sea.

See topic Courts.

SOCIAL INSURANCE:

Pay Related Social Insurance (PRSI) contributions are payable earnings less allowable superannuation contributions up to amount shown below. Figures shown are for men and women at standard rate—this encompasses about 80% of population. Figures in parentheses after percentages are limits of income beyond which no further contribution is payable.

	%
Employer	12.20 (£25,800)
(9% where income under £9,000 p.a.)	
Employee	
PRSI	5.50 (£21,500)
* Health Levy	1.25 (no limit)
* Employment and Training Levy	1.0 (no limit)
	7.75

* Exempt where income less than £9,250 p.a.

Self-employed persons are liable to pay only 2.25% health contribution and employment levy on total income. There are provisions whereby self-employed are liable to social insurance of 5% on first £21,500 of income. See topic Taxation, subhead Income Tax.

STATUTE OF FRAUDS:

See topic Frauds, Statute of.

STATUTES:

Statutes passed in each year are subsequently published together in a single volume. No compilations or codifications exist, but there is an Index to the statutes passed between 1922 and 1985. Statutes, statutory orders and regulations and Index are published by Government Publications (Address: Sun Alliance House, Molesworth Street, Dublin 2).

SUPPLEMENTARY PROCEEDINGS:

See topic Executions.

TAXATION:

All taxation imposed by Oireachtas.

TAXATION . . . *continued*

Value added tax is imposed on wide range of goods and services. Standard rate is 21%. 12½% rate applies to cakes, crackers, wafers and other flour based bakery products and biscuits and also to works of art, antiques, literary manuscripts, general repair and maintenance, services, hairdressing and other personal services, driving lessons, cleaning services, immovable goods, building services, newspapers and tour guide services and to contract work on supply of finished goods only.

2.8% rate applies to flat rate farmers, supply of livestock and live greyhounds and hire of horses. 21% rate applies to concrete blocks and ready to pour concrete, petroleum gas, adult clothing and footwear, farm management services, and services not subject to VAT at other rates. Certain activities are exempt such as certain lettings of immovable goods, medical services, insurance services, certain banking activities, public transport, certain agency services, funeral undertakings.

Customs and excise duties are applied at varying rates to wide range of commodities. Following Ireland's accession to EU, customs duties between Ireland and other member States have been largely eliminated.

Automobiles.—See topic Motor Vehicles.

Income Tax.—(Individuals) Income tax year is from Apr. 6 to Apr. 5 of following year. Income tax is imposed on incomes, profits, salaries and emoluments of all kinds irrespective of source from which derived in case of persons both domiciled and resident in Ireland. Foreign income, excluding U.K. income, is not chargeable in hands of non-domiciled residents except to extent that such income is remitted into Ireland. Persons making annual or regular payments of annuities, patent royalties, etc. must also deduct tax and account for same to Revenue.

Unmarried individuals are entitled to tax deductible personal allowances of £2,650 and additional £800 where individual is employee. Married couples, whether with one or two incomes, have double these personal allowances and double rate bands. Other deductions include dependent relative £110, old age £200, medical expenses over £100 (individual), £200 (family), additional £2,500 for one parent family, medical insurance premiums, blind person etc. After above deductions, income is taxable as follows:

First	£9,400 (£18,800 for married couples)	at 27%
	Balance	at 48%

In addition, employees must pay "Pay Related Social Insurance" contributions on income as follows:

PRSI	5.5% (on first £21,500)
PRSI Health Levy	1.25% (no limit)
Employment/Training	1% (no limit)

The Business Expansion Scheme allows tax deduction of up to IR£25,000 per annum (available separately to husband and wife) which may be claimed for investment in certain manufacturing and grant aided companies. Relief also extends to certain approved tourism activities. Maximum amount of relief allowed to individual in a lifetime is no longer limited to any amount. Shares must be held for five years to avoid partial clawback.

Employees who purchase shares in their employer company or 75% subsidiary can claim once off tax deduction for cost up to £5,000.

Employees of certain companies may receive ordinary shares up to value not exceeding £10,000 per annum under approved profit share scheme without charge to income tax.

Tax deductions are available to individuals up to maximum of £25,000 per annum for investments in qualifying Irish film companies. Where shares are held for over three years, relief is ignored for Capital Gains Tax. Tax deductions are also available up to £25,000 per annum for individual's investment in new Irish company engaged in manufacturing certain service trades or research and development projects. Relief is subject to full employment condition.

Corporation tax is charged at rate of 30% on first £50,000 and thereafter 38% on both income and chargeable gains. Tax payable is reduced if company has any income qualifying for reduced rate of tax. For each £77 dividend received by resident individual he is chargeable to income tax on grossed up (at 23%) equivalent viz. £100 and is entitled to tax credit of £23. (This tax credit is reduced to 1/18th of net dividend for companies subject to tax at 10%.) Resident companies are not liable to corporation tax or income tax on dividends on ordinary shares received from other resident companies. Self assessment system applies whereby companies are required to make tax payment six months after accounting year end based on their calculation of their final tax liability and to file tax return within nine months of end of accounting period. Interest penalties may apply to noncompliant taxpayers.

Double Taxation Relief.—Ireland has double tax agreements with Australia, Austria, Belgium, Canada, Cyprus, Czech Republic, Denmark, Finland, France, Germany, Hungary, Italy, Japan, Republic of Korea, Luxembourg, Netherlands, New Zealand, Norway, Pakistan, Portugal, Russia, Spain, Sweden, Switzerland, U.K., U.S., Zambia. Treaties with Greece, Israel, Mexico and Poland are under negotiation.

Tax Relief.—Effective tax rate of 10% applies to trading income derived from manufacturing and certain other services carried out in Ireland by companies, whether resident or nonresident to 31 Dec. 2010. Tax credit for resident individuals on dividends paid out of such profits is 1/18th.

10% corporation tax rate has been extended to certain research and development companies, repairing of ships, engineering services, computer services, qualifying shipping activities, trading houses, repair or maintenance of aircraft and related components, certain film production, certain meat and fish processing, certain mail order operations if carried on at Shannon Airport, advertising income arising in course of production of newspapers and processing of meat owned by intervention agency. Company may claim deduction, of up to £350,000 per annum in respect of investing in qualifying Irish film companies.

International Financial Services: 10% corporation tax rate has been extended to certain operations to be carried on Customs House Dock area of Dublin by companies licenced to do so by Minister for Finance, and extends to these operations to 31 Dec. 2005.

Activities which companies may be licensed to carry on include: (1) Provision of services of type normally provided by bank in ordinary course of its trade, in relation to transactions and foreign currencies; (2) global money management; (3) international dealings and foreign currencies, futures and options denominated in foreign currencies; (4) dealings in bonds, equities and similar instruments denominated in foreign currencies; (5) insurance and related activities; (6) provision of services of processing, control, accounting, communication, clearing, settlement or information storage in relation to financial activities.

To qualify for 10% corporation tax rate licensed services must be provided to persons not ordinarily resident in State.

Companies may also be licensed to carry on development or supply of computer software for use in activity referred to at (6) above.

Mining companies get free depreciation for cost of plant and machinery, allowances for abortive exploration, annual depletion allowance and up to 120% allowance of cost of exploration. Allowance available for expenditure incurred by person on rehabilitation of site of qualifying mine following closure of mine.

Profits or gains from sale of stallion services or from occupation of woodlands are exempt from tax.

Depreciation allowance may be deducted in computing profits; there is single rate annual wear and tear allowance of 15% (10% in year seven) given on straight line basis for plant and machinery provided after 1 Apr. 1992. This applies to both new and second hand plant and machinery. In general no accelerated allowances are available. However, tax depreciation up to 100% is available in relation to (1) commercial buildings in designated urban areas (with exceptions in Dublin) and (2) new plant and machinery used by qualifying service companies in Customs House Docks area or in Shannon Customs Free airport. If allowance exceeds profit of year, balance may be carried forward and set off against profits of subsequent years.

Profits or gains arising out of publications, production or sale of original and creative work written, composed or executed either solely or jointly by individual in State and not elsewhere are exempt from income tax, provided that Revenue Commissioners determine either that work has cultural or artistic merit or is generally recognised as having cultural or artistic merit. "Work" means either book or other writing, play, musical composition, painting or other like picture or sculpture. Relief now extended to individuals who, though not resident in State, are ordinarily resident and domiciled in State and not resident elsewhere.

Patent royalties arising to residents from patents devised in State by those residents are exempt from income tax and corporation tax and patent dividends paid to resident individuals on certain qualifying shares are also exempt from Irish income taxes. This relief is restricted where royalties are from connected persons.

Ireland has adopted EEC Directive on UCITS. In addition such collective investment undertakings established in Ireland are exempt from income tax and capital gains tax as are Investment Limited Partnerships. Withholding tax at standard rate would apply to most payments to Irish residents unless reduced or exempted under double Taxation Treaty.

Special tax exempt government securities may be subscribed for by certain foreign controlled companies trading in Ireland.

Company may claim deduction up to £200,000 p.a. (£600,000 max over three years) in respect of investing in qualifying Irish film companies. Total annual investment limit of up to £6 million for company and its connected companies. Corporate investment in any one film company cannot exceed £2 million and where in 12 month period total of investments made by company and its connected companies exceeds £2 million, excess can only be invested in film companies with budget of less than £4 million.

Annual Wealth Tax.—None.

Anti-Avoidance.—Finance Act 1989 introduced general anti-avoidance provisions which can allow Revenue look through transactions entered into primarily for tax avoidance reasons. There are also specific anti-avoidance provisions in Irish law.

Capital Gains Tax.—Capital gains are chargeable at 40% on excess of value of disposals over value on Apr. 6, 1974 (or later date of acquisition) as indexed for inflation. Exemptions include principal private residence (save where sale price exceeds current use value), first £1,000 (£2,000 for married couples) of gain each year, sale of certain chattels, certain futures contracts, government stocks. Reduced rate of 27% was introduced in 1994 Finance Act for sales of certain ordinary shares by individuals. Nonresidents are liable only on gains derived from disposal of Irish land, minerals and business assets and exploration rights on Irish continental shelf. Capital gains tax is self assessment tax and severe penalties can be applied where liabilities are understated.

Residential Property Tax.—Annual Residential Property Tax is imposed at rate of 1.5% of excess of market value over £94,000. Household income must also exceed £29,500 per annum. Tax reduced for a number of children up to maximum of ten by T x c/10 where T = Tax and c = number of children. Territoriality rules are by reference to his domicile (not his residence).

Capital Acquisitions Tax.—Charged on gifts and inheritances of all types of property with aggregation in both cases back to June 2, 1982. Tax free thresholds are: Spouse and children, £178,200; near relatives, £23,500; others £11,880 (indexed annually in line with inflation). Single threshold and band of reduced rates applies to each recipient in respect of all benefits from all donors etc. Rates for inheritances are on progressive scale from 20% to 40%, gifts are taxed at three-quarters of these rates and agricultural relief applies at flat rate of 75%. Gifts or inheritances of certain businesses operating for profit in Ireland are relieved here. Test of chargeability is domicile of donor, situation of assets or proper law of disposition. Inheritance or gift from spouse is exempt. Capital acquisitions tax is self assessment tax and severe penalties can be applied where values are understated.

Probate Tax.—Tax will be charged at rate of 2% on net value of all estates over £10,000 passing under will or intestacy in case of deaths occurring after 17th June, 1993. £10,000 exemption threshold will be indexed and marginal relief also applies. Probate tax will be allowed as expense for inheritance tax purposes.

Stamp Duty.—Ad valorem stamp duty is payable on agreements, deeds, transfer of stocks and shares, promissory notes, contract notes, etc. Under Finance Act, 1991

TAXATION . . . *continued*
instruments executed after 1 Nov. 1991 stamp duty is compulsory. Some of rates are: Leasing agreement for lease if term under 35 years, 1% of annual rent; if term over 35 years and under 100, 6%; if term over 100 years, 12%; transfers of stock and marketable securities, 1% of marketable value; certain transfers to young farmers, 1% of market value. If only legal title to shares passes (not beneficial interest) that transfer will be exempt from fixed duty of £10. 1% duty imposed on electronic transfer of shares. Market makers entitled to purchase shares without liability to stamp duty.

Rates on conveyance or transfer on sale of lands, tenements and hereditaments, or on lease with payment of fine, vary.

Rate of stamp duty is as follows:

	Where principal value of consideration exceeds	and does not exceed	Rate %
—	—	£ 5,000	Nil
—	£ 5,000	£10,000	1
—	£10,000	£15,000	2
—	£15,000	£25,000	3
—	£25,000	£50,000	4
—	£50,000	£60,000	5
—	£60,000	—	6

Rate is 50% of foregoing on voluntary transfer between certain classes of relatives. Intergroup transfers may qualify for 2% ad valorem rate. Exemption may be granted in relation to certain company reconstructions. There is no stamp duty on new house or flat which qualifies for government grant and in respect of which certificate of reasonable value has issued.

Documents under seal must be stamped within 30 days of their date. Failure to stamp documents within stipulated time renders responsible party liable to heavy penalties. Documents not stamped cannot be produced in evidence in any Court of Law except in criminal matters.

See also topic Social Insurance.

TRADEMARKS:

Law relating to trademarks is contained in Trade Marks Act, 1996 which defines trademarks, grounds for refusal of registration, effects of registered trademark and provides for infringement, registration, assignment and licensing, surrender, revocation, invalidity, collective marks and certification marks.

Trademark may be registered in respect of "any sign capable of being represented graphically which is capable of distinguishing goods or services of one undertaking from those of other undertakings". Trademark may in particular consist of "words (including personal names), designs, letters, numerals or the shape of goods or of their packaging". Trademarks will be precluded from registration if they do not fulfil above requirements or are devoid of any distinctive character, or consist exclusively of signs or indications which may serve, in trade, to designate kind, quality, quantity, intended purpose, value, geographical origin, time of production of goods or rendering of services or other characteristics of goods or services or if they are, inter alia, contrary to public policy or morality. In addition, trademarks which consist exclusively of signs or indications which have become customary in current language or in bona fide and established practices of trade will not be registered as trademarks. Trademarks will not be refused registration for any of aforementioned reasons if it can be shown before date of application for registration, trademark has acquired distinctive character as result of use made of it.

Trademark can also be precluded from registration if it is identical to earlier trademark or in certain cases similar to earlier trademark and is registered in respect of similar or identical goods or services.

Trademark may be registered for period of ten years and may be renewed for further periods of ten years.

Application for registration of a mark must be made by proprietor or his lawfully authorized agent in the prescribed form supported by statutory declaration as to use, etc. Application must be accompanied by: (a) Representation of the mark on or affixed to a sheet of strong white paper of foolscap size or 29 to 34 c.m. by 20 to 22 c.m. headed "Representation of Trade Mark accompanying application by . . . . . . (here insert full name, trading style and address of applicant) dated . . . . . . 19. . . ." and signed at foot by applicant or his authorized agent; (b) three additional copies of the representation and particulars above mentioned on similar sheets headed "Additional representation of Trade Mark"; (c) full name and address of the agent (if any); (d) prescribed fee or fees or evidence of payment thereof. Applications for registration of same mark in different classes are treated as separate and distinct applications.

Address: 45 Merrion Square, Dublin 2.

Council Regulations (EC) No. 40/94 on Community Trade Mark have been implemented by Ireland. Regulations provide alternative to National trademark filing in European Union by enabling Community Trade Mark ("CTM") to be registered in respect of all EU Member States. CTM registration has registration period of ten years from date of filing of application and may be renewed for further ten year period.

The Madrid Protocol relating to International Registration of Marks of June 27, 1989 has also been implemented by Ireland. Protocol sets out procedure for obtaining Madrid Agreement Trade Mark. Under procedure resident of member country must first obtain registration in their home country. Immediately, or at anytime thereafter, he can make application to World Intellectual Property Organisation in Geneva through his national office to extend his national registration to those countries who are members of Protocol.

Assignment.—Subject to certain restrictions, a trademark is assignable and transmissible either in connection with or independently of goodwill of a business. A certification trademark, however, is not assignable or transmissible without consent of Minister for Enterprise and Employment.

TRANSPORT:

Under Road Transport Act, 1986, quantitive restrictions on carriage of goods for reward were removed. Freight carrier licences can be obtained once all E.C. requirements for access to occupation of road haulage operator are complied with.

Operator conditions are controlled by E.C. Mechandise Road Transport Regulations, 1977 as amended. Every haulier is required to hold Road Freight Certificate before being issued with merchandise licence. Road Freight Certificate is issued by Department of Transport, Energy and Communications after examining applicant's reputation, financial standing and professional competence.

TREATIES:

European Union (EU) came into being on 1st Nov. 1993 and includes European Community, resulting in change in terminology. However "European Community" or "EC" will be used when referring to specific regulation or directive adopted by Commission.

By virtue of a Treaty of Accession, Ireland became a Member of European Economic Community, European Coal & Steel Community and European Atomic Energy Community on Jan. 1, 1973. European Economic Community's Common Commercial Policy applies as regards Ireland's Trade relations with nonmember countries. In 1987, Ireland ratified Single European Act which amended constitutional Treaties of E.C. and set about establishing internal market. On Nov. 23, 1992 Massricht Treaty was ratified by Ireland but will not come into effect until signed by all Member States. This Treaty introduces new powers and policy areas including Economic and Monetary Union, European Citizenship, Foreign and Security policy, Consumer policy, Education and Heath.

Bilateral agreements between Ireland and various other countries have been entered into. These include agreements for avoidance of double taxation with respect to taxes on income, entered into with various countries. See topic Taxation, subhead Double Taxation Relief. There is also an agreement with U.K. in respect of death duties.

See also Selected International Conventions section.

UNIT TRUSTS:

Regulated by Unit Trusts Act, 1990. Provides for establishment of new and enhanced arrangements for control of unit trust schemes, in line with international practice. Central Bank has authority of vetting and approving or rejecting unit trust schemes (and advertising relating to schemes). Act provides criteria for deciding whether or not to accept scheme. Competence and sufficiency of financial resources are guiding principles. Appeal lies to High Court.

WILLS:

Valid will may be made by a person who has attained age of 18 or is or has been married, and is of sound mind.

Will or codicil must be in writing and must be signed at foot or end thereof by testator or by some other person in his presence and by his direction, and such signature must be made, or acknowledged by testator in presence of two or more credible witnesses present at same time, who must attest and subscribe will in presence of testator. If witness, or husband or wife of witness, is left legacy, execution of will is valid, but legacy will fail. Probate of will may be granted to executor by probate court on expiration of 14 days after death of testator.

Will is valid as regards form if it complies with law of (a) Place where it was made; (b) country of nationality possessed by testator either at time of making will or of his death; (c) place where testator was domiciled or had his habitual residence either at time of making will or of his death; (d) place where immovables are situated as far as they are concerned.

See also topics Descent and Distribution; Taxation, subhead Probate Tax.

ISRAEL LAW DIGEST

(The following is a list of all Topics, including cross-references, covered in this Digest.)

ISRAEL LAW DIGEST

Revised for 1997 edition by

YAACOV SALOMON, LIPSCHÜTZ & CO., Advocates of Haifa and Tel-Aviv.

See topics Law Reports, Codes, Etc.; Statutes.

ABSENTEES:

Apart from Absentees' Property Law, 1950 which deals basically with local problem of care and custody of property belonging to persons who left country at time of 1948 war, there are no specific provisions regarding absentees. Power of attorney may be given for all purposes and, if executed abroad, should be authenticated. See topic Acknowledgments.

Under Protection of Deposited Property Law, 1965 where management or control of property has been committed to another, written notification thereof in form set out in Law, must be given to Administrator General if ten years have elapsed from authorisation or appointment.

ACKNOWLEDGMENTS:

Any deed, power of attorney or other instrument in writing made or executed in any place outside of Israel may be proved in any civil cause or matter in Israel if authenticated (a) before an ambassador, minister, chargé d'affaires or secretary of an embassy or legation, or any consul, vice-consul, pro-consul or consular agent of Israel, and attested by a certificate under the hand of such officer and his official seal, or (b) before a notary public and attested by a certificate under his hand and notarial seal and authenticated by any Israel officer mentioned under (a). (Evidence Ordinance [New Text] §33). Certain public documents such as court and administrative documents and notarial acts, are exempt from this requirement because Israel is party to Convention Abolishing the Requirement of Legalisation for Foreign Public Documents. See also topics Treaties; Affidavits.

ACTIONS:

Civil procedure is governed by Civil Procedure Rules, 1984. In general, courts will only exercise jurisdiction over persons within territorial limits of state and assumption of jurisdiction will depend on validity of service of process. Rules give a list of events in which courts may grant leave to serve outside jurisdiction. Foreign claims are proved in same way as local claims. Foreign law is a question of fact and is proved by evidence of an expert in law in question. See also topics Death; Limitation of Actions; and Practice.

Limitation of.—See topic Limitation of Actions.

Death.—See topic Death.

ADMINISTRATION:

See topics Executors and Administrators and Descent and Distribution.

ADOPTION:

Adoption is permitted subject to an order of competent district court. Procedure to be followed is set out in The Children Adoption Law, 1981, and in Civil Procedure Rules. See topic Practice. Interest of child to be adopted is given paramount consideration. Adopted child must be under 18 years of age. Normally adoption of a child will not be allowed if adopting parents live abroad or intend to take child abroad. Secrecy is observed and neither natural parents nor adopting parents know identity of each other unless otherwise ordered by court. Religion of child and adoptive parents must be same (procedure for conversion of child in certain instances set forth in law). 1996 amendment establishes special procedure and recognition of special agencies for adoption of children from foreign countries.

Surrogacy Law (1996).—Surrogacy agreements must be approved by special surrogacy commission. Surrogate mother must be (i) unmarried (this requirement may be waived under certain circumstances); (ii) not relative of any of biological parents; (iii) of same religion as biological mother. Law deals only with situation in which no biological material is contributed by surrogate. Seven days after birth court order declaring parentage of newborn is sought. Under special conditions surrogate may withdraw from agreement.

See also topic Descent and Distribution.

ADVERSE POSSESSION:

Land Law 1969 has virtually abolished whole of existing Ottoman legislation and there are now no provisions relating to acquisition of title by adverse possession. See also topic Limitation of Actions.

AFFIDAVITS:

The jurat, which is a memorandum in regard to the place, time and person before whom the affidavit is made, should be without interlineation, alteration, erasure or obliteration, immediately at the foot of the document to be sworn, and towards the side of the paper, and should be signed by the person administering the oath, at the side of the date of the swearing and the place where the document or the instrument is sworn, and should state that the document or the instrument was sworn before the person administering the oath and that warning was given that document was executed under penalty of perjury. See also topic Acknowledgments.

The last paragraph of the affidavit should use words to the following effect: I swear by Almighty God (or I solemnly and sincerely declare and affirm) that this is my name and signature, and that the contents of this, my affidavit (or affirmation of declaration, as the case may be), are true.

In case of a declaration, there should be added the following words: I make this solemn declaration conscientiously believing the same to be true. Declarations may be signed before any advocate authorized to practise in Israel and have same force as an affidavit.

AGENCY: See topic Principal and Agent.

ALIENS:

Except in regard to elections, aliens are under no disability. Aliens wishing to enter Israel must secure a Traveller's Visa. See topic Constitution and Government, subhead Citizenship.

Corporations Owned or Controlled by Aliens.—Nonresidents may buy and sell Israeli shares provided payments made through authorised dealer, generally bank. Otherwise there are no restrictions on ownership or control of Israeli corporation by alien.

ARBITRATION:

Now governed by Arbitration Law, 1968. All disputes may be submitted to arbitration. No particular form of submission is required, except that submission must be in writing. Award may be enforced by leave of court in same manner as a judgment or order of court to same effect. Award may be set aside if it has been improperly procured, or if arbitrator has misconducted himself or award is evidently bad. Court will usually stay action brought in dispute which it has been agreed should be submitted to arbitration. Where international convention to which Israel is party, applies to arbitrators, court will stay action, in accordance with such convention. Schedule is attached to law containing rules relating to procedure of arbitration which will apply unless contrary intention appears in agreement.

A foreign award is enforceable as a local award and may be relied upon in any legal proceedings. In order that a foreign award may be enforceable in Israel, it must have been (a) made in pursuance of an agreement for arbitration which was valid under the law by which it was governed, (b) made by the tribunal provided for in the agreement or constituted in manner agreed upon by the parties, (c) made in conformity with the law governing arbitration procedure, and (d) has become final in the country in which it was made, and (e) is in respect of a matter which may lawfully be referred to arbitration under the law of Israel, the enforcement thereof not being contrary to the public policy or the law of Israel.

See also topic Executions.

ARCHITECTS:

Under 1958 law all architects must be entered in a register. Qualification: (a) Diploma of Technion, Technical High School; (b) registration abroad entitling to work as architect; (c) actual work for 12 years and examination.

ASSIGNMENTS:

Under Assignment of Obligations Law, 1969, right of a creditor, including a conditional or a contingent right, may be assigned without consent of debtor, may be of whole or part of debt and may be conditional or by way of charge. Debtor retains same rights against assignee as he had against assignor and if he pays assignor before receiving notice he is exempt from further payment. Debtor can also assign debt in whole or in part to another with consent of creditor.

ASSOCIATIONS:

The following forms of corporate associations are recognized: (a) partnerships; (b) companies; (c) cooperative societies; (d) societies.

Partnerships.—A partnership is defined in Partnership Ordinance (New Version), 1975 as relation which exists between persons carrying on business in common with view to profit. Partnerships are either general or limited.

A partnership formed in Israel may not consist of more than 20 persons. Every partnership formed in Israel must be registered with the Registrar of Partnerships, to whom certain particulars are to be supplied. A small registration fee is payable.

Partners of a general partnership are liable jointly and severally for all debts of the partnership. A limited partnership consists of one or more general partners who are liable for all debts, and one or more limited partners who are not liable for the debts of the firm beyond the amounts contributed by them as capital. A corporation may be a limited partner.

See also topic Business Names.

Companies.—See topic Corporations.

Cooperatives or Cooperative Societies.—A society which has as its object the promotion of thrift, self-help and mutual aid among persons with a common economic need, can be registered as a cooperative society.

No member is entitled to hold more than one-fifth of the capital. Registration fees are nominal.

Non-Profit Associations.—Association having two or more members for nonprofit purposes may be registered with Registrar of Non-Profit Associations, provided regulations contain provision for annual meetings, presentation of audited accounts and proper supervision of activities. Registration fee is payable. (Non-Profit Associations Law 1980).

ATTACHMENT:

An application for an attachment may be made in all civil actions whether in contract or in tort. It must be based on a written document or other satisfactory proof as to reasonableness of claim, in which an amount of money is claimed.

An application for attachment may be made prior to or simultaneously with institution of civil proceedings. It can be granted ex parte or in presence of the respondent. It

See Topical Index in front part of this volume.

ATTACHMENT . . . *continued*
must be supported by an affidavit. A bond or other security is invariably required. Real and personal property may be attached. Property attached may include monies due or property held by third party.

Except in special circumstances such as perishables, property attached cannot be sold before final judgment in action.

Third party claims in opposition to attachment can be heard upon motion in proceedings.

Respondent may obtain release of an attachment against adequate security.

See topic Executions.

ATTORNEYS AND COUNSELORS:

Chamber of Advocates Law of 1961 regulates admission of members to Israel Bar. Israel Bar has been constituted as recognised entity by virtue of 1961 Law, and it vested in elected bodies of members of Bar right to admit members to Bar, to regulate discipline and make other appropriate provisions affecting practice of law in Israel.

Only persons who have qualified as lawyers, are residents of Israel, and have reached age of 23 may be admitted to Israel Bar. Persons who qualify as lawyers may be graduates of Law Faculty or qualified college in Israel or persons who are admitted to a foreign Bar and practiced abroad for not less than two years and/or are graduates of foreign law school. Normal period of apprenticeship prior to admission to local Bar is now 12 months from date of fulfillment of requirements for graduation with reductions for foreign lawyers related to prior experience. There are special provisions for apprenticeship preliminary to admission to local Bar.

A licence to practice as an advocate is renewable annually against the payment of an appropriate fee.

A foreign advocate or attorney may not appear even for the purposes of a particular case, unless he was nominated to defend a foreign citizen accused of a capital punishment crime, and was approved by the Ministry of Justice.

There is a special registration for pleaders before the Rabbinical courts. All advocates may be inscribed on this list upon paying a registration fee.

Under Patents Law, 1967, with leave of court, patent agent has right to plead in patent actions, on nonlegal point.

The Israel Bar which assists foreign lawyers seeking local counsel; Jerusalem address, telephone and telefax numbers: The Israel Bar, 1 Shopen Street, Jerusalem 92190, Israel, Telephone: 972-2-660271, Telefax: 972-2-610062. Tel-Aviv address, telephone and telefax numbers: The Israel Bar, "Beit Hapraklit", 10 Daniel Frisch Street, Tel-Aviv 64731, Israel, Telephone: 972-3-6918691, Telefax: 972-3-6918696. Haifa address, telephone and telefax numbers: The Israel Bar, 21 Herzl Street, P.O. Box 4997, Haifa 31049, Israel, Telephone: 972-4-673397, Telefax: 972-4-673398.

BANKRUPTCY:

The principal law governing bankruptcy proceedings is Bankruptcy Ordinance (New Version) of 1980, which follows substantially English Bankruptcy Acts of 1914 and 1926.

A debtor is liable to be declared bankrupt and to have his property administered under the Bankruptcy Law upon committing any of the following acts, which are termed Acts of Bankruptcy: (1) If he makes a fraudulent gift or transfer of his property, or any part thereof; (2) if he makes any transfer of his property, or any part thereof, or creates any charge thereon which would be void as a fraudulent preference if he were adjudged bankrupt: (3) if, with intent to defeat or delay his creditors, he departs out of Israel, or being out of Israel remains out of Israel or departs from his dwelling house or absents himself from his usual place of business or abode; (4) if any of his property has been attached and sold in the execution of the decree of any court; (5) if he files in the court a declaration of his inability to pay his debts or petitions to be adjudged bankrupt (debts in such case must exceed NIS.10,000 due to at least two creditors); (6) if he gives notice to any of his creditors that he has suspended, or that he is about to suspend payment of his debts; (7) if creditor has obtained final judgment against him for any amount, and execution thereon not having been stayed, has served on him in Israel or by leave of court elsewhere bankruptcy notice requiring him to pay judgment debt, or to secure or compound for it, and he does not within seven days after service of notice (or in case service is effected out of Israel, then within time limited) either comply with requirements of notice or satisfy court that he has counterclaim, set-off or cross demand which equals or exceeds amount of judgment debt, and which he could not set up in action in which judgment was obtained.

The expression "debtor" includes any person of not less than 18 years of age of whatever nationality who at the time when any act of bankruptcy was done or suffered by him: (a) was personally present in Israel; or (b) ordinarily resided or had a place of residence in Israel; or (c) was carrying on business in Israel personally, or by means of an agent or manager; or (d) was a member of a firm or partnership which carried on business in Israel.

A creditor is unable to present a bankruptcy petition against a debtor unless: (a) the debt owing by the debtor to the petitioning creditor, or, if two or more creditors join in the petition, the aggregate amount of debts owing to the several petitioning creditors amounts to NIS.50,000, (b) debt is liquidated sum, and (c) act of bankruptcy on which petition is grounded has occurred within three months before presentation of petition. It is also required that debtor be domiciled in Israel, or within a year before date of presentation of petition that debtor (a) has ordinarily resided, or (b) had dwelling house, or (c) place of business, or (d) has carried on business personally or by means of agent or manager, or (e) is or has been member of firm or partnership of persons which has carried on business by means of partner, agent or manager in Israel.

A creditor's petition must be verified by affidavit of the creditor or of some person on his behalf having knowledge of the facts.

At the hearing the court requires proof of the debt of the petitioning creditor, of the service of the petition, and of the act of bankruptcy. A creditor's petition cannot, after presentment, be withdrawn without the leave of the court.

BANKS AND BANKING:

No banking business may be transacted in Israel except by a bank registered under provisions of Companies Ordinance. A foreign company may transact banking business if registered as a foreign company under Ordinance.

Bank may not operate in Israel unless licensed by Governor of Bank of Israel, under Banking Law (Registration) 1981, subject to compliance with Banking Ordinance 1941, as am'd. Purchase and sale of controlling rights in banks require permit of Governor. Banks Law provides for fulfilment of certain conditions preliminary to registration especially by fixing minimum of authorized and paid-up capital of banks operating in Israel. There are also provisions in regard to returns to be furnished. Under Bank of Israel Law 1954, which constituted State of Israel Bank—The Central State Bank—Bank of Israel is given certain powers in regard to control of banking institutions, especially in respect of liquidity, grant of credits, reserves, and rates of interest. 1976 amending law provides for discharge of liabilities, postponement of payments, addition of interest and linkage differences when banking services are disrupted by labour disputes. Banking Law (Service to Customer) 1981 places obligation on banks to give customers proper banking services with penalties for misleading or unfair actions. Rules governing use, validity and rights and obligations of issuers and holders of credit cards have been embodied in new law adopted June 1, 1986.

BILLS AND NOTES:

Principal statute governing Bills and Notes is Bills of Exchange Ordinance (New Version) 1957 (as amended) which follows substantially English Bills of Exchange Act of 1882.

Inland and Foreign Bills.—An inland bill is one which is, or on its face purports to be (a) both drawn and payable within Israel, or (b) drawn within Israel on some person resident therein. Any other bill is a foreign bill.

Inland bills must be stamped before execution. Foreign bills can be stamped after execution, before presentation for payment. Bill of exchange which has been dishonoured by nonacceptance can now be executed by summary procedure whereby bill of exchange, promissory note or cheque may be executed as though judgment had been given. Amount stated in bill shall be collected in accordance with 1968 Execution Amendment Law with addition of interest so fixed therein, and if no interest is fixed therein, with addition of interest at rate fixed in Adjudication of Interest Law 1961 from date of payment of bill or from date of its presentation for payment. Person wishing to execute bill shall file application to Execution Office supported by affidavit verifying facts stated therein. Debtor may oppose application and Chief Execution Officer shall stay application and refer matter to court. For purposes of hearing in court, opposition shall be regarded as application for leave to defend in summary proceedings under Civil Procedure Regulations 1984. When bill has been dishonoured by nonacceptance, or by nonpayment, notice of dishonour must be given to drawer and each indorser, subject to limited exceptions. Notice of dishonour may be given either to party himself, or to his agent in that behalf. It must be given within a reasonable time, which normally is three days after dishonour of bill.

The provisions in regard to presentment for acceptance, acceptance, and issue of bills in a set do not apply to promissory notes.

The provisions in regard to presentment for payment apply to promissory notes, only where the promissory note is in the body of it made payable in a particular place, in which case it must be presented for payment at that place, in order to render the maker liable.

Limitation of Actions.—No action on a bill of exchange, cheque or promissory note can be maintained against any party thereto, other than an indorser, after expiration of seven years, or against an indorser after expiration of two years from time when cause of action first accrued to the then holder against such party. Where a bill is payable after sight, presentment for acceptance is necessary in order to fix maturity of instrument. When a bill payable after sight is negotiated, holder must either present it for acceptance, or negotiate it within a reasonable time, provided always that a bill payable after sight must be presented for acceptance within six months of its date, or such shorter period stipulated for either by drawer or by an indorser, or such longer period not exceeding 12 months as may be stipulated by drawer. Failure in regard to presentment discharges drawer and all indorsers prior to holder.

A bill must be presented for payment in accordance with the following rules: (a) where a bill is not payable on demand, presentment must be made on the date it falls due; (b) where a bill is payable on demand, then presentment must be within a reasonable time after its issue, in order to render the drawer liable and within a reasonable time after its endorsement, in order to render the indorser liable. Presentment must be made at a reasonable hour, on a business day, at the proper place, excluding therefore legal holidays. The legal holidays include the State holidays and certain religious days of Jewish, Moslem and Christian communities.

Conflict of Laws.—Where a bill drawn in one country is negotiated, accepted or payable in another the rights, duties and liabilities of the parties are determined as follows: (1) Validity of the bill as regards requisites of form is determined by the law of the place of issue; validity of a supervening contract (e.g., acceptance, endorsement, etc.) is determined by the law of the place where such contract was made. (2) Interpretation of the drawing, endorsement or acceptance is determined by the law where the contract was made, provided that where an inland bill is indorsed in a foreign country the endorsement must, as regards the payer, be interpreted according to the law of Israel.

BROKERS:

There is limited legislation in regard to brokers. Brokers must be licenced by the District Commissioner. Licences are renewable annually. A tariff of brokerage fees for licenced brokers is fixed by law. The usual fees range from 1% to 5%.

BUSINESS NAMES:

Under the Registration of Business Names Ordinance 1935, every individual or firm carrying on business under a business name, i.e., name which does not consist of true surname of individual, or of true names of all partners, must register name as business name. Particulars required to be furnished under Ordinance have to be furnished

See Topical Index in front part of this volume.

BUSINESS NAMES . . . *continued*
within 15 days after person or firm commences business under business name. Nominal fee is payable.

CHATTEL MORTGAGES:

See topics Mortgages; Pledges.

CHATTELS:

See topic Moveables.

COMMERCIAL REGISTER:

No special registration required but see topics Business Names; Corporations; Licences.

CONSTITUTION AND GOVERNMENT:

A formal Constitution of State of Israel has not yet been promulgated. Present Constitution is based on Declaration of Establishment of State of Israel, dated 14th May, 1948, on Law and Administration Ordinance, 1948, and on Transitional Law of 1949. By a resolution of 13th June, 1950, Knesset resolved to impose upon Constitution, Law and Justice Committee the task of preparing a draft constitution. Constitution would thus be built up chapter by chapter. So far, 11 such chapters have become law: Basic Law—The Knesset (1958), Basic Law—Israel Lands (1960), Basic Law—President of the State (1964), Basic Law—The Government (1968), Basic Law—The State Economy (1975), Basic Law—The Army (1976), Basic Law—Jerusalem Capital of Israel (1980), Basic Law—State Investigator (1988), Basic Law—Freedom of Activity; and Basic Law—Respect of Man and His Freedom. Further Basic Law (1980) substituted reference to principles of Jewish Traditional Law for reference to U.K. common law and equity as prescribed by §46 of Provisional Order in Council 1922 now repealed. (Basic Law—Appointment of Judges [1984]).

The Knesset.—Basic Law—the Knesset, and Knesset Election Law, 1959 combine all previous laws in reference to sovereignty and elections of Knesset, the legislature of Israel. Knesset is elected by all Israeli citizens over age of 18 years in direct, national election by party list. Knesset consists of only one chamber, in which there are 120 members. Term of Knesset is four years. Elections take place on same day all over country and election day is a public holiday. Limits in reference to election propaganda are provided by law, and State officials, army officers, judges, etc., are not allowed to participate in election campaign. Recent amendment forbids those party lists from standing for election which call for negating of Israel's Jewish or democratic character, or which incite racism.

President of Israel is elected by Knesset for a period of five years. 1963 Law forbids holding of office of President for more than two consecutive periods of five years.

Government consists of Prime Minister and Ministers of State. Prime Minister is elected directly by all Israeli citizens over age of 18, in national elections. Elected Prime Minister then selects ministers of his Government. Government which does not enjoy confidence of Knesset must resign. All powers which were formerly vested in British Crown or Mandatory Government, are now vested in Government of Israel, and are exercised through various Ministers of State. Balance is created by empowering majority of members of Knesset to vote nonconfidence in Prime Minister. Latter, in certain circumstances and with consent of President can order dissolution of then sitting Knesset and holding of new elections.

Law and Administration.—Laws which existed on date of establishment of State of Israel on 14th May, 1948, continue to be effective insofar as they are not inconsistent with establishment of State, and insofar as they have not been abrogated or modified by laws passed since establishment of the State of Israel.

Citizenship.—The Law of Return, 1950, as amended, sets forth entitlement of Jew to acquire Israeli citizenship. For purpose of this Law, Jew is (1) anyone born of Jewish mother or who converts to Judaism and (2) who is not member of another religion. Under Citizenship Law, 1952, as amended, Israeli citizenship is acquired in one of following ways: (1) Any Jew who has emigrated or emigrates to Israel and expresses his desire to settle there, may acquire Israeli citizenship unless (a) he ceased to reside in Israel before July 14, 1952 or (b) being a foreign citizen he makes or has made a declaration that he does not desire to be an Israel citizen and in case of an infant, his parents have made such a declaration; (2) former Palestine citizen becomes an Israel citizen if he was resident in Israel on July 14, 1952 and fulfils certain other conditions; (3) any person born in Israel is an Israel citizen if his mother or father is an Israel citizen; (4) stateless person born in Israel after setting up of State may acquire nationality by filing a request to such effect between his 18th and 21st birthdays provided he has resided in Israel five years continuously prior to application; (5) Israel citizenship may also be acquired by naturalization, conditions being (a) residence in Israel at time of and for three out of five years prior to application, (b) intention to reside permanently in Israel, (c) some knowledge of Hebrew language and (d) renunciation of any other citizenship. An infant who is a resident of Israel or one of whose parents is an Israel citizen may apply for grant of citizenship. Israel citizen living abroad may renounce his citizenship. Citizenship acquired by naturalization, may be lost in certain circumstances. Save in case of naturalization, Israel citizenship does not require giving up of any former citizenship.

CONSUMER PROTECTION:

Consumer Protection Law of 1981 forbids dealer in goods or services to mislead consumer by act or failure to act, in writing or verbally in any material matter affecting transaction, inter alia re quality, nature, quantity and type of goods and/or services, measure, weight, form, components, date of delivery of goods or supply of services.

Dealer is likewise forbidden to exploit in any way, reduced circumstances, physical or mental deficiency, ignorance, language, lack of experience or to exercise undue influence to induce transaction on unreasonable or abnormal terms.

Dealer is obliged also to disclose material defects known to him.

Misleading advertisements, or packaging are forbidden.

Detailed Regulations govern credit sales, interest calculation, marking of goods on package and advertising directed at reaching minors.

Representative action (class action) can, with permission of court hearing matter, be submitted by consumer or consumer organization.

CONTRACTS:

Israeli Law broadly follows English rules of common law and equity. There are also relics of Turkish laws and there is a growing body of legislation on contracts. Contract is formed by offer and acceptance. To great extent Israeli legislation has either codified English Common Law or borrowed from models such as American Uniform Commercial Code. One notable departure is absence of any requirement of consideration as basis for contract. (The Gift Law 1968 however retains concept of consideration where gift is defined as ownership of property otherwise than for consideration.) What is paramount under Contracts Law 1973 is intention of parties to enter into agreement.

Several laws have replaced Turkish legislation and lay down general rules in respect of various types of contract. These are Agency Law 1965, Guarantee Law 1967, Pledges Law 1967, Bailees Law 1967 and Sale Law 1968. It is always possible to contract out of these Laws.

Contract Law.—Contracts (General Part) Law, 1973, contains codification of general part of law of contract, which broadly follows principles of English Law of Contract which have hitherto been accepted by courts. However, there are some departures from English law, e.g., consideration is no longer required to create enforceable contract. Law came into force on Jan. 1, 1974.

See also topics Consumer Protection; Landlord and Tenant; Mortgages; Moveables; Pledges; Principal and Agent; Restrictive Trade Practices; Sales.

Excuses for Nonperformance.—Contract is void in case of fundamental mistake by one of parties to contract, illegality and impossibility of performance. Impossibility must be literal impossibility. Presence of a material misrepresentation, duress or undue influence may make contract voidable by non-offending party.

Notices Required.—Notice of cancellation of contract for fundamental breach must be given within reasonable time after party becomes aware of breach. If breach is not fundamental, party in breach is given period of grace to remedy breach and if necessary notice of breach is given within reasonable time of elapse of such period. Period of grace is not required to be notified in writing. (Law of Contracts [Remedies for Breach of Contract] 1970 §§7-8).

Notice is required for set-off in case of money debts owed by one party to another in same transaction whether liquidated or not, and if not in same transaction, in case of liquidated debts only. (Law of Contracts [General Part] 1973, §53).

Purchaser of goods must give immediate notice to vendor after inspection required to be made on delivery if goods are found not to be as ordered, or as soon as defect discovered if concealed, otherwise purchaser has no claim against vendor. (Law of Sale 1968, §14).

Vendor must give notice to purchaser of any third party claim against goods supplied which he knew of or should have known of before delivery. (Law of Sale 1968, §18).

Applicable Law.—English rules of conflict of laws apply and "proper law of the contract" is applicable law: If parties choose a law in contract, this will almost invariably be applicable law. As regards contracts for sale of goods Uniform International Commercial Code applies from Aug. 18, 1972.

Government Contracts.—There are no special forms and Government is generally liable for its contracts and can be sued on them although injunction and specific performance are not available against State. Obligatory Tenders Law (1992) requires Government companies and bodies to carry out public tenders as condition for contracting.

Remedies for breach of contract have been given statutory force by Contracts (Remedies for Breach of Contract) Law 1970. Subject to provisions of Law, injured party may claim enforcement or rescission of contract and/or damages. Enforcement is similar to equitable remedy of specific performance and is granted except where contract is incapable of performance, where enforcement requires compelling carrying out of personal work, where enforcement requires unreasonable amount of supervision by court or it is inequitable in circumstances of case. Rescission is permissible in case of fundamental breach but where breach is not fundamental, reasonable time must first be given to party in breach to remedy breach. Damages are granted for injury caused by breach and its consequences and which party breaking contract foresaw or should have foreseen as a probable consequence of breach at time contract was made.

Breach of Contract.—Supreme Court has summed up 1970 Law regarding relief on breach of contract (a) that breach of contractual condition, including date of payment, agreed as being "basic" is fundamental breach; (b) on fundamental breach injured party may, and on ordinary breach, he must give an extension which other party may use to fulfil his contractual obligation within reasonable time of grant of extension; (c) right to regard contract as void and must be exercised within reasonable time after lapse of such reasonable period, in case of ordinary breach or immediately in case of fundamental breach; (d) right to regard as void, revives if extension given, even if not obligatory by law, after lapse of reasonable extension period. Supreme Court has also held that in cases where contract is not voided, injured party is entitled to profits realized by party in breach as consequence of breach.

Form.—In general, form of contract is immaterial but certain contracts need to be in writing in order to be enforceable, in particular contracts relating to land and to lending of money and partnerships and agreements with building contractors.

Contractors' Agreements.—1974 law regulates work undertaken by a contractor who is not an employee of person ordering work. It regulates liability of contractor to repair defects, contractor's right to refuse delivery until paid according to agreement, and liability to pay contractor.

Distributorships, Dealerships and Franchises.—There is no specific legislation which regulates distribution and marketing contracts, dealerships or franchises. These contracts are regulated by different legislative enactments, such as Law of Contract, Agency etc.

See Topical Index in front part of this volume.

CONTRACTS . . . *continued*

Contracts on these subjects which do not expressly state period of time during which they will be in force can be revoked at any time by one party communicating to other notice of revocation or termination, given in advance, stipulating reasonable period of time until termination will take effect. Question of reasonableness is decided by courts based on period of time during which contract was in force prior to termination, investments by parties, etc.

Israeli Supreme Court ruled that exclusive distributor to whom exclusive rights were granted in certain area, is not capable of preventing third parties, who purchased their products from source other than original supplier or manufacturer, from distributing their products in same area.

Israeli courts will not normally force parties to continue relationship of principal and distributor, marketing agent or franchisee but will award damages to injured party in case of unjustified termination or insufficient notice.

Warranties.—§11 of Law of Sale 1968 provides that vendor fails to fulfil his obligations under sale agreement if only part of goods or larger or smaller quantity than agreed upon is delivered, if article supplied differs in kind or description from agreement, if article lacks quality or characteristics required for normal or commercial use thereof or for special purpose for which agreement implies it was purchased, or if article is not, by reference to type, description, quality or characteristics, according to sample or specimen submitted by vendor, unless so submitted without any undertaking of conformity to sample. If vendor does not within reasonable time of receiving notice from purchaser, remedy deficiency in fulfilment of his obligations, purchaser may claim specific performance, rescission or deduct from price payable value of deficiency. (§28 of Law of Sale).

CONVEYANCES: See topic Assignments.

COPYRIGHT:

English Copyright Act of 1911 is incorporated into Israeli Copyright Ordinance.

Nature of Copyright.—Copyright is sole right to produce or reproduce work of literature, music, drama or art or any substantial part thereof in any material form in public. Copyright in lecture exists in delivery. If work is unpublished, it is sole right to publish it wholly or partially and includes sole right to produce, reproduce, perform or publish any translation of work. Copyright exists in conversion of dramatic work into novel or vice versa; and in making of any record, perforated roll, cinematograph film or other contrivance by means of which literary, dramatic or musical work may be mechanically performed or delivered. Publication of any work means issue of copies of work to public. Any unauthorised person who performs above acts infringes copyright. According to 1953 Copyright Amendment Ordinance, copyright in unpublished work exists where author was at time of creation national or resident of Israel.

Infringement.—Copyright in work is infringed when person without copyright owner's consent does anything, sole right to do which, is conferred on owner. Thus copyright is infringed when unauthorised person sells work or lets it for hire or by way of trade exposes or offers it for hire; or where he distributes work either for trade or in manner that prejudices owner of copyright; or when he exhibits work by way of trade in public; or when he imports for hire or sale any work which to his knowledge infringes copyright; or where he for his private profit knowingly permits theatre or other place of entertainment to be used for performance of work without copyright owner's consent.

There are the following exceptions to copyright infringements: (a) Fair dealing with any work for purposes of private study, research, criticism, review or newspaper summary; (b) use by author of work of any mould, cast, sketch, plan, model or study made by him where he is not copyright owner, provided that he does not repeat or imitate main design: (c) making paintings, drawings, engravings or photographs of work of sculpture if permanently situate in public place; (d) publication of non-copyright matter for bona fide use of schools as long as not more than two passages from works by same author are published within five years and source from which passages are taken is acknowledged; (e) publication of report of lecture delivered in public unless printed notice of prohibition of publication is given; (f) reading or recitation in public by one person of any reasonable extract from any published work.

Term of copyright is for life of author and for 50 years from Jan. 1st after his death. Same position obtains in case of any anonymous or pseudonymous work.

Ownership of Copyright.—Author of work is first owner of copyright therein except: (a) In case of engraving or photograph where plate or original was ordered by some other person and was made for valuable consideration in pursuance of that order where person who orders original is first owner; (b) where author was in employ of some other person under contract of service and work was done in course of his employment, employer (in absence of any contrary agreement) is first owner. This position does not obtain where work is some contribution to newspaper, magazine or periodical where (unless there is contrary agreement) ownership of copyright remains vested in author.

Assignment.—There are no special forms for assignments or licences nor does copyright require registration.

Civil Remedies.—Where there is infringement, owner is entitled to injunction, damages or otherwise as may be conferred by law for infringement of right. Costs are in absolute discretion of court. In action for infringement plaintiff is presumed to be owner unless defendant puts existence of copyright or owner's title in issue. Even if damage resulting from infringement is not proved court may award compensation of not less than NIS 5,000 and not more than NIS 10,000 for each infringement. (Copyright Ordinance §3A).

Copyright Owner's Rights.—All infringing copies and plates used or intended to be used for production of such copies are deemed to be property of copyright owner who may take proceedings for recovery of possession or conversion, except as regards architectural restriction where interdict or injunction cannot be obtained or where demolition cannot be ordered. Infringing structure is not deemed to be property of copyright owner.

Prescription of Action.—According to Prescription Law of 1958 action for copyright infringement expires after seven years from date of infringement.

Protection of Foreign Works.—Where convention relating to copyright protection has been concluded between Israel and another country, or where Israel has acceded to convention, Minister of Justice may direct that works for which protection is required by such convention shall be protected. Israel is signatory of Stockholm B, Brussels and Unesco Conventions. Protection granted by Minister shall not exceed any protection were such work to have been published in Israel. Work published simultaneously in Israel and several other countries shall be considered as having been first published in Israel provided that there is no "colourless" publication.

Privacy.—By an amending Statute of Law of Civil Wrongs, use of name, connotation picture or voice of a person for commercial purposes, constitutes a civil wrong (a tort) rights to relief being given to person affected and after his death to his heirs.

Moral Right.—By 1981 Amendment, author of work has moral right in accordance with Berne Convention to have his work published without distortion, defect or alteration prejudicing its value, or his good name. Infringement of this right is compensated even if financial damage not proved.

Performer's Rights.—1984 Law grants performers, including actors, singers, musicians, dancers or other performers protection for 25 years against recording, broadcasting, televising, sale, renting, import or possession of such recording etc. for commercial purposes without consent of performer. If performance protected is given in course of performer's employment, protection is granted to employer.

CORPORATIONS:

Principal law concerning companies is Companies Ordinance, (New Version), 5743-1983. From day on which company has been formed in accordance with date appearing on certificate of association, company assumes all legal rights, duties and acts permitted by law. Any seven or more persons may form public company, and any two or more persons, but not more than 50, private company. Both classes of companies must register memorandum and articles of association with Registrar of Companies. Objects of company are set out in memorandum which is company's charter. Any act of company not within objects set out in memorandum is ultra vires. Distinction has been drawn in Companies Ordinance between ultra vires acts and acts in which company directors act outside scope of their authority. Where servant of company acts outside scope of his authority on behalf of company, such acts have no validity vis-a-vis company, unless subsequently authorised by general meeting of company or by decision of board of directors where director has acted outside scope of his authority. Should company wish to change objects as determined by memorandum of association, such change may now be effected by special resolution and comes into force 21 days after adoption of resolution subject to rights of objection of minority shareholders. Articles set out internal regulations of company. Unless particular set of articles is filed, sample articles contained in Second Schedule of Companies Ordinance govern internal management of company. Great elasticity is possible in drafting of articles and it is common to include preemption rights and various devices for protecting interests of minority shareholders.

Companies may be: (a) Limited by shares, (b) limited by guarantee, or (c) unlimited. In a company limited by shares, liability of members is limited to amount, if any, unpaid on shares respectively held by them. In a company limited by guarantee, liability of members is limited by memorandum to such amount as members may respectively thereby undertake to contribute to assets of company in event of company being wound up. Company not having any limit on liability of its members is an unlimited company. Company limited by shares is by far most common form of company.

Companies Ordinance provides for split vote whereby shareholders may vote one way for portion of their shares and other way for rest of their shares at company meetings.

Directors and officers owe duty of care and good faith to company and must disclose any personal interest in contracts of company. Company whose articles of association expressly permit same may insure liability of directors and officers and indemnify them, in certain specified circumstances.

Companies Ordinance has been amended to require companies, whose securities, i.e.: shares, debentures, warrants, etc., were offered to public by prospectus and which are held by public, to include as members of their Boards of Directors, individuals known as "public directors" who are otherwise not connected with company or with interested parties. Appointment of said individuals requires approval of special committee, provided for by relevant amendments and composed of (1) judge, appointed by Minister of Justice after consultation with President of Supreme Court, (2) chairman of Securities Authority (see also topic Securities) and (3) chairman of Tel-Aviv Stock Exchange Ltd. By said amendments to Companies Ordinance, Boards of such companies are also required to establish control committees, which have extensive review and supervisory powers and are composed of not less than three members of Board, including all of public directors, and excluding chairman of board, managing director, general business manager, comptroller, secretary or any other officer employed by company.

Registration fees are payable in form of registration fees and capital duty. Every company must file annual return with Registrar of Companies containing statutory information in regard to share capital, charges and directors. Public company must also file accounts.

Foreign Company.—Companies Ordinance defines foreign company as being all companies and associations, except partnerships which have been formed or registered outside Israel. Number of members is now unspecified. Foreign company which establishes place of business in Israel, has to be registered as foreign company. Annual return must be filed.

Application for registration by foreign company has to be made within one month from establishment of place of business and has to be accompanied by following documents: (a) Certified copy and Hebrew translation of charter, statutes or memorandum and articles of company; (b) list of directors; (c) names and addresses of some one or more persons resident in Israel authorized to accept on behalf of company service of processes and any notices required to be served on company; (d) certified

See Topical Index in front part of this volume.

CORPORATIONS . . . *continued*
copy of power of attorney enabling some person ordinarily a resident in Israel to act for company in Israel. Fee NIS. 330, plus publication fee, or in case of corporation not constituted for purposes of profit fee of NIS. 110, is payable on registration of foreign company.

Government Companies Law 1975.—Regulates formation, management and winding-up of companies in which State has more than half voting power or right to appoint more than half directors. Law provides for compensation for minority shareholders in companies which become subject to Law, appointment of directors on behalf of State and of managing directors and appointments to government companies of accountants, legal advisers and internal comptrollers. Resolutions of government companies on certain matters require government ratification. Some of provisions of Law also apply to companies in which State has not more than half voting power or right to appoint not more than half directors. By amendment adopted May 27, 1986, various requirements of this Law may be waived by Government if necessary to enable offering abroad of shares of Government company.

See also topics Associations; Securities.

COURTS:

The courts of Israel consist of the following: (1) Magistrates' Courts, which deal with civil matters in which the subject matter is of NIS.1,000,000 or less, and recovery of possession and partition of immovable property of any value, and in criminal matters with contraventions and misdemeanours. Claims not exceeding NIS. 5,000 where claimant appears in person may be dealt with under simplified procedure. Minister of Justice may, by Order, empower Magistrates' Court to act as Court of Local Matters and deal with defined matters, mainly municipal and local laws and offences. (2) District Courts, which have jurisdiction in all matters save as expressly vested in any other courts, e.g., magistrates' courts, and serve as Appellate Courts for Magistrates' Courts decisions. There are five District Courts, one in each of following cities: Jerusalem, Tel-Aviv, Haifa, Beer Sheva and Nazareth. Admiralty jurisdiction formerly vested in Supreme Court, is now vested in district court sitting in Haifa. There is right of appeal to Supreme Court. (3) Supreme Court, which has jurisdiction as High Court of Justice to which application in nature of mandamus, petition of right, habeas corpus and any other petition against Government, or government officer or any other public authority can be made and also as Court of Appeal, i.e., appellate tribunal from decisions of district court. (4) Municipal Courts, which have jurisdiction over any offences against municipal regulations or bylaws and over certain other specified minor offences. (5) Anti-profiteering courts are attached to each magistrates' court and district court. Tribunal is composed of professional judge or magistrate, and two members of public. (6) Rent Tribunals constituted under 1954 Tenant Protection Law, consisting of magistrate and two members of public, assess rent and value of services in relation to tenancies. (7) By Labour Courts Law 1969 court was set up to deal with all matters arising from employer/employee relationships including national insurance claims. Special Juvenile Tribunals were constituted for first time in 1955. (8) Administrative Courts—The Administrative Courts Law (1992) governs operation of these courts from whose decision appeal lies, of right, to District Courts. Since 1957 Chief Justice may order criminal case to be reheard either by Court of Appeal or by district court if new facts have come to light, another person has been convicted for same offence, or evidence relied on has been declared false or forged. Chief Justice can also decide to rehear any matter decided by Supreme Court if it involves question of importance, difficulty or novelty.

The religious courts of several recognized religious communities have jurisdiction in matters of marriage and divorce of residents. In other matters of personal status these courts have jurisdiction with consent of the parties concerned. The religious courts have no jurisdiction over foreigners except by consent of all parties.

Courts are empowered by Legal Assistance Foreign States Law 1977 to collect testimony, seize documents or articles, conduct searches or carry out other legal proceedings at request of legal authority of foreign country. All such proceedings are to be conducted according to Israel Law. Court is entitled to refuse request for such aid if it is convinced that proceedings are of political character. Law does not apply to extradition proceedings prior to trial or serving of sentence.

See also topic Labour Relations.

CRIMINAL LAW:

Punishments Law 1977 effected comprehensive codification of criminal law and came into force on Apr. 1, 1978. New general and preliminary section came into force on Aug. 8th, 1995, dealing with basic tenets of criminal responsibility. Criminal procedure is codified in Criminal Procedure Law (Consolidated Version) 1982.

Magistrates' Courts can deal with crimes for which penalty is a fine only or imprisonment up to seven years. All other offences are within jurisdiction of district courts. In respect of limited offences, private complaint may be filed, otherwise Attorney-General or his representative is in charge of criminal proceedings on behalf of state.

Courts have jurisdiction to release on bail persons charged with any offence except one for which penalty is death or life imprisonment or in respect of certain offences against security of state.

Capital punishment for murder was abolished in 1954, except in respect of a limited number of offences under Nazis and Nazi Collaborators (Punishment) Law, 1950 and it is still in force under Genocide (Prevention and Punishment) Law 1950 and in respect of treason under §96 of Punishments Law. Law Forbidding Denial of the Holocaust 1986 provides penalties of imprisonment (up to five years) for persons convicted of denying occurrence of Nazi holocaust or publishing praise of and/or identification with acts committed by Nazi regime. 1995 Public Defence Law establishes Public Defence Bureau intended mainly for indigent defendants.

See also topic Limitation of Actions.

CURRENCY:

Unit of currency is Israel New Shekel (NIS). Currency Law of 1985 changes old currency, Israeli Shekel (IS) to New Shekel, with banking system converting to new currency on Jan. 1, 1986. One thousand IS equals one NIS. Since 1955 the Bank of Israel is the central state bank and is the issuing bank of the Government. Dealings in foreign currency are authorized only through approved banks and there are limitations on the export of foreign currency.

Exchange Control is now governed by Currency Control Law 1978 and Currency Control Regulations 1978, as amended from time to time.

CUSTOMS:

See topic Taxation, subhead Customs Duty.

DEATH:

The Declaration of Death Law implements the United Nations Convention on the subject of declarations of death of persons who disappeared in Europe during the Nazi regime. The same law also provides for declarations of death in a case of persons dying a natural death or through accident and of whom all traces have been lost for more than two years. Application by an interested person, as defined by the Law, is to be made to the competent court, which is the Jerusalem District Court. (Book of Laws, No. 93, of 13.3.53).

A copy of death certificate of a person dying in Israel is obtainable on application to the local authorities of the area in which the death took place.

Actions.—On death of any person any cause of action in respect of a civil wrong subsisting against or vested in him survives against or, as case may be, for benefit of his estate.

Where death is caused by a civil wrong and such person would, had death not ensued, have been entitled at time of his death to recover compensation in respect of bodily injury caused to him by such civil wrong, the husband, wife, parent and child of such deceased person may recover compensation from person responsible for such civil wrong.

These laws, like all other laws, apply equally to foreigners.

See also topic Limitation of Actions.

DEEDS: See topic Land.

DEPOSITIONS:

See also topics Acknowledgments; Affidavits.

For Use Within Israel.—The court or a judge may at any time order that any particular fact or facts be proved by affidavit, or that the affidavit of any witness be read at the hearing, on such conditions as the court or judge thinks reasonable. Where it appears that either party bona fide desires the production of a witness for the court's examination and that such witness can be produced, an order will not be made authorizing evidence of the witness to be given by affidavit.

Affidavits must be in the first person, divided into paragraphs and confined to such facts as the deponent is able of his own knowledge to prove, except on interlocutory applications, in which a statement of the deponent's belief may be admitted provided that the grounds thereof are stated.

Within Israel for Use Elsewhere.—Under Legal Assistance to Foreign States (Consolidated Version) Law, 5737-1977, court may, at request of foreign judicial authority, submitted in form and manner prescribed by regulations, order taking of evidence, production and seizure of documents or other articles, carrying out of search or performance of any other legal act, all subject, unless otherwise provided in this Law, to provisions of any law applying in Israel to preformance of these acts. Court may permit witness to be examined by a representative of party to foreign proceedings, if court is satisfied that such representative in competent to examine witness in foreign country. Certain restrictions apply. Minister of Justice is charged with implementation of Law and is authorized to make regulations as to any matter relating to such implementation. In accordance with such authority, Minister of Justice promulgated Regulations for the Enforcement of the Hague Convention 1970 (Taking of Evidence), 5737-1977. Regulations specify required content of request for taking of evidence. Letter of Request should be submitted to Director of Courts in Jerusalem, who will direct same to appropriate court.

Under the Extradition Ordinance, depositions or statements on oath taken in a foreign state, and copies of such original depositions or statements and foreign certificates or judicial documents, stating the fact of conviction may, if duly authenticated, be received in evidence in proceedings for extradition.

Outside Israel for Use Within Israel.—On the application of any party to any civil proceedings, the court may make an order for examination upon oath before any person in any place outside jurisdiction of any witness, and court may give directions as to matters connected with examination. Person directed to take any examination may administer oath and report to court on examination, and conduct of any witness.

DESCENT AND DISTRIBUTION:

Comprehensive succession law was enacted in 1965—Inheritance Law of 1965. Former limitations on power of testamentary dispositions in respect of certain classes of immovables were abolished (see topic Wills). Subject to any testamentary dispositions, following are legal heirs entitled to succession: (1) Spouse of deceased; (2) children and their descendants and parents of deceased and their descendants.

Spouse is entitled to movable property, including passenger vehicle and contents of home and, as to remainder of estate: (1) If deceased left children or their descendants, or parents—one-half; (2) if deceased was survived by siblings or their descendants or grandparents—two-thirds; provided, however, that if at time of death of deceased, spouse had been married to deceased for three years or more and lived with him in apartment included, wholly or partly in estate, spouse takes whole apartment or share of deceased therein and two-thirds of estate. If deceased was not survived by any of above-named relatives, except spouse, spouse inherits entire estate.

State succeeds in absence of relations.

Adopted child is entitled to same share as natural child. New provisions are embodied in 1965 law entitling needy spouse, needy child or needy surviving parents to maintenance out of estate. Court is entitled to allow widow or widower a one-time grant or periodical maintenance.

DESCENT AND DISTRIBUTION . . . *continued*

Maintenance in respect of children may be granted until they reach age of 18 and in special cases up to 23 years of age, and to parents for life.

Administrator may be appointed by court to administer estate, and court may confirm as administrator an executor appointed by will.

Creditors have to be satisfied first before any distribution is made to heirs.

Spouse, children or parents who lived with deceased in his place of residence are entitled to continue to reside in same premises as lessees of legal heirs for such duration and subject to such terms as may be settled with heirs or as settled by court.

Competent court is entitled to deal with estate of any person who resided in Israel on date of his death or has left property in Israel.

Applicable law is law of residence of deceased on date of his death, except in respect of assets which devolve in accordance with lex situs. Competent court is district court (civil court) where deceased resided at time of his death, or in case of nonresident court having jurisdiction where any assets of deceased are situated in Israel.

Religious courts may exercise jurisdiction when all parties consent to such jurisdiction.

See also topic Marriage.

DESIGNS: See topic Patents.

DISPUTE RESOLUTION:

No significant legislation.

DIVORCE:

Rabbinical Courts have exclusive jurisdiction in regard to divorce where both parties are Jews, and are either domiciled in Israel or Israeli citizens. Christian recognized Religious Courts have exclusive divorce jurisdiction in regard to Christians who are Israeli citizens. Moslem Religious Courts have exclusive divorce jurisdiction in regard to Moslems who are Israeli citizens or foreigners who, under law of their nationality, are subject in such matters to jurisdiction of Moslem Religious Courts.

Law of Jurisdiction in Dissolution of Marriage in Special Cases, 1969, authorises Chief Justice to direct that an application for divorce (which is not in jurisdiction of any Religious Court) be dealt with either by a Civil Court or a Religious Court. As a result, it is now possible in case of mixed marriages where parties belong to different religious communities, for marriage to be lawfully dissolved. Law also repealed limitation of jurisdiction in divorce cases of foreigners.

Maintenance.—By 1972 Law to ensure payment of maintenance where judgment for maintenance is given in favour of a spouse, a minor child or a parent, resident in Israel, party entitled may apply to be paid by National Insurance Institute, thereby saving himself necessity of execution proceedings. Amount payable is sum adjudged, subject to overriding maximum fixed by regulations. Rights under judgment are subrogated to Institute which may recover from defendant under judgment. Apart from right to maintenance legal separation is not recognized.

Division of Property of Spouses in Divorce.—In absence of agreement each spouse is entitled by 1973 Law of Financial Relations between Spouses to half of total property of both spouses excluding such property as either had before marriage or received as gift or by way of inheritance during marriage or non-assignable rights or property which parties agreed should not be taken into consideration.

ENVIRONMENT:

Environmental legislation in Israel is extensive and includes Abatement of Nuisances Law, Hazardous Substances Law, Planning and Building Law, Water Law, laws governing Prevention of Sea Pollution and regulations adopted pursuant to said laws. These laws are administered primarily by Minister of the Environment. With respect to radiation, standards of International Radiation Protection Agency have been adopted. Environmental legislation sets emission standards, standards for disposal of hazardous wastes, limitations on noises, etc. Standards of U.S. Environmental Protection Agency have been adopted in certain areas (such as with respect to nitrogen emissions) while in others (such as those dealing with particle emissions and sulfur dioxide emissions) standards are similar to those in Germany. As a condition for obtaining building permits for industrial plants, power plants, etc., Planning and Building Law requires submission of plan-specific environmental impact statements to authorities, based on guidelines promulgated by Minister of the Environment. In addition Businesses Licensing Law includes provisions related to environmental matters, which must be satisfied as condition for receiving license to operate business.

EXCHANGE CONTROL:

See topics Currency; Foreign Trade Regulations; Investment Law and Incentives.

EXECUTIONS:

Execution Law 1967 provides for various methods of enforcing judgments and for securing defendant's property during course of an action (see topic Attachment). Judgment debtor can be detained or prevented from leaving country if Chief Execution Officer considers he intends to impede execution. There is power to attach movable property but certain items such as foodstuffs for subsistence of debtor and family for 30 days, vital household effects and clothes, religious articles and trade implements are exempt. Attached property may be sold after seven days from date of attachment. Immovable property may also be attached and sold after 30 days. Dwelling house is exempt unless it can be shown that debtor has somewhere else to go. Agricultural land required for subsistence is also exempt. There are also provisions for attachment of property in hands of a third party which includes debts due to judgment debtor. There are certain exemptions, most important being wages up to a certain amount. In certain limited circumstances a debtor, who has not, after an inquiry into his means, paid the ordered instalments of his debt, can be arrested. Further form of execution commonly used is appointment of a receiver similar in nature to remedy of equitable execution used in Anglo-Saxon systems.

By virtue of a 1968 amendment to Law, bill of exchange may be enforced directly by execution without obtaining judgment.

Execution of Foreign Judgments.—Under Foreign Judgments Enforcement Law 1958, foreign judgment may be enforced in Israel either by action thereon before a district court or by grant of an exequatur issued by a district court. A "judgment" for this purpose means any judgment or order given by a court outside Israel in any civil proceedings, whereby a sum of money is made payable and includes an award in any arbitration, if award is, in pursuance of law enforced in place where it was made. It is enforceable in same manner as a judgment given by a court in that place. Judgment to which an exequatur has been accorded is executory in Israel. There are certain conditions required for enforcement, particularly reciprocity and that judgment was given according to rules of natural justice.

By amendment to above Law in 1977, foreign judgment will be recognized by Israel Court only if following conditions are satisfied: (a) Agreement with country where judgment was given; (b) Israel undertook by such agreement to recognize judgments of same class; (c) such undertaking applies only to judgments enforceable by Israel Law; (d) all conditions of agreement are fulfilled.

By same amendment debts in foreign currency may be paid in that currency or in Israel currency at rate of exchange in force at time of payment.

Special provisions in regard to the enforcement of foreign awards are contained in the (Arbitration) Foreign Awards Ordinance of 1934. The provisions of this ordinance apply only in respect of territories which have made reciprocal provisions. There is as yet no provision for the reciprocal enforcement of awards between Israel and the United States, but it would seem that an award issued and confirmed in the United States may be enforced in Israel under the Enforcement of Foreign Judgment Rules.

EXECUTORS AND ADMINISTRATORS:

See also topic Descent and Distribution.

An administrator may be appointed on the application of any person entitled to an interest of the estate. An administrator is personally liable at the instance of persons beneficially entitled for any wrong committed by him in the course of his administration. An administrator is required to give security, whilst an executor may be exempted from furnishing any security for the due administration of the estate. Executors or administrators are required to file returns in regard to their administration and the discharge is obtained on proper application after the conclusion of the administration or by leave of the court even before the winding up of the estate. The court will, on the application of an administrator, give such direction as may from time to time be required as to the administration of the estate.

The application for probate of a will or for the appointment of an administrator of an estate of a deceased person is made by petition to the court having jurisdiction in the area where the deceased had his last usual residence or place of business; and if the deceased had no place of residence or place of business in Israel, then the petition may be addressed to the court within whose area any part of the estate is to be found.

EXEMPTIONS:

The following are exempt from attachment: (1) a minimum income sufficient to provide the debtor with the necessities of life; (2) things necessary for the support, clothing and lodging of the family of the debtor; (3) machinery and implements used by the debtor in exercising his trade; (4) amount of salary of employees per month (different for single and married persons), but not more than 80% of earnings; (5) dwelling house of debtor unless reasonable substitute dwelling is available.

FOREIGN EXCHANGE:

See topics Currency; Foreign Trade Regulations; Investment Law and Incentives.

FOREIGN INVESTMENT:

See topic Investment Law and Incentives.

FOREIGN TRADE REGULATIONS:

Exchange Control Regulations were imposed during World War II. Although Regulations of 1941 were substantially relaxed, dealings in foreign currency and export of foreign currency are controlled by regulations. Contracts with nonresidents required to be approved by Controller of Foreign Exchange. Tendency in recent years has steadily been a relaxation in control and the streamlining of procedures. Similarly, while for many years all imports were subject to import licences due to exchange control and for protection of local industry, present tendency is towards liberalization of imports including elimination of necessity for import licences on an ever-increasing number of goods and materials. Treaties of friendship and commerce have been concluded with many countries and are renewable annually or at other regular intervals. In Nov. 1977 necessity for import licences was virtually abolished.

Israel has concluded trade and customs agreements with European Economic Community.

See also topics Currency; Investment Law and Incentives; Taxation.

Free Trade Zone.—1985 Law establishes Southern Port City of Eilat as Free Trade Zone with substantial reductions in taxes on goods and services purchased by residents and tourists. Income tax benefits and employers' tax benefits were also granted under Law establishing Zone, but abolished under 1990 tax reform and made subject to new set of rules under Income Tax Ordinance.

See also topic Taxation.

FRAUDS, STATUTE OF: See topic Contracts.

GARNISHMENT:

See topics Attachment; Executions.

GUARDIAN AND WARD:

Legal Capacity and Guardianship Law of 1962 governs appointment and duties of guardians. Legal acts of persons under 18 and other equally incapacitated persons are subject to ratification by court and where property rights are involved to consent of

GUARDIAN AND WARD . . . *continued*

court. Management of affairs of and care of legally incapacitated persons is entrusted to guardian, subject to general supervision of court. Jurisdiction is vested in District Court but religious courts have jurisdiction if all parties so desire. Law of domicile applies but court has powers over incapacitated person living in Israel or over legal acts performed in Israel relating to property of incapacitated person.

HIRE:

See topic Landlord and Tenant.

HOLIDAYS:

The following are public or legal holidays for the purpose of the Bills of Exchange Ordinance: Independence Day (also day of rest); Jewish holidays (Passover, first and last days, Pentecost, New Year's, two days, Day of Atonement, and First and Eighth day of Feast of Tabernacles); Christian holidays (New Year's Day—according to both Gregorian and Julian calendar, Ascension Day, Christmas Day, and Easter Monday); Moslem holidays (Shaker Bairam, three days, Qurban Bairam, four days, and Maulid al Nabi, one day).

There are also legal rest days. The Jewish rest days are the days mentioned above under "Jewish holidays," as well as Saturdays. These need not be the rest days for non-Jews, as they may rest on their respective holidays and other religious days.

Election day is a public holiday.

HUSBAND AND WIFE:

See topics Divorce; Marriage.

IMMIGRATION:

Substantial rights are granted to new immigrants including income tax concessions, customs and purchase tax exemptions on personal and household effects, investment assistance and housing facilities.

See also topic Constitution and Government, subhead Citizenship.

INFANCY:

Age of majority of both sexes is 18. Parents of a minor (a person under 18) are natural guardians. Natural guardians or any guardians appointed by court may consent to or ratify a contract made by a minor but unless made with such consent or until ratified, contract may be repudiated by minor or by his guardians or by Attorney General. Consent or ratification need not be in writing.

Certain acts of a guardian, such as transfer of real property, charges or mortgages, gifts, donations, guarantees and transactions between a minor and his guardian or his parents, require the approval of court.

An infant is represented in court by his guardian. Court may appoint a guardian ad litem.

Adoption.—See topic Adoption.

See topic Guardian and Ward.

INSURANCE:

The 1981 Insurance Contracts Law has basically legislated much of common law position and now governs law of Commercial (as opposed to State) Insurance in Israel.

Scope.—Law regulates law pertaining to life insurance; personal accident; sickness and disability insurance; regular commercial insurance; and vehicle insurance. (However, 1970 Motor Vehicle Insurance Ordinance is still applicable.) Law does not however apply to Maritime Insurance where 1863 Ottoman Maritime Trade Law still applies (insofar as it has not been repealed). Law does not apply to air insurance, nor does it apply to re-insurance treaties.

1981 Law repeals 1976 Law dealing with rights of third parties but incorporates protection of third parties in case of insolvency of insured. 1981 Law also repeals 1904 Ottoman Insurance Law which dealt with property insurance.

1981 Law provides that should one of parties wish to cancel contract in accordance with said Law or by virtue of conditions of contract, contract is terminated 15 days after notice has been sent to other party.

Claim for insurance payment prescribes three years after occurrence of event insured against.

1981 Law applies concurrently with 1951 Insurance Business (Superintendence) Law. Latter regulates and limits carrying on of insurance business in Israel, deals with grant of licences, lodging of returns by insurance companies and payment of deposits by persons engaging in insurance business in Israel.

See also topics Labour Relations; Consumer Protection.

INTEREST:

Under law of 1957, rate of interest chargeable is restricted. Minister of Finance may by order approved by Finance Committee of Knesset (Israel Legislature) fix maximum rate of interest chargeable in respect of commercial transactions of various categories. Where repayment is linked to index, maximum permitted rate is 13%. Courts are authorized to reopen usurious transactions and penalties are provided in case of any breach of law.

INVESTMENT LAW AND INCENTIVES:

The Encouragement of Capital Investment Law 5719-1959 ("ECIL").—This law, as am'd, provides incentives for capital investments. It succeeds earlier legislation with respect to encouragement of investments. Substantial reliefs and exemptions from income tax are allowed by ECIL. ECIL provides program under which Investment Center ("Center"), established pursuant to ECIL, may grant status of "approved enterprise", "approved asset", "approved investment" or "approved loan", to subject of investment plan approved by Center ("approved plan").

Foreign currency invested through approved plan and profits earned thereon may be repatriated in foreign currency by foreign investor.

Several types of legal entities may be approved as owners of "approved enterprise". Until recently Center's policy with regard to foreign individual and corporate investors was to require that their investment be made through Israeli corporation. However, recent influx of foreign construction companies into Israel led Center to consider granting approvals under ECIL directly to foreign corporate investors.

In order to provide appropriate taxation for this new approach, ECIL was amended in Feb., 1992, to provide for 15% "branch tax" on income of foreign corporations owning "approved enterprise". Amendment authorizes Income Tax Commissioner to forego branch tax if satisfied that income subject to tax was reinvested in corporation's business in Israel.

ECIL has undergone major revisions in recent years. Currently, ECIL provides owners of "approved enterprises" with several alternative sets of benefits, "standard", "alternative", "government guarantee", and "combined", which are summarized as follows:

(a) Sets of Benefits under ECIL.—"Standard" set of benefits focuses primarily on extending government grants to investor and lowering his tax rate. "Alternative" set of benefits provides investor with complete tax holiday in lieu of government grants. "Government guarantee" set of benefits focuses primarily on government guarantees granted to investor for amounts borrowed by him, coupled with tax incentives. "Combined" set of benefits provides investor with combination of government grants, government guarantees and certain tax incentives.

"Standard" set of benefits consists of grants computed as percentage of total capital invested in approved enterprise. Percentage varies in accordance with "development zone" in which enterprise is located, and type of enterprise. In addition to grants under ECIL, Center gives "capital grants", as percentage of investments made in "approved enterprise". Following table describes current rates (in percentages) of above grants:

DEVELOPMENT ZONE	INDUSTRY		HOTELS		OTHER TOURISM ENTERPRISES	
	ECIL	CAPITAL	ECIL	CAPITAL	ECIL	CAPITAL
A	30	4	12	13	5	13
B	15	2	12	7	5	4
Other	0	0	12	1	5	0

In addition to said grants, owner of "approved enterprise" is entitled to tax benefits. Major tax benefit is lower tax rate on profits of enterprise and on dividends paid out of such profits (if owner is corporation). Corporate tax rate is reduced from ordinary 36% rate to 25%. Withholding tax on dividends distributed by corporation is reduced from ordinary 25% rate to 15%.

All grants are received subject to meeting terms of approval issued by Investment Center.

(b) Enhancement of Tax Benefits to Foreign Investors.—Amendment to ECIL enhanced above tax benefits when foreign investors form substantial portion of owners of corporation, which in turn owns "approved enterprise". Tax rate on such corporation is lowered gradually as function of increase in foreign investor's holding thereof. In addition, period for which tax benefits are granted is extended in case of corporations with substantial foreign investment.

Following table summarizes tax rates imposed on corporations, substantial portion of whose owners are foreign investors:

Percentage of Foreign Investment in Taxable Year	Maximum Rate Year of Tax
49 - less than 74	20%
74 - less than 90	15%
90 or more	10%

Percentage of foreign investment is defined in relation to five different rights: (1) rights to profits, (2) voting rights, (3) rights to appoint directors, (4) percentage of share capital plus shareholders' loans to corporation, and (5) percentage of share capital only.

If foreign investors have more than 50% of second, third and fifth type of rights, then second and third rights are not taken into account in calculating percentage of foreign investment in taxable year.

As indicated above, tax rate for corporations that do not have above-mentioned amount of foreign investment is 25% (under "standard" set of benefits).

(c) Duration of Benefits.—As with tax rates, duration of benefits also varies according to whether or not corporation is substantially owned by foreign investors. Corporations not substantially owned by foreign investors enjoy "standard" set of tax rate benefits for seven years. Dividends from income entitled to benefits are taxed at only 15% for 12 years.

Corporations with more than 25% foreign investment are entitled to tax rate benefits under "standard" set of benefits for ten years, and special tax rate for dividends paid from benefit entitled income applies in such case with no time limitation.

Above rules apply both to corporations entitled to gradually reduced tax rates (i.e. corporations with 49% or more foreign investment) and to corporations having substantial foreign investment which is less than 49% (i.e. corporations with more than 25% and less than 49% foreign investment whose income is subject to tax rate of 25%).

For purposes of duration of incentives, more than 25% foreign investment threshold is calculated by method slightly different from that used in computing foreign investment for purposes of entitlement to the gradually reduced tax rates.

Corporation meeting said threshold is defined as "foreign investment corporation". "Foreign investment corporation" which meets certain timing requirements with regard to approval of its "approved enterprise" is defined as "foreign investors corporation". Only "foreign investors corporation" is entitled to gradually reduced tax rates, provided that percentage of foreign investment reaches at least 49% (see table above). Under certain circumstances, duration of tax rate benefits may be extended by Center

See Topical Index in front part of this volume.

INVESTMENT LAW AND INCENTIVES . . . *continued*
for additional five years for corporations having more than 74% foreign investment (calculated in same manner as more than 25% threshold for purpose of definition of "foreign investment corporation" is calculated. See above).

(d) "Alternative" Set of Benefits.—Only legal entity which is entitled to "alternative" set of benefits under ECIL is corporation owning approved enterprise. Such corporation must forego grants and tax benefits under "standard" set of benefits described above. Instead, such corporation is granted complete tax holiday for period which varies in accordance with development zone in which enterprise is located.

Periods of tax holiday are as follows:

DEVELOPMENT ZONE	PERIOD OF TAX HOLIDAY (YEARS)
A	10
B	6
Other	2

Tax holiday for enterprises located in other zones may be extended to four years under certain circumstances. After expiration of period of tax holiday, corporation is entitled to tax benefits under "standard" set for remainder of term of benefits. Corporation owning enterprise in "Other Zones" may also enjoy "alternative" set of benefits (even though it has no entitlement to grants under "standard" set of benefits). Under "alternative" set of benefits, if dividends are paid out of exempt income, distributing corporation is taxed at rates equal to tax rate which would have been imposed had corporation not chosen "alternative" set. In addition, withholding tax is imposed on shareholder. Only corporations expecting high profits in their early years of operation and planning reinvestment of such profits should choose "alternative" set of benefits.

(e) New Sets of Benefits.—In 1990, two additional alternative sets of benefits were added to ECIL. Corporation owning "approved enterprise" which has capital invested in its stock at least equal in value to 30% of sum of approved investment plan and exceeding certain minimum amount, may qualify for these two new sets of benefits. Special rules make it possible for partnerships and cooperative societies to enjoy two new sets of benefits with regard to extensions of existing "approved enterprises".

"Government Guarantee" Set of Benefits.—Under this program qualified corporation may receive government guarantee for amounts borrowed by corporation up to 70% of approved investment plan. Guarantee is up to 75% of amount of loan (85% in case of certain start up expenses). As to tax benefits, corporation may elect either "standard" set of benefits or "alternative" set of benefits. However, if it elects former, it must forego government grants and if it elects latter, and in addition (a) enterprise is not located in development zone A or B and (b) corporation forgoes government guarantees, then period of tax holiday is extended to four years.

"Combined" Set of Benefits.—Under this program corporation entitled to two new sets of benefits may elect, if it has industrial enterprise or industrial building, to receive reduced grants under "standard" set of benefits and reduced government guarantee under "Government Guarantee" set of benefits. Reduced rates are as follows:

(1) With regard to industry—

DEVELOPMENT ZONE	LEVEL OF GRANTS		LOANS (GOVERNMENT GUARANTEES 75%-85% OF AMOUNT OF LOAN)
	ECIL	CAPITAL	
A	17	4	49
B	5	2	63
Other	—	—	—

(2) With regard to hotels—

DEVELOPMENT ZONE	LEVEL OF GRANTS		GOVERNMENT GUARANTEES
	ECIL	CAPITAL	
A	—	13	57
B	—	7	63
Other	—	1	69

(3) With regard to other tourism enterprises—

DEVELOPMENT ZONE	LEVEL OF GRANTS		GOVERNMENT GUARANTEES
	ECIL	CAPITAL	
A	—	13	57
B	—	4	66
Other	—	—	—

Note: Accurate combined rate of grants and guarantees is always 70%.

Corporation electing "combined" set of benefits may not enjoy benefits of "alternative" set of benefits i.e., tax holiday, but it may enjoy lower tax rate under "standard" set of benefits.

(f) Accelerated Depreciation.—Granted under all sets of benefits.

(g) Preventing Foreign Investment Erosion Due to Currency Devaluation.—Certain corporations with foreign shareholders which had "approved enterprises" as of certain date can still elect to use, for dealing with income from such enterprises, certain accounting methods which assure that foreign investment is not eroded due to Israeli currency devaluations. Generally, today, to achieve above purpose, "foreign investment corporations" may elect to handle their tax accounting in U.S. dollars.

The Encouragement of Investment (Capital Intensive Companies) Law, 5750-1990.—This law, ("Law") adds to array of investment incentives. Tax benefits under Law apply to Capital Intensive Corporations. Capital Intensive Corporations ("CIC") are corporations with paid-up capital of at least $30 million, of which 75% or more is employed in qualifying activities. In addition, all shareholders of CIC must be nonresidents and purpose of CIC must be to engage in business in qualifying activities or invest in Israeli corporations engaged primarily in said activities.

"Qualifying activities" are establishing or expanding industrial, agricultural, tourism, transportation, building, water, energy, communication or computer enterprises and performing research and development in aforementioned areas. Tax benefits provided by Law are: (1) 25% tax rate on "real capital gain" from disposition of stock or fixed assets used in qualifying activity. (2) 15% tax rate on ordinary income derived from qualifying activities. (3) 15% tax rate on dividends from distributing company engaged primarily in qualifying activities. (4) Special tax regime which applies to distribution of dividends—25% withholding tax is imposed on recipient shareholder. However, upon distribution, CIC receives refund for corporate tax paid by it. Refund amounts to full 25% of corporate tax when shareholder is subject to full 25% withholding rate. If withholding rate is reduced by treaty then refund to CIC is reduced correspondingly so that combined tax rate will always be 25%. (5) No further taxes are imposed on CIC or its shareholders.

Duration of benefits under Law is 30 years.

Since CIC may also enjoy benefits under ECIL, and since combined tax rate on 90% or more foreign-held corporation and its shareholders is only 23.5% (10% on "foreign investors corporation", and 15% on distributed dividend), main benefits of Law are as follows: (a) Ability to enjoy reduced tax rates for substantial period of time after period of ECIL benefits will have expired. (b) Shift of tax burden from corporation to its shareholders, which may enable individual shareholders to receive foreign tax credits in their countries of residence, for what otherwise would be underlying corporate tax credited only to corporate shareholders. (c) Reduced capital gains tax upon disposition of investment (such reduced rate is not available under ECIL).

In addition, Law is very beneficial to corporations not entitled to benefits under ECIL.

The Encouragement of Industry (Taxes) Law 5729-1969.—This Law extends several tax benefits to Industrial Corporations. Industrial Corporation is corporation, income of which consists 90% or more of income from industrial enterprise owned by it. Industrial enterprise is enterprise activities of which consist principally of manufacturing activities.

Tax benefits provided include: accelerated depreciation of intangibles, deduction of expenses borne in issuing stock for trade on stock exchange, possibility to file consolidated tax return with certain other industrial corporations or certain corporations holding industrial corporations.

§16A of Income Tax Ordinance.—This section authorizes Minister of Finance to grant refund of Israeli income tax to nonresidents, to extent that latter do not receive foreign tax credit for Israeli tax, in their country of residence. Advance commitment by Minister of Finance that he will exercise his said authority should be secured.

Incentives for Research and Development ("R&D").—Main incentives for performing R&D in Israel include those under (a) Encouragement of Research and Development in Industry Law, 5744-1984, (b) general tax law, (c) special tax regime for CIC's, and (d) BIRD Foundation Program.

(a) Encouragement of Research and Development in Industry Law, (5744-1984) ("ERDL").—Certain benefits for encouragement of R&D are granted under provisions of ERDL.

ERDL regulates awarding of grants, loans and tax benefits to those carrying out R&D schemes which have received proper authorization. Schemes eligible for authorization under ERDL are generally yearly or multi-year schemes that result in development of know-how, processes or methods for production of new products or new processes or in substantive improvement of existing products or processes. Main benefits granted by ERDL are: (a) Grants, calculated as specified percentage of R&D expenses. Percentage of expenses granted is between 5% and 66%, according to nature of R&D, level of sales or exports made by taxpayer, area of country where R&D scheme is performed, etc. (b) Authorized loans, granted instead of above-mentioned grants. (c) Tax relief to scientific workers employed in accordance with authorized schemes.

ERDL also provides for royalties which promoter is obliged to pay to Israeli Treasury from sales of developed product.

(b) Tax Benefits under General Tax Law.—Tax benefits are granted under general tax law with regard to R&D expenses. Certain R&D expenses may be deducted on current basis, even if they are of capital nature. (See also topic Taxation, subhead Income Tax.)

(c) Special Tax Regime for CIC's.—See subhead The Encouragement of Investment (Capital Intensive Companies) Law, 5750-1990, supra.

(d) BIRD Foundation.—Israel-United States Bilateral Industrial R&D Foundation provides funding for joint ventures between Israeli and U.S. firms for performance of industrial R&D, aimed at developing new product or process.

Additional Incentives to Special Activities.—In addition to above, specific incentive schemes are granted to investors engaged in certain special activities. These may be tax or other incentives to activities in construction, agriculture, oil exploration, film production, investments in securities traded on Tel Aviv Stock Exchange ("TASE") and international trade.

(a) Construction.—ECIL provides tax benefits to investors in construction if at least 50% of building space is rented for residential purposes during specified time period. Benefits include imposition of low tax rates provided under ECIL on both "real capital gain" realized at time of sale of building and on rental income, accelerated depreciation and other benefits. In Feb., 1992, new legislation generally expanded benefits to investors in construction. Among major changes are increase in annual rate of depreciation from 10% to 20%, ability to partially or totally shift tax benefits associated with

See Topical Index in front part of this volume.

INVESTMENT LAW AND INCENTIVES . . . *continued*
construction between developer and purchaser of building, shortening of minimum required rental period and ability to apply law to portions of buildings.

With regard to foreign corporations investing in construction main feature of new legislation is imposition of "branch profit tax" at rate of 15%. Unlike comparable "branch tax" provision adopted under ECIL, such tax may not be waived.

New legislation also provides new tax regime with regard to real estate corporations ("REC's"). New regime applies if certain conditions are met, including: (a) REC is "Real Estate Association" under Land Appreciation Tax Law 5723-1963 i.e. it owns primarily real estate. (b) REC is approved by Income Tax Commissioner for purposes of new regime. (c) All of stockholders are nonresident individuals at time they purchased stock. (d) None of stockholders owns 5% or more of stock of REC. (e) Number of stockholders is at least 50. (f) Main activity of REC is construction, leasing or selling of buildings. (g) REC owns at least 50 apartments. REC may be either foreign or domestic corporation. If REC meets requirements described above, neither purchase of stock in REC nor disposition thereof is subject to tax. Under normal circumstances, purchase of stock in "real estate association" is subject to purchase tax and disposition thereof is subject to land appreciation tax. Disposition of residential units by individuals may be exempt under Land Appreciation Tax Law 5723-1963. But this exemption is limited by number of apartments owned or disposed of by individual during given period of time. Exemption from tax under new regime is not limited and thus may present attractive vehicle for nonresident individuals to purchase apartments in Israel.

Finally, new legislation deals with investments in real estate through entities listed on TASE or through investment funds. First, new legislation provides exemptions from purchase tax and from land appreciation tax upon purchase and disposition of units in partnerships listed on TASE, whose main activity is construction or leasing of apartments (before this amendment similar exemptions were granted only to purchase and disposition of stock in corporations). Second, new legislation enables investment funds to invest in real estate and provides tax principles relevant to such investment.

(b) Agriculture.—Encouragement of Capital Investments in Agriculture Law, 5741-1980 ("ECIAL") provides special tax and other incentives for investments in agriculture made according to "approved plan". Incentives include lower tax rate on income generated by "approved agriculture enterprise", accelerated depreciation, capital grants and other incentives. In Mar., 1992, new legislation introduced "alternative" set of benefits for investments in agriculture which is very similar to "alternative" set of benefits under ECIL (see above) i.e. main feature is complete tax holiday.

(c) Oil Exploration.—Special tax benefits are granted under Income Tax Regulations (Deductions from the Income of Owners of Oil Rights), 5716-1956 and Income Tax Regulations (Principles for Computing Tax because of the Holding and Sale of Participation Units in an Oil Exploration Partnership), 5749-1988, to persons engaged in oil exploration in Israel or holding units in oil exploration partnerships, which units are traded on TASE. Eligible partnerships are partnerships which spend most of their expenses in oil exploration and development and are approved by Income Tax Commissioner. Benefits include current deduction of exploration costs and substantial depletion deduction.

(d) Film Production.—Special tax benefits are granted under Income Tax Regulations (Deductions from Income of Investors in a Film in Israel) 5750-1990, to holders of units in film production partnerships, which units are traded on TASE. Eligible partnerships are partnerships which are engaged solely in production of film and which have rights to income from film at reasonable level compared to their share of production costs. Tax benefits include current deduction of production costs spent in Israel and deferral of recognition of certain income from sale of film.

(e) Investments in Securities Listed on TASE.—Exemption from capital gain tax on disposition of stock listed on TASE is described below. Similar exemption is provided for other types of securities. These incentives are granted only to persons not engaged in investment in stock exchange as business activity. However, either first listing of stock on TASE or first sale of said stock is not exempt from tax. Exemption is not available to taxpayers who are subject to Income Tax Law (Adjustment for Inflation), 5745-1985.

(f) International Trade.—Under ECIL foreign corporation based in Israel and engaged in international trade which does not include import to or export from Israel, may be granted by Minister of Finance reduction or even complete exemption from Israeli corporate tax. Same reduction or exemption may apply to dividends distributed by said corporation to foreign stockholders. In addition, capital gains of corporation from sale of assets located outside Israel and capital gains of foreign stockholders disposing of their stock in corporation may also be exempted.

JUDGMENTS:

Enforcement of Foreign Judgments.—By a law of 1958, judgments of foreign courts are enforceable if they were given in the foreign country by a court having jurisdiction to act, and are final and not subject to appeal, and their contents are not in contradiction to the laws of Israel or public policy in Israel and they are capable of execution in the country in which they were given. The jurisdiction is based upon mutuality and special rules have been provided. See topic Executions.

LABOUR RELATIONS:

Employment Agencies Law 1996 requires that employment agencies be licensed. Manager of agency must (1) have at least three years experience in field; (2) show that in past five years he has not committed any crimes of moral turpitude. Also agency must present bank guarantee, guaranteeing its financial obligations towards its employees. Employment conditions must be specified in written agreement. Agency may not demand fees for its services from employee. Employment of foreigners or by foreigners requires special permit.

Wages.—1958 Wage Protection Law provides that wages must be paid in cash. Other modes of payment are allowed only under collective agreement; only small portion may be paid in food and lodging. Payment must be directly to labourer. Fixed amount is free from attachments. Time for payment fixed and if delayed, additional sum is payable. This rule was made applicable to compensation for dismissal by 1977 Amendment. Debts due from labourer to employer can be deducted only within limits. 1976 Sickness Pay Law provides for payment of 75% of normal wage in case of sickness for period up to 1½ days for each month of service, unless provided otherwise under Collective Agreement. The Minimum Wage Law (1987) forbids payment of wages below specified levels. The Equal Wages for Male and Female Employees Law forbids discrimination in this area.

Employment of Children.—Employment of children and young persons is governed by Law of 1953 Relating to Employment of Youth and Apprenticeship Law of 1953. Employment of persons under age of 14 is forbidden. Minister of Labour has power to prohibit or limit employment of infants in specific occupations or to fix age for employment in certain employments. Minister may also fix work hours and conditions of employment.

The employment of women is also strictly governed by the Employment of Women Law 1954, which restricts the employment and working hours and makes provisions for the protection of women employed in the various undertakings. Maternity leave is also granted to adoptive mother. Vacation without pay is granted to natural mother, as well as to her husband.

The Law for Equal pay for Men & Women—1996.—This law is aimed at prevention of discrimination between men and women who are employed by common employer in virtually identical positions. Law provides procedure for taking action against discriminating employers. Such action may be initiated by labour unions, women's rights movements and employee.

National Insurance Law (Consolidated Version) 1995 as amended contains comprehensive code in regard to payment of old age pensions, payments in respect of compensation to workmen injured by accident, maternity payments, unemployment payments, death benefits and child allowances.

National Insurance Law provides for old age pensions to males of over 65 and females over 60 or 70 and 65 respectively in relation to high-income workers and for compensation in respect to death or injury during work both to workmen and to independent earners. It also provides certain benefits in respect to childbirth and burial expenses. Law is administered by National Insurance Board which levies fixed premium on all residents. Premiums vary according to income and premiums due from employed persons are deducted by employers from their salaries.

Assurance of Income Law, 1980 provides for persons resident in Israel who are unable to work or support themselves sufficiently and who are not eligible for benefits under National Insurance Law. All claims are subject to specific conditions.

National Employment Service.—By the 1959 law, employment agencies have been erected on a national basis and no labourers may be employed except through those agencies, with the exception of certain highly specialized professions or administrative employment. 1976 amending law provides youth occupational guidance and requires notification of dismissals of ten or more employees at one time.

Equal Employment Opportunity Law, 1988 now makes it unlawful for employer to discriminate between his employees or between those requesting work, because of their sex, marital status or status as parents, as regards: (1) Receipt of employment; (2) conditions of employment; (3) promotion; (4) education or vocational training; (5) dismissal and severance pay. See also subhead Wages, supra.

Collective Agreements.—Collective agreements may be entered into between an employer or an organization of employers and between organized labour, regarding conditions and terms of work. Labourers rights under such agreements cannot be waived, and the Minister of Labour may extend its application.

Labour Disputes.—There is no provision in regard to compulsory settlement of disputes between employers and labourers, but the Department of Labour has power to assist the employers and labourers in the settlement of their industrial disputes and it normally intervenes in such disputes with a view of securing an amicable settlement. In case of labour disputes provision is made for settlement by mediation, the mediator possessing far-reaching powers to assemble the parties and ascertain the nature of the dispute. Certain matters are passed to compulsory arbitration, the decision of the arbitrators being binding. There is now a Labour Court which deals with labour disputes.

Under Civil Wrongs Ordinance (New Version) 1963, as amended, employer is liable for acts of his employee if he authorized or ratified act or if it was committed by servant in course of his employment.

By Amendments to Law of Settlement of Labour Disputes, following limitations were introduced on right to strike: (a) By §5a of 1969 Amending Law a 15 day notice must be given of any intended strike both to Commissioner of Labour Relations and to employer; (b) by §37 b-d of 1972 Amending Law, special provisions governing public service were introduced. Term "public service" includes labour relations in service of Government, municipalities and local councils, health services, primary and higher education, aviation, oil, water and electricity. In a public service a strike declared without legal notice above-mentioned or whilst a collective agreement is in force is (with few exceptions) an "unprotected strike." Participation by individual labourer in an unprotected strike deprives him of protection granted by Collective Agreements Law to effect that a participation in a strike does not constitute a breach of personal agreement of labourer. Person causing labourers to participate in an unprotected strike is liable for procuring a breach of contract. Labour Courts are entitled to issue an injunction prohibiting individual labourers to participate in an unprotected strike. By amending law 1976, Labour Courts are empowered to order proportionate wage reduction in case of unprotected "go-slow" strike in public services. See also topic Banks and Banking.

See also subhead National Insurance Law, supra.

Compensation for Dismissal.—By a 1963 law an employee who has worked continuously for a minimum period of one year with same employer in same job is entitled on dismissal to compensation amounting to a sum equal to one month's pay for each full year of service. No compensation is payable if employee is dismissed for dishonesty. In certain cases, such compensation may be paid even where employee resigns of his own accord, e.g., for health reasons. Female worker who leaves her employment within nine months after birth or adoption of child by her in order to attend to such child is entitled to compensation. The Wage Protection Law provides for surcharge of 20% per month for failure to timely pay compensation for dismissal.

See also subhead Wages, supra.

LABOUR RELATIONS . . . *continued*

Right of Dismissal.—Supreme Court, as High Court of Justice, set aside a judgment of Labour Court of Appeal ordering an employer to continue employing an employee whom he had dismissed. Rule that court does not order specific performance of a contract of personal employment, is not affected by fact that employment is governed by a collective agreement.

Labour Courts.—By a 1969 Law, special Labour Courts were created and given exclusive jurisdiction in all matters dealing with or arising from labour relations.

There are now five District Labour Courts located in Jerusalem, Tel-Aviv, Haifa, Beer Sheva and Nazareth, as well as State Court in Jerusalem. In every Court there are professional judges and two members of the public, one nominated by employers' association and one by employees' association. In State Court there are three professional judges and two members of public appointed as above. District Courts have exclusive primary jurisdiction in all matters between employers and employees and in collective agreement disputes arising from a special collective agreement (i.e., one dealing with one or a limited number of employers). State Court has primary jurisdiction in disputes arising from general collective agreements (i.e., agreements covering all employers of a certain category) and an appeal jurisdiction from District Court. Both courts have criminal jurisdiction too.

There is no appeal from State Court. It is subject however to a limited "High Court jurisdiction."

Trade Unions.—Supreme Court refused to interfere with decision of Labour Association not to create a trade union consisting of workmen of one branch in certain towns. Labour Association is a voluntary body and, hence, law courts would refrain from interference with a decision, which prima facie constitutes a valid exercise of Association's discretion.

LAND:

Under the "Basic Law—Land of Israel 1960," all the lands which belong to the State Development Authority or J.N.F. are considered as the lands of Israel, the ownership whereof cannot be assigned either by sale or by any other way. Land includes land, houses, buildings and all other appurtenances belonging thereto. Under the Land of Israel Law, 1960, several transactions in reference to these lands are exempted from the prohibition of transfer. There are seven permissible transactions wherein transfer of ownership of lands belonging to State of Israel can be effected. Special authorities were created in order to manage lands and to supervise execution of provisions of law.

Law regarding rights in land is now virtually codified by Land Law, 1969. Ottoman and Mandatorial laws regarding land have not been totally abolished. They are still in operation regarding: (1) Statute of Limitations for unsettled land (§§20 and 78 of Ottoman Land Law of year 1274 of Hegerrah); (2) various laws pertaining to lands belonging to religious trusteeships (§162 Land Law); (3) transfers of land and obligations to transfer land executed prior to effective date of law (Jan. 1, 1970) and (4) any right in land existing prior to effective date of law, Ottoman Law still prevails. By §8 of Land Law, obligation to transfer land must be in form of written document. Equitable rights in land have been abolished, although law itself fashions such rights. (§9). In Occupied Territories, Ottoman, Mandatorial, Jordanian Law applies.

Owner of land has right to claim possession against wrongful occupier. Joint tenancies may only be over an undivided whole. Any joint tenant may require dissolution of joint tenancy which may be carried out by agreement or by order of court. Court may order partition or sale.

Settlement.—Land registration now covers most of country however, unsettled lands exist in parts of entire country, as well as in various other urbanized areas. Occupied Territories are not settled at all.

Cooperative Houses.—Cooperative Houses Law has been repealed but has been incorporated in Land Law. It facilitates registration of separate dwellings in a jointly-owned house and regulates rights between owners. Urban housing in Israel is largely based on cooperative housing.

Sale of Apartments Law 1973 came into force on 1/10/73 and provides that a sale of an apartment which has been built or is about to be built must be accompanied by a specification in a form prescribed by Minister of Housing. Any deviation from specification or from applicable town planning regulations is regarded as a noncompliance conferring upon purchaser all rights under Sales Law 1968. (See topic Sales.)

Special provisions apply to sale of an apartment in a condominium house or in a property designated to be registered as a condominium house requiring all relevant details as to management of house. Default in attaching specification is punished with considerable financial penalty.

See also topic Sales, subhead Sale of Flats.

Securing Purchasers of Apartments.—By 1974-76 Law of Sale (Apartments) (securing investments of apartment purchasers) vendor or lessor by lease for more than 25 years, of an unbuilt apartment, may not receive from purchaser more than 15% of purchase price unless he gave purchaser bank guarantee securing refund of all monies paid, in event of non-delivery of apartment to purchaser as agreed, or has insured himself with an authorised insurance company against such event, with purchaser as beneficiary under policy, or has transferred ownership or long lease of apartment to purchaser or encumbered same in his favour. Alternatively, vendor may give to purchaser security by way of registering notice of warning at office of Land Registry in favor of purchaser.

Transfers.—In order to register transaction in Land Registry, there must be filed in connection therewith certifications regarding Betterment Tax, Acquisition Tax, Property Tax (which latter tax applies only with regard to unimproved lands, but not including agricultural lands, cultivated and used as such) and authorization from Local Authority. Immovable property can only be transferred by execution of a deed which has to be signed either at competent Land Registry in Israel or before any lawyer in Israel who authenticates signatures on deed. Deed is executed before District Land Registrar, when appropriate fees must be paid. Transferee's title is entered on Register in substitution for title of transferor. All transfers of immovable property must now be reported for Betterment Tax purposes. Transfer and registration of settled land is effected under Torrens System, whereas unsettled land is registered under Deed of Title System.

Development Authorities' lands may be leased in perpetuity (or for automatically renewable periods of 49 years) in lieu of outright sale of said land which is prohibited under Basic law: Land of Israel 1960.

Recuperation Areas Authority.—By 1973 Statute this authority is set up and authorised to recommend that a certain area having qualities that would attract persons recuperating, be declared a recuperation area, of one of various categories, and any restrictions on undertakings within area. It can also encourage research, advance level of services of existing recuperation areas, encourage housing, supervise and generally regulate exploitation of area. This law contains full supplementary provisions regarding effect of such declaration, and any ensuing rights and liabilities. There is also law dealing with repair of buildings and maintenance thereof.

Radio and Television Aerial Masts.—Local Authorities (Radio and Television Aerial Masts) Law 1975 empowers local authorities to limit number of radio and television aerial masts on buildings and to require erection of central masts on apartment buildings with compensation for persons aggrieved and financial penalties for infringements. Permits should be obtained from local building authorities.

See topic Taxation. See also topics Adverse Possession; Landlord and Tenant; Limitation of Actions; Mortgages.

LANDLORD AND TENANT:

Land Law 1969 requires written document and registration in Land Registry to effect lease if for more than five years or with option to renew beyond five years. Registration not required for lease of dwellings or business premises unless for period exceeding in all ten years. Subject to agreement lease may be charged with mortgage or easement and tenant may transfer lease or sublet. See also subhead Hire and Loan Law 1971, infra.

Duties of landlord to provide services and effect repairs are laid down in Tenants Protection Law 1972. This Law also consolidates previous legislation regarding control of rentals and protection against eviction for tenants of residential and business premises occupying under leases prior to Aug. 20, 1968 which have expired or who paid key-money. Protection extends to surviving spouse, children or parents who occupied premises with tenant at least six months prior to decease. Protected tenant continues to hold on terms of expired lease as varied by agreement or by Law. Rights of inheritance of protected tenant are limited in accordance with provisions of §§20-30 of Law (i.e., can have one transfer of rights and in certain circumstances second transfer, but no more).

Rentals of premises within Law may not be increased except within the limits fixed by Regulations issued periodically. In event of dispute between landlord and tenant, local Rent Tribunals have power to fix rental. Regulations state that regarding certain types of business premises, ceiling for rent will not apply.

Outgoing tenant is entitled to share of key-money to be paid by incoming tenant, amount of which depends on whether his tenancy began before or after 1958, period of occupation and whether he himself paid key-money. Special procedure is provided to settle outgoing tenant's share if disputed.

Law ceases to apply to premises falling vacant and does not apply to buildings completed and let after 1968, nor to buildings of Approved Undertakings (see topic Investment Law and Incentives).

Principal grounds for eviction of protected tenant are nonpayment of rent, breach of original lease justifying eviction, wilful damage, use of premises for unlawful purpose, molesting neighbours, premises required for own purposes or rebuilding by landlord, public body requiring premises for public purpose. In last two cases alternative accommodation must be provided.

Hire and Loan Law 1971.—Law in respect of hire applies to both moveables and immoveables where contrary intention does not appear in agreement. Object hired must comply with specifications in agreement unless lessor knew otherwise at date of agreement or lessee did not notify lessor of unsuitability within reasonable time. Lessor has liability to repair. Where object hired is a chattel, lessor may exchange defective chattel so as to comply with his obligations. Where repair not carried out, lessee may repair and debit lessor with expense or reduce rent in accordance with defect. Where object leased is land and lessee cannot use it for reasons connected with land or access thereto, he is not liable to pay rent. Lessee must give lessor facilities to inspect and repair. Lessor may assign his rights but must notify lessee. Lessee may not assign without lessor's consent, but if lessor unreasonably withholds consent, in case of land lessee may assign without lessor's consent, and in case of any object court may order transaction.

See also topic Sales, subhead Sale of Flats.

LAW REPORTS, CODES, ETC.:

There are official law reports of cases in Supreme Court and in district courts and there are also official reports of cases in rabbinical courts and certain specialised reports such as tax cases.

Certain branches of the law are codified and may be found in books of Mandatory Ordinances and Israeli Statutes. See also topic Statutes.

LEGISLATURE:

See topic Constitution and Government.

LICENCES:

Business Licencing Law of 1968, replacing pre-State legislation empowers Minister of Interior in consultation with Minister of Health to issue Orders requiring certain businesses to obtain licences in order to ensure proper environmental and health conditions, prevention of public nuisances and observation of Town Planning regulations, public safety, prevention of pollution and diseases in livestock. Special provisions are laid down for sale of intoxicating liquors and public entertainments. Comprehensive list of businesses requiring licence has been drawn up in Registration Order of 1973 covering close to 200 kinds of business. Licencing authority is local government or such authority as Minister of Interior may determine. Fine or imprisonment is

See Topical Index in front part of this volume.

LICENCES . . . *continued*
imposed for noncompliance. Companies pay double fine. Court may order temporary or permanent closing of business convicted for noncompliance.

See also topic Foreign Trade Regulations.

LIENS:

There are various forms of liens which basically follow English Law. Maritime liens are provided by Shipping (Vessels) Law 1960.

LIMITATION OF ACTIONS:

Actions must be brought within following periods after respective causes of action, including civil wrongs, accrue: (a) in respect of a debt or chattels, within seven years; (b) in respect of unregistered land, 15 years. There is now no limitation period in respect of registered settled land. (c) parties may agree in writing, in separate document, to extend period in case of land, and either to extend it or shorten it in case of movables.

Supreme Court decided in 1955 that suits for specific performance are not barred by any limitation period, but only by laches (delay causing damage).

See topics Bills and Notes; Insurance; also topic Adverse Possession.

In respect to crimes the following are the periods of prescription: felonies, ten years; misdemeanours, three years; contraventions, one year. Period of prescription runs from date of commission of offence or from date of last step taken in investigation or prosecution of offence in question in respect of felonies or misdemeanours; and in respect of contraventions, from date of commission of offence.

Time limits for bringing of actions under Nazis and Nazi Collaborators (Punishment) Law 1950 and under Genocide (Prevention and Punishment) Law 1950 were abolished in 1966.

Customs prosecutions must be instituted within five years.

Lost Property Law of Return.—By a new law of 1973 which came into force on Aug. 31, 1973, a person finding lost property must either return it to its owner or notify police and may keep property or deliver it to police unless police require such delivery, in which case he must comply with requirement. If owner has not been found within four months, he is presumed to have forfeited ownership, in which case it passes into finder's ownership. If, however, finder did not notify police it becomes State property. Previous owner may, however, within a year redeem lost property on paying its value at time of redemption. Goods liable to destruction or live stock may be sold after notifying police and provisions of Law apply to proceeds.

MAINTENANCE:

See topic Divorce, subhead Maintenance.

MARRIAGE:

Matters of marriage are considered as matters of personal status, which are within exclusive jurisdiction of Rabbinical religious courts in respect of all Jews and religious courts of other denominations in respect of non-foreigners who are members of respective recognized religious communities. In respect of foreigners, who are not Jews, their national law applies, and local courts will recognize as valid any marriage which is valid according to national law.

General consuls, vice-consuls and any other competent consular authority may officiate at marriages where at least one of the parties is of the consul's nationality.

No marriage of a girl under 17 is permitted unless court orders otherwise in special circumstances.

Every marriage must be registered by person performing marriage. Registration is effected by filing a copy of record with District Commissioner of district where marriage is performed. Failure to register involves considerable penalties.

Financial Relations Between Spouses.—1973 Law which came into force on Jan. 1, 1974 provides that spouses may regulate their financial relations by an agreement which requires approval by District Court or by Religious Court having jurisdiction in matters of marriage and divorce of spouses. Failing such an agreement, financial relations and ownership of property of spouses will be regulated as follows: (a) Entry into marriage or its subsistence do not affect spouse's ownership rights and do not confer upon either spouse any right in other spouse's property or any liability for other spouse's debts: (b) upon dissolution of marriage whether by divorce or by death of one spouse, each spouse is entitled to half of total property of both spouses excluding such property as either had before marriage or received as a gift or by way of inheritance during marriage or non-assignable rights or property in respect of which parties agreed that they are not to be taken into consideration. In event of death of a spouse, his heirs succeed to his rights under Law.

Law further contains provisions as to details of assessment of value, of preventing attempts of alienation in order to defeat provisions of law, and confers extensive jurisdiction upon court in application of provisions. Law does not affect such jurisdiction as is conferred upon Religious Courts but these Courts must apply provisions of Law unless both parties agreed to be judged by Religious Law. Law makes necessary amendments in Law of Succession in order to secure spouses rights according to provisions of this Law.

See also topic Divorce.

MINES:

Mines and minerals are the property of the state and their exploitation is governed by the Mining Ordinance of 1925, as amended. Licences for prospecting or exploring mines or for minerals may be obtained from the competent government department, and concessions are granted by the State. Mining rights or mining leases are obtainable on terms to be agreed with the State.

Oil.—The Oil Law of 1953 provides for prospecting and mining licences and regulations in regard to exploitation of mineral resources in Israel, particularly in respect of prospecting for oil and oil concessions.

National Energy Authority.—Set up by 1977 law to plan, develop and regulate sources and consumption of energy in Israel, taking over Governmental functions under Mining Ordinance and Petroleum Law.

See also topic Taxation.

MONOPOLIES AND RESTRAINT OF TRADE:

See topic Restrictive Trade Practice.

MORTGAGES:

Immovable property may be mortgaged to secure any debt or obligation. Mortgage of immovable property requires registration at District Registry in which land is situate. Mortgage on immovable property not registered is not valid. Mortgage on land is realized by order of court or of Execution Office. Any provision denying mortgagor right to repay loan at any time is invalid.

Any mortgage pledge or charge created by company and not registered with Registrar of Companies within 21 days is void against a liquidator or any creditor.

For mortgage of chattels see topic Pledges.

Israel ships may be mortgaged by documents executed: (a) abroad, before an Israel diplomatic or consular delegate and approved by him; (b) in Israel, before Registrar of harbour of registration of ship. Mortgages must be recorded with Registrar of Ships. Mortgage on a ship is foreclosed or executed by order of Admiralty Court.

MOTOR VEHICLES:

Motor vehicles have to be licensed annually. Drivers are also licensed biennially by reference to type of vehicle driven. Age limit is $17^1/_2$, in respect of all vehicles other than motorcycles. Age limit in respect of motorcycles is 16. All vehicles must carry third party insurance. Transfers of vehicles are effected by Deed of Sale recorded with licensing authority. Identification marks are applied to various types of vehicles, by reference to registry offices. Speed limit is 50 kilometres in built-up areas, 80 kilometres in open country and 100 kilometres (at present restricted to 90 km) on fast motorways. There is detailed road-code and substantial penalties for breaches. Security belt law enacted.

Certain restrictions apply temporarily in regard to the transfer of vehicles as a result of present war conditions. Normally bona fide transactions are approved. Special provisions apply in regard to public vehicles including omnibuses and taxis, and their transfer is substantially restricted.

MOVEABLES:

Moveables Law 1971 grants to owner of moveables same rights against wrongful possession and trespass as Land Law 1969 grants in respect of immoveables. Joint ownership is over undivided whole with right to claim partition. See topic Landlord and Tenant.

NATIONAL SERVICE:

The Security Service Law, 1959, replaces all previous laws in this connection. Under the provisions of the law, every male resident of Israel from the age of 18 to 26 must serve 30 months compulsory service in the Army (extended by Order to 36 months), and from age of 27 to 29, 24 months.

Unmarried women from the age of 18 to 26 must serve 24 months. In the Reserves, every man up to the age of 39 years must serve one month per year and from the age of 40 to 49 years, 14 days per year. Unmarried women and married women without children up to the age of 34 years must serve one month per year. All soldiers on the reserve list are paid partly by the Army and partly by their employers.

NOTARIES PUBLIC:

All existing laws and regulations governing Notaries Public have been repealed by a 1976 Notaries Law. Notary must be Israeli citizen, member of Bar, who practises as an advocate in Israel 15 years or, if he is 65 years of age, or is a new immigrant, ten years. New law defines authority of notary, lays down procedure to be followed and code of professional ethics, confers on his confirmations status of lawfully sufficient proof of their contents; and enumerates acts which must be confirmed by him. Notary may be tried in an action before disciplinary courts of Bar, with appeal to Supreme Court. Israel diplomatic and consular representatives overseas are authorised to act as Notaries.

PARTNERSHIPS: See topic Associations.

PATENTS:

Patent Law was enacted in 1967.

Application.—An inventor or any person deriving title to an invention under him, whether product or process which is new, useful and susceptible of industrial or agricultural application may apply for grant of patent. Patent is granted to person who first validly applied for it in Israel, except that where owner's application for protection has already been filed in one of Convention countries, date of foreign application is deemed to be date of application filed in Israel, if application in Israel has been filed within 12 months after filing of other application.

Patent application is filed at office of Registrar of Patents in Jerusalem, and may be filed through an attorney.

Term of a patent is 20 years from date of application for patent provided that renewal fees are paid on their due dates.

Certain exploitation rights are reserved in favour of persons who prior to application date, have in good faith exploited invention in Israel.

Concept of novelty applied is that of universal novelty.

Opposition and Revocation.—Opposition to grant of a patent may be made within three months from date of publication of application in Reshumot (Government Official Gazette).

Patent may be revoked by Registrar on grounds on which opposition to grant of patent may be made, namely that invention is not patentable or that opponent and not

See Topical Index in front part of this volume.

PATENTS . . . *continued*
applicant is owner of invention or if there exists another reason for which Registrar is entitled to refuse application in accordance with provisions of Law.

Licences may be granted by patentee. A licence under a patent is not effective in respect of any party other than parties to licence unless licence has been registered.

Certain rights are reserved to State in respect of use of patents which are required for security of State. Appropriate Minister may permit exploitation of patent by Government departments if it is necessary to do so in interest of defence of State or maintenance of essential supply and services. However, when such permission is given, owner of invention is entitled to compensation whether in form of royalties or otherwise, as detailed in Law. If Registrar is satisfied that owners of a patent have a monopoly which is misused he may grant a licence to exploit patent to a person who has applied for and paid prescribed fee, provided application is filed after expiration of three years from date on which patent was granted, or four years from date of filing of patent application, whichever is later.

Compulsory licence may also be ordered if it is necessary to assure public of a reasonable quantity of medical supplies. Detailed provisions are contained in Law in regard to factors to be taken into account in granting a compulsory licence, conditions of licence including payment of royalties.

Patents are assignable. Patentee may also charge patent or income thereof. Assignment and charge have to be registered.

Designs can be registered under Patents and Designs Ordinance of 1925 as am'd in respect of one or more class or classes of goods. A certificate of registration is granted by Registrar. On registration of a design proprietor of design is entitled to copyright in design for five years, and period may be renewed from time to time for five years up to three cycles of five years each.

An amendment to Ordinance brings Israel law in line with Hague International Convention for Protection of Industrial Property to which Israel has now become a signatory. A design may no longer be eliminated from Register because it is in use abroad, and not in Israel. Registration in Israel of a patent or design registered abroad receives preference over an application registered after date of foreign application, if registered in Israel within 12 or six months respectively after registration in any of signatory countries of convention. (Book of Laws, No. 99, of 12.6.52).

PLEDGES:

Law of pledges is contained in a law with effect from Oct. 1, 1967.

Pledge is a charge on chattel as security for debt and creditor may recoup from pledge if debt not discharged. Pledge is created by agreement between debtor and creditor. Pledge serves as security for interest, costs and damages due from debtor. Debtor may repledge chattel to a further creditor, but prior creditor takes precedence; if, however, prior creditor agrees, later creditor may have equal rights (pari passu).

Any profits from pledge are subject to pledge unless agreed otherwise.

In case of nonpayment, execution is obtained by court order, except in case of banks where such order is not required.

On cessation of debt, rights of pledge terminate and debtor may demand return of pledge.

PRACTICE:

Consolidated and revised Rules of Court in civil actions came into effect on Oct. 1, 1984. Actions are commenced by a statement of claim, answered by statement of defense. English procedure is closely followed with rights of request for further particulars, discovery of documents and interrogatories. New rules provide for preliminary settling of issues by court where necessary. Procedure in cases against Government is same as for other cases.

PRESCRIPTION:

See topics Adverse Possession; Limitation of Actions.

PRINCIPAL AND AGENT:

Comprehensive code covering law of principal and agent was recently promulgated as Agency Law of 1965. Law sets out duties and rights of agents. No special formality is required to establish any agency relationship, and agent may be granted unlimited or limited authority. Corporation may be appointed as agent.

Power of attorney authorising person to act as agent in respect of lands or rights in land must be in writing and in certain cases, especially if irrevocable, copy of power of attorney has to be deposited with Land Appreciation Tax Authority and may be subject to payment of Land Appreciation Tax.

Person entrusted with possession of assets or their management, is required, if ten years have passed since grant of authority, to advise Administrator-General of existence of the power or authority. No transaction relating to immovables may be given effect by virtue of power of attorney after expiration of ten years from date of appointment, except with authority of appointor or with leave of court.

Agents for purchase of military equipment of all kinds for Israel Army or Defence Ministry may not receive commission unless permit granted by Defence Minister.

REAL PROPERTY:

See topic Land.

RECEIVERS:

A comprehensive code in regard to liquidators is contained in the Companies Ordinance in respect of winding up of companies. Receivers may be appointed in pending proceedings by way of interlocutory remedy or by judgment. Receivers may also be appointed under a debenture according to its terms. Receivers appointed by a court are officers of the court and must submit certain periodical returns and obtain the discharge from the court. See also topic Executions.

RECORDS:

The only system of formal records is the recording at the District Land Registry of land dispositions, including sales, exchanges, leases exceeding three years and mortgages. There is a limited system of recording of documents before the Public Notary (power of attorney and pledges), and for registration of ships (transfers of ships and mortgages), registration of patents and designs, and registration of trade marks. See also topics Patents; Shipping; Trademarks and Tradenames.

REPORTS: See topic Law Reports, Codes, Etc.

RESTRICTIVE TRADE PRACTICE:

Under Restrictive Trade Law, 1988, replacing prior law of 1959, every "restrictive arrangement", or agreement (i.e., any arrangement or agreement which includes restrictive instructions in reference to price, profits, division of market, quantity or quality of goods) must be registered and receive approval thereof by court, or exemption from compliance with law, from appraiser appointed by Government to oversee restrictions on trade. Failure to comply with provisions of this law constitutes offense punishable by two years imprisonment or heavy fines for each day that offense continues. This law also defines and deals with monopolies and provides that monopolist may not refuse to supply commodity or service, in respect of which monopoly exists.

SALES:

Sales Law 1968 governs sales of all assets whether movable or immovable but may be contracted out. Usage of parties or of trade may govern sale. Seller is bound to deliver property and transfer ownership therein, delivery being by putting property at disposition of purchaser. If no time is set for delivery there is an implied condition of reasonable time and delivery takes place at place of business of seller. Seller does not fulfil his duty if he does not deliver amount ordered or property of a different nature than that ordered or which does not comply with sample or to accepted usage or which in any other way does not comply with contract. Purchaser may not rely on such unsuitability if he knew of it at time of signing of contract. Purchaser has a duty to inspect property on receipt and must advise vendor immediately of unsuitability. In case of latent defects in goods, purchaser has two years within which to give notice of unsuitability.

Remedies are same as for ordinary breach of contract. In case of unsuitability, purchaser also has right of deduction from price.

International Sale of Goods.—Sale (International Sale of Goods) Law 1971 adopted, for Israel, Uniform Law on International Sale of Goods. Law is now in force.

Purchaser's Bona Fides.—Rule that a bona fide purchaser of movables in ordinary course of vendor's business, acquires clear ownership, is not affected by fact that said movable was pledged and notice was entered in Register of Pledges. Bona fides for purpose of law of sales, is not necessarily excluded by omission to examine Register of Pledges, even if such omission is negligent.

Sale of Flats.—Special 1974 Law regulates mode of securing monies paid by a purchaser of a flat to seller by providing that if purchaser pays more than 15% of price of flat, seller must either give purchaser a bank guarantee securing all sums paid if for any reason transfer cannot take place, or obtain a policy of insurance from an insurance company covering liability to repay in such a case to purchaser sums paid by him or mortgage flat or a proportional part of area on which it is to be built to secure such repayment or enter a note of sale in Land Registry books provided no mortgage is registered, or transfer ownership to purchaser.

Law provides penalties for breach of this provision.

Protection of Consumers Law 1981 provides penalties for exploitation and misleading of customers in sales and services for private purposes. Customers are to be given full and correct information, regarding goods sold and price thereof in credit and instalment sales.

Real Estate Agents Law-1996.—All practicing real estate agents must pass qualification examinations and be licensed by Real Estate Agents Registrar. Agents licence may be revoked if he does not abide by rules of law which inter alia strive to maintain minimal code of ethics.

Price Control.—Price Control Law of 1996 applies to various goods to be specified in Minister's ordinances, whose offices deal, or are concerned with, said goods. These goods must belong to at least one of following categories: (i) their price is not normally controlled by market forces due to monopolistic nature of manufacturer or purchaser; (ii) their manufacture or sale is supported by Government funds; (iii) are deemed "Vital Commodities"; (iv) are scarce; (v) control of their price is instrumental in inflationary control. Where Minister is responsible for such regulated goods, he may establish maximum prices and profits for sale of such regulated goods.

Debits Card Law 1986 regulates use of credit and debit cards issued mainly by banks and extensively used for consumer payments and bank withdrawals.

See also topic Contracts.

SEALS:

There is no necessity for seals on private instruments. Corporations are required to have an official seal which is to be fixed on deeds and other documents which by virtue of the statutes of the particular corporation require the corporate seal.

Municipal corporations have a corporate seal. The seal of the State of Israel is affixed to particular instruments of a very special class. The Minister of Justice is in charge of the State Seal.

SECURITIES:

Under Mutual Investment Trust Law, 1961, company, objects of which are to make as trustee mutual investment in securities, must have certain minimum amount of paid capital and must be connected with another company which will deal with securities.

Securities Law 1968 sets up a Securities Authority to watch over interests of public investing in securities. Offer of securities to public is forbidden except by way of a prospectus permitted by Authority. Law imposes civil liability on directors and experts

See Topical Index in front part of this volume.

SECURITIES . . . *continued*
to purchasers in respect of contents or prospectus. Any person purchasing securities relying on an erroneous statement in prospectus has a right of rescission within a reasonable time. Provisions of law also apply to securities in Israeli companies offered abroad. Authority has power to waive provisions of law in respect of securities of a company registered abroad if satisfied that laws of country of registration adequately safeguard Israeli investors.

By 1981 Amendment "insider trading" by persons holding 10% or more in corporation where shares issued to public or dealt in on Stock Exchange, and by persons holding position in such corporation giving them access to inside information becomes criminal offence punishable by imprisonment or fine; excepted are bona fide transactions, e.g. purchase of qualifying shares, transactions by trustee, liquidator, receiver, transactions by bona fide written contract.

1984 Law protects savings invested in approved savings schemes, Government bonds, provident funds and insurance policies issued in Israel, by forbidding Government expropriation or deterioration of conditions of such savings as to amount and date of redemption, rate and due date of interest, linkage basis and rate of tax.

SHIPPING:

A substantial part of the shipping law was embodied in the Shipping (Vessels) Law 1960 dealing primarily with shipping registration and ships' mortgages. Certain parts of the (English) Merchant Shipping Act 1894 have been applied and still apply to Israel.

Ministry of Communications is in charge of maritime matters including the enforcement of the shipping laws. See also topic Mortgages.

Under Ports Authority Law of 1961, Ports Authority was constituted as a separate legal entity and, pursuant to said law, control of ports and their management is vested in Ports Authority.

Shipping (Sailors) Law 1973 regulates conditions necessary to become a sailor both of Israeli and non-Israeli citizens. It provides means of supervision and disciplinary action. Council is appointed to plan, control and supervise examinations. Law defines authority and rights of captain, and regulates his duties both on land and on high seas. It also regulates discipline, and work distribution, salary and other rights of crew and deals with offences.

Encouragement of Employment of Israeli Sailors Law-1996.—Israeli shipping companies dealing in international shipping are encouraged to employ Israeli crew members through tax incentive which, in effect, reimburses shipping company with income tax paid in respect of their salaries.

STATUTES:

Statutes are published regularly in Official Gazette and there are annual volumes.

TAXATION:

Income Tax.—Income Tax Ordinance was codified in 1961. New version of Ordinance brings up to date and incorporates in a comprehensive code the provisions of 1947 Ordinance and subsequent amendments.

Income tax is payable on income of any person arising in, derived from or received in Israel from any business, profession or employment as well as from dividends, interest and linkage differences, annuities, rents, premiums, royalties and other profits or gains. Special provisions impose tax on gains from share redemption, bond-washing, waiver of debts, stock options, fringe benefits of employees and imputed interest. Noncapital business expense of obtaining income is deductible, including depreciation on cost of business assets (see also subhead Companies Tax, infra), interest and linkage differences on business loans. Deduction of travel and entertainment expense is restricted. Special regulations determine amounts of personal expenses of foreign experts which are recognized as deduction.

As from 1/1/87 tax and accounting year is calendar year instead of year to Mar. 31, except for four classes of assessees who may apply for special period of assessment.

All businesses and professions are required to keep accounts in accordance with rules. Noncompliance involves penalties and loss of tax benefits under law.

Expenses (including capital expense) on approved research projects in industry, agriculture, transport or energy allowed as deduction. If project not approved, expense allowed in three equal annual instalments from year of outlay.

Beginning in 1990 benefits for R & D and other expenses (e.g. investments in movie production, oil exploration etc.) limited by total ceiling to be provided annually by Minister of Finance with regard to all taxpayers combined. (See also topic Investment Law and Incentives.)

Rates.—Individuals pay tax on taxable income at progressive rates, i.e.: 15%, 30%, 45% and 50% (earned or rental income). Amounts charged at each rate are adjusted periodically for index changes. Reduced rates may be charged on pay for shift work in industry and to residents of certain settlements. Reduced rate up to 35% ceiling applies to interest on certain index linked deposits. As from 1990 benefits on pay for shift work limited to low-income workers. Tax credits are allowed for resident taxpayer and wife. As from 1995 above-mentioned also applies to residents of Territories who are not Israeli citizens. (Said taxpayers are subject to Israeli taxation on income sources in Territories if entitled to Israeli citizenship under Law of Return 5712-1952.) Additional credits allowed for new immigrants and for soldiers entering industry, agriculture, construction or hotels at end of compulsory military service. From 1996 special additonal credit applies to women.

Tax credit of 35% is allowed for donations to recognized charitable bodies, subject to ceiling of lower of 30% of chargeable income or NIS. 327,000 (for tax year 1995), or together with Research and Development deductions (see catchline Exemptions, infra) 50% of chargeable income before Research Investment deduction. As to companies and cooperative societies, see catchline Exemptions, infra.

Exemptions.—The following persons and institutions are exempt from income tax either totally or partially: municipal and local councils; public institutions for promotion of religion, charity, education and charitable trusts; pension funds: cooperative societies not deriving their income from nonmembers; blind and certain handicapped persons in respect of earned income not exceeding certain ceiling or other income not exceeding certain ceiling; diplomatic representatives and consular officers in regular service of foreign states in respect of salaries and emoluments payable for such services provided such foreign state grants similar relief to Israel; war invalids, victims of hostile action or Nazi persecution and dependents of deceased members of fighting services in respect of pensions payable by government; temporary resident in respect of income derived from sources abroad, provided he did not reside in Israel for more than six months in year preceding to year of assessment and does not intend to stay permanently in country; linkage differences received by individuals on sale of assets, compensation on expropriation of assets, cancellation of sale of assets, claims for damages, private loans to another individual, provided such linkage differences are not liable as trade or professional income; linkage differences on Government loans not held for trading; linkage differences on loans made to company by controlling shareholder (shareholder having 5% of certain rights) under certain circumstances; nonbusiness exchange differences on individual's foreign currency deposits if not business income; on loan from nonresident; on foreign currency deposits of payments by nonresidents on account of share purchases; income of nonresident from employment in Israel is exempt for limited period and sum if employed by foreign employer; new residents in respect of income received from abroad for first seven years of residence; nonresidents in respect of interest on certain types of securities and loans, income from investments in foreign currency in securities quoted on Tel-Aviv Stock Exchange provided investor receives no double taxation relief or if Double Taxation Agreement with investor's country allows "tax-sparing"; monthly payments received by Gentiles who saved Jews during Holocaust; linkage differentials on Index linked deposits made by individuals or trust funds provided such linkage differentials are neither part of individuals business income nor derived from deposits which must be registered in his business records; trust fund income derived from exchange rate differentials on bond redemption provided bond is foreign security; payment received by orphan whose state was caused by violent act commited by family member. See also topic Investment Law and Incentives. *Note:* Above list of exemptions is incomplete. Rents from lease of residential apartments are exempt from tax up to ceiling.

All arrears of tax are charged with interest and linkage differences which are not allowed as deductions from income. Interest and linkage differences are allowed on overpayment and are exempt from tax.

National Health Insurance Law.—In 1994 National Health Insurance Law ("NHIL") was adopted. NHIL imposes direct tax based on employee's individual monthly salary up to certain amount. Rate of tax under NHIL ranges from 3.1% to 4.8%. All residents are permitted to choose health maintenance organization ("HMO") from which they wish to receive services and HMO's are paid in accordance with standard approved tariff. Exemptions granted for instance to those who were recognized by "Yad Veshem" Institute as Jewish saviours provided they reside in Israel.

Companies Tax.—Israel imposes income tax on taxable income of corporations. Generally speaking, taxable income is computed in manner common to most developed tax systems of the world. Concept which directs Israeli taxation of transnational transactions is mixture of territorial principle and of taxation on worldwide basis.

Corporate tax rate is 36%. Dividend distributions to individuals are taxed at rate of 25%, withheld at source. Withholding rate may be reduced by tax treaties. Under United States-Israel Tax Treaty, said rate is reduced under certain circumstances. There is special tax regime relating to capital gains tax which derives from fact that in Israel substantial portion of nominal "capital gain" may be attributed to inflation and devaluation of Israeli currency. (See catchline Negating Effect of Inflation on Tax Accounting, infra.) Because of relatively high rate of inflation from which Israeli economy suffers from time to time, Israel developed very sophisticated legal mechanism to avoid on one hand taxation of inflationary gains and on other hand abuse of tax system by claiming ordinary deductions based on inflationary financing without corresponding recognition of ordinary income. (See catchline Negating Effect of Inflation on Tax Accounting, infra.) Extensive new legislation entered into force in 1994, enabling tax-free transfers, mergers and splits.

Negating Effect of Inflation on Tax Accounting.—Nominal tax accounting has serious adverse effects during period of rapid inflation. Beginning in early 1980's, and, with regard to foreign investors, beginning in late 1970's, Knesset (Israeli legislature) has tried to solve this problem. Several attempts at finding solution have been made and currently main body of law dealing with problem is Income Tax Law (Adjustment for Inflation), 5745-1985 (referred to as "Law").

This highly complicated Law was introduced in 1985 as Temporary Measure for tax year 1985 replacing Income Tax Law (Taxation in Inflationary Conditions), 5742-1982. 1986 Amendment extended Law beyond tax year 1985. 1987 Amendment made Law permanent measure except that Finance Minister with approval of Knesset Finance Committee may announce, within three months of any given tax year, that this Law does not apply to said tax year.

Two major problems that Law attempts to redress are following: (1) Erosion of taxpayer's equity invested in current assets during period of high inflation. Such equity is likely to be eroded if taxpayer's nominal gain from sale of such assets is taxed at ordinary tax rates. (2) Loss of government tax revenues resulting from full deduction of nominal inflation-linked interest expenses incurred on debt used to finance acquisition of long-term assets. Sale of such assets is subject to special capital gains tax regime largely negating effect of inflation by limiting tax on gains resulting from inflation (accumulated until 1/1/1994) to mere 10%. Taxpayers would therefore enjoy windfall if they were allowed to deduct full, nominal amount of their inflation-linked interest payments against income taxed at ordinary rates.

Law attempts to solve these two problems by protecting that portion of taxpayer's total equity invested in current assets while offsetting deductibility of nominal interest on that portion of taxpayers liabilities attributable to investments in fixed assets.

This is accomplished by granting taxpayer additional deduction with regard to equity invested in current assets, while imputing additional income to taxpayer with regard to its debt financed fixed assets.

Calculation of these amounts is accomplished as follows:

Taxpayer must calculate his "total capital" which consists of "sum of capital" minus "sum of fixed assets". These sums are based on balance sheet figures of capital and fixed assets as of beginning of tax year. List of items to be taken into account in

See Topical Index in front part of this volume.

TAXATION . . . *continued*
calculating each sum appears in Supplements A & B to Law. Special adjustments are made to reflect differences between financial accounting and tax accounting. In addition "total capital" includes figures reflecting changes in "sum of capital" and "sum of fixed assets" during tax year. If "total capital" is positive figure it is "protected" against erosion by inflation, by allowing deduction equal to "total capital" multiplied by increase in cost of living index during tax year, up to 70% of taxable income (excess may be carried forward). Protection is needed because positive "total capital" means that capital has been invested in current assets. If "total capital" is negative figure it is multiplied as above and result is added to income because it means that fixed assets have been debt-financed and, while all financing expenses including their inflationary element (linkage differences) are fully deductible, inflationary element of appreciation of fixed asset (accumulated until 1/1/1994) is taxed only at 10%.

Law and regulations thereunder provide mechanism to ensure that depreciation deductions retain their real value even during inflationary period. Law and regulations supplement, and in many cases replace, depreciation rates and/or systems provided under other tax laws.

Law provides for adjustment of closing inventory values and of advances from customers and to suppliers, but application of these provisions has been postponed.

Law provides that Stock Exchange gains may be taxed even if not realized, and that if value of securities owned by taxpayer does not increase at rate equal to rate of inflation taxpayer is "punished" for investing protected capital and/or for debt-financing purchase and carrying of such securities. "Punishment" takes form of including in income difference between value of said securities, and said value increased at rate of inflation, and value actually attained. Law overrides exemption normally provided for Stock Exchange transactions, and exemption in case of listing of stock in industrial corporations.

Special deduction is provided to compensate taxpayers for erosion of current earnings.

Above rules apply to vast majority of companies and to vast majority of partnerships and individuals required to maintain and report on double entry system. Less complex rules apply to other taxpayers and many taxpayers are not subject to Law at all (e.g. taxpayers who do not claim financing expenses and are not subject to reporting under double entry system).

Foreign owned companies and partnerships may be exempt from application of Law by electing to report their income in foreign currency under set of Regulations protecting them from effect of inflation.

Capital Gains Tax.—Capital gains are taxed under special tax regime provided for in Income Tax Ordinance which in effect taxes real gains at regular income tax rates and gains resulting from inflation at flat rate of 10% for inflationary gains accumulated before 1994, and exempts such gains accumulated after 1994. Rate of 35% applies to real gains on sale of foreign securities by trust fund.

Briefly, in calculating capital gain tax due "purchase price" (cost minus depreciation deductions) of asset is divided by cost of living index at time of purchase, and multiplied by cost of living index at time of resale. This is called "adjusted purchase price". That part of profit on sale, which equals difference between original purchase price and adjusted purchase price is called "inflationary sum" and is taxed at rate of 10% of such difference for inflationary sum accumulated before 1994 and 0% for inflationary sum accumulated thereafter. Foreign residents are entitled to calculate "inflationary sum" based on currency of investment. Balance of profit on sale is called "real capital gain" and is taxed at regular tax rates (corporate or individual). Where asset sold was acquired by inheritance after 31 Mar., 1981, cost of original purchase by deceased is taken for calculating profit on sale. Amounts spent on improvements of asset sold are deductible and brought into calculation of adjusted purchase price after index adjustment.

Capital gains on sale of stock traded on Tel Aviv Stock Exchange Ltd. ("TASE") are exempt from tax except for gains in certain first sales after registration of stock for trade. Exemption does not apply to taxpayers subject to Income Tax Law (Adjustment for Inflation). Similar exemptions apply to sales of certain stock of Israeli companies listed and traded on overseas stock exchanges. Nonresidents are exempt from 10% tax on "inflationary sum" on all sales of stock (even if not traded), provided they calculate "inflationary sum" based on currency of investment.

Similar tax regime (i.e. separation between "inflationary sum", taxed at 10% or exempt, and "real capital gain", taxed at regular rates) is provided by Land Appreciation Tax Law, 5723-1963 for taxation of capital gains upon disposition of interests in real estate or real estate companies.

Double Taxation.—Agreements are in force with U.K., Sweden, France, (new treaty entering into force 1/1/97), Finland, Germany, Denmark, Norway, Austria, Singapore, Holland, Italy, Belgium, Canada, Jamaica, South Africa, Hungary, Poland, Japan, Czech Republic, U.S.A., China, and Ireland. Agreements are in force with China, Ireland (France-new treaty). (Treaties with Phillippines, India, Thailand, Greece, Russia and Turkey signed but ratified only by Israel.) Mutual exemption has been agreed with many countries with regard to shipping and aviation profits. Unilateral relief may also be granted in certain circumstances.

Estate Tax.—Repealed in relation to estates of persons deceased after 31/3/81. Capital Profit Tax and Land Appreciation Tax Law adjusted so that profit on sale of asset inherited after 31/3/81 includes increment accrued during lifetime of deceased. See subhead Capital Gains Tax, supra. Estate Tax Law was completely abolished in Dec. 1987.

Property Tax.—As from 1/4/81 Property Tax is charged only on market value of unimproved land, but not agricultural lands designated as such or used as such by owner who owned land as of 1/1/1995. Valuation date is Dec. 1 of preceding year. As from 25/7/1995 temporary measures grant certain exemptions as incentive to rapid building of residential apartments.

Purchase tax may be applied by the Minister of Finance to certain commodities and services. It has been applied to large range of commodities at percentage of wholesale price.

Land Appreciation Tax.—Imposed on sales of land, house property and rights in land (including lease of ten years or more and also lease of less than ten years when relating to state lands). This tax is calculated on substantially same basis as Capital Gains Tax (see subhead Capital Gains Tax, supra). As from 10/7/78 sale of private dwellings exempted provided owner has not made exempt sale in previous four years, or has not had two residential apartments in previous four years. Special temporary measures for tax years 1992-1994 expands considerably exemptions for sale of residential apartments. Temporary measure extended until 30/6/1995. Purchase tax of up to 5% is imposed on purchase of real property. Regarding purchase of apartment and agricultural lands, there is progressive purchase tax starting from 0.5% until 31/12/1996.

Betterment Levy is payable in event there has been advantageous change in building rights which increase value of property, as result of official rezoning. Rate of levy is 50% of betterment. Levy is payable on issue of building permit or on disposition of property.

Value Added Tax (VAT).—It was imposed in Israel from July 1, 1976. Tax is charged on all taxable transactions in Israel and on imports to Israel. Taxable transaction includes sale of asset or supply of services by taxable person in course of his business and also sale of asset used by taxable person in course of his business. Taxable person is person who sells asset or supplies services in course of his business. Isolated transactions of commercial nature and any sale of real estate to taxable person other than financial institution or nonprofit organization are also included.

Tax is paid by taxable person as percentage of sale price of asset sold or of service supplied and amount of tax is included in invoice given to customer. Customer in his turn may if he himself is taxable person deduct tax included in invoice and paid by him from amount of any tax which he himself has to pay on sales or services supplied by him. If customer is not taxable person he cannot set off tax which he paid at time of purchase or receipt of services against any other VAT.

Rate of tax presently in effect is 17%. There are number of transactions exempted from tax such as letting of living accommodation for period not exceeding ten years, letting of any property for key money, transactions of business with annual turnover of less than certain amount (adjusted for inflation) sale of assets where tax paid when assets were purchased could not be set off and import of goods exempt from customs duty by virtue of international treaties and import of goods for diplomatic staff insofar as exempt from customs.

Certain other transactions are not charged with tax and are described as "zero-rated." These include goods imported by person entitled to purchase them free of Purchase Tax, e.g. an immigrant, hotel accommodation and services including car-hire supplied to foreign tourists, purchase of air and sea tickets (and land tickets to bordering countries), air and sea transport, sale of specified fruit and vegetables. Minister of Finance was authorized to determine as "zero rated" sale of goods to bodies contributing to Palestinian Authority, as long as such goods are destined for development or humanitarian, noncommercial purposes in Territories. Where taxable person has effected zero-rated transaction as distinct from an exempt transaction, he is entitled to set off any VAT paid by him in connection with any purchases made or services provided by him in connection with such zero-rated transaction.

Financial institutions such as banks and insurance companies are taxed VAT on different basis, namely on percentage of their income chargeable to tax under the Income Tax Ordinance and also on percentage of total salaries and wages as assessed to income tax. Present rate is 17%. Nonprofit organizations are also liable to VAT on amount of salaries and wages paid by them unless such amount is below threshold adjusted for inflation. Present rate is 8.5%.

Employer's Tax.—Employer pays tax on payroll. Exemption granted to industrial undertakings within Encouragement of Industry (Taxes) 1969 Law, farms, companies where 70% of goods sold are exports of Israel industrial or agricultural products, hotels, housing construction, certain computer services companies and certain R & D funds. Tax is paid together with income tax deducted from payroll by employer. Eilat employers exempted in respect of workers employed in Free Trade Zone. (See topic Foreign Trade Regulations, subhead Free Trade Zone.) Currently rate is set at 0% for all employers except public institutions, not for profit organizations and entities treated as the State, which are subject to 4% tax.

Municipal Rates.—Under Municipalities and Local Authorities Ordinances local governments impose tax on buildings and occupied land. Tax is based on area of chargeable assets, location, use and type of building and is payable annually by occupier. Arrears are charged with interest and linkage differences. In recent years increases in rates have been limited by special laws. Reductions are granted for some tenants based on age or social condition.

Stamp Duty.—A comprehensive system of taxes in the form of a stamp duty is fixed by the Stamp Duty on Documents Law, 1961, which provides for stamps to be affixed on certain classes of documents. Rates of duty are either fixed or ad valorem.

Customs Duty.—Customs are payable in respect of import of commodities subject to substantial list of exempted articles. Duty is either fixed or ad valorem. Many tariffs subject to limitations under General Agreement on Tariffs and Trade with European Economic Community, and under Free Trade Area Agreement with U.S.

Israel has concluded trade and customs agreements with European Economic Community and customs duties have been progressively reduced on imports from member nations as from 1/1/87. Israel has concluded Free Trade Area Agreement with U.S. under which customs duties have been progressively reduced. Products must be of Israeli origin to enter U.S. under F.T.A.A. which means certain percentage of value added must be of Israeli source. Israel has concluded customs agreement with EFTA countries.

Eilat—Free Trade Zone.—By 1985 Law exemption from customs duty, purchase tax, excise, levies and customs deposits on imports from abroad and from Israel, also from V.A.T. except electronic equipment, dishwashers, clothes driers, deep freezers and private cars. Special income tax benefits and employer's tax benefits were provided by 1985 Law in respect of work performed in Eilat and to residents of Eilat, but abolished in 1990 tax reform and made subject to new set of rules under Income Tax Ordinance.

Implementation of Agreement Concerning Jericho and the Gaza Strip (Economic Arrangements and Miscellaneous Provisions) Law (5735-1994).—This law

TAXATION . . . *continued*
was enacted in Dec., 1994 to implement economic arrangements between State of Israel and Palestine Liberation Organization ("PLO"), based on Jericho and Gaza Strip Agreement. Law and Agreement (concerning Preparatory Transfer of powers to the Palestinian Authority) provides, inter alia, arrangements concerning employment of Palestinian workers in Israel, "customs envelope" of Israel over relevant territories and other matters of direct and indirect taxation.

Implementation of Agreement Concerning Preparatory Transfer of powers to the Palestinian Authority (Amendments of Law and Miscellaneous Provisions Law) (5736-1995) enacted in May 1995, to implement arrangements concerning preparatory transfer of powers and responsibility to Palestinian Authority, as provided by Agreement, signed between Israel and Palestinian Authority in Aug. 1994. Law provides arrangements concerning transfer of tax revenues to Palestinian Authorities which taxes have been collected by Israel on activities of residents of Territories who are not citizens. Law also discusses other tax affairs such as supply of information concerning residents of Palestinian Authority to Palestinian Authority.

TRADEMARKS AND TRADENAMES:

Under Trade Marks Ordinance (New Version), 1972, trade marks are registered with Registrar of Trade Marks. Trade mark is defined as mark used upon or in connection with goods for purpose of indicating that they are goods of proprietor of such mark by virtue of manufacture, selection, survey, or dealing with or offering for sale. Trade marks capable of registration must consist of characters, devices or marks or combinations thereof which have distinctive character. Application for registration is advertised, and opposition may be made within three months of advertisement. Period of duration of trade mark rights is seven years from date of registration, but this period may be renewed for 14 years from expiration of original registration, or of last renewal.

Under Trade Mark Ordinance, trade mark may be transferred even if goodwill connected therewith is not transferred. Further, licence to use trade mark may be granted by owner of mark. Such licence is subject to registration with Registrar of Trade Marks. In addition, following Lisbon Treaty of 1958, use of name of place of origin with reference to quality may be protected if product originates from such place and its qualities are connected therewith.

Under §16 of Ordinance, introduced in 1965, Registrar may, subject to certain qualifications, allow registration of mark registered in its country of origin, notwithstanding that it might not otherwise qualify for registration.

Tradenames.—See topic Business Names.

TREATIES:

Civil Procedure.—Israel is party to Convention on Service Abroad of Judicial and Extrajudicial Documents in Civil or Commercial Matters, and to Convention on Taking of Evidence Abroad in Civil or Commercial Matters. (Regulation for the execution of the Hague Convention [Civil Procedure] 1954).

Israel is party to United Nations Convention on Recognition and Enforcement of Foreign Arbitral Awards.

Extradition Treaties.—Israel has signed following bilateral Extradition Treaties: Belgium (1956), Italy (1956), Luxembourg (1956), Netherlands (1956), France (1958), Switzerland (1958), South Africa (1959), United Kingdom (1960), Austria (1961), U.S.A. (1961), Sweden (1963), Canada (1967), Swaziland (1970), Fiji (1972) and Australia (1975).

Double Taxation.—§196 of Income Tax Ordinance empowers Minister of Finance to issue Order giving effect to Treaty made with another State for Relief of Double Taxation, regardless of anything contrary thereto in Ordinance. For list of countries parties to double taxation treaties with Israel, see topic Taxation, subhead Double Taxation.

Customs Duty.—Israel is party to General Agreement on Trade and Tariffs (GATT), and to many Conventions affecting customs duties of which principal ones are Convention concerning creation of International Union for Publication of Customs Tariffs (Brussels) effective 1956, Lisbon Names of Origin Convention effective 1966, Brussels Convention on Nomenclature for Classification of Goods in Customs Tariffs effective 1970, Kyoto Convention for Simplification and Harmonisation of Customs Formalities effective 1977. Israel has signed customs, trade and free trade area agreements with EEC, U.S.A. and EFTA countries. (See also topic Taxation, subhead Customs Duty.)

Public Documents.—Israel is party to Convention Abolishing the Requirement of Legalisation for Foreign Public Documents.

Many bilateral treaties affecting aerial and maritime navigation, commerce, tourism, economic, scientific and cultural cooperation have been signed and are published in Official Treaties Gazette.

TRUSTS:

Nature of trusteeship, duties of trustees, formation of private trusts, charitable trusts and public trusts are defined in Law of Trusteeship 1979.

Trusteeship is defined as relationship to asset requiring trustee to hold such asset or act on behalf of beneficiary or for any other object. Trusteeship may be created by law, by agreement with trustee or by deed of charitable trust, which must be in writing signed in presence of notary or created by will in writing, or bequest under will. If trust is of public nature, registration (with Registrar of Trusts) and publication required. Law also provides for creation of companies for advantage of community requiring licence from Minister of Justice, approval as public institution for tax purposes, declaration by court that its objects are charitable; registration is necessary.

Duties of trustees and supervisory powers of courts are referred to in Law generally, but more detailed regulations are laid down for trusteeship in special cases, e.g. under Law of Inheritance, Law of Guardianship and Legal Capacity.

Trust (Mutual Investment Funds).—Mutual Investment Funds Law of 1961 allows establishment of mutual investment funds. It regulates constitution of the fund and its operations and, subject to compliance with provisions of the law, exempts income of the fund from company tax, and the income tax does not exceed 25%. Income derived from the realisation of securities of an approved mutual fund is free from income tax.

WAREHOUSEMEN:

There are no special provisions in regard to warehousemen, except in respect to licensed warehouses approved by the Director of Customs. There are two classes of licensed warehouses, viz., (a) general warehouses to be used for the warehousing of goods generally, and (b) private warehouses to be used only for the warehousing of goods which are the property of the licensee. Licensed warehouses are only warehouses in which dutiable goods may be warehoused prior to the payment of the duty.

General rules as to bailment are now governed by Bailees Law, 1967.

WATER:

Under the Water Law, 1959 the State acquired ownership of all the water resources in the country. The law entitles all persons to use water only in accordance with the provisions of the law. The objects of the law are to preserve water supplies, to prevent their decrease and pollution and to utilise the water resources for development purposes of the country.

WILLS:

Detailed provisions in regard to capacity to make a will and appropriate form of will are now contained in Inheritance Law 1965.

Will may be in writing or may be made verbally. Holograph will need not be attested. Any other written will must be signed by testator in presence of two witnesses at least. Witnesses must confirm execution of will by testator in their joint presence.

Will may be declared or signed before judge or registrar of civil court or before judge of religious court.

There is no limitation on right of disposition by will. Earlier limitations were abolished.

Capacity to make will is determined by law of place of residence of testator at time will is made, but will is valid in form if made in accordance with Israeli law or in accordance with law of place where it was made or law of residence of deceased when will was made or at time of his death. When testator is not a resident of Israel, will is valid if it is in accordance with form recognised by national law of deceased.

ITALY LAW DIGEST

(The following is a list of all Topics, including cross-references, covered in this Digest.)

ITALY LAW DIGEST

Revised for 1997 edition by

STUDIO LEGALE BELTRAMO, Attorneys at Law of Rome, Italy.

(Abbreviations used are: C. C.—Civil Code; C. C. P.—Code of Civil Procedure; C. N.—Code of Navigation; P. C.—Penal Code; R. D.—Royal Decree; D. M.—Ministerial Decree; D. L. L. T.—General Lieutenant Decree; G. P.—General Provisions of Civil Code; D. L.—Law Decree; D.L.L.—Legislative Decree; D. P. R.—Decree of President of Republic; D.P.C.M.—Decree of President of Council of Ministers)

Italy is member of EU. See also European Union Law Digest.

ABSENTEES:

Should any person fail to appear at place of his last domicile or residence and no news thereof be available, interested parties or heirs of such person may obtain from court the appointment of an administrator to transact absent person's business. (C. C. 48). Declaration of absence may be obtained from court in event of protraction of absence for two years or more. (C. C. 49). Upon issuance of said declaration heirs, under will or at law, may be granted temporary possession of absent person's estate. (C. C. 50). Those that have thus been granted temporary possession of estate may not dispose of it, but they may retain income therefrom to a varying extent depending upon degree of kinship with absentee. Should absentee return or evidence be found that he is alive his estate must be restored, but those in temporary possession may retain any and all benefits legitimately accrued to them until that time. (C. C. 56). See also topic Death.

ACKNOWLEDGMENTS:

Documents are acknowledged by notaries public. See topic Notaries Public.

Authentications.—Authentication of acknowledgment taken in Italy of documents to be used within Italy is no longer required. (D. P. No. 678, Aug. 2, 1957). Acknowledgment taken in Italy, of documents to be used abroad, can be authenticated by proper Ministry and by Foreign Affairs Ministry. Acknowledgment taken abroad, of documents to be used within Italy must be authenticated by local Italian Consul or by local authority with Apostille of "Convention de La Haye du 5 Octobre 1961" when applicable. U.S. is party to Convention.

ACTIONS:

Courts must decide all civil cases on the basis of law; however, in certain cases, upon request of parties, they may decide on basis of equity (C.C.P. 114). Rules governing procedure of civil actions are set forth in Code of Civil Procedure. Civil actions are commenced normally by service of summons. Special actions (especially in matters of urgency) are commenced by filing an application with the competent court. Parties must be represented before the courts and magistrates (except the lower magistrate, Conciliatore) by an attorney who acts by virtue of a proxy.

Foreign law, if embodied in statutes, is proved by producing copy of the statutes, as contained in official publications (Official Gazette, Codes, etc.). If foreign law is not statutory, it is proved by production of cases, law reports and opinions.

Foreign claims are proved by written evidence or by testimony (see topic Depositions).

See also topics Courts; Limitation of Actions.

ADMINISTRATION:

See topic Executors and Administrators.

ADOPTION:

Persons wishing to effect adoption when adoptee is of age must: (a) Have no legitimate descendants, (b) be at least 35 years of age, and (c) be at least 18 years older than adoptee. Under exceptional circumstances, tribunal may grant authority for adoption even though adopter be only 30 years of age. (C.C. 291).

Persons wishing to effect adoption when adoptee is under age must: (a) Be married for three years or more, (b) not be judicially or de facto separated, (c) be able to educate and support adoptee, (d) be no less than 18 years and no more than 40 years older than adoptee. (Law May 4, 1983, Nr. 1984).

Children born out of wedlock may not be adopted by their parents.

Consent Required.—Adopter's and adoptee's consent is required, but if adoptee is under age of 18, Juvenile Court must declare that adoptee may be adoptable. Such declaration is subject to ascertaining that parents of adoptee died or cannot be found or refused to appear in Court or showed to be unable and unwilling to assist and support adoptee. Same declaration is not required in special circumstances, such as adoption by relatives or persons living with adoptees before death of parents, etc. If adoptee is over age of 12, he must be personally interviewed by court; if he is between age of 14 and 18 his consent is required. In case of adoption of person over age of 18, if adoptee or adopter are married, assent of other spouse is also required and in any event adoptee's parents' assent is also necessary. (C.C. 296-297). Failing such consent adoption can be authorized by court if same is proved to be in interest of adoptee.

Jurisdiction upon adoption proceedings pertains to tribunal or Juvenile Court of district where adoptee resides.

Name.—Adoptee takes surname of adopter and adds his own to it. If adoptee is under age or was born out of wedlock and was not recognized by his natural parents, he takes only adopter's name. If adoption is made by husband and wife adoptee takes surname of husband. (C.C. 299).

Revocation.—Adoption may be revoked: (a) By adopter on grounds of unworthiness of adoptee when latter has made attempt upon life of adopter, his spouse, his ascendants or descendants, or if adoptee has been found guilty of crime in their respect, involving prison term of no less than three years. Death of adopter at hands of adoptee give rise to legitimate claim on part of those persons who would have had title to adopter's estate in absence of adoptee; (b) by adoptee on same grounds stated above.

Effect of Adoption.—Adoptee, when he is over 18, maintains all his rights and duties towards his original family, except that guardianship (patria potestas) is vested unto adopter. No civil rights arise between adopter and adoptee's family and likewise between adoptee and adopter's family. If adoptee is under age of 18 he acquires status of legitimate son of adopter and all relations with his family of origin cease to exist, except for prohibition to marry natural relatives.

Except upon specific approval of appropriate authorities adopter and adoptee may not marry each other. (C.C. 87).

Adoptee enjoys same rights of inheritance from adopter as legitimate child (see topic Descent and Distribution) but he does not enjoy any right of inheritance from family of adopter. (C.C. 576).

Special Adoption.—Special rules are set forth by Law No. 184 of May 4, 1983 for adoption of foreigners under age or for adoption by foreigners of minor Italian children.

Entry of minor foreigners in Italy for adoption is subject to consent of judicial authority of country or origin of adoptee, legalized by local Italian consulate, or to consent of Italian Ministry of Foreign Affairs and Ministry of Internal Affairs.

D. M. June 28, 1985 provides for principles and criteria to grant authorisation to nonprofit entities, having legal personality, to deal with organization and promotion of adoption of foreigners under age.

ADVERSE POSSESSION:

Acquisition of title through possession of real estate inconsistent with title of another is subject to the following: (a) possession is not protected if acquired by means of fraud or violence; and (b), possession usually continues uninterrupted for 20 years or for ten years, but in latter case only if real estate was acquired in good faith from one not owner, by appropriate instrument duly recorded. (C.C. 1158–1159).

AFFIDAVITS:

Affidavits as used in Anglo-Saxon legal system are not customary in Italy, only exception being in connection with certifications of vital statistics and personal status matters (such as date and place of birth, residence, nationality, status of single, married or widow, birth of a son, death of husband or wife or parent or sons, accomplishment of military service, registration in public lists), as well as with succession matters where—probate system being unknown in Italy—an affidavit must be filed certifying: (a) In cases of intestacy, to absence of a will and to existence and identity of heirs at law; (b) when a will exists, to fact that there are no heirs other than those mentioned in will. Such affidavits are sworn to either before a magistrate (pretore) or before a notary public, mayor or town clerk ordinarily by four persons or, in specific cases, by interested party, and constitute full evidence in respect of allegations contained therein.

AGENCY: See topic Principal and Agent.

AIR LAW:

Ownership, registration and operation of aircraft is regulated by Second Part of the Code of Navigation (see topic Shipping) which, subject to certain amendments, has been in force since 1942. Aircraft is classified as "registered movables", i.e. as personal property that, like vessels and motor vehicles, is subject to certain publicity and registration requirements.

Ownership of aircraft is evidenced by certificate of matriculation issued by Minister of Transport. Title to and other property rights in aircraft must be recorded for public notice purposes in register maintained by Ministry of Transport and known as Registro Aeronautico Nazionale (National Aircraft Register). Hence, any transaction capable of constituting, extinguishing or transferring title to, or any other property or security rights in, Italian aircraft can be asserted against third parties only if properly recorded in National Aircraft Register.

Save as stated under subhead Financing/Leasing infra, aircraft can be registered in National Aircraft Register only if it is owned by Italian State, or Italian public entity, or by Italian nationals or by company incorporated and having its main office in Italy. For registration in name of company, two conditions must obtain: (1) that no less than two-thirds of share capital of company is held by Italian nationals; and (2) that two-thirds of directors (including managing director) and general manager are Italian nationals.

Italy is party to most international conventions on uniform air law among which are: Warsaw convention of 1929 on carriage by air (and related Hague Protocol of 1955); Chicago convention of 1944 on international air navigation; Geneva convention of 1948 on recognition of rights in aircraft; Rome convention of 1952 on surface damages by aircraft to third parties; Tokyo convention of 1963 on infringements and other acts committed on board aircraft.

Any agreement submitted to National Aircraft Register in connection with initial recording or transfer of title to or any other property or security right in aircraft must, if written in foreign language, be accompanied by sworn Italian translation.

See Topical Index in front part of this volume.

AIR LAW . . . *continued*

Airworthiness/Operations.—Registro Aeronautico Italiano (Italian Aircraft Register) is technical agency, quite distinct from National Aircraft Register. While, as mentioned, National Aircraft Register records title to and other property rights in aircraft, Registro Aeronautico Italiano is in charge of verifying fitness of aircraft to fly and to be used for particular type of service. Register issues Certificate of Airworthiness, which must be kept with aircraft at all times, and makes periodic checks of fitness of aircraft.

Registro Aeronautico Italiano is also charged with performance of investigations in connection with air accidents.

Operation of regular airlines on preestablished routes is subject to license granted by Decree of the President of the Republic. As a rule, license may be accorded only to persons or companies possessing prerequisites to own aircraft registrable in National Aircraft Register.

All crew members must obtain licence for performance of their individual services and must be chosen from personnel registered in lists kept by special agency known as "Ente Nazionale della Gente dell'Aria". However, Decree-Law No. 560, dated Dec. 30, 1992 (implementing EC Directive No. 91/670) provides for mutual recognition of professional licences granted within EU territory. Accordingly, European citizens who have been granted licence in their home countries may apply to Italian Ministry of Transport for its confirmation.

Mortgages/Liens.—Mortgages on aircraft are established by agreement and must be recorded in National Aircraft Register. To obtain such recording agreement must be in form of either notarial instrument ("atto pubblico") or notarised private writing. Notation of mortgage must be made on aircraft's matriculation certificate.

Mortgage can be taken as security for any financial obligation of owner of aircraft or of any third party, secured by owner.

In addition to preventing mortgage from being asserted against third parties, failure to record in National Aircraft Register affects very validity of security as between mortgagor and mortgagee.

Unless mortgagee's rights are satisfied or mortgagor provides alternative security as directed by court of competent jurisdiction, aircraft against which mortgage has been recorded cannot be cancelled from National Aircraft Register.

Financing/Leasing.—(a) Subject to nationality requirements referred to under heading Ownership/Registration, purchase of aircraft by Italian residents may be secured by mortgage on aircraft.

There are no significant foreign exchange restrictions in Italian system, so that no previous consent is required with respect to external borrowings or deferred sales arrangements.

(b) As mentioned, it is still basic rule, under Art. 751 of Code of Navigation, that registration of aircraft in National Aircraft Register can only be made in name of aircraft's owner and that owner must be either Italian national or juristic person meeting certain nationality requirements. It follows that Italian lessee, not being owner of aircraft, cannot register it in its name and, conversely, foreign lessor could not proceed with registration in absence of Italian nationality qualifications.

However, pursuant to amendment to Art. 751, Italian licensed airline operating regular flights on preestablished routes may from time to time be authorised by ad hoc decree of Minister of Transport to register aircraft in its name in National Aircraft Register when it has exclusive and actual availability of aircraft, even though not being its owner.

In this case both National Aircraft Register and matriculation certificate must, in addition to usual information, contain reference to legal basis (other than ownership) on which registration has been effected. Thus, since lessee operating licensed airline has full availability of leased aircraft, latter can be registered in National Aircraft Register. If lessee is not licensed regular airline operator he can, upon appropriate application, obtain from Ministry of Transport authorisation to use aircraft under lease agreement not exceeding term of three years and providing for lessee's right to purchase aircraft at expiration of lease. When lessor is company having its main office outside Italy authorisation is granted for maximum term of 12 months, and may be renewed once for equal period.

ALIENS:

Alien or stateless person, whose father or mother or one of whose direct ascendants in second degree were citizens by birth, becomes citizen of Italy: (a) if he enters active military service for Italian State and prior thereto declares that he intends to acquire Italian citizenship; (b) if he accepts public employment from State, even if abroad, and declares that he intends to acquire Italian citizenship; (c) if upon reaching majority he has resided legally in territory of Republic for at least two years and declares within one year after reaching majority that he intends to acquire Italian citizenship.

Alien or stateless spouse of Italian citizen acquires Italian citizenship after six months if he resides in Italy or three years after date of marriage, provided there was no dissolution or annulment of marriage and no divorce or separation, upon presentation of specific documentation as required by Art. 1 of D. P. R. No. 362 of Apr. 18, 1994.

Application may be denied if applicant has been found guilty of certain political crimes or of crimes for which law provides punishment maximum of which is not less than three years' imprisonment.

Citizenship may be granted by presidential decree on favorable opinion of State Council and recommendation of Minister of Internal Affairs to: (a) alien whose father or mother or direct ascendant within second degree was citizen by birth, or who was born in Republic and in both cases, has legally resided in Italy for at least three years; (b) alien who is of age and is adopted by Italian citizen who after adoption resides legally in Italy for at least five years; (c) alien who has been in Italian government service for at least five years, even if abroad; (d) alien who is citizen of member state of European Community and has legally resided in Italy for at least four years; (e) stateless person who has legally resided in Italy for at least five years; (f) alien who has legally resided in Italy for at least ten years.

In exceptional and special cases Government may grant citizenship to persons not having above requisites. (Law No. 91 of Feb. 5, 1992).

See also topic Immigration and European Union Law Digest, topic Internal Market, subheads Free Movement of Workers and Freedom to Provide Services.

Corporations Owned or Controlled by Aliens.—Italian corporations may be, in general, owned or controlled by aliens without limitations. Italian corporations owning and operating aircraft or vessels, however, must be under control and management of Italian citizens; furthermore, Italian corporations engaging in motion pictures production are not eligible for certain government subsidies unless their management is entrusted to Italian citizens.

See also topic Real Property.

APPEAL AND ERROR:

Any judgment rendered in first degree may be appealed to next higher court. Against a second degree judgment an appeal may be filed with supreme court (Court of Cassation) but only on points of law. Second degree judgment may also be appealed before same court which issued it when: (1) it is result of *dolus* of one of parties against other; (2) it is result of false testimony or evidence; (3) after judgment new essential documents are found which a party was prevented from exhibiting before because of force majeure or of an act of the other party; (4) there is an error in fact, resulting from the documents; (5) judgment is inconsistent with another judgment between parties; (6) judgment is result of *dolus* of magistrate.

ARBITRATION:

Arbitration proceedings may be instituted in all controversies except in certain special matters such as those concerning personal status, domestic relations, certain labour disputes which must be brought before ordinary courts and, in general, those concerning rights which parties have no power to dispose of. (C. C. P. 806).

Arbitrators to a controversy must be odd in number and unless otherwise provided by parties, their procedure and awards made in Italy are governed by Italian law.

Proceedings for voidance of arbitration awards may be instituted before civil courts on certain specific grounds, e.g., when arbitrators have exceeded sphere of jurisdiction conferred upon them by parties.

New rules recently enacted (C.C.P. 832-840) apply to international arbitration and recognition and enforcement of foreign arbitral awards. Above mentioned provisions are without prejudice to applicability of international conventions, infra.

Awards may also be contractual in nature if so provided by parties in arbitration agreement. In such case, award is binding as a contract between parties but is not enforceable unless a judgment has been entered upon award.

Pursuant to New York Convention of June 10, 1958, to which Italy is a party, awards rendered abroad are recognised in Italy regardless of parties' nationality or domicile. Since Italy ratified said Convention without adopting possible limitations foreseen by Art. 1.3 thereof, awards rendered abroad are recognised in Italy even if rendered in a country which is not a party to Convention and if subject matter of dispute is not of a commercial nature.

Italy is also a party to European Convention on International Commercial Arbitration signed in Geneva on Apr. 21, 1961 and to Convention on settlement of investment disputes between states and nationals of other states signed in Washington on Mar. 18, 1965. Moreover, Italy is a party to previously existing international Conventions on arbitration. (Convention of Geneva dated 24th Sept., 1923, Convention of Geneva of 26th Sept., 1927 and Convention of New York of 10th June, 1958). See also Agreement of Sept. 26, 1961, supplementing Italian-U.S. Treaty of Friendship, Commerce and Navigation of Feb. 2, 1948.

ASSIGNMENTS:

Rights, credits, debts and choses in action may be assigned by contract. The formal requirements of such instruments are the same as for normal transfers of rights, having regard to what rights are in fact transferred. Certain rights, such as those relative to maintenance or support, are not assignable. Rights as to which dispute is pending before court cannot be assigned to judges, clerks, process servers, lawyers, and notaries discharging their functions within jurisdiction of that court. (C.C. 1261).

Notice to a debtor or his acceptance thereof are necessary for the assignment of rights to become fully effective and operative in debtor's respect, but the latter's consent is not required. (C. C. 1264).

Assignment of debts or contracts by a debtor or one party to a contract are of no effect on the creditor or the other party unless their consent thereto is previously obtained.

Assignor is answerable to the assignee for the existence of his title at the time when the assignment is effected, but normally he has no liability as regards the debtor's solvency.

Assignment for Benefit of Creditors.—A debtor may assign the whole or part of his assets to his creditors, but the assignment is operative only in respect of those creditors who have agreed thereto and is void unless it is made in writing. The creditors may dispose of the assets assigned to them as they see fit and share in the proceeds of the liquidation thereof in proportion to their respective credits, but the debtor retains the right to control the management and receive the accounts relative thereto. The creditors may not levy execution on the debtor's assets other than those assigned until the liquidation of the latter has been completed. (C. C. 1977-1986).

Assignment of Receivables to Banks, Factoring Companies and other Financial Intermediaries.—These assignments are regulated by Law No. 52, Feb. 21, 1991 (as am'd by D.L.L. No. 385, Sept. 1, 1993) when following conditions occur: (a) assignor is entrepreneur; (b) assigned receivables arise from contracts entered into by assignor within course of his business; (c) assignee is bank, factoring company or other financial intermediary, whose by-laws include assignment of receivables. Assignees must be registered in Register held by Bank of Italy. Bank of Italy may exercise supervision powers on correct exercise of assignment activities.

ASSOCIATIONS AND FOUNDATIONS:

Associations and foundations can be granted status of legal entities by decree of President of Republic or, for specified categories of institutions operating within limits of province, by decree of prefects. (C. C. 12). Associations and foundations having

See Topical Index in front part of this volume.

ASSOCIATIONS AND FOUNDATIONS . . . *continued*
status of legal entities cannot purchase real property nor accept gifts or legacies unless authorized by same authorities. (C.C. 17). As to companies, see topic Corporations and Partnerships.

ATTACHMENT AND SEQUESTRATION:

There is "sequestro convenzionale" (attachment ex contractu) which corresponds to the American-English sequestration in contracts; that is, a species of a thing in controversy is deposited by two or more persons with a third person, who binds himself to restore it, when the litigation is over, to the party to whom it has been adjudged. (C. C. 1798).

Another form is the "sequestro giudiziario" whereby the court authorizes the seizure: (1) of real or personal property, title to which is controversial, and (2) of books, ledgers, documents, samples or any other thing which may be used as evidence of a credit. (C. C. P. 670).

The third form of sequestration ("sequestro conservativo") may be authorized by the court upon the creditor's demand whenever the creditor has founded reasons for suspecting that the guaranty of his credit may be prejudiced. (C. C. P. 671). This form of attachment may be granted by the court without hearing the debtor. Both as regards "sequestro giudiziario" and "sequestro conservativo," the creditor must, however, institute regular proceedings for the confirmation of the attachment, in event precautionary measure has not been granted in context of pending litigation, by serving debtor writ of summons within 30 days maximum from effecting such attachment. No lien or preference in respect of other creditors is created by attachment.

AUTOMOBILES:

See topic Motor Vehicles.

BANKRUPTCY:

Only traders (persons or concerns ordinarily engaged in business of medium or large dimension) are subject to or can invoke bankruptcy law. He who is not able to discharge his obligations or pay his debts is in state of insolvency and may be declared bankrupt at his own instance or at instance of one or more creditors, or by civil tribunal of its own motion. Provisions in this matter are set forth in Bankruptcy Law (R. D. Mar. 16, 1942, No. 267), but for procedure of extraordinary administration (for which see subhead Extraordinary Administration, infra).

The appointed judge and a trustee (receiver) are the administrators of the bankruptcy. The trustee acts under the direction of the appointed judge, designated by the tribunal, and he is specifically charged with the assessment of the assets and liabilities of the bankrupt. A committee of from three to five creditors surveys the administration of the bankruptcy.

Gifts and donations made by bankrupt within two years prior to bankruptcy are null and void. Abnormal transactions and payments made within two years prior to bankruptcy are declared null and void, unless other party can prove that he was not aware of insolvency of bankrupt. Normal transactions and payments made one year prior to bankruptcy are also declared null and void, if receiver proves that other parties were aware of insolvency of bankrupt.

After status of assets and liabilities has been assessed bankrupt may file an application for a settlement (concordat) with his creditors. If proposed settlement is not approved by creditors or if, after approval, it is defaulted by bankrupt, then regular winding up follows (alienations, collections, distributions, etc.).

Claims are submitted to appointed judges and, if accepted, included in an official list. When list is completed and assets are sold, claims are settled in following order: (1) preferential claims are paid in full (claims of mortgages, pledges, tax collectors' claims, social insurance agencies' claims, labor claims); (2) all ordinary claims are settled pro-rata with remaining funds.

Preliminary Concordat.—Any merchant, individual or company, who (a) has been in business for at least two years, (b) has not been declared a bankrupt during the five preceding years, (c) has never been sentenced for bankruptcy and (d) has not yet been judicially declared bankrupt, may ask for a meeting of his creditors and upon furnishing serious guaranties, real or personal, offer to pay not less than 100% of his preferred debts and 40% of his non-preferred debts or alternatively offer all his property to the creditors in payment of his debts, provided that such property is valued at no less than above percentages of his preferred and non-preferred debts.

The tribunal, by a decree not subject to appeal, decides whether the application may be accepted, and if it is, it orders a meeting of creditors to be held before a judge within 30 days and appoints trustee to take care of administration of assets. Concordat must be approved by majority of voting creditors, representing two-thirds of total amount of claims. If tribunal ratifies concordat, decision binds every creditor.

Controlled Administration.—A merchant, individual or company, in temporary financial difficulties may, in order to safeguard the interests of his creditors, apply to the tribunal for the control of his business operations and for the administration of his assets for a period not to exceed two years. If, on or before expiration of two years, debtor produces evidence to effect that he is in position to fulfil his obligations to creditors, then proceedings are stopped. If, on other hand, controlled administration proves fruitless, then declaration of bankruptcy is issued by tribunal.

Forceful Administrative Liquidation.—Insurance companies, banks, certain companies controlled by State, consortiums and other special legal entities may not be subject to normal bankruptcy proceedings and, in case of insolvency, they are liquidated by commissioner appointed by court.

Extraordinary Administration.—Persons or concerns in insolvency status are submitted to extraordinary administration by one or three commissioners under control of Ministry of Industry (rather than bankruptcy) whenever their debts towards credit and social security institutions exceed 76,906,000,000 lire and five times corporate paid in share capital, provided that employees are no less than 300.

Extraordinary administration is resolved by court or, when employees' wages are unpaid for more than three months, by Ministry of Industry. It can be extended to parent companies, subsidiaries, affiliates or companies that have lent amount exceeding one third of their assets to company in extraordinary administration.

Extraordinary administration procedure is aimed at safeguarding continuance of business of insolvent company and employment of its personnel by allowing commissioner to continue trading and to transfer all or part of business to third parties. (Law 95 of Apr. 3, 1979, as am'd).

Penal Sanctions.—The debtor who has ceased making his payments and finds himself in any of the following conditions is declared a "simple bankrupt" and may be punished by from six months to two years imprisonment: (a) If his personal expenses or those of his family exceeded his income according to his financial conditions; (b) if he has spent a large part of his income in gambling or manifestly imprudent operations; (c) if, for the purpose of delaying bankruptcy, he has used other ruinous means; (d) if he has caused further prejudice to his financial condition by abstaining from applying for a bankruptcy declaration or by any other grave fault; (e) if he has failed to discharge the obligations agreed to in a previous concordat; (f) if during the three years preceding the bankruptcy declaration he has not kept the books and papers prescribed by the law or has kept the same in an irregular or incomplete manner and has failed to appear before the referee, or trustee or committee of creditors. An entrepreneur who continues to resort to credit dissimulating his insolvency may be punished with imprisonment up to two years.

A bankrupt is guilty of "fraudulent bankruptcy" if he has made false entries in his books, destroyed or hidden assets, set forth in his books or declared himself debtor of sums not due. Those guilty of fraudulent bankruptcy may be punished by imprisonment from three to ten years.

BILLS AND NOTES:

Drafts or promissory notes must be dated and it must be specifically stated therein whether it is a promissory note (cambiale) or a bill of exchange (lettera di cambio). It must have written therein the sum to be paid, date of maturity and place of payment, and must be signed by drawer or maker with his name and surname. (R. D. Dec. 14, 1933, n. 1669).

Provisions in promissory notes for payment of interest are of no effect except in payments by sight and at a certain time after sight. Promissory notes may be endorsed by one or more persons and all are individually liable for payment of same. Payment may be guaranteed by any person, even by the endorser, who must sign his name and the word "avallante" or "per avallo" and is liable if acceptor or maker and the assured endorser fail to pay.

If note is not paid the same must be protested by an authorized officer within two days after day of maturity. Notes can be enforced by summary execution. Notice of protest must be sent to endorser and to drawer within four days from day of protest, otherwise endorser is not subject to summary execution proceedings.

Promissory notes which do not comply with the stamp tax law are valid in all respects except that they cannot be enforced by summary execution. Forms of promissory notes bearing the appropriate stamp duty are available for purchase. The limitation for actions on promissory notes against acceptor is three years from the day of maturity, for actions against drawer and endorser it is one year from the day of the protest. Any endorser who has paid note or against whom an action for redress is instituted by another endorser, has action for redress against drawer and any prior endorser; limitation of foregoing action is six months from day of payment or, alternatively, from day when above-mentioned action for redress was commenced. If limitation terms have expired, action for unjust enrichment may be brought against acceptor, drawer or endorser.

Law No. 43 of Jan. 13, 1994 introduced new instrument called "cambiale finanziaria" which is payable to order and issued in series by companies, entities and enterprises and having minimum amount of Lire 100 million per note with maturity of not less than three months and not more than 12 months from issue date. As to legal requirements and applicable provisions, this instrument is equivalent to ordinary promissory note; it can be endorsed only with clause "without guarantee" or equivalent; it must contain wording "cambiale finanziaria", other elements required by law for promissory note and indication of return of any kind agreed upon.

Issue of "cambiali finanziarie" is considered "collection of savings" pursuant to provisions and subject to limitations of Banking Law.

CHATTEL MORTGAGES:

Personal property may not be mortgaged in Italy. The practical effects of chattel mortgages are, however, obtained by means of pledges (C. C. 2784-2807), which become valid and operative upon physical possession of the property passing to the creditor or to a trustee appointed by both parties. The pledge must be evidenced by a duly registered written instrument if the credit which it secures exceeds the sum of 5,000 lire, and the creditor who holds such a pledge is entitled to preference over other unsecured creditors on the proceeds of the sale of the pledged property, but he may in no way appropriate this property; nor can the creditor use or otherwise dispose of the pledged property without the pledger's consent.

CITIZENSHIP:

See topic Aliens.

COLLATERAL SECURITY:

See topic Chattel Mortgages.

COMMERCIAL REGISTER:

All those (inclusive of individuals, partnerships and corporations) who exercise activity organized for production or exchange of goods or services shall be registered in register, called "Registro delle imprese". (C.C. 2188). Rules for implementation of above Register—which is instituted within structure of each Chamber of Commerce—have been issued pursuant to Art. 8 of Law No. 680, Dec. 29, 1993 (see D. P. R. No. 581 of Dec. 7, 1995). In preceding period Register was substituted, for business carried out by companies (inclusive of partnerships and corporations), by records kept by special offices of Tribunals.

CONFLICT OF LAWS:

Regulated by Law No. 218, May 31, 1995:

See Topical Index in front part of this volume.

CONFLICT OF LAWS . . . *continued*

(a) Status and competency of persons are governed by their national law. (art. 20).

(b) Corporations, associations, foundations and any other private or public entity are regulated by law of State where their procedure of constitution has been perfected. Italian law is however applicable if main office or main business of such entities are located in Italy. (See topic Corporations and Partnerships, subhead Foreign Corporations.)

(c) Personal property (movables) and real properties (immovables) are governed by law of place of their location. (art. 51).

(d) Inheritance is governed by national law of deceased at time of death. However, testator may, by testament, expressly choose applicability of law of State where he is resident. (art. 46).

(e) Formalities for execution of testament are governed by law of place where instrument is executed or by national law of testator or by law of State where testator is resident or domiciled at time of execution or death. (art. 48).

(f) Gifts are governed by national law of donor at time of donation. However, donor may, by express declaration inserted in or attached to instrument of donation, choose applicability of law of State where he is resident. (art. 56).

(g) Formalities for execution of gifts are governed by law applicable to them or by law of State where instrument is executed. (art. 56).

(h) Obligations ex contractu are governed by Rome Convention of June 19, 1980 (made effective by Law No. 975, Dec. 18, 1984) without prejudice to other applicable treaties. (art. 57). Noncontractual obligations are governed by law of place where they arose. (arts. 58, 61, 62).

(i) Personal relations between husband and wife of different citizenship are governed by law of State where their matrimonial life is mainly located. (art. 29). Patrimonial relations between husband and wife are governed by law applicable to their personal relations; however, parties may agree in writing to apply law of State where at least one of them is resident. (art. 30).

(j) Personal relations between parents and children are governed by national law of children. (art. 36).

(k) Prerequisites, constitution and revocation of adoption are governed by national law of adopting person or persons (if common) or by law of State wherein both adopting persons reside, or mainly conduct their matrimonial life at time of adoption. However, Italian law shall always apply when adoption of minor which attributes to him status of legitimate child is applied for to Italian court. (art. 38).

Patrimonial and personal relations between adopted and adopting person/persons and their relatives are governed by national law of adopting person or persons (if common) or by law of State wherein both adopting persons reside or mainly conduct their matrimonial life. (art. 39).

(l) Foreign law is not applicable if its effects are contrary to public order. In this case, alternative foreign laws shall be applied if provided by above-mentioned rules or, in their absence, Italian law shall be applied. (art. 16).

(m) Italian jurisdiction shall apply when defendent is domiciled or residing in Italy or has authorised representative in Italy. (art. 3). However, parties may agree in writing to derogate from Italian jurisdiction in favor of foreign court or foreign arbitrator provided that dispute concerns rights which may be disposed of by parties. (art. 4).

CONSTITUTION AND GOVERNMENT:

Established by the Constituent Assembly on Dec. 22, 1947.

Basic Principles.—Italy is a democratic republic, founded on work. The sovereignty belongs to the people, according to the forms and limits of the Constitution. (art. 1). All citizens have equal social dignity and are equal under the law without discrimination for sex, race, language, religion, political opinions, personal or social status. (art. 3). The State and the Catholic Church, within their order, are independent and sovereign. Their relations are regulated by the Lateranensys Pacts. (art. 7). All religions and confessions are free under the law. The juridical status of the foreigner is regulated by the law, according to international treaties and rules. The foreigner, who in his country cannot have the effective exercise of the democratic liberties guaranteed by the Italian Constitution, has the right of asylum in the Republic's territory. No extradition of a foreigner is allowed for political crimes. (art. 8-10). Italy repudiates war as an offensive instrument against the liberty of other peoples. On an equal footing with the other States, Italy admits limitations to her sovereignty necessary for peace and justice among nations. (art. 11).

Civil Rights.—Personal liberty and domicil are inviolable, except where arrests, searches or seizures are officially authorized by the judiciary. (art. 13). Freedom of speech, writing, press, movement, meeting and association are safeguarded. (art. 16 to 21). Every person may act in a lawsuit for the protection of his rights and interests. (art. 24). No one may be held criminally liable except under a law enacted before punishable crime is committed. (art. 25). Criminal liability is personal. An accused person is not deemed guilty until the final judgment is passed. (art. 26).

Economic Rights.—The Republic protects labor in all forms and applications and takes care of the formation and professional elevation of the workers. (art. 35). The worker has right to a wage in proportion to the quality and quantity of his work, and in every case the wage must assure to him and to his family a free and dignified existence. (art. 36). Compensation, unemployment insurance, old age benefits are established. (art. 38). Organization of "unions" is free. But the organization must be on a democratic basis, and the unions must register with the local or central offices of the government, according to law. (art. 39). The right to strike is recognized, within the limits established by law. (art. 40). Private initiative is free. (art. 41). Private ownership is recognized and safeguarded, but property may be expropriated against payment of an indemnity where the public interest so requires. (art. 42).

Political Rights.—All citizens of major age (18 years), men and women, are electors. The ballot is personal, equal, free and secret. Its exercise is a civic duty. (art. 48). All citizens have the right to form or join a political party. (art. 49). They have the right to petition the Chambers (Chamber of Deputies and Senate). The defense of the Fatherland is a sacred duty of the citizen. Military service is obligatory within the limits established by the law. (art. 52). Every citizen is obliged to contribute to the public expenses according to his ability to pay. (art. 53).

Parliament consists of two Chambers (Houses): Chamber of Deputies and Senate of the Republic. (art. 55). Chamber of Deputies is elected by direct, universal suffrage: one deputy for every 80,000 inhabitants. All electors who have reached age of 25 years on election day are eligible for Deputy. (art. 56). Senate of the Republic is elected on regional basis. Each Region elects one Senator for every 200,000 inhabitants. No Region can have less than six Senators. Val d'Aosta Region has only one Senator. (art. 57). Senators are elected by direct, universal suffrage. Electors for Senate are those who have reached 25 years of age. Electors who have reached 40 years of age are eligible for Senator. (art. 58). Former Presidents of Republic are de jure Senators for life. (art. 59). Both Chamber of Deputies and Senate are elected every five years. (art. 60). Further to referendum aimed at abrogating prevailing electoral law, new electoral procedure was enacted in 1993 for election of both Chamber of Deputies and Senate according to which Deputies and Senators shall be elected on basis of single-member consistency and in compliance with partial majority system (proportional system still applies to election of 25% of members of the two Houses). Said procedure substituted for former system based on proportional system. Legislative function is exercised collectively by the two Chambers (Deputies and Senators). (art. 70). Laws are promulgated by President of the Republic. (art. 73). Before promulgating, President may ask Chambers to reconsider; but if Parliament again approves law, promulgation is mandatory. (art. 74).

The President of the Republic is elected jointly by the two Chambers (Parliament). Three delegates from every region participate in election. The ballot is secret and a majority of two-thirds of the assembly is required. After a third ballot an absolute majority is sufficient. (art. 83). To be elected President of the Republic a citizen must have reached 50 years of age. (art. 84). The President is elected for the term of seven years. (art. 85). Whenever the President of the Republic cannot fulfill his functions, the same are exercised by the President of the Senate. In case of permanent impediment or death or resignation of the President of the Republic, the President of the Chamber of Deputies orders the election of a new President of the Republic. The President of the Republic is the head of the state and represents the national unity. He orders the elections of the new Chambers; authorizes the presentation of the bills by the government; promulgates the laws; orders the popular referendums according to the constitution; appoints the state officers; is the Chief of the Armed Forces; declares the state of war following the deliberations of the Chambers; is the chairman of the Superior Council of the Judiciary; gives pardons and reduces penalties. (art. 87). He may dissolve either or both Chambers. (art. 88). In order to be valid his acts must be countersigned by the proponent minister and in case of laws by the President of the Council also. (art. 89).

The Government of the Republic consists of the President of the Council, of the Ministers and they form together the Council of Ministers. The President of the Council is appointed by the President of the Republic, who appoints also the Ministers under the proposal of the President of the Council. (art. 92). The Government must ask and obtain a vote of confidence from the Chambers.

The Judiciary.—Justice is administered in the name of the People. (art. 101). The judicial power is vested in the ordinary justiciary. Extraordinary or special justiciaries may not be created. (art. 102). The Council of State and the other administrative judiciaries are qualifed to adjudicate on matters concerning the protection of the individual interests from the action of the executive and also the civil right in the cases indicated by law. The Court of Accounts has jurisdiction on the matter of public accounts. (art. 103). The Military Tribunals in war time have the special jurisdiction established by the laws; in peace time they have jurisdiction only for military crimes perpetrated by members of the Armed Forces. The Judiciary constitutes an autonomous order, independent from any other power. The appointments, transfers, promotions, disciplinary provisions, removals, relative to judges are vested in the Superior Council of the Judiciary, whose chairman is the President of the Republic. (art. 105).

Constitutional Court decides on controversies relative to constitutional legality of laws, on conflicts of jurisdiction between the powers of the State, and of the Regions or among the latter; on the indictments against the President of the Republic and the Ministers. (art. 134). The Constitutional Court is composed of fifteen judges appointed as follows: one-third by the President of the Republic; one-third by Parliament and one-third by the Supreme Judiciaries. Their term is 12 years. When the Court declares the constitutional illegitimacy of a law, the latter ceases to have effect the day following the publication of the decision. There is no appeal against the decisions of this Court. (art. 137).

Regions, Provinces, Municipalities.—Republic is divided into Regions, Provinces, and Municipalities. Regions are autonomous institutions with own powers and functions; regions of Sicily, Sardinia, Trentino-Alto Adige, Friuli e Venezia Giulia, and Val d'Aosta enjoy a special autonomy. (arts. 114 to 116). Provinces and Municipalities are autonomous institutions and represent decentralized subdivisions of State.

Amendments of the Constitution may be adopted by each Chamber in two successive resolutions at least three months elapsing between the first and the second such resolution. The second resolution must be carried by an absolute majority of the members of each Chamber. (art. 138). But the republican form cannot be subject to constitutional revision. (art. 139).

CONTRACTS:

Under Italian law "a contract is the agreement of two or more parties to establish, regulate or extinguish a patrimonial legal relationship among themselves". (C.C. 1321). There is general power in all competent persons to freely enter into contractual agreements, limited only by public policy and unlawful motives. There is also general power in same persons "to make contracts that are not of the types that are particularly regulated, provided that they are directed to the realization of interests worthy of protection according to the legal order". (C.C. 1322).

The necessary requisites of a contract are: (1) agreement of parties, to be reached as described below under subhead Formation of Contracts; (2) causa, which is economic reason for contract. Unlawful causa will affect validity of contract. Causa is unlawful

CONTRACTS . . . *continued*
when contrary to mandatory rules, public policy or moral or when contract constitutes means for evading application of mandatory rules; (3) object, which must be possible, lawful, determined or determinable (C.C. 1346); (4) form, when prescribed by law under penalty of nullity (e.g.: contracts that transfer ownership of immovables must be made by public act or private writing).

Parties may condition effectiveness or termination of contract upon future and uncertain event (respectively suspensive and resolutive condition) and may also set forth initial or final time limit.

Formation of Contracts.—Contract is formed when he who made offer has knowledge of acceptance of other party (C.C. 1326); acceptance which does not conform to offer is equivalent to new offer. Both offer and acceptance may be revoked provided, as to latter, that revocation comes to knowledge of offeror before acceptance and, as to former, that if performance in good faith is begun by acceptor offeror is bound to indemnify him for expenses and losses sustained.

Parties in conduct of negotiations and formation of contract must conduct themselves according to good faith, subject to being exposed to pre-contractual liability.

Dissolution of contracts providing for mutual counterperformance may occur: in case of important nonperformance of its obligation by party who has already received counterperformance. However, nonperformance may be excused by supervening impossibilty of performance, by all cases of force majeure and in event that, due to extraordinary and unforeseeable facts, performance has become exceedingly burdensome.

Dissolution of contracts may also occur when parties have agreed to insert in contract express resolutive clause (C.C. 1456) providing that contract will be resolved if specified obligations is not performed in designated manner, or when time fixed for performance by one of parties must be considered essential in interest of other (C.C. 1457). Another case of dissolution of contract occurs when other party serves on defaulting party written notice to perform within appropriate time, declaring that, unless performance takes place within such time, contract shall be deemed dissolved. (C.C. 1454).

Nullity of Contracts.—Contract is void if contrary to mandatory rules, if one of requisite set out above is missing, if causa is unlawful, if motives common to both parties of contract are unlawful, if object lacks in requisites listed above and in any other case estblished by law. (C.C. 1418). Relevant action is not subject to prescription and can be submitted by anyone who has interest in it or can be declared ex officio by court.

No validation of void contract is possible unless provided by law. Nevertheless, void contract can produce effects of different contract of which it has requisites of substance and form, whenever, considering objective sought by parties, it must be deemed that they would have wished it if they had known of nullity. (C.C. 1424).

Voidable Contracts.—Contract is voidable if one of parties was legally incapable of contracting, if it was incapable of understanding or intending and such contract results in grave prejudice to it, provided that other party acted in bad faith. (C.C. 1425). Furthermore, annulment of contract can be demanded by contracting party whose consent was given by mistake, extorted by duress or obtained by fraud. (C.C. 1427).

Action for annulment can only be submitted by those persons in whose interest it is established by law and within five-year period.

Rescission of Contract.—Contracts entered into in state of danger (i.e.: unfair conditions because of necessity, known by other party, of saving itself or others from present danger of serious personal injury) (C.C. 1447) or entered into at unfair conditions and such disproportion being result of state of need of one party of which other availed itself for its advantage (C.C. 1448) can be rescinded upon demand of injured party and within one year period from formation (C.C. 1449).

Applicable Law.—Obligations ex contractu are governed by Rome Convention of June 19, 1980 (made effective by Law No. 975, Dec. 18, 1984) without prejudice to other applicable treaties. See topic Conflict of Laws.

Government contracts are, as a rule, awarded on basis of bids, while system of direct negotiations is admitted exceptionally, in view of particularity of contract. Contracts are normally entered into on basis of general conditions and specifications and performance bond is usually required.

CONVEYANCES: See topic Deeds.

COPYRIGHT:

The protection of copyrights is governed by Law No. 633 of Apr. 22, 1941. The author of creative pieces in the fields of science (including computer software), literature, figurative arts, music, architecture, theater, cinema, radio and television has exclusive right to publish and to exploit his works. (art. 12). These rights include reproduction in any way and by any means (art. 13), performance in public (art. 15), broadcasting (art. 16), trading (art. 17), translation and adaptation (art. 18) of protected works. Aforesaid rights may be purchased, sold, transferred or assigned (art. 107) independently one from another. Furthermore, author, as well as his heirs, has "moral right" on his works, i.e., right to assert his authorship and to restrain anyone from altering works in manner prejudicial to his honour or reputation. (art. 20). Such right is of personal nature, not transferable and not subject to time limitations.

Duration of protection of economic (as opposed to "moral") rights is throughout life of author and for 50 years after his death. (art. 25). Such duration for motion pictures is 50 years from date of first public exhibition of picture. (art. 32). However, duration of protection of economic right for all works will be extended to 70 years as result of implementation of EC Directive No. 98 of Oct. 29, 1993.

New works need not be deposited for them to be protected under the Law, but a register is in use, and registration is the normal procedure followed. Certain works must be registered in order to be protected (records, photographs, etc.). (art. 106).

The Copyrights Law applies only to Italian citizens or residents. Protection of foreign works is subject to reciprocity and is often governed by International Conventions. Works of American citizens or residents are protected now in Italy under the Universal Copyright Convention which came into effect in Italy under Law July 19, 1956, No. 923.

See also European Union Law Digest, topic Copyright.

CORPORATIONS AND PARTNERSHIPS:

These are dealt with in arts. 2247 to 2554 of Civil Code, as amended or supplemented by D.P.R. No. 1127 of Dec. 29, 1969; Law No. 216 of June 7, 1974, D.P.R. No. 30 of Feb. 10, 1986; D.L.L. No. 127 of Apr. 9, 1991 and other legislation. Many amendments or additions were made to comply with EC Directives.

Different forms of corporations and partnerships are provided for therein, as shown in following breakdown:

Società per Azioni.—This is the form that is closest to the American concept of a corporation. Certain formalities must be complied with in connection with incorporating one. The Memorandum and Articles of Association must be executed before a notary public and the Tribunal having jurisdiction over the district must ratify them. The capital subscribed by the shareholders cannot be less than 200,000,000 lire and shares are nominal. At moment of formation incorporators (or upon capital increase participating shareholders) are required to pay at least 30% of subscribed capital. Each shareholder's liability is limited to shares subscribed by him unless he is sole shareholder, in which case such sole shareholder is liable without limitation in case of insolvency of company for obligations of company which arose in period in which shares are shown to have belonged to such sole shareholder. Each share carries one vote. Preferred shares may be issued entitling to privileges in connection with distribution of company's profits, and in reimbursement of capital upon dissolution of company, but they may in no event carry more than one vote and may be limited in voting rights. Companies whose shares are listed in Stock Exchange may issue saving-shares without voting rights in amount not exceeding 50% of corporate capital. Saving-shares may be issued to bearer. There is generally no limitation as to amount of capital that may be subscribed by foreigners or to foreigners being directors or officers of company. See topics Aliens; Foreign Investments.

Shareholders' meetings are "ordinary" and "extraordinary". In order to attend meeting shareholders must deposit their shares with company or designated bank at least five days before date of meeting. "Ordinary" meetings deal, on majority vote of those present, with approval of annual accounts, appointment of directors and auditors, and with such other matters as are reserved to their jurisdiction by articles of association or submitted to them by directors. Ordinary meeting must be convened at least once a year within four months from end of fiscal year. "Extraordinary" meetings deal with changes in articles of association, issuance of debentures and appointment of liquidators; their resolutions are valid if passed by holders of more than half of capital stock, but different quorums and majorities may be provided for by articles of association.

Management of company is vested in one or more directors, appointed by ordinary shareholders' meeting for maximum term of three years. Appointment may be renewed.

Each company must have a Board of Auditors (Collegio Sindacale) composed of at least three members (individuals, partnerships or companies) chosen from Register of Official Auditors and appointed for period of three years, whose duties include examination of administration of company and of its books, certification of balance sheets, etc. (C.C. 2397-2409, as supplemented and am'd).

Companies having their shares quoted in stock exchanges and holding companies whose capital exceeds 10,000,000,000 lire must file accounts, minutes and other data with Stock Exchange and Securities National Commission and are subject to investigation by such Commission. In said companies some of main tasks normally performed by board of auditors are entrusted to auditing firms. (See topic Securities.) Other special regulations for companies whose shares are listed on Stock Exchange are laid down by Law No. 216 of June 7, 1974 (as am'd), by D.P.R. No. 136 and No. 138 of Mar. 31, 1975 and by Law No. 904 of Dec. 16, 1977. Companies whose capital exceeds 2,000,000,000 lire (or 3,000,000,000 lire for more than ten funds) may be authorised by Ministry of Treasury to establish and operate open investment funds; companies whose capital exceeds 5,000,000,000 lire may be authorized by Ministry of Treasury to establish and operate closed investment funds (required capital is 7,000,000,000 lire if companies apply for establishing and operating both closed and open investment funds). These companies are subject to several restrictions and to control of Bank of Italy, of Stock Exchange and Securities National Commission, and of Ministry of Treasury. (Law No. 77 of Mar. 23, 1983, as am'd by D.L.L. No. 83 of Jan. 25, 1992 for open investment funds and Law No. 344 of Aug. 14, 1993 for closed investment funds).

Societa a responsabilità limitata.—It is equivalent of German G.M.B.H. and does not substantially differ from preceding form in that shareholders have limited liability, except: (a) company's stock must not be less than 20,000,000 lire; (b) each share is called "quota," no certificate thereto being issued by company, and company's charter may provide that they are untransferable. Otherwise shares may be negotiated through assignments recorded in company's books; (c) no board of auditors is required for company of this type unless company's stock is of 200,000,000 lire or more. Company may be organized by unilateral act and may have only one quotaholder. Under certain conditions, and in case of insolvency, sole quotaholder is personally liable above company stock for company's obligations; sole quotaholder, however, is not personally liable if he is individual.

Società in accomandita per azioni and *Società in accomandita semplice.*—These involve combination between limited and unlimited liability of partners, "soci accomandanti's" liability being limited to their share, whereas "soci accomandatari" are liable jointly and without limitation.

Società in nome collettivo.—This is a general partnership whose members have unlimited liability for its obligations. The memorandum of association containing all the partnership's and individual partners' relevant data must be deposited with the Registrar of Business Enterprises. The powers and duties relative to the operation of the partnership may be conferred upon one or more of the partners who are answerable to the other partners.

Società semplice.—This is simplest form of partnership in that it requires no formalities. Unless otherwise provided by agreement between partners, and such agreement

See Topical Index in front part of this volume.

CORPORATIONS AND PARTNERSHIPS . . . *continued*
is made public or known to third parties, operation of partnership, which however may not engage in industrial or commercial activities, is conducted severally by each of partners, each having full and unlimited liability for obligations of partnership.

Finally there are two forms that stand out by themselves; these are:

Associazione in partecipazione.—This is practically a capitalization deal that may be formed as a result of one party ("associante") agreeing to accept the contribution ("apporto") of another party ("associato") against a share in the profits. The "associante" retains the operation of the business. The "associante" acquires all rights and assumes all obligations with third parties, but the "associato" may be made to share in the losses in direct proportion to his shares of the profits, although in no event may his losses exceed the value of his contribution.

Società Cooperative.—Cooperative Societies may be incorporated with a limited or unlimited liability, but the Society's name must bear a qualification as to whether it is a limited or unlimited cooperative. They are subject to several restrictions and government controls, such as that their board of directors may on determined grounds be ousted by the appropriate government authorities and replaced by a commissioner appointed to carry on the business, or by a receiver entrusted with winding it up.

Each of the partners may not hold more than 80,000,000 lire worth of shares and these may be assigned only with consent of board of directors whose approval is also required for admission of any new member. Such limit is of 120,000,000 lire for Societies operating in agricultural fields or formed for work or production purposes.

Special provisions are set forth in respect of transformation, merger and split off of companies. (C. C. 2498-2504-decies).

Foreign corporations are regulated by law of State where procedure for constitution has been perfected, in particular in respect of: juridical nature; name; constitution, transformation and dissolution; capacity; organs' powers and organization; representative powers; members' rights, duties, access and exclusion; liabilities for corporations' obligations; consequences of breach of law and by-laws. (Art. 25 of Law No. 218 of May 5, 1995). However, Italian law will be applicable if corporation's main office or main activities are located in Italy. Corporations organized in foreign countries which establish in Italy one or more branches with permanent representation must comply with provisions of Italian law in respect of deposit and registration of articles of association, publication of their balance-sheet and of names of representatives, and of operation of their business. (C. C. 2506-7-8-10). See topics Aliens; Commercial Register; Foreign Investments; and European Union Law Digest, topic Corporations.

Taxes.—See topic Taxation, subhead Direct Taxes, catchlines Legal Entities Income Tax (IRPEG) and Local Income Tax (ILOR).

COURTS:

Giudice di Pace (Justice of Peace) only has jurisdiction in civil matters involving movable property whose value is not in excess of 5,000,000 lire, or involving circulation of vehicles or boats and not exceeding 30,000,000 lire in value, and in certain special proceedings. (C.P.C. art. 7).

Pretura (Praetor, Magistrate's Court) has civil jurisdiction up to 20,000,000 lire, penal jurisdiction in cases involving up to four years imprisonment and/or fine and certain specific offences. It has exclusive first instance jurisdiction over all labor matters and certain special proceedings. (C.C.P. art. 8).

Tribunali Civili e Penali (Civil and Penal Tribunals) have general jurisdiction, civil and penal, and appellate jurisdiction as to praetor's and Justice of Peace's judgments.

Corte d'Appello (Court of Appeals) has appellate jurisdiction over judgments of tribunals. A section of this court is named Corte d'Assise (Court of Assize) for trial by jury of the gravest penal proceedings. A Corte d'Assise d'Appello (Appeal Court of Assize) has been set up in 1951 to deal with appeals from judgments of the Corte d'Assise.

Corte di Cassazione (Court of Cassation) is the supreme judicial court of final resort. Its jurisdiction is confined to matters of law, taking the facts as found by the lower courts.

Corte Costituzionale (Constitutional Court).—See topic Constitution and Government, subhead Constitutional Court.

Tribunali per i Minorenni (Juvenile Courts) have jurisdiction over minors for adoption, affiliation, and for crimes committed by minors.

Tribunali Amministrativi (Administrative Courts).—There are a number of administrative courts having jurisdiction over specific matters.

Admission to the judiciary—except for Justice of Peace—takes place by national contest among doctors of jurisprudence, and post is for life.

CRIMINAL LAW:

Criminal law is controlled by the Penal Code. Criminal Procedure is regulated by the Code of Penal Procedure. See topic Constitution and Government, subhead Civil Rights.

CURRENCY:

Legal currency is the Italian lira. Bank of Italy holds a monopoly on issuance of currency notes. Foreign Exchange Control Office (Ufficio Italiano di Cambi) exercises limited control on transactions between residents and nonresidents and/or involving foreign currency. Nonresident foreigners when in Italy are practically subject to no control at all or currency restrictions.

See also topic Foreign Investments.

CURTESY:

Does not exist in Italy. Wife and husband have the same rights as to inheritance. See topics Descent and Distribution; Dower and Dowry.

CUSTOMS:

Imports from foreign countries are subject to custom duties and in some cases to a special import licence. Rates of duties, which vary depending on categories of goods, are set forth in Customs Tariff. European Union imports are subject only to very limited administrative duties. Italy is a party to General Agreement on Tariffs and Trade.

See also European Union Law Digest, topic Customs Duties.

DEATH:

If a person remains absent from his domicile or residence and gives no news for ten years then a presumption of death arises and this is declared by the court on the application of the heirs of the absent person. Presumptive death may be declared irrespective of the prior declaration of absence. (C. C. 58). See topic Absentees.

A presumption of death arises also in the following cases (C. C. 60): (a) Of persons who have disappeared in the course of war operations or have been taken prisoner by the enemy, no news of them being forthcoming after two years from the Peace Treaty or three years after the cessation of hostilities; (b) of persons who have disappeared as a result of an accident, no news from them being forthcoming for two years from the date of the accident.

Upon the issuance by the appropriate court of the declaration of presumptive death the heirs succeed in the estate and the deceased's spouse may remarry (C. C. 63-65) but the new marriage is declared void if the person declared dead should return or evidence be found that he is alive (C. C. 68). If the person declared dead should return or evidence be found that he is alive, then the estate must be returned to him in the condition in which it is at such time. Such person may also recover the price accruing from the sale of property (if the price is yet due) or the new property into which such price may have been invested. (C. C. 66).

Under the special provisions of the Code of Navigation, in case of disappearances arising from sea or air accidents the appropriate port or consular authority issues a statement. If such statement is positive as to the death, same is declared to all effects; if the statement contains only a presumption then the normal provisions outlined above apply.

Actions for Death.—There are no special procedures concerning actions for death. Any person who suffered damages as a consequence of a wrongful death may claim the same through ordinary action.

Death certificates cannot be obtained by mailed request but an application prepared on appropriate stamped paper must be actually filed with the office of vital statistics of the place where deceased died. Usually the procurement of such certificates is handled by specialized agencies with branches or correspondents throughout the country.

DECEDENTS' ESTATES:

See topics Descent and Distribution; Executors and Administrators; Wills.

DEEDS:

Conveyances of real estate, easements, leases or partnerships for over nine years, perpetual or life incomes, settlements and other contracts provided by the law in order to be valid instruments must be in writing. (C. C. 1350). All instruments relating to the creation or assignment of rights with respect to real property must also be recorded in the books of the Conservatore dei Registri Immobiliari (Recorder of Mortgages). Acts subject to said recording are those specified by law. (C. C. 2643). See also topic Taxation, subhead Indirect Taxes, catchlines Registration Tax and tax on capital gain from transfers of real property (INVIM).

DEPOSITIONS:

When depositions are to be taken outside of the country, a request (letters rogatory) is sent by the court through the Foreign Ministry, to the Italian Consulate of the state or place where witness is living. Testimony is taken directly before the Italian consul (when witness is an Italian citizen) or transmitted by the consul to the proper authority in the foreign state (when witness is a foreigner). (C. C. p. 204).

Italy is party to Convention on the Taking of Evidence Abroad in Civil or Commercial Matters signed in The Hague on 18 Mar. 1970.

DESCENT AND DISTRIBUTION:

In case of intestacy estate devolves in this order to: (a) Lawful descendants; (b) lawful ascendants; (c) collaterals; (d) natural relatives; (e) husband or wife; (f) the State. (C. C. 565).

The parents are succeeded by their legitimate children who share equally. (C. C. 566). Legitimate or natural children include those legitimized and those adopted. (C. C. 567). If decedent has no children, brothers, sisters or descendants thereof, his father and mother inherit in equal shares. (C. C. 568). If there are no children, parents, brothers or sisters or descendants thereof, half of the estate goes to ascendants of the paternal line and the other half to ascendants of the maternal line. But if the ascendants are not of the same degree, inheritance goes to the nearest kin. (C. C. 569).

If there are no children and no parents or other ascendants, brothers and sisters inherit in equal shares. Half-blood brothers and sisters are entitled to half of the share taken by the full-blood brothers and sisters. (C. C. 570). If decedent leaves only parents and full-blood brothers and sisters, all inherit per capita, provided that the share of the parent or parents shall in no event be less than one half. If there are half-blood brothers and sisters each one inherits half of the share inherited by the full-blood brothers and sisters. (C. C. 571).

If decedent leaves no descendants, parents or other ascendants, brothers and sisters or their descendants, inheritance goes to the nearest kin, without distinction of line, but inheritance cannot go beyond the sixth degree. (C. C. 572). If natural child dies without children or spouse, his estate goes to parent who recognized him. If he was recognized by both parents, estate goes to them in equal proportions. (C. C. 578). If natural child dies without leaving children or parents, his spouse inherits all the estate. If there are parents, inheritance goes: two-thirds to his spouse and one-third to his parents. (C. C. 579).

Surviving spouse is entitled to one half of estate if there is only one child or one-third if there are two or more children. (C. C. 581). Surviving spouse is entitled to two thirds if there are only legitimate ascendants or brothers and sisters or both. (C. C. 582). However ascendants are in any event entitled to one fourth of estate. Should

See Topical Index in front part of this volume.

DESCENT AND DISTRIBUTION . . . *continued*

there be no children, ascendants, brothers or sisters, surviving spouse inherits entire estate. (C. C. 583). Spouse who has not been held responsible for separation by final decree has same inheritance rights as nonseparated spouse. If spouse has been held responsible for separation by final decree, he/she is entitled to life annuity if at time of other spouse's death he/she received only from spouse support allowance. Life annuity can in no event exceed support allowance. (C. C. 585).

When there is no kin entitled to the inheritance, the State inherits. (C. C. 586).

Non-donable Shares.—Where a will exists, the following limitations as to disposition of the estate must be complied with by decedent who is survived by legitimate children, legitimate ascendants, natural children or spouse, having due regard to the fact that: (a) Adopted children have the same rights as legitimate children, and (b) there is a right of representation in favor of the descendants of legitimate or natural children. (C. C. 536).

As regards children reserve portion (the portion that cannot be freely disposed of by testator) is one-half of decedent's estate if only one child is left or two-thirds if children left are two or more. (C. C. 537). If decedent does not leave legitimate children, but legitimate ascendants, the reserve is one-third of estate. (C. C. 538).

Reserve in favor of surviving spouse is one half of estate of other spouse if no children are left.

When decedent leaves children and his spouse, if there is only one child, portion of estate reserved to latter is one-third, another third goes to surviving spouse. When children are two or more, portion of estate reserved to surviving spouse is one fourth and that reserved to children is one half of estate. (C. C. 542). Surviving spouse is in any event entitled to lifetime use of family home and furnishings, if owned by decedent or by husband and wife jointly. (C. C. 540).

When decedent leaves only legitimate ascendants and his spouse, latter is entitled to one half of estate, and ascendants to one-quarter of estate. (C. C. 544). There is no reserve for spouse against whom final decree of separation has been issued unless he was granted alimony. In this case he is entitled to lifetime annuity that, in any event, cannot exceed alimony. (C. C. 548). See topics Affidavits; Executors and Administrators; Wills.

DISPUTE RESOLUTION:

Alternate dispute resolution is limited to arbitration (see topic Arbitration).

DIVORCE AND SEPARATION:

Grounds for Divorce.—Either spouse may obtain a divorce on any of following grounds: (1) When other spouse has been sentenced to life imprisonment or to imprisonment for more than 15 years; (2) when other spouse has been sentenced to imprisonment for any period of time as a consequence of serious crimes against other spouse or certain other members of family or as consequence of certain serious crimes against third parties; (3) when other spouse has been acquitted on grounds of mental insanity from crimes against other spouse or certain other members of family; (4) when husband and wife have been living apart for at least three years since separation hearing, as result of judgment of separation issued by court; (5) when husband and wife have been living apart as matter of fact since at least two years before Dec. 18, 1970; (6) when other spouse has carried out actions referred to in (2) above (except for case of injuries to other spouse and/or certain other members of family), although this has not resulted in his being convicted; (7) when spouse is foreign national and has obtained abroad divorce or annulment of marriage, or has remarried; (8) when there was no marital intercourse and (9) when judgment certifying change of sex has become final.

Jurisdiction and Proceedings.—Application for divorce must be filed with court of place of residence of defendant or, if defendant resides abroad, with court of place of residence of plaintiff or, finally, should both spouses reside abroad, with any Italian court. Judgment granting divorce provides also for custody of children and for alimony from husband to wife or vice versa, according to circumstances. Alimony obligation ceases in case of remarriage of spouse in whose favor it was granted.

Name.—Final judgment of divorce is registered in public vital statistics records and woman loses right to use husband's surname, unless specific authorisation is granted by court to add such surname to her maiden family name, whenever she has specific interest for herself or for her children; after such registration each spouse may remarry. (Law No. 898 of Dec. 1, 1970 as am'd by Laws No. 436 of Aug. 1, 1978 and No. 74 of Mar. 6, 1987).

Annulment of civil or non-Catholic marriages is granted by civil courts, of Catholic marriages by Ecclesiastical Courts in conformity with Lateran Treaty executed between Italy and Vatican on Feb. 11, 1929. Grounds for annulment are substantially: (a) Infirmity of mind of either spouse; (b) either spouse's consent having been extorted by use of violence or being result of an error in identity; (c) either spouse's impotentia coeundi antecedent to marriage and unknown to other spouse.

Separation, a mensa et thoro, between husband and wife may be granted because of any reasons rendering unbearable their life in common or being prejudicial to education of children. (C. C. 150-151). Separation may also be based on mutual consent to be expressed before court and ratified by same. (C. C. 158). Subsequent cohabitation between parties to a separation voids decree of separation. (C. C. 157).

DOWER AND DOWRY:

Property of spouses acquired after marriage are under a joint ownership (comunione). Income accruing from properties must be used for support of family. (C. C. 177-197). Management of joint property pertains to husband and wife severally. Extraordinary management and disposal of joint ownership pertain to husband and wife jointly. However, an agreement may be entered into between spouses to keep all respective properties separate. In this case neither spouse acquires any rights in property of other, whether personal or real as a result of marriage, except for rights of each of them to a distributive share of estate of deceased spouse. (C. C. 215-219). See topic Descent and Distribution. Husband and wife or a third person may constitute a family patrimony which cannot be alienated and income therefrom goes to family. (C. C. 167-171).

ENVIRONMENT:

In Italian environment legislation general definition of environment is actually missing. Hence, regulation of whole matter can be inferred from individual pieces of legislation which have been enacted to regulate specific fields. It must be pointed out that Ministry of Environment exists since 1986, having been established by Law No. 349 of July 8, 1986 for "the promotion, conservation and recovery of environmental conditions consistent with the basic interests of the public and with the quality of life, for the recovery and the improvement of the national patrimony and the preservation of the national resources from pollution." Ministry of Environment shall, in agreement with Regions, draw up and realize plans to reduce pollution.

Protection of natural environment is granted by Law No. 1497 of June 29, 1939 and by Law No. 394 Dec. 6, 1991 which sets forth basic rules to realize "protected areas", register of which has been laid down by Ministerial Decree of 1991. Several parks and natural reserves exist all over Italian territory. As to protection of flora and fauna several international conventions and EC Directives apply. Same objectives are pursued by sanitary laws of 1934, legislation on electric power plants of 1933 and law on fishing of 1931 as amended in 1955 and 1968, art. 6 whereof prohibits fishing by explosives and electricity and throwing into water of any substance able to benumb or kill fishes or other water animals.

Water pollution is governed by Law No. 319 of May 10, 1976, as amended and supplemented by Laws No. 544 of Aug. 10, 1976 and No. 690 of Oct. 8, 1976; by Legislative Decree No. 133 of Jan. 27, 1992 which implemented several EC Directives (464/76, 176/82, 513/83, 156/84, 491/84, 347/88, 415/90). Law No. 319 of 1976 provides that discharge of any sewage or waste into waters (rivers, lakes, sea, etc.) is subject to prior license by Provincial Authorities and/or by Ministry of Merchant Navy and that discharge waters must not exceed maximum pollution standards laid down in detailed provisions annexed to law, subject to periodic revision. Legislative Decree No. 133 of 1992 provides that discharges of waters of industrial plants and those flowing into public sewer systems must be previously authorized by Province if containing one or more dangerous substances listed in annex to law. Province makes controls over discharges made pursuant to prevailing laws. Infringements of law provisions are punishable by up to three years' imprisonment, while violation of conditions set forth in discharge licenses are punishable by up to two years' imprisonment.

In addition, mention should be made of large number of international Conventions to which Italy is party and which are aimed at establishing international cooperation to prevent water pollution. Among others, Convention for the protection of the Mediterranean Sea signed in Barcelona on Feb. 16, 1976 and ratified by Law Jan. 25, 1979 No. 30, Convention for the prevention of sea pollution due to discharge of waste signed in London, Mexico City, Moscow and Washington on 29th Dec., 1972 and ratified by Law No. 305 of May 2, 1983 and Brussels Convention on liability for damages arising from pollution caused by hydrocarbons signed on Nov. 29, 1969 and ratified by Law Apr. 6, 1977 No. 185. See also topic Shipping.

Air pollution is governed by Law No. 615 of July 13, 1966, known as anti-smog law, which is aimed at preventing and restraining pollution arising from heating systems (see also Decree of the President of the Republic No. 1391 of Dec. 22, 1970), industrial plants (see also Decree of the President of the Republic No. 322 of Apr. 15, 1971) and from circulation of motor vehicles (see also D.P.C.M. of Mar. 28, 1983 setting out maximum limits of polluting elements in air, to be surveyed applying methods provided for by Decree of Ministry of Environment of Apr. 15, 1994). For these purposes, territory of Italy is divided into two controlling zones (A and B) by Decree of the Minister of Health.

As to heating systems, law sets forth certain technical and building prerequisites for those having power exceeding 30 Kcal/h; as to emission from motor vehicles, it is set forth that they may not exceed certain limits set out in applicable rules, while as to industrial plants, it is provided that they must have devices able to reduce dangerous emissions. Pollution deriving from industrial plants is also subject to provisions set forth by Decree of the President of the Republic No. 203 of May 24, 1988 which implemented EC Directives 80/779, 82/884, 84/360, 85/203.

As to protection of ozone layer, mention should be made of Law No. 549 of Dec. 28, 1993 and EC Reg. No. 3093 of Dec. 15, 1994.

Air pollution is also regulated by several international conventions (Geneva Convention on long-distance air pollution through borders, signed on Nov. 13, 1979 and ratified by Law No. 289 of Apr. 27, 1982 and Vienna Convention for the protection of the ozone layer, signed on Mar. 22, 1985 and ratified by Law No. 277 of July 4, 1988) to which Italy is signatory.

Smoking in public places is forbidden pursuant to Law No. 584 of Nov. 11, 1975 and advertising tobacco is also prohibited by Law No. 165 of Apr. 10, 1962.

Acoustic pollution is governed by Law No. 447 of Oct. 26, 1995.

ESCHEAT: See topic Descent and Distribution.

ESTATES: See topic Real Property.

EXCHANGE CONTROL:

See topics Currency; Foreign Investments.

EXECUTIONS:

Titles for execution are (C. C. P. 474): (a) Final decisions and other special orders issued by courts; (b) promissory notes and other payment orders; (c) documents drawn by notary public concerning obligations to pay sums of money. In order to execute above titles it is necessary to obtain a copy of them with a special certification of enforceability, issued by competent court. (C. C. P. 475).

Execution can affect both movable and immovable property of debtor, on basis of a special procedure, which is concluded by public sale of said property (C. C. P. 503) and payment of creditor (C. C. P. 510).

See Topical Index in front part of this volume.

EXECUTORS AND ADMINISTRATORS:

There is nothing in the Italian legislation which corresponds to the American probate court. Estates vest directly into the heirs. There are provisions for guardians, and executors may be named. The succession opens at the moment of decedent's death in the place of his last residence. (C. C. 456).

Testator may name one or more executors. They must be persons capable to contract. Minors are excluded. (C. C. 700). Testator may grant to executors the right to take immediate possession of the estate, but such possession cannot exceed the period of one year from date of executor's acceptance. Court may extend period by one more year only once. If there are infants, absentees or persons deprived of civil rights among heirs, executor, upon notice, must cause property to be sealed and make inventory of same in presence of heirs. At end of administration, executor must account. All expenses in connection with administration of estate are chargeable to estate. (C. C. 703-705-709-712).

The heir entitled to receive the property of a decedent may obtain same from the executor by furnishing him a sum of money sufficient to pay legacies or by furnishing him evidence of having satisfied them as directed by testator in his will. (C. C. 709). Italian death duties are payable on world-wide estate except when deceased at time of death was domiciled abroad. In this case death duties are payable only on such portion of estate, as is located in Italy.

EXEMPTIONS:

The following property is exempt from levy: Beds, wearing-apparel, kitchen utensils, nuptial rings, household movables, dining tables and chairs, wardrobes, cases, except when of great artistic value, refrigerators, heating stoves, gas or electric stoves, washing machines, letters, registers, family papers, books, tools, machines and other trade instruments, fuel and food needed by debtor's family for one month. Salaries can be levied only to extent of one-fifth thereof except in special cases. (C. C. P. 514-515-545).

FIDUCIARIES:

See topics Executors and Administrators; Trusts.

FOREIGN CORPORATIONS:

See topic Corporations and Partnerships, subhead Foreign Corporations.

FOREIGN EXCHANGE:

See topics Currency; Foreign Investments.

FOREIGN INVESTMENTS:

In keeping with deregulatory process in foreign exchange matters, Law No. 43 of Feb. 7, 1956 has been repealed and investments of foreign capital fully liberalised. As a rule, no authorisation of Italian Currency Control Authorities is any longer required for foreign loans, guarantees and foreign trade transactions.

FOREIGN TRADE REGULATIONS:

Italy is a signatory of Convention Relating to a Uniform Law on the International Sale of Goods of Wien of Apr. 11, 1980, which has become effective on Jan. 1, 1988.

See topic Foreign Investments; also topic Currency.

FRAUDS, STATUTE OF:

The following contracts are void unless they are in writing and subscribed by the parties: sales of immovables, contracts of co-ownership of immovables, contracts establishing or cancelling easements and other rights in immovables, leases for more than nine years, settlement agreements, etc. (C.C. 1350).

Oral testimony is in general not sufficient to prove contracts exceeding 5,000 lire in value. (C. C. 2721).

FRAUDULENT SALES AND CONVEYANCES:

Creditors may void assignments made by debtors in order to defraud them. (C. C. 2901).

GARNISHMENT:

A third party is summoned to appear before a praetor and either personally or by attorney must state what goods or money is in his possession or he owes to the defendant. If he refuses to appear or to make any declaration or if objections arise about the latter, the praetor decides within the limit of his jurisdiction or remits the parties to the tribunal for a hearing and decision. In the meanwhile the garnishee is bound to keep the money or the goods in his possession as a judicial trustee. When a third party owes money which may be exacted immediately or within 90 days, the money is, by the praetor, assigned to the creditors. Otherwise the goods or credits are sold in the interest of the creditors by a public judicial auction. (C. C. P. 543-554).

GIFTS:

Donatio inter vivos must be made by a notarial instrument executed in presence of two witnesses and must be accepted by donee in same act or in a subsequent public instrument. (C. C. 782). Small gifts of movables are valid without public instrument, provided there has been actual delivery thereof. Moderate value of gift must be evaluated according to financial situation of donor. (C. C. 783). Gift can be revoked for ingratitude or as result of birth of children to donor. (C. C. 800). Gifts of real property to legal persons are null and void unless authorized by Government. (C. C. 17). See also topic Conflict of Laws.

HOLIDAYS:

Generally, holidays are not computed in the time for payment. For instance if a note falls due on Sunday or on a statutory holiday, payment is due on the next business day. (R. D. Sept. 27, 1941, art. 96).

Following is list of recognized public holidays: All Sundays, Jan. 1, Apr. 25, Labour Day (May 1), Mon. after Easter, Assumption Day (Aug. 15), All Saints' Day (Nov. 1), Conception Day (Dec. 8), Christmas Day, Dec. 26. (Law No. 259 dated May 27, 1949, as am'd by Law No. 54 dated Mar. 5, 1977).

HOMESTEADS:

No exemptions with respect to or restraints on alienation of homesteads.

HUSBAND AND WIFE:

The wife may alienate, donate, collect and transact business without the consent of her husband. (Law July 17, 1919, No. 1176).

Marital property can be governed by a contract (matrimonial articles). Where no such contract is executed as is the prevailing custom in the country, each spouse maintains full control of his/her property acquired prior to marriage, and is not answerable for other spouse's debts or obligations. (C. C. 167-168). See topics Dower and Dowry; Marriage.

IMMIGRATION:

Tourists wishing to stay in Italy for less than three months are not subject to specific permits. For longer stays, permit (sojourn permit) must be obtained from police authorities. Foreigners wishing to work in Italy must also obtain permit from Labor Office and special visa at Italian Consulate before entering Italy. Aliens who are not EU nationals cannot enter Italy for study or work purposes without passport and, if required, visa.

Police shall deny access to aliens who do not prove to have adequate means of support. (Law No. 39, Feb. 28, 1990). D. L. No. 269 of May 17, 1996 (still to be converted into Law) states that aliens who are not EU nationals can obtain sojourn permit of two years-duration, provided they have been offered work for open-ended period.

Italy is signatory of International Convention of Strasbourg dated Feb. 5, 1992 on participation of aliens in local public life, ratified by Law No. 203, Mar. 8, 1994.

See also topic Aliens and European Union Law Digest, topic Internal Market, subheads Free Movement of Workers and Freedom to Provide Services.

INCOME TAX: See topic Taxation.

INFANCY:

Age of majority is 18 for both sexes. (C. C. 2).

A minor is represented jointly by his father and mother or his guardian or by parent who has exclusive parental authority over minor; these have also management of his goods and properties. (C. C. 320).

Extraordinary contracts and transactions concerning minor and his properties are to be authorized by the "Giudice Tutelare" or by Tribunal (C. C. 320) and in absence of authorization may be voided upon request of parents having parental authority, minor or his heirs (C. C. 322).

INHERITANCE TAX: See topic Taxation.

INSOLVENCY: See topic Bankruptcy.

INTEREST:

The legal rate of interest is 10%. Any different rate must be evidenced in writing. (C. C. 1284).

INTESTACY: See topic Descent and Distribution.

JUDGMENT NOTES: See topic Bills and Notes.

JUDGMENTS:

The decisions emanating from a judge in Italy are of three classes:

(a) Ordinanze.—All orders in the course of a suit on the instance made by one party with citation of the other party or ex officio.

(b) Decreti.—Orders made on instance of a party without summoning the other or ex officio.

(c) Sentenze.—Decisions or opinions based upon facts and points of law (judgments). A judgment is "contumaciale" if rendered by default; "parziale" (interlocutory) when given in the course of the suit upon some intermediate object, without finally deciding the suit.

There are not, in the Italian law system, all the specifications and definitions of judgments provided in the American statutes. The decision is given upon the facts and the demands brought by the parties.

Foreign Judgments and Arbitration.—

Awards.—Foreign judgments are granted through summary proceedings (delibatio) given full executive force by the Court of Appeal in whose jurisdiction execution is sought, provided, however, that the following prerequisites are met: (a) That the foreign judgment has been rendered by a court having jurisdiction over the matter according to the principles of the Italian law on jurisdiction; (b) that the foreign law has been complied with with respect to service of summons, and reasonable notice has been given for the defendant to enter an appearance; (c) that the parties appeared before the court in conformity with the foreign law or that default was duly assessed and declared under the provisions of the said law; (d) that the judgment is final according to the foreign law and that it does not conflict with another judgment rendered by an Italian court; (e) that no parallel suit between the same parties instituted prior to the foreign judgment's becoming final is pending before an Italian court; (f) that the judgment is not contrary to Italian public policy.

If the foreign judgment was rendered by default or if it falls under the provisions of Section 395 C. C. P. (fraud, forgery or gross mistake in fact), the Italian court reviews also the merits of the case and, according to its findings, either grants execution or renders an independent judgment.

JUDGMENTS . . . *continued*

Arbitration awards made in foreign countries, when foreign arbitrations are allowed by Italian law, are subject to the same provisions as apply to foreign judgments provided, however, (a) that such awards do not concern disputes that cannot by Italian law be settled by arbitration, and (b) that they comply with requirements of 1958 New York Convention on Arbitration. See topic Arbitration.

Pursuant to enactment of Law No. 218 of May 31, 1995 on conflict of laws, previous regime of exequatur of foreign judgments (see topic Conflict of Laws) will be deeply amended. From Oct. 1, 1996, foreign judgment will be recognized in Italy without resort to any proceedings when: (i) judge who pronounced it could take cognizance of case in accordance with principles on jurisdictional competence obtaining in Italy; (ii) document introducing proceedings was made known to defendant pursuant to provisions of law of place where proceedings were held and essential rights of defense were not infringed; (iii) parties entered appearance in conformity with laws of place of proceedings or their failure to appear was declared in conformity with that law; (iv) judgment became res judicata in accordance with law of place where it was pronounced; (v) it is not contrary to another judgment rendered by Italian judge and which became res judicata; (vi) no proceedings are pending before Italian judge for same matter and between same parties which were initiated prior to foreign proceedings; (vii) its provisions do not produce effects contrary to public policy.

Recognition of foreign arbitration awards is subject to filing of application with Presiding Judge of Court of Appeal of place of residence of other party (or, if such party is not resident of Italy, with Presiding Judge of Rome Court of Appeal) together with certain documents. Foreign award is declared enforceable by decree (against which opposition may be filed) except when: (i) dispute could not be settled by arbitration under Italian law; or (ii) award contains provisions contrary to Italian public policy.

JURISDICTION:

The rules on jurisdiction in civil matters are set out in the Code of Civil Procedure and it is outside the scope of this digest to render any summary thereof. The following rules are, however, of interest to foreigners:

Voluntary Waiver of Italian Jurisdiction.—Jurisdiction of Italian courts can be waived by agreement in favor of foreign jurisdiction provided that such derogation is evidenced in writing and that dispute relates to rights which parties may dispose of. (See 1958 New York Convention on Arbitration, 1968 Brussels Convention on Jurisdiction and Enforcement of Judgments in civil and commercial matters, and 1988 Lugano Convention on jurisdiction and enforcement of judgments in civil and commercial matters.)

Italian Jurisdiction over Foreigners.—A foreign national may properly be summoned before an Italian court if, inter alia: (1) he is a resident of or domiciled in or has a representative in Italy specifically authorized to appear in court or has accepted Italian jurisdiction (provided such acceptance is evidenced in writing or defendant enters appearance without alleging lack in jurisdiction); (2) criteria, set forth in §§2, 3 and 4 of Title II of 1968 Brussels Convention on Jurisdiction and Enforcement of Judgments in civil and commercial matters apply, even if defendant is not domiciled in territory of contracting state, when one of matters covered by scope of convention is involved.

LABOR RELATIONS:

This matter is covered by Arts. 36 to 40 of Constitution (see topic Constitution and Government, subhead Economic Rights), by Book Five of Civil Code, by special laws concerning employment agencies, social insurance, labor trials and assistance, by collective (i.e., trade union) bargaining and by usage; by Law No. 300 of May 20, 1970 as amended new provisions have been enacted with respect to hiring of workers and protection of their freedom and honour. Said provisions also pertain to rights of labor unions and to unions' activities within places of employment.

Categories of Employees.—Employees are classified into executives, intermediates, clerks and workmen. (C.C. 2095).

Hours of work cannot exceed, in general, 48 hours per week. All employees are entitled to one day of holiday per week, and to period of vacation every year. (C.C. 2109).

Wages.—May be determined by time or by job. They cannot be lower than minimum provided by collective bargains.

Labor Unions.—Recognized under Italian Constitution. (art. 39). They may enter collective bargains which, when ratified by Labor Ministry, are compulsory for all employers and employees of category, regardless of their membership in respective associations or unions.

Dismissal.—Subject to notice which varies according to category of employees and duration of employment. (C.C. 2118). However, enterprises, except for few cases, cannot dismiss any of them without "giusta causa" or "giustificato motivo", i.e., specific reason of complaint. (C.C. 2119; Law No. 300 of May 20, 1970 and Law No. 604 of July 15, 1966 as am'd). Reason of complaint must be notified to employee in writing and five days term must be given for employee's answer. Only after receipt of such answer or elapsing of five days term can dismissal be validly notified to employee. If existence of "giusta causa" or "guistificato motivo" is denied by court, employer may be ordered to reinstate dismissed employee, or to pay indemnity. However, for enterprises with more than 15 employees, reinstatement of employee is mandatory, unless employee requests payment of indemnity. Special provisions regulate collective dismissals.

Severance Bonus.—All employees are entitled to severance bonus in proportion to length of employment, payable upon termination of same.

Trial Period.—Valid only if agreed in writing or stated in writing in hiring letter. See also European Union Law Digest, topic Labor Law.

Public Sector.—Labor relations and related matters like, for instance, payment of severance allowances or pensions, are in general differently regulated in public as distinguished from private sector. However, major reform of public sector was started by Legislative Decree No. 29 of Feb. 3, 1993, subsequently amended and followed by several decrees for its implementation. Reform was mainly aimed at abolishing privileges accorded to public employees, and to establish uniform rules for public and private employment even though certain differences will necessarily be maintained, in view of official role played by public employees. New collective bargaining system for public sector has also been established. This reform is still on way to completion.

Strike.—It is right recognized by Constitution and "can be exercised within the limits set forth in the laws which regulate it". (Art. 40 of Constitution). For time being there is no law governing this matter save for Law No. 146 of July 12, 1990 which has introduced some control and regulations for strikes affecting public services deemed to be essential to community.

Pensions.—Public compulsory pension system is funded through mandatory contributions paid by employers and in part, but also through employers, by employees. Upon satisfaction of certain requirements, pensions are payable for old age retirement; or for retirement after certain number of years of employment; or for disability. Social allowance ("pensione sociale") is also payable, upon satisfaction of certain requirements, as extreme remedy, regardless of payment of any kind of contributions by or on behalf of person to whom it is paid. Legislative Decree No. 124 of Apr. 21, 1993 introduced supplemental pension funds which may be established in addition to public compulsory pension system. Major overall reform was approved by Parliament on Aug. 8, 1995 (Law No. 335) by which not only these supplemental pension funds have been implemented but age for retirement has been raised as well. Such reform also introduced new methods of pension computation together with gradual abolition of early retirement.

LANDLORD AND TENANT:

Leases in General.—Term of lease cannot exceed 30 years. Lease agreement need not be in writing unless term exceeds nine years, in which case agreement must be in written form and cannot be asserted against third parties unless recorded in books of Conservatore dei Registri Immobiliari (Recorder of Mortgages). Subleasing is permitted subject to contrary provisions in lease agreement.

Lessor's Main Obligations.—Lessor must: (1) Deliver property to lessee in good state of repair; (2) keep it in condition such as will be suitable for use agreed; (3) ensure its peaceful enjoyment throughout lease.

Lessee's Main Obligations.—Lessee must: (1) Take delivery of property and observe diligence of bonus pater familias in using it for agreed purposes; (2) pay rent on dates agreed; (3) return property to lessor upon termination of lease in same condition as originally delivered, subject to normal wear and tear.

Loss or Deterioration of Property.—Lessee is liable for loss or deterioration of property, even as result of fire, unless he proves that loss or deterioration occurred for reason not imputable to him.

Improvements.—Lessee is not entitled to compensation for his improvements to property unless such improvements were consented to by lessor.

Term.—Leases for specified term terminate at expiration thereof without notice. Leases for indefinite term terminate upon giving by either party to other of notice agreed or required by custom. If upon termination lessee is left in possession of property, lease is deemed to have been renewed for indefinite period.

Special Legislation.—Ordinary rules set forth in Civil Code in respect of leases were affected for many years by special legislation consisting mainly of rental freezing and forceful extension of lease agreements. New legislation (Law No. 392, "The Fair Rental Act") was enacted on July 27, 1978, which substantially affects lease of commercial and residential premises. Main features of new legislation are as follows: (a) Residential leases cannot last less than four years, and commercial leases cannot last less than six years; (b) subject only to certain exceptions and except as otherwise agreed by parties, rent for residential premises must be in annual amount not exceeding 3.85% of current value of premises as determined on basis of certain parameters related mainly to size, location, age and condition of premises; this requirement does not apply to leases entered into after 11th July, 1992 and relating to residential premises built after that date.

Agricultural Leases.—These are governed mainly by special legislation and by Law No. 203 of May 5, 1982. Agricultural leases cannot last less than 15 years and rent cannot exceed amount determined on basis of parameters established from time to time by governmental commission.

LAW REPORTS: See topic Statutes.

LEGISLATURE:

See topic Constitution and Government.

LICENSES:

Among Governmental licenses are: licenses (abilitazioni) for the exercise of intellectual professions (architects, engineers, doctors, etc.); driving licenses; passports; licenses for operating motor vehicles; licenses to carry weapons; licenses to operate bars and places of entertainment; licenses for discharge of sewage waters, etc.

Licenses to operate stores, trade licenses, etc. are issued by local Chambers of Commerce and by municipalities.

LIENS:

The debtor's property is the common security of his creditors, who therefore have an equal right on the same, excepting the case of legitimate preferred or privileged claims. Preference is established by privileges (liens), chattel mortgages and mortgages. (C. C. 2740-2741).

Privileges on movables are: (1) General privilege covering the entire property of the debtor as security for judicial expenses, undertaker's expenses, sickness expenses, wages, professional fees, food, state's credits for taxes etc.; (2) special privilege, covering only determinate movables, as security for custom duties on merchandise, taxes on rent, lease, pledges, hotel bills, carrier's fares etc. (C. C. 2751-2755); (3)

LIENS . . . *continued*
special privilege which may only be taken by banks as security for medium or long term loans and may only cover certain present and future movables (such as existing or future plants and works, raw materials, stock, assets purchased with proceeds of medium or long term loan in respect of which special privilege is intended to be granted, existing or future receivables arising from sales of all assets listed in art. 46 of D.L.L. No. 385 of Sept. 1, 1993).

Privileges on immovables are those arising from judicial expenses (art. 2770); from land tax and other taxes due to the State, to the Provinces, to the Municipalities (art. 2771); from payments due to the State for licences or contributions (art. 2776-2775).

LIMITATION OF ACTIONS:

Actions must be brought within ten years with the following principal exceptions (C. C. 2946-2962):

Five Years.—Actions to recover damages, annuities, incomes for life, rent or interest due; actions on partnership agreements.

Three Years.—Actions by employees and teachers (under salary for a period over a month) professional men or notaries; actions on pledges on ships or promissory notes.

Two Years.—Actions to recover damages arising from the driving of vehicles.

Eighteen Months.—Actions against carriers if shipment was made elsewhere than in Europe.

One Year.—Actions to recover broker's commission; actions against forwarders; actions to recover damages by reason of collision of ships, insurance on shipping or breach of chartering contract; actions against carriers if the shipment was made in Europe.

See also topics Adverse Possession; Bills and Notes.

MARRIAGE:

Both spouses must be 18 years old. But marriage at age of 16 years may be permitted by decree of court.

Marriage can be celebrated only after due publication of the bans by the appropriate officer. (C. C. 93).

Widow may remarry 300 days after death of her husband. The same period must elapse in case of annulment (except for impotence) or dissolution of the marriage. (C. C. 89).

Marriage is prohibited between certain categories of persons, such as: (1) Ascendants and legitimate or natural children; (2) affinities of the same line; (3) lawful or natural brother and sister; (4) affinities of the same degree; (5) uncle and niece or aunt and nephew; (6) an adopter and person adopted or their descendants. (C. C. 87). Marriages indicated Nos. (4) and (5) may be permitted by the appropriate authorities. (C. C. 87).

Marriage can only be proved by certified extract from the records of the Office of Vital Statistics. (C. C. 130).

Marriage by proxy is permitted to soldiers in time of war and also when one of the spouses resides abroad and serious motives exist as assessed by the Attorney General. The proxy must be made by a public instrument. The marriage cannot be celebrated after 180 days have elapsed since issue of the proxy. (C. C. 111).

A foreigner who wants to marry in Italy must present to the Office of Vital Statistics an affidavit from the competent authorities of his country (practically his local consul), stating that according to his law there is no impediment to the marriage. (C. C. 116).

By virtue of the Concordat between the Vatican and Italy, February 11, 1929, as amended on Feb. 18, 1984, marriage may be celebrated by Catholic minister and must be notified to Office of Vital Statistics. Non-Catholic marriages are celebrated by appropriate municipal officers (mayor, etc.). Annulments of matrimony pronounced by ecclesiastical authorities must be approved by decree of Supreme Tribunal of Signature and then filed for execution before court of appeals, which orders recording of judgment in records of Office of Vital Statistics. See topic Divorce and Separation.

MARRIED WOMEN:

See topics Husband and Wife; Marriage.

MONOPOLIES AND RESTRAINTS OF TRADE:

No Italian law made specific provisions for antitrust rules until enactment of Law No. 287 of Oct. 10, 1990 entitled "Rules for the Protection of Competition and Market". Law No. 287 substantially parallels arts. 85 and 86 of EEC Treaty as well as Council's Regulation No. 4064 of Dec. 21, 1989 concerning mergers and acquisitions having community dimension, by prohibiting within Italian domestic market arrangements among undertakings such as may prevent, restrict or alter free competition. It applies both to private and to public undertakings as well as to those with prevalent State participation, which are significant portion of Italian market. See topic Unfair Competition and European Union Law Digest, topic Monopolies and Restraint of Trade.

MORTGAGES:

Mortgages attach to real property only and to registered movables, such as vessels, aircraft and automobiles. There are three kinds of mortgages: legal, judicial and voluntary. (C. C. 2808).

The legal mortgage is created by law and attaches among others to (a) the property sold as security to the seller against the buyer's failure to fulfil the obligations arising from the sale, (b) property of co-heirs, partners and other co-partitioners as security for payment of adjustments required as result of partition; (c) property of criminal defendant, as security to State in respect of expenses of trial, recovery of damages thereof, etc. (C. C. 2817). Judicial mortgage is that which attaches to property of one against whom judgment is rendered. Voluntary mortgage is originated by agreement entered into between parties as evidenced by written instrument. Mortgage must clearly set forth sum of money secured. Priority of mortgage is determined by date of its filing in office of register of mortgages. It continues as lien for 20 years, and unless renewed prior to expiration of this period it loses any priority it might have had on other liens which have attached to property since filing of mortgage. (C. C. 2847). Mortgage can be cancelled by limitation, or release or satisfaction by creditor. Release must be expressly stated in writing by creditor. (C. C. 2878, 2879). See topic Chattel Mortgages.

MOTOR VEHICLES:

There exists a presumption of guilt upon the drivers of motor vehicles as a result of which they are liable for all damages caused by the operation thereof, unless they can prove having done everything possible to avoid causing the damage. Where more than one vehicle is involved in accident, presumption of liability is shared equally among the drivers thereof. The owner of a motor vehicle is liable jointly and severally with the driver unless he can prove that the vehicle was being operated against his will. (C. C. 2054).

Compulsory third-party liability insurance is governed by Law No. 990 of Dec. 24, 1969 as amended, which (a) institutes obligation of insurance for third-party liability upon all owners or users of licenced vehicles, (b) in case of accident grants damaged party direct action against insurer.

Highway Code.—New highway code has been adopted by D.L.L. No. 285 of Apr. 30, 1992 (as am'd) implemented by D.P.R. No. 495 of Dec. 16, 1992.

NEGOTIABLE INSTRUMENTS:

See topic Bills and Notes.

NOTARIES PUBLIC:

In Italy notaries have the qualification and standing of public officials whose organization and functions are similar to those of the French system. A notary must be a University graduate of law in order to be admitted to pass a special competitive examination which is a prerequisite of his subsequent appointment to his office by the appropriate court. The number of notaries is limited and each can practice only within a determined district (Collegio notarile). To be admitted to practice each notary is also required to give a bond. Each notary must keep a record of all instruments drawn before and acknowledged by him and is specifically required to keep the originals of the deeds drawn by him. On his death all documents on file in his office are delivered to a Notarial Archive maintained under State supervision. He issues certified copies of documents on file in his office. He is empowered to take affidavits under oath but only jointly from a minimum of four deponents and as to matters of common knowledge. See also topic Acknowledgments.

PARTNERSHIP:

See topic Corporations and Partnerships.

PATENTS:

Patents are governed by R. D. No. 1127, June 29, 1939, as amended and supplemented by R. D. No. 1411, Aug. 25, 1940 (regarding patents for models and industrial designs) and D. P. R. No. 338 of June 22, 1979. In addition, D.L.L. No. 198 of Mar. 19, 1996 has been enacted to make Italian legislation consistent with compulsory provisions of Trips Agreements.

Objects of the patents are all new inventions, which may have industrial exploitation. (art. 12).

Application for patents must be filed with "Ufficio Italiano Brevetti e Marchi" by inventor or his heirs. (art. 27). Patents have duration of 20 years, from date of application. (art. 4). (Patents applied for prior to Aug. 21, 1964 had duration of 15 years.) All rights relative to and deriving from patents are freely assignable and transmissable. Patent's assignments and licenses must be recorded with "Ufficio Italiano Brevetti e Marchi" (art. 66) to become enforceable against third parties (art. 68).

Italy is member of existing International Convention on patent protection (so-called "Union de Paris," last revised at Stockholm July 14, 1967, ratified under Law No. 424, Apr. 28, 1976) and is signatory of International Convention regarding deposit of models and industrial designs (so-called "Arrangement de La Haye" last revised in Geneva on Aug. 29, 1975 and ratified by Law No. 37, Jan. 25, 1983).

See also European Union Law Digest, topic Patents.

PERPETUITIES:

Generally they are prohibited. When the property is vested, the same goes into the exclusive possession of the other person without any limitation as to disposition. A benefit may be granted to a third person for the usufruct, but only for life, or for 30 years in case of legal person.

PLEDGES: See topic Chattel Mortgages.

POWER OF ATTORNEY:

See topic Principal and Agent.

PRESCRIPTION: See topic Limitation of Actions.

PRINCIPAL AND AGENT:

Mandate (Power of Attorney).—The mandate is a contract whereby one party agrees to effect one or more transactions on behalf of another. (C. C. 1703). The agent or attorney in fact is empowered to carry out not only the transactions which he has been specifically authorized to do but also to perform any other acts that may be required in order to fulfil the mandate. (C. C. 1708). The agent, however, may not exceed the powers conferred upon him by the principal without incurring personal liability, but the principal may subsequently ratify such ultra vires acts.

The agent may, however, depart from the instructions originally received when confronted with unforeseen circumstances as a result of which the approval by the principal of a different course of action may be reasonably expected. (C. C. 1711). The agent may not entrust others with the performance of the mandate without the authority of the principal; if he does, he is answerable for the acts of such substitutes. (C. C.

PRINCIPAL AND AGENT . . . *continued*

1717). A mandate terminates on the following grounds, viz., (a) when its duration has expired or the object for which it was intended has been achieved, (b) when it has been revoked by the principal or renounced by the agent, or (c) when either the principal or the agent has died or become incompetent. (C. C. 1722). In the cases referred to under (b) above, the principal and the agent are respectively liable for damages to the other if the revocation or renunciation of the mandate was unjustified.

A mandate given also in the interest of the agent or of third parties is irrevocable.

The formal requirements of the instrument evidencing the power of attorney must be the same as those that are required for the transactions which are the object of the power of attorney. (C. C. 1392). Powers of attorney executed abroad must be authenticated. See topic Acknowledgments.

Contract of Commission.—When the agent is appointed with the understanding that he must undertake the principal's business under his own name, without using his principal's name, there is the so-called "contratto di commissione." The principal is called "committente" and the agent "commissionario." The effect of this contract is that third persons cannot sue the principal and vice versa. The "committente" must give the "commissionario" the commission (commissione), that is, a percentage on the business transacted. (C. C. 1731-1736).

Sales Agency.—By sales agency agreement, agent undertakes permanently to promote making of contracts for account of principal within specified territory. Exclusivity is implied. Agent is entitled to commission on contracts successfully concluded and to severance allowance upon termination equal to one year of commissions computed on average of last five years. Sales agency agreements may be entered into only with such persons or companies as are only enlisted on register of professional agents ("agenti o rappresentanti di commercio") kept by appropriate Chamber of Commerce. (C.C. 1792-1793, D.L.L. Sept. 10, 1991 No. 30).

REAL PROPERTY:

The Italian Civil Code divides all properties into "beni immobili" (immovables) and "beni mobili" (movables). The former correspond to real property. (C. C. 812-819).

Beni immobili are lands, whatever is erected on land, trees, crops, rivers and springs.

There are no restrictions on foreigners and nonresidents for purchase, ownership or sale of real property.

REPLEVIN:

"Azioni possessorie" are those actions which lie to regain possession not only of movables (personal chattels) but even of immovables, whose possession has been taken unlawfully. The action must be brought within one year from the dispossession. The recovery or the reintegration is ordered by the praetor upon summons, without stay and swiftly against any person even against the owner of the goods. (C. C. 1168-1170).

REPORTS:

There are no official reports in Italy with exception of judgments of Constitutional Court which are published on "Gazzetta Ufficiale della Repubblica Italiana." See topic Constitution and Government, subhead Constitutional Court. Reports are voluntary. Usually jurisprudential reports are contained in reviews edited by well known jurists. Following is a list of most authoritative reports: Il Foro Italiano, La Giurisprudenza Italiana, Il Massimario delle Decisioni Civili della Corte di Cassazione, Il Foro Padano, La Rivista Penale, La Rivista di Diritto Commerciale, La Rivista di Diritto Internazionale.

Laws and statutes are published by Government in "Gazzetta Ufficiale della Repubblica" and in "Raccolta delle Leggi e Decreti della Republica d'Italia."

SALES:

Seller's principal obligations include delivery of goods or other property sold, transfer of all ownership rights, warranties that goods or property have qualities promised or necessary for proper use, and are exempt from defects. (C. C. 1476).

Buyer's principal obligation is payment of price. (C. C. 1498). When defects are discovered, buyer may request either voidance of sale or reduction of price. (C. C. 1492). In case of voidance of sale, seller must return consideration received, as well as interest thereon, and, in any event, buyer is entitled to damages. (C. C. 1494).

Sale may be rescinded on account of "lesione enorme" in price; that is, when price agreed upon is less than one-half equitable price, and in effecting purchase, buyer took advantage of state of need of seller. (C. C. 1448).

Warranties.—Unless parties have expressly agreed otherwise, seller is by law bound to hold purchaser harmless from eviction, in form of redress of damages in addition to reimbursement of purchase price. (C. C. 1483). Purchaser summoned by third party, who claims to have rights with respect to goods sold, must, however, in turn summon seller, otherwise he forfeits warranty.

Seller is furthermore bound to warrant that goods sold are exempt from defects. (C. C. 1490). Purchaser must notify seller of any possible faults within eight days from date of discovery of same, under penalty of forfeiture of claim. Statute of limitation for related action is one year from delivery. (C. C. 1495). Also, such warranty can be contractually excluded, provided there is no bad faith by seller. (C. C. 1490-1491). See also European Union Law Digest, topic Product Liability.

Notices Required.—See subhead Warranties, supra.

Applicable Law.—See topic Contracts.

International Sale of Goods.—United Nations Convention on Contracts for the International Sale of Goods, in force on Jan. 1, 1988. See topic Treaties and Part VII, Selected International Conventions.

SALES AGENCY:

See topic Principal and Agent, subhead Sales Agency.

SEALS:

In instruments, seals of witnesses are not required, except in notarial deeds of gift (atti di donazione).

SECURITIES:

General.—By Law No. 216 of June 7, 1974, as repeatedly amended and supplemented, Stock Exchange and Companies National Commission (Commissione Nazionale per le Società e la Borsa, commonly referred to as "CONSOB") has been established. Its main functions and powers are: to establish stock exchange calendar, to authorize operations of companies engaging in intermediation for trade of securities (SIM, q.v.), to approve systems of quotation and price listing of securities, stocks, bonds, etc., to investigate into companies whose shares are listed on stock exchange and to authorize listing of shares of new companies, to establish regulations for and to authorize public offerings of securities.

Insider Trading.—Persons holding confidential information acquired by reason of their office or profession are prohibited from engaging in securities transactions or recommending them or disclosing information to third parties. (Law No. 157 of May 17, 1991).

Intermediation.—Law No. 1 of Jan. 2, 1991 replaced old system under which securities were traded through intermediation of individual stock exchange brokers, with new system pursuant to which such intermediation can be exercised solely by special companies known as SIMs (Società di Intermediazione Mobiliare) or by authorized banks. Intermediation includes trading, placement, consultancy, management, solicitation and distribution of securities. Hedging and swap transactions must also be channeled through SIMs, authorized banks, or open investment funds, unless they are made as principal with SIMs or authorized banks. SIMs must be organized as "Società per Azioni" or "Società in Accomandita per Azioni" (see topic Corporations and Partnerships) with minimum capital from 600 million to 3 billion lire depending on activities authorized to be carried out (Regulation of Bank of Italy dated July 2, 1991) and are subject to registration in special register under CONSOB's authorization and supervision.

Public Offerings.—Those who wish to proceed through public offering with purchase, sale or offer for subscription and exchange of securities such as shares, debentures whether convertible or not or other instruments or rights or otherwise solicit public savings shall notify CONSOB, publish prospectus and observe rules laid down by Law No. 216 of June 7, 1974, as amended and supplemented, and by CONSOB Regulations. Those who wish to proceed through public offering with sale or offer for subscription, whether or not with view to listing, of securities such as shares, convertible debentures or other instruments or rights entailing acquisition of voting rights shall comply with additional rules set out by Art. 1-8 of Law No. 149 of Feb. 18, 1992 and comply with specific rules and procedures laid down by CONSOB.

Those who wish to purchase or exchange securities listed in stock exchange or traded on so-called "restricted market" such as shares, convertible debentures or other instruments or rights entailing acquisition of voting rights, as well as those who wish to takeover listed company shall comply with additional rules set out by Art. 9-37 of Law No. 149 of Feb. 18, 1992 and comply with specific rules and procedures laid down by CONSOB.

Reporting.—Any acquisition or variation of participation exceeding 2% in company listed on stock exchange or 10% in non-listed company must be reported to CONSOB, Bank of Italy and to company that shares were purchased within 48 hours after completion of transaction. (Law No. 216 of June 7, 1974 as am'd by Law No. 149 of Feb. 18, 1992).

SEPARATION: See topic Divorce and Separation.

SEQUESTRATION:

See topic Attachment and Sequestration.

SHIPPING:

This matter is governed by Code of Navigation, enacted by Royal Decree No. 327, dated Mar. 30, 1942. Specific matters are governed by specific statutes, among which, fisheries, special credit to shipping enterprises, and certain aspects of crew employment contracts and connected topics.

Ships may fly Italian flag, provided they are owned, to an extent of two-thirds at least, by Italian nationals, Italian public bodies or Italian authorized companies. (art. 143, C. N.). Italian ships must be recorded in special registers, kept by appropriate administrative authorities. (art. 146, C. N.). Whenever nationality requirements no longer exist, ship must change its flag (art. 156-162, C. N.) and be stricken off register (art. 163, C. N.). By ruling of Government, foreign companies and natural persons may be authorized in specific instances to own ships flying Italian flag. (art. 144, C. N.). Further provisions are given as to seaworthiness of ship (art. 164-168, C. N.) and documents of navigation (art. 169-178, C. N.). Master of a ship may act as registrar of births, marriages and deaths taking place on board (art. 203, C. N.), subject to particular conditions and regulations.

Title to property of a ship may be acquired by construction (art. 232, C. N.) or contract; more co-proprietors may organize a peculiar kind of unlimited partnership (società di armamento fra i comproprietari) (art. 278-286, C. N.). Specific provisions are laid down in Code for contracts of lease of a ship (art. 376-383, C. N.), affreightment (art. 384-395, C. N.) carriage of persons (art. 396-418, C. N.) and carriage of goods (art. 419-468, C. N.), which must be all in writing. Bills of lading (art. 460, C. N.) are issued either for carriages in a general ship, or under charter-party.

Code further governs general average (art. 469-481, C. N.) collision (art. 482-488, C. N.), and salvage (art. 489-513, C. N.); law of marine insurance is rather different from general provisions on insurance of Civil Code (art. 514-547, C. N.). Ships may be mortgaged (art. 565-577, C. N.), upon filing of deed of mortgages in register where ship is recorded (art. 569, C. N.); liens are granted for specific credits upon ship, freight (art. 552-560, C. N.), and cargo (art. 561-564, C. N.).

See Topical Index in front part of this volume.

SHIPPING . . . *continued*

Pleasure boats are subject to compulsory insurance similar to that provided for vehicles (see topic Motor Vehicles). Law No. 50, dated Feb. 11th, 1971, has introduced a simplified administrative regime concerning construction, registration and operation of pleasure boats. Air navigation is governed by second part of Code. (art. 687-1037, C. N.). (See topic Air Law).

Italy is party to most international conventions on uniform shipping law, including, inter alia: Brussels conventions of 1910 on salvage and collision; Brussels convention of 1924 on bills of lading (and Brussels Protocols of 1968-1979); Brussels convention of 1926 on maritime liens and mortgages; Brussels convention of 1952 relating to arrest of sea-going ships; London convention of 1954 against pollution of hydrocarbons at sea; Geneva convention of 1958 on high seas; Brussels convention of 1969 on civil liability for oil pollution damage (including 1976 Protocol); Brussels convention of 1971 on the establishment of an international fund for compensation for oil pollution damage; L.D.C. Dumping Convention of 1972 on the prevention of the sea pollution caused by dumping; London Convention of 1973 for the prevention of pollution from ships, (including 1978 Protocol); London convention of 1974 on safeguard of human life at sea (including 1978 Protocol); Montego Bay convention of 1982 on the law of the sea; London convention of 1989 on salvage.

STATUTES:

All Italian law is embodied in statutes. The fundamental statutes are the five codes (civil code, code of civil procedure, penal code, code of penal procedure, code of sea and air navigation). In addition, several Unified Texts of law exist which contain a codification of various statutes relating to one specific matter.

All other matters are governed by individual statutes. All statutes are published in the Official Gazette of the Republic.

Laws other than those establishing taxation, approving state budget, amnesties or international treaties may be repealed as a consequence of a referendum.

TAXATION:

Taxes are divided in Italy into two broad categories: direct and indirect taxes.

Direct taxes are regulated by D.P.R. No. 917, Dec. 22, 1986 and are:

Personal Income Tax (IRPEF) is imposed on net income produced in Italy or elsewhere deriving from any sources accruing to any person even if residing outside Italy (nonresidents, however, are taxable only on income produced in Italy or related to property located in Italy).

Certain incomes such as of minor children are deemed to be taxpayer's and are added to latter's income. Taxable income is divided, depending on source, as follows: from immovable property, capital, employment, business enterprises and other sources.

Aggregate taxable income results from sum of net incomes pertaining to each category, after deduction of expenses incurred for production thereof as well as of certain taxes, social security contributions, and few types of other expenses. 27% of amounts paid as premiums on life, accident insurances, and as non-compulsory social security contributions, not to exceed 2,500,000 lire, interest on mortgage loans, not to exceed 7,000,000 lire, medical and funeral expenses, school and university fees may be deducted from tax due.

Relief is granted for support of wife, children and close relatives, by deducting from tax due a fixed amount for each person. Credits are available, to some extent, for taxes paid in foreign country where income is produced. A few types of occasional income (such as proceeds from sale of a going business, value of new shares gratuitously assigned to shareholders, termination of employment severance bonus), are taxed separately at average rate applicable to taxpayer for two preceding years. Tax rates apply to successive income brackets as shown in following table:

Income (million Lire)				*Rate*
Up to	7.2			10%
From	7.2	To	14.4	22%
From	14.4	To	30	27%
From	30	To	60	34%
From	60	To	150	41%
From	150	To	300	46%
Over	300			51%

Legal Entities Income Tax (IRPEG) is imposed on net aggregate income (including capital gains) accruing in Italy or abroad, to corporations and other private or public legal entities, having their registered or administrative office or main business in Italy, and on net aggregate income (including capital gains) accruing in Italy to companies and bodies, whether legal persons or otherwise, not having their registered or administrative office in Italy.

Taxable income is profit resulting from profit and loss account, to be prepared according to rules established by tax laws. Expenses and costs necessary for production of income are deductible.

A five year carry-forward is permitted for losses incurred. Credits are available to some extent for taxes paid in foreign country where income is produced.

IRPEG is levied at rate of 37%. Taxable income of legal entities which do not carry out business activities, is limited to that deriving from immovable properties, interest on capital and occasional business activities.

Financial Law No. 724 of Dec. 23, 1994 reserves presumed income to all companies which are non-operative (so-called "società di comodo") irrespective of whether their operations cease or not, provided that company has less than five employees and less than 800,000,000 lire proceeds. For such companies IRPEG shall be levied on presumed income equal to 2% of company's net assets increased by financings made available by shareholders and third parties and destined to company's fixed assets and, in any case, to not less than 8,000,000 lire. Company may, however, rebut such presumption by proving to tax authorities that, for extraordinary and objective circumstances, actual income has in fact been less.

Local Income Tax (ILOR) is imposed at rate of 16.20% on income of any kind produced in Italy accruing to persons (other than employees or professionals, who are not organized as enterprise), to any type of companies, partnerships, and associations. For tax purposes income accruing from business activities and services carried out abroad, without permanent establishment, is deemed to be produced in Italy. Income deriving from salaries and professional fees from holding of interest in companies or other entities subject to IRPEG (legal entities income tax) and income taxed by flat withholding are not subject to ILOR. Most of rules established for assessment, deductions, allowances, etc. of IRPEG and IRPEF apply also to this tax. Special deduction of up to maximum of 16,000,000 lire is granted to physical persons for income deriving from self-employment, operation of enterprise and land exploitation when taxpayer contributes with his work to production of such income.

Assessment of Direct Taxes.—An annual return on a special form shall be filed each year by taxpayer either between May 1 and June 30 of subsequent year, or one month after deadline for approval of balance sheet (when taxpayer is taxed on balance sheet basis), setting forth annual income and other information on taxpayer's standard of living. Also foreign corporations not having office or permanent establishment in Italy must file their tax return in respect of income produced in Italy or related to property located in Italy, indicating name and address of representative.

Tax returns are subject to review by tax authorities, who have broadest powers of investigation (also with banks, under certain circumstances) and may, whenever appropriate, assess actual income. Authorities' right to assess income taxes is normally prescribed if notice of assessment is not served by Dec. 31, of fifth year following year in which relevant return was submitted (period is six years in case of omitted return). Omission to file tax return or to report all income is punished by fines and, in some instances by penal sanctions.

Withholding of direct taxes is provided, with few exceptions in respect of income deriving from salaries and wages, pensions, compensation for services and brokerage, professional fees, interest and income from capital, dividends and prizes, interest in respect of bonds and similar securities. Withholding on dividends is, as a rule, applicable at rate of 10% on account of tax eventually due, or 32.4% as final tax only when recipient is not resident or is legal entity not subject to IRPEG tax. Foreign recipient is under special circumstances entitled to partial refund of taxes on dividends paid in his country. Pursuant to D.L.L. No. 239, Apr. 1, 1996 payments of interest in respect of bonds, notes, receipts and coupons will not be subject to witholding in Italy to extent that payments are made: (1) to Italian legal entity (with certain exceptions); or (2) to nonresident legal entities and nonresident individuals (provided, inter alia, they are resident in countries with which Italy has entered into anti-double taxation treaty). Any payment of interest in respect of bonds, notes, receipts and coupons made to other entities or individuals not meeting requirements set forth by D.L.L. No. 239 will be subject to witholding tax of 12.50% as final tax or on account of tax eventually due when recipients are public or private entities, different from companies, not carrying out commercial activities.

Generally, tax withheld is credited against ultimate tax liability of recipient.

Tax on Capital Gains.—Gains arising from sale or transfer of shares, bonds, warrants or other securities will be subject to Art. 81 of D.P.R. No. 917, Dec. 22, 1986, as modified by D.L. No. 27, Jan. 28, 1991 (converted into Law No. 102, Mar. 25, 1991). Capital gains (net of capital losses) realized by individual shareholders on shareholdings which exceed 2% of share capital of listed company, 5% of unlisted company, or 10% of entities whose capital is not divided into shares, are subject to tax at flat rate of 25% (analytical taxation). If shareholdings are lower than these percentages, seller or transferor has option to choose, in event sale is implemented through authorized intermediaries, between payment of capital gains tax either on described analytical basis, or on synthetic flat basis (i.e. at rate of 15% to be applied on sale price, regardless of gains or losses).

If seller or transferor is not Italian resident, consideration should be given to applicable double taxation treaty, taking into account that treaties can be derogated from if provisions set forth in Italian domestic legislation are more favorable to taxpayer.

Indirect taxes are levied on transfers of property or wealth as well as on consumption of goods and services. Main indirect taxes are: Added value tax (I. V. A.), inheritance and gift tax, registration tax.

Added Value Tax (I. V. A.)—This tax has replaced turnover tax (I. G. E.) as of Jan. 1, 1973. Tax is levied on proceeds received by business firms, corporations and professional men for goods sold or services rendered within Italy and for goods imported from abroad. Entrepreneur or professional man is allowed to deduct added value tax charged to him by his suppliers from I. V. A., levied on amounts he receives from his clients; therefore, burden of this tax will ultimately rest upon final buyer or client. Ordinary rate of I. V. A. is 19% reduced to 9% or 4% for most food, agricultural products, houses in certain circumstances and other essential items.

I. V. A. is not applicable to transactions of a financial nature, loans made by banks, change of foreign currency, sales of shares and securities, sales of business, leases of immovable property, city transports, hospital services, schooling when recognized by State, etc.

Inheritance and Gift Tax.—All properties, both within State and abroad, belonging to residents or only within State if belonging to nonresidents, are subject to inheritance and gift tax.

This tax is split in two parts. First part affects whole estate. Rates thereof are progressive as follows: up to 250,000,000 lire exempt; from 250,000,000 lire to 350,000,000 lire 3%; from 350,000,000 lire to 500,000,000 lire 7%; from 500,000,000 lire to 800,000,000 lire 10%; from 800,000,000 lire to 1,500,000,000 lire 15%; from 1,500,000,000 lire to 3,000,000,000 lire 22%; over 3,000,000,000 lire, 27%. Second part is payable in addition to first part only when heir or legatee or donee is not straight relative or spouse of deceased or donor and affects single shares devolved. Rates of this part are based on principle that closer kinship between deceased or donor and his successors or donee, smaller tax payable. There are three classes in this part as follows: (1) in favour of brothers and sisters and straight relatives of spouse: up to 100,000,000 lire, exempt; from 100,000,000 lire to 250,000,000 lire, 3%; from 250,000,000 lire to 350,000,000 lire 6%; from 350,000,000 lire to 500,000,000 lire 10%; from 500,000,000 lire to 800,000,000 lire 15%; from 800,000,000 lire to 1,500,000,000 lire 20%; from 1,500,000,000 lire to 3,000,000,000 lire 24%; over 3,000,000,000 lire, 25%. (2) Between other relatives up to fourth degree and spouse's

See Topical Index in front part of this volume.

TAXATION . . . *continued*
relatives up to third degree for amounts as above: 3%, 5%, 9%, 13%, 19%, 24%, 26%, 27%. (3) Between other, more distant relatives and strangers: for amounts as above, 6%, 8%, 12%, 18%, 23%, 28%, 31%, 33%.

See subhead Double Taxation, infra.

Registration Tax.—This tax applies to all deeds and contracts made in Italy having a civil, commercial and judicial nature, to verbal agreements of lease of immovables located in State and of transfers or lease of business located in State, to incorporations or transfers of foreign companies in State and capital increases thereof, as well as to deeds made abroad, concerning transfer of immovable property, real estate or other rights and leases of immovables located in State. This tax may be proportional or in a fixed amount according to nature of act involved. If act refers to goods or services already subject to I. V. A., this tax will be applied in fixed amount.

Proportional rates, which are based on "value" (which in many instances is subject to assessment by tax authorities) of contract, vary from minimum of 0.50% to maximum of 15% according to type of contract.

Tax on Capital Gain from Transfers of Real Property (INVIM).—This tax affects land as well as buildings and is levied on basis of capital gain realised through transfers of real property or in case of donation or inheritance on basis of appreciation in value from purchase to gift or inheritance. Rates vary from 3% to 30%. This tax also applies, every ten years, to appreciation in value of immovables owned by real estate companies. Following imposition by D.L.L. No. 504, Dec. 30, 1992 of new Municipal Tax (I.C.I.) on immovable property (see below), INVIM has been abolished effective from Jan. 1, 1993. However, INVIM will still be payable until Jan. 1, 2003 in respect of capital gains which have accrued up to Dec. 31, 1992.

Tax on Immovable Property Imposed by Municipalities (ICI).—This tax affects immovable property located in State, including property which is instrumental to exercise of enterprise or which is object of business activity of enterprise. ICI is due by owner, or holder of usufruct, use or habitation right, even if nonresident. It is fixed and imposed by Municipalities where real property is located and is levied on basis of value of real property as resulting from cadastral registers. Rates vary from 0.4% to 0.7%. Amounts payable for ICI are not deductible from taxpayer's income for purposes of determining taxable base for IRPEF and IRPEG.

Double Taxation.—There are several anti-double taxation treaties between Italy and other countries. Treaties between U.S. and Italy cover income (Law No. 763 of Dec. 11, 1985) and inheritance (Law No. 943 of July 19, 1956) taxes. Treaty does not apply to local income tax (see subhead Direct Taxes, catchline Local Income Tax (ILOR), supra). Under this Treaty, individual, corporation or other entity of one of contracting States shall not be subject to taxation by other contracting State in respect of its industrial and commercial profits unless it is engaged in trade or business in such other State through permanent establishment situated therein. Inter alia Treaty broadly provides, subject to certain qualifications, that royalties, accrued from sources within one contracting State to resident or corporation or other entity of other contracting State are exempt from taxation in former State. Income from real property is taxable in State where such property is situated. Compensation for personal services including salaries (other than governmental salaries) and professional fees are, subject to certain qualifications, taxable in State where such services are rendered.

TRADEMARKS:

Trademarks are governed by R.D. No. 929, June 21, 1942 as amended and supplemented by D.L.L. 480\1992, implementing EC Directive of Dec. 21, 1988.

All new words, designs, sounds and/or emblems which may be able to identify products or goods on market may be registered as trademarks and are protected upon such registration for renewable period of ten years from date of application. Under certain conditions, de facto use of unregistered trademark is also protected.

Applications for registration must be filed with "Ufficio Italiano Brevetti e Marchi" (art. 25) by person who has right to obtain it or by his heirs. Trademarks must be used actually within five years from their registration, and their use may not be suspended for period of more than five years, without losing protection. (art. 42).

To become enforceable against third parties, assignments and licences of trademarks must be recorded with "Ufficio Italiano Brevetti e Marchi". (art. 51).

Italy is signatory of existing International Convention on trademarks protection (so-called "Union de Paris", last revised at Stockholm, July 14, 1967, ratified by Law No. 424, Apr. 28, 1976), of "Madrid Arrangement for the International Registration of Trademarks" (last revised at Madrid, June 27, 1989, and ratified by Law No. 169, Mar. 12, 1996).

EU trademarks are governed by Reg. No. 40\1994, Dec. 20, 1993.

TREATIES:

Apart from the strictly political treaties, Italy is a signatory of many multilateral conventions: Convention for protection of children, 1902; Convention concerning marriage and divorce, 1902; Warsaw Convention on Air Transport, 1929; Universal Copyright Convention, 1952; Convention concerning industrial property, 1883; Convention concerning trademarks, 1891; Convention concerning bills of exchange and promissory notes, 1930; Convention concerning the recognition and enforcement of foreign arbitral awards, 1958; Convention concerning the law applicable to trusts and their recognition, 1985; Convention concerning conciliation and arbitration, 1994; etc.

There are also many bilateral agreements of commerce and navigation inter alia with U.S., Austria, Belgium, France, Germany, Spain, Sweden, Switzerland, U.S.S.R.

International Sale of Goods.—United Nations Convention on Contracts for the International Sale of Goods, in force on Jan. 1, 1988. See topic Sales and Part VI, Selected International Conventions.

See also topics Foreign Trade Regulations; Shipping; Taxation; Arbitration.

See also Selected International Conventions section and European Union Law Digest.

TRUSTS:

A trust, in the technical sense and in the manner contemplated in America, does not exist in the Italian legal system because a beneficial title different from the legal title is unknown to Italian law. By different means the same results as those of American trusts can be often obtained, for anybody may appoint an attorney or an administrator for dispositions directed to benefit a third person. But the main difficulties arise in the cases of trusts established by will and testament. Testator cannot, by will, leave his estate to a person, directing him to transfer the property to a third person except where such directions are made in respect of sons of testator's sons or of brothers and sisters or of charitable bodies.

The deceased may appoint by will an administrator to take care of the estate left to his children during their minority, but the property remains irrevocably in the children's possession from the date of their father's death, and the administrator cannot alienate any part of the estate without a special authorization of the court.

Italy is also party, to Convention of the Hague of July 1, 1985, on law applicable and recognition of trusts, which has come into effect on Jan. 1, 1992 by Law No. 364 of Oct. 9, 1989.

UNFAIR COMPETITION:

The law on unfair competition (concorrenza sleale) is primarily based on judicial decisions interpreting the Code. Under §§2598 to 2601 C. C., the use of another firm's distinctive name, the use of symbols for the purpose of confusing customers, spreading rumors as to the quality or value of a competitor's goods, or the doing of any act not in conformity with the normal ethical standards of business is prohibited. A cease and desist order, as well as damages, may be obtained by the successful plaintiff. See topic Trademarks and European Union Law Digest, topic Monopolies and Restraint of Trade.

WILLS:

A will cannot be made by one who has not attained majority (18 years) or is not mentally competent (C. C. 591), or by one who was for any reason incapable of understanding or intending at moment when he made will.

A will may be holographic or notarial and in this latter case it may be secret or public. Finally a will may be special.

(a) A holographic will must be entirely handwritten, dated and signed by the testator. (C. C. 602).

(b) A public will is drawn before a notary public in the presence of two witnesses. (C. C. 603).

(c) A secret will may be written by the testator or by a third person. If it is written by the testator, it must be signed at the bottom. If written partly or wholly by third persons or mechanically, it must be signed by the testator at the bottom and initialed on every page. In either case it must be sealed up and handed to a notary in the presence of two witnesses. The notary draws up a statement to the effect that the will has been handed to him, and such a statement must be signed by the testator, the witnesses and the notary. (C. C. 604-605).

(d) Special wills are those made during prevalence of contagious diseases or in case of public calamity or accident. Such wills become void after three months have lapsed since cessation of the extraordinary circumstances under which they were made. (C. C. 609). Special wills are also those made on the high seas or on board an aircraft (C. C. 611-616) and those made by soldiers in zones of war operations. Such wills become void when three months have lapsed since the testator has returned to a place where an ordinary will can be drawn up. (C. C. 618).

Whoever is in possession of a holographic will must deposit the same with a notary public for publication as soon as he knows that the testator is dead. The publication is made by the notary, who draws up a certificate thereof in the presence of two witnesses. (C. C. 620).

A secret will must be opened and published by the notary as soon as he receives notice of the death of the testator, in the presence of two witnesses. (C. C. 621).

The notary who has received a public will must communicate the existence of the same to the heirs as soon as he has knowledge of the testator's death; the same communication to heirs must be done by the notary after the publication of an holographic or secret will. (C. C. 623).

Wills executed by two or more persons in the same instrument in favor of a third person or for mutual benefit (survivorship clause) are prohibited. (C. C. 589). See topic Descent and Distribution.

JAPAN LAW DIGEST

(The following is a list of all Topics, including cross-references, covered in this Digest.)

JAPAN LAW DIGEST

Revised for 1997 edition by

BLAKEMORE & MITSUKI, of the Tokyo Bar.

(Abbreviations used are: B. L. for Bankruptcy Law; C. for Constitution; C. C. for Civil Code; C. L. for Copyright Law; C. C. P. for Code of Civil Procedures; C. E. L. for Civil Execution Law; Com. C. for Commercial Code; C. T. for Code of Trusts; C.P.E.L. for Civil Preliminary Execution Law; C. T. L. for Court Law; F. E. C. L. for Foreign Exchange and Foreign Trade Control Law; L. B. N. for Law of Bills and Notes; L. C. for Law of Checks; L. C. L. for Limited Corporation Law; P. L. for Patent Law; T. L. for Trademark Law.)

ABSENTEES:

Subject to such restrictions as may be imposed under foreign exchange controls, nonresidents are permitted to own and utilize property to same degree as residents. Authority may be exercised by proper power of attorney.

Care of property, if not specifically entrusted by voluntary act of owner, can be directed by court order. (C. C. 25). Persons assuming control over property without legal duty are held responsible to strict standards of conduct. (C. C. 697).

Service of process may be made on agents in respect to matters within their scope of authority.

Escheat follows in event of absence of known heirs of sufficiently close relationship to permit inheritance and of eligible persons having special connections with decedent. (C. C. 959).

ACKNOWLEDGMENTS:

Formality of acknowledgment is not, as a rule, essential to validity of an instrument. However, acknowledgment of notary authenticates the performance of a legal action and the identity of acting parties, and thereby affords to an otherwise private instrument a presumption of genuineness which is similar to that of an official document. Acknowledgment of original articles of incorporation in case of organization of joint stock corporations and limited corporations is made mandatory by statute. (Com. C. 167; L. C. L. 5). Frequently instruments to be recorded are both drafted and certified by notaries. See topic Notaries Public.

At present time, acknowledgments for use in U.S. or by U.S. citizens or corporations may be taken before American consular officials and certain designated Army officers. Acknowledgments for use in other countries usually may be taken by diplomatic representatives of those countries who are accredited to Japanese government.

Japan is party to Convention Abolishing the Requirement of Legalisation for Foreign Public Documents. (See topic Treaties.)

ACTIONS:

Service of process is not essential for establishment of jurisdiction and is in all cases court's responsibility. Service can be made by registered mail, by bailiff's personal service or deposit at home or office, by publication, and through Japanese consular officials in foreign country. (C. C. P. 160 through 180). Evidence may be obtained from overseas by letters rogatory or by means of testimony taken before Japanese consular officials commissioned by court. (C. C. P. 264). See topic Depositions. Documents prepared by governmental officials within scope of office, even officials of foreign government, are presumed to be authentic, but authenticity of private documents, including depositions taken by private attorneys, must be proved. (C. C. P. 323, 324). Foreign law is presumed to be within court's knowledge. In case of uncertainty court obtains expert testimony or makes inquiry directly of public or private organization competent to respond. (C. C. P. 262, 310). Japan is party to certain conventions relating to civil procedures. (See topic Treaties.)

See also topic Bills and Notes.

ADMINISTRATION:

See topic Executors and Administrators.

ADOPTION:

Ordinary Adoption.—Any person attaining majority may adopt another person, provided person to be adopted is not lineal ascendant or older than adopting party. (C. C. 792, 793). Married person may adopt or be adopted either jointly with spouse or acting alone but in general with consent of spouse. (C.C. 796). However, married person may not adopt minor except jointly with spouse. (C. C. 795). Consent of Family Court is generally required in adoption of minors. (C. C. 798). Adoption may be dissolved through judicial dissolution (1) Upon grounds of malicious desertion, (2) where it is unknown whether party to adoption is dead or alive for three years or more or (3) for any other reason making difficult continuation of adoptive relationship. (C. C. 814). Adoption may also be dissolved upon mutual consent of parties.

Special Adoption.—Family Court may create special adoptive relationship if deemed especially necessary for benefit of person to be adopted where special certain circumstances supporting such adoption exist, after taking into consideration outcome of period of custody by adopting party of person to be adopted, which period shall be, in general, six months or more. (C. C. 817-2, 817-7, 817-8). Other requirements are: (1) Adopting party shall be married person (C. C. 817-3) 25 years of age or older (C. C. 817-4), and in general (2) husband and wife shall jointly adopt (C. C. 817-3), (3) person to be adopted shall be under six years of age (C. C. 817-5) and (4) natural parents of person to be adopted shall give consent to adoption (C. C. 817-6). Once special adoptive relationship is created, legal family relationship between adopted person and natural parents and other relatives by blood ceases to exist. (C. C. 817-9). Special adoptive relationship may be dissolved only by Family Court if deemed especially necessary for benefit of adopted person where certain conditions warranting such dissolution are met. (C. C. 817-10).

Applicable Law.—In case of adoption in Japan involving divergent nationalities, requisites for adoption and its dissolution are determined by law of country of adopting party. If law of country of adopted party requires consent of that party or third party, permission of public authorities or other disposition for adoption, such requirements must also be met. (Horei 20).

AGENCY: See Principal and Agent.

ALIENS:

Supported by strong constitutional guarantees, an alien is now afforded virtually all rights of a Japanese except those of political nature. In general aliens are permitted to own property and to contract without governmental approvals but cannot practice professions of quasi-public character. Aliens must register at municipal offices having jurisdiction over their places of stay within 90 days from entry. (Alien Registration Law 3). Entrance into country is subject to governmental approval except for members of U.S. Armed Forces, U.N.'s agencies, diplomats, consuls and their dependents, and public officials of foreign governments and international organizations recognized by Japan. Alien has equal access to courts, but in case of certain kinds of tort actions against Japanese government, he is equally treated only if country of his nationality extends same right to Japanese nationals. (State Tort Claims Act 6). By virtue of Security Treaty between U.S. and Japan and Administrative Agreement in implementation thereof, alien members of U.S. Armed Forces, including civilian components, together with dependents, are subject to criminal jurisdiction of Japanese courts under certain circumstances, and to civil jurisdiction of Japanese courts in all instances apart from execution of judgments of Japanese courts rendered on claims arising out of performance of official duty.

Acquisitions of real estate or rights related thereto by nonresident aliens involve prior notification, except for those for office, factory, residence or certain other uses. In case of certain extraordinary circumstances such acquisition may be made subject to approval. (F.E.C.L. 20 through 23).

Corporations owned or controlled by aliens are regarded as "foreign investors" for purpose of inward direct investments including acquisition of shares. (F.E.C.L. 26). See topic Foreign Investments. See also topic Corporations, subhead Foreign Corporations.

ASSIGNMENTS:

Assignment of property right, whether real or personal property, may be made by means of agreement between parties. (C. C. 176). However, in order for assignment to be effective against third persons, assignment of immovables must be recorded, and those of movables must be accompanied by delivery. (C. C. 177, 178). Obligations may be assigned if their character renders assignment possible, unless parties have expressed contrary intention. (C. C. 466). Specifically named obligee must give notice of assignment to obligor or secure his consent in order to assert assignment against either obligor or other third party. Notice of assignment or consent to assignment must be in writing and bear officially confirmed date in order to assert assignment against third party other than obligor. (C. C. 467).

ASSIGNMENTS FOR BENEFIT OF CREDITORS:

See topic Bankruptcy.

ASSOCIATIONS: See topic Corporations.

ATTACHMENT AND INJUNCTIONS:

Attachment is available before judgment (or even before institution of an action) upon proof (a) of existence of creditor's claim for money, and (b) that satisfaction of judgment will be impossible or extremely difficult unless attachment occurs. (C. P. E. L. 20). Attachment normally is issued ex parte without examination of or notice to debtor and as general rule requires posting by creditor of bond to secure debtor. (C. P. E. L. 14). Attachment order may be attacked by debtor on ground that it was issued without any reason, that it has been rendered unnecessary by change in circumstances, and that action on principal claim was not instituted within proper and prescribed period of time. (C. P. E. L. 26, 37, 38). Attachment may be dissolved by deposit of prescribed amount in cash. (C. P. E. L. 22). Same general procedures apply to injunctions.

ATTORNEYS AND COUNSELORS:

Jurisdiction over Admissions.—Practicing attorney in Japan (Bengoshi) must be admitted by Japan Federation of Bar Associations (J.F.B.A., Nichibenren) and local bar association. Foreign attorney who has practiced law in his/her own country for five or more years may be admitted by J.F.B.A. to practice only his/her country's law in Japan.

Eligibility.—Graduates of Legal Training and Research Institute (L.T.R.I.), and others qualified under Art. 5 of Japanese Practicing Attorneys Act (J.P.A.A.), such as former judges of Supreme Court, professors of law faculties who have served for five years or longer and ones who, after passing Bar Examination, served as legal officers or prosecutors for five years or longer, are eligible to be admitted by J.F.B.A. (J.P.A.A. 4, 5, 6). One who has been sentenced to imprisonment or other severe criminal punishment, has been found guilty by Court of Impeachment of Judges, has been disciplined by J.F.B.A. or other professional associations, or has been found to be

See Topical Index in front part of this volume.

ATTORNEYS AND COUNSELORS . . . *continued*
incompetent or quasi-incompetent, or bankrupt, cannot be admitted by J.F.B.A. (J.P.A.A. 6).

Educational Requirements.—Except for those qualified under Art. 5 of J.P.A.A., it is necessary to be graduate of L.T.R.I. Only successful candidates of uniform Bar Examination are admitted to L.T.R.I.

Examination.—Uniform Bar Examination is held once a year by National Bar Examination Administration Commission under supervision of Minister of Justice.

License.—When practicing lawyer is first admitted by J.F.B.A., registration fee of 60,000 yen must be paid. There are annual membership fees for J.F.B.A. and local bar association membership fees must be paid as long as one is practicing law. Amount of fees varies from case to case.

Disbarment or Suspension.—In case of violation of J.P.A.A. disciplinary committee of J.F.B.A. will decide whether to give warning or to prohibit lawyer from practicing law for maximum of two year term, or to have lawyer removed from J.F.B.A. and to strike his/her name from J.F.B.A. register, depending upon violation of J.P.A.A. (J.P.A.A. 56, 57).

Unauthorized practice of law for compensation is prohibited and subject to criminal punishment. (J.P.A.A. 72, 73, 74).

Professional Association (Corporation).—There is no statutory authorization for formation by lawyers of professional associations or corporations.

Exclusion.—Testimony of attorney regarding privileged communications with client is excluded.

Contact Address and Phone Number of J.F.B.A.—1-1-1 Kasumigaseki, Chiyoda-ku, Tokyo 100, Japan, phone number 81-3-3580-9841, Fax number 81-3-3580-2866. There are 52 local bar associations. Each local bar association's contact address and phone number can be obtained by contacting J.F.B.A.

BANKRUPTCY:

Term "insolvency" as used in Bankruptcy Law has restricted meaning of simply debtor's inability to make payments. (B. L. 126). Joint stock company's inability to pay its debts without resulting great difficulty in continuing its business also forms basis for institution of extensive reorganization processes under Company Reorganization Law. (Company Reorganization Law 30). Fear of insolvency on reasonable ground can be basis for still other reorganization procedures under Commercial Code. (Com. C. 381).

Petitions.—Bankruptcy proceedings are instituted through petition to district court having jurisdiction over principal place of business or legal residence of debtor who may be either natural person or juridical person. (B. L. 105). Petitions may be made by creditors or by debtor himself. (B. L. 132). In case of legal person its director or liquidator also may make petition. (B. L. 133). Ground for bankruptcy is debtor's inability to make payments, or (in case of legal person) excess of liabilities over assets. (B. L. 126, 127). Debtor's suspension of payments on debts is treated as prima facie evidence of inability to make payments.

Administration.—Upon adjudication of bankruptcy, court appoints a receiver, orders report of claims and requires assembly of creditors. (B. L. 142). Assembly of creditors may appoint advisers to receiver, grant allowances to debtor, make decisions regarding continuation of business operations, and consent to important acts in liquidation of bankrupt estate. (B. L. 170, 194). As consequence of adjudication of bankruptcy, bankrupt person is immediately deprived of control over such of his property as is subject to legal attachment. (B. L. 6, 7).

Outstanding Obligations.—Obligations of bankrupt to third parties become due upon adjudication of bankruptcy. (B. L. 17). If performance of both parties to outstanding bilateral contract has not been completed, receiver may rescind such contract or demand performance by opposite party after performing bankrupt's obligation. (B. L. 59). Opposite party to bilateral contracts may call on receiver to make election regarding performance or rescission, and in event of failure of answer within reasonable period, rescission is presumed. (B. L. 59).

Powers of Receiver.—Power to administer and dispose of bankrupt estate belongs exclusively to receiver. (B. L. 7). Receiver represents bankrupt estate in litigation. (B. L. 162). Application may be made to him for restoration of property of third persons and also for payment of preferential claims against bankrupt estate in general or existing in regard to specific items of property included therein. He also may institute action to disapprove legal acts of debtor taken before issuance of adjudication of bankruptcy which were intended to prejudice creditors. (B. L. 72).

Preferential Payment.—Lien holders, mortgagees or pledgees on specific property included in bankrupt estate are entitled to be satisfied separately from such property outside receiver's control and to participate in bankruptcy proceedings only to extent of any deficiency. (B. L. 92 through 96). Persons whose own property has come under receiver's control as bankrupt estate can regain such property from his control. (B. L. 87 through 91). Certain tax liabilities of bankrupt person can be paid by receiver outside of bankruptcy proceedings. (B. L. 47, 49). After these preferential treatments and payments are completed, lien holders on general property of bankrupt person receive distributions preferentially from bankrupt estate ahead of ordinary creditors. (B. L. 39). Receiver may deny and restore to bankruptcy estate repayments by bankrupt persons to creditors at certain time prior to occurrence of insolvency or application filed for bankruptcy or those simply prior to adjudication of bankruptcy if mala fide on part of repaid creditor is proven to affect adversely other creditors. (B. L. 72 et seq.).

Illegal Preferences.—See subheads Powers of Receiver and Preferential Payment, supra.

Termination.—Normally bankruptcy proceedings are terminated with distribution of assets to creditors. Distributions may be intermediate, final or supplemental. (B. L. 256 et seq.). However, decree in bankruptcy may be dissolved with consent of all creditors. (B. L. 347 et seq.). Bankruptcy proceedings also may be ended upon judicial finding that value of bankrupt estate is not sufficient to repay costs of liquidation. (B. L. 353, 145). When value of bankrupt estate is less than 1,000,000 yen a simplified form of procedure called "petty bankruptcy" may be followed in which court decisions replace many actions of assembly of creditors. (B. L. 358 through 366).

Disabilities of Bankrupt Persons.—A person against whom an adjudication of bankruptcy is outstanding is subject to certain losses of rights, such as right to hold public office, and to practice law. However, these disabilities may be removed by court decree of rehabilitation in event of full payment of indebtedness, decision of discharge, or lapse of ten years without being punished for fraudulent bankruptcy. (B. L. 366-21, 367).

Composition.—Compulsory composition is provided whereby debtors may apply to a court with alternative plan for continuation of business and thereby halt bankruptcy proceeding. (B. L. 290 et seq.). Decisions for compulsory composition made by majority of creditors present at assembly of creditors holding three-fourths of total obligations of debtor are binding upon other creditors. (B. L. 306, also see 332).

Reorganization.—A reorganization proceeding permits creditors and shareholders of joint stock corporations to present plan for reorganization of company to court for approval. Decisions made by majority (usually from one-half to four-fifths) of each class of creditors, shareholders or mortgagors are binding upon all persons within that class. (Company Reorganization Law, also see Com. C. 381 through 403).

Foreigners.—Bankruptcy procedures apply uniformly to Japanese and foreigners, provided that a Japanese is afforded reciprocal treatment by law of country of foreigner concerned. Effect of bankruptcy adjudications is limited to property found in Japan, both in cases of Japanese and foreigners. (B. L. 2, 3).

BILLS AND NOTES:

In Japan bills (Tegata) are classified as bills of exchange (Kawase Tegata) and promissory notes (Yakusoku Tegata) and are distinguished from checks (Kogitte). Japanese law in regard to bills, notes and checks is in conformity with Geneva International Conventions on Uniform Law of 1930 and 1931.

Bills of Exchange.—

Essential provisions of a bill of exchange are: (1) Expression "bill of exchange" in body of instrument, (2) unconditional order for payment of fixed sum of money, (3) name of drawee, (4) designation of maturity, (5) designation of place for payment, (6) name of payee, (7) date and place where bill of exchange is drawn, and (8) signature of drawer. Lack of any of above-mentioned elements is fatal except that: (a) Payment is deemed to be at sight when no maturity is designated, (b) if no place of payment is designated but name of drawee is accompanied by place, such place is, unless otherwise indicated, deemed to be place of payment and residence of drawee, and (c) place of issue is deemed to be stated address of drawer. Bill of exchange may be payable to drawer, his order, or for account of third person. (L. B. N. 1 through 3).

Endorsements may be either in blank or contain a designation. They must be unconditional. Even though not drawn to order, every bill of exchange may be transferred by endorsement. Acceptance and payment is guaranteed by endorsement. (L. B. N. 11 through 13, 15).

Presentment for acceptance of bills payable at expiration of fixed period after sight must occur within one year after date of issuance. Presentment must be at residence of drawee and at a time prescribed by drawer or endorsers. (L. B. N. 21 through 23).

Acceptance may occur simply from signature of drawee on face of instrument. When bill is payable at expiration of fixed period after sight, acceptance must be dated. Acceptance may be for part of sum payable, but must be unconditional. Third party may guarantee payment of bill—act accomplished simply by his signature on face of instrument. (L. B. N. 25, 26, 30, 31).

Payment of bill of exchange may be: (1) At sight, (2) at expiration of fixed period after sight, (3) expiration of fixed period after issue date, and (4) at fixed date. (L. B. N. 33). Bill of exchange at sight is payable on presentment and presentment must occur within one year of date of issuance. (L. B. N. 34). Holder of bill of exchange payable on fixed date or at expiration of fixed period after issue date or sight must present for payment within two business days following due date. (L. B. N. 38). There are no days of grace. (L. B. N. 74). Unless specially provided payment is to be in currency of country where payment will occur, although rate of exchange and similar matters may be specified. (L. B. N. 41). Words prevail over figures in event of discrepancy as to amount, and as between more than one amount in either figures or words, smallest sum is deemed sum payable. (L. B. N. 6).

Recourse may be had by holder of bill of exchange against endorsers, drawer and other parties if payment has not been made at maturity. Holder has similar right before maturity: (1) If there has been total or partial refusal of acceptance, (2) if drawee has become bankrupt, or (3) if drawer (of nonacceptable bill) has become bankrupt. (L. B. N. 43). Default must be established through an officially authenticated instrument. Except for bill of exchange payable at sight, protest for nonpayment must come within two business days after bill is payable. (L. B. N. 44). Holder must give notice of nonacceptance or nonpayment within four business days, and endorser must relay information to person from whom he received bill within two business days following date of notice. (L. B. N. 45).

Liability of persons signing bill is not affected by invalidity of one or more signatures of other persons thereon. (L. B. N. 7). Person signing bill as agent is personally bound if lacking in authority. (L. B. N. 8). Both acceptance and payment are guaranteed by drawer, although by specific provision in bill the former responsibility may be escaped. (L. B. N. 9).

All drawers, acceptors, endorsers and guarantors are jointly and severally liable to holder who may proceed individually or collectively in any order. (L. B. N. 47). Holder's recovery includes amount of unpaid bill, interest at 6% per annum from maturity, and expenses. (L. B. N. 48, 49). Upon expiration of time limits set for presentment for protest or presentment for payment, holder loses rights of recourse against all parties other than acceptor. (L. B. N. 53). Presentment prevented by vis major or legal prohibition may be made at later date after termination of cause for delay. (L. B. N. 54).

Capacity of person to bind himself is determined by law of the country of his nationality, except that person lacking capacity nevertheless is bound if his signature is affixed in a country wherein he would have capacity. (L. B. N. 88). Acts performed by

See Topical Index in front part of this volume.

BILLS AND NOTES . . . *continued*
Japanese in foreign countries are valid as against other Japanese if in accordance with Japanese law. (L. B. N. 89). Laws of foreign country will govern in regard to obligations of acceptor as well as formalities for protest, when location of payment or act of protest is in that foreign country. (L. B. N. 90, 93).

Claims of holder arising out of bill of exchange expire three years from date of maturity as against acceptor, and one year from date of protest as against endorsers and drawer. Claims of endorser against other endorsers expire six months from date of payment or suit by endorsee. (L. B. N. 70).

Promissory Notes.—Essential provisions of a promissory note are: (1) Expression "promissory note" in body of instrument, (2) unconditional promise to pay fixed sum of money, (3) designation of maturity, (4) designation of place for payment, (5) name of payee, (6) date and place of issuance, (7) signature of maker. (L. B. N. 75). As in case of bills of exchange, lack of essential elements renders instrument invalid save in certain exceptional cases. (L. B. N. 76). Rules governing bills of exchange are made applicable by analogy to promissory notes. (L. B. N. 77).

Checks.—Essential provisions of a check are: (1) Expression "check" in body of instrument, (2) unconditional order to pay fixed sum of money, (3) name of drawee, (4) designation of place of payment, (5) date and place where check is drawn, and (6) signature of drawer. (L. C. 1). Lack of enumerated elements renders check invalid, except in instances similar to those governing bills of exchange. (L. C. 2). Check must be drawn on banker holding funds at disposal of drawer. (L. C. 3). Check is payable at sight. (L. C. 28). It must be presented for payment within ten days after issuance if in country of issuance, within 20 days if place of issue and payment are in same continent, and 70 days when places are in different continents. (L. C. 29). Crossed check may be paid by drawee only to banker or to customer of drawee. (L. C. 38).

Claims of holder against endorsers, drawer and other parties to check expire six months from last day of period in which presentment must be made, and claims of parties to check other than holder, such as endorsers, against other parties, such as other endorsers, expire six months from date of payment by or suit against such claimants. (L. C. 51). There is no acceptance. (L. C. 4). Subject to above-mentioned differences, provisions of law governing checks are similar to those pertaining to bills of exchange.

Special simplified civil procedures are provided for certain actions arising out of bills, notes and checks. (C. C. P. 444 through 463). Evidence in special procedures is exclusively documentary, except for testimony of parties regarding authenticity of instrument and fact of its presentation. In these procedures, defendant's cross-action is not allowed. Plaintiff may shift to ordinary procedures at any time during trial. No appeal is allowed from final judgment that issues under special procedures, but losing party has opportunity to have case retried under ordinary procedures. A monetary judgment on bill, note or check, whether issuing after ordinary or special procedures, always is accompanied by provisional execution order. (C. C. P. 196). Actions may be brought in court having geographical jurisdiction over place of payment designated on instrument, in addition to court of jurisdiction over place where obligor resides or has an office. (C. C. P. 2, 4, 6).

Revenue stamps must be affixed to bills and notes (but not checks) having face amount of 100,000 yen or more by drawer. Stamp tax rate varies with face amount. If amounts are stated in foreign currency, flat rate of 200 yen is applied. Failure to affix revenue stamps does not affect validity of documents, but does expose obligated party to criminal sanctions.

Choice of law rules are provided in Law of Bills and Notes and Law of Checks. (L. B. N. 88 through 94; L. C. 76 through 81). Form of any legal act in respect to bill and note is governed by law of place where instrument signed. (L. B. N. 89; L. C. 78). Validity of acceptance of bills of exchange or issuance of promissory notes is governed by law of place where instruments are payable. (L. B. N. 90). Validity of other acts in respect to bill or note, such as endorsement is governed by law of place of signature affixed. (L. B. N. 90; L. C. 79).

CHATTEL MORTGAGES: See topic Mortgages.

COMMERCIAL REGISTER: See topic Records.

CONCILIATION:

Japanese jurisprudence possesses a highly developed system of conciliation whereby disputes are settled under court supervision but through nonjudicial methods. Parties may request application of conciliation procedures prior to institution of formal actions, and court also may order resort to conciliation at any time in course of formal proceedings, when it appears that such procedures might result in proper settlement. (Civil Conciliation Law 2, 20). Conciliation procedures are simple and relatively inexpensive. Conciliation panel consisting of judge and two or more individuals of good standing hears contentions of both sides and explores possibility of settlement. (Civil Conciliation Law 5 through 7). When agreement satisfactory to both parties is obtained, it has binding and enforceable effect which is similar to compromise accepted by court. (Civil Conciliation Law 16; C. C. P. 203). Conciliation is widely used.

CONSTITUTION AND GOVERNMENT:

Japan was under occupation of Allied Powers from Sept. 2, 1945 to Apr. 28, 1952, during which time a new Japanese Constitution replaced Meiji Constitution of 1889. New Constitution retains institution of monarchy, but defines imperial role as devoid of governmental power except on purely ceremonial matters. (C. 4, 7). A Diet of two houses is declared to be supreme organ of state and sole law-making agency. (C. 41, 42). This Diet selects from among its membership Prime Minister who heads and names Cabinet. (C. 66, 67). Majority of Cabinet in turn must be named from Diet members. (C. 68). Cabinet resigns upon vote of nonconfidence or of rejection of confidence of House of Representatives, except when House is dissolved within ten days thereafter. (C. 69). Independent judiciary headed by Supreme Court is given power of judicial review over legislative and executive acts. (C. 76, 81). Selections to Supreme Court are made by Cabinet, but appointees are subject to recall vote of public at next general election and at ten-year intervals. (C. 6, 79). Elaborate bill of rights is contained in Constitution, as well as unique provision renouncing war. (C. 9, 10 through 40).

At present, the Japanese Cabinet consists of a Prime Minister, Ministers of Justice, Foreign Affairs, Finance, Education, Welfare, Agriculture, Forestry and Fisheries, International Trade and Industry, Transportation, Posts and Telecommunications, Labor, Construction, Home Affairs and various Ministers of State. Japan is divided into prefectures which in turn are subdivided into municipalities. Both prefectures and municipalities possess certain powers of self-government which are determined by Diet. (C. 92, 94).

CONTRACTS:

A contract is a legal act which creates an obligation by agreement of two or more persons. Both natural and legal persons may be parties to contract. A number of standard forms of contracts, namely, gift, sale, exchange, loan for consumption, loan for use, lease, employment, contract for specific work, mandate, bailment, partnership, life annuity and compromise, are governed by special provisions of Civil Code. Number of standard forms of commercial transactions, namely, sale, account current, undisclosed association, brokerage, commission agency, forwarding agency, carriage, deposit and insurance, are governed by special provisions of Commercial Code. However, these provisions may be modified by agreement of parties to contract.

Formation.—A contract arises through acceptance of an offer. An offer which recites a fixed time for acceptance cannot be withdrawn before termination of stated period. (C. C. 521). Dispatch of acceptance gives rise to contract, as also does occurrence of act which can be deemed declaration of intention to accept offer. (C. C. 526). Conditional acceptance of contract offer constitutes both refusal and counter-offer. (C. C. 528). Certain special provisions are applied to commercial transactions. (Com. C. 507 through 509).

Effect.—Either party to bilateral contract may refuse performance until other party tenders performance, except in situations where obligation to perform has not yet accrued. (C. C. 533). Once created, rights of third parties cannot be extinguished by actions taken by original parties to contract. (C. C. 538). In case of contract for establishment or transfer of real right in specified property, when property is lost or damaged for reasons or cannot be performed for intervening cause not attributable to assignor, loss falls on assignee. (C. C. 534).

Rescission.—Right of rescission may arise out of terms of contract, or by operation of law. Normally its exercise is preceded by a formal demand for performance made on delinquent party. (C. C. 541). Rescission serves to restore matters to state in which they were prior to formation of contract. (C. C. 545). Usually it is effected by declaration of intention to opposite party, although this formality is not required in all cases. (C. C. 540). Rescission does not preclude a demand for damages. (C. C. 545). Each of multiple persons who constitute a single party to a contract must join in notice of rescission and each must receive notice of rescission from opposite party. (C. C. 544).

Excuses for Nonperformance.—With exception of monetary obligation, nonperformance for reasons not attributable to responsibility of obligor, such as force majeure, can be invoked as a defense for nonperformance. (C. C. 415, 419). Unless specifically prohibited by law, such as that of contract for carriage by sea, parties can limit responsibility for nonperformance by special agreement. (C. C. 420; Com. C. 739; International Carriage of Goods by Sea Act 15).

Applicable Law.—Validity of contract is determined by law of place expressly or implicitly chosen by parties. In event of no choice governing law is that of place of act of creation of contractual relationship. (Horei 7).

Government Contracts.—In order to produce budgetary conformity, certain special statutory requirements exist for contracts to which government, either national or prefectural, is a party. These provisions generally take form of regulations of actions of government contracting officials, such as requiring competitive bidding, use of written contracts and inclusion therein of certain matters required by law, plus performance bonds of at least 10% of amount of contract, which they may waive under certain circumstances. (National Accounting Law 29 through 29-12).

Distributorships, Dealerships and Franchises.—There are no special rules applicable to formation and termination of these types of business arrangements. However, there are several judicial precedents where court decided in favor of distributor by restricting termination by seller without cause, although no rules or criteria for such decisions have been established.

CONVEYANCES: See topic Deeds.

COPYRIGHT:

Creation.—Copyright is afforded automatically without application or grant from government upon creation of object in literary, scientific, artistic or musical field except for certain categories of materials whose free republication is in public interest (as for example, statutes, orders or ordinances of public authorities, official government publications, court decisions, etc.). (C. L. 2, 10, 13). Included are choreography, pantomimes, architectural works, maps, motion pictures, photographs and computer programs. Compilation and data base works can also be copyrighted. Similar to European concept of droit moral, moral rights are afforded to author to protect him from unauthorized use of his work not released to public. (C. L. 18). Moral rights also cover rights to identify author and rights against unauthorized alteration of copyrighted objects and their titles. (C. L. 19, 20). Copyright holder has rights to copy, perform in public, broadcast, recite in public, exhibit, screen, translate and adapt copyrighted objects and to request payment for private use of copyrighted objects by digital audio or visual machines. (C. L. 21 through 27). Transfer or pledge of copyright takes no effect against third persons unless registered at Ministry of Education or agent designated by Ministry of Education for computer program. (C. L. 77).

Neighboring rights are afforded to performers, phonographic record producers and broadcasters. Performer's rights include exclusive rights to record (both audio and video) or broadcast performance, to lease to public commercial phonographic records

See Topical Index in front part of this volume.

COPYRIGHT . . . *continued*

of performance which were first sold no more than 12 months before, to request payment for use of commercial phonographic records of performance for broadcast and to request payment for lease to public of commercial phonographic records of performance after 12 months of first sale. (C. L. 91 through 95-2). Phonographic record producer's rights include rights to reproduce phonographic records, to lease to public commercial phonographic records which he produced and which were first placed on sale no more than one year before, to request payment for use of commercial phonographic records for broadcast and to request payment for lease to public of commercial phonographic records after one year of first sale. (C. L. 96 through 97-2). Broadcaster's rights include rights to reproduce or rebroadcast programs, and to transmit or communicate television programs to public using facilities to enlarge images. (C. L. 98 through 100).

Duration.—Copyright protection continues for lifetime of author and for 50 years after his death, 50 years after publication if published under a nom de plume or 50 years after publication for works published as product of organization. Copyright protection for motion pictures and photographs lasts 50 years after publication. (C. L. 51 through 55). Moral rights are exercisable only by author. (C. L. 59). However, immediate family of deceased author may petition for injunction or for appropriate measures to recover honor of deceased against infringer of deceased author's moral rights. (C. L. 60, 116). Duration of neighboring rights is 50 years from Jan. 1 next following first performance, first phonographic recording or first broadcasting, as case may be. (C. L. 101). Periods of duration of copyright count from Jan. 1 next following death, creation or publication, as case may be. (C. L. 57).

Publication.—Copyright holder may create publication right, which is exclusive right to print and distribute original text. Unless otherwise agreed, holder of publication rights must publish within six months after receipt of manuscript and must keep in print if such would be normal in publishing business. (C. L. 81). If holder of publication rights fails to abide by these obligations, copyright holder may rescind publication rights. (C. L. 84). Unless otherwise provided, publication right expires after three years from first publication. (C. L. 83). Publication right is not effective against third persons unless registered at Director-General of the Agency for Cultural Affairs. (C. L. 88).

Limited assignment of portions of general copyright is possible. (C. L. 61). Thus, all or each of attributes of general copyright such as reproduction rights, translation rights, performance rights, etc. may be assigned. (C. L. 21 through 28, 61, 63).

Infringement of copyright not only gives rise to rights to injunction and damages, but also, if infringement is of moral rights, rights to petition for appropriate measures for recovery of author's honor accrue. (C. L. 112, 115 through 118). Infringement also constitutes criminal offense. (C. L. 119, et seq.).

Copyright Treaties.—Japan is party to Berne Convention, UNESCO Treaty, Convention for Protection of Producers of Phonograms against Unauthorized Duplication of Their Phonograms and International Convention for the Protection of Performers, Producers of Phonograms and Broadcasting Organizations.

CORPORATIONS:

Legal personality may be acquired by means of procedures outlined in Civil Code, Commercial Code, or special acts of legislation, as well as by means of special legislative charter. Although legal persons are classified in many ways such as private and public, or for profit and for public welfare, all are grouped together for convenience under title "corporations."

Legal Persons Under the Civil Code.—Civil Code recognizes two categories of legal persons (often termed juridical persons) which are organized in public interest—associations (Shadan) and foundations (Zaidan). Association is formed by a group of persons, and is governed by articles of association prepared at time of its organization. (C. C. 37). Foundation is aggregation of property which has been set aside and dedicated to particular purpose through act of endowment. (C. C. 39). Both associations and foundations must be organized with approval of competent authorities in connection with religious worship, teaching, charity, art, or some similar public purpose. (C. C. 34). Operations of both are subject to supervision of competent authorities, and legal existence of both may be terminated upon completion of dissolution which may be caused upon occurrence of any event specified in articles of association or endowment, or bankruptcy or annulment of approval for incorporation, or fulfillment of objective provided in articles of association or endowment or impossibility of such fulfillment. Associations may also be dissolved by resolution of general assembly of members or when no member remains. (C. C. 67, 68). Normally general assembly of members of an association elects directors while directorate of a foundation may either be self-perpetuating (if so provided in original act of endowment) or appointed by court. (C. C. 37, 40). Both associations and foundations can act only through legally authorized officials, and both are liable for damages for acts committed by officials in course of conduct of their duties. (C. C. 44, 53). If any damage has been done to other persons by act beyond scope of business, members and directors having supported resolution for such matter and directors and other representatives having carried it out shall be jointly and severally liable for damage compensation (C. C. 44).

Business corporations are legal persons organized under Commercial Code and related acts.

Three classes of business corporations or companies are provided by Commercial Code—partnership corporations (Gomei Kaisha), limited partnership corporations (Goshi Kaisha) and joint stock corporations (Kabushiki Kaisha). A special act provides for a limited corporation (Yugen Kaisha) which closely resembles joint stock corporation. (L. C. L.). Each may be organized without special act of government approval through compliance with legal conditions of formation and subsequent registration. All business corporations must establish principal office and register that fact as well as subsequent creation of branch offices. All four varieties of business corporations are subject to judicial dissolution, and as legal persons, all may sue and be sued.

Partnership corporations (Gomei Kaisha) are fundamentally different from Anglo-American partnerships in that new and independent legal personality results from this form of commercial association. (Com. C. 53, 54). Partnership corporation is formed through articles of incorporation which state, among other items, value of contribution to be made by each member of corporation and are signed by each member. (Com. C. 63). Although one or more managers may be appointed through majority vote of members, each member (unless otherwise provided in articles of incorporation) has both right and duty to administer any of affairs of corporation. (Com. C. 70). All members must consent to alteration of articles of incorporation and to transfer of interest of any individual members. (Com. C. 72, 73). Individual members are prohibited from conducting business which competes with that of corporation or assuming official position in a competing concern unless with consent of other members of corporation. (Com. C. 74). All members are jointly and severally liable for obligations of firm in event of insufficiency of assets. (Com. C. 80). Admission to corporation is accompanied by liability for all obligations incurred prior thereto. (Com. C. 82). Members may withdraw at end of any business year with six-month prior notice from partnership corporation whose term is for indefinite period or for life, or from any partnership corporation at any time if unavoidable reasons exist. (Com. C. 84). Membership may be terminated upon consent of all members, or upon death, bankruptcy, adjudication of incompetency and expulsion of individual concerned. (Com. C. 85). Member's failure of contribution constitutes a reason for expulsion. Expulsion requires judicial process. (Com. C. 86). Withdrawing members are entitled to compensation for services rendered and contributions made to partnership corporation. (Com. C. 89). Partnership corporation itself may be dissolved upon expiration of term or happening of any other cause of dissolution provided in articles of incorporation, consent of all members, amalgamation, diminishing of membership to one, bankruptcy or court order. (Com. C. 94). Liquidation is accomplished through legally outlined procedures and under court supervision. (Com. C. 116 et seq.).

Limited Partnership Corporations (Goshi Kaisha).—Limited partnership corporation resembles partnership corporation in most respects but differs in that members may have either unlimited or limited liability for corporate obligations. (Com. C. 146). Liability status of each member must be specified in articles of incorporation, and members with limited liability must make their contributions in form of money or property. (Com. C. 148, 150). Members with unlimited liability have rights and duties of representation similar to those of members of partnership corporation, while member with limited liability, although unable to act on behalf of corporation, is entitled to inspect and supervise. (Com. C. 151, 153). Termination of membership by all members of either category is ground for dissolution. (Com. C. 162).

Joint Stock Corporations (Kabushiki Kaisha).—This form of corporate organization is most common in business circles and one which most closely resembles Anglo-American stock company or business corporation.

Incorporation requires formulation by one or more promoters of articles of incorporation which provide business object, trade name, number of shares authorized to be issued, number of shares to be issued at time of incorporation (not less than 1/4 of number of shares authorized to be issued) and number of these shares categorized by par value and nonpar value shares, par value per share of par value shares, seat of principal office, manner of giving corporation's public notices, and name and residence of each promoter. (Com. C. 165, 166). Par value per share of par value shares and issue price per share of nonpar value shares to be issued at time of incorporation must be not less than 50,000 yen. (Com. C. 166, 168-3). Other matters, such as corporation's duration, special benefits to promoters, contribution in kind, property to be taken over upon incorporation, various classes of shares (preferred, common or deferred and voting or nonvoting), etc., are optional, but not effective unless stated in articles of incorporation. (Com. C. 94, 168, 222). Acknowledgment of articles of incorporation by notary public is mandatory. (Com. C. 167). Capitalization must be ten million yen or over. (Com. C. 168-4). Incorporation occurs upon registration which follows inaugural meeting of shareholders. (Com. C. 188). Liability of promoters resulting from acting as promoters in course of incorporation may continue after incorporation. (Com. C. 193). Only promoters are permitted to make payment for stock by property contributions subject to court confirmation of its delivery and valuation. However, if value of contribution is not more than one-fifth of capital and not more than five million yen, or if contribution is marketable securities or real estate evaluated by licensed real estate appraiser and certified by attorney, court confirmation is not required. (Com. C. 168, 172, 173, 181).

Shares may be par value or nonpar value shares, which may in general be exchanged with each other by resolution of board of directors, or upon request of stockholders unless prohibited by articles of incorporation. (Com. C. 199, 213). Shares must be nonbearer form. Unless otherwise provided by articles of incorporation, shareholders who do not wish to possess certificates may require corporation not to issue certificates for their shares. If in such case share certificates have already been issued, such certificates must be returned to corporation. (Com. C. 226-2). Shares are freely transferable, but articles of incorporation may make transfer of shares subject to board of directors' consent. When such consent is not given to specifically proposed transfer, transfer is consummated by procedures provided by Commercial Code. (Com. C. 204, 204-2 through 204-5). Transfer of shares may be effected simply by delivering share certificates, but cannot take effect against corporation unless registered in stockholders' registry. (Com. C. 205, 206). Corporation cannot acquire its own shares nor hold as pledgee its own shares representing more than 1/20 of all the then outstanding shares, and joint stock or limited corporation with more than 50% of its shares or contributions directly or indirectly held by corporation cannot acquire shares of such parent corporation, other than in exceptional circumstances wherein corporation must dispose of them immediately or at proper time. (Com. C. 210, 211-2). In 1994, three exceptional circumstances in which corporation may acquire its own shares were added: (1) in case of transfer to its employees (Com. C. 210-2); (2) in case of redemption (Com. C. 212-2, 290); and (3) in case of request for board of director's consent for transfer of shares (Com. C. 210-2, 212-2, 204-3-2, and 210-3).

Holder of fractions of share constituting 1/100 of share or its multiples ("fractional share") is registered in fractional stockholders' registry unless he desires not to be so registered. Holder of fractional shares is entitled to certain limited rights as provided by Commercial Code or certain other limited rights if so provided in articles of incorporation. In no event can voting right at general assembly of stockholders be granted. (Com. C. 230-2 through 230-9). Fractional shares emerge in cases of issuance of new shares to shareholders, consolidation or split of shares by corporation of which

CORPORATIONS . . . *continued*

par value per share of shares or net assets per share on latest balance is 50,000 yen or more.

New shares within number of shares authorized to be issued may be issued at any time by resolution of board of directors or, if articles of incorporation so provided, by stockholders. Issuance of new shares to nonstockholders at particularly favorable price is subject to special approval of stockholders. (Com. C. 280-2). Subscription rights to new shares may be made transferable if subscription warrants are issued. (Com. C. 280-2, 280-6-3).

Stockholder's Liability.—Once subscription price is paid, subscriber becomes stockholder, and, together with successors or assignees, is not personally liable for debts of corporation. (Com. C. 200).

General assembly of stockholders which is principal organ of corporation is held once each fiscal term in regular sessions and upon call in extraordinary sessions. (Com. C. 234, 235). At regular sessions this assembly approves balance sheet, income statement and disposition of profit and loss, except that in case of corporation having stated capital of 500,000,000 yen or more, or having total liabilities of 20,000,000,000 yen or more on latest balance sheet ("large size corporation"), balance sheet and income statement, when approved by board of directors, board of auditors and accountant auditor, are not required to be approved by general assembly of stockholders. (Com. C. 283; Law for Special Measures to Commercial Code in respect of Auditing, etc. of Joint Stock Corporations 16). Each stockholder has one vote for each share. However, corporation is not entitled to vote in respect of its own shares, and neither joint stock corporation nor limited corporation more than 25% of whose outstanding shares or contribution is directly or indirectly held by another joint stock corporation is entitled to vote in respect of its shares in such other joint stock corporation. (Com. C. 241). Stockholders holding two or more shares on behalf of others may cast split votes by giving prior notice. (Com. C. 239-2).

Quorum for general assembly cannot be less than one-third of outstanding shares for election of directors or auditors. (Com. C. 256-2, 280). In case of amendment of articles of incorporation, capital decrease, issuance of new shares to nonstockholders at particularly favorable price, issuance of bonds convertible into stock on particularly favorable conversion terms to nonstockholders, merger, transfer of whole or important part of corporation's business or acquisition of whole of business of another corporation, and certain other major resolutions, quorum is more than one-half of outstanding shares in absence of stricter requirement in articles of incorporation. (Com. C. 375, 280-2, 341-2, 408, 245, 343). Quorum for other situations may be provided specially in articles of incorporation. In absence of special provisions in Commercial Code or articles of incorporation, quorum for resolutions is more than one-half of outstanding shares. Except for certain major resolutions which by statute require two-thirds majority vote, resolutions are adopted by simple majority of votes cast, in absence of special provision in articles of incorporation. (Com. C. 239).

Minority stockholders holding not less than 3% of outstanding shares for preceding six months are entitled to call general assembly of stockholders, with court permission. (Com. C. 237). Stockholders holding not less than 1% of outstanding shares or 300 shares for preceding six months may propose matters to be discussed at general assembly of stockholders. (Com. C. 232-2).

Board of directors takes charge of execution of business operation and supervises performance by individual director of his duties. (Com. C. 260).

Directors must be three or more in number, elected at stockholders' assembly, may hold office for term not in excess of two years (with certain exceptions), and must appoint one or more representative directors from among themselves to represent corporation. (Com. C. 255, 256, 261). Corporation is bound as against third persons acting in good faith for acts done by director with title of president, vice president, senior managing director or managing director even though he is not representative director. (Com. C. 262). Cumulative voting is available for election of two or more directors unless otherwise provided in articles of incorporation. (Com. C. 256-3).

Auditors (Kansayaku) who should not be confused with independent public accountants must be at least one in number, are elected at stockholders' assembly and hold office for term ending upon adjournment of regular assembly of stockholders for last settlement of accounts within three years after assumption of office. (Com. C. 273). Auditors of corporations (excluding those whose stated capital does not exceed 100,000,000 yen and total liabilities are less than 20,000,000,000 yen on latest balance sheet) are entitled to attend board of directors' meetings, have supervisory authority over performance of duties by directors and have duty to examine business and financial condition of corporation and its subsidiaries and financial statements and business report to be submitted to stockholders' assembly and also to report on them. (Com. C. 260-3, 274, 274-3, 275). Large size corporation must have three or more auditors at least one of whom must serve on full-time basis and, at least one of whom must be individual who has not served as director or been employed as manager or in another position by company or subsidiary during past five years, and in addition, accountant auditor (Kaikei Kansanin), who must be independent certified public accountant and be elected at stockholders' assembly. (Law for Special Measures to Commercial Code in respect of Auditing, etc. of Joint Stock Corporations 2, 3, 18). Accountant auditors investigate financial statements of corporations and submit report thereon to directors and board of auditors. (Law for Special Measures to Commercial Code in respect of Auditing, etc. of Joint Stock Corporations 13).

Bonds (straight, convertible or secured, or with warrants to subscribe for new shares) may be issued by, in principle, resolution of board of directors. (Com. C. 296). There is no limitation on issuance of bonds. Company that issues bonds must nominate commissioned company for bond holders ("shasaikanrikaisha"), to handle receipt of payments, etc. and to protect rights and interests of bond holders. Bonds with warrants to subscribe for new shares may be issued if issue price of shares to be issued upon exercise of such warrants does not exceed principal amount of such bonds. Such warrants may be transferred either with or separately from such bonds, according to their terms. (Com. C. 341-8). Assembly of bondholders may adopt resolutions, with court approval, on matters not provided by statute but which prejudice their interests. (Com. C. 319).

Statutory reserves consist of capital surplus reserve and earned surplus reserve. Capital surplus reserve includes portion of issue price not to be credited against stated capital. (Com. C. 288-2). Such portion is limited to excess over par value or (in case of issue of nonpar value shares at time of incorporation) excess over 50,000 yen and in no event can exceed one-half of issue price. (Com. C. 284-2). At least one-tenth of distributions paid from profits for each fiscal term and interim cash distribution must be set aside as statutory earned surplus until accumulated amount reaches one-fourth of stated capital. (Com. C. 288). Statutory reserves can be used only for replenishing of deficiencies in stated capital or for capital increase by transfer to stated capital. (Com. C. 289, 293-3).

Dividends for fiscal term can be declared only to extent of amount of net assets, less following: (i) Stated capital, (ii) statutory reserves (capital surplus reserve and earned surplus reserve), (iii) amount of earned surplus reserve required to be retained for fiscal term, (iv) excess, if any, of unamortized deferred accounts for business commencement or for research and development over aggregate of amounts referred to in (ii) and (iii) and (v) total amounts entered on assets side of balance sheet regarding treasury shares acquired and held by corporation. (Com. C. 290). In addition, corporation which closes its accounts only once a year may, if articles of incorporation so provide and certain other conditions are met, make interim cash distribution to stockholders by resolution of board of directors. In case of interim cash distribution, net assets are calculated by reference to latest balance sheet, but adjusted to reflect any subsequent dividend and earned surplus reserve set aside in respect thereof and in respect of proposed interim cash distribution, provided that interim cash distribution may not be made where risk exists that at end of that current fiscal term there might not be any excess of net assets over aggregate amount referred to in (i), (ii), (iii), (iv) and (v) above. (Com. C. 293-5).

Amendment of articles of incorporation, except as hereinbelow mentioned, requires two-thirds majority vote of stockholders present at general assembly of stockholders. (Com. C. 343). If preferred stock is outstanding, special consent of general assembly of preferred stockholders also is required for amendments to articles of incorporation which are adverse to their preferred stockholder interests. (Com. C. 345). In order to amend articles of incorporation so as to require board of directors' consent to transfer of shares by stockholder, affirmative vote is required by majority of stockholders who hold not less than two-thirds of outstanding shares, either voting or nonvoting. (Com. C. 348).

Reorganization processes may occur under special legislation or under Commercial Code provisions. Under Commercial Code, reorganization may be ordered by court if there appears danger of insolvency. This order may be issued upon application of director or auditor of corporation or its major creditor or minority stockholder. (Com. C. 381). In course of reorganization court may intervene and impose restrictions. (Com. C. 386).

Dissolution may occur because of expiration of time or any other event provided in articles of incorporation, amalgamation, bankruptcy, court order of dissolution, and decision of general assembly of stockholders. (Com. C. 404). Except in case of amalgamation and bankruptcy, dissolution is followed by liquidation in which court may take special steps to protect interests of creditors and stockholders. (Com. C. 417 et seq.).

"Unit" Share System.—Listed corporation existing as of Oct. 1, 1982 is required to adopt "unit" share system if par value per share of its shares or its net assets per share on latest balance sheet is less than 50,000 yen. Number of unit shares is that obtained by dividing 50,000 yen by par value, or such other number as corporation may determine by its articles of incorporation as far as statutory requirement is met. Unlisted corporation existing as of Oct. 1, 1982 may adopt this system determining in its articles of incorporation number of unit shares in compliance with same requirement. Certificates for shares representing fractions of one unit ("unit fractional shares") are issued only in certain limited circumstances, wherein unit fractional shares are transferable. Holder of unit fractional shares may require corporation to purchase such shares and purchase is consummated by procedures provided by Supplementary Provisions to Law Partially Amending Commercial Code, etc. He is entitled to exercise certain limited rights which do not include voting rights. At date yet to be specified by law, one unit of shares wll be consolidated into one share by operation of law. (Supplementary Provisions to Law Partially Amending Commercial Code, etc., 15, 16, 18, 19).

Limited corporations (Yugen Kaisha) resemble private companies or family corporations in English law. A limited corporation is created through execution of articles of incorporation which state object, trade name, capitalization, value of unit of contribution, name and residence of each member, number of units of contribution made by each member and principal office. Total number of members may not exceed 50. (L. C. L. 6, 8). Capitalization must be 3,000,000 yen or over. (L. C. L. 9). Each unit of contribution must be at least 50,000 yen, and transfer of unit by member to nonmember requires resolution of approval at general meeting. (L. C. L. 10, 19). Directors are elected at general meeting, and represent corporation in business matters. Directors are prohibited from engaging in competitive business activity. (L. C. L. 11, 27, 29, 32; Com. C. 254). In most respects powers and pattern of organization of limited corporation are similar to that of joint stock corporation.

Other Legal Persons.—Certain acts of special legislation afford legal personality to associations and organizations as distinct from provisions of Civil or Commercial Codes. Trade associations and labor unions are examples. In addition, public law provides that many public agencies, such as municipalities, have legal entity. In a few instances Diet has enacted special charters for public corporations such as The Bank of Japan.

Subsidiaries of Foreign Corporation.—See topic Foreign Investments.

Foreign Corporations.—Except for treaty provisions, the only foreign bodies recognized as legal persons in Japan are states, administrative divisions of states, and commercial companies. (C. C. 36). However, a recognized foreign legal person enjoys same rights and capacities as similar legal person does under Japanese law, unless treaty or law provisions are to contrary. (C. C. 2, 36). At present time such treaty or law provisions are nonexistent.

Foreign corporation doing business in Japan upon a continuing basis must register its place of business, name and address of its legal representative, law under which it has been established and various related facts following procedures similar to those used by Japanese corporations in registering branch offices. (Com. C. 479). Until such

CORPORATIONS . . . *continued*
registration has been accomplished, foreign corporation is not authorized to engage in business, and any person violating such provisions is jointly liable with corporation. (Com. C. 481). Failure to engage in business within one year, engaging in business for illegal purpose and continuing violations of criminal laws in defiance of warnings issued by Minister of Justice are grounds for issuance of court order for termination and liquidation of business office. (Com. C. 484). Fines not to exceed 1,000,000 yen are provided for various infractions of registration requirements. (Com. C. 498).

Establishment of branch in Japan or substantial change in kind or business purpose of branch in Japan by foreign corporation (excluding financial and public utility corporation) is categorized as inward direct investment under Foreign Exchange and Foreign Trade Control Law, and ex post facto report must be filed or, in exceptional cases of investment from certain countries or for certain industries, prior notification must be filed. Remittances to and from branch office can be made freely unless special method of payment is involved and subject to possible restriction under extraordinary circumstances. See topics Foreign Exchange and Foreign Trade; and Foreign Investments.

COSTS:

The successful party generally recovers costs although these may be apportioned at court's discretion. (C. C. P. 89-91). Nonresident plaintiff may be required to provide security to cover potential costs unless he is national or corporation of country which is party to Convention Relating to Civil Procedures of Mar. 1, 1954 having made no reservation. (C. C. P. 107). Filing fees for civil actions are relatively high and are based upon amount of relief.

COURTS:

Supreme Court, high courts, district courts, family courts and summary courts comprise the judicial institutions in Japan. There are no local or special courts in Japan. (C. 76, C. T. L. 2).

Supreme Court consists of a Chief Justice who is appointed by Emperor upon designation by Cabinet and 14 Associate Justices who are appointed by Cabinet, subject to recall public vote at next general election and at ten-year intervals. (C. 79, C. T. L. 5). Court operates through petty benches of three or more justices except that grand bench of all justices acts in cases involving constitutional questions and cases referred from petty bench requiring change in established precedents when petty benches have expressed different opinions, when opinions of justices in petty bench are equally divided, or when petty bench deems it proper for grand bench to handle case. (C. T. L. 9, 10; Rules Concerning Disposition of Judicial Business of Supreme Court 9). Court's consideration of appeals is limited. By constitutional provision it has rule-making power over procedures and practice, which is interpreted as being subordinated to statutory enactments. (C. 77).

With minor exceptions high court's function is purely appellate, and for many cases its decisions are final. High court normally operates through panels of three judges. (C. T. L. 16, 18).

District courts constitute principal trial courts. They exercise general jurisdiction over all civil and criminal actions not specifically given to other courts. However, they, together with summary courts, have jurisdiction over civil actions concerning real property even if claims involved are not more than 900,000 yen. (C. T. L. 24, 25). Normally district court maintains a number of branches, which are territorial. District court sits both as collegiate court of three judges and through single judge, depending on nature and importance of case involved. (C. T. L. 26).

Family court parallels district court and has jurisdiction over domestic matters and juvenile delinquency cases and criminal actions involving protection of juvenile interest. (C. T. L. 31-3).

Summary court handles minor civil actions involving claims of not more than 900,000 yen, and criminal actions in which punishment is limited to not more than three years imprisonment for certain types of cases and to fine or lesser penalty. (C. T. L. 33). Single judge of summary court has broad latitude in conduct of trials. (C. T. L. 35).

CURRENCY:

Legal currency is yen. Its exchange rate has been floating since Feb. 13, 1973.

CURTESY:

Does not exist in Japanese law.

DEATH:

Family court may, on application of interested party, issue an adjudication of disappearance when it is unknown for seven years whether absentee is living or dead or for one year in case person has been missing in war zone, has been on board a vessel which has sunk, or otherwise has encountered perils which might have been cause of death. (C. C. 30). Person whose disappearance has been adjudicated is deemed to have died at expiration of seven-year term referred to above or at extinguishment of perils referred to above. (C. C. 31). Such adjudication of disappearance can be revoked by court upon proof that individual is living or died at time different from that determined previously. (C. C. 32). Death reports also may be made through administrative findings in case of unusual disasters.

Death certificate of Japanese national may be obtained from municipal office having custody of deceased's family register. (See topic Records.) Although foreigners have no family register records certificate can be obtained from municipal office of area where foreigner died stating that notification of death has been duly received. American consulate will furnish "Report of Death" free of charge to any interested party if deceased was an American citizen, and not a member of Armed Forces and also will provide information, when available, as to Japanese government office from which certification may be obtained. Practice of other consulates in Japan is not uniform and some do not furnish death certificates in respect to their nationals.

Actions for Death.—Separate actions for wrongful death may be brought by heirs and by near relatives. Despite old precedents to contrary, general tendency of recent court decisions is to regard right to claim damages for mental anguish and suffering as a property right subject to inheritance. (C. C. 710, 887, 889, 890). Right given to parents, spouse and children of deceased includes compensation for mental anguish. (C. C. 711).

Simultaneous Death.—Simultaneous death is presumed by statutory provision when it is not clear that anyone among many could have survived. (C. C. 32-2).

DEEDS:

Although title to immovables, as with all other forms of property, may be transferred simply by means of agreement between parties, registration is necessary if this fact is to be set up against third parties. (C. C. 176, 177). Abstracts of title and title searches, in American sense, do not exist, and ownership normally can easily be determined from registration record, although not decisive. (Real Property Registration Law). See topic Records.

DEPOSITIONS:

Under exceptional circumstances where cause exists to believe that witness may not appear at trial or will (in criminal cases) be exposed to pressures likely to induce a change of statement, testimony may be "perpetuated." (C. C. P. 343; Code of Criminal Procedures 179). Parties usually are afforded opportunity to attend interrogation of witness or to submit questions in advance to examining judge. (C. C. P. 349; Code of Criminal Procedures 157). Testimony so taken may be used in criminal cases only when direct testimony is not possible or when witness gives conflicting testimony. (Code of Criminal Procedures 321).

Testimony for use in foreign countries is available through letters rogatory only when these are forwarded to Japanese court through diplomatic channels on reciprocal basis and are accompanied by full Japanese translation. Present official interpretation of Japanese law is that depositions may not be taken before foreign consular officials in Japan, unless otherwise specifically provided in consular treaty such as that with U.S.A.

DESCENT AND DISTRIBUTION:

Single system of succession applies to all estates, regardless of sex or family status of ancestor or successor, and to property of all descriptions.

Order of succession, as am'd on Jan. 1, 1981, is as follows: (1) Children; (2) lineal ascendants; (3) brothers and sisters. (C. C. 887, 889). When child of deceased is survived by lineal descendant or when brother or sister of deceased is survived by child, such descendant or child is entitled to share per stirpes in estate of ancestor. (C. C. 887, 889). Surviving spouse always is regarded as a successor and takes one-half share when children (or their lineal descendants) are co-successors, two-thirds share when lineal ascendants are co-successors, and three-fourths share when brothers and sisters (or their children) are co-successors. (C. C. 890, 900). Two or more lineal descendants or lineal ascendants or brothers and sisters share equally. (C. C. 900). An illegitimate child receives one-half of the share of legitimate lineal descendant, and half-brothers and sisters receive one-half of share of full brothers and sisters. (C. C. 900).

Special Contribution.—Special contribution by any co-successor to maintenance or increase of decedent's properties shall be valued by co-successors' agreement, deducted from estate prior to partition between co-successors and added to share of successor making contribution. Family court shall determine value in absence of agreement by co-successors. (C. C. 904-2).

Acceptance or Renunciation.—Within three months after becoming aware of commencement of succession, a successor must either unconditionally accept estate, accept it conditionally (i.e., with a reservation that obligations and legacies of ancestor will be paid only to extent of property acquired by reason of the succession) or renounce it entirely. (C. C. 915, 920, 922, 938). If no decision is expressed within three months, unconditional acceptance is presumed. (C. C. 921). When succession is accepted conditionally, public notice to creditors and legatees must be given within five days, and at least two months must be allowed for submission of claims against estate. (C. C. 927).

Separation of Property.—A creditor or legatee may apply within three months from date of succession for separation of succession property from successor's own property. (C. C. 941).

Co-successors acquire ownership in common (C. C. 898) and estate may be partitioned among co-successors on basis of their respective share by their mutual agreement. If they fail to reach agreement, family court decides manner of partition upon application of any co-successor. (C. C. 907). If so specified by ancestor, partition of estate may be suspended for five years or less. (C. C. 908).

Disinheritance.—Ancestor may disinherit presumptive successor in case of cruelty, gross insult or misconduct on part of successor, with permission of family court. (C. C. 892).

Gifts inter vivos to successors in connection with marriage or adoption are to be included within estate of succession, unless a contrary intention is expressed by ancestor. (C. C. 903).

Prior Law.—Civil Code provisions before amendment of Jan. 1, 1981 are applied to successions which took place on or before Dec. 31, 1980.

DISPUTE RESOLUTION:

Mandatory Dispute Resolution.—Japanese law does not have system whereby dispute shall be referred to alternative dispute resolution procedure, except that domestic disputes, such as divorce, and certain other disputes, including those concerning rent for land leases or building leases, shall first be subjected to conciliation procedures.

Voluntary Dispute Resolution.—Forms of voluntary dispute resolution under Japanese law include arbitration and conciliation.

Agreement to settle disputes between parties by means of arbitration, either in Japan or in foreign country, precludes parties from bringing suit in court to resolve disputes

See Topical Index in front part of this volume.

DISPUTE RESOLUTION . . . *continued*
that are covered by agreement. Arbitration award rendered either in Japan or in foreign country has same effect as final and conclusive decision of court (C. C. P. 800) and is made enforceable in Japan when it is endorsed by Japanese court in form of "enforcement judgment", which is granted without reexamination of merits of award (C. C. P. 802). Japan is party to Convention on the Execution of Foreign Arbitral Awards (Geneva Convention) and Convention on the Recognition and Enforcement of Foreign Arbitral Awards (New York Convention).

Conciliation.—See topic of Conciliation.

Also system of settlement before summary court with no lawsuit being filed is noted. Either of parties who made out-of-court settlement may, with agreement of other party, apply to summary court for enrollment of settlement agreement into court record. When registered in court record, settlement has same effect as final and binding decision of court. (C. C. P. 356).

DIVORCE:

Divorce may be either consensual or judicial.

Consensual divorce is obtained through the entry upon Family Register Record (see topic Records) of mutual agreement of parties to divorce. (C. C. 764, 739). No formalities are required unless a dispute arises as to custody of children or division of property, in which case a referral is made to family court. (C. C. 766, 768).

Judicial divorce is of two categories, that obtained through formal trial and that through a process peculiar to Japan called conciliation.

In case of formal trial, an action is instituted in district court upon grounds of (1) Unchastity, (2) malicious desertion, (3) where other spouse is not known to be dead or alive for not less than three years, or (4) incurable insanity. Court may dismiss action for divorce if all circumstances call for continuance of marriage. Court also may grant divorce in absence of any of above grounds upon finding of grave reasons which make difficult continuation of marriage. (C. C. 770).

Conciliation procedures permit voluntary submission of divorce action to family court which, after investigation, is authorized to confer on divorce agreement acceptable to parties, formal judicial sanction equivalent to adjudicated decree of divorce. (Domestic Matter Adjudication Law 21). No particular grounds must be alleged or proved to obtain divorce by conciliation.

Alimony as such is not recognized, although lump sum settlements which have similar objective may be granted by court. (C. C. 768).

In case of foreigners, divorce is governed by law of country of parties if they have same nationality. If they have different nationalities, it is governed by law of habitual residence of parties if they have same habitual residence. If they do not, it is governed by law of place most closely associated with parties. However, in case either party is Japanese having habitual residence in Japan, Japanese law governs. (Horei 16).

DOWER: Does not exist in Japan.

ENVIRONMENT:

On Nov. 19, 1993 "Environment Protection Act (E.P.A.)" was implemented. E.P.A. stipulates policies for protection of environment and clarifies responsibility of central and local governments, business entities and citizens for preservation of environment. Government shall state basic policies in order to promote protection of environment comprehensively and systematically (E.P.A. 15), shall state standards concerning air, water and soil pollution and noise (E.P.A. 16), and shall instruct local governments to make plans to prevent pollution in areas in which such plans must be implemented (E.P.A. 17). Central and local governments shall have environment committees to deal with matters regarding protection of environment (E.P.A. 41, 43) and environmental pollution measures committee shall be established by Prime Minister's office (E.P.A. 45). Central government or local government may take measures to ensure that those whose activities caused necessity for implementation of environmental protection projects shall share financial burden. (E.P.A. 37). Under Environment Protection Act, there are many laws and regulations which put actual policies into practice, such as Environmental Pollution Dispute Settlement Act, Air Pollution Prevention Act, Noise Control Act, Regulation on the Special Measures to Protect the Ozone Layer, Water Pollution Protection Act, Promotion of Use of the Recycling Source Act, Regulation of Waste and Disposal, etc.

Contact Address and Phone Number of Environmental Agency.—1-2-2 Kasumigaseki, Chiyoda-ku, Tokyo 100, Japan; phone 81-3-3581-3351. There are 47 local government environment committees. Each local government environment committee's contact address and phone number can be obtained by contacting each local government or above phone number.

EXCHANGE CONTROL:

See topic Foreign Exchange and Foreign Trade.

EXECUTIONS:

Execution follows from judgment of court, from settlement made in court or through conciliation procedures, from court order of payment or decree for provisional execution or from certain categories of contracts which provide for payment of fixed amount of money or securities and which are executed before notary public. (C. E. L. 22). (See topic Notaries Public, subhead Officially Authenticated Instrument). In all of above cases, however, execution certificate which certifies as to existence and maturity of obligation, must be obtained either from clerk of court issuing order or notary public certifying as to contract. (C. E. L. 25 through 27). Execution is conducted by bailiff or court, according to nature of claim or property. (C. E. L. 2, 3, 44, 113, 122, 143, 167).

Claim of a monetary nature may be satisfied through seizure of cash, seizure and sale at auction of property in debtor's hands, or through court order for assumption of management of real property. (C. E. L. 43, 112, 134). Obligations calling for surrender of particular item of property may be satisfied by seizure and transfer to creditor and obligations requiring merely legal action may be ordered by court. (C. E. L. 168, 169, 173). Specific performance is not available for obligations which can be performed only by debtor or through his inaction. See topic Garnishment.

Creditors entitled to execute their monetary claims by themselves and certain other specified creditors may apply for share in distribution of sales proceeds of real property, vessels and airplanes during period specified by court. (C. E. L. 49, 51, 121 and Civil Execution Rules 84).

Holders of preferential rights and pledgees may apply for share in distribution before seizure of cash or before receipt by bailiff of sales proceeds of movables. (C. E. L. 133, 140).

See also topic Preferential Rights.

Exemptions from Execution.—See topic Exemptions.

EXECUTORS AND ADMINISTRATORS:

Executor may be appointed by will, by person commissioned to do so by will, or by family court. (C. C. 1006, 1010). Person nominated may receive proper compensation for services rendered, but may not serve if declared bankrupt or incompetent. (C. C. 1009, 1018). Upon refusal of designated executor or in event of failure of testator to nominate an executor, appointment is made by family court. (C. C. 1010). If more than one executor is selected, dispositions are made by majority vote, unless a contrary intention was provided in will. (C. C. 1017). Failure of proper discharge of duties is grounds for removal of executor. (C. C. 1019).

Administrators of estates, in Anglo-American sense are virtually unknown, since heirs usually assume control immediately of all estates in event of intestate succession. See topic Descent and Distribution.

EXEMPTIONS:

Exemptions from execution are following: clothing and household equipment needed by debtor; food and fuel for debtor and his family for two month period; cash not exceeding 210,000 yen; implements and tools of technicians, laborers, farmers, and other varieties of professional men; three-fourths (in principle) of income derived from pensions and remuneration of workmen; seals, decorations and awards, genealogical materials and objects of worship; unpublished manuscripts or unrevealed inventions; and school books. (C. E. L. 131, 152 and Civil Execution Enforcement Ordinance 1).

In addition court is empowered to provide additional exemptions when necessary to afford debtor proper means with which to recoup himself. (C. E. L. 132, 153).

FOREIGN EXCHANGE AND FOREIGN TRADE:

Foreign Exchange and Foreign Trade Control Law is major act of legislation and by its amendment which became effective on Dec. 1, 1980, its coverage has been broadened so that it covers transactions theretofore covered by Foreign Investment Law. Wide areas are regulated by Law such as: (1) Payments directed abroad, payments to or receipts of payment from "exchange nonresident", and settlements of account between "exchange resident" and "exchange nonresident"; (2) transactions between "exchange resident" and "exchange nonresident" concerning creation, modification or liquidation of claimable assets arising from deposit, trust or monetary loan or guaranty or contract providing for purchase of foreign means of payment or claimable assets; and transactions between "exchange resident" and another "exchange resident" concerning creation, modification or liquidation of claimable assets payable in foreign currency arising from such contracts; (3) acquisition by "exchange resident" of foreign securities from "exchange nonresident"; acquisition by "exchange nonresident" of securities from "exchange resident"; issuance or flotation by "exchange resident" of securities in foreign country or of foreign securities in Japan; issuance or flotation by "exchange nonresident" in Japan of securities, and in foreign country securities expressed or payable in Japanese currency; (4) acquisition by "exchange resident" of immovables in foreign country or rights related thereto or acquisition by "exchange nonresident" of immovables in Japan or rights related thereto; (5) receipt and payment of funds between office in Japan of corporation and its office outside Japan; (6) certain service contracts between "exchange resident" and "exchange nonresident"; (7) acquisition of shares of Japanese corporation by "foreign investor" and its consent to substantial change in business purpose of Japanese corporation in which it has not less than one-third of issued shares; (8) establishment of branch, etc., in Japan or substantial change in its kind or business purpose; (9) conclusion of technology introduction contract between "exchange resident" and "exchange nonresident"; and (10) export and import trade, including export and import of means of payment, securities, and precious metals. (F.E.C.L. 16 through 55). "Exchange residents" mean all natural persons who have their permanent place of abode or who customarily live in Japan, and also juridical persons (corporate bodies, enterprises) having their seat or place of administration in Japan. Branches, local offices and other offices in Japan of exchange nonresidents are considered to be exchange residents irrespective of whether or not they have legal authority to represent "exchange nonresidents" and even if their headquarters are located abroad. "Exchange nonresidents" mean all persons, natural or juridical, other than "exchange residents".(F.E.C.L. 6). By virtue of various rules and regulations issued thereunder, general rules prescribed by Foreign Exchange and Foreign Trade Control Law and many restrictions have been eased, and by above-mentioned amendment to Law restrictions have been eased further.

See topic Foreign Investments.

FOREIGN INVESTMENTS:

Foreign Exchange and Foreign Control Law regulates transactions set forth below.

Acquisition of Shares.—For regulatory purposes manner of share acquisition is divided into two types: (a) Inward direct investment and (b) portfolio investment.

Inward direct investment type of share acquisition by foreign investors involves report, or in exceptional cases prior notification and possible issuance of recommendation of or order for alteration of contents or suspension of notified share acquisition. Foreign investor is defined to include exchange nonresident individual, foreign corporation, any corporation one-half or more of whose issued shares are directly or indirectly held by exchange nonresident individuals or foreign corporations, and any juridical person majority of whose directors or of whose officers having authority to represent it are nonresident individuals. Foreign investor desiring to acquire shares of

See Topical Index in front part of this volume.

FOREIGN INVESTMENTS . . . *continued*
Japanese corporation must in principle file ex post facto report with Minister of Finance and ministers having authority over business concerned (collectively "competent ministers"). In case shares to be acquired are listed on stock exchange or are designated by government as similar to listed shares, this report or prior notification is not required, unless ratio of holding by single foreign investor of shares (including both presently held and to be newly acquired) is 10% or more. Prior notification must be filed with competent ministers in exceptional cases of investment from certain countries or for certain industries, in which cases foreign investor must withhold share acquisition for (generally) 30-day period. Competent ministers may extend above 30-day period to as much as four months in rare cases when they deem it necessary to consider whether, if shares were acquired as notified: (a) Safety of Japan would be impaired, maintenance of public order would be disturbed or public safety would be hindered or (b) smooth operation of Japanese economy would be very harmfully influenced, or whether it is deemed necessary to alter contents of share acquisition or suspend it: (a) in order to treat notified share acquisition on substantially equal basis with treatment of Japanese investors in country to which foreign investor belongs and with which Japan has not concluded treaty concerning direct investment or (b) because whole or part of notified share acquisition is found to fall into category of capital transactions for which approval must be obtained in view of use of funds and other factors. If competent ministers are convinced that there are grounds for apprehension, they may within above four-month period (or five-month period if extended in case of necessity) recommend that foreign investor alter contents of or suspend notified share acquisition. Foreign investor who has accepted recommendation within ten days after its receipt may acquire shares in compliance with recommendation before elapse of above waiting period. If recommendation is not accepted or no acceptance reply is given, competent ministers may, but only within above four- or five-month period, order alteration of contents or suspension of notified share acquisition. (F.E.C.L. 26, 27, Supplemental Provisions of F.E.C.L. 2, 3).

Portfolio investment type of share acquisition involves prior notification but not recommendation of or order for alteration or suspension. However, in case of certain extraordinary circumstances portfolio investment may be made subject to approval. In particular, exchange nonresident (including foreign corporation) desiring to acquire shares from exchange residents must in principle file notification in advance with Minister of Finance. This notification is not required if share acquisition is made from or through Japanese or foreign securities company designated by Minister of Finance acting as intermediary, commission broker or agent. Alteration of contents or suspension of notified portfolio investment cannot be recommended or ordered. However, Minister of Finance may impose obligation to obtain approval but only in rare cases when he deems that: (a) Maintenance of balance of international payments of Japan would become difficult, (b) foreign exchange rate of Japanese currency might suddenly change or (c) movement of substantial funds to and from Japan would threaten Japanese financial market and/or capital market, and that it would become difficult to attain purpose of Law if portfolio investment were without restriction. (F.E.C.L. 20 through 22).

Technology Introduction Contracts.—Any exchange resident desiring to conclude, renew or alter terms of contract with exchange nonresident (including branch, etc., in Japan of exchange nonresident) under which nonresident transfers industrial property rights or other rights concerning technology, establishes rights to use these rights or advises on technology concerning operation of business ("conclusion, etc. of contract") must file in principle report within 15-day period after date of conclusion, etc. of contract with Minister of Finance and ministers concerned (collectively "competent ministers"), and in certain instances when technology is related to those kinds of technology designated by competent ministers, and if: (a) consideration for contract exceeds 100,000,000 yen, or is not fixed, (b) contract involves transfer, etc. of intellectual property right from resident in exchange for receiving technology, or (c) nonresident holds not less than 50% of shares of resident, must file prior notification with competent ministers, and withhold notified conclusion, etc. of contract for 30 days (or shortened period). Such notification is not required if branch, etc., in Japan of exchange nonresident concludes, renews or alters contract covering technology developed independently by branch, etc. Competent ministers may extend above 30-day period to as much as four months if they deem it necessary to consider whether, if notified conclusion, etc. of contract were carried out: (a) Safety of Japan would be impaired, maintenance of public order would be disturbed or public safety would be hindered, or (b) smooth operation of Japanese economy would be very harmfully influenced. If competent ministers are convinced that grounds for apprehension exist, they may recommend that parties alter whole or part of terms of contract or suspend conclusion, etc. of contract. Such recommendation can be made only within above four-month period (or five-month period if extended in case of necessity). Time and manner of carrying out conclusion, etc. of contract by parties having accepted recommendation and of issuance of order of alteration or suspension against parties not having accepted recommendation are same as stated in inward direct investment type of share acquisition above. (F.E.C.L. 29, 30, 31).

Repatriation Right.—Validation granted under abolished Foreign Investment Law for acquisition of shares and conclusion of technology introduction contract carries right to withdraw profits and repatriate investment subject to such conditions as may be imposed therein or as provided in Law. Under Foreign Exchange and Foreign Trade Control Law, which makes overseas payment generally free from any regulation, such right is not specifically provided. However, obligation to obtain approval for payment of dividends on and repatriation of investment in shares and royalties under technology introduction contracts may be imposed if it is deemed necessary for faithful performance of treaties or other international agreements concluded by Japan. (F. E. C. L. 16). In addition, in cases of sudden and substantial changes in international economy, if emergency exists, competent ministers can suspend such payments, delaying them for period specified by Cabinet Order. (F. E. C. L. 9).

FOREIGN TRADE REGULATIONS:

Foreign trade is regulated by Foreign Exchange and Foreign Trade Control Law. Export of goods is permitted with minimum of restrictions, insofar as it is consistent with objective of Law. (F. E. C. L. 47). Export of goods of certain type, or to certain destination, or under certain method of transaction or settlement may be subject to approval from Minister of International Trade and Industry. (F. E. C. L. 48). When Minister of International Trade and Industry deems it urgently necessary, he may place embargo by specifying type or destination of goods for period not exceeding one month. (F. E. C. L. 51). Import of goods may be subject to approval in certain circumstances for purpose of sound development of foreign trade and national economy. (F. E. C. L. 52).

See topics Foreign Exchange and Foreign Trade; Foreign Investments.

FRAUDS, STATUTE OF:

Although Japan has no specific statute of frauds, certain forms of expression of intention, such as wills and corporate instruments, must be in writing or executed before notaries. (C. C. 969, 970, 972; Com. C. 167).

GARNISHMENT:

Outstanding claim of debtor may be attached by his creditor through court order of garnishment which prohibits garnishee from discharging his obligation to original debtor, and also forbids debtor to dispose of or accept payment for obligation. (C. E. L. 145). Payment in violation of this court order cannot be set up against garnisher.

Exemptions from garnishment are as stated under topic Exemptions.

HOLIDAYS:

Legal holidays are: Jan. 1, Jan. 15, Feb. 11, Vernal Equinox, Apr. 29, May 3, May 5, July 20, Sept. 15, Autumnal Equinox, Oct. 10, Nov. 3, Nov. 23 and Dec. 23. In case any of these days falls on Sun., next Mon. becomes legal holiday. When day other than Sun. or holiday falls between two legal holidays, such day becomes holiday.

When final day for performance of legal obligation, or making of designation, delivery, or act of execution falls on legal holiday, or Sunday, period of time is extended through following day, either through specific provision of law or custom. (C. C. 142; Com. C. 520; L. B. N. 72, 77; L. C. 60; C. C. P. 156; Code of Criminal Procedures 55; Law of National Taxation General Rules 10).

In addition to legal holidays, Jan. 2, Jan. 3, Dec. 31 and Sats. are bank holidays.

HUSBAND AND WIFE:

Wife has full legal capacity, and rights and obligations equal to her husband to participate in care, support and education of children. (C. 14, 24).

Property.—Prior to marriage husband and wife may provide for property relationship different from that fixed by law, but such special provision cannot be set up against their successors or third persons unless registered. (C. C. 756).

Property relationship provided for by aliens is governed by law which governs effect of marriage. However if husband and wife in document signed by them choose law of country or place of habitual residence of husband or wife or law of location of immovables, that chosen law governs. Property relationship provided for pursuant to law of foreign country cannot set up judicial acts in Japan and properties in Japan against bona fide third persons. In such case property relationship as between third persons is governed by Japanese law. Notwithstanding foregoing, property relationship contract entered into pursuant to law of foreign country can be set up against third persons if such contract is registered. (Horei 15).

Legal property system requires husband and wife to share expenses of married life, and to assume mutual liability for acts pertaining to household matters. Notice to third person of contrary intent, however, relieves noncontracting spouse from obligation. (C. C. 760, 761). Property acquired by either spouse prior to marriage continues to be his or her separate property. (C. C. 762). Property may be acquired separately by either spouse in course of marriage, although upon divorce division of property acquired by joint efforts of spouses may be ordered regardless of location of formal legal title. (C. C. 762, 768). Property whose ownership is not clear is presumed to be owned by husband and wife jointly. (C. C. 762).

Contracts between husband and wife may be cancelled in so far as not injurious to rights of third persons. (C. C. 754).

Japanese married to alien may change family name to spouse's by reporting to ward office within six months after marriage.

IMMIGRATION:

Alien's authorized period of stay varies with his immigration status and is renewable with some exceptions and limitations. Three-year commercial visa may be given to aliens who engage in business in Japan. Instructors at educational institutions, aliens who are sent by foreign religious organization to engage in religious activities in Japan, foreign news reporters and aliens who are invited by a public or private Japanese organization for provision of advanced or specialized industrial technologies may also be given three-year period of stay. Students, researchers and skilled laborers normally are admitted on year by year basis. Tourists and other aliens who intend to stay for short period may be given 90 day visa. Minister of Justice has discretionary powers to authorize other statuses and periods of stay up to three years.

Entry-check, procedures for status change or renewal, and deportation process are provided in Immigration Control and Refugee Recognition Law. For registration requirements, see topic Aliens.

Japan is party to Convention Relating to Status of Refugees of July 28, 1951.

INFANTS:

Age of majority is 20 for both sexes. (C. C. 3).

Emancipation occurs upon marriage. (C. C. 753).

Disabilities.—Minor can act only with consent of legal representative (parents, in absence of parents, guardian). (C. C. 818, 819, 839, 841 through 846). Contracts made by minor without legal representative's consent are revocable until ratified. (C. C. 4). However, if proved that minor made use of fraudulent methods to make opposite party believe he had capacity, such contracts are irrevocable. (C. C. 20). Minor has full capacity in respect to transactions concerning property for which disposition has been authorized, to transactions within scope of business for which minor has been given

INFANTS . . . *continued*
full authority or acts of merely discharging liability or obtaining rights without incurring any obligation. (C. C. 4 through 6).

Ratification of contract of minor is made only by legal representative until minor attains majority, and after majority minor can ratify his own contract. Opposite party to contract may demand from minor, after majority, answer within period not shorter than one month as to whether he ratifies it and, in absence of reply within period, ratification is conclusively presumed. (C. C. 19).

Actions.—Minor may sue or be sued. However, in actions, minor must be represented by legal representative. (C. C. P. 49).

Service of process in action against minor must be made on his legal representative. (C. C. P. 165).

Wages.—Minor has right to claim directly and independently wages for his labor. (Labor Standards Law 59).

INJUNCTIONS:

See topic Attachment and Injunctions.

INSOLVENCY: See topic Bankruptcy.

INTEREST:

Loan interest rates may not exceed 20% per annum if principal is less than 100,000 yen, 18% if 100,000 yen or over and less than 1,000,000 yen, and 15% if 1,000,000 yen or over. If not specified, rate is 5% per annum on civil transactions and 6% on commercial transactions. (C. C. 404; Com. C. 514; Usury Law 1).

According to court precedents, if interest has been paid voluntarily at rates over above maximum rates, excess is deemed to have been applied toward principal repayment.

If interest for one year or more is not paid despite payment request, it may be added to principal of obligation and compound interest may be charged. (C. C. 405).

Contract for or actual receipt of interest at rates exceeding limits prescribed in Law Concerning Control on Acceptance of Contributions, Deposits and Interest Rates, Etc. is punishable. (Law Concerning Control on Acceptance of Contributions, Deposits and Interest Rates, Etc. 5).

Under this Law, maximum permissible interest rate to be charged by money-lending traders is 0.2% per day for three years from Nov. 1, 1983, 0.15% per day thereafter until Oct. 31, 1991 and 0.1096% per day thereafter.

Subject to certain requirements, interest paid voluntarily to money-lending traders at rates over maximum rates under Usury Law but not exceeding maximum permissible rates under Law Concerning Control on Acceptance of Contributions, Deposits and Interest Rates, Etc. is deemed to be valid interest notwithstanding provisions of Usury Law. (Law of Restrictions, Etc. on Money-Lending Business 43).

JOINT STOCK COMPANIES:

See topic Corporations.

JUDGMENTS:

Final judgment issued by a foreign court is recognized as binding only when: (1) Jurisdiction of foreign court is not denied by Japanese law or treaties, (2) if defeated party is Japanese subject, service was made on him by other means than publication, or he appeared without such notice, (3) judgment is not contrary to public order and good morals of Japan, and (4) foreign government reciprocates through recognition of Japanese judgments. (C. C. P. 200). Execution of final and conclusive foreign judgment meeting with above conditions is possible only when competent Japanese court has affirmed validity of that judgment in special action. (C. E. L. 24). Full reciprocity does not exist with U.S.A. by treaty, but reciprocity will be afforded upon proof of recognition of Japanese judgments in foreign jurisdiction.

LABOR RELATIONS:

Rules of employment must be established by every employer of ten or more workers in compliance with minimum standards of law. (Labor Standards Law 89). Establishment of such rules requires first a presentation to representative employees and then filing with Prefectural Labor Standards Supervising Office. Such rules must deal with wage programs and scales, working hours, time off, holidays, paid vacations, discharge, and to extent that these are customary in line of business concerned, with retirement allowances, safety, sanitation, accident compensation, etc. (Labor Standards Law 89, 90).

Labor agreements are made between company and lawfully organized union. When labor agreements become applicable to at least three-fourths of regular workers of plant, their terms then become applicable to all workers. (Labor Union Law 17). Normally content of labor agreements resembles that of rules of employment. Labor agreements do not require government approval. Injunctions and suits for civil damages are available for breaches of agreements. Labor agreements may be for three years or less and, unless term is provided therein, may be terminated by at least 90 days notice. (Labor Union Law 14, 15, 17).

Labor practices in Japan make the provisions of retirement allowances and substantial bonuses a virtual necessity. Employers also normally provide a wide range of benefits including medical and housing facilities. Employers are prohibited from setting off wages against advances to employees or requiring employees to deposit funds with employers. At least 30 days notice or pay in lieu of notice is necessary for discharge. (Labor Standards Law 17, 18, 20).

See also topic Infancy.

LAW REPORTS, CODES, ETC.:

See topics Reports, Statutes.

LEGISLATURE:

See topic Constitution and Government.

LICENSES:

See topic Patents. Licensing of industrial know-how cannot be registered but is regulated as element of foreign investment. See also topics Foreign Exchange and Foreign Trade; and Foreign Investments.

LIENS:

Lien is right of retention of object (movable or immovable), which is security for obligation created in relationship to that object. (C. C. 295). It affords lien holder initially right to deprive owner of possession until obligation is performed and right to apply for auction sale of property concerned to collect his claim, although he has no priority in distribution of sales proceeds. Provisions concerning auction sale for enforcement of preferential rights are applied to auction sale applied for by holder of lien. (C. E. L. 195). See topic Preferential Rights. Holder of lien arising out of commercial transactions is entitled to priority over general creditors in event of bankruptcy of debtor. (Com. C. 51, 521, 557, 562, 589, 753; B. L. 93). Retention of possession is essential for most types of liens. In case of immovables possession under lien is valid by virtue of possession alone and therefore constitutes exception to usual requirement for registration of real rights. In commercial transactions, scope of lien is extended to give possessor power of detention pending satisfaction of any commercial claims. (Com. C. 521). Lien holder is entitled to apply fruits of retained object toward satisfaction of outstanding indebtedness in priority to other creditors, and to repayment for sum of necessary expenses or improvements. (C. C. 297, 299). However, he may not use, lease, pledge or encumber object without consent of owner. (C. C. 298). Lien may be extinguished through offer of reasonable security in substitution thereof. (C. C. 301).

LIMITATION OF ACTIONS:

Statutes that establish time limitations on institution of litigation operate automatically, and such time limitations cannot be extended even upon consent of both parties. Such limitations differ from extinctive prescription (see topic Prescription) whereunder assertion must be made in litigation in order to be effective; also effect is retroactive. (C. C. 145, 144). Rights to damages, reduction of purchase price and cancellation of sales contract for seller's warranty are subject to one year limitation of actions. (C. C. 564 through 566).

LIMITED PARTNERSHIP:

See topic Corporations.

MARRIAGE:

If parental consent is obtained marriage may be effected by males who have attained age of 18 and females who have attained age of 16. (C. C. 3, 731, 737). Both males and females who have reached age of majority (20) may marry without parental consent and guardian's consent is not required for marriage of incompetent. (C. C. 738).

Prohibited marriages consist of those between lineal relatives, collateral blood relatives within third degree of relationship, and marriage of adopted children to lineal ascendants by adoption. (C. C. 734 through 736). Woman may not remarry until six months following dissolution or annulment of previous marriage. (C. C. 733). No restrictions exist regarding marriage between Japanese and aliens.

Ceremonies of religious nature, although customary, are not required and produce no legal effect.

Marriage occurs upon acceptance for registration of notification of marriage signed by both parties and witnessed by two persons. (C. C. 739). Act of acceptance by family registrar of notification of marriage must be preceded by his finding that no legal bars to creation of marriage exist. (C. C. 740). Despite record status, marriage is invalid if parties lacked an intention to marry because of mistaken identity or other reason. (C. C. 742).

Annulment may occur upon showing of existence of any other legal bar except failure of parental consent. (C. C. 743 through 748). Through act of marriage, minors automatically attain majority. (C. C. 753).

In case of marriage between persons of different nationalities, capacity for marriage is determined by law of parties' respective countries. (Horei 13). Form and manner of celebration is determined by law of place of marriage. However, marriage in compliance with form and manner of law of either party's country is valid, except for case where marriage took place in Japan and either party is Japanese. (Horei 13). Effect of marriage is governed by law of country of parties if they have same nationality. If they have different nationalities, it is governed by law of habitual residence of parties if they have same habitual residence. If they do not, it is governed by law of place most closely associated with parties. (Horei 14). Customary practice in Japan is for marriages between foreigners to be registered with Japanese authorities after their religious or consulate marriages have taken place in Japan.

MONOPOLIES AND RESTRAINT OF TRADE:

Private monopolization, unreasonable restraint of trade and unfair business practices are prohibited under Law Relating to Prohibition of Private Monopoly and Methods of Preserving Fair Trade ("Anti-Monopoly Law"). However, many types of activities are exempted by special statutes, particularly in regard to rationalization of medium and small domestic enterprises. Extent of these exemptions narrows actual scope of Anti-Monopoly Law, but these exemptions have been reduced since 1965. Fair Trade Commission of five members enforces provisions of this Law. Its findings are subject to review by Tokyo High Court. Commission checks business transfers, mergers, shareholding status (including that of foreign firms) and international agreements, all of which are subject to certain restrictions. Certain types of international agreements for period of one year or more and certain types of continuous sales or export and import agreements must be reported by Japanese party to Commission which screens them in order to confirm their compliance with its standards.

MORTGAGES:

In order to avoid complicated and time-consuming mortgage foreclosure procedures, provisional registration on basis of conditional sale or preliminary transfer of ownership in lieu of performance of monetary obligation is widely used for purpose of securing performance of obligation. Law Concerning Security by Means of Provisional Registration provides protection for debtors under such arrangement against undue profits of creditors.

Mortgage is encumbrance on specific item of property whereby creditor obtains preferential position in regard to settlement of obligation out of proceeds which could be realized from sale of the property, but without obtaining transfer of title or possession. (C. C. 369). Mortgages can be created only for purpose of securing performance of obligation which must be specifically described. Under Civil Code, mortgages may be created only on real rights of ownership, superficies, and emphyteusis, of immovables, although special legislation provides for mortgages on standing timber, ships, factory foundations, mining rights, fishing rights, agricultural implements, aircraft and automobiles, subject to these being duly registered with a competent agency. With respect to movables, on which mortgages may not be created, title may be transferred for purpose of security (Joto Tampo). Courts recognize such transfer as valid security. Mortgages may be created to secure specific obligation or unspecified obligations arising from series of transactions or same kind of transactions with obligor. (C. C. 369, 398-2).

Mortgage rights extend to fixtures and items attached to mortgaged property, as well as to funds or substitute items which constitute consideration for sale of, or compensation for damage to, the mortgaged property. (C. C. 304, 370, 372).

Recording, although not legal requirement, is virtually essential since through this means alone can mortgage be asserted against third party having due interest in mortgaged property. (C. C. 177).

Priority as between mortgages on same item of property is determined by dates of registration. (Real Property Registration Law 6).

Assignment of mortgage to another creditor independently of obligation which it secures is possible, but in order to assert against principal debtor or mortgagor as well as their related parties of interest, consent of principal debtor must have been obtained or notice must have been given. (C. C. 375, 376).

Discharge.—Third party who purchases mortgaged property may discharge mortgage by paying proper amount to mortgagee. (C. C. 377).

Foreclosure.—Mortgage is enforced through application to a district court for auction sale of mortgaged property. (C. C. 387; C. E. L. 181 through 188). Provisions concerning auction sale of real property are generally applied to auction sale for enforcement of mortgage. (C. E. L. 188). Only that portion of interest on an obligation which has become due in previous two-year period may be satisfied from proceeds of mortgage sale in priority to third parties' claims, unless registration of interest followed maturity of obligation which it secures. (C. C. 374).

Mortgage certificates may be issued by registration offices in regard to land, buildings or superficies. These certificates incorporate and combine both mortgage and obligation secured thereby, and are negotiable instruments. They are irrevocable, and are transferred by endorsement. System of mortgage certificates was introduced in 1931 but has been used only to a very slight extent.

MOTOR VEHICLES:

With certain exceptions, such as motor vehicles used by national and local governments, U.S. military personnel or foreign diplomats, all motor vehicles used on road must carry liability insurance covering up to 30,000,000 yen. For personal injuries arising from operation of motor vehicles, injured party may claim damages not only from drivers, but also, in many cases, from owners, those for whose benefit vehicles were driven or those who controlled operation of vehicles. In latter cases, exoneration is possible only if defendant proves that he and driver paid due care to operation, that injury was caused by intentional or negligent acts of injured person or third party other than driver, and that no mechanical defects existed in vehicle. (Law No. 97 of 1955, Art. 3).

Holder of international driver's permit issued pursuant to Geneva Convention on Road Traffic may drive motor vehicles in Japan during one year period following his entry into Japan. (Road Traffic Law 107-2).

Japan is member of Convention on Road Traffic of 1949.

See also topic Taxation.

NEGOTIABLE INSTRUMENTS:

See topic Bills and Notes.

NOTARIES PUBLIC:

Notaries are officials whose principal functions are preparation and authentication of instruments.

Notaries may act only in localities for which they are licensed, and are liable for damages which result from intentional or negligent acts performed in course of duty.

Instruments which notary prepares must be in Japanese language and must not provide for void or illegal act. Notary may act only on behalf of parties personally known to him or those whose identity is proved by official certificate as to seal or officially issued certificate of identification, such as passport or alien registration in case of foreigner, or those whose identity can be established by two persons with whom notary is personally acquainted.

Officially authenticated instrument is document either prepared or authenticated by notary in course of his official duties. Officially authenticated instrument has two qualities which distinguish it from private documents. As result of formalities under which it was executed, it carries strong presumption of validity which resembles that accompanying official record or official document. Also, when purport of instrument is a claim for delivery of a fungible or payment of a fixed sum of money or transfer of fixed amount of negotiable securities, instrument itself is sufficient to obtain an immediate execution against obligor if statement is made therein that obligor, at time of preparation of instrument, agrees to execution in event of default. (C. E. L. 22). Officially authenticated instrument prepared in one locality has force and effect in other parts of Japan, but similar instruments prepared in other countries may not form basis for execution.

Copies of officially authenticated instruments are preserved by notaries and may be inspected by officials or parties of interest.

PARTNERSHIP:

Anglo-American institution of partnership is not known to Japan. Two categories of associations, namely, partnership corporations (see topic Corporations) and informal associations (Kumiai) as provided in Civil Code, have many features similar to partnership.

An informal association is created when several parties contract to contribute to common undertaking. (C. C. 667). One or more managers may be designated, and thereafter managers who are also members may not resign or be removed without cause. (C. C. 672). Association acts through majority vote of its members or managers but every member or manager is empowered to transact ordinary affairs on behalf of association, unless objections are raised by other members or managers. (C. C. 670). Profits and losses are shared in proportion to respective contributions of members unless otherwise provided in partnership contract, although creditor may exercise rights equally against each member if he has no knowledge of actual ratio of assumption of loss. (C. C. 674, 675). Claims of association against third party cannot be offset by latter's claims against individual members. (C. C. 677). When duration of association is not fixed, or is fixed to last during lifetime of member, any member may withdraw at any time, except when this withdrawal would prejudice association. (C. C. 678). Membership also expires by death, bankruptcy, incompetency, and expulsion. (C. C. 679). Upon termination of membership, accounting must be made between association and withdrawing member. Dissolution of association occurs when object of its creation has been accomplished, or becomes impossible of attainment. (C. C. 682). Upon dissolution, affairs of association are liquidated and assets distributed. (C. C. 685 through 688).

PATENTS:

Patent rights come into existence by registration with Patent Office. (P. L. 66). Foreigner residing or doing business in Japan applies for patents on same footing as Japanese, while right of application of foreigner living abroad is governed by reciprocity principle or by treaty, and "one year rule" of International Convention applies. Nonresidents applying for patents or taking formal actions relating to patent rights must be locally represented. (P. L. 8). Both licensed attorneys and patent agents may perform this representation.

Patentability is afforded to new "high grade" inventions of articles or of processes of an industrial nature (i.e., relating to productive industry in the broad sense), except things potentially injurious to public order, morals or health. (P. L. 32). With certain exceptions, inventions publicly used or known in Japan, inventions described in publication distributed in Japan or any foreign country before application for patent or inventions described in prior patent application are not regarded as new. (P. L. 29, 29-2, 30). If several applications are made on different days on same invention, first application is entitled to patent. If multiple applications are made on same day, no applicant is entitled to patent on invention unless agreement is reached among applicants as to who is entitled to patent on invention. (P. L. 39).

Applications for patents are made to Patent Office in Japanese. From July 1, 1995, patent applicant may file specifications, drawings and abstracts in English subject to condition that applicant submits Japanese translation within two months from filing date. On request of patent applicant or other interested parties, patent application is examined by examiners of that office. (P. L. 48-2). Request for examination must be made within seven years following patent application. (P. L. 48-3). Examiners rule on substantial questions of patentability. On Jan. 1, 1996, post-grant opposition system was introduced. (P. L. 113). Under post-grant opposition system, any party can raise objection within six months after public notice of granting of patent. With respect to patent applications which were filed before Jan. 1, 1996, pre-grant opposition system applies. Under pre-grant opposition sytem, within three months after publication of examined application, objection may be filed by any person. Patent application is disclosed to public in Patent Gazette upon elapse of 18 months from patent application. (P. L. 64). Public disclosure entitles patent applicant to claim compensation equivalent to normal royalty from any infringer, this claim being exercisable only after publication following examination. (P. L. 65).

Patent Office jurisdiction covers decisions in respect to: (1) Appeals from decisions of examiners who refuse issuance of patents, (2) invalidity of patents, (3) amendments of specification or drawings involved in application for which patent was granted. (P. L. 121, 123, 126). Actions contesting such decisions may be instituted in Tokyo High Court. (P. L. 178).

Scope of patent is determined on basis of description of scope in application. Interested person may apply for Patent Office's opinion as to scope of patent, which opinion is advisory and not binding on court. (P. L. 71).

Term of patent rights is 20 years from date of application (effective on July 1, 1995). This is applicable for both patent rights and patent applications which are effective on that date. Term of patent may be extended for maximum period of five years, by application, where patented invention cannot be used for two years or more for reasons of development of data for government registration required under Agricultural Chemicals Control Law or Pharmaceutical Affairs Law. (P. L. 67). As property rights, patents are subject to transfer, inheritance, pledge, etc., but all such acts except inheritance cannot take effect unless registered. (P. L. 98). Consent of all other co-owners is necessary for co-owner of patent to license patent or to assign or transfer co-ownership. (P. L. 73). Transfer of right to apply for patents is recognized. (P. L. 33). Once acquired, patents may be terminated through various processes such as invalidation by Patent Office or abandonment.

Patent licenses consist of "exclusive licenses" and "ordinary licenses." Exclusive license arises only from contract and requires Patent Office registration. (P. L. 77, 98). Exclusive license affords exclusive rights of use even as against patent owner; also licensee can seek injunctive relief and civil damages for injury to his own interest. (P. L. 77, 100, 106). Ordinary license may arise from contract, from compulsory order of

PATENTS . . . *continued*
Director General of Patent Office or Minister of International Trade and Industry, or from operation of law (such as employer's right to use his employee's invention under certain circumstances). (P. L. 35, 78 through 83, 92, 93). Ordinary licensee cannot act to enjoin infringement but may probably sue for damages. Registration of ordinary license although not required affords certain benefits, primary being firm confirmation of licensee rights. Without such registration, holder of ordinary license arising from contract has no rights against third party who is recorded assignee of patent. (P. L. 99).

Compulsory license may be granted by Director General of Patent Office in case patented invention has not been appropriately worked more than three consecutive years in Japan or by Minister of International Trade and Industry in case it relates to public interest. (P. L. 83, 93). Owner of improvement patent may also request a license to patent on which his own patent is based. (P. L. 92).

Employee rights are protected by Patent Law which renders void assignments or exclusive license commitments made in advance of invention, in case where invention is not an "in service" invention. An "in service" invention is defined as one which belongs to scope of employer's business and is related to employee's performance of his past or present duty. Employee is entitled to reasonable consideration in case of a subsequent exclusive license or assignment to employer of an "in service" invention. (P. L. 35).

Utility model rights are related to patents but are governed by separate statute. (Utility Models Law). A new invention, which is not required to be as "high grade" as that subject to patent but has a practical utility in regard to form, composition or assembly of goods, can be registered, and owner afforded protection similar to that held by patent holder. Utility model rights last for six years from date of application. (Utility Models Law 15). Unlike patents, utility model is registered without going through process of Patent Office examiner examining merits. In order to exercise utility model rights, registrant must apply to Patent Office for search report on prior arts and give warning to alleged infringer together with such report. Utility model may be invalidated by Patent Office through invalidation action to be filed with Patent Office by interested party. Alleged infringer who has filed invalidation action may apply to court to stay pending infringement suit against him/her. When utilization of patent requires concurrent use of utility model, license may be required of holder of utility model right.

Designs also are afforded legal protection through process of registration similar to that followed with patents. (Design Law). Design to be recorded must be of new variety and of industrial nature, and must relate to form, pattern, coloring or combination thereof of goods. Designs are distinguished from utility models and patents in that they may concern ornaments instead of objects having practical use. Unlike patents, however, design is registered without publication although preceded by examination both of merits and of formal regularity before registration. Registration of design may be challenged on ground of lack of statutory requirements. Design rights are valid for 15 years following registration. (Design Law 21).

Improvements in plant species and circuitry of semiconductor integrated circuit are afforded certain legal protection through process of registration. (Law 115 of 1947 and Law 43 of 1985).

Patent Treaty.—Japan is party to Patent Cooperation Treaty done at Washington, June 19, 1970 and Agreement on Trade-Related Aspects of Intellectual Property Rights (Jan. 1, 1995).

PLEDGES:

Pledge is a real right (i.e., a right in a thing) created by contract and is form of encumbrance on property on which creditor obtains possession of right or object as security for an indebtedness and thereby gains preferential position over general creditors in regard to proceeds which can be realized from sale of property by auction. (C. C. 342). In general, any item of property, movable, immovable, or obligation, may be pledged, although specific statutory prohibitions exist in respect to certain specific rights or objects. (C. C. 343; Com. C. 850; Agricultural Land Law 3, 5, etc.). Except in case of pledges arising out of commercial transactions, pledgor may not contract before maturity of obligation for acquisition of ownership by pledgee or for disposition of ownership by means other than those provided by law. (C. C. 349; Com. C. 515). A thing once pledged may be re-pledged or, in case of immovable, may be used by pledgee for his own benefit. (C. C. 348, 356). In return, pledgee must answer for all changes in object and in case of an immovable, may not demand repayment of sum of management expenses nor demand interest for claim secured. (C. C. 348, 357, 358; however, see 299). Pledges of movables require a continuation of possession by pledgee in order to be set up against third party. (C. C. 352). Pledges of immovables are limited to ten years, subject to another ten years renewal. (C. C. 360). When claim is subject of pledge, notice must be given to obligor or his consent obtained in order for pledge to be set up against obligor or third party except in cases of shares of stock. (C. C. 364). Pledgee may collect a pledged claim directly. (C. C. 367). When object pledged is warehouse receipt if payment is not made when due, holder of instrument for pledge must protest according to procedures applicable to bills of exchange. (Com. C. 609). After one week from day of protest, holder may demand sale by auction of goods deposited in warehouse. (Com. C. 610). If sale is insufficient, satisfaction may be obtained from endorsers or debtor. (Com. C. 613). Recourse against endorsers may be made if application for sale of goods is made within two weeks from protest. (Com. C. 614).

Enforcement of pledges requires auction sale of property concerned (C. E. L. 181, 189, 190) in same manner as enforcement of preferential rights. (See topic Preferential Rights.)

PREFERENTIAL RIGHTS:

Preferential right is a real right (i.e., a right in a thing) which affords its holder a position superior to other creditors in respect to satisfaction of obligation from either entire property of debtor or from some particular item of his property. (C. C. 303). It arises by operation of law rather than by agreement. All preferential rights are specifically provided by statute. (C. C. 306 through 328). Their enforcement requires auction sale of property concerned. (C. E. L. 181, 189, 190). Provisions concerning auction sale for execution of judgment of court (see topic Executions) are generally applicable in enforcement of preferential rights. (C. E. L. 181, 189, 192).

General preferential rights are those which attach to all of property of debtor. Those provided by Civil Code arise in regard to: (a) Expenses incurred for common benefit of all creditors in connection with preservation, liquidation or distribution of debtor's property, (b) last six months of wages for servants, (c) funeral expenses of debtor or of relatives for whose support he is liable, and (d) last six months' supply of comestibles, and firewood, charcoal and oil necessary for debtor, his servants, and his relatives living with him and to whom he owes a duty of support. (C. C. 306 through 310). Order of priority of above-mentioned preferential rights is that given. However, as between these rights and special preferential rights, latter prevail. (C. C. 329). Order of recourse to property of debtor in enforcement of general preferential rights is (1) movables, and (2) immovables which are not subject of special security. (C. C. 335).

Special preferential rights differ in respect to movables and immovables. Preferential rights may exist in respect to following categories of movables: (1) Movables which belong to or are attached by lessee to land or buildings (i.e., fixtures), movables employed in use of land, and fruits of land which remain in possession of lessee, (2) baggage in possession of hotel, in respect to bill of guest, servants and animals, (3) luggage in possession of carrier, in regard to fare of traveler, cost of transportation of luggage and other miscellaneous expenses, (4) bonds deposited by public official, in respect to obligations arising as result of negligence in performance of his duty, (5) movables in respect to costs of their preservation, (6) movables in respect to purchase price for which they were acquired, (7) fruits derived from land for period of one year, in respect to seeds, seedlings and fertilizer supplied for use on land, and similar right to silk products in case of supply of silkworms or mulberry leaves, and (8) fruits or manufactured articles which are product of labor, in respect to agricultural wages for one year, and for industrial wages for three months. (C. C. 311 through 324). Priorities between special preferential rights pertaining to same movables are set by statute, although in certain instances knowledge of prior right serves to disqualify holders of an otherwise superior right which was created later. (C. C. 330).

Special preferential rights pertaining to immovables are ranked as follows: (1) Money necessary for their preservation or for enforcement of rights required for their preservation, when registered immediately; (2) work done by artisans, engineers, or contractors, in regard to increase in value effected thereby when registered in advance of performance; and (3) sale price with interest, if registered at time of a contract for sale. (C. C. 326, 337, 327, 338, 328, 340). See topic Shipping.

PRESCRIPTION:

Japanese concepts distinguish extinctive prescription, acquisitive prescription and limitation of actions. Prescription must be asserted to obtain court recognition and its benefits cannot be waived in advance. (C. C. 145, 146).

Period for extinctive prescription is ten years in case of obligations in general, five years for obligations arising from commercial transactions, and 20 years for all other rights excluding ownership. (C. C. 167; Com. C. 522). However, following special terms are provided: (1) Five years for obligation to deliver money or other things which will become due periodically once a year or at shorter intervals, or monetary claim in general of or against government; (2) three years for obligations in favor of doctors, construction engineers, contractors, etc.; (3) three years for tort liability after awareness of damage and identity of tortfeasor; (4) two years for obligations in favor of lawyers, notaries and bailiffs when arising out of their duties (dated from completion of services) or five years in regard to performance of any particular service by such persons; (5) two years for obligations in favor of producers, wholesalers, retailers, masters and teachers, etc.; (6) one year for obligations for wages of workers by month or lesser period and professional entertainers, freight charges, for rooms and lodgings, rent of movables; (7) one year for claims arising from general average or from collision between ships, etc.; and (8) six months, one year and three years for various liabilities arising out of bills, notes and checks. (C. C. 167 through 174, 724; Com. C. 798; L. B. N. 70, 77; L. C. 51). See topic Bills and Notes.

Interruption of prescriptive period results from: (1) Demand, such as occurs through judicial action which is not dismissed or withdrawn, participation in bankruptcy, or formal demand notice if followed within six months by institution of action; (2) seizure, attachment or injunction; and (3) acknowledgment. (C. C. 147 through 156). Prescription which has been interrupted commences to run anew from time when cause of such interruption was concluded. (C. C. 157).

Suspension of effects of prescription may also occur for six months following recovery of capacity or appointment of guardian, if minor or incompetent had no legal representative during six months preceding end of prescriptive period. (C. C. 158, 159). Likewise actions between husband and wife may be brought within six month period following divorce. (C. C. 159-2). Prescription also is suspended in respect to inherited property until six months after confirmation of successor, selection of administrator for property, or adjudication of bankruptcy. (C. C. 160). When natural calamity has prevented interruption of prescription, prescriptive period does not mature until two weeks following removal of the impediment. (C. C. 161).

Acquisitive prescription, such as affords ownership, has 20-year term in respect to possession of property in general, and ten-year period when possession initially was acquired in good faith. (C. C. 162, 163). See topic Limitation of Actions.

PRINCIPAL AND AGENT:

Valid declaration of intention by agent, made within scope of his authority and with showing that he acts for a principal, binds or accrues to benefit of principal. (C. C. 99). Similar declaration of intention made in absence of revelation of principal, as a general rule, binds only agent unless opposite party knows or should have known of principal's relationship. In commercial transactions, principal is bound but opposite party may demand performance of contract from agent if he does not know of principal's relationship. (C. C. 100; Com. C. 504). In noncommercial transactions, contract made as agent by one without authority is not valid against principal unless ratified. (C. C. 113). Opposite party may request ratification within reasonable time and has right of cancellation until ratified. (C. C. 114, 115). When authority cannot be provided or

PRINCIPAL AND AGENT . . . *continued*
ratification obtained, agent is bound at option of opposite party either to perform or to pay damages. (C. C. 117).

Role of agent may be assumed by person who has no legal capacity. (C. C. 102). Unless specified, powers of agent are limited to performance of acts of preservation, utilization or improvement which do not change fundamental nature of object of agency. (C. C. 103). Creation of a subagency is not permitted except with permission of principal or where unavoidable reason exists. (C. C. 104). No agent may act for both parties unless so authorized, or unless in discharge of obligation. (C. C. 108). Person who has represented to third parties creation of agency relationship is responsible for acts done by ostensible agent within ostensible scope of authority. (C. C. 109). If agent acts beyond his authority and opposite party has reasonable grounds to believe agent is acting within his authority, principal is responsible for such act by agent. (C. C. 110). Agency ceases with: (1) Death of principal (except when principal dies in case of commercial agency), (2) bankruptcy, death or adjudication of incompetency of agent, and (3) upon completion of term provided by contract. (C. C. 111; Com. C. 506).

Product Liability.—Product Liability Law ("P.L.L.") took effect on July 1, 1995. P.L.L. provides for special rules to be applied to case of product liability in preference to general negligence principle under Civil Code, which otherwise would apply. Under P.L.L. party which manufactured, processed or imported product as business ("manufacturer") is made liable for damages if product which manufacturer delivered, i.e., released to market, injured another party's life, body or property because of "defect" in product, i.e., lack of safety which product is supposed to provide. Also, liable under P.L.L. in same way as "manufacturer" are (a) party which placed its name, mark or other feature on product to represent that party is "manufacturer" of product, (b) party which made representation on product which would mislead others that party is "manufacturer" of product and (c) party which is comparable to "manufacturer" under circumstances. Manufacturer or deemed manufacturer shall be exempt from liability under P.L.L. (a) in case where defect could not have been discovered in light of state of scientific or technical knowledge at time when product was placed in market or (b) in case where product was used as part of raw material of another (primary) product, where defect in part or material was result of design directed by primary manufacturer and where manufacturer or deemed manufacturer was not negligent regarding defect.

Right to damages under P.L.L. shall be extinguished by prescription after three years from time that injured party or his/her legal representative became aware of injury and of party who is liable under P.L.L. Also, action for damages under P.L.L. is not available ten years after manufacturer or deemed manufacturer delivered product, except for action for damages caused by material harmful to human health when it is accumulated in human body or for damages which can be recognized after certain incubation period, for which ten-year period shall be counted from time that damages are recognized.

REAL PROPERTY:

No property rights can be created other than those provided for in Civil Code or other laws. (C. C. 175). Following are rights that exist: (I) Ownership (Shoyuken) is complete property right: "fee"; (II) possession (Senyuken) is a condition which will be protected against parties without rights. Possession is presumed bona fide and legal; (III) superficies (Chijoken) is right to use land of another for purpose of owning structures or trees thereon; (IV) emphyteusis (Eikosakken) is right to use another's land for cultivation or grazing; (V) servitude (Chiekiken) is right to use another's land for benefit and convenience of one's own land and corresponds to an easement in American law; (VI) commonage (Iriaiken) is based on old custom whereunder residents of a village use a forest or plain in common. (C. C. 180, 206, 265, 270, 280). There are four types of security interests in property: (A) Lien (Ryuchiken) which is form of possessory lien; (B) preferential right (Sakidori Tokken), which is statutory lien; (C) pledge (Shichiken), and (D) mortgage. (C. C. 295, 303, 342, 369). See topics Liens; Preferential Rights; Mortgages; Pledges.

Certain provisional or contingent rights may be regarded as quasi-property rights in that they can be recorded. Examples are an enforceable promise to sell and resell an immovable. Although lease is not yet considered property right, trend in recent legislation and litigation is to give it similar qualities. (C. C. 605; Land Lease and Home Rent Law 2, 10, 31). However, its continuing classification as contractual obligation still produces inability of lessee to assign or sub-lease without lessor's permission, although lessor will not be able to withhold permission unduly if lessee assigns to another lease together with building on leased land. (C. C. 612; Land Lease and Home Rent Law 19). Also lessee cannot record lease without consent of lessor. Owner of recorded building on leased land can assert lease against person acquiring title to land, and lessee of house who has been delivered possession of house can assert his lease against person acquiring title to house, even though lease itself is unrecorded. (Land Lease and Home Rent Law 2, 10, 31).

With regard to alien ownership of real estate, see topic Aliens.

RECORDS:

Registration offices under Ministry of Justice are located in all parts of Japan and maintain records relating to property and commercial matters. Family register records, although also under general supervision of Ministry of Justice, are maintained separately at every municipal office and are in custody of local officials. Registers of patents, trademarks, designs and utility models are kept by Patent Office in Tokyo.

Real rights in immovables subject to registration include ownership, superficies, emphyteusis, lease, and reversion. Certain forms of encumbrances on immovables, such as pledge, mortgage, and preferential right, may also be placed on record. (Real Property Registration Law 1). Although unrecorded real rights are actionable as between parties to their creation, they must be placed on record to be set up against third persons. (C. C. 177). Same is true of rights of ownership in vessels. (Com. C. 687). A peculiar feature of Japanese law permits a separation of ownership of buildings from land on which erected and can result in maintenance of separate records regarding buildings. (C. C. 86). A provisional registration system affords protection against subsequent transfers of property to third parties through recording of contractual arrangements or incomplete assignments. (Real Property Registration Law 2, 6, 7).

Commercial matters upon which registration is required are: business names, seals, business activities by minors, guardianship, managerial positions and details relating to incorporated concerns. (Commercial Registration Law). Provisional corporate name system affords protection against use of name by other person during interim period of moving principal office, incorporation procedures, and change of trade name or business purpose. (Commercial Registration Law 35, 35-2). Registration must be made both at principal and branch offices. (Com. C. 10). Foreign corporation is prohibited from doing business on continuous basis prior to registration of first business place in Japan. (Com. C. 479, 481). Valid registration of designated facts normally provides defense against third parties. (Com. C. 12).

Registration is required of contracts between husband and wife in respect to their property if terms of contracts are other than as provided by law. (C. C. 755, 756).

Injunctions prohibiting disposition of registered rights and attachments of registered property as well as adjudications of bankruptcy and commencement of reorganization procedures are also recorded. (C. E. L. 48, 175, 180; B. L. 119 et seq.).

REPORTS:

Judicial decisions are persuasive but not formally binding as precedents. Selected cases from the Supreme Court and inferior courts are published.

SALES:

Nature.—Sale is form of contract created when one person agrees to transfer property right to another party and other party agrees to pay price for it. (C. C. 555). Where option contract does not provide option period, option grantor may urge option grantee to exercise option by giving reasonable option period. (C. C. 556). When neither party has yet begun to perform contract of sale in which bargain money (Tetsuke) has been given, purchaser may rescind contract of sale by forfeiting that sum and conversely vendor may rescind by refunding double amount of bargain money. In both cases, further claims for damages are barred. (C. C. 557).

Warranties.—Following warranties exist in respect to sales, and even express provision for freedom therefrom will not release vendor if his liability arises out of facts of which he had knowledge but did not reveal to purchaser or if breach results from creation or assignment of rights by vendor to third persons: (1) Vendor has an obligation to acquire and transfer to purchaser right of third person which has been made subject of sale. (C. C. 560, 572). Failure on part of vendor to perform entitles purchaser to rescind contract, and to receive damages if he had no knowledge, at time of contract, that the particular right did not belong to vendor. Vendor has similar right to rescind, upon payment of damages, if he lacked knowledge, at time of contract, of fact that he did not possess that right. (C. C. 561, 562). (2) Purchaser may demand reduction in price if thing sold is deficient in stipulated quantity, or if vendor is unable to transfer full right because part thereof belongs to another person. Or, if purchaser having acted in good faith would not have bought remaining part alone, he may rescind contract. A reduction in price or rescission still leaves vendor liable for damages to purchaser acting in good faith. (C. C. 563, 565). All rights to obtain reduction, to rescind, or to damages, must be exercised within one year of purchaser's knowledge of fact, if he acted in good faith or one year from day of contract if he acted in bad faith. (C. C. 564). (3) If object of sale is subject to a superficies, emphyteusis, servitude, lien or pledge, or contains latent defect of which purchaser had no knowledge at time of contract, purchaser may rescind contract, providing encumbrance or defect prevents attainment of objective for which contract was made; otherwise purchaser has right for damages alone. Both recovery of damages and rescission are barred one year after purchaser obtains knowledge of fact. (C. C. 566, 570). (4) If purchaser loses ownership of an immovable as result of exercise of preferential right or mortgage covering the property, he may rescind and claim damages as well. (C. C. 567).

Price.—Expenses in connection with sales must be borne equally by both parties. (C. C. 558). Date fixed for delivery of object of sale is presumed to be date of payment. (C. C. 573). Fruits of a thing sold but not delivered belong to vendor. Purchaser is liable for interest on purchase price from date of delivery, unless another date for payment has been provided. (C. C. 575). If right is asserted by third party in respect to subject of a sale, purchaser may refuse to pay whole or part of purchase price unless vendor furnishes suitable security. (C. C. 576). If preferential right exists or a right of pledge or mortgage is registered in respect to immovable which is subject of sale, purchaser may refuse to pay purchase price until encumbrance is removed. (C. C. 577).

Repurchase.—This is type of security device in which vendor of immovable may, by special provision in sale agreement, be provided with right of repurchase, through exercise of which he may rescind sale through repayment of purchase price plus expenses. Unless contrary provision is made, fruits of an immovable and interest on purchase price are deemed to offset one another in event of repurchase. (C. C. 579). Term in which repurchase is possible cannot exceed ten years, and in absence of a specifically provided term, repurchase must occur within five years. (C. C. 580). When creditor of vendor seeks to exercise vendor's right of repurchase, purchaser may retain ownership of property by discharging vendor's obligation out of excess value of property over and beyond purchaser's price plus expenses and returning any remaining excess to vendor. (C. C. 582). If one co-owner has sold his share in an immovable with provision for repurchase, and immovable later is partitioned, former co-owner (vendor) may repurchase that part of the property received by purchaser in division. (C. C. 584). If purchaser received payment upon later auction of co-owned immovable, vendor (former co-owner) may assert a claim to extent of proceeds less purchase price. (C. C. 584).

Resale.—In case of a sale between merchants, if purchaser refuses or is unable to accept delivery of subject of sale, vendor may deposit it or may sell it at public auction after notifying buyer to accept it within reasonable time. Perishable goods may be sold without notification. Vendor has right to appropriate whole or part of proceeds of sale to satisfaction of purchase price but must deposit remainder with government deposit office. (Com. C. 524). If, according to nature of sale or any declared intention of

SALES . . . *continued*
parties, object for which contract was made cannot be attained unless performed at fixed time or within a fixed period, and such time has elapsed, other party is deemed to have rescinded contract unless he demands performance immediately. (Com. C. 525).

Inspection and Rescission.—As between merchants, purchaser must examine object of a sale without delay upon taking delivery, and must notify seller of any defect or shortage in quantity. Failure to take action provided above prevents purchaser from rescinding contract or demanding reduction in price or damages. Immediate notification also must be given in situations where hidden defects are discovered within six months, if purchaser is to preserve similar rights. Bad faith on part of vendor, however, removes purchaser's obligation to give immediate notification in cases mentioned above. (Com. C. 526). When purchaser rescinds, custody of object of sale is at expense of vendor. When there is danger of loss or deterioration of object of sale following rescission, purchaser must obtain order of court and sell goods at auction; proceeds of sale shall be placed in public deposit or kept in purchaser's custody and vendor given immediate notice of auction sale, if he does not reside or do business in same area as purchaser. (Com. C. 527). Similar rules apply when delivered goods differ from those ordered or are delivered in excessive amount. (Com. C. 528).

Notices Required.—No written notice is required for claim of nonconformity against seller after delivery.

Applicable Law.—Choice of law rules follow those of contracts in general (see topic Contracts) but with regard to passage of title, law of location of property governs. (Horei 7, 10).

SEALS:

Extensive use is made of seals in Japan, and most petty transactions are consummated through seals rather than signatures. Certain categories of important seals may be registered at municipal office of possessor or at registry office of corporate representative. Once registered, municipal office or registry office will issue certificate of seal, which may be used to identify person attaching seal to instrument. Although some form of consular verification often is required for special transactions, foreigners may substitute signatures for seals.

SEQUESTRATION:

Court may issue ancillary attachment order for purpose of preservation of enforcement of monetary claims or restraining order for purpose of preservation of rights which are liable to change and adversely affect interests of litigant. (C. P. E. L. 20, 23).

SHIPPING:

Principal features of shipping and maritime law are contained in Book IV of Commercial Code, Law of Ships, Ship Registration Rules, Marine Collisions Prevention Act, Ship Employees Act, Ship's Tonnage Act, Maritime Transportation Act, International Carriage of Goods by Sea Act, Act relating to Limitation of Liability of Owners, etc. of Ships, and other ordinances and regulations issued incidental thereto.

Ships have Japanese nationality if they belong to Japanese government, to Japanese citizens or commercial companies whose principal offices are in Japan and whose directors are Japanese or to legal persons whose principal office is in Japan and whose legal representatives are Japanese. (Law of Ships 1). A roster of ships at Maritime Office contains information regarding type, name, port of registry, construction and tonnage of all Japanese ships, except those of less than 20 tons gross and sailing boats. (Com. C. 686; Law of Ships 4, 20). In addition, records relating to ownership and rights in vessels of 20 tons gross or over are to be found at registration office having jurisdiction over home port of ship. Registration of ships produces results similar to registration of immovables. See topic Records.

Matters relating to use of ship are decided by majority of votes based on value of interest of each co-owner. (Com. C. 693). Any owner dissenting to extensive repairs or a new voyage may require co-owners to purchase his interest. (Com. C. 695). Any owner, except ship's husband, may transfer his interest without consent of co-owners, but should transfer of interest or loss of nationality by co-owner result in loss of Japanese nationality by ship, other co-owners may either purchase interest at reasonable price or have interest sold at auction. (Com. C. 698, 702). Profits and loss are apportioned at end of each voyage. (Com. C. 697). Sale in course of voyage transfers profits and losses to purchaser unless otherwise specified. (Com. C. 688).

Ship's husband may represent owners on all matters except: (1) Transfer, (2) lease or mortgage, (3) insurance, (4) new voyages, (5) extensive repairs, and (6) borrowing money. (Com. C. 700). Ship's master has authority to do all acts necessary for voyage (subject to certain limitations while ship is in home port), but may not, except in order to defray expenses necessary for continuance of voyage: (1) Mortgage ship, (2) borrow money or (3) sell or pledge whole or part of cargo (subject to certain exceptions when done in interest of cargo owner). If ship becomes unrepairable in course of voyage, master may sell it by auction. Limitations on master's authority will not bind third persons acting in good faith. (Com. C. 712 through 715, 717). Shipowner has no liability for damages to money, negotiable instruments and other valuables unless these are declared by consignor. Successive participants in carriage are jointly and severally liable for damage to cargo. (Com. C. 578, 579, 766).

Act relating to Limitation of Liability of Owners, etc. of Ships adopts system of limiting amount of damages arising during voyage which must be paid by liable shipowners, etc., structured to conform with Convention on Limitation of Liability for Maritime Claims, 1976. Limits of total liability of shipowner or his employees are: (a) Where claims are for loss of life or personal injury to passengers of ship, amount of 46,666 Units of Account (Special Drawing Rights as defined by International Monetary Fund) multiplied by authorized number of passengers or 25,000,000 Units of Account, whichever is less; and (b) where all claims are for property damage, 167,000 Units of Account plus, where applicable, 167, 125 and 83 Units of Account for each ton from 501 to 30,000 tons, from 30,001 to 70,000 tons and in excess of 70,000 tons, respectively. In other cases limits of liability are provided in patterns similar to (b), but amounts are approximately three times those in (b). Salvors and their employees are now eligible for limitation of liabilities. Certain claims are excepted from limitation and certain kinds of conduct bar limitation.

Liability of consignee for freight and other expenses arises upon receipt of cargo. Failure to accept cargo empowers shipowner to deposit. (Com. C. 753, 754). Also shipowner may, in event of failure of payment of charges, and with approval of court, sell cargo at auction for two-week period following date of delivery, as long as no third person has acquired possession. (Com. C. 757).

Full charterer may rescind carriage contract before commencement of voyage, upon payment of one-half of freight. (Com. C. 745). Part charterer who rescinds independently before commencement of voyage must pay full amount of freight, less freight earnings from other sources. (Com. C. 748). Damages or expenses occurring from disposition by master to save ship or cargo from a common danger are shared by all persons of interest in accordance with stated rules of general average. (Com. C. 789). Liability of contribution in case of general average is limited by value remaining at time of arrival of ship or delivery of cargo. (Com. C. 790, 791). Salvage is recognized, amount being determined by court on basis of circumstances. (Com. C. 800, 801).

Preferential right exists against ship, her appurtenances and unpaid freight for voyage for: (1) Expenses of a sale of ship and her appurtenances at public auction and expenses of preservation after commencement of proceedings for public sale; (2) expenses of preservation of ship and its appurtenances at last port; (3) fees and dues payable for ship in respect to voyage; (4) pilotage and towage; (5) expenses for assistance in distress and salvage and for ship's portion of any general average; (6) obligations which have arisen from necessity of continuing voyage; (7) obligations in favor of master or other mariners arising out of contract of hiring; and (8) obligations arising from sale or building and outfitting of ship effected prior to commencement of voyage, and for outfitting, supplies and fuel for her last voyage (Com. C. 842); and (9) claims for compensation of damage arising during voyage subject to possible limitation under Act relating to Limitation of Owners, etc. of Ships (Act relating to Limitation of Owners, etc. of Ships 95). Priority exists in order given, except that in cases (4), (5), and (6), later claims take precedence over earlier claims and later voyages over earlier voyages. (Com. C. 844). Assignee of ship must, after registering assignment, call on holders of preferential rights for notification within one month. Preferential rights take precedence over mortgages and last for one year following creation. (Com. C. 846 through 849).

Under Japanese International Carriage of Goods by Sea Act, preferential right against ship and her equipment is given to person who has right to claim compensation for damages to cargo arising within scope of master's duties when contract of carriage has been made with reference to whole or part of a ship and charterer in turn makes a contract of carriage with third person. Priority given to this preferential right is in same order as (9) above. (International Carriage of Goods by Sea Act 19).

Oil Pollution Damage Compensation Law implements International Convention on Civil Liability for Oil Pollution Damage, 1969 and its supplementary Convention to which Japan is party.

STATUTES:

The principal codes are the Constitution, Civil Code, Criminal Code, Commercial Code, Code of Criminal Procedure, Code of Civil Procedure and Civil Execution Law. Provisions of special statutes when applicable will supersede general codes but not Constitution.

TAXATION:

Taxation is both local and national. Limits both as to extent of local taxes and as to categories of local taxes are imposed by national law. Ad valorem taxes are levied on real property of various categories. There is no special personal property tax with certain exceptions.

Income tax is payable by individuals domiciled or resident in Japan ("resident" persons accompanying or attached to U.S. Armed Forces are exempt) in respect to all income although certain exemptions are allowed to residents of not more than five years who do not intend to reside permanently in Japan. Income of nonresidents is also taxable to extent derived from sources within Japan. Top bracket income tax rate is 50% for net income of over 30,000,000 yen. Also taxes of 20% are payable under Income Tax Law by nonresident individuals and corporations in respect to most types of Japanese source income, such as royalties, interest on loans, and dividends. Foreign tax credit may be obtained in accordance with certain formulae and under certain conditions. Under tax convention between Japan and U.S.A., rates of tax on royalties, interest and dividends paid to U.S. residents or corporations, having no permanent establishment in Japan, are: (1) 10% on royalties; (2) 10% on interest with certain exceptions; and (3) 15% on dividends; provided, however, if U.S. corporation owns 10% or more of shares of Japanese corporation, tax rate on dividend paid on such shares is reduced to 10% with certain exceptions. See subhead Special Taxation Measures, infra.

Inheritance tax is payable by: (1) recipients domiciled in Japan at time of inheritance; (2) recipients domiciled elsewhere but who acquire assets located in Japan through inheritance. Top bracket inheritance tax rate is 70% for taxable amounts of over 2,000,000,000 yen. Surviving spouse is exempt from tax that would accrue on decedent's net estate up to net estate value of 160,000,000 yen or if greater his or her statutory share of decedent's net estate. (Inheritance Tax Law).

Gift tax is payable by: (1) recipients domiciled in Japan; (2) recipients domiciled elsewhere but who acquire assets located in Japan. Top bracket gift tax rate is 70% for taxable amounts of over 100,000,000 yen. (Inheritance Tax Law).

Corporation tax is payable by Japanese corporations, including almost all types of juridical persons, such as those having religious, educational, medical and social welfare objectives, as well as labor unions, and also including informal associations having no status as legal entities but having representative. (See subhead An Informal Association under topic Partnership). Partnership under Anglo-American concepts thus is not subject to corporation tax, although its partners are individually subject to income tax. Foreign corporation is liable to corporation tax only for Japanese-source income. Uniform tax rate of 37.5% applies to income of business corporation having capital exceeding 100,000,000 yen. With respect to business corporation with capital

TAXATION . . . *continued*
not more than 100,000,000 yen and informal association without status as legal entity but with representative, tax rate is 28% for taxable income up to 8,000,000 yen and 37.5% for taxable income in excess of 8,000,000 yen. For other types of corporations, uniform rate of 27% applies. Foreign tax credit may be obtained in accordance with certain formulae and under certain conditions.

Consumption tax at rate of 3% is levied on all, with certain exceptions, sales and leasing of assets and provision of services effected in Japan for compensation by business enterprises and foreign goods received from bonded areas. Export transactions are exempt from consumption tax. Consumption tax must be paid by business enterprises and those who receive deliveries of foreign goods from bonded areas. Small enterprises stipulated by law are exempt from taxation.

Liquor and gasoline taxes are levied at rates provided by law.

Stamp duties are payable on documents enumerated by statute, which include certain deeds or contracts, bills and notes, share certificates and certain other investment securities, articles of incorporation, merger contract deeds, bills of lading, warehouse receipts, receipts of money, bank deposit books, etc. Amount runs from 200 yen to 600,000 yen per taxable document. (Revenue Stamp Tax Law).

Registration and franchise tax is payable in respect to matters required or permitted by law to be registered and various franchises, permits, designations and certain certificates with respect to one's qualifications. In general, tax runs from 1,000 yen to 300,000 yen or 0.1% to 5%. (Registration and Franchise Tax Law).

Local Tax.—There are separate prefectural and municipal taxes. Prefectural taxes are inhabitants' tax, enterprise tax, real property acquisition tax, entertainment tax, golf course tax, automobile tax, etc. Municipal taxes are inhabitants' tax, fixed assets tax, etc. Inhabitants' tax is payable by both natural persons and corporations and is calculated at specified rate of amount of income in case of natural persons or at specified rate of corporation tax in case of corporations, in addition to small head tax. Enterprise tax is also payable by both natural persons and corporations. Standard rates of fixed assets tax and real property acquisition tax are 1.4% and 4%, respectively. Automobile is subject to tax running from 7,500 to 111,000 yen per year. In addition, acquisition of automobile is subject to automobile acquisition tax at 3% of purchase price. (Local Tax Law). Furthermore, automobiles are subject to automobile weight tax which is imposed in accordance with types of automobiles and their weight. (Automobile Weight Tax Law).

Special Taxation Measures.—Various forms of favorable treatment in taxation or tax exemptions are provided in Special Taxation Measures Law for purpose of stimulating capital investment and developing important and useful industrial techniques, etc. They include: separate taxation on interest and dividends and reduced tax rates thereon; recognition of accelerated or inflated depreciation on certain machinery; special treatment of income derived from certain overseas technological transactions. Law introduced, effective Apr. 1, 1986, inter-company transfer pricing rules covering cross border transactions between Japanese company and its foreign affiliated company which include sales, purchase, loan, technical assistance and consultation transactions, etc. Under these rules transactions are deemed to have been consummated at arm's length transaction price. Also, Law introduced, effective Apr., 1992, thin capitalization rules which are somewhat similar to earnings stripping rules for debt-to-equity ratio in excess of 3 to 1.

Tax treaties for purposes of avoidance of double taxation and prevention of evasion from taxation have been concluded and are effective with Australia, Austria, Bangladesh, Belgium, Brazil, Bulgaria, Canada, Czech Republic, Denmark, Egypt, Finland, France, Germany, Hungary, India, Indonesia, Ireland, Israel, Italy, Luxembourg, Malaysia, Netherlands, New Zealand, Norway, Pakistan, People's Republic of China, Philippines, Poland, Romania, Russia, Singapore, South Korea, Spain, Sri Lanka, Sweden, Switzerland, Thailand, Turkey, U.K., U.S.A., Vietnam, and Zambia.

TRADEMARKS AND TRADE NAMES:

Trademarks are any written characters, designs, signs or combinations thereof or any combinations of these and colors which are used to distinguish merchandise as being manufactured, worked upon, certified or dealt with by a person. (T. L. 2). However, only trademarks registered through a process of application to Patent Office are entitled to be protected as trademark rights under Trademark Law. Registration is not permitted of trademarks which are not distinctive, which resemble marks of international organizations, governmental insignia, red cross mark, which are apt to be injurious to public morals, or which resemble registered or widely known trademarks for same or similar goods. (T. L. 3, 4). Service mark is made registrable starting Apr. 1, 1992.

Trademark rights continue for ten years commencing on date of registration, with subsequent ten-year renewals possible. (T. L. 19). Trademark rights can be transferred independently from transfer of business. Trademark licenses are authorized. In case trademark designates more than two categories of goods, trademark right may be transferred separately for each of designated goods. Transfer of trademark right, which must be preceded by public notice in daily newspaper, cannot take effect without registration. (T. L. 24, 35). Consent of all other co-owners is necessary for co-owner to assign or transfer co-ownership or to license trademark.

In case registered trademark conflicts with previously registered design or previously created copyright, such trademark cannot be used without consent of owner of design or copyright. (T. L. 29). Infringement of a trademark exposes party to injunction, action for damages and criminal prosecution. (T. L. 36 through 38, 78). Any person may file application with Patent Office for invalidation of registration of trademark which fails to satisfy requisites for registration. (T. L. 46). Also application for cancellation of a trademark can be filed for reason of improper use either by its owner or by licensee and for nonuse of more than three years. (T. L. 50, 51). A foreign trademark may be registered in Japan.

Trade Names.—Recording of trade name at registration office affords registrant protection against registration of same or similar name by third persons in municipal area for same business. (Com. C. 19). Temporary recording of trade name is available to business corporation in advance of change of its seat of principal office, trade name or business object, or in advance of its incorporation. Infringement may be enjoined and damages recovered. (Com. C. 20). Trade name of business corporation must indicate category of corporation. (Com. C. 17). Trade name of individual may be transferred or inherited in connection with business, but no transfer can be set up against third persons unless recorded. (Com. C. 24). Trade name continues on record until cancelled, upon showing of two year period in which name has not been used. (Com. C. 30, 31).

TREATIES:

Treaties or agreements that relate to commerce are in effect with the following: Greece (1899), Spain (1901 and 1915), Sweden (1911), Switzerland (1911), Denmark (1912), France (1912, 1964 and 1995), Germany (1928), Netherlands (1913), Finland (1926), Turkey (1934), Uruguay (1940), Iran (1941), U.S.A. (1953), Canada (1954), Cambodia (1956), U.S.S.R. (1956, 1958 and 1991), Norway (1957), Australia (1957 and 1977), India (1958), New Zealand (1958), Ethiopia (1958 and 1968), Yugoslavia (1959), Malaya (1960), Cuba (1961), Pakistan (1961), Peru (1961), Benelux (1962), Indonesia (1963), U.K. (1963), Haiti (1963), El Salvador (1964), Argentina (1967), Central African Republic (1968), Malta (1968), Mexico (1969 and 1996), Bulgaria (1970), Rumania (1970), Ivory Coast (1970), Malawi (1970), Zaire (1971), People's Republic of China (1974), Congo (1975), Hungary (1976), Poland (1980), Philippines (1980), Albania (1988), Mongolia (1990), Israel (1993) Czech Republic (1994), Republic of Turkey (1994), Republic of Singapore (1995) and Vietnam (1995).

Japan is a signatory to Convention on Settlement of Investment Disputes between States and Nationals of Other States of Mar. 18, 1965, Convention on Service Abroad of Judicial or Extrajudicial Documents, Convention Relating to Civil Procedures, Convention on Recognition and Enforcement of Foreign Arbitral Awards, Convention Abolishing the Requirement of Legalisation for Foreign Public Documents, Convention on Elimination of All Forms of Discrimination against Women and Marrakesh Agreement Establishing the World Trade Organization.

See also Selected International Conventions section.

Copyright Treaties.—See topic Copyright.

Patent Treaty.—See topic Patents.

Tax Treaties.—See topic Taxation.

TRUSTS:

One of the unusual features of Japanese jurisprudence is a codified law of trusts which is modeled on Anglo-American concepts but modified to conform with principles of continental law. Trust rights are sui generis, being neither real rights nor obligations, although weight of authority regards them as being in the nature of obligations. Although trusts may be created by operation of law, this is a rare occurrence, and in practice they arise from private acts and agreements. (C. T. 1, 2). Essential parties to trust are creator, trustee and beneficiary, although trust inspector whose duty is to check upon trustee may be appointed either by creator or by court. (C. T. 4, 7, 41).

Trust property may consist of movables, immovables or obligations. Causes of action may not be object of trust, and trusts created to defraud creditors are also prohibited. (C. T. 11, 12). As protection to third parties, act of creation of trust must be placed on record at appropriate office if involving real property, patents, mining rights, shares of stock, etc. Also, fact of trust must be noted upon negotiable instruments. (C. T. 3).

Trust may be created by will, in which case court may supply certain deficiencies which would prove fatal to establishment of trust relationship between living persons. (C. T. 2).

Trustee has duty to separate trust property from property owned by him personally and administer trust property in accordance with stated purposes of trust. (C. T. 1, 28). Unless otherwise provided he may not resign as trustee except with consent of beneficiary and creator, or upon bankruptcy, incompetency, removal by court for cause, etc. (C. T. 42, 43, 46, 47). Liability of trustee is that of good and faithful custodian, plus certain additional responsibilities to interested parties for restitution and replacement of property improperly removed. (C. T. 27, 29, 31). Unless specifically provided, trustee serves without compensation. (C. T. 35). Disposition of property in trust by trustee contrary to purpose of trust may be cancelled by beneficiary. (C. T. 31). Except for professional trustees, trustees are under supervision of court. (C. T. 41).

Public trusts are limited to objectives provided for foundations (see topic Corporations). (C. T. 66). In their administration consent of administrative agencies frequently is required, over and beyond conventional court supervision. (C. T. 67 et seq.). Special categories of trust companies are authorized by law and because of public interest in their operations, they are subjected to addtional controls and responsibilities.

WILLS:

Persons 15 years or older may, if possessed of testamentary capacity, make will. (C. C. 961, 963). Incompetent may make will during lucid interval and with attendance of two or more physicians who attest his lucidity at time of making. (C. C. 973). By means of will, testator may acknowledge an illegitimate child, create trust and dispose of property, etc. (C. C. 41, 781, 964, etc.).

Execution.—Civil Code provides form and ceremonies which must be used, and recognizes holographic wills, wills drafted by notaries (see topic Notaries Public) and secret wills, envelopes of which are acknowledged by notaries. (C. C. 967 through 970). In addition, certain exceptional situations are enumerated in which different formalities may be applied, such as oral will at deathbed which is reduced to writing, acknowledged by three witnesses and confirmed by registration with a court within 20 days, and wills made in quarantine or aboard ship. (C. C. 976 through 982).

In foreign countries, Japanese consul may perform functions of notary in regard to wills. (C. C. 984).

Testamentary Disposition.—Testator may dispose of any portion of his estate, but disposition in excess of legally secured portions of heirs is subject to later adjustment upon demands from heirs other than brothers and sisters. (C. C. 1031). For purpose of calculation of value of estate, gifts made within one year of death or gifts made in

WILLS . . . *continued*
anticipation of death may be included. (C. C. 1030). Legally secured portions in estates, as provided in Civil Code as am'd effective on Jan. 1, 1981 are: (1) one-third for all of successors in case where they are all lineal ascendants, and (2) one-half in other case, such as when spouse alone is successor and when successors are all lineal descendants or spouse and lineal descendants. (C. C. 1028).

Legacies may be burdened and in turn may be renounced by legatee. (C. C. 986).

Governing law as to existence and effect of wills is law of country of testator at time of execution, and rescission of wills is governed by law of country of testator at time of rescission. (Horei 26). Wills are deemed effective if lawfully made in accordance with any of (1) Lex loci actus; (2) lex patriae; (3) lex domicili or law of place where testator maintained permanent residence at time of establishment of will or testator's death; or (4) in case of will concerning real property, lex loci rei sitae of property. (Law concerning Choice of Laws in respect to Formalities of Wills 2).

See Topical Index in front part of this volume.

KOREA LAW DIGEST REVISER

Kim & Chang
Seyang Building
223 Naeja-Dong, Chongro-Ku
Seoul 110, Korea
Telephone: 82-2-737-4455
Fax: 82-2-737-9091/3
Email: http://www.kimchang.co.kr.; http://203.240.196.11

Reviser Profile

History: Kim & Chang, one of the first law firms in Korea, was founded in 1973 by Young Moo Kim, a 1970 Juris Doctor recipient from Harvard Law School, and Soo Kil Chang, former judge and Director of Korea Bar Association. Since that relatively recent beginning, the firm has grown to over 150 professionals and a support staff of over 400. Kim & Chang is the largest law firm in Korea and the recognized leader in providing specialized legal services for international transactions involving Korea. The continuing philosophy is to provide the responsive, high quality, across the border legal services required by their clients.

Firm Members: All of our lawyers graduated from prestigious Korean universities and have passed the rigorous Korean Bar Examination. Further, many have done post-graduate legal studies abroad and have had work experience in major international firms overseas. To assist in serving our clients, the firm also includes 30 resident expatriate foreign legal consultants with substantial international experience. All of our Korean lawyers are fluent in English, and many of our professionals have facility in other languages, such as Japanese, French, German, Chinese and Russian.

Areas of Emphasis: Kim & Chang is a full service firm which has developed departmental specialization. To ensure efficient teamwork, to mobilize resources for complex projects and to promote specialization, the firm is divided into the following departments in line with the principal areas of our practice: Corporate, Securities and Banking, Merger and Acquisition, Tax, Labor, Real Estate, Insurance, Trade and Foreign Exchange, Maritime, Litigation and Arbitration, Overseas Investment and Intellectual Property. In addition to these principal departments, Kim & Chang has other specialized sections that deal with legal matters such as civil contracts, military contracts, fair trade law, environmental law, advertising and press law, and specific industry-related law. Members of these departments work in close cooperation to provide each client with access to the special expertise of all departments.

Client Base: The firm represents a number of major multinational companies. Kim & Chang also serves numerous medium and small foreign clients doing business in or with Korea, as well as major Korean clients.

Significant Distinctions: Major distinctions of firm members include: Young Moo Kim, former member of the Foreign Capital Deliberation Committee of the Ministry of Finance, and commissioner of the Korea Trade Commission and former Nonstanding Commissioner of Securities and Exchange Commission; S. K. Chang, former judge, former Vice President of the Korean Patent Lawyers Association and former Vice President of the Seoul Bar Association, President of the Korean Intellectual Property Research Society, Inc. and director of the Korean Bar Association; and J. H. Lee, former Executive Director of the Korean Bar Association, former judge, former Vice President of the Seoul Bar Association, former member of the Fair Trade Committee and former Executive Director of the Korea Legal Center; H. C. Hyun, former Minister of Legislation and former Ambassador to the United Nations and Ambassador to the United States of America, and currently member of U.S.-Korea 21 Century Council, member of U.S.-Korea Business Council and member of Korea Foreign Trade Association Advisory Board for Global Trade Policy; S. M. Cha, former Administrator (Head) of the Office of Patents Administration and former Assistant Minister of Trade and Industry and currently member of National Assembly; Y. T. Suh, former Commissioner of National Tax Administration and former Minister of Construction, currently Member of National Policy Advisory Committee and Chairman of International Fiscal Association; C. P. Jhong, former General Counsel for Asian Development Bank; Kihwan Kim, former Vice Minister of Trade and Industry of Korea and former member of Monetary Board and currently Chairman of the Board of Korea Trade Promotion Corporation ("KOTRA"). Kim & Chang attorneys actively participate in the national legislative and policy making process by sitting on various judicial, administrative, and governmental advisory committees. Firm members have contributed numerous publications to international law journals and publications. Firm members are also engaged in various pro bono and civic activities.

REPUBLIC OF KOREA

(The following is a list of all Topics, including cross-references, covered in this Digest.)

REPUBLIC OF KOREA

Revised for 1997 edition by

KIM & CHANG, of the Seoul Bar

(Abbreviations used are: A.L. for Arbitration Law; B.N.A. for Bills and Notes Act; C.C. for Civil Code; C.C.P. for Code of Civil Procedure; C. Crim. P. for Code of Criminal Procedure; C. for Constitution; C.L.A. for Conflict of Laws Act; C.O.A. for Court Organization Act; B.L. for Bankruptcy Law; Com. C. for Commercial Code; C.R.L. for Company Reorganization Law; L.D.A.L. for Labor Disputes Adjustment Law; L.M.D.L. for Labor Management Council Law; L.S.L. for Labor Standards Law; L.U.L. for Labor Union Law; S.E.L. for Security Exchange Law; F.E.M.L. for Foreign Exchange Management Law; F.C.I.L. for Foreign Capital Inducement Law; C.A. for Copyright Act; T.A. for Trademark Act; R.T.L. for Road Traffic Law; M.V.C.L. for Motor Vehicles Control Law; E.E.C.A. for Exit and Entry Control Act; M.R.F.T.A. for Monopoly Regulation and Fair Trade Act; U.C.P.L. for Unfair Competition Prevention Law; C.P.A. for Consumer Protection Act; P.A. for Patent Act).

ACKNOWLEDGMENTS:

Formal acknowledgment is not usually necessary to validate instrument. Acknowledgment of notary does, however, authenticate identity of parties, verify required performance of party and creates presumption of genuineness to private instruments similar to official documents. Acknowledgment of articles of incorporation of stock and limited corporations is mandatory. (Com. C. 292, 543[3]). In civil actions, some papers submitted to court require acknowledgments. (C.C.P. 81[2], 326[1]). Recorded instruments are usually written and certified by notaries. See topic Notaries Public.

Acknowledgments for use in other countries usually may be taken by diplomatic representatives of those countries who are accredited to Korean government.

Authentication.—Private documents must be authenticated unless acknowledged by opposite party. (C.C.P. 328). In civil procedure practice, however, documents submitted to court need to be authenticated irrespective of whether they are private or not. (C.C.P. 330). Documents prepared by public officials, including foreign public officials in exercise of their duties evidenced by form and purport thereof, or private documents bearing signature or seal of principal or representative, shall be presumed to be authentic. (C.C.P. 327, 329). Authenticity of document may be proven by comparison of handwriting or seal impressions or, more generally in civil procedure, by witness. (C.C.P. 330).

Seals.—Most transactions in Korea are consummated by use of seals rather than signatures. Some seals may be registered with municipal office of owner (registry office in case of commercial transactions). Certificate of seals may be issued as to such seals. For foreigners, signatures may substitute seals although some kind of consular verification is required. (Foreigner's Signature and Seal Act).

ACTIONS:

Submission of Controversy.—All actions, except small claims, value of which is not more than 10,000,000 Won, must be commenced by filing complaint before courts or institutional arbitration. (C.C.P. 226). Complaints will not be accepted unless required fees have been paid. Fees or stamp taxes are proportionate to value of dispute (in court action, approximately half or one hundredth) and increases for appeal. When complaint involves corporate parties, documents such as certified copy of company register must accompany complaint in order to identify corporate parties. When complaint is filed by lawyer representing plaintiff, he must submit power of attorney establishing his authority. Small claims as defined in Special Legislation may be submitted to court by stating cause of action to court clerk. Complaint must be sufficient to identify parties to controversy, remedies sought for, and factual and legal arguments in support thereof. (Small Claims Trial Act). Rectifications in statements of facts or in causes of action are usually allowed without procedural limitations on manners or timing. But, in event that any complaint or defense is presented late intentionally or by gross negligence by either party, and is deemed to cause delay in concluding litigation, court may, upon motion or its own authority, render ruling in rejection thereof. (C.C.P. 138).

Confession.—Under Code of Civil Procedure, confession refers to statement of party or parties to admit fact which is adverse to himself or themselves. Court is bound by confession in finding facts and is not able to find facts contrary to confession.

Admission of Plaintiff's Claim.—If defendant admits plaintiff's claim legally and factually and such statement is described in court file, it is deemed to be final and conclusive for judgment which is not subject to ordinary appeal.

Waiver of Plaintiff's Claim.—If plaintiff waives and denies claims unconditionally and if such statement is described in court file, it is deemed to be final and conclusive for judgment. In that respect, waiver of claim is different from withdrawal of case.

Practice.—Civil practice is regulated by Code of Civil Procedure and various regulations issued by Supreme Court.

Sovereign Immunity.—Foreign countries and foreign diplomats are precluded from being litigated against unless they consent to be sued.

Intervention.—Third person not originally party to suit may intervene. (C.C.P. 65). Typical intervention occurs where third person claiming interest in subject matter brings claims against both parties to pending action. Intervenor may be made to join or assist one party in pending action. Where subject matter in pending action would allow intervention by third party and when he did not intervene, parties may notify third party of litigation. Notice generally binds third party by decision made in case vis-à-vis notifying party even when third party did not intervene in action. (C.C.P. 79).

Joinder.—All persons may join in one action as plaintiffs or defendants if rights or liabilities which are object of suit are common to two or more persons or are based on same ground in facts and law. (C.C.P. 61). Concept of necessary and indispensable party for purpose of joinder or nonjoinder is generally not applicable to proceedings in Korea. Third party practice is not known to Korean judicial system.

Severance creates two or more independent lawsuits, terminating in separate, final and enforceable judgments. Court may sever lawsuit without application from parties. Some lawsuits cannot be severed due to their nature (called "necessary common lawsuit"). (C.C.P. 63). Although lawsuit is severed, jurisdiction of lawsuit remains unchanged. Severance may be cancelled at any time. (C.C.P. 131).

Class actions do not exist under Korean law. However, legislation covering class actions and collective suit is under preparation by government.

ADOPTION:

Person other than minor may adopt another person. (C.C. 866). Married persons must be joined by their spouse to adopt. If married person is adopted, he or she must obtain his or her spouse's consent. (C.C. 874). Consent of adopted person's parents is generally required for adoption, and if parents or other lineal ascendants do not exist and minor is to be adopted, consent of guardian is required. (C.C. 870, 871). Adoption may be dissolved upon mutual agreement of parties. (C.C. 898). Adoption may also be dissolved through judicial proceedings: (1) If either adoptive parent or child has committed acts of gross negligence, impairing reputation of family or squandering family fortune; (2) if either party has been extremely maltreated by other or by his lineal ascendants; (3) if any lineal ascendant of one party has been extremely maltreated by other party; (4) if adopted child is not known to be alive or dead for three years or longer; or (5) if there is any other significant cause making it difficult to maintain adoptive relationship. (C.C. 905). With respect to adoptions involving different nationalities, requisites of each party are determined in accordance with respective law of nationality of such party, and effect of adoption and its dissolution are determined in accordance with law of adopting party's nationality. (C.L.A. 21).

ALIENS:

Aliens are persons not of Korean nationality or of no nationality. Aliens are now afforded virtually all rights of Korean with certain restricted exceptions. In general, aliens are permitted to own property and to contract without governmental approval but cannot practice professions of quasi-public character (e.g., law and public accounting). Alien may not own mines or register aircraft or vessel in Korea. Acquisition of land or rights related thereto require government approval or report. (Alien Land Acquisition Act). Fishery business license requires consent from National Assembly. Alien having no residence in Korea may not enjoy patent rights, with certain exceptions.

Aliens must register with immigration office having jurisdiction over their residence within 90 days from entry. Entrance into country is subject to governmental approval except for members of U.S. Armed Forces, UN's agencies, diplomats, consuls and their dependents, and public officials of foreign governments and international organizations recognized by Korea. By virtue of Agreement under Art. 4 of Mutual Defense Treaty between Republic of Korea and U.S. regarding Facilities and Areas and Status of U.S. Armed Forces in Republic of Korea, alien members of U.S. Armed Forces, including civilian military components, together with dependents, may be subject to criminal jurisdiction of Korean courts with respect to crimes committed in Korea which are punishable under Korean law. Aliens have equal access to courts in bankruptcy, compulsory composition proceedings and certain tort actions against Korean government; they are equally treated only if country of their nationality provides same treatment to Korean nationals.

Corporations owned by or controlled by aliens are regarded as "foreign investors" for purpose of inward direct investments including acquisition of shares, restrictions on acquisition and registration of mines, land, aircraft, vessels, fishery business licenses and patent rights. See also topic Corporations, subhead Foreign Corporations.

ALTERNATIVE DISPUTE RESOLUTION:

Alternative dispute resolution mechanisms are scattered in individual statutes and are mandatory or voluntary depending on provisions therein.

Voluntary Dispute Resolution.—Voluntary dispute resolutions take one of following three forms: mediation, conciliation and arbitration:

Arbitration.—Party or parties in dispute may petition for arbitration, outcome of which is binding on both parties. See also topic Arbitration and Award.

Mediation.—Party or parties in dispute may petition for mediation. Outcome of mediation is not binding on either party. Mediation takes one of following forms: negotation, independent expert appraisal, moderation and facilitation. Labor Dispute Adjustment Act (Arts. 18 through 21) and Environmental Pollution Damages Dispute Adjustment Act (Arts. 18 through 20) provide for mediation.

Conciliation.—Voluntary conciliation and other similar dispute resolution mechanisms are provided for in many statutes: Environmental Injuries Dispute Adjustment Act, Labor Dispute Adjustment Act, Insurance Business Act, Copyright Act, Securities Exchange Act, Medical Services Act, Construction Business Act, Male and Female Equal Employment Act, and Dairy Farm Promotion Act.

Civil Conciliation Law (1990) was enacted for purpose of utilizing conciliation as means of ADR since even though there exist conciliation systems in number of statutes it is seldom used.

Under Civil Conciliation Law, party may petition for conciliation to court. (C.C.L., Art. 2). Court to which lawsuit was filed may transfer case to conciliation if it deems such action necessary. (C.C.L., Art. 6). Judge in charge of conciliation may handle case himself or form committee to do so; provided, in case that parties request for committee, conciliation shall be handled by conciliation committee. (C.C.L., Art. 7). Judge in charge may investigate facts and evidences in appropriate manner at his discretion if he deems necessary to hear testimony of parties in dispute or interested

See Topical Index in front part of this volume.

ALTERNATIVE DISPUTE RESOLUTION . . . *continued*

parties. (C.C.L., Art. 22). Judge in charge may at his discretion terminate conciliation proceedings if he finds that nature of dispute is not suitable for conciliation or that party in dispute has petitioned for conciliation for improper reasons. Parties may not appeal ruling of termination of conciliation proceedings. (C.C.L., Art. 26). Conciliation is completed when parties record their agreements and settlement in writing. (C.C.L., Art. 29). Outcome of conciliation embraces enforceability equal to that of court settlement. (C.C.L., Art. 29). Petition for conciliation shall suspend statute of limitation. (C.C.L., Art. 35). Proceeding fees shall be paid by both parties if conciliation is reached in absence of any agreement as to such, and proceeding fees shall be paid by petitioning party if conciliation is not reached. (C.C.L., Art. 37).

Other Means of Alternative Dispute Resolution.—In addition to arbitration, mediation and conciliation, there are other means of dispute resolution within formal procedures.

Summary procedure under Code of Civil Procedure: with regard to claim based on monetary payment or on delivery of certain quantity of any other fungibles or negotiable instruments, court may, upon motion of creditor, issue payment order, to which debtor may raise objection within two weeks.

Summary procedure under Special Act Concerning Summary Proceedings for Civil Cases: joint law office prescribed by provisions of Art. 9 of Act or notary public may draw notarial deed on note, check or slip affixed thereto authorizing it to be immediately executable, which is regarded as writ of execution against drawer and endorser.

Compromise (court settlement): there are two types of compromise. Under first type, party to civil dispute may file motion, before lawsuit is actually filed, for settlement before district court located in place where general forum of other party exists, by setting forth allegations and ground for claim as well as actual circumstances of dispute. (Code of Civil Procedure, Art. 355). In event that settlement is not reached, party may apply for institution of suit. Under second type, where lawsuit is already in progress, compromise negotiations may be initiated either by parties or court at any stage of oral argument. In both types of compromise under Code of Civil Procedure, where agreement has properly been entered into protocol, compromise has same effect as final and conclusive judgment.

Mandatory Dispute Resolution.—Non-exhaustive list of Korean laws which require some form of nonjudicial dispute resolution mechanisms before parties resort to arbitration or litigation is as follows: State Compensation Act (Art. 16 requires claimant for damages against government entity to confront responsible party before appropriate committee and prohibits bringing dispute to courts until such conciliation procedures are certified to have been unsuccessful), Domestic Affairs Adjudication Act (Art. 50 requires that before proceeding may be adjudicated by courts, conciliation procedures must be applied for, and in case parties fail to petition for conciliation, family court shall return case to conciliation, unless court accepts that parties cannot be summoned or case cannot be settled by conciliation), Act concerning Fairness of Subcontracting Transactions (Art. 24 requires that conciliation commission shall confirm or conciliate case referred by Fair Trade Commission), Consumer Protection Act, and Mining Business Act.

ARBITRATION AND AWARD:

Written agreement to submit any controversy thereafter arising between parties or any existing controversy to arbitration is enforceable. Furthermore, dispute under arbitration agreement is not allowed to be litigated. (A.L. 3). There is only one institutional arbitration body, Korean Commercial Arbitration Board. Arbitration award has same legal effect as that given to judgment but may be enforced only after enforcement judgment is made by court. Enforcement judgment will be entered unless any of following prescribed grounds for cancelling or vacating award are found: (1) When selection of arbitrators or arbitration proceeding was contrary to provisions of Arbitration Act or arbitration agreement; (2) when either party was legally incapable of selecting arbitrators or following course of arbitration proceedings or when parties were not lawfully represented in proceedings; (3) when award directs actions that are prohibited by law; (4) when parties were, without justification, not heard or no reasons for award were given; or (5) when causes for bringing retrial as prescribed in Code of Civil Procedure exist.

Korea, party to UN Convention on Recognition and Enforcement of Foreign Arbitral Awards of June 10, 1958, will enforce arbitration award rendered in another party country.

ASSIGNMENTS:

Assignment of property may be made by agreement between assignor and assignee and, for real property, registration of transfer of title, and, for personal (tangible) property, delivery of possession. Assignment of credits will be effective upon agreement between assignor and assignee; however, to be effective against obligor assignor must give notice of assignment to such obligor or have his consent. (C.C. 450 [I]). Notice of assignment or consent must bear officially confirmed date in order to assert assignment against third parties other than obligor. (C.C. 450 [II]).

ATTACHMENT:

Attachment of chattels, real estate, or accounts receivable is effected upon judgment or enforcement judgment of arbitral award as first step of execution of judgments. Where it is shown to satisfaction of court that without provisional attachment execution of future money judgment might be frustrated or rendered difficult, provisional attachment may be granted prior to judgment. Security deposit for protection of respondent is usually required to be paid before court issues order. Amount of deposit is within court's discretion and ranges between one third and one eighth of amount sought to be protected by provisional attachment. See also topic Injunctions.

ATTORNEYS AND COUNSELORS:

Persons who are graduated from Judicial Research and Training Institute attached to Supreme Court are admitted to practice in any court of country after registering with Korean Bar Association. (Lawyers Act 7). In order to be admitted to Judicial Research and Training Institute, one must pass national bar examination. (Lawyers Act 4).

Minister of Government Administration may decide details of national bar examination. (Presidential Decree for National Bar Examination 2). In recent years, national bar examination was held once a year and number of those successfully passing national bar examination was not more than 300. However, such figure is expected to be increased by 100 per year, until it reaches 1,000, under judicial reform plan.

There are various examinations for licenses to practice as scriveners, patent agents, tax agents, customs agents, admiralty counselors, or realtors. Attorney is entitled to practice in any legal area without separate license. Attorney Disciplinary Committee censures, suspends or removes from office any attorney for professional misconduct, malpractice, fraud, deceit, crime, or misdemeanor.

When group of attorneys satisfies certain requirements and obtains license from Minister of Justice, they may perform duties of notary public. Attorneys may also incorporate their business pursuant to procedures and requirements prescribed in Lawyers Act. (Lawyers Act 30 through 48).

Minister of Justice has authority to issue lawyer's license to foreign lawyer when it is deemed appropriate. (Lawyers Act 6). Foreign lawyer who is granted lawyer's license as mentioned above may practice law in Korea with permission of Minister of Justice, only in cases where his country recognizes qualifications of and permits legal practice by Korean nationals qualified as lawyers. However, foreign lawyer shall in no case handle matters other than those related to foreign laws.

Contact addresses, phone and facsimile numbers of national and major local bar associations are as follows: (1) Korean Bar Association, address: 1553-1, Seocho-dong, Seocho-ku, Seoul, Korea, telephone: (02) 522-3761/6, facsimile: (02) 522-3767; (2) Seoul Bar Association, address: 1553-1, Seocho-dong, Seocho-ku, Seoul, Korea, telephone: (02) 522-9811/7, facsimile: (02) 522-9819; (3) Pusan Bar Association, address: 1, 2-ka, Bumin-dong, Seo-ku, Pusan, Korea, telephone: (051) 244-3735/6, facsimile: (051) 241-7366.

BANKRUPTCY:

Insolvency in bankruptcy means inability to make debt payments. (B.L. 116). Stock company's inability to pay debts but continue in business are grounds for reorganization.

Petition.—Bankruptcy process is begun by submitting petition to district court having jurisdiction. (B.L. 96). Petitions may be made by debtor or creditors. (B.L. 122). Petition of juridical person may be submitted by its director or liquidator. (B.L. 123). Debtor's failure to make debt payments is prima facie evidence of his inability to make payments and grounds for adjudication of bankruptcy. (B.L. 116). Juridical persons may be bankrupt when liabilities exceed assets. (B.L. 117).

Administration.—After adjudication of bankruptcy, court appoints receiver, orders listing of claims, and sets up meeting of creditors. (B.L. 132). Creditors may appoint advisers, grant allowances, decide whether to continue operating business and consent to important acts of liquidation of estate. (B.L. 170, 184, 187, 188). Consequently, bankrupt is immediately deprived of control over his property involved in bankruptcy proceedings. (B.L. 6, 7).

Outstanding Obligations.—Debtor's obligations to third parties become due and owing as of adjudication of bankruptcy. (B.L. 14). If debtor and another party to contract have not completed performance, receiver may complete debtor's performance and demand other party to fulfill its obligation or may cancel contract. (B.L. 50). Other party may demand election by receiver of performance or rescission. Failure to answer within reasonable period creates presumption of rescission. (B.L. 50).

Power of Receiver.—Receiver has exclusive power to administer and dispose of bankrupt estate. (B.L. 7). Receiver is bankrupt estate representative for litigation. (B.L. 152). Restoration of third person's properties and payments of preferential claims are accomplished by application to receiver. Receiver may also institute actions to avoid and annul acts of debtor intentionally prejudicial to creditors taken before adjudication of bankruptcy. (B.L. 64).

Preferential Payment.—Lien holders, pledgees or mortgagees of specific property in bankrupt estate may receive satisfaction from property independently of bankruptcy proceeding and may be involved in bankruptcy proceedings only to make up deficiencies. (B.L. 84 through 88). Person whose property has not come under receivership as part of bankrupt estate can get it back. (B.L. 79 through 83). Receiver can pay certain taxes independent of bankruptcy proceedings. (B.L. 38, 40). Lien holders on general property have next level of priority to receive distributions before ordinary creditors. (B.L. 32). Receiver declares payments made to creditors by bankrupt within certain period prior to, or after insolvency or filing of application for bankruptcy, and restores them to estate; also any payments made in bad faith purposely to adversely affect other creditors. (B.L. 64 et seq.).

Termination.—Distribution of assets to creditors terminates bankruptcy proceedings. Creditors may unanimously consent to dissolution of bankruptcy proceeding. (B.L. 319 et seq.). Bankruptcy proceedings may also be terminated if costs of liquidation are greater than value of bankrupt estate. (B.L. 135, 325). Petty bankruptcy may be used for estates less than 5,000,000 Won in which court makes decisions usually made by assembly of creditors and is generally simplified. (B.L. 330 through 338).

Disabilities of Bankrupt.—Person against whom adjudication of bankruptcy is pending loses certain rights. Full payment of indebtedness, discharge, or lapse of ten years absent fraud will allow court to remove all disabilities. (B.L. 358, 359).

Composition.—Debtors may present to court plans for continuing of business and stop bankruptcy proceeding. (B.L. 262 et seq.). Majority of creditors holding three-fourth of total obligations of debtor can decide on compulsory composition and all other creditors must comply. (B.L. 278, also see 304).

Foreigners of countries that allow reciprocity for Koreans in bankruptcy procedures are treated in same manner as Koreans. Bankruptcy adjudications affect only property found in Korea, to both Koreans and foreigners. (B.L. 2, 3).

BILLS AND NOTES:

Korea is in conformity with Geneva International Conventions on Uniform Law of 1930 and 1931.

See Topical Index in front part of this volume.

BILLS AND NOTES . . . *continued*

Bills of Exchange.—Bill of exchange must contain: (1) Term "bill of exchange", (2) unconditional order for payment of specified sum of money, (3) name of drawee, (4) maturity (payment is deemed to be at sight when no maturity is stated), (5) designation of place for payment (unless otherwise stated, place of payment is deemed residence of drawee), (6) name of payee, (7) date and place drawn if absent deemed address of drawer, and (8) name and seal, or signature of drawer. Bill of exchange may be payable to drawer, his order, or for account of third person. (B.N.A. 1 through 3).

Indorsements must be unconditional but may have designations or be in blank. All bills of exchange may be transferred by indorsement. (B.N.A. 11 through 13, 15).

Bills payable at specified period after sight must be presented for acceptance within one year after date of issue at residence of drawee. Drawer or indorsers prescribe time of presentment. (B.N.A. 21 through 23).

Name and seal, or signature of drawee on face of instrument is deemed as acceptance. Bills payable at specified period after sight must have dated acceptance. Acceptance must be unconditional but may be only for part of total sum payable. Third parties may guarantee bills or notes by signing and sealing on their face or tag. (B.N.A. 25, 26, 30, 31).

Bills of exchange may be paid: (1) At sight, (2) at specified period after sight, (3) at specified period after date of issue, and (4) at specified date. (B.A. 33). Sight bills of exchange are payable on presentment within one year of issue date. (B.N.A. 34). Bill of exchange payable on specified date or period after issue or sight must be presented for payment on due date or within two business days after due date. (B.N.A. 38). There is no grace period. (B.N.A. 74). Bills of exchange payable in currency other than currency of place of payment, may be paid in currency of place of payment. Exchange rate will be that on day of maturity or payment. (B.N.A. 41). Words prevail over figures, and smallest amount is amount payable. (B.N.A. 6).

Indorsers, drawer and guarantors are liable on bill of exchange if payment is not made at maturity or before maturity in events of: Total or partial refusal of acceptance; drawee becoming bankrupt or insolvent; or drawer of bill of exchange prohibited from presentment for acceptance becoming bankrupt. (B.N.A. 43). Instrument to prove default must be officially authenticated. When bill becomes payable nonpayment must be protested within two business days from due date, except for sight bills. (B.N.A. 44). Notice of refusal of acceptance or payment must be given to drawer and endorser within four business days, indorser must notify party from whom he received instrument within two business days of indorser's receipt of notice. (B.N.A. 45).

Invalid signatures on instrument do not remove liability of persons who actually signed bill. (B.N.A. 7). Agent signing bill is personally liable if he had no authority to do so. (B.N.A. 8). Drawer guarantees acceptance and payment, but may disclaim guarantee of acceptance. (B.N.A. 9).

Drawers, acceptors, indorsers and guarantors have joint and several liability. Holder may sue each individual without regard to order of liability or join all in one action. (B.N.A. 47). Holder may recover any amount unpaid on bill, 6% per annum interest from date of maturity, plus expenses. (B.N.A. 48, 49). If time limit for presentment for protest or payment passes, holder has no recourse against any party except acceptor. (B.N.A. 53). Presentment prevented by vis major or any other legal prohibition may be made after cause for delay has terminated. (B.N.A. 54).

Capacity is determined according to law of party's nationality, but he may still be bound if he signed in country wherein he had capacity. (C.L.A. 34). Formal acts required for bill of exchange, promissory note or check are governed by law of place where it is signed. Checks may follow requirements of law of place of payment. (C.L.A. 36). Obligations of acceptor of bills of exchange and issuer of promissory notes will be governed by law of place of payment. Obligations on checks will be governed by law of place of signing. (C.L.A. 37).

Holder's claims on bill of exchange against acceptors lapse three years from date of maturity, and against indorsers and drawers are actionable only one year from date of protest. Claims of indorser against other indorsers and drawer are actionable six months from date of payment or commencement of action by indorsee. (B.N.A. 70).

Promissory notes must, with certain exceptions, contain: (1) Term "promissory note", (2) unconditional promise to pay specified sum of money, (3) maturity date, (4) place of payment, (5) name of payee, (6) date and place issued, (7) name and seal, or signature of maker. (B.N.A. 75). Rules governing bills of exchange apply mutatis mutandis to promissory notes. (B.N.A. 77).

Bills of Lading.—Carrier must, upon demand by charterer or shipper, furnish him with bill of lading in one or more parts after receipt of goods carried. Carrier must, upon demand by charterer or shipper, furnish him with shipped bill of lading in one or more parts after loading of goods, or shall show effect of such loading on bill of lading mentioned in preceding sentence. (Com. C. 813[I][II]). Carrier may authorize master or any agent to furnish bills of lading or show above effect mentioned in preceding sentence. (Com. C. 813[III]).

Bill of lading must contain following particulars and be signed and sealed by issuer: (1) Name, nationality and tonnage of ship; (2) type, weight or volume of goods, types, number and marks of packages, noted in writing by shipper; (3) external appearance of condition of goods; (4) full name or trade name of charterer or shipper; (5) full name or trade name of consignee; and notify party; (6) port of loading; (7) port of discharging; (8) freight; (9) place where and date when bill of lading was made; and (10) if bill of lading has been made in two or more parts, their number. (Com. C. 814).

At designated port of discharging, master may not refuse to deliver goods carried, even though holder of only one of two or more parts of bill of lading demands such delivery. If holder of only one of two or more parts of bill of lading has taken delivery of goods carried, other part or parts shall lose their effect. (Com. C. 816). At places other than designated port of unloading, master may not deliver goods carried except upon receipt of all parts of bill of lading. (Com. C. 817). If two or more holders of bill of lading have demanded delivery of goods carried, master must without delay deposit goods with competent authority and dispatch notice thereof to each holder who has demanded such delivery. (Com. C. 818).

As to goods deposited with competent authority, holder of bill of lading to whom bill of lading was handed over earliest from assignor of bills of lading common to all holders, may exercise his right in preference to other holders of bill of lading. In regard to bill of lading delivered to absentee, time when bill of lading has been dispatched will be deemed as time when it has been handed over. (Com. C. 819).

Checks must contain: (1) Term "check", (2) unconditional order to pay specified sum of money, (3) name of drawee, (4) place of payment, (5) date and place where check is drawn, and (6) signature and seal of drawer. (Checks Act 1). Absence of any element invalidates check with certain exceptions as in bills of exchange. (Checks Act 2). Check must be drawn on bank with funds controlled by drawer. (Checks Act 3). Check must be payable at sight and presented for payment within ten days after issued. (Checks Act 28, 29). If presented for payment outside country but on same continent of place issued it must be within 20 days, 70 days if on different continents. (Checks Act 29). Crossed check may be paid by drawee only to banker or to customer of drawee. (Checks Act 38).

Holder's claims against indorsers, drawer and guarantors lapse six months from last day when presentment must be made. Claims of other parties lapse six months from date of payment or commencement of proceedings. (Checks Act 51). Checks are not accepted. (Checks Act 4). All other rules governing checks coincide with those governing bills of exchange.

Person who may become drawee of check shall be governed by law of place of payment. Even if check is invalid because person who may not become drawee according to law of place of payment has become drawee, obligation arising from signature which was affixed in another country in which there is no such law shall not be affected. (C.L.A. 35).

Days of grace, whether legal or judicial, are not permitted. (Checks Act 62).

Warehouse Receipts.—Warehouseman must, upon demand by bailor, furnish him with warehouse receipt. (Com. C. 156[1]). Warehouse receipt shall contain following particulars, and be signed and sealed by warehouseman: (1) Description, quality, quantity of goods bailed, and description, number and marks of packages; (2) full name or trade name, place of business or domicile of bailor; (3) place of storage; (4) storage fee; (5) period for storage, if such has been fixed; (6) amount insured, period of insurance, full name or trade name, and place of business or domicile of insurer, in case goods bailed have been insured; and (7) place where and date when warehouse receipt has been made. (Com. C. 156[2]). Holder of warehouse receipt may return such instrument and may demand warehouseman to divide goods bailed and furnish him with warehouse receipt in respect of each portion of goods thus divided. (Com. C. 158).

If, even in cases where goods bailed have been pledged by means of warehouse receipt, pledgee has given his consent, bailor may demand return of part of goods bailed even prior to maturity of debt. In such case warehouseman shall enter on warehouse receipt description, quality and quantity of goods thus returned. (Com. C. 159).

CHATTEL MORTGAGES:

See topic Mortgages.

COMMERCIAL REGISTER:

Commercial matters to be registered shall be entered in Commercial Register maintained by court having jurisdiction over locality of place of business. (Com. C. 34). Business names, seals, business activities by minors, guardianships, managerial positions, and details relating to corporate matters must be registered (Commercial Registration Regulations). If foreign company intends to engage in commercial transactions in Korea, it shall effect same registration as that of branch office of company incorporated in Korea either of same nature or of kind which it most closely resembles, and also register full name and permanent residence of representative and governing law under which it had been incorporated. (Com. C. 614). Foreign company may not engage in commercial transactions on continuing business until it has affected above registration. (Com. C. 616). Valid registration may provide defense as against third parties. (Com. C. 37).

CONSTITUTION AND GOVERNMENT:

Constitution.—Korean constitution was adopted on July 17, 1948 after emancipation from Japanese rule and has since been amended nine times. It declares principles of human rights and provides for basic principles of organization and administration of government. Korea is declared to be democratic republic. Sovereignty is held by people and all governmental authority is derived from people. (C. 1). Legislative power is bound by Constitution; executive and judicial power are bound by law. Korean nationals of both sexes who have reached 20 years of age qualify to vote on referenda or elections pursuant to statutes. (C. 24).

Legislative power is exercised by National Assembly. Members of National Assembly are elected in general, direct, and popular elections every four years. (C. 40 through 42). To pass bill, attendance of majority of members on register and concurrence of majority of members present are required. (C. 49). President may veto any bill passed by National Assembly for reconsideration. If National Assembly repasses bill with more than half of members on register in attendance and with concurrence of two-thirds or more of members present, bill becomes law. (C. 53).

Executive Power.—President is chief of state and heads Executive Branch which is vested with all executive power. (C. 66). President is elected by general, direct, and popular elections held every five years. (C. 67, 70). No person can be elected President more than once. (C. 70).

President is vested with substantial and independent powers to initiate and implement government policy. Among President's important powers are command of National Armed Forces, taking of emergency measures at time of financial or economic crisis subject to ex post facto approval of National Assembly, proclaiming martial law, appointing important public officials including ministers and judges of Supreme Court and right of pardon. (C. 74, 76 through 79, 104).

Judicial Power.—Judges are granted independent position. They are bound solely by Constitution and law and are not subject to any other orders or oppression. (C. 103). Judges, other than Supreme Court judges, are appointed by Chief Justice of Supreme Court; their term of office is ten years. Supreme Court justice's term is six years. (cc. 104, 105). Courts have authority to declare any decree or executive act

See Topical Index in front part of this volume.

CONSTITUTION AND GOVERNMENT . . . *continued*
unconstitutional or unlawful and void. Authority to declare statutes passed by National Assembly unconstitutional and void, however, is vested in Constitutional Court. (C. 111).

Law.—Korean law is based on Civil Law system. Laws are codified and court precedents are not granted official status as law.

International Law.—Treaties which Korea has entered into with other states and generally recognized rules of international law have same effect as domestic statutes. (C. 6).

CONTRACTS:

Contracts create legal obligations by agreement between two or more parties. Legal entities as well as natural persons have power to contract. Civil Code provisions govern many standard contract forms: Gift, sale, exchange, loan for consumption, loan for use, lease, employment, contract for specific performance, mandate, bailment, partnership, life annuity, and compromise. Many standard commercial transactions are governed by special Commercial Code provisions: Sales, current accounts, undisclosed associations, brokers, agency commissions, forwarding agencies, carriers, deposits, and insurance. Parties may modify these forms.

Formation.—Contract exists when offer is accepted. Offer specifying period for acceptance shall expire unless offerer receives notice of acceptance within such period. (C.C. 528). Offer which does not specify period for acceptance shall expire within reasonable period. (C.C. 529). Contract arises when acceptance is sent. Any act which can be deemed declaration of intent to accept will also give rise to contract. (C.C. 532). There is no conditional acceptance, only refusal with counter-offer. (C.C. 534).

Effect.—Obligation to perform in either party to bilateral contract arises when opposite party tenders performance, unless such obligation has not yet accrued. (C.C. 536). In case of contract under which one party is obligated to perform its obligation to benefit of third party beneficiary, original contracting parties cannot take away vested rights of third party beneficiary. (C.C. 541). In contract to create or transfer real rights in identified property if that property is lost or damaged or performance becomes impossible due to intervening causes not attributable to assignor and assignee, assignor absorbs loss. (C.C. 537).

Rescission.—Right of rescission may be included in contract, or be implied by law. Formal demand for performance is usually required before rescission. (C.C. 544). Rescission restores parties to same condition they were in prior to contract. (C.C. 548). Declaration of intention to rescind is made to opposite party, though not always required. (C.C. 543). Rescission does not extinguish right to damages. (C.C. 551). Each individual of group of persons who make up single party to contract must either send or receive notice of rescission. (C.C. 547).

Excuse for Nonperformance.—Nonperformance, except for payment of money, may be excused if causes are not attributable to or responsibility of obligor. (C.C. 390, 397). Parties may limit liability for nonperformance except where specifically prohibited by law.

Conflict of Laws.—According to provisions of Conflict of Laws Act, issue of execution and enforceability of contract is to be decided by law expressly or implicitly chosen by parties. In absence of such choice, those prevailing in place where act creating contractual relationship takes place will apply; rights to chattels or real estate are governed by law prevailing in place where subject asset is located; legal effect on assignment of credit is to be decided by law prevailing over debtor's domicile; and most admiralty issues including ownership of vessel are to be decided by law of country where vessels concerned are registered. (International Private Law 9, 12, 14, 44).

Set-off.—If two persons have obligations to each other of same subject-matter, both of which have become due, each obligor may set-off amount corresponding to extent of his obligation, unless nature of obligation does not so permit. (C.C. 492). Set-off is effected by manifestation of intent to opposite party; such manifestation may not be conditional nor limited in time. Obligations are presumed to be extinguished, by manifestation of intent, to extent they are set off. (C.C. 493). However, if obligation has arisen from intentional tort or is prohibited from attachment, may not be set off. Obligor of obligation garnished by creditor of obligee under such obligation may not set off obligation against any after-acquired claim against obligee. (C.C. 496 through 498).

Government contracts contain certain statutory requirements for competitive bidding, use of written contracts with specifically required provisions, and performance bonds. (Law regarding Agreements to which Government is Party 4 through 12, Enforcement Decree thereunder 4 through 53).

COPYRIGHT:

New Copyright Act (C.A.) was enacted by National Assembly in Nov. 1995 and took effect on July 1, 1996. Following information is based upon new C.A.

Upon creation of works, as that term is defined in C.A., copyright is established. (C.A. 4-10).

Protection of Foreign Works.—Copyright protection will be granted to foreigner under following conditions: (1) If foreign work is entitled to protection under any treaties which Korea has entered into or signed; and (2) if work is authored by one who resides in Korea or incorporated entity which has main office in Korea; and (3) if foreign work is first published in Korea or is published within 30 days after works were first published in foreign country. Retroactive protection is adopted for foreign copyrights published prior to Oct. 1, 1987. (C.A. 3).

Copyright Treaties.—Korea acceded to Universal Copyright Convention on July 1, 1987, effective on Oct. 1, 1987.

Duration.—In principle, author's property right shall subsist for term of 50 years after his death. (C.A. 36). Author's property right in anonymous or pseudonymous works, if pseudonym is not widely known, shall subsist for term of 50 years after its release. (C.A. 37).

Limitation of Author's Property Rights.—Author's property rights are limited to some extent in certain circumstances as provided in C.A. 22-35, e.g., where works are reproduced in judicial proceedings (C.A. 22), where works are used for purpose of school education (C.A. 23), etc.

Compulsory Licensing.—Anyone may use another's work with approval from Minister of Culture in certain circumstances as provided in C.A. 47-50, e.g., where consent to use of work is not obtainable because property right owner of published works is unknown or his abode is unknown, in spite of reasonable efforts to determine them (C.A. 47), where broadcaster who intends to broadcast released work for public interest has negotiated property right owner, but no agreement has been reached (C.A. 48), etc.

Neighboring Rights.—Stage performance, phonograph records, and broadcasts are entitled to protection for 20 years under C.A. as neighboring rights. Foreigners may enjoy all three neighboring rights under amended law. (C.A. 61-73).

Infringement.—Copyright holder may make claim for cessation of infringement, may demand destruction of infringing articles (C.A. 91), and may claim damage compensation (C.A. 93) against infringer. Author may make claim for any action necessary to restore his reputation against anyone who has infringed author's personal rights. (C.A. 95).

Penal Provisions.—Certain types of acts which are deemed to be in violation of C.A. are subject to criminal punishment. (C.A. 98-103).

Protection of Computer Program Works.—C.A. provides that provisions necessary to protect computer program works shall be provided in special law. (C.A. 4). Thus, special law entitled "The Computer Program Protection Act" (CPPA) was amended in Nov. 1995 and effective as of June 6, 1996. Amended CPPA grants protection for foreign computer programs created prior to July 1, 1987. Right equivalent to copyright is granted to author of computer program for 50 years from year immediately following year of publication or if program has not been published within 50 years of creation, 50 years from year immediately following year of creation.

CORPORATIONS:

Legal persons must come into existence in accordance with provisions of Civil Code, Commercial Code, special acts of legislation, or special legislative charter. (C.C. 31). Although classified as private and public, or for profit and for nonprofit, etc., they are grouped together for convenience under title "Corporations".

Legal Persons Under Civil Code.—Civil Code has two kinds of legal entities or juridical persons, associations and foundations. Natural persons may form association through articles of association and managed by directors elected by general assembly. (C.C. 40, 58). Foundation is created by endowment of property for particular purpose and managed by self-perpetuating or court appointed directorate. (C.C. 43). Both may be incorporated as legal persons subject to permission of competent authorities dealing with science, religion, charity, art, social intercourse or other nonprofit enterprises. (C.C. 32). Both act only through authorized representatives, and are liable for acts done by them if within scope of their duties. (C.C. 35, 59). Damages incurred as result of ultra vires act are joint and several liability of those members, directors and other representatives who have acted or supported resolutions for such ultra vires acts. (C.C. 35). Both associations and foundations may be dissolved upon expiration of period of duration, fulfilment of objectives or impossibility thereof, occurrence of any cause of dissolution specified in articles of incorporation, bankruptcy, or annulment of permission for incorporation. Associations may also be dissolved if no member remains, or by resolution of general assembly. (C.C. 77).

Companies, and legal persons organized under Commercial Code, are associations incorporated for purpose of engaging in commercial transactions and acquisition of gains. (Com. C. 169). Four kinds of companies are provided for by Commercial Code: Partnership Companies (hapmyong-hoesa), Limited Partnership Companies (hapchahoesa), Stock Companies (chusik-hoesa), and Limited Companies (yuhan-hoesa). If organized in compliance with all legal preconditions and properly registered no government approval is necessary.

Partnership companies create new and independent legal entities. (Com. C. 170, 171). Partnership companies are created by articles of incorporation with signature of each member stating value of respective contribution. (Com. C. 179). Managers are appointed by majority vote. Additional members must see to administration of company's business; however, articles may remove this duty. (Com. C. 200). Consent must be unanimous for changes in articles of incorporation or transfer of any individual member's share. (Com. C. 197, 204). Members may not conduct or assume official position in competing business without consent. (Com. C. 198). Members have joint and several liability for obligations in excess of company's assets. (Com. C. 212). Members subsequently admitted to company incur liability for all prior obligations. (Com. C. 213). Members may, with six months notice, withdraw from partnership at end of any fiscal year if company was established for indefinite period or for life of partner. Also members may withdraw at any time should unavoidable circumstances exist. (Com. C. 217). Membership may be terminated upon occurrence of any causes specified in articles of incorporation such as unanimous consent, death, adjudication of incompetency, bankruptcy, and expulsion. (Com. C. 218). Failure to make contribution is cause for expulsion which requires court order. (Com. C. 220). Withdrawing members must be paid for services rendered and reimbursed for contributions. (Com. C. 222). Partnership company may be dissolved upon expiration of prescribed term or occurrence of any cause of dissolution specified in articles of incorporation such as unanimous consent, loss of all except one member, merger, bankruptcy or by court. (Com. C. 227). Court supervises liquidation. (Com. C. 245 et seq.).

Limited partnership companies resemble partnership companies but differ in liability each member has for company obligations. (Com. C. 268). Liability of each member must be provided in articles of incorporation, and those with limited liability may not make their contribution in form of personal services or credit. (Com. C. 270, 272). Members with unlimited liability have responsibilities as in partnership company. Members with limited liability may not represent company, but may inspect and supervise its operations. (Com. C. 273, 277). Loss of all members of either class requires dissolution. (Com. C. 285).

See Topical Index in front part of this volume.

CORPORATIONS . . . *continued*

Stock companies are most common in business circles. Incorporation through articles of incorporation must be drawn by three or more promoters. Articles must state business objective, trade name, total number of shares authorized, amount of each share, total number of shares to be issued at time of incorporation, address of principal office, manner of giving company's public notices, and full name and domicile of each promoter. (Com. C. 288, 289). Following must be in articles to have legal effect: Company's duration, special promoter benefits, contributions in kind, property to be acquired upon incorporation. (Com. C. 227, 290). Articles of incorporation must be acknowledged by notary public. (Com. C. 292). Company comes into existence after court approval upon registration or upon registration after first meeting of shareholders when there are shareholders other than promoters. (Com. C. 299, 300, 308, 309, 311 through 314, 316, 317). Incorporation does not limit liability of promoters from acts in course of incorporation. (Com. C. 322). At time of incorporation, stock may be received for property contribution. Court must confirm property's value and delivery. (Com. C. 299).

Capital of stock company must be 50,000,000 Won or greater, and divided into shares. Only par value shares may be issued and each share should be of equal value of at least 5,000 Won. (Com. C. 329). Shares are usually nonbearer but articles may provide for bearer certificates. (Com. Co. 357). Those holding nonbearer shares and not wanting certificates may request that certificates not be issued and return any certificates already issued. (Com. C. 358-2). Company may issue two or more classes of shares which differ in respect to distribution of profits, interest, or surplus assets. Such particulars and numbers of each class of shares must be determined by articles of incorporation. (Com. C. 344). Transfer of shares may be restricted, requiring board approval under articles of incorporation. (Com. C. 335). Transfer before issuance of share certificates is not effective against company (this does not apply more than six months after incorporation or payment for new shares). (Com. C. 335). Company cannot purchase its own shares nor hold them as pledgee in amount exceeding 1/20 of total number of shares issued and outstanding. Company more than 40% of whose shares are held by another company (parent company) cannot acquire shares of such parent company, except in special circumstances as where company must dispose of shares immediately. (Com. C. 341, 341-2, 342, 342-2). Transfer of shares becomes effective upon delivery of certificates. However, nonbearer shares must be registered in stockholders' registry to be treated as transferred by company. (Com. C. 336, 337).

Authorized shares may be issued at any time by resolution of board of directors unless articles of incorporation require resolution of stockholders. (Com. C. 416). Each stockholder has preemptive rights to new shares according to number of shares he owns, and such rights may be made transferable by resolution of board of directors or, if articles of incorporation so provide, by stockholders. (Com. C. 416, 418). Transfer of preemptive rights to new shares must be done by delivery of subscription warrant. (Com. C. 420-3).

Stockholder's Liability.—After subscription price is paid, stockholder has no other personal liability for obligations of company. (Com. C. 331).

Organs of stock company are general meeting of stockholders, directors, board of directors, and auditors. General meeting of stockholders may resolve only matters provided for in Commercial Code or articles of incorporation. (Com. C. 361). Ordinary general meeting must be convened at least once each fiscal term and extraordinary general meeting may be convened whenever necessary. (Com. C. 365). Each stockholder has one vote for each share. However, company is not entitled to vote its own shares. Company more than 10% of whose issued shares are held by another company or by both parent and subsidiary company or subsidiary company is not entitled to vote its shares in such other company or parent company. (Com. C. 369, 434). Split votes may be cast with prior notice. (Com. C. 368-2).

Resolutions are adopted by simple majority of shares present, which should be at least one-quarter of total number of shares issued and outstanding. (Com. C. 368). Major resolutions require two-thirds majority of shares present, which should be at least one-third of total number of shares issued and outstanding (e.g., amendment of articles of incorporation, capital decrease, merger, transfer of whole or important part of company's business, taking over business of another company, dissolution, or removal of directors or auditors [Com. C. 374, 385, 415, 434, 438, 518, 522]). (Com. C. 368).

Proxies.—Shareholder may vote by proxy. Proxy statements must be filed with general meeting to establish power of representation. (Com. C. 368). Proxy holders may be limited to shareholders by articles of incorporation but representing others' voting rights shall not be prohibited or compelled.

Board of directors' duties include execution of business, appointment or removal of managers, establishing, moving or closing branch offices, and supervision of performance of individual directors. (Com. C. 393). Resolutions of board of directors are adopted by majority vote if more than one-half of all directors are present unless articles of incorporation have stricter requirements. (Com. C. 391).

There must be three or more directors, elected at general meeting by stockholders, and may each hold office for term usually not to exceed three years. (Com. C. 383, 384). One or more directors with authority to represent company must be appointed from among directors by resolution of board or, if articles so provide, by stockholders. (Com. C. 389). Company has liability for any acts of director who has used any title such as president, vice-president, chief director or managing director though not authorized representative if third party acted in good faith. (Com. C. 395). No director may, without consent of general meeting of stockholders, effect transaction for himself or third persons or become partner (other than limited) or director of another company in same kind of business. (Com. C. 397).

There must be at least one auditor, appointed at general meeting of stockholders. In selecting auditors, individual stockholder although owning, may not vote more than 3% of total number of issued voting shares. (Com. C. 409). Auditors serve until adjournment of ordinary general meeting of stockholders for final settlement of accounts held within three years from assuming office. (Com. C. 410). Auditors may not concurrently assume office of director, manager or other employee of company or subsidiary of company. (Com. C. 411). Auditors may attend board of directors' meetings, can supervise directors' performance of duties, may at any time require directors to file business report, and may examine business and financial condition of company. Auditors may request to board that general meeting of stockholders be convened. Auditors of parent company have power to examine business and financial conditions of subsidiary. (Com. C. 391-2, 412-2, 3, 4). Auditors have duty to report on and examine financial statements and business reports prepared by directors issued to general meeting. (Com. C. 413).

Amending articles of incorporation requires two-thirds majority vote present, which should be at least one-third of total number of shares issued and outstanding and at general meeting of stockholders. (Com. C. 434). If, company has issued two or more classes of shares, and certain class of stockholders is prejudiced by proposed amendment, resolution of meeting of such class of stockholders is required in addition to that of general meeting of stockholders. (Com. C. 435).

Statutory reserves are capital and earned surplus reserves. Capital surplus reserve is amount applied to stated capital and is limited to excess of issue price over par. (Com. 459). Ten percent of cash dividends paid out of profits each fiscal period must be credited to statutory earned surplus account until such account is one-half value of stated capital. (Com. C. 458). Statutory reserve funds can be transferred to stated capital to raise it or remove deficiences. (Com. C. 460, 461).

Dividends to extent net assets exceed stated capital, statutory reserves (capital surplus reserve and earned surplus reserve), and required amount of retained earned surplus reserve may be declared each fiscal period. (Com. C. 462). Company can pay dividends with new shares by resolution of general meeting of stockholders. Stock dividends cannot exceed one-half of total sum of dividends. (Com. C. 462-2).

Bonds may be issued by resolution of board of directors. (Com. C. 469). Value of bonds may not be greater than four times stated capital and statutory reserves. (Com. C. 470). Company may issue convertible bonds and bonds with warrants to subscribe for new shares. (Com. C. 513, 516-2). Bondholders may call assembly to adopt resolutions with court approval if their interests are being prejudiced unless provided otherwise in Commercial Code. (Com. C. 490).

Company may be dissolved by expiration of term in articles of incorporation, merger, bankruptcy, court order and resolution of general meeting of stockholders. (Com. C. 517). Except in merger court supervised liquidation follows dissolution. (Com. C. 531 et seq.).

Limited companies are created by two or more members not exceeding 50 who jointly execute articles of incorporation which provide business object, trade name, name and residence of each member, capitalization, value of each unit of contribution, number of units of contribution made by each member, and principal office. (Com. C. 543, 545). Capitalization of 10,000,000 Won or greater and at least 5,000 Won per unit of contribution are required. (Com. C. 546). Transfer of units to nonmember must be approved by general meeting. (Com. C. 556). Directors, elected by general meeting, are company's business representatives. Directors may not compete against business of company. (Com. C. 397, 547, 562, 567). Limited company is otherwise similar to stock company.

Other Legal Persons.—Certain acts of special legislation distinct from Civil or Commercial Codes may create associations and other legal entities such as trade associations and labor unions. Municipalities are also legal entities. Special charters for corporations such as The Bank of Korea have been passed by National Assembly.

Foreign corporations are those which have addresses abroad or are incorporated in compliance with foreign laws. There are no provisions in Civil Code about foreign corporations but generally they enjoy same rights and powers as similar domestic corporations under Korean law, absent treaty or provisions to contrary; for example, foreign corporations cannot enjoy mining rights (Mining Law 6), and cannot acquire real property rights (excluding mortgage) without permission of Minister of Construction and Transportation (Alien Land Acquisition Act 6).

Commercial Code provides for foreign companies in detail. Foreign company which intends to engage in commercial transactions must appoint representative in Korea, establish business office and, in respect to establishment of its office of business, register office in same manner of registration as that of branch office of same or similar kind of company incorporated in Korea. Company which establishes its principal office in Korea or whose chief objective is to carry on business in Korea must, even though incorporated in foreign country, comply with same provisions as company incorporated in Korea. (Com. C. 617). Foreign company must also register law under which it had been incorporated, as well as full name and permanent residence of its representative in Korea. (Com. C. 614). Until registered, foreign company cannot engage in commercial transactions and persons doing so are jointly and severally liable along with company. (Com. C. 616).

Failure to commence business within one year after registration, engaging in illegal business, and acting in contravention of law, decree, good moral or other social orders by representative or any other person administering affairs of company are grounds for issuance of court order for termination and liquidation of business office. (Com. C. 619, 620).

Except as otherwise provided, foreign company is deemed to be company formed in Korea either of same nature or kind which it most closely resembles, insofar as other laws apply. (Com. C. 621).

COSTS:

Costs of suit shall be borne by party defeated although these may be apportioned at court's discretion. (C.C.P. 89 through 92). Co-litigants shall bear costs in equal proportions. (C.C.P. 93). If plaintiff has no domicile, office or place of business in Republic of Korea, court shall, upon motion by defendant, order plaintiff to furnish security for costs except where defendant, knowing that there is cause for which security should be furnished, has pleaded orally on merits of case, or made statement in preliminary proceeding, he may no longer make motion for security. (C.C.P. 107, 108). Also court may, on motion of party without means to defray costs, grant aid in litigation except in instances where prospects of losing case are obvious. (C.C.P. 118).

COURTS:

Courts are classified into following six kinds: Supreme Court, high courts, district courts, family courts, patent courts and administrative courts. However, patent courts and administrative courts will be established in Mar. of 1998. (C.O.A. 3).

COURTS . . . *continued*

Supreme Court consists of Chief Justice appointed by President and 13 Associate Justices whose terms are six years. Only Chief Justice is prohibited from reappointment. (C. 104, 105). Supreme Court is highest court for cases (C.O.A. 11, 14). However, controversies that by their nature are conflicts between existing laws and Constitution shall be determined by Court of Constitution.

Appeal from decisions by military courts are heard by Appellate Military Courts with last appeal available to Supreme Court. Appeals from decision by single judge of district court fall under jurisdiction of collegial department of district court paneled by three judges. Appeals from decision by first level of collegial department of district courts are heard by three judges of High Courts which also function as court of first instance for administrative action and which also decide such other cases as are designated by law. Appeals from decision by second level of district courts or appeals from decision of High Courts are heard by Supreme Court. (C.O.A. 26 through 28).

District courts have both criminal and civil jurisdiction. There is no right to jury in any Korean court. In civil actions, depending on amounts involved case will be heard by single judge or by three judge collegiate body in first instance. Based on severity of applicable statutory punishment, criminal case in like manner can be tried either by single judge or by three judge collegiate body. District courts are primarily courts of general original jurisdiction, except in cases under exclusive jurisdiction of other specialized courts.

Chief Justice may cause judges to handle small civil claims and charges of misdemeanor. These minor cases are handled by summary proceedings. District court also has jurisdiction over various noncontentious cases such as reorganization or liquidation of business corporations, and registration of real property and corporate matters. Bankruptcy and conciliation proceedings also come under district courts' jurisdiction. (C.O.A. 29 through 36).

Family court is specialized court dealing with family affairs as well as juvenile delinquency. (C.O.A. 37 through 40).

Appeal and Error.—In civil actions, parties who are dissatisfied with decision by first level of courts have liberty to bring appeal without cause. Trial by appellate courts is to some extent de novo and appellate court conducts new fact finding based on evidence already submitted in first level of courts as well as evidence newly submitted to appellate court.

Appeal from decision by appellate court to Supreme Court must be based on errors in law or causes which are prescribed as absolute grounds for reappeal. (C.C.P. 393, 394).

General Forum.—Civil suit is basically subject to jurisdiction of court located at place of general forum of defendant; general forum of person shall be determined by his domicile. However, if person has no domicile in Republic of Korea, or his domicile is unknown, general forum shall be place of his residence, and if he has no place of residence, or his residence is unknown, it shall be determined by his last domicile; if ambassador or minister or any other citizen of Korea who enjoys extraterritoriality abroad has no general forum it is deemed place where Supreme Court is located; general forum of legal entity is its principal place of business, or if there is no such place, domicile of principal person in charge of its affairs is its general forum; general forum of Republic of Korea shall be place of government office that represents Republic with regard to suit, i.e., Ministry of Justice or place where Supreme Court is located.

Special Forum.—Suit against person who continues to work in office may be brought before court which has jurisdiction over place where such office is located; suit regarding property right may be brought before court of place of residence or of performance; suit on bills or checks may be brought before court of place of payment; suit regarding property right against crew may be brought before court of place of registry of vessel. Suit regarding property right against member of armed forces or its civilian component may be brought before court of place where military office and/or installation is located, or at place of registry of military vessels; suit on property right against person who has no domicile in Korea, or whose domicile is unknown, may be brought before court of place where subject matter of claim or security therefor, or any attachable property of defendant is situated; suit against person maintaining office or other place of business may, if it concerns business affairs of such office or place of business, be brought where it is situated; suit concerning vessel or voyage against owner, or any other person utilizing vessel may be brought before court of place of registry of vessel; suit based on claim against vessel or any other claim secured on vessel may be brought before court of place where vessel is located; suit by company or any other association against its member, or by member against another member may, if based on his status as member be brought before court of place where general forum of company or association is located; suit regarding tort may be brought before court of place where act was committed. Suit for damages due to collision of vessels, including aircraft, or any other accident at sea may be brought before court of place where damaged vessel first touched after accident; suit relating to salvage may be brought before court of place where salvage was effected or place where salvaged vessel first touched after salvage; suit relating to immovables may be brought before court of place where object is located; suit relating to registration may be brought before court of place where registration office is located; suit relating to succession right, testamentary gift, or any other act that takes effect by death may be brought in court of place where general forum of deceased was located at time of commencement of succession; in following cases, immediately superior court common to all courts concerned shall, upon motion of parties or concerned courts, designate jurisdictional court by ruling: (1) If court having jurisdiction is legally or actually unable to exercise jurisdiction; or (2) if jurisdictional district is not clear. No appeal may be made against ruling as mentioned above. Parties to suit may agree to first instance jurisdictional court. When defendant proceeds orally to merits of suit or makes statements in preliminary proceedings without questioning wrong jurisdiction in court of first instance, said court shall have jurisdiction. Thereon, court may conduct examination of evidence upon its own authority to establish jurisdiction.

Korea has no long-arm statute. Case may be transferred to another court based on causes prescribed in law.

CURRENCY:

Legal currency is Won. (F.E.C.A. [I]). In May 1964, Korea adopted unitary floating exchange rate system pegged to U.S. dollar in place of fixed rate system. Korea government introduced special basket pegged system on Feb. 27, 1980. Special basket consists of Special Drawing Right basket and unique trade weighted basket. In Mar. of 1990, special basket pegged system was replaced by market-average foreign exchange rate system. Market-average system determines daily exchange rate based on exchange rates and volumes in interbank market.

CURTESY:

Does not exist under Korean law.

DEATH:

Adjudication of Disappearance.—Missing person may be declared dead by court through adjudication of disappearance proceedings commenced on application by interested party or prosecutor. In order for court to declare missing person dead, it is necessary that no information has been received whether such person is living or not for five years. However, if person had been missing in war zone, on vessel which sunk, or on aircraft which crashed, or otherwise through perils which might have caused his death, necessary term of missing is one year after event has transpired. (C.C. 27). Person declared dead is deemed to have died upon lapse of such five or one year period. (C.C. 28). If it has been proved that person against whom declaration of disappearance has been made is alive or died at time different from that prescribed above, court shall, upon application of person himself, any party interested, or prosecutor, annul declaration of disappearance. In such case, all effects of deemed death such as inheritance and dissolution of marriage become null and void retroactively. Any act done in good faith after declaration of disappearance and prior to revocation, however, remain valid. Person who acquired property in good faith as direct result of declaration should return property to extent that he still remains enriched. Person who has acquired property in bad faith, however, should return such property together with interest thereon and pay any damages. (C.C. 29). As long as missing person is not declared dead by adjudication of disappearance, such person is presumed live. See topic Divorce.

Simultaneous Death.—In event that two or more persons died of same peril, it is presumed that they died simultaneously. (C.C. 30).

Actions for Wrongful Death.—Person who wrongfully causes death of another must pay damages to deceased's heirs and close relatives, such as spouse, parents and children. Such damages may include lost earnings of deceased and mental anguish and sufferings of both deceased and his close relatives. (C.C. 750 through 752).

DEPOSITIONS:

See topic Discovery.

DESCENT AND DISTRIBUTION:

Rules governing descent and distribution apply to property of all descriptions including real estate and personal property. Orders of succession are as follows: (1) Lineal descendants; (2) lineal ascendants; (3) brothers and sisters; and (4) other relatives within fourth degree of consanguinity. Presence of relatives in previous order excludes rights of relatives in more distant order. If there are two or more persons standing in same rank, those nearest in degree of kinship would have priority. Persons belonging to same order and standing in same degree of kinship share rights equally. (C.C. 1000). If lineal descendant, or brother or sister of deceased, who would have become successor had he or she been alive, has died or has become disqualified before opening of succession and there exists his or her lineal descendants, such lineal descendants receive share which would have been distributed to their lineal ascendant if ascendant had been alive or qualified. (C.C. 1001). If there exist such successors as deceased's lineal descendant or his lineal ascendants, wife of deceased becomes co-successor in same order of succession as his lineal descendants or his lineal ascendants.

Legitimate Portions.—Co-successors equally share in estate except that inheritance portion of wife of deceased shall be that of lineal descendants plus 50% thereof or that of lineal ascendants plus 50% thereof in case she succeeds jointly with lineal descendants or lineal ascendants respectively. (C.C. 1009). If any of co-successors has received from deceased gift or testamentary gift and value of gifted property is short of his share in succession, he shall be entitled to shares in succession within limit of such shortage. (C.C. 1008). Each successor is, however, provided with certain legally secured portions of estate taking precedence over donee's testamentary gift. Legally secured portions of successors are as follows: (1) As for lineal descendant or spouse of person succeeded to, one-half of legal inheritance portion; (2) as for lineal ascendant or brothers and sisters of person succeeded to, one-third of legal inheritance portion. (C.C. 1112).

Acceptance or Renunciation.—Successor may within three months from time he learned opening of succession, effect acceptance, either absolute or qualified, or renunciation. However, such period may be extended by court upon application of person interested or public prosecutor. Successor may make survey of property to be succeeded to before effecting such acceptance or renunciation mentioned above. (C.C. 1019).

Successor shall be deemed to have effected absolute acceptance if he has taken act of disposition with regard to property succeeded to, or if he has failed to effect either qualified acceptance or renunciation within three months from time he learned opening of succession, or if he has concealed or fraudulently consumed, or failed on purpose to enter in inventory property succeeded to after having effected qualified acceptance or renunciation. (C.C. 1026).

Partition of Estate.—If there exist two or more successors to property, they own property succeeded to in common. Person succeeded to may by will determine mode of partition of estate succeeded to, or forbid partition for period not exceeding five

See Topical Index in front part of this volume.

DESCENT AND DISTRIBUTION . . . *continued*
years from time of opening of succession. Except cases mentioned above, co-successors may, at any time, effect partition of estate succeeded to by their agreement. (C.C. 1012, 1013).

Separation of Property.—Obligee of property succeeded to, or testamentary donee, or obligee of person succeeded to, may within three months from time of opening of succession, apply to court for separation of property succeeded to, from inherited property of successor. As long as successor has not recognized or renounced pertinent succession, application may be filed with court for separation of property even after period mentioned above elapsed. In case where separation of property has been ordered, right and duty of successor to deceased with respect to property shall not be extinguished. (C.C. 1045, 1050).

DISCOVERY:

Court may, if it considers that there are such circumstances which would make it difficult to have evidence available unless examination thereof is conducted beforehand, examine evidence upon motion of parties. (C.C.P. 346). Motion for preservation of evidence may be made even where it is impossible to designate counter-party, in which case, court may appoint special representative for prospective counter-party. (C.C.P. 349). Motion for preservation of evidence shall be made to court of instance in which such evidence is to be used in case of pendency of litigation, and, to District Court having jurisdiction over place of residence of person to be examined or person possessing document or place where object to be inspected is located if litigation has not yet been instituted. (C.C.P. 347). Expenses regarding preservation of evidence shall be part of costs of suit. (C.C.P. 354). Even if witness has been examined in preservation of evidence procedure, he/she should be examined at hearing again if any party applies for such. (C.C.P. 354-2).

Party to suit may apply to court for order of production of documentary evidence addressed to person in possession thereof. Holder of document shall not refuse to produce it in following cases: (1) When party himself possesses document which he has referred to in suit; (2) when applicant is entitled to demand of holder of document delivery or perusal thereof; (3) when documents have been made out for benefit of applicant, or concerning legal relation between applicant and holder thereof. (C.C.P. 315, 316). Court shall, in case it deems motion for order of production of documents well founded, order holder of documents to submit them. (C.C.P. 318). In case party does not comply with order for production of documents, court may deem that allegations of other party relating to such documents are true. In case third-party fails to comply with order for production of documents, court may impose fine on him not exceeding 500,000 Won. (C.C.P. 320, 322). In case party, with object of preventing use by other party of document which he is ordered to produce, destroys same or otherwise renders it unfit for use, court may deem that allegations of other party relating to such document are true. (C.C.P. 321).

Depositions.—In principle, taking of evidence by court through examination of witness is made in course of trial by sitting judges. However, court may have witness submit written statement notarized by notary public in lieu of examining him/her at court, when it considers testimony by means of written statement sufficient in light of nature of case or facts to be proven. It must be provided that opposite party does not raise any objection thereto. (C.C.P. 281-2).

Although Korea is not party of any international treaty on juridical mutual assistance, Korean courts investigate evidence for use in foreign courts upon request of foreign courts under following conditions: (1) Government which foreign court belongs to should guarantee to provide Korea with equal legal assistance upon request of Korean court regarding same or similar matters; (2) there should be no probability that investigation may impair good health or public morals of Korea; (3) foreign court should make request through due diplomatic route; (4) request should be in writing which makes clear parties to suit, substance of claims, kind of evidence, and in case of interrogation of witness, name, nationality and domicile or residence of witness and contents of interrogation; (5) request should be accompanied by translation into Korean; (6) government which foreign court belongs to should guarantee payment of expenditures in investigation. (International Juridical Cooperation Act 12).

Interrogatories.—Interrogatories as discovery device relating to set or series of written questions drawn up for purpose of being propounded to party, witness, or other persons having information of interest in case are not recognized in Korean judicial system. Inquiries to opposite party may only be made through court to extent that they are deemed appropriate by court for clarification of arguments. Interrogatories may be propounded to third party through court as means of taking evidence when third party has information of interest to case.

DISPUTE RESOLUTION:

See topics Courts and Alternative Dispute Resolution.

DIVORCE:

Divorce may either be made by mutual consent or granted by court.

Divorce by mutual consent becomes effective through entry in Family Register Record after confirmation by family court of mutual agreement of parties to divorce. (C.C. 834, 836). Measures necessary for fostering children shall be decided by mutual consent. If mutual agreement has not been reached or is impossible, either party may petition court to decide on appropriate measures necessary for fostering children. (C.C. 837).

Divorce may be granted if one party institutes action against other party upon grounds of: (1) Unchastity, (2) malicious desertion, (3) extreme maltreatment by other party or his lineal ascendants, (4) extreme maltreatment of instituting party's lineal ascendants by other party, (5) if it is unknown whether other party is living or dead for three years or more, or (6) any other significant cause rendering continuation of marriage difficult. (C.C. 840).

When action for divorce is filed, court-administered pretrial procedures for conciliation should generally be followed. If divorce agreement is reached in such procedures, it will have same effect as court decision. If such agreement is not reached, court will hold trial and decide. (Domestic Matter Procedure Act. 50, 59, 60).

Even in cases where alimony is not awarded, one spouse may still demand partitioning of assets. If agreement is not reached with respect to partitioning of assets, family court shall decide on amount and method of partitioning considering amount of assets acquired through efforts of both parties and other circumstances. (C.C. 839-2).

Divorce involving foreigner is governed by law of husband's nationality at time facts forming grounds for divorce arose, but divorce cannot be granted unless Korean law also recognizes those facts as grounds for divorce. (C.L.A. 18).

DOWER:

Does not exist in Korea.

ENVIRONMENT:

Laws and Regulations.—Environmental issues are addressed by following laws: Basic Environmental Policy Act and its Enforcement Decree, Liability for Environment Improvement Expenses Act, Environment Pollution Damage Dispute Adjustment Act, Natural Environment Preservation Act, Noise and Vibration Regulation Act, Water Environment Preservation Act, Noxious Chemical Substance Control Act, Atmospheric Environment Preservation Act, Sea Pollution Prevention Act and its Enforcement Decree, Wastes Control Act, and Act Relating to Promotion of Economy and Reutilization of Resources.

Basic Environmental Policy Act (BEPA) sets forth general principles, fundamental policies, and administrative framework for environmental preservation and remediation. BEPA is merely declaratory in nature; however, other acts and decrees related thereto specify detailed regulation of matters related to environmental issues. Enterprises are required to take measures necessary for preventing environmental pollution and cooperate with government policies and regulations. (BEPA, Art. 5). BEPA contains general principle, viz., polluter pays principle, which is that anyone who causes environmental pollution must bear costs of restoring environment. (BEPA, Art. 7). Government is mandated to set environmental standards (BEPA, Art. 10) and investigate situations of environmental pollution (BEPA, Art. 15). Minister of Environment (MOE) is obliged to establish every ten years government long-term comprehensive plan for preserving environment. (BEPA, Art. 12). MOE may restrict any utilization of land and installation of facilities in special countermeasure area (Decree, Art. 5), which is designated by MOE (BEPA, Art. 22). Also, MOE may designate environmental influence zone. (BEPA, Art. 23). BEPA adopts strict liability standard for harm caused by environmental pollution, which applies to civil liabilities under all Korean environmental laws. (BEPA, Art. 31). When there is more than one business place, and if it is impossible to find which business place causes damage to environment, then each enterprise should indemnify for it jointly and severally. (BEPA, Art. 31). Arts. 36 to 38 establish Environmental Preservation Committee, Environmental Preservation Advisory Committee, and Environmental Preservation Association.

BEPA requires that, in certain situations, environmental impact statement be submitted to MOE before new project that may affect environment is begun. BEPA requires any entity, public or private, intending to construct project that can affect environmental quality (e.g., urban development, industrial sites, apartment complexes, or energy resource developments), to assess environmental impact and seek comments from MOE in advance.

Atmospheric Environment Preservation Act (AEPA) regulates emission of pollutants and odor into air. Noise and Vibration Control Act (NVCA) regulates generation of noise and vibration. Water Environment Preservation Act (WEPA) regulates effluents released into surface waters. WEPA does not apply to groundwater contamination, which is regulated by BEPA. Sea water is protected and governed by Sea Pollution Prevention Act (SPPA), which regulates oil, poisonous liquid substance, etc. and wastes discharged into sea from ships and sea facilities. When ocean atmosphere is damaged by discharge of oil or poisonous liquid substance, government can recover amount corresponding to damage from person who is responsible for such discharge. (SPPA Arts. 4-6, newly added by Law 4559, Nov. 30, 1995). Pollutants regulated under AEPA include sulfuric oxides, nitric oxides, carbon monoxide, and particulates, whereas pollutants regulated under WEPA include biochemical oxygen demand, chemical oxygen demand, floating material, chrome, copper, and zinc. AEPA and WEPA prime ministerial decrees set emission and effluent standards. AEPA and WEPA require permits from local government prior to installation of facilities that will emit air pollutants or discharge wastewater, provided that such facilities meet certain standards, such as size or capacity. (AEPA, Art. 10 and WEPA, Art. 10). AEPA and WEPA are enforced through administrative, criminal, and civil sanctions. Criminal penalties set by these laws include imprisonment for not more than seven years or fines not exceeding 50 million Won, depending on type of violation. (AEPA, Arts. 55 to 60, and WEPA, Arts. 56 to 61).

Waste Management Act (WMA) regulates generation and discharge of solid wastes. Noxious Chemical Substance Control Act (NCSCA) regulates manufacture and importation of virtually all chemicals, whether harmful or not. NCSCA requires that any business that manufactures, distributes, holds, stores, or transports toxic substances register with MOE. (NCSCA, Art. 10). Ministry of Labor (MOL) provides technical guidelines and environmental standards that are necessary to protect workers' safety and health. MOL has jurisdiction over Industrial Safety and Health Law (ISHL).

General Supervision.—Minister of Environment (MOE) has jurisdiction over environmental laws. MOE may appoint environmental supervisors or delegate his authorities to directors of regional environment offices. Address of MOE is 1, Chungang-dong, Kwacheon-city, Kyungki-province, Republic of Korea.

EXECUTIONS:

Execution or realization of secured interests held by mortgagees, lien holders, pledgees, or Chonse-Kwon holders (special type of statutory lease involving key money for lease) are made generally through auctioning chattels or real estate secured. Such auction procedure is conducted by court according to Code of Civil Procedure upon application from secured creditors. (C.C.P. 724 through 735).

Code of Civil Procedure provides various means of execution of judgments. In order to execute judgment or other enforceable instruments, judgment creditors in general must obtain certification of enforceability on face of certified copy of judgment. (C.C.P. 479). Movable assets of judgment debtor are seized and auctioned off by court

EXECUTIONS . . . *continued*
bailiff. Credits owned by judgment debtor are attached, and collected by or transferred to judgment creditors by court decrees. Execution on real estate or immovable properties of judgment debtor is effected by attachment and public sale by court decree.

Arbitration awards or foreign judgment may be executed after local court permits execution by issuing enforcement judgment. (C.C.P. 476). Settlements made and recorded in court or special types of payment orders by court are enforceable and executable. Based on special legislation, settlements between parties to pay sum of money, securities or fungibles, and promissory notes or checks notarized and confirmed that immediate execution is possible by notary public, are enforceable upon acquiring certification of enforceability from notary public without requiring judgment. (C.C.P. 519).

Judgment requiring specific performance by debtor may be enforced by employing others to do required performance in place of debtor and holding judgment debtor responsible for costs. (C.C.P. 692). Specific performance which by nature may not be performed by anyone other than judgment debtor himself may not be specifically enforced. If judgment debtor fails to do as ordered, judgment creditor can apply to court to fix appropriate period to make performance and to order, in case judgment debtor defaults performance within period, to make reparation of certain amount in proportion to period of delay or in lump sum immediately.

Fieri facias shall be granted when judgment has become final and conclusive or when provisional execution order has been given. (C.C.P. 480).

EXECUTORS AND ADMINISTRATORS:

Testator may by will appoint executor or commission third-person to designate one. If no designated executor exists or designated person refuses to accept designation, heirs become executors. If heirs refuse or are unable to serve, court may appoint executor upon application of person interested. (C.C. 1093 through 1096). If more than one executor exists, conduct of their duties shall be decided by majority, provided that each executor is entitled to do acts of preservation. (C.C. 1102).

Executor has right and obligation to manage property which is subject matter of testamentary gift and to perform acts necessary to carry out will. (C.C. 1101). Executor by designation or appointment shall be deemed to be representative of heirs. (C.C. 1103).

FOREIGN EXCHANGE:

Foreign Exchange Management Law ("F.E.M.L.") is most comprehensive act controlling contractual relationship, settlement method, payment and receipt, etc. between "residents" and "nonresidents". ("Residents" means all natural persons who have their domicile or residence in Korea and also juridical persons having their main office in Korea. [F.E.M.L. 3-1-12]. Branches, local offices and other offices in Korea of nonresidents are considered to be residents irrespective of whether or not they have legal authority to represent "nonresidents" and even if their main office is located abroad. "Nonresidents" means all persons, natural or juridical, other than "residents". [F.E.M.L. 3-1-13].)

Amendment to F.E.M.L. was made in 1992 whereby F.E.M.L. adopted new system of regulating foreign exchange transactions, i.e., so-called "negative system". Additional amendment to F.E.M.L. including amendment to enforcement decree and regulations, whose contents have not been determined as yet and which are expected to include little deregulation, will be effective from June 1, 1996. Under this negative system, transactions between resident and nonresidents are generally permitted, unless specifically subject to prior approvals from different foreign exchange authorities such as Ministry of Finance and Economy, Bank of Korea or foreign exchange banks as enumerated by enforcement decree and regulations depending on contents of transaction. There are two kinds of such prior approvals. First, approval is required for some proposed underlying transaction itself. Second, remittance authorization is required in some transactions at time of payment pursuant to underlying transaction. Failure to obtain foreign exchange approval does not affect validity of transaction between parties. However, in case where foreign exchange approvals of transactions are required, without such approvals, remittance of foreign exchange will not be permitted. Failure to obtain requisite foreign exchange approval is also criminal violation under F.E.M.L. and subject to substantial fines and/or imprisonment. (F.E.M.L. 30 through 34).

FOREIGN INVESTMENT:

Person, natural or juridical, who intends to invest in Korea must report its investment to Ministry of Finance and Economy ("M.O.F.E.") or Bank of Korea and obtain acceptance of such report from M.O.F.E. or, one of foreign banks authorized under F.C.I.L. to receive such reports, or must obtain approval of its investment. (Foreign Capital Inducement Law ["F.C.I.L."] 7). Investment is permitted in all except following fields: (1) Business which undermines national security or maintenance of public order; (2) business having negative effect on national economy; (3) business which results in infringement of laws of Korea (F.C.I.L. 3). M.O.F. should approve investment by foreigners within 15 days and through consultation with appropriate ministers concerned with that type of business depending on type of business or accept report thereof within five days. However, in certain complex cases, period during which M.O.F.E. should determine whether to approve foreign investment or not will be increased to 30 days. When foreign investors acquire additional shares through merger of company, amalgamation or partition of shares, change of reserves to capital, etc., they must report to Minister of Finance and Economy. (F.C.I.L. 8). Upon completion of investment procedures foreign investors must register with M.O.F.E. as Foreign Invested Enterprise. (F.C.I.L. 12). Business is subject to regulation by Korean government. Certain tax benefits are granted for five years to foreign investors and companies invested in by foreigners if certain criteria are met. However, such tax benefits have been and will be gradually reduced pursuant to Korean government policy.

Korean and juridical person who entered into any technology inducement agreement such as license agreement with foreigners or changed contents of previously reported agreement must report to relevant ministry and obtain acceptance of such report from that ministry under F.C.I.L., or must obtain approval of such agreement from foreign exchange bank under F.E.M.L. Agreement becomes enforceable when report is accepted by relevant ministry or approval is issued by foreign exchange bank. Royalties received by foreign party are exempt from income and corporation taxes for five years if technology meets high technology criteria. (F.C.I.L. 24).

Repatriation Right.—All dividends of foreign investors, proceeds from sale of shares, or royalties from technology inducement agreements may be repatriated. (F.C.I.L. 4). Other rights of foreign investors related to investment in Korean industry are same as Koreans. (F.C.I.L. 5, 6).

FOREIGN TRADE REGULATIONS:

Foreign trade in Korea is basically regulated by Foreign Trade Law (F.T.L.) and Enforcement Decree and regulations thereof. With certain exceptions, international trading business is required to be registered in Korea under F.T.L. (F.T.L. 7). Only registered trading company can apply for export license or import license for actual export of Korean goods or import of foreign goods. Consequently, if non-registered manufacturer or end-user wishes to export Korean goods or import foreign goods, actual exportation or importation must be done through existing registered trading company which charges, in general, commission for such services. However, there are some exceptions where non-registered trading companies can obtain export or import license. (F.T.L. 9).

Exportability and importability of item is regulated by Export and Import Notice and Consolidated Notice issued by Ministry of Trade, Industry and Energy under F.T.L. (F.T.L. 19). Export and Import Notice generally classifies three levels of export and import status: (1) Automatic approval items, meaning that product in question may be freely exported or imported subject to normal export or import licensing requirement; (2) restricted approval items, meaning that product may be exported or imported subject to recommendation, confirmation or approval from designated ministry or industry association; and (3) banned items. (F.T.L. 18). Notices adopt Harmonized Commodity Description and Coding System for classification of items.

F.T.L. also establishes import damage relief system whereby imports can be restricted if damage to any domestic industry concerned occurs. (F.T.L. 32 through 36).

FRAUDS, STATUTE OF:

Korea has no statute of frauds, however certain items, such as wills and articles of incorporation, must be in writing or executed before notaries according to specific statutes. (C.C. 1068, 1069; Com. C. 292).

GARNISHMENT:

As means of execution of money judgment, outstanding credits of judgment debtor may be attached by judgment creditor through court order of garnishment, which prohibits garnishee from discharging debts to original debtor and also forbids judgment debtor from disposing of or accepting payment for credit. Payment made in violation of garnishment order will not have legal effect against garnisher.

HOLIDAYS:

Government holidays are: Sundays; Jan. 1 and 2 (New Year); 30th day of 12th lunar month and 1st and 2d day of 1st lunar month (Lunar New Year Holidays); Mar. 1 (Samiljeol—Mar. 1 Independence Movement); Apr. 5 (Arbor Day); 8th day of 4th lunar month (Budda's Birthday); May 5 (Children's Day); June 6 (Memorial Day); July 17 (Constitution Day); Aug. 15 (Liberation Day); 14th, 15th and 16th day of 8th lunar month (Choosuk—Thanksgiving); Oct. 3 (National Foundation Day); and Dec. 25 (Christmas). Mandatory holidays of private sectors are one day per week (customarily, Sun.) and May 1 (Labor day), but many private companies are also closed on above government holidays.

HUSBAND AND WIFE:

Property.—Husband and wife may make property agreement prior to their marriage. Such agreement is not valid as against their successors or third parties unless it is registered prior to marriage and cannot be altered during marriage without court's consent. (C.C. 829). Absent such agreement, property acquired by either spouse prior to marriage continues to be separate property. Property may be acquired separately by either spouse during marriage. If it is not clear which spouse owns which property, it is presumed to be owned jointly by husband and wife. (C.C. 830). Each spouse may separately manage, use, and take profit from own property. (C.C. 831).

Living expenses for cohabitation of husband and wife must be borne by both parties, unless otherwise agreed to by both parties. (C.C. 833). Husband or wife is granted authority by operation of law to represent other in daily household matters. Each spouse is jointly and severally liable for legal obligations entered into by other with respect to daily household matters unless third party is otherwise notified in advance. (C.C. 832). Contracts between husband and wife may be cancelled by either spouse at any time but may not prejudice rights of third parties. (C.C. 828).

Personal relations between husband and wife are ruled by principle of equality of rights. Married women have no disabilities. Husband and wife should cohabitate, support, and aid each other, provided that each spouse should tolerate living apart if justifiable cause requires temporary separation. (C.C. 826). Marriage does not have any effect on family name of either spouse. (Family name of Korean national cannot be changed.)

Conflict of Laws.—Marriage is governed by law of husband's nationality. Property relationship between husband and wife is, however, governed by law of husband's nationality in effect at time of marriage. (C.L.A. 16, 17).

See also topic Marriage.

IMMIGRATION:

Aliens require entry visa for entering Korea specifying period of stay and purpose of stay. (E.E.C.A. 7, 10). Minister of Justice has power to grant entry visa, but most short period visas (up to 90 days) are delegated to Korean consuls stationed outside of Korea. (E.E.C.A. 8). However, aliens of some countries who enter Korea for tourism may enter Korea without visa and stay up to 90 days. (E.E.C.A. 7). Aliens entitled to stay in Korea for more than 90 days must report and register residence with local

IMMIGRATION . . . *continued*
Immigration Office. (E.E.C.A. 31, 32). Aliens can stay in Korea up to period specified in entry visa but such period is extendable with some exceptions. (E.E.C.A. 17, 25). However, aliens who enter Korea with short-period entry visa or without visa may not obtain extension of period of stay for more than 90 days. Status and period of stay vary according to alien's activity or purpose in entering Korea. (E.E.C.A. 10, 17).

INFANTS:

Minority lasts until person reaches 20 years of age. (C.C. 4).

Emancipation takes place upon marriage. (C.C. 826-2).

Disabilities.—Minors must have consent of legal representative (parent or guardian) unless such act is advantageous to minor. (C.C. 5, 909 through 911, 928 through 938). Contracts made by minor without such consent are revocable. (C.C. 5). If minor uses fraudulent methods to induce another party to believe he has capacity to contract, such contract is irrevocable. (C.C. 17). Minor has full capacity: (1) In disposition of property, for which authorization has been given by legal representative; (2) in acts of business, for which authorization has been given by legal representative; or (3) in entering employment contracts as employee. (C.C. 6, 8; L.S.A. 53).

Ratification of contract of minor is made by his legal representative prior to or by minor after having attained majority. Other party to contract may demand revocation or ratification by legal representative or minor who has attained majority within period designated by party not shorter than one month. In absence of reply within such period, ratification is deemed to have been made. (C.C. 15, 140, 143).

Actions.—Minors may sue and be sued. In legal proceedings, minor must have legal representative. (C.C.P. 51). For example, service of process in action against minor must be made on his legal representative. If child does not have sufficient intellectual capacity to comprehend consequences of his actions parents or guardian may be held liable for damages. (C.C. 753, 755).

Wages.—Minor has right to make claim for payment of wages for his labor independently. (L.S.L. Law 54).

INJUNCTIONS:

Injunctions and Provisional Attachments.—Provisional or pretrial injunction is available before judgment or before suit is commenced upon establishing prima facie case concerning: (1) Existence of petitioner's legal right supporting action or inaction to be ordered and (2) necessity to preserve status quo; to prevent substantial damages on lasting relation of right; or to avoid imminent violation thereon or conspicuous damages. (C.C.P. 714). Provisional injunction is usually issued without inter partes hearings, upon payment of security deposit into court by petitioner for protection of respondent.

Respondent in provisional injunction may: (1) Bring appeal causing court to review merits of case, (2) bring motion seeking cancellation of injunction by establishing special circumstances justifying cancellation, or (3) request court to direct petitioner to bring suit for decision on merits of case (usually within ten days). First two alternative actions are usually heard and decided by judge(s) who initially issued injunctive order. In case petitioner fails to bring suit, court will cancel injunctive order issued. Above rules generally apply to provisional or pretrial attachment, under which assets owned by respondent will be attached and prevented from being disposed. Usually court would not require petitioner to demonstrate necessity warranting provisional attachment if petitioner establishes claim to be protected. Provisional attachment order is usually issued in ex parte proceeding.

INSOLVENCY:

See topic Bankruptcy.

INSURANCE:

No one may operate insurance business without license obtained from Minister of Finance and Economy under Insurance Business Act. Insurance Business Act regulates by-laws and business operating manual of insurance companies, terms of insurance policies, development and sale of insurance products, calculation of premium rates and premium reserve, assets utilization, etc. Opening, removing, or closing of office, or operation of insurance business abroad are also regulated. Qualifications and duration of offices for officers of insurance companies are also determined by law. Minister of Finance and Economy has right to require insurance companies to make reports or to change their business operating manual. Insurance Supervisory Board established under Insurance Business Act supervises business of insurance companies and administers insurance guarantee funds and capital deposit financed by insurance companies. Foreign insurance company may conduct business in Korea after obtaining license.

INTEREST:

Agreement on payment of interest and interest rate is valid and enforceable unless it violates usury law. Absent agreement on interest rate, rate of 5% per annum is applicable to normal private transactions (C.C. 379) and of 6% per annum to commercial transactions (Com. C. 54). Statutory interest at rate of 25% per annum is payable from time when court judgment is given ordering payment of money. (Special Law on Expedition of Court Proceedings, Etc. 3).

Usury applies only to obligations to pay money. Contract for interest at rate over 25% per annum is subject to upper limit of 25% per annum. (Interest Limitation Law 1).

JUDGMENTS:

Civil Action.—Final judgment must be rendered upon completion of trial. (C.C.P. 183). Court may, however, when it has concluded hearings on part of suit, render final judgment as to that part. (C.C.P. 185). Also interlocutory judgment may be issued when trial on independent means of attack or defense, or any other intermediate issue has been concluded. (C.C.P. 186). Same shall apply to cause of action where there exists dispute concerning both cause and amount thereof.

Foreign Judgments.—Korea does not adhere to any multilateral or bilateral treaties concerning enforcement of foreign judgments. Thus, enforceability of foreign judgment is determined solely by reference to local statutes. Foreign judgment is enforced in Korea through obtaining enforcement judgment from Korean court in whose jurisdiction defendant has domicile or assets. (C.C.P. 476).

Foreign judgment must meet following requirements in order for enforcement judgment to be obtained: (1) It must be proven that foreign judgment is final and conclusive (C.C.P. 477[II] Item 1); (2) judicial power of court rendering judgment must not be denied by law or treaty (C.C.P. 203, item 1). Korea has no express provision in any law or treaty which denies all or any part of judicial power of any foreign court. It is established that item (2) relates to situation where exercise of jurisdiction by court rendering judgment was inconsistent with general rules of civil procedure concerning jurisdiction. Since there is no Korean statutory law on jurisdiction in action involving foreigners, commentators and courts take view that jurisdiction in international litigation should be decided by mutatis mutandis application of provisions of local procedural law in light of general purpose of procedural law (to treat parties in action fairly; to minimize cost; etc.). Korean courts recognize jurisdiction of Korean court over foreign defendant when parties have agreed to such jurisdiction. Korean courts, inter alia, will apply above rules in reviewing basis for exercise of jurisdictional power by foreign court; (3) defendant named in judgment, if he was Korean national (at commencement of such action), was either served with summons necessary to commence procedure by means other than publication, or voluntarily appeared (C.C.P. 203, Item 2); (4) judgment is not in violation of good morals or social standards of Korea (C.C.P. 203, Item 3). This test will be applied by examining judgment as well as reason for such adjudication; (5) there is guarantee of reciprocity (C.C.P. 203, Item 4). Supreme court has ruled that foreign country is deemed to guarantee reciprocity when such country recognizes force of Korean judgments by provisions of its laws or treaties without reviewing merits thereof, under same or more generous conditions as Korean laws would recognize foreign judgment under art. 203 of Code of Civil Procedure. If foreign judgment does not meet these requirements, motion for enforcement judgment will be dismissed. (C.C.P. 477[II]).

LABOR RELATIONS:

Labor Standards Law (L.S.L.) provides legal minimum labor standards in Korea. L.S.L. applies to all employers regardless of number of employees, however, employers having less than five employees are subject to only certain provisions of L.S.L.

Hours of labor are limited to eight hours per day and 44 hours per week with certain exceptions. At least one day off per week is required. (L.S.L. 45).

Wages and Salaries.—Amount of wage is determined by individual employment agreement or collective bargaining agreement. Attachment of right to receive wage is limited to protect livelihood of laborers. (C.C.P. 579). In accordance with L.S.L. employer cannot set off wage by debt which employee owes to him. (L.S.L. 25). Wages and salaries are preferred claims having priority over other creditors of employers except for claims secured by mortgages or pledges. (L.S.L. 30-2). Wages must be paid directly to employees, in full, in legal tender. (L.S.L. 36). With certain exceptions, wages must be paid once per month or more frequently on fixed day. (L.S.L. 36[2]).

Leave.—One-day monthly leave with pay and annual leave with pay (period thereof varies depending on attendance and period of service) are required. (L.S.L. 47, 48). One day menstruation leave per month with pay must be granted to female employees. (L.S.L. 59). Maternity leave of 60 days must be given to pregnant employees. (L.S.L. 60).

Child Labor.—With certain exceptions, minors under 13 years of age may not be employed. (L.S.L. 50). Females or minors under 18 years of age may not be employed in occupations detrimental to their morality or health. (L.S.L. 51).

Severance allowances must be paid to employees having worked for not less than one year in amount of not less than 30 days' average wage per each year of consecutive years employed. (L.S.L. 28).

Discharge.—Employers may not discharge employees without just reasons. (L.S.L. 27). With certain exceptions, at least 30-days notice, or pay in lieu thereof, is necessary for discharge. (L.S.L. 27-2).

Rules of employment in compliance with minimum standards of law must be established by every employer of ten or more workers. (L.S.L. 94). Establishment of such rules requires presentation of rules to more than half of employees or chairman of labor union which consists of more than half of employees and then filing with Ministry of Labor. If rules of employment are amended adversely to interest of employees, employer is required to obtain employees' consent to such amendment. (L.S.L. 95) Such rules must deal with wage programs and scales, working hours, time off, holidays, paid vacations, discharge, retirement allowances, safety, sanitation, accident compensation, and other matters applicable to all employees. (L.S.L. 94).

Occupational Injuries and Diseases.—Employers must, at their expense, provide medical care for employees suffering from occupational injury or illness. (L.S.L. 78). Employers must pay compensation in amount provided for in L.S.L. for loss of wages, physical impairments, or death due to occupational illnesses. Employers having five or more employees must subscribe to industrial accident compensation insurance with certain exceptions.

Insurance.—Object of Industrial Injury Compensation Insurance Act (I.I.C.I.A.) is to protect employees by compensating for damages caused by occupational disasters and establishing or administrating insurance facilities necessary for such compensation. (I.I.C.I.A. 1).

Proprietor of enterprise shall automatically become insurer. (I.I.C.I.A. 7). Insurance allowances shall be as follows: Allowances for treatment and recovery, leaves, inconvenience, permanent physical impairment, mental anguish suffered by family members, and funeral expenses. (I.I.C.I.A. 38). Premiums to be paid by employers are product of total compensation multiplied by factor set by Ministry of Labor for applicable industry.

Labor Unions.—Employees have right of self organization, to form, join or assist labor unions, to bargain collectively through their own representatives. Rights of

LABOR RELATIONS . . . *continued*
governmental officials and employees working at state-run enterprises, defense industries, and public utilities which have serious impact on national economy may be restricted or denied with respect to labor unions.

Collective bargaining agreements are made between employer or employer's organization and lawfully organized union. When collective bargaining agreements become applicable to at least one-half of regular workers of plant, their terms then become applicable to all regular workers of that plant. (L.U.L. 37). Those parts of rules of employment or employment agreement in violation of terms provided in collective bargaining agreements are null and void. (L.U.L. 36). Collective bargaining agreements may be for two years or less (collective bargaining agreements concerning wages may be for one year or less). (L.U.L. 35).

Unfair Labor Practice.—It is unfair practice for employer to: (1) Discharge or discriminate against employee because employee became member of labor organization or is about to organize labor union; (2) require employees or potential employees not to join company union or to join company union which represents less than two thirds of total employees; (3) refuse to bargain collectively with employees' representatives; (4) interfere with or dominate employee organization; (5) pay administrative expense of labor organization; and (6) discharge or disadvantage employee because he has participated in collective action or has notified governmental agency of fact that employer committed above violations. (L.U.L. 39). Commission of unfair labor practices by employers may be punished by imprisonment or fines. (L.U.L. 46-2).

Labor Disputes.—Labor Disputes Adjustment Law (L.D.A.L.) provides matters necessary to settle disputes between employer and employees. (L.D.A.L. 1). Employees who are employed in national or local government or national defense industry cannot initiate labor disputes. (L.D.A.L. 12). It is unlawful for employees who are engaged in labor disputes to resort to violence to influence resolution of dispute. (L.D.A.L. 13). Occurrence of labor disputes must be reported to labor authorities who shall conduct conciliation and mediation. (L.D.A.L. 16 and 18-29). Act of dispute may not be commenced during cooling-off period of ten days after dispute was reported (15 days in case of business deemed vital to public interest). (L.D.A.L. 14). If labor disputes are not resolved, Labor Committee shall arbitrate them if: (1) Both parties jointly apply for arbitration, (2) either party applies for arbitration pursuant to collective bargaining agreement, or (3) administrative agency demands arbitration or Labor Committee itself determines that dispute, which involves business which is vital to public interest, must be arbitrated. (L.D.A.L. 30).

Labor Management Council is organized within each business in accordance with Labor Management Council Law (L.M.C.L.) for purpose of improving welfare of employees and to help sound development of business. (L.M.C.L. 3, 4). Council consists of three to ten representatives of employer and employees. Council may debate on following affairs: (a) Improvement of productivity and welfare of employees, (b) prevention of disputes between employer and employees, (c) educational training of employees, (d) disposal of grievances of employees, (e) security, health care, and other affairs regarding improvement of labor conditions, and (f) other affairs regarding cooperation between employer and employees. (L.M.C.L. 20). Agreement of two-thirds of members present is necessary to pass resolution. (L.M.C.L. 13). Central Council is established under guidance of Minister of Labor which consists of representatives of employer, employees, and public interests. (L.M.C.L. 28).

Unemployment compensation exists in Korea through Unemployment Compensation Insurance Act which is effective from July 1, 1995. Under National Welfare Pension Law, company which has five or more employees must join government administered national pension program. Currently, employee and employer each contribute 2.0% of employee's monthly salary and employer will additionally contribute 2.0% to be transferred from mandatory severance pay reserves. Such figure will ultimately be 3.0% respectively from 1998. Amount transferred to national pension fund will be deducted from final amount of severance payment mandatorily payable to employees.

Minimum Wage Law provides minimum wage system. Currently, employers with ten or more employees must pay at least 1,275 Won per hour, and 10,200 Won per day. Minimum wage system may possibly apply to all enterprises and workplaces in future.

Equal Employment Treatment for Males and Females Law provides plan for enhancing welfare of female employees and establishment of Female Employees Committee. It also prohibits discrimination against women in regard to employment, training opportunity, assignments, wages, promotions, retirement, and dismissal with punishment of fine and imprisonment in case of violations.

Handicapped Persons Employment Promotion Act provides that employer shall perform several statutory obligations in order to enhance welfare of handicapped persons, including employing certain ratio of handicapped persons where employer maintains 300 or more employees.

LAW REPORTS:

See topic Reports.

LEGISLATURE:

See topic Constitution and Government.

LIENS:

Liens.—Lien is statutory right to retain possession of movable until certain credit owed is paid. There are two different types of liens created under Civil and Commercial Code; in former credit secured by lien should be related to object; in latter object must be owned by debtor but not necessarily related to debt owed. There are no other types of liens such as supplier's lien or equity liens. Certain statutory right of receiving payment from proceeds of certain objects in priority over general creditors must be differentiated from liens.

Lien affords holder right to deprieve owner of possession and maintain possession until payment obligation is performed and affords holder right to apply for auction sale of concerned property for collection of debt owed. Retention of possession is essential for most types of liens. See also topic Mortgages.

LIMITATION OF ACTIONS:

Lapse of time mostly affects substantive rights rather than procedurally barring actions. When prescribed period under extinctive prescription lapses during inaction by creditor, claim is deemed extinguished. Prescription as above does not serve as bar to action but may be asserted in litigation to defeat claim. There are statutes establishing time limitations on institution of litigation and such statutes are checked ex officio by court. This statute of limitation may not be extended by agreement between parties.

Personal Property.—If person possesses personal property with intent to own for ten years or more peacefully and openly, he shall acquire ownership of such property. (C.C. 246 [I]). If possession by such person commences in bona fide manner and without negligence, ownership shall be acquired after five years have elapsed. (C.C. 246 [II]).

See also topics Prescription; Real Property.

MARRIAGE:

Marriage becomes effective upon acceptance by family registrar of notification of marriage signed by both parties and two witnesses having attained majority. (C.C. 812). Ceremonies are, although customary, not required. Despite record status, marriage is invalid if parties lacked intention to marry. (C.C. 815). Supreme Court precedents generally take position that even if notification of marriage has not been made, effects similar to those of marriage are created if it is deemed that parties in fact maintain marital relationship.

Required age for marriage is 18 years for males and 16 years for females. (C.C. 807). Minors need consent of their parents or guardian.

Prohibited Marriages.—Important prohibitions are: There can be no marriage between those of same surname with common origin; between lineal relatives; between relatives within eighth degree of consanguinity. (C.C. 809, 815). No marriage can be entered into by person who presently has spouse. Woman cannot remarry for six months following dissolution or annulment of her previous marriage. (C.C. 810, 811).

Annulment may be made upon showing of existence of any legal defect (e.g. violation of any prohibition previously discussed). (C.C. 815 through 825).

Foreign Laws.—Requirements for marriage are determined by laws of parties' respective nationality. Manner of marriage is, however, determined by law of place of marriage. Nevertheless, Korean nationals in foreign states may marry by filing report of marriage with Korean ambassador or consul stationed in that foreign country. Effect of marriage is determined by law of husband's nationality. (C.L.A. 15, 16).

See also topic Husband and Wife.

MONOPOLIES AND RESTRAINT OF TRADE:

Unfair Trade Practices.—No enterprise shall engage in any of following or any act Fair Trade Commission ("FTC") deems detrimental to fair trade and publicly announces such as constituting unfair trade practice: (1) unreasonably refuse to transact with or discriminate against certain parties; (2) unreasonably engage in activities designed to eliminate competitors; (3) unreasonably induce or coerce competitor's customers to deal with oneself; (4) unreasonably take advantage of one's bargaining position in transacting with others; (5) transact with others on terms and conditions which unreasonably restrict business activity thereof; and (6) use advertisements or make representations that are false or which may deceive or mislead consumers with respect to enterprise, its goods or services. (M.R.F.T.A. 23). Enterprise which has committed unfair trade practices is subject to civil, administrative or criminal sanctions. (M.R.F.T.A. 24, 24-2, 56, 67).

Market Abuse.—Enterprises which meet criteria provided for by Presidential Decree for "market-dominating" enterprises shall not engage in any of following acts of abuse: (1) Unreasonably fixing, maintaining, or altering price of goods or services; (2) unreasonably controlling sales of goods or services; (3) unreasonably interfering with business activities of others; (4) unreasonably interfering with entry of new competitors; and (5) substantially restricting competition or damaging interest of consumers. (M.R.F.T.A. 3.).

Restriction on Business Combination and Economic Concentration.—Enterprises which meet criteria provided for by Presidential Decree must report acquiring or holding 20% or more outstanding shares or equity investment of another firm to FTC within 30 days of date of acquisition. Those intending to merge, take over, lease all or substantial part of another firm, or to establish new firm leading to substantial restraint of competition must report to Fair Trade Committee and must wait 30 days before acting. (M.R.F.T.A. 7, 12). Cross capital investment among affiliates of designated conglomerates is prohibited. (M.R.F.T.A. 9). Capital investment in other companies by company belonging to designated conglomerate is limited to 25% or less of net assets of company in question. (M.R.F.T.A. 10). Extension of loan guaranties by company belonging to designated conglomerate to its affiliates is limited to 200% or less of its own capital. (M.R.F.T.A. 10-2).

Collaborative activities designed to undertake any of following are, in principle, prohibited: (1) Fixing, maintaining, or altering prices; (2) determining terms and conditions for sale of goods or services, or terms and conditions for payment; (3) restricting production, delivery, transportation, or sales of goods or services; (4) restricting sales territory or trade of customers; (5) restricting new establishment, expansion of facilities, of installation or equipment for production of goods or services; (6) restricting type or specifications of goods at time of production or sale; (7) establishing new companies or the like in order to manage or control major parts of business collaboratively; and (8) interfering with business activities of others. (M.R.F.T.A. 19).

Restrictions on International Agreements.—No enterprise or trade association (with some exceptions) shall enter into international agreement or international contract which constitutes undue collaborative activities, resale price fixing or unfair trade practices, as defined by relevant guidelines.

See Topical Index in front part of this volume.

MORTGAGES:

Mortgage is encumbrance on specific item of property whereby creditor obtains preferential position in order to settle obligation out of proceeds which could be realized from sale of property without transferring title or possession. (C.C. 356). Mortgages may be created only on real rights of ownership. They may be established on real and personal property which may be registered with court or public registration office. Therefore, along with real estate, there may be mortgages on timber, ships, factory foundations, mining rights, fishing rights, agricultural implements, aircraft and automobiles. Additionally, some movables may be included in mortgage with registrable property; equipment may be object of mortgage together with land and factory building or as part of vessel. Movables on which mortgage may not be created may have security interest created by transfer of title ("Yangdo Tambo": title being put in name of creditor while obligor retains possession). Mortgages may be created to secure specific or unspecified obligations arising from series of similar transactions with obligor. (C.C. 357). Mortgage rights extend to fixtures and items attached to mortgaged property, as well as funds or substitute items which constitute consideration for sale of, or compensation for damage to mortgaged property. (C.C. 358, 359, 370, 342). Both recordation and agreement between parties are required to make mortgage legally enforceable. Priority of mortgages on same property is determined by sequence order of registration. (Real Property Registration Law 5). Mortgage may be assigned together with obligation it secures, but not independently. (C.C. 361). If obligation secured is fully performed or otherwise ceases to exist, mortgage becomes invalid whether there has been deregistration or not. Third party who purchases mortgaged property may discharge mortgage by paying proper amount to mortgagee. Foreclosure of mortgaged property shall be made through sale by auction. Proceeds shall be applied first to cover expenses of sale, and second, to cover mortgages in order of their priority. Court may take into account any nonperformance of obligation or impairment of collateral by creditor and thereby adjust liability of obligor.

MOTOR VEHICLES:

Drivers' licenses are required. Minimum age is 18 years. License is valid for life, but licensee is required to take aptitude test once every five years. Aliens with international drivers' license may drive in Korea for up to one year after their first entry. (R.T.L. 68, 70, 74, 80).

Vehicle Registration.—Every vehicle driven in Korea must be registered with competent local authority. Registration plate must be attached to vehicle and must be of prescribed size. All vehicles registered in Korea are subject to periodic mechanical inspections. (M.V.C.L. 4, 10, 41).

Transfers.—Transfer of title to vehicle does not become effective until transfer is entered on vehicle register. (M.V.C.L. 5).

Tax.—Registration tax is to be paid for registration on vehicle register of any vehicle not operated in transportation business. Acquisition tax is to be paid for any acquisition of vehicle. Vehicle tax is to be paid every six months during period in which vehicle is owned by person. (Local Tax Law 124, 132-2, 196-6).

Liability.—Victim or his heirs may claim damages for personal injuries or death arising from operation of motor vehicles not only from drivers, but also, in most cases, from owners for whose benefit vehicles were driven or those who controlled operation of vehicles. Exoneration is possible only if defendant proves in case that victim is not passenger, that he and driver took due care, that injury or death was caused by intentional or negligent acts of victim or third party other than driver, and lack of mechanical defects in vehicle, and in case victim is passenger, damage or accident is caused solely by victim's intentional acts or suicide attempt. (Act for Assurance of Paying Damages Caused by Motor Vehicles 3). Driver is criminally liable for death or injuries caused by his intentional or negligent acts subject to exception explained below.

Insurance coverage on motor vehicle of prescribed amount per person is compulsory for damages caused by operation of motor vehicle. Insurance coverage amount is between 15,000,000 Won and 60,000,000 Won in case of death, and 15,000,000 Won in case of injury. (Act for Assurance of Paying Damages Caused by Motor Vehicles, §5). Comprehensive insurance is available from Korean insurance companies to cover all liability to third persons caused by operation of motor vehicle. If such insurance has been obtained, criminal liability is exempted for injuries caused (not including death) except in cases of gross negligence as specified in statutes (e.g. driving by person not licensed). (Special Measure Law for Handling Traffic Accident 3, 4).

NOTARIES PUBLIC:

Notaries public are appointed by Minister of Justice and they are public officials of district public prosecutor's office. Notaries public, upon commission of party or other persons, prepare and authenticate instruments, deeds signed by private citizens, or articles of incorporation of company.

Notaries may act in localities where they are licensed to act and are liable for damages which result from their intentional or negligent acts performed in course of discharging their duties. Documents prepared or authenticated by notaries carry strong presumption of authenticity. When purport of instrument is claim for delivery of fungible or payment of sum certain or transfer of negotiable instruments, instrument itself is sufficient to obtain immediate execution against obligor if statement is made therein that obligor, at time of preparation of instrument, agrees to execution in event of default.

Under special legislation, practicing attorneys practicing in group may obtain license to act as notaries public. Lawyer's professional corporation is entitled to act as notary public.

PARTNERSHIP:

Partnership becomes effective when two or more persons agree to carry on joint undertaking by making mutual contribution thereto. Money, property, or services may be made object of contribution. (C.C. 703).

Affairs of partnership are conducted by majority of partners or, if several managers have been designated, by such managers. But ordinary affairs may be conducted by any partner or any manager acting alone, unless objections are raised by other partners or managers. (C.C. 706). One or more managers may be designated by partnership contracts or be elected with affirmative votes of more than two-thirds of all partners, and thereafter, managers who are also partners may not resign without due reason or be removed without unanimous consent of other partners. (C.C. 708).

Value of profit and loss to be shared is proportional to each partner's contribution in absence of specific agreement between partners. But creditor who was not aware of proportion of liability among partners at time when his claim arose may exercise his right against each partner in equal shares. (C.C. 711, 712). Debtor of partnership may not set off his claim against partner from his obligation to partnership. (C.C. 715).

When duration of partnership is not fixed, or is fixed at lifetime of partner, each partner may retire at any time. However, such partner may not, in absence of any unavoidable reason, retire at time which would be unfavorable to partnership. Even when duration of partnership is fixed, each partner may retire, if any unavoidable reason exists for doing so. (C.C. 716). Partner is deemed to have retired also in event of death, bankruptcy, adjudication of incompetency, or expulsion. (C.C. 717). Accounts between retired partner and other partners are based on status of property of partnership at time he retires, but accounting of matters not yet completed at that time may be made when completed. (C.C. 719).

Causes for dissolution of partnership are fulfilment of object of creation, impossibility of such fulfilment, or expiration of duration set by partnership contract. Upon dissolution, affairs of partnership are liquidated and assets distributed proportionally to each partner's contribution. (C.C. 721 through 724).

PATENTS:

Korea is member country of Paris Convention for Protection of Industrial Properties ("Paris Convention") and Patent Cooperation Treaty. Patent rights become effective when patent application is granted by and registered with Korea Industrial Property Office ("KIPO"). Foreigners residing or doing business in Korea may also apply for patent with KIPO. Nonresident foreigners may also apply for patents based on Paris Convention or if foreign country allows grant of patents to Korean nationals. (PA 25). Foreign applicants may claim priority on basis of foreign filing by making filing in Korea within one year from first foreign application date and satisfying procedural requirements. Nonresidents taking action involving patent rights are required to be represented by local patent attorney.

Patentable inventions must be ones which are "highly creative results of a technical idea utilizing the laws of nature" (PA 2), and be novel and inventive. However, following types of inventions are unpatentable: (i) inventions relating to substances which can be manufactured by transforming atomic nuclei; and (ii) inventions which are likely to injure public order, morality or health. (PA 32). With certain exceptions, inventions publicly used or known in Korea, or disclosed in publications distributed anywhere in world prior to filing date of patent application therefor, are unpatentable for lack of novelty and/or inventiveness. (PA 29).

Inventions concerning articles which involve lower degree of ingenuity may be protected as utility models, which have duration of 15 years being five years less than that of patent (see infra). Patent application may be changed into utility model application or design patent application and vice versa.

When several applications are made for identical inventions, first application is entitled to patent regardless of which applicant first conceived or completed invention. (PA 36). If multiple applications are made for identical invention on same date, applicant chosen by agreement among competing applicants will be entitled to patent, and, in absence of such agreement, none of the applicants will be entitled to patent. KIPO under direction of Minister of Trade and Industry, is responsible for receiving and processing patent applications, granting patents, conducting trials for cancelling, invalidating or confirming scope of claim of patent and reviewing appeals from rejection of applications. Korea adopts so-called "domestic priority claim system" wherein benefit of earlier filing date of co-pending national application can be claimed in subsequent application if such subsequent application is made by same inventor(s). (PA 55).

Applications obviously relating to national security or falling within fields indicated by defence agencies cannot be filed in foreign countries without government approval. (PA 41).

Patent application is subject to substantive examination by examiners only when request for examination thereof is filed. Such request may be filed by its applicant or any third parties and must be made within five years after filing. In absence of request for examination during such period, application lapses. (PA 57, 59).

Unless sooner published or rejected, every patent application will be subject to early publication in Official Gazette of Early Patent Publication 18 months after filing date (or priority date, if convention priority is claimed) for purposes of inviting comments from public. Applicant for patent is entitled to claim damages from infringers irrespective of giving written warning to them after application is disclosed through publication. This claim is based on early publication and can only be exercised when application is published for granting of patent. (PA 64 and 65).

Appeal from final rejection of patent application may be filed within 30 days from date on which final rejection is served. (PA 167 and 168). If such appeal is brought and amendment/correction to specification, claims and/or drawings of application are made within 30 days from date appeal was filed, Appellate Board of KIPO must return application file to examiner who rejected application so that he can reconsider or reexamine application based on amendment/correction. If examiner decides to allow application, he must withdraw his rejection. If he does not find reason to withdraw his rejection, then Appellate Board will consider application. (PA 173-175).

Once any grounds for rejection are overcome, patent application will be published for public inspection and opposition purposes in Official Gazette of Patent Publication for two months. After publication, patent applicant is given rights equal to patentee, with certain limitations. (PA 68).

Term of patent is 20 years from date of application. Patent rights, being property rights, may be transferred, inherited or pledged, etc., but all such acts except inheritance take legal effect only upon registration. (PA 101). Patent term may be restored up to five years from expiration of original term, depending on nature of invention involved, pretesting and other variables. (PA 89-92 and 95). Patents may be subject to

See Topical Index in front part of this volume.

PATENTS . . . *continued*
invalidation for various causes, such as wrongful patenting or nonworking by means of trial initiated by interested party and/or by examiners.

Employees are granted certain right in "in service" inventions. (PA 39 and 40).

Patent may be licensed exclusively or nonexclusively. Exclusive license gives licensee exclusive rights for patent (even excluding patentee). Nonexclusive license may contain limitation on time and territory.

Patentee or its exclusive or nonexclusive licensee may not work his patented invention if such working would require use of another's prior patent, registered utility model or registered design unless consent of prior patentee, etc. is obtained or unless nonexclusive license is granted as result of trial therefor. (PA 98). In order to obtain nonexclusive license by means of such trial, owner of later patent must prove that later invention represents significant technical progress over prior invention. (PA 138[2]).

If patented invention has not been worked for more than three consecutive years in Korea without justifiable reason, person who wishes to work patented invention may require patentee or its exclusive licensee to negotiate for grant of nonexclusive license. If no agreement is reached or no consultation is possible, person who wishes to work invention may petition Commissioner of KIPO to render mediation decision granting nonexclusive license. Upon filing of such petition, Commissioner must serve duplicate copy of petition on patent holder, giving him opportunity to reply. Official decision on petition must specify: (i) Scope of nonexclusive license to be granted, if any, and (ii) royalty to be paid by licensee and manner and time for payment thereof. Decision must take into account comments and views of Industrial Property Council of KIPO. Failure to pay royalties as required can result in cancellation of decision. If nonexclusive licensee fails to work patented invention within scope of nonexclusive license, Commissioner may, on motion by interested party or on his own motion, cancel decision, resulting in termination of nonexclusive license. (PA 107-116).

Applicant for international patent under PCT may submit its application translated into Korean to KIPO up to 20 months from earliest priority date in order to enter national phase in Korea.

PLEDGES:

Pledge is real right created by contract and delivery. Creditor obtains possession as security for indebtedness and gains preference to proceeds from sale by auction over general creditors. (C.C. 329 through 355). Any item of personal property or property right may be pledged with some statutory prohibitions. Except for pawn shops, pledgor may not agree before obligation becomes due and owing for any disposition of pledged property other than that provided by law. (C.C. 339). Pledges of movables require continuous possession by pledgee and pledgor may not hold item on behalf of pledgee. (C.C. 332). When claim is being pledged obligor must be notified or his consent obtained to make pledge valid against such obligor or third party. Pledgee may collect pledged claim. (C.C. 353). Negotiable instrument must be endorsed upon delivery to establish pledge. (C.C. 350). Pledge may be satisfied by sale by auction or upon appropriation with reason upon application to court. (C.C. 338).

PRESCRIPTION:

Legal concept in Korea distinguishes extinctive prescription, acquisitive prescription, and limitation of action.

Extinctive Prescription.—In general, claims lapse over ten years. Monetary claims arising from commercial transactions lapse over five years. However, property rights other than ownership and claim lapse over 20 years. (C.C. 162; Com. C. 64). Claims mentioned hereafter shall lapse if not exercised within three years: (1) Interest, support fees, salaries, rent, and other claims for delivery of money or other things made within one year; (2) claims of medical practitioners, midwives, nurses and pharmacists, in respect to medical treatments, professional services, or dispensation of medicines; (3) claims of contractors, engineers, and persons engaging in planning or supervising works, in respect of execution of works; (4) claims against attorneys, patent agents, notaries, public accountants, and judicial scriveners for return of documents kept in connection with their duties; (5) claims of attorneys-at-law, patent agents, notaries, public accountants, and judicial scriveners, in respect to their services; (6) prices of products and merchandise sold by producers and merchants; and (7) claims of artisans and manufacturers, in respect to their work.

Extinctive prescription for tort liability shall lapse three years after claimant becomes aware of damages and identity of tortfeasors or ten years after tort was committed. Claims mentioned hereafter shall lapse if not exercised within one year: (1) Right to claim for lodging, food, admission fees, price of articles of consumption and disbursement thereof, rental fees, and entertainment; (2) claims for renting clothing, bedding, funeral necessaries, and other movables; (3) claims for wages of manual workers and public performers and price of articles supplied by them; and (4) claims of owners of school properties, keepers of boarding schools, teachers, for education, clothing, food, and lodging of pupils and apprentices.

Extinctive prescription is two years for claims arising from collision between ships, etc.; and six months, one year and three years for various liabilities arising out of bills, notes and checks. (C.C. 163, 164, 766; Com. C. 842, 848; B.N.A. 70, 77).

Prescriptive period may be interrupted by: (1) Acknowledgment, (2) seizure, attachment, or injunction, or (3) demand, including demands by judicial actions following formal demand notice given six months earlier and which are not dismissed or withdrawn. (C.C. 168 through 177). Prescription commences to run anew upon conclusion of interruptive causes. (C.C. 178).

If minor or incompetent had no legal representative during last six months of prescriptive period, effects of prescription may be suspended for six months following recovery of capacity or appointment of guardian. (C.C. 179, 180). Likewise, actions between husband and wife may be brought within six months following divorce. (C.C. 180). Prescription regarding inherited estate is also suspended for six months after confirmation of successor, selection of administrator for estate, or adjudication of bankruptcy. (C.C. 181). When natural calamity has prevented interruption of prescription, prescriptive period does not mature for one month following removal of impediment. (C.C. 182).

Acquisitive prescription in general is 20 years for person who has peacefully and openly possessed immovable property with intention to own and ten years for person who has possessed it peacefully, openly with intention to own, in good faith and without negligence and has registered as being owner. Prescriptive period for movable property is ten years for person in possession of it peacefully and openly with intention to own and five years for person who possesses in good faith and without negligence. (C.C. 245, 246).

Limitation of Actions.—Time limitations on institution of litigation operate automatically, and cannot be extended for any reason. Such limitations are not retroactive as in case of extinctive prescription. (C.C. 167). Rights to damages, reduction of purchase price, and rescission of sales contract for seller's warranty are subject to one year or six months limitation of actions. (C.C. 573, 575, 582). See also topic Limitation of Actions.

Set-off.—See topic Contracts.

PRINCIPAL AND AGENT:

Agent acting within scope of his authority for his principal, binds such principal by any valid manifestation of intent. (C.C. 114). Unless other party knows or should have known of agent's status he binds only himself personally. In commercial transaction, principal is nevertheless still bound and performance by agent may additionally be demanded. (C.C. 115, Com. C. 48). Noncommercial contracts made by agent acting beyond her authority bind agent but not principal until ratified. (C.C. 130). Ratification may be requested within reasonable period and until ratified contract may be cancelled by other party at any time. (C.C. 131, 134). When only agent is personally bound other party may demand either performance or damages. (C.C. 135).

Individual with no legal capacity may be agent. (C.C. 117). Unless otherwise provided, agent may only perform acts of preservation or improvement of object of agency but may not alter it. (C.C. 118). Agent may not appoint subagent without consent of principal unless unavoidable reason exists. (C.C. 120). One may not be agent for both sides of legal act without consent, but performance of existing obligations is not subject to foregoing. (C.C. 124). Person who holds somebody out as authorized agent to third parties is responsible for acts done by apparent agent within his apparent authority. (C.C. 125). If agent acts outside scope of his authority but third party reasonably believes agent has authority, principal is bound by acts of agent. (C.C. 126). Death of principal (other than in case of commercial transactions) or agent, bankruptcy, or adjudication of agent's incompetency, completion of terms of contract all terminate agency relationship. (C.C. 127, Com. C. 50).

Commission merchant is person who effects sales or purchases of goods or of valuable instruments in his own name for account of another person. By sale or purchase effected for his principal, commission merchant directly acquires rights and incurs obligations with regard to other party to transaction. (Com. C. 102). Goods or negotiable instruments which have been received by commission merchant from his principal, or acquired through sales and purchases, shall be deemed to belong to principal insofar as relationship between principal and commission merchant, and creditors of commission merchant are concerned. (Com. C. 103). As relationship between principal and commission merchant is mandate, commerical merchant owes general duty to properly manage affairs entrusted to him with due care. Also he is under special obligations stipulated in Commercial Code. (Com. C. 104, 105, 106, 108). Commission merchant has right to demand remuneration, right of retention, right for deposit and auction of subject matter, and right to intervene. (Com. C. 61, 67, 91, 107).

PROCESS:

Service of process in litigation is made ex officio only by court and, in principle, by personal service through court sheriffs or by mail. (C.C.P. 161 through 165, 173). Service of process to party represented by attorney will be made to attorney of record. (C.C.P. 166, 167).

Supplementary Service.—In case person on whom service is to be made is not at place of service, document may be delivered to clerk, employee, or cohabitant who has sufficient intellect. If person who is to be served documents, has, without justifiable reasons, refused receipt thereof, such documents may be left behind at place where service is to be effected. (C.C.P. 172). In case service cannot be effected by means of supplementary service described above, court clerk may dispatch document by registered mail. (C.C.P. 173).

Method of Service in Foreign Country.—Service to be effected in foreign country shall be effected upon entrustment thereof by presiding judge to Korean Ambassador, Minister or Consul stationed therein or competent government authorities of that country. (C.C.P. 176).

Service by Publication.—In event that domicile, residence or other place of service of party is unknown, or it is deemed impossible or ineffective to effect service in foreign country, presiding judge may, upon his own authority or upon motion of parties, order service by public notice. Service by publication shall be made by placing document to be served in custody of court clerk and by putting up notice to that effect on bulletin board of court. (C.C.P. 179, 180).

Agent for Service of Process.—If party to litigation does not have domicile, residence, place of business, or office in jurisdiction of relevant court, he shall designate place for service and agent for service of process in such jurisdiction and make report thereof to court. (C.C.P. 171). Designation of process agent may be reported to court only after court proceedings have commenced.

REAL PROPERTY:

Only property rights provided for in Civil Code or other laws including customary laws can exist (C.C. 185) and include following: (i) Ownership (fee simple); (ii) possession, superior to parties without rights and is presumed bona fide and legal; (iii) superficies are right to another's land while owning structures or trees on it; (iv) servitude is right of use of another's land for benefit and convenience of one's own land; (v) deposit lease (chonse-gwon) is right to use and take profits from immovable owned by another person in accordance with nature of immovable, by taking possession of immovable and upon payment of lease deposit; and (vi) commonage is based on old custom of use of forest or plain in common (C.C. 192, 211, 279, 291, 302, 303).

REAL PROPERTY . . . *continued*

There are two types of security interest in property: (a) Possessory liens, and (b) mortgage. (C.C. 320, 356). See topics Liens; Mortgages.

Certain provisional or contingent rights such as future sale or repurchase are quasi-property rights and can be recorded. Lease is not considered property right. (C.C. 621, Law of Protection of Lease of House 1). Lease cannot be recorded without consent of lessor. Owner of recorded building on leased land can demand without record lease from individuals who acquire title to land. (C.C. 622).

Tenancy in common is form of ownership whereby each owner holds undivided interest in property. If property is owned jointly by two or more persons in proportion to their share, ownership thereof shall be joint-ownership. (C.C. 262). Joint-owners are entitled to dispose of their own shares and may make use of or take profits of whole of that which is owned jointly in proportion to their share. (C.C. 263). Each joint-owner shall pay expenses of administration and bear all other charges relating to property jointly owned in proportion to his share. (C.C. 266). No joint-owner may dispose of or make any alteration in property jointly owned without consent of other joint-owners. (C.C. 264).

Adverse Possession.—If person possesses real property with intent to own for 20 years or more, peacefully and openly, he may acquire ownership of such property by making registration thereof. (C.C. 245 [I]). Person who is registered as owner of real property and possesses such property for ten years or more, peacefully and openly, in good faith and without any fault or negligence related to such possession shall acquire ownership of such property. (C.C. 245[II]).

Alienation of Property (Restrictions on).—Real property is transferred by agreement between parties upon registration of transfer of title in court (or registration office of court). (C.C. 186). Personal property is transferred by agreement between parties upon transfer of possession. (C.C. 188).

Condominiums.—Separate ownership of individual units is permitted for multiple-unit buildings (e.g., apartment). Unit owners have joint ownership of common portion with other owners and also have undivided interest in right to use common portion. In addition, unit owner also has right to use land on which building is located. Such undivided interest in common portion and land may not be disposed of separately from ownership of unit. (The Law relating to the Ownership and Management of Multiple-unit Building).

RECORDS:

Registration offices are established under courts to maintain records relating to property including ships and commercial transactions and are located throughout Korea. Family register records are maintained at municipal office in custody of local officials. Patent Office in Seoul maintains registers of patents, trademarks, designs, and utility models.

Real rights in immovables requiring registration include ownership, superficies, deposit lease (Chonse-gwon) and mortgage. Real rights in immovables may be created by registration of such rights with relevant record office. In Korea, separation of ownership of buildings and land upon which it is erected and maintenance of separate records thereof is possible. Provisional registration system affords protection against subsequent transfers of property to third parties through recording of contractual arrangements or incomplete assignments.

Records are required of injunctions prohibiting disposition of registered rights, attachments of registered property, adjudications of bankruptcy, and commencement of reorganization procedures.

See also topic Commercial Register.

REPORTS:

Supreme Court periodically publishes decisions it made and also publishes important decisions made by lower courts. Decisions by courts are also published in various private publications.

SALES:

Nature.—Sale is contract for transfer of property rights in exchange for purchase price. (C.C. 563). Unless otherwise dictated by agreement or custom, transfer and payment must be made simultaneously. (C.C. 568). Unless otherwise agreed by parties, when neither party has begun to perform contract of sale in which earnest money has been paid, purchaser may rescind contract of sale by waiving that sum and vendor may rescind by refunding double that amount. This bars further claims for damage. (C.C. 565).

Warranties.—Following warranties are made in sales, and even express disclaimers will not release vendor if he had knowledge of defects but did not reveal them to purchaser or if breach results from rights given to third persons by vendor (C.C. 584): (1) Vendor must acquire from third persons and transfer to purchaser all rights that are subject of sale (C.C. 569). If vendor fails to perform, purchaser may rescind contract, and receive damages if at time of contracting he did not know that right did not belong to vendor. Vendor may also rescind, if he did not know that he did not possess such right, but must pay damages (C.C. 570, 571); (2) purchaser may request lower price if goods are not up to stipulated quantity, or if vendor cannot transfer all rights. He may rescind contract if (in good faith) he would not have entered into contract if he had such knowledge. However, vendor is still liable for damages if purchaser acted in good faith. (C.C. 572, 574). All these rights must be exercised within one year of purchaser's knowledge of fact, if he acted in good faith or one year from day of contract if not (C.C. 573); (3) if object of sale is subject to superficies, servitude, registered lease right (chunse-kwon), pledge or lien, or contains defect of which purchaser had no knowledge at time of contract, purchaser may rescind contract if it thwarts purpose for which contract was made; otherwise purchaser may only seek damages. Damage claims and rescission are not allowed after one year from discovery (C.C. 575, 580); (4) if purchaser loses ownership of immovable as result of exercise of preferential right or mortgage or registered lease right (chunse-kwon) covering property, he may rescind contract and claim damages as well (C.C. 576).

Price.—Expenses of sale are divided equally between parties. (C.C. 566). Fruits of thing are vendor's even after purchase but before delivery. Absent credit arrangement purchaser must pay interest on purchase price after delivery. (C.C. 587). If third party asserts right to goods purchaser may refuse or withhold payment until vendor provides suitable security. (C.C. 588).

Repurchase.—Vendor may, by special provision in sale contract have right to repurchase goods through repayment of purchase price plus expenses or other agreed amount. Unless otherwise agreed, upon repurchase, fruits of immovable and interest on purchase price are deemed to offset one another. (C.C. 590). Right to repurchase cannot exceed five years for immovables and three years for movables, and in absence of specifically provided term, repurchase must be within such corresponding periods. (C.C. 591). When creditor of vendor seeks to exercise vendor's right of repurchase, purchaser may retain ownership of property by paying to vendor's creditor debt owed by vendor, value of property exceeding purchase price, and expenses. Remaining sum, if any, must be paid to vendor. (C.C. 593). If one co-owner has sold his share in property with provision for repurchase, which is later partitioned, former co-owner (vendor) may repurchase that part of property received by purchaser in division. If purchaser receives payment upon auction of co-owned property, former co-owner (vendor) may assert claim against proceeds. (C.C. 595).

Resale.—Between merchants, if purchaser refuses or is unable to accept delivery, vendor may deposit goods or sell goods at public auction if vendor has given purchaser notice and waited for reasonable period thereafter. Perishable goods may be sold without notification. Vendor must deposit proceeds of sale after deduction of expenses with government deposit office but has right to proceeds of sale for satisfaction of purchase price. (Com. C. 67). If purpose for which contract was entered into cannot be fulfilled unless performed at specified time or period, and it has lapsed without performance of one party, other party is deemed to have rescinded contract unless he immediately demands performance. (Com. C. 68).

Inspection and Rescission.—Between merchants, purchaser must examine goods upon delivery, and give notice of all defects or shortages if he later wishes to rescind, claim damages, or price reductions. Vendor must be notified immediately of hidden defects found within six months, if purchaser also wishes to preserve those rights. There is no requirement of immediate notification if vendor has acted in bad faith. (Com. C. 69). When purchaser rescinds, goods are to be kept or deposited at expense of vendor. If goods may lose value or deteriorate after rescission, purchaser must obtain court order and sell goods at auction; proceeds must be deposited or kept by purchaser in his custody under approval of court. Vendor must be notified immediately of auction sale, if he does not reside or do business in same area as purchaser. (Com. C. 70). Similar rules apply to goods differing from or more than those ordered. (Com. C. 71).

Notices Required.—In general, no written notice is required for claim of nonconformity against vendor after delivery (however, see subhead Inspection and Rescission, supra).

Applicable Law.—Conflicts of Laws Act rules follow rules of contracts in general (see topic Contracts) but with regard to transfer of title, law where property is located governs. (C.L.A. 12).

Consumer Protection.—Consumer Protection Act ("C.P.A.") provides administrative power to protect consumers and provides for mediation of disputes by Consumer Protection Board. Civil remedies must be pursued through general principles of existing civil law. Manufacturers, importers, or packagers are required to mark goods with any necessary information. (C.P.A. 16). Competent government agency may order or implement collection, destruction or other measures with respect to goods which may cause harm to consumers. (C.P.A. 17-3).

Installment Sales.—Any sale in which payments are made in installments, usually monthly, is installment sale. Subject goods may be delivered upon final payment of total purchase price. However, they are usually delivered prior to payment of initial installment or upon payment thereof.

Seller may take certain steps to assure full payment by purchaser. Seller usually retains title to subject goods until payment of purchase price is made in full and then he transfers it to purchaser upon receipt thereof. If payment of installments is delayed seller can terminate purchase agreement and demand return of subject goods. Also, if any installment payment is missed seller can accelerate remaining installment payments and demand lump sum payment of remaining purchase price. Seller must try to avoid actions against public order or abuse of rights. (C.C. 103, 2).

Fraudulent Sales.—If obligor willfully prejudices property rights of obligee by transferring rights to goods to subsequent purchaser who is aware that such transfer is prejudicial, obligee may apply to court to have such sale rescinded. Sale for purpose of defrauding creditors (e.g. sale at price substantially undervalued) may be declared void by court and property returned.

SECURITIES:

Regulation and Registration.—Securities and Exchange Law ("S.E.L."), Enforcement Decree and various regulations thereunder regulate securities business in Korea. Administrative functions are given to Ministry of Finance and Economy ("MOFE"), Securities and Exchange Commission ("SEC") and Securities Supervisory Board ("SSB"). MOFE is given powers to approve establishment of securities companies (S.E.L. 28), branches of foreign securities companies (S.E.L. 28-2), to supervise businesses of, and to receive reports from SEC, SSB and Korea Stock Exchange ("KSE") (S.E.L. 126, 141, 142, 116 and 117, etc.). SEC is given wide power of registration of securities and securities issuers; it may issue necessary regulations and order investigations into violations of SEC regulations and orders and review and resolve various matters. (S.E.L. 118 et seq.). Under instruction and supervision of SEC, SSB enforces resolutions of SEC, supervises and inspects securities companies and other security related institutions. (S.E.L. 130, et seq.). Securities are defined as government bonds, municipal bonds, bonds issued by statutory juridical entities, corporate debentures, certificates of capital contribution issued by statutory juridical entities, stock certificates, instruments representing preemptive rights, certificates or instruments issued by foreign government or foreign companies having same nature as

See Topical Index in front part of this volume.

SECURITIES . . . *continued*

foregoing certificates or instruments and being designated by MOFE, beneficial certificates issued by trust companies or investment trust companies. (S.E.L. 2[I], E.D. of S.E.L. 2-2).

Companies wishing to list securities other than exempt securities on exchanges, companies which have not listed securities on KSE ("non-listed companies") and intend to make public offering of securities other than exempt securities, non-listed companies wishing to merge with listed companies, non-listed companies wishing to have their securities other than exempt securities, traded at over-the-counter market, companies in course of being incorporated wishing to make public offering of securities other than exempt securities, and companies designated by SEC which meet certain criteria as is prescribed by Enforcement Decree must be registered with SEC in advance. (S.E.L. 3). With certain exceptions, if total amount of offering or selling of securities is over amount prescribed by decree of Minister of Finance and Economy, issuers of securities, before publicly offering or selling securities issued or to be issued, must file registration statement with SEC in advance. (S.E.L. 8). This is not applicable to certain securities including government bonds, municipal bonds, bonds and share certificates issued by statutory juridical entities.

Tender Offers.—With certain exceptions, offerors of tender offers outside exchanges to unspecified persons for stock certificates, instruments representing preemptive rights and convertible bonds issued by listed companies and companies registered with SEC ("registered companies"), which would result in offeror (including his family and other people having special relationship with offeror) beneficially owning 10% or more of total shares issued and outstanding must file tender offer disclosure statement with SEC prior to tender offer, send copy of such statement to issuer of subject securities, and make public notice in two or more daily newspapers. (S.E.L. 21 and 22, Enforcement Regulation of S.E.L. 6). SEC may order offeror to follow terms, conditions and method of purchase determined by SEC. (S.E.L. 23[III]).

Proxy Solicitation.—Solicitor of proxies with respect to listed stock certificates must, on or prior to solicitation, provide solicitees with reference documents prepared as provided by SEC and at same time file copies of reference documents and form of proxy with SSB. (S.E.L. 199, E.D. of S.E.L. 85, Paras. 1 and 3). Form of proxy must include box-type ballot to permit stockholders to choose between approving and disapproving each item to be discussed in shareholders' meeting. (E.D. of S.E.L. 85[II]). See also topic Corporations.

Shareholding Restrictions.—With certain exceptions, one may not hold beneficial ownership of shares issued by public judicial entity in excess of: (i) Number of shares held, at time of registering if more than 10% of total shares issued and outstanding (*Note.*—10% ownership limitation is scheduled to be repealed on Jan. 1, 1997) or (ii) number of shares held prescribed in articles of company within limits of 3% of total shares issued and outstanding. (S.E.L. 200, Paras. 1 and 2). Anyone holding shares in excess of above limitation may not exercise voting rights of excess shares. (S.E.L. 200[III]). SEC may order such shareholders to rectify shareholding position. (S.E.L. 200[III]). With certain exceptions, one who holds beneficial ownership of 5% or more of total issued and outstanding shares of any listed company must submit report thereon to SEC and KSE. (S.E.L. 200-2).

SEC may set restrictions on foreigners' acquisition of securities issued by listed corporations or registered corporations. (S.E.L. 203, E.D. of S.E.L. 87-2[I] and [II]). Unless otherwise approved by SEC, foreigners wishing to buy or sell listed securities must do so through exchanges. (E.D. of S.E.L. 87-2[III]).

Secured Bonds.—Secured bond is bond which has security. Because it is impracticable to provide specific security for each bond holder, Secured Bonds Trust Act enacted Jan. 20, 1962 enables company to provide collective security. Bond issuing company acting as trustor, and trust company acting as trustee, execute trust agreement. Trust agreement obligates trustee to acquire security, to maintain same on behalf of all bond holders, to enforce security, and to distribute foreclosure price to bond holders pari passu according to their credit amount. (Secured Bonds Trust Act 60, et seq.).

SEQUESTRATION:

Court may issue orders for provisional or prejudgment attachment in order to enforce monetary claims or restraining orders in order to preserve rights which may adversely affect interests of litigant.

SHIPPING:

Primary features of shipping and maritime law are contained in Part V of Commercial Code and other laws (e.g., Ship Act, Ship Registration Act, Seaman's Act, Marine Transportation Business Act, Maritime Transportation Industry Fostering Act).

Ships are of Korean nationality if they belong to: (1) Korean government, (2) Korean national, (3) corporation incorporated under Law of Korea where more than half of equity capital and more than three fifths of directors (including representative directors) of company are Korean nationals (representative director shall also be Korean national), and (4) company whose principal office is in Korea and whose legal representatives are Korean. Register of Ships at Korean Maritime and Port Administration contains information concerning type, name, port of registry, ownership, and tonnage.

Records relating to ownership and rights in vessels of gross tonnage of more than 20 tons can be found at registration office of home port of ship. (Ship Registration Law 2, 3, 4). See also topic Records.

Liability of consignee for freight and other expenses arises upon receipt of cargo. If consignee fails to accept cargo, shipowner becomes entitled to deposit cargo with competent authority or deliver cargo to custom's office or other place permitted by authorities as prescribed by laws and regulations. (Com. C. 803). Shipowner may, in case of failure to pay for freight etc. with approval of court, sell cargo at auction even after date of delivery, but within 30 days from such date, in order to receive freight and other incidental expenses, so long as third party has not acquired possession thereof.

Charterer of entire ship may rescind contract at any time before commencement of voyage if he pays one-half of freight. Part charterer may, upon agreement of all charterers, rescind before commencement of voyage but must pay entire amount of freight. Damages and expenses resulting from disposition by master to save vessel or cargo from common danger are shared among interested persons in accordance with rules of general average contribution. General average contribution and loss shall be determined based upon remaining value of ship and cargo at time and place of ship's arrival and remaining value of cargo at time and place of unloading of cargo. (Com. C. 836).

Regarding limitation of shipowner's liability, Commercial Code adopts basic features of International Convention for Unification of Certain Rules of Law in Regard to Collisions (Brussels, Sept. 23, 1910); International Convention for Unification of Certain Rules of Law Relating to Assistance and Salvage (Brussels, 1910); International Convention on the Limitation of Liability for Maritime Claims (1976) (new enactment for procedure for Limitation of Shipowner's Liability); and International Convention for Unification of Certain Rules of Law Relating to Bills of Lading, (Brussels, 1924) and its 1968 protocol although Korea is not signatory thereto. Korea is signatory to International Convention on Civil Liability for Oil Pollution Damage of 1969; International Convention in the Establishment of an International Fund for Compensation for Oil Pollution Damage, 1971 (new domestic legislation to incorporate the two conventions).

Maritime lien extends to ships, appurtenances thereof, and unpaid freight for: (1) Legal expenses incurred in interest of creditors, expenses incurred in respect to auction sale of ships and their appurtenances, taxes levied on ships in respect to voyage, pilotage and towing fees, and cost of maintenance and survey of ship and its appurtenances at last port; (2) claims arising from contract of employment of mariners and other employees of ship; (3) salvage remuneration and general average contributions; (4) indemnities for damages caused to navigational institutions, harbour facilities or navigable ways by collision between ships or any other accident, for loss of lives or for personal injuries to mariners or passengers, and for damages caused to cargo and luggage.

TAXATION:

Korean taxes are classified into national taxes imposed by central government and local taxes imposed by local authorities. National taxes are composed of internal taxes (which are composed of income tax, inheritance tax, gift tax, corporation tax, value added tax, special excise tax, assets revaluation tax, excess land profit tax, excess profits tax, liquor tax, telephone tax, stamp tax, securities transaction tax, agricultural and fishery communities special tax), education tax, traffic tax, and customs duties. Local taxes are composed of acquisition tax, registration tax, license tax, inhabitant tax, property tax, composite land tax, automobile tax, farmland tax, slaughterhouse tax, horse race tax, tobacco sales tax, city planning tax, community facility tax, area development tax, and workshop tax. Taxpayer's tax liabilities are specified in relevant tax laws, enforcement decrees, and enforcement regulations.

Income tax is payable by resident individuals in Korea upon their worldwide income, while income of nonresidents is taxable only to extent derived from Korean sources. Income is classified into global income, retirement income, capital gains income, and timber income. Global income is composed of interest, dividends, real estate income, business income, salaries and other income. Global income tax rate is progressive from 10% to 40% and applies to total of global income components. Top global income tax bracket of 40% is applied to annual global income over 80,000,000 Won. Inhabitant Surtax makes top effective tax rate 44%. Tax liabilities on retirement income, capital gains income and timber income are determined apart from global income tax liabilities using tax rates ranging from 10% to 75%. Inhabitant Surtax is also imposed upon these taxes. Retirement income, capital gains income, or timber income of nonresidents is taxed in same manner as residents. Global income of nonresidents who maintain domestic place of business (similar to "permanent establishment") or earn income from real estate are also taxed in same manner as residents. If nonresidents do not maintain domestic place of business and if they do not earn income from real estate, global income of nonresidents is taxed through withholding method. Withholding tax rate differs depending upon nature of income. 25% withholding tax rate is applied to interest, dividends, royalties, and other income earned by nonresidents; 2% for business income and income from leasing vessels, aircraft, etc.; 20% for certain personal service income; 10% of transaction price or 25% of profit, whichever is less, on income from transfer of securities; 10% to 40% for salaries. Inhabitant tax amounting to 10% of income tax is also withheld as surtax. Withholding tax rates modified by tax treaties are applied to income of nonresidents of country with which Korea has entered into tax treaty. Foreign tax credit may be obtained in accordance with certain formulae and under certain conditions. Income Tax Law specifies various nontaxable income, exemptions from income tax, income deductions and income tax credits.

Inheritance tax is payable by residents who acquire property by inheritance and by nonresidents who acquire property located in Korea by inheritance at rates ranging from 10% to 40%. Top inheritance tax bracket of 40% is applicable to taxable base exceeding 550,000,000 Won. Certain deductions and credits are specified in Inheritance Tax Law.

Gift tax is payable by residents who acquire property by gift, and by nonresidents who acquire property located in Korea by gift, at rates ranging from 10% to 40%. Top gift tax rate of 40% is applied to taxable base exceeding 300,000,000 Won. Corporations except for nonprofit corporations, are not subject to gift tax. Rules on gift taxes are specified in Inheritance Tax Law.

Corporation tax is payable by juridical persons under Corporation Tax Law. Noncorporate associations and foundations are also liable for corporation tax only upon income accruing from profit-making businesses. Foreign corporations are subject to corporation tax to extent of their Korean source income. Nonprofit corporations and foreign corporations are not liable while domestic profit corporations are liable to pay corporation tax upon liquidation income. Corporation tax rate of 16% is applied to income up to 100,000,000 Won. Income exceeding 100,000,000 Won is subject to rate of 28%, which has one exception discussed below. Nonprofit corporations are subject to corporation tax at rate of 16% for income up to 100,000,000 Won and at rate of 25% for income exceeding 100,000,000 Won. Inhabitant Surtax affects maximum rate. Up

See Topical Index in front part of this volume.

TAXATION . . . *continued*
until Dec. 31, 1996, agricultural and fishery communities special tax will be additionally levied at rate of 2% for income exceeding 500,000,000 Won per year. Special added tax on capital gains is also levied as corporation tax at 20% or 40% upon income accruing from transfer of real estate. Inhabitant Surtax is imposed, and makes maximum effective rate to be 44%. Foreign corporations which maintain domestic place of business or earn real estate income, or timber income are taxed in manner similar to domestic corporations. If foreign corporation does not maintain domestic place of business, it is subject to Korean taxation upon its domestic source income through withholding, except for corporation tax liability upon real estate or timber income, which is determined in same manner as domestic corporations. Foreign corporations earning real estate income or timber income, however, are subject to Korean taxation in same manner similar to domestic corporations regardless of whether they maintain domestic place of business or not. Withholding corporation tax rate applicable to foreign corporations is similar to withholding income tax rate applicable to nonresident individuals. 25% of withholding tax rate is applied to interest, dividends, royalties, and other income; 2% to business income and income from leasing vessels, aircraft, etc.; 20% to certain personal service income; 10% of transaction price or 25% of profit, whichever is less, to income from transfer of securities. Inhabitant tax amounting to 10% of corporation tax is also withheld as surtax. Withholding tax rates are also modified by tax treaties. Foreign tax credits may be obtained in accordance with certain formulae and under certain conditions.

Value-added tax ("VAT") is imposed upon supply of goods, services, and importation of goods at rate of 10%. Businesses are required to collect and pay to government VAT collected from purchasers (output VAT). VAT paid by businesses to vendors (input VAT) is deducted from output VAT or is refunded by government. VAT imposed upon importation of goods is collected by customs authorities. Certain goods such as basic life necessities, land, coal, books, and services such as education, financing, and social welfare are exempt from VAT. Goods for exportation, services provided outside Korea, international transportation by ships and aircraft, and certain goods or services supplied for foreign exchange earnings are subject to zero-rate VAT.

Special excise tax is imposed upon sales of jewelry, manufacture and sales of air conditioners, refrigerators, TV's, audio and visual equipment, passenger cars, pianos, etc., importation of above goods, and management of casino, golf course, ski resorts, etc., at rates ranging from 10% through 150%. Education tax amounting to 30% of special excise tax is imposed as surtax.

Customs duties are imposed upon goods imported. Average basic customs duties rate for 1995 is about 8%. Actual customs duties are modified by temporary customs duties, anti-dumping customs duties, retaliatory customs duties, emergency customs duties, adjustment customs duties, countervailing customs duties, beneficial duties, price parity customs duties, and tariff quotas. VAT rate of 10% is also levied. Special excise tax or liquor tax are also levied, on such taxable imported goods. Customs Duties Law specifies certain exemptions.

Penalty taxes are generally imposed under relevant tax laws for failure to file tax return within date due, failure to pay within date due, and failure to comply with obligations specified in tax laws. For example, penalty tax defined in Corporation Tax Law is as follows: Failure to file corporate tax return or to comply with obligation to maintain books or records results in penalty tax amounting to 20% of calculated tax or 0.07% of gross revenue of fiscal reporting period, whichever is greater. (In this case, penalty tax for under-reporting income discussed below is not assessed.) If tax base in corporate tax return falls short of amount that should have been declared, penalty tax for under-reporting income of 10% of calculated tax attributable to under-reported income is imposed. Failure to pay tax results in penalty tax of either 10% of amount or at interest rate of 0.04% per day for two years from due date and 0.03% per day for over two years from due date of corporation tax unpaid, whichever is greater. Failure to withhold taxes at source or to pay withholding tax to government results in penalty tax of 10% of tax not withheld or unpaid. Failure to publish balance sheet results in penalty tax of 1% of calculated tax or 0.004% of gross revenue, whichever is less (this penalty tax is not applied to foreign corporations). Failure to submit disbursement documents clearly to tax authorities results in penalty tax of 3% or 0.3% of amount disbursed. Apart from penalty taxes under each relevant tax law, person who evades taxes through fraudulent or unjust actions is subject to imprisonment up to three years and/or fines up to three or five times amount of tax evaded under Tax Criminal Punishment Law. Tax Criminal Punishment Law additionally specifies imprisonment up to one, two or three years and/or fines for failure to meet obligations specified in tax laws. Under Specified Criminal Additional Punishment Law, person who evades taxes in amount exceeding 500,000,000 Won per year may be subject to imprisonment for five years or more or for life. Person who evades taxes in amount from 200,000,000 Won to 500,000,000 Won may be subject to imprisonment for three years or more.

Special taxation measures are provided in Tax Exemption and Reduction Control Law for fiscal policy purposes. They include provisions for nontaxable income, tax credit, income deductions, tax exemptions, and tax refunds for public corporations, small enterprises, defense industries, overseas businesses, etc. Tax Exemption and Reduction Control Law is effective through Dec. 31, 1998. Foreign Capital Inducement Law provides tax benefits for corporation tax, income tax, certain local taxes, customs duties, VAT, special excise tax, and surtaxes thereon, applicable to foreign invested enterprise projects where equity investment is made by foreign investors for foreign loan and foreign technology provided. Such benefits are granted to foreign investor, foreign invested enterprise, foreign loan provider, and foreign technology provider under certain conditions, e.g. high technology.

Tax Treaties.—As of Jan. 1, 1995 tax treaties to avoid double taxation and to prevent fiscal evasion are effective with Australia, Austria, Bangladesh, Belgium, Brazil, Canada, China, Czech Republic, Denmark, Egypt, Fiji Island, Finland, France, Germany, Hungary, India, Indonesia, Ireland, Italy, Japan, Luxembourg, Malaysia, Mexico, Mongolia, The Netherlands, New Zealand, Norway, Pakistan, Philippines, Poland, Romania, Singapore, Spain, Sri Lanka, Sweden, Switzerland, Thailand, Tunisia, Turkey, U.K., U.S.A., and Vietnam. Such tax treaties provide foreign corporations or individuals with protection against Korean taxation with respect to corporation taxes, income taxes, and surtaxes thereon.

Amended tax return can be made by taxpayers before tax authority sends tax payment notice to taxpayers, in order to eliminate errors or complete omissions contained in tax returns which were filed originally. Amended tax return system is not available for local taxes and customs duties. Amended tax return eliminates penalty tax liability upon under-reporting of tax base by 50% if amended tax return is filed within six months after filing deadline of original tax return.

Tax appeals on administrative and judicial levels are available in Korea. Tax appeal on administrative level is prerequisite for appeal on judicial level. First level administrative appeal of national tax claiming illegal or improper administrative disposition or lack of necessary administrative disposition must be filed with Tax Office or Regional Office of National Tax Administration (Customs Office, in case of customs duties) within 60 days (90 days, if taxpayer has address outside of Korea) after taxpayer learns of administrative disposition. Taxpayer may omit first level appeal and file second level appeal directly to National Tax Administration (Office of Customs Administration, in case of customs duties) within same deadline applicable to first appeal. If first level appeal was made, second appeal must be made within 60 days after taxpayer receives or is deemed to have received decision of first level appeal. Third level administrative tax appeal must be filed with National Tax Tribunal within 60 days after taxpayer receives or is deemed to have received decision from National Tax Administration. Instead of lodging administrative appeal mentioned above, taxpayer may file appeal with Board of Audit and Inspection within 60 days (90 days, if taxpayer has address outside Korea). Local tax appeal procedures on administrative level are similar to those described above, except for administrative authorities in charge of tax appeal and deadlines. If final administrative disposition is not satisfactory after exhausting all appeals on administrative level, taxpayer can proceed to judicial level appeal within 60 days after taxpayer receives or is deemed to have received decision from National Tax Tribunal (Ministry of Internal Affairs or Provincial Authorities in case of local tax) or from Board of Audit and Inspection. Judicial appeal is available on two levels, i.e., High Court and Supreme Court.

TORTS:

Any person who causes damage to another intentionally or negligently by any unlawful act shall remedy such damages. (C.C. 750). Elements of tort action are: Negligence or intent; breach of legal duty; and injury or damages. Damages to body, freedom, honor, property, or life of another may be compensated by payment of money. Guardian (or parent) who is liable for supervising mentally incompetent person (including infants) shall be liable for damages such person causes. (C.C. 755). Employer is liable for his employee's tort if employee is acting within scope of his employment. (C.C. 756). Joint tortfeasors are jointly and severally liable. (C.C. 760).

TRADEMARKS AND TRADENAMES:

Trademarks.—Newly revised Trademark Act was promulgated in Dec. of 1995. Enforcement to commence on Jan. 1, 1996. Following explanation is based on newly revised Trademark Act. Trademark rights are obtained only when trademark is registered. (T.A. 41). Anyone who wishes to register trademark may file registration application with Korea Industrial Property Office regardless of whether trademark has actually been used. Materials which substantiate use of trademark thus need not be submitted when new application is filed. However, proof of use must be submitted when renewal application is filed. (T.A. 42[II][ii]). Further, trademark registration is subject to cancellation through trial brought by interested party if owner or its registered licensee has not used trademark on any of designated goods for any three consecutive years before cancellation hearings (trials) are brought. (T.A. 73[1][iii]).

Further, Korea has adopted national classification system regarding goods and services. This classification system includes 53 classes for goods and 12 classes for services. Applicant must classify goods or services to be covered by mark in appropriate class using national classification system and must also describe goods or services in detail on item by item basis. (T.A. 10).

Term of trademark right is ten years and may be renewed for subsequent ten year period. (T.A. 42). Trademarks may be transferred. (T.A. 54).

If owner of registered trademark permits another to use their trademark for six months or longer without registering this party as exclusive or non-exclusive licensee, interested party can bring cancellation action against registration. (T.A. 73[1][i]). Registration of exclusive or non-exclusive licensee is accomplished by submitting trademark license agreement executed by parties to Korea Industrial Property Office. Further, if trademark license agreement does not provide for royalty payments, no government approval is required. Only royalty-bearing trademark licenses must be approved by government authorities in accordance with Foreign Exchange Management Law and Foreign Capital Inducement Law.

Trade Names.—Individual may use business name or not, but business organization must use trade name to conduct its trade. (Com. C. 179[ii], 270, 289[I][ii]). Trade name need not include name of proprietor or refer to type of business involved. However, trade names of business organizations must include descriptor as prescribed in Commercial Code, such as joint stock company, etc., and such descriptors may only be used when actually applicable. (Com. C. 19, 20). Company can do business only under single trade name. (Com. C. 21). None may use trade name which is likely to cause confusion, with trade name of another for improper purposes. Civil liability may arise from such activity. (Com. C. 23).

Trade names may be registered with civil district court having jurisdiction over main and/or branch offices of business. Registration in one judicial district cannot be used to attack or prevent registration of similar trade name in different district. (Com. C. 22, 23). Transfer of trade name must be registered in commercial register to be enforceable against third parties. (Com. C. 25).

TREATIES:

International Conventions.—Treaties duly concluded and promulgated in accordance with Constitution and generally recognized rules of international law have same effect as domestic laws of Korea. (Const. 6[1]).

See Topical Index in front part of this volume.

TREATIES . . . *continued*

Agriculture and Food.—Constitution of the United Nations Food and Agriculture Organization (16/10/45), International Agreement for the Creation of International Office of Epizootics in Paris (25/1/24), International Plant Protection Convention (6/12/51), Constitution of International Rice Commission (13/3/48), International Cotton Advisory Committee (9/9/39), Wheat Trade Convention, 1971 (20/2/71), Constitution of Afro-Asian Rural Reconstruction Organization (31/3/62), Agreement establishing Food and Fertilizer Technology Center for Asian and Pacific Region (11/6/69), Charter of Asian Vegetables Research and Development Center (22/5/71), International Sugar Agreement (7/10/77), Convention Placing International Poplar Commission within framework of Food and Agriculture Organization of United Nations (19/11/59), Agreement Establishing International Fund for Agricultural Development (13/6/76), International Sugar Agreement, 1977 (7/10/77), Convention on the Conservation on the Living Resources of the South-east Atlantic (23/10/69), Plant Protection Agreement for the South East Asia and Pacific Region (27/2/56), International Sugar Agreement, 1984 (5/7/84), International Tropical Timber Agreement, 1983 (18/11/83), Wheat Trade Convention, 1986 (14/3/86), International Sugar Agreement (20/3/92), Convention on International Trade in Endangered Species of Wild Fauna and Flora (3/3/73), International Wheat Agreement, 1962 (19/4/62), Wheat Trade Convention (30/11/67), International Sugar Council Resolution Number One Extension of the International Sugar Agreement, 1973 (30/9/75) Acceptance of the Resolution Number Two for Further Extension of the International Sugar Agreement, 1973 (7/3/77), Grains Trade Convention, 1995 (7/12/94).

Atomic Energy.—Statutes of International Atomic Energy Agency (26/10/56), Agreement on Privileges and Immunities of International Atomic Energy Agency (1/7/59), Treaty Banning Nuclear Weapon Tests in Atmosphere in Outer Space and under Water (5/8/63), Regional Cooperative Agreement for Research Development and Training Related to Nuclear Science and Technology (12/6/72), Treaty on Non-Proliferation of Nuclear Weapons (6/13/68), Convention on the Physical Protection of Nuclear Material (29/12/81), Reservation to paragraph 2 of Article 17 of Convention on the Physical Protection of Nuclear Material (29/12/81), Regional Co-operative Agreement for Research, Development and Training Related to Nuclear Science and Technology, 1987 (12/6/87), Agreement to extend the Regional Co-operative Agreement for Research, Development and Training Related to Nuclear Science and Technology, 1987 (4/12/92), Agreement on the Establishment of the Korean Peninsular Energy Development Organization.

Aviation.—Convention on International Civil Aviation (7/12/44), International Air Services Transit Agreement (7/12/44), Protocol to Amend Convention for Unification of Certain Rules relating to International Carriage by Air Signed at Warsaw on Oct. 12, 1929 (28/9/55), Protocol on Authentic Trilingual Text of Convention on International Civil Aviation (24/9/68), Convention on Offenses and Certain Other Acts Committed on Board Aircraft (14/9/63), Convention for Suppression of Unlawful Seizure of Aircraft (16/12/70), Convention for Suppression of Unlawful Acts against Safety of Civil Aviation (23/9/71).

Culture.—Constitution of United Nations Educational, Scientific and Cultural Organization (16/11/45), Statutes of Bureau of International Education (25/7/29), Statutes of International Center for Study of Preservation and Restoration of Cultural Property (12/56), Agreement Establishing Cultural and Social Center for Asian and Pacific Region (1/8/68), Convention Establishing World Intellectual Property Organization (14/7/67), Amendment to the World Intellectual Property Convention (28/9/79), Convention on the Means of Prohibiting and Preventing the Illicit Import, Export and Transfer of Ownership of Cultural Property (14/11/70), Patent Cooperation Treaty (19/6/70), Convention relating to International Exhibitions and Protocol to amend the Convention Signed at Paris on 22nd November 1928 relating to International Exhibitions (19/5/87), Universal Copyright Convention as revised at Paris on 24 July 1971 (24/7/71), Protocol 1 Annexed to the Universal Copyright Convention as revised at Paris on 24 July 1971 concerning the Application of that Convention to works of Stateless Persons and Refugees (24/7/71), Protocol 2 Annexed to the Universal Copyright Convention as revised at Paris on 24 July 1971 concerning the Application of that Convention to the works of certain International Organizations (24/7/71), Universal Copyright Convention (24/7/71), Convention for the Protection of Producers of Phonograms against Unauthorized Duplication of their Phonograms (29/10/71), Notification in terms of Article V bis 1 of the Universal Copyright Convention as revised at Paris on 24 July 1971 (24/7/71), Regional convention on the Recognition of Studies, Diplomas and Degrees in Higher Education in Asia and the Pacific (16/12/83), Convention for the Protection of the World Cultural and Natural Heritage (16/11/72), Agreement concerning the Establishment of the International Institute for Central Asian Studies (8/7/95).

Customs.—Customs Convention on Temporary Importation of Packings (6/10/60), Customs Convention Concerning Facilities for Importation of Goods for Display or Use at Exhibitions, Fairs, Meetings or Similar Events (8/6/61), Customs Convention Concerning Welfare Materials for Seafarers (1/12/64), Customs Convention on A.T.A. Carnet for Temporary Admission of Goods (6/12/61), Customs Convention on Temporary Importation of Professional Equipments (8/6/61), Convention Establishing Customs Cooperation Council, with Annex and Protocol (15/12/50), Convention on Valuation of Goods for Customs Purposes (15/12/50), Convention on Nomenclature for Classification of Goods in Customs Tariffs (15/12/50), Convention Concerning Formation of an International Union for Publication of Customs Tariffs, Regulations of Execution, and Final Declarations (5/7/1890), International Convention to Facilitate the Importation of Commercial Samples and Advertising Material (7/11/52), Customs Convention on the International Transport of Goods under cover of TIR Carnets (14/11/75), Customs Convention on the Temporary Importation of Scientific Equipment (11/6/68), Customs Convention on the Temporary Importation of Pedagogic Material (8/6/70), International Convention of the Simplification and Harmonization of Customs Procedures (18/5/73), Annex concerning the Temporary Storage of Goods (Annex A2) (18/5/73), Annex concerning the Customs Warehouses to the International Convention on the Simplification and Harmonization of Customs Procedures (18/5/73), Customs Convention on Containers, 1972 (2/12/72), Annex A1 (Annex concerning Customs Formalities prior to the Lodgement of the Goods Declaration) to the International Convention on the simplification and Harmonization of Customs Procedures (18/5/73), Annex E1 (Annex concerning Customs Transit) to the International Convention on the simplification and Harmonization of Customs Procedures (18/5/73), Amendment to the Annex of the Convention on Nomenclature for the Classification of Goods in Customs Tariffs (30/6/77).

Diplomatic and Consular Relations.—Vienna Convention on Diplomatic Relations (18/4/61), Optional Protocol to Vienna Convention on Diplomatic Relations Concerning Compulsory Settlement of Disputes (18/4/61), Optional Protocol to Vienna Convention on Diplomatic Relations Concerning Acquisition of Nationality (18/4/61), Vienna Convention on Consular Relations (24/4/63), Optional Protocol to Vienna Convention on Consular Relations Concerning Compulsory Settlement of Disputes (24/4/63), Optional Protocol to Vienna Convention on Consular Relations concerning Acquisition of Nationality (24/4/63).

Disputes Settlement.—Convention on Settlement of Investment Disputes between States and Nationals of Other States (18/3/65), U.N. Convention on Recognition and Enforcement of Foreign Arbitratal Awards (10/6/58), Agreement Establishing an Economic Cooperation Centre for the Asian and Pacific Region (19/6/70), Agreement for Registry of Scientific and Technical Services for the Asian and Pacific Region (16/7/71).

Economic and Technical Cooperation.—Fundamental Clauses of United Nations Economic and Social Commission for Asia and Pacific (28/3/47), Articles of Agreement of the International Development Association (26/1/60), Convention on Asian Productivity Organization (14/4/61), Constitution of Colombo Planning Council for Technical Cooperation (9/50), Paris Convention for Protection of Industrial Property (20/3/1883), United Nations Industrial Development Organization (UNIDO) Charter (8/4/79), Charter of the Asian and Pacific Development Center (1/4/82), Memorandum of Understanding to confer upon the Committee for Coordination of Joint Prospecting for Mineral Resources in Asian Offshore Areas Status as an Intergovernmental Organization (29/7/87), Convention on the Organization for Economic Co-operation and Development (14/12/60), Decision of the Counsil Establishing a Development Centre of the Organization for Economic Co-operation and Development (23/4/92).

Environment.—Convention on the Conservation of Antarctic Marine Living Resources (20/5/80), The Antarctic Treaty (1/12/59), Convention on the Prohibition of Military or Any Other Hostile Use of Environmental Modification Techniques (10/12/76), Vienna Convention for the Protection of the Ozone Layer (27/5/92), Montreal Protocol on Substances that Deplete the Ozone Layer (26/5/92), Amendment to the Montreal Protocol on Substances that Deplete the Ozone Layer (10/12/92).

Finance.—Articles of Agreement of International Monetary Fund (22/7/44), Articles of Agreement of International Bank of Reconstruction and Development (22/7/44), Articles of Agreement of International Finance Corporation (25/5/55), Agreement Establishing Asian Development Bank (4/12/65), Agreement Establishing Asian Reinsurance Corporation (11/12/76), Agreement Establishing the African Development Fund (29/11/72), Agreement Establishing the African Development Bank (4/8/63), Agreement Establishing the European Bank for Reconstruction and Development (14/1/91).

Fisheries and Law of Sea.—Agreement for Establishment of Indo-Pacific Fisheries Council (26/2/48), International Convention for Conservation of Atlantic Tunas (14/5/66), International Convention for Regulation of Whaling (2/12/46), Protocol to International Convention for Regulation of Whaling (19/12/56), Convention on Future Multilateral Cooperation in the Northwest Atlantic Fisheries (24/10/78), United Nations Convention on the Law of the Sea (30/4/82), Convention for a North Pacific Marine Science Organization (PICES) (12/12/90), Convention on the Conservation and Management of Pollack Resources in the Central Bering Sea, Agreement Relating to the Implementation of Part XI of the United Nations Convention on the Law of the Sea (28/7/94).

Health and Tourism.—Constitution of World Health Organization (22/7/46), Statute of World Tourism Organization (27/9/70), Convention (No. 73) concerning the Medical Examination of Seafarers (29/6/46).

Humanitarian Law.—Geneva Convention for Amelioration of Condition of Wounded and Sick Members of Armed Forces in Field of Aug. 12, 1949 (12/8/49), Geneva Convention for Amelioration of Condition of Sick, Wounded and Shipwrecked Members of Armed Forces at Sea of Aug. 12, 1949 (12/8/49). Geneva Convention Relating to Treatment of Prisoners of War of Aug. 12, 1949 (12/8/49), Geneva Convention Relating to Protection of Civilian Persons in Time of War of Aug. 12, 1949 (12/8/49), Convention for the Exemption of Hospital ships, in Time of War, from the Payment of All Dues and Taxes Imposed for the Benefit of the State (21/12/04), Convention(II) with Respect to the Laws and Customs of War on Land (29/7/1899), Convention(III) for the Adaptation to Maritime Warfare on the Principles of the Geneva Convention of August 22, 1864 (29/7/1899), Convention on the Prohibition of the Development, Production and Stockpiling of Bacteriological (Biological) and Toxin Weapons and on Their Destruction (10/4/72), Treaty on the Prohibition of the Emplacement of Nuclear Weapons and other Weapons of Mass Destruction on the Sea-bed and the Ocean Floor and in the Subsoil Thereof (11/2/71), Protocol for the Prohibition of the Use in War of Asphyxiating, Poisonous or Other Gases, and of Bacteriological Methods of Warfare (21/1/90), Convention on Assistance in the Case of a Nuclear Accident or Radiological Emergency (19/6/18), Convention relating to the Status of Refugees (3/12/92), Protocol Relating to the Status of Refugees (3/12/92), Protocol Additional to the Geneva Conventions of Aug. 12, 1949 and relating to the Protection of Victims of International Armed Conflicts (Protocol I) (19/6/77), Protocol Additional to the Geneva Conventions of Aug. 12, 1949 and relating to the Protection of Victims of Non-International Armed Conflicts (Protocol II) (10/6/77).

Human Rights.—Convention on Prevention and Punishment of Crime of Genocide (9/12/48), Convention on Political Rights of Women (31/3/53), Convention for Suppression of Traffic in Persons and of Exploitation of Prostitution of Others (21/3/50), Final Protocol to Convention for Suppression of Traffic in Persons and of Exploitation of Prostitution of Others (21/3/50), International Convention on Elimination of All Forms of Racial Discrimination (21/12/65), Convention on the Elimination of All

See Topical Index in front part of this volume.

TREATIES . . . *continued*
Forms of Discrimination against Women (18/12/79), International Covenant on Economic, Social and Cultural Rights (10/4/90), International Covenant on Civil and Political Rights (10/4/90), Convention on the Elimination of All Forms of Discrimination against Women Article 16, Paragraph 1 (15/3/91), The Constitution of International Labour Organization (9/12/91), Convention on the Rights of the Child (20/11/91), Convention concerning Labour Inspection in Industry and Commerce (11/7/47), Convention concerning Employment Policy (9/7/64), Convention against Torture and Other Cruel, Inhuman or Degrading Treatment or Punishment (10/12/94).

Law.—Statute of the International Institute for the Unification of Private Law (15/3/40), Constitution of the Eastern Regional Organization for Public Administration (20/6/58).

Legal Counselling.—Statutes of Asian-African Legal Consultative Committee (15/11/56).

Maritime Matters.—International Convention on Load Lines (5/4/66), International Convention for Safety of Life at Sea (17/6/60), Convention on Inter-Governmental Maritime Consultative Organization (6/3/48), Convention on International Hydrographic Organization (3/5/67), Convention on International Regulations for Preventing Collisions at Sea (20/10/72), International Convention on Civil Liability for Oil Pollution Damage (29/11/69), International Convention for Prevention of Pollution of Sea by Oil, 1954 (12/5/54), International Convention for Safe Containers (2/12/72), Convention on Code of Conduct for Liner Conveyances (6/4/74), Protocol to the Treaty concerning the Permanent Neutrality and Operation of the Panama Canal (7/9/77), International Convention for the Safety of Life at Sea, 1974 (1/11/74), Protocol of the 1978 Relating to the International Convention for the Safety of Life at Sea, 1974 (17/2/78), International Convention on Tonnage Measurement of Ships, 1969 (23/6/69), United Nations Convention on the Law of the Sea (30/4/82), International Convention for the Prevention of Pollution from Ships, 1973 and Protocol of 1978 relating to the International Convention for the Prevention of Pollution from Ships, 1973 (2/11/73, 17/2/78), International Convention on Standards of Training, Certification and Watchkeeping for seafarers, 1978 (7/7/78), Convention on the International Maritime Satellite organization (INMARSAT) (3/9/76), International Convention on the Establishment of an International Fund for Compensation for Oil Pollution Damage (8/12/92), Protocol to the International Convention on Civil Liability for Oil Pollution Damage, 1969 (8/12/92), International Convention on Maritime Search and Rescue, 1979 (17/4/79).

Meteorology.—Convention of World Meteorology Organization (11/10/47).

Narcotic Drugs.—Protocol for Limiting and Regulating Cultivation of Poppy Plant, Production of, International and Wholesale Trade in, and Use of Opium (23/6/53), Protocol Amending Single Convention on Narcotic Drugs, 1961 (25/3/72), Convention on Psychotrophic Substances (21/2/71), Single Convention on Narcotic Drugs, 1961 (30/3/61).

Nationality.—Convention Relating to Status of Stateless Persons (28/9/54), Single Convention on Narcotic Drugs, 1961 (30/3/61).

Patents.—See topic Patents.

Privileges and Immunities.—Convention on Privileges and Immunities of Specialized Agencies (21/11/47), Convention on the Privileges and Immunities of the United Nations (9/4/92).

Postal Matters.—Constitution of Universal Postal Union and Final Protocol (10/7/64), Additional Protocol to Constitution of Universal Postal Union (14/11/69), Second Additional Protocol to Convention of Universal Postal Union (5/7/74), General Regulations of Universal Postal Union and Final Protocol (5/7/74), Universal Postal Convention and Final Protocol (26/10/79), Postal Parcels Agreement and Final Protocol (26/10/79), Money Orders and Postal Traveller's Checks Agreement (5/7/74), Asian-Oceanic Postal Convention, Final Protocol and Detailed Regulations (27/11/75), Agreement concerning Transfer to and from Postal Cheque Accounts and Supplement Dealing with the Negotiation through Postal Cheque Account of securities made preamble at Postal Cheque Office (11/7/52), Agreement concerning Postal Parcels and Final Protocol (11/7/52), Agreement concerning Postal Money Orders and Postal Travellers' Cheques (11/7/52), Agreement concerning Insured Letters and Boxes and Final Protocol (11/7/52), Agreement concerning Cash-on-Delivery Items (11/7/52), Amendment Asian-Oceanic Postal Convention (17/11/70), Giro Agreement (27/7/84), Cash-on-Delivery Agreement (27/7/84), Subscriptions to Newspapers and Periodicals Agreement (7/27/84), Constitution and General Regulations of the Asian-Pacific Postal Union and Asian-Pacific Postal Convention, its Final protocol and its Detailed Regulations (4/12/85). Fourth Additional Protocol to the Constitution of the Universal Postal Union (28/1/91), General Regulations of the Universal Postal Union (28/1/91), Universal Postal Convention and Final Protocol (28/1/91), Postal Parcels Agreement and Final Protocol (28/1/91), Agreement concerning Postal Money Orders (28/1/91), Giro Agreement (28/1/91), Cash-on-Delivery Agreement (28/1/91), Agreement between the Government of the Republic of Korea and the Universal Postal Union concerning the Organization of the 21st Universal Postal Congress (18/9/92), General Regulations of the Asian-Pacific Postal Union (11/12/92), Asian-Pacific Postal Convention (11/12/92), Postal Parcels Agreement (14/9/94), Fifth Additional Protocol to the Constitution of the Universal Postal Union (14/9/94), Universal Postal Convention and Final Protocol to the Universal Postal Convention (14/9/94), General Regulations of the Universal Postal Union (14/9/94), Money Orders Agreement (14/9/94).

Public Administration.—Constitution of Eastern Regional Organization for Public Administration (20/6/48), Charter of the United Nations (24/9/91), Statute of the International Court of Justice (24/9/91).

Space and Astronauts.—Treaty on Principles Governing Activities of States in Exploration and Use of Outer Space Including the Moon and Other Celestial Bodies (29/12/66), Agreement on Rescue of Astronauts, Return of Astronauts, and Return of Objects Launched Into Outer Space (19/12/67), Convention on International Liability for Damage Caused by Space Objects (29/3/72), Convention on Registration of Objects Launched into Outer Space (12/11/76).

Telecommunications and Satellites.—International Telecommunication Convention (25/10/73), Optional Additional Protocol to International Telecommunication Convention on Compulsory Settlement of Disputes (25/10/73), Agreement Establishing Interim Arrangements for Global Commercial Communications Satellite System, Special Agreement and Supplementary Agreement on Arbitration (20/8/64), Agreement Relating to International Telecommunications Satellite Organization and its Operating Agreements (20/8/71), Regional Agreements Concerning Use by Broadcasting Service of Frequencies in Medium Frequency Bands in Regions 1 and 3 and in Low Frequency Bands in Region 1 (22/11/75), Final Acts of World Administrative Radio Conference for Planning of Broadcasting Satellite Service in Frequency Bands 11.7-12.2 GHz and 11.7-12.5 GHz (13/2/77), Protocol on INTELSAT Privileges, Exemptions, and Immunities (19/5/78), Constitution of Asia-Pacific Telecommunity (27/3/76), Agreement Establishing the Asia-Pacific Institute for Broadcasting Development (12/8/77), International Telecommunication Convention (6/11/82), Optional Additional Protocol to the International Telecommunication Convention (6/11/82), International Telecommunication Convention (1965) and related Protocol (Final Protocol, Additional Protocols and Optional Protocol) (2/11/65), Final Acts of the World Administrative Radio Conference for Planning of the Broadcasting Satellite Service in Frequency Bands 11.2-12.2 GHz (in Regions 2 and 3) and 11.7-12.5 GHz (in Region 1).

Terrorism.—International Convention against the Taking of Hostages (17/12/79), Convention on the Prevention and Punishment of Crimes against Internationally Protected Persons, Including Diplomatic Agents (14/12/73).

Trade and Commerce.—Long-term Arrangement Regarding International Trade in Cotton Textiles (9/2/62), Protocol for Accession of Republic of Korea to General Agreement on Tariffs and Trade (2/3/67), Geneva Protocol (1967) to General Agreement on Tariffs and Trade (30/6/67), First Agreement on Trade Negotiation Among Developing Member Countries of Economic and Social Commissions for Asia and Pacific (31/7/75), International Convention to Facilitate Importation of Commercial Samples (7/11/52), Protocol Relating to Trade Negotiations with Developing Countries (8/12/71), Arrangements Regarding International Trade in Textiles (20/12/73), International Tin Agreement (1/3/54), Agreement on Interpretation and Application of Articles XVI and XXIII of the General Agreement on Tariffs and Trade (12/4/79), Agreement on Technical Barriers to Trade (12/4/79), Protocol Supplementary to the Geneva Protocol (1979) to the General Agreement on Tariffs and Trade (22/11/79), Agreement on Implementation of Article VII of the General Agreement on Tariffs and Trade and the Protocol thereto (12/4/79, 1/11/79), Arrangement Establishing the International Textiles and Clothing Bureau (13/12/83), Agreement on Implementation of Article VI of the General Agreement on Tariffs and Trade (GATT Anti-Dumping Code) (12/4/79), Protocol Extending the Arrangement Regarding International Trade in Textiles (31/7/86), Agreement on the Global System of Trade Preferences among Developing Countries (13/4/88), Protocol Maintaining in Force the Arrangement Regarding International Trade in Textiles (9/12/92), Third International Tin Agreement (9/12/66), Fourth International Tin Agreement (15/5/70), Case-on Delivery Agreement (14/9/94).

Traffic.—Convention on Road Traffic (19/9/49).

Treaty Law.—Vienna Convention on Law of Treaties (22/5/69).

Weights and Measures.—Meter Convention (20/5/1875), Convention Concerning Creation of an International Office of Weights and Measures, Regulations and Transient Provisions (20/5/1875), Convention Establishing International Legal Metrology (12/10/55).

Bilateral treaties number more than 1,037.

WILLS:

Persons 17 years or older may make last will and testament. (C.C. 1061). Even incompetent may make will during lucid interval in presence of physician who will attest to his lucidity at that time. (C.C. 1063). Testator may, in his will, acknowledge illegitimate children and dispose of property, etc. (C.C. 859, 1074, etc.).

Execution.—Civil Code provides required forms and formalities for holographic wills, wills by voice recording, wills drafted by notaries, and secret wills (envelopes of which are acknowledged by notaries) are all recognized. (C.C. 1066 through 1069). If will cannot be made in one of four forms due to illness or any other extenuating circumstances, oral will may be made in presence of two or more witnesses provided that it is transcribed by witness. (C.C. 1070).

In foreign countries, Korean consul may perform functions of notary in regard to wills. (Act Concerning Notarial Acts by Diplomatic Missions Abroad 3).

Testamentary Disposition.—Testator may dispose of any portion of his estate, but disposition in excess of legally secured portions of heirs is subject to adjustment upon demand from heirs. (C.C. 1115). For purpose of calculating value of estate, gifts made within one year of death or gifts made in anticipation of death may be included. (C.C. 1114). Legally secured portions of estate are: (1) One-half for spouse or lineal descendants, and (2) one-third for lineal ascendants or brothers or sisters. (C.C. 1112). See topic Descent and Distribution.

Legacies may be burdened and in turn may be renounced by legatees. (C.C. 1074, 1088).

Governing law of existence and effect of will is law of testator's nationality when executed and revocation of will is governed by law of testator's nationality at time of its revocation. Alternatively, wills may effectively be made in forms prescribed by law of place of execution. (C.L.A. 27).

WITNESSES:

Anyone can be examined as witness except privileged information may be subject to limitations. (C.C.P. 275). Persons who served or are serving as President, Chairman of National Assembly, Chief Justice or chief of Constitutional Court may not be examined without his/her consent as witness concerning matters related to official secrets. (C.C.P. 275). Courts must obtain approval from National Assembly or State Council in order to examine witness who was or is member of Assembly or Council when examination relates to official secrets. (C.C.P. 277, 278). Lawyers, patent attorneys,

WITNESSES . . . *continued*
notaries public, certified public accountants, licenced tax accountants, medical persons, pharmacists, or persons having legal duty of secrecy, or priests or other persons engaged in religious services can refuse to testify concerning information acquired in professional capacity and any person can refuse to testify with regard to information relating to technological or vocational secrets unless they are released from obligation to keep secret. (C.C.P. 286).

Subpoenas.—Subpoena must contain names of parties, summaries of inquiry and explanation of applicable punishment in case of failure to abide by subpoena. (C.C.P. 281). Witness who fails to appear at time and place as directed by subpoena may be liable for court costs and/or punishable by civil fine. (C.C.P. 282). Courts may cause witness to be forcefully brought before courts by issuing writ. (C.C.P. 283).

Oath is affirmation of truth of statement which renders one willfully asserting untrue statements punishable for perjury, and is administered only by judges.

REPUBLIC OF LATVIA LAW DIGEST

(The following is a list of all Topics, including cross-references, covered in this Digest.)

REPUBLIC OF LATVIA LAW DIGEST

Prepared for the 1997 edition by

KLAVINS, SLAIDINS & LOZE, of the Bar and of the Republic of Latvia, the New York Bar, the Connecticut Bar and the California Bar

(Abbreviations used are: CL, Civillikums, Civil Law of the Republic of Latvia, adopted on Jan. 28, 1937 and reinstated by the Law "On the 1937 Civil Law of the Republic of Latvia" (adopted Jan. 14, 1992), and amended on July 7, 1992; Dec. 22, 1992; May 25, 1993; June 15, 1994; Dec. 15, 1994; and Aug. 9, 1995. CPK, Civilprocesa Kodekss, Code of Civil Procedure of the Republic of Latvia, adopted on Dec. 27, 1963 (amended since May 4, 1990 on Oct. 2, 1990; Oct. 23, 1990; Aug. 13, 1991; Sept. 3, 1991; Nov. 27, 1991; Apr. 7, 1992; Jan. 20, 1993; Apr. 27, 1993; Feb. 23, 1995; and Sept. 13, 1995.)

PRELIMINARY NOTE:

The Republic of Latvia, independent from 1918 until 1940, was forcibly occupied in 1940 by the U.S.S.R. Supreme Council of Latvian S.S.R. declared Republic's de jure independence on May 4, 1990 and reinstated fundamental provisions of Republic's prewar constitution. De facto independence took effect on Aug. 21, 1991 when Latvian Saeima declared renewed independence. In 1995 Latvia became member of Council of Europe and signed Association Treaty with European Union. Pursuant to this Treaty and to Law "On the European Treaty Signed in Luxembourg on June 12, 1995" (adopted Aug. 3, 1995) Latvia has undertaken gradually to harmonize its legislation with that of European Union.

ABSENTEES:

During absence abroad, person may delegate authority to any person having full legal capacity by granting person delegated universal power of attorney. (See topic Principal and Agent.)

If absentee has not designated representative, last court having personal jurisdiction over absentee may appoint curator to protect and manage absentee's assets upon request of interested person and in event of necessity. Curator does not have right to decide any but most urgent matters. (CL, §§217, 370 et seq., §1502; CPK, §267 et seq.).

ACKNOWLEDGMENTS:

See topic Notaries Public. Republic of Latvia is party to Hague Convention Abolishing the Requirement of Legalization for Foreign Public Documents (Oct. 5, 1961).

ACTIONS:

Any person or legal entity, whether or not citizen of Republic of Latvia, may sue or be sued in Latvian courts subject to rules of procedure. Rules governing procedure in civil and administrative actions are set forth in Code of Civil Procedure. All actions are commenced by filing statement of claim with competent court. Appropriate venue generally is defendant's domicile or seat. Appropriate venue also may be following: place of tort, place of performance, situs of real property, or place of company's branch or representative office, if litigation involves business of such branch or representative office.

Court costs are determined by schedule set forth in Code of Civil Procedure. (CPK, §80). Attorneys' fees are determined by fee schedule adopted by Council of Sworn Attorneys pursuant to §54 of "Law on Attorneys in the Republic of Latvia" (adopted Apr. 27, 1993, not am'd), unless client agreement with attorney provides otherwise. Losing party has to bear all costs, including court costs and fees for witnesses and experts, as well as winning party's attorneys' fees, up to amount equaling 5% of successfully litigated sum. (CPK, §§90, 91).

Republic of Latvia is party to following treaties regarding judicial actions: Hague Convention on Questions of Procedure in Civil Matters (Mar. 1, 1954), Hague Convention Abolishing the Requirement of Legalization for Foreign Public Documents (Oct. 5, 1961), Convention on the Service Abroad of Judicial and Extrajudicial Documents in Civil or Commercial Matters (Nov. 15, 1965), Convention on the Taking of Evidence Abroad in Civil or Commercial Matters (Mar. 18, 1970). See also topic Courts.

ADOPTION:

Adoption of minor is permitted if adoption is in minor's best interests and if adoption will result in true parent-child relationship. Adoption of person who is no longer minor is permitted if such parent-child relationship has already been established. Upon adoption, adopted child and its descendants acquire same personal and property rights as children born in adopted parents' marriage. Adopted child's relationship with its natural parents ends, unless provided otherwise in adoption contract. However, adopted child retains any rights to pensions, support and similar payments to which it is entitled at time of adoption. (CL, §162 et seq.).

ALIENS:

In Latvian legislation term "aliens" is attributed to foreigners, i.e., foreign citizens, and apatrides, i.e., persons without citizenship.

Legal status of aliens is regulated by constitutional law "Human and Citizen Rights and Obligations" approved on Dec. 10, 1991, Law On Citizenship, approved on July 22, 1994, Law "On Immigration and Residence of Foreigners and Apatrides in the Republic of Latvia", approved on June 6, 1992, as well as other specific laws.

Noncitizens may own any property, except land and other natural resources which may be owned solely by citizens.

Noncitizens do not have to serve in mandatory state service and they are not allowed to own arms.

Noncitizens do not have voting rights, they cannot take state offices and they are not allowed to establish political parties.

Noncitizens have equal rights with citizens with respect to profit gaining activity, establishment of public organizations and entering of employment relations with employer and individual rights.

Noncitizens must obtain residence permits and labor permits.

Person who becomes citizen of Latvia may not have double citizenship. If Latvian citizen, in accordance with foreign laws, may also be simultaneously considered citizen of respective foreign country, in legal relations with Republic of Latvia he is deemed to be only citizen of Republic of Latvia.

ANTI-TRUST LAWS:

See topic Monopolies and Restraint of Trade.

ARBITRATION AND AWARD:

Disputes arising from civil matters may be submitted to arbitration where provided by Latvian law, bilateral or multilateral international treaties or parties' agreement. Parties may submit any dispute to arbitration, except for matters of labor law and family law. Agreement to arbitrate must be in writing. Awards may be enforced after court has issued writ of execution with respect to award granted by arbitral tribunal. Republic of Latvia is party to New York Convention on the Recognition and Enforcement of Foreign Arbitral Awards (June 10, 1958).

ASSIGNMENTS:

Any claim may be assigned to third party, including conditional, future and uncertain claims. However, claim may not be assigned if such claim, pursuant to statutory law or parties' agreement, hinges upon creditor's person, or if claim's contents would completely change upon assignment to third party. There are no formal requirements for agreement effecting assignment of contractual claim. Notice to debtor is advisable to prevent bona fide debtor from discharging debt by payment to assignor, because before such notice assignor retains right to claim payment from debtor. Debtor retains all objections against claim. (CL, §1798 et seq.).

ASSOCIATIONS:

Associations exist in form of "public organizations" or nonprofit organizations. Public organizations are governed by Law "On Public Organizations" (adopted Dec. 15, 1992, am'd on Apr. 6, 1993; May 11, 1993; Nov. 11, 1993; Apr. 5, 1995). Ten or more natural persons or legal entities may unite in public organization to achieve certain goal, purpose of which cannot be making profit. Specific laws apply to unions, political organizations, and religious organizations. Public organizations established and operating abroad may form branches in Latvia, if goal, characteristics and charter of such organizations do not violate constitution and laws of Republic of Latvia. Public organization acquires status of legal entity upon such organization's registration with Ministry of Justice. Nonprofit organizations are governed by Law "On Non-Profit Organizations" (adopted Dec. 17, 1991, am'd on May 11, 1993 and Aug. 24, 1995). Nonprofit organizations acquire status of legal entity upon registration with Register of Enterprises. Nonprofit organizations may use any income only for purposes declared in organization's charter.

ATTACHMENT:

At any time before or during legal proceedings, plaintiff may request court to take measures to secure object of claim. Plaintiff must prove to satisfaction of court that if such measures are not taken, execution of judgment will be more difficult or impossible. Court, at its discretion, may, among other measures, attach debtor's property or bank accounts, prohibit debtor from disposing of his property, or prohibit other persons from making payments owed to debtor. (CPK, §137 et seq.).

BANKRUPTCY:

Bankruptcy is included in Law "On Insolvency and Bankruptcy of Enterprises and Companies" (adopted Dec. 3, 1991, am'd by Regulations No. 18 of Jan. 4, 1994 and Law of Aug. 24, 1995).

Bankruptcy is defined as involuntary transfer or liquidation of insolvent enterprise for purpose of acquiring resources to satisfy lawful claims of creditors. Therefore, insolvency ruling made by court is one necessary pre-condition to bankruptcy.

In event that during insolvency proceeding court declares that enterprise has gone bankrupt (cannot cover all of its proven debts; there is no possibility of rehabilitation of enterprise; and there is no settlement reached by all creditors), and if number of creditors is more than three, tender board shall be created. This is institution elected by creditors for management of corpus of assets to be sold. In event that number of creditors is less than three, court shall delegate functions of tender board to court appointed administrator. Creditors retain right to request that court appointed administrator be replaced. Tender board shall report to court and to creditors' meeting.

Among its other functions, tender board has right to submit claims to invalidate transactions concluded by bankrupt enterprise with third parties or in favor of third parties during one year time period prior to date on which enterprise was declared insolvent, if any such transactions have caused any loss to creditors.

All creditor claims against bankrupt enterprise must be submitted within three months from date of publication of court's ruling that enterprise is insolvent. No later than two weeks after period for submission of claims has expired, tender board must convene creditors in order to review submitted claims. All claims which are reviewed and which are not rejected are viewed as binding on all participants and may not be appealed. Such claims are to be satisfied from property of bankrupt without dispute. Claims which are rejected may be submitted for further review by court, provided that submission is made within two weeks time from date on which claim has been rejected by creditors' meeting.

See Topical Index in front part of this volume.

BANKRUPTCY . . . *continued*

In accordance with Law "On Entrepreneurial Activity" (adopted Sept. 26, 1990, am'd on May 14, 1991; May 12, 1992; Jan. 12, 1993; Feb. 23, 1993; Apr. 27, 1993; May 11, 1993; May 18, 1993; Feb. 24, 1994; June 15, 1994; Mar. 29, 1995; Nov. 2, 1995; and by Regulations No. 129 of Apr. 10, 1996), debts to creditors of enterprise which is in liquidation (including liquidation after bankruptcy) must be satisfied in following sequence: (1) claims by employees; (2) taxes and other payments to State and municipal budgets; (3) unpaid amounts to agricultural suppliers for product; (4) certain payments to social security institutions; (5) expenses related to remedy of damages to surrounding environment, recultivation of land and renewal of forests; (6) claims secured by mortgage, in accordance with mortgage priority; (7) claims of creditors who have timely submitted such claims; and (8) debts owed to other creditors.

See topic Insolvency.

Note: There is draft replacement Bankruptcy Law under consideration by Saeima (Parliament), but has not yet been adopted.

CHATTEL MORTGAGES:

See topics Liens, Pledges.

COMMERCIAL LAW:

Note: Draft Commercial Code has been under consideration by Saeima (Parliament), but has not yet been adopted.

See topic Contracts.

COMMERCIAL REGISTER:

Register of Enterprises is administrative state institution which within territory of Republic of Latvia registers enterprises (entrepreneurial companies), their affiliates and representative offices, as well as all changes in basic documents of their operation. Operation of Register of Enterprises is based on Law "On the Republic of Latvia Register of Enterprises", adopted on Nov. 20, 1990, am'd on May 14, 1991; Apr. 7, 1992; Oct. 5, 1995; and by Regulations Nos. 116 of Apr. 9, 1996; 130 of Apr. 10, 1996.

Register of Enterprises operates under purview of Ministry of Justice. Register of Enterprises is managed by chief state notary public who is appointed and dismissed by Cabinet of Ministers upon proposal of Minister of Justice. Register of Enterprises performs: (1) state registration of enterprises; (2) state control over compliance of foundation and operation documents of enterprises with laws of Republic of Latvia; (3) uniform state record of enterprises; (4) giving information regarding enterprises. Upon registration of enterprise Register of Enterprise issues to entrepreneur registration certificate. Entrepreneurial company is deemed to be founded, but enterprise established upon date of their registration.

Following information must be entered into journal of Register of Enterprises regarding each enterprise: name of enterprise, main and additional types of activity, term for which enterprise is founded, date of signature of Charter, address, amount of share capital, shares in joint stock company or shares in limited liability company and their nominal value, name, surname, address and citizenship of members of Supervisory Board and Board of Directors, as well as directors, and names, surnames and positions of those officials and participants of agreement companies who are granted signatory rights. Journal of Register of Enterprise is permanently stored document. All documents as stated by Law "On Entrepreneurial Activity" and laws which regulate forms and types of entrepreneurial activity must be submitted for registration. Notary public of Register separately considers each application and within 30 days after date of submission of documents informs applicant in writing regarding passed decision, by issuing applicant document on registration of enterprises or motivated refusal, if enterprise is not registered.

All amendments to be registered shall be submitted to Register of Enterprises by enterprises within 15 days after date decision was passed. Register of Enterprises must review foundation documents of enterprises within 15 days after date of their submission. If enterprise does not receive refusal within 30 days it shall be deemed to be registered. Person may appeal refusal of registration at court.

Any legal or natural persons have right after payment of state fee to receive information from Register of Enterprises regarding any enterprise (entrepreneurial company), as well as certified extracts and copies of documents.

CONSTITUTION AND GOVERNMENT:

Based on Satversme (Constitution) of Feb. 15, 1922 (am'd by Laws of Mar. 21, 1933; Jan. 27, 1994; June 5, 1996) Latvia is independent democratic Republic. Sovereign power of Republic of Latvia is exercised by Latvian people. Territory of Republic of Latvia consists of regions of Vidzeme, Latgale, Kurzeme, and Zemgale.

Fundamental rights and freedoms of citizens and of all persons are codified in Law "Constitutional Law: Rights and Obligations of Citizens and Persons" (adopted Dec. 10, 1991, am'd on Mar. 30, 1995).

Legislative Power.—Unicameral Saeima (Parliament) consists of 100 representatives of Latvian people. Representatives are elected in general, equal, direct, secret and proportional elections. All citizens of Republic of Latvia who have reached 18 years of age are entitled to vote. Saeima is elected for term of three years. Saeima, among other powers, has power to pass laws, amend constitution, ratify international treaties, approve state budget, confirm appointment of judges and elect President.

Executive Power.—President is formal head of state, but carries no political responsibility for his actions. All of President's decisions additionally have to be signed by Prime Minister or relevant minister who assumes all responsibility for such decisions. President is elected by Saeima in secret elections by 51 or more votes by Saeima members for no more than two consecutive terms of three years each (change to four years is under consideration). President represents Republic of Latvia internationally and signs international treaties upon Saeima's approval, and may suggest legislation and dismissal of Saeima.

Supreme executive body is Cabinet of Ministers. Cabinet of Ministers consists of Prime Minister and 12 ministers appointed by Prime Minister. Prime Minister, who is appointed by President, and Cabinet of Ministers must receive vote of confidence of Saeima's majority. Cabinet of Ministers submits to Saeima's authority.

Judicial Power.—While constitution provides that all citizens are equal before law and courts, Law "On the Power of the Courts" (adopted Dec. 15, 1992, am'd on Dec. 16, 1993; June 15, 1994; Apr. 6, 1995; Sept. 28, 1995; Dec. 21, 1995; May 23, 1996) provides that all persons, regardless of citizenship, are equal before law and courts and have equal rights to protection by legal system. Judges are independent and submit to no authority except for that of law. Supreme Court Judges are appointed by Saeima for life terms.

Constitution provides for constitutional court, structure and responsibilities of which are based on Law "On the Constitutional Court" (adopted June 5, 1996). Based on Law "On the Power of the Courts" (see supra), judicial power is exercised by rajonu tiesas (District Courts), apgabaltiesas (Regional Courts), Augstākā tiesa (Supreme Court), and Satversmes tiesa (Constitutional Court). Law further provides that Republic of Latvia guarantees independence of courts and rights of person to defend his or her rights. Court hearings are public. See also topic Courts.

CONTRACTS:

Civil Law contains general principles applicable to all contracts (CL, §§1401-1911), as well as specific provisions applicable only to certain type of contract, such as sale, barter, lease, etc. (CL, §§1912-2346). Offer, acceptance and mutual consent are required for validity of contract, consideration is not. Contracts are void or voidable in following cases, among others: if entered into by person lacking legal capacity (CL, §1409); if contract is mere simulation, unless such simulation is related to illegal defrauding of innocent third party (CL, §1438); if contract was entered into based on fraud or duress (CL, §§1461, 1467); if party's misconception of contract's object is so fundamental that party cannot be deemed to have consented to contract (CL, §§1445, 1447); if contract's object does not and will not exist or is completely indefinite (CL, §§1413, 1417, 1454); or if contract's goal is illegal or immoral or intended to circumvent legal provisions (CL, §§1415, 1592).

Offer and Acceptance.—Offeror is bound by offer for time period determined by offeror. If offeror has not specified time period, offeror is bound until offeree is deemed to be delaying his response. Courts decide whether offeree procrastinated in given case. In commercial matters offeree is deemed to be procrastinating if such offeree has not responded as soon as possible. (CL, §1538). Between absent parties, contract is concluded at time acceptance is expressed, regardless of when offeror receives notice of acceptance. (CL, §1537). Silence may neither be deemed to mean acceptance nor rejection of offer, unless provided otherwise by law. (CL, §1530).

Form.—Contracts can be executed in following forms: (1) orally or implicitly; (2) in writing; (3) certified by sworn notary public; or (4) confirmed by registration in Land Book. Oral contracts are valid unless law provides for certain form. Contract lacking such form is not in effect. Each party is entitled to withdraw from contract unilaterally until contract is executed in required form. However, if law provides only for written (not notarial) form, and if parties have agreed orally on contract's essential elements, each party has right to demand of other execution of corresponding contract in required form. Real property rights acquired by contract can be exercised only after execution of notarially certified request to register such right in Land Book and after registration in Land Book. (CL, §§1473-1494).

Repudiation.—Civil Law explicitly provides that contract, once concluded, obliges parties to perform their respective contractual duties, and neither special difficulty nor complications arising at later time are grounds for repudiation of contract. One party may not withdraw from contract without other party's consent even if other party does not fulfill its contractual duties. (CL, §§1587, 1588).

Excuses for Nonperformance.—No liability for nonperformance arises if performance becomes impossible by accident (for reasons beyond parties' power) or by force majeure. (CL, §§1774, 1775). However, party in default bears risk of accidental loss or damage. (CL, §1661). In sales contracts, buyer bears risk of accidental loss or damage of object to be sold during time period between conclusion of contract and delivery of object to buyer, with certain exceptions. (CL, §§2023, 2024). (See topic Sales.)

Applicable Law.—In determining laws governing given contract, Latvian courts will respect parties' express agreement as to choice of law. Choice of law is in effect to extent that mandatory provisions of Latvian law are not circumvented. If parties have not agreed on choice of governing law, Latvian court is to assume that governing law shall be that of jurisdiction in which contract is to be performed. If place of performance cannot be determined, court is to apply law of country in which contract was executed.

Questions regarding contract's formal validity are governed by law of jurisdiction in which contract was executed or of jurisdiction of place of performance. Form of contracts with respect to real property located in Latvia is governed only by Latvian law.

Foreign law is not to be applied if foreign law conflicts with Latvian ordre public or mandatory provisions of Latvian law. Provisions of Civil Law dealing with conflicts of law (CL, §§7-25) apply where not provided otherwise by international treaties. Latvia is not party to UN Convention on Contracts for the International Sale of Goods (Apr. 11, 1980). (See topic Treaties.)

CORPORATIONS:

In accordance with laws of Republic of Latvia, "corporation" is union of physical persons or legal entities for purpose of business. Corporation may be established based on charter approved by founders or concluded agreements, defining also rights and obligations of corporation and its participants (shareholders) and manner of corporate management.

Limited Liability Companies.—One of most wide-spread types of businesses is "limited liability company" (Republic of Latvia Law "On Limited Liability Companies", approved on Jan. 23, 1991). Such company is liable for its obligations to extent of its entire property and its participants are liable for obligations of company to extent of property invested into company. Share capital of limited liability company consists

CORPORATIONS . . . *continued*

of property invested by its participants, which may be in form of monetary (any currency), nonmonetary and intellectual property, as well as securities. Minimum share capital is LVL 2,000.

Limited liability company may be established by one person; maximum number of participants is 50. If number of participants exceeds 50, company must be reorganized into joint stock company within two years, or it must cease its existence.

Charter of limited liability company must state name of company, its location, purposes of its activities, aims, term of existence; information regarding participants; size of share capital, value of share, number of shares, procedure of disposal of shares and manner of increase and reduction of share capital; relationship between company and its participants; management structure of company, number of members in company's executive body and inspection body, procedure of their election, rights and obligations; legality of participants' meeting; procedure of preparation, inspection and approval of annual reports; regulations regarding distribution of profits; manner of establishment of reserve and other capitals (funds); procedure of change of owners of shares in share capital; procedure of reorganization and liquidation of company; other regulations which would be necessary for company pursuant to its specific activities.

Company acquires status of legal entity from moment of its registration with Republic of Latvia Register of Enterprises.

Governing structures of company are participants meeting and executive body (Board of Directors, Directorate, Administration, etc.).

Participants meeting of company is supreme governing body of company. Participants carry out their rights to participate in management of company through participants meeting. Company participants have voting right only upon complete investment of their shares and upon their recording in Register of Participants no less than ten days prior to participants meeting. Each share entitled to one vote at meeting unless charter provides that larger number of shares entitled to one vote. Number of votes of participant corresponds to number of shares held by participant. Charter may envisage limitations of voting rights to separate participants who own large number of shares.

Company participants meeting is authorized to adopt resolutions if more than 50% of its share capital is present. In order to adopt resolutions regarding amendment to company charter (except change in share capital) and liquidation of company, quorum is required which consists of no less than three quarters of company share capital. If company is established by two founders, participation of both is required.

Company activities are managed by its executive body (Board of Directors, Directorate, Administration, etc.). Manner, functions and competence of company management is provided in company charter. Members of executive body are elected for period of three years and they may be reelected.

After approval of company's annual report and balance sheet at participants meeting, no less than 5% percent of net profit, depreciation deducted, must be transferred to reserve capital (reserve fund) until this fund equals 1/3 of share capital of company. With regard to use of remaining sum, participants meeting makes decision and determines size of dividends payable to participants. Dividends are calculated only with respect to fully invested shares.

Joint stock company (Republic of Latvia Law "On Joint Stock Companies" approved on May 18, 1993 as am'd) establishes its share capital through issue of respective number of shares or bonds at their nominal value in return for payment. Contrary to limited liability companies, shares issued by joint stock company are classified as securities.

Similarly to limited liability company, joint stock company is liable for its obligations to extent of all of its property and its shareholders are liable for obligations of company to extent of property invested into company. Number of founders of joint stock company may be no less than three, except case when sole founder is state, local government or foreign company.

Minimum foundation share capital for joint stock banks is LVL 2,000,000, for life insurance companies LVL 1,000,000, for other insurance joint stock companies LVL 500,000, stock exchange companies LVL 100,000, joint stock pawnshops LVL 10,000, other joint stock companies LVL 5,000.

Joint stock companies must invest registered share capital within five years, required registered share capital for joint stock banks is LVL 3,000,000, for life insurance companies LVL 2,000,000, for other insurance joint stock companies LVL 1,000,000, stock exchange companies LVL 250,000, joint stock pawnshops LVL 10,000, other joint stock companies LVL 25,000.

Share capital of joint stock company may be formed through investment of money (foundation share capital must be paid only in money), nonmonetary investment, intellectual property and securities quoted by stock exchanges.

Upon establishment of joint stock company, shareholders, among other documents, must prepare charter which should state name of joint stock company and its registered address, status of company, purposes of its activities and aims, information regarding founders; term of existence of company; size of foundation share capital, classes and number of shares, procedure of disposal of shares and manner of increase and reduction of share capital; size of registered share capital; number of members of management and inspection bodies of company, number of sworn auditors, procedure of election of sworn auditors and liquidators, rights and obligations; procedure of calling of general meetings of shareholders and manner of decision making, scope of general meetings; procedure of preparation, inspection and approval of annual reports; regulations regarding distribution of profits; calculation and payment procedure of dividends and other matters.

Company acquires status of legal entity from moment of its registration with Republic of Latvia Register of Enterprises.

Governing structures of company are general meeting of shareholders, Supervisory Board and Board of Directors. If there are 50 or less shareholders, it is possible that company does not establish Supervisory Board. For financial and crediting joint stock companies Supervisory Board is compulsory.

General meeting of shareholders of company is supreme governing body of company. Shareholders carry out their rights to participate in management of company through general meeting of shareholders. Company's general meeting of shareholders is authorized to adopt resolutions if more than 50% of its paid in share capital is present. Company shareholders have voting right only upon their recording in Register of Shareholders no less than ten days prior to general meeting of shareholders. Holders of shares of public issue acquire voting rights at general meeting as of moment of acquiring title to these shares. Each shareholder enjoys voting right pursuant to sum total of nominal value of all voting shares held by him.

With some exceptions, general meeting of shareholders adopt resolutions with simple majority of present shareholders with voting rights.

After approval of company's annual report general meeting of shareholders determines use of net profit of company. General meeting of shareholders determines sums to be transferred to capitals and reserves of joint stock company, to be dedicated to social needs, charity and other purposes, as well as size of dividends payable to shareholders.

Dividends are calculated only with respect to fully invested shares.

Partnership (Republic of Latvia Law "On Entrepreneurial Activity", approved on Sept. 26, 1990) is union of entrepreneurs which is established based on agreement executed by its founders. In accordance with executed agreement, participants of partnership invest property in partnership. Partnership is not liable for obligations of its participants which do not refer to company operation. Contrary to limited liability company and joint stock company, partnership is not separate legal entity. Two types of partnerships exist, general partnerships and limited partnerships.

General partnership unites several participants who are jointly and severally liable for obligations of partnership with their property and proportionally to share invested in partnership.

Limited partnership is partnership which unites participants of which one or several general partners are jointly and severally liable for partnership obligations with their property and proportionally to share invested in limited partnership, while other participants (limited partners) are liable for partnership's obligations only to extent of their investment.

Foreign investors (Republic of Latvia Law "On Foreign Investment" approved on Nov. 5, 1991) may engage in corporate activities in Latvia through establishment of limited liability companies or joint stock companies as well as through use of permanent establishments (permanent representative offices) in Latvia. (See topic Foreign Investment.)

COURTS:

Following courts exist in Republic of Latvia:

Satversmes tiesa (Constitutional Court) is specifically provided for in constitution and structured as provided by Law "On the Constitutional Court" (adopted June 5, 1996).

Based on Law "On the Power of the Courts" (adopted Dec. 15, 1992, am'd on Dec. 16, 1993; June 15, 1994; Apr. 6, 1995; Sept. 28, 1995; Dec. 21, 1995; May 23, 1996), courts of first instance in matters of civil, criminal and administrative law are rajona tiesas (District Courts). Code of Civil Procedure provides that all matters not assigned by law to higher court are within jurisdiction of District Courts. In civil matters, this includes claims for up to Ls 5,000. Five apgabaltiesas (regional courts) function as courts of appeals for matters decided by District Courts, but function as courts of first instance for following civil matters: adoption matters, matters regarding protection of patents and annulment of trademark registrations, disputes regarding title to real property, claims exceeding Ls 5,000, and bankruptcy matters. (CPK, §119).

Augstākā Tiesa (Supreme Court), located in Riga, is final court of appeals in all matters and court of first instance where specifically provided by law.

See also topic Constitution and Government.

CURRENCY:

National currency is Lats (Ls or LVL), which equals 100 santīmi. Central bank, Latvijas Banka, was established by Law "On the Bank of Latvia" (adopted May 19, 1992, not am'd) and granted monopoly rights to issue national currency.

CUSTOMS DUTIES:

This topic is governed by Law "On Customs Duties (Tariffs)" (adopted Sept. 29, 1994, am'd on Sept. 7, 1995; Oct. 5, 1995, Oct. 26, 1995; and Nov. 6, 1995). Tariffs currently applicable to given product are listed in Appendix 1 to aforementioned law.

Tariff rates vary according to trade agreement in force with given country. Rate of export tariffs is 0% for following countries, with which Free Trade Agreement is in force: Czech Republic, Estonia, member states of European Union, EFTA states, Lithuania, and Slovakia.

Export duties average 15% for countries with most-favored-nation status, based on various Agreements on Trade and Economic Cooperation. This is currently case with Armenia, Australia, Azerbaijan, Belarus, Canada, China, Cuba, Georgia, Hungary, India, Iceland, Kazakhstan, Kyrghyz Republic, Moldova, Poland, Romania, Russian Federation, Tajikistan, Turkmenistan, Ukraine, U.S.A., Uzbekistan and Vietnam.

Export duties average 20% for all other countries.

Import and export duties vary according to type of goods in question.

DEATH (PRESUMPTION OF AND ACTIONS FOR):

Court having jurisdiction over missing person's last domicile can declare missing person dead upon request of interested party or of absentee's court-appointed curator. This request can be made if ten years have elapsed since end of year in which information about now missing person was last heard. If missing person was 70 years or older, such period is reduced to five years. Court arranges for public notice in newspapers requesting missing person or third persons having knowledge of missing person to report to court. If court does not receive further information, it declares missing person dead by judgment. (CL, §377 et seq., CPK, §254 et seq.).

Missing person may be declared dead according to above provisions if missing person's last domicile was in Latvia. If person has left property in Latvia, Latvian provisions apply to this property even if missing person was not domiciled in Latvia. (CL, §10).

See Topical Index in front part of this volume.

DEPOSITIONS:

Code of Civil Procedure provides for witnesses' testimony and taking of evidence before Latvian courts, but contains no provisions regarding taking of evidence abroad. However, Latvia is party to Hague Convention on Taking Evidence Abroad in Civil or Commercial Matters (Mar. 18, 1970).

DESCENT AND DISTRIBUTION:

Decedent's estate consists of decedent's real and movable property, rights, and obligations at time of decedent's death. Estate is legal entity and may acquire rights or undertake obligations.

If decedent does not provide otherwise by testament, following statutory rights to intestate succession take effect:

Surviving spouse becomes decedent's heir regardless of marital property regime in effect during marriage. Surviving spouse receives share equal to each child's share, if there are fewer than four children. If there are four or more children, surviving spouse receives one-fourth of estate.

Right to intestate succession is based on blood relationship or adoption and does not extend to in-laws. Decedent's relatives inherit in certain order that is based on kind and proximity of relationship. Four classes of heirs are: (1) all direct descendants, (2) decedent's parents, siblings and children of siblings, if such sibling died before decedent, (3) decedent's half-siblings and children thereof, if such half-sibling died before decedent, (4) remaining more distant sideline relatives. Member of lower class does not become heir if any member of higher class is still alive. (CL, §398 et seq.).

Above provisions apply to estates located in Latvia. Estate's assets may be distributed to heirs residing abroad only after statutory rights of all heirs residing in Latvia have been satisfied. (CL, §§16, 17).

Rights of aliens to inherit real property currently still are restricted by Law "On Land Reform in the Cities of the Republic of Latvia" (adopted Nov. 20, 1991) and Law "On Land Privatization in Rural Areas" (adopted July 9, 1992).

See also topic Wills.

DIVORCE:

Court may grant divorce upon request of one spouse only in following cases: (1) if other spouse threatens health or life of spouse requesting divorce, (2) if other spouse has left spouse requesting divorce more than a year ago, (3) if other spouse suffers from long-lasting serious mental illness or contagious disease, (4) if other spouse has committed criminal act or lives in such manner that continuation of marital relationship would cause undue hardship, (5) if conjugal relationship has unsalvageably disintegrated, and (6) if married couple has lived separately for three continuous years. Divorce may be granted upon request of both spouses, but not earlier than one year from date of marriage. (CL, §69 et seq.).

Upon request of interested person, marriage may be annulled on following grounds: lack of registration, lack of legal capacity, and in cases of consanguinity. (CL, §59 et seq.).

Above provisions apply if Latvian court is to grant divorce or annul marriage, regardless of spouses' citizenship. Divorce or annulment by foreign court will be recognized in Latvia, except for cases in which reasons for divorce or annulment do not correspond to Latvian law and if such reasons conflict with Latvian ordre public. (CL, §12).

EXCHANGE CONTROL:

There are no foreign currency exchange controls applicable to repatriation of profits from Latvia.

EXECUTIONS:

Execution in civil matters is granted on basis of court judgments, court-approved settlements, arbitral decisions, decisions by commissions in labor disputes, and decisions by other tribunals and commissions established by law. Judgments by foreign courts are governed by international treaties (see topic Treaties). Foreign judgment must be submitted for execution in Latvia within three years of its becoming unappealable under law of country in which it was rendered.

Court having jurisdiction over domicile of debtor grants writ of execution (izpildu raksts) based on judgment or other decision listed above.

Court may grant writ of execution from date such judgment or other decision has become unappealable under Latvian law and for ten years thereafter. In such writ, court decides whether execution will be effected by attachment (arests) and sale of debtor's property; garnishment of debtor's salary, pension, stipends, or other sources of income; or by other methods provided by law. Based on writ of execution bailiff (tiesu izpildītājs), after notifying debtor of commencement of execution proceedings and granting debtor five day grace period within which to fulfill judgment voluntarily, proceeds to execute judgment. (CPK, §345 et seq.).

EXECUTORS AND ADMINISTRATORS:

Testament is executed by executor (testamenta izpildītājs) named therein. If testator has not named executor, heir named in testament functions as executor. If testator has not named heir, competent court appoints administrator (aizgādnis-term administrators in Latvian designates court-appointed trustee in insolvency matters).

Executor has rights and obligations specified in testament. If testament contains no such specifications, executor's obligation is only to ensure that testator's last will is realized. As there is no division of law and equity, executor does not acquire title to estate. Executor has neither right nor obligation to manage estate's assets, if testator has not specifically provided for such management. If, however, heir designated in testament has not yet accepted inheritance, or if testator has named no heirs, executor manages estate's assets until competent court has appointed administrator.

If statutory heirs of decedent who has not left testament, or testamentary heirs of testator, are known, have legal capacity and can be contacted, court does not take measures for estate's administration, unless one of heirs expressly so requests. Court must designate administrator on its own in following cases: if one or all of heirs are not known or cannot be contacted, if heirs have not accepted inheritance, if one of heirs lacks legal capacity, or if it is known that estate is burdened by debt and creditors' rights are endangered. (CL, §§616 et seq., 660 et seq.).

FOREIGN EXCHANGE:

Business of purchase and sale of foreign currency cash in Republic of Latvia is permitted to companies (enterprises) registered in particular manner and only upon receipt of license issued by Bank of Latvia.

Person authorized by Bank of Latvia is entitled to inspect places where foreign currency cash is sold and bought. (Republic of Latvia Bank of Latvia Resolution No. 164, dated Aug. 17, 1995).

FOREIGN INVESTMENT:

In accordance with Republic of Latvia Law "On Foreign Investment in the Republic of Latvia" (approved on Nov. 5, 1991; amendments on Feb. 23, 1993; June 16, 1994; Mar. 9, 1995; and Jan. 5, 1996), foreign investors are entitled to engage in entrepreneurial activity in Latvia by means of establishment of limited liability companies or joint stock companies. "Foreign investors" mean foreign physical and legal persons established abroad or international organizations registered abroad which invest assets for purpose of entrepreneurial activity in Republic of Latvia.

Company with foreign investment in Republic of Latvia may be established by foreign company as sole founder.

Foreign enterprises (corporations) may establish representative offices in Latvia which are not entitled to engage in entrepreneurial activity within territory of Latvia.

In order to engage in entrepreneurial activity, foreign enterprises (corporations) may use their permanent representative offices (permanent establishments) in Latvia. In this case, permanent representative offices of foreign enterprises (corporations) must be registered as permanent taxpayers in the Republic of Latvia and registered with Republic of Latvia Register of Enterprises.

Law "On Foreign Investment in the Republic of Latvia" states that if future laws of Republic of Latvia impair conditions of investment, for period of ten years that legislation shall be applied to foreign investment which was in effect at moment of that investment.

Foreign investors may repatriate their profits from Republic of Latvia after payment of all taxes provided for in laws of Republic of Latvia.

No import duties shall be imposed on property imported to Republic of Latvia as foreign investment and which is not intended for sale.

After settlement of obligations to creditors, foreign investor may freely remove its investment in Republic of Latvia enterprise from Republic of Latvia.

If international treaties regarding foreign investment entered into by Republic of Latvia specify other provisions than Law "On Foreign Investment in the Republic of Latvia", provisions of international treaty shall be applied.

Investment protection treaties are currently in force with following countries: Austria, Czech Republic, Denmark, Estonia, France, Israel, Canada, Great Britain, Lithuania, Netherlands, Norway, Poland, Finland, Switzerland, Taiwan, Germany, Vietnam and Sweden.

Investment protection treaties are not yet in force, but have been signed with Belgium, Luxembourg, Greece, Portugal, Spain, U.S.A. and Uzbekistan.

FOREIGN TRADE REGULATIONS:

Latvia does not apply licenses and quotas to imports and exports. Foreign trade is regulated only by import and export tariffs. See topic Customs Duties. See also topic Foreign Investment.

Free Trade Agreements are currently in force with Czech Republic, Estonia, member states of European Union, EFTA states, Lithuania, and Slovakia. Latvia has signed Association Treaty with European Union. For countries with which agreements on favorable terms of trade are in force, see topic Customs Duties.

FRAUDS, STATUTE OF:

Republic of Latvia has no Statute of Frauds, but see topic Contracts.

GARNISHMENT:

Attachment of monetary debts may be effected by court decree, pursuant to which persons owing payments to debtor must withhold certain percentage of such payments and transfer such withheld payments to creditor, up to amount of creditor's claim. (CPK, §400 et seq.).

HOLIDAYS:

Based on Law "On Holidays and Commemoration Days" (adopted Oct. 3, 1990, am'd Apr. 6, 1995; Sept. 21, 1995), following are legal holidays in Republic of Latvia: Jan. 1 (New Year's Day), Good Friday, Easter, May 1 (Labor Day, Convocation of the Constituent Assembly of the Republic of Latvia), June 23 (Midsummer's Eve), June 24 (Midsummer's Day), Nov. 18 (Independence Day—Proclamation of the Republic of Latvia in 1918), Dec. 25, 26 (Christmas), Dec. 31 (New Year's Eve).

HUSBAND AND WIFE:

If spouses do not agree otherwise by contract, each spouse retains separate ownership and management of assets owned by that spouse before marriage. Assets acquired jointly or by one spouse with financial or other assistance of other spouse during marriage become joint marital property. Both spouses are responsible for fulfilling contracts into which one or both spouses entered and object of which was related to family household. If spouses live separately, spouse not responsible for separation is entitled to financial support from other spouse, unless spouse requesting support avoids supporting him- or herself for no important reason. If real property is separate marital property, this fact must be registered in Land Book.

By contract, spouses can agree on system of separate marital property or of joint marital property. Separate marital property means that even during marriage, all property remains separate. One spouse may not manage, use or dispose of other spouse's property without other spouse's permission.

HUSBAND AND WIFE . . . *continued*

Joint marital property means that even property acquired before marriage becomes spouses' joint property. In contract establishing joint property, spouses agree whether one or both spouses will manage property. If real property is spouses' joint property, this fact must be registered in Land Book. Joint property regime ends upon spouses' agreement or by court decision, or upon death of one spouse, divorce, or bankruptcy of one spouse. Restrictions on spouse to dispose of other spouse's property are effective as against third parties only if restriction is registered in marital property register at spouses' domicile. (CL, §89 et seq.)

Above provisions apply if spouses' domicile is in Latvia. If spouses' property is located in Latvia, Latvian law applies to such property, even if spouses' domicile is not in Latvia. (CL, §13).

INFANTS:

Minority lasts until person reaches 18 years of age. Minors have no legal capacity. As contracts entered into by persons lacking legal capacity are void, minors must be represented by parents or guardians. If both parents have died, one of grandparents is appointed as guardian. Parents can appoint guardians for their children by testament. If parents have not done so and if there are no grandparents, competent court appoints guardian. Guardian appointed by parents' testament or by court manages minor's assets and is responsible to court. (CL, §219 et seq.).

Person's legal capacity is determined by jurisdiction in which person is domiciled. If person has several domiciles and one domicile is in Latvia, person's legal capacity is determined by Latvian law. Legal capacity of legal entity is determined by jurisdiction in which entity's seat is located. (CL, §8).

INSOLVENCY:

Insolvency is governed by Law "On Insolvency and Bankruptcy of Enterprises and Companies" (adopted Dec. 3, 1991, am'd by Regulations No. 18 of Jan. 4, 1994 and Law of Aug. 24, 1995).

Insolvency is defined as inability of enterprise to pay its debts, as established by court in manner described in this law, as well as entrepreneur's own admission. Debtor may be acknowledged as insolvent if debtor cannot fulfill those payment obligations which have come due. Insolvency may be presumed if debtor has interrupted making payments for period in excess of three calendar months.

Insolvency is considered to be established as follows: (1) if debtor admits to court or to one or more creditors, whether in connection with claim raised against debtor or independent thereof, that property of debtor is insufficient to cover all debts; (2) if while enforcing claim against property of debtor it becomes clear that property will be insufficient to cover all debts and court confirms as reasonable documentary evidenced submission of creditor that remaining property of debtor is insufficient to satisfy creditor's claim (creditors may make such submissions to court regardless of when term for fulfillment of debtor's obligations concludes); and (3) if debtor who has not properly fulfilled debtor's obligations performs acts which give rise to reasonable doubts by creditors regarding possibility to collect on debts (examples of such acts which are stated in law are unknown whereabouts and large scale transfer of property).

Enterprise itself or creditor (or group of creditors) may initiate insolvency proceedings. State enterprise and municipal enterprise insolvency may also be initiated by appropriate governmental institution. Insolvency of insurer may also be initiated by request of State insurance supervision inspection.

There is no separate insolvency or bankruptcy court, and insolvency matters are heard in general court system. Jurisdiction is in those courts where the legal address of debtor is identified.

In insolvency proceeding court must determine whether (1) settlement agreement is possible between debtor and creditor; (2) it is possible to begin rehabilitation activities; (3) it is possible to establish creditor administration. After such determinations, court must make its ruling. If court determines that property of enterprise is insufficient to fully pay all submitted and unquestionable claims, and settlement agreement or rehabilitation of enterprise or establishment of creditor administration is impossible, enterprise is declared bankrupt and sale of enterprise property is begun.

Court must publish any decision to declare enterprise insolvent, or to establish creditor administration, and all other creditor claims must be submitted within three months from date of publication.

After debtor is declared insolvent by court, and until appointment of creditor administration, court appoints administrator (trustee) who is accountable to court and to creditor's meeting. Court appointed administrator manages insolvent enterprise, including collection and preservation of assets, preparation of insolvent enterprise's balance sheets, contact with creditors. Administrator may alienate property of insolvent enterprise only if goal of such activity is to satisfy creditor interests.

Creditors' meeting has right to review work of court appointed administrator, and may consent to continued work of administrator or request that court appoint different administrator. Creditors' meeting may decide on any issue within its competence regardless of number of creditors present at meeting, provided that all creditors have received ten day advance notice of meeting. Decisions are made at creditors' meetings by majority vote of those present, and number of votes is determined proportionate to total amount claimed by each creditor.

Creditor administration has goal of avoiding liquidation of insolvent enterprise and renewing its financial stability. Creditor administration is established by court decision, with approval of creditors representing three-fourths of total amount of claims. Upon establishment of creditor administration, this administration assumes all management of insolvent enterprise in accordance with goals of administration as stated in court decision by which it is established. Creditor administration concludes its work with ruling of court one year after its date of establishment, unless its term is extended by court upon request by creditors' meeting.

Settlement agreement may be achieved at any stage during insolvency process, provided that actual division of debtor's property has not yet begun. Subject to few exceptions, settlement agreement will be approved by court if two-thirds of all creditors, and creditors representing no less than three-fourths of total amount of claims, have agreed to proposed settlement.

If neither creditor administration is established, nor settlement agreement made, court will request debtor's view on whether rehabilitation of debtor is possible. If debtor submits rehabilitation plan and court accepts such plan, court will set time period for rehabilitation (not to exceed 18 months; for agricultural enterprises two years) and will suspend court actions during this time period. In one year's time from start of implementation of rehabilitation plan, at least 40% of amount of valid claim made by each creditor must be repaid.

See topic Bankruptcy.

Note: There is draft replacement Insolvency Law under consideration by Saeima (Parliament), but has not yet been adopted.

LABOR RELATIONS:

Labor laws of Republic of Latvia apply to all employees and employers, irrespective of their status and form of ownership, if labor relations are based on employment contract. (Art. 65 of Labor Law Code of Latvia [LLC]).

Employment contract is written agreement between employee and employer pursuant to which employee undertakes to fulfill certain work in compliance with internal work regulations and directions of employer; employer undertakes to ensure salary and labor conditions as described in labor laws, collective agreement, upon mutual agreement of parties.

Employer is entitled to enter into employment contracts with citizens of Republic of Latvia, permanent residents of Latvia; foreigners and apatrides (persons without citizenship), if they have residential permit which entitles them to work. Persons under 15 years of age are not allowed to be employed in permanent work. School students of age of 13 years and older may be employed in easy work which is not harmful either to their health or morals in time free of studies. Such work may be undertaken only upon consent of parents or guardians.

Term of employment contract is determined upon mutual agreement by employer and employee. Term may be for indefinite period; for definite period; and for period required for fulfillment of definite work.

Upon entering into employment contract, employer may determine trial term for employee, in order to clarify whether employee suits assigned position. Trial period must be stated in employment contract. Trial period is not imposed on persons under age of 18 years. Trial term may not exceed three months, excluding period of temporary disability and period of time of absence of employee due to plausible reason. If trial term provided for in employment contract has expired, but employee continues to work, it must be acknowledged that employee has passed trial and future termination of employment contract at initiative of employer may occur only in compliance with general regulations.

All employees are entitled to annual vacations without impact on their work place (position) and average earnings.

Duration of annual vacation is determined in amount of not less than four calendar weeks, not counting state holidays. Vacation during first year of employment may be allocated to employee only after employee has been employed at respective enterprise, company or institution not less than six months without interruption. Vacations for second and subsequent employment years may be allocated at any time during year in accordance with vacation schedule set by employer. Compensation of vacation time in money is prohibited, except in those cases when employee is dismissed and has not used vacation.

Employees who are entitled to additional vacation are as follows: those who work in hazardous or hard work conditions; women who have three or more children under age 16; women or other persons who raise handicapped child. Length and manner of allocation of additional vacation are provided for either in collective agreement or upon mutual agreement between employer and employee. Employer may allocate to employee unpaid vacation by reason of family conditions or any other important reason.

Employment contract may be terminated if parties agree thereon (item 1, Art. 30, LLC), if term of employment contract has expired (item 2, Art. 30, LLC), if employee is called up or if employee enters state service (item 3, Art. 30, LLC); at employee's initiative (Art. 31, LLC); at employer's initiative (Art. 31, LLC) or at request of trade union of employees (Art. 38, LLC); if employee is moved to another enterprise upon his/her consent (item 5, Art. 30, LLC); if employee begins to work in an elected office (item 5, Art. 30, LLC); if employee refuses to move to other work in another area together with employer (item 6, Art. 30, LLC); if employee refuses to continue to work because employment contract provisions have been substantially changed (item 6, Art. 30, LLC); if employee is not elected to office for subsequent term (item 6, Art. 30, LLC); if court judgment has become effective by which employee is deprived of liberty (item 7, Art. 30, LLC); if violations of Republic of Latvia laws have been stated upon entering into employment contract (item 8, Art. 30, LLC); if employment contract does not comply with requirements of Republic of Latvia laws (item 8, Art. 30, LLC).

Employee is entitled to terminate employment contract at employee's own initiative, giving one month prior written notice.

Employment contract may be terminated at employer's initiative, if enterprise, institution or organization is liquidated (item 1, Art. 33, LLC); if enterprise, institution or organization reduces number of employees (item 2, Art. 33, LLC); if employer states that employee does not have sufficient professional skills, or if employee cannot proceed with respective work by reason of health (item 2, Art. 33, LLC); if employee, without any plausible reason, fails to fulfill obligations under employment contract or internal regulations (item 3, Art. 33, LLC); if employee has been sick for more than four months in succession (pregnancy and childbirth vacation is not included in this period), except cases when law provides for longer period without impact on work place (item 5, Art. 33, LLC); if employee is restored to work place which employee has been occupying before (item 6, Art. 33, LLC); if employee has been in work place under influence of alcohol, narcotics or drugs (item 7, Art. 33, LLC); if property of employer has been plundered (petty larceny included) (item 8, Art. 33, LLC); if heads of state authorities, management or local government enterprises and institutions, deputies thereof and chief accountants have not fulfilled their work obligations (item 1, Art. 254, LLC) or if their activity has been deliberately contrary to interests of state provided for Republic of Latvia laws (item 1, Art. 254, LLC); if employee at whose

See Topical Index in front part of this volume.

LABOR RELATIONS . . . *continued*
direct disposal are values in form of money or goods, has acted illegitimately and thus lost confidence of employer (item 2, Art. 254, LLC); if executive of state authorities, local government institutions or employee who is responsible for child-raising functions has committed immoral offense (item 3, Art. 254, LLC).

LAW REPORTS, CODES, ETC.:

All law is codified. No case law or law by precedent exists. Official texts of codified statutory law, treaties, administrative regulations etc. are published in Latvijas Vēstnesis (The Latvian Herald).

LEGISLATURE:

See topic Constitution and Government.

LICENSES:

License is required for certain kinds of entrepreneurial activity pursuant to §§31 and 32 of Law "On Entrepreneurial Activity" (adopted Sept. 26, 1990, am'd on May 14, 1991; May 12, 1992; Jan. 12, 1993; Feb. 23, 1993; Apr. 27, 1993; May 11, 1993; May 18, 1993; Feb. 24, 1994; June 15, 1994; Mar. 29, 1995; Nov. 2, 1995; and by Regulations No. 129 of Apr. 10, 1996), to secure state's interests. Activity may not be commenced prior to submission of license to Register of Enterprises. §32 of Law authorizes Cabinet of Ministers to determine types of entrepreneurial activity for which license is required. Regulations No. 321 of Oct. 31, 1995 (am'd on Nov. 21, 1995 by Regulations Nos. 356 and 361; on May 14, 1996 by Regulations No. 168; and on June 20, 1996 by Regulations No. 216) issued by Cabinet of Ministers contains detailed and exhaustive list of these activities and denotes institution responsible for issuing respective license.

Activities requiring license include, among others: insurance operations; buying, processing, manufacture and sale of precious metals and stones and goods made from them; operation of lotteries and gambling facilities; stock brokerage; investment company operations; manufacture and sale of medicine and other pharmaceutical products; production and sale of tobacco products and products containing alcohol; land, air, water and rail traffic services; wireless connection services; postal services; detective and private security services; certified auditing services; land surveying; legal and notaries' services; production and sale of weapons and explosives; construction and sale of gas lines; exploitation of minerals and other subterranean resources; commercial passenger transportation services within regional or city boundaries; international tourism services; operation of tourist lodgings (hotels, motels, campsites etc.); construction of buildings; fishery; trading with plant protection products; and others.

Following private practices are permitted only with license from respective professional society: medicine, veterinary medicine, teaching, building and construction design, civil engineering, and law.

Banking operations and buying and selling of foreign currency require license from Latvijas Banka (Central Bank of Latvia). "Credit Institution Law" contains further requirements regarding licenses for banking operations.

LIENS:

Civil Law states that parties may agree on securing liabilities by agreement penalty, guarantee or security deposit. (Art. 1691 of Civil Law).

Agreement Penalty.—In accordance with Civil Law, if parties agree on agreement penalty, party which fails to fully or partially fulfill its obligations must pay agreement penalty, even in cases when termination of agreement has not caused losses to other party. Amount of agreement penalty is stated by mutual agreement between parties and it is not limited to amount of losses which may be anticipated in event of nonfulfillment of agreement. If debtor partially fulfills obligations, agreement penalty must be paid by debtor in full amount. (Art. 1721 of Civil Law). In event of nonfulfillment of agreement creditor may only claim either fulfillment of agreement or payment of agreement penalty, if agreement does not state otherwise. (Art. 1718 of Civil Law).

Guarantee.—Civil Law states that guarantee is established on basis of written agreement. (Art. 1695 of Civil Law). Liability of guarantor corresponds to liability of primary debtor, therefore it may not exceed amount of primary debt.

If creditor raises claim against guarantor, guarantor may demand that creditor first direct claim to debtor, but only if such provision is stated in guaranty document. Claim can promptly be made against guarantor if debtor is absent or if insolvency of main debtor is proved or if auction is opened on his property. (Art. 1703 of Civil Law). In response to creditor's claim guarantor may use all objections which debtor might have against creditor. (Art. 1701 of Civil Law). If guarantor satisfies creditor, claim rights against debtor are transferred to guarantor in amount that has been paid to creditor.

Security deposit is paid by one party to another party upon execution of agreement not only as evidence of final execution of agreement but also as security for its fulfillment. (Art. 1725 of Civil Law).

Security deposit rights are only established upon actual delivery. Security deposit may be given not only in money, but in other valuables as well. When agreement which is secured by security deposit is fulfilled, security deposit can be either refunded to payer or included in his fulfillment of agreement. If agreement is not fulfilled because of fault of payer of security deposit, payer loses right to return of security deposit, but if agreement is not fulfilled by party which has received security deposit, receiver must refund same to security deposit payer in double amount. In addition, party at fault must compensate other party for its losses. Bank guarantees must be registered with Latvian Central Bank in order to take effect.

LIMITATION OF ACTIONS:

Actions based on contractual claims after limitation period has passed are not only barred as matter of procedure, but as matter of substantive law. Civil Law provides that such claims cease to exist after lapsing of limitation period. However, if debtor has fulfilled claim after limitation period has lapsed, he cannot demand restitution. General limitation period for contractual claims is ten years, unless provided otherwise in specific context. In particular, shorter limitation periods apply to claims arising from contracts involving delivery of goods, if goods are defective: claims for withdrawal from contract and claims for reduction of purchase price expire in six months and 12 months, respectively, from date of contract's execution. (CL, §§1633, 1634). Claims registered in Land Book are not subject to any limitation period. Reminder to, or admission by, debtor of claim suspends passing of limitation period. (CL, §1893 et seq.).

MARRIAGE:

Spouses must both be at least 18 years of age. Spouse less than 18, but at least 16 years of age can marry with his or her parents' or guardian's consent. Marriage is prohibited if court has declared spouse to be without legal capacity due to mental illness. Marriage also is prohibited between relatives related in direct line, between full or half siblings, between persons of same sex, between adopted parents and children, or where marriage would result in bigamy. (CL, §32 et seq.).

These provisions apply if marriage is entered into in Latvia. (CL, §11).

§15 of Law "On Acts Regarding Civil Status" (adopted Oct. 21, 1993, am'd June 17, 1996), aliens must have valid visa at time of marriage—marriage alone cannot be sole basis for extending visa at time of marriage. To marry in Latvia, aliens also must present proof from competent foreign authority certifying that no legal barriers to marriage, in particular, previous marriages, exist.

MONOPOLIES AND RESTRAINT OF TRADE:

This topic is governed by Law "On Competition and the Restriction of Monopolies" (adopted Dec. 3, 1991, am'd on Apr. 6, 1993). This law applies to all entrepreneurs, enterprises, legal entities and natural persons doing business in Republic of Latvia. Monopoly is defined as situation in which enterprise producing goods or offering services is in position, alone or together with others, to influence competition on Latvian market.

To promote competition and supervise implementation of above law, Monopoly Supervision Committee of Republic of Latvia ("Committee") was established by Cabinet of Ministers Regulation No. 481 of Nov. 12, 1992. Committee may give binding orders to cease monopolistic activity or unfair competition. If enterprise does not follow such orders, Committee may request competent court to demand liquidation or reorganization of such enterprise.

Law prohibits enterprise that has attained monopoly from forcing on business partner conditions not related to relevant contract's subject matter or which limit business partner's freedom of activity. Also prohibited is any understanding among enterprises that could result in weakening of competition in Latvian market. Following are prohibited regardless of effect on market: market division by territory, client group or other principles, price-fixing and agreeing on supply quota, object of which is creation of artificial demand, boycotts or any agreement that results in monopoly position of one or several enterprises.

Where merger or acquisition would result in control of 25% or more of product or service group in Latvian market, enterprise must request Committee's permission. Permission is deemed to have been granted if Committee does not prohibit merger or acquisition within 30 days.

No physical person may simultaneously be director, board member or in another leading position of two or more enterprises if basic activity of these enterprises is similar and if enterprises could be competitors in Latvian market.

Unfair competition, as more closely defined in aforementioned law is prohibited and punishable where so provided by Latvian Criminal Code.

Following activities constitute unfair competition: activities which result in commercial advantage of one enterprise by harming reputation of another enterprise; presenting distorted picture of competitor's enterprise, production or market activities; discrediting competitor without reason or misleading public about competitor's products. In addition, illegal competition is constituted by copying appearance or packaging of competitor's products; falsifying facts of production; or obtaining, using or publishing scientific, technical, production or commercial information without owner's permission.

MORTGAGES OF REAL PROPERTY:

Mortgage (hipotēka) on real property is form of pledge (ķīla). (CL, §§1279, 1367-1380). General provisions applicable to pledges both on movable objects and on real property are set forth in CL, §§1278-1339.

All pledges, including mortgages, must be based on claim which pledge is to secure. (CL, §1280). In case of nonperformance of claim, creditor secured by pledge is entitled to seek satisfaction from sale of pledged property. (CL, §1278).

Mortgage is established by agreement, by testament, or by court judgment. (CL, §1304). Mortgagee may exercise rights only after registration of mortgage in Land Book. (CL, §1368). See also topic Real Property. Mortgage is registered only in definite amount and only with respect to definite parcel of real property. Mortgagor must be registered as property's owner. (CL, §1373).

NOTARIES PUBLIC:

Operation of Notaries Public is regulated by Law "On Sworn Notaries Public" (adopted on June 1, 1993, am'd on June 17, 1996). Sworn notaries public are appointed for life term by Minister of Justice upon recommendation of Council of Sworn Notaries of Republic of Latvia. Sworn notaries public must be citizens of Republic of Latvia, must have law degree, and must have acquired relevant experience by working as assistant to notary public or by performing any other legal work. Sworn notaries public are members of legal system operating within designated jurisdiction of regional court.

Direct supervision of operation of sworn notaries public is performed by regional court in whose jurisdiction respective notary public is located.

Main task of public notaries is to prepare certifications by certifying acts (notarial deeds), to certify compliance of copies and translations with original documents, to certify signatures, to certify that person is alive, to certify presence or non-presence of counterparts for execution of legal transactions or performance of other duties, to certify contents of safes and other storages, to certify time of presentation of documents, to certify statements of claims.

NOTARIES PUBLIC . . . *continued*

Furthermore, duties of public notaries include legal consultations, preparation of acts, including agreements, acceptance of money, securities and documents for storage, preparation of projects for distribution of property.

Several of sworn notaries' functions can also be performed by assistants to sworn notary.

Acts and certifications prepared by sworn notaries public are public documents.

PARTNERSHIPS:

See topic Corporations.

PLEDGES:

Civil Law states that pledge is creditor's right to debtor's property based on which this property secures creditor's claim. In event of debtor's failure to fulfill obligations pledge must secure to creditor satisfaction of his claim. Pledge can be established on movable object (possessory pledge), immovable object (mortgage) as well as nonphysical object (rights).

Possessory pledge is established by debtor transferring movable object into possession of creditor. (Art. 1340 of Civil Law). In order to establish pledge rights debtor must be entitled to freely dispose of pledged object. Pledgee must, while pledge is at his disposal, maintain it as his own property. Pledgee may not use object pledged to him without special permission to do so. (Art. 1248 of Civil Law).

If movable or immovable accretion object is transferred as pledge into possession of creditor, in accordance with Civil Law it is deemed to be pledge of use. With regard to pledge of use creditor has not only right but also obligation to collect accretion. (Art. 1362 of Civil Law).

Mortgage grants to creditor right to immovable property only after its registration with Land Book. (Art. 1367 of Civil Law). Mortgage is only registered with Land Book in definite amount of money and for specific immovable property. (Art. 1373 of Civil Law). Record in Land Book must be made only upon approval of mortgagor. Mortgage may be established as security for claim which in future may arise in respect of credit granted to debtor. If debtor alienates immovable property to third person mortgage right remains effective. (Art. 1379 of Civil Law). Upon paying off of mortgage respective record must be made in Land Book, without which payoff of mortgage is not effective in respect of third persons. If several creditors have rights to one mortgage their right to receive satisfaction from mortgage must be satisfied in order of priority as mortgages have been recorded in Land Book.

Any pledged object is responsible for necessary expenses incurred by creditors for its maintenance and storage. (Art. 1292 of Civil Law).

Creditor has right to search for satisfaction from pledge and sell it if debtor fails to pay off underlying debt within set term. Creditor has no right to keep pledge as his property. (Art. 1334 of Civil Law). Creditor may only sell pledge for freely determined price if debtor has granted him right to do so. If creditor does not have such rights pledge may only be sold at auction through mediation of court. (Art. 1321 of Civil Law).

PRESCRIPTION:

See topic Limitation of Actions.

PRINCIPAL AND AGENT:

Civil Law provides for following three kinds of power of attorney based on agency contract: "special" power of attorney granted for distinct and specific matters, "universal" power of attorney covering all of principal's matters, and "general" power of attorney, covering all matters of certain kind or category.

Principal is bound by agent's actions only if agent has acted within limits of power of attorney granted to agent. Actions taken in transgression of powers granted to agent are void. Third parties may claim damages for losses in such cases only from agent.

Power of attorney expires upon (1) mutual agreement, (2) completion of certain matter for which power of attorney was granted, (3) principal's or agent's revocation of agency contract between them, (4) death of principal or agent, (5) expiration of time period specified in power of attorney. (CL, §§1515-1518, 2289-2317).

PRIVATIZATION:

Procedure of privatization of state and local government property objects is provided for in Law "On Privatization of State and Local Government Property Objects", approved on Feb. 17, 1994.

Purpose of privatization is by means of changing owner of state or local government property object to create beneficial environment for operation of private capital in interests of development of Latvia's national economy and to narrow activities which are performed by state and local governments as entrepreneurs. State or local government property objects which are subject to privatization are enterprises, companies, real property, portions of these enterprises, companies, real property which are owned by state or local government. State or local government owned property object may be privatized together with parcel of land if this is property of state or local government. Together they constitute one object to be privatized.

Privatization of state and local government property may be performed applying following privatization methods: (1) sale of state or local government property object (also capital shares) to privatization subject; (2) investment of state or local government property object as nonmonetary investment into entrepreneurial company which has private capital; (3) increase of share capital of state or local government charter company by attraction of private capital.

Any physical or legal person may be privatization subject which is authorized to acquire personal and/or real property in Latvia. In course of privatization of state or local government property object, neither state, nor local government, nor state or local government charter company, nor charter company share capital of which contains 25% or less of private capital, may be privatization subject. Privatization Agency performs privatization of state property objects in name of state. Local government property objects are privatized by local government property privatization commission. Payments for property objects must be made in (1) Lats, (2) privatization certificates.

Any physical or legal person is authorized to initiate privatization of state property object in accordance with requirements of aforementioned law. Resolution itself regarding delivery of state property objects to be privatized is adopted by Cabinet of Ministers. Right of first refusal as to property object to be privatized shall be enjoyed by: (1) that privatization subject in ownership of which plot of land is on which object is located, if more than half of territory occupied by object to be privatized is located on this plot of land; (2) lessee of state property object to be privatized if he has been leasing whole object to be privatized for period exceeding one year and owner of land has not executed right of first refusal.

Above persons acquire right of first refusal if they apply within two months after date when announcement regarding commencement of privatization of state property object has been published. In order to determine purchaser of state property object auction may be organized in form of tender or open auction.

New owner of privatized object is responsible for guarantees of employment of labor and investment commitments which new owner has undertaken under agreement.

Privatization Agency or local government have right of return purchase with regard to privatized object if purchaser fails to use object for purposes and in manner described in agreement.

Privatization Agency or local government retains right of first refusal with regard to privatized object if privatization subject resells respective object. Term of use of right of first refusal as described in agreement may not be less than three years after date of signing delivery and acceptance act of object.

New owner of privatized object has right of first refusal to purchase parcel of land owned by state or local government on which this object is located, unless owner of object enjoys right to purchase this parcel of land in accordance with Civil Law and other laws. Owner of parcel of land is obliged to enter into lease agreement with new owner of privatized object. Any disputes regarding terms and conditions of lease agreement are considered by court.

Privatization of residential premises owned by state and local governments is determined by Law "On Privatization of State and Local Government Owned Residential Buildings", approved on June 21, 1995. This law determines procedure of privatization of state and local government owned residential buildings and purpose is to develop real property market and to promote putting in order of residential buildings, protecting interests of inhabitants. There exists two types of privatization: privatization of entire residential building through privatization of apartments which is lengthier process, and assignment of apartments in ownership which is quicker and allows owners of apartments to freely dispose of their apartments. Persons who are entitled to privatize apartments, commercial premises, artist studios, as well as one-apartment and multi-apartment buildings are as follows: (1) owners of privatization certificates: citizens of Latvia, noncitizens and persons who have obtained permanent residency permits; (2) owners of privatization certificates: legal entities who are entitled to purchase land in accordance with existing laws, except state, local governments and companies in which state or local government owned capital shares separately or in aggregate exceed 50%. Payment for privatized object shall be made in privatization certificates and Lats.

REAL PROPERTY:

Ownership of and other rights pertaining to real property must be registered in Zemesgrāmata (Land Book). Registration confirms title to and other rights in connection with real property. "Land Book Law" (adopted Dec. 22, 1937, am'd on Mar. 30, 1993 and by Regulations No. 121 of Apr. 9, 1996) provides that registration is effected after formal request for confirmation of given right to real property. Power of attorney for such request to confirm by registration must be certified by sworn notary public.

Buildings erected on and connected to land are deemed to be part of land and owned by owner of land. However, separate ownership of buildings is possible based on agreement between respective owners. (CL, §§968, 969).

Leases terminate upon change in ownership of leased premises. (CL, §2168). However, if lease is registered in Land Book, new owner is bound by lease for its intended term.

Rights to real property are determined by law of jurisdiction in which real property is located. If real property is located in Latvia, form and contents of acquisition, change in contents or termination of real property rights is determined by Latvian law, regardless of which persons are parties to agreements and where agreements were made. Same applies to form and contents of contractual rights on basis of which rights to real property are be acquired, amended or terminated. (CL, §18).

Rights of aliens to acquire or inherit real property currently still are restricted by Law "On Land Reform in the Cities of the Republic of Latvia" (Nov. 20, 1991) and Law "On Land Privatization in Rural Areas" (July 9, 1992).

RESTITUTION AND DENATIONALIZATION OF PROPERTY:

Restitution and denationalization of property is related to property reform in Latvia. Its purpose is to restore ownership rights of former owners or their heirs to land, buildings and enterprises which were nationalized or otherwise dispossessed under Soviet regime. In Republic of Latvia this issue is regulated by following laws: "On Denationalization of Buildings in Republic of Latvia" (adopted Oct. 30, 1991, am'd on Mar. 31, 1994; July 28, 1994; Aug. 23, 1995; and by Regulations No. 87 of Apr. 2, 1996), "On Restitution of Buildings to Their Lawful Owners Thereof" (adopted Oct. 30, 1991, am'd Mar. 31, 1994; May 23, 1996), "On Restitution of Ownership Rights to Enterprises and Other Property Objects" (adopted Mar. 30, 1993; am'd on Oct. 6, 1994 and by Regulations No. 125 of Apr. 10, 1996), "On Restitution of Property to Religious Organizations" (adopted May 12, 1992, am'd on Jan. 13, 1994; Oct. 27, 1994), "On Land Privatization in Rural Areas" (adopted July 9, 1992, am'd on Apr. 27, 1993; Dec. 16, 1993; Dec. 8, 1994; Oct. 5, 1995; June 12, 1996; and by Regulations No. 9 of Jan. 5, 1996), "On Land Reform in the Cities of the Republic of Latvia" (adopted Nov. 20, 1991, am'd on Mar. 31, 1994; Nov. 24, 1994; Oct. 12, 1995; and by Regulations No. 8 of Jan. 5, 1996). These laws apply to real property objects constructed prior to July 21, 1940. In accordance with Latvian legislation, term of application of former owners or their heirs and term of submission of documents evidencing affinity have expired (June 1, 1996), however, in each particular case this term may be renewed or extended by court decision. Restitution of title to above

See Topical Index in front part of this volume.

RESTITUTION AND DENATIONALIZATION OF PROPERTY . . . *continued*

objects and return of properties is still going on in Republic of Latvia until completion of arrangement of ownership rights and registration of all title to real properties in Land Book.

SALES:

General contractual principles contained in Civil Law (CL, §§1401-1911; see topic Contracts) apply to sales contracts, unless specified otherwise in provisions on sales contracts (CL, §§2002-2090).

Any object or right with respect to which ownership rights can be transferred can be object of sales contract, including movable and real property claims, and rights. Seller promises to deliver object to buyer, and buyer promises to pay agreed consideration. Rights to movable and real property are not transferred by sales contract itself, which only creates obligation on seller to confer ownership of object on buyer. Title to movable property passes to buyer upon delivery. Title to real property is transferred upon registration in Land Book. (See topic Real Property.)

Object of sales contract must exist in reality and be so definite that no doubt can arise about its identity. If doubt can arise, contract is deemed not to have been concluded. (CL, §2007).

Upon conclusion of sales contract, even if sold object has not yet been delivered to buyer, buyer bears risk for accidental loss or damage of object. (CL, §2023). Foregoing does not apply if, among other exceptions (listed in CL, §2024), seller has agreed to bear risk until delivery to buyer, if loss or damage can be deemed to be seller's fault, or if seller is in default.

Following provisions are contained in CL, §§1593-1634, and apply to any contract in which one party delivers object to another party for money, including, in particular, sales contracts; seller is held liable if third party obtains title to sold object before delivery, or if item has hidden defects, or lacks any of characteristics that can be assumed or have been explicitly confirmed by seller. (CL, §1593). This applies regardless of whether or not this issue is addressed in contract. (CL, §1594).

Seller is liable not only for defects known to seller, but also for hidden, unknown defects. This does not apply to (1) minor defects that do not impede intended use of object; or (2) defects known to buyer. Seller is liable only for defects that existed before conclusion of contract. Seller is liable in any case for defects nonexistence of which seller explicitly confirmed. (CL, §§1612-1616). Although seller, by agreement, can exclude above-mentioned liability for defects, liability cannot be excluded if seller acted with malicious intent. (CL, §1617).

Consequence of seller's liability in case of malicious intent or express confirmation of given characteristic of sold object is that buyer can demand consequential damages. In all other cases of defects, buyer can choose only between rescission of contract and reduction of purchase price. (CL, §1620). Right to demand rescission of contract expires six months from date of contract's conclusion or from date seller gave explicit warranty. Right to demand reduction of purchase price expires one year from these dates. (CL, §§1633, 1634).

Consumer protection is governed by Law "On the Protection of Consumers' Rights" (adopted Oct. 28, 1992).

TAXATION:

System of taxes and duties in Latvia is regulated by umbrella Law "On Taxes and Duties", adopted on 02.02.95 (amended by law of 06.06.96). Taxes and duties system consists of: (1) state taxes; objects on which such taxes are imposed and their tariffs are stated by Saeima (Parliament), (2) state duties which are imposed in accordance with this law, other laws and regulations of Cabinet of Ministers, (3) municipality duties which are imposed in accordance with this law and binding regulations issued by council of each municipality. In Latvia there are following state taxes: personal income tax, company income tax, property tax, land tax, value added tax, excise tax, customs tax, natural resources tax, drawing and games of chance tax, social tax.

Personal Income Tax.—Law "On Personal Income Tax", adopted on 11.05.93 (amended by following Laws of 14.01.94, 27.10.94, 01.03.95, 31.05.95). Personal income tax is imposed on profit earned by natural persons and it consists of: (1) salary tax which is calculated and paid on income received by employee from employer; (2) patent payment which is advance payment required by municipalities for performance of specific types of commercial activity; (3) tax on income from entrepreneurial activity, if such income is not subject to company income tax, from individual work, property and other sources. Tax is calculated and paid to budget in two manners: in advance, including by means of salary tax and patent payment, and also by making annual income declaration. Tax is paid by: (1) natural persons—residents, who during taxation period have earned income in Republic of Latvia and/or abroad. Foreign natural persons are considered to be residents, if they stay in Republic of Latvia for 183 days or more within any period of 12 months which starts or ends within taxation year; (2) natural persons—nonresidents, who during taxation year have earned profit in Latvia; (3) natural persons—owners of individual enterprises, also private farms which during taxation period (calendar year) have earned income on which company income tax is not imposed. Annual income of payer is total of all money, material value and services received during taxation period. Annual tax rate imposed on taxable income is 25%. If taxpayer's annual income on which tax is imposed exceeds 60,000 lats, then 25% tax rate is imposed on amount of 60,000 lats, but tax rate of 10% is imposed on those amounts exceeding 60,000 lats.

Company Income Tax.—Law "On Income Tax of Enterprises", adopted on 09.02.95 (amended by laws of 12.10.95, 29.02.96). Payers of company income tax are as follows: (1) domestic enterprises which perform entrepreneurial activity, public and religious organizations and institutions financed from state budget which earn profit from commercial activity—residents; (2) foreign enterprises, entrepreneurial companies, natural persons and other persons—nonresidents; (3) permanent representative offices (permanent establishments) of nonresidents. With regard to residents, taxes are imposed on profit earned in Latvia and abroad during taxation period. Tax rate is 25% of this profit. With regard to permanent representative offices, tax is imposed on independently earned profit within taxation period in Latvia and foreign countries. Tax rate is 25% of this profit. With regard to nonresidents, tax is imposed on profit earned from entrepreneurial activity or activities related thereto in Latvia. Tax is withheld from payments which are made by residents and permanent representative offices to nonresidents, including to natural persons if no personal income tax has been withheld from such payments. Tax rates are from 5 to 25% depending upon type of income.

Social Tax.—Law "On Social Tax" adopted on 01.11.95 (amended by laws of 08.02.96, 05.06.96). Social tax is paid by: (1) employers—natural or legal persons who employ employees and are considered to be residents; (2) persons—residents, who are engaged in legal work relationship with employer—resident; (3) persons—residents who are engaged in legal work relationship with employer—nonresident; (4) self-employed persons. Social tax is imposed on socially insured person's work income irrespective of form in which income is received. Social tax rate is 38% of this taxable income. Social tax is paid proportionally by employer and employee as follows: currently 33% is paid by employer and 5%—by employee. Law provides for reduction in social tax rate each year by 1%, also leveling proportions paid by employer and employee, until Jan. 1, 2001, when tax rate will be 33% and which will be paid by employer and employee in equal portions.

Value Added Tax.—Law "On Value Added Tax" adopted on Mar. 9, 1995 (amended by laws of 26.10.95, 25.04.96). Value added tax is imposed on: supply of goods, rendering of services, import of goods, self-consumption performed within country by person on which this tax is imposed. Person on which this tax is imposed is natural or legal person, and groups bound by agreement to such persons and are registered or were to be registered as value added taxpayers. If total value of goods supplied or services rendered by those persons or groups of persons on which tax is imposed has reached or exceeded 10,000 lats within previous 12 months, they must register as persons on which value added tax is imposed. Value added tax rate is 18% of value of goods (also imported) supply, services and self-consumption on which tax is imposed.

Excise Tax.—Law on "Excise Tax" adopted on 12.12.90 (amended by laws of 11.07.92, 28.10.92, 30.03.93, 14.10.93, 28.07.94, 02.03.95, 16.05.96 and 13.06.96). Excise taxpayers are legal and natural persons who sell self-produced and imported alcoholic beverages, tobacco products, gold and other precious metals, automobiles, gas and diesel fuel. Alcoholic beverages and tobacco products must be marked with specific excise marks. Excise tax is not imposed on goods which are exported and it is not withheld from transit cargo transportation and from reexport.

Property Tax.—Law "On Property Tax" adopted on 18.12.90 (amended by laws of 03.09.91, 11.12.91, 30.03.95). Property tax is paid by natural and legal persons as well as foreign natural and legal persons on their property which is located within territory of Republic of Latvia. Tax is imposed on basic assets and unfinished construction objects. Property tax is not imposed on properties owned by natural persons, if these properties are not used for entrepreneurial activity. Property tax rates are from 0.5% to 4% depending upon value of property. Also related is land tax. Law "On Land Tax" adopted on 20.12.90 (amended by laws of 09.04.91, 17.03.92, 04.05.93, 26.10.95). Land taxpayers are legal and natural persons who own land or have been granted its use. Average land tax rates for each specific location of land are stated in appendices of law.

Natural Resources Tax.—Law "On Natural Resources Tax" was adopted on 04.10.95. Taxpayers are all legal and natural persons who in territory of Republic of Latvia (or continental shelf) extract natural resources on which taxes are imposed, or who release into environment pollutants on which taxes are imposed, or who sell or import goods and products harmful to environment and have received required permit (or should have received permit) to perform such activities. Tax is calculated in accordance with appendix to law.

Drawing and Games of Chance Taxes and Duties.—Law on "Drawing and Games of Chance Taxes and Duties", adopted on 16.06.94 (amended by law of 28.09.95). This tax is paid by enterprises which have received special license for organization and maintenance of drawing and games of chance.

Customs Tax.—Law "On Customs Duties (Tariffs)", adopted on 29.09.94 (amended by laws of 07.09.95, 05.10.95, 26.10.95, 06.11.95 and 08.07.96). Customs tax is paid by natural and legal persons who import to Republic of Latvia or export from Republic of Latvia goods or other objects. Customs tax is calculated based on following: (1) customs value of goods or other objects; (2) customs tariffs which are based on harmonized system of describing and coding of goods and combined nomenclature; (3) origin certificates of goods and other objects stated in this law and international agreements. Import customs duties and export customs duties are divided as follows: (1) basic tariff; (2) tariff which is applied to trade with countries having most favored nation regime with Latvia; (3) tariff which is applied to trade with countries with which free trade regime exists; (4) tariff which is applied to countries to which Latvia has granted trade advantages.

Annual Duties for Transport Vehicles.—Law "On Annual Duties for Transport Vehicles", adopted on 22.12.94. Duties are paid by all legal and natural persons having transport vehicles registered in their name in Republic of Latvia. Duties are paid each year prior to annual technical inspection of transport vehicle.

TREATIES:

Republic of Latvia is party to, inter alia, following international treaties:

General.—International Monetary Fund and International Bank for Reconstruction and Development—IMF (July 22, 1944); Convention on the Establishment of the International Civil Aviation Organization (Dec. 12, 1944); Constitution of the World Health Organization—WHO (July 22, 1946): Convention on the International Maritime Organization (Mar. 6, 1948); Statutes of the Council of Europe (May 5, 1949); Convention Establishing a Customs Cooperation Council (Dec. 15, 1950); European Convention on Culture (May 6, 1954); Convention on the Law of Treaties (May 23, 1969); Convention on the International Maritime Satellite Organization—INMARSAT (Sept. 3, 1976); European Charter of Regional Self-Administration (Oct. 15, 1985); European Energy Charter (Dec. 17, 1994).

Human Rights.—Convention on the Prevention and Punishment of the Crime of Genocide (Dec. 9, 1948); Convention on the Political Rights of Women (Dec. 20, 1952); Convention on the Nationality of Married Women (Feb. 20, 1957); International Covenant on Civil and Political Rights (Dec. 16, 1966); International Covenant

See Topical Index in front part of this volume.

TREATIES . . . *continued*
on Economic, Social and Cultural Rights (Dec. 16, 1966); Convention on Abolishing the Discrimination of Women (Dec. 18, 1979); UN Convention on the Rights of the Child (Nov. 20, 1989).

Consular and Diplomatic Relations.—Vienna Convention on Diplomatic Relations (Apr. 18, 1961); Vienna Convention on Consular Relations (Apr. 24, 1963).

International Cooperation in Legal Matters.—Hague Convention on Questions of Procedure in Civil Matters (Mar. 1, 1954), Hague Convention Abolishing the Requirement of Legalization for Foreign Public Documents (Oct. 5, 1961), Convention on the Service Abroad of Judicial and Extrajudicial Documents in Civil or Commercial Matters (Nov. 15, 1965), Convention on the Taking of Evidence Abroad in Civil or Commercial Matters (Mar. 18, 1970).

Arbitration.—New York Convention on the Recognition and Enforcement of Foreign Arbitral Awards (June 10, 1958).

International Transportation and Trade.—Protocol amending the Warsaw Convention of October 12, 1929 on the Unification of Some Rules Concerning International Aviation Transportation (Sept. 28, 1955); International Convention on Contracts for the International Carriage of Goods by Road—CMR (May 19, 1956); Convention on Contracts for the International Carriage of Passengers and Baggage by Road—CVR (Mar. 1, 1973) and its Protocol of July 5, 1978; International Convention on a Harmonized System for the Description and Codification of Goods (June 14, 1983).

Environment.—Helsinki Conventions on the Protection of the Baltic Sea Environment (1974 and 1992); Convention Regarding Wetlands of International Significance (Feb. 2, 1971); Vienna Convention on the Protection of the Ozone Layer (Mar. 22, 1985) with Montreal Protocol (1987); Basle Convention Regarding the Transportation Across Borders and Removal of Hazardous Waste (Mar. 22, 1989); Rio de Janeiro Convention on Climate Changes (May 9, 1992); Rio de Janeiro Convention on Biological Diversity (May 9, 1992).

Protection of Intellectual Property.—Paris Convention for the Protection of Industrial Property Rights (Mar. 20, 1883), as revised at Stockholm (July 14, 1967); Madrid Convention on the International Registration of Trademarks (Apr. 14, 1891), as revised at Stockholm (July 14, 1967); Berne Convention for the Protection of Literary and Artistic Works (Sept. 9, 1886), as revised at Stockholm (July 14, 1967); Washington Patent Cooperation Treaty (June 19, 1970).

Taxation.—Treaties for avoidance of double taxation are currently in force with following countries: Canada, Czech Republic, Denmark, Estonia, Finland, Iceland, Lithuania, Netherlands, Norway, Poland and Sweden. Treaties for avoidance of double taxation are not yet in force, but have been signed, with Belarus, France, Germany, Great Britain, Kazakhstan, U.S.A., and Ukraine.

Investment protection treaties are currently in force with following countries: Austria, Canada, Czech Republic, Denmark, Estonia, Finland, France, Germany, Great Britain, Israel, Lithuania, Netherlands, Norway, Poland, Sweden, Switzerland, Taiwan and Vietnam.

Investment protection treaties are not yet in force, but have been signed with Belgium, Luxembourg, Greece, Portugal, Spain, U.S.A. and Uzbekistan.

Free Trade.—Free Trade Agreements are currently in force with Czech Republic, Estonia, member states of European Union, EFTA states, Lithuania, and Slovakia. For countries with which agreements on favorable terms of trade are in force, see topic Customs Duties.

Agreements Among Baltic States.—Following agreements, inter alia, are in force among Latvia, Estonia and Lithuania: Free Trade Agreement, Protocol On a Single Visa Area, Agreement On a Mutual Visa Free Traveling Procedure, Agreement on Cooperation Regarding the State's Frontier Guards, Agreement On Mutual Assistance in Customs Matters. Latvia, Estonia and Lithuania have signed Agreement on Free Trade Regarding Agricultural Products.

TRUSTS:

Trusts within meaning of law of equity are not known in Latvian law, since there is no distinct system of equity comparable to that known in Common Law. Similar aims can be reached by civil law constructs such as guardians, administrators, and executors. Law of descent and distribution does not provide for division of title comparable to division between trustee and holder of equitable right under Common Law.

WILLS:

Wills (testaments) and contracts of inheritance are governed by Civil Law. Minor may make valid testament if minor is at least 16 years of age. Testament may be executed as public testament before notary public, local court or before Latvian Consul abroad before two witnesses. Private testament must be in writing and made before two witnesses who also must sign testament. However, if testator has written and executed testament in his own hand, testament is valid without witnesses.

Heirs are deemed to have accepted inheritance if they do not expressly reject inheritance within time period determined by testator or, if testator has not determined such time period, within one year of being informed of opening of probate proceedings.

Testator may dispose of all of his property by testament; however, his statutory compulsory heirs must receive their respective statutory shares of estate. Compulsory heirs are surviving spouse and direct descendants, and, if above do not exist, testator's living parents. Compulsory shares are determined by number of compulsory heirs alive. Compulsory statutory share equals half of such heir's intestate share (see topic Descent and Distribution).

Testator may name legatees with respect to separate items of estate; such legatees, without becoming heirs to estate as whole, have right to demand receipt of items from heirs or executor. (CL, §422 et seq.).

Rights of aliens to inherit real property currently still are restricted by Law "On Land Reform in the Cities of the Republic of Latvia" (Nov. 20, 1991) and Law "On Land Privatization in Rural Areas" (July 9, 1992).

LEBANON LAW DIGEST

(The following is a list of all Topics, including cross-references, covered in this Digest.)

LEBANON LAW DIGEST

Revised for 1997 edition by

KHAIRALLAH & CHAIBAN of the Beirut Bar.

(C. O. C. indicates Code of Obligations and Contracts; C. C. P., Code of Civil Procedure; C. C. T., Code of Commerce; C. C. M. Code of Maritime Commerce; C. P., Penal Code; C. P. P., Code of Penal Procedure; C. A. L., Lebanese Air Code; I. C. W., International Code of Warsaw [Air].)

PRELIMINARY NOTE:

Since its severance from the Ottoman Empire in consequence of the First World War, the Republic of Lebanon has enacted a series of Codes, a Code of Obligations and Contracts, a Code of Civil Procedure, a Code of Commerce, Penal Code, Code of Labor, Code of Social Security, and has shown a marked progressive tendency to keep up with the social and economical developments of modern life. Very little remains from the old Ottoman Law. The Personal Status Law and Domestic Relations are still governed by the Canon Law, each community having its own canon courts and codes.

ABSENTEES:

(References below are to the Law of Inheritance, promulgated June 23, 1959, affecting the estates of non-Moslems such as Christians and Jews.)

The death of the absent may be decreed in the following cases: (1) if absent for ten years in circumstances where destruction is generally presumed, as the case of a soldier who fails to return during ten years after the end of a war; (2) if he attains the age of 100 years and it is not known whether he is alive or dead. (Art. 34). In the preceding cases the court will only decree death after exhaustive investigations have been made, and advertisements inserted in local, and whenever possible in foreign newspapers designated by the court, especially in the country where the absentee is presumed to reside, and then six months after the latest advertisement. (Art. 35).

Property of the Absent.—The heirs of the absent may enjoy the use of the property, but may not perform any acts translative thereof, or establish a servitude thereon until five years have passed after issuance of the decree. (Art. 36). The distributive share of the absent in the estates of others, or legacies made to him, will be held in suspense for five years after the decree certifying his death; then the share or legacy will revert to the heirs of the decedent or testator. (Art. 37). If the heir is absent and has no agent to represent him, the judge, in chambers, upon the recommendation of the "Mukhtar" (a civil servant of the state) of the locality, or a relation of the absent, will order the taking of an inventory of the estate. (Art. 115). The assets are then handed over to the heirs present upon furnishing bond for the share of the absent; but if they refuse to furnish bond, the valuables are deposited in a bank, and the remainder of the property is delivered to a custodian to administer for the benefit of all. The custodian may be required to furnish bond. (Art. 116). If one or more of the heirs present ask for settlement of the estate, and it is possible to ascertain the domicile of the absent, the court will serve notice on him and give him sufficient delay to appoint an agent. If he then should fail to appear or appoint an agent, the settlement of the estate would be made in the presence of the custodian. If the domicile is not known, he will be served in the manner prescribed in the Civil Procedure Code (publication), and then the custodian will represent him. (Art. 117). The judge may issue a decree in chambers for the sale of perishable goods and may order the share of the absent therein and in the cash assets to be deposited in a bank. (Art. 118).

See also topic Executors and Administrators, subhead Settlement and Partition, catchline Settlement of Estate When Heirs are Unknown.

ACKNOWLEDGMENTS:

Acknowledgments may be made before a notary public. Identity of acknowledger is established by an identity card, issued to each inhabitant by Ministry of Interior, or by testimony of two identifying witnesses, or notary public's statement that acknowledger is personally known to him. Copy of instrument acknowledged is kept in archives of notary public, and another copy is given to acknowledger for use wherever necessary. Instruments acknowledged in this way are admitted to record or received in evidence without further proof.

Authentication for use outside the country requires the authentication of the notary's signature by the Ministry of Justice and the Ministry of Foreign Affairs, and the visa of the consular officer of the country where the instrument is to be used.

Documents acknowledged before a notary, which are intended for use in Lebanon, should be made and executed in accordance with the lex loci. The notary's signature must be certified by the competent authority (such as the county clerk in the United States). The signature of the competent authority must be certified by a Lebanese diplomatic or consular officer.

ACTIONS:

Limitation of.—See topic Limitations, Statute of.

ADMINISTRATION:

See topic Executors and Administrators.

AGENCY: See topic Principal and Agent.

ALIENS:

An alien is a person who is not a Lebanese citizen.

Visitors.—Visitors are allowed to make a temporary stay in the country: the length of stay depends upon nature and object of visit. Visitors desiring to make an extended stay must obtain residence permits from Sûreté Générale.

Aliens Desiring to Work in Lebanon.—Aliens desiring to work in Lebanon should obtain in advance an authorization from Ministry of Social Affairs, all with the exception of artists, who should obtain the permit from Sûreté Générale. In the sense of the statute, artists are persons who appear in an artistic manner in establishments which dispense alcoholic beverages, or where shows are given accompanied by music. (Art. 13). Foreign merchants who desire to establish themselves in Lebanon should submit evidence of bank guarantee equal to amount determined by Ministry of Social Affairs before they can obtain permit. Permit is subject to an annual tax. Citizens of U.S.A., U.K., the Swiss Confederation, France, Italy and Iraq are freed from this requirement. (Decree No. 6613, May 11, 1961; Decree No. 6931, June 16, 1961; Decree No. 7155, July 17, 1961). At beginning of each year Minister of Social Affairs publishes list of jobs and activities reserved to Lebanese citizens.

Acquisition of Real Property (Law No. 11614 of Jan. 4, 1969).—No alien, whether natural or moral person, can acquire inter vivos real property, or long term leases of over ten years, or very long term leases of over 20 years, without previous authorization granted by governmental decree. (Arts. 1 and 3). Exception is made of mortgages: Holder of mortgaged property may acquire mortgaged property at public auction provided he does not hold property thus acquired for more than two years; and provided, if he is not bank, that no holder than himself takes part in bidding at first public auction. (Art. 5). Every natural and moral person may acquire realty up to 10,000 square meters provided he starts to build on acquired property within period of two years after registration of land in Land Registry. (Art. 7). Authorizing decrees remain effective during one year after their publication in Official Journal and period is suspended during any litigation. (Art. 10). Subjects of Arab States and persons of Lebanese origin may acquire, without any authorization, buildings and realty to be built-up up to 5,000 square meters provided that area acquired in City of Beirut does not exceed 3,000 square meters, and provided they start building thereon within period of five years from registration in Land Registry. (Art. 3, as am'd by Law of Nov. 24, 1972). Deemed to be foreign companies are: Partnerships, limited liability companies which are not completely owned by Lebanese; Lebanese corporations (sociétés anonymes), and Lebanese sociétés par actions shares of which are not fully registered and owned by Lebanese. (Art. 2). Partnership, or limited liability company, or corporation (société anonyme, or société en commandite par action) which are deemed to be foreign by application of this law, may acquire without authorization up to 10,000 square meters for their own requirements, provided, in respect of partnerships and limited liability companies, majority of capital or majority of shares is owned by Lebanese and provided, in respect of corporations and sociétés en commandite par actions that at least one third of their shares are fully registered and owned by Lebanese. (Art. 3). These partnerships and corporations may also by special authorization and provided nature of their activities requires it, acquire up to 50,000 square meters of land. (Art. 11).

It is permissible to acquire realty exceeding area specified in Art. 11 for: Joint companies (sociétés mixtes) of general public interest or of touristic interest to capital or to activites of which State participates, foreign scientific, cultural and philanthropic institutions or associations, diplomatic and consular missions when same is necessary for their work. (Art. 14).

Every legal act contrary to this law is absolutely null and void, and parties thereto and all who participate in registration thereof are punishable by hard labor for time and penalty varying between value of realty and three times such value even if act is done under name of another person. (Art. 16).

Law is not retroactive. (Arts. 18, 19, 23).

Foreign Workers.—See topic Social Security.

Foreign Banks.—See topic Banks and Banking.

Corporations Owned or Controlled by Aliens.—See topics Banks and Banking; Corporations; Principal and Agent.

ARBITRAL AWARDS: See topic Judgments.

ASSIGNMENTS:

The consent of the debtor is not necessary for the assignment of a claim by the creditor to a third person, except where the law or agreement prohibits the assignment, or where the claim is unassignable by nature. The assignment of a chose in action is only possible with the consent of the debtor. As against third persons, and more particularly the debtor, the assignment exists only as of the date of the notice thereof made to the debtor or of his acceptance thereof in a notarial act. So long as these formalities are not accomplished, if the debtor pays the claim to the assignor, or to a previous assignee, he is discharged. The assignor warrants the existence of the claim at the time of the assignment, but not the solvency of the debtor, unless otherwise expressly stipulated. The assignee acquires all the rights and privileges of the assignor excepting those of a personal nature. (C. O. C. arts. 280-286).

ASSOCIATIONS:

Association is group of persons with non-lucrative aim. To form association, interest group must submit to Ministry of Interior its by-laws in duplicate with petition specifying name, object and head office of association; name, occupation, nationality and domicile of officers of association.

Foreign association cannot be established, or function in Lebanon before obtaining authorization from Minister of Interior after complying with requirements set forth in preceding paragraph.

Association may sue and be sued, may possess and administer property it holds, collect annual subscriptions from its members; own real property strictly necessary for accomplishment of its object. Foreign associations must comply with legislation in force governing acquisition of real property.

ASSOCIATIONS . . . *continued*

Association is deemed to be foreign when its head office is situated in foreign country; and also if situated in Lebanon it is affiliated with foreign institution; and if it is administered in fact by board having one-fourth of its members foreigners.

Association may be recognized as one of public interest and receive gifts, donations and legacies after approval of Government.

ATTACHMENT:

Creditor wishing to attach property of debtor must petition Chief of Bureau d'Exécution for order or writ of attachment; if claim is not evidenced by executory writ (titre exécutoire) creditor may be required to furnish bond, and must, within five days from issuance of writ, begin suit in confirmation of attachment and for its conversion into execution proper. (Arts. 866:876; 881:899; 900:917; 948:996 C.C.P.).

BANKRUPTCY:

Foreigners doing business in Lebanon are subject to the bankruptcy law on the same basis as Lebanese subjects. A foreign decree in bankruptcy may be enforced in Lebanon after obtaining the Exequatur.

BANKS AND BANKING:

Banking activities can be exercised by institutions established in form of Sociétés Anonymes. Foreign banking institutions which are considered in their country of origin as banks are not subject to this requirement. (Statute on Currency and Credit of Aug. 1, 1963, Art. 126).

All shares in Lebanese banks must be registered and owned in proportion of at least 51% by Lebanese citizens or by Lebanese corporations having at least 51% of their shares registered and owned by Lebanese citizens. Foreigners may own shares in Lebanese banks only if law of their country of origin gives same right to Lebanese. (Arts. 1 and 3 of Decree Law No. 87 of Sept. 16, 1983).

All foreign banks, which desire to open branch in Lebanon, must submit demand to that effect to Committee of Bank of Lebanon before they begin any publicity required by Decree of Dec. 30, 1926 and by Art. 29 of Code of Commerce. (Art. 130 as am'd by Decree Law No. 77 of June 27, 1977). Foreign banks may open branch in Lebanon only if law of their country of origin gives same right to Lebanese banks. (Art. 1 of Decree Law No. 87 of Sept. 16, 1983). Foreign banks may also be authorized to open representative offices in Lebanon, provided they do not deal with individuals but only with banks, financial institutions, companies, private and public bodies. Representative offices must file with Bank of Lebanon semiannual reports describing their activities; failure to do so entails withdrawal of license.

Committee has discretionary power to accept or reject demand taking into consideration public policy. (Art. 131 as am'd by Decree Law No. 77 of June 27, 1977).

Assets of foreign banks branches may consist of following: preestablishment expenses, equipment and furniture, built-in real property in Lebanon, Lebanese Government bonds or bonds guaranteed by Lebanese Government, and stock in Lebanese corporations wherein Lebanese Government is stockholder. Investment of branches in built-in real property is not subject to previous governmental decree authorizing acquisition of real property by aliens. (Art. 6 of Law 28/67 of May 9, 1967 as am'd by Decree Law No. 38 of Feb. 23, 1977).

If branch of foreign bank shall cease payment, creditors of branch operating in Lebanon shall have preference over other creditors of said foreign bank. (Art. 7 of Law 28/67 of May 9, 1967).

Mixed body has been created to guarantee deposits in banks (Art. 12) that do not exceed amount fixed by decree, when bank shall cease payments.

Special Laws Governing Banks that Cease Payment.—(Law No. 2/67, promulgated Jan. 16, 1967).

Shall be deemed to have ceased payment: every bank that declares that it has ceased payment, or that shall fail to pay a debt owing by it to Bank of Lebanon, or that shall draw a check on Bank of Lebanon without provision, or if it did not provide sufficient provision to cover a debit balance resulting from a clearing chamber operation. (Art. 2). Every bank may demand competent court for application of provisions of law either before cessation of payment, or during period of ten days that follow cessation. (Art. 3). Every creditor likewise may demand application of this law to any bank that shall cease payment of its commercial debts, or that consolidates confidence in it by unlawful means. (Art. 4).

Competent court shall immediately appoint a temporary manager to manage routine work, and will then examine demand in Deliberation Chamber, and if it grants demand, it will appoint an administrative committee of six to ten persons to take place of bank's board of directors, and by such an appointment administration of person appointed temporarily shall cease. (Arts. 5-7).

Administrative committee assumes powers of board of directors that has been relieved, and will represent creditors. (Art. 10). If it appears to administrative committee in period of six months that bank is in a condition to resume its operations, it will submit matter to court for a decision to call shareholders to elect a new board of directors; but if it appears that bank is not in such a condition, it will be placed under liquidation which shall be effected by a liquidation committee.

All property belonging to members of board of directors of bank that has ceased payment, as well as property belonging to Controllers of Accounts shall be deemed attached provisionally without necessity of a court decision. (Art. 13). Measures taken against bank shall not obstruct action against those responsible for operations of bank pursuant to provisions appertaining to bankruptcy with regard to their civil and penal responsibility. (Art. 14).

Banking Free Zone.—Banking free zone was created by Decree No. 29, dated Feb. 5, 1977 with respect to nonresident banking accounts in foreign currency. Accrued interest on such accounts is not subject to income tax.

BILLS AND NOTES:

Bills of Exchange.—A bill of exchange must be dated and contain an order to pay a certain sum of money, the name of the drawer, time and place of payment, consideration, place where drawn, name of the drawee, and whether it is the first, second, third or fourth copy. On the due date, the drawer must have made "provision" for its payment, equivalent to at least its amount. Acceptance presupposes "provision" and is considered sufficient proof of such in receipt to endorsers. The drawer and endorsers are jointly liable. The acceptor becomes primarily liable even though the drawer becomes bankrupt before its acceptance. Acceptance must contain the word "accepted" and be signed, and it cannot be conditional. It must be made on presentation, or at least 24 hours thereafter. There are no days of grace. Bills falling due on a holiday are payable on the next succeeding business day. Endorsements must be dated. Antedating an endorsement is forgery. All persons whose signatures appear on a bill of exchange, and acceptors are jointly liable.

Bills of exchange may be presented for acceptance until date of maturity. Bills made payable at a certain date after sight must be presented for acceptance within a maximum of one year from their date unless otherwise provided for by drawer. Presentation for payment should be made on due date. Protest for nonacceptance must be made within period required for presentation to acceptance, or in case presentation was made last day, within following 24 hours. Protest for nonpayment must be made within two working days following due date. Protest for nonacceptance releases holder from presentation for payment and from protest for nonpayment. Failure to observe all above periods does not release drawee, but releases endorsers and drawer who proves that provision existed on due date. Action of holder against drawee must be brought within a period of three years from date of maturity, and his actions against endorsers and drawer within a period of one year. Actions of endorsers against each other, and against drawer must be brought within six months from date payment was made by endorser or action is brought against him by holder.

Promissory notes are subject to the rules governing bills of exchange as regards maturity, liability, endorsement, payment, protest, and rights and duties of the holder. They should be dated and signed by the maker, and contain an order to pay a certain sum of money, the name of the payee, time and place of payment, and the consideration.

Checks.—A check should contain word "check" and unconditional order to pay a certain sum of money, name of drawee, place of payment, date and place where drawn, and signature of issuer. There must be "provision" at time of issue. Absence of "provision" renders drawer liable to criminal proceedings. (See subhead Penalties for Issuing Checks without Provision, infra.) Check may be drawn in favor of a specified person or to his order or to bearer, and must be drawn on a banker. It must be payable at sight, and should be presented for payment within eight days if place of issue and payment are in Lebanon, within 20 days if place of issue is in one of neighboring countries, or in Europe, or in one of Mediterranean countries, and within 70 days if place of issue is in some other country. Crossed checks may be presented for payment only through a bank. Actions of holder against endorsers and drawer must be brought within six months from termination of period of presentation. Actions of endorsers against each other and against drawer must be brought within six months from date payment was made by endorser or action is brought against him by holder. Action of holder against drawee must be brought within a period of three years from termination of period of presentation.

Penalties for Issuing Checks without Provision.—(Law No. 30/67, promulgated May 16, 1967).

Persons issuing checks without provision, or without sufficient provision, or who withdraw part or all of the provision after issuing a check, or who order nonpayment of a check for a cause other than loss of check or bankruptcy of holder are liable to a penalty of three months to three years prison, and a fine of 50,000 to 200,000 Lebanese pounds, together with face value of check and damages. (Art. 1).

Whoever accepts a check knowing that it is without provision is liable to same penalty. (Art. 2).

Drawee is obliged to pay value of check even after expiration of delay for presentation. (Art. 3).

CHATTEL MORTGAGES:

Chattel mortgages exist in a limited number of cases provided for by special acts. Chattel mortgages may be taken on motor vehicles (see topic Motor Vehicles); on ships (Arts. 61-72 C.C.M.); on airplanes (Art. 19 C.A.L.). However, these chattel mortgages have no effect even between parties thereto unless they are registered in special registry provided for purpose. (Art. 20 C.C.M.; Art. 19 C.A.L.).

Law of Mar. 27, 1963 constitutes within certain conditions a lien in favor of sellers of chattels sold on instalment, and evidenced by a notarized contract. Such liens are not valid for more than two years, and cannot be enforced against a bona fide assignee of the mortgage.

It is to be noted that chattel mortgage does not give mortgagee right to take possession of mortgaged chattel; he only has right to demand sale of mortgaged article at public auction, and to participate in bidding.

COLLATERAL SECURITY: See topic Pledges.

COMMERCIAL ESTABLISHMENTS:

(Law No. 11, promulgated July 11, 1967).

A commercial establishment consists of nonmaterial and material elements, comprizing firm name, trade name, lease, clientelle and business site. (Art. 15). Contracts affecting commercial establishment must be evidenced in writing, and they cannot be enforced against third parties unless registered in Register of Commerce. (Art. 3). Establishment may be sold or assigned (Arts. 5-21); it may be mortgaged (Arts. 22-28); attached (Arts. 29-36). Contracts for its management by an agent, or by a simple employee, or by an independent management in guise of a lease thereof by a person with a view to operating same for his own account, are permissible. (Arts. 38-46).

COMMERCIAL REGISTER:

Commercial Register is kept in records office of court of first instance. Merchants, companies and corporations doing business in Lebanon must be registered in Register of Commerce.

COMMERCIAL REGISTER . . . *continued*

Full information concerning capital, nature of business, persons in charge of management and having right to sign for firm are noted in Register. (Arts. 22-29 C.C.).

Registration is carried out by a petition submitted by person responsible for business, or his agent, to Registrar of Records Office of Court of First Instance where business is located. Unless otherwise specifically provided for in Code of Commerce, Registration should be carried out within period of one month of date of act or fact that needs to be registered. (Art. 31 C.C.). Failure to carry out registration within period specified subjects person responsible therefor to a fine ranging from 50 Lebanese pounds to 1,000 Lebanese pounds (Art. 37 C.C. as am'd). Any false information wilfully submitted for registration subjects responsible person to a fine ranging between 250 and 5,000 Lebanese pounds. (Art. 38 C.C. as am'd). These penalties are applicable without prejudice to fact that any information registration of which is required by law under pain of nullity cannot be enforced against third parties. (Art. 39 C.C.).

CONSTITUTION AND GOVERNMENT:

Lebanon as a Republic came into existence in 1920, and was endowed by the French High Commissioner under the Mandate with a Constitution similar to that of France. Under this Constitution the powers in the state are three, Legislative, Judical, and Executive.

Legislative power is vested in the Chamber of Deputies. There is at present no second chamber. The deputies are elected by universal suffrage, and their mandate is for four years. At present there are ninety-nine deputies. The Chamber enacts the laws on the proposal of the deputies or the Council of Ministers.

Judicial Power.—See topic Courts.

Executive Power.—President of Council of Ministers is appointed by President of Republic who has to consult with President of Chamber of Deputies. He is Head of Government and responsible with his Ministers to Chamber of Deputies.

President of Republic is Head of State. He is elected by Chamber of Deputies for period of six years and may not be reelected until expiration of six years thereafter. He may preside over Council of Ministers whenever he wishes but has no voting right. He signs laws and treaties with approval of President of Council of Ministers. He is Head of Armed Forces and Guardian of Constitution and of Independence, Unity and Safety of State.

For transitory period, representation in Chamber of Deputies, appointment of Ministers and holding of high office are based on religious affiliation. Seats in Chamber of Deputies are provided in proportion to number of various communities, equally shared between Christians and Moslems.

Constitutional Council.—Control of constitutionality of laws, and settlement of disputes regarding election of President of Republic and of Deputies are vested in Constitutional Council.

CONTRACTS:

Excuses for Nonperformance.—Force majeure; extinction of principal obligation entails extinction of accessory obligations and of mortgages given as guarantee; prescription; impossibility of execution. (Arts. 254, 290, 291, 341, C.O.C.).

Applicable law is law agreed upon between parties, provided contract is not contrary to public policy of state.

If contract contains no express agreement as to law applicable, court will seek to ascertain intention of parties, and will decide accordingly.

Normally, law applicable is that of country more closely connected with contract. Where contract is one for sale of real property, law applicable is law of situs of property.

Government Contracts.—Only contractors inscribed on List of "Accepted Contractors" are permitted to make offers for government contracts. For enterprises of a large magnitude, international bids are called for. With offer, contractor must deposit a sum equivalent to 3% of total amount of works involved. Certified check on a recognized bank is acceptable.

COPYRIGHT:

See topic Protection of Commercial, Industrial, Literary and Artistic Property.

CORPORATIONS:

Founders must be three or more in number. They are jointly responsible for the engagements taken, and the disbursements made before the constitution of the society. (C. C. 79).

Incorporation.—Except for number of activities for which authorization of government is still required by special laws and regulations (e.g., banking, insurance), corporation (société anonyme) is now constituted without such authorization. By-laws must be deposited and registered with notary public; same procedure applies to any amendment to by-laws. (C. C. 80 as am'd).

Corporations constituted for exploitation of public service must have one-third of capital in name of Lebanese subscribers; these shares may not be ceded to other than Lebanese citizens. (C. C. 78 as am'd).

Corporations constituted for exploitation of banking activities must have one-half of capital registered in name of Lebanese subscribers; these shares may not be ceded to other than Lebanese citizens. (Art. 132 of Statute on Currency and Credit as am'd by Decree Law No. 77 of June 27, 1977).

Head Office.—Every corporation founded in Lebanon must have its head office in Lebanon and is always of Lebanese nationality despite any clause to contrary. (C. C. 78 as am'd).

Capital cannot be inferior to 30,000,000 Lebanese Pounds, all subscribed. (C. C. 83 as am'd).

Reserve.—The board of directors must constitute a reserve fund by setting aside 10% of the net profits realized, and keep doing so until the reserve fund shall be equivalent to one-third of the capital. (C. C. 165).

Publication of Notice.—Before any appeal for subscriptions can be made to public, notice must be inserted in Official Journal, in one local newspaper and in one financial paper, bearing signature and address of each of founders, and indicating, among other things, name and seat of corporation and of its branches, its object, period, capital, number of directors and their fees, conditions requisite for the distribution of dividends. (C. C. Art. 81 as am'd).

Stock.—The minimum face value of each share cannot be inferior to 1,000 Lebanese pounds. (C.C. 84). Contributions made in kind must be valued by an expert designated by the President of the Court of First Instance. (C. C. 86). There are no founders' shares. (C. C. 103).

Bonds.—Corporations may issue loan-bonds, as well as bonds convertible into stock at option of bondholders. (C. C. 103 as am'd). Bonds so issued may not exceed in total twice amount of capital of issuing corporation, as it appears, in last approved balance sheet. (C. C. 124 as am'd).

Increase of Capital.—In the event of increasing the capital, the shareholders have a right of preference to subscribe the projected increase proportionally to the shares held by them, unless the general assembly convened for the purpose should decide otherwise. (C. C. 112, 113).

Directors.—Board of directors consists of not less than three and not more than 12 members of whom majority must be Lebanese, unless otherwise provided for by special laws. (C. C. 144 as am'd). Original directors named in by-laws of corporation hold office for five years; those elected by general assembly, for three years. (C. C. 149 as am'd).

Dissolution.—The loss of the reserve fund and one-half of the capital will bring about the dissolution of the society.

Limited liability companies (Legislative Decree No. 35, promulgated Aug. 5, 1967, as annex to Code of Commerce, Book II, Sec. VII) are formed between partners whose number may not be less than three or more than 20. Partners may not be charged with losses beyond their contribution to the capital. In case of devolution of shares by way of inheritance, number of partners may exceed 20, but not beyond number of 30. (Arts. 1 and 5).

Limited liability companies may engage in any commercial enterprise other than insurance, economic, savings, regular air transport, banking and investments for others. (Art. 4).

Capital.—Minimum capital is 5,000,000 Lebanese pounds divided into equal shares. (Art. 7). It should be completely paid up. Shares of partners may not be converted into notes capable of circulation, and company may not issue for its own account by way of open subscription or promissory notes any movable property or promissory notes, or founders shares (Art. 3) under penalty of prosecution for fraud (Art. 36). Contributions to capital may be either in cash or specific objects, and in latter case, specific objects must be appraised in same manner as in societes anonymes (Art. 9), and partners contributing specific objects and first directors are jointly liable to third parties for period of five years commencing with formation of company for any improper appraisal of specific objects (Art. 10), and any person who through maneuvers appraises specific objects at a figure exceeding by 20% their real value will be liable for fraud (Art. 35).

Capital may be increased by vote of partners who represent at least three-fourths of capital. (Arts. 26 and 27). Assembly of partners representing same majority may diminish capital, always provided such diminution safeguards rights of third parties. (Art. 29).

In event of a loss equivalent to at least three-fourths of capital, partners should take a resolution by a majority of three-fourths either to dissolve company, or to reduce capital by an amount equivalent to loss; if they fail to do so, any person having an interest may petition court for dissolution of company. (Art. 33).

It is permissible for partners representing three-fourths of capital to cede shares to a nonpartner; however, preference is given to company, or to one or more partners to purchase such shares. (Art. 15).

Capital must in its entirety be paid up and deposited in a bank chartered by government.

Name is determined by object of Company, or by name of one or more of partners provided there is added thereto phrase "limited liability," and provided capital is named, all under penalty of holding partners fully responsible without any limit, and to a fine varying between 100,000 to 300,000 Lebanese pounds. (Art. 6).

Formation.—Company may be formed by an ordinary or by an official deed duly recorded in Register of Commerce (Art. 2) and it is subject to same publicity as société anonyme (Art. 10). Company is not deemed to be duly constituted until distribution of shares among partners and determination of number of shares held by each of them, until shares are fully paid up and sum is deposited in a bank (Art. 8).

Management is entrusted to one or more directors from among partners, or others determined by by-laws of company, or by a subsequent deed, and that for a definite or an indefinite period. (Art. 16). Director or directors are clothed with powers which are requisite and necessary for management of company. (Art. 16). Director or directors may not be dismissed without a plausible cause; otherwise they may demand damages for unjust dismissal. (Art. 16). Director or directors may not withdraw sums deposited in bank in name of company before it is recorded in Register of Commerce (Art. 8) under penalty of fraud (Art. 35). Director or directors are responsible severally or jointly to company and to third parties for any contravention of provisions of legislative decree and by-laws for their mistakes, and any partner may bring action any clause in by-laws to contrary notwithstanding. (Art. 19).

General assembly is convened annually to pass on and approve acts of directors and budget and inventory, and whenever necessity calls, by a summons given by director or auditor, if there is one, and if they fail, any partner may petition court for designation of a person to convene assembly. (Arts. 21 and 23).

Every partner has so many votes as shares he holds or represents. No partner may appoint a proxy other than a partner, unless by-laws authorize same. Resolutions are passed by votes of partners representing at least one-half of shares, and if such majority is not attained, resolution may be passed by a second assembly summoned subsequently, and by a simple majority of capital it represents whatever it may be. (Art. 25). However, changing nationality of company or forcing of a partner to

CORPORATIONS . . . *continued*
increase his contribution to capital, or his obligations to company requires a unanimous vote, and no amendment of by-laws is permissible except by a majority representing three-fourths of capital. (Art. 26).

Auditors.—Partners shall designate one or more auditors if: (1) Their number is over 20; (2) capital exceeds 50,000,000 Lebanese pounds; (3) required by one or more partners representing at least one fifth of capital.

Holding Companies (created by Decree Law No. 45 of June 24, 1983).—Holding company is corporation objects of which are limited to following: Own shares in corporations and limited liability companies within and without Lebanon; participate in formation of corporations and limited liability companies, manage same, lend money and give its guarantee to same; own patents, licenses and trademarks and lease same to establishments within and without Lebanon; own chattels and real estate required by its activities (subject to law on acquisition of real property by foreigners: See topic Aliens, subhead Acquisition of Real Property).

Holding companies may not lend money to companies operating in Lebanon if their participation in equity of same is less than 20%.

Holding companies may not own directly participation exceeding 40% in capital of more than two companies operating within Lebanon in same industrial, commercial or noncommercial field if such ownership is meant to defraud law on monopolies (see topic Monopolies and Restraints of Trade); this limitation does not apply to investments without Lebanon.

Capital of holding companies may be expressed in foreign currency.

Board of directors of holding companies must include minimum of two Lebanese members, but its president may be foreigner and need not have work permit if he is nonresident.

Holding companies must have a registered office, but need not have place of business, in Lebanon; they must appoint at least one resident Lebanese auditor, and must keep their books and file their tax returns in accordance with Lebanese law. (For income tax, see topic Taxation, subhead Holding Companies.)

Off-Shore Companies (created by Decree Law No. 46 of June 24, 1983).—Off-shore company is corporation objects of which are limited to following: Negotiate and sign contracts concerning operations and deals to be performed without Lebanon on goods and materials located abroad or in customs free zone; use free zone facilities for storage and reexport of imported goods; lease offices in Lebanon and own real property required for its activities (subject to law on acquisition of real property by foreigners: See topic Aliens, subhead Acquisition of Real Property); make studies and give consultations at request of nonresident establishments, to be used without Lebanon.

Off-shore companies may not engage in any industrial, banking, insurance or holding business, or carry out any commercial operations within Lebanon other than those listed in their objects as above defined.

Off-shore companies must, upon registration in register of commerce, produce as security bank guarantee in amount of 10,000,000 Lebanese pounds issued by one of banks accepted in Lebanon.

Requirements regarding board of directors, auditors and bookkeeping are similar to those mentioned for holding companies. (See subhead Holding Companies, supra.)

For income tax, see topic Taxation, subhead Off-Shore Companies.

Foreign corporations (Sociétés anonymes) and partnerships having a silent partner, whose capital is evidenced by shares of stock (sociétés en commandite par action), before they can open up branches or agencies in the Lebanese Republic are required to submit to the Lebanese Administration a declaration, backed by their by-laws, and by their charter or act of incorporation. They should likewise name a duly authorized agent or agents to speak in the name of the corporation and represent it in all matters. Any subsequent modifications in the by-laws or charter, and any change of the agent or agents should be notified to the Administration.

All corporations (sociétés anonymes), and limited liability companies, whether Lebanese or foreign, doing business in Lebanon by means of branch office or agency established on Lebanese territory, must appoint Lebanese attorney-at-law paid on basis of yearly retainer fee. (Art. 63, of Law No. 8/70 of Mar. 11, 1970 as am'd by Law No. 18/78).

Foreign corporations must be registered at the clerk's office of the Court of First Instance.

Failure to comply with the preceding requirements will expose the delinquent foreign corporation to incapacity to appear as plaintiff before the courts, and the payment of a fine. Foreign corporations that comply with these requirements are treated in all respects on a footing of equality with national corporations and societies.

Foreign insurance companies (Decree No. 9812 of May 4, 1968) cannot do business in Lebanon unless authorized by Decree issued by Ministry of National Economy. No authorization may be granted unless following conditions are complied with: (1) Foreign insurance company should be a corporation (société anonyme) with a fully paid capital of at least 100,000,000 Lebanese pounds or its equivalent in foreign currency, Lloyd's Group and Mutual Funds are exempted from this condition (Art. 4); (2) petition submitted to Ministry of National Economy must be accompanied by its by-laws, charter or act of incorporation, an exposé of its intended activities, a certificate establishing amount of paid-up capital, a certificate establishing deposit of required bond, a certificate proving that Lebanese insurance companies are permitted to do business in foreign countries to which they belong, a balance sheet for financial year preceding date of petition (Arts. 3, 4); (3) company should have capacity to do same kind of business in its own country; (4) it should elect domicile in Lebanon; (5) it should submit for approval of Ministry of National Economy name of its duly authorized Agent to represent it in all matters (Art. 4). Any subsequent modification in declaration or in documents submitted as well as any change of agent should be notified to Ministry of National Economy. (Art. 5).

Free Exchange.—See topics Foreign Exchange; Foreign Investments.

Income Tax.—See topic Taxation, subhead Tax Holiday.

COURTS:

Judicial Power.—There are three degrees of courts, viz., Courts of First Instance, Appeal, and Cassation-Revision.

Courts of First Instance are of two kinds: (1) Sole Judge Courts having jurisdiction of all civil actions, real and personal, with exception of bankruptcies, under 10,000,000 Lebanese pounds. All actions under 800,000 Lebanese pounds are final and not open to any appeal. (2) District Courts of First Instance, one in each of the Five Districts of Lebanon: consisting of three judges. These Courts have general jurisdiction in all civil matters not specifically attributed to the sole Judge Courts of First Instance.

Courts of Appeal, five in number, one for each District. Composed of three Judges. These courts have authority to pass on questions of fact and questions of law.

The Cour de Cassation-Revision passes on questions of law exclusively.

Criminal Courts.—In criminal cases there are degrees viz., the Criminal Court of First Instance. Appeal is taken therefrom directly to the "Cour de Cassation". Trial by jury does not exist. This court passes on questions of fact, and applies the law.

Administrative Courts.—Claims against the government and the administrative departments are decided by a special court called "Conseil d'Etat".

See also topic Labor Relations.

CURRENCY:

Monetary unit is Lebanese pound. (Art. 1). Pending determination of its value in relation to gold standard, its value in relation to U.S. dollar is fixed at rate of the dollar on open market. Only State Bank, Bank of Lebanon, may issue bank notes with unrestricted legal tender value. Paper currency in actual circulation is 50, 100, 250, 500, 1,000, 5,000, 10,000, 20,000, 50,000 and 100,000 pound notes. Coins in actual circulation are 25, 50, 100, 250 and 500 pounds. Foreigners when in Lebanon are not subject to any control, or currency restrictions. Lebanese nationals and residents may keep foreign currency up to any amount. (Law Aug. 1, 1964).

See also topics Corporations; Foreign Investments.

CUSTOMS DUTIES:

Goods entering Lebanon are subject to a customs duty calculated in the basis of ad valorem value of the goods, or in their weight, depending on nature of the goods. Generally, valuable goods are taxed ad valorem—luxury articles, precious metals, jewelry, etc., but bulky, heavy goods are taxed by weight. Automobiles are taxed on weight or ad valorem depending on which is more advantageous to Treasury. Goods necessary for Lebanese industries are generally exempt.

DEATH:

There is no presumption of death. In the case of long absence of a person, oral testimony may be received, though not conclusively, to the effect that all such person's contemporaries in the locality have died.

Certificates of death may be obtained from the Department of Vital Statistics, Ministry of Interior. However, such certificates are generally given upon presentation of a power of attorney from a party entitled to same. It is more expeditious to obtain certificates through a local attorney.

Actions for Death.—See topic Limitations, Statute of.

DECEDENTS' ESTATES:

See topic Executors and Administrators.

DEPOSITIONS:

The Lebanese courts, by comity, will execute letters rogatory. If issued by an American court, these should be transmitted through the ordinary diplomatic channels. A more expeditious way is to send a commission to the American Consulate General in Beirut. The power of the courts and the American Consulate is more limited than under the Anglo-American practice.

DESCENT AND DISTRIBUTION:

The Moslem Community—Devolution of Property Owned in Fee.—The heirs at law are called in the following order:

(1) Those Having a Legal Reserve.—The quantum of the legal reserve is fixed and must be satisfied before the residue of the estate can be distributed. The following are the legal reservists and their reserve.

(a) The Father.—In the presence of male descendants, son, son of a son, how low soever, one-sixth of the estate. In the presence of sole female descendants, daughter, daughter of a daughter, one-sixth as legal reservist and two-sixths as residuary. In the presence of two or more female descendants, one-sixth as legal reservist, and one-sixth as residuary. In the absence of any male or female descendants, the father takes the entire estate.

(b) The Mother.—In the presence of descendants, or of two or more brothers and sisters, one-sixth of the entire estate, and in their absence, one-third thereof. In the absence of descendants and of two or more brothers and sisters, but in the presence of husband and wife, one third of the residue after the husband or wife has received his or her legal reserve.

(c) The Grandfather.—In the absence of the father, the grandfather takes the legal reserve of the father, with the following difference, however: (x) In the presence of the father, the father's mother has no legal reserve, but with the grandfather, she has; (y) in the presence of the father and a husband or wife, the father's mother receives one-third of the residue after the payment of the legal reserve of the husband and wife; with the grandfather, she receives one-third of the entire estate.

(d) The Grandmother.—One-sixth of the estate. She is barred by the mother.

(e) The Sister German or of the Whole-Blood.—If sole, one-half of the entire estate; if two or more and no male heir, two-thirds thereof. If she comes with male heir (brother german), the male gets double the portion of the female. If she comes with the sole daughter, the daughter takes her legal reserve of one-half of the estate, and the

DESCENT AND DISTRIBUTION . . . *continued*

sister german the residue. If she comes with two daughters, the two daughters receive two-thirds and the sister german takes the residue. If she comes with the daughter and the daughter of a predeceased son, the daughter receives one-half, the daughter of the one one-sixth and the sister german the residue. If she comes with a son, or the son of a son, how low soever, or with the father or grandfather, how high soever, she is barred.

(f) The Consanguine Sister.—If sole, one-half of the estate, if two or more, two-thirds thereof. If she comes with the consanguine brother, the male gets double the portion of the female. If she comes with the daughter, or the daughter of a son, these receive their legal reserves and the residue goes to the consanguine sister. If she comes with two or more sisters german, or with the son, the son of the son, the father, the grandfather, or the brother german, she is barred.

(g) The Daughter.—If sole, one-half of the estate; if two or more, two-thirds thereof. If she comes with the son, the male gets double the portion of the female.

(h) The Daughter of the Son.—If sole, one-half of the estate; if two or more, two-thirds thereof. If she comes with the son of the son, the male gets the double of the portion of the female. She is barred by the two daughters unless she comes with a male heir, or unless she comes with the son of the son, she is likewise barred by the son.

(i) Children of the Mother from a Former Marriage.—If sole, one-sixth of the estate, if two or more, one-third thereof. They are barred by descendants and by male ascendants. The distinction between the portions of the male and the female does not exist here.

(j) The Husband.—In the absence of any children, one-half of the estate; in their presence, one-fourth thereof.

(k) The Wife.—In the absence of children, one-fourth of the estate, in their presence, one-eighth thereof.

(2) Universal Heirs or Residuaries.—These are the consanguine relations who inherit the entire estate in the absence of legal reservists, or who take the residue after the legal reservists have been paid.

(3) Reversionists.—These are the legal reservists who receive the remainder of the estate, each in proportion to his or her legal reserve, in the absence of residuaries.

(4) Uterine Heirs.—These are the relations of the decedent who do not belong to the class of legal reservists, or to the class of universal heirs or residuaries, as the son of the daughter, son of a sister, father of the mother.

(5) Legatees.—For that portion of their legacies which exceeds the one-third of the estate.

(6) The State.—In the absence of all these foregoing heirs, the estate escheats to the state.

Devolution of Miri and Wakf Lands.—Miri lands are state domains. Wakf is mortmain. In both of these classes the dominium plenum is in the state, while the legal possession and use, together with the right to transmit to heirs, and to alienate inter vivos are in the tenant. The Miri lands and Wakf devolve on the heirs in the following order: (1) The children, male and female, share and share alike; (2) the grandchildren, male and female, share and share alike, per stirpes; (3) the father and mother; (4) brothers and sisters german or of the whole blood; (5) brothers and sisters consanguine; (6) brothers and sisters uterine; (7) the surviving spouse.

The children of a predeceased son or daughter inherit by representation the part of their predeceased parent. The father and mother, if they come concurrently with the children and grandchildren, have a legal reserve of one-sixth. The surviving spouse, if he or she comes concurrently with the heirs of the first class, has a legal reserve of one-fourth, and if with the heirs of the second class, one-half.

Non-Moslem Community—Christians and Jews.—The Inheritance Law of June 23, 1959, introduced new legislative provisions for the Christians and Jews. (Citations under the subhead are to Articles thereof). It placed the sexes on a footing of equality, established the right of representation, and amended the distributive share of the surviving spouse.

Classes of Heirs.—Under the new law heirs are divided into three classes: (1) the issue and their issue in line descending; (2) father and mother and their ascendants; (3) brothers and sisters and their issue. (Art. 14).

Legal Reserves.—Legal reserves have been established as follows: One-sixth to the parents and the survivor of them. (Art. 19); one-fourth to the surviving spouse in the presence of issue; one half to the surviving spouse in the absence of issue and the presence of father, mother, brothers and sisters; five-sixths to the surviving spouse in the presence of grandparents only; the whole in the absence of any of these heirs. (Art. 20).

The residue, after deduction of funeral expenses, debts and legacies, is distributed as follows: (1) issue and their issue in line descending (Art. 15); (2) the father and mother in the absence of issue, in equal shares; and if either predeceases the decedent, his or her share passes to his or her issue by representation; and in the absence of issue, the share passes to the other parent. If both parents predecease the decedent, their shares pass to their issue, but among such issue the right of representation is limited to the issue of the predeceased brother or sister (Art. 16); (3) in the absence of issue and parents and their issue, the estate passes to the grandparents in equal shares, the share of a predeceased grandparent passing to his or her issue by representation; and in the absence of such issue, to the grandparent on the same side, paternal or maternal; and in the absence of paternal and maternal grandparents, to their issue. (Art. 17).

Adopted Child.—The adopted child is treated on a footing of equality with the legitimate child. (Art. 23).

Illegitimate Child.—The illegitimate child inherits from the person who voluntarily acknowledges its parenthood. Its distributive shares is fixed as follows: (1) one-fourth of the portion of legitimate child in the presence of legitimate issue; (2) one half, in the presence of legitimate parents and brothers and sisters and their issue; (3) three-fourths, in the absence of these and the presence of other legitimate heirs; (4) the entire estate in absence of legitimate heirs. (Art. 24).

Posthumous Child.—Inherits if born within 300 days of the demise of the decedent.

Determination of Heirship.—The heirs are determined in a proceeding of "Devolution of Succession." If several persons perish in the same accident, the court will determine the dates of their respective deaths, taking into consideration the attending circumstances, age, physical condition and other relevant considerations. If it is not possible to determine the dates, all are deemed to have perished simultaneously. (Art. 6).

Nationality.—Difference of nationality is no impediment to inheritance if the national law of the alien accords reciprocal treatment to Lebanese citizens. (Art. 8). Difference of religion is an impediment (Under the Moslem Shar'i Law, a Moslem cannot inherit from a Christian, and vice versa.).

Escheat.—The estate escheats on the failure of heirs.

DISPUTE RESOLUTION:

Mandatory Dispute Resolution.—There exists no mandatory dispute resolution except in matters regarding labor relations (see topic Labor Relations, subhead Labor Disputes).

Voluntary Dispute Resolution.—Parties with full legal capacity may always agree to submit disputes to arbitration. For enforcement, original of arbitral award must be recorded in Records Office of Court of First Instance within which jurisdiction arbitration was carried out. Enforcement is granted by order of President of said Court.

For foreign arbitral awards see topic Judgments, subhead Exequatur of Foreign and International Arbitral Awards.

DIVORCE:

Divorce is governed by the Canon Law. Each community has its canon or ecclesiastical courts. Causes differ with the different communities. No uniform civil law is possible owing to the presence of so many religions and religious courts, each guarding jealously the privileges and rights enjoyed from times past.

Moslem Community.—The majority is Sunnite and follow the Hanafi Rite. The law concedes to the husband the right to dissolve the marriage. He can, therefore, put an end to the marriage at his uncontrolled option (the wife may do so only if the husband has conferred such power on her in the marriage contract, which is rarely, if ever, done). The dissolution of the marriage by the husband's own act is called Talak, repudiation, divorce. Talak is of two kinds, Raj'ai or revocable, which permits the husband to resume the conjugal relations, and Ba'en or irrevocable or absolute. A divorce which is revocable in its inception becomes irrevocable if the 'Iddat (period of probation, three menstrual periods) is allowed to elapse without the husband having revoked his act either expressly or tacitly. Divorce is effected by the husband making a declaration of the following sentence thrice at one and the same time: "I have divorced thee," or by saying at one and the same time: "I have divorced thee thrice."

Apart from the dissolution of the marriage by the husband's own act, the law allows the dissolution in certain cases by a decree of the court. Such dissolution is called "furkat." If furkat is decreed for a cause imputable to the wife, it has the effect of annulment.

Remarriage.—A woman who is divorced is prohibited from marrying within three menstrual periods or, if pregnant, until she gives birth to a child, and if past the age of menstruation, within three months from the divorce. The husband who divorces his wife cannot remarry her until she has been married to another man, and such second marriage has terminated after consummation (tahlil) and the period of probation ('Iddat) on account of her second marriage has elapsed.

As to dower in case of dissolution of marriage or separation, see topic Dower.

Children.—Custody of children of tender years, boys until the age of seven, girls until nine, is accorded of the wife. These ages passed, custody is given to the husband.

Catholic and Maronite Communities.—Communities under the jurisdiction of the Church of Rome. Jurisdiction is in the canon, or ecclesiastical courts of the Catholic and Maronite communities. The applicable law is the Canon Law of the Church of Rome, under which the marriage is indissoluble. Annulment or separation may be had in certain cases.

Protestant Community.—Jurisdiction is in the canon courts of the community. Law applicable is the personal status of the Protestant community.

Causes of Divorce.—(1) Adultery; (2) incurable insanity of either spouse; (3) attempt against the life of either spouse by the other; (4) adoption by either spouse of a religion other than the Christian religion; (5) five years absence; (6) refusal by either spouse to cohabit with the other for a period of five years continuously, without a legitimate cause.

Action may not be maintained where: (1) The offense was committed by procurement, or with the connivance of the plaintiff; (2) the offense has been condoned either expressly or tacitly; (3) the action was not commenced within six months after the discovery of the offense charged, or five years after its occurrence.

Separation.—Separation forever or for a limited time may be granted for cruel and inhuman treatment or unsafe and improper conduct which renders the continuance of married life insupportable. Damages are awarded in the discretion of the court to the party in whose favor the decree is rendered.

Children.—The court may make directions for custody of the children pending the action and thereafter. If they are of tender years and the wife is unworthy, the court may entrust the custody of the nearest relative on the father's side.

Remarriage.—The guilty party may not remarry for five years following issuance of the decree. After the expiration of this period, he or she may remarry only with a special decision of the court which rendered the decree, and provided his or her conduct has been exemplary. A divorced woman may not remarry within nine months from the issuance of the decree or, if pregnant, until she gives birth to the child.

Greek Orthodox Community.—The husband may sue for divorce for the following causes: (1) Discovery that the wife is not a virgin; (2) wilful destruction by the wife of the husband's seed; (3) if the wife sleeps outside of the conjugal home, attends banquets or bathes with men in mixed baths, all against the husband's orders; (4) if she goes to the races, theaters, or gambling halls surreptitiously or against the husband's orders; (5) adultery; (6) refusal for three years to obey a court order to cohabit with the husband; (7) refusal to obey the husband's repeated orders not to visit a special person or house.

The wife may sue for divorce for the following causes: (1) Impotence of the husband; (2) if he accuses her of adultery and fails to prove the charge; (3) if the husband encourages the wife to prostitution; (4) if he neglects her for three years; (5)

See Topical Index in front part of this volume.

DIVORCE . . . *continued*
adultery of the husband in the conjugal home and refusal by the husband to mend his ways.

Both husband and wife may sue for divorce for the following causes: (1) Incurable insanity; (2) joining the monastic orders; (3) attempt by either spouse against the life of the other; (4) sentence of imprisonment for five years or more for a defamatory offense; (5) adoption of another religion.

Remarriage.—Both may remarry; however, the wife may not do so before the expiration of four months.

Aliens.—Foreigners are subject to their national laws in matters of divorce, separation, alimony, and the custody of the children. All actions are brought before Civil Courts. Duly certified copy of national law must be submitted to court.

DOWER:

Dower (mahr) is a sum of money to which the wife becomes entitled by the marriage. The right of the wife thereto is perfected on consummation of the marriage or valid retirement (khulwa Sahiha). In case of dissolution of marriage by the husband or separation for some cause attributable to the husband (see topic Divorce) the dower becomes due and payable to the wife.

ENVIRONMENT:

Ministry of Environment, organized by Decree No. 5591 of Aug. 30, 1994, includes five departments, namely: Administration, Protection of Nature, Protection of Inhabited Environment, Prevention of Consequences of Technology and Risks of Nature, Intervention and Repression.

Hunting is regulated by order No. 110/1 of May 18, 1995 meant to protect all kinds of birds and land animals.

ESCHEAT: See topic Descent and Distribution.

EXCHANGE CONTROL:

See topic Foreign Exchange.

EXECUTIONS:

There are several forms: "Saisie arret" to attach debts, sums of money of personal property, belonging to the debtor and held by third persons; "saisie immobiliere," which operates on realty owned by the debtor; "saisie brandon," which operates on growing crops; "saisie conservatoire," resorted to as a safeguard to prevent the debtor from disposing of his property and rendering any judgment which may be recovered by the creditor of little or no value. It operates on all property owned by the debtor. Each of these forms has its special procedure, which is formalistic and complicated.

See also topics Judgments; Garnishment.

EXECUTORS AND ADMINISTRATORS:

There is no procedure which corresponds exactly to probate and the grant of letters of administration. The estate vests directly in the heirs, who administer it themselves.

Moslem Community.—The competent court is the Shar'i court, which upon the petition of an heir or a creditor will render a decree designating the heirs and their distributive shares. The heirs administer the property. If voluntary partition is not possible, partition is made by the court, and the transfers of realty registered in the Land Registry.

Non-Moslem Communities—Christians and Jews.—(References below are to the Law of Inheritance, promulgated June 23, 1959 affecting estates of Christians and Jews.) The succession is opened at last domicile of decedent irrespective of where property is situated. A married woman is deemed to have the same domicile as her husband; a minor, at the domicile of his guardian, and in the absence of a guardian at the situs of the bulk of the property. (Arts. 2, 3).

Settlement of the Estate at Request of a Party in Interest.—The competent court is the court of the place where the succession or estate is opened. It has jurisdiction over the making of the inventory, the distribution of the assets, and the partition of the estate among the heirs and persons having a right therein. (Arts. 93, 95).

The inventory may be made: (1) upon the petition of an heir, or a person having a right in the estate, or the executor; (2) if among the heirs or the persons having a right in the estate there is a minor who has lost his father, or if he is a person lacking capacity, or an absent one who has no agent to act for him. (Art. 94). The petition is heard by the judge of the court of first instance in chambers: objection to his decree may be made by any person who is harmed thereby. The opposition to the decree does not suspend the operation of inventory taking if the petitioner for the taking of same furnishes the necessary bond. The court may demand a bond from the person making the opposition. (Art. 95). The inventory is taken by an expert appointed by the judge. (Art. 96).

Settlement and Partition.—When the inventory is taken, the judge summons the heirs and persons having a right in the estate to appear before him on a fixed date with the evidence of their title or right, and a declaration as to whether or not they accept the inheritance. (Art. 98). If the parties in interest agree to remain in a state of indivision, the court will order the delivery of the assets to those entitled thereto against their receipt. Special legacies are paid to the legatees. Creditors may attach the property held in common, and reserve the right to pursue the heirs and legatees in proportion to their shares and legacies. (Art. 99). If one of the heirs demands partition, a notice is published in the Official Journal and one or more newspapers, and a copy thereof is posted at the door of the court or at some place near the domicile of the decedent, inviting all the parties in interest and the creditors to submit evidence of their rights within six months of the insertion of the notice in the Official Journal. (Art. 100). Upon the expiration of this delay, the court will summon the parties in interest and creditors to a meeting to discuss an amicable settlement (Art. 101), which if arrived at, the judge will confirm by decree rendered in chambers; if no settlement is arrived at each party having a claim must bring action within a delay which the court will fix (Art. 102). If action is commenced within the delay fixed, the judge will set a date for a hearing to examine whether or not to suspend the settlement and partition. (Art. 103). If the settlement pursues its course, the heirs may agree among themselves to partition the estate in the manner they may choose. (Art. 104). If they do not agree, the judge will draw up a plan for partition, calling in expert opinion if necessary. If the plan is approved, the judge will confirm it by decree rendered in chambers. (Art. 105). If one of the heirs rejects the plan, he will be asked to submit his opposition thereto, and the judge will render a judgment that shall not be open to any appeal or other recourse. (Art. 106). If the property does not lend itself to partition, it is sold at public auction. (Art. 107).

Settlement of Estate When Heirs are Unknown.—When the heirs are unknown, the "Mukhtar" (Civil officer of the Administration) of the locality where the decedent was domiciled notifies the court of the death, and the judge will render a decree in chambers for settlement of the estate. (Art. 110). After taking of the inventory, the court will deposit cash and other valuables in a bank, and deliver the remainder to a custodian to administer the same. The custodian or administrator may be required to furnish bond. Perishable goods are sold and the proceeds deposited in the bank. (Art. 111). If after five years no heirs present themselves, the judge will decree in chambers the delivery of the property to the State. (Art. 112). The custodian or administrator renders an account of his administration to the court, which will fix his fee, pay the same, and order the delivery of the residue to the State. (Art. 113). If thereafter an heir appears, he may claim the estate from the State. (Art. 114).

Settlement of Estate When One of Heirs Is a Minor or Lacks Capacity.—In such cases, the court on its own motion or upon information may decree the settlement of the estate. (Art. 119). It may appoint a guardian. (Art. 120). After taking inventory, proper measures are taken to safeguard the interests of the minor and the incapable, and then if no heir demands it, the court will determine if settlement is to be proceeded with, and the share of the minor and/or the incapable will be deposited in a bank. (Art. 121). If the judge finds it to the interest of the minor and/or the incapable to partition the estate, the guardian will represent his ward; however, all the contracts he may execute must be ratified by the judge. (Art. 122).

Executors.—The powers of the executor may be defined by the testator, and if same are not so defined, the executor will administer the estate, pay the debts and legacies and deliver other property according to the terms of the will. (Art. 82). If several executors are designated, they will act jointly unless otherwise specified in the will; all are jointly responsible for the assets of the estate. (Art. 83). The heirs may not dispose of the assets, or interfere with the administration in the presence of an executor. (Art. 85). Actions are brought against the executor. (Art. 86). The executor must promptly notify his acceptance of the charge to the heirs, give them a statement of the assets and liabilities, and inform them of the date of the settlement of the estate. (Art. 87). The heirs may demand the submission of yearly accounting if the period of services is long. (Art. 89). An executor may not be released of responsibility for his administration. (Art. 90). If the executor's fee is not fixed by the testator, he may demand a reasonable fee. (Art. 91).

The executor may be dismissed upon the complaint of an heir for failure to perform his duties, or if he becomes unfit for the performance of the same. (Art. 92).

In all cases, whether the person dies testate or intestate, the procedure consists of a party in interest—heir, next of kin, or creditor—petitioning the court for a decree determining the heirs and the distributive share of each. For Christian and other non-Moslem Communities competent court is Civil Court; for Moslem Community it is Shar'i.

If a person dies intestate, the administration is in the hands of the heirs and the distributive share of each will serve a copy of same on the Land Registrar for transfer of real property. If person of non-Moslem Community dies testate, Decree of Devolution of Succession will certify presence of will, and distribution of estate pursuant to testator's wishes. Will is then deposited together with certified copy of Decree of Devolution of Succession in Bureau d'Execution for execution according to its tenor. If there are minors, or if there is any contest, matter is referred to court.

EXEMPTIONS:

Following are exempt from seizure: (1) State property; (2) property belonging to foreign states; (3) rights attached to person of debtor; (4) private correspondence; (5) rights of author over his literary and artistic creations before publication; (6) wakfs; (7) bedding of debtor and his family and their necessary clothing, and objects necessary for exercise of worship; (8) consumables, combustibles and income necessary for maintenance of debtor and his family for two months; (9) equipment and tools relating to, and books necessary for debtor's profession or trade up to value of 10,000 Lebanese pounds; (10) implements and instruments used in teaching or practice of arts and sciences up to value of 10,000 Lebanese pounds; (11) one cow or six sheep or ten goats and food sufficient for them for two months; (12) alimony allowed by courts, family allowance, allowance for high cost of living, and sums granted to workers and employees as matter of aid; (13) end of employment compensation for civil servants and their retirement fees; (14) sums of money or articles given or bequeathed under condition that they shall not be seized or disposed of, during period of maximum of ten years from date on which beneficiary enters into possession of same (only persons who become creditors of beneficiary after expiration of this period may seize such sums or articles); (15) provisions for commercial bills and notes in circulation; (16) ships ready to sail unless debt concerns pending voyage; (17) commercial establishments as whole (unless pledged) or their intangible elements, always provided bankruptcy provisions are observed.

EXEQUATUR: See topic Judgments.

FOREIGN CORPORATIONS: See topic Corporations.

FOREIGN EXCHANGE:

There is no restriction on the importation or exportation of foreign currency. Lebanon enjoys a regime of free exchange.

FOREIGN INVESTMENTS:

There are no restrictions on foreign investments. Foreigners whose investments are made by converting their national currency into Lebanese currency may repatriate

FOREIGN INVESTMENTS . . . *continued*

them in same or other foreign currency. Dividends and profits derived from investments made in new productive enterprizes, or in enterprizes already in operation, may be taken out of country without any let or hindrance or limitation as to time and amount. In case of disinvestment, proceeds may be repatriated in any foreign currency in circulation in the country.

Lebanon is party to Convention with European Common Market Countries for Commercial Exchange and Technical Collaboration.

Guarantee of New Investments.—Decree Law of Jan. 15, 1977 has created National Institute for Guarantee of New Investments against risks of war and warlike operations, civil war, civil commotions, riots and revolutions. Only material losses resulting directly from above-mentioned risks are covered, provided they exceed 5% of total guaranteed amount. Institute receives from insured premium not to exceed annually two per mil of insured amount. Duration of insurance contract is one year renewable at option of insured for similar period(s) up to maximum of ten years. Institute undertakings are guaranteed by State.

See also topics Aliens; Corporations; Currency; Industrial Establishments.

FOREIGN TRADE REGULATIONS:

See topic Foreign Investments.

FRAUDS, STATUTE OF:

In civil contracts oral testimony is not sufficient to prove a claim amounting to over 500 Lebanese pounds. This rule does not apply to commercial transactions, or when a material fact is involved, as in cases of quasi contract, or where there is a commencement of proof in writing, or where it is not possible for the creditor to obtain written evidence, or where the creditor proves to the satisfaction of the court that the written evidence was lost, or where fraud to Law is involved. In all these cases, oral testimony is admissible regardless of the amount. (Arts. 254-257 C.C.P.).

GARNISHMENT:

Garnishment is applicable to all personalty (including sums of money, but excluding deposits in banks due to banking secrecy law) belonging to debtor and in possession in hands of garnishee. (Art. 881 C.C.P.). Creditor must petition judge presiding over Bureau Executif for garnishment order. (Art. 882 C.C.P.). If debt is not liquid, presiding judge will make provisional estimate of sum due. (Art. 883 C.C.P.). Decree denying garnishment may be appealed from. Garnishment order, or provisional estimation of sum due, may be revoked by judge at demand of one of parties after hearing both parties to litigation. (Art. 885 C.C.P.). Garnishee must within five days of service of garnishment order, submit to Bureau Executif declaration showing sum or personalty belonging to debtor in his possession. Failure to do so without reasonable excuse makes him responsible personally for sum forming basis of garnishment. (Arts. 888-890 C.C.P.).

HUSBAND AND WIFE:

Husband and wife have their separate estates. The wife has full control of her property and can manage it without any assistance or interference from her husband. She can sell it, lease it, mortgage it or dispose of it by will or otherwise as she pleases without consent of her husband.

IMMIGRATION: See topic Aliens.

INDUSTRIAL ESTABLISHMENTS:

(Law No. 30 promulgated Aug. 15, 1967 for Organization and Development of Industrial Establishments.)

Definition.—All industries run by motor force and employing five employees, and value of motor equipment exceeds 50,000 Lebanese pounds, and intended for transformation of first materials in semi-manufactured or fully-manufactured products, or intended for transformation, or assemblage of semi-manufactured into fully manufactured articles or for repairing of manufactured articles or parts thereof, or for preparation of articles, or for packing them or preserving them, are deemed to be industrial establishments. (Art. 1).

Declaration of Foundation.—All persons, or companies intending to establish a plant in sense of Art. 1 must submit a declaration to Ministry of National Economy giving following information: Name, nature of ownership, name of owner of establishment, situs of plant, head office, kind of industry, area of land and of building, their value and value of equipment and machinery, nature of materials employed, capital and other details pertaining to work. (Art. 2).

Person making declaration shall wait three months from date of submission of declaration, before commencing work. (Art. 3).

Any alteration whatsoever in factory shall be subject to a declaration made before execution of same. (Art. 5).

Petitioner for creation of a new industrial establishment must submit with declaration a technical study of project to a special bureau. Special bureau must give its opinion within three months, and if it appears to it that project is sound and advantageous, it will give its observations about extent and conditions of protection to be given to it by authorities: but if it appears to it that project does not comply with requirements, and it gives an adverse opinion, and if notwithstanding such an opinion project is executed, it will be deprived of any assistance or protection. (Art. 6).

Ministry of National Economy, pursuant to proposition of Minister of National Economy, may prevent establishment of new plants in any field of industry. (Art. 7).

Any contravention of Art. 5 subjects contravener to a fine of 100,000 to 500,000 Lebanese pounds.

INFANTS:

The age of majority is 18. (C. O. C. art. 215).

(References below are to the Law of Inheritance, promulgated June 23, 1959, affecting the estates of non-Moslems such as Christians and Jews.)

Illegitimate Children — Acknowledgment. — Parenthood of an illegitimate child may be established by voluntary acknowledgment, or by a declaration embodied in the birth certificate pursuant to the requirements of the registration of vital statistics, or in a notarial act. Voluntary acknowledgment is not permissible after the child attains the age of majority. (Art. 24). Voluntary acknowledgment binds only the person making it. (Art. 25). If either spouse acknowledges an illegitimate child in the marriage act, when the child is born before the solemnization of the marriage, the presence of such an illegitimate child will have no effect upon the rights of the other spouse and the issue of the marriage. (Art. 26). It is permissible for the illegitimate child to establish its paternity before the competent court in the following cases: (1) forceful carrying off, or rape, if pregnancy occurs during such period; (2) fraudulent inducement as in the case of abuse of authority, promise of marriage; (3) if there is a commencement of proof in writings from the alleged father embodying an unequivocal acknowledgment of paternity. (Art. 27). It is not permissible: (1) if it is proved that during the legal period of pregnancy the mother's conduct was bad, or if she had relations with another person; (2) if the alleged father during the period of pregnancy was not in a position to be the father because he was away, or was suffering from an accident. (Art. 27). The action may be brought by the child only, and if an infant, by the mother even though she be a minor. In the latter case the action must be brought within two years from the date of delivery. If the action is not brought during the minority of the child, the child may bring it within the year immediately following its majority; the delay will be two years following majority if the mother fails to acknowledge the child during its minority, or if she is incapable. (Art. 28). The child may trace its maternity before the competent court. The action, however, will not be heard unless brought within two years following the child's majority. Oral evidence is not admissible unless there is a commencement of proof in writing, or if there is a convincing presumption. (Art. 29). See also topic Descent and Distribution.

See also topic Executors and Administrators, subhead Settlement and Partition, catchline Settlement of Estate When One of Heirs Is a Minor or Lacks Capacity.

INSOLVENCY: See topic Bankruptcy.

INTEREST:

Legal rate of interest is 9%.

INTESTACY: See topic Descent and Distribution.

INVENTIONS (PATENTS):

See topic Protection of Commercial, Industrial, Literary and Artistic Property.

JUDGMENTS:

Foreign Judgments (Art. 1009 to 1022 C.C.P.).—Foreign judgments may not be executed until they are clothed with exequatur. However, pending grant of exequatur they may be used as evidence, or as a means for precautionary measures such as inscription of an annotation on title deeds, judicial custody, demand of trustee in bankruptcy of debts owing to bankrupt estate, or intervening as a party in actions of bankrupt, precautionary attachment, attachment in hands of third parties.

Petition for exequatur is equivalent to an action for confirmation of attachment, or of a debt. (Art. 1010 C.C.P.).

Judgments rendered by foreign administrative or penal bodies and courts are not subject to this law unless they embody a civil obligation, and then only to extent of such civil obligation. (Art. 1011 C.C.P.).

Foreign judgments in matters of capacity, personal status, and those rendered as a matter of grace upon simple petition of a person without summoning other parties in interest (Ordonnance sur Requête) do not need exequatur for their execution in Lebanon unless they are subject to any pending dispute or opposition where rendered. Examples of such judgments or decrees: Processes of recording or rectifying a record, radiation of entries in records of Lebanese vital statistics, or domestic relations. (Art. 1012 C.C.P.).

Petitions for exequatur are made directly to President of Civil Court of Appeal of domicile of defendant, or of his residence if his domicile is unknown, or of situs of property upon which execution is to be enforced; otherwise they must be made to President of Civil Court of Appeal at Beirut. Order of President of Court of Appeal granting or refusing exequatur may be appealed from before Court itself. (Art. 1013 C.C.P.).

Any court may give effect to foreign judgment used as evidence in matter pending before it, provided conditions of Arts. 1014 and 1015 C.C.P. are fulfilled; it may also grant such judgment exequatur if expressly requested by either party. (Art. 1020 C.C.P.).

Conditions for Grant of Exequatur.—(1) Judgment must be rendered by a court of competent jurisdiction under laws of country where rendered, always provided such competence is not based on nationality of plaintiff only; and in case of two foreign judgments on same subject rendered by two foreign sovereignties, exequatur will be granted to judgment which conforms with rules laid down by Lebanese law regarding international competence. (2) Judgment must have acquired status of res judicata, and be executory under law of country where rendered. However, the exequatur may be granted to gracious decrees (Ordonnance sur Requête) and to interlocutory judgments if executory in country where rendered. (3) Defendant must have been served with process, and been granted right to defend himself. (4) Judgment must have been rendered in name of state whose laws permit execution of Lebanese judgments through similar procedures or otherwise. (5) That they are not contrary to public policy of state. (Art. 1014 C.C.P.).

It is not permissible for Lebanese courts seized with a demand for exequatur to reexamine foreign judgment on merits at request of defendant except in following cases: (1) If it is established that foreign judgment has been rendered on instruments which were subsequently deemed or declared to be false; (2) if subsequent to rendering of judgment pertinent and decisive documents are discovered whose production has been withheld or obstructed by either party; (3) if judgment contains contradictory statements in decision rendered; (4) if it is established that laws of country where

See Topical Index in front part of this volume.

JUDGMENTS . . . *continued*
rendered order a revision on merits of judgments rendered by Lebanese courts before granting exequatur. (Art. 1015 C.C.P.).

Causes for Refusal of Exequatur.—Grant of exequatur will be denied in following cases: (1) If in same dispute a final judgment has been rendered by a Lebanese court; (2) if in same dispute and between same parties an action is pending before a Lebanese court, which was commenced before action which led to foreign judgment. (Art. 1016 C.C.P.).

Necessary Documents.—Party petitioning for exequatur must submit following documents: (1) Duly authenticated copy of judgment, which must satisfy and embody all conditions imposed by laws of country where rendered, which establishes its validity; (2) documents establishing that judgment is executory in country where rendered; (3) duly authenticated copy of summons addressed to defaulting party if judgment is rendered by default, and of service of same upon him; (4) translation of these documents into Arabic, the official language, duly legalized pursuant to Lebanese law. (Art. 1017 C.C.P.).

Exequatur of Foreign and International Arbitral Awards (Arts. 793 to 797 and 814 to 818 C.C.P.).—Foreign and International Arbitral Awards are given effect and are granted exequatur, provided party wishing to use same produces evidence of their existence, and they are not clearly contrary to public policy. Party seeking exequatur must produce original copy of award together with original of agreement to arbitrate, or true copy of both documents legalized by arbitrators or any other competent authority, and duly translated into Arabic.

Exequatur is granted by order of Court of First Degree of Beirut for awards rendered without Lebanon.

Exequatur may only be refused for following reasons: (1) Award was rendered without agreement to arbitrate, or such agreement was null or had lapsed; (2) award was rendered by arbitrators who have not been appointed in conformity with provisions of applicable law; (3) award covers dispute which is outside scope of arbitral agreement; (4) parties have not been guaranteed right to defend themselves; (5) award does not contain statement of parties' demands and defenses, or does not indicate name of arbitrators or grounds on which it was rendered, or is not dated and signed by arbitrators; (6) award is contrary to public policy.

Order granting or refusing exequatur may be appealed from. However, order granting exequatur may only be appealed from for following reasons: (1) Award was rendered without agreement to arbitrate, or such agreement was null or had lapsed; (2) award was rendered by arbitrators who have not been appointed in conformity with provisions of applicable law; (3) award covers dispute which is outside of scope of arbitral agreement; (4) parties have not been guaranteed right to defend themselves; (5) award is contrary to international rule of public policy.

Exequatur of Foreign Writs of Execution (Arts. 1023 and 1024 C.C.P.).—Exequatur may be granted if such writs satisfy following conditions: (1) That they are given by official who is competent under lex loci; (2) that they satisfy formal requirements of lex loci; (3) that they do not contravene public policy; (4) that they are executory under lex loci.

LABOR RELATIONS:

Labor relations are governed by two forms of contracts, individual contracts freely entered into between employer and employee, and collective contracts.

Law of Sept. 2, 1964, instituted collective conventions. These are negotiated and entered between employers and labor unions. (Art. 1). All unions and employers who enter into the collective conventions, and all members of the groups that adhere thereunto are bound by the provisions thereof. (Arts. 12 and 13). Duration of collective convention is two years, renewable for a similar period. (Art. 7).

Labor Disputes.—Disputes between employer and employee, as individuals, are settled by a special court called Arbitration Labor Council, which is composed of three members, a judge, who presides, a representative of the workers, and a representative of the employers. (Art. 77, Labor Code). Judgments rendered by Council are final and not open to any appeal. (Art. 80).

Collective disputes between employer and employees are settled by a special committee composed of nine members, presided over by a judge. (Art. 49; Law Sept. 2, 1964). Award rendered is final and not subject to any appeal. (Art. 61; Law Sept. 2, 1964).

Hours of Labor.—Maximum number of hours for workers of both sexes, over 16 years of age, with exception of agricultural work, is 48 hours a week. (Art. 31, Labor Code). This may be increased or decreased by a decision of Ministry of Social Affairs. It may be increased by employer to 12 hours a day provided notice is given to Ministry of Social Affairs, and provided employees and workers are paid an addition of 50% per extra work hour. (Art. 33). Children under 16 years of age cannot be made to work over seven hours a day. (Art 23).

Child Labor.—It is not permissible to employ children under eight years of age. Children under 13 cannot be employed in any mechanical or manual industries, or toolsome work at night, between 8 P.M. and 5 A.M. from May to Sept., and 7 P.M. to 6 A.M. from Oct. to Apr. (Art. 26). Children between 13 and 16 cannot be employed in mines, industrial ovens, explosives, soldering metals, manufacture of alcoholic beverages, painting by Duco process, and other hazardous trades. (Annex 1, Labor Code).

Female Labor.—Females cannot be employed in industrial plants at night, or in any of the hazardous trades set forth in Annex 1 of Labor Code, same as adolescents.

Labor Unions.—Labor unions are recognized by Labor Code (Art. 83) and unions may confederate with approval of Ministry of Social Affairs. (Art. 86). Unions are controlled by government which may dissolve them for contraventions of the duties imposed upon them or for any ultra vires acts. (Art. 105).

Wages and Salaries.—Minimum wages are fixed at 200,000 Lebanese pounds a month, payable for employees monthly, and workers fortnightly. (Art. 47). Wages earned and unpaid at termination of service may be claimed within two years, otherwise they will be barred by prescription. (Art. 351, C. O. C.). In case of bankruptcy of employer, unpaid wages of last year of service are privileged and take priority after debts to FISC, judicial costs and legal mortgages. (Art. 48, Labor Code).

Notice of Termination of Service.—Either party to a contract of employment may terminate same at any time provided he gives notice of termination to other party. Period of notice is one month if less than three years service; between three years and six years, two months; between six and 12 years, three months; over 12 years, four months. Notice must be in writing. Failure by either party to give notice subjects him to payment of a special compensation equal to salaries employee would have earned had such notice been given. Any misuse by either party of his right of termination subjects him to payment of an additional compensation to be assessed by courts. (Art. 50 of Labor Code as am'd by Decree No. 9640 of Feb. 6, 1975).

Indemnity on Termination of Service.—Rights and obligations of employee upon termination of service are governed by Code of Social Security of Sept. 23, 1963. Upon termination of service, employees are entitled to an indemnity provided they have served for a period of 20 years, or that they suffer from an ailment that diminishes their usefulness by 50%, or if they attain age of 60, if male, and 55, if female, and for unmarried women if they marry. (Art. 50). Indemnity is fixed at one month's pay for each year of service. An additional one-half month's pay is granted for each year of service over 20 years. (Art. 51). Indemnity is paid by Department of Social Security, and borne by employer and paid by him to Department. Contribution to be paid by employer has been determined at 8.50% of month's pay. (Art. 71).

Foreign employees who do not benefit from Lebanese Social Security Plan are entitled to receive upon termination of their service by their employer an indemnity equal to one month salary per year of service calculated on basis of last salary received. If termination is caused by employee no indemnity is due.

Family Allowances.—Married employees are entitled to family allowance paid to them by employer on behalf of Department of Social Security. Contribution to be paid by employer has been determined at 15% of that part of month's pay that does not exceed three times minimum wages. (See subhead Wages and Salaries, supra.) Family allowance paid by employer is deducted from contribution to Social Security.

Medical and Maternity Insurance.—Employees enjoy medical and maternity insurance covering 70% of costs, and provided by Social Security. Contribution to be paid has been determined at 13% of that part of month's pay that does not exceed twice minimum wages.

See also topic Social Security.

LAW REPORTS, CODES, ETC.:

See topics Reports; Statutes.

LEGISLATURE:

Regular Sessions.—Lebanese Parliament holds two regular sessions. First session starts on Tues. following 15th day of Mar. and continues until end of May. Second session starts on Tues. following the 15th day of Oct. and continues until end of year; this second session is limited to discussion of the budget before the discussion of any other subject. (Art. 32 of the Constitution).

Special or Extraordinary Sessions.—President of Republic may call Parliament for an extraordinary session by a Presidential Decree indicating the beginning of the session and its termination, and the subjects to be discussed. President of Republic is bound to call Parliament for an extraordinary session if he is requested by majority of members of Parliament. (Art. 33, Constitution).

LICENSES:

See topics Aliens, Corporations, Foreign Investment, Industrial Establishments, Motor Vehicles.

LIENS:

Liens may be contractual as in pledges (gages) and "antichresse" and "nantissements" (C. O. C. Law No. 46/L, art. 1, Arrete 3339, arts. 91, 100, 101), or they may arise out of contracts as in the following cases: Ready money sales, where the vendor has a lien until the price is paid (C. O. C. 407, 408); sales on credit, where the vendor may retain the thing sold if the vendee becomes bankrupt, is unable to pay or has diminished the value of the security (C. O. C. 410); vente a remere, or sale with right to repurchase, if the purchase price is not refunded (C. O. C. 473); bailments (C. O. C. 571, 582); transport (C. O. C. 686); freight, where the captain has a lien on the freight; mortgages (art. 120, Arrete 3339); workman who works with materials of others (C. O. C. 677); stolen goods bought at the market or from a merchant dealing in similar goods until payment of the price paid (C. O. C. 309). See also topic Chattel Mortgages.

LIMITATIONS, STATUTE OF:

Civil Cases—Realty.—Distinction must be made between realty that has, and has not, been surveyed (cadastre). For realty that has been surveyed and recorded in the Land Registry, there is no prescription, and adverse possession, no matter how long, cannot give title. For realty that has not been surveyed, the period is five and 15 years, depending on certain conditions in the title.

Civil Cases—Personalty.—As a general rule actions are barred by the lapse of ten years. Exceptions: Five-year rule for the following: arrears, interest, dividends, rent (rural and urban), and generally all prestations payable annually or at shorter periods, actions issuing from the partnership contract. Two-year rule, among others, for the following: professors, servants and workmen, for services and wages; hotel keepers, for board and lodging; physicians, lawyers, contractors and engineers, for services rendered.

Commercial Cases—Bills of Exchange, Notes to Order.—All these, whether made by merchants or by nonmerchants, are deemed to be commercial, three years.

Commercial Cases — Checks. — For actions against drawer and endorsers, among endorsers, and by endorsers against drawer, six months; against drawee, three years. (C. C. 442).

LIMITATIONS, STATUTE OF . . . *continued*

Insurance.—Two years. (C. O. C. 985).

Civil actions for damages based on felony are open to injured party and his heirs and next of kin, but are barred by lapse of ten years. (Art. 438, C. P. P.).

Civil actions for damages based on misdemeanor are barred by lapse of three years. (Art. 439 C. P. P.). See, however, subheads infra.

Civil actions for damages based on contraventions are open to heirs and next of kin, but are barred by lapse of one year. (Art. 440 C. P. P.).

Carriage by Air.—Actions against carrier in case of injury to persons are barred by lapse of ten years (Art. 10, C. A. L.), except contracts subject to Convention of Warsaw where the statute is two years (Art. 29:1, I. C. W.). Actions for injury to goods are barred by lapse of one year (Art. 70, C. A. L.), and for contracts subject to Convention of Warsaw, two years (Art. 29:1, I. C. W.).

Carriage by Sea.—Actions against carrier are barred by lapse of one year. (Art. 231, C. C. M.). Collision actions are barred by lapse of two years. (Art. 244, C. C. M.). Actions against insurer are barred by lapse of two years. (Art. 380, C. C. M.).

Motor Accidents.—If there is a contract of carriage, action against the carrier in case of injury to persons is barred by lapse of ten years. Action for injury to goods is barred by lapse of one year. (Art. 687, C. O. C.). If there is no contract of carriage, actions against wrongdoer based on delictual negligence are barred by lapse of three years; but action against owner of motor vehicle is barred by lapse of ten years.

Persons Entitled to Claim Damages.—Actions for damages are open to injured party and to his heirs and next of kin.

LIMITED LIABILITY COMPANIES:

See topic Corporations.

LITERARY AND ARTISTIC PROPERTY:

See topic Protection of Commercial, Industrial, Literary and Artistic Property.

MARRIAGE:

Marriage is governed by the Canon Law. Each community has its own law. However, irrespective of specificity of law governing each community, each of parties to contract of marriage has to produce to officer in charge of celebration pro nuptiae medical certificate showing diseases and impediments, if any, that may influence consent of other party; officer is bound to communicate contents of such certificates to parties concerned before celebration. (Decree Law No. 78 of Sept. 9, 1983).

Moslem Community.—Marriage is founded on contract, for which the consent of the parties is essential. Its validity does not depend on the observance of any religious rite or ceremony other than being witnessed by two properly qualified witnesses. In general, however, the contract is made before the ma'azoun.

Capacity.—Age, the male, 18; the female, 17. The male who has not completed his 18th year may marry with the authorization of the Cadi, and the female who has not completed her 17th year, with the authorization of the Cadi and the consent of the guardian. It is not permissible to marry a male infant who has not completed his 17th year or a female who has not completed her ninth year. It is not permissible to marry the insane except in case of necessity and with the authorization of the Cadi.

Plurality of Wives.—The Moslem law sanctions the predominance of the husband and concedes to a man the right to have more than one wife, not exceeding four, at one and the same time, provided he is able to deal with them on a footing of equality and justice.

Prohibitions and Impediments.—These are of a perpetual or a temporary nature. Perpetual prohibitions are based on consanguinity, affinity, or fosterage. Temporary impediments are: (1) Radical difference in religion, as between a Moslem and polytheist woman, until she embraces Islam; but a Moslem man may marry a Christian woman or a Jewess, but a Christian or Jew may not marry a Moslem woman; (2) two wives who are so closely related that if one of them had been a man, there could have been no marriage between them on account of relationship (a man cannot marry at the same time an aunt and niece or two sisters); (3) more than four wives at one and the same time; (4) a woman in the 'Iddat or period of probation. See also topic Divorce.

Catholic and Maronite Communities.—These are governed by the Canon Law of the Church of Rome. Marriage is solemnized by the authorized and ordained priest.

Protestant Community.—The marriage is a contract for which the consent of the parties is necessary. If either party is under age, the consent of the guardian is necessary. The ceremony must be performed by an authorized and ordained pastor of the church.

Conditions.—Both parties must: (1) Be mentally and physically competent; (2) be free from venereal diseases, consumption and incurable insanity; (3) have attained the age of marriage, 18 for the male, 16 for the female; (4) be not within the prohibited degree of relationship; (5) be not united by the bonds of a former marriage not yet dissolved; (6) if Christians, at least one of them must be a Protestant. An infant male who has not attained the age of 18 or a female that of 16, may be married in exceptional cases by a special court order. Each of the parties must submit a certificate from his or her spiritual chief that there is no impediment to the marriage, a medical certificate that he or she is free from the diseases enumerated above and from deformities which prevent the consummation of the marriage, and written consent of the guardian, if under age.

Greek Orthodox Community.—Marriage requires the consent of the parties and if under the age of consent (18 for a male, 15 for a female), the consent of the guardian is necessary. Marriage must be solemnized by a duly ordained priest.

Prohibitions.—Marriage is prohibited between blood relations in line ascending and line descending, and between godparents and godchildren; between collaterals in the fifth degree; the same prohibition in the case of relationship of affinity. Marriage between a man and a married woman with whom he has had sexual intercourse is forbidden. Marriage of ordained priests is forbidden.

Aliens are governed by his or her national law.

MONOPOLIES AND RESTRAINTS OF TRADE:

Official monopolies may be created for a limited period by a special law. (Art. 89, Constitution). Only official monopoly in existence is tobacco monopoly.

Dumping Law.—(Law No. 31, Aug. 5, 1967).

Articles imported into Lebanon for prices below wholesale prices in country of origin at time of importation, or for prices below price of same articles exported to other destinations, or for prices below cost of production plus a reasonable profit and cost of distribution, shall be subject to an impost, after investigation, over and above customs dues. Dumping impost shall be equal to value of dumping price, provided importation of article into Lebanon causes prejudice to existing Lebanese industry or hinders establishment of an industry in process of formation. (Arts. 2, 3, 4, 6).

Anti-Monopoly and High Cost of Living Law.—(Law No. 32, Aug. 5, 1967).

Every monopoly for production, purchase, or importation, or distribution of articles in Lebanon, which tends to curtail competition, and every act tending to corner market shall be deemed null and void. (Arts. 1, 2).

Whosoever shall undertake or attempt to undertake such acts is amenable to a term of prison from six months to three years, and a fine of 1,000,000 to 10,000,000 Lebanese pounds, or either of these penalties, and to confiscation of articles. (Art. 4).

See also topics Aliens, Corporations, Foreign Investments.

MORTGAGES:

Mortgages are of three classes: (1) contractual; these may be created by an instrument formally executed before the Land Registrar, or his auxiliaries (in localities where there is no Land Registry, the official in charge is the Sole Judge of the Court of First Instance); (2) legal mortgages; such as those accorded by law to a minor against the property of his guardian; the married woman against the realty of her husband for the dower; the state, municipalities and other public administrations, against the realty of their accountants and receivers; the vendor, barterer, and the party to partition, against the realty sold, bartered, or partitioned, when no contractual mortgage was made, for the price; the creditors and legatees of an estate; (3) judicial; arising from a judgment against a debtor.

The property subject to mortgage and the amount due must be specifically described and stated in the instrument. Mortgages have priority according to the date of their registration at the Land Registry. Mortgages may be canceled by releases formally executed before the Land Registrar or his auxiliary. A mortgage executed abroad cannot create a lien on property, but with a power of attorney may be given to a representative in Lebanon to make and record the mortgage. (Arrete 3339, arts. 120-143).

Mortgages may be released by cancellation in the Land Registry in the following cases: (1) extinction of the obligation which they guarantee; (2) formal renunciation of the mortgage. (Arrete 3339, arts. 150-157).

Antichresis is a contract by which the debtor places his creditor or a third person designated by the parties to the contract in possession of the debtor's realty, or a part thereof, by virtue of which the creditor may retain the same and collect its revenues until the debt is fully paid. (Arrete 3339, arts. 101-116).

MOTOR VEHICLES:

Vehicle License.—No motor vehicle can circulate without a special license to be delivered by Traffic Department. (Art. 117 of the Traffic Code). License is renewed once a year on payment of a special fee.

On registration, vehicles receive number plates. Colour of plates is black for private cars and red for taxis.

Operator's License.—No person is allowed to drive a vehicle without a driving license delivered by Department of Registration of Vehicles. (Art. 143). Lebanese driving licenses are not delivered to nonresidents. (Art. 149). License for persons over 50 is valid for five years, to be renewed on presentation of a copy of judicial record of operator and of a medical certificate of fitness. (Art.163). Minimum age for driving license is 18. (Art. 146).

Exempted from obligation of Lebanese license: Members of Armed Forces and Security Forces; persons in possession of a license of kind described in annex 9 of International Geneva Convention of Sept. 19, 1949; persons in possession of an international driving license; tourists in possession of a driving license delivered by their country, provided they have their license viséd, free of charge, by Department of Registration of Vehicles; and persons in possession of licenses delivered by countries with which there exists a special convention. (Art. 167).

Foreigners in possession of international licenses, of licenses of kind described in annex 9 of International Geneva Convention, may exchange their license for a Lebanese license, validity of which will not extend beyond validity of license exchanged. (Art. 168).

Sales.—Transfer of titles of motor vehicles has no effect with regard to third parties and State unless made at Registration Department by civil servant in charge of such formalities, and duly registered in a special register. (Art. 271).

Liens.—Motor vehicles can be pledged to a creditor without dispossession if pledge contract clearly provides for same. (Art 272). However, pledge has no effect with regard to third parties and State unless made at Registration Department by civil servant in charge of such formalities, and duly registered in a special register. (Art. 271). Pledge gives creditor a lien on motor vehicle. (Art. 4 of Decree No. 46/L of Oct. 22, 1932).

Traffic Regulations.—Drivers must keep to right unless they wish to overtake. (Arts. 5, 13 of the Traffic Code). Priority is given to ambulances, fire vehicles and vehicles of Security Forces. (Art. 29). When two vehicles meet at a crossing, vehicle coming from left must give priority to the other. (Art. 26).

Accidents.—There is a duty on operator of a car involved in an accident to give assistance. Operator who fails to do so will be arrested and fined. (Art. 566, Penal Code). In case of death or bodily injury penalties provided for in Arts. 564 and 565 of Penal Code will be increased by one-half. (Art. 567, Penal Code).

MOTOR VEHICLES . . . *continued*

Liability of Owner.—Person liable for accidents caused by a motor vehicle is the keeper, i.e., person who has intellectual use, control and direction of vehicle. (Art. 131 C. O. C.). Normally, owner is considered as being keeper of vehicle, but this is not always the case.

Masters are liable for accidents caused by their servants. (Art. 127, C. O. C.). Parents and tutors are liable for accidents caused by minor children living under roof and placed under their power. (Art. 126, C. O. C.).

Guests.—Guests injured are entitled to damages. There is no limitation to liability of owner or operator.

Insurance.—Insurance of third party liability covering physical injury is mandatory. (Decree Law No. 105 of June 30, 1977).

Foreign Vehicles.—Nonresident owners, members of touristic associations recognized by Lebanese Customs, may introduce their vehicles temporarily into Lebanon, free of charge (with exception of customs duty to be paid on gasoline), after obtaining a special circulation booklet to be delivered by said association. (Art. 238, Customs Code). This circulation booklet is valid for maximum period of one year. (Art. 239).

Nonresidents who wish to introduce their vehicles for a period not exceeding one month are exempted from having the special circulation booklet. (Letter No. 2611 of Nov. 12, 1964 of Supreme Council of Customs).

Actions Against Nonresident.—Nonresidents having a known residence or domicile are served with the process and proceedings by means of a registered letter return receipt requested. (Art. 362, C. C. P.).

If domicile of nonresidents is unknown the registered letter return receipt requested is sent to last known residence or domicile. If letter returns without notification, proceedings are served by advertisements in two local newspapers and posted on door of Court. (Art. 360).

Direct Actions.—There are no special provisions with respect to direct action against insurer. Actually, Lebanese Supreme Court is against direct action; Courts of Appeal and First Instance are divided on the subject.

NEGOTIABLE INSTRUMENTS:

See topic Bills and Notes.

NOTARIES PUBLIC:

Their duty is to draw up instruments, verify and make a record of all documents which the parties desire to make in authentic form, preserve the same on file as a record, and issue certified copies for execution; legalize translations of documents; receive deposits; protest notes; legalize wills and signatures; draw up powers of attorney, deeds and chattel mortgages.

PARTNERSHIP:

There are three kinds of partnership: (1) general partnership (societe en nom collectif); (2) special partnership (societe en commandite simple); (3) special partnership by shares (societe en commandite par action).

Partnerships are either commercial or civil according as the object thereof is commercial or other operations. The distinction is important in that only commercial partnerships may be adjudicated bankrupt.

A general partnership is formed by agreement between two or more persons, and carried on under a firm name and style containing the names of one or all of the partners, and followed by "& Co." The liability of the partners is unlimited.

A special partnership is formed by one or more general partners with unlimited liability, and one or more special partners, who are liable for the partnership debts only to the amount they have agreed to contribute, and who cannot participate in the management of the concern. If the special partner authorizes the use of his name as a member of the firm, he becomes a general partner with unlimited liability. The business is carried on under the firm name and style of the general partners or of one or more of them.

A special partnership by actions occupies a medial position between a simple partnership and a corporation (société anonyme). It is governed, however, by laws and regulations governing special partnership, and is carried on by general partners, who manage its affairs under supervision of a special committee appointed by shareholders. Profits are distributed in form of dividends. These partnerships, for their constitution, are subject to same rules governing constitution of corporations (société anonyme). (C. C. 234 as am'd). See topic Corporations, subhead Incorporation.

Partnership agreements must be deposited with the court; entered in a special register, and a special number given which must be printed on all letterheads, invoices and papers.

Limited Liability Companies.—See topic Corporations.

PATENTS:

See topic Protection of Commercial, Industrial, Literary and Artistic Property.

PERPETUITIES: See topic Wakfs.

PLEDGES:

If value of pledge exceeds 100 Lebanese pounds it must be established by a registered act, otherwise pledgee can claim no preference. In event of default in payment, creditor holding pledge may not dispose of it or appropriate it without a court order. Any convention between pledgor and pledgee which authorizes creditor to appropriate or dispose of thing pledged, without court order is null and void. Creditor may retain thing pledged until payment in full. (C. O. C. Law 45/L of Nov. 7, 1932).

PRESCRIPTION: See topic Limitations, Statute of.

PRINCIPAL AND AGENT:

Powers of attorney may be in a language other than Arabic, the official court language in the Republic of Lebanon, but in such a case they must be accompanied by a sworn translation before they can be used in judicial proceedings. The sworn translation is generally authenticated by a notary public. If executed in a foreign country, they must be viséd by Lebanese consular officer.

Commercial Representation.—(Law No. 34, promulgated Aug. 5, 1967).

Commercial representations are reserved to Lebanese natural or juristic persons; companies owned or controlled by foreigners are considered as foreign for purposes of Law, however exception is made regarding foreigners who were acting as commercial representatives before Feb. 12, 1975 or who may prove laws of their country authorize Lebanese nationals to act as commercial representatives. (Art. 1 as am'd by Decree No. 9639 of Feb. 6, 1975). Contract of representation must be in writing. It may restrict representation to one person; but in such case restriction is not binding on third parties unless recorded in Register of Commerce; no restriction is admitted in principle on foodstuff. (Art. 2 as am'd by Decree No. 9639 of Feb. 6, 1975). Contract of representation is deemed to be entered into for mutual benefit of contracting parties. It cannot, therefore, be annulled by unilateral act of principal, in absence of any mistake by representative, or in absence of any legitimate cause; otherwise representative will be entitled to indemnity for damage suffered by him, and also to lucrum cessans, so that if contract is for definite period, and period expires, he may in event of nonrenewal demand indemnity if his activities led to promotion of interests of principal. However, only loss of representative in Lebanese markets is taken into consideration. (Art. 4). Competent court in disputes arising out of contract is court of place where representative exercises his activities, to exclusion of all other courts, in spite of any agreement to contrary. (Art. 5). Law applies immediately on contracts in force on date of promulgation.

PROTECTION OF COMMERCIAL, INDUSTRIAL, LITERARY AND ARTISTIC PROPERTY:

Subject is governed by Decree 2385, Jan. 17, 1924, as revised by Decree 170, Dec. 6, 1937; Decree 177, Mar. 23, 1942; Decree 185, Apr. 16, 1943; Law, Feb. 26, 1946; Law, Dec. 10, 1946. Lebanon adhered to Berne Convention of Sept. 2, 1886, as revised by Rome Convention of June 3, 1928; it adhered to Paris Convention of Mar. 30, 1883, as revised by Brussels Convention of Dec. 14, 1900, Washington Convention, June 2, 1911, The Hague Convention of Nov. 26, 1925, and London Convention, June 2, 1934.

Inventions (Patents).—Petition should be addressed to Director, Office of Protection of Commercial, Industrial, Literary and Artistic Property, Beirut, by inventor, or his agent. (Art. 5). Petition should be accompanied by following documents: (1) Power of attorney duly executed and authenticated, and viséd by Lebanese Consul for use in Lebanon, if registration is to be made by an agent; (2) two copies of each of the following documents: (a) description of invention; (b) designs and drawings; (c) schedule of documents. (Art. 6).

Petition should be drawn up in Arabic, but petitioner may submit description of invention in foreign language, giving full name of inventor, his age, occupation, nationality, domicile, and those of his agent, if any; name and subject of invention; measurements in metric system. Petition should comprize only one invention. (Art. 7).

Fee for at least first year's registration should be paid in advance. (Art. 9).

Modifications, alterations, and additions to original invention are permissible, subject to supplementary fee. (Arts. 22, 23, 29).

Transfer, Assignment, and License.—Inventor may transfer, or assign, or license whole or part, or use, of the invention. (Art. 30). All transfers and assignments should be in writing, and registered at Office of Protection. (Art. 31).

Attachment.—Creditors may attach the right of inventor. (Art. 35).

Period of Protection.—Fifteen years.

Industrial Property (Sketches, Drawings, Models).—Materials with printed, painted, or woven designs and patterns, pictorial paper for mural decoration, models of dresses, cloaks, hats, caps, personal adornment trinkets, shoes, stays, socks and stockings, perfume phials and crystals, liquor bottles, cardboard containers, etc. may be protected. (Arts. 48, 50). Drawings and models should be deposited in Protection Office.

Petition should contain following details: Full name, domicile, nationality of petitioner, and same of agent if represented by one; number and quality of objects deposited, provided they do not exceed 100 for every deposit; period of protection desired. (Art. 53).

Petition must be accompanied by registration fee and two copies of description of each object; model of the seal stamped on containers. (Art. 34).

Trademarks and Tradenames.—Period of protection is 15 years, renewable for similar periods. (Art. 78).

Petition for registration should give following details: full name, domicile of petitioner, and those of agent if registration is made by one; nature of trade or industry; brief description of trademark or trade name with specimens of same; goods on which it is printed or woven; mention of registration in other countries; four copies of model specifying color and dimensions; original power of attorney if registration is made by an agent; brass cliché of trademark or trade name; one copy of certificates of registration in other countries. (Art. 79).

Petition must be accompanied by registration fee.

Literary and Artistic Property (Copyright).—Authors, composers, painters, designers, sculptors, engravers, etchers enjoy exclusive right of publication and reproduction of their work. They and their heirs and assigns alone have right to authorize translation or exhibition or reproduction in any form. (Arts. 138, 145). Protection accorded to creator of work during his lifetime, and 50 years thereafter to his heirs. (Art. 143).

Adherents to Berne Convention are protected within Lebanon without need of registration in Lebanon. (Art. 158).

Petition should give following details: Name and nature of work; name and address of author or creator of work, and those of his agent if necessary; three copies of publication; for paintings and statuary, three photographs taken from different positions; for cinematographic films, dances, pantomimes, three copies of pamphlet giving description of work. (Art. 160).

Petition should be accompanied by registration fee.

REAL PROPERTY:

See topics Aliens; Corporations.

REPORTS:

No official law reports. See also topic Statutes.

SALES:

The contract of sale is complete between the parties, and ownership passes the moment the agreement is concluded relative to the thing sold and the price. (C. O. C. 388). When goods are sold by weight, measure or number, the risk is borne by the seller until the goods have been weighed, measured or counted. (art. 390). In the case of goods that are sold subject to taste, the sale is not complete until the buyer has tasted and approved the goods. (art. 392). Sale of realty is not perfect until recorded in the land registry. (art. 393).

The chief obligations of the seller consist in the delivery of the thing sold and in warranting to the buyer peaceful possession and freedom from latent defects. (arts. 401, 428). Latent defects are those which render the thing sold unfit for the use for which it was intended, or which appreciably diminish its value. (art. 442). If the seller is aware of the defects, he is liable for the restitution of the price and for damages; if ignorant of same, he is only liable for the return of the price. (art. 449). The seller is not liable for patent defects, or those which the buyer was or could have easily discovered by the exercise of reasonable care, unless he declares that they do not exist. (art. 460).

The principal obligations of the buyer are the payment of the price and the taking of delivery of the thing sold. (art. 465). If he is troubled in his possession or finds himself in imminent danger of such trouble because of a previous sale of the thing by the seller to another, the buyer may keep the price until such trouble or danger of trouble shall cease. (art. 470). The buyer should take delivery at the time and place designated by the contract. In the absence of any stipulation to the contrary, the buyer must take delivery of the thing without undue delay. (art. 472).

In sales with an option or repurchase (vente à réméré), the option cannot be stipulated for a period exceeding three years: any longer delay is reduced to three years.

Notices Required.—When immovable property is concerned no notice is required by law, but buyer must file his action within 365 days from delivery. (Art. 463, C. O. C.).

When movable property is concerned, buyer must examine goods on delivery and notify seller with any patent defect within a period of seven days following delivery. If defects are latent or if buyer was prevented, by some cause, from examining goods, notification must be sent to seller immediately after discovery. (Art. 446, C. O. C.). In any case, action will have to be filed within 30 days. (Art. 463, C. O. C.).

Applicable Law.—See topic Contracts, subhead Applicable Law.

Warranties.—See beginning of topic, second introductory paragraph.

SOCIAL SECURITY:

(Statute of Sept. 26, 1963).

Social Security comprises insurance against sickness, maternity, accidents, professional injuries, family allowances and indemnities at termination of services.

Beneficiaries.—All workers including those engaged in agricultural enterprises enjoy benefits which statute confers.

Foreign Workers.—Foreign workers enjoy all benefits of the statute only if their national laws accord reciprocal treatment to Lebanese workmen, and provided they hold Lebanese permits. However, members of family of a foreign worker, who do not reside in Lebanon, do not enjoy benefits of the statute other than the indemnity given at termination of the service. (Arts. 9, 10).

STATUTES:

The laws of the Republic of Lebanon, generally, are codified, all with the exception of the Personal Status Law governing marriage, divorce, separation, filiation and guardianship, which are still governed by the Canon Laws of the various communities. In many instances, these have been codified.

The civil and commercial codes are based on the Ottoman and French Codes (the Ottoman Codes are practically translations of the old French Codes). In recent years, the Lebanese Code of Obligations and Contracts, Code of Maritime Commerce, Code of Commerce, Labor, and Social Security, were promulgated. In the absence of a text, the tendency of the courts is to apply the French Code, and to be inspired by French jurisprudence.

TAXATION:

Inheritance and Gift Taxes.—(Law No. 64, promulgated June 12, 1967).

Earlier Law concerning transfer tax on personal and real property has been amended as follows: Transfer tax imposed on all rights and personal and real property devolving upon others by inheritance, testament, wakf donation or any other mode with no return equivalent to its real value. (New Art. 1). Tax covers: (1) All personal and real property situated in Lebanon passing from a Lebanese or foreigner wheresoever he may be resident; (2) all personal and real property situated outside Lebanon and passing from a Lebanese residing in Lebanon; (3) all personal and real property situated outside Lebanon passing from a foreigner residing in Lebanon. This tax may be avoided by international conventions. (New Art. 3).

Exemptions.—40,000,000 Lebanese pounds to each of issue, husband and wife and father and mother; 16,000,000 Lebanese pounds unto each of other ascendants, brothers and sisters; 8,000,000 Lebanese pounds unto each of other heirs. There shall be added to exempted portion of issue 24,000,000 Lebanese pounds if issue is afflicted with a permanent ailment which prevents it from work, 1,600,000 Lebanese pounds per annum for each year or part of a year which separates it from completing 18th year; 16,000,000 Lebanese pounds to wife if child is married and 8,000,000 pounds unto each child under age of 18, always provided total does not exceed 40,000,000 pounds. (New Art. 9).

Rates.—

	Issue Husband & Wife	Father & Mother	Grand Parents Brothers & Sisters	Uncles Aunts Nephews Nieces	Others
Up to 30,000,000 Lebanese pounds	3%	6%	9%	12%	16%
Section between 30,000,000 and 60,000,000	5%	9%	12%	16%	21%
60,000,000 and 100,000,000	7%	12%	16%	21%	27%
Over 100,000,000	10%	16%	20%	26%	33%

Income Tax.—(Decree Law No. 14-4 of June 12, 1959 as modified by various amendments). Income tax is imposed on net profits realized in Lebanon during preceding year. (Art. 6). Net profit consists of all income subject to tax, after deduction of all expenses and burdens which exercise of commerce, industry or trade necessitates. These include: (1) Price of commodities and services rendered during year; (2) rent of premises; (3) interest on loans; (4) salaries, wages, compensation for dismissal from services, social security contribution; (5) reserve fund for dismissal from service; (6) premium of insurance for employees; (7) irrecoverable debts; (8) amortization of tangible fixed assets; (9) donations to charities within limit of 15,000 Lebanese pounds a year. Are not included: Taxes paid to foreign government on income earned in Lebanon (unless covered by treaty on double taxation), and losses incurred abroad by branches and agencies when head office of firm is in Lebanon. (Art. 7).

To determine amount of net profit subject to tax, taxpayer must submit declaration of real profits realized, or of gross income. In latter case administration fixes net profits subject to tax. Active partner in partnerships is personally responsible for submission of declaration. (Art. 10). Declaration of net profits is obligatory on following: (1) Partnerships, corporations (sociétés anonymes), limited liability companies, partnerships with silent partners (commandites), cooperative associations not exempted by special provision of law; (2) branches established in Lebanon by companies having their head office abroad; (3) factories and industrial establishments; (4) banking houses and exchange offices; (5) exporters and importers, commission agents, representatives of firms and factories, maritime, air and land travel agencies; (6) retail merchants employing more than four employees; (7) pharmaceutical and chemical depots; (8) hotels of first and second class; (9) theaters and cinemas of first and second class; (10) racing establishments; (11) flour mills other than those run by air and water power. (Art. 11).

If, in any year there shall be loss, same shall be carried to following year and deducted from its profits. (Art. 16).

Failure to submit declaration exposes defaulter to fine equivalent to 10% of tax for every month's delay, but accumulated sum shall not exceed 50% of total amount of tax.

Failure to keep regular books entails fine of 50% of tax.

Exemptions.—Each person is entitled to exemption equal to 3,000,000 Lebanese pounds, plus 1,000,000 Lebanese pounds if married, and 300,000 Lebanese pounds per male child under 18 years of age, or under 25 years of age if pursuing studies at university, or completely handicapped, and per female child whatever her age may be provided she is single, or widow or divorced, and dependant, within limit of maximum of five children.

Rate on Corporations, Limited Liability Companies and Special Partnerships by Share.—Income tax is paid on net profits at flat rate of 10%. For application of rate, dividends received as consequence of holding shares in other companies are deducted from profits, but remain subject to tax on dividends (see subhead Dividends, infra).

Rate on Physical Persons and Simple Partnerships.—After deduction of exemption, tax is paid on remaining profits at following rates (each partner in partnership is considered separately and taxed on his own share):

	Commercial and Non Commercial Trades
Up to 7,500,000 Lebanese pounds	3%
Section between	
7,500,000 and 18,750,000	5%
18,750,000 and 37,500,000	7%
Over 37,500,000	10%

Rate on Employees.—Each employer must submit list of his employees during preceding six months, with their salaries, wages and other increments and bonuses they may receive. (Art. 47). Employer deducts tax from salaries and wages, and is responsible for its payment to Treasury. Income tax on employees is assessed at following rates after deduction of exemption:

Up to 5,000,000 Lebanese pounds	2%
Section between	
5,000,000 and 15,000,000	4%
15,000,000 and 25,000,000	6%
25,000,000 and 75,000,000	8%
Over 75,000,000	10%

Dividends.—Distributed dividends of companies having their operation in Lebanon are taxed at flat rate of 5% (all profits made by foreign company out of its operation in Lebanon are considered as distributed dividends).

Stocks and Bonds.—All foreign stocks and bonds owned by individuals and companies residing in Lebanon, both Lebanese and foreigners, are taxed at flat rate of 5% of

TAXATION . . . *continued*
dividends distributed. Bank or any other person paying dividends in Lebanon shall deduct same and pay it to Treasury.

By Decree No. 5439 dated Sept. 20, 1982, interest paid on bonds issued by Lebanese corporations (see topic Corporations, subhead Bonds) are exempt from 5% withholding tax, but remain subject to income tax when received by other banking, financial or commercial institutions and included in their books as part of their income.

Tax Holiday.—Profits of newly established industrial establishments founded in Lebanon as of Jan. 1, 1980 are exempt from income tax for maximum period of ten years from start up of production, provided certain conditions are complied with; chief among which is condition that they are located in area which government wishes to develop, that they produce new articles and materials not produced in Lebanon before 1980, that value of new establishment, realty and fixtures invested in new plant and devoted to production, is not inferior to 50,000,000 Lebanese pounds, that total amount of profits exempted from tax during entire period of exemption does not exceed value of fixed assets (before amortization) invested up to date of start up of production.

Exemption is granted by governmental decree.

Industrial establishments founded before Jan. 1, 1980 may use up to 50% of their net profits, and for four consecutive years, to cover investments in new equipment meant to increase their production capacity, or in housing projects for their employees. Percentage may be raised to maximum of 75% of net profits if investment made in areas which government wishes to develop. Amount of investment is deducted from taxable profits.

Distributed dividends remain subject to special taxation (see subhead Dividends, supra).

Holding companies are exempt from income tax and from tax on distribution of dividends.

Holding companies are subject to fixed annual tax equal to 6% of that part of total equity (including reserves) that does not exceed 50,000,000 Lebanese pounds, 4% on that part between 50,000,000 and 80,000,000 Lebanese pounds, and 2% on that part that exceeds 80,000,000 Lebanese pounds, always provided that aggregate annual tax does not exceed 5,000,000 Lebanese pounds.

Holding companies remain however subject to following taxes: 6% on capital gain resulting from sale of assets within Lebanon (tax does not apply on sale of assets located abroad); 25% on earnings resulting from leases of establishments located in Lebanon, or of patents or other similar rights within Lebanon; 10% on management and service fees received from affiliate companies in Lebanon.

Off-shore companies are exempt from income tax and from tax on dividends. However, they are subject to payment of annual fixed tax of 1,000,000 Lebanese pounds and to tax of 6% on capital gain resulting from sale of assets within Lebanon.

TRADEMARKS AND TRADENAMES:

See topic Protection of Commercial, Industrial, Literary and Artistic Property.

TREATIES AND CONVENTIONS:

The treaties and conventions enumerated here are chiefly those bearing on legal and judicial relations.

Convention of Paris, Mar. 23, 1883, for Protection of Industrial Property, as revised at Brussels, Dec. 14, 1900, Washington, June 2, 1911, The Hague, Nov. 6, 1925, and London, June 2, 1934. Lebanon adhered July 19, 1939. (Decree 152 L. R.).

Convention of Berne for the protection of Literary and Artistic Property, as revised at Rome, June 2, 1928. Lebanon adhered June 28, 1934. (Decree 141 L. R.).

Convention with Western Germany for protection of Industrial Property. (Law of Aug. 10, 1955).

Charter of United Nations (International Court of Justice—Ratified by Lebanon, Sept. 25, 1945).

League of Arab States. Ratified by Law, Apr. 9, 1945. Treaty of Mutual Defence and Economic Co-operation between members of League of Arab States. (Law Dec. 5, 1952).

Treaty with Syria for Extradition of Criminals and Execution of Judgments. Feb. 25, 1951.

Treaty with Kingdom of Jordan for Extradition of Criminals and Execution of Judgments, Apr. 6, 1954.

Treaty with Yemen for Extradition of Criminals, Feb. 15, 1949.

Treaty with Iraq for Extradition of Criminals, 1929.

Convention for Rogatory Commissions with England, Feb. 7, 1922.

Treaty with Turkey for the Extradition of Criminals, 1932.

Treaty with Yugoslavia for Exchange of Penal Judgments, Feb. 24, 1953.

Treaty with Kuwait for Extradition of Criminals and Execution of Judgments. (Decrees No. 15743 and 15744 of Mar. 13, 1964).

Treaty with Belgium for Extradition of Criminals. (Law No. 33/64 of Nov. 17, 1964, supplemented by Decree No. 14805 of July 1, 1970).

Treaty with Tunis for Extradition of Criminals and Execution of Judgments. (Law No. 38/68 of Dec. 30, 1968).

Treaty with Italy for Execution of Judgments and Arbitral Awards and for Extradition of Criminals. (Decree No. 3257 of May 17, 1972).

Treaty with France on Double Taxation. (Decree No. 13673 of Aug. 23, 1963).

Point IV Convention with U.S.A., May 29, 1951.

Convention of Warsaw for Aviation as revised, Feb. 13, 1933 (through French High Commissioner), with complementary Convention of Guadalajara, Sept. 18, 1961 and The Hague Protocol of Sept. 29, 1955. (Decree No. 5194, Mar. 23, 1973).

Conventions on International Recognition of Right in Aircraft, signed in Geneva on June 19, 1948. (Law No. 11640, Jan. 9, 1969).

Convention of New York, June 4, 1954, on Customs Facilities. (Law No. 18, Dec. 26, 1970).

Convention of Vienna, 1961, on Diplomatic Relations. (Law No. 17, Dec. 26, 1970).

Convention of Chicago of 1944 on International Civil Aviation with New York Protocol of Mar. 12, 1971 and Montreal Protocols of May 27, 1947, June 14, 1954, Oct. 6, 1980.

Convention of Brussels of 1926 for the Unification of Certain Rules of Law Relating to Maritime Liens and Mortgages.

Convention of London of 1966 on Merchant Shipping.

Convention of London of 1954, as am'd in 1962, for the Prevention of Pollution of the Sea by Oil.

Convention on Repression of Unlawful Capture of Aircraft, signed in The Hague on Dec. 16, 1970.

Agreement of Chicago of Dec. 7, 1944 relating to transit of International Air Services.

Convention of Bruxelles of 1969 relating to Liability for Damages Caused by Oil Pollution.

Convention of Tokyo of 1963 relating to Offences and Certain Other Acts on Board Aircraft.

Air Transport Agreement between Government of Lebanon and Government of U.S.A. of Sept. 1, 1972.

International Convention Relating to Intervention on the High Seas in cases of Oil Pollution Casualties, signed in Brussels on Nov. 29, 1969. (Decree No. 9226, Nov. 12, 1974).

International Convention on the Liability of Operators of Nuclear Ships, signed in Brussels on May 25, 1962. (Decree No. 9228, Nov. 12, 1974).

International Convention on Repression of Unlawful Acts against Security of Aircraft, signed in Montreal on Sept. 23, 1971. (Decree No. 9227, Nov. 12, 1974).

Lebanese Government authorized by Law No. 13/75 of Apr. 5, 1975 to adhere to Brussels International Convention of 1924 for unification of certain rules of law relating to bills of lading, with amending Protocol of 1968.

Lebanese Government authorized by Law No. 14/75 of Apr. 5, 1975 to adhere to Brussels International Convention of 1952 for unification of certain rules concerning penal jurisdiction in matters of collision.

Lebanese Government authorized by Law No. 4/83 of Jan. 5, 1983 to adhere to United Nations Convention on the Carriage of Goods by Sea of 1978.

Lebanon is not party to Convention on Service Abroad of Judicial and Extrajudicial Documents in Civil and Commercial Matters. However, Lebanon adhered on Dec. 23, 1973 to Convention relating to Civil Procedure done at The Hague on Mar. 1, 1954, which includes number of provisions on service abroad of judicial and extrajudicial documents in civil and commercial matters.

Lebanon is not party to United Nations Convention on Recognition and Enforcement of Foreign Arbitral Awards.

Lebanon is not party to Convention on Taking of Evidence Abroad in Civil or Commercial Matters.

Lebanon is not party to the Convention Abolishing the Requirement of Legalisation for Foreign Public Documents.

Lebanese Government authorized by Law No. 294/94 of Mar. 10, 1994 to adhere to Brussels International Convention of Oct. 10, 1957 on Limitation of Shipowners' Liability.

Lebanese Government authorized by Law No. 387/94 of Nov. 10, 1994 to adhere to Basel International Convention of Mar. 22, 1989 on Control of Movement of Dangerous Waste Across Borders.

TRUSTS: See topic Wakfs.

WAKFS:

Wakf is a form of alienation made by the unilateral act of the grantor. It is constituted by the appropriation or tying up of certain property so that no proprietary rights may be exercised over the corpus, but over the usufruct only.

Kinds.—Wakfs are either charitable, or private or family wakfs. The former are settled on pious institutions, churches, mosques, schools, hospitals, rest houses for travelers, and the poor generally, or some other unfailing purpose of that character. The latter are meant for the grantor's family or descendants.

Amendment of the Law.—The law was amended by statute promulgated on March 10, 1947. Under the amendment, the charitable wakfs were left untouched, in that once properly created they are irrevocable and inalienable, except in certain cases and under special circumstances, they may be exchanged or sold by special court order. The private or family wakfs constituted after the promulgation of the new law are confined to two generations only, and when the grantor designates the beneficiaries specifically, to those designated who will be treated as one class. Further, the grantor may revoke the wakf wholly or in part, and may modify the terms and conditions, or change the beneficiaries, and upon the extinction of the two generations, or the death of the specifically designated beneficiaries, the wakf reverts to the grantor, if still alive, or to his heirs of the first and second generation, if dead.

Scope.—Outside of the limitations imposed on the private or family wakfs, the new law places no restraint on the grantor as to the nature of the uses he creates, or the disposal of the income. His directions are binding.

Conditions Required in Act Creating Wakf.—The creation of a wakf does not require the use of any particular terms, but the intention to settle property in perpetuity must be made clear. The wakf cannot be made conditional or contingent on a future event; it cannot be confined to a limited or terminable purpose, or for a particular period of time; it cannot be dependent on an option; there must be an intention, express or by implication, to settle property in perpetuity.

Conditions Required in Property Settled.—(1) It must answer to the description of tangible property in commerce (mal mutakawem); (2) it must be in existence and well determined at the time of the creation of the wakf; (3) it must be owned by the grantor; (4) it must be productive or capable of being used without the substance being consumed.

No question can arise with regard to the wakf of realty owned in fee, and of personalty permanently fixed to realty. The general rule would, therefore, exclude movable property including money. However, by consensus of opinion, a few specified articles (for example, books for mosques and churches), and such movables with respect to which a prevalent practice to make wakf has been established in the particular country in which the grantor resides, are exempted from the operation of the rule.

See Topical Index in front part of this volume.

WILLS:

Moslem Community.—A testator may dispose by last will and testament of one-third of his estate only. A legacy or legacies in excess of this one-third is reducible to the one-third unless approved by the heirs. A legacy to an heir is invalid, unless approved by the heirs.

Non-Moslem Communities—Christians and Jews (References below are to the Law of Inheritance, promulgated June 23, 1959).—Testator must be of sound and disposing mind and memory, and must have completed his eighteenth year. (Art. 39). Legacies may be made to heirs and nonheirs, and to the child conceived, provided there is no legal impediment. (Art. 40). A will made in the last sickness in favor of attending physician is invalid, unless physician is an heir: however, the will may be valid if the legacy is in payment of services due consideration being taken of the size of the legacy, the size of the estate and the value of the services rendered. (Art. 43). Legacy to an alien is not valid unless the national law of the alien accords reciprocal treatment to Lebanese citizens. (Art. 44). Legacies to places of worship, philanthropic institutions, educational and public establishments having legal capacity are valid. (Art. 46). Legatee must be designated by the testator himself; legacy to a legatee who cannot be determined at the time of testator's death is invalid. (Art. 48). Legacy of nude property to one person, and of the use to another is valid provided the use does not tie up the alienability of the property held in fee simple for a longer period than the life of the legatee and his issue. (Arts. 50, 51). Will partitioning the estate among the heirs, specifying the share of each is valid: however, if the legacy to any heir exceeds his distributive share in the estate, the excess is reduced to the portion thereof which may be disposed of by will. (Art. 49).

Testamentary Disposition.—The excess over the portion reserved for the issue, father, mother and surviving spouse is reduced to the quantum permitted by law. (Art 58). The reserve for the issue is 50% of the estate, to be divided equally among the living, share and share alike, the issue of a predeceased heir being given the share of their author by representation. (Art. 59). The reserve of the surviving spouse is 30% (Art. 60); that of the father and mother, 30%, share and share alike, and the entire 30% to the survivor of them (Art. 61).

In the presence of issue with the surviving spouse and the father and mother and the survivor of them, the reserve for the issue is 30%; that of the surviving spouse, 10%; that of the parents and the survivor of them, 10%. (Art. 62). In the presence of issue with a surviving spouse, or with the father and mother and the survivor of them, the reserve for the issue is 40%, that of the surviving spouse, or the father and mother of the survivor of them 10%. (Art. 63). If testator leaves a surviving spouse, father and mother or the survivor of them only, the reserve of the spouse is 20%, that of the father 15%, and that of the mother 15%. (Art. 64). If the legacies exceed the legal reserve, they are reduced to the level thereof: the demand for such reduction is only permissible to the heirs having a legal reserve and their universal heirs, and agents. (Art. 65).

To determine the legal reserve, there must be added to the net assets, after deduction of debts, the gifts inter vivos valued as at the date they were made. (Art. 66). If the legacy is of a Use, or an annuity, or of the nude property, the value thereof is estimated, taking into consideration the age of the legatee, his physical condition and other attending circumstances. (Art. 67). If the legacies exceed the sum which may be disposed of by will, or the portion thereof that remains after deduction of gifts inter vivos, the reduction is made without distinction between general and special legacies. (Art. 68).

Form and Execution.—Wills executed in Lebanon may be made in the official manner, or they may be holographic.

Official Form.—A will made in the official form must be drawn up by a Notary Public. (Art. 55). It must be filed with the Notary and mention thereof made in a special register.

Holographic Wills.—Holographic wills must be written, signed and dated entirely by the testator's own hand, and deposited by him personally, or by his special agent with the Notary Public, enclosed in an envelope, sealed with sealing wax, and the seal authenticated by the Notary Public, and an entry thereof made in the special register. (Art. 56).

Nuncupative Wills.—The will of a soldier on the battlefield may be made before an officer of the rank of lieutenant or above. It becomes null and void at the expiration of three months following the return of the soldier to a locality where the will could be made in the proper way. (Art. 57).

Revocation.—Testator may revoke his will wholly or in part. (Art 69). Revocation may result from the execution of a subsequent will, deed, or letter written by the testator's hand and deposited with the Notary Public. (Art. 70). A subsequent will which does not contain an express revocation may tacitly annul the provisions of the former will which are in contradiction therewith. (Art. 71). Revocation may result from the sale of the property bequeathed, devised, and up to the value of the thing sold. Such revocation may be upheld even though the sale is annulled for the absence of proper consent, or the return of the property bequeathed to the testator. (Art. 72). Revocation may be decreed at the demand of an heir or a legatee in the following cases; (1) nonperformance of the conditions of the will; (2) if the legatee commits a crime which bars him from the inheritance (Art. 73), always provided action is commenced within one year from the demise of the testator, or from the date on which the cause became known (Art. 74).

Lapse.—Legacies lapse in the following cases; (1) death of the legatee before the testator; (2) death of the legatee before the performance of the conditions of will during his lifetime; (3) return of the legacy by the legatee, or by his incapacity to receive the same; (4) destruction of the thing bequeathed during the lifetime of the testator. (Art. 75).

Acceptance of Will.—The legacy becomes binding by the express or implied acceptance of the will by the legatee. For the child conceived, the minor, and the person lacking capacity, acceptance may be made by the guardian. (Art. 77). It is permissible to accept the whole, or a part only, of the legacy, and it may be accepted by some legatees and rejected by others. (Art. 78). Acceptance takes effect as of the date of the testator's death. (Art. 79).

Children.—Children may not be deprived of their legal reserve in the estate. Children born after the execution of the will, or their issue if they predecease the testator, regardless of whether or not they are provided for in the will, receive their share of the legal reserve.

Foreign Executed Wills.—Wills executed without Lebanon may be drawn and authenticated pursuant to the provisions of the Lebanese law, or in the form in which official deeds and documents are authenticated under the foreign law (Art. 54); and they may be deposited with a Notary Public or a Lebanese consul. (Art. 56).

Foreign Probated Wills.—Decree probating the will may be granted to the executor if the foreign law grants reciprocal treatment to Lebanese decrees.

Probate.—Probate as understood by American courts, whereby attesting witnesses appear before the competent court officer to be examined is not a part of the procedure in Lebanon. The precautions attending the execution of the will, and deposit of same with the Notary Public, and entry thereof in the special register kept by the Notary Public render the examination of witnesses unnecessary. The will is executed according to its tenor by the Bureau Executif of the court. In the case of any opposition, the contest is heard by the Civil Court.

See also topic Executors and Administrators, subhead Settlement and Partition, catchline Executors.

LIECHTENSTEIN LAW DIGEST

(The following is a list of all Topics, including cross-references, covered in this Digest.)

LIECHTENSTEIN LAW DIGEST

Revised for 1997 edition by

RITTER, WOHLWEND, WOLFF, of Vaduz.

See topic Statutes.

ABSENTEES:

If for reasons of absence a person of age (see topic Infants) cannot act in an urgent matter nor designate a representative, furthermore if property is not taken care of because a person is continually absent with unknown abode or because of uncertainty as to heirs entitled to an inheritance, a curator (Beistand) is appointed by princely county court.

ACKNOWLEDGMENTS:

The form of acknowledgment is ruled by the law of the country, where the acknowledgment is taken. Acknowledgments taken in foreign countries to be used in Liechtenstein should be legalized by Swiss consulate, unless multilateral or bilateral treaties provide otherwise.

ACTIONS:

It is permissible to agree upon application of foreign laws for interpretation of contracts between Liechtenstein citizens and aliens. If Liechtenstein court is to decide about interpretation of such a contract, it has to apply foreign law agreed upon, so far as its provisions are not against public policy.

See also topic Limitation of Actions.

ADMINISTRATION:

See topic Executors and Administrators.

ADOPTION:

New Adoption Law enacted 1976. (LGBl. 1976/40; 1993/54).

Adoption becomes effective by agreement in writing between adopter and adoptive child and by court permission. If adoptive child is incompetent to act, he/she is represented by his/her legal guardian. Adoption by more than one person is only possible if adopters are spouses. With few exceptions, spouses may only adopt jointly. There must be reasonable cause for adoption.

Adoptive father must be at least 30 years of age and adoptive mother must be at least 28 years of age. Adoptive parents must be at least 16 years older than adoptive child.

Adopted child bears same relation to adopting parents and their kindred in all respects, including right of inheritance, as he/she would if he/she were natural child of such parents (subject to provisions on nationality). All rights and obligations as between adopted child and natural parents are extinguished by adoption.

ALIENS:

Rights and duties of aliens are equal to that of Liechtenstein citizens except in those cases where Liechtenstein citizenship is prescribed.

See also topics Citizenship; Real Property.

Corporations Owned or Controlled by Aliens.—See topic Partnership.

ASSIGNMENTS:

Assignment of personal property is effected by agreement about transfer of title of assignee.

Assignment of claims is, except where claims are transferred by virtue of law or by judicial act, effected by oral or written agreement between assignor and assignee. Notice to debtor is not required for validity of assignment but is advisable to prevent bona fide debtor from discharging his debt by payment to assignor.

For validity of assignments by way of payment between spouses and assignment by way of gift without handing over object, public document (öffentliche urkunde) is required.

ASSOCIATIONS: See topic Partnership.

ATTACHMENT:

Constitutes a provisional security measure provided for by Exekutions-ordnung LGBl, 1972/32 in order to protect creditor before effectuation of seizure or bankruptcy in execution proceedings.

Prerequisites allowable for all claims of private law including establishment of security by deposit money. Creditor may be a physical or juristic person. Attachable is any personal or real property of debtor situated in Liechtenstein and subject to seizure.

Grounds (Art. 274 of Executionsordnung) are: Debtor has no fixed domicile; debtor is suspected of avoiding his obligations by flight or removal of assets; debtor is in transit or at a fair or market but only for debts payable forthwith; debtor has no domicile in Liechtenstein; creditor has without success undertaken executions against debtor.

Indemnity.—Creditor is liable for damages resulting from unjustified attachment. Therefore, court may order security when granting attachment or later. Release of property from attachment will be granted by debtor against security.

Order of Attachment.—Creditor has to file petition with Liechtenstein court. Provided existence of claim and grant for attachment appeared to be credible, court will issue an "Order of Attachment." Debtor may oppose order of attachment within 14 days after receiving it.

Prosecution.—Creditor, in case he has not previously instituted court action or execution for his claim has to institute court action or execution proceedings within a period of time after receipt of document of attachment.

Alleged rights of third persons to attached property must be notified to court. Within 14 days after knowledge of attachment, owner of attached property must claim his property before court.

ATTORNEYS AND COUNSELORS:

Jurisdiction over admission to bar is vested in Liechtenstein Government.

Attorneys are governed by Law concerning lawyers dated Dec. 9, 1992, LGB1. 1993/41 and by rules of conduct issued by lawyers' association.

Eligibility.—Requirements to qualify as attorney are Liechtenstein citizenship and domicile in Liechtenstein, good standing, bar examination, and registration into list of attorneys kept by Liechtenstein Government.

Educational Requirements.—Applicant for bar examination must be holder of degree from university (law faculty) approved by Liechtenstein Government; two years clerkship, of these at least one year in law firm and six months at Liechtenstein Court; bar examination. Examinations are written and verbal on civil, criminal, constitutional and administration law.

Admission of Foreign Attorney.—

Admission Pro Hac Vice.—Admission of foreign attorney by Liechtenstein Government only for purposes of particular case, unless at least five Liechtenstein attorneys offer to take case.

Licenses and Authorized Practice.—Applicant who has passed examination and fulfils requirements (see subhead Eligibility, supra) is registered in list of attorneys kept by Liechtenstein Government.

Liabilities.—Attorneys are liable for neglect of duty.

Compensation.—Regulated by law; possibility of free agreement with client; no agreements as to de quota litis.

Discipline.—Liechtenstein Upper Court has jurisdiction over discipline of attorneys, possibility of appeal to Supreme Court.

Unauthorized Practice.—Prohibition of practice of law by individuals not admitted to bar (see subhead Admission of Foreign Attorney, supra).

Legal Professional Association.—Liechtensteinische Rechtsanwaltskammer (Law of Apr. 21, 1993; LGB1. 1993/72). President is elected for three years. Contact address is law firm of respective president, 1993-1996: Dr. Walter Kieber, 9490 Vaduz, Heiligkreuz 6. If foreign attorney seeks local counsel, association will send list of law firms but will not make recommendations.

BANKRUPTCY:

A new law (Konkursordnung) set in force at end of Sept. 1973.

Bankruptcy proceedings (Konkurs) are ordered by court in case of insolvency upon petition made by debtor or by any creditor. Suspension of payments is prima facie evidence of insolvency. As regards companies and estates of deceased persons, a bankruptcy order can also be obtained if liabilities exceed assets.

When ordering bankruptcy, court appoints a receiver (Masseverwalter), in whom bankrupt's assets are vested. Receiver is supervised by court.

All rights of lien or mortgage obtained by way of judicial execution or based on contracts expire on day when bankruptcy proceedings are opened, unless they were established more than 60 days before opening of bankruptcy proceedings. Any other right of lien or mortgage remains unimpaired by debtor's bankruptcy, subject, however, to receiver's right to impugn it.

Distribution of assets by receiver does not effect bankrupt's discharge, but a discharge can be obtained by way of judicial composition. Bankruptcy order having been issued, bankrupt may still apply for forced composition (Zwangsausgleich).

Composition with Creditors.—At request of an insolvent debtor, judicial composition proceedings (Nachlassverfahren) may be instituted by court. Upon institution of such proceedings, rights of lien or mortgage expire to same extent as in case of bankruptcy.

Subject to court's confirmation, composition becomes valid (and binding all creditors) if agreed upon by a qualified majority of creditors.

Special regulations are in force with regard to composition proceedings of bankers and banks.

BILLS AND NOTES:

Bills of Exchange (Wechselgesetz LGBl. 1971/51).—

Requirements as to Content.—(1) Designation as bill within text of document as drawn; (2) unconditional order to pay a determined sum of money; (3) name of drawee; (4) maturity; (5) place of payment; (6) name of person to whom or to whose order payment is to be made; (7) date and place of drawing; (8) signature of drawer.

Maturity.—Bill not mentioning maturity is payable at sight. Bill not mentioning place of drawing is deemed to have been drawn at place indicated with name of drawer written on bill or on a sheet attached to bill.

Transfer.—Delivery of bill with unconditional endorsement on bill or on sheet attached thereto, or with written assignment. If bill contains clause "not on order" or equivalent clause, transfer is effected only by delivery of bill with written assignment.

Presentment and Acceptance.—Bill may be presented for written acceptance by drawee at latter's place up to maturity unless prohibited in terms of bill; such prohibition is permissible only under certain conditions. Acceptance binds drawee for payment at maturity. Bill payable at sight must be presented within one year from date of drawing, unless otherwise stipulated. Bill has to be presented by holder on date of payment or on one of two following working days.

See Topical Index in front part of this volume.

BILLS AND NOTES . . . *continued*

Payment.—If a bill of exchange calls for a payment in a currency other than legal tender at place of payment, amount may be converted into local currency at rate of exchange prevailing on date of maturity. If debtor delays payment, holder has option to demand payment either at rate of exchange in force on date of maturity or at rate prevailing on day payment is actually effected. Value of foreign currency is determined according to commercial custom at place of payment. Drawer may, however, in bill itself prescribe rate of exchange to be applied in converting foreign currency.

Protest.—Bills not accepted or not paid must be protested in usual manner, unless protest is waived.

Recourse in Default of Acceptance or Payment.—Holder may exact payment from endorsers, drawer and others liable on bill, at maturity. This right also exists before maturity in case of nonacceptance, acceptor's insolvency or bankruptcy, or when execution on judgment against acceptor has been returned unsatisfied.

Any person paying bill has recourse against previous persons liable.

Days of Grace.—Not recognized, whether legal or judicial.

Limitation of Actions.—Actions are barred by statute of limitations. Periods: Any entitled persons against acceptor, three years after date of maturity; holder against endorsers and drawer, one year after due protest or if protest is waived one year after maturity; endorser against other endorsers and drawer, six months after date of payment or judicial enforcement.

Insofar as drawer and acceptor of a bill are unjustly enriched at expense of holder, they remain liable to latter, even when their liability has become extinguished by statute of limitations or because some formal requirements have not been complied with.

Revenue Stamps.—Nonaffixation of revenue stamps does not affect validity or negotiability but renders liable to tax penalties.

Conflict of Laws.—Capacity of a person to assume a liability on a bill of exchange is determined by law of country of his citizenship. If competency is denied by such law, liability nevertheless exists if signature has been given within a country according to laws of which person is competent. Form of contract on a bill of exchange is governed by law of country where contract is signed. Form and time limits for protests and form of other acts necessary for exercise or preservation of rights attaching to a bill of exchange are governed by law of country in whose territory protest is to be made or where act is to be performed. Effect of contracts on a bill of exchange of acceptor and maker of a promissory note are governed by law of place of payment. Effects of other contracts on a bill of exchange are governed by law of country where contracts were signed. Payment of a bill of exchange on maturity, calculation of dates for maturity and payment of a bill of exchange made out in foreign currency are governed by law of country where bill is payable.

Checks (Scheckgesetz LGBl, 1971/51/II).—Check must contain designation "check." Checks payable in Liechtenstein may be drawn only on banks. (Art. 3). Check cannot be accepted, it is payable on sight. Any provision to contrary is ineffective. If a check is "crossed," it may only be paid to a banker or to a customer of drawee. If a check is "especially crossed," it may only be paid to especially designated banker or to banker's customer if banker is himself drawee. Check may contain phrase: "only for accounting." In this case payment of check in cash is excluded.

Other Negotiable Instruments.—Law defines negotiable instrument (Wertpapier, papiervaleur, titolo di credito or cartavalore) to be a document to which a right is connected in such a way that such right cannot be exercised against debtor nor transferred to third persons without document. Such instruments may be issued in name of a specific creditor or payable to order of a specifically named creditor. Certain instruments are on order by virtue of law, such as bills of exchange, checks payable to a specifically named person, registered shares, instruments on goods (including warehouse receipts, warrants, bills of lading), mortgages issued on names. Instruments to bearer are frequently issued in Liechtenstein, especially for debentures and shares.

Transfer.—Full transfer may be effectuated only by delivery of instrument itself or means procuring power over instrument. No further requirement is provided for transfer of instruments to bearer. Further requirements for transfer, in case of an instrument on names, are a written declaration of assignment by transferor either on document itself or separately; in case of an instrument on order, either an endorsement on instrument or on a sheet attached thereto, or a written assignment on instrument itself or separately.

Defenses.—In any kind of negotiable instrument, debtor (obligor) has defenses (1) pertaining to validity and wording of instrument, (2) other defenses existing against immediate creditor.

In case of instruments to bearer or to order, other defenses of debtor based on legal relations between debtor and assignors are excluded, except in case of fraud; also excluded are defenses pertaining to validity of transfers, except that an instrument to order must show an uninterrupted chain of endorsements.

In case of instruments payable to named persons, additional defenses are possible based on legal relations between debtor and first creditor and all assignors; also defenses pertaining to validity of all transfers. See topic Assignments.

Special Kinds of Negotiable Instruments.—There are various forms of negotiable instruments showing only some of features described above. Instrument to order by law may be restricted as to transferability by endorsement, thereby assuming legal character of an instrument on names (so-called "recta-instrument"); instrument on names may have clause that debtor is entitled (but not bound) to perform to any holder of instrument (so-called "limping instrument on bearer"). Instruments to named persons or to order may be subject to special restrictions of transfer (so-called "vinculation"), e.g., in case of registered shares condition subsequent of consent of a corporate body according to bylaws.

CHATTEL MORTGAGES:

Known in Liechtenstein law only in very limited sense of pledging chattel by registration. See topic Pledges.

CITIZENSHIP:

By law of Nov. 2, 1960 (LGB1, 1960/23), revised on Aug. 2, 1974 (LGB, 1974/50), am'd on June 26, 1984 (LGB1, 1984/23) and on Oct. 14, 1986 (LGB1, 1986/104), right of citizenship is acquired by birth, marriage (not automatically), legitimation or admission. Requirements for admission are faculty of acting, assurance of homeright by Liechtenstein municipality and five years' residence in Liechtenstein. Citizenship is lost by resignation, legitimation, invalidation of marriage or deprivation. Latter can take place within period of five years after admission if requirements were not fulfilled, or at any time if admission was sought by fraud.

COMMERCIAL REGISTER:

Anyone carrying on commercially a trading, manufacturing or other business is obliged to register his firm in commercial register (Handelsregister). Legal entities such as company limited by shares, GmbH, Establishment, Trust and some foundations come into existence only if registered in commercial register.

COMMUNITY PROPERTY:

See topic Husband and Wife.

CONSTITUTION AND GOVERNMENT:

Liechtenstein is a monarchy upon a democratic basis. The state authority is divided between sovereign and subjects. A specialty of this monarchical constitution is the legislation initiative and the law-referendum by the nation.

The prime minister and his substitute are appointed by the sovereign for a period of six years upon suggestion of the parliament, which consists of 25 deputies and is chosen every four years according to the principles of the proporz (proportional) system.

A cabinet council of three ministers, chosen by parliament for a period of four years and ratified by sovereign, is associated with prime minister.

By virtue of the duty agreement with Switzerland an embassy has been established in Berne, Switzerland, and the foreign representation of Liechtenstein has been entrusted to the Swiss foreign department.

Commercial Treaties.—There is a postal agreement between Liechtenstein and Switzerland since 1922 and a duty agreement since 1924, under which the validity of commercial treaties entered into by Switzerland is extended also to Liechtenstein. The consular representation of Liechtenstein interests is in most cases taken care of by Swiss consulates.

COPYRIGHT:

Liechtenstein has adopted Berne International Agreement of 1886 and amendments of 1896, 1908 and 1948 and limitation of copyright has been fixed at 30 years after death of author. Acquisition of right does not depend on registration in a Public Register. It is acquired automatically by creation of a work of art as described by law.

CORPORATIONS: See topic Partnership.

COSTS:

Plaintiff, not resident in Liechtenstein, has to deposit security with court.

Costs of legal proceedings are calculated on number of court hearing hours, based on value in litigation.

Losing party has to refund costs to successful party.

COURTS:

In civil cases the princely county court decides in the first instance, the princely superior court in the second instance and the Princely Supreme Court in the last resort renders the final decision. All are located in Vaduz.

In criminal cases the princely county court decides violations, the jury offenses and the criminal court crimes. All are located in Vaduz.

In contentious administrative matters government decides in first instance, second instance is Verwaltungsbeschwerde-Instanz, in third instance Court of Administration renders final decision. All are located in Vaduz.

In constitutional matters Court of Constitution (Staatsgerichtshof) decides.

CURRENCY:

Legal currency is Swiss franc (SFr.). Swiss regulations regarding monetary, credit and currency policy within protection of Swiss coins and paper money are to be applied in Liechtenstein on basis of Currency Agreement entered on June 19, 1980.

DEATH:

If the death of a person is most probable because that person disappeared in grave mortal danger or has been absent for five years without some news, the court may be asked to declare that person as disappeared. If the disappeared person gives no notice within a year after official judicial invitation or if no news of him is received within this period, the court is authorized to declare such person as disappeared. Such declaration has the same legal effect as the death of such person would have.

DECEDENTS' ESTATES:

See topics Descent and Distribution; Executors and Administrators; Wills.

DESCENT AND DISTRIBUTION:

Intestate distribution is as follows: (a) Spouse and descendants of deceased, if any; (b) parents and brothers and sisters; (c) grandparents and their issue; (d) great-grandparents only.

Surviving spouse takes one-third if there are children, otherwise two-thirds.

Divorce cancels the intestate right of the surviving spouse.

If there is no next of kin the estate escheats to the state.

See Topical Index in front part of this volume.

DISPUTE RESOLUTION:

Mandatory Dispute Resolution.—Does not exist in Liechtenstein.

Voluntary Dispute Resolution.—

Arbitration.—According to Liechtenstein law (§§594-616 ZPO) every legal dispute which can be decided by regular court may also be decided by court of arbitration agreed upon by parties thereto. Every arbitration agreement has to be concluded in writing.

Number of arbiters is not limited. In case more than one arbiters are appointed, majority decides upon award to be rendered.

Action for annulment of award can be brought at competent regular court in specific cases itemized in law.

DIVORCE:

As provided by law of Dec. 13, 1973, Liechtenstein marriage act distinguishes between separation by mutual consent and separation without mutual consent on one hand and divorce on other hand. If parties agree on separation of marriage, they have to apply for judicial permission. Before granting legal separation, judge has to make two attempts to bring about reconciliation.

Separation without mutual consent and divorce may be granted for adultery, attempt against life, malicious desertion for over one year, and for other acts or behaviour on grounds of which living together has become intolerable.

Practice.—Petition for legal separation may be presented one year after contracting of marriage. Action must be brought within six months after first knowledge of offence by innocent party and in any case within five years after offence.

Petition for divorce may be presented three years after legal separation. If innocent party does not consent to divorce, petition must be dismissed. In this case divorce can only be granted after another two years without possibility of objection.

ENVIRONMENT:

There is no express law on protection of environment but protectionist provisions do exist in various other statutes such as law concerning waste disposal, law in respect of water protection, air purity law, forestry law and laws governing hunting and fishing. There is also nature protection statute and ancillary regulations issued by government under which various nature reserves have been created.

Pursuant to customs union between Principality of Liechtenstein and Switzerland (LGB1. 1923/24) certain provisions of Swiss statutes relating to environmental protection are directly applicable in Liechtenstein, for example several articles of Swiss law on protection of environment, ordinance regulating transportation of toxic waste, air purity ordinance, and noise prevention ordinance (LGB1. 1987/74).

General Supervision.—Within government there exists department for "Environmental protection, agriculture and forestry" which is in portfolio of deputy head of government.

EXCHANGE CONTROL:

Foreign Exchange Control.—See topic Currency and Switzerland Law Digest, same topic. See topics Foreign Investment; Foreign Trade Regulations.

EXECUTIONS:

Execution is granted upon judgments, settlements, as well as on grounds of an executable document. Movable property must first be seized in order to be realized upon according to legal regulations. Immovable property can be realized upon by sequestration or public sale.

EXECUTORS AND ADMINISTRATORS:

The compulsory institution of executors and administrators is not known in Liechtenstein. As a rule the administration of an estate is entrusted to the heir by the court until distribution. In exceptional cases the court may designate special trustees.

FOREIGN INVESTMENT:

There are no restrictions in Liechtenstein; only purchase of real estate (land and houses) requires a state consent which authorities are not obliged to grant. (Grundverkehrsgesetz, LGB1, 1975/5).

FOREIGN TRADE REGULATIONS:

Imports and Exports.—See Switzerland Law Digest, same topic and subhead, with following addendum: Since May 1995 Liechtenstein is member of European Economic Area (EEA).

FRAUDS, STATUTE OF:

See Austria Law Digest.

GARNISHMENT:

Attachment of outstanding debts of debtor is done by decree of court pursuant to which debt is assigned to creditor. This decree together with a garnishing order stating that debtor's debtor is forbidden to pay to his creditor, must be served upon debtor's debtor by court.

HOLDING COMPANIES: See topic Partnership.

HOLIDAYS:

Legal holidays are: Jan. 1; Jan. 6; Feb. 2; Mar. 19; Good Friday; Easter Monday; Ascension day; May 1; Mon. after Pentecost; Corpus Christi day; Aug. 15; Sept. 8; Nov. 1; Dec. 8; Dec. 25; Dec. 26.

HUSBAND AND WIFE:

Three relations regarding property are authorized: (a) Separation of property; (b) community of administration; and (c) community of property. To the latter two a public document is required which should show a donation to the community.

IMMIGRATION:

Residence and domicile permits are regulated on basis of agreements between Liechtenstein and Switzerland of Nov. 6, 1963 (LGB1. 1963 Nos. 38 and 39), by Swiss federal law of 1931, published in Liechtenstein Jan. 1990 (LGB1. 1990 Nos. 8 and 9) and various Liechtenstein statutory orders.

INFANTS:

Minority ends for both males and females on completion of 20 years of age.

Infants under age of 14 years are not subject to any prosecution under penal code. Minors on completion of 14 years and until age of 18 years are subject to special regulations of penal code.

Minor infants are represented by parent, if parents died or are deprived of parental power, by guardian appointed by court. Person under age of 21 years can transact business only with consent of his statutory guardian but may freely dispose of earnings acquired by himself.

INSOLVENCY: See topic Bankruptcy.

INTEREST:

The legal rate is 5%.

INTESTACY: See topic Descent and Distribution.

JOINT STOCK COMPANIES: See topic Partnership.

JUDGMENTS:

Judgments of foreign courts may be enforced in Liechtenstein in case of reciprocity.

Based on agreements between Switzerland and Liechtenstein (LGBl. 1970/4) and between Austria and Liechtenstein (LGBl. 1975/20), judgments in civil cases and judgments in arbitral cases are accepted in other country under certain circumstances and can be executed directly in other country.

LABOR RELATIONS:

Employers are not required to grant employees or their families any specific types of fringe benefits. Old age, disability insurance, family allowances and unemployment insurance are compulsory.

LAW REPORTS, CODES, ETC.:

See topic Statutes.

LEGISLATURE:

See topic Constitution and Government.

Legislative power is vested in Parliament.

Executive power consists of prime minister, and the four ministers of cabinet council.

LICENSES:

For establishing industrial or commercial enterprises a state consent is required (Liechtenstein Law 1916).

LIMITATION OF ACTIONS:

In civil cases statutory period is, as a rule, 30 years.

Principal exceptions: contestation of will, claiming of compulsory portion, revocation of donation for ingratitude, avoidance of contract because of error or fear, raising of damage claims. Right to enforce such claims expires at end of three years.

Some rights are even more limited in time (e.g., actions for libel, unless assault is involved).

MARRIAGE:

"Age of consent" is fixed at 20 for males and 18 for females. In order to contract marriage both parties must be capable of judgment.

Consent Required.—Minors or incapacitated persons wishing to marry must secure consent of their legal representative. In case of emergency consent may be secured by decision of court.

Prohibited Marriages.—Following impediments to marriage are provided by Liechtenstein marriage act: consanguinity, adoption and existing marital bond.

Ceremonial Marriage.—Civil ceremony is obligatory under Liechtenstein law.

Annulment.—Marriage may be annulled by court ex officio or upon application of injured party in following cases: where marriage was prohibited; where either party is physically or psychically impotent; where either party is not capable of judgment; where marriage was contracted without consent of legal representative; where either party was mistaken about identity of other; where consent of either party was obtained by fraud or by duress; where compulsory formality was omitted at time of marriage; where either party did not intend to establish community of life by marriage but to circumvent provisions on acquisition of Liechtenstein citizenship.

MARRIED WOMEN:

See topics Husband and Wife; Marriage.

MORTGAGES:

(Sachenrecht LGBl.1923/4).

MORTGAGES . . . *continued*

Debts may be secured by real estate either as a mortgage (Grundpfandverschreibung, Art. 296ff.), or as a mortgage certificate (Schuldbrief, Art. 319ff.), or as a land charge certificate (Gült, Art. 325ff.). Mortgage secures a determined, or undetermined, existing, future, or contingent debt. Mortgage certificate is a collateral security of a determined and unconditional bond. Land charge certificate secures payments due by present owner of a piece of real estate without any accompanying personal obligation. Mortgage certificate and land charge certificate are negotiable instruments issued to name or to bearer. They may be transferred by endorsement to name of purchaser and transfer of instrument or, for bearer certificates, by actual transfer of instrument. Certain exceptions provided, debtor may pay interest to former creditor unless he was informed of assignment. Capital must be reimbursed to person qualifying as creditor.

Certain exceptions provided, mortgages, mortgage certificates and land charge certificates become effective upon their entry in Real Register. Maximum amount must be stated in Swiss currency. Entries, including amendments and cancellations, are made only upon execution of a publicly authenticated document. Priority is established according to rank designated in Real Register, not according to date of registration. Stipulations can be entered in Real Register to effect that upon cancellation of a mortgage, mortgage certificate, or land charge certificate prior in rank, subsequent mortgages, mortgage certificates or land charge certificates may succeed in such rank.

When real estate is sold and buyer acknowledges his personal liability for debts secured by a mortgage or a mortgage certificate on such property, liability of original debtor terminates unless creditor files written objections with original debtor within one year.

Debts secured by mortgages or mortgage certificates or land charge certificates are not subject to statute of limitations. If debt is not paid in time, creditor may sell property by execution. Same includes all accessories such as, unless expressly stipulated otherwise, plant, hotel furniture, etc., also rents accrued since beginning of execution proceedings. Property gives security for capital, expenses necessitated by execution, interest of delay, outstanding interest for three years preceding last due date and outstanding interest since such due date. If there is more than one creditor, proceeds of sale are distributed according to rank of mortgage, mortgage certificate or land charge certificates.

Mortgages, mortgage certificates and land charge certificates are cancelled upon cancellation of their entry in Real Register or upon total destruction of piece of real estate given as security. Cancellation or return of instrument of a mortgage certificate or a land charge certificate can be requested upon reimbursement of capital.

MOTOR VEHICLES:

See Switzerland Law Digest.

NOTARIES PUBLIC:

Unknown in Liechtenstein. Legalizations, etc., are made by the princely county court. In special cases, arbitrator (Vermittler) can perform notarial functions.

PARTNERSHIP:

Law recognizes two different kinds of companies: First includes association, company limited by shares, limited partnership with share capital, joint interest company, limited liability company, reg. cooperative association, establishment, foundation; second comprises simple partnership, silent partnership, general partnership, limited partnership, general partnership, with limited liability. Belonging to either of above there is also known "Trust" ("Treuhandschaft") which has been adopted from Anglo-American law (see topic Trusts).

Founder and directors may be foreigners; there are no limitations as to their number. One member, however, of board of directors must be domiciled in Liechtenstein and must comply with certain professional qualifications. Minimum capital is Sfr. 50,000 for companies limited by shares and SFr. 30,000 for all other companies.

Companies of first class must be recorded in public commercial register, whereby they attain legal effect. Some foundations, e.g. family foundations, need not be recorded.

Owing to amendments to companies law of 1980, all companies running business according to commercial principles or companies whose statutory objects include such business must appoint auditing agency. Companies limited by shares always need auditing agency.

Holding and other companies which do not have real economic activity in Liechtenstein need not have office there but must be represented by firm or citizen residing in Liechtenstein.

Liechtenstein company is usually formed by Liechtenstein trustee for client. This procedure guarantees full anonymity to real founder. Forming of company only takes a few days.

PATENTS:

Liechtenstein forms joint patent territory with Switzerland. (LGBl, 1980 Nr. 31). Swiss patents are valid in Liechtenstein. Liechtenstein patent attorneys are admitted before Swiss and before European patent office. Liechtenstein is member of Munich patent treaty (European patent organisation) and can be nominated by any applicant, although nomination of either Liechtenstein or Switzerland will be considered sufficient to cover whole territory. Same applies to patent cooperation treaty of which Liechtenstein is also member.

PLEDGES:

(Sachenrecht Art. 365ff., LGBl. 1923/4).

Personal property is pledged by being delivered into possession of pledgee. Cattle may be pledged by registration in a special register and notification of office of execution of debts. Such pledges may only secure credits of certain institutions licensed by authorities in charge.

Claims are pledged by written agreement and, if desired, by notifying debtor. If such claim is established under a written agreement, same must be delivered into possession of pledgee. Negotiable instruments to bearer may be pledged by being delivered into possession of pledgee. Negotiable instruments to an individual name require furthermore an endorsement or an assignment in favour of pledgee. If, besides an instrument giving title to merchandise, separate warrants have been issued in order to evidence an existing pledge on merchandise, same must be given into possession of pledgee and notice thereof must be made on any other instrument giving title to merchandise. If shares are pledged, pledgor appears as shareholder in general meeting of shareholders. (Art. 390).

More than one pledge can be given on same property. To this effect pledgor must notify pledgee in writing and instruct him to deliver, upon payment of his debt, property to second pledgee. (Art 368). Pledgee may himself pledge property, but needs consent of pledgor. (Art. 369).

Pledge is not effective as long as it remains in exclusive power of pledgor.

Pledge is terminated when pledgee has lost possession or right to recover possession over pledge. Upon reimbursement of debt, pledgor can ask pledgee to return pledge to person entitled. If debt is not paid in time, pledgee may start execution proceedings or sell it, if specifically so agreed. Same includes accessories and, when claims have been pledged, as a rule, income deriving therefrom. Pledges give security for capital, interest, costs of execution and interest of delay. (Art. 373).

PRINCIPAL AND AGENT:

Power of attorney contracts can be made either verbally or in writing. Power of attorney can be general or special. In order to carry out certain business transactions (purchase and sale of articles, loan agreements, carrying on a lawsuit, signing a settlement, etc.) a power of attorney is necessary, which is given expressly for these kinds of transactions. For certain other transactions (gifts, company contracts, etc.) a special power of attorney is needed which is given for each separate transaction.

Lawsuit power of attorney must be given in writing; if made out in a foreign country, court can demand a notarial attestation of principal's signature.

Speaking generally, power of attorney expires at death either of principal or of agent; but a lawsuit power of attorney is not withdrawn at death of principal, nor a power of attorney made out by a merchant in mercantile trade.

Power of attorney can be withdrawn at all times by either principal or agent. Principal is, however, responsible to agent for all damages accruing to him in consequence of a premature withdrawal, and agent is responsible to principal for all damages accruing to him by reason of agent's prematurely ending power of attorney which was given him for purpose of completing transaction entrusted to him.

Where agent enters into a legal transaction with a third person who is aware that he is acting under a power of attorney, all rights and duties thereunder belong to and are imposed on principal. Agent who exceeds limits of his power of attorney or one who falsely pretends to act in behalf of a principal (falsus procurator) is responsible to third persons dealing with him in good faith, for all damages sustained, and in commercial transactions he can be compelled by third person to perform all obligations which he, in virtue of his supposed power of attorney, has incurred in name of supposed principal.

REAL PROPERTY:

Liechtenstein law distinguishes between immovable things, immovables (Grundstücke), tangible movable things, tangible movables (bewegliche Sachen or Fahrnis), and intangibles (choses in action [Forderungen or Obligationen] and negotiable instruments, bills and notes). A separate category of property are the so-called immaterial or industrial property rights, e.g., rights on patents, trademarks.

Immovables are: (1) land, (2) independent and lasting rights entered in Land Register, e.g., specific building leases (right in rem), right to springs, (3) mines (Sachenrecht/SR Art. 34). Ownership of immovables comprehends all buildings, plants and springs. (SR Art. 47). Disposition of an immovable made without reservations extends also to tangible movables which, according to local usage or intention of owner of immovable, are permanently provided for as to management, use or preservation, and brought in many ways into relationship to immovable for its service. (SR Art. 23/24). Restricted rights in rem on immovables include: servitudes (SR Art. 198), usufruct (SR Art. 216-253), land charges (SR Art. 254-264), mortgages (see topic Mortgages).

Effective in 1965 (LGBl, 1965/25) new law allowing ownership of a particular story or floor of a building was introduced and, in connection therewith, provisions concerning co-ownership have been adopted.

Acquisition.—There is a distinction between underlying legal ground (causa) for acquisition of ownership or restricted rights in rem on immovables and acquisition itself. Underlying legal ground gives an obligatory right of entry of ownership or of restricted right in rem into Land Register; only such entry brings right in rem into existence (principle of entry [into the Land Register]). There are certain exceptions of ipso jure acquisition of ownership or restricted rights in rem on immovables, e.g., in case of heirship, judgment, execution. In such cases, entry takes place as a mere declaratory measure, which however is a condition precedent for a disposition of right. For mortgages, principle of entry is as a rule fully applicable.

Entry in Land Register pertaining to ownership or to a restricted right in rem is only valid, if underlying legal ground is valid (principle of legality or of causality; SR Art. 626.) However, acquisition of ownership or of a restricted right in rem on immovables by an acquirer relying bona fide on an entry in Land Register is protected (principle of public faith of Land Register; SR Art. 625).

A kind of effect of rights in rem can be given to certain obligatory rights pertaining to immovables by way of "annotation" in Land Register (SR Art. 556), e.g., to right of preemption, of purchase, of repurchase, of ordinary lease, of usufructuary lease. Co-owners of an immovable have, by virtue of law without entry in Land Register, a right of preemption against any third person who has acquired a share in immovable.

Agreements for conveyance or encumbrance of immovables require for validity the form of a written contract and to get real estate requires registration in Land Register, without exception. (SR Art. 38).

Acquisition by Nonresidents.—Based on law acquisition of real estate by resident and non-resident aliens or by legal entities in which such have majority interest are to

See Topical Index in front part of this volume.

REAL PROPERTY . . . *continued*
be licensed by special commissions (Grundverkehrskommission). Permission for non-resident aliens or legal entities are not given. (Grundverkehrsgesetz, LGBl, 1975/5).

STATUTES:

The Liechtenstein Laws are published in Liechtenstein Law Gazette which appears as case may be. Summary of leading cases and court decisions is published quarterly in Liechtenstein legal paper (Liechtensteinische Juristenzeitung).

TAXATION:

Holding and domicilary companies only are subject to annual tax on capital of one per mille; based on company's own property, minimum SFr, 1,000 a year. No tax on profit, tax on earnings and tax on property have to be paid, except for companies whose capital is divided into shares; they pay 4% tax on dividends distributed and on liquidation surplus.

Double Taxation.—Liechtenstein has agreement for avoidance of double taxation with Austria only. (LGBl. 1970/37).

Value Added Tax.—Since 1995 value added tax is imposed at rate of 6.5% on most goods and services. Export are zero-rated. (LGB1. 1994/84).

TRADEMARKS AND TRADENAMES:

Trademarks and tradenames which are recorded at the patent office enjoy monopoly rights to be used only by the owner.

TREATIES:

See topics Judgments; and Constitution and Government, subhead Commercial Treaties; Taxation, subhead Double Taxation.

Liechtenstein is party to Convention Abolishing Requirement of Legalisation for Foreign Public Documents.

Since May 1995 Liechtenstein is party to Agreement concerning the European Economic Area (EEA).

TRUSTS:

Legal concept of trusts under laws of Liechtenstein is based upon Anglo-American trusts law. Trust is managed by one or more trustees on basis of instrument of trust which also gives trust its own name. In accordance with Anglo-American trust law, Liechtenstein trust does not have legal personality.

Special statute governs so-called "Treuunternehmen", trust enterprise, which is Liechtenstein adoption of so-called "business trust" or "Massachusetts Trust". Trust enterprise may be formed with or without legal personality and may be described as business association in terms of laws of Liechtenstein and has its own organization and its own capital (trust fund). It can be formed for either economic or other purposes (in which case it deviates from original concept). In deviation from rule governing trusts in general all liabilities arising out of legal existence and activities of trust enterprise are limited to trust fund.

WILLS:

A last will providing for the residuary estate is called "Testament," otherwise "Codicil."

Wills must be either holographic or at least personally subscribed by the testator. In the latter case three subscribing witnesses to the will are required; at least two of them must be present at the execution.

The testator must respect the forced heirship provisions, which compel him to give a certain fraction of his property to his children, if any, or otherwise to his parents. The "Pflichtteil" is equal to one-half of the intestate share. However, disinheritance is permitted in one of the following cases: Apostacy from Christianity; not supporting the testator in case of need; crime punished with 20 or more years in jail; or leading a life against public morals.

LUXEMBOURG LAW DIGEST

(The following is a list of all Topics, including cross-references, covered in this Digest.)

LUXEMBOURG LAW DIGEST

Revised for 1997 edition by

BONN & SCHMITT, of the Luxembourg Bar.

ABSENTEES:

When person has ceased to appear at place of his domicile or residence, and if his whereabouts are unknown, any interested party or public prosecutor ("ministère public") may apply to court ("juge des tutelles") to obtain judgment that such person is presumed to be absent. (C.C. 112). Court may appoint one or more relatives, or any other person, to represent absentee and to administer estate. Rights and duties of such representative are governed by same rules as those applying to guardianship of minors. (C.C. 113). If absentee reappears or if he provides information regarding his whereabouts, representative's mission ends and absentee takes over management of estate. (C.C. 118).

If more than ten years have passed since judgment of "presumption of absence", court may, upon motion by any interested party or public prosecutor, declare actual absence. (C.C. 122).

Judgment of actual absence has same legal consequences as death of absentee.

ACKNOWLEDGMENTS:

If foreign official acts and deeds are to be used officially in Luxembourg, signatures appearing therein must be certified by relevant authorities in country of origin, and signature of latter will have to be certified by Luxembourg consular or diplomatic officer. Luxembourg is party to several international conventions which simplify foregoing procedure for documents from Contracting States (Hague Convention of Oct. 5, 1961 [Luxembourg law of Mar. 14, 1978]; European Convention of June 7, 1968 [Luxembourg law of Mar. 14, 1978]; Athens Convention of Sept. 15, 1977 [Luxembourg law of Apr. 2, 1981]).

ACTIONS:

District court ("tribunal d'arrondissement") has full and common jurisdiction. District court consists of several specialized divisions.

In addition to district court, there are several specialized courts, with special jurisdictions, mainly administrative, labor law and social security courts.

If subject matter of case is valued in excess of LUF 200,000 case is heard by district court. Certain matters must be submitted to district court without taking into account amount involved. District court also hears appeals from decisions of Justices of Peace.

Jurisdiction of commercial courts (specialized division of district court) extends to (1) litigation relating to business transactions among traders, merchants and bankers; (2) litigation between shareholders or between members of board and shareholders of companies, if such litigation is related to business of their company; and (3) litigation involving any act of trade between any persons. (C. Com. 631). Commercial courts also deal with matters of bankruptcy. (C. Com. 635).

Justice of Peace ("Justice de Paix") has jurisdiction over matters valued at less than LUF 200,000, regardless of commercial or civil nature of litigation. Justice of Peace also has special jurisdiction in certain matters irrespective of amount involved.

Litigation that arises from labor relations is within jurisdiction of labor courts and labor courts of appeal.

Social security courts deal with social security matters.

Note: Administrative courts will be subject to major reform in 1996, introducing double degree of jurisdiction.

Litigation arising out of administrative decisions of State and other public authorities and agencies are brought, either directly, or after unsuccessful complaint to competent Minister, before Litigation Committee of Council of State ("Comité du Contentieux du Conseil d'Etat").

Actions may only be brought against individual administrative decisions; thus, general regulatory acts may not be challenged before Council of State.

Two legal actions are provided for by law: Action for annulment and action for reformation. Latter only exists if law specially provides for that possibility.

Unsuccessful party is ordered in judgment to pay costs. Sharing of costs is ordered when both parties are unsuccessful to some degree. As rule, costs are not very high; they include court costs, filing fees and registration tax for judgment. Each party has to support its own fees of counsel.

However, if court considers it inequitable that party have to pay certain costs, e.g. lawyers' fees other than those already included in legal costs, judge may order other party to pay such sum. (C.C.P. 131-1).

See topic Dispute Resolution, subhead Arbitration.

AFFIDAVITS:

Under Luxembourg law there is no general document under oath analogous to affidavit. Under certain conditions, written declarations from third parties may be submitted in court proceeding. (C.C.P. 274). Such declarations must relate to facts in which author of declaration was involved or of which he has personal knowledge. (C.C.P. 275-2).

AGENCY:

See topic Principal and Agent.

ALIENS:

Aliens have same rights and obligations as Luxembourg nationals, but exceptions to this rule may be created by law. (Const. 112). Status and capacity of aliens are governed by their national law.

Residence.—Aliens who wish to take up residence in Luxembourg for more than three months must apply for governmental license to do so by registering with local authorities of location of their residence. Such license is evidenced by delivery of foreign national identity card ("carte d'identité d'étranger"). Certain conditions must be met prior to delivery of such document, most important being valid work permit or business license. Nationals from EC Member States have right to reside in Luxembourg and need not obtain prior work permit or business license to do so. They will automatically be given residence permit, evidenced by residence card for EC nationals ("carte de séjour de ressortissant d'un Etat membre de la CEE").

Actions by Aliens.—Aliens suing in Luxembourg may be compelled, at request of Luxembourg-based defendant, to give sufficient surety to cover costs and damages to which plaintiff may be subject. (C.C.P. 166). Luxembourg is party to many bilateral and multilateral treaties which have abolished this requirement (Hague Convention of July 17, 1905 [Luxembourg decree of July 11, 1909], Hague Convention of Mar. 1, 1954 [Luxembourg decree of Mar. 30, 1956]).

Actions against Aliens.—Aliens may be sued in Luxembourg if they are domiciled in or residents of Luxembourg. Luxembourg courts will also accept jurisdiction if Luxembourg is place of performance of contract, in real estate matters if real estate is located in Luxembourg, in tort actions if tortious actions occurred in Luxembourg, or in bankruptcy matters if bankruptcy is declared in Luxembourg. International treaties may modify these rules.

Luxembourg courts will moreover accept jurisdiction in matters involving Luxembourg nationals even if underlying obligations have been assumed abroad with foreign national. (C.C. 15).

Corporations Owned or Controlled by Aliens.—There are no restrictions on basis of nationality of parties involved regarding ownership of Luxembourg corporation. Same is true as far as membership of board of directors and other corporate functions are concerned.

ALIMONY:

See topic Divorce.

ARBITRATION AND AWARD:

See topic Dispute Resolution.

ASSIGNMENT:

Basic rules regarding assignment of claims not embodied in negotiable instrument are set out in Civil Code. (C.C. 1689-1691). To make such assignment effective vis-à-vis third parties, assignment must be notified to debtor or be accepted by latter. Notification and acceptance may be made by notarial deed or simple contract. Assignment is valid between parties at exchange of consent.

ASSOCIATIONS:

Nonprofit organizations may be set up under law of Apr. 21, 1928, as modified in Feb. 22, 1984 and Mar. 4, 1994 ("Loi du 21 avril 1928 sur les associations et les fondations sans but lucratif, telle qu'elle a été modifiée par les lois des 22 février 1984 et 4 mars 1994").

Associations ("associations sans but lucratif") may be set up freely, and no governmental approval is required. Such governmental approval is, however, required for acceptance of gifts and donations, value of which exceeds certain threshold.

Fondations ("établissements d'utilité publique") are associations which pursue exclusively philanthropic, religious, scientific, artistic, social, sporting or international purpose. Foundations may be set up by notarial deed or by will. They must be authorized by grand-ducal decree prior to obtaining their full legal existence.

Associations and foundations are subject to three different taxes: Corporation tax, wealth tax and annual subscription tax.

Profits are basis of assessment of corporation tax. They are assessed on basis of regulations governing personal income tax, i.e., net worth comparison, taking difference between net assets at beginning and end of year.

Tax rates range from 20%, when taxable income does not exceed LUF 400,000, to 34% when taxable income is in excess of LUF 1,312,000.

Associations and foundations are subject to wealth tax on worldwide net worth. Tax rates range from 0.3% to 0.8%. In Luxembourg City, tax rate is 0.5%. However, both entities are exempted from corporation and wealth tax if they have religious, charitable or general public purpose.

If net value of their movable and immovable property exceeds LUF 1,000,000, associations and foundations must pay annual subscription tax of 0.12% on this value.

ATTACHMENT:

General prejudgment attachment ("saisie-conservatoire") exists only in commercial matters and is only granted where debtor may become insolvent. (C.C.P. 417).

Any creditor may, if existence of his claim is sufficiently established, apply to court to obtain prejudgment attachment of debtor's assets held by third parties. (C.C.P. 558).

There are other special types of prejudgment attachments, such as "saisie-gagerie" (C.C.P. 819), for conservation of tenant's furniture, "saisie-revendication" (C.C.P. 826), by which dispossessed owner claims property held by third party, and "saisie-foraine" (C.C.P. 822), by which creditor attaches personal property of nonresident debtors located in jurisdiction.

When enforcing final judgment, all real or personal property of debtor may be seized. Certain assets, which are enumerated by law, cannot be attached, or can only be attached in part, because of certain humanitarian considerations.

BANKING:

The Finance Act (Luxembourg law of Apr. 5, 1993 relating to financial sector) constitutes Luxembourg's general legal framework for all banking and nonbanking financial activities.

Act (most important provisions of former Banking Act of 1974 are maintained) implements provisions on EC banking passport and professional obligations of bankers

See Topical Index in front part of this volume.

BANKING . . . *continued*
and other financial intermediaries. Topics covered by statute are: conditions for access to financial sector; professional obligations in connection with banking and nonbanking financial activities; supervision, monitoring and control of banking and nonbanking financial activities; reorganization and liquidation of financial institutions; penalties for infringing rules set by Act. Annex lists activities to be considered as banking activities (same list as in Second EC Banking Directive).

BANKRUPTCY:

Only traders and commercial companies can be declared bankrupt. Trader is in state of bankruptcy if he ceases making due payments and has no more credit standing. (C.Com. 437). Bankrupt person must, within three days after having ceased payments, file declaration with register of commercial division of district court admitting insolvency. (C.Com. 440).

Bankruptcy will be declared upon such admittance. It may also be declared at request of bankrupt's creditors or on court's own motion. (C.Com. 442).

As from date of bankruptcy judgment, bankrupt may no longer administer his estate, and all transactions, as well as all payments made by him or to him, are null and void.

Same bankruptcy judgment also determines date of cessation of payments and following transactions, if carried out during such period or within ten days immediately preceding such period, will be null and void: all donations and all transactions where bankrupt receives grossly insufficient consideration; payments of unmatured debts; payments of matured debts not made in cash or negotiable instruments; all mortgages, pledges and other security rights for debts previously incurred. (C.Com. 445). Furthermore, all payments of matured debts, as well as all transactions with good consideration, which occurred during period of cessation of payments, may be voided, if other contracting party had actual knowledge of fact that bankrupt had ceased payments.

As result of bankruptcy judgment, all debts of bankrupt mature. (C.Com. 450). As of same date, interest will no longer accrue on unpreferred debts. (C.Com. 451).

Administration of bankrupt's estate is taken over by one or more court-appointed receivers. Actions of receivers are monitored by specially commissioned judge ("juge-commissaire"). (C.Com. 466).

Creditors are required to file declaration of their claims with registrar of commercial division of district court within maximum period of 20 days. This period of time may be extended for nonresident creditors. Declaration must contain full particulars of creditor and his claim. Receivers will examine claims filed which they may accept or dispute. If claim is disputed subsequent hearing will be held. If after such hearing claim remains still disputed, it will be submitted to court.

Creditors are informed of above proceedings by publications and advertisements, as well as by registered mail, once their identity is known.

After examination and discussion of claims, meeting of creditors is held, which will decide whether or not they will enter into settlement with debtor. If it is decided not to enter into settlement, receivers will liquidate estate by selling assets and paying off all bankruptcy expenses. Remaining assets will be divided equally among all unsecured creditors.

Special Procedures for Credit Institutions.—Credit institution which has ceased to fulfil its obligations and whose financial situation is wavering may be ordered to wind up its affairs by district court if public prosecutor or officials of Luxembourg Monetary Institute ("Institut Monétaire Luxembourgois" or IML) request such measures to be taken. Credit institution may further be wound up if previously granted delay of payment did not lead to improvement of institution's financial situation. Court then will appoint judge-commissioner and one or more trustees. Court may apply normal rules of bankruptcy, and accordingly it may fix within six months preceding bankruptcy date from which credit institution ceased to make due payments. Effects of bankruptcy will start at moment of court decision or at moment counterparty to transaction has knowledge of bankruptcy, and not retroactively at 0.00 am of day of court decision as in general law. Court chooses form of liquidation. As soon as liquidation is terminated, trustee produces statement of institution's assets, and court closes liquidation after due examination of documents submitted by commissioners appointed by court. Notice of voluntary liquidation by credit institution must be made to IML one month prior to notice for extraordinary shareholders' meeting called to consider such liquidation.

Law of May 3, 1996 has provided safe legal basis for bilateral and multilateral netting agreements between banks, other professionals of financial sector, UCITS and major companies in case of bankruptcy of one party. Set-offs carried out under such agreements remain valid after bankruptcy. Validity of close-out, anti-cherry-picking, connexity and default clauses is expressly recognized. Netting agreements made during period set for cessation of payments and covering immature debts are void.

BILLS AND NOTES:

Luxembourg is party to two Geneva Conventions of June 7, 1930 (Luxembourg law of Dec. 15, 1962) dealing, respectively, with uniform law on bills of exchange and promissory notes and conflicts of laws rules applicable thereto. Luxembourg is also party to Mar. 19, 1931 Geneva Convention on checks (Luxembourg law of Mar. 14, 1968, as amended by law of Jan. 16, 1987) dealing, respectively with uniform law on checks, and conflicts of laws rules applicable thereto.

There are no stamp duties on creation, payment or use of bills, notes and checks.

Certain formal requirements must be respected when creating bill of exchange. It must include words "bill of exchange". It must contain order to pay given amount, identity of drawer, maturity date, location where payment shall be made, identity of payee, and date and place of creation. It also must be signed by drawer.

Bills of exchange are transferable by endorsement. Endorsement is only valid if made without conditions. Endorsement can be to named endorsee or to bearer. Endorsers are liable for acceptance and payment of bill, but they may exclude subsequent endorsements, in which case they will only be liable towards their endorsee.

Holder of bill may request its acceptance by drawee until maturity. Acceptance results from drawee's signature on face side of bill or by word "accepted" or any equivalent word on bill. By accepting bill, drawee assumes personal commitment to pay at maturity.

Payment of bill may be guaranteed by third party or signatory acting as "aval". Such "aval" may be given on bill or on separate document. Guarantor must indicate who guaranteed party is, since otherwise guarantee will be deemed to be for benefit of drawer. Guarantor will be liable in same way as person who is beneficiary of guarantee.

Refusal of acceptance or payment must be established by formal deed ("protêt faute d'acceptation ou faute de paiement"). Holder must inform drawer and his endorsee of such refusal. Each endorser will in turn have to notify his own endorser.

Drawer, drawee, endorser or guarantors are jointly and severally liable towards holder, who may sue each of them separately or jointly. All actions are subject to certain time limits. Against drawer who has accepted bill, action must be brought within three years following maturity. Actions by holder against endorsers and drawer must be brought within one year from date of formal protest or maturity date.

Actions of endorsers against each other and against drawer must be brought within six months after payment or action against endorser for payment.

Promissory notes are governed by same basic rules as bills of exchange.

Checks must contain term "check". They are payable on demand. They must contain unconditional order to pay certain amount of money, name of drawee, place of payment, date and place of issuance of check, and signature of drawer. Drawee must be bank. Check may be payable to given person or to bearer. Checks may be transferred by endorsement unless such endorsement was excluded by drawee. Endorser guarantees payment of check unless he has excluded such guarantee. Endorser may also prohibit all further endorsements. Checks must be presented for payment after no later than eight days if drawn and payable in Luxembourg, 20 days if drawn inside Europe including Mediterranean, and 120 days if drawn elsewhere.

Checks may also be barred. Payment for such checks may only be made to banker or to client of drawee.

Drawing check in bad faith, where no sufficient funds are available for payment, constitutes criminal offense. Same is true if funds are withdrawn while check may still be presented for payment, or, even after expiration of time period provided for by law for presentation of check, if drawer fraudulently or in bad faith stops payment or withdraws funds necessary for payment.

CHATTEL MORTGAGE:

There are no chattel mortgages in Luxembourg, unless specifically provided for by law. Aircraft and ships can be mortgaged however.

Under certain conditions "floating charge" over business as going concern can be created ("gage sur fonds de commerce"). Charge may cover all assets of business, such as goodwill, trademarks, patents, lease contracts, business equipment and up to 50% of inventory. Parties may contractually agree exactly what will be charged. Receivables must be included expressly. This charge must be registered to become fully effective, no later than 15 days after contract was made.

Such floating charges may only be granted to bank and credit institutions approved by Luxembourg government.

COMMERCIAL REGISTER:

In each district court there is one register of commerce and companies ("registre de commerce et des sociétés"). It is open to public, and certified copies of any entries may be obtained upon payment of fees. All natural persons and legal entities pursuing commercial business activity must register. Failure to do so may be pleaded as defense to any court action brought by such person or entity, and is furthermore subject to fine.

Public offering of securities by domestic and foreign issuers must be preceded by filing of legal notice ("notice légale") with register, containing certain particulars regarding issuers and securities.

COMMISSIONS TO TAKE TESTIMONY:

See topic Depositions.

COMMUNITY PROPERTY:

Unless otherwise agreed upon by parties in marriage contract, community property includes all income of professional activity, interest and income of all assets, assets acquired during marriage. Assets that husband/wife owned prior to marriage, or acquired during marriage by inheritance or gift, do not form part of community property.

Right of administration and disposal rests with spouse via whom asset has entered community, except real estate. Spouse may not dispose of community property acquired or received by both spouses without consent of husband/wife. Action for annulment may be started by spouse who considers that other spouse has exceeded his powers in exercising right of disposal within two years after having knowledge of transaction.

CONSTITUTION AND GOVERNMENT:

Grand-Duchy of Luxembourg is constitutional monarchy. Its first constitution was established in 1841. Today's constitution dates back to 1868 and has been amended several times since.

Every five years, people elect members of Parliament (Chambre des Députés), which is main law-making body. Participation in these elections is compulsory.

Grand-Duke, a hereditary sovereign, is head of State. However, he exercises his powers in accordance with Constitution.

Country is governed by prime minister and his government, at present a coalition, which are responsible to Parliament.

There are three major political parties: Christian Democratic Party, Liberal Party, and Luxembourg Socialist Workers' Party.

All these parties are moderate parties and share same basic economic views. This has given Luxembourg tradition of political and social stability, as well as economic prosperity, which are unrivalled.

Judiciary.—According to art. 86 of Luxembourg Constitution, courts may only be created by law.

See Topical Index in front part of this volume.

CONSTITUTION AND GOVERNMENT . . . *continued*

Law of Mar. 7, 1980 on judicial system, as amended, regulates ordinary courts, which are constituted by professional judges, whereas several subsequent laws regulate special courts.

Judges are appointed for life.

CONTRACTS:

Distinction between Civil and Commercial Contracts.—General law of contracts is found in Civil Code. There is no separate comprehensive set of rules which defines and governs what are commonly called commercial contracts, although there are some commercial contracts that are governed by detailed legal rules. Contract may be commercial by its nature of because of commercial qualification of its author (contracts made in course of trade).

Same contract may be commercial for one party and civil for other; in this case, it is mixed contract, and civil law will apply to non-trader, and commercial law to trader. Jurisdiction of court is determined by status of defendant. If defendant is trader, it is commercial court; if defendant is non-trader, it is civil court.

Contracts Requiring Written Form; Registration; Notarial Deed or Other Formalities.—Under Luxembourg law, nearly all contracts are formed by agreement of parties concerned, and without any formality. Written form becomes necessary, however, for evidentiary reasons.

If contractual value exceeds LUF 100,000, contract must be in writing. For commercial contracts this rule is modified, since special rules of evidence will apply.

Some contracts require notarial deed for their validity, including marriage settlements and mortgage contracts.

Some contracts require particular form to be valid as against third parties, most important of such contracts being contract for sale of real estate. This contract requires notarial deed and must be registered and transcribed at mortgage registry office. Notarial deed and registration are required for formation of corporation, of partnership by shares ("société en commandite par actions"), or of limited liability company ("société à responsabilité limitée"). Such registration and transcription are separate and distinct from registration of trader with Trade Register, as set out above.

Sales Contracts: Special Requirements or Conditions.—Sales contracts require no special form other than written form necessary for reasons of evidence. However, law of May 19, 1961, regulates installment sales, to protect buyers from exorbitant charges.

According to Art. 1 of this law, it does not apply to contracts which are commercial for both parties and to sale of industrial or professional equipment for professional use. Decree of June 28, 1961, and decree of Apr. 14, 1965, further restrict application of this law. It applies only to sales having cash value of more than LUF 4,000 and of less than LUF 150,000.

Sales contracts between traders and non-professional buyers have also been largely affected by Law of Aug. 25, 1983, as amended, on consumer protection. Law intends to abolish any contractual disequilibrium arising out of inexperience or lack of knowledge of ultimate consumer. Clauses written into contract that exclusively benefit vendor are null and void.

Similarly, author of general conditions for sales contracts, i.e., vendor, may not include provisions for limited liability, withdrawal from contract, or compulsory recourse to arbitration, unless buyer has expressly accepted each one of these clauses in writing.

Elements of Fraud in Contracts.—Under Civil Code, consent is not valid if it has been obtained by error or if it has been extorted by duress or secured by fraud. (C.C. 1109). Fraud is ground for annulling contract only if means employed by one of parties were such that, without these means, other party would not have contracted. (C.C. 1116). These rules also apply to commercial contracts.

If there is obvious disproportion between performance of both parties to contract and if such disequilibrium is result of abuse of dominant position of one party and inexperience of other party, contract may be annulled or injured party's performance reduced. Burden of proof rests with injured party and annullment or reduction must be claimed within one year of conclusion of contract. (C.C. 1118).

Conflicts of Laws.—In absence of choice of law expressed by parties in their contract, Luxembourg courts apply to international contracts rules laid down in Rome Convention on law applicable to contractual obligations of June 19, 1980 (Luxembourg law of Mar. 27, 1986).

Consent; Offer and Acceptance.—Agreement is validly formed when offer has been made and accepted. Acceptance may result from silence, and need not always be expressed. It is matter of circumstances.

Permissible Subject Matter.—Subject matter of contract may include anything over which person may freely dispose (C.C. 1128), but may not however, be contrary to public policy or good morals, nor infringe any mandatory rules.

Performance.—Contracts must be performed faithfully. They must be fulfilled not only according to express terms of contract, but also according to all consequences which equity or common usage or very nature of obligation impose.

If one party does not perform its obligations, other party may seek to enforce contract in court or apply for termination of contract. If specific performance is not available, damages may be obtained.

Breach of contract, or termination or insufficient performance, entitles injured party to damages. Damages may be sought in court when party who violated contract refuses to pay damages stated in contract for such case, or when contract does not include amount of damages and parties cannot reach agreement on amount.

COPYRIGHT:

Copyright is protected by Luxembourg law of Mar. 29, 1972. This law covers all literary and artistic creations including computer software since law of Apr. 24, 1995. Copyright consists of exclusive right of author to publicly produce or reproduce his creation and to authorize production and reproduction thereof by third parties. Foreigners are treated in same way as Luxembourg citizens.

Luxembourg is signatory of most international conventions protecting copyright, including Berne Convention of Sept. 9, 1886, as amended (Luxembourg law of Nov. 19, 1974) and Universal Copyright Convention of Sept. 6, 1952 (Luxembourg law of June 13, 1955).

CORPORATIONS:

Types of Companies.—Luxembourg commercial companies are governed by law of Aug. 10, 1915, as amended.

All companies must have registered office ("siège social"), business name ("raison sociale" or "dénomination sociale") and specific business purpose ("objet social"). General and limited partnerships, joint stock company and limited liability company must have two or more partners.

There are no restrictions as to nationality of partners or as to their residence.

Commercial companies are formed by act of incorporation. For joint stock companies ("société anonyme"), limited partnerships by shares ("société en commandite par actions") and limited liability companies ("société à responsabilité limitée"), notarial deed is compulsory.

Publication in full of charter in official journal ("Mémorial") is required for joint stock company, limited partnership by shares, limited liability company, and cooperative society. For general and limited partnership it is sufficient to publish excerpt of charter. Amendments to charter must be published in same way.

General and limited partnerships are not restricted by legislation as to their system of management. However, in limited partnership management is reserved to general partners, whose role is same as that of general partners in general partnership. Silent partners may not take part in management of limited partnership.

In general partnership, if there is no contrary stipulation in charter, every partner represents legal entity, but decisions require consent of all partners. Charter often appoints one or more managers.

Management of cooperative society closely follows that of joint stock companies, but partners may freely regulate its management structure. In absence of any stipulation, law provides that company must be represented by director.

In limited partnership, liability of partners who take active part in its management is unlimited, whereas inactive or silent partner's liability is limited to amount of capital he has contributed to partnership.

In general partnership, partners are fully and personally liable.

In cooperative society, partners have unlimited liability, unless charter provides otherwise (which it generally does).

At formation of companies, tax of 1% is levied on invested capital. Joint stock companies are furthermore subject to annual subscription tax ("taxe d'abonnement") of 0.36%. Limited liability companies are subject to this tax at rate of 0.18%.

For income tax purposes, tax laws consider company as either personal company or capital company. Personal company has no separate existence under tax laws, and tax is levied upon individual partners according to their respective income from company. Capital companies, *i.e*, joint stock companies, limited liability companies, and limited partnerships by shares, are considered legal entities having separate existence and are subject to corporate tax on profits before distribution. Distributed profits are then subject to income tax at full rate applicable to recipient, if shareholder is Luxembourg resident. If he is not, only withholding tax is levied. Rate of this withholding tax is 15% and is reduced by most tax treaties.

Dissolution of any company may be effected on expiration of term fixed by act of incorporation, or if there is no extension of its term, by disappearance or impossibility of purpose of company. Dissolution may occur, too, if partners, according to formalities which differ from one company to other, agree to accelerate time of dissolution.

Joint Stock Companies ("Société Anonyme").—It is form usually adopted by foreign investors. It requires minimum capital of LUF 1,250,000 divided into shares, which are freely transferable unless corporate charter provides for certain restrictions. Shares may be in bearer form or registered form. Latter form is mandatory as long as shares have not been fully paid up. Capital must be subscribed entirely, but only 25% need be paid up at time of incorporation. Contributions that are not in cash must be valued by external qualified auditor. Company must have at least two shareholders. Liability of shareholders is limited to amount of their investment. Company is governed by board of directors, consisting of at least three members. Managing director, with day-to-day management powers, may be appointed by board. Statutory auditor must also be appointed. For companies meeting certain threshold figures, or engaged in certain types of activities (*e.g*, banking), annual accounts must be audited by qualified external auditors. Accounting standards are those imposed by EC rules.

Limited Liability Companies ("Société à Responsabilité Limitée").—Number of partners is restricted to 40. Partners' liability is limited to amount of their investment. Limited liability companies are run by one or several managers ("gérant"), who need not be partners.

If number of partners exceeds 25, law requires them to meet at least once a year in general assembly. Bylaws must mention date of this statutory general meeting. If there are fewer than 25 partners it is not legally necessary for them to meet at all; any resolution may be submitted to them for decision by mail and their vote may be expressed in writing. Resolution or proposed decision must be so clearly expressed as to make possible vote in negative or affirmative. If there are fewer than 25 partners, no statutory auditor is required. Capital of this type of company must be LUF 500,000 and shares must have nominal value of LUF 1,000 or multiple thereof. Shares must be subscribed and paid for in full. This type of company does not issue registered or bearer shares, but only participation certificates ("certificats de participation à personne déterminée"). Shares are personal and their transfer is subject to strict regulations.

Single Partner Limited Liability Companies.—1992 statute (Mémorial A 106, p. 3141) introduced limited liability company which is formed by one shareholder only. This law applies to small and medium sized enterprises.

Such company can either be formed at incorporation or by concentration of all shares in hands of one shareholder.

CORPORATIONS . . . *continued*

Holding companies must have as their sole object holding of participations in other Luxembourg or foreign companies, and management and development of such participations. Holding companies may not carry on any industrial or trading activity on their own. They may not have any establishment open to public. If company meets foregoing criteria, it will be taxed as holding company. As far as company law is concerned, holding companies are not special type of company and they may be organized as one of commercial companies described above, although practically they will mostly incorporate as joint stock company.

Main activities of holding company are: (1) Acquisition, management, exploitation and sales of participations in Luxembourg and in foreign enterprises; (2) acquisition, management and sale of official or private Luxembourg or foreign securities, producing interest income at fixed rate; (3) acquisition of patents and granting to other parties of licenses to make use of such patents. Proceeds of sales of patents should be reinvested in securities within one year. Nevertheless, isolated sale without reinvestment will not necessarily jeopardize holding company status; (4) granting of credit in all forms to companies in which holding company has participation, or to other parties to which it has conceded license to exploit its patents; (5) opening of accounts (for holding company's shareholders only) showing credit or debit balances. Ratio of subscribed capital (even if not fully paid up) and total credit balances (including bank and other borrowings, with exception of bonds) may not be higher than 1 to 3; (6) issuance to public of bonds or debentures; however, bond debt must not exceed ten times paid-up capital of holding company; (7) acquisition and holding of real property, but only insofar as such property is needed for holding company's own use. It may, however, hold interest in real estate company; (8) supervision of financial administration of companies in which it has interest and carrying out of technical and commercial control.

Financial holding companies are special holding companies allowed to collect funds in order to finance other companies within same group. They may also advance funds for unpaid invoices of group of companies, bills of exchange included.

According to tax authorities, group of companies encompasses all those companies united by substantial (minimum 25%) shareholding and common economic purpose, as well as all those companies that are mutually dependent and that are united under common name.

Financial holding companies must respect following conditions: (1) Holding company must be organized as joint stock company (société anonyme), as described above; (2) parent company or member companies of same industrial or financial group must appear as founders of holding company. In this connection, it should be observed that only companies in which group has majority participation can be considered as member companies; (3) shares must be in and remain in registered form; (4) shareholders must agree not to sell their interests in holding company to parties outside group, until all loans are fully repaid; (5) as result of administrative decisions, financial holding company would normally be expected to: (a) invest only in group companies, principally in shares, and (b) invest at least 25% of its subscribed capital; (6) financial holding company may use proceeds of its loans and its other funds only for benefit of enterprises in group. This provision must be taken up in statutes of holding company. Financial holding company may issue bonds in amount up to ten times its paid-in capital.

Taxation of holding companies is extremely favorable. Their tax base is net worth, not income.

On incorporation, registration tax of 1% on holding company's statutory capital must be paid.

During its lifetime only tax which will be levied is annual subscription duty of 0.2% on current value of securities issued. There are no other taxes. No taxes on profits or withholding taxes on distributed profits or interest apply.

For holding companies with statutory capital of at least LUF 1 billion, or equivalent thereof in foreign currencies ("holding milliardaire"), special rules of taxation, which under certain circumstances will be more favorable, will apply at company's option.

Sicav (Sicaf).—Sicavs ("société à capital variable") and Sicafs ("société à capital fixe") are special purpose companies, exclusive business purpose of which is to be investment funds, i.e., entities which collect investments from public and pool them with view to investing them on risk spreading basis. Their legal status is governed by Luxembourg law of Mar. 30, 1988 on collective investment undertakings. 1988 law, while creating special legal, regulatory and tax framework for these companies, expressly states, however, that, where it does not contain special provisions to contrary, rules of general corporate law of Aug. 10, 1915, as amended, continue to apply. Provisions that apply are primarily those relating to joint stock companies.

Sicavs are companies with variable share capital. This means that their capital varies constantly depending on their redemptions and issuances of shares. Sicafs have fixed share capital. In both instances, minimum capital required is 50 million Luxembourg francs or its equivalent in foreign currency. This minimum must be reached no later than six months following date of incorporation.

One-time capital contribution tax is payable by such investment companies at fixed rate of LUF 50,000. In addition, on yearly basis, these companies pay 0.06% subscription duty, which is levied on net asset value of their portfolio. It is payable quarterly in arrears. There are no other taxes on income or distributions, whether made to Luxembourg residents or foreigners.

While there are no restrictions based on nationality regarding operation of these companies, it is however legal requirement that central management of entity be in Luxembourg. Rationale behind this rule is to facilitate task of supervisory authorities ("Institut Monétaire Luxembourgeois", or IML), depositary bank and external qualified auditor in monitoring fund's activities. Following activities consequently must be undertaken in Luxembourg: fund accounting and bookkeeping; issue and redemption of units; and calculation of fund's net asset value. It is furthermore mandatory that share registers be kept in Luxembourg. All documents regarding entity (i.e., prospectus, notices, and financial statements) must be prepared in cooperation with Luxembourg authorities and must be mailed from Luxembourg.

Before beginning operations, all investment funds must obtain approval of IML, which monitors activities of Luxembourg-based investment funds.

During their existence, funds must provide periodic financial statements regarding their investment portfolio to IML and periodic accounts must be published for information to public. It is also requirement that each shareholder be provided with latest prospectus and appendixes at date of subscription. External qualified auditor, approved by IML, must furthermore be appointed to monitor activities of fund.

Besides forms of SICAV or SICAF, undertaking for collective investment may also choose form of "fonds commun de placement", i.e., unit trust or mutual fund (FCP).

FCPs are undivided coproprietorships of assets made up and managed according to principle of risk spreading on behalf of its unit holders who are liable only up to amount invested by them. Their rights and obligations, and investment rules, are all determined by FCP's management regulations. Such fund has no legal personality itself and therefore needs to rely on its management company to do business. Regulatory- and taxwise, same rules as for SICAVs or SICAFs apply.

Economic Interest Grouping (EIG) and European Economic Interest Grouping (EEIG).—EIG and EEIG have been created by two laws dated Mar. 25, 1991.

Aim of these groupings is to facilitate or to develop economic activities of their members and to improve or increase results of those activities. Therefore purpose of EIG and EEIG must be related to economic activity of their members. Such link is essential and distinguishes these groupings from company, which has much broader object, i.e., realizing and sharing profits.

Both have legal personality and their members are fully and personally liable.

There are no essential differences between EIG and EEIG. Members of EEIG must however originate from at least two Member States of European Community.

COURTS:

See topic Actions.

CURRENCY:

Luxembourg and Belgium have entered into monetary union, under which Belgian bank notes and coins are legal tender in Luxembourg. Issue of Luxembourg currency is limited. Monetary unit is franc and Luxembourg franc has same value as Belgian franc. Luxembourg has no central bank, and consequently Belgian central bank assumes some of these functions for Luxembourg.

Luxembourg has, however, its own financial monitoring body, "Institut Monétaire Luxembourgeois", or IML. IML's mission is varied. It is in charge of monetary matters. It monitors credit institutions, banks and nonbanking financial institutions. It also administers Luxembourg securities regulations.

Foreign exchange regulations are extremely liberal and there are no current restrictions on capital movements.

DEATH:

See topic Absentees.

Death certificate is delivered by registrar ("officier de l'état civil"), upon production of medical doctor's certificate evidencing such death.

Actions for Death.—Actions for death resulting from wrongful or negligent conduct may be brought by surviving spouse, descendants and ascendants, and other heirs. Damages may cover pecuniary loss, as well as loss of affection.

DECEDENT'S ESTATES:

See topics Descent and Distribution; Wills.

DEPOSITIONS:

Luxembourg has signed Hague Convention of Mar. 1, 1954 (Grand-Ducal Decree of Mar. 30, 1956) and Hague Convention of Mar. 18, 1970 (Luxembourg law of Mar. 19, 1977). Under 1954 Convention, public prosecutor's office ("procureur général" and "procureur d'Etat") receives and sends out rogatory commissions through diplomatic channels. Under 1970 Convention, rogatory commissions may be addressed directly to public prosecutor's office in Luxembourg ("Parquet général"). In accordance with possibility given in art. 23 of 1970 Convention, Luxembourg will not allow rogatory commissions that aim at pretrial discovery of documents. In certain instances, foreign rogatory commissions may be blocked by Luxembourg's banking secrecy rules. Indeed, directors, managers and employees of financial institution may not disclose confidential information, i.e. any information not publicly known, which they have gained knowledge of as result of doing business with customer, unless specifically authorized by law to do so.

DESCENT AND DISTRIBUTION:

Real and personal property are governed by same rules of inheritance. There is no right of primogeniture and no distinction between sexes. Certain persons may, however, be excluded from succession, e.g. murderers and attempted murderers of deceased. (C.C. 727).

According to Luxembourg's conflicts of laws rules, real property located in Luxembourg is subject to Luxembourg inheritance rules, and personal property is subject to laws of inheritance of last domicile of deceased.

Legal heirs include descendants, surviving spouse, ascendants and brothers and sisters. (C.C. 731). If there are no such heirs, estate goes to Luxembourg state.

Children, legitimate and illegitimate, and their descendants exclude all other heirs except for surviving spouse. (C.C. 745).

Surviving spouse may opt between share in estate, which may not be less than one quarter of estate, and usufruct of house and furniture in which spouses lived. Usufruct may be converted into capital if spouse remarries. (C.C. 767-1). Surviving spouse will inherit entire estate if there are no children and descendants. (C.C. 767-2).

If there are no children and descendants, and no surviving spouse, estate goes to brothers and sisters and parents of deceased, each being entitled to half of estate. If there is only one parent left, this share will be reduced to one quarter. If no parent survives, brothers and sisters will inherit all of estate.

If deceased leaves no brothers and sisters, all of estate goes to parents. If no parents are left, estate goes to ascendants.

DISPUTE RESOLUTION:

Arbitration.—Any matter person may contractually dispose of may be arbitrated. Law excludes from arbitration questions relating to legal status and capacity of person, matrimonial relations, divorce and separation, as well as matters regarding incapacity and absence of persons. (C.C.P. 1004).

Parties are free to make provisions for appointment of one or more arbitrators in arbitration agreement. In absence of such provision, arbitrators will be appointed according to rules of C.C.P. 1006.

Equally flexible approach has been adopted with regard to choice of rules of procedure. In absence of agreement by parties on this question, procedural rules normally applied by district court will apply. (C.C.P. 1009).

Unless parties have waived their right to appeal in arbitration agreement or since that time, awards may be appealed. (C.C.P. 1010).

Luxembourg is party to many of international agreements that deal with international commercial arbitration. It has ratified Geneva Protocol of Sept. 24, 1923 (Luxembourg law of July 29, 1930) on arbitration clauses, but only for commercial matters.

More recently, it has approved European Convention on International Commercial Arbitration, done at Geneva on Apr. 21, 1961 (Luxembourg law of Nov. 26, 1981), as well as Paris Agreement of Dec. 17, 1962 (Luxembourg law of Nov. 26, 1981) relating to its application. These two agreements, which contain detailed provisions on arbitration of disputes arising from international trade, came into effect in June 1982.

As far as recognition and enforcement of foreign arbitral awards are concerned, application for enforcement has to be made to Presiding Judge of district court. (C.C.P. 1028-1 and 1028-2).

Luxembourg has also ratified New York Convention on the Recognition and Enforcement of Foreign Arbitral Awards of June 10, 1958 (Luxembourg law of May 20, 1983).

DIVORCE:

Jurisdiction.—Request is submitted to court (Tribunal d'Arrondissement) of district of matrimonial home or defendant's domicile.

Aliens.—When both parties are aliens, divorce is only possible if allowed by their respective national law, or if parties have given up their domicile in their native country and have permanently settled in Grand-Duchy.

Types of Divorce.—Divorce may be by mutual consent or for specific cause:

Divorce by mutual consent (C.C. 275) must not be prohibited by one of parties' national law. Parties must have been married more than two years, and both must be over 23. Spouses agree on common settlement of their pecuniary interest, on their residence pendente lite, on alimony and on custody of children during and after proceedings.

Proceedings: Parties appear three times before president of court at intervals of six months and repeat their mutual consent to divorce. After one year, case is placed on calendar for hearing. At that point, court confirms that all legal requirements have been met, and grants divorce.

Divorce for Specific Cause.—Specific cause for which divorce is granted may be: (1) Abuse, cruelty or gross insult, when such acts constitute serious, and repeated violations of marital duties rendering marital state intolerable. (C.C. 229). Such acts include (i) adultery, (ii) violence, (iii) conviction for infamous crime, and (iv) desertion when not justified by serious grounds. Reprehensible conduct is examined by judge, having regard to social standing of parties. (2) Separation exceeding three years where spousal disunion cannot be remedied. (C.C. 230). (3) Separation in excess of five years due to mental insanity of spouse. (C.C. 231). Divorce may not be granted if it would result in serious material or moral suffering. When divorce is requested on grounds of C.C. 230 or 231, cost of proceedings is always borne by petitioner.

Proceedings: Request, which must be signed by lawyer, must be lodged with president of "tribunal d'arrondissement". Alleged wrongs must be outlined to court, and claims cannot be later modified during proceedings. In first stage claimant alone appears before president of court to confirm request. In second stage two parties are convened to appear in person, without assistance of their lawyer or counsel, before president of court who attempts to reconcile them. If conciliation fails, petitioner is granted authorization to go before court within three months. Normal proceedings then apply. Plaintiff may, if necessary, prove his case by all means, including hearing of witnesses. Counter-petitions are accepted, and divorce may be pronounced against either or both parties. Court's judgment granting or refusing divorce is appealable before higher court within 40 days of its notification. Case before appellate court will be granted expedited review.

Custody of Children.—Judge will make provision for temporary custody of children, according to parties' agreement, if any, or in best interests of children. When divorce is granted, parental authority and custody of children are awarded to either party or to third party, not necessarily member of family, in children's best interest.

Alimony.—President of court may make provision for temporary alimony according to parties' agreement. Court's decree granting divorce may award successful plaintiff alimony, which amount is determined having regard to defendant's revenue. Alimony is always revisable and revocable. Alimony ceases to be due to ex-spouse if such person lives together with third person or remarries.

Separation.—May be granted on same grounds as divorce. Private separation agreements are not accepted. Legal separation carries with it division of property. In case of reconciliation, after judgment granting separation, separation of property continues unless new matrimonial contract is signed. Reconciliation will be effective as against claims of third parties, only if special notary deed is signed and duly published.

Name.—Divorced woman cannot use her former husband's surname. However, use of husband's name during marriage being based only on custom and practice, divorced woman is not considered to "reacquire" her former surname. In certain instances, she may even be awarded by judgment authorization to continue using former husband's name.

Remarriage of Divorced Woman.—In case of divorce by mutual consent (C.C. 275) or on grounds of separation (C.C. 230, 231) woman may remarry after divorce has been confirmed by court. In other cases, same rule applies, provided 300 days elapsed since president of court's authorization to bring case before court, unless in meantime birth was given to child.

Dower.—This institution does not exist in Luxembourg. Under community property rules, wife is entitled to half of assets acquired by spouses during marriage with their joint revenue. Spouses may insert in their will clause by which disposable portion of their assets is left to last surviving party.

See topic Wills.

ENVIRONMENT:

Area Planning Law.—

(a) Types of Development Plans.—According to law of 11 Aug. 1982, governing conservation of nature and natural resources, every construction which is to be erected for purpose of housing, trade, industry or sports is subject to authorisation of Ministry of Environment. Authorisation will only be granted if construction falls within ambit of laws of 12 June 1937 (which govern town planning) and 20 Mar. 1974 (which governs national planning). Operating plans define special areas where construction can be erected.

Where municipalities do not have land-use plan, construction will only be authorised if erected in agglomeration, i.e. in centre of circle having radius of 100 metres within which are situated at least five permanently occupied habitations.

Besides above mentioned construction, which serve purpose of housing, trade, industry or sports, law distinguishes agricultural, gardening, market gardening, forestry, wine growing, piscicultural installations, or public utility undertakings. These buildings may be erected in natural environment, provided their purpose meets requirements of surroundings where construction is risk to conservation of nature.

According to law of 12 June 1937 every municipality subject to operating plan, i.e. with more than 10,000 inhabitants, must have building regulation (règlement des bâtisses). Law of 20 Mar. 1974 extended this obligation to all municipalities. Building regulation will determine character of construction and will provide for measures concerning conservation of sites and monuments from aesthetic point of view. All construction must meet with provisions of building regulations of relevant municipality.

Building regulations will also define monuments of artistic, historic or archeological value and places land-use plans designated as having special character from landscape point of view. In neighbourhood of these sites, new construction, extensions, billboards and other advertising facilities will be authorised only if they do not harm beauty of site. Besides these authorisations, it is understood that every construction needs separate building permit (permis de construire) from mayor (bourgmestre).

(b) Sanctions.—Law of 1982 on conservation of nature provides for fine of up to one million LUF and imprisonment from eight days to six months. Law compels court to confiscate machinery and tools used by contravener as well as vehicles used to infringe law. Court must also order, at expense of contravener, restoration of site within one year.

In practice, court may order, besides fine, confiscation of building equipment and demolition of construction illegally erected. Restoration of site in its previous state constitutes civil compensation of prejudice suffered by community.

Infringements of building regulations are punished by sanctions provided for by law of 12 June 1937, i.e., fine of up to LUF 500,000 and imprisonment from eight days to three months. Court may also order demolition of executed works and restoration of site, at expense of contravener.

Municipalities or, in their stead, State, may claim damages for prejudice suffered (partie civile). Although law governing land-use only gives courts mere possibility of ordering restoration of site, courts always order restoration, it being considered as only way to redress infringement.

Municipalities may also ask courts to order abolition of illegal works in penal proceedings; they also have the right to issue direct writ of summons (citation directe) against contravener.

Environmental Law.—Pursuant to art. 1 of law of 9 May, 1990 installations are subject to licensing requirements if they are potential source of risk of nuisance or may be harmful to health. Industrial or commercial installations, whose establishment or operation may involve risk or have adverse effect on safety, health or well-being of general public, neighbourhood, employees or environment are also subject to these requirements. Furthermore, every facility, activity or manufacturing process that may lead to simmilar risks is subject to licensing.

Determination of authorities responsible for granting license depends on classification of installation into one of three categories specified by law according to degree of risk involved.

Installations falling under category 1, such as chemical factories, must be licensed by Minister of Environment and Minister of Labour and are subject to "enquête commodo et incommodo" (see below).

Installations under category 2, such as e.g. bakery, are licensed by mayor (bourgmestre), whereas installations falling under category 3, such as e.g. hotel, must be licensed by above mentioned minsters, but without being subject to "enquête commodo et incommodo".

Application submitted to competent authority must include, in addition to name, occupation and residence of applicant, nature and location of installation, purpose of its operation and details on extent of production or nature of materials to be stored there. Applicant must also provide estimation of number of employees and list potential risks for their safety and health.

Additionally, he must supply information on use of water, air, water and soil pollution, noise levels, vibrations, radiation, nature, amount, treatment and disposal of waste and other by-products engendered during production. He must also provide evaluation of all other harmful effects on environment. Application must contain approximate data on measures designed to prevent or reduce harmful effects as well as potential risks for employees, surrounding neighbourhood, public and environment.

Authorisation of Minister of Environment and Minister of Labour will specify requirements to ensure protection for safety, health and well-being of public, surrounding neighbourhood, employees and environment (air, water, soil, noise level and waste).

ENVIRONMENT . . . *continued*

Authority issuing authorisation may require that installation be checked and approved on initial operation and in regular periods thereafter. Requirements of initial authorisation may be subject to continual review.

Subsequently imposed directives are possible.

Notification of project must be posted for two weeks in office of mayor at location of installation and in surrounding municipalities. It must also be published in four daily newspapers.

Objections can be filed by every citizen. Public discussion (enquête de commodo et incommodo) is held in community of location of installation, during which all objections will be heard.

Within 40 days of notification of authorisation (or non-authorisation) decision, any affected party, i.e., any person living in immediate vicinity of installation who can thereby claim personal and direct interest in decision, may appeal against decision.

Associations for protection of environment, which have been approved, have been recognised by Conseil d'Etat (highest administrative jurisdiction) in respect of their right to defend collective interests of affected individuals, provided association has got required approval by ministerial order.

Immediate neighbours and approved environmental associations also have right subsequently to ask competent authority to impose requirements on installations. They may even require deadline for fulfilling requirements already imposed.

Conservation Law of nature is governed by general law of 11 Aug. 1982 and many other laws on air or water pollution, waste or noise.

Objectives of law of 1982 are conservation of environment's character, variety and integrity, protection and restoring of landscapes and natural spaces, conservation of flora and fauna and their biotopes, upholding and improvement of biological balances, protection of natural resources against any damages, and improvement of structures of environment.

Law also deals with waste disposal, protection of woods and their biotopes.

For new installations subject to licensing requirements, authorisation will only be granted if installation meets all requirements provided for by statutes governing waste disposal, pollution, etc.

EXCHANGE CONTROL:

Since 1944, exchange control has been jointly organized with Belgium. In 1918 monetary association was created by Luxembourg and Belgium, leading to almost complete liberty of exchange between two countries. Since 1990, Luxembourg enjoys absolutely free movement of capital as last exchange control barriers have been waived. Some documentation must be provided to administrative authorities, but for statistical purposes only.

EXECUTIONS:

Under Luxembourg law, several methods of attachment are made available, depending on nature of property to be seized.

Rules Applicable to All Methods of Attachment.—Creditor must have evidence of indebtedness. Debt must be existing obligation; it may be future, but not contingent, liability. Certain property is not subject to attachment (C.C.P. 581-592), including: (1) Beds and clothing for debtor and his family, craftsmen's tools, or other property necessary for pursuit of trade; (2) alimony granted by court, by donation or will; (3) property given by will or donation under clause of immunity from attachment; and (4) portion of salaries, wages and pensions payable by state.

Money or Property Due to Debtor by Third Party ("Saisie-Arrêt").—Money or property held by third party may be due to debtor or belong to him. Attachment may be requested for conservation or execution.

Proceedings.—(1) If creditor has document acknowledging debt which is beyond doubt, e.g. established by judge or notary, seizure can be made directly by bailiff. (2) If creditor has no or weak documentary evidence of debt, e.g. private document, he must present petition to court of domicile of debtor or garnishee. With authorization of judge bailiff may then proceed to seize property. In both cases, debtor whose property has been seized must be advised and summoned within eight days following attachment. Garnishee must in turn be advised of summons within eight days.

Debtor's Personal Property ("Saisie-Exécution").—Debt must be liquid. One day at least before actual attachment proceedings, debtor must be served at his domicile with order to pay, together with notification of document acknowledging indebtedness.

Proceedings.—Seizure is executed by bailiff at domicile of debtor, with help of police if necessary. Debtor must be notified of attachment if it is made away from his domicile or not in his presence. Property may be seized in excess of alleged debt, but only property covering reimbursement of debt will be sold. Sale may only be made eight days or more after notification of attachment to debtor.

Debtor's Real Estate ("Saisie-Immobilière").—Addressed to real property only, this method of attachment follows strict rules. As in "saisie-exécution" debt must be liquid, and debtor must be served with documented order to pay before starting actual attachment proceedings.

Proceedings.—(1) Seizure is realized by service of document by process server 15 to 180 days after order to pay. Attachment is notified to seized debtor. (2) Attachment is registered on cadastral survey within 15 days after its notification. (3) Case must be brought before court within 15 days after registration, which authorizes or rejects attachment no earlier than 30 days and no later than 40 days subsequent. Sale must be made by adjudication.

Miscellaneous.—Special execution methods are provided for attachment of: (1) Private pensions and annuities; (2) fruits and crops ("saisie-brandon"); (3) tenant's furniture ("saisie-gagerie"); (4) foreign debtor's property ("saisie-foraine"); and (5) property to be recovered ("saisie-revendication").

FOREIGN EXCHANGE:

See topic Exchange Control.

FOREIGN INVESTMENT/FOREIGN TRADE:

International trade policy is within sole competence of EC authorities, although certain import regimes may be regulated directly by Member States.

Foreign investment is free in Luxembourg. Capital and income may be freely repatriated.

Luxembourg is Member State of Benelux Customs Union, European Community, and OECD.

FRAUDS, STATUTE OF:

In civil contracts, oral testimony is not admissible for claims exceeding LUF 100,000. (C.C. 1341). In commercial transactions such testimony is valid regardless of amount of claim. (C.Com. 109).

Unilateral undertakings to pay sum of money or to deliver specific thing must be signed by obligor who must as well write by hand sum or quantity. (C.C. 1326).

GARNISHMENT:

See topic Executions.

HOLDING COMPANIES:

See topic Corporations.

IMMIGRATION:

See topic Aliens.

INFANCY (CHILDREN):

In contracts and court actions, children must be represented by parent(s) exercising parental authority.

Age of majority for both sexes is 18. (C.C. 388 and 488). Child may be emancipated at 16 by court order. Emancipation is automatic upon marriage of child, which is only possible if authorized by parent(s) exercising parental authority. Emancipated minor enjoys full legal capacity, except that he cannot engage in commerce.

INVESTMENT FUNDS:

See topic Corporations.

JUDGMENTS:

Luxembourg has ratified Brussels Convention of Sept. 27, 1968 on jurisdiction and enforcement of foreign judgments concluded between member states of European Union, and Lugano Convention of Sept. 18, 1988, concluded with States of European Economic Area. Convention provides for simplified proceedings for recognition and enforcement of judgments rendered by signatory States' courts. Case is not reexamined.

Bilateral treaties have been signed with other countries, such as Austria. In absence of international treaty, procedure of enforcement must be carried out. It does not involve reexamination of case by court. (C.C.P. 546-3). Exequatur request must be lodged with President of "tribunal d'arrondissement" and will be granted only if: (1) judgment is enforceable in country where it was rendered; (2) judgment is not contrary to Luxembourg public policy; and (3) foreign court had jurisdiction in conformity with local, international and Luxembourg rules.

Arbitration Awards.—Foreign awards, like domestic ones, can only be executed upon enforcement order given by President of "tribunal d'arrondissement". (C.C.P. 1028-1). Proceedings and conditions are very similar to those requested for exequatur of foreign judgments.

LABOUR RELATIONS:

Right to work is guaranteed by Constitution. In accordance with such provision, state is under duty to adopt rules that assure work to everyone to largest extent possible.

Trade Unions.—They are organized along ideological lines, with socialist and Christian trade unions being most representative independent unions. White collar employees have their own union, and those active in banking sector usually affiliate with bank employees' union. All unions are moderate and effective in controlling their members. Membership has decreased over past years. Luxembourg's tradition of consensus politics integrates unions in periodic meetings together with employers and government. This has proved very successful in preventing labour disputes.

Work Permit.—Nationals of EC countries can freely work within territory of Luxembourg without work permit.

Prior to employment, all other foreigners must apply for work permit at National Labour Bureau, and undergo medical examination. Employer must certify that new person is needed and that no suitable candidate was found in national labour market.

Labour Contract.—Employment is normally of unlimited duration and must be evidenced in writing. In absence of written contract, existence and content of labour contract may be evidenced by any means, but contract is deemed to be for indefinite period of time, without possibility to prove contrary.

Labour contract for definite period of time is exceptional under Luxembourg law; it may only be entered into for performance of specific and temporary task. Term or at least minimal duration must be disclosed in contract, which cannot be cancelled before term except for gross negligence. Contract of limited duration can only be renewed twice, and has maximum duration of 24 months, including renewals.

Trial periods must be provided for in writing. Trial periods vary between two weeks and six months, with two exceptions: (1) trial period for unskilled workers may not exceed three months; and (2) trial period for employees whose monthly salary exceeds certain amount to be determined by decree (currently ca. LUF 120,000) may be 12 months at most. Trial period is not renewable. Labour contract may be terminated during trial period upon 15 days' to one month's notice. If contract is not terminated during trial period, it is deemed to be contract of unlimited duration as of first day of working relationship.

See Topical Index in front part of this volume.

LABOUR RELATIONS . . . *continued*

Employers' Obligations.—Within eight days of beginning of working relationship, employer must notify new hire to Coordination Centre of Social Security Institutions. Sickness and pension insurance are paid on equally shared basis by employer and employee, although accident insurance and State family allowances are exclusively supported by employer.

Working Time.—Limited by law to eight hours per day and 40 hours per week. However, blue and white collar workers can be asked to work up to nine hours per day as long as weekly working hours do not exceed 40 hours. Other derogations may be obtained with Ministry of Labour approval, if required for structural or technical reasons.

Overtime is allowed without prior approval if it does not exceed two hours per day. Overtime hours must be paid extra, i.e. + 25% per hour for manual workers, + 50% for office employees, and + 100% for minors.

Night work is prohibited for minors and expectant or breastfeeding mothers. Collective labour agreement must provide for salary increases of 10% or more for any night work.

Holiday.—Each employee is entitled to yearly leave of 25 days. Collective labour agreements may provide for additional holidays.

Extraordinary paid leaves are granted on certain occasions for: (1) death of parent or spouse (two days); (2) birth or wedding of child (two days); and (3) wedding of employee (six days).

Compensation.—There is no legal requirement as to amount of salary to be paid. However, (1) salary must not be less than minimum wages periodically determined by Government, and (2) it must be periodically adapted to wage index. Salaries must be paid at least once a month. Detailed salary statement must be remitted to employee.

Salaries must be paid in case of extraordinary leaves for family events (e.g. death of parent, birth of child). In case of sickness of white collar worker, salary is paid by employer during first three months of sickness absence, and then by health insurance for 52 weeks at most; (2) in case of blue collar worker, salary is paid by health insurance from first day of absence and for 52 weeks maximum. Similar rules apply to maternity leaves, which generally start eight weeks prior to birth of child and terminate eight weeks after birth. Upon her return, employer is compelled to reintegrate woman to her former job or to equivalent position.

Dismissal.—Prior to any dismissal, employer of more than 150 persons must meet with worker whose dismissal is envisaged for preliminary discussion. Worker must be called to meeting by registered mail at least two business days in advance. Notice must indicate reason for meeting as well as its date, place and time, and specify that employee may be accompanied by co-worker or trade union representative. If employer still wants to dismiss employee after meeting, employee must be notified of decision by registered mail, at earliest on day following meeting. This procedure applies both in cases of dismissal for serious fault and dismissal with notice period.

If less than 150 persons are employed, dismissal must simply be notified to employee by registered mail. Dismissal must be made upon following notice periods: (1) one month if employee has worked with same employer for less than five years; (2) four months if employee has worked five to ten years with same employer; (3) six months if working relationship existed for more than ten years.

If notice periods are not respected, employer must pay indemnity equal to employee's salary during period required for notice.

Indemnifications for dismissal must be paid to every dismissed employee who has been working for employer for more than five years. Indemnity varies in accordance with length of service, and ranges from one to 12 months' salary.

Retirement.—Minimum age that entitles employee to pension is 60 for women and 65 for men. However, smaller pension (pre-pension) may be paid out as of age of 55 and 60 respectively.

Early retirement schemes may be entered into upon special agreement with Ministry of Labour. Beneficiaries of this scheme must be at least 57 and may not execute any other paid or unpaid professional activity after early retirement. Pre-pension rights and duties cease when employee becomes entitled to normal pension.

LAW REPORTS; CODES:

Luxembourg law is organized in codified system with five main codes: Code Civil; Code du Commerce; Code Pénal; Code d'Instruction Criminelle; and Code de Procédure Civile.

All labor relations materials have been compiled in commercially published textbook. Another more recent compilation is Code Fiscal (tax code).

Other important laws are published in unofficial "Recueil des lois spéciales". Acts of Parliament and executive decrees are published in official journal, "Mémorial". Important court decisions are published in "Pasicrisie", issued four times a year.

LEGISLATURE:

See topic Constitution and Government.

LICENSES:

Business licenses are required for all commercial activities carried on in Luxembourg. (Law of Dec. 12, 1988). They are issued by Ministry of the Middle Classes. Some activities, especially in financial sector, require special licenses granted by Luxembourg Monetary Institute ("Institut Monétaire Luxembourgeois", or IML). General criteria to be fulfilled in all cases are professional experience or education and good standing.

LIENS:

Liens may be created by contract (see topics Pledges; Mortgages) or exist by operation of law. In cash sales, seller has lien until price is paid. (C.C. 1612). With deposits, depository has right to keep deposited assets until full payment of all fees and costs related to deposit is made. (C.C. 1948).

LIMITATION OF ACTIONS:

General period of limitation for actions is 30 years. (C.C. 2262). Time limitation to become owner of real estate held in good faith is ten or 20 years, depending on place of residence of actual owner. (C.C. 2263). There are numerous other limitation periods in civil matters.

General limitations period for rights and actions in commercial matters is ten years (C.Comm. 189), but statute of limitations may be shorter. Shorter limitation periods exist in labor matters, varying between six months and five years.

MARRIAGE:

Except in cases where Grand Duke grants special derogation for compelling reasons, man must be minimum of 18 years of age and woman must be at least 15 years old to be allowed to marry. Consent of parents is required for people marrying under age of 18.

Marriage is civil contract. Civil marriage must take place before religious marriage. (Const. art. 21).

Marriage is celebrated before mayor (or his representative) of place of residence of one of persons to be married. Couple may elect to have their respective rights over their assets governed by rules of Civil Code regarding matrimonial regimes, or by separate marriage contract entered into before notary public.

MONOPOLIES AND RESTRAINT OF TRADE:

Freedom of trade is protected by Luxembourg Constitution.

Monopolies and restraints of trade are governed by EC competition law as well as by law of June 17, 1970 on restraints of trade. Definitions therein are identical to those applicable under European Community law.

Committee, set up under 1970 law, advises Minister of Economy on agreements that may violate relevant law.

Minister may totally or partially prohibit arrangements that are in conflict with Luxembourg antitrust law. Legal actions in court can be started by public prosecutor in case of nonobservance of relevant decision of Minister.

MORTGAGES:

Mortgage is right (droit réel) in immovable property which guarantees execution of obligation. Mortgage is, by its nature, indivisible and exists fully on all of real estate employed to that end and on each and every portion of such real property. Mortgage remains on real property even if such property changes hands. Mortgage will exist only under circumstances and in forms recognized by law, which are legal, judicial and conventional mortgages. Legal mortgages result from law. Those provided for by civil law are not so relevant as those foreseen by fiscal law. Judicial mortgages result from judgments, but not from arbitration awards, unless latter have received judicial order of enforcement. Conventional mortgage is result of agreement and depends on form of contract. Notarial deed, properly registered, is required. Contracts made abroad cannot, in principle, create mortgage on real estate located in Luxembourg, except where special treaties might provide to contrary. Validity of conventional mortgage is subject to condition that notarial deed specify exactly nature and location of each element of real property owned by debtor which he agrees to mortgage. Each and all of debtor's actual property may be nominally subject to mortgage. Conventional mortgage further requires, in order to be valid, settlement of sum for which it has been given, this sum being certain and determined in deed. Between creditors, mortgages, be they legal, judicial or conventional, rank in order of their inscription at mortgage registry. Exception is made for certain fiscal debts which are secured by legal mortgage requiring no inscription. Mortgage is generally secured by its registration for period of ten years. Renewal is possible.

Law of June 14, 1966 provides for possibility to mortgage certain types of river boats. Such mortgages require notarial deed and must be registered with River Mortgage Registrar.

As for aircraft, Luxembourg has ratified Geneva Convention of June 19, 1948 on rights in aircraft. Law of Mar. 29, 1978 sets framework for aircraft mortgages, preferential claims and similar rights. It provides for registration with Registrar for aircraft mortgages.

MOTOR VEHICLES:

Liability insurance is required for all cars circulating in Luxembourg. Cars of residents must be registered with Ministry of Transportation. All rules to be observed by drivers circulating in Luxembourg have been compiled in Code de la Route.

PARTNERSHIPS:

Partnership is considered to be civil if its purpose is not commercial, if it is organized under art. 1832 of Civil Code and chooses one of forms outlined by that Code. (C.C. 1835 et seq.). Since buying of real estate for sale or lease and extraction of products from soil are not considered acts of trade, mining and real estate companies may be civil partnerships unless they adopt commercial form. Civil partnerships are separate judicial entities according to court decision of Mar. 11, 1875, and law of Sept. 18, 1933.

Partnerships are commercial if their intended purpose is to perform acts of trade. (Art. 1, Company Act of Aug. 10, 1915). Law recognizes six types of commercial partnerships, including those which are commercial by nature and partnerships whose subject matter is civil but that have adopted one of six forms of partnership. (Arts. 2 and 3, Company Act of Aug. 10, 1915).

In general partnership, if there is no contrary stipulation in charter, every partner represents legal entity, but decisions require consent of all partners.

The charter often appoints one or more managers.

In limited partnership, management is reserved to general partners, whose role is same as that of general partners in general partnership.

See also topic Corporations.

PATENTS:

Designs and Models.—New aspects of product having utilitarian function can be protected. Right is acquired by first deposit of claim in Benelux country. Benelux Convention on designs and models of Oct. 25, 1966 applies to all claims.

Inventions.—Governed by law of June 30, 1880 on patents. Temporary and exclusive rights are granted for each invention that is new, that is result of inventive activity and which has industrial application. Right to patent belongs to person who first registered his invention in accordance with law. Effect of patent is that, without authorisation of patent holder, invention cannot be applied, used or sold. Duration of patent is generally 20 years.

Luxembourg is member of Strasbourg Convention of Nov. 27, 1963 on unification of certain elements of patents, and 1971 Strasbourg Agreement on international classification of patents.

Trademarks.—Protected under Benelux Convention and uniform law of Mar. 19, 1962, as am'd by Protocol of Dec. 2, 1992, and Madrid Agreement of June 27, 1989 on international registration of trade marks. Exclusive right to trade mark is acquired by first deposit in Benelux or by international registration with International Bureau for Intellectual Property.

Industrial Property.—Luxembourg is party to Paris Convention of Mar. 20, 1883 on protection of industrial property.

PLEDGES:

To be valid, under civil law as well as commercial law, pledge must, besides consent to pledge, imply delivery of pledged object by debtor to pledgee or to specified third party holding in pledge for creditor. In commercial matters, delivery of carriage documents (bills of lading, way bills) is equivalent to delivery of object. Important example of pledge is pledge of business and its goodwill. Credit institutions wishing to accept such pledges generally must have permission of Government to deal with this branch of credit activity.

Law dated Dec. 21, 1994 provides that amount of secured debt no longer needs to be indicated in pledge deed. Moreover, law states now expressly that pledge can secure both present and future debts. Notification by bailiff of pledge to debtor of pledged claim is no longer required. Simple notification by mail is sufficient. As alternative, pledge may be accepted by debtor. Notification or acceptance may be done alternatively in authentic deed or in private deed.

Commercial pledges do not require notarial deed, and pledge may be established in conformity with procedure followed in sale of goods of similar nature.

Pledge is always accessory to contract. Termination of obligations under contract, for any reason, automatically releases pledge. Pledge may be released separately on waiver by creditor, merger of creditor's and debtor's rights, loss of pledged object or its delivery to debtor. Debtor's bankruptcy or death does not release pledge. Pledge of business and goodwill must be registered in mortgage registry. Registration must be renewed every ten years, and if not renewed it is barred by statutes of limitations. Non-renewal of registration is thus cause for release of pledge of business and goodwill.

When debt matures, creditor is not allowed to appropriate pledged object nor sell it at his option. Under civil law, creditor must obtain authorization from court to sell pledged object by auction or to take object in payment of amount determined by experts. Under commercial law, creditor must obtain authorization from president of commercial court either to sell pledged object by auction or by simple contract, unless place and manner of realization were previously agreed upon.

Pledge of Securities or of Sums of Money.—No registration or notification by bailiff is required to execute pledge of securities. Securities pledged do not have to be specified if all registered or bearer shares owned by debtor presently or in future are pledged to guarantee present and future claims of creditor. Unless otherwise agreed upon between parties, creditor must notify debtor by registered mail eight days prior to seeking enforcement of pledge.

Enforcement of pledge of securities which are quoted in official stock exchange or negotiated on regular market can be carried out after written notice to debtor and, if necessary, to third party, either by sale on stock exchange or market or by appropriation of pledged securities. Sale or appropriation must apply current price.

Securities which are not quoted or negotiated are sold on stock exchange in public sale by public officer.

Enforcement of money pledge may be carried out, if so agreed by parties, and after previous notice by registered mail to debtor, by set-off between pledged amount and claim due by pledgee to pledgor. If pledged amount is third party debt, such third party may be required at maturity to pay pledgee.

PRESCRIPTION:

See topic Limitation of Actions.

PRINCIPAL AND AGENT:

General principles of agency law are set out by Civil Code (C.C. 1984 et seq.). Law of June 3, 1994 provides detailed statutory rules for independent commercial agency contracts. Benelux Convention on Agency contains detailed provisions for this type of contract, but it has not yet come into force in Luxembourg.

In absence of specific statutory rules, it is recommended that parties determine their rights and duties contractually.

Extent of liability depends on nature of agent's relations with his principal. If agent is empowered to act in name and on behalf of principal, then latter is fully responsible for undertakings entered into by agent.

Law of July 1, 1988 provides that, unless otherwise agreed by parties, agency relationship terminates by discharge or resignation of agent, placing under guardianship of majors, bankruptcy or similar proceeding as well as death of principal or agent.

Under Law of June 3, 1994, commercial agent is defined as independent intermediary who negotiates sale or acquisition of goods, or negotiates and concludes transactions in name of and for account of another person. Agent is merchant person, subject to commercial law, and not employee. Agency contracts must be in writing and in two copies.

Agent must act loyally and in good faith in exclusive interest of principal. Law defines duties of agent and principal, and parties may not provide otherwise in contract. Law regulates agent's right to commissions and other remuneration.

At termination, agent is entitled to notice period and indemnity for termination. Noncompetition clauses with principal's business after termination must be in writing and limited as to geographic area, professional sectors and time (maximum 12 months). Law provides for cases of termination where such clauses cannot apply.

Representative under employment contract, subordinated to and supervised by his employer, is employee whose rights and duties are set forth by law on labor contracts of Mar. 24, 1989.

REAL PROPERTY:

Real property, e.g. land and buildings, may be acquired by accession (increase of existing land by act of nature), contract, inheritance or prescription (adverse possession, which must be continuous, public, unequivocal and peaceful). Transfers of real property interest by contract must be by notarial act and recorded in Mortgage Registry.

No restrictions on ownership of real property for foreigners apply. See topic Mortgages.

SALES:

Sales agreements are governed by arts. 1582 et seq. of Civil Code. They may be made by notarial deed or by private agreement. Sales contract is binding on parties and ownership rights pass to buyer at moment there is agreement as to price and assets, even though no delivery has taken place, nor price paid. Case law has decided that parties can provide that title is reserved in seller until purchase price is paid in full.

Price of sale must be determined by parties. According to case law, price must be bona fide, i.e., reasonably related to value of assets.

SHIPPING LAW:

Registration.—According to Luxembourg Shipping Act of Nov. 9, 1990, as am'd by law of June 17, 1994, all ships that operate under Luxembourg flag have to register with Record Keeper of Maritime Mortgages.

Supervision of maritime flag by "Commissariat aux affaires maritimes", which is department of Ministry of Transports.

Ships acquire Luxembourg nationality if they are registered under Luxembourg flag. Registration under Luxembourg flag supposes that ships are more than 50% owned by either natural persons who are citizens of European Union member State, or by companies whose principal place of business is located in EU-member State. In case of bare boat charter, significant part of management of ship must be carried out from Luxembourg.

Preferential Claims. Mortgages.—Registration of any agreement creating, transferring, declaring or terminating rights "in rem" with Mortgages Record Keeping Office is required by law for such rights to have any effect as against third parties. However, registration of such agreement is only possible if ship to which such conventions refer has itself been registered in Luxembourg.

Preferential creditors may either have preferential claims or mortgages. Preferential claims depend on nature of claims and always come first to mortgages. Claims remain preferential even if ship is sold to another person or if it changes its nationality.

Maritime mortgages may only be granted on specified ships and for fixed sum. Mortgages may be registered at any time during their existence, save for case of death or bankruptcy of debtor, sale or loss of nationality of ship.

Registration preserves mortgages for renewable period of ten years. Preferential order of maritime mortgages is determined by their date of registration, and if they have same date, by their registration number.

Maritime mortgages are exempt from any duty, except registrar of mortgages' salary.

Tax.—Shipowning companies will be liable to common corporate tax rate applicable to any Luxembourg corporation. Shipping companies may benefit from tax reductions available to Luxembourg companies for structural investments.

Sailors on Luxembourg registered ships are subject to special 10% tax on their income. Resident sailors will be taxed in Luxembourg as any other taxpayer residing in Grand-Duchy of Luxembourg.

Labour Law.—Except for traineeships, sailors must be aged 18 or more to be eligible for work on Luxembourg registered ship. Medical certificate is required from any sailor certifying that his physical condition is satisfactory and that his embarkation does not harm his own health or that of his co-sailors.

With limited exceptions, contracts of employment for definite period of time may not be terminated before expiration of set period. Contracts for indefinite periods of time can be terminated by each party, subject to giving notice and observing some procedural rules.

Luxembourg labour courts are competent to decide whether dismissals are abusive. Abusive dismissals give right to payment of damages by employer.

Working time on boat shall not exceed eight hours per day and 40 hours per week. However, collective labour agreements may provide for different working hours during week or over another time span than a week. In absence of collective labour agreement, more flexible working schedule may also be approved by competent minister at request of shipowner.

Wages of all persons employed on Luxembourg ships must be at least identical to minimum wages required by law for any other employee in Luxembourg.

Social Security.—Luxembourg social security protection is available to sailors of Luxembourg nationality or of country with whom Grand-Duchy has bi- or multilateral agreement on social security. For sailors of other countries, shipowner is required to sign insurance policy with private insurance company. Social security protection by country of residence or by private insurer must at least cover sickness, unemployment, pension, working accidents, professional diseases and motherhood. However, subject to approval by Luxembourg government, such sailors may also be covered by social security system of their country of residence, if such country gives social security protection at least equal to protection granted by Law.

See Topical Index in front part of this volume.

SHIPPING LAW . . . *continued*

Safety Requirements.—First registration will not be available in Luxembourg to ships older than 15 years. For ships of more than 15 years of age that are already registered in Luxembourg, their registration is conditional upon continued existence of class of ship in accordance with criteria of international classification companies.

Every shipowner must have protection and indemnity insurance that covers all damages that ship may cause. Insurance may only be issued by insurance companies that have their registered office in EEC and that can demonstrate professional experience. For ships carrying hydrocarbon oils, requirements are idential to those of 1969 Convention on Civil Liability for Oil Pollution Damage.

Maritime Companies.—New law of June 17, 1994, provides rules on creation under Luxembourg law of specific maritime companies, which must be approved by Government and whose corporate object is purchase, sale, charter or management of seagoing vessels, as well as financial or commercial operations thereto connected.

TAXATION:

Common tax law of Luxembourg is based upon taxability of world–wide income and assets of residents and taxability of certain income from Luxembourg sources or derived from permanent establishment in Luxembourg of nonresidents, as well as certain of their assets located in Luxembourg.

Transactions executed and services rendered in territory of Grand Duchy are subject to Value Added Tax at rates varying between 3 and 15%.

Personal Taxation.—Individual resident in Luxembourg is liable for income tax on his worldwide income, including certain capital gains. Individual is deemed to be resident if he stays continuously in Luxembourg for more than six months per year. Nonresident individual is liable for income tax only on Luxembourg source income. Income tax is levied on taxable income, after deductions, at progressive rates from 0 to 58%.

Inheritance Tax.—If last residence of deceased was in Luxembourg, all his assets are subject to inheritance tax except for real estate located outside Luxembourg. If last residence of deceased was not in Luxembourg, tax assessable on death is transfer tax, not inheritance tax, which is charged only on deceased's real estate in Luxembourg. No inheritance tax is due on transfers of property to ascendants and descendants of deceased, such as from parents to children. This exemption does not apply in case of transfer tax.

Rates of inheritance tax and transfer tax are progressive and vary from nil to 48% (including surcharge), according to degree of relationship between beneficiary and deceased and value of property inherited.

Corporate Taxation.—Resident company is liable for corporate income tax on its worldwide profits, subject to provisions of any relevant tax treaty. Top corporate tax rate in Luxembourg is 33% as basic rate, plus municipal business tax, plus 4% surcharge contribution to unemployment fund, amounting to total maximum rate of 40.29%.

Nonresident company is liable for corporate income tax only on specific types of income and capital gains arising in Luxembourg. Types of income that are taxable include business profits of branch or other permanent establishment of company in Luxembourg, interest from loans secured by Luxembourg real estate, and rental income from real estate situated in Luxembourg. Taxable capital gains include gains from disposal of Luxembourg branch assets and land and buildings in Luxembourg and gains from disposal of shareholdings in Luxembourg companies made within six months of acquisition where shareholding concerned exceeds 25%. Nonresident company is liable to withholding tax on dividends, interest from profit-sharing bonds, and royalties received from Luxembourg sources. This is usually final (definitive) tax but where such income arises through permanent establishment of company in Luxembourg it is subject to corporate income tax, credit being granted for withholding tax. Tax treaties frequently modify rules described in this paragraph, for example by reducing or eliminating withholding tax.

Nonresident company with branch in Luxembourg is liable for corporate income tax on all income earned through activities of branch or derived from assets held by branch as business property, regardless of its geographical source. Thus dividends, for example, received from third country on shares held by branch are subject to Luxembourg corporate income tax.

Taxes payable by new companies may be substantially reduced by following cumulative measures: (1) up to 25% exemption on taxable corporate income for companies supplying new services or producing new products in Luxembourg, for first eight years of operation; (2) 14% tax credit on investment in fixed assets, except land and buildings; and (3) 30% declining balance depreciation rate for production equipment.

Dividends and other distributions of profit paid by resident companies are subject to withholding tax of 25% on gross amount. No withholding tax is due if paying company is holding company or if dividends are paid to fully taxable resident company which owns at least 10% of paying company's share capital.

Tax treatment of dividends received by resident company depends on percentage of capital it holds in paying company.

If holding is less than 10%, dividends form part of recipient company's income for corporate income tax purposes. Dividends received from other resident companies are included gross of 25% dividend withholding tax that is applied in Luxembourg, this withholding tax being creditable against recipient company's corporate income tax liability. Amount included in taxable income in case of foreign dividends is net amount received plus that part of any foreign withholding tax deducted which is eligible for credit relief. Foreign withholding tax is often only partly creditable.

Subject to certain conditions, if holding of recipient company is 10% or more, dividends concerned are exempt in its hands from Luxembourg corporate income tax and municipal business tax on profits.

If holding is 25% or more, Luxembourg resident company will be exempt from charge of capital gains tax when disposing of shares held.

If Luxembourg resident company makes distribution to company resident in one of EC member states in which it has had direct holding of 25% over at least two years, no withholding tax is levied.

See also topics Corporations; Treaties.

TRADEMARKS AND TRADENAMES:

See topic Licenses.

TREATIES:

Luxembourg is, among others, signatory of Treaty of Rome (European Economic Community), Treaty of Paris (European Community of Steel and Coal), BENELUX Treaty, Treaty establishing Belgian-Luxembourg Economic Union, and General Agreement on Tariffs and Trade. It is member of NATO and United Nations.

Tax Treaties.—With Federal Republic of Germany (1958), Austria (1962), Belgium (1970), Brazil (1978), Bulgaria (1994), Canada (1989), China (1996), South Korea (1984), Denmark (1980), Spain (1986), U.S.A. (1962), Finland (1982), France (1958), Greece (1996), Hungary (1990), Indonesia (1995), Ireland (1972), Italy (1981), Japan (1992), Malta (1996), Morocco (1980), Norway (1983), Netherlands (1968), U.K. (1967), Romania (1996), Singapore (1996), Sweden (1983), the Czech and Slovac Republics (1992), Switzerland (1993).

With Iceland (1975), Soviet Union (1975), limited to avoidance of double taxation in respect of operation of ships or aircraft in international traffic.

With, Mauritius, Poland and Russia, treaties have been ratified, but are not yet in force.

WARRANTIES:

Seller must guarantee buyer against dispossession of property and latent defects. Buyer must bring defect to attention of seller as quickly as possible after discovery of defect. Courts determine time limit for bringing action in light of defect and personality, education and experience of buyer.

Liability for hidden defects arises even if seller was unaware of them. Courts have decided that professional sellers are deemed to know defects of goods sold by them and are liable for damages to buyers.

Applicable Law.—The Hague Uniform Acts on international sale of movables and on formation of international sales contracts of movables of July 1, 1964, as well as Rome Convention of June 19, 1980 on law applicable to contracts are applicable. Rome Convention confirms principles that have been applied by case law prior to Convention, including that parties are free to choose law governing international contracts subject to observing public order provisions. In some sales contracts, entered into outside Luxembourg with Luxembourg residents, Luxembourg consumer protection laws apply, in accordance with 1978 amendments to Brussels Convention on Judicial Competence of 1968.

WILLS:

Luxembourg Civil Code recognizes three forms of wills: holographic, notarial and mystic will.

Holographic will is not subject to any special form, but must be entirely handwritten, dated and signed by testator. (C.C. 970). Notarial will is set out by notary recording intentions of testator. It must be signed by two notaries or by one notary and two witnesses. (C.C. 973). Mystic will is written by testator or third party and handed over in sealed envelope to two notaries or to one notary and two witnesses who write down testator's declaration that document deposited in hands of notary or notaries is his will.

Minors under age of 16 and persons who are not of sound mind lack capacity to draw up wills. Testators can revoke their wills, either expressly or by subsequent wills containing provisions conflicting with those of first will.

Luxembourg applies Hague Convention of Nov. 19, 1957 on conflicts of law regarding form of wills.

MALAYSIA LAW DIGEST REVISER

David Chong & Co.
Suite 13A.01, 13A Floor
WISMA MCA, 163 Jalan Ampang
50450 Kuala Lumpur, Malaysia
Telephone: 263 2277
Fax: 263 2278
Singapore Office: OCBC Centre, #31-00 East Lobby, 65 Chulia Street, 0104. Telephone: 65 224 0955.
Fax: 65 538 6585. Email: dclaw@singnet.com.sq

Reviser Profile

History: David Chong & Co. was first established in 1984 in Singapore by David Chong Kok Kong, who is both a practitioner and an academic, having spent three years lecturing law at the National University of Singapore. David Chong & Co. was set up in Malaysia to provide support to its Singapore counterpart for all aspects of Malaysia law. The firm has expanded rapidly since its inception in Singapore and the David Chong & Co. Group currently has more than 50 lawyers spread over its offices in Singapore; Kuala Lumpur, Johor Bahru and Labuan (Malaysia); Suzhou (the People's Republic of China); Sydney (Australia); Yangon (Myanmar); and the British Virgin Islands.

Structure: The firm conscientiously recruits lawyers who are qualified in more than one jurisdiction, including Singapore, Malaysia, Brunei, England and Wales, Australia, the United States of America and the British Virgin Islands. Many of the lawyers are also fluent in Mandarin and Malay to help service the firm's ever increasing portfolio of clients in the Asian markets.

Services: The firm is a full service law firm with substantial experience in all areas of practice and comprises the following core departments: Corporate and Corporate Finance, Banking and Finance, Conveyancing, Tax, Intellectual Property, Trusts, Shipping and Litigation. The firm has developed expertise not only in the domestic market but also in regional and cross-border work in the Asia Pacific region including Australia, Cambodia, Cook Islands, Indonesia, Myanmar, Philippines, Thailand, Vietnam and India. The firm has also developed substantial expertise in off-shore financing in Labuan which is rapidly gaining popularity as a tax haven. To enhance its portfolio of services to its existing clients, the firm has expanded its offices to include one in Labuan. The firm has also developed strong ties with major banks and financial institutions in Malaysia in connection with off-shore financing projects.

Client Base: Clients include local and multinational corporations, private and public listed companies, banks (local and off-shore) and major financial institutions, insurance houses, property developers, manufacturers, traders, professional bodies and marine transport companies. The firm also has a large number of clients based outside Malaysia, primarily in Singapore, Japan, North America, Western Europe, Australia, the People's Republic of China and South-East Asia.

MALAYSIA LAW DIGEST

(The following is a list of all Topics, including cross-references, covered in this Digest.)

MALAYSIA LAW DIGEST

Prepared for 1997 edition by

DAVID CHONG & CO., Advocates and Solicitors, Kuala Lumpur, Malaysia.

See topic Statutes.

ABSENTEES:

Generally, in absence abroad, person may delegate authority to any person of full capacity, usually by way of power of attorney. As for company, as long as permitted by and in accordance with company's Memorandum and Articles of Association, its directors may empower any person as company's attorney to execute deeds on its behalf abroad. Power may be limited or unlimited as donor wishes.

Under Powers of Attorney Act (Act 424) (West Malaysia), in order for power of attorney to be valid, copy of power of attorney duly certified as "true copy" by Senior Assistant Registrar of (West Malaysia) High Court, or where original power of attorney has been deposited in Registry of Supreme Court in Singapore, office copy of such power of attorney, must be deposited in office of Senior Assistant Registrar of (West Malaysia) High Court.

ACTIONS:

Any person may sue or be sued as long as plaintiff is able to satisfy Malaysia courts that they have jurisdiction to hear matter. See topic Courts. If plaintiff resides outside Malaysia, he may be ordered by court to pay money into court as security for defendant's legal costs should plaintiff eventually fail to prove his claim.

Foreign Law.—Particulars of foreign law must be given if pleaded. Foreign law is to be proved as facts during trial. Experts can give oral evidence of foreign law. In absence of such evidence, Malaysia law will be applied. Exception is that Malaysia courts take judicial notice of all Public Acts passed by Parliament of U.K. and all local and personal Acts directed by it to be judicially noticed.

ADMINISTRATION:

See topic Executors and Administrators.

ADOPTION:

Governed by Adoption Act (Act 257) which does not apply to Muslims. Court may, subject to provisions of Act, make order authorising applicant to adopt child. Child is defined as unmarried person under age of 21 and includes female under that age who has been divorced.

Where application is made by two spouses jointly, Court may make order authorising adoption but otherwise no adoption order can be made authorising more than one person to adopt child.

Applicant must: (a) have attained age of 25 and be at least 21 years older than child; (b) must have attained age of 21 and be relative of child; or (c) be father or mother of child.

Adoption order requires consent of person who is parent/guardian of child or who is liable to contribute to support of child. Consent can be dispensed with by Court if: (a) in case of parent/guardian of child, he has abandoned, neglected or persistently ill-treated child; (b) in case of person liable to contribute to support of child, he has persistently neglected or refused to contribute; (c) in any case, person whose consent is required cannot be found, is incapable of giving consent or his consent is unreasonably withheld; or (d) in any case, in accordance with any written law relating to adoption of children for time being in force in any country any competent authority has given permission or granted licence authorising care and possession of child to be transferred to applicant.

Court, when making order, must be satisfied that: (a) consent of necessary persons has been obtained; (b) due consideration has been given to wishes of child taking into account age and understanding of child; (c) neither applicant nor person whose consent is required has made or received or agreed to make or receive any form of reward in consideration of adoption except such as court may sanction; and (d) if applicant had applied previously, there has been substantial change in circumstances.

Order cannot be made unless: (a) child has been continuously in care or possession of applicant for three consecutive months immediately preceding date of order; and (b) applicant has, at least three months before date of order, notified in writing officer of Social Welfare Department of State in which applicant is residing.

Upon making of adoption order, all rights, duties, liabilities and obligations of parent or guardian of child are extinguished and vest in, and are exercisable by and enforceable against, applicant.

ADVOCATES AND SOLICITORS:

See topic Attorneys and Counselors.

AFFIDAVITS AND STATUTORY DECLARATIONS:

Affidavit may contain only such facts as deponent is able of his own knowledge to prove.

Affidavit sworn for purpose of being used in interlocutory proceedings may contain statements of information or belief with sources and grounds thereof. Any document referred to in affidavit must be exhibited by attaching copy of document to affidavit.

Affidavit purporting to have affixed or impressed thereon or subscribed thereto, seal or signature of court, judge, notary public or person having authority to administer oaths in Commonwealth country (and in case of any other country, seal or signature of consular officer of Commonwealth country in testimony of affidavit being taken before it or him) may be admitted in evidence without proof of it being seal or signature of that court, judge, notary public or person.

Statutory Declarations.—Form of declaration is as follows:

I ... do solemnly and sincerely declare that ... and I make this solemn declaration conscientiously believing the same to be true, and by virtue of the provisions of the Statutory Declarations Act, 1960.

Subscribed and solemnly declared)
by the abovenamed ... at ..... in)
the State of ... this ... day of...)
19...)

Before me,

....

(Signature of President of Sessions Court, Magistrate or Commissioner for Oaths)

AGENCY:

See topic Principal and Agent.

ALIENS:

See topic Immigration.

APPLICABLE LAW:

See topic Constitution and Government.

ARBITRATION AND AWARD:

Local Arbitration.—Arbitration Act (Act 93) regulates all arbitrations conducted locally under Malaysia law except for matters stated below. Party may, before taking steps in legal proceedings commenced by other party brought in breach of arbitration agreement, apply to court to stay proceedings. Court may stay proceedings if satisfied that there is no sufficient reason why matter should not be referred in accordance with arbitration agreement, and that applicant was, at time when proceedings were commenced and still remains ready and willing to do all things necessary to proper conduct of arbitration. Award on arbitration agreement may, by leave of court, be enforced in same manner as judgment or order to same effect, and, where leave is so given, judgment may be entered in terms of award.

Act does not apply to arbitration held under Convention on Settlement of Investment Disputes Between States and Nationals of Other States 1965 ("Convention of 1965") or under United Nations Commission on International Trade Law Arbitration Rules 1976 and Rules of Regional Centre for Arbitration at Kuala Lumpur. Award made in arbitration held in conformity with said Convention and Rules, may be enforced in accordance with provisions of either Convention of 1965 or Convention on Recognition and Enforcement of Foreign Arbitral Awards 1958, as may be appropriate.

Convention of 1965 is given effect under Convention on Settlement of Investment Disputes Act (Act 392). Award made under this Convention may be enforced as if it were decree judgment or order of Court.

Foreign Awards.—Convention on Recognition and Enforcement of Foreign Arbitral Awards Act (Act 320) gives effect to New York Convention on Recognition and Enforcement of Foreign Arbitral Awards 1958. Convention award may be relied upon by party by way of defence, set-off or otherwise in legal proceedings in Malaysia.

ASSIGNMENTS:

Assignment of Contractual Rights.—Law on legal and equitable assignment of contractual rights similar to English law. Many such rights have been made assignable by specific statutes, such as Bills of Exchange Act (Act 204—negotiable instruments), Copyright Act (Act 332—copyrights) and Companies Act (Act 125—shares in companies).

Apart from such specific statutory provisions, law on legal (i.e. statutory) assignments is contained in Civil Law Act (Act 67) (Malaysia). Assignment of debt or other legal chose in action must be absolute, in writing, made under hand of assignor and must not purport to be by way of charge only. Express written notice of assignment must also be given to debtor, trustee or other person from whom assignor would have been entitled to receive or claim debt or chose in action. Assignment takes effect from date of notice. Such assignment is subject to all equities which would have been entitled to priority over right of assignee under law before 7 Apr. 1956 (for West Malaysia)/1 Apr. 1972 (for East Malaysia).

Failure to comply with formalities of Civil Law Act renders assignment void as legal assignment, but it may still be valid as equitable (that is, non-statutory) assignment. No particular form is required for valid equitable assignment. Transaction upon which assignee relies need not even purport to be assignment or use language of assignment. If intention of assignor clearly is that contractual right is to become property of assignee, then equity requires him to do all that is necessary to implement his intention.

Generally, assignee under legal assignment may sue upon assignment in his own name without joining assignor as party, whereas assignee under equitable assignment has to join assignor as co-plaintiff or co-defendant (except for absolute equitable assignment of equitable chose in action, where assignee can sue in his own name without joining assignor).

Rights that are incapable of assignment include rights under contracts which involve personal skill or confidence.

Assignment of Contractual Liabilities.—Similar to English law. Contractual liabilities cannot be assigned.

ASSIGNMENTS . . . *continued*

See also Contracts Act (Act 136) regarding person by whom promise is to be performed.

ASSOCIATIONS:

See topic Partnerships.

ATTACHMENT:

Attachment of property before judgment and after judgment made available under Debtors Act. (Act 256). Seizure of property before judgment may be sought after issuance of writ of summons, and order for seizure may be made in West Malaysia, Sabah or Sarawak ("State") if court is satisfied by evidence on oath that plaintiff has good cause of action against defendant and that: (a) defendant is absent from State and his place of abode cannot be discovered; (b) service of writ of summons cannot without great delay or difficulty be effected; or (c) defendant, with intent to obstruct or delay execution of judgment has, inter alia, removed, concealed, made away or about to remove, conceal or make away with his movable or immovable property.

ATTORNEYS AND COUNSELORS:

Governed by Legal Profession Act. (Act 166). Act applies throughout West Malaysia and is made applicable to Sabah and Sarawak with such modifications as Yang di-Pertuan Agong may, by gazetted order, make. Rulings are issued by Bar Council from time to time. Profession is fused, consisting of advocates and solicitors.

Admission.—To be admitted as advocate and solicitor of High Court of Malaya, person must be qualified person or articled clerk who has complied with conditions for admission stipulated in Act. "Qualified person" means person who: (a) has passed final examination leading to degree of Bachelor of Laws of University of Malaya or National University of Singapore (or its predecessors, University of Malaya in Singapore and University of Singapore); (b) is barrister-at-law of England; or (c) is in possession of such other qualification as may be declared by Qualifying Board, established under Act, and gazetted. In addition, he must be at least 18 years old, of good character, citizen or permanent resident of Malaysia and must have satisfactorily served in Malaysia prescribed period of pupillage for qualified persons.

Foreign Law Firms.—Person must either be citizen or permanent resident of Malaysia. Thus, foreign law firms are restricted from establishing presence in Malaysia.

AUTOMOBILES:

See topic Motor Vehicles.

BANKRUPTCY:

Law is contained in Bankruptcy Act (Act 360) (Malaysia). Bankruptcy proceedings may be brought against individuals under various grounds, most common where creditor serves bankruptcy notice and debtor has not complied with notice within prescribed time or is unable to resist notice debtor commits act of bankruptcy. (Bankruptcy notice may be issued by creditor who has obtained final judgment or final order against debtor for any amount and execution thereon has not been stayed; notice must be in prescribed form.) "Debtor" includes any person who at time when act of bankruptcy was commited, he: (a) was personally present in Malaysia; (b) ordinarily resided or had place of residence in Malaysia; (c) was carrying on business in Malaysia either personally or by means of agent; or (d) was member of firm or partnership which carried on business in Malaysia.

Creditor cannot present bankruptcy petition against debtor unless: (a) debt owed by debtor to petitioning creditor or to two or more petitioning creditors aggregates at least RM10,000; (b) debt is liquidated sum payable either immediately or at some certain future time; (c) act of bankruptcy relied upon must have occurred within six months before presentation of petition; and (d) debtor has requisite connection with Malaysia.

On court's issuance of receiving order, Official Assignee is appointed receiver of debtor's property which becomes divisible among his creditors.

BANKS AND BANKING:

Principal objects of Bank Negara Malaysia (Central Bank of Malaysia), are to: (a) issue currency in Malaysia and keep reserves safeguarding value of currency; (b) act as banker and financial adviser to Government of Malaysia; (c) promote stability and sound financial structure; and (d) influence credit situation to advantage of Malaysia (Central Bank of Malaysia Act). (Act 519). It oversees licensing and regulation of all activities of banks and financial institutions in Malaysia, other than offshore banks operating in international offshore financial centre of Labuan which are regulated and licensed by Labuan Offshore Financial Services Authority.

All institutions carrying on banking, finance company, merchant banking, discount house and money-broking businesses are required to obtain licences from Bank Negara Malaysia under Banking and Financial Institutions Act. (Act 372). Banks operating in Labuan are licensed and regulated under Offshore Banking Act. (Act 443) .

BILLS AND NOTES:

Bills of Exchange Act (Act 204) is substantially similar to English Bills of Exchange Act 1882 and Cheques Act 1957. Common law applies except where inconsistent with Act. Conflict rules are similar to those applicable in England.

BILLS OF SALE:

In general, chattel mortgages, other than mortgages and debentures registrable under Companies Act (Act 125), are governed by Bills of Sale Act (Act 268) which is applicable in West Malaysia only. Bill of sale as defined in Act is void unless for RM100 or more, made in prescribed form, truly sets forth consideration for which it was given and registered within seven clear days after execution thereof, or, if executed outside West Malaysia, registered within seven clear days after time at which it would, in ordinary course of post arrive in West Malaysia if posted immediately after execution thereof. Registration must be renewed at least once every 12 calendar months. Registered bills of sale are available for public inspection.

See also topic Chattel Mortgages.

CHARGES:

See topic Mortgages.

CHATTEL MORTGAGES:

Mortgages of chattel, except mortgages and debentures registrable under Companies Act (Act 125), are registrable under Bills of Sale Act (Act 268). Floating charges over chattels, charge over land or any interest therein and charge over ship or aircraft or share in ship or aircraft are registrable under Companies Act. This applies to property wheresoever situate for companies incorporated under Companies Act and to property in Malaysia for foreign companies registered under Companies Act. Such charges must be registered within 30 days after creation of charge (with extension of seven days for documents executed overseas). Otherwise charge is void against liquidator and creditors of company.

Mortgages of Malaysian-registered ships are also registrable under Merchant Shipping Ordinance. (Ord. 70). No additional written provisions for registration of aircraft mortgages.

See also topics Bills of Sale; Corporations.

COLLATERAL SECURITY:

See topic Pledges.

COMMERCIAL REGISTER:

Persons wishing to carry on business (i.e. every form of trade, commerce or other activity conducted for purpose of profit or gain) in Malaysia must seek registration either under Registration of Businesses Act (Act 197) or Companies Act (Act 125).

See also topics Corporations; Chattel Mortgages; Partnerships; Patents; Trademarks.

CONSTITUTION AND GOVERNMENT:

Malaysia is Federation consisting of: nine Malay States: Kedah, Perlis, Kelantan, Terengganu, Perak, Pahang, Selangor, Negeri Sembilan and Johor; Pulau Pinang and Melaka; Borneo states of Sabah and Sarawak; and Federal Territory of Kuala Lumpur and Federal Territory of Labuan. The nine Malay States, Pulau Pinang, Melaka and Federal Territory of Kuala Lumpur comprise West Malaysia; and Borneo States of Sabah and Sarawak, and Federal Territory of Labuan comprise East Malaysia. Malaysia has written constitution (Constitution of Federation of Malaysia). Any law, whether State or Federal, inconsistent with Constitution is to that extent void. See also topic Statutes.

The Monarch.—Yang di-Pertuan Agong is constitutional Monarch. Monarch's position is both hereditary and elective. Only Sultans of nine Malay States are eligible for election under system of rotation whereby each Sultan has chance of being elected unless he declines. Executive authority of Federation is vested formally in Yang di-Pertuan Agong but he must act in accordance with advice of Cabinet. Cabinet comprises members of Parliament, and is headed by Prime Minister.

Parliament.—Legislative power of Federation is vested in Parliament. Parliament consists of Yang di-Pertuan Agong, Dewan Rakyat (House of Representatives) and Dewan Negara (Senate). Members of Dewan Rakyat are directly elected by citizens. Dewan Negara is filled partly by appointees of Yang di-Pertuan Agong, and partly by members elected from State Legislative Assemblies. Enactments are presented to Yang di-Pertuan Agong for assent, but if not assented after 30 days, enactment is reconsidered in Parliament and presented again for assent. If enactment is not assented after 30 days of representation, it becomes law as if Yang di-Pertuan Agong had assented it. Dewan Negara only has powers to delay legislation, allowing Dewan Rakyat to reconsider its policies.

State Legislative Assemblies.—Legislative power of each State is vested in State Legislative Assembly. Each State has unicameral assembly consisting of ruler or governor, and members directly elected by people of that State. Ruler or governor acts on advice of Executive Council of that State, which is headed by Menteri Besar or Chief Minister. Bills passed by Assembly become law only upon assent of ruler or governor.

Judiciary.—Judiciary has four tiers comprising Federal Court, Court of Appeal, two High Courts (Malaya and Borneo), and Subordinate Courts. Judiciary is headed by Chief Justice Malaysia and Chief Judges of Malaya and Borneo. Judges of High Court and above are appointed until retirement at age 65, by Prime Minister in consultation with Chief Justice Malaysia.

See also topic Courts.

CONTRACTS:

Applicable Law.—Contracts Act (Act 136) is based on English law. Contracts must be made with free consent of parties competent to contract for lawful consideration with lawful object.

Excuses for Nonperformance.—Novation, rescission, alteration, dispensation, remittance, force majeure. Essentially same as English law.

Government Contracts.—Proceedings can be taken and enforced against Government. Such proceedings are governed by Government Proceedings Act. (Act 359).

Penalty.—Damages may be stipulated in contract in event of breach but if stipulation is by way of penalty then aggrieved party is only entitled to such compensation as Court considers reasonable.

Assignments.—See topic Assignments.

Privity.—Same as English law.

COPYRIGHT AND REGISTERED DESIGN:

Copyright.—

COPYRIGHT AND REGISTERED DESIGN . . . *continued*

Statute.—Copyright Act. (Act 332).

Treaties.—Malaysia is signatory to Berne Convention, hence nationals and residents of member countries enjoy copyright protection in Malaysia.

Protection.—Works covered under Act comprise literary (which includes dramatic works and computer programmes), musical and artistic works, sound recordings, films, broadcasts, and typographical format of published editions of work. Derivative works derived from these subject matters are considered "original works" and protected as such. No registration is required.

Copyright in literary, artistic and musical works ("works"), sound recordings and films extends to: (a) making reproductions in material form; (b) performing, showing or playing to public; (c) broadcasting; (d) communicating by cable; and (e) distributing copies to public by sale, rental, lease or lending, of whole work or substantial part thereof, either in its original or derivative form.

For broadcasts, copyright extends to recording, reproduction and rebroadcasting of substantial part of broadcasts, and performance in public of broadcasts before paying audience (for television broadcasts, includes right to take still photographs from broadcast).

For published editions of works, copyright is confined to right to make reproduction of edition.

For works (except photographs), copyright has duration of 50 years following death of author or following first publication, as case may be. For sound recordings and films—50 years from beginning of year following first publication. For television and sound broadcasts—50 years from beginning of year following first making. For published editions of work 50 years from beginning of year following first publication of edition.

Assignment.—Copyright may be assigned, but assignment must be in writing and signed by or on behalf of assignor.

Licence.—Copyright may be licensed either on exclusive or non-exclusive basis, and must be in writing.

Infringement of copyright takes place where, without permission of copyright owner, rights reserved exclusively to copyright owner is exercised by someone other than copyright owner. Person who imports article for purposes of selling, letting for hire or by way of trade offering or exposing for sale or hire, distributing article for purpose of trade or exhibiting article in public by way of trade or person who sells, lets for hire or by way of trade offers or exposes for sale or hire or exhibits article in public by way of trade and knows or reasonably ought to know that making of article was without consent of owner is liable for copyright infringement. Civil remedies include injunctions, damages or account of profits and delivery up of infringing copies and tools.

Registered Design.—

Statute.—United Kingdom Designs (Protection) Act. (Act 214). New Industrial Design Act will soon be passed.

Procedure.—No registration or reregistration in Malaysia is necessary. Registered proprietor of design registered in U.K. under Registered Designs Act 1949 enjoys in Malaysia like privileges and rights as though certificate of registration in U.K. had been issued with extension to Malaysia. Once new Industrial Design Act comes into force, applications for registration of designs can be filed locally.

Registrability.—To be registrable, design must satisfy following: (a) it must be new; (b) it must have eye appeal; (c) features of shape or configuration of design of article must not be: (i) dictated solely by function which article performs, or (ii) dependent upon appearance of another article of which article is intended by author to form integral part; and (d) appearance of article based on design must be material.

Rights.—Registered proprietor of design has monopoly over its use. No need to prove copying (cf copyright). Registration gives proprietor exclusive right: (a) to make or import: (i) for sale or hire, or (ii) for use for purposes of trade or business; or (b) to sell, hire or offer or expose for sale or hire, article in respect of which design is registered.

Duration.—Rights granted last for five years from date of registration but renewable for further periods of five years up to maximum of 25 years.

Infringement.—Person who does any of aforesaid acts reserved exclusively for registered proprietor without consent of proprietor is liable for design infringement. Civil remedies include injunctions, damages, and delivery up of infringing copies and tools.

Defence of innocence provided under Act i.e. registered proprietor of design is not entitled to recover damages in respect of infringement of copyright in design from defendant who proves that at date of infringement he was not aware nor had any reasonable means of making himself aware of existence of registration of design. Innocence defence does not affect plaintiff's right to injunction.

CORPORATIONS:

Governed by Companies Act. (Act No. 125).

Formation.—Two or more persons (including body corporates) may incorporate company. Apart from issuance of two shares, no minimum amount of authorised or issued share capital.

Limited/Unlimited.—Companies may be limited (liability of shareholders limited by shares or guarantee) or unlimited. Unlimited companies may be converted into limited companies but not vice versa.

Private company by its Memorandum and Articles of Association must restrict transfer of its shares, limit members to no more than 50 and prohibit invitation to public to subscribe for shares. Private limited companies must have words "Sendirian Berhad" or abbreviation "Sdn. Bhd." as part of its name.

Public company must not have above restrictions and may invite public to subscribe for shares and debentures by issuance of prospectus. Limited liability companies must have word "Berhad" or abbreviation "Bhd." as part of its name. Public companies may apply to be listed on Stock Exchange in accordance with Kuala Lumpur Stock Exchange listing requirements.

Listed companies are principally regulated by Kuala Lumpur Stock Exchange and Securities Commission, to whom applications have to be made for certain transactions such as injection of assets into listed company.

Registrar of Companies administers Companies Act. All statutory documents including Memorandum and Articles of Association, and concerning details of registered office, directors, amount of share capital, charges created over assets of company, are to be lodged with Registrar who also approves intended names of companies. Company must also file with Registrar annual returns setting out specified information including audited accounts, names of members, details of directors and paid-up share capital.

Administration of Company.—Essentially run by Board of Directors in accordance with Articles of Association. Certain matters are stipulated by Act as requiring approval of 75% of shareholders (for example, alteration in restriction of share transfer and alteration of Memorandum and Articles). Reduction in share capital requires Court order.

Secretary and Directors.—Company secretary and at least two directors must be locally resident.

Prohibited Acts.—Certain acts are prohibited by Act including provision of financial assistance by company for purchase of its own shares and in case of public companies, making loans to persons (including companies) connected with directors.

Foreign Companies.—Division 2, Part XI of Companies Act applies to foreign companies carrying on business in Malaysia and stipulates requirements including documents to be lodged with Registrar of Companies. Foreign companies must have registered office in Malaysia where all communications and notices may be served.

COURTS:

Superior Courts of Judicature.—Courts of Judicature Act (Act 91) establishes High Court, Court of Appeal and Federal Court.

High Court in Malaya and High Court in Sabah and Sarawak have jurisdiction to try all civil proceedings where cause of action arose, or defendant or one of several defendants resides or has his place of business, or facts on which proceedings are based exist or are alleged to have occurred, or any land, ownership of which is disputed, is situated within their respective local jurisdictions.

Court of Appeal has only appellate jurisdiction to hear and determine appeal against decision made by High Court except for several non-appealable matters.

Federal Court has jurisdiction to hear and determine appeals against decision made by Court of Appeal except for several non-appealable matters.

Subordinate Courts comprise Sessions Court, Magistrates' Courts and, in West Malaysia only, Penghulu's Courts. Sessions Courts and Magistrates' Courts have power to stay proceedings unless instituted in District in which cause of action arose, or defendant resides or has his place of business, or one of several defendants resides or has his place of business, or facts on which proceedings are based exist or are alleged to have occurred, or for other reasons desirable in interests of justice that proceedings should be had.

CURRENCY:

Local currency is Ringgit (RM).

See topics Banks and Banking; Exchange Control; Foreign Exchange.

CUSTOMS:

Customs duty is levied on certain categories of goods, including tobacco, liquors, motorcars and certain electrical goods. Applicable rates of customs duty and types of dutiable goods are found in Customs Act (Act 235) and its regulations. See also topics Foreign Investment; Foreign Trade Regulations.

DEATH:

Person is presumed dead if proved that he has not been heard from for seven years by persons who would have naturally heard from him if he had been alive.

Where two or more persons die in circumstances where uncertain who survived other, such deaths, subject to order of Court and for all purposes affecting right to title to property, are presumed to have occurred in order of seniority, so younger is deemed to have survived elder.

Married person may petition to Court to declare other party to marriage as presumed dead if petitioner has reasonable grounds for believing so. Party to marriage is presumed dead if continually absent for seven years and petitioner has no reason to believe that other person is living.

Executor or administrator of deceased may on behalf and for benefit of dependants commence action in name of executor or administrator within three years of death against person who by reason of his wrongful act, neglect or default caused death to deceased person. If no executor or administrator of deceased or no action is brought within six months after death by and in name of executor or administrator of deceased, action may be brought by and in name of all or any of persons for whose benefit executor or administrator could have brought it. This includes spouse, parent, grandparent, great-grandparent, child, grandchild or great-grandchild of deceased or person who is, or is issue of, brother, sister, uncle or aunt of deceased. Damages recoverable would include pecuniary loss to estate, bereavement and funeral expenses.

DEEDS:

Individuals.—Deed must be signed in presence of witness by party to be bound or by his attorney. Not necessary for deed to be sealed, so long as deed makes it clear on face of itself that it is intended to be deed.

Companies.—Common seal of company must be affixed in accordance with company's articles of association (usually in presence of two directors, or one director and one secretary). Individual authorised by company pursuant to power of attorney to execute documents under seal may execute them by signing for and on behalf of company and affixing his seal. See also topic Seals.

Attestation.—Generally, no attestation clause required unless deed contains power of attorney.

See Topical Index in front part of this volume.

DEEDS . . . *continued*

Consideration.—See topic Seals.

DEPOSITIONS AND DISCOVERY:

Obtaining Evidence for Local Courts Before Trial.—Court may, in any cause or matter where it appears necessary for purposes of justice, make order for examination on oath before judge or registrar or some other person, at any place, of any person.

Deposition of person examined pursuant to order of court may be received in evidence at trial of cause or matter if: (a) party against whom evidence is offered consents; or (b) court is satisfied deponent is dead, or beyond jurisdiction of court or unable from sickness or other infirmity to attend trial. Reasonable period of notice of intention to use such deposition must be given to other party before trial.

Where person to be examined on oath is out of jurisdiction, assistance from judicial authorities of country in which that person is to be examined may be sought by applying to High Court to issue letter of request to judicial authorities for evidence of person to be examined.

Obtaining Evidence for Foreign Courts.—High Court may make orders for examination of witnesses and production of documents.

Discovery.—During summons for directions after pleadings have closed, Court will order service of list of documents providing for discovery of documents.

DESCENT AND DISTRIBUTION:

In testacy cases, distribution of deceased's estate governed by properly executed will. In intestacy cases, distribution of movable property of deceased regulated by law of country in which he was domiciled at time of his death while that of his immovable property is regulated by Distribution Act (Act 300) (West Malaysia and Sarawak) and Intestates' Succession Ordinance (Ord.1/960) (Sabah). Sabah Ordinance is modelled on Intestates' Estates Act 1952 of England.

In effecting distribution in intestacy, if deceased is husband and leaves spouse but no issue, spouse gets half share of estate and balance half share will be distributed to parents if alive; if not, to brothers and sisters; if no brothers or sisters, then to grandparents. If there are no parents, brothers, sisters and grandparents, then spouse takes all. If deceased is wife and leaves spouse but no issue, spouse takes all.

If deceased is husband and leaves spouse and issue, wife gets one-third of estate and remaining share distributed equally between children. If deceased is wife and leaves spouse and issue, spouse takes all. If deceased leaves no surviving spouse, descendants or parents, estate will be distributed equally amongst deceased's brothers and sisters and in case any of them is dead, their descendants are entitled to share which he or she would have taken.

Grandparents will take whole estate in equal portions if no surviving spouse, descendants, parents, brothers and sisters or children of such brothers and sisters. Uncles and aunts take whole estate in equal portions if no surviving spouse, descendants, parents, brothers and sisters or children of such brothers and sisters or grandparents. If deceased leaves no spouse, issue, parents, grandparents, brothers and sisters, uncles or aunts, then granduncles and grandaunts take in equal shares.

Government is entitled to whole estate in default of distribution under foregoing rules.

Distribution provided under Act may be affected by Inheritance (Family Provisions) Act (Act 39) (Malaysia) which provides for maintenance of dependants in testacies and intestacies.

Law of Islamic Inheritance.—Rules of intestate succession set out above do not apply to Muslims. Distribution takes place only after legacies and debts, including funeral expenses, are paid out of property left behind by deceased.

If deceased is husband, and leaves no issue and no parent, widow gets one-quarter. If deceased is wife and no issue and no parent, widower gets one-half. If deceased husband leaves issue and no parent, spouse is entitled to one-eighth of estate. On other hand, widower is entitled to one-half of deceased wife's estate. Remaining share is distributed amongst children of deceased. Female children's share is generally half of male children's share.

If deceased leaves surviving spouse and no issue but parents, widower entitled to one-half of estate, and father and mother get two-thirds and one-third of remaining estate respectively. As for widow, she will be entitled to one-quarter share of husband's estate, and father and mother get two-thirds and one-third of remaining estate respectively.

If deceased leaves parents but no surviving spouse and no children, mother will get one-third and father will get remaining two-thirds. If deceased leaves parents and children but no spouse, each parent takes one-sixth share while remaining share will be distributed among children.

DIVORCE:

Law Reform (Marriage and Divorce) Act (Act 164) governs marriages, divorce and judicial separation. Cannot petition for divorce within two years of marriage. According to Act, court has jurisdiction to entertain proceedings for divorce, presumption of death and divorce, judicial separation or nullity of marriage if: (a) marriage has been registered under Act; or (b) marriage is deemed to be registered under Act, or was solemnised under law which expressly or impliedly provides that marriage must be monogamous; or (c) either of parties to marriage is domiciled in Malaysia at commencement of proceedings.

Either party to marriage may petition for divorce on ground that marriage has irretrievably broken down by reason of one or more of following facts: (a) respondent has committed adultery and petitioner finds it intolerable to live with respondent; (b) respondent has behaved in such way that petitioner cannot reasonably be expected to live with respondent; (c) respondent has deserted petitioner for continuous period of at least two years immediately preceding presentation of petition; or (d) parties to marriage have lived apart for continuous period of at least two years immediately preceding presentation of petition.

Two additional grounds of divorce not dependent upon irretrievable breakdown of marriage: (a) one party has converted to Islam, other party not so converted may petition for divorce; or (b) after two years of marriage, both husband and wife freely consent to divorce and present joint petition.

Court empowered to adjourn proceedings if reasonable possibility of reconciliation. Estranged spouses are encouraged to reconcile by being allowed to resume cohabitation for period not exceeding six months without prejudicing petition.

Petition for judicial separation may be presented to Court by either party to marriage on ground and circumstances set out above. Where Court grants decree of judicial separation, no longer obligatory for petitioner to cohabit with respondent. Judicial separation is no bar to petition for divorce.

Married person who alleges that reasonable grounds exist for supposing that other party to marriage is dead may present petition to Court to have it presumed that other party is dead and to have marriage dissolved. See topic Death.

When granting decree of divorce or judicial separation, Court has power to order division of assets acquired by them during marriage, payment of maintenance and custody of children of marriage.

Divorce in Islam.—Divorce in Islam, although permitted, is not encouraged. Divorce can be effected by Talak, Khu'lu or Fasakh. Divorce by Talak may be effected once husband utters words of divorce. Where husband does not agree to divorce wife but agrees to divorce by Khu'lu (redemption), Syariah Court may assess amount of payment to be made by wife according to her status and means. Husband will then have to pronounce divorce by redemption.

Either party may apply for and obtain decree of Fasakh (Divorce or Rescission by judicial decree) on any ground which is recognised as valid for dissolution of marriage by Fasakh in Islamic law which includes defects in either spouse such as insanity (whether intermittent or permanent), leprosy, vitiligo and dangerous contagious disease or apostasy of either spouse.

When registering divorce, President of Syariah Court has power to order: (a) division of harta sepencarian (assets acquired by them during marriage); (b) payment of maintenance during Iddah (period of continence) and payment of mutaah (consolatory gift) which wife is entitled to in event of divorce by Talak and Fasakh; and (c) custody of children of marriage.

EXCHANGE CONTROL:

Legal basis for exchange control is Exchange Control Act (Act 17) and Exchange Control Notices (known as ECMs) issued from time to time by Bank Negara Malaysia (Central Bank of Malaysia).

Residents require permission of Controller of Foreign Exchange before they can borrow from nonresidents in foreign currency equivalent of more than RM5 million. Specific prior permission of Controller is required for foreign borrowing of any amount in ringgit.

Payments by residents to nonresidents for any purpose are freely permitted, subject only to completion of Form P for individual remittance of more than RM100,000 and above or its equivalent in foreign currency.

Licensed offshore banks, offshore insurance entities and other offshore companies operating in Labuan International Offshore Financial Centre are declared as nonresidents for exchange control purposes, so that they can freely operate foreign currency accounts and move their funds into and out of Malaysia without being subject to exchange control monitoring.

See also topic Foreign Investment.

EXECUTIONS:

Writ of execution may be issued to enforce judgment. Most common form of execution proceedings is issuance of writ of seizure and sale of movable property of judgment debtor. Seizure and sale of immovable property are also available as form of execution of judgment. Seizure and sale of properties conducted by officers of Court.

Where judgment debtor is individual, judgment debt must be at least RM10,000 before bankruptcy proceedings may be brought against judgment debtor. Where judgment debtor is company, winding up proceedings may be brought against judgment debtor, if execution or other process issued on judgment is returned unsatisfied in whole or in part. See topic Bankruptcy.

Debts due to be paid to judgment debtor may be garnished as form of execution proceedings.Debt must be due and owing at time of garnishment.

EXECUTORS AND ADMINISTRATORS:

Upon death of person, whole of his real and personal property devolves to his personal representatives, who in case where he has left will are his executors and in case where he has died intestate are his administrators.

Appointment.—Executors are normally appointed by will. Administrators are appointed by court in case of intestacy, and in case of testacy where executor is not named in will.

Authority of Administrator and Executor.—Administrator obtains authority solely from grant of letters of administration. Until grant is obtained, administrator has no authority. Executor's authority stems from will. He has authority to conduct affairs of deceased, moment deceased dies. It is purely to lend authority and vest proper title that letters of probate are obtained.

Grant of Probate on Testacy.—Executors appointed under will can apply for Grant of Probate.

Letters of Administration on Intestacy.—Number of administrators who may petition for letters of administration cannot exceed four. If there is minority or life interest, then minimum of two persons required as administrators. If no such interest, one administrator will suffice. If trust corporation applies for letters of administration, then requirement of additional person is dispensed with.

Letters of administration are usually granted to next-of-kin in accordance with priorities to entitlement of estate under Distribution Act (Act 300) (West Malaysia and Sarawak) and Intestate Succession Ordinance (Ord. 1/960) (Sabah). Official Administrator may also administer estate if no application for letters of administration has been made, provided estate is worth less than RM50,000.

EXECUTORS AND ADMINISTRATORS . . . *continued*

Renunciation.—Executor or administrator may renounce his right to apply for letters of representation.

Grant of Probate and Letters of Administration.—Grant of Probate and Letters of Administration are normally given as matter of course once petition is filed.

Domicile.—Before granting letters of representation, court requires proof of domicile. Deceased's domicile will determine validity of his will or right of his personal representatives to apply for letters of representation and question of priorities between persons contending for letters of representation.

General Powers and Duties.—In addition to powers conferred by deceased's will, personal representative is also conferred certain powers in his capacity as trustee under Trustee Acts (Act 208) (Malaysia). Duties of personal representatives revolve around calling in estate's assets, determining beneficiaries and shares entitled to and thereafter distributing assets.

Assets and Liabilities.—Inventory of assets and liabilities of estate is first step to be taken by personal representatives to determine amount of estate duty payable and for purposes of distribution.

Creditors.—After calling in all assets of deceased and payment of funeral and testamentary expenses and estate duty, executor or administrator must ensure that debts of deceased are paid. Where estate is large, executor or administrator must place advertisement in Gazette or newspapers to give notice to all creditors that they ought to submit their claims within period stipulated, after which distribution will be made. If claim is not presented within time limited in advertisement, personal representative may distribute estate without being personally liable for debts which he had no knowledge of, but creditor may follow assets to beneficiaries.

Accounts.—Executor or administrator in winding up administration of estate must submit accounts for beneficiaries' perusal and approval before distribution.

Distribution.—It is duty of administrator in case of intestacy to distribute estate in accordance with laws on intestate succession, Distribution Act (Act 300) (West Malaysia and Sarawak) and Intestate Succession Ordinance (Ord. 1/960) (Sabah). In case of testacy, duty of personal representative to carry out terms of will. No distribution of estate until debts of estate are disposed of.

Resealing of Letters of Representation.—Grant of probate or letters of administration by Commonwealth country may be resealed by High Court. Once such grant is resealed, it has same effect as grant of probate or letters of administration of High Court.

FOREIGN CORPORATIONS:

See topic Corporations.

FOREIGN EXCHANGE:

Local currency, Ringgit, is freely convertible and is not pegged to any foreign currency. For monitoring purposes, Ringgit is usually compared to composite basket comprising currencies of Malaysia's major trading partners.

See also topic Exchange Control.

FOREIGN INVESTMENT:

Acquisition of Assets, Mergers and Takeovers.—Foreign Investment Committee ("FIC") was established in 1974, inter alia, to: (a) formulate policy guidelines on foreign investment in Malaysia; (b) monitor foreign investment, including foreign private investment; (c) coordinate and regulate acquisition of assets or mergers and take-overs of companies and businesses in Malaysia; and (d) advise Government on all matters concerning foreign investment.

Generally, guidelines issued by FIC state that following may be done only with prior approval of FIC: (a) proposed acquisition by foreign interest of substantial fixed assets in Malaysia; (b) proposed acquisition of interest, mergers and take-overs of companies and businesses in Malaysia by any means, which will result in ownership or control passing to foreign interests; (c) proposed acquisition of 15% or more of voting power by one or more foreign interest or associated groups, or by foreign interests in aggregate of 30% or more of voting power of Malaysian company and business; (d) control of Malaysian companies and businesses through joint-venture agreement, management agreement etc.; (e) merger or take-over of any company or business in Malaysia whether by Malaysian or foreign interests; and (f) any other proposed acquisition of assets and interest exceeding RM5 million, whether by Malaysian or foreign interests.

Acquisition of commercial properties and some industrial properties also require FIC approval.

Real Property.—Prior approval of relevant State Authorities is required before noncitizen or foreign company may acquire land or interest in land, other than industrial land, by way of disposal or effecting dealings with respect to alienated land or interest in land. However, no approval is required in respect of taking of charge or lien or lease by noncitizen or foreign company in respect of alienated land or undivided share in land. Where order for sale is made under National Land Code (Act 56), noncitizen of foreign company is not entitled to bid at sale where land is categorised "agriculture" or "building" or subject to condition that it be used for agriculture or building purpose without approval of State Authority.

Exchange Control.—Restrictions are placed on flow of capital in and out of Malaysia. In particular, restrictions are placed on dealings in gold, foreign currency, securities and debts, on payments in and outside Malaysia and on import into, export out of, transfer and settlement of property in Malaysia. These restrictions are mainly contained in Exchange Control Act (Act 17) and Exchange Control Notices issued from time to time by Bank Negara Malaysia (Central Bank of Malaysia). Restrictions imposed by Act, subject to limitations contained therein, apply to all persons notwithstanding that they are not in Malaysia and are not Malaysian citizens. See also topic Exchange Control.

Tax Incentives.—Foreign investment is encouraged. Various tax incentives are given for manufacturing, agriculture and tourism sectors. General incentives include granting of Pioneer Status and Investment Tax Allowance (ITA) to eligible companies. Eligibility is determined according to priorities termed as "promoted activities" or "promoted products" as determined by Minister of International Trade and Industry. Reinvestment Allowance is granted to manufacturing companies which incur qualifying capital expenditure for expansion of production capacity, modernisation and upgrading of production facilities and diversification into related products. Specific incentives are also granted for high-technology industries, strategic industries, export, research and development, training, industrial adjustment, small-scale companies, storage, treatment and disposal of toxic and hazardous wastes and Operational Headquarters status. In agricultural sector, incentives include agricultural allowance and deduction for capital expenditure on approved agricultural projects. Generally, other incentives include incentives for forest plantation projects, Infrastructure Allowance for projects located in Sabah, Sarawak and 'Eastern Corridor' of Peninsular Malaysia, tariff protection, exemption from import duty and raw materials/components, drawback of excise duty on parts, ingredients or packaging materials, drawback on sales tax on materials used in manufacture and exemption from import duty and sales tax on machinery and equipment.

FOREIGN TRADE REGULATIONS:

Customs duty is levied on some categories of goods, including tobacco, cigarettes, liquor and petroleum products imported into or exported from Malaysia. Applicable rates of customs duty and types of dutiable goods may be found in Customs Act (Act 235) and regulations made thereunder.

Areas specially designated for manufacturing establishments producing or assembling products essentially for export are known as Free Zones (FZ). Currently 12 FZs have been established. Goods exported abroad from FZs are not liable to customs duty.

Labuan and Langkawi are also designated free-trade zones. No export duty is payable upon goods exported from Labuan or Langkawi and no import duty is payable upon goods imported into Labuan or Langkawi other than petroleum and petroleum products and goods gazetted from time to time as dutiable by relevant Minister. However, customs duty is payable in respect of dutiable goods exported to Labuan or Langkawi from principal customs areas and dutiable goods imported from Labuan or Langkawi into principal customs areas in Malaysia, as if they were exports to or imports from abroad.

FRAUDS, STATUTE OF:

English Statute of Frauds Act inapplicable in West Malaysia. Parts of Act are probably applicable in East Malaysia though precise position uncertain because present statutes do not provide clear guidance on this issue. Case law on issue contributes to uncertainty.

FRAUDULENT SALES AND CONVEYANCES:

Conveyance of real property, to person or body (other than purchaser in good faith and for valuable consideration or person or body claiming through or under such purchaser), is generally liable to be set aside in case of fraud or misrepresentation to which person or body, or agent of person or body, was party or privy.

Fraudulent conveyance constitutes act of bankruptcy and, if made within six months preceeding presentation of bankruptcy petition, will be void against Official Assignee under doctrine of relation back, unless it is protected transaction under Bankruptcy Act (Act 360) (Malaysia) (certain bona fide transactions with third parties without notice of act of bankruptcy are protected).

Voluntary settlements, although not fraudulent, may be void or voidable under certain circumstances.

GARNISHMENT:

See topic Executions.

IMMIGRATION:

Governed by Immigration Act. (Act 155).

General.—Non-Malaysian citizen can enter Malaysia only if he has valid Entry or Re-entry Permit or name endorsed on Entry or Re-entry Permit of accompanying husband/father or if he has valid Pass or if specially exempted by Minister's order. He must not be prohibited immigrant.

Passes.—Director General may issue following passes for purpose of entitling person to enter and remain temporarily in Malaysia:

Employment Pass or Work Pass.—Employment Pass is required if foreigner wishes to take up employment under contract of service with Federal or State government or City Council or Municipality, or to take up employment under contract for minimum of two years with approved company or firm at monthly salary of at least RM1,200.

Foreign spouses of Malaysian citizens may apply for employment pass with evidence of their marriage and letter of appointment regardless of salary.

Work Pass necessary for person intending to work in Sabah. Following conditions must be satisfied: (a) he must be qualified to work or undertake employment in that particular trade, business or calling; (b) there must not already be unemployment in Sabah of persons skilled in that particular class of trade, business or calling; and (c) his taking up of such work and employment will generally benefit Sabah.

Dependant's Pass.—Wife and dependant children of Employment Pass holder may apply for Dependant's Passes to enable them to remain with him in Malaysia. Holder of Dependant's Pass is not allowed to engage in any form of paid employment in Malaysia without government's written consent.

Visit Pass.—May be issued to person wishing to enter Malaysia on social, business or professional visit, for temporary employment or as tourist. Dependant children may also apply for Visit Passes to accompany or join Work Pass holder in Sabah. Unless Minister has consented otherwise in writing, person holding Visit Pass as tourist or for purpose of social visit or as dependant child of Work Pass Holder cannot engage in any form of paid employment or in any business or professional occupation and cannot give political lectures, speeches, talks or engage in any political activity in Malaysia.

IMMIGRATION . . . *continued*

Student's Pass.—May be issued to person who has been accepted as student by recognised university or approved educational institution in Malaysia; or who possesses certificate issued by Minister charged with responsibility for education stating that it is desirable that he should be accepted as student at specified educational institution in Malaysia and that he has been so accepted.

Permanent Residence.—Entry Permits may be issued to foreigners wishing to acquire permanent residence in Malaysia. Re-entry Permits may be granted to Malaysian Permanent Residents who intend to re-enter Malaysia. Permanent residence granted to applicants on case-by-case basis in accordance with immigration policies of government.

Security Deposit.—Security by deposit or otherwise may have to be furnished as condition for issue of Pass, to ensure compliance with immigration provisions or conditions imposed in respect of Pass.

INCOME TAX:

See topic Taxation.

INFANTS:

Age of Majority.—Age of majority is 18 years.

Actions By or Against Infant.—Subject to certain exceptions, can only be commenced by next friend and defended by guardian ad litem.

Contracts with Infants.—Following common law, contracts generally unenforceable as against infant and voidable at option of infant, except contracts for necessaries (necessary goods and services supplied to infant) and contracts of apprenticeship, education and service. Such voidable contracts may be of two types: (a) binding on infant unless repudiated during minority within reasonable time of infant attaining majority; or (b) not binding on infant unless and until ratified after attaining majority.

Child (below 14 years) or young person (14 years and above but below 16 years) is competent to enter into contract of service otherwise than as employer and may sue without next friend or defend action without guardian ad litem. However, damages and indemnity not recoverable from child or young person for breach of contract of service.

Will made by infant not valid unless privileged will. Privileged will is one made by member of armed forces of Malaysia being in actual military service, or mariner or seaman (including member of naval forces of Malaysia) at sea.

INHERITANCE TAX:

See topic Taxation.

INSOLVENCY:

Corporate Insolvency.—Governed by Companies Act. (Act 125). Companies incorporated in Malaysia may be wound up either voluntarily or compulsorily by order of court. Voluntary liquidation proceedings may be carried out by members in which event company must be solvent in that it will be able to pay its debts in full within 12 months from date of resolution to wind up company. Compulsory winding up proceedings usually brought by creditors against company on grounds that company unable to debts of RM500 or more.

Individual Insolvency.—See topic Bankruptcy.

INTEREST:

General.—Interest is payable only when allowed by statute or in accordance with contract. No general prohibition on rate of interest that can be charged. However, simple interest not exceeding 12% or 18% per annum (for secured and unsecured loans respectively) may be charged by those carrying on business of moneylending pursuant to Moneylenders Act. (Act 400). Act does not apply to registered co-operative societies, licensed banks, licensed insurance companies, licensed pawnbrokers and companies licensed under Takaful Act. (Act 312).

Prejudgment.—Interest may be awarded by Court in respect of late payment of damages or debts.

Post-judgment interest is, subject to agreement of parties, at rate to be determined at discretion of Court.

JUDGMENTS:

Foreign judgments may, with leave of Malaysia High Court, be registered in Malaysia and enforced in same manner as judgment given by Malaysia High Court if judgment was obtained in court of country under ambit of Reciprocal Enforcement of Judgments Act. (Act 99). For foreign judgments not falling within ambit of Act, fresh proceedings must be commenced against judgment debtor on judgment in which event procedural and substantive rules on establishing jurisdiction and service of documents must be satisfied.

LABOUR RELATIONS:

Trade unions established after commencement of Trade Unions Act (Act 262) must be registered. Such trade unions fall within ambit of Industrial Relations Act (Act 177), which governs relations between trade unions and employers. Trade unions may claim recognition by employers and, upon being accorded recognition, may negotiate for collective agreements. Industrial Courts have power to deal with trade disputes under Industrial Relations Act.

Employment.—Governed by Employment Act (Act 265) and common law principles.

Scope of Act.—Act affords protection for "employees" defined as persons who have entered into contracts of service with employers and: (a) their wages do not exceed RM1,250 per month, irrespective of their occupations; or (b) they are engaged in occupations as listed in Act (generally involving manual labour, including artisans, apprentices, drivers, seamen and domestic workers) irrespective of monthly wages earned.

In above cases, employees' rights would be governed by contract of service, collective agreement with relevant trade union (if applicable), and Act. Terms or conditions in contract which are less favourable than those prescribed in Act or related subsidiary legislation are regarded as void to that extent, and more favourable terms and conditions of Act or related subsidiary legislation will be substituted for terms and conditions struck out.

Where person is not protected by Act, he must look to contract of employment and collective agreement (if he is trade union member) for rights under terms of his employment.

Termination of Contracts.—Contract of service for unspecified period of time is deemed to run until terminated by either party by written notice in accordance with Act. Period of notice required to be given is prescribed and varies depending on length of service with employer. Either party may waive requirement on notice. If contract of service is terminated without notice or adequate notice, either party is entitled to wages in lieu of notice or unexpired term of notice, as case may be.

In event of wilful breach of contract of service by any party, other party may terminate contract without notice. Employer can dismiss employee without notice on grounds of misconduct only after due inquiry. Employer also has option of downgrading employee or imposing other lesser punishment as employer deems just and fit.

If employee is not covered by Act and contract of employment is silent, termination is usually by reasonable notice following common law.

Absence without Reasonable Excuse.—Employee is deemed to have broken contract of service if he continuously absents himself for more than two consecutive working days without employer's prior leave, unless he has reasonable excuse and has informed or attempted to inform employer beforehand or at earliest opportunity during his absence.

Payment of Wages.—Generally, wages must be paid within seven days after last day of wage period in question. Employer is deemed to have broken contract of service if he fails to pay wages in accordance with Act.

Hours of Work, Holidays and Other Conditions of Service.—

(1) Hours of Work.—Subject to certain exceptions, employee has right not to work for more than: (a) five consecutive hours without period of leisure of at least 30 minutes; (b) eight hours a day; (c) spread over period of ten hours in a day; (d) 48 hours a week. Legal limit of working hours may be exceeded in emergencies. If overtime work is carried out, employee is entitled to overtime pay of at least 1.5 times his hourly rate of pay.

(2) Holidays.—Employee is entitled to paid holiday at ordinary rate of pay on ten gazetted public holidays in any one calendar year.

(3) Rest Days.—Employee is entitled to one rest day per week. Before commencement of month in which rest days fall, employer must give roster informing employee of rest days in that month. Employer may require employee to work on rest day in emergencies. Employee working on rest day is entitled to be paid at various rates of pay as set out in Act.

(4) Annual Leave.—Entitlement to annual leave commensurates with length of service. Employee who does not complete 12 months of continuous service in any year is entitled to prorated annual leave.

(5) Sick Leave.—Upon examination by doctor (whether appointed by employer or not, as case may permit) or dental surgeon, employee is entitled to paid sick leave as stipulated in Act and which varies depending on duration of service with employer, if no hospitalisation is necessary. If hospitalisation is necessary, employee is generally entitled to 60 days paid sick leave in each year.

(6) Termination, Lay-off and Retirement Benefits.—Employment (Termination and Lay-Off Benefits) Regulations 1980 enables employee to claim termination and lay-off benefits under certain conditions and prescribes method of calculating quantum of benefits. Minister may make regulations allowing for retirement benefits.

Employment of Non-Malaysian Citizens.—Under Employment (Restriction) Act (Act 353), non-Malaysian citizen must apply for and obtain valid employment permit before commencing employment, business, industry or undertaking in Malaysia.

Workmen's Compensation for Injury.—In general, Workmen's Compensation Act (Act 273) enables compensation to be claimed if workman (as defined therein) suffers personal injury by accident arising out of and in course of employment; or contracts prescribed occupational disease or injury either during employment or within specified time frame after cessation of employment, and disablement or death of workman results from disease.

LAW REPORTS:

Law reports published in Malaysia include Malayan Law Journal, All Malaysia Reports and Current Law Reports.

LANDLORD AND TENANT:

National Land Code (Act 56) (West Malaysia), makes distinction between lease and tenancy. Lease refers to letting of land for term exceeding three years and is registrable interest. Maximum term for which lease may be so granted is 99 years if it relates to whole of alienated land, and 30 years if it relates only to part thereof. Every lease has to be in prescribed form and registered with appropriate land Registry. Lease which is not registered is void as lease but nevertheless good and valid as agreement for lease and may be enforceable in equity by decree of specific performance.

Tenancy denotes letting of land for term not exceeding three years and is not registrable interest. It may, however, be protected by way of endorsement on register document of title. It can be granted orally or by way of written instrument in any form whatsoever.

For leases in Sabah and Sarawak, reference may be made to Sabah Land Ordinance (Cap. 68) and Sarawak Land Code (Cap. 81) respectively.

LEGISLATURE:

See topic Constitution and Government.

LICENCES:

Licences are required for activities such as conducting remittance businesses, futures trading, stock exchange trading, carrying out finance business transactions, establishing restaurant and entertainment centres, massage parlours, conducting import and export trade, selling and distributing liquor, conducting certain manufacturing activities, acting as travel agents, driving motor vehicles and conducting businesses as moneylenders or pawnbrokers.

LIENS:

Generally, liens may arise from common law, equitable, contractual or statutory sources.

Common Law Lien.—Legal lien is unassignable personal right of security exercisable by person in possession of goods against owner of goods, but with no power of sale. General lien entitles person in possession to retain goods until all claims or accounts against owner are satisfied. These liens arise only by general usage or by express agreement. Particular lien is right to retain chattels until owner pays charges incurred in respect of those chattels.

Equitable lien is equitable right to charge real or personal property of another until certain specific claims are satisfied. It does not depend on possession and holder of lien has power of sale. Equitable liens arise in particular relationships, e.g., partners, vendor and purchasers, or from course of conduct or express agreement of parties. Equitable liens arising from contract are registrable under Bills of Sale Act. (Act 268).

Contractual Lien.—It is matter of interpretation of contract what rights and obligations parties intended to arise from lien.

Statutory Lien.—It is question of statutory interpretation when such lien arises and what rights and obligations attach thereto.

Maritime Lien.—See topic Shipping.

LIMITATION OF ACTIONS:

Regulated by Limitation Act (Act 254) West Malaysia.

Three Years.—Compensation to family of person for loss occasioned by his death.

Six Years.—Actions founded on contract or tort including claim for personal injuries; actions to enforce award; actions for account.

Twelve Years.—Actions to recover land.

Disability.—Limitation periods above are extended for varying periods in case of disability.

Fresh accrual of action to recover debt or other liquidated pecuniary claim on acknowledgment or part payment of claim.

Fraud or Mistake.—Where action is based upon fraud of defendant, or right of action is concealed by fraud of defendant or action is for relief from consequences of mistake, period of limitation does not begin to run until plaintiff has discovered fraud or mistake, or could with reasonable diligence have discovered it.

Arbitration.—Above applies to arbitration.

Maritime Actions.—Limitation periods are provided for in Merchant Shipping Ordinance. (FMS Ord. 70).

Sabah and Sarawak.—Limitation Ordinance Reprint (Cap. 72) of Sabah and Limitation Ordinance Reprint (Cap. 49) of Sarawak list specific limitation periods for different actions.

MARRIAGE:

All marriages contracted in Malaysia must be monogamous and must comply with formalities laid down in Law Reform (Marriage and Divorce) Act. (Act 164). Act does not apply to Muslims or person married under Muslim law.

Prohibitions to marriage are: (a) cannot marry his/her grandparent, parent, child or grandchild, sister or brother, greataunt or greatuncle, aunt or uncle, niece or nephew, great-niece or great-nephew as case may be; (b) however, Hindu can marry under Hindu law or custom his sister's daughter or her mother's brother; (c) cannot marry grandparent or parent, child or grandchild of his/her spouse or former spouse; (d) cannot marry former spouse of his/her grandparent or parent, child or grandchild; or (e) cannot marry person whom he or she has adopted or by whom he or she has been adopted. Relationships of half blood are equivalent to relationships of full blood.

Each party intending to marry in Malaysia must notify Registrar of Marriages in district in which parties have been resident for period of seven days immediately preceding notice. Notice is to be posted by Registrar of Marriages until he grants his certificate or until three months have elapsed, whichever is earlier. Any person may lodge caveat against marriage. Registrar of Marriages only issues marriage certificate upon expiry of 21 days notice of intended marriage. Marriage licence is valid for six months from date of notice.

Chief Minister may, if he thinks fit, dispense with notice and grant special marriage licence authorising solemnisation of marriage between parties named in that licence. However he may only exercise his discretion if there is urgent need and good reason. Special licence is valid for one month from date of issue.

Solemnisation of marriage can take place any time during validity of marriage certificate. Solemnisation of marriage may be conducted by person authorised to do so including Malaysian Embassy, High Commission or Consulate.

Either party to marriage can petition for decree of nullity of marriage on ground that marriage is void in that: (a) either party was already lawfully married at date of marriage; (b) male under 18 years of age and female between ages of 16 and 18 years marries without special licence; (c) parties are within prohibited degrees as stated above; or (d) parties are not respectively male and female.

Marriage is voidable on following grounds: (a) non-consummation due to incapacity of either party; (b) non-consummation due to wilful refusal of respondent; (c) either party did not validly consent to marriage due to duress, mistake, unsoundness of mind or otherwise; (d) either party was suffering from mental disorder within meaning of Mental Disorders Ordinance (Ord. 31) or of such kind or to such extent as to be unfit for marriage; (e) respondent was suffering from venereal disease in communicable form at time of marriage; or (f) respondent was pregnant by some person other than petitioner at time of marriage.

Marriage will not be avoided where it will result in injustice to respondent, or petitioner with knowledge that it was open to him to have marriage avoided, led respondent reasonably to believe that he would not seek to petition to do so.

Muslim Marriages.—For marriage to be valid in Islam, there must be offer of marriage by one party which offer must be accepted by other party. Words must indicate with reasonable certainty that marriage has been contracted. There must be two witnesses who are sane and adult male Muslims.

Marriage may be solemnised by "Wali", "Kathi" or "Naib Kathi". Where "Wali" refuses his consent to marriage, bride may apply to "Kathi" who, if satisfied after due inquiry that consent was unreasonably withheld, may solemnise marriage and act as bride's "Wali".

MINES AND MINERALS:

Mines.—Petroleum Mining Act (Act 95) makes provisions with regard to mining for petroleum. These include restrictions on petroleum exploring and mining, and application for exploration licence. Act applies throughout Malaysia but in its application to Sabah and Sarawak only with respect to off-shore land.

Mining Enactments of various States regulate mining of minerals other than mineral oils in such states.

Mining leases must not infringe Malay Reservations Enactments of various States which restrict sale, lease and disposal of State land included within Malay Reservation in such states.

Minerals.—Mineral Ores Enactments of various States restrict purchase, treatment and storage of mineral ores (which do not include gold) in such states.

Gold Buyers Enactments of various States regulate purchase of raw gold in such states.

MORTGAGES:

In Malaysia, mortgages are created in form of charge.

Under National Land Code (Act 56) (West Malaysia), one may create legal/statutory charge in prescribed form over: (a) whole, but not part only, of alienated land; (b) whole, but not part only, of undivided share in alienated land; or (c) lease of alienated land, as security for repayment of debt, or payment of any sum other than debt, or payment of annuity or other periodic sum. Legal/statutory charge takes effect upon registration at appropriate land Registry. Subject to certain vitiating factors like fraud or forgery, registration confers indefeasible interest on chargee. Priority of charge may in appropriate circumstances be affected by device of tacking and postponement.

Noncompliance with National Land Code does not affect contractual operation of transaction which may then take effect as equitable charge. Court in exercise of its equitable jurisdiction may grant creditor specific performance of contract by ordering debtor to execute valid and registrable document of charge.

For lands in Sabah and Sarawak, registration provisions are contained in Sabah Land Ordinance (Cap. 68) and Sarawak Land Code (Cap. 81) respectively.

MOTOR VEHICLES:

Governed by Road Transport Act (Act 333) and related subsidiary legislation.

Classification of Motor Vehicles.—Construction, (unladen) weight limits, equipment, use and age of motor vehicles regulated by Act. Different requirements apply to various classes of motor vehicles. Third brake lights are compulsory for motor cars.

Registration and Licensing of Motor Vehicles.—Any person possessing or using motor vehicle in Malaysia must register it. Additionally, licence is required if motor vehicle is to be used in Malaysia. Valid third party insurance policy must, in absence of applicable exemptions, be in effect before licence can be issued. Grant of licence is also subject to condition that motor vehicle is roadworthy.

Tax is payable regularly in respect of motor vehicles in Malaysia.

Driving Licences.—Every driver of motor vehicle must possess valid driving licence. Before application for driving licence can be granted, applicant must satisfy one of following: (a) within one year before date of application, must have passed prescribed tests of competence to drive; (b) within three years before date of application, must have held driving licence issued by competent authority in Malaysia or Singapore; or (c) within three years before date of application, must have held driving licence issued by competent authority in any other country which has tests of competence to drive comparable to that prescribed under Act.

Driving licence issued under corresponding laws of country which is party, along with Malaysia, to treaty that purports to recognise domestic driving licences of contracting parties, is deemed to be driving licence granted under Act.

If driver's record, conduct or habits as driver establishes that it is not in interests of public safety for him to hold driving licence or that he is not competent to drive motor vehicle, then driving licence may be suspended for up to six months.

Person below 16 years is not allowed to drive motor vehicle on road and person below 17 years is not allowed to drive motor vehicle other than motorcycle or invalid carriage.

Use of Helmets and Safety Seat Belts.—Drivers and pillion riders of motorcycles are required to wear protective helmets. Use of safety seat belts by drivers and front seat passengers is mandatory.

Driving under Influence of Intoxicating Liquor or Drugs.—Driving while under influence of intoxicating liquor or drugs is offence.

Third Party Insurance.—Subject to certain exceptions, it is compulsory to insure all motor vehicles in use with respect to third party risks in Malaysia. Person using, causing or permitting another to use motor vehicle without such insurance coverage commits offence. Third party victim although not privy to insurance contract, has direct claim against insurer after obtaining judgment against motorist.

Commercial Vehicles.—Commercial Vehicles Licensing Board Act (Act 334) stipulates that licences have to be taken out for specified categories of commercial vehicles. Different conditions may be attached to various types of licences; in any event, all

See Topical Index in front part of this volume.

MOTOR VEHICLES . . . *continued*
licences carry conditions that commercial vehicle must be maintained in fit and serviceable condition and must comply with provisions on speed limits, unladen and laden weight limits and loadings.

NATIONALITY:

See topic Immigration.

NEGOTIABLE INSTRUMENTS:

See topic Bills and Notes.

NOTARIES PUBLIC:

Governed by Notaries Public Act. (Act 115).

Appointment.—Attorney-General is vested with power to appoint fit and proper persons to be notaries public to practise in West Malaysia or Sabah or Sarawak, or parts of these territories. Such persons must be practising advocates; or pleaders licensed before 1 Jan. 1956 under Pleaders and Petition Writers Enactment of State of Trengganu.

Attorney-General may appoint public officers as notaries public if no advocates are available for appointment in particular place.

If notary public is about to be absent from place of practice for more than one month, Attorney-General may appoint temporary notary public for up to 12 months. Temporary appointment lapses upon death or return to place of practice of notary public on account of whose departure temporary appointment was made.

Functions.—In general, notary public has and may exercise within place of practice all powers and functions ordinarily exercised by notaries public in England. But power of notary public to administer oaths or affirmations in connection with affidavits or statutory declarations, or to take or attest such affidavits or statutory declarations, is limited to certain situations as prescribed by Act.

PARTNERSHIPS:

Partnership Act.—Partnership subsists between persons carrying on business in common with view of profit and is regulated by Partnership Act. (Act 135). Common ownership or sharing of profits does not of itself create partnership.

Act governs nature of partnership, relationship of persons dealing with partners, relations of partners to one another and dissolution of partnership and its consequences.

Formation of Partnership.—Partnership of more than 20 members is forbidden if purpose is for acquisition of gain. Exception is when partnership is formed for purpose of carrying on any profession or calling which is declared by Yang di-Pertuan Agong to be profession or calling not customarily carried on by association or partnership incorporated under Companies Act (Act 125) or formed in pursuance of some other written law or letters patent.

Partner is agent of firm and has power to bind firm. Partners of firm are bound by acts done on behalf of firm unless otherwise agreed upon between all partners. In such case, such acts will not be binding on firm with respect to persons having notice of agreement.

Liability of Partners.—Every partner is jointly liable with other partners of firm for all debts and obligations of firm incurred whilst he is partner; and after his death, his estate is also severally liable in due course of administration for such debts and obligations, so far as they remain unsatisfied but subject to prior payment of his separate debts.

Taxation of Partners.—Partnership is not recognised in law as separate legal persona distinct from individuals who constitute it. Hence, for tax purposes, individual partners will be assessed on their respective shares of income.

Common Law Provisions.—Although Act contains provisions relating to creation and liability of partners, rules of equity and common law continue to apply save where inconsistent with Act.

PATENTS:

Statute.—Patents Act (Act 291) and Patents (Amendment) Act 1993 (Act A863).

Treaties.—Paris Convention. Accession to Patent Cooperation Treaty is being considered.

Procedure.—For domestic application, there are four stages: (a) Filing application in requisite form with prescribed fee. Application must contain: (i) request for grant of patent including statement justifying applicant's right to patent, (ii) specification containing description of invention, (iii) claim(s) defining matter for which applicant seeks patent protection and any supporting drawings, (iv) abstract which provides technical information concerning invention. If application is in order, filing date is given to application; (b) request for preliminary examination is filed within six months from date of filing of application; (c) applicant files request for substantive examination within 18 months from date of filing of application. Examiner will examine whether application complies with requirements of Act; (d) finally, patent granted if all is well.

Duration of Protection.—Grant of patent confers on owner exclusive right to exploit invention for 15 years from date of grant subject to payment of annual renewal fees from 12 months before date of expiration of second year.

Assignment/Licence.—Rights under patent or patent application may be assigned provided assignment is in writing and signed by or on behalf of parties to transaction. Licence may also be granted for working invention which is subject of patent.

Compulsory Licences.—Under certain circumstances, e.g. where there is abuse of patent monopoly rights, Act provides for grant of compulsory licences. Owner will then lose exclusivity of exploiting patent. Examples are nonproduction of patented product or non-application of patented process without any legitimate reason, or if pricing is unreasonably high.

Utility Innovations.—Act also provides protection for utility innovations. Innovation is valid for only five years from date of grant, extendable for two further periods of five years. Utility innovation means any innovation which creates new product or process or any new improvement of known product or process, which can be made or used in any kind of industry, and includes invention.

Infringement.—Patent is infringed if anyone without consent of proprietor makes, disposes of, offers to dispose of, uses or imports patented product or keeps it whether for disposal or otherwise. Same applies to patented process if unauthorised person uses it or does any of above acts in relation to product obtained by means of process. Remedies include injunctions, damages or account of profits, and delivery up.

PERPETUITIES:

See topic Trusts.

PLEDGES:

Bailment of Pledges.—Under Contracts Act (Act 136), bailment of goods as security for payment of debt or performance of promise is called "pledge". Bailor is called "pawner", and bailee is called "pawnee". Pawnee may retain goods pledged, not only for payment of debt or performance of promise, but also for interest on debt, and all necessary expenses incurred by him in respect of possession or preservation of goods pledged.

Pawnee may not, in absence of contract to effect, retain goods pledged for any debt or promise other than debt or promise for which they are pledged; but such contract, in absence of anything to contrary, is presumed in regard to subsequent advances made by pawnee.

Rights Relating to Pledge.—If pawner makes default in payment of debt or performance, at stipulated time, of promise in respect of which goods were pledged, pawnee may bring suit against pawner upon debt or promise, and retain goods pledged as collateral security, or give reasonable notice of sale. If proceeds of sale are less than amount due in respect of debt or promise, pawner is still liable to pay balance. If proceeds of sale exceed amount so due, pawnee is to pay over surplus to pawner.

If time is stipulated for payment of debt, or performance of promise for which pledge is made, and pawner defaults at stipulated time, he may redeem goods pledged at any subsequent time before they are sold, but he must also pay any expenses which have arisen from his default.

Where person pledges goods in which he has only limited interest, pledge is valid to extent of that interest.

Possession.—Person in possession of goods, bill of lading, dock-warrant, warehouse-keeper's certificate, wharfinger's certificate, or warrant or order for delivery, or any other document of title to goods, may make valid pledge of goods or documents subject to provisions of Act.

Suits by Bailee or Bailor against Wrongdoers.—If third person wrongfully deprives bailee of use or possession of goods bailed, or does them any injury, bailee is entitled to use such remedies as owner might have used in like case if no bailment had been made; and either bailor or bailee may bring suit against third person for such deprivation or injury.

Common Law and Equity.—Although Contracts Act (Act 136) contains certain provisions relating to pledges, rules of common law and equity continue to apply save where same is inconsistent with provisions of Act.

POWER OF ATTORNEY:

See topic Absentees.

PRINCIPAL AND AGENT:

Governed by common law. Generally, principal is bound by his authorised agent. Agent may be authorised expressly, impliedly or by estoppel or necessity. Agent acting outside scope of authority may be liable for breach of warranty of authority. Agent acting for undisclosed principal also personally liable.

See also topics Absentees; Partnerships.

PROCESS:

Service of Process Within Jurisdiction.—Writ must be served personally on each defendant or sent by prepaid A.R. registered post addressed to his last known address. Writ is deemed to have been duly served if defendant's solicitor indorses on writ, statement that he accepts service of writ on behalf of defendant or where defendant enters unconditional appearance in action.

Writ commencing action in respect of contract may also be served in accordance with terms of contract if contract provides that court has jurisdiction to hear and determine action in respect of contract or apart from such term, court has jurisdiction to hear and determine such action; and contract provides that, in event of action in respect of contract being begun, process by which it is begun may be served on defendant, or on such person on his behalf as may be specified in contract.

Above rules generally apply with necessary modifications to originating summons, notice of originating motion and petition.

Where action is against corporation, writ may be served: (a) by leaving copy of it at registered office (if any) of corporation; (b) by sending copy of it by registered post addressed to corporation at office, or, if there be more offices than one at principal office of corporation, whether such office be situated within Malaysia or elsewhere; (c) by handing copy of it to secretary or to director or other principal officer of corporation; or (d) for foreign company registered under Part XI of Companies Act (Act 125) by handing copy of it to, or sending same by registered post to, person authorised to accept service of process on behalf of foreign company.

Document may be served on corporation by leaving it at or sending it by registered post to registered office of company.

If it appears to court that it is impracticable for any reason to serve document personally on person, court may make order for substituted service of that document.

Service of Process Out of Jurisdiction.—Service of notice of writ and other originating process out of jurisdiction is permissible with leave of court in many

PROCESS . . . *continued*
instances provided in Rules of Court, i.e. essentially where defendant or claim has some connection with forum.

Service of Foreign Process.—Service of process required in connection with foreign civil proceedings may be initiated by letter of request from foreign court or tribunal requesting service on person in Malaysia received by Minister and which is sent by him to High Court with intimation that it is desirable that effect should be given to request.

If civil proceedings are pending before court or tribunal of foreign country, being country in which there subsists Civil Procedure Convention providing for service in Malaysia of process of tribunal of that country, letter of request may be from consular or other authority of that country requesting service on person in Malaysia of any such process received by Registrar. In both cases, letter of request must be accompanied by two copies in former case and one copy in latter case of English translation of process to be served.

REAL PROPERTY:

National Land Code (Act 1965) is main piece of legislation governing land matters in West Malaysia. It lays down law relating to land and land tenure, registration of title to land and of dealings therewith and collection of revenue therefrom.

Dealings recognised and capable of being created may be divided into those which are capable of registration and those which are not. Former consists of transfers, charges, leases and easements. Latter covers tenancies exempt from registration and statutory liens which are protected by way of endorsement and entry of lien holder's caveat respectively on register document of title. Noncompliance with requirements of Code does not affect contractual operation of transaction relating to alienated land or any interest therein.

Persons or bodies who are co-owners but who are not trustees or personal representatives hold as tenants in common (no right of survivorship). Only trustees and personal representatives may hold land as joint tenants (with right of survivorship).

Registered proprietors may subdivide, partition or amalgamate their lands. They may also apply for subdivision of certain kinds of buildings on their land into parcels, each to be held under separate strata or subsidiary title.

To curb speculation in property market, RM100,000 is levied on purchase by foreigners of building and agricultural land.

Land Registration.—Conveyancing system is registered (Torrens System). Title to property is registered at appropriate land Registry. Subject to certain vitiating factors, register is conclusive evidence of title.

Legislation governing land matters in Sabah is Sabah Land Ordinance (Cap. 68) and in Sarawak is Sarawak Land Ordinance (Cap. 81).

RECEIVERS:

See topics Bankruptcy; Executions.

SALES:

Sales are governed by Sale of Goods Act (Act 382) and other related statutes. Act is modelled on English Sale of Goods Act 1893.

Notices Required.—Generally, notices are not required under domestic sales law.

Applicable Law.—Generally, contract of sale is governed by law expressly or impliedly chosen by parties, unless choice is illegal, not bona fide, or against public policy. In absence of choice, contract is governed by law having closest and most real connection with transaction. Governing law applies to most contractual issues, including validity, interpretation and effect of terms.

Warranties.—Implied warranties are that: (a) seller has right to sell goods free from undisclosed encumbrances; (b) goods sold are of merchantable quality, except if defect has been revealed to buyer or if buyer has examined goods and ought to have discovered it; (c) goods are fit for buyer's purpose, provided that seller sells goods in course of business, and buyer makes known to seller particular purpose, unless buyer did not rely, or it was not reasonable for him to rely, on seller; (d) in sale by description goods correspond to description; and (e) in sale by sample, goods correspond to sample in description and quality, and that buyer will have reasonable opportunity to compare the two.

Hire-Purchase Act (Act 212).—Act applies to hire-purchase of specified goods. Implied warranties are in respect of: (a) title; (b) merchantability; and (c) fitness for purpose. Latter two terms will not be implied if owner informs hirer that goods are secondhand, and that warranties are excluded.

Consumer Protection.—No specific laws protecting consumers. Limited protection is provided by Price Control Act (Act 121) and Control of Supplies Act (Act 122). Under Standard and Industrial Research Institute of Malaysia (Incorporation) Act (Act 157), aforesaid Institute may provide safety standards (either mandatory or as guidelines) for specific products. It is offence under Trade Descriptions Act (Act 87) to apply false trade description to goods or to sell goods with false trade description.

SEALS:

Agreement under Seal.—For agreement under seal to be valid, there must either be consideration for execution of deed or agreement must come within § 26 of Contracts Act (Act 136) which provides that agreement made without consideration is void, unless: (a) it is expressed in writing and registered under law (if any) applicable for time being in force for registration of such documents and is made on account of natural love and affection between parties standing in near relation to each other; (b) if agreement is promise to compensate for something done; or (c) if agreement is promise to pay debt barred by limitation law.

Practice Relating to Company Seals and Seal Books.—Company secretary usually has custody of company common seal. Directors usually pass resolution each time common seal is to be affixed to document; usually common seals are affixed and attested to by two directors or director and company secretary or director and another person authorised to attest such affixation. Name of company (whether or not it is carrying on business under business name) must appear on its seal.

Where seal is frequently used, particulars of documents sealed may be entered in Seal Book.

See also topic Deeds.

SHIPPING:

Merchant Shipping.—Merchant Shipping Ordinance 1952 (FMS Ord. 70) regulates registration, mortgages, control of shipping, safety of shipping, construction, equipment and survey, manning, certification, masters and seamen, wreck and salvage and limitation of actions. Relevant statutes for Sabah and Sarawak are Ordinance 11/1960 and Ordinance 2/1960 respectively.

Ship Registration.—Under Merchant Shipping Ordinance 1952, Malaysia-registered ship must be owned by (a) Malaysian citizen; or (b) Malaysian company with majority Malaysian shareholding free of any trust or obligation in favour of non-Malaysian, and with principal office in Malaysia and management carried out mainly in Malaysia.

Malaysia-registered ship must be insured with Malaysian insurer under Insurance Act 1963. (Act 89).

Towage.—Private contract between parties.

Pilotage.—Regulated by Merchant Shipping Ordinance 1952. (FMS Ord. 70 of 1952).

Collisions.—Merchant Shipping (Collision Regulations) Order 1984 (PU.[A]438) gives effect to International Regulations for Preventing Collisions at Sea 1972 as amended.

Liens.—Maritime liens governed by common law. Statutory liens for rent and expenses of wharfinger and warehouseman provided under Merchant Shipping Ordinance 1952.

Pollution.—Regulated by Merchant Shipping (Oil Pollution) Act. (Act 515).

Carriage of Goods.—Carriage of Goods by Sea Act 1950 (Act 527) gives effect to Hague Rules.

Limitation and Exclusion of Liability.—Regulated by Merchant Shipping Ordinance 1952.

Admiralty.—Courts of Judicature Act 1964 (Act 91) provides that Malaysia High Court has same admiralty jurisdiction as High Court of Justice in England under United Kingdom Supreme Court Act 1981.

STATUTES:

Statute law in Malaysia comprises Federal law and State law. "Federal law" means: (a) any existing law relating to matter with respect to which Parliament has power to make law, being law continued in operation under Constitution; and (b) any Act of Parliament. "State law" means: (a) any existing law relating to matter with respect to which State legislature has power to make law, being law continued in operation under Constitution; and (b) law made by State legislature.

Laws made by State legislature are called Enactments, including those made by Malay States (see topic Constitution and Government) before 1957 and Federal Territory of Kuala Lumpur. Laws in Sabah, Sarawak and Labuan are referred to as Ordinances. Generally, Laws of Sabah would include references to Labuan. All revised laws enacted after 1 Jan. 1993 are designated by chapter ("Cap.") numbers.

Laws that are enacted by Parliament are referred to as "Acts" but those made between 1946 and 1957 are called Ordinances. With effect from 1 Jan. 1969, continuing series of numbers omitting references to year is used, e.g. Promotion of Investments Act (Act 327). Amendment Acts carry letter "A" prefixed to number, e.g. Promotion of Investments (Amendment) Act (A715).

With coming into force of Constitution (Amendment)(No.2) Act (Act A206) on 1 Feb. 1974, Federal Territory of Kuala Lumpur ceased to be part of State of Selangor and all powers and jurisdiction in or in respect of Federal Territory vested in Federation. All written laws existing and in force in Federal Territory before 1 Feb. 1974 continue to be in force therein until repealed, amended or replaced by laws passed by Parliament.

Similarly, coming into force of Constitution (Amendment)(No.2) Act (Act A585) on 16 Apr. 1984, Federal Territory of Labuan ceased to be part of State of Sabah and all powers and jurisdiction in or in respect of Federal Territory vested in Federation. All written laws, other than Constitution of State of Sabah, existing and in force in Federal Territory before 16 Apr. 1984 continued to have effect therein until repealed, amended or replaced by laws passed by Parliament.

Written laws of Selangor in force in Federal Territory of Kuala Lumpur before 1 Feb. 1974 and written laws of Sabah in force in Federal Territory of Labuan before 16 Apr. 1984, in their application to Federal Territories of Kuala Lumpur and Labuan, respectively, became federal laws.

TAXATION:

Income tax is payable by persons, including individuals, companies, trustees and bodies of persons, on income arising in or derived from Malaysia or remitted from overseas in respect of trade, business, profession, vocation or employment and dividends, interest, discounts, pension, charge, annuity, rents, royalties, premiums, and gains or profits from other sources. Exception: nonresident company may remit overseas income into Malaysia without tax liability attaching; resident company is likewise exempted, but with exception of business income from banking, insurance, and sea and air transport.

Unless exempted, payment of royalty and interest to nonresident person is subject to withholding tax of 10% and 15% respectively. However, no withholding tax if royalty or interest is attributable to business carried on in Malaysia by such person. Payment to non-resident for technical services, advice, assistance or use of property is subject to 10% withholding tax. Payment to nonresident contractor or professional under contract of service is subject to 20% withholding tax (15% for contract payment and 5% for tax payable by contractor's employees), and for nonresident public entertainer, 15%. These withholding tax rates are not absolute and some may be varied by double taxation agreements or under certain other circumstances. Dividends paid to nonresident are not subject to withholding tax but are subject to imputation tax.

See Topical Index in front part of this volume.

TAXATION . . . *continued*

Income tax rate for resident company is 30%. Malaysia adopts imputation system of taxation whereby tax paid on income of such company is imputed to benefit of its shareholders. Nonresident company is also taxed at same rate as resident company. No major differences in tax treatment for two except that resident company is generally able to qualify for tax reliefs afforded by double taxation conventions entered into by Malaysia with other countries whereas nonresident company is not. Tax rate of 30% also applies to income of trust and nonresident unincorporated body. Approved institutions of public or charitable character are exempted from income tax.

Individual income tax rate for resident individuals is based on graduated scale, with marginal rate from 0% to 32%. Various personal reliefs and rebates are available. Donations to approved charitable and public institutions are tax-deductible.

Nonresident employees, directors, partners, professionals, sole-proprietors, entertainers, artists, athletes and musicians are taxed at flat rate of 30% with no personal reliefs given unless otherwise provided for in double taxation agreement. Nonresident employees exercising employment in Malaysia for not more than 60 days are, however, exempted from tax. Remittances of foreign-sourced income into Malaysia by nonresidents are not subject to tax.

Income tax relief in respect of certain categories of income can be found in Income Tax Act (Act 53), and tax incentives for selected types of investments can be found in Promotion of Investments Act (Act 327).

Service tax is value-added tax levied on supply of prescribed services and prescribed goods by prescribed establishments or professional establishments in Malaysia. Prescribed services include most services provided by service industries and various professional fields. Prescribed goods are food, drinks and tobacco provided by prescribed establishments. Provision of prescribed services to territories outside Malaysia is zero-rated. Service tax rate is 5%.

Sales tax is generally levied on selected types of goods manufactured in Malaysia or which are imported for home consumption. Tax is borne by manufacturers and importers at rate of 5% or 15%, depending on class of goods in question. Wide range of goods are exempted from imposition of sales tax.

Stamp duty is imposed on specified class of instruments and may be for fixed amount or on ad valorem basis. For conveyance of land, duty is payable at progressive rate up to 4% of value; on sale of stocks and shares, 0.3% of value; on stockbroker's contract note, 0.15%. Exemptions from stamp duty are given for various specified transactions.

Estate duty is not payable on estate of deceased who died on or after 1 Nov. 1991.

Real property gains tax is capital gains tax levied on taxable gains from disposal of real property and shares in real property companies by residents and nonresidents pursuant to Real Property Gains Tax Act. (Act 169). Real property is deemed to include any right, interest or option over land. Taxable gain is difference between acquisition price and disposal price of real property but allowance is given for acquisition and disposal expenses. Tax rates are as follows:

Time of Disposition	Individuals	Companies
within 2 yrs of acquisition	30%	30%
in 3rd yr of acquisition	20%	20%
in 4th yr of acquisition	15%	15%
in 5th yr of acquisition	5%	5%
in 6th yr of acquisition and onwards	NIL	5%

Gains up to RM5,000 or 10% of profits (whichever is higher) is exempted from real property gains tax, as is any gain made on disposal of private residence by citizens or permanent residents (but given only on one-time basis). Other exemptions and part-exemptions are also provided for in Act.

Double Taxation.—Malaysia has double taxation agreements with more than 30 countries. With regard to countries with which no such arrangements are in force, unilateral tax credits may be available provided claimant is able to satisfy certain prescribed conditions.

TRADEMARKS:

Statutes.—Trade Marks Act (Act 175) and Trade Mark Regulations 1983 provide for, inter alia, registration of trademarks in respect of goods and services. These follow U.K. legislation closely.

Treaties.—Priority may be claimed for applications filed within six months from date of first application in "prescribed foreign countries" as approved by Minister of Domestic Trade and Consumer Affairs. Malaysia is also member of Paris Convention.

Definition.—Trademark is mark used or proposed to be used in relation to goods or services for purpose of indicating or so as to indicate, connection in course of trade between goods or services and person who has right, either as proprietor or as registered user, to use mark, whether with or without indication of identity of that person. Trademark may be device, brand, heading, label, ticket, signature, word, letter, numeral or any combination of these.

Registrability.—Trade Marks Register is divided into Parts A and B. To qualify for registration in Part A, mark must be distinctive i.e. "adapted to distinguish" goods or services from those of others. Mark must have some intrinsic quality which makes it distinctive. Mark must also contain or consist of at least one of following: (a) name of company, individual of firm represented in special or particular manner; (b) signature of applicant or predecessor of his business; (c) invented word or words; (d) mark which does not have direct reference to character or quality of goods or services; and which is not in its ordinary meaning, geographical name or surname; (e) any other distinctive mark.

Mark which does not qualify for registration in Part A may qualify for registration in Part B. To qualify for Part B, mark need only be "capable of distinguishing" one's goods or services. It is less stringent test than that for Part A. Registrar may have regard to extent to which mark is inherently capable of distinguishing goods or services and/or by reason of use of mark or of any other circumstances, mark is in fact capable of distinguishing as aforesaid.

Part A registration offers greater protection as original registration is, after seven years, considered valid in all respects unless registration was obtained by fraud, mark consists of scandalous design or matter which is likely to deceive or cause confusion or would be disentitled to protection in Court or would be contrary to law or morality. Part B registration can never become conclusive as to validity as it can still be opposed to and removed from Register after seven years.

Protection.—Upon registration of mark, it remains valid for initial term of ten years from date of filing of application, which term may be renewed for subsequent terms of ten years each.

Assignment.—Mark may be assigned with or without goodwill of business. Under Act, all assignments must be registered with Trade Marks Registry. If one or more marks are associated, they must be assigned as whole and not separately.

Infringement.—Plaintiff has recourse to civil remedies in form of damages, injunction, seizure of goods and discovery. If his mark is registered under Part A, plaintiff need only show that his mark is registered and that defendant used mark identical or so nearly resembling it as to be likely to deceive or cause confusion. If his mark is registered in Part B, plaintiff gets no relief if defendant establishes that use of mark is not likely to deceive or cause confusion.

Common Law Rights.—Act specifically preserves rights of action against person for tort of "passing off" and remedies in respect thereof. To succeed, plaintiff must show (a) goodwill or reputation in his mark or business; (b) misrepresentation made by defendant in course of trade which is calculated to injure plaintiff's goodwill or business; and (c) that damage has occurred or is likely to occur.

TREATIES:

Member of Association of South East Asian Nations (ASEAN) and World Trade Organisation (WTO). Malaysia has ratified International Centre for Settlement of Investment Disputes Convention (see Convention on Settlement of Investment Disputes Act - Act 392). Malaysia has trade agreements with Tunisia and Vietnam. It also has investment guarantee agreements with Austria, Belgium, Canada, Finland, France, Germany, Italy, Kuwait, Netherlands, Norway, Romania, Sri Lanka, Sweden, Switzerland, U.K. and U.S.A. These agreements cover matters like protection against nationalisation and expropriation, and compensation in such events. There are double taxation agreements with many countries (see topic Taxation).

See also Part VI of this volume for Selected Conventions to which U.S.A. and this country are parties.

TRUSTS:

Number of Trustees.—Trustees Act (Act 1949) limits number of trustees to four, except in case of property vested in trustees for charitable, religious or public purposes where there is no restriction on number of trustees.

Powers of Trustee.—These include powers expressly given by trust instrument and (generally, subject to any contrary intention expressed in trust instrument) powers conferred by Act, including following: (a) trustee for sale has power to sell or concur in selling all or any part of property; (b) trustees can give receipt which is good discharge. However, sole trustee other than trust corporation cannot give valid receipt for proceeds of sale or other capital money arising under trust for sale of land; (c) trustees can insure against loss or damage by fire any building or other insurable property to any amount, including amount of any insurance already on foot, up to full value of building or property, except where trust instrument forbids it or they are bound forthwith to convey building or property absolutely to any beneficiary upon being requested to do so.

Trusts under Torrens System.—Torrens System of registered conveyancing cannot be used to create trust over real property. This means that document creating trust cannot rely on registration to give effect to settlement. However, valid trust created outside register in conformity with trust principles may be protected by caveat or other means available under system.

WILLS:

Wills Act (Act 346) governs. Any person of sound mind may make will. Infant cannot make will, unless he is soldier in actual military service, or mariner or seaman at sea. See topic Infants.

Formalities of Execution.—Every will must be signed at foot or end thereof by testator, or by some other person in his presence and by his direction, and signature must be made or acknowledged by testator as signature to his will in presence of two or more witnesses present at same time, and those witnesses must subscribe will in presence of testator. Beneficiary or his spouse must not attest to execution of will.

Alterations, including obliteration and interlineation, made prior to execution must be authenticated by being referred to specifically in body of will itself, or placing signature or initials of testator and witnesses on will.

Revocation.—Will or part thereof may be revoked otherwise by another will or codicil duly executed, or by declaring intention to revoke it, and executed in manner in which will must be executed or by burning, tearing, or otherwise destroying will by testator, or by some person in his presence and by his direction, with intention of revoking it.

Foreign Wills.—Will is treated as properly executed if its execution conforms to manner required by Act or law in force in: (a) place where it was executed; or (b) place where testator was domiciled, either at time of execution or at death.

Allowance for Maintenance of Dependants.—Dependant of deceased may apply to Court for share of deceased's net estate for maintenance of that dependant under Inheritance (Family Provision) Act (Act 39) (Malaysia). If Court is satisfied that disposition of deceased's estate effected by his will is not such as to make reasonable provision for maintenance of that dependant, Court may order such provision to be made out of deceased's net estate as it thinks fit.

Act is not restricted to provisions in wills: application may be made in cases of intestacies as well. However, if surviving spouse had been provided for with not less

WILLS . . . *continued*
than two-thirds of income of net estate and where only other dependants are children, then no application can be made.

Persons for whom provision may be made are spouse, unmarried daughter, infant son or daughter or son who is, by reason of some mental or physical disability, incapable of maintaining herself or himself.

Court will on application made under Act have regard to any past, present or future capital or income from any source of dependant of deceased to whom application relates.

Application under Act must be made within six months from date on which representation in regard to deceased's estate is first taken out. However, Court will allow extension of time if Court feels that strict compliance with requirements of Act may prejudice interests of dependant.

Wills Made by Muslims.—In Islamic law, testator can bequeath only a third of his property with consent of his lawful beneficiaries. No one, however, can make bequest in respect of any legal Quranic heir. In other words, one cannot increase or decrease portions of those relatives whose portions are fixed in Quran nor can one deprive legal heir through bequest.

In East Malaysia position is different. Wills are governed by Muslims Wills Ordinance (Cap. 81) which provides for division of property made by will, and if there is conflict between Islamic law and division of property set out in will, provisions of will prevail.

See Topical Index in front part of this volume.

MALTA LAW DIGEST

(The following is a list of all Topics, including cross-references, covered in this Digest.)

MALTA LAW DIGEST

Revised for 1997 edition by

Rutter Giappone & Associates, of the Valletta Bar

Malta is an Associated Member of the EU and has filed formal application for full membership.

ABSENTEES:

Person absent abroad may generally delegate authority to any person of full capacity, usually by giving Power of Attorney. This is normally in written form and may be general or limited to particular scope.

In judicial matters if absent person of age cannot be summoned or in case of uncertainty as to heirs entitled to inheritance, judicial curator is appointed by Civil Courts.

ACKNOWLEDGMENT:

Documents are acknowledged by advocates or notaries public.

ACTION:

Courts must decide all civil cases on basis of law; however, in certain cases, upon unanimous request of parties, case may be referred to arbitration and decided on basis of equity. Rules governing procedure of civil action are set forth in Code of Civil Organisation and Civil Procedure (c. 12 of Laws of Malta). Civil actions are commenced normally by service of summons. All parties must be represented before courts by attorney except in case of Magistrates Courts (lower courts).

It is permissable to agree upon application of foreign laws for interpretation of contracts provided this is not against public policy of Malta.

ALIENS:

Rights and duties of aliens are basically equal to those of Maltese citizens except in case where Maltese citizenship is precluded and except in case of law relating to international offshore business.

See also topics Offshore Investment; Partnerships; Real Property.

ARBITRATION:

Malta Arbitration Centre is body corporate having distinct juridical personality set up under Arbitration Act 1996. Responsible for policy and general administration of affairs and business thereof is Board consisting of not less than five and not more than nine members appointed by President of the Republic acting on advice of Minister for Justice. Members of Board are persons having experience and capacity in international or domestic arbitration, conciliation and settlement of disputes, international trade, commerce, industry, investment and maritime affairs. Chairman and Deputy Chairman of Board must have practiced as advocates in Malta for period or periods amounting in aggregate to not less than 12 years. Attorney General is ex officio member of Board. Legal representation of Centre is on Registrar thereof, unless otherwise decided by Board.

Responsibilities of Centre are to: promote Malta as centre for international commercial arbitration; provide for conduct of international arbitration in Malta; encourage domestic arbitration as means of settling disputes; provide necessary facilities for conduct of arbitration; advise Government on above; perform any function supplementary or ancillary to above as well as any other function assigned to it under any law.

Centre together with Minister responsible for Justice has power through Board to make rules providing for: manner and requirements for registration of documents under Arbitration Act 1996; guidelines and optional models for drawing up arbitration clauses and agreements; any other matter in connection with which rules may be made under any provision.

International Commercial Arbitration is carried out according to UNCITRAL Model Law on International Commercial Arbitration.

Upon registration with Centre, foreign arbitration awards shall be enforced by Courts of Malta as though delivered in Malta.

ASSIGNMENTS:

Basic rules for assignment are set out in Civil Code.

Rights, credits, debits and causes in action may be assigned by written instrument. Formal requirements of such instruments are same as for normal transfer of rights, having regard to what rights are being transferred. Certain rights such as those relating to maintenance or support are not transferable.

Notice to debtor or his acceptance thereof are necessary for assignment of rights to become fully effective and operative in debtor's request, but latter's consent is not required.

Assignment of debts or contracts by debtor or one party to contract are of no effect on creditor or other party unless their consent thereto is previously obtained.

Assignor is answerable to assignee for existence of his title at time when assignment is effected, but normally he has no liability as regards debtor's solvency.

ASSOCIATIONS:

See topic Partnerships.

ATTACHMENT AND SEQUESTRATION:

The Code of Organisation and Civil Procedure provides for attachment of movable effects of one's debtor through warrants of sequestration granted by court either as precautionary measure at prejudgment stage or as means to effect execution of judgment already obtained.

In case of precautionary warrant, this may be authorised by court upon creditor's demand whenever creditor confirms on oath to have founded reasons for suspecting that guarantee of his credit may be prejudiced. This form of attachment may be granted by court hearing debtor, however, creditor must institute regular proceedings for confirmation of claim on which creditor justified attachment by filing writ of summons before competent court within ten working days from effecting such sequestration.

Executive warrant of sequestration is granted following definite judgment and precedes judicial sale of movable effects sequestrated.

No lien or preference in respect of other creditors is created by sequestration.

For attachment of immovable property see topic Mortgages (Hypothecs).

ATTORNEY:

Attorneys in Malta are called Advocates. No person may exercise profession of advocate in Malta without authority of President of Malta provided by warrant under Public Seal of Malta.

No person shall be authorized to obtain warrant unless: (a) he is of good conduct and of good morals; (b) he is citizen of Malta; (c) he has obtained academic degree of Doctor of Laws (LL.D.); (d) he has attended at office of practising lawyer for period of one year after completion of his academic course; (e) he possesses full knowledge of Maltese language; (f) he has been examined by two judges certifying that he is competent to act as advocate.

AUTHENTICATION:

Authentication of acknowledgment of documents taken in Malta to be used abroad can be effected by Minister of Foreign Affairs. Authentication of acknowledgment of documents taken abroad to be used within Malta must be effected by local Maltese Consul or by local authority with Apostille of "Convention de La Hage du 5 Octobre 1961" when applicable.

BANKRUPTCY:

Provisions regulating bankruptcy are set forth in Commercial Code (c. 13, Title III).

Only traders (persons or concerns ordinarily engaged in business) are subject to or can invoke bankruptcy law. One who is not able to discharge his obligations or pay his debts is in state of bankruptcy. Bankruptcy proceedings are instituted before Commercial Court either directly by trader himself or by any creditor.

Court shall in and by judgment declaring bankruptcy appoint one or more curators in whom bankrupt's assets are vested. Curator acts under direction of Court and is specifically charged with assessment of assets and liabilities of bankrupt.

Curator shall receive all sums due to bankrupt and may sue for any payments due to bankrupt. Curator cannot effect compromise except with authority of judge.

When debts are ascertained and their nature and extent determined Court then issues decree admitting or rejecting claims of creditors. All creditors, or majority of them (i.e. concurrence of majority of simple creditors present and 3/4 in value of proved debts) and bankrupt may reach settlement through reduction in creditors' claims or any other agreement not against law. Said settlement does not effect rights of privileged creditors who shall always be paid first.

If no settlement is reached property of bankrupt is sold. After sale of bankrupt's assets proceeds shall then be distributed to creditors according to their ranking: (1) Preferential claims are paid in full, (2) all ordinary claims are settled pro rata with remaining funds.

BILLS AND NOTES:

Law regulating bills of exchange, promissory notes and cheques is enunciated in Commercial Code. (§§260-272). Maltese courts rely heavily on English doctrine and case law for interpretation of relevant law.

Bill of exchange which fulfills all requirements brings parties within trading law, regardless of whether they are traders or nontraders, and whether or not bill was given in respect of purely civil transaction. Consequently, suits in respect thereof are brought before commercial courts.

Requirements as to Content.—(1) Unconditional order to pay determined sum of money; (2) name of drawee; (3) maturity; (4) place of payment; (5) name of person to whom or to whose order payment is to be made; (6) date and place of drawing; (7) signature of drawer.

Maturity.—Bill not mentioning maturity is payable on sight. Bill not mentioning place of drawing is deemed to have been drawn at place indicated with name of drawer written on bill or on sheet attached to bill.

Transfer.—Delivery of bill with unconditional endorsement on bill or on sheet attached thereto, or with written assignment. If bill contains clause "not on order" or equivalent clause, transfer is effected only by delivery of bill with written assignment.

Presentment and Acceptance.—Bill may be presented for written acceptance by drawee at latter's place up to maturity unless prohibited in terms of bill; such prohibition is permissible only under certain conditions. Acceptance binds drawee for payment at maturity. Bill payable at sight must be presented within one year from date of drawing, unless otherwise stipulated. Bill has to be presented by holder on date of payment or on one of two following working days.

Payment.—If bill of exchange calls for payment in currency other than legal tender at place of payment, amount may be converted into local currency at rate of exchange prevailing on date of maturity. If debtor delays payment, holder has option to demand payment either at rate of exchange in force on date of maturity or at rate prevailing on day payment is actually effected. Value of foreign currency is determined according to commercial custom at place of payment. Drawer may, however, in bill itself prescribe rate of exchange to be applied in converting foreign currency.

Protest.—Bills not accepted or not paid must be protested in usual manner, unless protest is waived.

See Topical Index in front part of this volume.

BILLS AND NOTES . . . *continued*

Recourse in Default of Acceptance or Payment.—Holder may exact payment from endorsers, drawer and others liable on bill, at maturity. This right also exists before maturity in case of nonacceptance, acceptor's insolvency or bankruptcy or when execution or judgment against acceptor has been returned unsatisfied.

Limitation of Actions.—Actions are barred by lapse of five years.

Revenue Stamps.—Not due.

Promissory notes must be dated and must set forth sum to be paid, name of party to whose order it is payable and time and place of payment.

Promissory notes are subject to rules relating to bills of exchange insofar as these concern maturity, endorsements, joint and several liability, payment, protest, rights and duties of holder.

Cheques must be drawn only on bank and must be paid at sight. Date of drawing must be stated. It may be drawn in favour of specified person or to bearer or to self.

Anyone who negligently or wilfully draws cheques without provision after he has drawn cheque or who instructs bank not to pay can be prosecuted under criminal law. (Criminal Code, c. 9 of Laws of Malta).

BROADCASTING:

The Broadcasting Act, 1991 makes provision for regulation of all sound and television broadcasting services in Malta. Broadcasting Authority has also been set up and its functions include that of issuing licences in respect of nationwide and community radio services and television services in Malta.

CHATTEL MORTGAGES:

See topic Pledge.

COMMERCIAL REGISTER:

There are number of public registers created by special laws to make certain information matter of public record. Anyone carrying on any business enterprises is obliged to register firm in relative commercial register. Legal entities such as commercial partnerships, limited liability company, trusts, only come into existence after duly being registered in their relative commercial register.

CONSTITUTION AND GOVERNMENT:

Malta is sovereign independent Republic with democratic Parliamentary System based on British model. Parliament consists of House of Representatives to which members are elected by universal suffrage every five years.

Basic law of Malta is written constitution (The Constitution of Malta) which effectively creates Republic and enshrines fundamental principle of balance of powers, rule of law, independence of judiciary and human rights.

Executive is composed of Cabinet composed of Ministers and Parliamentary Secretaries nominated by Prime Minister. Prime Minister, who is appointed by President of the Republic, is usually leader of party commanding greatest measure of support in House.

Malta enjoys civil law jurisdiction, however, most modern legislations including company, tax and maritime laws are generally modelled on their Anglo-American counterparts.

Judiciary is independent of Executive and of Legislature. Judges are appointed by Government; but they cannot be removed before retirement age except for proved inability to exercise their functions properly and following two thirds vote in House of Representatives.

Local Government.—Apart from national government (see topic Constitution and Government), by Local Councils Act, 1993, Malta has been divided into 67 localities each of which is administered as regards local affairs by Local Council consisting of from five to 13 counsellors (depending on population in each locality), one of whom is elected mayor. Elections of councillors will be held every three years. Councillors are elected by residents of each particular locality, while councillers then elect one of them as mayor.

CONTRACTS:

There are no essential differences between Maltese and Anglo-American law regarding validity of contracts. There is general power in all competent persons to freely enter into contractual agreements, limited only by public policy, illegal motives, and requirement that certain contracts be, (a) evidenced by writing, or (b) executed in presence of witnesses, or (c) acknowledged by notary public.

Applicable Law.—Obligations ex contractu are governed by law designated by parties, or failing such designation, by national law of parties if they belong to same country or by law of place where contract was entered into. Noncontractual obligations are governed by law of place where they arose.

Excuses for Nonperformance.—Nonperformance may be excused by supervening impossibility, by all cases of force majeure, and in event that, due to facts extraordinary and unexpected, performance has become exceedingly burdensome.

Government contracts are, as rule, awarded on basis of bids, except for system of direct negotiations in view of particularity of contract. Contracts are normally entered into on basis of general conditions and specifications and performance bond is usually required.

COPYRIGHT:

Protection of copyright is regulated by Copyright Act. (c. 196 of Laws of Malta).

Nature of Copyright.—Copyright consists in exclusive right to do, or authorise others to do, acts in relation to original work in question which are set out in Act namely literary, musical and artistic works, cinematographic films, sound recordings and broadcasts.

These rights include reproduction in any material form, communication to public, broadcasting or later rebroadcasting of whole work or substantial part thereof, either in its original form or in any form recognisably derived from original.

Copyright may be transmitted by assignment, by testamentary disposition and by operation of law, as movable property.

Copyright is conferred on every work eligible for copyright of which author, or in case of work of joint authorship, anyone of joint authors is, at time when work is made either Maltese citizen or is domiciled in Malta; or body corporate having legal personality under Laws of Malta.

Copyright in respect of literary, musical or artistic works, other than photographs, lasts for 25 years after death of author, in respect of cinematographic films and photographs for 25 years after work was first made accessible to public by owner of copyright, in respect of sound recordings for 25 years after recording was made and in respect of broadcasts for 25 years after broadcast took place. For joint authorship copyright runs from death of survivor irrespective of whether survivor is qualified person under copyright act.

Infringement.—Where any person infringes copyright in work he shall be liable, at suit of owner of such copyright, to payment of damages or to payment of fine not exceeding 500 Maltese Liri and to restitution of all profit derived from infringement of copyright.

CORPORATIONS:

See topic Partnerships.

COURTS:

There are four principal jurisdictions: civil, commercial, criminal and voluntary. Courts are divided into Superior Courts presided over by judges and Lower Courts presided over by Magistrates, depending on seriousness or gravity of cause. There is one Court of Appeal for all jurisdictions.

Constitutional Court is ultimate court to decide on actions challenging validity of laws, alleging violations of human rights or generally involving Constitution.

Administrative cases are normally dealt with through normal courts, but there is growing network of administrative tribunals with appeal (usually only on question of law) to Court of Appeal.

CURRENCY:

Unit of currency in Malta is Malta Lira which is made up of 100 Maltese cents. Central Bank of Malta has exclusive right to issue all Maltese money.

DEATH:

After lapse of three consecutive years from day person (known as absentee) was last heard of, any interested party may file application before court of voluntary jurisdiction requesting that any wills made by absentee be opened and provisional possession of property granted to any presumed heir under conditions court deems fit. If above continues for further period of six years any interested person may request court of voluntary jurisdiction to draw up formal certificate of death.

DEPOSITIONS:

As rule witnesses are examined in open court during trial of action "viva voce". Their deposition is taken by oath or solemn declaration. Evidence by "affidavit" is also permissable without prejudicing right of court to call deponent to appear in court for cross examination.

When depositions are to be taken abroad, Code of Organisation and Civil Procedure allows use of letters rogatory. These procedures are commenced in court and presented to Prime Minister for execution. Basically party making demand is to produce interrogatories reduced into writing and translated into language in which witness is to be heard. Both party making request and other party have right to be represented by consul abroad during examination of witness.

DESCENT AND DISTRIBUTION:

Rules of succession to real property and personal property are same. There is no doctrine of primogeniture. Persons who are incapable or unworthy of receiving under will (see topic Wills) are also incapable or unworthy of succeeding "ab intestato".

Order of intestate inheritance is as follows:

Regular Successions.—

Succession by Legitimate Descendants.—Children or their descendants succeed to their father and mother or other ascendants, without distinctions of sex, and whether they are issue of same marriage or of different marriages. They succeed "per capita" when they are all in their first degree; they succeed "per stirpes", when all, or some of them, take by representation. (Civil Code [§808]).

Succession by Legitimate Ascendants.—Where deceased has left no issue, nor parents, nor brothers or sisters, nor descendants from them, succession devolves upon father and mother of deceased in equal portions, or upon parent who may have survived him. Where deceased has left only ascendants in paternal and maternal lines, standing in equal degree, inheritance shall devolve, as to one moiety, upon ascendant or ascendants of one line, and, as to other moiety, upon ascendant or ascendants of other line. Where such ascendants stand in different degree, inheritance devolves upon nearest ascendant, without any distinction of line. (Civil Code [§§810 and 811]).

Where brothers or sisters of deceased, or descendants of predeceased brothers or sisters, whether of half or full blood, compete with father and mother, or, with one of them surviving, or, in default of both parents, with ascendants, or nearest ascendant, in any such case parents, ascendants, brothers and sisters shall succeed "per capita", and in equal portions; and descendants of brothers or sisters, whether of half or full blood, shall succeed by right of representation, "per stirpes".

Succession by Legitimate Collaterals.—If deceased has left neither issue, nor ascendants, his brothers and sisters, whether of half or full blood, and descendants of his predeceased brothers or sisters, of half or full blood, shall be entitled to succession. Brothers and sisters shall succeed "per capita", and their descendants by right of representation "per stirpes". On failure of descendants, ascendants, brothers or sisters, and descendants of brothers or sisters, succession devolves upon uncles and aunts, and then upon nearest collateral relation, in whatever line such uncles, aunts, or collateral relation may be. Succession between collaterals shall not extend beyond 12th degree.

DESCENT AND DISTRIBUTION . . . *continued*

Irregular Successions.—Illegitimate child has no right to succession of his parents, unless he has been legitimated by decree of court, or has been acknowledged either in act of birth or in any other public deed whether before or after his birth, or his filiation has been declared by judgment of competent court.

Legitimate children and descendants of predeceased illegitimate child may claim rights competent to such child.

Illegitimate child even though acknowledged or legitimated otherwise than by subsequent marriage, shall have no right over property of relations of either of his parents; nor shall such relations have any right over property of illegitimate child.

Where illegitimate child dies without leaving issue, or spouse, inheritance of such child devolves upon parent whose child, whether by legitimation, or acknowlegment or judgment of competent court, he is proved to be, or upon both parents, in equal shares, if, he is proved to be child of both of them. Where illegitimate child dies without issue, but is survived by spouse, inheritance shall devolve, as to two-thirds, upon surviving spouse, and, as to remaining third, upon father or mother of such child, or upon both father and mother in equal shares.

Rights of Surviving Spouse.—Where deceased spouse is survived by children or descendants legitimate or legitimated by subsequent marriage, surviving spouse shall only be entitled to usufruct of one-half part of estate of deceased.

Where deceased is not survived by such children or descendants but is survived by illegitimate children legitimated or acknowledged, surviving spouse shall be entitled to third part of property of deceased in full ownership. If deceased is not survived by illegitimate children but is survived by ascendants, or by brothers or sisters or their descendants, surviving spouse shall be entitled to one-half of property of deceased in full ownership. On failure of all persons mentioned, surviving spouse shall be entitled to whole of inheritance, after deducting therefrom such portion as may be competent to illegitimate children not legitimated nor acknowledged.

Rights of succession "ab intestato" shall not be competent to surviving spouse, if at any time of death of deceased party, spouses were separated from bed and board by judgment of competent civil court and surviving spouse had forfeited rights of succession. Where there is no kin entitled to inheritance, state inherits. (Civil Code [§830]). Maltese Parliament is currently discussing Family Law which inter alia contemplates widening of rights of surviving spouse.

DISPUTE RESOLUTION:

Mandatory Dispute Resolution.—All money claims not exceeding Lm100 are heard and determined by Small Claims Tribunal set up under Act bearing same name. Tribunal does not have jurisdiction to hear cases involving: questions of ownership of immovable property, or relating to easements, burdens or other rights annexed to such property, even though claim does not exceed Lm100; or causes of ejectment and eviction.

Tribunal is presided over by adjudicator who must be over 30 years of age, holds warrant of and has practiced as advocate for at least one year or as legal procurator for at least three years. He may not be member of House of Representatives, of Local Council, undischarged bankrupt, or have been sentenced to imprisonment for, or been found guilty of Crimes Against the Administration of Justice and other Public Administrations, Crimes affecting Public Trust, and Crimes affecting Public Trade.

Tribunal takes decisions principally in equity, although matters related to prescription decided upon according to law. Appeal lies from decision of Tribunal only: on any matter related to jurisdiction of Tribunal; on any question of prescription; where Tribunal has seriously infringed rules of impartiality and equity according to law and such shortcoming has prejudiced right of appellant; where Tribunal has not suspended proceedings where claim was sought to be avoided by way of defence, involving issue outside Tribunal's jurisdiction, or where it similarly failed to suspend proceedings where there was pending before competent court action outcome of which would have affected claim before Tribunal itself.

Voluntary Dispute Resolution.—Under Consumer Affairs Act 1994, consumer involved in dispute with trader regarding goods and services purchased or hired has recourse, if consumer so desires, to Consumer Claims Tribunal, which hears claims where value in dispute does not exceed Lm500. Tribunal can award up to Lm100 in moral damages caused by pain, distress, anxiety and inconvenience suffered.

Claim first made to Director of Consumer Affairs who will attempt to mediate between parties and help them reach agreement. If no agreement is reached, parties may present claim before Consumer Claims Tribunal against payment of small fee. Parties to case need not be represented by lawyer, although they may be so represented. This is intended to be quick and cheap way of obtaining redress.

See also topic Arbitration.

ENVIRONMENT:

Environment Protection Act, 1991, was enacted empowering Government to: (a) take all those measures, both preventive and remedial, that may be necessary for protection of environment of Malta; (b) collaborate with other governments and entities for protection of world environment; (c) take into account need to protect environment when deciding on economic or social matters; (d) disseminate in Malta knowledge about environment when deciding on economic social matters; (e) disseminate in Malta knowledge about environment; about pollution or threats of pollution, and facilitate help of all persons in protection of environment; (f) endeavour to apply scientific and technical knowledge and resources when deciding upon matters that affect environment; (g) endeavour that food and drink, land, sea and air be free of contamination from any toxic substances or from use of any unnecessary energy or from noise; (h) safeguard biological diversity of all species; (i) safegaurd common heritage of mankind. Civil action for damages as well as criminal punishments are provided for damages caused to natural, cultural and historical environment.

EXCHANGE CONTROL:

Law permits free repatriation of capital and earnings therefrom provided that capital was originally brought into Malta from outside sources. Earnings from legitimate business activities can also be freely repatriated. Exchange control permission or advice is however always necessary for such movement of funds.

In case of all offshore activities according to Malta International Business Authority, 1988 (see topic Foreign Investment), there are no restrictions on transfer of funds into or out of Malta.

EXECUTIONS:

Following grant title of execution (Code of Organisation and Civil Procedure [§253]): (a) judgments and decrees of Maltese courts; (b) public deeds received before notary public of Malta; (c) awards of arbitration made in accordance with procedure outlined in law for such arbitration (§968).

Execution can affect both movable and immovable property of debtor.

FOREIGN EXCHANGE:

See topics Currency, Exchange Control and Foreign Investment.

FOREIGN INVESTMENT:

Foreign investor seeking to do business in Malta may benefit from number of investment incentive laws regulating various sections of activity.

Onshore Industrial Investment.—Malta Development Corporation is national agency entrusted to promote industrial activity in Malta. (a) Incentives aimed at non-manufacturing projects as well as projects involved in manufacturing which is not export oriented, are laid down in Aids to Industries Ordinance 1959. Some of more important benefits are following: (i) investment allowance of 20% of original cost of plant and machinery invested during first three years; (ii) accelerated depreciation allowance for plant and machinery over six year period. This enables investor to claim up to 120% of sum invested in plant and machinery before arriving at its chargeable income; (iii) reduced rates of company tax where profits are utilized to finance increased investment. Net payable rate of 15% is possible where 60% or more of profits are to be reinvested. (b) Export orientated manufacturing companies are offered extremely competitive incentive package in terms of Industrial Development Act 1988. Qualifying companies are ones which carry out business consisting of: production, manufacture, improvement, assembly, processing, repair, preservation or maintenance of any goods, materials, commodities (including computer software) equipment, plant or machinery or rendering of services of industrial nature analogous to activities referred to in above paragraph, including repair, maintenance, commission installation, inspection or testing of plant, machinery or equipment.

Tax incentives include following: ten year income tax holiday to new companies exporting minimum of 95% of their production or services; Export Incentive Scheme (directed to companies that do not qualify for tax holiday status) granting income tax exemptions for additional profits resulting from increased export sales; tax free dividends relief from death and donation duties and customs duties payable on imported tools, machinery, etc.; investment allowance of 30% over and above actual cost of plant and machinery, and of 15% on industrial buildings and structures; accelerated depreciation enabling write off of plant and machinery over four years, and of industrial buildings and structures over 25 years; export promotion, research and development allowances; other benefits include soft loan programme, ready built factories at subsidized rents, training and management services grants, liberal policies on work permits, etc.

Companies may be wholly foreign owned and it is also possible for offshore company to hold shares in manufacturing subsidiary as long as it is sole owner of subsidiary.

FRAUDS, STATUTE OF:

Unless law expressly prescribes otherwise, verbal agreements have full binding force. Generally following transactions require written form: (a) agreement implying promise to transfer or acquire under any title ownership of immovable property or rights thereon; (b) transfer or assignment of rights; (c) any promise of loan for consumption; (d) suretyship; (e) lease for period exceeding two years in case of urban leases, or 14 years in case of rural leases; (f) civil partnership; (g) agreement relating to Promise of Marriage Law.

Any agreement implying transfer, acquisition or in any way effecting rights over immovable property must be incorporated in public deed.

FRAUDULENT SALES AND CONVEYANCES:

This is regulated by general provision of visa of consent under laws of contracts. See topic Contracts.

GARNISHMENT:

Where creditor under judgment or any other executive title, in order to obtain payment of debt owing to him, desires to attach in hands of third party moneys or immovable property due or belonging to his debtor, he may do so by means of garnishee order.

This order states amount due as well as title under which creditor sues out execution and expressly enjoins garnishee not to pay or deliver to debtor, or any other person, such moneys or things as may be in his hands, under penalty of payment of damages and interest.

Garnishee order is executed by delivery by marshal of copy thereof to garnishee. Copy of order is also served on debtor. Creditor may file judicial act calling upon garnishee to declare to Registrar what moneys or things, if any, belonging to person against whom order is issued he holds in his possession. Garnishee must within four days declare moneys or things held by him and pertaining to debtor. Default of declaration creates presumption of existence of funds or things. Declaration is made by letter to Registrar or by judicial act served on execution creditor.

Garnishee of his own accord, or else upon receipt of warrant of injunction to deposit issued on demand of execution creditor, lodges in court moneys or things attached by order. When lodging in court garnishee notifies both execution creditor and debtor.

Property not subject to attachment by garnishee order is following: (i) Salaries of any person employed in civil or military service of Government of Malta. (ii) Allowance of any person pensioned by Government. (iii) Charitable grants made by Government. (iv) Bequests made expressly for maintenance, if debtor has no other means of

GARNISHMENT . . . *continued*
subsistence (except if debt itself is not due in respect of maintenance). (v) Sums due for maintenance awarded "officio judicis" (if debt itself is not due in respect of maintenance). (vi) Sums due by civil or military departments of public service for price of works or supplies.

Notwithstanding above, if wife or minor or incapacitated child or ascendant of debtor sues husband, father or descendant (as case may be), for maintenance, court may either in judgment itself or in subsequent decree, order that specified portion of salary, allowance or bequest be paid directly to creditor. Service of such order on person who pays salary, allowance or bequest, is equivalent to garnishee order and such person shall pay creditor directly such part of salary, allowance or bequest specified in order. Court, however, cannot make such orders if debtor is officer or member of regular force of Malta, in which case creditor may only cause copy of order to be transmitted to authority concerned for their information.

(vii) Wages payable by employer to employee. However, if creditor states on oath in court that wages exceed Lm100 per month, court shall allow garnishee order on such excess unless employee shows to satisfaction of court that he needs such excess or part thereof for his or his family's maintenance, in which case court shall revoke garnishee order even with respect to such excess or part thereof.

Above does not apply (i.e. wages shall be garnisheed irrespective of whether these exceed or not Lm100 per month) if garnishee order was issued to ensure payment of maintenance due to wife or to minor or incapacitated child, or to ascendant of employee.

Garnishee order lapses on expiration of one year from issue thereof, unless court shall extend such time upon application by person suing out order.

Precautionary Garnishee Orders.—Such garnishee orders are issued prior or concurrently to lawsuit. However, action in respect of claim stated in precautionary garnishee order shall be brought by applicant within four working days from delivery to him of notice of execution of warrant or within ten working days after issue of warrant whichever is earlier. In default, order shall cease. What has been stated vis-à-vis executive garnishee orders regarding their effects, contents of order, mode of execution, declaration by garnishee, lodgement in court and property subject to such order applies to precautionary garnishee order.

Precautionary garnishee orders remain effective for six months unless extended. Notice of extensions are notified to garnishee.

IMMIGRATION:

Citizenship is exclusively regulated by Constitution of Malta.

Domicile is not defined in law, it denotes combination of facts. Maltese courts follow English principles in establishing concept of domicile.

Residence.—Law distinguishes between various types of residence status: (a) Non-residents: when visitor's stay does not exceed three months. He is entitled to purchase immovable property in Malta provided this is valued at over Lm15,000; (b) Temporary Residents: when Principal Immigration Officer grants permit to foreigner to reside temporarily in Malta. This is granted upon foreigner showing evidence that his income will enable him to live in country without becoming financial burden on Government; (c) Permanent Residence: when foreigner can show that he owns capital net worth of Lm150,000 worldwide or earns annual income of Lm10,000 and is prepared to purchase property in Malta worth minimum of Lm30,000 or rent premises at not less than Lm1,200 per annum.

Apart from above, temporary residence permit is automatically granted to expatriate employees working in Malta under valid working permit. This residence permit is normally made to coincide with foreigner's working permit.

INFANTS:

Age of majority is 18 for both sexes. (Civil Code [§157]). Minor who has attained age of 16 and who has been authorised to trade by parent to whose authority he is subject by means of public deed registered in Commercial Court (Commercial Code [§9]) shall in regard to all matters relating to his trade be considered as being of age (Civil Code [§156]). Infant is also emancipated by marriage.

Parent having paternal authority is administrator of property of his or her minor children. (Civil Code [§136]). Any minor whose parents have died or have forfeited paternal authority is subject to be placed under tutorship until he becomes of age or gets married. (Civil Code [§158]).

JUDGMENTS:

Enforcibility of Foreign Judgments.—Code of Organisation and Civil Procedure (§826) provides that any judgment delivered by competent foreign court may be enforced in Malta, in same manner as judgments delivered in Malta, upon request being made to Maltese court by means of Writ Of Summons.

By virtue of British Judgments (Reciprocal Enforcement) Act (c. 52 of Laws of Malta), judgment obtained from Superior Courts of U.K. may be registered in Malta upon request made by judgment creditor before Court of Appeal in Malta. This would also apply to countries within British dominion if equivalent reciprocal enforcement agreement has been agreed between Malta and any of those other countries.

By virtue of Maintenance Orders (Facilities For Enforcement) (c. 48 of Laws of Malta) maintenance order made against any person by any court in England or Northern Ireland shall be registered and enforceable in Malta through Civil Court, First Hall, upon transmission by secretary of state to President of Malta of copy of such maintenance order.

LABOUR RELATIONS:

Employer-employee relations are governed by number of labour and social security laws and regulations: The Conditions of Employment Act (c. 135 of Laws of Malta) governs inter alia basic conditions of employment, minimum number of hours of work, termination of employment, terminal benefits, minimum wages, minimum annual vacation, sick leave. According to this law, various industries have their own Wages Council which proposes regulations specifying conditions of employment within particular industries concerned.

Principal law regulating relations with Trade Unions in Industrial Relations Act, 1976. Workers are not required to join trade union and closed shop is not practiced in Malta. Collective agreements are common between unions and individual companies which are normally drawn for period of three years.

Disputes between employer and union or employer and employee are referred to Industrial Tribunal as constituted and regulated by Industrial Relations Act, 1976.

Employer-employee relationships are still subject to provisions of Civil Code in normal way apart from being subject to pertinent laws or agreements relating to their employment.

Under Social Security Act 1987, all persons in employment (including self-employed) must pay contributions to state for its social service system which includes benefits for: sickness and invalidity, unemployment, injury, maternity and death, as well as marriage grants, disablement gratuities and pensions and various other categories of pensions. Contributions, both those by employer and by employee, are paid together with and in same way as PAYE tax being deducted from wages and salaries.

Employees of offshore companies are exempt from paying any National Insurance Contributions (see topic Foreign Investment).

LAW REPORTS, CODES, ETC.:

There is official reporting of some of cases decided by various courts in Malta, but publication is not regular publication and has not been kept up to date.

LEGISLATURE:

See topic Constitution and Government.

LICENSES:

For establishing any type of industrial or commercial enterprise state consent is required.

LIENS:

See topics Pledge; Shipping.

LOCAL GOVERNMENT:

See topic Constitution and Government, subhead Local Government.

MARRIAGE:

(Marriage Act 1975. *Note:*—Maltese law in this field will undergo changes on approval of act amending Marriage Act and on enactment of Family Law which are presently being discussed in Parliament.)

Age of consent for both males and females is 16 years.

Marriage may be contracted either in civil form or in religious form, but always in accordance with provisions of Marriage Act. Recent amendment passed by Parliament on 31/1/95 provides that Catholic marriage celebrated in Malta shall as from moment of its celebration be recognized and have same effects as marriage celebrated in accordance with norms and formalities of Marriage Act.

Medical examinations and blood tests are not required. Marriage can be celebrated only after due publication of banns by Marriage Registrar.

Marriage is prohibited between certain categories of persons such as (1) ascendants and descendants in direct line, (2) brothers and sisters whether of full or half blood, (3) persons related by affinity in direct line, (4) adopter and person adopted or descendant or husband or wife of adopted person.

Marriage by proxy is permitted only if one of persons to be married is not present in Malta and in opinion of Marriage Registrar there exist grave reasons for permitting marriage to take place by proxy. Proxy shall cease to be operative 90 days after it is signed.

Annulment.—Marriage Act sets out grounds on which marriage is null and void "ab initio" namely (a) parties within prohibited degrees (supra); (b) either party under 16; (c) either party suffers from infirmity of mind at time of marriage; (d) existing prior marriage; (e) marriage lacks certain formalities but demand for annulment has to be made within two years of marriage; (f) if consent of either party (i) is extorted by violence or fear, or (ii) is excluded by error of identity of other party, or (iii) is extorted by fraud, or (iv) is vitiated by serious defect of discretion of judgment on matrimonial life or by serious psychological anomaly which makes it impossible for that party to fulfil essential obligations of marriage, or (v) is vitiated by positive exclusion of marriage itself on its essential elements or of right to conjugal act; (g) relative or absolute impotence of either party which must exist at time of marriage; (h) if either party subjects his or her consent to condition referring to future; (i) if either party did not have sufficient powers of intellect or volition to elicit matrimonial consent. Recent amendment now provides that "valid" marriage may be annulled on grounds that either party refused to consummate same. Furthermore exclusive competence has now been given to Ecclesiastical Tribunal when either party files petition for annulment of Catholic marriage before said tribunal.

When marriage is annulled children of that marriage are legitimate and spouse who was responsible for nullity of marriage is bound to pay maintenance to other spouse in good faith for period of five years unless latter gets married.

Divorce cannot be obtained in Malta. However, foreign divorce will be recognised if granted in country where either spouse is domiciled or of which he or she is citizen.

Separation from Bed and Board.—

Separations.—Court can grant separation a mensa et thoro on following grounds (1) adultery on part of other spouse (Civil Code [§§38, 39]), or (2) excesses, cruelty, threats or grievous injury against other spouse or against his or her children, or (3) marriage has irretrievably broken down (Civil Code [§40]).

Demand for separation based on last ground may not be made before expiration of four years from date of marriage. Separation may also be based on mutual consent to be expressed before court and ratified by same.

Separations may also be demanded if for two years or more one of spouses has deserted other without good grounds. (Civil Code [§41]). Subsequent cohabitation

MARRIAGE . . . *continued*
between parties to separation shall restore obligations of cohabitation and of maintenance. Any other effect of separation shall not cease except in virtue of public deed. (Civil Code [§64]).

Effects of Separation.—Spouse against whom separation is pronounced shall not as result of such separation be relieved from obligation of supplying maintenance to other spouse where such maintenance is due. (Civil Code [§54]). On separation being pronounced court shall on demand of either spouse direct cessation and liquidation of community of acquests even though it may have been established by contract.

When deciding in whose custody children shall be placed Court shall always be directed by better welfare of children. Other spouse who is not granted custody of children may be given right of access to them. (Civil Code [§57]).

MONOPOLIES:

Under Supplies and Services Act (c. 117) Government is entitled to restrict or limit any trading activity thus creating monopolies. Though Government intervention has been very limited, State was for some time prepared to grant monopolies to help set up new industries.

On its part State itself maintains virtual monopoly in certain fields, for example, trading of petroleum, water and electricity, telecommunication services, etc.

MOTOR VEHICLES:

Motor vehicle licence is required. Every vehicle must have number plates displayed front and rear.

Driver's license is required, which must be produced to police on demand. Person under 18 years of age may not operate motor vehicle. In Malta traffic must keep to left hand side of road. In case of any accident causing damage or injury to any person or vehicle or animal driver must stop and report accident to police and produce certificate of insurance to police within 48 hours.

It is not lawful for any person to use or permit another person to use motor vehicle on road unless there is in force in relation to user of vehicle such policy of insurance in respect of third-party risks as complies with Motor Vehicles Insurance (Third-party Risks) Ordinance (c. 165).

Visitor must hold international driving licence.

All cars rented in Malta are covered by fully comprehensive insurance.

In case of accident involving death or bodily injury and judgment is obtained against insured, then, notwithstanding that insurer may be entitled to avoid and cancel insurance policy, insurer has to pay sum adjudged by Court provided that insurer has notice of institution of proceedings by means of judicial act within seven days after conclusion of evidence of plaintiff in proceedings.

MORTGAGES (Hypothecs):

Mortgages (hypothecs) are of three classes: (i) Legal, that is, created by law in favour of specified persons in certain circumstances such as that belonging by law to wife on property of her husband for her dowry; (ii) judicial, arising from judgment against debtor; and (iii) contractual, that is, established by contract.

Hypothec can either be general or special one. General hypothec affects all property present and future of debtor, special hypothec affects only one or more of particular immovables of following kind: (a) things which are immovable by nature and products of such immovables so long as they are not separated therefrom; (b) right of usufruct over said immovables, during continuance of such right; (c) "dominium directum" over said immovables given on emphyteusis, and "dominium utile" over such immovables.

Whereas general hypothec attaches to property affected thereby only so long as such property does not pass into hands of third party, special hypothec has "abroit de suite" and thus it continues to attach to any immovable charged therewith into whosoever's possession such immovable may pass.

All hypothecs must be registered in Public Registry and they rank according to their date of registration. Registration may be reduced or totally cancelled either with consent of creditor given in public deed, or in virtue of judgment. Registration of provilege or hypothec in Public Registry shall cease to have effect after 30 years from date thereof unless such registration is renewed before expiration of said time.

Privileges.—Privilege is another right of preference which however always ranks prior to hypothec even if latter is registered at earlier date. Privileges may be either general, that is, extending over all property movable or immovable of debtor, or special, that is, affecting certain property movable or immovable. Whereas special privileges over movables and general privileges cease to exist if property so secured passes to hands of third parties, special privileges over immovables continue to have effect even when these are transferred to third parties.

Privileged debts over all property in general are: judicial costs, funeral expenses, death bed expenses, wages of servants and supplies of provisions which are indispensable for support of debtor and his family. Privileged debts over particular movables include amongst others: debt due to pledgee over thing which he holds as pledge, debt due to hotel keeper over affects of his guest, debt due for carriage of goods over goods carried. Amongst privileged creditors over immovables most important are: architects, contractors over immovable constructed for debts due to them in respect of expenses and price of their work.

Antichresis is devise in Maltese law which can only be created by virtue of writing whereby creditor acquires right to collect fruits of immovables belonging to his debtor, subject to his obligation of deducting annually such fruits from interest if any be due to him, and then from principal of debt. Creditor must also provide for maintenance and necessary repairs of immovable and pay ground rent, if any. Creditor does not become owner of immovable by mere default of payment at time agreed upon; however, in default of payment he may sue for sale of immovable by judicial auction. If creditor who holds immovable by way of antichresis, enjoys other rights of privilege or hypothec created on such immovable, he may exercise such rights as any other creditor.

MOTOR VEHICLES:

Motor vehicle licence is required. Every vehicle must have number plates displayed front and rear.

OFFSHORE INVESTMENT:

In 1988 Maltese Parliament laid down legal framework for development of Malta into reputable offshore financial centre.

The Malta Financial Services Centre Act, 1988 established Malta Financial Services Centre which acts as information liason between investors and government and more important still fulfills initial vetting and subsequent supervisory role. All companies other than overseas branches of foreign banks or insurance companies are registered as private limited liability companies under Commercial Partnerships Ordinance. Offshore company must in addition be registered with Offshore Authority.

Offshore Activity is defined by Act as "any business or other activity carried on from Malta in a foreign currency by persons and with persons not resident in Malta or with another offshore company or with an offshore trust."

Incentives vary depending on type of offshore company and proposed activity. For this purpose offshore companies are divided into trading and non-trading companies. Offshore trading companies may be banking companies, insurance companies and general trading companies. Non-trading company is one which expressly limits its objects to ownership managment and administration of property of any kind. For investors more conversant with common law vehicles of investment, establishment of Offshore Trust is also possible (see topic Trusts).

General trading companies may be set up with minimum capital of Lm500 (expressed in foreign currency) 20% paid up. Shareholders must be declared to Authority but need not appear on any public documentation, as locally licenced nominee companies may act as nominee shareholders. There are no restrictions on appointment of directors, provided that local nominee company acts as secretary or sole director of company.

Minimum paid up share capital for offshore banking company is USD 1,500,000, whereas for offshore insurance company it is USD 750,000. In both types of companies, there are no restrictions on appointment of directors, and there is no necessity for any nominee company appointment as case with general trading company.

In addition offshore banking and insurance companies are not bound by liquidity ratios, margins of solvency, reserve funds and asset margin requirements normally applicable to offshore banks. Authority must however satisfy itself that company is capable of properly conducting and supporting its business and of retaining sufficient asset resources and acceptable margins of solvency.

Offshore trading companies be they general, banking or insurance pay 5% tax on their self-assessed chargeable income. No tax is chargeable on any dividend, interest or other income paid by such companies to any persons not resident in Malta. In addition they are granted exemption from death and donation duties, stamp duties, customs duties on importation of company's requirements and of personal belongings of nonresident officers or employees of company. There is also freedom of exchange control.

Incentives accorded to offshore non-trading companies are even further encompassing. Non-trading offshore companies may be set up with minimum capital of Lm500 (expressed in foreign currency) 20% paid up. Beneficial owners need not be declared to Authority and total anonymity is possible. There are no restrictions on appointment of directors provided that locally licenced nominee company must act as secretary or sole director.

No taxation whatsoever is imposed, normal accounting and auditing requirements are not applicable and tax returns need not be filed.

Offshore companies can only be incorporated until 31/12/1996 and all offshore companies must be phased out by year 2004.

Malta has introduced, as alternative to these companies, International Trading Companies (see topic Taxation, subhead International Trading Companies) and new fiscal provisions in case of foreign income (see topic Taxation).

All rights, exemptions and privileges under Malta International Business Act 1988 are guaranteed and are tantamount to contractual obligation between Government and registered offshore company.

Freeport Activities.—Malta Freeports Act 1989 has designated customs free zone for utilization of freeport activities. Licences to operate in freeport are issued to Maltese registered companies by Freeport Authority. Incentives include exemption from income tax, death and donation duty, stamp duty, customs or excise duties on equipment, machinery, tools, material or other items brought into freeport by company, exemptions from social security contributions and freedom of exchange control. Expatriate employees are also granted beneficial tax status.

Foreign Trade Regulations.—See topic Treaties.

OMBUDSMAN:

Appointed by President of Republic upon resolution of House of Representatives supported by at least two-thirds of all members thereof. Term of office is of five years, with eligibility for reappointment for consecutive term. Cannot serve as: member of House of Representatives, local council, public officer nor take part in any professional, banking, commercial or trade union activity, or in any other activity for profit or reward while in office. Also cannot pursue any activity which might affect impartiality, independence or public confidence in his office.

Removed from office by President only upon proven inability to perform his functions and following demand by two-thirds majority of all members of House of Representatives.

Is responsible to resolve grievances involving: Government of Malta, including all Departments, Ministries and Authorities thereof as well as any Minister, Parliamentary Secretary, public officer and any member or servant of any other authority; any statutory body, partnership or other body in which Government or any of aforementioned bodies or combination thereof has controlling interest or effective control, including any director, member, manager or other officer of same; local councils or any committee thereof, mayors, councilors and members of staff; all actions of Malta

OMBUDSMAN . . . *continued*
Police Force (except any criminal investigation), of Public Service Commission and Armed Forces of Malta with some exceptions.

Cannot investigate: President, House of Representatives, Cabinet, Judiciary, certain commissions and bodies listed under Ombudsman Act, and in other limited cases specified under Ombudsman Act.

Right to complain to Ombudsman is remedy of last resort, is free of charge and must be made by person having personal interest in matter complained of.

PARTNERSHIPS:

All forms of business partnerships are regulated under Companies Act, Act XXV of 1995.

Three forms of commercial partnerships exist: (a) partnerships "en nom collectif"; (b) partnerships "en commandite"; and (c) partnerships "anonyme" or limited liability companies.

With regard to first two types of partnerships, law is based on continental (mostly Italian) pattern; while in case of limited liability company, law is to very great extent modelled on U.K. Companies Act 1995, U.K. Insolvency Act 1986, and EU Harmonisation Directives.

All commercial partnerships have to be registered with Registrar of Partnerships and when so registered acquire legal personality distinct from that of their members or shareholders.

Under Maltese law partnership must have at least two members or shareholders and its objects must be limited to commercial activities, although limited liability company which is private exempt (private company in which no body corporate is shareholder, holds any interest in or is director of that company) can be registered with one shareholder, or become single member company during its existence.

(a) Partnership "en nom collectif", originally known as "general partnerships" has been defined by law as partnership which operates under partnership name and has its obligations guaranteed by unlimited and joint and several liability of all parties, provided that no action shall lie against individual parties unless property of partnership has been discussed. (§6). Partnership name is limited to names of parties.

(b) Partnership "en commandite" is defined as partnership which operates under partnership name and has its obligations guaranteed by unlimited and joint and several liability of one or more parties, called unlimited parties, and by liability, limited to amount, if any, of any unpaid contribution, of one or more parties, called limited parties. (§50).

(c) Limited liability company, or corporation, is defined as partnership formed by means of capital divided into shares and having liability of its members limited to amount, if any, of unpaid shares respectively held by them. (§166).

Company may be public or private. Private company is one which restricts right to transfer its shares, limits number of its shareholders to 50, and prohibits invitation to public to subscribe for any shares or debentures.

Company is constituted by virtue of memorandum of association (Articles of Incorporation) which must contain following particulars: (i) whether company is public or private, (ii) name and residence of subscribers, (iii) name of company, (iv) registered office in Malta of company, (v) objects of company, (vi) details relating to share capital, (vii) number of, and names and addresses of first directors, manner of representation of company and name of first representative/s, (viii) name and residence of company secretary, (ix) period if any fixed for duration of company.

Subscribers may choose to regulate company by virtue of Articles of Association which is document signed by subscribers, registered together with memorandum. Alternatively, regulations contained in Companies Act 1995 may be made to constitute or supplement, as case may be, articles of company. These documents need not be incorporated in public deed.

Company may adopt any name that is not already in use but must end with words "Public Limited Company" or "PLC" in case of public company, or "Private Limited Company" or "Ltd." in case of private company.

Term "capital" as used in law has various different meanings: (a) Authorised share capital, is total amount of capital which company is authorised to issue by memorandum. On this value stamp duty is payable upon registration of company; (b) issued capital is that part of authorised share capital actually taken up or subscribed by shareholders, which cannot be less than Lm20,000 in case of public company, or less than Lm500 in case of private company. In case of foreign controlled company, minimum issued share capital is Lm10,000; (c) paid up capital is that part of issued capital which has been actually paid up by shareholders and must be not less than 25% for public companies and not less than 20% for private companies.

Shares may be of different classes having different voting, dividends and other rights as regulated in Memorandum and Articles of Company. All shares must be registered. Bearer shares are not permissible under Maltese law except in case of public companies.

Transfer of shares can be effected freely or as regulated by Articles of Association of Company.

Debentures and debenture stock is allowed under Maltese law.

Ordinary administration of company is entrusted to Board of Directors which is composed of one or more directors appointed by subscribers in general meeting in accordance with regulations set out in Articles of Association. Directors are authorised to exercise all powers of company which are not, by law or by Memorandum or Articles of Association reserved for company in general meeting. Directors, unless specifically required by Memorandum, need not be shareholders of company.

Law specifically requires individual to act as company secretary. There is no requirement that any shareholder or officer of company need be resident in Malta.

Company is required to hold first meeting of its members within three months from date at which it is entitled to commence business—this is called "statutory meeting". (§111[i]). Thereafter company is obliged to hold annual general meeting, and not more than 15 months should elapse between any two consecutive annual general meetings. "Extraordinary general meeting" can also be called at any time by directors upon requisition of such member or members holding not less than 10% of paid up share capital of company.

All shareholders are entitled to attend and vote at general meeting.

Procedures for calling of general meetings, for regulating procedure to be adhered to during these meetings, for regulating voting rights of shareholders are normally set out in Articles of Association of Company, and if not, regulations set out in Companies Act 1995 shall apply. As rule, unless otherwise regulated in Articles of Association, each share carries one vote and majority rule prevails.

In terms of law (§149), company is dissolved: (i) when company has resolved by extraordinary resolution that it be dissolved and consequently wound up by Court; (ii) when company has resolved by extraordinary resolution that it be dissolved and consequently wound up voluntarily.

Court will dissolve and wind up company where: (i) Company's business is suspended for 12 months uninterruptedly; (ii) company is unable to pay its debts.

Court will dissolve company where: (i) Number of its members is reduced below two and remains so for more than six months provided company is not single member company; (ii) number of directors is reduced below two in case of public companies, and below one in case of private companies, and remains so for more than six months; (iii) court is of opinion that grounds of sufficient gravity exist which warrant dissolution and consequent winding up of company; (iv) period of time for which company has been set up, if any, expires or event which under Memorandum and Articles sanctions winding up of company occurs and company before such expiry or occurrence or event, has not passed resolution to wind up voluntarily.

In case of voluntary winding-up, within 14 days from passing of resolution for dissolution and winding up of company, liquidator or officers thereof shall deliver notice of dissolution to Registrar for registration. Where company is dissolved by court, Registrar of Superior Courts shall forward copy of winding up order to Registrar for registration.

Companies Act 1995, contemplates also possibility of "overseas companies". Law allows that company which is registered or incorporated outside Malta to establish place of business in Malta by registering itself with Registrar of Companies by delivering to him: (i) authentic copy of deed of constitution of company; (ii) details of directors and secretary, if any; and (iii) names and addresses of one or more persons resident in Malta authorised to represent company in Malta.

Recent legislation in Malta (The Malta International Business Authority, 1989) has created new class of companies, namely offshore companies, which while retaining basic juridical characteristic features of Maltese company, differ in scope, application and attribution from Maltese company (see topic Offshore Investment).

PATENTS:

Patents are governed by Industrial Property (Protection) Ordinance (c. 29).

Object of patents are new industrial inventions or discoveries author of which is granted exclusive right of working same for his own profits. A number of inventions are not patentable, namely those relating to trades which are contrary to law, morals or public safety, those subject whereof is not production of corporal substances, those which are purely theoretical, and schemes relating to credit or finance.

Mode of Application.—Application for patent may be made by any person whether Maltese citizen or not. Applications for patent must be filed at office of Comptroller of Industrial Property. If complete specification is not produced with application, it may be produced within nine months from date of filing of application. In default application shall be deemed withdrawn.

Objections and Grants.—As soon as complete specification is accepted, Comptroller shall advertize acceptance by means of notice to be published three times in Government Gazette and in another newspaper. On expiration of two months and in default of lawful opposition patent shall be granted. During said time any person may give notice to Comptroller of opposition on any of following grounds: (a) that applicant obtained invention or discovery from him or from his legal representative, or (b) that patent had previously been granted in Malta for same invention; but on no other ground. Appeal may be entered to Court of Appeal on decision of Comptroller.

When patent is granted it shall be published in Government Gazette and its term is limited for 14 years from its date. However patentee may apply to Minister of Trade for extension for further term and in case of refusal he may appeal to Court of Appeal.

All rights relative to and deriving from patents are assignable and transmissible. Assignment shall not take effect, with respect to third parties, except from date of registration with Comptroller and has to be published in Government Gazette.

Trademarks are regulated by Part III of Industrial Property (Protection) Ordinance (c. 29).

Marks intended to distinguish product of any industry or articles of trade are considered trademarks provided they contain at least one of following particulars: (1) name of individual or firm represented in particular and distinctive manner, (2) signature of applicant, (3) distinctive device, mark, brand, heading, label, ticket or fancy word or words not in common use, or (4) word or words having no direct reference to character or quality of goods and not being according to ordinary signification surname or geographical name.

Marks and words referred to above must be different from those already legally used by other persons.

Applications to register trademark is to be presented to Comptroller of Industrial Property. Trademark must be registered for particular goods or classes of goods. Comptroller may on good grounds refuse to register trademark and in such case appeal lies from Comptroller to Court of Appeal.

Registration of person as proprietor of trademark shall entitle him to exclusive use of mark as from date of application. Such registration is for 14 years initially but may be renewed from time to time for periods of 14 years.

PLEDGE:

Pledge may only be created on movables including debts and rights over movable effects. Pledge of movable things is completed by delivery to creditor, or to third party selected by parties to contract, of thing pledged or of document conferring exclusive right to disposal of thing.

Although there is no need of any writing for constitution of pledge, in case where delivery cannot take physical form, pledge must result from public deed or private

See Topical Index in front part of this volume.

PLEDGE . . . *continued*
writing and (i) either notice of pledge is given by judicial act served on debtor of debt, or other right being pledged, or, (ii) such debtor has in writing acknowledged pledge.

Pledgee has right to retain thing pledged until debt is fully paid and if same debtor contracts another debt with same creditor subsequent to delivery of thing pledged, creditor, in absence of agreement to contrary, shall have, in respect of second debt, same rights on thing pledged as are competent to him in respect of prior debt.

Pledge confers to creditor right to obtain payment of thing pledged but law distinguishes between case when thing pledged is debt as distinct from case where pledged thing is any other movable thing. In former case pledgee is responsible for collection of such debt on maturity. He then has to place moneys or other things received either as agreed or failing such agreement, as court may determine. If debt secured by pledge is due pledgee may retain from any moneys received as aforesaid, amount sufficient to satisfy his rights and shall deliver remainder to pledgor.

If thing held on pledge is not money pledgee cannot dispose of such thing pledged in case of nonpayment but he may cause thing to be sold by auction under court's authority. However, if thing pledged has stock exchange or market price, court may, on creditor's application, order sale to be carried out by means of public broker, bank or other banking institution instead of by auction.

Apart from obligation to restore thing pledged when debt is extinguished, pledgee is also liable for loss or deterioration of thing pledged resulting from his negligence. Pledgor is bound on his part to refund to pledgee any expenses which latter may have incurred for preservation of pledge. Pledgee cannot either make use of thing pledged or sub-pledge without consent of pledgor. If pledgee abuses thing pledged, pledgor may demand that such thing be deposited with third party.

Pledge is deemed to be indivisible although debt may be devisible. If thing pledged bears interest or yields other profits, creditor shall appropriate such interest or profit to interest which may be due to him; if debt which is secured by pledge does not bear interest, then any interest of thing pledged shall be appropriated to capital.

PRESCRIPTION:

Generally all actions whether real, personal or mixed are barred by lapse of 30 years. (Civil Code [§2143]). In case of immovables held in good faith and under valid title prescriptive period is ten years. (Civil Code [§2140]).

Civil Code (§§2147-2160) provides various periods of limitation depending on object of action. Among more important are following: period of one year applies to actions of hoteliers or lodging houses for board and lodging and to actions of carriers by land or water for payment of their hire or wage; period of 18 months applies to actions of persons exercising any trade or mechanical art for price of their work or labour or materials supplied by them, to actions of creditors for price of merchandise, goods or other movable things sold by retail, actions of persons paid by year for payment of their salary, to actions of brokers for their brokerage fee, and to actions of any person for hire of movable things; period of two years applies to actions of builders of ships and other vessels and of contractors in respect of all works made of wood, stone or other material for works carried out by them or for materials supplied by them, to action of physicians, surgeons, advocates, notaries, architects, civil engineers and to other persons exercising their professions or liberal art for their fees and disbursements, to actions of attorneys or mandatories and to action of Government for payment of judicial fees, customs and other dues; period of five years to actions for payment of maintenance allowance or rent, for payment of interest or money lent, for restitution of money given on loan if loan not incorporated is public deed.

Actions for civil damages not arising from criminal offence are barred by lapse of two years, while if arising from criminal offence prescriptive period applicable to criminal offence applies to action for damages.

Actions for payment of any debt arising from commercial transaction or other cause, unless such action is otherwise regulated or results from public deed is barred by lapse of five years.

All executive titles are barred by lapse of three years from such time when they could have been executed.

Prescription is interrupted by judicial act filed in Court and served on party against whom it is sought to prevent running of prescription (§2128), by acknowledgment (§2133), and by payment on account (§2134).

PRINCIPAL AND AGENT:

This is regulated by Civil Code (§§1856-1890).

Mandate is contract whereby person gives to another power to do something for him. Except where expressly stated, mandate may be granted by public deed, by private writing, by letter, verbally or even tacitly. Contract is not perfected until mandatory has accepted mandate but this acceptance may be tacit or implied. Blank mandatory is possible if mandate granted by private writing. Mandate is gratuitous unless otherwise stipulated. Mandate is either special or general in which case it refers to acts of administration only. Power to alienate property, except such alienation falling within limits of administration, or to hypothecate property or to perform other acts of ownership must be expressed. Generally mandatory is presumed to be authorised to perform all that he deems necessary for carrying out of his mandate.

Mandate is terminated: by its revocation; by death, interdiction or bankruptcy of either mandator or mandatory; by termination of powers of mandator; by expiration of time during which mandate was to continue; by renunciation on part of mandatory.

Commercial agency is regulated by Civil Code (c. 13) which expressly states that except where otherwise provided by law, custom or agreement provisions relating to mandate in Civil Code (supra) apply to commercial agency.

All acts done by agent on behalf of principal, within scope of his authority, produce directly their effect whether in favour of or against principal. Agent is bound to furnish to third party all information regarding extent of authority conferred to him by principal, and any fake statement wilfully made by agent shall be considered commercial fraud.

Agent cannot transact with himself any business of his principal whether directly or indirectly without ratification of principal.

Where agency has been conferred in general terms, principal who withdraws agency may relieve himself from all liability towards third parties from any further acts done by agent by giving notice of such withdrawal by means of note filed in Commercial Court and causing such note to be published in Government Gazette and in other newspaper, and affixed in Exchange.

REAL PROPERTY:

Maltese Civil Code divides all properties into immovables (real property) and movables (personal property).

Real property consists of (i) property movable by nature such as land and buildings and springs of water; (ii) any movables annexed to tenement permanently to remain incorporated therewith; (iii) "dominium directum", usufruct, servitude, actions in respect of immovables and rights thereon and actions in respect of inheritance.

Real property may be acquired by accession, succession, prescription or contract.

Accession is right whereby owner of property acquires ownership of all that it produces or that becomes united to or incorporated with it, whether naturally or artificially. (Civil Code [§566]).

Succession.—See topic Wills.

Prescription is acquisition of ownership by any person who in good faith and under title capable of transferring ownership possesses immovable for period of ten years. (Civil Code [§2140]). Ownership may be acquired also even when there is absence of title or good faith after lapse of 30 years provided possession is continuous, public, unequivocal and peaceful. (Civil Code [§2143]).

Contract.—Acquisition of real property by contract is null if not made by public deed and registered at Public Registry by notary public. (Civil Code [§1363]).

Usufruct is real right to enjoy things of which another has ownership subject to obligation of preserving this substance with regard both to matter and to form. (Civil Code [§328]). Usufruct may be constituted either by law or by operation of man. In latter case it has to be constituted by public deed. Usufruct may be for life or for specified period and may also be conditional. (Civil Code [§331]).

Servitudes may be created by law for public or private utility; by contract or by prescription during period of 30 years under same conditions applicable to acquisitive prescription.

Acquisition of real property of foreigners is regulated by Immovable Property (Acquisition by Non-Residents) Act 1974.

Nonresident is defined as (i) any individual who is not citizen of Malta or who is not spouse of Maltese citizen; (ii) any association, corporate or otherwise, constituted in foreign country or has its principle place of business/residence abroad or if 25% or more of its share capital is owned by nonresidents

Nonresidents may purchase immovable property in Malta provided property to be used (i) as personal residence of applicant and family, or (ii) for approved industrial or tourist project.

Value of such property must exceed Lm15,000 and the nonresident must not own another property in Malta. Funds for acquisition of immovable property have to emanate from overseas. However, applicant may be granted loan from local banks provided that loan repayments are brought from overseas. Fee of Lm100 is payable to Government by applicant. On publication of deed of sale seller has to pay 13.6% sales tax.

REFERENDUM:

Law permits number of registered voters being not less than five and not more than ten to sign declaration proposing abrogative referendum. Proposal must be backed by at least 10% of total number of persons registered as voters for general elections in order that demand for referendum be accepted. Referendum may be held on all laws in Malta except Constitution of Malta and any provision thereof, European Conventions Act, and laws related to interpretation of statutes, general elections, fiscal matters, legislation giving effect to treaty obligations of Malta and bye-laws enacted by Local Councils.

Any person registered as voter or Attorney General on behalf of Government may file application in Constitutional Court requesting that referendum not be held on grounds that: number of persons having validly signed declaration was less than 10% of registered voters as required by law; provision relative to which referendum is demanded is one which cannot be subject of referendum; removal of provision to which referendum refers would render law incompatible with Constitution or European Convention Act; demand for referendum has been made before lapse of two years from date of previous unsuccessful referendum relative to same provision.

Referendum is valid only if 50%+1 of registered voters cast vote. Subsequent to successful referendum, President of Malta will issue Proclamation to effect that particular law to which referendum referred has been repealed.

SALES:

Sale is perfected when parties have agreed on object and price, although neither has been delivered and from that moment thing itself remains at risk and for benefit of buyer. Sale of immovable property, however, must be made by public deed and such contracts are binding on third parties only if recorded in Public Registry.

Promise to sell thing for fixed price shall not be equivalent to sale but if accepted it shall create obligation on part of promisor to carry out sale, or, if sale can no longer be carried out, to make good damages to promise.

All expenses of or incidental to contract of sale are at charge of buyer. However, in absence of agreement brokerage fees shall be borne by seller and buyer one-half each.

Principal obligations of seller are to deliver goods and to give certain warranties. If seller fails to make delivery at time agreed upon, buyer may elect either to demand dissolution of contract or to demand that he be placed in possession of thing sold.

Warranties.—Warranty which seller owes to buyer is in respect of quiet possession of thing sold and of any latent defect therein.

In absence of any express agreement there is implied warranty on part of seller warranting buyer against any eviction. Seller warrants buyer against latent defects only, and not against apparent defects which buyer might have discovered for himself. In said two cases buyer may elect either to restore thing and have price repaid to him or retain thing and have part of price repaid to him. If defects of thing were known to

SALES . . . *continued*
seller, he is not only bound to repay price received by him but he is also liable in damages towards buyers. Claims based on disturbance of quiet possession and latent defects must be brought in respect of immovables within one year as from day of contract and in regard to movables within one month as from day of delivery of thing sold. Where, however, it was not possible for buyer to discover latent defect of thing, said periods of limitation of action shall run only from day on which it was possible for him to discover such defect.

SHIPPING:

Legal Regime.—Main body of statutory maritime law is incorporated in Commercial Code and in Merchant Shipping Act (c. 234) (MSA) which later enactment is modelled on British Merchant Shipping Act. Number of international Maritime Conventions have been ratified by Malta including SOLAS 1974 and 1978 Protocol, International Load Line Convention 1966, International Tonnage Measurement Convention 1969, International Regulations for Preventing Collisions At Sea 1972, Convention for the Unification of Certain Rules relating to Assistance and Salvage at Sea 1910.

Regulatory Incentives.—MSA offers generous incentives to nonresident ship owners wishing to utilize Malta Flag. Shipping companies may be set up with minimum capital of Lm500, 20% paid up. Shareholders must be declared but there is no limitation on use of foreign trusts or corporations or shareholders. There are no restrictions on appointment of directors.

MSA accords exemption from income tax, death and donation duties and stamp duties if vessel exceeds 1,000 NRT. Specific exemption is necessary for smaller vessels. Shipping companies are exempt from exchange control if they are at least 80% foreign owned.

Crew Requirements.—Maltese registered vessels may be manned by officers and crew of any nationality. Local tax and social security contribution requirements are not applicable. Certificates of competence are to be provided within six months of registration.

Safety certification from internationally recognised classification society is necessary for registration. Vessels must comply with major safety conventions to which Malta is party (vide above) and with MSA provisions relatng to safety.

Carriage of Goods.—Main body of law is incorporated in the Commercial Code, MSA and Carriage of Goods by Sea Act 1954, as subsequently amended. Latter gives Hague Rules (appended as Schedule to Act) force of law.

Limitation of Liability.—MSA applies principles of Brussels International Convention relating to Limitation of Liability of Owners of Seagoing Ships.

Mortgages.—Provisionally or permanently registered vessels may constitute security through registration of mortgage on same. Mortgagee is treated very favourably by law. Mortgage constitutes execution title at law and in event of mortgagor's default, mortgagee is entitled to take possession of and sell ship or any share therein without necessity of lengthy court procedures. For purpose of security of actions and claims to which vessel is subject, ships are deemed to constitute separate and distinct assets within owner's estate. Mortgages rank high in list of debts accorded priority in event of distribution of proceeds of forced sale.

STATUTES:

All legislation in Malta is presently being recodified and updated under revised edition of Laws of Malta.

Legislation in Malta is first published in Government Gazzette before becoming operative.

STOCK EXCHANGE:

By Malta Stock Exchange Act, 1990 was established Malta Stock Exchange, institution which provides facilities for trading, purchase and sale of securities of quoted companies, corporate bodies and others issued by Government of Malta. Law, which basically follows EC Directives and Regulations in this field, provides inter alia for admission of licenced stockbrokers to membership of Stock Exchange, for confidentiality of Exchange Information, prohibition of insider dealing and for tax incentives for companies quoted on Malta Stock Exchange.

TAXATION:

Principal taxes under Maltese Law are following: Income tax (including tax on companies and tax on capital gains), death and donation duty, customs and excise duties, stamp duties (tax on documents and transfers), national insurance contribution, expenditure levy and number of other minor taxes, e.g., road tax on vehicles, etc. Malta has no property tax or wealth tax or municipal or local taxes. Sole taxing authority is Government of Malta and main taxes are assessed and administered by Commissioner of Inland Revenue.

Income Tax.—The Income Tax Act (c. 123) imposes tax upon income (including also capital gains) of any person (individuals or corporations), on following basis: (i) Income (and capital gains) arising in Malta is always subject to tax. (ii) Income (and capital gains) arising outside Malta is subject to tax if recipient is both domiciled and ordinarily resident in Malta, irrespective of whether such income is received in Malta or not. If recipient is either not ordinarily resident in Malta or not domiciled in Malta (or both) only income received in Malta is charged to tax.

Although Maltese system of tax is not schedular, following sources of income are specifically contemplated: Trade, business, profession or vocation, employment and offices, rental value of owner occupied houses, dividends, interest and discounts, pensions, charges, annuities or any other annual payments, rents and any other profits arising from immovable or real property, royalties, profit sharing in lieu of rentals in agriculture, sums realized under insurance against loss of profits, balancing charges (in respect of excess allowances for wear and tear), any distribution made on winding up of approved pension scheme, gains or profits of income nature not falling under any of above classifications. Fiscal year coincides with calendar year and assessment is on previous year basis. However permission in writing can be obtained by companies and other bodies to close accounts on day other than 31st Dec.

Foreign Source Income.—When income is divided from foreign source, relief from double taxation is extended so that company can practically ensure tax credit of 25% of tax due in Malta. Furthermore nonresident shareholders receiving dividends deriving from income originating from foreign source shall enjoy tax refund equivalent to 100% of tax paid by company in case of "participating holding company" and to 66.67% in case of all other companies. These measures have been introduced as alternative to offshore companies.

International Trading Companies.—Company registered in Malta engaged in carrying on any business activity from Malta with persons not resident in Malta and has its persons not resident in Malta and has its objects expressly limited to such activities and to such other acts as are necessary for its operations in Malta. Though company is liable for normal 25% company tax, nonresident shareholder will receive refund of about 30.83% of tax paid by company. This was introduced as alternative to offshore companies.

Individual Liability.—The Income Tax Act sets out number of rules for quantification of personal income from each source that is brought to tax. There are number of personal allowances which are granted to taxpayer by means of tax credit for tax due. Tax credit allowances vary according as to whether taxpayer is single or married and as to whether he is domiciled and ordinarily resident or not. Tax rates for computation of personal tax liability are on graduated scale reaching maximum of 35% where taxable income exceeds Lm4,100 (single person) or Lm5,000 (married person).

Since 1988 foreigners in possession of permit for permanent residence issued under Immigration Act 1970 are liable to income tax at flat rate of 15% on their chargeable income. Minimum liability after taking into account any double taxation relief to which such individual may be entitled is Lm1,000. Nonresidents whose stay does not exceed three months at any one time are not liable to tax. Temporary residents in possession of requisite permit are regarded as nonresidents for tax purposes.

Corporate Liability.—Taxable base of companies is same as that of individuals. Worldwide basis of taxation is thus applied to Maltese domiciled and ordinarily resident companies whether taxable income arises in Malta or elsewhere. Companies not ordinarily resident in Malta or not domiciled in Malta are liable for tax only on income received in Malta.

Companies pay income tax as fixed rate of 35% on net income. Net income is equivalent to aggregate income from all sources specified by law remaining after making allowance for exemptions and deductions admitted for expenditure employed wholly and exclusively in production of income.

Five deductions allowed by law are as follows: (i) Business expenses: these must be of noncapital nature but are not limited territorially. In case of no income, expense may be carried forward. (ii) Depreciation: allowance is made, initially and subsequently on wear and tear basis. (iii) Allowance is granted for debts that become bad during accounting period in question. (iv) Deduction is granted for legal and accountancy fees if paid in normal course of work and if necessary for running of business. (v) Rents paid for premises employed in generation of income also qualify as deduction.

Income Tax Act also provides for system of integration between tax paid by company on distributed profits and shareholders liability thereon. Upon distribution of dividend, Maltese registered or resident company is entitled to deduct tax from such dividend at rate paid by it (35%) on income out of which dividend is distributed. When dividend is taxed in shareholders hand, tax deducted by company is set off against shareholders' liability. Tax witheld by company is thus in effect payment on account of shareholders' liability.

All taxpayers be they individual or corporate are to file annual return of income containing such particulars, accounts and documentation as may be necessary to readily ascertain such persons' income. Return of capital assets owned on first of year of assessment is also required.

Death and donation duty has been repealed from Maltese legislation.

National Insurance Contributions.—The Social Security Act 1987 regulates collection and distribution of national insurance contributions. These are payable by employers and employees according to scale based on earnings.

Customs and Excise Duties.—Large variety of imported goods are subject to customs duties. Excise duties on other hand are levied on locally produced products, such as cigarettes, beer, soft drinks, etc.

Stamp Duty.—Some categories of commercial documents and legal documents as well as sales and other transfers (including transfers causa mortis) are subject to stamp duty levied under Duty on Documents and Transfers Act 1993. Ad valorem rates vary depending on class of documents/transfers involved.

Exemptions from above taxes are granted in terms of various investment incentive laws including, Industrial Development Act 1988, Malta International Business Activities Act 1988 (see topic Foreign Investment), Malta Offshore Trusts Act 1988 (see topic Trusts), Merchant Shipping Act (c. 234) (see topic Shipping), Malta Freeports Act 1989, etc.

Double Taxation.—Malta has signed Double Taxation Agreements with Australia, Austria, Belgium, Bulgaria, Canada, Denmark, Finland, France, Germany, Italy, Libya, Netherlands, Norway, Pakistan, Sweden, Switzerland, United Kingdom and U.S.A.

TREATIES:

Malta has Association Agreement with the European Economic Community (EEC). Most products manufactured in Malta enjoy unrestricted and tariff-free access to Common Market. Maltese Government submitted formal application for full membership in EEC in July 1990. Situation today is very similar to that obtaining vis-à-vis number of developed countries, such as U.S. and Canada, which classify Malta as developing country thereby granting preferential treatment to goods bearing Maltese certificate of origin. Malta is party to increasing number of Bilateral Agreements with countries such as Bulgaria, Turkey, Poland, Libya, Germany, U.S.S.R., Iraq, Czeckoslovakia.

TREATIES . . . *continued*

Malta has also signed Bilateral Investment Treaties with various countries such as Belgium, Germany, France, Italy, Netherlands, Libya, Switzerland and United Kingdom. Malta is also party to extensive array of Double Taxation Agreements (see topic Taxation).

TRUSTS:

Trusts are regulated by Trust Act 1988, which is broadly based on Jersey Trust Law.

Definition.—In terms of Act, trust exists where person called trustee, holds or has vested in him property under obligation to deal with that property for benefit of beneficiaries, whether or not yet ascertained or in existence, or for purpose which is not for benefit of trustee, or for both such benefit and purpose as aforesaid.

Trust whether created in Malta or abroad may qualify as offshore trust, provided that settlor and beneficiary are not resident in Malta and provided trust property does not include immovable property situated in Malta. It should be noted however that foreigner residing in Malta under permanent residence permit is regarded as nonresident for purposes of Act.

Creation and Registration.—Trust must be created by means of written instrument, whether by will or by unilateral declaration, and is subsequently registered with Malta International Business Authority. Initial registration formalities are complied with by filing with Authority certified copy of trust instrument and declaration by trustee that trust satisfies conditions of Act. Subsequent changes in trust deed must also be notified to Authority.

Trustees.—Only nominee companies licensed by Malta International Business Authority, to act as trustees for offshore trusts may be sole trustees; where trustees are more than one, one of such trustees shall be nominee company. Registration of trust may only take place through agency of such licensed nominee companies.

Trustee's duties may be defined in trust instrument but these cannot be excluded to extent greater than law provides. Trustees shall in execution of their duties and exercise of their powers and discretions act with prudence, diligence and attention of bonus pater familias and observe utmost good faith.

Other Features Of Trust.—Freedom to choose proper law. Proper law of trust is that chosen expressly or impliedly by settlor. In default Maltese Law applies.

Broad liberty of settlor to determine terms of trust. Discretionary trusts are also possible and "letters of wishes" are complied with. Protector arrangements are also recognised by Act.

Trust may continue for 100 years unless sooner terminated. Trusts for charitable purposes are not similarly restricted.

Fiscal and Regulatory Incentives.—Fee payable for registration of trust is Lm200. Tax is payable at fixed rate of Lm200 per year (on income of trust and its beneficiaries). Therefore no other tax on any other income is due by trustee and by its beneficiaries.

Trusts are exempt death and donation duties, stamp duties, custom duties and exchange controls.

No obligation to file any tax returns. Nominee company acting as trustee must however file annual declaration confirming that statutory conditions have been complied with.

Guarantees.—Rights, exemptions and privileges granted to offshore trusts are guaranteed for ten year period. Such guarantee is also applicable against retrospective action whether by legislation or otherwise.

Foreign Trusts.—Recent legislation, "The Recognition of Trusts Act", has codified various provisions from The Hague Convention on Trusts, so that foreign trusts are now recognized in Malta, and if registered with The Malta Financial Services Centre, foreign trust may appropriate all fiscal and other incentives applicable to Maltese Trust.

Foreign trust is trust whose proper law is other than Maltese law.

Proper law of trust is either chosen by settler or shall be deemed to be that law with which trust is most closely connected.

WILLS:

Will may either be public or secret. Public will is received and published by notary in presence of two witnesses. Secret will may be written out either by testator himself or by third person and then signed by testator. He shall deliver sealed document to notary or Court Registrar declaring on such delivery that document contains his will. Notary who receives secret will shall draw up act of delivery and this act shall be signed by testator, witnesses, and notary. Notary shall within four working days present such will to Court of Voluntary Jurisdiction.

Will made outside Malta shall have effect in Malta provided it is made in form prescribed by law of place in which will is made.

§592(i) of Civil Code provides for unica charta wills, i.e. wills made by husband and wife in one and same instrument; this is only instance where two persons can make joint will. Where such will is revoked by one of testators with regard to his or her estate, it shall continue to be valid with regard to estate of other. Secret unica charta wills are not allowed.

Persons over age of 18 years are capable of making will provided they are not illiterate, congenital deaf-mutes, interdicted persons on grounds of insanity and prodigality and persons who are not of sound mind at time of will. Persons over age of 14 but who have not completed their 18th year can only make remuneratory dispositions. On other hand persons unworthy of receiving by will include persons who killed or attempted to kill testator or charged him before competent authority with serious crime in spite of fact that they knew his innocence; persons who compelled or fraudulently induced testator to make or alter his will or prevented him from making new one or from revoking will already made, or suppressed, falsified or fraudulently concealed will. Any person who has been disqualified on any of said grounds can be rehabilitated by testator in subsequent will or by any other public deed. Members of monastic orders cannot dispose by will after taking their vows in religious order; nor can such persons receive under will except small life pensions.

Where testator leaves children or descendants surviving spouse cannot receive in ownership more than one-fourth of deceased's property. However, surviving spouse is entitled to usufruct of one-half part of deceased's estate. Law also provides for legitim which is portion of deceased's property which is reserved by law to descendants including illegitimate children or on their failure to his ascendants. Persons entitled to this "legitima portio" may be deprived thereof by specific declaration of testator in will on any of several grounds specified in law including inter alia case where descendant has refused maintenance to testator without reason or if descendant has been guilty of grevious injury against testator.

Legacies.—Any pure and simple legacy shall vest legatee, as from day of testator's death with right to receive thing bequeathed. Law provides for "legato di cosa altrui" and for legacies of life annuities and or pensions. Thing forming subject of legacy shall be presumed to have been bequeathed with its necessary accessories and in condition in which it shall be on day of testator's death. Any expense necessary for delivery or payment of legacy shall be charged to estate.

Testamentary Executors.—It shall be lawful for testator to appoint one or more testamentary executors but these must be confirmed by Court of Voluntary Jurisdiction, confirmation which would be forthcoming only after testamentary executor has entered into recognizance in records of court, with hypothecation of his property, to carry faithfully into effect testator's will and to render yearly account of his administration. Court may even require him to make up inventory. Pending procedure in confirmation executor may perform all that is necessary for preservation of estate. Testamentary executor may at any time renounce his office and he may also on good cause shown be removed from his office. In case of death, absence, renunciation or illness of only executor, execution of will shall vest in heirs unless court appoints some other person.

Revocation of Wills.—No person may waive power of revoking or altering any testamentary disposition made by him. Will may be revoked, wholly or in part, by subsequent will. Where subsequent will has not expressly revoked previous will or previous wills, it shall annul only such of dispositions contained in previous will or wills as shall be shown to be contrary to, or inconsistent with, new dispositions.

Provisions Common to Testate Successions and to Intestate Successions.—Action of demanding inheritance, or legacy or legitim shall lapse on expiration of ten years from opening of succession. No person is bound to accept any inheritance devolved on him; however renunciation cannot be presumed but may only be made by declaration filed in Court Registry. Heir who renounces testate succession forfeits all rights to intestate possession. Nevertheless his renunciation shall not operate so as to deprive him of right to demand any legacy bequeathed to him. Inheritance may be accepted unconditionally, or under benefit of inventory. Effects of inventory are that: (i) heir shall not be liable for debts of inheritance beyond value of property to which he succeeds; (ii) that he may free himself from payment of debts by giving up all property of inheritance to creditors, legatees and even to co-heir who does not similarly elect to give up the property; (iii) that his own property is not intermixed with property of inheritance, and that he shall retain his right to enforce payment of his own claims against inheritance.

Expenses of inventory and of account shall be at charge of inheritance.

Partition of inheritance may be demanded at any time. However, it shall also be lawful, by will, to suspend partition for time not exceeding five years.

See Topical Index in front part of this volume.

MEXICO LAW DIGEST REVISER

Curtis, Mallet-Prevost, Colt & Mosle
101 Park Avenue
New York, New York 10178-0061
Telephone: 212-696-6141
Fax: 212-697-1559
Email: CMP-NY@mcimail.com

Reviser Profile

The Firm began in 1830 when two practicing lawyers started a long line of lawyers and law firms extending in an unbroken chain up to the present time. In 1897, the firm name became Curtis, Mallet-Prevost & Colt; in 1925 it was changed to Curtis, Mallet-Prevost, Colt & Mosle. The Firm is now made up of approximately 120 lawyers, including experts who have published extensively on such diverse subjects as international money management, transnational contracts, state contracts, litigation against foreign states, sovereign immunity and the act of state doctrine, and the International Court of Justice. Its principal offices are in New York City. There are branch offices in Paris, London, Frankfurt Am Main, Hong Kong, Washington, D.C., Houston, Texas, Newark, N.J., and Mexico City. The Firm has five departments: Corporate and International; Litigation; Real Estate; Tax; and Trusts and Estates. The corporate and international department acts as general counsel to various public and private corporations and individual entrepreneurs. Clients are in the banking, insurance, securities, manufacturing, real estate and oil and gas industries. In addition, the corporate and international department frequently acts as special counsel to domestic and foreign clients, providing assistance in financing, know-how licensing, the negotiation and drafting of all types of contracts and instruments, counselling in all aspects of corporate law, and establishing the vehicles necessary to enable clients to conduct their domestic and foreign business activities. The Firm's international work permeates all areas of its practice and involves questions of private international law, foreign law and an unusual amount of public and quasi-public international law. Traditionally, much of the Firm's international practice has been concerned with Latin America. The Firm maintains its excellence in that area, with its Mexican affiliate, and also through the expertise of Latin American lawyers based in the New York office. The Firm's international practice has undergone a major expansion beyond Latin America to Europe, Africa and the Near and Far East. The Firm's litigation practice includes commercial litigation and arbitration, and white-collar criminal defense. It has substantial experience in civil aviation matters; it also has represented foreign States in transnational litigation and international arbitration arising out of acts of nationalization and alleged breach of economic development or natural resource supply contracts. Among the Firm's clients in real estate matters are institutional lenders and investors, real estate developers, both individual and corporate, foreign and domestic investors and syndicators. The tax department has substantial experience in all aspects of domestic and international business tax matters and real estate taxation. The matters the tax department deals with on a regular basis include: Taxation of foreign investments; the structuring of corporate transactions, including mergers, acquisitions, liquidations and reorganization; federal and state tax litigation; and tax planning for U.S. and foreign individuals. The trusts and estates department engages in general domestic trusts and estates practice and in tax planning for foreign persons wishing to invest in U.S. assets through offshore trusts and corporations. It represents individuals, trust companies, and banks acting as fiduciaries. It works for various charitable organizations located both in the United States and abroad including private foundations, museums, universities and hospitals. A group of fiduciary accountants with vast experience in the field assists the lawyers of the trusts and estates department. Curtis, Mallet-Prevost, Colt & Mosle has served as a Reviser for most of Latin American Law Digests since 1930.

MEXICO LAW DIGEST

(The following is a list of all Topics, including cross-references, covered in this Digest.)

MEXICO LAW DIGEST

Revised for 1997 edition by

CURTIS, MALLET-PREVOST, COLT & MOSLE, of the New York Bar.

(Abbreviations used are: C. C., Civil Code of Federal District; Com. C., Commercial Code; C. C. P., Code of Civil Procedure of Federal District. References are to articles of these Codes. See also topic Statutes.)

ABSENTEES: See topic Death.

ACKNOWLEDGMENTS:

Certificates of acknowledgment are unknown in Mexican law, since all documents which in the United States would ordinarily require a certificate of acknowledgment are executed before a notary public who certifies in the instrument itself to the facts which, in the United States, are usually expressed in a certificate of acknowledgment.

Documents executed in the United States should be acknowledged in the usual manner if they are to be used in Mexico. A certificate of the county clerk or other competent official as to the power of the notary to take the acknowledgment should be attached and a certificate of a Mexican consular or diplomatic officer should then be obtained to the effect that the signature of the county clerk or other official is authentic and that he is qualified to act. When the Minister of Foreign Relations of Mexico has attached a certificate regarding the qualifications of the consular or diplomatic officer the document may be recorded in the protocol of a Mexican notary by order of a competent court and is then duly recognized.

ACTIONS:

Actions for Death.—See topic Death, subhead Actions for Death.

Limitation of.—See topic Prescription.

ADMINISTRATION:

See topic Executors and Administrators.

ADOPTION:

A person over 25 years of age, free of marriage, and in full exercise of his civil rights may adopt one or more minors or an incapacitated minor or adult; in any case adopting party must be 17 years older than adopted. Individual exercising actual "Patria Potestad" must give his/her consent. Adopting party must prove: (a) Sufficient means to support them; (b) that adoption is beneficial to them; and (c) that he is person of good morals. Adopted party shall have rights and obligations of son. Husband and wife may also adopt when both agree to consider adopted as their own children, and when they are 17 years older than adopted. Adopted persons may use name of adopting party. Adoption can be revoked: (a) When both parties agree to do so, if adopted is over 18 years of age, and (b) in case of ingratitude of adopted. Ingratitude is deemed to exist when: (a) adopted commits intentional crime against adopting party or his family, or (b) if adopted brings criminal action against adopting party. (C. C. 390-410).

ADVERSE POSSESSION: See topic Prescription.

AGENCY: See topic Principal and Agent.

ALIENS:

According to Constitution of 1917 aliens have same individual guaranties as citizens. Guaranties are elaborately defined.

Aliens may not intervene in politics, and Federal Executive may require any alien to leave the country immediately and without trial in case his presence in Mexico is deemed undesirable. (Const., art. 33). Marriage in Mexico of aliens to Mexicans must be authorized by Department of Interior. Marriage and divorce must be authorized by Ministry of Interior. Entry of aliens is governed by General Law of Population of Dec. 11, 1973, as am'd and its Regulations of Aug. 31, 1992.

Naturalization is governed by Nationality Law of June 18, 1993.

Employment of Aliens.—(Labor Law, effective May 1, 1970 as am'd). Objective is to obtain equilibrium and social justice in labor-management relations; to work is both right and social obligation. These concepts are to be considered in interpreting law, and in case of doubt, interpretation most favorable to worker takes preference. In every enterprise or business at least 90% of workers must be Mexican. Technical and professional employments requiring special skills not available in country may be filled temporarily by foreign workers, but these may not be more than 10% of total number of workers engaged in each specialization area. Employer and foreign workers must be jointly responsible for training Mexican workers. Doctors on duty in factories or enterprises must be Mexicans. Provisions shall not be applicable to directors, administrators and/or general managers. Employment of aliens for maritime industries is prohibited.

Legal Rights for Foreigners to Reside in Mexico.—Art. 1 of Constitution of the United Mexican States provides that every person shall enjoy guarantees granted by that instrument; and principle of equality between nations—between Mexican and foreigners—is recognized in specific legislation.

Principle of equality between nationals and foreigners is subject to restrictions and limitations imposed by Constitution, regulatory laws that implement Constitution, and other legislation.

Migration to Mexico or entry for any purpose other than tourism is fraught with restrictions arising from statutes, administrative regulations, and internal policy. Latter, is fixed by Secretariat of Interior (Secretaria de Gobernación), General Bureau of Population (Direccion General de Población), and Department of Immigration (Departamento de Migración).

Immigration Categories.—Fact that alien is subject to these administrative proceedings points to differences between status of foreigner and that of citizen.

Foreigners are divided into three broad categories for purposes of immigration and according to which documentation is issued to them to legalize their presence in country. Each of these categories is further divided into sub-categories of immigration status.

General Law of Population establishes three general categories under which aliens may enter Mexico temporarily, or reside here as case may be, namely: (a) Nonimmigrant ("no-inmigrante"), (b) immigrant ("inmigrante"), and (c) one who has immigrated ("inmigrado").

Nonimmigrant Status ("No-Inmigrante").—Ten sub-categories included under this general heading are following:

1. Tourist ("Turista") status is extended to individual who comes to Mexico for pleasure, recreation or health or for activities of scientific, or artistic nature or to participate in sports. Maximum life of tourist permit is 180 days.

2. Individual in Transit ("Transmigrante") status is granted to individual simply passing through Mexico on transit visa. He is permitted limited period for stop-over en route to some other country.

3. Visitor ("Visitante") status is provided for individual whose purpose is to enter Mexico temporarily to engage in licit and honest activity for which he may be remunerated from source in Mexico or abroad. Such permit is granted for one year. However, if holder depends upon his own resources with which to live and which he has brought with him from outside of Mexico or from invested income generated by assets brought in and invested here or from any other income which has foreign origin; or if his activity in Mexico is of scientific, technical or artistic nature or if it pertains to sports, or similar activity, then in such event his visitante status pursuant to strict interpretation of law may be extended for four renewals of one year each.

4. Foreign Members of board of directors ("Consejero") of Mexican corporation entering to participate in board of directors and shareholders meetings may be granted visitors permit useful for attendance at such meetings. This temporary authorization is good only for one year; it may be extended four times. It provides for multiple entries and departures but no given sojourn in Mexico by holder of this status may exceed 30 days.

5. Alien Seeking Political Asylum ("Asilado Político") for protection of life and/or liberty may on occasion be admitted because he is suffering persecution by reason of political activity but only after Mexico carefully studies case. Such permit runs at pleasure of Gobernacion.

6. Student ("Estudiante") status is extended to individual approved to initiate, complete, or perfect studies in public institutions or private institutions whose programs are coordinated with National Educational Program or which have official authorization to operate. Annual extensions are issued with authority to remain in country during time required to complete his study program and to obtain documentation with respect to curriculum completed, provided that student may remain outside country during each year maximum of 120 days.

7. Refugee ("Refugiado") for alien seeking protection of his life, security or freedom because of violence, foreign agression, internal conflicts or violation of human rights in his own country.

8. Distinguished Visitor ("Visitante Distinguido") status is granted in special cases and in exceptional instances as matter of courtesy enabling recipient to enter and reside in Mexico; and its validity may run up to six months. This status may also be granted to those who are internationally recognized for their work in research or science, or in humanities or to journalists or other prominent individuals. Secretariat of Interior may extend life of such permit where it is deemed advisable.

9. Local Visitor ("Visitante Local").—Immigration officials may authorize alien calling at seaport or frontier city to enter provided that length of his stay on such permit may never exceed three days.

10. Provisional Visitor ("Visitante Provisional").—Secretariat of Interior is empowered to authorize as special exception disembarkation for period of up to 30 days for foreigner who wishes to stay in Mexico and who arrives at seaport or airport which is equipped for international services and where documentation held by foreigner lacks secondary (relatively unimportant) requisite to be valid for its holder to enter. In such special case deposit is required or bond must be posted to guarantee departure of alien from country in due course.

Immigrant Status ("Inmigrante").—Under this category entitled "Inmigrante" following eight sub-categories fall:

1. Individual Alien Sustained by Unearned Income ("Rentista" F.M. 2) sub-category is available to individual alien intending to live permanently and to be domiciled in Mexico who will rely for support upon resources brought with him into Mexico from outside country; from interest produced by investment here in certificates of deposit, credit instruments and/or bonds issued by government or by national banking institution or other sources which may be approved by Secretariat of Interior or finally, other permanent income from foreign source. Ministry of Interior may authorize "Inmigrante Rentista" to render personal services as professor or as scientist or to engage in scientific research and to function as technician where it deems such activity to be beneficial to country.

2. Investor ("Inversionista") sub-category is available to person immigrating to Mexico with intention to take up permanent domicile here bringing with him capital for investment in industry pursuant to Federal laws applicable to foreign investment and provided that investment contributes to economic and social development of nation and therefore is approved by Ministry.

See Topical Index in front part of this volume.

ALIENS . . . *continued*

3. Professional ("Profesional") status is granted for purpose of permitting given individual to practice his profession here. However, he must first register his professional degree or diploma with Bureau of Professions, Secretariat of Public Education, which must find it acceptable and approve it.

4. Confidential Personnel ("Cargos de Confianza") is classification applied to those individuals who are to serve in high level management capacity or other positions of trust and/or confidence in enterprise or institution established in Mexico, provided that in judgment of Secretariat of Interior there is no duplication in position or responsibility on staff of employer and that service which will be extended by given candidate for this status merits his being permitted to immigrate to Mexico.

Enterprise sponsoring individual seeking permit such as "Inmigrante" must have at least two-year operating history to qualify as such. Gobernacion is empowered to make exemptions although seldom does so.

5. Scientist ("Cientifico") status is granted to person who will direct or conduct scientific research, impart his scientific knowledge to others, prepare research personnel and do some teaching provided such activities are being conducted in interest of national development, in judgment of Ministry of Interior.

6. Technician ("Técnico") category is available to individual who is capable of carrying out applied research in field of production engaged in by his employer here or who is engaged to assume technical or special position provided capability required is not in judgment of Ministry of Interior available among current residents in country.

7. Family Members ("Familiares").—This status may be granted to dependent spouse of "inmigrante" or "inmigrado" or to dependent blood relative in direct line of descent of Mexican national and "inmigrante" or "inmigrado" without limit as to grade. Sons, daughters, nephews, grandchildren and brothers of "inmigrante" or "inmigrado" may also be admitted as "inmigrante familiares" as long as they are minors, unless they are students or if they are physically handicapped making it impossible for them to earn their livelihood.

8. Artists and Athletes ("Artistas y Deportistas") status is granted to artists and athletes to perform artistical and sport activities considered beneficial to country.

One Who Has Immigrated ("Inmigrado").—Each immigrant must renew his status at Ministry of Interior annually. At end of fifth year "inmigrante" is eligible to become "inmigrado" (one who has immigrated and acquired right to reside permanently in Mexico). In each case, however, applicant's situation is subject to review and appraisal by Ministry and every applicant must be specifically approved for this change in status. Neither annual renewals of "inmigrante" status nor final move to become "inmigrado" is automatically granted.

Under category "inmigrado" there are no sub-categories and no distinctions among them. This is status to which each foreign resident immigrant may aspire eventually to occupy. No matter sub-category group under which person may have been classified as "inmigrante", "inmigrado" status is one and same for all. "Inmigrado" is permitted to engage in any licit vocational activity anywhere in Republic (usually with exception of working as bartender).

"Inmigrado" may be absent from Mexico during 36 consecutive months without losing his or her status. Physical absence from Mexico in excess of 36 consecutive months results in forfeiture of said status; furthermore, accumulated absences in excess of five years over ten year period also cause extinction of status.

Administration of Immigration Law.—Granting of any immigration status, and issue of relevant documentation, are in fact and in law within discretion of Secretariat of Interior; they are not issued as matter of right. This is clear from General Law of Population, which stipulates that Gobernacion may deny aliens entry into Mexico or change of immigration status after entry when: (1) No reciprocity exists in matters of immigration between Mexico and country of applicant; (2) demographic interchange between Mexico and country of applicant is not in equilibrium; (3) quotas based on nationality, immigration category or vocational activities as fixed by Ministry of Interior have been filled; (4) granting of permit is deemed not to be in national interest; (5) conduct of applicant has not been in keeping with "morality and good customs"; (6) applicant has infringed Mexican law or regulation.

See also topic Foreign Investment.

ALIMONY: See topic Divorce.

ARBITRATION:

(C. Com. arts. 1415-1463). Law deals with domestic and international arbitration, and with recognition and enforcement of foreign arbitral awards. Any dispute arising out of specific legal relationship, when such dispute is under proper legal control of parties may be subject to arbitration. Arbitration agreement must be in writing, whether in form of arbitral clause in contract or in separate agreement. Invalidity of contract does not extend to arbitration clause contained therein, if reasons why contract is held invalid do not apply to such arbitration agreement. Arbitration agreement can be evidenced by any kind of document or by other means of communication which constitute record of agreement. Arbitrators may be empowered by parties to decide according to rules of law (en derecho) or ex aequo et bono (en conciencia). Number of arbitrators should be one unless parties have agreed on different uneven number.

Arbitrators have power to make provisional orders including interim measures of protection at request of either party, and to require any party to provide appropriate security in connection with such measures.

Mexico has ratified convention on International Commercial Arbitration, Panama 1975.

ASSOCIATIONS: See topic Partnership.

ATTACHMENT:

Attachments may be granted either before commencing an action or during the course of the same, in the following cases: (1) when there is reason to fear the defendant will abscond or conceal himself; (2) in an action in rem when it is feared that the defendant will conceal or injure the property; (3) in an action in personam when the defendant has no property other than that which is to be attached and it is feared that he will conceal or alienate it.

The plaintiff must prove his right to and the necessity for the attachment.

If the attachment is granted before the action is commenced, the plaintiff must give bond and the action must be begun within three days if the action is brought in the same place as the attachment is levied, plus an additional day for every 20 kilometers if brought in another place. (Com. C. 1168-93).

Certain documents entitle the holder to bring what is termed an executive action, in which case the plaintiff is entitled, as a matter of right, to attach the defendant's property. He may also be entitled to this right as a precautionary measure, as noted above. The following entitle the holder to executive action and consequently to attachment: (1) An executive judgment or nonappealable award; (2) public instruments (see topic Public Instruments); (3) judicial confession of the debtor; (4) bills of exchange, drafts, notes, orders and other commercial paper, providing, however, that such instruments are properly executed (see topic Bills and Notes); (5) policies of insurance; (6) awards of experts designated in insurance matters if given before a notary, if not so given, a judicial declaration of the experts, acknowledging their signatures and genuineness of the award, must first be had; (7) invoices, current accounts and any other commercial contract signed and judicially recognized by the debtor. (Com. C. 1391; Code of Civil Procedure Art. 443).

BANKRUPTCY:

Persons engaged in mercantile pursuits and mercantile corporations and partnerships which suspend payment may be declared to be in state of bankruptcy. Suspension of payment is presumed to exist: (1) When payment in general of matured debts of a liquidated amount has been suspended; (2) when execution has been levied by a creditor and sufficient property to satisfy his claim has not been found; (3) when merchant conceals or absents himself or closes his establishment without leaving a person in charge to cover his debts; (4) in case of assignment for benefit of creditors; (5) when merchant employs ruinous, fraudulent or fictitious means to discharge or avoid discharging his obligations; (6) when merchant applies for a declaration of bankruptcy; (7) when merchant petitions for suspension of payments and same is denied, or when, if petition is granted, no agreement is reached with creditors; (8) when merchant does not comply with obligations contracted with his creditors in suspension of payments proceedings.

A merchant may be declared bankrupt within two years of his death or retirement from trade, if it is proven that payment of his obligations ceased before his death or his retirement, or within the succeeding year. The estate of a merchant may be declared bankrupt when it continues enterprise in which merchant engaged and reasons for bankruptcy occur. Bankruptcy of a partnership brings about bankruptcy of unlimited partners. Bankruptcy of a partner does not necessarily bring about bankruptcy of partnership.

There are three classes of bankruptcies: (1) fortuitous; (2) culpable; (3) fraudulent. Declaration of bankruptcy may be made by court directly in cases provided by law, or upon written petition of merchant himself, or of any of his creditors or of District Attorney. Merchant applying for a declaration of bankruptcy must file in court a petition duly signed by him or by his legal representative stating reasons for his financial situation; with his petition he must file: (a) his account books; (b) a balance sheet; (c) a list of names and addresses of all his creditors and debtors, showing nature and amount of respective debts, and a statement of losses and profits during last five years; (d) a description showing a valuation of all his real and personal property, securities, merchandise and rights of any kind; (e) an appraisal and valuation of business as a whole. Order of court making declaration of bankruptcy must contain: (a) appointment of a receiver and of an inspector (interventor); (b) order to bankrupt to present his books and a balance sheet within 24 hours, if not filed with petition; (c) provision giving to receiver possession of all properties and rights, bankrupt being deprived of administration and disposition thereof, as well as an order to mail and telegraph offices that all correspondence of bankrupt be delivered to receiver; (d) prohibition to effect payments or to make deliveries of property to bankrupt; (e) call to creditors to file their credits within 45 days from last publication of bankruptcy declaration; (f) call for a meeting of creditors to be held within a period of 45 days beginning 15 days after period for filing credits; under special circumstances meeting of creditors may be held within a maximum period of 90 days; (g) order to register bankruptcy declaration in Public Registry Office where merchant is matriculated; (h) date as of which declaration of bankruptcy is retroactively made effective. Appointment of receiver must be made in favor of institutions or individuals in following order: (a) Chambers of commerce and industry; (b) National Credit Corporation. Law contains enumeration of persons not allowed to be receivers, such as blood relatives within fourth degree, either of bankrupt or of judge in charge, etc. Receiver must post bond, satisfactory to court, within 15 days of his appointment. Receiver's rights and obligations are those required in general for proper preservation and administration of property entrusted to his care. Receiver must render accounts every three months, together with report of his administration.

Creditors are represented either by one, three or five inspectors, according to volume of property involved. Inspector or inspectors are temporarily appointed by court upon making bankruptcy declaration: creditors later at their meeting by vote appoint permanent inspectors. If inspectors are to be three in number, majority of creditors appoints two, and other is appointed by minority; if they are to be five majority appoints three and minority two. Inspectors act as a board and their decisions are taken by a majority of votes. Meeting of creditors is called by court; call must be served personally on inspectors, on bankrupt and on receiver; other creditors are notified by publication in accordance with law. Creditors may attend meetings in person or by proxy. Meeting is held irrespective of number of creditors attending and volume of credits represented. Each creditor has one vote and resolutions are approved by absolute majority, except in cases where law requires special majorities or a majority in interest. Meetings of creditors are presided over by judge.

Bankrupt is deprived of administration and disposition of his property and of properties which he may acquire during bankruptcy proceedings; he may not leave locality where proceedings are being conducted without permission from court; if he requests permission to go abroad, court must consult with inspectors before acceding. He retains administration and disposition of certain properties such as: (a) rights

See Topical Index in front part of this volume.

BANKRUPTCY . . . *continued*
connected with his person, such as civil or political status, although they may indirectly have a patrimonial value; (b) properties constituting homestead; (c) profits obtained after declaration of bankruptcy, through exercise of personal activities, etc. All acts of ownership and administration by bankrupt concerning property affected by bankruptcy are void from moment bankruptcy is declared. Court, upon a report by receiver and by interventor, may grant temporary support to bankrupt and his family and fix its duration and amount.

All debts of bankrupt fall due at once and cease earning interest; mortgage and pledge credits, nevertheless, earn interest up to extent of respective guarantee. Property in hands of bankrupt which has not been transferred to him by a legal and irrevocable title is returned to its rightful owner.

Creditors are paid in a specified order of preference and are divided into five classes: (1) singularly privileged creditors; among these are creditors for funeral expenses and for expenses in connection with last illness leading to death of bankrupt, if bankruptcy is declared after death, and workers and employees for salaries during year preceding bankruptcy; (2) mortgage creditors; (3) special creditors to whom Code of Commerce or a special law grants a special privilege; (4) common commercial creditors whose credits are derived from mercantile operations; and (5) creditors under Common Civil Law; latter two classes being paid pro rata.

State of bankruptcy may end: (a) by payment either of total of credits or of percentage allotted during proceedings: (b) by lack of assets sufficient for payment of necessary expenses in connection with bankruptcy proceedings; (c) by failure of creditors to appear within period for filing credits; if only one creditor appears court declares bankruptcy terminated, and creditor may sue for payment in customary manner; (d) by unanimous agreement of creditors whose credits have been accepted and recognized. At any time during bankruptcy proceedings after admission and approval of credits and before final distribution of assets, bankrupt and his creditors may enter into agreements. Petition for agreement may be filed by bankrupt, by inspectors or by receiver. Petition must be filed together with a detailed plan for distribution among creditors, guarantees and periods of payment, and any other data regarding agreement. In order to be approved, petition for agreement must maintain absolute equality among non-privileged creditors. Court calls a meeting of creditors for discussion and approval of proposal; privileged creditors are free to attend meeting or not, without thereby endangering their position; proposal is published in a newspaper of large circulation at location of court, three times at intervals of five days, last publication being made at least five days before date of meeting.

Fortuitous bankrupts may be rehabilitated if they make formal promise to effect payment of unpaid debts as soon as their situation allows. Culpable bankrupts may be rehabilitated if they pay their debts in full immediately after serving their penalty; if they do not pay in full, they may be rehabilitated three years after serving penalty. Fraudulent bankrupts may be rehabilitated only if they pay in full and three years have elapsed after serving respective penalty. (Law of Dec. 31, 1942 as am'd).

BILLS AND NOTES:

"Law of Credit Instruments and Transactions" of Aug. 26, 1932 (Ley de Títulos y Operaciones de Crédito as am'd).

Bills of exchange must contain: (1) Statement that instrument is a bill of exchange; (2) place where and date when executed; (3) unconditional order to drawee to pay a certain sum of money; (4) name of drawee; (5) place and date of payment; (6) name of payee; (7) signature of drawer or of person executing instrument at his request or on his behalf. Bill may be drawn payable: (1) At sight; (2) at a certain period after sight; (3) at a certain period after date; (4) on a certain date. If drawn payable at other times or when time of payment is not expressed, bill is payable at sight. If bill is drawn payable one or several months after date or sight, payment must be made on corresponding day of month of maturity; if there is no such day, on last day of such month. If time of payment is stated to be "at the beginning," "at the middle" or "at the end" of any month, payment must be made respectively on first, fifteenth and last day of month. Expressions: "Eight days" or "one week," "fifteen days" or "two weeks," "a fortnight" or "half a month" are understood to mean not one or two whole weeks but periods of eight or fifteen days, respectively. If due date is a holiday, bill must be paid preceding day. Intermediate holidays are included in count of periods. Bill may be drawn to order of drawer; if drawn against drawer it must be payable at a different place. Bill may not be drawn to bearer. Bill, note or check drawn payable to a designated person is considered drawn to his order, unless instrument or an endorsement contains the words "not to order" or "not negotiable."

Bill of exchange is transferable by endorsement, which may be made: (1) To transfer ownership of bill; (2) for collection or (3) as security. Regular endorsement must contain: (1) Name of endorsee; (2) signature of endorser; (3) nature of endorsement; (4) place and date; but only endorsement of checks under five million pesos may be in blank and if made to bearer it is understood to be in blank. Endorsement must be unconditional. Partial endorsement is ineffective. Endorsement must be written on bill or on a paper attached thereto. Endorsement transferring ownership of bill makes all endorsers of this kind jointly liable, but any endorser may avoid liability by inserting phrase "without recourse" or some equivalent. Drawer may not waive liability; he is responsible for acceptance and payment of bill.

Bill must be presented for acceptance at place and address stated thereon. Lacking such statement presentation for acceptance must be made at domicile of drawee. If various places are designated for acceptance, holder may present bill at any of them. Bill drawn at a certain time from sight must be presented for acceptance within six months after date; but any obligee may reduce, or drawer may extend, said period by so stating on bill. If a bill is not presented for acceptance within proper time, holder loses his rights against endorsers and drawer. Acceptance is effected by writing "I accept" or its equivalent but mere signature of acceptor is sufficient evidence of acceptance. Bill may not be accepted conditionally but may be accepted for part of amount.

"Aval" is a guaranty by one who is not a party to bill. It may be made on bill or on a separate paper attached thereto.

Bill must be presented for payment at place and time stated. If drawn at sight it must be presented within six months after date but any obligee may reduce, or drawer may extend, period by so stating on bill. Payment may be made in part; but holder must protest for unpaid balance and retain bill until complete payment is effected. Holder may refuse to accept payment before due date. There are no days of grace.

Bill of exchange should be protested for partial or total nonacceptance or nonpayment. Protest is made before a notary public or broker if there be any in place, and if not, before highest political authority. Protest for nonacceptance must be made within two days after presentation, but always before due date, protest for nonpayment must be made within two days after due date; bill payable at sight should be protested on presentation or within two days following. Bill protested for nonacceptance need not be presented for payment or protested for nonpayment. Record of protest should contain: (1) Literal copy of bill, including acceptance, endorsements, etc.; (2) fact of presentation and whether or not person who should have accepted or paid was present; (3) reasons for refusal to accept or pay; (4) signature of person against whom protest is made or statement of impossibility or refusal to sign if such be case; (5) place, date and hour of protest; (6) signature of person before whom protest is made.

Acceptor, drawer, endorsers and guarantors are jointly liable to holder for amount of bill, interest, costs of protest and all other legitimate expenses. Holder of a bill duly protested may exercise his right of action against all of persons signing, or against some or any of them. Any endorser who pays has same right against previous endorsers and drawer.

Last holder of a bill duly protested, as well as any endorser who pays same, may reimburse himself by: (1) Charging to, or asking credit in account from other obligees for amount of bill, interest and other costs; or (2) drawing at sight against said obligees for amount of bill, interest and other costs. In both cases respective notice or bill of exchange should be accompanied by original bill, a copy of protest and an account of costs, including those of new bill. (Law of Aug. 26, 1932, arts. 25-41, 76-169).

Promissory notes must contain: (1) Statement that instrument is a promissory note; (2) unconditional promise to pay a certain amount; (3) name of payee; (4) time and place of payment; (5) date and place of issue; (6) signature of maker or of person signing on his behalf. If no time of payment is stated, promissory note is payable at sight. If payable at a certain time after sight, promissory note must be presented within six months after date. Most of provisions with regard to bills of exchange concerning endorsement, payment, protest, etc., are applicable to promissory notes. (Law of Aug. 26, 1932, arts. 170-174).

Checks may be drawn only against banks or other credit institutions and must contain: (1) Statement that instrument is a check; (2) place and date of issue; (3) unconditional order to pay a certain sum; (4) name of drawee; (5) place of payment; (6) signature of drawer. Checks are always payable at sight and may be payable to a designated person or to bearer only when they are under five million pesos. Check must be presented for payment: (1) Within 15 days after date, if payable at place of issue; (2) within one month, if payable at different place within national territory; (3) within three months if drawn abroad for payment in Mexico; (4) within three months if drawn in Mexico for payment abroad, provided foreign law does not state different period. Drawer may not stop payment on check during above periods. Bank, if it has funds of drawer, must pay check or be liable for damages, which may not be less than 20% of amount of check. Bank may refuse payment if it has notice that drawer is in state of bankruptcy or suspension of payments. Check presented at clearing house is considered as presented to drawee. Check presented in time and not paid must be protested within two days after presentation, in manner of bill of exchange payable at sight. For failure to present or protest, holder loses his right of action against endorsers, drawer and their guarantors; but in case of drawer and his guarantors they must prove that they had made provision of funds for payment and that such funds were available at time when presentation or protest should have been made.

There are special provisions regarding "crossed checks," "checks to be credited on account of holder," "certified checks," "cashier's checks" and "traveler's checks"; and most of provisions with regard to bills of exchange concerning endorsement, payment, protest, etc., are applicable to checks. (Law of Aug. 26, 1932, arts. 175-207).

CHATTEL MORTGAGES:

Chattel mortgages may be given in shape of pledges in which pledged objects remain in possession of debtor. In such case pledge must be recorded in public registry (C. C. 2859) and rules relating to pledges (q. v.) apply. Industrial and agricultural loans may be secured by mortgage on prime materials, products, machinery, tools, crops, etc.; such mortgages must also be recorded. (Law Aug. 26, 1932, arts. 321-333). Mortgage of real property includes machinery and utensils used in conducting industry established thereon, animals required for cultivation of estate and animals on stock farms used for breeding purposes. (C. C. 750, 751, 2896).

CLAIMS:

See topic Executors and Administrators.

COMMERCIAL REGISTER: See topic Records.

COMMISSIONS TO TAKE TESTIMONY:

See topic Depositions.

COMMUNITY PROPERTY:

See topic Husband and Wife.

CONDITIONAL SALES:

See topic Sales (Realty and Personalty).

CONSTITUTION AND GOVERNMENT:

(Constitution of Feb. 5, 1917 as am'd).

Mexico is federal, democratic, representative Republic composed of States and Federal District, which are free and sovereign in all that concerns their internal government, but united in Federation according to constitutional principles. States have their own Constitution based upon federal constitution.

See Topical Index in front part of this volume.

CONSTITUTION AND GOVERNMENT . . . *continued*

Legislative power of Republic is exercised by Congress formed by Chamber of Deputies and Chamber of Senators. Chamber of Deputies is composed of representatives of nation, elected every three years. Chamber of Senators is composed of two members of each State and two of Federal District. Half of Chamber is replaced every three years. Executive Power is exercised by President elected by direct popular vote for six years and cannot be reelected. Judicial Power of federal government is vested in Supreme Court of Justice, in collegiate circuit tribunals and in district courts. States and Federal District have their own judiciary system for State and Federal District matters.

See topic Foreign Investment.

CONTRACTS:

In area of contracts as in other branches of civil law distinction between commercial and civil transactions must be continually borne in mind. Commercial Code contains special rules governing commercial contracts, principal purpose of which is to simplify procedure. Commercial Code provides that in mercantile transactions parties are bound in manner and terms upon which they appear to have obligated themselves and that validity of commercial transactions does not depend upon observance of definite formalities and requisites except: (1) In cases where code requires an agreement to be in form of a public document (for example articles of association of a corporation or partnership) or where special formality or solemnity is required to render it effective (as for example bills of exchange); and (2) that in case of agreements executed in foreign countries they must comply with formalities required in country of execution regardless of whether or not such formalities are required in Mexico. (Com. C. 78, 79). Commercial contracts may be evidenced by correspondence, contract being complete from time offer is accepted and by telegrams if that class of document has been agreed upon in writing between parties and if telegrams conform with conditions and conventional signs, if any, previously agreed upon. (Com. C. 80). Certain classes of commercial contracts are not perfected until a record of them is made before registered broker who is a sort of commercial notary (corredor). (Com. C. 82).

With modifications and restrictions established by Commercial Code, provisions of civil law governing civil contracts as they relate to capacity of parties, exceptions and causes which rescind or invalidate contracts, are applicable to commercial contracts. (Com. C. 81).

If contract consists of offer and acceptance made at different places, and time within which acceptance must take place is not stated in offer, offer is considered as remaining open and offerer bound for three days in addition to time necessary for regular passage of mail between two places or time deemed sufficient in case there are no public mails taking into account distances and facility or difficulty of communication, unless there is a mistake relating to fundamental motive of one of parties. If an acceptance is not absolute it is considered as a new offer. Contracts are void for mistake of law. Mistake of arithmetic is only subject to correction. (C. C. 1803-1823).

Certain contracts must be in writing, such as contracts agreeing to make a future contract, sales of real estate, leases, pledges, mortgages, etc. Writing must be in form of public instrument depending on value of real property sold or mortgaged calculated according to formula set forth in C.C. Also public instrument is required in lease of rural property when lease exceeds value set forth in C.C. (C. C. 1832, 2317-2320, 2406, 2407, 2860, 2917. See topic Public Instruments). Reference is made to Civil Code of various jurisdictions for provisions of law with regard to interpretation of contracts, classes of obligations, performance, extinction of obligations, rescission, etc., and special classes of contracts such as suretyship, pledge, bailments, loans, insurance, sales, leases, etc.

See topic Sales (Realty and Personalty).

CONVEYANCES: See topic Deeds and Registration.

COOPERATIVE SOCIETIES: See topic Corporations (Sociedades Anonimas).

COPYRIGHT:

(Law of Nov. 4, 1963, as am'd by Decree of Nov. 16, 1963, Decree of Dec. 30, 1981 and Decree of July 17, 1991).

By this law an author is entitled to: (1) Recognition of his quality as author; (2) right to oppose deformations, mutilations, or modifications of his work and any action detrimental to same or to author's honor and reputation, excepting scientific, literary or artistic criticism, and (3) right to use and exploit work.

Rights under (1) and (2) are personal, perpetual, inalienable, statute of limitations won't run and irrenunciable and pass to author's heirs or testamentary beneficiaries. Rights under (3) are assignable and include reproduction, exhibition, performance, etc. of work by any means, especially in manner established in International Treaties and Conventions to which Mexico is party.

Works Protected.—Protection is granted in respect to literary, scientific, juridical, didactic, musical, choreographical, pictorial, architectural, photographic, and cinematographic works; computation programs; works for broadcasting and television, and any other works which, by analogy, can be regarded as artistic or intellectual productions and as long as they are expressed in form of writing, engraving, or in any other objective and durable form capable of reproduction or communication to public by any means. These works remain protected, even without registration. Arrangements, compendiums, translations, versions, graphic characteristics, etc., having originality of their own are protected to extent of such originality. Articles on current events may be reproduced unless prohibited by special or general reservation. In all cases, when reproduced, source must be given. Fictitious or symbolical personalities in literary works having definite originality may be subject of protection. Law also protects advertisement to be broadcast by any means.

Duration.—Copyrights remain in force: (1) For life and 50 years after author's death. Then, or before if there are no heirs, they become public domain. (2) In case of posthumous works, term is 50 years from date of first publication. (3) If author remains anonymous for 50 years from first publication, right passes into public domain. (4) In case of joint authors, 30 year period begins upon death or last survivor. (5) In case of works owned by Federation, States and Municipalities duration is 50 years.

Notice.—Every copy of protected works must display phrase, "Derechos Reservados," or abbreviation "D.R.", followed by symbol "©", name and address of owner, and year of first publication. Absence of these requirements does not destroy copyright, but publisher may be liable. Name and address of publisher, number of copies and date of completion of printing must also appear.

Copyright does not extend to: (1) Industrial application of ideas; (2) use of a work by reproductions or representation on occasion of a current event, provided it is not for profit; (3) translations or reproductions in form of brief extracts from scientific, literary or artistic works in educational publications, or for criticism or scientific research; and (4) copyright by hand, typewriting, photography, microfilm, etc. of a published work, provided it is for exclusive use of person making copy.

Limitations of Author's Rights.—Publication of literary, scientific, educational or artistic works necessary or helpful to advancement of public education or national culture is considered matter of public interest. Federal Executive may restrict a copyright and authorize publication of a work: (1) when for period of one year there has been no copy available in Mexico City and in three of principal cities of country, and (2) when sold at a price which precludes general use. Special procedure with intervention of author is established for this purpose. Ten percent of value of retail selling price of edition is deposited in at disposal of author. If edition is to be distributed free of charge, 10% of cost applies.

After seven years from first publication, Department of Education may grant to any Mexican or resident of Mexico a nonexclusive licence to translate and publish a work in Spanish. Applicant must prove that after request he has not obtained authorization from author.

Registration.—Copyright Directorate of Department of Education is in charge of Copyright Register, in which are recorded: Works submitted by authors; agreements or contracts which in any manner confer, modify etc., patrimonial rights of author; powers of attorney to act before Copyright Directorate, etc.

In case of two petitions for registration of a work first applicant prevails without prejudice to other to contest it.

Documents originating abroad submitted as proof of rights do not require legalization, but must be translated into Spanish under responsibility of applicant.

Commercial or civil societies, institutions, academies, etc. can only hold copyrights as successors in title to physical authors.

Publication Contract.—"Edition" contracts do not entail alienation of patrimonial rights of owner of work.

Foreigners residing permanently or temporarily in Mexico enjoy same rights of national authors. If author is national of state with which Mexico has no treaty or convention, or if work is first published in country with which Mexico has no treaty, copyright is subject to reciprocity, protection lasting seven years. If at expiration of this period work has not been registered in Mexico, any person may publish it with permission of Department of Education. If after seven-year period author registers his work, he enjoys full protection, except regarding editions previously authorized.

Authors' Associations.—Law contemplates the creation of authors' associations, composed of individual Mexican authors and foreign authors resident in Mexico, and of one General Association of Authors, whose members are various individual associations throughout country. Functions of individual authors' associations are: (1) To represent their members before judicial and administrative authorities; (2) to collect and distribute fees or royalties for publication or performance of works of their members pursuant to authorization conferred on them by national authors, and without it when author has not collected royalties for period of two years. Law authorizes Association to collect royalties on behalf of foreign authors, without authority conferred on them, but distribution of such amounts is subject to principle of reciprocity; (3) to enter into publication contracts in matters of general interest for their members; (4) to make contracts with foreign associations; (5) to contract on behalf of their members pursuant to authority conferred on them. General Association of Authors acts as general representative of authors and their associations, exercises general supervision over production of Mexican intellectual works, represents Mexican authors in dealings with foreign associations, and acts as arbitrator in copyright matters.

Intellectual Property Commission (Comisión Intersecretarial para la Protección, Vigilancia y Salvaguardia de los Derechos de Propiedad Intelectual) is in charge of overseeing proper application, compliance with and enforcement of intellectual property law. Commission is empowered to impose "exemplary sanctions".

Treaties.—Mexico signed inter-American Convention on Copyright and Literary Property in Washington, June 22, 1946, which was promulgated by Presidential Decree of Oct. 3, 1947, and also ratified Universal Copyright Convention and became bound by it on May 12, 1957, and by Decree of Aug. 11, 1975, ratified revision of July 24, 1971 of this Convention made in Paris. By Decree of Sept. 20, 1974, Mexico ratified Act of Paris of Berne Convention for protection of literary and artistic works of July 24, 1971.

CORPORATIONS (SOCIEDADES ANONIMAS):

Caveat: As to corporations which have foreign participation, certain special requirements must be met. (See topic Foreign Investment).

Provisions relating to corporations are found largely in General Law of Commercial Companies, of July 28, 1934 as am'd.

Special permit from Secretary of Foreign Relations is required to organize any corporation. (Law of Dec. 23, 1993).

Name of Mexican corporation may be freely chosen, but words "Sociedad Anónima" or abbreviation "S.A." must appear at end of corporate name.

Organization.—Corporations are formed either by public subscription or by articles of incorporation executed by at least two persons and each should subscribe at least one share. Minimum capital of 50 million pesos wholly subscribed is required. When shares are to be paid in cash, 20% of value must be paid in, and if payment is to be made in property other than cash total value of shares must be paid in.

CORPORATIONS (SOCIEDADES ANONIMAS) . . . *continued*

Public Subscription.—In case of formation by public subscription following rules prevail:

(a) Promoters must file in Public Registry of Commerce a prospectus signed by them, setting forth proposed by-laws and stating: (1) Object, (2) name and duration of corporation; (3) capital; (4) whether or not capital shall be variable, indicating minimum authorized in case it be variable; (5) domicile of company; (6) manner in which administration is to be carried on and powers of directors; (7) manner of electing directors and designation of those entitled to sign on behalf of company; (8) manner of distribution of profits and losses among members; (9) reserve fund; (10) cases in which company must be dissolved before expiration of its term; (11) manner of liquidation; (12) what part of capital paid in; (13) number, par value and nature of shares into which capital is divided, but shares may be without par value; (14) manner and time in which balance of subscribed capital must be paid; (15) participation in profits allowed to promoters; (16) powers of stockholders' meetings and other provisions regarding voting rights.

(b) Subscriptions to capital stock must be taken on two copies of prospectus, duplicate copy being left with subscriber. In taking subscriptions, following must be stated: (1) Name, nationality and domicile of subscriber; (2) number, nature and value of shares subscribed and manner of payment; (3) what property, if any, other than money, is given in payment for shares; (4) date of subscription and statement by subscriber that he is acquainted with and accepts proposed by-laws.

(c) All shares must be subscribed within one year from date of prospectus unless shorter period is fixed therein.

(d) If at expiration of subscription period, whole capital stock is not subscribed, or for any other reason constitution of company is not concluded, subscribers are released and entitled to recover amounts paid in.

(e) Cash payments are made by deposits in credit institution designated in prospectus; and are delivered to company when constitution is perfected. Property given in payment for subscription must be deeded to company on its constitution.

(f) A stockholders' meeting is held after capital is subscribed and at least 20% of same is paid. At this meeting first payment of 20% of capital must be acknowledged, value assigned to various properties, other than cash, contributed in payment of stock is also approved, but persons contributing such properties may not vote on their value, profits reserved for promoters of company are discussed, first directors and inspectors (comisarios) are appointed, and those empowered to sign for company are designated.

(g) Minutes of the stockholders' meeting and by-laws are protocolized and registered.

Articles of Incorporation.—When public subscription is not resorted to, it is sufficient that articles of incorporation be executed as a public document by incorporators. Such articles must state: (1) Names, nationality and residences of incorporators; (2) object, name and duration of company; (3) capital of company, contributions in cash or in other property, specifying value of latter and manner in which determined, together with statement as to whether or not capital shall be variable, if variable minimum authorized capital should be indicated; (4) domicile of company; (5) manner in which administration will be carried on and powers of directors; (6) manner of electing directors and designation of those entitled to sign on behalf of company; (7) manner of distribution of profits and losses among members; (8) reserve fund; (9) cases in which company must be dissolved before expiration of its term; (10) manner of liquidation; (11) what part of capital paid in; (12) number, par value and nature of shares into which capital is divided, but shares may be without par value; (13) manner and time in which balance of subscribed capital must be paid; (14) participation in profits allowed to promoters; (15) powers of stockholders' meetings and other provisions regarding voting rights. Foregoing provisions and others which may be added constitute both articles of incorporation and by-laws. Articles of incorporation and amendments must be recorded in Commercial Registry on judicial order; petition must be filed before competent judge and summary proceeding follows.

Effect of Organization.—Corporation cannot be declared void after being registered, except when object or purpose is illegal or when carrying on illegal business; in this case, any person may apply for immediate liquidation of corporation, then debts of company must be paid and remainder of assets applied to indemnify injured parties and to public charity. In such cases persons in control of company, whether or not owning a majority of its shares, are secondarily and without limitation liable for illicit acts of company.

Shares of stock are generally of equal value and confer equal rights; but articles of incorporation may provide for different classes of shares with special rights for each class. Each share has one vote; but it may be agreed that some of the shares can be voted only at special meetings called for extraordinary purposes stated in law, such as increase or reduction of capital, changes of object, bond issues, etc.

Shares with limited voting power must be reimbursed in preference to common shares in case of liquidation of company, and their holders have right to oppose resolutions of stockholders' meetings and to examine balance sheets and books of company.

No shares may be offered for sale to public without an authorization from Federal Government, unless shares are listed in a stock exchange.

Shares cannot be issued for less than their face value and can be non-assessable only when fully paid. Subscribers and acquirers of shares not fully paid are responsible for unpaid balance; this liability expires in five years from date of transfer, and no action can be taken against transferor before action is taken against transferee. On due date of amounts owing for subscriptions of shares company may either bring action or have shares sold through broker; if in either case, and within one month after due date, no action is taken or sale of shares cannot be made, such shares are cancelled and capital reduced accordingly. Shares must be issued within one year from date of articles of incorporation or any amendment increasing capital.

Shares must be issued in form provided by law, and must bear dividend coupons which must be nominatives. Company must keep stock register for registered shares, and to all effects persons appearing in such register are considered as owners of such shares. Articles of incorporation may provide that transfer of registered shares can be effected only with authorization of board of directors, which may deny said authorization and designate buyer at market price. Transfers of registered shares otherwise than by endorsement must be noted on stock certificate. No issue of shares can be made until previous issues have been wholly paid. Corporations cannot acquire their own shares unless by judicial proceedings and in payment of corporate credits, in which case company must sell shares within three months after acquisition; if resale is not made within that period shares are cancelled and capital reduced accordingly. Shares acquired by company cannot be voted at meetings of shareholders. In case of reduction of capital through reimbursement to shareholders of price of their shares, shares to be cancelled must be drawn before notary public or broker.

Treasury stock may be issued for convertible bond or debenture issues only.

Corporations are allowed, when articles of incorporation so authorize, to issue "workers' shares" (acciones de trabajo) and "participating shares" (acciones de goce). Former may be issued to employees of company under special conditions and restrictions. Latter share in net profits after dividends have been paid on common shares.

Corporations cannot grant loans or advances on their own shares. Shares issued for property other than cash must be deposited with company during two years; if value of property then appears to be 25% less than its estimated value, shareholder is liable for difference and company has a preferred lien on deposited shares.

Management may be in hands of sole administrator or of board of directors elected by stockholders but who need not be stockholders. Law calls them mandatorios. There may also be managers appointed by stockholders or board of directors or sole administrator and removable by them at any time. When directors are three or more, articles of incorporation must determine rights of minority stockholders in their election, but in any event minority representing 10% of capital is entitled to at least one director whose appointment can only be revoked jointly with that of all other directors. Administrators, directors and managers must furnish bond as determined in by-laws or by stockholders; administrators and directors are liable as agents and in manner provided by law and in by-laws; they are also responsible to company for faithful performance of their duties.

Supervision of affairs of company is in hands of one or more inspectors called "comisarios," who may, but need not, be shareholders and who are appointed by shareholders; they must give bond and their responsibility is similar to that of directors. Comisarios shall demand from board or managers financial monthly report.

Shareholders' meetings are regular or special and are known as general assembly. They must be held at corporate domicile. Regular meetings are held at least once a year within four months after close of fiscal year. Special meetings may be held at any time to decide on matters specially enumerated by law, such as modification of articles of incorporation, bond issues, etc. Meetings are called by administrator, board of directors, or inspectors, and in some cases by holders of at least 33% of capital stock. Notice must be published at least fifteen days before date of meeting, unless a different period is provided in by-laws, in official newspaper of state where company is domiciled or in a newspaper of large circulation in said domicile; notice must contain agenda or statement of matters to be submitted; but these requisites may be omitted if all shares are found represented at time of voting. At least half capital must be represented, and resolutions adopted by meeting are valid when taken by a majority of shares represented. At special meetings at least three-fourths of capital stock must be represented and resolutions must be approved by shareholders representing at least half capital stock. Shareholders may appear by proxy in form described by by-laws; when by-laws do not provide, proxies must be in writing. They may not vote on matters in which they have an interest contrary to that of company. Directors, administrators and inspectors may not hold proxies or vote on approval of accounts or on matters affecting their personal responsibility.

Dividends may not be paid on common shares unless a dividend of 5% has been paid on shares having limited voting power. Articles of incorporation may provide that dividend on shares having limited voting power be larger than that on common shares. When shares are not fully paid, dividends may be paid only in proportion to part paid in. By-laws may provide for payment, during a period not exceeding three years from date of respective issue, of interest not exceeding 9% per annum on shares; this interest is charged to general expenses.

Reserve Funds.—At least 5% of net earnings must be set aside each year as a legal reserve fund until such fund amounts to one-fifth of capital of company. Reserve fund must be built up in same manner if depleted.

Stockholders at general meeting are authorized to set aside not more than 10% of net earnings as a further reserve fund for reinvestment in improvements or for promotion of corporate purposes.

Bonds and other obligations issued by corporations are payable to designated person or to bearer when registered at National Securities Registry. They may be in denominations of 100 pesos or multiples thereof. Holders of obligations of same series must have equal rights. Obligations must contain: (1) Name, nationality and domicile of holder when required; (2) paid-in capital, and statement of corporation's assets and liabilities are shown by balance sheet specially prepared for issue; (3) amount of issue, number of obligations and par value of same, (4) rate of interest; (5) time of payment of interest and principal, and periods, conditions and manner of amortization; (6) place of payment; (7) list of special guaranties, if any, with registration data relating thereto; (8) place and date of issue and date and number of registration entry in Registry of Commerce; (9) signatures of authorized officers of corporation; (10) signature of authorized representative of holders of obligations. No clause may be inserted providing for amortization by drawings at a price above par or with premiums, unless interest payable to all obligation-holders is in excess of 4% per year and periodical sum set aside for amortization and payment of interest is same during entire amortization period. No issue may be made for an amount greater than net assets of corporation as shown in balance sheet specially prepared for that purpose, unless issue is intended to provide value or price of property for whose acquisition or construction corporation has contracted.

Law permits corporations to issue convertible bonds or debentures and then they may issue treasury stock to cover issue. This stock is not subject to preemptive rights.

In connection with issue corporation must execute an instrument before a notary public, which must be recorded at registry office of place where property mortgaged, if any, is located, and also at registry office of domicile of corporation. Such instrument

See Topical Index in front part of this volume.

CORPORATIONS (SOCIEDADES ANONIMAS) . . . *continued*
must contain: (1) Name, object and domicile of corporation; (2) paid-in capital and a specially prepared balance sheet, certified to by a public accountant, showing corporation's assets and liabilities; (3) minutes of shareholders' meeting at which issue was authorized; (4) minutes of director's meeting at which authority was given to one or more persons to sign instrument and obligations; (5) amount of issue, number of obligations and their par value; (6) interest rate; (7) time of payment of interest and principal and periods, conditions and manner of amortization; (8) place of payment; (9) security, if any; (10) destination of proceeds of issue, when they are in excess of net assets of corporation; (11) designation of representative of obligation-holders, together with his declaration to effect that he (a) has verified net assets declared by corporation, (b) has verified existence and value of property mortgaged or pledged and (c) will act as depositary of proceeds of issue to be applied to acquisition or construction of property.

Representative of obligation-holders may not be a holder himself, and may be an individual or corporation; holders may remove him at any time; his duties and powers are enumerated by law, but they may be expressly increased by instrument of issue.

A majority of outstanding obligations constitutes a quorum at ordinary meetings of obligation-holders; decisions must be approved by a majority vote of obligations represented. Three-quarters of outstanding obligations must be represented and vote of a majority thereof is required to (a) designate or remove representative of obligation-holders or (b) to grant extensions to corporation or amend instrument of issue.

Obligation-holders themselves may sue corporation for payment of coupons, obligations due or drawn, or amortizations or reimbursements due or ordered, provided that no action by common representative is pending to same effect. Actions for payment of coupons and obligations prescribe in three and five years respectively. (Law of Aug. 26, 1932, arts. 208-228 as am'd).

The annual balance must be completed within three months after close of fiscal year and submitted to inspectors at least one month before date of stockholders meeting in which it is to be discussed. Annual balance with inspector's annual report must be at stockholders' disposition at least 15 days before meeting. Annual balance must show amount of capital, amount paid in and to be paid in, cash assets and accounts constituting assets and liabilities of company. It must be published in official newspaper of state in which company is domiciled, and certified copy must be deposited in Public Registry of Commerce.

Fiscal Obligations.—(Law of Dec. 30, 1981 as am'd). Accounting must be performed in accordance with Federal Fiscal Code. Business reflected in foreign money must be registered and converted into Mexican pesos according to official foreign exchange rate on that business day.

Dissolution may be effected: (1) On expiration of legal term; (2) by impossibility of carrying on principal object of company or when such object has been consummated; (3) by resolution of stockholders, taken in accordance with articles of incorporation and law; (4) when number of shareholders is reduced to less than minimum provided by law or when all shares are owned by one person; (5) on loss of two-thirds of capital stock. On dissolution of company, it must be liquidated by one or more liquidators.

Government Supervision.—In order to obtain authorization of Federal Government to offer shares for sale to public, company must consent that its investments and business be supervised by a committee representing Government, with power to call meetings of shareholders. This supervision is carried on through a permanent auditor appointed by committee and paid by company. (Law of Dec. 30, 1939, and Regulations of July 16, 1940, amended by Decrees of June 20, 1945, and Feb. 11, 1946).

Investment Companies.—"Law of Investment Companies," of Dec. 21, 1984, as am'd covers creation and operation of investment companies, requiring minimum capital fully paid. Authorization to organize must first be obtained from National Securities Commission. Approval of charter is required. Such companies are subject to regulation and control of National Securities Commission. Special rules are provided for taxation.

Law forbids foreign governments or foreign official agencies, either directly or through nominees, to own stock in this class of companies. Penalty for violation of foregoing is either forfeiture of capital stock to Mexican Government, or revocation of operating franchise. Maximum individual or juridical person's participation allowed is 10% of capital with exception indicated by law.

Cooperative societies (sociedades cooperativas) may be for purposes of consumption, production, or both. At least ten members are necessary for incorporation and operation, but their number as well as duration and capital of society may be unlimited. Liability of members may be limited or unlimited. Capital is represented by certificates, which cannot be to bearer. From yearly earnings 10% to 20% must be set aside as a reserve fund which may be limited but not less than 25% of capital of a producers' cooperative or 10% of capital of a consumers' cooperative. Fund of 2 per mil of gross income must be set aside as a social insurance fund. Incorporation is effected by document executed before municipal authority, or before a civil judge, notary public or broker; whereupon Ministry of Industry and Commerce grants authorization to do business. This ministry has inspection of cooperatives and may withdraw its authorization and order their liquidation. Management is vested in general meeting of members, a board of directors, odd in number but not exceeding nine, and a supervisory board, with an odd number of members not exceeding five.

Dissolution.—Cooperative society is dissolved: (a) By resolution approved by two-thirds of members; (b) when number of members is reduced to less than ten; (c) when its financial condition does not permit further operations; (d) when object of cooperative has terminated; (e) by withdrawal of governmental authorization. (Law of Jan. 11, 1938; Regulations of June 16, 1938).

Civil Companies.—Under Federal Civil Code or those of various states, civil companies may be organized with a profit motive although for purposes not strictly mercantile. Firm name must be followed by words "Sociedad Civil" (Civil Company). Their administration may be entrusted to one or more members, who will be secondarily liable, jointly and severally, for obligations of company; other members are liable only to extent of their capital contribution, unless otherwise provided in instrument of organization or company contract. New members may be admitted and a member may assign his rights only with prior consent of other members, unless otherwise provided in company contract. (C. C. 2688-2738).

Foreign corporations may not acquire ownership of land, waters or their accessions, nor obtain concessions to exploit waters unless they agree before Ministry of Foreign Relations to be considered as nationals with respect to such properties and not to invoke with regard to them protection of their governments. In no case may they directly own land or waters within 100 kilometers of frontiers and 50 kilometers of seashore. (Const., art. 27, par. I; Law of Dec. 31, 1925).

Foreign corporations legally constituted are juridical persons and may appear in court or before other authorities without previous registration, but in order to do business, they must register in Public Registry of Commerce. Registration can be obtained only on authorization from Ministry of Commerce and Industrial Promotion, which is granted on compliance with following requisites: (1) Company must prove that it was constituted in accordance with its national law, by filing authenticated copies of articles of incorporation and other corporate documents, and certification issued by Mexican diplomatic or consular officer in respective country, to effect that company was so constituted; (2) articles of incorporation and other documents must not be contrary to public policy provisions of Mexican law; (3) company must have authorized agent or branch in Mexico. Articles of incorporation and other corporate documents to be used in Mexico, must be protocolized by notary public on order of competent judge together with company's inventory or last balance sheet, if any, and power of attorney of person or persons who are to represent company in Mexico. For this purpose, copies of such documents should be certified before notary, whose authority should be proved by county clerk's certificate or certificate of such officer as customarily acts in such cases, and this certificate should be authenticated by Mexican consul or diplomatic agent; these documents are translated into Spanish on protocolization. All of said documents, after protocolization in Mexico, must be presented to and recorded in Public Registry of Commerce on judicial order. Foreign corporation must publish annually balance sheet vised by certified public accountant.

See also topics Aliens; Foreign Investment.

Organization and Registration Fees.—Tax is payable on execution of corporate papers of domestic civil (noncommercial) corporation or upon protocolization of those of foreign corporation. (Law of Federal Fees of Dec. 28, 1982 as am'd).

See also topic Partnership.

COURTS:

Jurisdiction is divided between federal and state courts much as under our U.S. law. Federal system is composed of a Supreme Court of Justice, circuit and district courts, Council of Federal Judicature, federal trial jury and state and Federal District Courts as indicated by Constitution. Federal courts have jurisdiction over: (1) All matters involving federal laws, and treaties; when private interests are involved, such cases may be tried at option of plaintiff in state courts with a final appeal to Supreme Court of Justice; (2) matters involving maritime law; (3) cases in which Mexico is a party; (4) actions between states or a state and Mexico, and disputes between federal and state courts; (5) actions between a state and a resident of another state; and (6) cases concerning members of diplomatic and consular service except (4) in which only Supreme Court has jurisdiction. Federal courts also have jurisdiction over controversies arising out of laws or acts of any authority which violate individual guarantees or restrict sovereignty of states, and out of laws or acts of any state authority which usurp federal authority; jurisdiction referred to in this sentence gives rise to appeals or "amparos," procedure and scope of which are treated in special legislation. (Const. art. 104, Law of May 25, 1995, Law of May 10, 1995).

CURRENCY:

(Monetary Law of July 25, 1931, as am'd, Decree of June 18, 1992.) Monetary unit is peso divided into 100 centavos. Only Banco de México may issue bank notes with unrestricted legal tender value. Foreign currency obligations to be paid in Mexico may be discharged by delivery of national currency at rate of exchange published by Banco de México on date when payment is made.

CURTESY:

Not recognized in Mexico.

CUSTOMS:

Customs are regulated by Customs Law of Dec. 13, 1995, and its Regulations of June 3, 1996.

CUSTOMS DUTIES:

See topic Taxation.

DEATH:

If person disappears leaving no one to represent him, judge, upon petition of interested party, or on his own motion, shall summon him by publication and shall take necessary steps to safeguard property. In general, after two years, he may be declared absentee; and six years thereafter, upon request of interested party, he may be declared presumptively dead. However, if person disappears in war, shipwreck, flood or similar disaster, he may be declared presumptively dead after two years as from disappearance, without being previously declared absentee. Should disappearance occur as result of fire, earthquake, railroad or air accident, and there is sufficient evidence that person who disappears was there, presumption of death may be declared six months thereafter. (C. C. 648-722).

All deaths must be recorded in Office of Civil Registry of municipality or district where death occurs. Death forms may be obtained by applying to Official of Civil Register having jurisdiction.

Actions for Death.—Each State has its own Civil Code. Under Civil Code for Federal District and Territories anyone acting illegally or against good customs is liable for damages caused to another. If death results from wrongdoing amount of indemnity shall be fixed by applying quotas established by Federal Labor Law according to circumstances of victim and compensation or wages by him received, with

See Topical Index in front part of this volume.

DEATH . . . *continued*
certain limitations and imputing minimum salary if none was being earned. In addition court may grant family of decedent special compensation which may not exceed one third of the above stated indemnity. But this additional compensation does not apply against government for death of public servants. (C. C. arts. 1910; 1915 and 1928).

DECEDENTS' ESTATES:

See topics Descent and Distribution; Executors and Administrators; Wills.

DEEDS AND REGISTRATION:

Sales of real property may be made by private documents signed by parties before two witnesses. If value of real property exceeds value set forth in C.C. sale must be in form of public document. (See topics Contracts and Public Instruments). All contracts transferring or modifying ownership, possession or enjoyment of real property or rights in rem must be recorded in Public Registry of Property. Otherwise they do not affect third persons. On execution of deed involving such contract, notary advises registrar, who makes annotation, and if deed is filed for record within one month after execution registration is effective from date of such annotation, otherwise it takes effect from date of filing deed. Since registration fees are based on amount involved, actual and not nominal consideration must be stated in contract. (C. C. 2317-2320, 3002, 3003, 3018; Regulations of June 21, 1940 and Decree of Dec. 26, 1973).

Deeds executed in foreign countries may be recorded if authenticated by Mexican Consul and Ministry of Foreign Relations of Republic and protocolized. See topic Acknowledgments.

DEPOSITIONS:

Letters rogatory must be legalized by Ministry of Foreign Relations. Letters rogatory are also sent from one town to another in Republic, through judges of locality. (C. C. P. 104-109).

DESCENT AND DISTRIBUTION:

(C. C. 1281-1294, 1599-1791).

Estate of decedent passes to his heirs by force of law when decedent has not left valid will, when having left a will part of property is undisposed of, and when person entitled to residuary estate dies before testator, renounces inheritance or is incapacitated to take. Order of inheritance is as follows: (1) If there are descendants, they inherit, but surviving spouse owning property of less value than portion of child receives amount sufficient to make up difference, and ascendants are entitled to food, clothing, shelter and assistance in case of sickness (alimentos) up to value of portion of one child, (2) if there are no descendants, ascendants receive one-half and surviving spouse one-half; (3) there being no descendants or spouse, parents or surviving parent receive estate; (4) in default of foregoing, ascendants inherit; (5) in absence of descendants and ascendants, surviving spouse receives two-thirds and brothers and sisters one-third; (6) in absence of descendants, ascendants and brothers or sisters, spouse takes all; (7) if there are only brothers and sisters, or nephews and nieces, they inherit, portion of deceased brothers and sisters being taken up by their children per stirpes; (8) in absence of all the foregoing nearest relatives inherit, up to fourth degree; (9) in certain cases woman with whom deceased lived as man and wife has a share in inheritance; (10) in absence of any other heir, estates goes to public charity.

If administrator has been appointed, heirs must enforce their rights through administrator, but if none has been appointed heirs may make their claims directly. Right to claim inheritance prescribes in ten years.

Acceptance of inheritance may be made expressly or by implication. Repudiation must be in writing before judge or by public instrument before notary if heir is not in place where proceedings take place. Neither acceptance nor repudiation may be partial or conditional. Right to inherit from person who is alive may not be transferred nor repudiated. Acceptance and repudiation once made are irrevocable, unless there exists a will unknown at time of acceptance of repudiation, which alters character or amount of inheritance. Every acceptance is understood to be made with benefit of inventory, that is on condition that an inventory be made of estate and that heir is not liable for debts beyond amount of inheritance.

DIVORCE:

(C. C. 266-291; C. C. P. 156, 674-682).

Grounds.—Under provisions of Civil Code of Federal District and Territories, divorce dissolves marriage and may be granted for: (1) Adultery; (2) fact that wife gave birth to child conceived before marriage and judicially declared illegitimate; (3) proposal of husband to prostitute wife or his receiving remuneration to permit such prostitution; (4) efforts of either spouse to make other commit a crime; (5) attempts to corrupt children and toleration of such corruption; (6) syphilis, tuberculosis or any other incurable chronic disease which is contagious and hereditary, and impotence arising after marriage; (7) incurable mental alienation; (8) unjustified abandonment of home for six months; (9) abandonment of home for reason authorizing divorce, if prolonged for over a year without institution of divorce action by absent spouse; (10) declaration of absence by reason of disappearance for over two years, and declaration of presumption of death; (11) cruel treatment, threats and grave insults; (12) refusal to support, where right to support exists and cannot be enforced; (13) slanderous charge by one spouse against other, of crime carrying over two years' imprisonment; (14) commission of nonpolitical, infamous crime carrying over two years' imprisonment; (15) habits of gambling, drunkenness or use of drugs, when they threaten family ruin or cause constant marital discord; (16) acts of either spouse against person or property of other, which in other circumstances would be punishable by at least one year's imprisonment; (17) mutual consent.

Procedure.—Action for divorce must be brought by innocent party within six months after learning facts justifying divorce. Competent court is court of marriage domicile, or in case of abandonment, domicile of party abandoned. Domicile implies permanent rather than temporary residence. During proceedings judge makes orders as to alimony and custody of children. When divorce is granted children are awarded to innocent party; if both are guilty, children are placed in custody of grandparents or of guardian; in cases 9-13 and 16, aforementioned, they return to other party after death of innocent party, generally infant children are left with mother until they are five years old; courts may, however, make special orders for benefit of children. In any case spouses must support and educate sons until they come of age and daughters until they marry, provided they live honorably. After divorce innocent wife is entitled to alimony while she remains unmarried and lives honorably, but innocent husband only if he is indigent and unable to work. Parties are free to remarry, except guilty party cannot marry for two years after divorce and in case of wife 300 days must have passed since cohabitation ceased.

Mutual Consent.—Divorce by mutual consent cannot be requested until parties have been married a year. If they are of age and have no children they may appear before official of civil registry. If they are not of age or have children they must file agreement in court regarding custody and support of children, alimony during proceedings and division of property. Judge summons parties for two hearings at intervals of about 15 days and attempts to reconcile them; if they insist on their petition and agreement filed secures rights of children, judge declares divorce. If proceedings remain in abeyance for over three months they are discontinued. If parties become reconciled they cannot again ask for divorce by mutual consent until a year has passed. Parties cannot remarry until a year after divorce.

Foregoing is summary of divorce laws in force in Federal District and territories. Each State of Mexican United States has its own divorce laws, most of which are similar to those of Federal District.

Annulment of Marriage.—See topic Marriage.

DOWER:

Not recognized in Mexico.

ENVIRONMENT:

(General Law on Ecological Equilibrium and Environmental Protection dated Dec. 23, 1987 and its regulations of June 6, 1988, Nov. 18 and 23, 1988).

Law governs environmental regulatory process which includes environmental protection, natural resource conservation, environmental impact statements and risk assessments, ecological zoning, and sanctions. Within environmental protection are air, water and hazardous waste pollution, pesticides, and toxic substances. Federal government has exclusive jurisdiction over activities that have environmental impact on two or more states, operations that involve hazardous waste, activities that affect environment within capital city, and procedures for prevention and control of activities that could pose environmental risk or emergency of serious magnitude. Environmental regulatory agency is Secretariat of Social Development whose main functions are environmental policy formulation and enforcement, urban planning and administration of National Solidarity Program. It carries out its environmental functions through National Institute of Ecology and Office of Federal Attorney General for Environmental Protection. National Institute of Ecology is responsible for developing regulations and technical environmental standards or "normas"; granting permits, licences and authorizations; ruling on environmental impact statements; and studying state environmental programs. Office of Federal Attorney General of Environmental Protection is in charge of enforcing environmental laws, regulations and standards; conducting audits and evaluations; imposing sanctions, and educating public on environmental issues.

Hazardous Waste.—Waste is considered hazardous when it is explosive, ignitable, corrosive, reactive or toxic. List of hazardous materials and waste is published in official gazette. Authorization and registration must be obtained before generating or handling hazardous waste. Generator is responsible for its elimination, including final treatment. They are requirements for areas and containers for storing hazardous waste. Authorization for importation of hazardous waste for reuse or recycling may be granted.

Air.—Law requires achievement of ambient air quality standards for specific pollutants. Stationary sources of emissions of pollutant elements must control emissions to maintain them within maximum permissible levels. Facilities with stationary source of emission must obtain operating license, which is valid indefinitely and contains mandatory conditions.

Water quality standards are established. Law restricts wastewater discharges through issuance of permits. Handling, treatment and disposal of wastewater is regulated. Special permit and registration is required to discharge pollutants to any body of water, other than to municipal sewer system. Mandatory conditions include discharge limits, sampling, analysis and reporting.

Environmental impact statements are required for construction of new facilities. Technical standards or "normas" which implement law and regulations and set forth requirements, procedures, conditions and limits must be complied with. Administrative or criminal penalties are imposed for violations of law. Criminal sanctions include fines and imprisonment, depending on whether hazardous material or waste, air pollution, or water pollution is involved. Administrative sanctions include fines, temporary or permanent closure of facility, arrest of company officials and revocation of permits, depending on gravity of offense, economic situation of party involved and prior violations.

ESCHEAT: See topic Descent and Distribution.

EXCHANGE CONTROL:

(Provisions of Nov. 9, 1991).

There are no exchange control regulations. Banco de México publishes daily official selling rate of foreign exchange for payment of foreign currency obligations which may be paid locally by delivery of national currency at this rate of exchange. Computation of official selling rate of exchange is based on daily prevailing selling rates for U.S. dollar calculated according to provisions.

EXECUTORS AND ADMINISTRATORS:

(C. C. 1679-1791).

In Mexican law word "albacea" includes both executors and administrators, and same general rules apply to both.

EXECUTORS AND ADMINISTRATORS . . . *continued*

Testator may name one or more executors in his will. In default of appointment by testator heirs may appoint executor by majority vote, majority being determined according to interests of heirs and not by numbers. If there is no such majority, court makes appointment. Same rules apply to intestate proceedings. When entire estate is to go to legatees and no executor is named in will, they appoint administrator. Testator cannot relieve executor from giving bond, but heirs may do so.

Executor must complete his work within one year from date of his acceptance or date on which suits regarding validity of will are terminated, but extension of another year may be granted by heirs representing two-thirds of estate. Accounts of administration must be approved by all heirs; dissenting heirs may bring action in accordance with Code of Civil Procedure. Testator may designate compensation of executor; in absence of such designation executor is entitled to 2% of net value of estate and 5% of profits produced by industry, and he may choose between these percentages and amount designated by testator. Heirs who did not agree to appointment of executor may appoint inspector to supervise his work, and in certain cases, as when there are absent heirs or legacies to public establishments, inspector must be appointed.

Claims may not be paid until after inventory has been prepared, except that funeral expenses, expenses of last illness, costs of administration and food, clothing, shelter and assistance in case of sickness (alimentos) may be paid before termination of inventory. If cash funds are insufficient executor may, with approval of heirs or of judge, sell personal or real property, all such sales to be made at public auction unless majority of interested parties determine otherwise. Unless insolvency proceeding is pending, creditors are paid in order in which claims are filed, but if there are preferred creditors who have not filed their claims, those who are paid must give security. Executor cannot pay legacies until he has set aside enough property to pay debts. Creditors who file their claims after payment of legacies may bring action against legatees only if there is not enough inherited property to pay their claims.

Partition is effected by executor after inventory and administration accounts have been approved. It may be suspended by agreement of interested parties. It must appear in public instrument (q.v.). Annuities are provided for by setting aside sums which capitalize them at 9%.

FORECLOSURE: See topic Mortgages.

FOREIGN CORPORATIONS: See topic Corporations (Sociedades Anonimas).

FOREIGN EXCHANGE:

See topic Exchange Control.

FOREIGN INVESTMENT:

Foreign Investment Law.—(Foreign Investment Law of Dec. 23, 1993 and its regulations). Foreign investors may freely purchase capital of Mexican companies, acquire assets, engage in new lines of business or manufacture new products and open, expand, relocate and operate establishments, except as specifically provided in Law.

Restricted Activities.—Following activities exclusively reserved to State: Petroleum and hydrocarbons, basic petrochemicals, radioactive minerals and production of nuclear energy, electricity, harbors, airports and heliport control and supervision, postal, telegraphic and radio-telegraphic communications, satellite communications, coining money and issue of currency and any other one expressly reserved by specific law. Following exclusively reserved to Mexican citizens or Mexican companies with clause excluding foreign participation: Radio, television other than cable television, land transportation, gas distribution, credit unions, development banks, to extent provided by special laws, and certain technical professional services. Foreign capital participation allowed: Telephones, explosives and firearms manufacturing, fishing, financial leasing, flu-vial transportation, cable television, insurance, financial institutions, foreign exchange houses, limited purpose financial institutions, corporations under Art. 12(b) of Securities Market Law, shares or fixed capital investment stock holding companies, printing and publication of newspapers, "T" series shares of companies owning real property for agriculture, ranching and forestry, commercial fishing, port management, harbor services related to interior navigation, maritime corporations as indicated by Law, services related to railroads and trains and supply of fuel and lubricants for shipping, aircraft or trains, up to maximum of 49%, financial group holding companies, banking institutions, brokerage houses up to 30%; domestic air transportation, private air transportation and specialized air transportation, up to 25% and production cooperatives up to 10%.

In certain sectors, permission has been given to gradually phase-in foreign investment. In case of manufacturing and assembly of parts, equipment and accessories for automobile industry, foreign investment limit is now 49%, but no limit will exist from 1999 onwards. No foreign participation is currently allowed in international land transport of passengers, tourist and cargo between points in Mexico but it will be phased-in so that by 2004, 100% foreign investment will be permitted. In telecommunications sector, foreign participation in videotext and pocket switching is limited to 49% without special approval, but will be without limit beginning July 1, 1995. In construction sector, Foreign Investment Commission (Cimisión Nacional de Inversiones Extranjeras) approval is required for foreign investment to exceed 49%, but no approval will be required from 1999 onwards. Foreign investment of more than 49% is permitted only with prior approval of Foreign Investment Commission on: certain port and maritime services, management of air terminals, private education, legal services, credit information services, securities rating services, insurance brokers, cellular telephones, construction of pipelines for transport of petroleum and its derivatives and drilling of petroleum and gas wells. Approval is also required for foreign investment of more than 49% in Mexican company whose assets at time of acquisition have value over amount annually determined by Commission. Law provides that prohibited investments may not be made directly or indirectly or through trusts, agreements, bylaws, pyramidization or any other method that grants forbidden control or participation. Other cases, maximum foreign investment in capital 49% and may not control management under any circumstances. National Commission on Foreign Investment may authorize higher percentage of foreign investment. In determining whether to authorize such higher percentage, Commission will consider following characteristics of investment: (a) effect upon employment and training; (b) technology provided; (c) compliance with environmental protection laws; (d) increase in local productivity.

Investment by foreigners with immigration status "inmigrados" deemed as Mexican investment, provided activity or geographic area not exclusively reserved to Mexicans or Mexican companies with clause excluding foreigners.

Foreigners, foreign companies and Mexican company without clause excluding foreigners cannot acquire ownership of land or water within 100 kilometers of borders or 50 kilometers of seacoasts, except beneficial interest in trusts. See catchline Trusts, infra. Foreign company cannot acquire ownership of land or water or concession to exploit water; foreign individual can acquire same via permit from Ministry of Foreign Relations, agreeing to comply with paragraph four, Art. 27 (I) of Mexican Constitution.

Acquisition of Established Companies or of Control Thereof.—Persons acquiring over 25% corporate capital or over 49% fixed assets require special authorization of Ministry concerned. Every acquisition by Mexican enterprise with foreign capital participation which is holding company of more than 25% of capital of another Mexican enterprise or by which holding company has actual control of said enterprise requires authorization. Leasing of business or assets essential to operations thereof deemed acquisition assets. Authorization necessary where management passes to foreign investors or where latter obtain power to control management and granted if in national interest and with approval of National Commission on Foreign Investment. Any act above realized without authority void. Increases in capital stock of existing companies are allowed provided that proportion between foreign and Mexican capital ownership is maintained at levels fixed when foreign investment law came into effect. However, as of May 17, 1989, within three years non-Mexican investors are authorized to purchase shares in existing Mexican companies notwithstanding that their aggregate participation exceeds 49% of capital thereof. However, such investors must invest in new fixed assets valued at 30% at least of net worth of fixed assets as reported in Treasury Ministry for last fiscal year and comply with other conditions established in Regulations. Acceptance of all such conditions is deemed to have been given by purchase of shares.

No authorization is required for opening or relocation of establishments dedicated to activities in industry, commerce and services: (1) In case of new establishments (a) opened and operated by maquiladoras (in-bond companies), (b) opened and operated by other companies, if investors undertake (i) to invest in fixed assets minimum amount equivalent to 10% of net value of fixed assets reported to Treasury Ministry for last fiscal year and (ii) to comply with other conditions established in Regulations, or (c) when they are operated by companies surviving mergers; and (2) in case of relocation of industrial facilities, provided that they are not relocated within or to growth-controlled geographical zones having the highest industrial concentration. Similarly, foreign investment in new fields of economic activity or new lines of products does not require prior governmental authorization if foreign investors agree to above conditions. Conditions are deemed accepted by initiation of above-described activities.

Trusts.—Mexican credit institutions may acquire title to immovable property and shares of Mexican companies holding title to real property located within 100 kilometers from borders or 50 kilometers from seacoasts for industrial or tourism activities. Ministry to consider economic and social aspects of project. Trustee may lease property up to ten years: duration of trust is up to 50 years, renewable. Upon termination, property must be transferred to Mexicans or Mexican corporation with clause excluding foreigners. Interest of beneficiary evidenced by immovable property participation certificates which are nominative, non-amortizable and entitle right to use and enjoy realty, receive aliquot part of proceeds of securities, rights or property and of net proceeds upon sale. Trusts may also be used to hold shares of Mexican companies involved in: (i) Maritime and air transportation, (ii) gas distribution, (iii) manufacture of secondary petrochemicals, (iv) manufacture of automotive parts and components, (v) mining, and (vi) other specifically regulated activities, such as fisheries and telecommunications. As regards activities referred to in (i) and (ii), all foreign ownership must be through Mexican trusts. For activities (iii) and (iv), direct investment is limited to 40%, while up to 60% may be held through trust, and in mining, direct investment is limited to 49% and remaining 51% may be held in trust. Such trusts, which require prior authorization, are authorized for duration of 20 years. Voting of shares in trust is done through technical committees, which, for companies engaged in maritime and air transportation and gas distribution, must have even number of Mexican and foreign members and member appointed by Ministry.

Foreigners may participate in Mexican public companies through acquisition of certificates of participation issued by Mexican trust institutions whose assets are composed of shares of Mexican companies. Such shares conveyed in trust must be of new "N" (neutral) series. Certificates of participation issued by trusts holding "N" shares entitle foreigners only to pecuniary rights, not to voting or administrative rights. Series "N" shares held in trust are not considered as foreign capital for purposes of foreign investment laws.

Application for authorization of foreign investment submitted to Executive Secretary of National Commission of Foreign Investment. Decisions of Commission remitted to corresponding Ministry and governmental agencies for issuance of specific authorization.

Prior permit from Ministry of Foreign Relations required for foreigners to acquire immovable property located outside "forbidden zone" (within 100 kilometers from borders or 50 kilometers from seacoasts), for incorporation of companies or amendment of charter.

All governmental offices are required to act within specified time-tables. Failure to do so is deemed to be authorization of investment for which approval had been sought.

Registration.—National registry of Foreign Investment is divided into three sections: Section First, for foreign individuals or legal entities, Section Second for companies and Section Third for trusts.

Foreign individuals or legal entities must apply for registration within 40 business days following date on which they purchase or lease assets pursuant to Art. 8 of Law; set up, open or operate enterprise, branch or agency; lease enterprise pursuant to Art. 8 of Law; and acquire beneficiary rights under trusts referred to in Regulations. Companies must apply for registration within 40 business days following date on which they had or should have had knowledge of direct participation or acquisition of their capital stock by foreign investors, indirect participation and acquisition through trust of their

FOREIGN INVESTMENT . . . *continued*
capital stock by foreign investors. Credit institutions, as trustees, must apply for registration within 60 business days following date: (i) Of execution of trusts with foreign beneficiaries, when purpose of trust encompasses acts, regulated by law, to be performed either by trustees or by beneficiaries; (ii) of execution of trusts when foreign investors acquire, (a) as beneficiaries, corporate or pecuniary rights on companies' shares, (b) rights to dispose of companies' fixed assets, and (c) rights to exploit company or its assets which are essential for its exploitation; (iii) of acts where foreign investors acquire beneficiary rights under trusts referred to in sections (i) and (ii) hereof.

All applications for registration must be filed in Spanish language, in triplicate, before Oficialía de Partes de la Secretaría de Comercio y Fomento Industrial. Documents initially drafted in foreign languages must be translated into Spanish prior to filing. Registrations produce their effects from date of application before Oficialía de Partes or from date application is sent by registered mail or fax.

Capital stock of corporations must be in nominative form where: Owned by Art. 2 persons and as required by law. Approval of Commission necessary for foreigner to obtain bearer stock and must convert same into nominative. This to be set forth upon stock certificate.

Penalties include no dividends paid as to companies required to register which don't do so or as to stocks required to be registered which are not. Such companies may be registered on initiative of government or any shareholder. Transaction contrary to Law, and failure to register make act null and void and nonenforceable in Mexico, with fine up to amount of transaction and if not assessable, up to 100,000 pesos. Administrators, directors, general managers, comisarios and members of board of overseers jointly liable for noncompliance. Notaries and brokers authorizing instruments contrary to Law, forfeit license to practice and officers of Public Registry lose employment. Simulated acts to circumvent Law, up to nine years in prison and fine.

FOREIGN JUDGMENTS:

(C. C. P. 604-608).

Judgments and other judicial decisions emanating from foreign courts have such force in Mexico when they are not against public policy in accordance with Code of Civil Procedure for Federal District, Federal Code of Civil Procedure and other applicable laws except as treaties may provide. Foreign judgments and decrees will be enforced only if: (a) They comply with regulations relating to letters rogatory; (b) they were not given in rem action; (c) judge or tribunal rendering judgment is competent in international sphere to try matter and render judgment on it compatible to local regulations; (d) defendant was personally summoned in action; (e) they are final judgments according to law of country of origin; (f) they are properly authenticated; (g) not same cause of action pending between same parties in Mexican courts. However, judge may refuse to enforce foreign judgment if it is proved that country of origin does not execute judgments and other judicial decisions in similar cases; (h) obligation to be enforced is not against public policy in Mexico. Such judgments are enforced by court which would have had jurisdiction if judgments had peen rendered in Mexico. Judgment must be duly translated, and both parties are heard as well as Government attorney. Appeal lies from decision of court. Court does not inquire into merits of judgment but merely determines its authenticity and whether it is enforceable under Mexican law. If foreign judgment cannot be fully executed, partial execution is allowed at request of interested party.

FOREIGN TRADE REGULATIONS:

Foreign Trade Law of July 17, 1993 and its Regulations on unfair foreign trade practices of Dec. 23, 1993.

See topic Monopolies and Restraint of Trade.

FRAUDS, STATUTE OF: See topic Contracts.

HOLIDAYS:

Jan. 1 (New Year's); Feb. 5 (Promulgation of Constitution); Mar. 21 (Juarez's Birthday); Maundy Thursday*; Good Friday*; May 1 (Labor Day); May 5 (Victory of General Zaragosa); Sept. 16 (Independence Day); Oct. 12 (Columbus Day); Nov. 2 (All Souls' Day); Nov. 20 (Anniversary of Revolution); Dec. 12 (Our Lady of Guadalupe's Day), Dec. 25 (Christmas).

*Many offices do not open at all during Holy Week; Sept. 1, President's Address to Congress is not an obligatory holiday but many offices close.

HUSBAND AND WIFE:

Federal Law.—Pertinent provisions in Civil Code for Federal District and territories may be summarized as follows:

Married persons must contribute to the purposes of marriage and assist each other. Wife must live with her husband, but if he takes up his residence abroad or in objectionable locality, courts may relieve her of this duty. Husband must support his wife and household, but if she has means or is engaged in a profession, business or other occupation, she must contribute up to one-half of expenses, and if husband is indigent and unable to work all expenses of home devolve on wife. Husband and wife have equal authority in home and must, by mutual agreement, provide for education and establishment of their children, and for administration of their children's property; in case of disagreement between spouses, court must try to bring about an agreement, failing in which court must determine what it deems best for children's interest.

Wife is in general charge of work to be done in home. She may exercise employment, profession or business, if same does not interfere with her household duties. If husband provides for household needs he may object to such activities and if wife insists courts may decide. Husband and wife who are of age may each appear in court, contract, and dispose of their separate property, without consent of the other, but wife requires judicial approval in order to make contracts with her husband, except contract of agency, and to be surety for her husband and assume joint liability with him. Sales between spouses are allowed only when there is separation of property. Gifts may be made by spouses to each other, but they may be freely revoked and are confirmed by death of spouses if they are not in conflict with marriage articles and do not prejudice rights of persons entitled to support.

In contracting a marriage, the parties must state whether they marry under system of conjugal partnership (community of property) or under that of separation of property. Before or after marriage, articles of marriage may be drawn up in form of a public instrument (q.v.) recorded in registry of property, to regulate manner in which property of spouses is to be held.

Conjugal Partnership.—Marriage articles setting up system of community property must state assets and liabilities of marriage partnership, what property and income is to be comprised therein, and who is to administer property and with what powers. In default of such regulation, rules relating to civil associations (see topic Partnership) are applied, according to which, if right of administration has not been limited to one partner, all partners have equal administrative rights.

Separation of Property.—If system of separation of property is adopted, each spouse has full administration of his or her own property and income. This system may be adopted before or after marriage, by voluntary act of spouses or by judgment of court. It may be total or partial and may relate both to property owned at time of marriage and that received afterwards.

Antenuptial gifts are those which one of parties gives to other prior to marriage and those which a third person gives to one or both parties in consideration of marriage. Such gifts between parties may not amount to over one-sixth of property of donor.

State Laws.—Law prevailing in most of other regions of Mexico is found in Civil Codes of various states, provisions of which are still similar to those of Civil Code which was formerly in force in Federal District and territories. More important provisions of that code may be summarized thus:

Husband is required to support wife. Wife must obey husband in domestic matters, education of children and administration of property. Wife who has property of her own is required to support husband when he lacks means and is unable to work. Wife is required to reside with husband wherever he establishes his residence, if he so desires, unless there is a different understanding in marriage contract. Court may excuse wife from transferring her residence to a foreign country. Husband is legal administrator of all property of marriage. If he is a minor, judicial authorization is necessary for alienation or encumbrance of real property, and guardian is required in judicial matters. Husband is legal representative of wife. She may not, without his written authority, appear in court either personally or through attorney, nor may she acquire or alienate property by contract or obligate herself without consent of her husband except in cases especially provided by law. Permission to litigate or contract obligations may be given generally or specially, and if husband is absent or unjustly refuses to give such permission it may be obtained from court. Wife requires judicial authorization to litigate or contract when both she and her husband are minors, and to enter into any contract with her husband other than a power of attorney. A woman who is of age does not need permission from her husband nor judicial authorization to defend herself in a criminal action to litigate with her husband to dispose of her property by will, or when husband is legally incapacitated or unable to grant permission because of illness, when they are legally separated and when she has a mercantile establishment. Illegality of wife's acts, based upon lack of permission by her husband or court, cannot be set up except by herself, her husband or their heirs, and in no case when husband has ratified her action.

Property and affairs of married persons may be managed either on theory of a conjugal partnership or under theory of separation of property. Conjugal partnership may be voluntary or legal.

A voluntary conjugal partnership is governed in accordance with agreement of parties made either before or during marriage. This agreement must be in form of a public document. (See topic Public Instruments). In so far as not specifically agreed upon rules for a legal partnership govern. Any agreement by which one of parties is to receive all earnings or by which one of parties is to be responsible for losses and common debts to a greater proportion than his share of capital or earnings is void. Creditors who do not know terms of agreement may enforce their claims as though partnership were a legal one, but parties in such case may adjust matter between themselves according to their agreement.

Legal Conjugal Partnership.—If there is no express agreement between the parties the marriage is understood to be a legal partnership. In such case each is the owner of the property which he owned prior to the marriage and property which he possessed and acquired title to by prescription during the marriage, and also of property acquired by chance, gift, inheritance or legacy during the marriage. Property acquired by either of the partners during marriage as the result of a profession or business or manual labor and the proceeds thereof, etc., is joint property. The ownership and possession of their joint property resides in both the husband and wife. The husband may alienate or encumber personal property without the wife's consent, but real property owned in common may not be encumbered or alienated without the consent of the wife. Each of the parties may dispose of half of the common property by will.

Separation of Property.—There may be a separation of property either by a public document entered into before or during the marriage or by judicial decree in certain cases. In such case each may administer his own property subject to certain limitations. For example the wife may not alienate real property or real rights without express consent of the husband or the court if he unjustly refuse. Property acquired in common during the marriage is treated as in the case of a legal partnership until divided, unless the share of each has been designated; debts contracted before marriage are paid out of the property of the debtor; debts contracted jointly during marriage are paid jointly; if contracted separately they are paid by the debtor.

Antenuptial Gifts.—The rules relating to such gifts are generally the same as those hereinbefore stated for the Federal District.

IMMIGRATION: See topic Aliens.

INCOME TAX: See topic Taxation.

INFANCY:

Majority begins upon attaining 18 years of age. Minor may be emancipated, and hence freely administer his property by: (a) Parental action, if minor is under 18; (b)

INFANCY . . . *continued*
judicial decree; and (c) minor's marriage. Emancipation once obtained is not lost. Even emancipated minor requires: (1) Judicial authorization to alienate, mortgage or encumber real property; (2) a guardian ad litem for judicial matters. (C. C. 641, 643, 646). Women under 14 years of age and men under 16 are not allowed to get married. (C. C. 237).

Parental authority is exercised over the person and property of unemancipated minors, in the following order, by: (1) Father and mother; (2) paternal grandparents; (3) maternal grandparents. Property of a minor child under parental authority is divided into: (a) Property acquired by his work; and (b) property acquired in any other way. The ownership, administration and usufruct (enjoyment and income) of property of the first class belong to the child. The ownership and one-half of the usufruct of property of the second class belong to the child. The administration and the other half of the usufruct belong to the person exercising parental authority. Guardians may be appointed for minors not under parental authority. (C. C. 412-415, 424-430, 449-452).

Contracts of minors, not emancipated, are voidable by them only; but they may be ratified at majority. (C. C. 2230, 2233).

INSOLVENCY: See topic Bankruptcy.

INTEREST:

Legal interest is 9% per annum. The parties may agree upon any other rate, but when the rate is unconscionable, the judge may, in special circumstances, reduce the interest to the legal rate. If a rate higher than the legal rate has been agreed upon, the debtor may, after six months from the date of the contract, and whatever be the stipulated maturity, cancel the debt on two months' notice by paying the principal and matured interest. Agreements in advance to compound interest are forbidden under penalty of nullity. (C. C. 2393-2397).

Art. 362 of Commercial Code provides that debtors who do not pay their debts must satisfy from day following maturity the interest agreed upon, or in its stead legal interest at 6% annually. For interest payable abroad, see topic Taxation.

INTESTACY: See topic Descent and Distribution.

JUDGMENTS: See topic Foreign Judgments.

LABOR RELATIONS:

Federal Constitution, Title VI provides for labor and social security. Therefore, Congress must formulate labor laws which apply to workers, daily laborers, domestic servants, artisans, and in general all labor contractors: maximum duration of work for day must be eight hours, in case of night work it shall be seven hours. Certain types of works are prohibited such as unhealthful or dangerous work for women and for minors under 16 years of age. Hiring of minors under 14 years of age is absolutely prohibited. However, persons over 14 and less than 16 years of age shall have a maximum work day of six hours. For every six days of work, there must be at least one day of rest.

During pregnancy women are not allowed to perform any physical labor that requires excessive effort. They have six weeks before and six weeks after birth of maternity leave and must receive full wages and retain employment and rights acquired under their particular labor contract. In general minimum wages must be sufficient to satisfy normal material, social and cultural needs of head of family and to provide for education of children. Equal wages shall be paid for equal work, regardless of sex or nationality. In general minimum wages are exempt from attachments and deductions. Workers are entitled to participation in profits of enterprises; but such profit-sharing does not imply power to intervene in management or direction of them. Wages must be paid in money; they cannot be paid in goods, drafts, promissory notes, or in any other object intended to substitute for money.

Employers are responsible for labor accidents and for occupational illnesses of workers, contracted due to or in performance of work. Employers must pay indemnification when death or permanent or temporary incapacity result as consequence of such accident. Employers and workers have right to organize unions, professional unions, professional associations, etc. for defense of their rights and interests.

As to social security it shall be organized according to following basis: in general it must cover work accidents, occupational illensses, maternity, retirement, disability, old age and death. Provisions of Federal Constitution have been object of extensive legislation. Social Security Law of Dec. 21, 1995 has retirement savings system in addition to social security system. Retirement system is mandatory, private pension plan funded by employer contribution equal to 2% of employee's base salary.

Federal Labor Code effective on May 1, 1970 as am'd. Code tends to increase benefits for workers, to guarantee working conditions and to improve relations with employers as well. In case of doubts arising from interpretation of provisions of Labor Code, most favorable interpretation and treatment to worker shall always take preference. Working day is defined in law as period of time during which worker is available to render services to employer. In case of full-time working day employer is required to grant minimum rest period of one-half hour. In case of overtime, compensation must be calculated according to following procedure: (1) First nine hours of overtime per week must be paid at twice normal salary rate, and (2) overtime in excess of such nine hours must be paid at three times normal salary rate. If for any reason worker is requested to work on Sun., he is entitled to additional compensation equal to 25% of normal salary rate. Rule is applicable even though employee has day off during week. Also, if worker is requested to perform services on holidays he must be paid three times normal salary rate.

There are special provisions for minors, if under 16 or 18 years of age, as case may be. They are not allowed to perform certain types of work, such as to sell liquor, to work in underground or submarine tasks, and in nonindustrial establishments after 10 P.M., and in any kind of industrial work during night.

Code allows six days vacation after first year of service and an additional two days for each year of service up to a maximum of 12 days. Additional compensation equal to 25% of normal salary rate must be paid during vacations.

Salary is defined to be remuneration that employers must pay to employees in exchange for their work. In general, employers are required to pay benefits, e.g., bonuses, severance compensation, vacations, etc. which are based mainly on salary; therefore, if salary is increased benefits are also increased. Wages are reviewed yearly by government.

Code establishes a compulsory annual bonus equal to 15 days salary which must be paid generally at end of year. If worker has worked for a shorter term, bonus must be computed proportionately to number of days effectively worked during that year and must be paid before Dec. 20 of each year. Besides compensations mentioned above workers are entitled to profit sharing in general.

One of employers' obligations is that they are now required to permanently or periodically give training courses to workers as well as to promote participation by them in recreational and sport activities, etc. In certain cases, concerns are required to furnish housing, which may be complied with either by constructing or renting houses to workers. Requisite applies only to companies with more than 100 workers, to companies with less than that number but located at a distance in excess of three kilometers from a village, and to companies which although located at less than three kilometers have inadequate transportation. Employment contracts may not be terminated when there is a period of service of more than 20 years except for serious reason. Code also sets forth in detail further provisions regarding additional compensation for special cases, contemplating number of years, preferences and type of services rendered. As to statute of limitations, workers in case of unjustified termination of employment have two month period within which to sue employer. However, in certain other situations statute of limitations runs from one month up to two years as case may be. Code also regulates matters such as workers' investigations and inventions, independent agents, work performed at home, domestic workers, and rights and duties of crews of ships and airplanes as well. Procedures for strikes, and indemnification in case of accidents, among other requirements are also comprehended in Code.

LEGISLATURE:

See topic Constitution and Government.

LIMITATION OF ACTIONS:

See topic Prescription.

LIMITED LIABILITY COMPANIES:

See topic Partnership.

LIMITED PARTNERSHIP: See topic Partnership.

MARRIAGE:

(C. C. 97-113, 139-161, 235-265).

Impediments to marriage: (1) Lack of age, when no dispensation is obtained; (2) lack of consent, when necessary, on part of those exercising parental power, guardians, or judge; (3) relationship by consanguinity in direct descending or ascending line, between brothers and sisters of whole or half blood, and between uncles and nieces, aunts and nephews of third degree, but in last mentioned cases a dispensation may be obtained; (4) relationship by affinity in direct line; (5) adultery between parties if proved in court; (6) attempts against life of a spouse in order to marry other; (7) duress; (8) incurable impotence, and chronic and incurable diseases which are also contagious or hereditary; (9) drug addiction, mental retardation and other disabilities; (10) existing marriage. Adopter may not marry person adopted or his descendants while adoption lasts; nor may guardian marry his ward or former ward, without obtaining dispensation from municipal president after approval of guardianship accounts. Woman may not remarry until 300 days have elapsed since dissolution of former marriage, unless she meanwhile gives birth, but in cases of nullity and divorce time may be counted from cessation of cohabitation.

Marriage cannot be contracted by males under 16 years or by females under 14. Minors below the age of 18 require consent of their parents, paternal or maternal grandparents, guardians, or court, as case may be. If ascendants refuse or withdraw their consent an application may be made to courts.

Marriage ceremonies are performed by official of civil registry. Persons desiring to marry must file a written application, together with parental consent when needed, a certificate signed by two witnesses showing that there are no impediments, a medical certificate that they are free of diseases which are impediments to marriage, and a statement as to whether they marry under system of community property or separation of property. Parties and witnesses acknowledge their signature before official of civil registry and ceremony is performed by him within eight days thereafter.

Marriages may be annulled: (a) For error as to person married; (b) in case of existence of any of impediments aforementioned; (c) if formalities required for marriage ceremony were not observed. In certain cases there is no limit to time in which annulment may be demanded, as in case of marriage within prohibited degrees. In other cases there are time limits; thus in case of error as to person, annulment must be demanded as soon as error becomes known; in cases of lack of age marriage is validated if there are children or if minor reaches majority without an action of nullity; in case of lack of consent by parents or guardians annulment action must be instituted within 30 days after they learn of marriage; in case of duress action must be instituted within 60 days after duress ceased. While marriage lasts it produces civil effects with respect to party who acted in good faith.

Foregoing is a summary of provisions governing marriage in Federal District and territories. Law on this subject prevailing elsewhere in Mexico is generally to be found in Civil Codes of the various states and is in general very similar to law in Federal District and territories.

MARRIED WOMEN:

See topics Husband and Wife; Marriage.

MINES AND MINERALS:

(Constitution, Art. 27, Law of June 24, 1992 and its regulations of Mar. 25, 1993; Law of Federal Fees of Dec. 28, 1982 as am'd).

See Topical Index in front part of this volume.

MINES AND MINERALS . . . *continued*

Under art. 27 of Constitution, nation is owner of all minerals and substances which exist in veins, strata, masses or beds, and constitute deposits of a nature different from the land.

Exploration, exploitation and processing of mineral deposits, except petroleum, all kinds of hydrocarbons, radioactive minerals, salt mines among others, are governed by Law of June 24, 1992 and may be carried out by (a) state and (b) private enterprises. In case of (a) Government must act through public mining entity to which state makes assignment of minerals located in specific zones and in case of (b) Government grants concession. Assignments and concessions are granted by Executive Branch through Secretaría Energia, Minas e Industria Paraestatal and refer only to minerals located on free lands, as opposed to those already granted or assigned and to national mining reserves. Assignments are granted to Consejo de Recursos Naturales, descentralized government agency.

Mining concessions may be granted only to Mexicans and Mexican corporations 51% or more of capital of which belongs to Mexicans whose corporate purpose is exploration or exploitation of minerals, legally domiciled in Mexico. Special concessions for exploitation of mines or minerals essential for development of Mexico, which must be considered as a part of national mineral reserve, may be granted only to Mexicans or to Mexican corporations issuing a series of shares of which at least 66% of capital belongs to Mexicans.

Term of assignment of mining concession for exploration is six years and is 50 years for concessions for exploitation, renewable if application is filed five years prior to expiration. Terms commence running from registration date.

Concessionaires are entitled to certain benefits as right to expropriate necessary land for installation, storage plants and other facilities, easement of access, power and water lines, use of subsoil waters, and others. Mining concession is subject to termination for lack of payment of corresponding tax; failure to carry out exploitation and works as provided by law and regulations within terms therein established. In case of change of capital structure of concessionaire by which legal proportion of capital which must be in hands of Mexicans or Mexican corporations, as provided by law, is not maintained; law grants 365 natural day period for regaining previous proportion, if changes are not made Secretaría will call for public sale of portion of foreign capital in excess of percentage established by law. Sale proceeds go to Consejo de Recursos Naturales.

There is a public registry of mines wherein must be recorded organization, modification and dissolution of corporations organized for exploration, extraction or processing of mineral substances; concessions and transfers and termination thereof and acts affecting same; contracts for exploitation of minerals and other contracts related to mining industry and to constitution of easements and expropriations to be made in relation with same; and resolutions related to national mineral reserve. Recording affects third parties from date of registration. Public mining registry may be examined by any person who may obtain certified copies of entries and existing documents.

Infractions of law are subject to fines and cancelation of concession or assignment.

Fiscal questions, mining taxes, exemptions, fees and liens are provided for by Federal Law of Fiscal Fees.

Petroleum.—(Const. art. 27, Law of Nov. 27, 1958 as am'd and its Regulations of Aug. 24, 1959 as am'd). By petroleum is meant any natural mixture of hydrocarbons which contain, accompany or are derived from it. Petroleum industry is a public utility enjoying preferential right to utilize surface with right to expropriation on payment of compensation.

Petroleum, hydrocarbons and basic petrochemical activities are exclusively reserved to State which exercises its right through "Petróleos Mexicanos" which is authorized to execute construction and services contracts with individuals or juridical persons.

Petróleos Mexicanos.—Decree of July 16, 1992 sets forth organic law of "Petróleos Mexicanos" which is Federal governmental agency domiciled in City of Mexico, F. D. whose purpose is to oversee and carry out strategic management of all state petroleum industry activities through its fully owned subsidiary enterprises: Pemex Exploración y Producción engages in exploration and exploitation of petroleum and natural gas; Pemex Refinacion engages in industrial refining processes; Pemex-Gas y Petroquimica Básica engages in processing of natural gas, natural gas liquids and artificial gas; and Pemex-Petroquimica engages in industrial petrochemical processes not included in basic petrochemical industry. Transportation, except between well and processing plant, storage and distribution of natural gas can be carried out by private enterprise. Petróleos Mexicanos is administered by Board which is composed of 11 members, six of them represent State (through Executive Power) and other five members are selected by oil workers union from among its active members. It must also have General Director. Law grants broad powers for organization, management and exploitation of its assets, that is to say that it can perform all types of transactions directly or indirectly related to oil, and petro-chemical industry. Further provisions of law regulate meetings, special meetings, quorum and type of majority required for resolutions taken by Board as well as rights and duties of general director and officers.

MONOPOLIES AND RESTRAINT OF TRADE:

(Const. 1917, art. 28; Federal Law of Economic Competition of Dec. 22, 1992; Regulations to the Organic Law on Monopolies of Dec. 19, 1931; Federal Law on Consumer Protection of Dec. 22, 1992 as am'd; Foreign Trade Law of July 17, 1993 and its regulations of Dec. 23, 1993 and Regulations on unfair foreign trade practices of Nov. 24, 1986 as am'd).

Constitutional basis for restriction of monopolistic practices is found in art. 28, which categorically states that in Mexico monopolies, monopolistic practices, State monopolies and tax exemptions are prohibited as well as prohibitions under pretext of protection to industry with exception of activities in such areas as mail, telegraph and radiotelegraphy; petroleum and other hydrocarbons, basic petrochemical; radioactive minerals and production of nuclear energy; and electricity. That article further directs that there shall be proscribed every concentration in hands of one or few persons of necessary consumer goods for purpose of obtaining increase in prices; every act that prevents or tends to prevent free competition in production, industry, or commerce, or services to public; every agreement or combination of producers, manufacturers, merchants, common carriers, or those engaged in any other service to prevent competition among themselves and to require consumers to pay exaggerated prices; and in general whatever constitutes exclusive and undue advantage in favor of one or more specified persons and to prejudice of public in general or of any social class.

Federal Law of Economic Competition regulates Art. 28 of Constitution with regard to economic competition, monopolies and competition and it is applicable to all areas of economic activity. All economic agents, including individuals or juridical persons, public, federal, state or municipal administrative agencies or entities, associations, professional groups, trusts or any other form of participation in economic activities are subject to provisions of Law. Its purpose is to protect competition and market freedom by means of preventing and eliminating monopolies, monopolistic practices and other restrictions upon efficient functioning of markets for goods and services. Law prohibits monopolies and state monopolies, as well as practices that, in accordance with terms of Law, diminish, damage or impede competition and market freedom in production, processing, distribution, commercialization of goods and services. Law considers monopolistic practices per se those contracts, agreements, arrangements or combinations of economic agents competing among themselves, whose purpose or effect is to: fix, raise, coordinate or manipulate prices, or exchange information with same purpose or effect; restrict supply of or not to supply goods and services; divide markets, allocate customers or suppliers; establish or coordinate bids or abstention from bids. These practices are void and subject to penalties. Subject to proof, Law also considers as monopolistic practices those acts, contracts, agreements, arrangements or combinations whose purpose or effect is or may be to displace wrongfully other market agents, substantially impede their access to markets, or establish exclusive advantages in favor of one or various persons, when they involve: establishing exclusive distribution of goods or services, resale price maintenance or other resale conditions, tying or reciprocity, conditioning transactions upon agreement not deal with third parties, unilaterally refusing to sell or supply to particular persons goods or services that are usually available and offered to third parties, group boycotts and any other act that wrongly harms or obstructs competition and market freedom in production, processing, distribution and commercialization of goods and services. Such activities are violations only if: alleged responsible person has substantial leverage over relevant market and activities are conducted with regard to goods and services that correspond to market in question. Relevant market is determined by availability of substitute goods or services, and possibility to secure supply from other areas. To determine whether economic agent has substantial leverage in relevant market it is considered: if economic agent may fix prices unilaterally or substantially restrict supply without competing agents being able to counteract such leverage; if there exist barriers to entry; if there exist competitors and their leverage; economic agent's and competitor's access to sources of supply; economic agent's recent course of conduct; and any other criteria established by regulations.

Concentrations are defined as mergers, acquisitions of control or any transaction through which companies, associations, shares, partnership interests, trusts or assets are concentrated, or transactions in general that are carried out among competitors, suppliers, customers or any other economic agents. Sanctions are imposed upon those concentrations whose purpose or effect is to diminish, damage or impede competition and market freedom with respect to equal, similar, or substantially related goods or services. Some concentrations require prior notice to Federal Competition Commission which is decentralized administrative agency of Ministry of Commerce and Industrial Development. Federal Competition Commission in charge of preventing, investigating and opposing monopolies, monopolistic practices and concentrations pursuant to terms of Law. Concentrations that obtain favorable resolution from Commission, including those as to which Commission takes no action within applicable time period, may never be challenged on basis of Law. Concentrations not requiring prior notification may not be challenged a year after their creation. Federal Competition Commission has autonomy to issue its rulings and it is empowered to impose sanctions consisting in fines and orders of suspension, correction or termination of activity or concentration in question. Law permits those who prove to Commission loss profits or damages incurred as result of monopolistic activity or unlawful concentration to bring judicial action to recover them.

Foreign Trade Law and Regulations on Unfair Foreign Trade Practices.—Law regulates and promotes foreign trade. Secretary of Commerce and Industrial Promotion is in charge of enforcement of law. Law protects local production from unfair practices of international trade imposing countervailing duties on import of foreign goods. Dumping and subvention are considered unfair practices when injure or have tendency to destroy or injure national production. Dumping is defined as import of foreign goods at lower price than normal price in place of origin, and subvention as direct or indirect incentives, subsidies, premiums or assistance of any kind granted by foreign governments to producers, manufacturers, or exporters of goods in order to make them more competitive at international market, with exception of those trade practices internationally accepted.

Consumer Protection Law.—Law is of public interest and deals with: Consumers right to be informed; promotions and sales; real estate operations; form contracts; general representations and warranties; credit operations; lack of performance; services, domicile sales and general regulations on subject. Procuraduria Federal del Consumidor is federal agency to protect consumers' rights and to research marketing of products.

See also topic Foreign Investment.

MORTGAGES:

(C. C. 2893-2943; C. C. P. 468-488).

Mortgages must specifically designate the property they affect. A mortgage of real property covers all articles comprised under that term. (See topic Real Property). Although not so expressed, a mortgage includes: (a) The natural accessions of the mortgaged property; (b) improvements made thereon by the owner; (c) movable objects permanently incorporated with the mortgaged property by the owner and which cannot be removed without damage to such objects or the property; (d) new buildings constructed by the owner on the mortgaged land. Unless otherwise stipulated the mortgage does not comprise: (a) Industrial fruits of the property, produced before the creditor demands the amount due; (b) rents matured when payment of the debt is demanded. The following cannot be mortgaged: (a) Pending fruits and rents apart from

See Topical Index in front part of this volume.

MORTGAGES . . . *continued*
the land producing them; (b) movable objects permanently placed in buildings for adornment, convenience or the service of some industry, unless mortgaged together with the building; (c) servitudes, unless mortgaged with the dominant tenement; (d) the right of ascendants to receive fruits from property of their descendants; (e) use and the right of habitation; (f) property in litigation, unless the bill of complaint has been provisionally recorded in the registry or the creditor acknowledges in the mortgage instrument that he is aware of the litigation.

Only a person able to alienate may make a mortgage and only property subject to alienation may be mortgaged. If the mortgaged property becomes insufficient to secure the debt, the creditor may demand that additional property be included in the mortgage, otherwise the mortgage may be considered matured. When several parcels are mortgaged to secure a debt it is necessary to specify what part of the debt is secured by each, and any parcel may be redeemed by paying the amount corresponding to it. When mortgaged property susceptible of division is subdivided the mortgage lien must be distributed among the parcels. Without the consent of the creditor the owner of the mortgaged property cannot lease it or agree to an advance payment of rentals for a period extending beyond the term of the mortgage.

If the debt exceeds amount calculated according to formula set forth in C.C. mortgage must appear in public instrument (q. v.); if it is smaller sum there may be private instrument before two witnesses; but in any case mortgage has no effect as against third persons unless recorded. As against third persons mortgage does not secure interest on mortgage debt for more than three years, unless longer time, not beyond time specified in law relating to prescription, was expressly stipulated and stipulation is on record in registry.

Voluntary mortgages are those entered into by agreement of the parties or constituted by the owner of the property. The mortgage credit may be assigned, provided the assignment be communicated to the debtor and recorded in the registry. If the mortgage is constituted to secure an instrument to order, it may be assigned by mere endorsement of the instrument; if it secures an instrument to bearer, it may be assigned by mere delivery. The mortgage exists for the period stipulated; if no time is designated it cannot last longer than ten years.

Necessary mortgages are mortgages which the law requires certain persons to give in order to secure their administration of property or the rights of certain creditors. Thus guardians may be required to give mortgages to secure their administration of the property of their wards and state or municipal administrators and collectors to secure the revenues collected by them.

Foreclosure is effected by a summary action. A formal announcement of the institution of the mortgage action is published by the court and recorded in the registry and the debtor is given five days to present his objections. There is an expert valuation of the property and an order of sale by public bidding, which is advertised. The lowest bid allowable is two-thirds of the valuation of the property. Bidders must first make a deposit of 10% of this amount. If there is no bidder the creditor may ask that the property be adjudicated to him for two-thirds of the valuation or that another sale be held in which the valuation is reduced by 20%. If there is still no bidder he may ask that the property be adjudged to him for two-thirds of the new valuation or be delivered to him in administration to pay himself with the income or that there be a third sale at which any bid will be received. At this third sale if the best bid is less than two-thirds of the valuation in the second sale, the debtor is given opportunity for twenty days to pay the debt or to present a higher bid. At any time up to the termination of the sale or the adjudication of the property the debtor may redeem the property by paying the debt and costs; later there is no equity of redemption.

The right to the summary foreclosure action prescribes in ten years, counting from the time it might have been instituted. The parties may agree that the property is to be adjudicated to the creditor at a price determined when payment of the debt is demanded, but not when the mortgage is signed.

NEGOTIABLE INSTRUMENTS:

See topic Bills and Notes.

NOTARIES PUBLIC:

(Notarial Law of Jan. 9, 1932; Law of Dec. 30, 1947, as am'd by Decrees of Dec. 21, 1950, Dec. 21, 1965 and Dec. 26, 1966).

Mexican notary is a public official whose duties are much more important than those of the notaries under U.S. system of law. Contracts and conveyances between private individuals, powers of attorney and wills which are required to be in the form of a public document (see topic Public Instruments) when entered into in Mexico, should be prepared by and executed before a notary public. Notaries are required to pass examinations before they are commissioned, and must furnish bond. They are required to keep protocol, which comprises originals of all documents which are executed before them. General archives are kept to which protocols of notaries pass after certain length of time. Instruments executed before notaries must be prepared with certain formalities and drawn in Spanish language. If parties do not know Spanish they must appoint interpreter, who takes oath before notary that he will faithfully perform his duties. If parties are not known to notary, their identity must be certified to by two witnesses known to notary, who must also certify as to their legal capacity.

Contracts, powers of attorney and other documents executed in foreign countries should be duly authenticated (see topic Acknowledgments) and translated and protocolized in the office of a notary by order of a competent court in order to receive full recognition in Mexico.

Notary has no fixed term of office and may be removed from office only for cause.

Authentic copies of documents executed or protocolized before a notary may be presented as evidence in any court. (See topic Public Instruments). Notaries shall issue to each party a first copy of the notarial document and may issue second or further copies, provided third parties are not prejudiced, but such second or additional copies are not admissible in executive proceedings, unless issued by order of a court after notice given to the interested parties.

PARTNERSHIP:

Governed by law of July 28, 1934 as am'd (General Law of Commercial Companies) which applies to whole nation.

All partnership agreements must be in form of public documents (see topic Public Instruments) which must be recorded in Public Registry of Commerce. All partnerships are regarded as legal entities.

General partnership (sociedad en nombre colectivo) is a partnership in which all partners have unlimited and joint liability towards third persons. As between partners liability of one or more may be limited to a certain amount. Only name of partners may appear in firm name; when names of all are not used, firm name may consist of name of one or more with addition of words "y compañía" or other similar expression. Any person whose name appears in firm name, is liable as if he were a partner. In case firm name has been used by another partnership whose rights and obligations have been transferred to partnership, word "sucesores" must be added to firm name; likewise when name of a former partner is used in firm name.

Management of partnership may be entrusted to one or more administrators, who may or may not be partners; when administrators are not designated, all of partners have a voice in management. Administrators are appointed and removed by vote of majority of partners; any partner has right to separate from partnership when in spite of his opposing vote a non-partner is appointed administrator. A partner who has been appointed administrator can be removed only by judicial order if partnership agreement forbids his removal.

Partnership agreement can be modified only by unanimous consent of all partners, unless it authorizes modification by a majority; in this case minority has right to withdraw. Partners may not assign partnership rights, nor may new partners be admitted without consent of all other partners, unless partnership agreement allows such assignment and admittance by majority vote.

Administrators may not sell or mortgage real property of partnership without consent of a majority of partners, unless such sale or encumbrance constitutes principal object of partnership or a natural consequence thereof. Administrators may grant powers of attorney for carrying on specified partnership business, but in order to delegate duties vote of a majority of partners is required; in this case dissenting minority has right to withdraw from partnership if delegate is a non-partner. Firm name may be used by all administrators unless partnership agreement limits said use to one or more. Resolutions of administrators must be adopted by a majority and in case of a tie, partners decide. Resolutions of partners are also adopted by majority but partnership agreement may provide that such majority be computed by interest; if any one of partners holds a majority interest, vote of another partner is necessary. Partners not in administration may appoint an inspector and have right to examine books and accounts of partnership. Capital may not be distributed prior to dissolution and liquidation of partnership, unless otherwise agreed.

Capital of all kinds of partnerships may be variable; in this case expression "de capital variable" must be added to firm name. Capital may not be reduced to less than one-fifth of original capital.

Partnership agreement may be rescinded in respect of any of partners for: (a) Use of firm name or capital for own business; (b) violation of partnership agreement; (c) violation of legal provisions governing partnership; (d) fraudulent and deceitful acts; (e) bankruptcy, interdiction or incapacity to carry on commercial business.

Simple limited partnership (sociedad en comandita simple) is one in which one or more of partners are subject to unlimited and joint liability for partnership obligations, and one or more of partners are responsible for debts and losses only to amount of capital which they have subscribed. Name of partnership must include name of one or more of general partners; when all of names of general partners do not appear in firm name, words "y compañía" or other similar expression are added. Firm name must conclude with words "sociedad en comandita" or abbreviation "S. en C." Names of special partners must not appear in firm name. Any person whose name appears in firm name, is responsible in same manner as general partners. Special partners are also liable to same extent as general partners when expression S. en C. or words it represents are omitted. Special partners have no voice in management of company; if they intervene in any respect they are responsible to third persons together with general partners. However, in case of death or inability of administrator a special partner takes his place if partnership agreement does not provide manner of substitution, but in this case special partner can act only during one month from date of said death or inability and merely to perform urgent acts or take care of mere administration. Interests of special partners may be represented by shares in which case partnership is a "sociedad en comandita por acciones" (limited partnership with shares). Many of provisions regarding general partnerships are applicable to limited partnerships.

Sociedad en Comandita por Acciones (Limited Partnership with Shares).—This is legal entity which has aspects of both joint-stock company and partnership and is able to transact business, acquire real and personal property, and sue and be sued in its own name. It is composed of one or more general partners who have subsidiary, though unlimited, liability with company, and one or more limited partners responsible only to extent of their contributions.

Capital is divided into shares of stock; shares of general partners have to be registered and may not be transferred without consent of all of general partners and two-thirds of limited partners.

Name of firm may be composed of names of one or more of general partners, followed by words "y Compañía" (and Company). If not all general partners are included, name must also be followed by the words "Sociedad en Comandita por Acciones", abbreviated to "S. en C. por A."

Limited partners may not participate in administration of company. Organization, management and liquidation are governed by company rules, with some exceptions.

Asociación en Participación.—This is contractual arrangement between two or more individuals or enterprises for realization of one or more business transactions. There is no legal entity, nor may association operate under name. Managing associate receives capital from contributing associates and underlying agreement provides how profits will be distributed. Managing associate operates in his own name and is liable for debts of business, whereas contributing associates are liable only up to amount of

PARTNERSHIP . . . *continued*
their respective contributions. Association is to be based on written contract, which may modify some of basic rules expressed above.

Sole Proprietorship.—Individual person, including foreign individual with proper immigration permit, can do business in his name as sole proprietor and is personally responsible for losses of enterprise. Business has no legal personality.

Business Associations.—In Mexico, business enterprises are not only permitted, but are legally required to organize themselves into associations. Twenty firms in any particular industry may create national industrial association or chamber; for commercial chamber minimum is 50.

Limited liability companies (sociedades de responsabilidad limitada) are formed by members who are liable only for amount subscribed by them. They have some characteristics of a corporation and some of a partnership. Participations may not be represented by negotiable certificates, either to order or to bearer, and are transferable only in cases and in manner prescribed by law. Firm name must include name of one or more members, and must conclude with words "Sociedad de Responsabilidad Limitada" or abbreviation "S. de R. L." Failure to add said expressions to firm name makes members responsible without limitation. This type company may not have more than 50 members. Capital may not be less than 3 million pesos and must be divided into parts which may be of different class and value, but which in any case must be of 1,000 pesos or multiples thereof.

These companies cannot be constituted by public subscription, nor without total subscription of capital, nor without payment of at least 50% of each participation. Members cannot assign their interest and no new members may be admitted without consent of majority of members, unless company agreement provides for consent of higher percentage of members. No member may own more than one participation. When member makes further contribution or acquires all or part of interest of another associate, his participation is increased, unless participations are entitled to different rights, in which case they are held separately. Participations may not be divided unless in manner and cases provided by law.

Management is in hands of one or more managers who need not be members, who may act temporarily or for an indefinite period, and whose appointment may be revoked any time. Resolutions of managers are adopted by majority, unless it is stipulated that they must act jointly, in which case vote must be unanimous. Members act through general meetings at which resolutions are approved by vote of a majority representing at least half the capital, unless company contract or instrument of organization agreement requires larger proportion. General meetings have power to: (a) Discuss, approve, modify or reject balance sheet for preceding fiscal year; (b) declare dividends; (c) appoint and remove managers; (d) appoint council of inspectors, if any; (e) decide on division or amortization of participations; (f) modify company agreement; (g) consent to assignments of participations and admission of new members; (h) decide on increases or reductions of capital; (i) dissolve company; (j) exercise other powers which may be provided for by law or by company contract. Meetings are held at least once a year at company domicile. Modification of company agreement must be approved by at least three quarters of capital; except any change of object of company or increase of obligations of members requires unanimous vote of all members.

Company agreement may provide that members shall have a right to receive interest not exceeding 9% per annum on contributions; this right is limited to period long enough to allow company to perform acts and works necessary to carrying on of business, and may not exceed three years. This interest is charged to general expenses.

Foreign Partnerships.—Requisites before qualifying to do business are same as those provided for foreign corporations. See topic Corporations (Sociedades Anonimas).

PATENTS:

(Law to Promote and Protect Industrial Property of June 27, 1991 as am'd and regulations of Nov. 18, 1994).

Instituto Mexicano de la Propiedad Industrial is government agency in charge of industrial property matter.

New inventions susceptible of industrial application, including processes and products, are patentable. Following, among others, are not patentable: (i) uncovering of anything which already existed in nature; (ii) computation programs; (iii) surgical treatment methods; (iv) artistic works; and (v) variations of known products. Owner of patent may sue for damages any person who exploits patented process or product without owner's approval.

Patents are granted for period of 20 years, counting from application date.

Application may be filed by inventor, by his causahabiente (beneficiary) or by representatives of either. Prior application date in other country is recognized provided that application is filed within terms set forth in applicable international treaties. When there is no applicable international treaty, recognition is granted provided that application is made within 12 months after filing date of application in other country.

Law establishes general rules for granting of licenses and transfer of rights conferred by patents. Transfer of rights to be effective vis-à-vis third parties, must be registered. When patented invention is not exploited for industrial or commercial purposes by owner of patent during three years counting from granting date or four years from application date, whichever is later, third parties may request to grant "compulsory license" (licencia obligatoria) to exploit patented invention. When patented products are imported, such importation is regarded as effective exploitation of respective patent.

Patents expire, and therefore fall within public domain: (i) at end of term stated in Law; (ii) when annual fees are not paid; or (iii) for lack of exploitation.

Models are defined as objects, implements, apparatus or tools which, as result of modification in their disposition, structure, or configuration, have different function with regard to integral parts thereof or present different advantage as far as their utilization is concerned. Models may be registered for term of ten years counting from application date.

Industrial designs include both drawings and industrial models. Drawings must be related to industrial product. Industrial models must serve as basis for manufacturing of industrial products. Industrial designs are registrable for term of 15 years, commencing on application date.

Trade secret is defined as confidential information of industrial or commercial application that provides competitive or economic advantage to owner. Information considered trade secret must be expressed in documents, laser discs, microfilm films, by electronic or magnetic means or similar instruments.

Conventions.—Convention for the Protection of Industrial Property, Paris, Mar. 21, 1883, Stockholm Revision of July 14, 1967; Patent Cooperation Treaty with Regulations, Washington, June 19, 1970; Agreement on Trade-Related Aspects of Intellectual Property Rights, Marrakesh, Apr. 15, 1994.

PETROLEUM: See topic Mines and Minerals.

PLEDGES:

Pledges may be given of personal property and of crops to be garnered at a specified time. In the latter case pledge must be recorded in public registry. Object pledged must be delivered to creditor physically or constructively. Constructive delivery is understood to exist when there is agreement to leave object with a third person or when it is left with debtor either by agreement with creditor or because of express authorization by law. When pledge is left with debtor, contract has no effect as to third persons unless recorded in public registry. Recording may be effected only if property is clearly identifiable. Pledge contract must appear in writing; if a private writing, it must be in duplicate. Contract is not effective as to third persons unless date can be proved by registry, by public document or in some other conclusive manner. If object pledged is lost or deteriorates without fault of creditor, latter may demand another pledge or payment even before maturity. If debtor does not pay at maturity creditor may apply to a judge for sale of pledge at auction in accordance with rules provided in Code of Civil Procedure, but parties may agree that sale be made extrajudicially. Debtor may suspend sale by paying debt within 24 hours from suspension.

There are special rules regarding commercial pledges. In commercial pledges, if value of pledged articles or securities depreciates to less than amount of debt plus 20%, creditor may apply to judge for a sale of pledge. (C. C. 2856-2892; Law Aug. 26, 1932, arts. 334-345).

POWER OF ATTORNEY:

See topic Principal and Agent.

PRESCRIPTION:

(C. C. 1135-1180).

Acquisition of property or rights by virtue of possession or extinction of obligations by failure to require performance is called prescription.

Periods of prescription in commercial transactions are provided in Commercial Code and commercial laws, and consequently apply to whole nation. Prescription in commercial matters begins to run from date upon which an action might have been brought. It may be interrupted by any class of judicial proceedings for purpose of requiring debtor to recognize obligation or renew documents evidencing same. Prescriptive periods in which right to enforce an obligation is lost vary according to nature of action. More important are: (1) Actions to reclaim ownership of vessels, ten years; (2) actions arising out of articles of incorporation and partnership and out of operations of corporations and partnerships as between them and their members and between members, actions against liquidators of companies and partnerships, actions to collect principal of corporate bonds, five years; (3) actions to collect bills of exchange, promissory notes and coupons of corporate bonds, even though such documents were issued abroad, actions on warehouse certificates, actions based on maritime loans, three years; (4) actions by retail merchants on credit sales, except in case of accounts current, actions by commercial employees to recover salaries, actions arising out of contracts of transportation, actions against brokers for obligations arising out of their duties, actions against issuers of travelers' checks, actions derived from insurance contracts, many actions relating to admiralty matters, one year; (5) actions on checks, six months. In cases where shorter period is not established by Commercial Code, period is ten years. (Com. C. 1038-1048; Law Aug. 26, 1932, arts. 165, 192, 207, 227, 250, 258).

In matters not covered by Commercial Code, civil codes of various jurisdictions govern. In general, law of Federal District is as follows: Acquisition of property or rights by adverse possession is called positive prescription. Extinction of an obligation by failure to require performance is called negative prescription. Prescription already run can be waived, but not right to prescription in future. Government and municipalities are considered same as private individuals with respect to prescription of property, rights or actions susceptible of private ownership.

In order to acquire property by positive prescription, possession must be under claim of ownership, quiet, continuous and public. Real property is acquired by prescription: (1) In five years when held in good faith; (2) in five years when possession has been recorded in public registry; (3) in ten years even though held in bad faith. Periods designated in first and third cases aforementioned are extended by one-third if an interested party shows that possessor of rural property did not cultivate it during greater part of time, or that possessor of urban property neglected to make repairs, as a result of which property remained unoccupied greater part of time. Personal property is acquired by prescription in three years when held in good faith and in five years without good faith.

Period of negative prescription for extinction of rights is ten years when no other period is designated by law. Many actions prescribe in different periods, among them, following: (a) Actions for pensions, rents or other periodic payments, actions for accounting or to enforce liquidated obligations resulting from an accounting, five years; (b) actions for fees, salaries, wages or other compensation for services, actions of merchants for goods sold to persons not for resale, actions of hotel keepers for price of lodging and food, actions for libel or slander or for damages caused by persons or animals for whom defendant is liable, actions for civil liability for illicit acts which do not constitute crimes, two years.

Prescription does not run against incapacitated persons unless guardian has been appointed. It does not run: (a) Between ascendants and descendants while parental

PRESCRIPTION . . . *continued*
authority lasts, as to property to which descendants are entitled; (b) between husband and wife; (c) between incapacitated persons and guardians while guardianship lasts; (d) between co-owners or co-possessors; (e) against persons absent in public service; (f) against soldiers in active service in time of war.

Prescription is interrupted: (a) If possessor is deprived of possession for over a year; (b) by institution of suit or judicial demand, unless same is withdrawn or overruled; (c) if person in whose favor prescription is running expressly or tacitly acknowledges right of person against whom it is running.

PRINCIPAL AND AGENT:

(C. C. 2546-2604, C. Com. arts. 273-308).

An agency may be oral, it may appear in private writing with two witnesses and in public instrument, or in private instrument before two witnesses with all signatures acknowledged before notary or other authority, depending on amount involved and limit of power. Powers of attorney for appearing in court must be given by public instrument.

In order that the power of attorney may be unlimited it need only state that it is given with general authority and with such special authority as must be specifically granted according to law; general powers of attorney for administration need only state that they are given for general administrative purposes; and general powers for acts of ownership may also be in general terms; in these three cases if the authority of the agent is to be limited, the limitations must be expressed. The document must transcribe the entire text of C. C. Art. 2554. The agent cannot institute an action to enforce obligations contracted in the name of the principal, unless authority for this purpose is included in the power of attorney. Also agent needs express authority to subscribe for bills of exchange, promissory notes, and other exchangeable documents to file amparo suits before courts and to delegate powers to third persons.

The contract of agency is perfected by express or tacit acceptance on the part of the agent. If a power of attorney is given to a professional man for acts of his profession, it is considered as accepted if not refused in three days. An agency is gratuitous only when expressly so agreed. The agent may delegate his powers if expressly authorized to do so. The principal must advance to the agent the funds required for the exercise of the agency.

An agency is terminated: (a) By revocation; (b) by renunciation on the part of the agent; (c) by death of principal or agent; (d) when either is declared incompetent; (e) by expiration of its term or conclusion of the business for which it was given; (f) in certain cases when the principal has disappeared. The principal may freely revoke the agency, unless the same was stipulated as a condition in a bilateral contract or as a means to comply with an obligation contracted; in these cases the agent also cannot renounce the agency. The appointment of a new agent for the same matter implies revocation as to the former agent from the day he is notified of the new appointment. Although the agency is terminated by the death of the principal, the agent must continue his administration until the heirs can look after the business, if a different course might cause damage. If the agent renounces the agency he must continue acting until the principal can appoint another agent if damage might otherwise be caused.

PUBLIC INSTRUMENTS:

Documents executed before a notary and the notarial copies of such documents are considered public instruments. The law further designates numerous other documents as public instruments, among them documents issued by public officers in the discharge of their functions, documents, registers, etc., in the public archives and certifications thereof, certificates issued by officials of the civil registry, court records, etc. (C. C. P. 327-345, 411-417). In commercial matters public instruments also include mercantile contracts executed before mercantile brokers ("corredores") and certified by them. (Com. C. 1237). Most contracts of the more important kind are required to appear in a public instrument. (See topic Contracts.) Public instruments constitute full proof against parties and authorize institution of summary proceedings. (C. C. P. 443).

REAL PROPERTY:

The following are considered real property: (1) Land and the constructions thereon; (2) plants and trees unseparated from the soil and the fruits thereon which have not been separated by harvesting or regular cutting; (3) objects attached to a building in such manner that they cannot be separated without deterioration to the building or to the object; (4) statues, paintings and other ornamental objects placed on real property in such manner as to reveal the owner's intention to attach them permanently; (5) dove-cotes, bee-hives, fishponds and similar objects when the owner keeps them as a permanent part of the property; (6) machines, instruments and implements devoted by the owner of the property directly and exclusively for the industry conducted thereon; (7) fertilizers and seeds required for cultivation of the property; (8) electric apparatus and accessories attached to the land or buildings, unless otherwise agreed; (9) springs, pools, cisterns and water courses, aqueducts and pipelines for liquids or gases; (10) animals for breeding purposes on rural property devoted to cattle raising, and working animals indispensable for the cultivation of the property while devoted to that object; (11) dry-docks and other constructions which, though floating, are intended to remain at a fixed point in a river, lake or coast; (12) rights in rem on real property; (13) rolling stock of railroads, telephone and telegraph lines and radio stations. (C. C. art. 750).

The owner of real property owns the surface and whatever exists thereunder, subject to servitudes, police regulations, the mining laws (see topic Mines and Minerals) and article 27 of the Constitution of 1917.

RECORDS:

Public Register of Property.—All contracts transferring or modifying ownership, possession or enjoyment of real property or rights in rem must be registered in order to affect third persons. (C. C. 3002 et seq.). See also topic Deeds and Registration.

Commercial Register.—Corporate charter and its amendments, issuance of stock, and dissolution of commercial corporations must be registered. General and special powers of attorney must be registered. Individual merchants must register documents relating to their capacity to do business and family documents relating to their estate. Ship ownership must also be recorded in this register. (Com. C. 18, et seq.). See subheads Organization, Foreign Corporations, and Organization and Registration Fees, under topic Corporations.

Civil Register.—Birth and death, marriage and divorce, adoption and guardianship must be recorded in this register. (C. C. 35, et seq.).

There are various other registers such as Importers and Exporters Register and Taxpayers Register.

SALES (Realty and Personalty):

(C. C. 2248-2326; Federal Law on Consumer Protection of Dec. 22, 1992).

In general a sale is perfected between the parties when they have agreed as to the object of the sale and the price, although neither has been delivered. Sales reserving the right to repurchase are prohibited; but it may be stipulated that the seller shall have a preferential right to purchase at the same price offered by a third person, when the buyer wishes to sell the object; such right must be exercised within three days after notice of the third person's offer in the case of personal property, and within ten days after such notice in the case of real property.

It is legal to make installment sales with the condition that the sale shall be deemed rescinded if any installment is not paid. Such a condition is effective against third persons who may have acquired the object sold providing such object is real property or is some kind of personalty which can clearly be identified, and provided the condition is recorded in the public registry; but it is not effective against third persons acting in good faith, when the property is not susceptible of clear identification. In case of such rescission the buyer and seller must restore to each other the objects and amounts they have received, but the seller may demand rental for the object and an indemnity for its deterioration, both such rental and indemnity to be determined by experts, and the buyer may demand interest on the money paid to the seller.

It may also be stipulated that the seller retains the title until the price is paid and such a stipulation is effective as to third persons if it is recorded in the registry and the objects can be identified clearly. In such case the seller cannot sell the property to another until expiration of the period for paying the price and the buyer is meanwhile regarded as a lessee. If the property is retaken by the seller, the rules hereinbefore stated for retaking property sold on installments will be applied.

Mexico has enacted Federal Law on Consumer Protection that regulates consumer sales. Moreover it has created Public Office to deal with these matters.

International Sale of Goods.—United Nations Convention on Contracts for the International Sale of Goods, in force on Jan. 1, 1988. See Part VII, Selected International Conventions.

SHIPPING:

(Navigation Law of Dec. 23, 1993).

Legal acts related to national ships while in foreign waters are subject to Mexican law in whatever is compatible with the application of its own laws by the foreign state, and foreign vessels in territorial water are subject to Mexican laws.

Navigation and shipping are under jurisdiction of federal authorities. Mexican vessels must be registered in special registry. Mexican corporations and individuals may own Mexican vessels. National Maritime Public Registry shall also record acquisition, transfer or lease of any vessel; concessions to establish maritime and port installations or shipyards, drydocks and repair docks and other maritime and port services; incorporations and bylaws of maritime corporations, sale or encumbrances of same, as well as any contract which said corporations execute as public document; mortgages or other encumbrances on ships. There are provisions governing vessels and their crews and maritime contracts including leases, charter contracts, sales, insurance and averages.

STATUTE OF FRAUDS: See topic Contracts.

STATUTES:

Certain of general laws are of national scope, such as Commercial Code and Laws of Mines, Patents, Petroleum, Trade Marks, Copyrights, Railroads, Labor, Credit Institutions, Ways of Communications, Banks and Public Lands, etc. Each state has its own Civil Code, Penal Code, Code of Civil Procedure and Code of Criminal Procedure. There is also a Civil Code, a Penal Code, a Code of Civil Procedure and a Code of Criminal Procedure for Federal District and territories. All state Codes above mentioned are very similar to Codes of Federal District and territories but they often vary in details. In this digest, Civil Code, Commercial Code and Code of Civil Procedure of Federal District and territories have been followed in matters covered by them. The possibility of different provisions in corresponding Codes of any particular state must, however, be borne in mind.

TAXATION:

Caveat.—Mexico modifies its tax legislation last week of Dec. each year in connection with Federal Budget Law. This occurs after this digest has already been published. Consequently, some rates and provisions herein contained might not be accurate for year this edition is distributed, although correct as to previous one.

Federal Fiscal Code promulgated by Decree of Dec. 30, 1981, as am'd and its Regulations of Feb. 28, 1984 as am'd comprises provisions for surcharges on delinquent payments, penalties, collection procedures, appeals, statute of limitations, and other regulations applicable to various taxes. Code includes number of provisions taken from other specific laws which are considered of general application for all taxes, such as those referring to geographic and economic zones considered as part of national territory, rules for sales of assets, fiscal year, obligations to keep accounting records, procedures for guaranteeing payment of pending taxes in case of liquidation, basic conceptual definitions of sales transactions, and issuance of proper documentation and authority of Ministry of Finance to estimate income.

Income Tax (Law of Dec. 30, 1980 am'd and its Regulations of Feb. 28, 1984 as am'd.)—Subject to tax are: Individuals or juridical persons who: (1) Are residing in Mexico, on all incomes, regardless of source; (2) are residing outside country, with permanent establishment or fixed base of operation in Mexico, on income ascribed to latter; (3) are residing outside Mexico, on income from Mexican sources different than

TAXATION . . . *continued*

above. Whenever taxable income has its source abroad, income tax applied by country of origin will constitute credit, within certain limitations. Juridical persons residing in Mexico owning at least 10% of capital of foreign company may credit not only taxes paid on dividends but also taxes assessed and paid on its profits in said foreign country. Taxpayer who is not in position to take full credit for taxes paid to foreign country given five-year carry over of such excess foreign taxes, provided certain requirements are met. Tax brackets and amounts in pesos in income tax law are indexed on quarterly basis.

Main taxes established by Law are: (a) Tax on legal entities; (b) tax on nonprofit organizations; (c) tax on individuals; (d) tax on Mexican source income of nonresidents.

(A) Tax on Legal Entities.—Applicable to juridical persons which carry out business activities related to commerce, industry, agriculture, livestock and fishing activities, as defined in Law. These rules apply also to decentralized agencies doing business activities as well as to permanent establishments in country of foreign taxpayers residing abroad and to credit institutions.

Rates.—Tax liability is figured: Rate applicable to tax result in fiscal year is 34%. Tax result shall be determined by obtaining taxable income, which represents difference between gross income of such year and authorized deductions from gross income, minus fiscal losses from other fiscal years. From amount resulting, 50% is reduced if taxpayer is dedicated exclusively to agriculture, livestock or fishing activities; 25% if taxpayer dedicated to foregoing activities engages in industrialization thereof or combines such activities with commercial or industrial activities not producing more than 50% of gross income. If taxpayer is dedicated exclusively to publishing books, reduction is 50%.

Deductions permitted, among others: Purchase of merchandise and other raw materials, finished or semi-finished products used by taxpayer in order to produce other merchandise; expenses; investments; difference between final and initial inventories of fiscal year, when initial inventory is larger, in case of taxpayers engaged in livestock business; casualty losses due to Acts of God or force majeure; uncollectible credits; contributions to funds for research and technology development when complying with rules established in Art. 27 of Law; creation or increase of reserves for pension or retirement plans complementary to ones established by Social Security Law; interest.

Law permits depreciation and amortization of tangible fixed assets and of intangible assets, deferred charges and expenses. Law allows straight-line depreciation of buildings, machinery and equipment and straight-line amortization of intangible assets, deferred charges and expenses. Accelerated depreciation may be authorized by Secretariat of Finance and Public Credit.

Taxpayers may opt for immediate deduction of tangible fixed assets in year when utilization thereof starts or in following year. Law sets forth percentages of cost allowed for this deduction according to type of asset. Excess of said percentages is nondeductible in any case whatsoever. Assets must be utilized permanently in country, but outside metropolitan area and other areas as indicated by law.

No deduction is allowed for: Income taxes paid on behalf of taxpayer or third parties; profit-sharing by workers, members of board and others as provided by law; indemnification, seniority and similar reserves for employees except as provided by law; losses due to merger, capital reduction or liquidation of entities in which taxpayer had interest or stock; entertainment expenses; interests paid to individuals and to nonprofit organizations; losses derived from sale of assets which investment is not deductible in accordance with Law; presents offered to clients except when directly related to rendering of services; per diem or travel expenses except for meals, lodging, transportation and kilometer allowance outside 50 kilometers around company's premises; value added tax; tax on assets; employee's portion of social security fees paid to Mexican Social Security Institute except those of minimum wage workers, etc. Losses of operation may be carried over for period of five subsequent years. Note, however, this deduction is personal to taxpayer who suffered loss, not being usable by another juridical person even as consequence of merger. Nevertheless, in case of mergers surviving company may amortize its losses incurred up to moment of merger against taxable profits deriving from same types of business from which loss was incurred.

In certain cases, Secretariat of Finance and Public Credit may estimate gross income and determine tax profit by applying certain coefficients established for each kind of activity.

Consolidated Income Tax Returns.—Main advantage in these provisions is possibility of deducting currently, at consolidated level, tax losses incurred by controlled companies, in proportion to holding companies' ownership of total capital of such controlled companies. For this purpose, holding company for tax purposes is that company which: (a) Is resident of Mexico, (b) directly or indirectly holds at least 50% of shares with voting rights of controlled companies, and (c) in no case 50% or more of its shares with voting rights are owned by another corporation. 35% tax rate is applied to consolidated tax result. For this purpose, amount so included will be total tax result of all controlled companies and holding company itself, in accordance with certain rules contained in law.

In order to consolidate, Secretariat of Finance and Public Credit has to grant specific authorization. Holding and controlled companies must meet following requirements: (a) holding company must have written consent of each of controlling companies and (b) be obliged to prepare financial statements under provisions set forth in Fiscal Code of Federation. Following entities do not qualify for filing consolidated returns: Companies which are residents of foreign countries, credit institutions, insurance companies, auxiliary credit organizations, and brokerage and exchange houses. Additionally, nonprofit organizations or companies undergoing liquidation are not entitled to consolidating provisions.

(B) Tax on Non-Profit Organizations and Fixed Income and Common Investment Companies.—These rules apply to juridical persons who are not among those contemplated under Tit. II of Law (corporations and other organizations). Taxpayers will be those who own organization concerned. Said taxpayers are taxed on their corresponding individual income.

(C) Individuals are subject to.—

(a) Tax on Labor Income.—This tax applies to salaries of any kind and compensations pursuant to rescission or termination of employment agreements. Following are included: Fees of administrators, corporate inspectors, directors, general managers, remunerations to officers and employees of Government.

Fees are treated as salaries when services are carried out on premises of person paying fees.

(b) Tax on Fees other than Labor Income.—Fees of professionals, artists, agents of credit institutions, insurance companies or custom houses when not rendering subordinate personal services. Individuals obtaining income from rendering of independent personal service may deduct necessary expenses and investments. Nonresident individuals with fixed base of operation in Mexico are subject to tax.

Professional associations are not taxable directly, but members are subject to tax, in proportion.

(c) Rental income derived from lease or sublease contracts and earnings from non-amortizable participation certificates. Individuals may deduct yearly predial tax, maintenance expenses, interest on loans used to buy or renovate real estate for residential rental property or they may take allowed standard deduction which is 50% of rental income. For other real estate rentals optional standard deduction is 35% of gross rents.

(d) Transfer of Goods.—Taxpayer with income derived from any transfer of goods except by cause of death, donation or merger of corporations; adjudications; expropriation; trust, must effectuate provisional payment on each operation, applying general rates to 20% of these profits and multiplying result by five, to determine amount of said provisional payment.

(e) Acquisition of Assets.—Provisional withholding of tax assessed on income herefrom shall be made at rate of 20% on income received from donations, treasuries, acquisition by prescription etc., without any deduction.

(f) Business Activities.—Income of individuals who carry out business activities derived from commerce, industry, agriculture, livestock and fishing activities shall be subject to tax rate of 20% of estimated profit; advance payments will be made monthly. Tax profit and tax results will be determined as in juridical persons. (See [A] above.) Among other deductions are: Refunds, discounts or allowances; expenses; investments etc. Individuals receiving income not exceeding ten times annual minimum wage of geographic area corresponding to Federal District as provided by law in previous calendar year, unless otherwise estimated by Secretariat of Finance and Public Credit, will only have to fulfill simplified requirements established in Art. 119-G of Law. Requirements for deductions are similar to rules applicable to juridical persons.

(g) Dividends and profits distributed by juridical persons resident in Mexico are taxable according to special rules of Tit. IV. Tax payment is absorbed by distributing entity.

Taxpayers may credit against tax assessed on individuals residing in Mexico, Mexican income tax paid by juridical persons decreasing dividend or profit in accordance with Art. 121 of Law. In this case income obtained must be added to other income of taxpayer in preparing his annual return.

(h) Interest from bonds, debentures, certificates of credit institutions, mortgage certificates, negotiable instruments, loans or other credits of credit institutions and auxiliary organizations, amortizable participation certificates in real property and ordinary participation certificates and proceeds deriving from hedging operations, paid by individual residents of Mexico or received by them are subject to withholding tax of 20% of paid interest when such securities are classified as traded among general investing public; otherwise, such interest income would be considered normal gross interest income, subject to regular individual tax rates.

(i) Income from prizes obtained by individuals residing in Mexico from lotteries, raffles, gambling and competitions of all kinds is taxed at final rate of 8% and 15%. These tax rates apply to gross income without deduction.

(j) Other income of individuals includes among others: Fees for guaranties; income from dividends received from residents outside Mexico; income from royalties for use or exploitation of author's rights by third parties except when derived from music and literature works; amounts received from special personal savings accounts with exceptions indicated by law; amount of debts forgiven by creditor or paid by another person; moratory interests and indemnification for damages. Income derived from premiums, bonuses, or gains on sale of bonds, securities or other similar credit instruments which are classified as traded among general investing public, are considered as interest subject to 20% tax, rather than regular tax on profits from sale of securities; however, gains on sales of such securities having maturity of more than six months are not considered as interest. Taxpayers will make provisional payment at rate of 20% of received income.

Among exempt incomes appear: Payments other than salaries received by employees of general minimum wage when not exceeding legal minimum wages established by labor law; limitation is imposed on exemption from tax of social welfare benefits granted in form of disability subsidies, educational scholarships, day-care centers, cultural activities, sports, and other activities of similar nature, whenever sum of both salaries and social welfare benefits exceed amount of seven times minimum wage of economic area of taxpayer, all such social welfare benefits in excess of one annual minimum wage of economic area of taxpayer are taxable; Social Security benefit pensions for retirement, disability, dismissal or by reason of employee's death; compensation for professional risks or sickness; bonuses to employees (up to limit established in §XI of Art. 77 of Law) at end of year; fees of foreign diplomatic and consular representatives, employees of foreign embassies, with citizenship of said represented country, members of scientific delegations etc.; interests paid by lending institutions when not exceeding annual 5% of deposit amount; income from inheritance income; income from sale of shares from publicly held investment companies; interest paid by banking institutions on savings accounts; from donations among spouses and children; amount equal to 20 times annual minimum wage of income derived from royalties for use or exploitation of author's rights by third parties except in case of individuals who, in addition to receiving royalties, receive from same pay or either fees or salaries, when within calendar year, royalties are received from single person and when royalties are paid for technical, scientific and educational books.

General deductions for individuals residing in Mexico are: Minimum wage salaries; medical and dental fees as well as hospital expenses incurred by taxpayer and his/her spouse, children or person living with him in concubinage when said persons did not receive more than minimum wage salary yearly; funeral expenses; donations to public services or charity institutions. Contributions to educational institutions are expressly

See Topical Index in front part of this volume.

TAXATION . . . *continued*
authorized except in case of donations made to cover tuition or fees for services, etc.; however, deduction is conditioned upon use of funds so contributed for investments in capital assets. Additional cross-references are made to sections of law covering corporations. Thus, deductibility requirements, will be consistent for both individuals and corporate entities.

Rates.—Individuals residing in Mexico are subject to rates ranging from 3% to 35% on taxable income.

(D) Tax on Mexican Source Income of Foreign Country Residents.—Tax, when such payments are made for his benefit or serve purpose of avoiding disbursement by nonresident, applies only to Mexican source income of foreigners and of Mexicans residing in foreign countries.

Payments made for account of foreign country residents are subject to tax. Salaries, commissions and fees for intermediation services rendered outside Mexico are not subject to tax.

Income tax is calculated on basis of specified rates applied to gross income received. Deductions are allowed on expenses and other disbursements made abroad when directly connected with business activity subject to Mexican taxation. Foreign country resident may elect to be taxed on income net of expenses provided it has qualified representative in Mexico, who meets following requirements: (a) He is resident of Mexico; (b) he retains for five years supporting evidence of tax paid by him on behalf of foreign country resident; (c) guarantees payment of any additional taxes. Representative is jointly liable with those he represents for payment of tax due.

Law sets forth specific rules for determining when certain categories of income will be considered Mexican source income subject to income tax. For instance: Salaries and other payments made by employer for personal services rendered within Mexico are subject to tax with some exceptions. Tax rates are 15% and 30% of gross income received and must be withheld by party making payment. Salaries and other payments for services made to consular and diplomatic representatives, employees of foreign embassies, members of scientific delegations, etc. are exempt from tax.

Professional fees and other payments for personal services rendered in Mexico are subject to tax at rates of 15% and 30% of gross income.

Salaries, professional fees and other payments are not subject to tax when paid to foreign country resident by individual or juridical entity without permanent place of business in Mexico or if such permanent place of business exists, if particular services are unrelated to such establishment. This exemption applies only when service is for less than 183 days in 12 month period.

Income from immovables located in Mexico is subject to tax at rate of 21% on gross income.

Rental income from movable goods used within country for commercial, industrial, agricultural, cattle growing and fishing activities is subject to tax at rate of 21% on gross income.

Income from distribution of dividends or profits by companies resident in Mexico is subject to withholding tax at rate of 35% of gross income without deduction when such dividends are actually paid in cash or kind and not at time dividends are declared.

Income from interest earned on capital deposited or invested in Mexico is subject to tax at following tax rates: (a) 15%, on interest payable to foreign governmental financial institutions and foreign banks, duly registered with Secretariat of Finance and Public Credit; (b) 21%, on interest paid by credit institutions to nonresidents not included above and interest earned on sales paid to foreign machinery and equipment suppliers; (c) 35% on other types of interest. Interest income is presumed to be Mexican-source if party paying interest is resident in Mexico, or if not resident in Mexico, such party has permanent place of business in Mexico or fixed base.

Interest exempted from Mexican taxation when paid on three or more year loan agreement on which interest is fixed for same period and loans are granted by financial institutions registered with Ministry of Finance.

Income from financial leasing of assets used in Mexico is subject to tax at rate of 15%, on amount of payments made reduced by portion considered as original amount of investment in accordance with Art. 48 of Law. Taxable interest income of nonresidents includes compensation for guarantee of loans; applicable rate of tax depends on who renders guarantee service, and nature of loan.

Gains on sale of bonds, securities, and other credit instruments (different from shares of stock), which are classified as traded among general investing public and have maturity of up to six months are also taxable as interest income, subject to 20% flat rate. Gains on sales of this type of securities having longer maturities are taxed in same manner as capital gains on shares. Gains on sale of securities through authorized securities exchange or on broad-based securities market pursuant to rules issued for such purpose, are exempted from tax.

With regard to premiums or gains on future contracts for foreign currencies, nonresident will not be taxed if transaction generating this type of income is directly related to imports or exports of tangibles other than foreign currencies.

Income from royalties paid for use of assets or rights in Mexico is subject to tax at following tax rates: (a) 15% as to royalties for use or temporary enjoyment of copyrights on literary, artistic or scientific works, including films, radio and TV recordings, drawings or models, plans, formulas or procedures, commercial, industrial or scientific equipment as well as for information regarding industrial commercial or scientific experiences and in general for technical assistance or transfer of technology; (b) 35% as to royalties for use or temporary enjoyment of patents, certificates of invention or improvement, trademarks and commercial names.

Income from services related to construction, installation maintenance of immovable goods performed in Mexico is subject to withholding tax at rate of 30% on gross income. Election is available for payment of tax at rate indicated in Art. 10 of Law on net income provided foreign country resident has qualified representative in Mexico.

Income from sale of immovable assets located in Mexico is subject to tax at rate of 20% on gross income. Election is available for payment of tax at rate of 35% on net gain provided sale is made in form of public deed to purchaser. When he is not resident of Mexico and has no qualified representative in Mexico, Mexican resident payor of goods or services of nonresident assumes tax responsibility arising from transaction. When real property is acquired by resident of foreign country for more than 10% below its appraisal value, difference is taxable income of nonresident. Amount of tax on income so obtained will be 20% of profit on acquisition, payable within 15 days after authorities advise nonresident of their assessment.

Income from sale of shares or negotiable instruments issued by companies organized under Mexican law, whether or not sale takes place in Mexico, is subject to tax at rate of 20% of gross proceeds. Election available for payment of tax at rate of 30% of net gain provided foreign taxes equal to or exceed 70% of effective tax in Mexico.

In similar terms to those provided for in real estate transactions, nonresident will be deemed to have realized taxable income in Mexico on purchase of capital stock, whenever amount paid on acquisition is more than 10% below appraisal value of such shares. Tax of 20% is payable on deemed profit.

Tax on Assets of Businesses.—(Law of Dec. 27, 1988 as am'd and its Regulations of Mar. 29, 1989 as am'd). Tax at annual rate of 2% of added value of assets is assessed to all legal entities and individuals doing business in Mexico including foreign enterprises with permanent establishment and nonresidents with regard to their local inventories to be transformed or which have been transformed by taxpayer subject to tax. Tax is assessed on average value of assets less average value of liabilities during year.

Added Value Tax (Law of Dec. 22, 1978 as am'd; Regulations Feb. 28, 1984 as am'd).—Applies to sales, use and temporary possession of goods, independent services rendered and to importation of goods and services.

Any person, corporation or economic entity engaged in above mentioned business activities, is subject to tax. Added value tax applies to production and marketing of goods but not to their exportation.

Rates.—General rate is 15%.

Credit against Tax.—Tax paid for importation of services and goods which are strictly necessary may be credited against value added tax due in proportion that tax paid on imported goods is creditable.

Exemptions.—Among others: gold; gratuitous services; public transportation not requiring federal permit or concession; life insurance.

Tax on Ownership and Use of Vehicles.—Regulated by Law on subject of Dec. 1980 as am'd. Amount of tax is determined according to specific kind of vehicle.

Local Income and Other Taxes.—Federal District and the several states have their own revenue laws, taxing several activities or products or incomes. Rates in States are similar. In addition there are excise taxes on products or activities.

Special Tax Incentives.—

Assembly Plants.—Customs Law, Regulations of June 3, 1996 and Decree of Dec. 20, 1989 as am'd grant tax incentives to assembly plants. Applicable to: (a) Machinery where total output exported, (b) local producer who exports all or part of production. Assembly plants are authorized to sell in domestic market up to 50% of value of exported annual production. Temporary and duty-free importation of goods for assembly and finishing of: (1) Raw and auxiliary materials; (2) machinery, apparatus, instruments and equipment; (3) spare parts; (4) tools and accessories for production and security, as well as manuals and blueprints; (5) containers, packaging material, labels and booklets; (6) computer, telecommunications and administrative equipment.

Free Zones and Perimeters.—(Arts. 136-142 of Customs Law of Dec. 13, 1996 and its Regulations). Industries located herein may import goods duty-free if not produced in such area except alcoholic beverages, beer, cigarettes, cigars and race horses, realize duty-free exports of goods produced, finished or manufactured and, may remit such products to rest of Mexico without being taxed on raw materials and components included therein. For tax purposes free zones and perimeters deemed separate from rest of Mexico; goods brought from abroad into such areas not deemed import into Mexico; goods sent from areas to rest of Mexico, deemed import; goods sent from rest of Mexico to areas, deemed export.

Customs Law.—Law of Dec. 13, 1995, and its Regulations of June 3, 1996, establishes that base for ad valorem duties is "normal" or free market value of imported merchandise, which must appear on customs declaration as described in arts. 64 and 66 of said Law. Art. 64 of said Law sets prices from which to determine normal value of merchandise which must reflect usual price of competition defined as that prevailing between independent buyer and seller in free market conditions. For purpose of speeding up foreign trade operations, Law provides for having taxpayer himself prepare declarations and determine amount of tax liability payable, subject to review by customs authorities, provided that those who customarily carry out foreign trade operations be registered in National Registry of Importers and Exporters. Special mechanisms are provided for purpose of promoting specified areas of economy, such as in-bond processing industry, procedures for industrial deposits in bond which provide advantage of not paying import duties on imported products which are subsequently included in exports of items produced in Mexico. Deposits in bond, are extended to local goods, as result such items may be considered as exported at time they are placed in bonded warehouse under control of customs authorities, and certain tax incentives may be received as from time of deposit. Important benefits are authorized for purposes of developing industrial parts, which are intended to promote industrial development and export of Mexican produced manufactured products.

TRADEMARKS AND TRADENAMES:

(Law to Promote and Protect Industrial Property of June 25, 1991 as am'd; and regulations of Nov. 18, 1994).

Law protects trademarks and commercial slogans and names. Translations into other languages of words which are not registrable may not be registered. Among others, following are not registrable: technical names; isolated letters; numbers or colors; geographical denominations; and titles of literary works. Trademark may not be extended to additional products or services other than registration.

Instituto Mexicano de la Propiedad Industrial is government agency in charge of industrial property matter.

Registered trademarks enjoy protection for term of ten years. Such term may be renewed for terms of ten years. If mark registration is requested by two or more persons, rules governing use, license and transfer of rights of trademark must be attached to application. Application date in country of origin of trademarks registered therein is recognized as provided by international treaties. If there are no international

See Topical Index in front part of this volume.

TRADEMARKS AND TRADENAMES . . . *continued*
treaties, such date is recognized if application is made within six months from application date in country of origin. Resolutions on registration of trademarks, as well as extension of terms thereof, are published in official newspaper.

Applications for extension of registration of trademark must be made by owner within six months prior to expiration date. If trademark is registered in order to protect two or more classes of products or services, extension of registration in any one of such products or services shall be effective to cover all other products or services if fees are paid for other classes.

Owner of trademark or pending application may grant license to use trademark, which license must be registered to be effective vis-á-vis third parties. Products sold or services rendered by licensee must meet same quality standards as products manufactured or services rendered by licensor. When license is registered licensee has right to institute legal proceedings to enjoin falsification, imitation or illegal use of trademark unless there is contrary agreement. Franchise (franquicia) exists under Law when technical knowledge and assistance is transferred along with license for use of trademark.

Rights deriving from mark application and trademark registration may be mortgaged or transferred pursuant to general principles contained in Civil and Commercial Codes. To be effective vis-á-vis third parties, transfer must be registered. For purposes of transfers of rights, Law regards registration of trademarks as "linked" (marcas ligadas) when such trademarks belonging to same person are identical and cover similar products or services or when such trademarks are similar to degree of confusion and apply to same products or services or to similar products or services. In such instances, owner of trademark must transfer all or none of marcas ligadas except when Instituto considers that marks are not linked upon explanation and request of owner to that effect.

Registration of trademark is null and void when trademark has been used abroad by person, other than party submitting application, prior to application made in Mexico and when such trademark is identical or similar to degree of confusion.

Commercial slogans are defined as "phrases or sentences purpose of which is to advertise to public commercial or industrial establishments or businesses, as well as establishments and businesses which provide services, to distinguish them from others of same kind." Registration of commercial slogan is granted for term of ten years counting from date of filing application. Such registration may be renewed for terms of ten years.

Commercial name of industrial or commercial business or establishment or of business or establishment for rendering of services is protected, without requirement of registration in those geographical areas where business or establishment has customers or in entire country if there is constant and significant advertising and promotion at national level. Anybody using commercial name may request publication thereof in official newspaper. Such publication establishes good faith in use of name. Effect of publication of commercial name lasts ten years counting from application date and can be renewed for terms of ten years.

Mexican State is owner of denomination of origin and such denomination of origin may only be used by means of authorization. Denomination of origin is defined as name of geographical area of country which identifies product as originally of such geographical area, when quality and characteristics of such product are due exclusively to geographical region including natural and human elements. Companies or individuals engaged in extraction, production or manufacturing of products linked with geographical areas may request authorization to use denomination of origin.

Authorization to use denomination of origin lasts ten years counting from application date, renewable for periods of ten years. Right to use denomination of origin may be transferred by licensee, but such transfer shall be effective vis-á-vis third parties as from moment of registration.

Federal Courts enjoy jurisdiction to determine criminal sanctions and fines established in Law, as well as to resolve disputes of mercantile or civil nature arising from application of Law. Fraudulent use of trademark on commercial scale and revealing and unauthorized use of trade secrets are crimes. Sanctions provided by Law are imprisonment and fines.

Conventions.—Convention for the Protection of Industrial Property, Paris, Mar. 21, 1883, Stockholm Revision of July 14, 1967; Agreement on Protection of Denominations of Origin and its international registry, Lisbon, Oct. 31, 1958; Agreement on Trade-Related Aspects of Intellectual Property Rights, Marrakesh, Apr. 15, 1994.

TREATIES:

Bilateral:

Canada.—Convention for avoidance of double taxation and prevention of fiscal evasion with respect to taxes on income. Signed on Apr. 8, 1991.

El Salvador.—Treaty on Enforcement of Criminal Judgments. Signed on July 14, 1993.

France.—Convention for avoidance of double taxation and prevention of fiscal evasion with respect to taxes on income. Signed on Sept. 21, 1992. Extradition Treaty and Treaty on Criminal Judicial Assistance. Both signed on Jan. 27, 1994.

Germany.—Convention for avoidance of double taxation and prevention of fiscal evasion with respect to taxes on income. Signed on Feb. 23, 1993.

Italy.—Convention for avoidance of double taxation and prevention of fiscal evasion with respect to taxes on income. Signed on July 8, 1991.

Korea.—Convention for avoidance of double taxation and prevention of fiscal evasion with respect to taxes on income. Signed on Oct. 6, 1994.

Netherlands.—Convention for avoidance of double taxation and prevention of fiscal evasion with respect to taxes on income. Signed on Sept. 27, 1993.

Spain.—Convention on Recognition and Enforcement of Judgments and Arbitral Awards in Civil and Commercial Matters. Signed on Apr. 17, 1989. Convention for avoidance of double taxation and prevention of fiscal evasion with respect to taxes on income. Signed on July 24, 1992.

Sweden.—Convention for avoidance of double taxation and prevention of fiscal evasion with respect to taxes on income. Signed on Sept. 21, 1992.

Switzerland.—Convention for avoidance of double taxation and prevention of fiscal evasion with respect to taxes on income. Signed on Aug. 3, 1993.

United Kingdom.—Convention for avoidance of double taxation and prevention of fiscal evasion with respect to taxes on income. Signed on June 2, 1994.

United States.—Agreement relating to interchange of fiscal information. Signed in Washington on Nov. 9, 1989 and its Protocol. Convention for avoidance of double taxation and prevention of fiscal evasion with respect to taxes on income. Signed on Sept. 18, 1992 and its Protocol. For complete list of U.S.-Mexican Agreements, see Treaties in Force, publication compiled by Department of State annually as of Jan. 1.

Multilateral.—Convention for the establishment of an Inter-American Tropical Tuna Commission. Signed at Washington on May 31, 1949. Ratified Jan. 13, 1964.

International telecommunication convention. Signed at Geneva on Dec. 21, 1959. Ratified Feb. 14, 1962. Instrument of ratification deposited May 4, 1962. Promulgated by Decree of June 25, 1964 (published in D. O. of Aug. 14, 1964). Mexico is also party to 1965 Convention which replaces earlier conventions between parties to later Convention.

Mexico promulgated Convention on Recognition and Enforcement of Foreign Arbitral Awards done in United Nations in 1958.

"Latin American Integration Association" LAIA created 1980 after dissolution of LAFTA.

"Latin American Economic Systems" SELA created in Panama 1975.

Inter-American Conventions signed in Panama on Jan. 30, 1975: On conflict of laws concerning bills of exchange, promissory notes and invoices; On International Commercial Arbitration; On Letters Rogatory; On the Taking of Evidence Abroad; On legal regime of powers of attorney to be used abroad.

UN Convention on International Multimodal Transport of Goods, both signed at Geneva in 1980.

Inter-American convention on general rules of private international law, signed at Montevideo in 1979.

Inter-American Conventions signed at Montevideo in 1979: On extraterritorial validity of foreign judgments and arbitral awards and On domicile of natural persons in private international law.

Inter-American Conventions signed at La Paz in 1984: On status and legal capacity of juridical persons in private international law and On international competence for extraterritorial validity of foreign judgments.

Multilateral Trade Negotiations The Uruguay Round, Final Act, Marrakesh, Apr. 15, 1994 and Agreement Establishing the World Trade Organization, Marrakesh, Apr. 15, 1994. Convention abolishing the requirements of legalization for foreign public documents, with annex. Signed The Hague on Oct. 5, 1961.

International Sale of Goods.—ONU Convention on Contracts for the International Sale of Goods in force since Jan. 1, 1988, signed at Vienna on Apr. 11, 1980.

TRUSTS:

In recent years Mexico has adopted, with substantial modifications and restrictions, some of the principles of the Anglo-American law of trusts. "Fideicomisos" (trusts) may be created by will or by trusts declared "inter vivos" with respect to any real or personal property and rights, except rights of a strictly personal nature. Trusts may be created for the lives of any number of beneficiaries or successive beneficiaries provided that they are in being at the grantor's death. Secret trusts and, in general, trusts where the beneficiary is a judicial person whose duration exceeds 30 years are prohibited unless they are charitable or educational in nature. Only banking institutions may act as trustees. (General Law of Negotiable Instruments and Credit Transactions of Aug. 26, 1932 as am'd).

WILLS:

(C. C. 1295-1598).

All persons may make wills except: (a) Minors below 16 years; (b) persons not of sound mind. All persons may take by will with certain exceptions such as: (a) Persons not conceived at the time of the death of the testator; (b) persons who were guilty of certain crimes or dishonorable acts towards the testator; (c) guardians with respect to their wards, unless the will was made before their appointment or after the minor came of age and the guardianship accounts were approved; the physician who attended the testator during his last illness and near relatives of the physician, namely, spouse, ascendants, descendants and brothers and sisters, unless such persons are also legal heirs; the notary and witnesses who signed the will and their near relatives; ministers of religion with respect to other ministers and other persons to whom they are not related within the fourth degree; likewise near relatives of such ministers with respect to persons whom the ministers attended during a last illness or as spiritual advisers; (d) aliens and corporations in so far as they are included in the disabilities established by the Mexican Constitution; (e) aliens whose national laws do not allow a Mexican to inherit; (f) churches and religious sects and institutions; (g) persons whom the testator appoints as executors or guardians and who decline the office without good cause or are removed for bad conduct. Such incapacities must be declared by a court in an action brought within three years after the incapacitated person has entered into possession of the property, except that incapacities established on the ground of public policy may be enforced at any time.

Conditional legacies are allowed, but a condition not to give or not to do is regarded as nonexistent, as also a condition not to attack the will under penalty of losing the legacy.

The testator may freely dispose of his estate, but must leave aliments to the following person if they have insufficient property of their own: (a) Sons below 21 or who are unable to work, and unmarried daughters who live honorably; (b) surviving widow while unmarried and living honorable, and surviving widower if unable to work; (c) ascendants; (d) in certain cases the woman with whom the testator lived as man and wife; (e) collaterals within the fourth degree if under 18 or incapacitated.

A testator may appoint an heir to inherit in case the heir first named dies before the testator or refuses the inheritance. Trust substitutions are forbidden; but the title to property may be left to one person and the usufruct for life to another, and a father may leave his property to a son with remainder to children of the son born before death of the testator.

See Topical Index in front part of this volume.

WILLS . . . *continued*

Wills are either: (1) Ordinary; or (2) special. Ordinary wills are: (a) Public open; (b) public closed or (c) holographic. Special wills may be: (a) Private; (b) military; (c) maritime or (d) foreign.

The following cannot be witnesses to a will: (a) Clerks of the officiating notary; (b) minors below 16 years; (c) persons not of sound mind; (d) blind, deaf or dumb persons; (e) persons who do not understand the testator's language; (f) heirs and legatees, and their descendants, ascendants, spouse or brothers or sisters, but the presence of a witness of this kind invalidates only the provision benefiting such person or such relatives; (g) persons convicted of forgery.

Public open wills are made before a notary and three witnesses. The testator declares his will before the notary and the witnesses, the notary draws up the will in accordance with the testator's wishes as a regular notarial instrument and reads it aloud, whereupon all sign, with a statement of the place, date and hour of signing. The notary issues a certified copy (see topics Notaries Public; also Public Instruments) which serves as an original in all estate proceedings. If a witness cannot write, another signs for him, but at least two must sign. If the testator cannot write, a fourth witness signs for him; only in extremely urgent cases can one of the first three sign for him. In the case of blind persons the will is read twice, once by the notary and once by a witness or other person. If the testator does not know the language of the country, he may write his will and the same is translated by two interpreters, the original remaining in notary's file.

Public closed wills may be written by the testator or by another person at his request. The testator must put his scroll on every page and sign the will; he must then have it sealed or enclosed in a sealed envelope, and exhibit the same to a notary in the presence of three witnesses, declaring that it contains his last will. The notary writes a statement on the envelope and such statement is signed by the testator, the witnesses and the notary. If the testator cannot sign, another person may sign the will for him and the testator must so declare in presenting it to the notary. Likewise someone may sign the statement on the envelope for him, and if a witness cannot write, another person may sign for the witness. When the will has been closed and the covering statement signed, the notary makes a note of the matter in his records. The testator may keep the will himself or leave it in the custody of another.

Holographic wills are those written in their entirety by the testator. Such a will can be made only by persons who are of age. Aliens may make holographic wills in their own language. The testator must himself write and sign the will in duplicate in longhand, stating the date, and must place his finger-print on every page. The original in a sealed envelope is deposited in the General Archives of Notarial Offices; the duplicate, also in a sealed envelope, is returned to the testator; each of the envelopes being provided with a statement signed by the registry official and the testator.

Private wills are emergency wills which may be made in certain cases where the testator is seriously ill and there is no time to call a notary, or where no notary is available. It is necessary that the testator be unable to make a holographic will. A private will must be declared before five witnesses or in cases of great urgency before three witnesses, and need not be in writing when the witnesses cannot write or when there is great urgency. The will is valid only if the testator dies of the illness or in the danger in which it was made or within one month after the cessation of the circumstances which authorized it.

Military wills may be made, orally or in writing, before two witnesses by soldiers on entry into action or when wounded in battle.

Maritime wills may be made in writing on board a Mexican vessel, in duplicate, before the captain and two witnesses.

Foreign Wills.—A will made abroad is considered valid if made in accordance with the laws of the country where made. Mexicans may make wills before Mexican secretaries of legation, consuls and vice-consuls, acting as notaries.

See Topical Index in front part of this volume.

MONGOLIA LAW DIGEST REVISER

The International Law Firm of
ARNBERGER, KIM, BUXBAUM & CHOY
Mongolian Business Development Agency
Room 112
Prime Minister Amar's Street
Ulaanbaatar, Mongolia
Telephone: (976)(1) 31-0711; (976)(1) 31-3492
Fax: (976)(1) 32-5102
Email: akbc@magicnet.mn

New York, New York Office: 100 Maiden Lane, 16th Floor, Suite 1600B, New York, New York 10038. Telephone: (212) 504-6109. Fax: (212) 412-7016.

Los Angeles, California Office: 515 South Flower Street, Suite 3500, Los Angeles, California 90071-2201. Telephone: (213) 236-4355; (310) 358-0344. Fax: (213) 426-6222; (310) 358-0226.

Reviser Profile

ARNBERGER, KIM, BUXBAUM & CHOY is an international law firm with offices on the east and west coasts of the U.S.A. (New York City, Los Angeles and San Francisco) and in Hong Kong, China and Mongolia. The Firm's international division maintains five offices inside China, including the capital at Beijing and the cities of Guangzhou (Canton), Shanghai, Shenzhen, and Xiamen. Each of the Firm's partners are recognized international practitioners, several of whom are prominent in their respective legal fields and some of whom have extensively published and frequently lectured on current legal issues. The Firm's attorneys include several prominent American, Asian and European-trained attorneys, along with attorneys who are of counsel to the Firm and assist it from associated offices in Tokyo, Seoul, Taipei, Bangkok, Jakarta and Sydney.

Established in 1969 the Firm traces its roots in Asia to 1972, when one of its attorneys became the first American attorney to represent foreign parties in China. It has since become one of the largest American firms in East Asia. The Firm's international practice is also supported by experienced attorneys in the Firm's state-side offices, who provide expertise and work closely to coordinate overseas representations with client management and in-house counsel in North America and Europe. The Firm opened the first foreign law office in Mongolia in 1992, and is active in legal work, including arbitration, in Russia and some Eastern European countries. The Firm's legal prominence in Northeast Asia is recognized in its appointment as the official Reviser of Martindale-Hubbell's *China* and *Mongolia Law Digests*.

The Firm's attorneys have handled challenging cross-border cases and international transactions, ranging from leading copyright infringement and antipiracy victories in China on behalf of foreign software and literary publishers, through the negotiation of natural resource concession rights in Myanmar (Burma), to obtaining one of the largest product liability settlements in the Commonwealth of the Northern Marianna Islands on behalf of Japan's largest construction contractor. The Firm undertakes numerous major transactional matters including drafting the first insurance joint venture contracts in China; establishing major power plant contracts, handling major loan agreements and leasing transactions and assisting in public offerings. The Firm handles numerous transactions on behalf of major international banks. The Firm also handles all corporate work and other legal work on behalf of overseas divisions of European, Asian and American corporations.

The Firm is active in the representation of parties in the U.S.A., including foreign parties doing business in the U.S. Attorneys in the American offices actively handle all aspects of domestic-based litigation, complex business transactions and corporate matters, securities and commodities, admiralty law, employment law and intellectual property transactions. Attorneys in the Firm's U.S. offices also routinely counsel businesses and entrepreneurs in their investment matters and day-to-day corporate and business activities. Attorneys in the Firm's U.S.-based litigation division routinely handle a variety of cases, including securities and commodities, breach of contract, employment discrimination, insurance disputes, marine law, product liability, unfair competition, and intellectual property infringement litigation. The Firm has handled appeals all the way to the U.S. Supreme Court, including a successful landmark case (*Butz v. Economou* 438 US 478, 1978). The Firm's U.S.-based attorneys are frequently called upon to represent clients in significant transactions, example of which includes the US$60 million acquisition of America's third largest ski resort by a major foreign investor and the first ever negotiated license of patent rights between the National Institute of Health and a major Japanese manufacturer. The Firm has been very active in securities and commodities compliance and litigation, as well as public offerings in the U.S.A.

The Firm's partners and associates bring extensive international and domestic legal experience that few firms of its size can equal. The Firm therefore offers the expertise and diversity of a big firm, while simultaneously providing the personalized service and responsiveness found in smaller firms. The Firm has thus been favored with a broad client base comprised of many of the world's foremost multinational companies from the U.S., Canada, Asia and Europe. Various attorneys of the Firm are admitted to practice in New York, California, and other U.S. jurisdictions, as well as in foreign jurisdictions such as China, Mongolia, Hong Kong, Japan, Korea, Thailand, Indonesia and Australia. In addition to English, attorneys of the Firm are fluent in numerous foreign languages, including Mandarin, Shanghainese, Hokkien, Cantonese and other Chinese dialects, Japanese, Thai, Indonesian Bahasa, Korean, French, Spanish and Swedish.

MONGOLIA LAW DIGEST

(The following is a list of all Topics, including cross-references, covered in this Digest.)

MONGOLIA LAW DIGEST

Revised for 1997 edition by

ARNBERGER, KIM, BUXBAUM & CHOY of Ulaanbaatar, New York and California bars.

PRELIMINARY NOTE:

Formerly a tightly controlled Soviet satellite, Mongolia embarked in 1990 on radical economic and political reform program intended to transform it from communist one party state to free-market multiparty democracy. Encouraged by changes in Soviet Union, citizens staged pro-democracy demonstrations in Winter of 1990 which led to Mongolia's first free elections in June of that year. Victorious democratic coalition, led by Prime Minister Byambasuren, pushed through radical reformist agenda of more than 25 new laws, as well as numerous amendments to existing legislation. Government goals included rapid privatization of more than 80% of economy, liberalization of foreign investment and trade policy, tax overhaul, banking reform, and enactment of new constitution protecting political freedom and human rights.

By early 1992, Mongolian economy was in free-fall. Government estimated that during 1991, GDP shrunk by 15%, and personal incomes fell by one half. Rationing of basic commodities became widespread. While economic problems partly resulted from upheaval wrought by Government's reform program, Soviet Union's collapse had crushing effects. Halt of Soviet foreign aid, which formerly made up as much as 30% of Mongolian GDP, was compounded by new Russian demands that all petroleum purchases be made in hard currency.

Reacting to perceived crushing effects of Byambasuren's reforms, voters returned former ruling communist party, KPRP, to power in July 1992 elections. Government, headed by Prime Minister Jasrai, publicly maintained its commitment to free market reforms but pledged to safeguard social justice during transition period.

Government maintained that review is necessary to remove lacunae and to insure consistency with new constitution, and has pledged to enact all reformist legislation pending before parliament prior to next elections. Presidential election took place in 1993, and president was reelected. Economy seemed to have bottomed out and 3% growth in GNP took place in second quarter of 1994. Reform continued in 1993 and 1994, albeit at somewhat slower pace. Mongolia appears to be both politically and economically stable, though unemployment remains high.

Presidential election took place in 1993 and President Punsalmaagiin Ochirbat was reelected, this time as candidate from the democratic opposition. Even after years of crisis, Mongolian economy showed in 1994 and 1995 some positive changes at the macroeconomics level, unemployment remained high and poverty grew among the population.

Under these circumstances the elections of June 30, 1996 swept from power the MPRP and the Democratic coalition composed of the two main former opposition parties formed the new Government in July 1996. One of the first moves of the newly appointed Prime-Minister M. Enkhsaikhan was to reduce the number of Ministries from 14 to 9 in an effort to put in place an efficient and cost-effective public administration. The Government committed itself to speed up the pace of reform and to end the state controlled prices on the electricity, oil products, telecommunications services and housing rentals.

Being a country in transition to market economy and democratization, Mongolia has been continually updating its legislation and adopted a whole range of laws since 1990.

ADOPTION:

Mongolian marriage law allows adoption of children, and grants adopted children to have same rights and duties in adopted home as natural children. (Art. 53). Children are eligible for adoption from date of birth up to age 16 (Art. 50), with some restrictions which vary with age. Final decisions regarding adoption are made by executive body of relevant local hural (legislative body) or executive body of district (in city). (Art. 48).

Following documents are required by local authorities for adoption: (1) permission of parents or custodian; (2) official application; (3) child's medical certificate; (4) certificate of marriage; (5) document of social security organization certifying home environment of adoptive family; (6) documentation of prospective parent's employment; (7) child's birth certificate and child's passport.

Foreign citizens and stateless persons are not permitted to adopt Mongolian children. (Art. 48 amendment to the law, 1996).

AGENCY:

Citizens and legal persons may exercise their rights and obligations through representation by other persons. (Civ. Art. 57). Persons who are working in interest of others but on behalf of self (master, executors of will, etc.) and persons who are authorized to undertake future transactions are not representatives. (Civ. Art. 58). Representative's authority must be based on law, administrative act, or trust documents. (Civ. Art. 59). If represented party agrees to transaction made by person without authority to represent or representative who exceeded scope of authority, transaction will be considered valid since it has been ratified. (Civ. Art. 59).

Letter of authority to act as agent must be certified by notary. (Civ. Art. 61). Letter of authority granted by legal person must contain signature and seal of leaders of organization; chief accountant or acting accountant must sign letter of authority dealing with receipt, transfers, etc. of money, and/or property of legal person. Regulations concerning granting letter of authority for banking transactions and foreign trade deals, as well as form of letter of authority, are specified in law. (Civ. Art. 62). Trust is created for no more than three years; letter of authority will be considered valid only for one year from date of issuance if term of action is not specified in letter of authority; and letter of authority will be considered null and void if date on letter of authority is not specified. (Civ. Art. 63).

Trustee must personally carry out activity for which he was entrusted, and if specified in letter of authority that activity may be carried out by other persons or if it is important to do so for interests of principal, then letter of authority may be transferred. (Civ. Art. 64). Term of transferred letter of authority must not exceed term of original letter of authority. (Civ. Art. 64). Principal has right to suspend letter of authority at any time, and entrusted party has right to refuse letter of authority. (Civ. Art. 65). If entrusted party does not know about expiration of letter of authority or is not able to know it, transactions made with third person will be valid. (Civ. Art. 65).

ALIENS:

Law on legal status of foreigners in Mongolia of Nov. 1993 became effective on Feb. 1, 1994.

Visas are required to enter, exit and transit in Mongolia except when they are covered by agreements between states for mutual exemption from visas.

Constitution of Mongolia provides that rights and duties of foreign nationals shall be based on principles of reciprocity.

Foreigners must be holders of valid foreign passport and must obtain permission from competent Mongolian organizations prior to visiting or residing in Mongolia. (Art. 21).

Law classifies foreigners into four categories depending on duration of their visit or residence in Mongolia: (a) foreigners travelling to Mongolia for up to 30 days are considered visitors; (b) foreigners visiting Mongolia for up to 183 days are considered temporary residents; (c) foreigners living in Mongolia for up to five years are considered long term residents; (d) foreigners living in Mongolia for private reasons are considered immigrants. Aliens who are criminal defendants or suspects considered to represent threat to national security or public order may be denied exit from Mongolia. (Art. 22).

There are quantitative restrictions on number of immigrants residing in Mongolia. Total of immigrants in Mongolia should not exceed 1% of total population of country and immigrants from any one country should not exceed 0.33%. (Art. 24).

Council on Foreign Nationals under Ministry of Justice is in charge of immigrant status. (Art. 25).

Foreigners arriving in Mongolia, except those who arrived at invitation of Governmental organizations or local administrations, must register with Police within ten days of their arrival. Registration request must be made through host organization or private person. Foreign immigrants must inform Police of changes in residence, family status or employment within seven days of change. (Art. 26).

ARBITRATION:

Arbitration Tribunal of Mongolia, operating under aegis of Mongolian Chamber of Commerce and Industry, was originally established in 1961 to resolve trade disputes between Mongolian state enterprises and those of other COMECON countries. In 1991, Arbitration Court expanded to consider all commercial disputes involving foreign trade, regardless of nationality of disputants.

New Foreign Arbitration Law, which entered into force on Dec. 15, 1995 provides that duties and functions of Foreign Trade Arbitration shall be exercised by Arbitration Court. (Art. 3.1 Foreign Arbitration Law).

Structure and Activities of Arbitration Tribunal.—Arbitration Tribunal consists of Chairman, General Secretary, and not less than 15 arbitrators. (Art. 3.4). Chairman and arbitrators are designated by Council of the National Chamber for period of three years. (Art. 3.5). General Secretary is designated by Council as well. (Art. 3.6).

Seat of Arbitration Tribunal is Ulaanbaatar (Art. 3.3) regardless of location of tribunal. Hearing is conducted in Mongolian unless both parties agree otherwise (Art. 15). Arbitration Court shall strive to reach decision within 60 days from date of acceptance of claim unless specific timing is set forth by treaties, regulations or agreements. (Art. 14.1).

Jurisdiction of Arbitration Tribunal arises from arbitration clause in contract or separate agreement on arbitration conducted by parties. (Art. 5.1).

If intergovernmental trade agreement provides for arbitration conciliation, arbitration agreement is considered as concluded in relation to contract concluded within above agreement. (Art. 5.2).

Arbitration settles disputes within arbitration clause or agreement arising: from international economic contracts and transactions between individuals and or legal entities, as well as disputes preceding contract formation (Art. 6.1); between national and foreign founders of economic entity with foreign investment that operate in Mongolia (Art. 6.2); between foreign legal entities (Art. 6.3).

Legal norms and usages abided during arbitration conciliation. Laws and regulations of country chosen by mutual agreement of parties or international treaties is abided by, or if parties have not so agreed, then laws and regulations of country to which one of parties belongs or international treaties. (Art. 8.1).

Arbitration Court abides by agreements concluded between parties, as well as usages of trade applicable to particular transaction. (Art. 8.2).

Commencement of Proceedings.—Proceedings commence upon receipt of plaintiff's claim and payment of arbitration costs. Claim shall specify names and addresses of parties, arbitration agreement or treaty, demands, supporting documents, statement of value of dispute. (Art. 9.1). Defendant files counterclaim conforming to same requirements. (Art. 9.3).

Arbitration costs consist of basic and additional costs. Fees of arbitrators and arbitration costs as certain percentage of amount of claim shall be basic costs. Additional costs incurred during tribunal (expenses of conducting expert examination, traveling expenses of arbitrators, etc.). (Art. 3.5). Basic costs range from 4% but not less than 300 USD for claims up to 10,000 USD and 31,000 USD plus 0.5% of total price of any amount exceeding 200,000 USD. (Resolution N30 of Finance Minister, 1996). In event that party withdraws claim before arbitration hearing, he is refunded 50% of fee. However, amount which shall be kept by tribunal shall not be less than 200 USD. (Resolution, Arts. 3, 4). If case is settled by one arbitrator, party is refunded 25% of fee. (Resolution, Art. 2).

See Topical Index in front part of this volume.

ARBITRATION . . . *continued*

Arbitration costs shall normally be borne by losing party. Where claim is partially satisfied costs are divided according to proportion of award. Losing party bears additional costs as well. (Art. 37).

Selection of Arbitrators.—Arbitration Panel normally consists of three arbitrators selected from group currently serving on Arbitration Tribunal. One arbitrator is selected by plaintiff, one by defendant in reply. These two arbitrators in turn select Chairman of Arbitration Panel. (Art. 16.2). Parties also have option of selecting sole arbitrator by joint agreement. (Art. 16.6). If parties fail to appoint arbitrator within 14 days from date of receiving notification arbitrator is appointed by Chairman of Arbitration Court. (Art. 16.3).

Challenge of Arbitrators.—If single arbitrator from Panel of three is challenged, merit of challenge is decided by other arbitrators. If challenge is directed against two arbitrators, or all arbitrators, merit of challenge is decided by Chairman of Arbitration Tribunal. Arbitrator may reject nomination if arbitrator feels there is conflict of interest. (Art. 18).

Either party has right to challenge experts or interpreters, if doubt arises as to their ability. Merit of such challenge is decided by arbitrators. (Art. 32).

Arbitration hearings are conducted in open session. If evidencing documents are related to state or secret organisation or individual or commercial secrets of parties, arbitrator may, on his own initiative or upon request of parties, conduct hearings in private. In this event, award shall be announced openly. (Art. 13). Proceedings are conducted in Mongolian language. If participants are not familiar with Mongolian language proceedings translated by interpreter. (Art. 12). Third party is entitled to file independent claim and participate in proceedings, if considers that his interests are infringed. (Art. 25). Parties may participate in proceedings through their representatives. (Art. 27.1).

Arbitration awards shall be made by majority of arbitrators in writing with all arbitrators signing award. (Art. 51.4). Arbitration awards are considered final and are to be voluntarily fulfilled by parties. Decisions not fulfilled voluntarily are enforced in accordance with legislation of Mongolia. (Art. 56.3). Enforcement of award in foreign country shall be regulated by international treaties and conventions. (Art. 56.4). Within 60 days after passing of award, arbitrator may, at his own initiative or at request of party, make additional award. (Art. 53.1). Party must make requests within 30 days of receiving award and shall notify other party thereof. (Art. 53.20).

Mongolia acceded to United Nations Convention on the Recognition and Enforcement of Foreign Arbitral Awards in 1995.

BANKING LAW:

New Banking Law, which entered into force on May 1, 1991, establishes two-tiered banking system consisting of Mongolbank (Central Bank of Mongolia) and various commercial banks, both public and private. All banks are prohibited from engaging in material production, insurance services and land market operations. (Art. 5).

Note: Revision of Banking Law and adoption of Law on the Bank Operations were on Agenda of Special Session of New Parliament in Aug. 1996.

Mongolbank performs traditional duties of Central Bank, including printing banknotes, ensuring stability of tugrik, determining minimum reserves required for commercial banks, carrying out unified interest rate policy, managing interbank and government lending, maintaining state gold and silver reserves, and supervising activity of commercial banks. It maintains 21 branch offices throughout Mongolia, and has assets of approximately 185 million tugrik. Although Banking Law authorizes Mongolbank to establish foreign branches (Art. 25), none yet exist. Foreign exchange transactions are carried out by State Bank of Mongolia.

State Great Khural is responsible for supervising Mongolbank, approving its annual balance sheet (Art. 21) and appointing its President (Art. 9).

Commercial banks may be publicly or privately owned, held domestically, in joint venture with foreign party, or be of wholly foreign origin. (Art. 27). Parties wishing to establish new commercial bank must possess start up capital not less than 50 million tugrik (Art. 33.2), and submit application and charter to Mongolbank. Mongolbank may refuse to authorize establishment of new bank if such bank does not appear economically viable, or if its statutes conflict with Mongolian Law. (Art. 30). All commercial banks must maintain level of reserves dictated by Mongolbank (Art. 35.2), and submit its annual financial statement (Art. 41).

State presently operates eight commercial banks, including State Bank of Mongolia (foreign exchange), Industrial Bank (loans to large enterprises), and Agricultural Bank. One private commercial bank has been established, and more are expected once privatization has been completed.

Foreign currency loans from government shall be made by Mongolian bank in accordance with approval of Ministry of Finance and Mongolian government.

According to Point Seven of Art. 11(7) of Mongolian Bank Law, only Mongolbank (Mongolian General Bank) can carry out Mongolian Government's loans. Therefore, approval by Mongolbank is not required for repayment of foreign currency loans.

As for other banks, according to Art. 9 of Rules of Foreign Exchange Control, only those commercial banks which are authorized to engage in foreign currency operations may issue loans in foreign currency. Under all circumstances, no approval from Mongol bank is required in making payment.

Legal opinion for Government loans is needed from Ministry of Justice, license (order) from Ministry of Finance. Government loans and foreign investment shall be done through Mongolbank.

BANKRUPTCY:

Bankruptcy Law which entered into force July 1, 1991 provides basic procedures for declaring firms bankrupt, dissolving them and protecting economic interests of their creditors.

Bankruptcy proceedings can begin either upon creditor's claim that debtor firm is insolvent or upon debtor's own report of insolvency. (Art. 5.1). Court gives official public notice within ten days of initiation of such proceedings. (Art. 5.2). After notice, creditors may make their individual claims up until date set by court for creditor's meeting. (Art. 8). To protect interests of creditors, certain transactions performed by firms in bankruptcy are legally invalid, including pledges, transfers or sales of property which are detrimental to interests of creditors, payments made before contractual due date and refusals by firm in bankruptcy to receive payment of debts. (Art. 10).

Judgment of Bankruptcy is issued when firm proves insolvent, and fails to pay debts owed to creditors on time. (Art. 7). In its judgment, court sets date for creditor's meeting (Art. 7) and orders bankrupt firm to halt all business activities (Art. 8). Under certain circumstances, court may postpone decision of bankruptcy. Court may delay judgment for three months upon its receipt of debtor's guarantee to pay creditors. (Art. 6.1.a). Court may grant one year abstension if interested person approved by creditors agrees to bind himself to reorganize insolvent firm. (Art. 6.1.b).

Creditor's meeting is organized by court to dissolve bankrupt firm. (Art. 11.1). Creditor's Council is then established by court or by creditors. Council recommends trustee to be appointed by court, discusses and approves trustee's suggestions on distribution of debtor's assets and supervises trustee's activity. (Art. 11.2). Upon appointment by court, trustee prepares detailed financial investigation of bankrupt debtor, secures remaining assets and gives opinion on distribution of property to Creditor's Council. (Art. 12.1). If Creditor's Council is satisfied with trustee's opinion, it approves opinion and trustee is discharged. (Art. 12.2). Disputes are resolved by court. (Art. 12.2).

Property is distributed to creditors according to trustee's approved opinion. Creditors failing to submit claim before judgment of bankruptcy cannot be involved in distribution of property unless court decides otherwise. (Art. 15.2).

Property in firm's possession upon judgment of bankruptcy, bankruptcy insurance payments and property returned to firm as result of Art. 10 are all considered distributable. (Art. 13).

If property of firm does not suffice to pay off all creditor's claims, employee wages, allowances and other compensations are paid first and remainder distributed among creditors. (Art. 15.1). In such situation, members of firm without limited liability are personally liable for debts of firm. (Art. 15.1).

CIVIL CODE:

Civil Code consists of six parts: General Provisions, Law of Property, General Grounds for Liability, Contract Liability, Liability Not Arising under the Contract, and Right of Succession. It establishes legal capacity for various categories of persons and defines legal person with rights and obligations. Statute of limitations on most civil actions runs for three years. (Art. 69). Provisions on agency, contracts, insurance, labor, real property, sale and purchase, securities, succession, and trespass to be found under respective topics in this Digest.

CONSUMER PROTECTION:

Consumer Protection Law which entered into force Jan. 27, 1991 is ambitious and wide ranging, regulating product information, quality and character of sales transactions. Although consumer protection is to be administered by executive boards of local hurals and state control organizations (Art. 10), enforcement has been lax. Most products presently produced by state enterprises fail to meet its standards.

Accurate and complete information must be supplied to consumers. (Art. 6.1). Producers and sellers (defined as any entity or individual offering products to consumers) must supply their names, addresses, trademark, price, product designation, use instructions and warranty information. (Art. 6.2). Seller is obliged to give consumer opportunity to confirm asserted qualities. (Art. 7.2). Sellers or manufacturers who give false information may be fined and forced to forfeit proceeds from sales of falsely marked products to state. (Art. 11.1.c).

Dangerous products, harmful to health of humans or environment, must meet established state quality standards and be registered at State Registry. (Art. 4.1.a.). Manufacture, sale, and import of such product is forbidden without certificate of quality issued by authorized quality control laboratory. (Arts. 4.1.c, 4.4.d). Producers and sellers are responsible for printing warning labels on packaging of such product (Art. 4.2), as well as including storage and use instructions (Art. 4.3). Sellers or producers who discover that they have distributed products which are harmful to health of humans or to environment must immediately notify Government, relevant state control organizations, and public. (Art. 6.4).

Perishable products may not be sold or traded after their date of expiry if they could become harmful to health of humans or environment. Penalty for failure to meet state quality standards in manufacture of dangerous products, failure to obtain certificate of quality, or sale of perishable products after date of expiry is fine of up to 50,000 tugriks and forfeiture of properly labelled dangerous products. Penalty for failure to include proper use and storage instructions is fine of up to 20,000 tugriks. (Art. 11.1.b).

Duress or unconscionability may render contract unenforceable. Sellers who secure consent of consumers to contract through abuse of official position, or threat of such abuse, may not enforce agreement. (Art. 7.3). Contracts which unconscionably injure interests of consumers are similarly unenforceable. (Art. 7.3).

Defective Goods.—Consumer who unknowingly buys defective goods may demand either reduction in price (Art. 5.2) or refund from seller (Arts. 5.3.a, 5.3.b). Seller who fails to notify customers of defects has obligation to replace defective goods at soonest date possible agreed upon by consumer (Art. 5.3.a), and must pay fine for each day replacement is delayed (Art. 11.2.a). Seller who sells goods with defects which could not be detected at time of sale has obligation to repair or replace such goods within time period agreed on by consumer. (Art. 5.3.b).

Consumer grievances are handled by relevant State Control Organizations. If seller refuses to present claim to Control Organization (Art. 9.2.a), consumer may appeal decision of Control Organization to civil court (Art. 9.2.b).

CONSTITUTION AND GOVERNMENT:

Following popular democratic reform demonstrations in winter of 1989, existing Soviet-style constitution of 1960 was amended in May of 1990 to provide for multi-party elections. After victory of democratic coalition in election of July 29, 1990,

See Topical Index in front part of this volume.

CONSTITUTION AND GOVERNMENT . . . *continued*

reformist Prime Minister Byambasuren appointed draft commission to prepare entirely new constitution based upon principles of democracy, human rights and rule of law. Draft committee worked closely with American and European advisors and proposed constitution based on European parlimentary model. Draft constitution was submitted to State Great Khural June 1, 1991, and was adopted with some modification on Jan. 13, 1992.

Highest organ of Mongolian State pursuant to new constitution is State Great Khural, unicameral parliment of 76 members. (Arts. 20, 21.1). Members are directly elected for term of four years. (Art. 21.2). Exact electoral procedure is specified by Election Law. (Art. 21.4). State Great Khural normally meets for two 75 day sessions per year (Art. 27.2), but under certain circumstances, extraordinary sessions may be called (Arts. 27.3, 27.4, 27.5). State Great Khural has power to enact and amend laws, set dates of Presidential and Khural elections, establish standing committees dealing with specific issues, and to appoint or remove Prime Minister. (Arts. 25.1, 25.6). State Great Khural also approves budget, decides whether to ratify international agreements, holds referenda, decides questions of war and peace, and declares national emergencies. (Arts. 25.7, 25.18).

Government, highest executive body of State (Art. 38), is comprised of Prime Minister and his/her cabinet members (Art. 39.1), who normally sit for four-year term (Art. 40.1). Candidates for Prime Minister are nominated by Great Khural. (Art. 33.1). Nominee who is elected by State Great Khural proposes cabinet which must be approved by both President and State Great Khural. (Art. 39). Government may be dissolved prematurely if Prime Minister or half of members of Government resign (Art. 43.2), or if Government receives vote of no confidence from State Great Khural.

Constitution holds Government accountable to State Great Khural (Art. 41.2), but it nevertheless has wide-ranging powers. Pursuant to constitution, government proposes social and economic development plan for nation, and outlines scientific and tehcnological policy. (Arts. 38.2, 38.3). It is also responsible for proposing state budget (Art. 38.2), protecting environment (Art. 38.2), ensuring national security (Art. 38.6), and protecting human rights while enforcing public order (Art. 38.7).

President is head of state, and is elected for four year term through two-stage election process. (Arts. 30, 31.1). Parties with seats in State Great Khural nominate candidates, who then appear on ballot for national direct elections. (Arts. 31.2, 31.3). Candidate receiving majority of votes wins (Arts, 31.4), otherwise two candidates with largest share of votes face each other in run-off election (Art. 31.5). Powers of President are limited in line with constitution's parlimentary model. President may veto legislation in part or whole, but veto may be overruled in State Great Khural by 2/3 majority. (Art. 33.1.1). President also has power to make law by presidential decree, but such decrees are only valid insofar as they are compatible with existing law. (Art. 34). Additional powers of President include status as Commander in Chief of armed forces (Art. 33.2) and power to conclude international treaties (Art. 33.1.4).

Judicial System.—Constitution provides that judicial power is vested only in courts (Art. 47), and that Judiciary be strictly independent and guided by law (Art. 49). General Council of Courts, overseeing board whose structure and membership are left unspecified, acts to maintain judicial impartiality as well as to nominate judges to courts. (Art. 49.4).

Supreme Court is highest judicial organ, and court of last resort for all criminal, civil and administrative matters. (Art. 38). Supreme Court, however may not make rulings which involve constitution. (Art. 50.4). Constitution provides for Chief Justice (Art. 51.1), but number of judges is not specified. Judges are nominated by President from pool of candidates put forward by General Council of Courts. (Art. 51.2).

Procurator General and deputies are nominated by President and are appointed with consent of State Great Khural. (Art. 56.2). Procurator supervises registration and investigation of cases, and represents State in court proceedings. (Art. 56.1).

Constitutional Court supervises implementation of constitution and makes judgment on violations of its provisions. (Art. 66). There are total of nine justices, each serving six year terms. (Art. 65.1). Three each are appointed by State Great Khural, President and Supreme Court. (Art. 65.1). Chairman is elected from among members for three year term by majority of votes. (Art. 65.3). Constitutional Court may decide to take case on its own initiative, or on basis of petition from citizen, State Great Khural, President, Prime Minister, Supreme Court or Procurator General. (Art. 66.1). If court finds that laws, Presidential decrees, referenda, official actions or international treaties violate constitution, it submits its decision to State Great Khural. (Art. 66.2). Judgments are final if matter relates to violation of constitution by Government officials, or grounds for removing Government official from office; in all other matters, Constitutional Court grants final review only if its decision is rejected by State Great Khural. (Art. 66.3). Laws, decrees, referenda, official actions and international treaties found unconstitutional by Court are invalid. (Art. 66.4).

Human rights and personal freedoms are strongly protected by new constitution, reflecting influence of both American Bill of Rights and European constitutions. Discrimination on basis of ethnicity, language, race, age, sex, social origin, property, occupation, title, religion, conviction and education are all forbidden. (Art. 14). Enumerated rights include: right to life (except where State proscribes capital punishment) (Art. 16.1); clean environment (Art. 16.2); possession of private property (expropriation prohibited) (Art. 16.3); choice of work (Art. 16.4); assistance in old age (Art. 16.5) and free medical care (Art. 16.6). State guarantees right to free general education (Art. 16.7); right to protect intellectual property (through copyrights and patents) (Art. 16.8); and right to vote upon reaching age 18 (Art. 16.9). Freedom of association (Art. 16.10), religion (Art. 16.15), speech (Art. 16.16) and freedom from unreasonable search and seizure (Art 16.13) are similarly protected. Citizens have right to approach court to protect their rights. (Art. 16.14). Once in court, they may not be compelled to testify against themselves, and they are innocent until proven guilty. (Art. 16.14). Citizens have duty to respect and abide by laws, pay taxes and to serve in army. (Art. 17.1).

Human rights of foreigners in Mongolia are governed by Mongolian law and treaties concluded with relevant foreign states. (Art. 18.2). State has power to limit those rights of foreigners not specifically protected by international treaty, provided such limitation is necessary to ensure national security. (Art 18.5). Foreigners fleeing political persecution will be granted asylum provided their request is reasonable. (Art 18.4).

Local government in Mongolia is divided into 18 aimags (provinces), and its capital city, Ulaanbaatar. Aimags are further subdivided into somons; somons into bugs. Capital city is divided into districts and horoos. Each aimag, somon and district, as well as capital city, is governed by local Khurals, or parliaments. (Art. 59). Local social and economic policy is made within these administrative units (Art. 62.1), so long as their decisions are made in conformity with constitution and State Law (Art. 62.2).

State authority in provinces is administered by governors at each administrative level who are nominated by relevant local Khural and appointed by State Government Office. (Art. 60). Governor insures observance of national laws (Art. 61.1) and has right to veto legislation proposed by local Khurals (Art. 61.2). Veto, however, may be rejected by majority vote from local Khural. (Art. 61.3).

CONTRACTS:

Contracts may be made orally, except those which must be in writing as required by law. (Civ. Art. 39). If parties dispute agreement made in violation of legal requirement of making contract in writing, transaction may be proved by other evidentiary instruments even though parties have forfeited right to proved by verbal evidence. (Civ. Art. 39). Contracts are made orally when: (1) parties have agreed on principal conditions of their transaction, (2) there is exchange of things used traditionally as performance and receipt, or (3) in case of one party's offer to perform, term fixed for response or ordinary term has expired. (Civ. Art. 40). Contracts in writing are completed when: (1) parties provide documents expressing their intent and execute said documents, (2) one party has received letter, cable, official paper (e.g. telex), or other document expressing intent of another who has accepted offer, or (3) contract is registered and certified by notary in accordance with law. (Civ. Art. 40).

Contracts under unclear conditions will be considered invalid when it is unknown whether circumstances for formation of rights and obligations connected with this transaction have been created or not. (Civ. Art. 55). Contracts under conditions that fail will be considered invalid when it is unknown whether circumstances for abatement of rights and obligations will be created or not. (Civ. Art. 55). If one person intentionally hinders creation of fixed conditions, these conditions will be regarded as created; if one person intentionally accelerates creation of fixed conditions, these conditions will not be regarded as created. (Civ. Art. 55).

Court may consider following contracts null and void: (1) those made as result of delusion; (2) made by means of fraud, violence or threat or under duress; (3) made deliberately to detriment of citizens or legal persons, as well as made by person not authorized to conduct such transactions; (4) made by underage person without permission of parents or guardians; and (5) made by person who has legal capacity but is unable to understand and control his activity during conclusion of transaction. (Civ. Art. 44).

Conclusion of Contract.—If proposal is addressed to indefinite persons and does not contain any other description, it must be considered to be request to make proposal. (Civ. Art. 161). If draft contract is sent with fixed term of response and other party responds in time, contract will be regarded as concluded. (Civ. Art. 161). Contract is considered concluded when it becomes clear from late response of draft contract by other party that response was made in fixed time, although other party received draft contract beyond expiration date of its offer and did not inform another party about its rejection. (Civ. Art. 161). In cases where offering party informed other party about late reception of response, reply must be considered potential offer for new draft contract. (Civ. Art. 161). If other party proposes in its reply to conclude contract in terms different from terms in draft contract, reply must be considered new draft. (Civ. Art. 161). Disputes arising during conclusion of contract must be settled by litigation or arbitration as specified in law or contract. (Civ. Art. 161). Unilateral contract must be executed in written form. (Civ. Art. 167). If one party of unilateral contract renounces contract, other party has right to bring lawsuit. (Civ. Art. 167). Party which evaded without any reason its responsibility under contract must redress losses caused to other party as result of its acts. (Civ. Art. 167).

Interpretation of Contract.—When interpreting contract, court must consider direct meaning of words in contract. (Civ. Art. 166). If meaning of one of terms is not clear, court must construe term by comparing it with other terms and general content of contract. (Civ. Art. 166). If impossible to define content of contract as specified above, actual intent of parties must be defined by taking into consideration purpose of contract. (Civ. Art. 166). One must consider discussions held before conclusion of contract, correspondence of parties, practices established between parties, business attitude, and other related circumstances. (Civ. Art. 166).

Types of Contract.—Parties may conclude liberal contract by providing for settling mutual disputes by means of accommodation. (Civ. Art. 168). Unnamed contract is contract with specific content expressing basic nature and form of contract, although it is not regulated separately by this law and not directly named. (Civ. Art. 169). In contract for benefit of third person, parties must come to agreement concerning execution of obligations for benefit of third party. (Civ. Art. 170). Civil Code also contains provisions on contract dealing with energy and other resources (Arts. 222-228), contract on credit (Art. 229), transportation (Arts. 313-320), storage (Arts. 344-355), etc.

COPYRIGHT:

See topics Intellectual Property; Patents.

CORPORATIONS:

See topics Partnership; Joint Stock Company.

COURTS:

Structure and procedure of Mongolian courts will radically change with passage of new court structure and Procedure Law soon to be passed by State Great Khural. New constitution of 1992 provides only general guidelines for structure and practice of courts, but clearly, old system based on Soviet model will be entirely discarded.

COURTS . . . *continued*
Constitution provides that judicial system shall consist of Supreme Court, aimag and capital city courts, somon, inter-somon and district courts. (Art. 48). Special courts such as criminal, civil, and administrative courts may be formed, but all fall under supervision of Supreme Court. (Art. 48). Proceedings are to be held publicly if possible. (Art. 54). Separate Constitutional Court is empowered to make judgments on violations of, or disputes involving, constitution. (Art. 64).

See also topic Constitution and Government.

CURRENCY:

See topic Banking Law.

Foreign Currency Control Act was adopted on May 12, 1994 and became effective as of June 1, 1994. Foreign exchange is defined as all transactions related to selling, buying, depositing, lending, transferring, placing, laying down as guarantee of, taking out of or into, Mongolia foreign currency. Permanent and temporary residents in Mongolia must deal only through MongolBank (Central Bank) and commercial banks authorised by MongolBank when selling, buying, raising or transferring foreign currency. (Art. 12). Use of national currency as well as other nonconvertible currencies in foreign exchange transactions is subject to regulations approved jointly by President of MongolBank and Minister of Finance. (Art. 9). MongolBank is in charge of Exchange Control. (Art. 8).

Income of permanent residents in Mongolia realized in foreign currency must be deposited or sold out to MongolBank or commercial banks within 60 days. This provision was reinforced by Regulations enacted by Ministry of Finance and MongolBank on June 10, 1996 to carry out all transactions and payments in Mongolia in National currency from July 1, 1996. Permanent residents are allowed to keep part of their foreign exchange as working capital. (Art. 12.3).

Mongolian nationals or permanent residents as specified in law must report capital investment abroad or loan or financial assistance granted to foreign countries to Ministry of Finance. Foreign currency may be carried in or out of Mongolia if it is declared to customs without restriction on amount. Government loans can be guaranteed by Minister of Finance upon authorisation of Government subject to ratification by Parliament. (Law on the International Treaties and Agreements). Economic entities holding state property or with prevailing state participation must be granted currency loan from abroad with permission of Ministry of Finance.

Permanent and provisional residents are allowed to open foreign currency accounts in commercial banks or in foreign bank branches operating in Mongolia. Art. 17 provides for confidentiality of information on currency reserves and business discretion. There are also provisions for enforcing this act which include fines, confiscation or compensation pursuant to law.

CUSTOMS:

Customs system is supervised by Customs General Administration, which controls frontier points, employs customs officials and collects fines and duties. All goods and vehicles must enter Mongolia through frontier points and pass through customs. Ulaanbaatar International Airport, Boikhoyn Cal (Sino-Mongolian Border) and Sukhbaatar (Russo-Mongolian Border) are presently only frontier points which handle wider international traffic. Customs Administration officials have authority to confiscate or to impose fines on illegally imported goods, as well as power to present certain violations to criminal courts for prosecution.

Duties.—Customs Law, which entered into force on Feb. 11, 1991, requires owners of goods to present documents which accurately reflect goods' value. (Art. 14.3). Small Khural (now State Great Khural) has power to set tariff levels. (Art. 14.2). As of Aug. 1992, uniform tariff of 15% is set on all imported goods not specifically exempted by Customs Law. No tariffs are set on exports.

Goods exempt from duty include capital goods imported by enterprises with foreign participation to be used for production in Mongolia (Art. 3.3.1), goods to enter special customs zones or bonded warehouses (Art. 3.2), and goods imported as part of humanitarian aid programs (Art. 3.4). Goods transiting Mongolia (Art. 3.7), or those dispatched by mistake (Art. 3.5) are also exempted.

DAMAGES:

If person trespasses against life, health, honor, prestige, reputation, or property of others, he must bear unlimited liability for that damage; and eliminate such trespass, unless such act was without fault, was trespass de jure, or did not exceed limits of necessary defense. (Civ. Art. 377). Court must determine quantum of liability. Liability for trespass caused by workers in scope of their employment must be borne by legal person for whom workers are working. (Civ. Art. 378). If trespass resulted from wrong decision or misconduct of State Organ of Administration and its officials or happened during preliminary investigation and examination by court officials and Procurator's office, no damages will be assessed in accordance with Art. 377. (Civ. Art. 378).

Possession of item which may cause public nuisance is answerable in damages and one committing nuisance is liable for damages; however, if damage is caused in emergency situation such as accident or force majeure, as well as by intentional action or omission, or gross negligence of victim, possessor of item should not be liable for damages. (Civ. Art. 379). If product or service caused damage to life, health, or property of other persons through defective production, design, or composition, or other circumstances, person who sold or produced product must compensate such damages. (Civ. Art. 380). If damage was caused by violation of rules for use and storage of that product, seller or producer will not be liable in damages. (Civ. Art. 380). Damages caused by juvenile must be removed by juvenile are responsibility of their legal representatives—parents or guardian, and if damage was caused by juvenile under direct control of special school, reformatory, and health organizations, these organizations must be answerable for damages. (Civ. Art. 381). If person without legal capacity caused damage due to mental disorder, damage must be compensated by guardian or organization exercising regular control over him or her. (Civ. Art. 382). Underage people themselves are liable for damages caused to others; if earnings and property of underage people are insufficient for payment of damages, their parents and guardians must make up deficiency. (Civ. Art. 383). Citizen is not answerable for causing damage to others if he was unable to realize consequences of action or exercise reasonable control over his action. (Civ. Art. 384). Person who lost capacity as result of taking alcoholic drinks and narcotic drugs will not be free of civil liability. (Civ. Art. 384).

Person who caused damage jointly must bear joint and several liabillity. (Civ. Art. 385). Person who caused damage to health of others is obliged to compensate for loss of income, wages, and other similar profits (not taken completely result of disablement and all expenses connected with damage to health such as care of victim, additional meals, artificial limbs, hosital expenses, etc.). (Civ. Art. 387). If victim does not have definite earned income, wages, and profits during disabiity, victim has right to demand compensation in accordance with lowest wages fixed by law for disabled. (Civ. Art. 387). If health of person up to 16 years old and without earned income, wages and profits was damaged, responsible person must compensate expenses connected with damage. (Civ. Art. 388). If health condition of victim is not improved after reaching age of 16, parents or guardians have right to demand compensation at lowest wages fixed by law for disabled. (Civ. Art. 388). If person up to 16 years old had regular earned income, wages, and profits before time when damage was done, compensation must be made in amount of income, wages, or profits lost. (Civ. Art. 388).

If victim died, parents or relatives, as well as children, have right to demand compensation for consequential expenses connected with burial and damages. (Civ. Art. 389). Compensation must be established by size of average monthly earnings of victim, not including portion which should be paid to those able-bodied people who were under guardianship of dead victim or those who have no right to compensation. (Civ. Art. 389). Pension for loss of benefactor not to be included in compensation for victim. (Civ. Art. 389). If action of juridical person who is obliged to make compensation for damage will be terminated and there is no heir to his right and duty, his property may be seized and transferred to state social insurance agency in order to grant compensation for victim as specified in Art. 31. (Civ. Art. 391).

If person spreads information defaming dignity, prestige, or business reputation of other person, that person is obliged to eliminate non-property damage with montary or other forms of compensation, whether or not there was property damage. (Civ. Art. 392). Court must determine amount of compensation for non-property damage at request of complainant by considering methods for distribution of defamatory information, scope of distibuted information, and physical consequences, and must oblige disseminator to discredit defamatory information by same means used for spread of defamatory information. (Civ. Art. 392).

If gross negligent act or omission of victim has affected trespass or increased amount of damage, amount of compensation may be reduced by taking into consideration circumstances. (Civ. Art. 394). Court may reduce amount of compensation by taking into consideration property of perpetrator, except damage resulting from intentional criminal act. (Civ. Art. 394). Person who was injured during rescue of other's property from possible danger has right to demand compensation from owner of that property or from person who enjoys right of ownership, use, and disposal of that property. (Civ. Art. 395).

Person who voluntarily purchased other's property is obliged to return said property to its owner or to person who has right of ownership, use, and disposal of that property, if initial purchase subsequently becomes invalid. (Civ. Art. 396). Person who purchased other's property by fraud must return income earned or income to be earned, as well as its benefits to its legal owner from time when property was purchased. (Civ. Art. 396). Person who purchased property in honest way is obliged to return that property to its legal owner from time he knew or should have known lack of legal basis of his purchase. (Civ. Art. 396). If bailee transfers to another party property as bailment due to ignorance of expiration of bailment, no one may make claim for property purchased by third party. (Civ. Art. 397).

DESCENT AND DISTRIBUTION:

Property and rights of testator may be inherited; succession must be executed by law or testament; succession can be changed only by will of testator; legal inheritors or inheritors by testament must be only citizens who are alive during death of testator or his children born after his death; and property must be transferred to State ownership as escheated property if there is no legal heir to property. (Civ. Art. 398). Right to inherit intellectual property must be related only to right to property which may be obtained by law or testament; rights to intellectual property may be kept for 50 years; and rights not specified in this article must be transferred to State. (Civ. Art. 399).

If court decides that testator, legal inheritor, or inheritor by will was murdered intentionally, or other intentional criminal acts became cause of death, guilty person must forfeit right to inherit by law or will. (Civ. Art. 400). Property must not be inherited by person who is under investigation for crime specified in this article until judicial decisions are effective. (Civ. Art. 400). Permanent residence of deceased testator will be place for hearing matters of succession, and if last permanent residence of deceased is not known, place where one can find all or most property will be considered place for commencing succession claim. (Civ. Art. 402).

Heirs-at-law include: (1) husband, wife, children, adopted children, children born after death, and parents or foster parents without capacity for work; (2) parents or foster parents with capacity for work, grandparents, brothers, and sisters if no one under (1) exists or they refuse succession; (3) grandchildren and great-grandchildren if their parents who had right to inherit were not alive when succession commenced; and (4) citizen who has no ability to work and was living with deceased before his death for over one year under guardianship of deceased. (Civ. Art. 403). If testator left all his property to another person, not less than two-thirds of property to be inherited must devolve compulsorily on testator's underage children, children without ability to work and under guardianship of deceased, parents, foster parents, and other legal heirs. (Civ. Art. 403 or 405). If beneficiary named in will dies before will was probated or he refuses inheritance, testator may appoint another beneficiary. (Civ. Art. 406).

Will must be made in writing and certified by Baga and Somon Administration head. (Civ. Art. 407). Place and date of execution must also be specified in will, which must be certified by notary office. (Civ. Art. 407). Will will be considered certified in following cases: (1) testament of serviceman certified by commander of that military unit and (2) testament of people detained in prison or employed in prison certified by

See Topical Index in front part of this volume.

DESCENT AND DISTRIBUTION . . . *continued*

chief of prison. (Civ. Art. 407). Administration of will must be executed by inheritor appointed by will, but testator may appoint another person in charge of administration of will. (Civ. Art. 410).

If heir who lived together with testator until his death did not inform within three months notary or Baga and Somon Administration head of his refusal to accept legacy, it will be considered as accepted. (Civ. Art. 412). If heir died and did not accept legacy, right to accept his part would be transferred to his heir. (Civ. Art. 413). Although heir may accept property to be inherited, not waiting for arrival of other heirs, he has no right to sell, give, mortgage, or leave within one year from date when legacy was commenced or until acceptance of certificate for right to withdrawal, but may incur following expenses from inherited property: (1) expenses for taking care of testator and for his funeral, (2) expenses for guardianship of person who was under guardianship of testator or who has right to get pensions from testator, (3) salary and expenses necessary for providing other payments, and (4) expenses for protecting inherited property. (Civ. Art. 414).

Heir may hand in his application for granting of certificate of right to legacy to notary office where legacy was opened or Baga and Somon Administration head in absence of such office. (Civ. Art. 415). Certificate of right to legacy must be granted to heir one year after application was filed. (Civ. Art. 415). If there is reliable document evidencing that there are no other heirs, then certificate may be granted beyond one year since legacy was filed. (Civ. Art. 415).

ENVIRONMENT:

State Great Khural (Parliament) enacted between 1994-1995 package of 16 laws on environmental protection. Although they establish a basic environmental legal framework, they do not establish by themselves complete procedures or standards and therefore, are to be completed by resolutions enacted by Government or Parliament. Main Agency in charge of environmental protection is Ministry for Nature and Environment was created in 1988. After Parliamentary elections in 1996, newly formed government assigned Ministry with travel and tourism policy developments. Package of laws relevant to environmental protection include following:

Law on Land, Law on Underground Resources, Law on Mineral Resources, Law on Protection of Livestock Genetic Fund and Health, Law on Air, Law on Hunting, Law on Protection from Toxic Chemicals, Law on Forests, Law on Natural Plants, Law on Water, Law on Natural Plant Use Fees, Law on Fees for Harvest of Timber and Fuelwood, Law on Hunting Reserve Use Payments and Trapping Authorization Fees, Law on Special Protected Areas. There are three other laws in drafting stage which include Law on Private Ownership of Land, Law on Land Fees and Law on Mineral Resource Fees.

Law on Environmental Protection is umbrella law for all environmental and natural resource laws in Mongolia. It established overall institutional structure and general rights and responsibilities to be implemented by various line ministries and local governments.

Land Law.—Purpose is regulation of possession and use of land by citizens, economic entities, organisations of Mongolia. It establishes seven categories of land, rights of each level of government, rights and responsibilities of land users, procedures for land assessment, land use contracts and land conservation.

Law on Special Protected Area was adopted in 1994 and became effective on Apr. 1, 1995. It is divided into eight chapters covering General Provisions, Strictly Protected Areas, National Conservation Parks, Nature Reserves, Monuments, Governmental Rights and Responsibilities, Land Use and Research, and Administrative Penalties. Purpose of Law is to regulate "use and procurement of land" for state protection, to preserve and conserve "original condition", to protect specific traits, unique formations, rare and endangered plants and animals, historic and cultural monuments, natural beauty, and to foster scientific research.

Law on Hunting.—Purpose is to "regulate the protection and proper use" of Mongolia's animals—mammals, birds, and fishes... "which have hunting significance". It contains three chapters covering general provisions, hunting and trapping of animals, and administrative penalties. Law classifies animals as "very rare", "rare" and "abundant" depending on their capacity to recover "and their ecological importance". Besides establishing categories of animals and hunting seasons, it further regulates hunting methods, ownership of animals, their domestication, monitoring, permits and fees, export of animals, and provides administrative penalties for violation of Act.

Law on Forests.—Purpose is to manage protection, proper use and regeneration of Mongolia's forests. Forest resources are property of state which has power to grant possession of them to local governments. Local governments may then grant citizens, economic entities and organizations rights to use forests and forest resources pursuant to contract or license. Citizens may also own timber and forest resources on land which they lease provided they pay relevant fees. Any trees planted by them on land they lease shall be their property.

Law of Water adopted in Apr. 1995. Contains four chapters which cover general provisions, creation of databank, institutional and management structure, protection measures, use, water contracts and administrative penalties. Law refers to surface, ground, and mineral waters.

Law of Toxic Chemicals.—Purpose is to regulate production, export, import, storage, trade, transport use and disposal of toxic chemicals. Toxic chemicals are divided into three categories—highly toxic, toxic, and mildly toxic. Law contains one chapter related to protection requirements.

Law on Natural Plants was adopted in its present form in Apr. 1995 and became effective in June of same year. It contains four chapters covering general provisions, plant protection and restoration, plant use, and fines for violation of law. Plants are classified according to their abundance and restorative capacity as very rare, rare or abundant. Law also establishes certain plant protection zones to limit impacts of commercial activities.

Law on Air was adopted in Mar. of 1995 and became effective in June of same year. It contains four chapters governing general purposes, administration, and information related to air quality, various measures for protection, and fines and penalties for violations.

FOREIGN INVESTMENT:

See also topic Taxation.

New Foreign Investment Law entered into force July 1, 1993 as part of legislative reform package which included overhaul of Tax Law. While similar in many respects to old Foreign Investment Law of 1990, new Law was drafted from beginning as part of integrated tax/investment package. It also gives more detailed regulations on use of and by foreigners and more specific regulations on labor regulation for foreign employers.

Pursuant to new Law, foreigners are permitted to invest in any branch of economy unless laws or regulations stipulate otherwise. (Art. 4.1). Most notable such prohibition is provided by Constitution of 1992, which forbids foreign ownership of land. (Art. 6.3). Foreign investment may take four forms: (1) establishment of wholly owned subsidiary or Mongolian branch of foreign entity; (2) direct investment by purchase of shares of publicly traded Mongolian enterprise; (3) establishment of joint venture with Mongolian partner and (4) purchase of licence or other rights for exploitation of mineral or petroleum resources in Mongolia. (Arts. 5, 6).

Governmental approval of foreign investments must be obtained from Ministry of Trade and Industry. To obtain approval prospective investors must submit special application package which should identify investors, describe subject matter and amount of investment proposed, describe form of investment and duration. (Art. 12.2). In addition to application investors should include evidence of their own financial solvency, legal identity, any articles of incorporation for proposed business entity, any marketing, management, technical or other plans and any necessary authorizations from other Mongolian state organs which might be required. (Art. 12.3). Upon receipt of application Ministry of Trade and Industry shall in 60 days decide whether to issue certificate of approval. (Art. 12.4). Approval may be withheld if Ministry finds that proposed activities would be inconsistent with existing legislation, environmental protection, public health or Mongolian technological standards. (Art. 12.8).

Protection of Foreign Investments.—According to foreign investment law, state may expropriate foreign investment only where such action is in accordance with due process of law and is performed on nondiscriminatory basis. (Art. 8.3). Foreigners are guaranteed full and prompt compensation for expropriated investments. (Art. 8.3). Value of such compensation is determined according to value of expropriated investments as measured from date of expropriation. (Art. 8.4). Foreign investors are guaranteed equal treatment under law for losses caused by force majeure. (Art. 8.5). Foreign investors also have following additional rights: (1) to possess use and dispose of property invested, including right to repatriate investments made for formation of registered capital; (2) to participate in management of entity in which it has invested; (3) to promptly remit abroad its share of profits, dividends and proceeds from sale of assets. (Art. 10.1).

Operation of Foreign Invested Business Entity.—

Obligations—Labor Policy.—While foreign invested businesses are required to recruit employees primarily from Mongolian citizens, Ministry of Labor may permit employ of foreign experts. (Art. 24.1). Mongolian social and labor regulations apply to all Mongolian citizens employed. (Art. 24.2). Foreign employers have right to transfer their salaries abroad after paying required income tax. (Art. 24.3).

Obligations—Land Use.—In conformance with Constitutional prohibition on direct foreign ownership of land, Foreign Investment Law provides that all entities with foreign investment gain use of real property through lease. (Art. 21.1). Relevant local hural and its presidium must approve such leases. (Art. 21.3). Leases must contain terms, duration, any necessary measures for environmental protection, other liabilities of lessor and lessee, as well as annual rent. (Art. 21.2). Responsibilities for lease in case of joint venture are borne by investors in proportion to their capital contributions. (Art. 21.4). Initial lease terms may not exceed 60 years, but lessee may extend lease once for up to 40 years, provided this is stated in initial terms of lease. (Art. 21.5). State has right to substitute or take leaseholds for specific State purposes, but foreign investors have right of prompt and adequate compensation. (Art. 21.7). If State determines that use of land harms public health, environment or national security, it may cancel lease.

Winding Up and Dissolution of Foreign Invested Business Entities.—Business entities must notify Ministry of Trade and Industry within 14 days of their decision to terminate operations. (Art. 17.1). Along with such notice, business entities must submit statements of appropriate authorities to certify payment of all debts and performance of all obligations. (Art. 17.2). Upon receipt of relevant documents, Ministry of Trade and Industry shall withdraw authorization for business (Art. 17.3), and instruct Department of State Taxation to remove name of enterprise from State Register (Art. 17.4). Should operation of business be terminated before dissolution, foreign investors are entitled to transfer abroad their share of profits after final settlement of all business debts. (Art. 17.5).

Taxation of foreign invested business entities is governed by both Foreign Investment Law and Economic Entity Income Tax Law of 1993. Foreign investors may take advantage of tax preferences offered by both laws.

Customs Duty and Sales Tax Preferences.—Foreign Investment Law provides that registered initial capital of foreign invested business entity is free from both customs duty and sales tax. (Art. 19.1). For all enterprises except for caterers or traders, customs duties are suspended for five years on raw materials imported to support production. (Art. 19.2).

Other Preferences.—Foreign investments which are entirely new (i.e. not established by purchasing shares of existing business) are eligible for following three preferences: (1) investments in priority infrastructure projects such as power or thermal plants, highways, air cargo, railways, basic telecommunications and civil engineering receive ten year tax holiday plus five year 50% tax reduction thereafter (Art. 20.1.1); (2) investments in mining and mineral processing (except precious metals), oil

FOREIGN INVESTMENT . . . *continued*
and coal, metallurgy, chemicals, machinery, and electronics receive five year tax holiday plus five year 50% tax reduction thereafter (Art. 20.1.2); (3) foreign invested business entities not referred to in the two cases above which export more than 50% of their production receive three year tax holiday (Art. 20.2). In all cases regardless of method of formation of foreign invested business entity, reinvested income is deductible. (Art. 20.4).

See also topics Economic Entities and Taxation.

Foreign Investment Law.—Minister of Ministry of Trade and Industry has confirmed following with Resolution no. 271 dated July 2, 1993 and its annex "The order of the organization, registration and liquidation of the economic entity with foreign investment." Enterprises with foreign investment are those which: (1) are comprised of 100% foreign investment; (2) are comprised of joint venture with Mongolian and foreign investment. Economic entity with foreign investment may make direct investment by way of purchasing with free currency dividends, shares and other securities of economic entities operating on territory of Mongolia, including dividends, shares and other securities sold by voucher of investment in line with privatization law of Mongolia, or may buy them with tugriks obtained from investment activity.

Economic entities and joint-venture enterprises shall be permitted to deposit and to make other transactions at Mongol Bank. Only state enterprises appear to be required to sell portion of their foreign currency to Mongol Bank. Fact that state entity invests state property in joint venture does not make joint venture corporation state enterprise.

Importation of Funds.—Evidence of importation of funds and evidence of importation of foreign currency and investment shall be granted by Ministry of Trade and Industry on basis of projects and documents of foreign investment, evidence shall be granted on basis of note from Customs Board. If cash and foreign currencies are imported evidence shall be granted by certificate of bank. Evidence of investment through bank is sufficient to satisfy MT and obtain FIL benefits.

INSURANCE:

Items for insurance may be property and material, and insurance must be made on voluntary basis and, if it is stipulated by law, may have form of obligatory insurance. (Civ. Art. 360). Insurer must be legal person having license for maintaining insurance activity by authorized body and in full accord with demands specified in law. (Civ. Art. 360).

Insurer is obliged to compensate all or some of losses caused to person who has concluded insurance contract pursuant to contractual provisions. (Civ. Art. 361). Insurer must compensate for agreed portion of losses if property is not insured for its complete price. (Civ. Art. 361). If insurance price mentioned in contract exceeds real cost of insured property, then insurance contract will not be valid for excessive part. (Civ. Art. 316). Insurance contract must be made in writing; otherwise contract is null and void. (Civ. Art. 316).

Insurer is obliged to provide insurance with timely and full insurance payments pursuant to contract for insurance and to compensate necessary expenses, directed at reducing size of damages. (Civ. Art. 362). When insurance was provided and insurance payments made, and insurance paid, insurer enjoys right to demand compensation for losses caused to insured by third party, after payment of losses to insured. (Civ. Art. 316).

INTELLECTUAL PROPERTY:

See topic Patents.

Art. 86 of Civil Code provides:

Intellectual property includes scientific discoveries, inventions, copyrights, product patents, new production methods, and trademarks. Scientific discovery is form of intellectual property which explains laws and phenomena of natural world. Invention is creation of method or machine relating to production or operation or product that has not been registered before and invented for first time relying on natural laws and revealing its principles. Design patent is new and specific solution relating to form or design of product which may be made by manufacturing method. New production method is concrete solution relating to new production method or process and organization of production process. Trademark is distinctive mark used by legal persons or citizens carrying on business for purpose of distinguishing their own goods and services from others. Common mark is trademark used by members of cooperative of legal persons under control of that cooperative.

Works protected by copyright include: (1) oral or written literary works; (2) architectural projects, sketches, plans, blueprints for construction of buildings; (3) performing arts such as ballet, gymnastics, and pantomime and all works relating to fine art; (4) plays, scenes, and musicals for theater; (5) films, scores, other works relating to cinematography; (6) photographs and other works relating to photography; (7) projects, sketches, models, and drawings for scientific and technical purposes; (8) computer programs and software; (9) audio, vocal, and video works; (10) works originating from previously created works; (11) other works expressing authors' intellectual and creative activity; and (12) prototypes of products to be manufactured.

Contract for use of intellectual property must be made in written form, and if it is specially stipulated in law, it must be registered with competent Government body. (Civ. Art. 286). Item of contract for use of intellectual property is discovery, new creation, innovation, model of product, trademark, and other works related to copyrights, which were formed, registered, and considered in line with rules fixed by law. (Civ. Art. 287). Contract for use of intellectual property must include form and method for use of property; size, frame work, term, right and obligation of parties; their responsibility; and other conditions. (Civ. Art. 287).

JOINT STOCK COMPANY:

See topic Partnership.

Joint stock company may be established by public offering of prospectus sponsored by promoters or by subscription of small number of persons. Name of joint stock company is followed by abbreviation "HK". (Art. 29).

Joint stock company established by public offering shall include in its prospectus information on type of production service activity; duration of activity; proposed amount of charter fund; par value, number and total value of shares to be issued; estimated amount of profit; any preferential rights enjoyed by promoters and starting and closing date for subscription. Person who sponsors and signs prospectus shall be deemed founder. (Art. 30). Subscriptions for shares is governed by rules and procedures set by Securities Commission. Shares are subscribed by way of application form prescribed by competent authority.

Application must bear name and surname of subscriber; name of organisation receiving application; par value; number and total value of shares being subscribed for, and date of subscription. Signing of application by subscriber, or his proxy, shall constitute subscription for shares. If offer is not fully subscribed within period set forth in prospectus, promoters may decide to extend closing date up to 30 days. Subscriber must pay in advance not less than 30% of total subscribed shares price within 30 days of closing date of subscription. This payment may be delayed once, for up to 30 days. (Art. 31). Company must meet following requirements before it is established: (1) offer is subscribed to amount commensurate with proposed amount of charter fund; (2) advance payment for share is completed in its entirety; (3) if company is to engage in production or service required special permission, then such permission must be obtained from competent authority. (Art. 32). If these requirements are satisfied, promoters shall call constituent meeting. Constituent meeting considers and decides following issues: (1) approval of resolution establishing company and amount of charter fund; (2) approval of articles of association; (3) appointment of Board of Directors and determination of their salaries and allowances; (4) appointment of auditor (auditing board) and determination of his salary and allowances (auditor is selected from list of chartered accountants); (5) preferential rights granted to promoters, if any; (6) compensation of expenses incurred by promoters in connection with establishment of company. (Art. 33.3). Meeting is valid if it is attended by simple majority of subscribers and resolutions will be valid if they are passed by simple majority of votes cast. Each subscriber is entitled to one vote at constituent meeting. (Art. 33.5). Joint stock company must formulate articles of association and specify following items: (1) name, location and address of company; (2) business scope; (3) term of its activity, if applicable; (4) amount of charter fund; (5) classes of shares, par value, number of each class of shares, and total value of shares; (6) management structure, supervisory and auditing bodies, and their powers; (7) other matters prescribed by this law. Promoters shall, within 14 days of adoption of articles of association by constituent meeting, present application to registry requesting registration. Articles of association to be certified by notary public.

Charter Fund.—Minimum size of charter fund is 30,000,000 tugriks. Initial charter fund is comprised of payments for subscription shares. Payment for shares to be made in cash or in form of contributed assets or intellectual property. Charter fund must be contributed in its entirety within one year of registration of company. (Art. 37). Competent expert shall verify whether estimated value of such contributions are accurate and whether appraised value corresponds to total value of shares so received, report of expert's findings to be presented and appended to articles of association. Within six months of incorporation of company, Board of directors and auditors examines appraised value stated in report of expert and may, if it is deemed necessary, review appraisal. If appraised value of contributions does not correspond to value of shares received in return for them, respective member shall make up difference in value in cash. (Art. 38). Joint stock company empowered to increase charter fund if existing shares are fully paid up. Increase in charter fund can be effected either by issuing new shares or by increasing par value of existing shares, unless articles of association state otherwise. Reduction of charter fund is effected either by cancelling shares and reimbursing payment or reducing par value of shares, unless articles of association state otherwise. (Art. 40).

General Meeting.—Company's supreme authority is general meeting and may exercise following powers and functions: (1) revise articles of association; (2) adopt regulations on increase or decrease of charter fund; (3) reorganise or dissolve company; (4) examine and approve financial and budget plan; (5) elect and replace directors and examine and approve reports of board directors; (6) appointment of members of auditing board from list of chartered accountants and decide matters regarding remuneration and examine and approve reports of auditing board. (Art. 42).

General meeting has quorum if members representing more than 50 of all voting rights attend. However, depending upon nature of business to be transacted at meeting and number of members of company, articles of association may prescribe minimum number of members to be present at meeting. (Art. 44). Resolutions shall be adopted by simple majority of members with voting rights. General meetings include regular meetings and irregular meetings. Regular meetings shall be convened by Board of Directors. Irregular meetings shall be convened either by Board of Directors or by members representing 10% or more of voting rights. Member may authorise, in writing, another person to attend general meeting as proxy.

Board of Directors.—Between general meetings, powers of general meeting shall be exercised by Board of Directors. Board of Directors must be composed of three members or more and their term of office shall be specified in articles of association. Persons other than members of company may be appointed to Board of Directors. However, majority of directors must be members of company. Articles of association shall specify whether member of Board of Directors can be elected to board or management of other partnerships or companies. Chairman of Board of Directors is appointed from among its members, unless articles of association state otherwise. Chairman of Board of Directors shall give notice of and register composition and any changes to Board with Registry. Registry makes such information public. Board of Directors may exercise following powers: (1) devise company's business plan; (2) determine structure of company's administration, salary pool and rules for remuneration; (3) appoint executive director of company and enter into employment contract with him; (4) determine limits of executive directors powers to dispose of company's assets; (5) supervise activities of executive director and internal affairs of company's administration; (6) convene general meetings; (7) present to general meeting its views regarding financial and budget reports and proposed alterations to charter fund; (8) report to general meeting at least once a year, and other powers set out in articles of association and law. (Art. 46).

Meetings of Board of Directors include regular and irregular meetings. Meeting has quorum if absolute majority of all members are present or if all three members who

See Topical Index in front part of this volume.

JOINT STOCK COMPANY . . . *continued*
constitute Board of Directors are present. Irregular meeting may be convened by chairman or member of Board of Directors. Resolution is passed by simple majority of votes of members present at meeting. Resolution is signed by chairman and sealed with company's seal. (Art. 47).

Executive Director.—Day to day business of company is administered by executive director within powers prescribed by articles of association and employment contract. Unless stated otherwise in articles of association, person other than member of company may be appointed as executive director. Executive director is entitled to serve as chairman of Board of Directors. Executive director may represent company and carry out all transactions relating to company's activities within power granted to executive director by Board of Directors. (Art. 50).

Auditing.—Auditor (auditing board) shall supervise activities of Board of Directors and financial affairs of company. Articles of association shall set terms of office of auditor. (Art. 52). Following persons are prohibited from serving as auditor: (1) unqualified person; (2) person who was member of Board of Directors or management of company that went bankrupt; (3) relatives of members of Board of Directors or management or who are under influence of management; (4) person who works for company or affiliated or subsidiary company. (Art. 53).

Auditors have following duties: (1) supervise activities of company's management; (2) determine whether activities of company are in compliance with law and articles of association; (3) determine whether accounts kept, formulation and presentation of balance sheet and reports, and payment of taxes are in conformity with law; (4) determine whether statements in company's books and records, correspond to those of balance sheet; (5) determine whether estimation of assets is accurate; (6) ascertain amount of cash, securities and pledges held at any given time, as is deemed necessary; (7) examine particulars of transactions and contracts relating to company's activities. (Art. 54).

Auditor is liable if he fails to perform duties. (Art. 57). Meeting of auditing board is held at least once every three months, unless articles of association states otherwise. (Art. 55). Auditors attend general meetings and meetings of Board of Directors as observers. If Board of Directors rejects matter presented by auditor or his request for general meeting to be convened to consider that matter, auditor shall be entitled to convene general meeting. (Art. 56). Shareholders may file claim in court with respect to activities of Board of Directors or auditors. Shareholder shall be liable for costs. If facts stated in claim are reasonable and of serious nature, court may order general meeting to be convened to discuss matter. (Art. 59).

Shares.—Company may issue two types of shares, depending upon rights they carry: ordinary shares or preferred shares. (Art. 62.1). Each ordinary share has voting right. (Art. 60.2). Preferred shares accord their owner priority rights with respect to dividends and return of assets but have no voting rights. Preferred shares shall not exceed 20% of charter fund. (Art. 62). Company may acquire its own shares, but amount shall not exceed 10% of charter fund. (Art. 64). Company which holds sufficient shares of another company so as to be able to control it shall be deemed parent company and company so controlled shall be deemed its subsidiary company. Company may issue debentures secured by amount of charter fund. Debentures shall bear: (1) name, address and business scope of company; (2) amount of charter fund and paid-up capital; (3) date upon which general meeting resolved to issue debentures; (4) number, par and total value of debentures, terms of interest payment and redemption; (5) type and amount of assets which serve as security or guarantee. Debentures may either be convertible or preferred. (Art. 66).

Finance, Accounts and Reports.—Company must keep following books and records: register of members which contains surname and name of each member, number, par and total value of shares he holds, and any changes in composition of shareholders; debentures book indicates number and amount of debentures issued, surname and name of their holders, payments made, and amount of debentures that have been redeemed; (3) register of each general meeting and its resolutions; (4) register of meetings and resolutions of Board of Directors; (5) register of resolutions of auditors' meetings; (6) record of debenture-holders' meetings and resolutions. (Art. 67.1). Company's secretary keeps all books and registers, except for register of debenture-holders. Secretary is appointed by Board of Directors and powers, duties, and liabilities are set out in articles of association. Person appointed at meeting of debenture-holders shall keep their records. (Art. 67.2). Shareholders are entitled to inspect registers or have them verified by experts. Shareholder shall bear expenses of such verification. (Art. 67.6). Company, in accordance with procedures set out in Accounting Law, shall produce and publish annual financial report. Financial report must consist of: (1) balance sheet; (2) account of profits and losses; (3) cash-flow statement; (4) account of accumulated profits; (5) any additional explanatory notes. Executive director is responsible for accuracy of financial report. (Art. 68). Report of Board of Directors on state of business affairs of company and on its views shall contain: report and recommendations on activities of management during fiscal year; research and result therefrom with respect to growth of company; coordination of activities between holding, subsidiary, and other companies; financial results and main economic indices of company; statistics on financial activity of company for past five to ten years. (Art. 74).

Reorganisation.—Companies may be reorganised by consolidation of several independent companies into new company or by merger of several companies in which one company absorbs others. (Art. 75). Board of Directors of companies participating in consolidation or merger shall produce joint documents (project). Project shall state following: (1) name, address and business scope of new company; (2) articles of association of new company or, in case of merger, amendments to articles of association of absorbing company; (3) shares, dividends, estimation of assets, and rate of conversion thereof; (4) ratio of companies' shares to assets and method for adjusting them; (5) commencement date for participating in profit distribution; (6) date as of which rights and duties of companies in consolidation or merger are to be transferred; (7) means of resolving matters relating to contracts and transactions involving holders of securities other than shares; (8) indication of special benefits or preferential rights, if any, to be granted to management of companies consolidating or merging so as to protect their interests. (Art. 76). Within four months of registration of project, Board of Directors shall ascertain composition and structure of assets and liabilities of companies participating in consolidation or merger. Final balance sheets of consolidating or merging companies and initial balance sheet of newly-formed company shall be drawn-up by date of registration of new company. (Art. 77). General meeting of each company adopts resolution authorising consolidation or merger and approving project. These resolutions must be certified by notary public. (Art. 78). Board of Directors of participating companies shall produce reports indicating shares, dividends, estimation of assets, rate of conversion thereof, as well as reason for merger or consolidation. Board of Directors of any participating companies or newly formed company may reexamine these reports or appoint competent expert. (Arts. 80, 81). Reorganisation of companies may be effected by dividing company into several companies or by separating new company from existing one. Members of these companies are entitled to reserve right to own shares. Board of Directors of participating companies shall produce project documents for division or separation. (Art. 84).

Limited liability company is defined as legal entity with charter fund divisible into shares, is liable for its obligations to extent of its entire assets and each member bears responsibility in proportion to his/her capital contribution. Abbreviation "HH" shall follow company's name. (Art. 87).

Company is established pursuant to founding contract with statements same as for partnership. Company shall have articles of association. (Art. 88.1). Company may have only single member. (Art. 88.2). Company meets following requirements before it is established: (1) at least 30% of monetary contributions have been deposited; (2) assets in-kind are contributed in full; (3) if company's business scope required special permission, such permission has been obtained; (4) constituent meeting has been convened and articles of association adopted. Contract and articles of association to be certified by notary public. (Art. 88.3). Minimum size of charter fund is 10,000,000 tugriks. Contributions of each member to charter fund may be of differing amounts. (Art. 89). Each share has voting rights. Shares are transferable, but consent of all members must be obtained before transfer. Transfer of shares effective from date of its registration in register of members. If member fails to make contribution within period of time specified in contract, that period may be extended by up to 30 days. If member fails to make his contribution within extension, he is then expelled from company and his shares may be sold to other persons. Every member has right of preemption. If shares are not sold within one year of expulsion of member, charter fund is reduced accordingly, but shall not then be less than minimum size of charter fund required by law. (Art. 91).

General meeting is company's supreme authority and has same powers as general meeting of joint stock company. Director and, if required, members of Board of Directors are appointed by general meeting. Person other than member of company may be appointed as its director. (Art. 92). Director is entitled to enter into any contract or transaction related to business of company. (Art. 94). Liability of director is determined by general meeting. Director is personally liable for any damages caused to members of company, or any other persons, by his illegal actions. (Art. 95).

LABOUR LAW:

Collective agreement parties are administration and trade union. These parties determine agreement's term, procedure of conclusion and implementation.

Usually enters into force upon its signing. Any provisions reducing effect of other Mongolian laws are void. (Art. 7). Collective agreements primarily deal with work and rest hours, training of workers, and granting of social security. Legislation of Mongolia and collective agreement itself determines liability for nonobservance of collective agreement. (Art. 10).

Contract of employment can be concluded by mutual accord, with or without fixed term. It can be extended by mutual accord, as well as by continued performance of worker. Administration cannot require worker to perform beyond contract's terms. (Art. 12). Worker's job shall be retained by duties in government body up to three months, regular annual leave, short term medical leave, pre- and post-confinement leave, participation in lawful strike, and if returning to work from injury or illness acquired through work. (Art. 14).

Combining of duties from one worker is allowed, as is assigning of one worker's duties to another. Workers may be temporarily transferred by administration to other posts. (Art. 15).

Contracts may be terminated by mutual consent, initiative of either party; expiration of contract; worker leaving for military service; criminal indictment of worker or by act of law. Termination by administration is allowed for reduction in number of personnel, and inadequate job performance by worker. Termination requires one month notice and in case of unlawful termination, replacement worker must be laid off. (Art. 20).

Administration shall generally pay to dismissed worker benefit equal to average wages of not less than one month.

When dismissing worker, administration must determine date of transfer and work and fix it in dismissal decision which will be last day of transfer of work. Administration must grant worker dismissal benefit and his work book among other things. (Art. 24).

Hours of Work and Rest Periods.—Work hours shall not exceed 46 hours/week, eight hours/day, 30 hours/week for 14-15 year olds and 36 hours/week for 16-18 year olds. (Arts. 25, 26).

Administration must investigate and remove any work hazards. Night hours are from 22:00 to 6:00 (10 p.m. to 6 a.m.) (Art. 24). Part-time work is allowable as is aggregation of hours of work. Overtime work is allowed in issues of national emergency, to prevent lack of power supply. Overtime cannot exceed two shifts running or four hours for two consecutive work days. (Art. 30). Workers are allowed rest and meal breaks as well as public holidays off from work. Suns. are nonwork days. (Art. 31).

Workers are allowed annual leave of 21 work days plus extra days depending on their overall length of service. Workers are also allowed short term leaves of absence. (Art. 35).

Remuneration of Labour, Guaranteed Payment and Compensation.—Workers wages are fixed by administration in accordance with government regulations. Worker receives double wages for overtime work and holiday work. (Art. 41). Worker receives

See Topical Index in front part of this volume.

LABOUR LAW . . . *continued*
full wages if output is defective through no fault of his own. Payments are made twice a month. Changes to payment schedules requires one month notice. (Art. 48). Deductions of wages can only be made under few circumstances. There is compensation in case of transfer to local assignment and during absence for valid reason. (Art. 51). Workers can get previous average wages during periods of reduced hours of work during time of transfer to another work due to health conditions and for wrongful dismissal or transfer. (Art. 54).

Labour Discipline and Material Liability.—Administration may adopt internal labour regulations and adopt sanctions and liability for those regulations in accordance with Mongolian Law. Liability for workers may be limited or full. Workers who are liable must compensate organisation. (Art. 57).

Labour Protection.—Administration may not commence undertakings which do not meet safety requirements. Administration must supply, free of charge, adequate safety equipment and clothing. (Art. 68). Workers may stop during unfavorable weather conditions. (Art. 69). Administrations must report any industrial accidents. Administration must examine health of workers, and cannot send workers into conditions hazardous to health. (Art. 71). Administration cannot discriminate against disabled person. (Art. 74). Administration shall compensate worker for losses if due to fault of administration. (Art. 75).

Employment of Women and Young Persons.—Administration may not dismiss pregnant women having children under two years old. (Art. 78). These workers may also be prohibited from night hours, overtime work and assigned trips. Mothers are allowed breaks for nursing infants as well as maternity leave and reduction of assigned work hours. (Art. 80).

Labour Dispute.—All labour disputes and appeals shall be settled in courts or by Labour Dispute Settlement Commission. Courts have power to reinstate workers. (Art. 88).

Supervision of Implementation of Labour Legislation.—Law empowers government, governors of all instances and organization to supervise implementation of labour legislation. (Art. 95).

PARTNERSHIP:

Law on Partnership and Company adopted on May 11, 1995, regulates establishment and registration, administration, supervisory and auditing structure, reorganisation and dissolution.

Partnership may be established in two forms: (a) partnership with full liability of all members or (b) partnership with full liability of some members. (Art. 3.1).

Partnership with full liability of all members is defined as organisation whose partners are jointly liable for partnership obligations with property they contributed to partnership and with their own personal property. Abbreviation "BB" shall follow name of partnership with full liability of all members. (Art. 19).

Establishment and Registration. Partnership is established on basis of foundation contract. Contract shall contain name, address of partnership; time period for conducting activity; names and addresses of persons authorised to manage and represent partnership; size and estimation of share of capital contributed by every member, method of estimation; principles for distributing incomes and losses; date of signature of contract; names, citizenship, addresses of members and any other provisions deemed necessary. Members shall file application for registration at Registry within seven days of contract approval. Contract shall be notarised. (Art. 20). Partnership shall be deemed to be founded as of date of its registration. Registry receives and examines application and, if it complies with requirements partnership is registered within seven days. (Art. 11).

Management. Every member has right to manage and represent partnership. Contract may designate one or several members who are authorised to manage and represent partnership. Management shall decide matters by majority of votes, bear responsibility for decisions jointly and regularly inform other members about their activity. Activities of members who are entitled to manage and represent are supervised by other members. Managers are relieved of their duties if other members consider them to be exercising their duty to manage improperly.

Rights and Duties. Members participate personally in activities of partnership and may not be member of another partnership or company. Apart from number of shares contributed to partnership every member has one vote. Amendments to contract and changing basis of activity is decided unanimously by members. Other issues are decided by simple majority of votes, unless stated otherwise in contract. (Art. 22).

New members may enter partnership and they shall enjoy same rights and duties as other members. Reasons for withdrawing from partnership may be expiration of term of contract or other conditions set out in contract. Reasons for excluding members from partnership may be proven incapability to exercise their duties under contract, or to contribute their share of capital, or serious breach of their duties under contract. Excluded member has right to appeal exclusion in court within 30 days of decision. Share capital which was contributed by member who is excluded or who has withdrawn is returned to him within three months unless provided otherwise in contract. (Art. 23).

Partnership profits or losses for each member shall be proportional to share of capital contributed to partnership. (Art. 24). Members have right to share capital they contributed after dissolution of partnership. Share capital distributed only after debts of partnership are fully settled. If property of partnership is insufficient to settle fully its debts, then personal property of members shall be used, in proportion to their contributions to cover debts. (Art. 25). When member withdraws, is excluded or becomes insolvent, or when heir of member, declared dead or missing, does not join partnership, partnership shall be dissolved. However, if such partnership is to continue with its activities, contract must be amended and those amendments registered at Registry. (Art. 26).

Partnership with full liability of some members is organisation in which at least one of members is wholly liable with both his contribution and own personal property for partnership obligations, while liability of other members is limited to amount of their contribution. Abbreviation "ZB" shall follow name of partnership with full liability of some members. (Art. 27).

Peculiarities of Partnership with Full Liability of Some Members.—Foundation contract shall specify individual liability of each member. Only members with full liability have right to manage and represent partnership or company. Members who bear liability according to size of their contribution may not themselves participate in activities of partnership. Changing number of these members shall not be reason for dissolution of partnership. However, if all members withdraw then partnership will be dissolved. Remaining members may decide to continue activities as partnership with full liability of all members. They shall revise foundation contract and reregister partnership.

PATENTS:

See topic Civil Code.

Mongolia ratified Paris Convention for Protection of Industrial Property in 1985 and became member of World Intellectual Property Organization in 1979. Patent law of Mongolia was adopted by Parliament on June 25, 1993 and became effective from Sept. 1, 1993.

Law is designed to govern relations arising from protection of rights of authors of inventions, industrial designs or innovations and of patent owners and from their use. (Art. 1). Inventions and industrial designs may be patented, while authors of innovations can be issued certificates. (Arts. 4, 7). Invention is defined as absolutely new solution relating to product or process; industrial design means absolutely new, original solution relating to appearance or form of article of manufacture that can be produced by industrial means; and innovation means solution which is new for given organisation, and relates to product, process or organisation of manufacturing process. (Art. 3).

Unpatentable subject matters include: (1) scientific discoveries, theories and mathematical methods; (2) computer programs and algorithms; (3) schemes, rules or methods for doing business, performing mental acts or playing games; (4) solutions contrary to public order, morality, environment or human health. (Art. 4). Law established Patent Office with authority to examine applications and issue patents and innovation certificates. Patent application by non-resident is to be made by patent agent practising in Mongolia. (Art. 6). Application must be in Mongolian. If it is filed in another language, translation must be provided by applicant within two months. (Art. 6.8). Application must contain request, description of invention, claim(s), abstract and where necessary drawings, and references. (Art. 6.3). Law makes distinction between inventions and innovations with regard to procedures to follow in order to issue patents and innovation certificates.

Patent Office reviews application based on examination report, and within nine months from filing date, makes decision whether patent is to be granted. When required, Patent Office may extend this period of time up to 12 months. If patent is granted it shall be published in Patent Gazette. (Art. 10). Patents for inventions and industrial designs are valid for term of 20 and ten years respectively, and innovation certificates are valid for term of five years starting from filing date of respective applications. (Art. 14).

Patented invention or industrial design may be exploited only with consent of patent owner. Right to patent for invention or industrial design which has been created in course of employee's official duties or contractual obligations shall belong to employer unless otherwise provided in contract. (Art. 15).

Exploitation of patented inventions or industrial designs are subject to license contracts which should be registered with Patent Office. (Art. 19). License contract must be confidential. Fees are payable to Patent Office for maintenance of patent and for registration of license contract. (Art. 24).

Appeal filed against results of examination of patent applications for inventions or industrial designs shall be examined and considered by Patent Office. Appeals and disputes on all other matters shall be considered and settled by court. (Art. 27).

PETROLEUM:

Development and exploitation of petroleum resources in Mongolia is governed by Petroleum Law of Feb. 13, 1991 and Petroleum Regulations which implemented law. State petroleum administration, Mongol Gazryn Tos (MGT), enters into contracts related to petroleum operations and supervises their implementation. According to Petroleum Law, all petroleum in Mongolia is exclusively property of State. (Art. 3). Foreigners may exploit petroleum resources on basis of production-sharing contracts. All such contracts must meet certain basic requirements, including: (1) technology used must extract minimum of 20% of field resources; (2) steps must be taken to develop domestic petroleum processing industry; (3) training for domestic labor must be provided; (4) environmental damage must be minimized; (5) petroleum data and information must be provided to MGT; and (6) safety measures must be taken to protect health of personnel, prevent accidents and avoid damage to property or land. (Art. 6). Once contract is approved by MGT and government, prospective foreign contractor must receive land tenure permit from local authorities and mine tenure permit from government. (Art. 7).

Permitted term of petroleum operations differs according to type of activity pursued. For petroleum exploration, MGT may grant exploration term of up to five years with possibility of two extensions of two years each. (Arts. 8.1, 8.2). Term for oil field development is set at 20 years, but if contractor installs additional industrial infrastructure such as processing facilities and pipelines, MGT may grant two extensions of up to five years each. (Arts. 8.3, 8.4).

Royalty, Taxation and Production Sharing.—Contractors shall pay State royalty set by government (Art. 9.1), and are subject to normal rates of taxation set by Mongolian Law (Art. 9.2). Cost recovery oil is set at 40%. (Art. 11). Contractor shall share with State negotiated percentage of remaining part of total production after deduction of cost recovery and royalty. (Art. 10.1). Contractor has right to export its share of petroleum (Art. 10.2), but under certain circumstances, MGT may request delivery for domestic consumption (Art. 10.3).

Contractors are exempt from customs duties on: (1) import of equipment and materials necessary for petroleum operations; (2) reexport of equipment temporarily imported; and (3) export of its share of petroleum out of Mongolia. (Art. 12).

PETROLEUM . . . *continued*

Disputes over property arising out of petroleum operations are settled by court unless otherwise provided by contract. (Art. 13.1). Disputes related to petroleum contract may be settled by request of parties in accordance with UNCITRAL arbitration rules. (Art. 13.2). See topic Arbitration.

Liabilities.—State shall confiscate equipment, other property and petroleum produced in event that unauthorized person conducts petroleum operations. (Art. 14.1). Serious violations of criminal nature are subject to jurisdiction of court. (Art. 14.1.1). Contractors undertaking operations contrary to Petroleum Law or any other law of Mongolia are liable for damage caused. (Art. 14.2). Damage resulting from any infringement of contractual obligations shall be compensated for by guilty party. (Art. 14.3).

PRIVATIZATION:

New Privatization Law effective as of May 1991, marked radical departure from socialist principles of state ownership. Eighty percent of state assets are targeted for privatization; state retaining monopolies only in utilities, defense, and health care. However, revision of Privatization Law and of methods of transfer of assets will be undertaken in near future by new Parliament.

Central Privatization Committee (CPC) coordinates transfer of assets, along with Local Privatization Committees (LPCs) based in each aimag. (Art. 5.2). Commission was transformed in Aug. 1996 into Committee on State Property.

Voucher System attempts to allocate state property equally among citizens. All Mongolians born prior to May 31, 1991 receive voucher in nominal value of 10,000 tugriks. (Art. 12). Voucher is further subdivided into three red coupons, worth 1,000 tugriks each and one blue coupon, worth 7,000 tugriks. Red coupons are used in privatization of small businesses. They are fully tradable upon receipt, and may be bought by foreigners. Blue coupons, used in privatization of large enterprises, are not tradable, except in swap operations at Mongolian stock market.

Small businesses having annual turnover of less than 3 million tugriks can be sold at auctions organized by relevant LPC. (Art. 14). Prices are set in red coupons, with employees of business for sale receiving 10% discount. (Art. 15.1). Citizens leasing property to be privatized have right to first refusal. (Art. 15.2). Foreign bidders at auctions are permitted. As of Aug. 1992, most small businesses were privatized.

Large enterprises having annual turnover greater than 3 million tugriks are first audited by CPC. (Art. 16). Bankrupt enterprises are closed, while solvent ones are converted to joint stock companies and their shares auctioned to public for blue coupons (Art. 17.19) on Mongolian stock market. Foreigners are not permitted to participate in initial auction, but may engage in secondary share trading at stock market once enterprises have been sold off.

Agricultural sector, including state farms and livestock cooperatives, selects method of privatization itself, but such method may not contradict Privatization Law. (Art. 21). All pasture land is to remain in public hands.

Disputes or disagreements with LPC or CPC: Property disputes arising from privatization are resolved by civil courts.

REAL PROPERTY:

There is private and public ownership of property in Mongolia; foreign states and their citizens, international organizations, and persons without citizenship may be owners, unless it is stated otherwise in law or international treaties of Mongolia. (Civ. Art. 74). Land, minerals, forest, water resources, wild animals of Mongolia are property owned by State, except any real estate owned by citizens of Mongolia. (Civ. Art. 87). Citizens of Mongolia may own land, except pasture land and land for common use and land employed for State's special needs. (Civ. Art. 87). State and Government bodies have authority to decide questions connected with land. In accordance with Land Law, Great People's Khural and Government of Mongolia, department in charge of land, other central bodies, and heads of city, aimag, somon and district local administration must settle issues connected with land and its exploitation. Non-property owner has right to use, own, and dispose of owner's property if he is given authority to act as proxy by owner and this authority does not contravene law. (Civ. Art. 88).

Land Use.—Land Law of Mongolia was adopted by State Great Khural (Parliament) on Nov. 11, 1994 and became effective on Apr. 1, 1995.

According to relevant provisions of Constitution and of Land Law, minerals, forest, water resources, and wild animals of Mongolia are property owned by State, except any real estate owned by citizens of Mongolia. Only citizens of Mongolia may own land, except pasture land and land for common use and land employed for State's special needs. Foreigners may lease and use land under conditions provided for by Law. Citizens cannot transfer land in their possession to foreign nationals by way of selling, bartering, donating or pledging or transferring to others for exploitation without permission from competent state authorities.

Residential lots granted to citizens may not exceed 0.05 hectares. Size of land granted to citizens of urban areas for gardening or vegetable planting or similar purposes may not exceed 0.1 hectares.

Government or local authorities have right to establish maximum size of land to be granted to individuals or economic entities for industrial or commercial purposes and to take decision over transfer of land property rights. Land lease contracts with foreign nationals or foreign entities are renewable by periods of up to five years. State owned land may be possessed by Mongolian nationals for up to 60 years. Contracts to this effect may be extended once for period not exceeding 40 years.

Common Ownership.—Two or more persons may jointly or individually own property and possess rights to protect their property. (Civ. Art. 89). Common property under partial ownership must be owned, used, and disposed of by owners according to their mutual agreement; disputes connected with this agreement must be settled by court. (Civ. Art. 90). Each partial owner of common property has right to transfer his part to others or to dispose of it in other ways. (Civ. Art. 90). If one of owners of common property of be owned partially sells or leases his own part, he should inform other owners and other owners will have first option to lease that parcel. (Civ. Art. 91). If other owners do not respond to party's notice of intent to sell or lease parcel within one month from date of his notice, selling party has right to sell or lease own parcel to another party. (Civ. Art. 91). If one of owners of common property owned partially sells or leases own parcel by failing to notify other owners, other owners may bring lawsuit against him within six months to demand damages. (Civ. Art. 91).

Partial owner of common property has right to demand separation of his own parcel from common property. (Civ. Art. 92). If partial owner of common property does not agree with other owners concerning severance of his parcel and quality of property, property will not be altered by agreement between parties as to severance of parcel, then partial owner may request court to sever his parcel from common property. (Civ. Art. 92). Common property includes all profits, fruits, and animals obtained as result of use of property, and if other owners do not agree, profits, fruits, and animals will be allocated according to each owner's parcel. (Civ. Art. 92). Family property is one form of property that is under common ownership (Civ. Art. 94), and special provisions apply to family property (Civ. Art. 95-99).

Life Interest of Land.—Citizens may obtain right to life interest in State property in accordance with law and may inherit right to life interest. (Civ. Art. 103). Citizens have right to life interest in land in conformity with purpose and conditions of time when land was transferred to them. (Civ. Art. 103). Citizens who have right to life interest in land and to inherit life interest may allow others to use land according to its purpose and conditions. (Civ. Art. 103).

Vacant Property.—When owner of property is not known, property must be transferred to proper local administration, which must register and protect vacant property. (Civ. Art. 125). If owner of property is not established within six months of registration and declaration, or owner refuses to receive property, property will be transferred to State. (Civ. Art. 125).

Leased Property.—Landlord is obliged to transfer property to tenant for temporary use, and tenant is obliged to pay for use of leased property. (Civ. Art. 230). Contract for lease of property over one year between citizens must be made in writing; contract must be in writing if one party is legal person, regardless of term of contract. (Civ. Art. 231). Real estate lease contract, apart from apartment houses, must be registered with Real Estate Registration Agency. (Civ. Art. 231). Property leasing contract must be concluded with or without fixed term; contract for fixed term must not be more than ten years. (Civ. Art. 233). Upon expiration of term, if tenant continues to use property and lessor does not object, lease contract will be considered extended for uncertain period of time. (Civ. Art. 233). Although parties to contract without specified term have right to terminate at any time, they are obliged to inform other party about termination three months beforehand. (Civ. Art. 233).

Lease of Apartment House.—Lessor is obliged to transfer ownership or right to own, use and dispose of ownership and use by lessee and his family members in apartment, hostel, flat, room, or tent suitable for living conditions, and lessee is obliged to use that dwelling house in accordance with purpose of lease to provide dwelling and also to make lease payments in timely manner. (Civ. Art. 243). Contract for renting apartment must be made in writing; otherwise, it is null and void. (Civ. Art. 244). Landlord is obliged to transfer dwelling house in time to ownership and use of lessee and to make necessary repair work if it is stipulated in law or contract. (Civ. Art. 245). Lessee has following obligations: (1) pay rent at time fixed by contract, (2) use apartment and grounds for common use in line with its purpose, (3) make necessary repair work at proper time if it is stipulated in law or by contract, and (4) follow other rules for use of apartment. (Civ. Art. 246). Contract of lease of apartment may be concluded with or without fixed term. (Civ. Art. 247). Citizen may own and use apartment house for life, and this right is heritable. (Civ. Art. 247). Contract of lease of apartment house must be terminated by its destruction in accordance with decision of competent organization. (Civ. Art. 260).

Lease of Property.—Lessor is obliged to transfer real estate or movable estate and right to own, use, and dispose of such property to lessee for maintaining business activity and for implementation of purpose specified in lease with proper conditions, date and payment for ownership and use. (Civ. Art. 265). Lessee is obliged to use property in line with law or contract and to pay rents for leased property. (Civ. Art. 265). Unless it is stipulated in law, right to own profits, productivity and young animals obtained as result of use of leased property must be defined by contract concluded between parties. (Civ. Art. 266). Property lease contract must be made in writing; real estate lease contract must be registered at Real Estate Registration Agency; otherwise, contract is null and void. (Civ. Art. 267). Parties must fix term for property lease contract by mutual accord, taking into consideration property conditions and purpose of lease. (Civ. Art. 268). When it becomes impossible to discharge obligation specified in contract by reasonable excuse, one party has right to demand reconsideration and abatement of contract. (Civ. Art. 269). Lessor is obliged to transfer to lessee property fitting conditions specified in contract, and unless it is stipulated in law or contract, to repair that property. (Civ. Art. 272). Lessor must be answerable for quality deficiencies of property not known during conclusion of contract which delays use of property. (Civ. Art. 272). Lessee is obliged to use leased property in accordance with contract terms; not to damage fertility of land, soil, productivity of cattle, and quality of property; rehabilitate property and make payments in fixed term unless it is stipulated otherwise and agreed in contract; repair property, unless otherwise stipulated in law or contract; and return property to lessor by calculating usual wear and tear of property. (Civ. Art. 273).

Land Use Fees.—Resolution no. 136 (Apr. 26, 1991) of Government of Mongolia establishes schedule of basic fees for land in Ulaanbaatar City and for land use prices. Price for one hectare of urban land is 4.5 million tugriks and this applies to Mongolian citizens, economic entities, or organizations. Price for one hectare of urban land is US$633,800 for foreign companies, etc., who must pay in foreign currency. Annual land fee is 10% of this basic fee. These prices are subject to some negotiation.

Basic time period for land lease under draft land law to foreign entity or joint venture with foreign investor is 60 years, but it may be extended one time for another 40 years.

Initial lease period may be for 99 years depending on complexity of project, whether it is built in special economic zone once established, and length of time before investor will earn back initial investment. (Art. 44.[1.2]).

REAL PROPERTY . . . *continued*

Foreign enterprise, organization, or citizen who invests in technology which promotes production and service areas necessary for development of country, or which promotes protection and conservation of nature by using technology not harmful to nature, may enjoy reduced land payment rates and, in some cases, may be able to use land free.

SALE AND PURCHASE:

In contract for sale and purchase, seller is obliged to transfer things contracted for to buyer, who must receive items contracted for and pay contractually specified price. (Civ. Art. 202). Contract for sale and purchase of real estate must be registered at Real Estate Registration Agency. (Civ. Art. 203). Parties may establish prices by mutual agreement; prices must be paid immediately after transfer of items. (Civ. Art. 204). If seller does not transfer property to buyer or transferred property does not meet contract terms, buyer has right to claim transfer of property specified in contract or to claim compensation for losses caused by delay of execution of contract, and may claim compensation for losses caused by contract termination. (Civ. Art. 205). If ownership right is transferred before transfer of property, seller is obliged to store that property until it is transferred to buyer. (Civ. Art. 207). If it is stipulated in contract, buyer must pay all expenses borne by seller for storing property. (Civ. Art. 206).

If seller does not inform buyer beforehand about defects in property, buyer has right to complain and make following claims to seller: (1) exchange defective property for property of proper quality, (2) remove defect free of charge, (3) reimburse any expenses incurred for removal of defects or encumbrances in property, and (4) reduce costs by proper amount or refuse to make payments in partial amount for certain period. (Civ. Art. 210). Instead of claims, buyer has right to suspend contract, return defective property to seller, and demand return of money paid for property. (Civ. Art. 210). If previous two methods are not sufficient to compensate damages, buyer has right to claim complete damages. (Civ. Art. 210). If seller can prove that defects in property were caused by buyer's violation of rules concerning transportation and use of property or by force majeure, seller may refuse to meet claims of buyer. (Civ. Art. 210). If defects of purchased property are disclosed by buyer after expiration of period specified in paragraph 4 of this article but within time products may be used, and if buyer can prove that defects were caused before purchase of property, buyer may enjoy right to claim as stated in this article. (Civ. Art. 210).

Seller is obliged to supply all property together with its components and spare parts in accordance with standards, specifications, and price list. (Civ. Art. 213). If seller does not completely deliver property in fixed term, buyer has right to refuse receipt of property and to demand compensation for losses. (Civ. Art. 213). If seller does not meet claim of buyer, buyer has right to bring suit against defects in property within six months from date of raising claim. (Civ. Art. 214). If it is impossible to fix date of raising claim or of receiving its reply, or reply was not given, period of limitations will start running from date when period of raising claim expires. (Civ. Art. 214).

If third person brings suit against buyer about recovery of property for reasons existing before sale, buyer is obliged to involve seller in settling case. (Civ. Art. 216). If claim of third party about recovery of property is satisfied, seller is obliged to compensate losses of buyer. (Civ. Art. 216). However, if buyer did not involve seller in settling case, of if seller was involved and seller could prove that he was able to convince buyer to maintain property, then seller will be free of this obligation. (Civ. Art. 216).

SECURITIES:

Under Securities Law (1994), "security" includes shares certifying rights to dividend or vote, debentures with maturity no less than one year issued by authorized organisations; government bonds and other instruments determined by Securities Commission as security in conformity with law. (Art. 3.1). Securities may be in material and nonmaterial forms; securities issued according to established rules are securities in material form and securities not issued, but existing in special registry (such as computer), are securities in nonmaterial form. (Art. 3.2). Rights evidenced by ordered security must be transferred by handing in that security to others; rights evidenced by named security must be transferred by following rules about transfer of claims; and rights evidenced by permitted security must be transferred by making proper notes in that security. (Civ. Art. 83).

Securities are issued by Government, governors of capital city and provinces upon approval of relevant local hural (legislative body) and companies registered as legal person in Mongolia. (Art. 4). Issuer may sell securities through public or private offering. In case of public offering issuer shall obtain registration from Security Commission. This requirement shall not apply to private offering. (Arts. 6.1 and 2). Within 30 days after receipt of registration statement, Commission shall decide whether to declare registration statement effective or deny it. (Art. 6.6). Issuer may place its securities directly in primary market or through underwriter. (Art. 6.7). Professionals who prepare documents for registration statement shall bear responsibility for their accuracy and adequacy. (Art. 6.13).

Authority supervising and regulating activities of participants of securities markets shall be Securities Commission. (Art. 19.1). Commission shall be composed of five members. Chairman is appointed by Prime Minister, one member by Minister of Finance, another by President of Central Bank and remaining two members who represent interests of companies operating in security market by appropriate Standing Committee of State Great Khural (Parliament). Members of Commission shall be approved by Parliament. (Art. 19.1 and 2). Commission reports to Parliament on its activity. (Regulation of Security Commission, Art. 5).

Any person, directly or indirectly owning 5% and more of total shares of any company shall report it to Commission within five days after such acquisition. Any person who intends to directly or indirectly own 20% of total shares of any company shall make tender offer. (Art. 9). Tender offers shall be made in accordance with Securities Law and regulations of Securities Commission. (Art. 9.1).

Securities market includes primary markets as well as secondary market where securities are traded. All participants in securities market (underwriters, brokers, dealers, clearing and settlement organisations, depository organisations, etc.) shall be granted licences to operate in securities market. All participants and issuers bear common duty of periodically reporting to Commission; publishing mid-term and annual financial reports which are verified by independent auditor; promptly furnishing accurate and adequate information to all interested parties; ensuring fair and transparent trading in securities. (Art. 12). Participants and issuers are prohibited from: engaging in any act of deception of public or making untrue statements of material fact in connection with public offering, purchasing or selling of security; omitting, concealing or refusing to make available any material facts except insider information which may affect price of security; being involved in any securities transaction using any deceptive mechanism or technique to artificially stabilize, increase or lower market price of any securities; being involved in any faulty transaction; making any hidden or double cross transaction.

Requirements in regard to Stock Exchange: authorized capital of Stock Exchange is contributed by brokers, dealers, and underwriters which have Commission's licence and by Government; issuers and investors represent at least 50% of members of Board of Directors of Stock Exchange. (Art. 13). Stock Exchange is entitled to organise trading in securities not prohibited by Commission, to make rules subject of Commission approval and to grant operating permissions to licensed brokers and dealers.

Securities Commission and Government have within their power rights to conduct inspection and investigation. If Commission determines that person is about to infringe upon this law and relevant legislative acts it is entitled to suspend or terminate his usage of clearing and settlement services and in case of establishment of his guilt it may bring suit in court and ask to freeze his bank accounts. If person considers decision of Commission groundless he can appeal to court. If Government considers that decision made by Commission infringes upon existing legislation it can suspend it and request Commission to revise it and in case of Commission's approval, Government is entitled to bring suit to court.

Administrative sanctions may be imposed upon violators of securities legislation if there is no case for criminal charges. Court shall decide all disputes in regard to transactions in securities markets. (Art. 26).

SUCCESSION:

See topic Descent and Distribution.

TAXATION:

General Law of Taxation, enacted Jan. 1, 1993, outlines tax system, including general principles of taxation and rights and obligations of taxpayers. It also establishes legislative grounds for administrative apparatus of taxation. State Great Khural is authorized to introduce, amend, or suspend taxes, as well as to set rates in all but a few cases. (Art. 18). State Tax Administration, division of Finance Ministry, collects revenue and controls implementation on administration of tax laws.

Sales tax was first imposed in Mongolia by State Sales Tax Law enacted Jan. 1, 1993. Domestically produced goods and services are taxed at 10% of sale price. (Art. 6.1). Taxes are collected by vendor and remitted to State Tax Administration. (Art. 10.2). Exports are exempt from sales tax. (Art. 6.2). Sales tax is imposed on imported goods when they cross frontier, importer being required to remit tax along with any customs duty. (Art. 10.1). For imports, sales tax base is defined by contract price plus freight and insurance. (Art. 5).

Individual income tax was entirely revamped by Income Tax Law enacted Jan. 1, 1993. Citizens or residents (defined as foreigners staying in Mongolia for 183 days or more) are taxed on income from both within and outside Mongolia. (Art. 3). Nonresidents present in Mongolia pay tax only on income from within country. (Art. 3.4). Taxable income includes wages, salaries, bonuses, most allowances, capital gains, rents, dividends and interest. (Art. 4). Rates are progressive, ranging from 2% in lowest bracket to over 35% in highest. Wages up to 24,000 tugriks, business trip expenses, insurance refunds and disability payments are exempt. (Art. 4). Self-employed persons whose income derives from processing grains and cereals receive credit of 50%. (Art. 4). Employers hiring disabled receive exemption proportional to percentge of disabled employees in work force. (Art. 4).

Economic Entity Income Tax.—

Taxpayers.—Companies, cooperatives, joint ventures with foreign participation, commercial banks, credit and insurance agencies are all considered taxpayers under Economic Entity portion of Tax Law of July 1, 1993. (Art. 3). Branch office of foreign entity is also considered eligible taxpayer, but only if it is engaged in for-profit activity. (Art. 4.2).

Taxable income is defined differently according to type of activity giving rise to income. Income derived from most commercial activity, including manufacturing, trade in good, commercial banking, insurance, financial servies and interest income is defined as follows: Documented direct expenses are generally deductible. This broad category includes salaries, material expenses, social insurance, capital depreciation, interest on loans, administrative expenses, vehicles tax, payments for use of natural resources and excise tax. (Art. 5.1.1). Number of items are noted as not being deductible, including investment (except for reinvestment of profit in certain foreign investments, see Foreign Investment Law), repairs and maintenence, insurance premiums paid to private insurers (premiums to State owned insurers are deductible), normal loss, write off debts and fines or penalties. (Art. 5.1.1). Income from other types of activities is defined as follows: Prior cost is deducted from sale price for determining income from sales of real and personal property as well as sales of shares. (Arts. 5.2, 5.3). Dividend and interest income is defined by toal income. (Art. 5.1.5). Expenses of participation may be deducted from income won in lottery. (Art. 5.1.4).

Tax Exemptions and Credits.—Income from manufacture and sale of prosthetic devices, artificial organs and food for infants is exempt from income tax. (Arts. 7.1, 7.2.3). Income earned as interest on government bonds is similarly exempt. (Art. 7.1.2). Tax preferences in form of credits are granted to encourage activity in undeveloped areas of economy. 50% tax credit is granted for all income derived from primary food processing and production. This includes production and processing of meat, milk, cereals and flour. (Art. 7.2.1). Employers of disabled receive credit based on proportion of documented disabled persons they employ. (Art. 7.2.3).

Enterprises organized by senior citizens which have work force made up of 70% or more of that group are granted 50% credit on earned income. (Art. 7.2.4). In addition

See Topical Index in front part of this volume.

TAXATION . . . *continued*
to these enumerated credits, Great State Khural has power to grant tax credits or preferences on ad hoc basis upon application of enterprise. To qualify for consideration, applicant's activity must result in substitute production of products currently imported, or bring new technology to relatively undeveloped geographical sectors. (Art. 7.3). For foreign investors, special tax preferences generally not available to Mongolian persons may be available (see Foreign Investment Law).

Tax rates vary according to type of activity giving rise to income. Most commercial activity is taxed progressively with provision that total income tax burden should not exceed 40% of income. (Art. 6.1.1). Rates range from 5% of income up to 300,000 tugrik to around 30% for income over 1.5 million tugrik. (Art. 6.1.1). Dividend income is taxed at 15%. (Art. 6.1.2). Income from sale of stock through exchange is taxed at 10%, while sales not cleared through market are taxed at only 2%. (Art. 6.1.3). Lottery winnings and income from rental of videos is taxed at 60%. (Art. 6.1.4). Income from sale of real property is taxed on sliding scale based on duration of ownership, with turnovers in two years or less taxed at 40% while turnovers which take more than five years are taxed at 20%. (Art. 6.1.5).

Art. 4, paragraph 5(d) of Individual Income Tax Law of Mongolia (1992), New Edition, amended 23 Nov. 1993, concerning Art. 10.6, General Tax Law:

Amount of Mohns Taxable Income	Tax Rate
8,001-16,000	2%
16,001-32,000	160 tugriks plus 5% of amount of income exceeding 16,000 tugriks
32,001-64,000	960 tugriks plus 15% of amount of income exceeding 32,000 tugriks
64,001-128,000	5,760 tugriks plus 27% of amount of income exceeding 64,000 tugriks
128,001-256,000	23,040 tugriks plus 40% of amount of income exceeding 128,000 tugriks
256,001 and above	72,240 tugriks plus 45% of amount of income exceeding 256,000 tugriks

Dividends are included in categorization of wages and similar enumeration.

Vehicle tax on all forms of transport is imposed by Transport Facilities and Vehicles Tax Law of Jan. 1, 1993. All persons, citizens or not, are required to pay quarterly tax for operation of motorcycles, buses, trucks, cranes, and tractors. (Arts. 4, 5, & 7).

See topic Damages.

TRAVEL ABROAD AND MIGRATION:

Art. 16 of Constitution proclaims right of citizens to travel and reside abroad and to return to home country. Law on travel abroad and migration was adopted on Dec. 24, 1993 and became effective as of Feb. 1, 1994. Under this law citizens of Mongolia have right to travel freely abroad except those who are defendants in criminal cases or criminal suspects, or who are involved in unresolved civil cases. Citizens who were involved in State security sensitive work may be suspended exit from Mongolia for three years from date of their separation. Citizens wishing to travel abroad must apply to Police to obtain passport for travel abroad. Passports should be issued within ten days from date of submission of application. Citizens residing abroad for more than six months must register with Mongolian diplomatic mission in that country.

TRESPASS:

See topic Damages.

WILLS:

See topic Descent and Distribution.

NETHERLANDS LAW DIGEST

(The following is a list of all Topics, including cross-references, covered in this Digest.)

NETHERLANDS LAW DIGEST

Revised for 1997 edition by

DE BRAUW BLACKSTONE WESTBROEK, Amsterdam, Eindhoven, The Hague, Rotterdam, Brussels, London, New York and Prague.
(topic Taxation revised by LOYENS & VOLKMAARS, The Hague).

(Abbreviations used are: B.W., Burgerlijk Wetboek, Civil Code; WvK, Wetboek van Koophandel, Commercial Code; Rv, Wetboek van Burgerlijke Rechtsvordering, Code of Civil Procedure).

The Netherlands is member of EU. See also European Union Law Digest.

ABSENTEES:

Absentee, defined as person who has left his residence, is unattainable or whose existence is uncertain, retains all rights and liabilities. If, however, necessary to provide for administration of absentee's property, or if necessary to have absentee represented in suit, district court of absentee's last place of residence (if in Netherlands or, otherwise, court of The Hague) may appoint "trustee" ("bewindvoerder") at request of interested party or upon demand of public prosecutor (§1:409 B.W.). Trustee may not, however, represent absentee in matter of family law unless expressly authorized by district court. Fee of trustee may amount to 5% of net proceeds of administered property unless court decides otherwise. Trusteeship ends by joint decision of former absentee and trustee, by notice of termination from former absentee to trustee or when death of absentee has been ascertained.

If absentee declared "presumably dead" by district court (see topic Death), heirs may exercise their legal rights but must return property if absentee returns.

ACKNOWLEDGMENTS:

Dutch law does not require acknowledgment of signatures on private instruments.

In notarial instruments parties thereto acknowledge before notary to have knowledge of contents of instrument, whereas signature of notary constitutes certification of signatures of parties.

Signatures on private instruments may be certified by notary, and, if required, signature of notary can be certified by foreign consular officers.

So called "apostille" is issued by clerk of court to certify signature of notaries and certain other officials on documents to be used in countries party to The Hague Convention of Oct. 5, 1961; those countries include most EEC countries and USA. For documents to be used in countries party to Convention only apostille and no certification by consular officers is available.

See also topics Consuls; Notaries.

ACTIONS:

No distinction is made between actions at law and suits in equity. Generally, litigation is initiated by summons to be served on other party by process server. Summons must contain all essential facts (particulars) upon which demand for relief or injunction is based. Classification by plaintiff of his demand as specific action is irrelevant and may be disregarded by court which may grant relief or injunction on other legal grounds provided that sufficient facts have been stated. In his complaint to court, plaintiff repeats or refers to statements in summons. Defendant, in his answer, has to give reasons for his defenses; he must compile his defenses of procedural nature and his substantive defense.

However, plea that court has no jurisdiction must, and few other pleas may, be filed separately before answer. After his answer defendant can no longer plead new defence of procedural nature. Usually, each of both parties then files one motion ("repliek" and "dupliek"). Oral pleadings may follow at request of one of parties. To lawsuit initiated by summons, strict rules of procedure and proof apply. Suit is completed by judgment ("vonnis"). (See topic Judgments.) No jury. No summary judgment practice.

Specific suits, particularly relating to family law, are initiated by petition filed with court, copy of which is sent by court's clerk by registered mail to other party. To those suits less strict rules apply and they are completed by order ("beschikking"). For other special proceedings see topics Bankruptcy (Moratorium); Divorce; Labor Relations.

In case of urgency, provisional injunction or other provisional measure may be obtained from president of district court by highly accelerated form of procedure ("kort geding") similar to French référé, without prejudice to rights in main action. Parties may do so unless law provides for other means of obtaining provisional measures (see infra). See topic Courts.

Distinction between civil and commercial actions has been abolished. Disputes about labor contracts are treated as civil actions.

If one of parties is government or government agency but action is based on contract or tort, action is treated as civil action and civil courts have jurisdiction.

Generally, however, complaints about decisions by central or local government or government agency are to be submitted to administrative agencies or administrative courts and kind of procedure is regulated either by act dealing with substantive law or by special act of administrative procedure. (See also topic Courts.) Determination of damages by expropriation is, however, subject to normal courts. In some administrative proceedings provisional measures may be obtained from Chairman of specific administrative court. In other administrative proceedings parties can only obtain provisional measures by way of "kort geding" as outlined in above.

If parties agreed to submit their disputes to arbitrators according to procedure provided for in §§1020-1076 Rv, only order from president of district court is required to make award enforceable as judgment of Dutch court. In all other cases award (classified as "binding advice") is treated as agreement of parties to abide by decision of person(s) to whom they submitted their dispute resulting in contractual obligation which, if not complied with, shall be submitted by legal action to normal courts.

Special Parties.—Suit is to be brought by and against guardian of infant, committee of judicially declared incompetent, trustee in bankruptcy (only financial matters). As to deceased's estate, suit under circumstances is to be brought by "executeur-testamentair", if any. In all other cases, estate is represented by joint heirs; process may be served on "executeur testamentair" or on last address of deceased; or, within one year of decease, upon any one of heirs. See topic Executors and Administrators.

Joinder.—If suit is brought against several defendants separately, each party may file motion for joinder if subject matters of suits are sufficiently connected. Besides, if between two parties several suits on same subject are pending each of them may move for joinder.

Intervention by interested third party who has interest at stake is permissible.

Third Party Practice.—Before service of any responsive pleading or any motion other than motion for lack of jurisdiction, defendant may move for leave to serve summons and complaint upon third party who is or may be liable to him or to plaintiff for all or part of plaintiff's claim against him.

Interpleader.—Analogous practice does not exist.

Stay.—Court fixes terms within which pleadings and motions have to be filed and extensions requested by any of parties.

Proof of Foreign Claims.—Foreign marriage, birth and death certificates and other official documents or records are permissible as documentary evidence; if state of origin is not party to Convention of The Hague of Oct. 5, 1961, legalization of documents by Netherlands consulate may be required.

Proof of Foreign Law.—Judge himself will have to determine meaning of foreign law, if applicable, but may ask information in this respect from parties; usually he therefore instructs (one of) parties to prove meaning of foreign law. This does not relieve him, however, from obligation to investigate foreign law on his own. In determining meaning of foreign law, judge strictly conforms to relevant rules. EEC law: under §177 EEC Treaty court of one of member states can ask Court of Justice for preliminary ruling regarding matters set out in §177 if court in question is of opinion that such is necessary to be able to decide case. If decision of court in question will not be subject to appeal court is obliged to ask Court of Justice for preliminary ruling whenever question regarding matters set out in §177 is raised unless case is so clear that court can consider it as beyond discussion what preliminary ruling would be. European Convention concerning supply of information on foreign law concluded between members of Council of Europe in 1968 was ratified by Netherlands effective 1977.

Limitation of.—See topic Limitation of Actions.

Actions for Death.—See topic Death, subhead Actions for Death.

See also topics Aliens, subhead Procedural Rules; Constitution and Government; Courts; Evidence.

ADMINISTRATION:

See topic Executors and Administrators.

ADMIRALTY:

See topic Shipping.

ADOPTION:

Adoption is effected by judgment of district court, at petition of adopters (married couple or survivor of couple, if clear that during marriage couple intended to request adoption).

On date of petition, marriage between adopters must have lasted five years or more, they must have cared for and educated foster child for at least one year, one of petitioners must already have been appointed child's guardian, difference in age between each adopter and child may not be less than 18 nor more than 50 years, and child must be of minor age. One may not adopt one's grandchild (legitimate or natural).

On date of petition mother of child, if she is not married, must have attained age of 16. Persons who legally are deemed to be child's parents must not have filed objections, at first petition of adopters. At second petition filed at least two years later, objection of parents may be disregarded.

Parent and stepparent may adopt child out of wedlock, or child from earlier marriage, if other parent has not filed objections. Requirement of five years of marriage of adopters and requirement of difference in age between adopters and foster-child do not apply in this case.

Adoption granted only if severance from legal parent(s) and ties with adopters are in child's best interest.

Court of domicile of child has jurisdiction, or if child has no domicile in Netherlands, court of child's actual residence in Netherlands or if child neither domiciled nor residing in Netherlands, court at The Hague.

Child younger than 12 can be heard by court. Child aged 12 or more must be heard by court before judgment. Child aged 15 or more must not have indicated objections.

By affirmative decision child obtains all rights and obligations of legitimate child of adopters and ties of family law with original parents and their family relations are severed, as from date when appeal against judgment can no longer be instituted, even if it would turn out afterwards that court was wrong when it deemed all conditions to have been fulfilled.

See Topical Index in front part of this volume.

ADOPTION . . . *continued*

However, child may demand revocation by petition made not earlier than two and not later than three years upon attaining age of majority. Revocation will be granted only if court is convinced of child's interest and of reasonableness of request, and by revocation all legal ties with adopters and their relatives are severed and those with original parents and their relatives renewed.

Special form of "legitimation" with same results as adoption is provided if parents of natural child marry, and father formally recognizes child as his own.

ADVERSE POSSESSION:

See topic Limitation of Actions.

AFFIDAVITS:

Dutch law does not provide for affidavits. However, foreign affidavits may be accepted in evidence by courts; their probative value is in discretion of courts which may prefer to have evidence taken by means of letters rogatory or by consular officer.

Although Dutch laws do not confer specific authority to notaries to administer oaths, it is generally accepted that notaries have such authority and foreign courts generally accept affidavits taken before Dutch notary.

There are treaties between Netherlands and various other countries for mutual assistance in conduct of legal proceedings.

See also topics Acknowledgments; Consuls; Notaries.

AGENCY: See topic Principal and Agent.

AIRCRAFT:

Netherlands have signed and ratified Convention of Warsaw of 1929 (and amendments including The Hague Protocol of 1955, Guadelajara Convention of 1961, Guatemala Protocol of 1971 [not yet in force] and Protocols of Montreal of 1975 [not yet in force]) on international carriage by air; Convention of Rome 1933 on precautionary arrest on aircraft (does not apply to overseas territories); Convention of Chicago 1944 (and amendments including Buenos Aires Protocol of 1968 and Montreal Protocols of 1975) on nationality of aircraft, etc.; Convention of Geneva of 1948 on international recognition of rights in aircraft; Tokyo Convention of 1963 on offenses and crimes committed on board aircraft; The Hague Convention of 1970 on the suppression of unlawful seizure of aircraft; Montreal Convention of 1971 on suppression of unlawful acts against safety of civil aviation.

Netherlands have not yet ratified Convention of Rome of 1952 concerning damage caused by foreign aircraft to third parties on surface. According to explanatory memorandum pertaining to Law on Enactment of Book 8, Civil Code, second part ("Invoeringswet Boek 8 Burgerlijk Wetboek, tweede gedeelte") parties concerned and insurers have to settle disputes themselves in compliance with Netherlands tort law.

European Conventions.—Paris Agreement of 1956 on Commercial Rights of non-scheduled Air Services (does not apply to overseas territories); Paris Agreement of 1960 on Certificates of air worthiness for imported aircraft; Brussels Convention of 1960 on cooperation for safety of air navigation (Eurocontrol) (including Brussels Protocols of 1970, 1978, 1981); Paris Multilateral Agreement of 1967 on establishment of tariffs for scheduled air services (does not apply to overseas territories); Geneva Multilateral Agreement of 1979 on civil aircraft trading; Brussels Multilateral Agreement of 1981 on "En Route" charges. As Member State to European Union (EU), Netherlands are also bound by regulations effective within EU. Some of most important directives are Directive 2407/92 (July 23, 1992) on licensing of air carriers, D. 2408/92 (July 23, 1992) on access for air carriers to intra-Community air routes, D. 2409/92 (July 23, 1992) on tariffs for air services, D. 2410/92 (July 23, 1992) amending D. 3975/87 (Dec. 14, 1987) and D. 2411/92 (July 23, 1992) amending D. 3976/87 (Dec. 14, 1987) both regarding application of rules on competition for undertakings in air transport sector, D. 95/93 (Jan. 18, 1993) on "slot" allocation on Community airports and D. 94/56 (Nov. 21, 1994) on aviation accident and incident investigations. Noteworthy is also European Commission Directive 1617/93 (June 25, 1993) which, under certain restrictions, allows Member States to jointly plan, coordinate and operate air services within Community, to negotiate tariffs for scheduled services within Community and to allocate "slots" on Community airports. There is proposal for Directive on access to groundhandling market at Community airports, and for Regulation on air carrier liability in case of accidents.

National Regulations.—Provisions regarding recording of rights in aircraft are laid down in "Wet Teboekgestelde Luchtvaartuigen" (Mar. 6, 1957, "Staatsblad" no. 72 and Amendment) and "Kadasterwet" (May 3, 1989, "Staatsblad" no. 186 and Amendments). "Wet Teboekgestelde Luchtvaartuigen" shall be replaced by new Title 15 ("The Aircraft") to Book 8, Civil Code (Means of Traffic and Transport). Title 15 shall be supplemented by Title 16 (Operation of Aircraft) and Title 17 (Accidents) in the future.

Air transport regulations have been laid down in "Wet Luchtvervoer". (Sept. 10, 1936, "Staatsblad" no. 523 and Amendments). If "Wet Luchtvervoer" deviates from applicable provision of Warsaw Convention, Convention prevails.

Public law provisions are: "Luchtvaartwet" (Jan. 15, 1958, "Staatsblad" 47 and Amendments), covering, inter alia, issuance of air transport licenses; "Luchtvaartongevallenwet", (June 18, 1992, "Staatsblad" 705), regarding aircraft accident and incident investigations; "Regeling Toezicht Luchtvaart" (Jan. 22, 1959, "Staatsblad" 67 and Amendments), containing rules as to registration of aircraft, certification, licenses, airworthiness and safety requirements; "Wet Luchtverkeer" (June 18, 1992, "Staatsblad" 368 and Amendments), on air traffic; "Luchtverkeersreglement" (Dec. 18, 1992, "Staatsblad" 697), concerning air traffic control. Provisions regarding enforcement of rights in aircraft and precautionary arrest on aircraft are included in §§584a-584r Rv and §§729-729e Rv respectively.

ALIENS:

Visas are needed for entry for citizens; but agreements with many countries allow visitors to enter without visa or other formalities for stay for specified purposes or for limited period of time in some cases (including U.S.) without restrictions.

Aliens Act (1965, rev. 1994) regulates admission and expulsion of and control on aliens. Furthermore it sets conditions for granting and withdrawal of permits to stay for longer than three months, permits to establish residence and granting and withdrawal of status of refugees. From decisions taken by local authorities or Minister of Justice in general aliens have right to ask for revision to Minister of Justice. During revision procedure expulsion is suspended, when Minister of Justice is of opinion that revision has reasonable chance of success. When this is not case alien can apply for temporary injunction. In that case alien can apply for temporary injunction. Judicial appeal against Minister's decision must be lodged with district court of The Hague, which is dispersed over four other districts for this purpose. During appeal expulsion is not suspended, however temporary injunction may be sought. Aliens, when not in possession of legal documents entitling them to enter or stay in Netherlands, are according to Act subject to provisional imprisonment; in practice limited to those who claim refuge-status. Generally, alien is granted permit if he proves that his stay in Netherlands is in interest of Dutch society, or that his stay should be granted for urgent humanitarian reasons ("Klemmende redenen van humanitaire aard"). Generally, aliens must prove to be financially independent.

Extradition Act (1967) contains ratification of European Convention on Extradition (Paris, Dec. 1957) and Benelux Convention on Extradition (Brussels, June 1962).

Convention stipulates that extradition is possible for committed offences, punishable with one year or more imprisonment, in both extraditing country and country claiming extradition.

Netherlands reserves right to refuse extradition on humanitarian grounds. No extradition is granted where serious reason to believe that person, whose extradition is sought, will be persecuted for his religious or political views, his nationality or race. Extradition of Netherlands citizens is not possible.

Labour (by) Foreign Employees Act (Dec. 21, 1994) requires employer to obtain work-permit for employment of foreign employees. Employment without permit is misdemeanor and employer may be prosecuted. Certain categories, like residents of EU-countries are exempted. Permit is applied for at district labor office by employer with Central Board of Employment Office formally deciding. Grounds for refusal are refusal of alien's request for stay permit or existence of labor supply enjoying priority. Labour office must have been notified of vacancy at least five weeks before filing of request for work permit. More lenient policies apply with respect to international transfer of staff personnel. Applicants can ask for revision of refusal to Central Board. Judicial appeal is possible to district court which may also give temporary injunction.

Procedural Rules.—Generally private and commercial laws of civil and criminal procedure are same for aliens and Dutch citizens. For most aliens treaties provide that, as plaintiff, they are not required to post bond for costs of litigation and that, whether plaintiff or defendant, they enjoy benefit of legal aid system in same way as Dutch citizens. Basically Dutch courts have jurisdiction of any case instituted by Dutch citizens against any, even nonresident, aliens and vice versa, in respect of any obligation wherever contracted, provided that according to Rv §126 competent court is available (court must have jurisdiction over defendant's place of residence in Netherlands; if nonresident defendant, then over plaintiff's place of residence). Notice is by written summons. Conflict of law rules are based on nationality as well as on domicile. EEC Enforcement Treaty provides different jurisdiction rules for suits among residents of EEC countries, with exception of Portugal.

Corporations Owned or Controlled by Aliens.—No general disqualifications apply. Some provisions of Codes or of separate Acts or Royal Decrees have different rules for residents and nonresidents respectively instead of distinction citizen/alien. Others use both distinctions as factor. According to Dutch-American Friendship Treaty U.S. citizens are entitled to stay permit to develop enterprise in Netherlands in which they have invested minimum of Dfl 10,000,—or have share capital interest of at least 25%. See also topic Corporations, subhead Corporations Owned and/or Managed by Foreigners.

Under Nationality Act of 1984 Dutch citizenship is acquired by birth if one of biological parents is Dutch citizen, by adoption if one of adopting parents is Dutch citizen, by obtaining status of legitimate child of Dutch citizen or by nationalization. Immigrants can generally apply for citizenship after continued period of residence of five years.

Aliens who have married Dutch citizen can apply for citizenship after three years of marriage.

See topics Bankruptcy (Moratorium); Contracts, subhead Applicable Law; Corporations; Divorce; Foreign Investment; Labor Relations; Real Property; Taxation; Trade Register.

ALIMONY:

See topics Divorce; Exemptions; Husband and Wife.

ARBITRATION:

Arbitration as means of solving disputes is used regularly in Netherlands. Hence numerous standing arbitration committees in certain trades and standard rules of procedure and standard arbitration clauses for both national and international transactions, most importantly those of Netherlands Arbitration Institute (NAI) and Council for Arbitration in construction matters.

Civil and commercial matters may be submitted to arbitration with exception of matters not at parties' free disposition (e.g., matters relating to divorce, separation, care and control of minors, etc.) and matters under exclusive court jurisdiction.

Arbitration law is incorporated in Code of Civil Procedure. From Dec. 1, 1986, completely new set of regulations for arbitration applies.

Arbitral agreement may be agreement relating to existing dispute or arbitral clause intended for possible future disputes. Arbitrators must be in uneven numbers. Foreign arbitrators allowed under Dutch law. Arbitrators' acceptance of mission creates contract between arbitrators and parties.

Arbitrators can take interim measures, but attachment is national court's domain. "Amiable composition" (arbitrators bound only by general rules of public policy) must be specifically agreed to. Arbitral award must be in writing and reasoned and deposited at district court registry.

See Topical Index in front part of this volume.

ARBITRATION . . . *continued*

Arbitral award is only enforceable on application and granting of exequatur by president of district court. Award can only be annulled on limited grounds by courts, who may not rule on merits of case.

Netherlands are signatory to Protocol of Geneva of 1923 concerning arbitral clauses, Geneva Convention of 1927 on enforcement of foreign arbitral awards, New York Convention of 1958 on recognition and enforcement of foreign arbitral awards and Washington Convention of 1966 on the Settlement of Investment Disputes between States and Nationals of other States.

ASSIGNMENTS:

Assignability.—Personal rights and claims (i.e. rights and claims not on bearer or order) are assignable except for strictly personal ones and as far as not provided for otherwise by statute (e.g. claims for wages are assignable only to certain extent) or contract. Rights payable to bearer or order are always assignable.

Form.—Assignment of personal rights and claims is effected by notarial or informal deed of transfer followed by notice of transfer to debtor. If on date of drafting this deed, debtor exists but cannot be identified, assignment is deemed to have taken place on said date provided that notice of transfer is given expeditiously once debtor has been ascertained. Assignment of rights payable to bearer is effected by delivery of document embodying right to be assigned if alienator has possession and control of that document. Same applies to assignment of rights payable to order when document is under control and in possession of alienator, provided that document is also endorsed. When document embodying right is not under control and in possession of alienator, assignment is effected by deed of transfer followed by notice of transfer to debtor.

ASSIGNMENTS FOR BENEFIT OF CREDITORS:

Not known under Dutch law. See topic Bankruptcy (Moratorium).

ASSOCIATIONS:

Legal Entity.—Ordinary association ("Vereniging") is nonprofit organisation (§2:26 BW). Associations may be created merely by multilateral act. Such associations are restricted legal entities: those making third party commitments on behalf of association remain liable under certain circumstances even after their discharge along with association and association may not obtain title to registered goods or be appointed heir. Such restrictions do not apply if association either has full legal entity status by being created in first place by notarial deed or obtains such status by having articles of association incorporated in notarial deed. Limited concept of ultra vires applies: commitments to third parties by board are binding even if exceed association's purpose unless board can show third party knew or should have known that board exceeded purpose.

Other kinds of legal entities, provided for in BW, Book 2, are:

Cooperative society is association whose object it is to satisfy specific material needs of its members by means of entering into agreements with them in conduct of business which it operates to this end on behalf of its members. Business with third parties, if allowed by its articles, must be secondary to business with members. (§2:53-4).

Mutual insurance company is association whose object it is to enter into insurance contracts with its members in conduct of insurance business which it operates to this end on behalf of its members. Insurance business with third parties, if allowed by its articles, must be secondary to business with its members. (§2:53-4).

Limited Liability Companies (NV and BV) treated under topic Corporations, and ecclesiastical entities in §2:2.

See topics Corporations; Law Reports, Codes, Etc., subhead Recodification of Civil and Commercial Codes; Partnership; Records; Trade Register; Trusts, subheads Foundations, Fiduciaries.

ATTACHMENT:

Main Types.—Two main types of attachment have to be distinguished: (a) "Executoriaal beslag" and (b) "Conservatoir beslag".

Common feature, however, of both types of attachment is that after attachment attached property can no longer be disposed of to prejudice of attaching creditor.

"Executoriaal Beslag" (Attachment under Execution).—Act of seizing property, property rights or, in case of garnishment, debts owed to defendant, in possession of defendant or in possession of third party debtor to defendant, for satisfaction of claim of attaching creditor against defendant by virtue of judgment or notarial instrument, by which claim has been established.

See further topic Execution.

"Conservatoir Beslag".—Act of taking and holding into custody of law of property and/or money in possession of debtor or of third party who is owing this property or money to debtor (garnishment) for securing attaching creditor's right to seek recourse against this property and/or money.

Special Types.—Special types of "conservatoir beslag" are "revindicatoir beslag" (revindicatory seizure), which serves to secure right to possess or repossess goods or to prevent ship from sailing, "maritaal beslag" which serves to secure rights of spouses on marital community property while in divorce proceedings and "vreemde lingenbeslag" (foreign attachment), which serves to secure attaching creditor's right to seek recourse against property and/or money located in Netherlands of debtor without known residence within Netherlands.

Prior Permission.—In principle, conservatory attachment cannot be effected without prior permission of president of district court. To obtain permission attaching creditor has to supply summary proof of his claim and, in most cases, that debtor is about to frustrate attaching creditor's right of recourse or possession, e.g. by disposing of his property.

Period within which to Summon Defendant.—In all cases in which permission for conservatory attachment is asked after Jan. 1, 1992 and in which no principal claim is yet filed, president of district court shall only give permission under condition that attaching creditor shall institute legal proceedings against defendant to demand his principal claim within period to be fixed by president of district court; attachment becomes null and void ipso jure, if period is not observed.

In case principal claim is dismissed, and judgment concerned has become final and binding, attachment comes to end. If creditor appeals against judgment, attachment remains in force. In case principal claim is awarded, all conservatory attachments become "executoriaal beslag".

See further topic Execution.

Creation of Jurisdiction.—In general conservatory attachment does not create jurisdiction. However, in case of attachment of property in Netherlands of nonresident (foreign attachment) court will acquire jurisdiction also over principal claim. However, exclusive jurisdiction clause appointing foreign court should still be observed.

Goods Detained by Third Party (Garnishment).—In case of conservatory attachment of goods detained by third party or of debt due by third party to debtor writ of attachment is to be served on third party. This writ must, on pain of nullity, also inform third party where principal claim has been filed or within what period and where principal claim will be filed. Bailiff's notification of conservatory attachment, including writ of conservatory attachment, has to be served on debtor within eight days after date of garnishment. If period of eight days is expired, debtor is entitled to request president of district court to release attachment. When principal claim is filed after garnishment, writ of summons of principal claim has to be served on third party within eight days after date of introduction of principal claim. If this period is expired, attachment becomes null. As soon as four weeks have passed since garnishment, third party is obliged to inform bailiff who served writ of attachment or attaching creditor's attorney by extrajudicial statement what debts he owes defendant or which of defendant's goods are in his possession. If third party fails to meet this obligation, attaching creditor can institute legal proceedings against third party to demand payment of his principal claim. Subsequently, judgment obtained against debtor in respect of claim is to be served upon third party and latter is summoned to disclose any money due by him to debtor or any property of debtor in his custody and he is ordered either to make money or property available for execution or to surrender amount to which debtor was condemned.

Release.—Defendant may in proceedings before district court or (quicker) before president of district court obtain release of attachment on filing bond or on summary proof that principal claim is not valid or attachment was not necessary.

See also topics Execution, Exemptions.

BANKRUPTCY (MORATORIUM):

Any natural person and any private legal entity domiciled, residing and/or having place of business in The Netherlands may be declared bankrupt upon own request or upon request of creditor or public prosecutor.

Competent Court.—Court of debtor's domicile, residence or place of business has jurisdiction over petition for bankruptcy.

Bankruptcy will be pronounced only upon summary proof of debtor having actually suspended payment to at least two creditors. In case of adjudication of bankruptcy, appeal can be taken within eight days (fortnight for debtor not heard) by debtor, any creditor who has not petitioned for bankruptcy, or any person having interest.

Object of bankruptcy is debtor's estate at time he is declared bankrupt and property to be acquired by him during his bankruptcy except for, amongst others, wages and pensions if and so far as ordered by special judge ("Rechter-commissaris") and some social security payments; see topic Exemptions.

As result of bankruptcy: Debtor can no longer dispose of his property in The Netherlands to prejudice of creditors existing at time of adjudication of bankruptcy; claims of all creditors mature; separate attachments of debtor's property are annulled. In principle (absent appropriate treaty), foreign bankruptcy proceedings have no effect on debtor's assets in The Netherlands.

Administration.—On adjudication of bankruptcy member of court is appointed "Rechter-commissaris" who supervises administration and liquidation of debtor's estate by "curator" (trustee in bankruptcy/receiver) who is appointed by court, too. Receiver (or Clerk of Court) publishes judgment by which bankruptcy has been adjudicated, takes inventory of and collects and administers bankrupt's estate and with prior authorization of "Rechter-commissaris" he may continue bankrupt's business, appear in court or with arbitrators, sue and be sued, settle disputes out of court and/or realize bankrupt's property.

Validation of Claims.—Creditors can no longer take recourse against debtor's property separately except for those creditors who have special title to do so ("de separatisten") like mortgagee ("hypotheekhouder"), and pledgee ("pandhouder"). Creditors, who are not "separatist", have to file their claims with curator and to state thereby their rights of priority, if any. At meeting of creditors ("verificatievergadering") to be held at date to be fixed by "Rechter-commissaris" these claims and rights of priority are validated by "Rechter-commissaris". Before this meeting, receiver deposits with court for public inspection list of provisionally allowed and contested claims. If curator and/or creditor oppose validation of claim and/or right of priority at meeting this claim is referred to court. Bankrupt has to attend meeting.

Insolvency.—If meeting of creditors ("verificatievergadering") does not result in arrangement/composition approved by creditors or court, or if court nullifies arrangement, debtor is according to law in state of insolvency as from date of meeting or of court's ruling becoming final. When company is bankrupt, this company is thereupon in state of dissolution. Receiver settles entire estate. "Curator" has right to have mortgagee ("hypotheekhouder") and pledgee ("pandhouder") exercise their rights within reasonable time. However, "Rechter-commissaris" may grant extension.

Termination.—Bankruptcy can terminate in three ways: (1) Termination for lack of funds. If it appears that there are no funds for payments to creditors upon application of "Rechter-commissaris" court may terminate bankruptcy. This termination of bankruptcy does not affect creditor's claims. (2) Termination by arrangement. Debtor may offer arrangement ("accoord") before or in meeting of creditors. If accepted by creditors by vote qualified both in number of creditors and in amount of claims and subsequently approved of by court arrangement is binding upon all creditors except for

See Topical Index in front part of this volume.

BANKRUPTCY (MORATORIUM) . . . *continued*
creditors with right of priority. These latter creditors have to be satisfied in full unless they have taken part in voting on arrangement. Approval of arrangement by court terminates bankruptcy. Arrangement discharges bankrupt of all his debts. (3) Termination by distribution of funds of money collected and/or made by liquidation of bankrupt's property. Distribution will take place in order of priority of claims. Receiver may arrange interim distribution. If and as far as creditors do not receive payment they will retain claim.

See also topic Fraudulent Sales and Conveyances.

Moratorium ("Surséance van betaling").—Debtor who foresees he is not able to pay his creditors on short term may file petition with court for suspension of time of payment of his debt. Upon summary proof of his incapability to meet his debts on short term provisional suspension is granted. At same time administrator is appointed and meeting of creditors is ordered. Unless creditor or creditors being 1/3 of number of creditors and representing quarter of total amount of claims present at meeting oppose it court may grant definite suspension (maximum: 1 1/2 year's extension possible).

Privileged Claims.—Moratorium does not affect creditors whose claims are secured by mortgage, pledge, or other right of priority. They may still ask for payment in full. Others may no longer seek recourse against debtor individually and payments may be made to them only collectively and in proportion to each claim.

Administration.—Debtor may continue his business and administer and dispose of his estate in The Netherlands only with consent of administrator.

Termination.—Moratorium ends by: (a) Payment of all debts, (b) acceptance of arrangement and approved thereof by Court, (c) court decision to that effect. In latter case debtor may be declared bankrupt at same time if full payment to creditors is not to be anticipated.

BILLS AND NOTES:

Netherlands law was amended to comply with "Geneva Conventions" concerning bills of exchange and promissory notes (1930), and cheques (1931).

Bills of exchange must contain: (1) Term "wisselbrief" (i.e., bill of exchange) in language of document, (2) unconditional order to pay certain sum of money, (3) name of drawee, (4) date of maturity, (5) place of payment, (6) name of person to whom or to whose order payment must be made, (7) place and date of issue, (8) signature of drawer.

If any of above elements is lacking, document will not be bill of exchange, except as provided otherwise.

Maturity may be as follows: At sight; at certain date after sight; at certain date after date of issue; at certain date.

If bill of exchange does not contain provision on maturity, it will mature at sight. Bill maturing at sight or at certain date after sight may carry interest.

Drawer warrants that bill of exchange will be accepted and paid. Drawer must provide that drawee shall have funds for payment at maturity.

Transfer.—Every bill of exchange is transferable, by endorsement and delivery, except that bill of exchange "not to order" is transferable by assignment. Holder of bill will be considered to be lawful holder, if his rights are evidenced by uninterrupted series of endorsements, even if last endorsement is in blank, except if holder has acquired bill in bad faith.

Unless provided to contrary, endorser warrants acceptance and payment of bill of exchange.

Presentation for Acceptance.—Generally, holder can present bill of exchange to drawee for acceptance, prior to maturity. Word "accepted" should be noted on bill and acceptor should sign it. By acceptance, drawee makes commitment to pay bill at maturity.

Guarantee for Payment.—Third party can guarantee payment of bill of exchange, by writing "for aval" on bill and adding his signature.

Presentation for Payment.—Holder of bill of exchange must present it for payment within two working days of maturity.

Protest for Nonacceptance or Nonpayment.—Must be evidenced by means of authentic deed in due time.

Liability.—Drawer, acceptor, endorser and guarantor are jointly and severally liable to holder for payment.

Exchange Rate.—Bill of exchange payable in currency other than currency of place of payment, can be paid in currency of country of such place, at rate of exchange prevailing at maturity, except if provision for payment in certain currency has been made.

Forfeiture, Prescription.—Various terms must be observed, on penalty of forfeiture or prescription.

Promissory notes must contain: (1) Term "to order" or "promissory note" in language of document, (2) unconditional promise to pay certain sum of money, (3) date of maturity, (4) place of payment, (5) name of person to whom or to whose order payment must be made, (6) place and date of issue, (7) signature of issuer.

If any of above elements is lacking, document will not be treated as promissory note, except as provided otherwise.

Many provisions with respect to bills of exchange correspondingly apply to promissory notes.

Cheques must contain: (1) Term "cheque" in language of document, (2) unconditional order to pay certain sum of money, (3) name of drawee, (4) place of payment, (5) place and date of issue, (6) signature of drawer.

If any of above elements is lacking, document will not be treated as cheque, except as provided otherwise.

Cheque matures at sight.

Cheque must be drawn on bank holding funds at order of drawer. However, writing of uncovered cheque does not, by itself, constitute criminal offense. Cheque may be made payable to particular person with or without clause "to order", or to bearer.

Cheque is not subject to acceptance.

Transfer.—Cheque is transferable by endorsement and delivery, except that cheque "not to order" is transferable by assignment.

Presentation for Payment.—Cheque payable in country of issue must be presented for payment within eight days of date of issue. If cheque evidences that it is intended to circulate in another country, its term will be extended to 20 or 70 days respectively, if it will circulate in continent of issue or in another continent.

Other Means of Payment.—Most noncash payments in Netherlands are made through intermediary of bank- or giro-systems. Guaranteed bank cheques ("eurocheques") and credit cards have become popular as means of payment. All these instruments are subject to various legal provisions.

CHATTEL MORTGAGES:

See topic Pledges.

COMMERCIAL REGISTER:

See topic Trade Register.

COMMISSIONS TO TAKE TESTIMONY:

See topic Depositions.

COMMUNITY PROPERTY:

See topic Husband and Wife.

CONSTITUTION AND GOVERNMENT:

Netherlands is democratic constitutional monarchy. Present constitution dates from 1814 and had often been amended, lastly in 1995 on which occasion constitution was totally revised. Montesquieu's theory of separation of powers prevails.

Territorial/Administrative Subdivisions.—Major ones are: Provinces (12), Municipalities and drainage districts ("waterschappen"). Provinces and municipalities have popularly elected councils.

Executive Power.—Sovereign (now Queen) and Council of Ministers (together called Crown) constitute executive branch. Sovereign is head of Kingdom (Netherlands, Netherlands Antilles and Aruba, and has limited power and no political responsibility, Ministers being responsible for acts of Sovereign. Ministers, assisted by sub-Ministers ("Staats-secretarissen"), appointed by Royal Decree, head various ministries (in 1994: 13) and are individually responsible to Parliament but are not members of Parliament. Crown may initiate legislation in Parliament and may promulgate certain legislation as "Royal Decree" without consultation of Parliament (see subhead Legislative Power, infra). Chairman of Council of Ministers is Prime Minister, appointed by Royal Decree. Prime Minister coordinates work of Council of Ministers, which generally is based on coalition of two or more political parties. Prime Minister is not party leader.

Council of State.—Council of State ("Raad van State") consists of 30 members and several extraordinary members, all appointed by Crown. Sovereign is official chairman of Council of State. Advice of Council of State (plenary) is compulsory for practically all new acts, AmvB's (see subhead Legislative Power, infra) and ratification of treaties. Council of State advises Crown in disputes between governmental bodies and in cases of spontaneous annullment of governmental decisions contrary to law. Council of State acts through its Judicial Department on Administrative Disputes ("Afdeling bestuursrechtspraak") as administrative judge in appeal in disputes between Administration and citizens and between administrative bodies. In environmental matters of administrative nature it is judge in first and only instance. See topic Courts.

Legislative Power.—Main legislative body is Parliament ("Staten Generaal"), consisting of First Chamber (75 members chosen by popularly elected provincial councils) and Second Chamber (150 members chosen by universal suffrage), acting jointly with Government. First and Second Chamber can be dissolved by Royal Decree, ordering at same time new elections. Legislation by Parliament and Government is called Act ("Wet") having formal statutory force. Second Chamber of Parliament and Executive have right of initiative, but in practice, most bills initiated by Government. Bill passes plenary session of Council of State for advice and submitted to Parliament. After adoption by Second Chamber (debate in special committees; public debate in full session, attended by Ministers), same discussion and consideration take place in First Chamber on basis of bill as adopted by Second Chamber. Until adoption by Second Chamber amendments may be introduced by this Chamber and by Government. Both Chambers decide by simple majority with exception of special bills (mainly relating to Constitution: 2/3 majority). Bill becomes Act after adoption by Parliament and confirmation by Queen.

Legislation issuing from Queen and Government (Crown) alone is called "Algemene Maatregel van Bestuur" (AMvB), having same force as Statutes, provided penal sanctions and taxes must be based on Act. AMvB passes Council of Ministers, and Council of State in same way as bill. AMvB is issued by Crown in form of "Royal Decree" without consultation of Parliament. Ministers may exercise (delegated) legislative power through Decree ("Ministeriële Regeling"). Local authorities and other territorial or functional bodies, as well as statutory boards for trade and industry and some professions ("bedrijfschappen", "produktschappen") have regulatory powers ("verordeningen"). Legislation by local authorities must pass local representative bodies ("provinciale staten", "gemeenteraad", etc.).

Judicial Power.—Constitution provides for judicial power for adjudication of civil law disputes and of penal offences. Judiciary is independent of government and appointed by Crown to serve for life (maximum age 70). Judiciary does not pass on constitutionality of acts. Members of Supreme Court (Hoge Raad) are appointed by Crown after nomination by Second Chamber. Public prosecutors are formally appointed until revocation but in practice also until retirement age (65). See also topic Courts.

Civil Rights.—Except as above-noticed (see topic Aliens), all have equal rights to persons and property in Dutch territory. Human rights (prohibition of discrimination,

CONSTITUTION AND GOVERNMENT . . . *continued*
freedom of religion, press, association, assembly and demonstration, protection of privacy, physical freedom and privacy of communication) are guaranteed by constitution and can only be restricted by special laws. Self-executing provisions of human rights treaties, to which Netherlands is party (e.g., European Convention for the Protection of Human Rights and Fundamental Freedoms) are directly applicable and prevail over national laws.

Law.—Statutory law prevails. Judicial decisions (notably by Supreme Court) carry weight as interpretation of statutory law. Stare decisis rule does not exist. Dutch Civil Code is based on Napoleonic Code, but has developed since. New Civil Code entered into force Jan. 1, 1992. See topic Law Reports, Codes, Etc.

Laws are enforced by police. Prosecution of criminal offences set forth in Penal Code and various other laws (e.g. administrative or social-economic laws) by public prosecutors, who are hierarchically under Minister of Justice. So-called administrative sanctions (e.g. closing of enterprise, removal of illegal buildings) carried out by police at direction of administrative body charged with execution of law.

General Act on Administrative Law ("Algemene wet bestuursrecht"), which entered into force on Jan. 1, 1994, provides for general rules for Administration in respect of citizens, such as codification of general principles of proper administration, preparation of, participation in and publication of governmental decisions and procedural provisions regarding complaint and appeal.

Netherlands Antilles and Aruba.—Netherlands Antilles (abbreviated "the Antilles") and consisting of Caribbean islands Bonaire, Curaçao, Saba, St. Eustatius and St. Maarten and Aruba belong to Dutch Realm. Netherlands, Antilles and Aruba are equal partners in Kingdom of Netherlands. Dutch Sovereign is head of Kingdom, represented in Antilles and in Aruba by Governor. Under "het Statuut voor het Koninkrijk der Nederlanden" Antilles and Aruba enjoy autonomy except in matters of common concern with Netherlands (including defence, foreign relations and Dutch nationality). Antilles and Aruba have their own legislative assemblies ("Staten") elected by residents of Antilles and Aruba. Civil and commercial laws of Antilles and Aruba follow in general those of Netherlands, although Netherlands and both Antilles and Aruban corporate laws are growing apart to some extent because of adaptation of Netherlands corporate law to EEC directives, not incorporated by Antilles or Aruba in their legal systems. (See also topic Corporations, subhead Netherlands Antilles and Aruban Corporations.) Also Netherlands and both Netherlands Antilles and Aruban civil law is growing apart since new Civil Code, which entered into force in Netherlands on Jan. 1, 1992, is not enacted in Netherlands Antilles and Aruba. Some acts and treaties contain special clause that they apply equally to Netherlands and to Antilles and Aruba (Act is then called "Rijkswet"). Judgments of highest court in Antilles and Aruba ("Gemeenschappelijk Hof van Justitie van de Nederlandse Antillen en Aruba") in civil, commercial and criminal cases are, with minor exceptions, subject to appeal to Supreme Court of Netherlands in The Hague. (Act of July 20, 1961, as am'd by Acts of Dec. 18, 1963 and Dec. 12, 1985).

See also topic Courts.

CONSULS:

In countries mentioned in royal decree (Consulair Besluit) Netherlands consuls are competent to register births, marriages and deaths, to draw up instruments, for which Netherlands law requires notarial assistance, and to perform some judicial activities. Competence is limited to services for Netherlands citizens. Some States of U.S., Great Britain, Canada, Australia and South Africa belong to areas of above consular competence. Furthermore Netherlands consuls may issue visa for Netherlands to foreigners.

CONTRACTS:

As Distinguished from Other Sources of Obligations.—Together with unauthorized agency, undue performance and tort, contracts may result in legally enforceable obligations of one or more parties to give, to do or to refrain from doing something. B.W. Book 6 contains general principles of such obligations. B.W. Book 6, Title 5, gives general provisions for contracts and obligations resulting from contracts.

In general no special formalities are required for contract to be binding upon parties. There are, however, exceptions to this general principle, such as requirement of written contract, e.g. in case of hire-purchase (§7A:1576i B.W.), various stipulations in labor contract (not labor contract as such), requirement of notarial deed, e.g., in case of gift (§7A:1719), matrimonial contracts (§1:115 B.W.), incorporations (B.W. Book 2).

B.W. Book 7 contains provisions in respect of sale and exchange ("koop en ruil"), agency ("lastgeving"), commercial agency ("agentuur"), safe custody ("bewaarneming") and securityship ("borgtocht"). N.B.W. Book 7A contains provisions in respect of sale on deferred terms ("koop of afbetaling") and hire purchase ("huurkoop") of moveable goods, lease ("huur en verhuur"), employment agreement ("arbeidsovereenkomst") and contract work ("aanneming van werk"), non-trading partnership ("maatschap"), gift ("schenking"), loan for use ("bruikleen"), loan for consumption ("verbruikleen"), life annuity ("gevestigde of altijddurende renten"), aleatory contract ("kans-overeenkomst") and compromise ("dading").

B.W. Book 8 contains general conditions in respect of transport and specific conditions in respect of transport of goods ("goederenvervoer"), transport of natural persons ("personenvervoer"), maritime law ("zeerecht"), inland navigation ("binnenvaartrecht") and road-transport ("wegvervoersrecht").

§§15-951g W.V.K. contains provisions relating to contracts of business partnerships, contracts with brokers (merchandise and real estate), sales representatives, insurance brokers, stockbrokers, forwarding agents, carriers, signatories and holders of negotiable instruments, insurance, and some provisions in respect of maritime law and inland navigation.

Statutory provisions on special contracts may also be contained in special acts like those on copyright, on patents, on trademarks or in international conventions like those on transport by road, by railroad or by air and those on international sales of moveables.

Offer and Acceptance.—One is bound, irrespective of one's subjective intent, by such manifestation of intent as would reasonably justify understanding of other party that one assents to terms of agreement. Courts rule that offer is accepted at moment that offeror could reasonably be expected to take note of acceptance, which is later moment than deposit of acceptance in postbox.

Registration (voluntary) of contract at local tax authorities provides conclusive evidence of date of contract.

Pre-Contract Negotiating Obligations.—As negotiations near culmination, standard of good faith may under certain circumstances give rise to certain limitations to liberty of parties to withdraw from negotiations.

Competence of Parties.—See topics Infants; Husband and Wife.

Consideration.—Mutuality of consideration is not required. Person may undertake to give something, to act as agent for someone else, to take goods in custody, etc., without getting anything in return.

Offer is revocable except when offer includes specific term for acceptance or irrevocability otherwise follows from offer. If creditor and debtor agree that existing debt be discharged by paying less than amount due, payment of balance cannot be enforced. Contract whereby X promises to pay something to Y and Y, in return, undertakes to give something to Z, is generally valid and may be enforced by Z as third party beneficiary after his acceptance. In all these cases, deed or formal contract is not required.

Interpretation.—Courts not required under all circumstances to follow wording of contract when determining its meaning. What meaning parties could reasonably have attributed to clause and what parties may reasonably have understood from one another is decisive. Circumstances (e.g., course of dealing etc.) under which contract was concluded may also be considered. No formal parol evidence rule but similar principles followed in practice.

Annulment (Action for).—Possible where will of one of parties to enter into agreement was defective (i.e. entering into contract under threat, error, fraud, abuse of circumstances or in case one of parties is incompetent to contract).

Legality of Subject Matter.—If intended effect of agreement, i.e. obligations created for either party, would be contrary to law, good morals or public policy, agreement is in most cases null and void.

Underlying motives for making of contract, generally, do not count.

Nonperformance.—Code distinguishes between delay in performance, defective performance and nonperformance. Usually, final request of creditor for good performance within fixed period of time and debtor's subsequent default are required before aggrieved party can obtain remedy of damages (§§6:81-83 B.W.) or rescission of contract (§6:265 B.W.).

Remedies.—In case of default by one party, other party in general has choice of following remedies: (1) Specific performance, (2) specific performance with demand for supplemental damages, (3) demand for damages instead of performance, (4) demand for damages (expectation), (5) rescission of contract, (6) rescission of contract with demand of supplemental damages, (7) suspension of own obligations. Applicability of certain remedy depends on circumstances of particular case.

Liquidated damages and penalties must be agreed beforehand. Restitution for breaching party permitted. Immediate suit on anticipatory breach allowed. Obligation for injured party to limit damages.

Excuses for Nonperformance.—"Force majeure" or "cas fortuit" (§§6:74-78 B.W.). Defaulting party will be liable for claimed damages unless proves that failure to perform contractual obligations results from impossibility caused by facts or circumstances for which he cannot be held liable. (§6:74 B.W.). In other words, party is excused if nonperformance does not result from his fault and if he cannot be held liable for it by law, juridicial act or common opinion. Defence is banned if "force majeure" occurred when debtor was already in default (by delay or defective performance) unless in absence of such default damage would have occurred just as well. (§6:84 B.W.).

§§6:74-75 B.W. provide for excuse against claims for performance, damages and suspension in general, but not against claim for rescission.

If debtor who cannot be held liable for nonperformance derives benefit in connection with that nonperformance, creditor is entitled to damages by application of rules relating to unjustified enrichment. (§6:78 B.W.).

If contract comprises under term "force majeure" or "overmacht of toeval" any facts or circumstances which by law are not included, excuse of nonperformance is not based on §§6:74-78 B.W., but on contractual exclusion or limitation of liability. Whether and to what extent such excuse is admitted depends on court's construction of intention of parties and court's attitude towards standard contracts and also on restrictions imposed by public order; good morals and principles of reasonableness and fairness (§§6:2 and 6:248 B.W.) or on statutory restrictions applying to special contracts.

If contract provides for reciprocal obligations of each party, failure of party to perform entitles other party to demand rescission of contract by court or to rescind contract by written statement out of court.

In case of contract, other party's nonperformance may be invoked as excuse for nonperformance. (§§6:262-264 B.W., "exceptio non adimpleti contractus"). When, however, claimant cures his own nonperformance, defendant's excuse is barred.

Fundamental change of circumstances beyond control and original contemplation of parties give each of parties right to request that court shall alter results of contract or, entirely or partly, dissolve it. (§§6:258 B.W.).

Consumer Protection.—Specific provisions can be found in §§6:235-236 B.W. and throughout B.W. Book 7.

§§6:231-247 B.W. contain specific provision for general conditions. §6:225 B.W. provides specific rule on offer and acceptance of general conditions.

Government Contracts.—Except for public or administrative activities or employment contracts, government contracts under Netherlands law are contracts governed by private law of contracts and subject to jurisdiction of normal courts of justice. Netherlands government buys in accordance with Algemene Rijksinkoopvoorwaarden or A.R.I.V., and lets out works in accordance with Uniforme Administratieve Voorwaarden voor de uitvoering van werken or U.A.V.

See Topical Index in front part of this volume.

CONTRACTS . . . *continued*

Applicable Law.—On Sept. 1, 1992 Convention on the Law Applicable to Contractual Obligations (Rome, June 19, 1980) came into force for Netherlands. According to this Convention both parties are entitled (see §3) to make choice of law. If parties did not make choice of law, law of contract to be applied is law of country with which agreement has its closest connection. It is presumed that contract is most closely connected with country where party who is to effect performance which is characteristic of contract has its habitual residence or control administration at time of conclusion of contract. Other factors are also relevant to establish closest connection. (§4.2).

In derogation from principle of §4.2, §4.3 establishes presumption that country in which immovable property is situated has closest connection with any contract having as its subject matter right in that property or right to use it.

In derogation from principle of §4.2, contract for carriage of goods is presumed to be most closely connected with country in which carrier has his principal place of business at time of conclusion of contact if this country is also country in which place of loading or place of discharge or principal place of business of consignor is situated (see §4.4).

Special rules are applicable for consumer contracts and employment contracts.

According to §5 of Convention consumer contract is governed by law of country in which consumer has his habitual residence. According to §6, employment contract is governed by law of country in which employee habitually carries out his work in performance of contract, even if he is temporarily employed in other country.

Choice of law cannot deprive consumer or employee of protection afforded to him by mandatory rules of law which would be applicable according to §§5 and 6, in absence of choice of law.

From application of Convention are excluded: status of legal capacity of natural persons, succession, matrimonial and family relationships, negotiable instruments, arbitration and choice of court agreements, bodies corporate, agency, trusts, evidence and procedure, insurance and reinsurance.

Distributorships, Dealerships and Franchising.—

Distributorships.—Dutch law contains no specific provisions in respect to dealer and distribution agreements. General civil law is applicable. Distribution agreement is contract whereby manufacturer or supplier of goods or services enables independent contractor to resell these goods or services for his own risk and account. Examples of distribution agreements are exclusive distribution and exclusive purchasing agreements. Franchising can be qualified as form of exclusive distribution.

When distributor agrees to act as intermediary in conclusion of contracts for principal or to enter into contracts on behalf of and/or for account of principal, distribution agreement can be qualified as commercial agency. Specific provisions of Commercial Code are applicable (see topic Principal and Agent).

Franchising.—There are no Dutch laws which focus directly on franchising. Most franchising organisations in Netherlands are members of Dutch Franchising Association. In essence, franchise contract is contract whereby one party, franchiser, provides one or more other parties, franchisee(s), with right to use trademark name, secret commercial know-how or other distinguishing features, in sale of products or services.

EEC-regulations—Distribution and franchise agreements can be prohibited by §85.1 EEC-treaty. Commission of EEC has enacted several block exemptions i.e. regulations whereby certain categories of agreements are exempted as group. Because §85.1 EEC-treaty can be applicable to franchise or distribution agreement, it is of great importance to check whether agreement is in accordance with provisions of regulations. Relevant regulations are: 1983/83 of 22-06-1983 on application of §85(3) of treaty to categories of exclusive distribution agreements; 1984/83 of 22-06-1983 on application of §85(3) of treaty to categories of exclusive purchasing agreements, .4087/88 of 30-11-1988 on application of §85(3) of treaty to categories of franchise agreements.

COPYRIGHT:

Copyright Act of Netherlands is based, in principle, on Berne Convention, and follows provisions of Convention fairly accurately. Netherlands are also party to Universal Copyright Convention and, as of Jan. 7, 1995, to Agreement on Trade-Related Aspects of Intellectual Property Rights (TRIPs), so that, for all practical purposes, works made or published in most countries of world will be protected under Netherlands Copyright Law.

Copyright Act requires no notice, registration, deposit or any other formality for award or continuation of copyright. Copyright subsists in all manner of creative works. Act defines considerable numbers and categories of works, but protection not necessarily limited to these. Right continues 70 years after death of maker of work, or, in some cases, after its publication.

Protection against all unauthorized publication or reproduction is provided, including for example lending, reissuance of works broadcast via another broadcasting entity. Moral rights recognized to certain extent. Computer programs have been awarded copyright protection. (Mask works protected by separate act. See topic Patents, subhead Chips.) Act provides that one is entitled to oppose publication of one's portrait (including photos) if one has "reasonable interest". Fact that one is celebrity who can command payment for privilege of portrait's use has been held to be "reasonable interest".

Exceptions.—Limited incursions on copyright are accepted under Act, among which, for purposes of compilation; quotation; private use and educational. Renting is not considered incursion on copyright, provided equitable remuneration is paid.

Performing Artists; Producers of Phonograms; Broadcasting Organisations.—See subhead Neighbouring Rights, infra.

Assignment must be in writing and may be by will. Licenses may be in any form, including oral or even tacit.

Intermediary in exploitation of copyright in musical works is, by monopoly right created by Copyright Act, conferred upon two specific bodies set up for that purpose, BUMA and STEMRA, comparable to German GEMA.

See also topic Designs.

Neighbouring Rights.—Neighbouring Rights Act (NRA) came into force in 1993. From that date Netherlands has been party to Rome and Geneva Conventions (before 1993 protection was based on general principles of tort).

NRA grants exclusive rights to: (1) performing artists, (2) producers of phonograms and (3) broadcasting organisations.

Protection against unauthorised use (e.g. registration, reproduction, distribution, lending etc.) of performances, phonograms and broadcasts is provided. As regards secondary use of commercial records (e.g. broadcasting thereof), performers and producers are entitled to equitable remuneration. Neighbouring rights remain applicable for period of 50 years after date of performance, production of phonogram or broadcast.

Exceptions.—NRA contains exceptions similar to Copyright Act.

Assignment must be in writing except where inherited.

Intermediary.—New collecting agency, SENA, has been set up to collect remuneration for secondary use of commercial records.

Future Legislation.—*Note:* Several bills, serving to implement EU Law, are pending in Parliament. These bills are covering copyright and neighbouring rights. Subjects are: cable- and satellite transmission and introduction of payment of renumeration for photocopying.

CORPORATIONS:

N.V. and B.V.—Dutch law recognizes two main types of corporations: N.V. ("naamloze vennootschap" or "public company") and B.V. ("besloten vennootschap met beperkte aansprakelijkheid" or "private company with limited liability"). Both types are very similar, but there are a few important differences: (1) Shares of B.V. must be in registered form and no certificates for shares in B.V. may be issued, while N.V. may issue shares to bearer or in registered form and certificates may be issued for N.V. shares; (2) transfer of B.V. shares must be restricted by articles of association in either of two ways (or combination thereof): preemptive rights for other shareholders or transfer subject to approval of some corporate body, e.g. shareholders meeting or board of management; transfer of N.V. shares may or may not be restricted dependent on articles of association; (3) minimum capital for N.V. Dfl. 100,000 and for B.V. Dfl. 40,000.

In practice, B.V. form is more common form for family business and subsidiary companies, while public companies always have N.V. form. B.V.'s vastly outnumber N.V.'s.

Incorporation of N.V.'s and B.V.'s.—N.V. and B.V. companies are incorporated by execution of deed of incorporation ("akte van oprichting") by one or more persons in presence of notary. Incorporation is subject to declaration of nonobjection from Minister of Justice, which has to be obtained prior to execution of deed of incorporation. Such declaration may only be refused on grounds that, in view of intentions or past record of those who will determine or help determine company's policy, danger exists that company will be used for unlawful purposes, or that its activities will be carried on to detriment of creditors, or that articles of association are contrary to law or public order. For these purposes, Ministry examines draft instrument of incorporation and credentials of incorporators and initial managing directors ("bestuurders"). Ministry Directives give further details as to information Ministry needs to receive in order to enable it to examine credentials of incorporators, initial managing directors and supervisory directors. Directives also provide certain general guidelines as to contents of deed of incorporation, in particular as regards articles of association, which are contained in deed. If declaration of nonobjection is refused, any interested party has right of appeal.

Deed of incorporation must be in Dutch language and must be signed by incorporators or their proxies and notary.

Execution of deed of incorporation following receipt of declaration of nonobjection brings company into existence and company thereupon has legal personality. Managing directors however, remain jointly and severally liable to third parties for all acts binding company and performed during their term of office until: (i) Registration of company in Trade Register, (ii) payment of at least 25% of total par value of shares issued upon incorporation, and (iii) payment of at least Dfl. 100,000 (Dfl. 40,000 in case of B.V.) on shares issued upon incorporation.

It should appear from deed of incorporation how many shares and of what kind are issued to each incorporator. Each incorporator must take at least one share and together with others they must take so many shares that at least one-fifth of authorized capital is issued at time of incorporation. In deed of incorporation initial managing director(s) must be appointed.

Company must register with Trade Register immediately following incorporation. (See subhead Registration, infra.)

There is no organization tax but capital tax amounting to 1% of paid-up capital.

Amendment of Articles of Association.—With absolute majority of votes cast, unless articles require quorum and/or qualified majority, general meeting can resolve to amend articles. If existing articles forbid any amendment, general meeting can nevertheless amend by unanimous vote in meeting where entire issued capital is represented. If articles grant any right to anyone else than shareholders, amendment cannot deprive him of his vested rights, unless stipulated in grant. Convening notice must announce proposed amendment and complete text of amendment must be deposited at company's office for inspection by shareholders, from date of convening notice until meeting is closed.

Amended articles must be embodied in notarial deed and amendments have no legal force until Ministry of Justice has issued declaration of nonobjection, which may be obtained either prior to or after execution of deed of amendment, in contrast to incorporation where declaration must be obtained prior to execution of notarial deed.

Trade Register Act requires registration and deposit of complete text as amended.

Issuance of Stock.—Issue of N.V. shares requires resolution of general meeting or resolution of other corporate body (e.g. board of supervisory directors) which has received authority to issue shares either by means of provision in articles of association or through resolution of general meeting; grant of authority may be given for maximum of five years (renewable). Issue of B.V. shares requires resolution of general meeting, unless articles of association designate other corporate body. General meeting

CORPORATIONS . . . *continued*
can pass on its authority to issue shares to other corporate body. In case of B.V. there is no limitation as to certain period. Issuance of B.V. Shares and registered shares of non-listed N.V. further requires notarial deed.

Existing shareholders generally have preemptive rights in case of new issue, but there are important exceptions and restrictions to this rule.

If company is N.V., shares to bearer may be issued if fully paid up. If company is B.V., all shares must be made out in name of holder.

Concerning shares issued at incorporation against payment in Dutch legal tender or foreign currency bank statement must be produced in order to ensure that money is actually paid. With respect to shares issued after incorporation bank statement must only be produced in case of payment in foreign currency, in order to ensure that proper countervalue of amount in Dutch Guilders to be paid up is actually paid.

In case shares are paid up in kind upon incorporation or thereafter, description of assets and liabilities involved and valuation by auditor is required. Analogous rules apply if, within two years after company was registered in Trade Register, company acquires assets belonging to incorporator (or—if B.V. is concerned—incorporator or shareholder) or having belonged to such person as recently as one year before incorporation.

Different Kinds of Shares.—It is possible to create several classes of shares as well as preference and priority shares; holders of priority shares may have special rights, e.g. right to make nomination proposal for election of members of board of management or board of supervisory directors; holders of preference shares have special dividend rights.

Transfer of Stock.—Transfer of shares of N.V. is free unless limited by articles of association. Transfer of shares of B.V., however, is free only if transferee is husband or wife or next of kin of transferor or if transferee is another shareholder or B.V. itself, but articles may restrict these transfers as well. In other cases, articles must restrict transfer of shares (see subhead N.V. and B.V., supra).

Shares made out to bearer can be transferred only by actual delivery of share certificate. If delivery is effected for valuable consideration and transferee is in good faith, ownership passes to transferee even if transferor was not owner. If shares of listed N.V. are made out in name of holder, title to them can be transferred only by instrument of transfer followed either by written acknowledgment by N.V. after instrument has been submitted to N.V. or by service of instrument upon N.V. If certificates for shares in N.V. made out in name of holder have been issued, acknowledgment can be made in no other way than by endorsement on certificate or by replacing old certificate for new one.

All shares in B.V. must be made out in name of holder and no certificates of shares are permitted to be issued. Title to B.V. shares and to shares in non-listed N.V. is transferred by notarial deed. Transferee cannot exercise his shareholder's rights before company has been notified of transfer or has acknowledged transfer of its own accord.

Accordingly, transfer is not effected by entry in register of shareholders.

N.V. is required only to keep register of holders of shares made out in name of holder. B.V. is required to keep register of holders of all shares.

Rights of Shareholders and of Holders of Depositary Receipts Issued with Cooperation of Company.—(i) Right to attend general meeting of shareholders and to take part in discussions in person or by proxy applies equally to shareholders and to holders of depositary receipts, provided company co-operated in issuance of those depositary receipts. Such receipts are issued in exchange for shares by separate legal entity which undertakes to administer such shares in behalf of holders of depositary receipts. Separate legal entity exercises voting rights appertaining to shares in respect of which depositary receipts have been issued. Trust company frequently has legal form of "Stichting" (Foundation). (See topic Trusts, subhead Foundations.) Depositary receipts are called "certificaten" and are not to be confused with share certificates ("aandeelbewijzen"). (ii) Right to vote applies to shareholders only. Every shareholder has at least one vote. If capital is divided into shares of equal nominal values, any shareholder has as many votes as he has shares. If nominal amounts differ, smallest amount is unit, and number of units which can be comprised by sum total of amounts any given shareholder is holding determines how many votes he has. However, number of votes per shareholder may be limited by articles of association, provided that holders of equal amounts of shares must have equal number of votes, and provided that limitation may not be more favorable for holders of larger amounts of shares than for holders of smaller amounts. Further deviation from normal "one nominal share one vote" system is allowed provided that in such case no single shareholder shall have more than six votes (or if capital is divided in less than 100 shares, three votes). Cumulative voting is not allowed. With due observance of statutory restrictions and restrictions in articles of association, right to vote may be granted to pledgees ("pandhouders") and usufructuaries ("vruchtgebruikers") of shares. (iii) Every shareholder is entitled to share in profits. Separate legal entity which has issued depositary receipts collects dividends and other distributions as holder of shares in N.V. or B.V. and will pass dividends and other distributions on to holders of depositary receipts in accordance with its administration agreement with such holders. (iv) Any interested party can, on ground of violation of law, of articles, or of good faith, obtain from court annulment of resolution of general meeting of shareholders or of any other corporate body.

Shareholders' Liabilities.—Personal liability of any shareholder is generally limited to paying up in full nominal amount of shares, which liability does not cease by transfer unless exemption is granted by company.

Buy out Minority Shareholders.—Single shareholder or two or more group companies holding—on his/their own account—at least 95% of issued capital can buy out minority shareholder(s).

Management.—All executive authority and representation of corporation is vested in "Bestuur" (board of management) consisting of one or more managing directors ("Bestuurders") generally with equal individual authority to represent company vis-á-vis third parties unless articles of association provide that managing directors are only jointly authorized to do so. Articles of association may grant board of supervisory directors (see subhead Supervision, infra) right to approve certain actions of board of management but absence of approval does not affect validity of transactions entered into by company. In all matters where one or more members of board of management have interest conflicting with company's interest, supervisory directors must represent company unless articles provide otherwise or general meeting designates one or more different persons.

Board of management or its sole member is appointed by incorporators and, once corporation has been incorporated, by general meeting of shareholders, which also has authority to suspend and dismiss. If articles bind general meeting to nomination list, such list must contain at least two candidates for any vacancy (same applies to appointment of supervisory directors at nonstructural corporation) and nomination list loses its binding character if general meeting so decides by resolution passed with majority of at least two-thirds of votes cast representing more than half of subscribed share capital. However, at structural corporation, board of supervisory directors is entitled to appoint, suspend and dismiss members of board of management (see subhead Structural N.V. or B.V., infra).

Netherlands law provides detailed rules concerning liability of managing and supervisory directors in case of bankruptcy of company. If there has been mismanagement within three years before bankruptcy, members of boards may be held liable for entire deficit.

In case legal entity acts as managing director its managing directors are jointly and severally liable for any obligation such legal entity has as managing director.

Supervision.—Supervisory board is required by law only for structural corporations (see subhead Structural N.V. or B.V., infra). In other cases it is optional. In either case, law provides that its function must be to oversee conduct of affairs by board of management and general course of developments in N.V. or B.V. and enterprise(s) it operates and to assist board of management by giving advice. In exercise of this function, its members must be guided by interest of company and of enterprise(s) operated by it. Supervisory board is entitled to get in time from board of management all information which is required for proper exercise of its function. Articles may provide for additional tasks and powers.

When company is incorporated, first members of supervisory board must be appointed by deed of incorporation. Unless articles of non-structural corporation with supervisory board provide otherwise, members are appointed for indefinite period of time (but must retire when age 72 is attained) and any subsequent members are elected by general meeting. Articles may bind general meeting to nomination list (see subhead Management, supra).

Articles of such corporation may furthermore provide that one or more supervisory directors (not exceeding one-third of total number) may be appointed by other persons than general meeting. Power to appoint any supervisory director also entails power to suspend or dismiss. General meeting can terminate suspension at any time.

General meeting of shareholders exercises all authority not granted by law or under articles of association to others: right to appoint and dismiss members of board of management and supervisory board, to amend articles of association, to adopt annual accounts, to declare dividends, to file bankruptcy requests, to appoint company's auditor and to dissolve company (see, for differences, subhead Structural N.V. or B.V., infra). At least one general meeting of shareholders per annum must be held.

Meetings are convened by board of managing directors or by board of supervisory directors, but articles can grant this authority to others. Any group of shareholders and holders of depositary receipts issued with cooperation of company representing 10% of outstanding capital can require that general meeting of shareholders be convened by board of managing directors or by board of supervisory directors and in case of delay of meeting of more than six weeks apply to president of competent district court for authorization to proceed to convene meeting.

Voting.—See subhead Rights of Shareholders and of Holders of Depositary Receipts Issued with Cooperation of Company, supra.

Works Council.—Any enterprise employing 35 employees or more in Netherlands has to establish Works Council (Ondernemingsraad) under "Wet op de Ondernemingsraden". Ondernemingsraad ("OR") is elected for period of two years by secret ballot by all employees of enterprise and consists—absent contrary decision of OR—of three to 25 members according to number of employees it represents. Management and OR have to meet jointly regularly, at least six times a year, to discuss any matter which either management or OR deems to be important, as well as such items that under law have to be discussed, including at least twice yearly general trend of business of enterprise, which latter meetings have to be attended by board of supervisory directors or delegation thereof.

OR has to be consulted with regard to number of important decisions proposed by entrepreneur. These decisions include, among others, transfer of control over enterprise, closing down of enterprise, joint ventures with other enterprise, etc. In case advice of OR is in conflict with final decision taken, OR has right of appeal to special enterprise chamber of Court of Appeal in Amsterdam which may prohibit implementation of decision, but only if it determines that entrepreneur, in consideration of interests involved, could not in good reason have taken decision.

Without approval of OR, number of decisions concerning wages, pensions, shifts, hiring of personnel, seniority, complaints and education are null and void, if timely invoked by OR. In case approval is refused, entrepreneur has right of appeal.

Law provides in detail which information concerning business, structure and financial situation of enterprise has to be provided to OR. Furthermore, annual accounts have to be communicated to OR.

OR must be consulted in case of appointment or dismissal of manager of enterprise, but it has no right of appeal if its advice is neglected.

Finally, OR has (limited) right of veto with regard to appointment of members of board of supervisory directors of Structural Corporation (see subhead Structural N.V. or B.V., infra).

If enterprise employs less than 100 employees in Netherlands OR does not have all powers outlined above.

Structural N.V. or B.V.—Apart from distinction between N.V. and B.V. type of company, yet another demarcation line between different types of companies may be drawn. This division makes distinction between "normal" and "large" companies and is equally applicable to B.V.'s and N.V.'s. Large companies can be subdivided into "exempt" companies, "structure" companies and "mitigated structure" companies

CORPORATIONS . . . *continued*
depending on whether special management structure provisions do not apply or apply wholly or partly to them.

Civil Code contains number of general provisions solely relating to companies above certain size. Cumulative criteria for such company are: (1) It has issued capital and reserves totalling at least Dfl. 25,000,000; (2) it has (or dependent company has), pursuant to legal obligation to do so, formed works council; and (3) it and any dependent company together employ at least 100 persons in Netherlands. Dependent company is defined as: (1) Legal entity in which company or one or more dependent companies, by itself or together, furnishes at least 50% of issued capital; or (2) partnership, owning business registered in Trade Register, of which company or dependent company is fully liable partner.

If and so long as company meets these conditions, it is under obligation to file statement with Trade Register, indicating that company meets size requirements unless it is "exempt" company, as defined below. After company has filed above-mentioned statement during three consecutive years, it has to comply with special management regime under so-called "structure provisions" which are incorporated in Civil Code. This obligation ends three years after filing of such statement in Trade Register has ceased to be required and has been withdrawn.

Structure provisions basically provide for compulsory two-tier management system. Supervisory board ("Raad van Commissarissen") of at least three individuals must be established, to supervise activities of board of management.

See below for method of appointment of members of supervisory board of "large" company and powers of such supervisory board.

Two major exceptions to obligatory implementation of structure provisions:

In first place following "large" companies need not be registered as such and are therefore completely exempted ("exempt companies"): (1) Dependent company of another "structure" or "mitigated structure" company; (2) "pure" holding and financing company, provided that majority of employees of companies in its group are employed outside Netherlands; (3) company rendering administrative and financial services to companies referred to under (2) above and to affiliated companies; (4) company owned to extent of at least 50% under joint venture agreement by two or more structure or mitigated structure companies.

Second exemption ("mitigated structure companies") is only partial insofar as it permits articles of association to provide that, instead of supervisory board, general meeting of shareholders appoints and dismisses managing directors and adopts annual accounts. This only applies in case of those "large" companies which are owned to extent of at least 50%: (1) By legal entity employing majority of its employees outside Netherlands or dependent company thereof; or (2) under joint venture agreement, by two or more legal entities or companies of kinds referred to under (1); or (3) under joint venture agreement, by one or more legal entities or companies of kind referred to under (1) and one or more "structure" or "mitigated structure" companies.

Furthermore, above partial exemption is not applicable if majority of combined number of employees of company in question and legal entity or entities referred to in previous paragraph (employees of companies belonging to same group as such legal entity or entities being taken into account as their own employees) is employed within Netherlands. In other words, only those companies which have their "centre of gravity" outside Netherlands may opt for partial or "mitigated" structure regime.

Structural companies differ from normal types of N.V.'s or B.V.'s in various respects: (a) Board of supervisory directors is not appointed by general meeting of shareholders, but through co-optation by board of supervisory directors itself for period of four years (members appointed before date corporation obtains status of structural corporation remain members of board till that period has elapsed after such date if articles so provide), and may be reappointed up till age of 72 years; (b) before appointing new supervisory directors, procedure has to be followed including consultation of general meeting of shareholders and works council.

General meeting of shareholders, works council and managing board may nominate candidates; both general meeting and works council may veto nominations proposed by board of supervisory directors; veto only possible on limited grounds that consultation and nomination procedure has not been properly observed or that candidate is not suitable or that composition of board after election of vetoed candidate is improper. In case board still wishes to appoint vetoed individual, board must first seek to have veto declared unfounded by enterprise chamber of Court of Appeals in Amsterdam; (c) board of supervisory directors appoints and dismisses managing directors; (d) board of supervisory directors adopts annual accounts subject to approval of general meeting of shareholders which cannot amend annual accounts; (e) decisions taken by board of management in respect of following matters are subject to previous approval by board of supervisory directors: issue and acquisition of stock or bonds of company or of bonds issued by partnership of which company is fully liable partner; cooperation when depositary receipts are issued for shares; filing application for listing or withdrawal of listing of bonds or shares or depositary receipts at stock exchange; entering into or terminating lasting cooperation of company or dependent company with other corporation or as fully liable partner of partnership if such cooperation or termination is of vital importance; participation in another corporation by company or dependent company if investment represents 25% or more of value of capital and reserves, or substantial alteration in size of such participation; other investments of that order; amendments of articles of association; declaration of bankruptcy or application for moratorium of payments; dissolution of corporation; termination of employment of important number of employees of corporation or of dependent company; substantial changes in labor conditions of important number of such employees; reduction of issued share capital; (f) members of board of supervisory directors of structural corporation cannot be: (1) Employees of corporation; (2) employees of dependent companies; (3) representatives of unions involved in negotiating employment conditions for employees of corporation or of dependent companies.

Mergers/Take-overs.—Dutch law recognizes three types: (1) Take-over of assets, (2) take-over of shares, and (3) legal merger. (§§2:308-334 B.W.). First two types are not specifically dealt with in statutory law, so that general contracts law applies. Third type was introduced in 1984 as result of EEC Directive. Simplest form of legal merger involves one acquiring and one acquired corporation and leads to following result: (a) Assets and liabilities of acquired corporation are passing as whole by operation of law unto acquiring corporation, (b) all shareholders of acquired corporation (including those minority shareholders opposing merger) become shareholders of acquiring corporation or even, if so decided, of group-company holding directly or indirectly all shares of acquiring corporation, and (c) acquired corporation ceases to exist. Statute sets out detailed procedure to be followed and guarantees interests of parties involved (shareholders, creditors). Procedure starts with elaborate merger proposal by boards of management of both companies and must be approved by specified majority of shareholders. Legal merger is possible between Dutch legal entities of same kind (whereby N.V. and B.V. are considered to belong to same kind), and in certain circumstances between B.V. or N.V. and association or foundation.

Reports-Audit-Deposit-Disclosure.—Acts on Implementation of 4th and 7th EEC Directives with respect to annual accounts and annual reports of certain types of companies ("Acts") apply, inter alia, to N.V. and to B.V. They provide specific rules about subsidiaries, consolidated accounts, banks and insurance companies. (§§2:360-414 B.W.).

Scope.—Principles of law applicable before Acts are preserved as far as possible. Provisions of Act, however, are more detailed with respect to financial information to be set forth in balance sheet, profit and loss account and explanatory notes, as well as to valuation principles which should be used. By general administrative order, models of balance sheets and profit and loss accounts are prescribed. Acts also provide for rules about consolidation, annual report and additional data.

Currency.—Items in annual accounts and consolidated accounts may be expressed in foreign currency if international structure of group of companies concerned justifies it to do so.

Language.—Items in annual accounts must be written in Dutch language, unless general meeting of shareholders has decided on use of another language.

Publication.—As general rule, all companies must publish their annual accounts within eight days after adoption, or, in case of structural corporation, after approval thereof. Publication takes place through filing with Trade Register. Annual report and additional information must be published simultaneously with accounts.

Limitations.—Apart from power of Ministry of Economic Affairs to exempt companies for important reasons from obligation to draw up, present, adopt and publish annual accounts, Act provides for limitations of these obligations on basis of size of company's business. Small companies are allowed to draw up, present and adopt limited annual accounts. Annual report and additional data must be complete. Only limited balance sheet and limited explanatory notes must be published. Business of company is small, when at least two of three following conditions are fulfilled: (i) Value of total assets is not more than Dfl. 6,000,000; (ii) turnover does not exceed Dfl. 12,000,000; (iii) average number of employees is less than 50.

Medium sized companies are allowed to draw up, present and adopt profit and loss account according to rules applicable to small companies. Other financial documentation should be complete. Apart from balance sheet, on which some information may be left out and some items may be condensed, other financial documentation must be published according to way it should be drawn up. Business of company is medium sized when at least two of three following conditions are fulfilled: (i) Value of total assets is not more than Dfl. 24,000,000; (ii) turnover does not exceed Dfl. 48,000,000; (iii) average number of employees is less than 250. Other companies must draw up, present, adopt and publish complete financial documentation.

Auditing.—As general rule, annual accounts of medium sized and large companies must be audited. Small companies are exempted from this obligation.

Registration.—In addition to financial information referred to in previous paragraphs, following papers must be deposited for public inspection with Trade Register in whose district seat of company according to its articles is located: (1) Deed of incorporation including complete text of articles; (2) full text of following agreements made prior to formation: (a) concerning subscriptions imposing special obligations on company, (b) that ensure profit to incorporator or any person involved in formation of company, (c) concerning payment for shares by means other than in cash; (3) bank statement concerning shares issued at incorporation against payment in Dutch legal tender or foreign currency; (4) valuation by auditor (and in case of N.V. description of assets involved) in case shares are paid up in kind upon incorporation or thereafter; (5) bank statement concerning shares issued after incorporation against payment in foreign currency; (6) revised full text of articles after every amendment; (7) in case of dissolution of company: plan of distribution and account of liquidators. If business enterprise of company is located in other district than company's seat, deed of incorporation including complete taxt of articles and after any amendment revised full text of articles must also be deposited with Trade Register in whose district business enterprise is located.

Following information must be filed with respective Trade Register: (i) Name, seat, office address, business description, authorized, issued and paid-up capital of company; (ii) number of outstanding debt instruments; (iii) name of holders of shares which are not fully paid-up; (iv) names, addresses, powers, nationality, place and date of birth of managing and supervisory directors and holders of general powers of attorney, if any; (v) total of costs established and estimated by reason of formation of company and payable by company; (vi) if all shares are owned by one person or belong to marital community, name and residence of shareholder; (vii) if company meets criteria for structural company statement to that effect. Any change in relevant information must be reported to Trade Register within one week after change occurred.

Resolution of general meeting to dissolve company must be recorded in Trade Register together with particulars about liquidators.

Trade Register will arrange for publication of information on file and any changes therein in official government gazette ("Staatscourant").

With respect to any fact which is subject to requirement of deposit or registration, claim of third party, that he in good faith was unaware of it, is barred if fact had been published in official gazette unless third party proves that he acted within 15 days after publication and that when he acted he could not possibly have taken cognizance of publication.

On all instruments issued by company or to which company is party and on all outgoing letters, orders, order confirmations, invoices and other writings and all outgoing printed papers and all announcements made by company, except in form of telegrams, or cables or containing advertising matters, must be stated complete name

See Topical Index in front part of this volume.

CORPORATIONS . . . *continued*
according to articles, seat according to articles and, if capital is stated, always both amounts of issued and of paid up capital. In addition, there shall be stated in all letters, orders, invoices and offers Trade Register in which enterprise of company is registered and registration number. Noncompliance may be prosecuted by virtue of Act on Economic Offences.

Disputes.—§§2:335-343 B.W. contain rules to solve disputes within B.V. and closely held N.V. by providing for mechanisms by which (1) one or more shareholders holding at least one third of subscribed share capital can apply to competent court to force shareholder who is damaging interests of corporation to dispose of his shares and by which (2) shareholder who is damaged in his rights or interests by one or more of his co-shareholders to such extent that continuation of his shareholding cannot be reasonably expected, can apply to competent court to force such co-shareholder to acquire his shares.

Investigation into Company Affairs (§§2:344-359 B.W.).—If there are grounds to suspect that acts of mismanagement have been or are being done, order for inquiry can be applied for with specialized enterprise Chamber of Court of Appeal of Amsterdam, but application will be dismissed if it does not appear that applicant's objections have been communicated in writing to board of management and to supervisory board, and they have been given reasonable time to investigate matters and take sufficient steps. If trade union takes initiative, it must first ask written opinion of works council of enterprise of N.V. or B.V. Application can be made by: (a) One or more holders of shares or depositary receipts holding in aggregate not less than 10% of issued capital or par value Dfl. 500,000, whichever is lower; (b) trade union subject to certain conditions; (c) any natural or legal person to whom by articles or by contract such power has been given; (d) public prosecutor.

Committee of inquiry has far-reaching powers to make thorough investigation. Court determines which persons and/or entities will be allowed to inspect report of committee and may order deposit for public inspection in which case deposit will be advertised in official gazette. If mismanagement is established, court may take any of following measures: (a) Suspension or annulment of any resolution; (b) suspension or dismissal of any board member; (c) temporary replacement of any board member; (d) temporary deviation from designated provisions of articles; (e) temporary administration of shares by third party; (f) dissolution of N.V. or B.V. unless dissolution would harm interests of shareholders or employees or public interest.

Court can also postpone its final decision for such period as it determines if respective N.V. or B.V. undertakes to take necessary steps to terminate mismanagement and to undo or reduce its damaging effects as much as possible.

Dissolution.—N.V. or B.V. will be dissolved: (a) In cases provided for in its articles; (b) by special resolution of general meeting; (c) if after its adjudgment in bankruptcy, its insolvency is established or bankruptcy is lifted on ground of lack of assets; (d) by court in cases provided for in statutory law; (e) by decision of chamber of commerce if fails to fulfill certain administrative obligations.

Board of management acts as committee of liquidators unless other liquidators are appointed. Liquidators announce dissolution in official gazette and in national newspaper and have it registered in Trade Register. Words "in liquidation" must be added to name of company. For purpose of liquidation of its affairs, dissolved N.V. or B.V. subsists until liquidation is completed. Account of liquidators must be deposited for public inspection.

Other Provisions Affecting Application of Company Law.—Directives issued by Ministry of Justice, containing restatement of principal standards applied by Ministry when it is requested to issue declaration of nonobjection, which is legally required whenever company's articles are determined or amended.

"SER-Besluit Fusiegedragsregels 1975", as amended, containing kind of code of ethics to be observed in events of mergers, take-overs, and tender offers in order to protect shareholders on one part and employees on other.

"Fondsenreglement" (Stock Exchange Manual) which is compilation of conditions made by Amsterdam Association of Stockbrokers with which companies must comply in order to issue shares to public or obtain listing of their shares with Amsterdam Stock Exchange.

"Wet Toezicht Effectenverkeer" (Securities Trading Act) containing regulation of trade and brokerage in securities.

"Wet Toezicht beleggingsinstellingen" (Act on Supervision over Investment Institutions) containing provisions to protect investors who participate in investment companies.

Corporations Owned and/or Managed by Foreigners.—Ministry of Justice, in granting declaration of nonobjection, permits establishment of companies in Netherlands of which all shareholders and all members of managing and supervisory boards are aliens and nonresidents. There are no local burdens or disqualifications, which do not apply equally to domestic companies and foreign companies.

Domestic subsidiaries may be wholly owned by foreign parent, and all board members may be nonresident aliens. However, supervisory board members of foreign owned structural company cannot all be parent employees. See also topic Foreign Investment.

Certain nationality and residence requirements apply to companies engaged in banking, shipping or air transport.

Netherlands Antilles and Aruban Corporations.—Foreign entities and individuals frequently use Antilles as jurisdiction to organize finance, (investment) holding, patent holding, and real estate companies, activities of which companies are carried on exclusively outside Antilles. These "offshore-companies" may profit from certain tax advantages of treaties which limit or eliminate ability of country of source to levy withholding taxes on dividends, interest and royalties paid to Antillean company.

On Antilles form of corporate entity is N.V. ("Naamloze Vennootschap"), capital of which is divided into shares. (Code of Commerce, abbreviated "CC", §33). Shares may be in registered or bearer form. (CC §51). Nonvoting shares or shares which allow holder thereof to vote on limited number of subjects may be issued. Minimum issued share capital shall amount to Antilles florin 10,000 (approximately U.S. $6,000) with exceptions for banks and insurance companies. N.V. is managed by board of managing directors, consisting of one or more managing directors, who are appointed and can be dismissed by general meeting of shareholders. (CC §§103, 109, 111). Legal entity may be appointed managing director. N.V. is incorporated by one or more individuals or legal entities acting as incorporators, who execute deed of incorporation before notary. N.V. cannot come into legal existence until declaration of nonobjection to deed of incorporation or draft thereof has been obtained from Minister of Justice of Antilles. (CC §38). All shares in capital of N.V. can be held by one shareholder. Time needed for incorporation is about two weeks. Cost of incorporation varies between U.S. $2,000-3,000. To operate "offshore-company", N.V. must secure foreign exchange control license from "Bank van de Nederlandse Antillen", such license exempting N.V. from requirements imposed by §§17 and 18 of Foreign Exchange Control Ordinance 1940, as am'd. In addition, N.V. must obtain licenses for it to do business and for its managing directors to act as such under Regulation for Establishment of Enterprises of 1946, as am'd. All such licenses are ordinarily obtained as matter of routine if: (i) All N.V.'s shares are held by foreigners; (ii) its capital originates from foreign sources; (iii) its activities are conducted exclusively outside Antilles; and (iv) company must have representative on Antilles; upon incorporation such representative has to be managing director. N.V. must be registered with chamber(s) of commerce in territory/territories where its seat and its enterprise respectively are located. See also topic Constitution and Government.

Since June 1988 Aruba has apart from normal N.V. (with same characteristics as Antillean N.V.) so-called Aruba Exempt Company ("Aruba Vrijgestelde Vennootschap"), which owes yearly fixed amount to government, irrespective of amount of profit or loss.

COURTS:

National Courts.—Imposition of punishment provided for in statutory law and decision of all claims based on property rights, rights in rem, choses in actions and other private rights provided for in civil and commercial codes and special Acts, and, more generally, decision in all cases, which have not been specifically submitted to other specialized judiciary bodies, are under exclusive jurisdiction of general judiciary which consists of body of courts (three instances) stated below. Claims for damages or restitution based on contracts with or alleged torts of government or other public agencies are within jurisdiction of general judiciary. General judiciary is composed exclusively of lawyers with university degree. They are appointed for life (maximum age 70) and cannot be removed for political reasons. No cases are ever tried with jury. There are no commercial courts. It is noted that administrative chambers of district court decide upon administrative disputes (see subhead Special Courts and Proceedings, infra).

Proceedings in first instance are distributed between: (1) 62 cantonal courts ("Kantongerecht"), courts in first instance with limited jurisdiction where parties may argue own cases; (2) 19 district courts ("Arrondissementsrechtbank").

Cantonal courts (single judge) deal with: (a) Punishment of trespassers, (b) variety of measures required by family law, (c) choses in action if amount claimed does not exceed Dfl. 5,000 and collection of rents of any amount, (d) claims based on hire-purchase contracts, (e) demands for repair of buildings and for claims in connection with leases, (f) claims based on contracts of employment or on collective employment agreements or on principal and agent relation, (g) claims with respect to annulment of certain decisions by management by virtue of Works Council Act.

District courts have jurisdiction in first instance of all cases not specifically submitted to other courts. In district courts it depends on nature of case and/or its importance whether case submitted will be decided by single judge or three judges.

If prompt action is needed injunction can be obtained on very short notice from president of district court ("kort geding") during and even before or without institution of law suit about rights of parties. Judgment of president can not prejudice any rights in later lawsuit. After "kort geding" parties often refrain from law suit about rights of parties.

Second instance consists of appeal on points of fact or law and is generally allowed, unless excluded by statutory law (e.g. because of smallness of claim). Appeals from judgments of cantonal courts are handled by district court. Appeals in cases which in first instance were decided by district court are instituted with one of five courts of appeal ("Gerechtshof"). In exceptional cases, Netherlands Supreme Court acts as second instance.

Generally, courts of appeal decide appeals with three judges. Judgment of court of appeal on appeal from judgment of president of district court ("kort geding") does not prejudice rights of parties in litigation about main issue before court of first instance or appellate court.

Third instance consists of review only on points of law and on compliance with essential formalities by Supreme Court of Netherlands which merely adopts lower court findings of fact. Subject to such review are judgments in second instance and, if no second instance was admitted, judgments in first instance unless excluded by statutory law. If lower court based its judgment on "formal law" (Act made by Parliament and Crown), assertion that such act violates any provision of constitutional law is not admissible as ground for reversal of judgment. If, however, such act has been applied which in any respect violates provision of international treaty or convention, judgment can be reversed. Generally, grounds for reversal are: (1) Noncompliance with essential formalities and (2) violation of law of Netherlands or of Antilles, including (mostly unwritten) conflict of law rules. Violation of any applicable law of foreign country does not constitute ground for reversal by Supreme Court.

Special Courts and Proceedings.—Numerous acts (e.g. dealing with government control and administrative law regarding environment, town and country planning, education, public health etc.) provide for administrative procedures. Since Jan. 1, 1994 General Act on Administrative Law ("Algemene wet bestuursrecht") has come into force. Pursuant to this act, administrative disputes should be brought before administrative chambers of district court. Prior to this, however, complaint-procedure should be passed through in most cases. Appeals from decision of administrative chamber of district court are handled by "Judicial Department on Administrative Disputes" (Afdeling bestuursrechtspraak") of Council of State ("Raad van State"); see topic Constitution and Government. General decisions of (local) governments (e.g. so-called town or country plans) and decisions regarding environmental acts, are subject to

See Topical Index in front part of this volume.

COURTS . . . *continued*
direct appeal in first and only instance to Judicial Department on Administrative Disputes of Council of State.

Most rules of procedures of department of Council of State are set forth in Act of Council of State and General Act on Administrative Law.

Pending complaint procedure, appeal for administrative chamber of district court and department of Council of State, president of district court and chairman of department can be requested to take provisional measures or suspend appealed decree.

Enactment of General Act on Administrative Law has introduced more coherent system of administrative judicial protection in which department of Council of State ultimately decides upon most administrative disputes. However, special courts of appeal still exist for (i) matters regarding social security and staff-cases (Central Council of Appeal; "Centrale Raad van Beroep) and (ii) disputes on certain regulations for industry and business (Business Appeal Court; "College van Beroep voor het bedrijfsleven").

Objections against assessment of tax are in first instance lodged with inspector of taxes from whose decisions appeal can be made to specialized tax chamber of normal court of appeal in case of income and property taxes ("direct taxes"), tax on added value and some kinds of anti-pollution taxes. Second appeal to Supreme Court. Appeal against decisions by inspector about import duties must be instituted with Tariff Committee, instead of court of appeal. No appeal to Supreme Court from Tariff Committee decision.

In respect of violations of Act on Annual Accounts of Enterprises, some violations of Works Council Act and in respect of actions based on Act Revising Right of Investigation specialized Chamber of Court of Appeal of Amsterdam ("Ondernemingskamer") has exclusive jurisdiction subject to appeal to Supreme Court on matters of law. See topic Corporations, subheads Reports-Audit-Deposit-Disclosure; Investigation into Company Affairs.

Disputes about leases of land which in first instance are decided by mixed committee constituted of cantonal judge and of two specialists who may not be lawyers and who are not members of judiciary, are in second instance decided by mixed committee constituted of three members of Court of Appeal of Arnhem and two specialists who are not members of judiciary (so-called "Pachtkamer").

Benelux Court.—Concerning specific fields or rules of law, Belgium, Netherlands and Luxembourg, by virtue of Benelux Economic Union Treaty of 1958 commit themselves by special treaties to introduce into their national laws uniform provisions or uniform systems of statutory law and uniform regulations based thereon. Uniform interpretation of respective uniform laws and regulations is secured by provision in respective treaty granting exclusive jurisdiction for that matter to special Benelux Court provided for by Treaty of Mar. 31, 1965, which became operative on Jan. 1, 1974. Court is composed of nine judges (three from each state) and its sessions are held at Brussels. Questions of interpretation are submitted to Benelux Court by national court before which suit is pending. National court may do so upon initiative of party to suit or at its own initiative.

As of Jan. 1, 1975, Benelux Court has jurisdiction with regard to: (1) Benelux Uniform Trademark Act; (2) Benelux Uniform Act re Designs and Models; (3) fines imposed by national court on account of civil contempt, on party for indemnity of other party at whose complaint president of court had granted preliminary injunction or court had granted interlocutory or final injunction (Treaty of Nov. 26, 1973); (4) Benelux Uniform Act re mandatory insurance against liability caused by motor vehicles (Treaty of May 24, 1966). Pending are treaties and attached uniform acts re: (5) Agreements between principals and commercial agents (Treaty of Nov. 26, 1973); (6) penal clauses in private agreements (Treaty of Nov. 26, 1973).

Court of Justice of European Union.—Uniform interpretation of EU Treaty and EU regulations, etc. is similarly secured by exclusive jurisdiction of EU Court to which questions are referred by national courts relevant to issue of cases pending before latter courts. See European Union Law Digest.

Jurisdiction over Foreign States.—Courts only have jurisdiction over foreign states in matters concerning acts jure gestionis (acts in legal transactions of private law).

European Convention on State Immunity of May 16, 1972 is effective in the Netherlands.

See topic Actions.

CURRENCY:

Unit is guilder. Certain coins issued by State (to limited amount) and bank notes issued by Central Bank constitute legal tender.

Guilder is part of European Monetary System.

CURTESY:

There is no provision for curtesy in Dutch law.

CUSTOMS:

According to Rome Treaty of 1957 establishing European Union and time schedule agreed upon by state members, customs duties on trade between Common Market countries (Belgium, France, German Federal Republic, Italy, Luxembourg, the Netherlands, United Kingdom, Irish Republic, Denmark, Greece, Spain and Portugal) presently completely abolished. Sweden, Finland and Austria have joined EU as per Jan. 1, 1995. As from Jan. 7, 1996 Turkey forms customs union with EU under certain conditions. Customs rates applied by various member states on imports from countries outside EU are unified. Due regard is given to reciprocal lowering of rates suggested by President Kennedy.

Exemption from import duty can be obtained when imported goods after having been processed in the Netherlands are reexported or when imported goods or materials are used in the Netherlands for manufacturing products which are exported. However, this exemption does not apply in case of export to other EU countries. See also topic Taxation, subhead Turnover Tax. Payment of import duties on importation of goods from outside EU can be postponed, and avoided in case of reexportation out of EU, by storing goods under (administratively controlled) bonded warehouse-system.

Excise duty is levied on among others beer, wine, spirits, tobacco and mineral oils. See topic Foreign Trade Regulations.

DEATH:

If someone's death cannot be proven by death certificate, but his existence has become uncertain, interested parties can request that court order them to call upon missing person that he show that he is alive, and if such showing is not made, to declare that there is legal presumption that missing person has died. Time period, from departure of missing person or from latest news of his existence, has to be applied, i.e.: (a) Of five years or of (b) three years if person is missing in connection with war, natural disaster or other disaster, or (c) one year if missing person was member of crew or was passenger of vessel or airplane involved in accident.

In following cases someone's death can be established differently: If body of missing person cannot be found but, taking into account all circumstances, his death can be considered certain, court of The Hague can state, upon demand of public prosecutor or upon request of each interested party, that missing person has died: (a) If person has become missing in Netherlands; (b) if person has become missing while travelling on Dutch vessel or airplane; (c) if missing person was Netherlands national; (d) if missing person had his residence or domicile in Netherlands.

If person has died outside Netherlands and no death certificate has been made or can be submitted, court of The Hague, upon demand of public prosecutor or upon request of each interested party, can state that person has died: (a) If death has occurred while travelling on Dutch vessel or airplane; (b) if decedent was Netherlands national; (c) if decedent had residence or domicile in Netherlands.

Actions for Death.—Action for indemnification may be brought against defendant liable for death toward decedent (a) for reimbursement of funeral expenses and (b) for damages for loss of support; in principle no other compensation is granted. Damages for loss of support can only be claimed by: decedent's spouse or children; other relatives who were supported by decedent; persons who lived with decedent as family and were supported by him to extent that situation would have continued, and need support; person who lived with decedent as family and was supported by decedent's taking care of common household to extent that person must make other arrangements to take care of household. Extent of damages for loss of support depends on need of support and other circumstances. Action must be started within five years after plaintiff became aware of both damage and identity of defendant and in any case within 20 years after death. If decedent was killed by motor vehicle, law facilitates proof of other party's fault. Law does not make exceptions with regard to foreigners. Transportation law contains special rules with regard to actions for death. Liability of airline company towards passenger is generally limited to 250,000 gold francs (Warsaw Treaty of Oct. 12, 1929 as am'd by Protocol of Sept. 28, 1955; Air Transport Act ["Wet Luchtvervoer"]), though airline company's conditions often provide for higher amount. Statute of May 15, 1981 states that gold francs must be converted into IMF Special Drawing Rights in order to compute counter-value in Dutch guilders. In maritime law maximum amount of damages recoverable from carrier is limited to 300,000 Dutch guilders per passenger (§8:518 B.W.); further limits in proportion to holding capacity of ship may apply (Convention on limitation of liability for maritime claims, London, Nov. 19, 1976; 740a et seq. WvK).

DECEDENTS' ESTATES:

See topics Descent and Distribution; Executors and Administrators; Wills.

DEEDS:

See topics Notaries, Real Property, Mortgages, Wills, Corporations.

DEPOSITIONS:

Dutch law does not provide for depositions; for evidence by witness see topic Evidence. However, foreign depositions may be accepted in evidence; their probative value is at discretion of courts which may prefer to have evidence taken by means of letters rogatory or by consular officer.

Netherlands are party to Hague Convention on taking of Evidence Abroad in Civil or Commercial Matters of Mar. 18, 1970. (Statute of Dec. 11, 1980, §652). Proper Dutch Central Authority is "Officier van Justitie" at district court of Hague.

No other way to hear witness outside Netherlands is provided for other than by letters rogatory, transmitted to foreign court through diplomatic channels or to Netherlands consul in foreign country.

DESCENT AND DISTRIBUTION:

Intestate Succession.—In absence of a will (see topic Wills) there is one uniform rule of succession, applicable alike to realty and personalty.

Each of following classes of which one or more members is living takes to exclusion of subsequent classes: (1) Surviving spouse and children for equal parts; descendents of predeceased descendents share by representation; (2) parents, brothers and sisters of deceased for equal parts with minimum of one-fourth for each surviving parent; descendents of predeceased brothers and sisters take by representation. Shares of brothers and sisters and their descendents are divided equally, per stirpes, if all are of same marriage; if they are of different marriages, equally between paternal and maternal line of deceased with those of full-blood taking in both lines and those of half-blood in one line only. If no heirs are to be found in classes (1) or (2) estate is divided into two equal parts, each of which is distributed between ascendents or collaterals of father and mother, respectively, of deceased. In absence of any heirs (whether ascendents or collaterals) in either paternal or maternal line heirs of other line receive all of estate; (3) ascendents; proximate ascendent excludes more removed ascendents; (4) collaterals of equal degree but not further than sixth degree. Proximate collateral excludes more removed collaterals, but descendents of predeceased brothers and sisters of proximate collateral take share by representation. Representation takes place without restriction; (5) lacking surviving spouse, descendents or ascendents, and no collaterals capable of taking estate, estate escheats to State.

Posthumous Children.—Not excluded from heirship and share as if they were alive at time of death of deceased.

DESCENT AND DISTRIBUTION . . . *continued*

Adopted children are treated as children in blood of adoptors.

Illegitimate Children.—Take same position as legitimate children (but note that child is illegitimate child of father only if he has legally acknowledged child).

Distribution of Assets.—Debts need not be discharged before distribution is made. Heirs succeed deceased immediately in title to assets belonging to estate ("saisine") and are co-owners of such assets; they may distribute assets immediately among themselves. Creditors of estate, however, and legatees may oppose distribution until they are satisfied.

Heirs are at liberty to keep estate or any part thereof undistributed for any length of time. Any heir, however, may demand distribution unless there is agreement to have estate undistributed, which agreement cannot be made for more than five years. Formal distribution by notarial instrument is required only if one or more heirs are minors or otherwise do not have free disposal of their property. If real property forms part of estate it is common practice to effectuate distribution by notarial deed in order to facilitate proceedings at Title and Mortgage Register.

Determination of Heirship.—Probate proceedings are unknown. Heirship is generally determined by notary, who delivers certificate of inheritance (verklaring van erfrecht). Such certificate is generally accepted as sufficient proof of heirship. If heirship is contested parties may ask court for declaratory judgment.

Succession presumed accepted. Right to reject lost upon explicit or implicit indication of willingness to accept. Succession may be accepted either plain or under beneficium inventarii. Note, that estate, including its debts, devolves on heirs directly; upon plain acceptance heir becomes liable pro rata parte for all liabilities of estate; acceptance under beneficium inventarii prevents heirs from becoming liable to extent liabilities of estate exceed its assets. Minors and other persons not having free disposal of their property cannot accept other than under beneficium inventarii. Liquidation of estate which has been accepted under beneficium inventarii is subject to various formalities which are not required in case of plain acceptance.

DESIGNS:

Uniform Benelux Act on Designs and Models ("Act").—On Jan. 1, 1975, Act entered into force, creating uniform system of design protection for Belgium, Luxembourg, and Netherlands. Designs protected before Jan. 1, 1975 under existing national laws of these countries continue to enjoy protection existing before said date.

National Courts are competent in cases involving Act, but may refer to Benelux Court questions of interpretation of Act.

Design.—New appearance of utility product may be protected as design. Originality is no requirement, novelty alone is sufficient. Excluded from protection are aspects of appearance of product which are indispensable for achievement of technical effect.

Right to design is acquired by first application for registration, unless design is not new or application does not sufficiently disclose characteristics of design. Design is not new if either: (i) At any time during 50 years preceding application date design or design differing only in minor aspects, has been known to relevant industrial or commercial circles in Benelux, or (ii) identical or confusingly similar design has been registered previously.

Maximum period of protection of registered design is 15 years.

Cancellation and Infringement.—Nullity of registration may be invoked on grounds enumerated in Act. Most important ones are: (i) Design is not design as defined by Act, (ii) design is not new, or (iii) application insufficiently discloses characteristics. Owner of registered design may forbid manufacture, sale, etc. of identical or confusingly similar designs and claim damages. Unregistered designs are not protected and no unfair competition action against imitation can be instituted if registration of design has been omitted.

Copyright.—Design can be concurrently protected under copyright law, if sufficiently original. If design is registered, copyright protection after termination of design registration's effect continues only if notice to that effect is filed in Benelux Design Register.

Assignment and License.—Assignment of design must be in writing; for license of design no written statement is required. To have effect against third parties, assignment and license must be recorded in design register.

DISPUTE RESOLUTION:

In recent years alternative dispute resolution has become topical issue in The Netherlands. During year 1995 two initiatives have been taken aimed at introducing alternative methods for speedy resolution of conflicts. In June 1995 the Netherlands Mediation Institute (NMI, P.O. Box 30183, 3001 DD Rotterdam) was founded. It has published model mediation clauses, set of Rules for Mediation and Ethical Code for Mediators, and it keeps register of trained mediators. As per Sept. 1st, 1995 the Netherlands Arbitration Institute (NAI, P.O. Box 190, 3000 AD Rotterdam) has published model minitrial clause and set of Minitrial Rules.

Alternative dispute resolution in The Netherlands is solely on voluntary basis so far. There are no statutes or court rules requring litigation to be transferred to alternate dispute systems. Committee of experts is presently advising Minister of Justice on possible ways to introduce mandatory dispute resolution into Dutch legal system.

See topic Arbitration.

DIVORCE:

Ground.—Lasting breakdown of marriage only and exclusive ground for divorce and for legal separation. Guilt criterion abandoned. Defence that no lasting breakdown exists very unlikely to succeed: in case law, living apart for some longer period, or plaintiff consistently maintaining that in his/her personal view lasting breakdown exists, often considered signs of breakdown. If, in case of joint request, both parties assert lasting breakdown or if, in case of unilateral request, respondent does not deny breakdown, court will not investigate whether breakdown exists.

Legal Separation.—Granted for same ground as divorce. Institution retained for those whose religion prohibits divorce or who otherwise prefer legal separation. Separation proceedings mainly similar to divorce proceedings; see subhead Proceedings, infra. After three years of legal separation either party may request dissolution of marriage. This term may be shortened to at least one year in case of serious misconduct of other spouse. No term applies in case of joint request for dissolution of marriage.

Like divorce, legal separation terminates spouses' obligation to cohabit and leads to partition of community property. Legal separation has same consequences as divorce with regard to children born from marriage; see subhead Children, infra.

Legal separation only effective against third parties if separation has been registered in register of marital property.

Legal separation terminates in case of reconciliation of spouses. All effects of marriage revive. If judgment of separation had been publicized or registered, results of reconciliation cannot operate against third parties unless reconciliation has been publicized or registered likewise.

Action.—Divorce and legal separation are granted: (a) at request of either spouse; (b) at joint request of both spouses stating as their common opinion that lasting breakdown of their marriage has occurred. Pending suit at joint request either spouse may withdraw request.

"Prospective Allowance Defence".—If as result of requested divorce prospective allowances (pension rights, etc.) to other spouse would be lost or considerably reduced upon predecease of requestor, and defence is made hereof, divorce cannot be granted before reasonable and fair provisions have been made in this respect. No such provisions required, however, (a) in case of reasonable expectations that other spouse is capable of making sufficient provisions for him/herself; (b) if lasting breakdown for most part to be attributed to other spouse.

Alimony detached from guilt criterion and based on either party's need and financial means. At request of party who does not have and is not able to acquire sufficient income for living expenses, court may allow such party alimony, to be paid by other party, if latter has sufficient resources. Need for alimony of party may depend on circumstances such as length of duration of marriage, actual period of living together and standard of living during marriage.

Spouses may conclude agreement with view to divorce or separation on whether, and if so to what amount, one party will have to pay alimony to other party.

Alimony imposed by court or agreed upon by spouses may be altered by court in case of changed circumstances; such alteration may be excluded by written agreement of parties, but even then alteration is possible in event of essential change of circumstances causing unfairness.

Under Act of Apr. 28th, 1994, Stb. 1994, 324, alimony may be imposed by court for certain (finite) period of time and on certain conditions, but not for longer than 12 years after date of registration of judgment for divorce or dissolution in public record of marriages, births and deaths (see also subhead Proceedings, infra). Under same Act, all alimonies for infinite period of time, established by court or agreed upon from July 1st, 1994 onwards, end automatically after period of 12 years after date of registration of judgment. If marriage has lasted no longer than five years and no children have been born from marriage, this period is reduced to duration of marriage. Within three months after expiration of period, party entitled to alimony may request that court grant new period of alimony on grounds of fairness. Under same Act, party paying alimony as established by court or agreed upon before July 1st, 1994, may request court to end obligation to pay after it has lasted 15 years (though obligation cannot end within three years after said date).

Obligation to pay alimony ends at remarriage or cohabitation comparable to marriage of party entitled to alimony.

Children.—With regard to parental authority interest of child decisive. Court may, at its discretion, grant parental authority to either parent. Upon common request of parents, court may grant them joint parental authority.

Court may provide for visitation and information rights between minor child and parent without parental authority upon request of both parties or one of them. Only on few limited grounds, based on interest of child, may court refuse visitation rights. In such case court may still grant information rights to parent without parental authority. Before deciding upon request for visitation rights, court will hear minor if minor is aged 12 years or more. Court may also determine visitation rights according to minor's wishes. No statutory sanctions against nonobservance of right of visitation, but general sanctions can be used, though these are not always enforceable.

Court may change decision on parental authority and/or visitation rights upon request of one of parents, because of changed conditions. Child of 12 years or older will be heard by court.

Separation of Community Property.—If no marriage articles have been made, spouses are co-owners of all property which upon divorce must be partitioned into two equal parts. However, parties may expressly agree to partition in unequal parts; see also topic Husband and Wife.

Settlement of Pension Claims.—Under Act of Apr. 28th, 1994, Stb. 1994, 342, unless otherwise agreed in marriage articles or in agreement with view to divorce or separation, spouse, who has built up pension claims during marriage, is obliged to settle these pension claims with other spouse. As result of this settlement, other spouse obtains separate right towards pension fund to payment of part of pension.

Remarriage.—Immediately after divorce has taken effect (i.e. after judgment is registered in public record of marriages, births and deaths, see also subhead Proceedings, infra), either spouse may get married to third party. Former spouses may remarry each other. See also topic Marriage, subhead Requirements.

Jurisdiction.—In divorce and separation proceedings, Dutch courts have jurisdiction if, at moment when unilateral or joint request is filed, (a) both parties are Dutch citizens; or (b) either party has had permanent residence in Netherlands for 12 months, or Dutch party for six months. Upon joint request case is heard by court of either spouse's permanent residence. At request of one of spouses, case is heard by court of requestor's permanent residence, or if requestor lives outside The Netherlands, court

DIVORCE . . . *continued*
of respondent's permanent residence. If both parties live outside Netherlands, Court of The Hague has jurisdiction.

Proceedings are in writing, but with few exceptions, parties have to appear in court once. Until judgment (divorce and separation) has taken effect, each party may file request for provisional measures for duration of proceedings: provisional allocation of house to one of spouses, provisional assignment of minor children to one of spouses, provisional visitation rights, provisional alimony for children and/or other spouse. If provisional measures are requested, parties will have to appear in court.

Note: Judgment granting divorce or dissolution takes effect only as from date of registration in public record of marriages, births and deaths. Registration is made upon request of either party to competent record. If judgment is not registered within six months after it has become final, it is rescinded by law.

Foreign Divorce Judgment.—Under Act of Mar. 25th, 1981, regardless of nationality of parties, foreign divorce or separation is recognized in The Netherlands if granted after proper process by court or other authority having jurisdiction or if other party has acquiesced. If wife acquiesced, under certain conditions, dissolution of marriage effected by unilateral declaration of husband is recognized. Recognition of foreign divorce or separation effected prior to date of coming into force of Act (Apr. 10th, 1981) in accordance with case law or applicable international convention.

Foreign Parties in Divorce Proceedings in Netherlands.—Unless foreigners choose Dutch law to be applicable, they are, in principle, treated according to their common national law. In case common nationality of spouses has lost practical meaning (i.e. for one of spouses or for both of them real social connection with country of nationality is manifestly absent) or in case of different nationality, law of their common residence applied. If no common residence, Dutch law applied.

Annulment.—Each of spouses, ascendants of one of spouses, and public prosecutor may request annulment of marriage on several grounds. Person married to one of spouses may request annulment of (later) marriage of that spouse. Few other possibilities for annulment exist.

DOWER:

There is no provision for dower in Dutch Law.

ENVIRONMENT:

Legislation to preserve environment from pollution of soil, water and air has been enacted in recent years.

Numerous acts require companies to obtain licenses for all kinds of activities which may cause nuisance, damage or danger to environment or to neighbouring residential or business areas.

Generally licenses are subject to conditions, containing safety provisions, restrictions on kind or quantity of disposed substances, on method of disposal, etc.

Activities without obligatory license or in violation of conditions to license are considered criminal acts, punishable by fines and/or (when deliberately committed) by imprisonment of person responsible. Maximum fine in respect of environmental offenses has been increased to Dfl. 1,000,000, on 1 Apr. 1994. Third parties suffering damages by activities without or, in violation of, license can claim compensation in civil court procedure and/or compulsory closure of establishment.

Procedural rules for issue, withdrawal, alterations, appeal against such decisions and environmental impact statements are set forth by environmental control act (Wet milieubeheer), which entered into force on 1 Mar. 1993 and General Act on Administrative Law (Algemene wet bestuursrecht), which entered into force on 1 Jan. 1994. Former act is comprehensive act on environmental issues and requires most businesses to obtain license for construction and use of plants, machinery or installations, which may cause nuisance, danger or damage to third parties and environment. This act also empowers central authorities to impose levy on production or import of fuel. Furthermore, this act provides for compensation of damages as result of refusal of licenses, or conditions attached to licenses. Based on EC directive Environmental Impact Assessment (MER) is required before licenses be granted for projects with significant effects on environment. Additional procedural provisions in respect of MER of activities with trans-boundary consequences have entered into force in Apr. 1994. Act also regulates licences for disposal of waste, not only in respect of prevention, recycling, incineration and dumping but also in respect of international transport. Finally it regulates enactment of plan and policies regarding environment by public authorities.

At present following further legislation is enacted: act of noise nuisance (Wet geluidhinder), regulating restriction of noise by plants, roads, railways etc.; open water pollution act (Wet verontreiniging oppervlakte wateren), requiring license for disposal of waste water into open water. Act empowers central or local Government to impose levies on disposal of waste water; air pollution act (Wet inzake de luchtverontreiniging), regulating use of plants, machinery and installations, which may cause air pollution; soil protection act (Wet bodembescherming) relating to bringing in or on soil substances possibly damaging or polluting soil and to execution of works which might cause damage to soil. Act grants provincial authorities legislative powers for soil protected areas. Act empowers provinces and four largest cities to order polluter or owner of polluted soil or groundwater to clean up; it provides for recovery of cleaning costs from companies or persons responsible for pollution; nuclear energy act (Kernenergiewet), regulating by way of licenses any application of nuclear energy; pollution of sea by ships act (Wet voorkoming verontreiniging door schepen), referring to international treaty for prevention of pollution of sea by ships, London 1973; act on substances endangering environment: (Wet milieugevaarlijke stoffen), regulating import, packaging and labelling of substances, possibly dangerous to men and/or environment; subsoilwater act (Grondwaterwet), regulating retrieval and injecting of subsoil water; pesticide act (Bestrijdingsmiddelenwet), regulating trade in and use of pesticides; dangerous substances act (Wet gevaarlijke stoffen), regulating transport and disposal of dangerous substances. Legislation on mining (land and seabed) contains specific environmental regulations.

Strict liability for owner (possessor) of dangerous substances, whether in transport or not, and operator of dumping ground or drilling platforms has been enacted in Civil Code on 1 Feb. 1995.

General Supervision.—Decisions regarding environmental acts, e.g. decisions to grant or withdraw licenses or to impose administrative sanctions, are subject to direct appeal in first and only instance to Judicial Department on Administrative Disputes of Council of State. See also topic Courts, subhead Special Courts and Proceedings.

EVIDENCE:

Although evidence must be provided by parties, judge plays active role by allocating burden of proof and deciding on admissibility of evidence (except for documentary evidence which may be introduced without judicial permission). Generally, judge free in evaluation of evidence. Rule that illegally obtained evidence is excluded has not as yet been developed.

Evidence by Witness.—In principle, chamber of court before which suit is pending determines by interim judgment for which issues testimony of witnesses is required and who has burden of proof. Taking of testimony is usually delegated by chamber to single judge of court ("Rechter-Commissaris" or R.C.) unless parties jointly ask for testimony in chamber. Witnesses can be divided into two categories: litigants and others; differences between those e.g. with regard to conclusive force of testimony. Examination in chief, cross-examination and reexamination by attorneys of parties not permitted. Both R.C. and attorneys of parties may interrogate witness. It is however, at R.C.'s discretion, whether or not (and in what manner) to put questions.

Questions and answers are not recorded verbally; R.C. summarizes in terms R.C. considers relevant and dictates to secretary. Summary is read out to witness and submitted to witness for signature. R.C.'s report including summary is referred back to chamber.

Judge is free in evaluation of testimony by witnesses. Hearsay (testimonium de auditu) is admissible. See also topics Affidavits; Depositions.

Other Means of Evidence.—Apart from witnesses, most important are documentary evidence, evidence by experts and disclosure of books.

Documentary evidence: distinction made between "authentieke akten" (public instruments made by or in presence of public official, usually notary) and "onderhandse akten" (private writings).

Judge may appoint one or three experts, following choice of parties if they agree thereupon. Experts' report may be oral, but is usually written.

Judge may either at request of one of parties or on own initiative order party to disclose corporate records. Other party is allowed to comment on documents. If party does not obey court's order, judge can interpret such refusal to party's disadvantage.

Pretrial Evidence.—At request of one of parties, court may allow examination of witnesses or report by experts or inspection of premises without action pending. Party requesting such examination should have sufficient grounds to do so, usually to perpetuate testimony: for instance, if party intends to sue but fears that proof will be lost because of fading memory, illness, old age or imminent emigration of witness, or perishability of goods to be examined by experts. Also lawful to request examination merely to evaluate potential success in possible suit.

See also topic Actions, subheads Proof of Foreign Claims; Proof of Foreign Law.

EXCHANGE CONTROL:

No restrictions in effect. However, there are certain reporting requirements. See topic Securities.

EXECUTION:

Execution or enforcement of judgment or arbitral award. Measures of execution may also be taken by virtue of correctly drawn notarial deed.

Foreign judgment can be executed in Netherlands only upon leave ("exequatur") from district court where debtor is domiciled or execution has to be effected. However, exequatur can only be granted if execution of foreign judgment has been provided for in treaty or other international agreement. EEC Convention of Enforcement and Recognition of Judgments of Sept. 27, 1968 and Treaty of Lugauo of Sept. 16, 1988 now play important part in this field, as far as judgments in countries belonging to EEC are concerned.

Dutch arbitral awards can be executed upon order of president of district court where award has been filed. Foreign arbitral awards can be executed upon leave of president of district court where debtor is domiciled or execution has to be effected, irrespective of whether execution has been provided for in treaty.

Service of Judgment.—First step of execution is service of judgment on debtor by bailiff ("deurwaarder").

Means of execution may be divided into two categories: (a) Means which serve as incentive for debtor to give performance to judgment. Civil imprisonment and penal sum to be forfeited in case of noncompliance with judgment belong to this category; (b) means by which creditor himself brings about (legal) situation in which he would be if debtor would have complied with judgment. Examples of such means include: Seizure of debtor's property, subsequent public sale and distribution of proceeds by either bailiff (goods) or notary public (immovable property or ship). Other creditors showing valid claim may share in proceeds of sale. If proceeds do not allow full payment to all creditors distribution will take place either according to division, arranged between creditors, or, in case no agreement is reached, according to division determined by magistrate (Rechter-Commissaris); seizure by bailiff and bringing into creditor's possession of specified goods to which creditor has specific title, recovery of possession of such goods by bailiff and, if required with help of police; registration in proper public records of judgment condemning debtor to deliver ship or immovable property (instead of instrument that normally is entered into said record on delivery of ship or immovable property and that debtor refuses to sign or to file for registration) serves as alternative means of conveyance by way of execution of judgment to deliver.

EXECUTORS AND ADMINISTRATORS:

Executors may be appointed by will only. (See topic Wills.)

Their powers and duties are very limited in comparison with Anglo-American executor.

See Topical Index in front part of this volume.

EXECUTORS AND ADMINISTRATORS . . . *continued*

Executors may be given right to take actual possession over estate. Estate does not, however, devolve on executors but directly on heirs. Statute limits executor possession to one year unless otherwise provided in will.

Executors must make inventory and assist heirs in settling estate.

If executors have been granted right of possession they may claim assets of estate to be handed over to them and receive payments due to estate, administer estate and pay out legacies upon satisfaction of creditors. If legal heirs (see topic Wills) are entitled to estate or part thereof executors having been granted right of possession cannot take possession without prior consent of legal heirs.

Executor may sue on estate behalf. Claims may be brought immediately against estate. In first year, heirs can be sued collectively at last address of deceased.

EXEMPTIONS:

Object of attachment cannot be seized or only to limited extent: state owned property used for public service, tools of craftsman, means of education and study, wages, pensions, and social security payments like illness, invalidism, unemployment, welfare and old age payments, nontransferred copyright and strict personal rights like right of habitation. Most of these exemptions, however, do not apply to claim for alimony.

FOREIGN EXCHANGE:

See topic Exchange Control.

FOREIGN INVESTMENT:

Generally, foreign nationals and enterprises are given same treatment as Netherlands subjects in respect of engaging in commercial, industrial or financial activities including establishment of branches, formation of companies and acquisition of majority and even 100% interest in existing companies. All members of managing board may be nonresident aliens. Status of branch or subsidiary company of foreign investor is same as that of purely Netherlands branch or company.

Treaty of Friendship, Commerce and Navigation with U.S.A. (1956) contains general rules concerning admission and legal position of citizens of each country, possibility of carrying on trade, and how expropriation and social insurance are dealt with.

Investments in Netherlands by nonresidents are no longer subject to foreign exchange control.

Machines, apparatus and spare parts which non-EU company supplies to its subsidiary in The Netherlands or brings in as investment are not exempt from import duty, even if they have been manufactured by foreign company. See topic Customs.

Investment deduction is granted for investments in classified business assets if total amount of investments exceeds Dfl. 3,500 but not Dfl. 527,000 per annum. Investments less than Dfl. 1,000 are excluded. Deduction decreases if total amount of investment in one calendar increases. Sliding scale starts at 24% for small investments and decreases to 3% for large investments.

Apart from this investment deduction, cash grants may be granted if new businesses are established or existing businesses are expanded in certain designated area.

See also topics Aliens; Exchange Control.

FOREIGN TRADE REGULATIONS:

Respective legislation is based on principle of freedom of international trade, which has been restricted in specific circumstances and with respect to specific goods either by licensing, registration, or certification requirements, or by duties, levies or restitution systems.

The Netherlands is member state of EU, ECSC and Euratom Treaties.

By virtue of EC Treaty, member states form customs union covering all trade and comprising prohibition, as between these states, of customs duties on importation and exportation and all charges having equivalent effect. Member states have adopted common customs tariff for their relations with third countries. Moreover quantitative restrictions on imports or exports and all measures having equivalent effect are prohibited between member states. This also applies to products in free circulation in member state and originating in third country, as European Court of Justice held in case 41/76 (Donckerwolcke) (1976) ECR 1921. There are, however, some escape clauses in Treaty. See also European Union Law Digest, topic Customs Duties. With respect to ECSC products only part of this applies.

Netherlands is also member state of EEA Agreement between EU, ECSC, their member states and member states of EFTA. Contrary to EC Treaty, EEA Agreement does not constitute customs union. EEA Agreement constitutes free trade area in which only products originating in member states benefit from free circulation. Relevant provisions are very similar to equivalent provisions of EC Treaty.

Netherlands foreign trade regulations, implementing EU provisions, are mainly laid down in following Acts and secondary legislation: General Customs and Excise Act ("Algemene wet inzake douane en accijnzen"), and Act on Import and Export ("In-en Uitvoerwet") and Regulations thereunder. In addition, foreign trade may be restricted under Sanction Act ("Sanctiewet"), pursuant to decisions or recommendations from international bodies, notably United Nations Security Council, in interest of international peace and security. Furthermore foreign trade regulations in force in Netherlands are inserted in bi- and multilateral treaties, to which Netherlands are party. Number of treaty regulations are part of domestic law conferring rights and duties upon individuals.

See also topics Exchange Control and Foreign Investment.

FOUNDATIONS:

Foundation ("stichting") is legal entity created by notarial deed (either inter vivos or by will); it has no members and is governed by board. Foundations, may be used for social, cultural, scientific or charitable purposes; foundations may also be used for commercial purposes but their objectives may not include distributions to founders or directors or other persons except for social or charitable purposes. (2:285 B.W.). Foundations are not subject to corporate income taxes except for their entrepreneurial activities and commercially competitive activities. See also topic Trusts.

FRAUDS, STATUTE OF:

Netherlands has no Statute of Frauds. As rule, contracts are concluded by mutual consent (§6:217 B.W.) evidenced by offer and acceptance. Generally, there are no specific formalities required. However, certain contracts do require specific form. Contracts relating to loan of goods ("bruikleen and verbruikleen") for no consideration are only complete on delivery of goods (so-called "reële contracten"); other contracts require compliance with specific formalities. For instance: notarial deed is needed with respect to premarital contracts ("huwelijkse voorwaarden"); and contracts relating to hire purchase ("huurkoop") and noncompetition clause, in employment agreement, must be in writing and duly signed by parties. According to §3:39 B.W. contracts concluded without observance of required formalities are null and void, unless otherwise provided by law (see also topics Contracts; Deeds).

FRAUDULENT SALES AND CONVEYANCES:

Creditors whose recourses have been adversely effected by any juridical act like sale and conveyance by debtor, while debtor in performance of this act, to which he was not obligated, knew or ought to have known consequences, may annul this act by debtor. Annulment of acts other than by gratuitous title can only be invoked by creditor if those persons with whom debtor performed juridical act knew or should have known that prejudice to one or more creditors would result from it. This knowledge is, under certain circumstances, presumed in advance.

In Bankruptcy Act same rules apply with extension that payment by debtor, to which he was obliged, can also be annulled by curator if person whom debtor paid knew that at time of payment petition of bankruptcy had already been filed with court, or payment was result of arrangement between debtor and creditor, with object to give this creditor undue preferences over other creditors.

Creditor who challenges act on ground of prejudice annuls this act only for his own benefit and not to larger extent than is needed to make good prejudice he suffered.

Act of annulment is called "actio Pauliana". (§3:45 B.W.).

GARNISHMENT: See topic Attachment.

HOLIDAYS:

The legal holidays are Sundays, Good Friday, New Year's Day, Christmas Days Dec. 25 and 26, Easter Monday, Pentecost, Ascension Day, Liberation Day (May 5) and Queen's official birthday (Apr. 30). Banks and other offices are usually closed Sat. Process may not be served on legal holiday with exception of Good Friday. Time periods expire on next working day not being Sat. or holiday if last day of period falls on Sat. or holiday.

HOMESTEADS:

No provision for homesteads.

HUSBAND AND WIFE:

Changes in Statutory Law.—By Act of June 14, 1956, disabilities of married women were removed and matrimonial property law was revised accordingly. Act of 1956 applies to all spouses married since Jan. 1, 1957 and with respect to spouses who had married before, to their rights and obligations as from said date.

General Obligations.—Each of spouses has obligation towards other to be faithful, render all necessary assistance and maintenance, to care for and educate children and, unless there are weighty reasons not to do so, to form common household. In case of disagreement about place of residence, at request of one or both spouses, district court decides. Place of residence is determined by one of spouses in case other one has been placed under guardianship, or can or will not declare his/her will with respect to place of residence.

Marriage Property System.—From day of marriage community of property, consisting of all existing and future assets and liabilities of both spouses, is imposed by operation of law. Outside community of property remain only: (a) Gifts and bequests to spouse if so provided by giver or legator, (b) assets and liabilities especially attached to one of spouses, and (c) pension claims.

Spouses may deviate from this system by matrimonial property contract (see subhead Matrimonial Property Contract, infra).

Right of Disposal.—Unless otherwise provided by matrimonial property contract, each spouse generally has exclusive right of disposal of property which is part of community property from his/her side. If any asset of which one of spouses has exclusive right of disposal has been applied with his/her consent to other's business or profession, latter has exclusive right to use it within scope of business or profession but consent of both is required for disposition outside that scope.

If third party is not aware which spouse has right of disposal of any unregistered movable (including negotiable instruments made out to bearer), he may assume that holder of movable has that right.

Performance of obligations from acts concerning property by spouse who is not in possession of right of disposal of such property can be restrained by other spouse, which may result in obligation to repair damages by first spouse. Such liability, however, is part of community of property.

At request of one of spouses district court may in certain cases: (a) withdraw and entrust to requesting spouse right of disposal of all or part of community property; (b) cancel community of property of spouses.

Consent of both spouses required for: (a) Purchase of goods on instalment payment plan (unless goods mainly or only regarding business or profession by one of spouses); (b) transaction related to house in which they jointly or other spouse separately lives or to fittings and furnishings of such house; (c) gifts other than usual, not excessive gifts; (d) agreements by which liability under guarantee or other form of surety are incurred by spouse on behalf of third party, unless within scope of business or profession. If spouse acts without consent of other, provisions apply which enable other spouse to invoke invalidity of act by declaration to other party, unless other party acted in good faith or act concerned was gift. If spouse cannot declare his/her will or refuses consent, other spouse able to ask cantonal judge to decide. Both spouses are

HUSBAND AND WIFE . . . *continued*
jointly and separately liable for debts made in scope of normal housekeeping, including employment contract. Spouses are separately liable for other, separately contracted obligations. Creditors to such obligations have recourse against separate assets of contracting spouse as well as community property. Other spouse may prevent recourse against community property by indicating recoverable assets of contracting spouse to creditor.

Duties Between Spouses Relating to Household Expenses.—Spouses must provide each other with essentials. For payment of cost of household including care for and education of children, spouses have mutual obligation to apply income and property in following order: (1) Joint income (in sense of law of matrimonial property), (2) contributions from separate income in proportion of each spouse's income, (3) community property (in sense of law of matrimonial property), (4) contributions from separate property in proportion.

Court may determine otherwise at request by one or both spouses. Each of spouses has towards other during their marriage obligation to realize said contribution by furnishing monies and/or goods out of those assets of which he/she has exclusive right of disposal unless exempted by matrimonial property contract or unless special circumstances would make such contribution unreasonable. On ground of changed circumstances court may at any time, at request of one or both parties, interfere. Separation of households, caused by unreasonable behaviour of one spouse, ends obligation of other spouse to provide first with necessary payment of costs of living. Both spouses remain responsible for costs of care and education of children. Dissolution of any form of community is effected by: (a) Dissolution of marriage, death of one of spouses, disappearance of one of spouses followed by new marriage of other spouse, divorce; (b) separation from bed and board; (c) court's order; (d) respective agreement of spouses made during marriage in form of matrimonial property contract. Dissolution results in division into two equal parts, unless otherwise agreed in writing in advance.

After dissolution of community each of former spouses is 100% liable for those community debts for which he or she was previously liable and 50% liable for other community debts but after payment to creditor of more than his share he has recourse against other one.

Dissolution ends all legal, judicial and contractual administrative provisions. After dissolution spouses can only jointly act with regard to estate. However, provided he/she abandons his/her right from community of property, each of spouses has privilege to exonerate himself from liability in respect of such community debts for which, prior to dissolution, he was not liable. In respect of those debts for which he was liable, he is not exonerated. Heirs and residuary legatees of predeceased spouse have same privilege to be exercised within three months from date when informed of death, which term in special circumstances may be extended by court. Privilege lapses as soon as possible claimant of privilege has taken possession of or made away with any asset of community. If both spouses invoke privilege these provisions are replaced by obligation to liquidate community of goods. At request of one of spouses, court may order dissolution of community property on ground that other one is squandering community assets or by acts infringes upon applicant's right of disposal or without valid reasons refuses to inform applicant about community assets and liabilities and his administration thereof. Application is to be entered in public register and may be accompanied by seizure of assets.

Matrimonial Property Contract.—Such contract can be made prior to marriage or, subject to consent of court, during marriage. Contract must be executed before notary (see topic Notaries) and witnesses in form required by law. Otherwise, it is invalid. Contract cannot be invoked against third parties unless registered in public register of marital property held by court. Parties are free in determining their matrimonial property regime provided contract provisions: (a) Are not contrary to rules of law; (b) do not attribute bigger share of liabilities to spouse than his/her share of assets; (c) do not prejudice parental rights of spouses or rights accorded by law to surviving spouses.

Provisions governing legal community of property regime apply, insofar as contract does not deviate. Several possible matrimonial property systems (all containing some form of limited community of property), are provided explicitly in Civil Code but are relatively rarely used in practice. Complete separation of all community of property is most widely used. However, possibility of matrimonial property contract (whatever system) is hardly used. (1980:15%).

IMMIGRATION:

See topic Aliens.

INFANTS:

Persons under 18 are minors except if they are or have been married; (see also topic Marriage, subhead Minors and Wards).

Legal Acts.—Minor has no capacity to perform legal acts (inclusive of Court actions) on his own unless law provides otherwise. With consent of legal representative given (verbally or in writing) for particular act or (in writing) for specific purpose, minor who can be supposed to understand what he is doing is deemed to have capacity for performing that act, provided that legal representative had authority or was authorized to perform those legal acts for minor. If legal representative supplied minor with money for cost of living and/or study, minor is deemed to have capacity to apply money for that purpose. Minor has capacity to enter into employment with verbal or written authorization of legal representative which after four weeks' employment without objection on latter's part is deemed to have been given. In lawsuit based on employment contract minor can be party only with assistance of legal representative. Payment of wages or salary to minor discharges employer unless legal representative stipulated otherwise when consenting or has objected. Minor has capacity to act as agent for legal representative in latter's name and for latter's account without binding himself. If or insofar as incapacity has not been removed legal acts performed by minor can be annulled by legal representative or by minor himself after attaining majority.

Tort.—Minor under 14 cannot be held liable but his parents or guardian are liable. In respect of tortious behaviour of minor's of 14 or 15 years old, parents or guardian are liable next to minor unless parents or guardian prove that they cannot be blamed for not having prevented minor's behaviour.

Emancipation.—If minor has attained age of 16, court may at his request grant him capacity to collect and dispose of income, to lease personal and real property, to participate in company or partnership or to exercise profession or run a business, and if such grant ("handlichting") has been given, minor can sue and be sued independently. Minor cannot be authorized to dispose of registered goods (including real estate), securities, and claims secured by mortgages. If grant and scope of powers have not been published, it cannot be invoked against third party ignorant of it.

INSOLVENCY:

See topic Bankruptcy (Moratorium).

INTEREST:

Applicable interest rate is either legal interest or interest stipulated by agreement. Rate of legal interest is determined from time to time by government (most recently as per Jan. 1, 1992 at 12%, as per July 1, 1993 at 10%, as per Jan. 1, 1994 at 9%, as per Jan. 1, 1995 at 8%, as per Jan. 1, 1996 at 7% and as per July 1, 1996 at 5%). Interest rate stipulated by agreement may exceed legal interest provided this is not prohibited by law. Interest rate stipulated by agreement must be stated in writing.

In general in case of obligations to pay certain amount of money, damages caused by delay in payment consist only of legal interest as determined from time to time; in this case creditor does not have to prove any real damages.

Generally, legal interest is calculated as from date of summons to court, unless payment of debt due has been formally demanded in writing with explicit demand for legal interest from certain date.

Interest on borrowed monies extinguishes after five years so that interest must be demanded at each expiration date.

Compensation for, including interest on, consumers' credit may not exceed levels determined by ministerial decree by virtue of Act on Consumers' Credit.

INTESTACY:

See topic Descent and Distribution.

JOINT STOCK COMPANIES:

No parallel. See topic Associations.

JUDGMENTS:

Interim Judgments.—Before pronouncing final judgment, judge may render so-called interim judgment, which may have varying contents: (a) Ordering personal appearance of parties, e.g. to try and reach settlement; (b) ordering plaintiff or defendant to prove certain facts, by hearing witnesses; (c) ordering examination by experts; (d) providing day and hour for local inspection, etc.

Interim judgment ends part of dispute insofar as judge expressly sustains or denies part of claim.

Default judgment may be rendered against defendant who fails to appear, but proceedings may be reopened at his instance on payment of extra costs as long as judgment has not been executed. Term for reopening of default proceedings is 14 days and runs from: (a) Moment default judgment has been served upon defendant personally, (b) moment defendant performs act from which necessarily may be inferred that judgment or commenced term of 14 days has become known to him.

Foreign judgments, generally, are not enforceable but facts recited therein may, at discretion of court in Netherlands, be used as evidence. However, bilateral treaties with Austria, Belgium, Federal Republic of Germany, Great Britain, Italy and Suriname provide for reciprocal recognition and enforcement. Same holds for European Convention of Sept. 27, 1968, between Belgium, France, Luxembourg, Federal Republic of Germany, Italy and Netherlands (with accession treaties of Oct. 9, 1978 for Denmark, Ireland and U.K., of Oct. 25, 1982 for Greece, and of May 26, 1989 for Spain and Portugal). In respect of judgments pronounced and deeds executed on or after Feb. 1, 1973, provisions of said European Convention replace provisions of bilateral treaties insofar as some subject matters are dealt with: not covered by European Convention are listed subject matters like rights relating to birth, marriage, death, marital property rights, wills, decedent's estates, bankruptcy, social insurance, arbitration. Equal to European Convention is Lugano Convention of Sept. 16, 1988. In addition to Netherlands, relevant parties to Lugano Convention are Switzerland, Sweden, Norway and Finland. See also topic Divorce.

See also topic Arbitration.

LABOR RELATIONS:

General.—Dutch law with regard to labour relations is laid down in complex body of statutory regulations, which is rapidly changing, and in extensive case law. Following only gives bird's eye view of subject matter.

A. Employment Contracts.—Dutch Civil Code contains general rules on employment contracts. In practice, it may be difficult to distinguish between employment contracts on one hand and comparable contracts for (personal) services on other hand. Distinction, nevertheless, is important one, because many of statutory provisions for employment contracts are binding on parties, deviations therefrom being void.

Employment contract need not be in writing. Some obligations, however, are valid only if accepted in writing. Important example is so-called noncompetition clause, which is allowed, but which may be annulled or moderated by competent court, if equity so demands. Employer is furthermore obliged to furnish employee with document stating conditions of employment.

Other subjects dealt with in relevant title of Civil Code are: Forms and ways of payment of wages (special penalty in case of late payment), paid vacation (at least 20 days per year for full-time employee), consequences of illness of employee, testimonials, etc.

Full-time employees must be at least 16 years old. Employment with some exceptions forbidden for those under 15.

See Topical Index in front part of this volume.

LABOR RELATIONS . . . *continued*

Wages.—Civil Code does not contain specific provisions relating to level of remuneration. However, specific statute provides for minimum wages. For employees above 22 years of age minimum monthly gross remuneration presently is about Dfl. 2,100. If employee only works part-time pro rata reduction may be applied. For those under 23, minimum wage is lower, precise amount thereof depending on age of person concerned (e.g., minimum wage for 16 year old is 34.5% of minimum wage for 23 year old). Statute in question also provides for minimum vacation pay, to be paid annually and amounting to no less than 8% of income over past year.

Pensions.—There is no generally applicable law imposing obligation to grant pension rights; however, in some branches of industry participation in industry-wide pension plans is obligatory. If pension is provided, special, rather severe, rules for funding thereof apply to secure distribution under any circumstances.

Hours of Labour.—Dutch employee's working week tends to vary from 36 to 42 hours with trend to further reduction thereof. This is below statutory maxima (45 hours and 54 hours in overtime-situations). Specific rules concern minors.

Equal Pay.—Equal remuneration for man and woman for comparable jobs is imposed by statutory provisions.

Trial Period.—Parties may agree on maximum two-month trial employment period during which termination is at will. Trial period terms must be express and equal for employee and employer. Period may not be extended beyond two months. Trial period should be agreed upon explicitly prior to execution of work.

Termination. 1. Permit to Terminate.—In absence of mutual agreement or cause, employer may not terminate employment contract without permit from Regional Director of Regional Labour Office ("RLO"). Director has to balance interests of employer and employee. If permit is refused, contract cannot be terminated in valid way, and employer should continue to pay to employee his salary, etc. Especially in complicated cases, Director may need quite some time (varying from some months to half year or even longer) before rendering his decision. Although there are some applicable guidelines, it is quite often very hard to predict whether permit will be granted or not.

Termination. 2. Illness.—If employee is ill at moment that he is being given notice termination is void (unless employee has been ill for two consecutive years).

Termination. 3. Period of Notice.—B.W. provides very elaborate scheme for determining periods of notice to be observed by employers and employees. If there are no specific contractual rules, period will not be less than that between two successive wage payment dates, insofar as this period does not exceed six weeks. However, period of notice will be extended in any case by such factors as tenure and age, up to total of 26 weeks, e.g., employee over 58 with 13 or more years of service is entitled to period of notice of six months.

Termination. 4. Cause.—Above rules do not apply, if there is sufficient cause to warrant immediate cancellation of employment contract. Very serious misconduct should be present before such termination will be allowed; moreover, quite complicated formal rules have to be observed, e.g., cause must be stated explicitly and termination should be effected as soon as possible after it has appeared that there is cause. If these rules are not observed, cancellation is not valid, even if breach of contract in itself would have constituted sufficient cause.

Termination. 5. Compensation Payments.—Notwithstanding fact that employer has terminated contract of employee in accordance with above rules, compensation may be due, if dismissal is found to be "clearly unreasonable". This may be case if reason for termination is false or insufficient; it may also be case if financial effects of termination would otherwise be too hard on employee. Especially with regard to older employees, employees with long tenure and employees with high income, compensation payments are quite customary in The Netherlands.

Termination. 6. Further Remarks.—If contract is entered into for definite period of time it may expire automatically, and rules with regard to permit to terminate, period of notice and compensation payment do not apply unless observation of notice period is explicitely agreed upon between parties. However, this is not case if contract is renewed, albeit once again for definite period of time. Above rules do not apply either if court is requested to rescind contract "for important reasons"; however, in such case, compensation may be imposed by court. Rules with regard to permits to terminate do not apply to statutory managing directors of N.V. or B.V. For dismissal of members of Works Council special rules apply; for termination of their employment contract request shall have to be filed with Cantonal Court to rescind contract. In case of mass dismissals, special rules apply, providing for period of one month of suspension before request for permits to terminate will even be considered. Mass dismissal is present if employer wants to terminate 20 or more employees working in one region in period of less than three months.

B. Collective Labor Law.—Above is description of law relating to individual employment contracts. Picture would not be complete, however, without description of rules relating to labor-management relations.

Works Council.—Every enterprise employing 35 or more employees is obliged to have Works Council. Measures with regard to certain specific subjects cannot be taken without formal approval of Council. On most major subjects, such as all measures seriously affecting number of personnel employed in undertaking, Council has to be heard and be given chance to advise; if employer does not follow advice, appeal may be lodged with Business Chamber of Amsterdam Court of Appeal and decision will be annulled if employer is found to have acted unreasonably. As appears from its case law, Business Chamber is not likely to annul decision on material grounds but has annulled quite a number of decisions on grounds concerning procedure to be followed in obtaining Council's advice, especially concerning supply of relevant information to Council. See also topic Corporations, subhead Works Council.

Collective Bargaining Agreements.—Various Dutch unions hold quite strong position in the Netherlands. Although there are no specific rules relating to duty to bargain with unions, approximately 80% of Dutch working force is covered by collective bargaining agreements. Only 40% of employees, however, belong to one union or another, but employment conditions in collective agreements also have to be applied by unionized employers to nonmembers.

Number of unions are combined in federation called FNV which accounts for more than 50% of unionized employees. Collective bargaining agreement can be declared binding on nonorganized employees also, if certain conditions are fulfilled.

Strikes.—There are no Dutch statutory regulations on strikes. However, according to case law strikes are legal in principle. Injunction against strike can be obtained, if strike is being called although negotiations have not yet reached impasse or, if strike is in violation of collective bargaining agreement.

C. Social Security.—Dutch system of social security is one of most comprehensive (and most expensive) in world. Costs of system are borne by employees and employers alike; deductions up to almost 30% of gross salary have to be effected, and employer's share is somewhat bigger. Minor part of needed funds is provided by government. Premiums and benefits are only computed over amount not exceeding (approximately) Dfl. 69,000 on annual basis.

Unemployment Benefits.—Employee who, because of no fault of his own, is or remains unemployed is entitled to benefits which are 70% of his most recent salary for period of six months up to five and one-half years, depending on age and tenure with maximum of about Dfl. 50,000 per annum. For next two years employee is entitled to benefits which are 70% of statutory minimum wages. If employee is 57½ years or older when he becomes unemployed, latter benefits are continued for another one and one-half years.

Workmen's Compensation.—If employee is prevented from working for physical (or mental) reasons, he will receive compensation equal to 70% of his most recent salary not exceeding statutory maximum amount per day. During first year of inability to work, applicable criterion is whether or not employee is able to perform in his last job; if not, benefits are due to him. Thereafter, criterion is whether there is any work which he can reasonably be expected to perform; in this latter period, social security agencies may decide that employee in question is partly unable to work only and therefore is only entitled to reduced benefits. For statutes described here, reason for inability to work (illness, accident either on job or otherwise) is irrelevant. Benefits may continue for maximum period of six years.

Further Social Security.—Dutch employees earning less than approximately Dfl. 51,000 per annum are covered by compulsory healthcare system, under which most medical and related services are provided free, although recently (minor) own contribution has been imposed. Employees (as well as other heads of family) are entitled to certain children allowances. For all residents of Netherlands, old age pensions (about Dfl. 11,500 for individual and about Dfl. 16,500 for couple) are provided. Moreover, there are general schemes for widower's and orphan's benefits. There is also generally applicable statute covering costs of very long-lasting illness (treatment in mental hospitals for senility, etc.).

LANDLORD AND TENANT:

Law as to relations between landlord and tenant differs considerably as to: (a) Housing premises; (b) retail business premises; (c) "other" business premises; (d) agricultural sites; and (e) other real estate.

(a) Housing Premises.—Freedom to negotiate terms and conditions of contract severely limited in at least two respects: termination of contract and rental prices. For termination of contract, strict formalities apply (most important points being: notice to be given by registered letter or bailiff's writ and, if given by lessor, to contain reasons for notice). Notice by lessor does not terminate rental agreement if lessee remains in possession. Lessor must then file proceedings to terminate lease. Court is held to consider, as grounds for allowing action, only reasons advanced in lessor's notice to lessee. Court can order eviction, but only on one or more of limited number of grounds. Generally, these grounds are: (1) Unreasonable or improper conduct of lessee; (2) lessor urgently requires premises for his proper use, or if lessor is government agency, for purpose of implementing zoning plan; (3) premises have been temporarily let during lessor's absence, and lessor wishes to return. Law contains number of special provisions, protecting spouse, other members of household, and sub-lessees, from eviction when main rental agreement is discontinued.

(b) Retail Business Premises.—This is group of premises mainly consisting of shops, artisan's workshops, hotel, café and restaurant premises. Rental agreements must either be for less than two years, or for at least five years. For agreements of less than two years duration no further mandatory rules apply. For agreements of longer duration, lessee has option to prolong agreement to at least ten years. These agreements do not terminate upon lapse of their duration, but must be terminated by notice. Notice is subject to strict formalities: at least one year's notice by registered letter or bailiff's writ, and, if given by lessor: to specify grounds for notice. If notice is given by lessor, and lessee does not comply therewith, lessor must apply to court for termination order, much in same manner as described under subhead Housing Premises, supra. Notice by lessor after five-year term, is only viable in case of misconduct of lessee or urgent need, on part of lessor, to use premises himself for retail business purposes. In case of notice by lessor after ten-year term (or thereafter), court must balance parties' interests, but must allow action for termination if one or more of limited number of grounds is present.

Law provides that lessee who transfers his business to another, may ask court to substitute that other in his place as lessee.

(c) Other Business Premises.—For instance: offices, factories (but also all other buildings not covered under specific rules described under subheads Housing Premises, Retail Business Premises, or Agricultural Sites). Parties are free to agree on terms of contract. For termination of tenancy, by lessor, it is necessary that he summon lessee who has remained in possession to vacate premises, using registered letter with receipt, or bailiff's writ. Thereafter, lessee has limited time to submit request for prolongation of tenancy to court. Court can grant prolongation for maximum of three one-year periods.

(d) Agricultural Sites.—Agreements must be in writing, and must be approved by Board appointed for that purpose. Mandatory duration of agreement is at least six or at least 12 years, depending on whether premises include farm-building or not. Agreement is prolonged automatically for further six-year periods unless notice of termination is given by registered letter or bailiff's writ. Lessee may, when notice is given, submit request to court for prolongation of tenancy. Court must balance circumstances

See Topical Index in front part of this volume.

LANDLORD AND TENANT . . . *continued*
equitably in deciding whether to allow prolongation. In case of sale of agricultural sites, lessee has first refusal right to buy. Limited possibility for substitution of lessee by his successor in business.

(e) Other Real Estate.—Very limited category, including mainly nonagricultural sites without buildings. Examples: sportsfields, storage areas, parking lots. No mandatory provisions apply, parties are free to contract.

Rental Prices.—Though principal rule is that parties are free to negotiate rental prices as they see fit, in considerable number of cases price is subject to court, or other supervision. Most important instances are: For housing premises, rules vary, depending on value of premises. For more valuable premises, rental price may be amended to correspond to that of other, similar premises. For less valuable premises, lessee may request Rental Board ("Huurcommissie") to rule on fairness of agreed rental rate by reference to detailed valuation system concerning size, fittings, age, neighbourhood, etc. of premises and leading to fairly low valuations. Freedom to increase prices periodically is limited, and similarly supervised by rental board (Huurcommissie). Rents of publicly-funded housing have long been set by Ministry of Public Housing using similar valuation. Although this system was recently discontinued, large numbers of rental agreements are still based on conditions prescribed by Ministry. This situation will continue for some years to come. For retail business premises: either party may, if fixed period agreed upon (if any) has elapsed, or, if no fixed rental period continues to be applicable, each time contract has run for five years or series of five year periods, commence action to establish new contract price by reference to local rental conditions. For agricultural premises: parties may request revision of price at three year intervals. Initial approval of contract may be withheld if price is inappropriate. For all other nonagricultural business premises court that grants request for prolongation, may set price to be paid thereafter.

Note: For all kinds of rental agreements, law provides that sale of premises by lessor does not entail termination of rental agreement or of tenancy. In very limited number of cases this rule may be set aside in contract.

General.—Civil Code contains a number of provisions generally applicable to rental agreements, of which most important are: Lessor is responsible for damage resulting from visible or hidden defects in property; lessee may not sublet, unless otherwise provided or unless lessee wishes to sublet part of house he himself resides in; major maintenance and repairs are for account of lessor, minor repairs and day-to-day maintenance for account of lessee.

Civil Code rules just mentioned may be (and frequently are) set aside in contract forms.

See also topic Real Property.

LAW REPORTS, CODES, ETC.:

Codes.—Most essential parts of private and commercial law and civil procedure have been codified in Civil Code (Burgerlijk Wetboek; B.W.). Commercial Code (Wetboek van Koophandel; WvK) and Code of Civil Procedure (Wetboek van Burgerlijke Rechtsvordering; Rv) which were, in 1838, for greater part copied from or adaptations of French Codes.

They have been frequently amended and supplemented by Legislature. By 1938, 100 years later, 345 of original 2,030 sections of Civil Code had been amended or deleted and 209 sections had been added and body of private law outside Civil Code had become larger than Civil Code itself. Besides, gap between social and economic life in 1838 and modern times was bridged in practice by standard regulations and clauses replacing many non-compulsory statutory provisions and in litigation by unorthodox rulings of court.

Most essential parts of criminal law and criminal procedure have been codified in Criminal Code and Code of Criminal Procedure. These codes, in their present form, date from 1881-1886 and 1921-1929 respectively and have been frequently amended as well.

Recodification of Civil and Commercial Codes.—Project of recodification was started in 1947. Plans to replace both codes in stages by one Civil Code consisting of eight books (Draft New Civil Code: N.B.W.) were completed for largest part by Jan. 1, 1992.

Books 1 (natural persons and family law) and 2 (legal persons, company law) have been enacted and are in effect since 1970 and 1976 respectively.

Book 8 (transport) is in effect since Apr. 1, 1991.

Book 3 (general provisions as to property, rights in rem and obligations), Book 5, (rights in rem), Book 6 (obligations) and certain parts of Book 7 (nominate contracts) are in effect since Jan. 1 1992, together with related amendments of Code of Civil Procedure. Detailed transitional provisions apply. Rest of project is still under discussion.

Official Publications of Statutory Law and of Regulations.—All statutes and all regulations by Crown (i.e., Central Government) and some regulations by Ministers of Central Government are published in "Staatsblad" (abbreviated "Stb." or "S." with year and number). Other regulations are published in Official Gazette ("Staatscourant", abbr. "Stct.") or in official publications of lower governmental bodies. International conventions and treaties in "Tractatenblad", abbr. "Trb.". Above three publications are issued by Publishing Office "Sdu", Christoffel Plantijnstraat 2, 2515 TZ The Hague. Dutch text of European Communities regulations etc. is published in "Publicatieblad van de Europese Gemeenschappen" (Dutch-language edition of Official Journal of E.C.).

Law Reports.—There is no official reporting of Netherlands law cases, but there are number of unofficial reports.

Literal text of judgments (often abbreviated) is published in "Rechtspraak van de Week" (mainly civil cases Supreme Court; abbr. "R.v.d.W."); in "Kort Geding" (judgments in summary proceedings, abbr. "K.G."); in "Nederlandse Jurisprudentie", split in two series: N.J. (civil law [including arbitral awards] and criminal law) and A.B. (administrative law); in "Schip en Schade" (abbr. "S & S", shipping, transportation and fire insurance law); in "Verkeersrecht (traffic law, abbr. "V.R.") and in "Beslissingen in Belastingzaken" (taxation, abbr. "BNB").

In addition summaries or extracts in various forms of judgments and decisions relevant for their field of interest are published by numerous law reviews, such as "Nederlands Juristenblad" (general law review, official publications of Netherlands Lawyers Association, abbr. "N.J.B."), Kwartaalbericht NBW (general law review on [draft] New Civil Code), Weekblad voor Privaatrecht, Notariaat en Registratie (official publication of the Royal Civil Law Notaries' Association, abbr. Nederlands "WPNR", Tijdschrift voor Burgerlijk Recht (general law review on civil law, abbr. "NTBR"), "Ars Aequi" (for university students, abbr. "A.A." or "A.Ae."), "Sociaal Economische Wetgeving (social economic legislation, abbr. "SEW"), "Sociaal Maandblad Arbeid" (labor law, abbr. "S.M.A."), "de Praktijkgids" (inter alia, rental and labor law), "T.V.V.S." (law concerning companies and societies), "De Naamlooze Vennootschap" (company law, abbr. "De N.V."), "Weekblad voor Fiscaal Recht" (taxation, abbr. "WFR"), "Bijblad bij de Industriële Eigendom (industrial property law, abbr. "B.I.E."), "Tijdschrift voor Arbitrage" (arbitration, abbr. "TvA"), "Bouwrecht" (building and construction law), "De Gemeentestem" and "De Nederlandse Gemeente" (for municipalities), "Delikt en Delinkwent" (criminal law, abbr. "D.D."), "Tijdschrift voor Familie- en Jeugdrecht" (family and juvenile law, abbr. "F.J.R."). Judgments of Court of Justice of European Communities are officially reported in "Jurisprudentie van het Hof van Justitie" (Dutch language edition of European Court Reports).

Compilations and Treatises.—Increasing number of compilations is in loose-leaf form, with comments and references and purport to be regularly kept up-to-date by teams of authors. Sources of legal thought may be found in treatises, articles in periodicals and in notes under published court rulings. They have often considerable influence on courts and on legislature. Subjects like torts, good faith, reasonableness and fairness are largely judge-made law, compiled, classified and put in legal framework by authors who frequently make comparisons with drafts of New Civil Code and with laws of Belgium, Germany, France and occasionally Great Britain and U.S.A.

LEGISLATURE:

See topic Constitution and Government.

LICENSES:

In general, many (economic) activities are subject to licenses, permits or dispensations. Licenses (or dispensations) may be required under numerous acts, such as acts relating to: (a) Establishment of various kinds of enterprises and/or performance of various professions; e.g. establishment of hotels, cafes, restaurants, work and repair shops, retail trade; establishment of enterprises or practicing in branches like banking, insurance, transport (including transport by air and by water), installment trade, brokerage (real estate, insurance, stock), health-care, accountancy, legal profession; (b) agriculture and fishing; (c) mining (see topic Mines and Minerals); (d) trade and advertising; e.g., licenses may be required under acts on selling prices of goods and services, on import and export (see topic Foreign Trade Regulations), on organising of games of chance, on free-gift systems; (e) environmental protection; e.g. acts on pollution of open water, sea and air, noise pollution, on nuisance, on protection of soil, on (transport and) disposal of (chemical and other) waste and dangerous substances, on import, export, use and disposal of substances dangerous to environment, on trade and use of pesticides, on application of nuclear energy (see topic Environment); (f) protection of nature in general; (g) control and use of public rivers; (h) town and country planning, construction of buildings, and use of buildings for dwelling purposes; (i) (fire) arms; (j) broadcasting and telecommunication; (k) entry, stay and settlement of aliens (see topic Aliens); (l) driving motor vehicles (see topic Motor Vehicles); (m) termination of employment contracts (see topic Labour Relations).

Furthermore declaration of nonobjection from Minister of Justice is required for incorporation of two main types of corporations (see topic Corporations).

Apart from acts, issued by central government many regulations issued by local authorities (provinces, municipalities, drainage authorities) require licenses or permits.

To many licenses conditions may be attached. Generally both from grant or refusal (or withdrawal) of, as well as from conditions attached to licenses appeal is possible, with administrative agency or with administrative judiciary (see topic Courts). In many cases, not only applicants, but also interested third parties have right to appeal. General Act on Administrative Law (Algemene wet bestuursrecht), which entered into force on 1 Jan. 1994, provides for general procedural rules regarding participation, complaint, appeal and judicial review of Government decisions including granting of licences (see also topic Constitution and Government).

For licenses under industrial property rights, see topics Copyright; Patents; Trademarks; Tradenames.

LIENS:

In general, rule of "paritas creditorum" does apply. However, statutory law grants preference to certain groups of creditors in certain order. Some preferences are granted on specific goods only (for example preferences related to mortgage, pledge and costs of preservation of good), some on all goods of debtor (most tax claims, social security payments, claims of employees or former employees for wages and some pension payments).

LIMITATION OF ACTIONS:

Adverse Possession/Acquisition of Title by Prescription.—Rights in movables which are not registered property, and in claims payable to bearer or order are acquired by possessor by possession in good faith for three years without interruption. Rights in other property are acquired by such possession for ten years (acquisition by prescription). Good faith is assumed; contesting party has to show bad faith of possessor. If property has been in possession during statutory period, other rights to that property expire as result of statutory limitation of right of action (infra) and person in possession of property acquires rights in this property even if possession was not in good faith. Interruption or extension of limitation of right of action to terminate

LIMITATION OF ACTIONS. . . *continued*
possession (infra) interrupts or extends period for acquisition by prescription accordingly. Nonvoluntary loss of possession does not interrupt course of prescription provided possession is restored within one year or action installed within one year to that effect is successful.

Limitation of Actions.—Rights of actions are subject to limitation (also called extinctive prescription). In case of rights in personam right itself does not terminate by lapse of limitation period; nonenforcable right remains. In case of limited rights in rem prescription of right of action of holder of limited right against principal holder of property leads to revival of full title of latter to property involved.

Unless provided for by law otherwise rights of action expire by lapse of 20 years as from day following one performance can be claimed. Some special periods of extinctive prescription are:

Six months: annulment of termination of labour contract by giving notice of termination without prior consent of "regionaal directeur voor arbeidsvoorziening"; prescription period starts on date of notification of termination.

One year: annulment of resolution of meeting of shareholders by shareholder or third party interested; prescription period runs as from date of publishing resolution.

Two years: in case of purchase contract rights of actions and defences related to nonconformity of property sold and delivered; prescription period runs as from date on which notice of nonconformity has been given to seller; seller is to be notified on short term after nonconformity is discovered or reasonably should have been discovered.

Three years: annulment of legal act for reason of error/misrepresentation, fraud, threat, abuse of circumstances, prejudice to creditor's right of recovery or legal incapacity; prescription period starts on different dates; right of action for damages against producer of product as meant in EU product liability regulation of 25 July 1985; prescription period runs as from day after one victim knows or should have known of damage, defect and identity of producer; however, claim for damages becomes barred anyhow ten years after date on which product which has caused damage has been put into market; (see also subhead Extinction of Rights and Actions by Mere Operation of Law, infra).

Five years: right of action for performance of contractual obligation to hand over property or to do something; starting point of prescription period is date on which right has become claimable; right of action for payment of interest on sum of money, life rent, dividend, lease rent and all other amounts to be paid annually or even more frequently is subject to prescription five years after day following one on which amount involved has fallen due; right of action for indemnification or contractual fine; prescription period runs as from day following one on which victim knows both damage or claimability of fine and identity of debtor; claim for indemnification or contractual fine becomes barred anyhow 20 years—30 years in case of damage resulting from pollution of air, water or soil—after event which has caused damage or has made claimable fine; right of action for dissolution of contract for reason of breach of contract; prescription period starts as from day after one creditor has become familiar with breach of contract; dissolution becomes barred anyhow 20 years after breach of contract.

Contractual deviation from statutory terms of limitation of rights of actions is allowed. However, waiver of extinctive prescription not allowed before prescription has been completed.

Pleading of Limitation.—Limitation of actions must be pleaded. This may be done at any stage of proceedings before final judgment, appeal included. This right to plea limitation of actions can be renounced, expressly or implicitely, but only after full term as lapsed.

Interruption and Extension of Statutory Period of Limitation.—Limitation period is extended in certain cases because of special relationship between parties involved, e.g. between spouses, legal representative and incapable person represented by former, legal entities and their directors and between creditor and debtor who deliberately hides existence of debt or its claimability. Prescription will be completed not earlier than six months after expiration of ground of extension if right of action would become barred during existence of ground for extension. Limitation of action is interrupted by institution of legal action or by any other act of judicial recourse instituted in required form by person entitled to right of action. Prescription of rights of action to claim performance of obligation is also interrupted by written request for performance or by written communication in which creditor unequivocally reserves right to performance. Limitation of other rights of action is interrupted by written warning followed by act of judicial recourse (supra) within six months.

Limitation of right of action is interrupted if debtor by his words (explicitly) or by his act (implicitly) acknowledges existence of right whose protection is served by right of action.

Extinction of Rights and Actions by Mere Operation of Law.—In number of cases right/claim extinguishes because of elapse of time without appeal to it required; court by its own motion applies relevant rules. Not only right of action but also right/claim itself expires. Elapse of time cannot be interrupted or extended even by contract.

Some examples are:

Ten years: claim for damage based on product liability as provided for in EU product liability regulation of 25 July 1985, however only insofar as claim extinguishes by elapse of ten years after defective product has been put in circulation.

Five years: claim for alimony against alledged father of illegimate child; claim of shareholder for dividends.

Three years: revindication of stolen property; action for rescission of partition of estate of deceased or of other type of community property.

One year: some claims relating to international transport by ship.

Six months: some claims arising from labour and agency contracts; right of either party to render dissolution of marriage absolute by registration of decree; denial of father that child born in wedlock is his child.

Sixty days-six weeks: right of (unpaid) seller to recover possession of goods sold for cash (provided that they are still in same condition and have not been delivered for due consideration to third party acting in good faith), expires when simultaneously, six weeks have passed since right to payment of purchase price has become claimable and 60 days since day on which good concerned has been put into possession of buyer or someone else acting on his behalf.

Limitation of Action in Civil Litigation.—Normal judicial remedies are "opposition" (against judgment in default of defense), "appeal" and "cassation".

Judicial remedies can be instituted against "judgments" and "decisions or orders upon petition."

Judgments:

Opposition.—In general opposition against condemning judgment must be instituted within 14 days after service is made on defaulter personally by process-server or defaulter has carried out activities which show that he knows of judgment or its execution.

Appeal.—In general appeal is to be lodged within three months after day judgment has been passed. In case of judgment after summary proceedings term is 14 days.

Cassation.—In general cassation is possible only in case of judgment in appeal or final and conclusive judgment of first instance.

In general cassation must be entered within three months from day judgment has been passed. In case of summary proceedings, term is six weeks.

Decisions or Orders Upon Petition.—Especially in personal status and family matters decisions or orders are issued upon petition.

Opposition.—In general opposition against decision not possible.

Appeal.—In general appeal is to be lodged by party who made appearance in earlier proceedings within two months after date of decision; by other interested party within two months after service of final decision on him or he has gotten knowledge of that decision otherwise.

Appeal against decision authorizing execution of foreign judgment must be entered one month after date of decision.

Decisions on provisional measures in divorce case are not open for appeal.

Cassation.—Only party who appeared in Court in earlier proceedings can apply for cassation with Supreme Court within two months after date of final decision.

In case of decision authorizing execution of foreign judgment term is one month after date of decision in appeal.

Note: Above only main terms for judicial remedies are given; there are exceptions.

MARRIAGE:

Requirements.—Dutch law only acknowledges civil marriages, performed before registrar of marriages. Boys and girls under age 18 are not allowed to marry without dispensation of Minister of Justice unless both at least age 16 and girl being pregnant or having given childbirth. Marriage cannot be concluded if one party is so mentally disturbed that he/she does not understand meaning of statement. Only marriage between one man and one woman is recognized. Widow may not remarry until 306 days after husband's death, subject to four exceptions.

No prohibition of marriage on account of race, religion or nationality. No medical certificate is required.

Minors and Wards.—Minor may not marry without consent of those persons who by law are regarded as parents. If minor is under guardianship, consent of guardian is required as well. If such consent is not obtained it may be replaced by consent of court. Person who is under guardianship on ground of prodigality or abuse of alcohol may not marry without consent of guardian and supervising guardian which, if not obtained, may be replaced by consent of court. Person who is under guardianship because of mental disturbance, may not marry without consent of court.

Marriages prohibited between persons who either by natural ties or by adoption or are legitimately or illegitimately regarded as each other's ascendant and descendant or brother and sister. For weighty reasons, Minister of Justice may grant dispensation to those being brother and sister by adoption.

Formalities.—Notification of marriage is to be made by two parties in person at municipal registrar at residence of one of parties. If both parties have residence outside Netherlands and want to be married in Netherlands, registrar in The Hague may be notified, provided one party is Dutch national. Several documents have to be submitted, including certificate of birth of both parties, statement of names and addresses of witnesses (see infra), act of notification. In case one of parties is minor or ward: deed of consent (see subhead Minors and Wards, supra). If one of parties is foreigner: statement of police stating that foreigner has (made request for) residence permit (unless both parties have residence abroad). Sufficient documentary evidence of intention may replace personal appearance. Marriage may not be concluded within 14 days after date of act of notification, except for permission of public prosecutor for important reasons. If marriage is not concluded within one year after date of notification, new notification has to be made. Breach of promise to marry is no cause of action but in case act of notification of marriage has been made, relief can be granted for damaged proprietary interests within 18 months.

Marriage can be stayed by certain relatives, guardians and supervisory guardians if parties do not meet requirements or is spouse-to-be. Public prosecutor also can or, in certain circumstances, has to stay marriage. Marriage may not be concluded before stay has been cancelled, either by person invoking stay or by court. Marriage is concluded publicly by statement of two parties in person before registrar of marriages in city hall, in presence of at least two and at most four witnesses of age. Marriage certificate is supplied by and marriage is registered in local municipal register. Under special circumstances and subject to special requirements place other than city hall and marriage by proxy are possible. Marriage in church is permitted only after marriage before registrar of marriages and has no legal consequences.

Aliens may be married, provided one of them has permanent residence in Netherlands. This person must be registered in Gemeentelijke Basisadministratie, i.e. Local Administration. Both parties need a Declaration of conformation with Aliens Act. Apart from that normal statutory rules apply. However, documents required such as those evidencing identity, nationality, and single status may differ according to alien's nationality. Numerous bilateral treaties set forth general rules on marriage between aliens and Dutch nationals.

See also topics Aliens; Divorce; Husband and Wife.

See Topical Index in front part of this volume.

MINES AND MINERALS:

On-shore exploration and exploitation of coal, oil, natural gas and many other minerals are subject to concession awarded by Crown decree under Mining Act dating from 1810. Off-shore exploration and exploitation are governed by Continental Shelf Mining Act (1965), under which licence from Minister of Economic Affairs is required. Extensive, detailed provisions governing on-shore and off-shore exploration are laid down in various Crown Decrees and regulations of Ministry of Economic Affairs; pursuant to Upstream Licensing Directive (94/22/EEC) new competitive and nondiscriminatory procedure for issuing oil and natural gas licenses was introduced on June 5, 1996. In case of gas and oil production, state participation is regular feature by means of state-controlled company (Energie Beheer Nederland) which by Act holds 40% or 50% of gas interest. As per 1990 Dutch fiscal jurisdiction is extended to Dutch sector of continental shelf. Labour law concerning off-shore employees is governed by North Sea Mining Industry Employment Act (1992).

MONOPOLIES AND RESTRAINT OF TRADE:

This subject is governed by EU and ECSC Treaties, and in addition by 1956 Act on Economic Competition ("Wet Economische Mededinging") to extent that this Act is compatible with Community system. See also European Union Law Digest, topic Monopolies and Restraint of Trade.

EU competition rules applicable to enterprises may prohibit agreements, decisions and concerted practices (§85[1]) or abuse of dominant position (§86). In agriculture, application of these rules is somewhat limited. (EEC Regulation 26/62). Special rules apply to transport sector. In case 66/86, SAEED, concerning air transport, European Court of Justice held that national judges can directly apply Art. 86 if all conditions of this article are satisfied (see infra). ECSC Treaty contains specific rules for certain coal and steel products (not discussed below).

In deciding whether any particular transaction falls within §85(1) it is necessary to consider three aspects: (i) Whether there exists agreement, decision or concerted practice made between or observed by undertakings or by association(s) of undertakings, (ii) whether competition within Common Market may be prevented, restricted or distorted, and (iii) whether trade between member states may be affected thereby. §85(1) subparagraphs (a) to (e) illustrate certain particular agreements which commonly have as their object or effect restriction of competition within Common Market. These illustrations, however, are not exhaustive. Agreement may affect trade between member states if it appears, after consideration of its objective legal or factual elements, that agreement may reasonably be expected to exercise direct or indirect, actual or potential effect upon flow of trade between member states which may hinder creation of Common Market among those states and obstruct economic interpenetration aimed at by Treaty. In considering whether particular agreement falls within above definition, it is necessary to assess agreement within whole surrounding economic and legal context. Broadly speaking, agreements between parent and subsidiary or between subsidiary companies in same group, or subject to common control, fall outside §85(1), if subsidiary does not enjoy any real autonomy in determination of its course of action and agreement contains mere internal allocation of tasks.

Both European Commission and European Court of Justice specified on various occasions that §85(1) is only applicable to those agreements, decisions or concerted practices, which have appreciable effect on both competition and trade between Member States. European Commission issued notice concerning agreements of minor importance indicating that there is no appreciable effect if certain thresholds are met: joint aggregate turnover of all undertakings involved less than 300 million ECU and joint market share for products or services concerned on Common Market less than 5%. European Commission has adopted so-called effect doctrine when it comes to applying §85 to certain agreements and practices being operated outside territory of Common Market. Prohibition may apply if such agreements or practices produce their effect within EU. This doctrine has been endorsed by European Court of Justice.

If agreement falls within §85(1), two quite separate consequences follow. First, validity of agreement will be affected under civil law. §85(2) provides that any agreements prohibited pursuant to §85(1) are "automatically null and void". Under Dutch civil law infringement of §85(1) (and §86) constitutes tort and, hence, can give rise to liability for damages. Secondly, parties may be exposed to risk of European Commission taking proceedings under EC-Regulation 17/62 to enforce prohibition contained in §85(1) (and §86). Under §15(2) of that regulation, Commission may impose fines upon enterprises if they intentionally or negligently infringe Treaty. Under §3(1) thereof Commission may also require enterprises to bring to end infringements of Treaty. Under §16(1)(a) thereof such requirement may be enforced by imposition of penalty payments in respect of each day that infringement continues. Commission may also take provisional measures pending final decision. §14 of Regulation gives Commission right to hold investigation in enterprises.

European Commission is only body which has power to grant or refuse exemption pursuant to §85(3). Agreements, decisions or concerted practices in respect of which parties seek exemption ordinarily have to be notified to Commission. Unless Commission notified, no decision in application of §85(3) can be taken. Special procedures for notifying agreements and making applications for exemption and so-called "negative clearance" are contained in Regulation 17/62. Commission has exercised its powers to exempt "en bloc" under §85(3) certain categories of: exclusive distribution agreements (Regulation 1983/83), exclusive purchasing agreements (Regulation 1984/83), motor vehicle distribution and servicing agreements (Regulation 1475/95), specialization agreements (Regulation 417/85), research and development agreements (Regulation 418/85), franchise agreements (Regulation 4087/88), contracts in insurance sector (Regulation 3932/92) and for certain categories of technology transfer agreements (Regulation 240/96). Scope of two of these Group Exemption Regulations (417/85, 418/85) has been widened by Regulaton 151/93.

EEC-Regulation of 17/62 does not apply to transportation. Commission's powers to enforce prohibition contained in §85(1) (and §86) and to grant exemption pursuant to §85(3) are laid down in Regulation 1017/68 (for transportation by rail, road and inland waterway), in Regulations 4056/86 and 870/95 (for maritime transportation) and in Regulations 3975/87, 1617/93, 1618/93 and 3652/93 (for air transport and air transport services).

Commission issues decisions which are binding and notices which provide guidance for undertakings and indicate Commission's view on various matters relating to §85 (and §86). At present are to be mentioned: notices on exclusive agency contracts made with commercial agents (Dec. 24, 1962); on co-operation agreements (July 29, 1968); on imports of Japanese products (Oct. 21, 1972); concerning agreements of minor importance (Sept. 3, 1986) and concerning subcontracting agreements (Dec. 18, 1978), notice on co-operation between national courts and Commission (Feb. 13, 1993) and notice on application of EC competition rules to crossborder credit transfers (Sept. 27, 1995).

Conduct of kind prohibited by §86 requires presence of three factors: Existence of dominant position, abuse of that position and possibility that trade between member states may be affected by it. Commission has emphasized "over-all independence of behavior" as principal test of dominant position, which can only be satisfied by examining relative strengths of enterprises which compete in supply or acquisition of goods or services within particular market.

"Abuse" is thought to be objective criterion, which means that it may be brought about unintentionally. Abuse may be established irrespective of object of actions. It is economic effect that counts. Economic effect of abuse may consist of, basically: (a) market behaviour to disadvantage of third parties; or (b) action by which competitive structure of market is altered to disadvantage of third parties. Subparagraphs (a) to (d) of §86 illustrate kind of abuse which is prohibited. Illustrations are not exhaustive. From case law which has been developed by both European Commission and European Court of Justice it has become clear that §86 is applied on basis of its economic meaning rather than on its exact wording. Both "monopolizing" and "unfair trade practice" known in U.S. antitrust law seem to fall under scope of §86.

On Sept. 21, 1990 merger control regulation (4064/89) entered into force. Applies to mergers with community dimension. Latter criteria is decided on turnover of enterprises concerned. Below community dimension appraisal left to national authorities. Considered to be merger if enterprise(s) lose legal or economical independence. Merger must be notified to Commission within week of conclusion of agreement. Notice of Commission on distinction between concentrative and cooperative joint ventures (Dec. 31, 1994), notice on notion of concentration (Dec. 31, 1994), notice on notion of undertakings concerned (Dec. 31, 1994), notice on calculation of turnover (Dec. 31, 1994), notice on restrictions ancillary to concentrations (Aug. 14, 1990) and notice concerning assessment of co-operative joint-ventures under §85 (Feb. 16, 1993) contain further points of view regarding merger control of Commission.

Act on Economic Competition deals both with agreements between enterprises and dominant positions but does not apply to mergers and acquisitions. Act defines agreement in restraint of trade ("mededingingsregeling") as legally binding arrangement regulating competition between owners of enterprises. Minister of Economic Affairs must be notified of such agreements within one month after they have been entered into. Failure to notify is criminal offense, but does not render agreement void. There is no public notice of such notification, and "cartel register" is not yet open for public inspection. Exemption from registration requirement has been granted by decree for individual resale price maintenance contracts and agreements regulating economic competition exclusively outside Netherlands. Apart from some exceptions under Act agreements in restraint of trade are not null and void per se, but, on contrary, binding upon parties as any other contract is. However, if in opinion of Minister agreement is contrary to public interest ("algemeen belang") decree may be issued invalidating agreement. Such decrees are officially published. Managers of undertakings are subject to criminal proceedings if they act contrary to such decrees. Also agreement can be suspended pending inquiries by government.

As vertical price agreements, collective resale price maintenance is generally prohibited and invalidated by decree based on art. 9e of Act. Individual resale price maintenance is prohibited for certain consumer goods only. In June 1993, generic prohibition with respect to horizontal price agreements was enacted, followed by generic prohibition with respect to market sharing arrangements and bidding arrangements in June 1994. Each generic prohibition contains number of group exemptions and possibility for Minister to grant individual exemption in public interest. Minister may also declare agreement between majority of enterprises in specific sector of economy generally binding on all enterprises in that sector. Act further allows for injunctions, if, in opinion of Minister, dominant position of one or more enterprises in Netherlands market is present and effects contrary to public interest occur. Provisional measures may be taken by Minister. Some of injunctions provided for in Act are: Obligation to supply specified goods or to render specified services, and obligation to decrease prices. *Note:* In May 1996, draft of new Competition Act was sent to parliament. Ministry of Economic Affairs strives for enactment in mid 1997. New act will have strong resemblance to Community competition legislation in field of §§85 and 86, and in field of merger control.

MORATORIUM: See topic Bankruptcy (Moratorium).

MORTGAGES:

Mortgage is right over property for exclusive and express purpose of securing priority payment upon public auction in event that debtor fails to perform obligations. Mortgage may be vested to secure present obligations or mortgagor or third party, and future obligations as well.

Mortgageable Property.—Susceptable of mortgage are: (1) immovable property; (2) registered ships and other vessels; (3) aircraft; (4) limited rights in respect of mortgageable property like usufruct and similar rights in rem, like "erfrecht".

Mortgage deed must be in form of notarial instrument executed before Dutch notary. It must describe property, mention nature and amount of debt, or facts on basis of which debt may be determined, indicate parties, and may contain specific stipulations made by mortgagee such as restriction of mortgagor's power to lease mortgaged property, obligation to keep property insured, right of mortgagee to take over management of property in case of default of mortgagor, etc.

Power of attorney for creation of mortgage on behalf of mortgagee requires notarial instrument.

MORTGAGES . . . *continued*

Recording.—Any mortgage to be valid must be recorded in Title and Mortgage Registry for district where property is situated or where ship or aircraft is registered. See topic Records.

Priorities.—Creditors having claims secured by mortgage have priority on forclosure proceeds before other creditors and before taxes (except for real property taxes).

Among other mortgages rank of mortgage is determined by date of entry on record; mortgages entered on same date have same ranking.

Forclosure is effected in case of default of debtor by public auction of property before notary in district where property is situated.

If proceeds of sale are insufficient to satisfy secured obligations, mortgagee may proceed against other assets pari passu with all other unsecured creditors.

Bankruptcy of mortgagor or debtor does not affect mortgagee's right to forclose.

Upon request of either mortgagor or mortgagee president of court may order that forclosure is effected by private sale according to agreement to be approved by him.

Cancellation of mortgage is effected by notarial instrument upon satisfaction of creditor or otherwise at his discretion. If upon satisfaction creditor fails to cancel mortgage mortgagee may request court to order cancellation.

Upon forclosure of property cancellation of mortgage will be ordered by court at request of purchaser provided that forclosure took place with due observance of all legal requirements, and provided purchase price was paid in hands of notary.

Purchase price is distributed by notary to mortgagees according to priority.

Mortgages on Ships and Other Vessels.—Some special provisions apply. Mortgage on ship may be vested only if ship is registered in Register of Shipping. By change of nationality of ship obligations for which ship is mortgaged mature. Mortgagee is entitled to sell ship in any country where it is berthed.

Mortgage on Aircraft.—Similar provisions as for mortgage of ships apply.

MOTOR VEHICLES:

Drivers of motor vehicles living in Netherlands are required to have Netherlands drivers license. Foreigners starting to live in Netherlands should apply to local, municipal or provincial authorities for Netherlands drivers license as soon as possible after their actual establishment.

Minimum age for drivers license is 18 and license valid until age of 70. License should be renewed, however every ten years until driver has reached age of 60. After age of 60 has been reached, validity period will be shortened. Aliens may exchange national drivers license for Dutch license for same category motor vehicle, provided their existing license is still valid. Non-EU citizens may exchange foreign drivers license provided that they reside in Netherlands, and existing license is still valid.

Drivers licenses of American tourists issued in their home country are only recognized in Netherlands together with "International Driving Permit", to be obtained in their home country at American Automobile Association.

Motor vehicle with foreign registration plate to be used permanently in Netherlands is to be registered. For import of motor vehicle from EU-country V.A.T. and special tax on sale of passenger cars are charged; for import of motor vehicle from most non-EU-countries also import duty. Yearly registrations fee and quarterly or yearly use tax ("Motorrijtuigenbelasting") are dependent on vehicle weight and type.

Temporary use of foreign motor vehicle in Netherlands is, generally with maximum of one year, tax exempt.

Registration is subject to inspection of vehicle by inspectors of National Traffic Service ("Rijksdienst voor het Wegverkeer").

At transfer of motor vehicle, part II of document of registration ("kentekenbewijs") must be made out in name of acquirer. Acquirer must give to transferor signed indemnity release form, issued by post office. Transfer is registered via post office at National Traffic Service. No taxes due on transfer of motor vehicle by private persons. Purpose of Part III of document of registration is proof of property.

Insurance against third-party risks is compulsory. Principle of strict liability towards pedestrians and cyclists; action directly against insurer possible.

Motor vehicles more than three years old are subject to compulsory yearly inspection.

NEGOTIABLE INSTRUMENTS:

See topic Bills and Notes.

NETHERLANDS ANTILLES:

See topics Constitution and Government; Corporations.

NOTARIES:

Notary (notaris) is lawyer appointed by Crown to serve as public official within specified district. There are approximately 1,100 notaries in Netherlands. Duties of Dutch notary are different from those of notary public in Anglo-American jurisdictions: (a) For many legal transactions obligatory assistance of notary is required in form of notarial instrument. Such transactions include: incorporation and amendments to articles of association of legal entities, issuance, transfer and encumbering of registered shares (NV/BV), transfer and mortgage of real property and mortgage of registered vessels, wills, marriage settlements, liquidation of estates if e.g., minors are involved; (b) notarial instruments may also be drawn up for other legal transactions if clients so desire. Although law does not provide explicitly to that effect notary may, like common law notaries, notarize signatures; such notarisations receive full credit (see also topics Acknowledgments; Affidavits); (c) like general legal practitioners notaries may act as legal counsel to their clients on their request. However, notaries do not engage in any litigation.

Notarial instrument is document signed by parties thereto, or by their duly designated attorneys, and notary and if required two witnesses. Notarial instrument states: (1) Appearance of party or parties before notary, (2) exact wordings of statements by parties, (3) signature(s) of party or parties, (4) acknowledgment by notary of such signature(s) and notary's statement that requirements of law have been fulfilled, (5) date.

Subject to few exceptions law requires original of instrument to be kept in custody of notary and only certified copies may be given to party. Notarial instrument provides conclusive evidence of its date and of statements by notary and, between parties involved, of contents of their statements. Notarial instrument reciting claim may be enforced like judgment of court without any court procedure. On request of parties notarial instrument may be made out in foreign language provided that notary understands language; for certain instruments (e.g. incorporation and amendments to articles of association of legal entities) Dutch language is required.

See also topic Consuls.

PARTNERSHIP:

"Maatschap" is form of co-operation between two or more persons created by their agreement to make contributions (money, property or use of certain corporeal or incorporeal effects, labor or skill) as means for conduct of business or exercise of profession with purpose of profit-sharing.

Rights and liabilities ensuing out of activities or business transactions within scope of partnership can be subject to any kind of provision between partners, but provision that one partner is entitled to all profits is void. In principle all partners are entitled to manage partnership, unless contract between partners provides for managing partner(s) with special authority.

Liabilities of partnership (joint partners) bind individual partners for equal parts, as far as claims of creditors of partnership are concerned, unless contract has specified liability of individual partners. No liability of partnership exists if engaged in by partner outside scope of his authority.

Vennootschap onder firma, abbreviated "v.o.f." is "maatschap" created for joint conduct of business under common style. Each partner to v.o.f. is jointly and severally liable towards third parties and each partner individually binds co-partner(s) within scope of its object and of limitations of powers registered. Its formation must be embodied in written instrument, not necessarily executed before notary. Absence of instrument cannot be held out against third party. V.o.f. must be registered in Trade Register and limitations of powers of acting partner cannot be invoked by other partner(s) against third party if they are not evident from registration. According to case law creditors of partnership have priority over creditors of individual partners with respect to recourse against common assets.

Commanditaire Vennootschap, abbreviated "C.V." is "maatschap" created for conduct of business under common style if one or more partners abstain from activities in conduct of business. Such silent partner's liability is limited to amount of his contribution but any activity on his part may make him jointly and severally liable with active partner(s). If there is more than one active partner, relationship between these partners is governed by provisions related to v.o.f.

See also topics Associations; Corporations; Trade Register; Trusts.

PATENTS:

Obtainment of Patents.—Patents valid for Netherlands may be obtained through national filing of application, or through filing application under European Patent Convention. In either case, filing may be made pursuant to Patent Co-operation Treaty.

Subjects for Which and Persons to Whom Patents are Granted.—Patent is granted for new and inventive industrial product or process. Excluded from patent protection are varieties of plants, animals and essentially biological processes, with exception of microbiological processes and products thereby obtained. Product or process is not new when it was either publicly accessible in any manner, prior to day on which patent application was filed, or was described in unpublished Netherlands, European or Patent Cooperation Treaty patent application, filed prior to date of application for patent, provided Netherlands is designated in such application when it is published. Priority of 12 months may be invoked for applications filed in country of Paris Convention.

Applicant is deemed to be inventor. However applicant is not entitled to patent in case: (a) He derived invention from another person; (b) he is employee, and invention falls within scope of his work; (c) product or process has been invented by several persons who have agreed to work together; (in this case, co-inventors may apply jointly).

Persons who may claim title to patent or application in applicant's place, in three instances just mentioned, have maximum of two years after date of grant of patent in which they may enter that claim. Rights of third parties acquired in good faith in meantime are protected if certain conditions are fulfilled.

Obtaining National Patent.—As of Apr. 1, 1995, system of national patent filing has been substantially amended.

Applications must be filed in Dutch. Foreign applicants must elect representative address at offices of authorized patent agent.

Applicant must indicate, within 13 months, whether novelty search is required. If applicant foregoes novelty search, patent can be registered immediately. Registration leads to automatic grant of patent. Patent thus granted has limited period of validity of six years after date of application.

If novelty search is duly requested and performed, patent is also granted upon registration. Registration takes place after 18 months, unless applicant requests registration to be effected sooner. In that case, grant of patent takes place after both registration and novelty search have been effected. Patent obtained in this manner has maximum validity of 20 years after application date.

New national patent system does not provide for material examination of application on its merits. In granting patent, Bureau for Industrial Property therefore gives no ruling on patentability of subject matter of application. Third parties are free to dispute patentability of that subject matter in Court.

European Patents.—European patent is patent granted by virtue of European Patent Convention. Netherlands may be designated by applicant as one of countries for which his European patent is to apply. Patent Act is generally applicable to European patents also, in case Netherlands are designated, and same rights devolve to European patent as to "Netherlands" patent, provided that translation into Dutch language of

PATENTS . . . *continued*
European patent has been filed with Bureau for Industrial Property within three months after publication of granting of European patent. Main branch of Munich European Patent Office is established in The Hague (Rijswijk). Patentee cannot hold national patent and European patent for same subject matter. In that instance, national patent becomes ineffective as soon as corresponding European patent is definitely granted.

Patent Rights, and Obligations of Patentee.—National patents may be valid for period of six years or 20 years from application date, depending on application procedure chosen by applicant; see subhead Obtaining National Patent, supra. European patents have maximum validity of 20 years from application date. Assignment of patent or patent application must be in writing. For effect against third parties, assignment must be registered at Bureau for Industrial Property.

Patentee has exclusive right: (a) To manufacture, use, put into circulation, or sell, lease out, supply or otherwise deal in or, for any of said purposes, to offer, import or to keep in stock patented product and (b) to apply patented process and to perform activities mentioned under (a) using product directly obtained as result of patented process. Patentee may also oppose sale or supply of non-infringing goods, if intended for infringing use. Excepted from exclusive right of patentee, and therefore permitted, are: (i) Use for purposes of study or experimentation only, (ii) use aboard foreign ships or in other means of transportation, and (iii) prior user right, for persons who already applied invention in Kingdom before patent application was filed. Scope of patent is determined by contents of its claims, description and drawings serving to explain such claims. Reference is made to Protocol on Interpretation of §69 of European Patent Convention.

Patentee can grant license orally or in writing. Written license registered with Bureau for Industrial Property is valid against third parties. Compulsory license may be granted by Minister of Economic Affairs when required by public interest, or by court in case: (i) of insufficient exploitation of patent, or (ii) license is needed for use of younger patent.

Damages can only be claimed in case infringer knew that he infringed patent. Writ served upon infringer serves as constructive knowledge. Instead of damages court may award profits derived from infringement.

For patented products put into circulation in Kingdom effective date of patent (i.e. publication of grant or decision to grant, depending on which procedure applies), patentee may claim reasonable compensation (but no more) if certain conditions are fulfilled.

Patent can be declared invalid only on grounds specifically mentioned in Patent Act. Most important ones are lack of novelty, lack of inventive merit, and insufficient disclosure of invention.

Chips.—As of Nov. 7, 1987, Netherlands law provides specific protection for semiconductor topographies. Protection is obtained by depositing topography with Bureau for Industrial Property. Deposit must be effected within two years after topography has first been put to use. Period of protection is ten years, or 15 years for topographies which have never been put to use or deposited.

Mask Works.—See subhead Chips, supra.

Treaties.—Netherlands have ratified, inter alia, following treaties: (a) Stockholm text Paris Convention for Protection of Industrial Property; (b) European Patent Convention; (c) Patent Cooperation Treaty.

PERPETUITIES:

Dutch law does not contain rule against perpetuities as such. However, property and each limited right over property shall always be transferable, unless this is specifically precluded by law or by nature of right. Dutch law specifically allows vesting of interest in property after life of certain person under device of Fidei-Commis (see topic Trusts).

PLEDGES:

Pledge is, like mortgage, right of property for purpose of securing priority payment in event that debtor fails to perform obligations. Pledge may be vested to secure present obligations of mortgagor or third pary, and future obligations as well.

Susceptible of pledging are movable properties, both corporeal and incorporeal.

Pledge on corporal property and bearer documents is created by pledgor giving up possession to pledgee or third party.

Pledge on corporeal property and bearer documents may also be created by notarial deed, or by private deed date of which is certified by its registration, without property is given in possession to pledgee or third party; in such case pledgee may request possession of assets as yet in case of default or imminent danger of default by pledgor (See topic Chattel Mortgages.)

Pledge on incorporeal assets (e.g. receivables and shares) is effected in same way as transfer of such assets to third party; this normally includes execution of notarial or private deed and acknowledgment by or service upon third party against whom such property right may be exercised. However, property right to be exercised against third party may be pledged without such acknowledgment or service, provided pledge is created by notarial deed or by private deed date of which is certified by its registration (so called undisclosed pledge). Pledge on registered shares is effected (like transfer of registered shares) by notarial deed.

Obviously, pledge with possession of pledged assets for pledgee, respectively pledge with acknowledgment by or service upon person against whom property right is to be exercised provides better security, but often it is necessary to keep pledgor in possession of pledged assets (e.g. when he needs such assets, like stock or inventory, for his business purposes), or it is not desirable to disclose pledge to third parties against whom incorporeal asset (e.g. receivables) is to be exercised.

Pledgee of receivable is authorized to cash such receivable when due and payable.

Foreclosure.—In case of default pledgee is entitled to sell pledged property without court proceedings by public auction; securities listed on stock exchange or assets negotiable on market (e.g. commodities) may be sold without public auction with intermediary of broker. Upon request of either pledgor or pledgee president of court may order that foreclosure is effected in another way; president may also rule at request of pledgee that pledged assets will remain with pledgee for amount to be determined by president of court.

Proceeds of sale of pledged property shall go in payment of debt secured by pledge and any balance is to be refunded to pledgor. Pledgee has priority over other creditors (but not always taxes).

Bankruptcy of pledgor or debtor does not affect pledgees right to foreclose.

See also topic Mortgages.

PRESCRIPTION:

See topic Limitation of Actions.

PRINCIPAL AND AGENT:

General.—Terms principal and agent relate to agency being legal situation in which person (agent) performs legal acts on behalf and in name of other person (principal). Agency occurs in many fields of law. Civil Code provides for set of rules on representation by proxy (volmacht), part of which also applies to other types of agency. Civil Code also contains rules on specific types of agency, such as representation of company by directors and representation of partnership by partners, mandate (lastgeving), intermediation (bemiddeling), and commercial agency (agentuur).

Proxy can be oral or in writing, express or implicit as part of function/job and can be general for all matters or for specific matter. Businesses have to register certain proxies at local commercial register. Principal is represented by agent generally only if agent expresses to third party that he acts in name of principal and acts within limits of proxy. If agent acts without proxy or exceeding his (registered) proxy principal is only bound if principal consents, or, exceptionally, if principal's conduct or other circumstances attributable to principal caused other party to believe that agent had adequate power to represent principal. Businesses are bound by agent acting within his registered proxy even if registration is incomplete or incorrect unless other party is aware of incompleteness or incorrectness.

Agent acting without or exceeding his proxy is liable for damages.

Agent acting in name of principal still to be nominated has to inform third party of principal's identity within reasonable time failing which he is deemed to have acted on his own behalf, unless contract provides otherwise. Agent may act as counterpart of principal only if proxy has been specified in such detail that conflict of interest cannot arise.

Granting proxy does not deprive principal of capacity to perform by himself acts covered by proxy.

Main grounds of expiration of proxy are: termination of employment or duties of agent; lapse of time or fulfilment of condition; revocation; death, bankruptcy or guardianship of agent or principal. Proxy for benefit of agent or third party can be irrevocable or continuing after death or guardianship of principal.

Commercial Agency.—Commercial agents are defined as independent contractors who agree to act as intermediary in conclusion of contracts for principal or to enter into contracts on behalf of and for account of principal during specified period or for indefinite period of time and for commission. Civil Code is in line with EC-Directive 86/653 of 31 Dec. 1986 on self-employed commercial agents. Civil Code contains some provisions designed to protect commercial agent, including obligation for principal to pay agent upon termination compensation of up to one year's commission (based on average of last five years) in case agent has developed business and has thereby substantially increased value of principal's business, provided compensation is reasonable considering circumstances, in particular loss of commission.

REAL PROPERTY:

Land, everything that grows on or has been built on land and everything permanently affixed to, or destined for permanent service of, real property is deemed real property. Other property is movable.

Conveyance of ownership of real property takes place by notarial deed, executed by parties and notary, and subsequent entry of authentic notarial copy thereof in Title and Mortgage Register for district where property is situated. Buyer usually pays notarial fees. Joint ownership is possible. Special rules apply to ownership of apartments. Other (less encompassing) rights in rem on real property than ownership, e.g. "erfdienstbaarheid" (easements and servitudes), "erfpacht" (long lease), "opstal" (right to own buildings etc. on other person's land), "vruchtgebruik" (usufruct, right to use and to enjoy fruits of other person's property), are established and transferred by entry of notarial deed in Title and Mortgage Register. Lease of real property is subject to strict statutory provisions, tending to protect the position of lessee. Different rules exist for lease of agricultural property, housing, shops and small enterprises, other buildings. (See topic Landlord and Tenant.) Owners, persons entitled to other rights in rem, and tenants have action based in tort against factual infractions of their rights by third parties (e.g. squatters).

Free disposition of real property is restricted in certain rural areas. Municipalities have preemptive rights in certain town areas. Strict legislation on land and country planning forbids establishment of buildings without permit and limits other use of land. Permit should be in accordance with municipal zoning and building regulations (on location of buildings and use thereof as well as technical requirements). Several environmental laws restrict use of real property.

Netherlands law does not contain restrictions on ownership of real property by foreigners. Expropriation of real property against full compensation by central or local government is possible under Expropriation Act. Decision to expropriate is made by separate Act or requires approval by Crown. Compensation is determined by normal courts.

See topic Actions. See also topics Landlord and Tenant; Licenses; Limitation of Actions; Mortgages; Records; Sales; Taxation.

RECORDS:

Register of births, marriages and deaths is kept by officer of civil status appointed by central government in each municipality. (1:16-29 B.W.). Population register held by municipal authorities contains addresses and other particulars of residents. (Act of Apr. 17, 1887, §67). Central register of wills held by Ministry of Justice contains

See Topical Index in front part of this volume.

RECORDS . . . *continued*
complete record of all wills made in the Netherlands. (Act of Feb. 23, 1918, §124). The Hague district court keeps register containing facts relating to guardianship ("curatele"; 1:391 B.W.). Marital property registers are kept at each district court. (1:116 B.W.). Registers with respect to custody over minors are kept by each cantonal court. ("voogdijregister"; 1:244 B.W.). Register of bankruptcies are held at each district court. (§19, Bankruptcy Act). Each of 39 chambers of commerce keeps following registers: (1) Trade register in respect of (a) all business establishments in its district including branch establishments irrespective of legal form of owner or operator, (b) any limited company or closely held company domiciled in its district, (c) any cooperative society, (d) any mutual insurance company; (2) register of associations comprising (a) any association with unlimited status of legal entity, (b) any other association which by registration wants to limit personal liability of its board members; (3) register of "Stichtingen" in which foundations are registered.

See topics Associations; Corporations; Law Reports, Codes, Etc., subhead Recodification of Civil and Commercial Codes; Motor Vehicles; Trade Register.

Title and Mortgage Register kept by local registrars of real estate and mortgages contains rather complete record of ownership and rights in rem (including life estate) of real estate. (3:16-31, 84, 89, 98, 260-267, 274, 275 BW). Description of parcels of land and maps ("Kadaster") are kept by same registrar. Ships registers held locally by government officials contain particulars about sea-going and river vessels and rights in rem on them including mortgages. (8:193, 197, 783, 788 BW). Register of Dutch aircrafts kept by Kadaster of Rotterdam. (Act registered aircrafts, §2). Register of Patents (Patents Act 1910) is kept by Bureau of Industrial Property at The Hague under 1910 Patent Act. Benelux Register of Trademarks is held at The Hague under new Trademark Act. Register of Designs is held by Benelux Design Register at The Hague under Uniform Benelux Act on Designs and Models. There is no public register of copyrights.

REPLEVIN:

See topic Attachment.

REPORTS:

See topic Law Reports, Codes, Etc.

RESTRAINT OF TRADE:

See topic Monopolies and Restraint of Trade.

SALES:

B.W. Book 3, Title 2 and Book 6, Title 5 contain general provisions for conclusion and nullification of sales agreements. Book 7, Title 1 contains specific rules for sales agreements, which provide extended protection for consumer-buyer against professional seller ("consumenten-koop", i.e. consumer sales) as well as specific remedies in case of default for buyer and seller respectively.

Notarial deed, required for conveyance of ownership in case of sale of real property and registered vessels, is generally drafted to include all terms and conditions of sale. Hence, informal contract of sale preceding conveyance deed is generally, but misleadingly, referred to as "voorlopig koopcontract" (provisional purchase contract), although it is fully binding contract.

Sales agreement does not itself transfer ownership but creates obligation for seller to deliver sold goods and transfer ownership and for purchaser to pay price.

Under contract of sale without fixed price, buyer is obligated to pay reasonable price, as generally stipulated by seller. Unless agreed otherwise, price must be paid on delivery.

Unless otherwise agreed, costs of delivery are to be paid by seller, costs of collection of purchased goods, costs of deed of sale and costs of conveyance by buyer.

Buyer carries risk of loss of or damage to purchased goods from moment of delivery, unless he rescinds agreement or on valid grounds demands replacement of goods. If buyer does not cooperate with delivery, risk is transferred at moment of his default. But in case of fungible nonindividualized goods ("genuskoop"), risk is only transferred to buyer if seller has individualized goods and notified buyer thereof.

Remedies for non- or malperformance are generally alike for sales agreements and contracts in general. Delivered goods must be in conformity with what buyer may have reasonably expected on basis of agreement. Buyer must notify seller of difference with due speed after discovery. Buyer's claim regarding nonconformity expires two years after notification.

In case of nonconformity, buyer may demand: (a) delivery of any deficiencies, (b) repair of delivered goods, (c) replacement of delivered goods unless not warranted by too slight difference or goods are damaged by buyer's negligence, (d) damages (other than consequential damages) and (e) (under general contract law:) rescission of agreement. Seller is only liable for consequential damages if he knew of defect or guaranteed its absence. In case of consumer sales, professional seller may under (b) or (c) choose between repair (replacement) and restitution of purchase price to consumer-buyer.

In case of buyer's default in paying agreed price for purchase of delivered moveable non-registered goods, seller may revindicate goods by written notification to buyer, by which agreement is rescinded. Seller does not have this right if six weeks have passed since right to payment of purchase price has become enforceable and 60 days have passed since delivery of purchased goods to buyer.

In case of buyer's bankruptcy, same rule applies if trustee has failed to pay purchase price or provide security within reasonable time fixed by seller. Rule does not apply when ownership of goods has been transferred (other than gratis) to third party who did not reasonably have to expect that right of revindication would be exercised.

International sales of goods (Moveables)—Treaty of Vienna, Apr. 11, 1980 (ICSG) applies to international sales of moveable goods regardless of nationality of parties. Applicable (a) on contracts between parties having their habitual residences within different member-states or (b) when pursuant to general rules of international private law, law of one of member-states is applicable between parties.

Application of Treaty as from Jan. 1, 1992, replacing Uniform law on international sale of goods, adopted by Hague Treaty of July 1, 1964.

Sale with Payment by Instalments and Hire-Purchase.—Special provisions exist concerning "koop op afbetaling" (sale with payment by instalments), i.e., contract of purchase and sale at which parties have agreed that purchase price shall be paid in instalments, two or more of which shall become due after delivery of good to purchaser and "huurkoop" (hire purchase), i.e., contract of sale with payment by instalments at which parties have agreed that ownership of sold good shall not pass to purchaser by mere delivery of good, but only after buyer has paid all instalments.

Applicable Law.—Same rules apply as to contracts in general. Place where contract is concluded is not dominant factor. In absence of expressed or implied will of parties other factors like habitual residence of party performing most characteristic obligation may carry more weight.

Hague Treaty of Dec. 22, 1986, on conflict of law rules applicable on international contracts of sale, which is intended to be complement of Treaty of Vienna, Apr. 11, 1980 (ICSG), has not been ratified by Netherlands, although Netherlands is one of signatories. Reason is possible conflict and ambiguities in relation to Convention on the Law Applicable to Contracts and Obligations (Rome, June 19, 1980) which came into force for Netherlands on Sept. 1, 1992.

SEALS:

Dutch law does not provide for use of private seals.

SECURITIES:

The Act on the Supervision of the Securities Trade ("Wet toezicht effectenverkeer 1995") was amended effective Dec. 31, 1995 to implement Investment Services Directive (EC/93/22) and Capital Adequacy Directive (EC/93/6). Act defines "securites" as including shares, depository receipts, warrants, bonds, debentures, "futures" traded on exchange, options and similar rights.

Act contains provisions relating to:

(1) Offering of Securities.—First public issue in or from within The Netherlands is allowed only if securities are (to be) listed at authorized stock exchange in The Netherlands, or if certain information is made available, or if relevant securities consist of participations in investment institution registered in accordance with Act on supervision of investment institutions except with exemption or permission.

(2) Acting as Securities Intermediary or Portfolio Manager (collectively "Securties Institutions").—Except with exemption or permission, public offering or performing of services as securities intermediary or portfolio manager in or from within The Netherlands is prohibited.

This does not apply to performance of services as securities intermediary or portfolio manager by certain insurance companies, finance companies, investment institutions, credit institutions and securities institutions making use of "European passport", as specified in Act.

(3) Interests in Securities Institutions.—Except after consent of Minister of Finance it is prohibited to acquire, maintain or increase qualified interest (i.e. direct or indirect interest of 5% or more of shares or votes) in securities institution.

Securities institution concerned notifies Minister of Finance annually of persons or entities holding qualified interest, and has to notify Minister of Finance forthwith of any changes in such interest under or above 5, 10, 20, 33 or 50%.

(4) Organisation of Stock-Exchange.—Except after recognition by Minister of Finance it is prohibited to organise stock exchange in The Netherlands.

Act is accompanied by several decrees and further regulations, giving more detailed rules and describing several general exemptions to rules referred to above. In practice one of most significant of those exemptions regards exemption of prohibition described above under (1) in case offering of securities or services as intermediary or portfolio manager is made to professional traders or investors.

It should be noted that issue of debentures and other debt instruments in addition to provisions of Act on Supervision of Securities Trade, is subject to provisions of §82 of Act on Supervision of Credit System 1992 as well. Except from licenced banks and certain other institutions, it is prohibited for anyone to address public for purpose of raising money in ordinary course of business. Minister of Finance can give exemption or permission from this prohibition. Minister of Finance has given general exemption, by decree of Dec. 23, 1992, if debentures are denominated in amount larger than NLG 100,000 (or equivalent in other currency) or if it regards debentures that are issued in accordance with Act on Supervision of the Securities Trade.

Act on Supervision of Investment Institutions ("Wet toezicht beleggingsinstellingen").—Act prohibits soliciting or obtaining money or other goods as participation in investment institution that has not been licensed, or to offer participations in such investment institution, in or from within The Netherlands. Depending on form of investment institution: (i) investment company, (ii) investment fund, (iii) institution for collective investment in securities (referred to in EC Directive 611/85) based in The Netherlands, (iv) institution for collective investment in securities (referred to in EC Directive 611/85) based in other Member State of European Union, or in State which is party to Agreement on the European Economic Area, rules applicable to investment institutions vary.

Act Regarding Savings Certificate ("Wet inzake spaarbewijzen").—Act defines "spaarbewijzen" (Savings Certificates) as debt instruments to bearer on which no interest will be payable during term of instrument. Pursuant to par. 3 of Act transfer and acceptance of Savings Certificates, e.g., "commercial paper", is prohibited unless it is done through intermediary of either issuer of Savings Certificates or member of Amsterdam Stock Exchange.

Prohibition does not apply to transfer and acceptance by natural persons not acting in conduct of business or profession. Act does not apply to initial issue of Savings Certificates to first holder thereof. Act, however, may be applicable to subsequent sales and transfers of Savings Certificates by first and any subsequent holder. Act will not apply to transfer of Savings Certificates which takes place outside The Netherlands, provided that neither transferor nor transferee are residents or nationals of The Netherlands.

See Topical Index in front part of this volume.

SECURITIES . . . *continued*

The Act on Notification of Control in a Company Listed on the Exchange ("Wet melding zeggingschap in ter beurze genoteerde vennootschappen").—Natural or legal person who acquires or transfers shares in capital of company and who knows—or ought to know—that he has thereby acquired or transferred percentage of at least 5, 10, 25, 50 or 66⅔% of all of voting rights pertaining to issued share capital of that company is obligated to notify company and Minister of Finance thereof forthwith. Same holds if above mentioned situation results from establishment of termination of right of pledge or usufruct on shares in capital of company. Natural or legal person who acquires or transfers shares or certificates in capital of company and who knows—or ought to know—that he thereby holds or transfers interest of at least 5, 10, 25, 50 or 66⅔% of issued share capital of company is obligated to notify company and Minister of Finance thereof forthwith.

See topic Corporations, subhead Issuance of Stock.

SHIPPING:

§§8:160-740 jk B.W. sets forth maritime law legislation concerning merchant shipping, carriage of goods and persons by sea, collisions at sea, assistance and salvage, general average and limitation of liability and time limitation of claims. Legislation elaborated in decrees and regulations. Significant distinctions made between deep-sea and inland shipping. §§8:170-951 gk B.W. covers same subjects for inland shipping. Maritime law is not administered by special courts except in prize cases, of which Supreme Court has jurisdiction as prize court.

In Netherlands, maritime law, central figure is "reder", person using ship for deep-sea navigation (irrespective of whether he is owner or not) and either is master himself or one in whose service master is. In most cases "reder" and owner of vessel are same, but where owner is not "reder", owner in principle is not liable, provided always that claims arising out of exploitation of vessel are recoverable on vessel. (§8:215 ff B.W.).

Certain claims such as those arising out of labour contacts of master and crew, salvage fees, pilot fees, port, dock and canal, and other shipping does as well as claims on account of collision are deemed to have priority in relation to vessel even over ship's mortgage (or pledge). Certain priorities expire when vessel starts new voyage. (§8:210 ff B.W.).

Lien on cargo in favour of carrier is null and void. Carrier may, however, for as long as discharge of goods has not been completed, request that surety is provided for whatever is due to him on account of freight and/or contribution to general average. (§8:489 B.W.).

Netherlands party to: International convention on Bills of Lading of Brussels (1924) (as well as the modifications of 1968); International convention on collision between vessels of Brussels (1910); International convention on assistance and salvage of Brussels (1910); International convention on immunity of state owned ships of Brussels (1934); International convention on arrest of seagoing ships of Brussels (1952); International convention on limitation of liability of owners of seagong vessels (Brussels, 1957); International convention on collision in inland navigation (Geneva, 1960); Convention on civil liability for oil pollution (Brussels, 1969); Convention on establishment of international Fund for compensation of oil pollution damage (Brussels, 1971); York-Antwerp Rules 1950 and 1974.

STATUTE OF FRAUDS:

See topic Frauds, Statute of.

STATUTES:

See topic Law Reports, Codes, Etc.

TAXATION:

Most important taxes—all taxes on income, in particular—are levied on national level. There are taxes though which are levied by municipalities or other nonnational entities. Real estate tax is most important of these local taxes. Hereunder follows survey of national taxes which are of primary importance.

Personal income tax (inkomstenbelasting) based on Personal Income Tax Act of 1964. Individuals are taxed on income from certain sources, most important being: business or profession, employment and capital.

Capital gains in general are not taxed unless they are part of business or professional income. There is tax, however, on capital gains on "substantial share holdings".

Personal income tax is levied on progressive scale up to 60% which percentage is reached for parts of taxable amount above Dfl. 92,773 (1996).

Personal deductions depend, among others, on marriage, sharing household with another person or other persons, children's allowance. There are special rates in certain cases e.g., on occasion of discontinuation of business.

Subject to tax are residents of Netherlands and nonresidents but latter only on basis of certain income earned in Netherlands, in particular from Netherlands business or employment or from real estate in Netherlands.

Residents are taxed on their world-wide income. There is practice of tax authorities to allow certain foreigners working in Netherlands for foreign companies tax-free 35% allowance included in agreed salary during first ten years of their employment.

Corporate income tax (vennootschapsbelasting) based on Corporation Tax Act of 1969. Subject to tax are companies and certain other entities which are established or residing in Netherlands. Companies and certain other entities not established in Netherlands are taxed on account of certain income from Dutch sources, in particular, Dutch permanent establishment and real estate.

Corporate income is taxed at rate of 37% of first Dfl. 100,000, and 35% for excess. Rate of 37% may be decreased in near future to 35%.

Dividends received from another company (whether or not established in Netherlands), are in principle exempt from corporate income tax by virtue of participation exemption (deelnemingsvrijstelling). Most important conditions for application of participation exemption are following. In principle, recipient should hold at least 5% of shares of payor company. Foreign payor should be subject to income tax. Shares in foreign company should not be held as portfolio investment and generally not as inventory, except participation of at least 25% of shares or votes in company residing in member state of European Union.

Withholding Taxes.—Employer is obligated to withhold Wage Tax (loonbelasting) on wages paid to his employees. Tax is levied on basis of Wage Tax Act of 1964. Tax in principle is preliminary levy of personal income tax due by employee but for great majority of employees with no income from other sources tax in practice is final levy.

Company when distributing dividends has to withhold Dividend Tax (dividendbelasting). Tax is preliminary levy of personal or corporate income tax. Normal rate is 25%. Rate is lowered to percentages between 25 and nil by number of tax treaties. In certain situations exemption is granted.

There are no withholding taxes on other types of income, to wit, in particular, interest income or royalties (except for interest on profit sharing bonds).

Property tax (vermogensbelasting), levied under Property Tax Act of 1964. Individuals are taxed on their assets less liabilities as valued at beginning of year. There are number of assets which are exempted and there is certain amount tax exempt. Rate is 0.8%.

Turnover Tax (omzetbelasting).—Tax is levied under Turnover Tax Act of 1968. Act follows tax on value added system, obligatory in European Union under Sixth VAT Directive. Tax is due on importation of goods from outside EU, on acquisition by VAT-registered companies and legal entities of goods from other EU-countries, and on sale of goods and rendering of services in Netherlands. Tax is levied by tax authorities from importer, acquirer, seller or person or company rendering service (except in certain cases where such person is nonresident while purchaser/client is resident). In turn, such persons may invoice tax to purchasers/clients. Purchasers/clients at their turn may deduct on their turnover tax returns amounts so invoiced to them (or claim restitution thereof), if goods were delivered to them or services rendered to them in connection with their business (unless they perform so-called exempted services, including financial services). Foreign companies can appoint fiscal representative to fulfil Netherlands VAT-obligations. Regarding mail order firms specific provision applies. Final consumers cannot ask for deduction or restitution, except in certain cases of exportation. They finally bear tax burden. According to bill place where service is rendered will more often be at residence of client.

Ordinary turnover tax rate is 17.5%. There is reduced rate of 6% and reduced rate of nil. Registration of cars and motor vehicles is taxed with special motor vehicles tax.

Netherlands VAT is also due on purchase of new media of transportation (e.g. cars, pleasure boats) which are acquired from other EU Member States by individual persons who are resident in Netherlands.

Inheritance and gift tax (successierecht, schenkingsrecht and recht van overgang), based on Act of 1956 as substantially amended effective 1985. Tax is levied from heirs and other beneficiaries wherever they reside, of estate which belonged to person who was resident of Netherlands at time of his death. Dutch national is deemed to have had residence in Netherlands at time of his death if he had such residence within period of ten years before his death. Rates progress depending on degree of consanguinity and on amount inherited. There are exempted amounts based, also, on degree of consanguinity. Same rules apply to gift tax. Transfer of Dutch real estate by gift or death of nonresident is also subject to tax at regular rates. For purpose of gift tax, foreigner is deemed to have had residence in Netherlands at time of gift if he had such residence within one year of gift.

Miscellaneous.—Transfer tax (overdrachtsbelasting) is levied on transfer of real estate. Rate is 6%. Capital tax (kapitaalsbelasting) of 1% is levied on capital contributions to company. There are, of course, number of customs and excise duties. (See topic Customs.) There are also several pollution and other environmental levies. Stamp tax does not exist anymore. Stock exchange tax is abolished effective July 1, 1990.

Prevention of International Double Taxation.—in order to prevent, to certain extent, international double taxation, there is unilateral Decree on Prevention of Double Taxation (Besluit voorkoming dubbele belasting). Further, Netherlands are party to double taxation treaties concluded with many countries (among which, USA).

Netherlands Antilles.—Tax rates are low in Netherlands Antilles in number of cases. Act of 1964 (Belastingregeling voor het Koninkrijk) is aimed to prevent double taxation between Netherlands Antilles and Netherlands. Act was amended during 1985, in particular with respect to intercompany dividends.

For some more information on Netherlands Antilles, see topics Constitution and Government; Corporations.

TRADEMARKS:

Benelux Trademark Act (BTA).—On Jan. 1st, 1971, BTA entered into force. As of said date trademark laws of The Netherlands, Belgium and Luxembourg have been unified and one territory, as far as trademarks are concerned, has been created. BTA has been revised to conform with EC directive on harmonization of trademark law. As of Jan. 1, 1996, new BTA has entered into force.

National courts are competent in matters involving BTA, (arbitration is effectively excluded), but courts may refer to Benelux Court questions of interpretation of BTA.

Trademarks.—Any symbol distinguishing goods or (since Jan. 1st, 1987) services of enterprise can be trademark, with exception of shapes, if such shapes are determined by very nature of goods, produce technical result or influence essential value.

Right to trademark is acquired by registration and is valid for those goods or services for which trademark filed is registered. Unregistered trademarks are not protected and no infringement action based on unregistered trademark can be instituted. Registration of attachment or pledge of trademark is possible. Date of filing and not date of registration of trademark is decisive for moment right to trademark is acquired. Benelux Trademarks Office (branches in The Hague, Brussels, Luxembourg) may refuse to register sign if it does not meet legal definition of trademark (especially in case of lack of any distinctive character). In The Netherlands, appeal against refusal may only be filed with Court of Appeals of The Hague (within two months).

Correspondence address in Benelux is required. Trademark right remains valid for ten year periods, renewable indefinitely against payment of filing and renewal fees.

See Topical Index in front part of this volume.

TRADEMARKS . . . *continued*

Cancellation and Loss of Right.—Nullity of trademark registration (ex tunc) can be invoked on grounds enumerated in BTA, such as (i) complete lack of distinctiveness, (ii) misleading character, (iii) conflict with prior registration, (iv) filing was effected in bad faith. Right to trademark ceases to exist (ex nunc) inter alia (i) in case of nonuse during uninterrupted period of five years (but in general, this nonuse may be repaired if use has been resumed before relevant legal action has been brought); (ii) in case trademark has become generic through fault of proprietor (including acquiescence); (iii) in case of voluntary withdrawal or nonrenewal of registration.

Infringement.—Proprietor of trademark may oppose following kinds of use in economic intercourse: (i) any use of trademark for goods/services for which it has been registered; (ii) any use of trademark or corresponding sign for registered goods/services or similar goods/services, if this entails possibility of association between marks; (iii) any use, without valid reason of trademark known within Benelux, or of corresponding sign, for goods/services not similar to those for which trademark has been registered, if such use may entail unjustified benefit or other effect detrimental to trademark; (iv) any use of trademark or corresponding sign without valid reason, made not to distinguish goods/services, if such use entails unjustified benefit or other effect detrimental to trademark.

If proprietor of trademark accepts trademark infringement during at least five years, as general rule, he runs risk of losing his right of action (acquiescence).

Assignment and License.—Assignment of trademark must be in writing; for license of trademark no written statement is required. To have effect against third parties, assignment and license must be recorded in trademark register. Assignment need not be in conjunction with business in which trademark was used. Licensee has right to intervene in certain proceedings, instituted by proprietor, in order to claim compensation for damages directly sustained by him.

Collective trademark is symbol designated as such when filed, and distinguishing common features of goods/services from enterprises, which enterprises use trademark with consent and under control of proprietor. Together with trademark, regulation must be filed, setting out conditions for use, stating common features of goods/services which trademark guarantees, and specifying measures of control to be applied. In general, collective trademarks are subject to same rules as stated above.

Counterfeit.—Infringing goods and also materials used in production of infringing goods may be seized and claimed as property by trademark proprietor, or alternatively, proprietor may sue for destruction. These claims will be denied if infringement was not made in bad faith. Since Jan. 1st, 1993, comparable measures could be based on Anti-Counterfeiting Act. Infringer may be compelled to provide information concerning infringement.

Parallel Imports.—Exhaustion of rights is limited to European Union.

Treaties.—The Netherlands have ratified, inter alia, Paris Convention and Madrid Agreement.

TRADENAMES:

(Tradename Act entered into force Oct. 14, 1922, as am'd).

Use of name identical or similar to name or trademark which is already used by another enterprise is prohibited, if such use would confuse public. Assignment of tradename apart from enterprise is not allowed. Right to tradename is acquired by public use thereof, which need not be use in Netherlands. Foreign tradenames therefore are protected in Netherlands if name acquires reputation in this country and confusion would thus arise. Registration of tradename in Commercial Register not prerequisite for protection.

TRADE REGISTER:

(Trade Register Act of July 26, 1918 as am'd).

Trade Register is held by chambers of commerce. Enterprises which are established or have branch or agent authorized to contract in Netherlands or which are owned by legal entity established or with statutory seat in Netherlands must be registered with trade register held by chamber of commerce of district where enterprise, branch or agent is established.

Any limited company (N.V.), private company with limited liability (B.V.), cooperative society and mutual insurance company with statutory seat in Netherlands must be registered whether or not they have enterprise, branch or agent in Netherlands.

Particulars of and documents relating to enterprises, or legal entity must be filed on application to trade register, such as tradename used by enterprise, legal form of owner, directors if owner is legal entity, holders of proxy, agents, names of supervisory directors. All subsequent changes and additions must be registered within one week after changes or additions have occurred.

Third parties may rely in good faith on information and documents filed with trade register. Enterprise or legal entity may not prove inaccuracy or incompleteness of any such information or documents against third party who is ignorant of inaccuracy or incompleteness.

Responsible for supplying data for registration is owner or all co-owners of enterprise or if owner is legal person, any member of its managing board or person authorized by written power of attorney. If enterprise in Netherlands (e.g., branch establishment) is owned by nonresident natural or legal person, resident person in charge of daily management of Dutch enterprise is responsible as well. If foreign enterprise has no office or other establishment in Netherlands but is represented by agent in Netherlands having authority to bind owner by his act or signature, agent is also responsible for supplying data for registrations.

Supply of incorrect or incomplete data is penal offence with sanction of imprisonment or fine.

See topics Associations; Corporations; Law Reports, Codes, Etc.; Partnership; Records.

TREATIES:

Treaties become effective after explicit or tacit approval by parliament.

Self-executing provisions of treaties prevail over national acts and regulations.

Number of treaties to which Netherlands is party is too large to list. Some are mentioned where subject-matter is dealt with in this Digest. See topics Affidavits; Aircraft; Bills and Notes; Courts; Customs; Designs; Marriage; Monopolies and Restraint of Trade; Patents; Sales; Shipping; Taxation; Trademarks; Trade Register.

Treaties for reciprocal recognition and enforcement of foreign judgments are stated in topic Judgments under subhead Foreign Judgments.

Other examples are: United Nations Convention on Recognition and Enforcement of Foreign Arbitral Awards, signed at New York on June 10, 1958, Trb. 1959–5B ratified by Act of Oct. 14, 1963 Stb. 417, operative as from July 23, 1964; Convention on Service Abroad of Judicial and Extrajudicial Documents in Civil or Commercial Matters signed at The Hague on Nov. 15, 1965. Trb. 1966-91, ratified by Act of Jan. 8, 1975, Stb. 4, operative as from Jan. 2, 1976, Stb. 1976 by virtue of Royal Administrative Decree of Dec. 17, 1975, Stb. 693; Convention on Taking of Evidence Abroad in Civil or Commercial Matters signed at The Hague on Mar. 18, 1970; Trb. 1979–38, ratified by Act of Dec. 11, 1980, Stb. 652, operative as from June 7, 1981; Treaty of The Hague of Oct. 5, 1961 (Convention Abolishing the Requirement of Legalisation for Foreign Public Documents, "Apostille"). Trb. 1963, 28, ratified by Act of Mar. 10, 1965, Stb. 10.4, operative as from Oct. 8, 1965.

International Sale of Goods.—United Nations Convention of Contracts for the International Sale of Goods, in force on Jan. 1, 1992. See topic Sales and Part VII, Selected International Conventions.

TRUSTS:

Dutch law does not provide for trusts. However, for number of purposes for which Anglo-American trusts are being used analogous or similar devices are available, e.g.:

Fidei-Commis.—Subject to provisions in respect of forced heirship (see topic Wills) parents may provide in will that their estate will vest in child for life and thereafter in child's children (not necessarily born at time of testator's death), or that their estate will vest in brother/sister for life and thereafter in brother's/sister's children (not necessarily born at time of testator's death). In general child will be under obligation to keep estate together for grandchildren of testator.

Fidei-Commis de Residuo.—Subject to forced heirship provisions, any testator may provide in will that whatever heir will have received from his estate and will be left at time of death of heir will not devolve on his heirs but will be acquired by one or more persons (living at time of testator's death) designated in testator's will, or after such person's earlier death, will be acquired by such person's children, not necessarily born at time of testator's death. Heir has no obligation to preserve estate but may not dispose of by will; testator may determine that heir may not dispose of estate by donation inter vivos.

Administration ("bewind").—Subject to forced heirship provisions testator may provide that his estate or part thereof will be administered by administrator ("bewindvoerder") for specific period of time or during lifetime of heir.

Foundations ("stichting") are created by notarial deed (inter vivos or testamentary). They may be used for social, cultural, scientific or charitable purposes. Foundations also used to acquire capital stock of corporations against issue of depository receipts representing such stock to former stockholders who remain beneficiaries of such stock and continue to be entitled to dividends. Voting powers, however, will be exercised by foundation board. See also topics Corporations, subhead Rights of Shareholders and of Holders of Depositary Receipts Issued with Cooperation of Company; Foundations.

Trust by Agreement.—Exercise of certain rights under agreement may be conferred by parties to third party, "trustee", e.g., exercise of rights attached to bonds by trustee on behalf of all bondholders.

Fiduciaries.—Assets may be transferred to fiduciary acquiring legal title thereto. Fiduciary holds assets for beneficiaries as designated by fiduciary agreement and will distribute (net) revenues or transfer assets itself to beneficiary under conditions set forth in fiduciary agreement. It is not possible for fiduciary to designate beneficiaries at its own discretion (exception: foundation, but only for social and charitable purposes; see subhead Foundations, supra).

Foreign Trusts.—The Netherlands have signed and ratified The Hague Convention of 1986 on Trust, which has entered into force for the Netherlands on Feb. 1, 1996. If trust has been created which fulfils criteria of convention, it shall be recognized by Dutch courts.

See topics Descent and Distribution; Perpetuities; Wills.

WILLS:

Testamentary Capacity.—Wills made by minors under 16 and by persons of unsound mind are invalid. If spouses are married in community of property each spouse may dispose of undivided one-half of community property (see topic Husband and Wife).

Capacity to Benefit.—Any person benefiting from will must be living at time of testator's death. For exception, see topic Trusts.

Forced Heirship.—Testator may leave relatives entitled as legal heirs by force of law to certain portions of his estate, in which case testator cannot freely dispose of all of his estate. Only descendents are legal heirs, but only if they would have been heirs in case of intestacy.

Following parts of estate are reserved for legal heirs: if there is only one child: one-half of intestate portion of such child, if there are two children: two-thirds of their intestate portion, if there are three or more children: three-quarters of their intestate portion.

Descendents of predeceased children take per stirpes. Dispositions by will or even by gifts inter vivos made in contravention of forced heirship rules are valid, but may be reduced on demand by legal heirs. Surviving spouse and other interstate heirs may be excluded from estate in will either by express provision or by implication.

See Topical Index in front part of this volume.

WILLS . . . *continued*

Forms of Wills:

Notarial Wills.—Practically all wills are made in this form: testator describes his intention which is put in writing by notary and signed by testator in presence of notary and two witnesses, acknowledging signatures, execution, date and contents of will.

Mystic or Secret Will.—Testator draws up will himself and hands it, under sealed cover, to notary in presence of four witnesses stating that cover contains his last will. Protocol is drawn up by notary and written on outer covering and signed by testator, notary and witnesses.

Holographic Will.—Testator writes will himself in longhand and hands it, either open or under sealed cover, to notary in presence of two witnesses. Protocol is drawn up by notary on holographic will itself or on cover and signed by testator, notary and witnesses.

Codicil.—A few dispositions may be made by so-called "codicil" without intervention of notary; unlike what name codicil suggests it need not necessarily be supplemental to another will made earlier. Dispositions which may be made by codicil include: Legacies of specific jewelry or furniture and appointment of executor (see topic Executors and Administrators). Other assets like cash, real property, securities, claims etc. may not be bequeathed by codicil, neither may heirs be appointed by such instrument.

Codicils must be written in longhand, dated and executed by testator; witnesses are not required.

Oral wills are not valid.

Mutual wills, or wills executed in one instrument by two or more persons in favour of third party, are invalid.

Netherlands is party to Hague Convention of 1961 on conflicts of laws relating to form of testamentary dispositions (U.S. not signatory).

Revocation.—Will is by its definition revocable and any contracts which restrict freedom to amend or revoke will are null and void. Revocation must be in form of subsequent will or by special instrument drawn up by notary. Subsequent will which does not contain other provisions than revocation results in intestacy (see topic Descent and Distribution). Subsequent will which does not contain express revocation clause cancels in prior will only such provisions as are incompatible with those contained in subsequent will. Will made by individual being single is not annulled or revoked automatically by subsequent marriage.

Annulment.—Upon death of testator will may be annulled by court at suit of any interested party on grounds that it is defective in form or that testator was incapable or on plea that is was made through coercion or fraud.

Central Registry of Wills.—Notary is under legal obligation to give notice of any will drawn up by or deposited with him to Central Register of Wills. This notice does not specify contents of will, but merely fact that will was made and by whom. Upon death of testator Registar will inform (usually through intermediary of notary) interested parties on their request of existence of will and of name of notary in whose custody original of will is kept.

Probate.—See topic Descent and Distribution, subhead Determination of Heirship. See also topic Consuls.

NEW ZEALAND LAW DIGEST REVISER

Bell Gully Buddle Weir
Post Office Box 1291
I.B.M. Centre
171 Featherston Street
Wellington, New Zealand
Telephone: 64 4 473 7777
Fax: 64 4 473 3845
Internet Home Page: http://www.bgbw.co.nz
Auckland Office: The Auckland Club Tower, 34 Shortland Street, PO Box 4199.
Telephone: 64 9 309 0859. Fax: 64 9 309 3312. Internet Home Page: http://www.bgbw.co.nz
Manukau Office: Parkview Tower, 28 Davies Avenue, PO Box 76-333, Manukau City.
Telephone: 64 9 262 1979. Fax: 64 9 262 2045. Internet Home Page: http://www.bgbw.co.nz

Reviser Profile

Bell Gully Buddle Weir was formed by the merger in 1984 of Buddle Weir & Co of Auckland (1840) and Bell Gully & Co of Wellington (1860). Bell Gully & Co was appointed as Martindale-Hubbell Reviser for the 1939 edition which was the first year the New Zealand Digest was published. That firm and subsequently the merged firm of Bell Gully Buddle Weir has continued as Reviser. Today, Bell Gully is one of New Zealand's leading corporate law firms and acts for leading New Zealand publicly listed companies, the business and commercial sectors, government agencies, banking, insurance and financial institutions.

Bell Gully provides comprehensive assistance in foreign markets as well as advice to overseas investors and migrants seeking opportunities in New Zealand. The firm has strong international links spanning Australia, Asia, Canada, the United Kingdom, USA, Chile, Brazil and Argentina. Of particular importance has been the increasing focus of many of the firm's clients on the Asian region. In responding to this demand the firm has lawyers fluent in Mandarin, Korean and Indonesian dialects to complement Lex Asia, its directory and network of offshore law firms capable of representing its clients in their own country.

While proud of its past, the firm remains alert and committed to initiatives which will secure its future. In doing so it has concentrated its attention in two key areas—the expertise and commitment of its people and the quality of its service to and relationship with clients. Bell Gully's future performance is inextricably tied to excellence in both.

Areas of Practice:

Banking and Finance: The Banking and Finance group provides a comprehensive range of services to leading banks, sharebrokers, merchant and investment banks and other financial institutions, both in New Zealand and overseas.

Corporate and Commercial: Bell Gully works alongside many major companies providing commercially sound advice on all aspect of corporate and commercial law; from restructuring, mergers and joint ventures to flotations, investment, intellectual property and Maori incorporations.

Litigation: The firm's team of leading barristers and solicitors has a strong track record of successful dispute resolution across the full spectrum of commercial law. Bell Gully seeks to negotiate practical solutions as quickly as possible, avoiding protracted, costly litigation to arrive at commercial settlements.

Commercial Property: The Property group draws on multi-disciplinary skills in providing strategic advice to developers, investors and local authorities in commercial, industrial, rural and residential property transactions. The group advises on sale and purchase agreements, development project planning, leases and property management.

Tax: Bell Gully's tax lawyers advise on all aspects of New Zealand taxation, including tax litigation for corporations, local and national government entities. They also advise individuals in relation to both domestic and international transactions.

Special Interest Groups:

Underlying this broad grouping of expertise, the firm has developed a second tier of Special Interest Groups. These groups comprise teams of partners and senior staff who bring expertise in their core area to clearly defined industry sectors and other areas of commerce where detailed knowledge of the business environment is required.

Special Interest Groups encompass a wide range of commercial activity including Asian business, competition law and trade practices, computer industry and information technology, education, electricity sector, employment, energy sector, entertainment and sports law, environmental law and resource management, fishing, forestry, government relations, health, insurance, intellectual property, liquor and wine industry, Maori services, personal asset and tax planning, superannuation and telecommunications.

NEW ZEALAND LAW [illegible]

[illegible]

Wellington, New Zealand

[illegible]

Practice Profile

[illegible]

NEW ZEALAND LAW DIGEST

(The following is a list of all Topics, including cross-references, covered in this Digest.)

NEW ZEALAND LAW DIGEST

Revised for 1997 edition by

BELL GULLY BUDDLE WEIR of Auckland, Manukau and Wellington

ABSENTEES:

In absence abroad person may generally delegate authority to any person of full capacity or corporation by way of power of attorney. Power revoked upon donor becoming mentally incapable but power created under Protection of Personal and Property Rights Act 1988 will (if desired) endure after donor becomes mentally incapable. Power may be subject to conditions donor desires.

See also topic Taxation.

ACKNOWLEDGMENTS:

Execution of Instruments in New Zealand for Use Overseas.—Instrument executed in New Zealand for use overseas is commonly executed in presence of Notary Public or verified in his presence by person who witnessed execution of document (whether executed by individual or under seal of body corporate). In some cases (depending upon requirements of country in which instrument is to be used) execution or verification of signature and seal of Notary is authenticated by Internal Affairs Department with certificate to Ministry of Foreign Affairs and Trade which latter then certifies to diplomatic or consular representative of that country in New Zealand.

ACTIONS:

With some exceptions (e.g. defamation), on death of any person all causes of action subsisting against or vested in that person survive against or, as case may be, for benefit of estate.

Limitation of.—See topic Limitation of Actions.

Service of Foreign Process.—There are no special provisions for service of process of Commonwealth countries, and service may be effected under usual New Zealand Rules. Other foreign process is served by appropriate High Court by request transmitted through Secretary for Justice, unless convention is in force between New Zealand and country concerned, in which case application can be made, in standard form, to Registrar of the High Court at Wellington.

Proof of Foreign Law.—If it is considered by New Zealand Court that a foreign law is applicable to a particular dispute, that foreign law must be proved as question of fact. Evidence Act 1908, §39 allows receipt in New Zealand courts of official volumes of foreign statute law as prima facie proof of that law. Expert evidence is usually required.

ADMINISTRATION:

See topic Executors and Administrators.

ADOPTION:

Governed by Adoption Act 1955. Consent of all parents and guardians of child generally required. Consent of natural father may not be necessary if not married to child's mother at time of birth, not living with her in de facto relationship, and not involved with child since. Consent of parent or guardian dispensed with by Family Court in limited circumstances—unfit physically or mentally, abandoning child, neglecting child, persistent ill-treatment of child, persistent failure to maintain, failure to exercise duties and cares of parenthood. Consent can be subject to conditions as to religious denomination or practise.

Offence to give or receive payment or reward in consideration of adoption without consent of Court. Offence to publish advertisement indicating child available for adoption or that person desires to adopt or can make arrangements for adoption. Department of Social Welfare reports to Family Court on fitness of applicants and whether application will serve welfare of child.

Effect of adoption is that child deemed to be child of applicants as if born to them, and ceases to be child of natural parents for most legal purposes. Exceptions are in respect of forbidden degrees of marriage, nationality and race and citizenship, and any prior executed deed or will or intestacy or right thereunder.

New birth certificate issued for child. Any existing guardianship or maintenance or affiliation order ceases to have effect. Family Court reluctant to grant adoption if alternative arrangement (e.g. guardianship or custody order) will achieve same result without altering natural family relationships.

Adoption out of New Zealand, if legally valid according to laws of country where made, is deemed in New Zealand to have same effect as adoption made under Act in New Zealand.

Access to adoption records restricted. Adult Adoption Information Act 1985 gives limited rights of access to adopted person and birth parents, after referral to counselling. Adopted person or birth parent may place endorsement on file preventing access to identifying information.

AFFIDAVITS:

Affidavits of New Zealand court may be sworn in any Commonwealth country before any judge, court, notary public, commissioner of the High Court of New Zealand in that country, Commonwealth representative, or person lawfully authorised by laws of that country to administer oaths in that country. Where oath is taken by person or body other than Commonwealth Representative, that person or body must state in jurat or body of affidavit that he or it is lawfully authorised to administer oaths in country concerned.

In any other foreign country affidavit of New Zealand court may be sworn before any commissioner of the High Court of New Zealand, or before any Commonwealth representative exercising his functions in that country and allowed by laws of that country to administer oath. Where neither such commissioner nor Commonwealth representative is conveniently available in foreign country, affidavit may be sworn before any person lawfully authorised by laws of that country to administer oaths. In such cases affidavit should state that no such commissioner nor Commonwealth representative is conveniently available and that person taking oath is lawfully authorised to do so under local law. Court may require verification of authority.

There are no statutes allowing alternative to formal swearing although deponent may affirm rather than take oath.

See also topic Commissioners to Administer Oaths.

AGENCY: See topic Principal and Agent.

AIRCRAFT: See topic Carriage by Air.

ALIENS:

Restrictions on Ownership by Foreigners.—Subject to provisions of Overseas Investment Act 1973, Overseas Investment Regulations 1995 and Fisheries Act 1983, aliens may acquire, hold, and dispose of all real and personal property in New Zealand. Prior legislation restricting such dispositions, Land Settlement Promotion and Land Acquisition Act 1952 and Overseas Investment Regulations 1985, were repealed on Jan. 15, 1996.

Under overseas investment legislation, subject to certain exemptions, contracts for sale, leases for three years or more, and options for sale or lease, of land in New Zealand require prior consent by Minister of Finance and Minister of Lands, where: (a) purchaser, lessee or grantee not New Zealand citizen and not ordinarily resident in New Zealand, or is overseas company or body corporate, or is New Zealand company that is subsidiary of overseas company, or is New Zealand company controlled by overseas interests (each "overseas person"); and (b) where land is over 0.4 hectares and is part of certain islands, or contains or is next to reserves, historic or heritage areas, foreshore or lakes; or any land on other islands; or that together with any associated land exceeds five hectares or is worth $10,000,000 or more; or is any lake exceeding eight hectares in area.

Consent by Minister of Finance and Minister of Lands also required where overseas person acquires securities in any entity that owns or controls any land or interest in any estate in land (regardless of dollar value), that results in (A) land owning entity being owned or controlled by overseas persons or (B) overseas person acquiring 25% or more of ownership or control of land owning entity or increasing their ownership or control of land owning entity or increasing their ownership or control if overseas person already has 25% or more ownership or control.

Fisheries Act provides that no fishing quota be allocated to individual who is not ordinarily resident in New Zealand or to body corporate that is wholly or significantly controlled from outside New Zealand.

See topics Foreign Investment and Corporations.

Aliens are not qualified to enjoy parliamentary franchise or to own ship registered in New Zealand; but, provided they are not alien enemies, they may vote at municipal elections except where specifically disqualified by statute.

Rights of alien enemies are considerably restricted during the existence of a state of war.

See also topic Nationality.

Immigration.—New Zealand citizens have right to be in New Zealand at any time and do not require permit under Immigration Act 1987 to be or work in New Zealand. Persons other than New Zealand citizens may be in New Zealand only if such persons hold residence or temporary permit or are exempt under Act from requirement to hold permit. Persons other than New Zealand citizens may undertake employment in New Zealand if such persons hold residence permit, work permit or are holders of temporary permit giving authority to undertake employment or are exempt under Act from requirement to hold permit. No permit shall be granted to persons who: (a) Have been convicted at any time of any offence and sentenced to imprisonment for term of five years or more; (b) have been convicted within preceding ten years of any offence and sentenced to imprisonment for term of 12 months or more; (c) against whom removal order is in force; (d) have been previously deported from New Zealand or any other country; (e) are believed to have engaged in terrorism in New Zealand or are members of internal terrorist organisation; (f) are believed to have engaged in terrorism outside New Zealand or are members of international terrorist organisation; (g) are believed to be likely to engage in terrorism or commit offence against Crimes Act 1961 or Misuse of Drugs Act 1975.

Following persons are exempt from requirement to hold permit: (1) Persons on whom immunity is conferred by virtue of diplomatic status; (2) members of armed forces of any country, or crew of any craft used for transporting members of armed forces of any country to New Zealand, while: (i) members of that force are in New Zealand at request or with consent of Government of New Zealand, and (ii) members' presence in New Zealand is in ordinary course of members' duty or employment; (3) crew or passengers, on any seagoing craft carrying passengers or cargo in ordinary course of business and plying between any foreign place and New Zealand; (4) crew or passengers on any licensed foreign fishing craft; (5) crew on any commercial aircraft flying between any foreign place and New Zealand; (6) members or associates of any scientific programme or expedition of any contracting party to Antarctic Treaty within meaning of Antarctic Act 1960, or persons to whom §5 of that Act applies, while those members or persons are in Ross Dependency; (7) persons exempted by Mininster of Immigration by special direction; (8) classes of persons exempted under regulations made under Act. (Express time limits apply for circumstances set out in clauses (3), (4) and (5).)

Provision is made for deportation of persons threatening national security, suspected terrorists and certain non-New Zealand citizens if certain criminal convictions are entered against them. Persons falling within last category have right of appeal to special tribunal, while those ordered to be deported because of suspected terrorist activities or threat to national security have right of appeal to High Court.

See Topical Index in front part of this volume.

ALIENS . . . *continued*

In relation to persons suspected of being in New Zealand unlawfully, Act provides immigration officers with powers to require production of certain information, surrender of documents and application for removal order to be endorsed by District Court. Persons suspected of being in New Zealand unlawfully may be taken into custody by police and under removal order removed from New Zealand in certain specified circumstances. Persons named in removal order may appeal to Removal Review Authority.

Person applying for permanent entry permit may do so under general, business, family reunification or humanitarian categories. General category is assessed according to points system which allocates points to such factors as academic qualifications, relevant work experience and age. Full details of requirements under each category, and application forms, may be obtained from New Zealand Immigration Service, PO Box 4130, Wellington or from nearest New Zealand diplomatic post.

All persons entering New Zealand are required to produce on demand travel document (Passport or Certificate of Identity recognized by New Zealand Government).

See also topics Nationality; Corporations, subhead Foreign Corporations.

Corporations Owned or Controlled by Aliens.—Except as elsewhere indicated in this topic, there are no special provisions relating to corporations owned or controlled by aliens, as to issuing or raising of capital and as to filing of accounts. See topic Corporations. See also topic Monopolies and Restraint of Trade.

ARBITRATION AND AWARD:

Arbitration Act 1908 governs situation where parties agree to submit dispute to arbitration.

Arbitration (International Investment Disputes) Act 1979 implements Convention on the Settlement of Investment Disputes between States and Nationals of Other States.

Arbitration (Foreign Agreements and Awards) Act 1982 implements Convention on the Recognition and Enforcement of Foreign Arbitral Awards.

See topic Dispute Resolution.

ARREST:

Absconding debtors and persons guilty of contempt of Court may be arrested and/or imprisoned in some circumstances. Writ of sequestration is available by which property of contemnor may be seized. Imprisonment for debt has been abolished, except in specified circumstances where debtor may be imprisoned for period of up to one year under Imprisonment for Debt Limitation Act 1908 as amended by Imprisonment for Debt Limitation Amendment Act 1989.

ASSIGNMENTS:

Assignments of property the title to which cannot be transferred by delivery are usually effected by deed or other writing in accordance with special statutes. Any absolute assignment (not purporting to be by way of charge only) of any debt or other legal or equitable chose in action must be in writing under the hand of the assignor, and express notice in writing of the assignment must be given to the debtor, trustee, or other person from whom the assignor would have been entitled to receive or claim such debt or chose in action. Assignee takes subject to all equities existing between debtor and assignor at time of notice of assignment. Consideration is not required to validate statutory assignment. (Property Law Act 1952). Assignment which does not meet above conditions may still be enforceable as equitable assignment.

Assignments of book debts (other than certain hire purchase agreements) by individual ought to be registered in certain cases under Chattels Transfer Act 1924 in order to preserve enforceability against specified third parties. Assignments of book debts (other than certain hire purchase agreements) given by way of charge or mortgage by company must be registered under Companies Act 1955 by companies incorporated under that Act, or registered under Companies (Registration of Charges) Act 1993 by companies incorporated under Companies Act 1993 in order to preserve validity of assignment against liquidator or other creditors of company. See topic Chattel Mortgages.

ASSIGNMENTS FOR BENEFIT OF CREDITORS:

See topic Bankruptcy.

ASSOCIATIONS:

Any group of 15 or more persons associated for any lawful purpose (other than pecuniary gain) may be incorporated under Incorporated Societies Act 1908. All incorporated societies must register in Incorporated Societies Register. Incoporated societies may only carry out activities permitted by their objects. Members have no personal liability for debts, contracts, or other obligations of society unless incurred from operations involving pecuniary gain or as result of unlawful activities. On dissolution, surplus assets are disposed of in accordance with society's rules.

See also topic Partnership.

ATTORNEYS:

Person may act as barrister or solicitor in New Zealand provided he or she has passed prescribed examinations and becomes enrolled under Law Practitioners Act 1982. New Zealand Law Society is governing body of profession and is statutory body with objects and powers set out in that Act. Society's address is PO Box 5041, Wellington, New Zealand, telephone (64)(4) 472 7837, fax: (64)(4) 473 7909.

Governing body of Law Society is the Council, which is comprised of representatives from the 14 district law societies throughout New Zealand who are elected on basis which reflects numerical strength of each district society. Routine administration of Law Society is in hands of 12 person Executive Committee which meets monthly. In addition there are several standing committees and ad hoc committees which deal with areas of legal practice or specific issues.

AUTOMOBILES: See topic Motor Vehicles.

BANKING AND CURRENCY:

Reserve Bank is incorporated under Reserve Bank of New Zealand Act 1989. Reserve Bank is same body corporate as that incorporated under Reserve Bank of New Zealand Act 1964, and acts as central bank of New Zealand.

Reserve Bank's primary function is to formulate and implement monetary policy directed to economic objective of achieving and maintaining stability in general level of prices. 1989 Act continues to recognise Government's right to determine economic policy. Duty of Governor of Reserve Bank is to ensure that actions of Bank in implementing monetary policy are consistent with Government policy targets which are fixed from time to time.

Reserve Bank acts as lender of last resort for financial system if considered necessary to do so for purpose of maintaining soundness of financial system. Reserve Bank provides settlement accounts, advises Minister of Finance on matters relating to financial system and on foreign exchange, undertakes banking business of Government and provides to any person security registry services relating to financial securities. Reserve Bank has sole right to issue bank notes and coin in New Zealand.

Reserve Bank continues to have authority to register banks and to prudentially supervise them. There is no power to prudentially supervise nonbank financial institutions.

Only registered banks, representative offices and certain private savings banks can use word "bank" or derivatives in name. Reserve Bank shall not register any person as registered bank unless satisfied that business carried on, or proposed to be carried on, by applicant, consists of, or to substantial extent consists of, borrowing and lending of money, or provision of other financial services, or both. Reserve Bank must be satisfied with standing of applicant in financial market and its ability to carry on business in prudent manner.

Powers given to Reserve Bank (Governor General and Minister of Finance) for prudential supervision purposes are to be exercised for purposes of: (a) Promoting maintenance of sound and efficient financial system; or (b) avoiding significant damage to financial system that could result from failure of registered bank.

Under 1989 Act Reserve Bank has power to deal in foreign currency and may, on direction of Minister of Finance, influence exchange rates by dealing in foreign exchange within guidelines set by Minister. Minister may fix exchange rates for foreign exchange dealing by Reserve Bank.

Foreign Reserves.—Minister of Finance shall, in consultation with Reserve Bank, determine levels at which foreign reserves shall be maintained to enable Reserve Bank to exercise its powers. (1989 Act).

Exchange.—On Mar. 2, 1985 New Zealand changed its existing exchange rates by floating New Zealand dollar. Exchange rates are now determined by market forces and reflect demand for and supply of New Zealand dollars in foreign exchange markets.

Foreign Exchange Arrangements.—Foreign exchange facilities are provided by dealers in foreign exchange and enable any person or corporation to take out contracts for purchase or sale of specified amount of foreign exchange, at spot or at future dates. New Zealand Futures Exchange enables US$ and NZ$ futures contracts and NZ$ options to be purchased and provides any person or corporation with alternative hedging facilities.

Financial Transactions Reporting Act 1996.—Financial institutions are responsible for prevention and detection of money laundering and must verify customers, report suspicious transactions and keep records of financial transactions. Verification obligations arise when person requests to become facility holder or seeks to conduct occasional transaction which exceeds prescribed amount. Exceptions apply if another financial institution has verification obligation. Financial institution required to report transactions when financial institution has reasonable grounds for suspecting that transaction may be relevant to investigation or prosecution of money laundering offence or enforcement of Proceeds of Crime Act 1991 (provides for confiscation of proceeds of serious crime).

Financial institutions must keep transaction records (including amount, currency, date, parties and contact with other institutions) to enable reconstruction of transaction by police. Verification records kept for at least five years either in written form in English language, or readily accessible and convertible into written form.

Currency.—Since July 10, 1967 monetary unit has been dollar with 100¢ equalling $1.

See also topic Exchange Control.

BANKRUPTCY:

Law is contained in Insolvency Act 1967. Debtor commits an act of bankruptcy if: (a) Debtor makes disposition to trustee of his property for benefit of all or any creditors ("Disposition" is widely defined to include virtually any transaction by or with bankrupt including incurring obligations and making payments); (b) debtor makes fraudulent dispositions; (c) debtor attempts to delay or defeat creditors through absence from New Zealand, attempting to leave New Zealand, leaving New Zealand or attempts to avoid his creditors; (d) debtor fails to comply with bankruptcy notice served by creditor within 14 days; (e) debtor gives notice to any creditor that he has suspended or is about to suspend payment of debts; (f) at creditor's meeting (1) majority in number and value of creditors require filing of debtor's petition, or (2) debtor consents to file debtor's petition and does not do so within 48 hours; (g) possession taken under execution issued against him or property and judgment remains unsatisfied for seven days, but interpleader proceedings will delay time from running until determined; (h) writ of sale of his land has been directed and advertised and judgment remains unsatisfied for seven days; (i) return of nulla bona made to any execution levied on him or his property; (j) debtor conceals property with intent to prejudice creditors or prefer creditors; (k) debtor fails to account for trust monies held as trustee if court has made order to account which remains unsatisfied for seven days.

Proceedings may be instituted by debtor's petition or creditor's petition. Allegation by debtor that he is unable to pay his debts is sufficient to support debtor's petition. Liquidated debt not less than $200 and available act of bankruptcy within previous

BANKRUPTCY . . . *continued*
three months necessary to support creditor's petition. Two or more creditors may join to raise debt to $200.

On adjudication, property of bankrupt vests in official assignee. Bankruptcy relates back to filing of debtor's petition or first available act of bankruptcy. Property passing to official assignee comprises: (a) All property belonging to or vested in bankrupt at commencement of bankruptcy or acquired by or devolving on him before discharge; (b) capacity to exercise and take proceedings for exercising all powers in respect of property as bankrupt might have exercised for own benefit at commencement of bankruptcy or before discharge.

Property held by bankrupt in trust does not pass and bankrupt is entitled to retain necessary tools of trade to value of $500 and necessary household furniture and effects including wearing apparel to value of $2,000. Where bankrupt is purchaser under a hire purchase agreement official assignee may in certain circumstances introduce a buyer or settle bankrupt's obligations under Hire Purchase Act 1971. Detailed provisions render certain voidable transactions entered into by bankrupt within certain specified periods prior to adjudication.

Undischarged bankrupt may not enter into or carry on business alone or in partnership and may not be involved with business conducted by or on behalf of bankrupt. Undischarged bankrupt may not be director of company.

Discharge of bankrupt will be automatic upon expiration of three years from date of adjudication. Bankrupt can apply to court at any time for discharge. Assignee or any creditor (with leave of court) may object to discharge (automatic or otherwise) of bankrupt. If objection has been made bankrupt must be examined by assignee in court.

Person who is insolvent but not yet adjudicated bankrupt may make proposal to satisfy creditors. Provisional trustee is named to administer proposal and upon its acceptance by creditors he obtains court's approval to it. Court's approval precludes any creditor named in proposal from filing petition of bankruptcy or taking out proceedings to enforce debt without court's consent while proposal is in force.

Where debtor's total unsecured debts do not exceed $12,000 debtor or creditor may apply to District Court for summary instalment order whereby debtor undertakes to satisfy those debts.

Insolvent estates administered under Part XVII of Insolvency Act are subject to bankruptcy rules.

Official assignee is permanent official appointed by government and powers and duties are defined by statute.

BARRISTERS AND SOLICITORS:

See topic Attorneys.

BILLS AND NOTES:

Bills of Exchange Act 1908 is substantially reproduction of English Bills of Exchange Act 1882. As in England, rules of common law, including law merchant, save in so far as they are inconsistent with express provisions of Act, continue to apply to bills of exchange, promissory notes, and cheques. Conflict of law rules are same as English rules. Cheques payable into account of payee do not require endorsement.

CARRIAGE BY AIR:

International.—Carriage by Air Act 1967 gives force of law in New Zealand to Warsaw Convention, Hague Protocol (1955) and Guadalajara Convention (1961). The Carriage by Air Amendment Act 1990, passed by New Zealand Parliament but not yet in force, amends 1967 Act.

Internal.—1967 Act applies provisions of Hague protocol and Guadalajara Convention to carriage by air of passengers within New Zealand which is not international carriage. This part of Act is enforced. There are some variations from Convention. Claims for damages resulting from death or personal injury are covered by Accident Rehabilitation and Compensation Insurance Act 1992. Carriage of Goods Act 1979 covers any liability claimed for damage to baggage or cargo and gives carrier lien over unclaimed baggage and cargo. Carriage by Air Act varies time allowed for making claims.

CHATTEL MORTGAGES:

For purposes of Chattels Transfer Act 1924, "chattels" means any personal property that can be completely transferred by delivery, including machinery, crops, wool, stock and the natural increase of stock, and book debts. Chattels do not include motor vehicles within meaning of Motor Vehicles Securities Act 1989. Instruments given by individual affecting property in or right to possession of such chattels must be registered within 21 days (or 90 days if instrument is executed outside New Zealand) after execution in High Court Office of district in which chattels are situated. Provision is made for extending time for registration (subject to rights accrued in meantime) and registration must be renewed every five years. Failure to register within prescribed time makes instrument void against certain people (but not grantor).

Charges created by companies which if executed by an individual would require registration under the Chattels Transfer Act must be registered under Companies Act 1955 by companies incorporated under that Act or registered under Companies (Registration of Charges) Act 1993 by companies incorporated under Companies Act 1993.

Registration of instrument pursuant to Chattels Transfer Act is notice to all persons of instrument and of its contents.

Customary hire purchase agreements (as defined in Chattels Transfer Act) are valid for all purposes without registration (as are assignments thereof). Customary hire purchase agreement may be made only between conditional purchaser and manufacturer of or dealer in certain chattels listed in Act, must be in writing, and must be either bailment with option to purchase or conditional sale contract under which possession of chattel passes to purchaser, but property in chattel remains in vendor until final payment is made. Customary chattels are those usually sold on terms such as cash registers, refrigerators, radios, etc., but must be included in schedule to Act before they become customary chattels. Motor vehicles not customary chattels for purpose of Chattels Transfer Act.

Hire Purchase Act 1971 relates to retail agreements only and contains prescribed forms which must be strictly complied with. Act implies terms as to title, sample, fitness, quality, and description. No contracting out is permitted. Finance companies are responsible for statements, representations, warranties made by dealers and have statutory rights of indemnity against dealers. Rights of parties on repossession or voluntary return are determined on basis of resale value of goods. Vendor has duty to use all reasonable efforts to obtain best price. Statutory rebates are defined. See topic Contracts, subhead Credit Contracts Act 1981.

Motor Vehicle Securities Act 1989 governs registration of "security interests" affecting motor vehicles and establishes priority regime in respect of certain security interests. Registration of security interest is notice to all persons of its existence. When consumer purchases motor vehicle from dealer, any security interests will, in absence of express notice to consumer, be extinguished irrespective of registration. In other dispositions security interests will only be void for non-registration. See topic Motor Vehicles.

Ship Registration Act 1992 governs registration of ships and procedure for mortgaging ship or share in ship. Priority of mortgages is generally in order of registration.

COLLATERAL SECURITY:

See topic Pledges.

COMMERCIAL REGISTER:

No requirement to register other than provisions relating to companies (including overseas companies carrying on business in New Zealand), special partnerships and incorporated societies. No business register of names under which trading names able to be protected.

See topics Associations, Corporations and Partnership.

COMMISSIONERS TO ADMINISTER OATHS:

Judicature Act 1908 makes provision for appointment of Commissioners of High Court, who may be appointed to act in any country beyond jurisdiction for administering and taking any oath, affidavit, or affirmation in any proceeding pending in any superior or inferior court in New Zealand or in any proceeding within jurisdiction of any such court. Every oath, affidavit, or affirmation so taken is of same validity as if administered within New Zealand.

Commonwealth diplomatic representatives exercising their functions in any place outside New Zealand are given same powers by Oaths and Declarations Act 1957.

See also topic Affidavits.

COMMISSIONS TO TAKE TESTIMONY:

See topic Depositions.

CONDITIONAL SALES:

See topic Chattel Mortgages.

CONSTITUTION AND GOVERNMENT:

New Zealand is constitutional monarchy acknowledging Her Majesty the Queen as its Sovereign. It is member of British Commonwealth of Nations.

Its territory includes Cook Islands, Niue, Tokelau Islands, Kermadec Islands and a number of other islands inhabited and uninhabited. Cook Islands and Niue are now self-governing states in free association with New Zealand which remains responsible for their external affairs and defence. By Imperial Order-in-Council of 1923, Governor-General was appointed Governor of Ross Dependency and is empowered to make regulations for its government.

The Crown.—Governor-General represents Queen in New Zealand and holds in all essential respects the same position in relation to administration of public affairs as is held by Her Majesty in United Kingdom. Governor-General is appointed for five years by Her Majesty acting on advice of New Zealand Government. United Kingdom Government is represented in New Zealand by High Commissioner.

The Legislature.—Legislative power and authority reside in Parliament (General Assembly abolished by Constitution Act 1986) which consists of Sovereign in right and House of Representatives. Members of House of Representatives, who are known as Members of Parliament, are elected every three years. Elections are held once every three years and franchise is general. Electoral Referendum took place in 1993 which resulted in change from first-past-the-post (FPP) system set up by Electoral Act 1956 to mixed-member-proportional (MMP) system set up under Electoral Act 1993. MMP is proportional voting system under which there will be minimum of 120 Members of Parliament.

Each bill must be read three times in the House before it is placed before the Governor-General for his assent.

Assent of Governor-General as representative of Sovereign in right is necessary before bill becomes law.

The Imperial Laws Application Act 1988 specifies extent to which Acts of U.K. Parliament, subordinate legislation made pursuant to those Acts, and common law of England, are part of law of New Zealand.

The Statute of Westminster, 1931, an Act of the United Kingdom Parliament which abolished the right of that Parliament to legislate for the Dominions of the British Commonwealth of Nations without request and consent and which was adopted in New Zealand by Statute of Westminster Adoption Act 1947 ceased to have effect as part of law of New Zealand from Jan. 1, 1986. Constitution Act 1986 provides that no Act of U.K. Parliament passed after Jan. 1, 1986 shall extend to New Zealand as part of its law.

New Zealand Bill of Rights Act 1990. Act specifies basic human rights and fundamental freedoms in New Zealand. Act not entrenched and may be repealed by simple majority.

The Executive.—In accordance with British constitutional practice, main lines of government policy are determined by a Cabinet chosen by Prime Minister or Government Caucus. Under MMP coalition governments may result. Cabinet ministers must

CONSTITUTION AND GOVERNMENT . . . *continued*
be members of Parliament. Where legislative or executive powers are formally conferred on Governor-General he or she is advised by Executive Council which comprises members of Cabinet and, on occasions, other members of Parliament. Its functions correspond broadly to those of Privy Council in England.

The Judiciary.—High Court of New Zealand is superior court of first instance, possessing general jurisdiction. Both civil and criminal matters are within its purview, and it also combines therewith functions exercised in England by Probate, Divorce and Admiralty Divisions of High Court of Justice. From High Court appeal lies to Court of Appeal and thence to Judicial Committee of English Privy Council. As of mid-1996 New Zealand Government was proposing abolition of right of appeal to Privy Council and creation of new local appellate court.

Court of Appeal comprises Chief Justice and five other Judges, one of latter being President.

The Court of Appeal has both civil and criminal jurisdiction.

High Court holds sittings throughout country. Court of Appeal has power to do likewise.

The judiciary is free from the control of the executive. Appointments to the bench are made by the Governor-General on the advice of Cabinet, and the appointees cannot be removed from office except where an address from the House has been presented to the Queen or to the Governor-General.

Minor criminal jurisdiction and civil jurisdiction limited to claims not exceeding $200,000 are exercised by District Court. Jurisdiction can be extended by agreement. Legislation, effective July 1992, gave District Court wider original jurisdiction (including increased equitable jurisdiction and power to grant injunctions). Family Court, division of District Court, has jurisdiction over guardianship, matrimonial property, adoption proceedings and dissolution of marriage. Disputes Tribunal established under Disputes Tribunal Act 1988 has jurisdiction to hear claims in contract and tort that do not exceed $3,000 or $5,000 if both parties to dispute agree.

There are other specialised courts such as Youth Court and Employment Court. There are also a large number of administrative tribunals affecting many activities. There is no general legislation governing such tribunals. Where, however, power or right exercised by such tribunals falls within definition of "statutory power of decision" as widely defined in Judicature Amendment Act 1972 High Court has power to review exercise of, or refusal to exercise, that power.

CONTRACTS:

Much of New Zealand law of contract is similar to that of England and in many respects common law applies. There are number of statutes in force each relating to particular areas of law of contract. Principal features of contract statutes are their simplicity and broad discretion conferred on courts to grant relief.

Excuses for Nonperformance.—Same as under English law, except that Court has power to grant relief to a party to an illegal contract by virtue of Illegal Contracts Act 1970.

Applicable Law.—Parties may specify law to govern contract, if not then law of jurisdiction that has closest or real connection with parties or contract will govern.

Government Contracts.—No special requirements. Enforcement against Crown governed by Crown Proceedings Act 1950. Crown power to borrow restricted by Public Finance Act 1989.

Contractual Mistakes Act 1977 confers upon Courts and arbitrators power to mitigate arbitrary effects of mistakes, of certain kinds, which influenced one or more of parties to enter into contract and which resulted at time of contract in substantially unequal exchange of values or in conferment of benefit or imposition of obligation substantially disproportionate to consideration therefor. Mistakes of certain kinds are excluded.

Insurance Law Reform Act 1977 contains important provisions preventing insurer relying on misstatement in proposal unless certain significant matters are established. Provisions in insurance contracts requiring disputes to be referred to arbitration do not bind insured. Salesmen, etc., are deemed to be agents of insurer which is deemed to have notice of all material matters known to salesman.

Contractual Remedies Act 1979 sets out code of rules relating to remedies for misrepresentation and breach of contract which apply unless parties to contract have made other provision. Remedies in Act not applicable to sales of goods except in case of misrepresentation.

Consumer Guarantees Act 1993 provides that certain statutory guarantees are implied into sale of goods and services to consumers and establishes processes for enforcement of those guarantees.

See topic Sales.

Corporations (Investigations and Management) Act 1989, limits enforcement of contractual rights against corporation subject to statutory management. Statutory manager may suspend discharge of obligations under any contract without breaching or repudiating it. Statutory manager may exercise any power, privilege or right corporation has under any contract, and may terminate contracts of service or agency between corporation and its servants or agents.

Credit Contracts Act 1981, applies to credit contracts made on or after June 1, 1982 (provisions relating to oppression apply to contracts entered into before then), contains important provisions relating to disclosure of terms of arrangements whereby credit is granted and prohibits misleading credit advertisements.

Court may also reopen any credit contract which it considers is "oppressive". "Oppressive" is defined to mean oppressive, harsh, unjustly burdensome, unconscionable or in contravention of reasonable standards of commercial practice. Court has considerable remedial powers to provide relief to debtors under credit contracts which are oppressive.

Contracts (Privity) Act 1982, makes provision for enforcement by third party of promise made in its favour under deed or contract to which it is not party unless promise has been discharged or varied in accordance with contract or discretion of court or promise not intended to create obligation enforceable by third party.

Minors Contracts Act 1969, permits courts to enforce contract against or declare that contract is binding upon minor if contract is fair and reasonable in circumstances.

See topic Sales.

Distributions, dealerships and franchises, no statute law in New Zealand specifically applicable to these arrangements. Consideration must be taken of trade practices requirements of Commerce Act 1986. In particular, prohibition against actions whose purpose or likely effect is lessening of competition in market may have potential application to, inter alia, resale price maintenance provisions, exclusive dealing provisions and territorial restrictions provided for in contractual arrangements.

Protection of arrangements of this type is afforded by combination of registration of product and service trademarks under Trade Marks Act 1953 and prohibitions against misleading and deceptive conduct provided for by Fair Trading Act 1986 (expressly protecting both registered and unregistered trademarks) and in tort of passing-off.

See topic Sales.

CONVEYANCES: See topic Deeds.

COPYRIGHT:

Copyright in New Zealand now regulated by Copyright Act 1994 based on Copyright Designs and Patents Act 1988 (U.K.). Protection now expressly extended to new technologies such as computer programs, satellite broadcasts, cable programmes. Authors' moral rights greatly extended. Performance right also introduced. Border protection measures expanded. Copyright in articles written by journalists for newspapers etc. now owned by employer. Broadly speaking, copyright protection regime remains as under old Copyright Act 1962, but number of exceptions to infringement now provided or amended including those for educational establishments. Industrial designs are protected by copyright as well as by registration under Designs Act 1953.

Registration is not necessary for Copyright protection.

New Zealand extends protection to countries of Berne Convention and Universal Copyright Convention.

Copyright protection has been extended to nationals of variety of countries on basis of reciprocity of benefits.

Layout Designs Act 1994 provides for copyright style protection (without need for registration) in original layout designs or integrated circuits which are now expressly excluded from definition of "artistic work" in Copyright Act 1994.

CORPORATIONS:

New company legislation based on North American and, particularly, Canadian models, took effect on July 1, 1994. Companies now regulated by Companies Act 1955 ("1955 Act") if incorporated prior to July 1, 1994, or Companies Act 1993 ("1993 Act") if incorporated on or after July 1, 1994. Companies Reregistration Act 1993 requires 1955 Act companies to reregister under 1993 Act before July 1, 1997. Companies failing to reregister before this date will be deemed reregistered on July 1, 1997, and 1955 Act will be repealed.

1955 Act was amended by Companies Amendment Act 1993 ("1993 Amendment Act") to correspond with 1993 Act. Changes to 1955 Act include new directors' duties provisions, extended definition of "director" (see subhead Directors, infra), new directors' insurance and indemnification provisions, strengthened shareholder rights and remedies, new liquidation provisions (see subhead Liquidations, infra), simplified amalgamation provisions (see subhead Amalgamations, infra) and greater disclosure requirements.

1993 Act introduced concepts not incorporated in 1955 Act amendments. For example, 1993 Act companies do not have memorandum and articles of association, but may adopt constitution. 1993 Act itself contains rules concerning operation of companies, but companies may adopt constitution to alter or add to those rules to suit individual requirements. New solvency test governs distributions to shareholders. For example, company may not pay dividend to shareholders unless solvency test can be met. Companies able to repurchase own shares or provide financial assistance for purchase of own shares provided solvency test is met. Shares no longer have par value. Instead directors determine consideration for which shares are to be issued. Consideration must be fair both to company and existing shareholders. Requirement that companies have at least two shareholders has been removed and true "one-person" companies possible in which sole director is also sole shareholder. Distinction between public and private companies removed.

Amalgamations.—Means of amalgamating companies now simplified. Two or more companies may amalgamate and continue as one company which may be one of amalgamating companies or new company. Court approval for amalgamation is no longer required. There are two types of amalgamation under both Acts, namely: (1) "Long form amalgamation" primarily where companies proposing to amalgamate are not part of same corporate group; and (2) "short form amalgamation" where company wishes to amalgamate with direct or indirect wholly owned subsidiaries or where companies are directly or indirectly wholly owned by same company.

Capital.—Concept of share "capital" no longer applies with abolition of par value of shares. Raising of equity by companies registered in New Zealand by issue of shares to "overseas persons" restricted by Overseas Investment Regulations 1995. Regulations provide for Minister of Finance (through Overseas Investment Commission) to grant or refuse consent to specified transactions. Consent not required if: (a) issue of shares does not result in overseas person having a 25% beneficial interest in total shares of issuer, control of 25% of voting power of issuer or control of appointment of 25% or more of directors of issuer; or (b) neither value of shares to be issued or assets of issuer (and its subsidiaries if any) exceed $10,000,000 and New Zealand company does not own or have any estate or interest in specified classes of land. There are no restrictions on New Zealand companies borrowing overseas.

See topic Foreign Investment.

Cooperative Companies.—Certain classes of companies may be declared to be cooperative companies governed by Co-Operative Companies Act 1956. Legislation is pending to modify application of Companies Act 1993 to cooperative companies, and to create register of cooperative companies.

CORPORATIONS . . . *continued*

Directors.—Definition of "director" has been extended to include any person occupying position of director (by whatever name called). Person may be director for some purposes but not others. In general, following may be deemed to be directors: (a) any person in accordance with whose instructions director of company, or board, itself is required or accustomed to act; (b) any person entitled to exercise powers under constitution of company which would otherwise be exercised by board; (c) any person to whom power or duty of board has been directly delegated; and (d) under 1993 Act but not 1955 Act, shareholders given power by constitution to exercise power usually exercised by board, if shareholders in fact exercise that power or take part in deciding whether to exercise it.

Execution of Documents.—Common seal no longer required to execute documents, unless articles of association or constitution of company expressly requires.

See topic Seals.

Liquidations.—Statutory code relating to liquidation of companies has been simplified. Acts abolish distinction between voluntary and compulsory winding up and between solvent and insolvent winding up. Liquidator is no longer required to obtain court aproval or assent of "committee of inspection" before exercising certain powers. However, liquidators must now comply with more onerous reporting requirements. Court has express power to supervise liquidation and to make orders for enforcement of liquidator's duties.

See subhead Statutory Management and Receivership, infra.

Foreign Corporations.—Companies incorporated outside New Zealand are "overseas persons" within definition in Overseas Investment Regulations and as such require consent of Overseas Investment Commission to establish place of business in New Zealand or to carry on business in New Zealand.

"Overseas persons" that wish to carry on business in New Zealand for period of less than three months in any year need not obtain consent from Oveseas Investment Commission. There is general exemption for businesses whose total expenditure expected to be incurred prior to establishment of business is less than $10,000,000.

From July 1, 1994 any overseas company which was registered in New Zealand as branch under Part XII of 1995 Act is automatically deemed reregistered under 1993 Act. Now all overseas companies that commence "carrying on business" in New Zealand must apply for registration within ten working days of commencing that business. Term "carrying on business" is broadly defined, and there is no longer requirement that company have physical office in New Zealand. 1993 Act now applies to all overseas companies that administer, manage or deal with property in New Zealand, whether directly or through employees or agents.

Under 1993 Act, overseas companies carrying on business in New Zealand must now file annual return with Registrar of Companies. Registrar will nominate month during which return must be filed each year, and fee will be payable. In addition, notice of any alteration to registration details must be filed with Registrar within 20 working days of alteration. Failure to comply with these requirements may result in fine of up to $10,000.

Provided documentation required to be filed with Registrar is filed, overseas companies may, subject to Overseas Investment Act 1973, hold land as if company was registered in New Zealand. Consent of Minister of Finance and Minister of Lands is required for acquisition by overseas persons of specified classes of land, whether direct or indirect by way of share transfer, including land exceeding five hectares in area, land forming part of island (excluding North and South Islands), and land including or adjoining "sensitive land", such as foreshores, lakes and other specified areas.

Filing of Accounts.—Obligation of company to file accounts governed by Financial Reporting Act 1993. Issuers of securities to public and companies with assets of $450,000 or more, required to file financial statements complying with financial reporting standards. Act also requires overseas company to file financial statements, with auditor's report, with Registrar within 20 working days after signing of those accounts in accordance with laws prevailing in company's country of incorporation. No obligation for overseas company (except registered banks) to file separate accounts in relation to New Zealand operations.

Overseas Takeovers.—Consent under Overseas Investment Regulations 1995 is required for specified acquisitions of shares in New Zealand incorporated company by "overseas persons" (as defined) prior to such acquisitions taking place.

Consent to such acquisitions may also require consent of Commerce Commission under Commerce Act (see subhead Commerce Act 1986, infra).

Statutory Management and Receivership.—Corporations (Investigation and Management) Act 1989 provides for statutory receivership and management. Act allows statutory manager to take over management of company where company is operating fraudulently or recklessly, or where necessary to preserve interest of company's members or creditors, or for any other reason in public interest.

Receiverships Act 1993 relates to company receivers.

Takeovers.—Takeovers Act 1993 enacted to establish Takeovers Panel to recommend takeovers code to apply to takeovers of companies which are either parties to listing agreement with New Zealand Stock Exchange, or have 50 or more shareholders and $20,000,000 or more in assets. No takeovers code has been introduced as of May 1996.

Commerce Act 1986.—This Act contains provisions regulating anti-competitive conduct in relation to restrictive trade practices, monopolies, business acquisitions (or mergers and takeovers).

Some trade practices are absolutely prohibited, for example, price fixing between competitors, resale price maintenance, collective boycotts and misuse of market power. Other practices may also be prohibited if they have purpose, effect or likely effect of substantially lessening competition in market, for example, exclusive dealing, market sharing or output agreements.

Authorisations may be obtained from Commerce Commission for most restrictive trade practices on grounds of public benefit outweighing lessening of competition.

This Act deals with competition issues of mergers and acquisitions. Voluntary premerger notification system has replaced mandatory pre-merger notification provisions. Clearance or authorisation from Commerce Commission is required for any acquisition resulting in acquisition or strengthening of dominant position in market or substantial lessening of competition in market.

Securities Act 1978.—This Act contains extensive provisions relating to raising of investment monies from and issue of securities to public and imposes obligations as to information required to be given in such circumstances, particularly with reference to prospectuses. By virtue of Securities Amendment Act 1988 insider trading incurs substantial penalties and substantial security holders in public issuers must make full disclosure of their interests. Register of those interests must be maintained by public issuer.

COURTS:

See topic Constitution and Government, subhead, The Judiciary.

CRIMINAL LAW:

Apart from certain common law defences, criminal law is entirely statutory and has been so since enactment of Criminal Code Act 1893, an Act based on English Criminal Code Bill of 1880. Present law is contained in Crimes Act 1961. In addition to such jurisdiction as they possess in respect of indictable offences, District Court judges (and in certain cases justices of peace) have jurisdiction in respect of summary offences created by Justices of the Peace Act 1957, Summary Offences Act 1981 and Summary Proceedings Act 1957.

CURRENCY:

See topic Banking and Currency.

CUSTOMS (DUTY):

Customs Act 1966 governs import and export of goods to and from New Zealand. Tariff Act 1988 imposes tariff duties.

Duty has been historically high on wide range of imported goods (especially manufactured); since July 1, 1988 tariffs have been reduced on manufactured goods. Government retains extensive powers under Tariff Act 1988. See also topics Foreign Trade Regulations and Treaties.

DEATH:

There is no general statute relating to presumption of death. On application for probate, death certificate should be annexed to affidavit or there should be definite statement on oath that deceased died on or about specified date. If such evidence cannot be given applicant should place before Court evidence he has and obtain leave to swear to death. Where two or more persons have died at same time or in circumstances which give rise to reasonable doubt as to which of them survived other or others property of each person so dying shall devolve, unless contrary intention is expressed in duly executed will, as if he had survived other person or persons so dying and had died immediately afterwards. (Simultaneous Deaths Act, 1958). There is presumption of death after seven years continuous absence. Under certain circumstances this is defence to charge of bigamy. Dissolution of marriage is necessary, however, to remove all rights and obligations of marriage.

Official death certificates may be obtained by application to Registrar-General of Births, Deaths and Marriages, 191 High Street, PO Box 31-115, Lower Hutt and payment of applicable fee.

Actions for Death.—With minor exceptions, compensation rights are determined by Accident Rehabilitation and Compensation Insurance Act 1992. Where that Act does not apply claim for compensation for loss of support to dependents is possible under Deaths by Accident Compensation Act 1952 if accident due to negligence of person other than deceased. Action under Deaths by Accident Compensation Act must be brought within two years unless leave of court obtained.

DECEDENTS' ESTATES:

See topics Descent and Distribution; Executors and Administrators; Wills.

DEEDS:

In case of individuals, every deed must be signed by party to be bound thereby or by his attorney and attested by at least one witness who, if deed is executed in New Zealand, must add to his signature his address and occupation or description. No particular words of attestation are necessary. Formal delivery, sealing, and indenting are unnecessary, although principle of delivery of instrument as escrow still applies.

In case of companies execution of deeds is determined by Companies Act 1993 or Companies Act 1955 as amended by Companies Amendment Act 1993. From July 1, 1994 in case of all companies common seal will no longer be required and deed may be entered into on behalf of company in writing and signed under name of company by persons specified by Companies Act 1993 or by Companies Act 1955.

See also topic Corporations.

If attorney (either of individual or of company) signs certificate prescribed by Property Law Amendment Act 1975 immediately before or at any time after act is done, that is conclusive proof of non-revocation for persons dealing with donee of power in good faith for valuable consideration without notice of death of donor or other revocation. Certificate signed by officer of company which is attorney has similar effect.

See also topic Seals.

DEPOSITIONS:

For the purposes of proceedings in a New Zealand Court evidence may be taken abroad by means of commissions, special examinations, or requests to foreign Courts in lieu of commissions. Conversely, evidence may be taken on commission in New Zealand or by means of special affidavits or declarations made in New Zealand for use in proceedings before foreign tribunals. Evidence Amendment Act (No. 2) 1980 for "prescribed countries", allows taking of evidence in New Zealand on examination.

DESCENT AND DISTRIBUTION:

Real estate of any person who dies intestate as to such real estate is held by administrator upon trust for person who, if it was personal estate, would be entitled. Real and personal estate can therefore be treated together.

Administration Act 1969 generally reenacts earlier legislation so far as canons of descent and distribution upon intestacy are concerned and provides briefly as follows:

(1) **Intestate survived by a spouse:**

(a) If intestate also survived by issue of any degree who become indefeasibly entitled under statutory trust: Surviving spouse takes (i) personal chattels absolutely, (ii) $90,000 (with interest at 11% per annum from date of death) charged on residue, and (iii) one-third of residue absolutely. Issue take two-thirds of residue on statutory trusts.

(b) If intestate also survived by parent (or parents) but no issue who become indefeasibly entitled under statutory trusts: Surviving spouse takes (i) personal chattels absolutely, (ii) $90,000 (with interest at 11% per annum from date of death) charged on residue, and (iii) two-thirds of residue absolutely. Both parents surviving take one-third of residue in equal shares absolutely. One parent surviving takes one-third of residue absolutely.

(c) If intestate not survived by a parent, and no issue becomes indefeasibly entitled under the statutory trusts: Surviving spouse takes whole of estate (after payment of debts, etc.) absolutely.

(2) **Intestate not survived by spouse:**

(a) If intestate is survived by issue of any degree: Issue take upon the statutory trusts, but if no issue becomes indefeasibly entitled thereunder the distribution is the same as if no issue survived the intestate.

(b) If intestate is survived by a parent (or parents) but not by any issue, or if none of the surviving issue becomes indefeasibly entitled under the statutory trusts: Both parents surviving take whole residuary estate in equal shares absolutely. One parent surviving takes whole residuary estate absolutely.

(3) **Intestate not survived by a spouse or parent, and either not survived by any issue, or none of the issue surviving become indefeasibly entitled under the statutory trusts:**

(a) If intestate survived by a brother (or brothers), sister (or sisters), or issue of any degree of a deceased brother or sister: brothers and sisters (of full or of half blood) and their issue taking by substitution take whole residuary estate on the statutory trusts.

(b) If intestate is not survived by any of persons mentioned in (a) above or if though so survived none of them become indefeasibly entitled under statutory trusts, estate divided into two halves; one half on trust for maternal grandparents or grandparent, and if none such then for maternal uncles and aunts (of full or half blood); other half on corresponding trusts for paternal grandparent(s) or paternal uncles and aunts; issue of any degree of any deceased uncle or aunt takes share of that uncle or aunt by substitution; if no person takes absolutely vested interest in one half of estate, that half is held on trusts applying to other half of estate.

Bona Vacantia.—If no person mentioned in (1), (2) or (3) above becomes entitled to an absolute interest, the estate, in lieu of any right to escheat, vests in the Crown. The Crown may, however, make provision out of the estate for the dependents of the intestate and other persons for whom the intestate might reasonably have been expected to make provision.

Statutory trusts apply as regards three classes or primary stocks of relatives of the intestate, namely: (a) Issue, (b) brothers and sisters, and (c) uncles and aunts.

No person takes under statutory trusts unless he or she attains age of 20 years, or sooner marries. Rules of succession are provided in cases where statutory trusts fail.

Family Protection Act 1955 and Law Reform (Testamentary Promises) Act 1949 dealing with claims which certain classes of people may in certain circumstances make against estates of deceased persons apply to intestate estates.

DISPUTE RESOLUTION:

Mandatory Dispute Resolution.—New Zealand has no mandatory alternative dispute resolution regime which would require disputes to be subject of alternative resolution process prior to litigation.

There is legislation that encourages alternative dispute resolution, primarily mediation. That legislation includes:

Employment Contracts Act 1991 where parties may agree to have employment disputes mediated by member of specialist Employment Tribunal prior to adjudication of dispute.

Resource Management Act 1991 which deals with sustainable management of natural and physical resources. By consent mediation, conciliation and other procedures can be used to resolve disputes in specialist Planning Tribunal.

Disputes Tribunals Act 1988 which established Tribunal for resolution of claims less than $3,000. Tribunal will attempt agreed resolution prior to adjudication which, if successful, becomes order of Tribunal and enforceable in District Court.

Family Proceedings Act 1980 which provides for counselling and mediation for resolution of disputes arising out of marriage and child custody/access issues.

Residential Tenancies Act 1986 which provides for resolution of disputes between residential landlords and tenants by mediation if parties consent.

High Court Rules under which settlement conferences can be convened before judge at parties' request.

Voluntary Alternative Dispute Resolution.—Increasing use of alternative dispute resolution processes, primarily mediation, in commercial disputes.

Main organisations promoting use of alternative dispute resolution are Arbitrators' & Mediators' Institute of New Zealand and LEADR (Lawyers Engaged in Alternative Dispute Resolution). Both maintain panels of mediators and provide facilitation services to legal and commercial communities and general public.

Usual voluntary mediation process in New Zealand is: (a) Parties agree to attempt mediation and approach agreed mediator who arranges for them to execute mediation agreement that provides for procedure, confidentiality, mediator's indemnity and remuneration; (b) pre-mediation meeting (often between lawyers only) to take care of timing, venue, documents to be exchanged or given to mediator, identification of issues and other miscellaneous matters; (c) typical commercial mediation takes one day. Mediator will explain process and each party makes opening address. Mediator normally conducts series of joint and private sessions depending on progress towards resolution however no set procedure and importance given to flexible approach to allow parties to conduct mediation; (d) if resolution is agreed, parties (often by way of lawyers) draw up and sign binding agreement recording resolution prior to leaving mediation conference.

Other alternative dispute resolution processes such as minitrial and early neutral evaluation not unknown but do not enjoy same popularity as mediation which is now mainstream dispute resolution tool.

DIVORCE:

Family Proceedings Act 1980 applies.

Application to Family Court for dissolution of marriage may be made by either spouse where, at time of filing of application, at least one party to marriage is domiciled in New Zealand. Sole ground for dissolution will be that marriage has broken down irreconcilably, which ground shall be established only where court is satisfied that parties to marriage are living apart and have been living apart for period of two years immediately preceding filing of application.

Common law concepts of collusion and condonation etc., are no longer applicable.

Family Proceedings Act 1980 provides for recognition of overseas decrees of divorce or nullity where: (a) One or both of parties were domiciled in that country at time of order; or (b) that foreign court has exercised its jurisdiction on basis of: (1) residence for continuous period of not less than two years of one or both parties, or (2) nationality or citizenship, or (3) domicile of husband immediately prior to his desertion or deportation, or (4) domicile of husband as at date of agreement or order, or (5) in case of nullity of marriage, on basis of celebration of marriage in that country; or (c) decree or order is recognised as valid in courts of country in which at least one of parties to marriage is domiciled.

Family Court will not make order dissolving marriage unless satisfied arrangements made for custody, maintenance and welfare of every child of marriage under 16 years. There are limited exceptions to this. There may be ongoing liability for one spouse to maintain other after dissolution. This is to end after expiration of reasonable period.

ENVIRONMENT:

Resource Management Act 1991 provides statutory controls over use of land, air, and water, with overriding purpose to promote sustainable management of New Zealand's natural and physical resources. Focus is on effects of activities on environment, rather than using traditional zoning methods. To achieve this, hierarchy of documents sets out environmental policy, including: National Environmental Standards, National Policy Statements, National Coastal Policy Statements, Regional Policy Statements, Regional Coastal Policy Statements, Regional Plans, and District Plans. In addition, Act provides for system of resource consents, offences and penalties.

Crown Minerals Act 1991 provides for managed exploration of Crown owned minerals. It vests ownership of certain minerals in Crown, and provides for Minerals Programmes, exploration and mining permits, and access to land.

Hazardous Substances and New Organisms Bill, which is pending, is intended to manage or prevent harmful effects on people and environment of hazardous substances and new organisms. Management is aimed at ensuring maximum net national benefit. Bill prohibits importation, manufacture, development, field testing or any release of hazardous substance or new organism unless in accordance with Bill's procedures. Bill sets up new authority, Environmental Risk Management Authority (ERMA), which will administer Act, advise, monitor and review hazardous substances, and create registers. Bill introduced to New Zealand Parliament Nov. 1994, is expected to be passed by Parliament during 1996, however unlikely to come into force until regulations necessary have been passed, which could be in 1997.

Environment Act 1986 establishes office of Parliamentary Commissioner for Environment. Office has investigative and advisory role in relation to: systems and procedures used to manage allocation, use and preservation of natural and physical resources, any cause of adverse environmental effects, encouraging, collecting and disseminating information relating to environment, encouraging prevention and remediation to protect environment, and reporting its findings to New Zealand Parliament. Act establishes Ministry for Environment, which formulates policy on natural resource and ecosystem management, environmental planning and impact assessment, monitoring and pollution control. Primary goal of Act is ensuring that intrinsic values of ecosystems, value of environmental quality, Treaty of Waitangi, sustainability and intergenerational equity are taken into account in management of New Zealand's natural and physical resources.

Management of Crown owned natural resources governed by number of statutes, including Wildlife Act 1953, Wild Animal Control Act 1977, Reserves Act 1977, National Parks Act 1980, NZ Walkways Act 1975 and Conservation Act 1987. Conservation Act established Department of Conservation, which administers Crown owned natural resources.

Fisheries Act 1983 provides for fisheries. Fisheries Bill, currently before New Zealand Parliament, proposes integrating coastal fisheries and aquaculture with resource management regime through sustainable utilisation of New Zealand's fisheries resources.

Biosecurity Act 1993 relates to eradication and effective management of pests and unwanted organisms.

Other specific environmental protection has been provided in, for example, Marine Farming Act 1971, Ozone Layer Protection Act 1990, Marine Mammals Protection Act 1978, Marine Pollution Act 1974, Marine Reserves Act 1971, Maritime Transport Act 1994 and Antarctic (Environmental Protection) Act 1994.

Marine pollution see also topic Shipping.

See Topical Index in front part of this volume.

EXCHANGE CONTROL:

Remittances and receipts of foreign exchange are free from exchange control. In practice most foreign exchange dealing is undertaken through registered banks, although there is no legal impediment preventing any person or corporation dealing in foreign exchange.

New Zealand is member of World Bank, International Monetary Fund and International Finance Corporation.

See also topic Banking and Currency.

EXECUTIONS:

Judgments may be enforced in High Court by writs of sale, of possession, of sequestration, or by way of charging or garnishee order. Judgment debtors may be examined in Court as to financial means, (see High Court Rules, Second Schedule to Judicature Act 1908). District Court enforcement is similar but District Court has additional power to attach judgment debtor's salary or wages, (see District Courts Act 1947). Creditors may also use bankruptcy or liquidation proceedings. In certain circumstances Court may order arrest of defendant about to leave New Zealand with aim of frustrating plaintiff's action and obtaining of judgment (see Judicature Act 1908). See topic Arrest.

EXECUTORS AND ADMINISTRATORS:

On granting of probate or administration of estate of deceased person all his property, whether real or personal, and whether held by him beneficially or in trust, vests by force of Administration Act 1969, in his executor or administrator. Grant relates back to death of deceased. All real and personal property, with some limited exceptions, constitute assets for payment of debts.

Right to Administer.—In cases of intestacy the person most nearly related to the deceased is generally entitled to administration, but the Public Trustee is always entitled to be heard. The court will not make the grant to the Public Trustee where the person applying would, if the Public Trustee had not applied, have had a clear right to the administration.

Where an executor neglects to prove his testator's will or renounces probate within three months of his death, administration may be granted on application to any person interested in the estate or to the Public Trustee.

Estates of Nonresidents.—The New Zealand estate of a person dying abroad does not vest unless administration is granted in New Zealand. Probate or letters of administration (or an exemplification thereof) granted abroad require resealing in New Zealand, and the effect is to put the executor or administrator in the same position as if such probate or letters of administration had been originally granted in New Zealand. Nonresident executors or administrators are empowered to delegate their functions. Grant of administration to New Zealand resident ancillary to principal grant may be obtained in certain circumstances.

Commission of such amount as is just and reasonable in circumstances may be allowed by court to executor, administrator, or trustee on passing his accounts.

The rules of English law governing the rights and duties of executors and administrators generally apply. See England Law Digest.

EXEMPTIONS:

Levying of distress for unpaid rent is governed by Distress and Replevin Act 1908. Distress for rent from dwellinghouse now prohibited; exemption from creditor's remedies by way of execution limited to personal and family clothing, furniture and household effects, and tools or implements of trade, not exceeding in all $400 in value.

FACTORS: See topic Principal and Agent.

FOREIGN CORPORATIONS:

See topics Corporations; Exchange Control.

FOREIGN EXCHANGE:

See topics Banking and Currency; Exchange Control; Foreign Trade Regulations.

FOREIGN INVESTMENT:

Foreign investment, especially if introducing new technology or expertise or making other contributions to New Zealand's well-being is encouraged. New Zealand capital markets are open to any person or body corporate. Prior consent of Minister of Finance and Minister of Lands is required for all acquisitions (whether direct or indirect by way of shares) of specified land defined in Overseas Investment Regulations 1995. Apart from these exceptions only large investments (whether in land or other assets) generally involving investment of more than NZ$10,000,000 require consent.

See also topics Aliens; Exchange Control; Corporations, subheads Capital and Overseas Takeovers; and topic Licensing and Registration.

FOREIGN TRADE REGULATIONS:

Customs Act 1966 and Import Control Act 1988 allow Governor-General, by Order in Council, to prohibit or limit importation of any class of goods. Government now subjects all industry assistance policies to close scrutiny to encourage competition and economic efficiency. Customs Act 1966 gives Governor-General similar powers in regard to exports.

New Zealand is signatory to General Agreement on Tariffs and Trade.

See topic Treaties.

FRAUDS, STATUTE OF:

Statute of Frauds was repealed by Contracts Enforcement Act 1956 as to contracts made after Oct. 19, 1956. No contract to which this Act relates is enforceable by action unless the contract or some memorandum or note thereof is in writing signed by the party to be charged or by some other person lawfully authorised by him. Act relates to following contracts: (a) Every contract for sale of land; (b) every contract to enter into any disposition of land being disposition that is required by any enactment to be made by deed or instrument in writing or to be proved by writing; (c) every contract to enter into any mortgage or charge on land; (d) every contract by any person to answer for debt, default, or liability of third person. Act does not (a) apply to any sale by order of High Court or through Registrar of that Court, (b) apply to any alienation of Maori land by Maori being alienation that is required by Maori Affairs Act 1953 to be confirmed by Maori Land Court or to any sale of Maori land by order of that Court or (c) affect operation of law relating to part performance. "Disposition" is given very wide meaning. "Land" means any estate or interest, whether freehold or chattel, in real property.

See topic Sales.

FRAUDULENT SALES AND CONVEYANCES:

See topic Bankruptcy.

GARNISHMENT:

Any party to an action may at any time before judgment and by leave of court, on proof that other party is making away with his property or is absent from or about to quit New Zealand with intent to defeat his creditors or any party to action, or at any time after judgment without such leave as against other party against whom judgment has been obtained, issue out of court order charging: (a) Any estate or interest in land held by other party in his own name; (b) any debts due to him; (c) any right or interest of his in any partnership; (d) any shares held by him in any New Zealand company or overseas company having office in New Zealand in which transfers of shares may be registered; (e) any estate or interest in any land, moneys, shares, or other chattels, under any express or implied trust. (See High Court Rules, Second Schedule Judicature Act 1908; for District Court charging orders see District Courts Act 1947.)

New Zealand courts have jurisdiction to grant "Mareva" injunction restraining defendant from removing assets from jurisdiction or disposing of assets within jurisdiction.

HUSBAND AND WIFE:

Married Women's Property.—Law relating to matrimonial property and its division between spouses upon separation or divorce is contained in Matrimonial Property Act 1976. Act creates general rules, subject to important specified exceptions, for equal division of matrimonial property. One exception is, where court considers extraordinary circumstances would render repugnant to justice equal sharing of matrimonial home and family chattels, share of each spouse shall be determined in each case accordance with contribution of each to marriage partnership. (Contribution need not be monetary. Care of children, management of household, performance of work or services, are considered contributions in determining contribution, misconduct irrelevant unless gross and palpable and significantly affected extent or value of matrimonial property). Another exception is in event of marriage of short duration which is marriage of less than three years duration.

What Act defines as separate property is, again subject to important specified exceptions, outside jurisdiction of court. Matrimonial Property Rules 1988 prescribe procedure and forms for certain applications under Act. Act does not apply to de facto relationships.

Parties to actual or proposed marriage may subject to important formalities make written agreements with respect to status, ownership or division of their (including future) property. Such agreements are void if necessary formalities were not complied with or court is satisfied it would be unjust to give effect to agreement.

Married woman is capable of acquiring and holding property and disposing of that property as if she were femme sole.

Maintenance and Separation Orders.—Family Proceedings Act 1980 provides machinery for making of separation and maintenance orders in Family Court Division of District Court. Duty is imposed upon all legal advisers to promote reconciliation and conciliation. Procedures are also established for holding of mediation conference in attempt to resolve outstanding issues between husband and wife.

Any person may apply for separation order which may be made by Family Court if it is satisfied that there is state of disharmony between parties to marriage of such nature that it is not reasonable to require parties to continue or resume cohabitation.

During marriage each party is liable financially to maintain other to extent necessary to meet reasonable needs of other party. After dissolution of marriage, each party shall continue to be liable to maintain other party to extent that other party cannot, commensurate with family arrangements or responsibilities as defined, practicably meet whole or any part of those needs. Upon application, Family Court can order payment of periodic or lump sums. Provision is made for enforcement of such maintenance orders which includes charging and receiving orders. Procedures are established for enforcement of maintenance orders made in certain designated countries.

Domestic Protection Act 1982.—Where man and woman are or have been married or living together, either one may apply for nonviolence order or nonmolestation order against other, in respect of applicant or child of family. Applicants may also seek occupation order of family home.

IMMIGRATION: See topic Aliens.

INCOME TAX: See topic Taxation.

INFANCY:

Infant reaches majority at 20. (Age of Majority Act 1970). Minors Contracts Act 1969 renders contracts entered into by minor who has attained age of 18 years, life insurance contracts whereby minor over 16 years insures his own life, and contracts of service by minors, generally enforceable against minor unless court is satisfied that (a) Consideration for minor's promise or act was so inadequate as to be unconscionable; (b) any provision of contract was harsh or oppressive.

Other contracts entered into by minors under 18 are generally unenforceable against them but court has power to enforce them if fair and reasonable at time entered into.

All married minors have full contractual capacity regardless of age.

INFANCY . . . *continued*

Married minor irrespective of age and every minor of or over 18 years may make or revoke a will. Minors of or over 16 years may, with approval of Public Trustee or District Court make or revoke will. Also, infant of 16 years or more, with approval of Public Trustee, may dispose of life insurance policy or any interest therein by will.

Guardianship Act 1968 covers all questions related to custody, guardianship, wardship, and up-bringing of children. Family Court has primary jurisdiction under Act with some subsidiary jurisdiction in High Court and District Court. Overriding principle under Act that welfare of child paramount. Usual practice to appoint independent counsel representing child. Guardianship Amendment Act 1979 enacted provisions relating to enforcement in New Zealand of overseas court orders as to custody and access and as to enforcement overseas of such orders made by New Zealand Courts.

Father and mother are each a guardian of child. Unmarried mother is sole guardian in certain circumstances but father has right to apply. Both mother and father have right to apply to court on any matter affecting child. Child means a person under 20. Surviving parent has right to be appointed guardian to infant. Either parent has right to appoint testamentary guardian to act either alone or with surviving parent. Children, Young Persons and Their Families Act 1989 provides for children (under 14) and young persons (14 to 17) who are in need of care or protection or who offend against law and establishes Youth Courts and Commissioner for children.

Infant under ten years old cannot be convicted of any criminal offence. To obtain a conviction between age of ten and 14, it is necessary to show that infant knew act or omission was wrong or contrary to law.

Status of Children Act 1969 provides that for all purposes of law of New Zealand, relationship between every person and his father and mother shall be determined irrespective of whether father and mother are or have been married to each other and all other relationships shall be determined accordingly. In general, instruments and intestacies executed or arising before commencement of Act hold as though Act had not been passed.

See also topic Marriage.

INHERITANCE TAX: See topic Taxation.

INSOLVENCY: See topic Bankruptcy.

INTESTACY:

See topic Descent and Distribution.

JUDGMENTS:

Judgments of Superior Courts of U.K. are enforceable in New Zealand. Pursuant to Orders-in-Council made under Reciprocal Enforcement of Judgments Act 1934, judgments of superior courts of stipulated countries may be enforced in New Zealand. On assurance being given of substantial reciprocity of treatment in enforcement of New Zealand judgments, provisions of Reciprocal Enforcement of Judgments Act may be extended to judgments of any part of Her Majesty's Dominions, or judgments of any foreign country by Order-in Council. By virtue of §44 of Marine Pollution Act 1974 any judgment given by court in country in respect of which International Convention on Civil Liability for Oil Pollution Damage 1969 is in force, to enforce claim in respect of liability incurred under any provision corresponding to §32 of Marine Pollution Act 1974 (which relates to liability of shipowners) will have reciprocity in New Zealand.

Foreign judgments in personam constitute a good cause of action in New Zealand, as setting up a simple contract debt between the parties. Foreign judgment must be registered before it can be proceeded upon to recover any sum in any court in New Zealand. However, unregistered judgment may be recognised in proceedings based on same cause of action, and may be relied on for defence or counterclaim. Foreign judgment will not be registered if it has been wholly satisfied, or would be unenforceable in country it was given in. No foreign judgment whether from country to which Reciprocal Enforcement of Judgments Act applies or otherwise will be enforced unless court is satisfied that judgment is final and conclusive and that sum of money is payable thereunder. It will be deemed final and conclusive notwithstanding that appeal may be pending. There are various grounds upon which registration may, or shall, be set aside, such as lack of jurisdiction of original court. Under Judicature Act 1908 memorials of judgments of courts of any part of Her Majesty's Dominions, which are not enforceable under Reciprocal Enforcement of Judgments Act 1934, may be registered.

Guardianship Amendment Act 1979 enacted provisions relating to enforcement in New Zealand of overseas court orders as to custody and access and as to enforcement overseas of such orders made by New Zealand Courts.

LABOUR RELATIONS:

Department of Labour provides employment service, enforces safety, health and welfare regulations, maintains register of shops, offices and factories, collects and publishes information relating to employment, unemployment, wages, strikes. Department's inspectors have powers to inspect workplaces to ensure compliance with legislative requirements relating to wages, etc. In particular, Department of Labour provides inspectors who operate under Health and Safety in Employment Act 1992. Act repeals all preexisting major statutory provisions relating to health and safety of employees and has three major facets, imposing duties on employers, identifying roles of inspectors and establishing penalties for breach.

Employment Contracts Act 1991 replaced Labour Relations Act with effect from May 15, 1991. Employment Contracts Act makes major changes to industrial relations system. System of registered awards and agreements replaced with purely contractual regime of individual and collective employment contracts. Employment Contracts Act intended to facilitate move away from nationally set terms and conditions to enterprise based bargains.

Union membership voluntary. Preference in obtaining or retaining employment, by reason of union membership, prohibited. Unions have no special status under Act.

All contracts of employment covered by Employment Contracts Act which confers jurisdiction to deal with disputes about employment contracts on Employment Tribunals and Employment Court. Employee/employer relations cannot be conducted outside Act's provisions. Personal grievance procedures apply to all contracts of employment. Special remedies provided for employees in cases of unjustified dismissal, discrimination, sexual harassment including, if appropriate, general damages, reinstatement. Majority of enforcement action must be taken by employee(s) affected.

State Sector Act 1988 amalgamated labour relations in state sector with private sector from Apr. 1, 1988.

Holidays Act 1981 contains law relating to public holidays and to provision of annual holidays with pay for workers.

Parental Leave and Employment Protection Act 1987 makes provision for maternity, paternity and extended leave.

Social Security Act 1964 provides for superannuation, and for age, widows, orphans, family, invalids, miners, sickness, unemployment, emergency, medical and hospital and other related benefits.

Wages Protection Act 1983 and Minimum Wages Act 1983 define concept of wages and prescribe minimum rates. Minimum adult wage for person over 20 years is NZ$250 per 40 hour week. All wages earned by worker must be paid in cash except if paid by Crown, where wages may be paid by cheque, or as otherwise agreed, and without deduction except for taxation which is deducted from wages paid under PAYE system.

See also topic Taxation.

Accident Compensation.—Accident Rehabilitation and Compensation Insurance Act 1992 replaced Accident Compensation Act 1982 with effect from Apr. 1, 1992. New scheme moves from one predominantly funded by compulsory employer contributions to one where employer contributions are lower and balance is made up by deductions from earnings of employees and self employed. No lump sum payments, only earnings related compensation and limited medical expenses for injury by accident, are payable. Act is code and court proceedings for damages for personal injury (with certain exceptions) are expressly precluded in New Zealand, irrespective of negligence or fault by any party. In certain circumstances exemplary damages may be claimed. Generally, all claims under Act are made to Accident Rehabilitation and Compensation Insurance Corporation, however, there is provision for employers to be "exempt" and self insure for first 12 months coverage of any work accidents.

Privacy of Information.—Privacy Act 1993 came into force on July 1, 1993. Act affects almost every organisation in private and public sector that collects or holds or uses information about individual persons. To comply with Act most businesses need to implement procedures that regulate how they collect personal information, manner in which it is stored, how it is used and circumstances in which it may be disclosed to third parties. Provisions of legislation also impact on manner in which employers collect, store and disclose information in relation to their employees.

Discrimination.—Human Rights Act 1993 amalgamates and revises Race Relations Act 1971 and Human Rights Commission Act 1971. New grounds of unlawful discrimination are provided. Race Relations Act and Human Rights Commission Act prohibited discrimination on grounds of race, colour, ethnic or national origin, sex, marital status, religious or ethical belief and in area of employment, age. New grounds are disability, age (in areas additional to employment), political opinion, employment status and family status. There are new provisions on racial disharmony, sexual harrassment and racial harrassment. Special provisions relating to superannuation schemes deal with different treatment on grounds of age and disability.

LANDLORD AND TENANT:

Leases are governed by principles of contract, and by principles relating to grants of estates in land. Residential Tenancies Act 1986 applies to residential tenancies. Leases may be registered under Land Transfer Act 1952 but great proportion of leases are by unregistered deed. Leases for 20 years or more may constitute subdivisions and require local authority consent under Resource Management Act 1991. Landlord may levy distress for unpaid rent except where residential tenancy. Termination of leases is usually by expiry, forfeiture, determining event, surrender or merger. Property Law Act 1952 contains restrictions on, and provision for relief against, forfeiture. See also topic Real Property.

See topics Exemptions; Labour Relations (re discrimination).

LAW REPORTS, CODES, ETC.:

See topics Reports; Statutes.

LEGISLATURE:

See topic Constitution and Government.

LICENSING AND REGISTRATION:

Many business activities can only be carried on pursuant to licences or permits issued under statutes or regulations. Often the issue, control, and cancellation of licences are carried out by tribunals appointed under statute with or without rights of appeal to an appeal tribunal or High Court. Many businesses or professions, and persons engaged therein, must by statute be registered, and disciplinary power is often conferred upon controlling body. See also topic Constitution and Government, subhead The Judiciary (last paragraph).

LIENS:

Common law, equitable, and statutory liens are recognized. Common law liens may be general arising by operation of law or by contract or they may be particular. Examples of particular liens are those to which innkeepers and common carriers are entitled. Equitable liens arise from particular relationship between certain parties, such as between members of partnership. Statutory liens include those under Mercantile Law Act 1908 which confers liens on unpaid vendors, warehousers and shipowners, and those under Sale of Goods Act 1908, which confers lien on certain unpaid vendors. Wages Protection and Contractors' Liens Act Repeal Act 1987 provides for enforcement of liens over chattels. Contractual liens are also recognised by courts.

LIMITED PARTNERSHIP:

See topic Partnership.

LIMITATION OF ACTIONS:

Common law action for damages abolished in respect of personal injury by accidents occurring on or after Apr. 1, 1974 by Accident Compensation Act 1972; Act now replaced by Accident Rehabilitation and Compensation Insurance Act 1992 which came into force on Apr. 1, 1992; see topic Labour Relations, subhead Accident Compensation. However, exemplary damages under common law remain available. Limitation time for making claims to Accident Compensation Commission is generally 12 months of date of accident causing injury or death. Actions for recovery of land, except those brought by Crown in which case 60 years (§7, Land Act 1948), money charged on land and actions on deed must be brought within 12 years. Actions on simple contracts, merchants' accounts, tort (except personal injuries), to recover rent or to recover any sum recoverable by virtue of any enactment must be brought within six years. Actions under Fair Trading Act 1986 have three year limitations. Limitation periods extended in cases of disability, fraud and mistake and no limitation to actions for recovery of land tax or income tax.

MARRIAGE:

A licence will not be issued for marriages between persons either of whom is under 16. An infant of 16 years or over may not marry without the consent of both parents, guardians, or court, as case may be. Marriages within certain prescribed degrees of relationship are also prohibited in Second Schedule to Marriage Act 1955.

Notice of every intended marriage must be given by one of the parties to the registrar of the district within which one of the parties has dwelt for not less than three days, such notice containing full particulars of the parties and of the intended marriage. A declaration of the truth of the particulars in the notice must then be made, and party giving notice must also appear personally before registrar and declare that there is no impediment or hindrance to marriage. When registrar has issued certificate, marriage may be celebrated either before duly authorized marriage celebrant or before registrar. Any person may lodge with any registrar caveat against marriage of any person on grounds that marriage is one for which licence should not be issued.

In any case of marriage intended to be celebrated outside New Zealand under the Foreign Marriage Act 1892 (United Kingdom) or any new Act, or in any case of marriage between British subjects intended to be celebrated or contracted in the United Kingdom, one of the parties who has had his or her usual place of abode in a marriage district in New Zealand for not less than seven days beforehand may give notice of the intended marriage to the registrar of that district, the notice being required to contain full particulars of the parties and of the intended marriage. On being satisfied that there is no lawful hindrance to the marriage the registrar issues a certificate that the notice has been duly given. The same provisions as to consent to infants' marriages apply as in the case of marriages celebrated in New Zealand. Certain marriages abroad may be expressly declared valid in New Zealand as if solemnised in New Zealand in accordance with Act.

Pursuant to Status of Children Act 1969 relationship between person and his or her mother or father is determined irrespective of whether mother and father are or have been married to each other.

See topic Infancy.

MARRIED WOMEN:

See topics Husband and Wife; Nationality.

MONOPOLIES AND RESTRAINT OF TRADE:

Commerce Act 1986 is designed to promote competition in markets by prohibiting restrictive trade practices which substantially lessen competition. Price fixing and resale price maintenance are per se unlawful. Abuse of dominant market position is also prohibited under monopolisation laws contained in Act. Mergers and takeovers are prohibited if they are likely to result in acquisition or strengthening of any dominant position in market. Bare transfer of monopoly power is permitted.

Authorisations may be obtained from Commerce Commission for restrictive trade practices on grounds of public benefit. Clearances and authorisations may be obtained for business acquisitions on grounds of no acquisition or strengthening of dominance or countervailing public benefit. Right of appeal to High Court of New Zealand and, in limited circumstances, to Court of Appeal.

Territorial Sea and Exclusive Economic Zone Act 1977 claims for New Zealand territorial sea of 12 miles and exclusive zone of 188 miles beyond that. No foreign fishing craft is to be used for fishing within exclusive economic zone except in accordance with licence issued by Minister of Fisheries. Substantial penalties are provided for breach of Act. See also topic Shipping.

MORTGAGES OF REAL PROPERTY:

Virtually all private land is registered under Land Transfer Act 1952. Mortgage in order to be legal and not equitable must be in prescribed form, executed in prescribed manner and registered under Act. Order of registration determines priorities but priority may be varied by appropriate documents. Mortgages may secure further advances. Ownership is not transferred by mortgage of land. Registration is notice. Mortgage statutory charge. Equitable mortgages may be created by written agreement (deposit of title deeds alone is insufficient). Priority may be protected and notice given by caveat against title.

Powers of sale and entry into possession can only be exercised after giving one month's notice. Mortgagee in possession must comply with provisions of Property Law Act 1952. Mortgagee may buy in if sells through High Court.

Mortgage of land granted by company must also be registered with Registrar of Companies.

See also topic Real Property and topic Contracts, subhead Credit Contracts Act 1981.

MORTGAGES OF SHARES:

There are no statutory rules relating specifically to mortgages of shares. Mortgage of shares by individual is not registrable under Chattels Transfer Act 1924 as shares are not chattels for purposes of that Act. Mortgage of shares by company is not registrable under Companies Act nor Chattels Transfer Act. Mortgage of shares held by individual is therefore unregulated except by common law. Shares held by company may be mortgaged subject to general rules in companies legislation relating to charges over company assets.

See topics Corporations; Chattel Mortgages.

MOTOR VEHICLES:

Every motor vehicle must be registered, licensed annually and bear registration plate in front and rear. Vehicle must possess vehicle certificate of inspection, and owner must renew certificate every six months. Every driver must have license to drive. Extensive powers for making of regulations are conferred by Transport Act 1962 upon Executive Council.

Compensation for injuries received in motor accidents is assessed under Accident Rehabilitation and Compensation Insurance Act 1992. Owners of motor vehicles contribute to cost of scheme created by that Act. Motor Vehicle Dealers Act 1975 prohibits any person from carrying on business of buying, selling, exchanging or leasing motor vehicles without first obtaining motor vehicle dealers licence. All salesmen employed by motor vehicle dealers must be approved.

Motor Vehicle Securities Act 1989 appoints Registrar to establish and maintain register of "security interests" in motor vehicles. Act provides that in some circumstances where motor vehicle is purchased, acquired under hire purchase agreement or leased, any existing security interest will be extinguished. Priority regime for certain security interests is also established.

New Zealand is party to Geneva Convention on Road Traffic.

See also topic Sales.

NATIONALITY:

Citizenship Act 1977 consolidates and amends law relating to citizenship as originally set out in British Nationality and New Zealand Citizenship Act 1948; status of persons who are New Zealand citizens under latter Act is not affected. Every person born in New Zealand except for children of certain aliens holding diplomatic status or who are enemy aliens shall be citizen by birth although exception does not apply in case of children born after Jan. 1, 1978 if child would be rendered stateless. Every person born outside New Zealand after Jan. 1, 1978 shall be New Zealand citizen by descent if at time of his birth his father or mother is New Zealand citizen otherwise than by descent. Person shall be deemed to be child of New Zealand citizen if he has been adopted by that citizen pursuant to Adoption Act 1955. Any other person who has attained 18 years of age and is of full capacity may obtain citizenship by grant if he satisfies Minister of Internal Affairs that: (a) He has three years ordinary residence in New Zealand immediately prior to application (period may be reduced by Ministerial discretion in case of undue hardship); and (b) he is entitled to be in New Zealand indefinitely under Immigration Act; and (c) he is of good character; and (d) he has sufficient knowledge of responsibilities and privileges of New Zealand citizenship; and (e) he has sufficient knowledge of English language (this condition may be waived in case of undue hardship); and (f) he intends to continue to reside in New Zealand or work for Government overseas.

Citizenship may also be granted by Minister, without residence period, to any person: (a) Who is minor; (b) who marries New Zealand citizen and satisfies conditions (c) to (e) above and shows he will maintain association (other than through marriage) with New Zealand; (c) whose father or mother was at time of person's birth New Zealand citizen by descent; (d) in exceptional circumstances of humanitarian or other nature and if in public interest.

Act also provides for loss of citizenship in case of taking up other citizenship or if citizenship fraudulently obtained and for registration of aliens.

There are special provisions relating to persons of Western Samoan descent in Citizenship (Western Samoa) Act 1982.

See also topic Aliens.

NATURALIZATION:

See topics Aliens; Nationality.

NEGOTIABLE INSTRUMENTS:

See topic Bills and Notes.

NOTARIES PUBLIC:

Notaries exercise their functions in New Zealand. There is no statute law in New Zealand relating to notaries; English law applies. See topics Affidavits; Commissioners To Administer Oaths.

PARTNERSHIP:

The rules of common law and equity continue to apply except in so far as they are inconsistent with the Partnership Act 1908, which is, in main, declaratory of those rules.

In past, number of partners permitted in partnership carrying on business for gain was restricted to 25 (with some exceptions). From July 1, 1994, this restriction has been removed.

What is known as a "special partnership," which is similar to the "limited partnership" of English law, may be formed for the transaction of agricultural, mining, mercantile, mechanical, manufacturing, or other business (except banking and insurance). Such a partnership must be registered, and consists of general partners and special partners, the latter contributing to the common stock specific sums in money as capital, beyond which they are not generally responsible for any debt of the partnership.

A feature of the Act is the extent of the powers conferred on High Court to dissolve partnerships.

PATENTS:

Governed and regulated by Patents Act 1953 (as am'd 1994), and Patents Regulations 1954. Patents are granted for inventions. Term is now for 20 years. All procedures for extensions of term of patent have been repealed (subject to transitional provisions). Inventor or his assignee may apply. Three copies of specifications, claims and drawings are required but in nonconvention cases provisional specifications may be filed first if formal documents lodged within 12 months.

Application may claim priority from date of first filing in convention country if made within 12 months.

Novelty is essential. There can be no prior publication or use in N.Z. Obviousness will also be ground of refusal. Documents are examined and application must be in order for acceptance within 15 months from date of filing complete specification. Power of Commissioner to refuse application now restricted to case where invention contrary to morality. Previous grounds for refusal: that obviously contrary to well established natural laws, that use of invention contrary to law, or that invention is substance capable of being used as food or medicine which is mixture of known ingredients possessing only aggregate of their known properties or process of producing such substance by mere admixture, now removed.

After acceptance, acceptance is advertised in Patent Office Journal usually published monthly and opposition may be lodged within three months. Oppositions are decided by Commissioner subject to appeal to High Court.

There is no restriction on manufacture, sale or use of overseas patented article if no N.Z. patent. Otherwise patentee has exclusive entitlement. Patents may be assigned or licensed. In event of nonuse, compulsory licences may be granted. Note also Crown use provisions. Marking of articles with N.Z. patent number is not essential but failure may enable infringer to avoid damages.

In infringement proceedings for process patents for producing new products, purportedly infringing new product now deemed to be infringement unless and until defendant establishes its process is not that covered by patent.

Designs.—Governed by Designs Act 1953 and Regulations 1954.

PERPETUITIES:

Basically common law applies but Perpetuities Act 1964 introduced many improvements, e.g., (1) Woman who has attained age of 55 years or child under 12 years of age are now presumed for purposes of rule to be incapable of having a child; (2) unborn widow or widower possibility is abolished; (3) rule of remorseless construction is abolished; (4) High Court has power to reform disposition in certain circumstances; (5) wait and see rule is applied; (6) terminable fee becomes fee simple if it is not terminated within perpetuity period.

In general, perpetuity period is still a life in being plus 21 years but Act enables a settlor or testator to adopt a period not exceeding 80 years by specifying to that effect in instrument by which disposition is made.

PLEDGES:

The common law of pledges is still applicable, but the licensing and conduct of the business of pawnbrokers are dealt with by statute. Maximum rates of profit have been repealed by Credit Contracts Act 1981. See topic Contracts, subhead Credit Contracts Act 1981.

PRESCRIPTION:

See topic Limitation of Actions.

PRINCIPAL AND AGENT:

While basically common law there is Mercantile Law Act 1908 (virtually identical with English Factors Act).

An agent having in customary course of his business as such agent authority to sell, consign for sale, buy, or raise money on security of, goods, is known as "mercantile agent." Where such an agent is, with consent of owner, in possession of goods or their documents of title, any sale, pledge, or other disposition by him when acting in ordinary course of his business is as valid as if he was expressly authorized so to do by owner, provided purchaser takes bona fide, for value and without notice of agent's lack of authority. If goods are motor vehicles and security interests are registered over those vehicles pursuant to Motor Vehicles Securities Act 1989, purchaser is deemed to have notice of agent's lack of authority unless such authority is proved to exist. Powers so conferred on mercantile agent are in amplification and not in derogation of powers exercisable by him at common law.

There is also Secret Commissions Act 1910 and Real Estate Agents Act 1976. Secret Commissions Act provides penalties for agent who commits his principal to contract in which he has pecuniary interest, or for which he receives consideration from other party to contract. Latter Act provides for licensing of land agents, audit of their trust accounts and for fidelity guarantee fund. No land agent may recover commission unless he has acknowledgment of authority in writing whether made before or after contract.

REAL PROPERTY:

In general, apart from matters incidental to compulsory registration of land under Land Transfer Act 1952, law of real property in New Zealand is same as in England. Property Law Act 1952 consolidates law as to real property in New Zealand and embodies many of changes enacted by Law of Property Act 1925 (England).

The Land Transfer or Torrens system of title to land has now virtually superseded the old conveyancing system. Under the Land Transfer system the title of the owner is a certificate of title constituted by a page in a volume held in the District Land Registry. Legal owner retains duplicate certificate of title. All dealings (except private trusts and equitable dealings) are recorded in register which is, except in case of fraud, conclusive evidence of such dealings. Registration constitutes notice to all persons dealing with such land, and common law doctrine of constructive notice has no application. Title may now be gained by prescription of 20 years occupation in limited circumstances.

Foreign individual and corporation may become registered as proprietor of land in certain circumstances. See topic Aliens.

Joint Family Homes Act 1964 is designed to protect family home from creditors and grant it exemption from gift duty. Either or both spouses may settle their home upon themselves jointly under Act. Neither can separately alienate his or her interest. On death of either spouse home becomes property of survivor. Matrimonial Property Act 1976 gives some equivalent protection and exemptions.

Estate Duty Abolition Act 1993 abolished estate duty in respect of estates of persons who die after Dec. 17, 1992.

Protection of Personal and Property Rights Act 1988 gives High Court jurisdiction to appoint manager to manage affairs of incompetent people.

Treaty of Waitangi Act 1975 enables Maori inhabitants of New Zealand to claim compensation from Crown for injustices to Maori. Where land has been purchased from Crown-owned enterprise that land may be liable to be taken by Crown for return to Maori. Compensation is payable in respect of land taken. Liability is identified by memorial on title to relevant land.

The government of any foreign state is deemed to be and to have always been capable of being registered as proprietor of any estate or interest in land in the same manner as if it were a corporation, and any transfer or other instrument purporting to affect its land may be executed on behalf of the government of any foreign state by the senior representative in New Zealand of that state.

See also topics Taxation, subhead Tax on Property; Husband and Wife.

REPORTS:

Law reports include New Zealand Law Reports (NZLR) published by New Zealand Council of Law Reporting, New Zealand Town Planning Appeals (N.Z.T.P.A.), Tax Reports of New Zealand—(TRNZ); Family Law Reports—(NZFLR); New Zealand Administrative Reports—(NZAR); Conveyancing and Property Reports—(NZCPR); New Zealand Intellectual Property Reports—(NZIPR); District Court Reports—(DCR); and Butterworth's Company Reports—(BCR) all published by Butterworths; Trade and Competition Law Reports (T.C.L.R.), Criminal Reports of New Zealand (C.R.N.Z.), Family Reports of New Zealand (F.R.N.Z.) and Procedure Reports of New Zealand (P.R.N.Z.) published by Brooker and Friend; and New Zealand Bill of Rights Reports, (N.Z.B.O.R.R.). Summaries of cases appear weekly in Capital Letter, fortnightly in Current Law, and monthly in Recent Law.

RESTRAINT OF TRADE:

See topic Monopolies and Restraint of Trade.

SALES:

The Sale of Goods Act 1908 substantially reproduces the English Act of 1893, except that law relating to market overt is expressly excluded. The statute is practically a codification of the law on the subject and deals specifically with the formalities of the contract, the price, conditions and warranties, sales by sample, rights of unpaid sellers, and actions for breach of the contract.

A contract of sale may be made in writing (either with or without seal) or by word of mouth, or partly in writing and partly by word of mouth, or may be implied from the conduct of the parties.

Where goods are of perishable nature or where unpaid seller gives notice to buyer of intention to resell and buyer does not pay price within reasonable time, unpaid seller may resell goods and may recover damages from original buyer.

If a sale of goods is binding according to law governing contract of sale and to law of place where goods are situate at time of sale, sale will be upheld by New Zealand Court. Law governing the contract is determined by reference to intention of parties or to presumptions relating to place where contract was to be made or to be performed.

Layby Sales Act 1971 is deemed part of Sale of Goods Act 1908. Act excluded if sale is of motor vehicle and seller is dealer licensed under Motor Vehicle Dealers Act 1975 or price exceeds $1,000. Act entitles purchaser to statement of balance owing, to cancel contract and governs rights on cancellation and time when risk passes.

As to hire-purchase agreements, see topic Chattel Mortgages.

Where there is no remedy expressly provided by Sale of Goods Act 1908 law relating to remedies for breach of contract and misrepresentation is now governed by Contractual Remedies Act 1979 rather than common law.

Warranties on sale of goods are either expressed or implied under Sale of Goods Act 1908. Under this Act three conditions are implied after certain prerequisites are satisfied: (a) Correspondence with description; (b) fitness for purpose; (c) merchantable quality. In case of a sale by sample there is an implied condition that bulk shall correspond with sample in quality; that buyer shall have a reasonable opportunity of comparing bulk with sample; and that goods are not unmerchantable. Open to parties to exclude above conditions in their contract, except layby sales where Act does not allow contracting out unless conditions more favourable to buyer. An implied warranty or condition as to quality or fitness for particular purpose may be annexed by trade or usage. Certain warranties as to title are also implied in contracts of sale, namely: (a) implied condition on part of seller that he has right to sell goods; (b) implied warranty that buyer shall have and enjoy quiet possession of goods and; (c) implied warranty that goods are free from any charge or encumbrance in favour of any third party. There are currently no guarantees of quality imposed by law or usage.

Consumer Guarantees Act 1993 replaces implied conditions as to title, quality, fitness and correspondence with description and sample contained in Sale of Goods Act 1908 in case of supply of goods to consumers (customers purchasing for domestic use and not for business use or resale) and introduces additional guarantees, one of which is that goods are of acceptable quality. Goods will only be considered to be of acceptable quality if fit for all purposes for which goods of type in question are commonly supplied, have acceptable appearance and finish, be free from minor defects, be safe and durable and be what reasonable consumer fully acquainted with state and condition of goods would regard as acceptable having regard to such matters as nature and price of goods and representations made on packaging and by suppliers. Act also provides for guarantees in relation to services, including guarantees as to

SALES . . . *continued*
reasonable care and skill, fitness, time of completion and price. Procedures for enforcing statutory guarantees are created. Act cannot be contracted out of.

Door to Door Sales Act 1967 makes certain credit sale agreements, hire purchase agreements and hiring agreements in respect of sale of goods or provision of services entered into at premises other than vendor's premises unenforceable unless agreement is in writing, signed by purchaser and by or on behalf of vendor, contains a statutory statement dealing with purchaser's right of cancellation, contains statement of cost and details of credit received by purchaser, copy of agreement and form for use on cancellation is handed to purchaser at time agreement is made. Agreements that are subject to Act may be cancelled in all cases by purchaser within seven days entitling purchaser to return of all moneys paid, any trade-in and in certain cases compensation.

Unsolicited Goods and Services Act 1975.—Act provides if recipient does not agree to acquire or return goods and sender does not repossess them within stated time goods deemed gift. Contracts for supply of prescribed services made unenforceable unless recipient signs note complying with Act. Threats or demands for payment, and sending invoices, for unordered goods or services made offences.

Motor Vehicle Dealers Act 1975 requires car dealers to be licensed and salesmen to be registered or approved. Act imposes obligations on licensee in respect of sale of second-hand motor vehicles.

Motor Vehicle Securities Act 1989 provides that, in certain circumstances where motor vehicle is purchased any existing "security interest" will be extinguished. See topic Motor Vehicles.

Fair Trading Act 1986 dictates standards of consumer and product safety. Misleading and deceptive conduct, in relation to trade, is prohibited. False representations relating to wide range of descriptive aspects of those goods or services are also prohibited—i.e. quality, quantity, grade, previous history or usage, price, origin, approval, endorsement, etc. Certain unfair practices are also prohibited—trading stamp schemes, bait advertising, referral selling, pyramid selling schemes, etc. Penalties for infringement both civil and criminal—fines up to maximum of $100,000 for corporate liability and up to $30,000 for personal liability. Injunctive relief available to all litigants—remedy of corrective advertising available only to Commerce Commission, body given task of policing compliance with Act. Limited defences available to news media and restricted to reasonable mistake etc. Three year limitation period.

Minster can declare services safety standards.

See topic Contracts, subhead Credit Contracts Act 1981.

SEALS:

In case of individuals, sealing is not necessary for validity of any deed, but seals are sometimes used by individuals where document is intended for use overseas. Notaries Public continue to use seals.

In case of companies incorporated under either Companies Act 1955 ("1955 Act") or Companies Act 1993 ("1993 Act"), use of common seals is no longer required (unless articles or constitution of company provide otherwise). Companies incorporated under 1955 Act should retain common seal until articles are amended to delete references to common seal, or until company reregisters under 1993 Act. Given current uncertainty as to validity of documents executed under common seal, companies should generally dispense with use of common seal where possible.

See topic Corporations, subhead Execution of Documents.

SHIPPING:

Chief statute dealing with shipping and maritime transport in general is Maritime Transport Act 1994. Act contains ship safety provisions which came into force on 1 Feb. 1995. Maritime Safety Authority of New Zealand continues as organisation responsible for maintenance of and adherence to maritime safety standards.

Act also contains significant marine environment protection provisions, including measures relating to protection from oil spills and marine pollution. It is intended to repeal Marine Pollution Act 1974 in due course.

Owners of ships (and any other person for whose acts or omissions owner is responsible), salvors (and persons for whom they are responsible) and insurers of such persons are entitled to limit liability in respect of certain claims unless loss or damage arising from such person's personal act or omission was committed or omitted with intent to cause such loss or injury or recklessly and with knowledge that such loss or injury would probably result. Limit of liability can be claimed in respect of: (a) Loss of life or personal injury or loss of or damage to property occurring on board ship or directly connected with its operation or salvage; (b) loss or damage arising from delay; (c) loss or damage resulting from infringement of rights other than contractual rights directly connected with operation of ship or salvage; (d) claims in respect of raising, removal etc. of ships which have sunk or been wrecked; (e) claims in respect of removal, destruction or rendering harmless of cargo of ship; and (f) claims of person (other than person liable) in respect of measures taken to avert or minimize any loss, injury or damage for which person liable is entitled to limit liability.

Claims for salvage on contribution in general average, for oil pollution damage subject to Marine Pollution Act 1974 and claims in respect of nuclear damage are excluded.

Calculation of limits of liability is by reference based on tonnage of ship multiplied by "units of account" (being $NZ equivalent of International Monetary Fund Special Drawing Rights). Scale applicable is different for claims relating to loss of life or personal injury as opposed to other types of claim.

Carriage of Goods Act 1979 prescribes further limitations on liabilities. "Carrier of goods" liability is limited in amount to sum of $1,500 for each unit of goods lost or damaged or in case of contract "at declared value risk" for amount specified in contract. Carrier of goods will not be liable for any loss or damage to goods which results directly and without fault on its part from: (a) Inherent vice, (b) any breach of implied term that goods are fit to be carried and stored in accordance with contract or that goods are packed in manner in which they are tendered for carriage, (c) seizure under legal process, or (d) saving or attempting to save life or anybody in peril.

Sea Carriage of Goods Act 1940 applies to carriage of goods from New Zealand to any port outside New Zealand. Rules governing rights, immunities and liabilities of carrier are similar to those contained in schedule to Carriage of Goods by Sea Act 1924 (U.K.). Both Acts abolish undertaking to provide seaworthy ship which common law implied on part of shipowner. Admiralty Act 1973 prescribes jurisdiction in admiralty and in prize of New Zealand courts. See also England Law Digest, topic Shipping.

See also topic Carriage by Air.

Territorial Sea and Exclusive Economic Zone Act 1977 creates exclusive economic zone of New Zealand being, broadly, balance of seas from 12 mile territorial limit out to 200 miles from shore. Minister of Fisheries determines total allowable catch of fish within zone and what proportion thereof New Zealand fishing craft have capacity to harvest. Balance constitutes allowable catch for foreign craft. No foreign craft may fish within zone unless Minister has issued licence in respect of that craft. Fees for licences may be imposed. See also topic Monopolies and Restraint of Trade.

Antarctic Marine Living Resources Act 1981 gives effect to 1980 Canberra Convention on Conservation of Antarctic Marine Living Resources by prohibiting taking of marine organisms (living or dead) from Convention area without ministerial permission.

Driftnet Prohibition Act 1991 provides penalties in respect of driftnet fishing activities and implements Convention for the Prohibition of Fishing with Long Driftnets in the South Pacific.

Marine Pollution Act 1974 provides penalties in respect of oil or pollutant discharged into New Zealand waters; provides for civil liability of shipowners for pollution damage and regulates dumping and incineration of wastes.

See also topic Judgments.

Shipping Act 1987 provides for regulation of unfair practices as between shippers and carriers. Act is intended to promote fair competition in international shipping and provides procedures whereby Minister of Transport can investigate and regulate unfair practices. Act excludes parts of Commerce Act 1986 (which deals with competition and trade practices) from application to carriage of goods by sea from place inside New Zealand to place outside New Zealand.

Ships Registration Act 1992 governs registration of ships and procedure for mortgaging ship or share in ship.

STATUTE OF FRAUDS:

See topics Frauds, Statute of; Sales.

STATUTES:

The Statutes of New Zealand are published each year by GP Print Limited, as are also the New Zealand Gazette, which contains proclamations and Orders-in-Council, and the Regulations, which comprise all regulations made under the authority of statutes.

TAXATION:

Land tax has been abolished for land held on Mar. 31, 1992 and subsequently.

Sales tax was repealed from Oct. 1, 1986 when goods and services tax came into force, although excise tax is imposed on limited range of goods.

Goods and services tax is imposed by Goods and Services Tax Act 1985. It is similar to European value added tax. It applies to supply of all goods and services and is levied at rate of 12.5% on value of goods or services supplied; see §8.

Tax is payable on supply of nearly all goods and services. Two exceptions are for zero-rated goods and services and exempt goods and services. Zero-rating applies mainly to exported goods and services. There is no zero-rating of classes of goods. Exempt goods and services are mainly financial services and residential rents.

Income Tax.—Pay-as-you-earn system of collection has been adopted and applies to all salary and wage income of individuals. Various other withholding taxes apply—see catchline "Withholding Payments", infra. Other income is subject to system of provisional tax payments made in three instalments during financial year. Taxation Review Authority or High Court deals with objections to determinations made by Commissioner.

Rate for individuals is on sliding scale reaching maximum of 33% at $30,875 (proposed to be increased to $34,200 in 1996-97 and $38,000 in 1997-98). Low income rebate exists for taxpayers earning less than $9,500.

Rate for companies is 33¢ in dollar. Company dividends are taxable in hands of shareholders (except New Zealand companies in certain circumstances) and become part of shareholder's assessable income. Since Aug. 20, 1985 all distributions by company (except certain share repurchase but including bonus issues in lieu of dividends) are dividends. Scheme of full imputation for corporate distributions has applied from Apr. 1, 1988.

Accrual tax accounting rules relating to timing of deductions and recognition of income apply to all financial arrangements, that is, debt instruments or arrangements whereby money is obtained in return for payment, either present or future. Definition contains exclusions. Yield to maturity method of calculation must be used by holders of financial arrangements when ascertaining income to give discounted cash flow analysis to calculate yield on instrument. Yield is then applied in each compounding period to value of instrument at start of that period, in order to calculate interest which may be deducted or assessed in that period. When yield to maturity method is not appropriate, taxpayers will be required to use another appropriate and approved method. From Apr. 1, 1991, straight line method of accrual may be used by person holding or issuing financial arrangements totalling $1 million or less and accrual rates will not affect natural persons whose income does not exceed $70,000 p.a. or whose financial arrangements do not exceed $600,000 in value.

Note: Legislation has been enacted to deny deductions for payments to nonresidents if not enough information about payment is given to Inland Revenue Department. Also, partial deduction only is available for certain entertainment expenditure.

Government has enacted comprehensive legislation to subject to income tax New Zealand residents having 10% or greater interest in foreign companies controlled from

See Topical Index in front part of this volume.

TAXATION . . . *continued*
New Zealand, on their share of accruing income of those foreign companies (except in case of six specific countries). Legislation, generally applicable with effect Apr. 1993, also subjects to tax New Zealand residents on any growth in value of interests (of whatever size) in foreign companies, unit trusts, life insurance policies and superannuation funds (subject to certain exemptions). Where New Zealand resident has settled property on trust, all worldwide income of that trust is subject to New Zealand income tax and New Zealand resident is liable to meet such tax as agent for trustee unless trustee is resident in New Zealand at all times.

Excess retention tax applicable to dividend income of privately controlled investment companies has been abolished with effect from Apr. 1, 1990.

Nonresident withholding tax is payable on payments or distributions, to nonresidents, of dividends, royalties, know-how payments, and interest (including redemption payments on commercial bills). Persons making such payments are obliged to deduct withholding tax at source. On dividends, "cultural royalties" and interest if interest is not paid to "associated person", withholding tax is 30% for dividends and 15% for "cultural royalties" and interest, and no further New Zealand tax is payable by recipient. From other types of income subject to nonresident withholding tax, tax is minimum tax and is deductible from final assessment at rate calculated by reference to total income (including income not subject to nonresident withholding tax) of nonresident individual or company. Attached imputation credits will allow effective rebate of tax on dividends in some cases.

"Withholding payments", defined to include payments to nonresident contractors for services performed in New Zealand, for work in New Zealand on physical development projects or for supply for use in New Zealand of personal property or services, are subject to withholding of 15% of gross amount pending final determination of tax liability in New Zealand. Exemption may be sought on basis of satisfactory taxpaying history, application of reciprocal agreement on tax with nonresident's home state, etc.

Resident withholding tax applies to domestic payments of interest or dividends to New Zealand residents. In case of interest, only persons carrying on business are to be required to deduct withholding tax and many of those persons may receive interest income free of deduction. In case of dividends, exemption will continue to apply for inter-corporate dividends. Rate of withholding is 24% for interest and 33% for dividends (with credit given for imputation credits). Contributions to superannuation funds are subject to final withholding tax of 33%.

Superannuitant surcharge is imposed on government-provided superannuation when superannuitant's other income exceeds minimum level. Tax is calculated by formula according to amount of superannuitant's other income. Maximum tax is equal to amount of superannuitant's government-provided superannuation.

Fringe benefit tax is payable by employers on value of certain benefits (goods and services, low interest loans, vehicles for private use, and some subsidised transport) provided by employers to employees. No tax is imposed on employee who receives benefits on which employer pays fringe benefit tax. Rate of 49% applies from Apr. 1, 1989 but tax is deductible to employer.

Reciprocity with Other States.—New Zealand Government has entered into reciprocal agreements with U.S.A., Canada, U.K., Sweden, Japan, Singapore, Australia, Fiji, Malaysia, Germany, France, Philippines, Italy, Denmark, Switzerland, Belgium, Finland, Netherlands, Norway, South Korea, China, Ireland, Indonesia and India.

Agreements are based on "credit" system although some use "exemption" system in part. There are differences in each Double Tax Agreement.

Canadian agreement closely resembles agreement with U.S. Under Canadian agreement residents of New Zealand and Canada are exempt from taxation in other's territory if they are present within such territory for period not exceeding in aggregate 183 days in any year, in respect of personal services performed for persons resident in their own territory, provided profits or remuneration are subject to that territory's taxation. Tax payable in other territory on income derived from sources within such territory is allowed as credit to residents of Canada or New Zealand against tax payable in their own territory.

Industrial or commercial profits of New Zealand enterprise are not subject to taxation in Canada unless enterprise has a permanent establishment situated there to which such profits are attributable, and corresponding provisions are in force with respect to Canadian enterprises in New Zealand.

In New Zealand the credit allowed is lesser of (1) Tax imposed by country which has primary right to tax income, or (2) New Zealand tax on that income.

Tax on Property.—Profits derived by individuals or companies dealing in sale or disposition of real or personal property or who bought such property for purpose or intention of disposition are deemed to be assessable income. Profits derived by persons associated with persons dealing in land may also be deemed to be assessable income. Taxable profits can also arise from certain land betterment factors. There are exemptions for certain bona fide dispositions of properties occupied by individuals or companies. Capital gains tax has recently been studied by Government but Government has announced that no such tax will be introduced.

Death duty on estates of deceased persons was abolished by Estate Duty Abolition Act 1993 in respect of estate of any person who dies on or after Dec. 17, 1992.

Gift duty is imposed by Estate and Gift Duties Act 1968 on value of gifts made by person within any period of 12 months. No duty is payable where such gifts do not exceed value of $27,000 per annum in aggregate. Duty for gifts exceeding $27,000 in aggregate is as follows: (a) Exceeding $27,000 but not exceeding $36,000: 5% on excess over $27,000; (b) exceeding $36,000 but not exceeding $54,000: $450 plus 10% of excess over $36,000; (c) exceeding $54,000 but not exceeding $72,000: $2,250 plus 20% of excess over $54,000; (d) exceeding $72,000: $5,850 plus 25% of excess of $72,000. Charitable gifts are exempt from duty.

Annual budget is introduced about July and changes in tax rates usually take place from commencement of financial year which is Apr. 1.

Foreign Officials.—The Minister may exempt from any public or local tax diplomatic representatives of foreign states, high commissioners, foreign consuls, trade commissioners and their staffs resident in New Zealand solely for performance of official duties.

See also topic Treaties.

Absentees for tax purposes are individuals who do not have permanent place of abode in New Zealand and who are not present in New Zealand for 183 days or more in 12 month period. Tax liability of absentee generally depends upon: (1) Derivation from New Zealand of any income, (2) whether there is relevant double taxation agreement. 1981 Income Tax Amendment Act extends definition of New Zealand for purposes of Income Tax Act to include air and sea space above continental shelf where exploration or exploitation of natural resource involves activity on or in that water or air space.

Stamp duty is imposed by Stamp and Cheque Duties Act 1971 and (with effect from Mar. 17, 1988) only on conveyances and other instruments transferring or agreeing to transfer or lease commercial land and buildings. Basic rates are: conveyances of commercial land and buildings, 1% for first $50,000; $50,000 to $100,000 1.5%; excess over $100,000 2%; leases 40¢ per $100 annual rent. Stamp duty is no longer imposed on other instruments.

See also topic Real Property.

TRADEMARKS:

Governed by Trade Marks Act 1953 and Regulations 1954 which substantially follow U.K. counterparts. (See England Law Digest, topic Trademarks and Tradenames.) Recent Amendments made by Trade Marks Amendment Act 1994 widen definition of "trade mark", broaden scope of proprietor's protection and incorporate border protection measures. Note, however, significant transitional provisions. U.K. practice and interpretation is substantially followed. "Trade mark" means any sign capable of being represented graphically and capable of distinguishing goods and services of one person from another. May include shape of goods, shape of packaging and smells and sounds (if capable of being "represented graphically"). Marks for goods and services are registrable. Registration is not essential to use of mark but no Trade Mark Act action lies for infringement of unregistered mark. Common law remedy of "passing off" is not affected. To all intents, generally same restrictions as in U.K. apply to registrable marks except similar or identical mark is unable to be registered in relation to similar goods or services. Infringement also by use of identical or similar mark in relation to similar goods or services. Certification and defensive trademarks registrable. Convention applications must be made within six months of first application. Registration is for period of seven years followed by successive periods of 14 years. Trademarks are assignable with or without goodwill of business in goods in question and registered users are permissible. Register is divided into Part A and Part B as in U.K. Border protection provisions of Trade Mark Act enable proprietor to request Customs Department to detain goods with infringing marks.

Geographical Indications Act 1994 establishes registration system for protection of geographical indications for certain specified goods. Geographical indications are descriptions or presentations used to indicate geographical origin being county, region, locality or linear feature (river, road or similar geographical feature). Applications may be made for determination of geographical indication relating to geographical origin in New Zealand (via Surveyor General) or for non-New Zealand geographical indications (submitted in accordance with multilateral or bilateral international agreements). Commencement date of Act soon to be determined. No provision for tradename registration as in England.

See also topic Patents.

TREATIES:

New Zealand is party to bilateral trade and commerce agreements with number of countries. Most important treaty is New Zealand—Australia Closer Economic Relations Trade Agreement which provides for elimination of tariffs and quantitative import restrictions between two countries no later than 1995. New development, was conclusion in 1992 of Trade and Investment Framework Agreement with U.S.A. New Zealand is also party to bilateral agreements making provision for scientific and technological cooperation with other countries.

Agreements to avoid double taxation and fiscal evasion are in force. New Zealand has also concluded bilateral Investment Promotion and Protection Agreements. See topic Taxation.

New Zealand is member of World Trade Organisation.

New Zealand is member of Customs Cooperation Council and party to associated customs conventions, including International Convention on the Simplification and Harmonization of Customs Procedures.

New Zealand is also party to Asian Development Bank Agreement, Colombo Plan and Convention on the Organisation for Economic Co-operation and Development (OECD). It is member of U.N. (and related U.N. organisations), Commonwealth and European Bank for Reconstruction and Development, as well as being member of various regionally based organisations, including Asia-Pacific Economic Co-operation (APEC) and South Pacific Forum.

New Zealand is party to all of major U.N. human rights instruments, including International Covenant on Civil and Political Rights, International Covenant on Economic, Social and Cultural Rights and Convention on the Rights of the Child, Convention on Elimination of Discrimination Against Women, International Convention on the Elimination of All Forms of Racial Discrimination and Convention against Torture and other Cruel, Inhuman or Degrading Treatment or Punishment. New Zealand is also party to Operational Protocols to International Covenant on Civil and Political Rights.

New Zealand is party to Convention for Protection of National Resources and Environment of the South Pacific Region (SPREP Convention) and United Nations Framework Convention on Climatic Change, Convention on control of Transboundary Movements of Hazardous Wastes and their Disposal (Basel), London Convention on the Prevention of Marine Pollution by Dumping Wastes and Other Matter, Vienna Convention for the Protection of the Ozone Layer and Montreal Protocol on Substances that Deplete the Ozone Layer, Waigani Convention and Convention on Biological Diversity. New Zealand is also party to Antarctic Treaty and Protocol on Environmental Protection to the Antarctic Treaty, as well as Convention on the Conservation of Antarctic Marine Living Resources.

New Zealand is not party to Statute of The Hague Conference on Private International Law nor to Convention on Service Abroad of Judicial and Extrajudicial Documents in Civil or Commercial Matters, nor to Convention Abolishing the Requirement

TREATIES . . . *continued*
of Legislation for Foreign Public Documents. However, bilateral conventions providing for mutual legal assistance in respect of civil and commercial matters exist between New Zealand and 20 or so countries, and New Zealand has been party to Hague Convention on the Civil Aspects of Child Abduction since 1991. New Zealand now has legislation in place enabling it to conclude bilateral agreements or arrangements with other countries for provision of mutual assistance in criminal matters. New Zealand is party to 1958 United Nations Convention on Recognition and Enforcement of Foreign Arbitral Awards and to Convention on Settlement of Investment Disputes between States and Nationals of Other States.

New Zealand has bilateral extradition treaties or arrangements in force with large number of countries and is party to United Nations Single Convention on Narcotic Drugs and 1971 Convention on Psychotropic Substances.

New Zealand is also party to Berne Convention for the Protection of Literary and Artistic Works, Chicago Convention on International Civil Aviation, United Nations Convention on the Recovery Abroad of Maintenance, Treaty on the Non-Proliferation of Nuclear Weapons and South Pacific Nuclear Free Zone Treaty.

TRUSTS:

Trustee Act 1956 follows substantially Trustee Act 1925 of the United Kingdom with some modifications and extensions. See England Law Digest. However from Oct. 1, 1988 trustees may invest in any property, but are subject to new statutory duties from which they may contract out. Rules of common law governing rights and duties of trustees otherwise generally apply.

Only companies specially authorized by law can act as personal representatives of a deceased person. Trusts are not registrable under Land Transfer Act 1952, which affects legal interests only.

Public Trustee is authorized by statute to act as trustee under any will or settlement, and may accept appointment in conjunction with any other person. There is reciprocity of administration with Public Trustees of England and of other Commonwealth countries.

WILLS:

A will must be in writing, signed at the foot or end thereof by the testator or by some other person in his presence and by his direction, and such signature must be made or acknowledged by the testator in the presence of two or more witnesses present at the same time, and such witnesses must attest and subscribe the will in the sight and presence of the testator and of each other. It is practice to use attestation clause clearly indicating that these requirements have been complied with.

Wills Amendment Act 1977 provides that where person is divorced by any decree order or Legislative enactment recognised by New Zealand Courts any provision made by that person in his or her will in favour of other partner of former marriage shall unless contrary intention is expressed in will or any codicil thereto be null and void.

Status of Children Act 1969 abolishes illegitimacy in subsequently executed wills, but there are provisions to enable effect of Act to be negated.

See also topic Infancy.

Family Protection Act 1955 restricts freedom to dispose of property by will. That Act provides that if person dies leaving will without making therein adequate provision for proper maintenance and support of his or her wife, husband, children and, in certain circumstances, stepchildren, parents and grandchildren, court may on application order that such provision be made out of estate as it thinks fit. In general, application must be made within 12 months of grant of administration. "Children" includes illegitimate children and adopted children. Court has absolute discretion as to making of order. Provision made depends on size of estate and circumstances of applicant. Court will take into account material given it by administrators of estate who have duty to give to court information in their possession. Courts show little reluctance to make orders under Act.

Foreign Wills.—As regards realty, must be made (whether within or outside New Zealand) as required by law of New Zealand.

As regards movable property, held to be well executed if made outside New Zealand if made as required by: (a) Law of place where person was domiciled at time of his death; or (b) law of place where same was made; or (c) law of place where person was domiciled when same was made; or (d) law in force when same was made in place where person had his domicile of origin; and if made within New Zealand if made as required by: (a) Law of place where person was domiciled at time of his death; or (b) law of New Zealand; or (c) law of place where person was domiciled when same was made; and probate is granted or refused accordingly.

Law Reform (Testamentary Promises) Act 1949 provides that claims may be made against estates of deceased persons founded on services rendered deceased in his lifetime, where there was express or implied promise to reward claimant by testamentary provision. Claim is limited to extent to which deceased, by his will or otherwise has failed to remunerate claimant.

As to probate, see topic Executors and Administrators.

NICARAGUA LAW DIGEST REVISER

Curtis, Mallet-Prevost, Colt & Mosle
101 Park Avenue
New York, New York 10178-0061
Telephone: 212-696-6141
Fax: 212-697-1559
Email: CMP-NY@mcimail.com

Reviser Profile

The Firm began in 1830 when two practicing lawyers started a long line of lawyers and law firms extending in an unbroken chain up to the present time. In 1897, the firm name became Curtis, Mallet-Prevost & Colt; in 1925 it was changed to Curtis, Mallet-Prevost, Colt & Mosle. The Firm is now made up of approximately 120 lawyers, including experts who have published extensively on such diverse subjects as international money management, transnational contracts, state contracts, litigation against foreign states, sovereign immunity and the act of state doctrine, and the International Court of Justice. Its principal offices are in New York City. There are branch offices in Paris, London, Frankfurt Am Main, Hong Kong, Washington, D.C., Houston, Texas, Newark, N.J., and Mexico City. The Firm has five departments: Corporate and International; Litigation; Real Estate; Tax; and Trusts and Estates. The corporate and international department acts as general counsel to various public and private corporations and individual entrepreneurs. Clients are in the banking, insurance, securities, manufacturing, real estate and oil and gas industries. In addition, the corporate and international department frequently acts as special counsel to domestic and foreign clients, providing assistance in financing, know-how licensing, the negotiation and drafting of all types of contracts and instruments, counselling on all aspects of corporate law, and establishing the vehicles necessary to enable clients to conduct their domestic and foreign business activities. The Firm's international work permeates all areas of its practice and involves questions of private international law, foreign law and an unusual amount of public and quasi-public international law. Traditionally, much of the Firm's international practice has been concerned with Latin America. The Firm maintains its excellence in that area, with its Mexican affiliate, and also through the expertise of Latin American lawyers based in the New York office. The Firm's international practice has undergone a major expansion beyond Latin America to Europe, Africa and the Near and Far East. The Firm's litigation practice includes commercial litigation and arbitration, and white-collar criminal defense. It has substantial experience in civil aviation matters; it also has represented foreign States in transnational litigation and international arbitration arising out of acts of nationalization and alleged breach of economic development or natural resource supply contracts. Among the Firm's clients in real estate matters are institutional lenders and investors, real estate developers, both individual and corporate, foreign and domestic investors and syndicators. The tax department has substantial experience in all aspects of domestic and international business tax matters and real estate taxation. The matters the tax department deals with on a regular basis include: Taxation of foreign investments; the structuring of corporate transactions, including mergers, acquisitions, liquidations and reorganization; federal and state tax litigation; and tax planning for U.S. and foreign individuals. The trusts and estates department engages in general domestic trusts and estates practice and in tax planning for foreign persons wishing to invest in U.S. assets through offshore trusts and corporations. It represents individuals, trust companies, and banks acting as fiduciaries. It works for various charitable organizations located both in the United States and abroad including private foundations, museums, universities and hospitals. A group of fiduciary accountants with vast experience in the field assists the lawyers of the trusts and estates department. Curtis, Mallet-Prevost, Colt & Mosle has served as a Reviser for most of Latin American Law Digests since 1930.

NICARAGUA LAW DIGEST

(The following is a list of all Topics, including cross-references, covered in this Digest.)

NICARAGUA LAW DIGEST

Revised for 1997 edition by

CURTIS, MALLET-PREVOST, COLT & MOSLE, of the New York Bar.

(Abbreviations used are: C. C.—Civil Code; C. Com.—Code of Commerce; C. C. P.—Code of Civil Procedure. Numbers refer to articles in these codes.)

ABSENTEES: See topic Death.

ACKNOWLEDGMENTS:

Acknowledgments as customary in the United States are not used in Nicaragua, and documents requiring notarial authentication are executed as public instruments before notaries who retain the original in their file and issue certified copies. See topics Notaries Public; Public Instruments.

Documents executed abroad are accepted if executed in accordance with the laws of the respective country and authenticated by a diplomatic or consular officer of Nicaragua or, if none, of a friendly nation, but in cases where the Nicaraguan laws require a public instrument, no private writing will be accepted. (C. C. VI, XV; C. C. P. 1129-1131).

ACTIONS:

Actions for Death.—See topic Death, subhead Actions for Death.

Limitation of.—See topic Prescription, subhead Actions.

ADMINISTRATION:

See topic Executors and Administrators.

ADVERSE POSSESSION: See topic Prescription.

AGENCY: See topic Principal and Agent.

ALIENS:

Aliens in general have the same civil rights as citizens, and they can invest in any economic activity. (Const. art. 27, Immigration Law 153 of Apr. 22, 1993 and Aliens Law 154 of Apr. 30, 1993).

See also topics Descent and Distribution; Immigration; Mines and Minerals; Real Property; Records.

ALIMONY: See topic Divorce.

ASSIGNMENTS:

The assignment of a right or action is effected by delivery of the document evidencing the same, if any, or by a written instrument. Except when the document is subject to transfer by mere endorsement or payable to bearer, the assignment has no effect as to the debtor or third persons unless the debtor is notified thereof or accepts it. Notification may be made through a notary or judicial officer. The assignor of a credit document not subject to endorsement warrants the existence of the credit, but not the solvency of the debtor unless otherwise stipulated. (C. C. 2716-2747; C. Com. 230-232, 365-368).

ASSIGNMENTS FOR BENEFIT OF CREDITORS:

An assignment for the benefit of creditors is the voluntary abandonment by the debtor of all his assets, except those not subject to attachment, when in consequence of unavoidable accidents he cannot pay his debts. The creditors must accept the assignment unless the debtor is guilty of fraud or has dissipated his property, or has received deductions or extensions from the creditors. The assignment does not transfer the title to the property but only the right to dispose thereof. The debtor may be left in charge of the administration. The debts are extinguished only up to the amount obtained from the property assigned. (C. C. 2080-2091; C. C. P. 1809-1813, 1843-1858). See also topic Bankruptcy and Insolvency.

ASSOCIATIONS:

(Law 147 of Apr. 6, 1992).

Law regulates nonprofit organizations that can be organized by natural or juridical persons and at least five members are required. Associations legally established acquire juridical personality by legislative decree. Recording of their articles of association and decree of authorization is required. Articles of associations must contain name, domicile, purpose, term and name of its officers. Cancellation of authorization of associations is by legislative decree according to causes indicated by law and prior consultation with Ministerio de Gobernación.

ATTACHMENT:

On giving bond, precautionary attachments may be obtained with respect to the revenues, fruits or real property of the debtor, if the latter intends to take them away or alienate them, or if he is an alien, or if there is danger that they may deteriorate. The debtor may raise the attachment by giving bond. Likewise the claimant of a mine or of landed properties may demand judicial intervention in their management unless the defendant gives bond. An attachment may be issued without bond in summary actions based on certain documents designated in the law, such as documents executed before a notary, private documents judicially acknowledged, bills of exchange duly protested, judgments, etc. (C. C. P. 886-920, 1684-1842).

BANKRUPTCY AND INSOLVENCY:

(C. Com. 1047-1149; C. C. 2239-2334; C. C. P. 1843-1956).

Suspension of payments may be declared by the court on the petition of merchants who though possessing sufficient assets are unable to pay by reason of unforeseen circumstances. Extensions of time and other facilities will be granted to the extent approved by two-thirds of the creditors representing three-quarters of the debts, or three-quarters of the creditors representing two-thirds of the debts, and the same proportion of creditors may demand rejection of the suspension of payments. If there are no majorities in these proportions the judge may grant up to one year's extension. Certain debts are excepted, such as those guaranteed by mortgage or pledge, rentals, wages, etc.

Bankruptcy of merchants exists when they cease to make payments and do not enjoy the benefits of a suspension of payments. It may be declared on petition of the debtor or a creditor. The debtor thereupon becomes incompetent to manage his affairs and his debts mature, and, with certain exceptions, cease to bear interest. Bankruptcies are of three kinds: fortuitous, culpable and fraudulent; in the latter two cases the debtor is liable to prosecution under the Penal Code. The judge appoints a provisional receiver and calls a meeting of creditors at which a definitive receiver is appointed. The debtor may at any time make offers of settlement which take effect if accepted by the same proportion of creditors above designated in connection with suspension of payments, and approved by the court. Unless an agreement is reached the estate is liquidated. Nicaraguan property of a person declared bankrupt abroad must be applied in the first place to satisfy Nicaraguan creditors.

Insolvency relates to non-merchants and may be declared on the petition of a creditor on showing that the debtor's property is insufficient to pay his debts. Insolvency is presumed if the debtor cannot designate, or the registry of property does not show, sufficient property belonging to him on which an attachment can be levied. The rules relating to insolvency proceedings are similar to those relating to bankruptcy.

Fraudulent Transfers.—See topic Fraudulent Sales and Conveyances.

Privileged Credits.—See topic Liens.

BILLS AND NOTES:

(Negotiable Instruments Law approved by Legislative-Decree 1824 of June 11, 1971 as am'd by Law 620 of Mar. 18, 1977; and Law 24 of June 11, 1987).

Bills of exchange must show: (1) Name of bill of exchange within its text; (2) unconditional order to pay specific sum of money; (3) drawee; (4) due date; (5) place of payment; (6) payee; (7) if date and place of payment is not stated, bill is payable at sight. Bill may be payable: (a) At sight; (b) at certain time after sight; (c) at certain time after date; (d) at a fixed date; or (e) on several successive installment dates, with or without acceleration on default of one payment.

Endorsements may be made with or without recourse, but otherwise be unconditional, in full, to specific person or in blank or to bearer, in ownership or for collection or in guarantee or pledge.

Guarantee may be given to secure a bill through an "aval" which renders guarantor jointly and severally liable with party for whom given and subsequent endorsers. An "aval" is given on same bill or on a continuation sheet. Simple signature of a third party on front constitutes an "aval." Guarantee for "aval" is binding even if bill is not valid for incapacity of maker or other reason, except defects of form.

Presentment and Protest.—Bill payable at a certain time after sight must be presented for acceptance within one year after date unless drawer extended or shortened that period. Endorser may only reduce it. Drawee may demand a second presentation on day following first. Bill payable at sight must be presented for payment in one year after date, but period may also be extended or shortened by drawer and shortened by endorsers and drawer may stipulate that bill not be presented before a certain date which will then be starting point. Other bills must be presented for payment on due date or on two following working days. Bills must be presented for acceptance or payment, as case may be, at one of places indicated for payment. Presentment to a clearing house amounts to presentation for payment if not at sight. Presentment for acceptance or payment may be made to payee through a bank. Partial payment must be received after maturity date.

Failure to accept or pay must be established by a protest before a Notary Public. If for lack of acceptance or, if at sight, for lack of payment, protest must be made within period of presentment. In other cases, on any of two working days following due date. However, if presented through a bank, a notation on bill by bank, showing that it was not accepted or paid, substitutes for protest. If force majeure prevents presentment or protest periods therefor are extended but notice must be given, as stated below for event of dishonor, and a signed and dated notation thereof made on bill or additional sheet. Presentation and protest, if necessary, must then be made up on termination of obstacle but if this lasts more than 30 days, holder may exercise his rights without presentation and protest. Protest may be waived, but not presentation. Notice of dishonor must be given to drawer and immediate endorser within four working days. Each endorser must, in turn, give notice to his predecessor within two days.

Failure to present or to protest, when necessary, prejudices bill, except against acceptor or, if not accepted, against maker. Failure to give notice of dishonor does not, but it renders negligent party liable for damages suffered by his predecessors for up to value of bill.

Remedies.—Payee or holder in due course has an action on bill against drawer, guarantor for "aval," acceptor and endorsers who are jointly and severally liable therefor, plus interest, which may be agreed only in bills at sight or at period after sight, interest for period of default at agreed rate or 6% and expenses.

Action on underlying obligation, origin of bills, may be brought, provided that bills are returned or deposited with a bond or filed with action and that they were timely presented and protested, when necessary, and that they operated no novation. If this action is not available, action may lie against drawer, acceptor or endorsers, as case

See Topical Index in front part of this volume.

BILLS AND NOTES... *continued*
may be, for undue enrichment, within one year after right of action on bills has been lost or extinguished.

Promissory note to order must show: (1) Name of document within its text; (2) unconditional promise to pay a certain sum of money; (3) maturity, being otherwise payable at sight; (4) place of payment, being otherwise payable at place of issue; (5) name of person to whom or to whose order it is payable; (6) date and place of issue; (7) signature of maker. Most of rules related to bills of exchange are applicable to notes, maker taking place of acceptor. Note payable at a time after sight must be presented to maker who must endorse date of presentation. Upon refusal, protest is necessary to fix date.

Checks may only be drawn on banks with which drawer has an agreement and funds at his disposal and must be written in numbered forms supplied by drawee bank against a receipt or in other forms expressly authorized by same. Check must bear: (a) Name of drawee; (b) date and place of issue; (c) payee, stating or not that it is to his order or with clause "not to his order," or made "to bearer" or with no indication of payee, when it is deemed payable to bearer; (d) unconditional order to pay a specific sum of money written in letters and numbers or with stamping machine; and (e) signature of drawer or representative written by hand or, when authorized by bank, by special machine. Checks, even if postdated, are payable at sight and must be presented to drawee or a clearing house except within eight days, if payable at same place of issue; one month if at different place, within country of issue; and three months if issued abroad and payable in Nicaragua. Stop-payment orders are not valid, except when given after said periods and, in absence thereof, drawee may pay even if period has elapsed. Refusal to pay must be established by a protest or by a statement signed by drawee or clearing house that check was presented on time, and reason for denial of payment. Most provisions on bills of exchange apply to checks.

Law contains special provisions on crossed checks (payable to banks or a specified bank only); check to be credited on account, not payable in cash; nonnegotiable checks; certified checks; cashier's checks; circular checks (issued by authorized banks payable by any branch of drawer); traveler's checks; checks with stub for receipt (to be signed by holder upon collection); and checks issued by Treasury. Checks with "valor garantizado" (guaranteed checks) are specially regulated.

Conflict of Laws.—Capacity to issue, guarantee or endorse bills, notes or checks is governed by national law of obligor, but "renvoi" to other law is accepted; but if incompetent obligor is competent under law of place of execution, this law applies. Law of place of execution governs form of acts, but invalidity does not affect validity of later transactions related thereto, if said transactions are validly executed. Effects of obligations resulting from bills, notes, or checks are governed by laws of place where act creating obligation was executed. Form and periods for acceptance, payment, protest and other acts related thereto are governed by place where acts must be performed or executed.

CHATTEL MORTGAGES:

Personal property may be given in guarantee of unpaid part of purchase price or to secure payment of loan incurred to buy it. Chattel mortgage may be imposed on personal property belonging to another person if owner expressly consents to it. Personal property given in guarantee remains in custody of debtor. Contract must be in public deed or in private document acknowledged before notary public. Chattel mortgage may be canceled at any time by payment. Foreclosure action is summary. Statute of limitation for action arising from this contract is three years. (Law 146 of Mar. 20, 1992). As to ships and aircraft see topic Mortgages.

COLLATERAL SECURITY: See topic Pledges.

COMMUNITY PROPERTY: See topic Husband and Wife.

CONSTITUTION AND GOVERNMENT:

Constitution of Jan. 9, 1987 as am'd enacts principles of human rights, freedom and equality for Nicaragua. Government is democratic, republican, participatory and representative and is composed of: Legislative, Executive, Judicial and Electoral power. Legislative power is vested in national assembly whose members are elected for six year period. President and Vice-President are elected by direct vote for five year period. Judicial Power is vested in Supreme Court of Justice whose judges are designated by Legislative Power.

CONTRACTS:

See topic Principal and Agent, subhead Agents, Representatives or Distributors of Foreign Firms.

CONVEYANCES: See topics Deeds; Notaries Public; Public Instruments.

COPYRIGHT:

Copyright may be obtained on all kinds of literary, musical and artistic productions. In general, the privilege is perpetual for the author and his heirs; in the case of dramatic and musical compositions the right to present them publicly continues for the life of the author and 30 years thereafter. The right may be lost by prescription in ten years, and with respect to the presentation of dramatic works in four years. (C. C. 724-867). Nicaragua ratified Universal Copyright Convention on May 16, 1961.

CORPORATIONS:

(C. Com. 118-132, 201-286, 337-340).

Corporations may be formed by notarial instrument executed by two or more persons. The articles of incorporation must show: (1) Name and domicile of founders; (2) name and domicile of company; (3) object; (4) manner of electing directors, their term of office and manner of filling vacancies; (5) manner of electing supervisor or supervisors; (6) manner of calling and holding shareholders' meetings; (7) capital, stating value of contributions not in money, or manner of ascertaining same; (8) number, kind and value of the shares and whether registered or to bearer; (9) time and manner of collecting capital subscriptions; (10) advantages reserved to founders; (11) rules for drawing balances and calculating and distributing profits; (12) reserve fund; (13) duration, which cannot be indefinite nor exceed 99 years; (14) manner of forming majority; (15) persons representing company until election of directors. The by-laws must be approved by the shareholders and must state: (a) Powers of board of directors, board of supervisors, and shareholders; (b) supervision of acts of managers; (c) rights of shareholders to know how corporate funds are employed; (d) number of shareholders and amount of capital required at meetings to determine increase or decrease of capital or dissolution or modification of the company.

The corporation comes into being when the articles of incorporation and by-laws are registered in the mercantile registry, and these documents must also be published in the official newspaper. The corporation will not be registered: (1) If the founders are not honorable persons; (2) if the articles of incorporation do not contain the legal requisites; (3) if they contain provisions contrary to law, morals or public order; (4) if the by-laws are not approved as provided in the articles of incorporation or are not in accord with said articles; (5) if they do not offer the shareholders guarantees of good administration or opportunities to supervise the action of the managers, and the right to know how the corporate funds are employed. No corporation may begin operations until at least half the capital is subscribed and at least 10% of the cash capital is paid in. Companies holding a special privilege require approval of the President.

Corporations may also be formed by public subscription, for which purpose the founders publish a program and the corporation is constituted after all of the capital is subscribed.

Public sale of shares of stock or securities issued by corporations organized in country through advertisements, mail campaigns or public distributions of pamphlets or other means of propaganda must be registered with Superintendent of Banks and subject to regulations as provided by Law 15 of Apr. 9, 1970 which also governs investments made by corporations in investment companies.

Banking financing investment and insurance companies are subject to special laws.

Shares are registered and are transferred by endorsement and registration. Unless otherwise provided in the by-laws, a registered share not fully paid cannot be alienated without consent of the company, except by judicial sale, and in this case the company has the preferential right to buy. There may also be remunerative non-voting shares as compensation to the founders, but they cannot exceed 10% of the entire capital. Companies may purchase their own shares only in certain cases, and the shares purchased are considered amortized.

Dividends may be paid only from realized profits, but it may be agreed that during the period required for the enterprise to get under way, and designated in the by-laws, interest shall be paid at a specified rate.

Management.—Directors are elected by the shareholders or as provided in the articles of incorporation. They cannot do business with the corporation nor carry on the same business as the corporation unless authorized by the shareholders. Balances must be published yearly in the Government paper, but if the company was formed by public subscription, every six months. At least one-twentieth of the net profits must be set aside as a reserve until the same amounts to one-tenth of the capital. The shareholders elect one or more supervisors to watch over the administration of the company. If the corporation has a Government concession, the Government has the right of supervision.

Regular meetings of shareholders must be held at least once a year. No shareholder may represent over one-tenth of all the shares issued nor over two-tenths of the shares represented at the meeting. Unless otherwise provided in the by-laws, the presence of shareholders representing three-quarters of the capital and the vote of shareholders representing half the capital is required for extending or shortening the duration of the corporation, increasing or decreasing the capital, or otherwise modifying the articles of incorporation. Said changes must be approved by the judge and recorded in the registry of commerce. A corporation must be liquidated if it loses over two-thirds of its capital or becomes bankrupt, or if for over six months it has less than three shareholders and dissolution is requested by an interested party, or if it loses half its capital and the unguaranteed creditors request dissolution.

Foreign corporations must record their articles of incorporation and by-laws and the appointment of their agents. They must have a representative in Nicaragua with full power and annually publish in the official newspaper their balance and the names of the persons charged with their management. If their principal business is in Nicaragua and most of their capital is derived from there or their shareholders' meetings are held there, they are considered national companies.

COURTS:

Justice is administered by: (1) A Supreme Court which hears appeals from the courts of appeals and has various other functions in judicial matters; (2) courts of appeals which hear appeals from district judges and have other functions; (3) district judges having original jurisdiction in most civil and criminal matters; (4) local judges for minor civil cases and misdemeanors and who act as committing magistrates. (Law July 19, 1894, as am'd. See also Constitution of Jan. 9, 1987 as am'd).

CURRENCY:

(Monetary Law, Decree-Law 1-92 of Jan. 6, 1992 and Central Bank Law, Decree 42-92 of July 1, 1992 as am'd). Monetary unit is córdoba divided into 100 cents which is only currency in which promises of payment in Nicaragua may be agreed upon. However, promises in foreign money made abroad to be paid in Nicaragua or vice versa are legal, in many cases detailed in Law. Banco Central may issue bank notes which are legal tender.

CURTESY:

No estate by curtesy. See topics Descent and Distribution; Husband and Wife.

CUSTOMS:

Decree 942 of Feb. 1, 1982 regulates violations of customs laws. Central American Agreement on Tariff and Customs Regime and its Protocol establishes common regime that includes: Import tariff based on Brussels Nomenclature and ad valorem duties,

CUSTOMS . . . *continued*
law on customs value of merchandise and its regulations, uniform customs code and its regulations, regulations on tax exemptions.

DEATH:

If a person disappears a guardian or custodian may be appointed for his property. Four years after the absentee's disappearance, or six years if he left an attorney in fact, his presumptive heirs or legatees may petition for possession of his property, giving bond. Such petition may likewise be made after three years if the absentee disappeared in a battle, shipwreck, earthquake or similar calamity. Any security given is released and the possession of the property becomes final upon the expiration of 16 years, or 70 years after his birth. (C. C. 48-75).

Records of death are entered in the Civil Register. Death certificates are issued by the Official of the Civil Registry upon payment of a small fee fixed by local regulation.

Actions for Death.—There is no specific statute recognizing wrongful death action but this could be supported by the general provisions of Civil Code (arts. 2509 et seq.) on torts. Civil Aviation Code has some rules on death on occasion of air travel accidents. Civil actions out of tort are not usual and civil liability compensation out of crimes is usually sought in the criminal proceedings.

DECEDENTS' ESTATES:

See topics Descent and Distribution; Executors and Administrators; Wills.

DEEDS:

Deeds must be executed as public instruments before notary public. They are subject to taxes depending on value of the property. (C. C. 2534, 3935-3949, Decree 40-91 of Sept. 27, 1991). See also topics Notaries Public; Public Instruments.

DESCENT AND DISTRIBUTION:

In case of intestacy the estate passes to the following in the order given: (1) Legitimate children, with one-quarter share to natural children and grandchildren, if any, but in no case can the part of a legitimate child be less than that of a natural child; (2) legitimate ascendants with equal shares to spouse and natural children and grandchildren; (3) legitimate brothers and sisters with large shares to spouse and natural children and grandchildren; (4) natural children and grandchildren with half of estate to spouse; (5) natural parents and grandparents with half of estate to spouse; (6) spouse and natural brothers and sisters; (7) other legitimate collaterals to the sixth degree; (8) the municipality. A Nicaraguan heir of an alien has the same rights in the alien's estate as he would have according to the Nicaraguan law in the estate of a citizen of Nicaragua. (C. C. 998-1024).

See also topic Husband and Wife.

DIVORCE:

(C. C. 160-193; C. C. P. 1617-1622 and Leg. Decree 469 of Feb. 27, 1960).

Divorce dissolving the marriage bond may be granted for: (1) Pregnancy of wife in consequence of pre-marital illicit relations unknown to husband; (2) attempt of one spouse against life of other; (3) cruelty and grave insults; (4) adultery of wife; (5) concubinage of husband if notorious, or if in his own household, or if other circumstances constitute grave insult to wife; (6) abandonment; (7) absence for over five years without communicating with spouse; (8) separation for two years by judicial order or for five years without such order; (9) mutual consent. In the first seven cases the action may be brought only by the innocent spouse and only within one year after learning the facts.

The court of the conjugal domicile has jurisdiction in cases of divorce. The Code contains no requirement of residence for any specific period.

The judge may authorize the wife to leave the home or order the husband to leave it. The judge designates the alimony pendente lite to be paid by the affluent spouse to the needy spouse, and may in the final judgment grant alimony to the innocent spouse, which alimony is revoked when no longer needed. The children are awarded to the innocent spouse unless otherwise ordered by the judge; the mother always has the custody of the children until they reach seven years, unless the judge orders otherwise; in any case both parents are responsible for the support and education of the children. The public prosecutor is a party in all divorce proceedings.

For divorce by mutual consent the spouses must apply in writing and personally to the judge, who attempts to reconcile them at a hearing where both must necessarily appear in person or the proceeding is discontinued, and, if they insist, orders them to prepare an agreement as to custody of children and division of property. The judge thereupon declares dissolution of the marriage and his judgment is sent to the court of appeals for confirmation.

Separation without dissolution of the marriage may be decreed: (a) For the same reasons which are grounds for divorce; (b) for refusal of either spouse to support the other who is in need or to support the children; (c) by mutual consent. The same rules are applied as in an action for absolute divorce.

Law 143 of Jan. 22, 1992 regulates right to receive alimony and duty to pay it, bases of calculation and summary action to claim it, and causes for extinction of payment duty.

DOWER:

No dower right. See topics Descent and Distribution; Husband and Wife.

ENVIRONMENT:

(Decree 45-94 of Oct. 28, 1994).

Environmental impact statements are mandatory for projects having environmental impact, such as, mining, oil, gas pipelines, energy generating plants, ports, airports, railroads, roads, manufacturing plants, disposal of toxic waste and dams, among others. Failure to comply with obligation to prevent damage to environment, clean-up plans and with legal provisions are sanctioned with temporary or permanent closure of facilities.

EXCHANGE CONTROL:

(Decree 332 of Sept. 9, 1978, Decree 208 of Aug. 4, 1986 and Decree 42-92 of July 1, 1992). Proceeds from exports and foreign loans and from foreign investments, made under special law, must be sold through bank or authorized agent, following procedures established by Central Bank which will determine guarantee to be given for securing entrance of foreign exchange. Customhouses will not permit export without guarantee. Foreign exchange proceeding from other transactions may be freely disposed of. Central Bank, through other banks or authorized agents, sells at fixed rate of exchange, plus authorized commissions, foreign exchange necessary to pay for imports, intangible imports authorized by Bank, public debt, foreign debt, trips abroad up to amount established by Bank, and other similar expenses, all subject to regulations to be issued by Bank from time to time. Violations are subject to fine of 25% of transactions. Accomplices may be fined and subject to prison up to three years. (Decree 835 of Sept. 9, 1981). Decree 956 of Feb. 6, 1982 created tax on sale of foreign exchange for importation of certain items.

EXECUTIONS:

When an attachment has been levied and an order of execution is issued, perishable property is sold in the manner considered most advisable by the judge, mercantile effects are sold by a broker or a merchant appointed by the judge, and other personalty is sold at auction. Real property must be appraised, and a day is set for the auction, at which, unless the parties agree otherwise, no bid of less than two-thirds of the appraisal is accepted. If there are no bidders at this price, the creditor may demand that the property be adjudicated to him for two-thirds of the appraisal or that the judge reduce the appraisal by not exceeding one-third. In the latter case a new auction is held at which the lowest acceptable bid is two-thirds of the new appraisal. If there are still no bidders, the creditor may demand that the property be adjudicated to him for two-thirds of the new appraisal price, or delivered to him for administration, or be offered for sale a third time at any upset price designated by the judge. If the creditor does not demand such second or third sales the debtor is granted an extension of three years for payment of his debt, without interest. If the creditor requests administration of the property the debtor may demand a public sale without any upset price. After the property is sold, there is no equity of redemption. (C. C. P. 509-541, 1684-1796).

EXECUTORS AND ADMINISTRATORS:

(C. C. 1224-1433).

The testator may appoint as executor any person capacitated to obligate himself except the notary before whom the will is made. The will may empower the executor to sell real or personal property, but the executor cannot make use of this power except when indispensable for carrying out the will and with the approval of the heirs or the judge. The executor must give public notice to claimants against the estate. He continues in office for the time designated in the will; if no time is designated he continues for one year, but these terms may be extended by the judge. If there is no executor, the heirs are charged with carrying out the testator's wishes.

The estate vests in the heirs immediately upon decedent's death. The executor and the heirs have the duty of demanding the preparation of an inventory. Heirs must accept or refuse the inheritance without imposing conditions. Acceptance may be express or implied, but refusal must be express. Every acceptance is considered to be with benefit of inventory, that is, the heir is liable for the debts of the testator and other charges against the estate only up to the value of his share in the estate.

EXEMPTIONS:

The following property is exempt from attachment: (1) 95% of salaries and compensation if not exceeding 500 córdobas and the debtor has one close dependent who earns no salary; 90% of salaries and compensation not exceeding 1,000 córdobas and one-half the salary above that sum; (2) beds and necessary clothing of debtor, his wife and children; (3) professional books up to value of 16 córdobas; (4) implements to teach a science and art up to same value; (5) soldiers' uniforms and equipment; (6) tools of artisans and farmers; (7) food and combustibles of debtor's family for one month; (8) personal rights, such as habitation; (9) real property given or devised as not subject to attachment up to value appearing in appraisement made at time of delivery and judicially approved; (10) subventions to educational, charitable and similar establishments; (11) salary of soldiers and policemen, and pensions; (12) homestead recorded as such. (C. C. 2084; Laws Apr. 27, 1909, Jan. 16, 1920). The following are also exempt: (1) Wages of laborers and servants; (2) amounts for support; (3) periodical gift payments in so far as necessary for support of debtor, spouse and children; (4) amounts in savings banks and interest up to 40 cordobas; (5) life insurance policies; (6) payments to public works contractors except for salaries and materials furnished; (7) objects required for an art or trade, and implements, beasts of labor and materials required by a farm up to 48 cordobas; (8) household utensils; (9) property belonging to a service which cannot be stopped without obstacle to traffic or public hygiene, but revenues of such services may be attached; (10) easements, unless the ground is attached; (11) other property specifically exempted, such as property of municipalities and charity boards; (12) part of deposits in National Credit Bank. (C. C. P. 1703; Law Aug. 4, 1941; Law 468 of Feb. 27, 1960).

FORECLOSURE: See topic Mortgages.

FOREIGN CORPORATIONS: See topic Corporations.

FOREIGN EXCHANGE:

See topic Exchange Control; also topic Currency.

FOREIGN INVESTMENTS:

(Law 127 of June 19, 1991 as am'd by Decree-Law 2-92 of June 6, 1992 regulated by Decree 30-92 of June 10, 1992).

Law establishes foreign investor's rights and duties, and benefits and guaranties for foreign investment. Foreign investment may be freely convertible foreign currency, tangible assets, any form of technology, capitalization of loan, or reinvestment of

See Topical Index in front part of this volume.

FOREIGN INVESTMENTS . . . *continued*
profits. Foreign Investment Committee authorizes foreign investment and signed investment contract with foreign investor. Investment contract must include appointment of local agent, terms and conditions of investment, management and control of enterprise, and proceedings for solution of disputes regarding these matters and declaration that investor and investment are subject to local jurisdiction. There is no limit on participation of foreign investment nor in areas to invest. Existing tax regime is applied but exemption may be negotiated. Right to repatriate capital and dividends and to get foreign exchange and compensation in case of expropriation is guaranteed. All transfer of technology contracts must previously be approved. Foreign investment subject to former law may apply new regime.

FOREIGN TRADE REGULATIONS: See topic Exchange Control.

FRAUDS, STATUTE OF: See topic Public Instruments.

FRAUDULENT SALES AND CONVEYANCES:

Fraudulent acts of an insolvent debtor may be annulled on the petition of creditors, if the debtor contracted without a valuable consideration or if the person contracting with him was aware of his insolvency or was otherwise in collusion with him. Such annulment may be requested with respect to contracts executed within two years before the insolvency if the other party was closely related to the debtor by blood or marriage. In case of bankruptcy the following acts executed after the cessation of payments are void: (1) Acts without a valuable consideration; (2) payments of unmatured debts. The following acts executed after the cessation of payments are presumed fraudulent and may be annulled: (1) Alienations for a valuable consideration when the other party knew of the cessation of payments; (2) contracts where the consideration received was clearly inadequate; (3) payments of matured debts otherwise than in cash or commercial effects; (4) mortgages and pledges to secure previous debts. (C. C. 2020-2238, 2253-2263; C. Com. 1082-1086).

HOLIDAYS:

Jan. 1 (New Year's); Holy Week*; May 1 (Labor Day); May 27 (Army Day); July 14 (abrogation of Chamorro-Bryan treaty); Aug. 1 and 10 (St. Domingo); Sept. 14 (Battle of San Jacinto); Sept. 15 (Independence Day); Oct. 12 (Columbus Day); Nov. 1 (All Saints); Dec. 8 (Immaculate Conception); Dec. 25 (Christmas). (See Regulations of Art. 57 of Labor Code by Decree 196 of Jan. 15, 1976.)

* These are movable holidays.

HUSBAND AND WIFE:

(C. C. 105, 151-159, 1201-1209).

Husband and wife owe each other fidelity and mutual assistance. The husband must live with his wife and she with her husband and follow him wherever he fixes his residence, but these obligations are suspended if harm would result to either spouse. The spouses may either before or after marriage make agreements regarding their property, which agreements must be executed before a notary and recorded. Such agreements may be changed after marriage. In the absence of such an agreement each spouse may freely dispose of the property owned by such spouse at the time of marriage and that acquired thereafter in any manner.

Husband and wife may contract with each other and the wife does not require authorization by her husband or the court in order to contract or appear in court. The spouses are liable for the support and education of the children in proportion to their respective property.

The surviving spouse is entitled to a marriage portion of one-quarter of the estate of the deceased spouse, unless the surviving spouse is the owner of property, in which event the marriage portion is the difference between the value of such property and one-quarter the value of the estate. Everything received by the surviving spouse from the decedent's estate is credited to the marriage portion.

Community property system is optional in marriages in Nicaragua; persons married abroad under the rules of community property are still subject to such rules if they take up their domicile in Nicaragua unless they make new stipulations according to Nicaraguan legislation.

IMMIGRATION:

(Immigration Law 153 of Apr. 22, 1993, Aliens Law 154 of Apr. 30, 1993, Law 716 of Aug. 11, 1978).

Foreigners entering country must apply for a visa with Consul. Foreigners, after legal admission, with exception of tourists must get special identification document issue by local authorities.

For departure, foreigners must appear before Immigration Authority with their passport in order to obtain exit visas.

Aliens Law 154 establishes two special categories of residents: "Pensioned Residents" and "Investors Residents".

INFANCY:

(C. C. arts. 6-10, 244-282, 298-498, 2201-2219, 2472, Decree 1065 of June 24, 1982).

Minority ends at 21 except when the courts grant majority to a minor prior to that age. Contracts by males under 15 and females under 14 are void and, if over those ages, voidable.

Minors are subject to parental authority of legitimate father and mother or natural mother or, upon her death or absence of natural father who has recognized paternity. Parental authority includes custody, legal representation and administration of real and personal property of minor. In absence of parents guardian is appointed. Parents and guardians may receive fee of 5% to 20% of net income and have restricted powers of disposition.

Adoption is regulated by Decree 862 of Oct. 12, 1981.

INSOLVENCY: See topic Bankruptcy and Insolvency.

INTEREST:

The legal rate is that established for banking institutions in general by the National Bank of Development. Money loans by others than banking institutions may bear interest up to one and one-half times the legal interest. Interest cannot be compounded at periods of less than once a year.

Usury is punished by imprisonment and fine of ten times excess interest and obligations are void. (Decree Oct. 26, 1940 and Decree 121 of Oct. 23, 1979).

JUDGMENTS:

(C. C. P. 509 to 552).

Judgments constitute liens only upon property on which execution has been levied and after registration in public registry.

Foreign judgments have the effect provided by treaties; if there is no treaty, they have the same effect as is given to Nicaraguan judgments in the foreign country; if the foreign country does not execute Nicaraguan judgments, the foreign judgment cannot be executed in Nicaragua. If none of these rules apply, the foreign judgment will be executed in Nicaragua provided: (1) It was rendered in a personal action; (2) the obligation on which it is based is legal in Nicaragua; (3) the certified copy contains the requisites necessary in the foreign country so that it may be considered authentic, and those required in Nicaragua for its authenticity; (4) it was not obtained by default unless defendant was duly summoned; (5) it is not contrary to public order; (6) it is a definitive judgment in the foreign country.

LEGISLATURE: See topic Constitution and Government.

LIENS:

In insolvencies in general there are two classes of privileged credits: (1) Those affecting all properties of the debtor, such as judicial costs in the interest of the creditors, current taxes, funeral expenses, medical assistance for one month, minor wages for three months; (2) those affecting specific property, such as liens of (a) mortgagees and pledgees on articles mortgaged or pledged, (b) carriers on articles carried, for costs of transportation, (c) makers of personal property, on such property in their possession, for the price thereof, (d) landlords, on the fruits of the property, for the amount of the rental, (e) the Government and municipalities, for one year's back taxes. In bankruptcy the pledge and mortgage liens are first satisfied and thereupon the credits rank as follows: (1) Amounts due to Government; (2) judicial expenses; (3) funeral expenses; (4) expenses of last illness; (5) wages for six months; (6) rentals; (7) credits for support of debtor and family; (8) special privileged credits allowed by the Code; (9) general mercantile credits; (10) other credits. (C. C. 2335-2355; C. Com. 1109-1119).

LIMITATION OF ACTIONS: See topic Prescription.

LIMITED PARTNERSHIP: See topic Partnership.

MARRIAGE:

(C. C. 92-150; Law Feb. 14, 1933).

The marriage ceremony is performed by the district judge or local judge or by notary public who has been register at Supreme Court more than ten years. Marriages by proxy are allowed. No religious marriage may be performed unless there has been previous civil ceremony.

The following marriages are void: (a) Those of persons already married; (b) between ascendants and descendants by consanguinity or affinity, legitimate or illegitimate; (c) between brothers and sisters; (d) between the author of the death of one spouse or his accomplice, and the surviving spouse; (e) between a person convicted of adultery and the other party to the adultery. The following are causes for voiding the marriage: (a) Error or duress; (b) mental incapacity; (c) if the male is below 15 years or the female below 14; (d) impotence. However, these marriages are valid: (1) In case of error, duress or mental incapacity, if the parties continue living together one month after the defect is discovered; (2) if persons below the age of puberty live together one day after puberty is attained or if the female conceives; (3) in the case of impotence if no claim is made within one year. The following marriages, though valid, are prohibited and the parties are liable to punishment: (a) That of a male below 21 or a female below 18, without the consent of parents, grandparents or guardians; (b) that of a woman before the expiration of 300 days after the dissolution of a previous marriage; (c) between a guardian and ward before the guardianship accounts are approved; (d) marriages without due publication of edicts or exemption from such publication.

A marriage declared void, if contracted in good faith, produces civil effects with respect to the parties and children. If only one party acted in good faith it produces civil effects only with respect to that party and the children.

A marriage validly contracted abroad is valid in Nicaragua; if one of the parties was a Nicaraguan it is necessary that there was no violation of Nicaraguan laws relating to capacity for contracting marriage.

MINES AND MINERALS:

Decree 137 of Nov. 2, 1979 nationalizes mining sector, creating Nicaraguan Corporation for Development of Mines (CONDEMINA).

MONOPOLIES AND RESTRAINT OF TRADE:

Nicaragua does not have legislative regime for regulation of monopolies, mergers and other devices aimed at unfair restraint of trade.

Central American Regulations on Unfair Trade Practices of Dec. 12, 1995 implement principles established by Agreements of World Trade Organization. Central American governments may issue restrictive convenants to temporarily protect their local production from massive import of same or similar products that may cause pecuniary loss to local producers.

Consumer Protection Law.—(Law 182 of Nov. 1, 1994).

See Topical Index in front part of this volume.

MONOPOLIES AND RESTRAINT OF TRADE . . . *continued*

Rights granted to consumers under law are non-waivable and prevail over any other law, commercial practice or stipulation which opposes it. Law regulates relationship between supplier and consumer in any kind of goods and public or private services, including energy and water supply, sewer, telecommunications and postal services, ports, transportation and the like.

It also regulates advertisement, adhesion contracts, credit and door to door sales, and civil responsibility of suppliers.

MORTGAGES:

(C. C. 3771-3898; C. Com. 1024-1035; C. C. P. 1684-1796; Civil Aviation Law Sept. 19, 1956).

Mortgages must be executed in the form of notarial instruments and recorded in the public registry. Mortgages made abroad are valid if properly authenticated. Mortgages may be made on (a) real estate, its fruits, and rights in rem thereon and (b) ships and aircraft. The mortgage covers only three years back interest, unless the creditor causes other unpaid annuities to be expressly recorded, in which event third persons are affected only from the date of such record. Whenever the debtor makes a partial payment, he may demand a proportionate reduction of the mortgage.

When property encumbered by mortgage is sold at a public sale under execution, it is sold free of the encumbrance if the mortgage creditor was duly summoned; in such case the proceeds of the sale are devoted to the payment of liens in their order of preference. It is forbidden to stipulate that in case of nonpayment the creditor may take possession of the property, but the parties may waive the usual mortgage procedure and agree that the property be sold by judicial sale with an upset price designated in the mortgage instrument or assessed by experts. Mortgage foreclosures follow the general rules of summary actions and execution of judgments. After the sale there is no right of redemption.

Real property may be charged with a mortgage, divided in cedulas of 100 córdobas or multiples of that amount, signed by the property owner and the Registrar of Real Property. The liability for capital and accessories constitutes a charge of the property, the owner of which shall have no personal liability. (C. C. Art. 3888).

NOTARIES PUBLIC:

(Notarial Law, am'd by Decree 1290 of Dec. 15, 1966, Decree 658 of Feb. 24, 1981, Law 105 of July 14, 1990, Law 139 of Jan. 14, 1992 and C. C. 2364-2374).

Notaries require the authorization of the Supreme Court. A notary must have a proper diploma from a school authorized to grant it, must prove his reputation for honesty and good conduct, and must give bond. The following cannot be notaries: Those who are deaf or dumb or blind, or deprived of civil rights, or under indictment, or sentenced for any serious offense, or are bankrupts not discharged. Notaries may act anywhere in the Republic or even abroad if the parties are Nicaraguans or contract is to be performed in Nicaragua. In certain cases, district and local judges may act as notaries.

Instruments executed before a notary must be prepared with certain formalities. They must be in Spanish. Notary retains original document in protocol and furnishes parties with certified copies which have effect of originals in court. Documents certified by notary are invalid if they relate to matter in which notary, his wife, or his relatives within fourth degree of consanguinity or second of affinity, have interest, unless it be interest in corporation or unless all parties are relatives of notary and he had no direct interest.

PARTNERSHIP:

(C. Com. 118-200, 287-336; C. C. 3175-3292).

Commercial partnerships as well as civil partnerships are considered legal entities.

General partnership is one in which the partners are jointly liable without limit, for the debts of the partnership. It is formed by notarial instrument stating: (1) Names and domiciles of partners; (2) character of business; (3) firm name and designation of administrating partners; (4) capital contributed by each partner; (5) domicile of firm; (6) duration of firm. The firm name comprises the names of all the partners or the names of one or more of them adding the words "y Compaōnía." Unless the administration of the firm has been confided to specific partners, all have the power of management in person or by delegate. A partner may not on his own account engage in the same business as the partnership.

Limited general partnership is a partnership of the nature of a general partnership except that the liability of one or more partners is limited by the partnership articles. The firm name must be followed by the word "Limitada."

Limited partnership is the usual kind of a limited partnership in which one or more of the partners are special partners liable only for the amount of their contribution. The firm name must be followed by the words "en comandita." Ordinarily a special partner who allows his name in the firm name or engages in the management of the firm's business is jointly liable with the general partners. The participation of the special partners may be represented by shares.

Civil company is a company formed for purposes which the law does not consider commercial, such as agriculture, and is governed by special rules of the Civil Code. Unless expressly agreed otherwise, the partners are liable for the partnership debts only in proportion to their interest in the partnership.

PATENTS:

An inventor of a machine, apparatus, or method of fabrication or application useful for science or the arts may apply for a patent thereon, which is granted for a period of from five to ten years. Improvements on a patented article are entitled to additional patents, but not for more than the time lacking on the original patent. Application is made to the Ministry of Economy and samples, drawings or models must be filed. A small annual fee is payable. A patent is lost if not put in use within one year or abandoned for over one year, if the annual taxes are not paid, or the products are inferior to the sample filed. (Law Oct. 11, 1899, as am'd, and Law of Dec. 21, 1955).

PLEDGES:

The article pledged must be delivered to the pledgee or to some other person agreed on between the parties. As between the parties the contract is effective from the time of such delivery; as to third persons it must appear in a document executed before a notary or judge. In case of default the pledge may be sold in a summary judicial proceeding, or, if the parties have so agreed, by a third person at public sale. Any agreement allowing the creditor to appropriate the pledge is void. (C. C. 3728-3770; C. Com. 506-518). Pledges without delivery may be given to banks and national agencies for development on livestock (Law 21 of Mar. 31, 1959) and to others on farm and industry machinery and products or crops (Law of Aug. 6, 1937 as developed by Law 120 of Apr. 12, 1973).

PRESCRIPTION:

(C. C. 868-931; C. Com. 669, 670, 1150-1152).

The acquisition of property or rights by virtue of possession and the extinction of obligations by failure to require performance are called prescription. Prescription may be waived as far as it has run, but cannot be waived in advance. Real property belonging to the State may not be acquired by prescription.

Prescription is interrupted: (a) If the possessor is deprived of possession or enjoyment for over one year; (b) by express or implied recognition; (c) by law-suit unless the same is withdrawn or dismissed. Except in case of the extraordinary thirty year period mentioned below, prescription does not run: (1) Against minors or incompetents while they have no legal representative; (2) between parents and children under parental authority; (3) between guardians and wards; (4) against decedents' estates before the office of executor or administrator has been accepted; (5) against servants and laborers for their wages while they continue in the debtor's employ; (6) in favor of a debtor who has illegally impeded the action of his creditor.

Ownership is acquired by positive prescription, and requires possession based on a legal acquisition, and continued in good faith, quietly, uninterruptedly and publicly. Personal property is acquired by prescription in two years, but if the property was lost by the owner or taken from him by crime, possession for five years by a third person in good faith is required to establish ownership. Real property and rights therein are acquired by possession for ten years with good faith and under a legal acquisition, but ownership may be acquired by possession of 30 years without these conditions.

Actions.—Rights are lost by negative prescription and the prescriptive period varies according to the nature of the action. The action to enforce a right is extinguished by the prescription of the right. Some of the more important periods of prescription of actions are:

Ten years, actions to recover debts in general and civil actions not otherwise limited.

Five years, actions against administrators for rendition of accounts.

Three years, actions to recover interest, rents or pensions payable in periods of six months or more, actions against the acceptor of a bill of exchange, and mercantile actions for which no specific period is designated.

Two years, actions of judicial agents for salaries and fees, actions of principals against judicial agents for rendition of accounts, actions of teachers and physicians for fees, actions to recover salaries and wages, actions of contractors and artisans to recover price of work, actions of merchants for amounts due on sales not made for resale, actions of innkeepers to recover value of lodgings and food.

One year, actions for slander, actions to enforce rights in personal property, actions of holders of bills of exchange against drawer and endorsers, actions to recover interest, rents or pensions payable in periods of less than six months.

Six months, actions of endorsers among themselves or against the drawer.

PRINCIPAL AND AGENT:

(C. C. 3293-3389; C. Com. 398-459).

An agency may be conferred in writing or orally, but in court it can be proved by witnesses only in accordance with the general rules of evidence, and a private document will not be accepted when a public instrument is required. A power of attorney which is all-embracing (generalísimo) or general, must be granted by a public instrument. The former includes authority to alienate and encumber real property of all kinds, the latter merely grants authority to administer, and additional powers must be specifically expressed. A power of attorney for litigation confers general authority to carry on lawsuits, but specific authority is required for various special acts, such as to compromise, receive moneys, renew contracts, challenge, record in the registry of property, and delegate the power of attorney. A power of attorney for litigation otherwise than with respect to small amounts must be given in a public instrument.

An agent appointing a substitute is liable for the acts of the latter if he was not empowered to appoint a substitute or if the substitute is notoriously incompetent. An agency terminates by: (a) Termination of business or expiration of time for which given; (b) revocation by principal; (c) resignation of agent; (d) death, bankruptcy or declaration of incapacity of principal or agent; (e) cessation of principal in capacity in which he conferred agency.

If a mercantile agent wishes to refuse the agency given him, he must advise the principal as soon as possible and nevertheless take the necessary steps to protect the merchandise remitted to him. Factors must act in the name of their principals; if they do not they are personally liable and the person contracting with them may proceed either against the principal or the factor. The death of the principal does not terminate the factor's agency.

Agents, Representatives or Distributors of Foreign Firms.—Decree 227 of Dec. 22, 1979 regulates and defines distributorship agreements establishing grounds for termination of contract, indemnification and legal proceedings to recover same. Causes for termination or refusing to renew distributor or representation contracts without liability to foreign corporations are: any crime by distributor involving merchandise or interests of foreign principal; breach of distributorship contract; continued decrease in sale or distribution of merchandise due to negligence of distributor; acts for which distributor is responsible that prejudice introduction, sale or distribution of merchandise with which it has been entrusted and bankruptcy of distributor. Otherwise foreign principal must indemnify distributor.

See Topical Index in front part of this volume.

PUBLIC INSTRUMENTS:

A public instrument is a document executed before a notary public or other competent public official. It is proof of the purpose of its execution and of its date, and the declarations made therein are proof against the parties and their successors. The law requires numerous contracts to be executed as public instruments, e.g., deeds of real property, mortgages, general powers of attorney, articles of incorporation and partnership, etc. Other documents are private documents. With respect to a third person a private document is effective only from the death of one of its signers, or the date on which it was recorded in a public registry, delivered to a public official or presented to a notary for authentication. A writing is required to prove an obligation of over eight córdobas. (C. C. 2364-2430).

REAL PROPERTY:

Civil Code governs real property in Nicaragua.

Contracts regarding real property must be by public instrument and registered in Registry of Property.

Only Nicaraguans and corporations in which more than 51% of capital belongs to Nicaraguans may own property in an area within 20 km. from borders.

Decree 782 of July 19, 1981 as am'd and its regulations regulate agrarian reform.

RECORDS:

There is a public registry of real property for recording real property rights and conveyances; a registry of mortgages for recording documents relating to mortgage rights; and a registry of persons for recording judgments relating to the capacity of persons, divorce, bankruptcy, etc., and marriage articles and similar documents. There is also a mercantile registry for registering merchants, articles of partnership and incorporation, mercantile powers of attorney, trademarks, conveyances of ships, etc. Furthermore there is a civil registry for recording births, marriages, deaths, guardianships, etc. (C. C. 499-595, 3935-3980; C. Com. 13-27; Decree 14 of Oct. 9, 1947; Decree 29 of Nov. 30, 1950; and Law 80 of Mar. 12, 1990).

There is also a Central Registry of Civil Status, which issues identity cards. All Nicaraguans must have this ID card. Foreigners must request document equivalent to above from immigration authorities. (Decree Law 154 of Apr. 30, 1993).

REDEMPTION: See topics Executions; Mortgages.

SALES (Realty and Personalty):

(C. C. 2530-2731; C. Com. 341-368).

Between parties a sale is perfected when an agreement is reached as to the thing sold and the price, though neither has been delivered. If goods are sold by weight, count or measure, the sale is not perfected until they are weighed, counted or measured. In sales of real estate with designation of area and specification of a unit price, an adjustment must be made if a different area is found, but the purchaser may rescind the sale if the difference exceeds one-twentieth; in case an upset price was specified, no adjustment is required unless the difference exceeds one-twentieth, and the purchaser may rescind if an increase in the price would result.

The seller is not obliged to deliver a thing sold until the price is paid, unless a term was granted for payment, nor even in that event if the buyer becomes insolvent. Unless otherwise stipulated, the seller guarantees the title and warrants against hidden defects which render the thing sold useless or diminish its value to such an extent that the buyer would not have bought it. Personalty cannot be sold with reservation of the right to repurchase, and in case of real property, the right to repurchase cannot be reserved for over three years.

In mercantile transactions if no period is stipulated for delivery, the seller must have the merchandise at the disposal of the buyer in 24 hours. The buyer must make claim in writing within five days after delivery to him for differences of quantity or quality, and within 30 days for hidden defects. For the purpose of bringing suits on these grounds he must make a protest before a notary public, with two witnesses. The existence and amount of the differences must be determined by the judgment of experts.

SEALS:

Seals are not used in private contracts. Public instruments have most of the effects of sealed instruments in the United States.

SHIPPING:

The more important admiralty provisions are found in the Code of Commerce, Arts. 735-1046. Nicaraguan vessels must be registered in the mercantile registry. Conveyances abroad must be executed before a Nicaraguan consul and recorded in the registry of the consulate. Vessels of over 20 tons may be mortgaged and the mortgage may be assigned by endorsement authenticated by a notary public or captain of the port and recorded in the proper registry.

Decree 1104 of Sept. 20, 1982 and its regulations of Oct. 28, 1982 and Jan. 12, 1984, protect national merchant marine.

Vessel registrations are granted in accordance with Regulation 326 of Jan. 10, 1983.

STATUTES:

The principal codifications are the Civil Code, Code of Civil Procedure, Code of Commerce, Penal Code, Code of Criminal Procedure, Mining Code, Labor Code and Notarial Law. The current laws appear in an official newspaper called "La Gaceta."

TAXATION:

Legislative Decree 713 of June 28, 1962, as am'd and Decree 30-90 of July 28, 1990, and Decree 8 of Apr. 8, 1967, establish principles and rules (withholding, prescription, penalties, etc.) applicable to various taxes, including payment of taxes in foreign currency.

Income Tax.—(Law 662 of Nov. 26, 1974 most recently am'd by Decree 70-90 of Dec. 22, 1990; Accord 35-91 of June 7, 1991. Regulations by Decree 26 of June 25, 1975 as am'd). All income derived from assets located, services rendered and business done in Nicaragua or having effect therein is subject to tax, regardless of where income is received. Presumed income is based on taxpayer's net worth or net receipt applies when regular reported net income is less than presumptive amount established by law of 4% of net worth at last day of preceding tax year. Presumed income may be reduced in cases authorized by law.

Among incomes exempted are workers' compensation, certain insurance proceeds, lottery prizes from Popular Lottery; certain interests, all social security payments.

Gross income includes income derived from work, services, sales, business, gains for transfer of personal or real property, gifts, inheritance, lottery and similar items. Tax is paid on net income. Net income is gross income less deductions allowed by law. Losses may be carried forward for four years. Some payments are subject to withholding tax at source, among them, salaries over 5,000 córdobas, purchases of goods, construction works, lease and services in general at 3%.

Individuals are taxed at rates ranging from 7% to 30% and juridical persons at flat rate of 30%. Dividends paid to nonresidents are subject to 5% final withholding tax and profits paid to parent company by local brands, paid regular income tax plus 5% withholding tax.

Tax on Real Property.—(a) (Decree 3-95 of Jan. 31, 1995). Tax is levied on real property owned by individuals and juridical persons with net value over 40,000 córdobas at rate of 1% of market value. Tax is paid to municipalities where properties are located. (b) (Decree 36-91 of Aug. 19, 1991). All acts involving real property originally acquired from Government or its institutions or municipalities with construction over 100 square meters are subject to 100% tax on its recorded value. Tax is paid in advance, once per property, and notaries public must indicate payment of tax in all notarial deeds related to any of abovementioned properties.

Tax on Ownership and Use of Vehicles.—(Decree 6-93 of Jan. 10, 1993). Amount of tax is determined according to specific kind of vehicle.

Value Tax.—(Decree 1531 of Dec. 21, 1984 as am'd and its Regulations of Dec. 28, 1984). Goods circulated within country, importation of goods into country, transfer of real property, works, leasing, rendering of services within country are subject to this tax. Tax shall be levied on net price obtained by deducting from amount of invoice discounts or other reductions made according to commercial usage. General rate is 15% for services rendered by hotels, restaurants, night clubs, rental, insurers and other similar services, telecommunications. Transfer of real property, except mortis causa and merger of companies, movies, and transfer of used motor vehicles are taxed 5%. International air transportation and hospital and medical services are taxed 6%; professional and technical services are taxed 10%.

Consumer's Tax.—(Decree 23-94 of May 19, 1994).

Consumer's tax is applied to sales of specific and detailed list of items running from occasional 5% to 50%, payable on price of sale, if national product, or 5% to 80% on CIF price, if imported. In certain cases, consumer's tax applies under special rules.

Stamp Tax.—(Decree 136 of Nov. 11, 1985 as am'd). Tax is imposed on contracts, public documents, promissory notes and other documents and instruments specified by law, executed or issued within country and executed or issued abroad to take effect in Nicaragua. Tax rates vary for different transactions from flat rates to specified percentages.

Export Promotion, Decree 37-91 of Aug. 21, 1991 as am'd by Decree 22-92 of Mar. 20, 1992 regulated by Decree 23-92 of Mar. 20, 1992, grants special benefits to export of traditional and nontraditional products outside Central American area. Imports of raw materials and capital goods are exempted from duties and taxes, under temporary importation system. Exporting companies of nontraditional products may enter into export contract with Government and receive income tax exemption up to six years, and "certificado de beneficio tributario" (tax payment certificates) equivalent to percentage of value of exported goods, for period up to six years. Certificates are negotiable bearer instruments.

Free Zones.—(Decree 46-91 of Nov. 13, 1991 regulated by Decree 31-92 of June 10, 1992). Free zones can be publicly owned and administered by "Corporación de Zonas Francas" or privately owned and administered by corporation created for that purpose called "Empresa Operadora de Zonas Francas". Such corporation must be authorized by "Comisión Nacional de Zonas Francas". Free zones must be created for production and exportation of goods and services. They are exempted from all taxes, including municipal tax.

TRADEMARKS AND TRADENAMES:

(Central American Convention for the Protection of Industrial Property, 1968).

Trademarks comprise any sign, word, expression or any other graphic or material means which because of its special characteristics can clearly distinguish products, merchandise or services of person or corporation.

Trademarks are classified as industrial or manufacturers' marks, commercial marks and service marks.

Industrial or manufacturers' marks are those that distinguish goods produced or processed by specified manufacturing or industrial enterprise.

Commercial marks are those that distinguish goods commercial enterprise sells or distributes regardless of who produces them.

Service marks are those that distinguish activities of enterprises devoted to satisfaction of general needs by means other than manufacture, sale or distribution of goods.

Use or registration of following as trademarks is prohibited: (1) National flags or their colors, if latter appear in same order and positions as in former, coats-of-arms, insignia or distinguishing marks of contracting states, their municipalities and other public bodies; (2) flags, coats-of-arms, insignia, devices or denominations of foreign nations unless authorization from respective government has been obtained; (3) flags, coats-of-arms, insignia, devices, denominations or acronyms of international agencies of which one or more contracting states are members; (4) names, emblems and devices of Red Cross and of religious or charitable bodies legally recognized in any of member states of this Convention; (5) designs of coins or notes that are legal tender in territory of any of contracting parties, reproductions of securities and other commercial documents or of seals, stamps, or revenue stamps, or revenue stamps in general; (6) signs, words or expressions that ridicule or tend to ridicule persons, ideas, religions or

See Topical Index in front part of this volume.

TRADEMARKS AND TRADENAMES . . . *continued*
national symbols of third party states or international agencies; (7) signs, words or expressions, contrary to good morals, public order or good usage; (8) names, signatures, family names and portraits of persons other than person filing application without their consent or, if deceased, consent of their closest ascendants or descendants; (9) technical or common names of products, goods or services when they are intended to protect articles or services included in genus or species to which such names refer; (10) terms, signs or locutions that have passed into general use and which are used to indicate nature of products, goods or services, and qualifying and gentilitial adjectives. Trademarks that have become popular or widespread subsequent to their registration shall not be regarded as having passed into general use; (11) figures, denominations or phrases describing products, goods or services that are to be protected by trademarks or their ingredients, qualities, physical characteristics or use for which they are intended; (12) signs or indications that are used to designate type, quality, quantity, value or season of preparation of products or goods or of provision of services, unless they are followed by designs or phrases that particularize them; (13) usual and current form of products or goods; (14) plain colors considered separately, unless they are combined or accompanied by elements such as signs or denominations having particular or distinguishing character; (15) containers that are in public domain or have come into common use in any of contracting states and, in general, those that are neither original nor novel; (16) mere indications of origin or denominations of origin, except as set forth in item (b) of Art. 35; (17) distinguishing marks already registered by other persons as trademarks for products, goods or services included in same class; (18) distinguishing marks that by reason of their graphic, phonetic or ideological similarity may mislead or result in confusion with other trademarks or with commercial names, publicity expressions or symbols already registered or in process of being registered, if it is intended to use them to distinguish products, goods or services included in same class; (19) distinguishing marks that may mislead by indicating false source, nature or quality; (20) maps. These may, however, be used as elements of trademarks if they represent country or origin or source of goods which they distinguish.

Registration is mandatory for chemical, pharmaceutical, veterinary and medicinal food products. Term of registration is ten years subject to renewals for equal periods. Licenses must be registered.

International Mark Classification applies. Fees are: Registration of each mark or name, $50, and of propaganda slogans or signs, $25; renewal, $50; transfer, $10; any certificate or document, $5.

TREATIES:

Nicaragua is among others, a party to following: Convention on Private International Law (Bustamante Code), Havana, 1928; Multilateral Trade Negotiations, The Uruguay Round, Final Act, Marrakesh, Apr. 15, 1994 and Agreement Establishing the World Trade Organization, Marrakesh, Apr. 15, 1994.

Bilateral.—Treaty of friendship, commerce and navigation, and protocol. Signed on Jan. 21, 1956 with U.S. One significant clause is that in commercial matters citizens of both countries receive same treatment as nationals, in each country; Agreement relating to investment guaranties under §413(b)(4) of Mutual Security Act of 1954, as am'd, with U.S.

Multilateral.—General Treaty on Central American Economic Integration and its Protocol; Agreement establishing Central American Bank for Economic Integration.

Also see topic Copyright.

TRUSTS:

Trusts as they exist in the common law are unknown in Nicaragua, but the freedom of contract often makes it possible to create relationships similar to trusts.

USURY: See topic Interest.

WILLS:

(C. C. 932-997, 1025-1223).

Wills may be made by all except (a) males below 15 and females below 14, (b) persons not in possession of their faculties or declared mentally incapacitated and (c) persons unable to express their will orally or in writing. The following cannot be witnesses: (a) Minors below 18; (b) those mentally incapacitated; (c) persons who are blind, deaf or dumb; (d) persons convicted of crime carrying loss of civil rights, or convicted of forgery or perjury; (e) nonresidents; (f) persons who cannot understand the language of the testator; (g) the writer of the will and the wife, employees, servants or relatives within the fourth degree of consanguinity and second of affinity of the officiating notary; (h) in the case of open wills, the heirs and legatees and their spouses and relatives within the fourth degree of consanguinity and second of affinity, unless the legacy be of a specific chattel or of an unimportant amount. Wills are common or special. Common wills comprise the open and the closed will.

Open wills are made before a notary public and three witnesses who see, hear and understand the testator and of whom at least two know how to read and write. The will is drawn up by the notary in his protocol, stating the place, date and hour of execution; it must be read aloud by the notary to the testator in the presence of the witnesses; and all sign, or if the testator or a witness is unable to sign another signs for him and the notary so certifies. If the testator is in immediate danger of death and there is no notary in the locality he may declare his will before five witnesses, and in case of an epidemic a will may be made before three witnesses over 16; in such cases the will may be oral or in writing, but it becomes void two months after the danger or epidemic ceases or three months after the death of the testator, unless the will be proved before a competent judge.

Closed wills may be written by the testator or another person, expressing the place and date; they must be signed by the testator; and every page must be signed by him if written by another, or bear his scroll if he wrote the will himself. The will is enclosed in an envelope which is sealed; and the testator declares before a notary and five witnesses that the envelope contains his will. The notary writes a statement of such declaration on the envelope and all sign.

Special wills are military wills made by soldiers and naval wills made on Nicaraguan vessels at sea. They may be made before certain officers and require only two witnesses.

Foreign wills are accepted as valid if made in the form required by the respective foreign country and if the authenticity of the instrument is duly proved. A Nicaraguan or an alien domiciled in Nicaragua may likewise make a will before a Nicaraguan consul or diplomatic officer.

Testamentary Dispositions.—The testator may freely dispose of his estate, the only obligatory provisions he must make being (a) provisions for the support of his needy descendants and ascendants and (b) the marital fourth pertaining to the surviving spouses. Legacies to religious institutions are void in so far as they exceed one-tenth of the estate, nor can more than one-tenth be left for masses. Certain persons cannot receive legacies, such as: (1) The guardian in certain cases; (2) the teacher who was in charge of a minor testator; (3) the physician or priest who attended the testator in his last illness; (4) the accomplice of an adulterous spouse; (5) the notary before whom the will was made or the person who wrote it; (6) the descendants, ascendants, spouses, brothers and sisters and brothers-in-law and sisters-in-law of such persons; but remunerative legacies are permitted in cases (2) and (3), also legacies to the spouse or legal heirs of the testator. By reason of indignity the right to be an heir is denied to those who: (1) Killed or attempted to kill the author of the inheritance; (2) obliged the testator to make a will or modify it; (3) prevented him from making or revoking a will or destroyed, concealed or altered a later will.

See Topical Index in front part of this volume.

NORTHERN IRELAND LAW DIGEST

(The following is a list of all Topics, including cross-references, covered in this Digest.)

NORTHERN IRELAND LAW DIGEST

Revised for 1997 edition by

C. & H. JEFFERSON, Solicitors of the Supreme Court of Judicature, Belfast.

(Statutes are cited by reference to their Short Title [if any] and by the regal year and chapter number, except Statutes of Northern Ireland Parliament passed after Dec. 31, 1942 which are cited by calendar year and chapter. Statutes of Parliament of United Kingdom, Parliament of Ireland passed prior to 1801, and Parliament of Northern Ireland from 1921 to 1942 are distinguished by having "[U.K.]," "[Ir.]" and "[N.I.]" inserted after their respective citations. Measures of Northern Ireland Assembly are cited in same manner as Statutes passed by Northern Ireland Parliament after Dec. 31, 1942. S.R. & O. refers to United Kingdom Statutory Rules and Orders. S.R. & O. [N.I.] and S.R. refer to Northern Ireland Statutory Rules and Orders passed up to Dec. 31, 1973 and from Jan. 1, 1974, respectively. All subordinate legislation cited by calendar year and number. Orders in Council [Statutory Instruments passed between Apr. 1, 1972 and Dec. 31, 1973; and after July 17, 1974] are cited by calendar year and number [e.g. "1982, S.I. No. 1534 (N.I. 17)"]. [See topic Constitution and Government.] O. and r. refer to Orders and Rules of Supreme Court (Northern Ireland) (Revision) 1980 (1980, S.R. No. 346).

Northern Ireland, as part of United Kingdom, is member of EU. See also European Union Law Digest.

ABSENTEES:

There are no special provisions relating to rights or liabilities of persons residing out of Northern Ireland or who have departed therefrom or relating to the care of property, process agents or escheat.

Process Agent.—No duty to appoint agent for service of process. When defendant by his solicitor undertakes in writing to accept service and enters an appearance all obligation as to service of writ of summons is waived or dispensed with, and such an undertaking remains in force for six years. (0.9.r.1). Once undertaking is given, defendant is bound by authority he has given to his solicitor. Parties may agree that service of writ shall be good if made in a particular way unless such agreement involves asking court to do something which by rules it is forbidden to do. Person without jurisdiction can contract to have domicile for purpose of being sued within jurisdiction and service on agent named in contract to accept service is good, but agreement between parties cannot give court jurisdiction to do that which is forbidden by rules. (British Wagon Company v. Gray, [1896] 1 Q.B. 35).

Escheat.—County court has jurisdiction to hear and determine any action for recovery of land (irrespective of amount of annual value) where (a) At least six months rent of land remains unpaid and (b) tenant has deserted or otherwise abandoned land leaving any premises thereon unoccupied or land not farmed in accordance with rules of good husbandry. (Art. 12[3] County Courts [N.I.] Order, 1980 [1980, S.I. No. 397 (N.I. 3)]). Landlord of premises to which Business Tenancies (N.I.) Order 1996 (1996 No. 725 [N.I.5]) applies must satisfy Lands Tribunal that: (a) He has taken all reasonable steps to communicate with person last known to him to be tenant, and has failed to do so; (b) during period of six months ending with date of application neither tenant nor any person claiming under him has been in occupation of premises comprised in tenancy or any part thereof; and (c) during said period no rent has been payable by tenant, or if rent payable has not been paid. Lands Tribunal may order tenancy to determine from date of order. (1996 N.I.5 Art. 37).

ACKNOWLEDGMENTS:

Acknowledgement within Northern Ireland.—Acknowledgement of any instrument may be made in Northern Ireland before Commissioner for Oaths (§1 Commissioner for Oaths Act 1889, 52 & 53 Vict., c. 10 [U.K.]); officers of court performing duties in relation to court and authorized by judge may administer oaths required for any purpose connected with their duties (52 & 53 Vict., c. 10, §2). Every solicitor holding valid practising certificate has all powers of Commissioner for Oaths, but may not exercise such powers in proceedings in which he is acting or interested. (Solicitors [Northern Ireland] Order 1976 [S.I. No. 582 (N.I. 12) Art. 78]). Commissioner for Oaths is entitled to fee of £5 per signature to be sworn on affidavit, declaration or instrument in writing and fee of £1 per signature on each additional exhibit. (Commissioners for Oaths [Fees] Order 1993, [1993 S.R. No. 418]).

Acknowledgement without Northern Ireland.—Acknowledgement of any instrument may be made outside Northern Ireland for purpose of any cause or matter in Northern Ireland or for purpose of registration of any instrument in any part of U.K. may be taken or made in any place out of Northern Ireland before any person having authority to administer oath in that place, but in case of person having such authority otherwise than by law of foreign country, judicial and official notice shall be taken of his seal or signature affixed, impressed, or subscribed to or on any such oath or affidavit. (52 & 53 Vict., c. 10, §3). Every British ambassador, envoy and minister, charge d'affaires, and secretary of embassy or legation exercising his function in any foreign country, and every British consul, general, vice-consul, acting-consul, proconsul and consular agent exercising his function in any foreign place may in that country or place administer any oath and take any affidavit and also do any notarial act which any notary public can do within Northern Ireland and every oath, affidavit and notarial act administered sworn or done by or before any such person shall be as effectual as if duly administered, sworn, or done by or before any lawful authority in any part of Northern Ireland. Any document purporting to have affixed, impressed, or subscribed thereon or thereto seal or signature of any person authorized by this section to administer an oath in testimony of any oath, affidavit or act being administered taken or done by or before him shall be admitted in evidence without proof of seal or signature being seal or signature of that person or of official character of that person. (52 & 53 Vict., c. 10, §6).

The Statutory Declarations Act 1835 (5 & 6 Will 4, c. 62 [U.K.]) enables any non-litigious act or thing to be proved or evidenced by a declaration.

Voluntary declarations may be taken for purpose of confirming written instruments or allegations or proving execution of Deeds or other matters (§18).

The declaration must be in form prescribed in the Schedule to the Act (§20) as altered in title by §68, Conveyancing and Law of Property Act 1881 (44 & 45 Vict., c. 41 [U.K.]). Within United Kingdom declarations may be made before any justice of the peace, notary public or other officer authorized to administer oaths. Justice of the peace must take the declaration without any fee. Commissioner in Northern Ireland entitled to fee as above. (1988 S.R. No. 249). Outside U.K. every British Ambassador, Envoy, Minister Charge D'Affaires and Secretary of Embassy or Legation exercising his function in any foreign country and every British Consul-general pro-consul and consular agent acting consular general, acting vice-consul and acting consular agent exercising his powers in any foreign place may in that country or place administer any oath or take any affidavit and also do any notarial act which any Notary Public can do within U.K. (Commissioner of Oaths Act 1889, 52 & 53 Vict. c. 10 [U.K.], §6[1] am'd. Commissioner for Oaths Act 1891, 54 & 55 Vict. c. 50 [U.K.], §2).

General Requirements as to Taking.—Officer taking acknowledgement must know and have satisfactory evidence that person making acknowledgement is person described in and who executed instrument and must satisfy himself that person who is going to swear the oath thoroughly understands what he is going to swear to. A commissioner for oaths who is a party to any proceedings or interested therein or is solicitor, agent or correspondent of any party thereto or is clerk to a partner of any solicitor or persons concerned or interested cannot act as a commissioner in any such proceedings. (52 & 53 Vict., c. 10, §1[3]).

General Requirements of Certificate.—(1) If acknowledgement is taken within Northern Ireland or out of Northern Ireland by Northern Ireland Officer, no authentication is necessary and any document purporting to have fixed, impressed or subscribed thereon or thereto, seal and signature of any person authorized to administer an oath in testimony of any oath, affidavit or act being administered, taken or done by, or before him, is admitted in evidence without proof of the seal or signature being seal or signature of that person or of official character of that person. (52 & 53 Vict., c. 10, §6[2]).

(2) If acknowledgement is taken out of Northern Ireland, signature of foreign official authorized by law of his country to take oaths requires verification by High Court of his country. Certificate of president and clerk of county court in U.S. verified by its seal has been accepted. Certificate of British Vice-Consul as to authority of person before whom oath is taken is accepted without affidavit.

Married Woman.—No special requirements in case of.

Corporations.—No special requirements except those contained in articles and memorandum of association.

Effect of Acknowledgement.—Every oath, affidavit and notarial act administered, sworn or done by or before any person authorized to administer oaths in a foreign country is as effectual as if duly administered sworn or done by or before any lawful authority in any part of U.K. (52 & 53 Vict., c. 10, §6[1]).

Proof by Subscribing Witnesses.—Any attesting witness to the execution of any will or codicil, deed or instrument in writing or any other competent person can verify and prove the signing, sealing or delivery of any such will, codicil, deed or instrument by a solemn declaration in writing. (Statutory Declarations Act 1835, 5 & 6 Will. 4, c. 62, §16).

Forms.—The following is the form of statutory declaration prescribed by statute.

Form

I (name of declarant) of etc. do solemnly and sincerely declare that (here set out statement of facts to be proved in numbered paragraphs) . And I make this solemn declaration conscientiously believing the same to be true and by virtue of the provisions of the Statutory Declarations Act. 1835.

Declared at . . . . }
This day of }

Signature of Declarant

Before me . . . .

(Signature of Commissioner or Magistrate)
A Commissioner for Oaths (or Justice of the Peace for . . . .)

Stamp.—A declaration requires no stamp.

ACTIONS:

Action means litigation in a civil court for recovery of individual right or redress of individual wrong, inclusive in its proper legal sense of suits by Crown.

For purposes of Judicature (N.I.) Act, 1978 (1978, c. 23 [U.K.]), §120, "Action" means civil proceedings commenced by writ or in such other manner as is prescribed by Rules of Court and does not include criminal proceeding by or in name of Crown. Subject to any statutory provisions and to R.S.C. 1980 (1980, S.R. No. 346) civil actions in High Court may be commenced by writ of summons, originating summons, originating motion, or petition (O.5, r.1).

Equity.—Legal and equitable remedies are enforced by same court but nature of legal as opposed to equitable rights is unchanged. Rules of equity prevail subject to express provisions of any other Act and generally in all matters not particularly mentioned.

See Topical Index in front part of this volume.

ACTIONS . . . *continued*

Forms of Action.—Forms of writs are prescribed by O.6, r.1. Forms of originating summonses and originating motions are prescribed respectively by O.7, r.2; and O.8, r.3. Petitions must conform to requirements in O.9, r.2.

Condition Precedent.—Due performance of all conditions precedent need not be alleged. If defendant contends that a condition precedent has not been duly performed he must state specifically what that condition was and plead its nonperformance. But allegation which is of essence of cause of action is not condition precedent and must still be pleaded in the statement of claim. e.g. in action for dishonoured cheque notice of dishonour must be averred.

Parties.—

Government Departments and state officials may sue and be sued in manner prescribed by statutes relating to them but right to sue and liability to be sued is limited.

Ambassadors cannot be sued here (7 Anne c. 12. [U.K.]). Immunity extends to other members of embassy and to servants of ambassador and to members of official staff. Exemption from local jurisdiction can be waived with consent of sovereign or official superior.

Business Name.—See topic Commercial Register.

Corporations must sue and be sued in their corporate title or registered name as case may be.

Foreign sovereigns and states recognised by Her Majesty's Government are admitted to sue here in name by which recognised. Court will not entertain action by foreign state for enforcement of revenue law against its own subjects; similarly as to political or penal laws. A person contracting as agent for foreign government cannot be sued in absence of his principal.

Joinder of parties.—Two or more persons may be joined together in one action as plaintiffs or defendants with leave of court, or where: (a) If separate actions were brought, some common question of law or fact would arise in all actions; and (b) all rights to relief claimed in action arise from same transaction or series of transactions. (O.15, r.4).

Intervention.—Persons interested may by consent and on submitting to jurisdiction, attend on summons in action to which they are not parties and they will be bound thereby, but can generally only be insisted upon (1) In a representative action where intervener is one of class whom plaintiff claims to represent, (2) where proprietary rights of intervener are directly affected by proceedings, or (3) in actions claiming specific performance of contracts where third persons have an interest in manner in which contract should be performed. If foreigner seeks to intervene he may have to give security for costs.

Interpleader.—Relief by way of interpleader may be granted where person seeking relief (applicant) is under liability for any debt, money, goods or chattels for, or in respect of which he is, or expects to be, sued by two or more parties (claimants), making adverse claims thereto. (O.17).

Joinder of Causes of Action.—Plaintiff may in one action claim relief against same defendant in respect of more than one cause of action: (a) If plaintiff claims, and defendant is alleged to be liable, in same capacity in respect of all causes of action; or (b) if plaintiff claims or defendant is alleged to be liable in capacity of executor or administrator of estate in respect of one or more of causes of action and in his personal capacity but with reference to same mistake in respect of all others; or (c) with leave of court. (O.15, r.4).

Splitting Causes of Action.—Defendant may at any time apply to court or judge for order confining action to such causes of action as may be conveniently disposed of together. (O.15, r.5).

Consolidation.—Where two or more actions are pending in same court division, court may consolidate actions on appropriate terms if (a) some common question of law or fact arises in both or all of them; or (b) rights to relief claimed therein are in respect of or arise out of same transaction or series of transactions; or (c) there is some other good reason. (O.4, r.5).

Stay of Proceedings.—Court retains inherent power to prevent vexatious oppressive or unreasonable proceedings or those in which there is clearly no cause of action or equity. This jurisdiction is discretionary to be exercised by court if it thinks fit and its general jurisdiction to stay proceedings in proper cases is not limited by Rules of Supreme Court.

Application to stay must be made in court in which action is pending.

Lis Alibi pendens.—Where one action is a foreign action court may act in one of three ways: (1) Put party suing to his election, (2) stay suit in this country, or (3) restrain plaintiff from proceeding in foreign country or institution of proceedings in foreign country. Balance of inconvenience is not sufficient grounds for stay; defendant must show that continuance of action would work an injustice because it would be oppressive or vexatious or an abuse of power of court and that stay will not cause injustice to plaintiff.

Abatement and Revival.—Where party to action dies or becomes bankrupt but cause of action survives, action shall not abate by reason of death or bankruptcy. (O.15, r.7). Where at any stage of proceedings, interest or liability of any party is assigned or transmitted to or devolves upon some other person, court may, on ex parte application, make that other person party to action. (O.15, r.7). If after death of party, no new party is substituted, court may, on application of other party, order that action will be struck out unless it is proceeded with. (O.15, r.9). If death terminates cause of action or interest of party, action (save where otherwise provided by law) is at end.

Foreign Judgment.—Judgment by any court of competent jurisdiction may be sued on in High Court of Northern Ireland. (O.71). Foreign judgment that is contrary to public policy or that is founded on cause of action which is not recognisable in Northern Ireland law will not be enforced, general principle being that only judgments that rest upon principles of universal acceptance will be enforced. Judgment must be final and conclusive binding rights and liabilities of parties. Foreign court must be competent to entertain sort of case which it did deal with and to require defendant to appear before it; and proceedings must not offend against Northern Ireland views of substantial justice though there may be difference in procedure.

Foreign judgment (Reciprocal Enforcement) Act 1933 23.Geo. 5, c. 13 (U.K.). Queen may direct that provisions of the Act which relate to registration of foreign judgments may extend to any foreign country which is prepared to give reciprocity of treatment to judgments given in the superior court of U.K. A judgment of superior court of foreign country may be registered provided it is final and conclusive and there is payable thereunder a sum of money not being in respect of taxes, fines or penalties. (§1). Extended to France (S.R. & O. 1936 No. 609); Belgium (S.R. & O. 1936, No. 1169).

Application to register may be made within six years of date of judgment, but not if it has been wholly satisfied or if it could not be enforced by execution in country of original court. (§4, O.4[b]). Broadly speaking foreign judgment when registered can be treated as if it were judgment of a Northern Ireland Court (§2 [1]). If expressed in currency of foreign country it is treated on basis of rate of exchange prevailing on date when it was given in original court. (§2 [iii]). Interest and reasonable costs of registration may be added to judgment when registered. (§2 [vi]). Cases in which registration of judgment may be set aside are specified in §4 of Act as are circumstances in which country of origin is deemed to have and not to have had jurisdiction. §8 of Act defines circumstances in which foreign judgment is to be recognised.

Proof of Foreign Law.—Foreign Law Ascertainment Act 1861 (24 & 25 Vict., c. 11 [U.K.]) provides for ascertaining law of foreign country or state and applies only to countries with which conventions under Act have been made. British Law Ascertainment Act 1859 (22 & 23 Vict., c. 63 [U.K.]) provides for ascertaining of law as administered in any part of Her Majesty's Dominions.

Limitation of.—See topic Limitation of Actions.

Small Claims.—See topic Courts, subheads Inferior Courts of Northern Ireland, County Courts and Courts of Summary Jurisdiction.

Prohibited Actions.—Court has power to prevent vexatious, oppressive or unreasonable proceedings or those in which there is clearly no cause of action or equity. This jurisdiction is discretionary and exercised by court "if it shall think fit" (see §27[5] Supreme Court of Judicature Ireland Act 1877, 40 & 41 Vict., c. 57 [U.K.]).

Administration.—See topic Executors and Administrators.

Direct Action Against Insurers.—See topic Motor Vehicles, subhead Direct Actions.

ADMINISTRATION:

See topic Executors and Administrators.

ADOPTION:

Legal adoption in Northern Ireland regulated by Adoption Act (Northern Ireland) 1967 (1967, c. 35) and Adoption (Northern Ireland) Order 1987 (1987 S.I. No. 2203 [N.I. 22]). On application of person domiciled anywhere in U.K. and resident in Northern Ireland or domiciled, but not normally resident, in Northern Ireland, court may make adoption order authorizing applicant to adopt infant. Applicant must be (a) mother or father of infant, or (b) 21 years of age and relative of infant, or (c) 25 years of age. Order will not be made on joint application of two spouses unless (a) one of applicants is mother or father of infant or one is 21 years of age and relative of infant or is 25 years of age and (b) other is 21 years of age. In absence of special circumstances order will not be made in respect of female infant in favour of sole male applicant. (1967, c. 35, §2).

Consent Required.—Adoption order not made in any case except with consent of every person who is a parent or guardian of infant, and on application of one of two spouses, except with consent of other spouse. Consent to making of adoption order may be given generally or in respect of adoption by specified person, and unconditionally or subject to conditions with respect to religious persuasion in which infant is to be brought up. (§4). Consent of mother is of no effect if given within six weeks of birth of infant. If parent or guardian does not attend in proceedings on application for purpose of giving consent a document signifying consent is admissible as evidence of that consent without further proof of signature, but only if document is attested by a justice of the peace where it is executed in U.K. or if executed outside U.K. if attested by (a) any person for time being authorized by law in place where document is executed to administer oath for any judicial or legal purpose, (b) a British consular officer, (c) a notary public, or (d) if person executing document is serving in any of regular armed forces of crown, an officer holding a commission in any of those forces. (1967, c. 35 §§5, 6 and S.R. & O. 1969, No. 288). Court has power to dispense with consent where it is satisfied that person whose consent is to be dispensed with has abandoned, neglected or persistently ill-treated infant, is incapable of giving consent, cannot be found, has persistently failed to discharge obligations of parent, or unreasonably withholds consent, or in such other cases as court thinks fit. (§5).

Conditions Precedent.—No adoption order will be made unless infant is at least 19 weeks old and has been continuously in care and possession of applicant in Northern Ireland for at least thirteen weeks immediately preceding date of order, where applicant is relative or infant is placed with applicants by adoption agency or in pursuance of High Court Order. Otherwise Order will not be made unless child is at least 12 months old and during preceding 12 months has lived with applicant. Before making order court must be satisfied that (a) all necessary consents have been obtained and that person consenting understands nature of consent, (b) order made will be for welfare of infant, due consideration being given to wishes of infant, (c) that applicant has not received or agreed to receive, and that no person has made or given or agreed to make or give to applicant, any payment or other reward in consideration of adoption (§7[1]) except payment to welfare authority in respect of expenses reasonably incurred, payments sanctioned by court or certain payments to or by registered adoption society (§35).

Effect of Adoption.—Once order is made all rights, duties, obligations and liberties of parents or guardians of adopted infant in relation to future custody, maintenance, upbringing and education of infant are extinguished, and all such rights, duties, obligations and liabilities vest in and are exercisable by and enforceable against adopter as if adopted infant were an infant born to adopter in lawful wedlock. Where two spouses are adopters they stand to each other and to infant as they would if they had been lawful father and mother of infant, and adopted infant stands to them in same relation as to a

ADOPTION . . . *continued*
lawful father and mother. (§16). Adopter and infant are within prohibited degrees of consanguinity for purposes of law relating to marriage.

If adopted person or adopter or any other person dies intestate in respect of any property (other than property limited in tail or subject to an entailed interest under a disposition made before order) that property devolves in all respects as if adopted person were child of adopter born in lawful wedlock. (§19). In any disposition of property (including wills and codicils) after adoption order any reference to child or children of adopters includes adopted person, any reference to child or children of adopted person's natural parents is construed as not being reference to adopted person and any reference to person related to adopted person is construed as reference to person who would be related to him if he were child of adopter born in lawful wedlock and were not child of any other person, although in each case this is subject to a contrary intention appearing in disposition. (§18).

Restrictions on Sending Infants Abroad.—Without authority of court order no person may take or send an infant who is a British subject out of Northern Ireland to any place outside British Islands with view to adoption of infant (whether in law or fact) by any person not being parent or guardian or relative of infant.

Provisional adoption order may be granted by court to person not domiciled in Northern Ireland who intends to adopt infant under law of or within country in which he is domiciled and for that purpose desires to remove infant from Northern Ireland. Application may be made to High Court or alternatively to any county court within jurisdiction of which either applicant or infant resides at date of application or, if applicant not ordinarily resident in Northern Ireland, to any county court in jurisdiction where applicant resides at date of application. Normal adoption rules apply except that child must be continuously in care and possession of applicant in Northern Ireland for at least six, rather than three, consecutive months preceding date of provisional adoption order. (§38).

Registration of Adoption Orders.—Every adoption order contains a direction to Registrar General to make an entry in Adopted Children Register which contains particulars of name, sex, date and country of birth of infant and particulars of adopter and adoption order. Index may be searched and certified copies of entries therein obtained.

Effect of Revocation of Certain Orders.—Where person adopted in pursuance of order has subsequently become a legitimated person and order is then revoked, such revocation does not affect operation of law in relation to an intestacy which occurred or disposition made before revocation.

Extended Powers of Court.—Convention relating to adoption of children was concluded at Hague in 1965 and as result provisions of Adoption (Hague Convention) Act (Northern Ireland) 1969 (1969, c. 22) were enacted giving court power to make adoption order on application of person resident in Northern Ireland, being a U.K. national or national of a Convention country, or person resident in Convention country being U.K. national, in respect of unmarried infant under 18 years of age who is a U.K. national or national of a Convention country and resides in Northern Ireland or a Convention country. (1969, c. 22, §1). Provision also made therein for recognition of foreign adoptions and adoption proceedings. (§§4-7).

AFFIDAVITS:

Affidavit for use in Northern Ireland may be sworn in the United Kingdom, Colonies or Commonwealth, before any judge, notary public, or any person authorized to administer oaths there. In foreign countries it should be sworn before the British Consul and if sworn before a notary public, or person authorized by law to administer oaths there, the authority of such person must be verified, i.e., a certificate must be annexed that the person before whom affidavit is sworn is authorized to administer oaths in the country in which it is sworn. This certificate must be signed by a British Consul or Vice-consul or verified by seal of foreign court. No such verification is required when the person before whom the affidavit is sworn derives authority to administer oaths in such country from a British source. Affidavits for use in the High Court in Northern Ireland must be written, typewritten or printed in black ink, on foolscap paper, bookwise, with a margin on the left side.

Affidavits sworn for the purposes of any provisions of the Registration of Deeds Acts, or for the purposes of the registration of any document or transaction in the registry of deeds may be sworn as mentioned above as well as before one of the following persons: (a) If sworn in Northern Ireland before Registrar of Deeds, or Assistant Registrar, or before notary public, commissioner for oaths or justice of the peace having authority or jurisdiction in the place where the oath is administered; (b) if sworn in any other part of the British Isles, before notary public or commissioner for oaths having jurisdiction in that part or before any court or judge lawfully authorised to administer oaths in such part; (c) if sworn in any part of the Commonwealth outside the British Islands, before a judge of any court of record, the mayor of any incorporated city or incorporated town under common seal of such city or town, or notary public under his official seal; (d) if sworn in any other place, before a judge of a court of record or court of comparable status under seal of such court, mayor of any city or incorporated town under common seal of such city or town or a consular officer, or notary public under his official seal. (§2(1) Registration of Deeds (Amendment) Act 1957 [1957, c. 20]).

Form

An affidavit is commenced with title of action, e.g.: In the High Court of Justice in Northern Ireland 19. . No. . . (in Court Index), Queen's Bench Division (or Chancery Division). (In Chancery Division add, "In the matter of the Estate of . . . . Deceased (or as the case may be), Between A. B. Plaintiff, and C. D. Defendant." The full name, place of abode and description of the deponent must then be stated, e.g., "I, (Full Names) . . . . of . . . . (Address) . . . . County in the State of . . . . United States of America, (description) . . . . make oath and say as follows:" Then the facts to be deposed to should be set out in the first person in paragraphs numbered consecutively.

An affidavit must be confined to facts within the deponent's own knowledge and must contain an averment that such facts are within his own knowledge except on interlocutory motions where statements as to his beliefs with the grounds thereof may be admitted. Affidavits containing alterations or erasures cannot be filed or read without leave of the court, unless such alterations and erasures are initialled by the officer before whom the affidavit is sworn.

Jurat.—The jurat must follow close at the end of the affidavit to preserve its continuity and must state date when and place where it was sworn. The deponent must sign his usual signature, or make his mark, at left of jurat, not beneath it, and signature and full official character and description of person before whom affidavit is sworn, his official seal of office attached should follow immediately after jurat in form as follows:

(Signature of Deponent) { Sworn by the deponent . . . . (Name) at . . . . (Place) . . . . on the . . . . day of . . . . 19. .)

Before me,

(Seal) (Signature of Officer) (Title of Officer)

If the deponent appears to officer taking the affidavit to be illiterate or blind, officer must certify in jurat that affidavit was read in his presence to deponent, that deponent seemed perfectly able to understand it, and that deponent made his signature in presence of the officer. The jurat is sworn as follows:—

Form

The mark of X (Deponent's name) — Sworn by the deponent . . . . . . (Name) . . . . . . at (place and date as above) . . . . I having first truly distinctly and audibly read over the contents of the above affidavit to the said deponent who seemed to perfectly understand the same and made his mark thereto in my presence.

Before me (etc. as above).

Exhibits.—A document may be referred to in an affidavit either as an exhibit, thus: "the said letter is now produced and shown to me and marked with the letter 'A,' " or if not as an exhibit, thus: "hereunto annexed." In the former case the officer before whom affidavit is sworn must enquire whether the deponent has seen the document and is aware of contents thereof: in the latter case document should be annexed to affidavit at time it is sworn and is filed with it.

Every exhibit referred to in an affidavit must be marked with a short title of the cause or matter, and must be distinguished by some mark placed upon it, and must be signed and identified by the officer before whom affidavit is sworn, or certified by him to be the document referred to as follows:—

Form

(Title of Action)

This is the Exhibit marked "A.B." (or "A.B.1.") referred to in the Affidavit of X.Y. sworn in this action (if Chancery, "Matter" not "Action") this . . . . day of . . . . 19. ..

Before me,
(Name and Title of Officer.)

AGENCY: See topic Principal and Agent.

ALIENS:

Power to legislate with respect to aliens, nationality or immigration excluded from competence of Northern Ireland Assembly by Northern Ireland Constitution Act 1973. (1973, c. 36 [U.K.] Sch. 2). See topics Constitution and Government; Immigration; see also England Law Digest.

Corporations owned or controlled by aliens.—There are no disqualifications applying to corporations owned or controlled by aliens, but catalogues, trade circulars, show cards and business letters of companies must state, inter alia, nationality of directors and managers, if not British. (1960, c. 22, §192). Corporation's register of directors and secretaries, as well as documents required to be lodged with Registrar of Companies and Friendly Societies with respect to directors and secretaries on incorporation and thereafter, must state, inter alia, nationality of directors and usual residential address of directors and secretaries. (Arts. 21, 297 and 298 The Companies [N.I.] Order 1986 [1986 S.I. 1032] [N.I. 6]).

See also topic Corporations, subhead Foreign Corporation.

ARBITRATION:

All references to Arbitration Act (N.I.) 1937 (c. 8) unless otherwise stated.

Under Act arbitration not mandatory. Act governs arbitration pursuant to Arbitration Agreement between parties. §30(1) defines Arbitration Agreement as written agreement to refer present or future differences to arbitrators whether arbitrator named therein or not.

Subject to contrary intention expressed in Arbitration Agreement, reference under Arbitration Agreement is irrevocable except by leave of Court and has same effect as Court Order. (§1[1]). With leave of Court, arbitration award can be entered as judgment and have same effect as Court Order. (§16). Subject to contrary intention expressed in Arbitration Agreement provisions in schedule one of Act apply to arbitration. (§1[2]).

Any provision in Arbitration Agreement that parties shall pay own costs whatever outcome void unless Arbitration Agreement entered into after dispute, which is subject of arbitration, has arisen. (§23[R]).

If party commences Court proceedings in respect of matter agreed to be referred to arbitration, any party to such proceedings may after appearance and before delivering any pleadings or taking other steps in proceedings apply to Court to stay proceedings and Court may order arbitration. (§4).

Arbitrators.—Court may appoint arbitrator in default of agreement between parties or if arbitrator refuses to act, dies or incapable of acting. (§5).

Arbitrator may seek Court determination of any question of law or award or part of award. (§22[1]).

Where arbitrator has misconducted himself or proceedings or where arbitration or award improperly procured Court may set aside award. (§7[2]).

See Topical Index in front part of this volume.

ARBITRATION . . . *continued*

Limitation.—Limitation (N.I.) Order 1989 (S.I. 1989/1339 N.I.[11]) together with any other limitation provision apply to arbitration as they apply to action (Art. 72 S.I. 1989/1339 N.I. [11]) (see topic Limitation of Actions).

Foreign Arbitration Awards.—Recognition and enforcement governed by Part II Arbitration Act 1950. (14 Geo. 6 c. 27U.K. [U.K. Legislation: See England Law Digest]).

Consumer Arbitration Agreements.—May be unenforceable by party acting in course of business against consumer who is not acting in course of business. (Consumer Arbitration Agreements Act 1988 [1988, c. 21] [U.K. Legislation: See England Law Digest]). *Note:* §1(3)(1988, c. 21) overrides §4.

ASSIGNMENTS:

Assignments of legal choses in action are governed by §87 of Judicature (Northern Ireland) Act, 1978 (1978, c. 23 [U.K.]). Any absolute assignment by writing under hand of the assignor (not purporting to be by way of charge only) of any debt or other legal chose in action of which express notice in writing has been given to the debtor, trustee or other person from whom assignor would have been entitled to claim such debt or chose in action, is effectual in law (subject to equities having priority over right of assignee) to pass and transfer from date of such notice: (a) The legal right to such debt or thing in action; (b) all legal and other remedies for the same and (c) power to give a good discharge for the same without concurrence of assignor. Provided that if debtor, trustee or other person liable in respect of such debt or thing in action has notice (a) that assignment is disputed by assignor or any person claiming under him, or (b) of any other opposing or conflicting claims to such debt, or thing in action, he may either call on persons making claim thereto to interplead concerning the same or pay the debt or other thing in action into court.

This section enables legal assignments of legal things in action to be made so that assignee can sue in his own name without joining assignor as a party. Assignments of this kind need not be for valuable consideration but must be of the whole debt and not of a part thereof and written notice to debtor or trustee of the fund is essential.

Assignments of life assurance must be by deed in accordance with the Policies of Assurance Act, 1867 30-1 Vict., c. 144 (U.K.).

Equitable assignments both of legal and equitable things in action are recognized as valid; in such assignments the formalities of the statute need not be complied with, but must be complete so that the assignee can demand payment from the debtor. The equitable assignee cannot sue in his own name and must join assignor to proceedings. Notice in writing to debtor should be given, as priority of assignee's rights depends on date of such notice and he is entitled to be paid out of fund in order in which he gives notice to debtor or other person by whom fund is distributable.

ASSIGNMENTS FOR BENEFIT OF CREDITORS:

By Insolvency (N.I.) Order 1989 (S.I. 1989/2405 [N.I. 19]) any instrument whether under seal or not made by, for, or in respect of affairs of debtor for benefit of his creditors generally or made by, for, or in respect of affairs of debtor who was insolvent at date of execution of instrument for benefit of any three or more of his creditors, otherwise than in pursuance of law relating to bankruptcy, is deemed to be deed of arrangement to which Part VIII, c. I, S.I. 1989/2405 (N.I. 19) applies.

The following classes of instruments in particular are included: (a) Assignments of property; (b) deeds of and agreements for a composition; and in cases where the creditors obtain control over the debtor's property or business; (c) a deed of inspectorship entered into for the purpose of carrying on or winding up the business; (d) a letter or license authorizing the debtor or any other person to manage, carry on, release, or dispose of the business with a view to paying all debts and (e) any agreement entered into for the purpose of carrying on or winding up the debtor's business or authorizing the debtor or any other person to manage or carry on release or dispose of the debtor's business with a view to the payment of his debts.

Deed of arrangement is void unless it bears ad valorem duty stamp and is registered within seven clear days after its execution, if executed in Northern Ireland, or if executed abroad, within seven days after time at which it would, in ordinary course of post arrive in Northern Ireland, if posted within one week after execution thereof.

Deed for benefit of creditors generally is void unless before expiration of 21 days of registration it receives assent in writing of majority in number and value of creditors. No creditor is bound to join in such deed unless he thinks proper. Trustee must file statutory declaration that requisite majority of creditors have assented at time of registration or if deed is assented to after registration within 28 days thereof.

See also topic Bankruptcy and Insolvency.

ASSOCIATIONS: See topic Partnership.

ATTACHMENT:

Relevant legislation is Judgments Enforcement (N.I.) Order, 1981 (1981, S.I. No. 226 [N.I. 6]) as amended by The Judgments Enforcement (Attachment of Debts) (Northern Ireland) Order 1983 (1983 S.I. No. 1904 [N.I. 22]) and The Judgments Enforcement [Amendment] [Northern Ireland] Order 1986 (1986 S.I. No. 1166 [N.I. 11]). All references to statutory provisions are to provisions contained in 1981 Order. (1981 S.I. No. 226 [N.I. 6]).

Attachment of Earnings.—Where debtor is in receipt of income, Office may, on application of creditor, make attachment of earnings order requiring person to whom order is directed (employer) to make out of debtor's earnings such payments as may be specified on weekly, monthly or other basis, taking into consideration debtor's resources and needs. (Art. 73). Before making such order, Office has power to require debtor to furnish, within specified period: (i) Name and address of any person by whom earnings are paid to debtor; (ii) specified particulars of his earnings, anticipated future earnings, resources and needs; (iii) particulars for purpose of identifying debtor to his employer. Office may also require employer to furnish particulars of debtor's earnings.

See topics Executions; Judgments; Garnishment.

BANKRUPTCY AND INSOLVENCY:

Regulated by Insolvency (N.I.) Order 1989 (S.I. 1989/2405 [N.I. 19]) and Insolvency Rules (N.I.) 1991 (S.R. 1991/No. 364). Unless otherwise stated citations refer to Insolvency (N.I.) Order 1989.

Corporate Insolvency.—

Company Voluntary Arrangements.—Company may conclude effective arrangement with its creditors and shareholders. Arrangement may be proposed even after company has gone into liquidation or administration. If not in liquidation or administration directors propose arrangement. If authorised insolvency practitioner acting as directors' nominee is of opinion that there is some prospect of arrangement being approved, he will state that meeting of creditors and shareholders should be convened to consider proposal. For arrangement to be approved by creditors there has to be 75% majority in value in favour of it. Shareholders' approval is given by simple majority. Approved arrangement binds every person who was given notice of meeting to consider proposal. Nominee under obligation to report outcome of meeting to court, creditors and shareholders. Person whose function is to carry out arrangement is supervisor. Supervisor may apply to court for directions. (Part II).

Administration Orders.—Court can make Administration Order to place management of insolvent company in hands of Administrator. Court will do so if satisfied, inter alia, that order would ensure survival of company in whole or in part as going concern or more advantageous realisation of company's assets than in winding up. Application is by petition to court either by company, all its directors, creditors or supervisor and must be supported by affidavit. Effect of application for Administration Order is that no steps can be taken in legal actions, executions against company or its property or to enforce any security over company's property without leave of court. Once administrator appointed, directors must submit statement of company's affairs verified by affidavit to him. Administrator has full management powers of administration, including authority to call meetings of creditors. (Schedule I). Administrator must supply such information, including purpose statement and statement of affairs, to enable creditors to decide whether to approve proposal. Administrator must report outcome of meeting to court and if proposals approved, administrator must account for all his receipts and payments at regular intervals to Registrar of Companies, court and creditors. (Part III).

Administrative receiver is receiver or manager of company's property appointed under charge. Appointment not valid until receiver accepts. Receiver must notify company and advertise notice of appointment, and within 28 days send similar notice to all creditors. Powers conferred on receiver include power to carry on business. (Schedule I). Receiver must report to creditors within three months after appointment and send to Registrar of Companies and to all creditors report on events leading up to appointment, details of property being disposed of, amount owed to debenture holders and preferential creditors and amount (if any) likely to be available for unsecured creditors. Copy of report must also be laid before meeting of company's unsecured creditors within three months. (Part IV).

Winding up of company may be voluntary or by High Court. (Part V).

Members Voluntary Winding Up.—Shareholders of company resolve to put company into liquidation in circumstances other than its insolvency.

Creditors Voluntary Winding Up.—At meetings convened by directors of company, shareholders and creditors resolve to wind up company by reason of its insolvency, appoint liquidator and liquidation committee. At least seven days notice of meeting must be given to creditors. Notice must also be advertised. Creditors' meeting must be held not more than 14 days after shareholders' meeting. At creditors' meeting shareholders nominate qualified insolvency practitioner (infra) to act as liquidator. If more than one nominated, creditors decide on vote. Creditor is only entitled to vote if, as unsecured creditor, he is present or represented by proxy, his claim is not unliquidated and he has lodged claim. Voting is by reference to value of creditors' claims. Liquidator must advertise his appointment and notify Registrar of Companies. Liquidator must given all creditors within 28 days of meeting copy of Statement of Affairs and report on meeting. Liquidator must also call annual meetings of shareholders and creditors to keep them informed and must call final meeting of shareholders and creditors to approve his account before company can be dissolved.

Winding up by High Court.—Petition may be presented if company has by special resolution resolved that company should be wound up by Court; or company is unable to pay debts; or it is just and equitable that company be wound up. Company is deemed to be unable to pay its debts if it fails to comply with statutory demand (infra) or if its liabilities (including contingent and prospective liabilities) exceed its assets. Procedure to hearing of petition same as for bankruptcy; individual insolvency (infra) with following exceptions: (i) petition and demand must be served personally on director or authorised person at debtor company's registered office, (ii) petition must be advertised in Belfast Gazette not less than seven business days before hearing and not less than seven business days after service and (iii) petitioner or solicitor must lodge at court at least five business days before hearing prescribed certificate showing compliance with Rules together with copy of advertisement. Any creditor who has given notice to petitioner can appear on hearing of petition. On hearing of petition, Court may make winding up order and its discretion is unfettered. It is usual, if majority of creditors in value support petition, that order will be made. Court usually orders costs of petitioner be paid by company out of its assets in priority to all other claims including preferential and secured. Official Receiver serves sealed copy of order upon company and advertises it.

Antecedent Transactions.—If company goes into liquidation, any disposition of its property after date of presentation of petition is void.

Provisional Liquidator.—If necessary to protect company's assets prior to hearing of petition, court can on application of company, petitioner or creditor, appoint Official Receiver or authorised insolvency practitioner (infra) as provisional liquidator.

Statement of Affairs.—Directors or other officers are obliged to submit Statement of Affairs verified by Affidavit to Official Receiver within 21 days of order or appointment of provisional liquidator. Statement is in prescribed form.

Examination.—Official Receiver or liquidator may make application to Court for public or private examination of former officers of company. Application must be accompanied by report. Court may also order private examination of any person thought to have information relating to property of company.

See Topical Index in front part of this volume.

BANKRUPTCY AND INSOLVENCY . . . *continued*

Appointment of Liquidator.—Unless or until someone else is appointed liquidator, Official Receiver is liquidator. Only authorised insolvency practitioner can act as liquidator. Official Receiver must decide within 12 weeks after date of winding up order whether or not to summon meeting of creditors and contributories to choose alternative liquidator, of which 21 days notice given. Notice must also be advertised. Resolutions are passed on majority in value of creditors and contributories presented personally or by proxy. Creditors can only vote if debts liquidated and not secured. Contributories vote in accordance with articles of association. Creditors can also resolve to establish liquidation committee, but committee cannot be established when Official Receiver is liquidator. Any creditor (other than secured creditor) who has lodged satisfactory proof of debt is eligible for election. Committee's role is primarily supervisory, but it also must sanction certain acts of liquidator. Quorum for committee meeting is two.

Bankruptcy—Individual Insolvency.—

Bankruptcy Proceedings.—High Court alone has jurisdiction in bankruptcy proceedings.

Creditor's Petition.—To found petition for bankruptcy of debtor, creditor must show that (i) debt owed above bankruptcy level, currently £750, (ii) debt is for liquidated sum, (iii) debtor appears unable to pay debt or appears to have no reasonable prospect of being able to pay debt and (iv) debtor domiciled or personally resident or carries on business in Northern Ireland on day petition presented or at any time in previous three years. Failure to comply with statutory demand in prescribed form (Forms 6.01 to 6.03, S.R. 1991 No. 364) served personally upon debtor within 21 days of service or to apply within 18 days to have demand set aside is sufficient proof that debtor unable to pay debt or appears to have no reasonable prospect of being able to pay it. Petition in prescribed form (Forms 6.07 to 6.11, S.R. 1991 No. 364) must be verified by affidavit in prescribed form (Form 6.15, S.R. 1991 No. 364) and be accompanied by affidavit of service of demand and Official Receiver's receipt. Sealed copy of petition must be served personally on debtor at least 14 days before hearing of petition. Substituted service by post can be ordered by court. Affidavit of service of petition must be filed in court immediately after service. On hearing of petition, creditor must satisfy court that debt still owing. Court may order that bankruptcy order be made if satisfied debt not paid (nor secured or compounded for) or if debt due in future, and debtor has no reasonable prospect of being able to pay it when due. Bankruptcy order will not be made if court satisfied debtor able to pay all his debts or if debtor made offer to secure or compound for debt which has been unreasonably refused. If made, sealed copy of order sent to debtor and adjudication advertised in local newspapers and Belfast Gazette. Debtor can oppose petition by giving notice to petitioner and court specifying grounds of objection. Petitioner can withdraw petition or apply to have petition dismissed by filing supporting affidavit in court. (Parts VIII to X and Part 6 S.R. 1991 No. 364).

Debtor's Petition.—Debtor may present own bankruptcy petition on ground unable to pay debts. Petition must be accompanied by statement of affairs in prescribed form. Court may make bankruptcy order on hearing. If liabilities less than small bankruptcy level currently £20,000 and assets exceed minimum level, currently £2,000 then bankruptcy order must not be made. Instead court may appoint insolvency practitioner (infra) to prepare report on whether voluntary arrangement possible. (Part IX, c. I).

Voluntary Arrangement.—Individuals can make voluntary arrangement with creditors whereby creditors agree to accept dividend on their debts or allow debtor time to pay. It is essentially private arrangement. Insolvency practitioner acting as debtor's nominee applies to court for moratorium during which nominee considers debtor's proposals. Court considers proposals and nominee's report and directs whether creditors meeting should be held. Debtor's proposals either accepted, modified or rejected at creditors meeting. Court makes order approving voluntary arrangement and proposals implemented by supervisor (can be nominee). (Part VIII, c. II).

Restrictions in Bankruptcy.—Any disposition by bankrupt of his property after date of presentation of petition is void. Once order made, creditor has no remedy against person or property of bankrupt and may not commence legal action against him without leave of court. (Part IX, c. II).

Statement of Affairs.—Bankrupt obliged to submit statement of affairs in prescribed form verified by affidavit to Official Receiver within 21 days of order. If fails without reasonable excuse, guilty of contempt of court. (Part IX, c. II).

Public Examination.—Official Receiver must apply to court if he wishes bankrupt to be publicly examined on oath. Official Receiver, trustee and any creditor who has tendered proof in debt can ask questions at examination. (Part IX, c. II).

Creditors' Meeting and Appointment of Trustee.—Official Receiver must decide within 12 weeks after making of bankruptcy order to call creditors' meeting to appoint trustee. If no meeting called, Official Receiver is trustee and must give notice to court and creditors. No person can be appointed as trustee unless he is authorised insolvency practitioner (infra). (Part IX, c. III).

Proofs of Debt.—Every creditor must submit claim in prescribed form to Official Receiver or trustee to prove debt as soon as possible after adjudication. Official Receiver cannot declare dividend until he has examined every proof of debt. Creditor dissatisfied with Official Receiver's decision, can apply to High Court (Part IX, c. IV).

Discharge.—If person not previously bankrupt within last 15 years or has not been made criminally bankrupt, automatic discharge at expiry of three years from bankruptcy order is granted. If certificate of summary administration in force (liabilities less than £20,000) period is two years. Right to automatic discharge can be suspended on application of Official Receiver to court. After five years, bankrupt can apply to court to be discharged. (Part IX, c. I.).

Certificate of Discharge.—Court must, at request of bankrupt, issue certificate of discharge. Bankrupt is released from all obligations in respect of pre-bankruptcy liabilities with exception of fraud, fines and damages for negligence in respect of personal injury.

Annulment.—Court can annul order if it appears at any time that order ought not to have been made or that debts and expenses of bankruptcy have all been paid or secured to satisfaction of court since order.

Insolvency practitioners are licenced on authorisation by recognised professional body or competent authority appointed by Department of Economic Development. (Parts XII and XIII).

Debtors may also carry an arrangement in bankruptcy in which the proceedings are the same as in a bankruptcy, save that sittings are held in private, only the creditors and their solicitors attending, and the name of the arranging debtor is not, as a general rule, published in the daily newspapers nor is publication made in the official Gazette. Proceedings in court are reported anonymously.

Failure of the debtor to carry out an arrangement constitutes an Act of Bankruptcy.

Preferred Debts.—Parts V and XI of Insolvency (Northern Ireland) Order 1989 (1989 S.I. No. 2405 [N.I. 19]) provide in distribution of property of bankrupt there must be paid in priority to other debts: (a) Debts due to Inland Revenue on account of deductions of income tax paid during 12 months next before date of order of adjudication of bankruptcy ("relevant date"); (b) debts due to Custom and Excise in respect of Value Added Tax referable to period of six months next before relevant date; (c) certain social security contributions owed by debtor; (d) any sum owed by debtor to which Schedule 4 Social Security Pensions (Northern Ireland) Order 1975 (1975 c. 15) applies (contributions to occupational pension schemes and state scheme premiums); (e) any amount owed by debtor to person who is or has been employee of debtor payable by way of remuneration for period of four months next before relevant date and does not exceed maximum amount as specified by Department of Economic Development (at present £800); (f) amount owed by way of accrued holiday remuneration in respect of any period of employment before relevant date irrespective of whether employment was terminated before or after relevant date; (g) any amount which is ordered (even after relevant date) to be paid by debtor under Reserve Forces (Safeguard of Employment) Act 1985 (1985 c. 17) and is so ordered in respect of default by debtor before that date in discharge of his obligations under that Act as does not exceed such amount as may be specified in order by Department; (h) any sums due at relevant date from debtor in respect of levies on coal and steel production under European Community legislation.

Foregoing debts rank equally among themselves and must be paid in full unless property of bankrupt is insufficient to meet them, in which case they abate in equal proportions.

See also topic Fraudulent Sales and Conveyances.

BILLS AND NOTES:

Power to legislate with respect to negotiable instruments, except insofar as they may be affected by powers of taxation, is excluded from competence of Northern Ireland Assembly by Northern Ireland Constitution Act 1973. (1973, c. 36 [U.K.] Sch. 2). (See topic Constitution and Government.) Law of Northern Ireland is same as law of England. See England Law Digest, topic Bills and Notes.

CHATTEL MORTGAGES:

Mortgages of chattels except those executed by limited companies, which require registration under the Companies Order (see topic Corporations) or by credit unions, which require registration under Credit Unions (Northern Ireland) Order, 1985 (1985, S.I. No. 1205 [N.I. 12]) must be in form prescribed by Bills of Sale (Ireland) Act (1879); Amendment Act 1883 (46-7 Vict., c. 7 [U.K.]). There are two classes of bills of sale. First comprises absolute bills of sale, to which Bills of Sale (Ireland) Act (1879) (42-3 Vict., c. 50 [U.K.]) applies, and second comprises bills of sale given to secure payment of money and principal Act and amending Act are construed together.

An agreement, whether intended or not to be followed by the execution of any other instrument, by which a right in equity to any personal chattels, or to any charge or security thereon, is conferred, is a bill of sale. A bill of sale by way of security made or given in consideration of any sum under £30 is void. Every bill of sale must set forth consideration for which it was given.

What May be Mortgaged.—The Bills of Sale Acts relate only to personal chattels which come under one or other of four classes of things: (1) Goods, furniture and other articles capable of complete transfer by delivery; (2) growing crops when assigned or charged separately from the land; (3) fixtures when assigned or charged separately from the land; and (4) trade machinery, which for the purposes of the Acts is to be deemed personal chattels.

The subject matter of bills of sale by way of security is restricted by certain provisions of the amending Act which require in order that a bill of sale by way of security should have effect against persons other than grantor, that the personal chattels to which it relates should be specifically described in the schedule annexed to the bill of sale, and that grantor should be the true owner of such personal chattels at time of its execution. These provisions are subject to certain exceptions in the case of growing crops, fixtures, plant and trade machinery.

Although an instrument purporting to assign by way of security property other than personal chattels is void as a bill of sale, it may nevertheless be valid as regards property not deemed to be personal chattels within the meaning of the principal Act.

After Acquired Property.—A bill of sale by way of security is void except as against grantor in respect of any personal chattels specifically described in the schedule thereto of which the grantor was not the true owner at time of execution of the bill of sale. But the rules imposed by the amending Act with regard to the true ownership at the time of the execution of the bill of sale, and to the specific description of chattels in the schedule are subject to exceptions (1) in the case of growing crops separately assigned or charged, where such crops are actually growing at time when bill of sale was executed and (2) in case of fixtures separately assigned or charged, plant, or trade machinery, when they are in substitution for like fixtures, plant, or trade machinery which are specifically described in the schedule. And bills of sale, if in the statutory form, of such growing crops, and bills of sale with a schedule contemplating the substitution of fixtures, plant, or trade machinery for those assigned, will be valid against third parties as well as against grantor, although grantor was not the true owner of such growing crops or substituted articles, and although they are not specifically described in the schedule.

Requisites of Instrument.—A bill of sale must truly set forth the consideration for which it was given and a bill of sale made or given by way of security for payment of money by a grantor thereof is void unless in accordance with the form in the Schedule to the amending Act annexed. A bill of sale must be complete in itself and if it has to be read with some collateral agreement it is not in accordance with the statutory form.

CHATTEL MORTGAGES . . . *continued*

The names of the respective parties must be filled up with addresses and descriptions. Some consideration must be inserted. The form requires that a fixed sum shall be secured, and a bill of sale cannot be given by way of indemnity, the amount ultimately payable being uncertain nor can future advances be included. It must contain an agreement to repay the principal sum at a certain stipulated time or times. Every bill of sale given by way of security must have annexed thereto or written thereon a schedule containing an inventory of the personal chattels comprised in it. The name, address and description of the attesting witness or witnesses must be stated. Where registration is made void by failure to comply with the statutory requirements a bill of sale given by way of security is void in respect of the personal chattels comprised therein.

Execution of instrument by the grantor of a bill of sale by way of security must be duly attested by one or more creditable witnesses, not being parties thereto.

Filing.—Bills of sale given by way of security must be registered within seven clear days after the execution thereof or if executed in any place out of Northern Ireland then within seven clear days after the time at which it would, in the ordinary course of post, arrive in Northern Ireland if posted immediately after execution thereof. The bill of sale with every schedule or inventory thereto annexed or therein referred to and a true copy of such bill and of such schedule or inventory and of every attestation of such execution of such bill of sale together with an affidavit containing certain required particulars must be presented to the Registrar and the copy bill of sale and affidavit must be filed with him. The affidavit presented to and filed with the Registrar must prove the following facts: (1) The due execution and attestation of the bill of sale; (2) the residence and occupation of the grantor and of every attesting witness; and (3) the true date of execution of the bill of sale. The affidavit may be sworn before a master of the High Court or a Commissioner of Oaths.

Re-Filing or Extension.—The registration of a bill of sale must be renewed once at least every five years and if a period of five years elapses from registration or renewed registration of a bill of sale without a renewal or further renewal, as the case may be, the registration becomes void. The renewal by a registration is effected by filing with the Registrar an affidavit stating date of the bill of sale and of the last registration thereof and the names, residences and occupations of the parties thereto as stated therein and that the bill of sale is still a subsisting security.

Seizure.—Grantee cannot seize or take possession of the goods except for the causes specified in the amending Act. Possession may be taken for any one or more of those causes even though no express power of seizure is conferred by the bill of sale. Personal chattels assigned under a bill of sale given by way of security, are not liable to be seized or taken possession of by the grantee for any other than the following statutory causes: (1) If grantor makes default in payment of the sum or sums secured by the bill of sale at the time therein provided for payment; (2) if the grantor makes default in performance or any covenant or agreement contained in the bill of sale or necessary for maintaining the security; (3) if grantor becomes bankrupt; (4) if grantor suffers the goods assigned by the bill of sale or any of them to be distrained for rent, rates or taxes; (5) if grantor fraudulently either removes or suffers the goods or any of them, comprised in the bill of sale, to be removed from the premises; (6) if grantor does not, without reasonable excuse, upon demand in writing by grantee produce to him his last receipts for rent, rates and taxes; and (7) if execution is levied against the goods of grantor under any judgment at law. No power of seizure can be given for breach of agreements differing from the causes of seizure within the Act and to make seizure lawful the conditions of the Act must be observed.

Satisfaction or Discharge.—Where a debt secured following a bill of sale has been satisfied or discharged the Registrar may order a memorandum of satisfaction to be written upon any registered copy of the bill. Leave to enter up satisfaction may be obtained ex parte on a consent signed by the person entitled to the benefit of the bill of sale, attested by witnesses and verified by an affidavit being produced to the Registrar and filed in the Central Office. Where consent cannot be obtained an order to enter up satisfaction may be obtained on summons in chambers.

Form

This Indenture made the . . . . day of . . . ., between A. B. of . . . . of the one part, and C. D. of . . . . of the other part, witnesseth that in consideration of the sum of £. . . now paid to A. B. by C. D., the receipt of which the said A. B. hereby acknowledges (or whatever else the consideration may be), he the said A.B. doth hereby assign unto C. D., his executors, administrators, and assigns, all and singular the several chattels and things specifically described in the schedule hereto annexed by way of security for the payment of the sum of £ . . ., and interest thereon at the rate of . . . per cent, per annum (or whatever else may be the rate). And the said A. B. doth agree and declare that he will duly pay to the said C. D. the principal sum aforesaid, together with the interest then due, by equal . . . . payments of £. . . on the . . . . day of . . . . (or whatever else may be the stipulated times or time of payment). And the said A. B. doth also agree with the said C. D. that he will (here insert terms as to insurance, payment of rent, or otherwise, which the parties may agree to for the maintenance or defeasance of the security).

Provided always, that the chattels hereby assigned shall not be liable to seizure or to be taken possession of by the said C. D. for any cause other than those specified in section seven of the Bills of Sale (Ireland) Act (1879) Amendment Act, 1883.

In witness, &c. . . . .

Signed and sealed by the said A. B. in the presence of me, E. F. (add witness' name, address, and description).

Sale by Mortgagee.—Chattels seized under a bill of sale given by way of security must before removal or sale remain on the premises where seized until after the expiration of five clear days from the day they were seized, within which time of five days from the seizure the grantor may apply for relief.

COMMERCIAL REGISTER:

Regulations governing use of business names by firms and individuals are contained in Business Names (Northern Ireland) Order (1986 S.I. No. 1033 [N.I.7]). Citations unless otherwise indicated refer to that Order and Articles thereof.

"Notes for Guidance on Business Names and Disclosure of Business Ownership" available from Companies Office.

Who Must Comply.—Order applies to any person who has place of business in Northern Ireland and carries on business in Northern Ireland under name which: (a) in case of partnership does not consist of surnames of all partners who are individuals and corporate names of all partners who are bodies corporate; (b) in case of individual does not consist of his surname; (c) in case of company, being company capable of being wound up under Companies (N.I.) Order 1986, does not consist of its corporate name (see subhead Registration of Company Names, infra and topic Corporations). (Art. 3[1]).

Permitted Additions.—Legislation does not apply to persons (either partners or individuals) to whose names are added forenames or initials or recognized abbreviations of forenames; or in case of any addition merely indicating that business is carried on in succession to former owner. (Art. 3[2]).

Prohibitions.—Persons to whom legislation applies must not, without written approval from Department of Economic Development ("Department"), carry on business in Northern Ireland under name which would be likely to give impression that business is connected with H.M. Government or any district council; or which includes certain prohibited words or expressions, including (but not limited to) references to Crown or royalty, or any foreign or Commonwealth government; or is misleading; or contains expression "British" (unless business is of substantial size and importance). Certain terms, including "co-operative" and "building society" are prohibited. Names including "bank", "banking", "investment" or "trust" are permitted only where circumstances are justified.

Disclosure of Names.—All business letters; written orders for goods or services; invoices; receipts; and written demands for payment of business debts sent out by businesses to which Order applies must bear, in legible characters: (a) In case of partnership, name of each partner; (b) in case of individual, his name; (c) in case of company, its corporate name; and (d) in relation to each person so named, address within Northern Ireland for service of any documents relating to business. (Art. 6[1]). Notice containing aforementioned information must be prominently displayed in any premises where business is carried out and to which customers or suppliers of goods have access. (Art. 6[2]).

In case of partnership of more than 20 partners it is sufficient to maintain list of names and addresses, to be made available on request, at principal place of business, provided all documents bear address and note to effect that list of names and addresses is available at principal place of business for inspection. (Art. 6[3]).

Penalties Arising from Default.—Any person contravening requirements as to disclosure of names and addresses, without reasonable excuse, is guilty of offence and liable to fine on summary conviction not exceeding £400 and further fine for continued default. (Art. 9).

Any legal proceedings arising from contract made in course of business and brought by any person, firm or company who has failed to comply with requirement to disclose names and addresses must be dismissed if defendant shows: (a) That he has claim against plaintiff arising out of same contract which he has been unable to pursue by reason of plaintiff's default; or (b) that he has suffered some financial loss in connection with contract by reason of plaintiff's default; provided that courts can permit proceedings to continue if satisfied that it is just and equitable so to do. (Art. 7).

Registration of Company Names.—Generally, see topic Corporations.

Registrar of companies maintains index of names of: (a) All companies within meaning of Companies (N.I.) Order 1986; (b) certain unincorporated bodies to which Art. 667 Companies (N.I.) Order 1986 applies; (c) limited partnerships registered under Limited Partnerships Act, 1907 (1907, c. 24 [U.K.]); (d) companies within meaning of Companies Act, 1985 (1985, c. 6); (e) societies registered under Industrial and Provident Societies Act (N.I.) 1969 (1969, c. 24) or Industrial and Provident Societies Act, 1965 (1965, c. 12 [U.K.]).

Registration of Certain Names Prohibited.—Approval of Department is required for use of any name likely to give impression that company is connected with H.M. Government or any district council, or includes any word or expression specified in regulations made under Art. 5.

CONSTITUTION AND GOVERNMENT:

Northern Ireland forms part of the United Kingdom of Great Britain and Northern Ireland.

In 1920 the Parliament of the United Kingdom (which included Irish members) passed the Government of Ireland Act, which provided for the division of Ireland into Northern and Southern Ireland. Northern Ireland was to consist of the Counties of Antrim, Armagh, Down, Fermanagh, Londonderry and Tyrone and the Boroughs of Belfast and Londonderry; and Southern Ireland was to comprise the remainder of the island. The Act provided for separate Parliaments in North and South, and for a Council of Ireland to deal with matters in which both parts had a common interest.

The legislative powers of both Irish Parliaments were limited, certain powers and services being reserved for the Council of Ireland and others for the Parliament of the United Kingdom, which was to continue to include Members representative of both North and South. Laws in force in Ireland at the commencement of the Act were to continue in force, subject to the Act and to alteration or repeal by the new Parliaments in so far as their powers would extend.

The Government of Ireland Act 1920 (10-1 Geo. 5, c. 67 [U.K.]), took effect only in Northern Ireland. First Northern Ireland Parliament was opened on 22nd June, 1921. United Kingdom Parliament by Irish Free State (Agreement) Act, 1922 and Irish Free State (Consequential Provisions) Act, 1922 ratified an agreement with Southern Irish Political leaders whereby whole of Ireland was to be self-governing dominion under name of Irish Free State. Northern Ireland was to have an option of retaining its status in Government of Ireland Act, which option was in due course exercised.

In 1949 as result of Irish Free State resolving to become a Republic and secede from Commonwealth, United Kingdom Parliament passed Ireland Act 1949 (12, 13-14, Geo. 6, c. 4 [U.K.]). Section 1(2) of that Act provided "It is hereby declared that Northern Ireland remains part of His Majesty's dominions and of the United Kingdom and it is hereby affirmed that in no event will Northern Ireland or any part thereof cease to be part of His Majesty's dominions and of the United Kingdom without the consent of the Parliament of Northern Ireland."

See Topical Index in front part of this volume.

CONSTITUTION AND GOVERNMENT . . . *continued*

This principle is embodied in The Northern Ireland Constitution Act 1973. (1973, c. 36 [U.K.]). §1 provides that Northern Ireland should not cease to be part of U.K. without consent of majority of people ascertained by a poll. Northern Ireland parliament in form provided for by Government of Ireland Act 1920 (10-1 Geo. 5, c. 67 [U.K.]) was prorogued in 1972. There followed under Northern Ireland (Temporary Provisions) Act 1972 (1972, c. 22 [U.K.]) a period of direct rule by British Parliament at Westminster. Executive powers were exercised by Secretary of State and laws made by Order in Council.

The Northern Ireland Constitution Act 1973 (1973, c. 36 [U.K.]) replaced Government of Ireland Act 1920 (10-1 Geo. 5, c. 67 [U.K.]) and established a new constitution.

Act stated that Northern Ireland Parliament should cease to exist and should be replaced by Assembly. (1973, c. 36 [U.K.] §31). Northern Ireland Assembly Act 1973 (1973, c. 17 [U.K.]) provides for Assembly consisting of 78 elected members. Offices of Governor of Northern Ireland and of Attorney General for Northern Ireland were abolished. Attorney General for England and Wales is by virtue of that office Attorney General for Northern Ireland. (1973, c. 36 [U.K.] §10). Attorney General appoints Crown Solicitor for Northern Ireland whose service is available to any Minister or Department of Government of N.I. or U.K. (1973, c. 36 [U.K.] §35).

Present Position.—Unpopularity of some actions of elected Assembly Executive caused such political unrest that Executive was forced to resign and Assembly was prorogued by Order in Council in May 1974 and later dissolved. Secretary of State appointed two Ministers of State and three Parliamentary Under-Secretaries to be political heads of various Government Departments and Offices formerly headed by members of Northern Ireland Executive.

Northern Ireland Act 1974 (1974, c. 28 [U.K.]) provides for dissolution of Northern Ireland Assembly and provides for elections and holding of Constitutional Convention in Northern Ireland for purpose of considering what provision for Government of Northern Ireland is likely to command most widespread acceptance. Convention elected and dissolved after final report rejected by Westminster. Period specified in N.I. Act 1974 (1974 c. 28 [U.K.] §1) for which temporary provisions for government of Northern Ireland contained in 1974 c. 28 (U.K.) Sched. 1 should continue, extended until July, 1995.

Meanwhile laws are made by Order in Council and Secretary of State acts as Executive. These arrangements are temporary and Northern Ireland Constitution Act 1973 (1973 c. 36 [U.K.]) and Northern Ireland Assembly Act 1973 (1973 c. 17 [U.K.]) remain on Statute Book.

Representation at Westminster.—Northern Ireland is divided into 17 parliamentary constituencies, each returning one Member to U.K. House of Commons.

Representation in European Assembly.—European Assembly Elections Act 1978 (1978, c. 10 [U.K.]) provides for election of three members (§2) by single transferable vote system of proportional representation (§3) to represent Northern Ireland in European Assembly. (First elections held in 1979.) Franchise as for U.K. parliamentary elections. See European Union Law Digest, topic Constitution and Government.

Legislation.—Laws may be made by Measures of Assembly enacted by being passed by Assembly and approved by Her Majesty in Council. Measures shall have same force and effect as Acts of U.K. Parliament. (1973, c. 36 [U.K.] §4). Any matter may be subject of legislation except those listed in schedule 2 of The Northern Ireland Constitution Act 1973 (1973, c. 36 [U.K.]) as being solely within competence of U.K. Parliament, or those listed in schedule 3 which are indefinitely reserved by U.K. Parliament. Consent of Secretary of State is required before measures are submitted to Her Majesty in Council.

Excepted Matters.—Crown; U.K. Parliament; international relations; armed forces; nationality; taxes; appointment of judges; elections; coinage and bank notes. (1973, c. 36 [U.K.] Sched. 2).

Reserved Matters.—Matters relating to courts and legal profession; matters relating to maintenance of public order; criminal law; powers of arrest and detention; police; Assembly and its powers; trade with any place outside Northern Ireland except Republic of Ireland; navigation; civil aviation; postal services. (1973, c. 36 [U.K.] Sched. 3).

Where a measure purports to deal with an excepted or reserved matter, consent of Secretary of State is required before submission to Her Majesty in Council, which consent shall not be given unless measure is ancillary to other provisions dealing with excepted or reserved matters, i.e., if it is necessary or expedient for making those other provisions effective. (1973, c. 36 [U.K.] §5). Measures to which Secretary of State has consented must then be laid before both Houses of U.K. Parliament before being submitted to Her Majesty in Council. (1973, c. 36 [U.K.] §6).

Any measure, any Act of Parliament of Northern Ireland, any relevant subordinate instrument shall to extent if it discriminates against any person, or class of persons, on ground of religious belief, or political opinion be void. (1973, c. 36 [U.K.] §17). No Act shall be treated as discriminating if made for purpose of safeguarding national security. (1973, c. 36 [U.K.] §23). Standing Advisory Commission on Human Rights advises Secretary of State on adequacy of law for preventing discrimination on grounds of religious or political belief, and in providing redress for persons aggrieved. (1973, c. 36 [U.K.] §20).

E.E.C. European Communities Act 1972 (1972, c. 68 [U.K.]) provides that all such rights, powers, liabilities, obligations and restrictions created or arising by or under treaties forming E.E.C., and all remedies and procedures provided for by treaties must be recognized and available in law, and be enforced, allowed and followed accordingly. Provision is made for Her Majesty by Order in Council to make regulations in order to implement any obligations arising out of membership of E.E.C., and this power may be delegated to designated Ministers, including Ministers of Northern Ireland Government. Such regulations must be treated as Acts of Parliament. (1972, c. 68 [U.K.] §2). See European Union Law Digest, topic Constitution and Government.

Relations with Republic of Ireland.—Northern Ireland executive authority may: (a) Consult on any matter with any authority of Republic of Ireland, and (b) enter into agreement with such authority in respect of any transferred matter. (1973, c. 36 [U.K.] §12).

Northern Ireland Parliamentary Franchise.—Under provisions of Electoral Law Act (Northern Ireland) 1962 (1962, c. 14) a person is entitled to be registered as a parliamentary elector for any constituency returning a member to Parliament of Northern Ireland if he or she is a British subject, 18 or more years of age, not subject to any legal incapacity, and was born in Northern Ireland (or, alternatively, has resided continuously in U.K. for a period of seven years ending on qualifying date) and either (a) was residing in constituency on qualifying date and had resided in constituency or elsewhere in Northern Ireland for a period of three months ending on qualifying date; or (b) was on qualifying date occupying business premises in constituency and occupied those or other premises in constituency—or one or more than one other constituency in Northern Ireland—throughout three months immediately prior to qualifying date; or (c) is wife or husband of a person entitled to be registered in respect of above business premises qualification; or (d) was on qualifying date a member of Forces or a person employed in service of Crown in a post outside U.K., or a merchant seaman, and made a declaration that but for such service he or she would have been residing at an address in constituency; or is wife of such a person and is residing outside U.K. to be with her husband.

United Kingdom Parliamentary Franchise.—Under the provisions of the Representation of the People Act, 1949 (11-2 Geo. 6, c. 65 [U.K.]), a person is entitled to be registered as a parliamentary elector for any Northern Ireland constituency returning a member to the Parliament at Westminister if that person is a British subject or citizen of the Irish Republic of 18 or more years of age and not subject to any legal incapacity to vote, is resident at an address in that constituency on the qualifying date, and has resided at that address (or at any other address or addresses in Northern Ireland) for a period of three months ending on the qualifying date.

There are also included in the register the names of persons qualified as above but whose 18th birthday is after Sept. 16 and on or before the following May 1. Such persons are entitled to vote at any election, for which the register is used, held after Oct. 1 in that year.

In addition, a person who would ordinarily have been resident at a specified address in a constituency in Northern Ireland may be registered in respect of a service qualification if: (a) he or she is a member of the Forces; or (b) he or she is a person employed in the service of the Crown in a post outside the United Kingdom; or (c) she is the wife of a person having a Service qualification and is residing outside the United Kingdom to be with her husband.

Elections.—Persons entitled to vote on poll for election of members of Assembly are those who would be entitled to vote on polls held at general election to Parliament of Northern Ireland. Each vote is single transferable vote, that is a vote capable of being given so as to indicate voter's order of preference for candidates for election as members for constituency, and capable of being transferred to next choice when vote is not required to give a prior choice necessary quota of votes or when that choice is eliminated owing to a deficiency in number of votes given for a prior choice. (1973, c. 17 [U.K.]). Secretary of State has power by Order to make any provision concerning election and in particular provision concerning holding of any election, frequency, method of voting, counting and transferring votes. Same system applied to Convention elections.

Civil Service.—The Civil Service of Northern Ireland is in general organised on the lines of the Imperial Civil Service. It was staffed at its inception by the transfer of civil servants employed in Imperial Departments and this nucleus was supplemented by ex-service candidates recruited locally.

General control.—Regulation of Service falls within common law executive power of Crown and, as such is exercisable by Secretary of State for Northern Ireland, (§8). Power was exercised in certain important respects by Orders made by Governor dated Feb. 28, 1923 and July 11, 1923, nominating three Civil Service Commissioners to perform, in relation to Civil Service of Northern Ireland, functions similar to those performed by Imperial Civil Service Commission in relation fo Civil Service of U.K. Latter order also provided that Department of Finance should make Regulations for controlling conduct of Civil Service, and prescribing classification, remuneration and other conditions of service of all persons employed therein whether permanently or temporarily.

CONTRACTS:

Common law rules govern generally but certain subjects have been codified e.g. Bills of Exchange Act 1882, (45 & 46 Vict., c. 61 [U.K.]), see topic Bills and Notes: Sale of Goods Act, 1979 (1979, c. 54 [U.K.]), as amended by Sale of Goods (amendment) Act 1994 (1994, c. 32 [U.K.]), Supply of Goods (Implied Terms) Act 1973 (1973, c. 13 [U.K.]), see topic Sales; Marine Insurance Act 1906 (6 Edw. 7, c. 41 [U.K.]). A collection of statutes regulates gaming and wagering contracts. Common law relating to carriage of goods by land has been considerably modified by Carriers Act 1830 (11 Geo. 4 and 1 Wm. 4, c. 38 [U.K.]), and carriage of goods by rail, sea and air is regulated by statutes. Certain statutes such as Infant Relief Act 1874 (37 & 38 Vict., c. 62 [U.K.]) and Married Women's Property Acts 1882 to 1907 (47 & 48 Vict., c. 14 am'd 7 Edw. 7, c. 18 [U.K.]) affect capacity of parties to contract. See topic Infants, subhead Ratification of Contracts.

Restrictions on freedom of contract are contained in Moneylenders Acts (N.I.) 1900 to 1933 (1933, c. 22); Rent and Mortgage Interest Restriction Acts (N.I.) 1920 to 1956 (1956, c. 10, §63 [iii]); Air Corporations Acts 1949 and 1953 (2 & 3 El.2, c. 7, §4 [iii] [U.K.]); Transport Acts (N.I.) 1948 to 1960 (1960, c. 11, §2 [ii]); Borrowing (Control Guarantee) Act 1946. (10-1 Geo. 6, c. 14 [U.K.]; Import of Goods (Control) Order 1940, S.R. & O. 1940 No. 873 as am'd made under 2 & 3 Geo. 6, c. 69 (U.K.); Wages Council Act (N.I.) 1945 (c. 21).

Form of contract.—As general rule simple contract need not be reduced to writing.

Written evidence of contract is required to prove (1) promise by debtor to pay debt barred by statute of limitations (Statutes of Frauds Amendment Act 1828, 9 Geo. 4, c. 14, §1 [U.K.]); (2) bills of exchange, promissory notes and other negotiable instruments which must be reduced to writing and signed by parties thereto (Bills of Exchange Act 1882, 45 & 46 Vict., c. 61, §3 [U.K.]); (3) contents of marine insurance (Stamp Act 1891, 45 & 46 Vict., c. 39 [U.K.]); Marine Insurance Act 1906, 6 Edw. 7, c. 41 [U.K.]); (4) sale or transfer of registered ships or shares therein (Merchant Act 1894, 57 & 58 Vict., c. 46 [U.K.] §5 [ii]); (5) contract of sale of land and memorandum thereof must be signed by party to be charged or his lawfully authorised agent (Statute of Frauds

CONTRACTS . . . *continued*
[Ireland] 1695, 7 Wm. 3, c. 2, §2 [Ir.]); (6) any promise to answer for debt default or miscarriage of another (7 Wm. 3, c. 12, §2 [Ir.]).

Excuses for Nonperformance.—(a) Impossibility and frustration: common law rules of frustration have been am'd by Frustrated Contracts (N.I.) Act 1947 (c. 2); (b) exception clauses: common law rules governing exclusion of liability am'd by Unfair Contract Terms Act 1977 (1977, c. 50 [U.K.]); (c) mistake; (d) breach by other party; (e) renunciation; (f) prevention of performance by promisee; (g) where innocent misrepresentation has become term of contract (Misrepresentation Act [Northern Ireland] 1967 [1967, c. 14]).

Applicable Law.—Essential validity (as distinguished from formal validity), interpretation and effect of contract and rights and applications of parties to it are governed with certain exceptions by proper law of the contract i.e. law which parties have agreed or intended to govern or which they may be presumed to have intended. Prima facie proper law of contract is presumed to be lex loci contractus.

Legality of contracts.—Contract illegal by its proper law or by law of country where it is to be performed, lex fori, will not be enforced in Northern Ireland. Contracts which have their proper law are illegal in Northern Ireland if contrary to Northern Ireland ideas of public morality or even if any part of them is so contrary.

Discharge of contracts.—A contract which has been discharged, (otherwise than by performance) in accordance with or by means of operation of its proper law is discharged also in Northern Ireland so that no further action will lie upon it, but a contract which is still binding and subsisting by its proper law may nevertheless not be actionable in Northern Ireland because the plaintiff's remedy is barred by statute of limitations and this being a matter of procedure is for the lex fori.

Government Contracts.—No special provisions apply.

Distributorships, Dealerships and Franchises.—No special provisions apply.

COPYRIGHT:

Power to legislate with respect to copyright excluded from competence of Northern Ireland Assembly by Northern Ireland Constitution Act 1973. (1973, c. 36 [U.K.] Sch. 3). See topic Constitution and Government.

Statutes of U.K. Parliament therefore apply. See England Law Digest, topic Copyright.

CORPORATIONS:

Companies (Northern Ireland) Order 1986 (1986 S.I. No. 1032 [N.I. 6] as am'd by 1989 S.I. No. 2404 [N.I. 18]; 1989 S.I. No. 2405 [N.I. 19]; 1990 S.I. No. 593 [N.I. 5] and 1990 S.I. No. 1504 [N.I. 10]) governs incorporation, formation, operation, and winding up of companies limited by shares and by guarantee and unlimited companies. Unless otherwise indicated citations refer to Companies (Northern Ireland) Order 1986 and Articles thereof. Companies may be public companies or private companies. (Art. 12).

General Supervision.—Department of Economic Development, Netherleigh, Massey Avenue, Belfast BT4 2JS and Companies Office, IDB House, Chichester Street, Belfast BT1 4LE.

Purposes.—Companies may be formed for purposes of profit or charity. Purposes must not be contrary to criminal law. Objects of company are set out in memorandum which is company's charter. Acts not within scope of "objects clauses" in memorandum are ultra vires.

Name.—

Name of public company must end with words "Public Limited Company" or "PLC", (Art. 35).

Name of private company must end with "Limited" or "Ltd" (Art. 35) except for certain companies exempt from requirement (Art. 40).

Fee of £40 to register change of name.

Business Names (Northern Ireland) Order (1986 S.I. No. 1033 [N.I.] 7) applies to name of company carrying on business in name other than its corporate name. See topic Commercial Register, subhead Who Must Comply.

Term of Corporate Existence.—Perpetual.

Incorporators.—Any two or more persons associated for lawful purpose may by subscribing their names to memorandum of association and otherwise complying with requirements of Order in respect of registration, form incorporated company with or without limited liability. (Art. 12). No restriction as to citizenship or residence.

Memorandum and Articles of Incorporation.—

Memorandum of association stating name of company, objects and registered office (Art. 13[1]) must be signed by each subscriber in presence of at least one witness (Art. 13[5]) and delivered to registrar of companies (Art. 21). Memorandum of company limited by shares or guarantee must also state liability of members is limited. (Art. 13[2]). Memorandum of company limited by guarantee must state amount members guarantee. (Art. 13[3]). Memorandum of company with share capital must state amount of share capital and state against name of each subscriber number of shares be taken. (Art. 13[4]).

Articles of association (rules governing internal regulation of company) may be filed by company limited by shares and must be filed by company limited by guarantee or unlimited and must be signed by subscriber to memorandum each in presence of one witness (Art. 18); if articles not filed Table A of Order (as prescribed by regulations made by Department of Economic Development) applies. (Art. 19).

Filing of Memorandum or Articles.—Only one copy of memorandum and articles must be delivered to registrar of companies. (Art. 21).

Incorporation Tax or Fee.—Fixed registration fee of £50.

Filing Fees.—Fee of £20 on filing annual return.

Licence to do Business.—Certificate of incorporation issued by registrar of companies. (Art. 24).

Organization.—Company must (1) in each calendar year hold annual general meeting, (2) hold its first annual general meeting within 18 months of incorporation and (3) not more than 15 months must elapse between one such meeting and next. (Art. 374). Other organization is set out in articles.

Paid in Capital Requirements.—No requirement for private companies. Authorised minimum capital for public company is £50,000. (Art. 128).

Amendment of Articles or Memorandum.—

Objects clause in memorandum may be altered by special resolution. (Art. 15). (For special resolution, see Art. 386.)

Articles may be altered by special resolution. (Art. 20 as am'd 1990 S.I. No. 1504 [N.I. 10] Art. 46[2]).

Increase or Decrease of Authorised Capital Stock.—Companies having capital may increase or decrease capital by resolution at general meeting. (Art. 131). Public companies may not decrease capital below authorised minimum. (Art. 127).

By-Laws.—See subhead Memorandum and Articles of Incorporation, catchline Articles of Association, supra.

Stock.—No restriction as to classes, preferences, etc. Share is personal estate. Shares must be numbered unless all shares of particular class are fully paid up and rank pari passu. (Art. 192).

Stock Certificates.—Within two months of allotment, or of date when transfer of stock is lodged with company, company must complete and have ready certificates for shares issued or transferred. (Art. 195). Certification by company is prima facie evidence of title to shares in transferor named in certificate. (Art. 194).

Transfer of Stock.—Most transfers in practice fall within ambit of Stock Transfer Act (Northern Ireland) 1963 (1963 [N.I.], c. 24) which allows single form of transfer for fully paid shares in any company within ambit of Act except unlimited companies and companies limited by guarantee. It need only be signed by transferor. For transferors outside ambit of Act must consult articles of company in which stock is being transferred.

Issuance of Stock.—Issue of stock to public by private company prohibited. (Art. 91). No allotment of stock by public company unless minimum amount stated in prospectus is subscribed. (Art. 93). Minimum amount must be received within 40 days of first issue of prospectus. See further Arts. 90-98 of Order. Company issuing prospectus must comply with Arts. 66 to 73 and must comply with Stock Exchange requirements. Copy of every prospectus issued by or on behalf of company or in relation to intended company, signed by all directors and intending directors or their agent authorized in writing must be delivered to registrar of companies on or before publication (Art. 74) and comply with Art. 75.

Stock Transfer Tax.—None.

Stockholders.—General rule is any person can become stockholder. Persons may become members (1) by subscribing to memorandum or (2) by agreeing to become member either by applying for allotment of shares or by taking transfer from member. Person may cease to be member by (1) transfer, (2) forfeiture, (3) surrender, (4) sale by company under its lien, (5) death, (6) winding up of company and (7) expulsion. Existing shareholders have pre-emption rights on new allotments. (Art. 99).

Stockholders' Action.—Three types of action exist: (1) Personal action by shareholder; (2) representative action on behalf of group of shareholders; (3) derivative action brought on behalf of company.

Member may petition courts (1) when subjected to unfairly prejudicial conduct (Art. 452), (2) for company to be wound up on just and equitable ground (Art. 479[9]). Rules governing availability of derivative action are complex (see Foss v. Harbottle [1843], 2 Hare 461).

Stockholders' Liabilities.—In company limited by shares liability is limited to amount unpaid on members' shares. Past member is only liable for one year after membership ceases. (Art. 468). In other companies liability is unlimited except for company limited by guarantee where amount of guarantee is limit of liability.

Stockholders' Meetings.—Subject to Art. 374A there must be one annual general meeting (Art. 374). Members may requisition extraordinary general meetings. (Art. 376). Requisition must (1) state reason for meeting, (2) be signed by owners of one tenth of share capital or one tenth voting right (if not limited by shares), (3) be deposited at company's registered office. Notice requirements vary depending on type of meeting called. (Art. 377). Proxies may be appointed if company has share capital. (Art. 380).

Voting Trusts.—Can be created but uncommon in Northern Ireland.

Directors.—All public companies must have at least two directors and private companies at least one. (Art. 290). Directors' appointments in public companies must be approved at general meeting. (Art. 300). Directors of public company must be under age 70 except with approval of general meeting after special notice of resolution. (Art. 301). No restriction as to citizenship or residence. Directors need not be shareholders unless articles so provide. Director's service contract for over five years in public company cannot be created without resolution of approval at general meeting. (Art. 327).

Directors' Meetings.—Directors must act at meetings unless articles give them power to act otherwise. Due notice of meeting must be given to every director. Meetings may be held anywhere. Quorum of directors is usually fixed in articles.

Powers and Duties of Directors.—Director owes fiduciary duty to company to act bona fide in interest of company, not to act for collateral purpose and duty of care and skill.

Directors are generally given wide ranging powers of management under articles.

Statutory duties of directors of public company include duty (1) to convene extraordinary general meeting when net corporate assets are half or less of called-up share capital (Art. 152), (2) to disclose details of compensation to director on take-over (Art. 322), (3) to disclose directors' interest in corporate contracts (Art. 325) and in shareholdings in own company (Art. 332).

Liabilities of Directors.—

Civil liability to company to account for any company property misappropriated or profit diverted (Art. 584 and Common Law) or to creditors if fraudulent trading (Art. 583 and Art. 177 [1989, S.I. No. 2405 (N.I.19)]) or wrongful trading proved (Art. 178, 1989, S.I. No. 2405 [N.I.19]) in course of winding up.

Criminal liability includes liability for untrue statements in prospectus (Art. 80), liability for concealing name of creditor on capital reduction (Art. 151). Wide range of criminal offences directors may be liable for in Companies Order.

Officers.—Include directors, managers, secretary and may include solicitor if appointed at salary or auditors if formally appointed by articles or under Art. 392 as am'd (1990 S.I. No. 1504 [N.I. 10] Arts. 53-58). Secretary must be appointed in accordance with Art. 291.

CORPORATIONS . . . *continued*

Liability of Officers.—No provision in articles or contract may exempt officers for liability in respect of negligence, breach of duty or trust to company. (Art. 318). In winding-up officer may be liable in damages for misfeasance. (Art. 584). Various criminal offences in Order, e.g., Arts. 585 and 401.

Registered Office.—Must be stated in memorandum and located in Northern Ireland. (Art. 13 and Art. 295 as am'd [1990 S.I. No. 1504 (N.I. 10) Art. 71]).

General Powers of Corporation.—Express powers are set forth in objects clause of memorandum. Anything reasonably incidental to attainment or pursuit of any express objects of company will, unless expressly prohibited, be within implied powers of company. Where company's memorandum states that company's object is to carry on business as general commercial company, object of company is to carry on any trade or business whatsoever and company is empowered to do all such things as are incidental or conducive to carrying on of any trade or business. (Art. 14A). Subject to Art. 45 as am'd (1990 S.I. No. 1504 [N.I. 10] Art. 44) contract which is ultra vires company and beyond its powers is absolutely void. Ultra vires rule does not affect transaction decided on by directors dealing with person acting in good faith (Art. 45 and Art. 45A as am'd [1990 S.I. No. 1504 (N.I. 10) Art. 44]) nor catagories of wrong, e.g., crime or tort, for which company can be vicariously liable.

Dividends.—Must only be declared out of profits available for purpose. (Art. 271). (See also Arts. 272, 273.)

Sale or Transfer of Corporate Assets.—Directors must disclose any interests in contracts with company. (Art. 325). No director to buy substantial cash asset of company without resolution of company in general meeting. (Art. 328).

Books and Records.—Company must (1) keep minutes of general and directors' meetings (Art. 390); (2) full accounting records (Art. 229) at registered office; (3) account books open to inspection by company's officers (Art. 230); (4) make annual return to registrar of companies (Art. 371); (5) keep register of members (Art. 366) at registered office open to members free and others on payment (Art. 364).

Reports.—Subject to Art. 260 company auditors must report to members on accounts and on balance sheet and profit and loss account. Directors must prepare profit and loss account or if company is not trading for profit income and expenditure account (Art. 235), report stating matters and particulars required by Art. 243 and must (except on certain unlimited companies) in respect of each of company's financial years deliver to registrar company's accounts (Art. 246) which comprise balance sheet, profit and loss account, group accounts of holding company (if any), auditors report and directors' report (Art. 247). Every member and holder of company's debentures must receive copy of company's accounts.

Registration of Mortgages.—Every mortgage or charge created by company and being:

(1) *Mortgage or charge* (a) for purpose of securing any issue of debentures, (b) on uncalled capital of company, (c) created or evidenced by instrument which, if created by individual would require registration as bill of sale, (d) on any land, wherever situate, or any interests therein, (e) on any book debt of company;

(2) *Floating charge* on undertaking or property of company;

(3) *Charge,* (a) on calls made but not paid, (b) on ship or any share in shop, or (c) on goodwill, on patent or licence under patent or trademark or on copyright or licence under copyright is void against liquidator and any creditor of company unless received by registrar of companies for registration within 21 days after date of charges creation (Arts. 402-403) except in case of charge created out of U.K. comprising property outside U.K. which must be received by registrar of companies within 21 days of date instrument or copy could in due course of post if dispatched with due diligence have been received in Northern Ireland (Art. 405). Copies of all mortgages or charges must be kept at company's office and open to inspection of members and creditors of company. (Art. 414).

Mergers, Takeovers.—Miscellaneous provisions contained in Arts. 421, 422 and 423 as amended by Part III of Companies (Northern Ireland) Order 1989 (1989 S.I. No. 2404 [N.I. 18]). Also City Code on Takeovers and Mergers implemented by City Panel available from: Secretary Panel on Takeovers and Mergers, Stock Exchange Building, London.

Insider Dealing.—Restrictions contained in Company Securities (Insider Dealing) (Northern Ireland) Order 1986 (S.I. 1986 No. 1034 [N.I. 8]) as amended (Part III [1989 S.I. No. 2404][N.I. 18]).

Corporate Insolvency.—See topic Bankruptcy and Insolvency, subhead Corporate Insolvency.

Foreign Corporation.—Company carrying on business in Northern Ireland but incorporated outside it is required under penalty to file: (1) Certified copy of its charter, statute, or other instrument constituting or defining its constitution; (2) list of its directors; and (3) name and address of person resident in Northern Ireland authorised to accept service of process or any notices required to be served on company. Every such foreign company must also file such statement of its affairs as is required to be filed by public companies incorporated in Northern Ireland. (Art. 641). They must also comply with Arts. 642 to 648.

Insurance Corporation.—Companies Order provides considerable restriction on insurance business in conjunction with Insurance Companies Act 1982. (1982, c. 50).

Inspection.—Order contains provisions for inspection of corporation affairs by Department of Economic Development inspectors on application of minimum number of members. (Art. 424). Further extensive powers allow Department to conduct "informal" investigation of books and papers of company. No formal reason for such investigation need be given.

Taxation.—See topic Taxation. See also European Union Digest, topic Corporations.

COURTS:

Constitution, jurisdiction and administration of Northern Ireland courts substantially altered and amended by Judicature (Northern Ireland) Act, 1978. (1978, c. 23 [U.K.]). Any reference in this topic to section of statute without reference to statute by name or chapter number shall be reference to Judicature (Northern Ireland) Act, 1978. See also European Union Law Digest, topic Courts.

House of Lords.—Judicial functions of the House are largely governed by constitutional practice. It has a certain original, as well as appellate, jurisdiction. Appointment and position of the Law Lords and constitution of the appellate tribunal are dealt with by Appellate Jurisdiction Acts, 1876-1949 (39 & 49 Vict., c. 59 [U.K.], 50 & 51 Vict., c. 70 [U.K.], 3 & 4 Geo. 5, c. 21 [U.K.], 19 Geo. 5, c. 8 [U.K.], 10-1 Geo. 6, c. 11 [U.K.]).

In noncriminal matters, appeals lie from Court of Appeal in Northern Ireland to House of Lords only with leave of House of Lords (39 & 40 Vict., c. 59 [U.K.], §§3, 4, 11-2, 40 & 41 Vict., c. 57 [U.K.], §§65 & 68, 13 Geo. 5, Sess. 2, c. 2 [U.K.], §1, sch. 1, 20 & 21 Geo. 5, c. 45 [U.K.], §18, 8 & 9 El. 2, c. 65 [U.K.], §§1[c], 18[2]).

In criminal matters, defendant or prosecutor may appeal with leave to court below or to House of Lords either from Court of Appeal in Northern Ireland or from any decision of divisional Court of Queen's Bench Division. Leave to appeal is not granted unless it is certified by court below that point of law of public importance is involved and it appears to court that point ought to be considered by House. (20 & 21 Geo. 5, c. 45 [U.K.], §§6 & 20 am'd 8 & 9 El. 2, c. 65 [U.K.], §§1, 18 sch. 2).

Supreme Court of Judicature of Northern Ireland consists of Her Majesty's High Court of Justice in Northern Ireland ("the High Court"); Her Majesty's Court of Appeal in Northern Ireland ("the Court of Appeal"); and Her Majesty's Crown Court in Northern Ireland ("the Crown Court"). (1978, c. 23 [U.K.] §1).

The High Court consists of Lord Chief Justice of Northern Ireland, as President, and 11 judges. (§2). High Court has three divisions, namely: (a) Chancery Division; (b) Queen's Bench Division; (c) Family Division. (§5). All High Court judges may sit in any division. (§6). Principle matters over which High Court has jurisdiction include:

Chancery.—Administration of trusts, charitable or private; administration of estates of deceased persons; enforcement of mortgages and charges; construction of wills and other documents; questions of title to land; dissolution of partnerships; administration and winding up of joint-stock companies; taking of accounts; rectification, setting aside, or cancellation of deeds and other documents; specific performance of contracts; registration of title to land.

Queen's Bench.—Hearing of bail applications in criminal matters; applications for writ of habeas corpus; applications for judicial review of administrative decisions, seeking such forms of relief as order of mandamus, order of certiorari, declaratory judgment; exclusive jurisdiction in admiralty matters. (§30). Hears civil appeals from county courts and common law proceedings, such as claims for damages for breach of contract; damages for injuries to person or property; damages for nuisance, libel, slander.

Family.—All matters concerning dissolution of marriage; annulment of marriage; judicial separation; jactitation of marriage; adoption; wardship; custody of children and matrimonial property proceedings; applications under §17 of Married Women's Property Act, 1882 (for declaration as to rights of applicant spouse to matrimonial property).

Court of Appeal consists of Lord Chief Justice, as President, and three Lords Justices of Appeal. (§3). Every judge of High Court deemed judge of Appeal Court in exercise of its criminal jurisdiction (§6[2]), with proviso that no judge may hear appeal against his own judgment in lower court. Every matter before Court of Appeal is heard by three judges together, unless Lord Chief Justice directs that two judges hear appeal. (§36). Court of Appeal by Judicature (N.I.) Act, 1978 (1978, c. 23 [U.K.] §34) incorporates jurisdiction previously exercised by Court of Appeal and Court of Criminal Appeal, together with additional jurisdiction conferred by Act.

Civil Jurisdiction.—Court of Appeal has power to review decisions of High Court on points of law. May also hear appeals from county courts and petty sessions courts on points of law. Further appeal lies from judgment of Court of Appeal in civil matters to House of Lords, where statutes permit. Such appeal must be on point of law of general public importance.

Criminal Jurisdiction.—Persons convicted on indictment may appeal to Court of Appeal: (a) Without leave, on point of law; (b) with leave of Court, or on certificate of trial judge on question of fact, or on some other sufficient ground; (c) only by leave of Court against sentence (if not fixed by law); (d) automatically, if convicted by judge sitting without jury under Northern Ireland (Emergency Provisions) Act, 1978. (1978, c. 5 [U.K.]).

Court of Appeal sits in Belfast unless, by special direction of Lord Chief Justice, session is held at some other place in Northern Ireland.

Crown Court is superior court of record (in common with High Court and Court of Appeal) and was created by Judicature (N.I.) Act, 1978. (1978, c. 23 [U.K.] §4). Jurisdiction exercisable by Lord Chief Justice, as President, any judge of High Court or Court of Appeal, or any county court judge. (§4[1]).

All proceedings on indictment are tried by single judge with jury in Crown Court, except terrorist offences (see subhead Emergency Provisions, infra). Crown Court business may be conducted at any place in Northern Ireland. Act creates two-tier system by which certain cases, or classes of cases, are allocated to judges of High Court or Court of Appeal, and other cases or classes of cases to county court judges. (§47). Lord Chancellor has directed that serious offences such as treason and murder must be heard by judges of High Court or Court of Appeal.

Inferior Courts of Northern Ireland.—These are county courts and courts of summary jurisdiction (magistrates' courts). These courts are intended to provide localized judicial system of speedy operation to deal with minor criminal and civil matters. County courts are presided over by county court judges and (in more minor cases within courts' jurisdiction) District Judges. Minor criminal, quasi-criminal and civil matters, and initial stages of more serious criminal cases, are dealt with by Resident Magistrates in courts of summary jurisdiction.

County Courts.—Controlling legislation is County Courts (Northern Ireland) Order, 1980. (1980, S.I. No. 397 [N.I. 3]).

By County Courts Divisions Order (N.I.) 1983 (1983, S.R. No. 96), Northern Ireland is divided into seven county court divisions, each with several venues at which court sits on regular basis at least four times per year (more frequently in Belfast).

There must be at least one county court judge for each division. Currently 13 in Northern Ireland. Judges appointed by Crown on recommendation of Lord Chancellor. Judges for Divisions of Belfast and Londonderry are known as Recorders.

See Topical Index in front part of this volume.

COURTS . . . *continued*

County courts have jurisdiction in cases of libel and slander where damages claimed do not exceed £3,000, and in all other cases of disputes between party and party where sum, damages or penalty claimed does not exceed £15,000. Their jurisdiction also embraces all cases—irrespective of amount of damages or penalty—which have been remitted from High Court.

The court can also deal with ejectments, subject to a limitation of the annual value or rent of the lands and can decide equity matters, the jurisdiction being restricted as a rule in cases where land is involved by the annual value, which may not exceed £500, and in other cases by sum involved, which must not exceed £15,000. Equity jurisdiction of County Court includes such matters as applications under Trustee Act, (Northern Ireland) 1958; proceedings for maintenance and advancement of infants under Guardianship of Infants Act, 1866; making of adoption orders under Adoption Act (Northern Ireland), 1967; partition suits; and proceedings under Married Women's Property Acts. Its probate jurisdiction is limited to suits where assets do not exceed £500 in annual value (if land) and pure personalty does not exceed £15,000. To this court are also assigned criminal injury cases, and certain cases arising under Increase of Rent Acts and Settled Land Acts.

By Art. 30 of 1980, S.I. No. 397 (N.I. 3), as am'd by County Courts (Financial Limits) Order (N.I.) 1993 (1993, S.I. No. 282), actions in which amount claimed or value of specific chattels claimed does not exceed £3,000 are heard before District Judge, whose decisions have same force and validity as those of county court judges. Claims of up to £1,000 are dealt with by District Judges by way of informal arbitration but jurisdiction of these "Small Claims" courts excludes certain matters, i.e., ownership of land, defamation, claims in respect of personal injuries, claims arising from road traffic accidents.

Appeal from decisions of county court judges or District Judges on facts of cases lies to High Court. (1980, S.I. No. 397 [N.I. 3]; Art. 60). Alternative right of appeal on points of law by way of "case stated" to Court of Appeal. (1980, S.I. No. 397 [N.I. 3]; Art. 61).

By Art. 48 of Matrimonial Causes (N.I.) Order, 1978 (1978, S.I. No. 1045 [N.I. 15]), County Courts have jurisdiction to hear undefended divorces, regardless of amount of money or value of property involved.

Courts of Summary Jurisdiction.—Petty sessions courts have jurisdiction to hear and determine summarily minor criminal and quasi-criminal cases and certain minor civil disputes. Courts are held weekly in each of 26 petty sessions districts (which correspond to local government districts) but daily in Belfast. Jurisdiction derived mainly from statute. Main statute is Magistrates' Courts (N.I.) Order, 1981. (1981, S.I. No. 1675 [N.I. 26]). On civil side, powers include ejectments (if property let at rent not exceeding £110 per year), recovery of small debts not exceeding £100, and trespass; but they have no powers to deal with disputes over title to land. By 1978, c. 23 (U.K.); §97(2), Crown may, by Order in Council, abolish civil jurisdiction of petty sessions courts and confer it on county court District Judges.

Petty sessions courts have jurisdiction to decide whether prima facie case exists against persons charged with indictable offences; and powers under Domestic Proceedings (N.I.) Order, 1980 (1980, S.I. No. 563 [N.I. 5]) to grant separation orders, maintenance payments and custody of children in matrimonial disputes (see topic Divorce, subhead Judicial Separation).

Emergency Provisions.—Northern Ireland (Emergency Provisions) Act, 1973 (1973, c. 53 [U.K.] as am'd by Northern Ireland (Emergency Provisions) (Amendment) Act, 1975 (1975, c. 62 [U.K.]), consolidated by Northern Ireland (Emergency Provisions) Act, 1978 (1978, c. 5 [U.K.]) and subsequently amended by Northern Ireland (Emergency Provisions) Act, 1987 (1987, c. 30 [U.K.]) provides for trial of certain terrorist offences at Belfast Crown Court (1978, c. 5 [U.K.]; §6, as am'd by 1978, c. 23 [U.K.]). Offences in question are either created by statutes themselves or are existing common law or statutory offences listed in schedules to emergency legislation and known as "scheduled offences." (See 1978, c. 5 [U.K.]; Schedule 4.) Offences are tried before single judge with no jury (1978, c. 5 [U.K.]; §7) but in certain cases where scheduled offences do not involve terrorist element (i.e., domestic murder) offence can be "descheduled" by certificate of Attorney-General and tried before judge and jury (1978, c. 5 [U.K.]; §6).

Cases under emergency legislation may be tried by any judge of Supreme Court. County court judges can, at request of Lord Chief Justice, hear such cases with all jurisdiction, powers and privileges of Supreme Court judges (1978, c. 5 [U.K.]; §6) except general power to grant bail. Bail may be granted by judge of Supreme Court or by county court judge trying particular case only if he must adjourn that particular case. (1978, c. 5 [U.K.]; §2[1]).

Court of Justice of European Communities.—Where question concerning validity and interpretation of Treaty of Rome establishing E.E.C. or of any acts of institutions of Community is raised before domestic court of Tribunal it may refer matter to Court of Justice to give ruling. Where that court is highest domestic jurisdiction in sense that there is no remedy or appeal against its decision that court must bring matters before Court of Justice of European Communities as provided by Article 177, Treaty of Rome as ratified by European Communities Act 1972. (1972, c. 68 [U.K.]). See European Union Law Digest, topic Courts.

CURRENCY:

Power to legislate with respect to coinage, legal tender or negotiable instruments (including banknotes) excluded from competence of Northern Ireland Assembly (except as far as negotiable instruments may be affected by exercise of powers of taxation) by Northern Ireland Constitution Act 1973. (1973, c. 36 [U.K.] Sch. 2). See topic Constitution and Government.

Unit of currency is Pound Sterling which is divided into 100 pence. Bank of England banknotes (£5, £10, £20, £50) are legal tender in Northern Ireland. In addition, banknotes issued by various provincial banks (i.e. Bank of Scotland, Northern Bank, Ulster Bank) are widely circulated and accepted. Coins minted by Royal Mint (1p, 2p, 5p, 10p, 20p, 50p, £1, and special commemorative £2 and 25p "crowns") are legal tender. Banknotes and coins of Republic of Ireland are not legal tender in Northern Ireland.

CURTESY:

Abolished by Administration of Estates Act (Northern Ireland) 1955. (1955, c. 24).

CUSTOMS:

Power to legislate with respect to customs (reserved matter) excluded from competence of Northern Ireland Assembly by Northern Ireland Constitution Act 1973. (1973, c. 36 [U.K.] Sch. 3). Northern Ireland is integral part of U.K. of Great Britain and Northern Ireland with no internal customs between Britain and Northern Ireland. (See topic Constitution and Government.) Customs duty payable on certain goods crossing border between Northern Ireland and Republic of Ireland, which is U.K.'s only land frontier.

All Acts of U.K. Parliament on this topic apply to Northern Ireland unless their application is expressly or by implication excluded. See England Law Digest, topic Customs. See also European Union Law Digest, topic Customs Duties.

DEATH:

The common law rules apply, viz.: Where a person has been absent and not heard of for upwards of seven years from the time that he was last known to be living, by a person who would have heard had he been living, then he is presumed to be dead; but there is no legal presumption that he died at any given time within the seven years.

Survivorship.—Where several persons perish in same disaster, there is, in absence of evidence on the point, no presumption as to order in which they died or that they died at the same time. Onus probandi lies on party who asserts survival, or concurrent decease, or predecease.

Actions for Death.—Fatal Accidents (N.I.) Order 1977 as am'd by Sch. 6 of Administration of Justice Act, 1982 (1982, c. 53 [U.K.]) and Damages for Bereavement (Variation of Sum) (Northern Ireland) Order 1990 (1990, No. 2576) provides that whenever death of person is caused by wrongful act, neglect or default, and act, neglect and default is such as would (if death had not ensued) have entitled party injured to maintain action and recover damages in respect thereof, person who would have been liable if death had not ensued, is liable to action for damages notwithstanding death of person injured. Such action is for benefit of: (i) Wife or husband; (ii) former wife or husband; (iii) any person living in same household for two years as husband or wife; (iv) any parent or other ascendant; (v) any person treated by deceased as his parent; (vi) any child or other descendant; (vii) any person treated by deceased as child of deceased's marriage; (viii) any brother, sister, uncle or aunt of deceased (or issue thereof) (Art. 2[2]) and is brought by and in name of executor or administrator of deceased (Art. 4[1]). If no executor or administrator, or no action brought within six months of death by and in name of executor or administrator, action may be brought by and in name of all or any persons for whose benefit executor or administrator could have brought it. (Art. 4[2]). In assessing damages under Fatal Accidents Order (as am'd) benefits which have accrued or will or may accrue to any person from his estate or otherwise as result of his death must be disregarded (Art. 6[1]), and no account taken of widow's remarriage prospects (Art. 5[3]). Contributory negligence reduces damages recoverable to same extent as for any claim under §2(1) of Law Reform (Miscellaneous Provisions) Act (N.I.) 1948 (1948, c. 23). (Art. 7).

The Law Reform (Miscellaneous Provisions) Act (Northern Ireland) 1937 as am'd by Sch. 6 of Administration of Justice Act, 1982 (1982, c. 53 [U.K.]) provides that on death of any person all causes of action subsisting against or vested in him shall survive against or, as case may be, for benefit of his estate excluding causes of action for defamation. Where cause of action survives for benefit of estate of deceased person damages recoverable for benefit of estate of that person: (a) Do not include any exemplary damages; (b) do not include any damages for loss of income in respect of any period after person's death; and (c) where death of that person has been caused by act or omission which gives rise to cause of action, are calculated without reference to any loss of gain to his estate consequent on his death except that sum in respect of funeral expenses may be included. No proceedings are maintainable in respect of cause of action in tort which by virtue of Act has survived against estate of deceased person unless: (a) Proceedings against him in respect of that cause of action were pending at date of his death; or (b) proceedings were taken in respect thereof not later than six months after his personal representative took out representation. Where damage has been suffered by reason of any act or omission in respect of which cause of action would have subsisted against any person if that person had not died before or at same time as damage was suffered there is deemed to have been subsisting against him before his death such cause of action in respect of act or omission as would have subsisted if he had died after damage was suffered. Rights conferred for benefit of estates of deceased persons are in addition to and not in derogation of any rights conferred on dependents of deceased persons by Fatal Accident Acts.

Criminal Injuries (Compensation) (N.I.) Order 1977 (S.I. Mo. 1248[N.I. 15]) provides for payment of compensation by Secretary of State to victims of violent offences in Northern Ireland and to dependants of deceased victims (Art. 3[1]). Where person dies as result of criminal injury, being violent offence, arrest or attempted prevention of crime, and where incident is reported to police within 48 hours and notice of intention to apply for compensation is served on Secretary of State within 28 days, application for compensation may be made within three months of notice of intention by spouse or other dependant. (Art. 4[1]). Secretary of State determines amount payable in respect of pecuniary loss resulting from death; expenses incurred as result of death; and other expenses resulting directly from death. (Art. 4[5]). Any pension, gratuity or social security benefit payable in consequence of death is deductible (Art. 5[3]) but compensation is payable without regard to widow's remarriage prospects (Art. 5[6]) or to Fatal Accidents (N.I.) Order 1977 or to Part III of Law Reform (Miscellaneous Provisions) Act (N.I.) 1937 (Art. 7[2]). No compensation payable to anyone who is or ever was member of illegal organization or who is or has ever engaged in terrorism. (Art. 6[3]). Appeal against Secretary of State's determination can be made to County Court within six weeks of determination. (Art. 14[3]).

Death certificates of persons dying on or after Jan. 1, 1922, may be obtained from Registrar-General, Oxford House, Chichester Street, Belfast; fee £5.50.

See Topical Index in front part of this volume.

DEEDS:

Deeds must be signed, sealed and delivered and should be executed in the presence of two respectable witnesses who, in addition to signing their names, should subscribe their full addresses and descriptions, businesses or occupations. Seals of Bodies Corporate to be affixed in presence of at least two witnesses who sign their names.

Document signed by director and secretary or two directors of company and expressed to be executed by company has same effect as if executed under company's common seal. Document executed by which on face of it is clearly deed has effect, upon delivery, as deed and is presumed to be delivered upon being executed. (Art. 46A, 1990 S.I. 1504 [N.I. 10]).

Recording.—With exception of leases not exceeding 21 years where actual possession goes with the lease a memorial of all deeds, whether voluntary or for valuable consideration and whether creating a legal or equitable interest can be registered in Registry of Deeds. (Registration of Deeds Act [Northern Ireland] 1970 [1970, c. 25]).

Conveyances Compulsorily Subject to Registration are: (1) Conveyances of any estate for charitable uses which are void unless registered within three months after their execution (7 & 8 Vict., c. 97 [U.K.], §16); (2) certificate of appointment of bankrupts assignees must be registered within two months (20 & 21 Vict., c. 60, [U.K.], §269); (3) instrument executed by tradesmen or shopkeepers in Northern Ireland charging their goods after their death for their widow and children must be registered within four months after execution to bar creditors (5 Geo., c. 4 [Ir.]); (4) charging order for and advances under Land and Property Improvement Acts and other statutes (10 & 11 Vict. c. 32 [U.K.], §§ 21, 52, 21 & 22 Vict., c. 72, §51, 28 & 29 Vict., c. 88, §§6 & 7).

The Memorial must comply with provisions of Schedule 1 of 1970 Act (1970, c. 25) and must contain date when instrument perfected; names, addresses and occupations or descriptions of all parties and witnesses to instrument; and must specify land affected by instrument with name of street and county borough if land situated in a county borough; or county, barony and townland if land situated elsewhere, together with name of village and town where applicable.

Memorial need not be signed, sealed or attested, in case of any document lodged for registration. (§5 Registration of Deeds [Amendment] Act [Northern Ireland] 1967 [1967, c. 30]).

In case of wills registration is no longer possible. (§2 Registration of Deeds [Amendment] Act [Northern Ireland] 1967 [1967, c. 30]).

It is sufficient proof of execution of document if execution by grantor under document is attested by two witnesses who subscribe their names, address, and occupations or descriptions to document, and so execution of document need not be proved by affidavit.

Stamp Tax on Deeds.—See topic Taxation.

DEPOSITIONS:

The court or a judge may where it appears necessary for the purposes of justice make any order for examination on oath before judge or any officer of court, or any other person, and at any place, of any witness or person and may empower any party to any such cause or matter to give such deposition in evidence therein on such terms as court or judge may direct. (O.39, r.1).

Obtaining Evidence Out of the Jurisdiction.—Court has discretion in every case and before it will grant an application for leave to examine a witness out of the jurisdiction, it must generally be satisfied that (1) the application is made bona fide, (2) the issue in respect of which the evidence is required is one which the court ought to try, (3) the witnesses to be examined can give evidence material to the issue, (4) there is some good reason why they cannot be examined here, (5) examination abroad will be effectual.

Evidence out of the jurisdiction may be obtained: (a) By appointment of a special examiner (O.39, r.2) or in case of country with which convention has been made, by examination of witnesses before British consular authority in that country (O.39, r.2); (b) by letters of request (O.39, r.3), which method is available for all countries, but not employed in U.S., which prefers method (a).

The examination takes place in the presence of the parties, their counsel and their solicitors or agents, and the witnesses are subject to cross-examination and re-examination. (O.39, r.8).

Depositions taken before an officer of the court, or before any other person appointed to take the examination, are taken down in writing by or in the presence of the examiner, not ordinarily by question and answer, but so as to represent as nearly as may be the statement of the witness, and when completed must be read over to the witness and signed by him in the presence of the parties, or such of them as may think fit to attend. If the witness refuses to sign the depositions, the examiner must do so. (O.39, r.11).

When the examination of any witnesses is concluded the original depositions, authenticated by the signature of the examiner, must be transmitted by him to the Central Office of the Supreme Court and there filed. (O.39, r.11).

The person taking the examination under these rules may make special report to court touching such examination and conduct or absence of any witness or other person thereon, and court or judge may direct such proceedings and make such order as, on report, they or he may think just. (O.39, r.13).

Except where otherwise provided or directed by the court or a judge, no deposition may be given in evidence at the hearing or trial without consent of the party against whom it is offered, unless the court or judge is satisfied that deponent is dead, beyond the jurisdiction of the court, or unable from sickness or other infirmity to attend the hearing or trial, in any of which cases the deposition certified as above is admissible in evidence, saving all just exceptions, without proof of the signature to such certificate.

Obtaining Evidence For Foreign and Dominion Tribunals in Civil and Commercial Matters.—Laws of this country do not prohibit foreign, colonial or dominion courts or tribunals from obtaining, without request to or intervention of, the authorities or courts of Northern Ireland. A foreign court may make an order appointing a consular officer or some other suitable person as examiner to take evidence and special examiner may be appointed by a Dominion or colonial court but attendance of a witness before any person so appointed as examiner is entirely voluntary, examiner has no compulsory powers, and if witness refuses to attend aid of Northern Ireland courts must be invoked.

Courts or Tribunals in Foreign Countries.—Court or judge may, upon ex parte application of any person shown to be duly authorized to make the application, make an order appointing an examiner and ordering attendance of a witness within the jurisdiction before such examiner to take his testimony in relation to civil or commercial matter pending before foreign tribunal. (Foreign tribunals Evidence Act 1856).

The Northern Ireland court must be satisfied that: (i) Court of origin is a court of competent jurisdiction (certificate by ambassador or other diplomatic representative of foreign country that court is a court of competent jurisdiction according to laws of that country to hear and determine subject matter of the proceedings will normally be considered sufficient evidence by Northern Ireland and of the matter so certified); (ii) application relates to a civil or commercial proceeding pending in that court; and (iii) such court is desirous of obtaining, with the assistance of Northern Ireland court, evidence of a witness in this country. A certificate under hand of ambassador, minister, or other diplomatic agent of any foreign power received as such by Her Majesty or in case there is no such diplomatic agent, then of consul general, or consul of any such foreign power at London, that any matter to which an application is made under Act is a civil or commercial matter pending before court or tribunal in country of which he is diplomatic agent or consul having jurisdiction in the matter so pending, that such country is desirous of obtaining testimony of the witness or witnesses to whom application relates, is evidence of matters so certified, but where no such evidence is produced other evidence to that effect is admissible. (Foreign Tribunals Evidence Act 1856, §2). Where it is made to appear to court or a judge by commission rogatoire, or letters of request, or certificate signed in manner certifying to the effect mentioned in §2 of Act of 1856, or by such other evidence that court or judge may require, that foreign court is desirous of obtaining testimony of any witnesses here, such order may be made as may be necessary to give effect to intention of Act in conformity with §1 thereof. In practice desire of foreign tribunal to obtain evidence frequently takes form of issue by tribunal of commission rogatoire or of letters of request addressed to courts of this country.

Application to Northern Ireland court to take evidence for use in foreign court is made either (i) by agent in Northern Ireland of one of parties to proceedings in foreign country; or (ii) by Crown Solicitor without intervention of agents.

(i) *Application by Agent of One of Parties.*—Commission rogatoire, letters of request, or certificate of diplomatic representative that the evidence is required, is either sent direct to agent or through diplomatic channel and Foreign Office to Master of Supreme Court. Agents are rarely appointed in respect of convention countries. Evidence is usually taken in accordance with convention procedure and application is made to court by Crown Solicitor without intervention of agents for parties. If documents are received by Master, notification to this effect is sent to solicitor whose name appears thereon as appointed agent. Examination may be ordered to be taken before any fit or proper person nominated by person applying or before one of officers of court or such other qualified person as to court or judge may seem fit. In absence of any special directions in order for examination, procedure in High Court applies, i.e., in accordance with O.39.

Unless otherwise provided in order for examination, examiner before whom examination is taken must, on its completion, forward it to Master (Queen's Bench and Appeals) and on receipt thereof Master must certify it for use out of jurisdiction and forward depositions so certified, and commission rogatoire or letter of request, if any, to Her Majesty's Secretary of State for Foreign Affairs for transmission to foreign court or tribunal requiring same.

(ii) *Application by Crown Solicitor.*—Where commission rogatoire or letter of request is transmitted to Supreme Court by Her Majesty's Secretary of State for Foreign Affairs, with intimation that it is desirable that effect should be given to same without requiring application to be made to court by agents in Northern Ireland of any of parties to action or matter in foreign country, Master must transmit same to Crown Solicitor, who may thereupon, with consent of Her Majesty's Treasury, make such applications and take such steps as may be necessary to give effect to such commission rogatoire or letter of request. (O.70, r.3). Similarly, if letter of request is received by Master from consul general in London of foreign country with which civil procedure convention has been concluded it is also transmitted by Master to Crown Solicitor to be dealt with under provisions of convention and Rules of Court without intervention of agents to parties if none have been appointed.

When depositions are forwarded repayment is claimed of expenses incurred in respect of allowances to witnesses and examiners' fees. No court fees are charged nor is repayment claimed in respect of services of Crown Solicitor.

Courts or Tribunals in Her Majesty's Dominions.—Where upon an application court or judge is satisfied that any court or tribunal of competent jurisdiction in H. M. Dominions has duly authorized by commission, order or other process, the obtaining of testimony in, or in relation to any action, suit or proceeding pending in or before such court or tribunal, the court or judge may order the examination before person or persons, and in manner and form directed by such commission, order or other process, of such witness or witnesses accordingly; and court or judge by same order or any subsequent order may command attendance of any person to be named in such order for purpose of being examined or producing documents. (Evidence by Commission Act 1859).

It is essential that party desiring evidence instruct a solicitor in this country to take steps for execution of the letter of request from court out of the jurisdiction but within Her Majesty's Dominions and if letter of request is received through official channels name and address of solicitor who has been appointed as agent should be supplied.

Procedure on application is similar to that set out in case of letters of request from foreign tribunals. (O.70). Application is made ex parte to Queen's Bench Division on affidavit to which letter of request is exhibited. Depositions, when completed and received by Master, are certified as provided and are forwarded to Dominion or Colonial Office as case may be for transmission to court of origin. Any sum in respect of payment of fees, disbursements and expenses should be sent by party desiring evidence direct to solicitor appointed as agent and not through medium of Northern Ireland Court.

Where a Dominion or colonial court has appointed an examiner in Northern Ireland to take evidence, it is not necessary to apply here for appointment of an examiner but only to apply to High Court for an order to enforce attendance of witness; and an order if so made, takes the place of subpoena and disobedience thereto is deemed contempt of court. In such cases, depositions are returned by examiner to court requiring them as directed in order appointing him.

DEPOSITIONS . . . *continued*

De Bene Esse.—Court has jurisdiction where it is necessary for the purpose of justice to make an order for examination de bene esse of witnesses upon an ex parte application, the order being taken by applicant at his peril, and subject to risk of being discharged on sufficient grounds. (26 Ch. D.1).

Perpetuating Testimony.—Any person who would under the circumstances alleged by him to exist become entitled upon the happening of any future event, to any honour, title, dignity or office, or to any estate or interest in any property, real or personal, the right or claim to which cannot by him be brought to trial before the happening of such event, may commence an action to perpetuate any testimony which may be material for establishing such right or claim.

Witnesses may not be examined to perpetuate testimony unless an action has been commenced for purpose. (O.39, r.15).

DESCENT AND DISTRIBUTION:

By Administration of Estates Act (N.I.) 1955 (1955, c. 24), where deceased died intestate on or after Jan. 1, 1956, same rules of succession apply to real and personal property. All estate to which such deceased person was entitled for estate or interest not ceasing on his death and as to which he dies intestate, after payment of all debts, duties, testamentary and funeral expenses, is distributed as follows (figures of £125,000 and £200,000 below having been inserted by Administration of Estates [Rights of Surviving Spouse] Order [N.I.] 1993 [1993, S.R. No. 426] and applying to estates of persons dying after Dec. 1, 1987):

Surviving Spouse.—(A) Takes the personal chattels; (B) if intestate leaves neither issue, nor parents, nor brothers, nor sisters, nor issue of deceased brothers or sisters takes the whole of the estate; (C) if intestate leaves issue, takes, in addition to the personal chattels, (a) where the net value of the remaining estate does not exceed £125,000 whole of remaining estate, (b) where net value of remaining estate exceeds £125,000 sum of £125,000 free of all duties, charges, and costs, with charge upon remaining estate for that sum with interest thereon at 6% per annum from date of death until date of payment together with: (i) where only one child of intestate also survives, one-half of any residue left of remaining estate, after providing for that sum and interest thereon; (ii) where more than one child of intestate also survives, one-third of any residue left of remaining estate, after providing for that sum and interest thereon. (D) If intestate dies leaving no issue, but leaves parents or brothers or sisters, or issue of deceased brothers or sisters takes, in addition to personal chattels, (a) where net value of remaining estate does not exceed £200,000 whole of remaining estate, (b) where net value of remaining estate exceeds £200,000 sum of £200,000 free of all duties, charges and costs, and charge upon remaining estate for that sum with interest thereon at 6% per annum from date of death until date of payment together with one-half of any residue left of remaining estate after providing for that sum with interest thereon. In relation to estate of person dying after Mar. 2, 1970 but before Aug. 2, 1973, for "£125,000" mentioned above, read "£2,250"; for "£200,000" read "£7,500". (Family Provision Act [N.I.] 1969 [1969, c. 38, §1] and 1970, S.R. & O. [N.I.] No. 29). In relation to estate of person dying after Aug. 1, 1973, but before Jan. 1, 1978, for "£125,000" read "£7,500" and for "£200,000" read "£20,000". (1973, S.R. & O. [N.I.] No. 199). In relation to estate of person dying after Dec. 31, 1977, but before June 1, 1981, for "£125,000" read "£25,000" and for "£200,000" read "£55,000". (1977, S.R. No. 283). In relation to estate of person dying after May 31, 1981, but before Dec. 1, 1987, for "£125,000" read "£40,000" and for "£200,000" read "£85,000". (1981, S.R. No. 124). In relation to estate of person dying after Dec. 1, 1987, but before Jan. 1, 1994, for "£125,000" read "£75,000" and for "£200,000" read "£125,000". (1987, S.R. No. 378).

Issue.—If an intestate dies leaving issue, his estate is, subject to the rights of the surviving spouse (if any), distributed, per stirpes, among such issue. (§8 A. E. A. [N.I.] 1955).

Parent.—If an intestate dies leaving no issue, his estate is, subject to the rights of the surviving spouse (if any), distributed between his parents in equal shares, if both survive the intestate, but if only one parent survives the intestate, such surviving parent, subject as aforesaid, takes the whole estate. (§9 A. E. A. [N.I.] 1955).

Brothers and Sisters.—(1) If an intestate dies leaving neither issue nor parent, his estate shall, subject to the right of the surviving spouse (if any), be distributed between his brothers and sisters in equal shares, and if any brother or sister predeceases the intestate, the surviving issue of the deceased brother or sister take, per stirpes, the share that brother or sister would have taken if he or she had survived the intestate. (2) If the intestate dies leaving neither issue nor parent, nor brother, nor sister, his estate is, subject to the rights of the surviving spouse (if any), be distributed, per stirpes, among the issue of his brothers and sisters. (§10 A. E. A. [N.I.] 1955).

Next-of-kin.—If an intestate dies leaving neither spouse, nor issue, nor parent, nor brother, nor sister, nor issue of any deceased brother or sister, his estate is distributed in equal shares among his next-of-kin. Where any uncle or aunt of an intestate (being brother or sister of a parent of the intestate), who would have been included among such next-of-kin, if he or she had survived the intestate, has predeceased the intestate, leaving issue who survive the intestate, such issue represent that uncle or aunt, and by such representation take, per stirpes, the share that uncle or aunt would have taken as next-of-kin if he or she had survived the intestate. Representation of the next-of-kin is not admitted amongst collaterals except in the case of issue of brothers and sisters of the intestate and issue of uncles and aunts of the intestate. Subject to the rights of representation mentioned above, the person or persons who at the date of the death of the intestate stand nearest in blood relationship to him, are taken to be his next-of-kin. (§§11, 12 A. E. A. [N.I.] 1955).

Relatives of half-blood are treated as and inherit equally with relatives of whole-blood in the same degree. In default of any person taking the estate of an intestate under the foregoing provisions, the estate passes to the Crown as bona vacantia. (§§14, 16 A. E. A. [N.I.] 1955).

N.B. "Personal chattels" means carriages, horses, stable furniture and effects, motor cars and accessories, garden effects, domestic animals, plate, plated articles, linen, china, glass, books, pictures, prints, furniture, jewellery, articles of household or personal use or ornament, musical and scientific instruments and apparatus, wines, liquors and consumable stores, but does not include any chattels used at the death of the intestate for business or professional purposes nor money or security for money. (§45 A. E. A. [N.I.] 1955).

Inheritance (Provision for Family and Dependants) (Northern Ireland) Order, 1979 (1979, S.I. No. 924 [N.I. 8]).—Following death of any person domiciled in Northern Ireland, certain dependants, if not satisfied that reasonable provision has been made for them in deceased's will, or by intestacy provisions relating to deceased's estate, may apply to court for variation of relevant provisions. Following persons may apply: (a) Spouse of deceased; (b) former spouse who has not remarried; (c) any child of deceased; (d) any person who was treated as child of deceased's family; (e) any other person wholly or partly maintained by deceased immediately prior to deceased's death. (Art. 3).

If court is satisfied that reasonable financial provision has not been made for applicant, court can make any of following orders: (i) Order for periodical payments to applicant; (ii) order for lump sum payment; (iii) order for transfer of property; (iv) order for settlement of property for benefit of applicant; (v) order for acquisition of part of property by applicant; (vi) order for variation of ante-nuptial or post-nuptial settlement affecting applicant. (Art. 4).

In coming to its decision, court must have regard, inter alia, to financial resources of applicant; any physical or mental disabilities of applicant; and relationship between deceased and applicant.

Provision is made for granting of interim orders in case of great hardship (Art. 7) and for variation and discharge of orders (Art. 8). Except by leave of court, no application can be made after expiration of six months from grant of probate or letters of administration. (Art. 6).

DIVORCE:

Law regulating divorce, previously based on principle of "matrimonial fault" and governed by Matrimonial Causes Act (N.I.) 1939 (2 & 3 Geo. 6, c. 13 [N.I.]) has been replaced by system more closely akin to law of England, based on irretrievable breakdown of marriage. Governed by Matrimonial Causes (N.I.) Order, 1978 (1978, S.I. No. 1045 [N.I. 15]) and Family Law (N.I.) Order 1993 (1993 No. 1576 [N.I. 6]) and regulated by Matrimonial Causes Rules (N.I.) 1981 (1981, S.R. No. 184). Where any Art. or Rule is referred to without reference to Order or particular Statutory Rules, such Art. or Rule will be Art. of Matrimonial Causes (N.I.) Order, 1978, or Matrimonial Causes Rules (N.I.) 1981 as am'd by Matrimonial and Family Proceedings (N.I.) Order 1989 (1989 S.I. No. 677 [N.I. 4]).

Jurisdiction in matrimonial matters is exercised by Family Division of High Court or, where order made by Lord Chancellor is in force designating County Court sitting for any division as divorce County Court, County Court sitting for that division. (Art. 48). All County Courts have now been designated as Divorce County Courts, with jurisdiction to hear undefended divorces.

Domicile Requirements.—To give Northern Ireland courts jurisdiction to entertain proceedings for divorce or judicial separation: (a) Either spouse must be domiciled in Northern Ireland on date when proceedings commence, or (b) have been habitually resident throughout period of one year ending with that date provided proceedings in respect of same marriage are not pending elsewhere. (Art. 49).

Validity of divorce or legal separation obtained in country outside U.K. is recognised if: (a) Spouses had at time of proceedings both been domiciled in that country, or (b) divorce or separation is recognised under law of spouses' domicile or (c) one of spouses was at material time domiciled in that country and divorce or separation is recognised and valid under law of domicile of other spouse, or (d) neither of spouses having been domiciled in that country at material time, divorce or separation is recognised and valid under law of domicile of each spouse respectively. (Recognition of Divorces and Legal Separation Act, 1971 [1971, c. 53 (U.K.)]).

Sole ground for divorce at suit of either party to marriage is that marriage has broken down irretrievably. (Art. 3[1]). Court hearing divorce petition cannot grant divorce unless petitioner satisfies court of one or more of following "specified facts", namely: (a) Adultery by respondent; (b) behaviour by respondent of such kind that petitioner cannot reasonably be expected to live with respondent; (c) desertion of petitioner by respondent for continuous period of two years immediately preceding presentation of petition; (d) both parties having lived apart for continuous period of at least two years immediately preceding presentation of petition, and respondent consenting to divorce; (e) both parties having lived apart for continuous period of at least five years immediately preceding presentation of petition. (Art. 3[2]).

Limitation.—No divorce petition may be presented within two years of marriage. (1989 S.I. No. 677 [N.I. 4] Art. 3).

Parties.—Where in petition for divorce (or judicial separation) one party alleges other has committed adultery, he or she must make that person party to proceedings unless excused by court on special grounds from doing so. (Art. 53[1]). If court considers there is insufficient evidence against third party, it may dismiss third party from proceedings. (Art. 53).

Decree for divorce is at first "decree nisi" which is not made absolute, unless court fixes shorter period, until expiration of six weeks, during which time any person may show cause why decree should not be made absolute, and Crown Solicitor may intervene. (Art. 11).

Refusal of Divorce.—Court will refuse decree in following circumstances: (a) Where petitioner fails to satisfy court of one or more "specified facts" as in Art. 3(2); (b) where one or more specified fact proved, but court satisfied marriage has not broken down irretrievably; (c) where adultery is relied upon by petitioner, but petitioner having found out about adultery, both parties lived together for period exceeding, or periods together exceeding, six months (Art. 4[1]); (d) where five years separation alleged, if court satisfied respondent would suffer grave financial or other hardship, and it would in all circumstances be wrong to dissolve marriage (Art. 7).

Court may, at its discretion, refuse to dissolve marriage in following circumstances: (a) Where adultery is alleged, and respondent proves adultery committed with connivance of petitioner (Art. 4[2]); (b) where respondent consents to decree nisi after two years' separation only because he or she has been misled by petitioner (innocently or

DIVORCE . . . *continued*
deliberately) into doing so, court may rescind decree nisi (Art. 12[1]); (c) where decree nisi is granted on either two or five years' separation, decree absolute may be refused where court not satisfied financial provisions made by petitioner for respondent are reasonable and fair, or best in circumstances (Art. 12); (d) where court not satisfied about arrangement for welfare of minor children of marriage, may refuse decree absolute (Art. 44).

Reconciliation.—If at any stage of divorce proceedings court considers there is reasonable possibility of reconciliation, court may adjourn proceedings for as long as it thinks fit to enable attempts to be made to effect such reconciliation, but if parties resume cohabitation during such adjournment, no account shall be taken of that fact for purposes of proceedings. (Art. 8).

Financial and Property Considerations.—Matrimonial Causes (N.I.) Order, 1978, as amended by Family Law (N.I.) Order 1993, contains wide range of detailed provisions for division of matrimonial property, including money, between parties to dissolved marriage, and for future maintenance of less financially secure party (whether wife or husband).

Maintenance Pending Suit.—On petition for divorce, nullity, or judicial separation, court can make order requiring either party to marriage to make to other such periodical payments for maintenance, beginning with date of presentation of divorce petition and ending on determination of proceedings, as court sees fit. (Art. 24).

Financial Provision Orders.—On granting decree of divorce, nullity or judicial separation, court can make any one or more of following orders: (a) Order for periodical payments; (b) order for secured periodical payments; (c) order for lump sum payment or payments; (d) order for periodical payments to person named in order for benefit of child of family, or directly to said child; (e) order for secured periodical payments to person named in order for benefit of child of family, or directly to said child; (f) order for lump sum payment or payments to person named in order for benefit of child of family, or directly to said child. (Art. 25). Clauses (d), (e) and (f) do not apply to children of family who have attained age of 18 years unless undergoing fulltime education. (Art. 31).

Property Adjustment Orders.—On granting decree of divorce, nullity, or judicial separation, court can make any one or more of following orders: (a) Order that party to marriage transfers to other party, to any child of family, or to such person as specified in order for benefit of child of family, any property specified; (b) order that settlement of specified property be made for benefit of other party to marriage and of children of family; (c) order varying any ante-nuptial or post-nuptial settlement (including one made by will or codicil); (d) order extinguishing or reducing interest of either of parties to marriage under any such settlement. (Art. 26). Clause (a) does not apply to children of marriage who have attained age of 18 years, unless undergoing full-time education. (Art. 31).

Considerations to Which Court is to have Regard.—Court has duty, in deciding whether to exercise its powers under Arts. 25 or 26, to have regard to all circumstances of case, including following matters: (a) Income, earning capacity, property and other financial resources of each party; (b) financial needs, obligations and responsibilities of each party; (c) standard of living enjoyed by family before breakdown of marriage; (d) age of each party and duration of marriage; (e) any physical or mental disability of either party; (f) contributions made by each of parties to welfare of family, including contributions made by looking after home or caring for family; (g) value to either party of any benefit (for example, pension) which dissolution or annulment of marriage would adversely affect.

Court's duty is to exercise its powers under Arts. 25 and 26 so as to place parties, as far as is practicable, and, having regard to their conduct, just to do so, in financial position in which they would have been if marriage had not broken down and each had properly discharged his or her financial obligations and responsibilities towards other. (Art. 27[1]).

In deciding whether to exercise its powers under Arts. 25 or 26 in relation to child of family, court has duty to consider all circumstances of case including following: (a) Financial needs of child; (b) income, earning capacity (if any), property and other financial resources of child; (c) any physical or mental disability of child; (d) standard of living enjoyed by family before breakdown of marriage; (e) manner in which child was being educated or trained.

Court's duty is to exercise its powers so as to place child, so far as is practicable, in financial position in which child would have been if marriage had not broken down and each party had properly discharged his or her financial obligations and responsibilities towards him. (Art. 27[2]).

Commencement of Proceedings for Relief.—Where petitioner seeks such financial or property relief as is mentioned in Arts. 24, 25 and 26, such application shall be included in petition. Applications by respondent shall be included in answer to petition. Applications by either party if not so made require leave of court. (Art. 28).

Duration of Financial Provision Orders.—No order for periodical payments or secured periodical payments can extend beyond death or remarriage of benefiting party. After dissolution or annulment of marriage, no party can apply for financial provision order or property adjustment order after remarrying. (Art. 30).

Children.—Where petition for divorce, nullity or judicial separation has been presented to court, and there are children of family under 16 years (or undergoing full-time education or training) reference must be made to suitably qualified person to consider possibility of conciliating parties to marriage, and for report on children and suitability of any arrangements made or proposed by either party for their welfare. (Art. 43[1]). Where suitably qualified person reports that arrangements for children are unsuitable, or if for any other reason court sees fit, court can appoint guardian ad litem to safeguard interests of children for purposes of proceedings. (Art. 43[3]).

Court will not make absolute decree of divorce or nullity or grant decree of judicial separation, unless court, by order, declares itself satisfied: (a) That there are no children to whom this legislation applies; or (b) that satisfactory arrangements have been made for children; or (c) it is impracticable for party or parties to make such arrangements; or (d) that circumstances make it desirable for decree to be granted or made absolute without delay, despite fact that no satisfactory arrangements have yet been made. (Art. 44).

Custody and Committal Orders.—Court can make any order as it thinks fit for custody and education of any child of family under age of 18 before or on granting decree, or at any time thereafter; and also if proceedings are dismissed. (Art. 45[1]). Where court grants or makes absolute decree of divorce or grants judicial separation, it may include in decree declaration that either party is unfit to have custody of children of family. (Art. 45[3]). Where it appears to court that there are exceptional circumstances making it impracticable or undesirable for any child to be entrusted to either party or to any other individual, court can make order committing care of such child to Department of Health and Social Services. (Art. 46).

Remarriage.—Either party may remarry after decree has become absolute, unless appeal is pending.

Judicial Separation.—Petition for judicial separation may be presented to court by either party on ground that any of five "specified facts" as outlined above (see Art. 3[2], subhead Sole Ground, supra) exist. Court is not concerned whether marriage has broken down irretrievably. If court satisfied of existence of one or more specified fact, it must grant decree of judicial separation.

Petty Sessions Courts have jurisdiction under Domestic Proceedings (N.I.) Order 1980 (1980, S.I. No. 563 [N.I. 5]) as amended by Family Law (N.I.) Order 1993 to grant either party to marriage order for financial provision on ground that other party to marriage: (a) Has failed to provide reasonable maintenance for applicant; or (b) has failed to provide, or to make proper contribution towards, reasonable maintenance for any child of family; or (c) has, since date of marriage, committed adultery; or (d) has behaved in such way that applicant cannot reasonably be expected to live with respondent; or (e) has deserted applicant.

Petty Sessions Court may make any one or more of following orders for financial provision: (a) Order that respondent shall make to applicant such periodical payments, and for such term, as may be specified in order; (b) order that respondent shall make to applicant such lump sum as may be so specified; (c) order that respondent shall make to applicant for benefit of child of family to whom application relates, or to such child, such periodical payments, and for such term, as may be so specified; (d) order that respondent shall pay to applicant for benefit of child of family to whom application relates, or to such child, such lump sum as may be so specified.

If there is child of family under age of 18, Petty Sessions Court has power to make order regarding: (a) Legal custody of such child and (b) access to any such child by either party to marriage or any other person who is parent of that child. Court shall not dismiss application or make final order for financial provision until it has decided whether to exercise its power regarding legal custody and access.

Nullity of Marriage.—Effect of decree of nullity is that there was no marriage at all, whether it was void or voidable. Marriage can be declared void ab initio on following grounds only: (a) Parties are within prohibited degrees of relationship; (b) either party is under 16 years; (c) by reason of noncompliance with any statutory provision or rule of law governing formation of marriage; (d) at time of marriage either party was already lawfully married; (e) parties not respectively male and female; (f) in case of polygamous marriage entered into outside Northern Ireland, that either party was at time of marriage domiciled in Northern Ireland. (Art. 13).

Marriage is voidable on following grounds only: (a) Marriage not consummated owing to incapacity of either party; (b) non-consummation owing to wilful refusal of respondent; (c) lack of valid consent to marriage by either party (i.e., through duress, mistake or unsoundness of mind); (d) where either party, though capable of valid consent, was suffering (continuously or intermittently) from mental disorder within meaning of Mental Health Act (N.I.) 1961 (1961, c. 15) of such kind or to such extent as to be unfitted for marriage; (e) at time of marriage, respondent suffering from venereal disease in communicable form; (f) at time of marriage respondent pregnant by another party (Art. 14).

Court cannot grant decree of nullity unless satisfied petitioner was at time of marriage ignorant of facts alleged, and that proceedings were instituted within three years of marriage. (Art. 16).

Presumption of Death.—Any married person who alleges reasonable grounds exist for presuming other party dead may present petition to High Court for dissolution of marriage. Fact that for seven years or more other party to marriage has been continually absent from petitioner and petitioner has no reason to believe other party has been living within that time shall be evidence that other party is dead. High Court can then grant decree of presumption of death and dissolution of marriage. (Art. 21).

Publication of any particulars, in any newspaper or periodical, other than (1) Names, addresses and occupations of parties and witnesses, (2) concise statements of charge and defence, (3) submissions on any point of law, (4) judgment of court and court's observations in giving judgment; in relation to any judicial proceedings for dissolution or nullity of marriage is prohibited by Matrimonial Causes (Reports) Act (Northern Ireland) 1966. (1966, c. 29).

DOWER:

Abolished by Administration of Estates Act (Northern Ireland) 1955.

EXCHANGE CONTROL:

Power to legislate with respect to coinage, legal tender or negotiable instruments (including banknotes) excluded from competence of Northern Ireland Assembly, except insofar as negotiable instruments may be affected by exercise of powers of taxation. (Northern Ireland Constitution Act 1973 [1973, c. 36, Sch. 2]). See topic Constitution and Government.

EXECUTIONS:

Jurisdiction relating to enforcement of judgments is vested in Enforcement of Judgments Office (which is part of Northern Ireland Court Service under control of Lord Chancellor) and is exercised by designated officers in accordance with Judgments Enforcement (Northern Ireland) Order, 1981 (1981, S.I. No. 226 [N.I. 6]) as amended by The Judgments Enforcement (Attachment of Debts) (Northern Ireland) Order 1983 (1983 S.I. No. 1904 [N.I. 22]) and The Judgments Enforcement [Amendment] [Northern Ireland] Order 1986 (1986 S.I. No. 1166 [N.I.]1). All references to statutory provisions are to provisions contained in 1981 Order. (1981 S.I. No. 226 [N.I. 6]). Any

EXECUTIONS . . . *continued*
reference to Art. number in this topic is reference to 1981 Order unless contrary is indicated.

Order applies to judgments for recovery of money in civil proceedings (including those given outside Northern Ireland, but enforceable in Northern Ireland under any statutory provision); possession of land (including warrant for possession after conviction of squatter); delivery of goods and payment of lump sums under Domestic Proceedings (Northern Ireland) Order, 1980 (1980, S.I. No. 563 [N.I. 5]; Art. 4).

Applications for enforcement must be made within 12 years from judgment, and after six years leave of Office is required. (Art. 17).

Powers of Office.—For purposes of enforcement, Office may: (a) Make enforcement orders (Art. 13[a]); (b) issue custody warrants (Art. 13[b]); (c) issue summonses for attendance and examination of debtors as to their means, and other persons who may be able to give evidence as to debtors' means (Art. 13[c]); (d) conduct examinations as to means of debtors (Art. 13[d]); (e) receive monies in respect of payments of whole or part of amounts payable under judgments lodged for enforcement (Art. 13[e]); (f) stay enforcement of proceedings in Office (Art. 13[f]); (g) set aside, discharge or vary its own orders (Art. 13[g]); (h) issue notices and certificates of unenforceability (Art. 13[h]); (i) dismiss applications for enforcement (Art. 13[i]); and (j) make administration orders (Art. 13[j]).

Orders.—Where application has been accepted, Office may, at its discretion, make any of following orders which have force and effect of High Court orders: (a) Instalment order where it appears debtor will have means to satisfy judgment by instalments (Art. 30); (b) order of seizure by which certain property of debtor may be seized but not including, inter alia, such furniture, bedding, household equipment as appears essential for domestic purposes of debtor, spouse and dependants; and tools and implements of debtor's trade to value of £200 (1983, S.R. No. 150); (c) order charging land, which confers power of sale on application to court for possession (Arts. 46-52); (d) charging order on funds, stocks or shares, having effect so as to require that all dividends or interests accruing be paid to owner of charge (Art. 58); (e) debenture order, requiring debtor who has beneficial interest in debenture to make payment to creditor of principal or interest or both (Art. 61); (f) stop order in respect of funds, shares or stock held in debtor's name in court (Art. 62); (g) restraining order, where debtor has share in private company, restraining company from paying dividend to debtor or dealing with shares in any other way (Art. 66); (h) partnership order requiring partner's interest in property to be transferred to Office (1890, c. 39); (i) order appointing receiver by way of equitable execution against debtor (Art. 67); (j) attachment of debts order attaching all debts due to debtor for purpose of satisfying judgment debt (Art. 69) and Art. 72 as am'd); (k) order for payment by garnishee to creditor (Art. 70); (l) attachment of earnings order (requiring employer to make available such payments out of debtor's earnings as Office directs, in order to pay off judgment (Art. 73).

Certificate of Unenforceability.—Where it appears after examination of debtor that judgment cannot be enforced within reasonable time, Office may issue notice of unenforceability and, after giving debtor and creditor opportunity of being heard, may grant certificate of unenforceability. Where granted, no further application for enforcement is accepted unless certificate is set aside on application of any creditor who can establish that debtor has, or is about to have, assets which can be made amenable to enforcement. Grant of certificate constitutes act of bankruptcy. (Arts. 19-21). (See topic Bankruptcy and Insolvency.)

Appeal.—Any person aggrieved by order or decision of Office may appeal to High Court or, in certain cases, to Court of Appeal. (Art. 140).

EXECUTORS AND ADMINISTRATORS:

Executor or administrator must collect all assets of decedent, and discharge all his liabilities. One year is allowed for this purpose, and a legatee cannot without the leave of the court sue for payment of his legacy until after one year from decedent's death.

Real and personal estate to which a deceased person who died on or after Jan. 1, 1956, was entitled to an estate or interest not ceasing on his death, notwithstanding any testamentary disposition, devolves upon and vests in his personal representatives for distribution.

Personal representatives are not bound to publish for creditors, but, as a general rule, this is done in order to safeguard the personal representative against any personal liability for debts of decedent of which he has no notice.

Executor or administrator may be required by High Court as precondition to issue of grant to provide surety. (Art. 17 Administration of Estates [N.I.] Order 1979 No. 1575 [N.I. 14]).

Once a grant of probate or letters of administration has been obtained the remainder of the administration is usually carried out without the supervision of the court; but if unusual difficulty arises, a personal representative, a creditor or a legatee may apply to the court for an order for administration, and when such order is made the entire administration is carried out in the Chancery Division.

An executor may retain a debt due by the decedent to himself, out of the assets; even where the estate is insolvent an executor may retain his debt in full (out of the assets actually passing through his hands) as against a creditor in equal degree.

Personal representatives are not allowed any statutory fees, nor may they charge for their services unless authorized by the will to make professional charges.

As to inheritance tax, see England Law Digest, topic Taxation.

EXEMPTIONS:

Special Cases.—No execution can be issued against a foreign sovereign or a person subject to diplomatic immunity unless privilege is waived. No person is individually liable under any order for payment by Crown or any government department or any officer of Crown as such for money or costs. (Crown Proceedings Act 1947, 10 & 11 §6, c. 44 [U.K.]).

Rolling stock or plant of railway company exempt from execution. (Railway Companies Act 1867, 30 & 31 Vict. c. 137 [U.K.] §4).

Exemptions from Execution.—Wearing apparel and bedding of judgment debtor or his family and tools and implements of his trade not exceeding in whole value of £200 are exempt from liability to seizure under any execution. Judgment or order against member of Her Majesty's military (Army Act 1955, 3 & 4 Eliz. 2, c. 18 [U.K.] §185) or airforce (Airforce Act 1955, 3 & 4 Eliz. 2, c. 19 [U.K.] §185) cannot be enforced by levying execution against his arms, ammunition, equipment, instruments or clothing used for military or airforce purposes, or in respect of debt due for maintenance of wife or child of person subject to Naval Discipline Act against any person, pay, arms, ammunition, equipment, instruments or clothing.

Substitution.—Debtor who does not possess articles specifically exempted may not hold money or other property in lieu thereof.

FOREIGN EXCHANGE:

See topic Exchange Control.

FOREIGN INVESTMENT:

Industrial Development Board for Northern Ireland, I.D.B. House, 64, Chichester Street, Belfast, is responsible for all matters relating to establishment of new, or expansion of existing, industrial undertakings in Northern Ireland. Information about facilities for industrial development in Northern Ireland may also be obtained from: Industrial Development Board for Northern Ireland, Ulster Office, 11, Berkeley Street, London, W1X 6BU; or from Industrial Development Board for Northern Ireland, British Consulate General, 150 East 58th Street, New York, NY 10155. Industrial Development Board offers special assistance and generous grants to encourage industrial development under Industrial Development (N.I.) Order, 1982.

Industrial Development Board was established by 1982 Order. Functions of Board are to advise Head of Department of Economic Development generally on formulation and implementation of its industrial development policy. Department, through Board, has wide powers (subject to approval of Department of Finance and Personnel) to carry on, establish, develop, promote, assist and maintain any industrial undertaking for purposes of development or assistance of economy; promotion of industrial efficiency; and provision, maintenance or safeguarding of employment in Northern Ireland. Department may provide financial assistance, by arrangement with Department of Finance and Personnel, where such assistance is likely to provide, maintain or safeguard employment in any part of Northern Ireland. Department may also give financial assistance for research and development and for marketing of products.

Department may provide premises for industrial occupation, do anything required to develop land for industrial use, including erection of buildings and construction of access roads, and provision of fixtures and fittings. Department may give financial grants toward new machinery or plant. Grants of 20% are available in respect of industrial machinery; computers for business use; hire of machinery, plant or computers; renting of buildings needed for certain industrial processes; and mining activities.

FOREIGN TRADE REGULATIONS:

Northern Ireland Assembly cannot legislate on trade with any place outside Northern Ireland, except so far as trade may be affected by exercise of its powers of taxation, or by regulations made for sole purpose of preventing contagious disease, or for protection of traders from fraud. Northern Ireland Constitution Act 1973. (1973, c. 36 [N.I.]). See topic Constitution and Government.

All acts of the United Kingdom Parliament apply to Northern Ireland unless their application is expressly or by implication excluded. See England Law Digest, topic Foreign Trade Regulations. See also European Union Law Digest, topic Foreign Trade Regulations.

FRAUDS, STATUTE OF:

No action shall be brought: (1) to charge a person on any special promise to answer for the debt, default or miscarriage of another; or (2) to charge any person upon any contract for the sale of lands or any interest in same, or for any lease thereof for more than three years; unless in these cases the agreement or some note or memorandum thereof be in writing and signed by the party to be charged or someone by him lawfully authorized. (Statute of Frauds [Ireland] 7 Will. 3, c. 12, §2).

See also topic Sales.

FRAUDULENT SALES AND CONVEYANCES:

Transaction made by any company or person (whether or not bankrupt or insolvent) at undervalue for purpose of putting assets beyond reach of person making or who may make, claim against such company or person, or of otherwise prejudicing interests of such company or person in relation to claim, may be set aside on application of Official Receiver or trustee or victim of transaction to High Court. (Insolvency [N.I.] Order 1989, [S.I. 1989 No. 2405] [N.I. 19] Art. 367-369). Court may make such order as it thinks fit to restore position and to protect interests of victims of transaction. Interests of bona fide third parties are however protected.

Where bankrupt has within six months of presentation of bankruptcy petition (or five years in case of transaction at undervalue or two years if given to associate of bankrupt) given preference to any person, Court may, on application of trustee make such order as it thinks fit to restore position. Person preferred must have been creditor or surety or guarantor for debts or liabilities of bankrupt. If preference constituted transaction at undervalue given within two years of presentation of petition or is given to associate, insolvency of bankrupt is presumed at time of preference. Otherwise, trustee must prove insolvency. Interests of bona fide third parties are protected. (Art. 313, S.I. 1989/2405 [N.I. 19]).

Any conveyance, mortgage, delivery of goods, payment, execution or other act relating to property made or done by or against company within six months before commencement of its winding up which, had it been made or done by or against individual within six months before he became bankrupt, would be deemed in his bankruptcy fraudulent preference, is in event of company being wound up deemed fraudulent preference of its creditors and invalid accordingly. Any conveyance or assignment by company of all its property to trustees for benefit of all its creditors is void. (The Companies [N.I.] Order 1986 [S.I. 1986 No. 1032][N.I. 6] Art. 571).

See Topical Index in front part of this volume.

GARNISHMENT:

Creditor who has obtained judgment for sum of money may apply to Enforcement of Judgments Office for garnishee order attaching all debts due to judgment debtor from any person (garnishee) within jurisdiction for purpose of satisfying amount recoverable on foot of judgment or part thereof. (Judgments Enforcement [Northern Ireland] Order 1981 [1981 S.I. No. 266 (N.I. 6) Art. 69]). If garnishee upon service on him of order does not within specified period either pay required amount to Enforcement of Judgments Office or show cause why order should not be enforced creditor may proceed to enforce order as if it were judgment. If liability disputed office may determine issues or may direct any issue or question to High Court. (1981 S.I. No. 226 [N.I. 6] Art. 70). Order may be made attaching money in bank or other deposit taking institutions standing to credit of debtor. (1981 S.I. No. 226 [N.I. 6] Art. 72 and 1983 S.I. No. 1904 [N.I. 22] Art. 3[1]). Clerical and administrative costs of institutional garnishees in complying with attachment of debts order are deducted from debt which is subject of order. (1981 S.I. No. 226 [N.I. 6] Art. 72 and 1983 S.I. No. 1904 [N.I. 22] Art. 4 and 1986 S.I. No. 1166 [N.I. 11] Art. 3).

HOLIDAYS:

Jan. 1, Mar. 17 (St. Patrick's Day), Good Friday, Easter Monday, 1st Mon. in May, Spring Holiday, last Mon. in May, July 12, last Mon. in Aug., Christmas Day, Boxing Day (Dec. 26) and Dec. 27 are bank holidays on which all banks and Stock Exchange are closed.

HUSBAND AND WIFE:

A married woman is free to contract and is subject to the bankruptcy laws as if she were a feme sole. She can hold property free from any liability for her husband's debts and may dispose of same as she wishes. He is liable on foot of his wife's contracts for necessaries, e.g., food, clothes, medical fees, and articles for the home. The wife has implied authority to pledge his credit for such necessaries; but if a husband gives a wife a housekeeping allowance such authority may be cancelled.

Prior to 1938, property could be left or given to a married woman subject to the proviso that she be restrained from anticipating or alienating it during coverture. Such a provision in a deed or will made before 1938 is still operative but in any instrument executed since that date is void.

Actions.—In actions by or against married woman joinder of husband is unnecessary. Wife can sue husband in contract and tort.

Desertion and Nonsupport.—Any married woman whose husband has deserted her or has been guilty of wilful neglect to provide reasonable maintenance for her or for any of her children under age of 16 years (or under age of 18 years if receiving full-time training or education) whom he is legally liable to maintain may apply to court of summary jurisdiction for order that husband shall pay to wife personally or for her use to any officer of court or any third person on her behalf weekly sum and in any case where there are children under age of 16 years weekly sum in respect of each child.

If in the opinion of court of summary jurisdiction matters in question between parties would be more conveniently dealt with by High Court, court of summary jurisdiction may refuse to make order under Domestic Proceedings (N.I.) Order, 1980. (1980, S.I. No. 563 [N.I. 5]).

IMMIGRATION:

Power to legislate with respect to nationality, immigration and aliens as such is excluded from competence of Northern Ireland Assembly by Northern Ireland Constitution Act 1973. (1973, c. 36, Sch. 2). (See topic Constitution and Government.) Law relating to immigration governed by Immigration Act 1971 (1971, c. 77 [U.K.]) as am'd by British Nationality Act, 1981 (1981, c. 61 [U.K.]); and, with respect to citizens of Member States of European Economic Community, by Treaty and Regulations of E.E.C. See European Union Law Digest, topic Internal Market, subheads Free Movement of Goods; and Free Movement of Workers and Freedom to Provide Services.

European Economic Community.—Until Jan. 1, 1978, Safeguarding of Employment Act (N.I.) 1947 (1947, c. 24) generally restricted employment under contract of service in Northern Ireland to Northern Ireland workers except under permit issued by Department of Manpower Services. Act no longer applies, and is superseded by provisions of E.E.C. Treaty. Treaty provides for free movement of workers within member states and states that "any discrimination based on nationality between workers of the Member States as regards employment, remuneration and other labour conditions" must be abolished. (Art. 48[2]). Subject to limitations justified on grounds of public policy, public security and public health, workers have right: (a) To accept offers of employment in another member state which have actually been made; (b) to move freely within territory of member states for this purpose; (c) to stay in member state for purpose of employment in accordance with provisions governing employment of nationals of that state laid down by law, regulation or administrative action; and (d) to remain in territory of member state after having been employed in that state, together with relatives living with them. These provisions do not extend to professions, employment in public service, banking, insurance (except reinsurance) and transport.

Channel Islands, Isle of Man, Republic of Ireland.—Arrivals from these places are excluded from control under Immigration Act 1971 for most purposes. Entry into U.K. via these places may be restricted. (1971, c. 77, §9 and Sch. 4).

Overseas Arrivals.—

§2 of Immigration Act, 1971 (1971, c. 77 [U.K.]) as am'd by §39(2) of British Nationality Act, 1981 (1981, c. 61 [U.K.]) confers right of abode in U.K. on: (a) British citizens; (b) Commonwealth citizens having right of abode under 1971 Act (i.e. by birth, adoption, naturalization or marriage).

British citizens defined in Part 1 of 1981 Act as including: (i) Those born in U.K. to parent who is British citizen or settled in U.K.; (ii) foundlings; (iii) persons born in U.K., one of whose parents subsequently becomes settled in U.K. or becomes British citizen or has lived in U.K. for ten years from birth; (iv) children adopted by order of U.K. court; (v) children born overseas, if at least one parent is British citizen (otherwise than by descent) or British citizen in Crown service. Persons may also be registered as British citizens in certain circumstances. (§§3-10). British Nationality (Hong Kong) Act 1990 (1990, c. 34 [U.K.]) provides for acquisition of British citizenship by selected Hong Kong residents, their spouses and minor children.

§3 provides that persons who do not have right of abode require leave to enter U.K., which may be given for limited or indefinite period and which may be subject to conditions restricting employment or occupation in U.K. or requiring registration with police, or both. Section provides for system of immigration rules to administer Act and defines circumstances in which such persons may be deported (i.e., breach of conditions attached to entry; or if Secretary of State considers deportation to be conductive to public good).

INFANTS:

Age of Majority.—From Jan. 1, 1970, person, either sex, attains majority at 18, whether 18 reached before or after that date (Age of Majority Act [Northern Ireland] 1969 [1969 c. 28]).

Emancipation.—No special statutory provisions.

Disabilities.—In general an infant has no power to contract except for necessaries.

Ratification of Contracts.—Infants may ratify all contracts after majority. No writing needed. By Minors' Contracts (Northern Ireland) Order, 1988 (1988, S.I. No. 930 [N.I. 9]) minors can ratify otherwise unenforceable contracts on attaining majority. Order also provides for guarantees of contractual obligations entered into by minors to be enforceable against guarantors.

Actions.—Infant may sue by guardian if any or next friend. No court appointment needed. Guardian ad litem or next friend may upon request be appointed by the court to protect the interest of any minor or person unborn, unascertained or under disability in any suit relating to property in which such person may be or may become interested.

Torts.—Infant is liable for torts. Negligence of parent or custodian not imputed to infant.

INSOLVENCY:

See topic Bankruptcy and Insolvency.

INTEREST:

Judgments for money carry interest at 12% from their date (Judgments Enforcement [N.I.] Order, 1981 [1981, S.I. No. 226 (N.I.6)]), but 15% as from 19 May, 1985 (1985, S.R. No. 102. County Court (Amendment) Rules (Northern Ireland) 1993 made under S.I. 1980 No. 397 reduces rate of interest to 8% on decrees.

Extortionate rates of interest, whether in relation to money-lending or any other form of credit agreement other than those made with body corporate or with partnership of bodies corporate, are not permitted by Consumer Credit Act 1974. (1974, c. 39 [U.K.] §§137-140). There is no longer maximum permissible rate of 48% interest per annum. If debtor alleges credit bargain is extortionate, it is for creditor to prove contrary. "Extortionate" is defined as "grossly exorbitant" payments where ordinary principles of fair dealing are grossly contravened. (§138[1]).

JOINT STOCK COMPANIES:

(See topic Corporations.)

The principal class of unincorporated company is that formed under the Chartered Companies Acts 1837, Section 2 of which empowers the Crown by letters patent under the Great Seal to grant to any company or body of persons associated together for any trading or other purposes although not incorporated by such letters patent, any privileges which according to the rules of the common law it would be competent for the Crown to grant to any such company or body of persons by any charter of incorporation. The individual liability of members of such a company may be restricted by the letters patent.

JUDGMENTS:

Where a judgment or order directs a person to pay any money or deliver up or transfer any property, real or personal, to another, he is bound to obey such judgment or order upon being duly served with same, without demand.

Enforcement.—Money judgment may be enforced through Judgments Enforcement (N.I.) Order, 1981 (see topic Executions), or registered as mortgage against lands under Judgment Mortgage Act 1850, or if amount of judgment, including debt and costs, is £750 or over, bankruptcy proceedings may be instituted. Judgment for recovery or delivery of possession of land may be enforced by writ of possession. Mandatory order or injunction may be enforced by writ or sequestration or order for attachment for contempt of court.

Foreign Judgments.—Foreign judgments for fixed amounts can be enforced by action in the courts of Northern Ireland and cannot normally be re-opened provided the defendant was present in the jurisdiction of the foreign court when the proceedings were begun or submitted to it, e.g., by defending the foreign proceedings.

There are reciprocal arrangements for enforcing judgments of EEC member states. See European Union Law Digest, topic Judgments.

Under the Administration of Justice Act 1920, judgments obtained in many parts of the British Commonwealth can be registered in the High Court if the court thinks it just and convenient and provided application is made within 12 months. Under the Foreign Judgments (Reciprocal Enforcement) Act 1933, a judgment for a fixed amount obtained in India, Burma, Belgium or France can be registered in the High Court as of right within six years. On registration a foreign judgment may be enforced in the same manner as judgments of the High Court of Northern Ireland. Certain formalities regarding application for registration and notice to the debtor must be observed and power is given to the court to cancel registration on certain grounds.

There are reciprocal arrangements for enforcing judgments of EEC member states. See European Union Digest topic Judgments.

LABOUR RELATIONS:

Department of Economic Development administers services in connection with trade disputes, trade boards, labour exchange, factories and workshop, national health and unemployment insurance and matters relating to labour and employment generally.

Hours of Labour.—The number of hours which can be worked in shops during each day and each week is governed by Shops Act (N.I.) 1946. (1946, c. 7 [N.I.] am'd 1990, S.I. No. 246 [N.I.2]).

Nighttime employment of women, which means any woman aged 18 years or over is governed by Hours of Employment (Conventions) Act 1936. (26 Geo. 5 & 1, Edw. 8, c. 22 [U.K.], §1).

Contracts of Employment and Redundancy Payments Act (N.I.) 1965 (1965, c. 19) requires a minimum period to terminate employment and requires employers to give written particulars of terms of employment. It also provides for making of redundancy payments by employers, to full-time employees with at least two years continuous employment with employer or associated employer after age of 18.

Wages.—Practice of paying workmen wholly or partly in kind instead of cash is illegal; Truck Act (Ir.) 1815 (17 Geo. 1, c. 8 [Ir.]) and Truck Acts 1851 to 1896 (59-60 Vict., c. 44 [U.K.], §12). But if employee requests his employer by notice in writing to pay wages by payment into employee's bank account; by postal order; money order; cheque; any document issued by customer of bank which, though not a bill of exchange, is intended to enable a person to obtain payment from that bank of sum mentioned in document, and in any of these cases employer agrees, payment is good. (Payment of Wages Act [Northern Ireland] 1970 [1970, c. 12, §1]). Deductions from wages are also restricted by Wages (N.I.) Order 1988 (1988, S.I. No. 796 [N.I.7] Arts. 3–6) and payment of wages in public houses is prohibited (55 Geo. 3, c. 19 [U.K.], §§64-5). Preferential payment of wages is provided for in bankruptcy (c. 17 [N.I.]) and in winding up of companies (1960, c. 22, §287). Computation of wages of piece-workers is dealt with by Factories Act (N.I.) 1965, c. 20, §135.

In accordance with Fair Wages Resolution passed by Northern Ireland House of Commons on Feb. 11, 1947, Government contractors are required to pay rates of wages and observe conditions of employment not less favourable than those fixed for the district by voluntary negotiating machinery or arbitration. Similar conditions are usually attached to local authority contracts.

Wages councils, each comprising such number of persons appointed to represent employers and workers respectively as Department may specify, established by Wages (N.I.) Order 1988 (1988, S.I. No. 796 [N.I.7]). Wages councils empowered to makes wages orders prescribing minimum renumeration application to all time and piece workers within scope of wages council. (1988, S.I. No. 796 [N.I.7] Art. 15, Sch. 3).

Child Labour.—A person not over compulsory school age is deemed to be a child for purpose of enactments relating to employment of children and young persons. (Education Act [N.I.] 1947, c. 3, §54). Local authorities have power to restrict or prohibit employment of children (1947, c. 3, §§55, 56). Children and Young Persons Act (N.I.), 1968 c. 34, imposes restrictions on times child may he employed (§37[1]) on nature of employment (§37[2]) and children are prohibited from employment in any factory.

Employment of children, who are defined in Factories Act (N.I.) 1965, c. 20, §84(2) as persons who have not attained upper limit of compulsory school age within meaning of Education Act (N.I.) 1947, c. 3, §116, and young persons, defined as persons who have ceased to be children but have not attained age of 18 (1965 [N.I.] c. 20, §176), is governed generally by Factories Act (N.I.) 1965 (1965, c. 20, §§84-5) and Employment (Miscellaneous Provisions) (N.I.) Order 1990 (1990, S.I. No. 246 [N.I.2]).

Female Labour.—Woman or girl must not be employed within four weeks after child birth (Factories Act [N.I.] 1965, c. 20, §85) and as to their employment in factories generally see Factories Act (N.I.) 1965 (1965, c. 20, §§85 and 115-117 am'd 1990, S.I. No. 246 [N.I.2]). By Equal Pay Act (N.I.) 1970 (1970, c. 32) as am'd by Equal Pay (Amendment) Regulations (N.I.) 1984 (1984, S.R. No. 16) provisions are made to prevent discrimination, as regards terms and conditions of employment, between men and women employed on like work or work of equal pay.

Labour Unions.—Trade union is temporary or permanent organisation which consists mainly of workers and whose principal purposes include regulation of relations between such workers and employers or employers' associations or, which consists mainly of affiliated constituent group of such organisations or their representatives. (Industrial Relations [N.I.] Order 1976, S.I. No. 1043 [N.I.16] Art. 2). Industrial Relations (N.I.) Order 1993 (S.I. 1993/2688 [N.I. 11]) is made only for purposes to which §54(1) of Trade Union Reform and Employment Rights Act 1993 applies, amends law relating to employment rights and constitution and jurisdiction of industrial tribunals and abolishes right to statutory minimum remuneration.

Trade Union Acts (N.I.) 1871 to 1958 (1958, c. 30, §2[ii]) do not affect: (1) Any agreement between the partners as to their own business; (2) any agreement between an employer and those employed by him as to such employment; (3) any agreement in consideration of sale of goodwill of a business or of instruction in any profession, trade or handicraft. (Trade Union Act [1871], 34-5 Vict., c. 31 [U.K.], §23).

Purposes of any trade union are not, by reason merely that they are in restraint of trade deemed unlawful, so as to render any member liable to criminal prosecution for conspiracy or otherwise or so as to render void or voidable any agreement or trust (34-5 Vict., c. 31 [U.K.] §§2, 3) but nothing in Trade Union Act 1871 enables any court to entertain legal proceedings instituted with object of directly enforcing or recovering damages for breach of any agreement: (i) Between members of a trade union as such concerning condition on which any members for the time being of such trade union shall or shall not sell their goods, transact business, employ or be employed; (ii) for payment by any person of a subscription or penalty to a trade union; (iii) for application of the funds of a trade union, (a) to provide benefits to members, (b) to furnish contributions to any employer or workman not a member of such trade union in consideration of such employer or workmen acting in conformity with the rules or resolutions of the trade union, (c) to discharge any fine imposed by sentence of a court of justice; (iv) between one trade union and another; (v) for the breach of any bond to secure the performance of any of the above mentioned agreements. But such agreements are not thereby rendered unlawful (34-5 Vict., c. 31 [U.K.], §4) and if a union's purposes are not in restraint of trade or otherwise unlawful proceedings for direct enforcement of all its agreements can be taken in same way as they could have been taken before Trade Union Act 1871 ([1909] 1 K.B. 901.). There is no obstacle to proceedings for a declaration of rights or an injunction to restrain breach of an agreement, even though such proceedings may have the indirect result of keeping the agreement in force. (1905 A.C. 256). A member can recover damages for wrongful expulsion against some trade unions though some doubt remains whether such damages are recoverable from an unregistered union. ([1956] A.C. 104).

Trade union immunity from tort actions in respect of inducing breach of contract, interference with performance of contract, and intimidation and conspiracy provided action was in contemplation or furtherance of trade dispute is provided. (1976, S.I. No. 1043 [N.I.16] Art. 64). Industrial Relations (N.I.) Order 1987 (1987, S.I. No. 936 [N.I.9]) make provision for civil proceedings by and against trade unions (Art. 16) and abolishes certain trade union immunities (Art. 17). Where trade union found liable in proceedings in tort, except negligence, nuisance or breach of duty which has resulted in personal injury or breach of duty relating to use of property, upper limit of amount of damages which may be awarded is specified. (1987, S.I. No. 936 [N.I.9] Art. 18). Limit on damages dependent upon number of union members. (1987, S.I. No. 936 [N.I.9] Art. 19).

Friendly Societies Acts (N.I.) 1896 to 1958 (1958, c. 19, §2) except as regards insurance of young children, Industrial and Provident Societies Acts (N.I.) 1893 to 1955 (1955, c. 18, §12[ii]), and Companies Acts (N.I.) 1960 (c. 22) do not apply to a Trade Union (34-5 Vict., c. 31 [U.K.] §5; 39-40 Vict., c. 22 [U.K.] §2; 1948, c. 22, §§6-7; 1960, c. 22, §403[ix]) and registration of a trade union under any of those Acts is void.

Trade Union Acts contain no provision for settlement of disputes except those relating to an alleged breach of political funds rules. (Trade Union Act 1913, 2 & 3 Geo. 5, c. 30 [U.K.] §5[i] sch. 1).

Labour Disputes.—Department under statutory powers derived from Conciliation Act (59-60 Vict., c. 30 [U.K.] §§1-6) and Industrial Courts Act 1919 (9-10 Geo. 5, c. 69 [U.K.]) affords assistance for settlement of differences or disputes so as to avoid stoppages at work by conciliation, arbitration and formal enquiry. Both Acts provide for arbitration by consent of parties and Department may refer disputes to conciliation either by single arbitrators or board of arbitrators but awards are not legally binding on parties. Department is also empowered to appoint court of enquiry or committee of investigation into a dispute. Report of court of enquiry has to be laid before Parliament.

Machinery for avoidance of strikes and lockouts is provided by Emergency Powers Act (N.I.) 1926 (16-7 Geo. 5, c. 8) under which strikes and peaceful persuasion are not offensive (§2[i]). Immunity conferred in respect of picketing in restricted circumstances. (Industrial Relations [N.I.] Order 1982, S.I. No. 528 [N.I.8] Art. 18).

Industrial Relations (N.I.) Order 1976 (S.I. No. 1043 [N.I. 16]) establishes labour relations agency which has function of promoting improvement of industrial relations in field of collective bargaining. Agency exercises advisory function in respect of trade disputes, recognition of trade unions, and industrial relations training. Part 3 confers rights on employees in relation to "unfair dismissal" where contract of employment is terminated or not renewed in which case employer may be asked to show reason for dismissal. Complaints are presented by employees to industrial tribunal which has powers to provide for reinstatement and/or compensation.

Industrial Relations (No. 2) (N.I.) Order 1976 (S.I. No. 2147 [N.I. 28]).—This Order confers rights on certain employees in relation to guarantee payments (Art. 3), suspension on medical grounds (Art. 9), dismissal on grounds of pregnancy (Art. 14) and maternity in general (Arts. 14-31), trade union membership and activities (Art. 33), time off work (Arts. 37-42), insolvency of employer (Art. 43 am'd 1976, S.I. No. 1043 [N.I.16] Arts. 16-17), itemised pay statements (Art. 44) and terms and conditions of employment (Art. 48). Remedies are provided for breaches of these rights. Order also provides for disclosure to trade union representatives by employers of certain information for purposes of collective bargaining (Art. 50) and requires Labour Relations Agency to issue Codes of Practice in relation to conduct of industrial relations (Art. 55).

Industrial Relations (N.I.) Order, 1982 (S.I. No. 528 [N.I. 8]) introduces miscellaneous amendments to law relating to trade unions and employees' rights. Provision is made for secret ballots among trade union members. (Arts. 3-5). Order enables industrial tribunals to award compensation to persons unreasonably prevented from joining, or unreasonably expelled from, trade union (Arts. 6-7); amends law relating to "closed shops" (Art. 8); amends standard of determination of fairness in claims for compensation made by dismissed employees. Decisions of industrial tribunals must now be based on principles of equity and substantial merits of case. (Art. 9). Arts. 18 and 19 introduce restrictions on immunity of trade unions from legal liability where unions organize "secondary picketing" of businesses not directly involved in trade dispute.

Unemployment Compensation.—Unemployment benefit is payable under Social Security (N.I.) Act 1975 (1975, c. 15 as am'd). National insurance benefits system makes provision for unemployment, sickness or disability, widowhood, retirement and industrial injury. Most of these benefits depend on claimant satisfying contribution conditions.

There are four classes of contributions: Class 1—paid by all employees earning over Lower Earnings Limit which gives access to all contributory benefits; Class 2—paid by self-employed persons which gives access to all contributory benefits except unemployment benefit; Class 3—may be paid voluntarily by persons not otherwise liable wishing to secure widows' and retirement pensions; Class 4—additional contributions paid by all self-employed persons where profit and gains exceed specified limit as amended by §§3, 4 Social Security (Contributions) Act 1994.

Unemployment benefit payable to insured persons under pensionable age, 65 for men, 65 for women, and subject to special conditions to those in that class who have reached but are not more than five years over pensionable age and have not retired from work. (1975, c. 15, §14 am'd Social Security [N.I.] Order 1989, S.I. No. 1324 [N.I.13] Sch.1). Claimants must satisfy contribution conditions, be capable of work and be deemed available for employment (1975, c. 15, §§14 and 17) and must be actively seeking employment (1975, c. 15, §17 am'd 1989, S.I. No. 1342 [N.I.13] Art. 12 and Social Security [Unemployment Sickness and Invalidity Benefit] [Amendment No. 2] Regulations [N.I.] 1989, S.R. No. 364 Reg. 12[b]). Benefit is not payable for first three days (1975, c. 15, §14) and lasts for one year. To requalify person must be in employment for

LABOUR RELATIONS . . . *continued*
13 weeks out of 26 weeks preceding claim. (1975, c. 15, §18 am'd 1989, S.I. 1342 [N.I.13]).

Person who has lost employment may be disqualified from receiving employment benefit (a) for as long as stoppage continues, if employment lost through stoppage of work due to trade dispute at his place of employment unless he proves he is not participating in or financing or directly interested in trade dispute (1975, c. 15, §19[i]), or, (b) for period up to 26 weeks if employment lost as result of misconduct or he left it without good cause, or (c) employment or training refused without good cause when offered (1975, c. 15, §20 am'd 1989, S.I. 1342 [N.I.13] Art. 14 and 1989, S.R. No. 364 Reg. 7[b]), or (d) person failed to take reasonable steps to get suitable job when told about one (1975, c. 15, §20).

Fair Employment (N.I.) Act 1976 makes discrimination on grounds of religion or politics unlawful in field of employment, training and conferment of qualifications. Positive duty is conferred on employers to provide equality of opportunity. Fair Employment Commission ("F.E.C.") established by Fair Employment (N.I.) Act 1989. (1989 c. 32). Duty to identify and keep under review patterns and trends of employment in Northern Ireland. Power to carry out investigations and make directions to employers and require undertakings which may be appealed to Fair Employment Tribunal. Decision of Fair Employment Tribunal may be referred to Court of Appeal. Employer employing more than ten employees required to register with F.E.C. and complete monitoring return containing such information about employees of employer as may be prescribed by F.E.C.

Sex Discrimination (N.I.) Order 1976 (1976, S.I. No. 1042 [N.I.15] am'd Sex Discrimination [N.I.] Order 1988, S.I. No. 1303 [N.I.13]) makes discrimination in employment on grounds of sex or marriage unlawful. Order establishes Equal Opportunities Commission whose function is to work towards elimination of discrimination and promotion of equality of opportunity between men and women.

Employment Subsidies Act 1978 (1978, c. 6 [U.K.]) authorizes Department of Manpower Services, if in its opinion unemployment remains high in Northern Ireland, to set up schemes (with approval of Department of Finance) for making payments to employers to enable them to retain workers or take on extra workers, and generally to maintain or enlarge their labour force.

Health and Safety at Work (N.I.) Order, 1978 (1978, S.I. No. 1039 [N.I. 9]) provides legislative framework to promote, stimulate and encourage high standards of health and safety in places of employment. General purposes of Order are to: (1) Secure health, safety and welfare of persons at work; (2) protect persons other than persons at work against risks to health or safety arising out of or in connection with activities of persons at work; (3) control keeping and use of explosive, highly flammable or otherwise dangerous substances. Order includes duty on employee to take care for health and safety of himself and other persons at work (Art. 8) and duty on all persons not to interfere, intentionally or recklessly, with anything provided in interests of health and safety (Art. 9).

LAW REPORTS, CODES, ETC.:

See topics Reports; Statutes.

LEGISLATURE:

See topic Constitution and Government.

LICENCES:

Licenses are required by the following: Bookmakers and bookmaking offices (1953, c. 24, §§9-14; 1957, c. 19, §§2-4, 6-14; 1959, c. 26, §1); moneylenders (1953, c. 24, §38); pawnbrokers (1954, c. 30, §5); general dealers (3 Edw. 7, c. 44 [U.K.], §§1, 2[i], 12; 1954, c. 4, §1); and for horsebreeding (16-7 Geo. 5, c. 30 [N.I.], §§2, 3, 12) theatres and music halls (17-8 Geo. 5, c. 2 [N.I.] §12[i] sch. 2), cinematograph exhibitions (1959, c. 20, §§3, 6, 8 and sch.), dog racing (1946, c. 22, §§2, 5), fishing vessels (14 & 15 Geo. 6, c. 30 [U.K.] §8), air transport (8-9 Eliz. 2, c. 38 [U.K.] §§1-3), and to deal in game (18 & 19 Geo. 5, c. 25 [N.I.] §4[i]), sell eggs (1957, c. 27, §§1, 2, 5), produce and sell milk and milk products (1958, c. 31, §1), manufacture ice cream (1958, c. 27, §20), produce and keep petroleum or natural gas (18 & 19 Geo. 5, c. 52 [U.K.] §§1, 5; 8 & 9 Geo. 5, c. 52 [U.K.] §2; 20 Geo. 5, c. 13 [N.I.] §§1, 23), produce dangerous drugs (14-5 Geo. 6, c. 48 [U.K.] §2), manufacture new explosives (38 & 39 Vict., c. 17 [U.K.], §6), operate flax scutch mills (1954, c. 14, §§12, 14), sale of intoxicating liquor (1971, 19 & 20 Eliz. 2, c. 13, am'd by 1977 No. 1277 [N.I. 13.] and S.I. 1987/1277 [N.I.13]).

Excise licences are required by Customs and Excise Act 1952 (15 & 16 Geo. 5 and 1 Eliz. 2, c. 44 [U.K.]) for brewing of beer (§125, sch. 2), to manufacture sugar, glucose, saccharine, invert sugar (§§210-11), matches (§220), mechanical lighters (§221; 1 & 2 Eliz. 2, c. 34 [U.K.] §§3[iv], 35[vii] sch. 3, pt. 1; 8 & 9 Eliz. 2, c. 44 [U.K.] §§7, 79, sch. 8, pt. 3); to manufacture or deal in tobacco and snuff (§175, sch.5), to grow or cure tobacco in U.K. (§178) and by makers of vinegar (§225), dealers in manufacture of and retailers of sweets (§139), and by persons keeping or using stills or retorts (§226), makers, mixers of and retailers of methylated spirits (§116-7), dealers in beer, wine and spirits (§146; 4 & 5 Eliz. 2, c. 54 [U.K.] §2[iii]; 17 & 18 Geo. 5, c. 21 [N.I.] §5; 18 & 19 Geo. 5, c. 9 [N.I.] §1; 1957, c. 9, §12[ii]), and by distillers, rectifiers and compounders of spirits (§93-9).

LIENS:

Common law rules apply.

LIMITATION OF ACTIONS:

Governed by Limitation (N.I.) Order 1989 (1989 No. 1339 [N.I. 11]) which consolidates Limitation Acts (N.I.) 1958-1987 and provides that any proceedings, except proceedings by Crown (1) for recovery of any tax or duty or interest thereon or any fine or penalty due in connection with any tax or duty, or (2) for forfeiture under any statutory provision, or (3) in respect of forfeiture of any ship or interest in ships; must be brought within following periods after accrual of cause of action: This list contains more common types of proceedings only: there are others to which special time limits apply.

Sixty Years.—Action by Crown to recover foreshore.

Thirty Years.—Actions brought by Crown to recover any land or claiming sale of lands which is subject to mortgage or charge.

Twelve Years.—(a) Action upon instrument under seal other than to recover (1) arrears of rent charged or convention rent, or (2) any principal sum of money secured mortgage or other charge, or (3) arrears of interest in respect of any sum or mortgage secured by mortgage or other charge, or (4) arrears of annuity charged on personal property; (b) action to enforce award where arbitration agreement is under seal; (c) action to recover debt created by Art. 25(2) or Art. 474 of Companies (N.I.) Order 1986; (d) action (other than by Crown) to recover any land; (e) action to recover future interest in land by person entitled to preceding estate or interest; (f) action to redeem land by mortgagee of which he has been in possession for 12 years; (g) action to recover any principal sum of money secured by mortgage or charge on land or personal property (other than ship); (h) action in respect of right in nature of lien for money's worth in or over land for limited period not exceeding life; (i) action in respect of any claim to personal estate of deceased person or to any share or interest in such estate whether brought under will or intestacy.

Six Years.—(a) Action founded on simple contract; (b) action founded on quasi-contract; (c) action to enforce award where arbitration agreement is not under seal; (d) action to recover any sum recoverable by virtue of any statutory provision, other than (1) debt created by Art. 25(2) or Art. 474 of Companies (N.I.) Order 1986, or (2) amount recoverable under §1 of Civil Liability (Contribution) Act 1978; (e) action founded on tort other than (1) action claiming damages for libel or slander, (2) action claiming damages for negligence, nuisance or breach of duty where damages consist of or include damages in respect of personal injuries; (f) action upon judgement; (g) action in respect of further conversion of chattel after expiration of six years from accrual of action in respect of original conversion; (h) action brought or distress made to recover arrears of rent charge or damages in respect thereof; (i) action to recover arrears of annuity charged on personal property or damages in respect thereof; (j) action to recover arrears of conventional rent or damages in respect thereof; (k) action to recover arrears of interest payable in respect of any principal sum of money secured by mortgage or charge on land or personal property or to recover damages in respect of such arrears; (l) action against trustee to recover money or other property or in respect of any breach of trust but no period of limitation shall apply to action against trustees where (l) claim is founded on any fraud or fraudulent breach of trust to which trustee was party or privy or (2) claim is to recover trust property or proceeds thereof still retained by trustee or previously received by trustee and converted to his own use.

Normal limitation period for contract of loan is six years, but where contract of loan is made which provides no fixing date for repayment and loan is not expressly made repayable on demand, limitation period will only start to run when written demand for payment is made to borrower by or on behalf of creditor.

Three Years.—All actions for damages for negligence, nuisance or breach of duty where such damages consist of or include damages for personal injuries. Such actions cannot be brought after expiration of three years from: (a) Date on which cause of action accrued; or (b) date of knowledge (if later) of person injured of following facts: (1) that injury in question is significant; (2) that injury is attributable to act or omission giving rise to cause of action; (3) identity of defendant and (4) if it is alleged that act or omission was that of person other than defendant, identity of that person and additional facts supporting bringing of action against defendant. If injured person dies before expiration of three year period, cause of action survives for benefit of estate of deceased under Law Reform (Miscellaneous Provisions) Act (N.I.) 1937 (1937, c. 9 [N.I.]) for three years from: (a) date of death; or (b) date of personal representative's knowledge of facts listed above.

Actions under Fatal Accidents (N.I) Order 1977 (1977 [N.I.] 18) cannot be brought after expiration of three years from: (a) Date of death; or (b) date of knowledge of person for whose benefit action is brought.

Actions for damages in respect of defective products by virtue of any provisions of Part II of Consumer Protection (N.I.) Order 1987 (1987 [N.I.] 20) may not be brought after expiration of ten years from relevant time, other than action in which damages claimed consist of or include damages in respect of personal injuries to plaintiff or any other person or loss of or damage to any property, which may not be brought after expiration of three years from whichever is later, namely (a) date on which cause of action accrued; or (b) date of knowledge of injured person, or in case of loss or damage to property, date of knowledge of plaintiff or (if earlier) any person in whom cause of action was previously vested.

Judicial Discretion.—Where in cases involving actions for damages for negligence, nuisance or breach of duty in respect of personal injuries to any person or in cases involving action under Fatal Accidents (N.I.) Order 1977 or Consumer Protection (N.I.) Order 1987, it appears to Court that it would be equitable to allow action to proceed having regard to effect on both parties, Court may direct that above provisions are not to apply. (Art. 50).

Two Years.—Action to recover contribution by virtue of §1 of Civil Liability (Contribution) Act 1978 (1978 c. 47 [U.K.]) may be brought within period of two years from date of original settlement or Court judgment in respect of which contribution or indemnity is sought. (Art. 13).

Persons under Disability.—(I.e.: infant or person of unsound mind) where right of action accrues to person under disability, action may be brought at any time before expiration of six years from date when person ceased to be under disability or died, whichever event first occurred, except for (a) actions for personal injuries; or (b) action for libel or slander, where relevant period is three years.

Interruption of Statutory Period.—On acknowledgment in writing signed by the person making the acknowledgement there is a fresh accrual of the right of action in the case of actions (a) by any person (other than a mortgagee) to recover land; (b) by mortgagee to recover land; (c) by incumbrancer claiming sale of land; (d) in respect of personal right in or over land such as a right of support; (e) to recover debt; (f) claiming personal estate of deceased person.

LIMITATION OF ACTIONS . . . *continued*

An acknowledgment of title to any land by any person in possession thereof binds all other persons in possession during the ensuing period of limitation. On part payment there is a fresh accrual of right of action in the case of an action (a) by mortgagee to recover land; (b) by incumbrancer claiming sale of land; (c) to recover debt; (d) claiming personal estate of deceased person.

Fraud and Mistake.—Where (a) an action is based on the fraud of the defendant or his agent or any person through whom he claims or his agent; or (b) the right of action is concealed by the fraud of any person the period of limitation does not begin to run until the plaintiff has discovered the fraud or could with reasonable diligence have discovered it except that no action can be brought to recover or enforce any charge against or set aside any transaction affecting any property which has been purchased for valuable consideration by a person who is not a party to the fraud and did not at the time of the purchase know or have reason to believe that any fraud had been committed.

Where an action is for relief from the consequence of mistake the period of limitation does not begin to run until the plaintiff has discovered the mistake or could, with reasonable diligence, have discovered it.

Pleadings.—The statute of limitations must be pleaded in order to take advantage thereof.

MARRIAGE:

The word "marriage" as understood by Northern Ireland courts means voluntary union for life of one man and one woman to the exclusion of all others, as understood in Christian countries.

Polygamous Marriages.—Apart from divorce jurisdiction, Northern Ireland courts will usually treat polygamous marriages, valid according to law of the domicile, as binding in matters of property, legitimacy and succession.

Evidence of Ceremony.—Where usual evidence of a valid marriage is not forthcoming or is not readily available, in civil suits, if there is evidence of a ceremony of marriage having been gone through followed by cohabitation of parties, everything necessary for validity of marriage will be presumed in the absence of decisive evidence to the contrary, even though it may be necessary to presume grant of a special license.

Requisites for Valid Marriage.—(1) Age: Each party must have attained age of 16 years. (2) Mental Capacity: Each party must have mental capacity to marry. Lunatics cannot marry, nor can persons of unsound mind (not so found by inquisition or certified as a lunatic) unless he understands nature of contract or marries during a lucid interval. (3) Prohibited Degrees: Each party should be outside prohibited degrees of affinity and consanguinity which are those annexed to Book of Common Prayer subject only to exceptions contained in Family Law (Miscellaneous Provisions) (N.I.) Order 1984 as amended by Family Law (N.I.) Order 1993 (1993 No. 1576 [N.I. 6]). (4) Subsisting Marriage: Neither of the parties may be married to someone else if valid marriage is still subsisting (see also topic Divorce). (5) Free Consent and Understanding: Each party should consent to intermarry with a proper understanding of the contract. (6) Each party must be competent to perform marital intercourse (see also topic Divorce). (7) Ceremonies of marriage must be performed in due form: Marriages must be celebrated either (a) according to rites of Roman Catholic Church, (b) according to usages of Presbyterians, (c) according to usages of Quakers and Jews, (d) under Registrar's Certificate or licence, (e) special licence.

British Marriages Abroad.—Marriages abroad by British subjects may be validly contracted in three ways (1) under common law i.e., solemnised before a Priest either of the Church of England or the Church of Rome, (2) by lex loci contractus, (3) under Foreign Marriage Act 1892 §1, which provides that all marriages between parties of whom at least one is a British Subject, solemnised in manner provided in Act, in any foreign country by or before a marriage officer who include a British Ambassador, or Minister accredited to country in question, or a prescribed officer to solemnise marriages in embassy or legation, British Consuls, a governor, high commissioner, resident or other consular officers. Marriages may be solemnised abroad in accordance with the Act during hours of 8 A.M. and 6 P.M. Marriage (Extension of Hours) Act 1934.

Marriages solemnised by a Chaplain serving with any part of H.M. Forces in any foreign territory are, subject to certain provisos, valid.

There are no restrictions on marriage with foreigners.

Annulment.—See topic Divorce.

MINES AND MINERALS:

Property in all minerals existing in natural condition and in all mines for working of such minerals is vested in Department of Economic Development (Mineral Development Act [N.I.] 1969 [1969 c. 35], §1). Mines or minerals already vested in that Department (§3), Crown (§4), or which are property of any religious denomination or educational institution (§5) or which were being lawfully worked or developed by any person on Dec. 18, 1969 are excepted (§7). Owner of estate in possession in mines and minerals excepted by §7 must apply to Department for registration of that estate. (§8). Compensation is paid, subject to conditions, by Department for mines and minerals so vested under §1.

N.I. services in connection with coal and metalliferous mines and quarries are administered by Department of Economic Development, which has power to hold inquiries which it thinks necessary to ensure compliance with statutory obligations (Mining Industry Act, 1920 [10-11 Geo. 5, c. 50]). Mines of coal, stratified ironstone, shale and fireclay are governed by Mines Act (N.I.) 1969 (1969, c. 6); Coal Mines Regulation (Amendment) Act, 1917 (7 & 8 Geo. 5, c. 8); Coal Mines Act, 1919 (9 & 10 Geo. 5, c. 48); Mining Industry Act, 1920 (10 & 11 Geo. 5, c. 50); Coal Mines Act, 1931 (21 & 22 Geo. 5, c. 27); Under Mines (Working Facilities, etc.) Act (Northern Ireland) 1926 (16-17 Geo. 5, c. 9) [N.I.]).

Operation of Mines.—Every mine must be under management of one manager who is responsible for control and direction of that mine, and every owner or agent of any mine must appoint such manager to exercise personal daily supervision. Without approval of Department no person may act as manager for more than one mine. Every manager must be 26 years of age and holder of first class Certificate of Competency as awarded by Board for Mining Examinations. There must be in every mine at least two shafts or outlets with which every seam which is being worked shall have communication. Where two or more parts of mine are worked separately, owner or manager may give notice in writing to inspector of division (see subhead Inspection of Mines, infra) and thereupon each part will be treated as separate mine. Notice of any new shaft or seam must be given to Department of Economic Development in writing two weeks before shaft or seam is opened. (1959, c. 17, §§20, 21).

Safeguarding Employees.—Provisions as to safety regarding ventilation; safety lamps; fencing and securing shafts and outlets; travelling and haulage roads and refuge holds; securing and propping of roofs and sides; signalling and telephones; fencing of dangerous machinery and boilers; electricity; explosives and dust are contained in §§22-97 of Mines Act (N.I.) 1969 (1969, c. 6). Provision of suitable sanitary conveniences, washing accommodation, and sprays when silicious rock is being drilled is also required. On application of Attorney General, High Court may by injunction prohibit working of any mine in which there is breach of safety provisions of any of relevant Acts.

Inspection of Mines.—Inspection is governed by Mines Act (N.I.) 1969 (1969, c. 6) and inspectors are appointed by Department of Economic Development. They have power to make any inspection, examination or inquiry as may be necessary to ensure that regulating Acts are complied with, and they are obliged to make periodic reports to Department of Economic Development as to condition of mines. Owners of mines, their servants or agents are under duty to furnish means required by inspector for entry, inspection, examination and exercise of any of his powers. Plan of mine and its ventilation must be kept and produced for inspector if required. Notice must be given to appropriate inspector of any accident in mine which results in loss of life. Workmen employed in mine may, at their own cost, appoint two of their number, or any two persons who have had more than five years mining experience, to inspect mine.

Prospecting Licence.—Where mines and minerals are vested in Department, that Department may, subject to any rights conferred upon any other person by any lease or licence granted by Department, either enter on land and do whatever is reasonably necessary for purposes of searching for those mines or grant to any person licence to do what Department is authorized to do. (1969, c. 35, §11). Before doing so Department must advertise in Belfast Gazette and in at least one newspaper circulating in locality where land is situated. (§11).

Abandoned Mines.—Notice of any abandoned shaft or seam must be given to Department of Commerce, and owner of any abandoned mine must ensure that top or entrance of every shaft or outlet is surrounded by structure of permanent character which will prevent accidents. Any unfenced abandoned shaft may be deemed nuisance under Public Health Acts.

Taxes.—Income from mines is taxed under Schedule D Case 1. Reliefs for certain capital expenditure, treatment of demolition costs, etc., see Finance Acts (15-16 Geo. 6 & 1 Eliz. 2, c. 10, §305; 2-3 Eliz. 2, c. 44, §21).

MONOPOLIES AND RESTRAINT OF TRADE:

Law on this subject is practically same as in rest of U.K. Common-law rules apply subject to statutory provisions contained in Acts of U.K. Parliament which extend to Northern Ireland. (See England Law Digest, topic Monopolies and Restraint of Trade. See also European Union Law Digest, topic Monopolies and Restraint of Trade.)

The common-law rule is that all interference with individual liberty of action in trading and all restraints in themselves, if there is nothing more, are contrary to public policy and therefore void, unless justified by the special circumstances of a particular case. It is sufficient justification if the restraint is reasonable in the interests of the parties concerned and in the interest of the public. ([1894] A.C. 535, 565).

At Common Law (1) a combination of two or more persons wilfully to injure a man in his trade is unlawful and if it results in damage to him is actionable; (2) if the sole purpose of the combination is not to injure another but to forward or defend the trade and those who enter into it then no wrong is committed and no action will lie although damage to another ensues. ([1925] A.C. 700, 711, 712; [1942] A.C. 435). However, the purposes of any trade union are not by reason merely that they are in restraint of trade unlawful so as to render void or voidable any agreement or trust and a court cannot entertain any legal proceedings instituted with the object of directly enforcing or recovering damages for the breach of any agreement between members of a trade union as such, concerning the conditions on which any members for the time being of such trade unions shall or shall not sell their goods, transact business, employ or be employed or any agreement made between one trade union and another (Trade Union Act 1871, 34 & 35 Vict., c. 31 §§3, 4[1], [4]).

The Monopolies and Mergers Commission is established by Fair Trading Act 1973 (1973, c. 41 [U.K.]) and is reconstitution of former Monopolies Commission. Functions are broadly those of Monopolies Commission, but with certain significant changes and new functions. Main functions (section numbers being references to Fair Trading Act 1973) are: (a) To investigate and report on monopoly references made by Director General of Fair Trading ("Director") or Secretary of State (§54); (b) to investigate and report on newspaper merger references made by Secretary of State (§61); (c) to investigate and report on other merger references made by Secretary of State (§72); (d) to investigate and report on effect on public interest of specified practices referred to it by Secretary of State (§78); (e) to investigate and report on restrictive labour practices referred to it by Secretary of State (§79). For purposes of Act, monopoly situation exists in relation to supply of goods of any description if at least one quarter of all goods of that description supplied in U.K. are supplied by or to one and same person or one and same group of interconnected bodies corporate; or where two or more persons together supply at least one quarter of goods of that description and thus prevent, restrict or distort competition; or where one or more agreements are in operation, result or collective result of which is that goods of that description are not supplied in U.K. at all. (§6). Act also applies to supply of services. (§7).

Restrictive Trade Practices Act 1976 and 1977 (1976, c. 34 [U.K.] and 1977, c. 19 [U.K.]) together with Restrictive Practices Court Act 1976 (1976, c. 33 [U.K.]) consolidate and re-enact Restrictive Trade Practices Acts 1956-1973 using simpler terminology. (Where any section number is hereinafter referred to, it shall be reference to 1976, c. 34 [U.K.] unless otherwise described.)

See Topical Index in front part of this volume.

MONOPOLIES AND RESTRAINT OF TRADE . . . *continued*

Director General of Fair Trading (position established by 1973, c. 41 [U.K.]) has duty of preparing, compiling and maintaining register of agreements which are subject to registration under 1976 Act, and is given wide powers of obtaining information with regard to restrictive trading agreements. (§1). Part One of Act generally provides for registration and investigation.

Act applies to agreements (whenever made between two or more persons carrying on business within U.K. in production or supply of goods, or in application to goods of any process of manufacture, whether with or without other parties) being agreements under which restrictions are accepted by two or more parties in respect of any of following matters: (a) Prices to be charged, quoted or paid for goods supplied, offered or acquired, or for application of any process of manufacture to goods; (b) prices to be recommended or suggested as prices to be charged or quoted in respect of resale of goods supplied; (c) terms or conditions on, or subject to which, goods are to be supplied or acquired; (d) quantities or descriptions of goods to be produced, supplied or acquired; (e) processes of manufacture to be applied to any goods, or quantities or descriptions of goods to which any such process is to be applied; or (f) persons or classes of persons to, for, or from whom, or areas or places in or from which goods are to be supplied or acquired, or any such process applied. (§6). All such agreements must be registered with Director. (§1). Restrictions relating to following matters are disregarded: (1) Certain restrictions or information provisions relating to coal or steel (§9[1]); (2) any terms relating exclusively to goods supplied or processed under agreement for supply of goods or for processing (§9[3]); (3) terms by which parties agree to comply with standards approved by British Standards Institution, or standards prescribed or adopted by any trade association or other body approved by Secretary of State (§9[5]); (4) licences or assignments of patents or registered designs provided that only restrictions excepted relate to invention or articles made by use of it or articles to which design is applied (Sch. 3, Para. 5); (5) certain agreements between two persons for exchange of "knowhow" (Sch. 3, Para. 3); (6) certain agreements relating to trademarks (Sch. 3, Para. 4); (7) agreements under which all restrictions (as described in §6[1]) relate exclusively to export of goods and to certain other transactions in relation to goods taking place outside U.K. (Sch. 3, Para. 6).

Trade Associations are defined as a body of persons (whether incorporate or not) which is formed for purpose of furthering trade interests of its members or of persons represented by its members. (§43[1]). Where agreement is by trade association it is treated as though it were made between all persons who were members or represented by members and all these persons are under duty to register agreement. (§8[1]).

The Restrictive Practices Court consists of five judges and up to ten members appointed by the Lord Chancellor by virtue of knowledge of and experience in Industry, commerce and public affairs. (1976, c. 33 [U.K.] §§1-3). Court can sit in divisions anywhere in U.K. and has jurisdiction to declare whether or not any restrictions registered (with limited exception in favour of restrictions relating to transactions outside U.K.) are contrary to public interest. Jurisdiction is exercisable on application of Director whose duty it is to proceed in respect of all registered agreements.

There is a presumption that a restriction accepted in pursuance of a registered agreement is contrary to public interest but it is open to any party to satisfy the court that a particular restriction is not contrary to public interest by proving one or more of the following circumstances: (a) that the restriction is reasonably necessary, having regard to the character of the goods to which it applies, to protect the public against injury (whether to persons or to premises) in connection with the consumption, installation or use of those goods; (b) that the removal of the restriction would deny to the public as purchasers, consumers or users of any goods other specific and substantial benefits or advantages enjoyed or likely to be enjoyed by them as such, whether by virtue of the restriction itself or of any arrangements or operations resulting therefrom; (c) that the restriction is reasonably necessary to counteract measures taken by any one person not party to the agreement with a view to preventing or restricting competition in or in relation to the trade or business in which the persons party thereto are engaged; (d) that the restriction is reasonably necessary to enable the persons party to the agreement to negotiate fair terms for the supply of goods to, or the acquisition of goods from, any one person not party thereto who controls a preponderant part of the trade or business of acquiring or supplying such goods, or for the supply of goods to any person not party to the agreement and not carrying on such a trade or business who, either alone or in combination with any such other person, controls a preponderant part of the market for such goods; (e) that, having regard to the conditions actually obtaining or reasonably foreseen at the time of the application, the removal of the restriction would be likely to have a serious and persistent adverse effect on the general level of unemployment in an area, or in areas taken together, in which a substantial proportion of the trade or industry to which the agreement relates is situated; (f) that, having regard to the conditions actually obtaining or reasonably foreseen at the time of the application, the removal of the restriction would be likely to cause a reduction in the volume or earnings of the export business which is substantial either in relation to the whole export business of the United Kingdom or in relation to the whole business (including export business) of the said trade or industry; (g) that restriction is reasonably required for purposes connected with maintenance of any other restriction accepted by parties, whether under same agreement or under any other agreement between them, being restriction which is found by court not to be contrary to public interest upon grounds other than those specified in this paragraph, or has been so found in previous proceedings before court; or (h) that restriction or information provision does not directly or indirectly restrict or discourage competition to any material degree in any relevant trade or industry and is not likely to do so; and that restriction is not unreasonable having regard to balance between those circumstances and any detriment to public or to persons not parties to agreement (being purchasers, consumers or users of goods produced or sold by such parties or persons engaged or seeking to become engaged in trade or business of selling such goods or of producing or selling similar goods) resulting or likely to result from operation of restriction. (§10).

Where any restrictions are found by the court to be contrary to the public interest the agreements are void in respect of those restrictions and the court upon application of Director may make order restraining any person or party to agreement who carry on business in U.K. from giving effect to or enforcing agreement in respect of those restrictions or from making any other agreement to like effect. (§2). Court may also restrain trade association from making any recommendations.

Competition Act 1980—see England Law Digest, topic Monopolies and Restraint of Trade, subhead Competition Act 1980.

Resale Price Agreements.—It is unlawful for two or more persons carrying on business in the United Kingdom as suppliers of goods to make or carry out an agreement for the enforcement of conditions as to resale prices whereby withholding supplies refusing trade terms or imposing penalties or setting up trade courts and dealers in goods cannot make or carry out any agreement or arrangement by which they impose sanctions on suppliers who do not impose or enforce resale price maintenance conditions. This applies to associations and recommendations by suppliers of or dealers in goods and are treated on the same basis as agreements. Contracts for the sale of goods between two parties containing undertakings by the purchaser in relation to the goods sold and by the vendor in relation to other goods of the same description are exempted (1956, c. 68 [UK] §24) and no criminal proceedings lie in respect of any contravention of section but civil proceedings are available to Crown for injunction or other appropriate relief and also to individuals.

Nothing in the act interferes with the right of an individual supplier to enforce any contractual term as to resale prices against a party to a contract and the right of action of such a supplier is available against any person (though not a party to the sale) who acquires the goods with notice as if he had been a party to the contract. (1956, c. 68 [UK] §25). Condition as to amount of discount which may be allowed on resale of any goods or as to price which may be paid on resale of any goods for other goods taken by way of exchange is treated as condition as to price at which goods may be re-sold. (1956, c. 68 [UK] §26).

MORTGAGES OF PERSONAL PROPERTY:

See topic Chattel Mortgages.

MORTGAGES OF REAL PROPERTY:

A mortgage can be either legal or equitable.

Legal mortgage is one duly executed by deed or memorandum in writing, the legal interest in the lands or chattel passing to the mortgagee or lender.

Equitable mortgage can be effected by merely depositing the title deeds or other evidence of ownership with the mortgagee, no formal transfer document being executed. In this case the legal interest remains with the mortgagor while the equitable interest passes to the mortgagee.

Registration.—Mortgages of land should be registered in the registry of deeds. See topic Records. Mortgages executed by limited companies should be registered in Registry of Companies and Friendly Societies, Belfast—see topic Corporations.

Remedies of the mortgagee are:

(a) Foreclosure and sale, i.e., calling in the security. In this event the subject of the Mortgage must be sold and if a greater amount than the mortgage debt is recovered the mortgagee becomes trustee for the balance to the mortgagor.

(b) The mortgagee may enter into possession of mortgaged lands and take the rents and profits thereof. The accounting required is so strict that it is generally considered best to avoid this remedy where possible.

(c) Appointment of a receiver. The safest method is to apply to the Chancery Division of the Supreme Court or to the County Court if the matter is within the County Court jurisdiction (see topic Courts) to have receiver appointed. Receiver will enter into possession, receive rents and profits and account for them to Court.

Assignment.—Mortgages may be assigned in any of the ways in which they may be created.

Redemption.—The usual method of recording redemption is to endorse a short memorandum of satisfaction on the mortgage instrument. This, of course, should be registered in the registry of deeds if the mortgage was so registered.

MOTOR VEHICLES:

Law relating to motor vehicles and road traffic governed generally by Road Traffic (Northern Ireland) Order, 1981 (1981, S.I. No. 154 [N.I. 1]), Road Traffic Amendment (N.I.) Order 1991, subordinate legislation passed thereunder; and by Finance Act 1991. Any reference to Art. number is reference to 1981 Order.

Department of Environment is empowered to make regulations as to use, construction, equipment and speed of vehicles (Arts. 28; 50-52) and to authorise use on roads of special vehicles, etc. (Art. 29). Department can by Order prohibit and restrict driving of vehicles or classes of vehicles on specified highways (Art. 22) and impose restrictions as to driving over bridges and erection of notices (Art. 29). Road authority has power to make bylaws prohibiting or restricting waiting of vehicles in public roads. (Art. 21).

Vehicle Licence.—Vehicles must be licensed annually for use on public roads except, inter alia, fire engines, ambulances, invalid carriages. Licence duties levied by Department of Environment. Licence must be exhibited on vehicle. Law in Northern Ireland same as law in England.

Identification Marks.—Every new vehicle must be registered with Department of Environment and index mark and registration number of vehicle must be exhibited on flat rectangular plate or flat rectangular surface forming part of vehicle, on front of and on back of vehicle in vertical position. Identification marks must not be obscured. Law in Northern Ireland same as law in England.

Operator's Licence.—Driving licences are issued only after applicant has passed test of competence. (Art. 11). No person under 17 years may drive motor vehicle on public roads (exceptions: motorcycles, invalid carriages, certain other vehicles). (Art. 4). Provisional licence may be issued to any person over age of 17 years to enable him to undergo test of competence for full licence. (Art. 8). Provisional licence holders restricted to 45 miles per hour maximum (Art. 9) and must not drive on motorways. Provisional licence continues for six months unless revoked or surrendered. (Art. 5). Driving licences granted in Great Britain are valid in Northern Ireland. (Art. 17).

Title.—Registration Book containing particulars of the vehicle in respect of which a licence has been issued, is issued to every owner.

Sales.—On a sale or change of ownership of vehicle owner must deliver Registration Book to transferee or other new owner and forthwith notify change of ownership to

MOTOR VEHICLES . . . *continued*
registration authority and transferee must before using vehicle insert his name and address in appropriate part of Registration Book and deliver it to registration authority. On change of address owner must enter particulars of new address in space provided in Registration Book and forthwith deliver Book with such particulars entered in it to Council by whom vehicle is registered who will note change of address.

Liens.—There are no special provisions with respect to liens on motor vehicles.

Operation Prohibited.—Driving without licence (Art. 3) or while disqualified from holding licence (Art. 167) is prohibited. Person cannot obtain licence who is suffering from following diseases and disabilities: epilepsy, certain forms of mental disorders or mental defects, liability to sudden attacks of disability, giddiness or faintness, inability to read at distance of 25 yards in good daylight six figures of white or grey on black background of same size and arrangement as those prescribed for identification mark of motor car.

Size and Weight Limits.—Regulated by Motor Vehicles (Construction and Use) Regulations (N.I.) 1989 (1989, S.R. & O. [N.I.] No. 299).

Equipment Required.—Regulated by Motor Vehicles (Construction and Use) Regulations (N.I.) 1989 (1989, S.R. & O. [N.I.] No. 299).

Lights Required.—Regulated by Road Vehicles Lighting Regulations (N.I.) 1969 (1969, S.R. & O. [N.I.] No. 214) as am'd by 1971, S.R. & O. (N.I.) No. 72.

Inspection.—Goods vehicles and public service vehicles are subject to inspection. (Arts. 57 and 64).

Traffic Regulations.—Operators must comply with traffic signs in Road Traffic (Traffic Signs) Regulations (N.I.) 1966 (1966, S.R. & O. [N.I.] No. 23) as am'd by 1970, S.R. & O. (N.I.) No. 276.

Accidents.—Driver involved in accident must: (a) Stop; (b) give his name and address and name and address of vehicle owner if different, and its identification marks to police on demand, or to any person who on reasonable grounds requires him to do so; and (c) if for any reason he does not give these particulars, or if anyone is injured, report accident to police station or to policeman as soon as possible, giving information listed in (b) and producing certificate of insurance. (Art. 175).

Liability of Owner.—Driver is presumed to be servant or agent of owner. (Art. 207). Common law rules of liability of master for torts of his servants or agents apply.

Guests.—There is no limitation of liability of owner or operator for injury to guests.

Insurance.—Users of motor vehicles must be insured against third party risks or give security. (Art. 90, as am'd by Motor Vehicles [Third Party Risks] Regulations [N.I.] 1994 [No. 46] made under S1 1981 No. 154 [N.I.]).

Foreign Vehicles and Nonresidents Operators.—Motor Vehicles (International Circulation) Act 1952 (15 & 16 Geo. 6 & 1 Eliz. 2, c. 39. [U.K.]) enables Her Majesty's Government to give effect to U. N. Convention on road traffic signed in Geneva on Sept. 19, 1957, to Art. 4 of Agreement regarding status of forces of parties to North Atlantic Treaty signed in London, June 19, 1951 and to further international agreement on road traffic. Attorney General may make provisions in relation to Northern Ireland for any purpose for which provision may be made in relation to Great Britain. (15 & 16 Geo. 6. & 1 Eliz. 2, c. 39 [U.K.] §2). Following Orders still in force: Motor Car (International Circulation) Order 1930 (1930, S.R. & O. No. 968) as am'd by Motor Vehicles (International Circulation) Order 1957 (1957, S.R. & O. No. 1074); Motor Vehicles (International Circulation) Regulations 1957 (1957, S.R. & O. No. 1246).

Actions against Nonresidents.—No special provisions exist with regard to service of process and proceedings on nonresidents but leave of court is required to issue and serve a writ of summons out of the jurisdiction.

Direct Actions.—Third parties are given direct rights against insurers in cases of insolvency of insured (Art. 100), and where insurance policy is voidable through fraud (Art. 98).

NOTARIES PUBLIC:

Their appointment extends during the pleasure of the Crown by whom appointments are made and not for any fixed term. When any document for use in the United States is executed before a notary public the notary's signature should be verified by the American Consul in Belfast.

PARTNERSHIP:

With certain excepted corporations and associations (53-4 Vict. c. 39, §1[2]) partnership is relation which subsists between persons carrying on business in common with a view to profit (Partnership Act 1890, 53-4 Vict. c. 39 [U.K.], §1[1]). It may be general (1890, 53-4 Vict. c. 39) or limited (Limited Partnership Act 1907, 7 Ed.7 c. 24 [U.K.]). Generally, law of partnership is law of contract.

General Partnership.—

Formation.—Contract of partnership requires no particular form. In determining whether partnership does or does not exist regard must be had to following rules: (1) Joint tenancy, tenancy in common, joint property, common property, or part ownership does not of itself create partnership as to anything so held or owned, whether tenants or owners do or do not share any profits made by use thereof; (2) sharing of gross returns does not of itself create a partnership whether persons sharing such returns have or have not a joint or common right or interest in any property from which or from use of which returns are derived; (3) receipt by a person of share of profits of business is prima facie evidence that he is partner in business, but receipt of such a share or of a payment contingent on or varying with profits of business does not of itself make him a partner in business and in particular (a) receipt by person of debt or other liquidated amount by instalments or otherwise out of profits of business does not of itself make him partner or liable as such; (b) contract for remuneration of servant or agent of person engaged in business does not make servant or agent a partner or liable as such; (c) receipt by widow or child of deceased partner of portion of profits by way of annuity does not of itself render that person a partner or liable as such; (d) advance of money by way of loan to person engaged or about to engage in business on a contract with that person that lender shall receive a rate of interest varying with profits, or shall receive share of profits does not of itself make lender a partner or liable as such with person carrying on business provided that contract is in writing and signed by or on behalf of all parties thereto; (e) person receiving by way of annuity or otherwise a portion of profits of business in consideration of sale by him of goodwill of business is not by reason only of such receipt partner in business or liable as such. (53-4 Vict. c. 39, §2).

Name.—Persons who have entered into partnership with one another are called collectively a firm, and name under which their business is carried on is called the firm name. (53-4 Vict. c. 39, §4[1]). See topic Commercial Register.

Rights and Liabilities of Partners Inter Se.—Mutual rights and duties of partners, whether ascertained by agreement or defined by statute, may be varied by consent, express or inferred, of all partners. (53-4 Vict. c. 39, §19). All property, rights, and interests in property originally brought into partnership stock or acquired on account of firm are called partnership property and must be held and applied by partners exclusively for purposes of partnership in accordance with partnership agreement. (§20[1]). Unless contrary intention appears property bought with money belonging to firm is deemed to have been bought on account of firm. (§21). Land or heritable interest therein is treated as personal or moveable estate as between partners or representatives or heirs of deceased partner. (§22). Partnership property cannot be taken in execution for a separate judgment against one partner but court can make order where one partner is judgment debtor charging his share. (§23). All partners are entitled to share equally in capital and profit of business and must contribute equally towards losses of capital or otherwise sustained by firm. (§24[1]). Firm must indemnify every partner in respect of payments made and personal liabilities incurred by him in ordinary conduct of business of firm or in preservation of business or firm property. (§24[2]). Payments and advances beyond agreed subscribed capital made by partner entitled to interest at 5% per annum. (§24[3]). Partner not entitled to interest on subscribed capital before ascertainment of profits. (§24[4]). Every partner must take part in management of partnership business. (§24[5]). No partner entitled to remuneration for acting in partnership business. (§24[6]). No person can be introduced as a partner without consent of all existing partners. (§24[7]). Save changes in nature of partnership all differences connected with partnership business may be decided by a majority of partners. (§24[8]). Partnership books must be kept at place of business of partnership and every partner may inspect and copy them. (§24[9]). Expulsion of one partner not possible by majority unless agreement to that effect. (§25). Where partnership of no agreed fixed term, any partner may determine partnership on giving notice of his intention to all partners at any time. (§26). After expiration of fixed term and in absence of new agreement, continuance of partnership is presumed to be on old terms. (§27). Partners bound to render true accounts and full information to other partners of all matters affecting partnership and must account to firm for private profits made from transactions concerning partnership or its property. (§28-9). If partner competes with firm without consent of other partners, he must pay over all profits so made. (§30). An assignment by partner of his share does not entitle assignee to interfere in management of partnership or to inspect books and assignee merely entitled to assignor's share of profits. (§31).

Rights and Liabilities of Partners as to Third Persons.—Every partner is agent of firm and other partners for purpose of partnership business and acts of partner in doing usual business of firm bind firm and partners. (53-4 Vict. c. 39, §5). Not so if partner no authority to act and fact known to third party. Instrument relating to business of firm executed in firm name or in manner showing intention to bind firm by partner or other authorized person not being a partner, binds firm and all partners. (§6). If any person, not being a partner, suffers loss or injury through wrongful act or omission of partner acting in ordinary course of business, firm is liable to same extent as partner who has acted or omitted to act. (§10). New partner is not liable to creditors of firm for debts incurred prior to his becoming a partner but retiring partner continues to be liable for debts incurred before retirement, although he may be discharged from such liability by agreement. If a person, not being a partner, holds himself out to have authority as a partner, he is liable as a partner to anyone who has given credit to firm on strength of representation. (§14). Admissions or representations made by partner in ordinary course of business is evidence against firm.

Dissolution.—Subject to agreement, partnership is dissolved (a) On expiration of fixed term; (b) on completion of undertaking for which partnership entered; (c) on notice from one partner; (d) on death of partner; (e) on bankruptcy of partner; (f) where partner suffers his share to be charged for separate debt; or (g) when event occurs rendering continuance unlawful. May also be dissolved by court on application of one partner where another partner (a) Becomes of unsound mind; (b) is incapable of performing partnership contract; (c) is guilty of conduct prejudicially affecting business; (d) wilfully or persistently commits breach of partnership agreement. (53-4 Vict. c. 39, §32-5). Can also be dissolved when partnership can only be continued at loss or when court considers dissolution just and equitable. Notice of dissolution may be advertised in Belfast Gazette and thereafter all persons dealing with firm are deemed to have notice of change of partnership constitution. Authority of partners continues after dissolution for purposes of winding up. (§38). Every partner entitled to have partnership property applied in payment of debts and liabilities of firm and to have surplus assets applied in payment of what may be due to partners after deducting what may be due from partners to firm. (§39). Where remaining partners carry on business of firm with its capital and assets without final settlement of accounts between firm and outgoing partner then, subject to partnership agreement, outgoing partner is entitled to such share of profits made since dissolution as court may find attributable to use of his share of partnership assets, or interest at 5% per annum on his share. (§42). If option to purchase share of outgoing partner is given by agreement to and exercised by remaining partner, outgoing partner not entitled to further share of profits. In settling accounts on dissolution, losses including deficiencies of capital must be paid out of profits, capital and then by individual partners in proportion in which they were entitled to share profits. Assets must be applied (a) In paying debts; (b) in paying partners what is due from firm for advances; (c) in paying partners what is due from firm for capital. Residue is divided in proportion in which profits are divisible.

Limited Partnership.—Limited Partnership Act 1907 (7 Ed.7 c. 24) authorizes formation of partnerships in which liability of partner to creditors of firm is limited to fixed amount representing capital invested by him. Limited partnerships rare in Northern Ireland. On becoming a limited partner stated amount contributed to firm and partner not liable for firm's debts beyond that amount. Privilege of limited liability may

PARTNERSHIP . . . *continued*

be lost. (§4[3], §6). Must be one or more general partners liable for all debts and obligations of firm and one or more limited partners. Must be registered or becomes general partnership. Registration effected by delivering to Registrar of Companies, Department of Commerce, form of application to have partnership registered as limited partnership setting out particulars of firm, partners, business and term, if any, partnership entered into, accompanied by statement of contributions made by partners and requisite fees. To give effect to any change in partnership, change must be advertised in Belfast Gazette otherwise change of no effect. Limited partner must not take part in management of partnership business, and can not bind firm. If he does, he is treated as a general partner (7 Ed.7 c. 24, §6).

PATENTS:

Power to legislate with respect to patents or designs is excluded from competence of Northern Ireland Assembly by Northern Ireland Constitution Act 1973. (1973, c. 36 [U.K.]).

Law of patents has been considerably changed by Patents Act, 1977. It establishes new system of domestic law, gives effect to EEC Patents Convention and sets up new Patents Court. Minor amendments to 1977 Act by Copyright, Designs and Patents Act 1988. (1988, c. 48 [U.K.]). Except where contrary is indicated, reference to statutory provision is reference to 1977 Act. (1977, c. 37 [U.K.]).

Transitional Provisions.—Patents granted and applications for patents made before June 1, 1978 remain governed by Patents Act, 1949 but subject to certain amendments of which most important relate to duration. Patents granted before June 1, 1967 still run for 16 years with limited right to extension. Patents granted between June 1, 1967 and June 1, 1978 will run now for 20 years but without right to extension. Unless contrary appears all further references under this topic are to law established by Patents Act, 1977.

Patentability is now elaborately defined. Invention is not patentable unless it is new, involves inventive step and is capable of industrial application. (§1[1]). Number of inventions are never patentable, particularly scientific theories, aesthetic creations, computer programmes and biological processes except for those involving microbiology. (§1[3]).

Application for patent may be made by any person whether British citizen or not. Patents are granted primarily to inventor or joint inventors but may also be granted to any person entitled to legal interest in invention in U.K. at time of invention. They may also be granted to successors in title of either class of persons. (§7).

Mode of Application.—System of provisional protection under 1949 Act has been replaced for new applications by system of priority dates. Generally, priority date is date of filing of application at Patent Office. Priority may be gained if documents filed contain indication that patent is being applied for, applicant is identified, invention is described and filing fee paid (§15), even though documents do not fully comply with Act and Patent Rules, 1978. But such application will be treated as withdrawn unless within overall period of (generally) three and one-half years, requirements as to claims and abstracts are complied with and preliminary examination and search and substantive examination are both requested. Thus, although priority may sometimes be gained without full compliance with Act and Rules, it will almost always be necessary to file prescribed proper documents later. Formal application must be in prescribed form containing request for grant of patent, specification describing invention, abstract giving technical information and claim or claims. Claim or claims serve to delimit precise nature and extent of invention being patented. If patent is granted in respect of any claim or claims, it is their wording which forms basis of subsequent infringement proceedings. Consequently, they must be carefully and precisely drafted. (§14). Official searches made on application are now divided into two stages of preliminary examination and search and substantive examination, (§18). Two fees are payable.

Objections and Grant.—In contrast to 1949 Act objections are not receivable except by third parties as to whether they are entitled to patent invention in question. However, any person may lodge written observations as to whether invention is patentable at all. (§21). If Patent Office decides that application complies with Act and Rules, patent is granted upon payment of fee. It takes effect from date of publication in Official Journal and runs 20 years from date of filing of application. (§25). Renewal fees must be paid at end of fourth year from filing and every year thereafter or else patent ceases. (§25).

Revocation.—Third party may apply to court or comptroller of Patent Office to revoke patent on any of following grounds, but no other: (A) Invention was not patentable; (B) patent was not granted to person entitled to make application. Ground (B) can only be invoked by person who has obtained prior finding of court or comptroller that he was person truly entitled to patent invention. Further, except in cases of fraud, ground (B) cannot be invoked unless proceedings which produced that finding were commenced within two years of grant of patent; (C) specification of patent does not disclose invention clearly and completely enough for skilled person to perform it; (D) matter disclosed in specification of patent extends beyond that disclosed in application for patent as filed; (E) protection conferred by patent has been extended by amendment which should not have been allowed. (§72).

Infringement.—Right to sue for infringement does not arise until patent is published and only in respect of acts after publication. Broadly, infringement may be defined as commercial use of or dealing with patented product or process without consent of proprietor of patent. In case of process there is no infringement unless user or dealer knew or ought to have known that his acts constituted infringement. (§60). Defendant to infringement action can rely on any ground of defence common to all actions but he may only attack validity of patent on grounds available upon application to revoke. Usual relief granted to successful plaintiff is injunction coupled with damages or account of profits. (§61). Damages or account will not be ordered against defendant honestly and reasonably ignorant of patent. (§62). Failure to register transaction passing property in patent, license or sub-license within six months or if six months was too short as soon as practicable, also bars right of transferee to damages or account. (§68), Although secret prior user is no longer ground for revocation, bona fide prior use may be continued without constituting infringement.

Registration.—System of registration has been extended by 1977 Act. Grants, assignments, mortgages, vesting assents and court orders in relation to patent licenses and sub-licenses are all registrables. Priority of claims in respect of such property depends upon order of registration unless earlier unregistered transaction was known to person claiming under later register transaction. (§33).

Licenses.—To use or deal with patent can of course be negotiated with proprietor in ordinary way. There is also system of compulsory and semi-compulsory licensing. Under latter, proprietor who is perfectly willing to grant licenses on such terms as comptroller may decide are reasonable can at any time apply to have entry in register to effect that licenses under patent are available as of right. If applicant for license as of right cannot agree on terms with proprietor they will be settled by comptroller. If declaration filed by patent owner, licence of right under transitional provisions in Schedule 1 cannot be had for medicinal use of patented product and such other uses as Secretary of State may specify by Order. (1988, c. 48, §29). Applications for settlement of terms for licences of right available under transitional provisions in Schedule 1 made more than one year before relevant patent becomes subject to licence of right provisions not permitted. (1988, c. 48 §294). Under former, any person may at any time after three years from grant apply to comptroller for compulsory license upon such terms as are reasonable. Possible grounds for application are that: (A) Invention can be worked commercially in U.K. but it is not being worked at all or to fullest practical extent; (B) U.K. demand for patented product is not being met on reasonable terms or is being met to substantial extent by imports; (C) commercial working of patent in U.K. is being prevented or hindered by imports of patented production of products produced by patented process; (D) injury to commerce and trade of U.K. by reason of refusal of licenses on reasonable terms; (E) injury to commerce and trade of U.K. by reason of imposition of conditions by proprietor. Finally Crown has certain right to patented inventions compulsorily upon such terms as may be agreed or as may be ordered by court. (§48).

Invalidity of Certain Contracts.—Under both 1977 and 1949 Acts certain restrictive convenants in connection with patented material are rendered void. More important are new provisions protecting rights of employees to their inventions as against their employers. These apply to persons mainly employed in U.K. and to persons attached to place of business in U.K. who are not mainly employed anywhere or whose place of employment cannot be determined. (§43). Employee's invention is his own unless made in course of usual or special duties in circumstances where he might reasonably be expected to make invention or unless invention was made in course of his duties and these duties and his responsibilities were such that he had special obligation to further his employer's interests. In those cases invention is his employer's but he is entitled to compensation to be assessed by court or comptroller. (§40). Any contract diminishing those various rights is to that extent unenforceable.

International Element.—One of major purposes of 1977 Act was to bring U.K. law into line with EEC Patent Convention. Broadly, any EEC patent is to be treated as patent under 1977 Act. (§72). Patent Cooperation Treaty is older system applying to many countries, including U.S. Applications to patents offices of countries adhering to treaty establish earlier date for U.K. purposes provided that application to U.K. Patent Office is filed within 12 months of filing of foreign application and declaration is made specifying earlier application.

Court.—1977 Act abolished Patents Appeal Tribunal and replaces it by Patents Court which is part of Chancery Division of High Court of Justice. (§96).

Patent Agents.—Applications to and proceedings before Patent Office are generally made and conducted by patent agents. (§114). They are not lawyers in strict sense but are highly skilled in relevant law and practice. They are governed by Chartered Institute of Patent Agents, Staple Inn Buildings, London WC1.

PERPETUITIES:

Common law rule applies to all instruments taking effect prior to Mar. 26, 1966.

Perpetuities Act (N.I.) 1966 (1966, c. 2) alters rule against perpetuities in relation to instruments taking effect after Mar. 26, 1966. Disposition (§16) is not void for remoteness until such time (if any) that interest disposed of cannot vest within perpetuity period; until then it is treated as if it were not subject to rule against perpetuities (§3[2]). Period not exceeding 80 years instead of any other period may now be chosen as perpetuity period applicable to a disposition under rule against perpetuities (§1[1]) except a disposition consisting of conferring of an option to acquire for valuable consideration any interest or land where period is 21 years (§10). Where disposition is made in exercise of special power of appointment any period of years specified in instrument creating power will apply for purpose of any disposition made under it. (§1[2]).

In considering validity of any limitation it is now presumed that a male can only have a child at age of 14 years or over and that a female can have a child between ages of 12 and 55 years, but in case of living person evidence may be given to show that he or she will or will not be able to have child at time in question. (§2).

Where disposition is limited by reference to attainment by any person or persons of a specified age exceeding 21 years and it is apparent at time disposition is made or it becomes apparent at a subsequent time (a) that disposition would (otherwise) be void for remoteness, but (b) that it would not be void if specified age had been 21 years, disposition is vested for all purposes as if, instead of being limited to age in fact specified it had been limited by reference to age nearest that age which would, if specified instead have prevented disposition from being void. (§4[1]).

Where it is apparent at time disposition is made or becomes apparent at subsequent time that inclusion of any persons being potential members of a class or unborn persons who at birth would become members or potential members of class, could cause disposition to be treated as void for remoteness they are deemed for all purposes of disposition to be excluded from class unless their exclusion would extinct class. (§4[4]).

No disposition is treated as void for remoteness by reason only that interest disposed of is ulterior to and dependent upon an interest under a disposition which is void. (§6).

Rule against perpetuities does not invalidate a power conferred on trustees or other persons to sell, lease, exchange or otherwise dispose of any property for full consideration, or do any other act in administration (as opposed to distribution) of any property. (§8).

See Topical Index in front part of this volume.

PLEDGES:

A pledge consists of delivery of goods or chattels by one party (the bailor) or another party (the bailee) as security for the payment of a debt and upon the understanding that the article or articles delivered are to be returned on payment of the debt within the time fixed therefor, if any. The rights and duties of the bailor and bailee are governed by the common law. The bailee may sell the pledge in default of repayment. If more than one article is pledged all must be redeemed at the same time.

PRESCRIPTION:

See topic Limitation of Actions.

PRINCIPAL AND AGENT:

Common law rules apply generally; the principal is responsible for the acts of his agents. An agent acting for an undisclosed principal is personally liable. In order to make the principal liable, however, it must be shown that the agent was acting within the scope of his employment. If agent acts outside scope of his authority principal is liable if he is shown to have ratified and adopted action of agent, in which case ratification relates back to time at which agent acted, provided that at time of acting agent professed to be an agent; and that at that time principal was competent to act as such.

REAL PROPERTY:

There are four different classes of freehold estates: (1) Estate in fee simple; (2) estate in fee tail; (3) estate for life; and (4) estate pur autre vie.

Leasehold interests are classified by common law as being less than freehold, and are generally referred to as a term of years. They are not real property. Equitable estates are recognised.

A joint tenancy arises whenever land is conveyed or devised to two or more persons without any words to show that they are to take distinctive and separate shares. But if the grant contains words of severance the result is the creation of a tenancy in common. A tenancy in common will be presumed (a) where money is advanced on a mortgage by two or more persons; (b) where joint purchasers of land provide the purchase money in unequal shares; and (c) where land is bought by partners.

Rule in Shelley's case is recognised.

There are no restrictions on ownership of real property by aliens. (British Nationality Act 1948, 11 & 12 Geo. 6, c. 56 [U.K.]) and Status of Aliens Act 1914, 4 & 5 Geo. 5, c. 17. [U.K.], §17).

See topics Descent and Distribution; Executors and Administrators; Limitation of Actions; Wills.

RECORDS:

Dealings in freehold and leasehold registered land (i.e. leases for term greater than 21 years) must be registered under Land Registry Act (N.I.) 1970. (1970, c. 18 as am'd by Registration [Land and Deeds] [N.I.] Order [1992, S.I. No. 811]).

All deeds transferring interest in land not subject to 1970 Act may be registered in Registry of Deeds. Purchasers are deemed to have notice of all previous registered dealings with land.

See also topic Wills.

REPLEVIN:

Common Law rules govern.

REPORTS:

The Northern Ireland Law Reports are published under the superintendence and control of the Incorporated Council of Law Reporting for Northern Ireland which is composed of representatives of the bar and the solicitors' profession. In practice the English reported cases are consulted and followed.

SALES:

Regulated by Sale of Goods Act, 1979 (1979, c. 54 [U.K.]) am'd by Sale of Goods (amendment) Act 1994 (1994, c. 32 [U.K.]) which repeals and reenacts Sale of Goods Act, 1893 (56-7 Vict., c. 71 [U.K.]) and those sections of Supply of Goods (Implied Terms) Act 1973 (1973, c. 13 [U.K.]) which amended 1893 Act. Except where contrary is indicated, reference to statutory provision is reference to 1979 Act.

Contract of sale may be either absolute or conditional. Where the property in the goods is at once transferred from the seller to the buyer the sale is absolute; but if the transfer of the property in the goods is to take place at a future time or subject to some condition (to be fulfilled thereafter) the contract is merely an agreement for sale or conditional sale.

The seller may reserve the right of disposal of the goods until certain conditions are fulfilled. Until fulfillment (notwithstanding delivery to a carrier or shipper for the purpose of transmission to the buyer) the property in the goods does not pass to the buyer until the conditions are fulfilled.

When goods are shipped and by the bill of lading the goods are deliverable to the order of the seller or his agent, the seller is prima facie deemed to reserve the right of disposal. Where the seller of goods draws on the buyer for the price and transmits the bill of exchange and bill of lading to the buyer (together) to secure acceptance or payment of the bill of exchange, the buyer is bound to return the bill of lading if he does not honour the bill of exchange and if he does not honour the bill of exchange and wrongfully retains the bill of lading the property in the goods does not pass to him.

Unless otherwise agreed the goods remain at the seller's risk until the property therein is transferred to the buyer, but when the property is so transferred the goods are at the buyer's risk whether delivery has been made or not. This rule is subject to the proviso that if delivery has been delayed through the fault of either buyer or seller the goods are at the risk of the party in fault as regards any loss which might not have occurred but for such fault.

Where the seller is authorised to send the goods to the buyer, delivery of the goods to a carrier or shipper for transmission to the buyer is prima facie deemed to be a delivery of goods to the buyer. But goods are liable to be stopped in transit and the buyer is only deemed to have accepted the goods when he intimates to the seller that he has accepted them, or when the goods have been delivered to him, and he does any act in relation to them which is inconsistent with the ownership of the seller or when after a lapse of a reasonable time he retains the goods without intimating to the seller that he has rejected them. Goods may, by arrangement, be accepted conditionally and the acceptance may in such case be withdrawn on failure of condition. A resale by the buyer is strong evidence of acceptance. Where goods which he has not previously examined are delivered to the buyer, he is not deemed to have accepted them unless and until he has had a reasonable opportunity of examining them, and (unless otherwise agreed) when the seller tenders delivery to the buyer the seller is bound, on request, to afford the buyer a reasonable opportunity of examining the goods.

Where the seller is bound to send goods to the buyer but no time for sending them is fixed, the seller must send them within a reasonable time, which is always a question of fact.

Delivery of goods and payment of price (unless otherwise agreed) are concurrent conditions.

Warranties are collateral to main purpose of contract and breach gives right to damages but not repudiation of contract. Breach of condition may entitle buyer to treat contract as repudiated unless he elects to treat such breach as breach of warranty. (§11[2]). Whether stipulation is condition or warranty depends in each case on construction of contract and stipulation may be condition, though called warranty in contract. (§11[3]). In absence of contrary intention appearing, stipulations as to time are not deemed to be essence of contract.

Unless contrary intention is shown in contract there is (a) implied condition that seller has right to sell goods or in case of agreement to sell that he will have right to sell at time property is to pass (§12[1]), (b) an implied warranty that buyer will have and enjoy quiet possession of goods (§12[2]), (c) an implied warranty that goods are free from any charge or encumbrance in favour of any third party not declared or known to buyer when contract made. (§12[2]).

In case of sale by description there is an implied condition that goods correspond with description. (§13).

Sale of goods shall not be prevented from being sale by description by reason only that, being exposed for sale or hire, they are selected by buyer. (§13[3]).

Generally there is no implied warranty or condition as to quality or fitness for any particular purpose. Where seller sells goods in course of business there is implied condition that goods supplied under contract are of merchantable quality except: (a) As regards defects specifically drawn to buyer's attention before contract, or (b) if buyer examines goods before contract, as regards defects which that examination ought to reveal; goods deemed to be of reasonable quality if they are as fit for purpose for which goods of kind are normally bought as it is reasonable to expect having regard to any description applied to them, price and all other relevant circumstances. (§14). Where seller sells goods in course of business and buyer makes known any particular purpose for which goods are being bought, there is implied condition that goods are fit for such purpose except where circumstances show that buyer does not rely on seller's skill and judgment. Implied condition or warranty may be annexed to sale by usage. (§14).

Where any right, duty or liability arises by law under contract for sale it may (subject to Unfair Contract Terms Act, 1977 - see subhead Unfair Contract Terms Act 1977, infra) be negatived by express agreement between parties or by course of dealing or usage but any attempt to exclude §§12-15 of 1979 Act are void in case of consumer sale, and in any other case are not enforceable to extent that it is shown that it would not be fair or reasonable to allow reliance on such agreement.

Notices Required.—Unless otherwise agreed where goods are delivered to buyer and he refuses to accept them having right to do so, he is not bound to return them to seller but it is sufficient if he intimates to seller that he refused to accept them. (§36). No particular form is essential. It is sufficient if he does any unequivocal act showing he rejects. ([1875] L.R. 10, C.P. 391).

Consumer Credit Act (U.K.) 1974 protects consumers in respect of transactions involving hire or sale by credit in respect of: (a) Control of credit grantors, information to which consumer is entitled before selecting which form of credit he will avail himself of, (b) his rights during course of agreement, (c) his rights in default of or termination of agreement. Act applies where debtor is individual and where amount of credit does not exceed £5,000. See England Law Digest for further details.

Unfair Contract Terms Act 1977.—This Act (1977, c. 50 [U.K.]) imposes further limitations on extent to which civil liability for breach of contract, or for negligence or other breach of duty, can be avoided by means of contract terms. Basically applies only to business liability (arising from breach of obligations or duties arising in course of business). Act prevents exclusion or restriction of liability for death or personal injury resulting from negligence. (§21). Where party to contract deals as consumer or other party uses written standard form of contract, liability for breach of contract cannot be excluded or restricted except insofar as contract term satisfies statutory requirement of "reasonableness". (§3). Act provides guidelines for determining reasonableness (§11 and Sch. 2) and includes relative strength of parties' bargaining positions. Act also outlaws unreasonable indemnity clauses in contracts where one party is consumer (§4); restates existing protection for sale of goods and consumer credit (§6); and brings service contracts within its ambit. (§7). Part III contains provisions relating to international contracts.

Supply of Goods and Services Act, 1982.—This Act (1982, c. 29 [U.K.]) sets out terms to be implied in contracts for transfer of property in goods; contracts for hire of goods; and contracts for supply of services. Contracts for transfer of property in goods does not include contract for sale of goods. Contract for hire of goods does not include hire purchase agreement. Implied terms in both of foregoing include: (i) Transferor has right to transfer; (ii) transferee will enjoy quiet possession of goods; (iii) goods will correspond with description; (iv) goods to be of merchantable quality; (v) goods to be reasonably fit for purpose made known to transferor by transferee; (vi) quality of bulk supply must correspond with quality of sample. Implied terms in contracts for supply of service are: (i) Supplier will carry out service with reasonable care and skill; (ii) supplier will carry out service within reasonable time; (iii) supplier will be paid reasonable amount. Where right, duty or liability arises in any of above contracts, it may be

SALES . . . *continued*
negatived or varied by express agreement subject to provisions of 1977, c. 50 (U.K.). Implied terms listed in 1982 Act cannot be excluded or restricted by parties to contracts. (§11).

Consumer Protection Act 1987 (1987, c. 43 [U.K.]).—Part II of Act introduces general safety requirement for all consumer goods. Also empowers Secretary of State to make specific safety regulations. All goods must be reasonably safe; what is reasonable is to be determined by court. Parts I and III of Act govern respectively product liability and misleading price indications.

Applicable Law.—The cardinal principle is that law applicable to contract is that by which parties intended it to be governed. In absence of any other indication of intention of parties law of contract is lex loci contractus but this is not conclusive as tenor of contract may show that parties to contract intended it to be governed by lex loci solutionis.

Stipulations and terms of contract must be construed according to the lex loci contractus. Questions of evidence belong to lex fori.

SEALS:

Deed must be signed and sealed. It must have seal fixed or impressed upon or attached to it. Not necessary that particular kind of seal be used. Not every document under seal is deed, e.g., award, certificate of admission to learned society, letters of ordination.

SEQUESTRATION:

Mode of execution available against one who has disobeyed order of court. It empowers sequestrators to enter on lands of defendant and receive rents and profits and to take possession of his personal property until he complies with order. With court's leave they may sell personal property and pay proceeds into court.

SHIPPING: See England Law Digest.

STATUTES:

Statute Law Revision (N.I.) Acts are passed by U.K. Parliament at regular intervals to amend and repeal obsolete legislative provisions affecting Northern Ireland. Latest Acts passed in 1973 (1973, c. 55 [U.K.]) 1976 (1976, c. 12 [U.K.]) 1980 (1980, c. 59 [U.K.]) and 1986 (1986, c. 12 [U.K.]).

The Statutes Revised (Northern Ireland) contain in 16 volumes public and general statutes of Ireland, England, Great Britain, U.K. and Northern Ireland up to 1950 (am'd to 1954) which affect Northern Ireland. Chronological table of Statutes affecting Northern Ireland covering legislation to Dec. 31, 1989, published by Her Majesty's Stationery Office in 1990. Index to Statutes in Force in Northern Ireland covering legislation to Dec. 31, 1990, published in 1993 also by H.M.S.O. Latest edition (18th) of Index to Northern Ireland Statutory Rules and Orders in force on Dec. 31, 1988 (showing statutory powers under which they were made) published by H.M.S.O. in 1991.

TAXATION:

Government of Ireland Act, 1920 (1920, 10 & 11 Geo. 5, c. 67) established Exchequer and Consolidated Fund for Northern Ireland and vested wide powers of taxation in Parliament of Northern Ireland, while reserving to United Kingdom Parliament most important fields of taxation, including income tax, corporation tax, capital gains tax and customs duties. Parliament of Northern Ireland legislated in respect of estate duty, stamp duty, general betting duty, pool betting duty, duty on gaming machine licenses and duty on licenses for mechanically-propelled vehicles.

Northern Ireland Constitution Act, 1973 (1973, c. 36 [U.K.]) provides for continuation of Consolidated Fund but not Exchequer. Northern Ireland Assembly has considerably fewer powers of taxation than Parliament of Northern Ireland. By Schedule 2, Para. 8 of 1973 Act, taxes levied under any law applying to U.K. as a whole; taxes previously levied by Parliament of Northern Ireland; and taxes "substantially of the same character" as those taxes are "excepted matters" and therefore excluded from competence of Northern Ireland Assembly. However, by §14 of 1973 Act (and Schedule 1 of Northern Ireland Act, 1974) certain powers remain with Secretary of State to impose taxes in areas not deemed to be "excepted matters".

§15 of 1973 Act provides for payment to Consolidated Fund of Northern Ireland of proportionate share of tax revenue of U.K.

§16 of 1973 Act permits additional sums to be paid by United Kingdom Parliament into Consolidated Fund of Northern Ireland and permits Secretary of State to pay out such sums as are authorised by United Kingdom Treasury.

See topic Constitution and Government.

For details of taxes applicable to Northern Ireland as part of U.K., see England Law Digest, topic Taxation.

TRADEMARKS AND TRADENAMES:

See Trade Marks Act 1994. (1994, C26[UK]).

Tradenames.—See topic Commercial Register.

TREATIES:

By Northern Ireland Constitution Act 1973 (1973, c. 36[U.K.] Sch. 2) international relations, including treaties, making of peace or war, neutrality, and connected matters are "excepted matters" outside competence of Northern Ireland Assembly. There are three exceptions: (a) Agreements relating to surrender of fugitive offenders between Northern Ireland and Republic of Ireland; (b) exercise of legislative powers in connection with European Communities Act 1972 (1972, c. 68 [U.K.]); and (c) powers under §12 of Northern Ireland Constitution Act. By §12 Northern Ireland executive authority may consult on any matter with any authority of Republic of Ireland and enter into agreements or arrangements with such authorities in respect of any transferred matter. Assembly may by measure give effect to any such agreement and may transfer to any authority designated by or constituted under any such agreement or arrangement any functions otherwise exercisable by Northern Ireland authority. See topic Constitution and Government.

International Conventions.—As integral part of U.K., Northern Ireland adheres to international conventions and treaties to which U.K. as whole is party. See Selected International Conventions section.

TRUSTS:

Law regulating trusts and trustees is contained in Trustee Act (N.I.) 1958 (1958, c. 23); Trustee Investment Act (N.I.) 1961 (1961, c. 62); Trustee Investments (Additional Powers) (N.I.) Order 1983 (1983, S.I. No. 772) and large body of decided case law.

A trust may arise from an infinite variety of circumstances, in fact, on any occasion in which one person is placed in a fiduciary relationship to another. It may be called a confidence reposed in a person with respect to property of which he has possession or over which he can exercise a power to the intent that he may hold the property or exercise the power for the benefit of some person or object.

Trusts are either: (1) Express, i.e., created by the actual terms of some instrument or declaration; or (2) constructive or implied which arise when property to which no express trust is for the time being attached is acquired or held by a person under circumstances which render him bound in equity to hold it in trust for the the benefit of some person or object.

Express trusts may be either executed or executory. An executed trust is where the terms of the trust are designated by the instrument or declaration creating it. An executory trust is where the instrument or declaration by which it is created directs the subsequent execution of an instrument defining the trust.

A precatory trust is one created by expressions of confidence, request or desire that property will or shall be applied for the benefit of a definite person or object.

A secret trust is where property is in law given to a person either absolutely or upon an indefinite trust but there has been an undertaking by him or an understanding between him and the donor that it shall be applied for the benefit of some person or object.

Apart from the above, trusts may arise when one person receives money from or on behalf of another without apparent reason. In this case a resulting trust arises in favour of the donor or in favour of the person on whose behalf the money was paid. If, however, the donee stands in special relationship to the donor a presumption of complete gift may arise, e.g., husband paying a sum of money to wife or a person paying money to or for the benefit of another to whom he stands in loco parentis.

There are certain restrictions governing trusts in favour of charities and corporations.

Trustees have whatever discretion is given in the instrument creating the trust; otherwise they are bound to act with the utmost care and diligence and will under certain circumstances be held personally liable for any loss resulting from their own carelessness.

The investments which may be made with trust funds are limited by statute, unless otherwise provided for in the trust instrument.

A trustee may be called upon to account through the court at any time by a fellow trustee or a beneficiary.

WILLS:

Citations, unless otherwise indicated, refer to Wills and Administration Proceedings (N.I.) Order 1994 (S.I. 1994/1899 N.I. 13). This Order governs execution of wills, made on or after Jan. 1, 1995. Person under age of 18 cannot make valid will unless, either they are or have been married (Art. 4[1]) or such will is privileged will of person in actual military service (S.I. Wills [Soldiers and Sailors] Act 1918 [7 & 8 Geo. 5 c. 58]).

Testamentary Disposition.—Person may dispose of all estate by will (Art. 3), executed in accordance with The 1994 Order. (See subhead Execution, infra.) Restrictions in mortmain abolished. (Repeals Mortmain Act [N.I.] 1960 (1960, c. 20]) and see topic Perpetuities. If court considers operative dispositions of deceased's estate, whether by will or rules or intestacy, do not make reasonable provision for specified dependants, it may make order for maintenance out of estate on application, within six months of grant of administration, of those dependants. (Inheritance [Provision for Family and Dependants] [Northern Ireland] Order, 1979 [1979, S.I. No. 924 (N.I.8)]). But person may enter contract by which part or whole of estate will be bound and beneficiaries under will become trustees.

Execution.—Art. 5 requires that for will to be validly executed, it must meet certain requirements, (a) it is signed by testator, or by some other person in his presence and by his direction; and (b) it appears from will or is shown that testator intended by his signature to give effect to will; and (c) signature is made or acknowledged by testator in presence of two or more witnesses present at same time; and (d) each witness, in presence of testator (but not necessarily in presence of any other witness), either (i) attests testator's signature or testator's acknowledgment of his signature and signs will, or (ii) acknowledges his signature.

Attestation.—No form of attestation necessary. (Art. 5[2]).

Revocation.—Even if will is expressed to be irrevocable such expression is of no effect and will may be revoked.

Marriage.—Will is revoked by testator's lawful marriage unless will made in exercise of a power of appointment when property appointed would not in default of appointment pass to testator's personal representatives. (Art. 12). Where it appears from will that at time it was made testator expecting to be married to particular person and testator intended will should not be revoked by marriage, will not revoked by marriage to that person. (Art. 12[3]). Where, after testator has made will, marriage dissolved or annulled, gift to former spouse takes effect as if former spouse had died on date marriage dissolved or annulled. (Art 13[1]). Art. 13(1) will not take effect if any contrary intention appears from will. (per Art. 13[3]). No will revoked by presumption of intention on ground of alteration in circumstances. (Art. 14[2]).

Voluntary Revocation.—Will revoked by subsequent will, properly executed; by some writing, declaring intention to revoke will, executed in accordance with Art. 5 or by testator, or some person in his presence and by his direction, burning, tearing or otherwise destroying will with intention of revoking. (Art. 14[1]).

Revival.—Will may be revived by re-execution or by properly executed codicil showing intention to revive it. (Art. 15).

Witnesses.—Gift by will to person who witnesses will, or spouse of any such person, void (Art. 8), but only if witness signs will (Art. 8[3]). Executor may be witness (Art.

WILLS . . . *continued*
10) and will not void because witness incompetent to be admitted witness to prove execution (Art. 7).

Foreign Executed Wills.—Will is valid in Northern Ireland if execution thereof conforms to internal law in force in country where it was executed, or in territory in which testator domiciled at his death, or in state of which testator was a national. (Wills Act 1963 [U.K.] [1963, c. 44]). To procure probate of will of person domiciled in U.S., or abroad, it is necessary to appoint corporation or person in Northern Ireland as attorney to extract grant. Court will follow foreign grant and exemplified copy of will properly legalised should be forwarded to attorney in Northern Ireland.

Copies of Wills proved after year 1955 can be obtained from Principal Probate Registry, Belfast. Copies of wills proved prior to that date can be obtained from Public Record Office, Belfast.

See also topic Descent and Distribution.

NORWAY LAW DIGEST REVISER

Advokatfirmaet STABELL DA
Haakon VII's Gate 2
P.O. Box 1364
VIKA N-0114 Oslo, Norway
Telephone: 47-2201 6400
Fax: 47-2201 6401
Email: hq@stabell.no

Reviser Profile

History: The firm was established in 1991 through a merger of reputable medium sized law firms with long tradition in different areas of practice: *Stabell Heiberg & Co, Tellmann Ramm & Co, Strøm Sandaker & Co and Elde & Co.*

As of 1994 STABELL has grown into an organisation of 19 partners and in total 26 fee earners, making STABELL one of the largest Norwegian law firms.

Today STABELL reflects a combination of compatible legal skills and clients, establishment of a flexible organisation to service our clients nationally and internationally, adjusted to increased demand for services and diversified skills, at the same time being a better base for development of internal professional skills and specialisation.

Areas of Emphasis: STABELL emphasises high accessibility of professional legal assistance, realising the importance of close partner attention to all clients. The firm has founded a team player concept with clients and are known to give good personal service and new referrals immediate and relevant attention. STABELL is a full service firm with strength in Norwegian and international corporate law, banking and securities, tax, media, building and construction, insurance, property, agricultural law and litigation.

Client Base: STABELL's clients include large corporations in building and construction, insurance, finance, media, property developers, trade, industry and travelling as well as state or community owned companies and institutions.

Firm Activities: All partners and associates participate in internal professional study groups to ensure that the lawyers of the firm are professionally qualified and up to date. All lawyers of the firm are members of the Norwegian Bar Association. Several of the partners are strategically involved with the business community, being members of Boards of a number of corporations and charitable institutions.

NORWAY LAW DIGEST

(The following is a list of all Topics, including cross-references, covered in this Digest.)

NORWAY LAW DIGEST

Revised for 1997 edition by

Advokatfirmaet STABELL DA, Oslo.

See topics Law Reports and Statutes.

ABSENTEES: See topic Death (Presumption of and Actions for).

ACKNOWLEDGMENTS:

In most cases signature to documents needs no attesting by witnesses, but deed of conveyancing, mortgages and other documents to be recorded with real estate registry or ships registry need for that purpose and also other documents for purpose of execution need special attesting by two witnesses, lawyer or sheriff. They can also be signed before notary public. When documents have to be signed abroad for use in Norway, signature will usually have to be signed before notary public whose signature will need legalization by Norwegian consul.

ACTIONS:

Appraisement of evidence is free and informal. Written contracts, letters and other documents are suitable as proof. Court depositions may be taken. Depositions may also be taken abroad. Procedures are regulated by treaties with other countries.

Proof of foreign law may be given by producing text of statutory law, textbook on same or opinion by outstanding lawyers.

See topics Courts; Death (Presumption of and Actions for), subhead Actions for Death.

Limitation of.—See topic Limitation of Actions.

AFFIDAVITS:

If foreign lawyers require service of affidavits in Norway procedure laid down in convention with relevant country should be adhered to.

ALIENS:

The legal position of aliens is in general the same as that of Norwegian citizens.

Alien must have passport to enter Norway, except citizens of Denmark, Finland, Sweden and Iceland.

Aliens from non-EEA countries need prior permit to take up permanent residence or to seek employment in Norway. EEA-citizens must register with local police after arriving in Norway. This does not apply to citizens of Nordic countries.

Alien ownership of property, see topics Real Property; Aviation; Shipping.

See also topics Continental Shelf, Immigration, Licences, and Real Property.

ALIMONY: See topic Divorce.

ARBITRATION:

(Act of Aug. 13, 1915, Ch. 32). All disputes relating to matters over which parties may legally dispose freely, can be settled by arbitration. An arbitration agreement must be made in writing. Parties are free to agree upon procedure and arbitrators. Award is binding on parties and may be enforced without further recourse to courts. Arbitration clauses are very frequent in all Norwegian shipping documents but are also used in other contract relations.

ASSIGNMENTS:

Claims may be transferred by agreement. Advice must be given to debtor to prevent him from making payment to transferor and to safeguard assignment against transferor's creditors. Transferror is responsible for existence of claim and his ownership thereof, but not for solvency of debtor.

ASSOCIATIONS: See topic Corporations.

ATTACHMENT:

Goods may be seized by court order if debtor's behavior indicates that execution will otherwise be unavailing. It is not necessary that the claim should be matured, but seizure may be made subject to security and on the condition that action must be brought within a term fixed by the court. Provisional seizure must be registered and then gives protection against debtor's transactions, but does not give any preference as against other creditors or any protection against subsequent execution or bankruptcy proceedings.

See also topic Executions.

ATTORNEYS AND COUNSELORS:

To obtain licence to practice one must: be 20 years old, hold cand.jur. degree (five-six years), have two years relevant practice, complete 46 hour course given by Bar Association and litigate three cases before courts. Attorneys must be covered by NOK 5,000,000 insurance.

Attorney with at least one year practice may, after satisfactory performance in two cases before Supreme Court, be licensed to litigate before Supreme Court.

Norwegian Bar Association (Den Norske Advokatforening); Kristian Augustsgate 9, 0164 Oslo, telephone (47) 2203 5050, fax (47) 2211 53 25.

Foreign attorneys may obtain permit to advise clients in foreign and international law. Courts may on individual basis allow foreign attorneys to litigate before courts.

Attorneys from EEA-countries may represent clients in Norway. If knowledge of Norwegian language is satisfactory, attorney may litigate before courts. With lack of language skills EEA attorney must perform with aid of Norwegian attorney. To obtain ordinary Norwegian licence EEA attorney must pass test on knowledge of Norwegian law.

AVIATION:

Legal aspects of aviation are codified in Act of Parliament, dated June 11, 1993. Act legalizes, inter alia, Warsaw Convention of 1929 with amendments in accordance with Hague Agreement of Sept. 28, 1955.

Registration of aircraft requires Norwegian ownership. To qualify company must be registered in Norway and two thirds of share capital must be owned and voted by Norwegian citizens. All members of board of directors must be Norwegian.

Norwegian aircrafts may not be owned by aliens. Aircraft owned by company is considered Norwegian owned when two thirds of share capital is owned and voted by Norwegian citizens or entities with similar status.

Liability.—Carrier is responsible for injuries to passengers, limited to 100,000 SDR. Owner is responsible for injuries to third parties. No need to prove negligence.

Time Bar.—According to §10-29 of above Act claims are barred by elapse of two years after aircraft's arrival at destination or after scheduled time of arrival when voyage was interrupted.

BANKRUPTCY:

(Bankruptcy Act of June 8, 1984). Debtor who is unable to meet his liabilities is obliged to file petition for bankruptcy, and under certain circumstances creditor may present bankruptcy petition against debtor, in which case proofs may be required before bankruptcy court.

Trustee is appointed, assets are registered and claims are called within three to six weeks. Notice for claim has to be given before bankruptcy court and creditors must prove before court if necessary.

Claims are paid in following order: (1) Fees and costs; (2) claims coming into existence during administration; (3) certain wages; (4) certain taxes and duties; (5) ordinary claims. Where claim is secured by mortgage, property covered has to be sold and proceeds are first applied to mortgage debt.

See also topic Fraudulent Sales and Conveyances.

Composition.—Debtor may obtain composition with creditors before going into bankruptcy. If he offers to pay at least 50% of unsecured debts, acceptance by at least $^3/_5$ of creditors representing $^3/_5$ of liabilities is sufficient; but if he offers less than 50%, there must be acceptance by at least $^3/_4$ of creditors representing $^3/_4$ of liabilities. Composition must be approved by court. Approval will not be given for offer less than 25%.

BILLS AND NOTES:

Norway is a party to the Geneva Conventions of June 6, 1930 and Mar. 19, 1931, concerning uniform law on the subject of bills of exchange and cheques. Two acts of May 27, 1932, establish conformity with the conventions. These acts have also incorporated the international rules as to conflicts of law on this subject, agreed on by the parties to the said conventions.

Bill of exchange (Act of May 27, 1932) must contain express indication that it is a bill of exchange and must show: Amount for which drawn; names of payee, drawer and drawee; time when and place where issued and to be paid. Time for payment must be on certain day after sight or after issue.

Bill may be transferred by indorsement which must be written thereon. Every indorser is responsible to all subsequent holders for acceptance or payment of bill unless he excludes personal liability by adding the words "ikke til ordre" (not to order) or the like.

Any holder of bill may present it for acceptance and if it is not accepted may have bill protested. Holder may also have bill protested for nonpayment, which must be done during two weekdays after day for payment.

No revenue stamps are to be affixed.

Cheque (Act of May 27, 1932) must be drawn on a bank only, must contain express indication that it is a cheque and must show: Sum to be paid; to whom and by whom payment is made; place of payment; day of issue; and signature of issuer. Cheque may be issued to bearer or to a specified person. Endorser of cheque is subject to same liability as endorser of bill of exchange.

A cheque can be revoked by the drawer before payment but when unduly revoking he is liable to penalty. Overdraft also subjects drawer to penalty. No stamps or taxes are payable on cheques.

Other instruments are divided into two groups: negotiable instruments and simple instruments, the former negotiable in same way as bills of exchange. (Act of Feb. 17, 1939).

A bill is negotiable when issued to bearer or to a person mentioned by name with the affix "or order"; when it specifically states that it is negotiable or when it gives mortgage in real property, registered vessels and aircrafts.

CHATTEL MORTGAGES:

See topic Mortgages.

COLLECTIONS:

Collections are arranged at fees varying from NOK 248,- to NOK 12,375,- or under certain conditions actual cost if higher. Collection fees are paid by debtor provided previous notice. In case creditor is foreigner, however, additional fees may be charged to creditor. If collection does not result, creditor will be responsible to collector for fee. As general rule, it is to be observed that Norwegian lawyers are not allowed, according to rules and ethics of The Norwegian Bar Association, to undertake case on

See Topical Index in front part of this volume.

COLLECTIONS . . . *continued*
percentage of proceeds or "no cure no pay" basis. Fee will be computed on basis of work spent on case and also with regard to value of interests at issue. Contingent agreements may however be entered into in special cases.

COMMERCIAL REGISTER:

Commercial companies have to be entered in central company register (Enhetsregisteret). Registration and current changes of Charter and Members of Board require use of particular form and that signature of Board members are witnessed by attorney or two laymen. It is advisable to contact Norwegian lawyer when entries in register are necessary.

CONFLICTS OF LAW: See topic International Law.

CONSTITUTION AND GOVERNMENT:

Norway is a hereditary democratic Kingdom. The Norwegian Constitution was promulgated May 17, 1814, and is based on Montesquieus principle of partition of power. It has been subject to a number of alterations, one of most important innovations being the introduction of "Parliamentarism" in 1884 (Parliament's right to discharge ministry).

The Government can be sued before the ordinary courts.

Executive power is vested with King in Council. Both men and women have accession to throne of realm. Council p.t. consists of 16 (including prime minister) ministers. Minister must be Norwegian citizen.

Legislature.—Parliament consists of two sections: "Lagtinget," consisting of one-fourth, and "Odelstinget," of three-fourths of members of Parliament. Parliament has 165 members. Any member of Parliament must have passed 18 years of age, and must have been domiciled for at least ten years in Norway.

Any proposed law must pass "Odelsting" as well as "Lagting." If both of them have treated it twice without having reached any agreement, it is submitted to the whole Parliament in plenum.

Judiciary.—The judges are appointed by the King in Council for lifetime. They are independent of administration and Parliament. See topic Courts.

It is within the province of the courts to decide whether a law passed by Parliament is in conflict with the Constitution.

CONTINENTAL SHELF:

(Act of Mar. 22, 1985). Right to submarine petroleum resources is vested in state. King in Council may, on conditions to be further stipulated, grant production licences. Production licence may be granted to body corporate established in conformity with Norwegian legislation and registered in Norwegian register of business enterprises or to company from European Economic Area (EEA). Such licence entails exclusive right to exploration for petroleum, exploration drilling and production of petroleum within delimited areas. Licensee becomes owner of petroleum which is produced. Rules on oil production provide for royalty ranging from 8% (for less than 40,000 barrels per day) and up to 16% (for 350,000 barrels per day) provided plan for development and operation (PDO) was approved prior to 1 Jan. 1986. Currently no royalty is levied on natural gas. In addition municipal and government tax is levied at rate of 28% and special tax at rate of 50%. Production licence is initially granted for six years and may be prolonged for up to 30 years upon relinquishment of half licence area. Further prolongation may be granted when justified by special reason. Licence to explore and exploit for submarine natural resources other than petroleum may be granted by government.

Delimitation of continental shelf between Norway and U. K. is settled by agreement of Mar. 10, 1965 between the two countries. Basis of agreement is principle of medium line. Similar agreements with Denmark and Sweden were entered on Dec. 8, 1965 and July 24, 1968.

Act introducing 200 nautical miles economical zone round coast was passed by Parliament on Dec. 17, 1976. Act does not influence shipping or aviation over zone nor does it influence Act on continental shelf. It does however restrict fishing in these waters to Norwegian citizens or citizens of countries listed in decree of Dec. 27, 1976 by Ministry of Fishing.

CONTRACTS:

Contracts are binding upon parties unless performance is contrary to public order. Normally no specific form is required and even verbal agreements are in principle valid. Reasons for invalidity are fraud, lack of intention on behalf of one of the contractors noticeable to the other contractor, mental deficiency, minority and stipulating of unreasonable prices or conditions.

Excuses for nonperformance of an otherwise valid contract are de facto and economical force majeure. Further nonperformance may in some cases be excused in accordance with doctrine of rebus sic stantibus.

Applicable Law.—Normally Lex Loci Contractus.

Government Contracts.—Ministries or directories in accordance with instructions from Government are normally entitled to bind Government. Contracts of minor importance entered into by subordinate official authorities are also normally binding on Government provided authority in question acts in accordance with ministry instructions.

Larger contracts for goods and services must in general only be entered into after tender procedure.

Distributorships, Dealerships and Franchises.—(Act on Price Regulation Measures of June 11, 1993, No. 66 and Act on Competition of June 11, 1993, No. 65). Appropriate authority is Competition Authority.

CONVEYANCES: See topic Deeds.

COPYRIGHT:

(Act of May 12, 1961). An author has the exclusive right of using his work in any way and for any sort of publishing. This applies as a rule to all kinds of intellectual productions, literature, lectures, cinema, music, painting and designs, sculpture, handicrafts, as well as data software. Upon author's death, ordinary rules of inheritance apply to such rights. No translation may be published without consent of person who has copyright. Author may convey his right of publishing totally or partly. Period of author-rights ends with expiration of 70th year after author's death. This applies to productions by Norwegian citizens, and to works by foreign citizens if either work is first made public in Norway, or according to reciprocal agreement between Norway and country in question. In any case copyright lasts for at least ten years after first publishing. Norwegian copyright is enjoyed by persons domiciled in Norway as well as by foreigners, provided their intellectual work is published in Norway within 30 days after having first been published abroad. Further, copyright may be extended to foreign citizens to same degree as enjoyed by persons domiciled in Norway by international agreement and on condition of reciprocity. Such agreement exists with U.S.A. and numerous other countries, among them those who, like Norway, are parties to Berne Convention.

No registration is required to obtain copyright. There are no formal requirements for giving assignments or licences.

CORPORATIONS:

All sorts of private and public corporations and associations for purposes of religion, philanthropy, trade, profession, labor (trade unions) etc. may be formed. Charter would be necessary for most of these corporations.

Companies with limited liability (joint stock companies) are regulated by Joint Stock Companies Act of June 4, 1976. As of Jan. 1, 1996 distinction between small and large joint-stock companies, so-called private and public limited companies, has emerged. Main difference between these kinds of joint-stock companies is that only public limited companies can offer shares for public subscription by obtaining shareholders' funds and through quotation on Stock Exchange. Public limited companies use abbreviation ASA while private limited companies use AS. Public limited companies must possess share capital amounting to at least NOK 1 million. Private limited companies must have share capital which amounts to NOK 50,000. Each share must be in equal amount and issued to specified shareholder.

If legal requirements for establishment have not been complied with, registrar shall refuse registration. Subsequent alteration in registered particulars must be registered.

When share is fully paid share certificate must be issued or shareholding entered in Central Register of Securities. Share transfers must be covered by contract notes. Share transfer must be entered in share register of company or in Central Registry of Securities, as case may be.

Board of directors may consist of three or more members of which one-half must be domiciled in EEA-countries. If share capital is less than NOK 1,000,000 number of board members may be reduced to one but then at least one deputy is required.

In companies with more than 30 employees, employees may demand to be represented on Board.

Companies with more than 200 employees shall have corporate assembly with not less than 12 members of whom one third is elected by employees and two thirds by annual general meeting. Main function of assembly is to elect board directors of whom one third normally are elected among employees.

Resolution for voluntary dissolution can be passed only by general meeting with consent of two-thirds of shareholders representing two-thirds of represented capital.

Companies must send annual accounts including directors' and auditors' reports to Central Register of Accounts.

Company must have one auditor who must be registered or authorized. Company's chief executive officer must be domiciled in EEA country.

Limited and unlimited partnerships are regulated by Company Act of June 21, 1985.

Most corporations and all companies and partnerships must be entered in appropriate public register.

Foreign Corporations.—See topics Aliens; Continental Shelf; Licences.

COURTS:

Boards of Conciliation are established in every town and parish. No lawyer may represent parties before Board of Conciliation unless other party has been given prior notification.

Courts of First Instance are either called "byrett" (town court) or "herredsrett" (county court).

In every jurisdiction are special divisions for probate, bankruptcy and enforcement. Duties of such divisions are performed in country districts or small towns by ordinary judge, in larger towns by special judge.

Town and county courts also deal with appeals against judgments of Board of Conciliation.

Courts of Appeal "Lagmannsretten".—There are six, one each for East, South, Southeast, West, Mid and North-Norway. Court of appeal is for individual case set with three judges. Two or four assessors are called when demanded by one of parties or when court deems fit. Appeal from town or county courts are dealt with where amount or value involved is at least kr. 20,000.

Supreme Court "Høyesterett".—This court has its seat in Oslo and is headed by Chief Justice of Norway. For individual case Supreme Court is set with five judges. Number of decisions are made by Judicial Select Committee of Supreme Court, which is set with three judges. Supreme Court deals with appeals from Courts of Appeal and in special circumstances directly from Courts of First Instance.

Criminal justice is administered by the same courts that handle civil lawsuits, viz. courts of first instance, Courts of Appeal, and the Supreme Court. In criminal case proceedings number of judges may differ from those of civil case proceedings.

See Topical Index in front part of this volume.

CURRENCY:

Monetary unit is Norwegian Crown (krone). Currency exchange is controlled by Act dated July 14, 1950. See topic Foreign Exchange.

CURTESY:

No right corresponding to "Curtesy" exists in Norway. As to the right of the surviving husband or wife to hold the joint estate for lifetime, see topic Husband and Wife.

CUSTOMS DUTIES:

Customs duties are levied by Government on most kinds of goods imported to Norway in accordance with list of charges which are revised every year. Rates are mainly based upon value and vary considerably.

23% value added tax is levied in addition.

For imports originating from EEA countries customs are now abolished except for certain agricultural products.

DEATH (PRESUMPTION OF AND ACTIONS FOR):

(Act of March 23, 1961). If a person has disappeared under such conditions that it is not reasonable to doubt he is dead, the judge of the Probate Court may decide that the person shall be considered dead. Otherwise presumption of death has to be established by court proceedings. Judgment that missing person be deemed dead may be obtained in case of unexplained absence for period of ten years. Person missing in connection with specific fatal event which created serious danger to his life, may be deemed dead after one year's absence. When it thus has been established that person is to be considered or deemed dead, his estate is normally wound up by Probate Court.

Actions for Death.—Civil action lies in favor of all persons who were supported by victim. Action to be brought within three years of death. Amount recoverable is not normally limited. Courts will estimate and allow damages according to circumstances in each separate case. See also topic Limitation of Actions.

DECEDENTS' ESTATES:

See topics Descent and Distribution; Wills.

DEEDS:

Transfer of real property must be entered in land register (see topics Real Property; Records) to be effective against third parties or creditors of vendor, and such purchase deed must bear certificate from either a notary public, a lawyer or two witnesses confirming that vendor is of age and has signed in their presence. Close relatives and employees of purchaser cannot confirm vendor's signature on deed. As to stamp duty, see topic Real Property.

Similar rules apply to ships and aircraft. No stamps payable.

DEPOSITIONS:

The proper Norwegian Court will examine witnesses upon request of a foreign court if such request is made through diplomatic channels to the Norwegian Ministry of Justice. Qualified Norwegian lawyer can also examine witnesses upon such request. Outside Norway for use in Norwegian Courts depositions are normally taken at request of Norwegian court in question by nearest Norwegian consular officer. See topic Actions.

DESCENT AND DISTRIBUTION:

The Law of Succession (of Mar. 3, 1972) has following classes of inheritors: (1) Children and other issue; (2) parents and their issue; (3) grandparents and their issue, but not remoter than their children and grandchildren. A nearer class of inheritors excludes more remote classes, and any person entitled to inherit will, with certain modifications, exclude his issue.

Surviving consort takes one-fourth if there are issue of decedent, one-half if there are no issue but father or mother or brother or sister or their issue, otherwise the entire estate. If there was community of goods (see topic Husband and Wife), only half the common estate is inherited, the other half falling to the surviving consort by virtue of his or her ownership. Recent change in law has granted surviving consort right to receive minimum of 4 G (annually revised bases for entire social benefit system) if there are issue of decent and 6 G in all other cases. This means that all smaller estates with values of respectively 8 G or less or 12 G or less will be taken over in whole by surviving consort. (1 G equals NOK 41,000 as of 01.05.1996.) See also topic Husband and Wife.

If there are neither heirs nor surviving consort nor a will, government takes entire estate.

Illegitimate children inherit from their mother on equal terms with her children born in wedlock. They also inherit from their father if they were born after Jan. 1, 1917. Paternity is established after legal proceedings in court. If alleged father admits paternity, however, County Governor will merely issue decree to that effect.

DISPUTE RESOLUTION:

Mandatory Dispute Resolution.—Conciliation before Board of Conciliation is mandatory in most civil cases. If proceedings fail board may at request of party pass judgment. During court proceedings judges may attempt conciliation.

Specific conciliation requirements apply to certain family and labour relations cases.

At request of party certain cases may be decided by certain panels. This applies e.g. to consumer, banking and patient liability matters. Generally rulings are not binding.

Voluntary Dispute Resolution.—Parties may agree to minitrials in front of ordinary courts. Claims arising out of criminal offences may be made subject to conciliation by Conflict Board.

Arbitration may take place on ad hoc basis or before established panels, e.g. Oslo Chamber of Commerce and Permanent Technical Panels. Ad hoc mediation and conciliation solutions are also seen.

See also topics Arbitration; Courts, subhead Boards of Conciliation.

DIVORCE:

(Act of July 4, 1991).

Either party who refuses to continue cohabitation may demand decree of separation. When decree of separation is given, divorce is granted after one year. Divorce is granted when cohabitation is discontinued for two years notwithstanding no decree of separation is given. Divorce may be granted without previous separation in some cases, e.g. severe threats, physical abuse etc.

Usual courts have jurisdiction. However, parties can agree to submit matter to County Governor for decision without court proceedings.

Conciliation before public arbitrator is compulsory in some cases.

See topic International Law.

Alimony may be decreed in favor of one of the parties, if this party cannot furnish such maintenance out of his own income.

Custody of children is based on what solution will be best for child. Mother is, however, often given custody of children—especially if children are young.

DOWER:

No rules apply. If given, donor may decide that dower shall be married woman's separate estate. See also topic Husband and Wife.

Dower is subject to inheritance tax. See topic Taxation.

ENVIRONMENT:

Among most important enactments in Norwegian environmental legislation is Pollution Control Act which states that all pollution is forbidden unless permission is given specifically or in law or regulation. Other important enactments are Product Control Act, Planning and Building Act, Nature Conservation Act, Outdoor Recreation Act and Cultural Heritage Act. Extensive regulations pursuant to law.

General Supervision.—

Ministry of Environment.—Highest authority in environmental matters lies with Ministry of Environment which is divided into five following departments: Department for Organisational and Economic Affairs; Department for Nature Conservation and Cultural Heritage; Department for Water Waste Management and Industry; Department for International Co-operation, Air Management and Polar Affairs; Department for Regional Planning and Resource Management; Address: Myntgaten 2, P.O. Box 8013 Dep., N-0030 Oslo, telephone: +47 22 24 90 90, telefax: +47 22 24 95 60.

State Pollution Authority.—It is responsible for measures against products and substances that are hazardous to environment or to health. It monitors atmospheric and aquatic pollution and oversees emergency services for oil pollution and other acute pollution. It administers Pollution Control Act and Product Control Act. Address: Strømsveien 96, P.O. Box 8100 Dep., N-0032 Oslo, telephone: +47 22 57 34 00, telefax: +47 22 67 67 06.

Directorate for Nature Management.—It is responsible for implementing nature management policy in Norway. Its authority derives from various acts and regulations e.g. Nature Conservation Act, Outdoor Recreation Act. Address: Tungsletta 2, N-7005 Trondheim, telephone: +47 73 58 05 00, telefax: +47 73 91 54 33.

Norwegian Polar Research Institute.—It is central government institution for mapping survey and practical and scientific investigation of polar regions. Address: Middelthuns gate 29, N-0368 Oslo, telephone: +47 22 95 95 95, telefax: +47 22 95 90 00.

Directorate for Cultural Heritage.—It is responsible for implementing policy relating to overall protection of Norway's cultural heritage. Its responsibilities are set out in Cultural Heritage Act. Address: Dronningens gate 13, P.O. Box 8196 Dep., N-0034 Oslo, telephone: +47 22 94 04 00, telefax: +47 22 94 04 04.

EXCHANGE CONTROL:

See topics Currency; Foreign Exchange; Licences.

EXECUTIONS:

Execution is levied pursuant to: A judgment, an order given by the board of conciliation, an accommodation made before such board or a court; a legal arbitral decision; written and certified acknowledgments of debt; and some other cases specified in the Executions Act of June 26, 1992. Debtor's goods of any kind may be taken in execution according to such judgment, etc. Through execution, creditors get mortgage on real property or in chattels. No handing over of articles mortgaged is necessary. Any execution must be registered in order to be valid against competing creditors. Goods must either be sold at public auction or by assistant appointed by court. When real property is sold at such public auction, all incumbrances which are privileged before claim must be covered, and rest of sales sum is paid out to creditor. Bonds and claims may be taken in execution. Documents are handed over to bailiff and debtor is prohibited to pay his debt to original creditor. Execution is performed in towns by special officers of execution, in country by sheriff.

After judgment is given and before execution may be obtained, or in case the losing party has made an appeal to the court of appeal, the claim of a creditor may be protected through a temporary seizure called "arrest" (attachment). Such attachment is performed in the same way and has the same legal effect as an execution, but the creditor has no right of sale till the judgment of the appeal court is given. See topic Exemptions.

EXECUTORS AND ADMINISTRATORS:

(Act of Feb. 21, 1930).

If at least one heir of age takes over full responsibility for debts, no administrator or executor is required by law to have estate settled.

Absent heirs, whose address is known, must, as a rule, have particular information of the succession. If the residence of such heirs is unknown, they are most frequently called through an advertisement to appear, but nonappearance does not deprive them of their right as heirs.

By leaving the winding up of the estate to the court the heirs avoid responsibility for the debts. If the probate court does not interfere the heirs may divide the estate

EXECUTORS AND ADMINISTRATORS . . . *continued*

between themselves if they undertake responsibility for the debts, but a creditor of the deceased is entitled, within six months, to claim the winding up of the estate by the court if he can establish that his chance of being paid would be reduced by the succession.

Within six weeks of receipt of legal notice, creditors may be called to prove their claims.

Appointment.—An executor can be appointed by will of deceased. Appointment must be approved by Probate Court. Executor must deposit security and acts under control of court.

EXEMPTIONS:

Under Act of June 8, 1984 every debtor has right to exemption of certain articles and assets such as personal belongings, unpaid salary, cash and bank deposits necessary for support of debtor and his family.

FOREIGN CORPORATIONS: See topic Corporations.

FOREIGN EXCHANGE:

Exchange control is governed by Exchange Control Act of 14 July 1950 and Royal Decree of 29 July 1955, with later amendments. It is administered by Ministry of Finance, but day-to-day management is carried out by Bank of Norway and other banks licenced by it.

Exchange control applies to both residents and nonresidents in respect of all currency transfers to and from Norway. Any person having permanent residence or habitual abode in Norway and any legal entity having base there, is regarded as resident for exchange control purposes. This definition does not accord with that in use for tax and social security purposes.

After many years with extensive regulation, which were based on principle that all transactions are forbidden unless they are allowed, new principle was introduced in new regulations which took effect July 1, 1990. According to new rules all transactions are now allowed, unless they are explicitly forbidden.

As result of EEA Agreement Norwegian companies and individuals may now make direct foreign investments, borrow in foreign currency, enter into forward exchange contracts, open accounts in foreign banks, purchase and sell life insurance and shares in companies.

See also topics Currency; Licences.

FOREIGN INVESTMENTS: See topic Licences.

FOREIGN TRADE REGULATIONS:

Foreign trade has been regulated since World War II by Acts of Dec. 13, 1946. During recent years, however, imports and exports have continually become freer and at present bulk of traded goods is free listed. Main items still under some formal control are vessels.

Norway is party to EFTA (European Free Trade Association), and from 1994 Norway is party to Agreement on the European Economic Area, which establish free movement of goods, services and establishments within EU/EFTA states. See topic Customs Duties.

FRAUDS, STATUTE OF:

As a rule, oral contracts have the same force as written; but a few contracts (e.g., marriage settlements) must be in writing.

FRAUDULENT SALES AND CONVEYANCES:

Every transaction which is fraudulent against the creditors may be declared void under the principle of invalidation adopted by most Western European countries in accordance with the principles of Roman law (Actio Pauliana).

GARNISHMENT: See topic Executions.

GUARDIAN AND WARD:

(Act of Nov. 28, 1898). Adults who are physically or mentally strongly handicapped may by court decree be declared incapable of managing his (her) own affairs, in which case a guardian is appointed. See also topic Infants.

HOLIDAY:

Legal holidays in Norway are New Year's Day, Maundy Thursday, Good Friday, Easter Monday, Ascension Day, White Monday, Dec. 25 and 26, May 1 and National Day, May 17.

Certain times expiring on a holiday may be extended to the following weekday. This provision applies to time for presenting cheques and all processual times. Holidays are not included in the lay-days, and they do not start running on a holiday.

Employees are entitled to 25 workdays, Sat. included, paid holidays per annum. Employees above 60 years of age are entitled to 31 days paid holiday. (Act of Apr. 29, 1988).

HOMESTEADS:

No homestead exemption.

HUSBAND AND WIFE:

(Act of July 4, 1991).

There may be a community of goods or separate property under a marriage settlement. In the absence of any agreement to the contrary community of goods is the rule. Marriage contracts must be put in a special form, called "ektepakt."

The property of both consorts at the time of marriage and the property they may acquire after the marriage is community of goods. Each consort has the right to dispose of the goods which he or she has brought into the community. By a divorce, a separation, or by the death of one of the consorts, the community acquired during marriage, is divided equally between consorts or between surviving consort and heirs of deceased one. However, by divorce or separation each of consorts may claim separate property of goods he or she has brought into marriage or later has brought into community by gifts or heritage.

Without the consent of the other consort, real property, belonging to the community of goods, may not be alienated or mortgaged if it serves as the common residence of the consorts or is attached to the industry of one of them. Movables may not be alienated or pledged without the consent of the other consort if the said movables belong to the common furniture or necessary toils.

If one of the consorts essentially diminishes the community of goods through mismanagement or neglect, compensation may be given the other consort for the loss when the community is divided.

By "ektepakt" (marriage settlement or contract) made previous to or after the marriage, the estate may be declared wholly or in part as the separate property of one of the consorts.

A donation from a third person may be on condition that the articles bestowed be the separate property of the receiver. In his will a testator may leave part or all of his estate to be the separate property of the heir in question, which also applies to hereditary shares, falling to issue under the law. Goods superseding separate property are separate property. Profits of separate property are separate property.

A marriage contract must be written, certified by two witnesses and signed by the parties. In order to acquire legal effect in relation to a third party such marriage contracts must be registered.

In relation to third parties each consort is during married life entitled to make dispositions on the responsibility of both, if the said dispositions are the usual ones for the household or bringing up the children. Each consort is responsible, both with the part of the community over which he has the right of disposing and with his separate property, for liabilities resting on him, whether they date from before or after the marriage.

Donations between consorts must be through a marriage contract, in order to render them valid. This, however, does not apply to ordinary gifts according to the economic situation of the giver.

Surviving consort has the right to continue possession of community property. For separate property special provision to same effect may be made in marriage contract. If deceased consort leaves issue of previous marriage the right is subject to their consent. (Act of Mar. 3, 1972).

IMMIGRATION:

Aliens may remain in Norway without specific permission up to three months. EEA nationals can apply for extended permission to remain in Norway within expiry of this period. Non-EEA nationals must apply for such extended permission before entering Norway. Provided applicant is not punished for crimes, permission is normally granted for periods up to one year.

Non-EEA nationals seeking paid employment in Norway must have permission from police. Permissions may be granted in special cases (wife and children of aliens already living and working in Norway, refugees, scientists, artists, technical experts, etc.). Applications to be sent prior to travelling to Norway to local Norwegian Embassy or Consulate. Exemption for foreigners with at least one Norwegian parent.

These rules also apply to temporary entry of technical and industrial personnel, etc.

After three years in Norway aliens may apply for general and unlimited permission to remain in country and to take paid employment.

After seven years uninterrupted residence in Norway aliens may apply for Norwegian citizenship.

INFANTS:

Minors below age of 15 may not be punished for criminal offences or—normally—held liable for damages. Parents may be held liable for damages caused by minors below 18 years.

Age of majority is 18. Agreements entered into by minor are invalid. Parents or, in their absence, appointed person act as guardian. Guardian has limited command of minor's property and income. (Act of Apr. 22, 1927).

INSOLVENCY: See topic Bankruptcy.

INTEREST:

(Act of Dec. 17, 1976).

Claims which are not paid on maturity carry 12% interest from date of maturity. Where no such date has been established creditor may claim payment in writing in which case interest accrues from one month after request for payment has been sent.

Interest on debt which is owed for purchase of consumer goods is also 12%.

INTERNATIONAL LAW:

Norwegian law on conflicts of laws applies domicile as the test of personal rights, i.e., when the legitimacy, sanity, capacity, marriage or divorce of a person is the subject of inquiry. The succession to the movables, as well as the immovables of an intestate, is as a rule governed by the law of his domicile.

The Norwegian concept of domicile does not coincide with the English. According to Norwegian law it is easier to acquire a domicile of choice.

The validity of a contract is governed by the proper law of the contract.

Norwegian courts have jurisdiction in all cases where defendant is domiciled in Norway, also in respect of an immovable situated outside Norway. In a divorce case Norwegian courts have jurisdiction even if only plaintiff resides in Norway, provided the spouses had their last joint domicile in this country. There is emergency jurisdiction to help Norwegian plaintiffs if divorce in country where defendant resides is unobtainable or connected with extreme difficulties.

JOINT STOCK COMPANIES:

See topic Corporations.

JUDGMENTS:

Judgments must state a time limit within which execution may not be levied, in ordinary cases two weeks and in some special cases three days from the service of the judgment. A judgment given by the Supreme Court of Appeal may be enforced at once.

Judgment for the plaintiff may be given both in the board of conciliation and in the courts of first instance, if the defendant does not appear.

Courts are entitled to order loser of court case to pay all reasonable court costs incurred by winning party.

Foreign Judgments.—The effect of foreign judgments depends upon treaty with the country where the judgment was rendered. Such treaties exist between Norway and other countries parties to EEA (Lugano convention). Norway is signatory to The Hague Treaty of 1954, exempting citizens of signatory countries from deposit of costs and making foreign judgments for costs enforceable. As to civil claims foreign judgments based on agreed venue may also be binding.

JURISDICTION: See topic International Law.

LABOR RELATIONS:

Pay and other conditions are to large extent settled by agreements between Employers Association and Unions who hold a strong position.

Employee may not be discharged unless facts justify termination of his employment. Infringements entitle employee to compensation which is assessed by courts under consideration of economical loss suffered, conduct of employee and employer and circumstances in general. (Act of Feb. 4, 1977, §62).

After retirement old age pension is usual but not compulsory. Government old age pension is payable after retirement at age of 67.

LAW REPORTS:

Statutory laws are reported in the Norwegian Law Gazette (Norsk Lovtidende) as soon as they are passed.

Every two years University of Oslo publishes a near complete set of all statutory laws in force in Norway. Latest issue covers laws passed 1685-1995. Supplementary issue published every alternating two years.

Judgments by Supreme Court are reported in "Norsk Retstidende." Judgments of principal interest passed by inferior courts are reported in "Rettens Gang." Both these publications are published by Norwegian Bar Association. Judgments in maritime cases passed by courts in Scandinavia are reported in "Nordiske Domme i Sjöfartsanliggender" published by Nordisk Skibsrederforening, Oslo.

See also topic Statutes.

LEGISLATURE:

See Constitution and Government, subhead Legislature.

LICENCES:

Licences are required for a number of activities such as land transportation, banking, mining, conveyance of real property and stockbroking. Licences are often only issued to EEA subjects.

Industrial manufacturing normally requires no licence. See however subhead Real Property, infra.

Real Property.—Acquirement of real property by aliens requires generally Government licence. According to statutory law passed by Parliament in 1974 licence will to large extent also be required for EEA citizens. See topics Real Property; Continental Shelf.

LIENS:

Factors, warehousemen, hotel-keepers, and carriers have lien upon goods for their charges. Persons making improvements, repairs, etc., upon personal property in their possession have a lien thereon for work done and material furnished. Solicitors have a lien upon documents in their possession for their charges. Certain third parties have liens upon ship and cargo for number of claims against shipowner. There is lien for taxes and number of rates and duties.

Mechanics' lien on real property does not exist in Norway.

LIMITATION OF ACTIONS:

One year: Claim related to ground transportation.

Two years: Claims against air carriers for injuries to passengers and damage to goods; see topic Aviation, subhead Time Bar.

By act of May 18, 1979 actions are limited as follows:

Three years: All claims unless otherwise stated.

Ten years: Claims for which written acknowledgment of debt has been issued, pension, alimony and some other claims.

Twenty years: Bank deposits.

It should be noted that many claims under Admiralty Law are barred earlier than stated above, time bar in some cases being as short as six months.

Time within which action must be brought is reckoned from first day creditor may demand payment.

Acknowledgment of liability by debtor keeps debt alive, and destroys effect of statutory limitation.

Contractual Limitation.—Agreements which have effect of excluding statutory limitations are not valid. After claim has arisen debtor may accept prolongation of time limits for three years at a time, but not for longer period than ten years altogether.

LIMITED PARTNERSHIP: See topic Partnership.

MARRIAGE:

(Act of July 4, 1991).

No person, who has not completed his 17th year, may enter into marriage without consent of his parents and royal permission. One who is declared incapable of managing his/her own affairs may not enter into marriage without guardian's consent. One who is suffering from contagious venereal disease may not enter into marriage unless other person is informed and doctor has guided them about hazards of disease. No marriage may be entered into by: Persons related in direct ascent or descent; brother and sister.

Marriage is solemnized by church wedding or contracted before the magistrate. Two witnesses must be present.

There are no restrictions on marriage with a foreigner.

Two persons of same sex may register as cohabitants. As general rule such registration produces same legal effects as entering into marriage. (Act of Apr. 30, 1993).

MONOPOLIES AND RESTRAINT OF TRADE:

Certain nationalization of private enterprises has taken place throughout years. Thus sale of wines and liqueurs is reserved to State Wine Monopoly; railways and voice telephony and telecommunication infrastructure are run by state-owned companies.

In principal all private enterprises may be subject to expropriation by passing adequate laws. Owners are, however, according to constitution entitled to full compensation. Such compensation is normally fixed by court assessment. Profit arising out of expropriation is taxed to the extent of about 28% unless reinvested in other enterprise.

Norway is member of EFTA and party to EEA Agreement.

MORTGAGES:

(Act of Feb. 8, 1980).

Real Estate.—Mortgage on real property is obtained through agreement or execution. Mortgage through agreement or execution must be registered in order to obtain legal protection in relation to third party; but registration is not necessary in case of liens. Priority of several mortgages is subject to time of their registration, mortgage first registered has precedence of all others. If debt is not duly paid, property mortgaged may be sold at public auction or by assistant appointed by court. Mortgage deed requires no stamp, but must be certified like deed (see topic Deeds) to be entered in register.

Chattel.—As main rule chattel may only be mortgaged by handing over to mortgagee. Industrialists, traders and business people may, however, also mortgage chattel used in business. This may be done by mortgaging chattel together with real estate and having deed registered in real estate register. Alternatively, mortgaging of chattel may take place separately, in which case mortgaging should be registered in Chattel Mortgage Register.

Similarly, ships, aircrafts and busses may be mortgaged as hitherto by entering deed in appropriate register.

MOTOR VEHICLES:

There is a special Motor Vehicle Act of June 18, 1965, containing provisions for the size and fittings of motor vehicles, the entry, examination and registration of such vehicles, drivers and driving and duties payable on such vehicles.

Special provisions are issued for motor vehicles belonging to foreigners. Foreign travelers wanting to bring their cars with them to Norway should obtain a green card from their insurance company which covers liability in Norway. If such card is not available in homeland, a compulsory liability policy must be subscribed, via customhouse at place of entry. See subhead Liability, infra.

Liability is regulated by an act dated Feb. 3, 1961 which instead of personal liability for owner or driver institutes compulsory third party insurance for all vehicles. Third parties are entitled to compensation (unlimited for bodily injuries) even if neither owner of vehicle nor driver has been inadvertent.

NOTARIES PUBLIC:

There are no special notaries public in Norway; ordinary judges of courts of first instance and sheriffs perform duties of notary public.

PARTNERSHIP:

(Act of June 21, 1985).

Unlimited partnership ("ansvarlig selskap") consists of partners who are personally responsible, jointly and separately, for partnership liabilities. Creditors may sue any of partners, but no judgment pronounced against such partner is binding on partnership as such or other partners. In case of bankruptcy partnership estate forms a separate estate in which creditors of partnership have a preference to those of several partners.

Limited partnership ("kommanditselskap") consists of some partners whose liability is unlimited and some partners whose liability is limited to amounts they have agreed to bring into the business as their share of the capital. Limited partners are liable to partnership creditors for amount of agreed contributions to capital which has not been paid in.

Commercial partnership must be entered into The Register of Business Enterprises.

PATENTS:

In accordance with Patents Act of Dec. 15, 1967, patents may be granted for new inventions which can be industrially utilized. Applications for patents are filed in "Styret for det Industrielle Rettsvern" (Patent Office) in Oslo, accompanied by enclosures required. Applications on file are made accessible to public 18 months after application/priority date. Applications are subjected to formality and novelty examination. Novelty requirement is absolute. Upon acceptance, applications are laid out for three months for public inspection and opposition. Only inventor or his legal successors is entitled to patent. Patent term is 20 years from date of filing of application, against payment of annuities, accrued annuities being payable only after grant of patent. Applicant not resident in Norway must be represented by agent residing in

PATENTS . . . *continued*
realm. Law suits concerning validity of patent shall be brought before City Court of Oslo.

Patents Act is in harmonization with corresponding Acts in Denmark, Finland and Sweden. Envisaged system of Nordic patent application is not enforced.

Norway is party to Paris Convention EEA Agreement, in which principle of EEA consumption of rights applies.

PLEDGES: See topic Chattel Mortgages.

PRESCRIPTION: See topic Limitation of Actions.

PRINCIPAL AND AGENT:

For principal and agents in general, provisions are given in the Act of May 31, 1918. Special provision concerning commissions, commercial agents and commercial travelers (commercial clerks) are given in Acts of June 30, 1916 and June 19, 1992.

Contract made by agent in name of principal and within limits of agent's power binds principal. If third party knew that agent acted outside his power, contract does not bind principal. The agent is responsible for his power being in order. There are special provisions with regard to revocation of the agent's power, death of principal or agent, bankruptcy of one of the parties, etc.

REAL PROPERTY:

Real property is land with accessories (like fences, trees, etc.). House built upon hired land is real property. No right in land can be legally acquired in relation to a third party, unless the title issued for the purpose of creating such right has been entered into the Land Register of the jurisdiction where the property is situated. Title is subject to 2.5% stamp duty.

Acquisition of real estate by persons living outside Norway will in certain instances be regulated by licensing laws.

RECORDS:

There are a number of public records. Land titles and all encumbrances on land, as mortgages, etc., are recorded in the land register of the jurisdiction where the property is situated. There is a land register at every court of first instance. Anybody who has an interest in the registrations may inspect the records relating to the particular parcel of land.

Other registers are The Register of Business Enterprises for commercial partnerships, limited partnerships and corporations, accounting register, ship registers, boat register, population register, register for aeroplanes and motor vehicles, and marriage contract register for their respective purposes.

Central Coordinating Register for Legal Entities coordinates company information from various official registers.

REPORTS: See topic Law Reports.

SALES:

Property in chattel may be transferred without any formality; and payment of purchase is not essential for transfer of ownership.

The Purchase Law of May 13, 1988, applies unless stipulations to contrary have been agreed upon or is consequent on commercial customs. Some of stipulations in law may not be altered to detriment of buyer when seller is professional and articles sold are consumer goods bought for personal use. This applies inter alia to delay on behalf of seller and to faults attached to object sold. In absence of agreement as to price, buyer must pay price demanded by vendor, unless same is unreasonable. Vendor must deliver goods sold at place where he had his residence or place of business at time of purchase.

If goods sold are not delivered in due time, and delay is not due to buyer's conduct or to accident for which he bears the risk, buyer may choose whether he will demand delivery or repudiate contract. If delivery is delayed, vendor may be liable for damages. If buyer fails to pay purchase money at maturity, vendor is free to choose whether he will uphold or cancel contract, but if delay is of no considerable importance contract may not be cancelled. If bargain is cancelled by vendor he may claim damages from buyer. In absence of proof of additional loss having been suffered, damages will be fixed at amount, by which purchase money exceeds price of goods of nature and quality similar to that of goods sold at time when delay began. If buyer omits in due time to send for or to receive goods sold, seller may be bound to take care of goods, and if necessary to sell them on account of buyer. Seller may claim compensation for his expenses, for which he has a lien on the goods.

If specific article purchased proves defective, buyer may repudiate contract and claim damages. If the purchase regards articles of special description and goods delivered are defective, buyer may repudiate the contract or demand proper delivery or a proportional reduction of purchase price. Under special circumstances vendor may be liable for damages, even though he is not to blame.

If, after conclusion of bargain, buyer goes into bankruptcy or negotiations have been opened as to a composition, seller has a right of stoppage in transitu even though goods were sold on credit.

Conditional Sales.—Movables may be transferred with an agreement that the buyer shall not acquire title until the full purchase price is paid. Sales on installment plan are governed and restricted by the Conditional Sales Act of June 21, 1985.

Notices Required.—Notice of nonconforming delivery is required to protect right against seller. Notices required to reserve rights for parties need not be in writing but written notices are preferable as containing proof of notice. In transactions between traders and industrialists notices reserving rights must be given without delay, otherwise without undue delay.

Warranties.—Whether or not a sold article is defective is dependent upon stipulations in contract and according to common law upon circumstances in each specific case such as purchase price, nature of purchased article, usual specification of same, property of sample presented prior to bargain, etc. Numerous leading judgments by Supreme Court give further guidance.

Applicable Law.—Normally Lex Loci Contractus.

International Sale of Goods.—United Nations Convention on Contracts for the International Sale of Goods, except part II and sales between Nordic countries, in force on Aug. 1, 1989. See topic Treaties and Part VII, Selected International Conventions.

SEALS:

No special rules regarding seals.

The use of a seal on a private document or a contract has no legal effect to its validity.

SEQUESTRATION: See topic Executions.

SHIPPING:

Maritime Act of Norway is dated June 24, 1994. Norway is party to various international Conventions entered into in Brussels on such subjects as Bills of Lading (the Hague Rules), Salvage, Limitation of Shipowners' Liability (of 1957), Collisions, Stowaways and Maritime Liens (of 1967).

Norwegian ships, to be entitled to carry national flag, must be exclusively owned by Norwegian subjects or by a corporation domiciled in Norway, whose board mainly consists of Norwegian subjects domiciled in Norway, and of whose capital six-tenths must be held by Norwegian subjects. Exemptions may be granted.

Master has legal competence to bind owner in matters concerning upkeep and running of vessel.

Owner's liability is limited in cases of accidents.

The law contains detailed provisions with regard to the owner's liability in connection with bills of lading and damage to goods. The effect of non-responsibility clauses in bills of lading is regulated by the Hague Rules.

There are a number of liens on ship and cargo peculiar to maritime law, particular liens being enumerated in maritime code (e. g., claims for wages of master and crew, salvage money, average, etc.).

By act of June 12, 1987, alternative ship register, Norwegian International Ship Register, has been established. This makes it possible to employ foreign seamen at salaries corresponding to salaries in seamens' homeland.

STATUTE OF FRAUDS: See topic Frauds, Statute of.

STATUTES:

The Civil Procedure, the Criminal Procedure and the Penal Law are codified. Regarding the civil law there are a number of special statutes but no general codification, although special parts are codified, e. g., the Inheritance Act, Marriage Act and Taxation Act.

See also topic Law Reports.

TAXATION:

There are two categories of taxable income—ordinary income and personal income.

Ordinary Income Tax is levied on net income which includes income derived from employment (salaries) and business, capital gains, interest and other capital proceeds. Capital costs and capital losses are only deductable in computation of ordinary taxable income. Ordinary income tax rate is 28%.

Personal Income Tax is levied on individual's gross income derived from employment or self-employment and pensions. Personal income tax rate varies from 9.5% to 13.7%.

Social Security Tax is payable at three different rates—3% (pensions), 7.8% (salaries) and 10.7% (self-employed). See also subhead Payroll Tax, infra.

Highest overall income tax for employees is 49.5%. Individuals who are self-employed are assessed at maximum rate of 52.4%.

Payroll Tax is payable by employer. Rate is 14.1% of gross wages and salaries. Payroll tax is deductable to employer. Exemption from liability to pay payroll tax and social security tax may be granted for employer as well as employee if latter is covered by similar foreign government pension and health service schemes.

Wealth Tax is assessed at progressive rates varying from 1% to 1.5%.

Corporation Tax is levied at flat rate of 28% (ordinary income tax rate). Individual shareholders who are actively participating in company are taxable for computed personal income from company if they own at least 2/3 of shares or are entitled to at least 2/3 of company's profit/dividend. Norwegian corporations do not pay wealth tax. Dividend from Norwegian corporations to shareholders resident in Norway is in practice not taxable. Dividend received from foreign corporations is taxable as ordinary income at 28%.

Withholding Tax on dividend from shares in Norwegian corporations is payable by shareholders domiciled abroad. Tax rate of 25% is levied unless otherwise is stipulated in tax treaty between Norway and country in question (see topic Treaties). Withholding tax shall be withheld by Norwegian corporation.

Value Added Tax (VAT) is payable at rate of 23% on all commercial sales of goods and most services. VAT is deductible until final consumer. VAT is refunded to retailers, merchants, factories etc. who instead normally have to pay 7% investment tax on most investments inside country. VAT is not charged on export sales.

Inheritance Tax ranges from 0 to 30% depending upon remoteness of heir and amount of his inheritance share.

Petroleum Tax.—Offshore oil production is subject to special state tax in accordance with decision to be made by Parliament each year. (Petroleum Tax Act of June 13, 1975, No. 35). For 1996 tax rate is 50% (which comes in addition to 28% ordinary income tax). See also topic Continental Shelf.

TAXATION . . . *continued*

Other Taxes.—In addition to taxes mentioned above there are number of special taxes collected by state or municipality such as property tax and luxury tax on different types of goods.

Payment of Taxes.—Ordinary income tax, personal income tax and social security tax is estimated and paid in same fiscal year as income is earned. Final assessment is taking place in subsequent year on basis of tax return filed by taxpayer. Capital tax is assessed on basis of taxpayer's financial position Jan. 1 in year in which taxes are assessed. Payment of taxes may be enforced by execution or sequestration.

TRADEMARKS AND TRADENAMES:

(Act of Mar. 3, 1961).

Trademarks and tradenames may be protected either by use or by registration. Trademarks are legally defined as comprising also service marks (such as a ship-owner's house flag), specific types of packages and slogans. A foreigner enjoys same legal protection as a native, but he may only register trademarks which are registered by himself in his own country. This rule does not apply to parties to Paris Convention of 1883 as revised in Stockholm 1967. Further, he must be represented by an agent residing in Norway, who can be summoned and appear in court on his behalf. A registered trademark is protected for ten years and registration may be renewed for ten years at a time. EEA consumption of rights applies. Lawsuits concerning validity of trademarks and names are heard and decided by city court of Oslo. Norway being a party to Nice Convention of 1957, has introduced International Classification of Goods for Trade Marks including services. Trade Marks Act is in harmonization with corresponding Acts in Denmark, Finland and Sweden.

TREATIES:

Treaties aiming at avoiding double taxation have been entered into between Norway and a number of foreign countries such as Australia, Austria, Belgium, France, Great Britain, Holland, Ireland, Italy, Japan, Scandinavian countries, U.S.A. and Germany. See topic Foreign Trade Regulations.

Norway is party to agreement on European Economic Area (EEA), Convention on Service Abroad of Judicial and Extrajudicial Documents in Civil or Commercial Matters, Convention on Taking of Evidence Abroad in Civil or Commercial Matters, and United Nations Convention on Recognition and Enforcement of Foreign Arbitral Awards, Convention Abolishing the Requirement of Legalisation for Foreign Public Documents, Convention on the Civil Aspects of International Child Abduction, Convention on jurisdiction and enforcement of Awards in Civil and Commercial Matters (Lugano convention). Norway is also member of OECD.

International Sale of Goods.—United Nations Convention on Contracts for the International Sale of Goods, except part II and sales between Nordic countries, in force on August 1, 1989. See topic Sales and Part VII, Selected International Conventions.

TRUSTS:

Trusts within the meaning of equity are not known in Norway.

WILLS:

(Act of Mar. 3, 1972).

Any person who leaves issue may dispose by will of only one-third of his estate, remaining two-thirds, up to kr. 1,000,000 per share for children and kr. 200,000 per share for grandchildren, devolving upon issue as their portio legitima. Person can reduce inheritance of surviving spouse through will if spouse is informed of its contents before death of testator. Surviving spouse has, however, right to minimum inheritance of approximately NOK 164,000 if person leaves issue, and NOK 246,000 if person leaves no issue.

Majority is not required by law for making a will, but a will made by a person under 18 years old is not valid unless confirmed by the King. Ordinarily a will must be made in writing in presence of two witnesses, subject to certain formalities prescribed in law.

A will may be altered or repealed, but such alteration or repeal must be done in the forms of a will.

A will made abroad according to the rules of a foreign country is valid in Norway even though said rules do not conform to Norwegian law.

PAKISTAN LAW DIGEST REVISER

Surridge & Beecheno
Finlay House, 3rd Floor
I.I. Chundrigar Road
Karachi 74000, Pakistan
Telephone: 92 21 242 7292-4
Fax: 92 21 241 6830

Reviser Profile

History: The firm was founded in 1948 in Karachi by two British Barristers, Charles Surridge and Peter Beecheno. Both the founding partners had a family history of legal practice in Rangoon (Burma) going back to the middle of the last century. In 1951 Campbell Gallaher came from England to join the firm as managing partner. Over the years the firm expanded and inducted several Pakistani partners and opened branch offices in Lahore and at Chittagong in then East Pakistan. The firm now has five partners and about twenty associates and has its principal office at Karachi and a branch office at Lahore.

Areas of Emphasis and Growth: The firm undertakes all forms of Civil and Commercial work both Contentious and Non-contentious. Its particular strengths are advice on and implementation of Foreign Investment Proposals, Corporate Law, Commercial Contracts, Building and Engineering Contracts, Admiralty and Shipping, Intellectual Property, Petroleum Laws, Banking and Finance and Aviation.

Client Base: The firm has a wide-ranging corporate clientele including international financial institutions, banks, pharmaceutical companies, oil companies and airlines. In addition the firm is the Karachi representative of a number of P & I Clubs based in the United Kingdom and Japan. The firm also has a corresponding relationship with major New York and London firms. For a list of representative clients please see the firm's entry in the Martindale-Hubbell Law Directory.

Firm's Activities: All partners and associates are members of the Bar Association and High Court Bar Association of Karachi and Lahore. A number of the firm's partners actively participate on the committees of the major clubs in Karachi and also assist and advise by their presence on the boards of various charitable institutions.

Significant Distinctions: A number of the partners are directors on the boards of some of Pakistan's largest public companies and the firm regularly represents its clients before the High Courts and the Supreme Court of Pakistan.

PAKISTAN LAW DIGEST

(The following is a list of all Topics, including cross-references, covered in this Digest.)

PAKISTAN LAW DIGEST

Revised for 1997 edition by

SURRIDGE & BEECHENO, Advocates and Solicitors, Karachi.

See topics Reports; Statutes.

ABSENTEES:

Persons resident outside Pakistan can institute suits against persons resident within, or apply for Letters of Administration to estates here or, under section 13 of Civil Procedure Code seek to have judgments obtained outside Pakistan enforced in Pakistan. Likewise suits may be brought against persons resident outside Pakistan and judgments obtained enforced against the judgment debtor's property within Pakistan.

Care of Property.—There are no special provisions but absentees may appoint an attorney under Powers of Attorney Act 1882 to deal with their property.

ACKNOWLEDGMENTS:

A certificate of an officer attesting an instrument that the person executing it acknowledged it to be his voluntary act is not a legal requirement in Pakistan. As to authentication of documents, see topic Affidavits, subhead Affidavits Sworn Abroad.

ACTIONS:

Proof of Foreign Claims.—A foreign claim may be proved in same manner as a local claim. Where a claim is to be proved by evidence of a foreign witness, such evidence can be taken on commission if Pakistani Court concerned issues a commission or letter of request to the foreign court.

Proof of Foreign Law.—Foreign law may be proved either by evidence of a person specially skilled in it or by direct reference to books printed or published under authority of the foreign Government. A man will not be accepted as competent to prove foreign law unless he is a practising lawyer, or has held some official position which presumes a knowledge of that law or has special knowledge of that law acquired from practical experience.

§94 of Qanun-e-Shahadat Order, 1984 dispenses with proof of genuineness of every book purporting to be printed or published under authority of government of any country and to contain any of laws of that country, and of every book purporting to contain reports or decisions of courts of such country.

Limitation of.—See topic Limitation of Actions.

AFFIDAVITS:

An affidavit is written statement on oath made before person competent to receive it and for production in Court. Affidavits sworn within Pakistan must embody title of the suit, or other proceeding, and complete identification of deponent as to name, religion, age and residential address as e.g., the following.

Form

I, ... son of . . . . . ., ... (state religion) adult aged . . years, residing at . . . . make oath and state:

Affidavit must be on facts within deponent's knowledge.

Deponent must be identified to commissioner of oaths by an advocate or registered court clerk. An affidavit is sworn before commissioner of oaths or first class magistrate in district court or commissioner for taking affidavits or deputy registrar in High Court.

Stamp.—Affidavits for immediate use in court and also affidavits in support of applications need not be stamped. Other affidavits must carry Rs. 10/—stamp.

Affidavits sworn abroad must be sworn before notary public and must then be legalized by Pakistan Embassy or Consulate as case may be.

ALIENS:

Aliens are defined in Pakistan Citizenship Act 1951, §2 (as Amendment Act 1952) to mean persons who are neither citizens of Pakistan nor Commonwealth citizens who have status of Commonwealth citizen under British Nationality Act, 1948 and British Protected person under same Act.

Alien visitors must register with the police within 24 hours of arrival and also, if they move about from area to area, in each area to which they go.

Acquisition of Citizenship.—Every person is deemed to be a citizen of Pakistan (1) whose parents or grand parents were born in territories now included in Pakistan and who after August 14, 1947 has not been permanently resident outside Pakistan, or (2) who had any parent or grand-parents born in territories included in India on March 31, 1937 and who has been domiciled at commencement of Pakistan Citizenship Act 1951 in Pakistan or in territories now included in Pakistan, or (3) who is a person naturalized as a British subject in Pakistan and has before the date of commencement of the Pakistan Citizenship Act 1951 renounced citizenship of the United Kingdom and of any foreign state; or (4) who before commencement of said Act migrated to territories now included in Pakistan from any territory in the Indo-Pakistan subcontinent and who migrated with intention of settling there permanently.

Furthermore, every person born in Pakistan after commencement of said Act is citizen of Pakistan by birth unless (1) such person's father possesses at time of his birth such immunity from suit and legal process as is accorded to an envoy of an external sovereign accredited in Pakistan and is not a citizen of Pakistan or (2) his father is an enemy alien and the birth occurs in a place then under enemy occupation. A person may also acquire citizenship by naturalization or by incorporation of new territory.

Under the §2 Pakistan Citizenship (Amendment) Ordinance 1972, dual nationality is permissible where a person who being a citizen of Pakistan, is also citizen of U.K. and Colonies or of such other country as Federal Government may, by notification in official gazette specify in this behalf.

Under Pakistan Citizenship (Amendment) Act, 1973, §8(2) a subject of State of Jammu and Kashmir who, being under protection of a Pakistan passport, is resident in U.K. or such other country as Federal Government may, by notification in official gazette, specify in this behalf, shall, without prejudice to his rights and status as a subject of that State, be deemed to be, and always to have been, a citizen of Pakistan.

Married women do not in most cases acquire the status of Pakistani Citizens when their husbands do.

Any alien woman married to a citizen of Pakistan or to a person who but for his death could have acquired such citizenship as above (see subhead Acquisition of Citizenship, supra) is entitled to make application to Federal Government, and, by taking oath of allegiance and obtaining certificate of domicile, she may be registered as citizen of Pakistan whether or not she is 21.

Registration.—A person who has ceased to be a citizen of Pakistan under Pakistan Citizenship Act 1951, §1, or has not renounced his dual nationality, where such renunciation is required by law, or has been deprived of his citizenship, is not entitled to be registered as citizen except with previous consent of Federal Government. Minors may be registered as citizens of Pakistan by their guardians and become citizens from date of their registration.

Under National Registration Act, 1973, every citizen of Pakistan, whether in or out of Pakistan, who has attained age of 18 years shall get himself, and a parent or guardian of every citizen who has not attained that age shall get such citizen, registered in accordance with provision of Act. (§4). Under §5 Registrar-General shall cause to be issued to every citizen, who has attained age of 18 years and registered himself under §4, an identity card. Identity card is subject to be called for inspection by Registration Officer or any gazetted officer under control of, and authorized by, Registrar-General. Identity card shall be surrendered on death of holder or within 60 days of holder ceasing to be a citizen. No citizen who has attained age of 18 years but does not possess or produce an identity card shall be granted a passport, permit or other travel document for going out of Pakistan and he will further not be allowed to vote.

Penalties for offences under Act are a fine not exceeding Rs. 50, or in default of payment of fine, simple imprisonment for a period not exceeding 15 days.

Under §10 any person who (a) being a person employed for purposes of this Act, publishes or communicates to any person, otherwise than in ordinary course of such employment, any information acquired by him in course of employment, or (b) having possession of any information which to his knowledge has been disclosed in contravention of Act, publishes or communicates that information to any other person, shall be punishable with imprisonment with term which may extend to six months, or with fine which may extend to Rs. 1,000, or with both, provided that nothing in this section shall apply to any publication or communication of information made: (i) for purpose of any criminal proceedings, or (ii) to any gazetted officer authorized by Federal Government or Registrar-General.

Deprivation.—If any certificate of domicile or naturalization was obtained by fraud, false representations or concealment of any material fact deprivation of citizenship will be by order of Federal Government. Furthermore, a certificate of naturalization may be revoked for acts of disloyalty, trading with enemy in wartime, imprisonment for 12 months or over within five years of naturalization or continuous absence for seven years unless the absence was in service for the Government or an international organization of which Pakistan at any time during that period was a member, or where the person has registered annually at the Pakistan Consulate or Mission as prescribed.

Other Rights.—Suits may be brought by alien enemies residing in Pakistan with permission of central government and other aliens may sue, without permission. (Civil Procedure Code, §83). However, it has been held by High Court in cases arising during and after Indo-Pakistan war of Sept. 1965 that an alien enemy is neither competent to institute a suit nor can he continue suit. He is not competent during continuance of hostilities to file an appeal or to continue appeal or execute a decree obtained by him. However, if a suit is filed against an enemy defendant he is not only entitled to defend suit but he is also entitled to file an appeal if a decision is given against him during continuance of hostilities. He is, however, debarred from executing any benefit derived by him in such litigation.

Corporations Owned or Controlled by Aliens.—See topics Corporations (Companies), subheads Foreign Companies, and Owned or Controlled by Aliens; and Foreign Investment.

ASSIGNMENTS:

All rights in moveable or immoveable property are assignable by way of gift, hire, lease or sale by §30 of Trustees and Mortgagees Powers Act 1866 a person may transfer to himself and another person or persons or corporation any moveable property that is by law assignable, as if he were transferring the property to another. Any actionable claim (chose in action) other than debt secured by mortgage of immoveable property or hypothecation or pledge of moveable property or beneficial interest in property not in possession of claimant, which actionable claim would be recognized in court of law as entitling relief to creditor, may be transferred. Such transfer must be in writing and signed by transferor or his duly authorized agent and can be with or without consideration.

Sale of tangible immovable property over value of Rs. 100 or of reversion can only be effected by registered assignment. Where value of such tangible immovable property is under Rs. 100 it can be effected by mere delivery.

ASSIGNMENTS . . . *continued*

A gift (transfer without consideration) must be made within lifetime of donor. A donor may also dispose of, in expectation of death, any moveable property that he could have disposed of by gift. A gift by a Muslim, which is called Hiba can be either of immoveable or moveable property without consideration and by word of mouth but in the case of immoveable property the donee must take possession of the property.

Insurance policies are assignable unless the Policies themselves provide otherwise. In the case of Life Policies this can only be done by a deed of transfer or an endorsement on policy which must be attested by a witness. A Marine Policy can be assigned either before or after the loss occurs.

Effect of assignment is to create an interest for assignee, in the assigned object. No greater rights can be created than those which existed in the tranferor.

Mere right to sue cannot be transferred nor can the salary of a public officer either before or after it has become payable.

ASSOCIATIONS:

Associations, clubs and societies are usually unincorporated and without shares; they have no legal entity and cannot sue or be sued on contracts made in their own name or on their behalf. Liability generally falls on office bearers.

Societies for scientific, charitable, educational and similar purposes may be incorporated under the Societies Registration Act 1860.

Formation.—Any seven or more persons may incorporate by subscribing to and filing a memorandum of association with Registrar of Joint Stock Companies.

Rights and Powers.—All those necessary to attain objects.

Property of such societies if not vested in trustees, vested in governing body and in all proceedings property described as that of trustees or governing body.

Actions.—May sue or be sued in name of president or other officials as determined by rules and regulations of society. Judgments enforced against property of society and not against that of officials.

Dissolution.—By vote of three-fifths of members and all necessary steps must be taken for disposal and settlement of property according to the rules. If no rules, then as governing body finds expedient. In event of dispute adjustment of affairs may be referred to court. Where any provincial government is member of society, no dissolution without its consent.

Professional Associations.—No statutory authorization necessary but Pakistan Bar Council constituted by Legal Practitioners and Bar Councils Act 1973 which came into force in Feb. 1973.

Co-operative and religious societies formed under Co-operative Societies Act 1925 and Religious Societies Act 1880 respectively.

See topic Partnership.

ATTACHMENT:

Rules regarding attachments governed by Code of Civil Procedure 1908.

Actions in Which Allowed.—Attachment orders made both in execution of decree and before judgment. Orders for attachment before judgment may be made in all except following actions: For recovery of immovable property; for foreclosure, sale or redemption in case of mortgage of or charge on immovable property; for determination of any other right or interest in immovable property; and for attachment of any agricultural produce in possession of agriculturist, or attachment or production of such produce. Order only made before judgment if defendant has failed to show cause to contrary or to furnish security. Provided however, attachment before judgment is not to affect rights existing prior to attachment, of persons not parties to suit nor bar any person holding decree against defendant from applying for sale of property under attachment in execution of such decree.

Property once attached before judgment, may not be reattached in execution of decree.

Where holder of decree for possession of immovable property or purchaser of any such property sold in execution of decree is resisted or obstructed by any person in possession of property he may make application to court and court shall investigate matter. All questions as to right, title or interest in or possession of immovable property shall be adjudicated upon and determined by court and no separate suit shall lie for determination of any such matter.

Courts Which May Issue Order.—All courts including industrial and tax tribunals, except Small Causes Court.

In Whose Favour Given.—In favour of plaintiff when made before judgment and in favour of decree holder to enforce execution. In both cases may be given in favour of nonresident or foreign corporations.

Grounds.—Order for attachment may be made before judgment if court satisfied that defendant with intent to obstruct or delay execution of decree that may be passed against him is about to dispose of whole or part of his property or is about to remove whole or part of his property from local limits of jurisdiction of court. Order for attachment after judgment made only to enforce decree.

Proceedings to Obtain.—Application of plaintiff or decree holder is necessary, together with affidavit and schedule specifying property to be attached.

Attachment Bond.—Judgment debtor may be required to furnish attachment bond to effect that he will not dispose of property in question and will endeavour to satisfy decree.

Levy.—Both moveable and immoveable property is subject to attachment.

Lien.—Decree holder has lien over property attached.

Release of Property.—Attachment withdrawn on dismissal of suit; where decree is satisfied or where other security furnished to satisfaction of court.

Sale.—Court can order sale only after judgment but pending execution of decree. Property attached may be sold only after public notice and proclamation of sale issued. Moveable property may be sold after 15 days of proclamation, and immoveable property after 30 days. Where immoveable property sold in execution of decree, person owning it or having an interest in it, may within 30 days of sale apply to have sale set aside on depositing in court (1) 5% of purchase money for payment to purchaser, and (2) decretal amount specified in proclamation of sale for payment to decree holder. Where immoveable property sold in execution of decree, decree holder or other person entitled to a rateable distribution of assets, or where their interests are affected by such sale, may within 30 days of sale apply to court to set aside sale on grounds of material irregularities or fraud in publicizing or conducting sale.

Claims of Third Persons.—Where property attached any person with interest in property may prefer a claim or make objection to attachment which must be investigated by court. Where claim or objection is rejected, person may institute suit to establish such claim. Limitation period is one year from date of attachment order.

See topic Executions.

ATTORNEYS AND ADVOCATES:

The four provinces of Pakistan have High Courts at Karachi, Lahore, Peshawer and Quetta. High Court of Sindh exercises original civil jurisdiction for district of Karachi for suits valued over Rs. 500,000. All district courts elsewhere in Pakistan exercise unlimited original civil jurisdiction.

Advocates.—The Legal Practitioners and Bar Council Act, 1973 governs all matters regarding advocates in the four provinces of Pakistan.

General.—Act envisages single class of practitioners, namely advocates, abolishing all previous distinctions between advocates, solicitors, pleaders, etc. Under this Act Pakistan Bar Council and Provincial Bar Councils for each province were constituted with tenure of five years.

Function of Pakistan Bar Council and Provincial Bar Council: (1) to prepare and maintain common roll of advocates whereby advocates registered on roll of Bar Council of one province are entitled to practise in every province of Pakistan; (2) to admit persons as advocates entitled to practise before High Court/Supreme Court; (3) to entertain and determine cases of misconduct against advocates of High Court/ Supreme Court; to award punishment; (4) promote and suggest legal reforms and provide legal aid etc.

Qualifications for Membership of Pakistan Bar Council.—Person is qualified if: he has been on roll of advocates of Supreme Court maintained by Provincial Bar Council, has been advocate for not less than ten years from filing of nomination papers and cleared all dues payable to Pakistan Bar Council. (§11.A).

Persons Who May Be Admitted as Advocates.—Barristers who have been called to Bar in England or persons who were enrolled as advocates of High Court in any area which before 14 Aug. 1947 was comprised within India may be enrolled as advocates of any Provincial Bar Council on payment of necessary dues.

To qualify as advocate in Pakistan today, candidates must obtain law degree of Pakistani University, or Bachelors Degree in any subject other than law from University in Pakistan or from University outside Pakistan recognized by Pakistan Bar Council and degree in law from a like University. (§26).

Citizenship and Other Requirements.—It is not necessary to be citizen of Pakistan to be enrolled as advocate, provided that person is national of any other country who has resided in Pakistan for period of not less than one year immediately preceding day on which person applies for admission. Consequently, such national may be admitted as advocate if citizen of Pakistan duly qualified is permitted to practise law in that other country. Advocates must also have completed age of 21 years. (§26).

To Qualify as Advocates Of High Court.—Primary conditions for admission as advocates of High Court are: practice for period of not less than two years as advocate, vakil or pleader before subordinate courts in Pakistan or practice outside Pakistan as advocate before any High Court specified in this behalf by Pakistan Bar Council and payment of enrollment fee and fulfillment of such conditions as may be prescribed by latter. (§27).

Advocates of Supreme Court.—Such persons must make application for enrollment as advocate of Supreme Court addressed to Chairman of Pakistan Bar Council. (§106). Admission is governed by Rules made by Supreme Court. Person is qualified for enrollment as advocate of Supreme Court if: he has been enrolled as advocate in High Court for not less than ten years; has been certified by Chief Justice of Pakistan and Judge of High Court and is fit and proper person to appear and plead as advocate before Supreme Court.

Advocate on Record.—Advocate of five years standing in Supreme Court shall be qualified to be registered as Advocate on Record on making application in this behalf. Provisions relating to enrollment of advocates contained in Supreme Court Rules shall mutatis mutandis apply to registration of Advocates on Record. No advocate other than Advocate on Record shall be entitled to act for party in any proceedings in Court regarding procedural matters. It is Advocates of Supreme Court and not Advocates on Record that appear and plead on behalf of party.

BANKRUPTCY: See topic Insolvency.

BANKS AND BANKING:

Nationalised Pakistani banks being denationalised by sale of shares and transfer of management to private sector bidders and/or employees. Government also allowing applications, in accordance with certain criteria, to set up new commercial banks including with foreign participation. Investment banks also allowed to be set up with foreign participation.

See topic Islamic Laws.

BILLS AND NOTES:

Bills of exchange (including cheques) and promissory notes are regulated by Negotiable Instruments Act, 1881.

Inland Instrument and Foreign Instrument.—An inland instrument is a promissory note, bill of exchange or cheque drawn or made in Pakistan payable in or drawn upon any person resident in Pakistan. Any other instrument is a foreign instrument.

Maturity.—Maturity of a promissory note or bill of exchange is date at which it falls due. Every promissory note or bill of exchange which is not expressed to be

BILLS AND NOTES . . . *continued*
payable on demand, at sight or on presentment is at maturity on third day after day on which it is expressed to be payable. When day on which a promissory note or bill of exchange is at maturity is a public holiday, instrument is deemed to be due on next preceding business day. Expression "public holiday" includes Fridays and days declared by Federal Government by notification in Official Gazette to be public holidays.

Holder in due course is a person who for consideration becomes possessor of a promissory note, bill of exchange or cheque if payable to bearer, or payee or indorsee thereof, if payable to order, before it became overdue, without notice that title of person from whom he derived his own title was defective and holds bill free of deffects of title or prior parties and may enforce payment against all parties liable on bill. A holder who derives his title through a holder in due course, and who is not himself a party to any fraud or illegality affecting the negotiable instrument, has all the rights therein of that holder in due course as regards acceptor and all parties to instrument prior to that holder. Every party to a bill is deemed to have become a party thereto for value and each holder is prima facie deemed to be a holder in due course.

Presentment for acceptance is necessary when a bill is payable a certain number of days after acceptance, or after sight. Presentment for acceptance is absolutely necessary in case of such bills to fix date of payment. Also, where a bill expressly stipulates that it shall be presented for acceptance, it must be presented for acceptance before it can be presented for payment. A bill of exchange is said to be dishonoured by nonacceptance when the drawee, or one of several drawees not being partners, makes default in acceptance upon being duly required to accept the bill, or where presentment is excused and the bill is not accepted, where drawee is incompetent to contract, or acceptance is qualified, the bill may be treated as dishonoured.

Where there are several persons, not being partners, liable on the negotiable instrument as makers, acceptors or drawees, as case may be, and no place of payment is specified, presentment must be made to them only.

Presentment for Payment.—Promissory notes, bills of exchange and cheques must be presented for payment to maker, acceptor or drawee thereof respectively, by or on behalf of holder in manner provided in law. In default of such presentment, other parties thereto are not liable thereon to such holder.

Where authorised by agreement or usage, a presentment through the post office by means of a registered letter is sufficient.

Exception.—Where a promissory note is payable on demand and is not payable at a specified place, no presentment is necessary in order to charge maker thereof nor is presentment necessary to charge acceptor of a bill of exchange.

Notice of dishonour must be given in case of dishonour by nonacceptance or nonpayment by the holder thereof or some party thereto who remains liable thereon to all other parties whom holder seeks to make severally liable thereon, and to some one of several parties whom he seeks to make jointly liable thereon.

When a bill of exchange is dishonoured by nonacceptance drawer or any indorser to whom such notice is not given is discharged, but rights of holder in due course subsequent to omission to give notice are not prejudiced by that omission.

When a bill of exchange is dishonoured by nonacceptance and notice of dishonour is given, it is not necessary to give notice of a subsequent dishonour by nonpayment, unless the bill is, in the mean time, accepted.

Stamp Duty.—Under §35 of Stamp Act 1899, no instrument chargeable with stamp duty shall be admitted in evidence, acted upon, registered or authenticated unless such instrument is duly stamped. This defect cannot be rectified in case of bills of exchange, and promissory notes, but in case of other such instruments this defect can be rectified by payment of proper duty and specified penalty.

Foreign unstamped notes and bills if invalid in the foreign country are invalid in Pakistan, and are never admissible in evidence in Pakistan.

Conflict of Laws.—If a negotiable instrument is made, drawn, accepted or indorsed outside Pakistan but in accordance with law of Pakistan, the circumstance that any agreement evidenced by such instrument is invalid according to law of country wherein it was entered into does not invalidate any subsequent acceptance or indorsement made thereon within Pakistan.

Where there is no provision to contrary in the contract, legality and validity of the instrument or of its acceptance or negotiation is governed by law of the place where instrument was made, drawn, accepted or negotiated. Law of place where instrument is payable determines liability of the parties, duties of holder with respect to presentment for acceptance or payment, date of maturity of instrument, what constitutes dishonour, all questions relating to payment and satisfaction including the currency and rate of exchange at which instrument is to be paid.

Law of any foreign country regarding promissory notes, bills of exchange and cheques is presumed to be same as that of Pakistan unless and until contrary is proved.

CHATTEL MORTGAGES:

Charges over moveable property can be created by way of hypothecation or by way of pledge. In the latter transaction possession of the goods is transferred whereas in a hypothecation possession of the goods is not transferred.

After-acquired Property.—Deed of Hypothecation can also be drawn up to include after-acquired property but this has to be done specifically.

Stock in Trade.—Hypothecation may cover floating stock and in cases where, for instance money is advanced to a trading company provisions to cover this stock are incorporated in the hypothecation.

Future Advances.—Can be covered by a hypothecation. It is also possible to provide that while any part of the debt is unpaid the whole security will continue as a security and not be diminished proportionately.

Formalities.—Instrument must be signed by both parties to it and where one of parties is a Company, in accordance with the articles of association, but if a hypothecation is witnessed it requires mortgage stamp duty. (See topic Mortgages, subhead Stamp Duty.)

Registration.—Is optional under §18 of Registration Act, 1908 Act XVI, but in case of company, unless particulars are filed under §121 of Companies Ordinance, 1984 such chattel mortgage shall be void against liquidator and any creditor of company.

COMMERCIAL REGISTER:

Registration not compulsory except for joint stock companies.
See topic Partnership.

COMPANIES: See topic Corporations (Companies).

CONSTITUTION AND GOVERNMENT:

First Constitution was promulgated in 1956 whereby Pakistan became a Republic within Commonwealth of Nations, whereas originally it had been a Dominion with Governor-General as its chief executive. This Constitution was abrogated in Oct. 1958 but country was governed as nearly as possible in accordance with abrogated Constitution. A new Constitution was promulgated in 1962. This Constitution was abrogated in 1969 but country was governed as nearly as possible in accordance with 1962 Constitution. On 10th Apr. 1973 National Assembly passed present Constitution, effective 14 Aug. 1973.

On 5th July 1977 General Zia-ul-Haq Chief of Army Staff proclaimed Martial Law and assumed Office of Chief Martial Law Administrator. Superior Courts continued to function as before. Certain parts of Constitution relating to fundamental rights were suspended, but otherwise Pakistan was governed as nearly as may be in accordance with Constitution of 1973.

By Provisional Constitution Order 1981 all laws made by authorities since inception of martial law were declared valid and President and CMLA were always to have had power to amend Constitution.

By Establishment of the Office of Wafaqi Mohtasib (Ombudsman) Order 1983 office of Ombudsman has been created to investigate complaints of maladministration against government functionaries, upon complaints by aggrieved persons and other specified institutions. Ombudsman has wide ranging remedial powers but if his orders are not complied with he may only refer matter to President who, in his discretion, may direct that they be duly implemented. Ombudsman has powers of civil court in many specified matters and no court has jurisdiction to stay or grant injunction against any order of Ombudsman or to question validity of any order or action taken by Ombudsman. Person aggrieved by order of Ombudsman may make representation to President.

By Revival of Constitution of 1973 Order, 1985, provisions of constitution as amended by order to stand revived on such dates as President may appoint. Amended Constitution still provides that President is Head of State and holds office for term of five years from day he enters upon his office; however General Mohammad Zia-ul-Haq appointed President for five years from Mar. 23, 1985.

By Constitution (Eight Amendment) Act, 1985 all President's orders, ordinances, and martial law orders and regulations, including Referendum Order 1984 (pursuant to which referendum was held, and General Mohammad Zia-ul-Haq became President), Revival of Constitution Order 1985, Constitution second and third amendment Orders 1985 and all other laws made between July 5, 1977 and Dec. 30, 1985 were validated by Parliament; and all orders made, proceedings taken, and acts done by any authority, or person between July 5, 1977 and Dec. 30, 1985, in exercise of powers derived from above-mentioned enactments were ratified, and cannot be called in question in any court on any ground whatsoever. On Dec. 30, 1985 General Zia-ul-Haq issued last Martial Law (Pending Proceedings) Order, 1985. Pursuant to which all Martial Law Orders and Regulations made on or after July 5, 1977, except for 32 Order and Regulations specified in Schedule to said Order, were cancelled.

By Proclamation (withdrawal of Martial Law) 1985 General Mohammad Zia-ul-Haq revoked Proclamation of July 5, 1977 and repealed laws (Continuance in force) Order 1977, and Provisional Constitution Order 1981. Offices of Chief Martial Law Authority, and martial law authorities of various zones, and Military Courts were abolished. Fundamental rights under Constitution revived, and Constitution of 1973 as amended by Constitution (Eight Amendment) Act 1985, and jurisdiction of courts stand fully restored.

Executive authority of Federation now vests in President and is to be exercised by him either directly or through officers subordinate to him. There is to be cabinet of Federal Ministers, with Prime Minister at its head to aid and advise President. Cabinet appointed by President from, and directly responsible to, National Assembly.

Executive authority of each Province now vests in Governor and is to be exercised by him either directly or through officers subordinate to him. There is to be cabinet of Provincial Ministers, with Chief Minister at its head to aid and advise Governor. Cabinet appointed by Governor from, and directly responsible to, Provincial Assembly.

Amended constitution also provides for Parliament (called the "Majlis-e-Shoora") consisting of two houses to be known as National Assembly and Senate. National Assembly now consists of 207 Muslim members with ten additional seats for representatives of religious minorities and, until expiration of ten years or holding of third general election to National Assembly, whichever is later, 20 additional seats for women. Senate now consists of 87 members, of whom 14 shall be from each of four provinces, eight shall be from Federally Administered Tribal Areas, three from Federal capital, and five from "Ulema" (religious scholars), technocrats and other professionals. Term of National Assembly is to be five years and that of members of senate six years, approximately half of them retiring every three years. Qualifications and disqualification for membership of Majlis-e-Shoora enhanced.

Islamic Democratic Alliance ("Islami Jamhoori Ittehad" or "IJI") electoral alliance of nine parties swept polls in Federal elections and in Punjab province and was able to form coalition governments in other provinces. Mr. Nawaz Sharif, President of IJI elected Prime Minister 6th Nov. 1990.

See also topics Courts; Islamic Laws; Legislature.

Economic Policy.—IJI Government has announced policy of deregulation; denationalisation and privatisation in reversal of "Economic Reforms" of 1970s. During 1991 there has occurred substantial deregulation of industrial controls, exchange and payment controls and partial deregulation of capital issues particularly as regards foreign investment in industrial undertakings and issue and transfer of securities

See Topical Index in front part of this volume.

CONSTITUTION AND GOVERNMENT . . . *continued*
pertaining thereto. Privatisation Commission set up to sell off Government's interest in number of public sector corporations. Government is also encouraging infrastructure development on BOT principles with generally unrestricted foreign participation in power generation, highways, airports, seaports and telecommunications, and has also allowed airlines and shipping lines to be licensed for operations alongside existing public sector operators. Protection of Economic Reforms Ordinance, enacted to give legal protection to these reforms.

See also topics Corporations (Companies); Exchange Control.

CONTRACTS:

The law relating to contracts which is to a great extent based on the Common Law of England is to be found in codified form in the Contract Act 1872. Previously this Act had contained sections on the sale of goods and on the Law of Partnership. Subsequently in 1930 and 1932 respectively these sections were repealed and separate Acts covering these subjects passed. Amongst the main differences between the Act and the Common Law are the provisions of the Act to the effect that a third party's actions may constitute sufficient consideration for the performance of promise and that past consideration is good consideration. (§2). Promisee may also dispense with, or remit wholly or in part, performance of promise made to him or may extend time for such performance or may accept instead of it any satisfaction which he thinks fit. There is however nothing corresponding to enforceable document under seal without consideration. See, however, §25 of Contract Act (Act IX of 1972).

Contract with a minor is void. For purposes of contract persons under 18 are minors.

Agreement to contracts obtained by force, fraud or undue influence are voidable at option of person coerced, defrauded or influenced. The consideration must be permissible by law. Illegal contracts, wagering contracts and contracts against public policy cannot be enforced. Contracts in restraint of trade are void to extent of the restraint except where made on the sale of goodwill of business, when a reasonable restraint upon the Vendor will be enforced. Principle of negotiorum gestor is also recognized and person benefitting must make some sort of payment to the other.

Excuses for Nonperformance.—When a contract consists of reciprocal promises to be simultaneously performed, no promisor need perform his promise unless promisee is ready and willing to perform his reciprocal promise.

When a contract contains reciprocal promises and one party to contract prevents other from performing his promise, contract becomes voidable at option of the party so prevented, and he is entitled to compensation from the other party for any loss which he may sustain in consequence of nonperformance of the contract.

When a contract consists of reciprocal promises such that one of them cannot be performed or that its performance cannot be claimed till other has been performed, and promisor of the promise last mentioned fails to perform it, such promisor cannot claim the performance of the reciprocal promise, and must make compensation to the other party to the contract for any loss which such other party may sustain by the nonperformance of the contract. An agreement to do an act impossible in itself is void. Contract to do an act which after contract is made becomes impossible, or by reason of some event which the promiser could not prevent, unlawful, becomes void when the act becomes impossible or unlawful.

If parties to a contract agree to substitute a new contract for it, or rescind or alter it, original contract need not be performed. Where a person at whose option a contract is voidable rescinds it, the other party thereto need not perform any promise therein contained in which he is a promisor.

If any promisee neglects or refuses to afford the promisor reasonable facilities for performance of his promise, the promisor is excused by such neglect or refusal as to any nonperformance caused thereby.

Measure of Damages.—On breach of a contract proper measure of damages is loss sustained by injured party naturally following as consequence of breach.

Contract without Consideration.—In four instances a contract even without consideration is valid. Firstly, where agreement is in writing and is based on natural love and affection, secondly, where agreement is to compensate person who has performed some act voluntarily for promisor or done something which promisor would have been legally obliged to do, thirdly, where it is promise in writing to pay time-barred debt, and, lastly, where there is contract of agency.

Applicable Law.—In absence of an express intention to contrary the proper law of a contract is presumed to be law of country where contract is made, and, where contract is made in one country and is to be performed wholly or partly in another country, the law of the country where performance is to take place. Parties to a contract are free to choose its proper law subject to the qualification that contract should have a substantial connection with the country the law of which is chosen and that there should be no reason for avoiding the choice on grounds of public policy.

Where parties have not expressed any intention the proper law is inferred from terms and nature of contract and from general circumstances of the case. Proper law governs the material or other essential validity of the contract as well as its interpretation, effect and discharge. Formation of the contract is governed by the law which would be the proper law if the contract were validly concluded. Capacity to contract is governed by law of country with which the contract is most closely connected. Formal validity is governed by law of country where contract is made or by the proper law.

Government Contracts.—There are no special requirements to be observed when contracting with Government. General law of contracts applies.

Distributorships, Dealerships and Franchises.—These are governed by general law of contracts and agency.

COPYRIGHT:

This is governed by Copyright Ordinance 1962 which came into force in Feb. 1967 as am'd. by Copyright (Amendment) Act 1992.

Nature and Term of Copyright.—Copyright is property and is exclusive right to do or authorise others do such acts in relation to original work in question as are set out in §3 of Ordinance.

Literary, Dramatic or Musical Work including Computer Software.—Copyright in these works extends to acts of reproducing work in any material form; publishing or performing it in public; producing, reproducing, performing or publishing any translation; making adaptation of work; using work in cinematographic work or making record of it; communicating work by radio or loudspeaker. Term of copyright is 50 years from beginning of calendar year next following year of author's death if his true name is published or 50 years after publication of work if true name not published, provided that where identity of author is published before expiry of this 50 year period copyright will subsist until 50 years after his death. For joint authorship, copyright runs from death of survivor.

Artistic Work.—Copyright in artistic work extends to acts of reproducing work in any material form; publishing it; using it in cinematographic work; televising it or adapting it. Term of copyright is as above.

Cinematographic Work including Video Films.—Copyright here extends to acts of copying it; broadcasting it or causing it to be seen or heard in public. Term of copyright is 50 years from beginning of calendar year next following year in which work is published.

Record.—Copyright here extends to making any other record embodying same recording; using record in sound track of a film; causing record to be heard in public and broadcasting it on radio. Term of copyright is 50 years from beginning of calendar year next following year in which work is published.

Rights of Broadcasting Companies.—Broadcasting companies can authorise re-broadcasting of their broadcasts; fixation of their broadcasts and copying of such fixations. These rights exist until 25 years from beginning of calendar year next following year of first broadcast.

Rights in Published Editions of Works.—Publisher enjoys rights of making or authorising making by photographic or other process of copies intended for sale in commerce of typographical arrangement of edition. Such rights subsist for 25 years from beginning of calendar year next following year in which edition first published.

Owner.—Author of a literary, dramatic, musical or artistic work is entitled to copyright except where work is commissioned or done during course of employment or done for Government or for an international organisation, when person who commissioned or employer or Government or international organisation is owner.

Term of copyright of Government or international organisation extends to 50 years from beginning of calendar year next following year of publication.

Term of Copyright of Posthumous or Unpublished Work.—In case of posthumous work 50 years from beginning of calendar year next following year of publication. If work whose author's identity is known is not published within 50 years after death of author, such work shall fall into public domain after 50 years from beginning of calendar year next following year in which author dies. Where author's identity unknown, and work not published within 50 years of creation, work falls into public domain after 50 years from beginning of calendar year next following year of creation.

Copyright (Amendment) Act 1973.—Because of effect of §10(2A) of Copyright (Amendment) Act 1973, copyright shall not subsist in original literary, dramatic, musical and artistic works, cinematographic works and records as respects its reprint, translation, adaptation or publication, by or under authority of Federal Government, as textbook for purposes of teaching, study or research in educational institutions.

Assignment.—Owner or prospective owner of future copyright can assign either wholly or partially, generally or subject to limitations and either for whole or part of term of copyright. Assignments must be made in writing and signed by owner or duly authorised agent. Assignment can also be made by testamentary disposition and where unpublished work is disposed of by will, it is inferred that copyright also passes unless contrary intention is expressed in will.

Copyright assigned in respect of unpublished work reverts to owner if such work remains unpublished for period of three years from date of assignment.

Relinquishment.—Owner can relinquish all or any rights comprised in copyright by giving notice in prescribed form to Registrar of Copyrights who must publish this notice. Relinquishment will not affect any rights existing prior to date of notice.

Registration of Copyright.—Author, publisher or owner of any copyright may make an application to Registrar in prescribed form and upon payment of prescribed fee for registration in Copyright Office. Assignments and licences can also be registered. Register of Copyrights is prima facie evidence of particulars entered therein and documents or extracts certified by Registrar and sealed with seal of Copyright Office are admissible in evidence. Certificate of registration is prima facie evidence of subsistence of a copyright and that person named in certificate is owner thereof.

Performing rights societies must, within prescribed time and in prescribed manner, prepare, publish and file with Registrar statements of all fees, charges or royalties which it proposes to collect for grant of licences or for public performance of works in respect of which it has power to grant licence. Failure so to do results in society being unable to commence any action or proceeding to enforce any remedy for infringement except with consent of Registrar. Objections to any such fees, charges, royalties, etc., can be lodged at Copyright Office and must be referred to Copyright Board for decision.

Copyright Board has jurisdiction to determine disputes between licensing bodies and persons claiming licenses and hear objections to any fees, charges, royalties or licensing schemes. When determining such disputes and hearing such objections, Board has all powers of a civil court under Code of Civil Procedure in respect of summoning, enforcing attendance of and examining any person on oath, receiving evidence on affidavits, issuing commissions for examination of witnesses or documents, requisitioning any public record or copy thereof from any court or office.

Infringement.—Owner or exclusive licensee of a copyright may sue on an infringement and is entitled to all such remedies by way of injunction, damages, accounts and otherwise as are or may be conferred by law for infringement of a right. Both civil and criminal actions are provided for infringement of copyright. If defendant proves that at date of infringement he was not aware of copyright or had reasonable grounds for believing copyright did not subsist, plaintiff is not entitled to any other remedy except injunction and decree for profits made by defendant by sale of infringing copies as court may deem reasonable. In any action, author or publisher named is, until contrary is proved, presumed to be author or publisher. Copyright owner is deemed to be owner

See Topical Index in front part of this volume.

COPYRIGHT . . . *continued*

of any infringing copy and may sue for recovery of possession thereof or in respect of conversion thereof. All offences under Ordinance are cognizable and non-bailable.

There is no infringement in use of any literary, dramatic, musical or artistic work for purpose of research, private study, criticism or review or reporting of current events. Use in judicial proceedings, reporting in newspapers of an address of a political nature unless such report is prohibited, reading or recitation of an extract in public, publication, reproduction or adaptation for use in educational institutions, or quoting of extracts for purpose of examination questions is not infringement. Amateur performances before a nonpaying audience or for benefit of religious, charitable or educational institution of any literary, musical or dramatic works is not infringement. There is no infringement of an artistic work if it is used for private or critical purposes or as a background to a film or television broadcast or if a photograph, painting, drawing or engraving of an architectural work is published.

Registrar may, upon application by owner or his agent and upon payment of prescribed fee and after making necessary enquiries, order that copies made out of Pakistan or work which would be an infringement if made in Pakistan shall not be imported. Copies in respect of which order made deemed to be goods of which import has been prohibited or restricted by Sea Customs Act and provisions of that Act will apply accordingly.

International Copyright.—Federal Government may by notification direct that all or any of provisions of this Ordinance may apply to foreign works provided that reciprocal arrangements exist in foreign country for protection of works entitled to protection under Ordinance.

CORPORATIONS (COMPANIES):

Law relating to corporations (or "companies" as they are called in Pakistan) is chiefly contained in Companies Ordinance, 1984 which repeals Companies Act, 1913. Effective date for coming into force of majority of provisions was Jan. 1, 1985.

General Supervision.—Duties of registration of companies and enforcing Ordinance are vested in Registrars, Additional Registrars, Joint Registrars, Deputy Registrars or Assistant Registrars of Joint Stock Companies who maintain offices in Karachi, Lahore, Peshawar, Quetta, Multan and Hyderabad. Corporate Law Authority ("CLA") also constituted by Federal Government, with wide powers of investigation of affairs of companies. CLA may in pursuance of findings of such investigation apply to court of law for any number of specified sanctions against company, including dismissal of any officer of company or direction to directors to carry out requisite changes in management or accounting policies. In addition, courts have jurisdiction in certain matters relating to Ordinance.

Formation.—Incorporated company, with or without limited liability, is formed in case of public company by seven or more persons, or in the case of private company by two or more persons, subscribing their names to a Memorandum of Association thereby agreeing to take at least one share each in company, and by otherwise complying with requirements of Ordinance as regards registration. Memorandum must state name of company with "Limited" as last word in its name in case of public limited company and parentheses and words "(Private) Limited" as last words in its name in case of private limited company; province in which registered office will be situated; objects of company; (in case of company limited by shares) that liability of members is limited; and amount of authorized share capital and its division into shares of fixed amount. Company may be limited by guarantee.

Name.—Name of company must not be identical to, or closely resemble, that of existing company or (without CLA's consent) contain any words denoting patronage of or in connection with any past or present, Pakistani or foreign, Head of State or Government or any international organisation. Name which is inappropriate or deceptive or designed to exploit or offend religious susceptibilities is also prohibited. Ordinance lays down procedure whereby company can change its name.

Registration of Articles.—A company limited by shares (to which the succeeding paragraphs exclusively relate) may also register articles of association signed by subscribers to memorandum setting out the company regulations. A company may adopt the specimen articles contained in Table A in First Schedule to Ordinance, which will in any case be deemed to be regulations of company in so far as its registered articles do not exclude or modify them.

Stamp Duty and Registration Fees.—Memorandum and articles of a company (which must be printed) are required to be stamped in accordance with Stamp Act 1899, and a fee based on amount of the authorized capital is payable to Registrar. There is no capital duty as such.

Certificate of Incorporation.—On registration of memorandum and articles together with certain prescribed returns. Registrar will issue certificate of incorporation, upon which subscribers (with such other persons as may become members of the company) become a body corporate with perpetual succession and common seal.

Public and Private Companies.—A private company is a company which by its articles restricts right to transfer its shares, limits number of its members to fifty and prohibits any invitation to the public to subscribe for shares. All other companies are public companies. Many provisions of Ordinance do not apply to private companies, and certain provisions do not apply to private companies unless they are subsidiaries of public companies.

Commencement of Business.—Except in case of private company, a company cannot commence any business or exercise any borrowing powers unless shares have been allotted to an amount not less than the minimum subscription; every director has paid full amount on shares taken or contracted to be taken by him; no money is or may become liable to be paid to applicants for shares owing to failure to obtain permission for shares to be dealt in on stock exchange; declaration that above conditions have been complied with has been filed with Registrar and Registrar has issued certificate to commence business; and either prospectus inviting public to subscribe for shares has been filed with Registrar or, if no prospectus is issued, statement in lieu of prospectus.

Alteration of Memorandum and Articles.—A company may alter its memorandum to change place of its registered office to another province or (to limited extent) with respect to its objects, and may alter or add to its articles, by special resolution, but any such alteration of memorandum must be confirmed by CLA. Particulars of all above alterations must be reported to Registrar.

Share Capital.—Shares of no par value are not permitted. All shares issued by company must be fully paid up. Company limited by shares may only have ordinary share capital which may be subdivided into different classes. Shares in company are moveable property transferable as provided in company's articles. Certificate under common seal of company is prima facie evidence of title of member to shares specified therein. Company is required to keep register of members and, if it has more than 50 members, index of members. No notice of any trust can be entered on register of members. Application for registration of transfer of shares can be made by transferor or transferee by delivering to company stamped and executed instrument of transfer along with scrip. Transfer of share of deceased member can be made by his legal representative. Member may confer on his spouse, parents, siblings or children right to acquire his shares in event of his death and such person(s) shall be entitled to such shares to exclusion of all others. Company cannot buy its own shares nor those of public company of which it is subsidiary. No company (except private company not subsidiary of public company) can give any financial assistance in connection with purchase of any of its shares. Where share capital of company is divided into several classes of shares, and rights attached to any class of shares are varied, holders of not less than 10% of shares of that class may apply to court to have variation cancelled. Company, if so authorized by its articles, may alter conditions of its memorandum so as to increase its share capital by issue of new shares; consolidate and divide its share capital into shares of larger amount; convert its shares into stock and vice versa; subdivide its shares into shares of smaller amount than fixed in memorandum; or cancel shares not taken or agreed to be taken by any person.

General Meetings.—A public company must hold general meeting of its members, called "the statutory meeting" not less than three months nor more than six months from date on which it became entitled to commence business, at which members may discuss formation of the company and the statutory report. This report, certified by the directors and the auditors of the company, must be circulated to the members and filed with the Registrar prior to the meeting. A company must hold an annual general meeting within 18 months from date of its incorporation and thereafter at least once a calendar year, within six months from close of financial year, not more than 15 months intervening between meetings. All other general meetings are extraordinary general meetings.

Quorum, Voting and Proxies.—Unless articles of company provide for larger number, two members in case of private company and five members in case of public company, personally present at meeting, and representing not less than 25% of total voting power of company either of their own account or as proxies, constitute quorum; each member has, except in case of appointment of director, votes proportionate to paid up value of shares carrying voting rights held by him according to entitlement of class of such shares; on poll votes may be given personally or by proxy; proxy must be member of company unless articles of company provide otherwise. Minutes of all general meetings (and directors meetings) must be kept.

Resolutions.—An ordinary resolution is passed by a simple majority. Special resolution is passed by three-quarter majority of such members entitled to vote as are present in person or by proxy at meeting for which 21 days notice must be given to members of intention to propose resolution as special resolution, provided that, if all members entitled to attend and vote so agree special resolution may be passed at shorter notice. Copy of every special resolution must be filed with Registrar. Distinctions between special and extraordinary resolutions is removed.

Directors.—Every private company must have at least two directors and every public company must have at least seven directors to be elected by members of company in general meeting on basis of cumulative voting system. Member may cast as many votes as is equal to product of shares held by him and number of directors to be elected and may cast all his votes in favour of any one or more candidates. Every director must hold at least one share in company. In addition articles of company may provide for holding of qualification shares by director. Normally, Corporate Law Authority imposes such condition for permitting company to issue shares. Companies (Issue of Capital) Rules 1996 impose conditions on issue of capital in respect of: (i) companies proposing to offer share capital to public; (ii) listed companies proposing to increase share capital through right or bonus issue; (iii) all companies proposing to issue shares for consideration other than cash; (iv) certain persons offering shares for sale to public. All directors of company can hold office for maximum period of three years only. Director cannot assign his office but, with approval of board, may appoint alternate director to act for him during his absence for period of not less than three months from Pakistan. No company except private company may make, guarantee or provide any security in connection with loan to director or partner, spouse or minor child of director. Director cannot hold any office of profit under company without consent of company in general meeting and he cannot enter into contracts of sale or purchase with company without consent of board. Ordinance lays down certain grounds upon which office of director shall be vacated and company may at any time, by resolution in general meeting, remove any director provided that resolution shall not be deemed to have been passed if number of votes in favour of it is not less than: (i) Minimum number of votes cast for election of director at immediately preceding election of directors, in case of removal of elected director, or (ii) total number of votes computed in manner in which votes are computed for election of directors divided by number of directors for time being, in case of removal of persons appointed as first directors of company or to fill casual vacancy on board. Director must disclose nature of any interest he may have in contracts entered into by him with company and cannot vote on any contract in which he is interested.

Managing Agents.—Appointment of managing agents prohibited except in certain limited cases. No company may appoint sole purchase, sale or distribution agent without approval of CLA. Penalty for contravention of these provisions is imprisonment of up to two years and/or fine of Rs. 100,000.

Mortgages and Charges.—Every mortgage or charge by a company affecting its assets is void against any creditor of the company unless notice thereof in the prescribed manner is given to Registrar.

See Topical Index in front part of this volume.

CORPORATIONS (COMPANIES) . . . *continued*

Execution of Documents.—Instruments not executed by a company under its common seal may be executed under the hand of an attorney of the company duly authorized by writing under its common seal.

Books and Returns.—Ordinance contains detailed provisions as to maintenance by companies of books of accounts, registers and other documents, and as to filing returns with Registrar giving notice of changes in board, shift of registered office, allotment of shares etc.

Winding-up.—Company may be wound up by court if: (a) It resolves to do so by special resolution; (b) it fails to file the statutory report or hold statutory meeting or any two consecutive annual general meetings; (c) it fails to commence business within one year from date of its incorporation or suspends its business for one year; (d) number of its members is reduced below statutory minimum; (e) it is unable to pay its debts; (f) it is carrying on unlawful or fraudulent activities or business not authorised by its memorandum or which is oppressive to any of its members or is run by persons who fail to maintain proper accounts or commit fraud in relation to company or who refuse to act according to its constitution or Ordinance; (g) being listed with stock exchange, it ceases to be so listed; or, (h) in court's opinion it is just and equitable that company should be wound up. Company may be would up voluntarily: (a) When period (if any) fixed by articles for duration of company expires; (b) if it resolves to do so by special resolution; or, (c) if it resolves by special resolution that it be voluntarily wound up. When company has resolved to wind-up voluntarily, court may order that winding-up will continue subject to court's supervision.

Foreign Companies.—Before company incorporated abroad can open branch in Pakistan it is necessary for permission of Board of Investment, Prime Minister's Secretariat, to be obtained. Further, issue of shares to nonresidents requires permission of Corporate Law Authority and of State Bank of Pakistan. Protection of minority shareholders is normally achieved by suitable provisions in Articles which under Companies Ordinance, 1984 can only be altered by special resolution requiring 3/4 majority. Special resolution is also required for reduction of issued share capital.

Every company incorporated outside Pakistan must, within one month of establishing a place of business in Pakistan, file with Registrar a copy of its charter or memorandum, address of its principal or registered office, a list of its directors, chief executive and secretaries, name and address of principal officer of company in Pakistan, names and addresses of one or more persons authorized to accept service of process and notices on behalf of company, and address of its principal place of business in Pakistan. Any change in any of matters aforesaid must be reported to Registrar, and company must file with Registrar each year its annual balance sheet and profit and loss account.

Capital Issues (Continuance of Control) Act 1947 has been repealed but this does not affect consent given by Federal Government or licences issued under §3 of Act.

Foreign Exchange Regulation Act 1947.—No shares or debentures in a company registered in Pakistan may be issued or transferred to a person who is not a resident of Pakistan (which expression is defined to include a foreign national who is for the time being resident in Pakistan and a company registered in Pakistan which is controlled directly or indirectly, by a person resident outside Pakistan) without permission of State Bank of Pakistan. However, State Bank has given general permission for certain categories of transactions for which no prior permission is required. Issues or transfer of shares of industrial companies (other than specified industries) quoted on Stock Exchange now allowed if price paid is not less than stock exchange price on date of sale. Disinvestment likewise permitted and disinvesting foreign investor permitted to repatriate proceeds provided not in excess of quoted price on date of transaction. Likewise issue or transfer of shares in private or public unquoted companies permitted if consideration paid is not less than "break-up" value as certified by chartered accountant. Likewise upon disinvestment in favour of resident repatriation of proceeds not exceeding break-up value certified by chartered accountant permitted. No restriction on foreign control, percentage of foreign ownership or transfer between nonresidents in foreign exchange outside Pakistan even for non-industrial companies. All issues required to be supported by evidence of remittance to issuing company in Pakistan. All transactions to be reported to State Bank and tax on capital gain, if any, required to be deducted.

Owned or Controlled by Aliens.—A company in which 50% or more of the shares are subscribed by a foreign national would be regarded as a company controlled by a person resident outside Pakistan. Foreign-controlled companies engaged in manufacturing and oil distribution exporting at least 50% of their products entitled to borrow for working capital without limit; in other cases up to 100% of their paid up capital, free reserves, undistributed profits and unremitted dividends as disclosed in latest balance sheet. Such companies engaged in manufacturing also permitted to raise rupee capital requirements from local banks or financial institutions. Except for the restriction above, corporations controlled by aliens are treated on the same basis as Pakistani controlled companies.

Companies (Appointment of Legal Advisers) Act 1974.—Under §3 every company shall appoint at least one legal adviser on retainership to advise such company in performance of its functions and discharge of its duties in accordance with law.

Retainer in respect of a legal adviser appointed by a company shall not be less than Rs. 350 per mensem.

An advocate may represent three companies as legal adviser and a registered firm may represent product of three and total number of partners of firm.

Under Companies (Appointment of Legal Advisers) (Amendment) Act 1975 companies with a paid-up capital of Rs. 500,000 have been bound by law to appoint legal advisers with retainer fee of Rs.350. Under Companies (Appointment of Legal Advisers) Act 1974, law was applicable to firms having paid-up capital of Rs.1,000,000.

An advocate means an advocate entered in any roll under provisions of Legal Practitioners and Bar Councils Act 1973.

See also topics Exchange Control; Foreign Trade Regulations; Industrial and Investment Regulations; Price Control; and Islamic Laws.

COURTS:

Highest Court in country is Supreme Court of Pakistan which sits at Rawalpindi and hears both civil and criminal appeals from various High Courts. There is one High Court for each Province. Supreme Court of Pakistan and Peshawar High Court have in relation to Provincially Administered Tribal Areas of Chitral, Dir, Kalam, Swat and Malakand Protected Area, same jurisdiction as in relation to other areas of North West Frontier Province. High Courts are superior Courts of Record. High Court of Sind hears original civil cases originating from Karachi District and being of value of more than Rs. 500,000, and appeals from civil and criminal courts of province. Other High Courts do not have original civil jurisdiction.

The subordinate courts can be divided into two broad divisions, the District Courts for civil matters and the Sessions and Magistrates Courts which deal with criminal matters. The District Courts consist of the Court of the District Judge, which hears civil cases and also a certain amount of appellate matters, both civil and criminal, and the lower courts of Additional District Judges and Subordinate Judges. The pecuniary limit of such courts in Karachi is Rs. 500,000, while at other places district judge or senior civil judge has unlimited pecuniary jurisdiction. There is also Small Causes Court where simple money suits within pecuniary limit which varies from place to place are heard. Pecuniary limit in Karachi is Rs. 5,000. On criminal side are Sessions Courts and Magistrates Courts, latter being subdivided into three classes, first, second and third.

See also topics Foreign Trade Regulations; Islamic Laws; Constitution and Government.

CURRENCY:

Under §24 of State Bank of Pakistan Ordinance 1955 the Bank has the sole right to issue bank notes for periods fixed by Federal Government.

Rupees and paisas are legal tender in Pakistan; 100 paisas are equivalent to one rupee. Notes used are of value of Rs. 1/—, Rs. 2/—, Rs. 5/—, Rs. 10/—, Rs. 50/—, Rs. 100—, Rs. 500/— and Rs. 1,000/—.

Rate of exchange is linked to basket of currencies and rate is fixed on daily basis against U.S. dollar by State Bank of Pakistan and vary according to transaction.

CUSTOMS:

The Customs Act 1969, as am'd by The Prevention of Smuggling Ordinance 1977 Ch. VI (Amendment of Customs Act 1969), consolidates and amends law relating to levy and collection of customs duties and also provides for other allied matters. This Act repeals (a) The Sea Customs Act 1878, (b) Inland Bonded Warehouse Act 1896 and (c) Land Customs Act 1924.

Central Board of Revenue which is Chief Customs authority may appoint officers of Customs or may entrust, either conditionally or unconditionally any functions of any officer of Customs under this Act to any officer of Federal or Provincial Government.

Under Act, Federal Government has power from time to time by notification to prohibit or restrict bringing or taking by air, sea or land goods of any specified description into or out of Pakistan. Contravention of this section would make goods liable to detention and confiscation by Customs authorities.

Act provides for levying of customs duties at rates prescribed under Finance Act, passed annually or under any law for time being in force on: (a) Goods imported into or exported from Pakistan; (b) goods brought from any foreign country to any Customs Station and without payment of duty there transshipped or transported for, or hence carried to and imported at, any other Customs Stations; and (c) goods brought in bond from one Customs Station to another.

Federal Government has general power to exempt from customs duties any goods imported into or exported from Pakistan.

Central Board of Revenue has power to declare certain places as Customs Ports or Customs airports or Land Customs Stations.

Federal Government may by special order in each case recording such circumstances exempt any goods from payment of whole or any part of customs duties chargeable thereon. Under S.R.O. 1972 Federal Government exempted samples of no commercial value from whole of customs duty leviable thereon on export from Pakistan.

Where goods are imported only temporarily with a view to subsequent re-exportation, Chief Customs authority has power to exempt them from duty subject to such limitations and conditions as it sees fit to impose on such goods either by generally prescribed rules or in any particular case by special order.

Where prescribed goods of such class or description which are intended to be used in production, manufacture, repair or refitting are imported into Pakistan, Chief Customs authority with previous sanction of Federal Government and subject to such terms and conditions as it sees fit to impose, may either exempt goods from duty or authorise repayment in full or in part of duty already paid.

Where goods capable of being easily identified are imported into Pakistan and upon which customs duties have been paid on importation are exported to any place outside Pakistan seven-eighths of such duties shall be repaid as drawback, subject to following conditions: (a) Goods are identified to satisfaction of an officer of Customs not below rank of Assistant Collector of Customs at same Customs Station, through which goods had been imported; and (b) goods are entered for export within two years of date of their importation as shown by records of Customs House or if such time is extended by Central Board of Revenue or Collector of Customs for sufficient cause within such extended time. Provided that Collector of Customs shall not extend time beyond three years of importation of such goods.

Federal Government has powers to make rules according to which repayment of duty as drawback will be allowed on such goods as are taken into use between importation and re-exportation.

Any conveyance entering Pakistan from any place outside Pakistan must call or land in first place at a Customs Station and deliver within 24 hours import manifest to appropriate Customs Officer.

Penalties for offences in above act range in specified cases to a maximum fine of Rs. 10,000, confiscation of conveyance and/or goods, a penalty not exceeding ten times the value of goods and/or imprisonment not exceeding six years on conviction before a Magistrate.

See Topical Index in front part of this volume.

CUSTOMS . . . *continued*

By Import of Goods (Anti-Dumping and Countervailing Duties) Ordinance 1983 additional duties may be levied on specified goods where: (a) Export price of goods are less than normal value and/or (b) country of origin or export has provided any subsidy or other financial assistance for manufacture or export of the goods.

By Import of Goods (Development Surcharge) Ordinance, 1984, development surcharge of three rupees and 50 paisa per ton is to be levied and collected on all goods other than food grains, fertilizers and petroleum products, imported through Karachi customs port.

DEATH:

Presumption of.—Under §124 of Qanun-e-Shahadat Order, 1984 where missing man is dead or alive, and it is proved that he has not been heard of for seven years by those who would naturally have heard of him if he had been alive, burden of proving that he is alive is shifted to person who affirms it.

In case of commorientes or persons dying in a common disaster or calamity, the old English rule governs which recognizes no presumption either of survivorship or of contemporaneous death, and treats matter as one of fact to be decided on the evidence. Therefore, party on whom onus lies of proving survivorship of one individual after another will fail if he has no evidence beyond the presumption that from age or sex that individual must have struggled longer against death than his companion.

Action for.—Where death of a person is caused by a wrongful act, neglect or default even amounting in law to a crime, and act, neglect or default is such as would, (if death had not ensued) have entitled injured party to maintain an action and recover damages in respect thereof, under Fatal Accidents Act 1855 such an action or suit may be brought by and in name of a successor, administrator or representative of the deceased person for benefit of wife, husband, parents and children, including grandparents, grandchildren and stepchildren.

In every such action court may award such damages as it thinks fit proportionately to loss suffered by the respective parties for whom and for whose benefit such action is brought, resulting from said death. Provided that not more than one action or suit is brought for and in respect of same subject matter, a claim for recovery of any pecuniary loss occasioned to deceased's estate by such wrongful act, neglect or default may be inserted in the action or suit.

Under Art. 21 of Limitation Act 1908 such action or suit if not brought within one year from date of death is barred.

DEPOSITIONS:

These may be taken in criminal cases by Magistrates and Sessions Judges and in civil matters by the civil judges. Provisions for this are to be found in Civil Procedure Code Order XVIII and Criminal Procedure Code, §353-§363. The maxim omnia praesumuntur rite acta esse applies to depositions and it will generally be assumed that, if signed by the judge or magistrate concerned, the contents thereof have been read over to the witness and checked. Where depositions are given in English the accused if he does not understand English, is entitled to a written interpretation of the contents which then forms part of the court record.

Depositions are either taken down by the magistrate or judge in his own hand or else a memorandum of the substance of the evidence is recorded by him, or failure to do this accounted for. The deposition should be read over to the witness, and if necessary, corrected.

De Bene Esse.—Under O. XVIII Civil Procedure in a case where it is feared that a witness is about to leave the jurisdiction, or other sufficient cause is shown to the court, a witness' evidence may be recorded immediately.

Dying declarations are admissible under §164 Criminal Procedure Code before a magistrate or judge.

Compelling Attendance of Witness.—Expenses of witnesses are paid into court by the applicant for summons, and summons to attend will subsequently be issued to witness named. Summons must specify time and place of attendance. Where expenses have been underestimated the court may direct the applicant to make up the sum. Where any witness fails to accept service, or having accepted service fails to appear and it seems to the court that such nonacceptance or nonattendance is deliberate, he may be arrested or his property attached.

Depositions outside the country may only be taken on commission or a letter of request.

A commission may only be issued to a competent foreign court in whose jurisdiction the witness resides.

Notice must be given to the other side and the other side must have an opportunity to cross-examine in person, by representation, or cross-interrogatories, when a commission outside the jurisdiction is executed.

Restriction on Local Use.—Depositions taken abroad are placed on same footing as depositions taken in Pakistan.

DESCENT AND DISTRIBUTION:

This is governed either by the personal religious law of the deceased or else by the Succession Act XXXIX of 1925. Hindus, Muhammadans, Buddhists, Sikhs and Jains are excluded under this Act and Parsis have a special chapter relating to them.

Where intestate has left a widow if he has also left lineal descendants, one-third of his property belongs to his widow and two-thirds to descendants, distribution amongst them inter se following certain prescribed rules.

If intestate left a widow and no lineal descendants but has left persons who are kindred to him and if his estate exceeds Rs. 5,000 the widow takes Rs. 5,000 outright. Of the residue, further one-half of this will go to his widow and one-half to the kindred again following certain prescribed rules for distribution amongst them. If the estate does not exceed Rs. 5,000 widow takes all.

If there are no lineal descendants or kindred, the widow inherits all. If intestate has left no widow, the property goes to lineal descendants or to kindered and if there is none, to state.

Rules for distribution where there are lineal descendants are that where there are surviving only children or a child or grandchildren or grandchild the property passes to them equally or him entirely. Where intestate leaves lineal descendents not all in same degree of kindred to him and those through whom the more remote are descended are dead the property is equally divided into shares corresponding to the number of lineal descendants who stood in the nearest degree of kinship to the intestate at his decease or who having been of like degree of kindred to him, died before him, leaving lineal descendants who survived him. One such share is allowed to each of the lineal descendants who stood in the nearest degree of kinship to the intestate at his decease, and one of such shares allotted in respect of each such deceased lineal descendant belongs to his surviving child or children or more remote lineal descendant as the case may be.

If there are no lineal descendants father of the deceased will inherit the property. If there is no father but mother and also brothers or sisters of the deceased and no child of any deceased brother or sister, the mother and each living brother or sister succeeds to the property in equal shares. Where there are children of any deceased brother or sister these children inherit per stirpes the share of their deceased parent. Where there are only the mother and a nephew or niece these take in equal shares or where there are more than one the nephews and the nieces take in equal shares the shares their respective parent would have taken if living at the intestate's death.

Where mother is the sole survivor she inherits the whole property.

Where intestate has left no lineal descendants nor any parents but brothers or sisters, estate will be distributed between them and the children of any deceased brother or sister will take per stirpes.

Where intestate has left neither lineal descendant nor parent, nor brother or sister, his property is divided equally between those of his relatives who are in the nearest degree of kindred to him.

Special rules exist for Parsi intestates as above stated.

Rules of intestate succession according to personal laws are very detailed. Not more than third of his property can be bequeathed by Muslim. Rules of succession further vary in Sunni and Shiah Schools of law, which are two main Schools of Muhammadan law.

DIVORCE:

Law relating to dissolution of marriage is governed partly by personal law and partly by statute law which apply to different religious communities. If one of parties is Christian question of divorce would be governed by Divorce Act 1869, as am'd by The Divorce (Amendment) Act 1975. Under Divorce Act 1869 both parties must be domiciled in Pakistan at time petition is presented and petitioner must be resident here. Jurisdiction to entertain petitions for divorce lies with High Court and also in District Court and decrees for dissolution under Act will be given as far as possible in conformity with principles and rules on which court for divorce and matrimonial causes in England acts.

Grounds for Divorce.—

Christian husband can ask for dissolution of marriage only on ground of wife's adultery, wife may seek dissolution on any of the following grounds: (a) Husband has changed his Christian religion; (b) he has gone through a form of marriage with another woman; (c) he has been guilty of incestuous adultery; (d) he has been guilty of marriage with another woman and committed adultery; (e) he has been guilty of rape, sodomy or bestiality; (f) he has been guilty of adultery with such cruelty as would have entitled his wife to divorce mensa et thoro; (g) he has been guilty of adultery coupled with desertion for two years.

Collusion or petitioner's own adultery will vitiate a petition but where such petition is dismissed on these grounds by District Court a similar petition may be presented to High Court. Adultery will be deemed to have been condoned where conjugal habitation has been resumed or continued. Relief can be granted to respondent on his or her application where respondent opposes petition and court will not be bound to pronounce any decree of dissolution where it finds that petitioner has been guilty of adultery, or unreasonable delay in presenting petition or cruelty to, or desertion or separation from, respondent. Every decree of divorce granted by District Court will have to be confirmed by High Court and such confirmation decreed by two or more Judges. The court may also hear additional evidence. Every decree for dissolution of marriage made by High Court not being a confirmation as above will be a decree nisi not to be made absolute less than six months from pronouncement thereof.

Where the parties are Muslim the contract of marriage under the Mohammedan Law may be dissolved in any one of following ways: (1) By husband at his will (2) by mutual consent of husband and wife, without intervention of a court; (3) by a judicial decree at suit of husband or wife.

Formerly any Mohammedan male of sound mind, who obtained puberty, could divorce his wife whenever he desired without assigning any cause by the pronouncement of talaq effected either orally or in writing.

Muslim Family Laws Ordinance 1961 has made some changes. By §7 subsection (1) of this Act, any man who wishes to divorce his wife must, as soon as may be after the pronouncement of talaq in any form whatsoever, give the Chairman notice in writing of his having done so, and must supply a copy thereof to the wife, a talaq unless revoked earlier, expressly or otherwise is not effective until expiration of 90 days from day on which notice under subsection (1) is delivered to the Chairman. Within 20 days of receipt of notice under subsection (1), Chairman must constitute an Arbitration Council for purpose of bringing about a reconciliation between parties, and Arbitration Council takes all steps necessary to bring about such reconciliation.

Woman married under Muslim Law is entitled to obtain decree for dissolution of marriage under Dissolution of Muslim Marriage Act 1939 on any one of the following grounds: (i) Whereabouts of husband have not been known for period of four years; (ii) she has not been maintained for period of two years; (iii) that husband has taken an additional wife in contravention of provisions of the Muslim Family Law Ordinance 1961; (iv) her husband has been sentenced to imprisonment for seven years or more; (v) her husband has failed, without reasonable cause, to perform his marital obligations for period of three years; (vi) her husband was, at time of marriage, and continues to be impotent; (vii) he has been insane for period of two years or is suffering from leprosy or virulent venereal disease; (viii) she having been given in

See Topical Index in front part of this volume.

DIVORCE . . . *continued*
marriage before age of 16, repudiated the marriage when she attained age of 18, or soon after, and the marriage had not been consummated during the previous period; (ix) husband treated her with cruelty; (x) on any other ground which is recognised as valid for dissolution of marriage under Islamic Law. No decree will, however, be passed under (iv) until prison sentence is confirmed nor under (i) for period of six months if husband enters appearance and satisfies court that he is prepared to perform his conjugal duties when court sets aside decree, and under (vi) court on application by husband must make order requiring husband to satisfy court within period of year that he has ceased to be impotent.

Renunciation by a married Muslim woman of Islam or her apostacy does not by itself operate to dissolve her marriage nor are her rights under Act affected.

Divorce by mutual consent is also possible between two Muslims.

See also topic Marriage, subhead Nullity.

Parsis are governed by Parsi Marriage and Divorce Act 1936 which lists several varied grounds.

By Amendment Act, 1975 (Act IV of 1976) jurisdiction has now been conferred solely on Court of Civil Judge, within local limits of whose jurisdiction husband and wife reside or last resided.

ENVIRONMENT:

Cornerstone of environmental legislation is Pakistan Environmental Protection Ordinance 1983. Pakistan Environmental Protection Agency (PEPA) headed by Director General and Pakistan Environmental Protection Council, consisting of federal and provincial ministers in charge of environment and urban affairs and headed by Prime Minister or such other person of repute as Prime Minister may nominate as chairperson have been established under Ordinance.

Ordinance requires environmental impact statement to be submitted to PEPA in respect of industrial activity, category, type or volume of discharges of air pollutants or wastes or area or class of public waters as may be prescribed by regulations. Detailed environmental impact statement has to be filed with PEPA by every proponent at time of planning project construction or completion whereof is likely to adversely affect environment.

Penalties for contravention or noncompliance of provisions of Ordinance, rules or regulations or any direction issued by PEPA is punishable with imprisonment for term which may extend up to two years or fine which may extend up to Rs. 100,000 or both, or in case of continuing contravention or noncompliance additional fine up to Rs. 10,000 per day.

Further legislation in form of draft bill of Pakistan Environmental Protection Act 1995 is in process of enactment. Proposed law will extend existing coverage and also provide more stringent penalties.

Land Improvement Loans Act 1883 provides for loans for improvement of land such as storage, supply or distribution of water, drainage, reclamation from rivers or other waters etc.

In addition there are various other federal and provincial statutes which regulate water and air quality, noise, toxic and harzardous substances, solid wastes and effluents, marine and fisheries, forest conservation, parks, wildlife and mineral development.

EXCHANGE CONTROL:

Exchange Control is regulated by the Foreign Exchange Regulation Act of 1947 as am'd by F.E.R. (Amend.) Act 1973 and covers payments and dealings in foreign exchange and securities and import and export of currency and bullion. No person except an authorized dealer may deal in foreign exchange without previous general or special permission of State Bank. This includes buying, borrowing, selling, lending or exchanging any foreign exchange with any person who is not an authorized dealer. No exchange is permitted except at rates authorized by State Bank. However effective Aug. 1991, under general permission of State Bank all individuals, companies including investment banks and registered firms may have and freely operate foreign currency bank accounts in Pakistan without restriction save that exports proceeds and earnings on account of services, commissions etc. may not be credited to such accounts. Foreign currency may now be held, exported and imported without restriction and such bank accounts are free from all other exchange control regulations. If foreign exchange is acquired from authorised dealer under general or special permission of State Bank for special purpose it must be used for that purpose and that purpose only or else sold to authorized dealer. Foreign national resident in Pakistan is deemed to be nonresident for purpose of Act. Federal Government has right to acquire foreign exchange by way of sale or assignment but not at price less than market rate of foreign exchange which is still exercised in respect of export proceeds and earnings of residents on account of services, commissions and the like. No acquisition can be made of any foreign exchange owned by authorized dealer and retained by him with permission of State Bank. Restrictions exist on import and export of gold or silver jewellery or precious stones. As regards transfer of securities to person resident outside Pakistan which, for this purpose, includes foreign national for time being resident in Pakistan and company registered in Pakistan which is controlled, directly or indirectly, by person resident outside Pakistan and control of Pakistani companies by such person, see topic Corporations (Companies), subhead Foreign Exchange Regulation Act 1947. Federal Government may acquire foreign securities in same manner as it may foreign exchange. No person resident in Pakistan may, except with State Bank permission, settle any property otherwise than by will, upon any trusts under which person who at time of settlement is resident outside Pakistan elsewhere than in territories indicated by State Bank will have interest in property, or may exercise power under said trust, and any such settlement or exercise of power is void to that extent.

Nonresidents are allowed to trade freely in Federal Investment Bonds (FIB's) and Treasury Bill (TB's) in secondary market through Special Convertible Rupee Accounts. Nonresident shareholders have choice of receiving dividends in US Dollars or in currency of country in which they reside if designated Authorised Dealer is maintaining account in that currency. Investment by nonresident (including overseas Pakistanis) are allowed on repatriable basis in corporate debt instruments viz Participation Term Certificates (PTC's) and Term Finance Certificates (TFC's) etc.

Foreign Exchange Bearer Certificates (FEBCs) denominated in Rupees may be purchased by any person in or out of Pakistan against payment in foreign currency. These are quoted on Stock Exchange at premium and may be purchased and encashed in foreign currency at prevailing rate of exchange. This enables Pakistan residents to access foreign currency and provides incentive to nonresident Pakistanis to obtain premium on their foreign currency earnings. FEBCs if retained (maximum of three years) carry annual return. Dollar Bearer Certificates (DBCs) also available for purchase by any person in dollars carrying return of 0.25% above 12 month U.S. dollar LIBOR quoted by Barclays Bank plc. London and may be encashed in dollars at any time. No limit on amount, no restrictions on possession, transfer, import, export and no taxation in Pakistan on FEBCs or DBCs.

Federal Government or State Bank may at any time by notification in Official Gazette direct owners of foreign exchange to make returns thereof to State Bank and supply particulars thereof. Federal Government may, by notification in official Gazette, direct citizens of Pakistan resident in Pakistan, or any class of such citizens, to make within such time, and giving such particulars as may be specified in notification, a return of any immoveable property or any industrial or commercial undertaking or company outside Pakistan, held, owned, established or controlled by them or in which they have any right, title or interest. Rights of entry and seizure exist in cases of suspected contravention of Act but action may be taken only on representation in writing supported by a statement on oath from informer, or subject to authorization in writing by Federal Government or State Bank a person may, for purpose of making an inquiry which he considers necessary for purposes of this Act, enter any place and call for and inspect any accounts, books or other documents kept in such place.

Contracts to avoid this act are invalid but not such contracts as make it a condition that State Bank permission be obtained and it will be an implied term of all such contracts that where anything is to be done that requires State Bank or Federal Government permission it need not be done unless such permission is granted. Legal proceeding to recover any amounts due are not however barred under the above provisions but no steps will be taken to enforce any judgement or order for payment except for the amount which the Federal Government or State Bank may permit.

Contravention of the Act can be punishable with two years imprisonment or fine or both, as well as confiscation of the property in respect of which the offence has been committed. Forum of such trial is either before a magistrate or an adjudication officer having the powers of a first class magistrate or a tribunal constituted by the Federal Government having these powers and appeal lies to the central government from an order of the adjudication officer or to High Court on appeal from the tribunal. Burden of proof rests with accused to show that he had permission to enter into the dealings or transactions, or to do the acts done.

See also topics Corporations; Foreign Trade Regulations; Industrial and Investment Regulations; Price Control.

Restriction on Repatriation of Foreign Funds Invested Locally.—See topic Foreign Investment.

EXECUTIONS:

Rules regarding execution governed by Civil Procedure Code 1908.

Decree may be executed by court which passed it or by court to which it is sent for execution. Court which passed decree may send it to another court for execution if judgment debtor: (1) Resides or carries on business within local limits of jurisdiction of other court; (2) has property within jurisdiction of other court; (3) has immoveable property within jurisdiction of other court and order is regarding sale of such property; (4) for any other reason recorded by court. All questions arising out of execution determined by court executing decree.

Decree against firm can be executed against: (1) Property of firm; (2) partners sued in their own names; (3) any person who has been individually served with a summons as a partner and has failed to appear; (4) in other cases against any other persons except aforestated with leave of court.

Where judgment debtor dies without satisfying decree, decree holder may apply to court for execution against legal representatives who are only liable to extent of deceased's property which is in their hands and is not already disposed of. Notice to representatives necessary.

Foreign decrees, including arbitration awards, may be executed in Pakistan if decree is from court of country with which Pakistan has reciprocal arrangements.

Kinds of Executions.—Court has wide powers to enforce execution by attachment and sale of moveable and immoveable property, including shares, securities, salary, negotiable instruments and debts, arrest and detention of judgment debtor.

Time for Issuance.—Execution application may be made immediately decree passed and warrant of execution may be served on judgment debtor without calling upon him to file objections except in case where decree is to be executed by detention and arrest of judgment debtor in which case notice is necessary. If notice issued more than one year after decree passed judgment debtor has right to file objections. Limitation period for execution 12 years from date of decree; may be extended in cases of fraud or force.

Stay granted at court's discretion if judgment debtor shows sufficient cause. Appellate court may grant stay where judgment debtor has filed appeal against judgment of trial court.

Lien.—Decree holder has lien on property attached.

Priorities.—Where immoveable property sold in execution of decree proceeds of sale applied as follows: (1) Defraying expenses of sale; (2) discharging amount due under decree; (3) discharging principal and interest due on subsequent incumbrances, if any; (4) rateably among holders of decrees for payment of money who have, prior to sale of property, applied to court which passed decree ordering sale for execution of decrees and have not yet obtained satisfaction.

See Topical Index in front part of this volume.

EXECUTIONS . . . *continued*

Satisfaction.—Where money payable under a decree is paid out of court or is otherwise adjusted in whole or part decree holder must certify payment or adjustment to court for record. Judgment debtor may apply to court notifying payment and/or adjustment and court after notice to decree holder must record such payment or adjustment if decree holder fails to show cause. Payment or adjustment not certified or adjusted is not recognised.

Sale.—Both moveable and immoveable property may be sold under court supervision upon decree holder showing sufficient cause. Sale usually effected by public auction. See topic Attachment.

Redemption.—Judgment debtor may offset sale by offering other security.

Supplementary Proceedings.—Judgment debtor may apply for appointment of receiver to collect sale proceeds when property attached is to be sold.

Body Execution. (Capias ad satisfaciendum).—Writ for arrest of judgment debtor may be issued if judgment debt not satisfied.

See topic Attachment.

EXECUTORS AND ADMINISTRATORS:

No right as an Executor can be established in any court of justice unless a court of competent jurisdiction in the provinces or capital of the Federation has granted probate of the will under which the right is claimed or has granted letters of administration with the will or with a copy of an authenticated copy of the will annexed. These rules apply only to wills made by Hindus, Buddhists, Sikhs or Jains and they are of classes specified in §57, clauses (a) & (b) of Succession Act 1925, and not at all to the wills of Muslims. (See topic Wills.) Where deceased was intestate and was Hindu, Muslim, Buddhist, Sikh or Jain or exempted person letters of administration may be granted to any person who, according to rules of distribution of estate applicable in case of such deceased, would be entitled to whole or part of such deceased's estate, in discretion of court as to which of these persons, if there be more than one, they will grant these letters. Failing such persons administration may be granted to creditor of deceased. Where deceased was not one of categories above-mentioned following are entitled to letters of administration in order of their entitlement: (1) Widow unless court sees fit reason to exclude her; (2) widow along with others entitled in absence of widow, in discretion of court; (3) if there is no widow, or she is excluded, than to those persons who would be beneficially entitled to estate according to rules of distribution of intestate's estate but where mother is one of these persons she alone is entitled to administration; (4) widower has rights of widow; (5) those who stand in equal degree of kindred to deceased are equally entitled to administration.

Probate may be granted to an executor appointed by the will and such appointment may be expressed or implied.

Capacity.—Probate or letters of administration cannot be granted to persons of unsound mind or minors nor to any association of individuals unless it is a company which satisfies the conditions made by the government. Grant of probate can be made to several executors simultaneously or at different times.

Special Kinds of Administration.—Administration with a copy annexed of authenticated copy of will proved abroad may be granted. In event of failure to accept or renouncing an executorship within the time limited for acceptance or refusal thereof, will may be proved and letters of administration with a copy of the will annexed may be granted to the person who would be entitled to administration in case of intestacy.

Universal legatees may be appointed where: (a) There is a will but no executor has been appointed; or (b) appointed executor refuses to act or is incapable of acting; or (c) executor dies after having proved will but before administrating estate of the deceased.

Rights of executorship and that of universal legatee may pass by succession.

Grant of letters of administration with the will annexed will not be made to any legatee other than an universal or residuary legatee before citation has been issued and published calling on next-of-kin to accept or refuse letters of administration. Where a person appointed executor has not renounced the executorship, provided that when one or more of several executors have proved a will, the court may, on death of the survivor of those who have proved, grant letters of administration without citing those who have not proved. When executor is absent, under S. 241, from the provinces in which application is made and there is no executor within the province willing to act, letters of administration, with the will annexed, may be granted to the attorney or agent of the executor limited until he obtains probate or letters of administration granted to himself.

In case of the minority of a sole executor or sole residuary legatee, letters of administration may be granted to minor's legal guardian for the period of minority. Similarly where a sole executor or a sole universal or residuary legatee or a person who would be solely entitled to the estate of the intestate is a minor or a lunatic letters of administration may be granted to the person to whom in the case such minor's or lunatic's estate has been committed by competent authority or if there be no such person to such other person as the court may deem fit.

Grants may be limited for purpose specified in the will or granted with an exception or for a remainder of the deceased's estate.

Grants may be altered, rectified or revoked by courts of competent jurisdiction.

FOREIGN EXCHANGE:

See topic Exchange Control.

FOREIGN INVESTMENT:

Government attaches great importance to inflow of direct foreign investment, particularly in areas where it brings advanced technology, managerial and technical skills and marketing expertise. Foreign investment is welcomed virtually without restriction in equity in manufacturing industry but has also been permitted in investment banking and other financial sector activities with Government approval and is being encouraged in power generation and other infrastructure development.

Foreign capital invested with Government approval is guaranteed repatriation facilities, and current profits thereon are remittable after payment of all taxes. In both cases formal permission of Exchange Control Department of State Bank of Pakistan is required.

Foreign Private Investment (Promotion and Protection) Ordinance, 1976.—Applies to all industrial undertakings in Pakistan having foreign private investment established with approval of Federal Government after Sept. 1, 1954.

"Foreign private investment" means investment in foreign capital by person who is not citizen of Pakistan or by company incorporated outside Pakistan, but does not include investment by foreign government or agency of foreign government.

§3: Federal Government may, consistent with national interest, for promotion of foreign private investment, authorise such investment in any industrial undertaking: (a) Which does not exist in Pakistan and establishment whereof, in opinion of Federal Government, is desirable; or (b) which is not being carried on in Pakistan on scale adequate to economic and social needs of country; or (c) which will contribute to: (i) development of capital, technical and managerial resources of Pakistan; (ii) discovery, mobilisation or better utilization of national resources; (iii) strengthening of balance of payments of Pakistan; (iv) increasing employment opportunities in Pakistan; or (v) economic development of country in any other manner.

§4: Where Federal Government sanctions an industrial undertaking having foreign private investment, it may do so subject to such conditions as it may specify in this behalf. When foreign private investment is by person who, being citizen of Pakistan, is also citizen of any other country, he shall deposit entire amount of repatriable foreign investment in foreign exchange account in Pakistan for its subsequent use for purchase of machinery and other fixed assets of undertaking.

§5: (1) Where Federal Government considers it necessary in public interest to take over management of an industrial undertaking having foreign private investment or to acquire ownership of shares of citizens of Pakistan in capital of such industrial undertaking, any agreement approved by Federal Government relating to such undertakings entered into between foreign investor or creditor and any person in Pakistan shall not be affected by such taking over or acquisition. (2) Foreign capital or foreign private investment in an industrial undertaking shall not be acquired except under due process of law which provides for adequate compensation therefor to be settled in currency of country of origin of capital or investment and specifies principles on and manner in which compensation is to be determined and given.

§6: Subject to provisions of Foreign Exchange Regulation Act, 1947 (VII of 1947): (a) Foreign investor in an industrial undertaking established after Sept. 1, 1954, and approved by Federal Government, may at any time repatriate in currency of country from which investment originated: (i) foreign private investment to extent of original investment; (ii) profits earned on such investment; and (iii) any additional amount resulting from re-invested profits or appreciation of capital investment; and (b) creditor of an industrial undertaking referred to in clause (a) may repatriate foreign currency loans approved by Federal Government and interest thereon in accordance with terms and conditions of said loan; Provided that nothing in this section shall affect terms of permission to make such investment granted to foreign investor before commencement of this Ordinance.

§7: Foreign nationals employed with approval of Federal Government in any industrial undertaking having foreign private investment may make remittances for maintenance of their dependants in accordance with rules, regulations or orders issued by Federal Government or State Bank of Pakistan.

§8: (1) Federal Government may allow such concessions to industrial undertakings having foreign private investment as may be admissible under any law for time being in force. (2) Foreign private investment shall not be subject to other or more burdensome taxes on income than those applicable to investment made in similar circumstances by citizens of Pakistan. (3) Foreign private investment shall be allowed all tax concessions which may be admissible on basis of any agreement for avoidance of double taxation which Government of Pakistan may have entered into with government of country of origin of such investment.

§9: Industrial undertakings having foreign private investment shall be accorded same treatment as is accorded to similar industrial undertakings having no such investment in application of laws, rules and regulations relating to importation and exportation of goods.

By §8 of Protection of Economic Reforms Ordinance, 1991 no industrial or commercial enterprise established or owned in any form by foreign or Pakistani investor for private gain in accordance with law and no investment in share or equity of any company, firm or enterprise, and no commercial bank or financial institution established or owned by any foreign or Pakistani investor shall be compulsorily acquired or taken over by Government.

To facilitate foreign investment in country, standard guidelines for payment of fees for technical know-how, royalties, have been prescribed. Ceilings on payments of royalties and technical fees have been abolished. Agreements falling within these prescribed limits do not need formal Government permission but have merely to be registered with State Bank of Pakistan. Entrepreneurs are free to contract foreign private loans/credits for financing foreign currency cost of industrial projects covered by Government's industrial policy on best possible terms and no approval is required for rate of interest, front end fees/ charges for cash loans and repayment period from State Bank. Loan agreements have to be registered with State Bank through bank and registration constitutes exchange control authority to that bank to make necessary remittances to lender on due date. Government is also open-minded on issue of quantum of foreign equity, which is decided on case by case basis where Government approval is still required.

See also topic Industrial and Investment Regulations.

FOREIGN TRADE REGULATIONS:

Imports and exports are chiefly controlled by annual Import Policy Order and Export Policy Order (made under Import and Exports (Control) Act 1950) which, in case of imports, sets out specific restrictions applicable to import of goods inter alia in form of "negative list". Items not on negative list or otherwise subject to any restriction may be freely imported, and except in certain specific cases, import licences have been abolished. However, 6% fee for privilege to import still required. Registration still required for importers and exporters under Registration (Exporters & Importers)

FOREIGN TRADE REGULATIONS . . . *continued*
Order 1993 with Export Promotion Bureau, Ministry of Commerce. Nominal registration fee is payable.

By Imports and Export (Control) (Amendment) Ordinance,1980 Federal Government have set up Commercial Courts with exclusive jurisdiction to deal with contravention by exporters of orders under §3 of Imports and Exports (Control) Act, 1950, relating to restrictions and control of exports. Commercial Courts can compel exporter guilty of contravention to deposit with court amount equivalent in court's opinion to damage suffered by foreign buyer as result of such contravention. These courts can also direct immediate compensation of such foreign buyer from revolving fund set up by Federal Government.

Amendment in Merchandise Marks Act 1889 requires that goods imported into or produced in Pakistan shall bear indication of country they were made in or name of manufacturer (with address). This only applies to classes of goods that government may by notification require to be so marked.

By rules made under Customs Act certificate of pre-shipment inspection and valuation of certain classes of imported goods is mandatory requirement.

See also topics Corporations (Companies); Exchange Control; Industrial and Investment Regulations; Price Control.

FRAUDS, STATUTE OF:

There is no statute of frauds in Pakistan, and under §11 of Contract Act 1872 all agreements are contracts if they are made by free consent of parties competent to contract, for a lawful consideration and with a lawful object and are not in the section expressly declared to be void. Provisions of the section do not affect any law in force in Pakistan by virtue of which a contract is required to be made in writing or in presence of witnesses or any law relating to registration of documents. Examples of such laws are Companies Ordinance, 1984 §§19 and 27 of which require memorandum and articles of association respectively of company to be in writing; Transfer of Property Act, under provisions of which sales, mortgages, leases, exchanges and gifts of immovable property and transfers of actionable claims must be in writing. Writing is also required for creation of trust by Trusts Act, in case of acknowledgment of barred debts by Limitation Act, in case of submission to arbitration by Arbitration Act.

Where a contract is not required to be in writing it is immaterial whether a clause is written, printed or typewritten. When written and printed clauses are inconsistent greater importance is to be attached to written clause.

GARNISHMENT:

Any person who has obtained a decree for any sum of money may apply to court that judgment has been obtained but decree is unsatisfied in respect of specified sum and that a third person (garnishee) owes money to judgment debtor.

Property Which May Be Reached.—All moveable and immoveable property.

Jurisdiction.—Garnishee must reside or property to be attached must be within local limits of jurisdiction of court issuing order.

Proceedings to Obtain.—On application supported by affidavit.

Practice.—Court may order garnishee to appear before court to show cause why he should not deposit money in court. Deposit by garnishee is valid discharge to garnishee.

HOLIDAYS:

Governed by Weekly Holidays Act 1942 which provides for persons employed in shops, restaurants and theatres. It declares that a shop will be entirely closed one day in every week and employees except anyone in a confidential or managerial position are entitled by law to one complete day's holiday, which will be day shop is closed unless employee's total period of employment is less than six days altogether or he has been allowed some other day completely free. Penalties under Act for Employer are Rs. 25 for a first offence and as much as Rs. 250 for a second offence. Weekly holiday Fri. as from July 1, 1977.

Public Holidays include the two main Muslim festivals of Id-ul-Fitar and Id-uz-Zuha which are fixed with reference to the lunar calendar, Ashura in the lunar month of Muharram and Id-e-Milad-Un-Nabi, as well as the anniversary of Quaid-e-Azam Mohammed Ali Jinnah's death (Sept. 11), Dec. 25 (which is both Christmas and the Quaid-e-Azam's birthday), Pakistan Day which is Mar. 23, and New Years day. Government holidays are compulsory but there are various other religious holidays which may or may not be given by individual employers, e.g., during the month of Ramzan all government offices and most other offices work Ramzan hours which are from 8 A.M. to 2 P.M. These hours are also the official summer hours for government offices and the courts.

HUSBAND AND WIFE:

Husband and wife are reckoned as separate persons and may freely contract either between themselves or individually as if they were unmarried. Suits in tort are maintainable between spouses.

§20 of the Succession Act 1925 further lays down that marriage neither entails accession to nor loss of property by married women. This section does not include in its operation Hindus, Muslims, Buddhists, Sikhs or Jains. Muslim women, however, by their personal law are equally protected.

Married Women's Property Act 1874 also excludes from its operation Hindus, Muslims, Sikhs, Buddhists and Jains, except when included specifically. Under it the wages, earnings or any separate property acquired by wife are protected and remain in her entire ownership.

Actions.—A married woman can sue in her own name to recover any wages or property belonging to her, as if she were unmarried and her husband need not be joined in the suit as plaintiff. Nor is he necessarily liable to be joined as defendant in any suit against her.

Debts.—A husband is not liable for his wife's pre-nuptial debts except where he undertakes to make payment of them. Nor is he liable for any debts she may contract after marriage except where these debts are contracted through his wife's agency, such as the supplying of necessaries to his house.

Maintenance.—A husband is responsible for maintenance of his wife and children and a court order may be obtained to force him to make an adequate allowance to his wife. Default in this respect renders him liable to a fine and also to simple imprisonment for a month or to both. No maintenance arrears can be claimed for a period over a year from the institution of the suit.

Insurance.—A wife may take out insurance for her husband's benefit. Insurance for her benefit will be deemed to be a trust in her favour and this section has been made applicable equally to Hindus, Muslims, Sikhs and Jains.

Additional Non-Liability of Husband.—A husband is not liable for his wife's breach of trust or where she is executrix for devastation, unless he has meddled with the Estate she is administrating.

HYPOTHECATION:

See topic Chattel Mortgages.

IMMIGRATION:

Entry into Pakistan—Passport Rule 1955.—To enter into Pakistan visa is generally required except in case of country which has reciprocal arrangements with Pakistan.

All foreigners entering the country (not being Commonwealth citizens) must register with police within 24 hours. If they wish to stay in Pakistan after expiry of their visa, they must obtain permission of Police Department.

Technicians, experts and industrial personnel may enter country under the general rules of entry, but their contracts of service in Pakistan must be approved by Investment Promotion Bureau of Ministry of Industries.

A foreign employee whose contract of service has been approved by Investment Promotion Bureau is entitled to remit 50% of his monthly salary up to ceiling of US$750 per month, which may in special cases be raised.

Emigration Ordinance 1979 regulates emigration of Pakistanis for employment abroad. Bureau of Emigration and Overseas Employment headed by Director General controls emigration and is responsible for welfare of emigrants. Protector of Emigrants fulfils same function in relation to particular district. Overseas Employment Corporation recruits Pakistanis for employment abroad. All other persons or agencies may only perform such recruitment, or advertise for such recruitment, if they possess licence from Federal Government.

Pakistani may emigrate if he can furnish proof of permission to work abroad such as employment visa issued by foreign employer or foreign government. Emigrant must appear before Protector of Emigrants and furnish him with any information required before emigrating.

Offences against this Ordinance are treated as criminal offences and tried by Special Courts created by Federal Government. Penalties include fine and imprisonment which may extend to five years.

Acquisition of Citizenship.—See topic Aliens.

INDUSTRIAL AND INVESTMENT REGULATIONS:

The Development of Industries (Federal Control) Act 1949 authorizes the Federal government to plan and regulate establishment of any new enterprise or development of any new or existing undertaking in any of industries specified in Schedule to Act and to otherwise make rules with regard to development of scheduled industries.

The rules governing these industries are set out in the Development of Industries Rules 1950.

Investment Regulations.—Projects for investment in manufacturing industry in Pakistan no longer are subject to sanction of any governmental authority except in case of certain specified industries in certain limited cases (see infra). List of specified industries now includes only: (a) Arms and ammunitions; (b) security printing; currency and mint; (c) high explosives; (d) radioactive substances; (e) alcoholic beverages.

Questions relating to income-tax reliefs and concessions, and remittance of dividends are dealt with respectively by Central Board of Revenue and State Bank of Pakistan.

Board of Investment, Prime Minister's Secretariat, assists would-be investors with information.

By Export Processing Zones Authority Ordinance, 1980, Federal Government is empowered to create Export Processing Zones in which industries will be set up and operated by sanction of Export Processing Zones Authority. Zones will be bonded customs areas and Federal Government may exempt them from any law in force in rest of Pakistan. Movement of goods from zones to remainder of country will only be in manner and extent specified by Authority. Authority is statutory corporation and will make master plan and phased master programme for development of zones. Industries will function according to conditions contained in letter of sanction issued by Authority.

See also topics Corporations (Companies); Exchange Control; Foreign Trade Regulations; Price Control.

INFANTS:

By the Majority Act 1875 the age of minority ceases for both sexes at 18 unless the minor has been made a ward of the court when it continues to age 21. Majority Act does not, however, effect minor's rights, under his personal law, during minority, of marriage, dower, divorce, and adoption.

Under Child Marriage Restraint Act 1929, however, minimum ages for marriage are for male 18 years and were for female 14 years. Family Laws Ordinance 1961 has now raised limit to 16 for females. Marriages contracted under these ages render parents or guardians of the minor, the major contracting party (if either of the parties is major, i.e., over 18) and the solemnizers of the marriage to penalties but marriage is not void.

Under Christian Marriage Act 1872 a minor is defined as a person who has not attained his or her 21st birthday.

See Topical Index in front part of this volume.

INFANTS . . . *continued*

For purpose of guardianship under Divorce Act 1869, children of Pakistani descent remain minors until their 16th and 13th birthdays respectively for males and females but for children of other descent minority continues till their 18th birthdays.

Actions.—Bringing or defending of suits by a minor is governed by Order XXXII of Civil Procedure Code. Every suit by a minor must be instituted in his name by a person called "next friend" of the minor, and a suit instituted directly by the minor may be struck off the file.

Where defendant is a minor, the court on being satisfied of the fact of his minority must appoint a proper person to be guardian ad litem for the suit for such minor. No person can be appointed guardian for a minor who has an interest adverse to that of the minor. Guardians ad litem must also be appointed for minors in petitions for letters of administration, and in any other matter in which the minor is directly or indirectly involved.

Contracts.—Minors cannot enter into valid contracts except in relation to marriage, divorce or dower.

INSOLVENCY:

Law of insolvency is governed in Karachi by Insolvency Act 1909; Provincial Insolvency Act 1920 applies elsewhere. Under Provincial Insolvency Act a debtor is held to commit an act of insolvency when: (i) he transfers all or substantially all his property to a third person for the benefit of his creditors; or, (ii) he transfers all his property with the object of defeating or delaying his creditors; or, (iii) where it is feared that he is about to abscond from the jurisdiction, or abandons his house or place of business or otherwise secludes himself so that he cannot be approached; or, (iv) where any of his property is sold in execution; or, (v) if he petitions to be adjudged an insolvent; or, (vi) makes an announcement that he has or is about to suspend payment of his debts; or, (vii) if he is imprisoned in execution of any decree against him.

Insolvency is deemed to commence from date of presentation of the petition.

For a creditor to bring a Petition against the debtor, the debt must be Rs. 500 or more and have become due. The act of insolvency complained of must have occured not more than three months prior to presentation of petition. A debtor may not present a petition to the court unless the debts amount to more than Rs. 500 or he is under arrest, or an order for attachment has been made and is subsisting against his property.

A debtor can be imprisoned in civil prison if he does not give security for his appearance. An interim order for the attachment of his property can be passed. An order for an arrest warrant to issue against him can also be made if it is shown that the debtor is committing various acts of bad faith.

After hearing of the petition for insolvency, the court may either dismiss it, or pass an adjudication order. Such an order brings the whole of the debtor's property into the receivership of the court and his debts are settled in the following order of priority: (1) State and municipal debts; (2) salary or wages of any clerk or salary in respect of work rendered to the insolvent not more than four months before the petition nor above Rs. 20; (3) secured creditors against their security; (4) expenses of administration; (5) unsecured creditors pro rata.

After an adjudication order the insolvent may apply for court protection against arrest. When a reasonable time has elapsed and the assets have been dealt with the insolvent may apply to court for discharge, but no absolute discharge will be given to him in the following circumstances: (a) The insolvent's assets are not of a value equal to 50 paisas on the rupee relating to the amount of his unsecured liabilities unless he satisfies the court that these circumstances are not his responsibility; (b) that he has omitted to keep proper account books in the business carried on by him within three years of his insolvency; (c) that he has continued to trade after knowing himself to be insolvent; (d) that he contracted any debt provable under Act without reasonable or probable grounds of being able to repay it; (e) that insolvent has failed to account satisfactorily for any loss on deficiency of assets; (f) that insolvent brought on insolvency by rash and hazardous speculations or by unjustifiable extravagance, or by gambling or by culpable neglect of his business affairs; (g) that insolvent has on any previous occasion been adjudged an insolvent or made composition or arrangement with his creditors; (h) that insolvent within three months prior to presentation of the petition gave undue preference to any of his creditors; (i) that insolvent has concealed or removed his property or any part thereof or has been guilty of any other fraud or fraudulent breach of trust.

An order for discharge does not release insolvent from: (a) Any debt due to the Crown; (b) any debt or liability incurred by means of any fraud or fraudulent breach of trust to which he was party; (c) any debt or liability in respect of which he has obtained forbearance by any fraud; (d) any liability under an order for maintenance of wife and children made under §488 Code of Criminal Procedure.

The debtor may be liable for any acts of fraud, making of false entries, wilful failure to perform duties imposed upon him, destruction of records, keeping or causing to be kept false books, to a year's imprisonment and this liability continues notwithstanding his discharge or the approval of any composition or scheme of arrangement.

Appeals can be preferred against any order of the court from a court subordinate to a District Court to the District Court whose order is final, provided that the High Court may call for the case to satisfy itself that the order in appeal was made according to law and may make such orders with respect thereto as it may think fit.

A person may also appeal from an original order of the District Court, to the High Court. Appeal must be taken to District Court and to High Court within 30 and 60 days respectively.

ISLAMIC LAWS:

On Feb. 10, 1979 two Ordinances came into force for purposes of providing punishments under Islamic Laws against offences of theft and adultery. Two more Ordinances dealing with manner in which punishment of whipping was to be carried out and amending second Schedule attached to Code of Criminal Procedure 1898, for purpose of facilitating enforcement of punishment of whipping and powers of authority to arrest in certain cases, also came into force on this date.

Under Ordinance VI of 1979, courts have now been empowered to award persons found guilty of offences of theft for first time punishment of "amputation of the right hand from the joint of the wrist" and for second time punishment of amputation of his left foot up to ankle and for third time and all subsequent occasions punishment of life imprisonment. Under Ordinance VII of 1979 courts have now been empowered to award persons found guilty of offence of "adultery" punishment of "stoning to death." Under Prohibition (Enforcement of Hadd) (Amendment) President's Order No. 12 of 1983, person found guilty of manufacturing and trafficing in opium, heroin, cocaine and other dangerous drugs "shall be punishable with imprisonment which is not less than two years and with whipping not exceeding 30 stripes and shall be liable to fine".

It may be noted however that punishments under both above Ordinances, i.e., VI & VII, are not ordinarily awarded but are subject to strict proof, e.g. in case of theft evidence of only those two witnesses is to be taken who are regarded fit by court in this behalf, meaning thereby that to qualify witnesses should have exemplary character themselves, both religion-wise and according to norms of society. In case of "adultery" requirement of witnesses as regards both their character and numbers is even stronger. Here four such witnesses are required to depose before court.

Besides above safeguards certain exceptions have also been provided in both Ordinances and provisions relating to lesser punishments have been incorporated in addition to stricter punishments. These lesser punishments are contained in Penal Code and now punishment of whipping has supplemented same.

Provisions regarding presence and examination by medical officers both before and at time of punishment are part and parcel of two Ordinances.

Government of Pakistan under Islamic Laws has also imposed complete "prohibition" in country. Prohibition under Central Laws has been supplemented by Provincial Ordinances which inter alia provide following: (a) That no member belonging to Muslim Community, be he citizen of Pakistan or any other country, would be allowed either to consume alcoholic beverages or sell, deal, keep or manufacture same; (b) all other persons whose religions allow consumption of alcohol, would henceforth be allowed to consume same only within four walls of their homes and not publicly; (c) strict punishments have been provided for violators of these regulations which include punishment of whipping.

By Constitution Amendment Order 1980 Federal Shariat Court replacing Shariat Benches of High Courts has been constituted. It consists of five members including Chairman who has rank of Supreme Court Judge while remainder have rank of High Court Judges. All five are appointed by President of Pakistan. Federal Shariat Court ("FSC") exercises noncontentious jurisdiction and may be petitioned by any citizen of Pakistan, Federal or Provincial Governments to examine any law except Constitution, Muslim personal law, law of procedure of any court or tribunal and, until May 1990, any fiscal law, or law relating to levy and collection of taxes and fees or banking or insurance practice and procedure. Court must decide whether it conforms to injunctions of Islam as contained in Holy Quran and Sunnah. If law is held to be repugnant to these injunctions it ceases to be effective from date specified and must be amended. FSC (Nov. 1991) struck down provisions relating to payment of interest in 22 laws and required amendment by 30 June 1992. Decision appealed to Supreme Court (Shariat Appellate Bench) by Government of Pakistan and others effect of which is to suspend operation of judgment until decision of Supreme Court.

By Banking Companies (third Amendment) Ordinance 1980 banks can now accept deposits on basis of participation in profit and loss of bank. Money so deposited will be invested by banks in business or transactions returns of which do not accrue to bank by way of interest. Person depositing money on this basis shall be entitled, subject to such general directions as State Bank may give from time to time in interest of monetary stability, to receive periodically share of profit of banking company arising out of such business or transactions and in event of loss, shall be liable to bear proportionate loss. In addition to above, banks can also accept deposits free of interest or return in any form and, until such time as government may determine, deposits can also be accepted on interest accounts.

By Circular dated June 20, 1984, of State Bank of Pakistan, issued under Banking Companies Ordinance, 1962, interest directed to be eliminated from banking system with effect from Jan. 1, 1985, in respect of finances provided by bank to Federal Government, Provincial Governments, public sector corporations and public or private joint stock companies, and with effect from Apr. 1, 1985, in respect of finances provided by bank to all other entities including individuals. As from July 1, 1984, all banks permitted to adopt alternative modes of financing listed in Annexure I to Circular, including profit and loss sharing, purchase of goods by banks and their sale to clients at appropriate mark-up in price on deferred payment basis, leasing, hire purchase, equity participation, purchase of participation term certificates, etc. Maximum and minimum rates of return or profit to be derived by banks from these transactions is to be determined by State Bank from time to time. As from July 1, 1985, no banking company to accept interest bearing deposits and all deposits to be on basis of participation in profit and loss of bank. These instructions have been implemented by Banking and Financial Services (Amendment of Laws) Ordinance, 1984, and Banking Tribunals Ordinance, 1984, has been enacted to provide for speedy recovery of finance provided by banks under these alternative systems. However these instructions are not to apply to on-lending of foreign loans or to foreign currency deposits.

By Zakat and Ushr Ordinance 1980, provision has been made for collection of Zakat and Ushr from Muslim citizens of Pakistan, or from companies, majority of whose shares are held by such citizens. Zakat is tax of 2½% on all assets, but compulsory deduction at source is only made from specified list of assets, including bank accounts, savings and investment certificates etc. On all other assets, Zakat is payable on self-assessment basis. Ushr is tax of 5% of produce from land. Zakat funds have been established at central, provincial and local level, and moneys in Zakat fund are to be utilised for specified purposes: For helping needy, orphans, widows, handicapped, and on public hospitals, educational institutions etc. Zakat councils, at central, provincial and lower levels have been created for administration and organisation of Zakat and Ushr collection and disbursement etc. Certain tax concessions are available on assets on which Zakat and Ushr has been paid.

By Zakat and Ushr (Amendment) Ordinance 1980, no compulsory deduction at source will be made from assets of person who files declaration in prescribed form, to effect that he is follower of one of recognized "fiqhs" and that his faith does not oblige him to pay Zakat in manner specified in Ordinance.

See Topical Index in front part of this volume.

ISLAMIC LAWS . . . *continued*

By Zakat & Ushr (Amendment) Ordinance, 1984, no Zakat to be charged on compulsory basis on assets which have been acquired against payment in foreign currency, or which are maintained in foreign currency and return on which and value on encashment, redemption or withdrawal which is payable in foreign currency.

The Modaraba Companies and Modaraba (Floatation and Control) Ordinance 1980 provides for setting up of Modaraba companies and carrying on of Modaraba business, which is defined to mean business in which person(s) participates with his money and another with his efforts and/or skill. Company can apply to Registrar (appointed under Ordinance) for registration as Modaraba company. Modaraba Company can then apply to Registrar for permission to float Modaraba business. Public participates by buying Modaraba certificates, Modaraba company shall subscribe in each Modaraba business floated by it to not less than 10% of total amount of Modaraba certificates offered for subscription, but remuneration of Modaraba company shall not exceed 10% of net annual profits. Registrar has powers of holding inquiries into running of Modaraba or of appointing administrator. Special tribunal may be constituted, with civil and criminal jurisdiction to hear claims and try offences, under Ordinance.

Evidence Act, 1872 repealed and replaced by Qanun-e-Shahadat Order, 1984. Majority of sections in new statute same as those of old Act. Certain changes have been made with view to bring law of evidence in conformity with injunctions of Islam. Under new statute all courts of law required to determine competence of witness in accordance with qualifications prescribed by injunctions of Islam, but where such witness is not forthcoming, court may take evidence of available witness. All accused persons, including accomplice made liable to cross-examination. Instruments pertaining to financial or future obligations must be attested by two men or one man and two women.

Under Constitution Islam is State religion and Art. 38 of Constitution states that State shall take steps to eliminate 'Riba' (which is generally accepted as being analogous to interest). Under Enforcement of Shari'ah Act 1991, Shari'ah is Supreme Law and Federal Government is required to set up commission to recommend measures, including suitable alternatives, by which economic system enunciated by Islam could be established in shortest possible time. Commission will oversee process of elimination of interest from every sphere of economic activity. However by §18 financial obligations and contracts made between National Institutions and Foreign Agency which as defined would cover almost all national and juridical persons are fully protected till alternative economic system is introduced.

JOINT STOCK COMPANIES:

See topic Corporations (Companies).

JUDGMENTS:

Judgment on Admissions.—Any party may, at any stage of a suit, where admissions of fact have been made, either on the pleadings, or otherwise, apply to the court for such judgment or order as upon such admissions he may be entitled to, without waiting for the determination of any other question between the parties, and court may upon such application make such order or give such judgment, as court may think just.

Judgment by Consent.—If it is proved to satisfaction of court that a suit has been adjusted wholly or in part by any lawful agreement or compromise, or where defendant has satisfied plaintiff in respect of whole or any part of subject matter of suit, court orders such agreement, compromise or satisfaction to be recorded, and passes a decree in accordance therewith so far as it relates to the suit.

Declaratory Judgments.—Any person entitled to any legal character, or to any right as to any property can institute a suit against any person who denies or is interested in denying his title to such character or right. Court may in its discretion make a declaration that he is so entitled, and plaintiff need not in such suit ask for any further relief. Court will, however, make no such declaration where plaintiff, being able to seek further relief than a mere declaration of title, omits to do so.

Judgment by Default.—If defendant does not appear when suit is called on for hearing, and it is proved that summons was duly served, court may proceed ex parte and pass an ex parte order.

Where defendant appears and plaintiff does not appear when suit is called on for hearing, court shall make an order that suit be dismissed, unless defendant admits the claim, or part thereof, in which case court shall pass a decree against defendant upon such admission, and where part only of claim has been admitted, shall dismiss the suit so far as it relates to remainder.

Revival.—First application for execution for a decree, to be within time, must be made within three years of decree. Subsequent applications must be made within three years from date of final order made on last application.

Foreign Judgments.—A foreign judgment is conclusive as to any matter directly adjudicated upon between the same parties or between parties under whom they or any of them claim litigating under the same title except: (a) Where it has not been pronounced by a court of competent jurisdiction; (b) where it has not been given on merits of the case; (c) where it appears on face of proceedings to be founded on an incorrect view of international law or a refusal to recognize the law of Pakistan in cases in which such law is applicable; (d) where proceedings in which judgment was obtained are opposed to natural justice; (e) where it has been obtained by fraud; (f) where it sustains a claim founded on a breach of any law in force in Pakistan.

Foreign judgment may be enforced by proceedings in execution mainly under §44A of Code of Civil Procedure 1908, but in other cases foreign judgment can only be enforced by a suit upon judgment.

§44A states: (1) Where certified copy of decree of any of superior courts of U.K. or any reciprocating territory has been filed in District Court, decree may be executed in Pakistan as if it had been passed by District Court. (2) Together with certified copy of decree shall be filed certificate from such superior court stating extent, if any, to which decree has been satisfied or adjusted and such certificate shall, for purpose of proceedings under this section, be conclusive proof of extent of such satisfaction or adjustment. (3) Provision of §47 shall as from filing of certified copy of decree apply to proceedings of District Court executing a decree under this section, and District Court shall refuse execution of any such decree, if it is shown to satisfaction of court that decree falls within any of exceptions specified in Clauses (a) to (f) of §13 which define cases in which a foreign judgment is not conclusive and are quoted first above. Also §14 states that court shall presume, upon production of any document purporting to be a certified copy of foreign judgment, that such judgment was pronounced by court of competent jurisdiction, unless contrary appears on record; but such presumption may be displaced by proving want of jurisdiction.

§47 defines the questions to be determined by court executing decree: (1) All questions arising between parties to suit in which decree was passed, or their representatives, and relating to execution, discharge or satisfaction of decree, shall be determined by court executing decree and not by separate suit. (2) Court may, subject to any objection as to limitation or jurisdiction, treat proceeding under this section as suit or suit as proceeding and may, if necessary, order payment of any additional court fees. (3) Where question arises as to whether any person is or is not representative of party, such question shall, for purposes of this section, be determined by court.

Award given in foreign state by arbitrators selected by parties cannot be equated to judgment given by foreign court and its validity is not open to attack on grounds mentioned in §13. Award pronounced in foreign state is not judgment within this section and no suit will in consequence lie on it even if it was filed in foreign court unless it was made a rule of court. However suit may be filed on award itself.

Where a foreign judgment is sought to be enforced in execution under §44A it will be open to the judgment-debtor to raise all objections which would have been open to him under §13 if suit had been filed on judgment.

Suit on foreign judgment in court governed by Code of Civil Procedure 1908 must satisfy conditions of §20 which states that suits should be instituted where defendant resides, or carries on business or personally works for gain or where cause of action wholly or in part arises.

Period of limitation for suit on foreign judgment in six years from date of judgment. (Limitation Act 1908, Schedule 1, Article 117). Pendency of appeal in foreign country will not bar a suit on foreign judgment, but if appeal results in decree dismissing appeal, appellate decree affords fresh starting point for limitation.

See also topic Executions.

LABOUR LAWS:

Major Central Acts and Ordinances which affect labour management relations in Pakistan are: (1) The Factories Act, 1934; (2) Payment of Wages Act, 1936; (3) Workmen's Compensation Act, 1923; (4) Minimum Wages Ordinance 1961; (5) Income Tax Ordinance, 1979; (6) Companies Profits (Workers Participation) Act, 1968; and (7) Industrial Relations Ordinance, 1969; (8) The West Pakistan Industrial and Commercial Employment (Standing Orders) Ordinance, 1968; (9) West Pakistan Shops and Establishments Ordinance, 1969; (10) The West Pakistan Employees Social Security Ordinance, 1965; (11) Workers' Children (Education) Ordinance, 1972.

Acts and Ordinances relating to mining industry in Pakistan are not included in the above list.

All these statutes are subject to frequent amendment.

Industrial Disputes.—Industrial Relations Ordinance, 1969, which came into force in Nov., 1969 and was am'd in 1970 and 1973, has further been am'd by Industrial Relations (Amendment) Act 1975 which deals with formation of trade unions, regulation of relations between employers and workmen and avoidance and settlement of differences or disputes arising between them. Ordinance does not apply to employees in Police, Armed Forces, Government administration, State television and radio, Pakistan International Airlines and Government printing Press. Industrial Relations (Amendment) Act 1973 has made substantial changes and improvements in Industrial Relations Ordinance, 1969 for betterment of workmen. Important changes introduced under this Ordinance are establishment of National Industrial Relations Commission. (§22-A). This Commission shall consist of not less than seven members including Chairman to be appointed by Federal Government. Main functions of Commission are to promote formation of trade unions of workers within same industry, federations of such trade unions and federations at national level and also to adjudicate and determine an industrial dispute to which an industry-wide trade union or a federation of trade unions is a party and any other industrial dispute which, in opinion of Federal Government, is of national importance and is referred to it by Government. Functions of National Industrial Commission also include registration of industry-wide trade unions, federation of such trade unions and federations at National level, to determine collective bargaining agent amongst said unions and federations, to try offences of unfair labour practices punishable under Industrial Relations Ordinance 1969, and to deal with cases of unfair labour practices specified in §§15, 16, 25a, 34 and to take such measures as are necessary to prevent an employer or workman from committing an unfair labour practice.

Amending Ordinance has also introduced a shop steward system to act as a link between labour and management. (§23-A). Shop stewards are to be elected by workmen at a secret ballot in a shop, section or department. Main function of shop steward is to act as a link between workers and employer, assist in improvement of arrangements for physical working conditions and production work in workshop, section or department and also to help workers in settlement of their problems either connected with work or with any individual grievance of a workman. According to §23-B of Ordinance workers employed in a factory employing 50 or more persons have been allowed participation in factory management to extent of 50%. For this purpose workers' representatives have to be elected to participate in factory management and minimun number of elected representatives is one. Law makes it obligatory on management of a factory, not to take any decision without advice in writing of workers' representatives in matters namely: framing of service rules, policy about promotion and discipline of workers, changing physical working conditions in factory, inservice training of workers and recreation and welfare of workers. New §23-B provides for joint management boards where factory is owned by company or if more than 50 persons are employed, in which workers' representation is 30% (management to be represented by directors/senior executives) to look after: (a) Improvement in production, productivity and efficiency; (b) fixation of job and piece rates; (c) planned regrouping or transfer of workers; (d) laying down principles of remuneration and introduction of new remuneration methods; and (e) provisions of minimum facilities

See Topical Index in front part of this volume.

LABOUR LAWS . . . *continued*
for such of workers employed through contractors as are not covered by laws relating to welfare of workers.

New provision (§25-A) has been inserted for redress of individual grievances according to procedure and time limit prescribed in said section.

Under Industrial Relations Ordinance 1969 workers and employers have been granted rights to establish and join associations of their own choice to draw up their constitutions, to elect their representatives in full freedom to organise their programmes, to establish and join any federations or confederations. §3 of Ordinance is intended to conform to requirements of ILO Conventions Nos. 87 and 98 which Pakistan has ratified.

§§15 and 16 of Ordinance also prohibit unfair labour practice on part of employers and workmen. Even threat to dismiss, discharge, remove from employment or injure a workman is an unfair labour practice. Intimidation, coercion, etc., of any officer of a collective bargaining agent is also an unfair labour practice. Workmen or unions are prohibited from canvassing for trade union membership or otherwise during working hours. Intimidation or coercion on an employer to sign a memorandum of settlement and to interfere in a ballot held under §22 are also unfair labour practices on part of workmen or their unions. Maximum penalty for employer for contravening provisions may be four years imprisonment and Rs. 5,000 fine and for workmen six months imprisonment and Rs. 200 fine.

Under §38A Federal Government may, whenever it considers necessary by notification in Official Gazette constitute a Wage Commission for fixing rates of wages and determining all other terms and conditions of service, in accordance with provisions of this Ordinance in respect of workers of a bank or such other workers as Federal Government may, by notification in Official Gazette specify.

Other important provisions: Limits application of conspiracy laws under Pakistan Penal Code and confers immunity on registered trade unions from certain civil suits; defines collective bargaining agent whose officers may represent workmen in any proceedings under Ordinance; provides for appointment of conciliator, arbitration, establishment of works councils to promote measures for securing and preserving good relations between employers and workmen; provides for establishment of Labour Courts and Labour Appellate Tribunals for adjudication of industrial disputes and other matters relating thereto; legalizes strikes and lock-outs as permitted under law except in public utility service like electricity, gas, oil, water, hospitals, post, telephone, telegraph, railways and airways etc., provides a penalty of up to one year imprisonment and Rs. 500 fine for first breach of a settlement, award or decision and similar penalties for other offences under Ordinance.

The Labour Laws (Amendment) Ordinance 1975 has added new §23C to Industrial Relations Ordinance 1969. It states: "(1) In every company employing 50 persons or more, the management shall, in the prescribed manner, set up a joint management board in which the workers' participations shall be to the extent of 33%. (2) The employers' representatives on the joint management board shall be from amongst the Directors or senior executives. (3) The joint management board shall look after the following matters, namely: (a) improvement in production, productivity, and efficiency; (b) fixation of job and piece rates; (c) planned regrouping of a transfer of the workers; (d) laying down the principles of remuneration and introduction of new renumerations methods, and (e) provision of minimum facilities for such of the workers employed through contractors as are not covered by the laws relating to the welfare of workers. (4) The joint management board may call for reasonable information about the working of the Company from its management and the management shall supply the information called for."

Factories Act 1934 regulates conditions of labour employed in a "factory" as defined in Act. This has been amended by Factories (Amendment) Act, 1973. One of amendments, makes all offences against Act, Rules and Order made thereunder as cognizable and bailable.

Act ensures that health and safety of labour are not ignored by factory owners. Chapter III of the Act requires employer to keep a minimum standard of cleanliness, ventilation, artificial humidification, lighting etc., and keep the building and machinery used by the factory in proper condition lest harm may be caused to labour. Vaccination and innoculation of each factory worker against such diseases and at such intervals as may be prescribed is made compulsory. Appointment of welfare officers by occupier or manager of every factory where not less than 500 workers are ordinarily employed is made compulsory.

In order to further ensure due observance of the conditions laid down in said Chapter III of Act, it provides for the appointment of inspectors who have been empowered to require the factory owners to fulfil the requirements of Act.

Every district magistrate is the inspector for the district in his jurisdiction. An appeal from the decisions of an inspector lies to the government concerned.

Besides making special provision regarding child and female labour, Act seeks to regulate daily and weekly working hours, weekly holidays, compensatory holidays, intervals of rest, overtime and shift working etc.

Chapter IV deals with working conditions of adults, Chapter V with conditions of work of children and adolescents. Children below 14 are prohibited to be employed.

Separate chapters have been devoted to "holidays with pay," "small factories," and "penalties and procedure."

Shops and Establishments Laws.—West Pakistan Shops & Establishments Ordinance 1969 regulates hours and other conditions of work and employment of persons employed in shops and commercial and industrial establishments. Ordinance has repealed Sind Shops & Establishments Act 1940, North West Frontier Trade Employees Act 1947, Punjab Trade Employees Act 1940, and Weekly Holiday Act 1942 in its application to provinces of Pakistan except tribal areas.

Ordinance primarily regulates daily and weekly hours of work, holidays, wages for overtime and leaves with pay in shops, commercial, industrial and other establishments. Children below 14 are prohibited to be employed.

Provisions for appointment of shops inspectors have been made in Ordinance. Inspectors are empowered to challenge any shop, establishment, etc., found guilty of breach of any mandatory provision of law.

Industrial and Commercial Employment.—This is governed by West Pakistan Industrial and Commercial Employment (Standing Orders) Ordinance 1968 as am'd by West Pakistan Industrial and Commercial Employment (Standing Orders) (Amendment) Act 1973.

This repeals Industrial and Commercial Employment (Standing Orders) Ordinance 1960, which was a Central Act applicable to both wings of Pakistan. Standing Orders lay down minimum terms and conditions of service which must be allowed to "workmen" by every employer of an industrial or commercial establishment as defined in enactments, provided such industrial or commercial establishment employs, or did employ on any day during preceding 12 months, 20 or more workmen.

Minimum terms and conditions of service given in schedule to Ordinance, in form of Standing Orders, cannot be changed except by way of improvement from workmen's point of view, for which it is made compulsory for employer to enter into a collective agreement with a trade union or a representative body of his workmen.

Standing Orders contained in Schedule are to be displayed to workmen in English and Urdu so that minimum terms of employment should be made known to them.

Non-observance of Standing Orders or any other provision of Ordinance by any "commercial establishment" or "industrial establishment" has been made punishable with fines or imprisonment or both.

Payment of Wages Act 1936 regulates payment of wages in certain "industrial establishments" as defined in Act. This has been amended by Labour Laws (Amendment) Act 1972 and Payment of Wages (Amendment) Act 1973.

Act casts responsibility of payment of wages to workmen upon employer or manager of establishment and regulates wage period and time for payment of wages. Act does not apply to wages payable in respect of a wage period which, over such wage period, average more than Rs. 1,000 a month.

Cuts imposed on wages on account of fines and various kinds of deductions and the circumstances under which these can be imposed have also been laid down in the act.

Special provisions have been made for: (1) deductions for absence from duty; (2) deductions for damage or loss to employer's property; (3) deductions on account of services rendered by employer; (4) deductions for recovery of advances; and, (5) deductions from wages for payment to cooperative societies and insurance schemes.

A single workman or a group of workmen, if aggrieved on account of non-payment or delay in payment of wages by employer or on account of a deduction made by him contrary to provisions of Act, can make an application within three years of time when deduction was made or payment was delayed or refused, to Commissioner appointed under Act. Appeal lies to District Court from a decision of Commissioner within 30 days of the directions given by Commissioner.

Inspectors appointed under Act have been empowered to check relevant books containing salary accounts to be maintained by employer.

For breach of certain provisions of Act, fines up to Rs. 500 may be imposed as punishment.

The Federal and provincial governments have made their own rules for proper functioning of Act in their respective jurisdictions.

Workmen's Compensation Act, 1923.—This has been amended by Labour Laws (Amendment) Act 1972 which has introduced some important changes. Schedules I and IV have been substituted and list of injuries and amounts of compensation have been revised and increased to provide substantial benefits to workmen.

There has been further amendment by Workmen's Compensation (Amendment) Act, 1973, and now workmen drawing wages up to Rs. 1,000 per month are covered by Act. Schedule II to Act gives a list of persons who are included in definition of "workmen." Act provides for payment of compensation by employer to his workmen injured during course of employment.

Compensation allowed by Act ranges between lump sum amount of Rs. 100 and Rs. 21,000 according to nature of injury and wages drawn by workmen concerned at time of receiving injury. Half-monthly payments at specified rates are payable in cases of temporary disablement for maximum period of five years.

The Act also lays down circumstances when employer will not be liable to compensate an injured workman.

Injuries have been defined under the Act to be mainly of the following kinds: (1) Injuries resulting in death of a workman; (2) permanent total disablement; (3) temporary total disablement; (4) permanent partial disablement; (5) temporary partial disablement.

Schedule I to Act gives list of injuries, a combination of two or more of which may constitute total disablement within meaning of Act. Loss of a limb or member of the body, is to be compensated according to the percentage loss of earning capacity as indicated in Schedule I.

List of diseases is given in Act which are recognized as occupational diseases.

Besides laying down provisions as to method of calculating compensation, Act provides details for payment of compensation to survivors in case of death of a workman resulting from injury received during employment.

Commissioners have been appointed under Chapter III of Act to entertain claims for compensation against employer from injured workmen. Commissioners' powers, procedure to be observed before them and provisions for appeals against decisions made by them are also laid down in this Chapter.

Under Chapter II of Act an injured workman is required to serve notice of his claim for compensation in the prescribed manner on employer and claim before Commissioner must be made within one year of time of receiving injury or date of death as case may be.

Special provisions have been made for keeping of an up-to-date record of fatal accidents by Commissioners and duty has been cast upon employers to furnish details regarding same to Commissioners. Employer is required to send periodic returns of compensation paid to injured workmen, to appropriate authority appointed by the government concerned.

Exhaustive rules have been framed by the central government under §32 of Act for smooth and efficient working of Act. Provincial governments observe separate rules.

Separate rules have been made by the central government for workmen's compensation returns and transfers of money due as compensation under Act.

Law of Trade Unions.—See subhead Industrial Disputes, supra.

LABOUR LAWS . . . *continued*

Income Tax Ordinance 1979.—Part I of Sixth Schedule relates to certain classes of provident funds which employer may establish for benefit of his employees.

Provident funds recognized by Commissioner of Income Tax have following advantages:

(1) To employer: (a) Employer obtains income tax relief on its contributions to fund; (b) employer is not liable for any fixed rate of interest (return to the member is governed by the actual return obtained on funds by trustees).

(2) To member employee: (a) Fund is in the hands of trustees; (b) members obtain income tax relief on their contributions to the fund; (c) when a member withdraws from fund he obtains entire balance free of tax; (d) circumstances in which a member can borrow against his contributions to the fund are clearly set out.

Minimum Wages Ordinance 1961.—Minimum Wages Ordinance which came into force on Sept. 29, 1961, provides for regulation of minimum rates of wages for workers employed in "industrial undertakings", as defined in Ordinance.

Ordinance provides for establishment of Minimum Wages Council by central government for advising central government and provincial governments on all matters relating to carrying out of provisions of Ordinance and other matters relating thereto. Ordinance also provides for establishment of Minimum Wages Board of provincial governments. According to scheme of Ordinance, Minimum Wages Board will, upon a reference being made by provincial government, recommend to such government after such enquiry as Board thinks fit, minimum rates of wages for workers employed in industrial undertakings in province. Upon receipt of recommendation of Board provincial government may declare minimum rate of wages for such workers and no employer may pay any worker wages at rate lower than rate declared under Ordinance. Any employer who contravenes provisions of Ordinance is punishable with imprisonment for term which may extend to six months or with fine which may extend to 500 rupees or with both. Board and Council may, for purpose of an enquiry under Ordinance, direct any employer to furnish such records, documents, information or do such other acts as Board, Council or Chairman may require.

Fringe benefits in Pakistan are not the subjects of legislation. These benefits are provided by collective bargaining agreement between unions and management as well as by judicial precedents which are based on practice prevailing in the region-cum-industry.

Fringe benefits which are generally provided to workmen in Pakistan include house, conveyance, medical, officiating and compensatory allowances, gratuity, pension, retirement scheme and provident fund.

Quantum of the benefit varies from industry to industry.

Special legislation in form of maternity benefits has been enacted for welfare of women employed in factories.

Bonuses in Pakistan in actual practice are no longer regarded as ex gratia payments. The industrial courts in the country allow claims for bonuses if there is an available surplus, and the workers have contributed substantially towards profits. For commercial and industrial concerns employing more than 20 "workmen" (as defined) cumpulsory bonus, related to profits, but compulsory maximum of one months salary, has to be paid, if profits are sufficient.

West Pakistan Employees Social Security Ordinance 1965, Ordinance No. 10 of 1965.—This extends to whole of Pakistan except tribal areas. This has been amended by West Pakistan Employees Social Security (Amendment) Act 1973. Contingencies covered by social security benefits are sickness benefits, maternity benefits, death grant, medical care during sickness and maternity, injury benefits, medical care in case of employment injury. All employees whose wages are up to Rs. 1,000 (instead of Rs. 500) per mensem are covered irrespective of their designation, status or nature of work.

All above benefits are available in case of any injury or accident or occupational disease arising out of and in course of employment. Sub-section 3 of §1 provides that it shall come into force at once but shall apply only to such areas, classes of persons, industries or establishments, from such date or dates and with regard to provisions of such benefits as Government may by notification specify in this behalf. Government has from time to time notified areas, classes of persons, industries and establishments etc. Ordinance deals with benefits in respect of sickness, maternity, death grant, medical care during sickness and maternity injury benefits, disablement pensions, disablement gratuity etc. This Ordinance has repealed Employee's Social Security Ordinance, 1962.

Control of Employment Ordinance 1965.—Ordinance is intended to control and check termination of service of essential personnel in industrial undertaking. Under Ordinance, three bodies have been constituted, namely: Manpower Board, Manpower Council and Manpower Tribunal. Manpower Board is most important.

Manpower Board is vested with wide powers. Section 5 defines functions and powers of Manpower Board. Board can control or regulate employment in any industrial undertaking, prohibit persons from accepting employment, lay down terms and conditions of service of persons employed or to be employed, etc.

Notified industries have to report to Board all situations which are vacant or likely to be vacant and employ such essential personnel and on such terms as may be directed by Board. No employer of notified industrial undertaking can fill any vacancy in which essential personnel are employed except with previous permission of Board.

Rules.—Rule 10 of Rules framed under this Ordinance is of general importance. Under this rule, no owner or manager of industrial undertaking is permitted to discharge or dismiss any person without previous permission in writing of Board.

Employers who have to comply with this Rule appear to be those who have received prior notice from Board requiring them to put up, before specified date, notices making known to employees provisions of this Rule and intimating place to which applications to Board may be addressed.

It is, however, not necessary for employer to obtain prior permission to discharge or dismiss his employee in cases of probationary period, employment for specific period, completion of piece of work for which employee was engaged, medical grounds or where employee has been guilty of gross insubordination, habitual absence from work or any other serious misconduct, etc. In all such cases employer has to give notice in writing to Board with reasons of discharge or dismissal within 24 hours of such discharge or dismissal.

It may further be mentioned that in cases where employer has to apply to Board for permission to discharge or dismiss, Board is required to communicate its order within 15 days of date of despatch of employer's application, failing which, Board's permission is deemed to have been given.

Phrases "industrial undertaking," "personnel" and "persons" have not been used with sufficient clarity in Ordinance and it Rules. These phrases in all probability refer only to "Notified Industrial Undertaking" and "Essential Personnel" respectively.

Breach of any of provisions of Ordinance or of Rules has been made a penal offence.

Companies Profits (Workers Participation) Act, 1968 came into force on 4th July, 1968 and extends to whole of Pakistan. This has been amended by Companies Profits (Workers Participation) Act, 1972. A substantial change made by Act is: payment by employer of 5% of profits of company every year to fund created for workers.

Under §3 of this Act every company to which scheme is applicable shall establish a workers participation fund in accordance with scheme given in schedule and company shall pay 5% of its annual profits to this fund. This scheme applies to all industrial undertakings where number of workers is 50 or more or if its paid-up capital is two million rupees or more or if value of its fixed assets is four million rupees or more.

Workers' Children (Education) Ordinance 1972 as amended by Workers' Children (Education) Act.—An Employer is obliged under Act in respect of a person employed in his establishment who is not earning more than Rs. 1,000 per month to pay to Provincial Government an education cess at rate of Rs. 100 per worker per annum in respect of establishments in which number of workers employed at any time during year is 20 or more. Provincial Government shall provide education free of cost up to matriculation examination to one child of every worker employed in an establishment referred to in §3.

Employees Old-Age Benefits Act 1976.—Applies to every industry or establishment wherein ten or more persons are employed directly or through any other person whether on behalf of himself or any other person, or were so employed on any day during preceding 12 months.

§9(1). Contributions payable every month by employer to Employees' Old-Age Benefits Institution in respect of every person in his insurable employment, at rate of 5% of his wages.

§22. Old Age Allowances: Insured person entitled to old age allowance at rates specified in schedule provided that: (a) He is over 55 years of age or in case of woman, 50 years, (b) contributions in respect of him were payable for not less than 15 years.

§23. Invalidism Benefit: Insured who sustained invalidism (i.e., condition other than that caused by employment injury as result of which insured person is permanently incapacitated to such extent as to be unable to earn from his usual or other occupation more than 1/3 of normal rates of earning in his usual occupation) shall be entitled to invalidism allowance at rate specified in schedule subject to conditions in §23.

§26. Right to invalidism and old age allowance is extinguished if claim is not made within 12 months from date it becomes payable, but Institution may condone delay if it was caused for reasons beyond applicant's control.

LABOUR RELATIONS:

See topics Labour Laws; Records.

LAW REPORTS, CODES, ETC.:

See topics Reports; Statutes.

LEGISLATURE:

Under 1973 Constitution, as amended by Revival of Constitution of 1973 Order, 1985 there shall be Parliament called "Majlis-e-Shoora" consisting of two Houses to be known as National Assembly and Senate. National Assembly shall consist of 207 Muslim members to be elected by direct and free vote; there shall be ten additional seats for representatives of religious minorities and for period of ten years or till holding of third general election whichever occurs later 20 additional seats for women. Senate shall consist of 87 members, of whom 14 shall be elected by each of four provincial assemblies, eight by members from Federally Administered Tribal Area in National Assembly, three shall be chosen from Federal Capital and five shall be chosen from "Ulema" (religious scholars), technocrats and other professionals. National Assembly shall be elected for five years. Senate shall not be subject to dissolution but its members shall hold office for six years, approximately half of them retiring every three years. If Bill is rejected or not passed within 90 days of receipt or passed with amendment by either House, it shall, at request of House in which Bill originated be considered in joint sitting and if Bill is passed in joint sitting, with or without amendment, by majority of total membership of two Houses it shall be presented to President for assent. Bill passed by Parliament can become law either on being assented to by President, or if President sends it to be reconsidered by both Houses in joint sitting, it is again passed, with or without amendment, by majority of total membership of both Houses, after which President must give consent. When National Assembly is not in session, President has power to make Ordinance which will be placed before National Assembly as soon as practicable and shall stand repealed at expiration of four months from its promulgation or earlier disapproval by Assembly. There are four provincial legislatures headed by governors, one each for provinces of Baluchistan, North West Frontier Province, Punjab and Sind consisting of 40, 80, 240 and 100 members respectively elected by direct and free vote; there shall be 23 additional seats reserved for minorities and for period of ten years or till holding of third general election whichever occurs later there shall be additional seats reserved for women equal to 5% of number of seats of each Assembly. Relationship between governors and provincial legislature is similar to that between President and National Assembly.

See also topic Constitution and Government.

See Topical Index in front part of this volume.

LICENCES:

See topics Foreign Trade Regulations; Industrial and Investment Regulations.

LIENS:

Lien is a right in one person to retain in his possession such property moveable or immoveable belonging to another until such time as claims of person in possession are satisfied. Lien, unless there is express provision to contrary, is not transferable and confers no right of sale on creditor without court intervention. Lien may be general, i.e., for a general balance owing to the creditor, or particular, i.e., a right over goods until certain demands are satisfied.

Carriers, unpaid sellers, hotel keepers, agents and all persons who are entitled to be paid for services rendered or for expending money for purposes of debtor have a right of lien on property in their possession belonging to debtor. Banker may have a lien over securities deposited with him for money due and in such cases bankers generally retain right to sell without recourse to debtor. Trustee has lien over trust property in respect of expenses lawfully incurred in connection with such property. Company may in its articles of association create lien over its own shares.

Right of lien is lost upon payment of debt, by tender of debt and by taking alternative security for debt.

LIMITATION OF ACTIONS:

Limitation is governed by the Limitation Act 1908. Actions must be commenced within the following periods:

Sixty Years.—Any suit by or on behalf of the central government, suits by a mortgagee for foreclosure and sale, against a mortgagee for redemption or to recover possession of immoveable property.

Thirty Years.—Against a depositary or pawnee to recover moveable property deposited, by a mortgagee to recover possession of the immoveable property from the mortgagor.

Twelve Years.—Inter alia, to recover a legacy or share in an intestacy, to establish a periodically recurring right, to enforce a charge upon immoveable property, to recover immoveable property mortgaged or bequeathed in trust which has been transferred for a valuable consideration, by a landlord to recover possession from a tenant, by a remainderman or reversioner for possession of immoveable property, generally for the possession of immoveable property or any rights therein not specially provided for.

Six Years.—For compensation for breach of a contract in writing registered, upon a foreign judgment, to obtain a declaration that an alleged adoption is invalid or valid, any suit for which no limitation is provided elsewhere in the Act.

Three Years.—Most actions arising in contract are within three years limitation including any breach of contract not specially provided for.

Two Years.—Suits against executors or administrators, for compensation for any malfeasance, misfeasance or nonfeasance independent of contract and not specially provided for.

One Year.—For wages, for price of food or drink supplied, for price of lodgings, to enforce a right of prescription, to set aside, inter alia, sale in execution of a decree, against the government to recover land acquired, money paid, challenged orders, for compensation for false imprisonment, by executors and administrators, for compensation for injuries under Fatal Accidents Act, or other injury, for compensation for malicious prosecution, libel and slander.

Six Months.—Under the Specific Relief Act.

Ninety Days.—For compensation for doing or omitting to do an act alleged to be in pursuance of any enactment for the time being in force.

Thirty Days.—To contest an award of the Board of Revenue.

Limitation need not be specifically pleaded as the courts must take cognizance of this.

Exclusion of Time.—Where at time of commencement of the period of limitation the person in whom right of action lies is under a disability e.g., where he is insane, a minor, or an idiot, time will not commence to run against him until disability ceases. Where a second disability commences before the first disability is over, time will run after second disability is over. Once time begins to run, however, subsequent disability will have no effect. Where the person dies still under a disability, his right of action passes to his legal representatives and time will commence to run from that date.

Public holidays and court holidays are excluded from the period of limitation.

In an appeal the time for obtaining a copy of the decree and judgment will also be excluded.

Where a plaintiff bona fide prosecutes his claim in a wrong court, the time of such prosecution will be excluded.

Extension of Time.—Where a defendant acknowledges a debt in writing during the period of limitation or makes a part payment of rent a fresh period of limitation will be computed from that date. (Limitation Act 1908, §19).

MARRIAGE:

Marriage, like divorce, is governed by different statutes and by personal customs for different communities. Under the Child Marriage Restraint Act minimum ages for male and female were respectively 18 and 14, but by Family Laws Ordinance 1961 minimum age for a female has now been raised to 16 years. No medical examination is required before marriage.

Christian marriages are governed by the Christian Marriage Act 1872. It applies where either one or both parties are Christians. Such marriages can be solemnized by any person who has received Episcopal ordination and according to the rites of that church, by a clergyman of the Church of Scotland, and by any minister of religion, marriage registrar or other licensed person. Marriage must, unless a special license is obtained, be celebrated between the hours of 6 a.m. and 7 p.m., and should normally be at a church unless special license is obtained or there is no church within five miles of the parties' residences. Notice must be given to the minister who is to solemnize the wedding, stating full names, status, profession, residential address and length of residence, if under a month, of the parties, and intended place of solemnization. Where one of parties is a minor consent in writing is also required of such person's parent or guardian and a copy of the notice and consent must also issue to Marriage Registrar unless the parents or guardians are not resident in Pakistan in which case no consent is required. This notice must be published both by the minister and by Marriage Registrar where it is sent to him and on the request of either party a certificate of notice given and a declaration made can be obtained from Registrar or minister, where no lawful impediment exists and the giving of such a certificate is not forbidden. Any person whose consent is necessary can forbid the marriage but the minister must examine the notice forbidding the marriage and satisfy himself that it is authorized. Where the marriage is to be solemnized by Marriage Registrar and consent is withheld, the parties may appeal on petition to District Judge. Marriages solemnized by Marriage Registrar are also governed by virtually similar rules.

Marriages must be solemnized within two months of issuance of a certificate of notice, otherwise, unless a certificate is reissued, the marriage will be void.

The marriage must be witnessed by two witnesses. Marriages must be registered and a register kept according to the rules under part IV of Act.

Special Marriage Act 1872 governs the marriages of persons who are not professing Buddhists, Christians, Hindus, Muslims, Parsis, Sikhs or Jains and also those persons who profess the Hindu, Buddhist, Sikh or Jain religion where such persons wish to marry out of their community into one of the remaining three communities. The minimum age under the Act is 18 for males and 14 for females and consent of the guardian or parents is required for the party who is under 21. No persons can marry who would have been unable to marry according to the laws of consanguinity or affinity under their personal law. No law of consanguinity operates however unless a relationship can be traced between the parties through some common ancestor who stands to each of them in a nearer relation than that of a great-great-grandfather or a great-great-grandmother or unless one of the parties is a lineal ancestor or brother or sister of some lineal ancestor of the other.

Marriages are solemnized before Registrars appointed for this purpose. Notice of marriage must be given and in absence of any objections can be solemnized after 14 days. Objections must be filed in court and if the court is in vacation Registrar must wait 14 days after opening of court so that objections can be lodged. A certificate of the filing of suit must be lodged with Registrar if he is to take cognizance that such objections have been made. Where such objections are frivolous, the person making them may be fined. The marriage must be solemnized before three witnesses and parties must sign a declaration in their presence and that of Registrar, stating that they are not professing Buddhists, Christians, etc., as above, or that being Hindu, Buddhist, etc., they will be marrying some person outside that community. Where either party is under 21, this declaration must also be signed by the father or guardian except where the party under 21 is a widow. The declaration must be countersigned by Registrar.

Marriages contracted under this Act are monogamous and dissolution of such marriages is governed by the Divorce Act 1869. See topic Divorce.

Issue of such marriage will be subject to the laws of consanguinity that governed the parties.

Rights of Hindus, Jains, Buddhists and Sikhs continue except rights to inherit any kind of religious position or status in their community.

Succession to property is governed by the Succession Act 1925.

A party's right of adoption ceases on marriage but the party's father may have the right to adopt where the party to such a marriage was an only son.

Other marriages are contracted under the parties' personal laws. Muslim marriages have been modified by the Family Laws Ordinance 1961 which provides that during the existence of one marriage no futher marriage may be contracted by the husband without prior permission of an arbitral commission or any other person so appointed having authority to grant or withhold such permission. No such second marriage is void, however, but the husband may be liable to a fine, or a year's imprisonment, or both. Muslim women can only marry Muslim men, but Muslim men can also contract marriages with Christian or Jewish women.

Nullity.—A marriage contracted under Christian Marriage Act and Special Marriage Act can be annulled for impotence at time of marriage continuing to date of presentation of the petition, as also in case of incapacity at the time of marriage, marriages between persons within prohibited degrees of consanguinity, and bigamy with respect to the second marriage. The children of a marriage contracted in good faith during the existence of a previous subsisting marriage are legitimate.

Marriage with a Foreigner.—There are no restrictions on marriage with a foreigner except on Government servants.

MINES, OIL FIELDS AND MINERAL DEVELOPMENT:

Regulation of Mines and Oil Fields and Mineral Development (Federal Control) Act 1948.—In exercise of powers conferred by §2 of 1948 Act, Pakistan Mining Concessions Rules 1949 and Pakistan Petroleum (Production) Rules 1949 were made. Former apply to all minerals other than petroleum and natural gas whereas latter apply only to petroleum and natural gas. Pakistan Petroleum (Production) Rules, 1949 repealed on Sept. 14, 1986 and replaced by Pakistan Petroleum (Exploration & Production) Rules, 1986.

1948 Act was amended by Regulation of Mines and Oil Fields and Mineral Development (Federal Control) (Amendment) Act 1976. By 1976 Act, following additional concessions have been granted: (1) Any provisions of rules made under §2, or of any amendment in Income Tax Act, 1922 (XI of 1922), hereinafter referred to as Act, made after effective date of agreement for grant of licence or lease to explore, prospect or mine petroleum, which are inconsistent with terms of agreement, shall not apply to extent of such inconsistency to company which is party to agreement. (2) Royalty shall be charged at fixed rate of $12^1/_2$% of well-head value and shall form part of sum of payments to Federal Government and taxes on income which shall neither be more than 55% nor less than 50% of profits or gains before deduction of "payments to the Government" referred to in sub-rule (2) of rule 4 of Second Schedule to Act, hereinafter referred to as said Schedule. (3) Before commencement of commercial production of petroleum, any expenditure on searching for, or on discovering and testing, petroleum deposit, or on winning access thereto allocable to surrendered area and to drilling

See Topical Index in front part of this volume.

MINES, OIL FIELDS AND MINERAL DEVELOPMENT . . . *continued*
of dry hole, shall be deemed to be lost at time of surrender of area or completion of dry hole, as case may be, for purpose of Second Schedule to Act. Such lost expenditure shall be allowed in one of two ways mentioned in sub-rule (1) of rule 2 of said Schedule. (4) In addition to net profits, amount charged in annual financial accounts on account of additional allowance admissible under rule 3 of Second Schedule to Act, and depreciation at such rate as may be agreed upon between President and licensee or lessee, which is company incorporated outside Pakistan, including its assignee, shall be allowed to be remitted and retained abroad, provided that aggregate amount of such additional allowance and depreciation does not exceed agreed percentage of investment in assets on which depreciation is charged. (5) Value of crude oil for purposes of royalty and income tax to be calculated on basis of price realised in transactions with purchasers other than subsidiaries or affiliates of licensee or lessee, including its assignee, and in case of transactions with subsidiary or affiliate, value shall be calculated on such basis as may be agreed upon between Federal Government and licensee or lessee. (6) Income derived by licensee or lessee from use of any surplus capacity of its pipeline by any other licensee or lessee shall be assessed on same basis as its income from petroleum produced by it from its concessions area. (7) Licensee or lessee which is company incorporated outside Pakistan including its assignee, shall be allowed to export its share of petroleum after meeting such portion of internal requirement of Pakistan as may be agreed upon. (8) Sale proceeds of share of petroleum exported by licensee or lessee which is company incorporated outside Pakistan, including its assignee, shall be allowed to be retained abroad and to be used freely by it, subject to condition that it shall bring back such portion of these proceeds as is required to meet its obligations under lease. (9) No customs duty or sales tax shall be levied on import of machinery and equipment specified in agreement for purposes of exploration and drilling prior to commercial discovery. (10) Concessionary consolidated rate of 5¼% customs duty ad valorem, including sales tax and any surcharge related thereto, shall be charged on import of machinery and equipment required for development of each commercial discovery until 24 months from effective date of mining lease granted with respect to each such discovery, and thereafter normal rate of customs duty, sales tax and any other duty shall be applicable. (11) Foreign nationals employed by licensee or lessee or its contractor shall be allowed to import commissary goods free of customs duty and sales tax to extent of $550 per annum, subject to condition that same shall not be sold or otherwise disposed of in Pakistan. (12) Foreign nationals employed by licensee or lessee or its contractor shall be allowed to import used and bona fide personal and household effects, excluding motor vehicles, free of customs duty and sales tax subject to condition that same shall not be sold or otherwise disposed of in Pakistan. (13) Foreign nationals employed by licensee or lessee or its contractor shall not be charged income tax for period of three years from date of their arrival in Pakistan in accordance with, and subject to provision of, clauses (xiii) and (xiiia) of subsection (3) of §4 of Act as in force on effective date of agreement with licensee or lessee. (14) Data in respect of areas surrendered by previous licensee or lessee shall be made available for inspection to prospective licensee free of charge. (15) Initial participation by Federal Government in exploration shall be to such extent as may be agreed upon between Federal Government and licensee.

MONOPOLIES AND RESTRAINT OF TRADE:

Undue concentration of economic power, unreasonable monopoly power and unreasonably restrictive trade practices are prohibited by a special enactment called Monopolies and Restrictive Trade Practices (Control and Prevention) Ordinance, 1970 came into force in Aug. 1971. Important provisions of Ordinance are (1) an undertaking the total value of whose assets is not less than 150 million rupees and which is not owned by public company, or is owned by public company in which individual controls at least 50% of equity will be deemed to have acquired undue economic power; (2) associate undertakings (as defined in Ordinance) which together produce, supply, distribute, or provide one-third or more of total goods or services in same market where they are competitors will be deemed to have acquired unreasonable monopoly power; and (3) where potential competitors have fixed purchase or selling price or imposed other restrictive trading conditions with regard to sale or distribution of any goods or provision of services or divided or shared markets for any goods or services, etc., will be deemed to have imposed unreasonably restrictive trade practices. Law is enforced by Monopoly Control Authority with power to conduct enquiries and issue orders, noncompliance with which may entail fine not exceeding 100,000 rupees. Any person aggrieved by order of Monopoly Control Authority can appeal against it to High Court. Certain undertakings are required to file returns for registration with Authority to facilitate enforcement of provisions of Ordinance and Rules framed thereunder.

Government Control.—Essential Commodities Distribution Order 1953 and Essential Supplies Act 1957, Essential Commodities Control Order 1965 and Price Control and Prevention of Profiteering and Hoarding Act, 1977 are enactments which enable Federal Government to control distribution and price of commodities therein specified. Number of these specified commodities is steadily decreasing as it is policy of Government to allow free play of market forces and to do away with price control.

MORTGAGES:

The law relating to mortgages has developed against the background of the anxiety of the government to protect farmers against unscrupulous moneylenders. This means that the remedies of a mortgagee are sometimes slower and less effective than would be desirable in a primarily commercial community and therefore full and careful drafting is absolutely essential to safeguard the mortgagee.

A mortgage is a transfer of an interest in specific immoveable property for the purpose of securing the payment of money advanced or to be advanced by way of loan, an existing or future debt or the performance of an engagement which may give rise to a pecuniary liability.

Kinds of Mortgages.—A simple mortgage is created where without delivering possession of the mortgaged property, the mortgagor binds himself personally to pay the mortgage money and agrees, expressly or impliedly, that failure to do so will give mortgagee a right to have mortgaged property sold, and to apply sale proceeds towards his debt.

A mortgage by conditional sale exists where mortgagor ostensibly sells the mortgaged property on condition either that if payment is not made by a certain date the sale will become absolute or else on condition that if payment is made buyer will transfer the property to the seller. These conditions have to be expressly written into the contract for sale.

A usufructuary mortgage exists where the mortgagor delivers, or undertakes to deliver, possession of the mortgaged property to the seller and authorizes him to retain possession until payment of the mortgage money and to receive the rents and profits in lieu of interest or partly in lieu of interest and partly in lieu the mortgage money.

Where the mortgagor binds himself to repay the mortgagee on a certain day and transfers the mortgaged property absolutely to mortgagee subject to proviso that mortgagee will retransfer it to mortgagor upon payment of the mortgage money as agreed, the transaction is called an English mortgage. This transfer may be with or without possession.

Where a debtor delivers to his creditor, or his agent in certain specified towns, documents of title to immoveable property, with intent to create a security thereon the transaction is called a mortgage by deposit of title deeds.

Any other mortgage is called an anomolous mortgage.

Registration is required where the property is valued at over Rs. 100 and all mortgages except by deposit of title deeds can only be effected by a registered instrument attested by two witnesses. Where the property is less than Rs. 100 in value and where the mortgage to be created is not a simple mortgagee the mortgage can be effected by delivery of the property.

Stamp Duty is worked out ad valorem. Stamp duty varies from province to province but is maximum of 8% of amount secured if possession is given and 3% of amount secured where possession is not given (in Sind) but only 1% for loans in Islamic mode of financing.

Priorities.—In general the first in time is first in rights but where a second mortgagee is induced to accept by the fraud, misrepresentation or gross neglect of first mortgagee, the prior mortgage will not take effect until after second mortgage.

If a mortgage made to secure future advances or the performance of an engagement or balance of a running account expresses the maximum to be secured thereby, a subsequent mortgage of the same property, if made with notice of the prior mortgage, will be postponed to the prior mortgage in respect of all advances or debts not exceeding the maximum though made or allowed with notice of the subsequent mortgage.

A first mortgagee buying the mortgaged land acquires rights of the mortgagor as against a second mortgagee.

Rights and Liabilities.—A mortgagor has the right after payment to redeem the mortgaged property, but where his interest is only a share in the property he is not entitled to redeem his share only, on payment of a proportionate part of the amount, except where the mortgagee or mortgagees has or have acquired the share of a mortgagor in the property. If mortgagor requires it mortgagee must transfer the property on redemption to a third person. Mortgagor has right to inspect documents, lease the property or commit waste unless the act is destructive or permanently injurious thereto or renders the security insufficient, i.e., reduces its value to less than one-third or where the property is buildings, one-half in excess of the amount due. Mortgagor is also entitled to any improvements without payment unless these improvements were necessary to prevent deterioration or under municipal direction. Mortgagor must defend mortgagee's title and possession; pay all public charges where the mortgagee is not in possession; where the mortgaged property is a lease, have paid all rents due and performed all covenants undertaken; and where the mortgage is a second mortgage, mortgagor will pay the interest, as and when it becomes due on each prior incumbrance and at the proper time discharge the principal.

After the mortgage money has become due, mortgagee has a right to foreclosure and sale but this right must be exercised before a decree has been made for redemption and the money deposited in court. The exercise of the power of sale without reference to the court is limited in most cases. Where mortgagee holds two or more mortgages executed by the same mortgagor if he brings a suit on one he must sue on all the others, too. His right to sue for the mortgage money arises when the mortgagor binds himself to repay same, where the mortgaged property is destroyed either wholly or partly or security is rendered insufficient, where the mortgagee is deprived of the whole or part of his security in consequence of the wrongful act or default of the mortgagor, or where the mortgagee in possession is not given quiet enjoyment of the property. A mortgagee must generally manage the property as man of ordinary prudence would manage it if it were his own.

Redemption.—Any person who has an interest in or charge upon the property mortgaged, the surety for the payment of the mortgage debt, a creditor of the mortgager who has in a suit for the administration of his estate obtained a decree for sale of the mortgaged property all have similar rights of redemption.

Deposit in Court.—Any time after payment becomes due mortgagor may deposit the amount owed in court and the court must issue notice to mortgagee of this payment. Mortgagee must then express willingness to accept the money deposited and himself deposit in court all documents in his possession of power relating to the property and will receive the money instead, while the documents will be handed over to mortgagor and all mortgagee's interest in the mortgaged property will be held to have ceased.

Corporate Mortgages.—See also topic Corporations (Companies), subhead Mortgages and Charges.

MOTOR VEHICLES:

Vehicle registration is required. Number plates must be displayed front and rear and must be of requisite size. Operations licence is required. Any person eligible to do so may apply to the licensing authority having jurisdiction in the area in which he ordinarily resides or carries on business for issue to him of a licence.

MOTOR VEHICLES . . . *continued*

Operation Prohibited.—(1) No person under age of 18 is allowed to drive a motor vehicle in any public place. (2) No person under age of 20 is allowed to drive a transport vehicle i.e., a public service vehicle, locomotive or tractor unless the latter two vehicles are used for agricultural purposes.

Licensing authority may revoke a licence when there are reasonable grounds for believing that holder of the license is by virtue of any disease or disability unfit to drive a motor vehicle.

Licensing authority has power to disqualify a person for a specified period from holding or obtaining a licence in certain cases viz: if person is habitual criminal or habitual drunkard, or the person has by his previous conduct as driver of a motor vehicle shown that his driving is likely to be attended with danger to public.

Transfers.—A certificate of registration containing a detailed description of the motor vehicle is issued by the registering authority. Within 30 days of transfer of ownership of any motor vehicle transferee must report transfer to registering authority within whose jurisdiction he resides and must forward certificate of registration to that registering authority together with prescribed fee in order that particulars of the transfer of ownership may be entered therein.

Insurance.—Any person using or permitting another to use a motor vehicle in a public place must be insured against third party risks.

Visitors to Pakistan having Carnet Registration may on reporting to the authorities obtain a free tax token for one month. On expiry of month visitors pay taxes normally imposed. Unless renewed by issuing authority for a further period, on expiry of Carnet Registration (usually valid for a year) visitor must pay relevant import duty on the vehicle and obtain fresh registration.

Visitors may not sell their motor vehicles in Pakistan until after two years from date of issue of the import permit by office of Controller of Imports and Exports. Then too vehicles may only be sold to non-Pakistani nationals and payment must be made in foreign exchange only. Customs duties must be paid prior to sale.

Nationals of Member States of International Convention holding international driving licences are permitted to use these licences until date of expiry when they may on application to licensing authority obtain a Pakistan driving licence.

Visitors from U.S. and nationals of states who are not members of International Convention may on basis of reciprocity obtain a Pakistan licence for duration of their stay in Pakistan on production of their respective driving licences.

NOTARIES PUBLIC:

There are at present two sorts of notaries public. Those who are appointed by the faculty in the United Kingdom who are empowered to do all things that it is usual for notaries public to do, such as enter protests from ships' masters, legalize documents, etc.; and those that are appointed under the Negotiable Instruments Act 1881 whose powers are limited to the powers delegated to them under that Act.

A new ordinance, namely, Notaries Ordinance 1961, was promulgated in June 1961 but has not been enforced so far throughout Pakistan but has been brought into force in West Pakistan except Tribal Areas with effect from Jan. 1966. This Ordinance would, inter alia, appoint notaries public in supersession of first of above-mentioned categories.

PARTNERSHIP:

Partnership is a status arising from contract between persons who have agreed to share the profits of a business carried on by all or any of them acting for all. A Partnership may be at will, for any duration specified, or for the prosecution of some particular and defined business.

Liability of the partners of a firm is joint and several. The firm is liable for individual acts of misfeasance and misapplication of money or goods by one of its partners.

Capacity.—No minor can be a partner but he may with consent of all partners be admitted to the benefits of the partnership. The minor's right of action against the partners will only arise when and if he desires to sever the connection between himself and them and his share will then be determined after valuation.

Registration is not compulsory but if done should include particulars of the firm's name, address of principal place of business and any other places of business, date of formation of the firm and date of joining of each partner and his address. This document should be signed and verified by all partners. Any alterations should be recorded. A firm which is not registered is not competent to sue on the basis of a debt amounting to more than Rs. 100.

Rights and Liabilities of Partners Inter Se.—Duties of a partner are to carry on business to the greatest common advantage of all and to indemnify the other partners for any loss caused by his own fraud. Other rights and duties may be created by contract and can be varied or restricted. By contract it may be provided that a partner be reimbursed for his part in the conduct of the business. A partner is entitled to be reimbursed for expenses incurred by him in the ordinary and proper conduct of the business or in an emergency but not where the emergency arose out of his own wilful neglect. Unless otherwise agreed by contract, each partner is entitled to an equal share in the profit of the firm. Consent of all the partners is required to any changes.

Change in the Constitution of the firm does not vary the rights and duties of the remaining partners. If after expiry of a fixed term of years for the existence of the firm the partners continue their business, the rights and liabilities inter se remain as before and where other enterprises are undertaken as additional ventures to the original undertaking, the same rights and duties that attended the original undertaking will continue to apply to the additional undertaking.

Rights and Liabilities of Partners as to Third Persons.—A partner is agent for the firm and his actions bind the firm but he cannot without express authority (i) submit a dispute to arbitration, (ii) open a bank account for the firm in his own name, (iii) compromise a claim without authority on behalf of the firm, (iv) institute a suit, (v) withdraw a suit, (vi) admit liability, (vii) acquire immoveable property or transfer the firm's immoveable property, (viii) enter into a partnership on behalf of the firm. However, by implied authority he may do all these things in an emergency to protect the firm from loss. Admissions by a partner are admissions by the firm and notice to one partner is notice to all except where it relates to a fraud committed by or with the consent of that partner.

Retirement from firm can be by consent; or by express agreement. Where a partner becomes insolvent, even if the partnership is not dissolved, he ceases to be a partner. Partner can also be discharged. A retiring partner can open a new business and carry on the same business as the firm from which he retired but he cannot use the firm name, represent the former firm or solicit orders from its customers. Reasonable agreements in restraint of operating such a new firm may be made and will be enforced.

Dissolution of the whole firm can take place by consent; adjudication of a partner, or the firm, as insolvent; or the happening of some event that makes pursuit of its purpose illegal. A firm will also be held to have been dissolved on the expiry of the express term of its duration or completion of its purpose. Liability of the firm and each individual partner after dissolution continues until notice has been given to the public of such dissolution.

PATENTS:

The law relating to patents is governed by the Patents and Designs Act 1911, and Patents and Design (Amendment) Ordinance 1983.

Applications for patents can be made by a person of any nationality according to the prescribed form. Applicant must be the first and true inventor of the invention or else an assignee of such person. Application should be accompanied by a provisional or complete specification plus documents supporting applicant's title where he is an assign. If a provisional specification is filed in the first instance, a complete specification must be filed within at most nine months. An extension of time may be granted but will not be for longer than a month at most. A patent is granted for 16 years but can be extended for a further period of five years if applicant can satisfy Controller that the granting of patent has not been sufficiently lucrative. In exceptional cases an extension of ten years or a period between five or ten years may also be granted.

Protection.—All inventions can be used in the interim period without prejudice to the patent and such protection is known as provisional protection.

Opposition.—After application is accepted by the Controller (which if not done within 15 months will mean that application is rejected) it will be advertised as accepted. Opposition can then be filed within four months only on one of the following grounds: (i) That opposer is the true inventor or assign thereof; (ii) that the invention described in the specification is the same as another invention filed elsewhere in the country which if granted will be prior in date to the grant of this patent; (iii) that the specifications are not clear; (iv) that the invention has been publicly used or been made publicly known in any part of Pakistan; (v) that the completed specification does not agree with the provisional specification and the invention described in the completed specification is one that is the subject of another application which if granted would be dated between the date of the second application and the filing of the completed specification. Controller will give notice to applicant of these objections and after four months following the advertising of acceptance he will give a decision. An appeal on this will lie to the central government.

Licenses.—After grant of a patent, application may be made for compulsory grant of license or revocation. If this application is refused by the central government appeal lies to High Court. Revocation cannot be ordered before four years have elapsed from the grant of a patent, nor, in any case, if the patentee gives satisfactory reasons to the government against such revocation. A grant can also be revoked on the following grounds: (i) Because a patent in respect of that invention already exists; (ii) that the grant was obtained by perpetrating a fraud; (iii) that applicant was not true inventor nor his assign; (iv) that no new improvement or invention step is involved; (v) that patent was obtained on a false suggestion or representation; (vi) that primary uses of invention are against law; (vii) that scope of invention is not clearly ascertainable.

Act also covers copyright of designs, and, subject to notification in official gazette, provides for reciprocal arrangements between Pakistan and foreign States for mutual protection of inventions and designs of applicants in those States.

PERPETUITIES:

No transfer of property can operate to create an interest which is to take effect after the life-time of one or more persons living at the date of such transfer and the minority of some person who shall be in existence at the expiration of that period, and to whom, if he attains that age, the interest created is to belong.

PLEDGES: See topic Chattel Mortgages.

PRESCRIPTION: See topic Limitation of Actions.

PRICE CONTROL:

Price control is regulated by government under Price Control and Prevention of Profiteering & Hoarding Act, 1977. Items affected thereby have been progressively reduced and at present direct control is exercised only in respect of few items. Full powers to regulate price, however, still lie with government and would be used if government felt prices were being inflated. Control also exists in relation to supply of essential commodities.

PRINCIPAL AND AGENT:

An "agent" is a person employed to do any act for, or represent, another in dealing with third persons. The person for whom such an act is done, or who is so represented is called the "principal."

Any person who is major and sane can employ a person as agent. No requirements as to sanity or majority are necessary in an agent for purposes of binding the principal to third parties but in such cases principal will not be able to enforce his rights against the agent. No consideration is needed between the parties and the authority can either be express or implied. Authority to do an act means implied authority to do every lawful thing supplementary to this act. If the authority is to conduct a business on

PRINCIPAL AND AGENT . . . *continued*
behalf of the principal, the agent may do all things incidental to this. Special powers lie with an agent in cases of an emergency to protect the interests of the principal.

Sub-Agents.—Any work personally to be done by the agent cannot be delegated by him, but otherwise he may, unless expressly forbidden to, delegate work to other persons who are then known as sub-agents. A sub-agent is responsible to the agent who is in turn answerable to the principal but third parties are bound directly to the principal. Where a sub-agent is appointed without authority he is in relation to the agent as an agent and the agent is, in relation to him, a principal.

Ratification.—Where a person acts for another the other can either expressly or impliedly confirm the actions provided he has knowledge of them. Partial ratification is not possible nor is ratification possible of an originally unauthorised action that injures a third party.

Termination of agency can be by revocation and by renouncing by death, insanity, or insolvency of the principal. Where the agent has an interest in the property forming the subject matter of the agency, the agency cannot be terminated to the detriment of such interest. Revocation is not possible by the principal with regard to acts already performed on his behalf. Where the agency was for a period of time and is revoked earlier, compensation becomes payable to the agent or where the agent is the person who terminates the relationship, to the principal. Reasonable notice should be given, and any acts done while there was no knowledge of the revocation will equally bind the principal. Where the principal dies, or becomes insane, the agent is bound to take all adequate steps to safeguard the principal's interest.

Rights and Duties.—An agent is required to show skill and diligence in conducting his principal's business, to communicate his actions to him and present accounts. Where agent deals on his own account in the business of agency without principal's consent, principal has a right to the benefits gained by agent. Agent has a right to be indemnified against the consequences of his lawful acts and acts done in good faith. He is entitled to be compensated for any injury caused by the principal's neglect. No agent is liable to carry out other than lawful orders of principal. Agent's duty is to pay sums received on principal's behalf though he may retain a portion out of these sums as retainer. An agent has a lien on principal's property for remuneration which becomes due when act to be performed is completed.

Third Party Rights and Duties.—Principal is bound to third parties by his agent's lawful and authorized acts. Where agent exceeds authority given to him and this is not ratified, principal is only bound to extent of authority he gave where the further transaction outside the agent's authority is separable from the authorized transaction. Otherwise he is not bound at all. Notice given to agent is notice to principal. Agent cannot, however, enforce a contract on his principal's behalf nor is he personally bound to third parties except where a contract exists to this effect or where the contract made by agent is for the sale or purchase of goods for a merchant resident abroad, or where agent does not disclose his principal's name, or where principal cannot be sued. Third parties have same rights and duties towards undisclosed principals as they would have had against the agents as principals but if the third parties can show that they would not have contracted with the principal had he been disclosed, they can refuse to fulfill the contract. An undisclosed principal cannot have greater rights against third parties than his agent would have had. Where an agent is personally liable, a person dealing with him may hold either him, or his principal, or both of them liable. Where a third party induces the agent or principal to act on the belief that the other only will be liable he is estopped by this representation and cannot sue the person so induced to act. A person falsely representing himself as an agent if his authority is not ratified is bound to make compensation for any loss or damage he has caused to third parties. Persons falsely contracting as agents where they are principals are not entitled to performance. Where principal induces belief that agent's unauthorized actions were authorized principal will be bound by his misrepresentation. Misrepresentation or fraud by agent acting in the course of his business will have same effect in agreements as if such misrepresentations were made, or frauds committed, by agent in matters which do not fall within his authority and do not affect his principal.

REAL PROPERTY:

Technically speaking there is no such classification of property in Pakistan. The contrast is not between real property and personal property but between moveable and immoveable property. There are no restrictions on ownership of immovable property in Pakistan by foreign controlled Pakistani incorporated companies; however foreign individual persons require prior approval of Home Department of relevant Provincial government or Federal Ministry of Interior in case of Islamabad Capital Territory.

See also topic Perpetuities.

RECORDS:

Power to make rules for the disposal of such records as are not in their opinion worth preserving lies with High Court over documents appertaining to High Court and to subordinate courts and with Chief Controlling Revenue Officer for the revenue courts. Of documents in the possession or custody of any other public officer, if these documents relate to the provinces then the provincial government or any other officer specifically appointed may deal with the disposal or retention of these. In any other case the central government or an officer especially appointed for this purpose may make such rules as to them may seem fit for the disposal of other documents. Where such rules are formulated, they must, where relating to a provincial government be subject to approval of such government and where relating to the central government be subject to its approval.

Employment records are governed by the Employment (Record of Services) Act 1951. This act applies to all persons concerned as employers or employees in such classes of employment and in such areas as the appropriate government may specify. An employee must keep a service book containing identification of the employee, name and other particulars of his or her employers, the period of employment, occupation rate of wages, leave taken and records of conduct and efficiency, and if the employee is male, a photograph. If such a book is kept prospective employers may ask for it to be produced. Employers may keep copies of such "service books" of their employees.

See also topics Corporations (Companies); Chattel Mortgages, subhead Registration; Labour Laws, subhead Workmen's Compensation Act, 1923; Marriage; Mortgages, subhead Registration.

REPORTS:

These are published here in a series of volumes by Law Department of Ministry of Law & Parliamentary Affairs. These publications cover post-partition period, i.e., from 1947 and also contain latest acts, ordinances and notifications. Revenue decisions are also published. There is also a more exhaustive private publication "The All Pakistan Legal Decisions" which contain reports of Supreme Court and High Court cases and from 1954 onwards have also contained latest acts, ordinances and notifications. There is also a private publication "Pakistan Tax Decisions" of revenue cases.

Authorities binding on the courts in Pakistan are judgments of the Supreme Court of Pakistan and Privy Council decisions pre-1950 and all Indian decisions before that date of courts of equivalent or superior status; persuasive authorities are decisions of the House of Lords, the Privy Council, the Indian Supreme Court, decisions of Indian High Courts, and decisions of Supreme Court of United States.

SALES:

A contract for sale of goods is governed by Sale of Goods Act 1930 and is a contract whereby seller transfers or agrees to transfer property in goods to buyer for a price. Such a contract may be conditional or absolute and may be effective immediately or in the future. A contract for future sale is an agreement to sell.

Formalities.—There must be an offer and acceptance of existing or future goods. The sale may be in writing or oral. If the goods have already perished, unknown to the seller, at the time of contracting then the contract to sell is void. If the goods perish before reaching the buyer the contract may be voidable.

Conditions and Warranties.—A condition is a stipulation that is essential to the contract while a warranty is a stipulation collateral to the main agreement. A condition may, and in certain cases, must be waived and treated as a warranty. This waiver becomes mandatory where goods have been partly accepted and are not severable. Implied undertaking or condition exists that seller has or will have the right to sell the goods. There is an implied warranty that buyer will have quiet enjoyment of the property and that the goods are free from encumbrances. It is a condition that where sale is by description or sample, the goods should correspond to the description or sample. There is no implied condition or warranty as to the fitness of goods sold for any particular purpose except where buyer makes known to seller such particular purpose and places reliance on seller's skill and judgment. If goods are generally sold by seller there is also an implied condition that they are fit for the purpose sold except where they are sold under their patent or trade name. Where sale is by description there is an implied condition that the goods will be of merchantable quality except where buyer examined the goods before purchase and the defects were not latent defects.

Transfer of Title.—Property passes in the goods when it is intended that it should pass. No better title can be passed than that of the seller unless the owner is precluded from denying seller's authority. A mercantile agent in possession, with consent, of goods can pass a good title to a bona fide purchaser as if expressly authorised so to do with the owner's consent. Similarly one of several joint-owners, in possession of the goods with the consent of all, can pass a good title to a bona fide purchaser. Where a seller has acquired goods under a voidable contract but which has not at the time he contracts been rescinded, a bona fide purchaser takes good title. Where a seller after sale retains possession of the goods and subsequently resells them to a third party, who is in good faith, that third party takes a good title. A buyer in possession after sale can also sell and a third party will take without notice of the original seller's lien, if any.

Delivery.—Unless otherwise agreed, payment and delivery are concurrent conditions though seller is not bound to deliver until buyer applies for delivery. Delivery should be made within a reasonable time at seller's expense. Where buyer rejects the goods he is not bound to return them physically to seller. Delivery is deemed to take place at time of the handing over of the goods to the carrier but seller must stipulate this.

Notices Required.—Unless otherwise agreed, where goods are delivered to buyer and he refuses to accept them, having the right so to do, he is not bound to return them to seller but it is sufficient if he intimates to seller that he refuses to accept them. Buyer is deemed to accept the goods when he intimates to seller that he has accepted them or when goods are delivered to him and he does any act in relation to them which is inconsistent with the ownership of seller, or when, after lapse of a reasonable time, he retains the goods without intimating to seller that he has rejected them.

Stoppage in Transit.—It is possible for an unpaid seller to take this action when buyer becomes insolvent. The duration of transit is calculated to last until buyer takes delivery from the carrier, even if after arrival of the goods at the appointed destination the carrier acknowledges to agent of buyer, or to buyer that he holds the goods on his behalf. It is a question of fact when goods are shipped as to whether the master is a carrier, or an agent of the buyer. The remainder of goods partly delivered can be stopped in transit.

Remedies of Seller.—Seller can sue for the price of goods even where delivery is not made, if the price was by contract payable on a certain date irrespective of delivery. He can also claim damages for nonacceptance of goods by buyer.

Remedies of Buyer.—Buyer can sue for damages for nondelivery. He can also sue for damages for breach of warranty, or for breach of a condition being treated as a warranty, or set up this breach in reduction of the price. Both these remedies can lie on the same breach where additional damage is incurred by buyer. Where either party repudiates the contract before date of delivery the other can sue immediately or wait until the contractual date comes around. Special damages and interest are also recoverable in certain cases.

Warranties.—See subhead Conditions and Warranties, supra.

See Topical Index in front part of this volume.

SHIPPING:

Principal acts applying to shipping include the British Merchant Shipping Act of 1894 (with regard to registration, mortgages, and various other matters) and the Maritime Conventions Act 1911 which provides that where both ships in a collision are to blame, both are to share expenses.

Merchant Shipping Act 1923 contains provisions relating to masters and seamen, certificates of competency, etc., the engaging and discharge of seamen, payment of wages, seamen's rights in respect to wages and modes of recovery allotment of wages, property of deceased seamen, and provisions as to health, hygiene and accommodation. There are also provisions regarding discipline, keeping of official logs, surveys, equipment of passenger and emigrant ships and rules about wrecks. There are special rules governing employment of young persons and rules regarding the pilgrim ships that carry passengers to Hijaz for pilgrimage.

Carriage of Goods by Sea Act 1925 incorporates the Hague Rules into the law of Pakistan for outward bills of lading. An express statement should be contained in every outward bill of lading or document of title as to the applicability of these rules. Carrier is bound to exercise due diligence to make ship seaworthy, properly to equip the ship and make the holds, etc., fit for the carriage of goods. Goods loaded must be clearly marked and a bill of lading giving all particulars should be handed to shipper. Neither carrier nor shipper will be liable for any loss caused by the unseaworthiness of the ship unless this was caused by want of due diligence on part of carrier. Defaults of others, fire, perils of the sea, act of God, war, latent defects, omissions of shipper, are listed, amongst other causes of damage, as causes for which carrier is not responsible. Carrier may surrender all or any of his rights. Special conditions in respect of special goods may be imposed and the scope of the above rules can be limited by contract, provided that the bill of lading is made nonnegotiable.

Merchant Shipping (Amendment) Act 1958 restricts right of Pakistani nationals to acquire seagoing ships, or to transfer or mortgage them to foreign nationals without consent of the central government.

Merchant Shipping (Amendment) Ordinance 1966 gives effect to rules of International Convention for Safety of Life at Sea signed at London in June 1960.

Admiralty Jurisdiction of High Courts Ordinance 1980, gives High Court extensive jurisdiction to hear admiralty cases relating to large number of specified questions or claims. In most cases, action in rem against ship will also lie.

See topic Constitution and Government.

SOVEREIGN IMMUNITY:

By State Immunity Ordinance 1981, foreign state is immune from jurisdiction of courts of Pakistan, except as specified. Exceptions include submission to jurisdiction by state and suits relating to commercial transactions, contracts of employment (where contract was made or work is to be wholly or partly performed in Pakistan), ownership, possession or use of property, patents and trademarks, memberships of corporate bodies (by state) arbitration (agreed upon by state), ships belonging to state, levy of customs duties, value added tax etc. Procedural requirements are also laid down. Government of Pakistan and Provinces are not immune from suit or other legal proceedings in courts in Pakistan.

STATUTES:

Law in force in Pakistan is based on English common law and except for the law of torts and personal law it is to be found in the various Federal and Provincial statutes and ordinances, and rules, regulations and orders framed thereunder from time to time. Recent enforcement of Islamic laws is also enacted by statute. (See topic Islamic Laws.)

All unrepealed Federal statutes and ordinances from 1836 to 1965 have been assembled and published by Ministry of Law & Parliamentary Affairs of Government of Pakistan in a set of 15 volumes under title "The Pakistan Code." These volumes have been amended up to May 1966. Federal as well as Provincial Acts, Ordinances, Rules, Orders and Regulations are first published in official Gazettes of Pakistan, and from 1954 have also been published in All Pakistan Legal Decisions, a private publication.

TAXATION:

Income tax is chargeable under provisions of Income Tax Ordinance 1979 ("Ordinance") which came into force on July 1, 1979. Income Tax ("Tax") is chargeable by reference to income of taxpayer ("Assessee") in previous year ("income year") which is either year ending June 30th or calendar year or such other year ending as may be permitted by Central Board of Revenue. Tax year known as "assessment year" runs from July 1st to June 30th. By Finance Act, 1991, extensive witholding tax provision enacted also turnover tax payable by companies and registered firms. CBR also enabled to prescribe scheme for payment of fixed tax by person maintaining small establishment to carry on business or profession.

For purposes of charge of tax and computation of total income all income is classified under following heads: (a) Salaries, (b) interest on securities, (c) income from house property, (d) income from business or profession, (e) capital gains, and (f) income from other sources.

Salaries.—This head covers all income received by way of salary, annuity, pension or gratuity, fees, commissions and perquisites or profits in lieu of or in addition to salary or wages.

Interest on Securities.—Income from interest receivable by person from any security of federal or provincial government or any debenture or other security issued by or on behalf of local authority or company is classified under this head. Standard withholding rate of 30% is applicable to such income except in case of interest on debentures issued by local authority or company for which recipient gets credit at time of his own assessment. Interest on Government Securities is exempt from tax.

Income from House Property.—Tax under this head is leviable in respect of annual rental value of property.

Income from Business or Profession.—This head applies to all income derived from commerical and industrial activities as well as from exercise of profession or vocation such as law, medicine, engineering, accountancy, etc. Income under this head is computed according to normal principles of accountancy after allowing deduction of business expenses. Losses are allowed to be set off against current income from all sources and where these are not completely absorbed in this manner can be carried forward for six years to be set off against further profits from same business profession or vocation. Six year time limit does not apply to unabsorbed depreciation allowance which can be carried forward indefinitely until it is completely set off against future profit. Special rules for computation of profits apply to undertakings engaged in exploration, production and extraction of oil, gas and mineral deposits as well as insurance business.

Capital gains derived from disposed of capital assets other than, inter alia, any stock-in-trade (not being stocks and shares), personal effects and land from which income derived by assessee is agricultural income, is charged under this head. Capital gains from sale of shares of public listed company is exempt from tax up to June 30, 1996.

Income from Other Sources.—Under this head all residual income from any source other than those listed above is included. This includes dividends, interest, royalties and fees for technical services. Dividend income received by assessee (not being company) from company is taxed at 10% as separate slice of income; likewise income from prize bonds (at 7.5%); interest/profit from banks, finance society or company profit on specified security issued by any of foregoing (at 10%) deductible at source. Tax on income of nonresidents from fees for technical services received under agreement entered into after 30th June, 1987 is charged at flat rate of 20%.

Personal Tax.—All individuals, unregistered firms, association of persons and every artificial juridical person other than company are liable to tax on their taxable income at rates set out in First Schedule to the Ordinance with minimum of 10% (of total income) where total income does not exceed Rs. 100,000.

Tax on Companies.—Super Tax and Surcharge abolished for companies from assessment year 1992-93. Company (corporation) pays tax at rate of 49%. Rates of tax to be progressively reduced as follows:

Assessment year	*Banking company*	*Public company other than a banking company*	*Other company*
1995-96	60%	36%	46%
1996-97	60%	36%	46%
1997-98 and thereafter	58%	33%	43%
1998-99	55%	30%	40%

Federal Education Fee levied on companies whose fixed assets exceed Rs. 50 million.

Tax on dividend received by public company is payable at rate of 5%, 15% in case dividends are received by foreign company and 20% in respect of private companies. Tax at rate of 10% and 15% is levied on bonus or bonus shares issued by public or private company respectively. However bonus shares issued by 30th June 1991 are exempt from tax. Nonresident air and shipping enterprises are taxed at flat rate of 3% and 8% respectively on their gross earnings.

Tax on Registered Firms.—Registered firms (partnership) are liable to pay super tax only at rates specified in First Schedule to the Ordinance. Share of income of each partner of registered firm is added to his other income if any and tax is levied on his aggregate income after deducting super tax.

Surcharge at rate of 10% of income and super tax is payable by all assessees whose total income exceeds Rs. 100,000. Income or classes of income and person or classes of persons enumerated in Second Schedule of the Ordinance are exempt from tax subject to conditions and to extent specified therein.

Double taxation agreements are in force between Pakistan and United States, Germany, Japan, United Kingdom, Sweden, Switzerland, Denmark, Austria, France, Ireland, Poland, Malta, Canada, Netherlands, Romania, Greece, Sri Lanka, India, Thailand, Philippines, Libya, Italy (air and shipping only), Iran (airlines only), Lebanon (airlines only), Saudi Arabia (airlines only), Belgium, Bangladesh, Norway, South Korea and Malaysia. Double taxation agreements being negotiated with Nigeria, Singapore and Turkey.

Stamp Duty.—Stamp Duty is leviable under Stamp Act, 1899 by provinces at rates which vary from province to province; Punjab rates adopted in Islamabad Capital Territory. All instruments chargeable with duty must be stamped before or at time of execution, and instruments executed abroad within three months of receipt in Pakistan. Certificate of Stamp Officer that full duty is paid or no duty is payable is conclusive.

No instrument chargeable with duty may be admitted in evidence unless it is properly stamped. A penalty may be imposed on all instruments which are not properly stamped to the extent of ten times the duty payable.

Rates of duty are fixed by provincial governments. Highest rate presently payable on any instrument is 9% ad valorem in Sindh, which is payable on conveyance of immoveable property.

See also topics Affidavits, subhead Stamp; Chattel Mortgages, subhead Formalities; Corporations (Companies), subhead Stamp Duty and Registration Fees; Mortgages, subhead Stamp Duty.

Sales Tax.—A single point sales tax at the general rate of 15% is levied on all goods imported into Pakistan or manufactured or produced in Pakistan. Certain articles are exempt from tax.

Estate duty abolished.

Wealth Tax.—In case of every individual, firm association of persons or body of individuals whether incorporated or not, and company it is levied at rate of 1/2% on first Rs. 500,000 of net wealth and proceeds at sliding scale up to maximum of 2 1/2% on balance of net wealth. Agricultural land to maximum value of Rs. 100,000 is exempt. Individuals, firms, associations of persons incorporated or unincorporated, and companies are all liable to this tax. Certain assets such as machinery and implements, growing crops, standing trees, properties held in trust, etc. are exempt.

Gift Tax.—By Gift Tax Act (Repeal) Order 1985 Gift Tax Act 1963 has been repealed, and as of July 1, 1985 no gift tax is leviable.

Capital Gains Tax.—Capital gains on immoveable property, which was payable under Provincial laws has been abolished as of July 1, 1986. Capital Value Tax

TAXATION . . . *continued*
payable in certain transactions relating to transfers of motor vehicles and immovable property if transferee not taxpayer.

See topic Islamic Laws.

TRADEMARKS AND PASSING OFF:

Trademarks may be acquired by any person claiming to be proprietor of a trade mark used or proposed to be used by him who is desirous of registering it. Nothing scandalous or likely to deceive, or hurtful to the religious susceptibilities of others, or contrary to law or morality can be registered. Use of chemical names is not permitted nor registration of identical or similar trade marks, but in the latter cases where there is honest concurrent user such registration may be permitted. Where proprietor claims to be entitled to exclusive use of any part of a mark, he may register the whole and the parts of the whole as separate trade marks. Each separate trade mark must however satisfy all conditions applying to it and all incidentals of an independent trade mark.

Registration.—Application is made to Registrar who may in first instance reject application in which case applicant can appeal to court. If application is accepted it is numbered and advertised so that opposition, if there is going to be any can be made. Unless opposition succeeds trade mark can be registered, with any such disclaimers as Registrar may think fit, and registration runs from date of application. A sealed certificate of registration will be issued to proprietor. Registration is for seven years and can be renewed. Where renewal fees are not paid mark can be removed but will be held to continue for purposes of barring other applications for registration of a similar trade mark for one year unless applicant can show that original trade mark had not been used for two years before removal and that no deception would result from his application.

Applications for registration are to be made to Registrar of Trade Marks, 67 Muslimabad, Dadabhai Naoroji Road, Karachi.

Government filing fees for single application for registration of a trademark is Rs. 400/—.

Effect of registration is to make infringers of trademark liable to action being taken against them. It gives proprietor exclusive right to the trademark. Registration is prima facie evidence of validity and after seven years it becomes conclusive evidence of this.

Registered User.—After a trademark has been registered application may be made for registration of registered users.

Assignment is possible for a registered or unregistered trademark but not where multiple rights would be created nor where exclusive rights would be created in different parts of the country in which case Registrar's approval is required.

Resale price agreement is not protected under Trade Marks Act.

Infringement occurs when a person not a registered proprietor thereof uses a trade mark or a mark deceptively similar to it in relation to same class of goods. Such action is punishable under Penal Code and also is actionable under provisions of Trade Marks Act. Unregistered trade marks are not protected by Act but have same rights under Penal Code. They are also protected under the common-law remedy against passing off. Passing off is actionable as a common-law tort.

Tradenames.—There is no provision in Pakistan for registration of tradenames.

Drugs.—Drugs Act 1976 regulates registration, import and export, manufacture and sale of drugs. Pakistan National formulary contains name of all drugs allowed to be imported, manufactured or sold. By Act, government has power to fix maximum prices of drugs and also to inspect, seize, analyse and punish importers and manufacturers of faulty drugs.

TREATIES:

Pakistan is a signatory to several multilateral and bilateral treaties, conventions and agreements concerning commerce, trade and foreign investment.

See topic Taxation, subhead Double Taxation Agreements.

TRUSTS:

Law relating to trusts (apart from *waqf* which is governed by Muslim Law, the relations between members of an undivided family which are governed by customary or personal law, and public or private religious or charitable endowments) is contained in Trusts Act 1882.

A trust under the Act may be created for any lawful purpose by a person competent to contract ("author of the trust") for the benefit of a person capable of holding property ("beneficiary") in respect of property transferable to the beneficiary which is not merely a beneficial interest under a subsisting trust. A trustee must also be a person capable of holding property and, if the trust involves the exercise of discretion, a person competent to contract. A trustee may accept or disclaim a trust.

Creation.—A trust of immoveable property must be declared by an instrument in writing signed by author of the trust or the trustee and, unless the instrument is a will, registered. No trust of moveable property is valid unless declared as aforesaid or unless ownership of the property is transferred to the trustee. In either case author of the trust must indicate with reasonable clarity: (a) an intention to create a trust, (b) purpose of the trust, (c) the beneficiary, and (d) the trust-property, and (unless the trust is declared by will or author of the trust is himself to be the trustee) transfer the trust-property to the trustee.

Duties and Liabilities of Trustees.—A trustee is bound to fulfil the purpose of the trust and, except as modified by consent of the beneficiaries, obey the directions of the author of the trust given at time of its creation; to acquaint himself with, and (where necessary) secure the transfer to himself of, the trust-property; to take steps for its preservation and deal with it as carefully as man of common prudence; to convert perishable trust-property into permanent and profitable property and to prevent waste; to keep accounts of the trust-property, and to observe impartiality as between several beneficiaries.

Rights and Powers of Trustees.—A trustee is entitled to possession of the instrument of trust and title deeds relating to the trust-property; to reimbursement of expenses and to recoup overpayments made to a beneficiary; to apply to the court for its advice or direction as to management of the trust-property; if empowered to sell the trust-property, to sell the same either together or in lots, by public auction or by private contract, and subject to such special conditions as he thinks fit; to vary investments; to apply property held in trust for a minor for the minor's maintenance, education and advancement; to give receipts for money and moveable property; to compound debts relating to the trust; and generally to do all acts for the realization, protection or benefit of the trust-property and for the protection and benefit of a beneficiary not competent to contract.

Disabilities of Trustees.—A trustee having accepted the trust cannot renounce it, unless so empowered by the instrument of trust, except with the court's permission or the consent of the beneficiary if competent to contract. The act contains restrictions on a trustee's right to delegate his office and prohibits a trustee from charging for his services unless so authorized in the instrument of trust, from using the trust-property for his own profit and from buying trust property.

Vacating Office of Trustee.—Office of trustee can be vacated only by the trustee's death or his discharge by the extinction of the trust, completion of his duties, by any means prescribed in the instrument of trust, by the appointment of a new trustee under the act, by consent of the beneficiaries if competent to contract, or by the court.

Appointment of New Trustees.—New trustee may be appointed by the person nominated in the instrument of trust or, if none, by author of the trust or the surviving or continuing trustees or the legal representative of the last surviving or continuing trustee or (with consent of the court) the retiring trustees or the last retiring trustee. Such appointment must be in writing under the hand of the person making it.

Extinction of Trusts.—A trust is extinguished when its purpose is fulfilled or becomes unlawful, when fulfilment becomes impossible or, being revocable, it is revoked. Except in case of a trust created by will, a trust can be revoked only when all the beneficiaries are competent to contract, with their consent; in exercise of an express power reserved to author of the trust; or, when the trust is for payment of debts of author of trust and has not been communicated to his creditors, at pleasure of author of the trust.

Investment.—Section 20 of Act lists the types of securities in which trust money must be invested (briefly, government stocks and first mortgages of immoveable property) unless the instrument of trust authorizes investment in other securities.

See also topic Perpetuities.

WILLS:

Making of a will is governed by the Succession Act 1925 and is based on the law in England. This does not, however, apply to Muslims and the law applicable to them is stated infra under subhead Muslims.

Capacity.—No one who is not a major or of sound mind can dispose of his or her property by will. Women, whether married or single may dispose of any property which they could have alienated or transferred during their lifetime. Physical handicaps do not bar a person from becoming a testator provided such handicaps do not prevent him from understanding the import of his actions. Insane persons may make a will during a lucid period. No person can make a valid will when he is in such a state that it may be presumed that he was incapable of knowing what he was doing. Aliens are not barred except as above by minority or insanity, from making wills. Domicile is the deciding factor under this law for the validity of a will.

Muslims.—The majority of the population being Muslim does not come within the purview of the above act. Such persons are governed by their personal law. Muslims are divided into two main communities, Sunnis and Shiahs, and the large majority of the Muslims in Pakistan are Sunnis of the Hanafi School. The remarks hereinafter made are therefore applicable only to them. The Shiahs are in a minority and are in themselves split up into several smaller sects, of which the Ismailis, with the Aga Khan as their religious head, are one. Every Muslim can dispose of his property by will if he is a major and not insane. The will can be either in writing or verbal. Not more than one-third of the estate can be disposed of by will in any case and no bequests may be made to persons who are heirs under the laws of intestate succession except with consent of all other heirs. Nor can more than one-third of the property be bequeathed without a similar consent. A Muslim will does not have to be proved and the taking out of a succession certificate is sufficient.

Limitation on Charitable and Religious Gifts.—No Person with any near relation can validly dispose of any property to religious or charitable uses except where the will was executed 12 months prior to his death and deposited within six months of execution in office of Sub-Registrar of Assurances.

Execution.—Ordinarily will must be in writing and signed by testator or some person on his behalf and in his presence. The signature must indicate that contents of the will were being approved. Signature must further be attested and the attesting witnesses must have seen the testator, or his attorney, sign in their presence or received an acknowledgement by testator of the signing of the will. Witnesses must each sign in presence of testator but need not sign in each other's presence.

Revocation.—A will may be revoked at any time during the testator's lifetime or amended by the addition of codicils. Marriage will usually revoke a will except where the will is privileged (see infra, subhead Privileged Wills). Deliberate destruction of the will with intent of revocation also serves to revoke the will.

Privileged Wills.—Any soldier, sailor or airman, if he is over 18 can make a will and such will is a privileged one. It can be either oral or in writing provided, if oral, it is declared before two witnesses. One month after the testator of a privileged will ceases to be in service, the will becomes void. Written wills do not require signature or attestation unless written in some one other than the testator's hand in which case they require signature. A privileged will may be revoked by a subsequent unprivileged will if that will is properly executed and clearly revokes the previous will.

Testamentary Gifts to Subscribing Witnesses.—No witness who is a beneficiary may take, but the will remains valid.

Foreign wills are governed by the law of domicile of testator except insofar as they relate to immoveable property in Pakistan. Foreign probate of such a will is proof of

See Topical Index in front part of this volume.

WILLS . . . *continued*
its due execution as far as the courts here are concerned, provided a properly authenticated copy of the will and probate are produced, notarial certification being sufficient. In other cases the court must satisfy itself of due execution of the foreign will. Probate cannot be granted of a foreign will executed within Pakistan relating only to property outside Pakistan.

Grant of foreign probate though evidence of due execution of the will is not sufficient for the grant of letters of administration here and application must be made to the courts. Law of testators domicile in this respect is not binding.

See also topics Executors and Administrators; Perpetuities; Trusts.

WORKMEN'S COMPENSATION LAW:

See topic Labour Laws, subhead Workmen's Compensation Act.

PANAMA LAW DIGEST REVISER

Icaza, Gonzalez-Ruiz & Aleman
Calle Aquilino De la Guardia No. 8
Edificio IGRA
Apartado 87-1371
Panama 7, Republic of Panama
Telephone: 507 263 5555
Fax: 507 269 4891; 507 264 2254
Email: igranet@pananet.com

Reviser Profile

History: The firm was founded in Panama City, Panama in the year of 1920 by Dr. Juan Lombardi, who had just retired as President of the Supreme Court of Justice of Panama and Dr. Carlos Icaza A., who had recently graduated as an attorney from Yale University. In the year of 1948, Dr. Francisco Gonzalez-Ruiz, who had graduated from the School of Law of the University of Paris, France, became a member of the firm and in the year of 1943, Dr. Roberto R. Aleman, who studied law in the Law School of Louisiana State University, Baton Rouge, Louisiana, joined the firm. After the death of Dr. Lombardi, the name of the firm was changed in the year 1950 to Icaza, Gonzalez-Ruiz & Aleman.

Areas of Emphasis and Growth: Icaza, Gonzalez-Ruiz & Aleman is engaged in the general practice of the legal profession with emphasis in the following areas: Administrative; Banking; Corporation; Distributorship, Agency and Franchise; Intellectual Property; Insurance; Litigation; Maritime and Admiralty; Oil and Mining; Taxation and Trusts. The firm is staffed with twenty lawyers with a support staff of more than one hundred employees.

Client Base: Icaza, Gonzalez-Ruiz & Aleman represents a substantial number of clients both local and foreign. Locally, the firm represents some of the most prestigious and important financial, banking, insurance and industrial concerns. Internationally, the firm represents some of the world's leading, financial, commercial, industrial and professional entities.

Firm Activities: The firm encourages the involvement and participation of its lawyers in civic and professional organizations. Memberships in some of the professional organizations are as follows: Panama Bar Association; Interamerican Bar Association; Panama Association of Industrial Property Law; Maritime Law Association of Panama; Interamerican Association of Industrial Property (ASIPI); United States Trademark Association (USTA); American Chamber of Commerce of Panama (AMCHAM); Banking Law Association; Multi-Law.

Management: A management committee of three partners scrutinizes and supervises the professional and administrative functioning of the firm.

Significant Distinctions: Major distinctions of the firm members include: Juan Lombardi, Member, Assembly of the Republic of Panama; Member of the Commission designated to draft the first Civil and Commercial Codes of the Republic of Panama, 1912; Chief-Justice of the Supreme Court of Panama, 1920. Carlos Icaza A., Alternate Judge of the Supreme Court of Panama. Member, National Council of Foreign Relations of the Republic of Panama. Francisco Gonzalez-Ruiz, Secretary of the Ministry of Government and Justice, 1941; Former Dean of the Law School of the University of Panama; Alternate Judge of the Supreme Court. Roberto R. Aleman, Editor-in-Chief, Louisiana Law Review, 1943; Chargé d'Affaires of Panama in Argentine; Advisor to Panama Delegation to General Assembly of United Nations, 1948; Special Ambassador, Canal Treaty Negotiation Commission, 1964-1968; Panama Ambassador in Washington, D.C., 1968-1970. Guillermo Jurado, Member, Assembly of the Republic of Panama, 1948-1952 and President thereof, 1948; National Economic Council, Republic of Panama, 1955-1962; Panama and Canal Zone (President, 1962) Bar Associations; National Council of Foreign Relations of the Republic of Panama. Mariano Oteiza, Counsellor of Panama Embassy in Washington, D.C. 1957; Vice-Minister and Acting-Minister of Foreign Relations 1958-1959; President, Rotary Club 1968-1969; Roberto R. Aleman H., Ambassador of Panama to the Kingdom of Belgium and Chief of Mission to the European Community 1990-1991; Alvaro A. Alemán H., Director of Internal Revenue, 1993-1994.

PANAMA LAW DIGEST

(The following is a list of all Topics, including cross-references, covered in this Digest.)

PANAMA LAW DIGEST

Revised for 1997 edition by

ICAZA, GONZALEZ-RUIZ & ALEMAN, of the Panama Bar.

(C. C. indicates Civil Code; C. C. P. indicates Code of Civil Procedure [or Judicial Code]; C. Com. indicates Code of Commerce; C. F. indicates Fiscal Code; C. T. indicates Labor Code; F.C. indicates Family Code; and see topic Statutes. All codes are cited by articles.)

ABSENTEES: See topic Death.

ACKNOWLEDGMENTS:

In Panama, certificates of acknowledgment in the form used in the United States and England are unknown.

The legal effect which in United States is secured by seals and acknowledgments is obtained in Panama by executing the document before a notary public in the form known as a public document or instrument. See topic Notaries Public.

Contracts, deeds, and other documents which require authentication by a notary public are executed with two witnesses before a notary, and made part of his protocol; that is to say, the original documents are kept in an official registry in the notary's office, and the interested party receives certified copies. The notary public testifies the execution of public and private documents; public documents become a part of the protocol while of private documents no record is left in the notary's office.

Foreign Acknowledgments.—Documents executed abroad, in conformity with law of country where executed, are entitled to recognition by Panama courts and administrative officials, with same force as in country where executed, if duly authenticated by diplomatic or consular representative of Panama.

Powers of attorney executed abroad must comply with 1976 Interamerican Convention on the Legal Regime of Powers of Attorney to be Used Abroad.

ACTIONS:

Limitation of.—See topic Limitation of Actions.

ADMINISTRATION:

See topic Executors and Administrators.

ADOPTION:

Any person of more than 18 years of age, may adopt any person, who is at least 15 years older than person adopted. In case of joint adoptions by spouses they must be at least of age, and younger of two spouses must be at least 15 years older than minor. Existence of descendants of person adopting does not preclude adoption.

Adoption must take place between persons of same sex, except in following cases: (1) any spouse adopts son or daughter of other spouse; (2) when both spouses adopt jointly third person. Adoption is prohibited: (1) of ward by guardian; (2) by spouse without consent of other; and (3) by parents of direct line and between brothers.

Minors under 18 years of age may be adopted in following cases: (1) when they lack father and mother; (2) if they are children of unknown parents; (3) if they have been abandoned; (4) if having father and mother or only one of two, they have consented; and (5) abused minors. Adoption: (1) gives adopted rights of legitimate child; (2) dissolves authority of natural parents; (3) makes adopted heir of adopter; and (4) entitles adopted to use adopter's surname.

Petition to adopt is filed with Sectional Minor Court.

Adoption may be rescinded on certain legal grounds.

AGENCY: See topic Principal and Agent.

AIRCRAFT:

National aircraft must be registered and owner must be citizen of Panama; if owner is juridic person and aircraft is to be used within Panama for cargo and passenger transport 60% of capital must be owned by, and management must be controlled by citizens of Panama. In cases of aircraft in international airline services under flag of Panama, 51% of capital must be owned by citizens of Panama. (Decree-Law 19 of Aug. 8, 1963).

Panama has ratified Convention of Chicago of 1944 (Law 52 of 1959) and Amendment Protocols of New York of 1971 (Cabinet Decree 121 of 1971) and of Vienna of 1971 (Cabinet Decree 28 of 1972) and of Montreal of 1980 (Law 16 of 1981) and has ratified Conventions (Air Piracy) of The Hague of 1970 (Cabinet Decree 13 of 1972) and of Montreal of 1971 (Cabinet Decree 59 of 1972) and has bilateral agreements with Belgium, Bolivia, Colombia, Cuba, Switzerland, U.K., U.S.A. and Venezuela. Aircraft flying through air space of Panama must hold proper certificates and documents of home country.

Aviation Code adopted by Decree No. 19 of Aug. 8, 1963, which incorporates as national law limitations of Warsaw and Rome Conventions. Cabinet Decree 13 of Jan. 22, 1969 amended Aviation Code and constituted Civil Aeronautic Authority Office as an autonomous institution with capacity to administrate all matters related to aviation and airports within Republic.

Civil Aviation Regulations were adopted by Resolution No. 111-JD of Nov. 16, 1996 in accordance with International Agreements subscribed by Federal Aviation Administration (FAA) and Organización de Aviación Civil International (OACI).

Panama adopted Protocol Complementary to the Montreal Convention on Air Piracy by Law No. 6 of 1996, and approved Montreal Convention of 1991 Marking Explosive Plastics for Detecton Purposes. National Airport Security Program (AVSEC) was adopted by Resolution No. 060-JD issued on Apr. 9, 1996 by Civil Aeronautic Department. Regulatons for construction and operation of airports within Republic of Panama are contained in Resolution No. 020-S.A.-96 dated Apr. 15, 1996.

ALIENS:

Under our Constitution, aliens enjoy same civil and commercial rights as citizens of Panama. Their life, honor and property are protected thereby, but may not own land located within 10 kms. from national borders (Const. art. 286) and their right to engage in some commercial activities is limited (Const. arts. 288, 289).

See also topics Foreign Investments; Corporations, subheads Foreign Corporations and Distributors and Sales Agents.

ASSIGNMENTS:

Assignments of credit rights or actions are only effective, as regard third parties, as of time its date may be fixed according to law. If transfer affects real property, from date of its filing for registration in Public Registry. Any debtor who pays his creditor, before having knowledge of assignment, is released from obligation. Principle of bona fide governs all relationships between assignor and assignee. Sale or transfer of a credit includes that of all accessory rights. Transfers of inheritance rights and credits in litigation are permitted.

ASSIGNMENTS FOR BENEFIT OF CREDITORS:

A debtor may assign all his property by either a public or private deed or instrument for the payment of his debts and the assignment must be accepted by his creditors, except in certain cases of fraud or where the creditors have previously made him allowances. This assignment in the absence of agreement to the contrary, only releases the debtor to the extent of the net value of the property assigned. The agreements between debtor and creditors must conform with the legal dispositions regarding meeting and preference of creditors. (C. C. 1062, 1500-4, 1653-67; C. C. P. 1812). See also topic Bankruptcy.

ASSOCIATIONS:

Right of association is granted in art. 39 of Constitution of 1972. Associations must be authorized by special laws or have approval of Executive. They are governed by Civ. Code 64-75 and Decree 26 of 1988. Decree No. 26 of 1988 was repealed.

ATTACHMENT:

Attachment is accomplished by the judicial deposit of personal property or a retention of moneys or values; by sequestration of real property. (C. C. P. 523, 1825).

These measures can be used either before or after complaint has been filed, but in either case party applying for attachment must furnish bond or security for costs and damages, and attachment obtained before action is commenced will be vacated if plaintiff does not file complaint within six days after attachment has been granted or if defendant has not been served complaint within three months of its filing and plaintiff has not requested service by publication, or if within 30 days of having received edicts for publication, he has not caused them to be published. Attachment will also be vacated on defendant giving bond or security, except in cases of real actions involving specific immovable or movable property and attachment has been directed against said property or when currency, credits or specific securities have been attached.

In executory proceedings, attachment is called "embargo."

See also topic Sequestration.

See also topic Courts, subhead Maritime Courts.

AUTOMOBILES: See topic Motor Vehicles.

BANKRUPTCY:

This subject is regulated by C. C. 1659-62 and Code of Commerce, Book 3rd, Law 43, 1919.

Kinds of Bankruptcy.—The bankruptcy may be: (1) Fortuitous; (2) culpable; (3) or fraudulent. In the latter two cases the bankrupt is liable to be prosecuted under the Penal Law.

Bankruptcy proceedings may be commenced by a merchant, by one or more of his creditors, or by the Public Prosecutor (Ministerio Publico) when the debtor has fled or is in hiding and has not left a representative to manage his affairs and fulfill his obligations.

A registered merchant who is unable to meet his obligations must call a meeting of creditors within two days after ceasing to make payments. This is done by presenting a petition to the court to be adjudged bankrupt. The debtor must state the reasons for his failure and make a statement of his financial condition and present a list of his creditors indicating the nature of their claims. He also must state the date in which he failed to make payments and present his account books.

When a creditor petitions for bankruptcy proceedings against a merchant the petition must state that he is a legal creditor, that his credit originates from acts of commerce, and that such credit is liquidated and demandable. When the debtor has fled without leaving a representative to manage his business and to attend the payment of his obligations, the creditor may demand the adjudication of bankruptcy even though the credit may not be due, but the creditor must prove to the satisfaction of the judge, that the debtor has failed in payment of his obligations or has maliciously disposed of all or great part of his property or has created incumbrances on it or tried to hide the same.

Effect of Declaration of Bankruptcy.—Upon the declaration of bankruptcy by the court, the debtor loses the administration and control of all his property except that which is not subject to attachment, but he retains a limited ownership. For the administration of the property of the bankrupt a receiver is appointed by the court, who assumes, for the benefit of the bankrupt estate, all the assets and liabilities and exercises all the privileges and rights of the bankrupt and holds all commercial agencies or representations which the bankrupt may have.

See Topical Index in front part of this volume.

BANKRUPTCY . . . *continued*

Bankrupt is not permitted to leave jurisdiction without permission from court. He is not a party in proceedings with regard to his property, but may appear in any matter concerning his person. He is precluded from exercise of civil rights granted by Constitution of Panama.

Upon the declaration of bankruptcy no interest is chargeable against the bankrupt estate, with the exception of secured credits.

Creditors outside of Panama in foreign countries cannot present their claims after two months from the date of the publication of the order of the court.

Composition.—The bankrupt may make a composition with his creditors at any stage of the proceedings, after examination and recognition of credits has been made, but not before. The agreement is made in a meeting of creditors. The court will approve the agreement if it is supported by majority of creditors. In order that an agreement between the creditors and the bankrupt be valid it must receive the majority of personal votes attending the meeting and that such majority shall represent three-fourths of the liabilities. None of the creditors can have more than one personal vote although he may represent several credits, and joint creditors will have only one personal vote. A creditor who assigns one or more of his claims to obtain more than one vote in the meeting will lose entirely the right to vote.

Property of Third Persons.—The property in the hands of the bankrupt which has not been transferred to him by a legal and irrevocable title is returned to its rightful owners.

Priorities.—Credits are classified as follows: (1) Credits with respect to personal property; (2) credits with respect to real property and real rights; (3) credits with respect to the balance of personal and real property. The rules of preferences are the following: (1) Credits with respect to personal property enjoy preference as follows: (a) Construction, reparation, conservation or price of the personal property in possession of the debtor up to the value of same; (b) credits guaranteed by pledge; (c) those guaranteed by bond or securities; (d) credits for carriage upon the price of goods, expenses and right of carrying, and keeping up to delivery; (e) credits for the price of the lodging upon the personal property of the debtor; (f) credits for seeds and expenses in cultivation, upon the crop for which those seeds were used; (g) credits for hiring and rents of one year upon the property and products of same. (2) Credits with respect to real property and rights enjoy preference as follows: (a) Credits in favor of the government upon the property of the contributors for taxes; (b) credits of insurance companies upon the property insured for the payment of two years' premium; (c) credits guaranteed by mortgage properly inscribed in the public register upon the mortgaged property; (d) credits properly noted in the public register by order of the court for embargoes, sequestration or execution of sentence upon the property so annotated, but only upon credits after the annotation. (3) Credits with respect to other personal and real property, enjoy preference as follows: (a) Credits in favor of municipality for taxes; (b) credits for expenses for administration of bulk of bankrupt estate; (c) credits for funeral of debtor, his wife and children under age if he lacks property of his own; (d) credits for medical attendance; (e) salaries and wages of employees for one year; (f) credits for advances made to debtor for him and his family for necessary articles, for period of one year; (g) credits for boarding during proceedings; (h) credits without special privileges found in public deeds or executed judgment if such judgment is based upon real litigation. Preference of these last two credits is established by their dates.

With respect to personal property, the proceeds are distributed pro rata among the creditors entitled to the same preferences, except as follows: Credits guaranteed by pledge have priority as to the pledged property; in case of bonds given to two or more creditors, such bonds take priority according to their dates; and with respect to crops credits for seeds, cultivation expenses and harvesting have preference over credits for hiring and rents.

Discharge.—The bankrupt may be discharged by the court without any petition if his bankrupt estate has been sufficient to pay all his debts except fraudulent ones. Culpable bankrupts are discharged upon proof of having suffered the penalty imposed upon them.

Foreign Declaration of Bankruptcy.—Except as otherwise provided in treaties, bankruptcy declared in a foreign country has no effect in Panama, until the judgment has been held enforceable by a local court. Even though the above requirement is not fulfilled preventive measures may be ordered against the property in Panama of the bankrupt if such measures are asked by means of rogatory commissions. In spite of the exequatur, the foreign declaration of bankruptcy will not affect the resident creditors of the bankrupt or their rights in his property within the Republic or abrogate contracts made with the bankrupt.

BANKS AND BANKING:

Regulated by Cabinet Decree No. 238 of 1970, which created National Banking Commission, as am'd by Law #93 of Nov. 1974. National and qualified foreign (see topic Corporations, subhead Foreign Corporations) bank companies must have a minimum paid-in capital, be beneficiary of a contingent credit, have a legal reserve and operate under one of following three types of banking licenses: General License to engage in banking business within or outside Panama (1,000,000 Balboas, minimum paid-in capital); International License to exclusively conduct foreign transactions from Panama (requirements are minimal; among them, must maintain 500,000 Balboas in National Bonds, free of encumbrances; this requirement has been constitutionally challenged); Representation License for foreign banks to establish local representative offices. Requirements vary on type of license. It is possible for foreign bank that obtains license in Panama to be administered by another bank already established in Panama. (Res. #16-89 adopted by National Banking Commission Oct., 1989). Numbered accounts similar to Swiss system are allowed. General License banks must pay Annual Tax of 25,000 Balboas. International License banks must pay annual tax of 15,000 Balboas. (Law No. 1 of Feb. 1985). In order for local bank to receive cash deposits in amounts over US$10,000 or in subsequent transactions amounting to less than US$10,000, but that will add up to US$10,000 or more during week, sworn declaration form must be completed and filed with bank.

See also topics Finance Companies; Trusts.

BILLS AND NOTES:

The Uniform Negotiable Instruments Act, translated into Spanish, was adopted by Law 52 of 1917.

Letter of credit must state the name of the payee, the limit of amount and the term for which issued, and must be signed by the issuing party and the payee. (C. Com. 944-956).

Lost instruments may be replaced by order of a competent court on due application and notice. Bond may be required. (C. Com. 957-974).

CHATTEL MORTGAGES:

Chattel mortgages are permitted on chattels which can be clearly identified. (Decree-Law 2 of 1955). In order to give notice to third parties such contracts must be recorded in the Public Registry Office. Chattel mortgages on the stock in trade are not permitted.

COLLATERAL SECURITY: See topic Pledges.

COMMERCIAL OR MERCANTILE REGISTER:

See topic Records.

COMMUNITY PROPERTY:

See topic Husband and Wife.

CONDITIONAL SALES: See topic Sales.

CONSTITUTION AND GOVERNMENT:

Panama is independent country. Its government is unitary, republican, democratic and representative, divided into three branches: Legislative, Executive and Judiciary, with separate powers.

Legislative body is called Legislative Assembly, whose members are elected for period of five years, by popular vote, one for each 30,000 inhabitants within electoral circuit, and another for residue of 10,000 inhabitants. At present there are 40 electoral circuits and 67 elected members of Legislative Assembly.

President is head of Executive Branch, elected by direct popular vote for term of five years.

Judicial Branch is composed of Supreme Court and Tribunals and Courts as are established by law. Members of Supreme Court are appointed by Executive Branch, with approval of Legislative Branch, for period of ten years.

CONTRACTS:

Contracts are governed as to nature, form, objects by general principles of Civil Code, but there are certain type of contracts which are deemed mercantile or commercial in nature, concerning which basic principles of contracts of Civil Code are applicable but are supplemented by provision of Commercial Code; and, in absence thereof, by commercial usage of each market place.

For validity of every contract there must be consent by persons having legal capacity to consent, object certain or object which is ascertainable, and consideration not contrary to law, public morals, or public order. Certain contracts must be in writing or executed by means of notarial document.

Franchise, Distributorship, Representation.—Are governed by general provisions of Civil and Commerce Codes and by Law No. 29 of Feb. 1, 1996. Specific provisions of Code of Commerce are: Brokers (arts. 107 to 127); commercial agents (arts. 100 to 106); commission agents (arts. 635 to 662); factors (arts. 603 to 617); transportation agents (arts. 728 to 739); mercantile power of attorney (arts. 580 to 602).

Note: Cabinet Decree No. 344 of Oct. 31, 1969, on contracts of agency, representation and distribution was declared unconstitutional by ruling of Supreme Court of Aug. 2, 1989.

Excuses for Nonperformance.—Where contract involves particular object, loss thereof discharges obligation provided loss occurs without fault of person required to deliver and before time for such delivery. (C. C. 1068).

In contracts in general, nonperformance or delay thereof is excused when performance is prevented by "unforeseen events" or events "impossible to avoid." (C. C. 990; 34-d). By "unforeseen events" is meant acts of God (force of nature) and by "impossible to avoid" acts of man, including Governmental actions or acts of enemies which prevent or delay performance.

Applicable Law.—As to external formalities, law of place of execution governs, but parties may follow pertinent law of Panama; however, when law of Panama requires a public instrument (notarial document), private documents have no force in Panama, even though valid where executed. (C. C. 7). By "private documents" is meant those in which notary or other authorized public official takes no part in execution.

Government Contracts.—They are governed by special provisions of Law 56 of Dec. 27, 1995, and certain provisions of Fiscal Civil Administrative and Penal Code. There must be public bids if official price exceeds US$250,000. When price is less than US$10,000 summary procedure to be determined by Ministry of Treasury and Revenue shall be followed to select contracting party. Call for offer of prices shall be made when official price is more than US$10,000 and does not exceed US$250,000.

CONVEYANCES: See topic Deeds.

COPYRIGHT:

Copyrights are governed by Law No. 15 of Aug. 8, 1994 and by Decree No. 261 of Oct. 3, 1995. They are granted for life of author and 50 years thereafter. Anonymous or pseudonymous works, as well as software and audiovisual works, are protected for 50 years as of date of publishing. Right to exploitation of copyrights is transferable and transfer must be made in writing. Copyrights must be registered in National Directorate of Copyrights (Ministry of Education). This Directorate may also apply

See Topical Index in front part of this volume.

COPYRIGHT . . . *continued*
administrative sanctions to copyright infringers. Civil and criminal actions before circuit courts may also be instituted against infringers.

Panama has also ratified Convention on Literary and Artistic Copyright, 1910; Convention for the Protection of Producers of Phonograms Against Unauthorized Duplication of their Phonograms, 1971; Interamerican Convention on Rights of Author in Literary, Scientific and Artistic Works; Convention Establishing World Intellectual Property Organization; Universal Copyright Convention as Revised in Paris, 1971; Convention Relating to the Distribution of Programme Carrying Signals Transmitted by Satellite, 1974; International Convention for the Protection of Performers, Producers of Phonograms and Broadcasting Organizations; 1886 Berne Convention for the Protection of Literary and Artistic Works, as revised in Paris on July 24, 1971 and amended on Sept. 28, 1979.

See also topics Patents; Trademarks and Tradenames; and Treaties.

CORPORATIONS:

Corporations are regulated by Law 32 of 1927, effective Apr. 1, 1927, and Law 9 of 1946.

Incorporation.—Two or more persons of full age, and any nationality, even though not residents of Panama, may form a corporation for any lawful purpose.

The persons desiring to form a corporation must sign an agreement of incorporation (pacto social) setting forth:

(1) The name and domicile of each subscriber.

(2) The name of the corporation, which may be expressed in any language, but must not be the same as, nor so similar to, the name of any other preexisting corporation as to lend itself to confusion, and must include a word, phrase, or abbreviation, indicating that it is a corporation and distinguishing it from a natural person or other form of association.

(3) The general object or objects of the corporation.

(4) The amount of the capital stock and the number and par value of the shares into which it is divided, both of which may be expressed in the currency of Panama, or in legal gold currency of any country, or in both, and if the corporation is to issue shares without par value the statements hereinafter referred to as to such stock (see infra subhead Shares and Capital).

(5) If there are to be shares of various classes, the number of each class and the designations, preferences and voting powers, and the restrictions, or requisites of each class, or a stipulation that such designations, preferences, etc., may be determined by a resolution of a majority of the interested stockholders or of a majority of the directors.

(6) The number of shares which each subscriber to the agreement of incorporation agrees to take.

(7) Domicile of corporation and name and domicile of its agent in Panama, who must be attorney-at-law or firm of attorneys admitted to practice in Republic of Panama. (Decree 147 of May 4, 1966). Resident agent is under duty to know client and keep enough information to identify client before competent authorities. This information shall be disclosed only upon petition filed by Public Prosecutor or member of Judicial Organ competent to take cognizance of narcotics' traffic, crimes or of money laundering arising therefrom, as result of proceedings already initiated in Republic of Panama, or under treaties for Mutual Legal Assistance.

(8) The duration of the corporation.

(9) The number of directors, which may not be less than three, and their names and addresses.

(10) Any other lawful provisions which the subscribers have agreed to.

The agreement of incorporation may be made in any place, in or outside Panama, and in any language. It may be in form of public deed or in other form, provided it is attested by notary public or by another official who is authorized to make attestations in place of execution.

If the agreement is not set forth in a public deed it must be protocolized in the office of a notary of Panama. If it has been executed outside of Panama it must, in order to be protocolized, be previously authenticated by a consul of Panama, or if there is no such consul, by the consul of a friendly state. If the agreement is executed in any language except Spanish there must be protocolized with it a translation thereof in the Spanish language, certified by an official or public interpreter of Panama.

Public deed or protocolized document setting forth agreement of incorporation must be filed for registration in Mercantile Registry, and incorporation is not effective with respect to third persons until agreement of incorporation has been registered. Law 1 of 1985 established US$150 annual franchise tax on all domestic and foreign corporations recorded in Public Registry of Panama applicable to both existing and new corporations. No other incorporation tax is levied upon corporations save registration fees which are charged at following rates: Minimum of US$75 when capital does not exceed US$10,000; 50¢ for each additional US$1,000 or fraction thereof on next US$90,000; 50¢ for each additional US$1,000 or fraction thereof on next US$900,000; 10¢ for each additional US$1,000 or fraction thereof when capital of company exceeds US$1,000,000. Should there be shares without par value, each such share is assigned value of US$20 as basis for computing registration tax. (Law 1 of 1985, Art. 5).

Amendment of Agreement of Incorporation.—A corporation formed under the Law of 1927 may amend its agreement of incorporation provided the amendments are in accordance with the provisions of the Law. Consequently, the corporation may change the number of its shares of stock or of any class of its stock outstanding at the time of such amendment; change the par value of the outstanding or subscribed shares of any class; change the outstanding or subscribed shares of a class having par value for the same or different numbers of shares of the same or a different class without par value; change the outstanding or subscribed shares of a class without par value into the same or different number of shares of the same or a different class having par value; increase the amount or the number of shares of its authorized stock; divide its authorized stock into classes; increase the number of classes of its authorized stock; change the designations of the shares, the rights, privileges, preferences, voting powers, and the restrictions or requisites.

An amendment of the agreement of incorporation must be made in the manner provided by the Law with respect to the execution of the agreement of incorporation.

Amendments made before shares have been issued must be signed by all persons who have signed the agreement of incorporation and by all who have agreed to take shares.

If shares have been issued the amendments must be signed: (a) By the holders, or their agents, of all the outstanding or subscribed shares entitled to vote, and have annexed thereto a certificate issued by the secretary, or an assistant secretary, of the corporation to the effect that the persons who have signed the amendment, in person or by agent, constitute all the holders of the outstanding or subscribed shares entitled to vote; or (b) by the president, or one of the vice-presidents, and the secretary, or one of the assistant secretaries, of the corporation, who must sign and annex to the instrument of amendment a certificate stating that they have been authorized to execute such amendment by resolution adopted by the owners, or their agents, of a majority of such shares and that such resolution was adopted at a stockholders' meeting held on the date fixed in such notice or waiver of notice thereof.

If the amendment alters the preferences of outstanding or subscribed shares of any class or authorizes the issuance of shares having preferences which are in any respect more advantageous than those of outstanding or subscribed shares of any class, the certificate referred to in (b) above must state that the officers of the corporation who signed the same were authorized to execute the instrument of amendment by resolution adopted by the owners, or their agents, of a majority of the shares of each class entitled to vote and that such resolution was adopted at a stockholders' meeting held on the date fixed in such notice or waiver of notice thereof.

If the agreement of incorporation provides that more than a majority of the outstanding or subscribed shares of any class is required in order to amend the same, the certificate referred to in (b) above must state that the amendment has been authorized in such manner.

Unless the agreement of incorporation, or the amendments thereof provide otherwise, each stockholder has a preferential right to subscribe for stock issued by virtue of an increase of stock in proportion to the number of shares owned by him.

The corporation may reduce its authorized capital stock by amendment of its agreement of incorporation, but no distribution of its assets may be made by virtue of such reduction, if it reduces the actual value of assets to less than the total amount of its liabilities, considering the amount of its reduced capital stock as part of such liabilities. In case of such reduction there must be annexed to the instrument of amendment a certificate under oath of the president or vice-president and the treasurer or an assistant treasurer stating that such reduction has not been effected by the distribution. Except in case of fraud the judgment of the board of directors as to the value of assets and liabilities is considered correct.

On increase of capital stock, recording tax is payable on the increase at the same rates as for original incorporation. See supra, subhead Incorporation.

Acquisition by Corporation of its own Stock.—Unless the agreement of incorporation provides otherwise, a corporation may acquire shares of its own stock. If such acquisition is made with funds or property which are not part of the surplus of assets over liabilities or of the net profits, the shares acquired must be cancelled by the reduction of the issued capital stock, but such shares may be resold if the authorized capital stock is not reduced upon cancellation thereof. The shares of its own stock acquired by a corporation with funds arising from its surplus or net profits may be held by the corporation or sold by it for its corporate purposes, and may be cancelled or reissued by resolution of the board of directors.

The shares of a corporation acquired by it, may not, directly or indirectly, be represented at a stockholders' meeting.

A corporation may not acquire its own stock with funds which do not arise from its surplus or net profits if by reason of such acquisition the actual value of its assets is reduced to an amount which represents less than the total amount of its liabilities, considering the reduced capital stock as part of such liabilities, but except in case of fraud, the judgment of the board of directors as to the value of assets and liabilities is considered correct.

General Powers.—Every corporation organized under the Law of 1927 has, in addition to any other powers specified in the Law, the following powers:

(1) To sue and be sued.

(2) To adopt and use a corporate seal and alter the same.

(3) To acquire, purchase, hold, use and transfer movable and immovable property of all kinds and to create and accept pledges, mortgages, leases, liens, and encumbrances of all kinds.

(4) To appoint officers and agents.

(5) To make contracts of all kinds.

(6) To make by-laws for the management and regulation of its affairs and property, for transfer of its shares and for calling of meetings of its stockholders and directors, and for all other lawful matters, provided such by-laws do not violate any existing laws or its agreement of incorporation.

(7) To carry on its business and exercise its powers in foreign countries.

(8) To dissolve in accordance with law, whether voluntarily or for other cause.

(9) To borrow money and contract debts in connection with its business or for any lawful purpose; to issue bonds, notes, bills or exchange, and other instruments of obligation (which may or may not be convertible into shares of the corporation) payable at a specified date, or payable upon the happening of a specified event, whether secured by mortgage or pledge or unsecured, for money borrowed or in payment for property acquired or for any other lawful object.

(10) To guarantee, acquire, purchase, hold, sell, assign, transfer, mortgage, pledge or otherwise dispose of or deal in shares, bonds, or other obligations issued by other corporations or by any municipality, province, state or government.

(11) To do whatever necessary in the accomplishment of the objects enumerated in its agreement of incorporation or in amendments thereof, or necessary or convenient for the protection and benefit of the corporation, and in general, to carry on any lawful business even if not similar to any of the objects specified in its agreement of incorporation or amendments thereof.

Shares and Capital.—A corporation created under the Law of 1927 has power to create and issue one or more classes of shares, with such designations, preferences, privileges, voting powers, restrictions or requisites and other rights as its agreement of

CORPORATIONS . . . *continued*
incorporation may provide, and subject to such rights of redemption as it may have reserved to itself in the agreement of incorporation.

The agreement of incorporation may provide that shares of any class are convertible into the shares of one or more other classes.

Shares of stock may have a nominal or par value. Such shares may be issued as fully paid and non-assessable, as partly paid, or without any payment having been made thereon. Unless the agreement of incorporation provides otherwise, fully paid and non-assessable shares having a par value, or bonds or shares convertible into such shares, may not be issued, in exchange for services or property which, in the judgment of the board of directors, are of a value less than the par value of such shares or of the shares into which such bonds or shares are convertible. It may not be stated in certificates for partly paid shares that there has been paid on account thereof an amount greater, in the judgment of the board of directors, than the value of what has actually been paid thereon. The payment may be in money, labor, services or property of any kind.

Except in case of fraud, the judgment of the board of directors as to values is considered correct.

Corporations may create and issue shares of stock without par value, provided there be set forth in the agreement of incorporation:

(1) The total number of shares that the corporation may issue;

(2) The number of shares, if any, with par value, and the value of each;

(3) The number of shares without par value;

(4) One or the other of the following statements: (a) That the capital of the incorporation shall be at least equal to the total sum represented by the shares with par value plus a determined amount with respect to every share without par value which is issued, and such amounts as from time to time, pursuant to a resolution or resolutions of the board of directors, are incorporated into the corporate capital; or (b) that the capital of the corporation shall be at least equal to the total sum represented by the shares with par value, plus the value which the corporation receives for the issue of shares without par value, and such amounts as from time to time pursuant to resolution or resolutions of the board of directors are incorporated into the corporate capital.

There may also be set forth in the agreement of incorporation an additional statement to the effect that the corporate capital shall not be less than the sum which is named therein.

Subject to the designations, preferences, privileges, voting powers, restrictions or requisites granted or imposed with respect to any class of shares, all shares of one class, whether with or without par value, are equal to the other shares of the same class.

A corporation may issue and sell the shares without par value, which it is authorized to issue for the amount which is prescribed in its agreement of incorporation; for such price as is considered fair in the judgment of the board of directors; for such price as from time to time the board of directors determines, if the agreement of incorporation so authorizes; or for such price as is determined by the holders of a majority of the shares entitled to vote.

All the shares without par value are deemed fully paid and non-assessable. The holders of such shares are not responsible, on account of such shares, to the corporation or to its creditors.

The price of the shares must be paid at such times and in such manner as the board of directors may determine. In case of default, the board of directors may elect to proceed against the defaulting stockholder to enforce payment of the part which he has failed to pay and to collect the damages which the corporation may have suffered, or to rescind the contract with respect to such stockholder, with the right in the latter case to retain for the corporation the amounts of the corporate assets which correspond to such stockholder.

In case it elects to rescind the contract with respect to the defaulting stockholder, and to retain for the corporation the amounts which correspond to him, the board of directors must give notice thereof to such stockholder at least 60 days in advance.

The shares which the corporation may acquire by virtue of the provisions of this article may be reissued and reoffered for subscription.

The certificate for shares must state:

(1) The recordation of the corporation in the Mercantile Registry.

(2) The corporate capital.

(3) The number of shares corresponding to the stockholders.

(4) The class of share, when there are various classes, as well as the special conditions, designations, preferences, privileges, premiums, advantages and restrictions or requisites which any of the classes of shares may have as against others.

(5) If the shares which the certificate represents are fully paid and non-assessable, this fact must be stated in such certificate; otherwise the amount which has been paid must be stated in the certificate.

(6) If the share be issued in the name of the holder, his name must be stated therein.

Shares may not be issued to bearer except when they are fully paid and non-assessable.

Shares represented by certificates issued in the name of the owner are transferable on the books of the corporation in accordance with what may be provided in that respect in the agreement of incorporation or in the by-laws. In no case does a transfer bind the corporation, until registration thereof in the Register of Stock.

If holder of certificate owes any amount to corporation, it may oppose transfer until amount owed is paid to it. In every case transferor and transferee remain solidarily liable for amounts which may be owed to corporation on account of shares transferred.

Bearer shares are transferable by mere delivery of the certificate.

If so provided in the agreement of incorporation, the holder of a stock certificate issued to bearer may cause such certificate to be exchanged for another certificate in his name for a like number of shares; and the holder of shares issued in the name of the owner may cause his certificate to be exchanged for another certificate to bearer for a like number of shares.

The agreement of incorporation may provide that the corporation or any of the stockholders shall have a preferential right to purchase the shares in the corporation which another stockholder desires to transfer. Other restrictions may be imposed upon the transfer of the shares, but a restriction which absolutely prohibits the transfer of the shares is void.

The corporation may issue new certificates of stock to replace those which may have been destroyed, lost or stolen. In such case the board of directors may require that the owner of the destroyed, lost or stolen certificate execute a guaranty to answer to the corporation for any claim or damage.

The agreement of incorporation may provide that the holders of any specified class of shares shall not be entitled to vote, or may limit or define such right with respect to the several classes of shares. Such provisions govern in all voting which may take place and in all cases in which the Law requires the vote or written consent of the holders of all of the shares or of a part of the shares.

The agreement of incorporation may also provide that the vote of the holders of more than a majority of any class of stock shall be required for specified purposes.

Voting Trusts.—One or more stockholders may agree in writing to transfer their stock to one or more trustees for the purpose of conferring upon them the right to vote in the name and stead of the owner, for a period fixed and upon the conditions stated in the agreement. Other stockholders may transfer their stock to the same trustee or trustees, thereby making themselves parties to such agreement. The certificates of stock so transferred must be delivered to the corporation and cancelled by it and new certificates issued in favor of the trustee or trustees, in which it must appear that they are issued pursuant to such agreement, and such facts must be noted in the register of stock of the corporation. In order that the foregoing provisions shall apply, an authenticated copy of the agreement must be furnished to the corporation.

Stock Register.—The corporation must keep at its office in Panama, or at such other place as the agreement of incorporation or the by-laws specify, a book to be known as the Stock Register (Registro de Acciones), in which must be noted (except in the case of shares issued to bearer) the names in alphabetical order of all stockholders, showing the place of residence, the number of shares held by each of them, the date of acquisition, and the amount paid thereon or that the shares are fully paid and non-assessable.

In the case of shares issued to bearer the stock register must state the number of shares issued, the date of issue and that such shares are fully paid and non-assessable.

Stockholders' Liability.—The holders of fully paid stock are not liable for the debts of the corporation. Other stockholders are liable to creditors of the corporation up to the amount unpaid on their stock, but no action may be brought against a stockholder for a debt of the corporation until judgment therefor has been obtained against the corporation and the full amount thereof remains uncollected after execution against the corporate property.

Dividends may be paid from net profits or surplus, but not otherwise, and may be declared and paid upon the basis of the amount actually paid upon partly paid shares. Dividends may be paid in stock when the directors so determine, provided such stock has been duly authorized and, if it has not theretofore been issued, there be transferred from surplus to capital an amount at least equal to that corresponding to the shares so issued.

Stockholders' meetings must be held in Panama, unless it is otherwise provided in the agreement of incorporation or by-laws.

Whenever under the provisions of the law the approval or authority of the stockholders is necessary notice of the meeting of stockholders must be given in writing and in the name of the president, vice-president, secretary or assistant secretary or of any person or persons authorized for the purpose by the agreement of incorporation or the by-laws.

The notice must state the purpose or purposes for which the meeting is called and the place and hour at which it is to be held.

The notice must be given at such time in advance and in such manner as the agreement of incorporation or the by-laws may provide; but if they do not otherwise provide, the notice must be given by delivery of the notice personally or by mail to each registered stockholder entitled to vote, not less than ten nor more than 60 days before date of meeting.

If the corporation has issued shares to bearer, the notice must be published in such manner as the agreement of incorporation or the by-laws provide.

Special meetings of stockholders may be called by the Board of Directors and must be called by the Board or the competent Circuit Judge upon demand of one or more stockholders whose shares represent at least $1/20$ of the capital stock. (Law 9 of 1946, reenacting C. Com. 420).

The stockholders or their legal representatives may waive in writing notice of any meeting either before or after the meeting.

Resolutions adopted at any meeting at which all the stockholders are present, in person or by proxy, are valid; and resolutions adopted at a meeting at which there is a quorum and notice of which has been waived by all absent stockholders, are valid for all purposes stated in such waiver, although the notice was not given in proper form.

If the agreement of incorporation does not otherwise provide, every stockholder is entitled to one vote for each share registered in his name, of whatever class and whether with or without par value. Unless the agreement of incorporation otherwise provides, board of directors may fix period, not exceeding 40 days, before date of each meeting of stockholders, during which no transfer of stock will be registered on books of corporation, or may fix date, not to be more than 40 days prior to date of meeting, as date on which stockholders (except holders of bearer shares) entitled to notice of and to vote at such meeting shall be determined. In such case, only stockholders of record on such date are entitled to notice of calling of meeting and to vote at such meeting.

In the case of shares issued to bearer, the bearer is entitled at stockholders' meeting to one vote for each share of stock entitled to vote, if he presents the corresponding certificate or certificates or proof of his right in the form prescribed by the agreement of incorporation or the by-laws.

At all meetings of the stockholders any stockholder may be represented by proxy, who need not be a stockholder, and who may be appointed by an instrument, public or private, with or without power of substitution.

Suits to invalidate resolutions adopted at stockholders' meetings must be instituted within 30 days. (Law 9 of 1946, reenacting C. Com. 418).

The agreement of incorporation may provide for cumulative voting at elections of directors.

See Topical Index in front part of this volume.

CORPORATIONS . . . *continued*

Directors.—The affairs of the corporation are managed by a board of directors, who must be of full age, may be of either sex, and need not be stockholders unless the agreement of incorporation so requires.

Subject to the provisions of the Law and of the agreement of incorporation, the number of directors is fixed by the by-laws, but there must not be less than three directors.

The directors are elected, and vacancies in the board are filled, in the manner provided in the agreement of incorporation or the by-laws, but, subject to such provisions, vacancies in the board, whether resulting from an increase in the number of directors or from any other cause, are filled by the vote of a majority of the members of the board. If directors are not elected at the time designated for that purpose, the directors in office continue to hold office until their successors are elected.

Subject to the provisions of the Law and of the agreement of incorporation, the board of directors has absolute control and full direction of the affairs of the corporation and may exercise all the powers of the corporation except those which the Law or the agreement of incorporation or by-laws expressly confer upon or reserve to the stockholders.

A majority of the members of the board is ordinarily necessary to constitute a quorum, but the agreement of incorporation may provide that a specified number, either more or less than a majority, shall constitute a quorum. The resolutions of a majority present at a meeting at which a quorum is present are the resolutions of the board.

The directors may adopt, alter, amend and repeal the by-laws of the corporation, unless otherwise provided by the agreement of incorporation or by the by-laws adopted by the stockholders.

If the agreement of incorporation or the by-laws do not otherwise provide, the board of directors may appoint two or more of their number to constitute a committee or committees, having all the powers of the board of directors in the direction of the affairs of the corporation, subject to the restrictions expressed in the agreement of incorporation, the by-laws, or the resolutions by which they were appointed.

If the agreement of incorporation expressly so authorizes, the directors may be represented and voted at meetings of the board of directors by proxies, who need not be directors and who must be appointed by an instrument, public or private, with or without power of substitution.

The directors may be removed at any time by the votes of the holders of a majority of the outstanding or subscribed shares entitled to vote in elections of directors. The officers, agents and employees may be replaced at any time by resolution adopted by a majority of the directors, or in any other manner prescribed by the agreement of incorporation or the by-laws. Also director or officer may resign as such and said resignation must be protocolized and registered in Public Registry Office. (Decree 204 of July 16, 1992).

If any dividend or distribution of assets be declared or paid which reduces the value of the property of the corporation to less than the amount of its liabilities, including the capital stock; or the amount of the capital stock be reduced; or if any statement or report be made which is false in any material point, the directors who have given their consent to such acts, with knowledge of the facts are jointly and severally liable to the creditors of the corporation for damage arising therefrom.

Officers.—A corporation must have a president, a secretary and a treasurer, elected by the board of directors, and may have such other officers, agents and representatives as the board of directors, the by-laws or the agreement of incorporation may determine, who must be chosen in the manner provided thereby.

The same person may hold two or more offices, if the agreement of incorporation or the by-laws so provide.

No person need be a director of the corporation in order to be able to be an officer thereof, unless the agreement of incorporation or the by-laws so provide.

Registration of the names of the directors, officers and anyone else holding general authority to represent the company is required; changes must likewise be recorded. To effect registration the necessary documents must be first protocolized with a notary public. Such documents may consist of the entire minutes of the directors or stockholders meeting, as the case may be, or an extract thereof containing the following data: (a) date of the meeting; (b) name of the chairman and of the secretary thereof, and if not the president and secretary of the company respectively, a statement of the reasons for others acting in their place; (c) in case of stockholders meeting, the number of shares represented and the relation thereof to the total outstanding shares, or a statement that all the shares have been represented; (d) in the case of a meeting of the board of directors, the names of all directors present or represented; (e) how notice was given or, if no notice has been given, the reasons therefor, whether by waiver or by presence at the meeting. The copy of the minutes of the meeting or the extract thereof must be certified by the secretary of the meeting or the chairman thereof. They must be protocolized preferably by the secretary of the company or in his absence by the president with a statement to that effect; in the absence of both, the registered agent or any other officer so authorized by the board of directors. (Decree No. 130 of June 3, 1948).

Sale of Assets and Rights.—Every corporation may, by virtue of resolution of its board of directors, sell, lease, exchange or otherwise dispose of all or part of its property, including its goodwill and its privileges, franchises and rights, upon such terms and conditions as its board of directors may deem expedient, if authorized by resolution of the holders of a majority of the shares entitled to vote thereon, adopted at a meeting duly called for that purpose, or by the written consent of such stockholders. The agreement of incorporation may, however, provide that consent of any class of stockholders is necessary in order to grant such authority.

If the agreement of incorporation does not provide otherwise, the vote or consent of stockholders is not necessary for the transfer of property in trust, or to encumber it by pledge or mortgage, as security for debts of the corporation.

Consolidation.—Subject to the provisions of the agreement of incorporation, two or more corporations organized under the Law of 1927 may consolidate so as to constitute a single corporation. The directors, or a majority of them, of each of such corporations desiring to consolidate may enter into an agreement to that effect, which they must sign, and in which they must set forth the terms and conditions of the consolidation, the mode of effecting it and any other facts and circumstances which may be necessary in accordance with the agreement of incorporation or with the provisions of the Law, as well as the manner of converting the shares of each of the constituent corporations into shares of the new corporation, and also any other details and lawful provisions which may be deemed desirable.

The agreement may provide for the distribution of cash, notes or bonds, in whole or in part, in lieu of the distribution of stock, provided that after such distribution the obligations of the new corporation, including those derived by it from the constituent corporations and the amount of capital to be issued by the new corporation, do not exceed the assets of the new corporation.

The agreement of consolidation must be submitted to the stockholders of each constituent corporation at a meeting thereof duly called especially for the purpose, at which the agreement must be considered and a vote taken as to whether it shall be adopted or rejected.

Without prejudice to the provisions of the respective agreements of incorporation, if the votes of holders of a majority of the shares entitled to vote in each corporation, are given in favor of the consolidation agreement, that fact must be set forth in a certificate of the secretary or assistant secretary of each corporation, and the consolidation agreement so approved and certified must be signed by the president or a vice-president and the secretary or an assistant secretary of each constituent corporation in the manner provided with respect to the execution of the agreement of incorporation.

The consolidation agreement so made must be presented at the Mercantile Registry for recording, as required in the case of agreements of incorporation and when recorded is the act of consolidation of said corporations.

When such agreement of consolidation has been made and recorded in the Mercantile Registry, each of the constituent corporations ceases to exist, and the consolidated corporation, so constituted, succeeds the extinguished corporations in all their rights, privileges, powers and franchises as owner and possessor thereof, subject to the restrictions, obligations and duties which corresponded to the constituent corporations respectively. The rights of creditors of the respective constituent corporations and liens upon their property are not prejudiced by the consolidation, but such liens affect only the property affected thereby at the date of making the agreement of consolidation. The debts and obligations of the extinguished constituent corporations bind the new consolidated corporation.

The agreement of incorporation of any corporation may prescribe additional conditions which must be fulfilled in order to consolidate the corporation with any other.

In the judicial or administrative proceedings to which the extinguished corporations or any of them have been parties, the new consolidated corporation continues as a party.

The liability of the corporations and their stockholders, directors or officers, as well as the legal rights and remedies of their creditors or of persons doing business with the corporations which are being consolidated, are not in any way to be impaired by the consolidation thereof.

Merger.—One or more Panama corporations may merge with one or more foreign corporations provided: (a) that foreign corporations be registered in Mercantile Registry (see subhead Foreign Corporations, infra); (b) that if foreign is surviving corporation same must remain registered in Mercantile Registry for five years after time of merger. During this period attorney-in-fact must be maintained in Panama duly authorized to receive service of process on behalf of corporation. Otherwise, service of process may be made to resident agent. (Law No. 32 of June 30, 1978).

Dissolution.—If the board of directors of any corporation subject to the Law of 1927 deem it advisable that the corporation should be dissolved, the board must propose, by vote of a majority of its members, an agreement of dissolution and within ten days thereafter must duly call or cause to be duly called a meeting of the stockholders having voting power, to decide upon the resolution.

If at the meeting so-called the holders of a majority of the shares entitled to vote upon the matter adopt a resolution approving the resolution for the dissolution of the corporation, a copy of such resolution of the stockholders, accompanied by a list of the names and residences of the directors and officers of the corporation, must be certified by the president or a vice-president, and the secretary or assistant secretary, and the treasurer or an assistant treasurer, and such certified copy must be protocolized and presented at the Mercantile Registry. When the copy has been presented, it must be published at least once in a newspaper in the place where is situated the office of the corporation in Panama, or if there be no newspaper in such place, in the Official Gazette of the Republic.

If all the stockholders having voting power thereon consent in writing to the dissolution, neither a meeting of the board of directors nor a meeting of the stockholders is necessary. In such case the document showing the consent of the stockholders must be protocolized, recorded in the Mercantile Registry and published as above stated. When these formalities are complied with, the corporation is deemed to be dissolved.

Every corporation whose existence expires by expiration of period of duration fixed in its agreement of incorporation or by dissolution, nevertheless continues for three years thereafter, for purposes of prosecuting judicial proceedings which may be deemed convenient, defending its interests as defendant, arranging its affairs, transferring and disposing of its property and dividing its capital; but in no case may it continue business for which it was constituted.

When the existence of a corporation expires by expiration of period of its duration, or by dissolution, directors act as trustees of corporation with powers to settle its affairs, collect its credits, sell and convey its property of all kinds, divide its property among stockholders, after payment of debts of corporation, and they have power to initiate judicial proceedings in name of corporation, with respect to its credits and property, and to represent it in proceedings which may be brought against it. In such case, directors are jointly or severally responsible for debts of corporation, up to amount of moneys and property of corporation of which they may have acquired possession and management.

Such directors are authorized to apply funds and property of the corporation to the payment of a reasonable compensation for their services and may fill any vacancy in their number.

See Topical Index in front part of this volume.

CORPORATIONS . . . *continued*

The directors, when acting as such trustees, make their decisions by majority vote.

Dissolution of a corporation may be ordered by a court for unlawful practices and for just cause upon demand of any stockholder; and the court may for good cause appoint liquidators. (Law 9 of 1946, reenacting C. Com. 524, 531).

Foreign Corporations.—A foreign corporation may have offices or agencies and carry on business in Panama after having presented at the Mercantile Registry for recording, the following documents:

(1) Deed of protocolization of its agreement of incorporation.

(2) Copy of its last balance sheet accompanied by a declaration of the amount of its capital utilized or intended to be utilized in business in Panama.

(3) A certificate that it is incorporated and authorized under the laws of the corresponding country, issued and authenticated by the consul of Panama in said country, or if there is no such consul, by the consul of a friendly nation.

(4) An excerpt of the minutes of the meeting wherein the then directors and officers were elected, executed by the secretary of the corporation.

(5) Appointment of business agent.

Foreign corporations acting within Panama and which have not complied with the above requirements may not initiate judicial or other proceedings before the courts or authorities of Panama, but may be sued in any proceeding before the judicial and administrative authorities, and are liable to a penalty of up to 5,000 balboas.

Foreign corporations recorded in the Mercantile Registry must present for record in the Mercantile Registry any amendments of their agreement of incorporation, or instruments of consolidation or dissolution which affects them.

Change of Domicile (siege social).—A foreign corporation may change its domicile (siege social) to Panama, if the country of incorporation permits such change, by filing with the Registry Office in Panama substantially the same documents as for qualifying. (Decree-Law 16 of Aug. 23, 1958).

Pre-existing Corporations.—Domestic or foreign corporations which, when the Law of 1927 came into effect, were established in Panama or had agencies or branches therein are governed by their deeds of incorporation, their by-laws and the laws in force at the time of their incorporation or establishment in Panama. But domestic corporations created before the Law of 1927 took effect may at any time subject themselves to its provisions, by resolution adopted by the stockholders and recorded in the Public Registry.

Stockholders of domestic corporations actually dissolved but not liquidated may, for the purposes of liquidation, avail themselves of the provisions of the Law of 1927, if so resolved by a number of stockholders not less than that which their by-laws require for determination upon dissolution of the corporation prior to expiration of the term fixed for its existence.

Distributors and Sales Agents.—Representation, agency and distribution of goods or services of foreign and national manufacturers or concerns in Republic of Panama are currently regulated by general provisions of Commercial Contracts contained in Title VII of Book I of Code of Commerce of Republic of Panama and by Law No. 29 of Feb. 1, 1996.

Under above cited legal frame, parties involved are free to agree to pertinent terms and conditions of said commercial relationships. Any controversy arising between manufacturer and representative, agent and/or distributor must be resolved before special civil circuit courts and Superior Court created by Law No. 29 of Feb. 1, 1996, and before Supreme Court, pursuant to special rules of proceeding created for first two instances by said law or through arbitration.

Mutual Fund Companies.—Cabinet Decree 248 of 1970 regulates operation of so-called mutual fund companies, their distributors and their sales agents. National and qualified foreign (see subhead Foreign Corporations, supra) mutual fund companies must be authorized by National Securities Commission to engage in mutual fund business, including sale of its shares and other securities, in Panama, have a minimum paid-in capital and maintain a guaranty deposit. Requirements vary for national and foreign companies.

Taxation.—See topic Taxation.

See also topics Partnership; Trusts.

COURTS:

There are six Superior District Courts, one Superior Family Court and one Superior Minors' Court. In civil, family and minors' cases, justice is administered by following tribunals:

Municipal courts, sitting in the districts or municipalities and having general jurisdiction in certain matters and with certain limits as to the amount in controversy.

Circuit Courts.—Sectional Family Courts having jurisdiction in domestic relations, marriage, separation, divorce and maintenance. Sectional Minors' Courts having jurisdiction in matters relating to paternity, maternity, adoption, guardianship and offenses committed by minors, sitting in capital of each province, having general jurisdiction: (a) in matters exceeding jurisdiction of municipal courts; (b) cases relating to adjudication of insanity, and bankruptcy, and appeals from municipal courts.

Superior district courts generally have jurisdiction in appeals from circuit courts. First District court hears civil cases, the Second District court, criminal and Third District court (created by Law No. 29 of Feb. 1, 1996) hears appeals from special circuit courts created by same law having jurisdiction on industrial property, copyright, consumer protection, free competition and monopolies cases. They all sit in First District in City of Panama; Third District court sits in Penonomé; Fourth, in David, and Fifth in Las Tablas. With exception of First and Second District courts, others hear both civil and criminal cases.

Superior Family Court having jurisdiction in appeals for Sectional Family Courts. Superior Minors' Court having jurisdiction in appeals from Sectional Family Courts.

Supreme Court, in the capital of the Republic, sitting in bank has jurisdiction (a) in constitutional questions; (b) in matters involving the interpretation of administrative acts; (c) in prize cases and (d) as trial court in certain criminal cases involving high officials.

First division has jurisdiction in recourse of cassation and bills of review, invalidation of judgments and appeals from the Superior courts.

Second division has jurisdiction in recourse of cassation and bills of review in criminal cases and in criminal appeals from the Superior courts; it also has original jurisdiction in certain criminal cases.

Third division has jurisdiction to determine legality of acts of the Executive branch of the Government and in controversies between the Government and private persons.

Fourth division has jurisdiction in miscellaneous matters, including the enforcement of foreign judgments. (Law 47 of 1956).

Probate Courts.—Probate jurisdiction is exercised by the circuit courts or the municipal courts according to the amount involved.

Labor Courts.—Sectional Courts sit in cities of several provinces and have general jurisdiction in labor cases. Two superior courts or tribunals sit as follows: one in capital of Republic, other in City of Santiago de Veraguas; both have jurisdiction in appeals from sectional labor courts.

Labor cases with certain limitations may be appealed to Supreme Court, which acts on behalf of Court of Labor Cassation which, although created by law, is not yet operational.

Boards of Conciliation and Decision created by Law No. 7 of 1975 have jurisdiction throughout Republic of Panama and have competence over dismissals; suits claiming labor benefits under B/1,500 and household employees' disputes. Decisions of Boards of Conciliation and Decision may be appealed before Superior Labor Tribunals in proceedings exceeding amount of B/2,000, or when sum of benefits and indemnifications that must be paid in lieu of reinstatement of employee including back wages, exceeds said amount. Decisions of Superior Labor Tribunals in these cases are not appealable. Actions concerning seamen enrolled in vessels in Panama registry may be filed before labor courts or maritime courts at option of seamen.

Maritime Courts.—Law No. 8 of Mar. 30, 1982 as modified and supplemented by Law No. 11 of May 23, 1986 has created Maritime Courts, sitting in City of Panama. Jurisdiction of Maritime Court shall extend to all causes arising from maritime commerce and maritime traffic within territory of Republic of Panama, its territorial sea, navigable waters of rivers, lakes and in waters of Panama Canal. Also to those arising elsewhere from maritime commerce and traffic, in following cases: (1) When actions are filed against vessel or its owner and vessel is attached within jurisdiction of Republic of Panama; (2) when Maritime Court has attached other property of defendant, even if he is not domiciled within territory of Republic of Panama; (3) when defendant is found within jurisdiction of Republic of Panama, and has been personally served with complaint of actions filed in Maritime Courts; (4) when one of two vessels involved is of Panama Registry or substantive law of Panama would be applicable by virtue of contract, or because so provided by Panama Law, or where parties had submitted, expressly or impliedly to jurisdiction of Maritime Court of Republic of Panama.

Law provides for attachment of vessels and other maritime property for following purposes: (1) To provide security and prevent that defendant secrete, sell, encumber or otherwise cause that property lose value or be wasted; (2) as means of acquiring jurisdiction; (3) to satisfy maritime liens on property attached.

See also topics Constitution and Government; Depositions and Executions.

CURRENCY:

National currency unit is "Balboa" at par with U.S. dollar, also legal currency. Panama has not issued paper currency. See also topic Foreign Exchange and Foreign Trade.

CURTESY:

The estate by curtesy does not exist in Panama. For rights of surviving husband see topic Descent and Distribution.

DEATH:

A person may be declared missing after two years have elapsed without his having been heard from, or if the same period has elapsed since the last news concerning him was received, or after five years, if the missing person shall have left some person in charge of his property. Presumption of death may be judicially declared after five years of the disappearance of the missing person or since he was last heard from, or 60 years from his birth. Upon final judgment, estate is probated as testate or intestate, as case may be. Should missing person reappear, or without such reappearance it is proved that he is still alive, he may recover his property in condition in which it may then be, but not products or income. (C. C. 50-60).

Application for death certificate should be made to Director-General del Registro Civil, Panama, Republic of Panama. Fee, including stamp paper, $4.20. Remittance should be made in Panama funds. See topic Records, subhead Vital Statistics.

Actions For Death.—There is no separate action for death. If death occurs as result of voluntary homicide, civil action lies against person responsible therefor (C. C. P. 1986); and if because of negligence only, then person responsible is liable under general negligence rule (C. C. 1644). Action may be brought only by decedent's spouse or relatives within fourth degree of consanguinity or second degree of affinity. Further, it is not clear if mental suffering can be computed as part of damages.

DECEDENTS' ESTATES:

See topics Descent and Distribution; Executors and Administrators; Wills.

See also topic Husband and Wife.

DEEDS:

A transfer of title to or any interest in real property must be by deed, called public instrument, which must contain a true statement of the consideration (not nominal), a true description of the property by bounds and nature of same, and if a building is conveyed the material of which constructed, the flights and the area in metric measurements. Both the grantor and the grantee must sign at the same time, with two witnesses and before a notary public. If one party is absent he must be represented by an attorney

DEEDS . . . *continued*

in fact. The signing of the deed takes place after the notary has read it to the parties in the presence of the witnesses. The original becomes part of the notary's protocol, and the parties receive certified copies, which must be accepted in place of the original by any court or authority. Real property duly recorded may be described by reference only to volume, folio and number of the Real Property Record.

In order that third persons may be bound to take notice of the transfer of real property rights, the deed must be recorded in the Public Registry.

The transfer of certain personal property rights is also made by deed with the same formalities.

DEPOSITIONS:

In civil cases part of the evidence is obtained: (1) by "testimonios prejudiciales" (questions and answers made before suit to third parties); (2) by "declaraciones" (depositions of witnesses). Depositions may be taken before regular period for testimony, if witness is of advanced age or about to depart to place of difficult access or when there are other special circumstances.

Letters rogatory, with copies of the questions to be asked, may be issued to another judge if the examination is to take place elsewhere. Letters rogatory without the Republic of Panama are transmitted through diplomatic and consular channels, or as provided by treaties.

Maritime jurisdiction established special rules for depositions patterned after U.S. Federal Rules of Civil Procedure.

DESCENT AND DISTRIBUTION:

Law of descent and distribution is contained in C. C. 628-693f, as superseded in part by Constitution adopted in 1972. (Const., arts. 55, 56).

In default of testamentary disposition, the bulk of the estate passes to the following in the order named: (1) descendants in equal parts; (2) ascendants (parents) excluding collaterals, in equal parts, or surviving parent takes entire estate; (3) collaterals in the order prescribed by C. C. 678-684.

Parents have the same obligations to their children, whether born in or out of wedlock, all children are equal in law, and have the same rights of inheritance. Proof of paternity (in case of children born out of wedlock) is to be regulated by Law 60 of 1946.

Adopted children have the same right of inheritance as other children.

Surviving spouse takes an equal portion with descendants and ascendants (parents). In the absence of descendants or parents the estate is divided into three parts; one for the surviving spouse; one for the paternal ascendants; and one for the maternal ascendants.

Escheat.—In the absence of heirs entitled to take, the municipality of the decedent's last domicile takes the entire estate.

Disability to Inherit.—The law enumerates various acts which render the guilty parties incapable of inheriting, such as killing of person from whom the guilty party would inherit, abandonment by children of their duties to their parents, etc.

Acceptance of Inheritance.—In order to be entitled to the inheritance the heir must accept the same. Acceptance may be expressed or implied, and may be unconditional or subject to certain conditions. Those who have not the free management of their property cannot accept or repudiate an inheritance.

In case of unconditional acceptance, the heir is liable for all the debts of the decedent, out of his own property as well as out of the estate which he accepts.

What Law Governs.—The estates of nationals or foreigners located in Panama pass according to the law of Panama even though the decedent is domiciled in a foreign country at the time of death. The right of inheritance is determined by the law of Panama, but a judgment or a decree of a foreign country according to the laws of such country will have legal force in Panama provided it is not in conflict with rights based upon Panama laws.

DESERTION: See topic Divorce.

DIVORCE:

The law of divorce is contained in Family Code 212-223.

Grounds.—Divorce may be granted for following causes: (1) attempt against life of spouse, their children or their stepchildren; (2) cruel treatment, psychic or physical, if it makes domestic peace and tranquility impossible; (3) out-of-wedlock sexual relationship; (4) attempt of one spouse to prostitute other; (5) attempt of husband or wife to corrupt or prostitute their children, or their stepchildren, or connivance for their corruption or prostitution; (6) absolute abandonment of duties of spouse and parent; (7) habitual or unjustified use of drugs or sedative substances; (8) habitual drunkenness; (9) actual separation for more than two years; (10) mutual consent, in following cases: (a) when complaint is filed more than two years from date of marriage, (c) when parties ratify their petition six months after date of presentation or filing in court thereof.

Domicile.—To obtain a divorce it is necessary to be domiciled in Panama. To acquire domicile, foreigners must comply with immigration laws and obtain necessary authorization from Ministry of Government and Justice.

Time to Sue.—An action for divorce on the grounds of: (a) causes (1), (2), (3), (4), (5), (7) and (8) must be brought within one year from happening of act furnishing ground for divorce; (b) cause (6) must be brought within two years from happening of act furnishing ground for divorce.

Remarriage.—Husband may remarry immediately after recording the decree of divorce in the Civil Registry. Wife may remarry immediately after recording of decree of divorce in Civil Registry, prior to scientific test certifying that she is not pregnant. Otherwise, wife may not remarry until 300 days after date of separation as determined by court, provided that divorce has by then been recorded in Civil Registry.

Decree of separation does not dissolve the marriage bond, but otherwise it has the same effect as a divorce except that the parties cannot remarry. See topic Husband and Wife.

DOWER:

There is no dower right in Panama. For rights of surviving wife see topic Descent and Distribution. See also topic Husband and Wife.

ENVIRONMENT:

Law No. 21 of July 9, 1980 prohibits discharge of any contaminating substances in country's navigable waters and territorial sea. This prohibition extends to all vessels registered in Panama's Ship Registry. Law No. 1 of Feb. 3, 1994 regulates protection, conservation, improvement, investigation and use of country's forests. This law declares of national interest all forest resources in country. In May 1995 law has been adopted to protect wildlife, imposing fines and imprisonment to infringers.

Following conventions have been adopted: Agreement for the Conservation of Biodiversity and the Protection of Wildlife Areas in Central America, signed in Managua, Nicaragua in 1992; United Nations Agreement on Climatic Changes, made in New York in 1992; Regional Agreement on Climatic Changes, signed in Guatemala in 1993; Regional Agreement on Transborder Movement of Dangerous Wastes, signed in Panama in 1992; Regional Agreement for the Management and Conservation of Natural Forest Ecosystems and the Development of Forest Plantations, signed in Guatemala in 1993.

See also topic Treaties.

ESCHEAT:

See topic Descent and Distribution. See also topic Husband and Wife.

EVIDENCE: See topic Depositions.

EXCHANGE CONTROL:

See topic Foreign Exchange and Foreign Trade.

EXECUTIONS:

Judgments for money are carried into effect by attaching property of the debtor. After judgment the judge must proceed upon petition as follows: (1) To notify the judgment; (2) to demand payment; (3) in case payment is not made, to obtain statement under oath from the debtor as to the property he has; (4) to attach his property declared by him or discovered by his creditor.

Attachment of property is made in following order: (1) Money; (2) jewelry; (3) credits in favor of debtor; (4) real property and its income; (5) salaries or pensions; (6) personal property in general; (7) any other things belonging to debtor not exempted from attachment. This order may be altered according to will and desire of creditor.

The valuation of the property is made by the judge with assistance of referees appointed by him.

After attachment the next step is the sale of the property that cannot be turned over to the creditor. The sale is held by the clerk after the necessary advertisement of sale and property. Bidders must file a bond in amount of 10% of total amount of property to be sold. Sale can take place for two-thirds of valuation. When nobody bids two-thirds another date will be set and bids for one-half will be accepted. If no bid for one-half is made, new sale takes place and property will be sold to highest bidder although his bid is for less than one-half of valuation.

The right to replevy is recognized but cannot be exercised by the person against whom the execution has taken place. Third parties may intervene to allege preferential rights but the sale will not be stayed unless the intervenor claims ownership based on a title of earlier date than the execution. (C. C. P. 1667-1757).

EXECUTORS AND ADMINISTRATORS:

The term used in Panama for executor is "albacea" and the law regarding "albaceas" is contained in C. C. 854-873.

A testator may appoint one or more executors. Persons who cannot contract obligations cannot be executors. Executors may be universal or particular. The office is voluntary, but an executor who resigns or declines without reasonable cause loses the legacy or bequest, made in his favor, provided he is not entitled to maintenance.

The office of executor cannot be delegated without express authorization from the testator.

Duties.—The testator may define the duties of the executor, but if he has not done so, then the executor must: (1) Pay the funeral expenses; (2) recognize the legacies; (3) look after the fulfillment of everything ordered by will and defend the will within or without the court; (4) take all steps in benefit of the conservation and custody of the property, with the intervention of the heirs. The executor must conclude his labor within one year from the date of his acceptance or from the date of litigations relating to the will. If the testator wants to extend the time he must so indicate, but in the absence of this indication it is deemed extended for six months more. The heirs and legatees may extend the time for any period, but if the decision is only by a majority, then the extension will be for six months.

Fees of the executor are fixed by the testator, but in the absence of this the court will fix them according to the bulk of the estate and the work involved.

The heirs act as administrators of the estate of a person dying intestate. (C. C. P. 1676).

EXEMPTIONS:

The following are exempted from attachment and execution: (1a) Minimum wage under law and pensions not exceeding $50; (1b) 85% of salary in excess of minimum wage (according to law) and pensions in excess of $50 earned by debtor; (2) beds and clothing of debtor, wife and children, and their furniture; (3) professional books to the amount of $5,000 at selection of debtor; (4) machineries or instruments used in

See Topical Index in front part of this volume.

EXEMPTIONS . . . *continued*
teaching of science or art to the amount of $5,000 at selection of debtor; (5) agricultural or mechanical utensils belonging to debtor; (6) food and fire to amount necessary for maintenance of family; (7) personal rights of use, and lodging and maintenance of debtor. (J. C. 1647). All salaries not exceeding $60 of single persons, or $100 of married persons, and all pensions from official sources are also exempt. (Labor Code 162; Law 132 of 1943 and Law 19 of 1957).

FIDUCIARIES:

See topics Executors and Administrators; Trusts.

FINANCE COMPANIES:

Natural or juridical persons, other than banks, insurance companies, cooperatives, mutual companies and savings and loans associations, engaged in making loans for personal or family purposes. Juridical or natural persons must have minimum paid-in-capital of B/150,000. Interest allowed is fixed by resolution of Ministry of Commerce and Industries between 1.5% and 2% per month depending on fluctuations in London Interbank Offering Rate (Libor). (Law No. 20 of Nov. 1986). Must pay annual tax equal to 2.5% of their paid in capital as of Dec. 31 of each year. Tax not to exceed B/ 12,500. (Law No. 1 of Feb. 1985).

FOREIGN CORPORATIONS: See topic Corporations.

FOREIGN EXCHANGE AND FOREIGN TRADE:

There is no control of foreign exchange. However, as preventive measure to control drug related money-laundering, in fashion similar to U.S. equivalent regulations, banks are required to report each transaction of more than US$10,000, and travellers into Panama are under obligation to report if they carry more than US$10,000 in cash or documents convertible "in cash".

FOREIGN INVESTMENTS:

See topic Investments.

FOREIGN TRADE ZONE:

Government has established a foreign trade zone (free zone) in City of Colon, where foreign goods may be imported, repacked, finished, or otherwise handled and then re-exported. Space will be rented at standard rates.

Operations within foreign trade zone are free of import and export taxes and all other national or provincial taxes with exception of taxable income derived from export operations, at fixed rate of 15%; but three equal advanced payments are to be made according to combined progressive tariff beginning at US$8,500 and up to US$500,000 for income in excess of US$120,000,000. Advanced payment is not to be made during first year of operations by enterprises to be established in Republic of Panama.

Agents handling merchandise within Free Zones shall pay US$8,500 as advanced tax for income earnings from reexportation of such merchandise, but tax shall be paid at fixed rate of 15% at end of fiscal period.

FOUNDATIONS OF PRIVATE INTEREST:

Foundations of private interest are governed by Law 25 of 1995, Resolution 201-847 of 1995 and Executive Decree 417 of 1995.

Incorporation.—One or more natural or legal persons may constitute Private Interest Foundation, personally or through third parties, in accordance with formalities set forth in Law 25. For such purpose it is required to constitute endowment devoted exclusively to purposes expressly contemplated in Foundation Charter. Initial endowment may be increased from time to time by founder of Foundation who shall be known as founder, or by any other person.

Foundation of Private Interest shall be governed by Foundation Charter and its regulations, as well as by provisions of Law 25 and of other legal provisions or regulations applicable thereto. Provisions of Title II of Book I of Civil Code shall not be applicable to these Foundations.

Foundations of Private Interest cannot pursue goals for profit. Nevertheless, Foundations may engage in mercantile activities in non-customary manner or exercise rights accrued from titles representative of capital of mercantile societies which are part of assets of Foundation; provided, however, that results or economic proceeds from said activities be devoted exclusively to purposes of Foundation.

Private Interest Foundation may be constituted to become effective from time of constitution or after death of founder, in any of following manners: (a) By private document subscribed by founder whose signature must be authenticated by Notary Public of place of its constitution. (b) Directly before Notary Public of place of its constitution.

Irrespective of manner used to constitute Foundation, formalities established in Law 25 for constitution of Foundations must be complied with.

In event that Foundation be constituted either by public or private instrument to become effective after death of founder, it shall not be required to comply with formalities prescribed in order to make will.

Foundation Charter.—Act whereby Foundation is constituted must embody following: (1) Name of Foundation set forth in any language of Latin alphabet, which shall not be identical or similar to name of another Foundation already in existence in Republic of Panama, in order that it may not lead to confusion. Name must include word Foundation to distinguish same from other natural or juridical persons of different nature; (2) initial assets of Foundation expressed in any currency of legal tender, which shall in no case be less than sum equivalent to B/10,000; (3) complete and clear designation of member or members of Foundation Council, which might include founder, setting forth their addresses; (4) domicile of Foundation; (5) name and domicile of resident agent of Foundation in Republic of Panama, which must be attorney-at-law or law firm, who must countersign Foundation Charter before it is filed for registration; (6) purposes of Foundation; (7) manner in which beneficiaries of Foundation are appointed, among which founder may be included; (8) reservation of right to amend Foundation Charter, whenever it is deemed advisable; (9) duration of Foundation; (10) use to be made of assets of Foundation, and manner in which same may be liquidated in event of dissolution; (11) any other lawful provisions which founder may deem convenient.

Amendments.—Foundation Charter, and also any amendment thereto, must be written in any language in letters of Latin alphabet and comply with formalities for registration of acts and titles in Public Register, to which end it must be first protocolized before Notary of Republic. If Foundation Charter, or amendments thereto, are not written in Spanish Language, they must be protocolized with translation made by authorized Public Interpreter of Republic of Panama.

Amendments to Foundation Charter, whenever allowed, must be effected and signed in accordance with provisions of Foundation Charter. Corresponding agreement, resolution or amendment thereof must set forth date on which it is issued, clearly identifiable name of person or persons subscribing same, and their signatures which must also be authenticated by Notary of place at which document is signed.

Registration Fees.—Every Foundation of Private Interest must pay registration fees and annual franchise tax equivalent to that established for corporations in Art. 318 and 318A of Fiscal Code.

Procedure and manner of payment, surcharge for arrears, consequences for lack of payment and all other provisions supplementary to legal principles aforementioned, shall be applicable to Foundations of Private Interest.

Juridical Personality.—Registration of Foundation Charter in Public Register will confer juridical personality to Foundation without necessity of any other legal or administrative authorization.

Registration in Public Register also constitutes notice to third parties. Consequently, Foundation may acquire and possess properties of all kinds, undertake obligations and be party in every type of administrative and judicial proceeding in accordance with provisions applicable thereto.

Upon Foundation acquiring juridical personality, founder or third parties who have undertaken obligation to contribute assets to Foundation, personally or at request of any other person with interest in Foundation, must comply with formalities to transfer to Foundation assets undertaken to be transferred.

When Foundation is constituted to become effective after demise of founder, same shall be deemed to have been in existence before demise of founder regarding donations that he or third parties have made to Foundation.

Assets of Foundation shall constitute assets separate from personal assets of founder, for all legal purposes. Therefore, they may not be attached, executed on nor be object of any action or security measure, except for obligations incurred or damages caused as result of fulfillment of purposes or objectives of Foundation, or for lawful rights of beneficiaries of Foundation. In no case shall Foundation be liable for personal obligations of founder or of beneficiaries.

Irrevocability.—Foundations will be irrevocable, except in following cases: (1) When Foundation Charter has not been recorded in Public Register; (2) when contrary is expressly set forth in Foundation Charter; (3) for any of grounds for revocation of donations.

In addition to provisions of foregoing article, transfers which are made to Foundations shall be irrevocable by person who made transfer, except if contrary is expressly provided in transfer thereof. When Foundation has been constituted to take effect after demise of founder, he shall have exclusive and unlimited right to revoke same.

Heirs of founder shall have no right to revoke Foundation, or transfers thereto, even in event that same had not been recorded in Public Register before demise of founder.

Existence of legal provisions in domicile of founder, or of beneficiaries, concerning hereditary matters shall not affect Foundation or its validity or prevent accomplishment of its purposes in manner provided in Foundation Charter or its regulations.

Creditors of founder or third parties have right to challenge contributions or transfers to Foundation when contribution or transfer amounts to fraudulent act against creditors. Rights of and actions by said creditors will be barred after three years from date of contribution or transfer of properites to Foundation.

Assets of Foundation may be derived from any lawful business, and may be constituted by present or future assets of any nature, sums of money or other properties which founder or third parties may also periodically incorporate into its assets. Transfer of properties to assets of Foundation may be effected by public or private document. However, if properties are real estate, such transfer must comply with provisions for transfer of real estate.

Foundation Council.—Foundation must have Foundation Council, powers and obligations of which shall be set forth in Foundation Charter or in its regulations.

Except in case where Council is juridical person, number of its members shall be not less than three.

Obligations of Foundation Council.—Foundation Council will be entrusted with fulfillment of purposes of Foundation. Except as might be otherwise provided in Foundation Charter, or in its regulations, Foundation Council shall have following general rights and duties: (1) To manage assets of Foundation, in accordance with Foundation Charter and its regulations; (2) to perform any acts, contracts and lawful business which might be convenient or necessary in order to fulfill purposes of Foundation; and to include in said contracts, agreements, or other instruments or obligation all of provisions and conditions which are necessary and convenient, which are compatible with purposes of Foundation, and which would not be contrary to law, morals, to good customs, or public order; (3) to inform beneficiaries of Foundation about status of its assets, as might be provided by Foundation Charter or its regulations; (4) to deliver to beneficiaries of Foundation assets or proceeds established in their favor by Foundation Charter or its regulations; (5) to perform all acts or contracts permitted to Foundation, by Law 25 and other legal or regulatory provisions applicable thereto.

Foundation Charter or its regulations may provide that members of Foundation Council may exercise their powers only with prior authorization of protector, committee or of any other supervisory body appointed by founder or majority of founders. Members of Foundation Council shall not be liable for loss of or impairment to assets of Foundation, nor for damages or injuries caused when aforesaid authorization has been duly procured.

See Topical Index in front part of this volume.

FOUNDATIONS OF PRIVATE INTEREST . . . *continued*

Except as otherwise provided in Foundation Charter or in its regulations, Foundation Council must render accounts for its management to beneficiaries; and, in its turn, to supervisory body. If neither Foundation Charter nor its regulations provide otherwise, account must be rendered annually. If no objection is made to account rendered within time required by Foundation Charter or its regulations, or within 90 days from date on which account is rendered, if nothing is provided therein, accounts would be deemed approved, and such time shall be stated in report of accounts rendered. After expiration of such time or upon approval of account, members of Foundation Council shall be released from liability for its management, unless they had not acted as ordinary prudent person. Such approval shall not release them from liability to beneficiaries or third parties interested in Foundation for damages caused by grave fault or fraud in management of Foundation.

Renewal Member of Foundation Council.—Founder may reserve right in Foundation Charter, for himself or for other persons, to remove members of Foundation Council, and also to appoint or add new members.

When nothing is provided in Foundation Charter or its regulations concerning right and/or causes for removal of members of Foundation Council, they may be removed by court in summary proceedings, for following causes: (1) When their interests are not compatible with interests of beneficiaries or of founder; (2) if they do not manage assets of Foundation with due care of ordinary prudent person ("Good Pater Family"); (3) should they be convicted for crime against property or public faith. In latter case indicted member may be suspended temporarily while criminal proceeding is pending; (4) due to incapacity or impossibility to perform purposes of Foundation, from time that such causes arise; (5) due to insolvency, bankruptcy or calling meeting of creditors.

Removal by court of members of Foundation Council may be requested by founder, and beneficiary or beneficiaries. If beneficiaries are incapacitated or under age, they may be represented by person having their custody or guardianship, as it may be the case. Order of court which decrees removal must appoint new members to replace former ones, who must be persons sufficiently capable, qualified, and of known good moral character to manage assets of Foundation in accordance with purposes established by founder.

Supervisory Bodies.—Foundation Charter or its regulations, may provide establishment of supervisory bodies, which might be constituted by natural or juridical persons, such as auditors, protectors of Foundation or other similar persons.

Powers of supervisory bodies shall be set forth in Foundation Charter or its regulations; and may include following, among others: (1) To supervise compliance by Foundation Council with purposes of Foundation, and with rights and interests of beneficiaries; (2) require Foundation Council to render accounts; (3) change purposes and goals of Foundation when it is impossible to achieve same or when their achievement would be highly costly; (4) to appoint new members of Foundation Council due to temporary or permanent absence or to expiration of term for which they were appointed; (5) to appoint new members of Foundation Council to replace original appointees in case of temporary or accidental absence; (6) to increase number of members of Foundation Council; (7) to ratify steps taken by Foundation Council set forth in Foundation Charter or its regulations; (8) to safeguard assets of Foundation and supervise compliance with their application to uses or objectives set forth in Foundation Charter; and (9) to exclude beneficiaries of Foundation and add others in accordance with what is provided in Foundation Charter or its regulations.

Dissolution of Foundation.—Foundation will be dissolved: (1) Upon arrival of day fixed for expiration of Foundation in accordance with Foundation Charter; (2) upon compliance with purposes for which Foundation was constituted or upon compliance thereof becoming impossible; (3) upon becoming insolvent, stopping of payments or upon calling of meeting of creditors by court; (4) due to loss or total extinction of assets of Foundation; (5) by its revocation; and (6) for any other cause set forth in Foundation Charter or in Law 25.

Every beneficiary of Foundation may challenge actions of Foundation which impair rights thereby conferred to them, denouncing such circumstance to protector or other supervisory bodies, if any; or if none, filing directly corresponding judicial claim before competent court in domicile of Foundation.

Exemption of Taxes.—Steps to constitute, amend or terminate Foundation as well as assignment, transfer or encumbrance of assets of Foundation and income from those assets or any other steps concerning same, are exempt from any tax, contribution, tariff tax, encumbrance or assessment of any type or denomination, provided that assets of Foundation consist of: (1) Assets located abroad; (2) money deposited by natural or juridical persons, whose income is not from Panamanian sources or is not taxable in Panama for any reason; (3) shares or securities of any kind, issued by companies whose income is not from Panamanian sources or is for any reason not taxable in Panama, even if such shares or securities are deposited in Republic of Panama.

Transfer of real estate, titles, certificates of deposit, securities, cash, shares made in compliance with purposes or objectives or extinction of Foundation, in favor of kin of founder within first decree of consanguinity, or of his spouse, shall also be exempt from all taxes.

Continuation of Foreign Foundation in Panama.—Foundations constituted in accordance with foreign law may agree to be governed by provisions of Law 25.

Foundations referred to in preceding article which agree to be governed by provisions of Law 25, must file continuation certificate issued by body which would be competent in accordance with its own provisions, and it shall set forth: (1) Name of Foundation and date of its constitution; (2) data of its registration or deposit in its country of origin; (3) express statement of its desire to continue its legal existence as Panamanian Foundation; (4) requirements provided by Art. 5 of Law 25 for constitution of Foundation of Private Interest.

Following documents must be accompanied to certificate containing continuation resolution and other requirements mentioned in preceding article: (1) Copy of original Foundation Charter expressing desire to continue in Panama, with any subsequent amendments thereto; (2) Power of attorney in favor of Panamanian lawyer in order that he take necessary steps to effect continuation of Foundation in Panama. Certificate of Continuation, and also accompanying documents to which Law 25 refers, must be duly protocolized and recorded in Public Register so that Foundation will continue its legal existence as Foundation of Private Interest in Republic of Panama.

In cases set forth in Art. 26 of Law 25, responsibilities, obligations and rights acquired by Foundation prior to change of domicile or legislation shall continue in force, as well as proceedings filed against it or ones filed by Foundation, without those rights and obligations being affected by change authorized by referred legal provisions.

Transfer of Panama Foundation to Jurisdiction of Another Country.—Foundations constituted in accordance with Law 25 and also properties which are part of its assets, may be transferred or be subjected to laws and jurisdiction of another country, as might be provided by Foundation Charter or its regulations.

Registration in Public Register.—Registrations concerning Foundations of Private Interest must be recorded in special section of Public Register known as "Section of Foundations of Private Interest".

To avoid undue use of Foundations of Private Interest, all of legal provisions of Executive Decree No. 468 of 1994 and any other provision in force to combat laundering of money from narco traffic, shall be applicable to its operations.

Secrecy and Confidentiality.—Members of Foundation Council and of supervisory bodies, if any, and also public or private employees who have knowledge of activities, transactions or operations of Foundations, must maintain secrecy and confidentiality at all times concerning same. Violations to such obligation shall be punished with imprisonment for six months and fine of B/.50,000, without prejudice to corresponding civil liability.

Provisions of this article shall be applied without prejudice to information which must be revealed to official authorities, and to inspections which they must conduct in manner established by Law.

Any controversy not subject to special proceeding established by Law 25 shall be resolved by summary proceedings.

Arbitration.—Foundation Charter or its regulations may provide that any controversy which may arise with Foundation shall be resolved by arbiters or arbitrators, and also procedure by which it must be governed. In event that such procedure has not been established, corresponding provisions of judicial code shall be applied.

FRAUDS, STATUTE OF:

Any agreement involving more than $500 must be in writing.

Written documents are classified as public and private documents. Public document is one made by public official in exercise of his duties. When it is made before notary public and forms part of notary's protocol it is called public deed. (C. C. P. 821). Private document is one made between parties without any official record thereof.

Agreements regarding personal property may be made by private document.

The following acts or agreements must be made by public instruments: (1) an act or contract dealing with any interest in real property, except the sale of crops in being or future; (2) leases for six or more years; (3) a marriage settlement; (4) an assignment or repudiation of an inheritance or of community property rights; (5) a power of attorney to contract marriage as proxy, a general power of attorney for litigation to administer property or to represent in an act which must be executed by public instrument or affects third parties; (6) an assignment of shares or right derived from an act executed by a public instrument. (C. C. 1131).

FRAUDULENT SALES AND CONVEYANCES:

In general all acts of commerce done with the intention to defraud creditors, when a person is bankrupt or insolvent, can be set aside on petition of the creditor, provided action is commenced within ten years.

An assignment for the benefit of creditors is regarded as a fraudulent conveyance unless made in accordance with the Civil Code.

A sale of property by a husband to his wife does not affect third person unless recorded in the Public Registry.

GARNISHMENT:

Property of debtor in hands of third person may be reached by order of sequestration or attachment describing it, subject to exceptions provided by law. See topics Exemptions; Attachment; and Sequestration.

HOLIDAYS:

National holidays, in addition to Sundays, are: Jan. 1, Jan. 9, Shrove Tuesday, Good Friday, May 1, Nov. 3, Nov. 10, Nov. 28, Dec. 8, Dec. 25, and day elected president takes office. (C. T. 46). If national holiday falls on Sun., following Mon. will be observed as holiday with pay. If on Sat., there is no effect. (C. T. 47).

See also topic Labor Relations.

HOMESTEADS:

There is no homestead legislation in Panama.

HUSBAND AND WIFE:

The law relating to husband and wife is in C. C. 110-3, 1162-1214 and in F.C. 77-197, 835.

The husband and wife are obliged to live together, be faithful and protect and respect each other. Maintenance must be furnished by husband and wife in proportion to means of each one. Spouses must decide which will be their domicile but in absence of agreement marital domicile will be that of husband or of wife according to circumstances in each particular case.

Married woman may engage in commerce without permit from her husband.

The wife needs no authority from the husband to appear in court. Marriage settlement may be altered any time during the marital relations.

Unless otherwise provided in prenuptial agreement, relationship between husband and wife on economic matters is regulated by Family Code for couples married on or after Jan. 3, 1995 when Family Code came into force. Such relationship between

See Topical Index in front part of this volume.

HUSBAND AND WIFE . . . *continued*
husband and wife married before date on which Family Code became effective is governed by pertinent laws and regulatons that were in force on Jan. 2, 1995.

Separate Property.—Unless otherwise provided in a prenuptial agreement, each spouse holds his or her own property and can dispose of same in the manner he or she wishes. The following property belongs to each spouse upon the dissolution of the marriage: (1) Property brought into the marriage; (2) the property bought with their own separate funds set aside in the marriage settlement; (3) should there be no marriage settlement, property bought for value by one of the spouses, presuming that the acquisition has been made from the private funds of said spouse; (4) property inherited; (5) property acquired before the marriage; (6) the real property which has replaced other property belonging to a spouse according to marriage settlement.

Community Property.—All other property is considered as community property and is distributed equally on dissolution of the marriage. The marriage may also be considered as a partnership if it is so stipulated in the marriage settle-ment. The following is partnership or community property: (1) Property acquired with community funds; (2) property acquired by industry, labor, wages or salary of either spouse; (3) income, rents or interest received from community property; (4) all property not identified as belonging to one of the spouses. (C. C. 1188, 1165).

The following obligations are charged to the partnership property: (1) All debts and obligations contracted during the marriage by either the husband or wife; (2) all interest from obligations affecting community property; (3) minor repairs and small expenses in preserving the property of either party, but major repairs to such property must be borne by the owner; (4) major and minor repairs to the community property; (5) maintenance of the family and the education of children of the marriage, and of the legitimate children of either party. The payment of debts contracted before marriage by either party is not chargeable to the community property.

The husband is the administrator of the community property, in the absence of an agreement to the contrary. He can sell or encumber the community property without the consent of the wife, provided the encumbrance is made in good faith without intention to defraud.

The spouse of an absentee may dispose of any property belonging to him or her, but not of community property or property which belongs to the absentee.

New Family Code was recently approved by legislative, now pending promulgation in Official Gazette by Executive branch. This Code, if promulgated, will affect present statutes.

IMMIGRATION:

Immigration is regulated by Decree-Law No. 16 of June 30, 1960, am'd by Decree-Law No. 13 of Sept. 20, 1965 and Law 6 of Mar. 5, 1980. Resident visas are issued to foreigners married to Panamanian citizens, investors and general managers of foreign companies established in Panama. Temporary visitor's visa is granted to foreign executives, which allows them to reside within Panama on yearly basis.

Prerequisite to visa application for foreign executives is procurement of work permit from Ministry of Labor. Under Art. 17 of Labor Code only 10% of employees may be foreign workers, 15% in case of technicians or specialized employees.

Law 9 of 1987, regulated by Executive Decree No. 62 of 1987, allows retired foreign workers with pension exceeding U.S. $500 per month to apply for residence visa. Panamanian passport is granted to those retired foreigners who deposit in National Bank of Panama amount of money which generates at least US$750 monthly in interest for five years. This visa offers tax advantages to applicants.

INCOME TAX: See topic Taxation.

INDUSTRIAL EXPORT ZONES:

Law No. 25 of Nov. 30, 1992 adopted series of incentives for creation of industrial export zones.

Some of tax incentives for companies, operating industrial export zone, are following: (a) Exemption from import tax and from tax on transfer of chattels applicable to introduction of machinery, equipment, spare parts and other material necessary for construction and maintenance of export zone. (b) Exemption from real estate tax applicable to land and buildings of export zone. (c) Exemption from income tax applicable to operation of zone during first ten years of operation. Among labor law incentives for companies operating industrial export zone are following: (a) Company may agree to work contract for definitive period of time of up to three years. (b) Company is under no obligation to have collective bargaining agreement during its first four years of operation. (c) Any fluctuation in export market which results in considerable loss of clients on markets will be deemed just cause of economic nature which will allow company to terminate labor relationship, provided prior approval is obtained from Labor Ministry. Executive Decree No. 1-D of Jan. 28, 1994 regulates various aspects of Law 25, 1992.

INFANCY:

Age of majority is 18; minors may be emancipated, but only by marriage. (Law 107 of 1973). Contracts by males under 14 and females under 12 are void and over those ages, if not emancipated, voidable. Voidable contracts may be expressly or tacitly ratified by minors within four years after age of majority. In absence of parents, guardian is appointed having legal representation of minor.

See also topic Adoption.

See topic Husband and Wife.

INHERITANCE TAX: See topic Taxation.

INSOLVENCY:

When a person, not a merchant, is unable to pay his obligations and his liabilities are greater than his assets, he may appear to the judicial tribunal to be declared insolvent. For further discussion see topic Bankruptcy.

INSURANCE:

Regulated by Law 55 of 1984. National and qualified foreign (see topic Corporations, subhead Foreign Corporations) insurance companies must have a minimum paid-in capital, maintain a guaranty deposit, be authorized by and operate under supervision of Insurance Commissioner. Insurance brokers' licenses are issued by Commissioner. Must pay annual tax, on basis of total assets as of Dec. 31, as follows: assets of B/10,000,000 or more, B/25,000; assets between B/5,000,000 and B/9,999,999, B/20,000; assets less than B/5,000,000, B/10,000. (Law No. 1 of Feb. 1985).

Law 72 of 1976 am'd by Law 28 of 1977 regulates reinsurance operations. Reinsurance companies must have minimum paid-in or allocated capital, as case may be, of not less than $250,000. Licenses are granted by National Commission of Reinsurance which supervises activities of companies through Insurance Commissioner.

INTEREST:

Legal rate is 6% per annum. In civil matters, maximum allowed is 9%; in mercantile transactions, maximum is 7%, but there are many exceptions. No maximum now set for loans by banks operating locally.

Acceptance of principal without reservation as to interest extinguishes obligation to pay interest.

Person charging monthly interest above that established by National Banking Commission (2% per month) is subject to penal punishment.

INTESTACY: See topic Descent and Distribution.

INVESTMENTS:

Under certain conditions government will grant exemption from many taxes to industries apt to develop natural resources of country and to those dedicated to assembling of finished products. Additional incentives are granted to industries that export all or part of their production. Such grants are made to corporations and resident foreigners on same basis as to nationals. (Law No. 28 of June 20, 1995).

Country has adopted relatively new law approved in 1994-1995 granting fiscal incentives to all sorts of tourist activities within Republic of Panama.

Important incentives are also granted for investments in agricultural sector, including cattle, most farming investments and for agricultural exports. (Law No. 2 of Mar. 20, 1986).

Incentives are granted for industries dedicated to the assemblage of raw materials and semi-finished goods into finished products. (Decree No. 5 of Jan. 19, 1979).

Ministry of Commerce and Industries is responsible for promoting national and foreign private investment in Republic of Panama. (Decree 13 of 1988).

Special regime has been established for creation and operation of Export Processing Zones. (Law 25 of 1992). Special labor relationship regime is established by virtue of Law Decree No. 1 of Jan. 11, 1996 and Law Decree No. 2 of Feb. 26, 1996.

Special regime has been created for operation of Oil Import Zones. (Decree No. 29 of July 19, 1992). In connection with this activity following regulations have been adopted: Cabinet Decree No. 38, 1992; Cabinet Decree No. 4, 1993; Cabinet Decree No. 14, 1993 and Decree No. 26, 1993.

Tourism.—Special incentive has been created by Law No. 8 of June 14, 1994, whereby tourist activities are promoted in Republic of Panama. This law has been regulated by Cabinet Decree No. 73 of June 14, 1994 which detailed incentive for investment in these activities.

JOINT STOCK COMPANIES:

Such companies, as understood in the United States, do not exist in Panama.

JUDGMENTS:

Judgments do not constitute a lien on property of judgment debtor as against third persons, except as to real property, when they have been recorded in Public Registry.

Foreign judgments have the force provided by treaty, or, in the absence of treaty provisions, the force that is given to Panama court judgments in the foreign country. If the courts of a foreign country refuse to carry on a Panama judgment, the judgments of that country have no force in Panama. If the foregoing rules cannot be applied, the foreign judgment will be enforced in Panama, if: (1) It was rendered on personal action, except as the law provides with respect to descent and distribution (see topic Descent and Distribution); (2) defendant was personally served in place where action was filed; (3) it was rendered on an obligation valid in Panama; and (4) it has been properly authenticated. (C. C. P. 1409-1411).

Law No. 8 of Mar. 30, 1982 which created maritime jurisdiction establishes that final judgments, arbitration awards, interlocutory judgments and orders decreeing protective measures rendered in foreign countries shall have in Panama force granted by international treaties and in absence thereof, they shall have same force granted therein to rulings rendered in Republic of Panama. If ruling has been rendered in country wherein by its jurisprudence Panamanian rulings cannot be enforced, it shall have no force in Panama.

LABOR RELATIONS:

Relations of employers and employees are regulated by a Labor Code adopted by Cabinet Decree 252 of 1971, which became effective Apr. 2, 1972. Code is divided in two parts: First contains substantive law—very detailed set of rules; and second sets up separate system of labor courts and procedure law.

When a national holiday falls on Sunday, the following Monday will be observed as a holiday with pay. If on Sat., there is no effect. (C. T. 47).

See topic Courts, subhead Labor Courts.

Minimum wage is provided by law. Amount varies according to nature of services and locality where performed. It is fixed periodically by Executive Decree (see Executive Decree No. 91 of Nov. 4, 1995). Special salary regime for seafarers and crew members to Panamanian Cruise Ships has been adopted by Executive Decree No. 4 of Feb. 25, 1994.

See Topical Index in front part of this volume.

LABOR RELATIONS . . . *continued*

Social Security.—Caja de Seguro Social (Social Security Fund) is an autonomous Government Agency which provides sickness, maternity, disability, workmen's compensation, old age benefits, widow's and orphan's pensions and funeral assistance. Social Security coverage is obligatory in certain districts and categories of workers: voluntary insurance with agency is also possible. Employer contributes 10.75% and employee, 7.25% levied on his wages. Cost of workmen's compensation is separate and borne entirely by employer.

See topic Taxation, subhead Education Tax.

LAW REPORTS, CODES, ETC.:

See topics Reports and Statutes.

LEGISLATURE:

See topic Constitution and Government.

LICENSES:

Licenses are required to carry on any industry and most trades. Retail trade can only be carried on by citizens of Panama and in limited cases by foreigners. (Const. art. 288). Sale of agricultural products, including cattle by breeder, does not require license.

There is no general requirement of special license for imports. However, license is required to import fire arms, explosives and drugs containing opium or cocaine. Then there is flat prohibition on other goods as instruments of war, counterfeit money, opium, pornographic literature and pictures. Plants and seeds may only be imported when specifically permitted.

See topic Taxation, subhead License Tax.

LIENS:

Mechanics' liens do not exist in Panama. Maritime liens or privileged credits affecting maritime property are established by C. Com. 1502-1511.

LIMITATION OF ACTIONS:

Periods after which some of more important rights of action are barred by running of Statute of Limitations are following: Actions relating to real property, 15 years; actions relating to personal property, six years; actions for alimony or rent, five years (Law 17 of 1961); tort actions, one year. Period with respect to commercial actions is generally five years, but some such actions are barred in one year. (C. C. 1668-1713; C. Com. 1649-53).

LIMITED LIABILITY COMPANIES:

See topic Partnership.

LIMITED PARTNERSHIP: See topic Partnership.

MARRIAGE:

The law relating to marriage is in F.C. 25.80.

A license is required for the performance of a religious marriage.

Prohibited Marriages.—The following conditions are a bar to marriage: (1) fact that male is under 16 or female is under 14 years of age, but marriage will be validated if they live together day after date of attaining majority, without filing complaint for annulment or if female conceives; (2) existing previous marriage. Marriages cannot take place between following: (i) Persons of same sex; (ii) relatives by consanguinity or adoption in direct descending or ascending line, and in collateral line up to second degree; (iii) relatives by affinity in direct descending or ascending line; (iv) person convicted as author or accomplice of murder or attempted murder against one of spouses, with surviving spouse. While proceedings are pending, marriage cannot take place. Marriage is prohibited to: (1) Minors, unless proper consent is given by parent or guardian; (2) women whose marriages have been dissolved, during period of 300 days after date of dissolution as determined by court, except if woman proves, with scientific test, that she is not pregnant; (iv) father or mother having children under paternal dominion without making judicial inventory of property of said children; (v) guardians and their descendants, with their wards, until accounts of guardianship are approved.

Annulment.—Marriages made in violation of any of the above-mentioned conditions and prohibitions can be annulled.

Foreign Marriages.—A marriage in a foreign country, which is valid according to the laws of such country or of Panama is valid in Panama.

MECHANICS' LIENS: See topic Liens.

MINES AND MINERALS:

(Decree-Law 23 of 1963 as am'd by Law 3 of 1988):

Mines and mineral concessions are governed by the Mining Code. The State is considered owner of all mines, but private persons may obtain right to work them. Precious stones and metals on the surface in open lands belong to first possessor. All persons except foreign states, certain governmental officials and incapacitated persons, may obtain mining concessions. Mines can be encumbered and transmitted like other real property, subject to the provisions of the Mining Code. Mining concessions expire by abandonment and failure to pay the taxes, but the right of the person is not terminated until it be so declared by competent authority.

Taxes, Royalties and Rentals.—The Mining Code provides for the payment of a surface tax, surface rentals and royalties. Surface tax and surface rentals are paid annually and in advance according to a tariff based on the class of minerals and the number of years of the concessions. The royalties are paid quarterly on a percentage basis according to the class of minerals.

MONOPOLIES AND RESTRAINT OF TRADE:

Provisions were adopted by Law 29 of Feb. 1st, 1996, against monopolies and restraint of trade.

Such provisions are not applicable to economic activities which Constitution and laws reserve exclusively to State; but are applicable to institutions and departments of State and to municipalities which are bound with compliance thereof insofar as economic activities reserved to State are not involved.

Underlying principles of law place specific emphasis in paramount protection of interests of consumer, by prohibiting activities which impair, restrict, diminish, prevent and otherwise infringe free competition and freedom to participate in production, processing, distributing, supplying, and trading in goods and services.

Law establishes what activities are deemed to constitute monopolistic practices, unfair trade competition, duties of State to take necessary measures to insure that goods sold and services rendered comply with requirements of quality, health and security; to offer programs of education, orientation, and information to consumer; to guarantee access to effective and expeditious administrative and judicial procedures; to enforce provisions of law; to promote and implement organization of consumer associations; to guarantee consumer with compliance of universally accepted rights of consumer.

Law creates Commission of Free Competition and Affairs of the Consumer, and provides for inquiries which could be made before it to determine whether act, contract, or practice constitutes monopolistic practice.

Law also establishes administrative and judicial procedure to insure compliance with law, provides for class actions and creates special court with jurisdiction in cases involving monopolistic and restraint of trade practices.

MORTGAGES OF PERSONAL PROPERTY:

See topic Chattel Mortgages.

MORTGAGES OF REAL PROPERTY:

Mortgages must be executed before a notary public in form of public instrument and recorded in Public Registry. Their date and effect are counted only from date of recording same. Mortgages made in a foreign country on property in Panama are valid if recorded in Public Registry. Each party to mortgage must appear in person before notary public. Instrument must describe property in detail.

The unrestricted right to mortgage property extends only to real property and real property rights. The following property, with restrictions may be mortgaged: (1) A building on the soil of another, if done without prejudice to the owner of the land; (2) the right to receive usufruct if the mortgage is cancelled when the thing, cause of the usufruct, terminates without will of the owner, but upon an involuntary event; (3) property already mortgaged if the mortgage is subject to prior mortgagors' rights; (4) railroads, tramways, channels, electric plants or any public utility if they are attached to land; (5) property belonging to wards if done according to the law; (6) property in litigation if the complaint has been previously recorded. The following property cannot be mortgaged: (1) Future rents and crops, if separated from the land producing the same; (2) personal property placed in buildings if not mortgaged with the building; (3) national and municipal obligations or obligations or shares of banks or companies of any nature; (4) real rights, to be acquired in the future, if they are not properly inscribed; (5) servitudes or easements if not mortgaged with dominant property; (6) use of dwelling; (7) mines without final title of concession, in spite of the fact that they are in own land. (C. C. 1566-1621).

Mortgage of vessels is governed by Code of Commerce, arts. 1512-1526.

MOTOR VEHICLES:

There is a national license tax collected by the municipalities. Rules and regulations for the operation of vehicles are issued by the President through the Ministry of Government.

Tourist automobiles are exempt from license requirements for a period not exceeding 90 days from date of arrival but vehicle must be registered with customs office.

NEGOTIABLE INSTRUMENTS:

See topic Bills and Notes.

NOTARIES PUBLIC:

(C. C. 1714-52). Notaries are public officials whose duties are much more important than those of notaries under the American laws. They must be attorneys. (Law 53 of 1961). They are appointed by the President for determined circuits.

Instruments executed before a notary public must be prepared with certain formalities and drawn in the Spanish language. The notary must set forth the Christian name and the surname, legal age, civil status, profession or occupation, and domicile of each party. He must certify that he knows the parties and witnesses and that they have legal capacity. It must appear that he has read the instrument to the parties and explained its legal force and effect. If the parties do not know Spanish they must appoint an interpreter ad-hoc to translate and sign with them. All public instruments executed before a notary public must have at least two witnesses. Parties to a notarial instrument receive formal certified copies which have the effect of originals and may be presented in court.

Consuls abroad are notaries and must keep a protocol as well as notaries in Panama.

PARTNERSHIP:

(C. Com. 249-358). Partnerships are considered as legal entities. Before doing business partnership agreement must be drawn up in public instrument, executed before a notary public, and recorded in Mercantile Registry. Fee for recording partnership articles is same as for recording articles of incorporation. (See topic Corporations, subhead Incorporation).

Unlimited partnerships (sociedades colectivas) are straight partnerships in which all partners have unlimited and joint liability. Such a firm must act under a firm name which must include the names of all the partners or of one or more, followed by the

PARTNERSHIP . . . *continued*

words "y Compañía," commonly abbreviated "& Cía." The name of a person not a partner cannot be used.

The partnership agreement must express the following: (1) Name and domicile of the parties; (2) partnership name; (3) object, duration of the company and the manner to compute the period of same; (4) amount of capital, explaining the share brought in by each partner, and if partially or totally paid, and the manner in which any unpaid balance is to be paid; (5) names of the partners who will manage the firm and use of the firm name; (6) statement of the contributions to the firm, whether in work, money, credits, or any other value with the valuation given to same; (7) percentage left for the reserve fund; (8) dates for inventories and distribution of profits; (9) the causes for the dissolution of the firm; (10) basis for the liquidation of firm and the manner for the selection of liquidators; (11) the form in which the publication of the firm will be made; (12) any other lawful agreement.

Limited Partnership.—The parties may provide in the articles of partnership that their liability is limited to amount of their contribution. (C. Com. 327).

Special Partnership.—"Sociedades en comandita" are partnerships in which one or more of the partners are subject to an unlimited and joint liability for the partnership obligations and one or more of the partners are not responsible for debts and losses except up to the amount of the capital they have subscribed.

The name of the firm must contain the name of at least one of the members of the firm, and immediately thereafter the indication that it is a limited partnership, the expressions commonly used being "S. en C.", "Limitada," or "Ltd." The names of special partners must not appear in the firm name, but only the names of the partners of unlimited liability.

The appointment of a manager is made by the majority vote of all the partners.

Foreign partnerships may do business within Panama if they record articles of copartnership in Mercantile Registry.

Limited Liability Company (Sociedad de Responsabilidad Limitada).—(Law 24 of 1966). This company has some of characteristics of a corporation and some of a partnership. Name of company must be followed by initials "S. de R. L." or its abbreviated for "Sdad. Ltda." Company may not have more than 20 members who are liable only to amount of their participation. Capital may not be less than B/2,000 nor more than B/500,000 and participations must be in amounts of B/100 or multiples thereof. Members are entitled to one or more votes according to amount of their participation. Resolutions are adopted by majority vote. Participations are not represented by negotiable certificates; may be assigned, but subject to preferential rights of other members. On death of member, his place is taken by his heirs, unless company agreement provides otherwise.

Individual Enterprise of Limited Liability.—When limited liability company is reduced to one member, it must be dissolved or converted into individual enterprise of limited liability. To form one of these enterprises, minimum capital of B/1,000 is required and inventory of all assets to be owned by enterprise. (Law 24 of 1966).

PATENTS:

Law No. 35 of May 10, 1996 in effect since Nov. 15, 1996 provides as follows:

Revalidation or confirmation patents have been eliminated. In order to be patentable, invention must be new, result of creative activity and susceptible of industrial use. Utility models must meet only novelty requirement and be susceptible to industrial use. Industrial designs need only to be new. Patents of products and processes are recognized, as well as patents for special use of product or of a not evident use thereof. Following, among others, are not deemed inventions: theoretical or scientific principles; discoveries, designs, projects, sketches, economic or business principles or methods; games; software programs per se; data presentation formats, and methods for surgical, therapeutical or diagnostic treatment. Following, among others, are excepted from patentability: vegetable species and animal species and breeds; biological material as it is found in nature; living matter of human body; vegetable varieties and essentially biological cases for obtainment or reproduction of plants, animals or varieties thereof, if they offend morality, integrity or dignity of human beings. Patents of invention shall have duration of 20 years from date application is filed. Registration of utility models shall have duration of ten years, not renewable, running from date application is filed. Registration of industrial designs shall have duration of ten years, running from date of deposit, renewable for five additional years. Industrial designs enjoy automatic protection for two years from first disclosure in Panama, without necessity of registration.

Documents required in order that number and date of deposit be assigned to patent application are: (a) Application setting forth name and address of petitioner, name of inventor and name of invention; (b) description of invention; (c) claims; (d) drawings (if applicable); (e) summary and (f) payment of tax and filing fees. Power of Attorney may be filed at later date. Priority may be claimed when Paris Convention, already ratified by Republic of Panama, enters into effect. Fourteen months after deposit, petitioner must request Industrial Property Office to render report on state-of-art, for which purpose it may submit reports prepared by national or international organisms. Eighteen months after deposit, and of examination as to form, patent application shall be published in Official Bulletin. After report of state of art is rendered, patent application is published, and any person may file objections, within period of two months. Industrial Property Office shall grant patent applied for, independently of contents of report of state of art and objections filed by third parties. Law does not contemplate for figure of compulsory licenses. Licenses are voluntary, and must be recorded, in order to be effective against third parties.

Law No. 41 of July 13, 1995 approved Paris Convention for the Protection of Industrial Property.

See topics Copyright; Trademarks and Tradenames.

PERPETUITIES: See topic Trusts.

PLEDGES:

Requirements for a valid pledge contract are: (1) That pledge is given to secure an obligation; (2) that thing pledged belongs to person pledging it; (3) that person pledging is capable of disposing of his property; (4) that pledged object be delivered to creditor or to a depository, but when pledge is of cattle, or of agricultural implements, owner of same may keep it subject to conditions of contract. In order to give notice to third persons such contract must be recorded in Mercantile Registry. All movable property can be pledged. Document of pledge must be acknowledged before Notary Public to be effective against third parties. When obligation is not canceled holder of pledge will apply to judge for sale of same. All baggage and articles brought into hotels by guests are considered as pledges of security for charges of innkeeper.

When livestock is pledged, pledgor may retain possession, but document must be recorded in Public Registry.

PRESCRIPTION: See topic Limitation of Actions.

PRINCIPAL AND AGENT:

(C. C. 1400-30; and C. Com. 580-634). An agent is required to adhere to the instructions of the principal and, if there are none, to proceed in the most prudent manner. He must account for everything he receives for the principal. He may delegate his powers, if not expressly prohibited from doing so, but is liable for the acts of substitution if there was no authority of delegation, or if his appointee is notoriously incompetent. In the absence of stipulation otherwise the principal must pay the agent a commission for all business done through him. In case of sale the commission will be on the amount of the sale. The agent cannot collect money or extend time of payment if not authorized to do so. When the commission is not stipulated it will be considered the usual commission paid in the place where the transaction took place. The agent is not entitled to reimbursement for expenses for his transportation unless there is an agreement to that effect. The principal must indemnify the agent for any damages caused from his negligence. The agent has the right to demand from his principal a copy of extract of the books regarding the transactions done through him.

The agency is generally conferred by power of attorney, which can be general or special. Power of attorney is drawn according to certain formalities of the law. Power of attorney made according to the formalities of the laws of a foreign country is valid in Panama, if authenticated by the Panama diplomatic or consular representatives or by means of Apostille of the 1961 The Hague Convention.

Persons presuming to act for others without authority are personally liable to the person to whom they misrepresent. If the person presumed represented ratifies or takes advantage of what has been done, the relation of principal and agent is established.

Power of attorney is terminated: (1) By revocation; (2) by resignation of agent; (3) by death, loss of civil rights, insolvency or bankruptcy of principal or agent.

According to legal opinion, a power of attorney coupled with an interest may not be revoked by principal and probably would not be revoked by his death. In commercial matters, death of principal does not terminate agency if failure of agent to act would jeopardize interests of principal; nor is the power automatically revoked by death of principal in case of a manager of a commercial or industrial establishment.

Power of attorney in civil matters, unless stipulated to contrary, is gratis; in commercial matters, remuneration to the agent is presumed.

REAL PROPERTY:

(C. C. 324-44). Practically the same distinction exists between real and personal property as in the United States. The things considered as real property are the following: (1) Land, buildings, roads and all sorts of constructions attached to the soil; (2) plants, trees and pending fruits while attached to the land; (3) everything permanently attached to the real property so that it cannot be separated without breaking or deterioration; (4) statues, paintings or other objects of use or ornament placed in such manner as to reveal the intention to make them a permanent part of the realty; (5) machinery, containers, instruments and tools required by the owner of the property for the industry or manufacture carried on therein; (6) beehives, dovecotes, fishponds and similar objects if attached to the property in a permanent manner; (7) fertilizer on land where it is to be used; (8) mines and quarries while the materials remain attached to the deposit; (9) dikes and floating constructions destined by reason of their object to remain at a fixed point of a body of water; (10) administrative concessions for public works, easements and other real rights on immovable property.

The owner of real property owns the surface and subsoil and whatever exists thereunder subject to easements and to the provisions of the mining laws, the law of waters and the police regulations.

Condominiums are permitted by Law #13 of Apr. 28, 1993, which superseded all prior provisions on Horizontal Property.

RECORDS:

The law regarding the recording of property and certain acts is contained in articles C. C. 1753-1802, and the recording and office for such purpose is regulated by following laws and decrees: Decrees No. 9 of 1920 and No. 117 of 1925; Decree-Law 41 of 1966; Executive Decree No. 47 of 1966; Law 47 of 1975; Laws No. 44 of 1976 and 50 of 1977; Decree No. 93 of 1976; Law No. 3 of 1979; Decrees 28 and 29 of 1979; Decree No. 8 of 1980; Law 14 of 1980; Decree 62 of 1980; Decree 203 of 1982. Office is called Public Registry and is subdivided into: (1) Registry of Property; (2) Registry of Mortgages; (3) Registry of Persons; (4) Microfilm Section (Mercantile) Registry; (5) special section for recording contracts regarding sale of pending fruits and personal property; (6) mining claims. Property Registry is for inscription of real property and any modification upon it. Mortgage Registry is for recording of mortgages on real property. Registry of Persons is subdivided into Civil and Mercantile; Civil Division is to record powers of attorney and sentences of courts, and Mercantile, articles of incorporation of companies, partnership deeds, etc. Mercantile Registry is to inscribe all acts of commerce that, according to law, must be recorded. All transactions that require inscription must be recorded to give notice to third persons and perfect title.

C. Com. 55 indicates all the documents or acts of commerce that must be inscribed.

The Registrar General is an officer of the court in the rank of Supreme Court Judge. He must furnish bond to cover damages for his negligence or incompetency.

On receiving a document it is examined to ascertain if it is in legal form. If mistakes are found, a period of time is allowed to correct them and in some cases registration

RECORDS . . . *continued*

may be refused at once. From the Registrar General's decision appeal is taken to the Supreme Court of Panama.

Vital Statistics.—Besides the Public Registry, there exists the Civil Registry for the inscription of marriages, births, deaths, etc. This is a separate and independent office, and the registrar is a semi-judicial official.

REPLEVIN:

Replevin (reivindicacion) is an action by the owner of a single thing, of which he is not in possession, against the actual possessor to surrender it to him. This action cannot be maintained against a third possessor who has recorded his property. Almost all real and personal property can be repossessed by replevin. The action must be brought by the owner, and against any possessor, with certain exceptions. (C. C. 582-96; C. C. P. 1574).

REPORTS:

The only court report officially published is the "Registro Judicial," which relates all the business done in the Supreme Court of Panama and the Superior Tribunals. The reports began in 1904.

Unofficial mimeograph copies of judgments and orders of Supreme Court were published monthly, until Apr. 1969. (Repertorio Jurídico).

RESTRAINT OF TRADE:

See topic Monopolies and Restraint of Trade.

SALES:

A sale of real or personal property is perfected and binding when the vendor and vendee have agreed upon the thing sold and the price thereof, though neither thing has been delivered; except that a sale of real property and rights and of an inheritance is not perfected until a public instrument is executed, but this exception does not apply to a sale of trees or pending fruits. In general the legal rules and principle of the Uniform Sales Act of the United States apply to law of sales in Panama. (C. C. 1215-88).

The expenses of the sale, unless otherwise agreed, are divided equally between vendor and purchaser. Sales of real property must be recorded immediately. In the sale of real property full description of same is required. See topic Deeds.

Conditional sales of personal property are permitted, provided the property can be clearly identified and the contract is recorded in the Public Registry Office. (Decree-Law 2 of 1955).

Notices Required.—There is no general provision in sale of goods with respect to notices, except that when goods have been delivered in container, purchaser may have three days within which to refuse acceptance because of damage or quality inferior to contract. Purchaser, on receipt, must assert condition that he is entitled to examination.

Warranties.—Vendor guarantees to vendee legal and peaceful possession of thing sold and that it has no hidden defects that will make it improper for its destined use, but vendor will not be responsible for obvious or visible defects if vendee could have easily noticed them by reason of his occupation or profession.

Applicable Law.—There is no provision as to law applicable; but it is assumed that local courts will apply law of Panama if contract, although made in foreign country, contemplates delivery in Panama.

SEALS:

Seals are used by the government departments but not by private persons. Public instruments executed before notaries, take the place of sealed instruments. Nevertheless juridical persons (corporations, churches, etc.) are using the seal, but it has not the effect that it has in the United States, but it is acquiring the effect of raising a presumption of being executed by the party stamping the seal.

SECURITIES:

Cabinet Decree No. 247 of 1970 created National Securities Commission and regulates sale to public of shares of corporations, other corporate securities, and sale of shares, bonds, or other evidences of indebtedness by mutual funds or evidences of ownership in such funds. Brokers and salesmen dealing in securities require a license issued by Commission. Decree No. 44 of 1988 authorizes creation of Stock Exchanges and regulates their installation and functioning. See also topic Corporations, subhead Mutual Fund Companies.

SEQUESTRATION:

This is a proceeding used before commencing or during any state of the suit against property of the defendant to ensure that such property of the defendant may not be put out of the reach of the plaintiff and that the plaintiff may be able to have something to secure satisfaction of a judgment in his favor. To obtain a decree of sequestration it is necessary that a bond be filed to answer for damages in case that the suit may not be successful. Any property, real or personal, owned by the defendant, whether in his possession or in the possession of some one else, can be sequestrated. The sequestration is almost like attachment and garnishment. (C. C. 375-98).

See also topic Courts, subhead Maritime Courts.

SHIPPING:

Principal features of maritime law and shipping regulations are covered by C. Com. 1077-1553, which lay down rules as to ownership and transfer of vessels, priority of liens thereon, rights and obligations of officers and crew, maritime contracts, bills of lading, marine insurance, average collision and shipwrecks. Limitation of liability of shipowners is governed by Law No. 8 of Mar. 30, 1982, Arts. 560-585, patterned after London Convention, 1976, on Limitation of Liabilities of Maritime Claims. Rights and obligations of officers and crew are also established in L.C. Arts. 251-278. For rules and regulations regarding registration of vessels see Panama Flag Laws No. 8 of 1925 and No. 54 of 1926. Executive Decree No. 106 of 1947, Decree No. 40 of 1954, Cabinet Decrees Nos. 45 and 331 of 1969, Law No. 11 of 1973, Decree No. 95 of 1974, Laws Nos. 5, 47 and 49 of 1975, Laws 39, 40, 50, 63 and 64 of 1976, Laws 55 and 56 of 1979, Laws 2 and 14 of 1980, Law 4 of 1983, Law 43 of 1984, Decree Law No. 17 of 1989.

Maritime laws of Panama are framed on old European laws, but are very favorable to steamship companies. No fixed schedule of wages or food is provided; Lloyd's and other ship surveyor certificate, including official annual inspection certificate, is accepted by Government. Annual tax is 10¢ per net registered ton. In addition there are following annual payments that must be made and which vary depending on size and type of vessel: Consular fees; inspection fees; fees to determine liability arising out of maritime chose in action and for participation of Government in international conferences and treaties. Vessels of foreign registry, chartered for period no longer than two years (renewable), may acquire Panamanian Registry without waiving such foreign registry provided country of registry allows it.

Likewise, vessels of Panamanian Registry chartered for period no longer than two years (renewable), may be registered in a foreign country without waiving Panamanian Registry, provided that such foreign country has a procedure similar to above.

Ship's mortgages are recognized as liens on the vessels. Registration fee is 10¢ per net registered ton of vessel with maximum limit of US$500. (C. Com. 1512 and C. F. 315). Law 14 of 1980 as am'd by Law 43 of 1984 provides for preliminary registration of ships' mortgages in Mercantile Registry. Decree No. 203 of 1982 provides for 24 hour service for preliminary filing of title deeds and mortgages to Panamanian registered vessels.

According to labor Code (Cabinet Decree 252 of 1971), 10% of crew must be Panamanians or foreigners resident in Panama married to Panamanian women or having Panamanian children. Clearance will not be given to vessels by local authorities or Panamanian consuls without justification for having less than such a percentage. Provisions of Labor Code are generally applicable to seamen.

Under Labor Code 263, articles of shipping must be signed in official forms prepared by Government and are governed by laws of Panama. However, in practice Government has permitted execution of shipping articles in accordance with prevailing nationality of seamen aboard a ship; and these articles are then attached to official forms issued by Government of Panama.

By means of Resolution No. 614-22-ALCN of Feb. 21, 1981, issued by Directorate General of Consular and Maritime Affairs, which came into effect on July 15, 1981, Republic of Panama adopted rules establishing requirements and procedures for issuance of certificates of competency to be granted to following officers serving Panamanian flag vessels: Master, chief engineer and deck and engine watchstanding officers and radio operator.

Under Resolution No. 614-308-ALCN of Dec. 31, 1982, issued by Directorate General of Consular and Maritime Affairs, which came into effect on June 1, 1983, there were adopted minimum manning requirements for Panamanian vessels.

Every Foreign Service vessel, at time of registering into Panamanian Merchant Marine must pay enrollment fee according to following rate: Vessels up to 2,000 GRT, US$500. Vessels from 2,000 up to 5,000 GRT, US$2,000. Vessels of 5,000 up to 15,000 GRT and more, US$3,000 plus US$0.10 for each Gross Registered Ton or fraction thereof in excess of 15,000 GRT up to maximum of US$6,500 in total.

Title deeds to vessels must be recorded in Mercantile Registry. Notarial translation and incidental expenses amount to approximately US$150. Law 12 of 1980 provides for preliminary registration in Mercantile Registry of title deeds to vessels.

Law 2 of 1980 provides the following: (a) Creates Directorate General of Consular and Shipping Department within Ministry of Finance and Treasury to oversee all aspects of Merchant Marine; (b) establishes two types of navigation patents, one provisional good for six months and regulation patent valid for two years in case of private recreation, sports or pleasure yachts and for four years in case of merchant vessels; (c) private recreation, sports or pleasure yachts in order to become registered, shall pay sole tax of US$1,500 every two years; (d) regulates requirements and procedures for deletion of vessels from Panamanian Registry; (e) US$1,000 if ownership is held by Panamanian Corporation or National.

Special fleet rebate tariff is established by Law No. 36 of July 6, 1995.

Regarding measurements and tonnage Panama has ratified International Convention on Tonnage Measurement of Ships, 1969.

National Port Authority created by Law 42 of 1974 as agency of government of Panama administers ports and traffic in jurisdictional waters.

STATUTE OF FRAUDS:

See topic Frauds, Statute of.

STATUTES:

Most of the legal provisions are codified. The important codes are Civil Code, Code of Commerce, Code of Procedure (or Judicial Code), Penal Code, Administrative Code, Mining Code, Fiscal Code, Sanitary or Health Code, Agrarian Reform Code, Aviation Code, Labor Code, Family Code, and Electoral Code. Family Code, which entered into force on Aug. 1, 1994 was enacted by Law No. 3 of May 17, 1994, am'd by Law No. 12 of July 25, 1994, superseded all prior legal provisions relating to family and minors, created Family and Minor's Lower and Appellate Courts, and prescribed rules of procedure by which they will be governed.

Governs the rights and obligations of spouses, equal rights of offsprings, and protection of minors. Family ties arise by consanguinity, affinity or adoption.

STAY OF EXECUTION: See topic Executions.

TAXATION:

The tax laws are found in the Fiscal Code of 1961 and amendments thereof.

Real Estate.—Scale (tariff) of taxes on real property is as follows: (a) 1.40% on any amount exceeding US$10,000 on assessed value of property to be taxed and up to US$20,000; (b) 1.75% on assessed value in excess of US$20,000 up to US$50,000; (c) 1.95% on assessed value in excess of US$50,000 up to US$75,000; (d) 2.10% on assessed value over and above US$75,000. (Art. 766 of Fiscal Code).

For purpose of taxation, rural real estate is valued at minimum of US$30 per hectare. (Law 63 of 1961).

See Topical Index in front part of this volume.

TAXATION . . . *continued*

Income tax is imposed on income from any source within Republic of Panama. Income tax is paid on progressive percentage scale up to maximum of 30% on any income of natural persons in excess of $200,000. No tax is paid on income of natural person which does not exceed $3,000. General deduction of $800 is allowed to each person; and of $1,600 on joint tax return of husband and wife.

There is flat income tax rate for corporations of 30% of net taxable income.

Dividends distributed by corporations deriving income from activities within Republic of Panama pay 10% tax which is withheld at source. Branches of foreign juridical persons must withhold 10% on their local taxable income, after deducting therefrom income tax payable in Panama. When shares are issued to bearer, then 20% tax is applied and also withheld source.

Following incomes are not considered as from sources in Panama and, hence, not subject to the tax: (a) income derived by a Panama office from invoicing at a higher price merchandise moving exclusively between foreign ports; (b) income of the Panama office from managing foreign operations; (c) dividends paid out of income not produced within the territory of Panama.

Exemptions.—Certain kinds of income are not subject to tax, more important being interest on Government bonds, on savings accounts and time deposits with banks operating within and outside Republic.

Capital Gain Tax.—There is no Capital Gain Tax as such; but profits obtained in sale of bonds, stocks, or other securities (with certain exceptions) are subject to income tax. Gains in sale of real estate are considered income, but computed on separate basis.

Estate Tax.—Law No. 22 of Dec. 30, 1985 has eliminated estate tax.

Gift Tax.—Law No. 22 of Dec. 30, 1985 has exempted from Gift Tax following: (a) Gifts of not more than $1,000; (b) gifts of real estate or titles, securities or shares of stock made in favor of spouse or relatives within first degree of consanguinity; (c) transfer in trust of real estate or titles, securities or shares of stock when cestui que trust is spouse or relative within first degree of consanguinity; (d) gifts to state, its autonomous institutions, municipalities and association of municipalities; (e) gifts to foster or organized institutions for social welfare and to education establishments constituted or to be constituted in accordance with Panamanian laws; or institutions or legal persons constituted exclusively for eleemosynary, educational or social welfare purposes; (f) homestead properties; (g) gifts in favor of persons unable to earn living by reason of physical or mental disability when such disability has been recognized by ruling of court and gift does not exceed $5,000; (h) acts referred to in Art. 35 of Law No. 1 of Jan. 5, 1984; (i) all other gifts when so provided in special laws.

Gasoline Tax.—There is an excise tax on refining and use of all motor fuel.

Carbonated Drinks Tax.—Tax established on sale of carbonated drinks and over syrups and concentrates utilized in production of carbonated drinks.

Cigarette Tax.—Tax is levied on national production, and foreign made is subject to custom duty.

Corporate Tax.—All Panama corporations must pay B/150 annual franchise tax within three succeeding months after date of registration and, thereafter, within three months after anniversary date of their registration.

Beer Tax.—Tax per liter is levied on production of beer.

Liquor Tax.—Taxes are levied on production of any potable liquids containing alcohol, amount being based on alcoholic content of beverages.

Education Tax.—Compulsory contributions for educational purposes are tax deductible. Employers contribute 1.25%, employees 0.75%, levied on their wages, and independent taxpayers 2% of net income.

License tax is imposed on net worth at flat rate of 1%; maximum tax is $20,000. See topic Licenses.

Sales Tax.—5% sales tax on transfer of ownership, lease and use of corporeal movable property, including importation of such goods. Among items exempted are transfers of goods mortis causa, donations; transfers in marriage settlement, contributions of partition of community property; transfer of negotiable instruments and stock certificates; sales made by farmers, poultrymen, cattle raisers of their respective products, or of similar products made in their natural state; export and re-export of goods; transfer of movable property within Panama free zones; operations affecting corporeal movable property within customs and storage deposits ownership of which is transferred by endorsement of documents; transfer of soft drinks already taxed; import and transfer of fuel and oil.

Stamp taxes are imposed on drafts, checks, receipts, accounts and acknowledgments of indebtedness, and legal business in the courts or the administrative branch of the government must be conducted on legal stamped paper. (Fiscal Code Art. 946, et seq.).

Among such taxes are the following:

10¢ for each $100 or fraction thereof of amount involved on action, contract, document or obligation for more than $10 not specially taxed and which relates to any matter of business subject to jurisdiction of the Republic. Same rate on receipts covering demandable obligations and not covered by any other provision of the law.

50¢ on each set of copies of bills of lading, consular invoices and declarations executed in the Republic covering merchandise for foreign ports.

Declarations for imports must bear a $1 stamp if value of merchandise imported is $10 or more. (Law 66 of 1961).

$10 on concession for exploitation of any kind of national or municipal properties, unless a certain value is specified, in which case tax is computed according to value.

$10 on proposal submitted to public powers for construction or repair of railways, ports, canals or other means of communications.

$10 on certificate or passport issued to foreigner for departure from the country.

$5 on certificate issued by Panamanian consular employee or diplomatic agent abroad.

$2 on each sheet of freight manifests, ships' crews and mess lists, customs declarations, requests for permission to discharge, pratiques and other documents which must be furnished in ports of the Republic for ships engaged in foreign commerce.

$2 on first authentication of signature of national official, and $5 in case of a foreign official on any document.

$2 on any document which does not or cannot, on account of its nature, state a specific amount, unless otherwise taxed. On tickets for travelling abroad by air $1 per coupon; by sea $4.

20¢ on clearance for ships or aeroplanes to depart.

1¢ for each $100 or fraction thereof of amount of draft drawn and payable outside the Republic and negotiated in the Republic.

50¢ plus 1% of total value on check, order for payment, draft or other document for $50 or more issued by a resident within the jurisdiction of the Republic against an institution in the Republic but not within its jurisdiction.

10¢ on all checks.

Stamp taxes are also imposed on foreign made perfumes, soaps, etc.

Law 1 of 1985 provides for stamp paper, US$4 per folio. In addition, most documents and petitions must bear 5¢ stamp.

Taxes on Vessels Enrolled under the Panama Flag.—See topic Shipping.

TELECOMMUNICATIONS:

General Provisions.—On Feb. 8, 1996, Law No. 31 was enacted whereby Telecommunication System within Republic of Panama is regulated.

Purpose of said Law is to promote private investment, expand access of people and improve quality of existing services.

Telegraphic services, radio broadcasting, and distribution of noninteractive television signals and radio amateur signals, were excluded from scope of application of law.

This law establishes three kinds of rights for concessionaries which must be stated in contract, and which are as follows: (1) price for right of concession; (2) annual rate of concession and (3) regulation fee as established by Regulating Entity. Such Regulating Entity is government institution that shall inspect administration of public services.

Law provides that communications are inviolable and cannot be intercepted or interfered with, nor content of communications can be released.

Telecommunication services shall be classified as follows: (1) Type A: Refers to those services that due to technical reasons are granted to limited number of concessionaires, under temporary exclusivity basis. (2) Type B: Rest of services which shall be freely granted under competition basis.

Regulating Entity shall grant and supervise concessionaires regarding use of frequencies assigned to telecommunications. Ministry of Government and Justice shall protect rights of concessionaries and shall not assign any frequencies that may interfere with those already granted.

Concession for Rendering Telecommunications Services.—Rendering telecommunication services shall help, in some cases, as established by contract, telecommunication network construction by concessionaire and use of radio electric frequency.

Major private and foreign participation in capital stock of companies engaged in telecommunication services exploitation is authorized. Under any circumstance, any foreign government or any company or consortium which have ownership, control or major participation in foreign government, may exploit, whether under its own basis or through intermediary, any of telecommunication services; or be shareholder or senior partner of such company.

Concessions shall have term of 20 years and extensions thereof cannot exceed equal term. Type A concessions shall be granted by Cabinet Council through public bid. Companies desirous to obtain concession, must prequalify pursuant to established procedure. To participate in bid stage, any company must be previously prequalified, however, companies that have not qualified but meet several conditions set forth by law, may associate with any other companies which have been prequalified.

Once Cabinet Council approves documents related for prequalified companies, Regulating Entity shall call for public bid which shall be governed by procedure established by rules of practice.

Type B concessions shall be granted, without any public bid, to any person who meets requirements established on this matter.

Rates and Prices.—Prices for telecommunication services offered on competition basis shall be fixed by concessionaires.

Regulating Entity may determine prices and rates provided that there is only one concessionaire rendering specific service, or when one or more services are subsidized; or whenever there are practices restricting competition.

Termination of Concession Contract and General Provisions.—State may terminate any contract by Administrative Resolution, provided that grounds exist for termination as established by law to rescind Type A concession. Such grounds are listed in Art. 47 of law, for example, non-authorized modification of object of concession, bankruptcy of concessionaire, and others.

C. V of law refers to all possible infringements, sanctions and procedures sanctioned by law.

Companies rendering telecommunication services shall require Type A Commercial License.

TOURISM:

Subject of tourism is governed by relatively new law adopted in mid 1994 and regulated in 1995 with purpose of adopting comprehensive development of all tourist activities within Republic of Panama. Law grants fiscal incentives and benefits to persons engaged in all of these activities which cover wide field such as establishment of hotels, motels, Apart Hotels (hotels with small apartments), restaurants, convention centers, etc.

In addition, zones of special interest for tourist development may be adopted and are granted even greater tax incentives.

TRADEMARKS, TRADENAMES AND SLOGANS:

New Industrial Property Law was enacted in Panama (Law No. 35 of May 10, 1996) and will be applicable as of Nov. 15, 1996. According to provisions of this new law, trademarks, business or commercial names and slogans may be protected, whether

TRADEMARKS, TRADENAMES AND SLOGANS . . . *continued*
applicant is national or foreign. Period of registration is ten years and registration may be renewed indefinitely for equal periods if application for renewal is filed within one year before and six months after expiration of term. Famous and notorious marks, as well as denominations of origin, are protected.

Applications for registration of trademarks no longer need to be based on foreign registrations or pending applications, and must be accompanied by following documents: (1) power-of-attorney with notarial acknowledgment as to existence and legal representation of applicant corporation, or with certificate of existence and good standing issued by competent authority of applicant's country; (2) affidavit of use of trademark, tradename or slogan; (3) six samples of trademark or drawing thereof; (4) receipt showing payment of government registration and publication fees; (5) priority claim, if any (Panama has approved Paris Convention). Same documents are required for applications for registration of slogans. Applications for collective and guaranty marks must also be accompanied by their regulations of use. Law contemplates 19 prohibitions for registration of mark. Application may be filed without power-of-attorney by posting refundable US$100 bond, but power-of-attorney must be filed within next two months after date of filing of application. Fee for registration or for renewal is US$100, plus 20% surcharge fee. It is necessary to file as many applications as classes to be protected with mark. Applications are published on Industrial Property Bulletin and oppositions may be instituted against them within following two months.

Business or Commercial Names.—Name of commercial, industrial or professional enterprise constitutes industrial property right. For registration of business or commercial name, following documents are required: (1) power-of-attorney with notarial acknowledgment as to existence and legal representation of applicant corporation, or with certificate of existence and good standing issued by competent authority of applicant's country; (2) affidavit of use of commercial name; (3) certificate issued by competent authority stating that applicant is engaged in commercial or industrial activities and is using name desired to be registered.

All documents coming from abroad must be certified with apostille of The Hague Convention or legalized by Panama consul.

Infringement of industrial property rights is punished with fines ranging from US$10,000 to US$200,000, together with suspension for three months of commercial or industrial license if infringer operates in Panama (or operating permit for companies established in Colon Free Zone or other free trade or export processing zones), seizure of infringing goods and of machinery used for infringement and with payment of compensation for damages caused. If infringer operates in Colon Free Zone or in any other free trade or export processing zones, fine will be equivalent to 25% of monthly commercial movement of company, but will never be less than US$75,000. Criminal actions may also be instituted and, if found guilty, infringer may be punished with up to two years imprisonment.

Opposition, cancellation, nullity and infringement proceedings, will be prosecuted before Circuit Courts, Superior Courts and Supreme Court, in accordance with rules of procedure established by Law No. 35 of May 10, 1996 and by Judicial Code.

Panama is member of General Interamerican Convention for Trademark and Commercial Protection (Law No. 64 of Dec. 28, 1934); of Convention establishing the World Intellectual Property Organization (Law No. 3 of Nov. 9, 1982) and of Paris Convention (Law No. 41 of July 13, 1995).

Law No. 41 of July 13, 1995 approved Paris Convention for the Protection of Industrial Property.

Business Names.—Name of a merchant or a business or a manufacturing firm constitutes a property right. Firm name, style or denomination of a firm doing business in any part of Panama can be protected by registration in Mercantile Registry, but only for locality where business is carried on. Exclusive right to use of name terminates with closing of firm or factory or stoppage of industry to which right refers.

See topics Copyright and Patents.

TREATIES:

No important commercial treaties. Panama has no tax treaties except with Costa Rica, Honduras, Nicaragua, Guatemala, and El Salvador excepting from custom duties certain products imported from or exported to said countries.

Panama has ratified following 1976 Interamerican Conventions: On Conflict of Laws concerning Bills of Exchange, Promissory Notes and Invoices; Conflict of Laws concerning Checks; International Commercial Arbitration; Letters Rogatory; The Taking of Evidence Abroad; and The Legal Regime of Powers of Attorney to be Used Abroad. It has also ratified 1981 Interamerican Extradition Convention; 1985 Interamerican Convention to Prevent and Punish Torture; 1991 Protocol to Interamerican Convention on Human Rights, relative to Abolition of the Death Penalty.

Panama has an agreement with U.S.A. whereby investments in Panama of U.S.A. nationals may be guaranteed by their government against war, expropriation and convertibility of currency risks. Panama is not party to: (1) Convention on Service Abroad of Judicial and Extrajudicial Documents in Civil or Commercial Matters; (2) Convention on Taking of Evidence Abroad in Civil or Commercial Matters; (3) United Nations Convention on the Recognition and Enforcement of Foreign Arbitral Awards.

Panama has ratified Treaty on Non-Proliferation of Nuclear Weapons and following Conventions: International Convention for the Safety of Life at Sea, 1948, 1960, 1966, 1974 and Protocol of 1978; International Convention for the Prevention of Pollution of Sea by Oil, 1954, Amendments of 1962 and 1969 and Protocol of 1978; International Convention on Load Lines, 1966, Amendments of 1971 and 1975; International Convention of Tonnage Measurement of Ships, 1969; American Convention on Human Rights "Pact of San Jose Costa Rica, 1969"; Convention on International Trade in endangered species of wild fauna and flora; Inter-American Convention on Rights of Author in Literary, Scientific, and Artistic Works; International Convention for Protection of Performers, Producers of Phonograms and Broadcasting Organizations; Convention relating to Distribution of Programme-Carrying Signals Transmitted by Satellite; Convention establishing World Intellectual Property Organization; International Convention for the Prevention of Pollution from Ships, 1973; Convention Abolishing the Requirement of Legalisation for Foreign Public Documents (Apostille), 1961; Agreement on Professional Readaption and Employment of Invalid Persons (General conference of the International Labor Organization, June 20, 1983—Law No. 18, Nov. 8, 1993); Convention of the United Nations Against Illicit Traffic of Drugs and Sicotropic Substances (Vienna, Dec. 20, 1988—Law No. 20, Dec. 7, 1993); Agreement on Civil Aspects of International Abduction of Minors (The Hague, Oct. 25, 1980—Law No. 22, Dec. 10, 1993); Agreement for the Constitution of the Interamerican Institute for the Research on the Global Change (Montevideo, May 13, 1992, Law No. 23, Dec. 10, 1993); Agreement of Air Transportation Between the Government of the Republic of Panama and the Government of the Russian Federation (Panama, Feb. 3, 1993—Law No. 25, Dec. 10, 1993—Ratification Instrument deposited Feb. 10th, 1994); Amendment of the Montreal Protocol Regarding Substances which Exhaust the Ozone Layer (June 29, 1990—Law No. 25, Dec. 10th, 1993—Ratification Instrument deposited Feb. 10, 1994); Charter of the International Union for the Preservation of Nature and the Natural Resources (Fontainebleau, France, Oct. 5, 1984—Law No. 26, Dec. 10, 1993—Deposit Instrument of Adhesion); Agreement for the Constitution of the Fund for the Development of Indian Communities of Latin America and the Caribbean (Madrid, Spain July 24, 1992—Law No. 27, Dec. 13, 1993—Ratification Instrument deposited Feb. 10, 1994); Law No. 2, May 16, 1994—Treaty Constituting the Central American Parliament (Guatemala, Oct. 2, 1987); Law No. 11, July 11, 1994—Convention of Mutual Legal Assistance relating to Traffic of Drugs between Great Britain, Northern Ireland and Republic of Panama (Mar. 3, 1993); Law No. 2, Jan. 12, 1995—Convention on Biological Diversity (Rio de Janeiro, June 15, 1995); Law No. 12, Apr. 20, 1995—Interamerican Convention concerning Violence against Women (Belem Do Para, Brasil, June 9, 1994); Law No. 13 Apr. 21, 1995—Regional Agreement concerning Border Transportation of Dangerous Waste (Panama, Dec. 11, 1992); Law 14, Apr. 21, 1995—Regional Convention to Maintain Natural Forest Ecosystems and develop Forest Plantations (Guatemala, Oct. 29, 1993); Law No. 18, May 5, 1995—"Washington Protocol" amending the Charter of the Organization of American States (Washington, Dec. 14, 1992); Law No. 19, May 5, 1995—"Guatemala Protocol" amending the Charter of the Organization of American States at the XIX Term of the Extraordinary Meetings of the General Assembly (Managua, June 10, 1993); Law No. 2, May 31, 1995—Approving the Additional Protocals 1 and 2 of the Geneva Convention of Aug. 12, 1949 on Confirmation and Development of Humanitarian International Rights Applicable to Armed Conflicts; Law No. 54, Dec. 18, 1995—Cooperation Agreement Between the Republic of Panama and the United States of Mexico to Repress Narcotraffic and Pharmaco Dependency. Panama, Mar. 8, 1995; Law No. 55, Dec. 22, 1995—Agreement for Mutual Assistance Between Panama and Colombia Concerning the Illegal Traffic of Drugs and Sicotropic Substances. Panama, Nov. 19, 1993; Law No. 15, Jan. 3, 1996—Air Transportation Agreement Between the Republic of Panama and China. Panama, Aug. 30, 1994; Law No. 22, June 8, 1995—Approving the Convention Whereby the Coordination Center was Created for the Prevention of Natural Disasters in Central America (CEPREDENAC). Guatemala, Oct. 29, 1993; Law No. 23, June 8, 1995—Interamerican Convention to Expedite Assistance in Case of Disaster adopted in Santiago of Chile, June 7, 1991 at the 21st Period of Ordinary Meetings of the General Assembly of the Organization of American States; Law No. 30, June 28, 1995—Convention of the Central American Commission to Eradicate Products, Traffic, Consumption and Use of Illicit Drugs and Sicotropic Substances. Guatemala, Oct. 29, 1993; Law No. 32, Interamerican Convention on Forced Disappearance of Persons. Belem Do Para, Brasil, June 9, 1994, at 24th period of meetings; Law No. 37, July 11, 1995—Convention for the Integration of Central American Production of Movies. Caracas, Nov. 11/89; Law No. 38, July 11, 1995—The Latin America Convention for the Joint Production of Movies; Law No. 39, July 13, 1995—Mutual Assistance Treaty on Criminal Matters Between Costa Rica, El Salvador, Guatemala, Honduras, Nicaragua and Panama, Guatemala, Oct. 29, 1993; Law No. 40, July 13, 1995—Agreement Between the Republic of Panama and Colombia on Measures to Prevent Deviations of Chemicals and Essential Substances. Panama, Nov. 19, 1883; Law No. 41, July 13, 1995—Agreement for the Protection of Industrial Property of Mar. 20, 1993. Revised: Brussels, Dec. 14, 1900; Washington, June 2, 1911; La Hague, Nov. 6, 1928; London, June 21, 1934; Lisbon, Oct. 31, 1958; Stockholm, July 14, 1967; Law No. 42, July 14, 1995—Agreement for Legal Assistance and Mutual Judicial Cooperation Between the Republic of Panama and Colombia. Panama, Nov. 19, 1993; Law No. 11, Jan. 3, 1996—Treaty on Social Integration of Central America. El Salvador, Mar. 30, 1995; Law No. 13, Jan. 3, 1996—Agreement for Settlement of Differences Concerning Investments Among States and Nationals of Other States. Washington, Mar. 18, 1965; Law No. 14, Jan. 3, 1996—Agreement on Security of the Personnel of the United Nations and Associated Personnel, Approved at the General National Assembly of the United Nations. Dec. 9, 1994; Law No. 16, Jan. 3, 1996—Agreement Constituting the South Center. Geneva, Sept. 1, 1994; Law No. 17, Jan. 3, 1996—Agreement for the Amendment of the Air Traffic Convention Between the Republic of Panama and the United States of America of 1949, Entered Into by Exchange of notes of the 12th and 13th of Jan. 1994; Law No. 18, Jan. 3, 1996—Commercial Agreement Between the Republic of Panama and the Republic of Poland. Panama, Nov. 14, 1994; Law No. 19, Jan. 8, 1996—Agreement Constituting the Multi-lateral Organization to Guarantee Investments. Seoul, Oct. 11, 1985; Law No. 20, Jan. 8, 1996—Agreement Constituting the Association of Caribbean States. Cartagena of Indies, Colombian Republic. July 24, 1994; Law No. 21, Jan. 8, 1996—Agreement Constituting the Organization of the Andres Bello Agreement of Integral Scientific, Technological, and Cultural Education. Madrid, Spain, Nov. 27, 1990; Law No. 22, Jan. 8, 1996—International Agreement on Tropical Woods. Geneva, Jan. 26, 1994; Law No. 38, Jan. 4, 1995—United Nations Convention on the Rights of the Sea. Montego Bay, Dec. 11, 1982.

See also topic Aircraft.

See also Selected International Conventions section.

TRUSTS:

Original law of trusts enacted in 1941 has been modified to make it more flexible. Law of trusts is now embodied in Law 1 of Jan. 5, 1984, regulated by Executive Decree 16 of Oct. 3, 1984, largely based upon laws of trusts as exist in Anglo-Saxon countries.

Trust may be created upon property of any kind, present or future. Cestui que trust may be settlor himself. Trust must be expressly declared in writing. Verbal, constructive or implied trusts are not valid.

TRUSTS . . . *continued*

Trust deed must contain, among other things specified in law, following: Complete and clear designation of settlor, trustee and beneficiary; sufficient designation of substitute trustees or beneficiaries, if any; description of property or of estate or portion thereof on which it is created; powers and duties of trustee. Trust deed might further contain such clauses which are not contrary to morals, laws or public order.

Trust inter vivos may be created by public or private deed. Trust mortis causa, by will. It may also be created by private deed, without formalities of will, in event that trustee is person authorized to engage in trust business. Trust is irrevocable unless otherwise expressly provided in trust deed. To affect rights of third parties, deed requires authentication by Panamanian Public Notary. However, trust on real property situated in Panama must be created by public deed and recorded in Public Register.

Assets of trust shall constitute separate estate from personal assets of trustee for all legal purposes, and cannot be attached or embargoed, except for obligations incurred into or damages caused by performance of trust, or by third parties when property has been transferred or withheld fraudulently and in detriment of their rights.

Designation of one or more nonexistent beneficiaries, or of class of beneficiaries, which are ascertainable, shall be effective provided one or more thereof shall come into existence or be ascertained during life of trust.

In case of revocable trusts, beneficiary and trustee may be replaced. Trustee may resign his office if it is expressly so authorized by trust deed; in absence of express authorization he may resign with judicial approval.

Trust deed may establish limitations to liability of trustee; but such limitations shall not release trustee from losses or damages caused by gross negligence or fraud.

Trustee might be removed by court through summary proceedings in presence of causes defined in law.

Trust is tax exempted when it involves: (1) Property situated abroad; (2) money deposited by natural or juridical persons whose income is not from Panamanian sources or taxable in Panama; or (3) shares of stock or securities of any kind, issued by corporations income whereof is not from Panamanian sources, although such monies, shares of stock or securities are deposited in Republic of Panama. Above exemptions are not applicable when property, money, shares of stock or securities are utilized in transactions not exempted from Panamanian taxes, unless they are invested in housing developments, urban developments or industrial parks in Panama, in which case profits from such investment are exempted of income tax.

Executive Decree No. 16 of Oct. 3, 1984 as modified by Executive Decree No. 53 of Dec. 30, 1985, regulates engaging in trust business as regards requirements, granting of license, guarantees, penalties and any other conditions to which trust companies, insurance companies, banks, attorneys and other natural or juridical persons engaged professionally and habitually in this business are subject to.

Regulatory power as to trust business resides in National Banking Commission. In addition to professional qualifications and experience in trust business, trust companies that engage in trust business in or from Panama must maintain available to Commission guarantee of US$250,000, consisting of unencumbered assets kept at all times in Republic of Panama.

Trust companies not exclusively engaged in trust business (such as banks or investments concerns) must maintain separate, over-all functional accounting between trust department and other departments.

No Panamanian company, unless licensed to do trust business, may utilize word "trust" or derivatives thereof in any language, or any other expression, either in their corporate name, corporate purposes, description, business denomination, invoices, letterheads, advertisements, notices or publications, implying that they are engaged in trust business.

Violation of secrecy in connection with trusts is penalized with internment or imprisonment of up to six months and fine of up to B/50,000.

Trust deed may establish governing law as either Panamanian or foreign.

VITAL STATISTICS: See topic Records.

WILLS:

The law regarding wills is contained in C. C. 694-853.

Any competent person may dispose of all of his or her estate freely by will, provided enough is left for the support and maintenance of children legally entitled to it until they attain majority or for life if they are crippled, and for the support and maintenance of legitimate parents, illegitimate mother and surviving spouse while they are in need of it.

Wills may be made by all persons, except those under the age of puberty, mentally incapacitated, civilly dead or unable to express their wills clearly. Wills are opened and published by the court of the last domicile of the testator.

Forms.—Wills, with respect to form, may be either common or special. The common may be holographic, open or sealed. Special wills may be maritime, military and foreign wills. The open will must be made before a notary public with all the formalities of the law. The sealed will may be made by any person ordered by the testator.

Witnesses.—The following cannot be witnesses to wills: (1) Minors; (2) persons not domiciled in the place making the will; (3) blind, deaf or dumb persons; (4) persons who do not understand the language of the testator; (5) persons mentally incapacitated; (6) persons convicted of forgery or perjury, and those deprived of civil rights; (7) clerks, employees or relatives of the notary; (8) in open wills the legatees or heirs. Three witnesses are needed.

Holographic wills can only be made by persons of legal age and to be valid must be written and signed in the testator's own handwriting, with the expression of year, month and day.

Open wills must be executed before a notary public with three witnesses. The will must be read aloud once, and in case of a blind testator twice, to the testator and the witnesses.

Closed or sealed wills are privately prepared by the testator and enclosed in a sealed envelope which the testator must, in the presence of a notary and three witnesses, declare to contain his will. On the envelope the notary makes a minute of such declaration and the same must be signed by all the parties. Blind persons are incapable of making closed wills.

Maritime wills are those made on board vessels. Maritime wills may be open or closed. If the vessel is a war vessel the will must be made before the commander and two witnesses. If executed on a merchant vessel the will must be made before the captain and two witnesses. Upon arrival in port, a copy of the will must be delivered to the diplomatic or consular representatives.

Military wills are those made by soldiers or police or any officer of either force while engaged in war or in commission. During battle a verbal will may be made in the presence of two witnesses.

Revocation.—Wills properly executed and rendered invalid by revocation by the testator. The revocation may be total or partial but no revocation can have effect unless made with the formalities required to make a will. A subsequent will revokes the prior one, if the testator does not express his will that the latter may remain in force in whole or in part.

Foreign Wills.—Citizens of Panama may make wills in a foreign country if they act according to the formalities of local law; and may in any case execute a holographic will. Foreign wills are valid in Panama if executed according to the law of the country where made.

See Topical Index in front part of this volume.

PARAGUAY LAW DIGEST REVISER

Peroni-Sosa & Altamirano
Post Office Box 114
Asunción, Paraguay
Telephone: 595 21 208 791
Fax: 595 21 22 242
Email: psa@prsa.una.py

Reviser Profile

History: The firm was founded in 1968 by Dr. Juan G. Peroni, Dr. Guillermo F. Peroni and Dr. Demetrio Ayala, under the name "Ayala & Peroni". Over the next decade the firm grew as its client base and areas of specialization expanded. In 1977 the name of the firm was changed to "Peroni-Sosa & Altamirano". The firm is presently staffed by 17 lawyers and 3 paralegals.

Areas of Emphasis: Peroni-Sosa & Altamirano offers a broad range of legal services for clients involved in international and local transactions in Paraguay. The firm's departmental specialization includes banking and financial operations; mineral resources and oil exploration projects; foreign investment; representation in general civil litigation; counseling before local government agencies and legislative bodies; and Intellectual Property matters.

Client Base: The firm represents local and foreign companies, governmental and multinational agencies.

Peroni-Sosa & Altamirano helped establish the local branches of several international banks, representing and handling on a daily basis their legal affairs in the country. The firm also represents financial institutions which do not have local offices, but which are involved in lending to agencies of the Paraguayan government and to local corporations.

In mining and oil exploration the firm has been instrumental in the granting of prospecting, exploration and exploitation concessions to several multinational companies.

Foreign companies and individual investors have used our services to establish themselves or to enter into joint ventures in Paraguay, for which purpose we have provided legal advice on incentives, coordination of feasibility studies, contacts with the government, and start-up of operations.

The representation of clients in the courts and before administrative agencies is an important concern of Peroni-Sosa & Altamirano and is a major part of the firm's activities. We have represented both plaintiffs and defendants in virtually every kind of civil and commercial litigation, including several landmark cases.

The firm has an Intellectual Property department, which is equipped with the latest computer and word-processing technology, covers every aspect of trademark, copyright and patent practice, and their commercial use within Paraguay by foreign and local companies.

Firm Activities: "Peroni-Sosa & Altamirano" encourages participation of its members in academic activities and professional organizations. Three partners currently teach courses at the Catholic University.

Paraguay's most important legal journal, *Revista Jurídica Paraguaya "La Ley"*, was founded in 1977 by Dr. Juan Guillermo Peroni, partner of the firm, who continues to be its director.

All partners and associates are members of the Colegio de Abogados del Paraguay. Some are also members of the International Bar Association, the Interamerican Bar Association, the American Society of International Law. Dr. Guillermo F. Peroni is past president of the Paraguayan American Chamber of Commerce.

Dr. Enrique A. Sosa was elected Minister of the Supreme Court in 1995, and took a leave of absence from the firm. Dr. Antonio Tellechea Solis is Dean of the Faculty of Law of Universidad Católica de Asunción.

Management: The firm is managed by a committee formed by the three partners, which monitors attorney performance, case management, client relationship, economic and technological development and firm growth.

PARAGUAY LAW DIGEST

(The following is a list of all Topics, including cross-references, covered in this Digest.)

PARAGUAY LAW DIGEST

Revised for 1997 edition by

PERONI-SOSA & ALTAMIRANO of the Asunción Bar.

(C.C. indicates Civil Code; C.de Proc. indicates Code of Procedure. All codes are cited by articles.)

ABSENTEES: See topic Death.

ACKNOWLEDGMENTS:

According to system in force where civil law prevails, contracts, deeds and other documents which require authentication by a public official are prepared by a notary or other authorized public official and made a part of his protocol; original documents are kept in an official register in office of notary or official. See topics Public Instruments, and Records.

Instruments executed in foreign countries, however, are given full recognition in Paraguay, if duly acknowledged in manner required in country where they were executed, authenticated by a consular or diplomatic agent of Paraguay, and authentication certified by Ministry of Foreign Affairs of Paraguay.

ACTIONS: See topic Prescription.

ADOPTION:

Governed by Law 903 and C.C.

Adoption equates adopted children with status of matrimonial children. No adoption by more than one person except when adopters are spouses or in case of adopter's death. Several minors, without sex distinction, may be adopted simultaneously or succesively.

Persons who cannot adopt: (a) Those affected by serious contagious illness; (b) those lacking economic resources; (c) those aged under 35 or over 60, except when adopters are spouses with minimum five years of marriage and have no children. Adopters must be at least 15 years older than adopted. Widows or single persons cannot adopt any one of opposite sex unless there is 30 years difference in age.

Spouses cannot adopt separately without other's consent except in case of divorce, separation, insanity declared by courts or absence with presumption of death.

To adopt minor over 16 years of age his consent as well as his father's or guardian's is required.

Adoption can be simple or complete.

Simple adoption grants adopted right to take adopter's surname. Kindred is limited to adopter and adopted and is revocable. Rights and obligations derived from natural kindred are not extinguished except those derived from patria potestas which are transferred to adopter.

In complete adoption, adopted and his descendants are adopter's heirs. It is irrevocable and grants adopted affiliation that replaces his original. All kindred with natural family is extinguished. Complete adoption is granted only in case adopted is orphan from father and mother, abandoned, of unknown parents, or when parents were deprived from patria potestas. Once complete adoption is granted, recognizance by natural parents or actions on filiation, are not allowed except those to prove marriage impediments.

ADVERSE POSSESSION: See topic Prescription.

AGENCY: See topic Principal and Agent.

ALIENS:

Foreigners enjoy same civil rights in Paraguay as Paraguayan citizens. They may do business, follow their trade or practice their profession, buy and sell real property, make wills and marry in conformity with law, and enjoy entire religious freedom. They are not obliged to become citizens or to pay extraordinary taxes.

Naturalization is granted to foreigners that have been living for a minimum of three years in country, during which time they must have worked continuously in a productive activity, and who can prove their good conduct both in country and in country of origin.

ASSIGNMENTS:

Assignments of credit rights or actions are only effective regarding third parties, from time date is fixed according to law. If transfer affects real property, from date of its filing for registration in public registry. Any debtor who pays his creditor, before having knowledge of assignment, is released from obligation. Principle of bona fides governs all relationships between assignor and assignee. Sale or transfer of a credit includes that of all accessory rights. Transfers of inheritance rights and credits in litigation are permitted and should be notarized.

ATTACHMENT:

In order to attach property in an ordinary civil action, one of following conditions must exist: (1) That debtor is not domiciled in Paraguay; (2) that debt is evidenced by certain written instruments; (3) that in case of action on bilateral contract, contract is in writing and complies with certain requirements as to its execution; (4) that debt is evidenced by mercantile books kept in due form; or, (5) when debt is subject to condition, that plaintiff proves that debtor is trying to dispose of, hide or remove his property, or that responsibility of debtor has decreased after obligation was contracted. Attachment will also be issued against specific property which is object of possessory action, an attachment will be issued at request of any of parties when facts are admitted which make out a prima facie case in their favor or when a favorable judgment has been obtained.

Party who obtains an attachment must give security for costs and damages. Attachment may also be issued with summary actions known as "Executory Actions."

BANKRUPTCY AND INSOLVENCY:

Law 154/69.

Bankruptcy declaration presumes insolvency of debtor. State of insolvency is manifested by one or more nonfulfillments of obligations that in court's criterian shows debtor as unable to pay his debt. Petition in bankruptcy can be filed by debtor, his inheritors or his creditors. Debtor can avoid declaration of bankruptcy by filing in court for a creditors' meeting. Debtor who engages in commercial activities and reaches a state of insolvency is obliged by law to file for bankruptcy or creditors' meeting. Court will decide whether to accept petition for a creditors' meeting or to declare bankruptcy. If creditors' meeting is accepted, court designates a trustee in bankruptcy who will review documentation submitted to him by creditors, for which purpose there is a term not less than 20 days and not more than 40 days. Creditors will be notified of court's admission of request by publication in one newspaper and by certified post, sent by trustee.

When requesting creditors' meeting debtor will continue administrating his business and assets. Creditors cannot continue or start summary action against debtor whose petition for creditors' meeting has been accepted by court, with exception of credits guaranteed by mortgages or chattel mortgages, or credits from salaried personnel as a consequence of a labor contract.

Debtor must present his payment proposal for consideration by his creditors in a special meeting called to this effect. Representation will be limited to those whose credits have been admitted and recognized by court. Creditors will vote to accept or turn down payment proposal submitted by debtor.

Only creditors authorized to vote are those with unsecured credits. Should a creditor with a privilege or guaranty vote, he automatically loses his privilege or guaranty.

Payment proposal is limited, in its scope, by law. If payment term is less than two years, debtor can propose a rebate of up to 50%; but if term exceeds two years, rebate shall not surpass 30% of credit. Maximum term authorized is four years.

If creditors turn down proposal, or, if accepted, court does does not confirm it, bankruptcy shall be declared.

Bankruptcy proceedings are similar to creditors' meeting procedure, but bankrupt is separated from administration of his business. Administration passes from bankrupt to trustee in bankruptcy to realize assets of bankrupt and make distribution of proceeds pro rata among unsecured creditors once secured creditors are paid off.

All capable persons, juridical or physical, can be declared bankrupt even if they have no commercial activities.

Bankruptcy of a corporation with a partner with unlimited responsibility provokes bankruptcy of this partner but does not provoke bankruptcy of those with limited responsibilities nor bankruptcy of corporations of which they form part.

Bankruptcy declared in a foreign country cannot be opposed to creditors domiciled in Paraguay over assets held by debtor in country.

When court declares a bankruptcy, it has to qualify actions of bankrupt. It can be considered casual, guilty or fraudulent. In last two cases, debtor will be prosecuted by the criminal courts.

BILLS AND NOTES:

See topic Drafts and Notes.

CHATTEL MORTGAGES:

Only one kind of chattel mortgage is recognized by law, that is recorded or registered pledge instituted by law. It is contract by which debtor assigns assets in guaranty of loan, without losing possession of them. Contract is registered and gives creditor privilege over all other creditors over those assets, as from date of recording. No subsequent pledge affecting same property may be executed by debtor, except with consent of creditor.

Recent jurisprudence gives employees' credits for salaries against a bankruptcy, privilege over one granted by chattel mortgage.

Certificate can be endorsed but endorsement has to be registered.

COMMERCIAL REGISTER: See topic Records.

CONSTITUTION AND GOVERNMENT:

Present Constitution was enacted in 1992. Paraguay is unitary, indivisible and decentralized Republic. There are legislative, judicial and executive powers. Legislature is composed of Senate and Chamber of Deputies. Legislature and President of country are elected directly every five years. Reelection for President is not permitted.

Judiciary is headed by Supreme Court composed of nine members and by courts established by law.

CONTRACTS:

Nature, form and object of contracts are governed by C.C.

Parties may freely determine their rights in contracts subject to compliance of coercive laws. Laws related to public policy and good customs may not be forsaken.

Contracts must be interpreted and performed in good faith.

Essential requirements of contracts are: Consent, object and form. Noncompliance of form in special cases results in nullity of contract.

Consent is expressed by offer and acceptance.

Contract is considered executed in place where offer is made.

Object of contract must be definite in respect to its kind. Future inheritances cannot be object of contracts.

See Topical Index in front part of this volume.

CONTRACTS . . . *continued*

Applicable Law.—Form of contract: (a) If parties are present, is ruled by law of place where executed; (b) if parties are absent but one of them signed private document, is ruled by law of place where signed; (c) if executed in different places, form is governed by law of place most favorable to its validity. Contracts executed in foreign country regarding real estate located in Paraguay must be recorded in public document and duly authenticated. Will only have effects once recorded with notary public and registered by order of competent court. Legal capacity is ruled by law of domicile. When contract is to be performed in Paraguay, validity or nullity of its object, substantial defects and capacity of parties to acquire rights is governed by C.C.

Distributorships, Dealerships and Franchises.—Law 194/93 governs relationships between foreign companies and firms (collectively, "Principal") and local representatives, agents and distributors (collectively, "Dealer") in Paraguay.

Definitions.—Representation is authority granted by contract to dealer to negotiate and carry out commercial transactions for promotion, sale or distribution of products or services provided by principal. Agency is contractual relationship whereby principal grants dealer authority to act as intermediary in negotiations or contracts with clients for promotion, sale or distribution of products or services, contemplating payment of commission. Distributorship is contractual relationship between principal and dealer for purchase or consignment of products, with objective of reselling same.

Form.—Dealer may be exclusive or of any other contractual form, under terms agreed to by parties.

Application of Paraguayan Law.—Parties may freely regulate their rights by contracts governed by Civil Code, waiver of rights recognized by Decree Law 7/91 is not allowed.

Termination Without Cause.—Principal may cancel, revoke, amend or refuse to renew representation, agency or distributorship, without statement of cause, but with obligation in such case to pay dealer minimum compensation pursuant to following criteria: (a) duration of relationship; (b) average gross benefits derived from relationship during last three years of activity.

Termination With Cause.—Representation, agency or distributor relationships may be cancelled, revoked, amended or not renewed for just cause, without obligation to pay compensation for following reasons: (a) noncompliance with contract clauses; (b) fraud or breach of trust on part of dealer; (c) inability or negligence of dealer in sale of products or services; (d) continued reduction of sales or distribution of products or services for reasons attributable to dealer; except if caused by quotas or restrictions on imports and sales, fortuitous events or force majeure; (e) any act attributable to dealer that affects or prejudices marketing, sale, or distribution of products or services; (f) conflict of interest due to representation, agency or distribution of products or services that may be in competition with products or services contemplated by relationship.

Prior to termination, principal shall require dealer cure cause invoked within term of 120 days. Noncompliance by dealer allows principal to exercise its rights immediately. Curing period not required if termination is related to fraud or breach. Stated causes shall be proved before Paraguayan courts or by arbitration if thus agreed; otherwise, cancellation, revocation, amendment or refusal to renew shall be deemed to be unjustified.

Purchase of Inventory.—At termination, dealer, regardless of compensation that may correspond, has option to sell to principal, its inventory at market price.

Jurisdiction.—Parties shall submit to territorial jurisdiction of courts of Paraguay. They may compromise in all patrimonial matters or submit to arbitration before or after suit is filed, provided that no judgment shall have been issued.

Evidence of Relationship.—From date of enactment of Law, documents and contracts shall be recorded in Public Registry of Commerce. Dealer who invokes relationship by virtue of acts occurred or documents granted prior to enactment of Law, may use all types of evidence established in laws, and particularly any of following: (a) letters of authorization from principal to act as dealer for promotion, sale or distribution of products and services; (b) purchase invoices evidencing that commercial operations have been carried out on basis of authorization, at least during two years prior to enactment of Law; (c) payment of commissions to dealer by principal for commercial operations carried out for at least two years prior to enactment of Law; (d) advertising by dealer incurred at his own account and expense indicating representation, agency or distributorship of goods and services in knowledge of but without opposition of principal; (e) payment or credit of commissions or compensation to dealer by principal for operations not carried out in their territory.

Excuses for Nonperformance—If event subsequent to execution of bilateral contract makes compliance impossible, without negligence of either party, reciprocal obligations extinguish. Had one party fulfilled its obligations consideration must be restored to him. When unpredictable and extraordinary circumstances make performance of long term excessively onerous for one party, it may claim rescission or amendment of obligations pending completion. Rescission will not be declared if claimant is guilty or if other party offers equitable amendment. In contracts accepted by one party without negotiation, adherent may be released of obligations or request amendment thereof. It is considered unfair to exclude or limit liability of dominating party; to authorize dissolution of contract or change of conditions or in any way deprive adherent of some rights without cause imputable to him; when exercise of contractual right of adherent is subject to other party's consent; to have adherent waive in advance any right based on contract to which he would be entitled in absence of such clause; to limit adherent's use of means of proof or place on him burden or proof (onus probandi); to subject adherent's right to whatever recourse available to condition or term or limit defenses or recourses in any procedure to which adherent would have been entitled; to authorize unilateral choice of competent jurisdiction.

COPYRIGHT:

Governed by C.C. and provisions of Law 94/25 and Decree-Law 3462/51 which cover and protect literary, scientific and artistic works. Public Registry for Intellectual Property is at Ministry of Education and Worship.

Protection covers author's life span and 50 additional years after death. There are no compulsory licensing provisions.

Works made by public officials or private sector employees related to their functions are considered to belong to State or employer.

Rights to literary, scientific and artistic works cannot be waived, transferred or sold, but their economic value or commercial exploitation can be transferred.

Copyrights may be obtained for foreign works with same rights as local works, but privilege does not extend beyond period provided by law of country where work was published. If period determined in local laws is shorter this prevails.

To obtain copyright two copies of work must be deposited at Registry. Foreign works are subject to same requirements when they have editor in Paraguay. Paintings or sculpture, sketches, and photographs must be deposited with data to allow identification. For films, script, dialogues, photographs and description of main scenes is required.

Registry publishes registration application for five days in local newspaper. If within a month nobody has claimed rights, Chief of Registry grants interested parties definite certificate of registration.

In case of counterfeit, author or owner may ask for embargo on work and claim damages and losses. Criminal action may also be filed.

Edition Contract.—Governed by C.C. Deals with reproduction, promotion and sale of literary, scientific or artistic works. Author or heirs have right to remuneration, unless express waiver. If remuneration is not agreed, courts fix it.

Editor is obliged to reproduce work in appropriate form without amendment, pay necessary expenses and take usual steps for success of sale. Editor fixes sale price but price should not cause limitation of sales.

If work is destroyed by unforseen accident while in editor's hands before edition, editor must pay author or heirs stipulated remuneration. If destruction was caused by negligence of editor or author, innocent party has right to damages.

Contract is extinguished if author dies or becomes incapable before concluding work. If important part has been completed, editor has right to it, except if agreement was that work would be published in full. In case of editor's bankruptcy, author may give work to another editor, unless he receives guaranty that edition will be made and obligations fulfilled.

CORPORATIONS (Sociedades Anonimas):

Under Paraguayan law, corporations (Sociedades Anonimas) are defined as mercantile companies. Corporations are liable for their obligations to extent of their assets. Participation of shareholders is represented by shares.

Corporate name must include Sociedad Anonima (S.A.).

Organization—Following conditions are indispensable for formation of corporation: (1) At least two shareholders; (2) capital stock must be completely subscribed; (3) corporation must have specified duration; (4) corporation may function once it is recorded in Public Registries.

Corporate By-Laws (Estatutos).—Following must be included in bylaws: (1) Full name, nationality, profession, civil status, domicile of shareholders, and number of shares subscribed by each one; (2) name of corporation and its domicile within country or abroad; (3) nature of business of corporation; (4) amount of capital subscribed and paid in; (5) nominal value of shares, and indication whether these are bearer or nominative; (6) value of assets incorporated in kind, if any; (7) basis on which distribution of profits will be made; (8) special privileges and rights, if any, conferred on founders; (9) dispositions regarding management and supervision, their respective powers and duties, and number of administrators; (10) powers conferred on stockholders' meetings, provisions regulating exercise of stockholders' right to vote, and procedure to take decisions at such meetings; (11) basis on which corporation is to be liquidated.

Formalities Required to Establish Corporation.—Shareholders must execute corporate contract in form of public instrument, with intervention of notary public.

Corporations acquire separate legal entity upon registration in Public Registry of Commerce.

Lack of registration will not make corporate contract void, but it may not be opposed to third parties. Shareholders, directors and any persons who have authorized acts, transactions and operations in corporate name prior to registration of corporation are jointly and severally liable for these.

Procedure for Establishment of Corporation by Public Subscription.—Corporation may also be established on basis of prospectus, which must indicate purpose and capital of company, principal provisions of bylaws, participation if any of promoters in profits of company, and date by which company will be established.

Prospectus must be rendered as public instrument, registered and published three times in important newspaper.

Subscription of shares must be made in public act or private contract certified by notary public. Name, nationality, civil status, profession, and domicile of subscribers, and number of shares subscribed must be given. Once subscriptions are made promoters must indicate when share capital must be paid in.

Date, within ten days from time deposit of paid-in capital was made, must be set for general meeting of suscribers to resolve if corporation will be incorporated. If affirmative, general meeting must decide and approve work of promoters, bylaws of corporation, valuation of assets in kind, if any, privileges reserved for promoters, and designate administrators and directors.

Decision of general meeting must be rendered into public instrument and registered. Promoters are jointly and severally liable for obligations to third parties made before corporation was incorporated.

Management and administration of corporation is exercised by one or more directors elected by shareholders' ordinary general meeting, or designated in incorporation documents. Their number is decided by general meeting if not specified in bylaws.

Directors need not be shareholders. They may be reelected, but appointment is revocable by Shareholders Meeting. Term of directors shall be for one fiscal year unless bylaws establish otherwise. Directors must be Paraguayans or foreigners with legal residence in country.

Directors may only engage in business transactions with their corporation under special circumstances. They are forbidden to execute any business on behalf of corporation not related to purpose for which it was formed.

See Topical Index in front part of this volume.

CORPORATIONS (Sociedades Anonimas) . . . *continued*

Corporate administrators are responsible to corporate creditors for negligence in their duty to safeguard integrity of corporation's assets.

Supervision.—One or more syndics must also be elected by ordinary general meeting to supervise management of corporation. They must be capable of performing duties assigned in bylaws, and domiciled in Paraguay. Bylaws shall determine duration of their terms, which may not exceed three fiscal years. Syndics may be reelected.

Syndics have following powers and duties: (1) Supervise administration and management of corporation, and participate without vote in general shareholders' and board of directors' meetings; (2) examine corporation's books and papers whenever they deem advisable, at least once every three months; (3) call extraordinary stockholders' meetings when they consider necessary and ordinary meetings when board of directors fails to do so; (4) ensure that corporation complies with all obligations under law, as well as with decisions of general meetings.

Responsibility of Administrators.—Administrators are not liable for obligations of company except in case of nonperformance of their duties, mismanagement, or personal violation of law, or corporate bylaws. In such instances administrators are jointly and severally liable to corporation and to third parties for their acts, but directors who opposed, voted against, or were not present when illegal acts were approved, are exonerated.

Shareholders' Meetings.—Called Asambleas Generales, may be ordinary or extraordinary, and must take place in corporate domicile.

Ordinary meetings must be called every year by directors or syndics, to consider and resolve following: (1) Annual report of directors, statement of accounts, balance sheet, distribution of dividends, syndic's report, and any other issue within their competence according to law and bylaws; (2) election of directors and syndics, and determination of their remuneration; (3) responsibilities of director and syndics, and their removal; (4) issue of shares.

Extraordinary meetings must be called by directors at any time, or by syndic when deemed necessary or convenient, or at request of shareholders representing 5% of corporate capital unless bylaws set other limits, to resolve following: (1) Change in bylaws; (2) increase or reduction of capital; (3) redemption, reimbursement or amortization of shares; (4) merger, transformation or dissolution of corporation; all matters related to liquidation and liquidators; (5) issue of debentures or exchange of these for shares; (6) issue of participation bonds.

Notice of meetings, including full agenda and any special requirements set forth in bylaws for participation, shall be published for five days, at least ten days before meeting. Should meeting not take place second meeting must be called within 30 days. Decisions on matters not listed in agenda are null and void.

To participate in meetings, shareholders must deposit share certificates with corporation or present certificate from bank holding shares, three days before meeting. Shareholders may be represented in meetings, but not by directors, syndics, managers or other employees of corporation.

Ordinary meetings on first call require quorum of shareholders representing majority of shares with voting rights; any number of shareholders forms quorum for second call. In both cases resolutions require absolute majority of votes present unless bylaws call for different majority.

Extraordinary meetings on first call require presence of shareholders representing 60% of shares with voting rights; on second call quorum is 30%. Bylaws may establish different quorums.

Shares.—Share certificates must be numbered, signed by one or more directors and, contain name of corporation, date and place of registration, amount of subscribed capital, number, par value and type of shares. Bearer share certificates may only be issued once they are paid in full; until that time, shareholders are given nominal provisional certificates and remain liable for payment. Bylaws may establish different kinds of shares with different rights, which may be nominal or bearer shares. Transfer of unusual shares may be subject to special conditions.

Corporation may acquire own shares when authorized by special general meeting, and such purchase may be made with liquid earnings provided shares have been paid-in fully.

Accounts.—Directors are required to prepare and present to syndics quarterly financial statements. These form basis of annual reports which must be presented to shareholders together with written approval of syndics.

Directors are also required to prepare each year inventory, detailed statement of account, report on its tenure, and whatever other documents are needed to show condition of corporation. Documents must be approved at shareholders' ordinary meeting.

Dividends.—Five percent of net profits must be set aside annually with purpose of creating reserve fund of not less than 20% of subscribed capital. Dividends may only be paid to shareholders out of corporation's net profits. Any infringement makes directors jointly and severally liable.

Issue of Debentures.—Law 772/79 and C.C. allow issue of debentures by corporations provided they fulfill certain requirements.

See also topic Foreign Investment.

Limited Liability Personal Company.—All persons capable of entering into commerce with certain capital may form limited liability personal company.

Assets that form part of capital will be separate and independent from personal assets belonging to physical person, and respond completely to company obligations. Physical person's liabilities are limited to company total capital except in cases of intentional damage, fraud or consciously disobeying law in which cases physical person will respond with all his personal assets. Companies must be created by public instrument which must include: (a) Name, surname, civil status, nationality, profession and address of physical person; (b) company name, which must always include name and surname of physical person followed by words: "Compaõnía Individual de Responsabilidad Limitada", meaning limited liability personal company, as well as amount of total capital and address of company; (c) specific purpose of company; (d) amount of assigned capital; (e) value attributed to each of goods; (f) designation of administrator; this post may be filled by same physical person or his representative. Such companies are commercial to all legal effects. Total amount of capital must be deposited at company start-up. Company will stop operating if one or more of following cases occur: (a) Events stated in charter; (b) by express wish of physical person; (c) death of physical person; (d) bankruptcy of company; (e) loss of 50% or more of declared capital.

CURRENCY:

National currency unit is "Guaraní." Banco Central del Paraguay has exclusive right to issue bank notes and mint coins; which are legal tender in all territory.

DEATH:

Death can be pronounced by judicial decision if person has disappeared during earthquake, shipwreck, air or terrestrial accident, fire or similar catastrophe, or armed conflict, when circumstances do not sustain reasonable doubt of survival.

Uncertainty due to lack of news in respect of life of disappeared person or absence from his domicile or last residence within Republic for period of four years is basis for presumption of death. Term is abbreviated to two years if disappeared person has not named representative to manage his estate.

Any person with legitimate interest in assets of deceased or Attorney General's office may file for judicial decision of disappearance.

Disappeared person's estate is provisionally distributed among heirs and legatees. After ten years of disappearance or after 70 years from his birth distribution becomes final.

DEPOSITIONS:

In civil cases part of evidence is obtained by: (1) "Posiciones," (questions and answers made during course of suit by one party to another); (2) "declaraciones" (depositions of witnesses). "Declaraciones" may be taken orally before regular period for testimony, if witness is of advanced age or about to depart to place out of country or when there are other special circumstances.

Letters rogatory, with copies of questions to be asked, may be issued to another judge if examination is to take place elsewhere.

DESCENT AND DISTRIBUTION:

According to C.C. applicable law of descent and distribution to Paraguayan or foreign heirs is law of decedent's domicile at time of death. Real estate located in Paraguay is governed by local laws. If proceedings for settling decedent's estate are initiated in Paraguay and also abroad, heirs domiciled in Paraguay receive from property located within it portion equal in value to property located in foreign country from which they were excluded by foreign law.

Estate of decedent is acquired by heirs either by will or by operation of law and is considered inherited as of decedent's death.

Physical persons already conceived have legal capacity to acquire assets by donation, inheritance or legacy but irrevocability of acquisition is subject to child being born alive and living for at least some instants after separation from mother's womb.

Heirs may waive inheritance within period of 150 days from date of real or presumptive death; if domiciled abroad period is 240 days. Acceptance is presumed to be made subject to inventory of estate. Estate accepted under benefit of inventory remains separate from heir's property with respect to debts and charges attributable to decedent's estate. In simple acceptance acceptor is obligated to pay debts and charges out of inherited assets and from his own, but on legacies only out of legated assets. Acceptance and waivers are irrevocable.

Determination of Heirship.—Heirs nearer in degree of kindred exclude others. Intestate heirs are called by law in this order: 1st: decedent's children and surviving spouse; 2d: ascendants and surviving spouse; 3d: surviving spouse; 4th: brothers and sisters and their descendants to fourth degree.

Right of Representation.—Descendants of heir who died before decedent occupy his place and inherit his portion of estate. Waiver may be made by his descendants. Descendants have unlimited right of representation. In collateral line it takes place only in favor of brothers' and sisters' children. Ascendants do not have this right.

Only part of decedent's estate may be disposed of freely by will. Compulsory heirs and percentage of estate they are entitled to are: Descendants, four fifths; ascendants, two thirds; surviving spouse, being neither descendant or ascendant, half; adoptant and adopted, half. Should there be different kinds of compulsory heirs highest percentage prevails.

Decedent's children, matrimonial or born out of wedlock, take equal shares in decedent's separate property and property belonging to conjugal partnership. Ascendants inherit only in absence of descendants.

Adopted children, in simple or full adoption, inherit from adoptant as do matrimonial children. In full adoption, adoptant inherits from adopted excluding natural parents except on estate received by adopted from his natural relatives, which are inherited by natural parents excluding adoptant. In simple adoption adoptant parents have same rights as natural parents.

Surviving spouse has right to inherit separate property. If there be descendants, portion equal to each of them; decedent's parents, either one or both, third portion; other ascendants, half; if neither descendants nor ascendants, total estate. Widow who has no children is entitled to one fourth of portion deceased spouse would have inherited from inlaws' estate. On community property should there be descendants or ascendants, surviving spouse has no right. (See topic Husband and Wife.) Surviving spouse is not compulsory heir if: Spouse was ill at time of marriage and dies of such illness within 30 days unless couple had been living together before; if spouse had been divorced by judgment as guilty party; if spouses had agreed to live separately or were in fact separated with no intention of living together.

Collateral relatives entitled to inherit are brothers or sisters and their descendants to fourth degree. Half blood brothers and sisters either matrimonial or born out of wedlock inherit half as much as those of whole blood.

If there is neither will nor intestate heirs estate is declared vacant and assets are transferred to State.

DESCENT AND DISTRIBUTION . . . *continued*

Out of court partition of inheritance is allowed if all heirs are of age and agree to partition. Partition must be judicial when: Incompetent heirs or emancipated minors are interested parties; decedent is declared presumptively dead and heirs have possession of estate; there are absent heirs or legatees whose existence is doubtful; third parties with legitimate interest oppose out of court partition.

Collation.—Value at time of legal action of assets donated to compulsory heirs by decedent during his lifetime may be brought into estate on demand. Donor may release heir of this obligation within limits of disposable portion. Following are not collatable: Expenses on food, health, descendant's education, customary or friendship gifts and amounts invested in life insurance policies.

DIVORCE:

Divorce is authorized by Law 45/91. There is no divorce without judgment of competent court. Law admits divorce by mutual consent after three years of marriage if both spouses are of age. Grounds for divorce are: (1) Attempt by one spouse on other's life; (2) immoral conduct of one of spouses or incitement to commit adultery, prostitution or other vices or crimes; (3) bad treatment, excessive cruelty or slanderous conduct and injury to reputation; (4) usual state of drunkenness or drug use, when affect matrimonial life, gambling when threatens family's economy; (5) permanent and serious mental disease, declared by court; (6) voluntary and malicious abandonment of family house by any of spouses, including lack of assistance to other spouse or children, or noncompliance of alimony for more than four months; (7) adultery; (8) separation for more than one year, without willingness to reconcile by any of spouses.

All evidence is allowed in divorce proceeding except deposition by spouses and testimonial evidence by their ascendants and descendants.

Reconciliation of spouses ends divorce proceedings. Spouses may remarry after 300 days of issuance of divorce decree.

See also topics Husband and Wife; Marriage.

DRAFTS AND NOTES:

Formal requirements of draft are: (1) Denomination of "Draft" inserted in text of document, in language in which it is made; (2) unconditional order of paying sum of money; (3) name of payor; (4) indication of date of payment; (5) place of payment; (6) name of payee; (7) time and place where it is issued; (8) drawer's signature.

Draft may be issued: (1) To order of drawer; (2) to order of drawee, or third person.

Liability of drawer towards drawee: Only if drawer did not provide sufficient funds to drawee; he guarantees not only payment of draft, but also its acceptance. Liability of drawee: If funds were provided, drawee is always liable to holder of draft. Anyone who signs draft on behalf of third person must be empowered to do so. Drafts may be drawn: (1) At sight; (2) at term after date; (3) at term after sight; (4) number of months after date; (5) number of days or months after date or sight. Lack of indication makes instrument sight draft. If there is any variation between what is written in num bers and in letters, latter shall be deemed valid.

Endorsements.—Drafts are always endorsable. Endorsement may be made to any person. Conditional endorsements are deemed not made and partial endorsements are null and void. Endorsers are jointly and severally liable for acceptance and payment unless otherwise stated. Valid endorsements may be made in blank, to bearer, stating beneficiary, as collateral, or endorsement giving power of attorney.

Protest.—Should be made before notary public and two witnesses. Failure to pay must be recorded next working day after draft was due. If this day is holiday or Sun. on next working day.

Notarial protest contains: Date, copy of draft with acceptances, endorsements, guarantees, and any other data; demand to drawee or person liable to accept or pay stating whether he was present or not; reasons for refusal or statement that none was offered; signature of protesting party or statement of impossibility. Lack of presentation in time, or of protest when necessary, prejudices bill against endorsers, drawers and other liable parties, but not against acceptor. Bill duly protested is sufficient evidence to request immediate embargo and subsequent sale of assets of person liable for payment.

Aval.—Guarantee third party gives in favor of persons liable for payment of draft. It must be written in same instrument, on back, after words "por Aval" or other similar words, signifying joint guarantee.

Promissory Notes.—Are ruled by same provisions as drafts. Maker takes place of acceptor.

Checks.—Following data must be inserted for validity of check: (1) Check number and account number; (2) date and place of issue; (3) order to pay sum of money; (4) bank against which it is drawn; (5) designation of place of payment; (6) signature. Checks must be presented to bank within 30 days after date. Law 941/64 establishes criminal responsibilities for issuing checks without sufficient funds available or written authorizaton from bank to overdraw account. This becomes applicable if drawer does not pay check in full 24 hours after having been notified, by certified telegram, that check was returned by bank. It is prohibited by law to receive postdated check.

EXECUTIONS:

Judgments for money are carried into effect by attaching property of debtor.

Attachment of property is made in following order: (1) Money; (2) jewelry; (3) personal property or livestock; (4) real properties; (5) credits or shares; (6) salaries or pensions.

After attachment, next step is sale of property. Sale is held by an auctioneer after necessary advertisement of auction sale. Bidders must file bond in amount of 10% of total amount of property sold. Sale must take place at fiscal valuation. When nobody bids, another date will be set after reduction of 25% of valuation or for two-thirds of same. In spite of reduction mentioned, if no bids are made, property will be sold without price limitation.

Third parties may intervene to allege preferential rights but sale will not be stayed unless intervenor claims ownership based on a title of earlier date than execution. (C.de Proc. art. 398-462).

EXECUTORS AND ADMINISTRATORS:

While estate remains undivided, administration is granted in common to heirs. Surviving spouse is administrator with other heirs collaborating. If spouse is incompetent or conflict of interest exists administrator is named by courts.

Testator may appoint one or more executors. If none appointed, heirs themselves execute provisions of will. Appointment of executor must be in one of forms required for wills but need not be in same instrument.

Persons incompetent to receive legacy can be executors. Heirs, legatees, witnesses to will, and notary before whom will was executed may also be executors.

Testator may define duties of executor. If testator makes no special provisions executor has all powers necessary to execute will. Appointment of executor does not deprive intestate heirs of possession of assets but enough property should remain in executor's possession to pay debts and legacies.

Executor can neither delegate his authority nor pass it on to his own heirs, but can act through representatives for whose actions he is fully liable.

Testator may have authorized executor to sell his property but sale may be made only if indispensable for executing will and all heirs agree or courts authorize it.

Executor has right to intervene in any action related to validity of will. Heirs may have executor removed because of incapacity or bankruptcy.

Executor is required to render account to heirs of his administration. When several executors are named, authority is executed by them in order they are named. If testator determined they act jointly they are jointly liable and any divergence must be resolved by courts. Executor's remuneration is fixed by courts and all expenses are chargeable to estate.

FOREIGN EXCHANGE:

Decree 216/89 and Central Bank Circular 9/89 established Free Fluctuating Exchange System for all imports and exports of goods and services, and for capital movements, including public and private financial payments. System is regulated by Central Bank of Paraguay by intervening in market, but rates of foreign currencies are determined by offer and demand. Import and export operations, payments of services in general and movement of private capital must be channelled through banks. Authorized Exchange Houses operate also in exchange market, buying and selling foreign currencies freely.

FOREIGN INVESTMENT:

Law 60/90 establishes incentives regime to encourage economic development, promote growth in production of goods and services, create employment opportunities, generate exports and substitute imports utilizing national resources, and incorporate efficient technology for increased and better use of national raw materials, labor and energy resources. Legal and fiscal framework allows national and foreign investors, without discrimination, to formulate investment projects, facilitating their full operational productivity.

Types of Investment.—Persons and legal entities may make investments and reinvestments in following manner: (a) In cash, in financing, in suppliers' credits or other financial instruments; (b) in capital goods necessary for development of approved investment projects; (c) in trademarks, drawings, models and industrial processes and other forms of transfer of technology subject to licensing; (d) in services and specialized technical assistance; (e) in form of leasing of capital goods; (f) in other forms as determined in regulations to be adopted by Executive Branch.

Capital goods, either imported or of local origin, must preferentially be new, of adequate technology, and in conditions of productive efficiency. Benefits contemplated are not extensive to goods and services for personal use or consumption.

Benefits.—Investment projects enjoy following benefits: (a) Total exemption from all taxes applicable to constitution, recording and registration of corporations and companies; (b) total exemption from all taxes applicable to issue, subscription or transfer of stock or shares provided for in company statutes or contracts; from all taxes on capital increase of companies or corporations, and on transfer of goods or beneficial rights subject to pecuniary valuation, that partners or shareholders pay-in to such enterprises as capital contributions contemplated in investment project; from all taxes applicable to issue, purchase or sale of bonds, debentures and other evidence of indebtedness of such corporations or companies; (c) total exemption from all taxes and charges applicable to foreign exchange transactions arising out of capital contributions or operations contemplated in investment project; (d) total exemption from customs duties and similar taxes, including specific Internal Revenue levies on imports of capital goods; (e) exemption from all requirements of special bonds in connection with importation of capital goods; (f) total exemption from all taxes and other levies on national or foreign loans, overdrafts, advances, suppliers' credits or financing; on chattel mortgages, mortgages and guarantees thereon; on renêwals, refinancing, extensions and amortizations thereof and on remittances and payments, within country or abroad of interest, commissions and principal applied to total or partial financing of investments contemplated in investment project, for term of five years; (g) exemption of 95% of income taxes over period of five years as of date of presentation of tax statement covering first year of production on income generated by investment project; (h) total exemption from all taxes applicable to beneficiaries of dividends and profits generated by investment project for term of five years; (i) total exemption from all taxes applicable on payments, accreditations or transfers of dividends, rentals, leases, profits, royalties, rights on use of trademarks, patents, industrial drawings and models and other forms of technology transfer subject to licencing to beneficiaries resident in country or not, for term of five years; (j) exemption from Stamp Tax applicable to acts, contracts, payments, receipts and promissory notes, related to investment project. Persons and legal entities reinvesting net profits are entitled to reduction of 50% of income tax. To qualify, reinvestment must be reflected in minimum increase of 30% of paid-in capital, in accordance with approved investment project.

Leasing of Capital Goods.—Foreign capital goods introduced into country and capital goods of national origin under leasing contracts enjoy same tax benefits under law and those applicable under System of Temporary Admission, during term of leasing contract, at which time contracts may be renewed, capital goods nationalized

See Topical Index in front part of this volume.

FOREIGN INVESTMENT . . . *continued*

or reexported. Businesses engaged in leasing of capital goods may apply for same benefits.

Leasing Register functions under General Directorate of Public Registers to register goods under leasing contracts, benefits granted, liens and other pertinent documents. Executive Branch regulates obligations and formalities of such Register.

Ships and aircraft of foreign registration, chartered or leased for period not exceeding two years, may be recorded in national register without prejudice to their original registration, provided country of original registration does so permit. Executive Branch regulates rights, obligations, formalities and benefits arising out of national registration.

General Provisions.—Beneficiaries must comply with all obligations and commitments assumed in approved investment project under penalty of cancellation of all or part of benefits granted. Detailed records of assets incorporated under investment project must be maintained in order to allow competent authorities to control their use and application.

Investment Council acts as advisory entity to Ministry of Industry and Commerce and Ministry of Finance. Membership is designated by Executive Branch with ministerial officials and representatives of private sector. Investment Council is chaired by representative of Ministry of Industry and Commerce and its members serve without remuneration. Investment Council is responsible for: (a) Advising public and private institutions on investments; (b) keeping record of applications filed and benefits granted; (c) counseling on issues related to investments not contemplated in present law.

Benefits are granted to applicant in each case by Ministerial Resolution executed jointly by Minister of Industry and Commerce and Minister of Finance. Ministry of Industry and Commerce supervises application and performance of economic development incentives; Ministry of Finance supervises all tax matters, but implementation by its departments is limited to overseeing compliance with Law, without further requirements.

Rights acquired by beneficiaries under Law are irrevocable, provided corresponding obligations are met.

FOREIGN TRADE REGULATIONS:

All importers and exporters must register as such and keep certain books of account. Most importations are subject to a system of import duties and ad valorem surcharges, unless expressly exempted therefrom. Special tariff concessions are granted to some products originated in member countries of Latin American Integration Association.

Import duties and surcharges are subject to constant revisions, and importations may at times be temporarily prohibited.

Exports are also subject to a system of surcharges unless exempt therefrom, pursuant to specific incentives and rebate programs.

HUSBAND AND WIFE:

Ruled by C.C. as modified by Law 1/92.

Rights and Obligations.—Husband and wife have same rights, obligations and duties, independent of monetary contribution to household.

Separate Property.—Each spouse is sole owner of following property: Those earned or inherited before marriage; those obtained by donation, inheritance, legacy or acquired by gift; those acquired for valuable consideration during marriage where title is previous to marriage; those obtained with own money or in exchange of assets owned by spouse; compensation for personal accidents, health insurance, personal injury or life insurace; author and patent rights; increase in value of personal property; pensions and life annuities in favor of one spouse prior to marriage; personal effects and family souvenirs, clothes, books and work tools; indemnity for damage to personal property; increase in value of personal property during marriage done with community property with right of compensation of other spouse.

Contracts.—Spouses cannot enter into contracts between them with regard to separate or community property but they may incorporate or become partners in companies of limited liability.

Domicile.—Place where spouses live together. Either spouse may temporarily abandon it to perform public duties, for work related reasons or other relevant personal matter.

Marriage Patrimonial Regimes.—Law recognizes following: (i) community property; (ii) differed participation and (iii) property separation. Patrimonial regime may be established by antenuptial agreement.

Community Property.—Property obtained during marriage. Spouses are subject to community property unless they agree to different system.

Community property includes; Earnings from work, commerce or profession of spouse; assets obtained by onerous title from common income; natural and civil fruit of community or separate property accrued during marriage; companies established during marriage; assets acquired through legal gambling, lottery or other. Both spouses have legal representation and administration of community property. Community property ends in following cases: divorce; marriage declared void; ordered by court; change of patrimonial system and death of one spouse.

Differed Participation.—That which each spouse manages, enjoys and disposes freely of separate and community property. At end of system each spouse acquies right to participate in profits obtained by other. Profits are divided equally.

Property Separation.—That which each spouse has use, administration and right to dispose his own property. Upon property separation, community property rights end.

See also topics Divorce; Marriage.

IMMIGRATION:

Requirements to obtain residence are: (1) Certificate of good behavior given by authorities from country of origin; (2) two photographs 4 x 4 cm.; (3) valid passport; (4) testimonial of job availability in country; (5) marriage certificate; (6) birth certificate. All documents must be certified by Paraguay Consul abroad. Authority in charge is Dirección General de Migraciones.

INFANTS:

Age of majority is 20. Minors may be emancipated: By marriage; by competent court judgment granted with minor's and parents' or guardian's consent enabling 18 year old minor to engage in business; by obtaining university degree. Emancipation is irrevocable.

Minors are subject to authority of both parents. In case of disagreement refering to practice of paternal authority court will decide under petition of party.

Parents have usufruct of their children's assets with certain exceptions, but cannot dispose of them without court authorization. In absence of parents guardian is appointed.

Contracts entered into by minors under 14 are null and cannot be ratified. If executed by minors over 14 but not emancipated they are voidable. Only minors may claim their nullity or ratify them once minority ceases.

INTEREST:

Punitive or compensatory interest on monetary obligations may not exceed maximum rates established by Central Bank, otherwise stipulation is considered null and void. 1990's Resolution No. 3 from Central Bank establishes that maximum interest rate will be considered from average of active rates applied by banks and other financial institutions, calculated monthly by Central Bank.

JUDGMENTS:

Foreign judgments have force provided for in treaties. In absence of a treaty, a foreign judgment may be executed if following circumstances exist: (1) that judgment was obtained in an action in personam; (2) that obligation on which action was based is valid according to Paraguay's law; (3) that decision be a final one and proper certifications and legalizations are complied with according to law of Paraguay; (4) that judgment has not been pronounced by default of condemned party.

LABOR RELATIONS:

Rules of labor law govern relations between workers and employers regarding subordinated and remunerated labor activity, either intellectual, manual or technical. Dependent intellectual, manual and technical workers; teachers of private educational institutions; persons exercising professional sports activities; labor unions of workers and employers of public sector; workers of State and Municipal institutions are subject to its provisions. (Art. 2 of Labor Code).

Following are not included in provisions of Code: Directors, managers, administrators, attorneys-in-fact, agents and other senior employees of firms who enjoy notorious independence in their work shall be independent of scope of application of Labor Code. In general all persons performing management and administrative functions with employers' express consent; (2) services performed occasionally such as friendly and good neighbour services; (3) public officials and employees of state central administration and personnel of autonomous state entities in charge of economic production of goods or public services; (4) those known as "extra-territorial", i.e. protected by diplomatic exemptions; (5) domestic service has its own regulations.

Labor Procedure Code establishes that jurisdiction cannot be delegated nor can competence be extended. Jurisdiction is exercised with respect to individual and collective legal labor conflicts in single, primary and secondary instances.

Working Hours.—Law imposes time limitations on labor: (1) (a) Daytime: eight hours per day or 48 hours per week. Daytime is from 6 a.m. to 8 p.m. (b) Nightwork: seven hours per day or 42 hours per week. Night time is from 8 p.m. to 6 a.m. (c) Mixed: 7½ hours per day or 45 hours per week. Includes parts of both, but less than 3½ hours of night time.

Additional working hours are allowed under special circumstances but they cannot exceed three hours per day, three days per week, or 57 hours per week, and must be paid extra. Not allowed for employees under 18.

Wages.—May be freely stipulated but cannot be less than legal minimum. May be paid by time units (month, fortnight, day or hour), by work units (either piecework, assignment or jobbing), by sales commissions or collection to account of employer and as percentage on future profits.

Labor Department sets minimum wages for workers in Republic according to areas and type of work performed based on cost of living studies made by National Council of Minimum Wages and by authorization of National Council of Economic Coordination and although law refers to areas, at present there is minimum wage for whole country.

Annual Bonus.—Law requires additional annual pay equivalent to one twelfth of earnings during year, provided they have worked full year with same employer. Bonus must be paid before Dec. 31.

Child Labor.—Right to work is acquired at 18. Minors over 15 and under 18 should have authorization to work issued by parents or guardian. Minors over 15 may only work: (a) At family enterprises not dangerous to their life, health or morals; (b) at trades doing work with intent of gaining knowledge of trade; (c) in agricultural and ranching activities under certain conditions.

Minors over 12 and under 15 may only work: (a) At family enterprises not dangerous to their life, health or morality; (b) at professional enterprises, performing work intended to acquire professional knowledge; (c) in agricultural and cattle activities under certain conditions.

Female Labor.—Women cannot perform any job dangerous to their life, health or morals. In case of pregnancy they are entitled to paid rest period of six weeks before and after giving birth. If more than 50 workers are employed in industrial or commercial establishment day care centers must be provided for children under two.

Discrimination.—Law forbids discrimination due to age, sex, nationality, religion or politics or trade union activities.

Labor Unions.—Law recognizes right of workers and employees, without distinction of sex or nationality, and without need of previous authorization, to freely establish organizations, purpose of which is to study, defend, develop and protect their professional interest, and also to improve social, economic, cultural and moral status of their associates. Labor unions may be formed by white-collar workers, manual

LABOR RELATIONS . . . *continued*
workers or mixed groups and may join in labor federations. Ratification and registration of labor unions and employer's associations must be authorized by Labor Department. Otherwise their acts are null.

According to Law guarantee of job tenure is granted to committee members in labor unions, federations and confederations duly registered and recognised by labor authorities as well as to workers conducting negotiations and transactions preparatory to recognition of labor union and those negotiating collective labor contracts or internal work regulations.

Labor Disputes.—National Constitution establishes rights and laws govern their exercise. National Constitution sets forth, in favor of all workers of public and private sectors, right to resort to strike in cases of conflict of interests. (Art. 98 NC). On the other hand, employers have right to lockout under same conditions.

Labor Code (Arts. 358/78 LC) recognizes right to strike, lawful exercise of which is restricted for protection of general interests and public services essential to community (Art. 128 and ending provision of Art. 98, NC).

Labor Code recognizes strike and lockout rights. Collective contracts may provide that parties will not take these actions, in event of labor disputes derived from application of law. To be legally acceptable strike should be intended to obtain acceptance of collective labor contract, or compliance therewith, or eventually negotiating acceptance of contract after it expires. Upon disappearance of mandatory arbitration and operation of Junta Permanente de Conciliación collective conflicts of economic nature are resolved directly by negotiation or through organs of voluntary mediation or before Courts.

Strike Declaration.—Following requisites must be met before implementing strike decision: This must be made by General Meeting of workers themselves of work place involved (Arts. 363 and 298, §[e] LC) who shall nominate members of Strike Committee in event that they do not have union to represent them.

Meeting shall comply with the following requirements: (a) Call pursuant to manner and anticipation set forth in statutes; (b) attendance of absolute majority, decisions being pursuant to favorable opinion of one-half plus one of those present; (c) duly drawn-up minutes of meeting (Art. 297, LC); (d) decision to be adopted by secret vote of participants in meeting (Art. 298, §[e], LC); (e) prior notice: notice of strike must be given 72 hours in advance to Labor Administrative Authority and employer; (f) Joint Commission: strikers and employers shall constitute joint commission to reconcile interests which in term of 72 hours shall seek agreement; in event of disagreement, matter shall be referred to Standing Commission on Conciliation and Arbitration (JPCA) of Ministry of Justice and Labor (Arts. 284 to 320, Labor Procedural Code) or to labor courts and tribunals. Arbitration is not mandatory but is recommended alternative for solution of collective conflicts; (g) legality or illegality of strike: Art. 378, LC, sets forth that any labor court may declare legality or illegality of strike pursuant to Art. 376, LC, which expressly sets forth instances of illegal strikes.

Workmen's Dismissal Compensation.—Dismissal is restricted after ten years of seniority.

Cause for dismissal must be evidenced in lawsuit.

Indemnification for lack of prior notice, depending on seniority: (a) Up to one year, 30 days' wages; (b) up to five years, 45 days' wages; (c) Over ten years, 90 days' wages.

Indemnification for seniority: 15 days' wages per year of service or fraction of six months.

Union representatives may not be dismissed unless for just cause evidenced in lawsuit.

Pregnant women may not be dismissed.

Dismissal of pregnant women is null and void.

Social Security System.—(Law 98/92). (1) Salaried workers, in conditions previously named; (2) apprentice workers; (3) personnel of autonomous State entities or mixed corporations, in charge of any economic operating of public service; (4) teachers and professors of primary, secondary, professional and language schools, private or public and on optional basis, independent workers, with respect to risks of accidents, illness and maternity; (5) same coverage for university professors in service of public and private institutions; (6) by Law 431/73, veterans, disabled and crippled ex-servicemen of Chaco War, wife and children under age, will receive, free of charge, in case of illness or injury, medical-surgical, odontological and pharmaceutical assistance, at public hospi-tals and at those pertaining to autonomous State entities; (7) diplomatic agents who employ persons to whom no exemption is applied, must comply with obligations imposed on employers by Social Security provisions of receiving State. Same for consular agents.

Social Security Institute (Instituto de Previsión Social-I.P.S.) is autonomous agency in charge of directing and administrating Social Security. It covers risks of illness or accidents for salaried personnel and dependents, maternity, accidents at work and professional illness, incapacitation, old age and death of salaried workers who render services or carry on job by virtue of verbal or written labor contract, whatever their age or salary earned. This institute is also in charge of retirements and supplementary pensions. Inclusion into Social Security System is mandatory. Infractions are generally fined. Moreover, if employer has not inscribed, nor communicated entrance of employee, nor contributed for him, in case of accident, or death by accident at work, he must be responsible before I.P.S. and pay amounts corresponding to pensions and other benefits.

Incidence of contribution on salary amount is 16.50% to employer and 9.50% to worker. Minimum base over which day laborers and workmen doing piecework must contribute, is amount corresponding to 18 days wages. In no case will contributions be calculated over amounts smaller than minimum legal wage.

Employers Liability.—Employers are not liable for accidents suffered by employees, even those resulting in death, as risk is covered by Social Security System which pays injury, disability or death indemnization.

LIMITATION OF ACTIONS:

See topic Prescription.

MARRIAGE:

Following conditions are bar to marriage: Minors aged under 16 unless special permit is granted by Minors Court, in special circumstances, from age 14 on; persons already married; person suffering chronic, contagious and hereditary disease; persons suffering chronic mental illness, even if temporary; deaf-mute, blind-deaf and blind-mute persons, when cannot freely express their will.

Minors between ages 16 and 20 need parental or guardian authorization to marry.

Cannot marry among themselves: ascendants and descendants in direct line; relatives with affinity in direct line; adopter and his descendants with adopted and his descendants; adoptive children among themselves and with biological children of adopter; person condemned for homicide, attempted homicide or accomplice of homicide of other spouse; kidnapper with kidnapped woman during kidnapping or within three months after it ends.

Validity of marriage requires that parties' consent be given before public official. Consent can be given through attorney; special power of attorney must indicate full personal data of person principal wishes to marry and shall expire after 90 days of authorization. For execution of marriage by granted power, one of contracting parties shall be present. (Law 1266/87).

Capacity of spouses, form and validity of marriage are ruled by law of place of marriage. Marriages executed in Paraguay are dissolved by death of spouse or divorce.

See also topics Divorce; Husband and Wife.

MINES AND MINERALS:

Art. 112 of Constitution determines that State has ownership of all hydrocarbons and solid, liquid or gaseous minerals found in natural state in country's territory, excepting stones or calcareous substances. State may grant concessions for prospecting, exploration and exploitation of deposits to individuals or private, public or mixed enterprises, for limited time. Concessions granted by Government require Legislative approval.

Oil and Gas Concessions.—Law 779/95 governs hydrocarbon concessions and establishes rights and obligations of parties. Concessions are divided into prospecting, exploration and exploitation phases. Requirements to apply for concession are: (a) demonstrate financial capacity and technical expertise; (b) establish local branch or subsidiary, designating legal representative; (c) present activities and investment program for prospecting and exploration phases; (d) present map of area with geographical coordinates.

Prospecting Permits.—Granted by Resolution of Ministry of Public Works and Communications, for one year renewable for another year, over 2,400,00 hectare area. Permit holder must post bond of US$75,000 approximately, and has preference to select one or more exploration lots in permit area.

Exploration Concessions.—Granted by contract with Government, for four years renewable for another two years, in 40,000 hectares lots to maximum area of 800,000 hectares. Concessionaire must post bond of US$.20 per hectare, and may convert into exploitation concession.

Exploitation Concessions.—Granted by contract, for 20 years renewable for another ten years, over area not to exceed 5,000 hectares. During exploitation stage concessionaire shall pay State following: (a) Land Fees: (i) one time fee of US$.30 per hectare, and (ii) progressive annual exploitation fees from US$.20 to US$2 per hectare; (b) royalties on production: (i) 100-5,000 barrels per day, 10%, (ii) 5001-50,000 barrels per day, 12%, (iii) over 50,001 barrels per day, 14%.

Mineral Concessions.—Law to govern mineral exploration presently before Congress. Meantime, Government has granted individual mineral concessions by contract approved by law, which establish rights and obligations of parties. Concessions are divided into prospecting, exploration and exploitation phases. Requirements to apply for concession are: (a) demonstrate financial capacity and technical expertise; (b) establish local branch or subsidiary, designating legal representative; (c) present activities and investment program for prospection and exploration phases; (d) present map of area with geographical coordinates.

Prospecting Phase is for one year renewable for another year, over 150,000 hectare area. Permit holder must post third party liability insurance of US$3,000,000, and has preference to select one or more exploration lots in permit area. Land Fees are US$.55 per hectare.

Exploration Phase is for two years renewable for another one year up to maximum area of 75,000 hectares. Concessionaire may convert into exploitation concession. Land Fees are US$1.30 per hectare.

Exploitation Phase Concessions.—Granted by contract, for 25 years renewable for similar period based on investment and production program, over area not to exceed 37,500 hectares. During exploitation stage concessionaire shall pay State following: (a) Land Fees of US$1.30 per hectare, and (b) royalties on production equivalent to 2.5% of FOB value.

MONOPOLIES AND RESTRAINT OF TRADE:

Art. 107 of 1992 Constitution forbids monopolies and artificial increase or decrease of prices which may restrain free market competition.

Government monopolies may be established by law as protection and exploitation of public utilities.

MORTGAGES OF REAL PROPERTY:

Mortgage cannot be placed on personal property, nor on right of usufruct or use and habitation, but when has to be placed on real property is extensive to all accessories so long as they are united to property, to all buildings erected on vacant land, to rents and results from insurance coverage. It is not divisible; properties mortgaged to secure debt are bound for whole amount and creditor may proceed against any or all of them. Only owner can mortgage property; joint owner may mortgage his share, but in case of partition, mortgage is applied on his share alone.

Mortgage must be made by a notarial act or public instrument. Instrument may be executed in a foreign country, and should be legalized and protocolized by order of civil court. They can be opposed to third parties as from date of recording in Public

See Topical Index in front part of this volume.

MORTGAGES OF REAL PROPERTY . . . *continued*

Registry of Mortgages or if a certificate of free disposability has been requested by a notary, up to 20 days from date of certificate.

Recording may be requested by grantor, grantee, and by anyone interested in security. Mortgages must be recorded every 20 years to be effective.

Debtor must not decrease value of mortgaged property; if he does so, mortgagee may require a deposit of an amount sufficient to make security good, and if negative may foreclose mortgage. Mortgages are foreclosed by brief, summary actions in C.de Proc.

Chattel Mortgages.—See topic Chattel Mortgages.

OIL AND GAS EXPLORATION AND EXPLOITATION:

See topic Mines and Minerals.

PARTNERSHIPS:

Limited Liability Company (Sociedad de Responsabilidad Limitada).—Company may use name of one or more partners preceded or followed by words: Sociedad de Responsabilidad Limitada or S.R.L. SRL can only be commercial, even if it undertakes civil activities. May not engage in banking, insurance, or savings/loans operations.

SRL may not operate unless contract has been registered in Public Registry of Commerce. Failure to do so creates unlimited responsibility of partners towards third parties.

Capital.—Represented by nominal non-endorsable quotas of Gs.1,000 or multiples thereof.

Incorporation.—SRL may be formed by two, but no more than 25, partners after subscription of company capital and payment in cash of at least 50% thereof. No minimum capital requirement, but must be adequate for type of business company will engage in. Export and import companies must meet certain requisites imposed by Central Bank. Company capital may also be incorporated in goods or fixed assets, which are transferred to company in constitutive documents or once company contract is recorded in Public Registry of Commerce. Partners remain jointly and severally liable towards third parties for value of goods and assets incorporated as capital.

If SRL has more than five partners, transfer of quotas to third parties must be approved by partners that represent 3/4 of capital; if less than five partners vote must be unanimous. Transfer of quotas among partners is unrestricted.

Partner wishing to transfer capital quotas must advise others, who must reply within 15 days. Assent is presumed if no opposition is made. Partner not able to obtain consent for transfer quotas may be authorized to do so by judge in summary proceedings. If opposition is deemed to be without cause other partners may acquire quotas under same conditions offered to or by third parties. Company may also acquire quotas with net liquid profits or by reducing its capital. Transfer of quotas must be made by Public Notary, and does not have effect until registered in Public Registry of Commerce.

Managers.—Administration and representation of SRL is charged to one or more managers (gerentes), who may be partners or not, and who have same rights and duties as directors of sociedades anónimas. There are no limitations to their terms.

Managers may not act on their own initiative in respect to any business transaction that is not included within objectives of company, nor can they assume representation of persons or commercial entities with similar business without express authorization of partners. Managers are jointly and severally liable to company and partners in case of bad management or violation of company charter.

All partners have right to take part in decisions of company. If SRL's charter does not determine how partners will reach decisions, rules of ordinary shareholder's meeting of sociedades anónimas will apply. Change of purpose, transformation, merger, or any other amendment to company's charter which imposes more responsibility to partners requires unanimous consent. Any other resolution by partners can be decided by vote of majority of capital. Each quota represents one vote.

Reserve Fund.—Five percent of actual net profits are required to be set aside annually with purpose of creating reserve fund of not less than 20% of company's capital.

Dissolution.—SRL is not dissolved by death, interdiction or bankruptcy of partners, or by dismissal of manager(s) named in contract, unless special dispo-sition stipulates contrary. Bankruptcy of company does not imply bankruptcy of partners.

Simple Partnership.—Any partnership that is not partnership as defined by Civil Code and does not have as object commercial activity is simple partnership. Commercial activities are following: (a) Any industrial activity whose purpose is to produce services and goods; (b) any activity as intermediary; (c) carriage; (d) banking, insurance or stock trading; (e) any other activity defined by merchant law as commercial activity. Any partnership that has as object commercial activity must be recorded in Public Register of Commerce. Law does not indicate any special form for this kind of partnership, but if partners wish to limit their liability they must show contract to third parties. Even if they do so partners who conduct business are subject to unlimited liability.

Commandite.—This partnership has two kinds of partners: (1) Those with unlimited liability, (2) those with limited liability, up to value of their shares (silent partners); firm name must contain at least name of one of active partners. When commandite does not show names of every partner, name must be followed by words "y Compaöoia". If silent partner adds his name to firm name he incurs unlimited liability.

General partnership rules are applicable to these companies if compatible.

Initial document of firm must indicate who are unlimited liability partners and who are silent partners. First administration and have same rights as partners of general partnership. Silent partners may not manage or do business in firm name, unless they are so authorized by special power of attorney. If they do so they have unlimited liability to third parties.

Joint-Stock Company.—As in commandite this partnership has same kind of partners. Unlimited liability partners have administration of partnership. Law of corporations is applicable where pertinent and not contrary to joint-stock company bylaws.

Shareholders named as administrators can only be removed by judgment rendered by competent judge, requested by general meeting of shareholders, representing at least 10% of paid-up capital.

General Partnership.—Partners have unlimited liability. Firm name must show name of one or more partners followed by words "Sociedad Colectiva" or "S.C.". Contract establishing firm must contain: (a) Partner's names, surnames and domiciles; (b) firm name; (c) partners who have administration of firm; (d) address of partnership and its branches; (e) partnership object, etc. When contract has been made by public instrument it must be recorded within 30 days. Partners cannot enter into business that is compatible with object of partnership unless duly authorized by other partners.

See topic Corporations (Sociedades Anôonimas), subhead Limited Liability Personal Company.

PATENTS:

New industrial products, new methods and new applications of established methods are patentable. Duration of patent is for 15 years, each patent paying an annual tax. Following are not patentable: (1) Discoveries, inventions or applications without industrial use, like plans and combinations for credit, finance, advertising and such; (2) discoveries, inventions and applications that are contrary to or an infringement of public order, national security or country's moral values; (3) medicines and pharmaceutical products are covered by laws and regulations dealing with this matter.

To obtain invention patent, following requisites are necessary: (1) Description of invention in duplicate; drawings and samples of models conforming to regulations must be presented with petition as well as fee established by law; (2) in case of chemical patent a sample for analysis should be included as well as sample for record purposes; (3) one copy of drawings should be on white paper and other on tracing paper; each drawing should be 33 cm. by 22 cm. with a margin of 15 mm. Improvements of inventions may be patented in same manner as original inventions and for period of original patent.

Patent rights can be ceded or transferred, but must be instrumented before a Public Notary and recorded in Patent Office.

For inscriptions of foreign patents it is necessary to indicate if patent has been recorded in country of origin, indicating date of recording. Petition has to be written in Spanish, or have pertinent translation enclosed.

For revalidation of patents by virtue of international treaties or conventions it is not necessary to present translation and legalization of patent documents; it is sufficient to mention country granting patent, number and date of approval and duration of patent right.

POWERS OF ATTORNEY:

See topic Principal and Agent.

PRESCRIPTION:

Prescription is governed by C.C.

Following rights and actions do not prescribe: Rights derived from family relations; action to attack null acts; action to demand partition of inherited property or condominiums that remain undivided; action of person declared presumptively dead to sue heirs for restitution of his property.

Actions must be brought within following periods after respective causes of action accrue:

Ten Years: For incapable person or his heirs against guardian to demand rendering of accounts and vice versa, period commences from date incapable person dies or incapacity ceases; those derived from right acknowledged by judgment; for petition of inheritance, period commences from date defendant took possession of inheritance; for collation of inheritance and all those not subject to lesser term.

Five Years: To demand accrued alimony pensions and price of rents; sums of money, not being principal, that must be paid annually or at shorter periods, i.e. interest; rights derived from relations between partners and with company; of company creditors to demand managers' liability.

Four Years: For heirs to demand reduction of estate of co-heir if it exceeds disposable portion, and action of reduction against third parties to safeguard heirs' legitimate portion; rights derived from endorsable or bearer documents; if they are payable at sight period commences on date of issue and if on time from due date.

Three Years: Rights derived from current account contract; merchants to demand price of goods sold to merchants; of indignity and disinheritance; period commences from date of decedent's death.

Two Years: To demand nullity of acts for error of fact, fraud, violence or intimidation (period commences from date violence or intimidation ceases or other vices are known); creditors to revoke contracts entered into by debtor in case of fraud: period commences from date creditors become advised and in any case five years after act was executed; to demand annullment of obligation incurred by incapable person without guardian's approval: period commences from date incapacity ceases; lawyers, engineers and all liberal professions to demand payment of fees; merchants to demand price of goods sold to non-merchants; liability derived from unlawful acts; partial or complete simulation, by parties to contract or by third parties: period commences from date third parties become aware of simulation and for contractual parties when supposed simulator intends to disavow simulation.

One Year: To cancel effects of donation or legacy by reason of ingratitude or indignity: period commences from date act is known by donator or decedent's heirs; owners of hotels, hospitals or similar entities for food, lodging and other related expenses; to demand payment of tuition in schools; auctioneers and brokers to demand payment of commissions; rights derived from transport contract: period commences from date passenger arrives or damage occurs or from date goods are or should be delivered, if transport began or ended abroad prescription is extended to 18 months; rights derived from insurance policy: period commences from date obligation is due, in life insurance prescription commences from date existence of benefit is known by beneficiary but may not exceed three years after damage took place.

Six Months: Purchaser to rescind contract or to be indemnified for non-apparent servitude which seller omitted to mention.

See Topical Index in front part of this volume.

PRESCRIPTION . . . *continued*

Three Months: Hidden damages action to cancel sales contract and to reduce price because of hidden defect.

Suspension of Prescription.—Prescription does not run against non-emanicipated minors, persons subject to interdiction because of mental illness, absentees and all other incapable persons during period they do not have guardian and six months after designation of guardian or until incapacity ceases.

Prescription is suspended: Between spouses; between person exercising patria potestas and minors subject to it; between guardian and minor or interdicted person until rendering of accounts is made; between companies or corporations and their managers while they are on duty; in favor of persons absent from country on public service. Suspension can be alleged only by person in whose benefit it is established. Period during which prescription is suspended is not counted.

Interruption of Prescription.—Prescription period before fact that brought about interruption is not counted. Prescription is interrupted by: Claim notified to debtor; presentation of title of credit at proceedings for settling estate of decedent or at creditors' meeting; acknowledgment of credit by debtor; by commitment between parties written into public deed to submit case to arbitrators or to amicable compounders.

Contractual Limitations.—Prescription in future may not be waived nor may parties agree to different period, but prescription already fulfilled may be waived explicitly or tacitly.

Pleading.—To claim prescription it must be alleged by person in whose favor it is established.

PRINCIPAL AND AGENT:

Powers of attorney which are to be presented in court, those for administration of property and those which concern public instruments or matters which should be in form of public instruments, must themselves be in form of public instruments.

General power of attorney only confers power of administration even though power gives authority to do any act when grantee deems convenient in course of administration. Special powers are necessary for following purposes: to make payments which are not in ordinary course of administration; to make contracts extinguishing obligations which existed at time; to submit suit to arbitration; to waive jurisdiction; to renounce rights which have been acquired by prescription; to renounce right to appeal; to renounce or remit debts gratuitously, except in case of bankruptcy of debtor; to do any act related to family's right which can be done by third parties; public document authorizing these acts must specify them and mention person to whom power is granted to make any contract for purpose of obtaining, transferring, waiving or extinguishing interest in real property; this paragraph does not include authorization to mortgage or transfer real property for debts preceding power; to make gifts except in cases of small sums to employees; to loan or borrow money unless business of administration consists of lending or borrowing, or unless it is absolutely necessary to borrow money to conserve property which is being administered; to lease real property for more than five years; to make grantee bailee, unless power refers to bailments or bailment or is made as result of administration of property; to allow grantee to become surety; to perform any sort of personal services; to form company; to accept inheritances and to admit obligations existing prior to granting of power.

Power is presumed onerous, except when contrary is agreed.

Power may be granted to minor 18 years old.

Special power for certain acts specifically determined must be limited to them and cannot be extended to similar acts which can be considered as natural consequence of those entrusted by grantor.

He may delegate power to another but is responsible for substitute, unless he has been given express authority to substitute, and is responsible when he has named a substitute who is notoriously incompetent or insolvent. Grantee may revoke a substitute at any time.

Power terminates by revocation; by renunciation on part of grantee; when duration of time for power is due or when either of parties is dead or has become incapacitated.

It is necessary that grantee and third persons know or should have known of termination of power in order to make it ineffective with regard to them. Everything that grantee does while he is ignorant of termination of power binds grantor.

Revocation occurs when grantor gives new power to another person for same purpose and grantee is notified of same. Granting of a special power revokes a general power insofar as it affects matters dealt with in special powers.

PUBLIC INSTRUMENTS:

Following are public instruments: (1) Notarial documents; (2) other instruments prepared by notaries or public officers in form provided by law; judicial proceeding and survey maps duly approved by judicial authorities; (3) judicial proceeding made as provided in laws of procedures; (4) bills of exchange accepted by Government or by official bank as its representative; (5) bills or any other credit document issued according to law; (6) registration on accounting books belonging to Public Administration; (7) registrations of public debts; (8) records of public registry; and (9) copies or photostatic copies of public instruments duly authorized.

Public instruments must be signed by interested parties who appear as having taken part in their execution. Following persons cannot be witnesses: Minors, even those emancipated; persons subject to interdiction or disability; blind persons; those who do not know how to sign; clerks of office and of other offices authorized to prepare public documents; spouse and relatives of public official to fourth degree of consanguinity and second degree of affinity; and those persons disabled by final verdict to be witnesses to public instrument.

Notarial documents must be in Spanish language. If person executing documents does not know Spanish language, document should be made in form of memorandum written in language known by parties and signed by them in presence of notary and authenticated by him. If not signed in his presence, authentication of signature must be certified by notary. It is then translated by official translator. Memorandum and translation are then placed in notary's protocol.

Notarial document must state its nature, object, names and surnames of persons executing it, whether or not they are of age, their family status, domicile, nationality, place, and date when it was signed, which may be holiday. If notary does not know parties, they must prove their identity with accurate legal document or two witnesses must identify them and document must include names, domicile or residence of witnesses. If parties are represented by agents, documents must state that power of attorney has been presented and it must be transcribed in notary's register along with document. If power has been executed in his own office, notary needs only refer to its place of record.

Notarial documents which do not state place and date of execution, name of person executing them, their signatures and which do not include power of attorney when executed by an agent and statement of presence of two witnesses and their signatures are void. Documents are also void which are not found in their proper place in notary's protocol.

Notary must give party who requests it, an authenticated copy of document. He may also give subsequent copies, but in case any of parties is required by document to do any act, he may only have subsequent copy by order of court.

REAL PROPERTY:

Ownership, possession and administration of real property and encumbrances thereon and their assignment are governed by C.C.

Condominium.—May be established by law, contract, will or legacy. Rules regarding partition of inheritance are applicable to partition of individualized real property.

Rights in rem on real property other than ownership and condominium are as follows:

Usufruct.—Consists of right to use and enjoy property belonging to another person without changing its substance. It may also attach to personal property.

Use and Habitation.—Consists of right granted by owner to take from land products which are necessary for sustenance of user and his family. When this right refers to house and its occupation it is called habitation.

Servitude.—Consists of temporary or perpetual right to use real property of another or exercise certain rights thereon or to prevent owner from exercising certain rights of ownership.

Mortgages.—See topic Mortgages of Real Property.

RECORDS:

General Direction of Public Registries. Law 879 and C.C. determine documents to be recorded and organization of public office.

Recordable Instruments.—Instruments that must be recorded are: Those establishing rights in rem on real property and vehicles, their amendments and extinguishment; attachments of such properties and personal inhibition against disposal; contracts between husband and wife concerning property rights; adjudication of community property after divorce or legal separation of spouses as well as divorce or legal separation judgment; title to ownership of vessels of more than six tons dead weight; mortgage on vessels, lease and attachment of vessels by judicial order and their cancellation.

Requisites for Recording.—Instruments to be recorded must be passed before notary public or granted by administrative or judicial decision.

Foreign Conveyances.—Acts executed abroad regarding real estate located in Paraguay will be valid if they are in form of duly legalized public instrument and will only produce effects after being recorded by notary public by order of competent courts and recorded with public registry.

Transfer of Decedent's Title.—Title to decedent's real estate is granted to heirs and legatees by competent local courts and must be recorded.

Commercial Registry.—Law 1034 determines persons and documents to be recorded: Merchant's business license; bylaws of corporations and companies engaging in commercial activities; individual enterprises of limited liability; books of commerce; powers of attorney granted for managing enterprise and its revocation.

Vital Statistics.—Law 58 creates Registry of Civil Status of Persons where births, recognizances and legitimations, marriages and deaths are recorded. In rural areas where there is no registry office, Justice of Peace is in charge of these records.

SALES:

A general condition not to resell is void but condition not to resell to specific person is valid. Condition to resell to vendor or to repurchase from buyer is void (Repurchase Agreement). Sale may be made with preferential right to purchase but only if buyer wishes to resell in which case vendor may have preferential right to buy within three days if personal property and ten days if real property. In case of sale by installments, if buyer has paid 25% of price or has introduced improvements that equal such value contract may not be canceled by vendor. All things that can be object of contracts can be sold, even if they are future things, if their sale is not prohibited by law.

TAXATION:

Governed by Law No. 125/91 and its regulations.

I. Taxes on Revenues.—

(A) Tax on Business Income:—

Taxable Income.—All income from Paraguayan sources derived or earned from commercial, manufacturing or service activities other than personal services: sale-purchase of real estate when activity is carried out as permanent business; use of assets, and other income shown on commercial balance sheets, excluding income from farming which is governed by specific rules applicable to sector; commercial partnerships, as well as foreign corporations or their branches, agencies, or business establishments in Paraguay; extractive industries such as mining and forestry, and certain farming activities (flower growing, forestry, bee keeping, poultry farming and others); consignment of merchandise; supply of certain services listed in law, which are subject to amendment and regulations.

See Topical Index in front part of this volume.

TAXATION . . . *continued*

Taxpayers.—Individual businesses, partnerships, associations, corporations and other private businesses; government-owned enterprises, decentralized government corporations, and mixed capital corporations; branches, agencies or businesses owned by foreign corporations. Corporations incorporated overseas shall pay tax on income paid or accredited to them. Individuals applying capital resources and personal labor jointly, for purpose of obtaining economic gain, except those involving strictly personal services or those engaged in farming.

Paraguayan Sources.—Business carried out, income obtained from goods located in or from entitlements used for gainful purposes in Paraguay; interest on securities and movable properties; technical assistance provided within country when utilized or applied in it; assignment of goods or rights when used even partially during agreed period, such as use of trademark or patent; international freight on goods carried to bordering countries or Uruguay deemed as 50% from Paraguayan sources. Other freight deemed 30% from Paraguayan sources.

Gross Income.—Defined as difference between total earnings and cost thereof. In sales, difference resulting from deducting from gross sales any returned goods, gratuities and price discounts as applied in local business usage or custom; in sale of fixed assets, difference between sale price and cost or revalued cost of assets, minus amortizations or depreciation allowed by law. Also: Proceeds from sale of movable property or real estate received in payment; proceeds from payments to partners or shareholders; any exchange rate differences resulting from transactions in foreign currencies; net benefits resulting from collection of insurance or indemnities; proceeds from any transfer of enterprises or business firms; interest on loans or investments (advances paid to partners or to employees are excluded as well as deposits placed in financial entities); any increase in net worth occurring during fiscal year other than that arising from revaluation of fixed assets or capital contributions or from exempt or nontaxable businesses.

Net Income.—Calculated by deducting from gross income all expenses incurred to obtain such income and to maintain source of income, provided they are real expenditures, duly documented, as follows: Taxes and social benefits excluding business income tax; operating expenses of business; personnel compensation; organization or incorporation expenses; interest and rentals or sums paid for assignment of assets and rights; losses suffered through casualties not covered by insurance; reserves or write-offs for bad debts; losses incurred as result of criminal acts; depreciation; amortization of incorporeal rights such as trademarks and patents; expenses and payments incurred overseas associated to taxable income from export and import operations; travel expenses, per diem, and other similar payments in cash or kind; gifts to State, municipalities and religious entities or to entities dedicated to social welfare or education, recognized by Tax Administration; professional fees and other compensation for personal services not subject to taxation; expenses and contributions paid to staff for health care, education, cultural development, or training. Losses incurred in any fiscal year may be set off against earnings generated in three following fiscal years.

Nondeductible expenses.—Interest on loans or advances from owner of business, partners or shareholders; penalties for tax offenses; earnings in any fiscal period retained in business as capital increases or reserve accounts. Amortization of payments for goodwill. Personal expenses of owner, partners or shareholders, and moneys drawn on account of future earnings. Direct expenses involved in earning nontaxable income. Value Added Tax (VAT).

Beneficiaries Not Domiciled in Paraguay.—Beneficiaries of Paraguayan sourced income domiciled abroad are subject to withholding tax, separately from their local branch or agency. Law establishes imputed profit margin to which rate is applied. Imputed profit margin varies as follows:

10% Rate: Insurance or reinsurance premiums; sales of travel tickets, radio message services, telephone calls and other similar services sent overseas from Paraguay; freight on international shipments.

15% Rate: Gross income earned by international news agencies; Gross income earned by leasing of shipping containers.

40% Rate: Rentals on motion picture films or television programs or those of any other projection medium.

50% Rate: Income earned from sources other than branches, agencies or businesses located in Paraguay.

100% Rate: Income earned by any other business arising from branches, agencies, or businesses located in country. Taxpayers may in such cases choose to pay taxes according to general rules governing tax by keeping adequate books of account for verification of expenses and income.

Presumptive Income.—Taxpayers who do not keep regular books of account run risk that Tax Administration may establish presumptive income on which to apply net income which in turn shall be subject to tax rate established by law. Taxpayers engaged in businesses character of which places difficulties to application of generally accepted accounting principles may request Tax Administration to apply tax regime based on presumptive income.

Revaluation of Fixed Assets.—Annual revaluation of fixed assets is mandatory and updated value shall result from applying to book value shown in previous fiscal year at percentage variation based on consumer price index as determined by competent government body.

Value of Inventories.—Merchandise in stock is carried on books either at cost of production, cost of acquisition, or at market cost at close of fiscal year, at taxpayer's option. Tax Administration may accept other systems of inventory valuation. Negotiable securities and valuables shall be booked at their market value at close of fiscal year. If not quoted on market, purchase price is used. Fixed assets and intangible assets are carried at purchase cost without prejudice of annual revaluation.

Reinvestment Exemption.—Benefits manufacturing and reforestation projects. In first case investment must be applied to installation, expansion or renewal of fixed assets devoted directly to production of manufactured goods; in latter case to forestation or to reforestation projects in rural areas. Investments must be in new productive assets or in case of imported assets which are in good condition and well maintained, suitable for manufacturing process. Reinvestments must be carried out in same fiscal period, extendable to following fiscal year. May not be distributed as dividends but kept in reserve account for capitalization. Value of reinvestments in excess of net income for fiscal period may be employed in future years. Companies reinvesting as indicated above, pay income tax at rate of 10% and are exempt from tax on remittances on earnings or dividends to beneficiaries not domiciled in Paraguay.

Branches or agencies of companies incorporated overseas shall keep accounts separate from those of their head office. Payments of interest, royalties and for technical assistance made by branches or agencies to their head office are deductible items for payors but taxable for payees.

Tax Rates.—Tax rate in general is 30%. Sums paid or credited to head offices by branches, agencies, or businesses located in Paraguay are subject to 5% tax. Income of individuals not domiciled in country, earned independently from that paid or credited on activities conducted by branches, agencies or businesses are subject to both tax rates above, limited to 5% in case of earnings or dividends.

(B) Tax on Farm Income.—Farming defined as business conducted for purpose of obtaining primary products, either vegetable or animal, by utilization of land, excluding business of handling, processing or treating farm products unless carried out by same producer.

Taxpayers.—Individuals; partnerships, whether incorporated or otherwise; associations, corporations and other private entities; government enterprises, self governing agencies, decentralized entities; individuals or corporations conducting taxable businesses, including corporations incorporated overseas and their branches and agencies.

Gross Income from Farming.—Income is determined on basis of presumptive income estimated at 12% of fiscal valuation of all real estate held by taxpayer under any title. Gross income is determined independently of whether or not exploitation actually takes place. National Cadastral Service determines annually fiscal value of land, excluding improvements and buildings, on basis of average prices prevailing on market during 12 months prior to every Nov. 1st.

Determination of Net Income.—Following is deducted from gross income: Expenses needed to produce and maintain income, up to 40% of gross income; value of any areas occupied by natural or planted forests and by permanent ponds; value of 20 hectares in case of properties under 100 hectares in area.

Tax Rate: 25% on net income as determined above.

(C) Small Businesses Tax.—This tax applies to commercial, manufacturing and service businesses other than personal services, conducted by individuals using their personal labor and capital to pursue economic gain, provided their total income in previous year did not exceed amount of Gs.37,208,310. Tax base is determined on basis of presumptions calculated on economic indicators according to taxpayer categories, allowing for factors such as salaries and wages paid, expenditures on utilities, rents, merchandise, raw materials and inputs purchased. Imputed profit margin is established for each business or trade. Tax rate varies between 1 and 4% according to category of each taxpayer.

II. Taxes on Capital.—

Real Estate Tax.—Applies to real estate property located in national territory, and taxpayers are owners or users thereof. When ownership is shared tax is paid by any one of owners.

Exemption.—Real estate owned by State and municipalities; real estate owned by religious entities recognized by competent authorities devoted on permanent basis to public service; lands declared to be historic national monuments, lands owned by recognized public welfare associations and in general any piece of land devoted to hospitals or public welfare services; real estate owned by foreign governments; real estate used as permanent premises by political parties and education, cultural, social, sports or labor unions whether owned or held in usufruct; properties of Chaco War veterans provided they or their surviving spouse live thereon; properties owned by Rural Welfare Institute and lands set aside for settlement by IBR; national parks and nature conservation reserves. In event of natural disasters such as floods land owners may request and government may reduce this tax by as much as 50%.

Tax Base.—Fiscal valuation of real estate as set by National Cadastral Service. Property values shall be increased until they match prices set by market following consumer price index, but increases shall not exceed 15% per annum. In case of rural properties any improvements or buildings shall not be computed in tax base.

Tax Rate: 1% of fiscal value per year, reduced by 50% in case of rural properties under five hectares in areas utilized for small scale farming.

III. Taxes on Consumption.—

(A) Value Added Tax (VAT).—Applicable to transfer of ownership of goods from one person or company to another; rendering of personal services and importation of goods. Excluded are personal services performed under employment.

Taxpayers.—Individuals providing personal services when their gross income in previous year exceeded Gs.17,509,793; individual businesses engaged in commercial, manufacturing or services businesses when their gross income in previous year exceeded Gs.37,208,310; partnerships and private entities in general; independent government entities, government enterprises and decentralized agencies engaged in businesses; importers of goods.

Origin of Tax Liability.—For sales of goods tax obligation arises upon delivery, issue of invoice or equivalent act, whichever happens first. For public services, on due date of invoice. For services, upon issuance of invoice or collection of full or partial payment for service, upon expiration of term for payment or upon termination of service. For items of personal consumption, at moment of purchase. For imports, at time register of entry of goods into Customs is opened.

Territoriality.—All sales of goods and services in Paraguay are taxable. In case of technical assistance when used or profited from in country; in case of assignment of rights or lease of goods, when used within national territory. In case of insurance and reinsurance when they cover risks within country or when goods or persons covered are situated in or residents of country.

Tax Base.—In transactions for consideration tax base is billed net price for goods or services. To establish net price and in determining price of goods used or consumed privately same rules apply as income tax, in addition to any special provisions. In case of imports, base is Customs value plus Customs duties in addition to other taxes applicable to delivery of goods (Customs and dock fees) and internal revenue taxes, but excluding value added tax.

Exemptions.—(1) Sale of Goods: Farm products in their natural state; foreign currencies, government or private bonds, securities including shares of stock; real estate;

TAXATION . . . *continued*
lottery tickets, betting slips; petroleum based fuels; goods received through inheritance; assignment of credits. (2) Services: Interest on government or private bonds; leases of real estate; financial intermediation business, including loans granted by overseas banks, except: Commissions earned by brokering purchase and sale of securities and as agents serving as payors of dividends, amortizations and interest; and commissions earned on issue and renewal of credit cards; sums earned by carrying out mandates and commissions unrelated with financial businesses; management of securities portfolios, debt collections, technical and administrative assistance, leasing movable goods; loans to and deposits in financial institutions authorized by Central Bank of Paraguay, and in cooperatives, Credito Agricola de Habilitación, Home Savings and Loan system, National Development Bank, and Fondo Ganadero. (3) Imports: Crude petroleum; travelers baggage; diplomatic service imports; goods to be applied directly to productive cycle in manufacturing or farming in projects benefitted by incentives offered under Law 60/90, except when such goods can be produced locally. Goods imported to render services are not exempted even if benefited by Law 60/90.

Liquidation of Tax.—Fiscal debit is sum of taxes accrued (invoiced as opposed to collected) by taxable transactions in each month. Fiscal credit is sum of taxes included in purchases of goods and services on local market during month, or on imports. Tax shall be liquidated on sum representing difference between fiscal debits and fiscal credits. Deduction of any fiscal credit is conditional on such credit arising from goods or services devoted directly or indirectly to transactions subject to taxation. Taxpayers rendering personal services may not deduct any fiscal credits arising from purchase of motor vehicles. When fiscal credit exceeds fiscal debits surplus may be carried over to future liquidations.

Tax rate is 10%.

(B) Selective Tax on Consumption.—Applies to imports of goods and to their first sale in case of domestic products. Importers and manufacturers of taxable domestic products shall be liable for tax.

For imports, taxable base is Customs value plus Customs duties and fees for services. For domestically manufactured goods taxable base is ex-factory price excluding VAT and this tax.

(C) Tax on Acts and Documents.—Applies to acts involving financial intermediation.

Amount of Tax.—2% per annum; loans of money or in kind and credits extended, as well as extensions thereof, granted by banks and financial institutions, 1.74%; bills of exchange, drafts, intercity bank checks, payment orders, letters of credit and in general any transaction involving assignment of funds within country, 1%; bills of exchange, drafts, payment orders, letters of credit and in general any transaction involving assignment of funds or currencies to overseas payees.

Banks and financial institutions and notaries public act as withholding agents for taxes on acts and contracts in which they take part.

TRADEMARKS AND TRADENAMES:

(Law 751/79).

Trademarks are symbols which distinguish products and services.

Following cannot be used as trademarks: (1) Letter words, names or symbols used by state and its entities; (2) form and color of products; (3) symbols or expressions contrary to law, public welfare, morals, customs, or that may induce error; (4) designations usually employed to indicate nature of products.

Title to trademarks passes to heirs of grantee and may be transfered freely, provided transfer is by public instrument and recorded at Office of Industrial Property. Protection of trademark lasts for ten years but can be renewed indefinitely upon payment of proper fees. Application for trademark must be accompanied by description in triplicate, indicating products or services to which it is to apply and class of object for which it is to be used. Legalized power of attorney is required when application is not filed personally by owner. When trademark is registered, certificate is issued to petitioner. Extract is published; opposition may be made within 60 working days of publication.

Owner of trademark may license its use by written contract, registered at Office of Industrial Property.

Use of trademark is not requirement for registration, validity or renewal.

Signatory member of Paris Convention since Jan. 1994.

Foreign trademarks to be protected must be recorded. Only owner or duly authorized agent may do so.

Misuse of trademarks is punishable by arrest. Attachment many be obtained by owner of trademark against articles which bear his trademark illegally.

WILLS:

Any person aged 18 years may dispose of his property by will. Testator may revoke his will at any time before dying. Law of testator's domicile at time of making his will determines his capacity to make will but validity of contents is determined by law of testator's domicile at time of his death.

Neither deaf mutes who can neither read or write nor persons insane at time of making of will may make valid will.

Mutual or joint wills in single document are null as well as those made in separate documents by two or more testators disposing reciprocally and mutually of their estates.

Contents of will must be expression of testator's wish. He cannot delegate or empower other person to make it. All dispositions subject to any condition or charge that are physically impossible or contrary to public interest are null.

Validity of will in respect to its form is governed by law in force at time of making will. Evidence of fulfillment of requirements must result from will itself and cannot be proved by other written documents nor by witnesses. Will made in Paraguay must conform to rules of Civil Code. If will is made aboard to have full effects in Paraguay it must be made in writing and signed personally by testator, according to law of place where executed.

Nullity of will defective in form nullifies all dispositions contained therein, but nullity of one disposition does not affect others. Dispositions in favor of persons who died before testator expires are null, but other dispositions are valid. Will lapses if at time of testator's death his child born after its execution is alive. If testator marries will executed before marriage lapses.

All physical and juridical persons have legal capacity to inherit by will subject to limitations established by law. Testator may create foundation in his will. Executors, heirs or Attorney General's office are required to apply to Executive Power for approval of such foundation.

If spouse who was not pregnant marries within 300 days after first marriage has been dissolved or annulled, she loses right to any legacies or other benefits granted by her first husband in his will.

Will to be valid must be signed by testator in his usual manner. Obvious alteration of signature annuls will.

Will, and any amendments and revocations shall be registered in Will Registry which is part of General Public Registry. Lack of registration will not invalidate will.

Notary who records or is in possession of will at time of testator's death must advise courts or interested parties. There are four forms of wills: Holographic will; will by public instrument; closed will; and military will.

Holographic Will.—To be valid must be entirely in writing of testator, dated and signed by him. If part of will, even with testator's authorization, is written by other person, will is null. Wills may be written in any language. Amounts and dates may be written in figures. Will is not invalid if place where it has been made is not stated or is erroneously stated.

All testator's dispositions made after his signature must be dated and signed by him. Will may be written in letter form or in domestic book. Testator may authorize his will with witnesses, seal or deposit it with notary or take any steps to secure his last will.

Will in form of public instrument must be executed before notary public in presence of three witnesses residing in place. Notary may not be relative of testator in direct line to any degree of consanguinity or affinity. Blind person may make will in form of public instrument but deaf, dumb, or deaf mute person who cannot make himself understood in writing cannot do so.

Testator may express orally his provisions to notary in presence of witnesses or deliver to him written document.

Will must state place and date of execution, names, residence and age of witnesses and whether it was dictated or prepared by testator himself. If testator does not understand Spanish language, presence of two interpreters to translate will into Spanish is necessary and will must be written in both languages. Will must be read in presence of witnesses and signed by testator, witnesses and notary. At least two wit nesses must be able to sign or one of them sign for another witness who cannot sign, and notary must so state.

Neither notary nor witnesses, their wives, or relatives up to fourth degree may take advantage of any disposition of will.

Closed Will.—Can be made by testator or another person on writing paper but all pages must be signed by testator. If he cannot sign, impediment must be stated and another person must sign for him.

Will must be delivered to notary in sealed envelope and in presence of five resident witnesses, stating that it contains testator's will. Notary certifies presentation on envelope and certificate is also signed by testator and all witnesses. At least three witnesses must be able to sign. Deaf person may execute closed will.

Military Will.—Sailors on ships of war and soldiers on campaign outside Republic, prisoners and camp followers, where there is no notary, may execute wills in writing before certain specified officers and required number of witnesses. Will is valid if testator dies within 90 days after extraordinary situation ceases.

Probate.—On testator's death, holographic will and closed will must be presented to courts of testator's last domicile. Any person who has interest in closed will may ask courts to open it. Courts take evidence, in presence of witnesses, of handwriting of testator in case of holographic will and if it is genuine, certify each page and order its recording.

Closed will cannot be opened by courts until notary and witnesses recognize their signature and that of testator. Then will is recorded. If notary and most of witnesses cannot appear before courts, evidence of handwriting is received.

Witnesses must have legal capacity to act as such, be known to notary and identified by him, understand language of testator and language in which will is written; they should be residents of place where notary is domiciled and must be of age. Neither ascendants nor surviving spouse or descendants of testator may be witnesses. Heirs, legatees, relatives of notary up to fourth degree, clerks of his office or servants may not be witnesses, nor those that are benefitted by will, nor blind, dear, mute or insane persons.

Registry.—By Law No. 105/90 Will Registry is created as part of General Public Registry Office, where all will granting must be recorded, as well as any alterations or cancellations. Noncompliance of recording does not invalidate will.

See also topic Descent and Distribution.

PERU LAW DIGEST REVISER

Curtis, Mallet-Prevost, Colt & Mosle
101 Park Avenue
New York, New York 10178-0061
Telephone: 212-696-6141
Fax: 212-697-1559
Email: CMP-NY@mcimail.com

Reviser Profile

The Firm began in 1830 when two practicing lawyers started a long line of lawyers and law firms extending in an unbroken chain up to the present time. In 1897, the firm name became Curtis, Mallet-Prevost & Colt; in 1925 it was changed to Curtis, Mallet-Prevost, Colt & Mosle. The Firm is now made up of approximately 120 lawyers, including experts who have published extensively on such diverse subjects as international money management, transnational contracts, state contracts, litigation against foreign states, sovereign immunity and the act of state doctrine, and the International Court of Justice. Its principal offices are in New York City. There are branch offices in Paris, London, Frankfurt Am Main, Hong Kong, Washington, D.C., Houston, Texas, Newark, N.J., and Mexico City. The Firm has five departments: Corporate and International; Litigation; Real Estate; Tax; and Trusts and Estates. The corporate and international department acts as general counsel to various public and private corporations and individual entrepreneurs. Clients are in the banking, insurance, securities, manufacturing, real estate and oil and gas industries. In addition, the corporate and international department frequently acts as special counsel to domestic and foreign clients, providing assistance in financing, know-how licensing, the negotiation and drafting of all types of contracts and instruments, counselling on all aspects of corporate law, and establishing the vehicles necessary to enable clients to conduct their domestic and foreign business activities. The Firm's international work permeates all areas of its practice and involves questions of private international law, foreign law and an unusual amount of public and quasi-public international law. Traditionally, much of the Firm's international practice has been concerned with Latin America. The Firm maintains its excellence in that area, with its Mexican affiliate, and also through the expertise of Latin American lawyers based in the New York office. The Firm's international practice has undergone a major expansion beyond Latin America to Europe, Africa and the Near and Far East. The Firm's litigation practice includes commercial litigation and arbitration, and white-collar criminal defense. It has substantial experience in civil aviation matters; it also has represented foreign States in transnational litigation and international arbitration arising out of acts of nationalization and alleged breach of economic development or natural resource supply contracts. Among the Firm's clients in real estate matters are institutional lenders and investors, real estate developers, both individual and corporate, foreign and domestic investors and syndicators. The tax department has substantial experience in all aspects of domestic and international business tax matters and real estate taxation. The matters the tax department deals with on a regular basis include: Taxation of foreign investments; the structuring of corporate transactions, including mergers, acquisitions, liquidations and reorganization; federal and state tax litigation; and tax planning for U.S. and foreign individuals. The trusts and estates department engages in general domestic trusts and estates practice and in tax planning for foreign persons wishing to invest in U.S. assets through offshore trusts and corporations. It represents individuals, trust companies, and banks acting as fiduciaries. It works for various charitable organizations located both in the United States and abroad including private foundations, museums, universities and hospitals. A group of fiduciary accountants with vast experience in the field assists the lawyers of the trusts and estates department. Curtis, Mallet-Prevost, Colt & Mosle has served as a Reviser for most of Latin American Law Digests since 1930.

PERU LAW DIGEST

(The following is a list of all Topics, including cross-references, covered in this Digest.)

PERU LAW DIGEST

Revised for 1997 edition by

CURTIS, MALLET-PREVOST, COLT & MOSLE, of the New York Bar.

Abbreviations used are: C. C. for Civil Code; C. Com. for Code of Commerce; C. C. P. for Code of Civil Procedure; Sup. Decree for Supreme-Decree. All Codes are cited by articles thereof.)

ABSENTEES: See topic Death.

ACKNOWLEDGMENTS:

Certificates of acknowledgment as generally used in the United States are unknown in Peruvian law. Contracts, deeds and other documents requiring authentication are executed before a notary public, who certifies in the instrument itself to the facts therein set forth.

Documents executed in foreign countries are given recognition in Peru if acknowledged according to the law of the foreign country and authenticated by a Peruvian consular or diplomatic officer. (Notarial Law 26002 of Dec. 7, 1992; C. C. P. 233-261).

ACTIONS:

Actions for Death.—See topic Death, subhead Actions for Death.

Limitation of.—See topic Prescription, subhead Limitation of Actions.

ADMINISTRATION:

See topic Executors and Administrators.

ADOPTION:

(C. C. 238, 377-385, 2087; Law Decree 25934 of Dec. 7, 1992 regulated by Sup. Decree 018-93-JUS of June 2, 1993).

Adoption is irrevocable and extinguishes legal bonds between adopted party and natural family, must be approved by judge. Adopting party must be of good reputation and at least 18 years older than adopted party. Consent is required from spouse of adopting party, from adopted party who is over ten years old, from parents if adopted party is under their "patria potestad" or where parents are curators; from tutor, curator and family council when adopted party is incompetent. Requires personal ratification of adopting party before judge where adopting party is foreigner and adopted party is under age. Adoption where parties are subject to different jurisdictions is governed by law of domicile of adopted party in matters related to his capacity, legal age, marital status, consent by parents or legal representatives, extinction of bonds with natural family and authorization to leave country. There are special requirements for foreign adopting parties.

ADVERSE POSSESSION: See topic Prescription.

AGENCY: See topic Principal and Agent.

ALIENS:

Aliens may not acquire or hold directly or indirectly lands, waters, mines and combustibles within a zone 50 kilometers wide along frontiers. Property acquired against such prohibition is forfeited to the Government. Likewise aliens may not acquire rural property in the border provinces or hold lands in the immediate vicinity of military posts. Aliens are generally exempted from military service and political duties, but may hold certain offices such as arbitrator, mining deputy and alderman.

Aliens in general have the same civil rights and duties as citizens both with respect to persons and property. They may do business, follow their trade or practice their profession, buy and sell real property, make wills and marry in conformity with law. Aliens may be allowed in country with temporary visa for up to 90 days and with resident visa for up to one year. Those with immigrant status can stay in country indefinitely. Aliens Law regulates admission, entrance, residency and expulsion of foreigners. Aliens may be expelled by resolution of Cabinet stating reasons for expulsion. Number of aliens in profession or industry cannot exceed 20%. Similarly, number of laborers as well as of employees, separately, may not exceed that proportion in any business or concern and salaries of foreign personnel must not exceed 30% of payroll. If employees are four or less, one can be foreigner. (Leg. Decree 689 of Nov. 5, 1991).

Rights of inheritance of aliens are governed by law of their domicile. (Const., art. 71, Alien Law Leg. Decree 703 of Nov. 5, 1991, Law Decree 25599 of June 30, 1992; C. C. 2046, 2100, 2101).

There is a special registry of aliens which issues identity cards for which fee and annual renewal fee are paid.

Special status is granted to foreign investors by Law 26174 of Mar. 22, 1993 regulated by Sup. Decree 009-93/RE of June 11, 1993.

See also topic Corporations.

ALIMONY: See topic Divorce.

ARBITRATION:

(Const. arts. 62, 63, Law 26572 of Jan. 3, 1996, Arts. 837-840 C.C.P.). Law deals with domestic and international arbitration, with recognition and enforcement of foreign arbitral awards and with arbitration in commercial and investment disputes between foreign party and Peruvian Government. Law distinguishes between domestic and international arbitration based on party's domicile. Any dispute arising out of specific legal relationship, when such dispute is under proper legal control of parties may be subject to arbitration, with exception indicated by law. Arbitration agreement must be in writing, whether in form of arbitral clause in contract or in separate agreement. Invalidity of contract does not extend to arbitration clause contained therein, if reasons why contract is held invalid do not apply to such arbitration agreement. Arbitration agreement can be evidenced by any kind of document or by other means of communication which constitute record of agreement. Arbitrators may be empowered by parties to decide according to rules of law (en derecho) or ex aequo et bono (en conciencia). Arbitrators may be national or foreign individuals in full enjoyment of their rights in instances where decision is ex aequo et bono; where decision is according to rules of law they must be lawyers and of legal age. Number of arbitrators should be three unless parties have agreed on different uneven number.

Arbitrators have power to make provisional orders including interim measures of protection at request of either party, and to require any party to provide appropriate security in connection with such measures. Deadline for arbitrators to issue award is 20 days counted from day evidence is submitted.

Peru has ratified following multilateral conventions: On Recognition and Enforcement of Foreign Arbitral Awards, New York 1958 and on International Commercial Arbitration, Panama 1975.

ASSIGNMENTS:

Assignment of right must be in writing and notified to debtor. Assignment of right carries with it securities or privileges thereof. Assignor of right guarantees its existence unless assignment is made without guaranty, but he is not responsible for solvency of debtor unless expressly stipulated. (Const. art. 2, §13; C. C. 1206-1217, 1435-1439; C. Com. 342, 343).

ASSIGNMENTS FOR BENEFIT OF CREDITORS:

Assignments for the benefit of creditors are governed by the bankruptcy law. See topic Bankruptcy.

ASSOCIATIONS:

Associations are nonprofit organizations that can be organized by natural or juridical persons. Associations legally established acquire juridical personality through recording of their articles of association, which must contain name, domicile, purpose and manner of administration. Meetings of members are called in cases provided in bylaws or at request of one-tenth of members. Association loses its existence in case of bankruptcy, and it may be dissolved by court decision at request of state's attorney in case its activities are contrary to public order or morals. (C. C. 80-98, 124-126, 2024 and 2025).

ATTACHMENT:

Provisional attachment may be granted either before bringing an action or during the course of the same, if the application is based on a document which is prima facie proof of the existence of the obligation and if the latter is not sufficiently secured. In case of attachment before suit the plaintiff must give bond and institute the action within ten days after the attachment if the suit is brought in the same locality; if it is brought elsewhere the court may allow a longer period depending on the distance. For suits to be instituted abroad an attachment may be issued if authorized by treaty. In actions in rem a provisional attachment may be granted if the plaintiff alleges sufficient grounds to fear the loss, destruction or deterioration of the object. The debtor is not notified of a provisional attachment nor allowed any recourse against the same until it is levied. The debtor may avoid or raise the attachment by paying the debtor giving bond.

An attachment may be issued in the course of executive actions, based on documents which authorize a summary proceeding such as: (1) Acknowledgments in court; (2) public instruments; (3) private instruments which have been specifically acknowledged; (4) bills of exchange, drafts, warrants, promissory notes, and checks; (5) any other document as provided by special laws. After attachment has been levied third party may intervene on ground that he is owner of property attached or has preferential credit. (C. C. P. 608-643, 693).

BANKRUPTCY:

(Law Decree 26116 of Dec. 28, 1992 regulated by Sup. Decree 044-93-EF of Mar. 18, 1993).

Petition for declaration of insolvency by "Comisión de Simplificación del Acceso y Salida del Mercado" ("Commission") may be made by debtor or its creditors. Debtor may file insolvency petition when its net worth has been reduced to one-third of its original value. Creditor may file insolvency petition when its outstanding credits exceed equivalent of 50 U.I.T. (Tributary Units). After hearing debtor and determining that it is insolvent, Commission will notify all creditors. Creditors are given period to file their claims and their credits are valued and classified. Creditors will hold meeting at which they will decide whether (i) to approve plan of reorganization, (ii) to approve agreement to dissolve and liquidate business or (iii) to seek judicial declaration of bankruptcy. Representative of Commission may be invited to creditors' meeting without right to vote. Agreements made at creditors' meeting require vote of creditors holding at least 70% of value of all claims.

Process of reorganization should not last more than one year, although this period may be extended by creditors' meeting. Unless bank, creditor or not of debtor, is appointed as trustee, debtor remains in possession of estate property and continues to operate business. Within 60 days from its appointment, trustee must propose plan of reorganization to creditors' meeting. Plan of reorganization will then be filed at competent court which will notify all other courts where any action had been brought

See Topical Index in front part of this volume.

BANKRUPTCY . . . *continued*
against debtor. From that date, all pending actions and debt obligations are automatically stayed. At any time during process of reorganization, creditors' meeting may agree to dissolve and liquidate business or to seek judicial declaration of bankruptcy.

If creditors' meeting agrees to dissolve and liquidate business, receiver will be appointed. Receiver will be empowered (i) to sell assets, (ii) to discharge debts, (iii) to extend payment terms, (iv) to refinance payment of debtor's obligations, and (v) to carry out necessary acts to dissolve and liquidate business.

If declaration of bankruptcy is sought, court will appoint bank as trustee. All pending actions against debtor will be joined to bankruptcy proceedings. Trustee will then classify all credits and attend to liquidation of business.

Trustee has power to avoid transfer of debtor's interest in property or incurring of obligation if transfer was made or obligation was incurred by debtor within six months prior to declaration of bankruptcy. Good faith transferee for value is, however, entitled to retain any property conveyed to him during that period.

For transactions invalid as to creditors of bankrupt, see topic Fraudulent Sales and Conveyances.

For preferential payments, see topic Liens.

BILLS AND NOTES:

(Arts. 557-562, Law 16587 of June 15, 1967).

Bills of exchange must state: (a) Name of "bill of exchange" ("letra de cambio") or its equivalent; (b) unconditional order to pay a specific amount of money; (c) drawee; (d) maturity date which may be: (1) at sight, (2) at a certain term after sight, (3) at a certain time after date, (4) on a certain date; (e) place of payment, but if not stated, place mentioned next to drawee's name applies; several payment places may be indicated and then choice is holder's; (f) payee; (g) date and place of issue; (h) name and signature of drawer. If maturity date is not stated, bill is payable at sight.

Bill may be drawn; (a) To order of drawer or to another person; (b) to be paid by third person; (c) to be paid by drawer, in which case no acceptance is necessary, term being computed from issue, if payable at certain term after sight; and (d) for account of another person. One or more counterparts of bill may be issued, stating on each whether it is a first or second copy, etc. If this statement is omitted, each counterpart is considered as separate bill.

Guaranty.—Payment of bill may be jointly secured in toto or in part by personal guaranty called "aval," given by third person in writing on same bill or additional sheet attached thereto, signed by guarantor after words "por aval" or other words signifying joint liability of signer with party for whom it is given. If this party is not mentioned, guaranty is deemed given for acceptor or drawer. Mere signature on back of bill constitutes an "aval." Guarantor who pays bill acquires any sureties covering it and rights of holder against person for whom aval was given and those liable to him.

Endorsements.—Bills of exchange, even if not to order, are transferable by endorsement. Unless there is a clause to contrary, endorser is liable for acceptance and payment, jointly with other endorsers, drawer, acceptor and guarantors. He may forbid further endorsements, in which case he is not liable to new endorsees. Endorsement must appear on bill or on separate sheet attached thereto, stating: (1) Endorsee; (2) kind of endorsement; and (3) name and signature of endorser. However, signature of endorser alone is sufficient and then any holder may insert there his name or negotiate bill without it, by delivery. Endorsement to bearer produces same effects of endorsement in blank. Endorsements may be made in guaranty of "for collection" or to person as "attorney-in-fact" or other similar expressions and then they do not pass title, but authorize collection and all acts related thereto. Endorsement "without recourse" or other expression of similar import destroys drawer's liability. Endorsement of bill after maturity is equivalent to endorsement in due course, provided that no protest has been made and that term therefor has not elapsed; otherwise it amounts to an assignment. Burden of proof that bill was prejudiced is on defendant who alleges it.

Acceptance.—Bill payable at certain time after sight must be presented for acceptance within one year of issue unless drawer has specified shorter or longer period. Acceptance is expressed by signature of acceptor, which may follow word "accepted" or other equivalent expression. Mere signature suffices. Presentation for acceptance of other bills is optional unless otherwise stated on it. If holder fails to present bill, when this is necessary, he loses his exchange action on same. Drawee may request that bill be presented again for acceptance on day following first presentation. His petition must appear in protest.

Due Date.—Bills at sight are payable on presentation, which must be made within one year after issue. Drawer may shorten or extend this period and endorsers may only shorten it. If drawer stated that bill should not be presented before certain day, term runs from that date. Bills drawn at one or several months after date or after sight mature on same day of issue in month in which payment is due, but if there is no such date in that month, then on last day of same. Words "eight days" or "fifteen days" are not equivalent to one or two weeks, but words "half a month" mean 15 days. Day of issue or presentation or acceptance is not included for computation of legal or conventional periods.

Payment should be made on maturity date. Holder cannot refuse partial payment even if bill was accepted for whole, but he may protest for balance. He cannot be compelled to receive payment before maturity. If bill is not presented for payment on its due date or if payment cannot be made for causes depending on holder, any one liable for bill may offer and tender in court amount thereof, at holder's cost.

Protest.—In case of failure to accept or pay bill, protest must be made by notary public or his secretary or by Justice of the Peace where there is no notary. Protest for nonacceptance should be made within term for presentation; and protest for nonpayment, within eight days after maturity, on a working day, before 7 P.M. If last day is holiday, term is extended to next working day. Protest must mention: (a) Place, hour and date; (b) name of holder; (c) name of payee and of any person acting in his stead in act of protest and his reply as to why drawee is not present; (d) text of bill; (e) signature of notary public or acting officer. Bill must be stamped with words "protested document" and must bear date and signature of notary or acting officer. Clauses waiving protest are ineffective.

Promissory notes must contain: (a) Title of "Promissory Note"; (b) place and date of issue; (c) unconditional promise to pay certain sum of money; (d) payee or person to whose order payment will be made; (e) maturity and place of payment; (f) name and signature of maker. Provisions regarding bills of exchange apply to promissory notes, except when inconsistent with nature of latter.

Checks must contain: (a) Number; (b) unconditional order to pay specific amount of money; (c) name and address of drawee bank; (d) place and date of issue; (e) signature of drawer. Checks are payable at sight and may be issued to bearer or to certain person or to his order. Check must be presented for payment within 30 days if issued in Peru and 60 days if issued in foreign country. No stop payment is allowed before applicable period has elapsed, except by order of court. In absence of valid stop order, bank may pay even after applicable period of presentation has elapsed. Drawer of check must have sufficient funds available in drawee bank. Bank refusing payment must, on day following presentation, place signed statement on check, indicating cause of refusal and date when check was presented. This statement is equivalent to protest which, however, may be made by holder, within period of presentation.

Letters of credit are issued from one merchant to another or to apply to a mercantile transaction. They must be: (a) Issued in favor of a definite person and not to order; (b) limited to a definite amount, or one or more indefinite sums not exceeding a definite limit. Letters of credit cannot be protested for nonpayment and the holder acquires no right of action on that account against the person issuing the letter. The letter may be annulled by notification to the holder and to the drawee. The holder must reimburse the person who issued the letter; in case of refusal a summary action lies and interest and costs are payable. The holder must use the letter within the period agreed or, if there is no agreement, within 12 months.

CHATTEL MORTGAGES:

Personal property not exempt from attachment may be given in guarantee of any obligation.

Chattel mortgages may be given in form of pledges in which pledged objects remain in possession of debtor. In such case pledge must be recorded in public registry and rules relating to pledges apply. (C. C. 1055-1090, 2043-2045).

Agricultural pledge is in practice a mortgage since the property pledged remains in possession of the debtor. The debtor must be engaged in agriculture or cattle raising. The following are subject to agricultural pledge: (a) Agricultural machines and instruments and any implement or thing devoted to rural exploitation; (b) cattle and farm animals and their products; (c) fruits of all kinds whether pending or cut; (d) timber cut or to be cut. The contract must appear in a public instrument when involving 50 soles or more; if the amount is smaller or there is no notary in the locality the contract may be made before a justice of the peace. The contract must be recorded in the real property registry and sufficient details must be stated to permit the identification of the property pledged. Without the written consent of the creditor the debtor can make no further contract regarding the pledged articles; but he may sell such articles in whole or in part if the creditor intervenes to receive the amount of his credit. If the price is less than the credit the creditor has a preferential right to acquire the property for such price, his credit continuing with respect to the balance. If the debtor makes contracts in violation of such prohibition the creditor may demand the sale of the pledge. The contract cannot stipulate an interest more than 4% higher than the bank interest nor can it stipulate that the creditor will acquire the pledge without public sale. In case of failure to pay, the pledge is sold through a broker if the articles are subject to quotation, otherwise the sale is effected at public bidding. Without the consent of the creditor the pledged articles cannot be taken away from the place where they were to be used when the contract was made. The law provides penalties for debtors who unlawfully abandon, sell or encumber pledged property. (C. Com. 315; Laws 2402 of Dec. 13, 1916, and 6665 of Dec 31, 1929).

Industrial Pledge.—Pursuant to Law of General Industry, any individual or corporation engaged in industrial activity may give industrial pledge on machinery, equipment, tools, means of transportation and rest of working elements, semi-processed goods, and any article manufactured or raw material keeping possession thereof. Document of pledge may be private document with signatures acknowledged before notary, and it must be recorded in Section of Industrial Pledges of Public Registry.

Objects pledged may not be removed without creditor's authorization from place of industrial exploitation. Any default of pledgor gives creditor right to sell object pledged. (C. C. 1055-1090, Law 2402 of Dec. 13, 1916, Law of General Industry No. 23407 of May 29, 1982 as am'd).

Industrial or mercantile pledge is especially dealt with in the Organic Law of the Industrial Bank of Peru for the protection of said bank. The details with regard to the contents of the pledge contract, the need of recording in the Mercantile Register and the procedure for enforcing payment of the obligation are substantially similar to those governing agricultural pledge above discussed. No third party action may be initiated against the bank when it seeks to foreclose on pledge. (Leg. Decree 202 of June 12, 1981).

COLLATERAL SECURITY: See topic Pledges.

COMMERCIAL REGISTER: See topic Records.

COMMISSIONS TO TAKE TESTIMONY:

See topic Depositions.

COMMUNITY PROPERTY:

See topic Husband and Wife.

CONDITIONAL SALES: See topic Sales (Realty and Personalty).

CONSTITUTION AND GOVERNMENT:

Constitution in effect was approved on Oct. 31, 1993.

Tit. I establishes people's rights. Peru is democratic, independent, sovereign and social republic. Its government is one, representative and decentralized.

Legislative powers are vested in Congress. Term of members of Congress is five years.

CONSTITUTION AND GOVERNMENT . . . *continued*

Executive Power is vested in President assisted by Cabinet. His term is five years, he may be reelected for additional period and elected again after expiration of one presidential term, and is elected by direct suffrage by more than half of votes validly cast.

Judicial Power is vested in Supreme Court of Justice and Lower Courts established in territory of Republic. There is no death penalty except in case of treason to country while in war and terrorism.

Tit. V refers to Constitutional Guaranties including habeas corpus right of action. Court of Constitutional Guaranties is composed of seven elected members. Its jurisdiction extends over territory of Republic. (Law 26435 of Jan. 6, 1995 as am'd).

CONTRACTS:

(Civil Code Arts. 312, 1351-1528, 2094, 2095; Commercial Code Arts. 1-15).

For contract to exist there must be legally capable parties, licit object, and legal form. Any contract lacking one of these requirements is not valid. Contracts obtained by fraud or mistake are void. Contracts are binding with respect to terms stated therein. Contracts must be executed and performed in accordance with rules of good faith and mutual intent of parties.

Any contract to succeed to property rights of person who has not died or whose death is not known, is prohibited. Contract related to community property between spouses is prohibited, except for granting of powers of attorney. Contracts required by law to be in form of public instrument grant parties right to compel other to execute said instrument. Contracts are governed by law of country in which they are executed. However, it is advisable to have contracts executed abroad authorized by Peruvian Consular official with formalities presented by Peruvian legislation.

Offer is not binding if it is made to person present without indicating any period of time and it is not immediately accepted (parties contracting by telephone are considered as present). If offer is made to absent person without naming period of time and sufficient time has elapsed for reply to reach person making offer, offer is not binding. Offer is not binding also, if made to absent person and reply is not received within stated fixed period and when before offer is received, or simultaneously with offer, withdrawal of offer is made known to offeree.

If acceptance is known too late by offeror, offeror shall immediately notify acceptor, under penalty of liability for damages. Late acceptance or any change made in offer when it is accepted, is proposal of different contract. If use of trade is not to require express acceptance contract is executed if offer was not refused. Acceptance is regarded as not existing if, prior thereto or together with it, withdrawal of acceptance becomes known to offeror.

Contract is not regarded as concluded as long as parties are not in accord as to all its parts.

Contracts made by letter or telegram are perfected from time acceptance was transmitted. Contract is considered concluded at place where offer was made. One of parties cannot demand performance if he himself has not complied or offered to comply. If after execution of contract one of parties incurs loss in assets sufficient to compromise or render doubtful performance to which he is bound, other party may refuse to perform his obligation until first party gives satisfaction as to his obligation or gives sufficient guaranties of performance.

Money given by one party to other is considered indication of conclusion of contract. Right to retract may be agreed to by parties. If party who gives money retracts, he loses money. If party who receives money retracts, he must repay it doubled. Money is considered as part payment of obligation, but, if by nature of obligation this is not possible, money given must be reimbursed at time contract is performed.

Anyone who makes stipulation in favor of third party has right to compel performance of obligation. Third party has same right after giving notice of acceptance to demand performance of contract and obligee may not exonerate obligor. Obligee may reserve right to replace third party named in contract, independently of latter's wishes, and of other contracting party. This stipulation in favor of third party may be made by "inter vivos" act or by "will".

Mercantile contracts are governed by Commercial Code and by uses of trade. These rules are supplemented by Civil Code. Peruvian law distinguishes between traders and non-traders. Traders are subject to special laws. Law of contracts is generic and applies to all contracts whether mercantile or otherwise. Commercial matters are following: Transfer of personal property for purposes of obtaining profit as permanent activity; operations of exchange; banking; brokerage; commercial paper operations; commercial agency and mediation; transportation; suretyship; corporate transactions; construction; maritime commerce. If contract is commercial as to one party it is deemed commercial as to all parties.

Applicable Law.—Parties may stipulate that contracts shall be governed by foreign legislation and jurisdiction, provided there exists link with said legislation, e.g., nationality of parties, place of performance, location of property, etc. However, said stipulation is not valid if contract refers to matters of exclusive jurisdiction of Peruvian courts, e.g., property located in Peru; contracts to be mainly performed in Peru. Contractual clauses entrusting foreign agencies with cognizance of differences which may arise in interpretation or performance of contracts and their settlement through arbitration are valid. Foreign law is not applied, however, by judge as matter of course, but must be introduced and proved in court by interested party.

Public Contracts.—(Const. art. 143, Sup. Decree 065 of July 19, 1985, Art. 167 of Law 23350 of Dec. 1981, Law 23407 of May 29, 1982).

Contracts executed with Government, State agencies and State enterprises are subject to special rules.

CONVEYANCES:

See topics Deeds; Notaries Public; Public Instruments.

COPYRIGHT:

(Const. art. 2, §8; Leg. Decree 822 of Apr. 23, 1996, C. C. arts. 18, 2093, Decision 351 of Dec. 17, 1993 of Cartagena Commission).

The law grants certain intellectual, moral and property rights to author, his successors or assignees, regarding scientific, literary and artistic works. Copyrights include all kinds of intellectual (including software), scientific, literary and artistic creations reproduced by any means. Law also protects translations, adaptations, musical arrangements and other transformation of private intellectual works; to protect these copyright works written authorization from original owner of work is necessary. Performers' rights are also protected. Literary and artistic works, performances and other productions are protected by law without requiring registration. Rights granted by the law last during author's lifetime and lifetime of author's spouse, children and parents and are extended for 70 years in favor of other heirs or legatees. Producer of a motion picture is protected for 70 years from first projection.

Among conventions joined are: International Convention for Protection of Literary and Artistic Works, Berne, Sept. 9, 1886; Convention on Literary and Artistic Property, Montevideo, Jan. 11, 1889; Convention on Literary and Artistic Copyright, Buenos Aires, Aug. 11, 1910; Universal Copyright Convention, Geneva, Sept. 6, 1952 and Paris revision of July 24, 1971; International Convention for the Protection of Performers, Producers of Phonograms and Broadcasting Organizations, Rome, Oct. 26, 1961; Convention for Protection against Unauthorized Reproduction of Phonograms, Oct. 29, 1971; Agreement on Trade-Related Aspects of Intellectual Property Rights, Marrakesh, Apr. 15, 1994.

CORPORATIONS:

(General Law of Societies, Sup. Dec. 003 of Jan. 14, 1985 as am'd; C. C. 2073, 2074).

Organization.—Charter and its subsequent amendments must appear in public instrument (see topic Public Instruments) which must be recorded in Mercantile Registry. Minimum of three persons and payment of at least one-fourth of capital are required to organize a corporation. This rule does not apply to corporations organized by state or its agencies, which are governed by law under which they are created.

Articles of incorporation must state name, citizenship, civil status, occupation and domicile of incorporators, and should include: (a) Name of company, which cannot be same as that of any other company, and which should be followed by phrase "Sociedad Anónima" or "S. A."; (b) object of business operations and domicile of company. Corporations organized in Peru have their domicile in Peru, except when their operations are conducted on foreign soil and domicile is established there; (c) duration; (d) date of commencing operations; (e) capital and number of shares in which it is to be divided, their par value and series. Bearer shares are not permitted; (f) unpaid capital and payment procedure; (g) description and value given to property contributed at organization; (h) rules for profit distribution; (i) special privilege, if any, granted to certain stockholders; (j) rules governing stockholders' meetings, board of directors and supervisory council ("Consejo de Vigilancia"); (k) minority representation on board and on supervisory council, which cannot be less than that established in law; (l) management; (m) when balance sheet should be submitted; (n) rules for increase or reduction of capital and for dissolution and liquidation of company; and (o) any other agreements. Also, corporations can be organized by public subscription. Promoters must make public prospectus containing all significant data, i.e., name, object, minimum capital subscription required, par value of shares, date for meeting of subscribers, which must be within six months from date of registration of prospectus in Mercantile Registry, etc. This meeting requires presence of absolute majority of all shares subscribed.

Founders.—In addition to their benefits as shareholders, founders can reserve for themselves a participation up to 10% of net profits for five years. Founders are liable for two years, commencing with date of constitution of company, for actions taken in period of organization.

Stock and Stockholders.—Capital must be represented by registered shares. Shares not representing capital are forbidden. No shares can be issued for less than their par value. Each share confers one vote. No stock can be issued before company's charter is recorded in Mercantile Registry. Provisional stock certificates must be issued as registered shares. Shares and transfers thereof are recorded in a special book. Ownership is determined by recorded inscription. Shares of all types must be numbered and are issued from stubs. Until shares are fully paid first subscriber and his assignees are liable for unpaid balance. This liability extends for three years following date of transfer. Shareholders are not liable beyond amount of subscribed shares. Company cannot purchase its own shares except from profits and for purpose of cancelling them, nor can it lend money on guarantee of its shares.

Stockholders' Meetings.—General assembly of stockholders holds ordinary and special meetings. Ordinary meetings are held, among other purposes, to approve balance sheet, elect members of board of directors, and of supervisory council (Consejo de Vigilancia), and to fix their salaries, to distribute profits. At special meetings, assembly, among other powers, exercises following: Removal from office of members of board and of advisory council, amending of charter and bylaws, increase or reduction of capital, dissolution of company. Meetings are called by board of directors when deemed necessary, or at request of shareholders representing one-fifth of capital. In case of refusal, petitioners can appeal to a local judge. Meetings are called by public notice in local paper where judicial notices are published, not less than ten days in advance of date set for special meetings and three days for ordinary sessions. Nevertheless, this requirement may be dispensed with when convening shareholders, representing totality of capital, consent to hold meeting. Quorum to hold meetings on first call requires representation of at least half of capital. On second call, any number of shares suffices. See subhead Amendment of Articles; Change of Capital, infra, for special quorum and voting requirements.

When a resolution is against law or interests of stockholders, it can be appealed before local judge by stockholders who had not attended meeting or who voted against it.

Directors are considered agents of company and have no joint or several liability so long as they act within limits of their authority and perform their duties with "diligence of a methodical merchant." Number of directors is determined in by-laws, as is term of office which cannot be for more than three years. They are elected and removed from office by stockholders. See subhead Stockholders' Meetings, supra.

CORPORATIONS . . . *continued*
Director need not be stockholder. For management purposes, board has duty to appoint a manager. Appointment of directors and powers conferred by company for any purpose must be recorded in Mercantile Registry. Directors must be Peruvian residents.

Minority Representation.—Companies not having a supervisory council must provide for minority representation on board of directors. To implement this each share confers as many votes as number of directors to be elected. Minority representation is not required when election of board is unanimous.

Supervisory Council (Consejo de Vigilancia).—This body has duty of watching over board's activities and company management in general. Its members are elected by stockholders. Companies with more than 50 shareholders or with capital over certain amount must have supervisory council, except when (a) its board of directors has been elected unanimously, or with vote of minority shareholders, or (b) when public accounting firm is in charge of auditing company's operations. All open stock companies and those corporations issuing debentures must have supervisory council unless public accounting firm is in charge of auditing company's operations.

Amendment of Articles; Change of Capital.—By resolution, at special stockholders' meetings, capital may be increased or reduced through issuance of new series of shares of stock when this action has been announced in call for meeting. Required quorum is two-thirds of capital on first call and three-fifths on second call. To adopt such resolution absolute majority of total paid-in capital is required. No increase of capital can be effected until full payment of previously issued stock has been made. Capital can also be increased by transferring available reserves to capital and issuing new shares to holders of outstanding shares in proportion to stock held by them or by increasing par value of outstanding shares of stock. Bonds and debentures can also be converted into shares. Same quorum and voting requisites are applicable to other changes of charter and by-laws. Changes which would impose new obligations on shareholders will not apply to those who had opposed them. If amendment consists of transferring company domicile to foreign country, or changing objects of corporation, or prohibiting assignment of shares, shareholders voting against such resolutions have right to withdraw from company and to be reimbursed. Reduction of capital with reimbursement to stockholders can only be implemented 30 days subsequent to third publication of appropriate amendment. Creditors can oppose such resolution. Stated capital must be reduced to extent of capital loss when such loss amounts to at least 50%.

Legal Reserve.—Companies with net income in excess of 7% of paid-in capital must set aside at least 10% of said income until reserve fund represents one-fifth of capital. See also topic Taxation, subhead Income Tax.

Dissolution.—Quorum and number of votes required for voluntary dissolution are same as those for amendment of articles (see subhead Amendment of Articles; Change of Capital, supra). However, in special circumstances, if such requirements cannot be complied with, stockholders can request local judge to act upon matter. Corporation may also be dissolved for following reasons: Expiration of term of company; losses which had reduced capital to less than one-third; merger; bankruptcy; continued inactivity of stockholders at their meetings; and ownership of all shares of stock by a single person. In this last case, dissolution can be avoided by admitting one or more shareholders within six months. Finally, Executive Power can request dissolution of corporation by Supreme Court when objects or activities of corporation are deemed to be against public order or morals. Executive Power may also order continued existence of company contrary to resolution for dissolution of same, when activity of company is believed to be in public interest. Liquidation is carried out in accordance with articles of incorporation, except as forbidden by law.

Open Stock Corporations.—Establishment and operation of open stock corporations (sociedades anónimas con accionario difundido) is regulated by Leg. Decree 672 of Sept. 23, 1991 as am'd and its regulations, Sup. Decrees 033-92-EF of Feb. 18, 1992 and 003 of Jan. 14, 1985.

Debentures.—As provided by General Law of Industries, industrial corporations and companies may issue debentures with in rem surety. For this purpose public document with intervention of trustee bank must be executed. Interest of said debentures shall be free from basic income tax on interest. Any offer to public may be made by means of prospect subject to proper regulations of same law. Trustee shall certify veracity of data contained in prospect and shall be liable for damages resulting from misrepresentation. (Law 23407 of May 28, 1982 as am'd).

Industrial Enterprises.—Law 23407 of May 28, 1982 called "General Law of Industries". See topic Taxation.

Fishing Enterprises.—Law Decree 25977 of Dec. 21, 1992 called "General Law of Fishery" and its regulations Sup. Decree 01-94-PE of Jan. 14, 1994 as am'd regulates fishing activities, specifying that hydrobiological species contained in jurisdictional sea up to 200 miles and in continental waters of Peru are in State's domain.

General Law of Fishery is comprehensive in scope, regulating most aspects of fishing industry and related activities. State as owner of hydrobiological resources may grant authorizations, fishing permits, licenses or concessions to exploit them. Such rights are not transferable. Any national or foreign individual or juridical person, whether private or of public nature may be beneficiary of exploitation rights. All fishing activities are subject to Peruvian law. Law classifies exploitation of hydrobiological resources into: Investigation activities, extraction, transformation, commercialization and services.

Special Corporations.—(C. Com. arts. 237 et seq.). There are special provisions for certain kinds of companies such as: (a) Credit companies; (b) banks of issue and discount; (c) railroad companies and public works companies; (d) general warehouse companies; (e) territorial credit banks; (f) insurance companies; (g) agricultural banks and companies.

Foreign corporations in order to do business in Peru must file and record in the mercantile registry: (a) Their articles of incorporation; (b) their by-laws; (c) a certificate of the Peruvian consul in the country of their origin stating that they are constituted and exist in accordance with the laws of such country; (d) the power of attorney of their representative. Any modifications of their articles of incorporation or by-laws must also be recorded. (C. Com. arts. 17, 21, 127, and Sup. Decree 003 of Jan. 14, 1985, arts. 15, 345).

Public corporations regulated by Law 24948 of Dec. 2, 1988 and its regulations. Guaranties in favor of Government or public corporations are regulated by Legislative Decree No. 215 of June 12, 1981.

Irregular Companies.—Relationship among stockholders and between them and third parties are regulated in arts. 385-397 of Sup. Decree 003 of Jan. 14, 1985.

Joint Ventures.—Contract must be in writing but does not require registration. (Sup. Decree 003 of Jan. 14, 1985).

COURTS:

Justice is administered by: (1) A Supreme Court of Justice, which hears appeals on points of law and has jurisdiction in certain other special cases; (2) superior courts, which are courts of appeal, one in each judicial district; (3) judges of first instance, who have original jurisdiction in most civil, labor, land, minors and criminal matters; (4) justices of the peace. (Organic Judiciary Law, Sup. Decree 017-93-JUS of June 2, 1993 t.o. 1993 as am'd).

CURRENCY:

(Const. art. 83, Law 25295 of Jan. 3, 1991 and Law of Central Bank 26123 of Dec. 29, 1992; C.C. art. 1237).

Monetary unit is Nuevo Sol (NS/.) divided into 100 céntimos. Only Banco Central de Reserva del Perú may issue bank notes which are legal tender. Obligations in foreign currency, unless stipulated to contrary, may be paid in national currency at exchange rate prevailing at time and place of payment.

CURTESY:

There is no estate by curtesy.

DEATH:

If a person disappears leaving no one to administer his property, guardianship of the property is ordered; temporary guardianship may be appointed at relative's or interested person's request, as provided by law, after 60 days of disappearance. Such guardianship ceases and rights of succession are granted to absentee's heirs upon expiration of ten years from disappearance or five years if absentee is over age of 80 years. If disappearance arises under circumstances indicating danger of death, above period is two years. (C. C. 47, 63-66, 70, 2069).

Deaths are recorded in the Civil Register of the district. Death certificates may be obtained by application to the office of the Civil Registry of the district where the death occurred.

Actions for Death.—Under Civil Code anyone who causes damages to another is liable. Compensation includes loss of profits, personal injury and moral damages. Rights given to family members of deceased include moral damages. (C. C. 1969-1988, 2097).

DECEDENTS' ESTATES:

See topics Descent and Distribution; Executors and Administrators; Wills.

DEEDS:

(Notarial Law 26002 of Dec. 7, 1992; C. C. 2008-2017).

Before notary enters deed in his records parties must prepare and sign minute of contract or instrument, when required by law notary himself may prepare minute at request of parties. Every deed must contain: (a) Place and date of execution and name of notary; (b) name, age, domicile and profession of parties; (c) whether they appear personally or by representative and in latter case reference must be made to power of attorney; (d) civil status and nationality of parties and statement as to whether they know Spanish; (e) statement that interpreter appears for party not knowing Spanish; (f) statement that notary knows parties and that minute of the document was filed when required; (g) identification of parties by two witnesses if not known by notary; (h) insertion of minute in full; (i) statement that notary read instrument to parties in presence of two witnesses and that they ratified same; (j) signature of persons appearing and notary.

Deeds must be written by hand in the notary's registry. There can be no figures, unknown characters, variations of hand writing, blank spaces, abbreviations, words stricken out or differences in ink. The notary retains the original in his files and issues certified copies which have the force of originals.

When the instrument involves a money obligation it must set forth the nature of such obligation, the amount of the debt, the interest and the property encumbered stating where the same is situated. In conveyances of real property the area must be stated, the value of the property, the date of the latest appraisal, if any, and the price in case of sales. Certain instruments are subject to record.

See topic Records; also topic Taxation.

DEPOSITIONS:

The evidence of witnesses in civil cases is taken on written or oral questions and cross questions. If the witnesses are not in the locality the judge may send letters rogatory to another judge to take the deposition. Letters rogatory from abroad to take testimony or for similar acts in Peru are complied with by Peruvian judges if legalized by a Peruvian consul. (C. C. P. 222-232).

DESCENT AND DISTRIBUTION:

In case of intestacy inheritance is distributed as follows in order stated: (1) Children and other descendants; (2) parents and other ascendants; (3) spouse; (4) collaterals by consanguinity of second degree; (5) collaterals by consanguinity of third degree; (6) collaterals by consanguinity of fourth degree; (7) government and public charity.

Surviving spouse is entitled to same share as a child; but such share is diminished by amount of spouse's interest in marriage community property. (See topic Husband and Wife.) If parents or ascendants inherit, spouse is entitled to same share as received

DESCENT AND DISTRIBUTION . . . *continued*

by them. However, former or separated spouse has no inheritance rights. (Const. art. 2 §§16 and 6, C. C. 660-685, 815-880, 2041, 2042, 2100, 2101).

DESERTION: See topic Divorce.

DIVORCE:

(C. C. 24, 348-360, 382, 2070, 2081, 2082).

Divorce dissolving the marriage bond may be granted for the following causes: (1) Adultery; (2) physical or mental distress; (3) attempt against life of spouse; (4) grave insults; (5) malicious abandonment of home for two years; (6) dishonorable conduct making life in common insupportable; (7) habitual and unjustified use of narcotics; (8) serious venereal disease contracted after marriage; (9) sentence after marriage to over two years imprisonment; (10) homosexuality after marriage; (11) separation by mutual consent after two years of marriage. In case of causes (1), (3), (9) and (10) action must be brought within six months after cause comes to knowledge of offended party and in causes (2) and (4) action must be brought within six months after cause was produced.

The Code contains no specific residence requirement. Domicile in Peru is presupposed.

A divorced wife cannot use her husband's name. The children are awarded to the spouse who obtains the divorce unless the judge considers that the children's welfare demands that they be awarded to the other spouse or to a third person. If both spouses are guilty the sons over seven years go to the father and the daughters to the mother. In any case both parents are required to support the children.

Alimony not exceeding one-third spouse's income is allowed innocent spouse if other spouse is guilty party and spouse has not sufficient property and cannot work. Indigent spouse, even if guilty, is entitled to assistance from other. Alimony ceases on remarriage of spouse receiving it. In special cases judge may award damages to offended spouse.

Separation may be granted for (a) causes (1) to (10) hereinbefore designated and (b) mutual consent. In the latter case the judge decides as to the awarding of the children and alimony, following the agreement of the parties as far as prudent. One year after the decree of separation, it will be converted into an absolute divorce on demand of either party. Period is six months for separation by mutual consent and for innocent party.

DOWER:

There is no provision for dower as known in American law.

ENVIRONMENT:

(Const. arts. 2, 22, 67 and 68, Environmental and Natural Resources Code Leg. Decree 613 of Sept. 7, 1990 as am'd; Sup. Decrees 016-93-EM of Apr. 28, 1993, 046-93-EM of Nov. 10, 1993, 01-94-PE of Jan. 14, 1994, 029-94-EM of June 7, 1994, and Law 26410 of Dec. 16, 1994).

Constitution establishes legal framework for environmental legislation granting to each person right to enjoy liveable and balanced environment and to demand environmental protection measures. Environmental and Natural Resources Code contains general rules for all productive sectors and considers environment and natural resources as national patrimony whose protection and conservation are of social interest. Legislation related to protection and conservation of environment and natural resources are of public interest. Code contains principles such as prevention and control of environmental pollution, reparation of damages, environmental impact assessments and land use planning. National Environmental Council is coordinating body for national environmental policy. Environmental protection for mining and metallurgy, oil, electric, fishing and agriculture areas are regulated by specific legislation. Administrative sanctions are imposed for violation of Code which includes fines; partial or total, temporary or permanent closure of facility and cancelation of operating license. Criminal sanction is imprisonment from one to four years as established by Criminal Code.

ESCHEAT: See topic Descent and Distribution.

EVIDENCE: See topic Depositions.

EXCHANGE CONTROL:

(Leg. Decrees 655 of June 8, 1991 and 668 of Sept. 11, 1991, Sup. Decrees 036-91-EF of Mar. 11, 1991 and 068-91-EF of Mar. 26, 1991).

There are no exchange control regulations. Prevailing exchange rate shall be determined by supply and demand. There is free possession, redemption and transfer abroad of foreign currency. Individual and juridical persons residing in Peru are allowed to have deposit accounts in foreign currencies in country and abroad.

EXECUTIONS:

Under a judgment ordering the payment of money, the defendant must make payment when he is formally notified of the judgment; if he fails to pay and there has been no previous attachment of his property, (see topic Attachment) attachment is levied on property designated by the creditor. If the property attached consists of securities to bearer it is sold through a broker designated by the judge or appointed by the parties. Other property is appraised by experts designated by the judge unless the parties have agreed on a value for the case of sale. The judge orders a sale at public bidding, which is held in his office if it affects real estate, vessels, jewelry or securities to bearer when not quoted or there are no brokers in the locality. A sale must be advertised at the place of trial in a newspaper for three days in case of personal property and six days in case of real property, for first sale and for subsequent sales terms are one and three days respectively; same publications are made in place where property is situated if different from place of trial. Debtor may make payment at any time before sale. No bids are accepted of less than two-thirds appraisal. If there are no bidders as many further sales as may be necessary are advertised, in each of which value of property is reduced by 15% for purpose of bidding. If at any sale no bidders appear creditor may request that property be adjudicated to him for two-thirds of appraised amount mentioned in last call for bids. There is no right of redemption. Credit remains alive insofar as not satisfied by execution. There are special provisions regarding fulfillment of obligations concerning delivery of personal property or obligations to do or refrain from doing specific acts. (C. C. P. 720-748).

EXECUTORS AND ADMINISTRATORS:

An executor may be appointed by will. If several executors are appointed they discharge office in order of their designation unless testator states that appointment is joint or assigns commission of each. If there is no executor heirs assume charge of estate and carry out provisions of will, but if they do not agree judge appoints administrator.

An executor must have the same capacity as an agent and not be incompetent to inherit. Banks may be executors. No one is obliged to accept the office, but after accepting he cannot resign without just cause.

Executor has duty to (a) arrange funeral of testator, (b) insure security of estate, (c) make an inventory, (d) administer estate, (e) pay debts and legacies, (f) defend will if it is attacked, (g) sell property for payment of debts, prior authorization of court is required, (h) execute terms of will. He ceases in office if he fails to begin work of inventory within 90 days after death of testator. His office expires when he has finished his work or when two years have elapsed, unless longer time was allowed him by testator or as indicated by art. 796. He is entitled to compensation designated by testator, and if none be designated to 4% of amount of inventory. He must render accounts to interested parties immediately after ceasing to act, even though relieved of this duty by testator, and also during his incumbency if ordered by judge on petition of interested party. (C. C. 778-797, 831-880).

EXEMPTIONS:

The following are not subject to attachment: (1) Household furniture and other goods; (2) items of personal use, books and food belonging to debtor and his relatives; (3) vehicles, machinery, tools and utensils used by debtor in his profession, occupation or studies; (4) decorations, uniforms of public officials and employees and weapons and equipment used by armed forces and police; (5) remunerations and pensions up to five procedural reference units, any amount over can be attached up to one third; (6) alimony; (7) goods used in temples; (8) tombs; (9) State assets. There are few exceptions. (C.C.P. art. 648).

FILING FEES: See topic Corporations.

FORECLOSURE:

See topics Chattel Mortgages; Mortgages.

FOREIGN CORPORATIONS: See topic Corporations.

FOREIGN EXCHANGE:

See topic Exchange Control.

FOREIGN INVESTMENT:

(Const. arts. 62-64, Legislative Decree 662 of Aug. 29, 1991 and 757 of Nov. 8, 1991, Sup. Decree 162-92-EF of Oct. 12, 1992, Sup. Decree 094-92-PCM of Dec. 28, 1992, Decision 291 and 292 of Mar. 21, 1991 of Commission of Cartagena Agreement).

Foreign investment is defined as foreign source contribution made by individuals or juridical persons. Direct foreign investment may be effected in form of freely convertible foreign currency, assets, capitalization of profits, conversion of debentures in shares, investment of profits entitled to repatriation, equity contributions of intangibles or in intangible technological contributions such as mark, industrial models, technical assistance, patented or unpatented technical know-how in form of physical goods, technical documents and instructions, and any investment to development country. Foreign investors have same rights and duties as national investors, therefore they may invest in all economic activities.

Foreign investors are authorized to buy shares from national investors and to acquire shares, participations or rights held by other foreign investors in national, mixed or foreign companies.

Investments of foreign individuals with legal residence in country may be considered national investment if they comply with special requirements including declaration to waive their rights to repatriate capital and remit profits abroad. Foreign investors are entitled to repatriate capital when they sell their shares, participations or rights or when company is liquidated. Foreign investors are allowed to transfer abroad 100% profits and repatriation of capital of direct foreign investment.

Direct foreign investment may be registered at National Commission of Foreign Investments and Technology (CONITE). Investment is automatically registered by filing appropriate documents. Registration is necessary for validity of foreign investor's rights. For transfer of registered direct foreign investment no approval is required, but notice must be given to CONITE.

Foreign and national investors may enter into contract with CONITE to enjoy up to ten year guarantees of legal stability related to: tax regime, free availability of foreign currency regime, and nondiscrimination rights. Contract must be executed prior to investment and investor must comply with requirement as provided by law. Investors contracting with state-owned entity may obtain Supreme Decree by which Government guarantees all obligations of state-owned entity.

Companies are classified as follows: (a) National company where more than 80% of capital belongs to national investors, provided that in opinion of competent authority, such percentage is reflected in technical, financial, administrative and commercial management of company. (b) Mixed company where between 51% and 80% of its capital belongs to national investors, provided that in opinion of competent authority, such percentage is also reflected in technical, financial, administrative and commercial management of company. (c) Foreign companies where less than 51% of its capital

See Topical Index in front part of this volume.

FOREIGN INVESTMENT . . . *continued*
belongs to national investors, or if, in case of higher national percentage such percentage is not, in opinion of competent authority, reflected in technical, financial, administrative and commercial management of company.

License agreements on transfer of technology and use and exploitation of foreign patents and trademarks must be registered with CONITE for purpose of payment of royalties. Agreements are automatically registered upon filing when payment of royalties is calculated on percentage of net sales or any other calculation form. Solution of conflicts and disputes arising from direct foreign investment or transfer of technology may be subject to arbitration.

Free Zones.—(Leg. Decree 704 of Nov. 5, 1991 as am'd by Leg. Decree 779 of Dec. 30, 1993). National or foreign individuals and juridical persons may be authorized to operate in free zones. There are four types of free zones: industrial, tourist, special commercial treatment and special development. Industrial free zones are created for promotion and development of industrialization of goods and services; and tourist free zones are created for promotion of national and foreign tourism. Investors in both zones are exempted from import duties, for 15 years; and from all Peruvian present or future taxes, except for contributions to social security; they are allowed to enter into temporary labor agreements, and their accounting may be kept in foreign currency. Special commercial treatment free zones are dedicated exclusively to commercial activities and are located on border and jungle areas. Entrance of goods to free zone are exempted from all Peruvian present and future taxes levied on sale of goods and are subject to import duty at special rate. Their accounting may be kept in foreign currency. Special development free zones are created for development of areas where located, for that purpose investors must enter into agreement with State for granting of benefits.

FOREIGN TRADE REGULATIONS:

See topic Exchange Control.

FRAUDS, STATUTE OF:

See topics Acknowledgments; Deeds; Public Instruments.

FRAUDULENT SALES AND CONVEYANCES:

Creditors have power to avoid gratuitous transfers which render debtor insolvent or impair creditors' ability to collect payment from debtor. Creditors have power to avoid transfers for value (i) if debtor's insolvency was notorious or should have been known by transferee, or (ii) transfer was fraudulently made for purpose of avoiding payment of future debt. However, good faith transferees for value are protected. (C.C. 195-200).

GARNISHMENT:

In general a debtor's property in possession of third persons may be attached.

HOLIDAYS:

Jan. 1 (New Year's); Maundy Thurs. (half holiday)*; Good Friday*; May 1 (Labor Day); June 29 (SS. Peter and Paul); July 28-29 (National Independence days); Aug. 30 (St. Rose of Lima); Oct. 8 (Angamos Combat); Nov. 1 (All Saints); Dec. 8 (Immaculate Conception); Dec. 25 (Christmas). (Leg. Decree 713 of Nov. 7, 1991 as am'd).

* These are movable holidays.

HOMESTEADS:

If member of a family has no debts, payment of which will be adversely affected, he may constitute "family home" on real property destined to be used by him or his family for agriculture, industry, or as a dwelling. Such home may not be alienated, mortgaged or encumbered; but up to two-thirds of any income derived therefrom is subject to attachment for taxes, judgment debts, and claims for support. Judicial approval is required for constitution of such family home and for its revocation (C. C. 488-501).

HUSBAND AND WIFE:

(Const. art. 5; C. C. 4, 36, 287-326, 2077-2080; C. Com. 6-12).

Spouses owe each other fidelity and assistance. They must live together unless health, life, honor or business of either would thereby be gravely endangered. Husband and wife may determine domicile and decide economic questions of family. Husband and wife must supply their family with necessaries of life according to their resources and situation.

The following is separate property of each spouse: (a) Property owned at the time of marriage or acquired during marriage if the consideration antedated the marriage; (b) gifts during marriage; (c) moneys paid for insurance. Each spouse has the free administration and disposition of his or her separate property, but if the wife does not contribute to the expenses of the marriage with the fruits of her separate property, the husband may demand the administration of all or part thereof on giving bond. The separate property of either spouse is not liable for the debts of the other.

Marriage creates a property community which cannot be renounced. The marriage community property comprises: (a) The income from the separate and the community property; (b) property purchased with community funds, though standing in the name of only one of the spouses; (c) property acquired by the work, industry or profession of either spouse; (d) improvements on separate property made at the cost of the community property or by the industry of either spouse. All property of the spouses is presumed to be community property until the contrary is proved.

Either spouse is representative of marriage partnership and may administer and alienate community property. For ordinary needs of home either spouse may represent marriage partnership, but if either abuses this power it may be limited by judge. Community property is liable for debts of marriage community. Income from each spouse's property is not liable for personal debts of other spouse unless it be shown that they were contracted for benefit of family.

The marriage community is terminated by (a) death of either spouse, (b) annulment of the marriage, (c) divorce, (d) separation of property, (e) declaration of absence or (f) legal separation of spouses. On such dissolution the separate property of each spouse is set aside and the balance is evenly divided between the spouses if they are living, as in the case of divorce, or between the surviving spouse and the heirs of the deceased spouse.

Wife may freely appear in court actions. Either spouse may exercise any profession or industry, and do any kind of work outside of home, with express or implied consent of other; and if one refuses consent other one may obtain authorization of judge if he/she shows that such measure is required by interest of marriage partnership or that of family. Husband and wife cannot contract with each other in matters related to community property.

INCOME TAX: See topic Taxation.

INDUSTRIAL PROPERTY:

C. C. arts. 18, 2093; Decisions 344 and 345 of Oct. 29, 1993 of Cartagena Commission; Leg. Decree 823 of Apr. 23, 1996; Sup. Decree 008-96-ITINCI of May 3, 1996.

Invention Patents.—Any person or corporation who invents or discovers or improves something of industrial application may obtain patent. Corporations may petition patents for inventions made by persons under their employment. Any invention of products or proceedings in any technology field which are novel, represent inventive step and are susceptible of industrial application. Invention is novel when it is not within state of art. Discoveries, scientific theories and mathematical methods; scientific, literary and artistic works; therapeutic, surgical and diagnostic methods among others are not considered inventions. Inventions contrary to public policy, morals and against life or health of people or animals and environment; on animal species and races and biological procedures to obtain them; inventions related to nuclear substances, to pharmaceutical products listed by World Health Organization as essential medicines; and related to substances composing human body are not patentable.

Patents are granted for 20 years from filing date. Patent gives exclusive right of exploitation, but compulsory license may be granted in case of declared emergency or national security reasons, and to guarantee free competition and avoid abuse of dominant position in market. Patent owner must exploit it, directly or by granting license in any member country of Andean Pact. Industrial production or commercialization of patented product, are considered exploitation of patent.

Industrial Designs and Utility Models.—Any new design or model which may be applied to industrial object may be registered as ownership of author if no publicity thereof in any form has been made before filing application. Registration grants exclusive rights for ten years. Utility models for new forms of objects or mechanism, provided they have practical use are registrable. Registration term is ten years from filing date. Provisions regarding patents are applicable to designs and models.

Trade Secrets.—Law also protects trade secrets and considers them as any confidential information that is valuable and provides competitive or economic advantages to owner. Information considered trade secret must be expressed in tangible form such as documents, microfilm films, laser discs or any other similar means.

Vegetal species are protected when they are novel, homogeneous, distinguishable and stable and generic designation has been assigned to them. When registered certificate of holder is issued for 15 to 25 years, depending on type of vegetal variety.

Trade-Marks and Commercial Services and Slogans.—Those signs visible and sufficiently distinctive and susceptible of graphic representation can be registered as marks. Trademark is any sign used to distinguish products or services produced or commercialized by one person from same or similar products or services produced or commercialized by another person. Slogans are words, sentences or captions used as supplement to trademark. Any person or corporation may apply for registration of tradenames or commercial services or slogans employed or to be employed in relation with economic activities. Item registered may be sufficiently distinctive. Combinations of colors, letters and numbers may be registered as trademarks. Executive Power may decree mandatory registration of tradenames for canned or bottled foods and pharmaceutical products. No registration may be granted to marks, denominations, signs and emblems of State or its agencies, or international organizations recognized by Peru, except if applied for by same; to usual or necessary shapes of products or denomination and color thereof; common words or their equivalent in common languages or descriptive denominations; marks which may be confused with others registered or pending registration; geographical names if their use may suggest origin; names of dead persons, except by their heirs, or names of historical personalities; title of literary, artistic or scientific works protected by copyright without permission of owner; marks contrary to law, those against public policy, denomination of protected vegetal varieties, those identical or similar to registered trade slogans and trade names provided under circumstances public may be confused; those that are reproduction, imitation, translation or total or partial transcription of distinctive signs, locally or internationally, well known, without taking into consideration classification of goods or services concerned; or because of similarity to well-known trademarks causes confusion to public independent of classification of goods and services for which registration is applied for. Registration of trademark grants ownership thereof and exclusive right to use it during ten years, renewable, if applied for within last six months. Owner of trademark may grant license to use or exploit it. Trademarks and commercial names can be cancelled for nonuse for consecutive three years by owner or licensee in any member country of Andean Pact.

Tradenames.—Those signs used to identify individuals or juridical persons regarding their economic activity. Even if name is not registered, law protects owner thereof for damages resulting from usurpation thereof if claimed within one year. Protection of tradename, whether registered or not, does not cover products manufactured by or dealt with by owner of name unless name is registered as trademark. Only owner of registered trademark may use it as name of his establishment, but name of establishment may not be adopted as trademark except by owner of establishment. Exclusive right to use of tradename ends with closing of establishment or termination of industry covered by name. Registration is granted for ten years and is renewable for additional ten year terms.

See Topical Index in front part of this volume.

INDUSTRIAL PROPERTY . . . *continued*

Collective Marks and Origin Denominations.—Producers or traders associations may register collective marks. Origin denominations belong to State who may grant right to use them for ten years, renewable.

Among conventions joined are: Convention for the Protection of Industrial Property, Paris, Mar. 20, 1883; Stockholm Revision of July 14, 1967 as am'd on Sept. 28, 1979; Convention on Patents and Trademarks, Montevideo, Jan. 16, 1889; Inter-American Convention for Protection of Patents and Trademarks, Washington, Feb. 20, 1929; Agreement on Trade-Related Aspects of Intellectual Property Rights, Marrakesh, Apr. 15, 1994.

INFANCY:

(C. C. 20-23, 42-46, 418-472, 502-563, 2070; Code of the Children and Adolescents, Law Decree 26102 of Dec. 28, 1992).

Infancy ends at the age of 18. Contracts of minors under 16 are void, and if over 16, voidable. Ordinarily, infants are subject to custody of their parents or guardians who have their legal representation and administration of property with limited powers of disposition. Parents exercising parental authority enjoy the usufruct of real and personal property with certain exceptions, of infant under 18.

INHERITANCE TAX: See topic Taxation.

INSOLVENCY: See topic Bankruptcy.

INTEREST:

(C. C. 1243-1250, 1663-1665).

Legal rate, in case there is no special agreement, is fixed by Central Bank.

Loans declaring receipt of money when in fact goods were delivered are considered sales.

Civil loans do not bear interest unless so agreed. Loans simulating receipt of larger sum than was actually received are limited to amount actually received.

Compound interest is prohibited, but interest may be compounded after a year in default by written agreement.

INTESTACY: See topic Descent and Distribution.

JUDGMENTS:

Judicial resolutions may be: (a) Decrees, when relating to mere procedural matters; (b) interlocutory decisions, when deciding incidental matters; (c) judgments, when deciding the action. Judicial resolutions must: (a) Set forth the facts and the law; (b) decide all matters in controversy and only such matters; (c) be based on the merits of the case and the law; (d) clearly state the decision. (C. C. P. 119, 127).

Foreign judgments have such force in Peru as is given them by treaty; if there is no treaty they have the same force as is given to Peruvian judgments in the country where rendered. In order that a foreign judgment be executed in Peru it is necessary: (a) That it does not decide matters of jurisdiction of Peruvian courts; (b) that it be not contrary to morals, good customs or Peruvian prohibitory laws; (c) that it be definite and unappealable in country where given; (d) that defendant was duly summoned according to laws of such country; (e) that foreign court rendering judgment is competent according to their law and with international principles; (f) that no same cause of action pending between same parties in Peruvian courts; (g) that judgment is not incompatible to another judgment previously rendered that fulfilled all requirements for execution; (h) that reciprocity is duly proved. (C. C. P. 837-840, C.C. 2102-2111).

LABOR RELATIONS:

(Const., Arts. 2, §§15, 22, 29; Civil Code Arts. 1755, 1764-1770; Commercial Code, Arts. 275-296; Law to promote employment, Leg. Decree 728 of Nov. 8, 1991 t.o. 1995 as am'd regulated by Sup. Decree 001-96-TR of Jan. 24, 1996; Law on labor contract with foreigners, Leg. Decrees 689 of Nov. 4, 1991 regulated by Sup. Decree 014-92-TR of Dec. 21, 1992; Law on compensation for period of services, Leg. Decree 650 of July 23, 1991 regulated by Sup. Decree 034-91-TR of Nov. 5, 1991; Law on profit sharing, Leg. Decree 677 of Oct. 2, 1991; Law on Collective Bargaining, Law Decree 25593 of June 26, 1992).

Under labor contract, worker offers to contribute to production by his personal labor, for specified or indeterminate time, in return for payment of wages. Labor contract whether individual or collective presumes payment of wages in money; maximum workday of eight hours; weekly rest period; prohibition of work by minors under 14 years of age; limitation on work of minors under 18; equal wages for equal work without distinction of sex; indemnity compensation for accidents; compulsory insurance; and intervention by Government to ensure enforcement of laws and regulations.

In case of dismissal without justified cause employer must indemnify worker with one month of salary for each year of service up to 12 years.

Any labor contract is null and void if it subjects employee to renunciation of any of benefits granted by labor social laws. Written labor contracts and labor contracts for fixed term must be authorized by Labor Department. Collective contracts are continually being concluded between labor unions and employers. Employers must maintain register of regulations, agreements, and labor contracts that govern their work centers.

Government guarantees freedom of labor. Anyone may freely engage in any profession, industry or occupation not contrary to morals, health or public security. Contract stipulations which restrict exercise of civil, political or social rights are prohibited. System of profit sharing by employees in earnings of enterprise is in effect. Laws on safety, health and hygiene are in effect. Also, there are regulations on minimum working conditions, indemnity for length of service and for accidents.

Foreigners may work in Peru subject to limitations. Only 20% of work force of enterprise may be composed of foreigners. Only 30% of total amount of salaries paid may go to foreign hands. These limitations are subject to exception for special cases. Every labor contract with foreigner is subject to approval by Labor Department. Labor contracts are for period up to three years and are renewable.

There are two systems of pension plans, National System of Pensions under government administration and Private System of Pensions. Employees have right to elect either system, both plans are funded by employer and employee contributions. Private system is managed by private corporations. (Law Decree 25897 of Nov. 27, 1992 as am'd). Private system of health in addition to public social security health system exist funded by contributions of employers and employees. Employees have right of electing either system. (Leg. Decree 718 of Nov. 8, 1991 t.o. 1995).

LAW REPORTS, CODES, ETC.:

See topics Reports, Statutes.

LEVY: See topic Executions.

LIENS:

(C. C. 1118-1131, 1055-1090; Law Decree 26116 of Dec. 18, 1992).

Liens are recognized for (a) the unpaid purchase price of real estate, (b) the cost of work or material furnished for the construction or repair of real property and (c) the value of property acquired in a partition with the obligation of paying compensation. Such liens are considered legal mortgages and their owner may require the execution of a public instrument acknowledging them for the purpose of recording such instrument in the public registry.

A creditor may hold as security property of his debtor which he may have in his possession, unless it was destined to be deposited with or delivered to a third person.

Creditor's claims are ranked in following order: (a) salaries and indemnities due to servants and employees; (b) support of debtor's family; (c) tax liabilities; (d) secured credits; and (e) other credits.

LIMITATION OF ACTIONS: See topic Prescription.

LIMITED PARTNERSHIP: See topic Partnership.

MARRIAGE:

(C. C. 234, 237, 239-294, 2075-2080).

Following may not marry: (1) Males and females below age of puberty but authorization may be granted by court if male is 16 and female 14, and in any case minor requires consent of his parents; (2) persons mentally ill, though having lucid intervals; (3) persons having transmissible chronic contagious disease; (4) deaf and dumb persons who cannot express their wishes unmistakably; (5) persons already married.

Following cannot contract marriage with each other: (1) Those related by affinity or consanguinity in direct line; (2) collaterals by consanguinity to third degree, but by court order third degree may be waived for good reasons and collaterals by affinity to second degree, where such relationship arose from marriage dissolved by divorce and former spouse is living; (3) adopter with person adopted, and their families in direct line or collaterals to third degree; (4) person condemned or under prosecution for death of spouse, with surviving spouse; (5) abductor with woman abducted.

Following marriages are likewise forbidden: (a) Of guardian, with minor or incompetent before accounts of guardianship are approved, under penalty of losing his compensation; (b) of widower or widow or divorced person without making inventory of property belonging to children, penalty being deprivation of usufruct of such property.

Persons desiring to contract marriage must apply to the mayor of the domicile of either party, or to the chief of the civil registry in the capital of the Republic or of a province. An announcement is posted for eight days and published once in a newspaper, but the mayor may for good reasons dispense with this requisite. If there is no opposition or the opposition is rejected, the marriage ceremony is performed by the mayor, or by such official, Catholic chaplain, or mayor of another town, as the mayor may delegate. Marriages having civil effects may likewise be performed by priests; priest must immediately send certificate of marriage to nearest civil registry.

Following marriages are void: (a) Those of persons mentally incapacitated; (b) those of deaf and dumb persons unable to express their wishes; (c) those of persons already married; (d) those of persons related by consanguinity or affinity in the direct line; (e) those of persons related by consanguinity to second and third degree, but judicial dispensation of third degree relationship; (f) those of persons related by affinity to second degree where relationship arose from marriage dissolved by divorce and ex-spouse is living; (g) those of person convicted or under prosecution for death of spouse, with surviving spouse; (h) those performed without intervention of competent official, except when parties acted in good faith. Following marriages may be annulled: (a) Where one of parties lacked age required by law, if action of nullity is brought on behalf of such party, but no action can be brought after minor has come of age or if female has conceived, and in any case contracting parties may confirm marriage when they come of age; (b) marriages between abductor and woman abducted; (c) where either spouse is absolutely impotent at time of marriage; (d) where one of parties was not in enjoyment of his mental faculties at time of marriage, or acted under duress, or was in error as to identity of other party, or was in ignorance of some defect of other party which would render living together insupportable, such as notoriously dishonorable life, sentence to over two years imprisonment, incurable contagious or transmissible disease, or defect which would endanger progeny. In cases mentioned in class (d) action may be brought only by aggrieved party within two years after marriage. If either spouse acted in good faith, voided marriage nevertheless produces civil effects with respect to such spouse and to children.

MARRIED WOMEN:

See topics Descent and Distribution; Husband and Wife; Wills.

MINES AND MINERALS:

(Const. art. 66, General Mining Law, Legislative Decree 109 of June 12, 1981, t.o. 1992 Sup. Decree 014-92-EM of June 2, 1992 as am'd; regulated by Sup. Decree 03-94-EM of Jan. 14, 1994 as am'd).

MINES AND MINERALS . . . *continued*

Mines in General.—Except petroleum and other hydrocarbons, mineral waters and guano, which are subject to special laws, mineral substances of all kinds in or under soil of national territory are governed by General Mining Law. Mineral deposits of any kind, including geothermic ones, belong to State and can not be alienated or acquired by adverse possession. Promotion of investment in mining activities is regarded as public interest. Exploitation of mineral and geothermic resources is done directly by State and by granting concessions to national or foreign natural or juridical persons with exception of certain government officials and their relatives. Law classifies mining activities into: (1) Informal prospecting (Cateo); (2) prospecting; (3) exploration; (4) exploitation; (5) general work; (6) processing (Beneficio); (7) refining; (8) commercialization; (9) transportation.

Informal Prospecting (Cateo) and Prospecting are free except on areas subject to prior private mining rights or excluded by resolution or on National Reserve areas or within areas subject to Special State Rights. They are also forbidden on property of public use, on fenced or cultivated land, on urban zones, archaelogical zones or zones reserved for national defense, as well as on mineral substances of national interest reserved by State.

Commercialization of mineral products, domestically and abroad, is free.

State may declare by law, reserve of certain mineral substances of national interest, also it may create National Reserve Areas on which mining rights will not be granted, to carry out directly or indirectly activities of exploration without prejudice to acquired mining rights.

Concessions.—Mining concessions are classified as follows: exploration, exploitation, processing (Beneficio), refining, general works and transportation and may be granted to individuals or juridical persons, national or foreign. Exploration concession grants holder right to explore mining substances within its perimeter. Exploitation concessions grant right to exploit same. Processing (Beneficio) concessions grant right to install and operate plants in order to extract or concentrate valuable part of aggregate of mining substances through physical, chemical and/or physico-chemical procedures. Refining concessions grant right to purify metals from products obtained during previous procedures. General work concessions grant right to offer auxiliary services to two or more concessions. Transportation concessions grant right to install and operate continuous transportation systems between mining center and port, processing plant or refinery.

Exploration and Exploitation Concessions.—Measure unit is square of one hectare. Concessions are indivisible and their extensions may range from 100 to 1,000 hectares, rectangular in shape with sides not to exceed one to ten in ratio, with some exceptions. Concessions on continental shelf are granted for extensions from 100 to 10,000 hectares. Concessions are: (a) Metallic and (b) nonmetallic.

Holders of mining concessions have rights and duties as stipulated by law, fee of US$2 per year and per hectare, for metallic substances and US$1 for nonmetallic substances paid at filing application, and during concession period. Minimum annual production is required, equivalent to US$100, per year and per hectare, for metallic substances and US$50 for nonmetallic substances, after completion of eight years of concession. In case of noncompliance, annual fee is increased.

Applicant of processing (Beneficio) or refining concessions must pay for registration rights plus, with respect to its capacity of production if it is less than 350 metric tons, 0.5 of U.I.T.; if 350-1,000 metric tons per day, 1 U.I.T.'s; if 1,000-5,000 metric tons per day, 1.5 U.I.T.'s; over 5,000 metric tons per day, 2 U.I.T.'s for metallic substances and for nonmetallic half rate.

Applicant of general work or transportation of minerals concessions must pay 0.003 of U.I.T. for each lineal meter of projected work for registration rights to Public Registry of Mining.

Concessions may be terminated by declaration of caducity, waiver, abandon, nullity and cancellation of mining rights. Pertinent inscription should be effected at Public Registry of Mining. It may declare them subject to new petition, except concessions for processing, general works, transport of minerals concessions which by nature could not be subject to new petition. Prior owner of concession and his immediate relatives cannot petition therefor in two years following declaration.

Law contains environmental protection regulations.

Taxation.—Concession holders in mining activities are subject to all taxes as indicated by art. 73 et seq. of Mining Law.

Incentives.—Law grants special benefits in order to promote private investment.

Executive power may guaranty by contract, tax stability for ten year period to holders of mining activities to obtain output of at least 350 metric tons a day and up to 5,000 metric tons a day and for 15 years over 5,000 metric tons, under conditions stipulated by law.

Hydrocarbons.—(Law 26221 of Aug. 13, 1993 regulated by Sup. Decree 055-93-EM of Nov. 17, 1993). Law creates PERUPETRO S.A., government enterprise of private law which may execute license or service contracts for exploration and exploitation of hydrocarbons with private developers under various stipulated arrangements by bid or individual evaluations. Maximum contract duration is 30 years for crude oil and 40 years for unassociated natural gas and condensates. Exploration phase, may not exceed seven years in either case. Contract term may be extended for up to ten additional years in case discovery turns out not to be commercial due to transportation problems. Foreign companies to execute contracts must be organized as branch or local company with domicile in capital city, have Peruvian citizen as agent and renounce all diplomatic recourse. Contracting parties have free disposition of hydrocarbons produced thereunder, such right may involve entire production or certain share of production. They may sell their share of production in domestic market or abroad and keep abroad all foreign currency proceeds derived from export or domestic sale. Export of hydrocarbons and by-products are exempted from duties. Government guarantees tax and exchange regime stability. Contracting parties are subject to regular income tax. Measures necessary for environmental protection are required. At termination of contract all equipment and installation must be turned over to Government. Disputes arising from execution of contracts may be subject to international arbitration.

MONOPOLIES AND RESTRAINT OF TRADE:

(Arts. 61, 63 and 65 of Constitution; arts. 3, 23, 33, 36 and 38 of Law 23407, General Industry Law of May 28, 1982); Leg. Decrees 668 of Sept. 11, 1991, 691 and 701 of Nov. 5, 1991 as am'd and 716 of Nov. 7, 1991 as am'd; Sup. Decree 133-91-EF of 1991 as am'd; Law 26122 of Dec. 29, 1992).

Any monopolistic practice, limitation, restriction or exclusivity in manufacturing and commercialization of goods and rendering of services is prohibited. All agreements and collusive practices impeding, distorting or limiting competition are also prohibited, as well as abusive exploitation of dominant position in domestic market. Law protects local production from unfair practices of international trade, imposing countervailing duties on import of foreign goods. Dumping and subvention are considered unfair practices. Dumping is defined as import of foreign goods at lower price than normal value in place of origin or of similar goods destined for consumption or use in country of origin in arm's-length transaction. Similar good is considered one with characteristics of quality, use, nature and function resembling imported good. Normal value is determined according to method indicated by law. Subvention is defined as direct or indirect incentives, subsidies, premiums or assistance of any kind, granted by foreign governments to producers, manufacturers, transporters or exporters of goods in order to make them more competitive on international market. Consumer Protection Law deals with consumers' rights to be informed; general representation and guaranties, products liability, credit operations, lack of performance, services, penalties for infringement of law and general regulations on subject. There are special regulations for advertisement of goods and services and for repression of unfair competition.

MORTGAGES:

(C. C. 1097-1122, 1956).

All real property which can be sold is subject to mortgage, but mortgages cannot be imposed on credits or leases. A mortgage may be constituted by a public instrument. Following are requisites of mortgage: (a) It must be constituted by owner having free disposal of property or by another duly authorized according to law; (b) lien must be of specific or determinable amount; (c) instrument must be recorded in real property registry; (d) it must secure specific or unspecified obligations. In order to secure documents transmissible by endorsement or to bearer mortgage instrument must also state: (a) Data relating to number and value of documents issued and secured; (b) their series; (c) date of issue; (d) time and manner of amortization; (e) designation of trustee; (f) other data to determine conditions of document; and furthermore, documents must be issued from stubbooks.

Preference among mortgages is decided by the date of registration. If the mortgaged property deteriorates so as to become insufficient, compliance with the obligation may be demanded before maturity. If the mortgage covers several parcels and the creditor forecloses on only one, in the possession of a third person, such owner may demand contributions from the owners of the other parcels. The right to impose second or further mortgages cannot be renounced. An agreement by which the creditor will become the owner of the property is void. Mortgages made abroad on Peruvian property are valid if recorded in Peru.

The vendor has a lien for the unpaid portion of the purchase price of real property. This and certain other liens are called legal mortgages and are subject to being recorded. See topic Liens.

Vessels are deemed real property and may be mortgaged under C. C. Art. 885 and Naval Mortgage Law 2411 of Dec. 30, 1916 with exception of art. 18 of Law 22202 of June 6, 1978. Aircraft may be mortgaged under Aeronautical Regulations, Sup. Decree 054-88-TC of Nov. 4, 1988 as am'd, Leg. Decree 670 of Sept. 13, 1991.

NEGOTIABLE INSTRUMENTS:

See topic Bills and Notes.

NOTARIES PUBLIC:

In order to be a notary it is necessary: (a) To be lawyer; (b) to be Peruvian by birth in full possession of civil rights; (c) to have no physical impediment; (d) to have good reputation; (e) not to have criminal record. Notaries are appointed by superior court of respective province and their number is restricted. They keep record in which they enter, in chronological order, public instruments executed before them. Their records are under judicial supervision. Instruments bear ordinal numbers; use of ciphers and unknown characters is prohibited, also variation of handwriting, blanks and abbreviations, and differences in ink. Notary retains original of instruments in his record and issues certified copies which have effect of originals. (Law Decree 26002 of Dec. 7, 1992).

PARTITION: See topic Real Property.

PARTNERSHIP:

(General Law of Societies, Sup. Decree 003 of Jan. 14, 1985).

Unlimited partnership (sociedad collectiva) is constituted by a public instrument (see topic Public Instruments) stating: (a) Name, nationality, civil status, occupation and domicile of partners; (b) firm name; (c) object of business; (d) duration; (e) capital and capital contribution of each partner; (f) firm's domicile and agreed places where its branches, if any, will be established; (g) administration system and powers granted to managers; (h) name of administrators; (i) any other legal agreements. Firm name must contain names of partners or some of them, followed by phrase "y compañía" or its abbreviation "S.C." Partnership articles must be recorded in Mercantile Registry, at which time firm becomes a legal entity.

Partners are jointly and severally liable for debts of partnership. If administration of company was not reserved to one or more of partners, they may all intervene in management. Limitations of powers of administrators do not affect third parties except when such limitations are recorded in Mercantile Registry or when it is proved that third party knew such limitations. All partners have right to supervise management. Resolutions of firm are adopted by majority vote, one partner one vote, but it may be agreed that vote will be in proportion of capital. In this case, if one partner represents

PARTNERSHIP . . . *continued*

more than half of capital, vote of another partner will be necessary to make majority. Industrial partners have no vote, except when vote is according to capital, in which case they have one vote equal to that of partner who represents largest capital.

Unless otherwise agreed upon, profits are divided in proportion to interest of each partner; partner who contributes his services is entitled to half of profits. If there is more than one industrial partner half is divided equally among them. Losses are proportionately distributed among capitalist partners only. When losses are greater than firm's capital, industrial partner shares losses in same proportion as that of capitalist partner who has smallest participation. No partner may convey his interest without consent of others. Partners may not carry on business similar to that of firm, unless authorized by other partners. Industrial partner cannot engage in other business of any kind without consent of firm.

Partnerships may terminate partially by failure of one or more partners to comply with partnership articles, culpable partner being excluded. Partnerships are totally dissolved by: (a) Expiration of term; (b) losses which reduce capital to less than one-third; (c) merger; (d) bankruptcy; (e) death or insanity of one of partners, except when charter contains provisions for continuation with other partners; (f) by resolution of Supreme Court. Regarding liquidation of partnerships, most of provisions concerning liquidation of corporations are applicable.

Limited partnership (sociedad en comandita) has two kinds of partners: general partners, who have unlimited liability, and special partners, who are liable only for amount they contribute. Firm name may contain only names of general partners, or of some of them. In any case, firm name must be followed by phrase "Sociedad en Comandita," or its abbreviation, "S. en C." Most of provisions relating to unlimited partnerships are applicable also to limited partnerships. Management is in hands of one of general partners, unless otherwise agreed upon, but special partners can also be appointed managers. Unless charter provides to contrary, appointment and removal of administrators require majority vote of general as well as of special partners. Except for above, special partners cannot take part in management and may examine status of administration only at time and in manner provided in partnership agreement; in absence of provisions in this respect, managing partners must supply necessary documents and annual balance sheet ten days before date set for approval of said balance.

Civil company is a company not formed for mercantile purposes. Company articles must appear in public instrument. Unless they provide otherwise every partner has power of administration, but requires authorization to alienate property of company (unless this is company's object), to impose liens thereon and to contract loans.

PATENTS:

See topic Industrial Property.

PERPETUITIES:

Entailments perpetually keeping property in one family and involving prohibitions of alienation were formerly permitted but are forbidden except for homestead (q.v.). Foundations for specific objects, however, are allowed, under general supervision of Government. (Const., art. 2, §13; C. C. 99-110, 127-129, 488-501, 882, 926).

PLEDGES:

A pledge contract involves the delivery of personal property to secure a debt and gives the pledge creditor a preferential right to be paid with the price of the pledged article; such preference ceases if the article leaves the custody of the creditor or of the third person appointed depositary. A pledge has no effect as to third persons unless it appears in a writing of indubitable date. On maturity of the obligation the creditor may demand a public sale of the pledge. Any agreement that the creditor may take the pledge in payment of the debt is void. (C. C. 1055-1083). See topic Chattel Mortgages.

PRESCRIPTION:

(C. C. 950-953, 1989-2007, 2091, 2099; C. Com. 953-965).

Prescription is a manner of acquiring the ownership of property or extinguishing a right of action by the passing of time.

Real property is acquired by prescription by continuous possession in capacity of owner for ten years and with legal title and in good faith, in five years. Personal property is acquired by continuous possession as owner for two years with good faith or for four years without good faith.

Limitation of Actions.—Rights of action are lost by prescription in different periods, depending on kind of action, most important being: (1) Actions in rem, actions on judgments and personal actions not otherwise limited, ten years; (2) actions of lawyers, physicians, teachers, hotel keepers, experts, surveyors, architects, artisans, servants and laborers for services rendered, three years; (3) actions for support and actions by minors or incompetents against their parents, actions to annul contracts for error, fraud or duress and actions to repair damages, two years. Period of prescription does not run: (1) Against minors or incompetents not under paternal care or guardianship; (2) between husband and wife during marriage; (3) between minors and their parents or guardians; (4) between incompetents and their guardians; (5) so long as it is impossible to make claim before Peruvian court; (6) between corporations and their administrator; (7) between man and common law wife.

Rights of action in mercantile matters are lost in the following periods: (1) Actions to collect dividends or participations in the capital of companies, five years; (2) actions against managers or directors of companies, four years; (3) actions based on drafts, promissory notes, checks, coupons and other commercial documents, actions to enforce liability of brokers, actions of partners or stockholders against the partnership or corporation and vice-versa, and actions arising from maritime insurance, three years; (4) actions arising from collisions, two years; (5) actions for services rendered or supplies furnished in connection with the construction, repair or provisioning of vessels, or in connection with their sale and custody, or regarding delivery of freight by land or sea, one year; (6) actions on bonds of agents or regarding the collection of freight and passage money, six months.

PRINCIPAL AND AGENT:

(C. C. 145-167, 1790-1808, 2036-2038; C. Com. 5, 50-63, 237-274).

A general power of attorney merely authorizes the agent to perform acts of administration; in order to alienate or encumber the property of the principal power must be expressly given in public instrument. Agency is compensated. Agent is obliged: (a) To discharge agency which he has accepted while it remains in effect; (b) to give notice to principal upon conclusion of business; (c) to follow instructions; (d) to render accounts. Agent is liable for acts of substitute appointed by him if appointment was without authorization or if he chooses notoriously incompetent person. Principal is obliged: (a) To reimburse agent for advances and expenses with interest and pay compensation stipulated; (b) to indemnify agent for losses caused by agency; (c) supply necessary means for performance of authorized acts.

An agency terminates by: (a) Revocation; (b) resignation of the agent; (c) death, incapacity or bankruptcy of the principal or agent; (d) termination of the business; (e) expiration of term. Appointment of new agent for same business is equivalent to revocation. Revocation takes effect from time former agent is notified. Agent who resigns must notify principal and continue to act until replaced, but he may cease in agency if he gives principal 30 days notice plus allowance for distance. So long as agent does not know of principal's death or that he should cease in agency for another reason, his acts as agent are valid.

PUBLIC INSTRUMENTS:

Public instruments are: (a) Documents authenticated by notaries according to law (see topics Deeds; Notaries Public); (b) documents issued or authorized by public officials in the discharge of their office. As evidence, copies of public instruments issued by notary or public official have the same value as originals. Public instruments are evidence of their execution and contents. Law designates numerous contracts which must appear in public instruments, including all contracts relating to alienation and encumbrance of real property, and documents which require recording in public registry.

Instruments written in foreign language must be presented with official Spanish translation in order to be accepted in evidence.

Private documents when acknowledged in court have the probative value of public instruments. When not acknowledged their value as evidence is subject to the discretion of the judge. (C. C. P. 233-261; C. C. 1411-1413).

REAL PROPERTY:

(C. C. 885-895, 938-946, 954-958, 993).

Following are considered real property: (a) Soil, undersoil and topsoil, mines and waters; (b) real estate; (c) mines granted to private persons; (d) ships and air-ships; (e) railroads and their rights of way; (f) wharves and dikes; (g) public service franchises; (h) real property rights subject to record in the public registry; (i) those indicated by law.

Ownership of real property comprises surface and also space below and above surface in so far as owner may find it useful to enjoy same. It does not comprise minerals or natural resources and archeological objects, which are governed by special laws. Floors of building may belong to several owners.

When property belongs to several persons any one may demand partition. Agreements not to divide cannot be made for more than four years but may be renewed. If no period has been stipulated four years is presumed. If property cannot be easily divided and there is no agreement among parties public sale is held and proceeds divided among owners, who have preferential right to purchase for same price.

Decree 25 of Mar. 6, 1959, regulates cooperative apartments.

RECORDS:

National System of Public Registries is comprised of: (a) Registry of Natural Persons, (b) Registry of Juridical Persons, (c) Registry of Real Property, (d) Registry of Personal Property and (e) other registries. (Law 26366 of Oct. 14, 1994 as am'd). (Decree Law 19893 of May 23, 1973, Sup. Decree 20 of Aug. 3, 1973, Decree-Law 20198 of Oct. 30, 1973, Leg. Decree 119 of June 12, 1981 and Law 23407 of May 29, 1982, Leg. Decree 667 of Dec. 9, 1991; C. C. 70-75, 2008-2045; C. Com. 16-32, Decrees Apr. 19, 1902, 2411 of Dec. 30, 1916, Law Decree 26127 of Dec. 29, 1992; Legislative Decree 110 of June 12, 1981, Supreme Decree 028-81-Em/SG of Sept. 23, 1981, Sup. Decree 027-82-EM/RPM of Aug. 11, 1982).

REDEMPTION: See topic Executions.

REPORTS:

The judgments and resolutions of the Supreme Court are annually published in an official publication called "Judicial Annals of the Supreme Court of Justice."

RESTRAINT OF TRADE:

See topic Monopolies and Restraint of Trade.

SALES (Realty and Personalty):

(C. C. 1364, 1366, 1484-1591; Law 6565 of Mar. 12, 1929, as am'd by Laws 6847 and 10666).

A sale is perfected when there is agreement as to the object and the price, although the object has not been delivered nor the price paid, but in the case of a sale of objects by weight, number or measure, the risk does not pass to the buyer until the objects are weighed, counted or measured or are placed at the buyer's disposal. The price may be left to the decision of a third person. In a contract of sale the period stipulated cannot exceed two years in the case of real property nor one year in the case of personalty; if nothing is stated these periods are understood. Unless otherwise stipulated each contracting party pays one-half the cost of the contract.

Certain persons are prohibited from purchasing certain property: (1) A public administrator may not buy property in his charge; (2) an agent, the property in his charge; (3) executor, property he administers; (4) judge, lawyer, notary or expert, property sold in suit in which they intervened; (5) President, Cabinet Ministers,

SALES (Realty and Personalty) . . . *continued*
assemblymen, congressmen and judges, national property; (6) Governors, national property in their jurisdiction.

The vendor must deliver the object sold, and warrants as to title and hidden defects. In sales of personalty, if the buyer fails to pay, the seller may dispose of the property without asking for rescission; if part of the price was paid the sale will be rescinded on petition of seller who should return amount received less compensation for damages.

If property is sold by area or contents the buyer must pay or the seller must return any excess, but if the difference exceeds one-tenth the buyer may elect to rescind the contract. Right to repurchase cannot be reserved for over two years.

In sales it is permitted to stipulate that the title shall not pass until the price is totally paid; in such event the parties must designate what part of the payments is to be considered as damages if the sale be rescinded for failure to pay the total price, but the judge may reduce the amount of the indemnity in view of all the circumstances.

A warranty is presumed even though not stipulated; the parties may agree otherwise, but such agreement is void if the defects are due to acts of the vendor. The parties may extend or restrict the ordinary rules regarding warranty.

A special law regulates the sale of personal property under the instalment plan in Lima, Callao and nearby coast towns. A registry is established to record such sales. The objects sold must bear numbers or marks permitting their identification. A person acquiring objects so registered cannot convey them without the cancellation of the registry unless a document showing the consent of the original vendor be attached; persons acquiring such objects without observing these requisites must return the objects to the original vendor who recorded the sale. If an attachment be levied on a registered object, the balance owing the original vendor is a first lien on the proceeds of the sale.

SEALS:

Seals are used by Government officers, courts, notaries public, etc. Documents issued by public officials must bear the seal of their office. Private persons, especially merchants, sometimes use seals but they produce no special effect and are equivalent to a signature. Public instruments (q.v.) have most of the effects of a sealed instrument in the United States. (C. C. P. 235, 236).

SEQUESTRATION:

When money, jewelry or credit instruments are attached they are deposited in the proper establishment or, when there is none, with a person designated by the judge. When salaries, pensions, revenues, fruits or credits are attached the judge may order that they be delivered to a depositary designated by the creditor or that the debtor retain them in his custody, at the option of the creditor. The person having their custody is considered as depositary with the rights and obligations of an administrator. The law designates the powers and obligations of administrators; in the case of rural properties, mines, vessels or industrial establishments a supervisor is appointed to watch over the administration. (C. C. P. 643, 654, 655, 661-673).

SHIPPING:

Legislative Decree 644 of June 22, 1991 eliminates restriction for routes and operation in international transport for domestic shipping firms. Domestic companies are those incorporated and registered in Peru. No limitation exists for full ownership of domestic shipping companies by foreign investor. Foreign shipping firms are excluded from cabotage, except in shipping along national border, in which they may participate subject to agreement. There is no reservation of cargo to domestic shipping companies. Participation of foreign companies in transport of Peruvian cargo is subject to reciprocity. In general, navigation and ports are governed by regulations of Merchant Marine and Port Captaincies contained in Supreme Decree 25 of Oct. 31, 1951 as am'd, which under Supreme Decree No. 4 of Jan. 19, 1961 applies also to lake navigation. Decree of May 13, 1966 as am'd also contains general rules regarding registration, navigability, sailing and other matters relating to vessels.

STATUTE OF FRAUDS:

See topics Acknowledgments; Deeds; Public Instruments.

STATUTES:

The laws of Peru are published in the official paper of the Government called "El Peruano," which appears daily; they are also officially published in annual publication called "Anuario de la Legislación Peruana." Official editions of codes and more important laws are occasionally issued. Most important are: Civil Code, Code of Civil Procedure, Code of Commerce, Stock Exchange Law, Penal Code, Code of Procedure in Criminal Matters, Mining Code, Taxation Code, Petroleum Law, Bankruptcy Law, Legislation of Customhouses, Legislation of Waters, etc.

TAXATION:

Sales Tax.—Leg. Decree 821 of Apr. 22, 1996 as am'd and its regulations. Sales of some personal property, construction contracts, specified services and importation of goods are taxed at 16% rate, with some exemptions established in law. Tax base is constituted by value of property sales, total income for services and CIF customs value.

Exportation of goods and services is not subject to this tax.

Tax exemptions are granted to industries, activities and services at jungle region. Transactions subject to this tax are also subject to 2% of municipal promotion tax.

Excise Tax (Impuesto selectivo al consumo) (Leg. Decree 821 of Apr. 22, 1996 as am'd and its regulations). Tax is levied on: Producer sales and importer of cigarettes, gas, wines, jewelry, yachts and recreation boats, gambling, race tracks, among others at rates ranging from 10% to 30%.

Tax on Real Property.—(Leg. Decree 776 of Dec. 30, 1993). Real property, including construction and fixtures, is subject to land tax. Rates are 0.2% up to 15 U.I.T.'s, 0.6% up to 60 U.I.T.'s and 1% on properties' value over 60 U.I.T.'s.

Income Tax.—(Leg. Decree 774 of Dec. 30, 1993 as am'd and regulations, Sup. Decree 122-94-EF of Sept. 19, 1994).

Object.—This tax is levied on income from Peruvian sources regardless of nationality of natural person or place of constitution of juridical person and on income earned abroad by residents of Peru. Peruvian source income is specifically defined in arts. 9 and 10 of Law. Export trade benefits related to merchandise produced, manufactured or purchased in Peru, even when it consists only of mere send off by agencies, branches, representatives or intermediaries to foreign countries always constitute Peruvian income. International activities such as transportation, communications, news services, insurance or reinsurance, film distribution and others, are subject to specific percentages to determine portion of income considered of Peruvian source.

Following are regarded as residents: (a) Peruvian nationals domiciled in Peru according to provisions of civil law; (b) foreign nationals with uninterrupted stay in Peru for at least two years, temporary absences of less than 90 days are disregarded; (c) Peruvian nationals performing public services for Government in foreign countries; (d) juridical persons organized in Peru; (e) branches and agencies in Peru of foreign concerns; (f) undivided estates when decedent was resident at time of death; (g) multinational banks; (h) irregular companies, associations and partnerships. New residents may submit to this law after six months' stay in country, having previously registered as taxpayers.

Persons and Entities subject to Tax.—(a) Individuals; (b) undivided estates; (c) juridical persons. Under latter are included among others following: (1) Corporations (sociedades anónimas) organized in Peru; (2) limited partnership (sociedades en comandita) organized in Peru; (3) cooperatives; (4) corporations with social ownership; (5) public corporations; (6) branches or agencies of foreign companies; (7) foundations and associations; (8) foreign societies of any kind receiving Peruvian income; (9) agricultural societies with social interest and agrarian cooperative societies of production.

Income of undivided estates is also regarded as income of single individuals until executors of heirs determine portion of each recipient.

Exemptions.—Not subject to this tax are: (a) Public sector, with exception of public corporations; (b) universities, educational and cultural centers; (c) legally established foundations with cultural, social or health purposes; (d) entities of mutual assistance; (e) rural communities; (f) native communities. Law grants exemption until Dec. 31, 2000 to: (1) Income, except from commercial activities of legally authorized nonprofit associations, foundations, including religious entities, if destined to their proper purpose and not directly or indirectly distributed; (2) interest on loans for economic development granted by international organizations or by foreign governmental insitutions; (3) rent from government-owned real estate; (4) salaries and other remuneration paid by foreign governments to officers of international organizations or foreign institutions as well as salaries to technicians for services rendered to Peru for assistance programs; (5) severance; (6) interest on loans granted to public sector except loans originated on cash reserve deposits (depositos de encaje) of credit institutions; (7) interest from savings deposits and any other deposit in local or foreign exchange; (8) fees of foreign professional sportsmen and athletic clubs not domiciled in Perú; and (9) royalties paid for technical, financial, economic or any other assistance rendered from abroad by international organizations or government agencies among others.

Gross income comprises all taxable income. In case of income derived from sale of property, gross income shall be difference between proceeds for sale and cost of property. Depreciation shall be deducted from cost whenever property involved is subject to depreciation.

Categories of Income.—Law establishes following:

(1) Income from Lease, Sublease and Transfer of Personal or Real Property.—Tax is levied on following: (a) Profit in cash or in kind from lease or sublease of real properties, including accessories; (b) value of improvements done by lessee or sublessee meaning profit to owner; (c) implied rent when owner himself occupies property, rate is 6% of property value when used as owner's residence; (d) income from lease or temporary assignment of personal or real property or intangibles.

(2) Income from Other Capital Investments (Interest, Royalties).—This category comprises: interest derived from loans, cedulas, bonds, debentures and any kind of credits as indicated by law (1), or from temporary or permanent assignment of trademarks; income from royalties, annuities and any compensation received in consideration of promise to forbear or not to do, but if promise relates to activities falling under other category income, latter applies; difference between amounts paid as premiums by insured and amounts paid received by same after agreed term elapses in life insurance and dotal policies, interest in excess payments received by members of cooperative societies, except those of laborers' cooperatives.

All transactions in cash or in kind originated by use or right to use patents, trademarks, designs, plans, secret formulas, author's rights for literary, artistic or scientific works, as well as any transaction obtained by industrial, commercial, or scientific information, are deemed as royalty arrangements.

(3) Industrial and Commercial Profits.—This category also includes income derived from commerce, industry, mining with certain qualifications, agriculture and cattle raising, forestry, fishing and other natural resources; from rendering services such as transportation, communication, hospitals, hotels, warehouses, banks, finance and insurance companies, brokers and other intermediaries; notary public fees; income derived from sale of real estate and any other income not included in other categories. Taxpayers with combined income from categories (3) and (4) are included in category (3).

Income of concerns or entities which are not corporations is attributed to owners or members thereof even if not distributed. Same applies to losses even if not charged to their accounts.

When corporation distributes dividends in kind, except its own shares, difference between market value and applicable basis of objects distributed shall be deemed profit or loss to corporation.

Individuals, juridical persons and undivided estates with income in this category up to certain amount may elect to be subject to special regime of income tax and be taxed at monthly rate of 3% of net income.

(4) Professional Fees and Income of Other Independent Individuals.—This category comprises income earned by professionals working alone or in association, and income of any other kind of independent workers and remuneration of members of boards of directors, attorneys-in-fact, promoters, executors, and the like.

TAXATION . . . *continued*

(5) Tax on Salaries and Other Remuneration.—This tax comprises: (a) Salaries received by employees except allowances for business trips; (b) pensions derived from work; (c) workers' profit-sharings whether liquid or proprietary; (d) income derived from laborers' cooperatives received by members; (e) income derived from services contracts, as stipulated by law.

Taxpayer may not deduct from gross income income tax paid by third party except when said tax is levied on interest of financing operations with foreign beneficiaries.

Deductions from Category (1) Tax.—20% of gross income and expenses for building improvements in fortuitous cases not covered by insurance.

Deductions from Category (2) Tax.—10% of gross income.

Deductions from Category (3) Tax.—Law allows numerous deductions among them: (a) Normal business expenses; (b) interest derived from loans and expenses incurred in obtaining it and cancellation of said loans within limits; (c) taxes levied on profit-producing activity; (d) insurance premiums; (e) losses deriving from acts of God; (f) depreciation of fixed assets and losses of goods, provided they are duly proven; (g) business organization expenses which may be deducted in first year, or within ten years; (h) amounts assigned to reserves and deductions ordered by Superintendency of Banking and Insurance as well as technical reserves by insurance companies; (i) losses from bad debts; (j) salaries and other remuneration of members of board of directors, up to 6% of net profits; (k) remuneration to stockholders in corporations to ascendants, descendants or spouse, provided they actually participate in management; (l) prospecting expenses of mining companies may be deducted in same year or redeemed under terms and conditions established by General Law of Mining; (m) royalties, fees and other expenses established by Regulations; (n) periodical fees and maintenance expenses by lessee in financial lease contracts.

Deductions from Category (4) Tax.—Taxpayer may deduct 20% of gross income, but no more than 24 tributary units (U.I.T.'s).

Deductions from Category (5) Tax.—Those who received income of Category (4) and (5) may deduct 7 tributary units (U.I.T.'s). Taxpayers with income of both categories may deduct once only.

Estimated Net Income for Nonresidents and for Branches and Agencies of Foreign Corporations.—Law provides for irrefutable estimate based on percentage of gross income in following cases: (a) Insurance activities, 7%; (b) lease of aircraft, 60%; (c) international transport and communication companies for services originating in Peru, 5%, except for air transport, 1% and sea transport, 2% or totally exempted by reciprocity; (d) news agencies for services rendered to Peruvian residents, 10%; (e) distribution of motion pictures, video-tapes, etc., 20%; (f) fees and remuneration for technical assistance obtained abroad from juridical persons, 40%; (g) exploration, development and transport of hydrocarbons, 25% and 15% when entered into by Peruvian residents; (h) 80% of gross income of freight companies, as indicated; (i) 20% of gross income for assignment of right for transmission of T.V. programs; (j) lease of ships, 80%; (k) lease of containers for sea freight transport, 15%.

Taxpayers domiciled in Peru shall add or set off results of several kinds of income obtained in Peru.

Rates.—

(A) Individual Residents.—On sum of all taxable income: Up to 54 U.I.T.'s (Tributary Units), 15%, and 30% on excess over latter sum.

(B) Individual and Undivided Estates Nonresidents.—On income from: pensions or remuneration for personal services rendered in Peru, royalties, and other rents, 30%.

(C) Resident Corporations and Legal Entities Deemed Juridical Persons.—Are subject to 30% rate.

(D) Nonresident Corporations.—(a) On income at their disposal from branches or agencies in Peru, 10%; (b) on interest from external credits not excluded from income tax, 1%, as provided by law; (c) on interest paid outside country by banks and financial institutions in Peru, 1%; (d) on income derived from lease of ships and aircraft, 10%; (e) on royalties and on any other income, 30%.

Income tax paid by juridical persons and branches, agencies or permanent establishment of foreign companies cannot be less than 2% of its net assets.

Transfer Tax (Alcabala).—(Legislative Decree 776 of Dec. 30, 1993). Tax is levied on transfer of realty, or rights on realty, at rate of 3% of adjusted transfer price. This tax must be paid by purchaser.

Special Treatment.—Law 23407 of May 28, 1982 as am'd, and its regulations, called "General Law of Industries" establishes basic legal provisions for promoting and regulating manufacturing. It covers most of manufacturing activities; primary processing activities of raw materials are not included, those are governed by extractive industry laws.

Law classifies companies based on size and location. By location companies are classified as centralized and decentralized. Centralized industrial companies are those established in Province of Lima and in constitutional Province of Callao. Decentralized company is one having its headquarters and over 70% of value of its production, of its fixed assets, of its staff and its payroll outside Lima and Callao. Tax incentives are designated to increase reinvestment in existing plants and direct new investments to areas outside Lima and Callao and there is also total tax exemption for companies working in border regions of Peru and in jungle. Individuals or companies considered to be domiciled in country for income tax purposes, which reinvest in industrial companies as provided by law are entitled to tax concession consisting of credit toward payment of their income tax. This credit should not exceed 60% of corresponding income tax due, in case of centralized industrial companies, or 70% of said tax when decentralized industrial companies are concerned. Credits are to be applied to fiscal year in which they are produced and if there is surplus it may not be reimbursed or carried forward to future years.

Centralized companies may allocate amount of reinvestment entitled to tax concessions to acquisition of fixed assets for modernization, enlarging productive capacity or arriving at better utilization of installed capacity, except case of goods that have been depreciated in country. Those companies are entitled to following tax concessions: (a) As of 1984 conversion to equity capital of revaluation surplus shall not be liable for payment of any tax, including that established by art. 24 of Law No. 23337; (b) they shall use as credit toward payment of their income tax sum attained by multiplying its average rate by 20% of outcome of following operations: (1) average annual number of stable workers over taxable year shall be determined, (2) figure obtained shall be multiplied by monthly minimum wage of metropolitan Lima for industry which is in effect at close of fiscal year in question.

Decentralized companies may carry out investment programs in accordance with Law to acquire fixed assets for setting up new industrial plants in decentralized, frontier or jungle areas; diversify its production, enlarge its production capacity, modernize its installations or obtain better utilization of its installed capacity.

Decentralized industrial companies may carry out approved reinvestment programs by importing used capital equipment, with governmental authorization.

Decentralized industrial companies have following tax concessions: (a) They may reinvest their profits in accordance with provisions of Law; (b) exemption of 50% of company capital tax; (c) as of 1984 conversion to equity capital of surplus shall not be subject to any tax, including that established by art. 24 of Law 23337; (d) amount resulting from multiplying average income tax rate by 40% of outcome of following operations shall be used as credit toward payment of income tax: (1) average annual number of stable workers over taxable year shall be determined, (2) figure obtained shall be multiplied by monthly minimum wage in effect in metropolitan Lima for industry at close of fiscal year in question; (e) exemption from payment of excise tax on transfers and of additional excise tax, in case of goods and furniture which are transferred for operation of company.

Industrial companies located outside province of Lima and constitutional province of Callao and within department of Lima are decentralized industrial companies which shall enjoy tax concessions provided by law in proportion of 75% of those granted to rest of decentralized companies, which in no case may be less than those awarded to centralized industrial companies.

Industrial conpanies established or which may be established in frontier and jungle areas shall be liable for payment of only contributions to Peruvian Social Security Institute and import duties and are exempted from all other taxes, in existence or to be established, including those requiring express exoneration.

See also topic Mines and Minerals, subhead Mines in General.

TRADEMARKS AND TRADENAMES:

See topic Industrial Property.

TREATIES:

Peru is a party, inter alia to following: Brussels Convention of 1924 on maritime transportation ratified by Supreme. Copyright Convention of Geneva 1952; Convention on Private International Law (Bustamante Code-Havana, 1928); Montevideo Treaty, 1980 (Latin American Integration Association); Cartagena Agreement (Andean Common Market); Interamerican Convention on International Commercial Arbitration (Panama, Jan. 30, 1975); Convention on the Recognition and Enforcement of Foreign Arbitral Awards (New York, June 10, 1958); Multilateral Trade Negotiations, the Uruguay Round, Final Act (Marrakesh, Apr. 15, 1994) and Agreement establishing the World Trade Organization (Marrakesh, Apr. 15, 1994).

See also topic Copyright.

TRUSTS:

(Leg. Decree 769 of Oct. 28, 1993, arts. 314-350).

Trust may be created upon property of any kind. Trust inter vivos must be by public deed and mortis causa, by will. Only banking institutions may act as trustees. To affect rights of third parties, trust on real property must be recorded in Public Register. Creditors may file petition of annulment of trust within statutory term when property has been transferred or withheld fraudulently and in detriment of their rights. In general, maximum term of trust is 20 years. Assets constitute separate estate from assets of trustee for all legal purposes, and cannot be attached or embargoed except for obligations incurred into or damage caused by performance of trust.

USURY: See topic Interest.

VITAL STATISTICS: See topic Records.

WILLS:

(C. C. 686-814, 2039, 2040, 2094).

Persons over 18 years of age may make wills. Dumb persons may make only closed or holographic wills, and blind and illiterate persons only wills by public instrument, which must be read to them twice. Peruvians abroad may make wills before Peruvian diplomatic or consular agent.

The following cannot be witnesses to a will: (a) Persons who are not in the exercise of their civil rights or who are blind, deaf or dumb, or who cannot read or write; (b) heirs and legatees mentioned in will, their relatives in direct line, spouse, brothers and sisters; (c) relatives of testator in direct line, brothers and sisters; (d) creditors whose only proof is statement in will; (e) spouse of officiating notary and his relatives to fourth degree of consanguinity and second of affinity, and his dependants; (f) spouse. Notary cannot be relative of testator in direct line nor collateral to fourth degree by consanguinity or second degree by affinity.

There are several kinds of wills: wills by public instruments, closed wills, holographic wills, naval wills.

Wills by public instrument are made before notary in presence of two witnesses knowing how to read and write. Notary writes will in his record and it is read by testator or some one designated by him, whereupon all sign.

Closed wills are signed by testator who encloses will in sealed envelope and declares before notary and two witnesses that envelope contains his will. Notary writes statement on envelope which is signed by all, and copies statement in his record, where it is again signed by all.

Holographic wills are written, dated and signed by testator in his handwriting. Such will must be registered within one year after death of testator.

Naval wills may be made by persons at sea before the captain and at least two witnesses. They are valid if the testator dies during the trip or within 30 days after arriving, and must be registered within one year.

WILLS . . . *continued*

Testamentary Dispositions.—Testators cannot freely dispose of their entire estate but only of such portion as they are not required to leave to the heirs designated by the law as obligatory heirs. Such heirs are the descendants, parents and spouse. Testator having descendants or spouse must leave them two-thirds of his estate and may dispose freely of only one-third; having ascendants must leave them one half of his estate and may dispose freely of only other half. Spouse's share is diminished by amount of spouse's interest in community property. (See topic Descent and Distribution.) Testator may disinherit obligatory heir for certain serious reasons involving unworthy conduct.

See Topical Index in front part of this volume.

PHILIPPINE REPUBLIC LAW DIGEST REVISER

Bito, Lozada, Ortega & Castillo
Post Office Box 781
Manila 1099, Philippines
Telephone: 63 2 818 2321 to 25
Fax: 63 2 810 3153

Reviser Profile

History: The firm was founded in 1901 by Oscar Sutro of San Francisco, California, U.S.A., with the support of his elder brother Alfred Sutro and E.J. Pillsbury, both partners of Pillsbury, Madison and Sutro based in San Francisco. Because of an earlier requirement that the name of any partner who ceases to be with the firm for any reason whatsoever should be dropped from the firm name, the firm name changed several times. Ross, Selph and Carrascoso was the firm name for many years. The present firm name was adopted in 1988. All partners were American until 1936 when the first Filipino partner was admitted.

Organization: The firm is located at the 5th and 6th Floors of Alpap I Building, 140 Alfaro Street, Salcedo Village, Makati City, Philippines.

It has 6 partners, 15 assistant attorneys and 35 nonlegal personnel like technical consultants, administrative and secretarial staff. The firm has an extensive and diversified general practice and corresponds with major foreign law firms. It is organized into several departments. The **Corporate and Commercial** department handles corporate formations, reorganizations and acquisitions, securities transactions, bankruptcy proceedings, and preparation of commercial agreements like agency, distribution, construction and manufacturing agreements. The **Litigation** department handles all types of commercial, civil and criminal litigation. The **International Business Transactions** department handles the establishment of subsidiaries, branch offices, regional offices of multinational companies, approval and registration of foreign investments, joint ventures, and international banking and lending transactions. The **Tax** department deals with the full range of corporate and individual taxation, tax planning, tax litigation and international transfer pricing as well as tax investigation. The **Labor** department handles all aspects of employer-employee relationships, labor disputes, pension and other employee benefits, and recruitment of overseas personnel. The **Admiralty** department handles all shipping, cargo and crew claims, collisions, salvage, preparation of charter party agreements, registration and mortgage of vessels, hull and P & I Club covered maritime cases. The **Intellectual Property** department deals with the registration of patents, trademarks, copyrights, technology transfers, and royalty agreements and with the prosecution of administrative, civil and criminal actions for infringement and/or unfair competition.

Each department is supervised by partners, who aside from general proficiency, have had training and experience in the field pertaining to such department.

Client Base: The firm clientele consists of companies engaged in agriculture, mining, oil exploration, manufacturing and marketing, offshore services, construction, manufacturing, shipping, aviation, insurance, banking, merchant banking, mass media, advertising, real estate development, and charities. Among these companies are General Motors Corporation, E.I. Du Pont de Nemours & Co., Kraft Foods Corporation, 3M Company, Imperial Chemical Industries Ltd., Schering A.G., IBM, Texas Instruments Inc., Amkor/Anam Industries and Protection and Indemnity (P & I) Clubs of shipowners. The firm also acts as legal adviser to the British and Swedish Governments.

Memberships: The firm is a member of the International Trademark Association (INTA) in New York, Association Internationale pour la Protection de la Proporiete Industrielle (AIPPI) in Brussels, Philippine American Chamber of Commerce in New York, European Chamber of Commerce in the Philippines (ECCP) in Manila, American Chamber of Commerce in the Philippines (AMCHAM) in Manila, Maritime Law Association of the Philippines (MARLAW), Asian Patent Attorneys Association (APAA) in Tokyo, Japan, Intellectual Property Association of the Philippines (IPAP) and Aviation Lawyers Association of the Philippines (ALAP).

Significant Distinctions: Diosdado Macapagal, President of the Philippines (1961-1965), Ricardo Paras, Chief Justice of the Supreme Court (1951-1961) and Amelito Mutuc, Ambassador to the United States (1962-1964) worked in the firm. The firm is the Reviser of the Philippine Republic Law Digest of the Martindale-Hubbell International Law Digest and Directory.

PHILIPPINE REPUBLIC LAW DIGEST

(The following is a list of all Topics, including cross-references, covered in this Digest.)

PHILIPPINE REPUBLIC LAW DIGEST

Revised for 1997 edition by

BITO, LOZADA, ORTEGA & CASTILLO, of Manila.

(The following abbreviations are used with reference to Codes and Statutes of the Philippines: R.A.C. indicates Revised Administrative Code of 1917; C.A. indicates Commonwealth Act; R.A. indicates Republic Act; C. of C. indicates Code of Commerce of Spain of 1886 promulgated in the Philippines on Aug. 6, 1888; C.C. [n] indicates Civil Code of the Philippines (R.A. 386) which took effect on Aug. 30, 1950; O.G. indicates Official Gazette; R.P.C. indicates Revised Penal Code which took effect on Jan. 1, 1932; R.C. indicates Rules of Court which took effect on Jan. 1, 1964; P.D. indicates Presidential Decree; L.O.I. indicates Letter of Instruction; G.O. indicates General Order; B.P. indicates Batas Pambansa; and E.O. indicates Executive Order. Acts and statutes are also referred to by their popular names.)

ABSENTEES:

A person is declared an absentee after lapse of two years without any news, or since receipt of last news, about him, or after five years if absentee left a person in charge of administration of his property. (C.C. [n], §384).

Care of Property.—An administrator is appointed by court, giving special preference to wife of absentee. (C.C. [n], §§383, 387). The administration ceases when: (1) Absentee appears personally or through an agent; (2) absentee's death is proved and his heirs appear; and (3) a third person appears claiming absentee's property. (C.C. [n], §389).

ACKNOWLEDGMENTS:

In the Philippines may be taken before following officers: Notary public, or any officer acting as notary public ex officio, such as clerks of Supreme Court, Regional Trial Court, Metropolitan Trial Judges, Municipal Trial Judges, Municipal Circuit Trial Judges, Chief of Division of Archives, Patents, Copyrights and Trademarks, etc. (A.C. §242).

Notary public must require person acknowledging an instrument who is liable to pay taxes on residence to exhibit his community tax certificate showing payment thereof. In addition, if person acknowledging is an alien, his alien certificate of registration must be exhibited.

In foreign country before ambassador, minister, secretary of legation, chargé d'affaires, consul, vice-consul, or consular agent of the Philippines acting within the country or place to which he is accredited; notary public or officer duly authorized by law of country to take acknowledgments of instruments in place where act is done.

When a party to the contract is an alien, in addition to his Community Tax Certificate, his Alien Certificate of Registration number, date and place of issuance thereof, and date of his last annual report must be stated in acknowledgment.

Forms.—*In the case of natural persons acting in their own right:*

Form

REPUBLIC OF THE PHILIPPINES)
PROVINCE/CITY OF . . . .) S.S.

BEFORE ME, a Notary Public, for and in the Province/City of . . . . . ., this . . . . day of . . . . . ., 199 . . ., personally appeared . . . . . . with Community Tax Certificates No. . . . . . . issued at . . . . . . on . . . ., and (if alien) Alien Certificate of Registration No. . . . . . ., issued at . . . . . . on . . . ., known to me and to me known to be the same person who executed the foregoing instrument and acknowledged to me that he executed the same as his free and voluntary act and deed for the uses and purposes therein set forth.

IN WITNESS WHEREOF, I have hereunto set my hand and affixed my notarial seal

this . . . . . . day of . . . ., 19. . . .

NOTARY PUBLIC
My Commission expires on Dec. 31, 199. . .
(Or other Official Authorized to
administer oath)

Doc. No. . . . .
Page No. . . . . . .
Book No. . . . . . .
Series of 1995.

In the case of corporations, after giving all data on residence tax certificates and alien certificate of registration as in above form, the text should continue: "in his capacity as . . . . . . of . . . . . ., with Community Tax Certificates Nos. C- . . . . and C-1 . . . . . ., issued at . . . . . ., and . . . . . ., on . . . . . ., 19. . . . and . . . . . ., 19. . . ., respectively, to me known and known to me to be the same person who signed the foregoing instrument and acknowledged to me that he executed the same as his free and voluntary act and deed and as the free and voluntary act and deed of the corporation which he represents, for the uses and purposes therein set forth."

In the case of deeds affecting real property, the following paragraph should be inserted between the first and second paragraphs of the above form: "I Further Certify that the foregoing instrument consists of . . . . . . pages, including this page; that it relates to a deed of (state whether sale, mortgage, release, etc.) over . . . . . . registered/unregistered parcels of land located in . . . . . ., Philippines; and that it was signed by the party/parties thereto and his/their instrumental witnesses at the bottom of the instrument and on the left hand margin of each and every other page thereof." This additional paragraph not required if the instrument consists of only one page.

In the case of chattel mortgages, the first paragraph, after data on alien and residence certificates, should read: "to me known and known to me to be the same persons who signed the foregoing chattel mortgage and affidavit as mortgagor and mortgagee and made oath to the truth of the said affidavit," etc.

Authentication.—An acknowledgment of a document or official record made outside the Philippines by a notary public, commissioner of deeds or other official authorized to take acknowledgments will not be admitted in evidence or recorded in the Philippines unless authenticated by an ambassador, minister, secretary of legation, charge d'affaires, consul, vice-consul or consular agent of the Republic of the Philippines resident in the jurisdiction where made.

Acknowledgments before notaries public for use in foreign countries are usually required to be authenticated by Clerk of Regional Trial Court in province where notary public is appointed, or, in case of notary public whose jurisdiction is confined to City of Manila, by Clerk of Regional Trial Court of Manila, and notarial certificates are also required to be authenticated by Executive Secretary to President of Philippines and consular officer of country in which acknowledgment is to be used.

ACTIONS:

See topic Courts; also topic Limitation of Actions.

ADOPTION:

Person of age and in possession of full civil capacity and legal rights may adopt provided he can support and care for his children, legitimate or illegitimate, in keeping with means of family. Adopter must be at least 16 years older than person to be adopted unless adopter is parent by nature of adopted or is spouse of legitimate parent of person to be adopted. Following may not adopt: (1) Guardian with respect to ward prior to approval of final accounts rendered upon termination of guardianship relation; (2) any person who has been convicted of crime involving moral turpitude; (3) alien, except former Filipino citizen who seeks to adopt relative by consanguinity; one who seeks to adopt legitimate child of his or her Filipino spouse; or one who is married to Filipino citizen and seeks to adopt jointly with his or her spouse relative by consanguinity of latter. Aliens not included in foregoing exceptions may adopt Filipino children in accordance with rules on intercountry adoption. Husband and wife must jointly adopt except when one spouse seeks to adopt his own illegitimate child; or when one spouse seeks to adopt legitimate child of his or her spouse. Following may not be adopted: (1) Person of legal age, unless he or she is child by nature of adopter or his or her spouse, or prior to adoption, said person had been treated by adopter as his or her own child during minority; (2) alien with whose government Philippines has no diplomatic relations; and (3) person who has already been adopted unless such adoption has been previously revoked or rescinded.

Written consent of following to adoption shall be necessary: (1) Person to be adopted, if ten years of age or over; (2) parents by nature of child, legal guardian or proper government instrumentality; (3) legitimate and adopted children, ten years of age or over, of adopting parent or parents; (4) illegitimate children, ten years of age or over, of adopting parent, if living with said parent and latter's spouse, if any; and (5) spouse, if any, of person adopting or to be adopted. Adoption shall have following effects: (1) For civil purposes, adopted shall be deemed legitimate child of adopters and both shall acquire reciprocal rights and obligations arising from relationship of parent and child, including right of adopted to use surname of adopters; (2) parental authority of parents by nature over adopted shall terminate and vested in adopters except that if adopter is spouse of parent by nature of adopted, parental authority over adopted shall be exercised jointly by both spouses; and (3) adopted shall remain intestate heir of his parents and other blood relatives.

If adopted is minor or incapacitated, adoption may be rescinded upon petition of any person authorized by court or proper government instrumentality acting on his behalf on same grounds for loss or suspension of parental authority. If adopted is at least 18 years of age, he may petition for judicial rescission of adoption on same grounds prescribed for disinheriting ascendant. Adopters may petition court for judicial rescission of adoption in any of following cases: (1) If adopted has committed any act constituting ground for disinheriting descendant; or (2) when adopted abandoned home of adopters during minority for at least one year, or, by some other acts, repudiated adoption. (E.O. 209).

Intercountry Adoption.—Any alien or Filipino citizen permanently residing abroad may file application for intercountry adoption if he/she has following qualifications and none of disqualifications:

"(a) is at least twenty-seven (27) years of age;

(b) is at least sixteen (16) years older than the child to be adopted at the time of the filing of the application, unless the applicant is the parent by nature of the child to be adopted or is the spouse of such parent by nature;

(c) has the capacity to act and assume all the rights and responsibilities to parental authority under his/her national law;

(d) has undergone appropriate counselling from an accredited counselor in his/her country;

(e) has not been convicted of a crime involving moral turpitude;

(f) is eligible to adopt under his/her national law;

(g) can provide the proper care and support and give the necessary moral values and example to the child and, in the proper case, to all his/her other children;

(h) comes from a country

(i) with whom the Philippines had diplomatic relations;

See Topical Index in front part of this volume.

ADOPTION . . . *continued*

(ii) whose government maintains a foreign adoption agency; and

(iii) whose laws allow adoption; and

(i) files jointly with his/her spouse, if any, who shall have the same qualifications and none of the disqualifications to adopt as prescribed above."

Intercountry adoption will only be resorted to if all possibilities for adoption of child under Family Code have been exhausted and it is in best interest of child.

AFFIDAVITS:

An affidavit is a statement of facts made in writing and under oath by a person before another who is authorized by law to administer oaths. Forms and solemnities of affidavits are governed by laws of country in which they are executed. But when they are executed before diplomatic or consular officials of Republic of Philippines in a foreign country, solemnities established by Philippine laws must be observed in their execution.

Uses of Affidavits.—They may be used to verify a pleading or paper in a special proceeding to obtain a provisional remedy, examination of witnesses, or stay of proceedings, or upon a motion and in any other case specially permitted by some other provisions of law. Evidence of the publication of a document, or notice required by law, or by an order of a court or judge, to be published in a newspaper, may be given by affidavit of the printer of the newspaper, his foreman, or principal clerk, annexed to a copy of the document or notice specifying the times when, and the paper in which the publication was made. If such affidavit be made in an action or special proceeding pending in a court, it may be filed with the court or the clerk thereof. In such case the original affidavit or a copy thereof, certified by the judge of the court or the clerk having it in custody, is prima facie evidence of the facts stated therein.

Form

Republic of the Philippines }
City/Province of . . . . } s.s.:

I, ..., after being sworn according to law, depose and say:
That (here set forth the declaration or declarations).

. . . .
Affiant

Subscribed and sworn to before me this . . . . . . day of . . . . . ., 19. . . ., in . . . . ., Philippines. Affiant exhibited to me his/her Residence Certificate No. . . . . . . issued at . . . . . ., Philippines, on . . . . . ., 19. . . . .

. . . .
Notary Public
My commission expires
Dec. 31, 19. . . . .

Doc. No. . . . . . .
Page No. . . . . . .
Book No. . . . . . .
Series of 19 . . . .

Affidavit as Evidence.—The law only concedes it the character of prima facie evidence of the facts stated therein, but such evidence is susceptible of impeachment, since all documents attest the facts that are the origin of and the date of their execution, but do not attest the veracity of the statements therein made.

Facts alleged against an accused in a criminal case cannot be proved by affidavits. Affidavits are admissible only in special cases relating to procedure and are simply prima facie evidence. The admission of an affidavit does not constitute error when those who signed it testify in court on what they had stated in the affidavit.

ALIENS:

Aliens in the Philippines are entitled to protection of life, liberty, and property. (118 U. S. 356). Due process of law, however, does not apply to political rights of aliens although it does govern in respect to their civil rights. (288 U. S. 549, 50 L.ed. 960, 33 Sup. Ct. 585). Undesirable aliens can be deported after prior investigation conducted by the President or his authorized agents and after informing alien of charge or charges against him and allowing not less than three days to prepare his defense. Said alien has right to be heard by himself or counsel, to procure witnesses in his own behalf and to cross-examine opposing witnesses. (A.C., §69, 38 Phil. 41). Knowingly and fraudulently evading payment of internal revenue taxes is ground for deportation. (R.A. 1093). "The Philippine Immigration Act of 1940" (C.A. 673), which took effect on Jan. 1, 1941, created Commission on Immigration & Deportation under supervision and control of Dept. of Justice.

Aliens are classified into immigrants and non-immigrants. (C.A. 673, §§9, 13). Immigrants are further subdivided into "quota" and "non-quota" immigrants. "Quota" immigrants must not exceed 50 of any one nationality or without nationality for any one calendar year.

To be admitted, immigrants must present an unexpired passport or official document in nature of passport issued by governments of countries to which they respectively and originally reside or other document showing their origin and identity as prescribed by regulations and valid passport visas granted by consular offices. (C.A. 613, §10).

Any alien who may not appear to examining officer at port of arrival to be clearly and beyond doubt entitled to land must be detained for examination in relation thereto by Board of Special Inquiry. (C.A. 613, §26).

A tax of ₱260 is collected for every alien over 14 years of age admitted in Philippines for stay exceeding 59 days. Tax is paid to Immigration Officer at port of entry. (C.A. 613, §31, as am'd by R.A. 749).

As a further step towards national security, "Philippine Alien Registration Act of 1941" was passed (C.A. 653) providing for compulsory registration and fingerprinting of resident aliens as well as aliens entering Philippines within 30 days after approval of Act. Accredited officials of foreign government recognized by Philippine Republic, or member of his official staff and family are exempt from registration and fingerprinting. "Alien Registration Act of 1950" (R.A. 562, as am'd by R.A. 578 and 751) provides for all resident aliens to register again within 120 days after approval of Act, by paying registration fee of ₱410. Thereafter, within first 60 days of every calendar year, all aliens must report to proper officer who will note fact on their original certificates, paying second registration fee of ₱110.

Political Rights.—Aliens cannot vote or hold public office.

Right to Engage in Various Occupations or Commercial Activities.—Aliens cannot engage in retail business (R.A. 1180) and in retail of rice or corn and by-products thereof (R.A. 3018). In bidding for government contracts like construction or repair of public works (C.A. 541) and purchase of articles for government (C.A. 138), preference is given to citizens of Philippines or to corporations organized under laws of Philippines 75% of capital stock of which is owned by such citizens. Overseas shipping business and construction of modern boats for overseas service shall be allowed to aliens provided 60% of capital of corporation organized under laws of Philippines is owned by citizens of Philippines. (R.A. 1407). No franchise, certificate, or any other form of authorization for operation of public utility shall be granted except to citizens of Philippines or to corporations organized under laws of Philippines at least 60% of capital of which is owned by such citizens. (§11, Art. XII, Constitution). Use, exploitation, and development of natural resources shall be limited to citizens of Philippines or to corporations 60% of capital of which is owned by such citizens. (§2, ibid). Aliens are excluded from ownership and management of mass media. Only citizens of Philippines or corporations or associations at least 70% of capital of which is owned by such citizens shall be allowed to engage in advertising industry. Participation of foreign investors in governing body of entities in such industry shall be limited to their proportionate share in capital and all executive and managing officers of such entities must be citizens of Philippines. (§11, Art. XII, ibid). Establishment of educational institutions, except those established by religious groups and mission boards and shall be owned solely by citizens of Philippines or corporations 60% of capital of which is owned by such citizens. (§4[2], Art. XIV, ibid). In financing companies, in case of corporations, 2/3 of all members of board of directors shall be citizens of Philippines while for partnerships, all managing partners shall be citizens of Philippines. (R.A. 5980). At least 70% of voting stock of any banking institution shall be owned by citizens of Philippines except where new bank is established as result of local incorporation of any of existing branches of foreign banks in Philippines or consolidation of existing banks in any of which there are foreign-owned voting stocks at time of incorporation. (P.D. 71). Under Investment Incentives Act, in case of registered enterprise engaged in preferred area of investment and duly registered with Board of Investments, 60% of capital stock shall be owned by citizens of Philippines and 60% of members of board of directors shall be citizens of Philippines.

Property.—Aliens cannot acquire by transfer or conveyance private land except in case of hereditary succession. (§7, Art. XII, Constitution). Mortgages of real property to aliens are allowed but alien mortgagees cannot take possession of mortgaged property during existence of mortgage except after default and for purpose of foreclosure, receivership, enforcement or other proceedings and in no case for period of more than five years from actual possession, and shall not bid or take part in sale of such real property in case of foreclosure. (R.A. 4887). No restrictions as to ownership of personal property.

Natural born citizen who has lost his Philippine citizenship and who has legal capacity to enter into contract under Philippine laws may be transferee of private lands up to maximum area of 5,000 square meters in case of urban land or three hectares in case of rural land to be used for business or other purpose. (R.A. 8179).

Anti-Dummy Law prohibits following acts: (1) In all cases in which any constitutional or legal provision requires Philippine or any other specific citizenship as requisite for exercise or enjoyment of a right, franchise or privilege, for any citizen of Philippines or of any other specific country to allow his name or citizenship to be used for purpose of evading such provision and for an alien to profit thereby; (2) to falsely simulate existence of minimum of stock or capital as owned by Philippine citizens in cases of corporations wherein Constitution or law requires that 60% of stock of which must be owned by Philippine citizens; (3) to lease, transfer, permit or allow any person or corporation not qualified under law to exploit or enjoy franchise, right, privilege or business, exercise of which is reserved to Philippine citizens or corporations 60% of capital of which must be owned by said citizens; and (4) to allow disqualified person to intervene in management, operation or control of business, whether as officer, employee or laborer, except technical personnel authorized by Secretary of Justice provided that election of aliens as members of board of directors engaging in partially nationalized activities shall be allowed in proportion to their allowable participation or share in capital of such entities.

Corporations Owned or Controlled by Aliens.—No foreign corporation or corporation formed, organized, or existing under any laws other than those of Philippines is permitted to transact business in Philippines or maintain by itself or assignee any suit for recovery of any debt, claim, or demand whatever, unless it has a license required by law.

See also topic Corporations, subhead Foreign Corporations; and topics Foreign Investments and Incentives; Retail Trade Law.

ALIMONY: See topic Divorce.

ARBITRATION:

The Arbitration Law (R.A. 876) permits parties to submit to arbitration to one or more arbitrators any controversy existing between them at time of submission and which may be the subject of an action, or parties to any contract may in such contract agree to arbitrate any controversy thereafter arising between them. Such submission or contract is valid, enforceable, and irrevocable, save upon such grounds for revocation of any contract. Such submission or contract may include questions arising out of valuations, appraisals, or other controversies which may be collateral, incidental, precedent or subsequent to any issue between parties. The arbitration must be in writing and subscribed by parties thereto.

The law is not applicable to controversies and to cases subject to jurisdiction of National Labor Relations Commission.

Power of Arbitrators.—Arbitrators can administer oaths, subpoena witnesses, issue subpoena duces tecum, decide relevancy and materiality of evidence offered, and grant rehearing.

ARBITRATION . . . *continued*

Award and Judgment.—The award must be in writing, signed, and acknowledged by majority of arbitrators. At any time within one month after award is made, any party may apply to court having jurisdiction for an order confirming award.

See topics Labor Relations; Dispute Resolution.

ASSIGNMENTS:

An assignment of credits and other incorporeal rights is perfected in the same way as the contract of sale. But an assignment of a credit, right, or action produces no effect as against third persons, unless it appears in a public instrument, or the instrument is recorded in the Registry of Property in case the assignment involves real property. The assignment of a credit includes all the accessory rights, such as a guaranty, mortgage, pledge or preference.

The assignor in good faith warrants existence and legality of credit at time of sale but not of solvency of debtor unless stipulated otherwise or that insolvency was prior to assignment and of common knowledge.

ASSIGNMENTS FOR BENEFIT OF CREDITORS:

A debtor may assign his property to his creditors in payment of his debts. This assignment releases the former from liability only to the net amount of the property assigned, except when the contrary is stipulated. The assignment operates as an abandonment of the universality of the property of the debtor for the benefit of his creditors, in order that such property may be applied to the payment of the credits. The initiative comes from the debtor, but it must be accepted by the creditors in order to become effective; a voluntary assignment cannot be imposed upon a creditor who is not willing to accept it. (37 O.G. 1444).

The assignment does not have the effect of making the creditors the owners of the property of the debtor, unless there is an agreement to that effect. The assignment gives to the creditors the right to proceed to the sale of the property, and to pay themselves in the amount which the proceeds of the sale permit and in the manner agreed upon. (8 Manresa, 322).

ASSOCIATIONS:

See topics Corporations; Partnership.

ATTACHMENT:

Writ of attachment may be had in any action brought for recovery of money or damages on a cause of action arising upon a contract or for fulfillment of an obligation: when defendant is about to depart from Philippines with intent to defraud his creditors; in an action for money or property embezzled, fraudulently misapplied or converted to his own use by defendant in a fiduciary capacity; in an action to recover possession of personal property unjustly detained, where it or any part thereof has been concealed, removed, or disposed of to prevent its being found or taken by applicant or an officer; when defendant has been guilty of fraud in incurring obligation upon which action is brought; when defendant has disposed of, or is about to dispose of, his property with intent to defraud his creditors; and in an action against nonresident defendant on whom summons may be served by publication. An attachment may be had at time of commencing action or any time thereafter.

In attachment case, a bond must be given to secure defendant against damage in an amount to be fixed by judge and not to exceed amount claimed.

Levy.—All orders of attachment must be served by an officer of the court.

The officer must attach and safely keep so much of defendant's property as will satisfy plaintiff's demands, unless defendant gives security, with sufficient sureties, in an amount sufficient to satisfy such demands, besides costs.

Real property standing on the records in the name of defendant or not appearing on the record, is attached by filing with the registrar of titles of land, for the province in which the land is situated, a copy of the order of attachment, together with a description of the property attached, and a notice that it is attached, and by leaving a similar copy of the order, description, and notice with the occupant of the property, if there is one.

Stocks or shares, or an interest in stocks or shares, of any corporation or company are attached by leaving with the president, or other head of the same, or the secretary, cashier, or other managing agent thereof, a copy of the order of attachment and a notice stating that the stock or interest of the defendant is attached, in pursuance of such order.

Debts and credits, and other personal property not capable of manual delivery, are attached by leaving with the person owing such debts or having such credits or other personal property in his possession or under his control a copy of the order of attachment and a notice that the debts owing by him to defendant, or the credits or other personal property in his possession or under his control, belonging to defendant, are attached in pursuance of such order.

In a criminal action the offended party may have the property of the defendant attached as a security for the satisfaction of any judgment that may be recovered from the defendant (a) when the defendant is about to depart from the Philippines; (b) when the criminal action is based on a claim for money or property which has been embezzled or fraudulently misapplied or converted to the use of the defendant who is a public officer, or any officer of a corporation, or an attorney, factor, broker, agent, or clerk, in the course of his employment as such, or by any other person in a fiduciary capacity, or for a willful violation of duty; (c) when the defendant has concealed, removed, or disposed of his personal property, or is about to do so; (d) when the defendant resides outside the Philippines.

Attachment in criminal cases is available only when the civil action for the recovery of civil liability arising from the offense charged is not expressly waived or the right to institute such civil action separately is not reserved.

Attachment may be discharged (1) when defendant gives a bond executed in favor of plaintiff equal to value of property attached; and (2) when defendant moves for an order of discharge on ground that attachment was improperly and irregularly issued.

Exemptions.—See topic Exemptions.

ATTORNEYS AND COUNSELORS:

Admission to practice of law is regulated by Rules 138, 139 and 139-B of Revised Rules of Court.

Member of Philippine Bar is commonly known as lawyer, attorney, attorney-at-law or counselor.

Eligibility.—Every applicant for admission to bar must be citizen of Philippines, at least 21 years of age, of good moral character, and resident of Philippines. He must produce satisfactory evidence of good moral character, and he must certify that no charges against him, involving moral turpitude, have been filed or are pending in any court in Philippines.

Registration as law student not required.

Educational Requirements.—Applicants for admission shall satisfactorily show that they have completed in authorized and recognized university or college (a) four-year high school course; (b) course of study prescribed for bachelor's degree in arts or sciences; and (c) four-year bachelor's degree in law.

Examination.—Examinations for admission to bar are given annually. Examinations are conducted by committee constituted by Supreme Court with Justice of Supreme Court as Chairman.

Admission Without Examination.—There are only two instances whereby persons are allowed to practice law without taking bar examination, to wit: (a) citizens of U.S.A. who, before July 4, 1946, were duly licensed members of Philippine Bar, in active practice in courts of Philippines and in good and regular standing as such may, upon satisfactory proof of those facts before Supreme Court, be allowed to continue such practice; and (b) Filipino citizens who are enrolled attorneys in good standing in Supreme Court of U.S. or in any Circuit Court of Appeals or district court therein or in highest court of any state or territory of U.S., and who can show by satisfactory certificates that they have practiced at least five years in any of said courts, that such practice began before July 4, 1946, and that they have never been suspended or disbarred. (§§3 and 4, Rule 138 Revised Rules of Court).

Foreign attorneys are allowed to practice as trademark or patent agents before Bureau of Patents, Trademarks and Technology Transfer, formerly Philippine Patent Office (which is not court) if they are registered to practice as trademark or patent attorneys in patent office of country where they reside, and proof of such registration to practice is submitted. Provided that patent office of such country allows substantially reciprocal privileges to those admitted to practice before Bureau of Patents, Trademarks and Technology Transfer.

Lien.—Attorney shall have lien upon funds, documents and papers of his clients which have lawfully come into his possession and may retain same until his lawful fees and disbursements have been paid, and may apply such funds to satisfaction thereof. He shall also have lien to same extent upon all judgments for payments of money and executions issued pursuant to such judgments.

Disbarment and Suspension.—Supreme Court, on its own motion or upon complaint under oath of another, may institute proceedings for removal or suspension of attorneys. Member of bar may be removed or suspended from his office as attorney by Supreme Court for any deceit, malpractice, or other gross misconduct in such office, grossly immoral conduct, or by reason of his conviction of crime involving moral turpitude, or for any violation of oath which he is required to take before admission to practice, or for wilfull disobedience of any lawful order of superior court, or for corruptly or wilfully appearing as attorney for party to case without authority so to do. Practice of soliciting cases at law for purpose of gain, either personally or through paid agents or brokers, constitutes malpractice. Court of Appeals and Regional Trial Courts may suspend attorney from practice and may recommend his disbarment by Supreme Court. Decisions of Court of Appeals and Regional Trial Courts suspending lawyer are to be elevated to Supreme Court which shall make full investigation of case and may revoke, shorten or extend suspension, or disbar attorney as facts may warrant. (§17, Rule 139-B, Revised Rules of Court).

Unauthorized Practice.—Generally, corporations are not allowed to engage in practice of law. No judge or other official or employee of superior courts or of Office of the Solicitor General, shall engage in private practice as member of bar or give professional advice to clients.

Professional Association.—Rule 139-A of Revised Rules of Court organized Integrated Bar of the Philippines, national organization of all lawyers included in Roll of Attorneys of the Supreme Court, and continued membership in this organization is requirement for lawyer to practice law.

AUTOMOBILES: See topic Motor Vehicles.

BANKRUPTCY AND INSOLVENCY:

The Insolvency Law of the Philippines (Act No. 1956) deals with suspension of payments, voluntary insolvency and involuntary insolvency. It is modeled after the Spanish Code of Commerce in its provisions for suspension of payment and after the Insolvency Act of California of 1895 and the Federal Bankruptcy Law of 1898 in its other provisions.

Suspension of Payments.—A solvent debtor who foresees the impossibility of meeting his debts when they respectively fall due may petition the court for a suspension of payment of his debts. If granted, a meeting of creditors is then held upon notice to them and, provided the required number of creditors agree to the proposal for the settlement of his debts made by the debtor, such settlement is declared binding upon all creditors. If the required number of creditors fail to agree the proceeding is terminated and the creditors are at liberty to enforce their legal rights.

Voluntary Insolvency.—An insolvent debtor, owing debts exceeding 1,000 pesos, may petition to be discharged from his debts.

Involuntary Insolvency.—Three or more creditors, who are residents of the Philippines, whose credits accrue in the Philippines, and whose credits aggregate not less than 1,000 pesos, may petition that debtor be adjudicated insolvent upon proper showing of one or more acts of insolvency as set forth in statute.

BANKRUPTCY AND INSOLVENCY . . . *continued*

Classification and Preference of Creditors.—Merchandise, effects, and any other property found among property of insolvent, ownership of which has not been conveyed to him by legal or irrevocable title, must be considered as property of other persons and must be placed at disposal of lawful owners. These include (1) dowry property remaining in hands of husband; (2) paraphernal property which wife may have acquired by inheritance, legacy or donation; (3) property and effects deposited with bankrupt or administered, leased, rented or held in usufruct by him; (4) merchandise in possession of bankrupt on commission, for purchase, sale, forwarding or delivery; (5) bills of exchange or promissory notes without indorsement remitted to insolvent for collection and all others acquired by him for account of another; (6) money remitted to insolvent, other than on current account, for delivery to a definite person in name and for account of remitter; (7) amounts due insolvent for sales of merchandise on commission and bills of exchange and promissory notes derived therefrom even when same are not made payable to owner of merchandise sold; (8) merchandise bought on credit by insolvent before actual delivery thereof and merchandise the bill of lading or shipping receipts of which have been sent to him after same has been loaded by order of purchaser and for his account and risk (in all these cases creditors of insolvent may claim merchandise so purchased by paying price thereof to vendor); and (9) goods or chattels wrongfully taken, converted, or withheld by insolvent.

Assignee.—In both voluntary and involuntary insolvency an assignee is elected by the creditors or appointed by the court to administer and liquidate the estate of the debtor and apply the proceeds pro rata to the payment of creditors.

The duly constituted family home of an insolvent may not be considered one of the assets to be taken possession of by the assignee for the benefit of creditors.

Discharge of Debtors.—At any time after three months after the adjudication of insolvency but not later than one year after such adjudication, the debtor may obtain an order discharging him from all unpaid obligations provided none of the fraudulent acts specified in the statute have been committed by him.

Receiver.—See topic Receivers.

BANKS AND BANKING:

Bangko Sentral ng Pilipinas is established as independent central monetary authority. It shall provide policy direction in areas of money, banking and credit. It shall have supervision over operations of banks and exercise regulatory powers over operations of finance companies and nonbank financial institutions performing quasi-banking functions. (R.A. 7653).

The General Banking Act (R.A. 337, am'd by P.D. 71) governs commercial banks, savings banks, mortgage banks, development banks, rural banks, stock savings and loan associations, and branches and agencies in Philippines of foreign banks.

Foreign banks may now operate in Philippine banking system through any one of following modes of entry: (1) by acquiring, purchasing or owning up to 60% of voting stock of existing bank; (2) by investing up to 60% of voting stock of new banking subsidiary incorporated under Philippine laws; or, (3) by establishing branches with full banking authorities. Foreign bank or Philippine corporation may own up to 60% of voting stock of only one domestic bank or banking subsidiary.

Only those among top 150 foreign banks in the world or top five banks in their country of origin as of date of application shall be allowed entry. However, Monetary Board shall adopt measures to: (1) ensure that at all times, control of 70% of resources or assets of entire banking system is held by domestic banks which are at least majority owned by Filipinos; (2) prevent dominant market position by one bank or concentration of economic power in one or more financial institutions with related interests; and (3) secure listing of shares of stocks in Philippine Stock Exchange of banking corporations established under first two modes of entry of foreign banks.

Non-Filipino citizens may become members of Board of Directors of bank to extent of foreign participation in equity of said bank.

Foreign banks authorized to operate under any of three modes of entry shall perform same functions, enjoy same privileges, and be subject to same limitations imposed upon Philippine bank of same category.

No foreign bank or banking corporation formed, organized, or existing under laws other than those of Philippines, can be permitted to transact business or maintain by itself or assign any suit for recovery of any debt, claim or demand whatsoever, until after it shall have obtained a license for purpose from Securities and Exchange Commission.

Residents and citizens of Philippines who are creditors of a branch or agency in Philippines of foreign bank have preferential rights to assets of such branch or agency.

No bank or banking institution shall enter, directly or indirectly, into any contract of guaranty or shall guarantee interest or principal of any obligation of any person, copartnership, association, corporation or other entity. However, this shall not apply to following: (a) Borrowing of money by banking institutions through rediscounting of receivables; (b) acceptance of drafts or bills of exchange; (c) certification of checks; (d) transactions involving release of documents attached to items received for collection; (e) letter of credit transactions, including stand-by arrangements; (f) repurchase agreements; (g) shipside bonds; (h) ordinary guarantees or indorsements in favor of foreign creditors where principal obligation involves loans and credits extended directly by foreign firms or persons to domestic borrowers for capital investment purposes; and (i) other transactions which Monetary Board may, by regulation, define as not covered by prohibition.

No director or officer of any banking institution shall, directly or indirectly, for himself or as representative of others, borrow any of deposits of funds of such bank, or be a guarantor, indorser, or surety for loans from such bank to others, or in any manner be an obligor for money borrowed from bank, except with written approval of majority of directors of bank, excluding director concerned. Monetary Board may regulate amount of credit accommodation that may be extended by banking institutions, to their directors, officers or stockholders.

Minor of seven years, able to read and write, with sufficient discretion, and not otherwise disqualified by any other incapacity, is authorized to deposit with and withdraw from banks without assistance of his parents and guardians. (P.D. 734).

P.D. 1034 authorizes establishment of offshore banking system in Philippines. Offshore banking refers to conduct of banking transactions in foreign currencies involving receipt of funds from external sources and utilization of such funds. Qualified to operate offshore banking units are banks organized under any law other than those of Philippines, their branches or subsidiaries. Local branches of foreign banks authorized to accept foreign currency deposits under R.A. 6426 may opt to apply for authority to operate offshore banking unit provided that upon receipt of corresponding certificate of authority to operate as offshore banking unit, license to transact business under R.A. 6426 shall be deemed automatically withdrawn. In issuing certificate of authority, following shall be taken into consideration: applicant's liquidity and solvency position; net worth and resources; management; international banking expertise; contribution to Philippine economy; and other factors such as participation in equity of local commercial banks and appropriate geographic representation. Bangko Sentral ng Pilipinas is authorized to collect fee of not less than US$20,000 upon issuing certificate of authority to operate and annually thereafter on anniversary date of such certificate.

Applicants shall submit to Bangko Sentral sworn undertaking of its head office or parent or holding company, duly supported by resolution of its board of directors, that, among others: (1) It will, on demand, provide necessary specified currencies to cover liquidity needs that may arise; (2) operations of its offshore banking unit shall be managed soundly and with prudence; (3) it will train and educate Filipinos in international banking and foreign exchange trading to reduce number of expatriates; (4) it will maintain in its offshore banking unit net office funds in minimum amount of US$1,000,000; and (5) it will start operations within 180 days from receipt of its certificate of authority. Operation and activities of offshore banking units shall be under supervision of Bangko Sentral.

BILLS AND NOTES:

Uniform Negotiable Instruments Act adopted.

Judgment Notes.—A provision in a note authorizing any attorney to appear and confess judgment against the maker in case of nonpayment at maturity, is invalid. (43 Phil. 444, 446).

CHATTEL MORTGAGES:

By a chattel mortgage, personal property is recorded in Chattel Mortgage Register as a security for performance of an obligation. If movable, instead of being recorded, is delivered to creditor or a third person, contract is a pledge and not a chattel mortgage. A chattel mortgage is not valid against any person except mortgagee, his executor or administrator, unless mortgage is recorded in Office of Register of Deeds of province in which mortgagor resides at time of making of same, or if residing without Philippines, in province in which property is situated. If property is situated in province other than that in which mortgagor resides, mortgage must be recorded in Office of Register of Deeds of both province in which mortgagor resides and that in which property is situated. (Act 1508, §4).

Payment of debts secured by a chattel mortgage may be enforced by foreclosure, judicial as well as extrajudicial, or by an ordinary action. Where debtor refuses to give up property, creditor must institute an action either to effect foreclosure directly or to secure possession as a preliminary to sale contemplated by law.

Penalty of imprisonment from one month and one day to six months or a fine amounting to twice value of property must be imposed upon (1) any person who knowingly removes any of mortgaged property to any province or city other than one in which it was located at time of execution of mortgage without written consent of mortgagee or his executor, administrator or assign; and (2) any mortgagor who sells or pledges personal property already pledged, or any part thereof, without consent of mortgagee written on back of mortgage and noted on record thereof in Office of Register of Deeds of province where such property is located. (R.P.C., §319).

Form.—The following is sufficient:

Form

This mortgage made this . . . . . . day of . . . . . ., 19. . . ., by A. B., a resident of the municipality of . . . . . ., Philippines, mortgagor, to C. D., a resident of the municipality of . . . . . ., Philippines, mortgagee, witnesseth:

That the said mortgagor hereby conveys and mortgages to the said mortgagee all of the following described personal property situated in the municipality of . . . . . ., Philippines, and now in the possession of said mortgagor, to wit:

(Insert specific description of property mortgaged.)

This mortgage is given as security for the payment to the said C. D., mortgagee, of promissory notes for the sum of . . . . . ., with interest thereon at the rate of . . . . . . per centum per annum, according to the terms of . . . . . . certain promissory notes, dated (insert dates), and in the words and figures following (insert copy of notes secured).

The conditions of this obligation are such that if the mortgagor, his heirs, executors, or administrators shall well and truly perform the full obligations above stated according to the terms thereof, then this obligation shall be null and void.

Executed at the municipality of . . . . . ., ..., this day of . . . . . ., 19. . . . .

A. B., Mortgagor.

IN THE PRESENCE OF:

(Two Witnesses)

We severally swear that the foregoing mortgage is made for the purpose of securing the obligation specified in the conditions thereof, and for no other purpose, and that the same is a just and valid obligation, and one not entered into for the purpose of fraud.

. . . .
A. B., Mortgagor

. . . .
C. D., Mortgagee.

(acknowledgment)

COMMERCIAL REGISTER:

Every owner of an establishment shall register in Bureau of Domestic Trade any name used in connection with his business other than his true name.

Registration fee is ₱110 for each name registered, renewable every five years; such renewal to be made during first three months following expiration of five-year period from date of original registration. (Act No. 3883, as am'd by R.A. No. 863).

COMMERCIAL REGISTER . . . *continued*

It is unlawful for any person to use or sign on any written or printed receipt, including receipt for tax on business, or on any written or printed contract not verified by a notary public, or on any written or printed evidence of any agreement or business transactions, any name used in connection with his business other than his true name, or keep conspicuously exhibited in plain view in or at place where his business is conducted, if he is engaged in a business, any sign announcing firm name or business name or style, without first registering such other name, or such firm name, or business name, or style, in Bureau of Domestic Trade together with his true name and that of any other person having joint or common interest with him in such contract, agreement, business transaction, or business. (Act. No. 3883, as am'd by Act No. 4147).

COMPROMISE AND SETTLEMENT:

A compromise is a contract whereby parties, by making reciprocal concessions, avoid a litigation or put an end to one already commenced. (C.C. [n], §2028). Court's approval is necessary in compromises entered into by guardians, parents, absentee's representatives and administrators or executors of decedent's estate.

There may be a compromise upon civil liability arising from an offense but it does not extinguish legal penalty. No compromise upon following questions is valid: (1) civil status of a person; (2) validity of a marriage or legal separation; (3) legal separation; (4) future support; (5) jurisdiction of courts; and (6) future legitime. A compromise covers only those objects definitely stated therein or implied by its terms and constitutes res judicata upon parties.

A compromise may be annulled or rescinded on grounds of fraud, mistake, violence, intimidation, undue influence or falsity of documents, or if it refers only to one thing to which one of parties has no right as shown by newly discovered evidence, or when a compromise was agreed upon and either or both parties are unaware of existence of final judgment, or when one of parties fails or refuses to abide by compromise.

See topic Dispute Resolution.

CONSTITUTION AND GOVERNMENT:

Republic of Philippines became independent republic on June 12, 1898. (R.A. 4166). On Feb. 2, 1987, new Constitution, which was enacted by Constitutional Commission of 1986, was ratified by majority of votes cast in plebiscite. It contains bill of rights very similar to bill of rights contained in Constitution of U.S. and it delegates functions of government to three branches, namely, legislature, executive, and judicial. Legislative power is vested in Congress of Philippines which consists of Senate and House of Representatives, members of which are elected directly by people. (§1, Art. VI, Constitution). Executive power is vested in President of Philippines who is elected by direct vote of people for term of six years. President is not eligible for reelection. In event of death, permanent disability, removal from office, or resignation of President, Vice-President shall become President to serve unexpired term. In case of death, permanent disability, removal from office, or resignation of both President and Vice-President, President of Senate or, in case of his inability, Speaker of House of Representatives, shall act as President until President or Vice-President shall have been elected and qualified. (§§1, 4, 8, Art. VII, ibid). Judicial power is vested in one Supreme Court and in such lower courts as may be established by law. Members of Supreme Court and judges of lower courts are appointed by President. (§§1, 9, Art. VIII, ibid).

Suffrage is exercised by citizens of Philippines who are at least 18 years of age and have resided in Philippines for at least one year and in place wherein they propose to vote for at least six months preceding election. No literacy, property, or other substantive requirement shall be imposed on exercise of suffrage.

Sources of Philippine Jurisprudence.—The jurisprudence of the Philippines is based partly upon Spanish law and partly upon the law of the United States of America and its several States. It is therefore partly a civil law and partly a common law system. It is a merger of the two. The Code of Commerce of Spain, which was made effective in the Philippines during the Spanish regime, is still in force, although many of its provisions have been modified or amended by special laws and the Civil Code of the Philippines. (R.A. No. 386). On the other hand, many statutes have been modeled after statutes adopted in the United States and the case law of the United States is cited and given persuasive effect.

CONTRACTS:

Contract is a meeting of minds between two persons whereby one binds himself, with respect to the other, to give something or to render some service. (C.C.[n] §1305). In onerous contracts the cause is understood to be, for each contracting party, the prestation or promise of a thing or service by the other; in remuneratory ones, the service or benefit which is remunerated; and in contracts of pure beneficence, the mere liberality of the benefactor. (C.C.[n] §1350). Contracts without cause, or with unlawful cause, produce no effect whatever. The cause is unlawful if it is contrary to law, morals, good customs, public order or public policy. (C.C.[n] §1352).

Excuses for Nonperformance.—Following are excuses for nonperformance of contracts: (1) When contract refers to obligation which consists in the delivery of determinate thing and latter is lost or destroyed without fault of debtor, and before he has concurred in delay; (2) when contract refers to a debt, and latter is condoned or renounced; (3) when contract refers to obligation and latter is merged in the characters of creditor and debtor in one and the same person; (4) when contract is novated; (5) when contract refers to service and latter has become so difficult as to be manifestly beyond contemplation of parties; (6) when object of contract refers to things outside commerce of men; (7) when object of contract refers to intransmissible rights or upon future inheritance except in cases expressly authorized by law; (8) when contract refers to services which are contrary to law, morals, good customs, or public policy; (9) when contract refers to objects which are not possible of determination as to their kind.

Applicable Law.—Law of place of making (lex loci contractus) governs formalities of contract. Both Civil Code and Code of Commerce follow lex loci contractus rule. Civil Code does not contain any conflicts rule respecting essential validity of contracts in general.

Government Contracts.—Construction projects shall generally be undertaken by contract after competitive bidding. However, projects may be undertaken by administration or by negotiated contract only where time is of the essence, or where there is lack of qualified bidders or contractors, or where there is conclusive evidence that greater economy and efficiency would be achieved through this arrangement subject to approval of Secretary of Transportation & Communications, Secretary of Public Works and Highways, or Secretary of Energy as case may be, if project cost is less than ₱1,000,000 and of President of Philippines, upon recommendation of Secretary, if project cost is ₱1,000,000 or more. Contract may be awarded to lowest prequalified bidder where bid complies with all terms and conditions in call for bid and is most advantageous to Government. To guarantee faithful performance of contractor, he shall, prior to award, post performance bond. (P.D. 1594).

Bureau of Equipment and other officers and employees of municipal and provincial governments and Philippine Government and of chartered cities, boards, commissions, bureaus, departments, offices, agencies, branches, and bodies of any description, including government-owned companies, authorized to requisition, purchase or contract or make disbursements for articles, materials, and supplies for public use, public buildings, or public works must give preference to materials and supplies produced, made and manufactured in Philippines. (C.A. No. 138, §1). Only unmanufactured articles, materials, or supplies of growth or production of Philippines, and only such manufactured articles, materials, and supplies as have been manufactured in Philippines substantially from articles, materials, or supplies of growth, production or manufacture, as case may be, of Philippines, must be purchased for public use and in case of bidding, subject to following conditions: (a) When lowest foreign bid, including customs duties, does not exceed two pesos, award must be made to lowest domestic bidder, provided his bid is not more than 100% in excess of foreign bid; (b) when lowest foreign bid, including customs duties exceeds two pesos but does not exceed 20 pesos, award must be made to lowest domestic bidder, provided his bid is not more than 50% in excess of the lowest foreign bid; (c) when lowest foreign bid, including customs duties, exceeds 20 pesos, but does not exceed 200 pesos, award must be made to lowest domestic bidder, provided his bid is not more than 25% in excess of lowest foreign bid; (d) when lowest foreign bid, including customs duties, exceeds 200 pesos but does not exceed 2,000 pesos, award must be made to lowest domestic bidder, provided his bid is not more than 20% in excess of lowest foreign bid; (e) when lowest foreign bid, including customs duties exceed 2,000 pesos, award must be made to lowest domestic bidder, provided his bid is not more than 15% in excess of lowest foreign bid. (C.A. No. 138, §3).

Whenever several bidders participate in the bidding for supplying articles, materials, and equipment for any of the dependencies mentioned in Sec. 1 of this Act for public use, public buildings, or public works, the award must be made to the domestic entity making the lowest bid, provided it is not more than 15% in excess of the lowest bid made by a bidder other than a domestic entity, as it is defined in Act. (C.A. No. 138; §4).

In construction or repair work undertaken by government, whether done directly or through contract awards, Philippine made materials and products, whenever available, practicable, and usable, and will serve the purpose as equally as foreign made products or materials, must be used in said construction or repair work, upon proper certification of the availability, practicability, usability and durability of said materials or products by Director of Bureau of Public Works and or his assistants. (R.A. No. 912).

Contract for supply to, or procurement by, any government-owned or controlled corporation, company, agency or municipal corporation of materials, equipment, goods and commodities shall not be awarded to any contractor or bidder, who is not a citizen of Philippines or a corporation or association at least 60% of capital of which is owned by Filipino citizens, except citizens, corporations or associations of a country whose laws or regulations grant similar rights or privileges to citizens of Philippines. In latter case native products and domestic entities shall be given preference in purchase of articles for Government. (R.A. 5183).

To upgrade government infrastructure projects, government devised schemes whereby private sector is encouraged to initiate and undertake such projects. It could be any of following: (1) "Build, Operate and Transfer scheme" whereby project proponent undertakes construction and financing of given infrastructure project and is allowed to operate said facility over fixed term but not over 50 years to recover its expenses and to receive returns on its investment and thereafter contractor transfers facility to government agency or local government unit; (2) "Build and Transfer scheme" whereby project proponent undertakes financing and construction of infrastructure project and after completion turns it over to government agency or local government unit concerned which shall pay proponent its total investment plus reasonable rate of return; (3) "Build-Own-and-Operate" whereby project proponent is authorized to finance, construct, own, operate and maintain infrastructure project from which proponent can recover its total investment plus reasonable return thereof; (4) "Build-Lease-and-Transfer" whereby project proponent is authorized to finance and construct infrastructure project and upon its completion turns it over to government agency or local government unit on lease arrangement for fixed term and after which ownership is automatically transferred to government agency or local government unit; (5) "Build-Transfer and Operate" whereby contract on infrastructure project is given by public sector to private entity which shall build facility on turn-key basis and upon its completion, title to said project is transferred to implementing agency but private entity operates facility; (6) "Contract-Add-and Operate" whereby project proponent adds to existing infrastructure facility; (7) "Develop-Operate-and Transfer" whereby project proponent is given right to develop property adjoining infrastructure project which is being undertaken by project proponent; (8) "Rehabilitate-Operate-and-Transfer" scheme whereby existing facility is turned over to private sector to operate and maintain same for fixed period; (9) "Rehabilitate-Own-and Operate" scheme whereby existing facility is turned over to private sector to refurbish and operate with no time limitation. (R.A. 6957 as am'd by R.A. 7718).

Distributorships, Dealerships And Franchises.—Franchises are granted by government to individuals or groups of individuals establishing corporation for operation of public utility. Constitution expressly vests upon Congress of Philippines power to grant franchise, certificate or any other form of authorization for operation of public utility which in no case shall be allowed longer than 50 years. (§11, Art. XII, 1987 Constitution).

See Topical Index in front part of this volume.

CONTRACTS . . . *continued*

Generally, contracts of distributorships, dealerships, and franchises involving domestic company are governed by laws on obligations and contracts instituted in Civil Code. Contracts of distributorship are governed by Civil Code provision on sales. Generally, contracting parties may establish such clauses, stipulations, terms and conditions they may deem covenient provided they are not contrary to law, morals, good customs, public order or public policy. Foreign companies can engage in wholesale activities but not retail because of Retail Trade Nationalization Law (R.A. 1180) which restricts retail activities to Filipinos or Philippine corporations or partnerships wholly owned and controlled by Filipinos.

Technology transfer agreements include such contracts that involved or entered into, by and between domestic company and foreign company and/or foreign-owned company, in addition to limitations set by law, such agreement is subject to rules and regulations on technology transfer agreements issued by Bureau of Patents, Trademarks and Technology Transfer.

All technology transfer agreements must be submitted for registration at Bureau of Patents, Trademarks and Technology Transfer office but following restrictive clauses in any technology transfer agreement are prohibited: (1) Those which restrict directly or indirectly export of licensed products under technology transfer arrangement; (2) those which restrict use of technology supplied after expiry of technology transfer arrangement; (3) those which restrict manufacture of similar or competing products after expiry of technology transfer arrangement; (4) those which require payments for patents and other industrial property rights after their expiration, termination or invalidation; (5) those which provide free of charge that major improvements made by technology recipient shall be communicated to technology supplier; (6) those which require that technology recipient shall not contest validity of any of patents of technology supplier; (7) those which restrict technology recipient in non-exclusive technology transfer arrangement from obtaining patented or unpatented technology from other technology suppliers with regard to sale or manufacture of competing products; (8) those which require technology recipient to purchase its raw materials, components and equipment exclusively, or fixed percentage of requirement, from technology supplier or person designated by him; (9) those which restrict research and development activities of technology recipient designated to absorb and adapt transferred technology to local conditions or to initiate R & D programs in connection with new products, processes or equipment; (10) those which prevent technology recipient from adapting imported technology to local conditions, or introducing innovations to it, as long as it does not impair quality standards prescribed by technology supplier; (11) those which require technology recipient to keep part or all of information received under technology transfer arrangement confidential beyond reasonable period; and (12) those which exempt technology supplier from liability for nonfulfillment of his responsibilities under technology transfer arrangement and/or liability arising from third party suits brought about by use of licensed product or licensed technology.

Technology transfer agreement has fixed term of ten years with no automatic renewal and royalty of 5% of net sales is allowed. Royalties in excess of 5% may be allowed upon prior approval of Bureau of Patents, Trademarks and Technology Transfer.

COPYRIGHT:

Copyrights may be registered for any of following: (a) Books, including composite and cyclopedic works, manuscripts, directories, and gazetteers; (b) periodicals, including pamphlets and newspapers; (c) lectures, sermons, addresses, dissertations prepared for oral delivery; (d) letters; (e) dramatic or dramatico-musical compositions; choreographic works and entertainments in dumb shows, acting form of which is fixed in writing or otherwise; (f) musical compositions, with or without words; (g) works of drawing, painting, architecture, sculpture, engraving, lithography, and other works of art; models or designs for works of art; (h) reproductions of works of art; (i) original ornamental designs or models for articles of manufacture, whether or not patentable, and other works of applied art; (j) maps, plans, sketches, and charts; (k) drawings or plastic works of scientific or technical character; (l) photographic works and works produced by a process analogous to photography; lantern slides; (m) cinematographic works and works produced by a process analogous to cinematography or any process for making audio-visual recordings; (n) computer programs; (o) prints, pictorial illustrations, advertising copies, labels, tags, and box wraps; (p) dramatizations, translations, adaptations, abridgments, arrangements and other alterations of literary, musical or artistic works or of works of Philippine Government; (q) collections of literary, scholarly, or artistic works or of works of Government of Philippines; and (r) other literary, scholarly, scientific and artistic works. (P.D. 49).

It is the exclusive right of a copyright owner: (a) to print, reprint, publish, copy, distribute, multiply, sell, and make photographs, photoengravings, and pictorial illustrations of the copyrighted work; (b) to make any translation or other version or extracts or arrangements or adaptation thereof; to dramatize it if it be a non-dramatic work; to convert it into a non-dramatic work if it be a drama; to complete or execute it if it be a model or design; (c) to exhibit, perform, represent, produce, or reproduce the copyrighted work in any manner or by any method whatever for profit or otherwise; if not reproduced in copies for sale, to sell any manuscripts or any record whatsoever thereof; (d) to make any other use or disposition of the copyrighted work consistent with the laws of the land.

Application for registration should be filed with National Library.

Copyright lasts during lifetime of creator and for 50 years after his death. In case of works of joint creation, period of 50 years shall be counted from death of last surviving co-creator.

Copyrights are not subject to levy and attachment.

Copyright privileges and protection have been extended to citizens of the United States by Proclamation No. 99 of the President of the Philippines. (44 O.G. 3717).

CORPORATIONS:

Corporation Code of Philippines (B.P. 68) classifies corporations into stock or nonstock.

Securities and Exchange Commission is charged with implementation of provisions of Corporation Code and promulgation of rules and regulations necessary to enable it to perform its duties, particularly in prevention of fraud and abuses of controlling stockholders, members, directors, trustees or officers.

Corporations may be formed for stated purpose or purposes. Where corporation has more than one stated purpose, articles of incorporation shall indicate which is primary purpose and which are secondary purposes. Only natural persons, not less than five nor more than 15 and majority of whom are Philippine residents may form corporation. Incorporator of stock corporation must own at least share of capital stock. Term of incorporation is 50 years and may be extended for additional periods of 50 years each by amendment of articles of incorporation. Number of directors must be not less than five nor more than 15 in case of stock corporations, nor more than 15 in case of nonstock corporations. Domestic corporations are organized by filing with Securities and Exchange Commission articles of incorporation specifying name, purpose, place of business, and term of incorporation, names of incorporators and directors, amount and kinds of capital stock, whether common, preferred or no-par value. It is required that "Inc." or "Corporation" be added after corporate name. Also, corporate name should not be identical or deceptively similar to that of any existing corporation. Principal office of corporation shall either be in city, municipality or province. Corporation must formally organize and commence transaction of its business within two years from date of incorporation, otherwise, its corporate powers not only shall cease but corporation shall also be deemed dissolved, except, if failure is not attributable to corporation. If, on other hand, corporation commenced transaction of its business but subsequently became continuously inoperative for minimum period of five years, Securities and Exchange Commission may suspend or revoke its corporate franchise.

Of authorized capital stock, 25% must be subscribed, and at least, 25% of total subscribed stock must be paid provided that in no case shall paid-up capital be less than ₱5,000 although §12 of Corporation Code provides that stock corporations shall not be required to have minimum authorized capital. Any contract for acquisition of unissued stock in existing corporation or corporation still to be formed shall be deemed subscription notwithstanding fact that parties call it purchase of shares. Articles of incorporation of corporations which will engage in business activity reserved for Filipinos and/or for corporations at least 60% of capital of which must be owned by citizens of Philippines shall provide that no transfer of stock or interest which will reduce ownership of Filipino citizens to less than required percentage of capital stock as provided by existing laws shall be allowed or permitted to be recorded in proper books of corporation and this restriction shall be indicated on all stock certificates issued by corporation.

There are no requirements regarding citizenship of stockholders, except that (a) 60% of stock in corporations organized in Philippines for purpose of engaging in operation of public utilities, (b) 60% of stock in corporations organized in Philippines for purpose of engaging in agriculture or mining, (c) 75% of stock in corporations organized for purpose of engaging in coastwise shipping trade, (d) 75% of stock in corporations organized for purpose of engaging in shipping trade on bays and rivers, (e) 60% of stock in corporations organized for purpose of engaging in fishing, (f) 60% in case of banks and banking institutions, (g) 100% in case of retail trade and rice and corn industry must be owned by citizens of Philippines, (h) 60% in case of financing companies, (i) majority of voting stock in corporations organized for purpose of engaging in underwriting of securities of other corporations, (j) 60% of stock in corporations engaged in preferred area of investment and duly registered with Board of Investments, and (k) 60% of stock in corporations engaged or proposes to engage in manufacturing, processing or exporting export products listed in export priorities plan or tourism priorities plan, or if not listed, at least 50% of its sales are export sales; or if service exporter, it is engaged or, proposes to engage in rendering services payable in foreign currency, in providing services to foreign tourists and foreign travelers in areas within Tourism Priorities Plan or in exporting television or motion pictures or musical recordings produced in Philippines. In all these classes of corporations, no alien may intervene in management, operation, administration or control thereof, whether as officer, employee or laborer therein, with or without remuneration, except technical personnel whose employment may be specifically authorized by President of Philippines.

Corporation commences corporate existence from date Securities and Exchange Commission issues certificate of incorporation; and thereupon incorporators, stockholders/members and their successors shall constitute body politic and corporate under name stated in articles of incorporation for period of time mentioned therein, unless said period is extended or corporation is sooner dissolved in accordance with law.

Management of corporation is vested in board of directors. Majority of directors of all corporations organized under Corporation Code must be residents of Philippines. At all elections of directors, there must be present owners of majority of outstanding capital stock, or if there be no capital stock, majority of members entitled to vote. Cumulative voting is provided for. Every director must own at least one share to qualify as director. No person convicted by final judgment of offense punishable by imprisonment for period not exceeding six years, or violation of Corporation Code, committed within five years prior to date of election, shall qualify as director or officer of corporation. Officers which corporations must elect at organization meeting are president, treasurer and secretary. Only president is required to be director of corporation. Any two or more positions may be held concurrently by same person except that no one shall act as president and secretary or president and treasurer at same time.

Every corporation incorporated under Corporation Code has power and capacity: (1) To sue and be sued in its corporate name; (2) of succession by its corporate name for period of time stated in articles of incorporation and certificate of incorporation; (3) to adopt and use corporate seal; (4) to amend its articles of incorporation; (5) to adopt by-laws, not contrary to law, morals, or public policy, and to amend or repeal same; (6) in case of stock corporations, to issue or sell stocks to subscribers and to sell treasury stocks; and to admit members to corporation if it be non-stock corporation; (7) to purchase, recieve, take or grant, hold, convey, sell, lease, pledge, mortgage and otherwise deal with such real and personal property, including securities and bonds of other corporations, as transaction of lawful business of corporation may reasonably require; (8) to adopt plan of merger or consolidation; (9) to make reasonable donations, including those for public welfare, or for charitable, cultural or similar purposes, provided that no corporation, domestic or foreign, shall give donations in aid of any political party or candidate; (10) to establish pension, retirement and other plans for benefit of its directors, trustees, officers and employees; (11) to exercise such other powers as may be essential to carry out its purpose or purposes; (12) to increase or decrease its capital stock; (13) to incur, create or increase bonded indebtedness; (14) to sell or otherwise

See Topical Index in front part of this volume.

CORPORATIONS . . . *continued*

dispose of all or substantially all of its assets; (15) to invest corporate funds in another corporation or business or for any other purposes; (16) to declare dividends, cash, stock or property; (17) to acquire its own shares; (18) to extend or shorten its corporate term; and (19) to enter into management contracts.

One or more stockholders of stock corporation may create voting trust for purpose of conferring upon trustee or trustees right to vote and other rights pertaining to shares for period not exceeding five years at any one time provided that in case of voting trust required as condition in loan agreement, voting trust may be for period not exceeding five years but shall automatically expire upon full payment of loan. No voting trust shall be entered into for purpose of circumventing law against monopolies and illegal combinations in restraint of trade or used for purposes of fraud.

Stock Certificates.—After the reconstitution of its records in accordance with existing laws, a corporation is now authorized to issue under certain conditions new certificates of stock in lieu of those which have been lost, stolen or destroyed, upon the registered owner or his legal representative filing with the corporation an affidavit setting forth, if possible, the circumstances as to how, when and where the certificates of stock were lost, stolen or destroyed, the number of shares represented by each certificate, the serial numbers of the certificates, and the name of the corporation which issued the same. Except in case of fraud, bad faith or negligence on the part of the corporation and its officers, no action may be made against any corporation which issued certificates of stock in lieu of those lost, stolen or destroyed.

Dividends.—Board of directors of stock corporation may declare dividends out of unrestricted retained earnings which shall be payable in cash, property or stock to all stockholders on basis of outstanding stock held by them.

Stock corporations are prohibited from retaining surplus profits in excess of 100% of their paid-in capital stock, except: (1) When justified by corporate expansion projects or programs approved by board of directors; or (2) when corporation is prohibited under any loan agreement with any financial institution or creditor, whether local or foreign, from declaring dividends without its/his consent; or (3) when it can be clearly shown that such retention is necessary under special circumstances obtaining in corporation.

Merger and Consolidation.—Two or more corporations may merge into single corporation which shall be one of constituent corporations or may consolidate into new single corporation which shall be consolidated corporation. Following shall be set forth in plan for merger or consolidation: (1) Names of corporations proposing to merge or consolidate; (2) terms of merger or consolidation and mode of carrying same into effect; (3) statement of changes, if any, in articles of incorporation of surviving corporation in case of merger; and with respect to consolidated corporation in case of consolidation, all statements required to be set forth in articles of incorporation for corporations organized under Corporation Code; and (4) such other provisions with respect to proposed merger or consolidation as are deemed necessary.

Appraisal Right.—Any stockholder shall have right to dissent and demand payment of fair value of his shares in following instances: (1) In case amendment to articles of incorporation has effect of changing or restricting rights of stockholders or class of shares, or of authorizing preferences in any respect superior to those of outstanding shares of any class, or of extending or shortening term of corporate existence; (2) in case of sale, lease, exchange, transfer, mortgage, pledge or other disposition of all or substantially all of corporate property and assets; and (3) in case of merger or consolidation. Appraisal right is also extended to any stockholder in case of investment of corporate funds in any corporation or business or for any purpose other than corporation's primary purpose.

Appraisal right is exercised by stockholder who shall have voted against proposed corporate action, by making written demand on corporation within 30 days after date on which vote was taken for payment of fair value of his shares. Failure to make demand within such period shall be deemed waiver of appraisal right. If proposed corporate action is implemented, corporation shall pay to such stockholder, upon surrender of certificates of stock representing his shares, fair value thereof as of day prior to date on which vote was taken.

If withdrawing stockholder and corporation cannot agree on fair value of shares, it shall be determined by three disinterested persons and findings of majority of appraisers shall be final. From time demand for payment of fair value of stockholder's shares until either abandonment of corporate action involved or purchase of said shares by corporation, all rights accruing to such shares shall be suspended except rights to receive payment of fair value thereof. If dissenting stockholder is not paid value of his shares within 30 days after award, his voting and dividend rights shall be restored. Right of stockholder to be paid fair value of his shares shall cease when demand for payment is withdrawn with corporation's consent, or if proposed corporate action is abandoned by corporation or disapproved by Securities and Exchange Commission or if Securities and Exchange Commission determines that such stockholder is not entitled to appraisal right.

Non-stock corporation is one where no part of its income is distributable as dividends to its members, trustees, or officers. Any profit which non-stock corporations may obtain shall be used for furtherance of purpose or purposes for which corporation was organized. Provisions governing stock corporations, when pertinent, shall be applicable to non-stock corporations, except as may be covered by specific provisions regarding non-stock corporations. Non-stock corporations may be formed for charitable, religious, educational, professional, cultural, fraternal, literary, scientific, social, civil service, or similar purposes, like trade, industry, agriculture, or any combination thereof.

Right of members to vote may be limited, broadened or denied to extent specified in articles of incorporation or by-laws. Membership in non-stock corporation, and all rights arising therefrom, are nontransferable. Termination of membership shall extinguish all rights of member in corporation or in its property.

Unless otherwise provided in articles of incorporation or by-laws, board of trustees, which may be more than 15, shall as soon as organized, so classify themselves that term of office of 1/3 of their number shall expire every year; and subsequent elections of trustees comprising 1/3 of board of trustees shall be held annually and trustees so elected shall have term of three years. Trustees thereafter elected to fill vacancies occurring before expiration of particular term shall hold office only for unexpired period. Regular or special meetings may be held at any place even outside place where principal office of corporation is located provided that proper notice is sent to all members and that place of meeting shall be within Philippines.

Close corporation is corporation whose articles of incorporation provide that all of its issued stock shall: (1) Be held by not more than 20 persons, (2) be subject to restrictions on their transfers, and (3) not be listed in any stock exchange or make any public offering. Any corporation may be incorporated as close corporation, except mining or oil companies, stock exchanges, banks, insurance companies, public utilities, educational institutions and corporations declared to be vested with public interest.

Articles of incorporation may provide for: (1) Classification of shares or rights and qualifications for owning same and restrictions on their transfers; (2) classification of directors; and (3) for greater quorum or voting requirements in meetings of stockholders or directors. Also, it may provide that business of corporation shall be managed by stockholders of corporation rather than by board of directors and that all officers or employees shall be elected or appointed by stockholders instead of by board of directors. Restrictions on right to transfer shares must appear in articles of incorporation and in by-laws as well as in certificate of stock.

Pre-emptive right of stockholders shall extend to all stock to be issued, including reissuance of treasury shares, whether for money or for property or personal services, or in payment of corporate debts.

If stockholders or directors are so divided respecting management of corporation's business that votes required for any corporate action cannot be obtained, Securities and Exchange Commission, upon written petition by any stockholder, shall have power to arbitrate dispute. In exercise of such power, Securities and Exchange Commission shall have authority to make such order as it deems appropriate, including order: (1) Cancelling or altering any provision contained in articles of incorporation, by-laws, or any stockholders' agreement; (2) cancelling or enjoining resolution or other act of corporation or its board of directors, stockholders, or officers; (3) directing or prohibiting any act of corporation or its board of directors, stockholders, officers, or other persons party to action; (4) requiring purchase at their fair value of shares of any stockholder, either by corporation or by other stockholders; (5) appointing provisional director; (6) dissolving corporation; or (7) granting such other relief as circumstances may warrant.

Any stockholder may compel said corporation to purchase his shares at their fair value, which shall not be less than their par or issued value, when corporation has sufficient assets to cover its debts and liabilities exclusive of capital stock. Any stockholder may, by written petition to Securities and Exchange Commission, compel dissolution of such corporation whenever any of acts of directors, officers or those in control of corporation is illegal, or fraudulent, or dishonest, or oppressive or unfairly prejudicial to corporation or any other stockholder, or whenever corporate assets are being misapplied or wasted.

Dissolution.—Corporation may be dissolved voluntarily and involuntarily. In case voluntary dissolution does not prejudice rights of creditors having claims against corporation, dissolution may be effected by majority vote of board of directors and by resolution adopted by affirmative vote of stockholders owning at least 2/3 of outstanding capital stock or of at least 2/3 of members. Copy of resolution authorizing dissolution shall be certified by majority of board of directors and countersigned by secretary of corporation. Securities and Exchange Commission shall thereupon issue certificate of dissolution. Where dissolution of corporation prejudices rights of creditors, petition for dissolution of corporation shall be filed with Securities and Exchange Commission.

In involuntary dissolution, Securities and Exchange Commission also has jurisdiction upon filing of verified complaint and after proper notice and hearing on grounds provided by existing laws, rules and regulations.

Franchise Tax.—There is no franchise tax on private corporations, but corporations which are granted special franchises by the Legislature must pay a franchise tax in accordance with the terms of the franchise. (Act No. 2711, §1508).

Special Classes of Corporations.—Educational corporations and religious corporations are governed by special laws.

Foreign Corporations.—No foreign corporation formed, organized or existing under any laws other than those of Philippines and whose laws allow Filipino corporations to do business in their own countries or states is permitted to transact business in Philippines until after it has obtained license to transact business in Philippines in accordance with Corporation Code and certificate of authority from appropriate government agency. Application for license to do business in Philippines must show: (1) Date and term of incorporation; (2) address of principal office of corporation in country or state of incorporation; (3) name and address of its resident agent authorized to accept summons and process in all legal proceedings; (4) place in Philippines where corporation intends to operate; (5) specific purpose or purposes of corporation which it intends to pursue in transaction of its business in Philippines; (6) names and addresses of present directors and officers of corporation; (7) statement of authorized capital stock and aggregate number of shares which corporation has authority to issue; (8) statement of outstanding capital stock and aggregate number of shares which corporation has issued; (9) statement of amount actually paid in; (10) such additional information necessary to enable Securities and Exchange Commission to determine whether such corporation is entitled to license to transact business in Philippines; (11) reciprocity certificate; (12) securities satisfactory to Securities and Exchange Commission to protect present and future creditors of corporation; and (13) agreement with Securities and Exchange Commission that service of summons or other legal process may be made upon it if foreign corporation shall cease to do business in Philippines or shall be without any resident agent.

Foreign banking, financial and insurance corporations shall, in addition to above requirements, comply with provisions of existing laws applicable to them. In case of all other foreign corporations, no application for license to transact business in Philippines shall be accepted by Securities and Exchange Commission without previous authority from appropriate government agency, whenever required by law.

No foreign corporation doing business in Philippines without license shall be permitted to maintain any action to court or administrative agency in Philippines but such corporation may be sued before Philippine courts or administrative tribunals on valid cause of action recognized under Philippine laws.

Without prejudice to other grounds provided by special laws, license of foreign corporation may be revoked or suspended by Securities and Exchange Commission on any of following grounds: (1) Failure to file its annual report or pay any fees; (2) failure

See Topical Index in front part of this volume.

CORPORATIONS . . . *continued*
to appoint and maintain resident agent in Philippines; (3) failure, after change of its resident agent or of his address, to submit to Securities and Exchange Commission statement of such change; (4) failure to submit to Securities and Exchange Commission authenticated copy of any amendment to articles of incorporation or by-laws or any articles of merger or consolidation within time prescribed; (5) misrepresentation of any material matter in any application, report, or other document submitted by such corporation; (6) failure to pay any and all taxes, imposts, assessments or penalties lawfully due to Philippine government; (7) transacting business in Philippines outside of purpose or purposes for which such corporation is authorized under its license; (8) transacting business in Philippines as agent of or acting for and in behalf of any corporation or entity not duly licensed to do business in Philippines; and (9) any other ground as would render it unfit to transact business in Philippines.

See also topic Aliens, subhead Corporations Owned or Controlled by Aliens; and topic Foreign Investments and Incentives.

COURTS:

Judiciary Act of 1948 (R.A. 296, am'd R.A. 1186, am'd R.A. 2613, am'd R.A. 5204) and Judiciary Reorganization Act of 1980 provide for following courts:

Supreme Court consists of Chief Justice and 14 Associate Justices. It may sit en banc or, in its discretion, in divisions of three, five, or seven members. All cases involving constitutionality of treaty, international or executive agreement, or law, which shall be heard by Supreme Court en banc, and all other cases which under Rules of Court are required to be heard en banc, including those involving constitutionality, application, or operation or presidential decrees, proclamations, orders, instructions, ordinances, and other regulations shall be decided with concurrence of majority of members who actually took part in deliberations on issues in case and voted thereon. Cases or matters heard by division shall be decided or resolved with concurrence of majority of members who actually took part in deliberations on issues in case and voted thereon, and in no case, without concurrence of at least three of such members. When required number is not obtained, case shall be decided en banc: Provided, that no doctrine or principle of law laid down by Court in decision rendered en banc or in division may be modified or reversed except by Court sitting en banc. (§4, Art. VIII, 1987 Constitution).

Supreme Court shall have following powers: (1) Exercise original jurisdiction over cases affecting ambassadors, other public ministers, and consuls, and over petitions for certiorari, prohibition, mandamus, quo warranto, and habeas corpus; (2) review, revise, reverse, modify, or affirm on appeal or certiorari, as law or Rules of Court may provide, final judgments and decrees of inferior courts in: (a) all cases in which constitutionality or validity of any treaty, international or executive agreement, law, presidential decree, proclamation, order, instruction, ordinance, or regulation is in question, (b) all cases involvng legality of any tax, impost, assessment, or toll, or any penalty imposed in relation thereto, (c) all cases in which jurisdiction of any inferior court is in issue, (d) all criminal cases in which penalty imposed is reclusion perpetua or higher, and (e) all cases in which only errors or questions of law are involved; (3) assign temporarily judges of lower courts to other stations as public interests may require. Such temporary assignment shall not exceed six months without consent of judge concerned; (4) order change of venue or place of trial to avoid miscarriage of justice; (5) promulgate rules concerning protection and enforcement of constitutional rights, pleading, practice, and procedure in all courts, admission to practice of law, integrated bar, and legal assistance to underprivileged; (6) appoint all officials and employees of Judiciary in accordance with Civil Service Law. Supreme Court shall have administrative supervision over all courts and personnel thereof.

Office of Court Administrator consists of Court Administrator and three Deputy Court Administrators with same qualifications as Justices of Court of Appeals. This office shall assist Supreme Court in exercise of its power of administrative supervision over all courts. (P.D. 828, am'd by P.D. 842).

Judicial and Bar Council is office under supervision of Supreme Court composed of Chief Justice; Secretary of Justice; representative of Congress; representative of integrated bar; professor of law; retired member of Supreme Court and representative of private sector. It has principal function of recommending appointees to Judiciary including Supreme Court.

Court of Appeals consists of Presiding Justice and 50 Associate Justices. It shall exercise its powers, functions, and duties through 17 divisions, each composed of three members. Court may sit en banc only for purpose of exercising administrative, ceremonial, or other non-adjudicatory functions. Majority of actual members shall constitute quorum for its session en banc. Three members shall constitute quorum for sessions of division. Unanimous vote of three members of division shall be necessary for pronouncement of decision or final resolution. Motion for reconsideration of its decision or final resolution shall be resolved within 90 days from time it is submitted for resolution, and no second motion for reconsideration from same party shall be entertained. Court of Appeals shall exercise: (a) original jurisdiction to issue writs of mandamus, prohibition, certiorari, habeas corpus, and quo warranto, and auxilliary writs of processes, whether or not in aid of its appellate jurisdiction; (b) exclusive original jurisdiction over actions for annulment of judgments of Regional Trial Courts; and (c) exclusive appellate jurisdiction over all final judgments, decisions, resolutions, orders or awards of Regional Trial Courts and quasi-judicial agencies, instrumentalities, boards or commissions, including Securities and Exchange Commission, Social Security Commission and Civil Service Commission except those falling within appellate jurisdiction of Supreme Court.

Regional Trial Courts are courts of general original jurisdiction in 13 Judicial Regions of Philippines. They exercise original jurisdiction: (1) In all civil actions in which subject of litigation is incapable of pecuniary estimation; (2) in all civil actions which involve title to, or possession of, real property, or any interest therein, where assessed value of property involved exceeds ₱20,000 or, for civil actions in Metro Manila where such value exceeds ₱50,000 except actions for forcible entry into and unlawful detainer of lands or building, original jurisdiction over which is conferred upon Metropolitan Trial Courts, Municipal Trial Courts and Municipal Circuit Trial Courts; (3) in all actions in admiralty and maritime jurisdiction where demand or claim exceeds ₱100,000 or in Metro Manila where such demand or claim exceeds ₱200,000; (4) in all matters of probate, testate or intestate, where gross value of estate exceeds ₱100,000 or, in Metro Manila where such gross value exceeds ₱200,000; (5) in all actions involving contract of marriage and marital relations; (6) in all cases not within exclusive jurisdiction of any court, tribunal, person or body exercising judicial or quasi-judicial functions; (7) in all civil actions and special proceedings falling within exclusive original jurisdiction of Juvenile and Domestic Relations Court and of Court of Agrarian Relations as now provided by law; and (8) in all other cases in which demand, exclusive of interest, damages of whatever kind, attorney's fees, litigtion expenses and costs or value of property in controversy exceeds ₱100,000 or, in such other cases in Metro Manila, where demand exceeds ₱200,000. (R.A. 7691). Regional Trial Courts exercise exclusive original jurisdiction in all criminal cases not within exclusive jurisdiction of any court, tribunal or body, except those now falling under exclusive and concurrent jurisdiction of Sandiganbayan which shall hereafter be exclusively taken cognizance of by latter. Also, they exercise original jurisdiction in issuance of writs of certiorari, prohibition, mandamus, quo warranto, habeas corpus and injunction which may be enforced in any part of their respective regions; and in actions affecting ambassadors and other public ministers and consuls. Regional Trial Courts exercise appellate jurisdiction over all cases decided by Metropolitan Trial Courts, Municipal Trial Courts and Municipal Circuit Trial Courts in their respective territorial jurisdictions. Such cases shall be decided on basis of entire record of proceedings had in court of origin. Supreme Court may designate certain branches of Regional Trial Court to handle exclusively criminal cases, juvenile and domestic relations cases, agrarian cases, urban land reform cases which do not fall under jurisdiction of quasi-judicial bodies and agencies, and/or such other special cases as Supreme Court may determine in interest of speedy and efficient administration of justice.

Metropolitan Trial Courts, Municipal Trial Courts, & Municipal Circuit Trial Courts.—Except in cases falling within exclusive original jurisdiction of Regional Trial Courts and of Sandiganbayan, Metropolitan Trial Courts, Municipal Trial Courts, and Municipal Circuit Trial Courts shall exercise exclusive original jurisdiction over all violations of city or municipal ordinances committed within their respective territorial jurisdiction; and exclusive original jurisdiction over all offenses punishable with imprisonment not exceeding six years irrespective of amount of fine, regardless of other imposable accessory or other penalties, including civil liability arising from such offenses, irrespective of nature or amount thereof provided that in offenses involving damage to property through criminal negligence they shall have exclusive original jurisdiction. Also, they shall exercise exclusive original jurisdiction over civil actions and probate proceedings, testate and intestate, including grant of provisional remedies in proper cases, where value of personal property, estate or amount of demand does not exceed ₱100,000 or, in Metro Manila where such personal property, estate, or amount of demand does not exceed ₱200,000 exclusive of interest, damages of whatever kind, attorney's fees, litigation expenses, and costs, amount of which must be specifically alleged provided that interest, damages of whatever kind, attorney's fees, litigation expenses, and costs shall be included in determination of filing fees, provided where there are several claims or causes of actions between same or different parties, embodied in same complaint, amount of demand shall be totality of claims in all causes of action; exclusive original jurisdiction over cases of forcible entry and unlawful detainer, provided that when defendant raises question of ownership in his pleadings and question of possession cannot be resolved without deciding issue of ownership, issue of ownership shall be resolved only to determine issue of possession; and exclusive original jurisdiction in all civil actions which involve title to, or possession of real property, or any interest therein where assessed value of property or interest therein does not exceed ₱20,000 or, in civil actions in Metro Manila, where such assessed value does not exceed ₱50,000 exclusive of interest damages of whatever kind, attorney's fees, litigation expenses and costs, provided in cases of land not declared for taxation purposes, value of such property shall be determined by assessed value of adjacent lots. These courts may be assigned by Supreme Court to hear and determine cadastral or land registration cases covering lots where there is no controversy or opposition, or contested lots value of which does not exceed ₱100,000. (R.A. 7691). In absence of all Regional Trial Judges in province or city, any Metropolitan Trial Judge, Municipal Trial Judge, Municipal Circuit Trial Judge may hear and decide petitions for writ of habeas corpus or applications for bail in criminal cases in province or city where absent Regional Trial Judges sit.

The following special courts have been created:

Court of Tax Appeals was created by R.A. 1125 and consists of a Presiding Judge and two Associate Judges, each of whom is appointed by the President, with the consent of the Commission on Appointments. The Court of Tax Appeals exercises exclusive appellate jurisdiction to review by appeal (a) decisions of Commissioner of Internal Revenue in cases involving disputed assessments, refunds of internal revenue taxes, fees or other charges, penalties imposed in relation thereto, or other matters arising under National Internal Revenue Code or other law or part of law administered by Bureau of Internal Revenue; (b) decisions of the Commissioner of Customs in cases involving liability for customs duties, fees or other money charges; seizure, detention or release of property affected, fines, forfeitures or other penalties imposed in relation thereto, or other matters arising under the Customs Law or other law or part of law administered by the Bureau of Customs.

Any party adversely affected by any judgment or final order of Court of Tax Appeals may appeal therefrom to Court of Appeals by filing seven legible copies of verified petition for review with said court and furnishing copies to adverse party and on agency a quo, within 15 days from notice of award, judgment or final order on denial of petitioner's motion for new trial or reconsideration. Proof of service of petition on adverse party and on court or agency a quo shall be attached to petition. (Supreme Court Circular No. 1-95).

Sandiganbayan was created by P.D. 1486 and revised by P.D. 1606 as amended by R.A. 7975. It shall sit in five divisions of three justices each. Presiding Justice and Associate Justices shall be appointed by President and cannot be removed from office except by impeachment upon grounds and in manner as provided for in constitution. Presiding Justice and Associate Justices shall have same rank, privileges, emoluments and be subject to same inhibitions and disqualifications as those provided for Presiding Justice and Associate Justices of Court of Appeals. Three Justices shall constitute quorum for sessions in division. Sandiganbayan shall exercise original jurisdiction in all

COURTS . . . *continued*

cases involving: (a) Violations of Anti-Graft and Corrupt Practices Act (R.A. 3019; R.A. 1379); and c. II, §2, Title VII of Revised Penal Code where one or more of principals accused are officials occupying following positions in government at time of commission of offense: (1) Officials of executive branch occupying positions of regional director and higher, otherwise classified at Grade 27 and higher, of Compensation and Position Classification Act of 1989, (2) Members of Congress and officials thereof classified at Grade 27 and higher, (3) members of judiciary without prejudice to provisions of Constitution, (4) Chairman and members of Constitutional Commissions, without prejudice to provisions of Constitution, and (5) all other national and local officials classified at Grade 27 and higher; (b) other offenses or felonies committed by public officials and employees in relation to their office; (c) civil and criminal cases filed pursuant to and in connection with Executive Order Nos. 1, 2, 14 and 14-A.

Sandiganbayan shall exercise exclusive appellate jurisdiction on appeals from final judgments, resolutions or orders of regular courts where all accused are occupying positions lower than salary Grade 27 or not otherwise covered by preceding enumeration. It shall also exercise exclusive original jurisdiction over petitioners for issuance of writs of mandamus, prohibition, certiorari, habeas corpus, injunction, and other ancillary writs and processes in aid of its appellate jurisdiction.

Military tribunals shall exercise exclusive jurisdiction in: (1) All offenses committed by military personnel of Armed Forces of Philippines while in active service; (2) crimes against national security and laws of nations; (3) espionage; (4) crimes against public order, namely: rebellion or insurrection, conspiracy and proposal to commit rebellion or insurrection, disloyalty of public officers or employees, inciting to rebellion or insurrection, sedition, conspiracy to commit sedition, inciting to sedition, illegal assemblies, illegal association; (5) violations of laws of firearms and explosives; (6) usurpation of military authority, rank, title and illegal use of military uniforms or insignia; (7) crimes against personal liberty; (8) rumormongering and spreading false information; (9) violations of decrees or orders where exclusive jurisdiction is specifically conferred upon military tribunals; (10) violation of Dangerous Drugs Act of 1972 (RA 6425); (11) swindling when committed in large-scale or by syndicate; (12) robbery committed by band or syndicate or when homicide and/or physical injuries have been committed by reason thereof; (13) murder committed by band or syndicate; (14) offense committed by detention prisoners detained in AFP detention centers by virtue of charges falling under exclusive jurisdiction of military tribunals (G.O. 49, as am'd).

CURRENCY:

Unit of monetary value in Philippines is peso, represented by sign "₱". Par value of peso shall not be altered except when necessary under following circumstances: (a) When existing par value would make impossible maintenance of balanced economy without depleting international reserve of Central Bank, or chronic use of restrictions on convertibility of peso into foreign currencies or on transferability abroad of funds from Philippines, or undue government intervention in or restriction of international flow of goods and services; or (b) when uniform proportionate changes in par values are made by countries which are members of International Monetary Fund; or (c) when operation of any executive or international agreement to which Philippines is party requires alteration in gold value of peso.

Bangko Sentral shall have sole power and authority to issue currency, within territory of Philippines. No other persons or entity, public or private, may put into circulation, notes, coins or any other object or document which may circulate as currency or reproduce or imitate facsimiles of Bangko Sentral notes without prior authority. Bangko Sentral has authority to investigate, make arrests, conduct searches and seizures in accordance with law, for purpose of maintaining integrity of currency. All notes and coins issued by Bangko Sentral shall be fully guaranteed by Government of Republic of the Philippines and shall be legal tender in Philippines for all debts, both public and private: Provided that coins shall be legal tender in amounts not exceeding ₱50 for denominations of ₱0.25 and above, and in amounts not exceeding ₱20 for denominations of ₱0.10 or less. (R.A. 7653). It is unlawful for any person to wilfully deface, mutilate, tear, burn or destroy, in any manner whatsoever, currency, notes and coins issued by Bangko Sentral. (P.D. 247).

By R.A. 4100, every provision contained in, or made respect to, any obligation contracted in Philippines with which purports to give creditor right to require payment in gold or in a particular kind of currency other than Philippine currency, is declared against public policy, null and void. This prohibition shall not apply to (a) Transactions where funds involved are proceeds of loans or investments made directly or indirectly, through bona fide agents, by foreign governments and international financial and banking institutions; (b) transactions affecting high priority economic projects for agricultural, industrial and power development as determined by National Economic Council which are financed by foreign funds; (c) forward exchange transactions entered into between banks or between banks and individuals or juridical persons; and (d) import-export and other international banking, financial investment and industrial transactions. With exception of enumerated cases, in which cases terms of parties' agreement shall apply, every other domestic obligation incurred, whether or not any provision as to payment is contained therein, shall be discharged upon payment in any currency which at time of payment is legal tender for public and private debts. If obligation was incurred prior to enactment of this Act and required payment in a particular kind of currency other than Philippine currency, it shall be discharged in Philippine currency measured at prevailing rates of exchange at time obligation was incurred, except in case of a loan made in a foreign currency payable in same currency in which case rate of exchange prevailing at time of date of payment shall prevail. (R.A. 529, am'd by R.A. 4100).

See also topic Foreign Exchange.

CURTESY:

There is no estate by curtesy.

CUSTOMS: See topic Taxation.

DEATH:

After an absence of seven years, it being unknown whether or not the absentee still lives, he is presumed to be dead for all purposes, except for those of succession. The absentee is not presumed dead for the purpose of opening his succession till after an absence of ten years. If he disappeared after the age of 75 years, an absence of five years is sufficient in order that his succession may be opened.

The following are presumed dead for all purposes, including the division of the estate among the heirs: (1) A person on board a vessel lost during a sea voyage, or an aeroplane which is missing, who has not been heard of for four years since the loss of the vessel or aeroplane; (2) a person in the armed forces who has taken part in war, and has been missing for four years; (3) a person who has been in danger of death under other circumstances and his existence has not been known for four years; (4) if married person has been absent for four years, present spouse may contract subsequent marriage if he or she has well founded belief that absent spouse is already dead. In case of disappearance, where there is danger of death under circumstances provided, absence of only two years shall be sufficient for present spouse to contract subsequent marriage. However, judicial declaration of presumptive death of absent spouse is necessary for purposes of contracting subsequent marriage by present spouse.

When two persons perish in same calamity such as wreck, battle, or conflagration, and it is not shown who died first, and there are no particular circumstances from which it can be inferred, survivorship is presumed from probabilities resulting from strength and age of sexes, according to following rules: (1) if both were under age of 15 years, older is presumed to have survived; (2) if both were above age of 60, younger is presumed to have survived; (3) if one be under 15 and other above 60, former is presumed to have survived; (4) if both were over 15 and under 60, and sexes be different, male is presumed to have survived; if sexes be the same, then the older; (5) if one be under 15 or over 60, and other between those ages, latter is presumed to have survived.

Actions for Death.—Civil liability based on wrongful death may arise from a crime or a quasi-delict.

Governing Laws.—Civil obligations arising from criminal offenses are governed by penal laws, subject to the provision of Civil Code on damages and human relations (1161 C.C.[n]), while civil obligations arising from quasi-delicts are governed by Arts. 2176-2194 of Civil Code and by special laws (1162 C.C.[n]).

Parties Entitled to Compensation and Parties Against Whom Action May Be Made.—Spouse, legitimate and illegitimate ascendents or descendants, and in certain cases, third persons entitled to support from deceased, may recover damages amounting to at least 3000 pesos in addition to compensation for loss of earning capacity and moral damages in certain cases. (2206 C.C.[n]).

Recent decisions have increased amount recoverable to at least ₱50,000. (People vs. Lugtu; Supreme Court En Banc Resolution dated Aug. 30, 1990).

Where the wrongful death is caused by a crime, obligation to indemnify devolves upon person (101 R.P.C.), or persons criminally liable, whether equally, if all are principals (109 R.P.C.), or severally, among principals, accomplices or accessories, or subsidiarily for those of other persons liable, such subsidiary liability to be enforced against the properties of principal, accomplice or accessory, in that order (110 R.P.C.), or their heirs (108 R.P.C.). Subsidiary civil liability may be enforced against certain persons, namely, (1) Those having authority or control over offender who is exempted by reason of minority, insanity (101 R.P.C.), and (2) employers, teachers, persons and corporations engaged in industry where offender is a servant, employee, pupil, workman or apprentice engaged in discharge of his duties (103 R.P.C.).

Where wrongful death is caused by a quasi-delict, obligation to indemnity is demandable not only for one's own acts or omissions, but also for those of persons for whom one is responsible. Father and, in case of his death or incapacity, mother, are responsible for damages caused by minor children who live in their company. Guardians are liable for damages caused by minors or incapacitated persons who are under their authority and live in their company. Owners and managers of an establishment or enterprise are likewise responsible for damages caused by their employees in the service of branches in which latter are employed or on the occasion of their functions. Employers are liable for damages caused by their employees and household helpers acting within scope of their assigned tasks, even though the former are not engaged in any business or industry. State is responsible in like manner when it acts through a special agent; but not when damage has been caused by official to whom the task done properly pertains, in which case what is provided in art. 2176 is applicable. Lastly, teachers or heads of establishments of arts and trades are liable for damages caused by their pupils and students or apprentices, so long as they remain in their custody. (2180 C.C.[n]).

In motor vehicles mishaps, owner is solidarily liable with his driver, if former, who was in vehicle, could have, by use of due diligence, prevented the misfortune. It is disputedly presumed that a driver was negligent, if he had been found guilty of reckless driving or violating traffic regulations at least twice within the next preceding two months. (2184 C.C.[n]). Manufacturers and processors of foodstuffs, drinks, toilet articles and similar goods are liable for death or injuries caused by any noxious or harmful substances used, although no contractual relation exists between them and consumers. (2187 C.C.[n]). Provinces, cities and municipalities are liable for damages for death of, or injuries suffered by, any person by reason of defective condition of roads, streets, bridges, public buildings, and other public works under their control or supervision. (2189 C.C.[n]). Proprietor of a building or structure is responsible for damages resulting from its total or partial collapse, if it should be due to lack of necessary repairs. (2190 C.C.[n]). Proprietors are also responsible for damages caused: (1) By explosion of machinery which has not been taken care of with due diligence, and the inflammation of explosive substances which have not been kept in a safe and adequate place; (2) by excessive smoke, which may be harmful to persons or property; (3) by falling of trees situated at or near highways or lanes, if not caused by *force majeure;* (4) by emanations from tubes, canals, sewers or deposits of infectious matter, constructed without precautions suitable to the place. (2191 C.C.[n]). Responsibility of two or more persons who are liable for a quasi-delict is solidary. (2194 C.C.[n]).

Limitation.—Responsibility for fault or negligence under Civil Code provisions on quasi-delict is distinct and separate from civil liability owing from negligence under

DEATH . . . *continued*
Penal Code. But plaintiff cannot recover twice for same act or omission of defendant. (2177 C.C.[n]).

Defenses.—Where death was caused by quasi-delict there can be no recovery where deceased's own negligence was immediate cause of his death. (2179 C.C.[n]). Obligation to indemnify ceases when persons obligated prove that they observed all the diligence of a good father of a family to prevent damage. (2180 C.C.[n]).

Where death was caused by a crime, there can be no recovery for damages by way of a civil action, where in a final judgment in a criminal case, there is a declaration that the fact from which the civil right might arise did not exist. (R.C., Rule 111, §2[b]).

Prescription.—Civil actions for wrongful deaths based on quasi-delict must be brought within four years (1146 C.C.[n]), while those based on a crime must be brought within five years (1149 C.C.[n]). If there is a final judgment of conviction of a crime, action based upon judgment must be brought within ten years from date of finality of judgment. (1144 C.C.[n]).

Applicability to Foreigners.—Penal laws and those of public security and safety are obligatory upon all who live or sojourn in Philippine territory, subject to principles of public international law and to treaty stipulations. (14 C.C.[n]).

DEBTOR AND CREDITOR:

Debt moratorium was declared unconstitutional as being unduly oppressive and hence is no longer in force. (Rutter v. Esteban, G. R. No. L-3708, promulgated May 18, 1953).

DEEDS:

Land must be conveyed by written deed. The names, surnames, civil status, citizenship, post office address and domicile of the contracting parties must be stated in the deed. It is also necessary to include the name of the wife or husband of the vendee, or show that there is no such person.

Recording.—In order to affect third persons, a deed must be recorded with the proper register of deeds. See topic Records. Deed must be presented for record in duplicate, one copy being returned with notation of registration.

DEPOSITIONS:

By leave of court after jurisdiction has been obtained, or without such leave after answer has been served, the testimony of any person, whether a party or not, may be used by any party for any purpose if (1) witness is dead; or (2) witness is out of province and lives more than 50 kilometers from place of hearing, or is out of Philippines; or (3) witness is unable to attend or testify because of age, sickness, infirmity, or imprisonment; or (4) that party offering has been unable to procure attendance of witness by subpoena; or (5) exceptional circumstances exist to allow use of deposition.

Within the Philippines depositions are taken before any judge, municipal judge or notary public on serving on adverse party notice of time and place of examination, together with affidavit showing that case is within provisions of law.

In a foreign state or country, depositions must be taken on notice before a secretary of embassy or legation, consul general, consul, vice-consul, or consular agent of Republic of the Philippines or before any person or officer as may be appointed by commission or under letters rogatory.

Deposition must be taken in the form of questions and answers, and it must be read to or by the witness and corrected by him in any particular, if desired, and must then be subscribed by the witness. No objection to the form of an interrogatory can be made at the trial unless the same was stated and recorded by the magistrate at the time of the examination, and objections are ruled on by the court at the trial. The commissioner must send the deposition to the clerk of the court in a sealed envelope or wrapper by mail or otherwise. It may be read at any stage of the action.

DESCENT AND DISTRIBUTION:

Succession pertains, in the first place, to the descending direct line. Legitimate children and their descendants succeed to the property of their parents and other ascendants, without distinction as to sex or age, and even if they should come from different marriages. An adopted child remains intestate heir of his parents and other blood relatives and he succeeds to property of adopting parents in same manner as legitimate child, but if he leaves no children or descendants, following rules must govern: (a) if adopted child is survived by his parents (legitimate or illegitimate) or legitimate ascendants and by his adopters, one half of estate goes to former and other half to adopters; (b) if he is survived by his spouse and illegitimate children and also by his adopters, one third goes to spouse, one third to illegitimate children and one third to adopters; (c) if he is survived by his illegitimate children and his adopters, one half goes to his illegitimate children and one half to his adopters; (d) if he is survived by his spouse and adopters, one half goes to his spouse and one half to his adopters; (e) if only adopters survive, they get entire estate; and (f) when adopters predeceased adopted and adopted died without any of heirs mentioned above, his collateral relatives will inherit under ordinary rules of legal or intestate succession. (Art. 190, E.O. 209).

In default of legitimate children and descendants of the deceased, his parents and ascendants inherit from him, to the exclusion of collateral relatives. In the absence of legitimate descendants or ascendants, the illegitimate children succeed to the entire estate of the deceased.

In the absence of legitimate descendants and ascendants, and illegitimate children and their descendants, whether legitimate or illegitimate, the surviving spouse inherits the entire estate, without prejudice to the rights of brothers and sisters, nephews and nieces, should there be any, in which case the surviving spouse is entitled to one-half of the inheritance and the brothers and sisters or their children to the other half.

If there are no descendants or ascendants, no illegitimate children and no surviving spouse, the collateral relatives within the fifth degree succeed to the entire estate of the deceased in the proportion established by law.

In default of persons entitled to succeed in accordance with the foregoing, the whole estate passes to the State. If a person legally entitled to the estate of the deceased appears and files a claim thereto with the court within five years from the date the property was delivered to the State, such person is entitled to the possession of the same, or if sold, to such part of the proceeds thereof as may not have been lawfully spent.

DISPUTE RESOLUTION:

Disputes and controversies in civil cases may be resolved prior to institution of court litigation or pending final resolution of case through compromise or arbitration.

Parties to compromise or those who submit their controversies to arbitration are bound thereto unless there is mistake, fraud, violence, intimidation or undue influence in which case, agreement may be annulled.

It is state policy in labor cases to promote and emphasize primacy of free collective bargaining and negotiations, including voluntary arbitration, mediation and concilliation as modes of settling labor or industrial disputes.

Mandatory Dispute Resolution.—In any civil action, parties and their attorneys are required to appear at pretrial conference before court to consider possibility of amicable settlement or of submission to arbitration. Any party who fails to appear at pretrial conference may be declared nonsuited or in default. (Rule 20, Revised Rules of Court).

Parties to collective bargaining agreement (CBA) are required to include in their agreement establishment of grievance machinery for adjustment and resolution of grievances arising from interpretation or implementation of their CBA and those arising from interpretation and implementation of company personnel policies. Grievances not settled before grievance machinery shall be automatically referred to voluntary arbitrator or panel of voluntary arbitrators. (Art. 260, Labor Code).

Cases arising from interpretation or implementation of Collective Bargaining Agreements and from interpretation or enforcement of company policies shall be disposed of by Labor Arbiter by directing parties to avail of grievance machinery and voluntary arbitration. Secretary of Labor and Employment may assume jurisdiction over disputes causing or likely to cause strikes or lockouts which will adversely affect national interests and certify same for compulsory arbitration.

DIVORCE:

Divorce in Philippines was abolished by new Civil Code (R.A. 386), which took effect on Aug. 30, 1950, and in its place legal separation is authorized. Petition for legal separation may be filed on any of following grounds: (1) Repeated physical violence or grossly abusive conduct against petitioner, common child, or child of petitioner; (2) physical violence or moral pressure to compel petitioner to change religious or political affiliation; (3) attempt of respondent to corrupt or induce petitioner, common child, or child of petitioner, to engage in prostitution, or connivance in such corruption or inducement; (4) final judgment sentencing respondent to imprisonment of more than six years, even if pardoned; (5) drug addiction or habitual alcoholism of respondent; (6) lesbianism or homosexuality of respondent; (7) contracting by respondent of subsequent bigamous marriage, whether in Philippines or abroad; (8) sexual infidelity or perversion; (9) attempt by respondent against life of petitioner; or (10) abandonment of petitioner by respondent without justifiable cause for more than one year. (Art. 55, E.O. 209).

No decree of legal separation shall be based upon stipulation of facts or confession of judgment. In any case, court shall order prosecuting attorney to take steps to prevent collusion between parties and to take care that evidence is not fabricated or suppressed. After filing petition for legal separation, spouses shall live separately from each other. Action shall be filed within five years from occurrence of cause and it shall in no case be tried before six months shall have elapsed since filing of petition. During pendency of action, court shall provide for support of spouses and their common children and shall give consideration to moral and material welfare of said children and their choice of parent with whom they wish to remain. It shall also provide for visitation rights of other parent.

Decree of legal separation has following effects: (1) Spouses shall be entitled to live separately from each other but marriage bonds shall not be severed; (2) absolute community or conjugal partnership shall be dissolved and liquidated but offending spouse shall have no right to any share of net profits earned by absolute community or conjugal partnership; (3) custody of minor children shall be awarded to innocent spouse, however, court shall take into account all relevant considerations, especially choice of child over seven years of age, unless parent chosen is unfit; and (4) offending spouse shall be disqualified from inheriting from innocent spouse by intestae succession. Provisions in favor of offending spouse made in will of innocent spouse shall be revoked by operation of law. After finality of decree of legal separation, innocent spouse may revoke donations made by him or her in favor of offending spouse, as well as designation of latter as beneficiary in any insurance policy, even if such designation be stipulated as irrevocable.

Reconciliation terminates proceedings for legal separation, if still pending, at whatever stage; and sets aside final decree of legal separation but separation of property and any forfeiture of share of guilty spouse already effected shall subsist, unless spouses agree to revive their former property regime. (E.O. 209).

DOWER:

Wife has no dower interest.

EMPLOYER AND EMPLOYEE:

See topic Labor Relations.

ENVIRONMENT:

General Supervision.—Primary government agency responsible for protection, conservation, management, development and exploration of environment and natural resources is Department of Environment and Natural Resources under executive branch of government.

It is composed of Department Proper, Staff Offices, Staff Bureaus, Regional Offices, Provincial Offices and Community Offices. Authority and responsibility for accomplishment of its objectives shall be vested in Secretary of Environment and Natural Resources who is appointed by President. (E.O. 292, s. of 1987).

National Pollution Control Decree of 1976 (P.D. 984) aims to prevent, abate and control pollution of water, air and land for more effective utilization of resources.

ENVIRONMENT . . . *continued*

Prohibited Acts.—No person shall throw, run, drain, or otherwise dispose of any organic or inorganic matter or any substance in gaseous or liquid form that shall cause pollution in any water, air and/or land resources of Philippines.

No person shall perform any of following activities without first securing permit from Bureau: (1) construction, installation, modification or operation of any sewage works or any extension or addition thereto; (2) increase in volume or strength of any wastes in excess of permissive discharge specified under any existing permit; and (3) construction, installation or operation of any industrial or commercial establishments or any extension, modification or addition thereof, operation of which would cause increase in discharge of waste directly into water, air and/or land resources.

Enforcement.—Environmental Management Bureau which is staff bureau of Department of Environment and Natural Resources is vested with powers and functions relating to environmental management, conservation and pollution control.

Penalties.—(1) Any person violating or failing to comply with any order or decision of Pollution Adjudication Board, or regulations issued by Bureau shall pay fine not exceeding 5,000 pesos per day for every day during which such violation or default continues; (2) any person violating any of prohibited acts shall be liable to pay not exceeding 1,000 pesos for each day during which violation continues, or by imprisonment from two years to six years, or both fine and imprisonment.

Prevention, Control and Abatement of Air Pollution Decree (P.D. 1181) aims to prevent, control and abate emissions of air pollution from motor vehicles to protect health and welfare of people and to prevent or minimize damage to property and hazards to land transportation.

Prohibited Acts.—(1) It shall be unlawful for any owner or operator of motor vehicle to allow it to discharge air pollutants at levels greater than acceptable pollutant concentration standards; (2) owner or operator of motor vehicle shall not use his vehicle or cause or allow it to be used unless such motor vehicle meets established emission standards; and (3) no imported or locally manufactured motor vehicle shall be sold, registered, or operated after effective date of implementing rules and regulations of P.D. 1181 unless it meets established emission standards as certified by Environmental Management Bureau.

Enforcement.—Environmental Management Bureau together with other government enforcement agencies shall be responsible for prevention, control and abatement of air pollution in traffic congested areas. Within Metro Manila, this law is being implemented and enforced by Metro Manila Development Authority.

Penalties.—Any person violating this decree and/or its implementing rules and regulations shall be liable to fine not exceeding 200 pesos, 500 pesos or 1,000 pesos for first, second and succeeding offenses respectively plus suspension of vehicle's certificate of registration in cases of third and succeeding offenses.

Marine and Pollution Decree of 1976 (P.D. 979) is aimed at preventing and controlling pollution of seas caused by dumping of wastes and other matter which create hazards to human health, harm living resources and marine life, damages amenities or interferes with legitimate uses of sea within territorial jurisdiction of Philippines.

Prohibited Acts.—It is unlawful for any person: (1) To discharge, dump or permit discharge of oil, noxious, gaseous and liquid substances and other harmful substances from or out of any ship, vessel, barge, or any other floating craft, or other man-made structures at sea, by any method, means or manner, into or upon territorial and inland navigable waters of Philippines; (2) to throw, discharge or deposit, dump, or cause, suffer or procure to be thrown, discharged, or deposited (either from or out of any ship, barge, or other floating craft or vessel of any kind, or from shore, wharf, manufacturing establishment, or mill of any kind) any refuse matter of any kind or description whatever other than that flowing from streets and sewers and passing therefrom in liquid state into tributary of any navigable water from which same shall float or be washed into such navigable water; and, (3) to deposit or cause, suffer or procure to be deposited material of any kind in any place on bank of any navigable water or on bank of any tributary of any navigable water, where same shall be liable to be washed into such navigable water, either by ordinary or high tides, or by storms or floods, or otherwise, whereby navigation shall or may be impeded or obstructed or increase level of pollution of such water.

Enforcement.—Philippine Coast Guard shall have primary responsibility of enforcing laws, rules and regulations governing marine pollution.

Penalties.—Any person who violates any of prohibited acts mentioned shall be liable for fine of not less than 200 pesos nor more than 10,000 pesos or by imprisonment of not less than 30 days nor more than one year or both fine and imprisonment.

Environmental Impact Statement System.—(PD 1586) Due to policy of state to attain and maintain rational and orderly balance between socio-economic growth and environmental protection, Environmental Impact Statement System was established requiring all agencies and instrumentalities of national government as well as private firms and corporations to conduct environmental impact assessment of any project or undertaking which may significantly affect quality of environment.

Prohibited Acts.—It is prohibited for any person, partnership or corporations to undertake or operate any project or area declared environmentally critical without first securing Environmental Compliance Certificate.

Enforcement.—National Environmental Protection Council shall have jurisdiction to undertake preparation of necessary environmental impact statements concerning declared environmentally critical projects and areas.

Penalties.—Any person, corporation or partnership found commiting prohibited acts, or terms and conditions of Environmental Compliance Certificate, or standards, rules and regulations issued by National Environmental Protection Council shall be punished by suspension or cancellation of its certificate and/or fine of not exceeding 50,000 pesos for every violation thereof.

Toxic Substances and Hazardous and Nuclear Wastes Control Act of 1990.—(R.A. 6969). This is aimed to regulate and keep inventory of importation, manufacture, processing, handling, storage, transportation, sale, distribution, use and disposal of all unregulated chemical substances and mixtures in Philippines including entry, storage or disposal of hazardous and nuclear wastes into country.

Prohibited Acts.—(1) Knowingly use chemical substance or mixture which is imported, manufactured, processed or distributed in violation of R.A. 6969 or its Implementing Rules and Regulations; (2) failure or refusal to submit reports, notices or other informations, access to records as required by R.A. 6969, or permit inspection of establishment where chemicals are manufactured, processed, stored or otherwise held; (3) failure or refusal to comply with premanufacturing and pre-importation requirements; and (4) cause, aid or facilitate, directly or indirectly, in storage, importation, or bringing into any part of Philippine territory any amount of hazardous and nuclear wastes.

Enforcement.—Department of Environment and Natural Resources shall be agency responsible in implementation of above purposes.

Penalties.—Penalty of imprisonment ranging from six months and one day to 20 years, depending on prohibited acts committed and fine ranging from 600 pesos to 4,000 pesos is imposed upon any person violating prohibited acts under R.A. 6969. If offender is foreigner, he or she shall be deported and banned from any subsequent entry in Philippines after serving his sentence.

If offender is corporation, partnership, association or juridical person, partner, president, director or manager who shall consent to or shall knowingly tolerate such violation shall be directly liable and responsible for act of employees and shall be criminally liable as coprincipal.

Administrative fines of not less than 10,000 pesos but not more than 50,000 pesos may be imposed by Secretary of Environment and Natural Resources upon any person or entity found guilty of violating R.A. 6969 and its Implementing Rules and Regulations.

National Integrated Protected Areas Systems Act.—(R.A. 7586). This is aimed at securing and maintaining perpetual existence of all native plants and animals through establishment of comprehensive system of integrated protected areas within classification of national park as provided for in constitution.

Prohibited Acts.—Following acts are prohibited within protected areas: (1) Hunting, destroying, or mere possession of any plants or animals or products derived therefrom without permit from Management Board; (2) dumping of any waste products detrimental to protected area, or to plants and animals or inhabitants therein; (3) use of any motorized equipment without permit from Management Board; (4) mutilating, defacing or destroying objects of natural beauty or objects of interest to cultural communities; (5) damaging, and leaving roads and trails in damaged condition; (6) squatting, mineral locating, or business enterprise without permit; (8) leaving in exposed or unsanitary conditions refuse or debris, or depositing in ground or in bodies of water; and, (9) altering, removing, destroying or defacing boundary marks or signs.

Enforcement.—National Integrated Protected Areas System is placed under control and administration of Department of Environment and National Resources whereby Protected Areas and Wildlife Division is created in each of its regional offices.

Penalties.—Any person violating this law or any of its rules and regulations will be fined in amount of not less than 5,000 pesos nor more than 500,000 pesos exclusive of value of thing damaged or imprisonment for not less than one year but not more than six years. Department of Environment and Natural Resources may also impose fines and penalties.

EXCHANGE CONTROL:

No statutory rule.

See topics Currency; Foreign Exchange.

EXECUTIONS:

Execution may not issue until judgment becomes final, and may issue at any time within five years after entry of judgment. In all cases, a judgment may be enforced after lapse of five years from entry, and before it shall have been barred by any statute of limitations, by an ordinary action. Sheriff must first attempt to satisfy a judgment out of the personal property of the debtor and then out of his real property. Execution may be made returnable at any time, not less than ten nor more than 60 days after its receipt by sheriff.

In enforcing execution against personal property, the officer must take possession thereof. In levying on real property, the officer must file with the register of deeds of the province in which the property is situated, a copy of the writ of execution, together with a description of the property levied on and notice of the levy, and a copy of the execution, description and notice must be left with the occupant of the property, if there is any.

Property sold under execution may be redeemed within one year thereafter.

A person indebted to the judgment debtor may pay to the sheriff the amount of his debt and the sheriff's receipt is a sufficient discharge for the amount so paid.

Exemptions.—See topic Exemptions.

Supplementary proceedings after execution was returned unsatisfied are provided, whereby the execution creditor may examine the judgment debtor under oath as to his property, business or financial interests. The examination may be made before the judge of the court issuing the execution or before a referee appointed by the court. Attendance of the party or witnesses may be compelled by an order or subpoena as in other cases. A receiver of the property of the judgment debtor may be appointed in a proper case. (R.C., Rule 39, §§38-43). Similar proceedings may be had while the execution is outstanding, if the judgment creditor shows by affidavit or otherwise to the satisfaction of the court that the judgment debtor has property which he unjustly refuses to apply to the satisfaction of the judgment.

EXECUTORS AND ADMINISTRATORS:

Regional Trial Courts have general jurisdiction over estates of decedents, whether testate or intestate, and appoint executors and administrators.

Married woman may act as executrix or administratrix.

Law requires courts to appoint residents only as executors or administrators.

Executor or administrator must file an inventory. Administration of an estate must be kept open at least six months, with exceptions noted below.

Rules of Court provide for publication and service in all matters requiring action as well as a final accounting and partition.

EXECUTORS AND ADMINISTRATORS . . . *continued*

Summary settlement of an estate, without appointment of administrator or commissioners, is allowed when gross value does not exceed 10,000 pesos.

A hearing shall be conducted in court having jurisdiction of estate not less than one month nor more than three months from date of last publication of a notice which shall be published once a week for three consecutive weeks in a newspaper of general circulation and thereafter, court will proceed for distribution of the estate.

When an estate has no debts and decedent has not appointed any one to partition estate and heirs are all of lawful age, they may, by agreement in writing, divide estate among themselves without court proceedings, regardless of amount or value of estate.

Right to attack sale or conveyance by decedent, see topic Fraudulent Sales and Conveyances.

Allowances.—The widow and minor children of a deceased person, if the amount of the estate permits, are entitled to an allowance from the estate pending liquidations, but such allowance may be deducted from their portion, in so far as it exceeds what they may be entitled to as fruits or income.

Claims.—On the granting of letters testamentary or of administration, the court must issue a notice requiring all persons having money claims against the decedent to file them, and fix the time for filing, which must be not less than six, nor more than 12 months after first publication of notice. Immediately after such notice is issued, executor or administrator must cause same to be published for three weeks and posted in four public places in the province and two public places in the municipality where decedent last resided. Executor or administrator must file in court proof that this has been done.

Claims must be filed within time limited in notice; otherwise they are barred forever, except that a claim not presented may be set forth as a counterclaim in any action by the executor or administrator against the claimant, and except that the court may, at any time before order of distribution is entered, for cause shown and on terms, allow claim not filed in time to be filed within a time not exceeding one month.

Claim may be filed by delivering same, with necessary vouchers, to clerk of court and serving copy thereof on executor or administrator. If claim is due it must be supported by affidavit stating the amount justly due, that no payments have been made thereon which are not credited and that there are no offsets to affiant's knowledge. If claim is not due or is contingent, it must be supported by affidavit stating particulars.

Within fifteen days after service of copy of claim on executor or administrator, he must file his answer admitting or denying the claim specifically and setting forth matters relied on to support admission or denial, or stating lack of knowledge sufficient to enable him to admit or deny. Executor or administrator must allege in offset any claim which decedent had against claimant, failing in which decedent's claim is barred. Copy of answer must be served on claimant.

Admitted claims are immediately submitted by the clerk to court, which may approve them without hearing or may order that heirs, legatees or devisees be notified and heard. Otherwise, on filing of answer or on expiration of time therefor, clerk must set claim for trial and notify both parties. Court may refer claim to a commissioner. Judgment of court approving or disapproving claim must be filed with record of the administrative proceedings, with notice to both parties, and is appealable.

Order of Payment if Estate Insolvent.—After paying the necessary expenses of administration, the debts of the estate must be paid in the following order: (1) Necessary funeral expenses; (2) expenses of last illness; (3) what is owing to laborers for salaries and wages earned and for indemnities due, for the last year; (4) taxes and assessments due to the government, or any branch or subdivision thereof; (5) debts due to the province; (6) other debts.

Compensation.—An executor or administrator shall be allowed the necessary expenses in the care, management, and settlement of the estate, and for his services, four pesos per day for the time actually and necessarily employed, or a commission upon the value of so much of the estate as comes into his possession and is finally disposed of by him in the payment of debts, expenses, legacies, or distributive shares, or by delivery to heirs or devisees, of 2% of the first 5,000 pesos of such value, 1% of so much of such value as exceeds 5,000 pesos and does not exceed 30,000 pesos, 1/2 of 1% of so much of such value as exceeds 30,000 pesos and does not exceed 100,000 pesos, and 1/4 of 1% of so much of such value as exceeds 100,000 pesos. But in any special case, where the estate is large, and the settlement has been attended with great difficulty, and has required a high degree of capacity on the part of the executor or administrator, a greater sum may be allowed. Lawyer acting as executor or administrator cannot charge estate for professional services. Fees fixed by will are in full satisfaction for services of executor. (R.C., Rule 85, §7).

EXEMPTIONS:

Following property is exempt from attachment and execution: (1) Debtor's family home constituted in accordance with Civil Code, or in the absence thereof, debtor's homestead in which he resides, and land necessarily used in connection therewith, both not exceeding in value ₱3,000; (2) tools and implements necessarily used by him in his trade or employment; (3) two horses or two cows, or two carabaos or other beasts of burden, such as debtor may select, not exceeding ₱1,000 in value, and necessarily used by him in his ordinary occupation; (4) his necessary clothing, and that of all his family; (5) household furniture and utensils necessary for housekeeping, and used for that purpose by debtor, such as debtor may select, of a value not exceeding ₱1,000; (6) provision actually provided for individual or family use sufficient for three months; (7) professional libraries of lawyers, judges, clergymen, doctors, school teachers, music teachers, not exceeding ₱3,000 in value; (8) one fishing boat and net, not exceeding total value of ₱1,000, property of any fisherman, by lawful use of which he earns a livelihood; (9) lettered gravestones; (10) all moneys, benefits, privileges or annuities accruing or in any manner growing out of any life insurance, if annual premiums paid do not exceed ₱500, and if they exceed that sum, a like exemption shall exist which shall bear same proportion to moneys, benefits, privileges, and annuities so accruing or growing out of such insurance that said ₱500 bears to whole annual premiums paid; (11) right to receive legal support, or money or property obtained as such support or any pension or gratuity from the government; (12) copyrights and other properties exempted by law. But no article or species of property herein mentioned are exempt from execution issued upon a judgment recovered for its price or upon judgment of foreclosure of a mortgage thereon. All property other than as hereinbefore stated is subject to attachment and execution.

FOREIGN CORPORATIONS:

See topic Corporations.

FOREIGN EXCHANGE:

Bangko Sentral is authorized to suspend or restrict temporarily sales of foreign exchange, and subject all transactions in gold and foreign exchange to license under §72, R.A. 7653. Pursuant to its charter, Bangko Sentral has issued regulations relating to operation of foreign exchange and trade control in Philippines. Digest of these regulations has been published by Bangko Sentral in order to assist firms and individuals in understanding exchange and trade control regulations. See also topic Currency.

FOREIGN INVESTMENTS AND INCENTIVES:

Omnibus Investments Code of 1987 (E.O. 226) incorporates all foreign investment laws and various incentive schemes administered by Dept. of Trade & Industry through either Board of Investments (BOI) or Export Processing Zone Authority (EPZA). It gives foreign and local investors complete information on all incentives which they may avail of, alternative incentive schemes available to them and requirements for registration of foreign investments without incentives.

State shall encourage private domestic and foreign investments in industry, agriculture, mining, forestry, tourism and other sectors of economy which shall: (1) Provide significant employment opportunities relative to amount of capital invested; (2) increase productivity of land, minerals, forestry, aquatic and other resources of country, and improve utilization of products thereof; (3) improve technical skills of people employed in enterprise; (4) provide foundation for future development of economy; (5) meet tests of international competitiveness; (6) accelerate development of less developed regions of country; and (7) result in increased volume and value of exports for economy. Also, State shall extend to projects which will contribute to attainment of these objectives, fiscal incentives without which said projects may not be established in locales, number and/or pace required for optimum national economic development. Fiscal incentive systems shall be devised to compensate for market imperfections, reward performance contributing to economic development, and be cost-efficient and simple to administer. Fiscal incentives shall be extended to stimulate establishment and assist initial operations of enterprise, and shall terminate after period of not more than ten years from registration or start-up of operation unless specific period is otherwise stated.

BOI, composed of seven governors: Secretary of Trade & Industry, three Undersecretaries of Trade & Industry to be chosen by President; and three representatives from other government agencies and private sector, shall be responsible for regulation and promotion of investments. Not later than end of Mar. of every year, BOI shall submit Investment Priorities Plan (IPP) to President. Under IPP prepared by BOI, preferred areas of investment are classified as either pioneer or non-pioneer. Upon registration with BOI, enterprise becomes registered enterprise in pioneer or non-pioneer preferred areas of investment. Pioneer enterprise is registered enterprise: (1) Engaged in manufacture, processing or production of goods, products, commodities or raw materials that have not been produced in Philippines on commercial scale or (2) which uses design, formula, scheme, method, process or system or production or transformation of any element, substance or raw material into another raw material or finished goods which is new and untried in Philippines or (3) engaged in pursuit of agricultural, forestry and mining activities and/or services including industrial aspects of food processing whenever appropriate, predetermined by BOI, in consultation with appropriate department, to be feasible and highly essential to attainment of national goal in relation to declared specific national food and agricultural program for self sufficiency and other social benefits of project or (4) which produces nonconventional fuels or manufactures equipment which utilizes nonconventional sources of energy or uses or converts to coal or other nonconventional fuels or sources of energy in its production, manufacturing or processing operations provided that final product will involve substantial use and processing of domestic raw materials, whenever available, taking into account risks and magnitude of investment. Non-pioneer enterprises shall include all registered producer enterprises other than pioneer enterprises.

Qualifications of Registrants.—To be entitled to registration under IPP, applicant must possess following qualifications: (1) If natural person, he must be citizen of Philippines; if partnership or any other association, it must be organized under Philippine laws and at least 60% of its captial should be owned and controlled by citizens of Philippines; if corporation or cooperative, it must be organized under Philippine laws, at least 60% of its capital stock outstanding and entitled to vote must be owned and held by Philippine nationals, and at least 60% of members of Board of Directors must be citizens of Philippines. If corporation does not possess required degree of ownership by Philippine nationals, it must establish following circumstances satisfactorily in order to qualify for registration under IPP: (a) It proposes to engage in pioneer project which cannot be adequately filled by Philippine nationals or applicant is exporting at least 70% of its total production, (b) it obligates itself to attain status of Philippine national within 30 years from date of registration or longer period depending upon export potential of project (registered enterprise which exports 100% of its total production need not comply with this requirement), (c) pioneer area corporation will engage in is one that is not within activities reserved for Philippine citizens or corporations owned and controlled by Philippine citizens; (2) it proposes to engage in preferred project listed in current IPP within reasonable period of time; or if not listed, at least 50% of enterprise's total production is for export or it is existing producer which will export part of production under certain conditions; or that enterprise is engaged or will engage in export of products bought from one or more export producers; or enterprise is engaged or will engage in rendering technical, professional or other services or in exporting television and motion pictures and musical recording made or produced in Philippines, either directly or through registered trader; and (3) it is capable of operating on sound and efficient basis and of contributing to national development of preferred area in particular and of national economy in general.

See Topical Index in front part of this volume.

FOREIGN INVESTMENTS AND INCENTIVES . . . *continued*

Rights and Guarantees.—Investors and registered enterprises are entitled to basic rights and guarantees provided in Constitution. Among other rights recognized by Government are: (1) Repatriation of investment; (2) remittance of earnings; (3) right to remit at exchange rate prevailing at time of remittance such sums necessary to meet payments of interest and principal on foreign loans and foreign obligations arising from technological assistance contracts; (4) freedom from expropriation of property represented by investments or property of enterprises except for public use or interest of national welfare; and (5) there shall be no requisition of property represented by investment or property of enterprises, except in event of war or national emergency.

Incentives.—BOI registered enterprises shall be granted following incentives to extent engaged in preferred area of investment: (1) Income tax holiday—full exemption for six years for pioneer firms and four years for non-pioneer firms from date of commercial operation, extendible for another year while registered expanding firms shall be entitled to exemption for income taxes proportionate to their expansion for period of three years from commercial operation; (2) additional deduction from taxable income equal to 50% of labor expenses for five years from registration; (3) tax and duty exemption on imported capital equipment and accompanying spare parts, under certain conditions; (4) tax credit on domestic capital equipment subject to certain conditions; (5) simplification of customs procedures for importation of equipment, spare parts, raw materials and supplies, and exports of processed products; (6) unrestricted use of consigned equipment provided re-export bond is posted unless equipment and spare parts have been imported tax and duty free; (7) employment of foreign nationals in supervisory, technical or advisory positions for five years from registration, extendible for limited periods with certain exceptions; (8) exemption from all taxes and duties on importation of breeding stocks and genetic materials within ten years from date of registration or commercial operation with certain conditions; (9) tax credit on domestic breeding stocks and genetic materials for same period as in (8) above subject to certain conditions; (10) tax credit for taxes and duties on raw material, supplies and semi-manufactured products used in manufacture of export products; (11) access to bonded manufacturing/trading warehouse system of registered export oriented enterprises; (12) exemption from taxes and duties on imported spare parts and required supplies and for consigned equipment; and (13) exemption from wharfage and any export tax, duty, import and fees. (E.O. 226 as am'd by R.A. 7918).

Registered Enterprises with Operations in Less Developed Areas.—Incentive are: (1) Automatic entitlement to incentives available to pioneer enterprises regardless of nationality; (2) additional deduction from taxable income equal to 100% of labor expenses for five years from registration; and (3) deduction from taxable income to extent of 100% of cost of necessary and major infrastructure and public facilities constructed.

EPZA-registered enterprises are also entitled to incentives available to BOI-registered enterprises. Additional incentives are: (1) Merchandise, raw materials, supplies, and other articles brought into export processing zone are exempt from taxes and duties subject to certain conditions; and (2) exemption from local taxes and licenses including real property taxes on production equipment or machineries.

Foreign business entity organized and existing under any laws other than those of Philippines whose purpose is to supervise, superintend, inspect or coordinate its own affiliates, subsidiaries or branches in Asia-Pacific region may be allowed to establish regional or area headquarters in Philippines subject to certain conditions, among which are following: (1) Its activities shall be limited to acting as supervisory, communications and coordinating center for its subsidiaries, affiliates and branches in region and (2) it will not derive any income from sources within Philippines and will not participate in any manner in management of any subsidiary or branch office it might have in Philippines. Regional or area headquarters shall be entitled to following incentives: (1) Exemption from income tax; (2) exemption from contractor's tax; (3) exemption from all kinds of local licenses, fees and duties; (4) tax and duty free importation of training materials; (5) importation of motor vehicles for expatriate executives and their replacement every three years provided taxes and duties are paid upon importation; and, (6) exemption from registration requirements. Expatriate executives are entitled to: (1) Multiple entry visa, valid for one year including spouses and unmarried children below 21 and exemption from payment of all fees and duties under immigration and alien registration laws; securing alien certificates of registration; and obtaining all types of clearances required by any government department or agency except notice of final departure and tax clearance from Bureau of Internal Revenue; (2) withholding tax of 15% on gross income received; (3) tax and duty free importation of personal and household effects; and (4) travel tax exemption. Foreign company which has established or will establish regional or area headquarters may be allowed to establish regional warehouses subject to following conditions: (1) Its activities shall be limited to serving as supply depot for storage, deposit, safekeeping of its spare parts or manufactured components and raw materials including packing and related activities; filling up transactions and sales made by its head offices or parent companies; and serving as storage or warehouse of goods purchased locally by home office of foreign company for export abroad; (2) it shall not directly engage in trade nor directly solicit business, promote any sale, nor enter into any contract for sale or disposition of goods in Philippines; and (3) it will not derive any income from sources within Philippines and its personnel will not participate in any manner in management of subsidiary, affiliate or branch office it might have in Philippines. Imported spare parts, raw materials and other items for use exclusively on goods stored, brought into regional warehouse from abroad to be kept and re-exported to Asia-Pacific and other foreign markets shall be exempt from payment of customs duty, internal revenue tax, export tax and local taxes.

Special investors resident visa may be issued to any alien who possesses following qualifications: (1) He has not been convicted of crime involving moral turpitude; (2) he is not afflicted with any loathsome, dangerous or contagious disease; (3) he has not been institutionalized for any mental disorder or disability; and (4) he is willing and able to invest US$75,000 in Philippines.

Foreign Investments Act of 1991 (R.A. 7042).—State shall promote and welcome investments from foreign individuals and juridical entities in activities which contribute to national industrialization and socio-economic development to extent that foreign investment is allowed in such activity by Constitution and relevant laws. Foreign investments shall be encouraged in enterprises that expand livelihood and employment opportunities for Filipinos; enhance economic value of farm products; promote welfare of Filipino consumers; expand scope, quality and volume of exports and their access to foreign markets; and/or transfer relevant technologies in agriculture, industry and support services. Foreign investments shall be welcome as supplement to Filipino capital and technology in those enterprises serving mainly domestic market.

Any non-Philippine national may do business or invest in domestic enterprise up to 100% of its capital provided it is investing in domestic market enterprise in areas outside Foreign Investment Negative List (FINL); or it is investing in export enterprise whose products and services do not fall within Lists A & B of FINL. It is also provided that country or state of applicant must also allow Filipino citizens and corporations to do business therein.

List of Investment Areas Reserved to Philippine Nationals or Foreign Investment Negative List.—(a) List A shall consist of areas of activities where foreign equity participation in any domestic or export enterprise engaged in any activity listed therein shall be limited to maximum of 40% as prescribed by Constitution and specific laws; and (b) List B shall consist of areas of activities and enterprises regulated pursuant to law which are defense-related activities, requiring prior clearance and authorization from Dept. of National Defense or which have implications on public health and morals.

Coverage.—Act covers all investment areas of economic activities except banking and other financial institutions which are governed and regulated by General Banking Act and other laws under supervision of Central Bank.

Existing enterprises which have been issued certificates of authority to do business or to accept permissible investments under E.O. 226, P.D. 1789 and R.A. 5455, whose activities are included in Transitory FINL or in subsequent Negative Lists, are allowed to continue same activities which they have been authorized to do subject to same terms and conditions stipulated in their certificates of registration.

Those whose activities have been previously authorized under E.O. 226, P.D. 1789 and R.A. 5455, and whose activities are not in Transitory FINL or in subsequent Negative Lists may opt to be governed by provisions of Act. Said enterprises shall be considered automatically registered with SEC upon surrender of their certificates of authority to BOI. SEC shall issue new certificate of authority upon advise of BOI.

Existing enterprises with more than 40% of foreign equity which have availed of incentives under any of investment incentives laws implemented by BOI may opt to be governed by Act. In such cases, said enterprises shall be required to surrender their certificates of registration, which shall be deemed express waiver of their privilege to apply for and avail of incentives under incentives law under which they were previously registered. Subject to BOI rules and regulations, said enterprises may be required to refund all capital equipment incentives availed of.

Special Economic Zone Act of 1995.—(R.A. 7916). Government aims to encourage, promote, induce and accelerate sound and balanced industrial, economic and social development in country by providing jobs in rural areas and increasing productivity and income of every individual and family living in these areas through establishment of special economic zones ("ECOZONES") that will effectively attract legitimate and productive foreign investments.

Special economic zones are selected areas which are highly developed or which have potential to be developed into agro-industrial, industrial, tourist/recreational, commercial, banking, investment and financial centers.

Any investor within economic zone whose initial investment shall not be less than US$150,000, his/her spouse and dependent children under 21 years old shall be granted permanent resident status within economic zone. Business establishments operating within ECOZONES shall be entitled to: (1) Fiscal incentives under P.D. 66 or E.O. 226; (2) tax credits for exporters using local materials as inputs as provided by R.A. 7844 (Export Dev't. Act of 1994); (3) exemption from taxes under National Internal Revenue Code; (4) goods manufactured by ECOZONE enterprise shall be made available for immediate domestic retail sales; and (5) additional deduction of 1/2 of value of training expenses incurred by ECOZONE enterprises in developing skilled or unskilled labor or for managerial or other management development programs.

To avail of all above incentives and benefits, business enterprises within ECOZONES must register with Philippine Economic Zone Authority.

ECOZONE enterprises are allowed to hire foreign nationals in supervisory, technical or advisory capacity not exceeding 5% of its workforce.

FRAUDS, STATUTE OF:

The following agreements cannot be proved except by writing, or by some note or memorandum thereof, subscribed by the party sought to be charged, or by his agent, or by secondary evidence of its contents: (a) an agreement that by its terms is not to be performed within a year from the making thereof; (b) a promise to answer for the debt, default or miscarriage of another; (c) an agreement made upon the consideration of marriage, other than a mutual promise to marry; (d) an agreement for the sale of goods, chattels, or things in action, at a price not less than 500 pesos, unless the buyer accepts and receives part of such goods and chattels; (e) an agreement for the leasing for a longer period than one year, or for the sale, of real property or of an interest therein; (f) a representation as to the credit of a third person.

FRAUDULENT SALES AND CONVEYANCES:

All contracts by virtue of which the debtor alienates property by gratuitous title are presumed to have been entered into in fraud of creditors, when the donor did not reserve sufficient property to pay all debts contracted before the donation. Alienations by onerous title are also presumed fraudulent when made by persons against whom some judgment has been rendered in any instance or some writ of attachment has been issued. The decision or attachment need not refer to the property alienated, and need not have been obtained by the party seeking the rescission. In addition to these presumptions, the design to defraud creditors may be proved in any other manner recognized by the law of evidence. Whoever acquires in bad faith the things alienated in fraud of creditors, must indemnify the latter for damages suffered by them on account of the alienation, whenever, due to any cause, it should be impossible for him to return them. If there are two or more alienations, the first acquirer first liable, and so on successively.

Contracts made in fraud of creditors when the latter cannot in any other manner collect the claims due them, are rescindable.

When there is a deficiency of assets in the hands of an executor or administrator for the payment of debts and expenses of administration, and it appears that the deceased in

FRAUDULENT SALES AND CONVEYANCES . . . *continued*
his lifetime had conveyed real or personal properties or a right or interest therein or a debt or credit with intent to defraud his creditors, or to avoid a right, debt, or duty of a person; or had so conveyed such property, right, interest, debt or credit, that by law conveyance would be void as against his creditors, and subject attempted to be conveyed would be liable to attachment or execution by a creditor of deceased in his lifetime, executor or administrator may prosecute to a final judgment an action for recovery of such real property, debt, credit, right or interest therein for benefit of creditors; and he may also, for like benefit, sue for and recover goods, chattels, right or credits fraudulently conveyed by deceased in his lifetime, with the intent stated; but no executor or administrator is bound to institute such proceedings unless creditors making the application pay such part of costs and expenses, or give security therefor to executor or administrator, as court judges equitable. (R.C. Rule 87, §9).

Bulk Sales.—The sale, transfer, mortgage or assignment of a stock of goods, wares, merchandise, provisions or materials otherwise than in the ordinary course of trade and the regular prosecution of the business, or of all or substantially all of the business or trade, or of all or substantially all of the fixtures and equipment used in and about the business of the vendor, mortgagor, transferor or assignor, is fraudulent and void as against existing creditors of the vendor, mortgagor, etc., unless the following conditions are complied with. At least ten days before the sale, transfer, etc., the vendor, mortgagor, etc., must furnish to the vendee, mortgagee, etc., a verified list of creditors and make a full detailed inventory of the property to be disposed of, giving cost price of each article. The said statement must be recorded with Bureau of Domestic Trade. Each creditor of vendor, mortgagor, etc., must be notified by mail of price, terms and conditions of sale, etc., and purchase money or mortgage money must be applied pro rata to payment of such creditors. Violation of bulk sales law is punishable by fine and imprisonment. Action to attack sale must be commenced within four years after discovery of fraud. (Act 3952).

GARNISHMENT:

Process in the nature of garnishment may be obtained by supplementary proceedings in aid of attachment or execution.

HOLIDAYS:

Thursday and Friday of Holy Week, Christmas Day and Sundays are legal religious holidays. The other legal holidays are: Jan. 1; Apr. 9; May 1; June 12; last Sun. of Aug.; Nov. 30; Dec. 30; and day appointed by law for holding general election. President may, in his discretion, proclaim any other day special public holiday.

When legal holiday falls on Sun., following Mon. shall not be holiday unless proclaimed special public holiday. (L.O.I. 1087). When the day, or the last day, for doing an act required or permitted by law falls on a holiday, the act may be done on the succeeding business day. (E.O. 292).

HUSBAND AND WIFE:

Husband and wife are obliged to live together, observe mutual love, respect and fidelity, and render mutual help and support. Husband and wife shall fix family domicile but in case of disagreement, court shall decide. Court may exempt one spouse from living with other if latter should live abroad or there are valid reasons for exemption. Exemption shall not apply if same is not compatible with solidarity of family.

Spouses are jointly responsible for support of family. Management of household shall be right and duty of both spouses. Either spouse may exercise any legitimate profession, occupation or business without consent of other. Latter may object only on valid and moral grounds.

Property Relations between husband and wife are governed in following order: (1) By marriage settlements executed before marriage; (2) by provisions of Family Code; and (3) by local custom. Future spouses may, in marriage settlements, agree upon regime of absolute community, conjugal partnership of gains, complete separation of property, or any other regime. In absence of marriage settlement, or when same is void, system of absolute community of property as established in Family Code shall govern.

In absence of contrary stipulation in marriage settlement, property relations of spouses shall be governed by Philippine laws, regardless of place of celebration of marriage and their residence except: (a) Where both spouses are aliens; (b) with respect to extrinsic validity of contracts affecting property not situated in Philippines and executed in country where property is located; and (c) with respect to extrinsic validity of contracts entered into Philippines but affecting property situated in foreign country whose laws require different formalities for its extrinsic validity.

If future spouses agree upon regime other than absolute community of property, they cannot donate to each other in their marriage settlement more than one-fifth of their present property. Donations of future property shall be governed by provisions on testamentary succession and formalities of wills. Every donation between spouses during marriage is void, except moderate gifts which spouses may give each other on occasion of family rejoicing. Prohibitions also apply to persons living together as husband and wife without valid marriage.

When man and woman who are capacitated to marry each other, live exclusively with each other as husband and wife without benefit of marriage or under void marriage, their wages and salaries shall be owned by them in equal shares and property acquired by both of them through their work or industry shall be governed by rules on co-ownership.

Spouse of age may mortgage, encumber, alienate or dispose of his or her exclusive property, without consent of other spouse, and appear alone in court to litigate with regard to same.

Administration and enjoyment of community of property shall belong to each other. In case of disagreement, husband's decision shall prevail subject to recourse to court by wife for proper remedy which must be availed of within five years from date of contract implementing such decision.

If one spouse is incapacitated, other spouse may assume sole powers of administration. These powers do not include disposition or encumbrance without authority of court or written consent of other spouse. Neither spouse may donate any community property without consent of other, however, either spouse may without consent of other, make moderate donations from community property for charity or on occasion of family rejoicing or family distress. (E.O. 209).

IMMIGRATION:

It was mutually agreed by Republic of Philippines and U.S. on Mar. 14, 1947 that U.S. have the right to bring into Philippines members of U.S. military forces and U.S. nationals employed under a contract with U.S. together with their families, and technical personnel of other nationalities (not being persons excluded by laws of Philippines) in connection with the construction, maintenance, or operation of bases. U.S. must make suitable arrangements so that such persons may be readily identified and their status established when necessary by Philippine authorities. Such persons other than members of U.S. Armed Forces in uniform must present their travel documents to the appropriate Philippine authorities for visas, it being understood that no objection will be made to their travel to Philippines as non-immigrants.

It was also mutually agreed that if the status of any person within Philippines and admitted thereto under the foregoing paragraph must be altered so that he would no longer be entitled to such admission, U.S. must notify Philippines, and must, if such person be required to leave Philippines by the latter government, be responsible for providing him with a passage from Philippines within a reasonable time, and must in meantime prevent his becoming a public responsibility of Philippines.

An alien coming to prearranged employment for whom issuance of a visa has been authorized in accordance with law, may be admitted in Philippines as a non-immigrant. Foreign nationals under employment contracts within purview of P.D. 66, their spouses and unmarried children under 21 years of age, shall be permitted to enter and reside in Philippines during period of employment of such foreign nationals provided: (1) Such aliens shall not remain in Philippines beyond period of employment authorized by Export Processing Zone Authority; (2) while in Philippines, they shall not seek any change in their admission status to any other non-immigrant status without first departing from country; and (3) they shall be subject to payment of usual visa and immigration fees. (L.O.I. 63). Aliens who are now in Philippines as non-immigrants and whose applications for immigrant visas were approved by Immigration Commissioner shall be allowed to acquire permanent residence without necessity of their visas provided that National Intelligence Security Authority of Armed Forces of Philippines and Commissioner of Immigration & Deportation shall find them qualified for permanent residence. Such adjustment of status may be allowed provided: (1) Subjects were properly documented at time of entry; (2) make proper application for adjustment of status; (3) qualified for admission as immigrants and are admissible as such; and (4) corresponding immigrant quota numbers are immediately available to such applications at time application is approved. (P.D. 419).

An alien is entitled to enter Philippines under and in pursuance of provisions of a treaty of commerce and navigation (1) Solely to carry on substantial trade principally between Philippines and foreign state of which he is a national or (2) solely to develop and direct operations of an enterprise in which, in accordance with Constitution and laws of Philippines he has invested or of an enterprise in which he is actively in process of investing, a substantial amount of capital; and his wife, and his unmarried children under 21 years of age, if accompanying or following to join him, subject to condition that citizens of Philippines are accorded like privileges in foreign state of which such alien is a national. (R.A. 5171).

It is unlawful for any individual to bring into Philippines or employ any alien not duly admitted by any immigration officer. Dismissal by employer before or after apprehension does not relieve employer of offense. (C.A. 613, am'd by R.A. 5701).

INCOME TAX: See topic Taxation.

INFANTS:

Emancipation takes place by attainment of majority. Unless otherwise provided, majority commences at age 18. Emancipation terminates parental authority over person and property of child who shall then be qualified and responsible for all acts of civil life, save exceptions established by existing laws in special cases. Contracting marriage shall require parental consent until age 21. (E.O. 209, am'd R.A. 6809).

INHERITANCE TAX: See topic Taxation.

INSOLVENCY:

See topic Bankruptcy and Insolvency.

INSURANCE:

Insurance Law of Philippines is contained now in Insurance Code of 1978 (P.D. 612, am'd P.D. 1141, am'd P.D. 1455, am'd P.D. 1460) and Civil Code. Insurance Code was taken verbatim from law of California, and courts may follow in fundamental points, at least, construction placed by California courts on California law. But when not otherwise specifically provided for by Insurance Law, contract of insurance is governed by rules of civil law regarding contracts.

Insurance Commissioner shall execute all laws relating to insurance, insurance companies and other insurance matters, mutual benefit associations, and trusts for charitable uses and have exclusive authority to regulate issuance and sale of variable contracts and to provide for licensing of persons selling such contracts, and to issue rules and regulations governing same. Any decision made may be appealed, unless otherwise specified, to Secretary of Finance. Insurance Commissioner shall have power to adjudicate claims and complaints involving any loss or liability for which insurer may be answerable under any kind of policy or contract of insurance, or contract of suretyship, or for which reinsurer may be sued under any contract of reinsurance it may have entered into, or for which mutual benefit association may be held liable under membership certificates it has issued to its members, where amount of any such loss or liability sued upon does not exceed ₱100,000 in any single claim, and any decision rendered shall have force of judgment.

No insurance company shall be authorized to transact in Philippines business of life and non-life insurance concurrently, unless specifically authorized to do so, provided that terms "life" and "non-life" insurance shall be deemed to include health, accident and disability insurance.

See Topical Index in front part of this volume.

INSURANCE . . . *continued*

Policy Provisions.—Life or endowment policy is required to contain, among others, a provision that policy shall be incontestable after it shall have been in force during lifetime of insured for period of two years from its date of issue or date of approval of last reinstatement, except for nonpayment of premiums and except for violation of conditions of policy relating to military or naval service in time of war, and except as to provisions relating to benefits in event of disability as defined in policy, and those granting additional insurance specifically against death by accident or by accidental means, as to additional insurance against loss of, or loss of use of, specific members of body.

Foreign Insurance Companies.—The Insurance Commission must require as a condition precedent to the transaction of insurance business in the Philippine Republic by any foreign insurance company, that such company file in his office a written power of attorney designating some person who shall be a resident of the Philippine Islands as its general agent, on whom any notice provided by law or by any insurance policy, proof of loss, summons and other process may be served in all actions or other legal proceedings against such company, and consenting that service upon such general agent shall be admitted and held as valid as if served upon the foreign company at its home office.

No foreign insurance company may engage in business in the Philippines unless possessed of paid-up unimpaired capital or assets and reserve not less than that required of domestic insurance companies; and no insurance company organized or existing under the government or laws other than those of the Philippines may engage in business in the Philippines until it has deposited with Insurance Commission, for benefit and security of its policy holders and creditors in Philippines, securities which are satisfactory to Insurance Commission, consisting of good securities of Philippines, including new issues of stocks of registered enterprises as this term is defined in R.A. 5186, to actual value of not less than minimum paid-up capital required of domestic insurance companies, provided at least 50% of such securities shall consist of bonds or other evidences of debt of Government of Philippines, its political subdivisions and instrumentalities, or of government-owned or controlled corporations and entities, including Central Bank. Total investment of a foreign insurance company in any registered enterprise shall not exceed 20% of net worth of said foreign insurance company nor 20% of capital of registered enterprise unless previously authorized in writing by Insurance Commissioner.

Tax on Receipts of Insurance Companies.—Every person, company, or corporation (except purely cooperative companies or associations) doing insurance business of any sort in Philippines is subject to a tax of 5% of total premiums collected, whether such premiums are paid in money, notes, credits, or any substitute for money. However, premiums refunded within six months after payment on account of rejection of risk or returned for other reason to person insured are not to be included in taxable receipts; nor is any tax required to be paid upon reinsurance by a company that has already paid tax, or upon premiums collected or received by any branch of a domestic corporation, firm or association doing business outside Philippines on account of any life insurance of insured who is a nonresident, if any percentage tax on such premiums is imposed by foreign country where branch is established nor upon premiums collected or received on account of any reinsurance, if risk insured against covers property located outside Philippines, or insured, in case of personal insurance, resides outside Philippines, if any percentage tax on such premiums is imposed by foreign country where original insurance has been issued or perfected; nor upon that portion of premiums received by insurance companies on variable contracts (§232[2] of P.D. 612) in excess of amount necessary to insure lives of variable contract owners (C.A. 466, am'd R.A. 6110, am'd P.D. 739, am'd P.D. 1994). Quarterly return of amount of gross sales, receipts and earnings shall be filed and tax due paid within 20 days after end of each taxable quarter. Agents for foreign companies not authorized to do business in Philippines are subject to double aforesaid tax, payable at same time and subject to same penalty for delinquency. Property owners who obtain insurance direct from foreign companies are subject to tax of 5% on premiums paid, and are subject to same penalty as insurance companies for failure to pay tax.

Tax on Life Insurance Companies.—Domestic life insurance companies and foreign life insurance companies doing business in the Philippines are no longer subject to normal corporate income tax. They are, however, subject to a 10% tax on investment income received from interest, dividends and rents from all sources, whether from or without the Philippines. Determination of total net investment income is provided for. Foreign life insurance companies not doing business in the Philippines are subject to tax as any other foreign corporation on any investment income received from the Philippines. (E.O. 37).

Stamp Tax on Insurance Policies.—See topic Taxation, subhead Documentary Stamp Taxes.

INTEREST:

Effective Jan. 1, 1983, Monetary Board of Central Bank suspended ceiling of interest rates that may be charged or collected on loans or forbearance of money, goods or credit. Rate of interest for loan or forbearance of money, goods or credits and rate allowed in judgments, in absence of contract as to such rate of interest, shall be 12% per annum. Rate of interest including commissions, premiums, fees and other charges on any loan or forbearance of money extended by pawnshop, pawnbroker or pawnbroker's agent, regardless of maturity, shall not be subject to any ceiling prescribed under Usury Law. (Central Bank Cir. 905).

Compound interest cannot be allowed except by agreement. Interest cannot be required to be paid in advance for more than one year.

Receipt of principal by creditor, without reservation with respect to interest, gives rise to presumption that interest has been paid. When judgment of court below is affirmed, legal interest is added to original judgment from date of former judgment until date of final judgment.

Usury.—Covenants and stipulations for higher rates of interest than are allowed by law are void, and usurers are subject to criminal prosecution.

INVESTMENTS AND INCENTIVES:

See topic Foreign Investments and Incentives.

JOINT STOCK COMPANIES: No legislation.

JUDGMENTS:

All judgments determining the merits of cases shall be in writing personally and directly prepared by the judge, and signed by him, stating clearly and distinctly the facts and the law on which it is based, and filed with the clerk of the court. Judgment by municipal or city judge need not contain findings of fact or conclusions of law.

Except in case of default judgment (see subhead Default Judgments, infra) judgment shall grant relief to which party in whose favor it is rendered is entitled, even if party has not demanded such relief in his pleadings.

Default Judgments.—If the defendant fails to answer within the time specified in the Rules of Court, the court shall, upon motion of the plaintiff, order judgment against the defendant by default, and thereupon the court shall proceed to receive the plaintiff's evidence and render judgment granting him such relief as the complaint and the facts proven may warrant. This provision applies where no answer is made, within the prescribed period to a counterclaim, cross claim, or third-party complaint. A judgment entered by default shall not exceed the amount or be different in kind from that prayed for in the demand for judgment.

Judgment on the Pleadings.—Where an answer fails to tender an issue, or otherwise admits the material allegations of the adverse party's pleading, the court may, on motion of that party, direct judgment on such pleading, except in actions for annulment of marriage or legal separation wherein material facts alleged in complaint must always be proved.

Foreign judgments have following effects: (1) in case of a judgment against a specific thing, it is conclusive upon title to thing; and (2) in case of a judgment against a person, it is presumptive evidence of a right as between parties and their successors in interest by subsequent title; but judgment may be repelled by evidence of a want of jurisdiction, want of notice to party, collusion, fraud, or clear mistake of law or fact.

LABOR RELATIONS:

National Labor Relations Commission shall be attached to Dept. of Labor & Employment for program and policy coordination only. It shall be composed of Chairman and 14 Commissioners. Commission shall have exclusive appellate jurisdiction over all cases decided by Labor Arbiters.

Labor arbiters exercise exclusive jurisdiction in: (1) Unfair labor practice cases; (2) termination disputes; (3) if accompanied with claim for reinstatement, those cases that workers may file involving wages, rates of pay, hours of work and other terms and conditions of employment; (4) claims for actual, moral, exemplary and other forms of damages arising from employer-employee relations; (5) cases arising from any violation of Art. 264 of Labor Code regarding prohibited activities, including questions involving legality of strikes and lockouts; and (6) except claims for employees compensation, social security, medicare and maternity benefits, all other claims arising from employer-employee relations, including those of persons in domestic or household service, involving amount exceeding ₱5,000, whether or not accompanied with claim for reinstatement. (R.A. 6715).

Hours of Labor.—Legal working hours for any employee in all establishments, whether for profit or not (except government employees, managerial employees, field personnel, members of family of employer who are dependent on him for support, domestics, person in personal service of another, and workers who are paid by results) shall not exceed eight in a day.

Any employee may be required by employer to perform overtime work in any of following cases: (1) When country is at war or when any other national or local emergency has been declared; (2) when it is necessary to prevent loss of life or property or in case of imminent danger to public safety due to actual or impending emergency; (3) when there is urgent work to be performed on machines to avoid serious loss or damage to employer; (4) when work is necessary to prevent loss or damage to perishable goods; and (5) where completion of work started before eighth hour is necessary to prevent serious obstruction to business of employer. Any employee required to render overtime work shall be paid additional compensation. (P.D. 850).

Weekly Rest Period.—Every employer shall give his employees a rest period of not less than 24 consecutive hours after every six consecutive normal workdays. (P.D. 850). Employer shall schedule weekly rest day of his employees, subject to collective bargaining agreement and to such rules and regulations as Secretary of Labor & Employment may prescribe, provided that preference of employee to his weekly rest day shall be respected by employer if same is based on religious grounds.

In case of force majeure, public emergencies, serious accidents and other exceptional cases as determined by Secretary of Labor & Employment, any employee may be required to work on his scheduled rest day even if it falls on Sun. or holiday, provided he is paid additional compensation of at least 30% of his regular wage. Where employees do not have regular working days by reason of nature of their work, they shall be entitled to additional compensation of at least 30% of their regular wage for work performed on Sundays and holidays. However, higher premium pay than that prescribed shall be paid by employer if stipulated in collective bargaining or other applicable employment contract. (P.D. 442).

Wages.—Effective May 1, 1996, all nonagricultural workers in Metro Manila shall receive minimum wage of ₱165 a day while for nonagricultural workers outside Metro Manila, wage rate varies from region to region. For all plantation agricultural workers, wage rate is ₱155 a day while non-plantation agricultural workers, ₱144.50 a day. For workers employed by export-oriented registered cottage and handicraft industry enterprises employing not more than 30 workers, wage rate is ₱151 a day for workers in Metro Manila and outside Metro Manila while for workers employed in cottage and handicraft industry enterprises employing more than 30 workers, wage rate is ₱153 a day for workers in Metro Manila and outside Metro Manila. In Metro Manila, for those employed by retail or service establishments regularly employing not more than ten workers, wage rate is ₱144 a day; for those regularly employing 11 to 15 workers,

LABOR RELATIONS . . . *continued*
wage rate is ₱161 a day and for those regularly employing more than 15 workers, wage rate is ₱165 a day. (R.A. 6727, am'd WO-NCR-1, 1-A, am'd WO-NCR-2 am'd WO-NCR-03, am'd WO-NCR-04).

Wages must be paid in legal tender, and it is unlawful to pay such wages in form of promissory notes, vouchers, coupons, tokens or any other form alleged as legal tender. Action to enforce any claim must be brought within three years, or else it is barred.

Employers are required to pay all their rank-and-file employees 13th month pay not later than Dec. 24 of every year. (Memo. Order 28).

Child Labor.—No child below 15 years shall be employed except when he works directly under sole responsibility of his parents or guardian and his employment does not in any way interfere with his schooling. Person between 15 and 18 years may be employed for such number of hours and such periods of day as determined by Secretary of Labor & Employment; however, employment of person below 18 years in undertaking which is hazardous or deleterious in nature shall not be allowed. No employer shall discriminate against any person in respect to terms and conditions of employment on account of his age. (P.D. 850).

Children below 15 years of age may however be employed in following instances: (1) When child works directly under sole responsibility of his parents or legal guardian and only members of employer's family are employed and his employment neither endangers his life, safety, health and morals, nor impairs his normal development; or (2) child's employment in public entertainment through cinema, theater, radio or television is essential but such employment contract must be concluded by child's parents or legal guardian with express agreement of child and approved by Department of Labor and Employment. In all these instances, following requirements should be complied with: (1) employer shall secure work permit from Department of Labor and Employment; (2) employer shall ensure protection, health, safety and morals of child; (3) employer shall institute measures to prevent exploitation or discrimination taking into account system and level of remuneration, and duration and arrangement of working time; and (4) employer shall formulate and implement continuous program for training and skill acquisition of child.

Employment of child models in all commercial or advertisements promoting alcoholic beverags, intoxicating drinks, tobacco and its byproducts and violence is prohibited. (R.A. 7610 as am'd by R.A. 7658).

Female Labor.—No woman, regardless of age, shall be employed, with or without compensation: (1) In any industrial undertaking between ten o'clock at night and six o'clock in morning of following day; (2) in any commercial or non-industrial undertaking other than agricultural between midnight and six o'clock in morning of following day; and (3) in any agricultural undertaking at night time unless she is given rest period of not less than nine consecutive hours. These prohibitions shall not apply: (1) In cases of actual or impending emergencies to prevent loss of life or property or in case of force majeure; (2) in case of urgent work to be performed on machineries to avoid serious loss which employer would otherwise suffer; (3) where work is necessary to prevent serious loss of perishable goods; (4) where employee holds responsible position of managerial or technical nature; (5) where nature of work requires manual skill of female workers and same cannot be performed with equal efficiency by male workers; (6) where women employees are immediate members of family operating establishment; and (7) under other analogous cases.

To insure safety and health of women employees, in appropriate cases, employer shall be required to: (1) Provide seats proper for women and permit them to use such seats when they are free from work and during working hours; (2) establish separate toilet rooms for men and women; (3) establish nursery in workplace; and (4) determine appropriate minimum age and other standards for retirement in special occupations.

No employer shall discriminate against any woman with respect to terms and conditions of employment on account of her sex. It shall be unlawful for employer to require as condition of employment or for continuation of employment that woman employee shall not get married or to stipulate that upon getting married woman employee shall be deemed resigned or separated, or to actually dismiss or discriminate against woman employee by reason of her marriage. (P.D. 850).

See topic Social Security, Subhead Benefits, catchline Maternity Leave Benefits.

Labor Organizations.—All persons employed in commercial, industrial, and agricultural enterprises, including religious, charitable, medical or educational institutions whether operating for profit or not, have right to self-organization and to form, join or assist labor organizations for purposes of collective bargaining. Exempted from joining are: (1) government employees; (2) managerial employees; and (3) employees of religious, charitable, medical or educational institutions not operating for profit provided latter do not have existing collective bargaining agreements. Security guards are now eligible for membership in any labor organization. (Philips Industrial Dev't. v. NLRC, 210 SCRA 339). Labor organization must be registered with Dept. of Labor & Employment to be legitimate labor organization entitled to: (1) Act as representative of its members for purpose of collective bargaining; (2) be certified as exclusive representative of employees; (3) own property, real or personal, for use and benefit of labor organizations; (4) sue and be sued in its registered name; (5) undertake activities for benefit of organization and its members, including cooperative, housing welfare and other projects not contrary to law; and (6) to be furnished by employer, upon written request, with his annual audited financial statements, including balance sheet and profit and loss statement, within 30 days from date of receipt of request, after union has been duly recognized by employer or certified as sole and exclusive bargaining representative of employees in bargaining unit, or within 60 days before expiration of existing collective bargaining agreement, or during collective bargaining negotiation. (R.A. 6715).

In organized establishments, when verified petition questioning majority status of incumbent bargaining agent is filed within 60 day period before expiration of collective bargaining agreement, Med-Arbiter shall automatically order election by secret ballot when verified petition is supported by written consent of at least 25% of all employees in bargaining unit to ascertain will of employees in appropriate baraining unit. To have valid election, at least majority of all eligible voters in unit must have cast their votes. Labor union receiving majority of valid votes cast shall be certified as exclusive bargaining agent of all workers in unit. In any establishment where there is no certified bargaining agent, certification election shall automatically be conducted by Med-Arbiter upon filing of petition by legitimate labor organization. (RA 6715).

Unfair Labor Practices.—It is unfair labor practice for employer: (1) To interfere with, restrain or coerce employees in their right of self-organization; (2) to require as condition of employment that person or employee must not join labor organization or withdraw from one; (3) to contract out services or functions being performed by union members when such will interfere with, restrain or coerce employees in their right of self-organization; (4) to initiate, dominate, assist or interfere with formation or administration of any labor organization; (5) to discriminate in regard to hire or tenure of employment or any term or condition of employment to encourage or discourage membership in any labor organization, unless there is closed shop agreement; (6) to dismiss or otherwise prejudice against employee for having given or being about to give testimony under Labor Code; (7) to violate duty to bargain collectively; (8) to pay negotiations or attorney's fees to union or its officers as part of settlement of any issue in collective bargaining; (9) to violate collective bargaining agreement. Only officers and agents of corporations, associations or partnerships who have actually participated in, authorized or ratified unfair labor practices shall be held criminally liable.

It is unfair labor practice for labor organization: (1) To restrain or coerce employees in their right of self-organization; (2) to cause or attempt to cause employer to discriminate against employee; (3) to violate duty, or refuse to bargain collectively with employer; (4) to cause or attempt to cause employer to pay or agree to pay money or other things of value, in nature of exaction for services not performed; (5) to ask for or accept negotiations or attorney's fees from employers as part of settlement of issue in collective bargaining; (6) to violate collective bargaining agreement. (P.D. 442). Only officers or agents or members of labor associations or organizations who have actually participated in, authorized or ratified unfair labor practices shall be held criminally liable. (B.P. 130).

Strikes, Picketing and Lockouts.—State encourages free trade unionism and free collective bargaining. Workers shall have right to engage in concerted activities for collective bargaining. Right of legitimate labor organizations to strike and picket and of employers to lockout, consistent with national interest, shall continue to be recognized provided that no labor union may strike and no employer may declare lockout on grounds involving inter-union and intra-union disputes.

In cases of bargaining deadlocks, certified bargaining representative may file notice of strike or employer may file notice of lockout with Dept. of Labor and Employment 30 days before intended date thereof. In cases of unfair labor practices, notice shall be 15 days and in absence of certified bargaining representative, notice of strike may be filed by any legitimate labor organization in behalf of its members. In case of dismissal from employment of union officers duly elected, which may constitute union busting where existence of union is threatened, 15-day cooling-off period shall not apply and union may take action immediately. Decision to declare strike must be approved by majority of total union membership in bargaining unit concerned while decision to declare lockout must be approved by majority of board of directors of corporation or association or of partners in partnership. (E.O. 111). In labor disputes causing or likely to cause strikes or lockouts adversely affecting national interest, Sec. of Labor and Employment may assume jurisdiction over dispute and certify same for compulsory arbitration. Such certification shall automatically enjoin intended or impending strike or lockout. President of Philippines, however, shall have authority to intervene at any time and exercise jurisdiction over any labor dispute affecting national interest in order to settle or terminate same. Before or at any stage of compulsory arbitration process, parties may opt to submit their dispute to voluntary arbitration. Secretary of Labor and Employment, National Labor Relations Commission or voluntary arbitrator shall decide dispute within 30 calendar days from assumption of jurisdiction or certification of dispute, which decision shall be final and immediately executory ten calendar days after receipt by parties. (RA 6715). Assumption of jurisdiction by President or Secretary of Labor and Employment and certification of dispute to National Labor Relations Commission shall be immediately executory unless restrained by proper authorities. (L.O.I. 1458).

National Health Insurance Act of 1995.—(R.A. 7875). National Health Insurance Program shall provide health insurance coverage and ensure affordable and accessible health care services for all Filipino citizens. Program includes sustainable system of fund collection, management and disbursements for financing availability of basic minimum package and other supplementary packages of health insurance benefits to progressively expanding proportion of population. It is limited to paying for utilization of health services by covered beneficiaries or to purchasing health services in behalf of such beneficiaries. It is prohibited from: (1) Directly providing health care services; (2) buying and dispensing drugs and pharmaceuticals; (3) employing physicians and other professionals for purposes of directly rendering health care; and (4) owning or investing in health care facilities.

Beneficiaries must be enrolled in program to entitle them to benefits and services provided by law. Following are considered enrolled in program: (1) All persons currently eligible for benefits under Medicare Program I, including SSS and GSIS members, retirees, pensioners and their dependents; (2) all persons eligible for benefits through health insurance plans established by local governments; (3) all persons eligible for benefits as members of local health insurance plans established by Philippine Health Insurance Corporation; and (4) all persons eligible for benefits as members of other government initiated health insurance programs.

Member whose premium contributions for at least three months have been paid within six months prior to first day of his or his dependents' availment shall be entitled to benefits of program.

Employees' Compensation and State Insurance Fund provides for tax-exempt employees' compensation program whereby employees and their dependents, in case of work-connected injury or death, may promptly secure adequate income and medical benefits.

Coverage is compulsory for all employers and their employees who are subject to coverage by Social Security System provided that in case of employee who is both covered by Social Security System and Government Service Insurance System, only his employment with latter shall be considered for purposes of his coverage. Coverage also extends to Philippine citizens employed abroad. All employers and their employees already registered with Social Security System shall not be registered again because they are automatically registered for coverage under Employees' Compensation.

See Topical Index in front part of this volume.

LABOR RELATIONS . . . *continued*

State Insurance Fund shall be liable for compensation to employee or his dependents except when disability or death was occasioned by employee's intoxication, willful intention to injure or kill himself or another and notorious negligence.

Contributions.—Initial monthly contribution of 1% of monthly salary credit to be paid by employers, which started Jan. 1975 and every month thereafter.

When covered employee dies, becomes disabled or separated from employment, his employer's contribution to pay monthly contributions shall cease at end of month of contingency and during such months that he is not receiving wages or salary.

Benefits.—

Medical Benefits.—Immediately after employee contracts sickness or sustains injury, he shall be provided by Social Security System during period of disability with such medical services and appliances as nature of his sickness or injury may require, subject to expense limitation prescribed by Employees' Compensation Commission.

Disability Benefits.—Any employee who sustains temporary total disability shall be paid by Social Security System cash benefit equivalent to 90% of his average daily salary credit, but not less than ₱10 nor more than ₱90 a day for continuous period not longer than 120 days. Payment of benefit shall bar recovery of sickness benefit under Social Security System for same sickness, injury or disability.

Any employee who contracts sickness or sustains injury resulting in permanent total disability shall for each month until his death, be paid by Social Security System during such disability, amount equivalent to monthly income benefit plus 10% thereof for each dependent child, but not exceeding five, beginning with youngest and without substitution provided that monthly income benefit shall be new amount of monthly benefit for all covered pensioners. Monthly income benefit shall be guaranteed for five years and shall be suspended if employee is gainfully employed or recovers from his permanent total disability, or fails to present himself for examination at least once a year upon notice by Social Security System.

Any employee who contracts sickness or sustains injury resulting in permanent partial disability shall for each month not exceeding period designated herein be paid by Social Security System during such disability income benefit equivalent to income benefit for permanent total disability.

Death Benefits.—Upon covered employee's death, his primary beneficiaries shall be paid amount equivalent to covered employee's monthly income benefit plus 10% thereof for each dependent child but not exceeding five, beginning with youngest and without substitution provided that monthly income benefit shall be guaranteed for five years. In absence of primary beneficiaries, his secondary beneficiaries shall be paid lump sum benefit equivalent to 60 times monthly income benefit. (P.D. 1368). Minimum death benefit shall not be less than ₱15,000. (P.D. 1692, am'd P.D. 1921).

Notice of Separation.—A contract of employment without a definite period may be terminated by employee by serving a written notice on employer at least one month in advance, or by employer by serving such notice to employee at least one month in advance or within a period equivalent to one-half month for every year of service, whichever is longer. If no notice is served, payment of an amount equivalent to employee's salary corresponding to required period of notice is sufficient.

Domestics.—House helpers cannot be required to work more than ten hours a day and are entitled to four days vacation each month with pay. If a domestic is unjustly dismissed, he must be paid salary earned plus that for 15 days by way of indemnity. If he leaves without justifiable reason, he forfeits any unpaid salary due him for not exceeding 15 days. Monthly minimum compensation for house helpers shall be (1) ₱800 in Manila, Quezon City, Pasay City, Caloocan City, Mandaluyong City, and municipalities of Makati, San Juan, Malabon, Navotas, Muntinglupa, Paranaque, Las Pinas, Pasig, Marikina, Valenzuela, Taguig and Pateros in Metro Manila and in highly urbanized cities; (2) ₱650 in other chartered cities and first class municipalities; and (3) ₱550 in other municipalities. Househelpers who are receiving at least ₱1,000 shall be covered by Social Security System (SSS) and be entitled to all benefits provided, thereunder. (R.A. 7655). Employer must furnish, free of charge to a domestic, suitable and sanitary quarters, as well as adequate food and medical attendance. Upon extinguishment of service, domestic may demand from employer written statements of nature and duration of services and efficiency and conduct of house helper.

See also topic Social Security.

LANDLORD AND TENANT:

Every lease of real estate may be recorded in the Registry of Property. Unless a lease is recorded, it is not binding upon third persons. Leases for one year or longer must be in writing under Statutes of Frauds. But where a contract made between owner of land and a lessee or tenant on share thereof has not been reduced to writing, or has not been set forth in a document written in a language known to lessee or tenant, the testimony of such lessee or tenant shall be accepted as prima facie evidence of the terms of a covenant or contract.

The lessee cannot assign the lease without the consent of the lessor, unless there is a stipulation to the contrary. When in the contract of lease of things there is no express prohibition, the lessee may sublet the thing leased, in whole or in part, without prejudice to his responsibility for the performance of the contract toward the lessor. The lessee may suspend the payment of the rent in case the lessor fails to make the necessary repairs or to maintain the lessee in peaceful and adequate enjoyment of the property leased.

If the lease was made for a determinate time, it ceases upon the day fixed, without the need of a demand. If at the end of the contract the lessee should continue enjoying the thing leased for 15 days with the acquiescence of the lessor, and unless notice to the contrary by either party has previously been given, it is understood that there is an implied new lease. If the lessee continues enjoying the thing after the expiration of the contract, over the lessor's objection, the former is subject to the responsibilities of a possessor in bad faith.

If the period for the lease has not been fixed, it is understood to be from year to year, if the rent agreed upon is annual; from month to month, if it is monthly; from week to week, if the rent is weekly; and from day to day, if the rent is to be paid daily. However, even though a monthly rent is paid, and no period for the lease has been set, the courts may fix a longer term for the lease after the lessee has occupied the premises for over one year. If the rent is weekly, the courts may likewise determine a longer period after the lessee has been in possession for over six months. In case of daily rent, the courts may also fix a longer period after the lessee has stayed in the place for over one month. Beginning Jan. 1, 1993 to Dec. 31, 1997, monthly rentals of all residential units not exceeding ₱480 shall not be increased by lessor by not more than 20% for first year; not more than 20% for second year; not more than 20% for third year; not more than 20% for fourth year; and not more than 20% for fifth year. Increases shall be cumulative and compounded. Rental shall be paid in advance within first five days of every current month or beginning of lease agreement unless contract of lease provides for later date of payment. Lessor cannot demand any advance rental but may ask for deposit not to exceed one month rental. (R.A. 7644). When lessor of house, or part thereof, used as dwelling for family, or when lessor of store, or industrial establishment, also leases furniture, lease of latter is deemed to be for duration of lease of premises.

The lease of a piece of rural land, when its duration has not been fixed, is understood to have been made for all the time necessary for the gathering of the fruits which the whole estate leased may yield in one year, or which it may yield once, although two or more years may have to elapse for the purpose.

Maximum period allowable for duration of leases of private lands to aliens or alien-owned corporations, associations or entities not qualified to acquire private lands in Philippines shall be 25 years, renewable for another 25 years upon mutual agreement of both lessor and lessee. (P.D. 471). However, foreign investors investing in Philippines shall be allowed to lease private lands for period not exceeding 50 years and renewable once for period not exceeding 25 years. (R.A. 7652).

Land tenancy on shares is governed by special laws, the stipulations of the parties, the provisions of partnership and by the customs of the place. The tenant on shares cannot be ejected except in cases specified by law.

If the lessee makes, in good faith, useful improvements which are suitable to the use for which the lease is intended, without altering the form or substance of the property leased, the lessor upon the termination of the lease must pay the lessee one-half of the value of the improvements at that time. Should the lessor refuse to reimburse said amount, the lessee may remove the improvements, even though the principal thing may suffer damage thereby. He may not, however, cause any more impairment upon the property leased than is necessary. With regard to ornamental expenses, the lessee is not entitled to any reimbursement, but he may remove the ornamental objects, provided no damage is caused to the principal thing, and the lessor does not choose to retain them by paying their value at the time the lease is extinguished. The lessor may judicially eject the lessee for any of the following causes: (1) When the period agreed upon, or the period fixed by the court, has expired; (2) lack of payment of the price stipulated; (3) violation of any of the conditions agreed upon in the contract; and (4) when the lessee devotes the thing leased to any use or service not stipulated. The ejectment of tenants of agricultural lands is governed by special laws.

LAW REPORTS, CODES, ETC.:

Following are law reports, codes, etc. of the Philippines: Lawyers Journal, Civil Code, Code of Commerce, Rules of Court, National Internal Revenue Code, Decision Law Journal, Land Reform Code, Revised Administrative Code, Revised Penal Code, Philippine Tax Journal, Official Gazette, Philippine Reports.

See also topics Reports; Statutes.

LEGISLATURE:

Legislative power is vested in Congress of Philippines which consists of Senate of 24 members elected at large and House of Representatives of not more than 250 members elected by qualified electors of districts into which country is divided. (§§1, 2, 5, Art. VI, Constitution).

Congress convenes once every year on fourth Mon. of July for its regular session, unless different date is fixed by law, and shall continue to be in session until 30 days before opening of its next regular session, exclusive of Sats., Suns., and legal holidays. President may call special session at any time. (§14, ibid).

LICENSES:

See topic Corporations, subhead Foreign Corporations; see also topic Aliens, subhead Corporations Owned or Controlled by Aliens.

LIENS:

There is no statute creating mechanics' liens in the Philippines. Under the Civil Code, those who furnish labor or materials for work undertaken by a contractor for a lump sum have no action against the owner except for the amount in which the latter is indebted to the contractor.

Any person who has done work on personal property is entitled to retain the same as a pledge until he is paid.

LIMITATION OF ACTIONS:

Actions to recover movables prescribe eight years from the time the possession thereof is lost, unless the possessor has acquired the ownership by prescription for a less period.

Real actions over immovables prescribe after 30 years. This provision is without prejudice to what is established for the acquisition of ownership and other real rights by prescription.

A mortgage action prescribes after ten years.

The following rights are not extinguished by prescription: (1) to demand a right of way; (2) to bring an action to abate a public or private nuisance.

The following actions must be brought within ten years from the time the right of action accrues: (1) upon a written contract; (2) upon an obligation created by law; (3) upon a judgment.

The following actions must be commenced within six years: (1) upon an oral contract; (2) upon a quasi-contract.

The following actions must be instituted within four years: (1) upon an injury to the rights of the plaintiff; (2) upon a quasi-delict.

The following actions must be filed within one year: (1) for forcible entry and detainer; (2) for defamation.

All money claims arising from employer-employee relations prescribe in three years.

LIMITATION OF ACTIONS . . . *continued*

The foregoing limitations are without prejudice to those specified in the Civil Code, in the Code of Commerce, and in special laws.

All other actions whose periods are not fixed in the Civil Code or in other laws must be brought within five years from the time the right of action accrues.

The time for prescription for all kinds of actions, when there is no special provision which ordains otherwise, must be counted from the day they may be brought. The time for prescription of actions which have for their object the enforcement of obligations to pay principal with interest or an annuity runs from the last payment of the interest or of the annuity.

The period for prescription of actions to demand the fulfillment of obligations declared by a judgment commences from the time the judgment became final. The period for prescription of actions to demand an accounting runs from the day the persons who should render the same cease in their functions. The period for the action arising from the result of the accounting runs from the date said result was recognized by agreement of the interested parties.

The period during which the obligee was prevented by a fortuitous event from enforcing his right is not reckoned against him.

The prescription of actions is interrupted when they are filed before the court, when there is a written extrajudicial demand by the creditors, or when there is any written acknowledgment of the debt by the debtor.

The war years and the period when the debt moratorium was enforced have been held to suspend running of period of limitations.

See also topic Death, subhead Actions for Death.

LIMITED PARTNERSHIP:

See topic Partnership.

MARRIAGE:

Marriage Law is found in Title I of Family Code (E.O. 209, am'd by E.O. 227), and in those provisions of Act 3613, as am'd, which have not been abrogated or repealed by Civil Code and Family Code.

Age of Consent.—Any male or female, 18 years of age or upwards, not under any of impediments in incestuous and void marriages from beginning and marriages void from beginning by reasons of public policy, may contract marriage. In case either or both of contracting parties, not having been emancipated by previous marriage, are between ages of 18 and 21, written consent of parent or guardian is necessary. When any contracting party is between age of 21 and 25, parental or guardian advice is necessary. Without such advice or if same is unfavorable, marriage license shall not be issued until after three months following completion of publication of application.

License is required, and on application therefor ten days notice must be given by local civil registrar before he will issue license, except in case of marriages in articulo mortis or at remote places. Marriages among Muslim or among members of ethnic cultural communities may be performed validly without marriage license provided they are solemnized in accordance with their customs or practices. Also, no license shall be necessary for marriage of man and woman who lived together as husband and wife for at least five years and without any legal impediment to marry each other. There are also exceptions in cases of foreigners and officers of U.S. Army or Navy, and where church requires banns, in which cases ten days notice is not required for issuance of license.

Ceremonial Marriage.—Marriages may be solemnized by: (1) Any incumbent member of judiciary within court's jurisdiction; (2) any priest, rabbi, imam, or minister of any church or religious sect duly authorized by his church or religious sect and registered with civil registrar general; (3) any ship captain or airplane chief in marriages in articulo mortis; (4) any military commander of unit to which chaplain is assigned, in absence of latter, during military operation; or (5) any consul-general, consul or vice-consul in marriages between Filipinos abroad. City and municipal mayors are now likewise authorized to solemnize marriage. (§§444 & 455, RA 7160).

Marriages shall be solemnized publicly in chambers of judge or in open court, in church, chapel or temple or in office of consul-general, consul or vice-consul except in cases of marriages contracted in point of death or in remote places in accordance with Art. 29 of Family Code, or where both parties request solemnizing officer in writing in which case marriage may be solemnized at house or place designated by them in sworn statement to that effect.

Marriage Certificate.—Person solemnizing marriage ceremony must issue certificate of marriage, in quadruplicate signed by contracting parties and attested by them, original copy to be given to contracting parties, duplicate and triplicate copies to be filed with local civil registrar where ceremony is performed, and quadruplicate copy to be retained by solemnizing officer. (Art. 23, E.O. 209).

When either or both contracting parties are citizens of foreign country, it shall be necessary for them before marriage license can be obtained, to submit certificate of legal capacity to contract marriage, issued by their respective diplomatic or consular officials. Stateless persons or refugees from other countries shall, in lieu of certificate of legal capacity, submit affidavit stating circumstances showing such capacity to contract marriage.

Marriages solemnized abroad, if valid in country where celebrated, are also valid in Philippines, except if: either or both parties did not have legal capacity to get married; marriage is immoral for being bigamous or polygamous; consent of one party is lacking because of mistake as to identity of other; one of parties at time of marriage was psychologically incapacitated to comply with essential marital obligations; marriage is incestuous; or marriage is void by reason of public policy.

Where citizen of Philippines is married to foreigner and latter thereafter obtains valid divorce abroad capacitating him or her to remarry, citizen of Philippines shall likewise have capacity to remarry under Philippine law.

Common law marriages are not recognized.

Annulment.—A marriage may be annulled upon various statutory grounds set forth in the Family Code.

MINES AND MINERALS:

All minerals, coal, petroleum and other mineral oils belong to State, and their disposition, exploration, development, exploitation or utilization is limited to Filipino citizens, or to corporations or associations at least 60% of capital of which is owned by Filipino citizens. Congress may, by law, allow small-scale utilization of natural resources by Filipino citizens. President may enter into agreements with foreign-owned corporations involving either technical or financial assistance for large-scale exploration, development, and utilization of minerals, petroleum, and other mineral oils according to general terms and conditions provided by law, based on real contributions to economic growth and general welfare of country. In such agreements, State shall promote development and use of local scientific and technical resources. (§2, Art. XII, 1987 Constitution).

Mineral prospecting, location, exploration, development and exploitation are of public use and benefit, and for which power of eminent domain may be invoked for entry, acquisition and use of private lands provided that any person or entity acquiring any right on such land after first publication of notice of any mining lease covering such land shall not be entitled to compensation. Subject to prior notification, prospectors or claimants of mineral lands shall not be prevented from entry into private lands by surface owners and occupants when prospecting or exploring provided that any damage done to property of surface owner shall be properly compensated. (P.D. 512).

No prospecting and location shall be allowed in: (a) Military or other Government reservations except where authorized; (b) mineral reservations; (c) lands covered by valid mining claims located and leases acquired, under previous mining laws and in accordance with this Decree; and (d) near or under buildings, cemeteries, bridges, highways, waterways, railroads, reservoirs, dams or any other public or private works unless authorized. (P.D. 1385).

Claim owner/lessee shall perform annual work obligations on his mining claims, value of which shall be that as shall be provided in regulations. For mining claims registered under P.D. 1677, annual work obligations shall start from date of recording. Holders of mining claims who have filed lease applications under P.D. 1214 shall perform annual work obligations on mining claims from date of filing of said applications, value of which shall be that as shall be provided in regulations. Such rate of work obligations may be increased at any time by Government after three months notice.

Application for lease of mining claims shall be filed with Director of Mines & Geo-Sciences within two years from date of recording, otherwise failure to do so would constitute abandonment of mining claims. No application for lease of mining claims shall be accepted unless accompanied by application fee and following: (a) Report under oath of licensed mining engineer or geologist to effect that mining claim is mineralized; (b) proof of compliance with required annual work obligations; (c) if application is filed by applicant's agent, certified copy of power of attorney granted by applicant; (d) if area applied for is public land covered by concessions or rights other than mining, written notice to permittee thereof; or requirements under P.D. 512, in case area is private land; (e) program of work proposed to be undertaken on area applied for; (f) proof of availability of technical competence and financial resources sufficient to develop claim; and (g) other documents as may be provided in regulations. Application form shall state full name, address, citizenship, civil status of applicant, his place and date of birth. (P.D. 1677).

Maximum area of mining claims which may be leased shall be: (a) In any one province: (1) to individuals, 500 hectares; (2) to mining partnerships or corporations, 5,000 hectares; (b) in entire Philippines: (1) to individuals, 1,000 hectares; (2) mining partnerships or corporations, 10,000 hectares. However, Director of Mines & Geo-Sciences with approval of Secretary of Environment & Natural Resources, may allow applicant to lease larger area not exceeding 10,000 hectares in any one province, depending upon nature of deposit, kind of minerals located, and other circumstances inherent in operation of mining claim justifying grant.

Mining lease contract shall grant lessee, his heirs, successors and assigns right to extract all mineral deposits found on or underneath surface of his mining claims covered by lease; to remove, process and utilize mineral deposits for his own benefit; and to use lands covered by lease for purpose specified therein provided Secretary of Environment & Natural Resources shall reserve right to grant and use easements in, over, through, or upon said claims as may be needed by other claim owners or lessees for right of way to enable them to have access to and/or facilitate operation of their mining claims.

Lessees are obligated to give preference to Philippine citizens in all types of mining employment insofar as such citizens are qualified to perform work efficiently; and to maintain effective programs of training and advancement commensurate with abilities of such citizens to perform satisfactorily operations involved. Lessees, however, shall not be hindered from using employees of their own selection, subject to provisions of C.A. 613, as am'd, for technical and specialized work which in their judgment and with approval of Director of Mines & Geo-Sciences requires highly specialized training in exploration, development or exploitation of mining claim provided that in no case shall each employment exceed five years and that no foreigner shall be employed as mine manager, vice-president for operations or equivalent managerial position, in charge of mining, milling, quarrying or drilling operation without passing government licensing examination or unless in special cases permitted by Director of Mines & Geo-Sciences for period not exceeding three years. (P.D. 463, am'd by P.D. 1902).

Areas containing radioactive minerals such as uranium, thorium and other elements occurring singly or in association with other minerals from which radioactive power and substances may be generated are open to mining location, registration, exploration, development and exploitation, and those who have discovered radioactive minerals and registered same with Bureau of Mines & Geo-Sciences and verified by Director of Mines & Geo-Sciences to be existing in sufficiently exploitable quantity shall be entitled to bonus of not less than ₱10,000. (P.D. 1101).

Mining claims and rights and other matters concerning minerals and mineral lands are governed by special laws.

Department of Energy absorbed powers and functions of Office of Energy Affairs and Energy Coordinating Council. Under this department are bureaus and services, like Energy Development Bureau; Energy Utilization Management Bureau; Energy Industry Administration Bureau; Energy Planning and Monitoring Bureau and Administrative Support Services, involved in formulation, implementation, planning and research, development and monitoring of programs and plans relative to utilization, exploration

MINES AND MINERALS . . . *continued*

and extraction of local energy resources. Department of Energy shall prepare, integrate, coordinate, supervise and control all plans, programs, projects and activities of Government relative to energy exploration, development utilization, distribution and conservation. Authority and responsibility for exercise of mandate of Department is vested with Secretary of Energy whose powers and functions are: (1) Establish policies and standards for effective, efficient and economical operation of Department in accordance with programs of Government; (2) exercise direct supervision and control over all functions and activities of Department, as well as its officers and personnel; (3) devise program of international information on geological and contractual condition obtaining in Philippines for oil and gas exploration; (4) create regional offices and such other service units and divisions; (5) create regional or separate grids as may be necessary and beneficial; and (6) perform such other functions as may be necessary and proper to attain objectives of law. It shall also perform non-price regulatory jurisdiction, powers and functions of Energy Regulatory Board. (R.A. 7638).

Energy Regulatory Board shall, after due notice and hearing: (1) Fix and regulate prices of petroleum products; (2) fix and regulate rate schedule or prices of piped gas to be charged by duly franchised gas companies which distribute gas by means of underground pipe system; (3) fix and regulate rates of pipeline concessionaires under R.A. 387 (Petroleum Act of 1949), am'd by P.D. 1700.

Power of National Power Corporation and electric cooperatives to determine, fix and prescribe rates being charged to their customers are now exercised by Energy Regulatory Board.

Government may directly explore for and produce indigenous petroleum. It may also indirectly undertake same under service contracts. Every contract shall, subject to approval of President, be executed by Energy Development Services after due public notice, pre-qualification and public bidding or concluded through negotiations. In opening contract areas and in selecting best offer for petroleum operations, any of following alternative procedures may be resorted to by Energy Development Services: (a) May select area or areas and offer it for bid, specifying minimum requirements and conditions; or (b) may open for bidding large area wherein bidders may select integral areas not larger than maximum; or (c) area may be selected by interested party who shall negotiate with Energy Development Services for contract.

In a service contract, service and technology are furnished by service contractor for which it shall be entitled to stipulated service fee while financing is provided by Government to whom all petroleum produced shall belong. If Government is unable to finance petroleum exploration operations or in order to induce contractor to exert efforts to discover and produce petroleum as soon as possible, service contract may stipulate that if contractor furnishes services, technology and financing, proceeds of sale of petroleum produced shall be source of funds for payment of service fee and operating expenses due contractor. Contractor, who may be a consortium, shall undertake, manage and execute petroleum operations. Contract may authorize contractor to take and dispose of and market either domestically or for export all petroleum produced subject to supplying domestic requirements of Republic of Philippines on a prorata basis.

Energy Development Services shall reimburse contractor for all operating expenses not exceeding 70% of gross proceeds from production in any year, provided, that if in any year operating expenses exceed 70% of gross proceeds from production, then unrecovered expenses shall be recovered from operations of succeeding years; pay contractor service fee, net amount of which shall not exceed 40% of balance of gross income after deducting Filipino participation incentive, if any, and all operating expenses.

Contractor shall have following privileges: (a) Exemption from all taxes except income tax; (b) exemption from payment of tariff duties and compensating tax on importations of machinery and materials required for petroleum operations provided that said machinery and materials are not manufactured domestically and will be used exclusively by contractor; (c) exemption from laws, regulations or ordinances restricting construction and operation of power plants for exclusive use of contractor and exportation of machinery and equipment when no longer needed; (d) exemption from publication requirements; (e) exportation of petroleum subject to prior filling prorata of domestic needs; (f) entry, upon approval of Energy Development Services, of alien technical and specialized personnel who may exercise their professions solely for operations of contractor.

Contractor shall be entitled to: (1) Repatriate over a reasonable period capital investment actually brought into country in foreign exchange or other assets and registered with Central Bank; (2) retain abroad all foreign exchange representing proceeds arising from exports accruing to contractors over and above (a) foreign exchange to be converted into pesos in an amount sufficient to cover, or equivalent to, local costs for administration and operations of exported crude and (b) revenues due Government on such crude; however Government and contractor may stipulate currency in which Government revenues arising under (b) above are to be paid; (3) convert into foreign exchange and remit abroad at prevailing rates no less favorable to contractor than those available to any other purchaser of foreign currencies, any excess balances of peso earnings from petroleum production and sale over and above required current working balances; and (4) convert foreign exchange into Philippine currency for all purposes in connection with petroleum operation at prevailing rates no less favorable to contractor than those available to any other purchaser of such currency. (P.D. 87 am'd by P.D. 469, am'd by P.D. 781).

See also topics Corporations; Monopolies and Combinations in Restraint of Trade.

MONOPOLIES AND COMBINATIONS IN RESTRAINT OF TRADE:

Revised Penal Code, Art. 186 (am'd R.A. 1956), makes it unlawful for any person: (a) to enter into any contract or agreement or take part in any conspiracy or combination in the form of a trust or otherwise, in restraint of trade or commerce or to prevent by artificial means free competition in the market; (b) to monopolize any merchandise or object of trade or commerce, or combine with any other person or persons to monopolize said merchandise or object in order to alter the prices thereof by spreading false rumors or making use of any other artifice to restrain free competition in the market; (c) being a manufacturer, producer or processor of any merchandise or object of commerce or an importer of any merchandise or object of commerce from any foreign country, either as principal or agent, wholesaler or retailer, to combine in any manner with other persons for the purpose of making transactions prejudicial to lawful commerce, or of increasing the market price in any part of the Philippines of such merchandise manufactured in or imported into the Philippines, or of any article in the manufacture of which such manufactured or imported merchandise is used. Penalty is higher if offense affects any food substance, motor fuel or lubricants, or other articles of prime necessity.

Any property possessed under any contract or by any combination mentioned in the preceding paragraphs, and being the subject thereof, shall be forfeited to the Government of the Philippine Islands. If the offender is a corporation or association, the president and each one of the directors or managers of said corporation or associations or its agent or representative in the Philippine Islands, in case of a foreign corporation or association, who shall have knowingly permitted or failed to prevent the commission of such offenses, shall be held liable as principals thereof.

MORTGAGES:

Mortgage is one of different kinds of guaranty recognized by law for insuring fulfillment of an obligation contracted either by same person who secures it or by a different person. A mortgage is either real estate mortgage or chattel mortgage. The instrument by which a mortgage is created should be recorded in Registry of Deeds. The creditor cannot appropriate for himself property mortgaged or dispose of same. The mortgagor, being owner of property mortgaged, can lease, sell or mortgage it again during pendency of contract of mortgage without affecting latter.

Form.—The following is sufficient as real estate mortgage:

Form

This REAL ESTATE MORTGAGE, made and executed this . . . . . . day of . . . . . ., 19. . . ., by A.B. Co., Limited, a sociedad anonima duly organized and registered under the laws of the Philippines, with its principal office in the City of . . . . . ., as Mortgagor, in favor of C. D., over the age of majority, a widower, and a resident of . . . . . ., ..., as Mortgagee.

WITNESSETH:

THAT WHEREAS the mortgagor is justly indebted to the mortgagee in the sum of . . . . . ., Philippine currency, as evidenced by its promisory note for said sum, in the words and figures following, to wit:

(Insert copy of Promissory Note.)

WHEREAS the mortgagor has agreed to secure the payment of said note by means of a good and valid mortgage upon that certain real property hereinafter described.

NOW, THEREFORE, for and in consideration of the premises and as security for the payment of the aforesaid note, the mortgagor has sold, transferred, and conveyed, and by these presents does sell, transfer and convey, by way of first mortgage, unto the mortgagee that certain real property, together with all the buildings and improvements thereon, situated in the Province of . . . . . ., P., and more particularly described as follows:

(Insert description.)

of which the said mortgagor is the absolute registered owner in accordance with the provisions of the Land Registration Act of the Philippines, its title thereto being evidenced by Certificate of Title No. . . . . . . of the Office of the Register of Deeds of the Province of . . . .

The mortgagor agrees, during the term and existence of this mortgage, to pay and discharge at maturity all lawful taxes and assessments laid or assessed upon the land herein and hereby mortgaged, and, in default thereof, the mortgagee may pay and discharge the same, and any and all sums so paid for such taxes or assessments shall bear interest at the rate of . . . . . . per annum, and shall be considered and held to be secured by this mortgage, and be a lien on said land herein mortgaged.

The conditions of this mortgage are such that if the said mortgagor shall well and truly pay or cause to be paid to the mortgagee the above mentioned promissory note according to the terms and tenor thereof, and shall well and truly pay and discharge at maturity all lawful taxes and assessments as aforesaid, then this mortgage shall be thereby fully discharged and of no further effect, otherwise it shall remain in full force and effect and be enforceable in the manner and form provided by law.

IN WITNESS WHEREOF, the A.B. Co., Limited, the mortgagor herein, has caused these presents to be signed by its General Manager, Y. Z., hereunto duly authorized, at . . . . . ., P., on the day and year first hereinabove written.

The A.B. Co., Limited
By Y. Z., General Manager.

In the Presence of:
(Signatures.)
(Acknowledgment.)

Foreclosure is by action filed in Regional Trial Court of province where land is situated. Debtor has three months after judgment of foreclosure in which to satisfy judgment; otherwise court may issue execution and cause property to be sold by sheriff at public auction to satisfy judgment. When so stipulated in contract, mortgage may be foreclosed extrajudicially under Act 3135, as amended. This Act requires that foreclosure sale be made under special power inserted in or attached to real mortgage. In case of extrajudicial foreclosure, mortgagor has right of redemption.

Private real property may be mortgaged in favor of any individual, corporation, or association, but mortgagee or his successor in interest, if disqualified to acquire or hold lands of public domain in Philippines, shall not take possession of mortgaged property during existence of mortgage except after default and for purpose of foreclosure, receivership, enforcement or other proceedings and in no case for a period of more than five years from actual possession and shall not bid or take part in any sale of such real property in case of foreclosure. (R.A. 4882).

Redemption.—There is no right of redemption after foreclosure sale except in cases falling under the provisions of Acts No. 2747, 2938 and 3135. In no case is redemption allowed after the sale of the mortgaged property has been confirmed by the court.

Deeds of trust are not extensively used, but a few deeds of trust have been executed in the Islands to secure bond issues, principally in connection with financing sugar centrals.

Pacto de Retro.—This is a form of conveyance with the right of repurchase by the vendor on or before a fixed date. It is used as a means to secure the payment of an

See Topical Index in front part of this volume.

MORTGAGES . . . *continued*

obligation. The vendee is entitled to possession under the pacto de retro, but he may lease the property to the vendor for an agreed rental. If the vendor fail to repurchase within the time fixed, the title is said to become "consolidated" in the vendee. The courts treat a pacto de retro as a mortgage when it is clear from the evidence that such was the intention of the parties.

Chattel Mortgages.—See topic Chattel Mortgages.

MOTOR VEHICLES:

Motor vehicles must be registered and licensed by Land Transportation Office and bear number plates. Drivers must be licensed, and license of professional chauffeur must bear his photograph. (R.A. 4136, as am'd).

Tourists or transients bringing their own motor vehicles may use same during but not after first 90 days of their sojourn in Republic provided that motor vehicles display number plates for current year of some other country or state, and provided that number plates with respective names and addresses of owners thereof be registered in Bureau of Land Transportation Office prior to operation of motor vehicles.

It is unlawful for any person to compel a change in course of an aircraft of Philippine registry while it is in flight or to compel an aircraft of foreign registry to land in Philippine territory or to seize control thereof while within said territory. Loading in any passenger aircraft operating as public utility within Philippines of any explosive or poisonous substance is also prohibited except if made in accordance with regulations issued by Civil Aeronautics Administration. (R.A. 6235).

Liability of Owner.—The owner of a private motor vehicle is solidarily liable with his driver if he, being in the vehicle, could have prevented the accident by the use of due diligence. If the owner was not in the motor vehicle, his liability ceases if he exercised the diligence of a good father of a family in the selection and supervision of his driver.

Every owner of a motor vehicle must file with the proper government office the bond to be executed by a government-controlled corporation to answer for damages which may be caused to third persons.

Guests.—There is no statutory restriction of liability for injury to gratuitous guest in car.

Actions Against Nonresidents.—No special provisions as to commencement.

NEGOTIABLE INSTRUMENTS:

See topic Bills and Notes.

NOTARIES PUBLIC:

Only qualified attorneys and certain public officials or persons qualified for the office of notary public may be appointed as notaries public. There must be at least one for each municipality. In the city of Manila notaries are appointed by Executive Judge, Regional Trial Court. In provinces they are appointed by judge of Regional Trial Court. Every notary must file oath of office. Various public officials are notaries public ex officio.

Notaries are usually appointed for a term of two years expiring on Dec. 31. Notary's authority is limited to province for which he is appointed, City of Manila being considered a province for that purpose.

A notarial seal is required. The law requires that each notary must keep a notarial register and show therein the nature of each instrument acknowledged or sworn to, date, number, and number of pages. Notarial registers must be archived in office of clerk of Regional Trial Court. Notarial fees are fixed by law. Notaries are under supervision of Regional Trial Court.

Notarial certificate must show date of expiration of commission.

PARTNERSHIP:

Under Civil Code which repeals provisions of Code of Commerce on partnership, a partnership may be constituted by two or more persons in any form, except when immovable property or real rights are contributed thereto, in which case a public instrument is necessary. Every contract of partnership having a capital of 3,000 pesos or more, in money or property, must appear in a public instrument, which must be recorded with Securities and Exchange Commission. Failure to record instrument does not affect liability of partnership and members thereof to third persons.

The partnership has a juridical personality separate and distinct from that of the partners, even though the contract of partnership may not have been recorded.

A contract of partnership is void, whenever immovable property is contributed thereto, if an inventory of said property is not made, signed by the parties, and attached to the contract of partnership.

Secret Partnerships.—Associations and societies, whose articles are kept secret among the members, and wherein any one of the members may contract in his name with third persons, have no juridical personality, and are governed by the provisions of law relating to co-ownership.

Limited Partnership.—This is formed by two or more persons under the provisions of the Civil Code, having as members one or more general partners and one or more limited partners. The limited partners as such are not bound by the obligations of the partnership. Two or more persons desiring to form a partnership are required to sign and swear to a certificate, which must state, among other things, the name of the partnership, adding thereto the word "Limited"; the character of the business; the location of the principal place of business; the name and place of residence of each member, general and limited partners being respectively designated; the term for which the partnership is to exist; the amount of cash and description of property contributed by each limited partner; and the extent of his participation in the profit. The certificate is required to be filed for record with Securities and Exchange Commission.

Dissolution and Winding Up.—On dissolution the partnership is not terminated, but continues until the winding up of partnership business is completed. The grounds for dissolution of a partnership are enumerated in the law, but on application by or for a partner the court can decree a dissolution under certain specified conditions. Dissolution terminates all authority of any partner to act for the partnership, except so far as may be necessary to wind up partnership affairs or to complete transactions begun, but not then finished.

PATENTS:

By Republic Act No. 165, as am'd, approved June 20, 1947, Patent Office was created. Any invention of new and useful machine, manufactured product or substance, process, or improvement of any of them, shall be patentable, unless it is contrary to public order or morals, to public health or welfare, or if it constitutes mere idea, scientific principle or abstract theorem not embodied in invention or any process not directed to making or improving of commercial product. Application for patent may be filed only by inventor, his heirs, legal representatives or assigns. Applicant who is not resident of Philippines must appoint agent or representative in Philippines upon whom notice or process relating to application may be served. If application is in order, Director shall issue patent in name of Republic of Philippines, under seal of Office, which shall be signed by him. Term of patent is 17 years from date it is issued, unless sooner revoked or cancelled on grounds specified in law.

An application for patent filed in this country by any person who has filed an application for same invention in a foreign country, which by treaty, convention, or law affords similar privileges to citizens of Philippines will be considered as filed on date it was filed in said foreign country, provided filing in Philippines is done within 12 months from earliest date on which any such foreign application is filed. No patent is granted for an invention which had been patented or described in a printed publication in this or any foreign country more than one year before actual date of filing of application, or which had been in public use or sale more than one year prior to such filing.

After two years from issuance of patent, Director may grant or compel granting of license under particular patent if it should appear that, without satisfactory reasons, patented invention is not being worked within Philippines; or demand for patented article in Philippines is not being met to adequate extent and on reasonable terms; or refusal of patentee to grant license would prevent establishment of any new trade or industry or trade or industry already established would be unduly restrained; or working of invention within Philippines is being prevented by importation of patented article; or if patented invention relates to food or medicine or manufactured products or substances which can be used as food or medicine, or is necessary for public health or public safety. (P.D. 1263).

A patentee whose rights have been infringed may recover damages sustained by reason of the infringement and may secure an injunction for the protection of his rights. Where damages can not be readily ascertained, patentee may be awarded a sum amounting to a reasonable royalty. Damages awarded may not be more than three times of actual damages.

Industrial Designs.—Any new and original creation relating to the features of shape, pattern, configuration, ornamentation, or artistic appearance of an article or industrial product may be protected as an industrial design by the author in the same manner and subject to the same provisions and requirements as relate to patents for inventions. The term of a design registration is five years from the date of registration, which may, on application, be extended to another five years.

Fees.—Administrative Order No. 1 issued by Bureau of Patents, Trademarks and Technology Transfer revised schedule of fees in filing applications for patents by categorizing applicants into small and big entities. Small entity is any business activity or industry, agribusiness and/or services whether single proprietorship, cooperative, partnership, or corporation, whose total asset is 5 million pesos or less; otherwise, it shall be considered as big entity.

Fees and charges are as follows: minimum of ₱200 as publication fee; ₱800 and ₱2,000 for invention patent of small and big entity, respectively; ₱550 and ₱1,200 for small and big entity, respectively for both utility model and design patent; ₱50 and ₱100 for small entity and big entity, respectively for each additional claim in excess of five claims if invention patent; ₱300 and ₱800 for small and big entity, respectively for each embodiment in excess of one design application; ₱500 and ₱1,000 for small and big entity, respectively for claim of convention priority in invention patent; ₱300 and ₱800 for small and big entity, respectively for both utility model and design patent; ₱500 and ₱1,000 for small and big entity, respectively for reissuance of application in invention patent; ₱100 and ₱300 for small and big entity respectively for conversion of invention patent to Utility Model; ₱100 and ₱500 for issuance of patent certificate for small and big entity respectively in invention patent and ₱100 and ₱300 for small and big entity respectively both in utility model and design patent. Annual fee for invention patent at beginning of fifth year—₱600 and ₱1,500 for small and big entity respectively; sixth year—₱900 and ₱2,000 for small and big entity, respectively; seventh year—₱1,200 and ₱2,500 for small and big entity, respectively; eighth year—₱1,500 and ₱3,000 for small and big entity, respectively; ninth year—₱1,900 and ₱4,000 for small and big entity, respectively; tenth-year—₱2,300 and ₱5,000 for small and big entity, respectively; 11th year—₱2,700 and ₱6,500 for small and big entity; 12th year—₱3,300 and ₱8,000 for small and big entity, respectively; 13th year—₱3,900 and ₱9,500 for small and big entity, respectively; 14th year—₱4,500 and ₱11,500 for small and big entity, respectively; 15th year—₱5,500 and ₱13,500 for small and big entity, respectively; 16th year—₱6,500 and ₱15,500 for small and big entity, respectively; 17th year—₱7,500 and ₱17,500 for small and big entity, respectively; for reinstatement of lapsed patent—₱800 and ₱2,000 for small and big entity in invention patent and ₱550 and ₱1,200 for small and big entity in both Utility Model and Design Patent; ₱3,000 and ₱6,000 for small and big entity, respectively in filing petition for compulsory licensing of invention patent while ₱1,500 and ₱3,000 for small and big entity, respectively is charged for Utility Model and Design Patent; ₱3,000 and ₱6,000 for petition for cancellation of invention patent if small and big entity respectively and ₱2,000 and ₱4,000 for cancellation of Utility Model and Design Patent of small and big entity respectively, ₱100 and ₱200 for each certification fee per patent in invention of small and big entity respectively and ₱75 and ₱150 for Utility Model and Design Patent if small and big entity respectively.

Technology Transfer Registry was established in Bureau of Patents, Trademarks & Technology Transfer of Dept. of Trade & Industry, which shall have following functions: (a) Formulate policies that would promote inflow of appropriate technology into preferred sectors of activity with focus on developmental and regulatory roles of

See Topical Index in front part of this volume.

PATENTS . . . *continued*

government in field of technology transfer; (b) establish standards on which to base relationships between parties to technology transfer arrangements, taking into consideration their legitimate interests and giving due recognition to needs of country for fulfillment of its economic and social development objectives; (c) encourage technology transfer arrangements where bargaining positions of parties are balanced to avoid abuses of stronger position and thereby achieve mutually satisfactory technology transfer arrangements; (d) measure extent of technology absorption and adaptation under technology transfer arrangements; and (e) perform such other functions as may be necessary for accomplishment of these objectives.

Technology transfer arrangements refer to contracts or agreements entered into by and between domestic companies and foreign companies and/or foreign-owned companies involving transfer of systematic knowledge for manufacture of product, for application of process or for rendering of service, including transfer, assignment or licensing of all forms of industrial property rights. (E.O. 133).

PLEDGES:

The following requisites are essential to the contract of pledge: that it be constituted to secure the fulfillment of a principal obligation; that the pledgor be the absolute owner of the thing pledged; that the person constituting the pledge have the free disposal of his property or that he be legally authorized for the purpose. In addition, the thing pledged is required to be placed in the possession of the creditor, or a third person by common agreement. Third persons who are not parties to the principal obligation may secure the latter by pledging their own property. It is also of the essence of this contract that when the principal obligation becomes due, the thing pledged can be alienated for the payment to the creditor. The creditor cannot appropriate the things given by way of pledge, or dispose of them. Any stipulation to the contrary is null and void.

All movables which are within commerce may be pledged, provided they are susceptible of possession. Incorporeal rights, evidenced by negotiable instruments, bills of lading, shares of stock, bonds, warehouse receipts and similar documents may also be pledged. The instrument proving the right pledged must be delivered to the creditor, and if negotiable, must be endorsed. A pledge is ineffective against third persons if a description of the thing pledged and the date of the pledge do not appear in a public instrument.

If the thing pledged is returned by the pledgee to the pledgor or owner, the pledge is extinguished. Any stipulation to the contrary is void. If subsequent to the perfection of the pledge, the thing is in the possession of the pledgor or owner, there is a prima facie presumption that the same has been returned by the pledgee.

The creditor to whom the credit has not been satisfied in due time, may proceed before a notary public for sale of thing pledged. Sale must be made at public auction, and with notification to debtor. If at first and second auction thing pledged is not sold, creditor may appropriate it, in which case he is obliged to give acquittance for his entire claim. Sale of thing pledged extinguishes principal obligation, whether or not proceeds of sale are equal to amount of principal obligation, interest and expenses in proper case. If proceeds of sale are more than said amount, debtor is not entitled to excess, unless it is otherwise agreed. If proceeds of sale are less, neither is creditor entitled to recover deficiency, notwithstanding any stipulation to contrary.

In pledges created by operation of law, after payment of the debt and the expenses of the sale, the remainder of the proceeds of the sale shall be delivered to the obligor. But a thing under a pledge by operation of law can be sold only after a demand of the amount for which the thing is retained. The public auction should take place within one month after such demand.

Pawnshops.—These are governed by special laws relating thereto, and subsidiarily by the provisions relating to pledges.

PRESCRIPTION:

By prescription one acquires ownership and other real rights through lapse of time in manner and under conditions laid down by law. (C.C. [n], §1106). Prescription runs against all persons having full civil capacity, even against: (1) Minors and other incapacitated persons who have parents, guardians or other legal representatives; (2) absentees who have administrators, either appointed by them before their disappearance, or appointed by the courts; (3) persons living abroad who have managers of administrators; and (4) juridical persons, except State and its subdivisions. (C.C. [n], §1108.). Prescription does not run between husband and wife, even though there be separation of property agreed upon in marriage settlement or by judicial decree. Neither does prescription run between parents and children, during minority or insanity of latter, and between guardian and ward during continuance of guardianship.

All things which are within commerce of men are susceptible of prescription, unless otherwise provided by law. Property of State or any of its subdivisions not patrimonial in character is not object of prescription. (C.C. [n], §1113). Persons with capacity to alienate property may renounce prescription already obtained but not right to prescribe in future.

PRICE CONTROL:

Price Coordinating Council consists of Secretary of Trade and Industry as chairman; Secretary of Agriculture; Secretary of Health; Secretary of Environment and Natural Resources; Secretary of Local Government; Secretary of Transportation and Communication; Secretary of Justice; Director General of National Economic and Development Authority; and one representative each from agricultural producer's sector, consumer's sector, trading sector and manufacturer's sector.

Sectoral representative of Price Coordinating Council shall be appointed by President for term of one year. Council shall meet every quarter or when President or Chairman convenes same.

Council shall have following functions: (a) to coordinate productivity distributions and price stabilization programs of government and develop comprehensive strategies to effect stabilization of prices of basic necessities and prime commodities at affordable levels; (b) make report to President and Congress of Philippines on status and progress undertaken by respective department as well as comprehensive strategies developed by Council; (c) advise President on general policy matters for promotion and improvement in productivity, distribution and stabilization of prices; (d) require from its members or any other government agency information necessary for assessing supply, distribution and price situation of any basic necessity or prime commodity; (e) publicize from time to time developments in productivity, supply, distribution and prices of basic necessities and prime commodities; (f) cause immediate dissemination of prevailing price or price ceilings imposed upon basic necessities or prime commodities whenever automatic price control over it is imposed; and (g) recommend to President imposition of price ceilings on basic necessities and prime commodities under certain conditions.

Automatic price control on prices of basic necessities and prime commodities can be imposed and are to last only for no more than 60 days, whenever following circumstances are present: (1) area is declared as disaster area or under state of calamity; (2) area is declared under emergency; (3) writ of habeas corpus is suspended in area; (4) area is placed under Martial Law; (5) area is declared to be in state of rebellion; and (6) state of war is declared in area. (R.A. 7581).

PRINCIPAL AND AGENT:

The provisions of the Code of Commerce governing agency have been repealed by the new Civil Code under which agency is presumed to be for a compensation. An agency is either general or special. An agency couched in general terms comprises only acts of administration, even if the principal should state that he withholds no power or that the agent may execute such acts as he may consider appropriate, or even though the agency should authorize a general unlimited management.

In certain specified cases and in any act of strict dominion, a special power of attorney is necessary. A special power to sell excludes the power to mortgage; and a special power to mortgage does not include the power to sell. A special power to compromise does not authorize submission to arbitration.

Third Persons.—So far as third persons are concerned, an act is deemed to have been performed within the scope of the agent's authority, if such act is within the terms of the power of attorney, as written, even if the agent has in fact exceeded the limits of his authority according to an understanding between the principal and the agent. A third person with whom the agent wishes to contract on behalf of the principal may require the presentation of the power of attorney, or the instructions as regards the agency. Private or secret orders and instructions of the principal do not prejudice third persons who have relied upon the power of attorney or instructions shown them. The agent is responsible not only for fraud, but also for negligence, which is to be judged with more or less rigor by the courts, according to whether the agency was or was not for a compensation.

When two persons contract with regard to the same thing, one of them with the agent and the other with the principal, and the two contracts are incompatible with each other, that of prior date must be preferred, without prejudice to the rules governing double sale of movable and immovable properties. If the agent has acted in good faith, the principal is liable in damages to the third person whose contract must be rejected. If the agent acted in bad faith, he alone is responsible.

If the agent had general powers, revocation of the agency does not prejudice third persons who acted in good faith and without knowledge of the revocation. Notice of the revocation in a newspaper of general circulation is a sufficient warning to third persons. The agency is revoked if the principal directly manages the business entrusted to the agent, dealing directly with third persons. A general power of attorney is revoked by a special one granted to another agent, as regards the special matter involved in the latter.

The agency shall remain in full force and effect even after the death of the principal, if it has been constituted in the common interest of the latter and of the agent, or in the interest of a third person who has accepted the stipulation in his favor. Anything done by the agent, without knowledge of the death of the principal or of any other cause which extinguishes the agency, is valid and fully effective with respect to third persons who may have contracted with him in good faith.

REAL PROPERTY:

The following are immovable property: (1) land, buildings, roads and constructions of all kinds attached to the soil; (2) trees, plants, and growing fruits, while they are attached to the land or form an integral part of an immovable; (3) everything attached to an immovable in a fixed manner, in such a way that it cannot be separated therefrom without breaking the material or causing deterioration of the object; (4) statues, reliefs, paintings or other objects for use or ornamentation, placed in buildings or on lands by the owner of the immovable in such a manner that it reveals the intention to attach them permanently to the tenements; (5) machinery, receptacles, instruments or implements intended by the owner of the tenement for an industry or works which may be carried on in a building or on a piece of land, and which tend directly to meet the needs of the said industry or works; (6) animal houses, pigeon-houses, beehives, fish ponds or breeding places of similar nature, in case their owner has placed them or preserves them with the intention to have them permanently attached to the land, and forming a permanent part of it, and the animals in these places are included; (7) fertilizer actually used on a piece of land; (8) mines, quarries, and slag dumps, while the matter thereof forms part of the bed, and waters either running or stagnant; (9) docks and structures which, though floating, are intended by their nature and object to remain at a fixed place on a river, lake, or coast; (10) contracts for public works, and servitudes and other real rights over immovable property.

RECEIVERS:

When a corporation or partnership has been dissolved, or is insolvent or in danger of insolvency, or a corporation has forfeited its corporate rights, a verified petition for appointment of receiver may be filed with Regional Trial Court showing that plaintiff has interest in properties or funds thereof and that same are in danger of being lost, removed, or materially injured, and upon sufficient evidence court may appoint receiver.

A bond with sufficient sureties must be given to secure the appointment of a receiver and a receiver must give bond for the faithful performance of his duties.

When it is made to appear in an action for foreclosure of a mortgage that mortgaged property is in danger of being wasted or materially injured, and in other cases where it is made to appear that property in which the plaintiff is interested is about to be lost, wasted or destroyed, and that the appointment of a receiver is the most convenient and feasible means of preserving and administering the property, a receiver may be appointed.

RECEIVERS . . . *continued*

The receiver is under the control of the court in which the action is pending.

Except in extreme or urgent cases, it is irregular for a court to appoint a receiver without giving the defendant an opportunity to be heard.

A receiver may be appointed in supplementary proceedings. See topic Executions.

A receiver may be discharged when it is made to appear that the necessity for a receiver no longer exists.

RECORDS:

All documents affecting land titles are registered with the register of deeds for the province in which the land is situated; in the cities of Manila and Baguio with the registers of deeds of said cities.

Mineral claims are registered with the mining recorder. The law provides for a mining recorder in each land district, but where no recorder has been designated the duties devolve upon the Secretary of the Provincial Board of the province in which the mineral claim is located. In the Mountain Province the mining recorder resides in the City of Baguio. (Administrative Code, §1848).

Vital Statistics.—The civil status of persons is recorded by civil registrars. There is a local civil registrar for each municipality and one for the City of Manila. All civil registrars are under the supervision of a civil registrar-general, who is the Director of Census & Statistics. (Act No. 3753).

Torrens System of registering land titles is in effect.

REDEMPTION:

See topics Executions; Mortgages; Sales.

REPLEVIN:

When the complaint in an action prays for the recovery of the possession of personal property, the plaintiff may, at the commencement of the action or at any time before answer, apply for an order for the delivery of such property to him. He must show by his own affidavit or that of some other person who personally knows the facts: (a) that the plaintiff is the owner of the property claimed, particularly describing it, or is entitled to the possession thereof; (b) that the property is wrongfully detained by the defendant, alleging the cause of detention thereof according to his best knowledge, information, and belief; (c) that it has not been taken for a tax assessment or fine pursuant to law, or seized under an execution, or an attachment against the property of the plaintiff, or, if so seized, that it is exempt from such seizure; and (d) the actual value of the property.

The plaintiff must also give a bond, executed to the defendant in double the value of the property as stated in the affidavit aforementioned, for the return of the property to the defendant if the return thereof be adjudged, and for the payment to the defendant of such sum as he may recover from the plaintiff in the action.

Upon the filing of such affidavit and bond the judge shall issue an order requiring the sheriff or other proper officer of the court forthwith to take such property into his custody.

If the defendant objects to the sufficiency of the plaintiff's bond, or of the surety or sureties thereon, he cannot require the return of the property; but if he does not so object, he may, at any time before the delivery of the property to the plaintiff, require the return thereof, by filing with the clerk or judge of the court a bond executed to the plaintiff, in double the value of the property as stated in the plaintiff's affidavit. If within five days after the taking of the property by the officer, the defendant does not object to the sufficiency of the bond, or of the surety or sureties thereon, or require the return of the property; or if the defendant so objects, and the plaintiff's first or new bond is approved; or if the defendant so requires, and his bond is objected to and found insufficient and he does not forthwith file an approved bond, the property shall be delivered to the plaintiff. If for any reason the property is not delivered to the plaintiff, the officer must return it to the defendant.

Third Party Claims.—If the property taken be claimed by any other person than the defendant or his agent, and such person makes an affidavit of his title thereto or right to the possession thereof, stating the grounds of such right or title, and serves the same upon the officer while he has possession of the property, and a copy thereof upon the plaintiff, the officer is not bound to keep the property or deliver it to the plaintiff, unless the plaintiff or his agent, on demand of the officer, indemnifies him against such claim by a bond in a sum not greater than the value of the property.

REPORTS:

The Philippine Reports, commencing from the time of the reorganization of the Supreme Court of the Philippines in 1901, contain the decisions of the Supreme Court.

Court of Appeals Reports, commencing from time of reorganization of Court of Appeals in 1936, contain decisions of Court of Appeals.

Decisions of Supreme Court and of Court of Appeals sitting en banc are now published in Official Gazette.

RETAIL TRADE LAW (R.A. 1180, am'd by P.D. 714):

Any act, occupation or calling of habitually selling direct to general public merchandise, commodities or goods for consumption, except if capital of a manufacturer, processor or laborer does not exceed ₱5,000 or if a farmer or agriculturist sells products of his own farm, or manufacturer or processor selling to industrial and commercial users or consumers who use products bought by them to render service to general public, or to produce or manufacture goods which are in turn sold by them, or hotel-owner or keeper operating restaurant, irrespective of amount of capital, provided restaurant is included in, or incidental to, hotel business, shall constitute retail business.

Retail business in Philippines is limited to Filipino citizens, and to associations, partnerships and corporations capital of which is wholly owned by Filipinos.

SALES:

The subject-matter of the contract must be a determinate thing and licit, and the vendor must have a right to transfer the ownership thereof at the time it is delivered. Things having a potential existence may be the object of the contract of sale. The efficacy of the sale of a mere hope or expectancy is deemed subject to the condition that the thing will come into existence. The sale of a vain hope or expectancy is void.

The goods which form the subject of a contract of sale may be either existing goods or "future goods," namely, goods to be manufactured, raised, or acquired by the seller after the perfection of the contract. Things subject to a resolutory condition may also be the object of the contract of sale. A contract for the delivery at a certain price of an article which the vendor in the ordinary course of his business manufactures or procures for the general market, whether the same is on hand at the time or not, is a contract of sale, but if the goods are to be manufactured specially for the customer and upon his special order, and not for the general market, it is a contract for a piece of work.

Price.—Gross inadequacy of price does not affect a contract of sale, except as it may indicate a defect in the consent, or that the parties really intended a donation or some other act or contract. If the price is simulated, the sale is void, but the act may be shown to have been in reality a donation, or some other act or contract. The fixing of the price can never be left to the discretion of one of the contracting parties. However, if the price fixed by one of the parties is accepted by the other, the sale is perfected.

Transfer of Ownership.—The contract of sale is perfected at the moment there is a meeting of minds upon the thing which is the object of the contract and upon the price. From that moment, the parties may reciprocally demand performance, subject to the provisions of the law governing the form of contracts. The ownership of the thing sold is transferred to the vendee upon the actual or constructive delivery thereof. The parties may stipulate that ownership in the thing shall not pass to the purchaser until he has fully paid the price.

When goods are delivered to the buyer "on sale or return" to give the buyer an option to return the goods instead of paying the price, the ownership passes to the buyer on delivery, but he may revest the ownership in the seller by returning or tendering the goods within the time fixed in the contract, or, if no time has been fixed, within a reasonable time. When goods are delivered to the buyer on approval or on trial or on satisfaction, or other similar terms, the ownership therein passes to the buyer (1) when he signifies his approval or acceptance to the seller or does any other act adopting the transaction, or (2) if he does not signify his approval or acceptance to the seller, but retains the goods without giving notice of rejection, then if a time has been fixed for the return of the goods, on the expiration of such time, and, if no time has been fixed, on the expiration of a reasonable time. What is a reasonable time is a question of fact.

Warranties.—Unless contrary intention appears, there is implied warranty that: (1) Seller has right to sell thing at time when ownership is to pass, and that buyer shall from that time enjoy legal and peaceful possession of thing; (2) thing shall be free from any hidden faults or defects, or any charge or encumbrance not declared or known to buyer. Implied warranty of seller, however, is not applicable to sheriff, auctioneer, mortgagee, pledgee, or other person professing to sell by virtue of authority in fact or law, for sale of thing in which third person has legal or equitable interest. (C.C. Art. 1547).

Risk of Loss.—Unless otherwise agreed, the goods remain at the seller's risk until the ownership therein is transferred to the buyer, but when the ownership therein is transferred to the buyer the goods are at the buyer's risk whether actual delivery has been made or not, except that: (1) Where delivery of the goods has been made to the buyer or to a bailee for the buyer, in pursuance of the contract and the ownership in the goods has been retained by the seller merely to secure performance by the buyer of his obligations under the contract, the goods are at the buyer's risk from the time of such delivery; (2) Where actual delivery has been delayed through the fault of either the buyer or seller the goods are at the risk of the party in fault.

Reservation of Security.—Where there is a contract of sale of specific goods, the seller may, by the terms of the contract, reserve the right of possession or ownership in the goods until certain conditions have been fulfilled. The right of possession or ownership may be thus reserved notwithstanding the delivery of the goods to the buyer or to a carrier or other bailee for the purpose of transmission to the buyer.

Where goods are shipped, and by the bill of lading the goods are deliverable to the seller or his agent, or to the order of the seller or of his agent, the seller thereby reserves the ownership in the goods. But, if except for the form of the bill of lading, the ownership would have passed to the buyer on shipment of the goods, the seller's property in the goods is deemed to be only for the purpose of securing performance by the buyer of his obligations under the contract. Where goods are shipped, and by the bill of lading the goods are deliverable to order of the buyer or of his agent, but possession of the bill of lading is retained by the seller or his agent, the seller thereby reserves a right to the possession of the goods as against the buyer.

Where the seller of goods draws on the buyer for the price and transmits the bill of exchange and bill of lading together to the buyer to secure acceptance or payment of the bill of exchange, the buyer is bound to return the bill of lading if he does not honor the bill of exchange, and if he wrongfully retains the bill of lading he acquires no added right thereby. If, however, the bill of lading provides that the goods are deliverable to the buyer or to the order of the buyer, or is indorsed in blank, or to the buyer by the consignee named therein, one who purchases in good faith, for value, the bill of lading, or goods from the buyer will obtain the ownership in the goods, although the bill of exchange has not been honored, provided that such purchaser has received delivery of the bill of lading indorsed by the consignee named therein, or of the goods, without notice of the facts making the transfer wrongful.

Lien.—Notwithstanding that the ownership of the goods may have passed to the buyer, the unpaid seller of the goods has: (1) a lien on the goods or right to retain them for the price while he is in possession of them; (2) in case of the insolvency of the buyer, a right of stopping the goods in transitu after he has parted with the possession of them; (3) a right of resale with certain limitations; and (4) a right to rescind, also with certain limitations. Where the ownership in the goods has not passed to the buyer, the unpaid seller has, in addition to his other remedies, a right of withholding delivery similar to and coextensive with his rights of lien and stoppage in transitu where the ownership has passed to the buyer. The unpaid seller's right of lien or stoppage in transitu is not affected by any sale, or other disposition of the goods which the buyer may have made, unless the seller has assented thereto.

Installment Sales.—In a contract of sale of personal property the price of which is payable in installments, the vendor may exercise any of the following remedies: (1) exact fulfillment of the obligation, should the vendee fail to pay; (2) cancel the sale,

SALES . . . *continued*
should the vendee's failure to pay cover two or more installments; (3) foreclose the chattel mortgage on the thing sold, if one has been constituted, should the vendee's failure to pay cover two or more installments. In this case, he has no further action against the purchaser to recover any unpaid balance of the price. Any agreement to the contrary is void. The same rule applies to contracts purporting to be leases of personal property with option to buy, when the lessor has deprived the lessee of the possession or enjoyment of the thing. In the foregoing cases, a stipulation that the installments or rents paid shall not be returned to the vendee or lessee is valid insofar as the same may not be unconscionable under the circumstances.

Plural Sales.—If the same thing should have been sold to different vendees, the ownership is transferred to the person who may have first taken possession thereof in good faith, if it should be movable property. Should it be immovable property, the ownership shall belong to the person acquiring it who in good faith first recorded it in the Registry of Property. Should there be no inscription, the ownership shall pertain to the person who in good faith was first in the possession; and, in the absence thereof, to the person who presents the oldest title, provided there is good faith.

Conventional Redemption.—This takes place when the vendor reserves the right to repurchase the thing sold. But the vendor cannot avail himself of the right of repurchase without complying with the stipulations which may have been agreed upon and without returning to the vendee the price of the sale and, in addition, reimbursing the vendee for the expenses of the contract, and any other legitimate payments made by reason of the sale, and for necessary and useful expenditures made on the thing sold.

Legal Redemption.—Legal redemption is the right to be subrogated, upon the same terms and conditions stipulated in the contract, in the place of one who acquires a thing by purchase or dation in payment, or by any other transaction whereby ownership is transmitted by onerous title.

Prohibited Transactions.—The husband and the wife cannot sell property to each other, except when a separation of property was agreed upon in the marriage settlements, or when there has been a judicial separation of property under Art. 136 of Family Code.

The following persons cannot acquire by purchase, even at a public or judicial auction, either in person or through the mediation of another: (1) a guardian, the property of the person or persons who may be under his guardianship; (2) agents, the property whose administration or sale may have been intrusted to them, unless the consent of the principal has been given; (3) executors and administrators, the property of the estate under administration; (4) public officers and employees, the property of the State or of any subdivision thereof, or of any government owned or controlled corporation, or institution, the administration of which has been intrusted to them, and this prohibition applies to judges and government experts who, in any manner whatsoever, take part in the sale; (5) justices, judges, prosecuting attorneys, clerks of superior and inferior courts, and other officers and employees connected with the administration of justice, the property and rights in litigation or levied upon an execution before the court within whose jurisdiction or territory they exercise their respective functions, and this prohibition includes the act of acquiring by assignment and applies to lawyers, with respect to the property and rights which may be the object of any litigation in which they may take part by virtue of their profession; (6) any others specially disqualified by law.

The foregoing prohibitions are applicable to sales in legal redemption, compromises and renunciations.

Notices Required.—A person to whom a document of title has been transferred, but not negotiated, acquires thereby, as against transferor, title to the goods subject to terms of any agreement with transferor. If the document is non-negotiable, such person also acquires right to notify bailee who issued the document of the transfer thereof, and thereby to acquire the direct obligation of such bailee to hold possession of the goods for him according to terms of the document. (C.C. [n], §1514). Unpaid seller may exercise his right of stoppage in transitu either by obtaining actual possession of the goods or by giving notice of his claim to carrier or other bailee in whose possession the goods are. Such notice may be given either to person in actual possession of the goods or to his principal. In latter case, notice to be effectual, must be given at such time and under such circumstances that the principal, by exercise of reasonable diligence, may prevent a delivery to buyer. When notice of stoppage in transitu is given by seller to carrier, or other bailee in possession of the goods, he must redeliver the goods according to directions of seller. (C.C. [n] §1532). An unpaid seller having a right of lien or having stopped the goods in transitu may resell the goods. However, where the right to resell is not based on perishable nature of the goods or upon an express provision of the contract of sale, giving or failure to give notice of intention to resell the goods must be relevant in any issue involving the question whether the buyer had been in default for an unreasonable time before the resale was made.

Applicable Law.—See topic Contracts, subhead Applicable Law.

SEALS:

Seals are not necessary except in connection with certain official and corporate acts.

SECURITIES:

Revised Securities Act (B.P. 178) defines securities to include: Bonds, debentures, notes, evidences of indebtedness, shares in company, preorganization certificates or subscriptions, investment contracts, certificates of interest or participation in profit sharing agreement, collateral trust certificates, equipment trust certificates, voting trust certificates, certificates of deposit for security, or fractional undivided interest in oil, gas, or other mineral rights, or, in general, interests or instruments considered to be "securities", or certificates of interests or participation in, temporary or interim certificates for, receipts for, guarantees of, or warrants or rights to subscribe to or buy or sell any of foregoing; or commercial papers evidencing indebtedness of any person, financial or non-financial entity, irrespective of maturity, issued, endorsed, sold, transferred or in any manner conveyed to another, with or without recourse, such as promissory notes, repurchase agreements, certificates of assignments, certificates of participation, trust certificates or similar instruments; or proprietary or nonproprietary membership certificates, commodity future contracts, transferable stock options, pre-need plans, pension plans, life plans, joint venture contracts, and similar contracts and investments where there is no tangible return or investment plus profits but appreciation of capital as well as enjoyment of particular privileges and services.

Securities and Exchange Commission.—This Act shall be administered by Securities and Exchange Commission which shall have jurisdiction, supervision and control over all corporations, partnerships or associations, who are grantees of primary franchises and/or license or permit issued by government to operate in Philippines, and in exercise of its authority, it shall have power to enlist aid of and to deputize agencies of government as well as any private institution, corporation, firm, association or person. (P.D. 1758).

No securities, except of class exempt under provisions of §5 of Act or unless sold in any transaction exempt under any of provisions of §6 of said Act, may be sold in Philippines unless registered and permitted to be sold as provided in Act.

On registration of securities with Commission, disclosing all information prescribed and payment of 1/10 of 1% of maximum aggregate price at which such securities are proposed to be offered; and after completion of publication is made; Commission finds that registration statement together with all other papers and documents attached thereto, is on its face complete and that requirements for protection of investors have been complied with, and unless there are grounds to reject registration statement as herein provided, it shall enter order making registration effective, and issue to registrant permit reciting that such person, its brokers and agents, are entitled to offer securities named in said certificate, with such terms and conditions as it may impose in public interest and for protection of investors. Every permit must state that issuance thereof is only permissive and does not constitute recommendation of securities permitted to be offered for sale.

Registration of Brokers, Dealers, and Salesmen.—No broker, dealer or salesman may engage in business in Philippines as such unless he has been registered as broker, dealer or salesman in office of Commission. Registration already granted may be revoked by Commission if, after reasonable notice and hearing, Commission determines that such applicant or registrant violated any provision of Act; or made material false statement in application for registration; or guilty of fraudulent act in connection with sale of securities; or demonstrated his unworthiness to transact business of broker, dealer or salesman.

Registration of Exchanges.—Any exchange may be registered with Commission as security exchange by filing registration statement in such form as Commission may prescribe. If it appears to Commission that security exchange applying for registration is so organized as to be able to comply with provisions of Act and its rules and regulations, and rules of exchange are just and adequate to insure fair dealing and to protect investors, Commission shall cause such exchange to be registered as securities exchange.

Margin Requirements.—To prevent excessive use of credit for purchase of carrying securities, Commission, in accordance with credit and monetary policies promulgated by Monetary Board, shall prescribe rules and regulations with respect to amount of credit that may be extended on any security other than exempted security. For extension of credit, such rules and regulations shall be based upon following standard: Amount not greater than whichever is higher of (1) 65% of current market price of security, or (2) 100% of lowest market price of security during preceding 36 calendar months, but not more than 75% of current market price. Monetary Board, however, may increase or decrease percentages, in order to achieve objectives of Central Bank during economic crisis.

Miscellaneous Provisions.—There are restrictions on borrowings by members, brokers, and dealers. Manipulation of security prices is unlawful. Manipulative and deceptive devices such as short sales or stop-loss orders, in contravention of rules of Commission, are prohibited. It shall be unlawful for any exchange to adopt artificial measures of price control of any nature whatsoever without prior approval of Commission. Also, fraudulent transactions and transactions on "over-the-counter markets" are considered unlawful.

SHIPPING:

Coastwise trade or shipping as a public utility is limited to citizens of Philippines and to corporations or other entities organized under laws of Philippines, 75% of capital of which is owned by citizens of Philippines.

The basic law on maritime commerce is Book III of the Code of Commerce. Its provisions cover vessels engaged in maritime commerce, or commerce by sea, whether foreign or coastwise; define the rights, duties and liabilities of persons who take part in maritime commerce; and treat of risks, damages, and accidents therein, as well as of proof and liquidation of averages.

Philippine Coast Guard shall be responsible for administration and enforcement of maritime laws, and registration and inspection of vessels.

It shall be unlawful for any person, association or corporation to establish, erect, or maintain any aid to maritime navigation without first obtaining authorization from Philippine Coast Guard, or interfere with any aid to maritime navigation.

The "Carriage of Goods by Sea Act," Public Act No. 521, 74th U. S. Congress, approved on April 16, 1936, was accepted and made applicable to the Philippines by Commonwealth Act No. 65, approved on Oct. 22, 1936. The acceptance, however, was made with a proviso that nothing in said Carriage of Goods by Sea Act must be construed as repealing any existing provision of the Code of Commerce which was then in force, or as limiting its application.

Any citizen of Philippines, or any association or corporation organized under Philippine Law, 60% of capital of which is owned by citizens of Philippines, engaged or which shall engage exclusively in overseas shipping business or in construction of modern boats for overseas service shall be exempt from payment of income tax derived from overseas shipping business for period of ten years from date of approval of Act, provided that entire net income after deducting 10% thereof for distribution of profits or declaration of dividends is reinvested for construction, purchase or acquisition of vessels and equipment. Amount reinvested shall not be withdrawn for period of ten years after expiration of period of income tax exemption. (R.A. 7471).

Maritime Industry Authority shall have jurisdiction and control over all persons, corporations, firms or entities in maritime industry. Its objectives are to: (1) Increase

SHIPPING . . . *continued*
production in various islands and regions of archipelago through provision of effective sea linkage, (2) provide for economical, safe and efficient shipment of raw materials, (3) enhance competitive position of Philippine flag vessels in carriage of foreign trade, (4) strengthen balance of payments position by minimizing outflow of foreign exchange and increasing dollar earnings, and (5) generate new job opportunities. (P.D. 474).

For development of Philippine overseas shipping, following are direct incentives: (1) Vessels which are duly registered in Philippines and which are owned or controlled, or chartered by Philippine nationals shall have at least equal shares as vessels of another country in carriage of international cargo between Philippines and that other country; and (2) shipping lines of third-countries shall be accorded opportunities to carry balance of international cargo on such bilateral trade which cannot be carried by such vessels of Philippines and that other country. (P.D. 806).

Common Carriers.—Under the provisions of the new Civil Code, common carriers are bound to observe extraordinary diligence in their vigilance over the goods and for the safety of passengers transported by them. They are held responsible for the loss, destruction, or deterioration of the goods, unless the same is due to any of the following causes only: (1) flood, storm, earthquake, lightning, or other natural disaster or calamity; (2) act of the public enemy in war, whether international or civil; (3) act or omission of the shipper or owner of the goods; (4) the character of the goods or defects in the packing or in the containers; (5) order or act of competent public authority. In all other cases, common carriers are presumed to have been at fault or to have acted negligently. A stipulation between the common carrier and the shipper or owner limiting the liability of the former for the loss, destruction, or deterioration of the goods to the degree less than extraordinary diligence is valid, provided it be: (1) in writing, signed by the shipper or owner; (2) supported by a valuable consideration other than the service rendered by the common carrier; and (3) reasonable, just and not contrary to public policy.

Law Applicable.—The law of the country to which the goods are to be transported governs the liability of the common carrier for their loss, destruction of deterioration.

Safety of Passengers.—A common carrier is bound to carry the passengers safely as far as human care and foresight can provide, using the utmost diligence of very cautious persons, with a due regard for all the circumstances. In case of death of or injuries to passengers, common carriers are presumed to have been at fault or to have acted negligently. Common carriers are liable for the death of or injuries to passengers through the negligence or willful acts of former's employees, although such employees may have acted beyond scope of their authority or in violation of orders of common carriers. This liability of common carriers does not cease upon proof that they exercised all diligence of good father of family in selection and supervision of their employees. Common carrier's responsibility cannot be eliminated or limited by stipulation, by posting of notices, by statements on tickets or otherwise. Contributory negligence of passenger does not bar recovery of damages for his death or injuries, if proximate cause thereof is negligence of common carrier, but amount of damages must be equitably reduced.

SOCIAL SECURITY:

Social Security Act (R.A. 1161, am'd R.A. 1792, am'd R.A. 2658, am'd R.A. 3839, am'd R.A. 4482, am'd R.A. 4857, am'd by P.D. 24, am'd by P.D. 177, am'd by P.D. 347, am'd by P.D. 735, am'd by P.D. 1202, am'd by P.D. 1636, am'd by E.O. 28, am'd by E.O. 102) provides for retirement, death, disability, and sickness benefits. Social Security System was created to carry out purposes of Act, under direction and control of Social Security Commission.

Coverage compulsory upon all employees not over 60 years of age on date of their employment and on employers on first day of their operation. Also covered are all self-employed persons earning ₱1,800 or more per annum. Effectivity of coverage of certain groups of self-employed shall be determined by Commission under such rules and regulations as it may prescribe. Philippine citizens recruited in Philippines by foreign-based employers for employment abroad may be covered by System on voluntary basis under such rules and regulations as Social Security Commission may prescribe. System commenced operations on Sept. 1, 1957.

Salary Bracket Number	Range of Compensation	Monthly Salary Credit	Monthly Contributions		
			Employer	Employee	Total
I	₱ 1- 149.99	₱ 125.00	₱ 6.40	₱ 4.10	₱ 10.50
II	150- 199.99	175.00	9.00	5.70	14.70
III	200- 249.99	225.00	11.40	7.50	18.90
IV	250- 349.99	300.00	15.20	10.00	25.20
V	350- 499.99	425.00	21.60	14.10	35.70
VI	500- 699.99	600.00	30.40	20.00	50.40
VII	700- 899.99	800.00	40.50	26.70	67.20
VIII	900-1099.99	1000.00	50.70	33.30	84.00
IX	1100-1399.99	1250.00	63.30	41.70	105.00
X	1400-1749.00	1500.00	76.00	50.00	126.00
XI	1750-2249.99	2000.00	101.30	66.70	168.00
XII	2250-2749.99	2500.00	126.70	83.30	210.00
XIII	2750-3249.99	3000.00	152.00	100.00	252.00
XIV	3250-3749.99	3500.00	177.30	116.70	294.00
XV	3750-4249.99	4000.00	202.70	133.30	336.00
XVI	4250-4749.99	4500.00	228.00	150.00	378.00
XVII	4750-5249.99	5000.00	253.30	166.70	420.00
XVIII	5250-5749.99	5500.00	278.70	183.30	462.00
XIX	5750-6249.99	6000.00	304.00	200.00	504.00
XX	6250-6749.59	6500.00	329.30	216.70	546.00
XXI	6750-7249.99	7000.00	354.70	233.30	588.00
XXII	7250-7749.99	7500.00	380.00	250.00	630.00
XXIII	7750-8249.99	8000.00	405.30	266.70	672.00
XXIV	8250-8749.99	8500.00	430.70	283.30	714.00
XXV	8750-OVER	9000.00	456.00	300.00	756.00

(Social Security Commission Res. No. 446 series of 1993)

Contributions.—Beginning as of last day of calendar month when employee's compulsory coverage takes effect and every month thereafter during his employment, employer must deduct and withhold from earnings of covered employee amount corresponding to his earnings during month in accordance with preceding schedule effective on Jan. 1, 1996.

Employer shall issue receipt for all contributions deducted from employee's compensation or shall indicate such deductions on employee's pay envelope.

Remittance of such contributions by employer shall be supported by quarterly collection list to be submitted to System at end of each calendar quarter.

Benefits.—Monthly pension shall be sum of average monthly salary credit multiplied by replacement ratio; and 1½% of average monthly salary credit for each credited year of service in excess of ten years. Monthly pension shall in no case be less than ₱1,000 nor paid in aggregate amount of less than 60 times monthly pension except to secondary beneficiary, provided that monthly pension of surviving pensioners as of Dec. 31, 1986 shall be increased by 20%.

Retirement Benefits.—Covered employee who has paid at least 120 monthly contributions prior to semester of retirement, and who: (1) Has reached 60 years and is not receiving monthly compensation of at least ₱300, or (2) has reached 65 years shall be entitled for as long as he lives to monthly pension provided his dependents born before his retirement of marriage subsisting when he was 57 years shall be entitled to dependents' pension. Covered member who is 60 years at retirement and who does not qualify for pension benefits shall be entitled to lump sum benefit equal to total contributions paid by him provided that he is separated from employment and not continuing payment of contributions to SSS. Monthly pension shall be reduced upon re-employment of retired employee who is less than 65 years old by amount equivalent to one-half his earnings over ₱300. Upon death of retired employee pensioner, his primary beneficiaries shall be entitled to 100% of monthly pension and his dependents to dependents' pension.

Death Benefits.—Upon covered employee's death, his primary beneficiaries shall be entitled to monthly pension and his dependents to dependents' pension provided that he has paid at least 36 monthly contributions prior to semester of death. If foregoing condition is not satisfied his primary beneficiaries shall be entitled to lump sum benefit equivalent to 35 times monthly pension. In absence of primary beneficiaries, his secondary beneficiaries shall be entitled to lump sum benefit equivalent to 20 times monthly pension. Minimum death benefit shall not be less than total contributions paid by him and his employer on his behalf nor less than ₱1,800 provided that beneficiaries of covered employee who dies without having paid at least three monthly contributions shall be entitled to minimum benefit.

Disability Benefits.—If permanent total disability occurs after he has paid at least 36 monthly contributions prior to semester of disability, he shall be entitled to monthly pension and his dependents to dependents' pension provided that if disability occurs before he has paid 36 monthly contributions prior to semester of disability, he shall be entitled to lump sum benefit equivalent to 35 times monthly pension. If disability is permanent partial, and such disability occurs before 36 monthly contributions have been paid prior to semester of disability, benefit shall be such percentage of lump sum benefit described above with regard to degree of disability. If disability is permanent partial, and such disability has been paid prior to semester of disability, benefit shall be monthly pension for permanent total disability payable not longer than period designated in schedule.

Maternity Leave Benefits.—Any female employee for whom at least three monthly maternity contributions in 12 month period immediately preceding semester of her

See Topical Index in front part of this volume.

SOCIAL SECURITY . . . *continued*

childbirth, abortion, or miscarriage have been paid and who is currently employed shall be paid daily maternity benefit equivalent to 100% of her present basic salary, allowances and other benefits or cash equivalents of such benefits for 60 days subject to following conditions: (1) that employee shall have notified her employer of her pregnancy and probable date of her childbirth which notice shall be transmitted to SSS; (2) payment shall be advanced by employer in two equal installments within 30 days from filing of maternity leave application; (3) in case of caesarian delivery, employee shall be paid daily maternity benefit for 78 days; (4) payment of daily maternity benefits shall be bar to recovery of sickness benefits for same compensable period of 60 days for same childbirth, abortion or miscarriage; (5) maternity leave benefits shall be paid only for first four deliveries after Mar. 13, 1973; (6) SSS shall immediately reimburse employer of 100% of amount of maternity leave benefits advanced to employees; and (7) if employee should give birth or suffer abortion or miscarriage without required contributions having been remitted for her by her employer to SSS or without latter having been previously notified by employer of time of pregnancy, employer shall pay to SSS damages equivalent to benefits which said employee would otherwise have been entitled to and SSS shall in turn pay such amount to employee concerned. (R.A. 7322).

Sickness Benefits.—Any covered employee who has paid at least three monthly contributions in 12 month period immediately preceding semester of sickness, and is confined for more than three days in hospital, or elsewhere, shall for each day of confinement or fraction thereof be paid by his employer or by System if such person is unemployed allowance equivalent to 90% of his average daily salary credit. Total amount of daily allowance shall not be less than ₱10 nor exceed ₱150, nor paid for period longer than 120 days in one calendar year, nor shall any unused portion of 120 days sickness benefits be carried forward and added to total period allowable in subsequent year.

Employee must have paid required contribution for at least a 12 month period. 100% of daily benefit paid by an employer must be reimbursed by System.

Funeral Benefit.—Funeral grant of ₱10,000 shall be paid to help defray cost of funeral expenses upon death of covered member, permanently totally disabled employee or retiree.

Private Benefit Plans.—Existing plans must be integrated with the System. Benefits already earned under such plans will not be impaired. Changes in the plan resulting from integration are subject to agreement between employees and employers concerned.

All contributions collected in payment of benefits made under the Act are exempt from any tax, assessment, fee or charge, and such payments are not liable to attachment, garnishment, levy or seizure before or after receipt by the person or persons entitled thereto except to pay any debt of the covered employee to the System.

Claims.—Filing, determination and settlement of claims are governed by rules promulgated by the Commission, whose decision becomes final 15 days after notice. Judicial review is permitted, after aggrieved party has exhausted remedies before the Commission.

STATUTE OF FRAUDS:

See topic Frauds, Statute of.

STATUTES:

The Philippines has a Civil Code, a Code of Commerce (insofar as its provisions have not been abrogated or repealed by special laws and the Civil Code), a Revised Penal Code, an Election Code, a National Internal Revenue Code, Rules of Court (almost entirely supplanting provisions of Code of Civil Procedure and provisions of Criminal Procedure), and Revised Administrative Code. Laws passed by Congress are published under title Republic Acts.

See headnote to this digest for abbreviations used herein.

Uniform Acts adopted are: Negotiable Instruments and Warehouse Receipts.

TAXATION:

The "National Internal Revenue Code of 1977" (P.D. 1158, as am'd) provides for: Income tax; estate and gift taxes; specific taxes on certain articles; privilege taxes on business and occupation; documentary stamp taxes; mining taxes; taxes on resources of banks and receipts of insurance companies; tax on corporate franchises; amusement taxes; charges on forest products; fees for sealing weights and measures; firearms tax; radio fees; tobacco inspection fees; and water rentals, and such other taxes as are or hereafter may be imposed and collected.

Administration of Code and collection of taxes are vested in Bureau of Internal Revenue, headed by Commissioner of Internal Revenue, and two assistant chiefs known as Deputy Commissioners.

Tax on Individuals.—

Citizens or Residents.—Tax is imposed upon taxable compensation, business and other income received from all sources by every individual, whether citizen of Philippines or alien residing in Philippines. Rate of tax for (1) purely compensation income—graduated from 1% on taxable compensation income if over ₱2,500 but not over ₱5,000 to 35% on income in excess of ₱500,000, and (2) Simplified Net Income Tax (SNIT) for Self-Employed and for Professionals Engaged in Practice of Profession—graduated from 3% on taxable income not exceeding ₱10,000 to 30% in excess of ₱350,000. (R.A. 7496).

Taxable compensation income includes all income payments received as result of employer-employee relationship and other income of similar nature, including compensation paid in kind, less allowable personal and additional exemptions. (R.A. 7498).

Social security benefits, proceeds of life insurance policies paid to heirs or beneficiaries upon death of insured, separation pay or any amount received by official or employee or by his heirs from his employer as consequence of separation from service of employer due to death, sickness or other physical disability or for any cause beyond control of official or employee shall be exempt from payment of income tax. (E.O. 37).

Retirement benefits, pensions, gratuities received by officials and employees, whether from Philippine or foreign government agencies and other institutions, private or public, in accordance with reasonable private benefit plan maintained by employer shall be exempt from payment of income tax provided that retiring official or employee has been in service of same employer for at least ten years and is not less than 50 years of age at time of retirement and that benefits granted shall be availed of only once. (E.O. 37).

Withholding Income Tax.—Collection at source of income tax on compensation paid on or after Jan. 1, 1954 is in force. It applies to all individuals deriving purely compensation income. Employer is constituted as withholding agent. Term employer embraces not only individuals and organizations engaged in trade or business, but organizations exempt from income tax, such as charitable organizations, clubs, social organizations and societies, as well as Government of Philippines, including its agencies, instrumentalities, and political subdivisions. Every employer making payment of compensation income shall deduct and withhold tax in amount computed in accordance with withholding tables prepared by Dept. of Finance and should be equal to tax due on employee's compensation income for entire year. Employee receiving compensation is entitled to withholding exemptions, but in order to avail of such, employee must file with his employer withholding exemption certificate. In case of change of status of employee as result of which he would be entitled to lesser or greater amount of exemption, employee shall, within ten days from such change, file with employer new withholding exemption certificate reflecting change. (R.A. 7497).

In case of married individuals, husband and wife shall be treated as separate units and shall compute separately their individual income tax based on their respective total taxable incomes provided that if any income cannot be definitely identifiable as income exclusively earned by either of spouses, same shall be divided equally between spouses for purposes of computing their respective taxable income. (R.A. 7497).

Exemptions are: ₱9,000 for single or married individual judicially decreed as legally separated with no qualified dependents; ₱12,000 for head of family; ₱18,000 for each married individual, provided in case one of spouses is deriving taxable income, only said spouse shall be allowed to avail of aforesaid basic personal exemption. Married individual or head of family shall be allowed additional exemption of ₱5,000 for each dependent; provided, that total number of dependents for which additional exemptions may be claimed shall not exceed four dependents; provided further, that additional exemption for dependents shall be claimed by only one of spouses in case of married individuals. Dependent means legitimate, recognized natural or legally adopted child chiefly dependent upon and living with taxpayer if such dependent is not more than 21 years of age, unmarried and not gainfully employed or if such dependent, regardless of age, is incapable of self-support because of mental or physical defect. Head of family means unmarried or legally separated man or woman with one or more dependents, one or both parents, or with one or more brothers and sisters living with and dependent upon him for their chief support, where such brothers or sisters are not more than 21 years of age, unmarried and not gainfully employed or where such brothers or sisters, regardless of age are incapable of self-support because of mental or physical defect.

For persons who are self-employed and who are engaged in practice of profession, taxable income includes taxable income received during taxable year from all sources except following: (a) foreign source gross income derived by nonresident citizen; (b) certain passive incomes, i.e. interest income/yield from Philippine currency bank deposits and deposit substitute instruments; royalties; prizes exceeding ₱3,000 and winnings (except Philippine Charity Sweepstakes winnings); dividends received from domestic corporation and share of individual partner in partnership subject to income tax (see subhead Income Tax on Corporations, infra); (c) capital gains from sales of shares of stocks; and (d) capital gains from sales of real property. In computing for net taxable income subject to SNIT, following direct costs are allowable as deductions: (1) Raw materials, supplies and direct labor; (2) salaries of employees directly engaged in activities in course of or pursuant to business or practice of their profession; (3) telecommunications, electricity, fuel, light and water; (4) business rental; (5) depreciation; (6) contributions made to Government and accredited relief organizations for rehabilitation of calamity-stricken areas declared by President; and (7) interest paid or accrued within taxable year on loans contracted from accredited financial institutions which must be proven to have been incurred in connection with conduct of taxpayer's profession, trade or business. For individuals (including professionals) whose cost of goods sold and direct costs are difficult to determine, maximum of 40% of their gross receipts shall be allowed as deductions to answer for business or professional expenses as case may be. (R.A. 7496).

Interest from Philippine currency bank deposit and yield from deposit substitutes and from trust fund; royalties, prizes and other winnings, whether received by citizen or resident alien from sources within Philippines shall be subject to final tax at rate of 20%. Dividends received from domestic corporations and share of individual partner in partnership subject to tax by citizen or resident alien from sources within Philippines are taxed at rate of 15% in 1986; 10% on Jan. 6, 1987; 5% effective Jan. 1, 1988 and 0% effective Jan. 1, 1989. (E.O. 37).

Nonresident citizens shall be taxed on their taxable income derived from all sources without Philippines as follows: 1% if not over US$6,000; US$60 plus 2% if over US$6,000 but not over US$20,000; US$340 plus 3% if over US$20,000. In computing taxable income, following deductions shall be allowed from gross income from sources without Philippines: (1) allowance for personal exemption in amount of US$2,000 if person making return is single or married person legally separated; or US$4,000 if married or head of family; and (2) total amount of national income tax actually paid to government of foreign country of his residence. (E.O. 37).

Nonresident alien is deemed doing business in Philippines if he stays in Philippines for aggregate period of more than 180 days during any calendar year. Nonresident aliens engaged in trade or business in Philippines shall be subject to tax in same manner as resident citizens and aliens on taxable income received from all sources within Philippines, except capital gains tax realized from buying and/or selling shares of stock of Philippine corporations listed in dollar or foreign currency board of exchange. Other nonresident aliens pay flat rate of 30% on their entire income from sources within Philippines. (E.O. 37).

Tax due must be paid at time return is filed but not later than Apr. 15 in case of residents of Philippines, whether citizens or aliens, whose income had been derived solely from salaries, interests, dividends, allowances, commissions, bonuses, fees, pensions, or any combination thereof. All other individuals not mentioned above, including nonresident citizens shall file their returns on or before Apr. 15. If tax due is in excess of ₱2,000 (US$200 in case of nonresident citizens), taxpayer may pay same in two

TAXATION . . . *continued*
equal installments, first installment at time return is filed and second installment on or before July 15. (E.O. 37).

In lieu of deductions from gross income, individual subject to tax on his taxable net income, other than nonresident alien, may elect optional standard deduction in amount not exceeding 10% of his gross income (B.P. 135).

Income Tax on Corporations.—Philippine corporations and partnerships, except general professional partnerships, are taxed at 35% upon taxable income from all sources within and without Philippines. All corporations, agencies or instrumentalities owned or controlled by government, including Government Service Insurance System and Social Security System are subject to income tax as imposed upon associations or corporations engaged in similar business or industry. Foreign corporations engaged in trade or business in Philippines are taxed at same rate on taxable income from all sources within Philippines. Foreign corporations not engaged in trade and business in Philippines shall pay tax equal to 35% of gross income received from all sources in Philippines, as interest, dividends, rents, royalties, salaries, premiums, annuities, emoluments or other fixed or determinable annual, periodical or casual gains, profits, income and capital gains. Nonresident cinematographic film owners, lessors or distributors are taxed at 25%; nonresident owners of vessels chartered by Philippine nationals are taxed at 4.5%; nonresident lessors of aircrafts are taxed at 8.5% and nonresident lessors of machineries and other equipment are taxed at 7.5%; interest on foreign loan received by nonresident foreign corporation and contracted on or after Aug. 1, 1986 are taxed at 20%; dividends received by nonresident foreign corporations from domestic corporation are taxed at 15% provided country in which said foreign corporation is domiciled shall allow credit against tax due from nonresident foreign corporation, taxes deemed to have been paid in Philippines equivalent to 20% which represents difference between regular tax (35%) on corporations and tax (15%) on dividends; capital gains realized by nonresident foreign corporation from sale, exchange or other disposition of shares of stock in any domestic corporation not traded through local stock exchange, tax is 10% if not over ₱100,000 and 20% if over ₱100,000; capital gains presumed to have been realized from sale, exchange or other disposition of shares of stock listed and traded through local stock exchange, tax is 1/4 of 1% based on gross selling price of shares of stock. (E.O. 37).

General professional partnerships are not subject to income tax but partners are liable for income tax in their individual capacity on their shares in partnership profits whether distributed or otherwise. In determining partner's distributive share in net income of partnership, each partner shall take into account separately his distributive share of partnership's income, gain, loss, deduction, or credit to extent provided by Tax Code, and each partner shall be deemed to have elected itemized deductions, unless he declares his distributive share of gross income undiminished by his share of deduction.

Domestic or foreign insurance companies are allowed to deduct from their gross income a special deduction in form of net additions required by law to be made within year to reserve funds provided released reserve is to be treated as income from year of release.

Every corporation subject to tax shall file, in duplicate, quarterly summary declaration of its gross income and deductions on cumulative basis for preceding quarter or quarters upon which income tax shall be levied, collected and paid. Tax so computed shall be decreased by amount of tax previously paid or assessed during preceding quarters and shall be paid not later than 60 days from close of each of first three quarters of taxable year. Final adjustment return covering total net income for preceding calendar or fiscal year, shall be filed on or before Apr. 15 or on or before 15th day of fourth month following close of fiscal year, as case may be. (P.D. 1705).

Exemption from tax is granted to corporations of classes usually exempted from income tax.

General professional partnerships are required to file a return of their income, stating items of gross income and allowable deductions and names and addresses and shares of partners.

Withholding of Tax at Source.—Withholding of final tax on certain incomes shall be withheld by payor-corporation and/or person and paid in same manner and subject to same conditions as provided in Tax Code. Finance Secretary may require also withholding of tax on items of income payable to persons (natural or juridical) residing in Philippines by payor-corporation and/or person as provided for by law at rate of not less than 2 1/2% but not more than 35% which shall be credited against income tax liability of taxpayer for taxable year. Withholding tax rate on interests or other payments on obligations with tax free covenant bonds is 30%. (E.O. 37).

Estate tax is graduated from 5% on net estate over ₱200,000 but not over ₱500,000 to ₱1,545,000 plus 35% of excess over ₱10,000,000.

For purposes of determining net estate subject to estate tax, following items are deductible from value of gross estate: (1) Expenses, losses, indebtedness and taxes, (2) property previously taxed, (3) transfers for public use, and (4) family home.

Tax is payable at time estate tax returns are filed which shall be within six months from decedent's death. (R.A.7499).

Gift tax is imposed on donor only. Tax for each year is computed, at rates hereinafter mentioned, on basis of total net gifts made during calendar year. Donor pays on net gifts to all beneficiaries at rates varying from 1.5% if net gift is over ₱50,000 but not over ₱100,000 to ₱558,750 plus 20% of excess over ₱5,000,000. Gifts to educational, charitable or religious corporation, institution, foundation, philanthropic organization or research institution are exempt from gift tax provided that not more than 30% of said gifts shall be used by such donee for administration purpose. Contributions in cash or in kind to any candidate, political party or coalition of parties for campaign purposes, shall be governed by Election Code, as amended. (R.A. 7499).

Tax is payable at time return of donor is filed which shall be within 30 days after date gift is made. (C.A. 466, am'd by P.D. 69).

Value-Added Tax.—All sellers of goods and services whose aggregate gross annual sales of articles and/or services exceed ₱500,000 will be covered by value-added tax (VAT), unless such sales are specifically exempt. Certain sales of goods and services are either zero-rated or exempted from VAT. VAT is imposed on each sale in Philippines of taxable goods and services and on imports to Philippines. VAT at rate of 0% or 10% is based on gross selling price of goods sold or gross receipts realized from sale of services. (E.O. 273).

Tax on Franchises.—There is collected in respect to all franchises on electric gas and water utilities tax of 2% on gross receipts derived from business covered by law granting franchise. (R.A. 7716).

Tax on Privately-owned Passenger Automobiles, Motorcycles and Scooters.—Additional tax on privately-owned passenger automobiles, motorcycles and scooters shall be paid by owner in amount based on shipping weight or factory weight of vehicle; however, owner of a private motorcycle and scooter shall pay a fixed additional tax of ₱15 and that of jeep, ₱20. (R.A. 5448, am'd R.A. 5470).

Documentary stamp taxes are imposed upon documents, instruments, loan agreements, and papers, and upon acceptances, assignments, sales and transfers of obligation, right, or property incident thereto. Among such taxes are: On bonds, debentures and certificates of indebtedness issued by any associations, company, or corporation, ₱1.50 on each ₱200, or fraction thereof, of face value; on original issue of certificates of stock, ₱2 on each ₱200 or fraction thereof of par value, or in case of non-par value, of actual consideration paid therefor; on sales, agreement to sell, memorandum of sales, deliveries, or transfer of due bills, certificates of obligation, or shares or certificates of stock ₱1 on each ₱200 or fraction thereof of par value of such bond, due bill, certificates of obligation, or stock, provided that in case of stock without par value, tax shall be equivalent to 25% of tax paid upon original issue of said stock, provided further that tax herein imposed shall be increased to ₱1.50 beginning 1996; on certificates of profits or interest in property or accumulations of any association, company or corporation, ₱0.50 on each ₱200, or fraction thereof of face value; on bank checks, drafts, etc. ₱1.25 provided that this tax shall be increased to ₱1.50 beginning 1996, on negotiable promissory notes, bills of exchange, etc., ₱0.30 on each ₱200 or fraction thereof, of face value; on acceptance of payment of bill of exchange, etc., ₱0.30 on each ₱200 or fraction thereof of face value on, if expressed in foreign currency, of Philippine equivalent; on foreign bills of exchange and letters of credit, ₱0.30 on each ₱200 or fraction thereof, of face value, or Philippine equivalent, if expressed in foreign currency; on life insurance, policies, ₱0.50 on each ₱200, or fraction thereof, of amount insured; on policies of insurance on property, ₱0.50 on each ₱4, or fraction thereof, of premium; on fidelity bonds, and other insurance policies, ₱0.50 on each ₱4 or fraction thereof of premium; on policies of annuities, ₱1.50 on each ₱200 or fraction thereof, of capital of annuity, or should this be unknown, then on each ₱200 or fraction thereof, of 33 1/2 times annual income; on indemnity bonds, except as may be required by legal proceedings, ₱0.10 on each ₱4 or fraction thereof of premium charged, provided tax herein imposed shall be increased to ₱0.30 on each ₱4 or fraction thereof beginning 1996; on each certificate of damage and on every certificate issued by customs office, marine surveyor, or other person acting as such and on each certificate of any description required by law or for purpose of giving information, ₱10; on warehouse receipts, ₱10 provided this tax shall be increased to ₱15 beginning 1996; on each Jai-Alai, horse race tickets, lotto or other authorized number game, ₱0.10 provided if cost of ticket exceeds ₱1; additional tax of ₱0.10 on every ₱1 or fraction thereof; on bills of lading or receipts from ₱1 to ₱10; on proxies, ₱10 and to be increased to ₱15 beginning 1996; on powers of attorneys, except acts connected with collection of claims due from or accruing to Government, ₱5; on leases and other hiring agreements, ₱3 for first ₱2,000 or fraction thereof and additional ₱1 for every ₱1,000 or fraction thereof in excess of first ₱2,000 for each year of term of contract; on mortgages, pledges, and deeds of trust, ₱20, when amount secured does not exceed ₱5,000 and on each ₱5,000 or fraction thereof in excess of ₱5,000 additional tax of ₱10; on deed of sale and conveyance of real property, ₱15 when value received or contracted to be paid for such realty does not exceed ₱1,000 and ₱15 for each additional ₱1,000 or fraction thereof in excess of ₱1,000; on charter parties and similar instruments, from ₱500 to ₱1,500 according to gross tonnage of ship and duration of charter. (R.A. 7660).

Mining Tax.—Locator, holder or occupant of any mining claim shall pay in advance from date of registration of claim in Office of Mining Recorder, and on same date every year thereafter an annual occupation fee of ₱2 a hectare or fractional part thereof, until lease covering mining claim is granted. For privilege of exploring, developing and disposing of minerals from lands covered by lease, there is imposed upon lessee on coal-bearing public lands, an annual rental of five pesos per hectare or fraction thereof for each and every year for first ten years, and ten pesos per hectare or fraction thereof for each and every year thereafter during life of lease. On all mineral lands of 1st, 2d, 4th and 5th groups provided under Mining Act, two pesos a hectare or fraction thereof shall be imposed as rental. On coal, royalty shall not be less than 20 centavos a ton of 1,016 kilograms, on gold, a royalty of 1 1/2% of actual market value, of annual gross output thereof and on all other minerals, a royalty of 2% of actual market value of gross output. There is imposed on actual market value of annual gross output of minerals produced from mineral lands not covered by lease, an ad valorem tax in amount of 2% of value of output, except gold which shall pay 1 1/2%. (C.A. 466, am'd by R.A. 6110, am'd by P.D. 69).

Final capital gains tax is imposed on net capital gain realized from (1) sale, exchange or other disposition of shares of stocks in any domestic corporation not traded through local stock exchange—10% on first ₱100,000 or less and 20% in excess of ₱100,000; (2) sale, exchange or other disposition of shares of stock listed and traded through local stock exchange—1/2 of 1% based on gross selling price of share or shares of stock; (3) sale, exchange or other disposition of real property located in Philippines classified as capital assets, including pacto de retro sales and other forms of conditional sales, by individuals, including estates and trust, is computed at rate of 5% based on gross selling price of fair market value prevailing at time of sale, whichever is higher. (E.O. 37).

Said capital gains tax shall be in lieu of tax imposed under §21 of Code and capital gains shall not be included in his gross income for purposes of computing taxpayers-sellers income tax liability. (B.P. 37).

Real estate tax in city of Manila is 1 1/2% of assessed value; in city of Baguio not to exceed 2% of assessed value; in municipalities from 1/4% to 1/2% of assessed value. Provincial real estate tax is from 1/8% to 3/8% of assessed value.

Additional tax of 1% on assessed value of real property in addition to real property tax regularly levied under existing laws is imposed. However, additional tax shall not be

See Topical Index in front part of this volume.

TAXATION . . . *continued*
collected if entire total assessed valuation of real property assessable to any person does not exceed ₱3,000, and total real property tax shall not exceed maximum of 3%. (R.A. 5447).

Residence tax is imposed annually according to wealth and income. Persons subject to tax pay ₱5 plus additional tax, not exceeding ₱5,000, according to schedule in Act. Corporations (including partnerships, associations, joint stock companies, etc.) pay ₱500 plus additional tax, not exceeding ₱10,000, according to schedule in Act. (R.A. 7160).

Specific tax on distilled spirits if produced from sap of nipa, coconut, cassava, camote or buri palm or from juice, syrup or sugar of cane, provided such materials are produced commercially in country where they are processed into distilled spirits, per proof liter, ₱4. If produced from raw materials other than those enumerated, per proof liter, ₱35. Also, ad valorem tax shall be collected equivalent to 60% of brewer's selling price. (R.A. 6956).

Manufactured Oils and Other Fuels.—There shall be collected on refined and manufactured mineral oils and motor fuels specific taxes which shall attach to following goods as soon as they are in existence as such: Lubricating oils and greases; processed gas; waxes and petroleum; denatured alcohol for motive power; naphtha, regular gasoline and other similar products of distillation; premium gasoline; aviation turbo jet fuel; kerosene; diesel fuel oil; liquefied petroleum; asphalts; bunker fuel oil and on similar fuel oils having more or less same generating power; and naphtha, when used as raw material in production of petrochemical products. (R.A. 6965).

Franchise Taxes.—See topic Corporations.

Tax on Receipts of Insurance Companies.—See topic Insurance.

Amusement taxes are imposed on proprietor, lessee or operator of cockpits, cabarets, night or day clubs, boxing exhibitions, professional basketball games, Jai-Alai, race tracks and bowling alleys. Rate consists of 18% in case of cockpits, 18% in case of cabarets, night or day clubs, 15% in case of boxing exhibitions, 15% in case of professional basketball games, 30% in case of Jai-Alai and race tracks, and 15% in case of bowling alleys, of gross receipts, irrespective of whether or not any amount is paid for admission. (P.D. 1959). Collection of amusement tax on paid admissions from proprietors, lessees, or operators of theaters, cinematographs, concert halls, circuses and other places of amusement was removed from Bureau of Internal Revenue and is now collected by provincial or city government under Local Tax Code.

Social Security Tax.—None. See topic Social Security for required contributions.

Sales Tax Reform Decree of 1985.—Sales tax has been reclassified into original sales tax and subsequent sales tax. Original sales tax is imposed on producers, manufacturers and importers on first sale of products involved. Subsequent sales tax is imposed on subsequent sales of articles. (P.D. 1991, am'd P.D. 2006, am'd P.D. 2031).

Uniform Taxes on Wireless Stations.—All persons, firms or corporations operating a wireless receiver and/or transmitting station for wireless reception and/or transmission of wordage, pictures or other matter intended for publication, either in the public press or by means of broadcast radio news, and not devoted principally to the reception and/or transmission of advertisements, are subject to the payment of the real property tax, the basic annual and additional residence taxes, and the income tax, which are in lieu of all other taxes. They are required to pay, in addition, such fees and charges as are or may be imposed by executive order or regulation, such as filing fees, construction permit and station license fees, and annual permit fees.

Customs Tariff Law of Philippines is embodied in Tariff and Customs Code of 1982 (P.D. 1464, as am'd) which covers rates of import duty, tariff rates and customs law.

No financial institution shall open any letter of credit covering imports unless applicant for such letter of credit deposits full amount of duties due on importation. Amount of duties due shall be based on declaration of applicant for letter of credit; importer subject to penalties prescribed by Code. (P.D. 1853).

In addition to any other duties, taxes and charges imposed on all importations into Philippines, there shall be levied and paid additional duty of 3% ad valorem. This additional duty shall also be levied and paid, even if importation is exempt under existing laws, except in following importations: (1) Those of government agencies or government-owned or controlled corporations with existing contracts, agreements or obligations with foreign countries, international institution, associations or organizations entitled to exemption pursuant to agreements of special laws; (2) those of diplomatic corps; (3) personal effects of returning Filipino diplomats; (4) those of bonded manufacturing warehouses; and (5) those of bonded smelting warehouses.

With respect to importations which are at present totally or partially exempt from customs duties and/or internal revenue tax under provisions of any general or special law, additional duty of 3% ad valorem shall be levied and paid, in addition to 5% customs duty imposed thereunder. (E.O. 860).

Tax Census Law (R.A. 2070 as am'd by R.A. 5268) provides for compilation and consolidation of data on properties, income and liabilities of residents over 21 years of age, corporations, partnerships, and other business concerns. Tax census is taken in Apr., once on or before 15th day in case of individuals and corporations using calendar year or on or before 15th day of fourth month following close of fiscal year in case of corporations using fiscal year.

TORRENS ACT: See topic Records.

TRADEMARKS AND TRADENAMES:

Trademarks, trade names, or service marks used to distinguish goods, business, and services of one from that of another may be registered with Patent Office (R.A. 166), provided they are actually in use in commerce in Philippines for not less than two months before application is filed, and that country of which applicant is a citizen grants by law similar privileges to citizens of Philippines. The certificate of registration remains in force for 20 years, provided affidavits are filed on 5th, 10th, and 15th anniversaries of issue of certificate attesting that mark or name is still in use, and if not in use, stating reasons for its nonuse.

Infringement.—Any person who, without consent of registrant, uses, sells, or advertises any reproduction, counterfeit, copy or imitation of a registered mark or trade name is guilty of infringement. Injunction may be obtained to prevent infringement and court may order infringing material to be destroyed.

No imported merchandise can be admitted entry in Philippines which copies or simulates mark or trade name registered in Philippines, or bears a mark or trade name calculated to induce public to believe that article is manufactured in Philippines, or that it is manufactured in a country other than place where it is in fact made.

A registered mark or tradename may be assigned, but the assignment must be in writing, acknowledged before a notary public or other officer authorized to administer oath, and certified under the hand and official seal of the notary or other officer. An assignment is void as against any subsequent purchaser for value without notice, unless the assignment is recorded in the Patent Office. When the assignment is executed in a foreign country, the authority of the notary or other officer shall be proved by the certificate of a diplomatic or consular officer of, or representing the interest of, the Government of the Philippines. No assignment executed in a foreign country written in a language other than English or Spanish shall be recorded unless accompanied by a verified English translation. No instrument will be recorded which does not, in the judgment of the Director, amount to an assignment, or which does not affect the title to the trademark or tradename to which it relates.

Rights of Foreign Registrants.—Subject to well defined exceptions, persons who are nationals of, domiciled in, or have a bona fide or effective business or commercial establishment in any foreign country, which is a party to any international convention or treaty relating to marks or tradenames, or the repression of unfair competition to which the Philippines may be a party, are entitled to the benefits and subject to the provisions of the Trademark Law to the extent and under the condition essential to give effect to any such convention and treaties so long as the Philippines continue to be a party thereto.

An applicant for the registration of a mark or tradename, who is not a resident of the Philippines, must appoint an agent or representative in the Philippines upon whom notice or process relating to the application or registration may be served.

Firm Name, etc.—A firm name, business name or style is required to be registered in Bureau of Domestic Trade, together with true name of owner thereof and that of any other persons having joint or common interest with him in firm or business in which name is used.

See topics Commercial Register; Patents, subhead Technology Transfer Registry.

TREATIES:

Philippines is among others, a signatory to following: (1) Convention on Recognition and Enforcement of Foreign Arbitral Awards, June 10, 1958; (2) Convention on Manufacturers' and Commercial Trademark with Kingdom of Belgium, Feb. 5, 1957; (3) Interim Trade Agreement with Switzerland, Oct. 26, 1946; (4) International Sugar Agreement, Dec. 4, 1958; (5) International Wheat Agreement, Nov. 8, 1963; (6) Trade agreement with SCAP acting in respect of occupied Japan, May 18, 1950; (7) Agreement on importation of educational, scientific and cultural materials, Nov. 22, 1956; (8) Protocol on trade relations with Swiss Confederation, Oct. 18, 1956; (9) Trade Agreement with Republic of Korea, Feb. 24, 1961; (10) Trade Agreement with Commonwealth of Australia, June 16, 1965; (11) Agricultural Commodities Agreement with U.S.A. under Title I of Agricultural Trade Development and Assistance Act, as am'd, June 25, 1957; (12) Agreement on Surplus War Property with U.S.A., Sept. 11, 1946; (13) Philippine Alien Property Agreement with U.S.A., Aug. 22, 1946; (14) Agreement with U.S. Information Service for transfer to Philippines of Radio Station KZFM, Oct. 4, 1946; (15) Agreement with U.S.A. regarding payment of public and private claims, Aug. 27, 1948; (16) Supplemental Agreement No. 3 with FAO of U.N. on technical assistance to government, Nov. 14, 1952; (17) Agreement entered into with U.S.A. for purpose of arranging for return to government of U.S. of residual total of peso funds purchased for dollars and advanced to national defense forces, Philippines, by U.S.-Ryukyus Command, Nov. 6, 1950; (18) Mutual Defense Treaty with U.S.A., Aug. 30, 1951; (19) International Convention on Recovery Abroad of Maintenance, June 30, 1956; (20) Vienna Convention on Diplomatic Relations, Nov. 15, 1965; (21) Treaty on Investments with Federal Republic of Germany, Mar. 3, 1964; and (22) Exchange of notes constituting agreement with U.S.A. supplementing Military Bases Agreement of May 14, 1947, for collection of taxes for sales of motor vehicles within Military Bases, Dec. 29, 1965.

Conventions for Avoidance of Double Taxation and Prevention of Fiscal Evasion with respect to Taxes on Income and Capital are in force with Denmark, Kingdom of Sweden, Republic of Singapore, United Kingdom of Great Britain and Northern Ireland, Canada, U.S.A, France, Pakistan, Australia, Japan, Belgium, New Zealand, Finland, Indonesia, Austria, Thailand, West Germany, Korea, Malaysia, Netherlands, Italy and Brazil. (Rev. Memo. Cir. No. 4-92).

Philippines is not a party to: (1) Convention on Service Abroad of Judicial and Extrajudicial Documents in Civil or Commercial Matters; (2) Convention on Taking of Evidence Abroad in Civil or Commercial Matters; and (3) Convention Abolishing the Requirement of Legalisation for Foreign Public Documents.

TRUSTS:

Trusts are either express or implied. Express trusts are created by the intention of the trustor or of the parties. Implied trusts come into being by operation of law. The principles of the general law of trusts, in so far as they are not in conflict with the Civil Code, Code of Commerce, the Rules of Court, and special laws, are accepted.

USURY: See topic Interest.

WILLS:

All persons who are not expressly prohibited by law may make a will. Persons of either sex under 18 years of age cannot make a will. In order to make a will it is essential that the testator be of sound mind at the time of its execution. To be of sound mind, it is not necessary that the testator be in full possession of all his reasoning faculties, or that his mind be wholly unbroken, unimpaired, or unaffected by disease,

WILLS . . . *continued*
injury or other cause. It is sufficient if the testator was able at the time of making the will to know the nature of the estate to be disposed of, the proper objects of his bounty, and the character of the testamentary act. A married woman may make a will without the consent of her husband, and without the authority of the court. A married woman may dispose by will of all her separate property as well as her share of the conjugal partnership or absolute community property.

Forms of Wills.—Every will must be in writing and executed in a language or dialect known to the testator. Every will, other than a holographic will, must be subscribed at the end thereof by the testator himself or by the testator's name written by some other person in his presence, by his express direction, and attested and subscribed by three or more credible witnesses in the presence of the testator and of one another. The testator or the person requested by him to write his name and the instrumental witnesses of the will, must also sign, as aforesaid, each and every page thereof, except the last, on the left margin, and all the pages must be numbered correlatively in letters placed on the upper part of each page. The attestation must state the number of pages used upon which the will is written, and the fact that the testator signed the will and every page thereof, or caused some other person to write his name, under his express direction, in the presence of the instrumental witnesses, and that the latter witnessed and signed the will and all the pages thereof in the presence of the testator and of one another. If the attestation clause is in a language not known to the witnesses, it must be interpreted to them. Every will must be acknowledged before a notary public by the testator and the witnesses. If the testator be deaf, or a deaf-mute, he must personally read the will, if able to do so; otherwise, he must designate two persons to read it and communicate to him, in some practicable manner, the contents thereof. If the testator is blind, the will must be read to him twice; once by one of the suscribing witnesses, and again, by the notary public before whom the will is acknowledged.

Holographic Will.—A person may execute a holographic will which must be entirely written, dated, and signed by the hand of the testator himself. It is subject to no other form, and may be made in or out of the Philippines, and need not be witnessed. In holographic wills, the dispositions of the testator written below his signature must be dated and signed by him in order to make them valid as testamentary dispositions. In case of any insertion, cancellation, erasure or alteration in a holographic will, the testator must authenticate the same by his full signature.

When a Filipino is in a foreign country, he is authorized to make a will in any of the forms established by the law of the country in which he may be. Such will may be probated in the Philippines. The will of an alien who is abroad has effect in the Philippines if made with the formalities prescribed by the law of the place in which he resides, or according to the formalities observed in his country, or in conformity with those which the Civil Code of the Philippines prescribes. A will made in the Philippines by a citizen or subject of another country, which is executed in accordance with law of country of which he is citizen or subject, and which might be proved and allowed by law of his own country, has same effect as if executed according to laws of Philippines.

Two or more persons cannot make a will jointly, or in the same instrument, either for their reciprocal benefit or for the benefit of a third person. Wills of this kind executed by Filipinos in a foreign country are not valid in the Philippines, even though authorized by the laws of the country where they may have been executed.

Witnesses to Wills.—Any persons of sound mind and of the age of 18 years or more, and not blind, deaf or dumb, and able to read and write, may be a witness to the execution of a will. The following are disqualified from being witnesses to a will: (1) any person not domiciled in the Philippines; (2) those who have been convicted of falsification of a document, perjury or false testimony. If a person attests the execution of a will, to whom or to whose spouse, or parent, or child, a devise or legacy is given by such will, such devise or legacy is void, but so far only as concerns such person, or spouse, or parent, or child of such person, or any one claiming under such person or spouse, or parent, or child, unless there are three other competent witnesses to such will. However, such person so attesting will be admitted as a witness as if such device or legacy had not been made or given.

Codicil.—In order that a codicil may be effective, it must be executed as in the case of a will.

Revocation.—A will may be revoked by the testator at any time before his death. Any waiver or restriction of this right is void. A revocation made outside the Philippines, by a person who does not have his domicile in this country, is valid when it is made according to the law of the place where the will was made, or according to the law of the place in which the testator had his domicile at the time; and if the revocation takes place in this country, it is operative if it is in accordance with the provisions of the Civil Code.

Allowance and Disallowance of Wills.—No will may pass either real or personal property unless it is proved and allowed in accordance with the Rules of Court.

POLAND LAW DIGEST REVISER

Altheimer & Gray
Suite 4000
10 South Wacker Drive
Chicago, Illinois 60606
Telephone: 312-715-4000
Fax: 312-715-4800
Warsaw, Poland Office: UL Nowogrodzka 50, 00-950 Warsaw, Poland. Telephone: (48 22) 629-8357; (48 22) 621-2219. Fax: (48 22) 628-3640.

Prepared in cooperation with Professor Dr. Hab. A. Calus, Chairman, Department of International Law, Central School of Commerce, Warsaw, Poland

Reviser Profile

History and General Description: Altheimer & Gray, founded in 1915, is a Chicago-based multinational law firm focusing on business transactions worldwide with offices in Chicago, Warsaw, Prague, Kyiv, Bratislava, Istanbul and Shanghai.

More than 200 attorneys serve both publicly and privately owned companies, including firms listed on the New York, London, Warsaw, Prague and American Stock Exchanges and traded on NASDAQ. Our clients include large manufacturing, service, distribution, retail, real estate development, hotel and financial organizations, emerging and mid-size businesses, and the governments of several Central and Eastern European countries. In many instances our firm has had relationships with clients for more than 50 years. We also enjoy extensive and close relations with key government ministries, based on reputation and professionalism of our attorneys.

The firm's attorneys are experienced in a variety of international practice areas and have assisted foreign clients in connection with investment in the United States and American and foreign clients in their direct investments and licensing of technology outside the United States. Our attorneys counsel clients on matters that include international joint ventures, eurocurrency/eurodollar financing transactions, international arbitrations, taxation, complex financing, real estate and construction projects, acquisitions and divestitures, finance and banking, securities, antitrust, environmental matters, patents, licensing, intellectual property, insurance and counseling emerging governments.

Attorneys in the firm have significant contacts and relationships with foreign governments, lawyers, banks and corporations in Eastern and Western Europe; Canada; Latin America; and the Far East, including Japan and the People's Republic of China.

Eastern European Experience: Altheimer & Gray has represented clients in connection with Central and Eastern European matters for over twenty years. In September, 1990 we became the first American law firm to open an office in Poland. Then, in December, 1991, we opened an office in Prague, Czech Republic and in July, 1993 we expanded once more with the opening of offices in Kyiv, Ukraine and in December, 1993 Bratislava, Slovakia. In January, 1994 we opened an office in Istanbul, Turkey. The majority of our attorneys in the European offices are multilingual nationals, fluent in English. Several American lawyers are resident in those offices, while a large core group of American attorneys divide their time between Chicago and European assignments.

The firm's practice in Central and Eastern Europe, serviced from our Warsaw, Prague, Kyiv and Bratislava offices, concentrates in the following areas:

Privatizations: The privatization of Polish, Czech, Slovak and Ukrainian companies represents a major segment of the firm's current practice in Central and Eastern Europe.

In Poland, Altheimer & Gray represented the acquiror in the first privatization in which a Western firm was permitted to purchase a controlling interest in a state-owned enterprise. Virtually every aspect of this transaction created precedents which have had an impact on subsequent privatizations. The firm has since been involved in numerous major privatizations representing either the purchasers, the Ministry of Privatization, the Ministry of Industry or the acquired company. The firm is also involved in the developing Polish securities market and has represented several companies in connection with initial public offerings of their stock, including the first offering of bank shares.

In the Czech Republic, Altheimer & Gray has been involved in numerous privatizations representing the acquiring company. The firm has also acted as a Senior Advisor to the Czech Republic Ministry of Privatization during the initial period of the first wave of large-scale privatization. In this position, the firm was actively involved in the review and negotiation of many significant privatization projects involving foreign participation presented to the Ministry in the first wave of large-scale privatization. The firm also provided assistance in connection with the establishment of uniform procedures to increase the efficiency of the privatization process. In addition, the firm was the principal draftsman of the original form purchase agreements which were accepted by the Fund of National Property during the first wave of large-scale privatization and which have been distributed by the Ministry of Privatization for use in privatization transactions involving foreign participation. These form agreements represent the Ministry's institutional position on numerous issues arising in the acquisition process.

In the Ukraine, Altheimer & Gray is active in privatization and joint venture transactions. The firm advises foreign purchasers in connection with some of the first privatization transactions to be completed. Our attorneys counsel both the foreign companies and the government from initial structuring of negotiations to the completion of a successful business transaction. Clients include multinational companies in the food processing, consumer products, oil exploration and refining, telecommunications, construction equipment and hotel industries.

In Slovakia, our attorneys address matters similar to those the firm addresses in the Czech Republic—privatization and acquisition transactions, foreign investments and joint ventures.

Our practice in the region focuses on meeting the needs of clients entering these emerging markets.

During the last six years in Central and Eastern Europe the firm has been involved in numerous privatization, acquisition, joint venture, securities and finance transactions.

Joint Ventures and Foreign Investment: The firm is representing numerous multinational corporations, real estate developers, hotel chains, investors and others in structuring joint ventures with Polish, Czech, Slovakian, Ukrainian and Turkish enterprises.

Real Estate Development: The firm is representing clients in major commercial, industrial and hotel real estate development projects. Advice is provided in a wide range of legal matters, including tax planning, structuring and documentation, leasing, financing, management and construction arrangements.

Banking and Finance: The firm has represented major U.S. and European money-center financial institutions and a consortium of European banks and Scandinavian banking firms in their respective establishments of banking, financing and leasing operations. The firm also represents major international multilateral financial institutions, investment funds and merchant banks in connection with their financing and investment activities in Central, Eastern and Southern Europe.

Insurance: The firm advises clients on foreign and domestic business and insurance requirements and risk management matters and counsels insurers and reinsurers on the area's evolving statutory mandates.

Taxation: Altheimer & Gray serves as tax counsel to numerous local and multinational clients, providing advice on all aspects of local tax law with respect to both transaction matters and on-going operations.

Altheimer & Gray's Support Systems: We offer clients direct communication links via modem with our Chicago, Warsaw, Prague, Kyiv, Bratislava, Istanbul and Shanghai offices. Our network system in the Chicago office allows us to offer 24-hour service. Altheimer & Gray's multi-lingual support staff is equipped with the latest technology.

POLAND LAW DIGEST

(The following is a list of all Topics, including cross-references, covered in this Digest.)

POLAND LAW DIGEST

Revised for 1997 Edition by

ALTHEIMER & GRAY, of the Illinois Bar, and Warsaw, Poland. Prepared in cooperation with Professor Dr. Hab. A. Calus, Chairman, Department of International Law, Central School of Commerce, Warsaw, Poland.

Abbreviations used are: C.C. (Polish Civil Code); C.C.P. (Code of Civil Procedure, Law of Nov., 1964, as amended, 1989 and 1990); Comm.C. (Commercial Code of 1934); and Monitor Polski official gazette.

The Republic of Poland is an associate member of the EU.

PRELIMINARY NOTE (AS OF JULY 1, 1996):

Poland is still undergoing legal reforms, particularly in areas of constitutional and business law. However, at least in business law area, all major legislation necessary to return to market economy has been introduced, either through new enactments since 1989 or through revival and amendments of pre-World War II legislation. Therefore, current changes can be described more as improvements to existing system than revolutionary changes.

Poland found itself in advantageous situation when appropriate groundwork for implementing free-market-economy principles was accomplished because of many pre-WWII laws, which remained in force. Following are principal regulations of such statutes effective from 1930's: (a) Commercial Code of 1934 ("Comm. C."), in relation to general partnership, limited partnership, limited liability company and joint stock company together with regulations on commercial register, (b) Check Law and Law on Bills of Exchange of Apr. 28, 1936, (c) Bankruptcy Decree and Decree on restructuring agreement proceedings of Oct. 24, 1934. Crucial issue in these areas is not implementation of changes and amendments but creation of conditions for effective application of already existing regulations.

In 1995 several new important legislative enactments were made. Revised Law on Acquisition of Land by Foreigners now allows for purchase of real estate without permit in certain circumstances. Revised Law on Companies with Foreign Participation provides for investments without permits in most areas of economy. Revisions to Foreign Exchange Law have further liberalized foreign exchange regulations and include provisions that ease transfer of foreign currency by foreigners abroad.

ABSENTEES (POWER OF ATTORNEY):

During their absence, persons may generally delegate authority to any person of full capacity. Exceptions prescribed by law or pursuant to legal transactions apply to citizenship, family status, and when required, personal activity. It is common to give power of attorney. Legal transactions executed within limits of representative's authority produce direct consequences for those represented. General power of attorney confers authority for all acts of ordinary management. Acts falling outside of ordinary course of business require power of attorney defining type of such acts; unless law requires specific power of attorney for particular transaction. If particular form is required to validate transaction, power of attorney to perform that transaction must be given in required form. Power of attorney may be revoked at any time unless principal renounces right to revoke on grounds justified by legal relationship underlying such power. (arts. 95-109 C.C.).

Power of attorney may be given to sue, accept service, or accept proceedings, and is strictly construed. Before courts, absentee may be represented by advocate, by legal counselor in economic matters, by person who is joint party to absentee in proceedings, by strictly defined family members, by person managing its property or business or by someone who is in relationship of permanent mandate, when object of proceedings is within limit of mandate. (art. 87, §1 C.C.P.).

ACKNOWLEDGMENTS:

Acknowledgments are taken before Polish notary public. If document prepared in Poland is to be used abroad and attested by foreign consular office, it should be acknowledged upon request of interested party in one of following ways: (1) authenticity of signature of judge and court secretary and authenticity of court's official seal appearing in court's document should be acknowledged by President of such court or judge authorized by him, (2) authenticity of signature of notary public and of official seal of notary public office on document should be acknowledged directly by Ministry of Justice, (3) authenticity of signature of sworn translator and his seal on document's translation should be acknowledged by President of higher court or person authorized by him. (¶12, Ordinance of Minister of Justice, May 25, 1970—Instruction on legal turnover with foreigners in civil and criminal matters).

In principle, Polish law does not require, for acknowledgment of official documents prepared abroad, that they be attested by Polish office abroad. Official foreign documents enjoy same force of evidence as official Polish documents. If document, however, concerns conveyance of property located in Poland, or its authenticity is doubtful, document should be acknowledged by Polish diplomatic mission or consular office, unless Poland's international agreement provides otherwise. (art. 1138 C.C.P.). Acknowledgment of foreign documents by Polish diplomatic and consular missions abroad is explicitly required in certain laws and regulations.

Poland is not party to Hague Convention of 1961 on Abolishing Requirements of Legalisation for Foreign Public Documents. Poland's international obligations in such matter result from: Hague Conventions of 1905 and 1954 Concerning Civil Procedure, or bilateral conventions.

ACTIONS:

Generally, any person, natural or legal, may sue or be sued in Polish courts if he or it is of capacity to be party in such process. Entities with "quasi-legal personality" of Polish Law, like commercial partnership, so far as they may be directly subjects of right and duties, also have "court capacity" and may sue or be sued either solely in their name or jointly with their partners or members. Rules governing procedure in civil actions are set forth in C.C.P.

Polish State and its agencies do not enjoy jurisdictional immunity within Poland. Unless otherwise regulated by law, actions against Polish State are brought against State Treasury. Any act in connection with legal proceedings brought by or against State Treasury is undertaken by authority of state organizational unit, activity of which is connected with claim, or by authority of supervising entity. (art. 67, §2 C.C.P.). (As to actions against foreign state, see topic Courts.)

Polish law, like other laws of continental European states, does not know action in equity. Legal proceedings in Polish courts may take form, depending on nature of case, of litigation or non-litigious proceedings. Litigation is commenced by filing complaint with court. Non-litigious proceedings may be conducted pursuant to general provisions or special provisions. C.C.P. provides for special proceedings in: personal actions, family actions, real property, inheritance, state actions, and court deposits. Service of process on defendant is accomplished ex officio by court. Before courts, parties need not be represented by advocate. Incapable person is represented by guardian. There are no special modes of proof of foreign claims. For proof of foreign law, see topic Foreign Law.

Appropriate Forum.—Appropriate venue is generally place of residence of defendant: for natural person, place where person remains with intention of permanent residence; for legal person, place of its seat. Venue for State Treasury is place of seat of state entity activity of which is connected with given claim. Seat of legal entity is place where its management is located, unless law or statute provide otherwise. Appropriate venue also may be: place of performance of contract; place where tort was committed; situs of real property; situs of assets; or place of corporation's branch if litigation involves such branch's business. If defendant is not domiciled in Poland, general venue is determined pursuant to place of his stay in Poland or, if such place is not known or is not located in Poland, last place of defendant's residence in Poland. On jurisdiction as to subject matter, see topic Courts.

Costs.—Losing party is required to refund to adversary all costs necessary to defend rights (costs of proceedings) upon adversary's demand. Necessary litigation costs of party represented by lawyer include compensation and expenses of his lawyer, court costs and costs of personal appearance of party required by court. Court decides costs in each decision ending litigation. Determination of costs by courts in civil cases is regulated by Law of June 13, 1967, as amended 1982 and 1991. Court costs include court fees and expenses. Court fees consist of entry and office fee. Expenses include, for example, fees of witnesses, experts, interpreters, appointed guardians and costs of telephone or telegraph announcements. Party filing documents subject to fees or giving rise to expenses is required to cover court fees unless law or court provides otherwise. Entry fee is percentage fee, unless regulations provide for established fixed fee or maximum or minimum fee. Amount of proportional entry fee is based on amount in controversy. In case of fees with maximum or minimum limits, there are two types of fees, temporary and final, which should be determined by court in decision which first ends litigation. Office fees are collected for executory acts, certifications, excerpts, experts and other documents released from files. Party which files motion which causes expenses to be incurred must post amount to pay such expenses. Amounts of entry and office fees are determined by Minister of Justice. Following are decrees currently in force: on determination of entry fees in civil proceedings, decree of May 17, 1993; on determination of office fees in civil proceedings, decree of Mar. 13, 1991, as amended July 28, 1991. Entry fee amounts to: in civil proceedings—8% of value of subject matter in controversy but not less than 10 zlotys; in economic disputes—8% of value up to 10,000 zlotys, from 10,001 up to 50,000 zlotys—800 zlotys and 7% from surplus over 10,000 zlotys; from 50,001 up to 100,000 zlotys—3,600 zlotys and 6% from surplus over 50,000 zlotys; over 100,000 zlotys—6,600 zlotys and 5% from surplus over 100,000 but not more than 100,000 zlotys. Court may waive fees on petition: of natural person stating facts of family status, property and income, on proof of detriment to person's ability to provide family necessities; or of organization with no legal personality, on proof of insufficient resources.

Lawyer's fee is based on value in controversy, usually percentage thereof. Contingency fees are considered unethical.

Security for Costs.—Unless otherwise provided for in law or in international agreements, aliens commencing civil action before Polish court must, upon defendant's demand, post security for defendant's costs. According to C.C.P. (arts. 1119 and 1120) alien need not post security if resident in Poland, or alien has sufficient property situated in Poland for securing costs, or reciprocity exists between Poland and country of which plaintiff is citizen, or action is based on agreement of Polish jurisdiction. Reciprocity exists with signatories of Hague Convention on Civil Procedure of 1954.

Limitation of.—See topic Limitation of Actions.

Lack of Jurisdiction.—See topic Courts.

AFFIDAVITS:

Statements or declarations reduced to writing and sworn to or affirmed before officer who has authority to administer oath or affirmation is unknown as item of special evidence in Polish law. Affidavit taken abroad or within Poland, like any written or printed declaration or statement of facts made voluntarily, may be used as evidence in court. In such case, court evaluates credibility and strength of evidence according to its

AFFIDAVITS . . . *continued*
own judgment based upon "comprehensive consideration of collected evidence material". (art. 233, §1 C.C.P.).

Under Polish law, provision permitting for use of affidavits is not necessary for execution of affidavit for foreign use before Polish notary. Affidavit may be executed in Polish and additionally in any other language spoken by notary or any other language if sworn translator thereof is present. Affidavit's effectiveness before foreign court depends on its compliance with requirements of respective foreign law.

AGENCY:

Representation under Polish law is general concept of acting on account of principal and corresponds to American agency law. Three types of contracts express agency concept in Polish law: contract of mandate, contract of agency and contract of sale-purchase on commission. Under contract of mandate, person accepting order is obliged to act on behalf of principal in specified legal transaction. (art. 734, §1 C.C.). Under contract of agency, person accepting order (agent) is obliged for fee (commission) to act as intermediary on permanent basis when concluding specific contracts on behalf of principal or to conclude such contracts in principal's name. (art. 758, §1 C.C.). Under contract of sale-purchase on commission, person accepting order (commission agent) is obliged for fee (commission) and within scope of his business to buy or sell movables on account of principal (commissioning party) but in agent's own name. (art. 765 C.C.).

See topic Principal and Agent.

ALIENS:

Law on Aliens of Mar. 29, 1963, as amended, defines alien as natural person who does not have Polish citizenship. (art. 1). Persons without citizenship are generally regarded as aliens. Legal person (i.e., corporation) with seat abroad has status of alien. Law of Mar. 24, 1920 on purchase of real estate by foreigners, as amended in 1988, regards as aliens any legal person having its seat in Poland but which is controlled, directly or indirectly, by alien natural or legal persons. Corporation of which at least 50% of equity capital is possessed directly or indirectly by aliens (legal or natural persons) is deemed to be alien corporation. Law of June 14, 1991 on Companies with Participation of Foreign Parties, as amended, defines "foreign subject" which embraces: legal persons having registered principal place of business abroad, natural persons domiciled abroad, and companies without legal personality established by such persons.

Law on International Private Law of 1965 states: "Aliens in Poland may have rights and obligations equal to Polish citizens except when laws indicate otherwise." Aliens have essentially same rights and duties as Polish citizens except with regard to voting rights or free social security.

Acquisition of real estate by foreigners requires foreign purchasers to apply for consent of Minister of Internal Affairs. See also topic Real Property.

Foreigner, having citizenship of two or more states, is treated as citizen of only one such state. Poland is party to International Convention on Certain Issues Regarding Conflict of Citizenship Laws and protocol thereto concerning statelessness, signed at the Hague in 1930.

Law of Feb. 15, 1962 on Polish Citizenship, as amended, provides that marriage of Polish citizen with person who is not Polish citizen does not alter his citizenship status. Change of citizenship by one spouse does not alter citizenship status of other spouse. (art. 3). Poland is party to International Convention on Citizenship of Married Women, signed in New York in 1957.

See topics Immigration; Foreign Investment; Taxation.

ALIMONY:

See topic Divorce.

ANTI-TRUST LAWS:

See topic Monopolies and Trade Restraints.

APPEAL AND ERROR:

Judiciary.—Judgments of trial court (courts of original jurisdiction) are appealable on legal or factual basis. (arts. 367, 368 C.C.P.). Appeal in civil case may be filed within two weeks from delivery of judgment and its justification to appealing party. (art. 371, §1 C.C.P.). There is only one regular stage of appeal. Appellate courts may: dismiss appeal, accept appeal and reverse lower court's decision in whole or in part and remand decision for second proceeding to court comprised of different judges (in specified instances, to different court) and can reverse lower court's decision and render meritorious decision, if case concerns violation of substantive law, or, in other types of violations, if, in connection with appellate proceeding, there is sufficient basis for resolution of issues. (arts. 387-90 C.C.P.). Higher courts (sad wojewodzki) serve as appellate courts for lower district courts. If higher court acts in first instance, then appeal is brought to appellate court. If significant legal uncertainty exists in appeal to higher or appellate court, court may refuse to render decision and instead present case to Supreme Court. Supreme Court can answer legal question or accept case for appeal. (art. 391, §1 C.C.P.). Pending appeal, execution of trial court judgment will be delayed (with some exceptions).

Administrative Appeals.—Decisions of administrative bodies are appealable. As general rule, supervisory entity reviews appeal. Appeal may be filed within 14 days from date of delivery of administrative decision to party, and, if decision is oral, from day it was announced. Detailing of grounds for appeal is not necessary. It is sufficient that it appears from appeal that party is not satisfied with decision. Specific provisions may prescribe other requirements as to content of appeal. Appeal is made to appropriate appellate entity through body that issued decision. Unless otherwise specified by law, decision is not executed before termination of time to file appeal, and filing of appeal in specified period postpones execution of decision. In cases where appeal is made by all parties, organ that rendered decision may set aside decision or modify it. Parties may appeal new decision. Appellate body may affirm decision, reverse it and, depending on degree to which facts were presented on appeal, render meritorious decision or remand case for review by organ of original jurisdiction. Appellate body may not render decision unfavorable to appellant unless original decision is clearly contrary to law or public interests. Decision of appellate body may be appealed to Supreme Administrative Court if it is contrary to law and all other administrative remedies are exhausted, or if appeal is brought by prosecutor's office. Appeal may be brought within 30 days from date of delivery of decision. Filing of appeal does not postpone execution of decision unless administrative organ or administrative court decides otherwise. In rendering judgment, administrative court is not confined to matters brought up on appeal. Administrative court may set aside decision and remand, or determine that it is invalid or contrary to law.

Extraordinary Appeal.—If decision is clearly contrary to law or interests of Republic of Poland, then Minister of Justice, First President of Supreme Court, Chief Prosecutor of Republic of Poland and Spokesman for Human Rights, and, in cases involving employment rights and social benefits, Minister of Employment and Social Policy, can bring extraordinary appeal from all binding final decisions. Extraordinary appeals are brought to Supreme Court. Party may also petition Minister of Justice or Chief Prosecutor to bring extraordinary appeal. Examination of extraordinary appeal from decision of Supreme Court is made by seven justices of Supreme Court. Extraordinary appeals from decision of Supreme Administrative Court are reviewed by five Supreme Court justices.

Clarification, Supplementation and Interpretation of Decisions.—Court, or if applicable, administrative body, may, on its own motion or at request of party to suit or proceeding, clarify in judgment or decision, inaccuracies, mistakes in writing or calculations, or other obvious errors in judgment or decision. Within 14 days from delivery or rendering of judgment or decision, party may also request court or administrative body to complete such judgment or decision in areas body was obliged to address in such judgment or decision. Such court or administrative body may resolve issues that were not addressed in judgment or decision or in separate judgment or decision.

Reinitiation of Proceeding.—In cases specified by law depending on type of proceedings (civil or administrative), one can request reinitiation of proceeding terminated by binding or final decision, when judgment was rendered or decision made as result of crime, or when judgment was based on falsified or forged document, and when, in connection with decision, evidence on which important conclusions as to facts were made turned out to be false. Reinitiation is barred after certain period of time unless party was precluded from acting or could not be adequately represented.

Arbitration awards are not appealable. See topic Arbitration and Award.

Source of Law.—Basic source of law for above-described matters is C.C.P. and Code of Administrative Procedure of June 14th, 1960 (as am'd).

See topic Courts.

ARBITRATION AND AWARD:

Contracting parties, within limits of their capacity to freely incur obligations, may take controversies concerning property rights to arbitration, excluding controversies concerning alimony or employment relations. Agreement to arbitrate must be in writing and signed by both parties. Agreement must indicate precisely object of controversy or relation which gave rise to claim. Agreement may include names of arbitrators involved, as well as one superarbitrator, or, if arbitrators have not been selected, petition may include number of arbitrators and way they are to be chosen. Until parties fulfill arbitration requirements, no parties may petition regular court. Agreement may indicate also foreign arbitral tribunal to which parties may bring dispute (jurisdiction of Polish regular courts is excluded). Validity of such clause depends upon at least one party having domicile abroad or operating business abroad to which claim relates, and also upon agreement being binding according to law applied in foreign forum. For Polish court to yield jurisdiction to foreign forum one party must object alleging exception before arguments have begun upon suit's subject matter.

Any person having full legal capacity to conduct legal transactions and fully possessed of public rights and citizenship rights may be arbitrator. State judges may not be arbitrators. Unless otherwise indicated in agreement to arbitrate, when one arbitrator or superarbitrator is not indicated or chosen, parties may ask lower regular court to appoint arbitrator and superarbitrator. Party may ask that arbitrator or superarbitrator be stricken upon same grounds as those for which judges are struck from hearing certain cases. Until arbitration has commenced, parties may prescribe procedure to be used during arbitration. When no procedure has been prescribed, arbitral tribunal may prescribe any procedure it deems proper. Arbitral tribunal is not bound by rules of civil procedure, but must establish all circumstances necessary to pass judgment on controversy before it. When making award, if there are parts of judgment on which required majority of votes cannot be reached, agreement to arbitrate ceases to be in effect. Awards of arbitral tribunal are passed by absolute majority vote of arbitrators (simple majority vote with all voting), unless agreement to arbitrate requires unanimity. Awards should include, among other things, reasons taken into account by court and basis for its award. There is no appeal from award of arbitral tribunal. Arbitral award has same legal effect as judgment of regular state court after state court declares its enforceability. Parties may request that award be quashed. Petition to quash can be taken to regular court within one month of receipt of award (when calculating this time period, calculation is different when petition is based upon argument for trial de novo). Bases upon which regular court may quash award of arbitral tribunal are precisely described in art. 712, §1 C.C.P. Reasons justifying decisions to quash include that: no agreement exists; one or more of parties have been denied possibility of protecting their rights before arbitral tribunal; award concerning party's rights is not logically formulated, contains contradictions or illegalities; decision is contrary to principles of "social coexistence" of Poland; procedural rules were not followed; or reasons exist which would be basis for instituting trial de novo in court proceeding.

Four arbitration panels normally operate: National Economic Chamber's Arbitration Court in Warsaw (general jurisdiction); International Court for Maritime and Intraland Disputes in Gdynia (limited jurisdiction); conciliatory court governing cotton disputes in Gdynia (limited jurisdiction); conciliatory court governing wool disputes in Gdynia (limited jurisdiction). Principles of arbitration of National Economic Chamber are

ARBITRATION AND AWARD . . . *continued*

based on rules of former college of arbitrators within Polish Chamber of Foreign Trade established in 1947.

Poland is party to several international arbitration conventions: U.N. Convention on Recognition and Enforcement of Foreign Arbitral Awards signed in New York June 10, 1958 ("U.N. Convention"); European Convention on International Commercial Arbitration signed in Geneva Apr. 21, 1961; and Convention signed in Moscow May 26, 1972 concerning arbitration of civil law controversies resulting from economic and scientific cooperation. In relation with states which are not parties to U.N. Convention, Poland is bound by provisions of Geneva protocol on arbitration dated June 23, 1923. In regard to arbitration initiated ad hoc, practice of Polish foreign trade is to invoke in agreements to arbitrate Arbitration Rules of United Nations Economic Commission For Europe and also invoke Arbitration Rules of United Nations Commission on International Trade Law (UNCITRAL).

Awards of arbitral tribunal have legal force of regular court's judgment. Executory judgment is made by lower or regular court of general jurisdiction over defendant. When jurisdiction cannot be established, parties should look to district where transaction is normally carried out. If winning party wants to execute award abroad, executory award is made by state court in whose district arbitral tribunal sat. Awards of arbitral tribunals pronounced abroad, if they are able to be executed, are self-executing if execution is provided for in international agreement. When arbitral award announced abroad is to be executed in Poland, higher court having jurisdiction over debtor will decide upon its executability. Alternatively, if such higher court cannot be located, then court to be referred to is court in which execution of foreign award is to take place. Both U.S.A. and Poland are parties to New York Arbitration Convention ("New York Convention"). Between those two countries, awards of arbitral tribunals can be executed without any problems.

ASSIGNMENTS:

Assignment of Claim.—Creditors may transfer claims to third persons without consent of debtor unless transfer would be contrary to law, contractual stipulation, or nature of obligation. Claim and all rights connected pass to buyer, particularly claims for unpaid interest. Contract of sale, exchange, donation or other contract obliges creditor to transfer claim to buyer unless specific provision states otherwise or parties otherwise agree. If claim is contained in writing, assignment of claim should be in writing. Notice to debtor is not required but it is advisable to prevent bona fide debtor from discharging his debt by payment to assignor. (arts. 509-518 C.C.).

Taking Over Debt.—Third persons may step into shoes of debtor, thereby releasing debtor from obligation. Debts may be assumed by contract between creditor and third person with consent of debtor or by contract between debtor and third person with consent of creditor. Consent of creditor is ineffective if creditor does not know that person taking over debt is insolvent. Contracts concerning assumption of debt must be in writing to be valid as must creditor's consent. Person assuming debts may assert all defenses of original debtor against creditor except for set-off defense from previous debtor's claim. If claim was secured by guarantee or limited right in rem established by third person, guarantee or limited right in rem ceases to exist at moment of assumption unless guarantor or third person expressly consents to continuation of security. (arts. 519-526 C.C.).

Assignment of any Property, Real or Personal.—See topic Sales.

ASSIGNMENTS FOR BENEFIT OF CREDITORS:

See topics Assignments; Bankruptcy and Restructure.

ASSOCIATIONS:

Association is voluntary union of unlimited number of persons, membership and membership fund which may change, that conducts joint economic activities in joint interest of its members. Association law is governed by Act of May 10, 1995 on Associations, as amended. Foreign citizens living in Poland may establish associations according to laws binding on Polish citizens. Foreigners living outside of Poland may become members of association whose charter accepts foreigners living abroad. Assets of association are private property of its members.

It takes at least ten individuals or three legal entities who want to establish association may adopt statute of association and file application for registration with registry court. Registry court approves registration after determination that statute is in accordance with law. National Association Council maintains registry of associations. Association gains legal personality at time of registration into registry.

Meeting of all members of association is association's supreme decision-making authority. Associations also must have governing board and supervisory board that acts as internal control.

Association's property consists of membership fees, gifts, inheritance, legacies, profits from association's economic operation, profits from association property and public charity. Associations may organize economic activity according to general rules defined by law. Profit from such activities serves to attain charter aims and cannot be divided between members.

ATTACHMENT:

To secure claim which can be brought to regular court or arbitration tribunal, court may issue temporary order if claim is credible and lack of security could deprive creditor of proper remedy. Issuance of temporary order is allowed in other cases when it is necessary to secure execution of judgment. Security of pecuniary claims is accomplished by: seizure of tangible property, work salary or assets, or other claims; compulsory real estate mortgage or pledge recorded in ship register; prohibition on sale or rental of real estate not having land register book, or for which land register book was lost or destroyed.

If object of security is not pecuniary claim, court issues order which it considers suitable, including orders envisaged to secure pecuniary claims. In choosing appropriate means of securing claim, court takes interests of parties into account in order to assure creditors' claims or proper protection of their rights and in order to avoid charging debtor more than necessary. When security receivership is established, it will be carried out according to provisions on receivership in process of execution from real estate, with reservation that debtor cannot be nominated as receiver.

ATTORNEYS AND COUNSELORS:

Polish legal professionals are divided into two categories: Advocates and Legal Counsels. Each of these professions is regulated by separate statute, both of 1982, and initially were intended to perform different roles in socialist economy. Advocates were intended to render legal services to individuals and Legal Counsels were to provide legal advice to then dominant state sector of economy. With decreasing role of state participation in economy and development of public sector, distinctions between character of legal practice by these two professions are sometimes blurred. There is ongoing discussion about unifying Advocates and Legal Counsels Bar. Presently, however, Advocates and Legal Counsels are still regulated by separate statutes and have in many instances different rights and obligations.

Advocates.—Goal of Advocate Bar is, pursuant to statute, to provide legal advice, protect civic rights and freedoms and participate in development and application of laws. Advocate Bar, consisting of Advocates and Advocate Trainees, is organized in form of self governing body. In order to be admitted to Advocate Bar person must: (a) be of good repute, (b) be Polish citizen enjoying full civic rights, (c) be law school graduate and (d) have participated in three year Advocate training and passed bar exam. Following persons are exempted from obligation to participate in Advocate training and passing bar exam: (a) professors of law and doctors with habilitation in legal studies, (b) persons who have been judges, prosecutors or notaries for three years, (c) persons who are qualified as judge, prosecutor or notary and have been employed as Legal Counsel for three years, and (d) persons who are qualified as Legal Counsels and have been employed for three years as such.

Advocates, in their practice, are only subject to laws passed by Parliament. While exercising their duties, they are entitled to same legal protection as judges and prosecutors and enjoy freedom of speech to extent determined by general character of their duties and limitations contained in laws. Advocate may be prosecuted for abuse of freedom of speech only in disciplinary proceeding. Advocates are obligated to keep confidential all information obtained in connection with performance of their services. Statute, subject to some exceptions, prohibits Advocate from entering into employment agreement. It also prohibits Advocate from rendering services in circuit where his/her spouse is employed by police or his/her relative works as judge or prosecutor. Advocate may not render legal services also if: he/she is married to person working as judge or prosecutor, he/she is more than 70 years old, has been legally incapacitated, or has been considered by Circuit Advocate Chamber permanently unable to perform his/her duties as Advocate. Advocate may refuse to provide legal services to person only for material reasons and has to inform such person of such reasons. Advocates' fees for representing clients before court are limited in amount pursuant to Regulations issued by Minister of Justice. Advocates perform their services either as members of Advocate cooperative, or, upon obtaining permit from Minister of Justice, may establish private practice. Advocate cooperatives, dominant when law on Advocates was adopted, have presently become exception. Majority of Advocates have established private practices.

All Advocates are members of Advocate self-government body—Circuit Advocate Chamber. Competencies of General Assembly of Circuit Advocate Chamber include (a) election of Circuit Advocate Council, Circuit Disciplinary Court, Circuit Supervisory Board and delegates to National Advocate Assembly, (b) approving budget of circuit, and (c) general supervision over activity of Circuit Advocate Council and Circuit Supervisory Board. Circuit Advocate Council is responsible for all matters not reserved for other Advocate organs including admitting new Advocates to bar. Circuit Disciplinary Court decides in disciplinary matters of circuit bar members. National Advocate Assembly (a) elects General Advocate Council, Upper Disciplinary Court and Upper Supervisory Board, (b) exercises general supervision over General Advocate Council and Upper Supervisory Board, and (c) has rule making power with respect to principles of professional conduct by Advocates and rules of Advocate self-government. Competencies of General Advocate Council include: (a) representation of Advocate Bar, (b) supervision of Circuit Advocate Councils, (c) determination of rules regarding training of Advocate Trainees, and (d) participation in preparation of laws and regulations concerning Advocates. Upper Disciplinary Court hears appeals from decisions of Circuit Disciplinary Courts. Advocate ceases to be member of Circuit Advocate Chamber upon: (a) death, (b) resignation, (c) becoming member of different Circuit Advocate Chamber, (d) employment in police, organs of justice administration, or as notary, (e) being drafted to military, (f) loss of Polish citizenship, (g) loss of civic rights or right to practice law resulting from court decision, or (h) disciplinary decision on expulsion from Advocate Bar.

Legal Counsels.—Goal of Legal Counsels Bar is, pursuant to statute, to provide legal services to state and cooperative enterprises, social organizations and companies with participation of state, cooperative capital or social organizations. It is widely recognized in practice that Legal Counsels may also render legal services to private companies and associations. In order to be admitted to Legal Counsel Bar, person must: (a) be of good repute, (b) be Polish citizen enjoying full civic rights, (c) have full legal capacity to undertake legal actions, (d) be law school graduate and (e) have participated in three year Legal Counsel training and passed bar exam. Following persons are exempted from obligation to have participated in Legal Counsel training and passing bar exam: (a) professors of law and doctors with habilitation in legal studies, (b) Advocates and persons entitled to be admitted to Advocate Bar, (c) persons who have been judges, prosecutors or notaries for three years, and (d) persons who are qualified as judge, prosecutor or notary and have been employed as Legal Counsel for three years. Persons who have been judicial, notarial or prosecutor trainees and who have passed applicable professional exam are exempted from obligation to participate in Legal Counsel training but must pass Legal Counsel bar exam.

Legal Counsels may provide legal services on basis of employment agreement or on basis of legal services contracts. Employer of Legal Counsel does not have right to influence contents of Legal Counsel's legal opinion. Legal Counsel does not have right to advise his client/employer in any matter in which he is party interested in outcome of such matter, or in disputes where he is Legal Counsel of other party or has such relations with other party which may influence outcome of dispute. While exercising

See Topical Index in front part of this volume.

ATTORNEYS AND COUNSELORS . . . *continued*
their duties, Legal Counsels are entitled to same legal protection as judges and prosecutors and enjoy freedom of speech to extent determined by need for such freedom arising under particular circumstances and limitations contained in laws. Legal Counsel may be prosecuted for abuse of freedom of speech only in disciplinary proceeding. Legal Counsel representing client before court is entitled only to compensation which is limited in amount pursuant to Regulations issued by Minister of Labor.

All Legal Counsels are members of Legal Counsel self-government body—Circuit Legal Counsel Chamber. Competencies of General Assembly of Circuit Legal Counsel Chamber include (a) election of Circuit Legal Counsel Council, Circuit Disciplinary Court, Disciplinary Officer, Circuit Supervisory Board and delegates to National Legal Counsel Assembly, (b) approving budget of circuit, and (c) general supervision over activity of Circuit Legal Counsel Council and Circuit Supervisory Board. Responsibilities of Circuit Legal Counsel Council include (a) representing professional interests of Legal Counsels in that circuit, (b) organization of professional training of Legal Counsels, (c) evaluation and supervision over quality of services rendered by Legal Counsels and Legal Counsel Trainees, and (d) cooperation with administration and other bodies in matters connected with application of law and rendering legal services. Circuit Disciplinary Court decides in disciplinary matters of members of circuit bar, brought by Disciplinary Officer. National Legal Counsel Assembly (a) elects General Legal Counsel Council, Upper Disciplinary Court and Upper Supervisory Board, (b) exercises general supervision over General Council and Upper Supervisory Board, and (c) has rule making power with respect to principles of professional conduct by Legal Counsels and rules of Legal Counsel self-government. Competencies of General Legal Counsel Council self-government. Competencies of General Legal Counsel Council include (a) representation of Legal Counsel Bar, (b) opining new laws, (c) supervision of Circuit Legal Counsel Councils, and (d) determination of rules regarding training of Legal Counsel trainees. Upper Disciplinary Court hears appeals from decisions of circuit Disciplinary Courts. Legal Counsel ceases to be member of Circuit Legal Counsel Bar upon (a) his/her application, (b) loss in whole or in part of capacity to undertake legal actions, (c) loss of Polish citizenship, (d) loss of civic rights resulting from court decision, (e) death, or (f) loss of right to practice law resulting from disciplinary or court decision.

AUTOMOBILE:

See topic Motor Vehicles.

BANKRUPTCY AND RESTRUCTURE:

Bankruptcy is regulated in Poland by Bankruptcy Decree of Oct. 24, 1934, as amended, which until 1990 was of marginal significance since bankruptcy of state enterprise was subject to separate provisions. Bankruptcy Decree applies to all business entities, including companies or enterprises established by foreign entities with exception of entities not subject to registration of economic activity pursuant to Law of Dec. 23, 1988 on Economic Activity, as amended.

Grounds for Bankruptcy Declaration.—General grounds are insolvency of particular business entity. Business entities are deemed insolvent when they fail to pay debts. Business legal entities and general partnerships in course of liquidation will be declared bankrupt when their property is not sufficient to cover debts. Bankruptcy declaration is to be proceeded by motion therefor, which may be filed directly by debtor or any one of his creditors. Duty to file motion for bankruptcy declaration in court rests upon each business entity which discontinues paying its debts or, in case of legal entities and commercial partnerships, upon its normal representatives or liquidators, if property of legal entity or partnership is not sufficient to cover debts. Motion is to be filed within two weeks from day of emergence of grounds for bankruptcy declaration (i.e., day of debt payment discontinuance or day when it was revealed that property is not sufficient to cover debts). Application for initiation of composition settlement proceedings waives requirement to declare bankruptcy. Person who failed to file motion is liable for resulting damages to creditor (liability of more than one person is joint and several). Motion is to include identification of debtor, location of debtor's enterprise or his other property as well as circumstances justifying motion and their genuineness. If bankruptcy declaration is required of creditor, he is to make his claim credible, if it is required of debtor, he is to submit balance sheet of his property and list of his creditors or indicate reasons why he cannot pay.

Competency of Court and Bodies Engaged in Bankruptcy Proceedings.— Proceedings for bankruptcy declaration are initiated in district court appropriate for area where main plant of debtor's enterprise is located. If debtor does not have his enterprise in Poland, proceedings are initiated in district court appropriate for area of debtor's domicile or seat or in case of lack of such domicile or seat in district court appropriate for area where debtor's property is located. Bankruptcy declaration decisions are adjudicated by three professional judges of business court, as part of district court. Court may require down payment for proceeding costs from creditor who filed motion for bankruptcy declaration. Prior to ruling on motion, court may, upon creditor's demand, hand down temporary orders appropriate to secure debtor's property. Court's decision on bankruptcy declaration includes identification of bankrupt, summons for creditors to produce claims within designated time and appointment of judge-commissioner and receiver in bankruptcy (it may be legal entity). Date of court's decision is automatically date of bankruptcy declaration. Decisions are publicly announced and delivered to bankrupt, his successor, receiver in bankruptcy and creditor who demanded declaration. After bankruptcy declaration, activities of bankruptcy proceedings are conducted by judge-commissioner with exception of those reserved for court. Judge-commissioner, among other specific activities allotted to him, will direct proceedings, supervise receiver in bankruptcy and specify activities that receiver in bankruptcy may not perform without his permission or consent of creditors' council. Receiver in bankruptcy takes over property by virtue of law, administers such property and carries out liquidation. Receiver in bankruptcy is entrusted with various duties: informing chamber of finance creditors with whose address he is familiar, and banks and institutions where debtor may have safes or deposited money or other property. Receiver in bankruptcy is entitled to demand necessary information concerning bankrupt's property from offices, institutions and other people in possession thereof. Receiver in bankruptcy reports his activities and submits adequately justified periodical as well as final financial reports. If receiver in bankruptcy does not fulfill his duties properly, he may be replaced by another. He is also responsible for damages resulting from careless carrying out of his duties. Receiver in bankruptcy is entitled to compensation, which is set by court upon recommendation of judge-commissioner according to amount of work accomplished as well as reimbursement for expenses caused by carrying out his duties.

Results of Bankruptcy Declaration.—Bankrupt is required to indicate and relinquish all property as well as commercial books, correspondence and other documents. Debtor is not allowed to leave place of residence without consent of judge-commissioner. Court may decide upon judge-commissioner's request or on its own to apply certain coercion measures in respect to bankrupt engaged or suspected to be engaged in activities aimed at concealment of property, its encumbrance with illusive obligations and generally making calculation of property more difficult. (Provisions of C.C.P. on execution of nonmonetary performances apply to foregoing.) As result of bankruptcy declaration, bankrupt loses ability to use and dispose of property belonging to him or it on day of bankruptcy declaration as well as acquired in course of proceedings (such property is called estate in bankruptcy). Legal actions of bankrupt concerning property included in estate in bankruptcy and undertaken after bankruptcy is declared are legally ineffective in respect to such estate. Anyone, however, who executed contracts with bankrupt may require return of objects that enhanced estate. Property not belonging to bankrupt is excluded from estate in bankruptcy and released to person entitled to it. If bankrupt transferred object which did not belong to him or it, and received reciprocal performance, it is to be relinquished to one entitled to it, providing it is included in estate in bankruptcy and separated from other property. Course of action is similar when object is transferred by receiver in bankruptcy. If receiver knew object is subject to exclusion, entitled persons may demand compensation as well. Monetary obligations of bankrupt which are not yet due become due on day of bankruptcy declaration. Nonmonetary property obligations are transformed on day of bankruptcy declaration into monetary obligations by virtue of law. In event of bankruptcy of one spouse, provided joint marital property established, or joint property of marital achievements, joint property is included in bankruptcy estate. Donations of bankrupt made within one year before motion for bankruptcy declaration is filed are ineffective in respect to estate in bankruptcy. Similarly, legal actions undertaken by bankrupt against consideration with spouse, relatives or kin (relation established pursuant to appropriate provisions) within six months before motion for bankruptcy declaration filed are also ineffective.

Bankruptcy Proceedings.—Further proceedings after bankruptcy is declared take place in declaring court. Court consists of three judges. Judge-commissioner may require creditor who filed motion for bankruptcy declaration to deposit down payment for costs of further proceedings. Announcements provided by bankruptcy law are displayed in court building and published in at least one popular daily newspaper. Judge-commissioner may, upon request of receiver in bankruptcy, also order placement of announcements in other domestic and international daily newspapers. Upon request of bankrupt or creditor, announcement is to be published in daily indicated by them and paid for by them. Court records are available for participants of proceedings and for everyone who can sufficiently justify need for making copies and excerpts. Receiver in bankruptcy, on his own motion or upon order of judge-commissioner initiates sealing of entire or part of bankrupt's property. Sealing is executed by court executive officer or notary public. Receiver in bankruptcy is to prepare inventory of estate in bankruptcy and estimate it as soon as possible. Inventory list is to be set up by receiver in bankruptcy or court executive officer or notary public upon his request. Both bankrupt and members of creditors council are to be notified and may be present at inventory preparation. Receiver in bankruptcy is to produce balance sheet or correct bankrupt's balance sheet based upon inventory list, other documents and estimation. After inventory is set up and balance sheet produced, receiver in bankruptcy is to carry out liquidation through sale of real and personal property, execution of claims from bankrupt's debtors and other bankrupt's property rights included in bankruptcy estate. Enterprise of bankrupt will be sold in its entirety if possible. Purchaser of enterprise is not liable for bankrupt's debts. Sale through bankruptcy proceedings bears same legal consequences as sale through execution. Judge-commissioner is to appoint creditors council, if necessary, or if creditors holding at least $1/5$ of total claim amount (which have been acknowledged or recognized as probable) so require. Creditors council is to assist receiver in bankruptcy, supervise him, examine state of funds in estate, grant permission for activities which may be carried out only pursuant thereto (e.g., further enterprise operation longer than three months from date of bankruptcy declaration or sale of rights or claims) and deliver opinions in other matters upon request of receiver in bankruptcy. Creditors council may demand explanations from receiver in bankruptcy, and examine books and documents concerning bankruptcy. Provided council is not established, all activities are to be assumed by judge-commissioner. During bankruptcy proceedings, creditor's assembly may be gathered. Such assembly is convened by judge-commissioner's announcement at least two weeks prior to gathering when law so requires or upon request of at least two creditors jointly holding not less than $1/3$ of total amount of acknowledged claims as well as in cases judge-commissioner deems necessary. Voting rights belong to participants holding acknowledged claims.

Proclamation and Recognition of Claim.—Each creditor of bankrupt willing to participate in bankruptcy proceedings, which is conditioned by recognition of claim, is to timely proclaim his claim to judge-commissioner regardless if secured by mortgage, pledge, or in any other way, subject to deduction or not. Proclamation is to be executed in writing (required contents and annexures are specified in law). Documents justifying proclamation are to be attached thereto in original or certified copy. Creditor domiciled abroad is to designate place of residence for purpose of deliveries. Immediately after period for claim proclamation expires, receiver in bankruptcy is to produce draft of list of claims. Prior to that, however, he is to summon bankrupt to file statement on proclaimed claims, with emphasis on issue of acknowledgment of claims. List is to be prepared according to law. Claims in foreign currency are to be listed after calculation into domestic currency. Draft of claim list is to be submitted to judge-commissioner who, after summoning and examination of both receiver in bankruptcy and bankrupt, decides on acknowledgment of entire or part of claim (or denial to acknowledge). Objections may be filed within two weeks from day of announcement of claim list. Objection must include facts and proofs justifying its filing. Court

BANKRUPTCY AND RESTRUCTURE . . . *continued*
decides on objection after trial. After judge-commissioner determines list of claims, bankrupt may reach settlement with non-preferred creditors if satisfaction of preferred and estate in bankruptcy creditors is secured or they consent thereto. Consent is to be granted in form of decision issued by judge-commissioner, who designates term for creditors assembly to which bankrupt, receiver in bankruptcy and creditors are summoned. Settlement is accepted by approval of majority of voting creditors holding together not less than two thirds of total amount of claims according to list established by judge. Settlement accepted by assembly is to be approved by judge.

Distribution of Estate Funds.—Art. 203 of Bankruptcy Law determines sequence of dues remittance in bankruptcy execution. Dues are divided into preferred and other claims. Preferred claims include such dues as costs of bankruptcy and settlement proceedings, dues arising from receiver's activities and out of contracts that were performed at receiver's request, taxes and other public fees due for two years preceding bankruptcy declaration, together with all additional dues, delay penalties and execution costs. Other claims include such items as claims, together with interest for year preceding bankruptcy declaration, with contractual compensation, trial and execution costs, penalties and court costs and dues stemming from donations and legacies. If amount to be distributed is not sufficient to cover all dues entirely, dues will be covered in their entirety in sequence of art. 203. If amount to be distributed is not sufficient to entirely cover all dues of same position, they are to be covered proportionally to amount of each of them. Receiver in bankruptcy is to prepare and submit to judge-commissioner plan of distribution, which is to include: (a) amount subject to distribution, (b) list of claims and rights of entities participating in distribution, (c) designated amount to which each participant is entitled as result of distribution, (d) indication of amounts to be paid and those to remain in court's deposit. Plan is carried out after its approval by judge-commissioner. After plan of last distribution is executed, court renders its decision on termination of bankruptcy proceedings. Such decision is announced and delivered to bankrupt, receiver in bankruptcy and members of creditors council.

Restructure.—On Feb. 3, 1993 Law on Financial Restructure of Enterprises and Banks (Restructure Law) was adopted. Main task of Restructure Law is to reduce insolvency problem of Polish debtors.

Restructure Law provides three types of financial restructure: amicable banking adjustment; public sale of bank's debts; purchase of shares of companies wholly owned by State Treasury in return for debts. Public sale of bank's debts means that bank is entitled to sell its due debts on pubic basis for their market value. Above mentioned public sale can be effected on auction basis, on public offer basis or on negotiated basis after public invitation. Intention of sale of due debts has to be announced in at least one of countrywide daily newspapers and in bank's and its branches seats as well as in debtor's seat ("Announcement Procedure"). Transfer of debts can be effected without debtor's approval, transfer cannot be effected in favor of debtor or any entity related or dominated by debtor. Dominant entity shall mean such position of entity where latter: (a) commands majority of votes in management bodies of another (dependent) entity including situation where this comes in effect of agreement with other authorized persons or (b) is authorized to appoint or recall majority of members of managing bodies of another (dependent) entity, or (c) where more than half of members of managing bodies of another (dependent) entity are at same time directors or executives of entity in question or entity linked to entity in question by relation of dependence.

Creditors who possess totally at least 30% of due debts in relation to state owned enterprise or State Treasury wholly owned company are entitled to apply for conversion of debts to shares, on condition that given obligation was assumed before June 30th, 1992, although this condition is not applicable to debts purchased on public sale of bank's due debts described above. In order to execute conversion of debts to shares, creditors place on application containing list of debts to appropriate enterprise or State Treasury wholly owned company and respectively to Minister of Privatization or other administrative body representing State Treasury. Providing that in one month's time from day when application was placed due debts have not been paid off, Minister of Privatization or other administrative body representing State Treasury shall announce, by way of Announcement Procedure intention of converting debts for shares, or send by mediation of entity operating brokerage firm to Securities Commission application for permission to float State Treasury wholly owned company's shares to public trading in order to convert shares for debts. In case when debtor is state owned enterprise, it has to be transferred to State Treasury wholly owned company prior to effecting actions mentioned in previous sentence. When Securities Commission's permission is granted, Minister of Privatization or other administrative body which represents State Treasury in company announces intention of converting debts for shares. Announcement has to be effected in way of Announcement Procedure.

As soon as debts are converted for shares, debtor's obligations connected with such debts expire. In case when during 30 days from day specified in announcement as deadline for submitting offers for conversion, parties do not agree upon conditions of such conversion, debtor shall be entitled to have claim against State Treasury, remaining shares owner, to convert his debts for shares provided that following principles shall be fulfilled if company's net book value does not show debit balance, creditor in return for obligations shall acquire part of company's equity in proportion equal to quotient of value of obligations against company's book assets, decreased by company's debts which were not converted to stocks, if net book value of company shows debit balance, obligations are subject to conversion into part of company's equity in proportion equal to quotient of obligation value against total value of liabilities of company as of date of balance sheet.

BANKS AND BANKING:

Banks in Poland consist of state banks, cooperative banks, state-cooperative banks and banks formed as joint stock companies. Primary Polish banking legislation is Banking Law of Jan. 31, 1989, as amended and Law on National Bank of Poland (NBP) of Jan. 31, 1989, as amended.

Founders of banks may be legal or natural persons. Except when founder is State Treasury, foreign bank or foreign banking institution, number of founders cannot be smaller than three legal persons or ten natural persons. Charter is granted to state bank by Council of Ministers. Charter of joint stock company bank is adopted by bank founders. Joint stock company banks may be established with consent of President of NBP given in consultation with Minister of Finance, and in conformity with provisions provided by Comm.C. Bank in form of joint stock company is obliged to inform NBP of any shareholder holding more than 10% of shares in capital and is obliged to obtain consent of NBP for transfer of shares as result of which one shareholder would have 20%, 33%, 50%, 66%, or 75% of votes at shareholder's meeting.

Basic activities of banks are accumulating of monetary resources, granting credits and loans, and making financial settlements. Rights of banks to possess foreign exchange assets and undertake operations with such assets as well as all other activities of banks are defined by bank's charter and subject to permit of President of NBP. Banks are obliged to maintain financial liquidity. Banks ensure proper protection of property received into custody. Banks may issue regulations which specify following: types of savings deposits and conditions for keeping savings accounts, types of credit granted and conditions of credit and loan agreements, conditions of providing safe-deposit boxes, and other banking services. Provisions of such regulations are binding upon parties unless rights and duties are otherwise stipulated by agreement.

Banks may grant guarantees and sureties to residents and foreigners according to their instructions and within limits. Guarantee must be in writing to be valid. While respective provisions of C.C. are applicable to bank guarantees, bank's obligation is always financial. Commission on granted guarantee or surety may be charged by bank in currency of guarantee or surety. Banks perform foreign exchange operations in accordance with principles specified in Banking Law, Law on NBP, foreign exchange law and in international agreements to which Republic of Poland is party. Banks perform financial and clearing services relating to international transactions in all forms permitted in international banking practice. Banks perform foreign exchange control within scope of provisions of foreign exchange law.

Joint stock company banks may be established by foreign persons or with their capital participation. Permit also specifies what portion of profit can be transferred abroad by foreign persons without separate foreign exchange permit. At no time, however, may such portion be less than 15% of total profit. Branch or representative office of foreign banks may be opened on territory of Republic of Poland subject to permit issued by Minister of Finance in agreement with President of NBP. This permit may also specify what portion of profit must be used for financial operations performed exclusively in Poland.

NBP is central State bank. NBP is managed by President of NBP, who is appointed and removed by Parliament upon motion of Prime Minister. Activities of NBP include issuing legal tender of Republic of Poland, granting refinancing credits to other banks, accepting deposits, carrying out monetary settlements, organizing operations in foreign currencies in accordance with provisions of foreign exchange law, performing cash service of State budget and activities as provided in Law on NBP.

See topics Corporations; Currency; Foreign Exchange.

BILLS AND NOTES:

Poland is party to Geneva Convention of June 7, 1930 concerning bills of exchange, and of Mar. 9, 1931 concerning checks. Polish law, like laws of all countries party to those conventions, sharply distinguishes between bills of exchange and checks. In fact, such matters are covered by two different laws, one dealing with bills of exchange of Apr. 28, 1936, and other dealing with checks of Apr. 28, 1936. Bills of exchange are based upon personal credit of parties while check drawn on bank is covered by adequate funds of maker at bank.

Bills of exchange law deals with two types of instruments. One is "drawn bill of exchange", corresponding to American bill of exchange; other is "own bill of exchange", corresponding to American promissory note.

Drawn bill of exchange must contain: (1) express designation as bill of exchange in any language in which bill is drawn, (2) unconditional order to pay sum certain, (3) name of drawee, (4) time of payment, (5) designation of place of payment, (6) name of person on whose behalf or on whose order payment ought to be made, (7) day and place of issuance of bill, and (8) signature of issuer. If one of above-mentioned requirements is missing, valid bill of exchange does not exist. There are, however, certain exceptions to these rules, most importantly that bill of exchange on which time of payment is absent, is considered payable at sight and bill of exchange on which place of issuance is missing is considered issued in place appearing next to issuer's name. Rules on drawn bills of exchange are applicable to own bill of exchange to extent not inconsistent with nature of own bill of exchange.

Bill of exchange may be drawn on issuer or on account of third party. Reservation of interests made by issuer is only effective on bill of exchange payable at sight or at certain time after sight. If amount is expressed in figures and words, words prevail in case of discrepancies. Validity of genuine signatures on instrument is not affected by invalidity of other signatures (e.g., in case of minority, forgery). Bills may come due at sight, at certain time after sight, at certain time after day of issuance or on certain date. Bills with another date of payment other than aforementioned or which are payable on consecutive dates are void.

Issuer of bill is liable for its acceptance and payment although his liability for acceptance can be eliminated. Unless eliminated, he has to pay to legal holder amount stated on bill discounted for payment before maturity.

Every bill of exchange can be transferred by endorsement. When issuer inserts words "not on the order", or other tantamount reservations on instrument, bill can be effectively transferred only by simple assignment. Endorsement must be unconditional. Conditions regarding endorsement are treated as if they were not written. Endorsement on bearer is regarded as endorsement in blank. Legal holder is regarded as anyone who has bill and shows his right with non-interrupted series of endorsements and last can be in blank. Persons against whom rights of bill of exchange are vindicated cannot bring to their own defense objections based on personal relations with drawer or with previous bill holders, unless holder, when acquiring bill of exchange, was consciously acting to cause damage to debtor.

Billholder, or any person who is in possession of bill of exchange, may submit it to be accepted by drawee in place of his domicile. By accepting bill of exchange, drawee is put under obligation to pay bill when payment comes due. Bill payment may be secured by guarantee for bill of exchange in its entirety or part of bill's amount.

See Topical Index in front part of this volume.

BILLS AND NOTES . . . *continued*

Holder of bill which falls due on certain day or at certain later time, or after sight, may submit it to be paid on first day or within next two days after bill falls due. Billholder is not required to accept payment before bill falls due. Drawee, when paying before bill falls due, does so at his own risk. Anyone who pays on due date is therefore relieved from obligation, unless he is acting upon deceit or displays gross negligence. Drawee is required to check chain of endorsements, but not signatures of endorsers. If bill was drawn up for currency which is foreign at place bill falls due, bill amount may be paid in domestic currency, according to its value as of payment date. Foreign currency value is established according to customs of place of payment. Drawer, however, may provide that amount paid is to be calculated pursuant to exchange rate, as such is set forth in bill.

Refusal of acceptance or payment must be confirmed by public statement called protest because of nonacceptance or nonpayment. Protest because of nonacceptance is to be executed in form that states bill must be submitted to be accepted. Protest because of nonpayment of bill to be paid on certain day, after certain time following such day, or upon presentment, is to be made within two business days following payment date. If drawee ceased to pay debts, or execution concerning his property was conducted unsuccessfully, billholder may exercise his recourse remedy only after submitting bill to drawee to be paid and after executing protest.

Billholder must, within four business days following protest, notify his endorser and drawer. Notification can be done by any method, even by simply presenting bill. Anyone who drew bill, accepted it, endorsed it or guaranteed it is jointly liable to billholder. Protest must be drawn up by notary public.

Holder of protested bill is entitled to amount of bill plus cost of protest and other expenses, 6% interest from date of maturity, and for bills issued and payable in Polish legal tender, statutory interest rate, and commission of not over 1/6% of amount of bill in case of absence of contract. One who cashes bill is entitled to be reimbursed for what he paid to previous holder plus his own expenses, plus 6% interest from payment date, and for bills issued and payable in Polish legal tender, statutory interest rate, and commission of not over 1/6% of amount of bill in case of absence of contract. Subject of recourse may, unless provided otherwise, execute his right by issuing new bill of exchange for one of jointly liable persons, paid at sight and in place of domicile of party liable in return.

Period of limitations for action against acceptor is three years, beginning with payment date. Claims of billholder against endorsers and drawer are subject to one year's limitation, starting from day of protest, executed in proper time. Claims of endorsers against each other and against drawer are subject to six month limitation, commencing day endorser redeemed bill, or he himself was sued on that basis.

Capacity of person to incur liabilities under bill is determined by law of his nationality unless such law declares another law to be applicable. Liability incurred by alien is, however, binding if incurred in country according to law of which liability would be valid. As to form of obligation, lex loci is applicable, but obligations of Polish nationals need only comply with requirements of Polish law. Substantive law applicable to obligations of acceptor is law of place of payment. Obligations of other persons signed on instrument is determined by law of country where signatures were affixed. Country of payment's law determines whether bill may be accepted only in part and whether holder must accept partial payment and measures which must be taken in case of loss or theft of bill. Law of place where bill was issued determines time within which recourse must be taken. Form and limitation of protest action are ruled by law of country in which protest is taken.

Checks should be drawn on banker, who has funds of issuer on deposit subject to order, according to express or implied contract entitling issuer to dispose of such funds through checks. Instruments issued without compliance with this provision are regarded as checks in spite of noncompliance. On checks issued and payable in Poland, only banker can be indicated as drawee. Order to pay, which does not correspond to this provision, is invalid as check. Check is not subject to acceptance. Check must contain: (1) designation as check in text of instrument in language of issuance, (2) unconditional order to pay sum certain, (3) name of person which ought to pay, (4) designation of place of payment, (5) designation of day and place of issuance of check, and (6) signature of issuer. If one of above-mentioned elements is absent, document is not considered check unless some exception foreseen by law exists. Checks are payable at sight and may be drawn on (1) indicated person with additional provision "to the order" or without it, (2) indicated person with additional provision not "to the order" or another provision of equivalent meaning, or (3) to bearer. Check without indication as to whom it should be paid is also considered check to bearer.

Check drawn on indicated person, with or without provision "to the order" may be transferred by endorsement, which should be unconditional. Endorsement to bearer is equivalent to endorsement in blank. Drawer or check's holder may disallow payment of cash for check by writing across its face words "transfer to the account" or another equivalent phrase. In that event, check may be used by drawee only for clearing of book account by crediting, clearing or debiting. Book account clearing bears effects equivalent to regular payment.

Checks drawn and payable in same country should be presented for payment within ten days after they are drawn. Checks drawn in country different from place of payment should be presented for payment within 20 or 70 days, depending upon whether drawing and payment place are in same or different parts of world. For this purpose, checks drawn in European countries and payable in country located on or across Mediterranean Sea are considered drawn and payable in same part of world. Starting day of terms specified above is day indicated on check as date of drawing. Revocation of check may be effective only after time to present check expires. Revocation of check payable in Poland may be also effective if check was drawn on name or "to the order," and sent by drawer directly to drawee and revoked before drawee fulfilled his obligation. If check has not been revoked, drawee may also pay after term for check presentment has expired. Check may be presented for payment even before date of issuance noted thereon. All parties whose obligations result from check are jointly liable in relation to checkholder. Checkholder may execute recourse against endorsers, drawer and other debtors if check was not paid when presented at proper time and refusal to pay was confirmed by protest, drawer's note on check, which shall be dated and state day of presentation, and/or statement of clearance chamber, dated and confirming that check was deposited for clearing at appropriate time, and was not redeemed. In general, payer has similar rights of recourse against previous endorsers as in case of bills of exchange.

Claims of checkholder resulting from recourse against endorser, drawer and other debtors is subject to six month limitation, starting from day of payment. Claims, resulting from recourse that debtors obligated to pay check have against each other, shall be subject to six month limitation, starting from day debtor redeemed bill, or he himself was sued on that basis.

Conflict of laws in case of checks is governed by similar principles as those for bills of exchange. Determination of who can draw upon check is governed in accordance with law applicable in country of check's payment. Laws of country where check obligations were incurred govern consequences of such obligations. Place of check's payment plays crucial role and determines, inter alia, following: (1) whether check may be paid only upon presentment, or some time after presentment and, what consequences are of affixing postponed date of issuance, (2) presentment terms, (3) whether holder is entitled to demand partial payment and whether he is required to accept it, and (4) whether drawer may revoke check or oppose its payment.

BROKERS:

Polish law does not recognize special type of broker contract. Legal basis for brokerage may be agency contract which is durable and commissioned. Maritime Code of Dec. 1, 1961 regulates maritime brokers and Laws of July 28, 1990 on Insurance Activities and of Mar. 22, 1991 on Public Turnover of Securities and on Trust Funds, as amended deals with insurance brokers and brokers employed by brokerage firm. Maritime brokerage firms act as intermediaries for monetary gain in transactions involving contracts of buying and selling, shipping, towage and maritime insurance. Maritime brokers may act as intermediaries for both parties. Maritime brokers must inform party when he decides to act on behalf of other party, and when he mediates he must take into account interests of both parties. Insurance and reinsurance brokerage may be conducted either by natural or legal person who has obtained permit from Minister of Finance.

Activities of securities broker within enterprise include conducting brokerage house and brokerage activities according to Law on Public Turnover of Securities and Trust Funds. Broker's activities include offering securities into public turnover, buying or selling securities on behalf of and on account of person giving commission, and holding securities on third party's order.

Brokerage house may be run by natural person, legal person or organizational entity without legal personality. If brokerage house manager is joint stock company, its capital stock may be composed only of registered shares. Conducting brokerage house requires permission of Securities Commission. If brokerage activities are to be undertaken by bank, bank has to organizationally and financially separate brokerage activities from its other activities.

Entity conducting brokerage activities in Poland is required to employ in brokerage activities persons who are authorized to engage in brokerage in Poland. Entity conducting brokerage house cannot simultaneously conduct other economic activity. Within limits of permit for conducting brokerage activities, entity may buy securities in its own name and on its own account with purpose of further reselling.

For management of portfolios of securities and giving investment advice brokerage house needs separate permit, which can also be granted to company not providing brokerage services. Such permit can be granted only if company employs licensed investment advisors.

Broker must be natural person fulfilling legally prescribed personal requirements. He must pass exam before examination committee for brokers and have been registered on list of brokers maintained by Securities Commission. Broker is obliged to conduct his activities according to fair practices and must particularly have in mind best interests of party giving him instructions. He is obliged to keep secret information received during brokerage activities. Investment advisors are also licensed by Securities Commission.

With respect to companies with foreign participation seeking to engage in real estate brokerage, see topic Foreign Investment.

CARTEL LAW:

See topic Monopolies and Trade Restraints.

CHATTEL MORTGAGES:

Polish law defines chattel mortgage as lien on movables without delivery of object to creditor or to third person. Establishing pledge on movable without delivery of item of personal property to creditor or third person on whom parties have agreed requires specific exception. Only exception is in favor of bank. Exceptions can be regarded as equivalent to chattel mortgages in common law. In order to secure credits given by bank, pledge on behalf of bank may be established on movables of pledgor while leaving them in possession of pledgor or third person. (art. 308 C.C.). Pledge remains in force regardless of any changes which object of pledge may undergo in process of transformation. In event object is combined with other objects, pledge attaches to those other objects as well. Contracts establishing such pledge must be concluded, under threat of invalidity, in writing and must define pledged object in manner corresponding to its characteristics. Contracts should be entered in register of pledges maintained by bank. Pledges commence with contract's registration.

Characteristics of chattel mortgages are similar to pledges on ships. According to Maritime Code, they may take two forms depending on whether ship is entered in ship register. Pledge on ship is entered in ship register and maritime mortgage is subject to law on mortgage. Maritime mortgage contracts should be in written form with notarized signatures. Pledge should be also entered in register. Pledge on ship which is not entered in ship register is subject to provisions of civil law concerning pledges on movables. It may be established as pledge with possession or without possession. (Maritime Code of 1961, arts. 64, 65).

COMMERCIAL LAW:

Until Apr. 23, 1964, when C.C. became effective, there was formal distinction between civil and commercial law. Commercial law was regulated by Comm. C.,

See Topical Index in front part of this volume.

COMMERCIAL LAW . . . *continued*
which was composed of two sections: one on "merchant" and one on "commercial activities". Introductory provisions of C.C. repealed many provisions of Comm. C. with exception of provisions concerning commercial partnerships, limited liability companies and joint stock companies. Provisions concerning tradename, procura (for explanation of this term see topic Principal and Agent) and commercial register also remain in force in respect to these companies. Provisions of Comm. C. (arts. 518-524 and 531) remain in force within scope of foreign trade. Law on introductory regulations of C.C. provided that in respect to foreign trade relations provisions of C.C. concerning written form for purposes of evidence do not apply, and moreover, that seller's liability for defects of sold property may be limited or excluded subject only to reservation that such limitation or execution is ineffective if seller deceitfully concealed existence of defect from buyer. Latter rule, however, lost its significance after reform of C.C. in 1990.

Despite recent rapid growth of number of business entities operated as enterprise pursuant to still effective Comm. C. regulations and Law of Dec. 23, 1988 on Economic Activity, state owned enterprises and cooperatives remain economically important legal form of enterprise operation. Consequently, law related to these entities plays important role in law of business relations.

Committee on Reform of Civil Law, operating with Minister of Justice, based reform of private law upon principal of unity of civil law, which results in departure from idea of formal separation of private law into two codes, civil and commercial. Reformed C.C. is intended to include general provisions typical for both civil and commercial code. On one hand, concept of entity which is entered into commercial registry because of type of its activity is incorporated, together with appropriate stipulations on registry, firm and commercial books, into provisions of C.C. On other hand, C.C. regulations are to be commercialized with respect to contractual obligations. New law on commercial companies is in preparation and should replace remaining provisions of Comm. C.

Legal foundation for state enterprise as legal entity operated in form of enterprise was Law of Sept. 25, 1981 on State Enterprises, as amended, and regulations of Council of Ministers of Nov. 30, 1981, as amended. Significant supplement to these acts were Law on Finances of State Enterprises and Law of Sept. 25, 1981 on Self-Governance of State Enterprises.

Legal status of cooperatives is based upon Cooperative Law of 1982, as amended, which is also being revised. Role of cooperatives in Polish law is to be maintained, but legal regulations should be adjusted to model that of countries with free-market economy.

There are two opinions about state enterprise as legal form of conducting business activities. Belief is that form cannot be reformed, in economic sense, for purposes of operating effective enterprise. Consequence of this idea is privatization. Another belief is that they may be subject to appropriate commercialization, which is necessary since they will remain common form for carrying out business activities in Poland. This results in permanent changes of regulations on state owned enterprises and financing, which are primarily aimed at transformation of state enterprises into joint stock company with State Treasury as sole stockholder.

Privatization endeavors were formally reflected in Law of July 13, 1990 on Privatization of State Enterprises, as amended, which provides for two methods of privatization: through liquidation of state enterprise or through its transformation into limited liability or joint stock company of State Treasury, which shall offer its stock for sale to third parties, including employees of such company.

Polish law on commercial relations consists of many separate regulations such as: law on bills of exchange and checks, bankruptcy law, banking law, insurance law, transportation law, law on industrial property, securities law and some chapters of air and maritime law.

See topic Privatization.

COMMERCIAL REGISTER:

In Poland many registers are maintained for economic matters: commercial register, register of cooperatives, state enterprise register and foreign enterprise register. Foreign enterprise register is maintained only for enterprises established and acting under Law of July 6, 1982 on principles of conducting economic activity in Poland by foreign persons and entities, which law is losing significance because as of Jan. 1, 1989 no new foreign enterprises may be established under it. Limited liability companies or joint stock companies established under Law of June 14, 1991 on Companies with Participation of Foreign Parties are registered in commercial register as other like domestic corporations. Commercial register operates according to order of Minister of Justice of July 1, 1934 and is maintained by regular court acting as register court for this type of activity. Commercial register is composed of three parts: Part A for personal commercial companies which are partnerships; Part B for domestic limited liability companies and joint stock companies; and Part C for foreign limited liability companies and foreign stock companies. Part C may have significance only to extent largely repealed provisions of 1928 and 1934 regulations, which allow foreign joint stock and limited liability companies to carry out activities in Poland, are applied in practice. Entering into register in case of joint stock and limited liability companies has constitutive effect in that it establishes legal entity.

Jurisdiction of register court is determined by location of enterprise. Commercial register, together with all documents filed, is open to public. Applications may be submitted to court in person or in writing. If submitted in writing, signatures of applicants should be confirmed by notary unless their signatures are already filed in register court. Power of attorney to complete application should also be notarized. Register court examines whether application and enclosed documents are in conformity with applicable provisions of law. Court may always examine if information given in application is true.

Notification of changes in circumstances which are subject to registration in commercial register should be provided within two weeks following such changes. Register court may, by means of fines, obligate entities to provide notification. Fine may be forgiven if demands of court are satisfied. If person obliged to notify court failed to do so despite proper request, register court may enter appropriate information ex officio.

Persons obliged to notify are jointly liable for damages resulting from failure to comply with notification requirements.

Since 1944, it is not necessary to publish all entries to register in Monitor Polski gazette. If there are no particular publication requirements, announcement of entries is accomplished by placing announcement on announcement board in court building and local administration office. Preparations are underway to establish special publication journal for announcements concerning economic relations. As for third parties acting in good faith, one cannot protect itself from inaccurate data entered into register. Public has right to examine register and documents during office hours under supervision of secretary and to obtain copies of documents and excerpts from records. On demand one can receive official certificate that certain entry does not exist or that application or document was not submitted.

Each partner of partnership has right and obligation to register partnership in commercial register, notwithstanding different provisions of partnership contract. Management board of limited liability company or of joint stock company must give notification of establishment of company in order to effectuate entry into commercial register. Entries include company name, seat and type of activity. In case of partnership, entries also include names of persons authorized to represent company and mode of representation. In case of capital companies, entries also include amount of founding capital, full names of members of management board and mode of representation. Contributions in kind should also be indicated. All changes concerning registered data should be entered in commercial register. When company establishes procurist ("prokurent"), it must enter fact of such establishment into register. (See topic Principal and Agent.)

In procedures before register court, there are fees imposed and collected. Fees include one-time sign up fee and office fee according to Minister of Justice's Regulation of Sept. 4, 1982, as amended, on Fees in Court Procedure Concerning Commercial Registration.

Register of state enterprises is maintained by economic court which is organizational unit of lower regular state courts. State enterprises acquire legal personality from moment of registration. Register of state enterprises is open to persons having legal interest, excluding data containing state and economic secrets. Register book established for state enterprises is composed of following chapters: "Identification of the Enterprise", "Organization of the Enterprise", "Property of the Enterprise", "Mergers", "Divisions", "Liquidation or Bankruptcy of the Enterprise". Director of enterprise, or his designated agent, is obliged to present application for entry to register. Application should include exact data necessary to fill each chapter of register.

Other registers in Poland are: (1) ship register, (2) patent register and (3) trademark register. Ship register is administered by Maritime Chamber having jurisdiction over ship's home port. Two other registers are administered by Patent Office of Republic of Poland.

CONSTITUTION AND GOVERNMENT:

Polish Constitutions.—Governmental Regulation of May 3, 1791 enacted "Constitution of May 3rd", as was noted in preamble, "for the good of society, for the preservation of freedom, for the saving of our nation and its borders." It was first modern constitution in Europe, and, after American Constitution, second in world. During period between World Wars, Poland had two constitutions: Constitution of Mar. 21, 1921 and Constitution of Apr. 23, 1935. After World War II, government acted under Constitution of Mar. 21, 1921, but new political system quickly found reflection in Constitutional Regulation of Feb. 19, 1947 on structure and powers of highest organs of government of Polish People's Republic. Constitution of Polish People's Republic adopted on July 22, 1952 was coronation of then existing political system. Constitution of 1952 was amended several times beginning in early 1980s. During time before "Round Table" discussions, post of Spokesman of Human Rights was created, as well as Constitutional Tribunal and State Tribunal. Most important changes were made after discussions by means of amendment of Apr. 7, 1989. Name "Republic of Poland" was restored, post of president and institution of senate were created. Further amendments were passed in 1989 and 1990. In 1992, "Little Constitution" was adopted. It introduced new arrangement of powers between legislative and executive branches of government, replacing old system of government with modified system stressing separation of powers and increasing role of executive branch, particularly role of President of Republic of Poland. "Little Constitution" does not cover Bill of Rights, which is still regulated by 1952 Constitution, as amended. Therefore, current Constitution consists of two separate enactments, one being Little Constitution and second 1952 Constitution dealing with Bill of Rights and judicial branch of government.

Separation of Powers.—Constitution is based on doctrine of separation of powers, where legislative branch makes laws, executive branch carries them out, and judiciary branch interprets them and adjudicates disputes.

Parliament.—Legislative power is vested in Parliament, which consists of two houses: Sejm and Senate. Sejm is highest organ of government, and highest representative body of people; it reflects nation's sovereign rights. Sejm passes laws, adopts resolutions describing fundamental direction of governmental activities and supervises activities of government and other organs of administration. Right to initiate legislation is reserved to members of Sejm, Senate, President and Council of Ministers. Sejm annually approves country's budget and releases government from having met budget for preceding year. Senate reviews laws, proposed budget laws and financial plans for government and has right to propose their amendments. Rejection by Sejm of amendment of law made by Senate requires absolute majority vote. Laws are signed by President who is responsible for their promulgation. President can address Constitutional Tribunal with request to determine compliance of law with Constitution, as well as refuse to sign law and, with explanation, return law to Sejm for reconsideration. Sejm consists of 460 members who are elected for term of four years. Senate consists of 100 senators who are elected for same term as Sejm.

Referendum may be called by Sejm or President with consent of Senate in order to decide matters of extraordinary importance. Results of referendum are binding if number of participants amounts to at least one half of persons entitled to vote.

CONSTITUTION AND GOVERNMENT . . . *continued*

President of Republic of Poland is highest representative of Polish nation in domestic and international relations. President is elected in popular election for five year term and may be reelected only once. Any Polish citizen over age of 35, who has full voting rights, can be elected to presidency. For violations of Constitution or laws and for crimes, President may be charged by State Tribunal. President ratifies and terminates international agreements. President must be authorized by Sejm to ratify international agreements relating to State borders, defensive alliances and ones which would significantly burden state finances or would necessitate change in law.

Constitutional Tribunal determines constitutionality of laws and other norm setting acts of government and also determines generally binding interpretation of laws. Decisions of Constitutional Tribunal on constitutionality of laws are reviewable by Sejm. Members of Constitutional Tribunal are selected by Sejm from outstanding members of legal community. Members of Constitutional Tribunal are independent and are only subject to Constitution.

State Tribunal determines liability of persons who hold highest public posts, as specified by law, for violations of Constitution and laws. State Tribunal may also determine criminal liability in connection with such violations, and for crimes committed in connection with exercise of public functions. Members of State Tribunal are elected by Sejm for term of Sejm. Chairman of State Tribunal is First President of Supreme Court. Judges of State Tribunal are independent and are only subject to laws.

Persons holding public posts may not engage in any economic activity. They may however be designated to manage or supervise State economic entities that is: State or communal enterprises and companies whose shares are held by Treasury of State.

Highest Control Chamber controls commercial, financial, organizational and administrative activities of State administration, enterprises and other organizational entities that are subject to such State administration, checks legality, effectiveness and dependability of such activities. Highest Control Chamber is subject to Sejm. President of Highest Control Chamber is elected and recalled by Sejm, with consent of Senate.

Spokesman of Human Rights guards rights and freedoms specified in Constitution and other laws. Spokesman of Human Rights is elected by Sejm, with consent of Senate, for term of four years.

Government.—Council of Ministers is main governmental body. President of Council of Ministers supervises Council of Ministers and all organs of governmental administration. President of Council of Ministers, Council of Ministers as a whole and Ministers, issue regulations and executive orders, on basis of laws and in order to implement laws. Council of Ministers, may also, if authorized by Sejm issue decrees with force of law, subject to control and promulgation by President. President of Council of Ministers is nominated by President, other members of Council of Ministers are nominated by President pursuant to proposal from President of Council of Ministers. Sejm approves nominations of members of Council of Ministers by absolute majority vote. Sejm may recall Council of Ministers.

Prosecutor's Office safeguards compliance with laws and oversees bringing of criminals to justice. Prosecutor's Office is subject to Minister of Justice, who acts as Chief Prosecutor.

National Council of Radio and Television safeguards freedom of speech and realization of rights of citizens to information and is to represent in radio and television popular interests. Members of National Council of Radio and Television are nominated by President, Sejm and Senate. State monopoly in radio and television has been abolished and private persons may operate radio and television businesses after obtaining concessions from National Council of Radio and Television.

Foundations of Governmental and Commercial Structure and Governmental Rights and Obligations of Citizens.—Republic of Poland is democratic country, implementing rules of social justice. Republic of Poland guarantees freedom of economic activity irrespective of forms of ownership; limitations of this freedom may only be imposed by laws. Republic of Poland protects ownership and right to inheritance and guarantees full protection of personal property. Condemnation is only allowed for public purposes and for adequate compensation. Specific constitutional rights and obligations include following: right to freedom of speech, publishing, assembling, meeting, demonstrating and of engaging in manifestations. Citizens of Republic of Poland have equal rights without regard to sex, place of birth, education, employment, nationality, race, beliefs or ancestry and social status. Polish citizens abroad are entitled to receive assistance from Republic of Poland. Citizen of Republic of Poland is to comply with Constitution and laws.

Regional Administration and Territorial Self-Governance.—Governor (wojewoda) is organ of state administration and representative of government in region. Voivod is state administrative organ at regional level, appointed and recalled by Prime Minister which functions as representative of government in region. Territorial self-governance is basic organizational form of public life at lowest level of administration. Commune (gmina) satisfies general needs of local public. Commune has legal personality and performs public tasks in its own name, according to rules determined by law. In area regulated by law, commune performs state administrative duties. Main organ of commune is council elected by residents of commune. Council elects other organs of commune. Commune has right to own real property and has other proprietary rights. All such assets and rights constitute communal property.

Electorial Laws, Regulations on Elections of Sejm, Senate and President.—Elections of Sejm, Senate and President are conducted by secret ballot. Every citizen over 18 years of age has right to vote, without regard to sex, nationality, race, belief, education, length of residency, ancestry, employment or wealth. Every citizen over 21 years of age may be elected to Sejm or Senate. Women have rights equal to men. Members of armed forces have same voting rights as civilians. Persons who are mentally disturbed or whose public rights have been suspended in court proceeding do not have right to vote. Candidates to Sejm, Senate and Presidency are named by political and social organizations and voters.

CONTRACTS:

Sources.—C.C. Book One, Title IV "Legal Transactions" with section: "General Provisions" (arts. 56-65), "Conclusion of Contract" (arts. 66-72), "Form of Legal Transaction" (arts. 73-81), "Defects in Declaration of Will" (arts. 82-88), "Condition" (arts. 89-94), "Representation" (arts. 95-109). Book Three "Obligations" with two kinds of titles: general and concerning separate type of contracts. In first group, most important are: Title I "General Provisions" (arts. 353-365), Title II "Plurality of Debtors and Creditors" (arts. 366-383), Title III "General Provisions Concerning Contractual Obligations" (arts. 384-396), Title VII "Performance of Obligations and Effects on Non-Performance" (arts. 450-497). In second group—Title XI "Sale" (arts. 535-555), Title XV "Contract for Work and Labor" (arts. 627-646), Title XVII "Lease and Tenancy" (arts. 659-709), Title XIX "Loan" (arts. 720-724), Title XX "Contract for Bank Account" (arts. 725-733), Title XXI "Mandate" (arts. 734-751), Title XXIII "Contract of Agency" (arts. 758-764), Title XXIV "Contract of Sale-Purchase on Commission" (arts. 765-773), Title XXV "Contract of Carriage" (arts. 774-793), Title XXVI "Contract of Forwarding" (arts. 794-804), Title XXVII "Contract of Insurance" (arts. 805-834), Title XXX "Contract of Storage" (arts. 853-859), title XXXI "Contract of Company" (arts. 860-875), Title XXXII "Contract of Suretyship" (arts. 876-887), Title XXXIII "Contract of Donation" (arts. 888-902). C.C. does not contain any reference to customary law. References to custom are of special character, e.g., according to art. 65, §1 "A declaration of will should be interpreted as required by the circumstances in which it was made, by the principles of social co-existence and established customs". In commercial relations, according to decisions of Supreme Court, established customs prevail over non-mandatory provisions. Reform of C.C. in 1990 introduced new provision concerning contractual freedom: Parties concluding agreement may freely determine their legal relationship as long as its contents or aim is not contrary to nature of relationship, law or principles of social coexistence. INCOTERMS—Definitions of International Chamber of Commerce are customarily used in trade.

Applicable Law.—(Law of Private International Law of Nov. 12, 1965).

Parties may choose any law to regulate their contract providing that such law is related to obligation. No such requirement exists with respect to contracts governed by Maritime Code of 1961, as amended and Air Law of 1962, as amended. Choice of law is also guaranteed by regulations of arbitration court, operating within National Economic Chamber. Full freedom of choice of law is professed both in practice and judicial decisions as well as doctrine.

If parties did not select law appropriate for given contract, following rules may apply: (1) Law applicable in seat of stock exchange or public fair, provided that contracts were concluded thereon. (2) Law of joint domicile, providing that parties have joint domicile. (3) If none of above-mentioned rules apply, law provides for specific rules relating to particular contracts. For example: For sales contract, law where seller has his seat; for agency, mandate, work and labor, transportation, forwarding and storage contracts, law where party receiving order has its seat or residence. (4) If none of specific rules is applicable, law of country where contract consummated. Freedom of choice of law does not apply to real estate contracts. In case of real estate, law of country in which it is located is applicable. (arts. 25-30).

Legal capacity is governed by party's national law. Legal capacity of legal entity is established according to law of country in which it has its seat. When transaction is conducted within scope of enterprise operation, law of enterprise's principal place of business governs legal capacity. If foreigner, who does not have legal capacity under his national law, concludes transaction, determination of his legal capacity is governed by Polish law, if required, in order to protect parties acting in good faith. (This rule is not applicable to legal transactions of family, guardianship and succession law.) Form of transactions is controlled by law governing underlying issue, but compliance with law of country in which transaction was concluded is also acceptable. (arts. 9, 10 and 12). (See topic Foreign Law.)

Formation of Contract.—Contracts may be concluded as result of offer and acceptance or of negotiations. Offers are declarations of intent to execute contract with specific person, specifying essential contract provisions. Offers stating period within which offeror will await reply is binding on offeror until period expires. If no period was specified, offers made in presence of another party, or by telephone or other means of direct long distance communications, cease to bind if not accepted immediately; offers made in other manner cease to bind if time expires in which offeror, in normal course of business, would receive reply sent without unreasonable delay. Public display of item at place of sale at specified price is offer of sale. Acceptance of offer made with reservation concerning change or supplementation of content is considered counter offer. Contract is considered concluded when offeror received declaration of acceptance; or, if such declaration was not required, when other party began performing contract. Announcements, advertisements, price lists and other information, directed to public or particular persons, are not offers, but invitations to begin negotiations. If parties conduct negotiations with aim of concluding specific contract, contract is concluded when parties reach understanding as to provisions which were objects of negotiations. If person conducting commercial activity received offer to conclude contract in framework of his activity from person with whom he has ongoing relationship, lack of answer is regarded as acceptance. General conditions, model contracts or regulations issued by party authorized by appropriate provisions, binds other party within provision limits if they were delivered when concluding contract. When use of such documents is customary it is sufficient that other party could have learned of their contents. Other general conditions, model contracts or regulations bind other party only when contents were previously agreed to be contents of contract. (arts. 66-72, 543, 385, 386).

Conditions of Validity of Contracts.—Contracts concluded by person without capacity to enter into legal transaction (minor under 13 years, persons mentally incapacitated) are void. However, when person concludes contract concerning ordinary, everyday matters, contract is valid when performed, unless contract injures person lacking capacity. Minors under 13 years and persons partially legally incapacitated, have limited capacity to contract. Where persons of limited capacity contract and incur obligations or dispose of rights, consent of person's statutory representative is required to validate contract. Contract concluded without required consent is valid if ratified by statutory representative. Person of limited capacity may ratify contract if full capacity is regained. Person who concluded contract with person of limited capacity may set period within which statutory representative must ratify contract; he is not bound after

CONTRACTS . . . *continued*

period passed without ratification. Full capacity to enter into legal transactions is acquired at 18 years of age. (arts. 10-22).

With certain exceptions, intent of person performing legal transaction may be expressed by conduct revealing intent (declaration of will). If law stipulates that legal transaction be written, legal transaction not in that form is invalid only if law so requires. If, by law, legal transactions must be in particular forms (e.g., notarized transaction), they are invalid if not in that form. This is not so where observance of form is required to produce specific consequences of such legal transaction. If requirement of written form is not observed and contract is not invalid, no evidence from witnesses or statements of parties concerning conclusion of contract are admissible in litigation. Exceptions are prescribed by law. C.C. provisions concerning written form for purposes of evidence do not apply to foreign trade transactions. In internal relations, such evidence is admissible if both parties express consent or if document makes fact of performing legal transaction probable. Courts may admit above-mentioned evidence, if due to particular circumstances of case, court deems it necessary. Legal transactions of great value must be in written form. If contract is in writing, supplementation, change, or termination by agreement by parties and renunciation, must be in writing. To observe written form, it is sufficient to sign document stating party's intent. Exchange of documents concludes contract if each document states one party's intent and is signed by that party. (arts. 60, 73-75, 77, 78).

Statement of intent made to another party for sake of appearance is invalid. In case of error as to essence of legal transaction, party may avoid legal consequences of statement of intent. If statement of intent is made to another person, avoidance of legal consequences is permissible in cases of error caused by that person, even if without fault, or if that person knew or easily could have known of error, this limitation does not concern gratuitous legal transactions. If error is intentionally caused by other party, legal consequences of statement of intent made under influence of error may be avoided even when mistake was not significant and when it did not concern content of legal transaction. (arts. 83, 84, 86).

Legal transaction inconsistent with law or designed to evade it, is invalid unless applicable regulation prescribes otherwise. Invalid provisions in legal transactions may be replaced by appropriate provisions of law. Legal transaction not consistent with principles of social coexistence is invalid. If legal transaction is partially invalid, rest remains valid, unless it appears from circumstances that transactions would not have been concluded without invalid provisions. Contracts for performance which is impossible are invalid. Parties who knew about impossibility of performance at time of contract and did not inform other party, must repair injury which other party sustained by concluding contract without knowledge of impossibility of performance. (arts. 58, 387).

Preliminary Contract, Contract for Benefit of Third Party, Contract of Donation.—Contract in which one or both parties bind themselves to conclude specific contract, must define essential provisions of future promised contract, and period of time within which it is to be concluded. If party bound to conclude contract evades conclusion, other party may demand redress of damages sustained. If preliminary contract meets requirements upon which validity of promised contract depends, particularly requirements as to form, party may bring action for conclusion of contract. (arts. 389, 390). If contract stipulated that debtor will fulfill obligation for benefit of third person, that person may demand that debtor fulfill stipulated obligation, unless contract provides otherwise. Stipulations regarding duty to perform obligation for benefit of third person cannot be withdrawn or altered, if third person declares to either party that he wishes to take advantage of stipulation. Debtor may raise objections based on contract against third person. (art. 393). In donative contract, donor obligates himself to gratuitously perform benefit to donee at expense of donor's property. Declarations of donor must be notarized to be binding. However, donative contracts concluded without being notarized become valid if promised performance was carried out. This rule does not override any provisions requiring observance of particular form for declarations by parties because of object of donation. (arts. 888, 890).

Rules of Fulfillment of Contracts.—Fundamental rule for performing obligations is principle of specific performance. This principle is seen in: priority of natural restitution over duty to compensate damage, introduction of duty to accept partial performance, limitation of right to refuse acceptance of performance because of debtor's delay, limitation of possibility of renouncing contract in event of mutual delay, and admissibility of substitute performance. Debtor must fulfill obligations in accordance with content and in manner corresponding to socio-economic purpose and principles of social coexistence; and, if there are customary practices, in manner consistent with customs. Creditors must cooperate in same manner in fulfillment of obligation. Debtors are obliged to display diligence required in relations of that type (due diligence). Due diligence is defined within framework and with consideration of professional character of that commercial activity. Creditors may demand debtor's personal performance only if this appears from content of legal transaction, law or character of performance. If debtor is obliged to provide generic goods and quality is not defined by appropriate regulations, or by contract, and does not appear from circumstances, debtor should deliver goods of average quality. (arts. 354-357, 362).

Debtors may be jointly or separately liable for entirety of performance satisfaction; satisfaction of creditor by any debtor releases rest (joint and several liability). Until creditor is completely satisfied, debtors remain jointly and severally bound. Obligation is joint and several by force of law or legal transaction. If several persons entered into obligation concerning common property, they are jointly and severally bound, unless agreed otherwise. Debtors liable under indivisible obligation are liable to perform as joint and several debtors. (arts. 366, 369, 370, 380).

Creditors cannot refuse to accept partial performance, even though entire claim has become enforceable, unless acceptance of such performance violates established interest. If place of performance is not specified, and does not appear from nature of obligation, it must be performed where debtor was domiciled at time contract was made. Pecuniary payment must be made at place of domicile or principal place of business of creditor at moment of such payment; if creditor changed place of domicile or principal place of business after obligation created, he bears extra cost of remittance caused by change. If obligation is connected with debtor's or creditor's enterprise, domicile or principal place of business of enterprise is decisive with regard to place of performance. If time for performance is not defined or apparent from nature of obligation, obligation must be performed upon demand. If debtor becomes insolvent or, if due to circumstances for which he is liable, security of claim has been considerably reduced, creditor may demand performance, regardless of stipulated time limit. Performance under mutual contracts must occur simultaneously, unless it appears from contract, law or decision of court that one party is obliged to perform its obligation earlier. If mutual obligations must be performed simultaneously, each party may withhold performance until other party performs. Contract is terminated by performance of agreement terms. (arts. 450, 454, 455, 458, 488).

Consequences of Nonperformance of Obligations (Breach of Contracts).—Debtor must redress damage resulting from nonperformance or improper performance of obligation. Debtor is in qualified delay if he does not fulfill obligation within stipulated time limit or, if time limit not specified, when he does not fulfill obligation upon demand by creditor. In event of qualified delay by debtor, creditor may demand redress of resulting damage, regardless of whether he performed. If, however, due to debtor's qualified delay, creditor has lost interest, either completely or to predominant degree, creditor is free to refuse performance and demand redress of damage resulting from nonperformance of obligation. (arts. 471, 476, 477).

If one party delays fulfilling obligation under mutual contract, other party may indicate appropriate additional time limit for performance, under condition that, in event of passing of time limit without performance, it may renounce contract. It may also demand, either without additional time limit, or after its passing without effect, fulfillment of obligation and redress of damage. If right to renounce mutual contract was stipulated in event of nonperformance of obligation within time limit, party entitled may renounce contract without designating additional time limit in event of delay by other party. This is also true where performance of obligation by one party after expi ration of time limit would have no effect on other party due to nature of obligation or purpose of contract intended by it and known to other party. Party renouncing mutual contract is obliged to return to other party everything received under contract; it may demand not only return, but also redress of damage resulting from nonperformance of obligation. (arts. 491, §1; 492; 494).

Persons obliged to pay damages are liable only for normal damages. Within above limits and without legal or contractual provision to contrary, redress of damages covers losses borne by injured persons as well as loss of profits. If injured party contributed toward occurrence or extent of damage, obligation to make redress is subject to appropriate reduction, according to circumstances and degree of fault of parties. Redress of damage may take place, either through restitution to former state or payment of appropriate sum of money, at option of injured party. If restitution to former state is impossible, or would entail excessive difficulty or cost to person liable, injured person's claim is limited to pecuniary payment. If redress of damage takes pecuniary form, amount of indemnity is determined according to prices in effect on date of assessment of indemnity, unless particular circumstances require that prices existing at another moment be taken as basis. (arts. 361-363).

If something defined generically is object of obligation, creditor may, in event of debtor's qualified delay, purchase at own expense same quantity of same type of goods or demand their value from debtor in both cases retaining claim for redress of damage resulting from qualified delay. When obligation consists of action, creditor may, while retaining claim for redress of damage, demand authorization by court to perform action at debtor's expense. Creditor is in qualified delay, when, without justification, he evades acceptance of offer of performance, refuses to perform act without which obligation cannot be fulfilled or declares to debtor that he will not accept performance. If creditor is in qualified delay, debtor may demand redress of resulting damage and place object of performance in court deposit. (arts. 479, 480, 486).

Contracts may stipulate that redress of damage resulting from nonperformance or improper performance of non-pecuniary obligation will take form of specified sum (liquidated damages) of payment. Debtor may not release himself from obligation by payment of liquidated damages without consent of creditor. Upon breach of contract, liquidated damages are owed to creditor in amount fixed regardless of amount of damage. Parties cannot demand indemnity higher than stipulated penalty unless parties agree otherwise. If obligation was substantially performed, debtor may demand reduction of liquidated damages. This is true when liquidated damages are flagrantly exorbitant. If merchant obliged himself in foreign trade to liquidated damages, he cannot demand reduction. If in commercial transaction contractual penalty was agreed, parties to contract cannot claim higher indemnity. (arts. 483, 484 C.C. and art. 531 Comm.C.).

Excuses for Nonperformance.—One premise of contract liability is that breach of contract results from circumstances for which debtor is liable. According to art. 471 "debtor is obliged to redress any damage resulting from non-performance or improper performance of an obligation, unless non-performance or improper performance was result of circumstances for which debtor is not liable." Debtor may not be held liable for breach of contract when he proves he is not responsible for breach. If nothing else appears from particular provision of law or legal transaction, debtor is liable for failure to observe due diligence. No person has liability whose breach of contract is due to act of God. Act of God is external event which cannot be foreseen or prevented (e.g., flood, earthquake, lightning striking). Incident is to be understood as event causing nonperformance or improper performance of obligation which occurred despite debtor's due diligence. Parties may determine by contract events which will be considered acts of God. Law itself makes debtor liable for certain fortuitous events, particularly when he is in qualified delay. Debtor may, by means of contract, accept liability for nonperformance of obligation owing to specified circumstances for which, by virtue of law, he is not liable. Stipulation, whereby debtor is not liable for damage intentionally caused to creditor, is not valid. (art. 473). If performance becomes impossible, due to circumstances for which debtor is not liable, obligation ceases to exist. If object of performance has been sold, lost or damaged, debtor is obliged to deliver anything gained in exchange for object as redress of damage. (art. 475).

COPYRIGHT:

Copyrights are regulated by Law on Copyright of Feb. 4, 1994 which has entered into force on May 23, 1994. Law has introduced new system of protection of copyrights in Poland. Scope of copyright covers any manifestation of creative activity of individual nature including, among others, works expressed in words, mathematical

COPYRIGHT . . . *continued*
symbols, graphical signs, literary, journalistic, scientific, cartographic works, computer programs, works of fine arts, photographic works, stringed musical instruments, industrial designs, architectural and urban works, musical works and works composed of words and music, works for stage and audiovisual works. Provisions of Copyright Law apply to works: (a) whose author or co-author is Polish citizen, (b) which were originally published in Poland (or simultaneously in Poland and abroad), (c) which were first published in Polish language, or (d) whose protection results from international agreements.

Copyright belongs to author unless specific regulations provide otherwise. Copyright Law differentiates between personal and proprietary copyrights. Personal copyrights encompass connection of author with work such as right to authorship to work, to sign with author's name, to inviolability of content or form of work, to decide when work shall be made publicly available for first time, to supervise method of use of work and to protect good name of work, which unless Law provides otherwise, is unlimited in time and not subject to repeal or transfer. Proprietary copyrights which encompass right of author to exclusive use and dispose of work in any field of exploitation and to receive compensation for use of such work, proprietary copyrights expire after 50 years from author's death from date of its first publication if author is unknown or such rights are owned by person other than author. Employer whose employee created work upon performance of his employment duties acquires proprietary copyrights to work.

Author's proprietary copyrights are transferable only in written form of agreement. Agreement for transfer of all works or works of particular kind of same author which are to be created in future is invalid.

Poland is party to Bern Convention of Sept. 9, 1886 on Protection of Literary and Artistic Works (as am'd Berlin, 1908, and Rome, 1928), Paris Act of Bern Convention signed in Paris on June 24, 1971 (with exclusion of arts. 1-21 and annex) and Universal Convention on Copyright of Sept. 6, 1952 signed in Geneva, verified version of which was signed in Paris July 24, 1971. Poland is party to bilateral treaty with U.S.A. signed Mar. 21, 1990 concerning business and economic relations (which has been ratified by both parties and will be effective 30 days following exchange of ratification instruments) in which Poland agrees to enact laws for protection of certain copyrights.

See topic Patents and Topographies.

CORPORATIONS:

Types and Sources.—Generally, concept of corporation corresponds in Polish law to concept of legal person. Polish law recognizes two main types of business corporations, joint stock company and company with limited liability. Joint stock company may be formed for all legal purposes (not necessarily business); company with limited liability can be formed only for economic activity. Polish company with limited liability is generally equivalent to close business corporation in American law. Shareholders of limited liability company are not liable personally for obligations of company with exception of tax obligations of company where shareholders are liable with all their personal property in such part in which shareholder is entitled to participate in division of profit. In Polish law, concept of "ultra vires" acts is unknown. Polish corporation is not restricted by enumerations in its document of creation. Its legal capacity to act after deletion of Art. 36 of C.C. (as of Oct. 1, 1990) appears to be unlimited. Basic source for both types of business corporations is Commercial Code of 1934: joint stock company (arts. 307-497), and company with limited liability (arts. 158-306). Position of aliens in formation of business corporation is established through Law of June 14, 1991 on Companies with Participation of Foreign Parties, as amended. Law of July 13, 1990 on Privatization of State Enterprises, as amended also introduced new provisions to Polish business corporation law.

Formation of Business Corporation.—Articles of incorporation in joint stock company are listed in charter which must be notarized. Joint stock company may be formed by at least three (natural or legal) persons; company with limited liability may be formed by one natural or legal person. If founder is State Treasury, joint stock company may be one-person company. Law of 1991 contains no limitation for foreigner or nonresident to establish one-person company with limited liability. Every corporation must have corporate name, which designation may be freely chosen. Important elements of articles of incorporation required by law are corporate name, time of existence, if limited, and amount of founding capital. Joint stock company must also include structure of managing and supervisory bodies. Corporation comes into existence by entry in Commercial Register.

Institutional Structure of Corporation.—Every business corporation must have two bodies: management board and shareholders' general meeting. Polish business corporation law recognizes two types of supervisory bodies: supervisory council and revisory commission. Joint stock company must have one of such supervisory bodies. Company with limited liability need not unless its founding capital exceeds 250 million zlotys and number of shareholders is greater than 50.

Mergers and Transformations of Companies.—Mergers of corporations can be accomplished through: (1) transfer of all assets of acquired corporation to purchaser in exchange for shares (or stock), which acquiring corporation issues (or assigns) to stockholders of acquired corporation; or (2) formation of new corporation (either joint stock or limited liability) to which assets of all merging companies are transferred, in return for shares or stock of new corporation. Resolution for merger complying with law, approved by qualified majority vote of shareholders (stockholders) is required, as well as appropriate notices. Assets of each merged company should be managed separately until all creditors whose interests arose before merger and who, in writing, demand payment before end of six months from last notice of intent to merge are either satisfied or given security. During time when assets are managed separately, premerger creditors are given priority over post-merger creditors. Comm. C. contains provisions on transformation of joint stock companies into limited liability companies and vice versa. Transformation does not result in any change in relations between corporation and third parties. Stated capital of new corporation may not be lower than stated capital of corporation being transformed. Therefore, if not all stockholders of corporation being transformed become stockholders in new corporation, additional capital must be paid in full in cash. Stockholders who do not participate in new corporation can, after registration of its transformation, demand pay out of amount equal to their respective shares, calculated according to special balance sheet prepared as one requirement of resolution on transformation. Specific provisions govern transformation of governmental enterprises into one-person capital corporations of State Treasury. Principal provisions are contained in Law of July 13, 1990 on Privatization of State Enterprises.

Dissolution and Termination of Corporations.—Dissolution of corporation can be caused by: (1) grounds included in statute or agreement of corporation, or in resolution of shareholders' general meeting on dissolution of corporation, or transfer of seat of corporation outside of Poland; (2) declaration of bankruptcy of corporation; and (3) other grounds enumerated in Comm. C. (for example, transformation, or merger). Dissolution of corporation occurs after liquidation. During liquidation, corporation retains its legal status. Liquidation is with addition of "in liquidation" to its corporation's name. Liquidators are of members management board unless statute or agreement of corporation or stockholders' resolution contains contrary provisions governing liquidators. If court decides that corporation should be liquidated, court can name liquidators. Liquidators must make balance sheet at beginning of liquidation. Comm. C. regulates liquidation proceeding, rules of paying creditors and division of assets of liquidated corporation. After completion of liquidation and approval of final accounts by general meeting of stockholders, liquidators provide liquidation statement to registry court, at same time depositing demand for removal of corporation from commercial register. Aims of liquidators are to terminate current business of corporation, obtain payments from creditors, perform obligations of corporation, and transform assets of corporation into cash. New business can be obtained only if necessary to terminate old business. Real property is sold at public auction, or to individuals only after resolution approving such sale is passed at stockholders' meeting and at price determined at such meeting.

Civil and Criminal Liability.—Member of management or supervisory body of corporation can be liable to corporation for damage that results from acts contrary to law or articles of incorporation. Member of management or supervisory body and liquidator should, when carrying out their functions, act as independent business persons and are responsible to corporation for all damage that results from lack of such care. Those who take part in formation of joint stock corporation or limited liability company and knowingly or negligently fail to comply with legal provisions, and cause damage to corporation, are obligated to remedy such damage. Suit for damages against members of management or supervisory bodies and liquidators can only be brought in jurisdiction in which seat of corporation is located. Statute of limitations is generally five years, but longer periods are applicable if damage results from crime or breach of law. Criminal liability can result from doing damage to corporation in formation and from causing damage to it while performing functions in management or supervising bodies, or as liquidator for which penalty is fine and up to five years' imprisonment, or in being member of management board or liquidator and not giving notice of corporation's bankruptcy despite existence of factors that determine bankruptcy under regulations, for which penalty is fine or up to six months' imprisonment or both.

See topic Foreign Investment.

COURTS:

Poland, as unitarian, nonfederal state, has single court system. Courts are divided into courts of general jurisdiction and special courts (e.g., military courts). Courts of general jurisdiction are comprised of appellate courts, voivodship (higher) courts and district (lower) courts. District courts deal with cases of criminal law, civil family law, guardianship law, labor law and social insurance law, with exclusion of matters delegated by statute to other courts. Following courts in Poland are of central character: Supreme Court, Supreme Administrative Court, Constitutional Tribunal and Tribunal of State. Legal bases upon which courts function are contained in following acts: Law on Common Courts of June 20, 1985; Law on Supreme Court of Sept. 20, 1984; Law on Supreme Administrative Court of May 11, 1995; Law on Constitutional Tribunal of Apr. 20, 1985; Law on Tribunal of State of 1982, C.C.P. of Nov. 17, 1964; Ordinance of Minister of Justice on Internal Regulation on Functioning of Common Courts of Nov. 19, 1987. All above acts have undergone many amendments.

Organization and Division of Competence Between Common Courts.— Appellate court is created for several voivodships and district court for one or more communes within boundaries of same voivodship.

Appellate courts are set up to decide on appeals from judgments of voivodship courts. In voivodship courts, separate structures (bureaus) have been set up for cases dealing with labor and social insurance law (labor and social insurance courts). Additionally, voivodship courts serve as courts of first instance in matters such as: protection of copyrights, patents and trademarks; claims arising from press law; and claims in which amount in controversy exceeds 2,000 zlotys. Voivodship courts adjudicate commercial (economic) matters with exception of those which have been restricted for jurisdiction by district or antimonopoly courts. Commercial (economic) cases are such which arise from civil law relationships between business entities, within limits of their economic activity. Following are also considered to be commercial cases: claims arising from contract of partnership; claims against economic entities for discontinuance of acts harmful to environment and/or payment of damages related to such, as well as prohibition or restriction of activities harmful to environment; and matters under jurisdiction of courts on basis of antimonopoly regulations.

District courts are trial courts for all ordinary cases except those which are specifically restricted to voivodship courts. In scope of economic or business matters, district courts adjudicate such matters as: claims in which amount in controversy does not exceed 2,000 zlotys; claims to issue order for payment adjudicated in writ of payment proceedings, regardless of value of amount in controversy, and other matters delegated to such courts by separate regulations. In district courts, separate family and juvenile divisions are set up (family courts) especially to deal with matters of family and guardianship law, proceedings in juvenile cases and proceedings involving persons addicted to alcohol.

Unlike voivodship courts, district courts may be divided into divisions depending on need. In case of such need, civil and criminal divisions are formed.

COURTS . . . *continued*

Commercial (economic) courts are autonomous organizational units which deal with economic matters created within framework of voivodship and district courts, which have their seat in cities where voivodship self-government bodies are located.

Antimonopoly court is autonomous organizational unit dealing with antimonopoly cases created within Voivodship Court in City of Warsaw.

Courts of Central Character.—Supreme Court is chief judicial organ of Republic of Poland. It supervises judicatory functions of common as well as all other courts and in particular over military courts and Supreme Administrative Court with exception of such central courts as Constitutional Tribunal or Tribunal of State. Specifically, Supreme Court deals with: extraordinary appeals against final judgment; passing of resolutions to clarify ambiguous laws or laws which have been applied by various courts in nonuniform manner and responding to questions of law pertaining to specific cases which cause ambiguities.

Generally, Supreme Court ensures uniform interpretation of law. Supreme Court is divided into Administrative Chamber, Labor and Social Insurance Chamber, Civil Chamber, Criminal Chamber and Military Chamber.

Supreme Administrative Tribunal sits in Warsaw as well as in regional centers created for one or more voivodships. Supreme Administrative Tribunal adjudicates claims against decisions of administrative authorities within boundaries and mode of procedure is specified in Code of Administrative Procedure of June 14, 1960 as amended, and in other specific regulations. Following decisions are not subject to appeal before Supreme Administrative Tribunal: (i) hierarchial relationship between organs of state administration, (ii) hierarchial relations within organs of state administration, (iii) non-appointment to high units, (iv) disciplinary matters, (v) matters involving issuing visas, (vi) belonging to competence of Patent Office, and (vii) matters belonging to jurisdiction of other courts.

Claim over decision of administrative authority may be filed by: private party, social organization which took part in administrative proceedings, or public prosecutor. Claim may be filed with Supreme Administrative Tribunal after ordinary administrative procedure has been exhausted, unless claim is filed by public prosecutor. Claim must be filed within 30 days of delivery or announcement of decision but in case of public prosecutor, term is six months. Claim is filed through state administrative agency which rendered appealed decision in last instance. (For information on Constitutional Tribunal and Tribunal of State, see topic Constitution and Government.)

Judges are appointed by President of Republic of Poland. Only Polish citizen who has reached age 26 and completed university legal education and post graduate court training and has passed judicial state examination may be appointed judge. Judges are irremovable from their posts, except for cases prescribed by law (e.g., President recalls judge from post on motion of National Court Council), judge has renounced his function or has reached age 65, although appointment may be prolonged to age 75. Judges, in performing their functions, are independent and subject only to law. In first instance, courts hear cases in panels of one presiding judge and two lay-judges unless specific provision states otherwise. All decisions outside of hearing are made by presiding judge without participation of lay-judges. President of court may order case heard by three professional judges if he feels it is justified by complexity of matter. Appellate court hears cases always with three judge panel, even if law allows to decide appeal in closed sitting. Economic matters are in first instance heard by one professional judge without presence of lay-judges if defendant has not answered statement of claim or has admitted it; or if amount in controversy does not exceed two million zlotys. President of court of first instance may rule any economic case to be heard by only one judge without participation of lay-judges. President may also rule any such case to be heard by three professional judges if he considers it important as precedent for future decisions. Supreme Court adopts resolutions in various prescribed panels; of three, five or seven justices; whole chamber; joint chambers; or whole assembly. Resolutions of whole assembly of Supreme Court, joint chambers or whole chamber, at moment of their adoption, acquire authority of so-called "legal principles". Seven judge panel may order that its resolution be given force of "legal principle".

Enforcement.—Compulsory enforcement of judgments and other court rulings belongs to jurisdiction of district courts and their executive officers. Executory acts are performed by executive officers with exception of those restricted to court. Judgments of foreign state courts or arbitration tribunals are enforced in same manner as judgments of domestic courts. (See topics Arbitration and Award; Judgments.)

Exclusive jurisdiction exists in matrimonial matters, relations between parents and children, and adoption, if both spouses have domicile in Poland, under condition that one of them is Polish citizen or has no citizenship. To exclusive domestic jurisdiction belongs: matters concerning legal incapacitation, declaring as presumably dead Polish citizen or person having no citizenship domiciled in Poland, and declaration of death occurring in Poland; matters pertaining to custody and guardianship over Polish citizen or one with no citizenship but has his domicile in Poland (court may refrain from performing guardianship over Polish citizen); and cases involving inheritance, if death occurred in Poland and decedent was Polish citizen at time of death. To exclusive jurisdiction of domestic courts belongs: matters concerning real property rights, possession of real estate in Poland, and arising from renting or leasing thereof except for claims for rent, and to other matters to extent decision affects real property located in Poland.

Lack of Jurisdiction.—Polish courts do not have jurisdiction over marital matters, matters arising from relations between parents and children and in adoption matters involving to foreign citizens not residing in Poland. Only under certain circumstances, Polish court may declare as presumably dead person of foreign nationality. (See topic Death [Presumption of and Actions for].) Full jurisdictional immunity is enjoyed by persons with diplomatic status. However, it does not apply to matters specifically enumerated in C.C.P. such as: matters of real property law pertaining to private immovable property located in Poland as well as inheritance, where persons enjoying immunity are not acting on behalf of state or any appropriate international organization; and matters related to professional or commercial activity of such persons undertaken by them in Poland outside their official functions. Persons who enjoy restricted jurisdictional immunity or functional immunity (e.g., consuls), may not be sued in Polish courts as to matters related to acts undertaken in their official capacity. Polish courts do not have jurisdiction over matters concerning real property or immovables or concerning possession of immovables located abroad. Generally, if express provision of law does not provide for jurisdiction of Polish courts in specific matters, Polish courts will not have jurisdiction unless: defendant has residence, domicile or seat in Poland at moment of service of process; defendant has property or property related rights in Poland; or dispute deals with subject matter situated in Poland, inheritance opened in Poland, or obligation which arose or is to be performed in Poland.

See topics Actions; Appeal and Error; Arbitration and Award; Commercial Register; Foreign Law; and Judgments.

CURRENCY:

Legal currency of Republic of Poland is Zloty. One zloty is divided into 100 grosz. Law of July 7, 1994 on Denomination of Zloty introduced new zloty that replaced old zloty (that will continue in circulation unitl Dec. 31, 1996). Greatest nominal value of banknotes is two million old zlotys. NBP has exclusive right to issue legal tender of Republic of Poland. Legal tender comprises bank notes (notes of NBP), coins in zloty, and grosz. Bank notes and coins issued by NBP are legal tender in Poland.

Value of bank notes, weight of coins, and dates of circulation are determined by President of NBP in consultation with Minister of Finance. President of NBP may withdraw from circulation specific kinds of legal tender. Upon expiration, tender ceases to be legal, and is subject to exchange in banks determined by President of NBP.

Principles of establishing and applying basic exchange rate of zloty in relation to foreign currencies are determined by Council of Ministers, and basic exchange rate of zloty is fixed by President of NBP in consultation with Minister of Finance and Minister of Foreign Economic Relations. Current exchange rates of foreign currencies in zlotys are published by President of NBP.

See topics Banks and Banking; Foreign Exchange.

CUSTOMS:

Customs Law of Dec. 28, 1989, as amended, consists of following chapters: "General Provisions", "Principles of Turnover of Commodities with Abroad", "Customs Value of Commodities", "Custom Free Areas and Custom Bonded Warehouses", "Customs Obligations", "Customs Proceedings", "Anti-Dumping Customs Duties", "Protection of Market Against Imports Threatening Economic Interest of Polish Producers", "Customs Administration", "Customs Agency" and "Transitional and Final Provisions". Poland is party to World Trade Organization (WTO).

Imported commodities are subject to customs duty, with exceptions provided by law. Duties are assessed in accordance with customs value. Customs value is transaction value, i.e. price actually paid (defined as aggregate payment to be paid by purchaser to seller for goods and includes all payments made or to be made as condition of sale) or due for goods to be transported into Polish customs territory, provided, however, that there exist no restrictions relating to disposition or use of products by purchaser, sale of price of goods does not depend on conditions or rendering of services value of which cannot be determined, purchaser shall not be entitled to certain portion of profit from further resale, disposition or future use of goods by purchaser is restricted, purchaser and seller are affiliated. If customs value cannot be determined based on its transaction value, such customs value is established on basis of separate pieces being transported or on identical or similar goods sold in Polish customs territory in larger amounts and in condition in which goods of which customs value is being established in arm's length transactions at time of transfer or within 90 days of such transfer less (1) margin customarily charged in connection with sale of such goods, (2) cost of transport and insurance, and (3) cost of transfer of such goods into Poland. Council of Ministers, by regulation, determines customs rates or suspends collection of customs duties in cases justified by economic or social needs. Minister of Foreign Economic Relations may, by order, introduce lump customs rates on imports by travellers or in postal turnover, when such action does not constitute economic activity. Customs Law contains list of circumstances under which imported commodities are exempt from customs duty. Minister of Foreign Economic Relations, according to type of commodities, may apply such measures as (1) restrictions on quantity and value of imported commodities, (2) deprivation or restriction of exemption in relation to travellers crossing customs border several times in calendar year. There are also exemptions from customs duty granted in conformity with reciprocity agreements concerning imports and exports of certain countries. Separate customs duties are set in compliance with specific agreements between Poland and EU, CEFTA and EFTA. Similar agreement establishing special customs treatment between Poland and EFTA countries is at present undergoing ratification procedure. Customs duty shall be assessed in accordance with state of commodities as of date of customs entry and on basis of rates in force on that day. (arts. 4, 10-14, 16, 17, 23, 24).

Customs value is price paid or price to be paid for commodity declared for customs clearance ("transaction value"). To transaction value are added following costs: (1) transport and insurance costs borne to border or port; (2) commission paid in connection with sales; (3) costs of containers, if in customs procedure they are treated as part of commodities; (4) costs of monies due and license fees which buyer had to pay as condition of sales; (5) costs of revenues or other profits from resale, utilization or other dispositions related to commodity, which directly or indirectly benefit seller; (6) costs connected with delivery, by buyer, free of charge or at price lower than market price, of objects or services utilized in connection with production or sales of commodities. From transaction value are deducted costs of transportation of commodities, including unloading, port fees and other fees connected with transport, as well as costs of insurance of commodities. Customs Law specifies special rules when transaction value cannot be established concerning assessment of customs value of commodities. (arts. 25-30).

Party exporting commodities is obligated to deliver and declare commodities to customs clearance area. Customs supervision and customs control is performed by customs officers. Goods type or quantity of which indicates their commercial character must be accompanied by, among other documents, original invoice, specification of product, where applicable, certificate of origin and/or import permits and Single Administrative Document. Customs body carrying on custom proceedings may (1) demand official translation of document in foreign language into Polish and (2) refuse

CUSTOMS . . . *continued*
acceptance of foreign document not legalized by Polish diplomatic representation or Polish consular office, when credibility of document arouses doubts or requirement of legalization results from separate provisions of law or agreement. Customs proceedings are carried on by head of customs office to which commodities are to be delivered. Anti-dumping procedure and protection of Polish market against import threatening interest of Polish producers is carried on by Minister of Foreign Economic Relations. Permits for establishment and conducting custom free warehouses, are carried on by President of Central Customs Office. Custom free areas are established by order of Council of Ministers. President of Central Customs Office, supervised by Minister of Foreign Economic Relations, is central body of State administration in customs matters.

Bilateral agreement signed Aug. 8, 1990 exists between Poland and U.S. on cooperation and mutual assistance between their customs services.

DEATH (Presumption of and Actions for):

Missing person may be declared dead if ten years have elapsed from end of calendar year in which, according to existing information, that person was still alive. If, however, at moment of declaring him dead missing person would have attained 70 years of age, period of five years is sufficient. Missing person cannot be declared dead before end of calendar year in which missing person would have attained 23 years of age. One who is reported missing during voyage by air or sea due to disaster to vessel or airplane or any other extraordinary occurrence may be declared dead after six months from day disaster or other extraordinary occurrence took place. If such disaster to vessel or airplane cannot be confirmed, running of six-month period commences one year following day vessel or airplane was to arrive at its port of destination or, if it did not have port of destination, two years following day it was last heard from. One who is missing as result of direct danger to life not envisaged above, may be declared dead after one year following day on which danger ceased or, according to circumstances, must have ceased. (arts. 29, 30 C.C.).

It is presumed that missing person died at moment specified in decision declaring him dead. Most probable is specified as moment of presumed death or, failing any data whatsoever, first day of period on which it becomes possible to declare person dead. If time of death was specified merely by date of day, end of that day is treated as moment of presumed death. If several persons lost their lives during common threat of danger to them, it is presumed they died simultaneously. (arts. 31, 32 C.C.).

Decision to declare death, if such person is Polish citizen or is domiciled in Poland, and does not have any other citizenship, is within exclusive jurisdiction of Polish courts. Polish court may also declare foreigner dead if person authorized to submit application is domiciled in Poland, or foreign citizen had his domicile in Poland. Declaration of death, if death took place in Poland, also belongs to exclusive jurisdiction of Polish courts. (art. 1106 C.C.P.). Law on International Private Law of 1965 stipulates that when Polish court declares missing person as dead, court must apply that person's home country law. According to Law on Birth, Marriage and Death Certificates of Sept. 29, 1986, in case of declaration of death of foreign citizen or declaration of such missing person as dead, death is registered in registry office which has jurisdiction over central district of Warsaw.

See topics Actions; Courts.

DEEDS:

See topic Mortgages.

DEPOSITIONS:

Legal assistance (obtaining evidence, delivery of certificates, providing information or explanations etc.) as well as service of court letters and documents in international civil law relationships are governed by arts. 1130-1136 C.C.P. This is supplemented by executory regulations: Decree of Minister of Justice and Minister of Foreign Affairs of Aug. 26, 1966 on principles and mode of requesting legal assistance by courts in international civil procedure, as well as ordinance of Minister of Justice of May 25, 1970 containing instructions regarding foreign legal relations in civil and criminal matters. Poland concluded several bilateral treaties pertaining to broadly defined legal assistance (encompassing service of letters and documents). Poland is also party to both Conventions Concerning Civil Procedure (Hague 1905 and Hague 1954) as well as to Convention Concerning Claims for Alimony From Abroad (New York 1956).

In cases of legal assistance, courts communicate with both courts and other government bodies of foreign states. They also communicate with Polish diplomatic and consular authorities through Ministry of Justice. Polish courts direct their requests for legal assistance, which is to be provided in countries which have adhered to Hague conventions, to appropriate foreign authorities of Republic of Poland. Diplomatic authorities performing consular functions, as well as consular authorities of foreign states in Poland, have right to address courts and executory officials directly. District courts and executory officials should, immediately after settling or clarifying matter, answer request which they received from consular authority of foreign state.

Polish courts provide broadly defined legal assistance on request of foreign courts and other foreign government bodies. In civil cases, requests are handled by district courts (in Polish language). If Polish court which has been requested to assist does not have jurisdiction over matter, it transfers request to appropriate court and notifies requesting body of transfer. If inaccurate or faulty address of person whom request concerns has been given, court should, ex officio, take measures to establish appropriate address.

Legal assistance may be refused by Polish court if: (a) act would be incompatible with fundamental legal principles of Republic of Poland or it would be prejudicial to its sovereignty, (b) performing requested action falls outside jurisdiction of Polish courts, or (c) state from which request for legal assistance originated refuses to provide legal assistance to Polish courts.

Acts requested by court or organs of foreign state concerning legal assistance by Polish court are performed in accordance with Polish law. Procedural law of requested country applies to form of action to be performed, obligation of witnesses to appear and testify, right to refuse to testify, permissibility and form of oath, conditions of valid service of letters and documents originating in foreign courts, etc. Court may, however, upon request of foreign court, apply to action requested form other than one prescribed by Polish law, if said form is neither forbidden by Polish law nor contrary to fundamental legal principles (public order) of Republic of Poland. In relationships with countries that are parties to Hague conventions, if letter rogatory specifies manner in which act should be performed, court performs action as requested unless it is contrary to law of requested country.

Polish law adopted principle that if court or organs of foreign states request that court deliver letter (document) to person in Poland, without supplying translation of that letter into Polish, it is to be delivered to addressee only if he agrees to accept it. Law also requires that addressee who refuses to accept delivery must be informed of legal consequences which may arise abroad from that act.

Documents and records created to satisfy request for legal assistance (e.g., confirmation of delivery, protocols, certificates, copies of court decisions) and received request, must be returned to court or other requesting organ of foreign state in same manner in which original request was received. Records concerning satisfaction of request must be returned, accompanied by transmittal letter which must be signed by president of court and bear official seal of court. If expenses are incurred in connection with providing legal assistance at request of court or other organ of foreign state, such costs are to be paid from budget of court and reimbursement demanded in currency of given state; applicable manner of currency conversion is to be indicated. Costs are not reimbursed if international treaty ensures providing of legal assistance free of charge or does not require transfer of expenses.

DESCENT AND DISTRIBUTION:

Statutory succession consists of rules governing descent and distribution. (arts. 931-940 C.C.). These are divided into following groups:

First Group.—Deceased's children and spouse are, by force of law, first appointed to inheritance; they inherit in equal shares. However, part passing to spouse cannot be smaller than one-fourth of entire inheritance. If child of deceased did not survive, his share passes in equal shares to his children. This provision is correspondingly applied to more remote descendants.

Second Group.—In absence of descendants of deceased, his spouse, parents, brothers and sisters are by force of law appointed to inheritance. Spouse who inherits concurrently with other persons from this group receives one-half of inheritance. Remaining parts are inherited in equal shares by brothers and sisters. If one parent did not survive opening of inheritance, his share passes half to other parent and half to deceased's brothers and sisters. If, aside from spouse, only parents or only brothers and sisters are appointed to inheritance, they inherit in equal shares whatever passes jointly to parents, brothers and sisters.

Third Group embraces three situations: (a) when there are no descendants, parents, brothers, sisters and descendants of brothers and sisters of deceased, entire inheritance passes to deceased's spouse; (b) when there are no descendants or spouse of deceased, entire inheritance passes to his parents, brothers and sisters and their descendants; (c) when there is neither spouse of deceased nor relatives appointed by force of law, inheritance passes to Treasury, his statutory heir.

Some Special Rules Concerning Spouse, Adoptee and Deceased's Grandparents.—Spouse inheriting by force of law concurrently with other heirs, excluding deceased's descendants who lived with deceased at moment of his death, may demand, above spouse's share of inheritance, household objects used by spouse when deceased lived jointly with spouse or used exclusively by spouse. Spouse is excluded from inheritance if deceased had filed for divorce due to spouse's fault and demand for divorce was justified. Exclusion of spouse from inheritance is decision of court.

Adoptee inherits after adoptive parents and his blood relatives, as if he were adoptive parent's child, and adoptive parent and his relatives inherit after adoptee, as if adoptive parent were adoptee's parent. Adoptee does not inherit from his natural ascendants and their relatives, and those persons do not inherit from him.

Deceased's grandparents, if they live in poverty and cannot obtain means of support due them from persons upon whom statutory duty of maintenance or alimony rests, may demand, from heir not charged with such duty, means of support in relation to their needs and value of his share of inheritance.

For discussion of legitimate portions, see topic Wills.

DISPUTE RESOLUTION:

General.—Polish law provides for dispute resolution only through judicial proceedings (see topic Courts) and arbitration (see topic Arbitration and Award). There are generally no statutes or rules for out-of-court proceedings such as mediation, fact finding or minitrials.

Mandatory Dispute Resolution.—Polish labor law provides special proceeding for Group Dispute Resolution, with respect to disputes that may arise between employees represented by trade union and employers. Employees are entitled to undertake strike, only if mediation proceeding provided for is exhausted.

Voluntary Dispute Resolution.—Polish Civil Code includes general regulation of conciliatory procedure in accordance with which parties may make reciprocal concessions in scope of legal relationship existing between them, in order to settle their claims, resulting from this legal relationship or ensure their performance or execution or prevent existing or possible dispute to occur. In result of conciliation procedure parties enter into agreement, which shall be enforceable according to general rules of law of contracts. There are special rules for termination of such agreement if parties conclude agreement acting under influence of mistake.

There is also special regulation for individual labor disputes. According to Polish Labor Code employee may submit claim to mediation committee before filing court suit. Such committees are special bodies elected by employer and union organization that is present in employer's enterprise.

DIVORCE:

Divorce is regulated by 1964 Family and Guardianship Code in arts. 56-60 and by C.C.P. in arts. 425-446. Poland is party to Hague Convention on Conflicts of Law and Jurisdiction relating to Divorce and Separation of June 12, 1902.

DIVORCE . . . *continued*

Divorce may be effectuated only by judgment of court. Court dissolves marriage by means of divorce. Husband and/or wife may demand divorce on grounds of irreconcilable breakdown of marriage. However, although such breakdown has occurred, divorce is not permissible if as consequence well-being of parties' common minor children would suffer in any way or if judgment to dissolve marriage by divorce would be contrary to principles of social coexistence. Divorce is also not permissible if demanded by party solely at fault for breakdown of marriage unless other party consents to divorce, or if denial of such consent is under particular circumstances contrary to principles of social coexistence.

In divorce decree, court decides which party, if any, is at fault for breakdown of marriage. Court does not decide upon fault if both parties mutually consent to no-fault procedure. Legal consequences of such judgment will be as if no party were at fault.

In judgment of divorce, court decides legal custody of common child as well as level of maintenance and care costs which each parent must bear. Court may award custody of child to only one parent, restricting parental custody of other to certain rights and obligations toward child.

Divorced party who as consequence of marriage had changed his or her former last name may, in course of three months from date on which divorce judgment becomes final, through declaration made in front of registrar, return to last name which party had borne prior to marriage.

Divorced party who was not proven to be solely at fault in breakdown of marriage may, under certain circumstances, demand that other divorced party provide means of support and sustenance in degree reflecting justified needs of entitled and financial abilities of obliged. If one party was proven to be solely at fault and divorce brings about substantial deterioration of material situation of party not at fault, court may, upon demand of latter, decide that party solely at fault is obliged to provide other with means of support within his or her justifiable needs even though latter may not be in dire circumstances. Obligation to provide means of support ceases in case of marriage of divorced party. However, if obliged is divorced party who was not found to be at fault in breakdown of marriage, obligation ceases after five years from moment of granting of divorce, unless court, due to exceptional circumstances, decides on demand of entitled to prolong five year term.

According to art. 18 of Private International Law Code of 1965, law of country of which both parties are citizens at time of initiation of divorce proceedings is applicable to divorce. In absence of common national law, law of country in which both parties are domiciled is applicable. If parties do not have domicile in same country, Polish law is applicable.

Note: At present draft of new law is being discussed in Polish Parliament which if accepted would introduce institution of separation.

In matters of jurisdiction see topic Courts.

ENVIRONMENT:

Legal framework for Environment Protection is described in Statute on Protection and Management of Environment of 1980, as amended, and Regulations issued thereunder. Statute describes obligations of administration and private persons with respect to environment protection, civil and criminal liability for violation of its provisions, and powers of administrative bodies supervising enforcement of environmental laws.

Protection of Lands and Mineral Resources.—Land i.e. its soil or its sculpture is, pursuant to statute, object of legal protection, and in case it is damaged or destroyed, it should be restored to its previous condition. High quality agricultural lands may not be used for nonagricultural and non-forestation purposes, including investment purposes. Persons conducting agricultural activity are obligated to use their lands so as to preserve their agricultural value. Persons not conducting agricultural activity are obligated to abstain from any actions which may contaminate land. Persons excavating minerals are obligated to take measures which are necessary not only to protect mineral resources but also land surface, and surface and underground waters. Person failing to observe duty to protect agricultural and forested lands may, in cases specified in statute, be subject to imprisonment.

Protection of Waters and Sea Environment.—Inland and sea waters have to be utilized in such manner so as not to destroy ecological balance and deteriorate their usefulness for people, animals, plants and state economy. Plans of all undertakings which may significantly influence water environment have to describe projected activity necessary to protect water environment. Voivods (see topic Constitution and Government, subhead Regional Administration and Territorial Self-Governance) may proscribe use of ships and other water vehicles on certain waters, if it is necessary for preservation of water environment. Persons who, undertaking ground works which influence waters, do not use means necessary to preserve ecological balance or do not observe legal requirements imposed on such works may be subject to criminal sanctions and fines.

Air Protection.—Aim of air protection is to prevent excessive concentration of air pollutants and to reduce their existing concentration. Businesses are obligated to use technologies which protect air from pollution and to monitor concentration of air pollutants. Person emitting air pollutants must apply for individual permit from Voivod for such emissions. Upon payment of fee, Voivod issues such permit, describing maximum level of emissions by applicant. Person who exceeds such maximum permitted level may be ordered to restrain from actions producing excess emissions. Users or internal-combustion engines have to ascertain that these engines do not emit air pollutants in excess of applicable norms. Voivods, in case of emergency, may temporarily proscribe emission of certain air pollutants or use of vehicles with internal-combustion engines. Person conducting business, who fails to monitor concentration of air pollutants, may be subject to criminal sanctions and fines. Persons exceeding permitted level of air pollutant emission may be fined. Persons responsible for contamination of air which might be harmful for humans or may cause significant environmental or economic damage may be imprisoned and fined.

Protection of Plants, Animals, Landscapes, and Special Protection of Plants in Cities and Villages.—Statute provides for general protection of plants and animals, necessary to preserve ecological balance in environment. Statute specifically prohibits destruction of plants which prevent soil erosion and destruction of plants or animals important for removal of effects of pollution. Persons must abstain from activities which endanger plants in cities and villages. Trees or bushes may, generally, be removed only upon permit from commune. Voivods may determine that certain areas should be particularly protected for their landscape or tourist value. Persons who destroy plants which prevent soil erosion, plants or animals important for removal of effects of pollution, damage trees, or breach provisions of Voivod decisions establishing landscape protection area, may be subjected to criminal sanctions and fines. Persons who remove trees of bushes without permit may be fined.

Protection of Environment Against Noise and Vibrations.—Voivod determines permissible level of noise or vibrations. Person producing noise or vibrations, exceeding level set by Voivod, must apply for individual permit from Voivod. Upon payment of fee, Voivod issues such permit, describing maximum level of noise or vibrations which may be produced by applicant. Person who exceeds such maximum permitted level may be ordered to restrain from actions producing excess noise or vibrations. Persons producing noise or vibrations in excess of permitted level may also be fined.

Environment Protection Against Wastes and Other Contamination.—Businesses which produce wastes are obligated to protect environment from any damage or deterioration caused by such wastes and have to make efforts to recycle such wastes. Statute prohibits imports of dangerous wastes. Other wastes may not be imported, unless imports are authorized by Main Inspector for Environment Protection. Statute also prohibits exports of dangerous wastes without permission of Main Inspector for Environment Protection. Transit of dangerous wastes through territory of Poland requires permit of Main Inspector for Environment Protection. Wastes which cannot be recycled should be stored, liquidated or disposed of, only in places which are designated for that purpose. Businesses which produce packages or other products which, after they are used, might pose threat for environment, have to determine method of such products' recycling, or if this proves impossible, of their disposal. Owners and users of houses, condominiums and other real properties are obligated to maintain their real property clean and free of any man made wastes and contamination. Persons failing to observe laws protecting environment from wastes and other contamination may be subject to criminal penalties and fines. Persons who, without proper authorization, import or export wastes and persons responsible for contamination of water, air or land which might be harmful for humans or may cause significant environmental or economic damage, may be imprisoned and fined.

Protection from Radiation.—Radioactive substances or equipment utilized for their production may only be used if there are sufficient safeguards protecting people and environment from radiation. Radioactive wastes may be recycled only in accordance with terms of decision by Voivod. Persons using or producing radioactive substances which may be harmful for humans or environment are obligated to monitor level of radiation to which they expose environment. Persons failing to observe legal requirements relating to protection of people and environment from radiation may be subjected to criminal penalties and fines. Persons responsible for contamination of water, air or land which might be harmful for humans or may cause significant environmental or economic damage may be imprisoned and fined.

Production of Machines and Other Technical Equipment.—Authors and producers of machines and other technical equipment are obligated to ascertain that such machines comply with environment protection standards. Producers are also required, if improper use of machine could be dangerous for environment, to place instruction of such machine describing its proper use. In some cases machine users are also responsible for proper use of their machines. Imported machines and technical equipment have to comply with Polish environment protection standards. If imported machines or technical equipment are determined to be harmful for environment, such imports may be temporarily suspended by Minister of Environment Protection, Natural Resources and Forestry acting in cooperation with other authorities. Persons designing or producing machines which may be dangerous for environment, persons selling machines without subjecting them to inspection for compliance with environment protection standards, and persons failing to examine periodically their machines for compliance with environment protection standards, may be subject to criminal penalties and fines.

Civil Liability for Damage of Environment.—Persons responsible for damage of environment are liable for such damage pursuant to general rules of civil liability contained in Civil Code. Person may be restrained from action, by court order, if such action is contrary to environmental laws and constitutes nuisance for its neighbors. Person may be restrained from action by administrative order if such action causes deterioration of environment.

Administration of Environment Protection.—Statute gives primary role in administration of environment protection to government administration supervised by Minister of Environment Protection, Natural Resources and Forestry. Self-government administration plays secondary role. Statute establishes Environment Protection and Water Management Funds which finance environment protection. It also establishes National Environment Protection Council—body responsible for creation of environment protection policy.

EXCHANGE CONTROL:

See topics Foreign Exchange; Banks and Banking.

EXECUTIONS:

District courts and court executive officers are competent in execution matters. All execution activities are carried out by court executive officers with exception of those reserved for courts alone. Motion to initiate execution is to be filed with appropriate court or court executive officer. In cases where execution ex officio is possible, it may be carried out upon demand of court of first instance which examined case, and later directed to appropriate court or court executive officer. In motion or demand for execution ex officio, performance to be executed and method of execution is to be indicated and executory document is attached thereto.

Executory document with writ of execution is basis for execution. Following are executory documents: (a) decision of court, as well as court settlement which is valid or subject to immediate execution, (b) arbitral award or settlement reached therein, (c) other decisions, settlements and acts which by virtue of law are subject to court

EXECUTIONS . . . *continued*
execution, (d) notary deed, in which debtor subjected himself to execution and includes duty to pay certain amount of money or execution of other exchangeable property quantitatively indicated in deed, or duty to release individually indicated object, when date of payment, execution or release is indicated in deed.

Special procedure is established for banks. Bank books and excerpts from these books certifying declarations of debtor, lifting of obligations, renouncement of obligations, confirmation of receipt of dues or confirmation of granting of credit, amount of such credit, interest on crdit and form of repayment are considered official documents and constitute basis for entries into Land Registry Books and public registries (see topic Mortgages). These documents together with declaration that obligations shown therein have become due are considered execution documents fully empowered, without necessity of obtaining writ of execution from court.

Executory document is basis for execution for entire claim it includes and from entire assets of debtor, unless it provides otherwise. Regulations determine in detail all object limitations of execution. Executory body is not entitled to examine justification and maturity of duty covered by executory document. Debtor must be notified at beginning of execution and provided with text of executory document together with description of method of execution upon first executory act. If place of debtor's stay is not known, court will appoint him guardianship ex officio if execution is to be initiated ex officio or upon creditor's request otherwise.

Execution from personal property must be undertaken by executive officer of court in district in which property is located. Execution on personal property commences with its seizure, which is done by registering it in seizure protocol. Seizure may be made when property is in possession of debtor or creditor who initiated execution. Personal property in possession of third parties may be seized only upon their consent to seizure, their admission that it is debtor's property or in other circumstances specified by law. Sale of seized property may not take place sooner than seventh day after day of seizure, unless law provides otherwise (e.g., property might be sold immediately after seizure in case it may soon get spoiled or its guarding or storage would cause excessive costs).

Execution of real property must be undertaken by executive officer of court in district in which property is located. Court execution officer summons debtor to pay his debt or otherwise he will start process of description and evaluation of property. Upon sending of summons to debtor, court's execution office is to send request to authority maintaining land registry books to make entry about initiation of execution or to file request for collection of documents. Real property is considered seized when summons is delivered to debtor. In relation to debtor to whom summons was not delivered and third parties, real property is considered seized when entry is made in land registry book or court execution officer's request to collection of documents is filed. Seizure includes real property and everything which, according to law, may be object of mortgage. Seized property is sold through public auction. Date of auction may be no earlier than one month from day of description and evaluation or before decision execution is based upon becomes binding.

If State Treasury is debtor, creditor, by presenting executory document, calls state organizational entity directly to effect performance. Such unit is required to effect performance confirmed by executory document. If executory document, drawn for certain amount of money, will not be executed within two weeks from day of delivery, creditor may request that court attach writ of execution to executory document, in order to carry out execution on bank account of appropriate state organizational entity. In case of nonmonetary performance, court, upon creditor's request, is to specify date for director of appropriate state entity to carry out performance and is to fine him if he fails to perform within specified time.

Executory proceedings are governed by arts. 758-1095 of second chapter of first part of C.C.P. Except regulation of execution from real and personal property, C.C.P. permits "execution from compensation for work", "execution from other claims and proprietary rights" and "execution from maritime vessels". Stipulations on execution of nonmonetary performances (arts. 1041-1059) are important among other executory proceedings regulations. Execution against debtor, who carries out business activity in form of enterprise, may take execution on profits acquired from such activity by establishing receivership over enterprise.

FOREIGN CORPORATIONS:

See topics Corporations; Foreign Investment.

FOREIGN EXCHANGE:

Foreign Exchange Law of Dec. 2, 1994, regulates principles of foreign exchange transactions and use of exchange rates, obligation of domestic persons to report property held abroad and of foreign persons to report property held in Poland, competence of entities in foreign exchange matters, and principles of controlling exchange.

Foreign exchange can be subject of property of domestic persons in Poland and abroad, as well as foreign persons in Poland. Domestic and foreign persons may carry out foreign exchange transactions subject to restrictions set forth in provisions of Law. Economic subjects are obliged to administer receivables due from foreign persons in manner ensuring immediate transfer from abroad of all foreign means of payment of such receivables. Domestic persons are obliged to administer foreign exchange values owned abroad in manner ensuring their immediate transfer from abroad. Domestic person who acquired foreign exchange values during his stay abroad is obliged to ensure transfer of such values from abroad within two months from date of return to Poland.

Economic subjects engaged in transactions abroad in goods, services and rights relating to intangible assets may not set periods of maturity of receivables that exceed three months from date of exporting of goods from Poland or from date of transfer of property or establishment of right, and, in case of provision of services, from date of making out invoice or other equivalent documents. Domestic persons are obliged to immediately resell foreign currencies and submit for purchase foreign exchange to bank authorized to carry out purchase associated with such obligation.

This obligation does not apply to: (1) natural persons who receive foreign means of payment from entitlement not connected with carrying out of economic activity or exercising free profession; (2) foreign diplomatic missions, consular offices, special missions and international organizations and other foreign representative offices enjoying diplomatic and consular immunities and privileges; (3) certain designated institutions; (4) domestic persons with respect to: (a) foreign means of payment purchased at licensed bank, (b) foreign means of payment that were left abroad with purpose of utilization on basis of foreign exchange permit, (c) foreign means of payment resulting from donations from foreign persons exempt from reselling on basis of foreign exchange permit, (d) foreign currencies accumulated on restricted accounts with exceptions of currencies to which beneficiary acquired right to dispose on its own account; (5) domestic persons engaged in exchange of foreign currencies as economic activity. (art. 6).

Foreign exchange permit is required for carrying out of following foreign exchange operations: (1) transfer abroad of foreign exchange values, with exception of: (a) transporting abroad by domestic natural persons and foreign natural persons of foreign means of payment, up to amount specified by Minister of Finance in general foreign exchange permit (currently 5,000 ECU), (b) transfer of foreign currencies abroad by domestic persons in order to meet their obligations with respect to foreign persons relating to purchase from such persons of goods located abroad or subject to economic transport from abroad, (c) transfer of foreign currencies abroad by domestic persons in order to meet their obligations with respect to foreign persons arising from agreements on provision of services, with exception of services performed in Poland to benefit of natural persons and meant to satisfy their personal needs, (d) transfer of foreign currencies abroad by domestic persons in order to meet their obligations with respect to foreign persons relating to purchase or establishing intangible rights, (e) transporting and sending abroad by foreign natural persons of foreign means of payments declared at entry for clearance at customs office and reflected in personal declaration confirmed by that office, (f) transfer abroad by persons not having residence or seat in Poland of foreign currencies purchased with Polish currency up to amount of net financial results of their branch and representative offices referred to of banks and insurance companies calculated on basis of account books maintained in accordance with applicable rules, (g) transfer abroad by foreign persons of convertible currencies stemming from free foreign accounts of such persons and foreign exchange not exceeding amount of such accounts, as well as foreign means of payment purchased by such persons with Polish currency stemming from those accounts, (h) transfer abroad for benefit of restricted persons foreign currencies stemming from restricted accounts with respect to which beneficiary has not acquired right to administer on his own account, (i) transport and transfer abroad by domestic persons of foreign exchange purchased at banks in order to meet obligations with respect to foreign persons relating to certain entitlement; (2) transfer of ownership of foreign exchange located in Poland between domestic and foreign person or transfer of claims or obligations where subject of performance of which is foreign exchange located in Poland with exception of following: (a) acceptance by domestic persons of donations of foreign exchange values from foreign persons, (b) administering of foreign exchange values in will and making dispositions in case of death in accordance with provisions of banking law, (c) purchase of foreign legal means of payment in banks by foreign persons with Polish currency from free foreign accounts of such persons, (d) sale and purchase of foreign currency from authorized entities; (3) carrying out of foreign exchange and currency services for population by persons other than bank authorized pursuant to provisions on National Bank of Poland, (4) granting by domestic persons to foreign persons of credits and loans in foreign exchange values, as well as drawing by domestic persons of such credits and loans from foreign persons including those connected with issuance and turnover in debt securities, with exception of commercial credits drawn from foreign persons provided, however, that terms of commercial credit shall not be less favorable than generally accepted in similar cases in international financial market and credited party shall inform National Bank of Poland about such credit, (5) establishment by domestic persons in favor of foreign persons of warranties and guaranties of fulfilling obligations where subject of which is foreign exchange values with exception of warranties and guaranties of fulfilling certain enumerated obligations as well as warranties and guaranties of repayment of commercial credits, (6) settling and making payments in foreign exchange values in Poland for acquired goods and real estate, rights to assets or for services rendered and for work, (7) opening and possession of bank account in foreign bank by domestic person with exception of natural persons during their stay abroad, as well as foreign diplomatic and consular missions, (8) acquisition by domestic persons of securities issued abroad and coupons from those securities, as well as interests and shares in companies or enterprises with seats abroad, as well as other rights of similar nature, in particular participation units in investment funds with seats abroad, (9) acquisition by domestic persons, by legal action, of real estate located abroad, (10) sale by banks of foreign means of payment for domestic means of payment to foreign persons and transfer abroad of foreign means of payment connected with such sale. (art. 9).

In accordance with Regulation of Minister of Finance of Jan. 26, 1996 on General Foreign Exchange Permit, domestic persons can transfer foreign exchange values to OECD member states and other countries with which Poland entered into agreements on investment protection in order to (i) puchase shares in companies with seats in such countries, provided, that number of such shares constitutes at least 10% of aggregate number of votes at shareholders meeting of such company; (ii) purchase or establish branch or enterprise; (iii) purchase real estate located aborad, provided such purchase is in connection with commercial activities carried out abroad, provided value of above-described transactions does not exceed equivalent of 1,000,000 ECU as of date of purchase. Domestic commercial companies may transfer abroad foreign currencies in order to purchase treasury securities or bonds, issued by enterprises or institutions with seats in countries that are OECD member states, that are admitted to public trading in such countries and maturity period of which is not less than one year, provided, however, that amount of such investment does not exceed equivalent of 1,000,000 ECU on date of purchase.

Generally, domestic commercial companies can obtain loans in exchangeable currencies with repayment term of at least five years, entered into in connection with permanent commercial relations reflected in particular by fact that lender shall be able to manage enterprise of borrower. This provision treats such loans as form of direct investment that is not subject to special permit. Regulation provides, however, that terms of such loan cannot be not less favorable than customary terms generally

FOREIGN EXCHANGE . . . *continued*

applicable in connection with such loans. Similar provision applies in case of granting of loans by domestic persons to foreign persons.

Furthermore, commercial companies may settle their respective obligations through mutual set-off, provided, however, that obligations are due and valid. All such transactions must, however, be registered with Bank Handlowy w Warszawie S.A. within 14 days from date of set-off.

Regulation permits companies with foreign participation to obtain loans in foreign currencies from such companies' foreign shareholders, provided that terms of such loan are not less favorable than customary terms generally applicable in connection with such loans. Similarly, domestic persons who are shareholders of foreign companies may grant loans to such companies in foreign currencies, provided that terms of such loan are not less favorable than customary terms generally applicable in connection with such loans and that loan (principal and interest) shall be repaid in currency in which it was granted or in another exchangeable currency.

Domestic persons are obliged to report to National Bank of Poland their property holdings abroad. Foreign persons are obliged to report property held in Poland, with exception of diplomatic representatives, consular officers and all other persons enjoying diplomatic privileges and immunities. National Bank of Poland is obliged to observe principle of secrecy of information concerning property holdings reported to it. (arts. 16, 17).

Administrative competence concerning foreign exchange is vested with Minister of Finance and National Bank of Poland, in consultation with President of National Bank of Poland, which issues by way of ordinance general foreign exchange permits, which are issued for all domestic or foreign persons or specified group thereof. National Bank of Poland issues individual foreign exchange permits. Principles of issuing such permits are determined by President of National Bank of Poland in consultation with Minister of Finance. Minister of Finance cooperates with President of National Bank of Poland in creating State foreign exchange reserves, and in defining principles of administering those reserves. President of NBP, in consultation with Minister of Finance, may define admissible amount of indebtedness and liability of foreign exchange banks in relation to foreign persons. (arts. 17-21).

Foreign Exchange Control.—Foreign exchange transactions and other operations for which Foreign Exchange Law requires foreign exchange permit are subject to foreign exchange control. Obligation to report property holdings is also subject to control. Minister of Finance and his subordinated organs, and in some instances customs administration and frontier guards, perform foreign exchange control in accordance with principles and procedures of financial control. Controlling organs are authorized to demand information concerning transactions and bank accounts denominated in foreign currency, with exception of information on savings deposits and on property holdings. Foreign exchange control is also carried out by: (1) National Bank of Poland—concerning foreign exchange operations effected by foreign exchange banks and domestic and foreign persons to whom foreign exchange permits for those operations have been issued, (2) banks—concerning foreign exchange payments and settlements effected by or through those banks, (3) customs administration—concerning frontier foreign exchange control and foreign exchange control of postal consignments, (4) frontier guards—concerning frontier foreign exchange control, when such guards are authorized to perform customs control, (5) postal administration—as concerning postal consignments registered for abroad. Frontier foreign exchange control is performed in accordance with principles and procedures for customs control. When requested to do so by entities performing foreign exchange control, domestic and foreign persons are obliged to offer oral and written explanations as well as to produce required documentation relating to foreign exchange control. Domestic and foreign persons exporting or importing foreign currency are obliged to report said value and, when requested to do so by organs performing foreign control, present foreign currency for control. (arts. 21-25).

See topics Banks and Banking; Foreign Trade and Foreign Investments.

FOREIGN INVESTMENT:

Basic legal acts governing direct business activity of foreign entities in Poland (or participation in such activity) include: (a) Council of Ministers decree of Feb. 6, 1976, concerning conditions, procedures, and issuing permits to foreign corporate bodies and individuals to establish representative offices in Republic of Poland for purpose of conducting business, (b) Law of July 6, 1982, as amended, on principles of Conducting of Economic Activity in Small Industry by qualified foreign parties and natural persons within Republic of Poland, and (c) Law of June 14, 1991 on Companies with Participation of Foreign Parties, as amended. Law of 1982 applies only to business activities conducted before enactment of Law of Dec. 23, 1988 on Economic Activity with Participation of Foreign Parties.

According to decree of 1976, permit is required for foreign individual or corporate body to establish representative office in Republic of Poland. Permit to conduct activities in foreign trade is granted by Minister of Foreign Economic Relations. Permits in other fields are granted by authorized minister in cooperation with Minister of Foreign Economic Relations. Foreign representative office may be established to conduct business in foreign trade, transport, tourism and cultural services. Entity may establish branch office or agency to conduct business, office of technical information to conduct activities in field of scientific and technical information, or supervisory office to supervise transactions between foreign entity and Polish foreign trade enterprise. Office may conduct business activity only within scope of its permit. Permit should be granted to foreign entities if justified by volume of turnover with Polish enterprises, institutions and corporations.

Polish law, except Law of 1982, allows foreign parties to conduct economic activity in Poland only through corporation established under Comm. C. and in accordance with Law of June 14, 1991 on Companies with Participation of Foreign Parties, as amended. "Economic activity" is defined as production, construction, trade and services conducted for profit. Such activity may be conducted either in form of limited liability, joint stock company established by Polish and foreign parties, or solely by foreign parties. Foreign entities may establish one-shareholder limited liability companies. Foreign parties are defined as legal persons having their registered seat abroad, natural persons domiciled abroad, and companies which have no legal personality established by persons.

According to Law of June, 14, 1991 on Companies with Participation of Foreign Parties, as amended, permits have to be obtained if shares or stocks in company are to be acquired by state-owned firm and this entity will make in-kind contributions of its business, real property or organized part of its business having capacity to engage in economic activity to cover cost of initial capital or if company enters into agreement or series of agreements pursuant to which it obtains right to use above described property of state-owned entity for more than six months or acquires title thereto. Finally, foreign entity has to comply with other laws or regulations that may require permit. Foreign investors and foreign entities forming limited liability or joint stock company only have to meet requirements set out in Comm.C. (rough equivalent of $1,500 for limited liability companies and $40,000 for joint stock companies). There is no minimum percentage foreign participation amount.

Minister of Finance may exempt company from corporate income tax if foreign entity contributes more than two million ECU's (roughly 2.75 million U.S. dollars at current exchange rates) and, additionally, when business activity is conducted in regions of high unemployment, or ensures introduction of new technological developments, or enables export of goods and services at rate of at least 20% of value of total sales. Only companies in which foreign entities have purchased or hold shares or stock prior to Dec. 31, 1993, are entitled to receive such tax exemptions.

Regulation of Council of Ministers on Deduction of Investment Expenses from Income and Reductions of Income Tax dated Jan. 25, 1994, as amended, applies to investment expenses incurred after Jan. 1, 1994. Regulation governs, inter alia, deduction of investment expenses from gross profit of both natural and legal persons. Regulation provides investment incentives to companies that generate profits within first three years of activities. Generally, investment expenses can be deducted up to 25% of total taxable income. However, taxpayers whose export earnings constitute over 50% of total earnings or in excess of equivalent of eight million ECU and taxpayers who incurred investment expenses in connection with purchase of machinery and equipment considered as fixed investments or licenses, patents and domestic scientific works can deduct such expenses up to 50% of their total income.

All profits as well as payments to foreign entity upon redemption of shares or liquidation of company can be transferred without separate foreign exchange permit. Furthermore, foreign entities are guaranteed indemnification for expropriation and for actions with equivalent results. Permits will be denied whenever business activity threatens State economic interests, State security and defense interests or protection of State secrets.

Contributions from foreign parties should be made in form of: (i) monetary contributions of foreign exchange deposited on unrestricted foreign exchange account of foreign exchange transferred from abroad through foreign bank or in zlotys purchased at authorized bank for foreign currency, or (ii) in-kind contributions, provided that contributed property is transferred from abroad purchased for exchange describe in item (i) hereof, or purchased for exchange inherited by foreign party.

There are no limitations regarding transfer of profit abroad.

Act of 10 June 1994 on Public Procurement contains general provisions requiring governmental bodies subject to Act to treat all offers equally and carry out procurement process in such manner as to discourage corrupt practices. Definition of government bodies includes practically all units of central and territorial governments and territorial self-government units and all institutions that spend public funds. Act permits procuring entities to apply domestic preferences (such as in connection with local construction projects, where procuring entities may require that all of entities involved, materials and products be domestic). Furthermore, pursuant to Regulation of 29 Dec. 1994 of Council of Ministers on Implementation of Domestic Preferences in Connection with Public Procurement, domestic entities geneally obtain 20% price discount on offers made in connection with construction services, deliveries and other services.

Act provides for five types of procurement proceedings: (1) unlimited tender, which is to be applied in most cases, and would be open to all vendors and suppliers who meet certain basic eligibility standards (Act includes requirements relating to conviction of crime in connection with procurement proceedings, default on public contract etc.); (2) limited tender which is permitted in certain specific circumstances for example, when cost of conducting unlimited tender would be prohibitive or goods or services required are highly specialised; (3) two-stage tender, involving making of offers without price in initial stage with price established after selection, to be used when it is impossible to define up-front technical approaches and quality of goods or services requested, if negotiations are necessary because of specialised nature of work involved or if procurement involves research, scientific opinions or other specialised services; (4) competitive negotiation which is used when unlimited tender has not resulted in any tender or in other limited circumstances; and (5) single source procurement which is used when only one supplier is capable of offering required goods and services.

Act established Office of Public Procurement, which oversees enforcement of Act and publishes public procurement bulletin in which procurements are announced.

See topics Aliens; Corporations; Investment Protection.

FOREIGN LAW:

In international conflicts of law, substantive laws of foreign countries may be applied in Poland. Polish conflict of law is codified in Law of Nov. 12, 1965 on International Private Law. It is composed of 38 articles, which are divided into 12 sections: "General Provision" (arts. 1-8), "Persons" (arts. 9-11), "Form of Legal Transaction" (art. 12), "Limitation of Actions" (art. 13), "Marriage" (arts. 14-18), "Consanguinity" (arts. 19-22), "Guardianship and Tutelage" (art. 23), "Ownership and other Rights in Property" (art. 24), "Obligations" (arts. 25-31), "Labor Relations" (arts. 32-33), "Inheritances" (arts. 34-35), "Final Provisions" (arts. 36-38). In procedural matters, applicable rule is lex forum.

General rules concerning application of foreign law include following: (a) Polish law must be applied if foreign law, indicated in Law of Nov. 12, 1965 on International Private Law as applicable to certain situation, requires application of Polish law; (b) if foreign national law, indicated in Law on International Private Law of Nov. 12, 1965

See Topical Index in front part of this volume.

FOREIGN LAW . . . *continued*

as applicable, requires applying other foreign law to given situation, it is to be applied thereto; (c) if more than one different legal system is applicable in state, law of Poland is to indicate applicable legal system; (d) foreign law may not be applied if its application contradicts basic principles of legal order in Republic of Poland; and (e) Polish law must be applied if factors indicating which foreign law is to be applied cannot be established, or contents of applicable foreign law are not known.

Several provisions regarding foreign law recognition are included in C.C.P. According to art. 1134, court facing application of foreign law may request Minister of Justice to give text thereof and to have foreign judicial practice explained. Court may also appoint experts to familiarize it with foreign law and foreign judicial practice.

(For domestic/foreign law conflict solutions in particular situations see appropriate subject entry.)

FOREIGN TRADE AND FOREIGN INVESTMENTS:

Poland has no foreign trade law per se. Foreign trade transactions are subject to same C.C. provisions as domestic transactions. Administrative foreign trade law consists of customs, regulations, and foreign exchange resolutions. According to Customs Law of 1989, as amended, "turnover of commodities with foreigners shall be allowed to each person on equal rights, preserving conditions and restrictions provided for by law and international agreements". (art. 3).

Turnover of commodities in foreign trade is banned where international agreements or separate provisions impose ban on possession, dissemination, or turnover of such commodities. Where international agreements or separate provisions stipulate that possession, turnover or dissemination of commodities depends on fulfillment of certain requirements, turnover may be subject to fulfillment of such requirements. Permits for importation and exportation of commodities are required when goods are: (1) commodities whose turnover requires license (radioactive materials, arms, petrol, alcohol and tobacco products); (2) commodities whose importation or exportation is subject to quota as to quantity or value, or as to which temporary restrictions are imposed; (3) commodities whose turnover is effected on basis of international agreements providing for clearance in clearing units adopted in foreign trade; (4) scientific technical documentation when exported; and (5) temporarily imported or exported means of production and means of transportation with exception of personal cars leased, hired or taken to use with view to performing economic activity, temporarily imported or exported; (6) advanced technology products, binary chemical substances, nuclear technology products, binary materials, turnover in which is specially controlled or limited on basis of international or bilateral agreements or which must comply with special requirements.

Minister of Foreign Economic Relations, in agreement with Minister of Industry and Trade, may assign quantitative and value quotas to commodities imported to Polish customs area, or exported. Minister of Foreign Economic Relations is to announce (a) list of commodities for which importation or exportation specifies quotas on quality, value, or time restrictions imposed by international agreements; (b) list of countries with which turnover of commodities is effected on basis of international agreement providing for clearance in clearing units adopted in foreign trade; and (c) list of advanced technology products, binary chemical substances, nuclear technology and products and binary materials. Council of Ministers may impose temporary restrictions on turnover of commodities abroad and import and export quotas, where required by trade policy, economic interest or national interest of State. (arts. 5-9 of Customs Law of 1989).

In Feb., 1994 Polish Parliament passed Law on Equalizing Fee for Certain Agricultural and Food Products Transferred from Abroad. Equalizing fee is payable in connection with import of agricultural and food products that are important to profitability of farms and restructuring of agriculture and are transferred into Poland in such quantities and on such terms that could cause harm to domestic producers of similar or identical products. Equalizing fee is in amount of difference between domestic and foreign prices of imported product. Equalizing fees are published in Office Journal of Ministry of Agriculture and Food Economy. Fees must be paid in addition to customs duties and other taxes imposed on imported product.

FOREIGN TRADE REGULATIONS:

See topics Foreign Exchange; Foreign Investment; Foreign Trade and Foreign Investments.

FOUNDATIONS:

Establishment and operation of foundations is governed by Law of Apr. 6, 1984, as amended. Foundation enjoys personality at law at moment of entry into registry. Until 1989, registry was handled by district court Warsaw-Praga. Since 1989, fourth division of business court in Warsaw district court took over registry responsibility. Registry is open and accessible to third parties.

Foundations may be established for realization of purposes corresponding with basic social and economic interests of Republic of Poland such as: health care, scientific development, education, culture and arts, social care and social security, environment and monument protection. Foundations may be established by natural persons regardless of citizenship and domicile, or legal entities located in Poland or abroad. Foundation must be located in Polish territory. Establishment of foundation, unless established in will, requires declaration of will filed in form of notarial deed. Declaration must include purpose of foundation and proprietary components aimed at its realization.

Founder is to set up charter of foundation specifying its name, location, assets, principles, forms and scope of foundation activities, composition and structure of management board, method of appointment and responsibilities and rights of board and its members. Charter may also contain other provisions, particularly those relating to conducting business activities by foundation, availability and conditions of merging with other foundations, change of charter or purpose and stipulations governing creation of other foundation organs. Founder may authorize another natural or legal person to set up charter. Notary fees should not be collected for preparation of act which contains exclusively declaration of will on establishment of foundation. No court fees should be assessed for proceedings aimed at registering foundation.

Management board directs foundation's activities and represents it before third parties. Where management board violates law, charter or purpose of foundation, court acting on motion of appropriate Minister or District Governor (wojewoda) may suspend management board and appoint receiver.

If foundation completes its objectives, or exhausts financial resources and assets, it is to be liquidated in manner specified in charter. If charter does not provide guidelines or if provisions are impossible to execute, liquidation decision should be made by court. In other cases, foundation liquidation may take place only if law so provides. If charter does not determine appropriation of remaining proprietary resources after liquidation, court is to issue decision on their designation, considering foundation purposes.

Business activity of foundation may be conducted by separate business entity established by management board or foundation itself; it may also take form of participating in company. Carrying out business activity by foundation itself requires separation of revenues and costs in order to assure proper record keeping. Foundation enjoys certain income tax exemptions because of transfer of income from business activity into realization of statutory purposes. Acquisition by foundation of money, other personal property or property rights in form of succession, legacy or donation is free of taxes on successions and donations.

FRAUDULENT SALES AND CONVEYANCES:

See topics Assignments; Bankruptcy and Restructure; Bills and Notes; Contracts.

GARNISHMENT:

See topics Attachment; Executions.

HOLIDAYS:

Legal holidays are Jan. 1 (New Year's Day), Easter Monday, May 1 (Labor Day), May 3 (Constitution Day), Corpus Christi Day, Aug. 15 (Ascension Day), Nov. 1 (All Saints' Day), Nov. 11 (Independence Day), and Dec. 25-26 (Christmas Days).

Time periods expire at end of next working day if last day of period would fall on holiday or Sun.; in case of Sats., time periods expire only on free Sats. Free Sats. are determined for every year separately.

HUSBAND AND WIFE:

See topics Descent and Distribution; Divorce; Infants; Marriage.

IMMIGRATION:

Visitors for business or pleasure may enter Poland with valid passport and visa, as tourists or for long term. Visas are available at Polish embassies and consulates. No visa required for nationals of Argentina, Austria, Belgium, Denmark, Finland, France, Germany, Great Britain, Holland, Italy, Luxembourg, Malta, Norway, Sweden and Switzerland. U.S. citizens may enter Poland without visa. Generally, invitations are required for citizens of Commonwealth of Independent States.

Alien may obtain residence permit in form of residency card. Residency cards are issued by proper authorities according to alien's intended place of residence.

Person performing job or rendering services, except temporary work for foreign employer, must obtain residence permit. Employment Law of Dec. 29, 1989 states that businesses can employ aliens who have obtained special permission from employment authorities of particular province. Such authorities should take into consideration present employment situation. If regulations condition working upon obtaining special permission from proper authorities, business firm must seek such permission.

Law of June 14, 1991 on Companies with Participation of Foreign Parties (see topic Foreign Investment) states that company with participation of foreign investors may hire employees without requiring employees to become citizens or residents of Poland, if company obtains permission from proper employment authorities of province. No such permission is required for persons delegated by foreign investor to perform work within company if they do not have direct employment contract with company.

Alien can obtain political asylum in territory of Republic of Poland from Ministry of Internal Affairs with consent of Ministry of Foreign Affairs. Alien can acquire Polish citizenship provided he has resided in Polish territory for at least five years. In special cases this requirement may be waived. Alien may be granted Certificate of Naturalization provided that person obtains documentation regarding dismissal or loss of previous citizenship. Polish citizenship granted to both parents is also extended to their minor children.

See topic Labor Relations.

INFANTS:

Legal standing of infant is regulated in arts. 62-113 of Family and Guardianship Code of Feb. 24, 1964 and arts. 8-22 of C.C. as well as arts. 453-458 and 568-584 of C.C.P.

Children remain under parental authority until age of maturity (i.e. 18 years of age). Both parents have parental authority, but in case of judicial establishment of paternity, father does not have such authority until granted in judicial decision establishing paternity. Parental authority may also be granted to father by guardianship court after establishment of paternity. District court serves as guardianship court except for minor's adjudication, in which event court for minors is appropriate. Adjudicated person's domicile determines exclusive jurisdiction of guardianship court. Where domicile cannot be determined, district court of Warsaw is competent.

Parental authority includes right and duty to take care of person and property of minor as well as to educate him. Minor under parental authority must obey his parents who are his legal representatives. If minor is under parental authority of both parents, each parent may act separately as minor's legal representative. Parents are obligated to administer with due diligence property of minor remaining under their parental authority. Such administration does not include minor's wages or property rendered to him to be freely used. Parents may not undertake activities exceeding scope of regular administration or grant their consent to minor without judicial permission. Parents are obligated for child support on behalf of minor, who is not able to live by himself, unless profits from minor's property are satisfactory to cover expenses of his living

INFANTS . . . *continued*

and education. In all other circumstances, only subject in need is entitled to alimony performances.

Law of Nov. 12, 1965 on International Private Law provides that legal relationship between parents and children is governed by child's national law (law of parent's citizenship). Establishment and denial of paternity or maternity are governed by child's national law as of moment of child's birth. Recognition of child is governed by law of country of which child is citizen. Recognition of conceived, but unborn child is governed by national law of mother. Child support performance between parents and children are governed by national law of person entitled to receive such performance (arts. 19, 20).

See topic Contracts, subhead Conditions of Validity of Contracts.

INTEREST:

Interest on money is due when it results from legal transaction, law, court decision or decision of other competent institution. If interest rate is not defined, statutory rate of interest is due. Statutory interest rate is defined by regulation of Council of Ministers. Regulation may prohibit reservation or collection of interest higher than that which is defined as maximum. Failing contrary reservation regarding date of payment of interest, interest is due at end of every year. When term of maturity is shorter than one year, interest is due simultaneously with payment in full. If debtor is late in fulfillment of performance, creditor may demand interest for period of delay even though he has not sustained damage and delay resulted from circumstances for which debtor is not responsible. If interest rate for delay was not fixed in advance, statutory interest is due. If, however, claim bears interest rate higher than statutory rate, creditor may demand interest for delay according to higher rate. In event of debtor's qualified delay, creditor may also demand redress of damages according to general principles. (arts. 359, 360 and 481 C.C.).

INTESTACY:

See topics Descent and Distribution; Wills.

INVESTMENT PROTECTION:

Poland is active in concluding bilateral agreements on protection and support of foreign investments. Such agreements were signed with following countries: Albania, Argentina, Australia, Austria, Belgium, Byelorussia, Republic of Bulgaria, Canada, China, Czech Republic, Denmark, Finland, France, Germany, Great Britain, Greece, Holland, Republic of Hungary, Indonesia, Israel, Republic of Kazakhstan, Republic of Korea, Latvia, Lithuania, Malaysia, Republic of Moldavia, Norway, Romania, Singapore, Slovak Republic, Spain, Sweden, Switzerland, Thailand, Tunisia, Turkey, the United Arab Emirates, Eastern Republic of Uruguay and Republic of Uzbekistan.

These agreements provide for fair and equal treatment of investments, most favored nation provisions, and other provisions relating to providing prompt, adequate and effective compensation for expropriation, which may only be conducted for public purpose and under due process of law.

Poland is party to similar bilateral treaty with USA signed Mar. 21, 1990 concerning business and economic relations (which became effective on Aug. 6, 1994).

Currently Poland is considering adopting Washington Convention of Mar. 18, 1965 on settlement of investment disputes between states and citizens of foreign countries.

See topics Copyright; Patents and Topographies.

JUDGMENTS:

In civil matters, Polish court has discretion over whether or not to recognize decision of foreign court where foreign court's decision is not subject to execution. Excluded from rule are foreign court decisions on nonfinancial matters of foreign citizens issued by court that has jurisdiction according to such person's home country law, unless such decision is to be basis for dissolution of marriage or for entry into registry of birth, marriage and death certificates, as well as land and mortgage registrations or any other register in Poland. Recognition of foreign judgment is subject to reciprocity. However, reciprocity is not necessary in matters which, according to Polish law, belong to exclusive jurisdiction of state where judgment was pronounced. Everyone who has legal interest may apply for recognition of foreign court's judgment.

Foreign court judgments in civil matters, which in Poland are subject to court jurisdiction and are executable, constitute executory document if execution is envisaged in international agreement. Foreign court judgments relating to claims for alimony in family matters are executory documents and will be executed in Poland without international agreement but under condition of reciprocity. Poland is party to Convention on Vindication of Alimony Claims Abroad signed in New York in 1956.

In cases involving foreign court judgments, decision is made by voivodship court (higher court) on which three professional judges sit. Recognition of foreign court's judgment is pronounced by either court which would have territorial jurisdiction over case: court in whose district it is situated, lower court which would have had jurisdiction, or, if neither court can be found, court having jurisdiction for City of Warsaw. Regarding enforceability, decision is made by court of domicile or principal place of business of defendant or, if no such court can be found, higher court in whose district execution is to take place. Once order of enforceability becomes final and valid, higher court will give effect to foreign court's judgment in execution order.

Execution orders concerning foreign court judgments are subject to certain requirements. Requirements may be documented in international agreement or, in absence of such requirements, Polish law requires that judgment be pronounced after international agreement comes into force and that judgment be subject to execution in state where it was pronounced. Execution and recognition of foreign court judgments depend upon fulfillment of six conditions described in art. 1146, §41 C.C.P. Among conditions are following: (1) judgment of foreign court must be valid and enforceable in state in which judgment was passed, (2) matter, in accordance with Polish law or international agreement, must not belong to exclusive jurisdiction of Polish court or of courts of third country, (3) parties must have had opportunity to defend themselves, (4) judgment must not be contrary to fundamental principles of legal order of Republic of Poland, (5) in matter in which Polish law was to be applied, such law must have been applied, or foreign law applied must not differ in material way from Polish law.

For execution of foreign arbitral awards see topic Arbitration and Award.

LABOR RELATIONS:

General.—Polish laws apply to all aspects of employment in firms with foreign participation or who employ foreign nationals. Polish law also governs social security and trade union activities.

Discharge.—Notice required to terminate employment contract concluded for unspecified period of time is: two weeks, if worker has been employed for period shorter than six months; one month, if worker has been employed at least for six months; and three months, if worker has been employed at least for three years.

Employer may not terminate contract with employee scheduled to reach retirement age in two years or earlier, or during holiday of employee and his excused absence at work. Regulations on termination of employment contract are also applicable in case of notice to terminate working and pay conditions.

Employment contract may be terminated without notice if employee: has committed offense or seriously neglected duties at work; has been deprived of license authorizing him to perform his job; has been unable to work for period longer than three months because of disease; or for unacceptable reasons has not been present at his workplace for more than one month.

Employment Contract.—Company may employ persons who do not have Polish citizenship nor permanent residence card, if approved by local state administration. If foreign partner delegates persons who are not bound by employment contract with company in which he is shareholder, such approval is not required.

Under Polish law, employee is person employed on basis of employment contract. Such contract may be concluded for either unspecified or specified time, or for execution of defined task. Permanent employment contracts may be preceded by temporary employment contract as probation. Probation cannot extend beyond two weeks, or in case of employees holding management posts, three months. Employment contract can be dissolved if agreement is reached between parties (one party gives notice of termination of employment contract, with termination suggested within specified time for notice or before time for termination specified in contract expires).

Wages.—For companies with foreign participation, rules applying to remuneration of employees are established in founding act (articles of incorporation) of employer or decided upon by its management. Wages are fixed and paid in zlotys.

Employees are entitled to take remuneration only for work performed. If work stoppage is not caused by fault of employee, remuneration is paid in accordance with his rank in wage scheme. If stoppage is caused by employee, he has no right to accept remuneration. Employee bears pecuniary responsibility for damages caused to his workplace as result of his failure to perform.

Wages of employees regarded as foreigners according to income tax law are liable to tax amounting to up to 45% of wage unless stated otherwise in international agreements binding in Poland. Income gained by foreigners residing abroad as result of membership on Management or Supervisory Board is taxed at fixed rate of 20%. Tax is ameliorated by Oct., 1974 Polish-U.S. Agreement designed to avoid double taxation, which agreement does not limit possibility of levying taxes when remuneration is paid by company having its seat or domiciled in state in which employment is exercised. However, Polish tax may be levied only on remuneration paid for work performed in Poland. See topic Taxation.

Employees designated as foreign persons in Foreign Exchange Law of Feb. 15, 1989, as amended, are allowed to purchase foreign currency in foreign exchange bank provided they have paid appropriate taxes. Foreign employee will be issued certificate by his company stating amount of foreign currency allowed to be purchased. Foreign employees are entitled to transfer foreign currency abroad without separate foreign exchange permit.

Hours.—Labor Code of 1974 governs employment hours. Maximum working time is eight hours per day and 42 hours per week. Working hours are fixed by employer. Number of overtime hours per employee must not be greater than four hours per day and 150 hours per calendar year. Aside from regular wage, employee working overtime is entitled to overtime allowance amounting to 50% of his wage for first two overtime hours per day, and 100% of his wage for subsequent hours.

Employees must be insured by company in state social security system. Insurance premium amounts to 45% of wages earned by employee and additional 3% of earned wages is payable to Labor Fund and 1% to Unemployment Fund. Premium is paid by employer.

Labor Unions.—Trade unions are legal in Poland. Group of ten people in plant is sufficient to initiate establishment of union. In event of collective labor disputes, case is submitted to conciliation committee elected by parties and subsequently to Public Arbitrator at common courts. If no solution is achieved, trade union may authorize strike, giving seven days' notice.

Group Layoffs.—If due to economical or organizational reasons in period not exceeding three months employment contracts are terminated with 10% of employees or at least 100 employees in enterprise employing over 100 employees, procedure of consultation with trade unions has to be followed and local employment agency has to be informed at least 45 days before planned terminations of employment contracts. Employees with whom employment contracts are terminated in such procedure are entitled to compensation amount of which depends on length of employment.

Unemployment Compensation.—Pursuant to Law of Oct. 16, 1991 on Hiring and Unemployment, unemployed persons are eligible to receive compensation if they meet certain personal requirements, register with regional employment office and continue to seek employment. Regional employment offices may require unemployed to receive additional training. Persons who fail to accept offer of employment, training or public works may be ineligible to receive compensation. Compensation is equal to 36% of average wage and is payable for up to 12 months.

LAW REPORTS, CODES, ETC.:

Poland is civil law country. Unlike common law countries, doctrine of stare decisis is unknown and thus no decisional or judiciary law (i.e., law by precedent) exists. Civil law is enacted system of law. Doctrine of Polish civil law was not favorable for customary law; no indication of such source of law is generally made in Polish system of law. However, customary law is acknowledged as important source of law, especially in foreign commercial relationships. Polish civil law acknowledges customs established in trade in certain environments and in certain goods or services. Though court decisions lack legislative force, it is impossible to negate court's influence on civil law interpretation. Of particular significance were Supreme Court's Guiding Principles for Judiciary issued upon motion of Minister of Justice, Public Prosecutor General or First President of Supreme Court. These guidelines interpret provisions in force and are binding upon courts. After last reform of Polish court system, Supreme Court may only pass resolutions explaining legal regulations. In all other cases, decision of higher courts is binding only in particular cases, and only if matter on appeal is remanded are lower courts bound by decisions of higher court. However, decisions of higher courts are frequently followed by lower courts because of their reasoning and persuasive force.

Polish civil law is in principle codified law. Efforts in unification and codification of Polish civil law were undertaken in years 1918-1939 after Poland regained its independence. In private law, most important achievements were Code on Obligation (1933) and Comm. C. (1934). These two codes were partially replaced in 1965 C.C. (Law of Apr. 23, 1964). Other important private law codes now in force include: Family and Guardianship Code (Law of Feb. 25, 1963), Labor Code (Law of June 26, 1974), Maritime Code (Law of Dec. 1, 1961), Air Law (Law of May 31, 1962). Procedure for settlements of civil law disputes is provided for in C.C.P. (Law of Nov. 17, 1964).

Poland has two official journals for publication of laws: Journal of Laws of Republic of Poland and Monitor Polski Gazette. Following legal acts are published in Journal of Laws: laws, decrees, regulations, international agreements entered into by Poland and government statements related to their enforcement, announcements (e.g., announcements regarding publication of uniform texts of normative acts), decisions of Constitutional Tribunal and other legal acts, which publication therein is provided by specific stipulation of law. Monitor Polski Gazette, on other hand, contains: resolutions of Council of Ministers, executive orders of ministers and other central offices issued in order to implement laws and decrees with reference to authority stated therein as well as other instructions, decisions, directives, circular letters and announcements of state authorities and central offices. Subordinate normative acts (instructions, circular letters, directives) issued by particular ministers are usually published in official gazette of ministry, e.g., Official Gazette of Ministry of Finance, Official Gazette of Ministry of Justice.

Law reports concerning civil law are published in monthly judgments of Supreme Court, Civil Law Division and Labor and Social Insurance Division. Institute of State and Law of Polish Academy of Science publishes Judgments of Polish Courts.

See topic Commercial Law.

LEGISLATURE:

See topics Constitution and Government; Law Reports, Codes, Etc.

LICENSES:

See topics Brokers; Foreign Exchange; Foreign Investment; Foreign Trade and Foreign Investments; Motor Vehicles; Patents and Topographics.

LIENS:

In certain circumstances, debtors enjoy right of lien, which authorizes them to refuse performance until creditor satisfies or secures execution of debtor's claim. According to C.C., it is relative right which is ineffective against third parties. It is restricted to debtor-creditor relationships and provided only in following circumstances: (1) Persons obliged to deliver another's property may retain it until all obligations are satisfied or security given for all claims to which they are entitled including refunds for expenditures made for damages caused. Rule not applicable when duty to deliver results from tort or where return of hired, leased or borrowed property is concerned. (art. 461). (2) Due to rescission of contract, parties are obligated to return already completed performance. Each will have right of lien until other offers to meet obligation or offers to secure claim for such return. This rule is applied upon dissolution or invalidity of mutual contract. (arts. 496, 497). (3) Lessor may object to removal of property through statutory right of pledge. Lessor retains it at own risk until rent in arrears is paid or secured. (art. 670, §1).

Commercial right of retention, provided for in Comm. C., applies in international trade relations and to relations among merchants (i.e., currently only in relations between commercial companies). According to Comm. C., both personal property as well as securities owned by debtor (also those owned by creditor in exceptional circumstances) and held pursuant to commercial transaction by creditor with debtor's knowledge (but which in time he is obligated to hand over) may be subject to retention. Right of retention serves as security for mature claims with exception of debtor's bankruptcy declaration, initiation of composition agreement proceedings or proceedings aimed at bankruptcy prevention, or situation where debtor abstains from payment or execution from personal property proves to be ineffective. In such cases, right of retention may be extended to secure unmatured claims. Creditor has right of retention as long as he has possession, or title is transferred to his name, or he can dispose of property through warrants. Commercial right of retention, unlike regular liens, is effective against debtor, his creditors and third parties who have acquired rights to retained property after commercial right of retention is established. Creditors are required to give notice of establishment of retention through registered mail or are otherwise liable for compensation. Creditor may not execute his right of retention after he receives reasonable security. Regulations on commercial pledges were repealed. Creditor obtains satisfaction from retained property pursuant to regulations on execution from movables and has priority over other parties who have right of lien (arts. 518-524 Comm. C.).

LIMITATIONS OF ACTIONS:

Except as otherwise provided by law, property claims are subject to limitation of time. Statute of limitations is defense that prevents claimant from enforcing right but does not extinguish obligation itself, and court cannot recognize "limitation of action" ex officio. Once statute of limitations has passed, person against whom claim is made may refuse to fulfill claim, unless he voluntarily renounces to invoke statute of limitations. Renouncement is not possible prior to running of statute of limitations. Thus, party performing obligation in spite of statute of limitations may not reclaim. Time-barred claim may be set-off, if at moment when set-off became possible, limitation period had not yet expired. Unless specific provision prescribes otherwise, term of limitation is ten years. For claims concerning periodical performance and claims connected with conducting of commercial activity, term of limitation is three years. Examples of shorter terms include following: (1) sale claims under warranty for physical defects, one year calculated from day when item is delivered to buyer; (2) claims resulting from contract for work and labor, two years from day work delivered, and if work was not delivered, from day on which, according to terms of contract, it was to be delivered; (3) claims of person who possesses bills of exchange against endorser or drawer of bill of exchange, one year counting from date of protest, in case of exception "without costs", counting from date of payment; (4) claims of endorsers between themselves and against drawer of bill of exchange, six months, counting from day on which endorser bought bill of exchange or was summoned before court because of controversy surrounding bill. Claim certified by valid court decision or other organ called to decide cases of given type or by arbitral award, as well as claims certified by settlement made before court or arbitral tribunal, are barred by limitation on expiration of ten years, even though period of limitation of claims of that type may be shorter. If claim certified in that manner requires periodical performances, claim for such performances due in future is subject to three year period of limitation.

Limitation periods cannot be altered by contractual agreement. Period of limitation commences running on day on which claim becomes enforceable. Case law does exist, when commencement of period of limitation is not clear. After interruption as to running of limitation, period of limitation starts anew. Running of limitation is interrupted as follows: by every act before court or other organ called to decide cases or enforce claims of given type or before court of arbitration, undertaken directly for purpose of vindicating, establishing, satisfying or securing claim; or by recognition of claim by person against whom claim exists.

MARRIAGE:

Marriage is regulated by Family and Guardianship Code of Feb. 25, 1964, Title I "Marriage". (arts. 1-61). Other sources of regulations in marriage matters are: C.C.P. (arts. 425-452, 567), Law on Registry where Birth, Marriage and Death Certificates are Kept of Sept. 29, 1986, c. VI "marriage contracting" (arts. 53-63 and arts. 14-18) of Law on Private International Law of 1965. Poland is party to Hague Convention of June 12, 1902 on Conflicts of Law Relating to Marriage and Convention on Consent to Contract Marriage, Lowest Marriage Age and Marriage Registration signed in New York on Dec. 10, 1962.

Marriage is contracted when man and woman jointly file with officer of birth, marriage and death certificates located in place of domicile of one of parties statement that they wish to enter into marriage relationship. Supervising authority, upon legitimate reasons, may allow parties to contract for marriage before head of another birth, marriage and death certificates office. Parties are also at liberty to have religious ceremony, but such ceremony is of no legal effect. Marriage cannot be contracted before expiration of one month from day parties, intending to get married, filed statement with head of birth, marriage and death certificates office in writing that they do not have knowledge of any circumstances excluding contracting thereof (this term may be shortened because of important reasons). Under special circumstances, court may permit filing of statement to contract marriage by representative. Certificate of representation must be in writing, notarized, and include name of person with whom marriage is to be contracted. Marriage is contracted in birth, marriage and death certificates office publicly and solemnly in presence of two mature witnesses. Marriage certificate is construed immediately after contracting thereof, according to Law on Registry where Birth, Marriage and Death Certificates are Kept. Minimum marriage age is 21 for man and 18 for woman. Under special circumstances, age requirement may be reduced by guardianship court to 18 for man and 16 for woman, providing circumstances indicate that marriage will be beneficial to future family and in accordance with social interests. Marriage may not be contracted by person totally legally incapacitated, including persons mentally ill or retarded; provided, however, that person is not totally legally incapacitated and his or her condition does not endanger future offspring, court may grant permission for marriage.

Marriage may not be contracted by person already married, between relatives in direct line, between siblings or between kin in direct line, unless, because special circumstances exist, court waives prohibition against marriage between kin. Additionally, marriage may not be contracted between adopter and adoptee.

Both parties in marriage have equal rights and duties. They are obliged to conjugal life, mutual assistance, faithfulness and cooperation on behalf of family they create. Spouses are required, according to their financial abilities, to satisfy needs of family they create. Both are jointly and severally liable for obligations incurred by one of them in transactions relating to satisfying family's needs. Statutory joint property of husband and wife, which includes their possessions, is established upon marriage contraction. Objects not included as joint property remain as individual property. Creditor of one spouse may demand satisfaction from joint property. Contractual extension, limitation or exclusion of statutory joint property is possible. Such contract may be concluded before marriage, but must always be in form of notarial deed. Form of marriage contract is governed by law of country in which contracted. In event of marriage outside Poland, compliance with form required by national law of spouses is only requirement. Same principles apply to nullification of marriage. Both personal and property relations, including conclusion, amendment or dissolution of marriage settlement, is governed by national law of spouses. Property relations resulting from marriage settlement is governed by national law of spouses as of day of conclusion of settlement. When spouses do not have common national law, law of place of their

See Topical Index in front part of this volume.

MARRIAGE . . . *continued*
domicile applies and when spouses have separate domicile, Polish law applies. Foreigner intending to contract marriage is required to file, with head officer of birth, marriage and death certificates office, document testifying to his ability to contract marriage according to his national law. If document is difficult to obtain, court may waive requirement to present such document in non-litigious proceedings, after establishing foreigner's ability to contract marriage according to own national law. Stateless person and person whose citizenship is impossible to determine is required to file document testifying to his ability to contract marriage according to law of country in which he is domiciled.

MINES AND MINERALS:

Geological and Mining Law of Feb. 4, 1994 governs rights to mineral deposits in Poland. All mineral deposits in Poland are State Treasury property and royalty payments must be paid for extractions. State Treasury's rights to mineral deposits do not include rights to land above such deposits. Based on license from appropriate authority, economic entities can obtain exclusive right to extract mineral within certain area for limited period of time. Economic entities that have extracted mineral have right to freely dispose of minerals unless granted license or other Polish laws provide otherwise.

Mining companies that have license to extract mineral deposits must present to land owner draft of agreement for use of land. If owner does not accept draft within one month, mining company may apply to mining authority for temporary permit to use land. Mining company must pay owner (possessor of land) compensation for entire period of temporary occupancy of land in amount equal to average yearly net income obtained from property during last five years. Compensation set forth in agreement between owner (possessor) of land and mining company cannot exceed above-mentioned compensation.

Mining companies are obliged to prevent mining damages, repair any damages and provide land reclamation on whole mining area at company's cost. Repair of damages is limited to restoration to former state. If water resources disappear or become useless for persons and for livestock as result of mining activities, compensation is to take form of new well or other means providing sufficient amount of water for persons and livestock, at least at existing level of water resources before damage. There is three year statute of limitations on claims arising from mining damages.

Building permit is required for mining construction. Mining authority determines technical conditions of mining activities. Activities of mining company are to be carried out in accordance with plan of activity confirmed by mining authority. Such activities must be controlled and supervised by persons who have authorization from mining authority. Mining companies must maintain updated geological and measure records. Mining authority is authorized to review these records.

MONOPOLIES AND TRADE RESTRAINTS:

In field of monopolies and trade restraints, two major sources of law exist in Poland: Law of 1993 on Preventing and Combating Unfair Competition ("Law of 1993") and Law of Feb. 24, 1990 on Preventing Monopolistic Practices ("Law of 1990"). Law of 1990 is widely applied in practice, especially against socialized sector of Polish economy (against state enterprises and cooperatives). Number of regulations were promulgated in connection with Law of 1990: decree of Council of Ministers of July 11, 1990 on requirements applicable to plan of intent to merge, transform or form commercial entities and decree of Minister of Justice of Apr. 13, 1990 on formation of antimonopoly court. Law of 1990 itself contains important amendments to C.C.P., adding provisions on antimonopoly procedure. (arts. 479^{28}-479^{35}).

Unfair Competition.—Law of 1993 contains broad provisions, according to which those who injure entrepreneur by means contrary to applicable regulations or established norms (such as commercial honesty), through libel or slander, through inducement of competitors not to perform duties, through falsely marking geographical origin of goods, through counterfeiting goods, through disclosure of secrets of technical or commercial enterprises, etc., must terminate such activities and redress damage caused and possibly provide compensation. Law of 1993 also separately covers such dishonest competition as (a) infiltration of client base of enterprise through any means that can cause persons to whom enterprise offers products, goods or services to falsely believe such enterprise is source of products, goods or services; (b) falsely representing enterprise in such fashion as to confuse customers as to association with competitor, wherever such competitor may exist; (c) dissemination of false information about competitor; (d) limiting access to market for competitors through sale of products or services below their cost of production, inducement of third persons not to sell or purchase from other enterprises, differentiated treatment of clients; and (e) advertising contrary to law or public order, misleading or comparative (unless it is true and contains information useful for clients). Commercial courts at local level have jurisdiction over disputes over civil claims based on law of combating dishonest competition. Foreign legal and natural persons benefit from Law of 1993 on basis of international agreements or on basis of reciprocity.

Anti-monopoly Practices.—Law of 1990 regulates rules and methods governing combating of monopolistic activities of commercial entities which have effect in Republic of Poland, as well as determines bodies which have jurisdiction to consider such matters. Law of 1990 lists in detail various types of monopolistic practices and describes particular effects of such actions. List includes: (a) imposition of onerous contract terms, giving commercial enterprise that imposes such terms unjustifiable profits; (b) tying arrangements which subject conclusion of one contract to acceptance or fulfillment of unrelated performance; (c) acquisition of shares or stock of corporations or assets of business entities, if such acquisition could result in severely weakening competition; and (d) combining by same person of functions of director, supervising council member, or audit commission member in competing business entities joint market share of which is more than 10%. Category of monopolistic agreements includes: (i) establishing, directly or indirectly, specific prices or method of pricing between competitors with respect to third parties; (ii) division of market according to territory, type of products or clients; (iii) agreeing on unified production, sales or purchases of goods; (iv) restricting market access or eliminating from market business entities not party to agreement; and (v) agreement by competitors on terms of contract to be concluded with third parties. Category of abuses of monopolistic position in market includes: (A) countering of evolution of conditions necessary for formation or development of competition; (B) market division; (C) preferential sales to certain customers; (D) refusal to sell if there are no alternative supply sources; and (E) dishonest actions effecting formation of prices, including resale costs, and selling below market price to eliminate competition. Monopolistic position occurs if business entity does not encounter serious competition on national or regional market. Dominant position is presumed when entity has 40% share of market. Entity which enjoys monopolistic position must not: (1) limit, despite its capability, production, sale or acquisition of products, especially if it would lead to price increases; (2) terminate sale of products leading to price increases; or (3) charge exorbinate prices.

With respect to first three above-mentioned types of monopolistic practices, rule of reason applies; i.e., that such actions are prohibited unless they are necessary to conduct commercial activities and do not significantly restrict competition. If monopolistic practices are found to exist, including those practices prohibited by law governing conduct of business entities that are monopolies, Anti-monopoly Office issues decision requiring termination of such practices and defines conditions of such termination. Agreements that violate regulations governing broadly defined monopolistic practices are, in full or in part, null and void. If, as result of monopolistic practices, prices were artificially inflated, Anti-Monopoly Office can issue decision to decrease prices. Anti-Monopoly Office can issue decision prohibiting performance of agreement that: (a) restricts types of products produced or sale of products or (b) contemplates combining sales or acquisition of products, if such agreement is contrary to interests of competitors or consumers. Anti-Monopoly Office prohibits performance of such agreement if it results in substantially limiting competition or precludes competition in market, and does not result in commercial benefits, such as (i) substantial decrease in cost of production or sale or (ii) increase in quality of goods.

Plan to merge or transform business entities is subject to review by Anti-Monopoly Office. Law requires that notification disclosing intention to acquire, or subscribe for, shares in business entity that results in obtaining or exceeding 10%, 25%, 33% or 50% of votes at shareholders meeting of shareholders of such entity be filed with Anti-Monopoly Office. Such requirement is conditioned upon value of annual sales of both entities, i.e. acquiring and target entities. Notification obligation arises if such value exceeds 5 million ECU in calendar year preceding year when notification on intention of acquisition is made. Office may, within two months from date notification is filed, issue decision prohibiting acquisition if involved entities, as result of proposed transaction, would obtain dominant position on market or would strengthen their dominant market position. Regulations governing formation of organizational structures of business entities are not applicable to natural persons. Governmental enterprises, cooperatives and commercial companies that have dominant position in market may be subject to division or dissolution if they limit competition or its formation. Once such conditions are found to exist, Anti-Monopoly Office may issue decision requiring division of enterprise or cooperative or dissolution of company, describing requirements and conditions of such division or dissolution. If found that business entity has dominant position in market, Anti-Monopoly Office may issue decision requiring it to limit business activities, prescribing conditions and terms of such limitation.

Anti-Monopoly Office is main organ of governmental administration, and, as such, subject to supervision of Council of Ministers. President of Anti-Monopoly Office, who is nominated and can be recalled by President of Council of Ministers, heads Anti-Monopoly Office. President of Anti-Monopoly Office can form separate branches of Anti-Monopoly Office and determine their seat, territorial and in rem jurisdiction. Business entities are required to comply with request of Anti-Monopoly Office to conduct investigation and aid in its completion. Authorized persons have, inter alia, right to: (a) enter into all locations of business entity under investigation; (b) examine all documents of entity under investigation; (c) demand explanation, including written, from employees of entity under investigation; (d) participate in collective meetings of members of entity under investigation; and (e) secure all documents and other evidence. Information obtained during course of investigation is considered secret.

Administrative proceedings envisioned in Law of 1990 are initiated by Anti-Monopoly Office or at request of person with standing. Persons who have right to commence proceeding in Anti-Monopoly Office include: (a) business entities whose interests were or could be affected by monopolistic practices, as well as branches of such entities; (b) control organs of State and society; (c) social organizations formed to protect consumer interest; and (d) organs of communes. Demand for commencement of proceeding is to be given in writing and must include reasons for such proceeding. Appeal from decision of Anti-Monopoly Office can be brought, within two weeks after delivery, to Higher Court in Warsaw (anti-monopoly court). Appeal proceedings are governed by C.C.P. provisions on proceedings in commercial matters. Anti-Monopoly Office may require decision to be immediately executed. It may also, in connection with decision, determine monetary fine to be paid to State Treasury. Law also permits imposition of monetary fine as sanction for failure to comply with terms of decision. See topic Courts.

MORTGAGES:

Mortgage is qualified right over real property and is attached to given claim as security. Most important role of mortgage is ability to attach secured claim to real property regardless of entity or person to whom it belongs. Mortgagee has priority for satisfaction before personal creditors of mortgagor unless creditors enjoy so-called "execution privileges". Institution of mortgage is governed by Law of July 6, 1982 on Land Registry Books and Mortgages. Perpetual license may also be object of mortgage, which encompasses buildings and equipment owned by perpetual user.

Entry into land registry book is necessary to establish mortgage. Mortgage secures only financial claims and may be set only as to certain amount of money. Satisfaction of mortgage is governed by provisions on judicial execution proceedings. Any other contractual agreement is invalid. Limitation of claim secured by mortgage does not alter right of mortgagee to satisfaction. Claims secured by mortgage may not be transferred without mortgage unless law provides otherwise; mortgage also may not be transferred without claim which it secures. Mortgage is established on entire real property, including accessories, and is maintained in its entirety until entire secured claim expires. Expiration of claim secured by mortgage results in mortgage expiration,

MORTGAGES . . . *continued*
unless specific regulations provide otherwise. If mortgage is deleted from land registry book without valid legal grounds, mortgage expires after ten years. Effectiveness of mortgage security renouncement is conditioned upon mortgage deletion from registry. In case of mortgage expiration, mortgagee is obligated to accomplish all necessary activities enabling mortgage to be deleted from registry.

Specific regulations concerning bank credits permit for documents issued by bank confirming granting of credit, amount of credit, interest on credit and terms of repayment to be entered into Land Registry Books to establish mortgage. These documents with declaration that provides obligation has become due, constitute execution documents without necessity to obtain writ of execution from court.

Two other mortgages exist in addition to regular type: mortgage to cover future debts and mandatory mortgage. Mortgage to cover future debts serves as security for claims for unspecified amount of money up to certain limit and usually secures existing or future claims resulting from given legal relationship or claims connected with mortgage claims, but not included in regular mortgage automatically by virtue of law. Mandatory mortgage is established upon unilateral demand of creditor to secure claim confirmed by executory document with writ of execution, specified in provisions on executory proceedings. On such basis, creditor may acquire mortgage on all real property of debtor.

See topic Real Property.

MOTOR VEHICLES:

Operator's license is required for operating motor vehicles in Poland. Minimum age is 17 years. License is valid for lifetime of licensee and must be produced to police on demand. Nevertheless, license may be suspended in case of violations regarding motor vehicles. Alien may drive within Poland for up to one year after first entry on basis of international operator's license, or, in certain cases, of valid home country license. Polish operator's license may be granted to alien on basis of international or home country license for same period of time for which original license was issued.

Vehicle Registration.—Every vehicle driven in Poland must be registered; registration plate must be displayed in front and rear and must be of requisite size. Registration tax is to be paid during time of registration. Registration card is issued by local authorities upon registration of vehicle and must be produced to police on demand; registration card is to be surrendered upon deregistration.

Transfers.—Registration book comes with vehicle. Upon registration of vehicle this book is issued by local registration authority, showing name of registered owner. On transfer of vehicle, book must be sent to authority for registration. Upon transfer, new registration card is issued by local authority.

Liability.—Registered owner of vehicle is liable for all injury or damage caused by operation, whether by negligence or not, if vehicle is used with his permission. Owner's strict liability is limited to certain amounts. Owner is not liable if he can prove that accident causing injury or damage was caused solely by other person's negligence.

Insurance is compulsory on motor vehicle against liability for injury or damages caused by operation of vehicle to third persons. Plaintiff is entitled to action directly against insurer.

Tourists who plan to drive while visiting Poland must have registration documents, driver's license, passport and international insurance certificate (green card).

In Poland, as in all of Continental Europe, drivers drive on right-hand side of road. International road signs are used. There are no "yield" signs. Turning right on red light is allowed only if there is flashing green arrow.

Minor motor vehicle traffic violations will result in citation fine, to be paid within two weeks.

NEGOTIABLE INSTRUMENTS:

See topics Banks and Banking; Bills and Notes; Brokers; Chattel Mortgages; Currency; Foreign Exchange; Interest; Pledges.

NOTARIES PUBLIC:

Legal position of notary in Poland was significantly changed in Law on Notaries, Law on Introduction of Law on Notaries Public and Amendment to Code of Civil Procedure and Law on Land Registry Book of Feb. 14, 1991.

Previous regulations on notaries public will remain effective for state notary offices until dissolution (two years from date law becomes effective) and to notaries public, other workers employed by them and individual notaries public, unless law provides otherwise.

Law on Notaries is divided into two parts: structure and notarial acts. Notary is appointed to perform notarial acts. In cases specified in law, notarial acts may be performed also by notary's assistant employed in notary office. Notary acts within scope of legal authority as person of public trust and enjoys protection of public functionaries. Notarial acts performed by notary according to law have power of official document. They must be executed in Polish. Notary may also perform same act in foreign language, using his own linguistic ability, if appropriate, or assistance of sworn translator. Notarial acts must be performed in notary office, unless nature of act or circumstances require otherwise. Notary must use official stamp with eagle effigy and may operate only one office. Minister of Justice maintains registry of notary offices and publishes list of such every year in Monitor Polski Gazette. Minister of Justice must after request of interested party and consultation with appropriate notary council appoint notary and designate his office. Only Polish citizens may become notaries. Law on Notaries (art. 115) specifies requirements to become notary public. Notary public is required to act according to oath and to constantly improve professional qualifications. He is obligated to keep secret circumstances of case with which he became familiar during performance of notarial acts, even after termination of his functions. Notaries must establish self-government, including notary chambers and State Notary Council and must have legal capacity. Supervision of notaries and self-government activity must be performed personally by Minister of Justice or through presidents of appeal courts or higher courts or other appointed individuals. Notary is disciplinarian responsible for professional misconduct or transgressions to seriousness and dignity of profession.

Notary is responsible for damages he causes during performance of notarial acts pursuant to C.C. provisions, and is required to be very diligent in performing notarial acts.

Following acts may be performed by notary: preparation of notarial deeds, preparation of certificates, delivery of statements, writing of reports, protests of bills of exchange and checks, safe-keeping of documents, money and securities, preparation of excerpts and copies of documents, drawing of drafts of acts, declarations and other documents upon parties' request, and performance of other activities as provided in separate regulations.

Acts and documents must be executed in clear and understandable manner. Notary public must refuse to perform activities contrary to law. If party participating in activities does not know Polish and translation is not attached thereto, notary is required to interpret text himself or use assistance of interpreter. Signatures on notarial deeds and notarized documents must be executed personally in presence of notary. If signature on document was not executed in presence of notary, signing person must, in presence of notary, confirm signature as his own, and this fact must be mentioned by notary in document. Documents of performed notarial acts must be transferred after five years from execution to deeds registry archives of appropriate district court for further safe-keeping. Notary may acknowledge following: authenticity of signature, compliance of copy or excerpt with submitted document, date of document presentation, and fact of someone being alive or his stay in certain place.

In cases stipulated by law, notary shall provide courts and other state authorities written information on documents prepared by him and excerpts thereof.

Notary shall be compensated for performance of notarial act according to agreement with parties involved, but may not receive more than maximum fee for appropriate act set in notary pay chart. Pay chart must be prepared by Minister of Justice in cooperation with Minister of Finance and after consultation with National Notary Council. Regulation of Minister of Justice of Apr. 12, 1991, as amended, includes notary fees. Notarial fee is established based on value of subject matter concerned: (1) up to 10,000 zlotys—3%; (2) exceeding 10,000 zlotys up to 20,000 zlotys—300 zlotys plus 2% of amount above 10,000 zlotys; (3) exceeding 20,000 zlotys up to 50,000 zlotys—500 zlotys plus 1% of amount above 10,000 zlotys; (4) exceeding 50,000 zlotys—800 zlotys plus 0.5% of amount above 50,000 zlotys. Total fee may not exceed 5,000 zlotys. There are different fees for specific acts, e.g. for preparation of will, maximum fee is 10 zlotys.

PARTNERSHIP:

Polish law contemplates three forms of partnership: civil partnership (arts. 860-875 C.C.), commercial partnership (arts. 75-140 Comm.C.) and limited partnership (arts. 143-158 Comm.C.). These forms are comparable to American partnerships. C.C. states, "by partnership agreement, partners bind themselves to strive to attain common economic objective by acting in specified manner, particularly by making contributions". (art. 860, §1 Comm.C.). According to art. 75, §1 C.C., "commercial partnership is company, which conducts in common name enterprise for profit in large size, and is not another commercial company". Ancient provisions determining which economic activity signifies conducting enterprise in larger size are no longer in force. In either form, formation of partnership is based on agreement, which must be in writing. Primary difference between civil and commercial partnerships is that latter must have formal corporate name, and must be inscribed into commercial register.

Civil Partnership.—Partner's contribution may consist of property, other assets or personal services, each of which is presumed of equal value. Unless otherwise stated in partnership agreement, each partner participates equally in profits and losses, regardless of type and value of contribution. While partners may be released from participation in losses, partners cannot be excluded from sharing profits. Partner cannot make disposition of his interest in common partnership property, nor of his interest in property's particular elements. For duration of partnership, partners cannot demand division of partners' common property, and no partner's creditor can demand satisfaction from partner's share in common property of partnership nor from his interest in property's particular elements. Partners are jointly and severally liable for partnership's obligations. Each partner is entitled and obliged to manage partnership's affairs. Each partner may manage affairs, which do not exceed scope of partnership's ordinary management, without partners' resolution. If, however, before conclusion of matter, any one partner objects to its being carried out, partners' resolution is needed. Failing agreement or resolution to contrary, each partner is authorized to represent partnership to extent he is entitled to manage its affairs. If partnership was formed for unspecified period, partners may withdraw by serving notice three months in advance of end of fiscal year and for sufficient reasons may serve notice without even observing notice requirements. If partnership was formed for specific period, contrary stipulation is invalid. If, in spite of expiration of specified duration of partnership, it persists with consent of all partners, it is treated as formed for unspecified period. For sufficient reason, each partner may demand court-ordered dissolution of partnership.

Commercial Partnership.—Commercial Code distinguishes two kinds of commercial partnership: commercial partnership and limited partnership.

Commercial partnership operates under name which includes last names of all partners or last name and at least first letter of first name of one or several partners with abbreviation standing for "partnership". Since regulations do not provide for specific form of abbreviation, it may be freely created. Word "partnership" is acceptable, although in business practice abbreviation "ska" has been widely adopted. For entry of commercial partnership into commercial register see topic Commercial Register.

Partnerships are able to acquire rights and incur obligation and to sue and be sued. Partnerships enjoy so-called "handicapped legal capacity". Rights and contributed property, as well as acquired property and property otherwise gained for partnership during its duration, constitute partnership's assets.

Each partner has right to represent partnership. Partner, however, may be excluded from right of representation or entitlement to represent partnership jointly with another partner or procurist (for explanation of term "procurist", see topic Principal and Agent). Deprivation of right to represent partnership against partner may only be

PARTNERSHIP . . . *continued*

accomplished in form of judicial decision. Partner's right to represent partnership extends to all transactions, including judicial proceedings, connected with operation of any business enterprise, including transference and encumbrance of real property and granting and revocation of procura (see topic Principal and Agent). This right cannot be limited with legal consequences against third parties.

Each partner is jointly and severally liable for partnership obligations with remaining partners and partnership itself. Joint liability is extended to entirety of assets and is also applied in case of bankruptcy. Anyone who joins already existing partnership is liable for obligations incurred prior to his entry and any contrary provision is without effect against third parties.

Each partner has right and duty to run partnership business, unless stated otherwise. Third parties cannot be contractually designated to run partnership business with exclusion of partners. Neither right of partner to personal inquiry about partnership's business standing and its level of assets, nor his right to personal examination of books and documents of partnership, can be limited. Each partner may handle business matters without prior resolution of partners, providing such matters do not exceed scope of ordinary partnership activities. Resolution, however, is necessary before activity is carried out when at least one partner objects. Running partnership business may be entrusted to one or several partners, which is equivalent to exclusion of remaining ones from such activities. Granting of power of attorney requires consent of all partners who enjoy partnership management rights and revocation may be effected by any one of them. Unanimity is required of all partners appointed to run partnership business for passing of resolutions on matters which do not exceed scope of common partnership activities. In cases that exceed such scope, unanimity of partners, even those excluded from running partnership business, is required. Partner who runs partnership business must not receive any compensation for his personal services. Right or duty of partner to run partnership business may be revoked by means of judicial decision if based on important reasons.

Partners' contributions are considered to be equal. Partners' contribution may consist of ownership, other rights (including right to use property or rights), or rendering of services. Partner is neither entitled nor obligated to increase his contribution; he has right to equal share of profit and shares losses in same proportion, regardless of type and amount of his contribution. Partner who only renders services as contribution does not share in losses. Other partners may also be exempt from obligation to cover losses if so stipulated in contract. Unless partnership is dissolved, no partner may require distribution of partnership assets. Partners must abstain from any activities contrary to partnership interests. In general, partners are prohibited from engaging in competing business or joining another partnership as partner or as management member in particular. If this prohibition is violated, each remaining partner may require delivery of profits gained by transgressing partner, as well as demand compensation, while still holding right to dissolve partnership or demand ousting of transgressing partner.

Occurrence of any of following events may result in partnership dissolution: reasons stipulated in contract, consent of all partners, declaration of partnership's bankruptcy, death or bankruptcy of one of partners, notice to terminate, or judicial decision.

Partnership is presumed extended for unlimited period of time if reasons for termination stipulated in contract occurred, but partnership still operates upon consent of all partners. Notice of termination of partnership established for unlimited period of time may be given by partner no later than six months before end of business year. Each partner may demand dissolution of partnership by judicial decision. Despite death or bankruptcy of partner and despite notification of termination by partner or his personal creditor, partnership may still exist between remaining partners, providing it is so stipulated in contract or agreed upon by remaining partners.

Upon occurrence of reason for dissolution, partnership must be liquidated, unless another method is agreed upon. All partners become liquidators, but are free to unanimously appoint themselves or others for this function. Liquidation is carried out under partnership name. Liquidator's duties include: termination of partnership business, enforcement of claims, fulfillment of obligations and sale of partnership assets (including option of public auction). New business transactions may be entered into only when necessary to complete old ones. Liquidators must prepare balance sheet at beginning and end of liquidation. Partnership assets must be sold to cover all outstanding obligations of partnership and appropriate amount must be held in reserve to cover other obligations. Remaining portion is divided between partners according to provisions of contract. If there is no contract, contributions must be paid off first, and surplus divided proportionally to partners' participation in profit distribution. If partnership assets are insufficient to cover debts and contributions, deficit must be divided between partners according to provisions of founding contract. If there is no contract, deficit must be divided proportionally to partners' participation in losses. Same proportions must be maintained for distribution among partners of portion of deficit of insolvent partner. Liquidators are to announce completion of liquidation to delete name of firm from registry.

Limited partnership is company, purpose of which is to run, under common firm name, revenue raising enterprise on large scale or farm under common firm name, is limited partnership if, with respect to debtors for partnership's obligations, at least one partner is responsible without limitation, and liability of at least one partner (limited partner) is limited. Unless stated otherwise in Commercial Code, provisions applicable to registered partnerships are applicable to limited partnerships. Execution of limited partnership agreement has to be done in form of notarial deed. Limited partnership is formed at moment of its entry into commercial register.

Limited partner is liable for limited partnership's obligations in relation to its creditors only to amount of partnership's founding capital. Limited partner is free from liability within limits of amount of contribution made to limited partnership's assets, with exception of tax obligation for which limited partner is liable with all his personal property up to his share in division of profit. In event that contribution is returned, in part or in whole, liability is reinstated in amount of value of returned contribution. With respect to creditors, in case contribution is reduced by losses, each payment made by partnership to limited partner before completion of contributions to original amount is considered to be return. Decrease in partnership sum does not have legal effect upon creditors whose claims have arisen before decrease is registered.

Person who becomes limited partner in existing limited partnership is liable for limited partnership's obligations which exist at time that his name is entered into commercial register. In event that limited partnership agreement is entered into with commercial entity which conducts enterprise, limited partner is also liable for obligations which arose during conduct of enterprise and exist at time of entry into commercial register.

Limited partner can only represent limited partnership pursuant to power of attorney. If he enters into transaction with third party without disclosing power of attorney, he is liable for such transaction without restriction. Contrary contract provisions do not have legal effect with respect to third parties.

Limited partner has right to demand annual balance sheet and to review books and documents to check their truthfulness. Pursuant to application of limited partner, registry court may, based on important reasons, require showing of balance sheet and giving of explanations, as well as allow him to review books and documents, at any time. Such rights of limited partner cannot be excluded or limited by agreement.

Unless agreement provides otherwise, limited partner does not have right or obligation to carry out limited partnership's activities. It is necessary to obtain limited partner's consent before carrying out matters outside scope of normal activities of limited partnership.

Limited partnership agreement must specify manner of division of losses and profits. In cases of doubt, limited partner participates in losses only to amount of set contribution.

Death of limited partner does not constitute grounds for liquidation of limited partnership. Heirs of limited partner should designate person who obtains his rights. Activities of remaining partners carried out before such designation are binding on heirs of limited partner. Division of shares of limited partner between his heirs is effective with respect to limited partnership only with consent of remaining partners.

PATENTS AND TOPOGRAPHIES:

Law on Inventions of Oct. 19, 1972, as recently amended governs inventions and patents in Poland. Other regulations in patent law area are as follows: Law on Patent Office of Republic of Poland of May 31, 1962; Law on Patent Agents of Jan. 9, 1993. Poland is party to Paris Convention on Protection of Industrial Property of Mar. 20, 1883, as amended, and by Act of Stockholm signed in Stockholm on July 14, 1967. Poland is party to bilateral treaty with U.S.A. signed Mar. 21, 1990 concerning business and economic relations (which has been ratified by both parties and will be effective 30 days following exchange of ratification instruments) in which Poland agrees to enact laws on certain trade matters, including protection of certain patents, copyrights and proprietary information.

Patentable invention is novel, not obvious, useful solution, technical in character. Solution is considered novel if it was not made public, publicly utilized or displayed in public in manner that would enable person to utilize solution. Patents cannot be obtained for: new varieties of plants and animals, biological methods of plant or animal cultivation; inventions which would be contrary to binding law or social norms; computer programs; nuclear products, or scientific principles and inventions.

Right to patent serves creator of invention. If more than one person created invention they jointly have right to patent. Right to patent for invention created during course of employment or execution of another agreement belongs to employer or commissioner, unless parties decide otherwise. If invention was created with help of economic entity, right to utilize invention for own use serves economic entity. In agreement parties may expend or limit this right.

Office of Patents of Republic of Poland ("Patent Office") has authority to grant patents and patent documents. Applications for patents are made at Patent Office and include application form, description of invention, summary of description and, if necessary, drawings. Patent Office announces decisions on patent applications after examination of whether: (a) patent application was properly completed; (b) application relates to technical solution; (c) invention is not outside scope of patent protection; (d) invention can be utilized; and (e) it is clear that invention is novel. From date of filing, third parties may review documentation only with consent of applicant. Patent Office may engage experts to review application. Experts are obliged to not disclose data contained in application. From date of publication, third parties may review description of invention, patent restrictions and drawings and, within six-month period, may direct comments on grounds why patent should not be granted to Patent Office. From time of publication invention is protected by temporary patent, unless application was withdrawn or Patent Office refuses to grant patent.

Party in proceeding before Patent Office is person submitting invention. In proceeding before Patent Office in matters involving, submitting, reviewing and sustaining protection of invention only Patent Agent may act as attorney. Foreign persons may act only through Patent Agent domiciled in Poland.

Priority to right to receive patent for invention is determined as of date of filing of application in Patent Office, except in following situations: (a) priority is determined as of date invention is publicly displayed domestically or internationally, if filing of application at Patent Office occurs within six months following such display; (b) according to provisions contained in international agreements, foreign citizens and foreign legal persons of countries that belong to International Union of Protection of Industrial Property, and citizens and legal persons of other countries if they have residency or chief business office or conduct substantial industrial or commercial enterprise in country that belongs to such Union, have priority to receive patent in Republic of Poland as determined by date when they first filed for patent in member state, if they file patent with Patent Office within 12 months from their original filing date.

Granting of patent is confirmed through conferring of patent document. Information relating to granting of patent or certificate of authorship is included in patent register. Patents are valid for 20 years from date of filing patent with Patent Office.

By obtaining patent, one receives right to exclusive use of invention and right to protection. Patent holder may not abuse his right especially through implementing monopolistic practices. Patent Office may demand from patent or license holder explanations as to usage of exclusive right. Patent for invention of production method also extends onto products obtained by this method.

See Topical Index in front part of this volume.

PATENTS AND TOPOGRAPHIES . . . *continued*

Person who in good faith used invention when priority is determined, may continue to use it in same scope in his enterprise free of charge. This right also serves person who prepared all necessary facilities for use of invention. These rights may be entered into patent register. Transfer of these rights may be conducted only together with enterprise.

Invention, usage of which exceeds scope of original patent awarded on basis of earlier priority (initial patent) may be subject of dependent patent. Dependent becomes independent on expiry of initial patent. Patent holder may apply for additional patent for improvements or supplements which have characteristics of invention, but may not be used independently. Additional patent expires together with basic patent. Right to patent and patent itself are transferrable and inheritable. Agreement to transfer rights must be in writing and dated, with date officially certified. Transfer of patent rights is effective with respect to third parties when such transfer is included in patent register.

Patent holder can license another party to use invention. License agreement for its validity must be concluded in writing. At request of interested party, license can be included in patent register. Unless license agreement provides otherwise, exclusive licensee entered into patent register has same right as patent holder to pursue claims for patent violations. Also, unless license provides otherwise, granting of license does not preclude ability of patent holder to use patent or grant other licenses to use patent. Such license is non-exclusive patent license. In absence of contrary provisions in agreement, licensee may use invention to same extent as licensor. Licensee may grant sublicense if he obtains permission from patent holder; otherwise, sublicensing is prohibited. Unless specified otherwise, licensor is obligated to give licensee all technical experience necessary for use of patent that licensor holds at time agreement is executed.

As result of proceeding, Patent Office may grant permission (mandatory license) to use invention that has been patented by another party, if: (a) use of invention is necessary to avert danger or eliminate conditions threatening security of State; (b) it has been ascertained that patent right is abused especially in instances where patent holder does not give access to products manufactured on basis of invention in quantities fulfilling social needs or patent holder prevents fulfilling of social needs through usage of invention being object of dependent patent (here initial patent holder may request permit for usage of dependent patent). Patent Office publishes decision on possibilities to apply for mandatory license. Award of mandatory license for reasons of not fulfilling of social need may not be awarded before lapse of three years from award of patent.

One who uses invention pursuant to mandatory patent is obligated to make appropriate payments (license fees) to patent holder. Scope and term of license, detailed requirements for license, amount of license fee, and method of payment should be specified in decision to grant mandatory license.

"Design" entitled to protection is new and useful technical design dealing with shape, build or structure of permanent object. Granting of right to protection is represented by protection certificate. Patent Office has authority to grant rights of protection and issue protection certificates. Information about granting of right to protection is included in protection register. By obtaining right to protection, one receives right to exclusive use of design in Poland. Right to protection is valid for five years from date of filing with Patent Office. Protection may be extended for another five years upon request from holder of right. Scope of protection is specified in protection provisions contained in description of protected design.

Patent Office maintains patent register and register of rights of protection of designs, for entries required by Law on Inventions. It is presumed that everybody has knowledge of entries in register. President of Patent Office determines rules governing maintenance of registers, requirements and procedure of making entries, review of registers and copying of copy of entry from registry. One-time registration charge and fees, to be paid at determined times during protection period, are to be paid in connection with protection of inventions and designs.

Foreign citizens and foreign legal persons are entitled to rights in connection with inventions based on international agreements binding on Republic of Poland or on principle of reciprocity.

Law on Inventions lists matters over which Patent Office adjudicates in commission (for example, nullification or termination of patent or right to protection for using design). Judges named by Minister of Justice sit on commission. Judges are selected from judges from higher court of City of Warsaw. Appeals from decisions of Patent Office and complaints about determinations of Patent Office are reviewed by Appeals Commission of Patent Office. Appeals Commission is composed of judges named by first President of Supreme Court from its Justices. Provisions on extraordinary appeal are applicable to legally binding decisions of Appeals Commission.

Integrated Circuit Topographies.—Law on Protection of Integrated Circuit Topographies of Jan. 27, 1993 governs protection and registration of integrated circuit topographies. Integrated circuit is one or more layer, three dimensional product created from semiconductor elements forming continuous layer, their mutual conductor connections and isolating spaces inseparably compressed, in aim of fulfilling electronic functions. Integrated circuit topography is three dimensional solution expressed in any form of layout, of elements, in which at least one is active element, and all or part of connections of integrated circuit.

Integrated circuit topographies may be registered with Patent Office of Republic of Poland if they are original, i.e. are result of creator's own intellectual work and are not commonly known at moment of filing for registration. Topographies which have been in commercial use before filing in Patent Office may be registered if period of commercial usage does not exceed two years.

Right to register with Patent Office serves creator and any person who on basis of written agreement acquired this right from creator. Protection is awarded on registration of topography. Registration is completed on day on which application containing motion for registration, material identifying topography and declaration as to date on which topography has been entered into turnover are delivered to Patent Office. Applicant is not obliged to disclose those parts of topography which are trade or production secret unless this is necessary to identify topography. Protection is awarded for period of ten years.

Person entitled to registration acquires exclusive right to: (1) reproduce topography; (2) use topography for trade purposes, import, production of copies or products containing such copies.

Person who used topography in Poland before topography was registered or first introduced into turnover, may continue to use this topography in same scope, in his enterprise, free of charge. This right also serves persons who at this time prepared all necessary facilities for usage of such topography. These rights may be entered into register on motion of interested party.

Mandatory licenses may be established by Patent Office for usage of topography to which another person is entitled on basis of registration if it (1) is necessary to prevent or avert state of national emergency; (2) has been established that right of exclusivity is abused in mannner contrary to public interest, especially through monopolistic practices. Person using topography on basis of awarded mandatory license is obliged to pay entitled person license fee of market value of license.

Foreign natural and legal persons benefit from provisions of this law on basis of international agreements or on basis of reciprocity. Foreign persons may act before Patent Office exclusively through attorney-in-fact who is domiciled in Poland.

See subhead Patent Agents, infra.

Patent agents are persons entitled to provide assistance with respect to industrial property rights, defined as procurement, maintenance and execution of rights related to objects of creative activity, intended for industrial use and to names and marks, which distinguish products and services in industrial or commercial activity, and to counteract unfair competition. Professional duties of patent agents in particular consist of: (1) preparation of applications to Patent Office for registration of industrial property rights; (2) participation on basis of power of attorney in proceedings before Patent Office, courts and other institutions which decide on matters of industrial property; (3) execution of agreements and performance of other activities on behalf of foreign and Polish persons.

Patent agents in order to practice their profession must be entered into register kept by Patent Office.

Patent agents are obliged not to reveal any information obtained in connection with their professional services, and may not provide services in matters, where conflict of interest may exist.

Persons domiciled in foreign country or having their seat abroad may act before Patent Office only through representation of patent agent domiciled in Poland.

See subhead Integrated Circuit Topographies; and topic Trademarks.

PLEDGES:

Pledge is security claim on movable good, referred to herein as "Movable" ("Pledge on Movables" [arts. 306-326 C.C.]) or transferable rights ("Pledge on Rights" [arts. 327-335 C.C.]). Movable secures right by which creditor may satisfy claim, regardless of whose property it has become, having precedence over personal creditors of owner of movable, except those with priority by force of law. Pledge may also be established in order to secure future or conditional claim. To establish pledge on movable, contract between owner and creditor must be entered into, and object must be delivered to creditor or to third person whom parties have stipulated. If movable is being held by creditor, contract itself is sufficient to establish pledge on movables. Contract to establish pledge on rights must be in writing with certified date, even if contract to transfer right does not require such form. If establishment of pledge on rights over claim does not take form of delivery of document or endorsement, written notice to debtor of claim by pledgor is required to establish pledge on rights. Pledge may be established on movables of debtor to secure credits of bank, but such movables must be held by debtor or third party.

If at moment of establishment of pledge, object of pledge is already subject to another property right, later-established pledge has priority over right established earlier, unless pledgee acted in bad faith. Stipulation by which pledgor obliges himself to pledgee not to dispose of or charge object of pledge before expiration of pledge is invalid. Satisfaction of pledgee from charge takes place according to provisions concerning court execution proceedings. Time limitations on claim secured by pledge do not override right of pledgee to acquire satisfaction of right attached. Transfer of claim secured by pledge also transfers pledge. If claim is transferred with exclusion of pledge, pledge expires. Pledge cannot be transferred without claim which it secures. If pledgee returns movable to pledgor, pledge ceases to exist, regardless of any stipulation to contrary.

Pledgee may perform any transaction and vindicate any claim, in order to preserve right attached by pledge. If enforceability of secured claim depends upon serving of notice by creditor, pledgor may serve notice without consent of pledgee. If claim secured by pledge is enforceable, pledgee may serve notice of right attached to claim and that fulfillment of pledge obligation attaches to object of performance. If pecuniary claim secured by pledge becomes enforceable, pledgee may demand that, in lieu of payment, pledgor transfer attached right to him, to extent of amount of claim secured by pledge. Pledgee may take his part of claim before pledgor takes part due him.

Pledges may arise by operation of law ("Statutory Pledges"). Statutory Pledges arise in similar ways as do Pledges on Movables. For example, Statutory Pledges arise in following situations: (a) lessors acquire Statutory Pledge of lessee's movables brought into leased property, unless such movables are not subject to seizure (art. 670); (b) tenants renting movables which aid in conduct of farm or enterprise acquire Statutory Pledge if movables are situated within area of property of tenancy (art. 701); (c) agents acquire Statutory Pledge of principal's movables received in connection with agency contract (art. 764); (d) commission agents acquire Statutory Pledge of items constituting commission sale items (art. 773); (e) carriers and forwarding agents acquire Statutory Pledge on shipments (arts. 790, 802); and (f) warehouses acquire Statutory Pledge on goods accepted for storage (art. 857).

PRESCRIPTION:

See topic Limitations of Actions.

PRINCIPAL AND AGENT:

Polish law distinguishes between direct and indirect agents. Agent acts on behalf of principal. Direct agent acts on behalf of disclosed principal. Indirect agent acts in their

PRINCIPAL AND AGENT . . . *continued*

own name and principal is undisclosed. Authorization to act as agent for principal may be based on law, on statement by principal (power of attorney), or on contract between agent and principal (see topic Agency). Indirect agent can act pursuant only to contract. Generally, representation by agent is permitted only in some cases. In field of family law, parties typically cannot act through agents.

Legal transaction consummated by direct agent within limits of his authority produces direct consequences for principal. When agent acts as indirect agent, neither undisclosed principal nor third person with whom agent dealt acquires any rights against or assumes any obligation of other.

General power of attorney confers authorization for all acts of ordinary management. For acts going beyond scope of ordinary management, power of attorney is required for particular act or transaction. If particular form is required to make legal transaction valid, power of attorney must be in such form. General power of attorney should be made in writing to ensure its enforceability. Any limitations placed on agent's authority by principal will not affect validity of transaction concluded by agent in name of principal. Power of attorney may be revoked at any time, unless principal, for reasons justified by legal relationship underlying agency, waived his right to revoke power of attorney. Authorization expires on death of principal or agent, unless otherwise stipulated in power of attorney. If person consummated contract as agent but did not have authorization to enter into transaction, validity of transaction depends on ratification by principal. If, after expiration of his authority, agent concludes transaction in name of principal within limits of original authorization, legal transaction is valid unless other party knew about expiration of authority or could easily have obtained such knowledge. Agent may appoint another agent for principal only when power of attorney sets forth such authority, or when law or legal relationship so authorizes. Agent cannot benefit from legal transaction entered into on behalf of principal unless power of attorney so stipulates, or if nature of legal transaction precludes, any possibility of infringing upon interests of principal. This provision is applied correspondingly, when agent represents both parties in transaction. (arts. 95-109 C.C.).

Polish law recognizes special class of powers of attorney called "prokura". Only principals which are commercial companies can establish prokura. Prokura confers upon agent authority to enter into all transactions inside and outside of court connected with conduct of enterprise, except sale of enterprise itself and disposal of real estate. It cannot be restricted by principal in its scope of authority relative to third persons except to restrict procurist to act only with another procurist (or principal or manager of corporation), or to limit procurist to one of several branch offices of principal. Prokura confers powers upon procurist tantamount to powers of principal himself. It must be recorded in commercial register and may be revoked at any time by principal; revocation also has to be registered in commercial register in order to notify third persons. (arts. 60-65 Comm.C.).

PRIVATIZATION:

Law of July 13, 1990 on Privatization of State-Owned Enterprises, as amended ("Privatization Law"), provides for transformation of state-owned enterprises into joint stock companies and making shares of such companies available to employees and public and for liquidation or selling of assets of state-owned enterprises. Privatization of enterprise may be initiated by enterprise director and employees' council or by President of Council of Ministers with approval of Minister of Ownership Transformations.

Once state-owned enterprise is transformed into joint stock company, shares of such company become property of State Treasury until they are made available to public. Company established through transformation acquires all rights and liabilities of state-owned enterprise, including those arising from employment arrangements. Final balance sheet of state-owned enterprise becomes opening balance sheet of new company. Joint-stock company must establish supervisory council, one-third of members to be elected by employees.

Sale of shares to public should occur within two years from date of registration of company. Shares may be sold by auction, through public offering and through negotiations following public invitation. Up to 20% of shares must be made available to company's workers on preferential basis at half-price. Employees' preferential right to acquire shares may be exercised within one year from date shares are offered.

Founding body of company, with approval of Minister of Ownership Transformations, may liquidate state-owned enterprise for (1) sale of entire enterprise or organized portions of assets of such enterprise; (2) contributing enterprise's assets or part of assets to company; (3) lease for stated period of time of entire enterprise or part of its assets. Liquidation decision is made by founding body on own initiative or upon request of employees' council of enterprise. Assets may be leased if (1) application for liquidation by lease is approved by employees' council and general assembly of employees; (2) assets of enterprise are contributed to corporation; (3) majority of employees of enterprise become shareholders of corporation after liquidation; (4) all shareholders of corporation are natural persons, unless Minister of Ownership Transformations provides otherwise; (5) amount of stock capital will not be lower than 20% of combined value of establishment fund and fund of liquidated enterprise.

Law of Apr. 30, 1993 on National Investment Funds and Their Privatization, as amended ("Fund Law") introduces formation of investment funds in form of joint stock companies established by State Treasury. State owned enterprises chosen by Council of Ministers will be contributed to these funds and transformed into joint stock companies. Authorities of fund are: Shareholder's Meeting, Supervisory Board, and Management Board. Contract may be entered into between fund and specialized managerial firm for management of fund. State Treasury will remain sole shareholder of shares transferred to funds until issuance of two types of share certificates is effected: compensation shares and regular share certificates. Compensation share certificates will be awarded to persons enumerated in Fund Law (civil servants, pensioners, judges, prosecutors) for free. Share certificates will be distributed between whole population of Poland and their cost may not exceeed 10% of average remuneration in country. Share certificates may be exchanged for equal number of shares in each established fund after fund's shares have been admitted to securities market.

REAL PROPERTY:

Real estate consists of land and buildings permanently connected with land or parts of such buildings, unless pursuant to regulations such buildings or parts constitute object of ownership separate from land. Reserving exceptions prescribed by law, buildings and other installations permanently connected with land, as well as trees and other plants from moment of planting or sowing, are considered part of land. Installations, purpose of which is delivery or removal of water, steam, gas, electrical current or similar installations, are not considered part of land or building if they form component part of enterprise or institution. Rights connected with ownership of real estate are also considered parts of land.

Real estate can be object of ownership. Owner (including State Treasury and communal estates) can grant perpetual usufruct. In establishing perpetual usufruct, similar provisions to those governing transfer of ownership of real estate are applied. Within limits defined by laws and principles of social coexistence and by contract, perpetual lessee may use land to exclusion of other persons. Within same limits, perpetual lessee may dispose of his right by sale or inheritance. Lease of State Treasury commune's land by perpetual lease is for 99 years. In exceptional cases, when economic purpose of perpetual leasing does not require leasing land for 99 years, it is permissible to lease land for shorter period. However, term must be for at least 40 years. Within last five years prior to expiration of period stipulated by contract, lessee may demand extension for further period of 40 to 99 years. Perpetual lessee may, however, make such demands earlier, if period of amortization of expenditures intended for land subject to lease is considerably longer than time remaining on lease. Refusal to prolong is permissible only in consideration of some important social interest. Contracts for prolongation of perpetual leases must be notarized. Perpetual lessee pays rent annually throughout lease period. Use of State Treasury land by perpetual lessee must be defined in lease. Lease may be terminated before expiration of specified period if perpetual lessee uses land in manner obviously incompatible with its contractual purpose and particularly if, contrary to contract, lessee fails to erect buildings or installations specified in agreement. In case of expiration of perpetual lease, lessee is entitled to compensation set out by contract for buildings or other installations erected by him or becoming his property and existing on date of returning land subject to lease. Absent contractual valuation of such compensation, compensation is in amount of one fourth of value of buildings and other installations existing on date land subject to lease is due to be returned. No compensation is due for buildings or installations erected contrary to contract provisions. Perpetual lessee is obliged to demolish them upon demand, restoring land to its previous state. (arts. 232-243 C.C.).

Acquisition of Real Estate by Foreign Persons.—Law of Mar. 24, 1920 on Acquisition of Real Estate by Foreign Persons, as amended, provides that acquisition of real estate by foreign persons may take place after permit from Minister of Internal Affairs has been granted. Minister of Internal Affairs grants permit after consultation with Minister of National Defense and, in event permit involves agricultural lands, consultation with Minister of Agriculture. Acquisition of real estate is defined by statute as any event resulting in transfer of ownership or transfer of right of perpetual usufruct to land. In practice during last several years, Minister has been issuing permits to applicants who meet eligibility criteria and comply with legal requirements described below.

Provisions of Law apply to all forms of acquisition of real estate, including contracts of exchange, sale or donation, in-kind contributions of real estate to founding capital of company and acquisition of right of perpetual usufruct to land. Execution of leases or rent agreements is not considered acquisition of real property. Statute requires foreign person to obtain permit in order to acquire shares in Polish company which holds ownership or perpetual usufruct rights to land, if such company thereby becomes controlled company, and, if in event that such company is already controlled company, if its shares are acquired by person other than its existing shareholder. Controlled company may obtain permit from Minister of Internal Affairs allowings its shares to be acquired in future by foreign persons.

Law defines "foreign person" as any of following: natural person who is not Polish citizen; legal person with registered seat outside of Poland; or legal person with registered seat in Poland, but controlled, directly or indirectly, by persons who fall into either of above-listed categories (term "controlled" is defined to mean as holding at least 50% of company's capital). Acquisition of real property in violation of statute is null and void. Law is not applicable to acquisitions of real property through intestate inheritance, and following categories of real estate acquisitions are exempted from permit requirement: (i) acquisition of and ownership right to apartment, (ii) acquisition of real property by foreign citizen holding permanent residency permit for at least five years, (iii) acquisition of real estate by foreign persons, married to Polish citizen, residing in Poland for at least two years, if such real property is considered spousal communal property, (iv) acquisition of real property from person who held ownership right or perpetual usufruct right to such property for at least five years and acquiring foreigner would have been entitled to intestate inheritance after such person, and (v) acquisition of undeveloped property by controlled company done in furtherance of its statute goals, if total area of real property located within city limits in Poland, acquired by such company does not exceed 0.4 hectares. Above exemptions to permit requirement do not apply in situations where acquired real property is located in border zone or if it is agricultural land with area exceeding one hectare.

Foreign person wishing to acquire real estate in Poland must file permit application which sets forth name and address of applicant and seller of real estate; description of real estate; terms of sale; evidence of existence of sufficient funds for purchase; explanation of purpose of purchase; and documentary evidence of applicant's connection with Poland (such as having registered seat in Poland).

Permit application has to be accompanied by following documents: written statement of seller(s) expressing intention to dispose of property and specifying legal form of transfer; excerpts from real estate and mortgage register concerning property to be acquired; documents certifying applicant's ties with Poland; documents setting forth right of applicant to conduct economic activity in Poland; and estimated value of property (this information may be provided to Minister after granting of promise to grant permit is given). Applicant must also pay certain application fees.

Decision of permit is issued by Minister no later than two months from date of filing of all of required documents. Permits issued by Minister are valid for one year (no

See Topical Index in front part of this volume.

REAL PROPERTY . . . *continued*
extensions may be granted) and specify name of acquirer, real estate to be acquired, minimum price for acquisition and any important terms of acquisition, such as special conditions that must be met before transaction can be entered into. Once application is approved, applicant is required to pay stamp duties in amount of 1% of value of property.

Zoning.—Law of July 7, 1994 on Zoning specifies scope and activities related to zoning of land and defining of methods of its use, assuming that development of ecological system should be basis of such actions, and also provides regulations and methods of resolving conflicts between interests of citizens, regional self-governing bodies and state in such matters. Zoning Law provides that local regional bodies ("gminas") shall designate zoning and define methods of use of land located within borders of given gmina. Zoning Law governs issuance of decisions on conditions relating to construction and use of location needed in connection for construction permit. In order to be valid, such decision must conform with provisions of local zoning regulations. Such decision must be issued by head of local regional body, major or president of city. Zoning Law provides that if terms of application for decision on conditions relating to construction and use of location confirm with local zoning ordinances, then person granting such decision cannot deny terms requested and, furthermore, granting of such decision cannot be conditioned upon applicant's fulfillment of certain additional services not provided for in regulations (such as payment of supplementary fees). Before granting construction permit, appropriate organ verifies whether proposed use of parcel or location confirms, inter alia, with regional zoning ordinances.

Construction Regulation.—Law of July 7, 1994 on Construction regulates design, construction, maintenance and tearing down of buildings and defines roles of state administrative bodies in this regard. Construction Law provides that generally construction may commence only once final decision permitting such construction has been granted. Construction proposal must meet requirements set out in decision on conditions relating to construction and use of location and must contain proposed use of location; architectural and construction details; declarations of appropriate entities relating to provision of utilities, if necessary; results of geological and engineering studies and geotechnical conditions relating to location of buildings, if necessary. Such proposal is approved in construction permit. Construction Law provides that Minister of Spacial Economy and Construction shall precisely define scope and form of construction proposal.

RECORDS:

See topics Acknowledgments; Associations; Chattel Mortgages; Commercial Register; Contracts; Corporations; Death (Presumption of and Actions for); Executions; Foundations; Marriage; Mortgages; Motor Vehicles; Notaries Public; Partnership; Patents and Topographies; Real Property; Sales; Trademarks.

REPORTS:

See topic Law Reports, Codes, Etc.

REPRIVATIZATION AND RESTITUTION:

Law on Reprivatization is in process of preparation. However, claims of Catholic Church have been recognized in Law on Relation of State to Church of May 17, 1989. Further developments will be reported.

SALES:

Sales are contracts, pursuant to which seller obliges himself to transfer ownership of particular object and buyer obliges himself to accept object and pay seller price. Objects can be movables (personal property) or immovables (real property). Provisions of C.C. governing sales are correspondingly applied to sale of energy and property rights. (art. 555). Property rights may be transferable real rights, such as perpetual lease, real servitude, pledge, or mortgage; rights in intangible goods such as copyrights, patent rights, or utility models rights; or rights of subrogation or assignment. In practice, sale can encompass bundle of several property rights, e.g., enterprise.

Parties to sales contract can specify items to be transferred. In absence of specification, following rules are applied: contract of sale, exchange, donation or otherwise obliges transfer of ownership to buyer, unless parties have decided otherwise; items defined only generically (fungibles) require actual transfer of possession to demonstrate ownership. Actual transfer of possession is also required for future contracts. (art. 155).

Price in sales contracts may be specified by indicating basis of calculation. If parties stipulate reasonable price, it is assumed that price at time and place of delivery is intended. Benefits, burdens and risk of accidental loss or damage pass to buyer at moment of delivery.

While sales contracts, as rule, do not require any special form, general contract law requires that if value of sale object is higher than amount specified by law, sale must be confirmed in writing. In certain cases, however, special form is required by law for sale to be valid. According to art. 158 "A contract for transfer of ownership in real estate must be in form of notarial deed".

If seller must deliver to place which is not place of performance, seller may deliver by entrusting item to carrier engaged in transporting such items. Buyer, however, becomes obliged to pay only after item has arrived and buyer has had opportunity to inspect item. Seller is obliged to furnish buyer with necessary legal and factual information, including instructions for use. If buyer is delinquent in payment, seller may store item at expense and risk of buyer, or may also sell item at buyer's expense. Seller must, however, first establish time limit during which buyer can pay, unless time limit is impractical because item may spoil or incur other damage. Seller is also obliged to immediately inform buyer of subsequent sale. If buyer is delinquent in payment on partial delivery, or if it is doubtful timely payments for remainder will be made, seller may withhold delivery of remainder, and designate appropriate time limit for buyer to secure payment after which, if no payment is made, he may renounce contract. (arts. 544, 546, 551, 552).

Statutory Warranties.—Seller is liable to buyer if sale item has defect diminishing its value or utility, is of insufficient quality, or was delivered to buyer in incomplete state ("warranty for physical defects"). Seller is also liable to buyer if ownership of sale item is partially or completely vested in third party. Seller is released from liability for warranty if buyer knew of defect upon execution of contract. If object is defined only generically, or object is to be produced in future, seller is released from liability for warranty, if buyer knew of defect at moment of delivery. Parties may extend, limit or exclude liability for warranty. However, in consumer contracts limitations or exclusions of liability for warranty are admissible only in cases provided for by specific regulation. Exclusions or limitations of liability for warranty are ineffective if deceitfully concealed defect from buyer. Seller is not liable for warranty claims for physical defects which arose after passing of risk to buyer, unless defects resulted from cause previously inherent in object. If object sold has defects, buyer may renounce contract or demand reduction of price. Buyer, however, cannot renounce contract if seller immediately declares his readiness to remedy defect. If defective objects are defined generically, buyer may demand delivery of equal amount of objects free of defects and cure of any damages resulting from delay. If items are specially designed and seller is producer, buyer may demand removal of defect, designating appropriate time limit for removal. If time limit passes without cure, buyer may renounce contract. Seller may refuse to cure defect if cure would require excessive cost. If buyer renounces contract or demands reduction of price, he may demand damages resulting from such circumstances unless defect results from circumstances for which seller is not responsible. In such latter case, buyer may seek damages only for damage which he sustained from entering into contract without knowing of defect's existence. If, when goods are shipped to another place, due to physical defect beyond seller's control buyer renounces contract or demands delivery of item free of defects, he cannot return them without previous consultation with seller and is obliged to arrange for storage at expense of seller, until seller, in ordinary course of business, is able to dispose of it as he considers best. (arts. 556-561, 566, 567).

Buyer loses his rights of warranty for physical defects if he does not inform seller of defect within one month of discovery; or if inspection is usual in given relations, if he does not inform seller of defect within one month after which he could have discovered it through due diligence or inspection. Minister of Internal Market may establish shorter time limit for notice of defects of perishables. However, in case of sale between persons involved in commerce, loss of right to warranty occurs if buyer did not inspect items within reasonable time, and did not immediately notify seller of defect and, in event defect came to light later, if he did not inform seller immediately after discovery. Dispatch of registered letter prior to expiration of time limit is sufficient for purposes of notification. Right to warranty for physical defects of items is not lost, in spite of nonobservance of either time limits for inspection or notice to seller about defects, if seller deceitfully concealed defect or assured buyer that no defects existed. (arts. 563, 564).

Buyers, against whom third persons vindicate claims concerning item sold, are obliged to immediately notify seller and ask him to join in suit. If buyer fails to do so, and third person obtains favorable decision, seller is released from liability for warranty of title, insofar as his participation in proceedings was necessary to demonstrate that third person's claims were completely or partially unjustified. If due to legal defect buyer is forced to deliver item to third person, contractual exclusion of liability for warranty does not release seller from duty to reimburse price paid, unless buyer knew rights of seller were in dispute or he purchased item at his own risk. (art. 574, 575).

Express Warranties (Guarantees).—If seller delivers to buyer written guarantee (express warranty) of quality, it is presumed that seller must remove physical defects or deliver free of defects, if defects are found within prescribed time limit. If no time limit is specified in guarantee, time limit is one year, calculated from day when item was delivered to buyer. If not otherwise provided for in guarantee, seller is liable only when defect arose from inherent product defect. Buyer who receives guarantee may enforce statutory warranty for physical defects only when seller does not fulfill, within appropriate time, duties stemming from guarantee. This limitation does not apply to duty to redress damages sustained due to defect's existence. Buyer enforcing claim resulting from guarantee must bring item, at seller's expense, to place indicated in guarantee or to place where item was delivered to him, unless it appears from circumstances that defect must be removed in place in which item was situated at moment of discovering defect. Seller must perform duties resulting from guarantee within appropriate time, and deliver item to buyer at seller's own expense, at place indicated in accordance with above-mentioned rules. Seller bears risk of any accidental loss of item from time of delivery to seller to its collection by buyer. If, in fulfilling guarantee, seller furnishes buyer with item free of defects, or has made substantial repairs to item sold, guarantee period commences from moment of furnishing new or repaired item. Otherwise, guarantee period is extended for period during which buyer could not use it. Time limit for enforcement of statutory warranty claims for physical defects must extend at least three months from expiration of guarantee period. Provisions concerning express warranty are also applied in cases where seller, who is not producer of item sold, gave buyer guarantee document drawn up by producer. In such event, buyer may enforce claims resulting from guarantee only against producer, and statutory warranty claims for physical defects only against seller. (arts. 577-582).

Sale by Installments.—Installment sales allow buyer to pay seller increments of purchase price over specified time period; and product delivery is made before complete payment. Buyer may pay installments before payment comes due. In event of prepayment, buyer may deduct amount corresponding to appropriate rate of interest of National Bank of Poland. Stipulation of immediate enforceability of unpaid price for delinquent installments must be made in writing and executed with contract of sale. Seller may renounce contract of sale if buyer is delinquent in at least two installments, and amount in arrears exceeds one-fifth of contract price. In such case, seller should designate any appropriate additional time limit for payment. But, if cure period passes without effect, seller will be entitled to renounce contract. Contractual provisions less advantageous to buyer are invalid and provisions equivalent to those presented above are implied instead. (arts. 583, 585, 586).

Conditional Sales.—If seller reserves ownership of movable item until payment is complete, it is presumed that transfer of ownership took place subject to condition

SALES . . . *continued*

precedent. If item is delivered to buyer, reservation of seller's ownership must be in writing, and is effective against buyer's creditors only if document has certified date. If seller reserves ownership, seller may demand any appropriate compensation for use or damage of item upon recovery. Sales on approval or with reservations of inspection are final subject to buyer's inspection and acceptance of item. If no time limit for approval or inspection is specified in contract, seller may designate appropriate time limit. If buyer accepts item without declaring approval or inspection period, and did not designate declaration before passing of term, it is presumed that buyer finds item to be acceptable. (arts. 589-592).

Restriction of Sales or Other Conveyances.—There are works of art and other cultural items whose removal from Poland is regarded as essential loss of Polish cultural heritage. Some of such goods cannot be objects of sale, others can only be sold subject to license to transfer such goods abroad. (See: Law of Preservation of Cultural Goods and Museums of 1962 [as am'd] and Regulations on Filing Applications and Issuing Certificates and Permits for Transfer of Cultural Goods Abroad [1965], Specification of Objects Not Being Cultural Goods [1965, 1967].)

Product Labelling and Warranties.—In accordance with Regulation of July 15, 1994 on Labelling of Foodstuffs, all packaged foodstuffs must be labelled in accordance with specific guidelines set forth in Regulation. Regulation of May 30, 1995 on Detailed Conditions of Concluding and Performance of Contracts with Participation of Consumers introduced obligation that all products sold should be marked with label in Polish language and contain information on function of product, manufacturer, importer or country of origin, energy consumption, possession of permit allowing for sale on market. Liability of seller for faults of product (inadequate quality) is established on basis of Civil Code and this Regulation. Seller is required to address customer complaints at retail outlet. Customer may demand refund of price, decrease of price, exchange of faulty product, removal of fault.

Certificates.—Law of Apr. 3, 1993 introduced obligation for domestic and imported products which may be hazardous or which serve preservation of life, health or environment to obtain safety mark issued by Polish Testing and Certification Centre. Services which may be hazardous or which serve preservation of life, health or environment must also obtain service safety certificate. Basis for evaluation of product or service are Polish standards. List of products and services for which obtaining of safety marks is obligatory is published by Director of Polish Testing and Certificate Centre. Products manufactured in accordance with Polish standards or standards established by international or regional organizations may obtain certificate of compliance with such standards or certificate of compliance authorizing marking of such products with compliance mark. Tests for obtaining safety mark are conducted by authorized laboratories. Payments for tests are made by applicants. Obligation to obtain safety mark does not relate to products manufactured according to individual orders, technical appliances which fall under regulations on technical inspection, planes, ships, pharmaceuticals and health services. Introduction of product or service onto market which does not but should contain safety mark is levied with fiscal penalty of 10% of proceeds obtained from sale. This penalty is collected by revenue office.

Product Standards.—Polish Standards established requirements, methods of testing and methods of performing other actions in particular in scope: work safety, life and environment presentation, basic quality characteristics common for groups of products, including technical and functional characteristics of products, materials, energy used on market and for production, main specifications, parameters and technical characteristics connected with quality, type, function of products, drafting of construction documentation and methods of approval of construction works, technical documentation. Application of Polish Standards is voluntary with exception of standards established by appropriate ministers as being obligatory and which in particular relate to presentation of life, health, work safety, environmental protection, and products ordered by state agencies.

International Sale of Goods.—Poland has signed United Nations Convention on Contracts for the International Sale of Goods, adopted in Vienna on Apr. 10, 1980. UNCITRAL will be ratified in near future.

See topics Contracts; Limitations of Actions.

SECURITIES:

Law of Mar. 22, 1991 on Public Trading in Securities and on Trust Funds, as amended ("Securities Law"), sets forth basic requirements governing public trading of securities in Poland. Securities Law establishes Securities Commission ("Commission") as main administrative body in charge of monitoring public trading in securities. Obligations of Commission include such tasks as ensuring observance of fair trade and competition in public trading and protection of investors.

Securities Law contains detailed requirements to be met by individual who desires to become broker. Such person must have capacity to perform legal actions, enjoy full public rights, cannot have been sentenced for crimes and must have passed brokerage examination before Examination Commission for Securities Brokers. Operation of brokerage firm, which may be performed by bank, is subject to permit from Commission, which permit specifies, inter alia, scope of firm activity, required amount of firm's initial capital and ratio of amount of credits in relation to such amount, and required ratio of initial capital to turnover. Commission has authority, in specified circumstances, to suspend or revoke such permit. Securities Law also establishes Brokers' Association ("Association"), in which membership by brokers is mandatory. Association's duties include representation of brokers and protection of their legal interests, cooperation with Commission and other bodies in drafting and enforcing law in field of public trading of securities and maintaining of professional standards of brokers.

Investment advisors are considered separate licensed profession. Employment of proscribed number of licensed advisors is prerequisite to operate trust fund, or brokerage house having permit to render investment advice or to manage portfolios of securities of their clients. Foreign advisors can get license in Poland after passing examination before Commission.

Public offering of securities requires permit from Commission. Offering is defined as offering for purchase, purchase or transfer of rights from issued securities if offer is to more than 300 persons or to unidentified addressee unless one of exceptions have been met, like offer is for shares to employees under provisions of Law of July 13, 1990 on Privatization of State-owned Enterprises or offer is to purchase shares in one-person State Treasury company covering not less than 10% of shares by one purchaser. Law specifies requirements prospectus must meet. Detailed requirements are included in separate regulation of Council of Ministers. Secondary public trading is to take place only on Stock Exchange (with few exceptions).

Securities Law regulates acquisition of large blocks of shares. Obligation to notify is placed upon holders of stock entitled to 5% and 10% of votes. Person intending to acquire shares of public company entitled to 25, 33 or 50% or more of total number of votes must notify Commission prior to transaction. Commission may prohibit acquisition. Acquisition of shares constituting 10% or more of votes shall be done by public tender only.

Trust funds are managed by trust fund corporations, which are supervised by Commission. Such corporations may be established only in form of joint stock companies. Securities Law provides that at least 90% of value of fund assets must be invested in securities admitted to public trading or in securities issued by State Treasury or National Bank of Poland and no more than 5% of value of fund may be invested in securities of single issuer.

Securities Law sets forth provisions regulating civil and criminal liability of issuer of securities, persons offering securities into public market, brokers and insiders. Issuers and persons offering securities into public market are liable for damages resulting from false or dishonest information contained in documents relating to securities, unless such persons and persons for whom they are responsible are innocent. Insider trading is criminal offense.

Bonds.—Law on Bonds of May 12, 1995 governs issuance, sale and purchase and redemption of bonds. Term "bond" has been defined as security issued in series, pursuant to which issuer states that he is debtor of owner of bond (obligee) and promises to perform obligation required in bond (redemption of bond). Pursuant to Law, following entities may issue bonds: entities with legal personality that conduct economic activities; autonomous regions (gmina) and associations thereof and city of Warsaw; other entities with legal personality that are authorized to issue bonds in accordance with other regulations. Banks are also authorized to issue bonds. However, this activity is further regulated by Act of Jan. 31, 1989—Banking Law. Law is not applicable to issuances of bonds by National Bank of Poland and State Treasury.

Obligation set forth in bond may be monetary or in kind. Monetary obligation requires that issuer of bond pay to bondholders principal amount of bond together with interest, as provided in terms of issuance. In kind obligation may require issuer to give bondholders right to portion of issuer's future profits or right to convert bond into shares of issuer, or preemptive right with respect to future share increases of issuer.

In accordance with Law, bond may be fully or partially secured or may be unsecured. Bond may be fully secured through any of following methods: placement of security interest or mortgage on property of issuer; guaranty by National Bank of Poland or other bank whose capital is equal to at least 10,000,000 ECU in Polish currency; guaranty by State Treasury; guaranty of foreign bank or international financial institution whose capital is equal to at least 10,000,000 ECU; guaranty of autonomous region (gmina), which is only applicable in case of bonds issued by gminas or associations thereof or commercial entities controlled by gminas or enterprises established by gminas.

Only entity that has been in existence for three consecutive fiscal years (and has prepared financial statements to present activities conducted during such time) may issue unsecured bonds, provided, however that share capital of such entity is equal to at least multiple of five and Commercial Code requirement governing minimal amount of share capital of given type of commercial entity. Law provides that issuer of bond is liable for obligations stemming from bond with all of its assets, while liability of guarantor is limited to amount of guaranty.

Bonds may be issued through public subscription or purchase offer made to no more than 300 individual investors. Law of Mar. 22, 1991 on Public Turnover in Securities and Trust Funds would govern public subscription and turnover in bonds. In case of public subscription detailed requirements concerning content of prospectus would have to complied with.

In order to protect interest of bondholders, Law created new entity in Polish law: bank trustee, which would function as legal representative of issuer. Law requires that issuer enter into agreement with trustee prior to commencement of issuance and material provisions of such agreement would have to be disclosed in prospectus or sale offer. In order to serve as trustee bank must have capital in amount of at least equivalent of 10,000,000 ECU in Polish currency and cannot, inter alia, serve as trustee for any other outstanding bond issue, cannot be debtor of issuer, members of management or supervisory organs of bank cannot be lenders of issuer, own more than 10% of shares of issuer.

Trustee bank is required to conduct periodic analyses of financial situation of issuer to analyze whether issuer is able to meet its bond obligations and is required to inform bondholders of financial situation of issuer before issuer fails to meet its bond obligations if situation creates significant risk that issuer will fail to meet its bond obligations. If trustee determines that issuer has failed to meet its bond obligations, it can, among other things, establish additional security for bond obligations, demand that issuer repay all of its obligations in full, file appropriate court claim against issuer or file bankruptcy declaration on behalf of issuer.

Law provides for penalties applicable to, inter alia, entities that issue bonds without complying with requirements of Law or who provide false or conceal information that could have material impact on determination of ability of issuer to meet its bond obligations.

SECURITY FOR COSTS:

Aliens commencing civil action before Polish court must, upon demand by defendant, post security for costs which defendant may incur in such action, unless otherwise stated by law or settled by international agreements. According to C.C.P. (arts. 1119 and 1120) such obligation does not exist when alien is resident in Poland or has sufficient property situated in Poland for securing costs, reciprocity exists between Poland and country of which plaintiff is citizen, or action is based on agreement of

See Topical Index in front part of this volume.

SECURITY FOR COSTS . . . *continued*
choice of Polish courts jurisdiction. (Reciprocity is considered to exist with signatories of Hague Convention on Civil Procedure of 1954.)

SEQUESTRATION:

See topics Actions; Attachment; Bankruptcy and Restructure; Executions; Judgments.

SHIPPING:

See topics Attachment; Brokers; Chattel Mortgages; Commercial Register; Customs; Foreign Trade and Foreign Investments.

STATUTE OF FRAUDS:

See topic Contracts.

STATUTES:

See topics Law Reports, Codes, Etc.; Commercial Register.

SUPPORT:

See topic Divorce.

SYSTEM OF GOVERNMENT:

See topic Constitution and Government.

TAXATION:

Income Tax.—Corporate Income Tax Law which came into effect on Feb. 15, 1992 applies to legal persons and organizations without personality at law, except for partnerships without personality at law. Taxpayers whose domicile or headquarters is located within Poland are liable to tax with respect to entirety of their income, irrespective of place where income has been earned. Taxpayers whose domicile or headquarters is not located within Poland are liable for tax only with respect to income earned within Poland.

Tax year is period of 12 consecutive full months. Where taxpayer does not choose otherwise, giving notice to relevant tax office, tax year must be calendar year. Tax payable is 40% of tax base. Income tax on income from dividends and other earnings obtained as part in profits gained by legal persons domiciled within Poland is 20% of earnings so obtained. Amount of tax paid on income from dividends and other earnings obtained as part in profits gained by legal persons domiciled within Poland is deducted from amount of tax assessed. Withholding tax on income obtained on copyrights or usage of production process or production, trade or scientific equipment or know-how is 20% of proceeds.

In determining income which constitutes tax base, following is disregarded: (1) earnings from sources located within Poland or abroad, not liable to income tax or exempt from such tax; (2) exempt earnings; and (3) costs incurred in obtaining earnings. Donations towards science, technology, education, culture are deductible from tax base up to 15% and donations towards public safety, religious worship and other charities are deductible from tax base, up to 10% of income. Aggregate amount of donations may not exceed 15% of income, however, donations to natural and legal persons and organizations lacking personality at law who pursue such objectives as part of their business operations and gifts to natural persons for whom such gift would constitute personal earnings are not deductible.

Monies received and other money values, including those arising from exchange rate differentials, value of earnings in kind, and value of free benefits obtained constitute earnings. Earnings do not include following, among other things: (1) payments collected or receivables recorded with respect to provision of goods and services to be effected in successive reporting periods, and also loans (credits) drawn with exception of capitalized interest; (2) sums of interest on receivables accrued but not received; (3) sums received on account of return of cooperative contributions, redemption of shares in business corporation, redemption of securities by issuer, and repurchase of units in trust funds, to extent constituting costs of earnings; (4) earnings obtained in order to establish or increase authorized capital in business corporation, membership fund in cooperative or organizational fund in insurance company, or, in trust fund companies, value of assets held by such funds.

Costs incurred to obtain earnings and operating costs of legal person constitute costs of earnings. Costs of earnings also include such items as (1) provisions for depreciation of fixed assets and intangible and legal assets (depreciation charges); (2) partial or total losses in fixed assets and operating capital caused by accidents with exception of port depreciated or covered by insurance proceeds; (3) expenditures for research and development, and experiments. Costs of earnings are deductible only for tax year to which they are related, i.e., costs of earnings incurred in previous years are deductible where related to earnings gained in tax year in question, or where such costs, specified by type and amount related to tax year in question, have been recorded although not yet actually incurred; where such recording is not possible, costs are deductible for year in which recorded.

Following, inter alia, may not be included in costs of earnings: (1) expenditures for acquisition of land or right of perpetual usufruct thereto, and expenditures for acquisition or production of other fixed assets and intangible and legal assets, where subject to depreciation; (2) expenditures for membership contributions in cooperative, shares in business corporation, other securities or units in trust funds established by taxpayer unless establishment of such fund is required by law; (3) deductions and payments to various kinds of funds established by taxpayer unless establishment of such fund is required by law; (4) interest on taxpayer's own capital invested in source of earnings; (5) gifts and donations; (6) one-time compensation for industrial accidents and occupational illness, and additional insurance contributions payable where working conditions have deteriorated; (7) fines and money penalties adjudicated in penal proceedings, treasury offence proceedings or administrative proceedings, and interest due on same.

Following are some items exempt from tax: (1) income from sale, in whole or in part, of real estate included within farm with exception of income from sale of land which loses its status as agricultural or forest land as result of such sale; (2) income from sale of real estate or of right of perpetual usufruct performed under environmen tal protection regulations; (3) income earned outside Poland by taxpayers whose domicile or headquarters is located within Poland, where international agreement to which Poland is part so provides; (4) income of taxpayers—other than state enterprises, cooperatives and business corporations—whose statutory objective constitutes activity in fields of science, technology and education (including higher education), culture, physical education and sports, environmental protection, support of civic initiatives involving construction of rural roads, telecommunications, water supply networks and other charitable works; (5) income of legal person not having their seat or management in Poland, obtained from activity concluded in Poland and financed from funds awarded by international financial institutions or means awarded by foreign countries on basis of agreements concluded with Polish Government.

Taxpayers must submit, without prior summons, declaration in standard form on amount of income (losses) obtained from beginning of tax year, pay to tax office monthly advances corresponding to difference between tax payable on income earned from beginning of tax year and sum of advances payable for preceding months.

See topic Foreign Investment.

Law on Personal Income Tax which came into effect Jan. 1, 1992 applies to all natural persons who permanently reside in Poland, those who remain in Poland longer than 183 days per year and those who reside abroad but whose source of income is in Poland. Tax is applicable to all income, regardless of source, received by natural person, except for income from general agricultural activity (which remains subject to agricultural tax), income from forestry activities, income taxable under inheritance and gift tax, and income obtained from activities which cannot be subject of legally binding contracts.

Income of married persons is taxed separately unless parties express contrary intent. If so desired, total income of spouses may be divided by two to obtain applicable basis for determination of tax rate, and tax calculated on that half is multiplied by two to determine total tax payable by both spouses.

Income Tax Law defines nine categories of sources of income (including employment, economic activity and real estate). If person obtains income from more than one source, subject of taxation is total amount of income derived from all sources, except for losses from taxable sources and enumerated costs of obtaining income. Sources expended for obtaining such income are deductible. Tax Law sets out over 40 categories of tax-exempt income including government awards, insurance payments and lottery winnings and sale of share of national investment fund, interest from savings accounts with exception of accounts held in connection with performed economic activity, interest and discount of State Treasury bonds.

Income Tax Law provides for progressive income tax rate ranging from 20% to 45%. Widening of spread of tax-scale is planned when average salaries increase.

Value Added Tax.—Law on Value Added Tax and Excise Duty, as amended ("VAT Law"), introduced as of July 5, 1993, replaced turnover tax. Goods and services as well as import and export of goods and services are subject to value added tax. Taxable persons are legal persons, organizational units without legal personality and natural persons (1) with principal place of business or place of residence in Poland, if they conduct activities in their own name and for their own account, in circumstances indicating intention of repeating such conduct, (2) conducting stockbroker activities, activities arising out of management of trust funds, activities arising out of management contract, job-order, intermediation, commission sale or other services of similar character, (3) subject to customs duty, irrespective of whether or not goods are exempted from customs or customs duty is suspended, (4) having principal place of business or place of residence abroad if they carry out sale of goods or supply services personally or through authorized person or with help of employees or with use of establishment or equipment serving purpose of production, commercial or service activity, (5) receiving imported services. Tax liability arises upon delivery, transfer, barter or donation of goods or provision of services or, if sale has to be confirmed with issue of invoice, at moment of issuance of invoice, but not later than seven days after goods were delivered or services performed. In respect to export of goods, tax liability arises upon confirmation by border customs office of carriage of goods abroad. In respect to import of goods, tax liability arises upon decision of customs office allowing shipment into Poland. Taxpayer should submit registration notice to revenue office prior to first performance of sale of goods or provision of services.

Following taxpayers are exempted from value added tax: (1) whose combined value of sale and value of export of goods and services in previous tax year did not exceed 80,000 zlotys, (2) who pay income tax in simplified lump sum form. Exempted taxpayers may give up exemption.

Turnover constitutes tax base. Turnover is amount due on account of sale of goods, less amount of tax; turnover is decreased by amount of proved, legally permitted and mandatory rebates (discounts, deductions, decreases, accepted claims), by value of returned goods, refunded unwarranted amounts and amounts of invoice corrections. Discounts reduce turnover when they are granted within one year of day of delivery of goods or supplying services. Discounts granted on account of guarantee or warranty reduce turnover even if they are granted more than one year from delivery of goods or supplying services. Tax rate is set at 22%; some goods and services listed to appendix to VAT Law are charged with 7% tax (e.g. goods used in forestry and agriculture, goods used in health care, food stuff, goods for children). Goods and services exempted from tax are, among others: products of meat packing industry, fish catch products, raw materials for dairy industry, products of forestry and hunting, agricultural services. For export of goods tax rate is 0%. Taxpayers have right to deduct from amount of output tax which they are liable to pay amount of input tax (sum of amounts of tax specified in invoices decreased by rebates) charged upon acquisition of goods and services by taxpayer. Settlement of input tax for month in which taxable person has not carried out taxable activity is effected in next period when output tax is charged. Where in settlement period amount of input tax exceeds amount of output tax, taxable person has right to deduct difference from output tax payable for future periods. Tax difference will be refunded by revenue office.

Taxpayers are required to calculate and pay tax for monthly periods, by 15th day of month following month in which tax liability arises to account of relevant revenue office. Taxable persons are required to issue invoice certifying sale of goods, its date,

TAXATION . . . *continued*

unit price without tax, sale value, amount of tax, amount payable and data concerning taxable person and buyer. Taxpayers are not required to issue invoices to natural persons who do not conduct economic activity. At request of natural persons they should issue simplified invoices. In simplified invoices tax may be calculated by applying to amount payable rate of 18.03%. Taxpayers rendering services on behalf of natural persons, not conducting economic activity, including services in scope of trade are obliged to record such services through fiscal cash registers, if value of turnover exceeds that which is stated in Law.

Sale of goods or services listed in appendix 6 to VAT Law, which includes among others engine fuels, equipment to operate games of chance and mutual betting, passenger cars, sea going yachts, high standard electronic equipment and video cameras, cosmetics and perfumes, alcohol, wine, beer, tobacco products, as well as excessive decrements or unaccounted for shrinkage of some excisable goods are subject to excise tax. Liable to pay excise tax are producers and importers of excisable goods; said liability arises irrespective of tax liability not later than on day on which goods leave premises of producer. Excise tax base is provided by turnover of excisable goods. With respect to import, excise tax base is their customs value plus due customs duty and import tax. Tax for producer and for importer, respectively, ranges from 95% and 1,900% for alcohol; 80% and 400% for engine fuels; 40% and 56% for passenger cars and 25% and 40% for other products.

Inheritance and Donation Tax.—Law on Inheritance and Donation Tax of 1983, as amended, does apply to acquisition through inheritance or donation of property located within Poland or by individuals being Polish nationals or permanently living in Poland. Tax is progressive up to 40% and depends on value of property acquired and family relation between donor (deceased person) and heir.

Import Tax.—Law on Import Tax levied on imported goods provides for 5% tax.

Local Taxes.—Law on Local Taxes and Tariffs, as amended, provides levying upon natural persons, legal entities and organizational units without personality at law following local taxes: (a) real estate tax, (b) tax on means of transport, (c) tax on keeping of dogs, and (d) local fees covering fee for trading on open market places, fee charged on tourists and fee for some official acts of local government authorities.

Tax and Social Security Charges on Wages.—Wage encumbrance placed upon employer, calculated in following pattern: 45% of wage (social security fund – "ZUS") + 3% of wage (Labor Fund) + 0.2% of wage (Unemployment Fund) which amounts to total of 48.2% of wage.

Tax of Sale of Securities in Public Trading.—Law on Tax of Sale of Securities in Public Trading of 1995 introduced tax on sale of securities in public trading, except for sale in initial public offering. Aggregate price paid by purchaser of securities constitutes tax base in exchange transactions. In off exchange transfers of shares listed on Exchange, tax base is equal to exchange price of shares as of date of sale and, if there was no session on such date, then price using last session prior to entering into sale agreement. In case of shares that are not listed on Exchange, then tax base is equal to price set forth in sale agreement. In Regulation of Feb. 23, 1995, as amended, Minister of Finance introduced temporary waiver of tax of sales of securities in public trading made between Feb. 27, 1995 to Dec. 31, 1995.

Stamp Duties.—Law on Stemp Duties of 1989, as amended, provides for payment of stamp duties in connection with proceedings before administrative bodies, execution of various contracts, preparation of certain documents and court decrees. Specific rates are provided in Regulation of Minister of Finance of Dec. 9, 1994.

Polish—U.S. Treaty.—Poland and U.S. signed treaty on prevention of double taxation on Oct. 8, 1974 based upon following principles: (a) in Poland—entities domiciled or with their seat located in U.S. may deduct from Polish tax due their corresponding amounts paid in U.S., (b) in U.S.—entities domiciled or with their seat located in U.S. may deduct from U.S. tax their corresponding amounts paid in Poland. U.S. companies holding in Poland at least 10% of shares in Polish companies may also deduct part of taxes paid by such Polish company from its proceeds. Deducted amount, however, may not exceed part of U.S. tax, which depends on taxpayer's net income from Poland or income from out of U.S. in relation to total net profit of taxpayer in same tax year.

Treaty also introduces several principles, such as: (a) dividend is taxed in country where seat of company is located and tax may not exceed: (i) 5% of gross dividend amount if receiver is legal entity controlling at least 10% of shares with voting rights of legal entity paying dividends or (ii) 15% of gross dividend amount in all other circumstances, (b) interest is not subject to taxation in country in which it was accrued, (c) license dues may be taxed in country in which they were accumulated but no more than 10% of their amount, and (d) capital proceeds are free from taxation in country in which they were accrued.

Poland is bound by bilateral international agreements on prevention and avoiding of double taxation with following countries: Albania, Argentina, Australia, Austria, Belgium, Bulgaria, Byelorussia, Canada, China, Denmark, Estonia, Finland, France, Germany, Great Britain, Holland, Hungary, Indonesia, Ireland, Israel, Italy, Republic of Korea, Latvia, Lithuania, Malta, Republic of Moldavia, Norway, Romania, Singapore, South Africa, Spain, Sweden, Switzerland, Thailand, Tunisia, Socialist Republic of Vietnam, the United Arab Emirates, and Republic of Zimbabwe.

TRADEMARKS:

In Poland, Law on Trademarks of Jan. 31, 1985, as amended, governs all matters of trademark law. Trademark is sign designed to distinguish goods or services of certain "natural or legal persons" authorized to carry out market activity in spheres of production, commerce and services (generally called "enterprises"). Such goods and services are distinguished from other similar goods and services produced by other enterprises. In particular, trademark may be word, design, ornament, color composition, plastic form, melody or other sound signal, or combination of such elements. (arts. 4 and 5).

Protection of trademark is acquired upon registration. Registered trademark receives "protection certificate". Patent Office of Republic of Poland administers registration process for trademarks and issues protection certificates. Registration of trademark may be conducted on behalf of enterprise and only for goods which are objects of market activity (here "goods" also includes services). In order to be registered, trademark should have sufficiently distinguishing features as determined under normal conditions of market economy. Registration of trademark must not infringe on personal and financial rights of third parties. Registration is also illegal when it includes inaccurate data, or illicit use of name and abbreviation of Republic of Poland. Symbol of Republic of Poland includes seal, colors and anthem of nation (same also relates to names and symbols of members of Paris Convention on Protection of Industrial Property). It is also unacceptable to register trademark for goods of same kind if (1) it is similar to trademark of another enterprise to such extent that under normal conditions of market economy it would cause confusion among consumers as to origin of merchandise, or (2) it is similar to trademark broadly known in Poland as symbol for another product if it would cause confusion among consumers as to origin of product. Apart from these two examples, trademark may not be registered if it includes description of geographic character or description of government of member of Paris Convention on Protection of Industrial Property, or if it describes municipality of state for goods that originate in that territory if use of trademark would confuse consumers. Above criteria of unavailability result from international agreements. (arts. 6-10).

In Republic of Poland, priority of receipt of right to protection by registered trademark belongs to Polish natural or legal persons, members of Paris Convention listed above, and also to natural and legal persons of other states who have interests in "industrial, commercial, service enterprises" in state that is member of Paris Convention. Priority extends to date of application for registration of trademark in state party to Convention, if application for registration of same trademark in Patent Office for same goods takes place within six months of such date, or according to date of public exhibition of goods marked with such trademark exhibition in Republic of Poland or in state belonging to Paris union, if application for registration of same trademark in Patent Office for same goods takes place within six months of such date. Priority may be transferred to another person. (art. 12).

Enterprise on behalf of which trademark is issued receives exclusive right to use trademark in market within whole territory of state for goods covered by registration. Right lasts ten years from date of correct application for trademark in Patent Office. Trademark protection may be continued beyond term on petition of authorized person for additional ten years. Protection of trademark registration may also be alienated. Contract for transfer of such protection should be in written form with fixed date. Such contract becomes enforceable against third parties from date of entry in register of trademarks. (arts. 13, 15).

Authorized person (authorized on basis of registration of trademark) may demand cessation of all trademark infringement or actions threatening infringement. Such person may also seek, according to general rules, remedy for damages in form of monetary compensation or ill-gotten profits. Whoever illegally introduces into commerce goods or services marked with trademark of another is subject to imprisonment of up to one year or fine. (arts. 20, 57).

Foreign natural and legal persons may benefit from rights under Trademark Law, and in accordance with international agreements binding Republic of Poland, on basis of reciprocity. Poland is party to Madrid Agreement concerning prosecution of illegal distribution of goods, signed in Madrid in 1891, as amended in Washington in 1911, and in the Hague in 1925. Poland is also member of Paris Convention on Protection of Industrial Property, signed in Paris in 1883, as amended in Washington in 1911, in the Hague in 1925, and in Stockholm in 1967.

See topic Patents and Topographies, subhead Patent Agents.

TREATIES AND CONVENTIONS:

Republic of Poland is party to, inter alia, following multilateral agreements:

General.—Bern Convention of Sept. 9, 1886 (as am'd Berlin, 1908, and Rome, 1928); Association Agreement between EU and Poland (1993); Statute of Council of Europe (May 5, 1949); Treaty on Establishment of European Bank for Reconstruction and Development (May 29, 1990); Accord Establishing World Trade Organization (Apr. 15, 1994).

International Cooperation in Legal Matters.—

Procedure.—Hague Convention relating to Procedure in Civil Matters (1905 and 1954); U.N. Convention on Recognition and Enforcement of Foreign Arbitral Awards (New York, June 10, 1958); European Convention on International Commercial Arbitration (Geneva, Apr. 21, 1961); New York Arbitration Convention; International Convention on Certain Issues Regarding Conflict of Citizenship Laws (Hague, 1930); Law on International Private Law of 1965; Poland is not party to Hague Convention of 1961 on Abolishing Requirements of Legalisation for Foreign Public Documents.

Intellectual and Industrial Property.—Bern Convention of Sept. 9, 1886 on Protection of Literary and Artistic Works (as am'd Berlin 1908, and Rome 1928); Paris Act of Bern Convention signed in Paris on June 24, 1971 (with exclusion of arts. 1-21 and annex); Universal Convention on Copyright of Sept. 6, 1962 signed in Geneva, verified in Paris, July 24, 1971; Paris Convention on Protection of Industrial Property (Paris, Mar. 20, 1883, as am'd, Stockholm, July 14, 1967).

Family.—Convention Concerning Claims for Alimony Abroad (New York, 1956); International Convention on Citizenship of Married Women (New York, 1957); Hague Convention on Conflicts of Law and Jurisdiction relating to Divorce and Separation (June 12, 1902); Hague Convention on Conflicts of Law relating to Marriage (June 12, 1902); Convention on Consent to Contract Marriage, Lowest Marriage Age and Marriage Registration (New York, Dec. 1962); Convention on Conflicts of Laws relating to Form of Testamentary Disposition (Hague, 1961).

Trade.—Paris Convention on Protection of Industrial Property (Paris, 1883, as am'd in Washington, 1911, Hague, 1925, and Stockholm, 1967); Geneva Convention of June 7, 1930 concerning Bills of Exchange and of Mar. 9, 1931 on Checks; United Nations Convention on Contracts for the International Sale of Goods (Apr. 10, 1980); Madrid Agreement Concerning Prosecution of Illegal Distribution of Goods (Madrid 1891, as am'd in Hague, 1925); Central European Free Trade Agreement (Dec. 21, 1992); European Free Trade Agreement (Dec. 10, 1992).

Tax Treaties—Avoidance of Double Taxation on Income and Property.—Poland is bound by bilateral international agreements on prevention and avoiding of double taxation with following countries: Albania, Argentina, Australia, Austria, Belgium,

TREATIES AND CONVENTIONS . . . *continued*
Byelorussia, Canada, China, Denmark, Estonia, Finland, France, Germany, Great Britain, Holland, Indonesia, Israel, Italy, Republic of Korea, Latvia, Lithuania, Malta, Norway, Singapore, Spain, Sweden, Switzerland, Thailand, Tunisia, Socialist Republic of Vietnam, the United Arab Emirates, Republic of Zimbabwe.

TRUSTS:

See topics Bankruptcy and Restructure; Wills.

WILLS:

Wills and contracts of inheritance are governed by C.C. (arts. 941-958 and 1047-1057).

Wills in General.—Disposition of property in case of death can only be made by will (testament). Will may contain disposition of only one testator. Only person with full capacity to enter into legal transaction may draw up will. Will cannot be drawn up by agent, it must be made by testator personally. Will is invalid if it was drawn up in absence of conscious or free decision-making or expression of intention; under influence of error justifying assumption that had testator not acted under influence of error, he would not have drawn up will with such content; or under influence of duress. Will must be interpreted so as to assure fullest possible fulfillment of testator's intentions. If will is ambiguous, interpretation fulfilling intent of testator's dispositions and giving them reasonable content must be followed.

Ordinary Wills.—Last will and testament can ordinarily be executed in three ways; (a) holographic will—testator may write his will in his own hand, sign it and affix date. However, lack of date does not render handwritten will invalid, if it does not give rise to doubts as to testator's capacity to draw up will, as to contents of will or as to mutual relationship of several wills; (b) notarial will—will may be drawn up by notary; and (c) oral will—testator may also draw up will by orally declaring his last will to chairman or other permanently office-holding member of local authority in presence of two witnesses. Testator's declaration is written down in protocol and dated as of time of writing. Protocol is read to testator in presence of witnesses. Protocol must be signed by testator, by person to whom will was declared, and by witnesses. If testator cannot sign protocol, it must be specified in protocol, together with reason for lack of signature. Deaf or mute persons cannot make will in such manner.

Emergency Wills.—If there is apprehension of early death of testator or if, due to specific circumstances, observance of ordinary form of will is not possible or impractical, testator may orally declare his last will in presence of at last three witnesses. There are special provisions for emergency wills during voyage on Polish ship or aircraft. Emergency wills expire six months from cessation of circumstances which justified non-observance of form of ordinary will, if testator is still living. Running period is suspended during time in which testator has no possibility of drawing up ordinary will.

Revocation of Will.—Testator may at any time revoke either entire will or any of its particular provisions. Only person with full capacity to enter into legal transaction may revoke will; it must be done personally, never through agent. Revocation of will may take place either by testator drawing up new will, or by destroying it with intent to revoke will, or stripping it of characteristics upon which its validity depends, or by making alterations in will, from which his intention to revoke its provisions is apparent. If testator draws up new will without specifying in it that he revokes previous will, only those provisions of previous will which are not compatible with contents of new will are subject to revocation.

Legitimate Portions of Inheritance.—Descendants, spouse and parents of deceased who would have been appointed to inheritance by force of law are entitled, if permanently disabled from work or minor, to two-thirds of value of share of inheritance which would have passed to them on statutory succession, and in other cases—half value of such legitimate share. If person entitled did not receive compulsory share due either in form of donation made by deceased, or in form of appointment to inheritance, or in form of legacy, he is entitled, against heir, to claim for payment of such amount of money as is needed to cover or to make up compulsory share. Deceased may deprive descendants, spouse and parents of their compulsory share by will (disinheritance), if person entitled to compulsory share persistently behaved in manner contrary to principles of social coexistence against deceased's wishes; committed intentional crime against his life, health or freedom or flagrant insult to him or one of persons closest to him; or persistently failed to fulfill his family duties to deceased. Cause of disinheritance of person entitled to compulsory share must be stated in text of will. Deceased cannot disinherit entitled person if he forgave him. Descendants of disinherited descendant are entitled to compulsory share, even though person disinherited outlives deceased. (arts. 991, 1008-1011 C.C.)

Contracts of Inheritance.—Contract over inheritance from living person is invalid, subject to exceptions stated in C.C. Statutory heir may, by way of contract with person he is to succeed, renounce his inheritance. Such contract must be concluded in form of notarial act. Contract of sale, exchange, donation or other contract binding heir to assign inheritance transfers inheritance to purchaser, unless parties have decided otherwise. Contract obliging assignment of inheritance must be concluded in form of notarial act. Same applies to contract transferring inheritance, which is concluded for purpose of performing previously existing obligation to dispose of such inheritance. Purchaser of inheritance succeeds to rights and obligations of heir.

Foreign Wills.—According to Law of Nov. 12, 1965 on Private International Law (art. 35) validity of will and other legal actions in case of death are determined by national law of testator at day of execution thereof. Compliance with form provided by law of state in which transaction was executed is also acceptable. Poland is party to Convention on Conflicts of Laws relating to Form of Testamentary Disposition signed in Hague on Oct. 5, 1961. Foreign will and each testamentary disposition is valid if its form complies with internal law of place where testator made it, or of nationality of testator, or of place of domicile of testator, or of place in which testator had his habitual residence, and, for immovables, of place where they are situated. See topic Descent and Distribution.

PORTUGAL LAW DIGEST REVISER

Dr. Nuno Reynolds Telles Pereira and Dr. Luís Miguel Sasseti Carmona with Dr. Martin J.H. Reynolds all of
Largo da Academia Nacional de Belas Artes, No. 16
1200 Lisbon, Portugal
Telephone: 351-1-346-2277; 342-8383
Fax: 351-1-346-5079

Reviser Profile

Note: The strict standards of lawyers' ethics in Portugal prevent us from publishing further information on our Reviser of the Portugal Law Digest.

PORTUGAL LAW DIGEST

(The following is a list of all Topics, including cross-references, covered in this Digest.)

PORTUGAL LAW DIGEST

Revised for 1997 edition by

DR. NUNO REYNOLDS TELLES PEREIRA and DR. LUIS MIGUEL SASSETI CARMONA with DR. MARTIN J.H. REYNOLDS, all of Lisbon.

C.C. (Civil Code); C.P.C. (Civil Procedure Code); C.C.C. (Code of Commercial Companies); D.L. (Decree-Law); IRS (Personal Income Tax); IRC (Corporation Tax); C.A. (Local Authority Tax); C. Pen (Criminal Code); Bankruptcy Code [Code of Special Proceedings for the Recovery of Business Enterprises and Bankruptcy].

See topic Statutes.

Portugal is a member of EU. See also European Union Law Digest.

ABSENTEES:

When necessary to provide for administration of assets of absentee whose whereabouts is unknown and who has no legal representative or attorney or latter is unable or unwilling to act, court will appoint provisional curator. (Art. 89 C.C.). After two years absence if absentee has no legal representative or attorney, or otherwise after five years, State Attorney or any interested party may apply for legal declaration of absence for purpose of absentee's heirs inheriting his estate. (Art. 99 et seq. C.C.). Presumption of death may be applied for by spouse not judicially separated, by heirs or by anyone having right to absentee's property dependent on his death (and whether or not administration of his assets has previously been provided for as above) after ten years from last news of absentee or after five years from his attaining age of 80 whichever may occur first, but never before expiration of five years from his attaining majority. (Art. 114 et seq. C.C.). Spouse of married absentee, may marry again after presumption of death has been declared. If absentee returns, his spouse's former marriage is considered as dissolved by divorce. (Art. 116 C.C.).

ACKNOWLEDGMENTS:

Documents executed abroad in accordance with local law for use in Portugal do not normally require notarial or Consular legalization (Art. 365-1 C.C.), and may be translated either by Consulate, or by Notary or sworn translator in Portugal. Powers of attorney for patent or trademark applications do not require any formalities.

However, it is generally advisable to legalise documents executed abroad, with Apostille of the Hague Convention of 5.10.1961 or at Portuguese Consulate.

ACTIONS:

Facts on which foreign claim may be based have to be proved in same way as facts on which any other claim may be grounded and foreign law, when applicable, must be proved by way of certificate issued by competent authority abroad and legalized by respective Portuguese Consulate or by expert witnesses acceptable as such to court.

Limitation of.—See topic Prescription and Limitation of Actions.

ADOPTION:

Adoption is effected by court decision (Art. 1973-1 C.C.) and may, as rule, be granted if: (1) Considered to be to real advantage of child; (2) based on lawful reasons; (3) not involving unfair deprivation of other children of adopter; (4) there is reasonable assumption that link like that of parent and child will be established between adopter and child (Art. 1974-1 C.C.). Child will be taken care of by adopter during certain time so that court can judge convenience of constitution of this relationship. (Art. 1974-2 C.C.). When child is over 14 his consent is required. (Art. 1981-1[a] C.C.). Depending on various circumstances, adoption can be complete, adopted in this case acquiring situation equal to other children in his new family and relation to his former family being extinguished (Art. 1986-1 C.C.), or restrictive in which case only certain rights and duties between adopter and child are established (Art. 1992 et seq. C.C.).

AFFIDAVITS:

Under law governing evidence, affidavits are not considered and it is not the practice in Portuguese courts and official bodies to accept such means of proof.

AGENCY: See topic Principal and Agent.

ALIENS:

Civil status and capacity of aliens as well as their family rights and duties and successions are, as a rule, governed by their personal law. (Art. 25 C.C.). Excluding political rights, aliens, as general rule, enjoy same rights as Portuguese citizens. (Art. 14-2 C.C.).

If residence visa is required, this must normally be applied for before entry into Portugal as transit visa cannot normally be changed into residence visa. EEC nationals enjoy special status regarding residence. (Decree-Law 60/93 of 3.3.93). In case of citizen of U.S. coming into Portugal, reference should be made to Portuguese Consulate. Decree-Law 59/93 of 3.3.93 provides new rules about entry, permanency and departure of non-EEC foreign nationals.

As a rule, non-EEC alien cannot be employed in Portugal without preliminary working visa obtained abroad and employer registering respective service agreement with Ministry of Labour in accordance with rules of Decree-Law 97/77 of Mar. 17, 1977.

EEC nationals are allowed to enter Portugal provided they are in possession of valid passport or identification document. EEC nationals must apply for residence card within three months of entry.

Portugal is party to Shengen Agreement.

Corporations Owned or Controlled by Aliens.—Foreigners are allowed to establish themselves in all economic sectors open to private enterprise with exception of such limitations as established in International Agreements to which Portugal is party. (D.L. 214/84 of 2.8.1984).

See also topics Corporations; Industries; Mines and Minerals; Nationality.

ALIMONY: See topic Divorce.

ASSIGNMENTS:

Credit or right may, as a rule, be freely assigned for a consideration or not, even without consent of debtor. There are special provisions forbidding assignment to certain persons of credits subject to litigation. (Art. 579-1 C.C.). As between assignor and assignee, right assigned passes by virtue of assignment contract, but debtor when he has not expressly agreed with assignment and third persons are not bound thereby until notice of assignment in authentic form has been given to debtor. (Art. 583-1 C.C.). Assignor guarantees to assignee existence and right to claim credit but solvency of debtor is only guaranteed by assignor to assignee if such guarantee has been expressly given in assignment contract. (Art. 587 C.C.). Party to a bilateral contract may assign all or any of his rights with agreement of other party unless otherwise contracted for. (Art. 424 C.C.).

ASSIGNMENTS FOR BENEFIT OF CREDITORS:

These assignments are not recognized by Portuguese law, unless all the creditors agree thereto.

New Code of Special Proceedings for the Recovery of Enterprises and Bankruptcy (D.L. 132/93 of 23.4.93) provides that, during recovery of enterprise phase, it is possible to assign property to creditors (Art. 88), or to constitute new company in order to exploit premises of debtor enterprise, in which case creditors' claims will be represented by holdings of capital in company (Arts. 78 et seq.).

ASSOCIATIONS:

Institutions of religious, cultural or sporting nature and other nonprofit associations enjoy juridical personality. Political parties must be approved by Constitutional Court.

See also topics Corporations; Partnership.

ATTACHMENT:

Judicial attachment of property and rights or other precautionary proceedings are permitted in certain cases as preservative or preventive measure, within a time limit before an action is commenced or in course thereof. (Arts. 619 to 622 C.C. and 402 et seq. C.P.C.). In debt cases judicial attachment can only be employed against defendant who is not registered as merchant. In execution proceedings on judgment attachment is preliminary to ultimate sale by court of property attached. In cases of copyright infringement and infringement of industrial property (trademarks, etc.), seizure of infringing goods may also be applied for.

Provision for Indemnity.—The applicant for an attachment or for precautionary proceedings must formally undertake to indemnify the other party for the damages he may suffer as a result of such attachment or precautionary proceedings if the other party is ultimately successful.

AUTOMOBILES: See topic Motor Vehicles.

BANKRUPTCY:

Bankruptcy laws are to be found in Code of Special Proceedings for the Recovery of Enterprises and Bankruptcy as approved by D.L. 132/93 of 23.4.93.

Bankruptcy regime is designed to be swifter and to give priority to possibility of recovering enterprise over its mere extinction under bankruptcy.

Recovery can be applied for whenever enterprise is considered still to be economically viable.

Methods for Recovery of Enterprises: (1) Concordata (composition), (2) creditors moratorium (acordo de credores), (3) financial restructuring, (4) management under court supervision.

Recovery of Enterprises can be applied for to courts by any creditor or Attorney General whenever debtor: (a) fails to fulfil one or more obligations which, bearing in mind amount involved, or circumstances of failure to fulfil, demonstrates debtor's incapacity to timely meet whole of its obligation; (b) disappearance of owner of enterprise or of its directors, without appointment of substitute, which results from financial difficulties of enterprise, or abandonment of premises where enterprise has its head office or main place of business; (c) dissipation of assets, fictitious creation of credits or any other anomalous act demonstrating intention to avoid fulfilling obligations.

If debtor enterprise is not deemed economically viable and any of situations referred to in (a), (b) or (c) above occur, any debtor or Attorney General can apply for bankruptcy. If (a) above occurs, debtor itself must within 60 days apply for recovery or bankruptcy depending on whether or not there are sound grounds for considering enterprise economically viable.

Bankruptcy can also be applied for by any creditor or by Attorney General, in event of death or ceasing of activity by debtor, within one year of any of acts referred to in (a), (b) or (c) above.

See Topical Index in front part of this volume.

BANKRUPTCY . . . *continued*

At any stage of liquidation of assets, creditors with certified credits amounting to at least 75% of credits, together with debtor can halt bankruptcy proceedings by way of extraordinary agreement, which requires confirmation by judge.

Once bankruptcy is decreed credits of State, Local Authorities, and Social Security lose their privileged status and become ordinary creditors, thus ranking equally with any other ordinary creditor.

Individual debtor not owning business enterprise can submit to court proposal aiming to reduce or reschedule its debts, so as to avert bankruptcy.

Once bankruptcy is decreed it causes immediate maturity of all outstanding obligations and suspends all interest, except on mortgages constituted prior to date of insolvency. It also deprives bankrupt of his civil capacity until his discharge.

From date of bankruptcy decree administration of bankrupt's estate is taken over by administrator appointed by court who is charged with liquidation. He is assisted or supervised by committee of creditors appointed by judge.

BILLS AND NOTES:

Portugal adhered to the Conventions signed at the Geneva Conference on June 7, 1930, providing for: (1) A uniform law for bills of exchange and promissory notes; (2) the settlement of certain conflicts of laws in connection with bills of exchange and promissory notes; and (3) general provisions with regard to bills of exchange and promissory notes. All these Conventions took effect in Portugal from June 21, 1934.

Portugal also signed similar Conventions at Geneva on Mar. 19, 1931, with regard to cheques, which took effect in Portugal from June 21, 1934.

Legislation covering issue of cheques without cover. (D.L. 454/91 of 28.12.91).

CHATTEL MORTGAGES: See topic Mortgages.

COLLATERAL SECURITY: See topic Pledges.

COMMERCIAL REGISTER:

Commercial Registry, which is governed by Commercial Registry Code, approved by D.L. 403/86 of 3.12.86, covers inscription of individual traders, with limited or unlimited liability, commercial and industrial companies, and merchant ships, and registration of juridical changes thereto. In addition, amongst others, resolutions required by law for acquisition of assets by company, promise of sale or charging of stock holdings in companies, except for shares, and debenture issues and respective official authorizations, change of head office, projects for merger and division of companies and company resolutions approving such projects, and reduction of companies' capital; resolutions maintaining control of company by other in group of companies and termination of such control. Also subject to commercial registration are certain proceedings affecting individual traders and commercial entities generally, commercial powers of attorney, establishment of branches of companies, commercial agency agreements, agreements forming complementary groups of companies, European groups of economic interest, etc. Relevant applications must be made by party concerned or legally appointed representative. Fines and imprisonment may be imposed for failure to comply with requirements, and uninscribed commercial or industrial companies are considered as being of unlimited liability and cannot invoke their trading capacity to third parties. Ships which have not been registered may not undertake any voyage.

Before registering with Commercial Registry, corporations, other bodies and individual traders must apply to National Registry of Corporate Bodies for permission to use chosen company name and for Identity Card.

COMMUNITY PROPERTY:

See topic Husband and Wife.

CONSTITUTION AND GOVERNMENT:

On Apr. 25, 1976, new Constitution of Republic of Portugal came into force. It was voted by Constituent Assembly thereafter extinguished. However, with view to protecting and guaranteeing maintenance of democracy main political parties reached revised agreement with Armed Forces prior to approval of new Constitution by Constituent Assembly. Political parties with representation in present Assembly of Republic, are following: Social and Democratic Centre—Popular Party (CDS-PP), Portuguese Communist Party (PCP) and its allies, Social Democratic Party (PSD) and Socialist Party (PS), latter having formed present government after winning Oct., 1995 General Elections.

In accordance with 1976 Constitution of Republic, power is exercised by President of Republic, Assembly of Republic, Government and Courts. Constitution was first revised in way to transform its "revolutionary" content into Western type text with view to better protecting private enterprise and property. Revolutionary Council was replaced by State Council and Constitutional Court. Constitution was further revised in 1989.

Judicial functions are carried out by normal judicial courts: special courts for judging crimes against State or other offenses are no longer permitted.

CONTRACTS:

Except when law specifically provides for any special formalities such as notarial public deed or written document duly stamped, contracts may even be verbal and can be proved by witnesses or other evidence. (Art. 405-1 C.C.).

Excuses for Nonperformance.—Apart from nonperformance due to force majeure, party to simulated contract or party who entered into contract under false pretenses or coercion may claim it to be null and void. (Arts. 240 et seq. C.C.). When due to error, consent given by one of parties does not correspond to what such party would normally and reasonably require or when there is error about identity of other party or object of contract, contracting party concerned has right to annul contract. (Arts. 247 and 251 C.C.).

Applicable Law.—As a rule it is for contracting parties to choose applicable law to contract. There are exceptions, e.g., with regard to contracts relating to real estate, concession rights, banking, insurance, etc. If chosen law, however, contains provisions considered to be contrary to Portuguese public policy, such provisions cannot apply. (Arts. 35 to 45 C.C.).

See also topic Courts.

Government Contracts.—As a rule these contracts are entered into as a result of public tenders terms and conditions of which include most of clauses of eventual contract governed by same laws as any contract between private entities.

Distributorship, Dealership and Franchises.—These contracts are not specifically provided for by Portuguese law, and therefore parties are free to regulate them, provided that basic legal principals and "general law of obligations" are respected. In specific case of Franchising, practice is to take into account "European Franchising Ethical Code", rules of "International Franchise Association", and decisions of European Court.

CONVEYANCES: See topic Deeds.

COPYRIGHT:

Law relating to copyright is contained in Decree-Law 63/85, of Mar. 14, 1985, and subsequent amendments substituting former Code of Copyright approved by Decree-Law 46,980 of Apr. 27, 1966 and subsequent alterations under which protection is afforded to authors of all intellectual works which are considered to be, amongst others, literary, artistic and scientific writings; lectures, lessons, speeches, sermons and other works of similar nature; dramatic or musical-dramatic works; choreographic works and pantomimes, stage execution of which is fixed in writing or in any other way; musical compositions whether with words or not; cinematographical works and those produced by any process similar to cinematography; drawing, painting, architecture, sculpture, engraving and lithographical works; photographical works and those produced by any process similar to photography; applied art works; pictures and geographical maps; projects, sketches and plastic works relating to geography, topography, architecture or sciences. Copyright exists during lifetime of author and another 50 years thereafter. It may be assigned for life interest, pledged, or attached in judicial proceedings.

Transfers of copyright, as also pledges and attachments thereof, are subject to registration.

Authors' names and noms de plume are also protected, subject to registration.

Portugal is a signatory to Berne Convention.

CORPORATIONS:

Decree-Law 248/86, of Aug. 25, 1986, created new form of undertaking, individual trader with limited liability, in addition to existing forms of commercial entities governed by commercial law, namely: Partnerships, limited partnerships, companies having stock capital in form of quotas, companies limited by shares, and cooperative societies. There is also form of association of interests known as "participation account" but association in this case concerns parties to account and not third persons.

In addition to above classification by form there is also classification according to object, such as banks, insurance companies, shipping companies, and companies having concessions from or contracts with State, in respect of which special authorities for their constitution or regulations for their functioning are necessary or applicable.

All banks and insurance companies as well as companies running basic industries such as transports, power production and distribution, pulp, cement, tobacco, except foreign owned, were nationalized in 1975; however, at present and as result of 1989 revision of Constitution new sectors have been opened to private enterprise, including banking and insurance. Several banks and insurance companies have as result been privatised.

There are two forms of limited liability corporation or company, namely companies having stock capital (sociedades por quotas) and companies having share capital (sociedades anónimas). There is also a form of limited partnership having share capital.

Companies Having a Stock Capital (sociedades por quotas).—The two outstanding legal features of the companies having a stock capital are: (1) The division of the capital into quotas or holdings of stock which may be of unequal amount; and (2) restriction of liability of stockholders to total amount of unpaid capital, that is, stockholder may, in certain circumstances, be called on for benefit of creditors to pay not only calls in respect of his own stock, but also of any stock in respect of which there is liability outstanding.

These companies may be constituted and function with minimum of two members, minimum capital of Esc. 400,000$00 and minimum holding of Esc. 20,000$00. They are extremely easy to manage. Holdings must be divisible by Esc. 250$00. (Arts. 197 et seq. C.C.C. as approved by D.L. 262/86 of 2.9.86).

Companies limited by shares (sociedades anonimas) are governed by more elaborate provisions (Arts. 271 et seq. C.C.C.) than stock companies above referred to. Five subscribers are necessary. Minimum capital is Esc. 5,000,000 represented by shares of minimum nominal value of Esc. 1,000$00 each. Administration of company is entrusted to board of directors who need not be shareholders supervised by financial board, or by board of directors with general council formed by shareholders and supervised by official auditor, whilst board of general meetings serves as kind of liaison between general body of shareholders and managing boards. It is function of this board to assume chairmanship and direction of general meetings of company. Unless shorter period established in statutes, term of office of board of directors and financial board is four years, reelection being permitted if specifically allowed by articles of association.

Debenture-holders may attend general meetings of shareholders, but have no right of address or vote. Shareholders holding number of shares insufficient to entitle them to vote may appoint one of them their representative to annual general meeting and to resolve as to manner in which such representative shall vote on behalf of group capital.

The annual report and accounts must be filed with competent Commercial Registry, and if company's shares are quoted on Stock Exchange they must also be published in Official Gazette.

CORPORATIONS . . . *continued*

A company may deal in its own shares and debentures if so authorized by its articles. Bearer shares may be subject to registration or deposit with bank.

Stock Exchange.—Stock Exchange Code was approved by D.L. 142-A/91 of 10.4.91, and has undergone several amendments latest being D.L. 261/95 of 3.10.95.

In both forms of company debentures may be issued subject to certain conditions. Directors, or, in case of companies having stock capital, managers "gerentes" whether or not they are share or stockholders are personally liable for unpaid taxes or debts due to State, and they are restricted as regards trading with company and carrying on similar business; trading year ends on Dec. 31 and accounts should be submitted for approval by quotaholders or shareholders before Mar. 31; from annual profits there must be set aside 5% for creation and maintenance of reserve fund up to 20% of nominal capital; legal acts affecting constitution of company must be published and registered; except for certain special industries there are normally no restrictions on foreign capital and management.

In all forms of company, resolutions may be passed unanimously in written form without need to hold general meeting.

Other types of companies have been object of specific regulations, inter alia: Leasing companies (Decree-Law 135/79 of May 18 and subsequent legislation) and investment companies (Decree-Law 342/80 of Sept. 2 and subsequent legislation). Object of former is to let immovables or equipment according to borrower's request, against agreed rentals. Object of latter is to perform financial operations, to promote new ventures, acquire shares and quotas in other companies and assist them. Regional Investment Companies, which may contribute to regional development, have been granted special status, including possibility of issuing shares and bonds to public in general.

Taxation.—Commercial companies and other collective entities (such as civil and professional persons associations) are now subject to IRC—income tax on collective bodies—which replaced former industrial tax. (IRC Code as approved by D.L. 442-B/88 of 30.11.88).

Tax is due by resident corporate entities on income obtained in Portugal. Nonresident corporate entities and those having permanent establishment in Portugal are generally subject to IRC on income obtained in country.

Depending on nature of income and on whether or not corporate entity is resident in Portugal IRC rate of tax may vary from 15% to 36%.

Depending upon company's location, municipal tax, at rate of up to 10% of corporate income may be charged.

Foreign Corporations.—Foreign holdings are subject to regulations contained in Code of Foreign Investments approved by Decree-Law 321/95 of Nov. 28, 1995. Except for certain specified activities, foreign corporations may freely do business in country. If, however, they establish any form of representation in Portuguese territory they are subject to taxation with regard to their activity in country in same way as any Portuguese company and should therefore register branch in Commercial Registry so that they have juridical personality and capacity to go to court.

See also topics Aliens; Commercial Register; Industries; Partnership.

COSTS:

Except in cases of recognised title to legal aid, costs (i.e., court fees) are payable by losing litigant to extent of his failure to succeed. Both parties, however, have to pay substantial part of estimated costs in advance as legal action proceeds. Lawyers are only liable for costs when acting with no forensic power of attorney.

Each party bears his own lawyer's fees, and successful party cannot recover these from losing party.

Pursuant to D.L. 387-B/87 of 29.12.87 aliens and stateless persons with habitual residence in Portugal are entitled to legal aid. Nonresident aliens are also entitled to such aid, provided that their respective countries afford same right to Portuguese nationals.

COURTS:

The courts are independent and the State is represented in them by Attorney General or one of his officials.

Parties may stipulate that certain case is to be submitted to courts of country of one of parties, or to international courts, with or without exclusion of others, as long as: (a) That court accepts appointment by parties; (b) it is considered to be of real interest to one or more parties involved; (c) it does not involve any problems concerning certain rights, immovables situated in Portugal, bankruptcy or insolvency of corporations head offices of which are situated in Portugal, or any questions related to labour matters; (d) this stipulation is in writing and has same form as contract it is supposed to protect. Otherwise, Portuguese Courts always have jurisdiction in case of contract which is to be performed in Portugal.

There are provisions for Arbitration in Law 31/86 of 29.8.86 and Arts. 1525 et seq. C.P.C. Arbitration can be voluntary or compulsory, by operation of Law. In disputes involving international commercial interests parties may appoint arbitrators and choose law to be applied in event of their not having been instructed to judge in accordance with general equitable principles.

CURRENCY:

Portuguese escudo in relation to sterling has been lately at rate of about 237 to pound and in relation to dollars at rate of about 158 to U.S. dollar. See topic Exchange Control.

CUSTOMS:

Inasmuch as in a concrete case a number of laws may be involved, it is not practicable to summarize the law on this subject with accuracy and sufficient brevity for inclusion herein.

DEATH:

Presumption of Death.—See topic Absentees.

Actions for Death.—Inasmuch as in a concrete case a number of laws may be involved, it is not practicable to summarize the law on this subject with accuracy and sufficient brevity for inclusion herein.

DECEDENTS' ESTATES:

See topics Descent and Distribution; Executors; Wills.

DEEDS:

Written documents may be authentic or private. Authentic documents are those duly issued by competent public authorities or by public notaries or other officials with similar functions; all other documents are considered private documents. Private documents are considered authenticated when confirmed by parties before public notary, as provided for in notarial laws. (Art. 363 C.C.).

Foreign Documents.—Authentic or private documents issued in foreign country, in accordance with its laws, carry same weight as evidence as would those of same nature issued in Portugal. If document is not legalized, and there are justified doubts about it or its acknowledgment being genuine, its legalization may be required. (Art. 365 C.C.).

See also topic Acknowledgments.

Authentic Documents.—Amongst authentic documents, "escrituras públicas" (public deeds written in books of notary and executed by parties thereto) are the more important and are required, inter alia, in case of: (1) Conveyances of immovables; (2) mortgages; (3) assignments and charges of mortgage debts; (4) assignments and charges of stock ("quotas") of quota stock companies; (5) commercial or industrial leases and leases subject to registration; (6) transfer of commercial and industrial establishments; (7) extrajudicial division of estate; (8) transfer and pledge of copyright; and many others.

Documents with notarial legalization are private documents in which handwriting and signature or only signature have been recognized by notary or his assistant as genuine.

DEPOSITIONS:

Depositions are only taken in Court or as preparation of a criminal case at Criminal Police and are one of strongest means of making evidence in judicial proceedings.

DESCENT AND DISTRIBUTION:

No distinction is made between realty and personalty for purposes of intestate succession.

Order of succession is as follows: (1) To surviving spouse and descendants per stirpes; (2) to surviving spouse and ascendants; (3) to brothers and sisters and to their descendants; (4) to collaterals not comprised in (3) down to fourth degree; (5) to State. (Arts. 2131 to 2155 C.C.).

Surviving spouse, descendants and ascendants are obligatory heirs, and testator subject to Portuguese law having such heirs may not freely dispose by will of more than one-third of his estate when nearest heirs are surviving spouse and one or more children (or issue of deceased children) or two or more children or surviving spouse and one or two parents; one-half when nearest is surviving spouse or one child (or issue of deceased child) or parents; one-third when nearest are ascendants other than parents. Any testamentary disposition in excess of these proportions is void as to excess. (Arts. 2156 et seq. C.C.).

Succession and executors powers are governed by personal law of deceased at time of death. (Arts. 62 et seq. C.C.).

DIVORCE:

Either of spouses may apply for divorce when other culpably fails in matrimonial duties when failure due to its seriousness and repetition jeopardizes possibility of life in common. (Art. 1779 C.C.). Spouses are mutually bound by duties of respect, faithfulness, cohabitation, cooperation and support. (Art. 1672 C.C.). Separation de facto during six consecutive years; absence when whereabouts of absentee is unknown for at least four years; and insanity of other spouse during six years when due to its seriousness jeopardizes possibility of life in common are also grounds of divorce. (Art. 1781 C.C.).

Grounds for judicial separation of persons and property (which does not dissolve marriage bond or dispense from duty of faithfulness) are same as those for divorce.

Divorce or separation of persons and property can also be applied for to court by mutual consent of both spouses. (Arts. 1775 et seq. C.C.).

Also, divorce by mutual consent can be obtained at Civil Registry. (Art. 1773 C.C.).

Judicial separation of persons and property may be converted into divorce at any time when applied for by both spouses or after two years by one. (Art. 1795-D C.C.).

Either party has right to apply for alimony in accordance with legal provisions.

DOMICILE:

Concept of domicile as known to American and English law is quite alien to Portuguese law. "Domicilio" signifies place or locality of habitual residence and affects principally jurisdiction and taxation.

DOWER: See topic Husband and Wife.

ENVIRONMENT:

According to Art. 66 No. 1 of Portuguese Constitution everyone is entitled to environment fit for a human, healthy and ecologically balanced life. It is for State, inter alia, on its own, or at request and with support of popular initiatives to prevent and control effects of pollution and prejudicial forms of erosion, to organise and promote biologically sound countryside, to classify and protect countryside and localities and to promote rational use of natural resources, safeguarding its capacity for renewal and its ecological stability. (Art. 66 No. 2 of Constitution).

Art. 52 No. 3 of Constitution confers on all, either individually or through associations for defence of interests in question, right of "Acção Popular" (Popular Action,

ENVIRONMENT . . . *continued*
i.e. kind of "qui tam action", on behalf of individual and also State) to promote and prevent cessation or judicial prosecution of offenses which involve deterioration of environment, as well as to apply for compensation on behalf of injured party or parties.

There are other provisions in Portuguese Constitution regarding Environment as for instance Arts. 81(n), 91, 96 No. 1(d), 96 No. 2, 168 No. 1(g), 229 No. 1(c), and 234 No. 1.

Portugal has enacted two Laws, "Lei das Associações de Defesa do Ambiente" (Law for Associations for the Defense of Environment) (Law 10/87 of 4.4.87) and "Lei das Bases do Ambiente" (Basic Law of the Environment) (Law 11/87 of 7.4.87), which grant citizens, inter alia, right to prompt and accessible judicial means of obtaining compensation for damage to environment, right to representation or to participation in State organisations for general defence of environment, right to consult and be informed by associations for defence of environment at central, regional and local administrative offices relating to variety of matters including studies on environmental impact.

Latest revision of Penal Code, which came into force on 1st Oct. 1995 introduced three new types of crime, namely crime of damage to nature (Art. 278 Penal Code); crime of pollution (Art. 279 Penal Code) and crime of pollution endangering community. (Art. 280 Penal Code).

Air Pollution Control.—Governed by Art. 1346 C.C. (Emission of Fumes); Art. 8 of Law 11/87 of 7.4.87 (Basic Law of the Environment); D.L. 89/90 of 16.3.90 (Regulations of Stone Quarries) and D.L. 352/90 of 9.11.90 (Protection and Control of the Quality of the Air).

Water Pollution Control.—Governed by Decree 5787-IIII of 10.5.19 (Law for Waters); D.L. 38382 of 7.8.51 (General Regulations of Urban Construction); D.L. 90/71 of 22.3.71 (Pollution of the Sea, Beaches and Shores); D.L. 70/90 of 2.3.90 (Regime of Property Belonging to the Public Water Domain and Supervision and Enforcement of Offences); D.L. 74/90 of 7.3.90 (Water Quality Rules); D.L. 93/90 of 19.3.90 (National Ecological Reserve) and Decree 37/91 of 18.5.91 (approves Agreement on Cooperation for the Protection and against Pollution of the Coasts and Waters of the North-West Atlantic).

Waste Disposal.—Art. 1347 C.C. (Prejudicial Installations); D.L. 13/71 of 23.1.71 (Construction of Building and Industrial Installations, Rubbish and Waste Waters Depot); D.L. 468/71 of 5.11.71 (The Law of Land Belonging to the Public Water Domain); D.L. 343/75 of 3.7.75 (Disciplinary Measures for Certain Operations to the Soil and Countryside); D.L. 488/85 of 25.11.85 (Solid Residues); D.L. 89/90 of 16.3.90 (Regulations of Stone Quarries); D.L. 121/90 of 9.4.90 (Transformation of Dangerous Residues and their Movement in Portugal); D.L. 186/90 of 6.6.90 (Evaluation of Environmental Impact); Portaria 624/90 of 4.8.90 (Rules for the Discharge of Urban Waste Waters); Portaria 809/90 of 10.9.90 (Rules for the Discharge of Residues from Slaughterhouses); Portaria 810/90 of 10.9.90 (Rules for the Discharge of Residual Waters from Pig Farms); D.L. 327/90 of 22.10.90 (Regulates Occupation of Land Burnt by Forest Fires); D.L. 352/90 of 9.11.90 (Protection and Control of the Quality of the Air); D.L. 88/91 of 23.2.91 (Storage, Collection and Burning of Used Oils) and Portaria 505/92 of 19.6.92 (Rules for the Discharge of Waste Waters from Tanneries).

Recycling.—Resolution of the Counsel of Ministers 2/93 of 7.1.93 (Use of Recycled Paper and Selective Collection of Obsolete Papers in Government Offices).

General Supervision.—"Ministério do Ambiente" (Ministry for the Environment), Rua do Século No. 51 2º, Lisbon; "Ministério do Equipamento Planeamento e da Administração do Território" (Ministry for Equipment Planning and Territorial Administration), Praça do Comércio, Lisbon; "Direcção Geral do Ambiente" (Directorate General of the Environment), Avenida Almirante Gago Coutinho, 30, Lisbon; "Direcção Geral do Ordenamento do Território" (The Directorate General of Planning of the [National] Territory), Campo Grande, 50, Lisbon; "Comissões de Coordenação Regional" (Regional Coordination Committees); the Lisbon Region is covered by the "Commissão de Coordenação da Região de Lisboa e do Vale do Tejo", Rua Artilharia 1, 33, Lisbon; "Instituto da Água" (Water Institute), Avenida Almirante Gago Coutinho, 30, Lisbon; "Instituto de Promoção Ambiental" (Institute for the Promotion of the Environment), Rua do Século, 63, Lisbon; "Instituto de Conservação da Natureza" (Institute for the Conservation of Nature), Rua da Lapa, 73, Lisbon.

ESCHEAT:

Unclaimed dividends, deposits and balances in account become the property of the state on the expiration of five or fifteen years according to the nature of the credit right. (Decree 10,474). See also Descent and Distribution.

EXCHANGE CONTROL:

D.L. 170/93 of 11.5.93 has liberalized import and export of funds.

New law designed to prevent "Branqueamento de Capitais" (money laundering) has been enacted by D.L. 325/95 of Dec. 2, 1995.

EXECUTIONS:

Judgments can be executed, through execution proceedings, when final and binding or when law provides that appeal brought against it does not suspend its execution. Judgment is final and binding when it ceases to be subject to appeal.

Documents enacted or authenticated by notaries, bills of exchange, promissory notes, cheques, invoice extracts and other documents can also be executed through execution proceedings. (Arts. 46 et seq. C.P.C.).

New form of summary enforcement of small debts, up to 250,000 Escudos, known as "INJUNÇÃO", has been created by Decree-Law 404/93 of 10.12.93. In order for "Injunção" to be granted, debtor will have to be validly served with notice of application, and has seven days to present his defence. If debtor does not pay, or does not present his defence, creditor can apply to court for execution of debt through execution proceedings.

EXECUTORS:

Property in estate does not pass to executor whose duties are to carry out instructions specifically given by testator within limits of law and, if no such instructions have been given, to (1) Look after funeral of testator and pay respective expenses and ceremonies as may have been indicated in will or, otherwise, in accordance with usages of place where deceased died; (2) see that terms of will are carried out and, if necessary, to uphold validity thereof before courts; (3) carry out functions of "head of the family" when will does not contain any provision to contrary and when deceased did not leave surviving spouse who shares in estate as an heir or is entitled to a moiety in property owned in common.

Functions of "head of the family" are to administer estate of deceased pending distribution of estate.

FORECLOSURE: See topic Mortgages.

FOREIGN DOCUMENTS:

See topics Acknowledgments; Deeds.

FOREIGN EXCHANGE:

See topics Currency; Exchange Control.

FOREIGN INVESTMENT:

Direct Foreign Investment is governed by D.L. 321/95 of Nov. 28, 1995, and is subject to registration with ICEP-Investimentos, Comércio e Turismo de Portugal, Av. 5 de Outubro 101/3, Lisbon, within 30 days. Foreign investment enjoys same rights and guarantees afforded to Portuguese investors, being eligible for same incentives.

Special rules apply to foreign investment that may affect Public Order, that is connected with production and trade of weapons, ammunition and war material, or that involves exercise of Public Authority. Projects of special interest to Portuguese economy and which are to be carried out by Portuguese companies with foreign investment, are eligible for "Contractual Regime" (Contract with the State) governed by Decreto Regulamentar ("Regulatory Decree") 2/96 of May 16, 1996.

See also topics Corporations; Exchange Control; Industries; Mines and Minerals.

FOREIGN JUDGMENTS: See topic Judgments.

FOREIGN TRADE REGULATIONS:

See topic Exchange Control. See also topic Industries.

FRAUDS, STATUTE OF: See topic Deeds.

FRAUDULENT CONVEYANCES:

Nullity of simulated agreement may be pleaded judicially at any time and by any interested party, even if simulation was fraudulent. (Art. 242 No. 1 C.C.).

However, nullity of simulation cannot be pleaded by simulator against bona fide third party, i.e. against someone unaware of simulation at time his rights were created. (Art. 243 Nos. 1 and 2 C.C.).

Declaration of Bankruptcy makes all bankrupts' debts immediately due, even if their maturity date has not yet occurred, and closes all current accounts. (Art. 151 Bankruptcy Code).

Agreements made by bankrupt after Declaration of Bankruptcy are invalid as against estate in bankruptcy, unless made for valuable consideration with bona fide third parties, in which case such agreements are only invalid as from date on which Bankruptcy Decree is registered. (Art. 155 No. 1 of Bankruptcy Code).

Debtor, who, with intention of prejudicing his creditors, deliberately allows himself to become insolvent and declared bankrupt, may be condemned to maximum of five years' imprisonment or to fine of up to 600 days of prison remission. (Arts. 227 et seq. Criminal Code as am'd by Decree-Law 48/95 of 15.03.95).

GARNISHMENT:

Precautionary proceedings permitted in certain cases as preservative or preventive measure, before action is brought, include procedure by which money or property of debtor in possession of third parties may be subjected to claims against debtor. (Arts. 381 et seq. C.P.C.). See also topic Attachment.

HUSBAND AND WIFE:

In absence of any antenuptial agreement, marriage regime before June 1967 is full community and after that date community only of after-acquired assets. (Arts. 1717 et seq. C.C.). Community in both cases lasts until marriage dissolved by death or divorce or until judicial separation of persons and property, or exceptionally of property only, is decreed. Each spouse is administrator of own property and of specified property owned in common; otherwise administration of property owned in common belongs to both spouses.

Husband and wife together are entitled to dispose inter vivos of movable property administration of which belongs to both jointly and apart from certain exceptions each is entitled to dispose of own or of common property of which he or she has administration. In general, except when marriage is with separation of property, husband or wife can only dispose of or lease immovable property and/or commercial establishments whether owned in common or otherwise with consent of other spouse. Insofar as Matrimonial Home is concerned, even in event of separation of property, consent of other spouse is required. (Arts. 1682 and 1682-A C.C.).

In Private International Law marriage regime is defined according to common national law of spouses at date of celebration of marriage or in default by law of spouse's common habitual residence at time of marriage or in default, law of first common matrimonial residence. (Art. 52 C.C.).

Deceased Husband or Wife.—Surviving spouse is entitled to maintenance out of income of estate. (Art. 2018 C.C.).

IMMIGRATION:

Foreign technicians and industrial personnel generally are only allowed to enter country to work if respective employer has previously registered service agreement with Ministry of Labour.

Special regime exists in respect of citizens of EEC Member States. See topic Aliens.

INDUSTRIES:

There are numerous regulations relating to establishment of new industries and new factories. When part of capital is foreign owned, rules contained in Code of Foreign Investments must be observed.

See also topics Aliens; Corporations; Mines and Minerals.

INFANCY:

Age of majority is 18 (Art. 130 C.C.), but minor is fully emancipated when he marries having attained 16 years of age.

Apart from some exceptions infants cannot enter into contractual obligations and are normally represented by their parents.

INSOLVENCY:

Governed by D.L. 132/93 of 23.4.93. See also topic Bankruptcy.

INSURANCE:

Governed by D.L. 102/94 of 20.04.94, pursuant to Directives 92/49 CEE of 18.6, 92/96/CEE of 10.11 and 91/674/CEE of 19.12.

Supervision of insurance business lies within competence of "Instituto de Seguros de Portugal".

INTEREST:

Apart from agreement and excluding those cases where special provision is made by law, interest does not run until debtor is formally notified that interest is claimed. Legal rate is established from time to time by government. Interest at rates up to 3% or 5% above legal rate can be agreed in loans depending on whether there is or is not guarantee in nature of mortgage. Interest also runs on items in current account where there is contract of current account, and on sums received by agent for remittance to his principal. Legal interest rate is at present 10% per annum. (Art. 559 C.C. and Portaria [Ministerial Order] 1171/95 of 25.9.95).

On commercial matters legal interest rate is 15% per annum. (Art. 102 of Commercial Code as am'd by Ministerial Order 1167/95 of 23.9.95).

INTESTACY:

See topic Descent and Distribution.

JUDGMENTS:

Foreign judgment must be examined and confirmed by Court of Appeal as Second Instance normally Judicial District Court of residence of person against whom judgment is used. Only thereafter can it be enforced in Portugal. (Arts. 1094 et seq. C.P.C.).

Portugal has ratified Lugano Convention of 16.9.88 relating to jurisdiction and enforcement of judgments in civil and commercial matters.

LABOR RELATIONS:

Collective labor contracts are binding at law for their duration on all workers and employers in particular trade or industry.

See topic Taxation, subhead Social Security.

LANDLORD AND TENANT:

Leases are generally classified as: (1) Residential; (2) commercial or industrial; (3) leases for professional activities; (4) agricultural. First three are basically governed by D.L. 321-B of 15.10.90. Residential leases are of two kinds: (a) For period of six months or one year automatically renewable, at tenants option. Landlord is entitled to yearly rent adjustments; (b) for fixed period of at least five years, which is not automatically renewable, but yearly rent adjustments are also possible. Each year government decrees maximum rate of increase of rents.

Commercial, industrial and leases for professional activities can also be for fixed term. (D.L. 257/95 of 30.9.95).

Agricultural leases cannot be made for less than ten years (seven years in some cases). (D.L. 385/88 of 25.10.88).

There is special regime for Forestry Leases. (D.L. 394/88 of 8.11.88).

LAW REPORTS, CODES, ETC.:

See topic Statutes.

LEGISLATURE:

See topic Constitution and Government.

LICENSES:

See topics Exchange Control; Industries; Mines and Minerals.

LIENS:

With respect to all credits in its favor, the State enjoys a privileged position over other creditors, whether secured or unsecured (Arts. 773 et seq. C.C.), except in event of bankruptcy where State loses such privilege (Art. 152 of D.L. 132/93 of 23.4.93).

LIMITATION OF ACTIONS:

See topic Prescription and Limitation of Actions.

LIMITED PARTNERSHIP:

See topic Partnership.

MARRIAGE:

Marriage celebrated abroad where one of spouses is Portuguese must be registered with Portuguese Consulate and subsequently with Central Civil Registry Department for marriage to produce effects in Portugal. (Arts. 1654 and 1664 et seq. C.C.).

MARRIED WOMEN:

See topic Husband and Wife.

MINES AND MINERALS:

The State owns all mineral deposits. (Art. 84 of Constitution). Licenses for prospecting are valid for five years for mineral deposits, and for three years for hydromineral or geothermal resources. (Art. 18 of D.L. 90/90 of 3.3.90). Before license has expired, definite concession can be applied for, which involves certain formalities. State may declare any given area closed to prospecting and grant exclusive licence to prospect to approved person or entity.

Subject to rules of Code on Foreign Investments, aliens may acquire mining concessions, but Mines Department must be satisfied as to identity of applicant and his having sufficient capital available to fulfill official work programme.

All transactions, such as sale, mortgage or lease of concessions, must have the previous approval of competent Minister in Government.

MONOPOLIES AND RESTRAINT OF TRADE:

See topic Restraint of Trade.

MORTGAGES:

A legal mortgage can be created over land and buildings, ships and motor vehicles as defined by Decree 21,087. Mortgage does not operate as a conveyance of property to mortgagee subject to an equity of redemption, but merely creates a legal charge which is enforced by sale through court on application for purpose.

Fixed plant and machinery are only covered by the mortgage where specifically referred to and described therein.

Priority of mortgages depends on date of registration.

MOTOR VEHICLES:

The law governing motor vehicles is contained principally in D.L. 54/75, and Decree 55/75 both of 12.2.75, Decree 130/82 of 27.11.82, and D.L. 522/85 of 31.12.85.

A licence (livrete) is issued by Technical Commission in whose records car is registered, and a Register of Automobile Property is kept for recording of ownership, mortgages, actions in rem, judicial attachments, transactions and charges on motor vehicles. A motor vehicle cannot be pledged but can be mortgaged. Insurance against third party risks is a condition precedent to registration of any mortgage or charge. Unpaid purchase price on sale enjoys a special legal charge or privilege on car, provided it is registered. On nonpayment of a secured credit, and on security being given by creditor, an order will be made for seizure of car.

Lorry and motor bus services are subject to special regulations.

NATIONALITY:

Portuguese nationality is attributable in accordance with Law 37/81 of 3.10.81, as am'd by Law 25/94 of 19.8.94, and D.L. 322/82 of 12.8.82, both as am'd by D.L. 253/94 of Oct. 20, 1994, to following persons:

(a) Children of Portuguese mother or father who are born in Portuguese territory, in territories under Portuguese administration, namely Macau and East-Timor, or born abroad whilst their Portuguese parent is in service of Portuguese State; (b) children of Portuguese mother or father born abroad who declare that they wish to be Portuguese; (c) persons born in Portugal with foreign parents, who have been legally resident in Portugal, for six or ten years (depending on whether they are nationals of former Portuguese colonies, or not), provided they are not in service of their own country and declare that they wish to be Portuguese; (d) persons born in Portuguese territory who have no other nationality.

Foreigners not born in Portugal may acquire Portuguese nationality by naturalization provided following requirements are met: they have legally resided in Portugal for six or ten years (depending on whether or not they are citizens of former Portuguese colonies); they are of full age; they are sufficiently acquainted with Portuguese language; they prove effective connection with Portuguese community and are of good repute; and finally if they are able to prove financial means to support themselves.

In some instances some of these requirements can be waived.

Foreigner who has been married to Portuguese citizen for more than three years may acquire Portuguese nationality if he/she declares they wish so to do during marriage.

NEGOTIABLE INSTRUMENTS:

See topic Bills and Notes.

NOTARIAL SERVICES:

Portuguese consuls abroad have notarial powers and can draw up and attest notarial documents and contracts.

See also topics Deeds; Principal and Agent.

NOTARIES PUBLIC:

See topics Acknowledgments, Deeds, Notarial Services, and Principal and Agent.

PARTITION:

Owners in common are at any time entitled to partition of property, unless community of property is in marriage, in legal association, or in common parts of a condominium in horizontal property. Co-owners may agree that property remains undivided for period not exceeding five years, renewable. (Art. 1412 C.C.).

PARTNERSHIP:

Principal characteristics of a Portuguese partnership are unlimited joint and several liability of partners for debts of firm, and possession by firm of a legal personality distinct from that of partners composing it. Death does not necessarily dissolve a partnership, but bankruptcy of firm involves bankruptcy of individual partners. Partnerships are subject to registration. (Arts. 175 et seq. C.C.C.).

See also topic Corporations, subhead Companies Limited by Shares.

Limited partnership is one in which the liability of one or some of the partners is restricted to a certain amount, the remainder being responsible without limit. Apart from the differences inherent in the limitation of liability, these associations are governed by the rules applicable to an ordinary partnership. The limited capital may be represented in the form of shares. (Arts. 465 et seq. C.C.C.).

PATENTS: See topic Trademarks and Patents.

PLEDGES:

To secure fulfilment of an obligation, debtor may constitute pledge of movables by delivering same for purpose, to creditor or to third party. Stock representing capital of stock company, and rights against transferable movables, may also, by special provision, be pledged. Pledges of rights are subject to formalities and publication under provisions to which rights themselves may be subject and are only allowed when rights pledged have as object movable and transmittable property. Pledge of credit is only effective after either through Court or otherwise notification to debtor or acceptance by debtor, unless article pledged is subject to registration, in which case it becomes effective upon registration. As rule, pledge must be sold by court so that creditor is paid out of respective proceeds. Parties may agree that sale be effected out of court or that article be adjudicated to creditor for value which court may establish. (Arts. 666 et seq. C.C.).

See also topic Motor Vehicles.

PRESCRIPTION AND LIMITATION OF ACTIONS:

Rights, as well as rights of action, may be lost by prescription, prescription period for former being 20 years (Arts. 309 et seq. C.C.), unless shorter period is specifically provided by law, e.g., for alimony pensions, rents, interest, dividends, etc. There are also procedural limitations on right to bring actions, e.g., actions on bills of exchange against acceptor must be brought within three years from date of falling due, this period not being subject to interruption as in case of prescription.

PRINCIPAL AND AGENT:

Relation of principal and agent is expressed in contract of "mandato" which is presumed in civil law to be gratuitous, where no remuneration is stipulated in contract and object thereof is not part of agent's regular business or profession. Amongst other duties, agent must comply with instructions of his principal, must give him information requested, must promptly inform his principal of execution of instructions or of reason for nonexecution, must render accounts and must deliver to his principal whatever he may have received in performing his duties. Principal is bound to supply his agent with necessary data to carry out instructions, to pay his agent agreed remuneration, if any, and to give him provision on account according to usages, to reimburse agent in respect of any expenses which agent may reasonably have considered necessary, with legal interest as from date they were incurred and to indemnify agent against any loss or damage arising therefrom, even if principal may not have been at fault. Acts in excess of agent's authority do not bind principal. (Arts. 1157 et seq. C.C.).

Contract between principal and agent is determined by (1) Revocation by either; (2) death or interdiction of either; (3) incapacity of principal if object of contract are acts which cannot be performed without intervention of curator.

In commercial law, agency agreement is governed by D.L. 178/86 of 3.7.86 as amended by D.L. 118/93 of 13.4.93, and is presumed to be for remuneration; its cancellation without proper cause gives rise to action for damages. Agent is entitled to lien on property of principal in his possession for purposes of agency.

Agent under contract of "mandato" may be entrusted with execution of his mandate without mention of his principal, contracting only in his own name. This is contract of "comissão" and is characterized by absence of privity between principal and person with whom agent contracts.

Powers of attorney written and signed by the donor whose handwriting and signature are recognized and certified by a notary, are valid. For certain purposes, such as alienating land and signing cheques, etc., the power of attorney must be either, written by notary or by grantor himself in presence of notary, who will subsequently attest both handwriting and signature of grantor. (Notarial Code as approved by D.L. 47619 of 31/3 and am'd by D.L. 67/90 of 1.3.90).

Powers of attorney issued to lawyers and contemplating forensic powers are subject to simplified certification formalities.

REAL PROPERTY:

See topic Records; also topics Acknowledgments; Deeds.

RECORDS:

All land is registrable and title can be verified by means of certificates from Land Registry.

Land Registry is governed by Immovable Property Registry Code as approved by D.L. 224/84 of 6.7.84 and as amended by D.L. 355/85 of 2.9.85 and Decree 60/90 of 14.2.90.

RESTRAINT OF TRADE:

Similar to existing EEC regulations, certain practices which may affect trade and competition are prohibited and subject to fines. Following are prohibited: (a) Agreements between undertakings, decisions by associations of undertakings and concerted practices adopted with view to preventing, distorting or restricting competition, such as: directly or indirectly fixing purchase or selling prices or other trading conditions; limiting or controlling production, distribution, technical development or investment; sharing markets or sources of supply; applying dissimilar prices or other conditions even though only occasionally; directly or indirectly refusing to buy or sell goods or services; making conclusion of contracts subject to acceptance of supplementary obligations; (b) any abuse by one or more undertakings of dominant position in market is also considered to be in restraint of trade; (c) further particular unlawful practices are also prohibited namely imposing either directly or indirectly minimum selling prices, except on certain goods or where officially authorised; applying dissimilar prices or conditions of sale to equivalent transactions; refusing to sell or provide services. (Competition Law, D.L. 422/83 of 3.12.83).

SALES:

Contract of sale is regulated by Arts. 874 to 938 of Civil Code and Arts. 463 to 476 of Commercial Code. Where thing sold is determined, property therein passes by virtue of contract, independently of delivery. Otherwise property does not pass until object is determined.

By Decree 19,490, on delivery of goods sold on credit, if bills of exchange are not issued, seller is bound to issue invoice accompanied by extract thereof which must be sent to buyer by registered letter or bearer within eight days of delivery and returned by buyer in like manner, agreed or corrected. Signed, or, where buyer has failed to sign, protested extract is indispensible for any action for price. Provisions relating to bills of exchange (see topic Bills and Notes) are applicable to extracts except where inconsistent therewith.

Warranties.—In principle vendor warrants suitability of goods for purchaser's purposes as known to vendor. Sales of goods against sample or of a recognized standard carry corresponding warranties, otherwise sales conditional upon examination by purchaser who must make quality claim within eight days of delivery. Claims for hidden defects must be made within 30 days of discovery and within six months of delivery.

In buildings, claims on hidden defects must be lodged within one year of discovery, warranty being valid for five years. (Art. 1225 C.C.).

Notices.—See subhead Warranties, supra.

Applicable Law.—See topic Contracts, subhead Applicable Law.

SHIPPING:

The substantive provisions of the maritime law are contained in the Act of Navigation of 1863, arts. 485 to 540 and 574 to 698 of Commercial Code as well as Decree-Laws 349/86, of Oct. 17, 1986 and 191/87 of Apr. 29, 1987. There are in addition numerous decrees regulating construction, equipment and general conditions of safety of vessels.

Questions affecting the property in, liens on, and mortgages of a ship are governed by the law of the ship's nationality.

Portugal is a signatory of Brussels Convention of Aug. 25, 1924, relating to bills of lading, and of Brussels Convention of Apr. 10, 1926, relating to privileges. See topic Corporations.

Maritime Courts were created by Law nr. 35/86, of Sept. 4, 1986.

STATUTES:

Foundations of substantive civil law are contained in Civil Code, in Commercial Code and in Code of Commercial Companies. Some matters of civil law such as lease contracts, labour relations and others, as well as many matters of commercial law such as bills of exchange, promissory notes and cheques, banking and credit regulations, insurance matters, etc. are contained in various other enactments, in form of Decrees and Laws.

Court procedure, both civil and commercial, is governed by Code of Civil Procedure approved by Decree-Law 44,129 of Dec. 31, 1961 which came into force on Apr. 24, 1962, and subsequent alterations.

Organization of judicial courts is contained in Law 38/87, of Dec. 23, 1987 as amended by Law 24/90 of Aug. 4, 1990. Notarial services are regulated by "Codigo do Notariado" promulgated by Decree-Law 207/95 of Aug. 14, 1995, as amended by Decree-Law 40/96 of May 7, 1996. There are also codes governing Land Registry, Commercial Registry, Civil Registry and Foreign Investment.

TAXATION:

There are three basic taxes on earnings: (a) IRS—personal income tax, (b) IRC—corporation tax, (c) CA—local authority tax.

IRS is due by individuals residing in Portugal and by nonresidents with income arising in Portugal. Tax is based on net profits of each category of income namely: (i) Salaries; (ii) earnings of liberal professions; (iii) agricultural, industrial or commercial activity when carried out by individuals; (iv) capital gains; (v) immovable property (rents received by owners); (vi) applied or invested capital; (vii) retirement pensions; (viii) gambling. Rate of tax is variable and on sliding scale, taking into consideration whether taxpayer is single or married and amount of earnings of each spouse, in latter case, percentagewise. In 1996 for net income of over 6,000,000 escudos, rate of tax is approximately 40%; for net income of up to 1,010,000 escudos rate is 15%. Interim tax rates are 25% and 35%.

IRS due by taxpayers whose earnings arise from exercise of liberal professions, earnings of immovable property, etc., are subject to withholding tax, generally on account at rate of 15%; interest on bank deposits is subject to 20% withholding tax.

IRC.—See topic Corporations.

With respect to taxes in arrears State enjoys privileged position over all other creditors whether secured or unsecured.

See Topical Index in front part of this volume.

TAXATION . . . *continued*

CA.—Local authority tax "Contribuição Autárquica".

Rate is 0.8% for rural property and between 0.8% and 1.0% for urban property although this may be altered each year by competent municipal assembly.

See also topic Domicile.

Other forms of taxation are:

Value Added Tax.—Known in Portuguese as "Imposto Sobre Valor Acrescentado" (IVA). This is similar to existing European Union "VAT" regulations, and was introduced by Decree-Law 394-B/84 of 26 Dec. 84 in order to replace transaction tax and other small indirect taxes. Following are subject to IVA: Supply of goods and provision of services against payment in territory, by taxable person; importation of goods. Unless specifically exempt, every taxable person whose annual income exceeds Esc. 1,500,000. Basic rate is 17% but in certain cases reduced rate of 5% is applicable.

S&GD—Succession and Gift Duty.—"Imposto Sobre Sucessões e Doações" is applied on sliding scale to value of asset(s) transferred on death or by gift inter vivos. Rates of duty depend on degree of relationship between deceased/donor and person receiving bequest legacy or gift.

Land Transfer Tax.—("SISA") is levied on value of: (a) Rural property at rate of 8%; (b) urban property and building plots at basic rate of 10%. (If exclusively for dwelling purposes, is exempted up to 10,400,000 escudos and rates of 5% to 26% for values of more than Esc: 10,400,000 to Esc: 28,900,000. If more than Esc.: 28,900,000, rate is 10%.)

Social Security.—Contribution is levied since Oct. 1, 1986 on all salaries or wages at rate of 23.75% payable by employer and 11% payable by wage earner. (Decree-Law 140-D/86, of June 14, 1986).

TRADEMARKS AND PATENTS:

The protection and registration of trademarks, tradenames, trade awards, and trade designs and models, patents of invention, patents of introduction of new industries, patents of introduction of new industrial processes, are dealt with under the general heading of Industrial Property which is governed by D.L. 16/95 of Jan. 24, 1995, which is in force since June 1, 1995.

Portugal is a signatory to the Convention of 1883 for the protection of industrial property and to the Conventions of 1891 for the international registration of marks and the suppression of false indications of origin.

Portugal is also signatory of June 19, 1970 Washington's Patent Cooperation Treaty, and of Munich Convention on European Trademarks of Oct. 5, 1973.

TREATIES:

Portugal is member State of European Community EEC. It also has commercial treaties with several other foreign countries and in some cases such as with Great Britain treaties to avoid double taxation. Portugal is also party to certain conventions on service and taking of evidence abroad on civil and commercial matters but not to United Nations Convention on Recognition and Enforcement of Foreign Arbitral Awards. See also Selected International Conventions section.

TRUSTS:

Not known to Portuguese law as a rule, but exceptionally provided for Madeira offshore interests according to Decree-Law 352A/88 of Oct. 3, 1988.

WILLS:

There are two principal kinds of will, public and sealed. (Arts. 2204 et seq. C.C.). Public will is one written in books of, and executed before, public notary in presence of two witnesses. A sealed will is handwritten and executed before notary and two witnesses and endorsed with formal notarial act of approval. (Arts. 116 to 126 of Notarial Code).

Joint wills are not permitted. (Art. 2181 C.C.).

Wills made abroad by Portuguese citizens in accordance with foreign competent law only produce effects in Portugal if form observed in their execution or approval was solemn. (Art. 2223 C.C.). Generally wills made abroad are deemed to be valid as to form if in accordance with law of place where made or with personal law of testator, either at moment of execution or at moment of death or in accordance with law to which local rule of conflicts of laws may refer matter. If, however, personal law of testator prescribes, at date of execution, observance of certain formalities, under pain of nullity or ineffectiveness, even though execution takes place abroad such formalities must be observed. (Art. 65 C.C.). Intrinsic validity of will of foreigner is governed by personal law of testator. (Arts. 62 and 63 C.C.). See topic Descent and Distribution.

ROMANIA LAW DIGEST REVISER

Hall, Dickler (Romania) SRL
World Trade Center
Bulevardul Expozitiei, nr. 2; Suite 2.25
78334 Bucharest, Romania
Telephone: (40) (1) 222-8888
Fax: (40) (1) 223-4444

New York Offices: Hall Dickler Kent Friedman & Wood, 909 Third Avenue, New York 10022. Telephone: 212-339-5400. Fax: 212-935-3121. 11 Martine Avenue, White Plains 10606. Telephone: 914-428-3232. Fax: 914-428-1660.

California Office: Hall Dickler Kent Friedman & Wood, 2029 Century Park East, Los Angeles 90067. Telephone: 310-203-8410. Fax: 310-203-8559.

Reviser Profile

History and General Description: Founded in 1934, Hall Dickler Kent Friedman & Wood is a New York-based general practice law firm best known for its work in several primary practice areas, which include: Corporate and Securities, Litigation, Intellectual Property, Taxation, Trust & Estates, Employment Law, Real Estate, Advertising, Marketing and International Law. The firm's Arts and Entertainment Law practice is based in Los Angeles, California.

Eastern European Practice: Hall Dickler Kent Friedman & Wood was the first major Western law firm to open offices in Romania, known as Hall Dickler (Romania) SRL, and is presently the only American law firm with offices in the country. The firm maintains a permanent Bucharest-based staff of ten, including American and Romanian attorneys and, in addition, offers the depth of Hall Dickler's operations in New York and Los Angeles. Bucharest regularly consults the Corporate, International Tax and Real Estate departments in New York in structuring multimillion dollar joint venture projects.

Hall Dickler represents the most important foreign and multinational investors in Romania. The firm advises major Romanian commercial companies involved in international transactions and provides ongoing assistance to foreign-owned companies and joint ventures already operating in Romania. Hall Dickler's expertise in economic, legislative and judicial issues, and its relationships with government officials, enables it to act authoritatively on a client's behalf.

A representative list of Hall Dickler's Bucharest clients includes: ABC Capital Cities (USA), Apple Computer Europe SA (France), Banca Ion Tiriac (Romania; the largest private bank in Romania), BASF Aktiengesellschaft (Germany), CanWest International (Canada), CelmagSPA (Italian steel company; the third largest foreign investor in Romania), Coca-Cola Company and the Coca-Cola bottlers (USA, Austria, Ireland & Turkey; collectively the largest foreign investor in Romania), Computer Associates (USA; software), Confex International SA (Romania; clothing manufacturer), Daewoo Group (Korea; potentially the largest foreign investor), DHL Romania, Digital Equipment (France), Daimler-Benz AG (Germany), Heineken BV (The Netherlands), Imhoos & Partners (Switzerland), ING Bank (The Netherlands), MI Drilling (USA; petroleum related services), Mars Inc. (Germany), RJ Reynolds (Switzerland), Royal Dutch/Shell Group (The Netherlands), Tarom SA (Romania's international airline), Young and Rubicam (USA) and many others. We list these names with their permission.

Hall Dickler's attorneys and the other consultants working with the firm are recognized among Romania's leading international commercial advisors. Hall Dickler's Eastern European practice is headed by Dr. Victor Tanasescu (Advocat and Member of the Bar of Bucharest), who was formerly Chief Counsel to the Romanian Ministry of Foreign Trade, where he supervised and participated in high-level international commercial matters involving Romanian and foreign businesses. He is one of a select group of Romanian arbitrators approved by the International Chamber of Commerce and has authored, co-authored, or edited approximately 25 books and studies concerning joint ventures, foreign investment, contractual relations, and licensing.

The attorneys and support staff at Hall Dickler (Romania) SRL are fluent in Romanian, French, English, Russian, Italian and German. The firm maintains a modern, fully-equipped and computerized office in Bucharest.

Hall Dickler's international practice involves counselling on Romania's national laws, as well as on such matters as the U.S. Foreign Corrupt Practices Act, the U.N. Convention on Contracts for the International Sale of Goods, and International Arbitration Arrangements. The firm assists inbound clients in compliance with Federal and State disclosure requirements and restrictions on U.S. acquisitions. Project investments are reviewed from the standpoint of insurance coverage under programs of agencies such as the Overseas Private Investment Corporation, and the Multi-Lateral Investment Guaranty Agency.

Hall Dickler also assists clients in obtaining financing for their projects from international financial institutions such as European Bank for Reconstruction and Development and the Export/Import Bank of the United States.

ROMANIA LAW DIGEST

(The following is a list of all Topics, including cross-references, covered in this Digest.)

ROMANIA LAW DIGEST

Revised for 1997 edition by

HALL DICKLER KENT FRIEDMAN & WOOD of the Bucharest, New York and White Plains, NY and Los Angeles, CA bars.

(Civ. Code indicates Civil Code; Civ. Pro. Code indicates Civil Procedure Code; Com. Code indicates Commercial Code; Fam. Code indicates Family Code.)

ABSENTEES:

Every natural person possesses rights and duties. (Romanian Constitution; Decree No. 31/1954 and Decree No. 32/1954, both modified by Law No. 4/1956; Family Code, as adopted by Law No. 4/1954 and subsequently modified; Decree No. 212/1974 for ratification of the International Agreement on Human, Civil and Political Rights; and Law No. 18/1990 for the ratification of the International Convention on Children's Rights). Person's capacity to exercise such rights and duties begins at birth and terminates at death. (Decree No. 31/1954 art. 7). Death may be ascertained directly, physically, or by court decision subsequent to judicial declaration that person is absentee (see also topic Death [Presumption Of and Actions For]).

Declaration of Absence.—Person missing from his residence may be declared absent in court, and curator named, provided that one year has passed since most recent recorded evidence demonstrating absentee to be alive. (Decree No. 31/1954 art. 16). Initiation of court action for declaration cannot be made prior to end of requisite one-year period.

One-year period is calculated as follows: (1) from date of most recently recorded evidence regarding absentee—relying on oral and written testimony; (2) if date of last sighting cannot be established with precision, then from last day of month when such recent evidence was recorded; or (3) from last day of year when such recent evidence was recorded. (Decree No. 31/1954 art. 17).

Declaration Procedure.—Procedure for declarations of absence is stipulated in Decree No. 32/1954. First, requests for declaration are made to Court located in absentee's last known domicile. (Decree No. 32/1954 art. 36 and Civ. Pro. Code art. 2 par. 1, modified by Law No. 59/1993). Second, President of the Court orders local council (city hall) and police to gather as much information as possible about absentee. (Decree No. 32/1954 art. 37). Third, request for declaration of absence is posted by judicial order at absentee's last known domicile and at city hall to allow those with relevant information to report it to proper authorities. President of the Court may also assign custodians in city hall with task of naming curator in conformity with Fam. Code art. 152. Curator will temporarily protect interests of absentee.

Within 45 days from posting of notice, public hearing is scheduled and following parties are called: person to be declared absent (at his last domicile), attorney (if applicable) or trustee (if no attorney exists) and representatives of city hall. Hearing takes place after conclusions of Prosecutor's Office are heard. Finally, public hearing is held to announce judicial decision, which is appealable to Court of Appeals within 15 days. (Civ. Pro. Code art. 284).

Once final, decision is posted for 30 days on door of court and of city hall in municipality where absentee last resided. Decision may be communicated to department of custodial authorities for purpose of naming curator, if this was not done at trial. (Decree No. 32/1954 art. 39).

Legal Effect.—Declaration of absence has no effect on absentee's rights and duties since that person is considered alive until final judicial declaration of death has been rendered. (Decree No. 31/1954 art. 19).

Naming curator for absentee or trustee for minors of absentee is not subject to declaration of absence since measures involving legal protection of persons and property require only actual existence of absence.

Foreign citizens declared absent pursuant to Law No. 105/1992 (regarding regulation of private international law relations) which stipulates that conditions, effects and annulment of decision assuming death or absence, as well as decisions regarding presumption of survival or death, are determined by current national law of absentee, or, in absence of identifiable laws, Romanian law will apply. (art. 16).

ACKNOWLEDGMENT:

Acknowledgment is declaration by which person affirms right or obligation alleged against him or fact which his opponent depends upon in legal procedure. It is unilateral act of free will which may constitute means of evidence. For example, debtor acknowledges debt or detainment of chattels or creditor acknowledges payment affirmed and made by debtor.

Acknowledgment is regulated by Civ. Code arts. 1204-1206, relating to indebtedness and payment. Procedural process for acknowledgment is regulated by section concerning administration of evidence, Civ. Pro. Code arts. 218-225.

To be effective, acknowledgment must be made according to following: (a) with awareness and free will, acknowledging importance and sincerity of act which may result in legal consequences against declarant; (b) as unilateral act of free will which is irrevocable, with exception of mistake of fact; (c) only made in relation to rights belonging to declarant and only by that party or by special mandate; and (d) it must be express and cannot be inferred by party's silence.

In addition, under Civ. Pro. Code art. 225, judge has right to imply that declarant's unjustified refusal to appear at interrogation, or to answer question at interrogation, constitutes acknowledgment.

Acknowledgment may be written or oral and can be made before judge or extrajudicially.

Written acknowledgment is subject to general laws concerning written evidence. (Civ. Code arts. 1171-1190; Civ. Pro. Code arts. 172-185).

Documents are considered means of executing acknowledgments, made with intention to produce legal results and to serve as previously established evidentiary material.

Oral, out-of-court acknowledgments cannot be used as evidence when agreement's subject cannot be proved by witnesses. (Civ. Code art. 1205).

ACTIONS:

Action enables party to obtain, in court, realization or recognition of rights and civil interests guaranteed by law.

Romanian Constitution grants individuals free access to justice in order to defend their legitimate rights, liberties and interests. Law may not restrain exercise of this right. (art. 21).

Besides right of plaintiff to file suit, action includes right of defendant to respond and defend himself and to file counterclaims. It also implies other activities and procedural possibilities, such as: right to ask for conservation (guarantee) measures, right to contest award through appeal or recourse (appeal, recourse) and right to request forced execution of award.

According to aim of claimant, actions may be regarded as following: (1) actions for realization of right; (2) actions for assessment of right; and (3) actions for constitution of rights. According to nature of claimed rights, actions may be personal (action for payment of sold merchandise), real (action for possession of a good) and mixed. Object claimed by action may be movable or fixed.

Summoning of Parties Before Court.—According to Civil Procedure Code art. 112, summons must contain, inter alia: (a) name and domicile of parties; (b) object of claim and if possible its value; (c) legal and factual basis of claim; (d) evidence; and (e) claimant's signature.

Generally, at trial level, proper venue and jurisdiction is granted in Law Court of territory where defendant's domicile is located. In cases of real estate litigation, jurisdiction is granted to Court where such real estate is located. If domicile of defendant is unknown, jurisdiction belongs to Court where domicile of plaintiff is located. In addition, Romania also has tribunals, appeal courts and Supreme Court of Justice. Material and territorial competence of courts is established by Civ. Pro. Code arts. 1-19. Role, composition and functions of courts and of Public Ministry, as well as status of magistrates, are provided in Law No. 92/1992, regarding organization of courts.

Actual summons, along with annexed documents, are provided to defendant. Within 30 days, defendant may submit answer which includes: (a) procedural exceptions regarding claimant's request; (b) legal and factual basis of answer contesting elements of plaintiff's claim; and (c) defendant's signature. (Civ. Pro. Code art. 115).

Written evidence must be attached to summons, as well as to defendant's answer. If witnesses are requested to appear before court, their names and addresses must also be included.

Court fees for issuing summons are established by Government Resolution No. 1295/1990, as amended and Government Ordinance No. 10/1993. Summons for claims requesting money damages are taxed by 8% of amount claimed if claim exceeds 25,000 lei; and 10% if claim exceeds 100,000 lei. Stamp duty for summons provided by Law No. 76/1992 regarding incapacity of payment is 10,000 lei, irrespective of value of debt.

International Private Law.—Law No. 105/1992 regarding settling of international private law relations also establishes procedural norms for actions involving foreign parties. (arts. 158-162). Such norms refer to procedural requirements, object and cause of action, modality of adjudicating civil action, and evidence that may be used in international private law actions, including administration of such evidence.

Romanian courts apply domestic procedural law in actions involving foreign citizens. Romanian law also determines whether legal issue pertains to procedural or substantive law. (Law No. 105/1992, art. 159). Capacity of each party to stand trial is governed by party's national law. (Law No. 105/1992, art. 158).

Object and cause of civil action are determined by law regulating background of legal relationship. Procedures applicable in trying parties are also determined by same law. (art. 160). Evidentiary material for proving legal act and proving capacity of written document which acknowledges legal act are provided by law of place where legal act was signed, or by law chosen by parties. Proof regarding facts is determined according to law of place where such facts occurred. (art. 161).

ADOPTION:

Requirements.—Adoption establishes kinship similar to that existing in natural kinship. Requirements for legally concluding adoptions are as follows: (1) Adoption must be made solely in interest of adoptive child (Fam. Code art. 66); (2) adoptive child must be minor—except where that person is now adult but was raised while minor by adoptive parents (art. 67); (3) adoptive parent must be of legal age (art. 117), and there must be age differential of at least 18 years between adoptive child and adoptive parent (art. 68). For well-founded reasons, age differential may be reduced—for example, married woman wishing to adopt who has not reached age of 18; (4) adoptive parents must provide consent, and if adoptive child is minor, child's natural parents must provide consent, as well as adoptive child if such child is at least ten years of age.

Adoption between brothers and sisters is not permitted, nor is adoption between spouses. (Fam. Code art. 67). Only one person may adopt child, except when both husband and wife adopt concurrently or successively. (art. 69).

Jurisdiction.—Courts of law have jurisdiction to rule on adoption applications. (Law No. 11/1990, as completed and modified in 1995). Application for adoption shall be submitted to court of law where adoptive parent resides. In case of orphan committed to child care institution, application shall be submitted to court of law where that institution is located. If application is made by foreign citizen or Romanian citizen domiciled abroad, it shall be submitted to court of law where adoptive child resides. If adoptive child is Romanian citizen domiciled abroad, application shall be submitted to Bucharest City tribunal. (art. 1 par. 4).

See Topical Index in front part of this volume.

ADOPTION . . . *continued*

In order to supervise adoptions, aid minors during adoption, and promote international cooperation in this area, Romanian Committee for Adoptions ("RCA") was founded. Foreigners and Romanian citizens domiciled abroad may only adopt children registered with RCA, who have not been placed for adoption or have not been adopted in Romania for at least six months prior to registration.

Application Documents and Procedure.—Following documents pertaining to adoptive child must be submitted with adoption application: (1) birth certificate in legalized form; (2) marriage or death certificate of natural parents in legalized form; (3) notarized declaration of consent given by natural parents or legal guardians; (4) medical certificate regarding minor's state of health; and (5) confirmation by RCA that minor has been registered in its register and will be permitted to enter and reside in adoptive state. (Law No. 11/1990 art. 4).

Following documents must be submitted by adoptive parent: (1) notarized written declaration indicating whether adoptive parent requests adoption with total application or one with restricted application (see Law No. 11/1990 as republished, art. 5); (2) birth and marriage certificates in legalized form; (3) certificates regarding adoptive parents' criminal records; (4) certificates pertaining to adoptive parents' state of health; (5) for foreigners or Romanians domiciled abroad, document issued by competent foreign authorities stating that such person may adopt child according to laws of foreign country; and (7) social inquest from competent foreign authorities containing opinion regarding requested adoption.

Application will be heard in council room before panel of two judges, representative of Public Ministry, persons stipulated under Fam. Code art. 70, Prosecutor, and in cases of international adoptions, representative from RCA. Those who have legitimate interest in adoption may intervene in proceeding. (art. 9). If adoptive parent or child is foreigner, each is subject to their national laws concerning basic conditions for concluding adoptions, provided they do not conflict with Romanian private international law (see Law No. 105/1992—§III). Adoption is approved by means of court ruling, subject to contest in accordance with Civ. Pro. Code.

Legal Effect.—Adoptive child receives name of adoptive parent. (Fam. Code art. 78). If spouses adopt child, child will have their common name and if spouses have different names they shall decide upon name.

Adoption is final on date court ruling becomes final. Adoption creates civil kinship which differs depending on whether adoption with restricted application or with total application has been granted. For adoption with restricted application, civil kinship is established between adoptive child, his descendants, and adoptive parents. However, kinship is not established between adoptive child, and relatives of adoptive parents. For adoption with total application, civil kinship is established between adoptive child, descendants of adoptive child, adoptive parents, and relatives of adoptive parents.

Request to nullify adoption may be submitted to court if in best interests of adoptive child (Fam. Code art. 81), and only by adoptive child, natural parents, or pertinent child care institutions. If adoption is declared null and void, adoptive child acquires former name, or may keep adopted name if well-founded reasons exist.

AFFIDAVIT:

Romanian law makes no specific provisions for affidavits. Under corresponding Romanian procedural law, sworn declaration with judicial evidentiary value is made only before judge presiding over civil or criminal case. However, if affidavit corresponding with foreign law is introduced in court, it may be used as evidence under Law No. 105/1992, concerning private international law relations, which provides that means of authenticating legal document, as well as its evidentiary value, are governed by laws of country where document was executed. Findings of fact are governed by law of country where affidavit is introduced.

Rulings on evidence presented in sworn declarations or affidavits (e.g. credibility of witness's testimony) are subject to Romanian procedural law.

To be introduced before Romanian court, affidavits must also be authenticated by respective foreign authorities and, subsequently, either by diplomatic mission or by respective country's consular office in Romania. Additionally, they must also be reviewed and stamped by Romanian Ministry of Foreign Affairs. It is not necessary to provide further authentication where respective countries have adopted reciprocity agreement with respect to documents formulated according to laws of each country.

AGENCY:

Definition.—Agency refers to legal relationship whereby agent is authorized to act on behalf of principal for some legal affair, binding principal with respect to third parties.

Authority and Classification.—Civil agency, relating to performance of civil acts, is regulated by Civil Code arts. 1532-1559. Commercial agency, which covers conducting business affairs on behalf of principal, is governed by Com. Code arts. 347-407.

Agency falls under several categories: (a) general, where it implies all operations (administrative acts) of concern to principal, or particular, when one or more specific acts are performed on behalf of principal; (b) representative, where agent acts nomine alieno, on behalf of principal, or nonrepresentative, when agent acts on principal's account without executing act in his own name, as is common in commercial context (e.g. shipping contract, consignment contract); (c) gratuitous (especially in case of civil agency), or for consideration (usually in case of commercial agency), unless otherwise stipulated.

Agency contract must meet same formality requirements as required for general contracts by Civil Code arts. 948-968 (e.g. capacity to conclude contract, valid consent, definite object, legal cause).

Agency contracts are consensual, becoming effective through simple agreement of parties, and may be written, verbal, or implied by law. (Civ. Code art. 1533). Usually, agency is granted through written instrument (power of attorney, authorization, delegation) in which powers and limits of agency are set forth. Notarized power of attorney is necessary if law requires that act be concluded by agent. In order to represent principal in Court, agent must be attorney.

Duties of Parties.—Agent has following duties: (a) To execute, in good faith, duties of agency according to contract and principal's reasonable instructions; (b) to provide evidence to principal that duties have been fulfilled according to mandate. (Civ. Code art. 1541, Com. Code art. 382).

Principal has following duties: (a) To put at agent's disposal means necessary for fulfilling agency (Com. Code art. 385); (b) to compensate agent as agreed (Com. Code art. 386); (c) to reimburse agent for reasonable expenses incurred while performing within scope of agency (Com. Code arts. 1547 and 1549).

Legal Effect.—In concluding legal act, agent establishes direct legal relationship between principal and third party, as if principal had acted directly. Unauthorized acts concluded by agent do not bind principal, except where principal ratifies act, expressly or as implied by law. (Civ. Code art. 1546). When ratification is provided, principal is responsible to third party, unless third party accepted execution of legal act knowing that it was beyond limits of agent's power. (Civ. Code art. 1545).

Termination.—Agency terminates upon: (1) revocation; (2) unilateral termination by agent; (3) death of either principal or agent; (4) court decree of interdiction; and (5) insolvency and bankruptcy of principal or agent. (Civ. Code art. 1552). Party which unjustifiably revokes agency and breaches its accompanying duties shall be responsible for damages. (Com. Code art. 391).

Private International Law.—According to Law No. 105/1992, law of state in which agent enjoys authority applies in agency relationships, even in absence of express agreement between agent and principal. If agent utilizes professional title in performance of his duties, law of jurisdiction where agent's professional office is located will apply. (art. 93). Relations between principal and third party are submitted, unless otherwise agreed, to law of jurisdiction where agent's professional office is located. (art. 95). In exercising authority, agent must also comply with laws of state where agency is peformed. (art. 97). Representation, concerning administrative acts or acts of alienation regarding immovable property, is governed by law of situs of property. (art. 100).

ALIENS:

According to Law No. 25/1969, aliens are foreign or stateless persons without Romanian citizenship who have same fundamental rights as Romanian citizens with exception of political rights, civil rights and those rights recognized by international agreements signed by Romania. (Law No. 25/1969 art. 1). General protection of aliens and their assets is guaranteed by Constitution art. 18.

As with Romanian citizens, aliens must exercise their rights and constitutional liberties in good faith without violating rights and liberties of others; and they must respect laws of Romania. (Constitution art. 54; Law No. 25/1969 art. 1).

Romania's national policy, which provides aliens with civil rights similar to those enjoyed by Romanian citizens, has certain restrictions. For example, aliens do not have rights to own real property. (Constitution art. 41). Also, aliens employed to work in foreign investment-related activities may not be employed in nonmanagerial positions, but only in managerial and specialty positions. (Law No. 35/1991 art. 31; Decree No. 9 of Dec. 3, 1989 repealed requirement for authorization of mixed marriages).

Aliens, whether individuals or businesses, have same procedural rights and obligations as Romanian individuals or businesses relating to Romanian legal actions. In court, foreign citizens benefit from procedures of private international law relations, exemptions or tax reductions, free legal assistance, equally and under same conditions as Romanian citizens, under reciprocity agreements between Romania and country of citizenship or domicile of parties at trial. Under these reciprocal arrangements, claimant with foreign citizenship cannot be required to post bail or any other guarantee on basis that he is foreigner, is not domiciled in Romania, or does not have place of business in Romania. (Law No. 105/1992, concerning regulation of private international law relations, art. 163).

ARBITRATION AND AWARD:

Provisions.—Arbitration is regulated by provisions of Book IV of Civ. Pro. Code arts. 340-370, as modified by Law No. 59/1993.

Main feature of Law No. 59/1993 is parties' contractual freedom, i.e., parties are free to use arbitration and, when choosing arbitration, to organize it as they wish. However, limitation placed upon parties choosing arbitration requires that they not elude laws concerning public order and good morals. (Civ. Code art. 5).

Composition of arbitration court is determined by interested parties, who decide whether litigation shall be adjudicated by one or more arbitrators. (Civ. Pro. Code art. 345). Arbitrators are appointed or replaced according to established conventions governing arbitration. (art. 347). Time, place and related payment of expenses of arbitration are established by parties. (arts. 353, 354, and 359, para. 1).

Several restrictions in Book IV bind parties: (a) provisions of art. 340, regarding capacity to establish arbitral convention and domain of litigations capable of being resolved by arbitration according to which only patrimonial litigation may be submitted to arbitration, provided that they refer to rights which parties can waive and (b) provisions of art. 358 regarding fundamental principles of arbitral procedure (equal treatment, observance of right to defense). Any infringement thereof constitutes grounds for annulment of arbitral convention.

Arbitration Decision.—New regulations establish in detail methods for adopting arbitral decision and its contents. (c. VII, arts. 360-360[3]).

Value and effects of arbitration involve three stages: (1) from its pronouncement, arbitration decision is obligatory for parties and becomes res judicata, without any other requirements; (2) from its communication, arbitration decision has effect of court's final decision (art. 363 par. 3); (3) once granted executory status by competent judicial body, arbitration decision constitutes executory title and may be executed in same manner as court decision (art. 368).

Termination.—According to art. 364, arbitration decision may be overturned for following reasons: (a) litigation was not capable of being solved through arbitration; (b) no arbitral convention existed or convention was null or inoperative convention; (c) arbitral court was not constituted in conformity with arbitral convention; (d) party was absent at hearing and summoning procedure was not legally accomplished; (e) decision was pronounced after expiration of arbitration time period provided by art.

ARBITRATION AND AWARD . . . *continued*
353[3] (i.e. five months from constitution of arbitral court, unless parties agreed otherwise); (f) arbitration court pronounced itself upon causes that were not required or did not pronounce itself upon required cause, or it awarded more than was requested; (g) arbitral decision did not include ruling and underlying motives, did not provide time and place of pronouncement, or is not signed by arbitrators; (h) disposition of arbitral decision includes dispositions that cannot be met; (i) arbitral decision infringes public order, good morals or imperative dispositions of law.

Competence to render decision in action for annulment belongs to judicial court immediately above those competent for arbitrations. Decisions in this instance may be contested only through appeal. (arts. 365-366).

Institutional Arbitration.—Book IV refers to institutional arbitration, i.e., arbitration organized by permanent institution of arbitration, which is form of arbitration aimed at facilitating resolution of litigations. For instance, International Commercial Arbitration Court of Bucharest which was founded in 1953 and reorganized by Decree 139/1990 regarding Chambers of Commerce and Industry. In other major cities of country, there are arbitration commissions affiliated with county Chambers of Commerce and Industry, which possess competence for adjudicating commercial litigations, provided parties have concluded arbitral convention.

International Arbitration: Recognition and Execution of Foreign Arbitral Decision.—In order to benefit from power of res judicata, foreign arbitral awards in Romania must be recognized in accordance with provisions of Law No. 105/1992 arts. 167-172, regarding regulation of international legislation relations.

Foreign arbitral decisions not carried out by those obliged to execute them, can be enforced within territory of Romania, in accordance with provisions of Law No. 105/1944 arts. 173-177, provided, inter alia, that: decision is final and not subject to appeal according to State where it was granted; court which granted award was competent to settle litigation; there is reciprocity regarding enforcement of foreign arbitral awards between Romania and that State.

International Conventions.—Romania is party to 1923 Geneva Protocol regarding arbitral clauses (ratified by Law of Mar. 21, 1925) and to 1972 Geneva Convention for Executing Foreign Arbitral Conventions (ratified by Law of Mar. 26, 1931). Romania is also party to following conventions: 1958 New York Convention for the Recognition and Execution of Foreign Arbitral Decisions (ratified by Decree No. 186/1961); European Convention of International Commercial Arbitration (Geneva 1961) (ratified by Decree No. 218/1961); Convention for Resolving Legal Actions Related to Investments (Washington 1965) (ratified by Decree No. 62/1975).

ASSIGNMENT:

Under Romanian law, assignments may have credit, debt or right as their object.

Assignment of credit is contract by which assigning creditor, or assignor, transfers his rights to receive credit to another person—assignee. Debtor of assignable credit, who is referred to as assigned debtor, is third party so that assignment is fulfilled without his participation. Assigned debtor continues to have obligations for which he is responsible to assignee, provided that assigned debtor is notified about assignment. Otherwise, assigned debtor shall continue to be responsible to assignor. Assignment is usually performed for valid consideration, and is regulated by Civ. Code sections relating to sales, art. 1391 et seq.

Since assignment is contract, it must meet all of conditions required for valid contract, as well as conditions pertaining to sales, payments, and donations. In principle, all credits are assignable, including but not limited to those credits which have amount of money as their object. Assignments are made by agreement between assignor and assignee. Generally, assignment may be confirmed by third party when debtor is given notice. Assignment of credit, nominative or upon order, is valid, regardless of whether or not notice is given, as it is made upon registration of assignment for purposes of expediency.

Legal Effect.—Goal of assignments is to transfer credit to assignee's property at its nominal value, including all rights assignor possessed in relation to assigned debtor. Assignee becomes creditor in lieu of assignor, taking over latter's rights to receive credit. Credit itself remains unchanged; it maintains it nature (civil or commercial), as well as guarantees (which ensure fulfillment of obligation and establishment of interest rate). Assignor guarantees existence of credit, and its validity, when assignment is executed. This legal guarantee is implied when there is no clause in contract which refers to guarantee, but is not operational where contract would have excluded obligation to provide guarantee. However, assignor guarantees neither debtor's solvency nor efficacy of credit guarantees, except if otherwise agreed upon, and then, only for debtor's solvency at time of assignment and only within limits of price received.

Assignment of debt is contract by which assigning debtor, obligor, transfers his debt obligations to assignee, who is then charged to fulfill obligor's duties to creditor, or obligee. Such assignment requires obligee's consent, since debt becomes personal contract governed by assignee's solvency and abilities as administrator. Assignment of debt is not regulated by Romanian legislation, but is permitted under principle of "freedom of conventions". Once obligee agrees to assignment of debt, resultant obligations are transferred from obligor, or former debtor, to delegatee. That delegatee may submit to obligee all exceptions to previous relationship between obligor and obligee, except those which are personal.

Assignment of right is transfer of right upon parties' will or in accordance with law, from initial holder of that right, assignor, to assignee. Example of assignment of right is assignment of industrial or technological rights such as patents. Assignment may be final or temporary, total or partial. In general, civil law provisions relating to sales are applied to assignments when there is no specific regulation.

ASSOCIATIONS:

Citizens are equal before law and public authorities with regard to privileges and discriminations (Constitution arts. 16-1, 137-1 c), and enjoy right to enter into associations irrespective of sex, race, nationality, religion, culture or origin. Association is governed by Law No. 21/1924 regarding legal persons and Decree No. 31 of 1954 relating to Natural and Legal Persons, as modified by Law No. 4/1956.

Associations.—Association is body of persons organized for specific purpose, having its own charter and general form, and procedural framework of company. It is agreement whereby many persons pool their property, material resources and activities, on permanent basis, to realize certain nonprofit purpose. Purpose of association may be purely theoretical, or it may represent general interests of group as whole or in part, or it may represent associates' personal non-patrimonial interests. (Law 1924 art. 32). Association's property (fees, gifts, inheritance, legacies, public charity, profits from association's economic operations) is limited to carrying out its express purpose, and may not be divided and claimed by individual associates.

Formation.—Association is formed by at least 20 members who must adopt charter, elect governing board, establish board's liability, formulate purpose of association, and select name of association and its head office. Upon recognition by competent court and registration at court register, association's legal existence is established. (Law No. 21/1924, art. 32). Some court decisions have held that members of associations may be legal as well as natural persons, but other courts have held that associations may be formed only by natural persons.

Rights and Powers.—Associations enjoy only rights and powers mentioned in its charter which are necessary for its stated purpose. (Law No. 21/1924).

Liabilities.—Associations may not depart from provisions of their charters and norms of public order, good morals and ethics. (Law No. 21/1924).

Actions.—Both association and its members may sue and bring actions against each other or against third parties. (Law No. 21/1924).

Dissolutions.—Association may be dissolved: (1) by decision of general meeting of its Board; (2) by expiration of term of duration; (3) when purpose has been effectuated or is no longer practicable; (4) by insolvency; (5) by absence of Board; (6) upon breach of charter's dispositions by associates; (7) when association's activity is illegal or contrary to public order, morals and ethics. (Law No. 21/1924).

Professional Associations.—All professional persons in Romania (e.g. physicians, chemists, engineers, research workers, artisans) are entitled to form professional associations.

ATTACHMENT:

Attachment is legal proceeding requested by creditor in which defendant debtor's property is seized to satisfy plaintiff creditor's demand. It serves to preserve property, making it unavailable for disposition, thereby guaranteeing repayment of debts. There are three types of attachments: (a) Guaranteed (Civ. Pro. Code arts. 591-595 and 597-601); (b) Judicial (art. 596); and (c) Executory (arts. 416, 417, 425).

Guaranteed attachment is initiated by request of creditor who has brought action in court for payment of debt. In some instances, creditor is required to post bond, such as when creditor has no written proof to back his claim. In this case, bond is valued at one-third of amount subject to litigation. Bond is also required in commercial litigation. (Com. Code art. 908). Attachment may also be requested (and bond posted) when no debt is due, but when debtor, by his own acts, has put his assurances in doubt or when there is danger that debtor might flee, hide his assets, or spend them. (Civ. Proc. Code art. 597).

It is not necessary to commence attachment action where debts result from landlord-tenant relationship. If request is admitted, attachment is simply made by judicial execution.

Guaranteed attachment is temporary and remains in effect until final decision is made at trial. Debtor may obtain possession of attached property if he provides guarantees (demonstrating he has means to pay debt) required by court. In commercial context, debtor has to provide total amount owed, including interest and expenses, before possession of property is granted. If creditor obtains executory title, guaranteed attachment becomes execution attachment. If debtor thereafter fails to meet his obligations, compulsory sale of assets may follow.

Should party seeking attachment lose on merits of case, guaranteed attachment terminates.

Judicial attachment is permitted in trials involving personal property, or possession, administration or use of common good. During trial, restrained property is usually entrusted for preservation and administration to third party.

Executory Attachment.—After creditor has obtained executory title for payment of debt, creditor may begin to trace movable assets of debtor. First stage involves identifying and attaching debtor's movable goods. If attachment summons remains unanswered, judicial executor may attach debtor's assets at debtor's residence or any place where debtor's movable assets are located, provided that no prior guaranteed attachment has been made. Attachment consists of making inventory of debtor's assets and impounding them. Debtor may retain possession of attached property, but he cannot depreciate or alienate it. If reasons exist to doubt credibility of debtor, goods will be sealed or removed.

ATTORNEYS AND COUNSELORS:

Legal activity in Romania is governed by Law No. 51/1995.

Practice of Law.—Profession of lawyer is free and independent; only members of Bar Association are entitled to practice law. (art. 1).

Bar Association consists of all lawyers in county or in City of Bucharest. (art. 43). In order to become member of Bar, applicant must be Romanian citizen and hold degree or doctorate in law. (art. 9). Also, candidates to enter Bar Association must pass examination in accordance with Law No. 51/1995, except in following instances: candidate holds degree of doctor of law or master of law; or candidate has practiced for at last four years as judge, prosecutor, or notary. Following passage of examination, candidates must practice for two years as apprentice and afterwards candidate must pass examination to be confirmed. (art. 15).

Legal profession may be practiced individually, in association, or in corporate bodies (civil professional companies). Individual lawyers may associate for joint practice, which does not alter rights of principals of associated offices. (art. 5). Law firm consists of two or more associated chartered lawyers who may employ lawyers on retainer. Terms of association shall be agreed upon by parties, in accordance with civil

See Topical Index in front part of this volume.

ATTORNEYS AND COUNSELORS . . . *continued*
law. Law firm and its employees may not render legal assistance to persons having conflicting interests.

Lawyer may conduct his activities through following means: legal opinions; legal assistance and representation before legal prosecutors and notarial institutions; defence by specific legal means of legitimate rights and interests of natural and legal persons in their relationships with public authorities, institutions and any persons; drafting of legal papers. (art. 3). In payment for services rendered, lawyer is entitled to fees and funding for all expenses incurred in interests of client. (art. 27).

Foreign Lawyers.—Member of foreign bar association may practice law in Romania without having Romanian citizenship, provided he fulfills conditions of Law No. 51/1995, and under terms of either mutual convention concluded by Bar Association of Romania with counterpart association of applicant's country of origin, or on one-time basis, jointly with Romanian lawyer. (art. 12).

When mutual convention governs, foreign lawyer shall be registered with Romanian Bar in jurisdiction in which his offices are located, which obligates such lawyer to fully observe rights and obligations deriving from Law No. 51/1995. (art. 10). Foreign lawyers or foreign law firms may register legal consultancy firms in Romania, for activities of commercial nature only, in association with Romanian lawyers. Foreign lawyers may not present conclusions, orally or in writing, before Courts of Law and other judicial bodies in Romania, except for Courts of Commercial Arbitration. (art. 10).

Status of Lawyer.—According to art. 12 of Law No. 51/1995 legal profession is incompatible with following: (a) salaried work in other professions; (b) occupations affecting dignity and independence of legal profession, or violating code of moral conduct; (c) direct commercial activities. (art. 12).

Practice of law is compatible with several other occupations: (a) member of Parliament (either chamber), counselor in local or county councils; (b) professor and researcher in legal field; (c) literary and press activities; (d) arbitrator, mediator or conciliator. (art. 13).

Lawyer's status is lost by occurrence of following: (a) written renunciation of right to practice legal profession, (b) death, (c) retirement, (d) exclusion from legal profession as disciplinary measure, (e) when final sentence is passed against lawyer for penal offence, which makes him unworthy of status of lawyer. (art. 23).

Lawyer's status is suspended in following instances: (a) in case of incompatibility, (b) during period of interdiction imposed by Court or disciplinary measures, (c) for nonpayment of taxes and duties to professional bodies, for period of six months from date due until full payment.

BANKRUPTCY:

Bankruptcy is regulated by Law No. 64/June 22, 1995 as published in Monitorul Oficial on June 29, 1995 and effective 90 days thereafter.

Law applies to natural persons or corporate entities that cannot meet their commercial commitments, and establishes procedure for recovery and payment of liabilities or liquidation of debtor's assets. (arts. 1-2).

Bodies authorized to apply such procedure are Court, Receiver, Administrator, Liquidator, Assembly of Creditors, and Creditors' Committee. (art. 4).

Court shall judge debtor's objections to creditors' petition, appoint Receiver, adjudicate requests to suspend debtor's activities, annul recent transfers of assets, approve restructuring plan or wind-up, to close proceedings. (art. 6).

Receiver shall affix seals, inventory debtor's assets and conservation thereof, set and chair meetings of Assembly of Creditors, examine claims and ensure their collection, receive and make payments, sell assets in debtor's estate. (art. 10).

Meetings of Assembly of Creditors shall be attended by two delegates of debtor's employees, who may vote regarding employees' receivables and other money rights. (art. 13).

Within 45 days from commencement of proceeding, creditors holding at least 50% of all claims may decide upon employment of Administrator to be appointed by Court. Administrator shall be chartered accountant or holder of academic degree in economics or law, with at least five years experience. (art. 17).

Administrator shall monitor financial operations, assist debtor in administration and conduct all or part of debtor's activities. (art. 18).

Procedure.—Preliminary petition may be filed by debtor, creditors or local Chamber of Commerce and Industry. Court shall reject petitions for reorganization from debtors that filed similar petition, or were subject of such petition submitted by creditors, in preceding five years. (arts. 19-23).

If, within five days of receipt of petition submitted by creditors, debtor contends that it is unable to make payments, Court shall call, within 30 days, meeting of creditors, debtor and local Chamber of Commerce and Industry.

Upon debtor's request, Court may require petitioning creditors to deposit, within five days, bail bond with maximum value of 30% of receivables.

Bail shall be returned to creditors if petition is accepted. If petition is rejected, bail may be used to cover damages suffered by debtor. If bail is not deposited on time, preliminary petition shall be rejected.

If Court finds debtor insolvent, proceeding shall continue. (art. 26). Claims shall be submitted within 60 days of date when Court sent first notice of petition.

Debtor must furnish Receiver and Administrator with all information required regarding its activity and assets, and list of payments and transfers of assets effected during 90-day period prior to petition. (art. 33).

Receiver or Administrator shall file detailed report with Court, within 30 days, regarding circumstances and potential liabilities of any administrator, manager, accountant, employee or other persons. (art. 35).

After commencement of reorganization proceeding, debtor's managers are forbidden to alienate debtor's shares they hold. (art. 37).

Debtor, creditors holding at least one-third of secured claims, or unsecured creditors holding at least one-third of unsecured receivables, associates of partnership and shareholders owning at least one-third of registered capital of joint stock company shall be entitled to propose reorganization plan.

Such plan shall provide for restructuring and continuation, sale of part of debtor's estate, or liquidation.

Expenses for drafting of plan and cost of acceptance proceeding shall be deducted from debtor's estate. (art. 55).

Once accepted, such plan shall be lodged with Court, published in Monitorul Oficial and made available to all parties concerned. (art. 62).

Not later than 30 days after publication of plan, Court shall call meeting of debtor, creditors, Receiver, and Administrator. Creditors with subordinate receivables and shareholders may attend meeting but may vote for plan only if plan provides for less favorable treatment than in case of liquidation. Only creditors to claims of which no objection has been raised may vote for plan. (art. 63).

Plan shall be acknowledged by Court provided at least two of categories of creditors accept plan, and all unsecured creditors shall be subject to equitable treatment. If no plan is acknowledged, Court shall order liquidation. (art. 64).

Funds obtained from liquidation shall be distributed with following priority: expenses related to liquidation; repayment of loans granted by banks during reorganization; secured claims; taxes, stamp fees, legal expenses, and wages; if debtor is natural person, amounts owed for room and board for prior six months and upkeep for himself, wife and children, as granted by Court; claims from labor contracts for previous six months; commercial acts conducted by Receiver or Administrator; administrative expenses of debtor's estate, debts resulting from continuation of debtor's activity; unsecured claims; shareholders' claims. (art. 106).

Upon closing, debtor shall be relieved of obligations unless debtor is found guilty of fraudulent bankruptcy. (art. 122).

Court may order that liabilities of corporations be borne by administrators, managers and accountants guilty of certain acts not limited to fraud. (art. 123).

BANKS AND BANKING ACTIVITY:

Banking activity in Romania is regulated by Law No. 33/1991 and Law No. 34/1991.

Romania's banking system consists of: (1) National Bank of Romania (NBR); and (2) commercial banks with state or private capital (foreign or domestic), which are established solely as joint-stock companies in accordance with Law No. 31/1990 concerning Commercial Companies, and with express authorization of NBR.

National Bank of Romania.—NBR is central bank, exclusively funded with state-owned capital. Its management is directed by Board of Administration chaired by President, who also serves as Governor of NBR. Upon motion by Prime Minister, Romanian parliament appoints Members of Board of Administration of National Bank, and its Governor, for eight-year terms. NBR is subordinate to Parliament and is authorized to regulate entire banking system by: (a) issuing rules with legal force; (b) establishing and managing monetary and credit policy; (c) carrying out commercial paper transactions for commercial banks; (d) granting credits and loans; (e) facilitating overdraft and refinancing credits; (f) performing clearing and current account services, supervision and banking control activities; (g) providing cash services to State budget to cover temporary deficits; (h) administering State Treasury on basis of agreements with Ministry of Finance; and (i) carrying out operations involving gold and precious metals, foreign exchange transactions and treasury bonds.

Commercial Banks.—In order to be registered and carry out activities in Romania, banking companies must obtain prior approval of NBR. Such approval may be withdrawn if banking company does not observe terms provided by law. Law No. 35/1991 concerning Foreign Investments, as amended by Law No. 57 of July 10, 1993, applies to commercial banks with foreign capital. Consequently, Romanian Development Agency (RDA) must approve investments made by these banks.

Minimum required share capital for banking companies is 8 billion lei, subscribed and paid in cash. Payment of 50% of share capital is mandatory at time of bank's incorporation, and capital must be fully paid within two years from date of incorporation. Banks are required to open current accounts with NBR, in which minimum reserves are maintained as additional guarantee for constituted deposits.

Commercial banks in Romania are established by public subscription of shares or on basis of Contract of Association (Articles of Incorporation), concluded by at least five shareholders who may be Romanian or foreign individuals or legal entities.

Irrespective of their designation (agricultural banks, banks for development, commercial banks, credit banks, or banks for foreign trade), commercial banks may only participate in commercial banking activities. Their scope of activity is to attract funds as deposits or nonnegotiable instruments, payable at sight or at fixed terms, as well as to grant credits and loans. Banks shall protect, guarantee and ensure deposits of their clients. In addition, banks may buy, sell and administer monetary assets, transfers of funds, clearing operations, and ensure proper protection of property received in their custody. Banks may undertake foreign exchange operations, external payments, open letters of credit, issue letters of guarantee, endorse bills of exchange, and trade with commercial paper and titles, in accordance with banks' by-laws and international norms. Banks may also act as dealers on foreign currency exchange market for sale or purchase of currency on behalf of clients.

Foreign exchange operations are carried out in accordance with Regulation for Foreign Exchange Operations, issued by NBR on May 4, 1992, which also provides procedure for NBR's supervision and control of foreign exchange operations.

Banks, with exception of NBR, may participate in establishment of other commercial companies (whose purpose is independent of banking operations). Participation is limited to amount up to 20% of social capital of commercial company.

Banks may not engage in transactions involving current and fixed assets, except for those transactions necessary to execute their claims, and may not purchase their own bank shares or use such shares to pay off their debts.

Foreign banks may establish subsidiaries and branches in Romania in compliance with above legislation, and with prior authorization of NBR. Incorporation documents of parent bank are required for establishment of subsidiaries and branches.

BILLS AND NOTES:

Drafts: Legal Provisions.—Bills and notes are regulated by Law No. 58/1934, as amended by Government Ordinance No. 11/1993. Law No. 58/1934 is based upon uniform provisions of Geneva Convention of June 7, 1930. Romania is not party to Geneva Convention.

See Topical Index in front part of this volume.

BILLS AND NOTES . . . *continued*

Based on art. 2 of Law No. 33/1991 regarding banking activity, National Bank of Romania has issued Norms No. 6/1994 regarding trade of banking companies and other credit companies with bills and notes, and Technical Norms No. 10/1995 regarding bills and notes. Under Order No. 138/1995, issued by Governor of the National Bank of Romania, following acts were adopted: Regulation No. 8/1994, Norms No. 6, 7 and 15/1994 and Technical Norms No. 9, 10 and 16/1994. Government Ordinance No. 11/1993 has been reestablished, with some amendments. As consequence, courts were entrusted with authority to grant executory power to bills and notes as well as checks, and court executors were granted power to draft protests, activity of notaries ceasing in this respect.

Formation.—According to Law No. 58/1934 art. 1, draft includes: (a) name of draft in its title; (b) unconditional order to pay determined amount; (c) name of person who must pay (drawee); (d) term; (e) place of payment; (f) name of person to whom or at order of whom payment must be made (payee); (g) date and place of issuance; (h) signature of person issuing draft (drawer).

Drawer is liable for acceptance of draft and its payment (art. 11). After its issuance, draft is presented, prior to its expiration, to drawee at his domicile for acceptance. (art. 24). Acceptance is written on draft as "accepted", or its equivalent, and is signed by drawee.

Acceptance and Obligations.—Signature of drawee on front side of draft is considered acceptance. (art. 28). Acceptance must be unconditional but drawee may limit his acceptance as to amount. If any other alterations are made to contents of draft while it is being accepted, it is considered refusal. (art. 29). By accepting draft, drawee undertakes to pay draft during its term. In case payment is not effected, owner of draft, has direct draft action against drawer for everything that is due. (art. 31). Refusal to accept is written by court executor in document entitled protest of nonacceptance.

Payment of draft may be guaranteed for entire amount or for part of it. Such guarantee may be given by third party or by signatory of draft. (art. 33). Guarantee is given on draft or in annex. It is expressed by words "for guarantee" or by any other equivalent expression, and is signed by person providing guarantee. Guarantor is obliged in same manner as person for whom he provided such guarantee. When guarantor pays draft, he acquires all rights that draft provides him against person for whom he provided guarantee, and against other debtors of draft. (art. 35).

Draft may be transmitted by endorsement. If drawer writes on draft words "not at the order" or equivalent expression, title may be transmitted only in form and with effects of ordinary assignment. (art. 13). Endorsement must be written on draft or in its annex and must be signed by endorser. Endorsement transfers all rights resulting from draft. (art. 16).

Holder of draft is considered legitimate owner, provided he justifies his right by continuous series of endorsements. (art. 18).

Drawee and his guarantors are directly obliged to pay draft. Endorser, drawer and his guarantors are indirectly obliged to pay. Persons against whom draft action was initiated cannot raise exceptions to owner on basis of their personal relations with drawer or former owners. (art. 19).

Payment.—Draft must be presented for payment on due date or within two days after such date, at place and address indicated in draft. (arts. 41-42). In case owner of draft encounters refusal to pay, such owner must request court executor to draft protest of nonpayment, which is necessary for owner to sue debtors (endorser, drawers and their guarantors), and to initiate forced execution against them.

If voluntary payment was not effected, owner, who performed formalities mentioned above, may obtain such payment from any debtors of draft by commencing legal action or by forced execution.

Draft may constitute executory title for capital and accessories. Granting of executory title upon draft is made by court having jurisdiction over place of payment or, by court having jurisdiction over domicile or head office of draft debtor or at choice of draft's holder or at address chosen for execution of draft. After granting of such executory title, summoning of execution is made; within five days after such summoning, debtor may contest execution. If debtor's contest is dismissed by final court decision, forced execution may be effected.

Promissory Note.—Promissory notes are regulated by Law No. 58/1934 arts. 104-107, regarding bills of exchange and promissory notes.

According to art. 104 of this law, promissory note must contain: (a) name of promissory note in its title; (b) unconditional promise to pay determined amount; (c) term; (d) place of payment; (e) name of person to whom or at order of whom payment must be made; (f) date and place of its issuance; (g) signature of subscriber.

Promissory note is subject to provisions regarding draft, insofar as they are not incompatible with nature of this instrument. (art. 106). Subscriber of promissory note is bound in same way as one who accepts draft. (art. 107). Unlike draft, however, promissory note does not include name of drawee, since drawer and drawee are one and same with subscriber.

Check.—Checks are primarily regulated by Law No. 59/1934, as amended by Law No. 83/1994 and Technical Norms No. 9/1994. Similar to draft, check establishes legal relations between three persons. However, check differs from draft in that it is not credit title, but only payment instrument. Based on art. 2(1) of Law No. 33/1991 regarding banking activity, National Bank of Romania issued Norms No. 7/1994 regarding trade using checks of banking companies and other credit companies. Checks are also regulated by Regulation No. 10/1994 regarding operations involving checks effected by banks.

According to Law No. 59/1934 art. 1, check must include: (a) name of check in its title; (b) unconditional order to pay determined amount; (c) name of person who must pay (drawer); (d) place of payment; (f) date and place of its issuance; (g) signature of subscriber.

Check may be issued only if drawer has cash availabilities, either as bank deposit or as credit given by drawee to drawer. (art. 3). Check stipulated as being payable to specific person may be transferred by endorsement, regardless of whether it mentions "at the order". (art. 15).

Payment of check may be guaranteed in whole or in part. (art. 26). Check may be paid on sight. Check issued in foreign country and payable in Romania must be presented within 30 days and if issued outside Europe, within 70 days. If check is payable abroad, presentation term will be dictated by local law. (art. 30).

International Private Law.—Law No. 105/1992, regarding settling of international private law relations, contains following provisions regarding drafts, promissory notes, and checks (arts. 127-138): (a) person who, according to his national law, does not have capacity to sign draft, promissory note or check, may be bound by such title if his signature was made in country where law considers him capable of being subscriber; (b) obligation undertaken by draft, promissory note or check is subject to formal conditions of law of country where obligation was subscribed. For checks, observance of formal conditions provided by law of country of payment is sufficient. (art. 128); (c) terms established for exercise of regressive action are determined, in relation to any subscriber, by law of country where title was issued (art. 129); (d) form and terms of contest, as well as formal conditions of certain documents necessary to exercise or conserve rights for draft, promissory note or check, are established by law of country where protest or another necessary document must be drafted (art. 130).

Law No. 105/1992 also contains provisions exclusively regarding either draft or promissory note, which are as follows: (a) effects of obligations of recipient of draft and subscriber of promissory note are subject to law of place where such instruments are due (art. 131); (b) law of place where instrument was issued establishes if owner of draft acquires right of credit over amount which occasioned issuance of such instrument (art. 132); (c) law of country where draft is paid establishes if acceptance may be restrained to part of amount, as well as whether owner of title is obliged to receive partial payment (art. 133).

As for applicable law regarding checks, Law No. 105/1992 provides following provisions: (a) law of country where check is due determines persons for whom such instrument may be drafted (art. 135); (b) law of country where obligations resulting from check were subscribed determines effects of such obligations (art. 137); (c) law of country where check is due determines following: if title must be drawn on sight or if it may be drawn after certain time on sight, as well as effects of post-dating; term of presentation; if check may be accepted, certified, confirmed or authorized and effects of such notations (art. 138).

CONSTITUTION AND GOVERNMENT:

Romania's Constitution, adopted on Nov. 21, 1991, sets forth fundamental rules and principles relating to, inter alia, economy, public finance, rights, liberties, duties of citizens, and obligations of branches of government.

Romanian state is characterized as: (a) national, sovereign, independent, unitary and indivisible; (b) democratic and social state, which warrants human dignity, rights, freedoms, justice, and political pluralism (art. 1-3 c); (c) provides national sovereignty which Romanian people exercise through representative government or by referendum; (d) divided into communities, cities and districts; (e) guarantees equality of its citizens irrespective of race, nationality, ethnic origin, language, religion, gender, political opinion, membership in party, estate or social origin (art. 4-2 c); (f) recognizes national minorities and guarantees right to preserve, develop and express ethnic, cultural, linguistic and religious differences (art. 6-1 c), including right to education in one's mother tongue (art. 32-3 c), according to principles of equality and nondiscrimination (art. 6-2 c); (g) allows contact with Romanians living abroad; (h) guarantees political pluralism; (i) it includes right to join trade unions; and (j) validates international agreements to which it is party ("the treaties ratified by the Parliament become domestic laws" [art. 11-2 c]).

Constitutional law is construed and applied in accordance with United Nations Universal Declaration on Human Rights (10 Dec. 1948) and with treaties signed by Romanian government. In case of conflict between international and domestic law, international law is supreme. (art. 20 c).

Protection of Private Property.—Constitution provides for right to own property, and right to maintain debts against State. (art. 41-1 c). Private property is protected irrespective of owner. Foreign citizens and stateless persons may not acquire property rights over land. (art. 41-2 c). Private property may not be expropriated, except where warranted by public necessity, as established by law, and with prior compensation. (art. 41-3 c).

Public Authorities.—Sovereign power is distributed among Parliament, Presidency, Government, Central and Local Public Administration, Judiciary, Public Ministry and Superior Council of Magistrates. Parliament makes laws, President promulgates them, Government carries them out and Courts interpret them and adjudicate disputes.

Parliament is supreme representative body of Romanian people and sole legislative authority. (art. 58-1 c). It is composed of Chamber of Deputies and Senate, which are elected to four year terms by universal, equal, direct, secret and free suffrage in accordance with electoral law. (art. 59-1). Both Senate and Chamber of Deputies are governed by their own rules of conduct. Chamber of Deputies and Senate work either in plenary or separate sessions, and there are two ordinary sessions per year. Extraordinary sessions take place at request of President of Republic, Permanent Bureau of each Chamber, or at request of at least one-third of number of deputies or senators.

Chamber of Deputies and Senate adopt laws, decisions and motions in presence of majority. Legislators may not be made to account for their votes or political opinions. (art. 71 c). Legislative initiative belongs to Government, deputies and senators, as well as to at least 250,000 citizens from at least one-fourth of country's districts (10,000 from each district). Parliament adopts constitutional, as well as ordinary laws. Laws or legislative proposals adopted by one chamber of parliament are sent to other for revision. Differences are mediated by common commission or are settled in joint debates.

Legislative Council of Romania functions as advisory body for Parliament. It unifies and coordinates all laws passed by Parliament and keeps official record of legislation of Romania. (art. 79-1).

President of Romania is elected by universal, equal, direct, secret and free suffrage. (art. 81). President's term of office is four years, commencing on date on which oath of office is taken. (art. 83-1).

President plays prominent role as representative of state and guarantor of national independence, unity and territorial integrity. President has following duties: to safeguard Constitution and proper functioning of state authorities; to act as mediator

See Topical Index in front part of this volume.

CONSTITUTION AND GOVERNMENT . . . *continued*
between state and society (art. 80 c); to propose candidates for Prime Minister and appoints Government based upon Parliament's vote of confidence; to dissolve Parliament if it refuses to grant Government vote of confidence within 60 days after first demand is made, but only after second demand is rejected; to conclude international treaties negotiated by Government and to submit them to Parliament for ratification; to issue Decrees.

Parliament may suspend President from his duties after consulting Constitutional Court.

Government.—Council of Ministers is executive branch of government, which effects domestic and foreign policies ratified by Parliament and exercises general management of public administration. (art. 101-1 c). Government consists of Prime Minister, Ministers and other members established by law.

Government adopts decisions necessary to carry out laws and orders. Government and each of its members are jointly liable for activities of Government. (art. 108).

Parliament is entitled to withdraw confidence in Government, by adopting motion of censure by majority vote of deputies and senators.

Judiciary.—Supreme Court of Justice and other courts established by law are charged with ensuring justice. Extraordinary courts may not be created.

Public Ministry.—Within judicial system, Public Ministry represents general interests of society and defends lawful order, and rights and liberties of citizens. Its functions are exercised by public prosecutors.

Superior Council of Magistrates is body of magistrates elected by Chamber of Deputies and Senate for four-year terms. It makes proposals to President for appointment of magistrates, prosecutors and magistrates' Council of Discipline.

Constitutional Court consists of nine judges, appointed for term of nine years. (art. 140-1). Three judges are appointed by President of Romania. (art. 140-2). Fundamental task of Constitutional Court is to rule upon constitutionality of laws before promulgation, upon notification by any of following: President of Romania, President of either Chamber of Parliament, Government, Supreme Court of Justice, number of at least 50 deputies or at least 25 Senators, as well as ex officio, upon initiatives to revise Constitution. (art. 144-a). Court is also imbued with power to adjudicate on constitutionality of Standing Orders of Parliament and laws and orders.

Economy.—According to Constitution, Romania's economy is based upon principle of market economy. (art. 134 c).

CONTRACTS:

According to art. 942 of Civil Code, contract is agreement between two or more persons intended to establish or to terminate legal relationship.

Sources.—Contracts are regulated in general by Civil Code of 1865. (arts. 942-985), primarily civil contracts: sale/purchase (arts. 1294-1404); exchange (arts. 1405-1409); leasing (arts. 1410-1490); company (arts. 1491-1531); agency (arts. 1532-1559); commodities (arts. 1560-1575); lease (arts. 1576-1579); deposit and conventional sequester (arts. 1591-1634); aleatory contracts (art. 1635); fide-jussio (accessory contract) (arts. 1652-1661); pledge or pawn (arts. 1685-1696), etc.

Commercial contracts and some special provisions applicable to them are provided for in Commercial Code of 1887: sale (arts. 60-73); carry-over (stock exchange contract) (arts. 74-76); current account (arts. 370-373); commercial agency and commission (arts. 374-412); transport contract (arts. 413-441); pledge (arts. 478-489); freight contract (arts. 557-591); passenger transport contract (arts. 592-600); maritime lease (arts. 601-615); maritime insurance (arts. 616-653).

Certain contracts are regulated by specific laws: commercial companies (Law No. 31/1990); insurance contracts (Decree No. 471/1971); management contracts (Law No. 66/1993), individual and collective labor contracts etc. There is also great variety of unspecified contracts adapted to specific situations.

Under Romanian law contract must be based upon autonomous will of parties, concept borrowed from French Civil Code of 1804. Generally speaking, Romanian model generally based upon European contractual law, inspired by French and Italian Civil Codes.

After 1989, traditional features of contract law were restored: (1) full contractual freedom to enter into contract; (2) right to choose one's contractual partner; (3) rights to establish contractual clauses and to choose its form; (4) once entered into, contract is fully enforceable (pacta sunt servanda); (5) basis of contract's binding force is constituted by free will of parties, and State may become involved at request of interested party to support execution of contract or to sanction its non-execution in court of law.

Types of Contracts.—Contracts may be consensual; solemn; or real:

Consensual contracts arise from simple voluntary agreement of parties without any formalities. Consensual contracts need not be in writing, although writing serves as proof of contractual relationship between parties.

Solemn contracts require execution of certain standard forms and must be based upon mutual agreement between parties. Nonobservance of authentic solemn forms (for which proper evidentiary foundation has been provided) will void contract. Examples of solemn contracts are contracts for sale of land, and contracts for mortgage.

Real contracts require delivery of good by one party to other. Examples of real contracts are lease, deposit, pledge, and transport of goods.

According to mutual or unilateral nature of obligations assumed by parties, contracts may be classified as:

Bilateral contracts in which parties are mutually obliged one in respect to other (Civ. Code art. 943), each of them simultaneously having both quality of creditor and quality of debtor (for instance, sale/purchase contract); or,

Unilateral contracts which bind single party, such as loan for pledge. (Civ. Code art. 944).

According to intent of parties, contracts may be classified as:

Contracts with onerous title (for valid consideration)—contracts in which each of parties intends to obtain benefit. (Civ. Code art. 945). Contract with onerous title is transferable, when obligation of one party is equivalent to obligation of other. (Civ. Code art. 947).

Gratuitous contracts arise when one of parties intends to obtain, without consideration, benefit for party with whom it is made. (Civ. Code art. 946).

Capacity.—Any natural or legal person has capacity to enter into contract, unless incapable according to law. (Civ. Code art. 949). See topic Infants.

According to Decree No. 31/1954, regarding natural and legal persons, civil capacity has dual aspect: use capacity (capacity to have rights and obligations); and exercise capacity (capacity to exercise rights and assume obligations through legal acts). Use capacity begins at birth of person and ends at death. Full exercise capacity is available at age 18. Minor who is 14 or older, has restrained exercise capacity. Person under judicial disability, because of mental disability, does not have exercise capacity and cannot enter into any contract for duration of disability.

Additionally, law provides special incapacities; spouses may not contract to sell anything to each other. (Civ. Code art. 1307). Legal entities may have only such rights as pertain to their object as established by law, by its contract or by its Statute. (Decree No. 31/1954 art. 34).

Formation of Contract.—Two acts are necessary for formation of contract: offer and acceptance.

Offer is voluntary statement proposing entrance into contract. In order to be valid, offer must be: (a) complete—include all essential elements of proposed contract, allowing voluntary agreement of parties to be performed by simple acceptance of offeror. Incomplete offer only has value of invitation to contract; (b) made with firm intention of offering party to obligate itself; (c) materialized in express act such as letter, telegram, telex transmission, or fax or by implied act, such as by presentation of merchandise; (d) when law requires specfic form (e.g. private signature or authentication) offer must comply with form; and (e) addressed to specific person or to general public.

Offer differs from promise to enter into contract because it is unilateral statement, rather than mutual legal act based upon voluntary agreement. For instance, owner of good agrees to sell his good to another person if latter expresses will to buy it. Thus, offer includes unilateral obligation, incumbent on owner of good. It is not offer nor sale contract, but only unilateral promise to sell. When both parties agree to enter, in future, into specific contract, then it is considered promise of contract, with mutual character.

Acceptance is voluntary statement made by offeree to offeror accepting conditions and formalities established by offeror. In order to be valid, acceptance must: (a) contain express statement of will; (b) coincide with offer; if offered party modifies offer's elements, establishing new conditions or making counter-proposals, it is considered counteroffer. Commercial Code expressly provides that "the conditional or limited acceptance is considered as a refusal of the first proposal and constitutes a new proposal" (art. 39); (c) originate from offeree; (d) constitute response within term established by offering party.

Offer and acceptance may be withdrawn (Com. Code art. 37), but only before offeror has received acceptance, which is moment when contract is concluded. Nonobservance of this requirement brings forth liability for breaching party, but does not affect contract enforceability. Valid cancellation is effective at moment it is transmitted to other party, regardless of when it is received.

Offer and acceptance may become void upon death of either party before conclusion of contract. Proposals or negotiations may be continued by successors, in name of deceased, through new offer or acceptance.

Contracts Concluded by Correspondence (Between Absent Persons).—Under Romanian law, voluntary agreement is realized and contract is signed when offering party has knowledge of other party's acceptance. (Com. Code art. 35). Receipt of acceptance is relative assumption that offering party has knowledge of acceptance.

Contract may be concluded before date indicated by acceptance (e.g., when party begins execution). (Com. Code art. 36). In order to conclude contract early, following conditions must be satisfied: (a) offeror must have requested immediate execution of contract; (b) offeror did not request prior answer; and (c) such answer is not necessary, according to nature of contract.

Void, Voidable Contracts.—

Agreement flaws are circumstances which may void contract because of flaws in manifestation of will of party: "The agreement is not valid when it is given by mistake, obtained by force or obtained by deceit." (Civ. Code art. 953).

Mistake of fact does not void contract, unless it is material error. (Civ. Code art. 954). Error regarding identity of contracting party constitutes agreement flaw only when that identity is material to contract (intuitu personae).

Coercion, as provided by Civ. Code art. 956, occurs when one party forces agreement upon another through use of fear or intimidation. In cases of coercion, contract is void for all parties involved. (Civ. Code art. 957). Mere knowledge or fear, with reasonable apprehension of violence, will not render contract void. (Civ. Code art. 958).

Deceit may void contract when deceitful means, used by one of parties, are of such nature that it is evident that but for deceit, other party would not have entered into contract. (Civ. Code art. 960).

Contracts entered into by mistake of fact, violence or deceit are not necessarily void, but open to voiding action.

Purpose of Contract.—Every contract must have purpose, creation of obligations constituting action to give (transmission of right to creditor), to perform, or not to perform (action of debtor).

Purpose of action of giving must comply with certain conditions: (1) it must be capable of being traded (Civ. Code art. 963); and (2) it must be determined or determinable (Civ. Code art. 964). Future object may form obligation. (Civ. Code art. 965).

Reason constitutes consideration for which party assumed its obligation. Obligation without purpose or based upon false or illegal purpose does not affect validity of contract. Additionally, contract is effective, even though reason is not expressed. Reason is presumed until proven otherwise. Reason is illegal when prohibited by law or when it is contrary to morals or public order. (Civ. Code arts. 966-968).

Effects of Contracts.—Contracts legally concluded have binding power between parties. (Civ. Code art. 969). Once contract is concluded, contractual obligations must

See Topical Index in front part of this volume.

CONTRACTS . . . *continued*

be executed accordingly, in good faith, as provided for by Civ. Code, art. 970, being binding not only for what is expressly provided, "but also for all consequences which the equity, the usage or the law have given to the obligation". Unilateral cancellation of contract is generally not admitted. (Civ. Code art. 969 par. 2). In cases provided by law or by contract, however, unilateral cancellation is possible (agency contract, deposit contract, etc.). Contracts do not generally affect rights of third parties: "The conventions have effects only between the contractual parties." (Civ. Code art. 973).

Interpretation of contracts is made according to common intention of both parties, and not according to literal sense of terms. When clause is ambiguous, it is construed in sense in which it may have effect (ut valeat), and not in sense that it does not have any (ut pereat). Clauses normally in contract are implied by law. All contract clauses are interpreted as part of whole, and each clause is given such sense as results from entire contract. When in doubt, contract is interpreted to benefit obliging party. (Civ. Code arts. 977-985).

International Private Law.—Law No. 105/1992 regarding settling of international private law relations determines the law applicable to contract (arts. 73-87), such as: (a) contract is subject to law agreed upon by parties; (b) choice of law applicable to contract must be expressed or must result from its content or circumstances; (c) parties may choose law applicable to entire contract or part of contract; (d) agreement regarding choice of applicable law may be modified by agreement of parties; (e) when parties cannot agree to choice of law, contract is subject to jurisdiction having most contacts. Such relations are considered to exist with law of state in which debtor of contract's action has domicile, residence, business, or head office, at time of contract. Contract regarding fixed asset or temporary right over fixed asset coincides with law of state where such asset is located; (f) if no such characteristics exist, law of place where it was concluded is chosen. If parties are located in different countries and have negotiated through exchange of letters, telegrams or telephone, contract is considered to be concluded in country of domicile or head office of party which originated offer; (g) existence and validity of parties' choice of law are determined by law they elected. If such law declares choice void, contract is governed by law indicated in letters (e) and (f) above; (h) existence and validity of contract contested by one party is determined according to law which would have applied if it was considered valid; (i) legal effects of silence of party are subject to national law of such natural person or law governing status of such legal person; (j) contract between parties having their domicile or head office in different countries is considered concluded when offeror receives acceptance; (k) foreign law applicable to contract includes its material law provisions; (l) contract is subject to form conditions established by law governing its substance. Contract is held valid from form point of view if parties, or their representatives, who are in different countries at time of contract's conclusion, have complied with formal conditions provided by law of either of these countries; (m) forms of publicity necessary to validate contract by which rights over goods are instituted against third parties are subject to jurisdiction where such goods are located.

COPYRIGHT:

New law, Law No. 8/1996 (hereinafter "Law"), regarding copyright, was passed by Romanian Parliament in Feb. 1996 and published in Monitorul Oficial No. 60 on Mar. 20, 1996, becoming effective 90 days from its publication. Law abrogated Decree No. 321/1956, with all its subsequent amendments, and any other contrary provisions.

Law contains 154 articles which are generally consistent with European Union regulations. Law provides for registration system of works in special ledger. However, intellectual works are acknowledged and protected whether they are published or not, because of mere fact that they have been created, whether completed or not.

Natural or legal entity that created work is its author. (Art. 3). In cases expressly provided by Law, natural or legal entities, other than author, may benefit by protection granted to author.

Author may be person under whose name work has been made known to public. Original works of intellectual creation in literary, artistic or scientific area, regardless of method of creation and specific form of expression, and independent from value and destination, may be copyrighted.

Author has exclusive right to: decide whether, how and when work is to be made known to public or used; claim recognition as author; decide under what name work is published; demand observance of integrity of work, oppose any change, retract work and seek compensation for damages. Retraction right is not applicable to computer programs. (Art. 10).

Copyright of literary, artistic or scientific work is effective once such work has been created, regardless of specific form or method of expression. Proprietary rights are valid for lifetime of author. After death, such rights are inherited according to civil law, for 70-year period (50 years in case of computer programs).

Author or holder of copyright may assign proprietary rights to another person on contractual basis, on exclusive or non-exclusive basis. Assignment agreement must set forth transferred rights, methods of exploitation, duration and extension of assignment, and remuneration of copyright holder. Assignment of proprietary rights regarding future work, is null and void. (Art. 39).

With regard to protection of computer programs, according to Art. 73 of Law, author of computer program benefits, inter alia, by exclusive right to authorize reproduction, translation, adjustment, arrangement, transformation and distribution of original or copies of computer program.

Authorized user of computer program may make archive or backup copy, without author's consent. Authorization of copyright holder is required when reproduction of code or translation of its form is indispensable in obtaining information required for inter-operation of computer program with other programs. Such information may not be used for purposes other than inter-operation, may not be supplied to other persons, unless communication proves to be necessary for such inter-operation, and may not be used for production or commercialization of computer program, expression of which is basically similar, or for any other act affecting author's rights. (Arts. 77-79).

Performing Artists' Rights.—Artist has exclusive proprietary right to authorize establishment of his performance, reproduction of such recorded performance, its dissemination, presentation in public place, adjustment of performance, and its broadcasting on radio or television. (Art. 98).

Recording Producers' Rights.—Recording producer has, among other rights, exclusive right to authorize import into Romania of legally made copies of its own recordings. Duration of proprietary rights of recording producers is 50 years, commencing on Jan. 1 in year following that when first recording was produced. (Art. 105).

Radio and television companies have exclusive proprietary right to authorize establishment of their own radio or TV programs, reproduction, broadcasting, transmissions to place accessible to public, and alterations of their own radio or television programs. (Art. 113).

Protection of Copyrights and Related Rights.—Romanian Copyright Office is solely responsible for monitoring, observing and controlling copyright legislation; it is specialized body subordinated to Government. It may exercise, upon author's request and expense, protective measures, observation and control of activities which may lead to violation of laws. (Art. 137).

Procedures and Penalties.—Violation of rights may result in civil, tort and penal liability. Authors may request courts to order assessment of violation, recognition of rights, claim damages, request application of any of following measures: remittance of returns from illicit acts or of goods resulting from illegal acts; destruction of equipment and means in possession of violator; confiscation and destruction of illegal copies; publication of court award in mass media at violator's expense. (Art. 139).

Penalties provided for various violations consist of imprisonment from two to five years, or fines ranging between 200,000 and 7,000,000 lei.

Application of Law.—Foreigners who are holders of copyrights or related rights enjoy protection provided by international conventions, treaties and agreements to which Romania is party, and in their absence, benefit from equal treatment with Romanian citizens, provided that latter shall benefit by same national treatment in respective states. (Art. 147).

Authors are entitled on original works or their authorized copies mention of reserved use, consisting of encircled symbol © and title, place and year of first publication.

Recording producers, performing artists and other holders of exclusive rights of producers and performing artists, are entitled to include on original or authorized copies of sound or audiovisual recordings or on their cover, mention of protection of their rights, consisting of encircled symbol ℗ and title, place and year of first publication.

Unless proved otherwise, exclusive rights claimed by symbols © and ℗ are assumed to exist and belong to persons who use them. (Art. 148).

CORPORATIONS:

Governing Law.—Area is regulated, in part, by 1887 Commercial Code and its subsequent modifications, Law No. 31/1990 concerning trade companies, Law No. 35/1991 modified by Law No. 57/1993, reprinted in 1993, concerning foreign investments, and Law No. 71/1994 for attraction of foreign investors in industry. There are also many Government Decisions in this area, such as G.D. 1323/1990 regarding impermissible activities, G.D. 331/1992 regarding sale of land, G.D. 19/1991 regarding tourism, G.D. 1279/1990 regarding insurance companies.

Types of Companies.—Companies may be founded as any one of following entities: (a) general partnership (societate in nume colectiv); (b) limited partnership (societate in comandita simpla); (c) limited joint-stock companies (societate in comandita pe actiuni)—combination of limited partnership, whose social capital is divided by shares—social obligations are guaranteed with social capital and general partners' joint and several liability, limited partners are liable only in proportion to their shares; (d) joint-stock companies (societate pe actiuni) whose social obligations are guaranteed with social capital—shareholders are liable only in proportion to their shares; (e) limited liability companies (societate cu raspundere limitata) whose social obligations are guaranteed by capital; associates are bound only to pay their shares. (Law No. 31/1990 art. 2).

Joint stock companies and limited liability companies are most frequently used by foreign investors (see also topic Partnership).

Company Formation.—Basic instruments necessary to create company are Contract of Association (Law No. 31/1990 arts. 8 par. 1. and 32 par. 1) and, for joint-stock companies and limited liability companies, Statute (similar to by-laws) (Law No. 31/1990 arts. 8 par. 1 and 32 par. 1). In cases of corporations with sole shareholder, only Statute is required. (Law No. 31/1990 art. 210 par. 4). Both Contract of Association and Statute must be authenticated by state notary.

Maximum of 50 associates may set up limited liability company, having social capital of at least 100,000 lei, divided into shares (social parts) of no less than 5,000 lei each. Contributions in kind may be maximum 60% of total social capital. (Law No. 31/1990 arts. 34 and 200). Minimum of five associates is necessary to set up joint-stock company, having social capital of at least 1,000,000 lei, divided into shares of no less than 1,000 lei, from which cash contributions to capital may be no less than 30% of entire subscribed capital. (art. 8 par. 3). If associate is foreign investor, its contribution to social capital must be at least U.S. $10,000 in order to achieve status and safeguards accorded to foreign investors. (Law No. 57/1993 art. 10).

By means of shareholder voting or company rules regarding organization and operation, shareholders are authorized to establish any rules, provided they do not prejudice public order and morals. Usually, companies have general assembly of shareholders, board of directors, president and officers designated by board of directors or by president. Indemnification of directors and officers takes place by decision of board of directors.

Elements of the Contract of Association and Statute.—Contract of Association of limited liability company must include elements mentioned in Law No. 31/1990 (e.g. names of partners, address of their residence or headquarters, capital subscribed and deposited, duration of company). Statute of limited liability company may contain other elements accepted by associates. Joint-stock company's Contract of Association must also include elements mentioned in Law No. 31/1990.

Any natural or legal persons may associate themselves and set up companies in order to carry out commercial operations. (Law No. 31/1990 art. 1 par. 1, Com. Code

CORPORATIONS . . . *continued*
arts. 3-6). Foreign natural and legal persons may establish companies individually or together with Romanian persons, in all sectors of industry, including: (a) exploration and exploitation of natural resources; (b) agriculture; (c) communications; (d) industrial and civil engineering; (e) research and technological development; (f) trade; (g) transport; (h) tourism; (i) banking; (j) insurance and (k) industry. Establishment is limited to newly established companies that must not infringe upon environmental protection, security interests, public order, or health and morals of nation. (Law No. 35/1991 art. 4 reprinted 1993).

Authorization and Registration.—After authentication by state notary and payment of social capital, company must obtain permission to operate from Tribunal of Justice. Once granted, Tribunal's permission must be published in Official Gazette, and thereafter, registered at Trade Register Office and with fiscal authority, which shall provide it with fiscal code. Publishing requirements must always be fulfilled. If requirements have not been met, any associate may demand their fulfillment or, if company has not yet been registered, its dissolution and liquidation. Once registered, however, companies become legal persons for time period specified by founders.

Aliens.—If founder of corporation is foreign national, it should obtain certificate of investor from Romanian Agency for Development. License for export and import of certain goods must be acquired from Trade Ministry.

Legal and natural foreign persons may also set up subsidiaries, branches and representations in country or abroad with integral foreign capital or in association with Romanian persons. Foreign persons are entitled to participate in increasing existing companies' social capital or in acquiring shares, social parts, bonds or other commercial notes of such companies.

Company Operations.—General Assembly may increase capital at any time, but may not decrease it below limit prescribed by law. Under Romanian law, dividends are considered quotas from actual profit paid to associate, in proportion to his shares. (Law No. 31/1990 art. 37). In addition, every company must keep ledger (cartea mare), diary and inventory (Law No. 82/1991; see also decision 704/1993 regarding accounts). Joint-stock companies must also keep register of shareholders, register of meetings and minutes of general assemblies, and of board of directors meeting, and register of minutes and findings made by auditors exercising their commission. (Law No. 31/1990 art. 127).

Annually, at least 5% of company's capital must be taken over to form reserve fund until it reaches one-fifth of total fixed capital of company. (Law No. 31/1990 art. 131 par. 1). Fund remains with company and is reinvested into company operations. Mergers are initiated by companies themselves, observing same formalities as those for incorporation. (Law No. 31/1990 art. 174).

Dissolution and Liquidation.—Company may be dissolved upon expiration of its term, decision of general assembly, bankruptcy, decrease of social capital or number of associates below minimum limit prescribed by law. Limited liability companies and general partnerships may also be dissolved by bankruptcy, disability, exclusion, retirement or death of associate, or if number of associates has been reduced to one associate and no contractual clause exists to continue company using legal heirs. (Law No. 31/1990 art. 169).

COURTS:

In Romania, judicial branch is separate and distinct from other branches of government. Courts have jurisdiction to hear all cases in areas of civil, commercial, labor, family, and administrative law, as well as any other domain over which they are empowered to adjudicate. (Law No. 92/1992 art. 2). Romanian judiciary consists of following: (a) Law Courts, (b) Tribunals of Justice, (c) Appellate Courts, (d) Supreme Court of Justice.

Several laws govern judiciary: Law No. 92/1992 for Juridical Organizations; Law No. 56/1993, Law of Supreme Court of Justice; Law No. 54/1993 for Organizations of Court and District Attorney Offices in the Military Field; Law No. 29/1990 regarding Administrative Courts.

Law Courts.—Local Law Courts function in every county, district and in each sector of Bucharest. They adjudicate all general trials and requests, except those rendered to courts of other jurisdictions. (Law No. 92/1992 arts. 20 and 21). Actions falling within jurisdiction of Law Courts are presided over in some cases by two judges (e.g. pension maintenance actions and patrimonial litigation among physical persons involving payments not in excess of 300,000 lei). Single judge presides over other actions, such as those concerning garnishment and labor litigations, not in excess of 100,000 lei. In criminal cases, single judge presides over actions for rehabilitation and most crimes in which punishment includes penalties or imprisonment of less than two years. (art. 22).

Tribunals of Justice.—Tribunals function in principal towns of each county and in Bucharest. All local Law Courts of county or of Bucharest are included in district of each Tribunal of Justice. Tribunals have jurisdiction to adjudicate following matters among others: adoptions, commercial matters where amount at issue exceeds 10 million lei, establishment of commercial companies, civil matters with value exceeding 150 million lei, intellectual property matters, actions regarding enforcement of foreign judicial awards.

Bucharest Municipality Tribunal is solely competent in following matters: registration of political parties, requests regarding annulment of invention certificate, granting of compulsory license, litigation regarding royalties due in certain cirumstances, adoption of Romanian citizen having his domicile outside Romania.

At trial stage, two-judge panel adjudicates actions filed directly with Tribunal. On appeal, Tribunals review initial decisions of local Law Courts. As courts of recourse (appeal), they also adjudicate petitions of recourse filed against Law Court decisions which may not be submitted on ordinary appeal. (Law No. 92/1992 art. 25). In such cases, three judges must sit on Tribunal. (art. 26).

Appellate Courts.—Each Appellate Court exercises its jurisdiction in district covering several Tribunals of Justice. (Law No. 92/1992 art. 27). There are 15 appellate courts in Romania.

At trial level, three-judge panel adjudicates actions under its direct jurisdiction, such as commercial disputes where amount in controversy is minimum of 10 million lei. As appellate courts, they hear initial decisions rendered by Tribunals of Justice. As courts of recourse (appeal), they review decisions of Tribunals on recourse (appeal), as well as other cases over which they have jurisdiction.

Supreme Court of Justice is competent to adjudicate following: appeals of awards of Appellate Courts and other awards, as provided by law: appeals "in the interest of the law" (for unitary interpretation of law, such awards thereby become "binding precedent"), any other matters provided by law, such as impeachment of all judges of Appellate Court, request for removal of case from one court to another, request for suspension of strike.

Decisions on high appeal or submitted as review of Appellate Court decisions are reconsidered by Supreme Court of Justice. In some cases, Supreme Court has jurisdiction to adjudicate cases at trial stage. It may also apply to Constitutional Court to rule on constitutionality of laws before they are promulgated.

Supreme Court is organized into five sections: civil, criminal, commercial, administrative and military, each having its own jurisdiction. Supreme Court panels consist of either three or seven judges, or all judges of Supreme Court of Justice. Administrative section of Supreme Court hears requests of any physical or legal person contesting administrative decisions or actions which contravene their legal rights. Court may overturn such decisions and provide for damages. Unless otherwise specified by law, Court must render decision regarding injured party's claim within 30 days after filing of request. Decisions rendered by administrative sections are within jurisdiction of Tribunals of Justice or Appellate Court in territory where plaintiff is domiciled.

Judges.—All judges are appointed by presidential decree based upon nominations from superior council of magistrates, and may not be removed once appointed. Judge must have following qualifications: (1) Romanian citizenship, (2) law school degree, (3) no criminal record, (4) knowledge of Romanian language and, (5) good state of health. Judges of Law Courts and Tribunals of Justice may remain in office until age of 65, judges on Appellate Courts may remain in office until age of 68, and judges on Supreme Court of Justice may remain in office until age of 70.

Jurisdiction.—According to Law No. 105/1992 concerning international law relations, Romanian courts have jurisdiction in following circumstances: (a) defendant or one of parties to trial has his residence, office or business in Romania; (b) claimant receiving alimony lives in Romania; (c) Romania is situs of contractual or noncontractual obligation; (d) railway station, street, port or airport where passengers or merchandise were loaded or unloaded is in Romania; (e) insured goods or place where risk was produced is in Romania; (f) last residence of deceased is Romania; or (g) personal property of deceased is in Romania.

In addition, Romania courts have jurisdiction: (1) regarding protection or custody of Romanian minors living abroad; (2) involving declaration of presumptive death of Romanian citizen (even if abroad at time of death); (3) between foreigners if they expressly agree to such jurisdiction; and (4) in cases of bankruptcy or any other legal procedure regarding cessation of payments in case of commercial company with its head office in Romania.

Romanian Courts are exclusively competent to settle matters such as: adoption of Romanian citizens or persons with no citizenship, both having their domicile in Romania, actions regarding inheritance if deceased person had last domicile in Romania, litigation having as object real property located in Romania.

CURRENCY:

Romanian national currency is leu (lei in plural form). Leu is divided into 100 bani. Due to inflation, bani are no longer used in currency exchange. Highest nominal value of lei is represented by 10,000 lei bills. National currency consists of bills and coins.

National Bank of Romania has exclusive right to issue legal Romanian currency. (Law No. 34/1991 art. 9). National Bank may withdraw any kinds of national legal tenders from market. (art. 17).

CUSTOMS DUTIES:

Governing Provisions.—Romanian customs regime is governed by following provisions: Customs Code adopted by Law No. 30/1978, Customs Rules approved by Decree No. 337/1981, Government Resolution No. 865/1990, amended by Government Resolution No. 269/1994, regarding customs regime applicable to natural persons, Government Resolution No. 673/1991, regarding Romanian customs tariffs for imports, amended by Government Ordinances No. 26/1993, approved and modified by Law No. 102/1994, and No. 14/1994, Government Resolution No. 732/1993, regarding modification of name and classification of goods in imports customs tariff, Order No. 3/1992, of Ministry of Economy and Finance, regarding introduction of "Declaration of Customs Value".

Additionally, Romania adheres to guidelines established by General Agreement on Tariffs & Trade ("GATT") and European Union ("EU"), as well as to commercial conventions signed by Romania through bilateral international treaties.

Present customs tariffs make distinction between imports and exports effected by legal persons as opposed to natural persons.

Customs Duties: Legal Persons.—Customs duties provided for by import tariffs are expressed in percentages and apply to value of imported goods expressed in lei. Duties collected by customs authorities are transferred to State budget.

Government Ordinance No. 26/1993 cites some generic categories of goods exempted from customs duties; other such categories are mentioned in special laws or resolutions arising from economic circumstances or social needs. In order to be declared exempt, goods must comply with certain conditions provided by law and they must be used solely for stated purposes of their importation.

Customs duties are based on customs value, determined and declared by importers who are obliged to submit customs declaration stating customs value.

Goods that may be imported are listed in tariff positions, importers being obliged to write these positions in customs declaration. Customs authorities verify if stated tariff positions are correct, then calculate duties and supervise payment of such duties to customs unit's account. Payment shall be made by documents securing payment. Goods are considered to be legally introduced in Romania upon basis of customs

See Topical Index in front part of this volume.

CUSTOMS DUTIES . . . *continued*
confirmation, which shall be in writing. Sometimes, such conformation is temporarily given before actual payment (for maximum 30 days) in case customs value cannot be determined at date of declaration and technical verification is required.

Customs value is established as provided in art. VII of GATT on basis of transaction's value plus: (a) transport expenses outside Romania; (b) loading, unloading and handling expenses related to transport outside Romania; and (c) insurance costs outside Romania.

Customs declaration and acknowledging documents that are drafted by customs authorities constitute executory title regarding customs duties.

Customs Duties: Natural Persons.—Customs regime applicable to natural persons is governed by special provisions which establish conditions and limits under which such persons may import or export goods and "ad valorem" tariff of 20% applicable to customs value of goods exceeding quotas established for each category of duty free goods. Natural persons shall declare their goods to customs authorities where customs value is established according to list containing single value for each item or group of items, established by Ministry of Finance. Some categories of goods are covered by special norms (vehicles, etc.).

Law has special provisions regarding duty exemptions, applicable to Romanian or foreign natural or legal persons in case of small border trade, or for persons sent abroad on work related to their employment, for persons moving from Romania or for foods products that can be taken abroad.

Contests and Violations.—Contests over application of customs import tariff, establishment of customs value and proper tariff position may be resolved by filing complaint with General Customs Department. Within 15 days after Department's reply, claim must be filed with competent court. Prescription period for customs duties is five years, commencing at date of registration of customs declaration.

Contraventions of customs regulations include: use of customs declaration based on false documents; failure to pay duties; failure to attend customs proceedings in due time; conducting specific operations without customs license; or use of transport documents containing erroneous dates. Violations discovered by customs authorities are certified in written minutes by chief of customs unit. Interested party may file complaint with specific customs unit contesting such minutes within 15 days. Within maximum of five days customs unit must then forward complaint to court with jurisdiction over territory where plaintiff's head office or domicile is located.

At proposal of Ministry of Finance and Ministry of Trade, Government may temporarily permit reduction in duties or exemption from duties for certain merchandise.

Government Resolution No. 228/1992, introduced antidumping fees or compensatory fees to protect national producers and domestic market from unfair competition resulting from import of some products at dumping or subsidized prices or export at prices below those of national market.

DEATH (PRESUMPTION OF AND ACTIONS FOR):

When circumstances surrounding death or disappearance are such that certainty of death of particular individual is not ascertainable by direct or physical evidence, person may be declared dead by court decision. There are two situations where declaration of death is rendered: (1) where it is preceded by declaration of absence; or (2) in exceptional circumstances where no previous declaration of absence has been issued.

Declaration of Death Preceded by Declaration of Absence.—Person declared absent may subsequently be declared dead by court decision. (Decree No. 31/1954 art. 16 par. 2). Three conditions must be met for declaration of death: (1) final court declaration of absence must be mailed at least 30 days prior to declaration of death (Decree No. 32/1954 art. 39); (2) four years must have passed since recording of most recent evidence indicating absentee to be alive; and (3) at least six months must have passed from posting of declaration of absence. Four-year period is calculated according to Decree No. 31/1954 art. 17 (see topic Absentees).

Declaration of Death Not Preceded by Declaration of Absence.—In exceptional circumstances, declaration of absence need not precede declaration of death, such as during war, railroad or aviation accidents, shipwrecks, earthquakes, floods, and revolutions. (Decree No. 31/1954 art. 16 par. 3). Presence of exceptional circumstance, and its date, may be proved by evidentiary means. However, one year must have passed since occurrence of event. (Decree No. 31/1954 art. 17).

Court declaration of death is stipulated in arts. 36-38 of Decree No. 32/1954 and is communicated to registry's office for inscription in its register. Decisions declaring death must include date of death. In cases where there is lack of sufficient evidence of death, date will be established as final day of period during which court declaration of death may be made. (Decree No. 31/1954 art. 18).

Determination of date of death pursuant to declaration opens succession (Civ. Code art. 659) and terminates natural person's capacity to exercise his rights and duties. In addition, declaration has retroactive effects so that absentee is considered to have died on established date, not when decision becomes final.

Annulment of Declaration.—Amending of initially established date of death is possible if proved that such date is inexact. (Decree No. 32/1954 art. 43, applied by assimilation as procedure for art. 18). If person declared dead is alive, annulment of declaration of death may be requested at any time. (Decree No. 31/1954 art. 20). In order to annul declaration of death, court action must be initiated with same judicial body which rendered declaration of death. (Civ. Pro. Code art. 2, as modified by Law No. 59/1993). Action may be initiated by any interested party. Upon commencement of action, public hearing will be held, during which parties and conclusions of Prosecutor's Office are heard. Once annulment is granted, decision is communicated to Population Department for necessary modifications in its register.

After annulment, person declared dead may request restitution of his belongings. (Decree No. 31/1954 art. 20). Relationship between person wrongfully declared dead and his heirs, as well as extension of heirs' obligation to return his property, depends upon their good faith. In absence of good faith on part of heirs, restitution damages will be awarded.

Relationship between person wrongfully declared dead and third persons who, for example, may have received property from heir, will be regulated in favor of recipient only if he obtained property in good faith and for valid consideration.

Annulment of declaration of death affects family relations. If spouse of person declared dead remarries, and declaration of death is annulled afterwards, second marriage remains valid, and first marriage terminates on date of conclusion of new marriage. (Fam. Code art. 22).

Presumption of survival has no application in Romanian legislation. If several persons died during same event, and survivorship cannot be established, they are considered to have died simultaneously. (Decree No. 31/1954 art. 21).

DEPOSITIONS:

Testimony of witnesses is subject to general provisions regarding administration of proof (Civ. Pro. Code arts. 167-171), as well as special provisions (arts. 186-200).

Law provides general guidelines for administration of evidence which prohibit following persons from acting as witnesses: (1) family members and relatives up to and including third degree; (2) spouses, even if separated; (3) persons declared by law as incapacitated; and (4) those found guilty of perjury. (Civ. Pro. Code art. 189).

In cases involving civil and divorce actions, family members and relatives mentioned above may serve as witnesses, with exception of descendants, as provided by law. (Civ. Pro. Code art. 190).

In event that legal action is delayed by refusal of witness to testify, art. 188 of Civil Procedure Code provides for possibility of issuing summons and lists applicable penalties from 500 to 3,000 lei, according to Law No. 59/1993 art. II, modifying Civil Procedure Code. In certain cases, penalties may be waived, subject to judge's discretion.

Following are required by law to maintain confidentiality of information received during performance of their duties, and thus, are excused from serving as witnesses (Civ. Pro. Code art. 191): those who perform religious services, doctors, midwives, pharmacists, attorneys and notaries public. Present or former public servants maintaining confidentiality of circumstances known to them while serving in their professional capacity, as well as those who may incriminate themselves or others by their testimony may also be exempt from serving as witnesses. (art. 189).

According to art. 193 of Civil Procedure Code, witnesses must be sworn in prior to their testimony, in person, before court. (art. 169).

Law prohibits use of rogatory letters for administration of evidence when: (1) administration of evidence is to be made in another city or locality; or (2) administration of evidence occurs by delegation, by court of same level or one of lower level (if court of same level does not exist).

Rogatory letters requested between Romanian court and foreign court, are effected by Ministry of Justice in accordance with conventions existing between the two countries. Details of existing bilateral conventions are maintained by Ministry of Justice and communicated annually to every Romanian court. Procedural requirements regarding witness' testimony in these situations is governed by Civil Procedure Code arts. 192-198. According to art. 142 of Civ. Pro. Code, if witness does not know Romanian language, authorized translator must be used, or in absence thereof, trustworthy person whose conduct shall be governed by provisions relating to experts. Judge may act as translator without having to take oath.

DESCENT AND DISTRIBUTION:

According to Romanian law as it relates to intestate succession, inheritance passes to deceased person's relatives in order of their degree.

Classes of Heirs.—

First Class.—Such class consists of deceased person's children and their descendants, irrespective of gender, and includes both marital children and legally recognized nonmarital children. (Civ. Code art. 669). Adopted children and their descendants are also members of this class, but their inheritance rights depend on whether adoption is fully effective.

Second Class.—This class is composed of privileged descendants and privileged collateral ancestors. If there are no heirs of first class, or if they are not eligible to inherit (i.e. they are guilty of serious act against deceased), or they reject inheritance, heirs of second class will stand to inherit, bypassing heirs of third and fourth classes. Privileged descendants are parents of deceased, either through marriage or adoption. Privileged collateral ancestors are brothers and sisters of deceased, together with their descendants. Brothers and sisters include those from within or outside marriage and from fully effective adoption. If privileged descendants or privileged collateral ancestors stand to inherit alone, they have right to total inheritance. Against privileged descendants, privileged collateral ancestors will take one-half or three-fourths of inheritance, depending on whether both or only one parent survives.

Third Class.—This class is composed of ordinary descendants (i.e. grandparents, and great-grandparents, of deceased). They stand to inherit after descendants, privileged descendants and collateral ancestors. Ordinary descendants may come either from within or outside marriage.

Fourth Class.—This is class of ordinary collateral ancestors consisting of uncles, aunts, and primary cousins of deceased. Such persons stand to inherit if no one stands to inherit from first three classes. Members of this class may come from within marriage or outside marriage.

General Principles of Legal Inheritance.—Heirs stand to inherit in order of their classes, regardless of degree of relatives. Living spouse, however, who is not part of any class of legal heirs stands to inherit against each class of heirs. Within same class, relatives of closer degree take precedence over those of more remote degree for purposes of inheritance. As part of second class (class of privileged ascendents and privileged collateral ancestors), parents of deceased (relatives of first degree) do not overtake brothers and sisters of deceased (second degree relatives), but share in inheritance. In case of succession representation, remote inheritant steps up in degree and replaces his deceased descendant, joining those heirs closer in degree by virtue of deceased descendant's share. (Civ. Code art. 664). Succession representation proceeds according to straight-line descent (art. 665) and includes descendants from brothers and sisters (art. 666). Class relatives of same degree inherit in equal shares, but in case

See Topical Index in front part of this volume.

DESCENT AND DISTRIBUTION . . . *continued*
of brothers and sisters from different marriages, brothers and sisters by both mother and father will take larger share than those only by one mother or father.

If there are no legal heirs or testamentary heirs, estate of deceased reverts to state.

Inheritance Rights of Surviving Spouse.—According to Law No. 319/1944, surviving spouse's right of inheritance depends upon whether that person was spouse of deceased at time of succession.

Surviving spouse has right to share in inheritance, but size of his share depends upon class of heirs against whom he takes. When surviving spouse takes with decedent's descendants, regardless of their number, surviving spouse receives one-fourth of inheritance. When surviving spouse takes against privileged descendants and collateral ancestors, he receives one-third of inheritance. When surviving spouse takes against ordinary descendants or ordinary collateral ancestors, such surviving spouse receives three-fourths of inheritance. If there are no legal heirs, or legal heirs are not eligible to inherit, or have rejected their inheritance, surviving spouse inherits entire estate of deceased.

Surviving spouse also has right to inherit furniture and objects from house shared by couple, as well as any wedding gifts, and retains this right unless he competes with heirs other than descendants of deceased. If there are descendants, these assets become part of estate. Surviving spouse has right to reside in house that is part of estate (Law No. 319/1944 art. 4), provided that spouse does not own second home and that his first is not includable in descendant's own inheritance. Habitation right of surviving spouse is temporary, and generally lasts until inheritance is divided, but at least until succession commences. If surviving spouse remarries before division of inheritance, habitation right lasts until date of remarriage.

DIVORCE:

Divorce is initiated by filing application in Law Courts (Fam. Code arts. 22, 26, 38, 39; Constitution art. 44 par. 2; Law No. 105/1992 regarding regulation of international private law relations, arts. 22 and 23). Under present draft of Fam. Code (following changes made in 1993 by Law No. 59) there are three methods for divorce: (1) divorce for well-founded reasons; and (2) divorce upon application of both spouses; and (3) divorce based on medical reasons.

Divorce for Well-Founded Reasons.—Divorce for well-founded reasons occurs when relations between spouses are gravely prejudiced and continuation of marriage is no longer possible. (Fam. Code art. 38 par. 2). Well-founded reasons include: (1) unjustified refusal of one spouse to live with other; (2) unjustified desertion of marital home; (3) adultery; (4) acts of violence; and (5) physiological incompatibility. Law Court may pronounce divorce against guilty spouse if evidence demonstrates that such spouse caused separation. Court can also permit divorce against both spouses if both have submitted divorce applications for well-founded reasons (see Fam. Code art. 608), or when evidence demonstrates that both are at fault. In such circumstances, court decision will not cite grounds for divorce if requested by both parties. (Civ. Pro. Code art. 617 par. 2).

Divorce Upon Application of Both Spouses.—Divorce may also be granted upon application of both spouses (Fam. Code art. 38 par. 2) if, as of date of submission of divorce application at least one year has passed since date of marriage, and there are no minor children from marriage. If such conditions are fulfilled, proof is not administered and court of law awards dissolution of marriage without pronouncing fault of either spouse. (Civ. Pro. Code art. 617 par. 3).

Divorce Granted for Medical Reasons.—Either spouse can apply for divorce when either spouse's state of health makes continuation of marriage impossible. (Fam. Code art. 38 par. 3).

Legal Effect.—Marriage is dissolved as of date on which Court decision becomes final and irrevocable (see Civ. Pro. Code art. 377 par. 2). Patrimonial effects of marriage as to third parties ceases on date when notation regarding divorce decision is made in Civil Status Register or, on date when third parties receive notice of divorce. (Fam. Code art. 39; see also Decree No. 278/1960, regarding civil status documents, arts. 14 and 24 and Law No. 105/1992).

Regarding use of post-divorce spousal names: (1) Spouses may agree that spouse who used other spouse's family name during marriage can keep such name after divorce; (2) in absence of agreement between spouses, court of law may grant this right for well-founded reasons, such as when spouse has become known in certain field and is recognized as personality under name of other spouse; (3) in all other circumstances, or court order, each spouse will use name used before marriage. (Fam. Code art. 40).

Alimony and Support.—Upon dissolution of marriage, divorced spouse has right to support if: (a) from time before or during marriage, spouse suffers from incapacity and cannot work as result; and (b) if, within one year from divorce, incapacity to work arises as result of circumstances related to marriage.

Alimony owed is equivalent to one-third of net income of spouse obliged to pay it, but is subject to needs of payee and means of payor. Alimony, together with child support, may not exceed one-half of net income of obliged party. (Fam. Code art. 41 par. 3).

If divorce is based upon fault of spouse requesting support, spouse at fault benefits from stipulations in Family Code regarding alimony for only one year from date of dissolution of marriage. (art. 41c).

In all cases, right to receive support ceases when recipient remarries. (Fam. Code arts. 2, 38, 39, 86, 89 letter a, 93, 94 par. 1-2, 95).

Child Custody.—Issues ancillary to divorce, such as child custody, child support obligations, and use of marital home, are decided mainly in accordance with minor's best interests. (Fam. Code art. 38 final par.). Status of minor children is determined according to Fam. Code art. 42. When deciding which parent receives custody of child, court takes into account interests of minor children, hearing directly from children if they are at least ten years of age, as well as hearing opinion of parents and of guardian authorities. Subject to court ruling, children may be placed in custody of relatives or other people, or with child-care institutions. Contribution of each parent to costs of support and education for children is also established by court. Agreement of parents as to payment of support is effective only if sustained by court (see also Fam. Code arts. 86, 93, 95, 97, 101, 107).

Parental rights are exercised by parent having custody of child. (Fam. Code art. 43). When child is assigned to such person, court will establish which parent shall administer property of child and represent child or acknowledge his acts. Person having custody over child has rights and duties uniquely relating to person of child. Other parent has right to have personal relations with child, and supervise child's upbringing, education and training. (Fam. Code; Constitution arts. 29 par. 6, 44 par. 1, 45, 46; Decree No. 31/1954 arts. 4-10).

Divorce procedure is governed by Civ. Pro. Code arts. 607-619. Divorce application must contain elements required for legal action (Civ. Pro. Code art. 82) and details regarding names of marital children, or of those who possess legal status of legitimate children.

Divorce application should be filed with court having jurisdiction over territory of last common domicile of spouses. If there was no such domicile, or if neither spouse resides there any longer, competence belongs to court having jurisdiction over territory where defendant is located. If defendant lives abroad, application must be submitted to foreign court having jurisdiction over territory where claimant is located. (Civ. Pro. Code art. 607).

According to Law No. 105/1992, regarding settling of international private law relations, divorce is governed by parties' national common law. If spouses have different citizenship, then common domicile rule is applied. (art. 20). If there is neither common citizenship nor common domicile, law of State where spouses had common residence, or with which spouses have in common closest relation, shall be applied. If one spouse was Romanian citizen at date of application for divorce and foreign law does not allow divorce or allows it under very restricted conditions, Romanian law shall apply.

ENVIRONMENT:

Primary provisions of Romanian legislation regarding environmental protection are as follows: Law No. 9/1973 regarding environmental protection; Order No. 623/1973 of Ministry of Health regarding Norms of Hygiene for Environmental Protection in inhabited areas; Law No. 18/1991 regarding Land; Government Resolution No. 457/1994, regarding organization and functioning of Ministry of Water Management, Forestry and Environmental Protection; Government Resolution No. 127/1994 regarding discovery of torts as to Norms for environmental protection and applicable penalties; Law regarding Environmental Protection, currently being considered by Parliament (already passed by Chamber of Deputies).

Soil Protection.—With regard to protection of soil, all landholders in Romania must observe following rules: (a) not to pollute land by storing, discharging or spreading wastes resulting from industrial, agricultural and other activities; and, (b) to perform works required by relevant authorities so as to prevent harmful effects of natural phenomena or ecomonic and social activities. Legislation regarding protection of soil has following purposes: maintain status of agricultural land; ascertain that land is used for agricultural purposes; ensure improvement of land quality.

Change in usage of agricultural land shall be approved only in certain cases provided by Law No. 18/1991 and only with prior approval of Ministry of Food and Agriculture.

Under Law No. 9/1973 and International Convention on Environmental Protection, ratified by Government Resolution No. 127/1994, both of which regulate environmental torts, landholders which fail to take cleanup measures and to develop lands which are not occupied in productive or functional manner within city bounds, may be penalized with fines between 100,000 and 250,000 lei. In compliance with Law No. 18/1991, landholders have right of property, as well as other real rights over land; de facto holder of land is liable for pollution of land and has legal obligation to immediately take adequate measures for its elimination.

Subsoil Protection.—According to Romania's Constitution, wealth of subsoil is public property exclusively. For works of public interest, public authorities may use subsoil of any real property, irrespective of its owner, with obligation to pay damages to owner.

Protection of subsoil is regulated by Law No. 9/1973, which prohibits disposal, evacuation, scattering or injection in subsoil of solid, liquid or gaseous residues, of radioactive substances etc., contents of which may lead to pollution of underground mineral water deposits. Tapping of natural resources within subsoil must avert pollution and prejudice, or, should latter be caused, reparations must be made.

Penal law makes reference to following crimes in connection with soil and subsoil protection: degradation of farm land, destruction and degradation of agricultural crops; obstruction of conservation measures.

Protection of Forests.—Legal status of forests is regulated by Forestry Code, enacted by Law No. 30/1962, as amended by Law 18/1991, Law No. 9/1973 and Decision of the Council of Ministers No. 2499/1969, which prohibits following: cutting of forest trees without having right to do so; appropriation of trees which are already cut; destruction of trees; unauthorized cattle grazing in forest areas; destruction of improvement works being performed in forests; transportation of wood without authorization and without certificate of origin; placement of industrial installations within or near forests; and vehicular traffic within forests, except as permitted on forest roads.

Maximum amount of wood to be exported from Romania is provided by law, on annual basis. Export of wood is strictly prohibited, unless exporter has authorization, issued by Ministry of Trade and Tourism with approval of Ministry of Waters, Forests and Environment. Such authorizations shall also provide maximum quantity allowed for export, and are granted on auction basis, provided that applicants produce contracts concluded with buyers.

Protection of Waters.—Legal status of water is regulated by following: Law No. 8/1974; Art. 135 of Romania's Constitution; Government Resolution No. 196/1991 regarding establishment of "Apele Romane" R. A. (Romanian Waters, Regie Autonome); Government Resolution No. 264/1991 regarding duties of Ministry of

ENVIRONMENT . . . *continued*

Environment for protection of waters; Government Resolution No. 1035/1990 regarding establishment of Regie Autonome of mineral waters; Law No. 17/1990 regarding legal regime of maritime waters; Law No. 9/1973.

Following acts are forbidden: (a) to release in water any kind of substances containing bacteria or microbes that may change chemistry of water and render it harmful for public health, flora, and fauna, or unsuitable for use; (b) to perform any works related to waters, without prior approval of competent authorities; (c) to use commercial enterprises without installations for water cleaning.

Violations of legal provisions regarding water protection are punishable with fines and/or imprisonment.

Protection of Atmosphere.—Regarding protection of atmosphere, legislation provides some obligations for state authorities and companies such as: to take measures for appropriate placement of factories and other economic units; to improve technologies; to recycle air-polluting wastes; and to use pollution-free means of transportation.

According to art. 77 of Law No. 9/1973, it is forbidden to release harmful substances in atmosphere in form of gas, vapor, aerosols, solid particles. Such actions are considered crimes and are punishable by fines or jail sentences ranging from three months to two years.

EXECUTIONS:

Code of Civil Procedure (Book 5, arts. 372-580) regulates following: forced execution, direct forced execution, execution of obligation to perform (including obligation to hand over assets), and indirect forced execution, where debt is recovered through sale of assets seized from debtor.

Creditor's rights and debtor's obligations relate to person: creditor may only value his right, and debtor is responsible only for personal debt.

Forced execution is fulfilled by bailiffs who function with courts of first instance and tribunals. (Law No. 92/1992 art. 110). They fulfill forced execution of civil dispositions from executory titles.

There are several forms of executory titles: (a) court decisions (final decisions, with temporary execution, and those issued by foreign courts); (b) notarial executory titles (Decree No. 387/1952, republished in 1959); (c) authentic notary documents, as well as promissory notes and checks granted executory status by State Notary (art. 4 of Decree No. 377/1960); (d) bank loan documents.

No decision or executory title may be executed until debtor has received acknowledgment together with summons and attached copy of title to be executed. Court's executor must give summons to debtor at least one day prior to any execution. (Civ. Pro. Code arts. 387-388).

If creditor allows six months to pass without fulfilling executory title, or without having initiated other formalities of seizure, execution may be set aside by interested party.

Forced execution concerns all debtor's movable and immovable assets, with certain exceptions allowed by law.

All assets belonging to natural persons may be seized except those assets considered of strict necessity for existence of debtor and of his family, and assets having strictly personal character, such as goods of domestic use, clothes, food, work tools, etc. (Civ. Pro. Code arts. 406-408). Salaries and other monetary rights of employee may be seized only up to sum which does not exceed one-half of net monthly salary of that employee, in following order of preference: (a) alimony obligations; (b) compensation for damages caused by death or injury; (c) payment of debts towards state issued out of duties and taxes; (d) compensation for damages to public property; (e) any other debts. (Civ. Pro. Code art. 409).

Compensation for temporary work incapacity, for employee's dismissal according to law and unemployment benefits, may not be pursued unless compensation constitutes damages caused by death and injury. Compensations granted in case of death, pregnancy and recovery therefrom, for taking care of ill child, damages or any other special destination indemnities and school scholarships may not be pursued for any kind of debts.

Like movable assets, immovable assets are seizable, but Civil Code provides several limits: (a) immovable assets of underage or restricted person may not be pursued prior to sale of all movable assets in his possession (Civ. Code art. 1826); (b) mortgaged immovable may be pursued with priority by mortgagor creditor (Civ. Code art. 1828); (c) two immovables owned by same debtor may not be pursued simultaneously, but successively (Civ. Code art. 1829); (d) immovables with annual revenue exceeding value of debt may not be seized. Naturally, debtor must produce evidence in this respect.

Concurrent Ownership.—Difficulties arise when debtor is not exclusive owner of assets subject to seizure. Pursuing such asset would constitute execution against third party that has no obligation towards creditor. Creditors may not seize and sell part owned jointly with debtor in immovable of legacy or of company. Rather, creditors must first request partition of immovables owned in common. This impediment does not occur if debtor's share in asset is established beyond reasonable doubt. (Civ. Pro. Code art. 490 par. 1).

With regard to legal status of assets owned in common by spouses, assets acquired during marriage by either spouse are, from moment of their acquisition, common to spouses. (Fam. Code art. 30). Spouses are liable with their common assets for expenses incurred in administrating any of common assets, for obligations contracted together, and for obligations contracted by any of spouses fulfilling ordinary material needs. If common creditors are not satisfied through common assets, they are entitled to seize spouses' private assets as well. (Fam. Code art. 34). Common assets may not be seized by creditors of one of spouses. After seizure of personal assets, creditor may request division of common assets. By division, assets attributed to each spouse will become private assets and may be object of forced execution by creditor.

Direct forced execution is execution in kind directed against object of obligation established by title to be executed.

When debtor is forced to hand over certain movable assets, bailiff must send debtor summons to return assets willfully; otherwise, court executor will seize asset from debtor and will deliver it to creditor. (Civ. Pro. Code art. 572).

In case of immovable asset, debtor is summoned to relinquish control over immovable within five days after having received summons. If he does not release immovable by this period, bailiff shall force debtor to do so.

Indirect forced execution in case of executory title having as object money debt concerns debtor's seizable movable or immovable assets by direct sale or auction. Sum of money obtained from sale of assets, after deduction of expenses, is used to satisfy creditor's debt. If there are several creditors, money obtained from sale of assets is divided in order to satisfy their individual debts, after preferential debts (e.g. those guaranteed by mortgage contracts).

EXECUTORS AND ADMINISTRATORS:

Upon death, person's estate is transferred to his successors. Successor may decline inheritance (Civ. Code art. 686), provided that he waives his rights no more than six months after date of death (art. 700). Waiver of inheritance must be express and effected through declaration at State Notary where succession was opened. (Civ. Code arts. 696-698).

Inheritance may be accepted when decedent's property becomes property of successor, in which case estate of decedent merges with personal assets of successor. Successor becomes responsible for liabilities of decedent's estate, not only within limits of decedent's own estate, but also within that of successor. Successor may accept inheritance "under benefit of inventory", thereby making himself responsible only for assets of decedent's estate. (arts. 704 and 714). Debts and obligations of estate are borne by all successors (i.e. those successors who inherit all or portion of decedent's estate—in which case they constitute legal successors or legatees). Legatees with title to specific asset are not obligated to bear debts and obligations of estate.

Testamentary Executor.—Usually, execution of will is performed by legal successors and universal legatees. However, testator may nominate one or more persons to serve as executor. (Civ. Code art. 910). In this case, State Notary must issue certificate acknowledging appointment. Function of testamentary executor is to supervise proper execution of will. Powers and objectives of testamentary executor differ, depending upon whether testator granted executor possession of movable assets, or "seisin". Executor without seisin supervises and controls execution of testamentary provisions, without actually executing provisions. (art. 916). Testamentary executor with seisin has right to execute testamentary provisions by obtaining possession of all or part of movable assets of testator. (Civ. Code art. 911). Seisin is granted for up to one year from date of testator's death. Executor has obligation to deliver movable assets to respective legatees. In event of insufficient funds to pay legatees, executor is obliged to request sale of movable assets to obtain necessary amounts. Testamentary executor also has right to cash in inheritance claims to movable assets. (art. 916 par. 3).

Testamentary executor has duty to carry out his obligations and to provide all relevant information related to administration of estate. (Civ. Code arts. 1539-1540).

FOREIGN EXCHANGE:

Legal Provisions.—Hard currency regime is primarily governed by following legal acts: Governmental Resolution No. 352/1991, regarding application of hard currency regime in Romania; Rule No. V/10.813/1994, regarding hard currency operations, issued by National Bank of Romania on basis of Law No. 34/1991, regarding Statute of National Bank of Romania; Ordinance No. 18/1994, regarding measures for enhancement of financial discipline of economic agents, followed and clarified by Instructions No. 1/Mar. 15, 1994, issued by National Bank of Romania and Ministry of Finance; Circular No. 13/Apr. 25, 1994 regarding hard currency control over collections resulting from exports; Circular No. 23/May 1995 for amendment of rules regarding hard currency operations, issued by National Bank of Romania.

Possession by Romanian and Foreign Citizens Entering Romania.—Possession of hard currency by Romanian citizens and their subsequent obligations were provided by Decree No. 210/1960; cancellation of art. 37 revoked all sanctions provided for possession and non-declaration of foreign currency. Rule No. V/10.813 provides that natural persons may enter Romania with equivalent in cash of US$10,000 per natural person and trip. To this end, natural persons include Romanian or foreign citizens, as well as natural persons representing legal persons. When entering Romania, natural persons are obliged to declare to customs any amounts exceeding US$1,000 and all travelers' checks. Such customs declaration, signed by customs, must be shown when exiting Romania in order to justify hard currency. Amounts exceeding US$10,000 are left in custody of customs authorities and will be returned to owner upon exiting Romania, at owner's request, if request is lodged within three years from date when amount was left in custody.

Besides maximum amount of US$10,000, natural persons may enter or exit Romania with travelers' checks, bank checks, credit cards and any other such banking instruments, expressed in hard currency. Natural persons cannot exit or enter Romania with amounts in cash in excess of 100,000 lei, except as provided in Circular No. 25/1994, issued by National Bank of Romania.

Exiting Romania.—As regards hard currency amount that may be taken out of Romania in cash, natural persons domiciled in Romania may exit Romania with maximum of US$1,000 per person and trip. Natural persons domiciled in Romania may take out up to US$5,000, based upon documents establishing that amount was cashed from bank or obtained following legal exchange against lei. Such amounts will be mentioned in customs declaration. Natural persons temporarily visiting Romania may leave Romania with same amount of cash as declared to customs when entering Romania.

Excess Amounts.—Amounts exceeding foreign currency limits are kept by customs authorities, according to procedure applicable for entry into Romania.

Norms No. 11/Dec. 18, 1992, issued by National Bank of Romania, establish modality of application of regulations regarding foreign currency sums that become State property according to law and procedure applicable in case such foreign currency sums are returned to legitimate natural persons. (art. 6). Government Ordinance No. 12/1994, modified arts. 31, 37, 38 of Law No. 32/1968 regarding establishment of and sanctions for contraventions, in sense that court procedure now allows appearance before court of officer who discovered violation and of any other person able to testify for resolution of matter.

See Topical Index in front part of this volume.

FOREIGN EXCHANGE . . . *continued*

Other Provisions.—Following persons are exempt from above-mentioned obligations: foreign citizens and their family members who are staff of diplomatic, consular and commercial representative offices of foreign states in Romania; foreign citizens who are officials with diplomatic passports, on temporary missions or transiting through Romania, as well as persons given diplomatic privileges, on basis of conventions to which Romania is party. However, such persons are not exempt from obligations regarding amounts in lei.

Currency legislation also includes general provisions establishing status of residents and nonresidents from hard currency point of view. Residents include following: (1) Romanian legal persons registered in Romania; (2) branches and subsidiaries of foreign companies, registered in Romania; (3) natural persons domiciled in Romania, regardless of their citizenship; (4) natural persons without citizenship who are domiciled in Romania; (5) diplomatic or consular missions, as well as other representative offices of Romania abroad, and their Romanian staff. Nonresidents include following: (1) legal persons not registered in Romania; (2) representative offices of foreign companies, which operate and are registered in Romania; (3) diplomatic and consular missions of other countries in Romania; (4) international organizations functioning in Romania and their staff; and (5) natural persons domiciled abroad who temporarily visit Romania for business or tourism.

Romanian Legal Persons.—In territory of Romania, payments, compensations, transfers, and other financial and capital transactions between legal entities and between legal entities and natural resident persons shall be made only in lei (Romanian currency). (Rules No. V/10.813/1994 of National Bank of Romania).

Hard currency operations may only be performed between resident and non-resident persons and only through accounts opened with Romanian banks authorized by National Bank of Romania. In areas having special customs regime, hard currency operations may also be performed between resident persons, provided that prior approval of National Bank of Romania is obtained.

Hard currency operations include: cashing, payments, compensations, transfers, credits, financial and capital transactions with movable or immovable valuables expressed in currencies of other countries or in composite currencies such as ECU, as well as operations in Romanian lei, which occur between resident and nonresident persons (as defined by point 4 of Rules).

Hard currency current operations include: (a) export and import of goods; (b) export and import of services; (c) medical, educational, business travel, and tourism expenses; (d) expenses of embassies and diplomatic missions or of international organizations or their representatives; (e) income from direct or portfolio investments or from capital and financial account operations; (f) current transfers representing taxes due to international organizations; (g) any transactions which are not capital and financial account operations, as provided by c. III of Rules.

Banks may grant credits in hard currency to resident legal persons only for import of goods and services. Romanian legal persons, regardless of their legal form and type of property, are obliged to collect, in hard currency, amounts related to export of goods, international execution of projects and sale of services, as well as those amounts related to any other international operations and transactions. Such amounts should be paid into accounts opened with commercial banks, either Romanian or foreign, authorized to operate in Romania.

Romanian legal persons, regardless of their legal form and type of property, are obliged to collect, in hard currency, amounts related to exports of goods, international execution of projects and selling of services, as well as those related to any other international operations and transactions, in accounts opened with commercial banks, either Romanian or foreign, authorized to operate in Romania.

Hard Currency Accounts.—Art. 4 of Government Ordinance No. 18/1994 provides for Romanian legal and natural persons (having status of business persons) to keep hard currency resources in foreign bank accounts only with prior authorization of National Bank of Romania. Hard currency capital and financial account operations are subject to approval of National Bank of Romania.

Amounts from inheritance, sums realized by foreign natural persons from sale in Romania of fixed assets, as well as pensions paid abroad by Romanian natural persons, are all subject to authorization of National Bank of Romania, through Currency Control Office, granted on basis of advice of Ministry of Finance, based on legal provisions and agreements signed by Romania with other countries. In order to obtain authorization, applicants must show documents proving source of amount for which transfer abroad is requested, as well as written proof from financial authorities that applicant does not have any unpaid debt in Romania representing taxes or other obligations towards State.

As for hard currency accounts of residents and nonresidents, Romanian legal persons may receive following: (1) hard currency collected from exports of goods; (2) hard currency from international execution of projects and sale of services, including hard currency advance amounts transferred by foreign partners for account of such operations; (3) contribution to capital subscribed in hard currency by foreign partners to commercial companies established in Romania and all subsequent increases of such capital; (4) sums in hard currency received as donation, aid or use clause for specific purposes expressly stated by donor; (5) banking credits received in hard currency; (6) sums of hard currency bought on banking currency market reserved to legal persons; (7) sums of hard currency realized by exchange houses and other commercial companies so authorized by National Bank of Romania; (8) dues of members, donations, aid received from within Romania or abroad by Romanian legal persons related to cultural or social activities or events; (9) commissions collected in hard currency; and (10) any other collections in hard currency resulting from relations with foreign natural or legal persons.

Payments may be effected from hard currency accounts of Romanian legal persons only as external payments of current account.

Operations of buying and selling hard currency by Romanian legal persons may be effected only through banking currency market intended for such persons, according to Norms of National Bank of Romania. Hard currency transfers between Romanian legal persons or between Romanian legal persons and accounts of Romanian natural persons are forbidden, but in latter case exception is made for payment of dividends in hard currency.

Resident natural persons may possess and use hard currency, and they may keep it in cash or in personal accounts opened with commercial banks authorized in Romania. Romanian natural persons who have hard currency incomes abroad may keep such amounts in accounts opened with foreign banks.

Nonresidents, either natural or legal persons, may open hard currency accounts with Romanian or foreign commercial banks authorized in Romania. They may use sums kept in such accounts without any restriction, and may transfer them to banks located abroad or exchange them for lei on Romanian hard currency market.

Diplomatic and consular missions of foreign countries in Romania, as well as nonresident legal persons registered in Romania which have lei incomes from lawful activities, may keep such lei resources in accounts opened with commercial banks authorized in Romania. With every new lei deposit, owner of account is obliged to supply written statement to bank, explaining source of lei. Such resources may be used only to effect lei payments in Romania.

Hard currency market is defined by Rules of National Bank of Romania as market, in which purchases and sales of hard currency are effected against Romanian currency. Annex 4 of Rules provides regulations to be observed for exchange operations. Following entities may effect exchange regulations: banks; foreign exchange houses established according to Law No. 31/1990; tourism companies authorized by National Bank of Romania. Participation on interbanking hard currency market is subject to authorization of National Bank of Romania.

In accordance with Law No. 34/1991, National Bank of Romania has following prerogatives: (a) regulate and supervise interbanking hard currency market; (b) authorize and supervise brokers of interbanking hard currency market; (c) participate on market in order to protect national currency; (d) publish daily rate of exchange of Romanian lei.

FOREIGN INVESTMENT:

Legal Framework.—Foreign investment regime is established by Law No. 35/1991, modified by Law No. 57/1993 and republished in Official Bulletin No. 185 of Aug. 2, 1993. Legislation provides guarantees and benefits to foreign investors and grants integral and unlimited use of returns of their investments.

Guidelines of this Law are as follows: (a) Principle of liberalization and promotion of foreign investment, involving elimination of restrictions and establishment of guarantees and benefits so as to create best possible regime for such investment. Law grants free access for foreign investments in all economic fields of activity (art. 4), through various realization modalities (art. 2), and by way of issuing substantial guarantees (arts. 5-11) and benefits (arts. 13-17). Governmental and administrative involvement within area of foreign investment is reduced to minimum, consisting of initial admission procedure required for foreign investors in Romania (arts. 18-23), as well as measures for guiding and encouraging foreign investors towards priorities of national economy, by granting supplementary benefits (arts. 14-16). Benefits have been granted, for example, by Law No. 66/1992 for foreign investors in domain of exploration and exploitation of oil and gas deposits and, by Law No. 84/1992 concerning free zone regimes. Recently, additional benefits have been granted by Law No. 71/1994 subject to condition that foreign investor contribution be minimum of US$50 million, cash, and to achieve production of integrated value of minimum of 60% and export minimum of 50% of annual production value; (b) principle of identical treatment of foreign investors. Thus, legal regime is same regardless of citizenship for natural persons, or nationality for legal persons (art. 11); (c) principle of national treatment, such that when foreign investment is confirmed, along with guarantees and special benefits it receives, it shall also be granted, in principle, same treatment as that provided to Romanian investors (with some exceptions mentioned below); (d) principle of stability of legal regime of foreign investments and application of most favorable legal regime. Legal regime established by Law No. 35/1990 applies to entire duration of foreign investment, unless subsequent law contains more favorable provisions. (art. 10).

Areas of Commercial Activity Open to "Foreign Investment".—As provided in art. 1 of Law No. 35/1991, foreign investment may be conducted through following activities: (a) setting up of commercial companies, subsidiaries or branches with wholly owned foreign capital or in association with Romanian natural or legal persons, according to provisions of Law No. 31/1990 regarding commercial companies; (b) increase of nominal capital of existing company or acquisition of social parts or shares in such companies, as well as bonds or other commercial instruments; (c) concession, leasing or management contracts; (d) acquisition of property rights over movable or fixed assets, or other real estate rights, with exception of property rights upon land; (e) acquisition of industrial and intellectual property rights; (f) acquisition of credit rights or other rights regarding services having economic value that are associated with investment; (g) purchase of production facilities or other buildings, except residences not related to investment; (h) formation of contracts regarding exploration, exploitation and production sharing of natural resources.

Concept of "Foreign Investor".—As provided in art. 3 of Law No. 35/1991, "foreign investor" means natural or legal persons, with their residence or head office abroad, which conduct investments in Romania, in any of forms provided by law.

Contribution of Foreign Investors.—As provided in art. 2 of Law No. 35/1991, foreign investor's contribution may consist of following items: (a) capital in free currency; (b) machines, equipment, transport means, components, spare parts and other goods; (c) services, industrial and intellectual property rights (patents, licenses, know-how, trade and factory marks, copyrights) knowledge and methods of organization and management; (d) revenues and profits deriving from activities conducted in Romania, as well as goods and values legally acquired, after payment of taxes and fees provided by law.

Restrictions on Foreign Investments.—Art. 4 of Law No. 35/1991 applies following restrictions to foreign investment: (a) it shall not violate norms concerning environmental protection; (b) it shall not interfere with Romanian security and national defense interests; (c) it shall not offend public order, health or morals.

Guarantees and Rights.—Foreign investments in Romania may not be nationalized or submitted to measures having similar effects, except in cases of public interest. In such instances, procedure provided by law must be observed and immediate and

See Topical Index in front part of this volume.

FOREIGN INVESTMENT . . . *continued*
adequate indemnity payment must be made corresponding to value of investment. (Law No. 35/1991 art. 5). Under Law No. 33/1994, regarding expropriation for public utility, adopted upon basis of art. 41 of Constitution, private property may not be expropriated unless for use of public utility, with fair and prior compensation.

Art. 9 of Law No. 35/1991 also grants foreign investors following rights: (a) to participate in management and administration of investment, according to contracts and statutes (by-laws); (b) to assign their contractual rights and obligations to other investors, either Romanian or foreign; (c) to transfer abroad entire annual profits, observing conditions of Romanian foreign currency regime, after payment of taxes, fees and other obligations provided by Romanian law. Profits due to foreign investors, in foreign currency or in lei, may be used to effect new investments in Romania, to buy Romanian goods or services, or they may be legally exchanged on financial market; (d) to transfer abroad amounts collected from copyrights, expert assistance, expertise and other services, according to existing contracts; (e) to transfer abroad amounts obtained from sale of shares, social parts, bonds or other commercial instruments, as well as amounts resulting from liquidation of investments, in observance of conditions of Romanian foreign currency regime; (f) to transfer abroad in agreed currency amounts obtained as indemnity in cases of expropriation, nationalization or other similar measures.

Incentives.—According to provisions of Law No. 35/1991, foreign investors are granted several customs, fiscal and profit incentives, such as: (a) exemption of customs duties for machines, machinery, equipment, transport means and any other imported goods necessary for investment, which constitute in-kind contribution or which are purchased with cash contribution of foreign investor to nominal capital or to increase of such capital (art. 12); (b) exemption of customs duties for period of two years, calculated from date when facility begins to operate or, as case may be, from date when activities start, for raw materials, consumable materials, imported spare parts and components, all of which are necessary for and are used in production (art. 13); (c) exemption of profit tax for period of two to five years, subject to field in which investment was effected (art. 14). If investment is effected by setting up of commercial companies, subsidiaries or branches with wholly-owned foreign capital or in association with Romanian natural or legal persons, exemption of profit tax is granted subject to condition that contribution of foreign investor, in cash and in kind, represents at least 20% of company's nominal capital, but not less than US$10,000. Foreign investments not meeting these requirements are governed by provisions of common law; and (d) reduction of profit tax by 50% or 25% after expiration of periods above-mentioned, in certain conditions provided by art. 15 of Law No. 35/1991 (if profit was used to enlarge and upgrade technical and material infrastructure, to protect environment, if at least 50% of realized products and services are exported, if new jobs are created, etc.).

Tax exemptions and reductions are only granted to commercial companies which registered with Register of Commerce prior to Jan. 1, 1995 and for which exemption period has not expired. (Government Ordinance No. 70/1994, published in Official Monitor No. 246 of Aug. 31, 1994).

Certification Procedure for Foreign Investment.—Conditions necessary to be considered "foreign investor" are provided in Law No. 35/1991 arts. 19-23. Foreign investors must file application with Romanian Development Agency ("RDA"), governmental institution specializing in promotion of foreign investment in Romania. Application shall have as annexes required documents—company contract and statutes, commercial contracts or other legal documents drafted according to requirements of Romanian law. RDA analyzes status of investor, field of application and manner in which investment is to be effected, as well as capital to be invested. (art. 19). RDA's reply must be communicated within 30 days from date of filing of application. If foreign investor receives no such communication within this 30-day period, it is considered that investment may be effected. (art. 21). Express or tacit confirmation of RDA is first step in effecting investment in Romania. (art. 22). Once such legal documents are completed and registered with Register of Commerce, foreign investor is entitled to apply to RDA for "certificate of investor", document establishing status of foreign investor before Romanian authorities, and which is used to evaluate associated rights.

Results.—Most frequently used form for effecting foreign investment in Romania is commercial company with partial or total foreign capital. Based upon data supplied by National Office of Register of Commerce (Statistical Bulletin No. 11/1994, page 4 and annex 8), number of commercial companies with foreign participation registered in Romania between Dec. 8, 1990, and Mar. 31, 1994, totals 29,848 with subscribed total capital of 287.9 billion lei, out of which US$541.5 million are subscribed in free currency, average for one commercial company being 9.6 million lei and, respectively, US$18,100.

In consideration of this data, it appears that volume of foreign investments in Romania, though increasing, is still at low level.

International Conventions.—To extent that international agreements and conventions regarding foreign investment, signed by Romania, do not provide otherwise, provisions of Law No. 35/1991 are applicable. (art. 34). This text acknowledges numerous international conventions signed by Romania in order to promote and mutually guarantee capital investments. Most recent bilateral agreements include those entered into between Romania and following nations: U.S.A., May 28, 1992 (ratified by Law No. 110/1992); Uruguay (Law No. 38/1991); Turkey (Law No. 9/1992); Greece (Law No. 90/1992); Israel (Law No. 91/1992); Finland (Law No. 113/1992); Australia (Law No. 6/1994); Thailand (Law No. 7/1994); Argentina (Law No. 39/1994); Switzerland (Law No. 40/1994); United Arab Emirates (Law No. 94/1994).

Romania is also party to Convention for the Settling of Claims Regarding Investments Between States and Persons from Other States, signed in Washington, D.C. on Mar. 18, 1965 (ratified by Decree No. 62/1975), and to Convention for the Constitution of the Multilateral Investment Guarantee Agency, MIGA, adopted in Seoul, South Korea on Oct. 11, 1985 (ratified by Law No. 43/1992).

GARNISHMENT:

Garnishment is procedure by which plaintiff creditor obtains, by judicial garnishee order, amounts owed to debtor by third person, garnishee. Garnishee is ordered to pay established amount directly to creditor. Garnishment may be ensuring or executory, and is regulated by Civ. Pro. Code arts. 452-462. There are two distinct procedural functions of garnishment: (1) serves to enforce execution of obligations; (2) provides guarantee for achievement of executory title.

Ensuring garnishment arises at request of creditor whose claim is ascertained by signed, written document which is object of court action. Creditor may be required to post bond for sum established by court. When no written document exists, bond is one-half value of amount claimed by creditor. Garnishment action commences with garnishment order, communicated directly to garnishee, which effectively makes total amount unavailable to garnishee for other uses. Garnishee may avoid garnishment by putting amount in question at creditor's disposal.

After creditor has obtained executory title, guaranteed garnishment may become executory garnishment through validation procedure. If legal action is rejected, garnishment order becomes obsolete and garnished sum becomes available for use. (Civ. Pro. Code art. 455).

Executory Garnishment.—Creditor who has obtained executory title may request garnishment order, provided that ensuring garnishment has not already been instituted. During validation stage of garnishment, parties are summoned (creditor, debtor and garnishee), and trial is conducted. If it is ascertained that all legal requests have been fulfilled, court will validate garnishment. At this point, garnishee becomes debtor of garnishing creditor, and is ordered to pay debt. This decision may be appealed. (Civ. Pro. Code art. 460).

GIFTS:

To be valid, gift must be made by authentic deed. (Civ. Code art. 813). Noncompliance with authenticity requirement voids gift. When gift contract is finalized by separate offer and acceptance, gift must be delivered within lifetime of donor. In addition, donee must have capacity to accept offer.

Minors and persons forbidden by court order do not have capacity to make gifts. (Fam. Code arts. 129 [1-3] and 133 [3] with reference to arts. 105 [3] and 147). Minors who have reached adult age cannot make gifts to their guardians until such guardians have been released from their duties to care for minor (except where guardian is minor's ascendant). (Civ. Code art. 809 and Fam. Code art. 140). Following do not have capacity to receive gift: (1) Unborn persons (Civ. Code art. 808) and companies which have not yet acquired legal existence; (2) doctors and pharmacists who treated donor for illness which caused donor's death, as well as priests who assisted donor in religious matter during donor's last illness (Civ. Code art. 810); (3) deaf or mute persons who cannot write, except in instances in which such persons are assisted by specially appointed person (Civ. Code art. 816 and Fam. Code arts. 152, 159).

Minors and others forbidden to make gifts have right to receive them. However, such gifts must be accepted in presence of their legal representatives (parents or guardians) and by their ascendants. (Civ. Code art. 815). Legal entities may also accept gifts, provided that subject matter of gift corresponds to scope of entity's activities. (Decree No. 31/1954 art. 34).

Since gifts are generally irrevocable, any clause or condition which may directly or indirectly infringe upon donee's use of gift, is incompatible with essence of gifts and is void. (Civ. Code art. 822).

Spousal Gifts.—According to arts. 826 and 937 of Civil Code, gifts between spouses are revocable at any time, regardless of whether revocation is made during or after marriage, or after death of donee. Such revocation need not involve court action and may be either express or implied.

Special Gift Categories.—(1) Secret gifts appear under guise of contract involving compensation and are valid if they meet all conditions set forth in Civ. Code arts. 813-814 (requirements of signature, notarization and donor competence). (2) Indirect gifts are legal acts which are made with intention to bestow benefit, but are realized on basis of another act other than gift. Indirect gifts need not be authenticated because they are valid if made according to procedural and substantive requirements for legal acts under which they are realized.

Renunciation of debt, by which creditor refuses right of credit, also qualifies as indirect gift.

Revocation.—Parties to gift contract may stipulate in contract that, under certain conditions, contract will be automatically rescinded.

In addition, gifts may be revoked even in absence of revocation clauses in contract in following instances:

(1) Ingratitude of Donee.—Ingratitude refers to attempts made by donee on donor's life, violent or grave injury caused by donee to donor, as well as donee's refusal to provide donor with food when requested. (Civ. Code art. 831). Revocation action ceases when donor or his heirs, having knowledge of ingratitude, forgives donee. Forgiveness is presumed when a year has passed after discovery of fact leading to revocation and donor or his heirs have not requested revocation within this period.

(2) Birth of Child to Donor.—Gifts are revoked by right when donor had no children at time of gift's making, but subsequently, living child was born to donor. Revocation due to birth of child may not be set aside by any contrary stipulation in gift contract. (Civ. Code art. 836).

HUSBAND AND WIFE:

Matrimonial system is governed by provisions of Fam. Code, enacted by Decree No. 32/1954.

Fam. Code art. 1 stipulates that in relations between spouses, husband and wife have equal rights. Patrimonial relations between spouses are founded on principle of equality between genders.

Common and Separate Assets.—Spouses may have two categories of assets: (a) those common to spouses; and (b) those owned separately. Generally, assets acquired during marriage by either spouse are common assets. (Fam. Code arts. 30-31). Common assets include those assets acquired by spouse individually, while married, even if that spouse's name is solely listed on document of acquisition.

Assets are common if acquired before divorce decision becomes final. (Fam. Code art. 39).

See Topical Index in front part of this volume.

HUSBAND AND WIFE. . . *continued*

Apart from assets acquired before marriage (Fam. Code art. 31[a]), following are considered separately owned by spouses: assets acquired during marriage by inheritance, legacy or donation (except when donor has stated that they shall be common); assets of personal use or for one spouse's work; assets acquired as awards or rewards; scientific or literary manuscripts, artistic designs and projects, inventions and innovative projects, and other similar assets; insurance or compensatory indemnification for damages caused to person; value representing or substituting asset owned separately by spouses. (Fam. Code arts. 1-3, 30, 32, 36, 139).

Under Romanian Constitution family is founded upon free consent of spouses to marriage and their full equality (art. 44), but principle of equality is not applied in separation of assets in case of divorce. Upon divorce, contribution of each spouse to acquisition of assets and their well-being is considered.

Agreements Limiting Right to Common Assets are Void.—Fam. Code aims at protecting common interests of spouses and family from inexperience of either spouse. For example, neither spouse may dispose of immovable common assets without express consent of other spouse.

System of common assets has imperative character, so that neither spouse, under influence of other and under appearance of serving interests of community, may be deprived of assets. Matrimonial agreements concluded in contravention of law are null.

Spouses may not agree to relinquish their equal rights to manage, use and dispose of common assets. Agreements may not provide that certain assets acquired during marriage are separately owned by one of spouses, nor remove common character of matrimonial assets by establishing one spouse's rights over them or their shares if those assets are divided. Also, one spouse may not donate common assets during marriage. For example, Supreme Court declared to be null and void agreements by which one spouse admits not having made any contribution in acquiring assets during marriage. (Decree No. 31/1960). Agreement attempting to increase community assets by diminishing assets of one spouse is also invalid. (Fam. Code art. 30 par. 2). Sales between spouses are not permitted in effort to prevent them from making irrevocable donations and to protect third parties against fraud. (Civ. Code art. 1307).

Donations between spouses are revocable, although other donations (see topic Gifts) are irrevocable legal acts. (Civ. Code art. 934). Donations may be executed between spouses only regarding assets owned separately by them, not with regard to common assets.

Effect of Marriage or Dissolution Thereof.—Patrimonial effects of marriage cease regarding third parties from moment divorce decision is registered with Civil Status Register or from date third parties are given notice by another. (Fam. Code art. 39 par. 2). As result, third parties may consider those assets acquired after dissolution of marriage as assets owned separately by spouses.

Supreme Court has established that asset acquired by one spouse after dissolution of marriage with money from other spouse represents asset owned separately by spouse who acquired it, other spouse having only credit against sum remitted during marriage.

Assets acquired during separation de facto of spouses are common. For such assets, Supreme Court (Civil Decision No. 1861/1982) established they are common, but situation de facto may determine smaller contribution for spouse who did not actually contribute to acquisition.

Marriage Terminated by Death.—In case of death of one spouse (Fam. Code art. 37: end of marriage by death of one of spouses or by court's decision declaring death of one of them), assets acquired up to date established by court decision as being date of death are common, and those acquired after this date are owned separately.

If court's decision declaring death is annulled, all assets acquired after established date of death are common, because neither marriage nor community of assets ceased. If former spouse of person declared dead has remarried, and new marriage is bona fide, community of assets from previous marriage is valid up to conclusion of new marriage.

Proof of Asset Status.—With regard to proof establishing ownership over assets, Fam. Code art. 30 par. 3 provides presumption with regard to community: "the feature of common asset is not to be proved". Until proved otherwise, asset acquired during marriage is considered common and spouse claiming to own asset separately must prove it.

Any probatory means is admitted in order to demonstrate that assets ar personal to one spouse. (art. 5 par. 1 of Decree 32/1954—derogation of principle established in Civ. Code art. 1191 forbidding proof with witnesses and presumptions regarding assets valued over 250 lei and whenever it is managed against or over amount stipulated in documents. Reason for derogation from common right instituted in Civ. Code art. 1191 is that of material and moral impossibility of elaborating upon documents [Civ. Code art. 1198]).

In case of marriage concluded before enactment of Family Code (Feb. 1, 1954), proof of asset owned separately by spouses may be made by any probatory means. (art. 5 par. 2 of Decree No. 32/1954). In case of marriage concluded after enactment of Family Code, proof towards third parties may be used only in conformity with Civ. Code art. 1191. In relations between spouses, proof about quality of asset owned separately may be made by any probatory means.

Obligations of Spouses.—According to Fam. Code art. 32, spouses are liable with their common assets for: expenses made in managing any of common assets; obligations contracted together; obligations contracted by any of spouses for needs of marriage; for prejudice caused by one of spouses to assets of public property (Constitution art. 135 par. 4) if by this they increased their common assets (see Constitution art. 41 par. 2 and Decision of Constitutional Court of Sept. 7, 1993 published in Official Gazette No. 232 of Sept. 27, 1993).

After seizing assets owned separately by debtor spouse, his personal creditor may require separation of common assets, but only to extent necessary to cover debt. Assets attributed following such separation become separately owned. (Fam. Code art. 33 par. 2, 3; Civ. Pro. Code arts. 372-580, modified through Law No. 59/1993).

Assets owned separately by spouses may be seized by common creditors, but only after first seizing common assets. (Fam. Code art. 34; Civ. Pro. Code arts. 372-580, modified through Law No. 59/1993).

Reciprocal Tacit Mandate.—Presumption of reciprocal tacit mandate is provided by Fam. Code art. 35: "the spouses together manage, use and dispose of common assets. Either spouse, exercising alone these rights is presumed to have the other spouse's consent." This presumption has relative character, as it can be overturned by proof to contrary.

Because presumption of tacit reciprocal mandate does not have absolute character, court is entitled to verify if spouse who participated in alienation of asset demonstrated disapproval by his behavior. However, right of bona fide third parties who deal with one spouse cannot be overlooked. If acquirer was of ill will, it must be proved, because presumption of good will prevails. (Civ. Code art. 1899 par. 2).

Exception from reciprocal tacit mandate are stipulated in Fam. Code art. 35 par. 2: neither spouse may alienate or mortgage common land or buildings without express consent of other spouse (see also Land Law No. 18/1991 arts. 45-51; art. 41 of Law No. 50/1991 regarding license for construction). Spouse who did not expressly consent to document regarding alienation or mortgage of land or construction may initiate annulment or claim, as other owner. In case of claim, express consent of other spouse is not necessary, because it benefits community of assets and, therefore, both spouses.

Although Fam. Code art. 35 par. 2 refers only to land and constructions, it is also applied in case of other immovables: (1) by destination (Civ. Code arts. 468-470); (2) by object (Civ. Code art. 471—usufruct of immovable goods, servitudes, actions of claiming immovables); or, (3) by right (Civ. Code arts. 493, 494). Fam. Code art. 35 par. 2 refers only to alienation by documents between living persons, not documents in case of death (i.e.: will).

Judicial practice also established exceptions to reciprocal tacit mandate, besides that stipulated by art. 35 par. 2, i.e. documents with gratuitous title between living persons, irrespective of fact whether they refer to movables or immovables. Exception to this limit, established by practice, is ordinary gifts (birthday gifts) and charity.

Division of Common Assets.—Common assets are divided between spouses upon dissolution of marriage (Fam. Code art. 36 par. 1), either by mutual agreement between spouses, or, in case of disagreement between spouses, by court order.

Common assets may be divided, totally or partially, during marriage by court order under special circumstances. For example, if spouse has no other resources to help needy child from previous marriage or if spouse has left domicile and has not consented to alienating some of common assets. (Fam. Code art. 36 par. 2).

Division of common assets during marriage may occur only in following cases: (1) at spouse's request; (2) at personal creditor's request (personal to either spouse); or (3) at seizure of assets of one spouse.

Assets divided during marriage become separately owned. (Fam. Code art. 36 par. 2). Undivided assets, as well as those acquired at later date, are common assets. (Fam. Code arts. 1-3, 30-35, 37-39).

With regard to separately owned assets, either spouse enjoys exclusive right to manage, use and dispose of separately owned assets, and either spouse may conclude legal documents during marriage with other spouse (excepting sales, Civ. Code art. 1307) or with third parties.

INFANTS:

Physical persons may exercise civil rights and fulfill civil obligations when they are of legal age, regardless of gender. Persons come of legal age when they reach age of 18. (Decree No. 31/1954 art. 8). However, minors who marry acquire full capacity to exercise their rights.

Prior Adult Consent for Execution of Legal Documents.—Persons who have reached age of 14 have limited capacity to exercise their rights: they may conclude legal documents provided that their parents or guardians consent. (Decree No. 31/1954 art. 9). Purpose of prior consent is to protect minors from deceit of third parties. (Fam. Code arts. 105 par. 2 and 133). It is necessary for minor to reach age of 14 at time of contract: simply having entered year when age of 14 will be reached is insufficient.

Persons between ages of 14 and 18 years may legally conclude some types of legal documents without consent of guardian or parent, including: (a) those documents which may be concluded before age of 14 (simple documents); (b) special deposits at CEC, Insurance and Savings Bank of Romania (see Decree No. 31/1954 art. 10 final par.); and (3) public administration documents, if they are not harmful. (Decree No. 32/1954 art. 25).

If minor has reached age of 16, he may dispose of half of his estate through use of will. (Civ. Code art. 807).

Following legal documents cannot be validly executed without prior consent of parent or legal guardian: (a) administrative documents; (b) contracts to repair or lease goods; (c) documents involving some type of disposition, such as alienation; and (d) documents encumbering property with real charge (e.g. mortgage or security).

Legal Obligations of Minors.—Minors are forbidden from making donations or guaranteeing obligations of others. Also, minors may not conclude legal documents with their guardians, or their guardians' spouses, direct relatives, or siblings. (Fam. Code arts. 128 and 133 par. 3).

According to norms of civil procedure, minors between ages of 14-18 may be subpoenaed personally or through their guardians. If minor has not yet reached age of 14, minor must be subpoenaed through legal representative, since law recognizes that minors under 14 do not have capacity (full or limited) to exercise their rights.

JOINT-STOCK COMPANY:

Law No. 31 of 1990 provides for establishment of joint-stock companies (hereinafter, "S.A.").

S.A. may be established in any field of activity: production, construction, transportation, commerce, import-export, and services. In some areas of activities, such as financial services, banking, brokerage and insurance, law expressly provides that companies established in such fields must be conducted through S.A. Foreign investment may also be conducted through S.A. in compliance with Law No. 35/1991 concerning foreign investments, and Law No. 31/1990 concerning commercial companies. (See also, topic Corporations.)

Irrespective of procedure used to incorporate S.A., share capital is represented by shares issued by company, which may be nominative or bearer shares. If contract of

See Topical Index in front part of this volume.

JOINT-STOCK COMPANY . . . *continued*
association does not provide for type of shares, they are considered to be bearer shares; shares which are not fully paid are nominative. Regardless of their type, shares have equal value. (art. 61).

Two procedures are utilized to incorporate S.A.:

(I) Simultaneous Constitution.—At least five shareholders, Romanian or foreign, legal or natural, may establish S.A. Contract of association of S.A., sets forth: establishment of S.A.; share capital; and, shareholders' subscription of shares issued by company.

At time of authentication of constitutive documents (contract of association and statutes) at State notary office, share capital paid must not be less than 30% of total subscribed capital. Contract of association will specify date on which subscribed share capital is to be fully paid. For S.A. composed of Romanian shareholders, capital must be minimum of 1 million lei. Foreign shareholders must contribute minimum of US$10,000. (Law No. 57/1993 art. 10).

(II) Public Subscription of Shares.—One or more founders must draft prospectus for stock subscription, as provided in art. 9 of Law No. 31/1990. It is not mandatory for founders to become shareholders of respective company. Prospectus must mention date established for closing of subscription, and must be signed by founders, authenticated at notary office, and filed with local Register of Commerce. Also, founders must file application for authorization to publish prospectus which must be granted by local court of Register of Commerce. After its authorization, prospectus for stock subscription shall be published in press.

Subscription of shares must be made on one or several copies of prospectus, certified by court which authorized its publication. Subscription must comprise name/denomination of subscriber, domicile or headquarters, number of subscribed shares, date of subscription and express statement that subscriber has knowledge of and accepts prospectus. (Law No. 31/1990 art. 11).

Upon closing of subscription, founders must convene constitutive assembly of shareholders by public notice in Official Monitor, published no less than 15 days from date of meeting. (art. 12).

Company is established only when entire share capital has been subscribed and if each subscriber has paid in cash 50% of value of subscribed shares. Shares representing in-kind contributions must be fully paid. Debts owed by third parties are not acceptable as consideration. (art. 13).

At constitutive meeting, each subscriber has right to one vote, irrespective of number of subscribed shares. (art. 17). If shares provided for by prospectus have not been fully subscribed, assembly may reduce share capital to level of subscription, eliminating shares not subscribed.

Constitutive assembly reviews existence of payments of share capital, approves contract of association and statutes of company, appoints authorized persons to authenticate documents, proceeds with incorporation formalities, and appoints administrators and auditors of company. (art. 21).

Rights and Liabilities of Founders/Promoters.—Promoting subscribers to contract of association, as well as those persons who have significant role in company's establishment, are considered founders/promoters.

Founders must deliver incorporation documents to administrators and are jointly liable for undetermined period of time to third parties for any noncompliance with legal requirements of incorporation procedure, as well as for obligations assumed at time of incorporation of company. Founders are responsible for expenses incurred for incorporation and do not have recourse against subscribers if company fails to be incorporated. (art. 27). Founders and initial administrators are jointly liable for full subscription of share capital and payment of in-kind contributions. (art. 28). Founders have right to receive quota of net profits of company, not exceeding 6%, which may not be granted for period of greater than five years from date of incorporation of company, irrespective of whether or not founders are shareholders of company. (art. 30).

Upon fraudulent dissolution of company, founders have right to request damages. Right to sue may be exercised within six months from date of general assembly of shareholders deciding upon such dissolution. (art. 31).

Shareholders' Rights.—Each share signifies one vote. (art. 67). Right to exercise their vote is suspended for those shareholders delinquent in making their payments. (art. 67).

Shareholders which did not participate in general assembly or those which voted against its decisions and requested recording of their opposition in minutes, have right to commence legal action contesting decisions of general assembly, within 15 days from date of publication of decisions in Official Monitor. (art. 90). At time action is initiated, plaintiff shareholder may request issuance of stay of execution of contested decision. (art. 91).

Shareholders who disagree with general assembly's decisions, concerning principal aim of company's objective, relocation of place of business or modification of legal form of company, have right to withdraw from company and obtain payment for their shares. Payment must be made in proportion with their participation in nominal capital, and in accordance with last approved balance sheet. At this time, withdrawing shareholders must deposit shares they possess. (art. 92).

Shareholders have right to receive dividends in proportion to their share participation in capital; if dividends are not received, shareholders have right to request restitution of shares, within three years from date of share distribution.

Every shareholder has right to submit complaint to auditors regarding items subject to audit. Auditors must verify such complaint and draft report for general assembly.

Liabilities.—Shareholders are obligated to pay all their debts toward company and to effectuate payments of capital in timely manner and in accordance with conditions stipulated in Contract of Association. Shareholder who is delinquent in making capital contribution is liable for damages incurred by company and, if contribution was made in cash, shareholder is also obligated to pay interest from date contribution should have been made. If shareholders fail to submit their remaining contributions when due, council of administration of company may file claim against shareholders for remaining contributions or void shares. (art. 66).

Shareholder who possesses conflict of interest against company must withdraw from activity which gives rise to conflict. In such cases, shareholder is liable for damages incurred by company, if without his vote, required majority would not have been met. (art. 85).

Administration and Control.—Administration of S.A. is effectuated by one or several administrators, who constitute Administration Council. Procedures for naming and replacing administrators, as well as obligations, rights and liabilities of administrators, are provided by Law No. 31/1990, §III, arts. 93-110, supplemented by Com. Code arts. 374-391 regarding agency.

Company administrators are liable for nonfulfillment of obligations. However, those administrators who declared in Administration Council Decision Register that they oppose such obligations, are not liable.

Internal control of company is secured by censor/control commission named by shareholders. Naming of such controllers, as well as their obligations and liabilities are regulated by Law No. 31/1990, §IV, arts. 111-117, supplemented by Com. Code dispositions regarding agency liability.

General assembly of shareholders has direct action against promoters, administrators, controllers and directors whose actions have prejudiced company. Suits commenced by shareholders or by general assembly against administrators, controllers, or promoters are usually brought in court with jurisdiction over territory where company has its principal place of business or where defendant is domiciled. Actions against administrators also rest with company's creditors, who may exercise action in event of bankruptcy of company.

Dissolution and Liquidation.—Such procedures are regulated by Law No. 31/1990 Title VI, arts. 169-173, respectively arts. 176-184 and 187-193. (See also, topic Corporations [Trade Companies].)

Following lead to dissolution of S.A.: (1) reduction of number of shareholders below five; (2) reduction of capital below 1,000,000 lei, or its equivalent in foreign currency; (3) expiration of duration of company. (Law No. 31/1990 art. 169).

Liquidation of S.A. is verified by Law Courts, which will also be responsible for naming liquidators. Any shareholder may oppose this action or contest final liquidation balance.

Court Actions.—S.A. can be sued by any party asserting claim against it, in accordance with established procedure stipulated in Civil Procedure Code. S.A. is represented in court by its legal representative, administrator or general director, or by person authorized by general director or general assembly to act as legal representative.

S.A. may sue any legal or natural person, or debtor, in asserting its rights in accordance with procedures established by Civil Procedure Code, and by special laws which regulate each case.

JUDGMENTS:

Recognition and Execution of Foreign Awards.—Legal regime pertaining to foreign awards is established by Law No. 105/1992 regarding settling of international private law relations, which sets forth following provisions regarding foreign awards: (a) their recognition, so as to benefit from authority of adjudicated matter (arts. 166-172); (b) approval of their forced execution, in event that they are not executed willingly by party bound by award; (c) their evidentiary relevance as to ascertained facts (art. 178).

For purposes of Law No. 105/1992, term "foreign award" means both legal acts of courts and notarized documents or any other documents issued by competent authorities of another country.

Full and Conditioned Recognition of Foreign Awards.—Law No. 105/1992 distinguishes between full legal recognition of foreign awards and recognition on condition that such awards comply with international norms.

Full legal recognition is granted to awards regarding civil status of citizens of country where such award was given, or if award was rendered in third country, it was subsequently recognized in country of citizenship of each party. (art 166).

Other awards may be recognized if following conditions are fulfilled: (a) award is final, according to law of country where it was made; (b) court which rendered it had jurisdiction to adjudicate matter according to its national laws; (c) there is reciprocity in recognizing foreign awards between Romania and country where such award was rendered. (art. 167). Romanian law does not require specific reciprocity, either legal or diplomatic, and therefore, de facto reciprocity is sufficient, existence of which is assumed until evidence to contrary is provided. (art. 6).

Recognition of foreign award may be refused only in specific cases, namely: (a) when award results from fraudulent procedure; (b) when award violates public order according to Romanian law; (c) when action has already been adjudicated and award rendered, even nonfinal, by Romanian court, or when matter is being adjudicated by Romanian court at time of foreign court's notice. (art. 168).

Recognition Procedure.—Request for recognition is processed by county court having jurisdiction over territory where party refusing to recognize award has its domicile or headquarters. Request must be filed together with: (a) copy of foreign award and (b) proof that such award is final. Additionally, request must include proof of service of process and notice of court action to party not present before foreign court, or any official act proving that summons and court act were acknowledged, in due time, by party against whom award was rendered. Request may also contain proof of any other act which indicates that foreign award follows all regularly observed conditions.

Execution of Foreign Award.—Foreign awards which are not willingly executed by parties obliged to execute them may be executed, at request of interested party, by court of territory where such execution is to be enforced. (art. 173 par. 1). In addition to provisions of art. 167, foreign award must be enforceable according to law of court which rendered it, and right to request forced execution must not violate three year statute of limitations. (art. 174).

Exequatur/Procedure.—Procedure approving enforcement of foreign award, currently called exequatur, is adversarial in-court procedure. Request must be accompanied by documents proving observance of above-mentioned international regularity conditions.

See Topical Index in front part of this volume.

LABOR RELATIONSHIP:

General Rules.—Right to work and right to choose one's place of employment are guaranteed by Romania's Constitution. Labor relationships are regulated by distinct legislation, modified since 1990 to adapt to Romania's new economic system.

Commercial companies, Romanian legal entities, irrespective of nature of their social capital, as well as subsidiaries, branches, representative offices, and agencies of foreign companies authorized to operate within Romania, may hire personnel on basis of individual or collective employment agreements. Each legal entity hiring personnel has obligation to register entity with Labor Office, which is subordinated to Ministry of Labor.

Authorities.—Persons who hire personnel within commercial companies are given authority to do so through statutes, joint venture agreement, or by decision of general assembly of shareholders. In general, General Director of company, or his representative, is responsible for hiring personnel. Employment conditions are established by Board of Directors.

Working Hours.—Romanian law has established five-day work week and eight-hour work day.

Employment.—Hiring of personnel is made on basis of individual employment agreement concluded for specific or indefinite period of time. Individual employment agreement includes data concerning employer and employee, nature of work, position and qualification, duration of employment, salary, other rights related to employment (bonuses, participation in profit, etc.), duration of holiday and indemnification granted, rights and obligations of both parties. Individual employment agreements are signed by both parties and registered with local Labor Office where company, branch, or subsidiary is located.

Labor Relations.—Commercial companies may negotiate with representative of employee or union regarding rules and general principles concerning labor relationship, remuneration, labor conditions, working program, and rights and obligations of each party to be included in collective employment agreement.

Salary is negotiated by parties and finalized in individual labor contract. Salaries are periodically indexed according to rate of inflation, respective normative act being published in Official Monitor. Commercial companies, regardless of nature of capital, are required to provide employees at least minimum guaranteed salary. Payment for overtime (above eight hours per day), as well as for work performed on weekends and holidays, should be paid with increase of 50% of base gross salary for first two hours of overtime, and with increase of 100% of base gross salary for overtime which is above two hours in normal work day, as well as for work performed during weekends and holidays. (Labor Code art. 120).

Other salary rights may be negotiated separately in individual labor contract, or may be included in negotiated salary, with mention of latter in individual labor contract or in collective work contracts.

Law also provides for right of employees to participate in distribution of company's net profits, limited to participation fund of 10%; establishment and approval of such benefit is within authority of shareholders' general assembly. Employees must also be provided with fringe benefits for special activities, vacation benefits, and holidays, as agreed to by company's executive council (Board of Directors).

Employees have benefit of annual paid vacation, duration of which may not be less than 18 days, and agreed upon indemnity for vacation must be equal to at least employee's monthly salary.

Expiration of Labor Contract.—Individual labor contracts terminate at initiative of employee who has given adequate notice. In general, notice of termination must be given 15 days prior to termination with respect to executive personnel, and 30 days with respect to employees with leadership functions. Such terms may be modified by internal company rules, through collective labor contracts or by mutual agreement of parties.

Individual labor contracts may terminate at initiative of employer. Causes and conditions for dismissal are not only those provided by applicable labor law, but also, those established by internal company guidelines. Notice for termination of individual contracts is same as those for group contracts.

Social Protection.—In Romania, persons who have reached age of 18 may be legally employed, and persons between ages of 16-18 years may be employed only with consent of parent or guardian. Adolescents may not be hired for hard labor, or for work involving toxic materials or noxious subterranean conditions.

Women benefit from special rights for pregnancy and post natal periods guaranteed by law. After giving birth, women have option of either one-year vacation for child care, with pay equal to 60% of salary, or post-natal vacation consisting of reduced working program of six hours for nursing for period of 6-12 months. During pregnancy and nursing period, women may not work in toxic environment and may not participate in hard labor.

Disabled persons benefit from labor conditions expressly provided by law, as well as from fees, tax exemptions and reductions. Companies which hire disabled persons benefit from tax and fee exemptions in proportion to number of disabled persons hired.

Employee Liabilities.—Employees are liable for damages incurred by company as result of their activity and are obligated to pay damages. Damages so caused are recovered from employee whether based on executory payment agreement, assumed by employee, or on court decision representing damages. Employee may contest such decision in court within 15 days from date of decision's announcement.

Association.—Law recognizes employee's right of freedom of association in unions or professional associations, as well as right to strike.

Labor Disputes.—Employees have right to contest company's executive decisions which violate their rights recognized by labor contract. Employees may contest decisions regarding dismissal which constitute abusive measure imposed by company. Employees's right to bring action in court may be personally exercised or exercised by union and professional associations.

LEGAL PROFESSION:

See topic attorneys and Counselors.

LEGISLATION:

Romanian Legislation.—In addition to Constitution, Romanian legal system includes following categories of laws: constitutional laws, organic laws and ordinary laws. Constitutional laws are those which amend Constitution. Organic laws govern electoral system, organization of Government, status of civil servants, legal regime of property and succession, general organization of education and other important areas. All other laws constitute ordinary laws. (See topic Constitution and Government).

If bill is passed by Parliament, it is sent to President of Romania for promulgation. Prior to its promulgation, President has one chance to request that Parliament reexamine law. Once signed, law is published in Official Gazette of Romania and becomes applicable at time of its publication or at date provided in document. (Constitution arts. 77-78).

In addition to their publication in Official Gazette, laws and other legal acts are published in monthly or quarterly collections.

In order to implement laws, Government issues resolutions and ordinances, within limits and conditions provided by special enabling law, which are published in Official Gazette of Romania. Until published, resolution or ordinance has no legal effect. (Constitution art. 107).

Within their specific domain of activity, ministries and other administrative bodies may issue various legal pronouncements subordinate to laws, such as: orders, instructions, rules, and norms. For instance, National Bank of Romania may issue regulations regarding gold and free currency operations on basis of art. 33 of Law No. 34/1991.

Observance of Constitution represents fundamental obligation. (Constitution art. 51). In order to guarantee supremacy of Constitution and conformity of laws with its provisions, Constitutional Court was established. (art. 152). This Court decides upon constitutionality of laws, Parliament rules, and Government ordinances. Court's decisions are compulsory and are published in Official Gazette of Romania. (arts. 140-145). Organization and functions of Constitutional Court are governed by Law No. 47/1992.

Legislative Council is special consultative body of Parliament. According to art. 79 of Constitution, Council authorizes legislative acts with view to systemize, unify and coordinate Romanian legislation, and maintains comprehensive records of Romanian legislation. Organization and functions of Legislative Council are regulated by Law No. 73/1993.

Present legislative system is undergoing extensive renewal requiring reevaluation of legal and institutional framework needed to support complex economic reform program. Presently, legislative system is characterized by coexistence of three categories of laws: (a) codes and laws adopted prior to 1944-1945; (b) laws adopted during communist regime; and (c) new laws, intended to revive and modernize old laws and codes, or replace laws adopted during communist regime.

In general, Romania's traditional legislative system was modeled after French and Italian models; similarities can be seen today in new laws. Furthermore, Agreement of Association between Romania and European Union and its OAV member states, signed in Brussels on Feb. 1, 1993 (ratified by Law No. 20/1993), includes following provision: "The parties acknowledge that one of the conditions for the economic integration of Romania in the Community is the harmonization of the present and future legislation of Romania with that of the Community. Romania will endeavor to gradually render its legislation compatible with that of the Community." (art. 69).

Codes.—Main regulations regarding entire branch of law are divided among codes.

Civil Code (Civ. Code) was modeled after French Civil Code of 1804 and became effective Dec. 1, 1865. It includes preliminary title, "General Considerations about the Effects and Application of Laws" (arts. 1-5) and following three books: Book I, "Persons" (arts. 6-460), which has since been abolished, as it constitutes object of 1953 Family Code (Fam. Code) and of Decree No. 31/1954 regarding natural and legal persons; Book II, "Goods and Methods of Changing Property" (arts. 461-643); and Book III, "Methods of Acquiring Property" (arts. 644-1914).

Romanian Commercial Code (Com. Code) was modeled after Italian Commercial Code of 1882 and has been in effect since Sept. 1, 1887. It contains four books: Book I, "General Considerations about Commerce" (arts. 1-489); Book II "Maritime Commerce and Navigation" (arts. 490-694); Book III, "Bankruptcy" (arts. 695-888); and, Book IV, "The Exercise and Duration of Commercial Actions" (arts. 889-971). Many sections of initial provisions of Commercial Code were incorporated into other laws such as Law No. 58/1934 regarding bills of exchange and promissory notes, Law No. 59/1934 regarding checks, Law No. 31/1990 regarding commercial companies, and Law No. 26/1990 regarding Register of Commerce.

Civil Procedure Code (Civ. Pro. Code) was modeled after French Code of 1806 and Code of Swiss Canton of Geneva, promulgated in 1819, and has been in effect since Dec. 1, 1865. It constitutes common law procedure in civil and commercial matters. Civ. Pro. Code contains seven books: Book I, "Competence of Courts" (arts. 1-40); Book II, "Contentious Procedure" (arts. 41-330); Book III, "General Provisions Regarding Noncontentious Procedures" (arts. 331-339); Book IV, "Arbitration" (arts. 340-371); Book V, "Forced Execution" (arts. 372-580); Book VI, "Various Procedures" (arts. 581-720); Book VII, "Final Provisions" (arts. 721-735).

Civil Procedure Code was substantially amended by Law No. 59/1992 (regarding, inter alia, competence of courts, methods of appeal, arbitration, regulation of divorce). Code was also amended by series of new laws, such as: Law No. 92/1992 regarding organization of courts, Law No. 56/1993 regarding Supreme Court of Justice, Law No. 29/1990 regarding administrative procedures.

Domestic Commercial Legislation.—In addition to provisions of Commercial Code, commercial activity is regulated by series of laws primarily adopted after Dec. 1989. For example, Law No. 15/1990 regarding reorganization of State commercial units as regies autonomes and commercial companies, Law No. 31/1990 regarding commercial companies, Law No. 26/1990 regarding Register of Commerce, Law No. 58/1991 regarding privatization of state-owned commercial companies, Law No. 35/1991 regarding foreign investments. Related laws were also adopted, such as: Law No. 12/1990 regarding protection of citizens against illegal commercial activities; Law No. 11/1991 regarding unfair competition; Decree No. 139/1990 regarding Chambers of Commerce and Industry; Law No. 84/1992 regarding free zones; Law No. 77/1994 regarding employee and management associations in privatizing commercial companies; Law No. 33/1991 regarding banking activity; Law No. 34/1991 regarding Statute

LEGISLATION . . . *continued*

of the National Bank of Romania; Law No. 47/1991 regarding establishment, organization and functioning of commercial insurance companies; Law No. 64/1991 regarding patents; Law No. 139/1992 regarding protection of industrial drawings and designs; Law No. 52/1994 regarding movable assets and commercial stocks; Law No. 15/1994 regarding amortization of fixed capital; and Law No. 66/1993 regarding management contracts.

Among laws of former regimes, following are still applicable: Decree No. 443/1972 regarding civil navigation; Decree No. 471/1971 regarding State insurance (including insurance contract); Law No. 118/1937 regarding functioning and police of Romanian Railways; Law No. 28/1967 regarding factory, trade and service marks; and Law No. 30/1978 regarding Customs Code.

International Conventions.—Romania is party to various multilateral international conventions, such as: Convention for the protection of industrial property (Paris, 1883); Convention for the unification of certain rules pertaining to international air transport (Warsaw, 1929); Additional Convention to the Warsaw Convention (Guadalajara, Mexico, 1961); Convention regarding international railroad transport (Bern, 1980); Convention regarding the regime of navigation on the Danube (Belgrade, 1948); Convention for the unification of certain rules regarding approach (Brussels, 1910); International Convention for the unification of certain rules regarding bills of lading (Brussels, 1924); International Convention for the unification of certain rules regarding privileges and maritime mortgages (Brussels, 1926); United Nations Convention regarding the transportation of goods on ships (Hamburg Rules) (Hamburg, 1978); York-Anvers Rules, adopted and supplemented at International Law Association Conferences (Anvers, 1877), including all subsequent amendments (applicable by virtue of Paramount clause); Convention regarding the contract for international transport of goods on highways (Geneva, 1956); International Convention for facilitating the importation of commercial samples and advertising material (Geneva, 1952); customs Convention regarding the international transport of goods covered by the TIR license (Geneva, 1959); customs Convention regarding the temporary transport of packaging (Brussels, 1960); European Convention regarding the customs tariff of pallets used in international transport (Geneva, 1960); Customs Convention regarding privileges granted for importation of goods intended to be displayed or used in exhibitions, fairs, congresses or other similar gatherings (Brussels, 1961); Customs Convention regarding temporary importation of professional material (Brussels, 1961); Customs Convention regarding ATA license for temporary admission of goods (Brussels, 1961); Customs Convention regarding temporary importation of scientific material (Brussels, 1968); Customs Convention regarding containers (Geneva, 1972); United Nations Convention regarding contracts for the international sales of goods (Vienna, 1980); Convention regarding prescription in the field of international sales of goods (New York, 1974); Convention regarding the recognition and execution of foreign arbitral awards (New York, 1958); European Convention regarding international commercial arbitration (Geneva, 1961); Convention for the settling of disputes regarding investments between states and persons from other states (Washington, 1965).

LEGISLATURE:

Parliament is supreme representative body of Romanian people and sole legislative authority of Romania. It is made up of Chamber of Deputies and Senate, whose members are elected to four-year terms by universal, equal, direct, secret and free vote.

Chamber of Deputies and Senate work in separate and joint sessions, and are convened together in two annual ordinary meetings. At request of President of Romania, two chambers are also convened in extraordinary meetings.

Citizens belonging to ethnic minorities, which have not garnered minimum number of votes required to be represented in Parliament, have right to one deputy seat per ethnic group. (Constitution of Romania art. 59).

Deputy or senator may not be held, arrested, searched or summoned for criminal or civil court action without prior approval of chamber. Legal jurisdiction in such cases belongs to Supreme Court of Justice. Also, deputies and senators may not be held legally responsible for votes or political opinions expressed by them during their mandate. (Constitution art. 70).

Parliament adopts constitutional amendments, organic laws and ordinary laws by majority vote. Organic laws govern, inter alia: (1) voting system, organization and functioning of political parties; (2) state of emergency, violations, penalties and execution of such penalties; (3) granting of amnesty or collective pardon; (4) organization and functioning of Supreme Council of the Magistrates, courts, Public Ministry and Financial Court; (5) statute of civil servants, administrative disputes, legal regime of property and succession; (6) labor rights, trade unions and social welfare; and, (7) religion.

Legislation is introduced by Government, deputies, senators and citizen's group of at least 250,000 voters. Citizens exerting their right to initiate legislation must have legal capacity and must originate from at least one-fourth of Romania's counties. In each county and in Bucharest, at least 10,000 signatures must be gathered to support such initiative.

Organic laws and decisions regarding rules of Chambers are adopted by vote of majority of each Chamber's members. Ordinary laws and decisions are adopted by vote of majority of each Chamber's attending members.

Laws are sent to President of Romania for promulgation, to be made within 20 days from receipt of such laws. Before promulgation, President may request Parliament to reexamine law or verify its constitutionality. If so requested, promulgation of law shall be effected within maximum of ten days after receipt of law, subsequent to its reexamination or to Constitutional Court's decision conferring constitutionality of such law.

Law is published in Official Gazette of Romania and becomes applicable at time of its publication or at date specified in its publication.

LIENS:

Concept of lien is derived from right of guarantee (such as pledge) or from privilege based upon concept of pledge (such as right of hotel owner or transport agent to hold goods of traveler until payment for accommodations is effected). (Civ. Code art. 1730). In order to establish lien, parties must execute contract which must be registered with Public Notary to be effective against third parties.

Lien is subject to privileged and mortgage creditors of relevant assets, whose privileges or mortgages arose after date when assets came into custody of holder.

Lien does not grant prerogative to claim assets which are in possession of another person. It operates only while goods are still in possession of holder; and ceases after assets are voluntarily returned.

Lien is indivisible, and therefore, applies to entire assets until full payment of debt. Holder is not entitled to civil interests in assets and cannot invoke such custody to obtain, by usucapio, ownership of assets.

MARRIAGE:

According to Family Code, as promulgated by Law No. 4/1954, subsequently modified, and Constitution of 1991, marriage is union between man and woman based upon free consent, monogamy, and contractual relationship as required by law. In order to give rise to its associated rights and obligations, marriage must be concluded in front of representative from register of births, deaths and marriages. (Fam. Code art. 3). Religious marriage ceremony may take place only after civil ceremony.

Requirements.—To be legally concluded, marriage must be between people of different sexes, and male must be at least 18 years of age and female 16 years. In special circumstances, such as pregnancy, female may marry at 15 provided that she possesses medical certificate and obtains special marriage license from local council (town hall). In addition, both future spouses should consent freely to marriage and both should inform other of their respective state of health. (Fam. Code arts. 16-17).

Marriage is denied or declared void if: (1) spouse is already married or is mentally incapacitated, mentally retarded or temporarily insane (art. 9); (2) parties are relatives in direct or collateral line to fourth degree (art. 6); (3) marriage is between adoptive parent and adoptive child (or their ascendants) (art. 7); (4) guardian wishes to marry minor under his ward (art. 8).

Marriage Declaration and Registration.—To marry, both parties must submit declaration of marriage (Fam. Code art. 12) at least eight days prior to marriage date. (Decree No. 278/1969 art. 22). Declaration must be submitted to registry for births, deaths and marriages for locality where marriage will occur. If one party lives in another town, declaration may be submitted to that town's registry, which will send declaration to first registry.

Marriage declaration must stipulate that: (1) parties wish to marry; (2) each party is aware of other's state of health; (3) there are no impediments to marriage; and (4) one party will take name of other, or use both last names. (Fam. Code art. 28).

Representative of registry determines that parties are of age, and that above-mentioned formalities are complete. Then parties submit their birth certificates, identity documents and medical certificates.

In exceptional cases, eight-day term may be reduced upon application to mayor and marriage may be concluded earlier. Exceptional cases include situations where child will be born within eight-day term, where prospective husband will be called to military duty, or when one of parties must leave to study or complete mission abroad.

Conclusion of Marriage.—Marriage document is issued by registry for civil status documents and signed by spouses and representative. Marriage may only be proved through this certificate. (Fam. Code art. 18).

Location where marriage is concluded is chosen by spouses according to their residence. (Fam. Code art. 11). Marriage of two Romanian citizens on board Romanian ship sailing outside of Romanian waters may be performed by ship's commander. (Decree No. 278/1960 art. 9). Marriage may not be concluded on airplane.

In order to conclude marriage, it must be possible for public to participate, but witnesses are not compulsory. Thus, it is possible for only spouses and registry representative to be present when marriage is concluded.

Marriage concluded in violation of norms regarding categorical impediments is null and void. (Fam. Code arts. 4-7[a], 9 and 16).

If consent to marry has been given through mistaken identity, deception or threat of violence, spouse may request annulment of marriage within six months from discovery of grounds for annulment. (Fam. Code art. 21).

For regulations concerning remarriage after marriage to person later declared dead, see topic Death (Presumption Of and Actions For).

Any person may oppose marriage between date of submission of marriage declarations and conclusion of marriage. Opposing statements are submitted in writing, stating reasons for opposition and providing proof if necessary. (Fam. Code art. 14). If challenge is well-founded, marriage will not be concluded and investigation will commence, followed by official report. If challenge is unfounded, representative of registry will proceed with marriage.

Conflict of Laws.—In Law No. 105/1992 regarding relations in international private law, rights acquired in foreign country are respected in Romania except when they violate public order. Art. 18 of Law No. 105/92 stipulates that basic conditions required to conclude marriage are determined by national law of each prospective spouse. If foreign law is more restrictive than Romanian law, the latter will govern where one spouse is Romanian citizen or marriage is concluded on Romanian soil.

Required formalities for marriage are subject to laws of state where marriage is concluded. (Law No. 105/1992 art. 19). Marriage of Romanian citizen abroad can be concluded before competent local state authority with jurisdiction or, in presence of diplomatic agent or consular clerk of Romania. Marriage concluded in presence of Romanian diplomatic agent or consular clerk is subject to procedural requirements of Romanian law.

MONOPOLIES AND RESTRAINT OF TRADE:

Legal Framework.—With regard to establishment of free, normal and fair market conditions, following regulations are in effect: (1) Law No. 15/1990 regarding reorganization of State economic units as regies autonomes and commercial companies (arts. 36-38); and (2) Law No. 11/1991 regarding restraint of unfair competition.

In addition to its domestic legislation, Romania is also signatory of following international conventions: (1) Convention of the Paris Union of March 20, 1883, for

See Topical Index in front part of this volume.

MONOPOLIES AND RESTRAINT OF TRADE . . . *continued*
protection of industrial property, as revised in Stockholm on July 14, 1967; (2) agreements signed in Brussels on Feb. 1, 1993, including: (a) European Agreement establishing an association between Romania, and the European Community and its member states (ratified by Law No. 20/1993); (b) Interim Agreement regarding trade and trade-related matters between Romania and the European Economic Community and the European Community of Coal and Steel (ratified by Law No. 16/1993).

Romania is also party to Agreement with the member states of the Free Trade European Association (ratified by Law No. 19/1993) and General Agreement on Tariffs and Trade (GATT) (ratified by Decree No. 480/1972).

Romanian legislation in this field is still in embryonic phase, but will subsequently be supplemented and enhanced so as to eventually acquire level of protection similar to that existing in EU, as mandated by Romania's Association Agreement with EU. (art. 67).

Domestic Legislation.—Arts. 36-38 of Law No. 15/1990, which are inspired by arts. 85 and 86 of Treaty of Rome of Mar. 25, 1957, regarding European Economic Community, provide major antimonopoly and unfair competition regulations.

Art. 36 forbids following practices amongst State-owned commercial companies or regies autonomes: (1) agreements or decisions of association between them; (2) establishment or imposition of monopoly or dumping prices; (3) limitation or control of production, retailing, technical development or investments; (4) division of markets or supply sources, application of unequal conditions to commercial partners for equivalent services; conditioning signing of contracts on acceptance, by partners, of additional services which, by their nature and according to commercial practices, are not related to object of such contracts; or (5) any other concerted practices capable of affecting trade which are intended to restrain competition, or to abusively exert dominant position upon market.

Art. 36 also forbids activities of economic agents or group of economic agents holding dominant market position, characterized by monopoly situation or by visible concentration of economic power, which could affect normal functioning of market in free competition conditions. Art. 38 excepts following from provisions of art. 36: agreements and decisions of association and concerted practices which contribute to enhancement of production and distribution of goods, promotion of competitive level of Romanian goods, appointments and services on foreign markets.

Additionally, interdictions provided in art. 36 do not apply to activities undertaken with exclusive monopoly title and which State reserves for itself on basis of art. 40 and other specific laws. According to art. 36, paragraph 2, violation of such interdictions are penalized according to provisions of civil or criminal law regarding unfair competition.

As provided in art. 37, legal actions contesting practices and actions restraining competition may be filed by any interested person, including: (1) party which incurred damages; (2) Public Ministry; (3) association for protection of consumers; (4) professional organizations, such as Chambers of Commerce and Industry; and (5) by any natural or legal person possessing claim for legitimate interest.

Trade Restrictions.—Romanian Constitution of 1991 provides that State must guarantee freedom of trade and protection of fair competition (arts. 134-2), and that all citizens have free choice of profession and place of work (arts. 38-1). Therefore, any person is entitled to become merchant, assuming that certain conditions are met, such as existence of civil capacity (minor or person under interdiction may not be merchant). Some positions, however, are not compatible with profession of merchant (judges, prosecutors, public servants, free professionals). Also, person sentenced for bankruptcy and subsequently declared unable to practice such profession may not be trader. (Com. Code arts. 881 and 882). As provided by Governmental Resolution No. 1323/1990, following activities, inter alia, cannot be object of commercial company: (1) activities which constitute, according to law, State monopoly; (2) manufacture or sale of drugs or narcotics in form other than medicine; and (3) activities which, according to criminal law, violate specific legal provisions.

Prohibition against representative or employee of merchant to undertake personal business similar to that of employer is provided for in legal provisions as well as in contractual clauses.

When transferring assets or funds acquired through commerce, seller may not enter into competition with buyer by operating similar business in same geographic area. Obligation exists even if not expressly provided in contract, resulting from obligation of seller. (Com. Code art. 397, Law No. 11/1991 art. 4, par. 1).

Monopoly.—Under Law No. 11/1991, Art. 4 para 2, contravention of such Law is sanctioned by amounts ranging between 5,000 and 20,000 lei.

With regard to penal liability, it is only applicable to physical persons (employee of legal person); penal action may be commenced upon complaint of victim, Chamber of Commerce and Industry, or another professional body.

International Private Law.—According to Law No. 105/1992, compensation claims based on act of unfair competition or another act which illegitimately restrains free competition are subject to law of jurisdiction where damages were produced. (art. 117). In alternative, at request of injured party, claimant may also apply either to law of state where such party has its head office (if unfair competition resulted from acts by that party exclusively) or law governing contract between parties, if unfair competition damaged relations between parties. (art. 118).

Romanian courts may order payment of damages for injury resulting from unfair competition, based on foreign law, only to extent established by Romanian law for similar injuries. (art. 119).

MORTGAGE:

Mortgage is real property guarantee, which does not require depriving owner of possession of property. (Civil Code art. 1746). Mortgage can be established by agreement of parties, in accordance with law. (Civ. Code art. 1749 par. 1). One who applies for mortgage must have capacity to alienate property. (Civ. Code art. 1769). Debtor may not mortgage property in which he has only future title. (art. 1775).

Mortgage contract must be in original form and must contain guaranteed sum and mortgaged property. (Civ. Code art. 1772). Mortgage must be recorded in special register book or in land book of state notary office of district where property is located. Recording mortgage protects creditors against third parties and it also creates record of degree of preference of mortgage. (Civ. Code art. 1778). Between two creditors of different degrees, one who recorded first will have priority over any subsequent creditor to full indemnification from value of mortgaged property. Recording preserves mortgage for 15 years. To renew mortgage, it must be registered again before expiration of its first term. (Civ. Code art. 1786 par. 1).

When debt has been satisfied, mortgage is terminated and deleted from register. If payment has been partial, recording is preserved by "reduction of the inscription".

Legal Effect.—Debtor as owned maintains possession of mortgaged property and it may be transferred to third party who takes subject to mortgage. (Civ. Code art. 1790). Mortgage creditor has preference right over other creditors.

Third party may commence special procedure for "cleansing" real property of mortgage, by which third party makes offer to pay debts and expenses of mortgage, so that price of property stipulated in sale contract is paid, or, until appraised amount of property is paid if transfer is by donation. If creditor accepts this offer and new owner pays mentioned price or makes sum available, real property is "cleansed" of mortgage. (Civ. Code arts. 1801-1818).

NOTARIES PUBLIC:

See topic Public Notaries.

PARTNERSHIP:

Natural and legal persons may form partnerships and commercial companies in accordance with Law No. 31/1990 regarding such companies, Commercial Code, and Law No. 26/1990 regarding Register of Commerce.

Commercial companies with headquarters in Romania are Romanian legal persons and may establish one of following companies:

(1) General Partnership ("Societate in nume colectiv"—S.N.C.).—Social obligations of general partnership are secured by registered capital contributed by all partners with unlimited liability. Its name must include at least one of partners and mention that it is partnership. (See topic Corporations [Trade Companies].)

As they have unlimited liability, none of partners may be party to another company which is either in competition with or has same object of activity as partnership, nor may they perform operations on their own or others' accounts without having other partners' agreement. Partners are jointly liable for partnership's obligations.

Commercial partnerships are authorized to operate by court located in jurisdiction where company has its principal place of business. (Law No. 31/1990 art. 4; Civ. Pro. Code art. 2). Partnership becomes legal entity from date of its incorporation in commercial register, and after publication in Official Monitor. Partnerships may establish branches or subsidiaries in locality where they have their principal place of business, either within Romania or abroad.

According to art. 169 of Law No. 31/1990, following conditions have effect of dissolving commercial partnerships and provide grounds for liquidation which may be requested by any partner: (1) expiration of partnership's term; (2) impossibility of realizing partnership's objectives; (3) decision of general meeting of partnership; (4) bankruptcy; (5) reduction of capital or decreasing capital below legal limit; (6) number of shareholders is reduced below five. (See topic Corporations [Trade Companies].) Dissolution of commercial partnerships must be registered in commercial register and publicized in Official Monitor, except when partnership expires due to expiration of its term of duration.

(2) Limited Partnership ("Societate in comandita simpla"—S.C.S.).—Social obligations of limited partnership are guaranteed by contributions of all partners to registered capital. Additionally, general partners are joint and severally liable, whereas limited partners are liable only in proportion to their contribution to capital. Company's name must include name of at least one of partners, as well as words "Limited Partnership". (See topic Corporations [Trade Companies].)

(3) Common Provisions.—Unless otherwise stipulated, assets brought to partnerships as contributions become its property. Partner who is delinquent in making contribution is liable for damages. If contribution is in cash, partner must pay established interest commencing with day when contribution should have been made.

Dividends are paid to partners in proportion to their contributions to capital. These contributions do not incur any interest.

(4) Limited Joint-Stock Company ("Societate in comandita pe actiuni"—S.C.A.).—Registered capital of limited joint-stock company is formed of shares. Its social obligations are secured by social capital. General partners have unlimited liability and limited partners are only obligated in proportion to their shares. Such company's name must include proper name which should differentiate it from other companies and also mention words "Limited Joint-Stock Company". Its capital may not be less than 1,000,000 lei and number of shareholders may not be smaller than five. Founders have unlimited liability to third parties both for failure to fulfill legal formalities provided for establishment of company and for obligations they assumed upon establishment. Capital is represented by shares issued by company, which may either be nominal or bearer. Nominal value of each share may not be smaller than 1,000 lei. Shares must have equal value, and confer equal rights to holders. (See also topics Joint-Stock Company and Corporations.)

(5) Joint-Stock Company ("Societate pe actiuni" —S.A.).—Social obligations of joint-stock company are secured by its registered capital. Shareholders are liable only in proportion to their shares, and company's name must contain proper noun so as to single it out from other companies, as well as term, "joint-stock company". Its capital must not be less than 1,000,000 lei, and number of shareholders no less than five. Registered capital is represented by shares issued by company, either nominal or bearer. Value of one share may not be less than 1,000 lei, and shares must be equal in value as they impart equal rights upon their holders. One share gives right to one vote during company's meetings. Shares are indivisible. (See also topics Joint-Stock Company and Corporations.)

(6) Limited Liability Company ("Societate cu raspundere limitata"—S.R.L.).—Social obligations of limited liability company are secured by registered capital, and shareholders are obligated only in proportion to their shares. Company's name must include title denominating its object of activity, as well as term "limited liability company". Registered capital may not be less than 100,000 lei,

PARTNERSHIP . . . *continued*
which is divisible into equal shares whose value may not be lower than 5,000 lei. Number of shareholders may not exceed 50. Contributions in kind to registered capital may not account for more than 60% of capital. If there is foreign participation, foreigner's contribution to social capital may not be less than US$10,000. When there is only one associate, said person has rights and obligations incumbent upon general assembly of shareholders. (See also topic Corporations.)

PATENTS:

In General.—Rights over inventions are recognized and protected by issuance of protective patent by State Office for Inventions and Trademarks (OSIM) in accordance with Law No. 64/1991, concerning invention patents, and by Government Decision No. 152/1992.

OSIM patent grants holder exclusive right of exploitation for duration of patent's validity which belongs to inventor or successors to such rights.

Invention may be patented under following conditions (1) it is new; (2) it results from activity involving invention; and (3) it has potential for industrial application. Inventions may constitute product, device, or method of production. Inventions contrary to public order and morals may not be patented.

Following may not be patented: ideas, discoveries, scientific theories, mathematical methods, computer programs per se, solutions with economic or organizational character, diagrams, methods of education and instruction, play systems, city planning, plans and methods subject to being systemized, physical phenomenons, culinary recipes, discoveries of aesthetic character.

Application Procedure.—Patent application must be made by authorized person or agent, with domicile or office in Romania. Patent applications to be filed with OSIM must be written in Romanian, and should contain identification and information pertaining to applicant, together with description of invention and, if necessary, explanatory drawings. Applicant must also file all public documents concerning invention, including copies of patents granted in other countries.

At OSIM's request or upon applicant's own initiative, claims, drawings or descriptions contained in application may be modified before final decision by OSIM is made. While application is pending before OSIM, applicant may seek advice of consultant knowledgeable in industrial property.

Fees.—Registration, publication and examination of patent application, as well as issuance of patent and maintenance of its validity, are subject to fees.

For entire duration of patent's validity, titleholder must pay annual fees for keeping patent current. Fees owed by foreign individual or legal persons are paid in foreign currency to OSIM. Nonpayment of fees may result in titleholder's loss of rights associated with patent.

Patent Rights.—Right to receive patent, which derives from registration of patent application, as well as rights associated with patent, may be transferred. Transfer may be made by assignment or by means of exclusive or non-exclusive license, as well as by legal succession or by will. Transfer imbues third parties with rights effective at date of registration at OSIM.

At request of any interested person, Bucharest Municipal Tribunal may issue compulsory license at expiration of four year term from date of patent application, or three year term from issuance of patent, whichever is longer, provided that invention was not utilized or not sufficiently utilized in Romania, and patent holder cannot justify its inactivity, and also, if agreement was not reached with such holder regarding transfer of rights. Compulsory licenses are registered with OSIM and produce effects from date of registration.

If it is determined that beneficiary of compulsory license did not fulfill its obligations to exploit invention, in accordance with established conditions, court may revoke license upon request of patent holder.

OSIM's decisions may be contested at this office by interested persons in three month term from communication. Violation of rights concerning inventions are punishable by law, applying sanctions and imprisonment.

Protection of Drawings and Industrial Models.—Law No. 129/1992 provides for protection of drawings and industrial models. Rights over drawings and industrial models are recognized and safeguarded by title of protection granted by OSIM which confers upon holder exclusive right of exploitation or use within Romania.

Applications to register drawing or industrial model must encompass following: (1) identification of applicant or author; (2) information regarding goods for which industrial model is destined to be incorporated; (3) summary description of elements of drawing or industrial model; and (4) ten graphic reproductions. Application materials must be submitted personally or by representative which has domicile or place of business in Romania.

Registration application for drawing, industrial model, photograph, or any other graphic representation is published within six months from date of registration in Official Bulletin of Industrial Property of OSIM.

Any interested person may make written objections to registration of representations which must be sent to OSIM within three months from their publication.

Registration of representations is subject to fees according to Law No. 129/1994. Nonpayment within terms provided by law hinders process, and may cause nonrecognition of priority and loss of holder's rights.

Period of validity of registration certificate or drawing or industrial model is five years from date of registration deposit and may be renewed for two successive periods of five years. For entire validity period of certificate, holder is required to pay fees to maintain certificate. Nonpayment of fees results in loss of holder's rights.

PLEDGE:

According to Romanian law, pledge is accessory contract by which debtor provides creditor with movable asset to guarantee debt. (Civ. Code art. 1685). Object of pledge may be tangible or intangible asset, such as claim that debtor has against another party. When pledge is tangible, asset is delivered to creditor or, upon agreement of parties, to third party charged with holding pledged asset until debt is paid. (art. 1688).

Pledge may be: (1) established by agreement of parties; (2) provided by law; or (3) awarded by court order. Pledges for debts in excess of 250 lei must be in written form and must include sum of debt and description of pledged assets. Writing must be registered by filing copy of it at state notary office (Civ. Code arts. 711, 719-720) to insure debt against third party creditors (art. 1680 par. 1). If pledged asset is intangible good, such as credit, then written pledge must be notarized as well as recorded, to make it good against all third parties.

If debtor does not pay debt, creditor may proceed to collect pledge, by requesting court order authorizing him to possess assets as compensation for debt. Alternatively, creditor may request sale of pledged goods to recover amount of original debt. (Civ. Code art. 1689).

As accessory contract, pledge shall terminate upon payment or cancellation of debt, voluntary delivery of pledged goods, or upon cancellation of pledge itself.

PRINCIPAL AND AGENTS:

General Rules.—In business situations, relations between principal and agent are usually established by mandate contract having as its object "negotiation of commercial business in the name and on behalf of the principal". (Com. Code art. 374).

Mandate may be either of following: (a) with representation—when agent has representative capacity, acting in name of principal; or (b) without representation—when agent acts on behalf of principal, but signs document on his own behalf (such as commission, or consignment). (See topic Agency.)

In case of mandate with representation, legal document signed by agent will yield direct legal effects for principal, as if latter personally signed such contract. Representation assumes existence of power of attorney given by principal. If scope of representation is general agent is empowered to sign all legal acts in interest of principal, except those strictly personal, and if special, agent is empowered to sign specific legal act(s). (See topic Agency.)

Agent is obliged to act solely within limits of powers granted by principal and must make known his quality of agency to third parties.

Representation in Commercial Transactions.—Merchant, either natural or legal person, may be assisted in his activity by various auxiliaries who either represent his interests or help him accomplish commercial operations. Such auxiliaries may be dependent (employees of trader) or independent (possessing quality of traders in their own right). First category includes delegates, commercial salesmen and commercial travelers. (Com. Code arts. 392-404). Second category includes brokers and commercial agents.

Delegates are empowered to operate their employers' business, either at same location or different location as that of employer. (Com. Code art. 392). Therefore, delegates are empowered to manage employer's company, at head office or at branch, and to act in name and on behalf of employer. Capacity of delegate to act as agent is general and lasts for duration of agency. He concludes and executes daily operations of unit that he manages, without having to request specific approvals for each operation. However, such rights may be restrained by agency agreement. When signing documents, delegate is obliged to add name of employer's company and make mention that he signs "by power of attorney". Legal provisions regarding delegates also apply to representatives holding power of attorney, who are empowered to sign only for specific purposes and who are not empowered to effect trade on regular basis.

Agency agreement regarding delegate must be registered in Register of Commerce. (Law No. 26/1990 regarding Registry of Commerce art. 21).

Commercial Salesmen.—According to Com. Code art. 404, commercial salesmen are delegates for retail sale of goods, at location of employer's business and under latter's supervision. Commercial salesmen possess right, at location of business, to conclude and sign commercial contracts, to request and collect payment for price of goods, providing valid receipt in name of employer.

Commercial travelers are empowered by employer "to negotiate or undertake operations regarding his business" (Com. Code art. 402), in locations other than those where employer's business is located. They are empowered to find clients and to collect offers and orders to be signed subsequently by employer. In such circumstances, commercial travelers have quality of agents, without representation powers, but may sign legal acts in name and on behalf of employer when empowered to act upon commercial transactions.

Mediators establish contact between parties willing to enter business transaction and facilitate such parties reaching agreement. Mediator does not have representation powers, and therefore, does not represent parties. He is entitled to commission, if contract is signed due to his intervention.

Commercial agents.—There are two categories of commercial agents: (1) those regularly empowered by one or more merchants to negotiate commercial operations, without having right to sign in their name; and (2) those regularly empowered by one or more traders to sign commercial contracts in their name.

Usually, commercial agents act in specific town or region for commission, investigating market and providing merchant with relevant information. They also keep deposited goods. Activity of commercial agent may be organized as commission company, agency or business office, under conditions provided by Com. Code art. 3.

Foreign Representative Offices In Romania.—Foreign companies may open their own representative offices in Romania on basis of authorization issued by Ministry of Trade, under conditions provided by Decree No. 122/1990. Issuance of authorization is subject to annual fee of approximately US $1,200. If representative office represents more than one firm, fee is increased by 10% for each specific firm.

International Private Law.—According to art. 93 of Law No. 105/1992, regarding settling of international private law relations, relations between principal and agent or mediator are governed by law of country where agent exerts his powers, unless otherwise agreed by parties. Relations between represented person and third parties are subject, unless otherwise agreed, to law of place where professional head office of agent is located. (art. 95). Methods by which agency powers are exercised must comply with conditions provided by law of country where such activities take place. (art. 97). Agency contracts enacted for administration or disposition of real property are subject to law governing situs of property. (art. 100).

See Topical Index in front part of this volume.

PUBLIC NOTARIES:

Public Notaries are governed by Law No. 36/1995 (published in Official Gazette No. 92/May 16, 1995) and can be State-owned or private.

Qualification.—In order to be permanent appointee, Public Notary must graduate from law school, and if practicing for two years, pass examination administered by Ministry of Justice (no exam being necessary if working as Notary Public, judge, prosecutor or attorney for five years). All Public Notaries must have following characteristics: Romanian citizens residing in Romania, full civil capacity, no penal charges in their criminal records, good reputation, and good health. To become Public Notary, request must be made to Ministry of Justice. After one is nominated as Public Notary, such person must register his office within 60 days with Court of Appeal of territory in which office is located. Public Notaries must take oath before Minister of Justice.

All districts have numerous State-owned Notaries. Territorial jurisdiction of local notaries corresponds to geographic district of respective local courts. (Government Decision Nos. 819/1992; 337/1993).

Authentication.—Public Notaries attest and certify deeds and other written original documents or copies under official seal, thereby giving such documents legal authority. (Law 36/95, Art. 16).

Seal.—Public Notaries apply notarial seal on all deeds to be notarized, confirming their authenticity.

Powers and Duties.—Public Notaries may acknowledge authenticity of signatures, dates of deed presentations, and existence and condition of some goods and chattels. Public Notaries must also keep books regarding registration of real estate, transfer of property, inscription of mortgages on debtor's real property, contests made against some promissory notes and returned checks, and records in some fields of maritime law. Public Notaries are vested with jurisdiction and authority to open inheritance procedures and issue inheritance certificates, except in cases of disputes arising between heirs. In addition, authentic wills are executed by Public Notaries. (Law 36/1995, Art. 8).

Territorial Extent of Powers.—Except in cases involving registration of real estate and other situations expressly provided for by law, every notary is qualified to draw up notarial acts for people, regardless of their district of domicile, or citizenship. (Decree No. 377/1960).

Expiration of Commission.—Public Notaries exercise their authority and jurisdiction, and possess right of official signature until date of resignation, retirement or dismissal. (Decree No. 377/1960).

Fees.—Law establishes taxes and fees imposed for services rendered by State-owned Notaries. (Decision No. 1295/1990 and Order No. 10/1993).

REGISTER OF COMMERCE:

Obligation to Register.—Law No. 26/1990 requires every business participant, natural or legal person, to register with Register of Commerce prior to commencement of business operations. Business participants who must register include: (a) natural persons operating commercial business; (b) commercial companies and their subsidiaries, branches, representative offices, and agencies; (c) "Regies autonomes" (autonomous administrations); and (d) cooperative organizations.

Content of Application for Registration.—Applications for registration and accompanying information are submitted on standard forms under conditions and terms provided by law and by "Methodological Norms" issued by Register of Commerce and applicable since Aug. 1, 1994.

Application for registration of natural persons must contain personal information and other information pertaining to person's commercial activities. Following information is needed for commercial companies: (1) information about founders, administrators, auditors, authorized agents (proxies) and about firm itself; (2) legal form and object of activity; (3) capital structure; (4) method of profit distribution; (5) requirements necessary to establish validity of general meeting's decisions; and (6) duration of company. Any changes to this information or to corporate statutes (by-laws) must be registered. Transfers or mortgage of commercial capital, declarations of bankruptcy, criminal prosecution of business participants, and termination of business must also be reported.

Judicial Control.—Registration in Register of Commerce is completed only after office agent examines application and only on basis of disposition provided by judge of Register of Commerce or, as case may be, by final court decision.

Functions of Register of Commerce.—Under Law No. 26/1990, Register of Commerce is official record of all business participants in Romania, and as such, possesses three primary functions: (a) to gather all essential and recent legal and economic information regarding person and economic activity of every business participant in order to provide "market transparency"; (b) to insure publication of this information, as required by law, whereby registrations and their specifications contained in Register are meant to be known by third parties, so as to prevent them from pleading ignorance to registrations. Law No. 26/1990 provides for register to be public and establishes manner of publicity (issuing copies of registrations, issuing certificates regarding registration or absence of registration of some specifications, etc.). Legal publicity made by Register of Commerce is completed by publishing registration and any changes to company contract or statutes in Romania's Official Bulletin, part IV; (c) to formally establish commercial company as legal person which, according to Law No. 31/1990, becomes effective from date of registration in Register of Commerce.

Organization; Fees.—There are total of 41 territorial offices of Register of Commerce which work in association with county Chambers of Commerce and Industry. National Office of Register of Commerce works with Romanian Chamber of Commerce and Industry and has authority to record all national registrations according to information provided by territorial offices.

Since date on which Registry of Commerce was established, Dec. 8, 1990, through Mar. 31, 1994, 380,500 firms have been registered, of which 343,300 were commercial companies, 953 were autonomous authorities, 4,052 were cooperative organizations, and 32,200 were natural persons.

Registration fees are established by Romanian Chamber of Commerce and Industry together with Ministry of Finance.

Register of Commerce is separately maintained from commercial registries, where business participants must keep accounting records according to Com. Code arts. 22-34 and Accountancy Law No. 82/1991, or from commercial company registries, instituted by Law No. 31/1990, regarding commercial companies (shareholders' register, company and general meeting decisions register, etc.).

SALES:

Provisions.—Sales are regulated by Civ. Code of 1865, and Commercial Code of 1887, which had as its model Italian Code of 1882. Civ. Code arts, 1294-1404 regulate sales of movable assets and immovable assets. Sales of immovables are regulated exclusively by civil legislation, whereas sales of movables may be regulated by commercial as well as civil legislation. (Com. Code arts. 60-73). Generally, provisions of Civil Code and that of Commercial Code are complementary in nature, and are applied only when contract has no stipulations on matter. Besides codes and special laws, there are applied usages (conventional norms), especially in commercial matters (usages of trade).

Contract for Sale of Goods.—Characteristic feature of commercial sales is intention to resell acquired good; intention which exists when good is acquired and accepted by other party.

Sales is consensual contract concluded by simple voluntary agreement between parties, without fulfilling any formalities and without remitting sold good or payment price when concluding contract. (Civ. Code art. 1295).

For sales to be effective certain conditions must be met: (1) contract must be validly concluded; (2) seller must own good; and (3) good must be itemized.

If goods are lost between moment of agreement and actual delivery to buyer, risk of their loss is borne by buyer, with buyer still having obligation to pay price. Contract may stipulate transfer of risks at moment of actual delivery of goods rather than at moment of sale.

In case of absent persons, contract is considered concluded from moment tenderer has acknowledged acceptance. (Com. Code art. 35). Acceptance is presumed acknowledged when offeror receives goods.

Seller's Duties.—According to Civil Code, seller has several important obligations: to deliver sold goods and to be responsible for eviction and defects. (art. 1313). Seller also has obligations of informing buyer and providing security.

Obligation of Delivery.—Civ. Code art. 1316 stipulates three forms of delivery for movable goods: (1) real delivery (effected through transferring material possession of good); (2) consensual delivery (when material delivery cannot occur at moment of sale, or when buyer is already in possession of good); or (3) symbolic delivery (when keys of building where goods are stored are turned over). In commercial matters, delivery occurs by transmission of good's representative titles (e.g. bill of lading and warrants).

Object of delivery must be good sold as it existed when contract was made. (Civ. Code art. 1324). Obligation to deliver good includes that of delivering its accessories (Civ. Code art. 1325), as well as obligation to preserve good until delivery. Delivery must occur, unless otherwise indicated, at location of sold good at time of sale. (Civ. Code art. 1319; Com. Code art. 59). Delivery expenses are seller's responsibility, and expenses related to taking possession are buyer's responsibility. (Civ. Code art. 1317).

Eviction Guarantee.—Seller is responsible for undisturbed ownership of good (eviction guarantee) and for defects in good. (Civ. Code art. 1335). As consequence, seller must guarantee that transmitted property is protected against third parties and against harm prior to delivery. Guarantee is seller's obligation to ensure buyer's undisturbed ownership.

Parties may agree to increase, decrease or abolish obligation of responsibility for eviction. (Civ. Code art. 1338). When seller is responsible for eviction, buyer has right to demand compensation for purchase price, judicial expenses and damages. (Civ. Code art. 1311). If buyer is only partially evicted, but eviction is material to contract, he may request annulment of sale. (Civ. Code art. 1347).

Guarantee for Defects of Goods.—Seller is responsible for hidden defects of sold good if defects render good unusable for its ordinary purpose, or its use is so diminished that it is assumed that buyer would not have bought, or paid same price for, good had buyer been aware of defects. (Civ. Code art. 1352).

Seller is responsible solely for hidden defects (those not apparent through reasonable inspection upon delivery). (Civ. Code art. 1353). Hidden defects should not be mistaken with good's nonconformity to contractual quality requirements. Hidden defects are also distinct from mistakes of fact as to substance, age, quality or market value of good. (Civ. Code art. 945).

When delivered goods are nonconforming, buyer may seek several distinct actions: (a) annulment (when buyer's consent was affected by error over substance of objects of contract) (Civ. Code art. 954); (b) rescission of sale (when goods stipulated in contract were delivered, but not with agreed quality); (c) diminishment of price proportional to defect. Buyer has right to ask for elimination of defect. If seller exercised bad faith and was aware of hidden defects, he is obliged to return money and to pay damages. (Civ. Code art. 1356).

In commercial sale contract, seller is responsible not only for hidden defects, but also for obvious defects of good during transport, provided that buyer denounces defects within two days after receipt of good.

Obligation to Inform Buyer.—It is seller's obligation to inform buyer upon all contracting conditions, uses, possible dangers, and necessary precautions associated with good. Obligation to inform begins in pre-contractual stage; seller must provide buyer with information he needs to make informed decision. During execution of contract, seller has obligation to provide buyer with all information related to assembly and use of goods.

Seller is responsible to buyer or third parties for damages caused by goods under normal use. Seller must check products he manufactures or sells, and inform buyer of potential dangers of good. Obligation to inform is regulated by Governmental Order No. 211/1992 regarding consumer protection, as modified by Law No. 11/1994.

See Topical Index in front part of this volume.

SALES . . . *continued*

Buyer's Duties.—Buyer's main obligation is to pay price. (Civ. Code art. 1361). Buyer also has duty to take possession of good and cover all related expenses. Price is paid at time and place stipulated in contract. If there are no stipulations, price must be paid when seller delivers good. (Civ. Code art. 1362).

Buyer must pay interest on overdue payments. However, buyer may withhold payment if his enjoyment of good is disturbed or if there is danger of eviction by claim of third party. (Civ. Code art. 1364).

Liability for Breach of Contractual Obligations.—Non-execution of contractual obligations has consequences stipulated in Civil and Commercial Codes. Non-execution exception exists whereby party is entitled to refuse to execute its own obligation if other party does not execute its correlative obligation. If buyer paid price, but seller refuses to deliver sold good, buyer has right to request annulment of contract, or taking over of good. If good has been delivered, and buyer has not paid price, seller may request annulment of contract. (Civ. Code art. 1365). Non-breaching party may force other party to execute contract, when possible, or to ask for annulment of contract, with damages. (Civ. Code art. 1021).

In commercial matters, if seller does not execute obligation to deliver good, buyer has right to buy good from market, under supervision of official agent. If buyer does not execute his obligation to take over good, seller has right to place it with registered trading house at buyer's expense, or to sell it by public auction. (Com. Code art. 68).

International Commercial Sales.—Same provisions apply to international sales contracts as apply to domestic sales. (Civ. Code arts. 1294 et seq.; Com. Code arts. 60 et seq.). Romania is party to Convention of the United Nations regarding contracts for international sales of goods, Vienna, Apr. 11, 1980 (ratified by Law No. 24/1991). It is also party to Convention regarding prescription in matters of international sales of goods, New York, June 14, 1974, as well as in Protocol modifying the Convention, Vienna, 1980 (Law No. 24/1992).

In commercial relations between Romanian and foreign enterprises, parties may adopt INCOTERMS Regulations, elaborated by International Chamber of Commerce in Paris, and, in relations with American market, Revised American Foreign Trade Definition (RAFTD, 1941).

International Private Law.—Law No. 105/1980 regulates laws applicable to private sale contract, giving priority to choice of law of parties. (art. 73). In absence of such choice, priority is given to legislation of State of buyer when concluding contract, or State of buyer's domicile or head office. (art. 88). As exception to provisions of art. 88, commercial sale contract is submitted to legislation of country where buyer has its bank account or its head office if: (a) negotiations took place and contract was signed by parties in that country; or (b) contract expressly stipulates that seller must execute his obligation to deliver goods in that country. (art. 89). Sales by auction, stock exchange or fairs are submitted to legislation of country where reception of goods took place, unless parties choose law of another jurisdiction. (art. 90). Legislation of country where reception of goods occurred establishes terms and procedures for verification of quantity and quality, as well as measures to be taken if goods are refused. (art. 92). In case of sale of land or buildings located in Romania, Romanian law shall apply.

SECURITIES:

Framework for securities market in Romania has been established through following legislation, inter alia: Law No. 52/1994 regarding securities and stock exchanges; Government Resolution No. 936/1994 regarding application of Law No. 52/1994; Government Ordinance No. 18/1993 regarding status of securities transactions effected through means other than stock exchange and organization of brokerage institutions, approved by Law No. 83/1994; Government Resolution No. 788/1993 regarding approval of Regulations governing public bidding for sale of securities, and Regulations governing licensing of brokerage companies and brokers; and Government Ordinance No. 24/1993 regarding organization of establishment and operation of open investment funds, and of investment firms as financial brokerage institutions.

Stock Exchanges.—According to Law No. 52/1994, stock exchanges shall be established as public institutions by decision of National Securities Commission ("NSC"). Minimum of five securities companies, authorised by NSC to negotiate on stock exchange, is necessary in order to set up stock exchange. (art. 44). Supervision and control of stock exchange shall be exercised by its General Inspector, who shall be appointed by NSC for period of five years, subject to his reappointment. (art. 45).

Only securities firms which are members of stock exchange may negotiate and conclude transactions on stock exchange, through their authorised agents. (art. 66).

Securities Brokerage Firms.—Brokerage of securities may be performed only by brokers/dealers authorized by NSC, acting through joint stock companies, whose object of activity is solely brokerage of securities. (Law No. 52/1994 art. 35, and Government Resolution No. 788/1993 appendix 11).

Brokerage of securities shall mean: (a) Purchase and sale of securities on behalf of clients; (b) purchase and sale of securities in one's own name; (c) guaranteeing placement of securities on primary and secondary bids; (d) conveyance of client orders with purpose of executing them through authorized brokers; (e) possession of clients' securities and/or equities with purpose of executing orders related to these; (f) administration of clients' individual portfolio investments; (g) safekeeping of clients' securities and/or equities for purpose of administering their portfolio investments, or for other purposes expressly authorized by regulations of NSC; (h) granting of credits for purpose of financing clients' transactions within limits set by National Bank of Romania, in consultation with NSC; (i) securities brokerage activities provided for by regulations of NSC.

According to provisions of Art. 4 of Appendix 11 to Government Resolution No. 788/1993, minimal subscribed and paid capital of securities brokerage firm may range between 50,000,000 to 300,000,000, depending upon activities undertaken. Such capital must be underwritten and paid entirely upon date of company's establishment. Any decrease or increase of capital requires prior approval of NSC.

Shareholders of brokerage company may be natural and/or legal Romanian and/or foreign persons.

Neither company nor its "significant shareholders" (i.e. those holding directly and alone, or through agency, together or in association with other persons, at least 5% of issuer's subscribed capital or at least 5% of total voting rights at issuer's General Assembly of Shareholders) may hold any ownership interest in other securities firms. However, members of Board of Administration or of Management Committee, as well as securities agents of securities firm, may hold shares in another such company only if their individual and corporate shares do not exceed 5% and 20%, respectively, of registered capital of such company, and provided that they are not elected members of management of such securities company.

Licensing of Securities Firms and Brokers.—Ordinance No. 18/1993 provides for establishment of NSC, which is responsible for regulating securities market in order to protect investors. Securities firm, established in form of joint stock company, must be licensed to operate by NSC, which requires submission of application form to NSC, which shall decide on licensing within 30 days from receipt of application.

For licensing of individual securities brokers/agents, securities firms shall submit applications to NSC, which shall pronounce on licensing application(s) within 15 days from its registration.

Licensing of securities brokers shall be temporary. Definitive licenses shall be issued to brokers after they have completed special course and/or passed relevant tests.

Natural persons shall not be authorized to perform as securities broker in their own name, but rather, must act on behalf of authorized securities firm. Individual brokers may not perform brokerage activities for more than one firm.

Public/Private Offerings.—According to Government Resolution No. 788/1993, securities may be sold in Romania through public or private offerings. Public offerings require authorization of NSC, as well as approval of Court. Issuer is responsible for providing relevant information in prospectus which must be true and accurate. NSC has 30 days from date of registration in which to approve or reject offering. Public offerings may be made either by offeror in form of direct placement, or by intermediary companies as intermediary placement.

Private placements must also be authorized by NSC, and may be made either directly by offeror or by intermediary.

Investors shall be entitled to access to certain, correct, sufficient information made public at proper time, in respect of securities, their issuers and issuers' market activity. NSC is responsible for drafting appropriate regulations in order for investors to have equal access to such information. (Law No. 52/1994 art. 79).

SEQUESTRATION:

Legal sequestration involves appointment by Court of person who is granted custody over movable or immovable goods during legal action, to insure preservation and administration of goods. (Civ. Pro. Code art. 596).

Court may delay sequestration until final settlement of legal action. Requests for sequestration are usually granted when there exists threats of damage or alienation to goods, or when co-owner is deprived of use. Mere existence of litigation over goods does not represent in itself reason to enforce sequestration; party seeking legal sequestration must demonstrate its necessity.

Legal sequestrator or administrator is authorized only to take conservative and administrative actions; he may cash revenues and debts and pay current debts or debts with executory title. Subject to approval of court which enforced sequestration action, administrator may also appear in court as legal representative of parties. Additionally, he must report to Court periodically about administration of goods. Goods are delivered to prevailing party upon resolution of legal dispute.

Security Sequestration.—This form of sequestration may be used when object of litigation is payment of sum of money. In order to prevent bad faith alienation of debtor's property which would endanger future forced execution, claimant may request security sequestration. This measure, regulated by Civil Pro. Code arts. 591-595 and 597-601, provides for sequestration of movable assets (located with debtor or third party) which may be sold if debtor does not fulfill his obligation.

To request security sequestration, debt must be due and acknowledged by written, enforceable document. Upon decision of court, creditor may be required to post bond. Creditors who do not produce written document evidencing debt are also entitled to request security sequestration, provided they post bond equivalent to one-third of claimed amount.

Security sequestration may be approved, even before payment of debt is due, under situations provided for in Civ. Pro. Code art. 597: (1) if debtor reduced guarantees provided; (2) did not offer promised guarantees; or, (3) if debtor is liable to flee, hide or waste his goods.

Security sequestration is enforced by court located in territory where debtor is domiciled. Sequestered goods remain in custody of debtor or, if latter cannot be trusted, in custody of third party. Sequestered goods cannot be forcefully sold prior to existence of executory title. (Civ. Pro. Code art. 601).

TRADEMARKS:

According to Romanian law, there are three types of trademarks: (a) manufacturing trademarks—manufacturing enterprises register their products; (b) commercial trademarks—commercial enterprises register goods in which they trade; (c) service trademarks—commercial enterprises register services they render.

Characteristics.—All three types of trademarks are distinctive symbols used by enterprises to distinguish their goods, works and services from identical or similar ones rendered by other enterprises.

Trademarks may include words, letters, numbers, graphic representations (plain or three dimensional), audio representation or other similar elements. Trademarks may not be used or registered when protected items: (a) are not sufficiently distinct from identical or similar goods, works or services, that are registered in Romania or protected by international conventions, except when registration is applied for or authorized by title holder of these trademarks; (b) constitute copy, imitation or translation of foreign trademark which is well-known in Romania for identical or similar goods, works or services; (c) constitute names which are customary (usual) names, necessary or generic for these products, works or services, or exclusively refer to time or place of manufacture or nature, destination, price, quality, quantity or weight of products; (d)

See Topical Index in front part of this volume.

TRADEMARKS . . . *continued*
include, without legal authority, names or portraits of political or administrative figures in Romania, denominations of administrative and territorial areas and organizations in Romania, imitations and copies of coats of arms, banners, orders, medals, emblems and badges, official symbols of marking, verification, quality control or guarantee; (e) include elements mentioned in paragraph (d) belonging to other countries or promulgated by international organizations if use of trademarks is prohibited by conventions to which Romania is party; (f) include false or misleading elements or are contrary to law, public order and rules of social conduct.

Foreign trademarks are subject to Romanian law based on international conventions to which Romania is party, and if none exist, based on reciprocity.

Procedure.—Any legal or physical person, Romanian or foreign, has right, according to Romanian law, to apply for registration to State Office of Inventions and Trademarks (Oficiul de Stat pentru Inventii si Marci—OSIM).

Application for registration to OSIM requires fulfillment of conditions prescribed by law. If such are fulfilled, application is registered by OSIM and subject to examination for formation of prescribed deposit which guarantees applicant, based on law, right of priority against other subsequent deposits commencing with date of application. Application which meets conditions of prescribed deposit is registered in register of trademarks.

If prescribed conditions for trademark registration are met and, if after term of three months from date of its publication in Official Gazette regarding trademarks, no sustainable objection is made trademark is registered in register of manufacturing, commercial or service trademarks and applicant receives registration certificate.

Trademark Rights.—Trademark registration confers upon holder right of exclusive use of trademark for term of ten years from date deposit was effected. At request of holder, registration of trademark may be renewed upon expiration of ten-year term.

Rights regarding registered or renewed trademarks can be conveyed in whole or in part, according to law. Rights regarding collective trademarks cannot be conveyed by enterprises receiving approval to use them.

Termination.—Trademark rights terminate when: (a) trademark holder expressly waives his rights by written declaration; (b) enterprise possessing trademark is liquidated, and rights regarding trademark are not conveyed or transferred to another enterprise; (c) term of trademark expired, and renewal formalities were not effected, as permitted by law; (d) trademark was canceled.

Fees.—For trademark registration and renewal, as well as for any other act or service rendered by OSIM regarding trademarks, fees are applied as prescribed by Government Resolution No. 274/1991. Fees for trademark renewal not paid upon expiration of ten-year term may be paid during following six months at rate increased by 50%. Nonpayment of fees due for trademark registration or renewal leads to loss of date of instituting deposits, and nonpayment of fees for invoking priority results in loss of right of priority. OSIM can grant, when justified, extension of payment due dates for fees prescribed by Government Resolution No. 274/1991, at rate increased by 70%.

TREATIES AND CONVENTIONS:

Romania is member of following organizations: Council of Europe; United Nations (UN); International Monetary Fund (IMF) and World Bank; International Bank for Reconstruction and Development (IBRD); International Finance Corporation (IFC); Multilateral Investment Guarantee Agency (MIGA); European Bank for Reconstruction and Development (EBRD); General Agreement on Tariffs and Trade (GATT); and Bank for International Settlements (BIS). It is Associate Partner of North Atlantic Treaty Organization (NATO), and is candidate to become member of European Union.

Multilateral Treaties and Conventions to which Romania is Party.—(1) The Convention of Geneva, regarding Uniform Law on Checks (1931); (2) Convention of Geneva for settling Conflicts of Laws in Check matters (1931); (3) Convention of New York on the Recognition and Enforcement of Foreign Arbitral Awards (1958) (with following reserve: "Romania will apply the Convention only for litigations which treat relations of contractual or noncontractual contracts which are considered as being commercial by the legislation. It will apply Convention to Recognition and Enforcement held on the territory of another contracting State. As to the awards held on a noncontracting State's territory it will apply Convention but on the basis of reciprocity agreed between Parties"); (4) European Convention of Geneva on International Commercial Arbitration (1961) (excepting Arrangement of Paris [1972] applying European Convention on International Commercial Arbitration); (5) United Nations Convention of Vienna on Contracts for International Sale of Goods (1980); (6) Convention of Washington Regarding the Settling of Litigation Arising from International Investments (1975); (7) Charter of Paris for a new Europe (1990); (8) Convention removing torture (1990); (9) Convention INMARSTAT (1990); (10) Convention EUTELSAT (1990); (11) Convention on Children's Rights (1990); (12) Convention of Basel on Transport of Dangerous Waste Materials (1991); (13) International Pact on Capital Punishments' Abolition; (14) Convention of Rome on the International Fund for Agricultural Development (FIDA); (15) Convention of Geneva relating to tin (1975); (16) Convention of Brussels regarding temporary import of Packages (1960); (17) Convention of Bern (as revised at Stockholm) on Literary and Artistic Works' Support; (18) Convention of Paris (as revised at Stockholm in 1967) regarding Industrial Property Support; (19) Arrangement of Madrid (as revised at Stockholm in 1967) regarding International Recording of Trade-Marks; (20) Convention relating to Imprescriptibility of War Crimes (1968); (21) Customs Convention of Brussels (1968); (22) Convention of Vienna relating to Diplomatic Relations (1961); (23) Convention of London regarding Protection of Human Life at Sea (1960); (24) Convention of Chicago regarding Civil International Aviation (1944); (25) Convention of Geneva regarding Transfrontier Atmospheric Pollution Over Long Distances (1979); (26) Convention regarding International Railway Transports (COTIF—1983); (27) International Convention relating to Railway Goods Transports (CIM); (28) International Convention relating to Travellers and Baggage Transport on Railways (CIV); (29) International Convention regarding International Transport of Goods on Roads (CMR); (30) United Nations Convention regarding Transport on Sea (1978); (31) Convention of London regarding to Sea Collisions (1972); (32) Cultural Convention of Europe (1991); (33) Conventions AELS and GATT; (34) Convention of Geneva relating to Commerce with Civil Airships; (35) Convention of Montreal relating to International Airships' Protection; (36) Convention relating to Statute of Refugees.

Mutual Promotion and Warranty of Investments.—Following countries are those with whom Romania has entered into treaties and conventions relating to mutual promotion and warranty of investments: Arab Emirates; Armenia; Canada; Czech and Slovak Republics; China; Egypt; France; Germany; Great Britain; Gabon; Israel; Indonesia; Hungary; Malaysia; Mauritania; Morocco; Netherlands; Russia; Senegal; Syria; South Africa; South Korea; Sri Lanka; Sudan; Switzerland; Tunisia; Turkey; and U.S.A.

Trade Conventions.—Romania has entered into trade conventions with following countries: Argentina; Bangladesh; Botswana; Brazil; Cameroon; Canada; Chile; China; Colombia; Costa Rica; Croatia; Cyprus; Ecuador; Egypt; Finland; France; Ghana; Greece; Guatemala; Guinea; India; Indonesia; Iraq; Kenya; Kuwait; Lesotho; Liberia; Libya; Malta; Mexico; Mozambique; Namibia; New Zealand; Nicaragua; Nigeria; Panama; Peru; Philippines; Portugal; Russia; Rwanda; Slovakia; South Africa; South Korea; Tunisia; Turkey; Ukraine; Uruguay; U.S.A.; Uzbekistan; Zambia.

WILLS:

Wills are regulated by Civ. Code arts. 800-812 and 856-931.

Generalities Regarding Wills.—Will is legal act by which individual, testator, anticipating death, disposes of all or part of his estate. It is unilateral, personal, solemn and revocable legal act.

Will contains dispositions, or legacies, of testator's estate at time of death, as well as other dispositions. Requirements for valid will include following: (a) capacity of testator to make dispositions; (b) free will of testator; and (c) valid cause of legal act. Under Civil Code provisions, wills must also be in writing. Nonobservance of legal requirements shall render will void.

Ordinary wills include following:

(a) Holographic Will.—Will which is entirely handwritten, dated and signed by testator. Proof of handwriting and signature of testator shall be obtained by comparison with other documents. (Civ. Code arts. 1178 and 1182).

(b) Authentic Will.—Will which must be authenticated by state notary according to law. (art. 860). In order to authenticate it, notary verifies testator's identity, reads will's content aloud in presence of testator, and asks testator whether contents represent his last will, if contents verified, testator signs will before notary.

Declarations made before authenticating notary and recorded in notary's authentication minutes can only be contested on grounds of forgery, but validity of these declarations may be contested by any means of proof.

(c) Secret Will.—Will written by testator or another person, signed by testator, closed, sealed and submitted to court for authentication is secret. Judge in receipt of will drafts minutes on separate piece of paper or on envelope containing will, certifying presence of testator, latter's declaration that will is his, and subsequently, both judge and testator sign and date minutes. (arts. 864-867).

Privileged Wills are created under following special circumstances:

(a) Maritime Will.—Drafted during sea journey by crew member or by passenger in front of ship's captain or his deputy, assisted by ship's administrative officer or his deputy.

(b) Military Will.—Drafted by commanding officer of unit assisted by two witnesses. If military man is wounded or ill, will shall be drafted by chief military doctor assisted by commanding officer.

(c) Will Executed During Epidemic (Contagious Disease).—Drafted by member of local council or mayor assisted by witnesses.

Privileged wills must be written and signed by testator in presence of two witnesses, and are valid only if testator died as result of such special circumstances provided by law. Military and epidemic wills are terminated within six months after cessation of event which prevented drafting ordinary will. (Civ. Code arts. 871-873, 876-878, 882). Corresponding figure for maritime will is three months.

Simplified Forms of Wills.—Simplified will can be created with bank deposits, containing testamentary clause which represents legacy with particular title.

Romanian citizens located abroad may create will either in form of holographic will, as provided by Romanian law, or in form provided by law of country where will is drafted. (Civ. Code art. 885).

Revocation of Legacy.—Revocation of will may be effected by testator or by court on account of actions perpetrated by legatee.

Voluntary revocation is accomplished by testator and may be of two kinds: express voluntary revocation, effected by testator either through will or authenticated document (Civ. Code art. 922); and tacit voluntary revocation, not expressly declared but resulting from actions of testator (art. 923).

Court revocation is sanction for blameworthy acts perpetrated by legatee against testator or his memory.

Disinheritance is testamentary provision by which testator prevents legatees from attacking will, excluding them from legacy or reducing them to legal residue. Disinheritance is void if it promotes illegal or immoral testamentary provisions.

Succession residue is that part of legacy which rightfully belongs, according to law, to reserve heirs, and thus, cannot be freely disposed of by testator. Reserve heirs are descendants of testator without limitation as to degree (children, grandchildren, great-grandchildren and children from outside marriage), privileged ascendant (father and mother), and surviving spouse. (Civ. Code arts. 841, 842; Family Code art. 63).

Successor's Unworthiness.—Legatee loses his legal or testamentary succession rights if found guilty of one of following acts: (1) attempted murder of testator; (2) libelous statements about testator; and (3) failure to disclose that testator was murdered. (Civ. Code art. 655).

Renouncement of Succession.—Renouncement occurs when legatee rejects succession rights offered to him. Renouncement may be effected expressly by declaration of

See Topical Index in front part of this volume.

WILLS . . . *continued*
renouncement before notary. (Decree No. 40/1953 art. 2). If renouncement to succession is not effected within six months from beginning of succession, such legatee shall be treated in same manner as other legatees. (See also topic Descent and Distribution.)

RUSSIAN FEDERATION LAW DIGEST REVISER

Holme Roberts & Owen LLC
Ulitsa Pokrovka #45
Riverside Towers
Kosmodamianskaya Nab., #52/1
Suite 9100
Moscow, Russia 113054
Telephone: 011 7 095 961 3000
Fax: 011 7 095 961 3001
Other Offices: London, Denver, Boulder and Colorado Springs, CO and Salt Lake City, UT.

Reviser Profile

Firm Overview.—Founded in 1898, Holme Roberts & Owen LLC ("HRO") is one of the oldest and largest law firms in the Rocky Mountain region of the U.S. Nearly 200 lawyers and 480 support staff serve clients domestically and abroad from offices in the U.S., Western Europe, and the former Soviet Union ("CIS").

HRO's U.S. domestic practice focuses on corporate matters, including mergers and acquisitions and securities; natural resources, including mining, oil and gas, and independent power production; telecommunications, with special focus on cable and multichannel television and telephony; project finance and banking; real estate; litigation; environmental and international. The firm has been serving companies with multinational interests for over fifty years. Its international practice team works out of four offices in the U.S. and offices in London and Moscow, assisting established and emerging companies, including multinational and domestic and both publicly and privately owned companies, from a broad spectrum of industries including telecommunications, high tech, financial services, biotech, mining, oil and gas, environmental, cable television, computer technologies, manufacturing, engineering, real estate, and media.

CIS Practice.—HRO has been assisting clients with CIS transactions since 1989, and opened its first CIS office in Moscow in mid-1993. In addition to several lawyers with substantial U.S. and European experience, HRO's Moscow office has four full time Russian-qualified attorneys, educated in Russia and the U.S. and fully fluent in Russian and English. The Moscow office is linked by a state-of-the-art telecommunications network to HRO's other international offices, enabling attorneys in various locations to work together, sharing expertise and jointly staffing assignments. This globally integrated arrangement provides HRO's clients with virtual round-the-clock service.

Corporate.—HRO's CIS practice over the last six years has focused on representing U.S. and European clients as well as Russian-American joint ventures on transactions and operations in Russian and various other republics, including drafting and negotiating contracts with Russian and western partners, employees, suppliers, banks and government agencies, completing pre-acquisition due diligence, and structuring joint stock companies and partnerships under Russian law. HRO serves as outside general counsel to various joint venture and wholly-foreign owned Russian legal entities and advises clients on director and management liability, shareholders' rights, corporate procedures and contract interpretation mandated by applicable Russian laws. When drafting contracts or foundation documents for Russian entities, HRO focuses on the dynamic nature of Russian law, devising strategies and terms to protect clients' interests today and also provide sufficient flexibility to support clients' goals and activities in the foreseeable future.

Securities Markets.—HRO has assisted western clients in acquisitions and restructuring of Russian open and closed joint stock companies, in large industry-specific and diversified portfolio investments, privatization and investment fund formations and acquisitions. The firm registered the first mutual fund in Russia. Its attorneys assist clients with stock issuance, prospectus registration, shareholder registration, registration and disclosure requirements for investments in Russia, bond and convertible debenture issuance, quality control and monitoring of the registrar organization, compliance with regulations for publicly traded companies, and compliance with specific securities regulations promulgated by the Russian State Property Committee and the Russian Securities Commission and Ministry of Finance.

Mergers & Acquisitions.—In post privatization era in Russia an investor has many investment options available among publicly traded and privately owned companies. Acquisitions are quickly becoming a preferred way to enter the market, expand on experience developed in a related industry, or takeover a successful competitor. HRO has extensive experience in acquisition and merger negotiations and documentation for companies in various industries ranging from telecommunications to mining, real estate development and financial services. Its clients' M&A projects are expedited through the firm's understanding and experience in Russian antimonopoly and securities regulations as well as corporate law. HRO remains on the cutting edge in M&A practice in the constantly changing legal and business environment in Russia. For example, HRO represented "Red October" in its successful defense against the first ever hostile takeover attempt in Russia, advised a client on taking a publicly traded company private, also a first in Russia, and has advised several clients on adaptation of western reorganization techniques to the Russian context.

Corporate Finance.—HRO has assisted numerous international and Russian clients with negotiation and documentation of financing through multilateral financial institutions, including the European Bank for Reconstruction and Development ("EBRD"), International Finance Corporation ("IFC"), and Russian American Enterprise Fund ("RAEF"). It also assists US-based clients in obtaining financing from the U.S. Oversees Private Investment Corporation ("OPIC") and the U.S. Export-Import Bank ("EXIM Bank"). Another rather unique aspect of the firm's practice involves assisting clients in obtaining financing in Russian capital markets, including use of western collateral to obtain preferential interest loans from Russian banks.

Due Diligence.—HRO's general corporate, corporate finance, securities, M&A, and real estate practice in the CIS is enhanced by the firm's substantial experience conducting due diligence for acquisitions and investment in Russia, ranging from simple corporate status due diligence, including assessment of company formation, share registration, and management and control, to complex reviews of compliance with industry specific legislation and regulations, government authorizations and licensing, status of share registers, labor matters and liabilities, litigation and administrative actions. The firm supplements its due diligence research, in part, through on-going contacts with relevant government agencies and legislative bodies.

Taxation and Currency Matters.—HRO's CIS practice group includes two attorneys with substantial experience structuring international transactions in a tax efficient manner. The firm also keeps up to date on current Russian domestic and international tax issues that affect clients' investment strategies in the CIS, including income and repatriation taxes, property taxes, VAT, payroll taxes and tax treaty relations between Russia and other countries. During 1992-1993 HRO advised the Legislative Committee of the Russian Parliament on possible impacts of new tax and other foreign investment legislation.

HRO monitors currency regulations for its clients to facilitate timely and cost effective repatriation of profits and compliance with banking regulations and local rules of payment. Understanding hard currency and local currency regulations is critical to successful business in the CIS. The firm assists clients in structuring their transactions and business relationships to comply with the intricate and often inconsistent capital movement regulations, investment licensing requirements and hard currency operations permits. The firm's Moscow office staff includes a currency regulations specialist who worked for the Hard Currency Department of the Central Bank of the Russian Federation prior to joining the firm.

Natural Resources.—HRO has over seventy years experience in natural resources and has assisted clients with natural resource projects in the CIS, including project finance, for over six years. The firm advises U.S., Australian, and Western European clients, as well as governments and companies based in the CIS on projects in mining, oil & gas, and timber development in Russia, Ukraine, Belarus, Kazakhstan, Azerbaijan, Uzbekistan, and Kirgyzstan.

Intellectual Property.—HRO's intellectual property practice includes trademark and trade name registration and contract support, software registration, trade secret protection, database and computer chip protection, copyright registration and support, exclusive distribution arrangements, and intellectual property licensing. HRO attorneys are part of the lobbying team for the trade secret and intellectual property sections of Part II of the new Civil Code, currently under consideration by the Russian Duma (Parliament).

Real Estate.—Real property ownership and leasehold laws have developed rapidly over the last several years due to the expanding need for investment in this area and desire for direct ownership by legal entities and individuals. HRO's real estate experience in Russia includes legislative compliance at federal and local levels, due diligence on title and ownership rights, compliance with construction regulations, preparation for government tenders in real estate privatization, structuring land and improvements leases, and structuring real estate investments to maximize profits and minimize tax. HRO also has substantial experience in utilizing domestic and foreign real property as collateral in secured project financing from Russian and multilateral lending institutions.

Environmental.—Russian environmental laws impose substantial liability on owners of polluting enterprises, especially in the natural resources, construction and infrastructure industries. Although these laws are only enforced sporadically, foreign investors often are singled-out for enforcement. HRO is one of the few Moscow firms that dedicates substantial resources to environmental practice, advising clients on their liability exposure and on ways to minimize and contain potential liability through pre-transaction negotiations and indemnifications. For clients seeking multilateral (EBRD, IFC, OPIC, EXIM Bank, RAEF) financing, HRO advises clients on how to comply with the environmental restrictions of such financing sources without jeopardizing the value of their investments.

Library & Online Research Systems.—Up-to-date monitoring of the ever changing Russian legal environment is HRO's number one priority. To this end, the firm has an extensive library of Russian and international legal publications, including regularly updated loose-leaf reference materials and periodicals. The firm also utilizes the on-line GARANT Legal Research System and the on-line USIS Legal Database in the Moscow office and several U.S. offices. It also receives Interfax business and legal publications on-line daily. Cutting edge legal research is also carried out through extensive contacts with relevant government agencies and legislative bodies, which gives the firm access to draft legislation and the opportunity to review upcoming developments before they become law.

Arthur Andersen.—Arthur Andersen reestablished operations in Russia in 1990 and has since grown to over 450 professionals in offices in Moscow, St. Petersburg and Novosibirsk. It provides a full range of audit, accounting, tax, business systems and educational services to both foreign investors and domestic organizations.

RUSSIAN FEDERATION LAW DIGEST

(The following is a list of all Topics, including cross-references, covered in this Digest.)

RUSSIAN FEDERATION LAW DIGEST

Prepared for 1997 edition by

HOLME ROBERTS & OWEN LLC, of the Colorado & Utah Bars, Moscow, Russia and London

(Taxation and Customs Topics prepared by Arthur Andersen, Moscow office).

Primary abbreviations used: RSFSR—Russian Soviet Federation of Socialist Republics; RF—Russian Federation; Konst. RF—Constitution of RF; GK RF—Civil Code of RF of Nov. 1994; GK RSFSR 1964—Civil Code of RSFSR of 1964; GPK RSFSR—Code of Civil Procedure of RSFSR of 1964; UK RSFSR—Criminal Code of RSFSR of 1960; UPK RSFSR—Code of Criminal Procedure of RSFSR of 1960; Civ. Fund—Fundamentals of Civil Legislation of RF of 1991; MinFin RF—Ministry of Finance of RF; MinJustice RF—Ministry of Justice of RF; MinForAff RF—Ministry of Foreign Affairs of RF; MinEc RF—Ministry of Economics of RF; GKAP RF—State Committee on Antimonopoly Policy and Support for New Economic Structures of RF; CBk RF—Central Bank of RF.

PRELIMINARY NOTE:

Following are full citations for each legislative source referred to in primary abbreviations above. Following certain citations is shortened version used for references in text. Constitution of RF adopted by popular referendum on Dec. 12, 1993 ("Constitution"); Civil Code of RF Part One and Part Two adopted correspondingly on Nov. 30, 1994 and Dec. 22, 1995 ("new Civil Code" as last amended on Feb. 26, 1966); Civil Code of RSFSR adopted by Supreme Soviet of RSFSR on June 6, 1964 as last amended on Dec. 24, 1992 ("Civil Code of 1964"); Code of Civil Procedure of RSFSR adopted by Supreme Soviet of RSFSR on June 11, 1964 as last amended on Dec. 31, 1995; Criminal Code of RSFSR adopted by Supreme Soviet of RSFSR on Oct. 27, 1960 as last amended on July 1, 1994; (new Criminal Code of RF has been adopted by Parliament of RF on May 24, 1996 and signed by President of RF, but not published yet); Code of Criminal Procedure of RSFSR adopted by Supreme Soviet of RSFSR on Oct. 27, 1960 as last amended on Aug. 27, 1993; Fundamentals of Civil Legislation of USSR and Republics No. 2211-1 adopted by Supreme Soviet of USSR on May 31, 1991 ("Civil Fundamentals"). "Subjects" of RF defined in topic Constitution and Government, subhead Federal Structure.

RF law is still skeletal, includes many inconsistencies within and between various codes, statutes and decrees, and is subject to varying interpretations by broad scope of administrative and judicial persons and entities weilding extensive discretion. Also, translation difficulties raise additional concerns regarding meaning of laws, and no official English translation of laws exists. To extent possible, this Digest reflects actual wording of laws without interpretation and without resolving inconsistencies, except as mandated by relative priority of RF laws.

ABSENTEES:

Upon application of concerned individuals, court may declare person missing when absent for over one year. Property of missing person transferred to custodian appointed by court. Material support for missing person's dependents and satisfaction of other obligations provided out of property placed in custodian's care. If person reappears, court rescinds missing person declaration and dissolves fiduciary administration of person's property. (GK RF Arts. 42-44).

Recognition as missing by court provides grounds for dissolution of marriage at registry office on spouse's initiative, as well as adoption of child without parental consent. See topics Death; Divorce.

ACKNOWLEDGMENTS:

See topics Seals; Notaries Public.

ACTIONS:

Costs.—Court costs in civil cases regulated by c. 7 of RSFSR Code of Civil Procedure and consist of state fee and court administrative expenses. (GPK RSFSR, art. 79). Amount of state fee determined by Law "On State Fees" of Dec. 9, 1991 as last amended Dec. 31, 1995, and depends on amount of claim and type of dispute. (Law "On State Fees," art. 4; GPK RSFSR, art. 83). Some claims and participants exempt from costs. For example, plaintiff exempt for claims related to labor relations, torts, alimonies, intellectual property rights and several others. (GPK RSFSR, art. 80). Court costs assessed on defendant in proportion to plaintiff's success on civil claim, but if plaintiff's claim disallowed in whole or part, plaintiff must pay portion of defendant's fees, proportional to percent of claim disallowed. Reasonable attorneys fees recoverable depending on circumstances of case. Misconduct by party may be sanctioned with fee to compensate other party's lost time. (GPK RSFSR, arts. 90-92).

Arbitration courts similarly assess costs proportional to success of parties on claim/defense. (Arbitration Procedure Code of RF of May 5, 1995 art. 95[1]). See topic Dispute Resolution. Cassation and appellate costs allocated in same fashion. (Id., art. 95[3]). If court finds misconduct by party (e.g., unreasonable refusal to consider settlement offer, failure to turn over documents), court may assess administrative expenses regardless of outcome. (Id., art. 95[3]). In criminal matters, indigent defendants have right to state paid attorney.

Limitation of Actions.—Civil actions generally must be commenced within three years. (GK RF, art. 196). Limitations period shortened or extended in certain statutory instances. (Id., art. 197). Parties may not contractually alter duration or application of limitations period. Period typically runs from day claimant learned or should have learned of violation. Where obligations have specific term for performance, period begins on expiration of such term. New Civil Code defines grounds for suspension of limitations period. (Id., art. 22). If foreign law applied, limitations period for relevant action established pursuant to that law. (Civ. Fund., art. 159).

Proof of Foreign Claims and Foreign Law.—Special procedures of Soviet era eliminated by amendments to Civil Procedure Code adopted by Supreme Soviet of RSFSR on June 11, 1964 as last amended Dec. 31, 1995 and adoption of new Code of Arbitration Procedure of May 5, 1995 ("APK RF"), which apply methods of proof for questions of fact when proving foreign law and claims. Courts may seek advice on foreign law from MinJustice RF and other RF institutions, competent organizations in foreign country or other experts. (Civ. Fund, art. 157[1], APK RF, art. 12[2]). RF law applied if foreign law not properly established (APK RF art. 12), or where foreign law not consistent with RF public policy (Civ. Fund, art. 158).

ADMINISTRATIVE LAW:

Primary source of administrative law and procedure in RF is Code of Administrative Violations ("KoAP RSFSR"), frequently amended since adoption on June 20, 1984 and last am'd Feb. 2, 1995. KoAP RSFSR defines violations punishable by fines, confiscations or other obligations in areas such as automobile operation, minor currency operations, hunting and disorderly conduct, and describes procedure for administrative appeal. (Id., art. 271). Rulings may be appealed to procurator (Id., art. 275) or court, trial court decision constituting final resolution of administrative dispute (Id., art. 266). Procedure in KoAP RSFSR also relevant to substantive violations under other federal laws.

Administrative decisions also potentially appealable pursuant to RF Law No. 4866-1 "On Lodging Complaints with Court of Law on Actions and Decisions Infringing Citizens' Rights and Freedoms" ("Law on Appeal"), adopted in most recent form Dec. 14, 1995. Citizen may apply for separate judicial review of acts of officials or government that citizen believes violate citizen's rights. (Id., arts. 1, 2). Collegial and individual administrative decisions potentially appealable to highest courts if citizen can show decision unlawful, and not just unfavorable exercise of administrative discretion. Appealable unlawful acts include violation or frustration of citizen's rights and freedoms, imposition of unlawful duties, liabilities or wrongful prosecution. (Id., Arts. 2-4). Constitution guarantees citizen's right to judicial review of administrative actions. (Konst. RF art. 46[2]).

ADOPTION:

RF Family Code ("FC") adopted Dec. 8, 1995 allows adoption of child under 18 years when in child's interests. (Family Code, art. 124). Adoption effective on decision of court. Adoption of child considered by court during special proceedings stipulated by civil procedural legislation. Rights and obligations arising from adoption attach upon court decision. Prospective adoptive parent(s) must be legally competent citizens over 18 years of age. Adoption subject to state registration. (Id., art. 125). Full rights and duties of natural child acquired by adoptive child, including rights of inheritance, family name and obligations to support ill or elderly parents. Confidentiality of adoptive status guaranteed. (Id., art. 139).

Adoption of Russian child by foreign citizens permitted when no possibility of placing child with Russian families residing in RF, or relatives, regardless of citizenship or place of residence.

ADVERSE POSSESSION:

Citizen or legal entity other than record owner may acquire ownership of property by possession of real property openly, continuously, and in good faith for 15 years or possession of personal property for five years. Adversely acquired ownership right to immovable and other property subject to state registration, arises from moment of state registration. Adverse possessor can tack prior period(s) of possession by parties to which he is legal successor. (GK RF, art. 234).

AFFIDAVITS:

Affirmations or declarations in written form, sworn to official having authority to administer oath, generally not received as evidence in Russian courts but Russian notaries may certify affidavits for use in international transactions and foreign or arbitral proceedings. (See, Fund. of RF Legislation on Notarization of Feb. 11, 1993; Comments to Regulations on London Court of International Arbitration of Jan. 1, 1990.)

AIRCRAFT:

USSR Air Code of May 11, 1983 governs Russian civil aviation activities, including all aircraft within borders of RF and all Russian aircraft traveling outside RF, unless otherwise provided by laws of country hosting such aircraft. (Id., art. 3). Russian Ministry of Transportation regulates and issues five year licenses for carriage of passengers and cargo, cargo handling, aircraft servicing, construction and operation of airports, and mail carrier operations. (Id., art. 5). Russian airspace and air traffic control overseen by RF Interdepartmental Commission for Use of Airspace and Air Traffic Control. (Decision of RF Government No. 1148 of Oct. 6, 1994).

ALIENS:

Aliens (foreign citizens and stateless persons) bear rights and obligations similar to those of RF citizens, as limited by federal law or international agreement. Political asylum granted in compliance with universally recognized norms of international law. (Konst. RF, arts. 62, 63). Visas required for every foreigner entering RF. Visa application must include certificate of absence of HIV infection. (Federal Law No. 38FZ art. 10, Apr. 12, 1995, Decision of Government of RF No. 1158, Nov. 25, 1995). Work permits for aliens issued by RF Federal Immigration Agency, pursuant to established quotas for employment in certain fields and total permissible number of foreign

See Topical Index in front part of this volume.

ALIENS . . . *continued*
employees. (Presidential Decree No. 2146 of Dec. 1993 "On Solicitation and Utilization of Foreign Labor in Russian Federation"). Work permit application must include decision of local authorities that foreign labor needed and draft contract including employment terms. Decision of local authorities based on priority employment right of RF citizens to employment. Permits generally issued for one year with extension at discretion of authorities for one additional year. Permits are nontransferable. Work permit requirements exempt high and managerial level officers and specialists working for firms with foreign participation, foreign citizens engaged in science and art projects under intergovernmental agreement, employees of embassies and consulates, student interns with Russian enterprises, journalists accredited in RF, instructors invited to academies and educational institutions and others. Subject to permanent residence in RF, aliens bear same income tax obligations as RF citizens. Aliens may wed in RF following procedure established by RF law.

See topic Marriage, subhead To Foreign Nationals.

ALIMONY:

See topic Divorce, subhead Alimony.

ARBITRATION AND AWARD:

See topic Dispute Resolution.

ASSIGNMENTS:

Assignment of claim generally permissible without consent of other party, to extent not inconsistent with law or contract, provided claim not inextricably connected with creditor such as alimony or personal injury claim. (GK RF arts. 382, 383). Debtor not obligated to assignee-creditor until assignor-creditor delivers documents evidencing assignment. Assignment must follow same formalities of execution, notarization and registration as transaction giving rise to debt. (Id., art. 389). Initial creditor liable to assignee for invalidity of transferred claim, but not for nonperformance by debtor, unless initial creditor contractually assumes suretyship for debtor's obligation to new creditor. (Id., art. 390). Debtor may not assign obligation to third party without consent of creditor. Formalities and procedure of debt transfer same as for assignment of claim. (Id., art. 391).

Assignment of Claim for Financing.—Current or future monetary claim may be assigned to obtain or secure financing. Person obtaining financing ("Customer") liable to person providing financing ("Financial Agent") for validity of claim assigned (GK RF, art. 827[1, 2]), but not liable for failure of debtor to fulfill claim (Id., art. 827[3]). Debtor obligated to pay claim to financial agent only after receiving written notification of assignment specifying claim and identifying financial agent. (Id., art. 830[1]).

If financing received for sale of claim, customer not liable to financial agent if amount received as claim less than price paid for claim. If claim assigned to secure customer's obligation to financial agent, latter must pay customer amount received from debtor in excess of claim secured to financial agent. If amounts received by financial agent from debtor less than amount secured by customer, latter must pay balance to financial agent, unless contract provides otherwise. (Id., art. 831).

If financial agent delivers claim to debtor, latter may claim set-off against amount owing on claim debtor has against customer under debtors' contract with customer, if set-off claim existed when notification on assignment of claim was received. (Id., art. 832[1]). However, debtor may not refuse to pay financial agent based on prohibition against assignment in contract between debtor and customer, unless agent was aware of prohibition: debtor's only recourse for such violation of prohibition against assignment is against customer. (Id., arts. 832-833).

ASSOCIATIONS:

New Civil Code divides all permissable types of Russian legal entities into three categories. First category includes business partnerships, companies and manufacturing and consumer cooperatives in which participants have broad ownership and management rights and obligations. Second category consists of state and municipally-owned unitarian enterprises and owner-financed institutes, in which participants have ownership rights or other rights in rem. Third category consists of public and religious organizations (associations), philanthropic and other foundations, and associations of legal entities (leagues and unions), in which founders and participants have no ownership rights. (GK RF art. 48). Organizations are further classified as commercial (organizations whose principal purpose is profit making) and noncommercial (organizations that do not regard profit making as principal purpose and do not distribute profit among participants). (Id., art. 50[1]).

Commercial organizations may be established as business partnerships, companies, manufacturing cooperatives and state and municipally owned unitarian enterprises. (Id., art. 50[2]). See topic Business Associations.

Noncommercial (Nonprofit) Organizations.—Noncommercial or nonprofit organizations ("NPOs") governed by new Civil Code and law of Jan. 12, 1996 "On Noncommercial Organizations" ("NPO Law"). NPO Law not applicable to consumer cooperatives. NPO is defined as organization with primary goals other than profit making that does not distribute profit among participants. NPO subject to registration with appropriate registration authorities. NPO may engage in entrepreneurial activities if consistent with objectives for which NPO established. NPO operates on basis of foundation documents (i.e. charter and foundation agreement) (NPO Law, art. 14), and in cases provided by law, on basis of general statute for respective type of NPO. (Id., art. 52[1]).

Consumer Cooperatives.—Associations of individuals and legal entities that pool contributions to meet common material and needs pursuant to cooperative's charter. (Id., art. 116). Members cover losses with additional contributions. Members jointly and severally liable for obligations of cooperative to extent of contributions. Court may dissolve cooperative for failure to satisfy obligations. (Id., art. 116[4]). Proceeds from cooperative's activities distributed among members pursuant to charter and applicable law. Law of June 29, 1992 "On Consumer Cooperatives", effective to extent not inconsistent with new Civil Code, further defines rights and duties of entity and members and provides guidance on cooperative governance.

Public and Religious Associations.—Voluntary associations of individuals sharing common interest to meet spiritual or other immaterial needs. Members do not retain rights in respect to property contributed, and are not liable for obligations of organization. (NPO Law, art. 117). Public Associations are governed by NPO Law and law of May 19, 1995 "On Public Associations" ("Public Associations Law"). Public Associations Law does not require registration, however optional registration available though MinJustice RF, and only registered public associations acquire status as legal entities. (Public Associations Law, art. 21).

Foundations.—Organizations without membership, established by individuals and/or legal entities by voluntary contributions for social, charitable, cultural, educational and other public purposes. (NPO Law, art. 7). Assets contributed become property of foundation. Founders not liable for obligations of foundation. Foundation must publish annual reports on use of assets. Procedure for management and formation of foundation defined by charter approved by founders. (Id.). Only court may liquidate foundation, upon petition of interested persons on grounds defined by statute. On liquidation, property remaining after satisfaction of creditor's claims used for purposes stated in foundation's charter.

Noncommercial partnerships created by individuals and legal entities for social, charitable and educational purposes. (NPO Law, art. 8). Partners make contributions to partnership. Partnership not responsible for liabilities of partner and partners not liable for obligations of partnership. (Id.).

Institutions and Unions.—NPO created and financed by owner to perform managerial, social, cultural and other noncommercial functions. Owner has secondary liability for obligations of institution. (Id., art. 120, NPO Law, art. 9). Unions of commercial and noncommercial associations may form to coordinate their entrepreneurial activities. Such unions are NPOs (Id., art. 11). Members of union retain autonomy but have secondary liability for union's obligations to extent stipulated in foundation documents (founders agreement and charter). (Id., art. 11[4]).

Members of union may use its services free of charge and may terminate membership at end of any fiscal year but retain secondary liability for obligations of union in proportion to their contributions for two years from date of withdrawal. Members may be expelled by decision of other members. New member admitted by unanimous consent, but admission may be conditioned on assumption of secondary liability for obligations of union incurred prior to admission. (Id., art. 12).

Charitable Organizations.—RF Law "On Charitable Activities and Charitable Organizations" of Aug. 11, 1995 ("Charitable Organizations Law," art. 6) created NPOs for purposes of carrying out charitable activities. Charitable organizations may be created in form of public associations, foundations, and institutions. (Id., art. 7). Charitable organizations may engage in commercial activities consistent with its declared purposes. (Id., art. 12).

ATTACHMENT:

Upon petition of parties or its own initiative, court may take measures to secure enforcement of claim if failure to take such measures could result in impediment to or impossibility of implementing court decision. (GPK RSFSR, art. 133). Attachment may include seizure of defendant's assets or funds in possession of defendant or third party; prohibition of certain actions by defendant; prohibition of certain property transfers between defendant and third parties and temporary prohibitions on certain alienations of property. (Id., art. 134). Attachment decision may be appealed. (Id., art. 139). Court may require plaintiff to provide security against possible losses of debtor resulting from attachment. (Id., art. 140).

ATTORNEYS AND COUNSELORS:

On Apr. 15, 1995, RF Government, on initiative of MinJustice RF, issued directives on rendering paid legal services in RF (RF Government Resolution No. 344, "Provisions on Licensing Activity of Rendering Paid Legal Services on Territory of RF") ("Resolution 344"). Previous regulation of legal practice concerned only Union of Advocates, nongovernmental, nationwide consortium of all local collegia or bar associations. ("Law on Union of Advocates in RSFSR", adopted [1980] and "Law on Advocacy in USSR", adopted Nov. 30, 1979). Only members of collegia are "advocates" for purposes of procedural codes and other rules defining requirements for trial counsel. Advocates have fairly exclusive right to appear in civil and criminal litigation and may engage in all other aspects of legal practice. Representation by non-advocates in trial matters substantially circumscribed by statute, but some exceptions exist. (E.g., in civil matters court may allow representation by non-advocate employees of organizations or other individuals [GPK RSFSR, art. 44], and trade-union representatives may appear in criminal cases [UPK RSFSR, art. 47]). Union of Advocates regulations remain important, since Resolution 344 exempts from licensing requirements members of Union of Advocates and other nongovernmental attorney organizations with charters of conduct approved by MinJustice RF. (Resolution 344, art. 1).

Licensing Requirements.—Resolution 344 requires all persons rendering paid legal services, unless exempted, to be licensed by MinJustice RF or appropriate local authority in jurisdiction where practice intended. (Id., arts. 1, 6, 7). License from MinJustice RF valid throughout RF, local licenses limited to territory of licensing authority. Local licensing authorities maintain attorney files, passed on to MinJustice RF. (Id., arts. 8-10). Licenses valid up to three years. (Id., art. 14). Inside legal counsel and members of collegia exempt from licensing.

Attorney must have diploma from RF law school and three years experience in legal practice. Unlicensed foreign lawyers may only provide paid legal services on law of country that issued their law diploma. (Id., art. 3). Legal entities licensed upon submission of notarized documentation of qualifications of each attorney intending to advise clients directly. (Id., art. 12). Foreign legal entities licensed by MinJustice RF. (Id., art. 7). License not transferable, and licensee must notify authorities of change to structure of entity or scope of practice (Id., arts. 21, 22).

Suspension/Annulment of License.—Attorney/firm licenses suspended for performance of paid legal services outside authorized territory, failure to report changes to registration data or violations of other license terms. (Id., art. 22). License annulled, and attorney/firm banned upon finding that license has been transferred, entity-licensee has been liquidated, solo practitioner's registration as individual entrepreneur has

See Topical Index in front part of this volume.

ATTORNEYS AND COUNSELORS . . . *continued*
terminated, or licensee failed to cure violations giving rise to suspension. (Id., art. 23). Decisions on licensing activities appealable to court. (Id., art. 27).

Admission to Patent Bar.—Citizen permanently resident in RF, higher legal education, four years legal experience in intellectual property matters and satisfactory score on qualifying examination required. (Regulations of RF Council of Ministers No. 122, "Regulations for Patent Attorneys" of Feb. 12, 1993).

BANKRUPTCY:

All commercial legal entities except budget financed enterprises (see topic Business Associations, subhead State Enterprises), consumer cooperatives and charitable or other foundations may be declared insolvent (bankrupt) by court, resulting in liquidation, if unable to meet creditor claims. (GK RF, art. 65[1]). With consent of creditors, entities may also declare voluntary bankruptcy. (Id., art. 65[2]). Grounds and procedures for judicial and voluntary bankruptcy provided in Law No. 3929-1 "On Insolvency (Bankruptcy) of Enterprises" of Nov. 19, 1992 ("Bankruptcy Law") and new Civil Code. (GK RF, art. 65[3]). Special rules apply to enterprises with state or municipal funding and commercial banks. (Bankruptcy Law, arts. 11, 14).

Proceedings.—Bankruptcy proceedings available are reorganization (either outside management or "rehabilitation"), liquidation (including forcible liquidation by judicial decision and voluntary liquidation by debtor under control of its creditors) and amicable settlement. Arbitration courts have sole jurisdiction of bankruptcy cases (Id., §I, arts. 1-3). Bankruptcy proceeding must be initiated by petition filed by debtor, creditor(s) or procurator (Id., §II, art. 4). Debtor's petition may be filed in anticipation of insolvency but may not be withdrawn once filed. (Id., art. 5). Creditor may file bankruptcy petition if debtor at least three months in default on financial obligation to creditor and fails to cure within one week of receiving written notice and demand from creditor. Procurator may file if evidence of willful or sham bankruptcy and on other grounds permitted by law. Any petitioner may request reorganization. (Id., art. 7).

Three arbitration court judges must consider bankruptcy petitions, pursuant to complex and technical statutory procedures. Court may institute bankruptcy proceedings, suspend bankruptcy and permit reorganization or refuse petition if debtor solvent. (Id., arts. 8-10).

Reorganization.—Outside management allowed only if real possibility to restore solvency through sale of debtor's property exists. Reorganization may only continue for 18 months, during which creditor claims are stayed. (Id., art. 12). Rehabilitation only permitted if solvency feasible through financial aid to debtor by owner or third parties. Creditor claims are not stayed during rehabilitation, which requires that at least 40% of creditors' claims be paid within 12 months. Rehabilitation limited to 18 months unless court extends for additional six months. (Id., art. 13).

Liquidation.—If reorganization unsuccessful, court determines insolvency and begins forcible liquidation using court-appointed receiver. From insolvency declaration, debtor prohibited from alienating property or paying obligations, except to secured creditors, unless otherwise agreed by creditors and court. Accrual of interest and penalties on debtor's obligations also cease. (Id., §IV, arts. 18, 30). Debtor's estate excludes property subject to lien. (Id., art. 26[4]).

Court may invalidate payments to creditors prior to determination of insolvency if payments occurred when debtor effectively insolvent and within six months prior to determination, or, even if payments made beyond six month period, if payments intended to harm other creditors and transferee parties aware of that intention. Court may also invalidate payments made to some but not all creditors when debtor effectively insolvent, if parties were aware of insolvency. Such invalidations do not apply to payments to secured and privileged creditors. (Id., art. 28).

Under Bankruptcy Law, assets of debtor's estate are applied to claims, after payment of bankruptcy expenses, in following priority: (1) tort claims by individuals; (2) wages of employees, pension fund liabilities and allowances, and amounts due under authorship and licensing contracts; (3) mandatory obligations to state funds; (4) claims of creditors; (5) claims of employee-shareholders or owners; (6) claims of other shareholder-owners; (7) all other claims. Creditors in priority categories (1)-(3) are deemed "privileged creditors". (Id., art. 30). Note that relative priority for creditor claims under bankruptcy provisions of new Civil Code (which is higher authority) differ, putting secured creditors in third category and omitting distinctions in categories (5) through (7) of Bankruptcy Law. If commercial bank or credit institution is liquidated, claims of individuals who are creditors of bank or credit institution are included in first priority claims. (GK RF, arts. 65[3], 64[1]). Upon distribution of debtor's estate, debtor deemed free of debt and, if debtor is entity, liquidated and stricken from State Register (see topic Commercial Register). (Bankruptcy Law, §IV, arts. 36-37).

Amicable settlement between debtor and creditors in fourth and following priorities permitted at any stage of bankruptcy procedures if approved by court and two-thirds of all creditors in those categories. (Id., arts. 40-41). Extrajudicial procedures also permitted, under which debtor may agree with some or all creditors on, e.g., deferred payments or debt rebates, or may agree on voluntary (extrajudicial) liquidation, with unanimous consent of and subject to control of all creditors. (Id., §VII, arts. 50-51). By Resolution No. 926 of RF Council of Ministers, of Sept. 20, 1993, Federal Agency on Insolvency (Bankruptcy) ("Agency") established as part of State Committee for Management of State Property.

Acts committed by debtor, creditor or others prior to or during bankruptcy proceedings, which are deliberate, incompetent or negligent and cause harm to debtor and creditors, deemed "wrongful acts" under Bankruptcy Law and subject to prosecution. (Id., §VI, arts. 44-48).

BANKS AND BANKING:

Banks governed primarily by law of Dec. 2, 1990 "On Banks and Banking Activity in RF", as most recently amended Feb. 13, 1996 ("Banking Law"). Bank is any legal entity licensed by CBk RF, including foreign entities, to solicit deposits and investments and conduct other types of banking activities. Banking Law also applies to credit institutions, which may perform certain banking operations. (Id., art. 6). RF banking system consists of CBk RF, credit institutions, branches and representative offices of foreign banks. (Id., art. 2). Banking Law outlines permissible banking activities and transactions. Banking operations with foreign currency subject to special licenses. (Id., art. 5). Banks may open branches and representative offices in RF and abroad. (Id., arts. 25, 35).

Bank Formation and Registration.—Bank formed on registration of charter and issuance of license by CBk RF. Law lists documents necessary for license application. (Id., art. 14). Registration and license void if charter capital not paid within one month of registration. (Id., art. 15). Minimum charter capital and reserve levels adjusted quarterly by CBk RF, and for second quarter of 1996, minimum charter-capital set at 12 billion rubles (approx. U.S.$2.5 million) for newly-established banks licensed to conduct operations in hard currency, and three billion rubles (U.S.$625,000) for banks licensed for limited banking activities and credit institutions. (Telegram No. 55-96 CBk RF of Apr. 17, 1996). CBk RF supervises banking activity and may impose sanctions including revocation of bank license for violation of banking laws. (Id., arts. 6, 9).

Confidentiality, Seizure and Garnishment.—All banks, including CBk RF, must guarantee confidentiality of account and deposit information, except for required disclosure to banking authorities, courts, and investigatory, auditing, and fiscal organs. Seizure and garnishment of money and other valuables kept in banks may be ordered by general or arbitration court or investigatory body such as tax police. Garnishment of account executed on specific writ issued by court or upon request of fiscal authorities as provided by applicable law. (Id., arts. 26-27).

Banks with Foreign Participation.—Under CBk RF Letter No. 14 of Apr. 8, 1993, "On Conditions of Establishment of Banks With Foreign Participation" ("Conditions"), banks with foreign participation are formed jointly by RF residents and nonresidents, established as RF legal entities solely by nonresident banks or as branches of nonresident banks. (Conditions, art. 1). CBk RF licenses banks with foreign participation upon consideration of financial position and business reputation of founders (with preference given to founders actively involved in operations with Russian banks), geographical representation of founders and relations between RF and founders' home country. (Id., art. 3). At least one foreign shareholder must contribute not less than ruble equivalent of U.S.$2,000,000 to charter capital. (Id., art. 4). Additional CBk RF license required for each new branch. (Id., art. 5).

Branches and affiliates of foreign banks permitted only if parent financially stable with solid domestic business reputation. Foreign bank must provide branch with charter capital of not less than ruble equivalent of U.S.$5,000,000. CBk RF may prohibit or limit foreign bank's present or future operations, if parent becomes unstable or branch incurs debts affecting bank's ability to satisfy claims of Russian clients and creditors. (Conditions, art. 6.3). Banks active in RF territory require permission of CBk RF to increase charter capital by nonresidents and for transfers of shares held by foreign persons or entities. CBk RF limits participation of foreign capital in RF banking system. Unclear if 1993 limit of 12% applicable to 1994 and 1995 fiscal years. (Id., art. 8).

Central Bank of Russia ("CBk RF").—Activities of CBk RF, nonprofit legal entity, governed by constitution and law "On the Central Bank" ("CBk RF Law") of Dec. 1, 1990 as most recently amended Dec. 27, 1995. CBk RF Law establishes legal status, objectives, functions, scope of activities, authority and operations of CBk RF. Charter capital and other property of CBk RF federally owned. (CBk RF Law, art. 2). CBk RF and federal/local governments not mutually liable unless obligations undertaken jointly. (Id., art. 2). Objectives of CBk RF include stability of ruble, unified federal monetary policy, development and improvement of banking system and facilitation of interbank settlements. CBk RF may issue regulations within its scope of activity, binding on all federal agencies and authorities, organs of state power, all legal entities and individuals, provided acts comply with federal laws. (Id., art. 4). CBk RF may not participate in capital finance or activities of other credit institutions unless specifically authorized by CBk RF Law. (Id., art. 7). Charter capital of CBk RF is 3 billion rubles (approximately U.S.$600,000,000). (Id., art. 9). CBk RF Chairman nominated by President and appointed by Duma. (Konst., arts. 83, 103). CBk RF Board elected by Duma. (CBk RF, arts. 11-13).

CBk RF may not grant credit to RF Government for financing budget deficit or purchase government securities upon initial issuance. (Id., art. 22). CBk RF authorized to engage in following operations with Russian and foreign credit institutions: granting secured loans for term not more than one year; buying and selling checks, bills of exchange and promissory notes with payment period not more than six months; buying and selling government securities on open market; buying and selling bonds, deposit certificates and other securities with term of repayment not more than one year; buying and selling foreign currency, and payment documents and obligations in foreign currency; buying, holding and selling precious metals and other currency assets; maintaining settlement and deposit operations; holding and managing securities deposited; issuing guarantees and conducting operations with financial instruments used for financial-risk management; and opening accounts with Russian and foreign credit institutions on RF territory and foreign states. (Id., art. 45). CBk RF prohibited from acquisition of shares of credit and other institutions, with certain exceptions. (Id., art. 48). CBk RF establishes and publishes official ruble exchange rates of foreign currencies (Id., art. 52), sets reserves for credit institutions and banks, establishes rules on maintenance of accounting records, and sets procedure for filing of accounting and statistical reports (Id., arts. 55, 56). Authorized to open representative offices in foreign states. (Id., art. 54).

BILLS AND NOTES:

Promissory Notes.—Supreme Soviet Resolution No. 1451-1 "On Bills and Notes" ("Resolution No. 1451-1") of June 24, 1991, readopted Regulation "On Bill of Exchange and Promissory Note" of 1931 ("1931 Regulation") as primary regulation on negotiable instruments, to extent consistent with federal law. Valid promissory notes or bills of exchange must be executed on special form, approved by Resolution No. 1451-1, containing following information: general designation of nature of instrument; place and exact date of execution; date payable (set date, on sight or at certain time after sight); and signature of payor. (Id., c. I, §§1, 2, 75). Regulation contains detailed procedure and rules regarding endorsement of bill of exchange (Id., c. II),

See Topical Index in front part of this volume.

BILLS AND NOTES . . . *continued*
acceptance (Id., c. III), available guaranty (Id., c. IV), payment and date of payment (Id., cc. V-VI), and claims for nonacceptance or nonpayment (Id., c. VII). Certain provisions governing bills of exchange apply to promissory notes. (Id., c. XII, §77).

Bill of foreign origin, made out in foreign currency and designating RF as place of payment, may be converted into Russian rubles at official exchange rate. Same procedure applies when bill executed in RF but payable abroad, presented for payment within RF. (Id., c. VI, §41). Bill transferred by endorsement on back of document. (Id., c. II, §11).

Nonpayment of bill must be certified by protest to notarial office, or if none available, to court of first instance. (Id., c. VI, §44). Drafter of negotiable instrument liable for payment without prior protest, but protest necessary to obtain remedy from parties subsequently liable. Action against original promisor on note or bill must be brought within two years of date of promise to pay. Promisee must file action against parties other than promisor who are jointly or collaterally liable on bill within nine months of promisor's refusal to pay. (Id., c. VI, §38).

Checks.—Regulations "On Checks" approved Feb. 13, 1992 by RF Supreme Soviet Resolution No. 2349-1 ("Check Regs"), govern formalities of execution and rights arising under checks. Valid checks must indicate nature of instrument, declaration of transfer of sum to payee from identifiable account, identification of currency of payment, date and place of execution and signature of payor. (Check Regs, art. 3). Check issued by legal entity must have seal of issuer. (Id., art. 4). Check may be transferred to third party personally or through endorsement. Check Regs contain rules on procedure for endorsement of check (Id., c. 3), payment on check (Id., c. 5), and consequences of nonpayment of check by payor bank (Id., c. 7). Checks made abroad and payable within RF subject to Russian law, except check form and obligations arising thereunder valid if check valid under laws of Russia or place of origin, and extent to which check binds foreign person determined by law of state in which payment requested. (Id., art. 32). Check must be presented for payment within six months of execution.

See topic Securities.

BUSINESS ASSOCIATIONS:

Legal entities (business organizations other than individual entrepreneurs, representative offices and branches of foreign companies) share certain common characteristics:

Formation, Name and Purposes.—Foundation documents of legal entities are charter and foundation agreement, approved and signed by all founders. Legal entities deemed established on date of state registration (Id., art. 51[2]) and must enter details of state registration, including company name, in Uniform State Register of Legal Entities, accessible to general public (Id., art. 51[1]). (See topic Commercial Register.) Foundation documents must include information prescribed by statute and may define purposes of legal entity, even when not required to do so by law. Legal entity must operate on basis of its foundation documents. Amendments to foundation documents become effective with respect to third parties. (Id., art. 52). Name of legal entity must refer to its legal status. Legal entity whose name is registered has exclusive right to use that name. (Id., art. 54).

Incorporators.—Founders and participants in legal entities may be individuals and other legal entities, unless founder is sole participant also owned by sole individual/entity. (Id., art. 98[6]). State and municipal authorities and bodies may not be participants unless otherwise stipulated by law. (Id., art. 66[4]).

Filing Fees and Licenses.—Presidential Decree No. 2270 of Dec. 22, 1993 grants local authorities right to set amount of state registration fee for registration for all forms of legal entities. (Id., 28). Legal entities may engage in activities for which license is required only upon receipt, within period specified, and until termination of required license. (GK RF, art. 49).

Rights and Obligations of Participants.—Participants in legal entities have right to participate in management, receive and have access to information on business activity, and participate in distributions of profits and liquidation proceeds. Participants obligated to make agreed contributions, refrain from disclosing confidential information, and act reasonably, in good faith and in best interest of legal entity. (GK RF, arts. 53[3], 57).

Liability.—Legal entities bear liability for their obligations to extent of their assets. (GK RF, art. 56[1]). With exception of general partners, and members of additional liability companies, liability does not extend to legal entity participants. Legal entities are not responsible for obligations of participants unless otherwise stated in foundation documents. (Id., arts. 56[3], 77, 80, 95). Vicarious liability extends to participants or parent companies when they cause bankruptcy of legal entities. (Id., art. 56[3]; JSC Law, art. 3[3]). General partners and additional liability company participants jointly and severally liable for company obligations. (GK RF, arts. 75, 95). See discussion of individual business organizations below.

Manufacturing Cooperatives.—Established by at least five citizens by charter to pool personal efforts and property contributions in business joint venture. (Id., arts. 107-108). Members may be vicariously liable for obligations of cooperative. (Id., art., 107[2]). Cooperative's assets allocated to shares of members or to indivisible funds, pursuant to charter. Cooperatives may not issue stock. Profits and liquidation assets distributed commensurate with members' contribution of efforts unless otherwise established in charter. (Id., art. 109). Procedures for and legal impact of management, withdrawal and expulsion of members, and reorganization and liquidation of cooperatives described in new Civil Code. (Id., arts. 111-112).

Joint Ventures.—Civil Code abolished joint venture as form of business organization. Term "joint venture" still used unofficially to describe enterprises with foreign capital participation.

Limited Liability Company ("OOO").—Limited liability company ("LLC" or "OOO") established by one or more individuals/entities (including foreign persons) pursuant to foundation agreement and charter, with charter capital divided into ownership shares. OOO may not have another company as sole participant, if such company owned by one individual or entity. Participants not liable for OOO's obligations, except jointly and severally liable to extent of unpaid portion of respective contribution obligations. Name of limited liability company must include words "limited liability". (GK RF, art. 87[2]). Legal status and obligations of OOO's and their participants defined in new Civil Code and special law on OOOs, not yet adopted. (Id., arts. 87-88).

Half of OOO's charter capital must be paid prior to date of initial registration, remainder within first year of operation. Charter capital may not fall below minimum to be determined by new OOO law (currently set at 1,000 times minimum month wage [approx. U.S.$15,180]). Reduction in charter capital or liquidation mandatory if, after second fiscal year, OOO's net assets drop below stated charter capital. Reduction of charter capital permitted after due notification of creditors. Increase in charter capital permitted after charter capital fully paid by participants. (Id., art. 90).

OOO has two-tiered management structure, consisting of members' meeting and executive body. Members' meeting has exclusive nondelegable authority on certain matters. (Id., art. 91). Each participant has right to withdraw at any time without consent and, on withdrawal, right to receive value of its share in charter capital, by method and within time stipulated by law and foundation documents. (Id., art. 94). Participants may transfer company interests to other participants without consent. Company must pay participant, in cash or kind, real value of participant's share, if charter prohibits sale of share to third party and other participants refuse to purchase share. (Id., art. 93).

Additional Liability Company ("ADO").—Similar to OOO, except participants in ADO jointly and severally liable for company's obligations, proportional to respective charter capital contributions. If participant becomes bankrupt, its liability for company obligations assumed by other participants in proportion to their respective contributions, unless different procedure for liability-sharing stipulated in foundation documents. (Id., art. 95).

Joint Stock Companies ("JSC").—JSC initially introduced by law "On Enterprises and Entrepreneurial Activity" of 1990 ("1990 Law") and Regulations of Cabinet of Ministers No. 601 ("Reg. 601") and RF Law No. 208-FZ "On Joint Stock Companies" ("JSC Law") of Dec. 26, 1990. New Civil Code and JSC Law supersede 1990 Law and Reg. 601.

JSC charter capital divided into shares. Participants not liable for JSC obligations and bear risk of JSC losses only to extent of value of their stock, except participants liable for JSC obligations to extent of unpaid contributions. JSC founders jointly and severally liable for obligations arising prior to registration, unless their actions subsequently approved by general meeting of shareholders. (JSC Law, art. 10[3]).

JSC may be open or closed. Stockholders in open JSC may transfer stock without consent of other shareholders. Open JSC may offer open subscriptions, selling stock without limitation except as regulated by federal law, but is subject to public disclosure obligations. JSC in which stock distributed only among shareholders or with their consent deemed closed. Shareholders in closed JSC have preemptive right to acquire stock sold by other shareholders. Closed JSC limited to 50 shareholders. (JSC Law, art. 7[2]).

Charter capital rules of JSC same as OOO except as follows: All shares must be issued to founders on establishment of JSC. (Id., art. 25[2]). Charter of JSC must provide amount of distributed shares and may state amount of authorized shares it can issue and distribute later. Law or charter may restrict quantity and total nominal value of stock held or maximum number of votes cast by any shareholder. Minimum amount of charter capital required for open JSC is 1,000 times minimum monthly wage and for closed JSC, 100 times minimum monthly wage. (JSC Law, art. 26). At least 50% of charter capital must be paid on registration and remainder during first year after registration. (Id., art. 34). JSC may increase charter capital by increasing nominal value of shares or by additional shares not exceeding amount of authorized stock by resolution of shareholders' meeting. Issuance of additional shares in excess of authorized stock requires respective amendment of JSC charter and registration of amendment. Charter may grant shareholders preemptive rights. Decrease in charter capital permissible after due notification to creditors, through decreasing nominal value of shares or JSC purchase of shares if so provided by charter. (Id., arts. 23-30).

JSC may issue preferred shares but not in excess of 25% of value of its charter capital, and may issue bonds subject to statutory restrictions. If JSC issues preferred shares of one or more types, its charter must provide amount of dividends and amount paid on liquidation for each type of preferred share. (Id., arts. 25, 32-33). JSC may only declare and pay dividends if: (1) charter capital paid in full; (2) value of net assets after payment of dividends not lower than charter capital and reserve fund; and, (3) if other conditions provided in JSC Law satisfied. (Id., art. 43). Authority of shareholders' meeting provided by law which JSC cannot amplify. (Id., art. 48). JSC Law outlines detailed procedure of organization and holding of shareholders' meeting and voting by shareholders. JSC must keep register of all shareholders in established procedure. (Id., art. 44). JSC with over 50 shareholders must have board of directors, whose scope of exclusive, nondelegable authority must be defined by charter. (Id., art. 65). Open JSC must publish certain corporate information including annual report and profit and loss statement. (Id., art. 92).

Representative Offices.—Foreign companies may establish direct commercial representations or service offices not recognized as separate legal entities. Representative offices accredited by RF Chamber of Commerce, MinFin RF or MinForAff RF, and enjoy certain tax and accounting benefits. (See topic Taxation.) Detailed requirements on establishment, registration and activity of representative offices in "Regulations for Establishment and Operation of Representative Offices of Firms, Banks, and Organizations in USSR", approved by USSR Council of Ministers Decision No. 1074 of Nov. 30, 1989 and still effective in RF.

Individual Entrepreneurs.—Both RF and foreign citizens may conduct entrepreneurial activity, without formation of legal entity. (GK RF, art. 23). Entrepreneurial activity is defined as ". . . independent activity conducted at one's own risk and designed for the systematic receipt of profit from use of property, sale of goods, performance of works or vending of services by persons registered as entrepreneurs". (Id., art. 2). Registration of entrepreneurs occurs within three days of receipt of completed application form and proof of registration fee payment by local and State Tax Inspectorates. (RF Presidential Decree No. 1482 "On Streamlining the State

BUSINESS ASSOCIATIONS . . . *continued*
Regulation of Enterprises and Entrepreneurs in the RF" of July 8, 1994, art. 2). Entrepreneurs must also comply with applicable licensing requirements, for example, sole practitioner attorneys must also obtain licenses from MinJustice RF. (See topic Licenses.) Registration may be denied by registering agency, or terminated by court decision, if entrepreneur provides incomplete or unreliable information, or upon bankruptcy declaration or entrepreneur's request. (Id.). In absence of express legislation, entrepreneurial activity subject to same legal constraints and privileges as legal entities. (GK RF, art. 23).

Individual entrepreneurs may voluntarily substitute payment of aggregate federal, regional and local taxes and fees for payment of single tax amount, if total receipts from previous year total less than 100,000 times minimum wage. (RF Law No. 222-FZ "On a Simplified System of Taxation, Accounting and Reporting for the Entities of Small Business" of Dec. 29, 1995). Entrepreneurs qualifying for simplified taxation system are also exempt from profit taxation. (Letter of State Taxation Service of RF No. VG-6-02/177 of Mar. 13, 1996). Individual entrepreneurs also required to register with pension fund and contribute 5% of their income. (RF Law No. 1998-1 "On Income Tax on Individuals" of Dec. 7, 1991). See topic Taxation.

Partnerships.—Law "On Enterprises and Entrepreneurial Activity" adopted in Dec. 1990, which introduced partnership concept, essentially replaced by partnership provisions in part 1 of new Civil Code. New Civil Code allows formation of general and limited partnerships. General partners may be individual entrepreneurs or commercial organizations and limited partners may be private citizens or any legal entity. Partnerships may not issue shares. (GK RF, art. 66).

Partners have statutory confidentiality obligation and rights to participate in management, receive information and participate in distributions of profits and liquidation assets. (Id., art. 67). Partnerships may hold interests in other companies and partnerships. Partner contributions may be money, securities, property rights and other rights subject to monetary valuation. Valuation of contribution is as agreed by partners unless law requires expert evaluation.

General Partnership.—Partnership whose participants engage in business activities on behalf of partnership and incur liabilities for its obligations to extent of their personal assets. Person may only participate in one general partnership. (Id., art. 69).

Rights and Liabilities of Partners Inter Se.—Partnership managed by unanimous consent of partners and each partner has one vote and entitled to act on behalf of partnership, unless founders' agreement provides otherwise. If founders' agreement provides for joint management, each transaction requires consent of all general partners. Management may be commissioned to one or several partners, pursuant to power of attorney issued by partners. (Id., arts. 71, 72).

Each partner must complete 50% of its contribution to charter capital by date of registration and balance within time stipulated in founders' agreement. Partners may not compete with partnership business without consent of other partners. If obligation breached, partnership may require breaching partner to compensate for resulting partnership losses or transfer any gains from competing transactions to partnership. (Id., art. 73).

Partners share profits and losses commensurate with ownership shares in charter capital, unless otherwise provided by founders' agreement or partner consensus. Agreement to exclude partner from profit or loss sharing prohibited. (Id., art. 74). Partner may withdraw from partnership on six months notice and receive value of partnership assets commensurate with partner's charter capital, unless founders' agreement provides otherwise. Transfer of partnership interest subject to consent of other partners. (Id., arts. 78, 79). Partners have fiduciary obligation to partnership. (Id., art. 53[3]).

Rights and Liabilities to Third Persons.—Partners jointly and severally liable for partnership obligations including obligations incurred prior to partner joining partnership. Withdrawing partner liable for obligations that arose prior to partner's withdrawal for two years after withdrawal. (Id., art. 75). Partnership may not rely on limitations on partner powers in founders' agreement in relations with third parties, unless third party knew or should have known of limitations at time of transaction. (Id., art. 72[1]).

Dissolution.—Partnership may continue after withdrawal or death of partner or other statutory termination event, if so stipulated in founders' agreement or agreement of remaining partners. (Id., art. 76[1]). Partnership liquidated on statutory grounds. (Id., arts. 61, 76, 81).

Limited Partnership.—Consists of both general and limited partners. Limited partners bear risk of partnership losses only to extent of their financial contributions and generally do not participate in management of partnership. Individual or entity may be general partner in only one limited partnership. Partner in general partnership may not be general partner in limited partnership, and general partner in limited partnership may not participate in general partnership. (Id., art. 82[1, 3]).

Name of limited partnership must include names of all general partners and words "limited partnership" or "partnership in commendam", or name of at least one general partner and words "and Co." and "limited partnership" or "partnership in commendam". If limited partner's name included in name of partnership, limited partner becomes general partner. (Id., art. 82[4]).

Rights and liabilities of general partners similar to general partnership. Limited partner may only participate in management pursuant to power of attorney. Management participation with power of attorney does not affect limited liability. Limited partner must remit contribution in return for partnership certificate, has right to agreed share of profits, right to withdraw and receive contribution at end of any fiscal year, right to transfer interest to third party without consent and certain preemptive purchase rights. (Id., art. 85).

Dissolution.—Limited partnerships liquidated upon withdrawal of all limited partners, unless general partners agree to reorganize into general partnership in lieu of liquidation. On liquidation, limited partners have preferred right over general partners to receive their contributions from partnership assets. (Id., art. 86).

Small Enterprises.—Law No. 88-FZ "On State Support of Small Entrepreneurship in RF" of June 14, 1995 ("SE Law") outlines methods and procedures for state support of small enterprises. Enterprise qualifies as "small" if commercial organization in which ownership interest of government enterprises and noncommercial organizations (see topic Associations) does not exceed 25%, ownership interest of legal entities which are not small enterprises does not exceed 25%, and average number of employees does not exceed statutory maximums. Current employee limits are 100 for industrial, transportation and construction establishments, 60 for scientific, technical services and agriculture, 30 for trade and public services and 50 for other industries. Registered individual entrepreneurs also treated as small enterprises. (Id., arts. 1-3). To qualify as "small", enterprise must register with appropriate authorities. (Id., art. 4). SE Law confirms RF commitment to provide support to small enterprises by creating beneficial financing terms, increasing availability of materials, and allowing simplified registration and specialized training. (Id., art. 5). RF announced similar intent in Federal Program of State Support to Small Enterprises adopted for 1994-95 by Resolution of RF No. 409 of Apr. 29, 1994.

Small enterprises enjoy favorable tax and bookkeeping regimes, and preferential tax treatment including exemption from profits tax during early years of certain activities. (RF Law No. 222-F2 "On Simplified Procedures of Taxation, Bookkeeping and Reporting of Small Enterprises of Dec. 29, 1995"). If tax laws providing less favorable treatment are adopted, small enterprise exempt from such adverse change during first four years of operations. (SE Law, art. 9). State Committee on Support and Development of Small Business established by Presidential Decree No. 563 "On State Committee on Support and Development of Small Entrepreneurship", of June 6, 1995 to implement government policy of supporting small enterprises.

State Enterprises.—New Civil Code defines state and municipally-owned unitarian enterprises as legal entities in which founders have ownership rights or other rights in rem. (GK RF, art. 48[2]). Unitarian enterprise is commercial organization with no ownership rights to property allocated to it. Only state and municipal entities may establish unitarian entities. (Id., art. 113[1]). Assets of state or municipally owned unitary enterprise belong to enterprise only by "right of economic authority" or "operational management" with state or municipality retaining ownership rights. (Id., art. 113[2]).

Unitarian enterprise based on right of economic authority established by resolution and charter adopted by duly authorized state or local authority. Owner of assets of enterprise not liable for obligations of enterprise unless vicarious liability rules apply. (Id., art. 114[8]; §1, art. 56[3]). Federally owned assets may be used to establish unitarian enterprise based on right of operational management (also known as federal budget financed enterprise), pursuant to charter approved by RF. (Id., art. 115[1-2]). Budget financed enterprise may have right to possess, use and dispose of property assigned to it, in accordance with its purpose, terms of owner's assignment and intended purpose of property (Id., art. 296[1]), but enterprise may only alienate assigned property with consent of owner, and must distribute revenues of enterprise as determined by owner of property (Id., art. 297). RF is vicariously liable for obligations of budget financed enterprise, if its assets prove insufficient. (Id., art. 115[5]).

RF and municipal entities liable for their obligations to extent of their property, other than such property assigned to legal entities established by right of economic authority or operational management. (Id., art. 126[1]). RF and municipal entities not liable for obligations of legal entities they establish except as provided by law or pursuant to guarantee RF assumes for legal entity. (Id., art. 126[3], [6]). Liability of RF in relations with foreign legal entities, nationals or countries is defined by RF Law on State Immunity. (Id., art. 127).

RF and municipalities may own property, including land and natural resources, and may assign property to state and municipally owned enterprises and institutions for possession, use or disposal. (Id., arts. 214-215). Transfer of property to ownership of citizens and legal entities in accordance with RF privatization laws. (Id., art. 217). See topics Associations; Privatization.

CITIZENSHIP:

Citizenship status determined by RF Law No. 1948-1 "On Citizenship in RF" of Nov. 28, 1991 ("Citizenship Law") and relevant treaties. In case of conflict, treaty controls. (Citizenship Law, art. 9). Russian citizens may have dual citizenship in other republics of former USSR and dual citizenship in foreign states if applicable treaty provides. (Id., art. 3; Konst. RF, art. 62). Diplomatic and consular services offered to RF citizens living abroad. (Id., art. 5).

Russian citizenship derives from various circumstances, including former USSR citizenship, Russian citizenship prior to Bolshevik Revolution of Nov. 7, 1917, birth, naturalization, restoration of citizenship, opting for Russian citizenship following territory transfer made pursuant to international treaty, and other events described in Citizenship Law. (Id., art. 12). Citizenship not affected by marriage or divorce between RF citizen and foreign national or acquisition by spouse of foreign citizenship. (Id., art. 6).

Citizenship by Birth.—Persons considered RF citizens by birth if born in RF, or one parent at date of birth was USSR citizen living permanently in RF, or parents are Russian citizens at child's birth regardless of place of birth, or in certain other circumstances. If parents unknown, child born in Russia is considered Russian citizen until missing parent(s) located, at which time citizenship determined. (Id., arts. 14-17).

Citizenship by Registration.—Upon application, persons with following qualifications may be registered as Russian citizens subject to certain limitations: spouse of RF citizen; born to parents who are USSR citizens (time limitations apply); stateless residency in RF for sufficient period; other circumstances related to national origin and/or statelessness within territory of former USSR. (Id., art. 18).

Citizenship by Naturalization.—Citizenship may be conferred on persons 18 and over and capable of work, regardless of origin, social status, racial or national background, sex, education, language, or religious, political or other convictions. Citizenship generally granted if applicant has established permanent residence in RF territory as foreign citizen or stateless person for five years, or uninterrupted residence for three years immediately prior to filing application. Residency requirement reduced by half for persons recognized as refugees by Russian law or treaty, persons with prior USSR citizenship, and persons who have demonstrated achievements in science, technology or culture or have professional qualifications desired by RF, or have established record

CITIZENSHIP . . . *continued*
of efforts to assist social development of RF. (Id., art. 19[1-3]). Naturalization denied to those who participate in forceful challenges to RF constitutional structure, political parties or other organizations engaged in activities incompatible with Russia's constitutional principles, or who have served sentences for acts prosecutable under Russian law. (Id., art. 19[4]). Applications and petitions to acquire, restore, accept or forfeit RF citizenship requires payment of state duties. (RF Law No. 226-fz "On State Duties" art. 6, of Dec. 31, 1995).

COMMERCIAL REGISTER:

Business and nonprofit organizations established in RF (hereafter "RF entities") must register to become legally effective. (GK RF, art. 51). Registration governed by Regulation "On Procedure of State Registration of Subjects of Entrepreneurial Activity" approved by Presidential Decree No. 1482 of July 8, 1994 ("Registration Procedure"). Registration Procedure defines documents necessary for registration and grounds for denial of registration. RF entities must generally register with local registration authorities. Additional registration on federal level, (with State Registration Chamber established pursuant to Regulation of MinEc RF "On State Registration Chamber with MinEc RF" of June 30, 1994 ["SRC Regulation"] required for enterprises with foreign investment in charter capital exceeding 100 million rubles and enterprises with foreign investment operating in energy and fuel industry, regardless of amount of charter capital).

Within ten days after registration RF entities must register with local tax service, which enters registration information in State Register of Enterprises. (Regulation of MinFin RF of Apr. 14, 1993 and State Tax Service of RF of Apr. 12, 1993 "On Procedure for Maintenance of State Register of Enterprises" ["Regulations on State Register"], arts. 8-9). Upon tax registration enterprise given registration number. (Id., art. 3). Enterprises with foreign investments must also be included in register for enterprises with foreign investments maintained by State Registration Chamber. (SRC Regulation, art. 3). Any change in entity's foundation documents registered with state authorities must also be reported to local tax service, which causes corresponding amendment in State Register of Enterprises. (Regulations on State Register, arts. 11-12).

RF Government Regulation No. 707 "On Procedure of Maintenance of Register of Financial and Industrial Groups of RF" of June 19, 1994 established separate register for financial and industrial groups in RF, maintained by RF State Property Committee.

CONFLICTS OF LAW:

Art. 15 of Constitution provides that where international treaty of RF conflicts with other RF law, treaty shall control. (Konst. RF, art. 15[4]). Art. 71(o) of Constitution established RF jurisdiction over conflicts rules. (Id., art. 71[o]).

Civil Fundamentals prescribe conflicts rules according to specific context in which action arises. In property disputes, title determined pursuant to law of forum in which property located at time of suit or when grounds for suit arose. (Civ. Fund, art. 164[1, 2]). If property transferred pursuant to contract, law of state where contract concluded controls. Title under freight contract executed abroad determined by law of forum from which goods are shipped. (Id., art. 164[3]). Parties may contract out of above provisions in favor of other controlling law.

Disputes over contract terms and validity usually resolved by norms of country where contract concluded. Locus of contract ascertained by reference to RF law. Contract may not be declared invalid if formalities comply with RF law. Formalities of contract concluded by RF citizens and legal entities, regardless of place of contract origin, governed by RF law, as are transactions involving immovable property situated in RF. Parties may usually select application of foreign law. (Id., art. 165).

In absence of contrary agreement, controlling law for assessment of obligations arising out of foreign economic transactions is law of forum where party acting in one of following capacities has residence or principal place of business: vendor, lessor, licensor, bailee, agent, carrier, forwarding agent, insurer, lender, donor, guarantor, pledgor. Otherwise, transaction governed by law of forum of party whose action was of essential importance to contract. Agreements establishing joint venture with foreign participation governed by law of country where enterprise founded. (Id., art. 166). Tort obligations construed with respect to law of forum in which tort took place. (Id., art. 167). Unjust enrichment cases similarly resolved. (Id., art. 168). RF Law No. 5338-1 "On International Commercial Arbitration", of July 7, 1993, requires Russian tribunals to recognize that choice of law clause refers to substantive law, and not just conflicts rules of country chosen. (Id., art. 28).

CONSTITUTION AND GOVERNMENT:

RSFSR, pursuant to Dec. 12, 1991 ratification of treaty creating Commonwealth of Independent States ("CIS"), adopted USSR laws and normative acts pending passage of new legislation. On Dec. 25, 1991, Supreme Soviet Council of Russia renamed Russian Soviet Federated Socialist Republic ("RSFSR") Russian Federation ("RF"). (RF Law "On Renaming the State of the RSFSR" of Dec. 1991). USSR and RSFSR acts remain effective in RF, but only to extent do not conflict with RF law and regulations. RF similarly adopted all obligations of USSR under international treaties. (MinForAff RF Letter No. 11/UGP, of Jan. 13, 1992).

Constitution.—Present RF Constitution adopted by popular referendum Dec. 12, 1993. (Konst. RF, §2[1]). Constitution envisions separation-of-powers between legislature, executive and judiciary. (Id., arts. 10, 80ff). Individual civil liberties (e.g. freedom of conscience [Id., art. 28], equal protection [Id., art. 20] and rights of criminal accused [Id., arts. 45-54]) guaranteed, as are "economic" rights such as ownership and entrepreneurship. (Id., arts. 34-37). Constitution assures citizens of affirmative "social" privileges, including rights to housing, medical care and sound environment.

Constitution contains supremacy clause. (Id., art. 15[1]).

Separation of Powers.—Legislative, executive and judicial branches operate independently to check encroachments on respective spheres of authority. (Konst. RF art. 10).

Legislative Branch.—Federal Assembly consists of two chambers, Federation Council and State Duma. Federation Council comprised of two representatives, one executive and one legislative official from each "subject" (as defined in subhead Federal Structure, infra) of RF. (Id., art. 95). Federation Council resolves, inter alia, matters of appointments, war powers, impeachment and states of emergency. (Id., art. 102). State Duma, comprised of 450 deputies, adopts federal legislation by simple majority for subsequent approval by Federation Council and President. (Id., art. 105). State Duma may override (by two-thirds majority) veto of Federation Council and may supersede Presidential veto if Federation Council also supports law by two-thirds vote. Legislative initiative vested in President, members of Federal Assembly, legislative organs of RF subjects, and in Supreme, Superior Arbitration and Constitutional Courts. (Id., art. 104).

Executive Branch.—Consists of RF President and "Government of RF" (i.e., federal ministries and committees). President directly elected for four two-year terms, and appoints ministers and committee chairpersons. President may bypass legislative approval by issuing mandatory orders and decrees, bypassing legislative approval for matters within executive jurisdiction and may dissolve State Duma under certain circumstances specified in Constitution.

Judicial Branch.—Consists chiefly of Constitutional Court, Superior and lower arbitration courts, Supreme Court and lower courts of general jurisdiction. Military and administrative tribunals also exist, and appeals from decisions of either may be heard in courts. Procurator's office oversees administration of justice, performing functions of criminal prosecutor, attorney-general and ombudsman for complaints of citizens. President submits nominations and proposals for removal of RF Procurator-General to Federation Council for approval. See topics Courts; Procuracy.

Federal Structure.—RF consists of 89 "subjects": 21 republics, six territories, 49 regions, two "cities of federal significance," 10 autonomous districts and one autonomous region. (Konst. RF, art. 65[1]). All 89 subjects have equal, plenary authority to regulate activities not preempted by federal law. (Id., arts. 5, 73). Beyond exclusive jurisdiction over such issues as national security, monetary policy, etc., federal government possesses joint jurisdiction with subjects on such questions as involving, for example, real property law, domestic relations and law and order. (Id., arts. 71-72). If conflict between federal and local authority on issue of joint jurisdiction, federal law controls. (Id., art. 76[5]). Status of RF subjects stipulated by Constitution adopted Dec. 12, 1993 and Federal Treaty as of Mar. 11, 1992, signed by RF subjects.

Pending comprehensive legislation defining spheres of federal and local power, existing federal laws and Presidential decrees control to extent consistent with Constitution and Federal Treaty. While most authority on questions of federalism is fact specific, Presidential Decree No. 2265 "On Guarantees of Local Self-Government in RF", of Dec. 22, 1993 ("Decree No. 2265") notes that decisions of local administration may be reversed by court order only. ("Decree No. 2265, art. 3). Decree also recognizes broad local autonomy in charter formation and distribution of government powers, which may be done by popular referendum. (Id., art. 4).

CONSULS:

Decree of USSR Supreme Soviet Presidium of June 25, 1976 defines authority and duties of RF consuls as including protection and sale of property of RF citizens dying abroad, acceptance of inheritance by RF citizens, search for RF heirs, formalizing adoption of Russian children resident outside RF, protection of Russian citizens in foreign jails, performance of notarial functions, including administration of decedents' estates, legalization of documents of authorities functioning within consular jurisdiction, and issuing Russian visas for admission of foreigners to RF. RF signed 1961 Hague Convention Abolishing the Requirement of Legalization for Foreign Public Documents on May 30, 1996. Consulates in U.S. located in Washington, D.C., New York, Seattle and San Francisco.

See topics Letters Rogatory; Treaties.

CONSUMER PROTECTION:

On Feb. 7, 1992, RF Law "On Consumer Rights" of Feb. 7, 1992 ("Consumer Law") set minimum standards for product quality and establishing producer liability and consumer rights and remedies. Consumer Law amended on Dec. 5, 1995. Consumer Law imposes liability for violations of quality standards and establishes procedures for consumers to exchange or obtain refund for low-quality merchandise. (Id., §II, arts. 18-26; §III, arts. 27-39). Private agreement between consumer and producer invalid if stipulated quality or consumer rights below statutory levels. (Id., art. 16.1). Consumer may also file grievance with GKAP RF. (Id., §IV, arts. 40, 41). Enforcement available through regional offices possessing authority of federal agency. Consumer unsatisfied with local remedy may sue in court. (Id., art. 17).

See topic Monopolies and Restraint of Trade.

CONTRACTS:

Contracts governed primarily by general law on obligations in Part I, §3 of Civil Code. (GK RF, cc. 9, 27-29). "General Provisions on Contract" in cc. 27-29, and by rules governing transactions in c. 9. (GK RF art. 420[2, 3]). Specific types of contracts governed by Part II of Civil Code.

Parties free to conclude contract even if relevant category of contract not expressly addressed in law, and may conclude contracts containing elements of different types of contracts (mixed contracts). (GK RF, art. 421[1, 3]). Contract deemed concluded upon agreement of parties to all material terms (i.e., those terms deemed material or necessary by law or by parties), in form required by law. (Id., art. 432[1]). Contract terms are as agreed by parties unless otherwise required by law, and if not agreed by parties are as provided in law or, if not so provided, as determined by customs of business applicable to such contractual arrangements. (Id., art. 421[4, 5]). Customs of business may be deemed to include model terms RF has published for specific categories of contracts. (Id., art. 427). Consideration not required, but parties must be legally competent and must act without fraud, threat, violence, or mistake. (Id., arts. 168-179).

Contract must comply with laws in effect when contract concluded. If law adopted later establishes binding rules different from those in effect at conclusion of contract, contract terms remain in force unless new law states it applies to contracts executed before new law was adopted. (Id., art. 422[2]).

CONTRACTS . . . *continued*

Form.—Contract may be concluded orally unless written form required by law. (Id., arts. 158, 159, 434). Specific forms, notarization and registration required for certain types of contract, e.g., contracts involving real property must be registered with proper authorities. (Id., arts. 131, 164). (See topic Real Property.) Additional requirements on form (e.g., use of official form or affixing seal) may be imposed by law or agreement. (Id., art. 160[1]). Failure to obtain notarizations or registrations required by law may result in invalidation of transaction contemplated by contract. (Id., art. 165).

Offer and Acceptance.—Contract deemed concluded upon receipt by offeror of offeree's acceptance of valid offer. Civil Code defines and describes legal impact of various factors relating to offer and acceptance, including irrevocability of offer, revocation of acceptance, impact of offers specifying period for acceptance, acceptance on conditions inconsistent with offer, and conclusion of contract through bidding procedures. (Id., arts. 435-445, 447).

Modification and Termination.—Contract may be modified or terminated by parties' agreement, by court on request of one party if other party commits material breach, or upon substantial change in circumstances from those prevailing at time contract concluded, unless otherwise provided by law or contract. Agreement to modify or cancel contract must be executed in same form as contract, unless otherwise stipulated by law, contract or business customs. (Id., arts. 450-453).

Categories of Contracts.—Special rules in new Civil Code apply to certain categories of contracts, including following:

"Cumulative contract" results if party has right to consideration for performing obligation, and "independent" if party obligated to grant something without receiving consideration. Contract presumed to be cumulative unless law or contract provides otherwise. (Id., art. 423). If cumulative contract fails to state price, price is that ordinarily charged under comparable circumstances for similar goods or services. (Id., art. 424[3]).

Contract of accession results if one party forced to accede to terms in other party's standard forms. Party that acceded may demand alteration or termination if contract deprives him of rights ordinarily granted under contracts of such category, limits liability of other party for violating its obligations, or contains other burdensome conditions which acceding party, acting reasonably, would not have accepted had it been allowed to participate in determining contract terms. Alteration or termination not permitted in relation to plaintiff's entrepreneurial activities, if acceding party knew or should have known conditions in contract. (Id., art. 428).

"Public contract" describes commercial organization's obligations when selling goods or services to general public (e.g., retail trade, common carrier, communications services, electric power, medical or hotel services). Commercial organization may not give preference to certain customers over others with respect to public contract, except as permitted by law. RF government may issue binding rules on conclusion and performance of certain public contracts (e.g., standard forms). (Id., art. 426).

"Preliminary contract" is agreement to conclude contract in future on terms provided in agreement. Party which concludes preliminary contract but unjustifiably evades conclusion of principal contract must compensate other party for losses incurred. (Id., arts. 429-445[4]). Special provisions also apply to contracts intended to benefit third party. (Id., art. 430).

Other.—Part II of Civil Code governs rules for additional types of contracts, including agreements used previously, such as purchase and sale, commission, exchange and gift contracts. It also contains rules for types of contract used in emerging market economy, including contracts for real estate sale (see topic Real Property), sale of enterprises (see topic Sales), energy supply, agency, various types of leasing, various banking activities, commercial concession (see topic Franchise) and management in trust (see topic Trusts).

COPYRIGHTS:

RF Law No. 5351-1 "On Copyright and Related Rights" of July 9, 1993 ("Copyright Law"), RF Law No. 3523-1 "On the Legal Protection of Computer Programs and Databases" of Sept. 23, 1992 ("Software Law"), and RF Law No. 3526-1 "On the Protection of Integrated Circuit Topology" of 23 Sept. 1992 ("Integrated Circuit Law") provide copyright protection in RF. Copyright Law is newer and more comprehensive than Software and Integrated Circuit Laws, and generally offers better and longer protection for programs, databases and integrated circuits. Copyright applies to any work of science, literature or art, including computer programs, that result from original creative endeavors in presentable form in RF, whether published or unpublished. (Copyright Law, arts. 5-6). RF copyright definition slightly stricter than international conventions which do not require creative element. Copyright not extended to public documents, national symbols, folk art or news stories. (Id., art. 8).

Registration.—Copyright attaches upon creation, and does not require registration. (Id., art. 9). Optional registration of computer programs, databases, and integrated circuits provided by Russian Agency for Legal Protection of Computer Software, Databases and Integrated Circuit Topology.

Duration of Protection.—Copyright generally endures for lifetime of author plus 50 years, with longer periods provided in certain circumstances. (Id., art. 27). Neighboring rights protected for 50 years from date of first legal disclosure. (Id., art. 53). Protection under Integrated Circuit Law limited to ten years, although integrated circuits protected by Copyright Law as well. Rights of authorship, name, and reputation last indefinitely. (Id., art. 27). Once copyright expires, work enters public domain and may be freely used without payment of royalties. (Id., art. 28).

Infringement.—On infringement, copyright holder may demand discontinuance of infringement, recognition as copyright holder, restoration of situation that existed before infringement and compensation for any losses, including lost profits. (Id., art. 49).

Conventions.—RF acceded to Berne Convention on Dec. 9, 1994 (with reservation that convention would not protect works already in RF public domain on date of convention's effectiveness on RF territory). Soviet Union acceded to Universal Copyright Convention on May 27, 1973, including additional protocols 1 and 2, obligations under which were assumed by RF on Jan. 13, 1992. Russia acceded to Convention for Protection of Producers of Phonograms Against Unauthorized Duplication of Oct. 29, 1971 on Dec. 9, 1993.

CORPORATIONS:

See topic Business Associations.

COSTS:

See topic Actions, subhead Costs.

COURTS:

Federal court system divided by subject matter competence into arbitration (commercial) courts, courts of general jurisdiction and Constitutional Court. Courts of general jurisdiction hear civil and criminal actions and may review administrative decisions. Economic disputes resolved at municipal, regional, republican and federal levels by courts of arbitration. Arbitration court system in RF differs from non-judicial dispute resolution mechanism commonly referred to as arbitration. (See topic Dispute Resolution.) RF Constitutional Court settles disputes concerning compliance of federal laws and normative acts with RF Constitution, jurisdiction of government bodies and individual liberties. Additional bodies adjudicating legal rights and duties include administrative tribunals, military courts, arbitral associations, justices of peace and, until recently, comrades' courts.

Operation and structure of court system established by following federal laws: "On Judiciary of RSFSR" of July 8, 1981 ("Judiciary Law"), "On Constitutional Court" of July 23, 1994 ("Const. Court Law"), "On Arbitrazh Court" of May 5, 1995 ("Arb. Court Law"), GPK RSFSR, UPK RSFSR, and APK RF. See also topic Actions, subhead Costs. Procuracy, regulation of judicial system, as well as civil, criminal and arbitrazh law and procedure within exclusive jurisdiction of federal government. (Konst. RF, art. 71[n]). Courts also established by subjects of RF. See topic Constitution and Government.

Constitutional Court.—Court's 19 justices provide conclusive interpretation of constitutional issues and may examine normative acts of state entities and agreements between them, including Presidential decrees, administrative/ministerial regulations and judicial declarations of highest courts. Court rules exclusively on questions of law. Interpretations of Constitutional Court binding on all judicial, legislative and executive authorities and all citizens and associations in RF. (Const. Court Law, art. 106). Right to apply for review held by: RF President, RF Government, both chambers of Federal Assembly (or one-fifth of deputies in either chamber), RF Supreme Court, RF Superior Court of Arbitrazh and legislative/executive organs of RF constituents. (Konst. RF, art. 125[2]).

Courts of General Jurisdiction.—System consists of municipal, regional, republican and federal courts. Jurisdiction includes all civil, criminal and administrative-appellate matters not within arbitrazh court competence. Highest court of supervision is RF Supreme Court. (Konst. RF, art. 126; Judiciary Law, art. 54). Military tribunals integrated into system of general courts, with final appeal justiciable in RF Supreme Court. (Judiciary Law, art. 1 with amendments).

Civil Matters.—Municipal or district courts review disputes concerning domestic and labor relations, property interests (within statutory limits) and other rights and duties arising from civil legislation. (GPK RSFSR, art. 113). Right to jury trial theoretically available but has not been implemented. (Id., art. 10). Higher courts of general jurisdiction may assume competence over any civil matter for first-instance review, and under certain provisions of GPK RSFSR and Judiciary Law (e.g., state secrets), are required to do so. (Id., arts. 114-117).

On personal jurisdiction, proper forum generally respondent's place of residence or, for legal persons, place of business or situs of property. (Id., art. 116). Suit may also be brought in jurisdiction where contract executed, harm caused or respondent has representative. (Id., art. 118). Parties may privately stipulate jurisdiction. (Id., art. 120).

Criminal Matters.—All criminal cases tried in municipal and district courts, except where subject matter specifically assigned by Criminal Procedure Code and military regulations to superior or military court. (UPK RSFSR, art. 36). Cases heard in higher courts include crimes against state, activity related to foreign relations and disrespect for police or court process.

Arbitrazh Courts.—Current system successor to quasi-administrative network tribunals called state arbitrazh, established in Soviet era to resolve conflicts between state enterprises and enforce government economic plans. Incorporated into judicial system in 1991, arbitrazh courts adjudicate so-called economic disputes between regulatory authorities, organizations and individuals engaged in entrepreneurial activity. Arbitrazh court system consisted of, in ascending importance, regional courts, courts of subjects of RF (see topic Constitution and Government) and RF Superior Court of Arbitrazh. (Arb. Court Law, art. 3). Arbitrazh system operates independently from general courts. Decisions of Superior Court of Arbitrazh binding on all other courts and government bodies. (Konst. RF, art. 127; Arb. Court Law, art. 7).

Personal jurisdiction generally based on location of respondent, but suit may be brought, for example, at place of performance of contract, where respondent has property and/or business operations (APK RF, art. 26), or in forum stipulated by parties (Id., RPK RF, arts. 26, 30). Actions challenging official and administrative actions must be brought in jurisdiction where government decision maker located. (Id., art. 29[3]).

Pursuant to new procedural code effective July 1, 1995, arbitrazh courts have jurisdiction over foreign and joint venture entrepreneurial entities and persons, parties previously assigned to general courts. Foreign persons (legal and natural) have equal procedural rights when bringing arbitrazh suits. (Id., art. 210). Arbitrazh courts recognize norms of foreign law upon presentation of adequate proof of contents by proponent. (Id., art. 12). (See topic Actions.) Bases for personal jurisdiction over foreign respondents include representative in RF territory, past or future contractual obligations on RF territory, causing property or other damage through activity in RF, unjust enrichment on RF territory, and causing damage to claimant's RF reputation. Parties may also privately stipulate as to forum. (Id., art. 212).

COURTS . . . *continued*

Appeal and Error.—Two variations of post-trial review available in RF: cassation and judicial supervision.

Courts of General Jurisdiction.—Provided that protest or complaint filed within ten days of civil court decision, cassation appeal to higher court available to any participant. RF procurator may also seek appeal. (GPK RSFSR, art. 282). Parties may raise new arguments in cassation court. (Id., art. 285). Cassation court may affirm, reverse and remand for reconsideration, or enter new judgment if additional collection and review of evidence not required. (Id., art. 305). Upon cassation decision or termination of period for review, judgment enters into legal effect and may not be appealed further (Id., art. 318), unless material, newly-discovered or unexpected circumstances arise. Decision with legal effect may otherwise only be challenged via petition to courts or procuracy. (Id., art. 319ff).

Arbitrazh Courts.—Participants in arbitrazh proceeding have right to appeal decision, within one month of receipt, for appellate review by trial court. (APK RF, arts. 146-147). Additional evidence may be introduced upon showing it could not be offered at trial. (Id., art. 155[1]). Claims not raised at trial barred on appeal. (Id., art. 155[3]). Appellate court may affirm, enter modified judgment or remand for reconsideration. (Id., art. 157).

Administrative Decisions.—See topic Administrative Law.

CRIMINAL LAW:

Criminal justice system operates under Soviet codes, as amended by legislation and Presidential decrees. (See topic Constitution and Government for applicability of Soviet law.) System governed by UK RSFSR and UPK RSFSR. Drafts of new substantive and procedural codes currently under legislative review.

Procedural Rights.—Rights comparable in many respects to "due process" accorded to suspects in U.S. in relation to arrest and detention (UPK RSFSR, arts. 11, 122), interrogation (Id., arts. 47, 52, 123; Konst., RF, art. 48[2]; MinJustice RF Letter No. 09-09/19-94, "On Procedure for Payment of Attorney Services by State" of Jan. 31, 1994), and search and seizure (UPK RSFSR, arts. 168, 169; Konst., RF, arts. 46[2], 50[2]). Presumption of innocence exists with all doubts resolved in favor of accused and accused has right against self-incrimination. (Id., arts. 49, 51[2]). Exclusionary rule and prohibitions on double jeopardy and ex post facto laws also in Constitution. (Id., arts. 50, 54[1]).

Substantive Criminal Law.—Present criminal code adopted in 1960 and amended numerous times, most notably by "1991 Fundamentals of Criminal Legislation in USSR and Union Republics" ("1991 Fund"). 1991 Fund eliminated ideologically-based crimes such as private enterprise and "anti-Soviet activity", but many hallmarks of Soviet era remain, for example, imposition of far more serious punishment for crimes against state property than crimes against persons. Sentences for crimes include fines, performance of labor and services for state, imprisonment (maximum sentence 15 years) and death penalty. Women, minors and senior citizens not subject to death penalty. (UK RSFSR, art. 23).

Economic/Commercial Crimes.—New forms of "white collar" crime, resulting from transition to market economy, addressed by rapid amendments of Code and frequent, often inconsistent, executive decrees. Since 1992, new provisions for criminal liability have arisen in RF Customs Code, Law on Hard Currency Regulation and Control, RF State Tax Service Letters; Law on GKAP RF, laws regarding trademark and product labeling, and commodities regulations. New codes expected to integrate and clarify implementation of such amendments and decrees.

Corruption.—President Yeltsin issued two decrees, Decrees No. 981 and No. 361 concerning corruption of governmental officials. Decree No. 361 of Apr. 4, 1992 prohibits government employees from engaging in entrepreneurial activity, using governmental position to assist private parties in return for compensation, and participating directly or indirectly in management of commercial companies. Violations result in termination and other liabilities. Prior to appointment to governmental position, person must present his tax declaration and information on his assets and liabilities. Decree No. 981 dated July 2, 1993 imposes restrictions on business travel by key governmental employees at expense of inviting party or other private party, except for business travel under international or intergovernmental agreements.

Organized Crime.—In effort to stem rising levels of organized crime, President Yeltsin, on June 14, 1994, issued Decree No. 1226 "On Urgent Measures to Protect Citizenry Against Gangsterism and Other Manifestations of Organized Crime". Federal Assembly previously rejected as unconstitutional law proposing similar potent steps. Presidential decrees generally have binding force, without legislative approval, to extent do not contravene RF Constitution, treaties and federal law. Decree No. 1226 allows detention for 30 days, without bail and before initiation of criminal proceedings, of persons suspected of gang-related activity, and allows investigative agents to audit finances, search residences and places of business and review all files of suspect, relatives, personal friends and business acquaintances. No bank and/or commercial secret inaccessible to authorities. Any information obtained in investigation admissible in cases appearing to involve organized crime. Decree, on its face, seems to contravene several criminal procedural rights and guarantees. Constitutional Court, which began functioning again in spring of 1995 after 18-month suspension, has yet to consider constitutionality of Decree.

Extradition.—Russian citizens on RF territory protected from extradition to other countries. (Konst., RF, art. 61[1]). U.S. and RF, despite increased cooperation on organized crime, have not formalized extradition treaty.

CURRENCY:

One ruble equals 100 kopeks. Presidential Decree No. 721 of May 16, 1996, mandates action by Government of Russian Federation and CBk RF to make Russian ruble fully convertible currency.

See topic Exchange Control.

CUSTOMS (DUTY):

Customs Code of RF ("TK RF") of June 18, 1993 describes organization of customs control, customs regimes for cross-border goods movements, free customs zones, types of customs payments, customs clearance procedures, customs exemptions and benefits, sanctions for violation of customs legislation, and dispute settlement procedures.

Principal customs regimes are import of goods for free circulation, reimport, transit shipments, bonded warehouses, duty-free shops, processing on customs territory, processing under customs control, and temporary importation. (TK RF, art. 23). Customs payments include customs duties (on import and certain exports), VAT on import, excise duties, customs clearance duty, miscellaneous charges for issuance of licenses or certificates, storage of goods and similar services. (Id., art. 110). Exemptions from customs duties found in relevant import or export tariffs and subject to frequent change. Level and applicability of duties depends on customs regime. Certain exemptions and benefits may be specifically provided by legislation. Federal law "On State Support to Mass Media and Book Publishing" No. 1991-FZ of Dec. 1, 1995, exempts periodical publications and book products connected with education, science, and culture imported into or exported from RF by editorial boards of mass media or by publishing houses from customs duties and fees. Paper, polygraphic materials and polygraphic carriers, audio and video materials, and technological and engineering equipment imported into RF by editorial boards of mass media, publishing houses, information agencies, television and radio companies, polygraphic enterprises and used for mass media and book products connected with education, science, and culture are also exempt from customs duties. These exemptions remain in effect until Dec. 31, 1998. (Federal law "On Supplementing the Law of the RF on Customs Tariffs" No. 185-FZ, Nov. 25, 1995).

Export Duties.—Resolution of the Supreme Council of May 21, 1993 established all export customs duties shall expire on Jan. 1, 1996. Once negotiations on admission of Russia to World Trade Organization commenced, was clear that Russia had to abolish export duties to obtain membership. President of RF ordered Government to abolish export customs duties on most types of oil-refining products and on certain types of timber products by Dec. 1, 1995. Further orders set Jan. 1, 1996 as date for reduction of rates of export customs duties on all other commodity groups except oil, gas and some other raw material goods. Federal Program of Export Development contains similar provisions and confirms necessity of decreasing or abolishing export duties for all goods.

As of Apr. 1, 1996, export duties on all goods except oil and gas were abolished. By July 1, 1996, export of oil and gas scheduled for export duties exemption. ("On the Abolition of the Export Customs Duties, the Change of the Rates of Excise on Oil, and the Additional Measures for Ensuring the Receipt of Returns by the Federal Budget" Law No. 479, Apr. 1, 1996).

Import Tariff (Duty).—Import tariff effective from May 10, 1995 on rates which do not increase and from July 1, 1995 in respect to most increases ("On Adoption of Rates on Import Duties" No. 454, May 6, 1995) changed in part by Decision of Government of RF No. 413 of Apr. 11, 1996 from May 15, 1996. Duty charged on basis of type of goods imported, with goods allocated to 97 categories listed in Classifier of Goods for Foreign Economic Activity of RF. (Ordinance of State Customs Committee of RF ["GTK RF"] "On Setting into Force of Second Edition of Classifier of Goods for Foreign Economic Activity of RF", Mar. 9, 1992). Basic rates established as percentage of customs value or in ECU per unit. Basic rates range from duty free to 100% for nearly pure alcohol, weapons, ammunition and accessories, tanks and other self-propelled armored vehicles. Basic rate can be adjusted depending on goods' place of origin. Goods originating in countries not included on list of countries granted most favored nation treatment charged double basic rate. (Ordinance of GTK RF No. 396, June 19, 1995). If goods originate in developed or least developed countries, users chart of preferences reduces basic rate correspondingly to 25 or 100%.

50% reduction in import duties may be applied to some items for period not exceeding five years, provided foreign suppliers are founders of enterprises producing similar goods in territory of RF using Russian raw materials and Russian labor, and such foreign suppliers make direct investments into industries of material production in RF amounting to not less than U.S.$100 million and not less than U.S.$10 million into charter capital of Russian importer, i.e., enterprise producing similar goods. This benefit provided by signing investment agreement between investor and Russian government. (Decree of President on "Additional Measures to Attract Foreign Investments into Manufacturing Industries of RF", art. 2, Jan. 25, 1995).

Enterprises with greater than 30% foreign ownership may import items for own needs and export products of own production, normally subject to licensing, without license. ("On Foreign Investments in RF", July 4, 1991, art. 25). After Sept. 1, 1994, this benefit granted only if specific enterprises obtain special certificates proving mentioned items fall under either "own needs" or "own production" categories. In June 1994, GTK RF strengthened mandatory certification procedures for imported goods, requiring proof of safety certification at time of customs clearance. Foreign investor exempt from customs duties for particular types of goods imported in connection with production-sharing agreements. (Law "On Production Sharing Agreements", No. 225-FZ of Dec. 30, 1995, art. 13).

VAT on Import.—All imports of goods currently subject to 20% VAT with few exemptions. Reduced rate of 10% VAT applies to selected foodstuffs, food raw materials and children's articles. VAT on imports calculated based on customs value of imported goods augmented by import duty and, if applicable, excise duty. Exports of goods exempt from VAT. Imports of certain listed technological equipment VAT free. (Ordinance of GTK RF "On Exemption from VAT and Special Tax of Imports of Certain Goods" of Apr. 13, 1995 [Ordinance of GTK RF, No. 248, Apr. 13, 1995.]). List of excise goods includes alcohol, spirits, wines, beer, other beverages, cigarettes and cigars, motor petrol, articles of jewelry with precious metals and parts thereof, articles of goldsmith's and silversmith's wares and parts thereof, articles of natural or cultured pearls, precious or semi-precious stones, and new and second hand automobiles. Excise rates set by Law No. 23-FZ of Mar. 7, 1996, "On Amending the Law of

CUSTOMS (DUTY) . . . *continued*
the Russian Federation 'On Excises'" as percentage of customs value of commodity or in ECU per unit of measurement.

Customs Clearance Fee.—Total of ruble and hard currency portion of customs clearance fee currently 0.15% of customs value of goods. (TK RF 95, art. 114).

Goods may be imported into RF free of customs duty if placed in customs warehouse. Temporary importation of goods allowed for two years with possible extension of term. (Id., art. 71). Temporary importation attracts monthly payments of 3% on basis of total taxes, duties and charges which would have been payable had goods been brought in for free circulation. (Id., art. 72).

Individuals entitled to import goods up to U.S.$2,000 and export goods up to 50 times minimum monthly wages (approximately U.S.$740) free of customs duties. (Ordinance of Government of RF of Dec. 23, 1993 "On Shipping in and out of RF of Goods not Designated for Production or Commercial Use", §2[a], ["Ordinance of Dec. 23, 1993"]). Certain nontaxable limits also set for postal shipments. If U.S.$2,000 limit (500 times minimum monthly wages for export) exceeded, unified customs duty of 30% (60% for export) levied on difference between actual value of goods and limit. Value exceeding U.S.$10,000 for import and 500 times minimum monthly wages for export will be additionally taxed at rates set forth for commercial import/export. (Id., §2[c, d]). Special rules apply to import of automobiles. (Order of GTK RF, No. 416 of Aug. 15, 1994). In compliance with TK RF art. 121 delay or extension of customs duties payment may be granted for not more than two months by GTK RF, subject to bank guarantees for sums of customs payments due. (Order of GTK RF, No. 580, Aug. 19, 1995).

DAMAGES:

Damages in RF arise out of breach of obligations involving both tort and contract duties. Party only liable for breach if at fault (intentional or negligent breach), unless law or contract provides otherwise, but breaching party must prove non-culpability. (GK RF, art. 401). Agreement in advance limiting one's liability for willful breach generally void. (Id., arts. 400[2], 401[4]). Damages awarded on basis of comparative fault. (Id., art. 404[1]). See topic Torts for culpability standards. Non-breaching party has duty to mitigate damages. (Id., art. 404). Damages made to person or property must be compensated in full by party that caused damage. (Id., art. 1064[1]). In certain cases, non-breaching party may obtain compensatory damages and expenses, as well as lost profits in amount no less than breaching party's unjust enrichment. (Id., arts. 15[2], 393[1-2]).

Parties may generally enforce penalty clauses, while retaining ability to recover any losses exceeding penalty. (Id., art. 394[1]). If liability was insured, breaching party must compensate non-breaching party difference between insurance compensation and actual amount of damages. (Id., art. 1072). Payment of penalty and compensation for losses does not necessarily relieve obligor from duty of specific performance. (Id., art. 396).

Rule of comparative negligence generally controls in torts, but strict liability applied to certain activities. Court, in evaluation of harm caused to claimant, may consider negilgence of individual who caused damage and adjust award accordingly, except where action predicated upon intentional tort. (Id., art. 1083[3]). Types of tort damages available include: compensatory, pain and suffering, lost wages, emotional distress and wrongful death. Amount of awarded damages indexed for inflation. (Id., art. 1091). While culpability may affect award of moral and other damages (see topic Torts, subhead Libel), punitive damages, per se, not available. If claimant was grossly negligent and person who caused damage was not at fault, amount of damages can be decreased or damages not awarded at all. (Id., art. 1083[2]).

Creditor must make claim against principal debtor before proceeding against party bearing secondary liability. (Id., art. 399). Employers and others liable in respondeat superior may recover separately from employees/agents or may implead them into claimant's action. (Id., art. 402). See topic Torts.

DEATH:

Presumption of death for missing persons arises five years after last news of whereabouts. Period reduced to six months following disappearance under dangerous circumstances or circumstances giving reason to suspect death in particular accident, and to two years from date of cessation of military operations following disappearance in military operations. Official death date of entry of court order declaring person dead. Reappearance after declared dead or discovery of residence cancels court declaration of death.

Person who reappears after declared dead may demand return of any property remaining in possession of person to whom property gratuitously passed after declaration of death, with exception of money and bearer securities from bona fide acquirer. (GK RF Item 3, art. 302, arts. 45-47). Persons to whom property of declared dead individual passed as result of commercial dealings, must return such property only if aware that individual presumed dead was actually alive when they acquired property at issue.

DEEDS:

See topics Sales, subhead Land Sales; Mortgages.

DEPOSITIONS:

In RF domestic litigation, judge conducts investigation analogous to pre-trial discovery, questioning witnesses and requesting preliminary offers of proof. (GPK RSFSR, art. 49). Formal depositions, serving functions similar to those in U.S. practice, do not exist in RF.

See topic Letters Rogatory.

DESCENT AND DISTRIBUTION:

In intestate succession, children (including adopted children), spouse and parents of decedent are first-category heirs, all taking equal shares in estate. (Civ. Fund., art. 154). Grandchildren and great-grandchildren of decedent receive parents' shares per stirpes. (GK RSFSR 1964, art. 532). Siblings and grandparents of deceased are second-category heirs, taking only if every potential first-category taker either rejects or is ineligible for gift. (Civ. Fund., art. 154). Disabled persons, dependent on decedent for not less than year prior to death, take share equal to those in category upon which estate descends. (GK RSFSR 1964, art. 532). Where there are no heirs-at-law or intestate takers, government takes by right of succession. (Id., art. 527).

See topics Wills; Executors and Administrators; Taxation.

DISPUTE RESOLUTION:

Disputes may be resolved in court (see topics Courts; Actions) or by alternative dispute resolution ("ADR") mechanisms. Most commonly used form of ADR in RF is voluntary commercial arbitration. Other forms of ADR not regulated by law and currently no mandatory dispute resolution.

Arbitration and Award.—Term "arbitration" has two meanings in RF laws. One defines type of court that deals with commercial disputes through purely judicial proceedings. (See topic Courts, subhead Arbitrazh Courts.) Other defines type of ADR mechanisms commonly called arbitration in western courts. Binding conflict resolution through both ad hoc and institutional arbitrations available on voluntary, contractual basis to foreign and Russian organizations with foreign trade, shipping and investment disputes.

Federal Laws.—Resolution of commercial disputes via ad hoc or institutional arbitration regulated by "Temporary Provisions On Treteysky (i.e., Arbitration) Courts for Resolution of Commercial Disputes" No. 3115-1 of June 24, 1992 ("Temporary Provisions"). Temporary Provisions provide detailed rules for domestic and international disputes and can be used for ad hoc arbitration. Resolution of international commercial disputes via ad hoc or institutional arbitration specifically governed by RF Law No. 5338-1 "On International Commercial Arbitration" of July 7, 1993 ("Arbitration Law") drafted on basis of UNCITRAL Model Law. Arbitration Law describes requirements for recognition of arbitral awards, execution and contents of forum clauses, composition of tribunals, procedural requirements and substantive challenges to award. Jurisdiction of arbitration limited to trade, investment and other types of commercial disputes submitted to arbitration on basis of written arbitration agreement. Arbitral decision, regardless of country of origin, recognized and executed by competent court in RF, if certain conditions met. (Arbitration Law, art. 35[1]). Exclusive grounds for nonrecognition include incapacity of party when arbitration agreement executed, invalidity of agreement in jurisdiction where dispute referred or decision rendered, lack of fair opportunity of losing party to be heard, decision rendered in manner violative of arbitration agreement, impropriety of subject matter for resolution by arbitration under RF law, and decision counter to RF public policy. (Id., art. 36). Petition for nonrecognition must be submitted to RF court within three months after receipt of arbitration decision by judgment debtor. (Id., art. 34[3]).

RF Chamber of Commerce and Industry oversees operation of International Commercial Arbitration Court ("ICAC") and Maritime Arbitration Commission which are only current Russian institutional arbitration entities. Procedural rules of ICAC effective May 1, 1995.

Treaties.—Conflicts between RF federal law and international treaties resolved in favor of treaty. (Konst., RF, art. 15[4]). U.S. and RF signed Bilateral Investment Treaty ("BIT") June 17, 1992 which obligates signatories to provide arbitral fora and recognize private arbitration agreements. UNCITRAL rules apply unless parties stipulate otherwise. (BIT, art. 8). Acknowledgment and execution of foreign awards also mandated under 1958 UN Convention on Recognition and Enforcement of Foreign Arbitral Awards, effective in USSR from Nov. 20, 1960 and enforced in RF pursuant to Decree of USSR Supreme Soviet Presidium of June 21, 1988.

Proof of Foreign Law.—See topic Actions.

DISSOLUTION OF MARRIAGE:

See topic Divorce.

DIVORCE:

Dissolution of Marriage.—Marriage may be terminated by divorce or death or presumption of death of spouse. (RF Family Code of Dec. 29, 1995, art. 16). If wife pregnant, or if less than one year has passed since birth of child, husband may not file for divorce without wife's consent. (Id., art. 17). After divorce, disabled husband or wife entitled to alimony from spouse with sufficient means, provided spouse became disabled before divorce or within one year prior. Wife retains right to alimony for duration of pregnancy and three years after birth. (Id., art. 90).

Marriage considered terminated upon filing notice and registration of marriage termination with Bureau for Registration of Acts Affecting Civil Status. Bureau entitled to register termination upon mutual consent of spouses, if no minor children, or presentation of court decree establishing presumption of death, insanity or criminal sentence of not less than three years. (Id., art. 19).

Dissolution of marriage effected by court order if spouses have common underage children. (Id., art 21). Court granting divorce determines custody and child support (amount of alimony), and, at request of one or both spouses divides marital property. Marriage terminated as of date of court decision.

Upon appearance of missing or presumed dead spouse, and cancellation of respective court decisions, marriage may be restored by registry office by joint application of spouses, unless other spouse has entered into new marriage. (Id., art. 26).

Marriage may be annulled by court if Family Code terms for entering into marriage are violated, including, without limitation, absence of voluntary agreement to enter into marriage or concealment of possession of venereal disease or HIV-infection. (Id., arts, 12-14, Item 3 of art. 15).

Alimony includes all familial support obligations, including material support for spouse, child maintenance, and support of elderly or infirm parents. (RF FC of Dec. 29, 1995, §§13-15). Amounts and procedures for alimony payments established by mutual written consents of spouses or other persons providing and benefitting from support (or legal representative of beneficiary). Agreed amount may not be less than minimum established by law. In practice, alimony terms usually set by court. Court may modify amount or release parent from support obligations for children. Adults

DIVORCE . . . *continued*
must support disabled parents requiring material assistance in fixed amount set by court. Repeated failure to meet alimony obligations punishable by up to two years in prison. (UK RSFSR, art. 122).

EMIGRATION:

USSR law "On Immigration/Emigration" of May 20, 1991 became effective in RF as of Jan. 1, 1993. Every RF cititzen has right to enter and exit RF upon presentation of external (international) passport. Passport valid for departure to all countries. Passports issued to citizens 18 or older by local internal affairs authority. Younger persons traveling with parent or adult included in adult's passport. Denial of external passport possible if applicant involved with state secret or contractual obligations, criminal charges or conviction, has given false statements, has outstanding military obligations, is involved in pending civil suit, has been deemed especially dangerous recidivist by court, or has been placed under administrative supervision by militia. Payment of state duties required for certain types of exits from RF, including: issue or extension of exit visa or foreign passport (or substitute document); additions of any kind (except above) to previously issued documents, and for issuance of new exit visa to replace lost or spoiled documents. (RF Law No. 226-FZ, "On State Duties", art. 6, Dec. 31, 1995).

See topic Immigration.

ENVIRONMENT:

Primary legislative act governing environmental control is RF Law on Environmental Protection passed Dec. 19, 1991 ("EP Law"). Various regulations issued by environmental agencies and authorities purport to implement and supplement this law; however, many uncertainties and gaps in regulations make many provisions of EP Law merely declaratory. Ministry of Preservation of Environment and Natural Preserves of Russian Federation ("Ministry") responsible for enforcing EP Law and coordination of activities of various governmental agencies in environmental protection area.

EP Law establishes jurisdiction of federal and local administration and special environmental authorities over environmental matters (Id., arts. 5-10) and confirms citizens' right to enforce EP Law through court actions and administrative complaints (Id., arts. 11-14). EP Law provides general rules on limits of pollution of various natural resources and establishes different types of payments for natural resource use and its pollution. (Id., arts. 19, 20). Pollution of natural resources regulated by imposing maximum limitations on quantities of pollutants discharged into environment. Such quantities established by special state authorities. (Id., arts. 25-34). EP Law envisions formation of environmental remediation fund, comprised of fines and environmental insurance premiums paid by citizens and enterprises (Id., arts. 21-23), ecological corps of experts (Id., art. 35), ozone and climate watch (Id., art. 56), and "green belts" around densely populated areas (Id., art. 54[5]). EP Law enforced through assessment of fines, criminal liability (Id., arts. 81), and incentive programs including tax privileges (Id., art. 15).

Certain activities in environmental protection area such as use, transportation, burial and destruction of industrial and other waste (except for radioactive materials) must be licensed pursuant to Government Regulation No. 168 of Feb. 26, 1996. Licenses issued by Ministry and its territorial agencies.

Environmental Due Diligence.—RF Law "On Environmental Due Diligence" of Nov. 30, 1995 ("Due Diligence Law") implements EP Law requirements on environmental due diligence ("EDD") for projects or activities that may adversely affect environment. (EP Law, art. 36). Given breadth of Due Diligence Law and absence of precise implementing regulations, potential impact on business activities in RF is difficult to estimate. Ministry responsible for developing procedures to implement Due Diligence Law.

Application.—Due Diligence Law applies to broad range of projects and activities and requires EDD performed for substantiating documentation for economic and other types of activity that might have direct or indirect environmental impact. (Id.). No specific exclusions from EDD review. Private activities subject to review include formation of Russian/foreign joint ventures, preparation of substantiating documentation for production sharing arrangements and technical documentation for new equipment, technology, materials, and substances. Although Due Diligence Law does not expressly refer to wholly-owned Russian companies, application of law to such companies anticipated. Existing operations exempt from Due Diligence Law, but EDD required for changes in operations, such as expansion into new territory, introduction of new technology, or modification of production facilities.

Types of EDD.—Due Diligence Law provides for both governmental and public EDD. Governmental EDD required by Due Diligence Law at federal or local level, depending on size of project. Negative determination results in project prohibition. Public EDD optional at request of citizen or public organization. Consequences of negative determination from public EDD not addressed by Due Diligence Law, but presumably results in project prohibition.

Procedure.—During EDD applicant must prove absence of potential ecological danger. Unfortunately, Due Diligence Law does not specify affirmative proofs necessary for favorable EDD determination. Following submission of applicant's documentation, Ministry prepares budget for EDD review. Applicant must prepay estimated EDD cost. Due Diligence Law does not require payment of additional costs if budget inadequate, nor refund of money not expended. EDD performed by committee of independent experts appointed by Ministry, who begin work within one month after submission of payment and documents, and must issue report within six months. Favorable report allows project to proceed, but failure to commence project within specified time requires new EDD. Unfavorable report, which must include explanations, prohibits project. Ministry may also direct banks not to finance project. Applicnat may file suit for judicial review of unfavorable decision and, if applicant prevails, new EDD conducted.

Penalties.—Applicant in violation of Due Diligence Law if: (1) fails to submit required documents, (2) falsifies materials submitted, (3) causes expert to prepare false opinion, (4) conducts project in violation of unfavorable EDD report, or (5) differently from manner described in project proposal. Penalties for violations assessed administratively. If high degree of adverse environmental impact results, criminal penalties may be imposed.

Forests.—RF Law No. 4613-1 "Fundamentals of RF Forest Legislation" of Mar. 6, 1993 established norms for use and protection of RF forests under supervision of State Forest Protection Service and local authorities. Citizens and enterprises have right to use wooded lands on payment of applicable fees and observance of regulations. Federal and local funds comprised of user fees and fines used to protect and maintain forests.

Economic and Fishing Zone.—Pursuant to RF Law No. 187-FZ "On Continental Shelf" of Nov. 30, 1995 ("Continental Shelf Law"), external boundary of continental shelf established at 200 nautical miles. (Continental Shelf Law, art. 1). Fishing within zone must be licensed by Federal Fishing Agency. Foreigners may fish in zone if permitted by treaty. (Id., arts. 10-12). One-year license issued for limited quota within certain territories, for harvesting specific resources. Licenses must comply with strict requirements. Foreign boats must notify relevant fishing agency on entrance and exit from fishing zone identified in license and may fish only in presence of RF officer. (Id., art. 14). Fees include license and use fee, penalties for exceeding quotas and remuneration for replacement of wasted resources. (Id., art. 40). Limitations relaxed for scientific and environmental research. (Id., arts. 23-30).

ESCHEAT:

See topic Descent and Distribution.

EXCHANGE CONTROL:

CBk RF implements foreign exchange control laws. Only banks licensed by CBk RF to perform foreign currency operations ("authorized banks") may purchase and sell foreign currency and operate foreign currency exchange offices in RF. (RF Law No. 3615-1 "On Foreign Exchange Regulation and Foreign Exchange Control" [of Oct. 9, 1992] ["Exchange Control Law"], §I, art. 1). Authorized banks may sell foreign currency to RF residents without limitations, provided resident not otherwise prohibited from receipt of foreign currency under applicable legislation.

All non-commercial foreign currency transfers and short term transactions (i.e. with repayment term less than 180 days) (defined as "current transactions"), and may be effected without [CBk RF] license. All other foreign currency transaction termed "Capital transfers" and subject to CBk RF licensing, except for transactions listed in Cbk RF Resolution No. 39 "On Change of the Procedures of Performance of Certain Currency Operations" (of Apr. 24, 1996). (Exchange Control Law, art. 1; Letter of CBk RF No. 352 "Central Provisions on Regulations of Foreign Currency Transactions on Territory of RF", [of May 24, 1992] §II, art. 4). Foreign currency transactions involving capital transfers include direct investments, portfolio investments, assignments of rights of ownership in real estate and other assets (including subsurface resources, land and other real property), deferral of payments for period exceeding 180 days on import transactions, loans where principal repayment term exceeds 180 days and all other currency transactions not defined as current transactions. (Exchange Control Law, §1).

Domestic sales of goods and services for foreign currency to individuals prohibited unless seller specifically authorized by CBk RF legislation. (CBk RF Instruction No. 11 of Jan. 20, 1993). Russian legal entities licensed by CBk RF to render hotel, bar and restaurant services, personal and luggage insurance, international transportation of passengers and luggage, international communications and tourism and certain other activities with foreign currency. All sales and purchases on RF currency markets must be executed by authorized banks. (Exchange Control Law, art. 4).

RF legal entities must convert 50% of foreign currency export revenues into Russian rubles, excluding dividends, revenues, loans and charitable contributions. (CBk RF Instruction No. 7 "On Procedure of Mandatory Sale of Hard Currency Received from Sale of Goods", [of June 29, 1992] with amendments, §I, art. 1). Foreign legal entities, individuals and other nonresidents of RF may operate with Russian rubles in RF territory. For capital transfers, parties may open and deposit foreign currency into type "I" (investment) accounts, and for current transactions, type "T" ruble accounts. (CBk RF Instruction No. 16 "On Procedure for Opening and Maintenance by Authorized Banks of Ruble Accounts for Non-Residents", [of July 16, 1993] §II, III). Russian legal entities required to state records in rubles at exchange rate on date of transaction. (Regulations "On Book Keeping of Assets and Obligations of Organizations", approved by MinFin RF Order No. 50 of June 13, 1995).

Transactions in violation of foreign currency regulations void and subject to fines established by law. (Exchange Control Law, art. 14).

EXECUTION OF JUDGMENTS AND AWARDS:

Judgements of foreign courts and arbitration tribunals executed pursuant to international treaty. Execution by treaty must be sought within three years of entry of judgment or award into legal effect in country where rendered. (GPK RSFSR, art. 437). Arbitral decisions enforced pursuant to U.N. (New York) "Convention on Recognition and Enforcement of Foreign Arbitral Awards" (see topic Dispute Resolution, subhead Arbitration and Award) and European Convention on Foreign Trade Arbitration of 1961 (effective in USSR on Jan. 7, 1964). Russian courts generally carry out judgments, orders and inquiries (e.g., regarding discovery matters) of foreign courts, provided execution will not threaten security of forum and court receiving order competent to administer it. (Id., art. 436).

For RF domestic litigation, execution usually available only after appeal period expired. (GPK RSFSR, art. 209; see topic Courts). Rapid execution available for satisfaction of alimony and wage claims, reinstatement at work or other matters court deems appropriate. (Id., art. 210). Court sends judgment debtor notice and request for consensual satisfaction of judgment. (Id., art. 356). If claim not met within stated period, court may seize and sell debtor's property, garnish wages, stipends, pensions and other revenues, or attach specific property of debtor, even if possessed by third party. (Id., art. 356). (See topic Exemptions for limitations on these procedures). For execution on property in arbitration proceedings, judgment creditor submits execution list and proof of nonpayment to officer of law. (Arbitration Procedure Code RF, art. 207; MinJustice RF Letter Nos. 06-73/54-94 and S1-7/OZ-476 of July 6, 1994).

If proceeds insufficient to settle creditor claims, satisfaction occurs pursuant to priority list. Claims are paid, pro rata within each class, in following order: (1) alimony, wages, lawyer's fees, intellectual property royalties and personal injury

See Topical Index in front part of this volume.

EXECUTION OF JUDGMENTS AND AWARDS . . . *continued*

judgments, (2) social insurance premiums and judgments for personal property damage, (3) taxes, insurance premiums and judgments for damage caused to state and public organizations, (4) secured claims to extent of value of pledge, (5) unsecured claims of state organizations and enterprises, (6) all other claims. (GPK RSFSR, arts. 418-425).

EXECUTORS AND ADMINISTRATORS:

Probate occurs at testator's last domicile or, if unknown, location of principal portion of assets. Limitations period for claims of creditors and intestate takers commences on date of testator's death. (Civ. Fund., art. 153[2]). Execution of will carried out by "heirs" (term used for both testate and intestate takers) designated in will. Testator may appoint non-heir as executor, if such person's consent indicated in will. (GK RSFSR 1964, art. 544). Executor has power to perform all acts necessary but cannot receive remuneration and must prepare accounting statements [for heirs] upon request. (Id., art. 545). To take, heir must unconditionally accept gift, by taking possession or filing acceptance declaration within six months of commencement of probate. Questions of creditors claims and identification of additional takers also resolved within this period, after which heirs issued certificates of right to inherit and may dispose of property freely. (Id., arts. 557, 558). Notary office or local administration appoints trustee or custodian where property requires special supervision (Id., art. 556), and designates administrator in event of intestacy.

EXEMPTIONS:

Where compulsory execution sought, debtor permitted to retain certain possessions including residence (provided judgment not on action brought by mortgagee), basic clothing, furniture and foodstuffs of debtor and family, and supplies essential for continued operation of farming or professional activities (provided judgment does not involve deprivation of right to engage in such activities). (GPK RSFSR, art. 369 & Appendix No. 1). GK RSFSR 1964, art. 411 discusses executions against, and exemptions of, state enterprises. See topic Execution of Judgments and Awards.

EXPROPRIATION:

See topic Foreign Investment.

FOREIGN EXCHANGE:

See topics Currency; Exchange Control.

FOREIGN INVESTMENT:

RSFSR Law "On Foreign Investments" (of July 4, 1991) ("Investment Law") permits foreign investors to participate in enterprises established in RF. "Foreign investment" defined as all assets, including intellectual property, invested by foreigners to derive profit. (Investment Law, art. 2). Investor may establish wholly-owned or joint venture enterprises, purchase property including securities and investment properties, purchase right to use land and other natural resources, participate in privatization, and conduct any business not prohibited by Russian law, including granting of loans, credits, property and property rights, Investors contributing more than U.S.$10 million to charter capital of Russian company and directly investing in productive RF industries entitled to make investment agreements with RF government. (Governmental Decision No. 751, "On Procedure of Conclusion and Implementation of Investment Agreements" [July 24, 1995]). Investors may be foreign legal persons, foreign citizens, foreign states or international organizations. (Id., arts. 1, 3, 4, 35-37). Enterprises with foreign investments may realize products, works and services in RF if certification issued or recognized by competent state agency. (Id., art. 22). Special foreign trade zones grant foreign investors and companies with foreign participation more favorable tax and regulatory conditions than are available to domestic enterprises. (Id., c. 7).

Investment Law guarantees protection of foreign holdings under conditions no less favorable than those granted Russian nationals, with few exceptions.

"Repatriation of Investments".—Foreign investors guaranteed unobstructed transfer abroad of foreign currency investment proceeds, after payment of taxes. (Id., art. 10). If received in rubles, profits may be reinvested or deposited in banks in RF, but such accounts not immediately transferrable abroad. (Id., art. 11). (For rules governing currency conversion, see topic Exchange Control.)

Presidential Decree No. 1466 "On Improvements in Working with Foreign Investment" (of Sept. 27, 1993) granted foreign companies certain privileges, but has not been implemented by Russian authorities. Decree exempts properly registered enterprises with foreign participation from more adverse requirements of new legislation for three years from date of registration and provides that limitations on foreign investment activity may be imposed only by federal law or presidential decree.

Expropriation.—Foreign investment not subject to nationalization, requisition or confiscation, except in special cases dictated by public interest (eminent domain). Upon nationalization or requisition, investors entitled to prompt, adequate and effective compensation. Investment disputes involving foreign participation may be settled by courts of arbitration or general jurisdiction. (Id., arts. 6-9). See topics Courts; Dispute Resolution. Additionally, U.S. and RF concluded "Bilateral Investment Treaty" of June 17, 1992, but RF implementing legislation not yet adopted.

"Investments in Natural Resources".—Federal Law No. 225-FZ "On Production Sharing Agreements" (of Dec. 30, 1995) ("PSA Law") establishes legal grounds for relationships between Russian and foreign investments in exploration, development and production of mineral raw materials in RF under production sharing agreements. Under production sharing agreements RF provides investor (Russian or foreign) with exclusive rights for exploration, development and production of mineral raw materials in subsoil area defined in agreement and operations related thereto on chargeable basis and for certain period; investor performs above operations at own risk. (PSA Law, art. 2). Production under agreement shared between RF and investor. (Id., art. 8). Under agreement, investor enjoys liberal tax regime and avoids other compulsory payments due under normal conditions. (Id., art. 13). Provisions of international treaties of RF prevail over PSA Law. (Id., art. 24). Information and Consulting Center for Promotion of Foreign Investments established and functions under MinEc RF. (Governmental Decision No. 657 of June 30, 1995).

FOREIGN TRADE:

Federal Law No. 157-FEZ "On the State Regulation of Foreign Trade Activity" (of Oct. 1995) ("Foreign Trade Law") determines basis of State regulation of foreign trade activity and contains procedures for Russian and foreign persons. "Foreign trade activity" defined as business activity in field of international exchange of goods, services, or intellectual property. (Id., art. 2). Foreign trade law includes principle of nondiscrimination among foreign trade [participants]. (Id., art. 4). Both Russian and foreign persons entitled to conduct foreign trade. State regulations include import customs and tariff regulations (see topic Customs [Duty]), quotas and licenses to effect quantitative restrictions on export and import, control over exports of armament, military equipment and dual application goods, and state monopolies on export/import of certain goods mandated by federal law. (Id., arts. 12-17). (Federal Program of Export Development adopted by RF on Feb. 8, 1996 and provides basis for abolition of export customs duties after Apr. 1, 1996.) Foreign legal entities may open representative offices to conduct foreign trade activities in RF. (Id., art. 30).

RF Law No. 4804-1 "On Export and Import of Cultural Resources" (of Apr. 15, 1993) restricts export of certain historical, scientific and cultural assets. RF Government Resolution No. 854 "On Licensing and Establishing Quotas for Export and Import of Goods (Services) in RF", of Nov. 6, 1992, as amended Mar. 16, 1996 identifies items subject to import quotas and licensing. State Customs Committee of RF Resolution No. 610 "On Licensing and Quota Allocation of Export and Import of Goods (Services) in RF" (of Dec. 12, 1992) regulates import of military hardware and technology. Specific legislative acts govern import of nuclear materials, medicines and precious materials. Imports must correspond to technical, pharmacological, sanitary, veterinary, phytosanitary and ecological standards. Complimentary federal and regional programs to be established to promote foreign trade. (Id., art. 24).

FRANCHISES:

Although no RF law uses term "franchise", c. 54 of GK RF describes Commercial Concession ("CC"), similar to franchise agreement in several respects. Under CC, one party (owner) grants other party (user) certain exclusive rights owned by owner, including owner's trademark or trade name and business reputation, in specific territory, for fee and for definite or indefinite term. (GK RF, art. 1027). CC agreement must be registered by agency which registered legal entity or individual entrepreneur acting as owner to be enforceable. (Id., art. 1028[2]). Subconcession is permitted if agreed by owner, but original user secondarily liable to owner for damages caused by subuser, unless otherwise agreed. (Id., art. 1029). Owner must transfer to user any licenses provided by CC. Unless otherwise agreed. owner must provide technical assistance and consulting, including training of user's personnel and control of quality of goods and services produced by user under CC. (Id., art. 1031). Owner may not control prices user charges for goods or services. (Id., art. 1033). Owner is secondarily liable to customers for poor quality of products or services sold by user. (Id., art. 1034). (See topic Consumer Protection.) Assignment by owner to third parties of rights licensed to user does not terminate CC. (Id., art. 1038). Law specifies certain events which cause termination. Prior termination of CC must be registered, but consequences of non-registration not stated. (Id., art. 1037).

FRAUDS, STATUTE OF:

Contracts must be in writing if: (1) between legal entities, or (2) between legal entities and individuals, or (3) between individuals involving value of at least ten times minimum monthly wages, or (4) as stipulated by law, (GK RF, art. 161). Failure to comply with required written form deprives parties of right to confirm transactions or terms by witness testimony, but not of right to cite written or other evidence. Where expressly provided by law or agreement, or if contract involves foreign economic transaction, failure to comply with provisions requiring written form invalidates contract. (Id., art. 162).

FRAUDULENT SALES AND CONVEYANCES:

Upon suit by victim, transactions concluded under false pretenses, coercion, threat, "ill-intentioned agreement", or concluded on conditions extremely disadvantageous to one party, may be deemed invalid by court. Wrongdoer must return proceeds of transaction in kind or compensate value in cash. Injured party must deliver to state any property it received from wrongdoer as part of fraudulent transaction. Wrongdoer must then compensate victim for actual damages incurred. (GK RF, art. 179). No law expressly applies to fraudulent conveyances.

GARNISHMENT:

Execution of civil judgment may be levied on wages, pensions, student stipends and other forms of debtor's income (GPK RSFSR, arts. 358, 385), but only in absence of sufficient property of debtor for full satisfaction of claims (Id., art. 380). Judgment debtor must respond to court inquiries as to wages received and must notify court promptly upon change in employment status. (Id., art. 380). Amount withheld may not exceed 20% of wages, except for claims arising from alimony and child support, tort damages and reimbursements for theft, where 50% may be withheld. (Id., art. 383). Most social benefits exempt from garnishment except under alimony, child support, personal injury, and death of family provider claims. One-time employment benefits generally exempt. (Id., arts. 386, 387). Attachment 1 to GPK RSFSR contains list of exempt property, in addition to monetary exemptions under arts. 386-387.

GUARDIAN AND WARD:

Trusteeship and guardianship used to protect rights and interests of legally incompetent persons and minors. Trusteeship established over children under age 14 and court certified incompetents. (GK RF, art. 32). Guardianship established over minors (age 14-18) and court-certified drug or alcohol abusers. (Id., arts. 31-33).

Trustees and guardians appointed and supervised by local administrative bodies at place of residence of ward. (Id., arts. 34-35). Trustee or guardian usually serves

GUARDIAN AND WARD . . . *continued*
without compensation and lives with ward. (Id., art. 36). Extensive rules govern management of ward's income and property. (Id., arts. 37, 38). RF Family Code provides additional rules for guardians and wards.

"Patronage" guardianship established by local bodies for legally competent persons who cannot exercise or protect their rights. Patronage guardians appointed and removed only on request of ward. (Id., art. 41). Property of ward disposed of and transactions handled by guardian with ward's consent according to trust or agency agreement between guardian and ward. (Id., art. 41[3]).

HOLIDAYS:

The nine public holidays in RF are Jan. 1-2, New Year; Jan. 7, Christmas; Mar. 8, Women's Day; May 1-2, Labor Day; May 9, Victory Day; June 12, Independence Day; Nov. 7, Revolution Day and Dec. 12, Constitution Day. If public holiday falls on weekend, holiday shifted to next business day. (RSFSR Code of Labor Relations, art. 65). Employer may not require work on public holidays. (Id.). Public holidays declared by presidential decree or federal law. Numerous days designated to commemorate events and professions which are not mandated public holidays.

IMMIGRATION:

Presidential Decree No. 2145 of Dec. 16, 1993, regulates immigration control, i.e., identification and registration of individuals coming from abroad, which is supervised by Federal Migration Service. RF Government Resolution No. 1020 of Sept. 8, 1994 authorizes Federal Migration Service to carry out deportations and prevent illegal immigration, establish legal grounds for granting asylum, consider applications and interview candidates for asylum, determine legality of presence on RF territory and exact fines for violations of visa regime. Federal Migration Service official actions may be appealed to superior officer or department. Pendency of appeal suspends effect of challenged act. Decision of RF Government No. 459 of May 15, 1995 introduced standard form of invitation to invite foreigners and stateless persons to RF. Entry into RF requires payment of duty under certain circumstances, including issue or extension of entry visa or identification card of alien, issue of invitation to foreign persons, issue or extension of alien residence permit, modifications or additions to previously issued entry documents and replacement of lost or spoiled documents. (RF Law No. 226-FZ "On State Duty" art. 6, of Dec. 31, 1995). On applying for Russian entry visa, foreigners and stateless persons must present certificate of absence of HIV infection. (Federal Law No. 38-FZ, art. 10, of Apr. 12, 1995, Decision of RF Government No. 1158, of Nov. 25, 1995).

See topics Aliens; Emigration.

INDUSTRIAL PROPERTY RIGHTS:

RF assumed Soviet Union's obligations under Paris Convention for Protection of Industrial Property ("Paris Convention") pursuant to MinForAFF RF Letter No. 11/UGP of Jan. 13, 1992. Paris Convention defines industrial property as patents, utility models, industrial designs, trademarks, service marks, trade names, indications of source, and appellations of origin, which RF protects under separate laws devoted roughly to those subject areas. Art. 15 of Constitution provides treaty provisions shall apply where RF law inconsistent. (Konst. RF, art. 15[4]). Trade names protected in RF as trademarks. Additionally new Civil Code recognizes certain information as "commercial secrets", if it has commercial value, cannot be freely obtained on legal grounds, information holder takes measures to protect confidentiality, and information not designated by law as information that cannot constitute commercial secret. (GK RF, art. 139[1]). Persons or entities who obtain commercial secrets illegally must reimburse holder for losses incurred. Disclosure of commercial secret by worker in violation of employment agreement or by contracting party in violation of contract subjects worker or contracting party to reimbursement obligation for resulting losses. (Id., art. 139[2]).

See topics Copyrights; Patents; Trademarks.

INFANTS:

RF citizens acquire full civil rights and legal capacity at age 18. In cases where law permits marriage before age 18, citizen acquires full status from moment of marriage, even if marriage dissolved before age 18. (GK RF, art. 21). If marriage invalid, court may deprive underage spouse of full legal capacity. Minors age 16 or over may claim legal capacity and attendant rights under employment contract or as sole entrepreneur, with consent of parents or guardian. Minors may attain status (emancipation) by decision of court, trustee or guardian agency. Parents and guardians not liable for obligations of emancipated minor. (Id., art. 27). Transactions on behalf of unemancipated minors between ages six and 14 must be executed by parents or guardians, except that such minors have right to effect certain minor transactions. Parents and guardians liable for transactions and harms incurred by minor under age 14, including those effected by minor independently, unless they can prove lack of fault for breach of obligation. (Id., art. 28).

INSURANCE:

Insurance in RF, excluding state social security, regulated primarily by c. 48 of new Civil Code, RF Law on Insurance No. 4015-1 adopted Nov. 27, 1992 ("Insurance Law") and RF Central Bank Regulation No. 32 of Dec. 15, 1995 ("Currency Regs"). All insurance is either voluntary (based on contract between insured and insurer) or compulsory (effected by operation of law). (GK RF, art. 927). Three permissible types of insurance are personal (life, health, etc.), property (including risk of loss, risk of injuries to others in connection with property) and liability insurance (including tort, contract and business liability). (Id., arts. 929-934).

Insurance contract must be in writing, and must state object of insurance, nature of event(s) giving rise to claim, amount of insurance, and term. (Id., arts. 940, 942). Insurance contract becomes effective on payment of first premium, unless otherwise provided by contract. (Id., art. 957). Amount of insurance payable under one or several insurance contracts for specific property or business risk may not exceed actual value of property or estimate of potential business risk at contract formation. (GK RF, arts. 947, 951). Value of insured property or business risk determined by insurer, assisted by expert evaluator if needed, at contract formation. (Id., art. 945). Insured has statutory obligation to take steps reasonably necessary to minimize possibility of damage to insured property, and duty to report increased level of risk to insurer who may then demand higher premium. (Id., arts. 959, 962; Insurance Law, art. 18). Conversely, insurer obligated to "reconclude" contract if insured "has taken measures to reduce risk". (Id., art. 17). Insurer relieved from obligation to pay claim if insured event intentionally caused by insured, or by nuclear explosion, military activity, social unrest or strike. (GK RF, arts. 963-964). But if insurer fails to pay justified claim within specific period, insurer incurs fine of 1% of amount due for every day of delay. (Insurance Law, art. 17).

Insurance Supervision.—Insurance activity in RF supervised by RF Federal Service for Supervision of Insurance Activity ("Rosstrakhnadzor"). (Insurance Law, art. 30). Rosstrakhnadzor licenses and maintains state register of insurers, sets minimum capitalization, audits insurer annual reports, and regulates insurance activity. (Id.). Insurers may be legal entities licensed to offer specific types of insurance. Restrictions imposed on operations of foreign insurers within RF (Id., art. 6), and are presently limited to 49% share in joint venture companies. Insurers must establish insurance reserves, maintain normative ratio between assets and obligations, and comply with statutory accounting and reporting procedures. (Id., arts. 26-29). Insurers may form noncommercial mutual insurance societies to pool assets against large risks. (GK RF, art. 968). Monopoly prevention and unfair competition in RF insurance market effected by GKAP RF. (Insurance Law, art. 31).

Agents and Brokers.—Insurers may engage agents or brokers, provided they are registered as individual entrepreneurs insurers and have filed notice of intent to carry out insurance intermediation ten days prior to commencing activities. (Insurance Law, art. 8[1-3]). Foreign insurance companies may not use brokers or intermediaries in RF, unless applicable international treaty so provides. (Id., art. 8[4]).

Foreign Currency Operations.—Currency Regs allow RF insurers to offer insurance and make settlements in foreign currency for enumerated reasons including insurance of: goods during import and export; carriage when conveyance will cross RF customs boundary; liabilities to nonresidents by RF carriers; resident crew members of RF carriers during international carriage; residents sent on official overseas missions; foreign currency cash and securities; real estate outside RF; and machinery of foreign manufacture purchased with foreign currency. (Currency Regs., art. 2). Cbk RF issues permits to insurers authorizing foreign currency settlements, and insurers must make quarterly reports of all such settlements made. (Id., arts. 2, 5).

LABOR RELATIONS:

Labor relations governed primarily by Code of Labor Relations of 1971 ("Labor Code") as last amended Nov. 24, 1995 ("KZoT RF"). Labor Code provides protective legal regime for employees, including labor contracts, workplace rules, social safeguards, labor disputes, leisure and vacation time, wages and entitlement. No concept of "at will" employment in RF. Employment assumed indefinite unless valid business reason requires employment for fixed-term. Terminations must be "for cause". Labor Code does not regulate independent contractors. Labor contract terms less favorable than Labor Code invalid (Id., art. 5) but Labor Code entitlements may be supplemented by employer or labor collective (i.e., employees of company) by contract. Foreign companies may employ Russian nationals, and Russian companies may employ foreign nationals authorized to work in Russia. (See topic Aliens.)

Collective Contracts and Agreements.—Law of Mar. 11, 1992 "On Collective Agreements and Contracts" as amended Nov. 24, 1995 ("CCA Law") governs both labor contracts between employers and employees of particular organization and collective agreements establishing terms and social guarantees for specific industries or territories. (CCA Law, art. 2). Terms of collective agreements binding on all employers to which they apply. (Id., art. 3). Conclusion of such agreements not obligatory but may be initiated by either employees' representative or employer pursuant to statute. (Id., arts. 6-8). Statute also regulates types, terms, enforceability and procedures for amending labor agreements and penalties for violations of agreements or CCA Law. (Id., arts. 25-28). Strikes permissible if no threat to state security. (RF Law "On Resolution of Labor Disputes [Conflicts]" of Oct. 9, 1989).

Individual Labor Contracts.—Labor contract defined as agreement between worker and enterprise under which worker obliged to perform work of certain qualification and specialization and enterprise must pay salary and provide working conditions required by labor laws and labor contract. (KZoT RF, art. 15). Employment preferences based on sex, race or ethnicity prohibited. (Id., art. 16). Fixed-term contracts (up to five years or for specific projects) may be executed if nature of work requires it, employee desires it, or it is required by law, (Id., art. 17). At expiration of fixed-term contract, contract may be renewed or terminated. If employment continues without notice of termination or renewal, contract converted into contract for indefinite employment. (Id., art. 30). Labor contracts must be in writing. If employee starts work without written contract, initiation of work creates implicit contract. (Id., art. 18). Employers may include in contract trial period of up to three months (six months in special circumstances) during which time employee may be terminated if unsatisfactory, and without notice or severance benefits. (Id., arts. 22-23). Otherwise, termination permitted on parties' agreement, expiration of term, conscription into military, unilateral termination by employee, for causes enumerated in Labor Code, consensual transfer of employee to another enterprise and other specifically enumerated reasons. (Id., arts. 29, 31-33, 37).

Work Week and Leisure Time.—Regular work week 40 hours with overtime allowed only in limited circumstances such as national defense work. (KZoT RF, arts. 42-45). Employers must offer part-time work to certain classes of employees, such as pregnant women, mothers with children younger than 14 and persons taking care of disabled family members. (Id., art. 49). Minimum vacation for nonpregnant persons who are older than 18, and not working in far north or abnormally dangerous conditions is 24 days per year. (Id., arts. 54-56, 67, 85).

Supervision and Control of Labor Law.—Compliance with labor law reviewed by Federal Agency of Inspection of Labor under RF Ministry of Labor ("Inspection Agency"), trade unions and technical-legal inspectorates attached to trade unions. RF

LABOR RELATIONS . . . *continued*
Attorney General and regional/local affiliates exercise supreme supervisory authority over prosecution of labor violations (see topic Procuracy). Pursuant to Presidential Decree No. 209 "On Supervision of Payment of Wages", Inspection Agency, together with tax authorities and tax police, must conduct inspections of enterprises to determine compliance with labor law requirements on payment of wages. Employers violating labor law subject to disciplinary sanction or administrative and criminal liability. (KZoT RF, art. 249).

LANDLORD AND TENANT:

Commercial and residential landlord-tenant relations governed by cc. 34 and 35 of new Civil Code.

Commercial Lease.—Subjects of lease include land, enterprises, buildings, equipment, transport vehicles and other non-consumable property. Lease failing to describe subject is invalid. (Id., art. 607). Lease with legal entity, or for term longer than one year must be in writing. Lease for immovable property subject to state registration. (Id., art. 609). Lessor liable for undisclosed property defects, and lessee may demand repair, reduction of rent, may repair and deduct cost from rent, or terminate lease. (Id., art. 612). Lessee must timely pay rent and use property only as specified in lease. Lessor must consent to sublease, which may not exceed lease term. (Id., arts. 614-615). Transfer of ownership right does not terminate lease, however termination of lease terminates any sublease. (Id., arts. 617-618). Parties may agree when and why lease shall terminate, or may ask court to terminate for certain enumerated events of material breach. (Id., arts. 619-620). Unless otherwise provided, lessee enjoys preferential right to renew lease on expiration, and is entitled to compensation for improvements made by lessee and approved by lessor. (Id., arts. 621, 623). Lease of building shall include transfer of right to use land directly beneath building, even if lessor does not own land. (Id., art. 652).

Residential Lease.—State lease of public housing stock grants lessee's family members equal rights and obligations with respect to premises. If lessee dies or moves out, lease may be concluded with remaining family member. (Id., art. 672). Habitability of residential premises determined pursuant to housing legislation. (Id., art. 673). Lease for residential premises must be in writing. (Id., art. 674). Sale of residential premises does not terminate lease. (Id., art. 675). Lessor obligated to provide vacant habitable premises, connected to utilities. (Id., art. 676). Long term lease (longer than one year) must name all individuals permanently living in premises. Unnamed adults may not live permanently in premises without lessor's consent, however lessee may accommodate temporary tenants for up to six months. (Id., arts. 677, 679-680). Residential premises may be used only for living. (Id., art. 678). Lessee may not rebuild or reconstruct without lessor's consent. (Id.). Unless otherwise provided, maintenance repairs are responsibility of lessee, major repairs are responsibility of lessor. (Id., art. 681). Term of residential lease may not exceed five years. (Id., art. 683). Lessee enjoys priority right to renew lease, unless lessor delivers three months notice of intent not to re-let premises for at least one year. If lessor fails to deliver notice, lease is deemed renewed on same terms for additional term. (Id., art. 684). Lessee may sublet residential premises, subject to maximum habitability limitations, however sublessee does not enjoy renewal right of priority. (Id., art. 685). Lessee may terminate lease with three months notice. (Id., art. 687). Court may terminate lease for failure to pay rent, destruction or non-habitability of premises, or lessee's continued disturbance of peace after lessor's warning. (Id.).

Financial leasing is purchase financing method whereby lessees/purchasers may obtain equipment, buildings or other non-consumable goods (except for land), on long term lease, or lease-to-own basis. Lessor may be seller, or third party with purchase money who buys object of leasehold and rents it to lessee. (GK RF, art. 666). Third party lessor must notify seller that property will be leased to lessee. (Id., arts. 665, 667). Financial lease may stipulate that lessor select property on lessee's behalf. Property must be transferred by seller directly to lessee. (Id., art. 668).

Claims by lessee arising from contract concluded between seller and lessor which concern quality and completeness of property, term of delivery, or other instances of seller's improper performance of contract may be submitted directly to seller. (Id., art. 670). Lessee also denied right to terminate contract of sale with seller absent lessor's consent. (Id.). Lessor and lessee are joint and several creditors, with regard to seller. (Id.). Lessor not liable to lessee for seller's failure to perform unless lessor selected seller or contract stipulates lessor's liability. (Id.).

LAW REPORTS, CODES, ETC.:

All RF laws must be officially published to take legal effect. (Konst. RF, art. 15[3]). Conflicts between laws and regulations resolved pursuant to hierarchy described in RF Constitution. Constitution is supreme law, followed, in descending order, by federal law, presidential decrees and executive/administrative regulations. (See topic Constitution and Government for relationship between federal and regional lawmaking.) Judicial decisions, in civil law tradition, are not binding precedent but are increasingly persuasive in lower court practice.

RF legal system is code driven, in civil law tradition. Principal codes are Civil Code, Civil Procedure Code, Criminal Code, Criminal Procedure Code, Arbitration Procedure Code, Labor Code, Land Code, Code of Marriage and Family and Code of Administrative Violations. Part I of new Civil Code adopted on Oct. 30, 1994. Part II adopted on Dec. 22, 1995. Drafts of new criminal and criminal procedure codes currently in legislative review.

Law Reports.—At present, newly adopted statutes, executive orders and regulations integrated in weekly publication "Sobranie Zakonadatel'stva" ("Collection of Legislation"). Prior to 1994, acts of legislature published in "Vedomosti" ("Registers") of Supreme Soviet and RF legislative organs. Executive acts predating mid-1994 can be found in "Sobranie Postanovlenii Pravitel'stva" ("Collection of Government Resolutions"), "Sobranie Actov Presidenta i Pravitel'stva" ("Collection of Acts of President and Government") and "Biulleten' Normativnykh Aktov Ministerstov i Vedomstov SSSR" ("Bulletin of Normative Acts of Ministries and Departments of USSR").

Judicial decisions, resolutions and explanations of highest courts published in "Biulleten' Verkhovnogo Suda" ("Bulletin of Supreme Court"), "Vestnik Vishego Arbitrazhnogo Suda Rossiiskoi Federatsii" ("Bulletin of Superior Arbitration Court of RF") and "Vestnik Verkhovnogo Konstitutsionnogo Suda Rossiiskoi Federatsii" ("Bulletin of Constitutional Court of RF").

"Collection of Treaties in Force" is compilation, with three-year delay, of conventions, treaties and bilateral agreements to which RF is signatory. Most recent agreements found in weekly executive and legislative registers, above, or in monthly Bulletin of International Treaties, currently in third year of publication.

Computer databases of Russian law and regulations compiled in Garant, Konsultant Plus, Kodeks and USIS services.

LEGISLATURE:

See topic Constitution and Government.

LETTERS ROGATORY:

Consular Convention executed June 1, 1964 by U.S. and USSR became effective June 13, 1968. Pursuant to special agreement, letters rogatory may be transmitted through Department of State for execution by RF court. Civil Procedure Code provides that Russian courts will, pursuant to federal law or international agreement, carry out decisions, orders and inquiries (regarding, e.g., documents and testimony sought) of foreign courts, provided execution will not threaten security of forum and court receiving order is competent to administer it. (Id., art. 436).

LICENSES:

Certain activities require licenses from government authorities. (GK RF, art. 49). Decision of RF No. 1418 "On Licensing of Certain Types of Activities", of Dec. 24, 1994 as amended May, June, Aug. and Oct. 1995 defines types of activities subject to licensing and corresponding issuing authorities. Licensing of some activities, including auditing, insurance and banking, governed by laws other than Licensing Regulations.

Transfer of licenses generally prohibited. Licenses must identify areas in which valid. License registered with licensing authority. Minimum license term three years. (Licensing Regulations, §5). License forms approved by MinEc RF. (Order No. 4, of Jan. 18, 1995).

Licenses may be suspended or annulled in following cases: licensee submits termination petition; license application contains unreliable data; licensee violates license terms; licensee disobeys orders of licensing authorities; and liquidation of licensee or termination of entrepreneurship registration. (Licensing Regulations, §9).

Decision to issue or deny license made within 30 days of receipt of application and supporting materials. Period may be extended up to 15 days, but in no case beyond 60 days from application date. (Id., §3). Denial must include reasons for denial. (Id., Procedures, §4). License must contain: name of issuing authority and licensee, type(s) of licensed activity term, any restrictions, registration number and issue date. (Id., §5). Approximately 200 RF regulations and laws apply to licensing of various activities.

For other rules on licensing, see topics Banks and Banking; Currency; Insurance; Mines and Minerals; Securities.

LIENS:

Addressed under topic "retention" in new Civil Code, RF law regards lien as right of creditor to retain goods of debtor held by creditor in event debtor fails to timely or satisfactorily perform obligations to creditor or reimburse losses. Retention may also secure claims between parties not directly connected with goods held. Creditor may retain goods even after legal rights to goods technically transferred by debtor to third party. Satisfaction of obligations against goods subject to lien similar to procedures for execution of pledge. (GK RF, arts. 359-360).

See topics Pledges; Mortgages.

LIMITATION OF ACTIONS:

See topic Actions.

MARRIAGE:

Men and women at least 18 years of age may wed one month after filing application with Bureau for Registration of Acts Affecting Civil Status. In special circumstances registry office may shorten or extend one month term. Rights and obligations of spouses attach on registration. (RF Family Code, Dec. 29, 1995, arts. 10-13).

Marriage prohibited when: one applicant already married, applicants related by blood, one applicant is adopted parent of other, or one or both applicants have been certified incompetent by court. (Id., art. 14).

Property.—Husband and wife have equal rights. (Konst. RF, art. 19). Wife may take husband's surname, or husband may take family name of wife. (Family Code RF, art. 32). Wife does not lose rights to property acquired before marriage. (GK RF, art. 256[2]). Spouses hold after-acquired property jointly. Property possessed by either spouse before marriage remains separate and may be alienated without consent of spouse. Property acquired by one spouse during marriage becomes joint property. Inheritances/bequests and gifts to one spouse do not become joint property. In event of dispute, court may fix spouses' shares, considering relative earning capacities. In property settlement, non-luxury items used solely by one spouse pass to that spouse without compensation to other. Luxury items retain joint property status in absence of formal agreement to contrary. Debts of either spouse are charged against joint property, unless incurred for clear personal benefit of one.

To Foreign Nationals.—RF Family Code requires persons married on RF territory to satisfy qualifications for marriage according to legislation of their respective countries of citizenship (or in case of stateless persons, of jurisdiction in which they are resident). Thus, if marriage would be illegal in person's own country, marriage will be illegal in RF. If person has dual citizenship in RF and other country, requirements of RF law apply. If person has dual citizenship in two non-RF countries, person may choose which law shall apply. (Id., art. 156). RF recognizes legal marriages performed outside RF. (Id., art. 158).

MINES AND MINERALS:

RF Law No. 2395-1 "On Underground Resources" of Feb. 21, 1992, as amended Mar. 3, 1995 ("Mineral Law") contains fundamentals of natural resources legislation and defines jurisdiction of RF over RF natural resources. "Subjects" (i.e., republics and regions within RF), authorized to issue laws regulating natural resources within scope of federal laws. (Id., art. 1-1). Subsurface resources remain state property (federal or local), but minerals and other resources extracted from subsurface may be both state and private property. Subsurface not subject to purchase, sale, gift, inheritance, deposit, pledge or any other form of alienation but rights to use underground resources may be alienated or assigned to extent transfer permitted by federal law. (Id., art. 1-2). Art. 6 of Mineral Law defines permissible use of natural resources. Production of radioactive raw material and burial of radioactive waste and toxic substances limited to state enterprises. (Mineral Law, art. 9).

Licenses.—License of right to use natural resources granted either for fixed term (up to five years for geological exploration; up to 20 years for mineral production; up to 25 years for combination of exploration and production) or unlimited term (for construction and operation of underground facilities unrelated to mine production, establishment of specially protected areas, etc.). Term of license to use natural resources based on feasibility study. Term of license commences on date of issue and may be extended at request of user. (Id., art. 10). License certifies right of holder to use natural resources for area, term and purpose specified in license. License identifies permissible activities, e.g.: geological exploration; development of mineral deposits; utilization of waste products from mining and related processing industries; use of subsoil for purposes other than mineral production; establishment of specially protected geological features; or collection of fine minerals, paleontological or other geological materials. (Id., art. 11). Resolution of RF Supreme Soviet "On Procedure for Licensing Use of Underground Resources" of July 15, 1992 ("Licensing Procedure") specifies procedure for licensing. Regulation "On Licensing Certain Types of Exploration and Exploitation Activities" approved by Resolution of RF Government of July 31, 1995 ("Geological Licenses Procedure") provides rules on licensing geological exploration and exploitation. Licenses issued as part of licensing agreement package or in conjunction with production sharing agreements, discussed under subhead Production Sharing Agreements, infra. License granted by decision of Russian Geological Committee ("GC") or its territorial subdivisions or as result of auction or tender. (Licensing Procedure, art. 2.2). License granted simultaneously with rights to use land. (Id., art. 4). GC may refuse to issue license for applications not in conformance with Licensing Procedure or if applicant deliberately submits incorrect information or fails to submit evidence of required financial and technical means to conduct effective and safe activities. GC issues licenses for minimum of three years, valid for whole RF territory, while subdivisions issued by licenses valid only within each subdivision. (Geological Licenses Procedure, arts. 10, 17).

Granting of License.—Under tender system, successful applicant must offer terms and technical solutions most likely to protect natural resources. Under auction system, license awarded to highest bidder. (Licensing Procedures, art. 10). §11 Licensing Procedures also addresses conditions for licensing right to use continental shelf and exclusive maritime economic zone.

Grounds for Termination of Right to Use Natural Resources.—Right terminated on expiration of license, waiver by licensee or occurrence of events that prevent further exercise of rights. GC may terminate, suspend or limit rights if use creates threat to health of people in work zone, licensee violates license terms, licensee systematically violates rules for use and protection of natural resources, force majeure circumstances or liquidation of licensee. (Licensing Procedures, art. 16). Grounds for revocation of license are: gross violations of tender or auction rules, failure to pay license fees, contravention of antimonopoly laws concerning natural resources; collusion between licensing and license applicants and other grounds provided by law. (Id., art. 17). Revocation of license subject to appeal.

Payments for Use of Natural Resources.—User fees include tender auction and licensing fees, fees for use and replacement of raw materials, excise, profits and other taxes, payments for land, marine areas and areas of territorial sea floors, and fees for geological information. Payments may be paid in cash, as portion of minerals produced or in form of works or services. (Id., art. 43). Instruction of MinFin RF No. 8 of Feb. 4, 1993, State Tax Service No. 17 of Jan. 30, 1993 and Federal Mine and Industrial Supervision Agency No. 01-17/41 "On Procedure for and Time Limits of Remittance to Budget of Royalties for Right to use Subsoil" of Feb. 4, 1993 describe procedures and set minimum prices for use of various types of natural resources. (Id., §4).

Production Sharing Agreements.—RF Law "On Production Sharing Agreements" of Jan. 11, 1996 ("PSA Law") permits negotiated production sharing agreements ("PSA") for exploration, extraction, transportation, processing, storage, use and sale or disposition of minerals. Subject to certain exceptions and grandfathering provisions, areas eligible for inclusion in PSA specified from time to time by subsequent law. (PSA Law, art. 2). Mineral Law continues to cover matters not preempted by PSA; PSA must be confirmed by license. (Id., art. 2). Parties to PSA (federal and regional RF governments and investor) may negotiate percentage of production to be allocated to (1) cost recovery, (2) royalties, taxes, duties and subsurface use payments, and (3) profit split between RF and investor as negotiated. (Id., arts. 3, 6, 8). Investor exempted from (1) other taxes (except profits tax, which is fixed at rate in effect on date of PSA, and social benefits taxes for Russian national employees), (2) VAT on imports of related goods and services and exports of production, and (3) hard currency conversion requirements. Investor may take production in kind and export free of quotas. (Id., art. 13). PSA Law purports to take precedence over any future RF law (federal or local), except environmental laws. Adverse economic effects of future tax or other laws which do not exempt PSA shall be borne by RF parties via subsequent reductions to their share of production. (Id., arts. 13, 17, 18). Investor to have access to pipeline transportation. (Id., art. 12). Investor may not transfer its rights without consent of RF party. In event of assignment, must reissue license to assignee. (Id., art. 16). Russian companies have preferential right to provide services and specified percentage of equipment must be of Russian manufacture. (Id., art. 7). Disputes may be settled by international arbitration (see topic Dispute Resolution). RF parties may waive sovereign immunity. See topic Environment, subhead Economic and Fishing Zone.

MONOPOLIES AND RESTRAINT OF TRADE:

RF Law "On Competition and Restriction of Monopolistic Activities on Markets" of Mar. 22, 1991 as amended ("Antimonopoly Law"), governs measures for prevention and curtailment of monopolistic activity and unfair competition. Antimonopoly Law applies to all arrangements which impact competition on RF markets, including activities and relationships of foreign and Russian legal entities and individuals, and agreements executed abroad, if such activity effects RF markets. (Id., art. 2[1]). Monopolistic practices and unfair competition in financial markets and involving commercial paper restricted by other RF laws. (Id., art. 2[3]). See topic Securities.

Antimonopoly Law prohibits dominant enterprises from withholding goods from market to increase prices, imposing unfavorable contract terms unrelated to purpose of contract (e.g., unreasonable demands for payment in foreign currency or purchases of large quantities), "tying" or conditioning execution of contract on acceptance of unwanted goods, establishing obstacles to market entry and violating pricing rules. (Id., art. 5). Collusion between enterprises forbidden if may result in restraint of competition. (Id., art. 2). Antimonopoly authorities may challenge agreement between competitors with joint market share exceeding 35%, price accords between competitors, market partitioning agreements and other concerted actions including refusal to contract with specific enterprises or restricting access to goods.

Definitions.—"Unfair competition" includes activities that restrict ability of enterprises to operate in market or produce and distribute goods. (Id., art. 4). "Dominant position" is position of enterprise in market for particular goods, that enables enterprise to restrict access to same market by competitors. Position generally considered dominant if single entity's share of goods on particular market exceeds 65%. (Id.). GKAP RF may set benchmark below 65%. Position not dominant if market share 35% or less. (Id.). Any operation aimed at preventing, restricting or eliminating competition to detriment of consumer, including abuse of dominant position, defined as "monopolistic activity". (Id.).

Price Controls.—Basic guidelines for determining if price has been "fixed" established by Provisional Procedural Recommendations of GKAP RF "Concerning Disclosure of Monopoly Prices" of Apr. 21, 1994. "Monopoly price" is price substantially above price under normal market conditions. RF Government Instructions "On Procedure of Price Control of Products Manufactured by Monopolistic Enterprises" of Dec. 29, 1991 established State Register of Monopoly Enterprises ("Register") under authority of GKAP RF and imposed price controls on certain goods produced in markets dominated by entities in Register.

Prices in RF generally determined by market forces, but new products of monopoly enterprises (i.e., those entities in Register) set in accordance with Provisional Instruction No. 2 as amended Dec. 31, 1992, issued by State Pricing Committee "On Procedures for Applying Free (Market) Prices and Tariffs on Industrial and Technical Products, Consumer Goods and Services". As of Jan. 1992, enterprises in Register must notify State Pricing Committee under MinFin RF of price increases with respect to any goods or services in which entity holds dominant position in local markets. ("Procedures for Regulation of Pricing of Monopolistic Products", adopted by MinEc RF and MinFin RF of Dec. 29, 1991, art. 8).

Antimonopoly Committee.—GKAP RF prevents and curtails monopolistic activity and unfair competition, assists in drafting antimonopoly legislation, and generally controls implementation of antimonopoly laws. (Antimonopoly Law, arts. 12, 17, 18). GKAP RF may compel dissolution of dominant entities. (Id., art. 19). GKAP RF must protect commercial secrets obtained during course of its activities. (Id., art. 15).

Prior approval of GKAP RF required for: (1) acquisitions exceeding 20% of voting shares in enterprises with certain levels of assets (not applicable to founders of entity at formation); (2) purchase or lease by entity or group of entities of primary means of production of another entity, if value of assets sold or leased exceeds 10% of transferor's asset value; and (3) acquisitions of controlling blocks of shares in target company. Prior approval of GKAP RF for such transactions necessary only if net value of assets of purchasing entity or entities ("Acquirer") exceeds 100,000 times minimum monthly wage, or Acquirer listed in Register as "dominant" i.e. with market share exceeding 35%, or Acquirer already has controlling interest in target enterprise. Procedure for obtaining GKAP RF approval in GKAP RF Order No. 145 of Nov. 13, 1995. Notice to GKAP RF also required within 15 days of registration of transaction in which asset value of Acquirer between 50,000 and 100,000 times minimum monthly wage. Transactions concluded in violation of those provisions may be invalidated by court on request of GKAP RF. (Id., art. 18). Applicant informed within 30 days of application to GKAP RF of approval or reasons for rejection of proposed transaction. (Id., art. 17).

Antimonopoly Register.—Pursuant to GKAP RF Regulation No. 60 of Oct. 10, 1991, state registry established for enterprises occupying dominant positions in goods and services markets. Threshold percentage of market share for inclusion in Register is 35% or amount determined annually by GKAP RF. Any conduct violative of antimonopoly laws may result in inclusion in Register. Enterprises may petition to be removed from Register on various statutory grounds.

Liability for Violations of Antimonopoly Legislation.—Failure to comply with order of GKAP or violation of antimonopoly laws after administrative penalty levied may result in criminal prosecution. Criminal penalties include up to three years corrective labor, substantial fines or restriction on business and other activity for up to three years. (Monopoly Law, arts. 22-26).

MORTGAGES:

RF legal framework for mortgages incomplete. RF Government adopted "Basic Provisions on Pledge of Immovable Property—Mortgage" on Dec. 22, 1993 as model for new mortgage legislation, and State Duma accepted first reading of laws "On Mortgages" and "State Registration of Rights to Real Property", but neither law adopted. Pledge section of new Civil Code includes provisions relevant to mortgages. May 1992 law "On Pledge" ("Pledge Law") includes chapter on mortgages, effective to extent consistent with new Civil Code. Moscow City Government issued Resolution

MORTGAGES . . . *continued*

No. 3356 "On Principles for Use of Pledge-Backed Financing in City of Moscow" of Apr. 25, 1995 ("Resolution") addressing financing of Moscow City real estate development projects through mortgage, and §1.1 of "Procedures for Using Pledge Backed Financing" (Attachment #1 to Resolution) recommends this procedure for enterprises in Moscow using mortgages. Resolution also approved model "Pledge Agreement for Real Property", i.e., mortgage (Attachment #7 to Resolution) which is widely used as basis for mortgage transactions in Moscow.

Pledge Law defines "mortgage" as pledge of buildings, construction projects, enterprises and other attachments, as well as land parcel itself or right to use land, and requires mortgage agreement be notarized and registered with local authorities in region where mortgaged property located. (Id., arts. 42, 43). Mortgage of enterprise extends to all property comprising enterprise, movable and immovable, unless otherwise provided by law or contract. Mortgage of building permitted only with simultaneous mortgage, under same agreement, of land site on which building located or of pledgor's right to lease site. Mortgage of land parcel does not include buildings and attachments of pledgor situated or being erected on mortgaged parcel, unless specifically included in agreement. (GK RF, art. 340). Execution of pledgee's claim on mortgaged real property, in absence of court order, permissible only on basis of notarized agreement between pledgee and pledgor, concluded after emergence of grounds for seeking levy of execution. (Id., art. 349[1]). Release of mortgage must be noted in register in which mortgage contract initially entered. (Id., art. 352[2]).

See topics Pledges; Real Property.

MOTOR VEHICLES:

Motor vehicles governed generally by RF Law No. 196-FZ "On Safety of Traffic" of Dec. 10, 1995 ("Traffic Law") and RF Law No. 1130 "Regulations for Licensing Activity in Sphere of Road Traffic" of Nov. 20, 1995 ("Licensing Law"). RF licensing of vehicles and drivers conducted by departments of Ministry of Internal Affairs State Traffic Inspectorate. (Licensing Law, art. 4). Potential drivers must meet age specifications for vehicle for which license sought, complete certified training program, and pass qualifying exams. (Traffic Law, arts. 25-27). Motorcycles and scooters ("category A") licensed and driven by individuals 16 years of age or older. Automobiles under 3,500 kilograms ("category B") and heavier passenger vehicles ("category D") with less than nine passenger seats require licensed drivers over 18 and 20 years, respectively. (Id., art. 25). Right to drive may be terminated due to expiry of license, ill health, or certain felony convictions. (Id., art. 28).

Commercial Transport.—Licensing of retail trade with trucks, buses, and special transport vehicles requires special application containing documentation of identity and structure of legal entity or natural person applying for license, state certification as legal entity, payment of application fee, taxation information, and physical inspection of business address. (RF Law No. 822 "On Approval of Regulations Licensing Retail Trade with Lorries, Special Transport Vehicles, and Buses", art. 3, Aug. 18, 1995). Retail transportation licenses nontransferable, with terms of three to five years. Licenses generally granted within 30 days from application. (Id.). License types include freight shipment ("S"), transport of passengers ("P"), forwarding services ("F"), maintenance of transport vehicles ("V"), and shipment of dangerous cargoes ("DC"). (RF Law No. 118 "Regulations for Licensing Carriage, Forwarding and Other Activities Connected with Transportation and Maintenance of Transport Vehicles in RF", art. 4, Feb. 26, 1992 with amendments).

Conventions.—USSR acceded to Convention on International Road Traffic of 19 Sept. 1949, under which drivers licensed in member states may drive legally in other member states with valid domestic driving permit plus International Driving Permit honored by all member states.

NOTARIES PUBLIC:

Role of notary in RF differs substantially from notary role in common law countries. Notaries engage primarily in drafting, registering and safeguarding wills, administering decedent's estates, supervising alienation of real property, authenticating documents, certifying powers of attorney and authenticating signatures. Consular offices abroad have similar and additional functions: e.g., certification of accuracy of translations, establishing persons as living, establishing place of residence, certifying identity of applicant in comparison with photograph, certifying time of deposit of documents, accepting deposits of money and securities, accepting documents and evidence for safekeeping and other notarial functions. (See topic Consuls.) RF signed to Hague Convention Abolishing the Requirement of Legalization for Foreign Public Documents of Oct. 5, 1961 on May 31, 1992.

RF Law "On Fundamentals of RF Legislation on Notaries" of Feb. 11, 1993 ("Notary Fund") allows for government employed as well as private practioner notaries. MinJustice RF registers both state and private notaries. In absence of notary, local executive may notarize documents. State notaries prohibited from operating for profit "in excess of established fee schedule". (Notary Fund, art. 1).

Same rights and obligations attach to state and private notaries, and documents certified by them have equivalent legal effect. Licensed notary who has not practiced for three years must re-qualify by exam. (Id., arts. 3-4). Notaries must not disclose information contained in documents they examine, except on request of court, procurator, examining official or arbitration court conducting criminal or civil proceedings. (Id., art. 5). Private notary who intentionally discloses notarial secret liable for damages caused. License may be revoked if notary violates law. (Id., art. 17). Notaries may set own fees for additional services not included in established fee schedule. (Id., art. 1).

PARTNERSHIPS:

See topic Business Associations.

PATENTS:

Patent Law of RF No. 3571-1, of Sept. 23, 1993 ("Patent Law") regulates property and relations arising in connection with development, legal protection and use of inventions, utility models and industrial designs. (Patent Law, art. 1). State Patent Agency of RF ("RosPatent") registers and issues patents. (Id., art. 2).

Patentability.—Inventions, utility models and industrial designs generally patentable if novel, inventive (representing development beyond existing technological level) and industrially applicable. (Id., arts. 4-6).

Registration.—All patent applications filed with RosPatent. If patent holder nonresident of RF or foreign citizen or legal entity, application must be filed by patent agent registered with RosPatent acting on behalf of applicant by proxy. (Id., art. 16).

Duration of Protection.—Patent valid for 20 years for invention; five years for utility model, which may be extended up to three years; or ten years for industrial design, which may be extended up to five years. All periods of protection effective from date patent application filed. (Id., art. 3).

Infringement.—If patent rights infringed, patentee may demand violator cease infringement and compensate for losses incurred. (Id., art. 14).

PERPETUITIES:

No limitations on disposition of property analogous to common law rule against perpetuities.

PLEDGES:

Pledge regulated by new Civil Code and, to extent consistent, RF Law "On Pledge" adopted May 29, 1992 ("Pledge Law"). Pledge gives creditor right to preferential satisfaction from pledged property before other creditors subject to exceptions provided by law fails. (Id., art. 334[1]).

Pledge agreement must be in writing, must state value of and indicate which party shall retain possession of pledged property, must be notarized if underlying agreement for which security given was notarized and must be notarized and registered if subject of pledge is immovable property. (Id., art. 339). If pledged property evidenced by security, security must be transferred to pledgee or deposited with notary unless agreement provides otherwise. (Id., art. 338[4]). Subject of pledge may be any property or property rights, including real (immovable) property, except personal claims inextricably connected with creditor (e.g., alimony), and other rights prohibited by law from being assigned. (Id., art. 336). Pledgor must own or have right of economic authority over property to be pledged. (Id., art. 335). Pledged property remains in pledgor's possession, unless otherwise provided by agreement. (Id., art. 338[1]). Pledged property left with pledgor identified by affixing markings evidencing pledge. (Id., art. 338[3]).

Unless otherwise provided by agreement, pledgee's rights extend to appurtenances of pledged property. Pledge shall extend to products and revenues received from use of property, to extent provided by agreement. (Id., art. 340[1]). In mortgage of land, pledge does not extend to buildings or fixtures situated on land, unless contract so provides. (Id., art. 340[4]). Agreement may extend pledge to prospective rights. (Id., art. 340[6]).

Pledge right arises on conclusion of contract or, if contract requires possession by pledgee, upon transfer of property to pledgee. (Id., art. 341). Rights and obligations of pledgor and pledgee in respect of pledged property defined by statute unless otherwise provided by contract. (Id., arts. 343-347). Agreements requiring that pledgee derive benefit and revenue from pledged property to repay secured obligation enforceable. (Id., art. 346).

Levy on pledged immovable property executed only pursuant to court order, unless otherwise provided in notarized debtor-creditor agreement concluded after grounds arise for seeking levy. (Id., art. 349[1]). Generally, levy on pledged movable property must be executed pursuant to court order, unless initial debt instrument or subsequent agreement provides otherwise. (Id., art. 349[2]). Pledged property on which execution has been levied sold at public auction according to statutory procedures. (Id., art. 350).

See topic Mortgages.

PRESCRIPTION:

See topic Adverse Possession.

PRESS REGULATION:

No limitation on press freedoms permitted, except as provided by law. (RF Law "On Mass Media" of Dec. 27, 1991 as amended ["Mass Media Law"], art. 1). Censorship forbidden (Id., art. 3), but forbidden to use mass media to commit crimes, disclose state or other secrets protected by law, incite attempts to seize power, change constitutional structure of state by force or inflame ethnic, class, social, religious intolerance or differences. Use of telephone, video and cinema to influence public subconsciousness forbidden. (Id., art. 4).

Mass Media Law outlines rules applicable to founders of mass media (Id., art. 7) and registration of mass media activity (Id., arts. 8-13) and defines basic rights of journalists (Id., art. 47). Journalists obligated to verify information transmitted, preserve confidentiality of material and sources, obtain consent to distribute personal information, and inform persons when they are being recorded. State guarantees journalist's right to perform professional activities, and to retain honor, dignity, health, life and property while doing so. (Id., art. 49).

Foreign Journalists.—Representative offices of foreign mass media established with consent of MinForAff RF unless international treaty provides otherwise. Foreign journalists register under Russian law and country of their abode, unless treaty provides otherwise. (Id., art. 55). MinForAff RF accredits correspondent. (Id., art. 48). If foreign states establish limitations on Russian correspondents, Russia may reciprocate.

PRINCIPAL AND AGENT:

Representation by agent permissible and enforceable. Agent acquires rights solely for principal, binding principal only. (GK RF art. 182). Agent may assign obligations to third party only if authorized by agreement or if circumstances demand substitution. (Id., art. 187). If agent acts outside scope of authority, only agent bound unless principal ratifies. Commercial representative is agent who permanently and independently represents business in normal course of business. Simultaneous commercial

See Topical Index in front part of this volume.

PRINCIPAL AND AGENT . . . *continued*
representation of multiple parties to single transaction permissible only with consent of parties represented. Commercial representation must be performed according to contract. (GK RF, cc. 49, 52). Notarized power of attorney required in some cases. (Id., art. 185).

PRIVATIZATION:

Privatization intended to shift ownership of state property to private sector and ensure widespread participation by RF citizens. RF privatization initiated by law "On Privatization of State and Municipal Enterprises in RF" adopted July 3, 1991 as amended ("Privatization Law"), which describes privatization procedure and types of privatized enterprises. Programs on Privatization ("State Program") issued by RF in 1994. 1992-94 contain more detailed rules. Privatization implemented in two stages for investment: (1) Initial voucher privatization in which RF workers received vouchers in newly privatized entities, followed by (2) cash privatization, in which whole enterprises sold to highest bidder.

State Program for 1994. State Program expands list of enterprises subject to privatization restrictions, expands scope of foreign participation and prohibits adoption of restrictions on privatization not specifically mentioned in 1994 Program. Conversion from voucher to cash privatization after July, 1994 effected by Presidential Decree No. 153r, "Main Provisions of State Program of Privatization of State and Municipal Enterprises in RF after July 1, 1994" of July 22, 1994 ("Main Provisions"), which was first proposed as federal law but rejected by Duma because it allowed sale of land on which privatized factories sat. (Voucher privatization continued for limited purposes during fall of 1994.) Main Provisions define mechanism for implementing 1994 Program through cash privatization. Enterprises generally allowed to retain 51% of proceeds from sale of their shares in cash privatization, except that enterprises whose privatization plans were approved before July 1, 1994 must be sold pursuant to State Program for 1994, and not Main Provisions. Permissible methods for privatization under Main Provisions include sales of shares through investment or commercial tenders and through stock auctions. State Program for 1994 continues rights of employees of privatized enterprises to gratis or preferred receipt of shares pursuant to one of three options selected by labor collective of privatized enterprise. Foreign participation in cash auctions implemented through authorized "I" (investment) bank accounts. See topic Banks and Banking.

Privatization supervised by RF State Committee for Management of State Property ("GKI RF"), which registers and approves privatization plans involving federally owned enterprises or others that require GKI RF approval under 1994 Program. Regional and municipal officers serve similar function for regionally and locally-owned property, subject to GKI RF review. RF state property fund holds enterprise interests following conversion of federally owned enterprises into joint stock companies and conducts privatization auctions. Same functions performed by regional and municipal property funds in relation to enterprise with authorized funds of 500 million rubles or less, and regionally and municipally-owned property.

State Program for 1994 lists state and municipal enterprises as to which (1) privatization is prohibited (over 40 categories of enterprises and assets, including natural resources, enterprises of historical value, railroads, television and radio centers, educational institutions and related infrastructure, large publishing houses and enterprises); (2) privatization requires decision of RF government or GKI RF or state administrative authorities; or (3) privatization is mandatory. Foreign participants subject to various additional restrictions listed in State Program for 1994, and must file notification with MinFin RF. Enterprise being privatized subject to approval from Antimonopoly Committee at RF or regional level and/or to file notice with MinFin, RF depending on percent of total interests being acquired by individual investors and percent of total interests being acquired in privatized enterprise.

See also topic Monopolies and Restraint of Trade, subhead Antimonopoly Committee.

PROCURACY:

RF Law No. 168-FZ "On Amending the Law 'On Procuracy of RF'" of Nov. 17, 1995 provides new version of law "On Procuracy of RF" ("Procuracy Law") and stipulates objectives and duties of procuracy. Procuracy established to supervise legality and admininstration of justice, protect rights of citizens through intervention in court and administrative proceedings, conduct criminal prosecutions, hear complaints (non-exclusive authority) of citizens as to rights violations, and serve other functions related to judicial process. (Id., arts. 1-3). Procurator's offices review implementation of laws and regulations by local legislative, executive and administrative bodies, as well as by legal entities, public organizations and officials. Procuracy cooperates with appropriate agencies in other states, participates in drafting laws and international treaties, concludes international treaties on judicial assistance (recognition and enforcement of civil judgments) and combats crime. Organization procedure regulated by Constitution and Federal Laws. (Id., arts. 1-3).

Procuracy is unitary structure, with local, regional, republican and other procurators forming hierarchy up to RF Procurator-General. (Id., art. 11[1]). Procurator-General appointed on nomination by RF President and dismissed by Federation Council. (Id., art. 12). Procuratorial supervision, including court practice, generally withdrawn in favor of principle of "separation of powers" and independence of procuracy. Procuracy entitled to supervise implementation of human rights and freedoms (Id., arts. 26-28), to investigate citizens' grievances against state agencies, court actions (Id., arts. 35-39), often during pendency of consideration or appeal, and may appeal question to RF Constitutional Court. Procuracy controls pre-trial investigations (Id., arts. 29-31), and may submit "protests" to highest RF courts requesting vacation of lower court decisions (Id., art. 36). Procurators have non-exclusive right of general supervision of implementation of laws by state agencies, legislative and local self-government organs, legality of administrative acts and may protest actions inconsistent with law. (Id., arts. 21-25).

See topics Administrative Law; Courts.

REAL PROPERTY:

Under RF law, real property equated with immovable property, generally defined as everything so tightly linked with land that it cannot be moved without causing damage incommensurate with essence of thing in question. Real property includes land sites, subsoil lots, isolated bodies of water, forests, buildings and structures, etc. (GK RF art. 130[1]). It also includes aircraft, seacraft, inland ships, spacecraft, certain enterprises, and other property defined as immovables by law. (Id., arts. 130-132). RF law permits citizens and legal entities, including state and municipal entities, to own any property they are not prohibited from owning by law. (Id., arts. 212-213). Land and natural resources not owned by citizens or legal entities defined as state owned. (Id., art. 214[2]). Individuals and entities which do not own certain property may still have rights in rem to property, including right of inheritable lifetime possession or right of permanent (perpetual) use of plot of land (Id., arts. 216, 265, 268), servitudes (Id., arts. 216, 274, 275) and rights of economic authority or operational management of property (Id., arts. 216, 294, 296). Co-ownership of property also permitted. (Id., art. 244).

Ownership and other rights in rem concerning real property, and limitations on and transfers and terminations of such rights, must be registered in uniform state register maintained by juridical agencies. Right of ownership acquired (as to newly created immovables, such as buildings) or transferred from moment of registration. (Id., arts. 131[1], 164, 219, 223). In cases provided by law, special registration, separate from state registration, may be required. (Id., art. 131[2]). Procedures for state registration established in accordance with new Civil Code and law regarding registration of real property rights (not yet adopted). (Id., art. 131[6]). Until adoption of such law, registration carried out by various authorities depending on type of real property (e.g., land transaction registered with offices of RF Committee on Land Resources). Failure to register real property rights and transactions generally invalidates right or transaction. (Id., art. 165). C. 18 of new Civil Code defines rights of ownership in rem to residential premises. (Id., arts. 288-293).

Termination of Real Property Rights.—Property ownership rights may be terminated pursuant to grounds and events stipulated by law. (Id., art. 235). Grounds for termination of ownership rights in and/or forcible removal of real property from its owner include levy of execution on land by court order (Id., arts. 237, 278), state buyout of private land site pursuant to eminent domain procedures (Id., arts. 279-283), confiscation of land used in manner which violates land use laws (Id., art. 285) and termination of ownership rights in mismanaged residential premises by local authorities (Id., art. 293). If land nationalized pursuant to new laws, state must compensate owner for losses incurred, including value of property. (Id., art. 306).

Foreign Ownership.—Legality of foreign ownership of real property in RF still unclear. Presidential Decree No. 1767 on "Regulation of Land Relations and Development of Agrarian Reform in Russia" of Oct. 27, 1993 expressly allows RF citizens and legal entities owning land to sell, mortgage and exchange land and contribute it to legal entities, including those with foreign participants. (Id., §1). However, RF Constitution allows "citizens" to own and alienate land, without mention of foreign citizens or companies. (Konst. RF, art. 35). Other RF real property laws do not expressly prohibit or allow foreign ownership, but 1991 law "On Foreign Investments in RSFSR", still in force, guarantees foreign investors same rights and privileges regarding investments as RF entities and individuals. (Id., art. 6). Commentators generally agree foreign ownership of real property permitted under RF law, but further clarification needed on permissible forms of ownership and applicable limitations.

Condominiums.—Presidential Decree No. 2275 "On Approval of Provisional Regulations on Condominiums" of Dec. 23, 1993 ("Condo Decree") defines condominium ("condo") as association of owners in single residential real estate complex, in which every member owns residential or nonresidential property. (Id., §1). Condo is nonprofit organization of residents/owners which acquires status and rights of legal entity from receipt of state registration certificate. Management and disposal of common property and activities of condo association, including restrictions on use of member contributions, governed by Condo Decree and condo charter. (Id., §8). Members of condo associations liable for debts of condo only to extent of investment and not responsible for obligations of other members. (Id., §7).

Condo, as entity, may not own real estate. All real estate acquired by condo in common ownership of members. (Id., §10). Management control vested in members, with voting weighted in proportion to total space owned by each member, and management board, answerable to members. Exclusive authority of member meeting and board defined in Condo Decree. (Id., §§22-25). Condo association liquidated on acquisition of all commonly owned real estate by one individual, physical destruction of real estate or court decision. (Id., §28).

See topics Adverse Possession; Land Sales; Landlord and Tenant; Mortgages.

Land Sales.—During Soviet era, private land ownership prohibited. All real property belonged to state and state enterprises. Present Constitution allows private, state and municipal ownership of land (Konst. RF, art. 9) and affirms right of RF citizens and entities to freely possess, use and dispose of land provided use does not violate rights and interests of others.

First attempt to privatize state land made pursuant to RF Law No. 4196-1 "On Right of RF Citizens to Private Ownership of Government Buildings and Residential Housing, Right to Land Parcels for Conducting Subsistence and Non-Commercial Farming Activity and Right of Sale of Such Parcels" of Dec. 23, 1992 ("Land Law"), which established right of citizens to own and sell land but limited use of land sold (i.e., to personal and subsistence farming, residential uses, etc.). Presidential Decree No. 503 "On Rules of Purchase and Sale of Land Parcels by RF Citizens" of May 30, 1993 ("Decree 503") prescribed mechanisms for such sales, requiring contract be notarized and registered by appropriate committee for land resources management. (Id., §7). Decree No. 1767, as amended Dec. 24, 1993, "On Regulation of Land Relations and Development of Agro-Reform in Russia" of Oct. 27, 1993 ("Decree 1767") clarifies rights and obligations arising from private land transactions, noting right of landowners to sell, transfer, inherit, pledge, lease, exchange, and contribute land to charter capital of corporations and partnerships, including those with foreign investment. Decree 1767 requires issue of certificate or deed of land ownership to each owner. Certificate entered in land register maintained by local land management committee.

REAL PROPERTY . . . *continued*

Presidential Decree No. 631 "On Sale of Land Parcels During Privatization of State and Municipal Enterprises" of June 14, 1992 permits land on which privatized enterprise being located to be acquired in context of privatizations with some exceptions. New Civil Code includes chapter on land ownership that will take effect on enactment of new land code. Local authorities authorized to issue regulations on land sale, for example, Resolution of Moscow Mayor No. 110-PBM "On Land Lease and Primary Form of Land Relations in Moscow" of Mar. 2, 1992 as amended, which prohibited private land ownership within city.

Contracts for sale of immovable property ("improvements") addressed in c. 30 of new Civil Code. (GK RF, arts. 549-558). Contracts must be in writing, must specify characteristics of improvement being transferred, price, and are subject to state registration. (Id., arts. 550-551, 554-555). Contract for sale of improvement simultaneously transfers right to use land beneath improvement. (Id., art. 552). If seller of improvement owns land beneath improvement, then land ownership transferred with sale of improvement. (Id.). Improvements may be sold without consent of third party land owner, and buyer shall acquire right to use land on same terms enjoyed by seller. (Id.). Sale of land beneath improvement leaves improvement owner right to use land beneath improvement. (Id., art. 553). Transfer of improvement must be evidenced by deed of transfer. (Id., art. 556). Contracts for sale of residential premises containing residents must include list of residents and their respective rights. (Id., art. 558).

REPLEVIN:

Owner entitled to reclaim property from unlawful possessor (GK RF, art. 301), but not from bona fide purchaser for value unless property lost, stolen or otherwise taken from his possession against owner's will. Recovery permitted in all cases where possessor acquired property without compensation from party without right to dispose of property. Money and bearer securities cannot be reclaimed from bona fide purchaser. (Id., arts. 302-303).

SALES:

Part I of new Civil Code contains general rules on transactions, obligations and contracts also applicable to sales. (GK RF, cc. 9-12, 21-29). Provisions on specific types of sale transactions found in Part II of new Civil Code. (Id., c. 30).

Sales contract includes any undertaking by seller to convey property or goods to buyer, if buyer agrees to accept and pay for same. General sales rules applicable to sale of securities, currency, property rights and sales of enterprises and immovable and movable property, unless otherwise provided by law. (Id., art. 454[1]). No particular form required for sales contract, unless subject matter requires it be written, notarized or registered with state authorities (e.g., contracts for sale of land). Parties generally free to determine contents of agreement unless law requires certain terms. Terms considered agreed on if contract specifies name and amount of goods to be sold. (Id., art. 455). See topic Contracts.

Price.—In absence of contract term or regulatory act establishing price, price set by reference to sales of similar goods under similar circumstances at time contract concluded. If neither contract, legislation nor business custom indicates period over which payment to be made, buyer obliged to pay promptly upon receipt of goods or title. (GK RF, arts. 424, 485). Buyer may pay in full or use credit. If buyer defaults on payments for goods sold on credit, seller may demand payment in full or return of unpaid goods and, unless contract provides otherwise, interest. Unless contract provides otherwise, goods sold on credit treated as pledge securing buyer's obligation to pay. (Id., art. 488). If contract provides that seller retain ownership of goods until buyer pays, buyer may not sell or dispose of goods before paying in full, unless special circumstances apply. (Id., art. 491).

Quality of goods must conform to standards set in contract. If contract omits reference to quality, seller must tender goods of usual caliber for purposes stated in contract or otherwise known by seller. If seller does not know intended use, tender should conform to standards for normal use. Where statute or regulation sets quality standards, parties cannot set lower requirements. (GK RF, art. 469). Sales contract may provide for warranty on goods sold. (Id., arts. 470-471).

Defects.—Buyer receiving defective goods not previously disclosed by seller entitled to substitute goods of proper quality, removal/repair of defects free of charge in reasonable time, compensation for expenses incurred in removing defects or discount in purchase price. If defects substantial, buyer may refuse performance and demand return of money paid for goods, or demand substitute goods of proper quality. (GK RF, art. 475). (See topic Consumer Protection.) If such remedies do not compensate fully, buyer may seek consequential damages and recover other costs incurred. (See topic Damages.) Seller liable for defects only if buyer proves defects appeared or causes of defects existed prior to transfer of goods. (Id., art. 476). Unless otherwise provided by law or contract, claims not permitted unless defects discovered within reasonable time not exceeding two years after transfer of goods. Warranty term controls if warranty provided. (Id., art. 477). Seller must notify buyer of rights of third parties to property sold. Failure to disclose third party rights entitles buyer to reduced price, rescission and/or damages unless buyer knew or should have known about third party rights. (Id., art. 460).

SEALS:

Seal generally not necessary for execution of contract. (GK RF, art. 160[1]). However, seal required for execution of certain documents (e.g., power of attorney issued by enterprise [Id., art. 185(5)] and certification of subject of pledge left with pledgor which requires seal of pledgee [Id., art. 338(2)]). Seal also necessary for notarization of documents issued by legal entity (e.g., financial documents, accounting documents). Company must have company seal (Law No. 208-FZ "On Joint-Stock Companies", of Nov. 24, 1995, art. 2), commonly used to validate or certify signature. Seal of company must contain its official name in Russian and place of registration. Seal may additionally indicate company name in any foreign language. State authorities may prescribe form of seal for certain companies (e.g., Resolution of Moscow Mayor "On Seals of Enterprises and Organizations of Moscow Construction Complex") of June 24, 1994.

SECURITIES:

Securities are documents which certify property rights, exercise and transfer of which may be effected only upon tender of such documents. (GK RF, art. 142). Recognized types of securities including stocks in corporate entities, government and nongovernment bonds, promissory notes, checks, depository certificates, derivative securities, and investment shares in mutual funds. (Presidential Decree No. 2063 of Nov. 4, 1994 "Government Regulations of Securities Market in RF" ["Decree No. 2063"]) Law "On Operations with Securities" of Apr. 22, 1996 ("Securities Law") also defines so called "issued securities" (Id., art. 2), that are placed through issues, and give holders equal right within one issue irrespective of the time acquired (Id.). Securities Law governs all matters related to issue and trade of "issued securities" and activities of professional investment institutions. (Id., art. 1). Securities Law classifies shares and bonds as "issued securities". (Id.).

Federal Securities Commission ("FSC") regulates securities market and activities of investment institutions. (Id., art. 40; Decree No. 2063, §6). Its functions include activities of state agencies involved in regulation of securities market, approving procedures for registration of issues by Russian and foreign legal entities and developing rules for licensing and conduct of professional activities on securities markets. (Securities Law, art. 42). MinFin RF has substantial jurisdiction over activities of securities market. (Instruction of MinFin RF No. 53 of July 6, 1992 "On Procedures for Execution and Registration of Transactions with Securities" ["Instruction No. 53"]). Jurisdiction of FSC and MinFin RF sometimes implementing legislation for Securities Law hopefully will clarify jurisdiction.

Forms of "Issued Securities".—"Issued Securities" may be: documentary securities registered in name of holder, non-documentary securities registered in name of holder, documentary bearer securities; non-documentary bearer securities. (Securities Law, art. 16). Documentary securities are certified by share or share certificate; non-documentary are certified by registration with securities registar.

Registration of Securities.—Securities Law art. 19 and MinFin RF Instruction No. 2 "On Procedures for Issuing and Registration of Securities in RF" of Mar. 3, 1992 ("Instruction No. 2") address registration of initial issue of securities. Instruction No. 53 outlines procedures for registration of transactions involving investment institutions and sales of securities. Securities Law requires registration of initial issue of securities, when placed through potentially unlimited number of investors, through placement among limited number of investors which exceed 500, and in cases when amount of issue exceeds 50,000 minimum wages. (Securities Law, art. 19). Initial issue may include issue on formation of joint stock company, for increase of charter capital or issue of bonds. (Instruction No. 2, §3). Procedure for initial issue through public offering includes approval and publication of prospectus, registration of securities and prospectus, and placement of securities. Procedure for closed subscription outlined in Instruction No. 2, §4. Art. 22 of Securities Law stipulates requirements for stock prospectus. Instruction No. 53 provides procedures for registration of transactions with securities and outlines rights and obligations of investment institutions with respect to registration. (Instruction No. 53, §§2.1, 3.3).

Securities registration implemented by agencies authorized by FSC. (Securities Law, art. 20). Currently registration implemented by MinFin RF and regional Departments of Finance. (Instruction No. 53, §5.1; Instruction No. 2, §5). Denial of registration for cause only and may be appealed to regular or arbitration court. (Securities Law, art. 21). MinFin RF maintains Uniform Register of Securities. (Letter of MinFin RF "On Publication of Uniform Register of Securities of RF of Dec. 2, 1992"). Issuer must file quarterly reports and statement on any material changes in financial status of company with registration authorities. (Securities Law, art. 23). Shares of closed companies registered with MinFin RF or regional Department of Finance, depending on size of issue. (Instruction No. 2, §5). Officers of company signing stock prospectus liable for misrepresentations in prospectus. (Id., §11). Term of offer for securities is limited in prospectus. Number of shares to be issued cannot exceed number of authorized shares of company as reflected in its charter. (Securities Law, art. 24).

Securities Sales.—Stock purchase price for initial issue must be equal for all purchasers. (Government Resolution No. 78 "Regulations on Issuance and Circulation of Securities and Stock Exchanges in RF" of Dec. 28, 1991. ["Regulation No. 78"], §35). Share price on secondary market established by market. Settlement for sale of shares cannot exceed 90 days. (Id., §1[4]). Debt financing for purchase of securities cannot exceed 50% of purchase price. (Id., §3.1). Title to securities registered in name of holder passes to buyer upon tender of share certificate to seller after registration; title to bearer securities passes to buyer upon tender of share certificate; title to non-documentary securities registered in name of holder passes to buyer upon registration. (Securities Law, art. 29).

Bonds.—Joint stock companies may issue bonds (including convertible bonds) for amount not to exceed authorized capital or, if secured, not to exceed security interest. Unsecured bonds may be issued no sooner than third year of incorporation of company. (GK RF, art. 102). Company should register prospectus for bond issue. Company may issue bearer bonds and bonds registered in name of holder. (JSC Law, art. 33).

Government Securities.—Consist of government obligations (Regulation No. 78, §3) and state treasury bonds (MinFin RF Letter No. 140 "Regulation for Procedure of Placement, Circulation and Payment of Treasury Bonds" of Oct. 21, 1994). Derivative securities defined by Regulation No. 78 as "any securities acknowledging right of their holder to purchase or sell in the future other forms of securities". (Id., §3).

Investment Professionals and Institutions.—Securities Law recognizes several types of professional entities engaged in securities transactions: brokers, dealers, asset managers, clearing operators, depositories and registrars. (Securities Law. c. 2). Regulation No. 78 still in effect also lists among professional investment institutions, investment consultant, investment company and investment fund. (Regulation No. 78, §15).

"Broker" acts as sale intermediary (agent), compensated through commission. (Securities Law, art. 3). "Dealer" engaged in securities trading in its own name by public announcement of purchase/sale price for securities with obligation to buy/sell securities at quoted prices. (Id., art. 4). "Asset management" involves trust management of securities, funds to be invested in securities and securities received or obtained in

See Topical Index in front part of this volume.

SECURITIES . . . *continued*

course of asset management. (Id., art. 5). "Clearing activities" include mutual settlements of securities trading. (Id., art. 6). "Depository" provides custodial services and/or registration of ownership rights. (Id., art. 7). "Registrar" maintains shareholder registers for joint stock companies. (Id., art. 8). Registrar cannot engage in other types of professional investment activities. (Id., art. 10). "Investment consultant" consults on issue and placement of securities. (Regulation No. 78, §17). "Investment company" organizes issue of securities and provides guarantees for placement with third parties, invests directly in securities, and performs other securities transactions on its own behalf. (Id., §18). (However, investment consultant and investment company are not among professional organizations that operate on Russian securities market as defined in Securities Law.) "Investment fund" issues shares to accumulate funds from investors to invest in securities and bank accounts. (Id., §19). Investment fund must be joint stock company and may not use more than 5% of charter capital for acquisition of securities issued by one entity nor acquire more than 10% of securities issued by one entity. (Presidential Decree No. 1086 of Oct. 7, 1992). Certain special funds may hold up to 25% of securities issued by one entity. (Presidential Decree No. 2284 of Dec. 24, 1993).

Investment institutions must obtain licenses from FSC. (Securities Law, art. 39). There are three categories of licenses: (1) for professional organizations to operate on securities market, (2) to act as registrar, and (3) to operate stock exchange. Procedures for licensing registrars are set in FCS Instruction No. 6 of Aug. 30, 1995.

Nominees.—Securities may be acquired and held by nominee. Nominee has no ownership rights in securities. Nominee may not commingle its assets with securities held as nominee. Nominee holder may not transact with securities it holds as nominee without instructions from own and nominee not responsible for noncompliance of owner with antimonopoly or tax laws. Upon instruction of owner, registrars must enter nominee holder in shareholder register. (Presidential Decree No. 662 "On Measures of Formation of All-Russian Telecommunication System and Rights of Owners of Securities in Deposit" of July 3, 1995; arts. 2-3). Relationship between nominee and owner and between nominee holder and registrar regulated by State Property Committee of RF. (Instruction No. 840-p of Apr. 18, 1994, §6, and State Property Committee of RF Instructions No. 2002-p of July 26, 1994).

Mutual Funds ("MF").—MF legal status is primarily regulated by Civil Code ("CC") of Russian Federation ("RF") provisions on trust management (arts. 209, 1012-1026), Federal Law No. 15-FZ of Dec. 26, 1995 "On Putting in Force Part Two of the Civil Code of the Russian Federation" (art. 4), Federal Law No. 39-FZ of Apr. 22, 1996 "On Securities Market", Decree of President of RF No. 765 of July 26, 1995 "On Additional Measures for Increasing the Effectiveness of the Investment Policy of the RF" ("PD"), Federal Commission on Securities and Capital Market Decisions ("FCS acts") and State Tax Service Letter No. NP-2-01/80N of Dec. 15, 1995 ("STS letter"). PD refers to MF as instrument for activating Russian Federation investment policy. MF is defined to be not legal entity but "property complex" managed in trust by management company ("MC"). MF could be of open or interval type and invest correspondingly, subject to limitations and proportions, provided by FCS acts No. 12, 13, 14, either in securities or securities, bank deposits, real estate and proprietary rights to real estate. By acquiring investment shares in MF ("MF shares"), investors (except State agencies) enter trust management agreement with MC and thus join MF investment activity (PD, arts. 1 & 5), performed by MC in compliance with MF Rules and Prospectus for MF shares issue. MF may start operation upon registration of MF Rules and Prospectus for MF shares issue with FCS (or state agencies authorized by FCS). MF Rules and Prospectus for MF shares issue must contain compulsory terms embodied in Model Rules and Prospectus worked out by FCS. (FCS acts No. 13, 14, 15). PD and FCS acts lists mandatory conditions for registration of MF shares prospectus, provides principals for redemption of MF shares and defines rights of MF investors. (PD, arts. 7-21). FCS acts lists mandatory conditions for registration of MF shares prospectus, provides principal rules for redemption of MF shares and defines rights of MF investors. (Id., arts. 7-21).

Investment Shares.—MF shares as securities certify right of MF investor, upon presentation, to demand redemption of shares for return determined on basis of value of assets of MF as of date of redemption. Procedure for issuing MF investment shares, share distribution, share circulation, maintaining register of shares proprietors and registration of prospectus are established by FCS. Term of offer for investment shares is not limited, therefore investment shares issue is not subject for tax on operations with securities. (STS letter, art. 9). Issue of derivative securities from investment shares is not allowed. (Id., art. 1). Management company—commercial organization, which manages MF property solely in interests of investors (PD, art. 5, FCS act No. 11 of 10.10.95) referring to its management company status and name of particular MF it is acting for in this capacity. MC not entitled to exercise any kind of activity other than activity involving trust management of MF or management of non-state pension funds' assets, investment funds or specialized investment funds of privatization, which accumulated private citizens' privatization vouchers. Management company's own capital is to be not less than one billion rubles (approximately—U.S.$200,000). Requires license for MF trust management. (PD, art. 6, FCS act No. 11 of 10.10.95). Liable for harm (not just losses) to investors resulting from negligence or from conflict of interest. (CC art. 1022, PD, art. 11). MC reimbursed for expenses incurred for MF management out of MF property and must publish MF audited financial. (PD, art. 16). Physical persons could be managers of or form executive body of MC if they have qualification certificate, issued by FCS. Legal persons are not allowed to bring about functions of MF's executive body.

Taxation MFs enjoy comparatively liberal tax regime and let investors release investments from double taxation. MC pays property tax for MF real estate. MC not liable for profit tax in respect of MF assets increase. (STS letter).

STATUTES:

See topic Law Reports, Codes, Etc.

TAXATION:

Corporate Taxation.—Under RF Law No. 2116-1 "On Taxation of Profits of Enterprises and Organizations" of Dec. 27, 1991 as last amended Feb. 12, 1996 ("Profit Tax Law"), profit tax imposed on Russian legal entities, foreign legal entities conducting entrepreneurial activities in RF through "permanent representations" (concept similar to permanent establishment under OECD model) (Id., art. 1), and other foreign entities receiving income from Russian sources other than through operation of permanent representation (Id., art. 10).

Russian legal entities taxable on taxable profits from all sources worldwide. (Id., art. 12). Foreign legal entities operating through permanent representations in RF taxable on taxable profits derived from activities of their representations in RF. (Id., art. 3[a]). In certain cases, authorities permitted to impute income to permanent representation where it is otherwise impossible to determine attributable income. This imputation generally 25% of expenses entity incurs to run its Russian activities. (Id., art. 3[c]). Profit tax on foreign legal entities receiving income from Russian sources other than through permanent representation (e.g., recipients of loan interest, dividends, royalties, rentals, service fees and management fees) collected through withholding at source ("withholding tax").

Withholdings made on repatriation of profits and other cross-border payments due in currency in which remittance effected. (Profit Tax Law, art. 10). General withholding tax rate 15% on dividend and interest payments, 6% on freight income and 20% on royalty payments in respect of copyrights and licenses, rental payments and other forms of income derived from Russian sources. Last category quite broad and includes lease payments, payments for management services and any other income arising from use of assets or performance of services in RF without existence of permanent establishment. Such income taxed on gross basis. (Instruction of RF Main State Tax Service ["GNI RF"] No. 34 "On Taxation of Profits and Income of Foreign Legal Entities", of June 16, 1995, §5.2). Double tax treaties, including those to which USSR was party and RF honors, may stipulate reductions in these rates.

New income notification requirements apply. While originally interpreted to control outflow of "passive" income from Russian Federation, from Jan. 1, 1996 notification of Russian sourced income requirement has also been recommended for notifying tax authorities of any Russian sourced "active" income of foreign legal entities which operate in Russia through representative offices. (State Tax Service Methodological Recommendations, No. NP-6-06/652, of Dec. 20, 1995).

Taxable profits largely determined by provisions of statutory accounting related to deductibility of specific costs. Provisions may differ significantly from U.S. GAAP (e.g., deductibility of interest restricted).

Tax year is calendar year. Enterprises established in last quarter of calendar year may include period of three months or less in subsequent calendar years filed. (MinFin RF No. 170 "Statutory Accounting and Financial Statements" of Dec. 26, 1994, §34 ["Regulation No. 170"]).

Rates.—Federal corporate profits tax rate 13%. (Profit Tax Law, art. 2[13]). Various regions may set profits tax rate up to 22% for most entities and up to 30% for banks, insurance companies, brokers and intermediaries. Thus, combined rate of 35% (13% federal and 22% regional) applies for most taxpayers. (Banking is taxed at 43% combined rate.) Higher rates can apply to certain entertainment and gaming activities. Entities having branches (not separate legal entities) in different regions of RF required to apportion taxable profits between those regions. Although no guidance on computation of tax liability released, law suggests property and number of employees be used as apportionment factors. (Id., art. 1[2]).

Excess Wage Tax.—Tax was imposed on employer, not employees, on "excess" salaries, meaning amounts in excess of six times monthly minimum salary, at profits tax rate applicable to enterprise. (Profit Tax Law, art. 2[13]). (See topic Wages.) Tax is abolished from Jan. 1, 1996.

Depreciation.—Tax depreciation same as book depreciation. Statutory rules on depreciation rates highly specific, extending to over 100 pages of rates. Ordinarily, depreciation given on straight-line basis on historical cost. (Regulation of Gosplan, MinFin RF "On Depreciation of Fixed Assets", of Dec. 29, 1990, art. 12).

Since Jan. 1, 1991, accelerated depreciation at twice normal rates available for certain production assets of Russian legal entities. Mid-size Russian legal entities (employing from 15 to 200 employees) may also use accelerated rates to expense 50% of historical cost of newly purchased production equipment with useful life of more than three years in first year of operation. (RF Government Regulation "On Accelerate Depreciation and Revaluation of Fixed Assets", §7). Low book value items of one million rubles and items with useful life of less than one year allowed to be expensed. (Regulation No. 170, §46).

Capital gains (difference between selling price and historical cost) included in taxable profit and taxed at applicable profits tax rate. Historical cost adjusted periodically to reflect inflation. (Profit Tax Law, art. 2[4]). Historical cost of tangible fixed assets adjusted in accordance with certain documents allowing revaluation of such assets. Revaluations have occurred in June 1992, Jan. 1994, Jan. 1995 and Jan. 1996.

Dividends from one resident company to another taxed at source at rate of 15%. Dividends from resident company to nonresident taxed at 15%, unless lower rate stipulated by relevant double tax treaty.

Social Charges.—Russian employers must make social security (5.4%), pension fund (28%), employment fund (1.5%), and obligatory medical insurance (3.6%) contributions. (RF Law "On Insurance Rates to Social Funds", of Mar. 30, 1993, art. 1, and subsequent laws extending insurance rates to 1994, 1995, 1996; Procedures "On Contributions to Pension Fund", of Dec. 27, 1991, art. 1). Total amount payable, deductible for profits tax purposes, equal to 38.5% of each employee's gross salary.

Although law not clear on whether foreign entities conducting business in RF required to pay these contributions, social fund's administration considers foreign entities responsible for social fund contributions for Russian employees. Position with respect to foreign employees less certain, but pension fund (covering bulk of contributions) has stated it does not expect contributions in respect of foreign individuals working for foreign legal entities or Russian legal entities with foreign participation based on Law "On Foreign Investments in RF", of July 4, 1991, art. 34.

Payments and Returns.—Russian companies, including those with foreign ownership, must submit quarterly and annual reports and balances to tax and statistical authorities. Quarterly filing due within 30 days after end of reporting quarter, annual filing by Apr. 1 of year following reporting year. (Ordinance on Statutory Accounting and Financial Statements of 26 Dec. 1994, in RF §76). Annual returns and balances of

See Topical Index in front part of this volume.

TAXATION . . . *continued*
open joint stock companies, enterprises with turnover exceeding 500,000 times minimum monthly wage and entities with foreign ownership subject to audit by Russian audit firm. (Government Resolution No. 7 "On Main Criteria of Activities of Economic Participants" of Dec. 7, 1994, §§1, 4).

Tax treaties to which former USSR was party currently honored by RF, with exception of treaty with Hungary terminated Jan. 1, 1994. Treaties between RF and U.S. and Poland are now in force. New Treaties between RF and Sweden, Ireland, South Korea, Vietnam, Bulgaria, Romania, Uzbekistan ratified and enter into force from Jan. 1, 1996. Treaties between RF and U.K., Turkey, China and Hungary signed, but await ratification by parties involved.

Former USSR had treaties with following countries: Austria, Belgium, Bulgaria, Canada, Cyprus, Czechoslovakia, Denmark, Finland, France, Germany, Hungary, India, Italy, Japan, Malaysia, Mongolia, Netherlands, Norway, Poland, Romania, Spain, Sweden, Switzerland, U.K. and U.S.

Individual Taxation.—Art. 1 of RF Law No. 1998-1 "On Income Tax on Individuals" of Dec. 7, 1991 defines resident as individual physically present in RF for 183 days or more in calendar year. Residents taxed on worldwide income but nonresidents taxed only on their Russian source income. Rules can be modified by tax treaties. Current law suggests narrow view of Russian source income as only income paid to individual by Russian entity (arguably, also income paid by permanent representation).

Tax on Russian source income normally paid by withholding at source at graduated rates for residents (Id., art. 9) and at flat 20% for nonresidents (Id., art. 17). Income from sources outside RF assessed on current year basis. (Id., art. 12). Income received in foreign currency converted to rubles as of date of receipt or, for earned income, as of last day of month earned. Income of married persons taxed separately: no joint filing. Benefits-in-kind taxable. Taxable benefit cash equivalent generally defined as market value of benefit provided. Certain exemptions apply to foreign citizens who are residents for income tax purposes, notably with respect to accommodation and official cars provided to foreigners. (Id., art. 2).

Rates.—Taxable income for 1996 taxed at following rates:

Taxable income (rubles)	Tax (%)	Cumulative tax (rubles)
Up to 12,000,000	12	1,440,000
12,000,001 – 24,000,000	20	1,440,000 + 20% as exceeds 12,000,001 but does not exceed 24,000,000
24,000,001 – 36,000,000	25	3,840,000 + 25% as exceeds 24,000,000 but does not exceed 36,000,000
36,000,001 – 48,000,000	30	6,840,000 + 30% as exceeds 36,000,000 but does not exceed 48,000,000
Over 48,000,000	35	10,440,000 + 35% as exceeds 48,000,000.

For most expatriates, little or no deductions available and tax rate close to 30%. However, fluctuations of exchange rate may result in different effective tax rate on foreign currency income. For example, in 1993-1994 effective rate much lower (closer to 15% in 1994) due to ruble devaluation. Deductions enjoyed by most expatriates in home countries not available.

Social Security Contributions.—Russian nationals employed in RF by Russian or foreign legal entities required to contribute 1% of gross salary to pension fund, withheld at source by employer. Contribution deductible in determining taxable income. Self-employed individuals must register with pension fund and contribute 5% of income. Compulsory home country social security contributions by foreigners also treated as tax deductible.

Deductions and Exemptions.—All taxpayers entitled to individual exemption and exemptions for dependents equal to minimum wage. Exemptions for dependent children available to both spouses. (Id., art. 3 §6[b]). Certain donations also exempt as ex gratia payments on leaving employment. Deductions of up to 5,000 times minimum monthly wage in any one tax year available for expenditure incurred by individuals on purchasing or constructing own housing. (Id., art. 3, §6[c]). Farming income and income received from sale of agricultural products from private plots not taxable. (Id., art. 3, §1[s, y]).

Capital Gains.—Effective from 1993, sums received from sale of apartments and country houses in excess of 5,000 times minimum monthly wage taxable. For other property, limit for exception 1,000 times minimum monthly wage. Alternatively, individual taxed on "net income" basis (i.e., sales price less documented expenses incurred in obtaining income). (Id., art. 3, §1[r]).

Investment Income.—Interest paid to individuals on deposits by Russian banks and certain other deposit-takers and interest paid on Russian (and former Soviet) Government bonds exempt from tax. No specific exemptions provided for dividends subject to income tax. For dividends received by employee of paying company, tax withheld at employee's marginal tax rate on salary. Dividends paid to other individuals received net of income tax withheld at rate determined as if gross dividend were individual's only income for year. Dividends reinvested in research and development funds exempt from taxation. (Id., art. 3, §1[2]).

Returns and Payments.—If taxpayer's only income is income from employment, subject to withholding tax at source, individual not required to complete income tax return. If there is further liability to tax and total income received during reporting year exceeds lowest tax bracket, return must be completed and filed by Apr. 1 of year following under review. No extensions of this deadline allowed. (Id., §39). If return late, penalty of 10% of tax due based on return may be charged. Criminal sanctions could also apply. (UK RSFSR, arts. 162[1], [2]).

Foreign individuals resident in RF, receiving income from abroad, must file annual returns declaring income recieved in year under review if total income received during reporting year exceeds lowest tax bracket. In first year of residence, must file preliminary returns estimating income. (GNI RF Instruction No. 8 "On Applying Law on Taxation of Income of Individuals" of Mar. 20, 1992, art. 57).

Other Taxes.—

Value Added Tax ("VAT").—VAT, effective in RF from Jan. 1, 1992, operates under standard credit-invoice system where amount of tax liability is difference between VAT collected from purchasers/clients and amount of VAT paid to vendors/suppliers. General rate 20% on sales of goods/services in RF. Taxable sales include majority of domestic sales of goods/services. Certain food products and children's goods subject to lower 10% rate. Exported sales and services and list of other specified supplies of goods/services exempt from VAT. (GNI RF Instruction No. 1 "On Calculation and Payment Procedure of VAT" of Dec. 9, 1991 ["Instruction No. 1"] c. 9, art. 13). As of Jan. 1, there are new rules for what are considered exports of services. For many services decisive consideration in regard to where services are provided is where economic activity of recipient of services is located.

In addition to VAT, special tax at rate of 1.5% was collected in similar fashion. Separate filing for VAT and special tax was required. Special tax abolished as from Jan. 1, 1996. (RF Law "On Special Tax" of Feb. 23, 1993, art. 1).

Accredited representative offices from approximately 90 designated countries (as well as accredited employees of representative offices) exempt from VAT on rental payments. (Instruction No. 1, c. 5, art. 13[x]). Tax authorities require VAT on foreign currency receipts be collected and remitted in foreign currency. This position arguably contradicts art. 3 of RF Law "On Currency Regulation and Control" of Oct. 9, 1992 but has not yet been challenged. Changes to VAT law introduced system of withholding and remitting VAT by Russian purchaser of goods and services sold on RF territory by foreign entity, not registered with tax authorities, through so-called reverse-charge mechanism. (RF Law "On VAT" of Dec. 6, 1991, art. 7[5]).

Tax on Securities.—Under art. 3 of law "On Taxation of Securities Transactions" of Dec. 12, 1991 following tax on securities applies from Jan. 1, 1992: On issue of securities, 0.8% of nominal value.

Excise duties on domestic sales of certain goods produced in RF effective from Jan. 1, 1992. Excise duties on imports implemented from Feb. 1, 1993. List of goods subject to duty includes alcohol, tobacco, cars, trucks with capacity of up to 1.25 tons, carpets, jewelry, diamonds, natural leather, fur clothing, yachts, hunting guns, car tires and gasoline. Excise rates differ for domestic products and imports. Rates are percentages of customs value and range from 10% for engine oil to 400% for nearly pure alcohol. Effective from Jan. 1, 1995 all imported goods subject to excise duties cleared through customs only if goods have specified excise duty stamps. (Decision of Government of RF No. 319 "On Introduction of Excise Duty Stamp" of Apr. 14, 1994, arts. 1, 5). With some exceptions, export sales exempt from excises.

Export Duties.—See topic Customs (Duty).

Tax on Property.—Business property tax levied on property belonging to Russian entities, including companies with foreign participation, representative offices and branches. Tax based on net value of fixed and intangible assets, inventories and expenses incurred as of certain dates. (GNI RF Instruction No. 33 "On Procedure of Calculation and Paying Property Tax" of June 8, 1995, §2, art. 2). Representative offices may use home country depreciation rates for purposes of property tax calculations. (GNI RF Instruction No. 24 "On Calculation and Payment to Budget of Tax on Property of Foreign Legal Entities Carrying Out Activity Via Permanent Representative Offices and Other Separate Subdivisions Based in RF" of Feb. 23, 1994, §2, art. 2). Assets excluded from tax include monetary assets, social and cultural assets, environmental protection assets, agricultural equipment, pipelines, electricity lines and land. Prepaid rent included. Under certain tax treaties, foreign enterprises without permanent establishment in RF may be exempt from tax, at least with regard to movable property (e.g., Double Tax Treaty USSR-Germany, USSR-Austria).

Maximum tax rate 2% (RF Law No. 2030-1 "On Property Tax of Enterprises" of Dec. 13, 1991, art. 6), but specific rates can be fixed by local authorities. In Moscow, rate for 1994 and 1995 was 1.5%, effective from Apr. 1, 1996 tax rate is 2% (however, certain categories eligible to tax benefits on this tax). In St. Petersburg rate for 1994 was 1% and rate from Jan. 1, 1995 is 2%.

Tax on Vehicles.—Taxes imposed on purchase of vehicles and on vehicle owners. Tax on purchase, applicable to legal entities but not individuals, defined as percentage of purchase price of vehicle excluding VAT, excises and customs duties (for imported vehicles), 20% for cars, vans and trucks and 10% for trailers and semi-trailers. Tax on vehicle owners applies to both individuals and entities and levied at rate of 1.3 rubles per engine horsepower. This tax is federal tax but rates can be increased by local regions. (RF Law "On Road Funds" of Oct. 18, 1991, arts. 6-7).

Road Use Tax applies to Russian companies, including companies with foreign participation, representative offices and branches from Jan. 1, 1992. Tax rate applies to gross sales of company excluding VAT and excises. For trading companies, both retail and wholesale, rate of 0.03% and for all other entities rate of 0.4% applies. This tax is federal tax but rates can be increased by local regions. (RF Law "On Road Funds" of Oct. 18, 1991, art. 5). Road Use Tax rate was increased to 2.5% of sales and 0.15% of trade turnover (previously 1.5% and 0.11%) for Moscow as of Apr. 1, 1996. (Changes to the Moscow Law No. 9-45 of May 25, 1994).

Transport tax, effective from Jan. 1, 1994, applies to all enterprises except state-financed, at rate of 1% based on total payroll. Tax decuctible for profit tax purposes. (Presidential Decree No. 2270 of Dec. 22, 1994, §25[b]).

Tax on Using Name "Russia" or "Russian Federation".—.05% tax on sales of trading companies, both retail and wholesale, and 0.5% tax on turnover of other enterprises charged for using words "Russia" or "Russian Federation" in name of any company. (RF Law No. 4737 "On Tax on Using Name 'Russia', 'RF'" of Apr. 2, 1993, art. 2).

Oil sales tax levied on companies carrying out domestic sales of oil products. Taxable base is wholesale price excluding VAT or, in case of entities buying and reselling oil products, difference between VAT exclusive sales and purchase prices. Tax rate is 25%. (RF Law "On Road Funds" of Oct. 18, 1991, art. 4).

Inheritance and gift tax charged on specified list of items inherited by or given to Russian individuals. List of items includes buildings, cars, jewelry, garages, currency values and securities. Uncertain if tax applies to gifts or inherited property located outside RF. Tax rates different for inherited property and gifts but vary from 3% to 40% of value of property. Rates depend on degree of relationships. (RF Law "On Inheritance Tax" of Dec. 12, 1991, art. 3).

Expense-based taxes are:

Advertisement tax—5% of expense (including indirect);

Transport tax—1% of annual salary fund (ASF) (which approximates [all inclusive] payroll for the year);

Educational establishments maintenance tax—1% of ASF.

See Topical Index in front part of this volume.

TAXATION . . . *continued*

Local Taxes.—Local tax authorities have significant powers to levy local taxes and determine rates of certain non-local taxes such as profits, road use (gross turnover based) and property (asset based) tax. While tax rates and bases of local taxes often determined or restricted by federal instructions, imposition of these taxes largely discretionary and overall tax burden can vary from region to region. In particular, some local authorities have responded to absence of profits among many Russian enterprises by levying taxes based on gross sales, thus yielding possibility of significant tax burdens even on loss making enterprises. Plans to limit taxation power of local authorities pending.

RF Tax Code currently discussed, adoption likely.

TORTS:

RF tort law found primarily in law of "obligations" in Part I and cc. 59 and 60 in Part II of new Civil Code. With some exceptions for moral damages (see subhead Libel, infra), tort liability generally requires culpability, with burden of proof on respondent to show no harm caused. (GK RF, art. 1064[2]). Harm caused to health or property of individual or legal entity must be compensated by tortfeasor, or if offender less than 14 years (plus in other exceptional cases) and if provided by law, then compensation by person who did not cause harm, such as parents of minor. Unless actions of respondent violate moral principles of society, harm caused with consent of claimant does not create liability for respondent. In cases provided by law, compensation required for harm caused by lawful actions. (Id., art 1064[1-3]). If danger of future harm exists, court may order respondent to stop or interrupt activity unless such termination against public interest. Such court action does not deprive individuals and legal entities from right to claim remedies. (Id., art. 1065). Employer liable for harm caused by employee during work. Government liable for harm caused by acts of its agencies, employees, prosecution and militia. (Id., arts. 1068-1070). Persons engaged in extrahazardous activities (operation of automobile included) face strict liability for damages caused, unless can establish harm result of force majeure or claimant grossly negligent. (Id., art. 1079). Contributory negligence not bar to recovery but considered in damages award, based on comparative fault. (Id., art. 1083). Wrongful death action available to persons in statutory class who can establish dependency on decedent at time of death. (Id., arts. 1088, 4089[2]). New Civil Code provides separate remedies rules for damage caused to life and health of individual (Id., arts. 1084-1094) and product liability (Id., arts. 1091-1095).

Libel.—Individual may petition court to demand retraction of data damaging individual's honor, dignity or business reputation, unless disseminator can prove information accurate. Such protection available posthumously. Libelous material disseminated through mass media must be retracted in same media, and injured party entitled to publication of rejoinder in same media. Defamed individual also entitled to demand compensation for losses and moral damages incurred as result of defamation. (Id., arts. 151-152, 1099). If moral harm results from dissemination of defamatory information discrediting individual's honor, dignity and business reputation, compensation of moral damages awarded regardless of fault of offender. (Id., art. 1100). Type of physical and emotional suffering taken into account by court when determining amount of compensation for moral harm. (Id., art. 1101). Rules protecting business reputation of individuals also applicable to business reputation of legal entities. (Id., art. 152).

Resolution of RF Supreme Court Plenum "On Some Issues of Application of Law on Compensation for Moral Damages" of Dec. 20, 1994 ruled that moral damage may include suffering caused by, inter alia, alienation of relatives and friends, inability to continue in social or work-related activity, exposure of family or medical secret, and injury to honor, dignity or business reputation.

See topic Damages for tort remedies.

TRADEMARKS:

Trademarks regulated by Law of RF No. 3520-1 "On Trademarks, Service Marks and Appellations of Origin of Goods" of Sept. 23, 1992 ("Trademark Law"). For legal protection trademark must be registered with RF Patent Agency (Rospatent). (Trademark Law, arts. 1, 8).

Duration of Protection.—If mark registered and trademark certificate issued, trademark owner has exclusive right to use and dispose of mark for ten years from date application received by Rospatent, with renewal for additional periods of ten years each. (Id., arts. 4, 16).

Infringement.—Trademark rights infringed if person without authorization manufactures, uses, imports, offers for sale or sells trademark or designation similar to trademark. (Id., World Intellectual Property Organization Trademark Law Treaty, art. 4). Infringement entails both civil and criminal liability. (Id., art. 46).

RF was an original signer of WIPO Trademark Law Treaty concluded in Geneva on Oct. 28, 1994.

TREATIES:

Pursuant to RF Constitution, norms established by international treaties have precedence over federal laws and acts. (Id., art. 15[4]). RF legislation and practice on implementation of international agreements conforms generally to provisions of Vienna Convention on Law of Treaties of May 23, 1969, brought into effect in USSR on July 13, 1986. Since demise of Soviet Union, RF has adopted all obligations of USSR under international treaties. (MinForAff RF Letter No. 11/UGP, Jan. 13, 1992).

International Agreements Effective in RF.—MinForAff RF publishes "Collection of Treaties in Force" compilation, with three-year delay, of conventions, treaties and bilateral agreements to which RF/USSR is signatory. Most recent agreements found in executive and legislative registers, published weekly, or in monthly Bulletin of International Treaties, currently in third year of publication.

Prominent treaties to which RF is signatory include: UN (New York) Convention on Recognition and Enforcement of Foreign Arbitral Awards of June 10, 1958 (effective in USSR on Nov. 20, 1960); UN (Vienna) Convention on Contracts for International Sale of Goods of Apr. 11, 1980 (effective in RF from Sept. 1, 1990, with some alterations as to contract formalities); Hague Convention the Abolishing Requirement of Legalization for Foreign Public Documents of Oct. 5, 1961 (signed by RF May 31, 1992) and Vienna Convention on Law of Treaties of May 23, 1969 (effective in USSR on July 13, 1986, with certain reservations as to jurisdiction of International Court of Justice, subsequently relaxed by USSR/RF legislation). Environmental, human rights and weapons accords comprise substantial portion of Soviet/RF treaty law.

Recent Developments.—Bilateral Investment Treaty between U.S. and RF executed by U.S. and RF on June 17, 1992, providing guarantees and dispute resolution provisions for foreign investment activities. On Nov. 3, 1994, RF Government declared intention to accede to Universal Copyright Convention, and on Dec. 9, 1994 acceded to Berne Convention for Protection of Literary and Artistic Works. RF has recently signed, or is preparing to sign, numerous other conventions, treaties and bilateral agreements, primarily in areas of customs, taxation and banking.

Commonwealth of Independent States ("CIS").—On Dec. 12, 1991, RF ratified Minsk Agreement creating CIS, accord later joined by total of 11 former republics of USSR. While CIS Member-States generally have adopted USSR legislation as foundation, they have full national sovereignty to amend or abolish laws and to enter into international compacts. By Protocol to Commonwealth Pact, CIS states have agreed to fulfill obligations of U.N. Charter. Most prominent CIS economic accord is Agreement on Cooperation in Sphere of Foreign Economic Activity, signed in Tashkent, Uzbekistan, on May 15, 1992. On July 6, 1992, CIS Members established Economic Court of CIS to be located in Minsk, Belarus.

For discussion of treaties on judicial cooperation and assistance, see topics Execution of Judgments and Awards; Actions. For discussion of double tax treaties see topic Taxation. Individual topics include references to subject matter treaties where appropriate.

TRUSTS:

Presidential Decree No. 2296 "On Trusts" of Dec. 24, 1993 introduced trust concept. (art. 21). New Civil Code identifies trust agreements as arrangement under which one party ("settlor of trust") gives another party ("trustee") property for certain period of time. Trustee manages property in trust for benefit of settlor of trust or third party designated by settlor of trust ("beneficiary"). (GK RF, art. 1012[1]). Trustee must perform transactions with property in trust on its own behalf, specifying in agreements that it is acting as trustee. (Id., art. 1012[2]). All types of property, movable and immovable, including but not limited to enterprises, securities, rights evidenced by securities, exclusive rights and property complexes may be subject of trusts. Monetary assets held in trust only when specified by law. (Id., art. 1013[1]). Settlor of trust must be owner of property held in trust unless otherwise provided by law. (Id., art. 1014). Trustee cannot be beneficiary under trust arrangement. (Id., art. 1015[3]). Trust agreements must specify property in trust, name(s) of beneficiary(ies), amount and form of fee payable to trustee, and term of agreement, which may not exceed five years. Trust agreement must be in writing and registered when provided by law. (Id., art. 1017). Trustee must hold property in trust separately from own assets and maintain separate balance sheet for trust operations. (Id., art. 1018).

WAGES:

Minimum wage established by law and binding on all employers. (RF Labor Code, art. 78). Precise amount set initially by RSFSR Law "On Increasing of Social Guarantees to Workers" of Apr. 19, 1991, RF Law "On Minimum Amount of Monthly Wage", indexed periodically for inflation. Federal Law No. 40-FZ "On the Increase of the Minimum Rate of the Remuneration of Labor" of Apr. 10, 1996 established minimum monthly wage at 75,900 rubles per month effective Apr. 1, 1996. Monthly wage must be paid twice per month. (RF Labor Code, art. 96). See topic Labor Relations.

WAIVER:

No provision of Russian law expressly affirms validity of waiver, but numerous provisions expressly prohibit or restrict validity of waiver, e.g., citizen's full or partial waiver of legal capacity void unless otherwise provided by law. (GK RF, arts. 9[2], 22[3]) and agreement between participants in partnership waiving right of participants to withdraw void. (Id., art. 77[27]). New Civil Code permits trust to be terminated if settlor of trust waives rights under trust, when provided by law. (Id., art. 1024[1]).

WILLS:

Testamentary instruments must generally be signed by testator and notarized to take legal effect. (Civ. Fund, art. 155[2]; GK RSFSR 1964, arts. 540-541). Testator has broad control over dispositions, may exclude almost any heir-at-law except minor (including adopted) children of testator and, to extent can prove inability to earn income, spouse, parents and sufficiently related or dependent disabled individuals. Such persons entitled to at least two-thirds of share they would have received in intestacy. (GK RSFSR 1964, art. 535; Civ. Fund, art. 155[3]). Household effects and furnishings remain with heirs-at-law who lived with testator for not less than one year before death. (GK RSFSR 1964, art. 533).

Devisees may refuse to accept devises in favor of other testamentary beneficiaries, heirs-at-law, government or other organizations. If designee refusing gift fails to designate substitute taker, share passes to other designees in will, other intestate takers or, if there are no other designees or heirs-at-law, to state. (Id., art. 550).

Revocation of will effected by declaration to notary office or local administration, writing new certified will stating intent to revoke and drafting certified will with different dispositive provisions which revoke prior will, fully or in part, to extent inconsistent. (Id., art. 543).

Testamentary designees must wait up to six months for rights of ownership in bequest, until executor ascertains all persons entitled to share in estate. Notary office issues heirs (term used for both testate and intestate takers) certificates of right to inherit six months after date probate opens. (Id., art. 558). Creditors of testator may file claims with executor or notary office within same six month period, and all

See Topical Index in front part of this volume.

WILLS . . . *continued*
testamentary beneficiaries (of specific, general or residuary gifts) equally liable for such claims, pro rata, to extent of gift. (Id., arts. 553-554).

Cash deposits in state banks, depending on charter or rules of institution, may be conveyed by simple execution of transfer order to be effective upon death. If order properly filed, bank account not considered part of testator's estate for any purpose.

No will specific provision of new Civil Code or Civil Fundamentals directly addresses requisites of testamentary capacity, including issues of duress or undue influence. These dangers presumably minimized by notarization requirement and new Civil Code provisions dealing generally with incapacity, fraud, duress and resulting invalidity of transactions in which these elements are found. (GK RF, arts. 177, 179).

See topics Executors and Administrators; Taxation.

SAUDI ARABIA LAW DIGEST REVISER

White & Case
1155 Avenue of the Americas
New York, New York 10036-2787
Telephone: 212-819-8200
Fax: 212-354-8113

and

Law Office of Hassan Mahassni
in Association with White & Case

Jeddah, Saudi Arabia Office: Al-Nakeel Center, 4th Floor, Madinah Road on Palestine Circle, P.O. Box 2256, Jeddah 21451. Telephone: 966 2 665 4353. Fax: 966 2 669 2996.

Riyadh, Saudi Arabia Office: Law Office of Hassan Mahassni, The Saudi Ceramic Company Building, 5th Floor, King Fahd Highway. Postal address: P.O. Box 17411, Riyadh, 11484. Telephone: (966 1) 464 4006. Fax: (966 1) 465 1348.

Reviser Profile

General Information: White & Case is an international law firm with offices in New York, Paris, London, Brussels, Stockholm, Helsinki, Moscow, Prague, Warsaw, Budapest, Tokyo, Hong Kong, Singapore, Bombay, Jakarta, Hanoi, Almaty, Tashkent, Bangkok, Istanbul, Ankara, Johannesburg, and Mexico City, associated offices in Jeddah and Riyadh, Saudi Arabia, and other U.S. offices in Washington, D.C., Los Angeles and Miami. White & Case was formed in 1901 and has approximately 650 lawyers worldwide. Among others, the U.S., French, Polish, Swedish, English, Mexican, Czech, Finnish, and Saudi Arabian nationalities are represented in the partnership.

White & Case offers corporate, banking, real estate, litigation and tax advisory services to clients in a broad range of industrial enterprises and financial and related services businesses who operate on a local, regional or global basis. The firm also has a number of complementary specialized practices, including mergers and acquisitions, environmental, broker/dealer regulation, ERISA and pension planning, executive compensation arrangements, intellectual property, transportation asset financing, computer law, trusts and estates, immigration, entertainment/communications and government contracting.

The Law Office of Hassan Mahassni is one of Saudi Arabia's oldest and most respected legal practices. The firm was established in 1970 by Saudi practitioner Hassan Mahassni and has offices in Jeddah and Riyadh. Mr. Mahassni is a partner at White & Case.

The Law Office of Hassan Mahassni's practice is both local and regional in scope and is focused primarily on corporate, commercial and financial transactions including project financings, engineering and construction contract documentation, joint ventures, mergers and acquisitions, secured, unsecured and Islamic-based financings, debt restructuring, bank regulatory work, and maritime, insolvency and intellectual property matters. Commercial litigation in all of Saudi Arabia's courts and administrative bodies, arbitration and labor law advice are also significant practice areas.

White & Case's network of offices in the major commercial centers around the world enables the firm to provide a consistently excellent standard of professionalism, client services, administrative support and efficiency to local, regional and international clients. The firm's lawyers are multilingual, multicultural in perspective and experienced in assisting clients with the legal issues arising out of complex domestic and cross-border transactions.

Practice Areas: White & Case offices around the world provide legal services in a variety of practice areas.

Lending and Financial: White & Case represents over seventy-five international and domestic banks in a broad range of secured and unsecured transactions, leasing and equipment financing, Islamic-structured financings, project financing, private placements, and municipal financing.

Sovereign Representation: The firm has represented more foreign countries in the areas of government borrowing and debt renegotiation than any other law firm in the world.

Privatization: White & Case has played a major role in a number of privatizations, including the first Turkish privatization and the development of Turkey's capital markets, the design and implementation of the Polish Mass Privatization Program, the largest cross-border privatization in Czechoslovakia to date, and a wide-range of privatization programs in Russia, Estonia, Latvia and other former states of the Soviet Union.

Mergers and Acquisitions: The firm advises on domestic and cross-border mergers, acquisitions and leveraged buyouts, takeover defenses, tender offer financing, and conducts takeover litigation.

Project Finance: The firm is an acknowledged leader in project finance and equipment finance, including energy-related projects such as cogeneration facilities, power plants and refineries, and aircraft and other equipment financing and leasing.

Securities and Capital Markets: The firm advises as to capital market transactions such as credit-enhanced facilities, structured receivables financing, money market preferred stock issues, domestic and Eurocurrency offerings, mortgage- and receivables-backed financings and swaps.

Corporate, Bank, Institutional and Private Client Representation: The firm has an extensive general corporate, bank regulatory and financial services practice, provides general local and international tax advice, and acts for private clients and fiduciaries.

Workouts and Bankruptcy: The firm represents lenders, borrowers, creditor committees and other participants in the adjustment of debt outside or inside of bankruptcy proceedings.

Real Estate: White & Case advises lenders, investors, owners and developers in a broad range of activities including acquisition, sale, leasing, planning, zoning, permitting, development, environmental audit, financing and other matters.

Litigation: This area includes administrative law, antitrust, trade regulation and unfair competition, international and domestic arbitrations, bank litigation, commodities, employment, environmental liability, product liability, securities and taxation litigation.

Environmental Law: The firm advises on regulatory matters, provides representation in compliance disputes, and counsels clients worldwide with respect to potential liabilities.

Intellectual Property and Computer Law: White & Case has a worldwide practice in all aspects of intellectual property and litigation, including patents, trade secrets, unfair competition, copyright, computer law and the counseling and negotiation of technology-related agreements and intellectual property licenses.

Engineering and Construction Law: The firm assists with all legal aspects of civil engineering and construction projects, including documentation, arbitration and litigation.

European Economic Community Law: White & Case actively participates in mergers and acquisitions, competition law, cross-border financings, capital marketing law, and local and transnational tax planning and intellectual property law within the EEC.

SAUDI ARABIA LAW DIGEST

(The following is a list of all Topics, including cross-references, covered in this Digest.)

SAUDI ARABIA LAW DIGEST

Revised for 1997 edition by

WHITE & CASE, of the New York Bar

and

LAW OFFICE OF HASSAN MAHASSNI

IN ASSOCIATION WITH WHITE & CASE, of the Saudi Arabian Bar.

(Abbreviations used are: BASR—Bankruptcy Avoidance Settlement Regulations; CCL—Commercial Court Law; DZIT—Zakat and Income Tax Department; GCC—Gulf Co-Operation Council; GTR—Government Tenders Regulations; H—Hejira; NIR—Negotiable Instruments Regulations; SAMA—Saudi Arabian Monetary Agency; Shari'ah—Islamic law; SLWL—Saudi Labor and Workmen Law; SR—Saudi Riyal; SRC—Saudi Regulations for Companies. Dates used throughout refer to the Hejira calendar followed by the corresponding Gregorian calendar dates. Saudi Arabian jurisprudence follows the Hanbali school of Islam. Saudi Arabia is a member of the GCC and the Arab League.)

ACKNOWLEDGMENTS:

Document executed before notary public in foreign jurisdiction which is required to be used in Saudi Arabia should have notary public's signature thereon authenticated by Saudi Consul in foreign jurisdiction, which typically requires one or more prior local authentications and counter-authentications in that jurisdiction. If not already executed in Arabic language, such document must thereafter be translated into Arabic by duly licensed translator and submitted to Ministry of Foreign Affairs in Saudi Arabia for further authentication. If such document is to be submitted to Saudi public notary or Saudi courts, further authentication by Saudi Ministry of Justice in Saudi Arabia will be required. Document may also be executed before foreign consul located in Saudi Arabia, followed by translation into Arabic, authentication by Saudi Ministry of Foreign Affairs and, if necessary, Saudi Ministry of Justice as aforesaid.

Certain types of documents such as Saudi limited liability company's articles of association, and real property title deeds and mortgages must be executed by and before Saudi notary public.

See topic Notaries Public.

ACTIONS:

Depending on subject matter of controversy, civil actions are brought before Shari'ah courts (primarily family law, and real property ownership and leasing matters), Boards of Grievances (disputes with public sector, general private sector commercial disputes, enforcement of foreign judgments, trademark, copyright and patent disputes, and foreign investment license disputes), Negotiable Instruments Offices (actions based on negotiable instruments), Commission for the Settlement of Banking Disputes (locally known as SAMA Committee) (banking related disputes other than those involving negotiable instruments), and Commissions for the Settlement of Labor Disputes (disputes arising under SLWL).

Most private sector commercial disputes may be submitted to arbitration under Saudi Arbitration Regulations regime (Royal Decree No. M/46 dated 12.7.1403 H. [Apr. 25, 1983] and Council of Ministers Resolution No. 7/2021/M dated 8.9.1405 H. [May 27, 1985]) which among other things mandates approval of arbitration agreement by Saudi court or tribunal which otherwise would hear dispute giving rise to arbitration, and further requires such court or tribunal to hear objections to arbitral award, and to ratify award prior to judicial enforcement thereof.

Under Shari'ah doctrines applicable in Saudi Arabia, Saudi court or tribunal will consider and apply only Saudi Arabian law, notwithstanding existence of contractual governing law clauses to contrary.

ALIENS:

In general, aliens have same civil rights as citizens. Aliens are subject to jurisdiction of Saudi courts and tribunals if they reside in Saudi Arabia, or if cause of action arose out of Saudi Arabian marriage, certain other family law matters, or if cause of action relates to Saudi Arabian assets, or obligations initiated or performed in Saudi Arabia.

Only citizens and, in certain limited circumstances, nationals of other GCC states are allowed to own real property. Only citizens and other GCC nationals may engage in commercial trading activities. Saudi entity having non-Saudi shareholders which is duly licensed under Foreign Capital Investment Code is allowed to own real property for corporate purposes subject to obtaining license from Ministry of Interior (Regulations for non-Saudis Taking Possession of Real Property in The Kingdom, Royal Decree No. M/22 dated 12.7.1390 H. [Sept. 13, 1970]), but in practice such licenses are infrequently granted.

Only Saudi citizens and other GCC nationals are permitted to hold publicly traded shares of Saudi joint stock companies.

Alien (other than GCC national) must obtain visa to enter, and must obtain permit to reside in, Saudi Arabia. Visas or permits are not granted upon arrival and must be obtained in advance. Visa and residence permit requirements are onerous, subject to change without notice, and strictly observed by authorities.

See topics Corporations; Foreign Investment; Marriage.

ARBITRATION:

See topic Actions.

ASSIGNMENTS:

As general rule, assignment of causes of action, claims, etc. is not enforceable under Shari'ah principles, but assignment of debts or monies is enforceable.

ASSIGNMENTS FOR BENEFIT OF CREDITORS:

See topic Bankruptcy.

ASSOCIATIONS:

See topic Corporations.

ATTACHMENT:

Attachment in advance of judgment is available upon application to court or tribunal having primary jurisdiction in respect of merits of action, or in urgent cases by application to Ministry of the Interior. (Precautionary Distraint of Property Regulations, Royal Decree No. M/4 dated 1.3.1410 H. [Oct. 2, 1989]; see also NIR, Art. 67). Attachment applications are required to be decided within 15 days of submission to relevant court or tribunal. Most movable and real property may be attached. (CCL, Royal Decree No. M/32 dated 15.1.1350 H. [June 1, 1931], Art. 572). Party seeking attachment is required to post security, usually guarantee of Saudi Arabian bank.

Plaintiff in civil action may in certain circumstances obtain order from relevant court or tribunal restraining defendant from traveling outside of Saudi Arabia prior to or during pendency of such action. Such restriction can usually be lifted by defendant's appointment of attorney-in-fact to appear in local legal proceedings and furnishing of security. In certain circumstances individual debtor may be imprisoned for nonpayment. (Private Rights Claims Regulations, Minister of Interior Resolution No. 20 dated 21.1.1406 H. [Oct. 5, 1985]).

BANKRUPTCY:

The Saudi Arabian Bankruptcy Code (CCL, Arts. 103-149) was enacted over 60 years ago and contemplates an age when commerce was undertaken by individual traders operating entirely within Saudi Arabia. Although drafted in terms of personal bankruptcy, it is generally accepted that Code also applies to corporate bankruptcies.

Bankrupt is defined in Code as "a person whose debts exceed his assets and who is thereby unable to discharge his liability for such debts." Code stipulates three categories of bankruptcy: "real", "negligent" and "fraudulent". "Real" bankrupt is defined as "a person who carries on trade with [sufficient capital]; who keeps proper books and does not spend lavishly but whose assets are lost through fire, flood or other natural causes . . . "Negligent" bankrupt is defined as "a person who . . . spends lavishly, fails to reveal to, or actively conceals from his creditors his insolvency and carries on trading until he exhausts his capital." "Fraudulent" bankrupt is defined as "an imposter . . . [who] practises tricks and intrigues with regard to his capital or makes false entries of imaginary debts . . . in his books . . . or keeps improper books . . ." Determination of what type of bankruptcy obtains in particular case is factual matter determined by competent tribunal which at present is Board of Grievances, Commercial Part.

Under Bankruptcy Avoidance Settlement Rgulations (Royal Decree No. M/16 dated 4.9.1416 H. [Jan. 24, 1996] incorporating Council of Ministers Resolution No. 129 dated 2.9.1416H. [Jan. 22, 1996]), commercial debtors (individual or corporate) may seek "amicable conciliation" with creditors through local chamber of commerce committees established for this purpose. If such conciliation is unsuccessful or if debtor believes such conciliation unlikely to succeed, BASR permits debtor to apply to Board of Grievances, Commercial Part, for order to convene "settlement procedures" with creditors under Board supervision to avoid application of Bankruptcy Code. BASR expressly provides that initiation of settlement procedures under its regime will stay litigation against debtor and will not result in acceleration of debtor's indebtedness. Settlement procedures under BASR require approval of at least two-thirds of holders of undisputed debt. In accordance with Shari'ah principles which would not permit discharge of debts by operation of law and without creditor's consent, BASR provides that creditors not joining settlement shall be repaid as determined by Board of Grievances. BASR expressly contemplates issuance of implementing rules covering procedural matters which at July, 1996 had not yet been promulgated.

BILLS AND NOTES:

NIR (Royal Decree No. M/37 dated 11.10.1383 H. [Feb. 24, 1964], as am'd by Royal Decree No. M/45 dated 12.9.1409 H. [Apr. 18, 1989]) regulates issuance and use of bills of exchange, order promissory notes and checks. NIR protest and notice provisions have been implemented. (Ministry of Commerce Resolution No. 487 dated 19.6.1411 H. [Jan. 5, 1991] and Explanatory Note). In private sector transactions, negotiable instruments may be prepared and negotiated in English language.

Jurisdiction over claims relating to negotiable instruments lies with Negotiable Instruments Offices, which are specialized adjudicating authorities operating under purview of Ministry of Commerce. In order for Negotiable Instruments Office to accept action on negotiable instrument for consideration, it must first satisfy itself that instrument in question meets appropriate tests therefor stipulated in NIR.

Bills of exchange must contain: (i) Words "bill of exchange", (ii) unconditional order to pay specified sum, (iii) name of drawee, (iv) date of maturity, (v) place of payment, (vi) name of payee, (vii) date and place of making, and (viii) signature of drawer.

Endorsements must be unconditional and partial endorsements are void. Endorsements in blank are permitted.

Bill of exchange may be drawn payable at sight, after specified period from sight, after specified period from making, or on specified day. Bill of exchange payable at sight is due upon mere presentation thereof and must be presented within a year from date of its making. Drawer may extend or shorten this period.

See Topical Index in front part of this volume.

BILLS AND NOTES . . . *continued*

Acceptance must be unconditional. Bill of exchange payable after specified period from sight must be presented for acceptance within one year from date thereof unless drawer extends or shortens this period.

Any mention of or term relating to interest in bill of exchange is deemed void.

Order promissory notes must contain: (i) Order stipulation or word "order", (ii) unconditional promise to pay specified sum, (iii) date of maturity, (iv) place of payment, (v) name of payee, (vi) date and place of making, and (vii) signature of maker.

Most of provisions in NIR relating to bills of exchange are expressed to be applicable to order promissory notes.

Any provision in note purporting to provide for alternative or successive dates of payability (such as acceleration for default clause) is considered of no effect. Demand order promissory notes must be presented for payment within one year after date of making thereof.

Checks must contain: (i) Word "check", (ii) unconditional order to pay specified sum, (iii) name of drawee, (iv) place of payment, (v) date and place of making, and (vi) signature of maker.

Checks must be drawn on bank, and may be expressed to be payable to bearer. Check made payable to specified person is negotiable by endorsement.

Checks are payable at sight. Use of undated, postdated or incorrectly dated checks is proscribed. Issuance of check without sufficient funds on account is criminal offense.

Under NIR, checks drawn and made payable in Saudi Arabia must be presented for payment within one month from date of making; checks drawn abroad and made payable in Saudi Arabia must be presented for payment within three months from date of making, although in practice these limitations are not usually strictly adhered to.

NIR contains provisions for certified and crossed checks.

CALENDAR:

Hejira calendar is official calendar. Hejira year is comprised of 12 lunar months, each having 29 or 30 days. Hejira year has 354 days. Minister of Commerce has directed that all Saudi entities (including Saudi entities with foreign shareholders) must have fiscal years based on Hejira calendar.

CHATTEL MORTGAGES:

See topic Mortgages.

COMMERCIAL REGISTER:

Each entity (including sole proprietorships, limited liability companies with non-Saudi shareholders, and branch offices of foreign entities) conducting business within Saudi Arabia is required to be registered with Ministry of Commerce (locally referred to as commercial registration) in appropriate geographical area in which such business is being conducted. (Commercial Register Code, Royal Decree No. 21/1/4470 dated 9.11.1375 H. [June 17, 1956] and Minister of Commerce Resolution No. 151 dated 17.8.1403 H. [May 29, 1983]).

Entity in respect of which license under Foreign Capital Investment Code has been issued must provide evidence of such license in order to obtain commerial registration.

Under commercial registration scheme, separate registration is required for head office and for branch offices of registrant. Upon due registration "commercial registration certificate" is issued which contains among other things registrant's name, address, its legal form, registered activities, name of manager(s) and directors, place and date of registration, and commercial registration number.

Commercially registered entity must include on all of its correspondence its address, commercial registration number and, in case of limited liability entity, amount of its paid-in capital.

See topics Corporations and Foreign Investment.

CONSTITUTION, GOVERNMENT AND SOURCE OF LAW:

In 1932, King Abdul Aziz bin Abdul Rahman Al-Faisal Al-Saud established The Kingdom of Saudi Arabia from Kingdoms of Hejaz, Nejd and their Dependencies. (Decree No. 2716 dated 17.5.1351 H. [Sept. 18, 1932]). Saudi Arabia is monarchy. Several decrees were generally understood to comprise basis of organization of government including: Organic Instructions of the Kingdom of the Hejaz (Aug. 29, 1926); Decree Constituting the Nejd a Kingdom and Uniting the Nejd with the Hejaz (Jan. 29, 1927); Decree Establishing a Council of Ministers (Dec. 29, 1931); Decree No. 2716 referred to above; and Decree No. 38 entitled Regulations of the Council of Ministers (May 11, 1958). During 1992, King Fahd bin Abdul Aziz Al-Saud issued three decrees which established formalized framework of government. First decree (Royal Decree A/90 dated 27.8.1412 H. [Mar. 1, 1992]), called Basic Law of Government, in 83 articles confirms among other things Saudi Arabia's monarchical structure and its adherence to Islam and Shari'ah, and addresses independence of judiciary and certain fundamental rights of citizens and residents. Second decree (Royal Decree A/91 dated 27.8.1412 H. [Mar. 1, 1992]) establishes and empowers appointed Consultative Council (Majlis al-Shoura) comprised of 60 members and speaker to express opinions on certain matters (such as general policy of state, interpretation of laws, and adoption of international treaties) referred to it by President of Council of Ministers. Consultative Council may also propose laws to be promulgated by King. Third decree (Royal Decree A/92 dated 27.8.1412 H. [Mar. 1, 1992]) covers internal governance of various regions of Saudi Arabia and provides among other things for establishment of Provincial Council for each province. In 1993 new rules governing Council of Ministers were promulgated. (Royal Decree A/14 dated 3.3.1414 H. [Aug. 20, 1993]). Council of Ministers recommends legislation to be issued by King.

Sources of Law.—Word "law" in Saudi Arabia is understood to refer to Islamic law (in Arabic, Shari'ah). All secular regulations are subject to and interpreted in accordance with Shari'ah precepts.

Shari'ah has four primary sources. First is Quran, which Muslims believe is word of God delivered to God's messenger, Prophet Mohammed. Quran contains numerous principles and guidelines for human behavior in both secular and religious life. Second is called "Sunna", and is comprised of that which Prophet Mohammed was reported to have said, done, or approved. (Quran, 59:7). Sunna expounds, elaborates and explains many of general rules of Quran. Third is called "Ijmah"—consensus of scholars. If at given time in history, all reputable Islamic scholars agreed on certain rule as being "Islamic" response to specific question, such agreement or consensus is treated as binding rule of Shari'ah. Fourth is "Qias", or analogy. Feature of Shari'ah, as of other legal systems, is that application of law to specific matter should apply equally to analogous matter, because similar cases should lead to similar results.

CONTRACTS:

Principles of contract in Saudi Arabia derive from Shari'ah and are not codified in any statute or civil code. Quran contains numerous references to commercial contracting principles; according to Quran, God has specifically commanded Muslims to honor their contracts. (Quran, 5:1).

Under Shari'ah there is considerable freedom to contract so long as purposes of contract are lawful. In Saudi Arabia speculation ("gharar") and unproductive gain or interest ("riba") are prohibited and thus contracts having either of these as elements would be unenforceable.

Written contracts are preferred but oral contracts, if properly witnessed or proved, are enforceable. (Quran, 2:282). Contracts with minors or incompetents are void.

Damages.—Only proven direct damages are awarded for breach of contract. Damages for lost opportunity or lost profits are considered speculative and would not be awarded. It would be unusual for Saudi court or tribunal to fashion injunctive relief or remedies.

Excuse for Nonperformance.—Generally speaking force majeure, undue hardship and impossibility are recognized grounds for nonperformance of contract.

Applicable Law.—Saudi court or tribunal would construe and apply only Saudi Arabian law as to matters in controversy before it, notwithstanding existence of contractual governing law clause to contrary.

Government Contracts.—Contracting with Saudi public sector is regulated by GTR (Royal Decree No. M/14 dated 7.4.1397 H. [Mar. 27, 1977] and Rules for Implementation of Tenders Regulations (Minister of Finance Resolution No. 2131/97 dated 5.5.1397 H. [Apr. 23, 1977]) which contain set of rules and procedures governing, among other things, public bid requirements, direct purchases, bid submission rules, contract award rules, contract conditions, delay fines, and means and terms of payment. Standard form of public works contract has been issued. (Council of Ministers Resolution No. 136 dated 13.6.1408 H. [Feb. 1, 1988]).

Public sector contracting parties typically require bid, performance and, where applicable, advance payment guarantees issued by approved banks or insurance companies. Under GTR, contractor is not permitted to stop performance of public sector contract even if public sector entity has breached its obligations under contract. (GTR Rules, Art. 29). Public sector contractor has liability for ten years from handover for any partial or total collapse of structure. (GTR Rules, Art. 30).

Contractors wholly Saudi-owned or owned not less than 50% by Saudi interests are shown perference in public sector contracts. (GTR, Art. 1[d]). Saudi manufactured goods are also shown preference as are goods manufactured in other GCC states or by entities having at least 51% Saudi or other GCC national ownership. (Council of Ministers Resolution No. 139 dated 25.6.1407 H. [Feb. 23, 1987]).

Wholly foreign-owned contractor or Saudi contractor having less than 51% Saudi equity ownership therein which has been awarded public sector contract must subcontract not less than 30% of value of contract to wholly Saudi-owned firms. (Council of Ministers Resolution No. 124 dated 29.5.1403 H. [Mar. 14, 1983] as clarified by Ministry of Finance Circular No. 5767/404 dated 9.11.1404 H. [Aug. 6, 1984] and Nos. 3/1742 and 3/1743 dated 12.3.1406 H. [Nov. 24, 1985], and Council of Ministers Resolution No. 145 dated 7.7.1406 H. [Mar. 17, 1986]).

See topics Corporations and Principal and Agent.

Distributorships, Commercial Agency and Franchises.—Contract evidencing these types of commercial relationships must be entered into with Saudi natural persons or entities wholly owned by Saudi interests in which all of entity's directors and officers authorized to bind entity are Saudi nationals. (Saudi Commercial Agents Regulations [Royal Decree No. M/11 dated 20.2.1382 H. (July 22, 1962), as am'd by Royal Decree Nos. 5 dated 11.6.1389 H. (Aug. 24, 1969) and 32 dated 10.8.1400 H. (June 23, 1980), and as supplemented by Rules for Implementation of Commercial Agents Regulations issued under Minister of Commerce Resolutions Nos. 1897 dated 24.5.1401 H. (Mar. 30, 1981) and 1012 dated 17.9.1412 H. (Mar. 10, 1993)]).

Ministry of Commerce has published standard forms of agency/distributorship and franchise contracts but use of such forms is not mandatory. However, Ministry of Commerce will generally require agency/distributorship/franchise contracts submitted to it in connection with registration of agents/distributors/franchisees to stipulate Saudi Arabian law as governing law. Under current Ministry of Commerce practice, arbitration under regime other than Saudi Arabia's (such as International Chamber of Commerce) may be provided in such agreements.

Terminated agent or distributor or franchisee does not have automatic or statutory right to termination compensation. Absent specific contractual provisions governing termination compensation, Shari'ah would mandate compensation to wrongfully terminated agent, distributor or franchisee only if actual damages could be proved to have been sustained on account of costs incurred in expectation of continuation of agency/distributor/franchise relationship with principal. Consequential and indirect damages are generally not damages for which party may be compensated under Shari'ah.

Compensation of commercial agents is not regulated.

Three person committee has been established by Ministry of Commerce to mediate commercial agency and distributorship disputes between parties to commercial agency, distributorship and franchise agreements. Such mediation is mandatory; if unsuccessful, disputants could arbitrate or litigate.

See topic Principal and Agent.

COPYRIGHT:

Copyright Regulations (Royal Decree No. M/11 dated 19.5.1410 H. [Dec. 17, 1989]) became effective in Jan., 1990.

COPYRIGHT . . . *continued*

Copyright Regulations cover all scientific, literary or artistic works expressed in writing, sound, painting, photography or motion. Motion pictures and sound recordings are omitted from that part of Copyright Regulations stipulating types of works protected, although these media are referred to elsewhere in Regulations. If this omission was oversight, rules for implementation of law which are expected to be issued in due course could provide clarification.

Copyright Regulations provide that works of foreign and Saudi authors are to be protected if they are published, acted or shown for first time in Saudi Arabia. Read literally, Copyright Regulations would thus appear not to extend protection in any practical sense to works of foreign authors since virtually no foreign works are publiced initially in Saudi Arabia. Clarification of this provision might also be included in such rules for implementation.

Copyright will in most cases be valid for lifetime of author plus 50 Hejira years from date of his death. Protection of sound and audio-visual works, photographic works and works in applied arts is limited to 25 Hejira years from date of publication. Duration of protection afforded to computer software is not specifically mentioned. For works owned and copyrighted by juridical entity, protection begins on date of publication but duration of such protection is unclear.

Violators of Saudi copyright are subject to fines and, if business, to closure for up to 15 days. Infringing works are subject to confiscation and destruction.

Saudi Arabia acceded in July, 1994 to Universal Copyright Convention as revised at Paris on July 24, 1971.

CORPORATIONS:

SRC (Royal Decree No. M/6 dated 22.3.1385 H. [July 20, 1965], as am'd by Royal Decree Nos. M/5 dated 12.2.1387 H. [May 21, 1967], M/23 dated 28.6.1402 H. [Apr. 22, 1982], M/46 dated 4.7.1405 H. [Mar. 25, 1985] and M/22 dated 30.7.1412 H. [Feb. 3, 1992]) provides for establishment, regulation, merger, liquidation and dissolution of general partnerships, limited partnerships, joint ventures, joint stock companies, partnerships limited by shares, limited liability companies, companies with variable capital, and cooperative companies. SRC expressly contemplates conversion of one type of entity into another. Subject to licensing and other restrictions outside of SRC, foreign entity can participate or invest only in joint venture, joint stock company or limited liability company. However, foreign entity engaged in professions may associate with Saudi professional to establish Professional Company under regulatory framework separate from SRC.

SRC also prohibits foreign companies from issuing or selling securities in Saudi Arabia unless prior approval of Ministry of Commerce is obtained.

Joint venture (SRC, Arts. 40-47) is unincorporated association in nature of consortium. If foreign entity is joint venture partner, it must either be licensed pursuant to Foreign Capital Investment Code and commercially registered or, if consortium is party to public sector contract, provisionally licensed by Ministry of Commerce. In most circumstances, joint venture is considered as de facto general partnership.

Joint stock company (SRC, Arts. 48-148) is entity with limited liability which is entitled to (but need not) issue stock to Saudi public. Stock ownership is evidenced by certificates which may be issued in bearer form. Classes of stock, including preferred shares, may be issued subject to certain restrictions. Unless otherwise provided in entity's constitutive documents and subject to certain exceptions, stockholders have preemptive rights.

Joint stock company is administered by board of directors comprised of not less than three members, each of whom must own not less than specified amount of stock. Annual meetings of stockholders are required.

Accounts of joint stock company must be audited by auditor duly licensed in Saudi Arabia.

Royal Decree is required subject to certain limited exceptions to incorporate joint stock company which holds government concession, or which is public utility company, company that will receive government subsidy, company in which government or other public sector entity will participate, or bank.

If joint stock company sustains losses in excess of three-quarters of its capital, directors must convene meeting of stockholders to determine whether to dissolve company or to continue to maintain its existence, and in either case public notice must be published indicating action taken.

Limited liability company (SRC, Arts. 157-180) is entity with limited liability having at least two and not more than 50 shareholders. Sometimes also referred to as limited liability partnership, it is most common vehicle for foreign investment in Saudi Arabia. Limited liability company cannot engage in insurance, savings or banking business.

Shareholders have statutory right of first refusal if shareholder wishes to sell his shares to third party. Shares in limited liability company confer equal voting rights. Share ownership is evidenced by entity's articles of association; share certificates are not issued. Profits need not be distributed in proportion to share ownership. Among other things, any proposed shareholders' action which increases financial liability of shareholders requires unanimous approval of shareholders.

Limited liability company need not have board of managers. If company has more than 20 shareholders, management board comprised of at least three shareholders must be formed. Annual meetings of shareholders are required.

Accounts of limited liability company must be audited by auditor duly licensed in Saudi Arabia.

If limited liability company sustains losses in excess of three-quarters of its share capital, shareholders must meet to determine whether to dissolve company or to continue to maintain its existence, and in either case public notice must be published indicating action taken. If shareholders determine to continue, company must be made solvent, failing which shareholders shall have joint personal liability for company's debts if company continues to trade.

Foreign Corporations.—Branch offices of wholly foreign owned entities are required to obtain foreign capital investment license pursuant to Foreign Capital Investment Code.

If foreign-owned entity is party to public sector contract and not otherwise licensed under Foreign Capital Investment Code, registration with Ministry of Commerce, locally known as temporary commercial registration or provisional licensing, is required in order to undertake such contract. (Ministry of Commerce Resolution No. 680 dated 9.11.1398 H. [Oct. 10, 1978]). Provisional licensing is available only in respect of public sector contracts, must be applied for within 30 days of signing such contract, and is valid only in respect of such contract for duration of such contract. Each time foreign entity obtains new public sector contract (even if its public sector contracts run concurrently), provisional licensing in respect of new contract must be obtained. By its terms, Resolution No. 680 applies to prime contracts as well as to subcontracts; in practice Ministry of Commerce exercises considerable discretion in administering provisional licensing scheme, and has limited provisional licensing to certain types of prime contracts.

Foreign-owned entity undertaking multiple public sector contracts may obtain "representative office" license from Minister of Commerce which would allow entity to establish office to supervise and coordinate its various administrative activities within Saudi Arabia. This license would be in addition to provisional licensing. Representative office is prohibited from directly or indirectly engaging in commercial activity. (Minister of Commerce Resolution No. 1502 dated 8.3.1400 H. [Jan. 26, 1980]).

Foreign-owned entity may obtain "technical and scientific services office" license from Minister of Commerce which would allow entity to establish office to offer technical and scientific services to distributors of entity's products, to conduct market and related surveys, and to undertake product research. Such office is prohibited from directly or indirectly engaging in commercial activity. (Minister of Commerce and Industry Resolution No. 1532 dated 6.6.1395 H. [June 15, 1975]).

Professional Company.—Saudi and non-Saudi entities engaged in "free professions" (such as engineering, law and accounting) may associate to establish professional company not subject to SRC under Professional Companies Regulations (Council of Ministers Resolution No. 16 dated 16.2.1412 H. [Aug. 28, 1991] and implementing rules therefor (Minister of Commerce Resolution No. 41 dated 8.1.1413 H. [July 8, 1992]) so long as 51% of capital thereof is owned by Saudi interests. Such entities require license issued by Ministry of Commerce, and do not provide limited liability to participants therein.

See topics Commercial Register and Foreign Investment.

CURRENCY:

Official currency is Saudi Riyal which is divided into 100 Halalas. Saudi courts and tribunals will enforce judgment in foreign currency.

DEATH:

Matters pertaining to death are subject to Shari'ah and largely administered and adjudicated by Shari'ah courts.

Writ of death is issued by Shari'ah court upon satisfactory proof of demise. For Muslims, such writ also contains designation of heirs as established under Shari'ah. (Quran, 4:11-13). As general principle under Shari'ah, people of different religions do not inherit from each other.

Typically designated heirs will appoint by means of duly notarized power of attorney one or more of their number to act as their attorneys-in-fact to deal with deceased's affairs. If no such power of attorney is issued, all such heirs must act jointly.

Under Shari'ah, powers of attorney and agency relationships are deemed revoked by death of grantor or principal, as case may be.

Actions for Death.—Under Shari'ah, party (as determined by Shari'ah court) directly responsible for wrongful death of another must pay diyah or "blood money". Amounts of diyah payable in circumstances of death or injury are fixed from time to time by Royal Decree. Obligation to pay and right to receive diyah apply also to non-Muslims.

See topic Descent and Distribution.

DEPOSITIONS:

Depositions and other detailed discovery devices are in general not feature of Saudi jurisprudence.

DESCENT AND DISTRIBUTION:

Matters pertaining to disposition of deceased's property are subject to Shari'ah and largely administered and adjudicated by Shari'ah courts.

Muslim may make will devising property to nondesignated heir so long as will does not dispose of more than one-third of his estate. At least two-thirds of Muslim decedent's estate must be distributed to designated heirs in specified percentages in accordance with Shari'ah. (Quran, 4:11-13). Non-Muslim is not considered as designated heir of Muslim.

Wills should be in writing and witnessed in accordance with Shari'ah requirements. Under Shari'ah, designated heir cannot be disinherited.

See topic Death.

DISPUTE RESOLUTION:

Mandatory Dispute Resolution.—By its nature Shari'ah favors and encourages amicable resolution of disputes by mediation, but this policy is effected primarily through voluntary means. Mediation is never binding on dissatisfied disputant which always has resort to applicable judicial or quasi-judicial dispute resolution forums.

See topic Actions.

Voluntary Dispute Resolution.—Under BASR, debtor may resort to mediation before committees established by local chambers of commerce. Ministry of Commerce has established committee to mediate disputes between commercial agents/distributors and their principals. In both instances, disputants are not foreclosed from seeking applicable judicial or quasi-judicial dispute resolution. Mediation is largely informal process and resort to formalized alternate dispute procedures and systems such as fact-finding and minitrials (as those terms are understood in Western common law jurisdictions) would be unusual.

Most private sector commercial disputes may be submitted to arbitration. Under Shari'ah, resort to arbitration requires agreement of disputants and cannot be mandatory.

DISPUTE RESOLUTION . . . *continued*

See topics Actions; Bankruptcy; and Contracts.

DIVORCE:

Matters pertaining to divorce, including alimony, custodial rights and child support are subject to Shari'ah and administered and adjudicated by Shari'ah courts. In divorce between Muslim and non-Muslim governed by Saudi Arabian law, non-Muslim's rights would be subject to Shari'ah principles which could have effect of circumscribing non-Muslim's property and custodial rights.

ENVIRONMENT:

Pollution control and related environmental regulation are responsibility of and enforced by Meteorology and Environmental Protection Administration (MEPA), established under Royal Decree No. 7/M/8903 dated 21.4.1401 H. (Feb. 2, 1981). MEPA has issued Environmental Protection Standards (General Standards) covering among other things ambient air quality, air pollution sources, receiving water guidelines, direct discharge performance and discharge pretreatment guidelines. (MEPA Document No. 1409-01).

EXCHANGE CONTROL:

At present time there are no exchange control regulations as to import or export of local or foreign currency or repatriation of funds, profits or capital after corporate dissolution.

SAMA has in past requested local banks to obtain SAMA's prior consent before: Inviting non-Saudi banks to participate in local syndicated SR financings; participating in syndicated SR financings arranged abroad; and participating in foreign currency syndicated loans to persons or entities not resident in Saudi Arabia. (SAMA Circular No. 5013/M/A/68 dated 1.4.1403 H. [Jan. 15, 1983]).

EXECUTIONS:

Upon final judgment of court or tribunal, execution can be levied on property of debtor except in respect of certain personal and professional necessaries. Debtor can be imprisoned for nonpayment of debts in certain circumstances.

EXECUTORS AND ADMINISTRATORS:

See topics Descent and Distribution; Death.

FOREIGN EXCHANGE:

See topic Exchange Control.

FOREIGN INVESTMENT:

Under Foreign Capital Investment Code (Royal Decree No. M/4 dated 2.2.1399 H. [Jan. 1, 1979]) and Rules for Implementation of Foreign Capital Investment Code (Minister of Industry and Electricity Resolution No. 323 dated 10.6.1399 H. [May 7, 1979]), foreign investment in Saudi Arabia is permited subject to obtaining foreign capital investment license. Administration of investment licensing scheme has in large part been delegated to Foreign Capital Investment Committee, comprised of representatives of various ministries headed by Deputy Minister of Industry and Electricity.

"Foreign capital" is broadly defined to include money and securities, assets in kind such as machinery and raw materials, and intangible property such as trademarks and patents. In order to qualify for investment license, foreign capital must be invested in "economic development projects" requiring foreign technical expertise as determined from time to time by Minister of Industry and Electricity. (Minister of Industry and Electricity Resolution No. 11/S/F dated 17.7.1410 H. [Feb. 12, 1990]).

Applicant for investment license may be natural person or juridical entity.

At present time, only foreign capital invested in foreign-owned branch office, or in share capital of either joint stock company or limited liability company will qualify for investment license. To date by far most common form of investment vehicle has been share ownership in limited liability company.

Licensing is not automatic and applicant must be able to demonstrate its expertise in particular area in which investment is sought. Once granted, investment license stipulates permitted corporate objects of entity subject to license. No change in corporate objects, share capital, shareholders or their respective interests in share capital can be made without prior amendment of investment license, which is matter of licensing authority's discretion.

Foreign shareholder of limited liability company or joint stock company with investment license is eligible for five Hejira year (in case of services project) or ten Hejira year (in case of industrial or agricultural project) holiday from Saudi corporate taxes if Saudi share capital ownership in relevant entity is not less than 25% of total share capital. Where previously licensed industrial entity increases its share capital in order to undertake expansion of production facilities, under certain circumstances another ten year tax holiday will be granted in respect of net profits of entity related to such expansion. (Minister of Finance and National Economy Resolution No. 3/3170 dated 2.12.1413 H. [May 23, 1993]).

Other investment incentives available to licensed foreign capital investment in industrial projects include access to low cost consessionary financing provided by The Saudi Industrial Development Fund (Royal Decree No. M/3 dated 26.2.1394 H. [Mar. 20, 1974], as am'd by Royal Decree No. M/71 dated 13.12.1394 H. [Dec. 27, 1975]), and possibility of protective tariffs, exemption from customs duties on imported machinery, spare parts and raw materials, and access to low-cost long-term leased land located in industrial estates of various municipalities (Regulations for the Protection and Encouragement of National Industries, Royal Decree No. 50 dated 23.12.1381 H. [May 27, 1962]).

In addition, entity subject to investment license which has Saudi shareholding therein of not less than 50% is considered to be Saudi entity for purposes of qualifying for preferential treatment as service contractor under GTR; in addition, if such entity has Saudi shareholding therein of not less than 51%, such entity would not be required to subcontract 30% of value of any public sector contract it obtains to wholly Saudi-owned entities.

It is unlawful for foreign natural person or entity to invest or otherwise trade in name of Saudi person or entity in order to avoid applicable doing business, licensing or registration requirements. (Regulations for the Combat of Cover-Up, Royal Decree No. M/49 dated 16.10.1409 H. [May 21, 1989] and Ministry of Interior Resolution No. 2144 dated 23.5.1411 H. [Dec. 10, 1990]).

See topics Contracts, Corporations, Foreign Trade Regulations, Principal and Agent.

FOREIGN TRADE REGULATIONS:

Saudi Arabia, together with Bahrain, Kuwait, Oman, Qatar and United Arab Emirates are members of The Gulf Co-Operation Council (GCC) whose stated purposes include coordination and unification of economic, financial and monetary policies and commercial, industrial and customs legislation of member states. (Joint Economic Agreement among the Members of The Gulf Co-Operation Council, Royal Decree No. M/13 dated 21.3.1402 H. [Jan. 16, 1982]).

See topics Currency and Foreign Investment.

FRAUDS, STATUTE OF:

Statute of frauds is not feature of Saudi jurisprudence.

FRAUDULENT SALES AND CONVEYANCES:

See topic Bankruptcy.

GARNISHMENT:

In certain civil proceedings, creditor who holds judgment against defendant may by application to relevant Saudi court or tribunal garnish monies owing to defendant by third parties or movable property of defendant in possession of third parties.

Property Which May Not be Garnished.—In respect of civil claim maximum amount of salary or wages that can be garnished is 10%. (SLWL, Art. 119). As matter of practice, entitlements due and owing by public sector to debtor cannot usually be garnished by private sector litigant.

IMMIGRATION:

Saudi Arabian-born issue of alien parents would not automatically be entitled to Saudi nationality. Saudi citizenship is granted to aliens only by Royal Decree.

See topic Aliens.

INFANTS:

Under Shari'ah, age of majority is reached when puberty has been attained together with evidence that person in question has ability to make responsible decisions. As matter of practice, age of majority in Saudi Arabia is considered to be 18. See NIR, Art. 7. Minor has no legal capacity to enter into or perform contracts.

Under SLWL, minimum age for employment is 13.

INSOLVENCY:

See topic Bankruptcy.

INTEREST:

Under Shari'ah as interpreted in Saudi Arabia, charging and payment of interest are prohibited. (Quran, 2:275-281 and 3:130). Although Saudi commercial banks and other enterprises in practice routinely charge and pay interest, no Saudi court or tribunal will award or enforce obligation to pay interest or obligation deemed to be in nature of interest.

See topic Contracts.

JUDGMENTS:

Foreign Judgments.—Board of Grievances has jurisdiction over applications for enforcement of foreign judgments. (Royal Decree No. M/51 dated 17.7.1402 H. [May 10, 1982]). Rules of Civil Procedure in respect of Board of Grievances (Council of Ministers Resolution No. 190 dated 16.11.1409 H. [June 20, 1989]) specify inter alia manner in which applications for enforcement of foreign judgments should be filed and heard, and specifically empower Board to issue its judgment enforcing foreign judgment if foreign state where such judgment was issued would afford reciprocal treatment to judgments of Saudi courts and provided nothing in foreign judgment (such as interest) contravenes Shari'ah.

Traditionally, Saudi Arabian courts would not enforce judgments of non-Saudi courts absent specific treaty providing otherwise. This was primarily on account of what were perceived to be certain Shari'ah constraints. Saudi Arabia is party to one such treaty signed in 1952 with six other original members of Arab League, namely, Jordan, Lebanon, Syria, Egypt, Iraq and Yemen. (Agreement for the Execution of Court Decrees dated 22.2.1372 H. [Nov. 10, 1952]). In rare instances foreign judgments have been enforced in Saudi Arabia under terms of Arab League Treaty.

During 1994, Saudi Arabia acceded to New York Convention on the Enforcement of Foreign Arbitral Awards, 1958 but invoked reciprocity reservation. (Royal Decree No. M/11 dated 16.7.1414 H. [Dec. 29, 1993]).

Actual enforcement of such judgments, like other domestic judgments in commercial civil cases, rests with Civil Rights Department of Ministry of Interior. (Private Rights Claims Regulations, Minister of Interior Resolution No. 20 dated 21.1.1406 H. [Oct. 5, 1985]).

LABOR RELATIONS:

SLWL (Royal Decree No. M/21 dated 6.9.1389 H. [Nov. 15, 1969]) governs relations between employers and employees in private sector. SLWL also provides for establishment of Commissions for the Settlement of Labor Disputes under jurisdiction of Ministry of Labor and Social Affairs to adjudicate labor-related controversies. Ministry also has Labor Offices in most localities which attempt to conciliate disputes prior to litigation. Labor unions are not permitted.

LABOR RELATIONS . . . *continued*

Both written and unwritten labor contracts will be enforced, and written contracts are routinely used. SLWL provides for non-mandatory "probationary period" of up to three months at commencement of employment relationship.

Duration of employment may have specified or unspecified term. In case of latter, either employer or employee may terminate same upon 30 days notice for monthly employees or 15 days notice for hourly, daily, weekly or other employees. If employer fails to observe this notice period, SLWL requires payment in lieu of notice.

If employment is terminated without "valid reason", terminated party is entitled to compensation determined by adjudicatory authority which in practice has traditionally awarded three-five months salary as termination damages.

Employee is entitled to "end of service" award upon completion of specified term labor contract or upon termination by employer of unspecified term labor contract. Under SLWL, that entitlement is equal to (i) one-half month's pay for each of first five years of employment and (ii) one month's pay for each subsequent year. Most recent rate of pay which in practice may include certain allowances payable to employee is required to be used in calculating such award. Award is also payable if employee is called to military service, if employee was leaving for reasons "of force majeure beyond his control" or, in case of female, if she resigns for marriage or childbirth.

If employee under unspecified term contract resigns, he is entitled to (i) one-third of award referred to in immediately preceding paragraph for corresponding time periods referred to therein, if his employment period is two or more years but less than or equal to five years, (ii) two-thirds of such award if his period of employment is more than five years and less than ten years, and (iii) full amount of such award if he resigns after ten years, in each case so long as employee gives 30 days prior notice of his resignation.

Wages are considered preferred debts and superior to other claims on employer's property.

Under SLWL, maximum work day is eight working hours or 48 working hours per week, not including prayers, breaks or meals. During fasting month of Ramadan, maximum is six working hours and 36 working hours per week. Overtime, weekend and holiday pay rates are mandated for all but employees in "positions of trust".

SLWL requires annual vacation of at least 15 days with full pay for each employee who has completed one year of service. This period is increased to 21 days when employee has completed ten continuous years of service.

LANGUAGE:

Official language of Saudi Arabia is Arabic. All correspondence, agreements with, and financial reports and tax returns submitted to, Saudi government and its instrumentalities must be in Arabic. In addition, all companies doing business in Saudi Arabia are required to keep their books of account in Arabic. Saudi courts and tribunals will consider and construe only documents submitted in Arabic or in Arabic translation as translated by duly licensed translator. All Saudi court or tribunal proceedings, as well as arbitration proceedings, must be in Arabic.

LAW REPORTS, CODES, ETC.:

All statutes and most (but not all) ministerial resolutions are published in official newspaper of record, *Umm Al-Qura*. Ministry departmental circulars are frequently unpublished. Few statutes have been officially translated into English.

Stare decisis is, in accordance with Shari'ah doctrines of equity and fairness, not feature of Saudi jurisprudence. Court and tribunal decisions are not published and not publicly disclosed, except that Board of Grievances, Administrative Part, has published in Arabic excerpts from some of its decisions related to public sector disputes and administrative law matters.

See also topic Constitution, Government and Source of Law.

LEGISLATURE:

See topic Constitution, Government and Source of Law.

LICENSES:

See topic Foreign Investment.

LIENS:

See topic Mortgages.

LIMITATION OF ACTIONS:

Under Shari'ah, specific periods of limitation are not recognized on grounds of equity and fairness unless any delay in enforcing rights itself had effect of prejudicing disputants, approach somewhat akin to doctrine of laches. Notwithstanding foregoing, various secular statutes do stipulate limitation periods. For example, claim against public sector entity arising out of public sector contract must be brought before Board of Grievances within five years from date on which cause of action first arose, absent "legal excuse". Under SLWL, claims must be brought within 12 months.

MARRIAGE:

Permission of Ministry of Interior is required for Saudi citizens wishing to marry aliens other than GCC nationals.

See topics Aliens and Divorce.

MINES AND MINERALS:

All natural deposits of petroleum, natural gas and derivatives thereof, and minerals and quarry deposits, are state's exclusive property, and exploitation thereof is regulated by Royal Decree.

Petroleum and mineral projects are specifically exempted from definition of "economic development projects" as defined in Foreign Capital Investment Code, and generally speaking SRC would not be applicable to entities formed to engage in petroleum and mineral sectors.

MONOPOLIES AND RESTRAINT OF TRADE:

By means of Royal Decree and requirement of industrial and foreign capital investment licensing, de facto monopolies or concentrations are effectively created. At present time, Saudi Arabia does not statutorily regulate monopolies or restrictive trade practices.

MORTGAGES:

Under Shari'ah, mortgage, pledge or lien on movable property is valid only if such property is delivered into possession of pledgee. Mortgages, pledges or liens on movable property are usually not enforceable as security devices absent such possession.

Ship Mortgages and Maritime Liens.—Saudi Ship Mortgage Regulations (Royal Letter of Assent No. 9/3/8469 dated 1.9.1374 H. [Apr. 22, 1955]) provide for creation, registration and enforcement of ship mortgages on Saudi flag vessels. However, in practice it is not often clear to what extent Saudi Ministry of Communications has actually implemented substance and procedures of these regulations.

Extent to which true maritime liens can be asserted against ship is unsettled, in part because of Shari'ah constraints as to movable property referred to above. Under CCL, crews' wages, expenses for necessaries and insurance premiums are stated to be privileged and ranked, while under ship mortgage regulations similar liens are provided; precise interplay of CCL and Ship Mortgage Regulations remains unclear.

Aircraft Mortgages.—There is no provision for creation, registration or enforcement of aircraft mortgages.

Real Property Mortgages.—This type of mortgage is permitted under Shari'ah and in practice Notary Public registers and records such mortgages both in registry kept for that purpose and by means of notation on title deed evidencing ownership of real property.

At present time, however, Notaries Public will not register or record mortgages in respect of real property where commercial banks are or are suspected by Notary Public to be involved, on grounds that such involvement implies that interest is feature of transaction. (Supreme Judiciary Council Decision No. 291 dated 25.10.1401 H. [Aug. 25, 1981]).

See topics Interest and Notaries Public.

NOTARIES PUBLIC:

Notaries public are considered to be highly important public officials who must have same qualifications as judges in order to serve. Notaries are well versed in Shari'ah. Notaries are appointed and are under supervision of Minister of Justice and Supreme Judicial Council (highest court in Shari'ah court system and forum for consideration of matters submitted to that body by King or Minister of Justice).

See topics Acknowledgments, Mortgages, Real Property.

PARTNERSHIP:

See topic Corporations.

PATENTS:

The Patent Regulations (Royal Decree No. M/38 dated 10.6.1409 H. [Jan. 17, 1989]) became effective in May, 1989. Owners of foreign patents may be entitled to obtain confirmatory or reciprocal patent under terms of Patent Law in that patent issuing authority, known as King Abdul Aziz City for Science and Technology, is authorized to decide whether to grant confirmatory patents which recognize priority of foreign patent pursuant to terms of any relevant international treaty to which Saudi Arabia is party. At present, Saudi Arabia is not party to any major international patent treaties, and it is unclear whether patent authority will actually grant confirmatory patents or, if so, on what basis.

Once issued, confirmatory patent is valid for 15 Hejira years from date of issue provided that holder has used same in either commercial or industrial capacity within two years of that date. If patent holder fails to use its Saudi patent within this period, issuing authority may license patent to another party if it can establish that it would use same. Holders of Saudi patents have right to file claim with "Patent Committee" against any person or juristic entity infringing on their patent. Decisions of Patent Committee may be appealed to Board of Grievances. Patent Committee is empowered to order cessation of infringing activities, to fine infringer and to award damages to patent holder.

PLEDGES:

See topic Mortgages.

PRINCIPAL AND AGENT:

Under Shari'ah, agency relationship (including granting of power to act as attorney-in-fact) is considered to be terminable at will by either principal or agent, notwithstanding contractual terms to contrary. In practice however, it is considered prudent to adhere to contractual termination provisions in accordance with terms thereof. In respect of natural persons, death also revokes agency.

Commercial Agents.—Non-Saudi natural persons or entities not wholly-owned by Saudis are (with certain exceptions in respect of other GCC nationals) prohibited from engaging in trading activities in Saudi Arabia. While "trading activities" in this context is not expressly defined in any Saudi legislation, in practice that term has been taken to mean import, sale of or trading in goods. Accordingly, it has been long-established practice for foreign manufacturers to appoint Saudi agents or distributors to trade and distribute their products in local market.

Under Saudi Commercial Agents Regulations (Royal Decree No. M/11 dated 20.2.1382 H. [July 22, 1962], as am'd by Royal Decree Nos. 5 dated 11.6.1389 H. [Aug. 24, 1969] and 32 dated 10.8.1400 H. [June 23, 1980], and as supplemented by Rules for Implementation of the Commercial Agents Regulations issued under Minister of Commerce Resolution No. 1897 dated 24.5.1401 H. [Mar. 30, 1981]), no person or entity may act as commercial agent or distributor unless Saudi natural person or entity wholly owned by Saudi interests in which all of its directors and officers

PRINCIPAL AND AGENT . . . *continued*
authorized to bind entity are Saudi nationals. Applicability of this legislation has been extended to franchising. (Minister of Commerce Resolution No. 1012 dated 17.9.1412 H. [Mar. 10, 1993]).

Commercial agents, distributors and franchisees must have valid commercial registrations and must also register with Ministry of Commerce each time agency/distributorship/franchise relationship is entered into. As part of such registration process, agent or distributor must submit its agreement with its non-Saudi principal to Ministry of Commerce which traditionally has taken expansive view of its ability to require substantive changes in that agreement. Such agreements which stipulate non-Saudi law as governing law will not be accepted.

Failure of Saudi agent or distributor so to register with Ministry of Commerce could result in fines and other penalties to such agent or distributor, but would not render agency or distributorship agreement invalid or otherwise subject non-Saudi principal to any penalties except that, in certain circumstances, principal not having registered Saudi agent or distributor could not participate as supplier in public sector tender.

See also topic Contracts, subhead Distributorships, Commercial Agency and Franchises.

Service Agents.—Under Decree Governing the Relationship between Foreign Contractors and Saudi Agents (Royal Decree No. M/2 dated 21.1.1398 H. [Dec. 31, 1977]), prior to tendering for or concluding public sector contract, non-Saudi contractor must have "Saudi service agent".

Agent must be Saudi natural person or wholly Saudi owned and controlled entity. While only express exceptions to this requirement are in respect of armaments contracts (see also Council of Ministers Resolution No. 1275 dated 12.9.1395 H. [Sept. 17, 1975]) and government-to-government contracts, in practice from time to time public sector entities stipulate in their tender documents for other types of contracts that no service agents are permitted.

Saudi service agent must not represent more than ten foreign principals and his compensation must not exceed 5% of value of contract.

See topic Foreign Investment.

REAL PROPERTY:

Ownership of real property is evidenced by title deeds. Real property records are kept manually and administered by designated notaries public who also register ownership and record transfer of real property and real property mortgages.

See topics Acknowledgments, Aliens, Mortgages.

SALES:

As general matter, Shari'ah mandates fair and equitable dealing among parties to sale contract. Saudi Arabia has not enacted comprehensive legislation relating to sale of goods. In absence of such legislation, sale contract should expressly include all material terms pursuant to which sale is made. Certain terms relating to title retention, repossession, remedies, disclaimers and limitation on liability, etc. may not be enforceable under Shari'ah.

Applicable Law.—See topic Actions.

Warranties.—Although under Shari'ah, certain basic warranties (such as merchantability and fitness for particular purpose) are arguably implicit, all relevant warranties should as matter of prudence be expressly included in sale contract.

SHIPPING:

Primary maritime legislation is Seaports, Harbors and Lighthouses Regulations (Royal Decree No. M/27 dated 24.6.1394 H. [July 14, 1974] as am'd by Minister of Communications Resolution No. 11 dated 12.2.1406 H. [Oct. 26, 1985]). Ministry of Communications oversees and administers maritime transport activities. Vessels and others entering, using or making use of Saudi Arabia's seaports are subject to GCC Rules and Regulations for Seaports which are published in English translation.

Saudi Flag.—In order to register vessel under Saudi flag, shipowner (or in case of bareboat charter registration, demise charterer) must be Saudi natural person, wholly Saudi-owned entity, or Saudi limited liability company having not less than 51% Saudi share capital. Owning entity must have headquarters in Saudi Arabia, Saudi national experienced in maritime transport as overall manager thereof, and at least two-thirds of its directors (including such manager and chairman) must be Saudi nationals residing in Saudi Arabia. Limited liability company with foreign capital invested therein must be duly licensed under Foreign Capital Investment Code.

Vessel Registration.—In order for Saudi flag vessel to trade, its owners must obtain maritime transport license (Minister of Communications Resolution No. 53 dated 24.3.1403 H. [Jan. 8, 1983]), requirements for which include evidence of applicant's foreign capital investment license (if applicable) and commercial registration. In addition, documentary requirements for appropriate type of registration must be complied with. At present time, there are four types of registration: Temporary, provisional/dual, provisional and permanent.

Under temporary registration, ship may be registered outside of Saudi Arabia by obtaining temporary certificate of registry from Saudi Embassy or Consulate abroad. Temporary registration is valid only for one voyage to enable vessel to proceed to her Saudi port of registry for provisional registration.

Provisional/dual registration is essentially bareboat registration scheme whereby foreign registered vessel which is demise chartered to Saudi demise charterer that otherwise satisfies all of nationality and related requirements applicable to actual owner, becomes registered under Saudi flag. Registration is only valid for duration of demise charter, and requires "original flag" of vessel to be relinquished during period of Saudi registration. Among requirements for this type of registration is notice from appropriate authorities of vessel's "original flag" stating that it has relinquished vessel for term of charter party. Saudi flag vessels demise chartered to foreign interests may also fly flag of another nation for duration of such demise charter, during which period Saudi registration will be suspended.

Provisional registration occurs when temporarily registered vessel first arrives at her Saudi port of registration, or when vessel at her Saudi port of registry comes under Saudi flag for first time. Vessel's presence in her Saudi port of registry is required. Documentation requirements are extensive. Upon completion of these requirements, provisional certificate of Saudi registry and trading certificate (which attests to validity of vessel's classification certificates) are issued, each with validity period of six Hejira months.

Permanent registration is available to provisionally registered vessels and must be applied for prior to expiration of provisional registration. Permanent registration is valid for five Hejira years and is renewable. Vessel must be at her port of registry to effect permanent registration. New trading certificate in respect of permanently registered vessel is issued on annual basis upon showing that all classification certificates are valid.

TAXATION:

Taxes are levied by central government. At present time no local or regional taxes have been imposed. Tax legislation is effected by Royal Decree, resolutions of Ministry of Finance and National Economy, and circulars issued by DZIT of that Ministry. Portions of this legislation are collected and occasionally published in English.

Principal taxes are income tax and Islamic tax known as Zakat. No property taxes, inheritance taxes or sales taxes are currently being levied.

Income tax is levied on non-Saudi persons or entities (including in respect of limited liability companies having non-Saudi shareholders) having income derived from Saudi Arabian sources. GCC nationals or GCC entities wholly owned by GCC nationals are generally considered to be Saudi persons or entities for taxation purposes. Income tax in respect of Saudi limited liability company with foreign shareholding is assessed on foreign shareowner's share of net income. If such tax is paid, there would be no further tax on dividends distributed to foreign shareholder.

Individuals.—Salary and benefits of non-Saudi employees are not subject to income tax at present. However, non-Saudi person deriving income from investments in capital of Saudi business enterprises (if not already subject to corporate income tax) or from professional activities or partnership profits is subject to income tax at following rates (assuming taxpayer is not Saudi resident):

	Annual Taxable Income	Tax Rate
On first	SR 1 — 16,000	5%
On next	SR 16,001 — 36,000	10%
On next	SR 36,001 — 66,000	20%
	SR 66,001 and upwards	30%

Companies.—Corporate tax is levied on net income. No distinction is made among types of business entities, and applicable tax on partnerships, joint ventures, limited liability companies and joint stock companies is computed on same basis. In determining taxable income, capital gains are considered as ordinary income. Gross income is determined using accrual method of accounting. Only depreciation based on straight-line method and according to rates established by DZIT may be deducted; in certain circumstances, higher rates can be negotiated.

Allocations of administrative or general overhead costs of foreign head offices are not allowed. Operating losses cannot be carried back or forward or used to offset profits of affiliates.

Corporate tax rates are as follows:

	Annual Taxable Income	Tax Rate
On first	SR 1 — 100,000	25%
On next	SR 100,001 — 500,000	35%
On next	SR 500,001 — 1,000,000	40%
	SR 1,000,001 and upwards	45%

In certain circumstances, such as when no tax return has been filed or DZIT determines such approach is appropriate, income tax will be assessed on "deemed profit" basis pursuant to which assumed percentage of taxpayer's gross revenues (such percentage is effectively never less than 15% and can reach 100%) is considered as net income subject to tax at above rates.

Under current DZIT practice, supply only contract whereby foreign company non-resident in Saudi Arabia furnishes goods or material to Saudi Arabia would not generate income subject to Saudi tax. However, supply contract that also provides for installation or other services rendered in Saudi Arabia would be taxable even as to supply component thereof.

Zakat.—This is Islamic tax on wealth and is levied on Saudi and GCC natural persons, wholly Saudi or GCC owned entities, and Saudi or GCC shareholders in limited liability companies. While calculation of Zakat is complex, rate is 2.5% of net worth for individual, and 2.5% of total capital resources of enterprise excluding fixed assets, long-term investments and deferred costs.

Withholding Taxes.—Saudi tax filers are required to make withholdings on certain payments paid to foreign entities which are not Saudi tax filers, and to pay such withheld amounts to DZIT. Such amounts represent foreign entity's Saudi tax liability. Failure so to withhold results in liability of Saudi tax filer for foreign entity's Saudi tax obligations. In many cases, amount required to be withheld is calculated by reference to deemed profit of 15% as to each payment made to foreign entity, although higher rates may be assessed (for management fees and royalties, rate is 100% at present).

Disputes arising out of final tax assessment are considered in first instance by Preliminary Objection Committee attached to DZIT, decisions of which can be appealed to High Appeal Committee if taxpayer pays full amounts in dispute or posts security prior to such appeal.

See topic Foreign Investment.

TRADEMARKS:

The Trademarks Regulations (Royal Decree No. M/5 dated 4.5.1404 H. [Feb. 5, 1984] as supplemented by Rules for Implementation of Trademarks Regulations issued under Minister of Commerce Resolution No. 94 dated 5.8.1404 H. [May 6, 1984])

TRADEMARKS . . . *continued*

permits person or company to register unique combination of letters, numbers, symbols or signs which are applied to certain category of goods or products in such way as to distinguish said goods or products from similar goods or products in marketplace.

Common descriptive names of products, emblems, insignias or flags of any state, religious symbols, or trademarks which are inconsistent with Islamic customs and values or which are deemed to be against Saudi public policy, cannot be registered. In addition, deceptive, confusing, or otherwise misleading marks may not be registered nor may marks showing image of person without that person's consent. Well known mark used by another person or company will also not be registered unless applicant can prove that it is owner of said mark.

Trademark registration is valid for ten Hejira years from date of application and is perpetually renewable for similar ten year periods. Owner of registered mark is not required to use said mark in order to maintain or renew registration, but evidence of such use is important in maintaining or defending action for infringment by another mark.

Applications for registration are filed with Ministry of Commerce, Trademarks Bureau. Decision against registrability is subject to appeal.

After initial review by Bureau, applicant must publish copy of mark and description of goods to be covered by same in official newspaper of record, *Umm Al-Qura*. Publication is followed by 90-day objection period during which owners of similar marks may make formal objection to registration of subject mark. Objections are filed in first instance with Ministry of Commerce, but may be referred to Board of Grievances. If no objections are filed registration of mark is issued within 90-180 days after expiration of objection period. Final registration, when issued, dates back to filing date of application for same.

Registration of trademark gives rise to legal but rebuttable presumption that registrant is owner of mark entitled to sole and exclusive use thereof. Five years of continuous, open and uncontested use of registered mark gives rise to irrebuttable presumption of ownership.

Trademark Law makes it unlawful for person fraudulently to use or imitate registered mark of another so as to deceive public or to knowingly trade in goods which have been labeled with false, misleading or imitated mark. Prior to filing of action, injured owner of registered mark may apply for seizure of infinging products, offending labels, letterhead, advertisements or other materials bearing infringing mark.

TREATIES:

Saudi Arabia is member of The Gulf Co-Operation Council and Arab League.

There is no reliable means of ascertaining all of treaties and conventions to which Saudi Arabia is party.

Certain of more significant treaties are set out below:

Multilateral.—Convention on the Settlement of Investment Disputes between States and Nationals of Other States, Washington, 1965; Agreement for the Creation of the Organization of Petroleum Exporting Countries, Baghdad, 1960; Agreement for the Establishment of an Arab Organizaion of OPEC, Beirut, 1968; Convention Establishing the Multilateral Investment Guarantee Agency, Seoul, 1985; Arab League Convention for the Enforcement of Judgments, 1952; Articles of Agreement of the International Monetary Fund, Formulated at the Bretton Woods Conference, 1944; Articles of Agreement of the International Bank for Reconstruction and Development, 1944; Articles of Agreement of the International Finance Corporation, Washington, 1955; Articles of Agreement of the International Development Association, Washington, 1960; Vienna Convention on Diplomatic Relations, Vienna, 1961; Treaty on Non-Proliferation of Nuclear Weapons, 1968; Convention for the Suppression of Unlawful Acts Against the Safety of Civil Aviation, Montreal, 1971. Saudi Arabia acceded in 1994 to New York Convention on the Enforcement of Foreign Arbitral Awards, 1958 and to Universal Copyright Convention as revised at Paris on July 24, 1971.

Bilateral.—(France) Convention on the Avoidance of Double Taxation with Respect to Taxes on Income and on Estates and Inheritance (with Protocol), Paris, 1982; (U.S.A.) Agreement on Guaranteed Private Investments, 1975.

WILLS:

See topic Death.

SCOTLAND LAW DIGEST REVISER

Digby Brown & Company
The Savoy Tower
77 Renfrew Street
Glasgow G2 3BZ Scotland
Telephone: 141-332-8899
Fax: 141-332-2920
Email: maildesk@digbybrown.co.uk
Website: http://www.digbybrown.co.uk/home.html
Edinburgh, Scotland Office: 7 Albyn Place, Edinburgh EH2 4NG Scotland.
Telephone: 131 225 8505. Fax: 131 225 8482.
Dundee, Scotland Office: Discovery House 5 Cowgate, Dundee DDI 2HS Scotland.
Telephone: 1382 322197. Fax: 1382 200180.

Reviser Profile

Background: Digby Brown & Co. was established in 1910 and is now a medium sized firm in Scotland. The firm comprises six partners, seven associates and four paralegals.

Areas of Practice: The firm specialises in civil litigation and in particular personal injury litigation. Separate partners are responsible for plaintiffs and defendants' litigation. Areas of emphasis and growth include Workmens Compensation Law, General Insurance Defense, Road Traffic Law, Malpractice, Products Liability Law. These areas cater for private clients who demand a high degree of specialisation. In addition to the foregoing the firm is able to offer a service to the general public on Real Estate, Wills and Estates, Matrimonial and Criminal Law.

Client Base: The major clients represented by Digby Brown & Co. are leading British Insurance Corporations as well as some of the largest Unions in the United Kingdom. In addition to this there is a large representation of individuals who rely on all aspects of our expertise for their legal needs.

Operating Area: Digby Brown & Co. have been based in Glasgow since 1910, serving one of the largest industrial cities in the United Kingdom. In order to provide a more efficient method of litigating complex cases, an office was opened in Edinburgh where the Supreme Court is situated. This has the additional advantage of allowing the firm to develop from its base in Western Central Scotland through to the East Coast of Scotland. Further expansion has seen the opening of an office in the North East in Dundee, close to the oil centre of Aberdeen.

Firm Activities: The firm takes an active interest in legal reform and further legal education. Members of the staff are involved in tutoring and lecturing both to lawyers and to students. The firm has particularly close links with the School of Law at Glasgow University.

SCOTLAND LAW DIGEST

(The following is a list of all Topics, including cross-references, covered in this Digest.)

SCOTLAND LAW DIGEST

Revised for 1997 edition by

DIGBY BROWN & CO., Solicitors, Glasgow.

See topics Constitution and Government; Reports.

Scotland is member of EU. See also European Union Law Digest.

ABSENTEES:

In absence abroad, a person may delegate authority to persons of full capacity. Power of attorney may be granted for special purpose or general power to conduct all absentee's affairs. Specific powers should be expressly conferred in deed. Power ends on absentee's return to country or death. Power also ends on subsequent senility of grantor, except where granted after 1st Jan. 1991.

ACKNOWLEDGMENTS:

Requisites of attested deeds are settled partly by statute, and partly by common law. When such requisites are complied with, there is legal presumption of authenticity. Solemn attested deeds require to be witnessed by two witnesses and designations of witnesses must be given and also date of subscription.

The practice of taking declarations by way of formal acknowledgment before justices or others is prohibited except where the person administering the oath has jurisdiction by statute. (Statutory Declarations Act, 1837).

Justices of the peace, notaries and others have, however, power to take any oath or acknowledgment required by laws of a foreign country to give validity to instruments or writings designed to be used in such foreign country.

There is no special form of acknowledgement of a signature. It is advisable to have any form of acknowledgment signed either by or before a British consul.

ACTIONS:

Jurisdiction.—Principles of jurisdiction in Scottish courts now contained in Civil Jurisdiction and Judgments Act 1982. Statute gives effect to European Community Convention of 27th Sept. 1968. Principal ground of jurisdiction is domicile of defender. Domicile is broader concept than residence. Implies habitual residence, substantial connection. Alternative grounds of jurisdiction include place of performance of obligation, of delictual event, of pursuers residence (in alimentary actions), of situation of moveable property which is subject matter of dispute. Exceptions to domicile as ground of jurisdiction arise where subject matter of action is right to heritable property, or validity of companies, partnerships, or associations.

Person may sue, be sued in Scottish courts subject to rules of procedure. Burden of proof is on party who asserts affirmative of issue.

Questions relating to evidence such as competency of witnesses and sufficiency of proof are matters of procedure governed by rules of courts.

Court of Session has exclusive jurisdiction in actions involving status. Jurisdiction for divorce actions has now been extended to Sheriff Court by Divorce Jurisdiction Court Fees and Legal Aid (Scotland) Act 1986.

Formation of courts, see topic Courts.

ADMINISTRATION:

See topic Executors and Administrators.

ADMIRALTY:

Jurisdiction of admiralty as regards prize, which was vested in High Court of Admiralty, is now incorporated within jurisdiction of Court of Session. Other functions of admiralty court are with exceptions exercised by sheriff courts. Jurisdiction in criminal matters being with High Court of Justiciary and other criminal courts.

ADOPTION:

Law consolidated by Adoption (Scotland) Act 1978. Adoption order may be made under statutes extinguishing parental rights and duties of natural parents and investing them in adopters.

Only children under 18 who are unmarried can be adopted.

Either married couple or one person can adopt.

Incest and Related Offences (Scotland) Act 1986 now treats intercourse between adoptive parent and child as incest.

Rights of Adopted Children.—See topic Descent and Distribution.

AFFIDAVITS:

English commissioners or others are not empowered to take oaths for us in the Scottish courts, which appoint special examiners to take the evidence of a witness who cannot appear in person. The statutory form is as follows:

Form

I, A. B., of ...... in the County of ...... do solemnly and sincerely declare that (here set out facts in numbered paragraphs). And I make this solemn declaration conscientiously believing the same to be true, and by virtue of the Statutory Declarations Act, 1835.

Declared at ......, in the County of ......,
this ...... day of ......, 19......, before me } A. B.

....
(Name and designation of Commissioner)

Affidavit should set forth all particulars contained in above style and must be signed by deponent and also by justice, magistrate or judge ordinary before whom it is emitted.

Words "who being solemnly sworn depones" are called jurat. Deponent must actually appear before justice, magistrate or judge ordinary and he must be sworn. Word "swear" must be used.

Admissibility.—As person against whom affidavit is used has no opportunity of cross-examining deponent, an affidavit is not admissible after death of deponent, or when he is abroad and refuses to give evidence before a commissioner of court.

AGENCY: See topic Principal and Agent.

ALIENS:

Aliens are persons born beyond the dominions of the Crown, of parents who are not themselves natural born subjects.

Property.—Alien may hold land and personal property as natural born subject and may transmit title. Heirs of alien succeed to such property. Alien cannot own British ship or hold shares therein.

Immigration.—The Immigration Act 1971 and British Nationality Act 1981, consolidate law relating to immigration and regulate rights of immigrants to enter U.K. The Immigration (Carriers Liability) Act requires carriers to make payments to State in respect of passengers brought by them to U.K. without proper documents.

ASSIGNMENTS:

Movable (personal) estate may be assigned, including policies of insurance. A form of assignation (Scottish technical term) is provided by statute.

An assignation conveys no higher or better right than the grantor possessed and all defenses competent against the assignor may be pleaded against the assignee.

Form.—The form prescribed is as follows:

Form

I, A.B. in consideration of &c., do hereby assign to C.D. his executors or assignees (or otherwise as the case may be) the bond (or other deed or property) granted by E. F. dated &c., by which (here specify any circumstances requiring to be stated in regard to nature of right assigned).

In witness whereof, (place and date of signing and names and designations of witnesses).

Intimation.—To complete legal effect of an assignation intimation is necessary. An assignation is validly intimated: (1) by a notary public delivering a copy thereof certified as correct to holders of the fund; (2) by a copy of assignation being transmitted by post to such holders; or (3) by the debtor endorsing an acknowledgment of intimation on the assignation. A certificate of the notary in first case and a written acknowledgment of receipt in second case will be sufficient evidence of intimation.

Policy of Assurance.—An assignation does not confer any right to sue for amount of policy until written notice of debt and of purport of assignation have been given to insurance company at its principal place of business. Date on which such notice is received by company regulates priority of all claims made under assignation. (Policies of Assurance Act, 1867).

Proper form of assignation is as follows:

Form

I, A.B. of &c., in consideration of &c., do hereby assign unto C.D. &c., his executors, administrators and assignees the within Policy of Assurance granted &c., (here describe the Policy) in witness whereof: &c.

ASSIGNMENTS FOR BENEFIT OF CREDITORS:

This is a recognized manner of dividing estate if a person be unable to meet obligations. Form used is by assignation to trustee for benefit of creditors. Deed must be assented to by creditors or debtor will not be discharged.

Court does not exercise supervision over trustee under a voluntary assignation except that his accounts are audited and his commission fixed by an officer of court if trust deed does not provide for these things being done by a committee of creditors.

ASSOCIATIONS:

Unincorporated bodies may sue or be sued in name of body. Judgments are valid against such bodies and individual partners. (Sheriff Court Act, Scotland, 1907).

Friendly societies which may have for objects, inter alia, payment of money in sickness and at death, while not incorporate, are regulated by, and registered under Act of Parliament. An Act of 1955 extends powers of societies and makes corresponding amendments for trade unions in relation to amounts payable on death. Friendly Societies Act 1974 consolidates Friendly Societies Act, 1896-1971.

ATTACHMENT (Arrestment):

Attachment is of two kinds: (a) where judgment has been obtained the attachment is made in execution; (b) where judgment has not been obtained, or debt is future, attachment is made in security.

Warrant is obtained from court and contained in judgment. In a depending action warrant is granted on ex parte application contained in summons, and property may be

See Topical Index in front part of this volume.

ATTACHMENT (Arrestment) . . . *continued*
attached prior to service in action. This procedure is known as arrestment on dependence of action. This applies alike to resident and nonresident.

Property Liable.—All movable goods belonging to debtor in hands of third parties or debts due to debtor can be attached. Ships are also attachable. Process of recovery prior to and following decree is governed by Debtors (Scotland) Act 1987. Wages are attachable in hands of employer who on receipt of appropriate schedule will make payments to creditor.

Release.—The judge before whom an action is pending may release attachment on such terms as to security as he may consider proper.

Damages.—Wrongful use of attachment renders user liable in damages if act has been malicious and without probable cause.

ATTORNEYS AND COUNSELORS:

Scottish Legal System recognises distinction between solicitor (Scottish term for Law Agent under Solicitors [Scotland] Act 1933) and advocate (member of Scottish Bar), two branches having developed separately.

Admission to Roll of Solicitors is achieved by obtaining Degree in Law, Legal Diploma and subsequent two years practical experience. On admission to Roll of Solicitors, solicitor is then required to take out Annual Practising Certificate. Main solicitors regulatory body is Law Society of Scotland. Its powers are based on Solicitors (Scotland) Act 1988. Headquarters for Law Society of Scotland are 26 Drumsheugh Gardens, Edinburgh, EH3 7YR, (Telephone Number 031-225-7411). Law Society, as one of its functions, appoints legal professionals and lay members to sit as Scottish Solicitors Discipline Tribunal who investigate complaints of professional misconduct and decide whether to censure or strike off solicitors from Solicitors Roll.

Term solicitor may be broadly interpreted to mean general legal practitioner, however, often many Scottish solicitors are specialists in their own field. Consequently Law Reform (Scotland) Act 1990 §§25-29 extended right of audience of solicitors from Inferior Court, such as Sheriff Court, to Superior High Court and Court of Session. This was previously exclusive domain of members of Faculty of Advocates. Individual solicitors have to satisfy requirements that they have necessary knowledge and expertise to qualify for this extended right of audience.

Faculty of Advocates is membership organisation for Scottish Bar. It is headed by Dean of Faculty and is based at Parliament House 1, Parliament Square, Edinburgh, (Telephone Number 031-226-2881). Advocates have rights of audience in nearly all courts and tribunals in Scotland. Distinction can be made between Junior and Senior Counsel, latter having many years of experience and are also known as Queens Counsel. In nearly all cases instructions should be through Enrolled Solicitor, particularly if litigation is contemplated in Scotland.

AUTOMOBILES: See topic Motor Vehicles.

BANKRUPTCY (Sequestration):

Law of Bankruptcy was codified by Bankruptcy (Scotland) Act 1985, and was further amended by Bankruptcy (Scotland) Act 1993. Creditor must now have debt of not less than £1,500 to petition for sequestration.

Formal bankruptcy is brought about by sequestration of debtor's estate in terms of which process such estates become vested in a trustee for creditors. Sequestration may be obtained by petition to Court of Session or to Sheriff Court of County where debtor resides or carries on in business.

Debtor can petition for his own sequestration if qualified creditor concurs in petition. He can also petition if his debt exceeds prescribed limit, he has not been sequestrated in previous five years, and he is either apparently insolvent or has granted Trust Deed with trustee having complied with certain requirements contained in Act.

Petition by a creditor can only be presented when it has been established by legal process that debtor cannot pay his debt. Further requisites are: (1) That debtor is subject to jurisdiction of Scottish Courts. (2) That creditors have debts of at least £1,500. (3) That formal evidence of insolvency be produced, and (4) that debtor has during year before presentation of petition, either resided or had place of business in Scotland.

On sequestration being awarded, interim trustee is appointed. If petition nominates such trustee, if Court is satisfied that person is qualified, he will be appointed interim trustee. Where no person is nominated in petition Government official entitled "Accountant in Bankruptcy" will be appointed interim trustee.

1993 Act introduced provision where debtor has no assets for summary administration of sequestration of debtor's estate. Statutory meeting is usually called to appoint permanent trustee, although this can be dispensed with in certain circumstances.

Trustee will report as to whether debtors assets will be sufficient to pay dividend.

Bankrupt will be discharged automatically after three years, although trustee may apply to Court prior to automatic discharge for extension if he has just cause to do so.

See also topics Assignments for Benefit of Creditors; Insolvency.

BILLS AND NOTES:

The law regarding bills of exchange is codified by the Bills of Exchange Act, 1882. As defined by the Act of Parliament a bill is an unconditional order in writing addressed by one person to another signed by the person giving it requiring the person to whom it is addressed to pay on demand or at a fixed or determinable future time a sum certain in money to or to the order of a specified person or to bearer. (§3).

To preserve right of recourse holder must duly present bill for acceptance and payment.

Every person whose signature appears on a bill is prima facie deemed to have become a party thereto for value and every holder is prima facie deemed to be a holder in due course. (§30).

Where a bill is payable after sight, presentment for acceptance is necessary in order to fix the maturity. (§39).

If drawee of a bill has in his hands funds available for payment, bill operates as an assignment of sum for which it is drawn in favor of holder from time when bill is presented to drawee. (§52-2).

On dishonor holder must at once give notice to drawer and each endorser, otherwise his right of recourse against them is discharged. Simple notice is sufficient in case of an inland bill; a notarial protest is necessary for a foreign bill.

A cheque is a bill of exchange drawn on a banker payable on demand. (§73).

A promissory note is defined as an unconditional promise in writing made by one person to another signed by the maker, engaging to pay, on demand or at a fixed or determinable future time, a sum certain in money to, or to the order of a specified person or to bearer. (§83).

Three days of grace are added to time of payment fixed by bill. Where last day of grace falls on Sun., Christmas Day, Good Friday, or day appointed by Royal Proclamation, bill is due and payable on preceding business day. When last day of grace is a bank holiday (other than Christmas Day or Good Friday) under Bank Holidays Act, 1871, or when last day of grace is a Sun. and second day of grace is a bank holiday bill is due and payable on succeeding business day. (§14).

Provided all statutory requirements have been given effect to, there is provided in Scotland a summary method for recovery, a protest being written out and signed by notary which being registered in court books, an extract is issued having effect of a judgment of court.

Period of limitation on a bill of exchange is six years, but thereafter debt may be proved by writ or oath of debtor.

Where a bill drawn on one country is negotiated, accepted or payable in another, its validity as regards requisites in form of bill is determined by law of place of issue and its validity as regards requisites in form of supervening contracts, such as acceptance, indorsement or acceptance supra protest, is determined by law of place where particular contract was made. But a bill issued outside of U.K. is not invalid merely because not stamped according to law of place of issue, and where such bill conforms, as regards requisites of form, to law of U.K., it may, for purpose of enforcing payment thereof, be treated as valid as between all persons who negotiate, hold or become parties to it in U.K. (§72).

BONDS:

See topic Mortgages of Real Property.

CHATTEL MORTGAGES:

Chattel mortgages are unknown. The law does not recognize any security over furniture or personal effects unless possession, actual or constructive, is transferred to the creditor. Retention of title claims in commercial contracts are frustrated if true intention is to create security over moveables.

COLLATERAL SECURITY: See topic Pledges.

COMMERCIAL REGISTER:

Under Registration of Business Names Act 1916, every firm carrying on business under name which did not consist of true surname of all partners or every individual carrying on business under name other than true surname or who had changed name required to register with Registrar of Business Names. All names had to be published in business documents and correspondence. 1916 Act was repealed and Register abolished by Companies Act 1981 which makes further provisions regarding permissible business names, public disclosure etc. See also topic Corporations, subhead Registration.

COMMISSIONS TO TAKE TESTIMONY:

See topic Depositions.

COMPANIES: See topic Corporations.

CONSTITUTION AND GOVERNMENT:

So far as this subject matter is concerned Scotland enjoys same constitution as England, and paragraphs under heading in England Law Digest may be read as equally applicable to Scotland. Similarly subhead Executive may be read as applicable to Scotland.

Scottish Law.—The law of Scotland consists partly of enacted law which has the authority of some body having legislative powers, partly of common law, which is recognized by the courts as binding on some ground other than express enactment. Enacted law may include a Royal proclamation or order; an Act of Parliament; an Act of Sederunt; an Act of Adjournal; a bye-law or regulation issued either by a department of the State or by some local authority or body having statutory powers. A statute may be either a public or general statute or a local or personal act. Acts of Sederunt are rules passed by the Supreme Court of Scotland. Acts of Adjournal are passed by the High Court of Justiciary for regulating procedure in that Court and in inferior criminal courts.

Judiciary.—House of Lords is ultimate court for appeals in Britain. Supreme Court in Scotland in civil matters is Court of Session sited in Edinburgh. High Court of Justiciary is supreme criminal court having a permanent session in Edinburgh but with provision for circuit or local courts. In practice High Court is permanently on circuit in larger towns. Sheriff Court is a court of first instance and has equal jurisdiction as to monetary value with Court of Session but latter has jurisdiction in certain cases denied to Sheriff Court involving status.

CONTRACTS:

Obligation arises from consent. Consideration is not necessary element. Gratuitous promise proved only by writ or oath of party making it. Courts will entertain action on contract only if patrimonial interest involved.

Power to Contract.—Lunatics and pupils (boys under 14, girls under 12) no power at all. Minors under 18 have power to contract, but contract may be reduced until he attains 22. Injury or harm must be proved (Enorm Lesion).

Children below 16 years of age now have no capacity as general rule to contract (as per The Legal Age of Capacity [Scotland] Act 1991 which came into force on 25th Sept. 1991); however, transactions which cause 16 and 17 year old substantial prejudice may be set aside by Court on application by young person.

See Topical Index in front part of this volume.

CONTRACTS . . . *continued*

Constitution of Contracts.—Some require no special form. Others must be entered in writing. Contracts relating to heritage except lease for less than one year require probative writing of both parties. Imperfect contract may be made binding by actions of parties.

Avoidance of Contracts.—Contract may be rendered void or voidable where consent obtained by improper means, or given under error in facts. Contract induced by violence is void. Also void where object is for furtherance of illegal purpose. Impossibility of performance may or may not render contract void. Doctrine of frustration excuses performance when impossibility caused independent from volition of contracting parties. See England Law Digest, topic Contracts, subhead Excuses for Nonperformance.

Rights of Third Parties.—Contract cannot impose liability on someone not party to contract. Third party may acquire right to sue on contract.

Statutes.—§4 Unfair Contract Terms Acts 1977 applies to consumer contracts in Scotland.

Distributorships, Dealerships and Franchises.—No special rules exist as regards formation and termination of these types of business arrangements, and normal rules of Contract Law will apply.

COPYRIGHT:

Copyright means the sole right to produce or reproduce original, literary, dramatic, musical and artistic work or to deliver lecture. It includes sole right: (a) to produce, perform or publish translations; (b) to convert dramatic work into novel; (c) to convert novel into dramatic work; (d) to make records or films or any contrivance by means of which work may be performed. (Copyright Act, 1911, §1). Copyright in design is provided for by the Registered Design Act, 1949. Both these Acts have been incorporated in the Copyright Act 1956 and the whole field widened to embrace modern trends in television and sound broadcasts, cinematograph, films, etc. Copyright, Designs and Patents Act 1988 has amended and consolidated law in this area. See also Cable and Broadcasting Act 1984.

CORPORATIONS:

Name "Corporations" is usually applied to municipal bodies, thus, Corporation of City of Glasgow, Corporation of City of Edinburgh. These municipal bodies were abolished by Local Government Scotland Act 1973 and replaced by two tier local authority bodies. Large authorities, called Regional Councils, of which there are nine, are subdivided into smaller authorities, called Districts, of which there are 50. Local Government in Scotland is presently under review and from 1 Apr. 1996 there will be in existence single tier system of Local Government, such councils dealing with all functions presently carried out by District and Regional Councils except for function of water and sewerage which will go to three separate quangos.

Under this head may also fall those companies created by Royal Charter, or by special Act of Parliament. Such bodies are all regulated by Terms of Charter or particular Act of Parliament.

Term applied to incorporated business organizations of limited liability is "companies." Law in regard to limited companies is contained principally in Companies Acts 1948-1981. 1948 Act is still principal Act 1967, 1976, 1980 and 1981 Acts follow. Law partly revised, mainly consolidated by Companies Act 1985.

Companies may be public or private. Under former system every company was public unless it satisfied certain requirements of private company set out in 1948 Act. 1980 Act introduces new system and reverses this. Public company must conform to certain specified minimum standards: (i) Minimum subscribed share capital £50,000; (ii) statement in Memorandum that it is public; (iii) name to include words "public limited company" or "plc"; (iv) minimum number of members, two.

Company which does not satisfy these requirements is private. Essential difference is that only public company may offer shares to public.

Registration.—The Business Names Regulations 1981 (also Company Business Names [Amendment] Regulations 1982) specify 79 separate words or expressions which require consent before use. Too like names are regulated; some names are prohibited either absolutely or conditionally.

Internal management of company is regulated by its articles of association. External management is regulated by its memorandum of association. Companies may adopt form of articles and memorandum as set out in Companies (Tables A to F) Regulations 1985 or as near thereto as circumstances admit.

Issue of Prospectus.—Where a prospectus is issued it must contain certain details of which the following may be mentioned: Number of deferred shares; names, descriptions and addresses of directors; minimum subscription; names and addresses of vendors; amount of purchase money; amount paid to promoter; and voting rights of classes of shareholders.

A company which does not issue a prospectus is not permitted to allot any shares or debentures unless prior to the first allotment there has been filed with the registrar a statement in lieu of prospectus, which must contain practically the same particulars as required in a prospectus.

See generally England Law Digest and European Union Law Digest.

COURTS:

Criminal cases dealt with by either District Courts, Sheriff Courts or High Court, depending on nature and seriousness of crime. Locus of crime bestows jurisdiction on court in particular geographical area.

Courts for civil business are supreme and inferior. Supreme Court, known as Court of Session, consists of 24 judges, together with temporary Judges appointed by Secretary of State. Eight judges sitting in two divisions with equal status, form Inner House or Appellate Courts. Eleven judges each sit in their own separate Courts, forming Outer House, and are known as Lords Ordinary. Remaining judge sits permanently on Law Commission. Inner House hears appeals from Outer House judges and from sheriff courts. In certain classes of cases an appeal lies from Court of Session to House of Lords. Until implementation of Law Reform (Scotland) Act 1990 (§§ 25-29) right of audience in High Court and Court of Session limited to members of Faculty of Advocates. Attorneys now permitted to appear.

Principal inferior courts are Sheriff Courts. There are six Sheriffdoms divided into Sheriff Court districts each of which has it's own courts. There is no limitation of amount which can be sued for in Sheriff Court. Sheriffs are provided for districts, appeal from whose decisions lies to Sheriff Principal. Each Sheriffdom has its own Sheriff Principal. Burgh, Police and Justice of Peace Courts which dealt with minor criminal matters have been abolished by District Courts (Scotland) Act 1975. Each District Council (see topic Corporations) is responsible for setting up and running District Courts. Further appeal in most cases is to the Court of Session.

Sessions.—Court of Session holds three sessions in year, dates being fixed by Act of Sederunt.

Sheriff Courts have winter session and summer session. There is a Christmas recess.

CURRENCY:

See England Law Digest. In addition, certain Scottish banks have right to make note issues, i.e. Royal Bank of Scotland, Bank of Scotland and Clydesdale Bank.

CURTESY:

Curtesy, or courtesy as it is spelled in Scotland, was name given to right of surviving husband to a life interest of heritable (real) property of his deceased wife, if he was father of a living child, which child would have been heir of wife. This right may not be defeated by will. (See also topic Descent and Distribution.) This right has been abolished as of 10/9/64 by Succession (Scotland) Act 1964.

CUSTOMS: See England Law Digest.

DEATH:

The Presumption of Death (Scotland) Act, 1977 contains provisions in relation to presumption of death of missing persons. Now any person with interest can raise action of declarator of death of missing person: (a) If there are reasonable grounds for supposing missing person has died or (b) if missing person has been absent for at least seven years and there is no reason to believe that he is alive. This procedure will be effective for all purposes including inter alia dissolution of marriage, succession to property, obtaining benefits due under insurance policies.

If death has occurred within last five years and date and place of death are known, local Registrar of Deaths can furnish a copy certificate. If wider search is required then application to Registrar of Deaths, Register House, Edinburgh, is necessary.

Actions for Death.—Civil action lies at instance of a spouse and ascendants and descendants of victim. Under Damages (Scotland) Act 1976 group of relatives entitled to claim is extended considerably. Right of damages is related to right of dependancy and support. Only spouse, parents, child (or person accepted as child of family by deceased) of victim are entitled to claim solatium. Negligence of party liable must be proved. That party can plead negligence or contributory negligence of victim to elide responsibility.

Parent of illegitimate child has right to recover damages and solatium in respect of death of that child as if child were legitimate.

Damages cover: (a) A sum representing loss of support which must be real at date of death, and (b) solatium, a sum representing injury to feelings of claimant caused by the death.

This law will apply to foreigners who would require to raise claim in Scotland if delict happened there and if defendants were subject to jurisdiction of Scotland.

As to time limits see topic Limitation of Actions, matter dealing with personal injuries.

DECEDENTS' ESTATES:

See topics Descent and Distribution; Executors and Administrators; Wills.

DEEDS:

Writing is required on obligations relative to land, conveyances, and leases for more than one year. Attested writings are subscribed by grantor in presence of two witnesses or acknowledged by him to them. If grantor cannot write, document may be subscribed by solicitor, notary public, or justice of the peace, or parish minister, before two witnesses who sign and testify to having heard document read and authority given to sign. (Conveyancing Act, Scotland, 1924). In Scotland "deed" does not connote a document under seal. See topic Records.

DEPOSITIONS:

Application may be made to court, before which action is pending, to have evidence of witness taken on commission. Usual grounds for application are that witness is resident abroad, proposing to go abroad, or is aged or infirm. Notice must be given except in case of extreme urgency, and names of persons to be examined should be intimated.

Written interrogatories may be ordered and it is in discretion of court whether evidence should be taken by interrogatories and cross interrogatories.

Witnesses Abroad.—Where evidence of any witness abroad is material application may be made to judge for letter of request to foreign tribunal within jurisdiction of which such witness is resident. On such letter of request being granted it is forwarded to Foreign Secretary for transmission to such foreign court.

Actions in Foreign Court.—Where Court of Session is informed that a foreign court is desirous of obtaining evidence of person resident in Scotland, an order may be issued ordaining such person to appear to give evidence. (Foreign Tribunal Evidence Act, 1856). Evidence will not be taken before a court but before a commissioner. (Case Baron De'Bildt, 1905, Frasers Reports 899).

Form.—The usual form of commission is as under:

Form

At . . . ., the . . . . day of . . . ., in the year . . . ., there was produced to A.B. (here name and design Commissioner) a Certified Copy Interlocutor, dated . . . ., pronounced by (name Judge) in the action pending before (name Court) at the instance of C.D., Pursuer, against E.F., Defender, whereby, inter alia, Commission is granted to the said Commissioner to take the oaths and examinations of witnesses in said action; of which Commission the said A.B. accepted, and made choice of G.H. to be his Clerk, and administered to him the oath de fideli administratione.

See Topical Index in front part of this volume.

DEPOSITIONS . . . *continued*

Thereafter compeared Pursuer and J.K. his Solicitor, as also the defender and L.M. his Solicitor (or as the case may be).

Compeared N.O. (designation and address) aged . . . ., who being solemnly sworn and interrogated as witness for Pursuer (or Defender) depones.

All which is true as the deponent shall answer to God (specifying corrections).

At the conclusion of the Proof the following docquet will be written:

What is contained on this and the . . . . preceding pages is the report of the Commissioner mentioned on the first page hereof.

Humbly reported by

. . . ., Commissioner,

. . . ., Clerk.

DESCENT AND DISTRIBUTION:

Distribution.—Net intestate estate, after deduction of rights enumerated under next headings, devolves in following order, without distinction between heritable (real) and movable estate, any surviving relative in an earlier group eliding completely any surviving relative in a later group; (1) Children; (2) either or both parents and brothers and sisters, one-half to parent or parents and one-half to brothers and sisters; (3) brothers and sisters; (4) either or both parents; (5) surviving spouse; (6) uncles or aunts, paternal or maternal line; (7) grandparent or grandparents, paternal or maternal line; (8) brothers or sisters of such grandparents; (9) ancestors of intestate remoter than grandparents, on both paternal and maternal lines, generation by generation successively and their collaterals coming before next remote generation.

There is therefore no distinction now by reason of age or sex. Two general principles apply to foregoing order of succession: (1) There is representation in all branches of succession, i.e., where any relative, who would, if alive, have been entitled to succeed to whole or part of estate predeceased leaving issue, such issue take share which deceased parent would have received if in life; (2) in case of collaterals, both those of full blood and those of half blood are entitled to succeed, but collaterals of full blood have preference. Collaterals of half blood rank without distinction as between those related through father or mother.

Husband and Wife.—Terce and courtesy abolished and new kind of rights known as "prior rights" created. These rights apply without distinction as between husband and wife, and arise only in cases of intestacy or partial intestacy. They cannot supersede will of deceased.

Succession (Scotland) Act 1964 relating to deaths on or after 10th Sept. 1964 made far-reaching changes in Law of Intestate succession in Scotland. These have been modified by §§(1) to (3) and Schedule (1) of Law Reform (Miscellaneous Provisions) (Scotland) Act 1968 as regards illegitimate children. §8 of 1964 Act gives surviving spouse ownership or tenancy to any one house owned or tenanted (other than under Rent Restrictions Act) by intestate provided that survivor is ordinarily resident therein at deceased's death. That also gave survivor furniture and plenishings belonging to deceased in any one house in which survivor was ordinarily resident at deceased's death. Maximum limits of £15,000 and £5,000 respectively replaced on house and furniture respectively falling under these provisions in certain cases, e.g. farmhouse, survivor received value and not house itself. These figures are now respectively £65,000 and £12,000. If furniture and plenishings exceeds £12,000 surviving spouse is entitled to such part thereof up to that value as he or she may elect.

From what was left after that right had been met, §9 of 1964 Act gave surviving spouse £5,000 if deceased was not survived by lawful issue and £2,500 if there was such issue of deceased. These amounts have now been increased to £35,000 and £21,000 respectively.

Legal rights of jus relicti and jus relictae remain unaltered with qualification that they are now calculated by reference only to net movable estate which remains after satisfying prior rights as above mentioned.

In addition to these prior and legal rights, surviving spouse may also have interest in net intestate estate as shown above. See subhead Distribution, supra.

Children.—Right of legitim remains unaltered with qualification that it is also calculated only by reference to net movable estate after satisfying prior rights above-mentioned. Now extends to illegitimate children. See subhead Illegitimates, infra.

New act also extends application of right by introducing representation. If child of deceased who would have had claim of legitim has predeceased leaving issue surviving, such issue may claim equally among them share of legitim to which parent would have been entitled on survivance.

Illegitimates.—Succession (Scotland) Act 1964 repeals Legitimacy Act, 1926 but substantially re-enacts its provisions. If mother of illegitimate child dies intestate and without lawful issue, such illegitimate child or issue of such succeeds to whole estate. If illegitimate child dies intestate without issue, or in case of woman without any illegitimate children or their issue, mother, if alive, succeeds to estate. By Law Reform (Misc. Prov.) Act, 1968, illegitimate child shares equally in estate with legitimate children of deceased person.

Adopted Children.—Prior to 1964 Act, adopted children had no rights in estate of adopting parent, only in estate of natural parents. (Adoption Act 1958). Under provisions of new Act, for all purposes relating to succession, adopted children are treated as children of adopter and not as children of any other person. They have right of legitim along with natural children of adopter, and right of succession of natural children.

Where succession by collaterals is involved, child adopted by two spouses jointly is treated as brother or sister of full blood in question with natural children, or other adopted children of spouse. If child has been adopted by only one of spouses, he or she is treated as brother or sister of half blood.

DESERTION: See topic Husband and Wife.

DISPUTE RESOLUTION:

At present alternative dispute resolution movement in Scotland is at very early stage of its development. Various professional bodies including Law Society of Scotland have instituted alternative dispute resolution forums but use of such facilities by potential litigants is entirely voluntary, and as yet not widespread.

Arbitration.—It has never been Law of Scotland that agreement to oust jurisdiction of Courts was invalid as contrary to public policy. Submission of certain kinds of disputes to arbitration may be rquired by statute (rare) or provided for in parties contract or may be adopted by parties when dispute arises in preference to resorting to litigaton.

Mandatory Dispute Resolution.—At present there are few statutory provisions in Scots Law requiring disputes which are brought before Courts to be referred to other bodies for resolution. Example of such provision is that any dispute between landlord and tenant of agricultural holding arising out of tenancy must be referred to arbitration (see Agricultural Holding [Scotland] Act 1949, §74).

Voluntary Dispute Resolution.—Statutory provision for voluntary dispute resolution includes intervention by ACAS (Advisory Conciliatory and Arbitration Service), body set up by statute to promote "good industrial relations", to facilitate resolution of individual and collective labour disputes. Under Employment Protection Consolidation Act 1978, §134 Conciliation Officer of ACAS has duty to endeavor to promote settlement of any individual complaint (unfair dismissal from employment etc.) and thus avoid need for determination of dispute of Industrial Tribunal hearing. Participation by parties in dispute in this process is entirely voluntary. In respect of collective labour disputes §§209 to 212 of Trade Union Labour Relations Consolidation Act 1992 provides for reference by ACAS, with consent of parties involved of any labour dispute to central arbitration committee or person appointed for purpose of arbitration. Decision of CAC or independent arbitrator is not legally binding on parties.

Other forms of alternative dispute resolution include Accord scheme instituted by Law Society of Scotland. This voluntary procedure provides alternative forum for resolution of disputes involving potential litigants. Involvement in process is entirely voluntary and only when agreement is reached is determination legally binding.

DIVORCE:

Under Divorce (Scotland) Act 1976 there is only one ground of divorce in Scotland, irretrievable breakdown of marriage. This is established by evidence of adultery, unreasonable behaviour, wilful desertion for two years, two years separation where defender consents to divorce, or five years separation where defender does not consent. Grounds for judicial separation are now same as for divorce. Under Act, either party may apply for financial provision on divorce, such application being for either periodical allowance, capital sum or for order varying any marriage settlement taking effect on or after termination of marriage. Act gives court power to counteract certain transactions designed to avoid claim for financial provision on divorce or aliment between spouses. Aliment can now be awarded in action for interim aliment to spouse living apart by consent even where there is no reasonable cause for nonadherence. Right of husband to cite his wife's alleged paramour as co-defender and right to sue paramour for damages are abolished. Expenses of action may still be awarded against alleged paramour in accordance with practice of court, if he or she intervenes in action.

Family Law (Scotland) Act 1985 outlines objectives of financial provision on divorce or nullity of marriage. Grants court power to transfer property between spouses, and regulate occupancy of matrimonial home. Creates rebuttable presumption that spouses own household goods in equal shares.

Domicile and Matrimonial Proceedings Act 1973 abolishes rule whereby a wife takes her husband's domicile automatically as a domicile of dependence and it makes consequential changes in law on dependent domicile of children. Changes are not limited to jurisdiction in consistorial cases. They are quite general in their scope and will apply for example in relation to succession, obligations, property income tax and estate duty.

DOWER:

A widow has a right, known as terce, to a life interest of one-third in any heritable estate belonging to her deceased husband where there are children of the marriage. Where there are no children the widow has a life interest in one-half of her husband's heritable estate. Terce abolished as of Sept. 10, 1964. See topic Descent and Distribution.

ENVIRONMENT:

This area of law is at present in state of transition. Environmental awareness and protection has come to forefront in last decade partly due to requirement to implement European Community legislation in this area. At present legislation and agencies involved overlap and conflict. First step in attempting to simplify legislation and regulatory bodies was taken with passing of Environmental Protection Act 1990. This deals with pollution in relation to air, land and water. However, other relevant legislation is for example, Nuclear Installation Act 1965 relating to radioactive material and licensing of such sites and Part Two of Food and Environmental Protection Act 1985 which deals with use of pesticides.

Responsibility for sewage and water has been removed from Local Authority control by Local Government Scotland Act 1994 to be brought under control of three unelected Public Authorities East, West and North of Scotland Water which are monitored by Scottish Water and Sewerage Customers Council.

The Environment Act 1995 created Scottish Environmental Protection Agency which has taken over function of National River Authority and Her Majesty's Inspector of Pollution. The Central Thrust of the Environmental Act 1995 is to set up one National Authority, more independent of Government, and instituting uniform approach to environmental protection. Prior to passing of this act responsibility for enforcing antipollution controls was split between various statutory bodies such as Local Authorities and National River Authority. SEPA now has remit of enforcing protection of quality of river water, air pollution matters involving prescribed processes and substances and waste regulation.

EVIDENCE: See topic Depositions.

EXCHANGE CONTROL: See England Law Digest.

EXECUTIONS:

Execution, being what is known as diligence on a decree, may proceed when days of charge or notice specified in decree or required by statute or common law have expired

EXECUTIONS . . . *continued*
without payment. Such execution may issue against heritable (real) estate or movable (personal) estate. Statutory provisions for implementation of diligence contained in Debtors (Scotland) Act 1987 include sliding scale of amount arrestable according to net income; rates amended from time to time in Law Reform (Scotland) Acts. Restrictions on items that can be seized (poinded) and sold in satisfaction of decree, e.g. essential household goods, tools of trade.

Execution against such heritable estate may proceed by what is termed inhibition, by which debtor is prohibited from disposing of or burdening his heritable property. Inhibitions prescribe in five years.

Execution may be used to attach all movables or land over which a security is held. Generally however heritable property is attached by sequestration. Movable property is attached by arrestment on decree followed by action of furthcoming. In terms of decree debtor's movables can be brought to sale by diligence known as a poinding.

EXECUTORS AND ADMINISTRATORS:

Executors are appointed by will of deceased, or, in intestacy, application is made to the court to make an appointment. In a competition of claimants the appointment of an executor is made in the following order: (1) a person having a general disposition of the estate in his favor such as a will; (2) the next of kin; (3) the widow; (4) a creditor; (5) a legatee. After Sept. 10, 1964 where widow or widower takes whole estate he or she has preference for appointment of executor.

A consul, vice-consul, or consular agent of a foreign country which extends similar privilege to this country, may apply for administration of estate of subject of such state dying in this country where no person is present entitled to administer such estate.

An executor appointed by will does not require to find security. In intestacy, security must be given to an amount fixed by the court.

FIDUCIARIES:

See topics Executors and Administrators; Trusts.

FORECLOSURE:

See topic Mortgages of Real Property.

FOREIGN CORPORATIONS:

See topic Corporations.

FOREIGN EXCHANGE:

See England Law Digest.

FOREIGN INVESTMENT:

See England Law Digest.

FOREIGN TRADE REGULATIONS:

See England Law Digest.

FRAUDS, STATUTE OF:

There is no Statute of Frauds in Scotland. Certain contracts must be in writing such as transactions affecting heritage, and leases for more than one year.

FRAUDULENT CONVEYANCES:

Fraudulent conveyances may be set aside under the bankruptcy statutes. See topic Insolvency.

GARNISHMENT: See topic Attachment (Arrestment).

HOLIDAYS:

Bank holidays in Scotland are New Year's Day, Christmas Day (or if they fall on Sun. the following Mon.); Good Friday; the first Mon. of May and Aug.; any day appointed by Royal Proclamation. (Bank Holidays Act, 1871).

HOMESTEADS:

There are no provisions as to exemption of property except of trifling extent in House Letting Acts.

HUSBAND AND WIFE:

A married woman may hold and dispose of property as freely as if unmarried. She may also sue actions at law without consent of husband. Husband is not liable for delict of his wife or for contract made by her. Parties have mutual obligation of support. Civil imprisonment still possible in case of wilful failure to pay sums decerned for as aliment. See also topic Descent and Distribution. Alimentary obligations set out in Family Law (Scotland) Act 1985.

Where title deed over matrimonial home is held in name of one spouse only, "non-entitled" spouse has occupancy rights which subsist until he/she freely and without coercion renounces them by affidavit. Court may also grant limited occupancy rights to "non-entitled" partner where unmarried couple are co-habiting. (Matrimonial Homes [Family Protection] [Scotland] Act 1981). See also topic Divorce.

IMMIGRATION: See England Law Digest.

INCOME TAX: See topic Taxation.

INFANCY:

Scotland, following Roman law, had two tier system capacity for people under age of 18. People (girls under 12 and boys under 14) generally had no capacity; their tutors acted for them. Minors (girls from 12 to 17 and boys from 14 to 17) had limited capacity. Transactions normally required consent of their curators in order to be valid. However, Age of Legal Capacity (Scotland) Act 1991 came into force on 25th Sept. 1991. Act sets out new rules in private law field in relation to legal capacity of people under 18 years old to enter into transactions having legal effect. Transaction is defined to include contact, promise, gift, consenting, bringing or defending legal proceedings and acting as executor or witness to signing of document. It establishes single tier system of upper age limit of 16. Children below 16 years of age have no capacity as general rule although there are a few exceptions. Their parents or guardians all have to act for them. Children aged 16 and 17 now have full legal capacity, but transactions which cause them substantial prejudice may be set aside by Court on application by young person. §1 (c) of Act sets out general areas where rules do not apply. Act does not have any affect to fields of crime and delict and does not alter any statutory age limits (such as being entitled to vote at 18); it also does not alter rules relating to appointment of curators bonis and ad litem or rights of parents under 16 towards their children.

The Law Reform (Parent and Child) (Scotland) Act 1986 makes fresh provision with respect to consequences of birth out of wedlock, rights and duties of parents, determination of parentage and taking of blood samples. Act grants equality of status to all persons whatever marital status of their parents. Law Reform (Scotland) Act 1990 §70 gives power to Courts to order party to provide blood sample on application of opponent. Failure to comply can be founded upon.

INSOLVENCY:

Insolvency at common law is condition of inability to meet debts or obligations.

Effects.—Every form of gratuitous alienation is forbidden. It is not necessary to show fraud either on part of grantor or grantee. Any creditor may challenge such transaction. Deeds, if gratuitous, made in favor of near relative or confidential friend, are presumed to be fraudulent. (Statute 1621 c. 18). All deeds conferring preferences on particular creditors to exclusion of general body of creditors are null. (Statute 1696 c. 5). Payments in cash are not affected, nor are transactions in ordinary course of trade. See also Bankruptcy (Sequestration).

The Insolvency Act 1986 consolidates enactments relating to company insolvency and winding up and enactments relating to insolvency and bankruptcy of individuals.

INTEREST:

There is no statutory rate of legal interest though it is custom of court to allow interest at 15% from date of service of proceedings. Interest can run on injury compensation from date injury sustained. Interest is due on bills and notes from date of presentation of bills payable on demand, and from maturity in other cases. (Bills of Exchange Act, 1880, Section 57). As general rule compound interest is not due.

Usury.—There is no usury law. Courts may give relief and reopen transactions between money-lender and borrower if amounts charged for interest and other expenses are excessive or transaction is harsh and unconscionable. (Moneylenders Act, 1900, §1). Interest exceeding 48% per annum prima facie harsh and unconscionable. (Moneylenders Act, 1927).

INTESTACY:

See topic Descent and Distribution.

JOINT STOCK COMPANIES:

Joint stock companies are not distinguished from companies. See topic Corporations.

JUDGMENTS:

Judgment is vouched by extract from books of court. The judgment authorizes execution. Provision is made for enforcing judgments obtained in English and Irish Courts. (The Judgment Extension Act, 1868). Foreign judgments are not recognized unless that foreign country has reciprocal agreements with this country for enforcement of judgments. In that event the foreign country plaintiff must constitute his claim by action in the Scottish court. See also topic Records.

Summary judgments may be entered in certain cases. See topics Bills and Notes; Records.

JUSTICES OF THE PEACE:

Office of justice of peace was founded by Statute 1587 c. 82. Certain administrative duties are performed by justices, such as taking of affidavits and signing of documents for persons unable to write. They have also judicial duties and now operate within framework of District Courts (see topic Courts).

LABOUR RELATIONS:

See England Law Digest.

LAW REPORTS, CODES, ETC.:

See topics Constitution and Government; Reports.

LEGISLATURE:

See topic Constitution and Government.

LICENSES:

See England Law Digest, topic Foreign Trade Regulations.

LIENS:

Recognized liens, more properly called retentions, are either general or special. A special lien arises in the course of a particular contract and operates as a security for fulfilment of counterpart. Retention of ship is competent for repairs not necessaries. There may be retention for carriage, for salvage, or by hotel keepers over property of guests. Persons bestowing labor and skilled workmen on contract locatio operarum have a similar right for price of labor on goods. An accountant is entitled to retain books.

A general lien extends beyond immediate transactions out of which possession has arisen and operates as a security for general balance of account.

See Topical Index in front part of this volume.

LIMITATION OF ACTIONS:

Various classes of debt are subject to limitations (properly called prescriptions) which are in respect of some classes absolute and in others conditional. In some cases the limitation absolutely cuts off and extinguishes the right. In others it merely limits the means of proof by which the right may be extinguished.

Holograph writings and holograph bonds are subject to 20 years limitation. (Statute 1669 c. 9). After that period authenticity must be established by debtor's oath.

Obligation on tutors and curators and wards to account or reimburse is presumed to be satisfied if ten years have expired. (Statute 1696 c. 9).

Cautionary (security) obligations are subject to limitation of seven years. (Statute 1695 c. 5).

Bills of exchange and promissory notes suffer six years limitation. (Statute 1783 c. 18). After expiry of that period document cannot be founded on, and action must be laid on the debt and established by proof other than the bill.

All bargains concerning movables, or sums of money provable by witnesses, are only provable by writ or oath if not sued for within five years of making the bargain. (Statute 1669 c. 9).

Merchants accounts, servants' wages, and house rents are subject to a three years prescription. (Statute 1519 c. 83). After expiry of three years, it is necessary to prove both constitution and subsistence of debt by writing or oath of debtor.

There is a general prescription, the negative prescription of 20 years applicable to obligations in general not specified above. In some cases, such as servitudes, it is 40 years. Foregoing have been largely replaced by Prescription and Limitation (Scotland) Act 1973 which deals with positive prescription (period of challenge reduced to ten years in respect of all recorded titles ex facie valid and not forgeries) with negative prescription (reduced to a new period of five years) applicable to nearly all commercial transactions (extinction of right of action instead of limitation of method of proof) and with positive servitudes and rights of way (now 20 years prescription). It is not possible to contract out of Act.

Various Acts designed for the protection of public authorities (including the Crown) have been repealed or amended by the Law Reform (Limitation of Actions) Act, 1954. Under Prescription of Limitation (Scotland) Act 1973 no action of damages in respect of personal injuries could be entertained by courts after three years from date of incident giving rise to claim, but Law Reform (Miscellaneous Provisions) (Scotland) Act 1980 gives power to courts to override this time limit if equitable to do so.

LIMITED PARTNERSHIP:

See topic Partnership.

MARRIAGE:

Marriage (Scotland) Act 1977 codifies existing legislation on constitution of marriage. Minimum age for marriage remains 16 and prohibited degrees of relationship are same as for England.

Act abolishes two of previous legal preliminaries to marriage ceremony: Proclamation of banns in church and issue of Sheriff's license. Now each party to any marriage (religious or civil) to be performed in Scotland must give notice individually to district registrar with evidence of date of birth and ending of earlier marriage. A 15 day period of continuous residence in district by one party is no longer required.

When giving notice of intended marriage party not domiciled in any part of U.K. is required, if practicable, to produce certificate of capacity to marry issued by competent authority in state of his domicile. This requirement does not apply if person has been resident in U.K. for two years immediately before submitting marriage notice. Party resident in another part of U.K. can submit approved certificate for marriage issued in that part and need not give any other notice. Provision is also made for such certificates to be issued to Scottish residents wishing to marry abroad.

List of marriage notices must be displayed at registration office and particulars entered in marriage notice book available for inspection by intending objectors.

When Registrar is satisfied there is no impediment to marriage (e.g., forbidden degrees, prior subsisting marriage, nonage, incapacity to understand nature of ceremony or consent to marriage, both parties of same sex, and in case of people domiciled abroad, impediment which would render marriage void ab initio under domicilary law) he will complete marriage schedule which is signed immediately after marriage by parties, both witnesses and celebrant.

Period between giving of notice and issuing by Registrar of marriage schedule will normally be 14 days.

No irregular marriage by declaration contracted after Jan. 1, 1941, is valid.

Foreign Marriages.—Marriage is recognized if constituted according to forms of country in which it is contracted.

Foreign Marriages Act. 1892.—Foreign Marriages Act affords facilities to British subjects for celebration of marriage abroad at house of a marriage officer (British Ambassador, Governor, Consul, &c.) or on board one of Her Majesty's ships on a foreign station.

Provision for Scottish resident who wishes to marry outside Scotland 1977 Act §7.

Prohibited Marriages.—Marriage within the undernoted degrees is forbidden: (1) ascendants and descendants to the remotest degree; (2) collaterals in first degree, i.e., brothers and sisters; (3) collaterals who stand in loco parentis, i.e., where one person is brother or sister to a direct ascendant of the other, thus a man may not marry his grandniece though as far removed in degree as are first cousins; (4) there is no difference between full and half blood; (5) the degrees prohibited in consanguinity are so in affinity. Marriage with deceased wife's sister is legal. Forbidden degrees are now specified in 1977 Act.

MARRIED WOMEN:

See topics Dower; Husband and Wife; Marriage.

MONOPOLIES AND RESTRAINT OF TRADE:

See England Law Digest.

MORTGAGES OF REAL PROPERTY:

Defined as a debt secured over land, or, in Scotland, a heritable security. Prior to Nov. 29, 1970, heritable security was created by bond and disposition in security, cash credit bond and disposition in security, or ex facie absolute disposition with relative agreement or back letter. Under such writs creditor acquired real or heritable security in addition to personal obligations of debtor. As from Nov. 29, 1970 heritable security may be constituted only in form of a standard security (see subhead Standard Security, infra) by virtue of Conveyancing and Feudal Reform (Scotland) Act 1970. All writs creating a heritable security required to be registered in Register of Sasines (see topic Records). Heritable securities constituted prior to Nov. 29, 1970 may subsist in their older forms for many years to come and may be assigned, discharged or enforced in accordance with law as it stood prior to said date, subject to modifications contained in 1970 Act. Remedies available to heritable creditor where debtor has failed to comply with notice calling up security (i.e., requiring payment of loan and interest) include: (a) Power of sale; (b) powers of entering into possession and rights incidental thereto; (c) powers to effect repairs, reconstruction or improvement of security subjects; and (d) foreclosure procedure whereby, in certain circumstances, creditor may with sanction of court become absolute proprietor of security subjects. Debtor in heritable security may dispose of subjects under burden of security, and whilst he remains in possession of subjects, he can perform all ordinary acts incidental to ownership, but creditor's security cannot be prejudiced by contracts outside ordinary powers of management into which debtor might enter without creditor's consent.

Standard Security.—New form for securing debt over land, i.e., heritable security, introduced by Conveyancing and Feudal Reform (Scotland) Act 1970, and use of which is compulsory as from Nov. 29, 1970. Rights and remedies of creditor and debtor under this form of security are generally those stated for older forms of security (mortgages) but with modified and simplified procedure laid down in said Act; also Act prescribes form of this security; its assignation and discharge, as well as certain statutory conditions to be imparted therein.

Limited Companies.—Where limited company borrows and grants heritable security, provision is made under Companies Acts for creation of a floating charge by registration of security writ in a special register (Register of Charges), purpose of which is creation of general security to creditor affecting whole property and assets of borrowing company.

MOTOR VEHICLES:

All motor cars must be registered. Registered number requires to be fixed to cars. Drivers must be licensed. License may be suspended and person disqualified from afterwards holding license if guilty of offense. Insurance is compulsory.

Driver must stop in case of accident. Body of legislation contained in Road Traffic Acts. And see England Law Digest.

NEGOTIABLE INSTRUMENTS:

See topic Bills and Notes.

NOTARIES PUBLIC:

No person can now be admitted as a notary public until he has been enrolled as a solicitor. (Law Agents Amendment Act, 1896). The commission is held from the Crown and is not limited in time. Women are entitled to obtain commissions as notaries.

Law Reform (Miscellaneous Provisions) (Scotland) Act 1990 §37 transferred office and function of Clerk to Admission of Notaries Public to council of the Law Society of Scotland, who are elected by solicitors in Scotland.

PARTNERSHIP:

Law as to partnership is codified by Partnership Act, 1890, which applies to U.K. Number of partners in private firm is limited to 20 save for partnerships of solicitors, accountants, stockbrokers or other kinds of partnership permitted by Department of Trade and Industry regulations. No partner can transfer his interest so as to introduce a new partner in his place without consent of other partners. Each partner is liable for whole debts and obligations of partnership and creditors having obtained judgment against partnership can enforce such judgment against estates of any or all of partners. Each partner has power to bind partnership in lines of partnership business. A firm is treated as a distinct legal person. When no term of duration has been fixed in a partnership contract any partner may determine partnership by giving notice of his intention to do so.

Limited Partnership.—A limited partnership may be registered but must contain one or more persons termed limited partners, contributing capital but who are not liable beyond the amount so contributed. A limited partner cannot take part in management, or he will be liable as an ordinary partner. (Limited Partnership Act, 1907).

PATENTS:

The Patents Act 1977 revises substantially patent system of U.K. Patent may be granted only if: (a) Invention is new, (b) it involves inventive step, and (c) it is capable of industrial application. Following are not "inventions": (a) Discovery, scientific theory or mathematical method, (b) literary, dramatic, musical or artistic work or any other aesthetic creation, (c) scheme, rule or method for performing mental act, playing game or doing business, or program for computer, and (d) presentation of information. Patent will not be granted for invention publication or exploitation of which might encourage offensive immoral or anti-social behaviour or for any variety of animal or plant or any essentially biological process for production of animals or plants not being microbiological process or product of such process.

Patent Office procedure is to be laid down by Patents Rules which will issue in form of Statutory Instruments.

Among more important changes are extension of term of patent to 20 years. Abolition of "provisional protection" and its replacement by system of claiming priority from earlier applications. Introduction of examination at application stage for inventiveness rather than mere novelty, abolition of many grounds of invalidity and abolition of practice of allowing patents for inventions which although new in U.K. had been known already abroad.

See Topical Index in front part of this volume.

PATENTS . . . *continued*

Recent measures taken to contend with technological advances include provisions to govern devices designed to circumvent copy—protection of works in electronic form, see Copyright, Designs and Patents Act 1988.

International Arrangements.—"Community patents" may be granted by European Patent Office and have contrary character throughout E.E.C. There will be transitional period of at least ten years when there will be "European Patents (U.K.)" which will be granted by European Patents Office but once granted will be equivalent to British Patents as far as U.K. is concerned. Act also introduces patents which will be governed by system of law based on European system but which will come solely under jurisdiction of United Courts and Patent Office. Application for such patent may be made in U.K. and "international application" may be made under Patent Cooperation Treaty under which single application for all cooperating countries is made to and initially processed by one of selected Patent Offices and then passed to Patent Offices of countries in which patenting is sought for further processing.

Infringement.—New Act includes statutory definition which can be summarized as unauthorized manufacture, working or use of patented product. Infringement may be prevented by interdict and damages may be claimed.

PERPETUITIES:

Perpetuities by which a succession of persons take a life interest are illegal. It is permissible to reserve life interest in movable estate in favor only of party in life at date of deed. Any such estate held in liferent by or for behoof of a party of full age born after date of such deed belongs absolutely to such person. (Trusts Act, 1921, §9).

Accumulations.—Certain prohibitions on accumulation of income to capital of trust. Thelluson Act 1800 as am'd.

PLEDGES:

Pledge is constituted by delivery on terms or conditions proved either by writing or by witnesses. The subject of pledge must be capable of delivery such as corporeal movables, goods, wares and merchandise. Debts may also be pledged when identified with the document as in bills and notes. Title deeds may be pledged as corporeal movables but not as carrying any interest in land. Right of property remains with pledgee and risk remains with him. Creditor has no right of use. The subject of pledge cannot be sold without order of court. (See also topic Principal and Agent.)

PRESCRIPTION:

See topic Limitation of Actions.

PRINCIPAL AND AGENT:

The principles of common law apply to matters relating to principal and agent. Where a mercantile agent, with owners' consent, is in possession of goods or of documents of title, any sale or pledge made by him is valid if person taking acts in good faith. (Factors Act, 1889, §2). Where a mercantile agent pledges goods in security for debt or liability due before time of pledge, the pledgee acquires no further right to the goods than the pledger himself had. (§4).

PRODUCT LIABILITY:

Law in Scotland which regulates liability of manufacturers for goods they produce is consolidated by Consumers Protection Act 1987. Part 1 of this Act implements Product Liability Directive (85/374/EEC) of European Union.

Important defence which was included under §4 is that state of scientific and technical knowledge at relevant time was not such that producer or products of same description might be expected to have discovered defects if it existed in his product while they were under his control.

Act does not allow any liabilities to be limited or excluded by any terms of contract. Act also extended strict liability to property damage as well as to death and personal injury caused by defective product where damage is worth at least £275.

REAL PROPERTY:

Scotland largely on feudal system. Vassal holds land under superior for payment of annual feuduty. Superior sets out conditions under which property may be held. Feu may be consolidated with superiority. Some land is held direct from Crown. Right over land without ownership may be created, e.g., servitude for benefit of adjacent land. System of registration of all conveyances in central record office. The Land Registration (Scotland) Act 1979 proposes new system of registration of title to land. See topic Records. Land may be conveyed to trustees. No bar on number of persons who may hold land.

See also topic Mortgages of Real Property. By Land Tenure Reform (Scotland) Act 1974 creation of new feuduties or similar payments from land is prohibited. Terms are provided for voluntary redemption of existing feuduties and such redemption is made compulsory on first sale occurring after Sept. 1, 1974.

RECORDS:

There is a very complete and reliable system of registration of deeds. Registration in public registers may be for execution, preservation or publication.

Execution.—Certain deeds such as formal bonds contain consent to registration for execution and following on such registration an extract of the deed may be obtained which warrants execution in same manner as judgment of court.

Preservation.—Neither consent nor warrant is necessary to record documents in Court Books for purpose of preservation. (Statute 1698, c. 4; Writs Registration Act, Scotland, 1868).

Publication.—This register applies to deeds dealing with heritable property. Such deeds must be registered. A General Register, kept at Edinburgh, is divided into separate divisions, one for each county. There are also certain Burgh Registers. Deeds may be transmitted by post. Deeds rank in order of registration. (Land Registers Act, Scotland, 1868).

The Land Registration Act 1979 establishes Land Register of Scotland. It is intended that gradual introduction of system of registration of interests in lands should replace recording of deeds in Register of Sasines as principal method of creating real rights in land.

Personal Registers.—The Register of Inhibitions and Adjudications contains notices of actions and legal diligence. (Land Registers Act, 1868).

Companies Register of Floating Charges.—See topic Mortgages of Real Property, subhead Limited Companies.

Defective Documents.—Law Reform (Miscellaneous Provisions) (Scotland) Act 1985 grants courts power to rectify defective documents where parties' intentions inaccurately expressed. Previously only Court of Session (see topic Courts) could reduce defective documents.

REPLEVIN:

This action is not so known. Specific property is recovered by action for delivery.

REPORTS:

Reports of cases are extant from very early times. Morrison's Dictionary contains decisions during year 1540. Reports are available almost without break from that time.

Court of Session.—Faculty Collection 37 vols., 1752 to 1841; Court of Session Second Series, 24 vols. 1838/1862; Third Series 11 vols. 1862/1873; Fourth Series, 25 vols. 1873/1898; Fifth Series, 8 vols. 1898/1906; Court of Session cases, continuing. (Publishers, Wm. Green & Son, Edinburgh, for Faculty of Advocates). Scots Law Reporter, 61 Vols. 1865/1927. (Publishers, John Baxter & Son, 39 Elden Street, Edinburgh). Scots Law Times, from 1893 on. (Publishers, William Green & Sons, Edinburgh). Current Law Reports from 1950 on. (Publishers, William Green & Sons, Edinburgh).

SALES:

Law of sale of goods is regulated by Sale of Goods Act, 1893 with important amendments contained in Supply of Goods (Implied Terms) Act 1973 and Consumer Credit Act 1974. Law of Sale of Goods has been consolidated by Sale of Goods Act 1979. Contract of sale may be made in writing, or by word of mouth, or partly in writing and partly by word of mouth, or may be implied from conduct of parties. Contract of sale may be either of existing goods owned and possessed by seller or goods to be manufactured or acquired by seller. Price may be fixed by contract or left to be fixed in manner agreed or determined by course of dealing. Where price is not so ascertained, buyer must pay reasonable price. Time of payment is not deemed to be of essence of contract. Where sale is of unascertained goods, property does not pass until goods are ascertained. Unless otherwise agreed payment and delivery are concurrent conditions. Remedies in cases of breach of contract are also prescribed.

Restrictions have been made by regulation on disposal of certain classes of goods particularly under Hire Purchase Agreements.

Warranties.—Sale of Goods Act sets out warranties as to quality of goods. When goods sold for particular purpose, implied conditions that goods are reasonably fit for said purpose. When goods bought by description from dealer in that class of goods, implied condition that goods of merchantable quality. May be implied warranty through usage of trade. Trades Description Act 1968 prohibits false trade descriptions.

Consumer Protection.—See England Law Digest, topic Monopolies and Restraint of Trade. Further protection given by Trades Description Act, 1968, Trade Description Act 1972, Supply of Goods (Implied Terms) Act 1973 and Consumer Credit Act 1974.

Notices Required.—Noncomformity with contract entitles buyer either within reasonable time to reject goods and treat contract as repudiated, or to retain goods and treat failure as breach and make claim for compensation or damages for defects. Rejection excluded by acceptance of goods.

Applicable Law.—Interpretation and effect and rights and obligations of parties are determined basically by contract itself. Court will look to intention of parties as set out in written contract. Therefore, law applicable is that which parties agree or intend should govern it. General rule that it is incompetent to contradict or qualify terms by extrinsic evidence, but, if necessary, reference may be had to writ or oath of parties. Illegal contracts (pacta illicita) cannot be enforced by action of either party.

SEALS:

Use of private seals has no legal significance except on share transfers. A deed to which a joint stock company is party is validly executed if sealed with common seal of company and subscribed on behalf of company by two directors or one director and secretary. Witnesses are not required. (Companies Act, 1948, §32[4]).

SHIPPING:

Law regulating ships and shipping is contained in Merchant Shipping Acts 1894-1979. To be deemed British ship, ship must belong wholly either to: (1) Natural born British subjects; or (2) naturalized subjects; or (3) bodies corporate established under laws of and having principal place of business in some part of dominions.

Registration.—Every British ship must be registered. Registry is made by Principal Officer of Customs of any port in Great Britain and by certain other officers in British possessions. In order that builder or purchaser of British ship may get it registered he must obtain a surveyor's certificate specifying tonnage, build and other identifying particulars, have ship marked for identification and draught, and subscribe a declaration of ownership, of his qualification, and of time and place of building. In event of first registry, builder's certificate must also be produced. On completion of registration, registrar issues a certificate adding name of master. Certificate is not subject to detention by reason of lien.

Ownership.—No notice is taken in registry of any trust. Registered owner has absolute disposal of ship or share. Property of ordinary vessels must be divided into 64 shares. Not more than 64 individuals can be registered at same time. Body corporate may be registered in corporate name.

Liability of Owners.—The first duty is to provide a sound and seaworthy ship and furnish a competent crew. Owners are liable for negligence and faulty navigation. Any person beneficially interested, otherwise than by way of mortgage, in ship or share of ship registered in name of another, is subject to all penalties as well as such registered owner.

See Topical Index in front part of this volume.

SHIPPING . . . *continued*

Provisions on limitation of liability of shipowners are materially altered by Merchant Shipping Act 1979, relevant sections of which when brought into effect will give force of law to Convention on Limitation of Liability for Maritime Claims 1976. Shipowner, without admitting liability, may apply to Court of Session to limit liability and to distribute amount determined among claimants.

Sale and Mortgage.—A registered ship or share can only be transferred by bill of sale containing description identifying ship. A ship may be made security for a loan. Mortgages must be registered. Preferences depend upon order in which securities appear on the Register. Disposal of ship or of shares beyond country of registry by way of mortgage or sale may be effected by certificate of sale and mortgage.

Charter Party.—A charter party identifies ship by name, master and tonnage, and contains implied obligations that the ship is seaworthy.

Master and Crew.—Master and mate of foreign going ship and home trade passenger ships must hold certificates from Department of Trade. It is not necessary that master be British subject. When vessel is abroad master is accredited agent of owners, in victualling and manning ship, and in ordering necessaries. He has lien over ship for wages. Right of wages and provisions begins when seamen commence work. Such right gives lien over ship.

Passenger and Emigrant Ships.—The regulation of vessels carrying passengers and emigrants is fully provided for in Acts.

See also England Law Digest.

SOLICITORS AND ADVOCATES:

See topic Attorneys and Counselors.

STATUTE OF FRAUDS:

See topic Frauds, Statute of.

STATUTES:

See topic Constitution and Government.

TAXATION:

Following taxes are imposed by United Kingdom Parliament and are collected throughout United Kingdom on a national basis. For notes on these taxes reference is made to England Law Digest: Income Tax; Value Added Tax; Stamp Duty; Corporation Tax; Capital Gains Tax; Capital Transfer Tax.

TRADEMARKS AND TRADENAMES:

At common law no one may copy a trademark, if purchasers may be induced to believe that they are getting goods made by the owner of the mark. The law is now codified by the Trade Marks Act, 1938.

Registration.—A register is kept at Patent Office wherein all registered trademarks are entered. No trust may be entered.

Marks must be registered in respect of particular goods or classes of goods and must contain or consist of at least one of the following particulars: (1) name of company; (2) signature of applicant or predecessor in business; (3) an invented word or words; (4) word or words having no direct reference to character or quality of goods; or (5) any other distinctive mark.

Application to register must be made in writing and on acceptance is advertised by registrar. Any person may object within time specified in advertisement. On registration a certificate is granted. No trademark may be registered which is identical with one belonging to a different proprietor.

Registration is for a period of seven or 14 years according to date of registration, but is renewable.

The person entered in register is entitled to enforce and protect right as in respect of other personal property, and has exclusive right to the trademark. Registration is prima facie evidence of validity. No registration affects right of person to use his own name.

Assignment.—A trademark, when registered, is assignable either in connection with goodwill of the business or not.

Cotton Marks.—Special provision is made for cotton marks, which are kept in a register at Manchester, known as the Manchester Branch.

International Agreements.—Provisions of Patent Acts as applied by orders in council apply to trademarks. See topic Patents.

Tradenames.—See topic Partnership.

TREATIES: See England Law Digest.

TRUSTS:

A trust can be created by any person who is legally capable of disposing of property, in regard to that property. Truster may confer upon trustee any legal powers he pleases. (Trust Act §§3 and 4).

Under the Trust (Scotland) Act 1961 it is now possible for special reasons to petition the court to vary purposes of trust.

Unlawful Trusts.—Trusts which are constituted for purposes which are illegal, or immoral, or contrary to public policy are unlawful and invalid, but to any deed, making reparation for harm done by an illegal or immoral act or contract, effect will be given.

USURY: See topic Interest.

WILLS:

A verbal legacy is effectual up to £100 Scots (i.e., £8/33), but otherwise writing is essential to validity of a will. Wills are revocable by granter at any time. Wills must be validly executed but do not require to be stamped. A will entirely in handwriting of testator and signed by him is effectual though not witnessed. If not written by testator, a will must be witnessed by two witnesses, whose designations and addresses must be written after their signatures or incorporated in body of deed.

No particular words or style are necessary to carry heritage; any words clearly indicating intention of testator are sufficient.

Probate.—This is known as confirmation. Sheriff of county in which deceased died has jurisdiction in matters of probate.

Children cannot be entirely disinherited by their parent's will. (See topic Descent and Distribution.)

Wills Executed Abroad.—Wills validly executed by foreigners, in accordance with the law of the place of execution, are valid in Scotland, although they do not conform to Scottish requirements. Confirmation of wills by foreigners resident abroad is issued by the Commissary Court (Sheriff Court) at Edinburgh.

The Wills Act 1861, §1, provides that every will made by a British subject outside of the United Kingdom is to be held, as regards movable estate, well executed if made according to forms required either by: (1) law of place where will made; (2) law of place where person domiciled at time will made; (3) law in force in that part of Her Majesty's dominions where person had domicile of origin.

A will so executed abroad will carry also heritage in Scotland. (Conveyancing Act, Scotland, 1874, §51; Foreign Jurisdiction Act, 1878; Colonial Probates Act, 1892).

See Topical Index in front part of this volume.

SINGAPORE LAW DIGEST REVISER

David Chong & Co.
OCBC Centre, #31-00 East Lobby
65 Chulia Street
Singapore 049513
Tel: 65-224-0955
Fax: 65-538-6585; 538-7559; 538-3570
Email: dclaw@signet.com.sg

Reviser Profile

History: David Chong & Co. was established in 1984 in Singapore by David Chong Kok Kong, who is both a practitioner and an academic, having spent three years lecturing law in the National University of Singapore. Since its inception, the firm has expanded rapidly and the David Chong & Co. Group currently has more than 50 lawyers spread over its offices in Singapore; Kuala Lumpur, Johor Bahru and Labuan (Malaysia); Suzhou (People's Republic of China); Sydney (Australia); Yangon (Myanmar) and the British Virgin Islands. The growth of the firm has paralleled Singapore's emergence as an international financial and commercial centre.

Structure: The firm conscientiously recruits lawyers who are qualified in more than one jurisdiction, including Singapore, Malaysia, Brunei, England and Wales, Australia, the United States of America, the People's Republic of China and the British Virgin Islands. Many of the lawyers are also fluent in Mandarin, Malay and some in Japanese, to help service the firm's ever increasing portfolio of clients in the Asian markets.

Services: The firm is a full service law firm with substantial experience in all areas of practice and comprise the following core departments: Corporate and Commercial, Corporate Finance & Securities, Banking and Finance, Conveyancing, Tax, Intellectual Property, Trusts, Shipping and Litigation. The firm has developed expertise not only in the domestic market but is also known for its expertise in regional and cross-border work in the Asia Pacific region including Malaysia, Australia, Cambodia, Cook Islands, Indonesia, Myanmar, Philippines, Thailand, Vietnam and India. To cater to increasing investment in China, the firm has also set up a China Practice Group (CPG) in its Singapore office. The CPG comprises both Singapore lawyers who are familiar with Chinese laws and Chinese legal advisers who are legally qualified in China.

Client Base: Clients include local and multinational corporations, private and public listed companies, banks (local and offshore) and major financial institutions, insurance houses, property developers, manufacturers, traders, professional bodies and marine transport companies. The firm also has a large number of clients based outside Singapore, primarily in Japan, North America, Western Europe, Australia, People's Republic of China and South-East Asia.

SINGAPORE LAW DIGEST

(The following is a list of all Topics, including cross-references, covered in this Digest.)

SINGAPORE LAW DIGEST

Revised for 1997 edition by

DAVID CHONG & CO., Advocates and Solicitors, Singapore.

References to "Cap." mean the Chapters of the Laws of Singapore.

ABSENTEES:

Person may delegate authority to person of full legal capacity by way of power of attorney setting out scope and nature of donee's powers and authorities.

Powers of Attorney can be made irrevocable for fixed period of time and if so, there is protection offered to purchaser from donee of such power of attorney. Powers of Attorney executed in Singapore or elsewhere, intended to be used in Singapore are in practice deposited in Registry of Supreme Court of Singapore; office copy of such Power of Attorney being so deposited is without further proof sufficient evidence of contents of instrument.

As long as memorandum and articles of association permit, company can by resolution appoint person to be attorney for corporation; and deed executed by such attorney binds company.

ACTIONS:

Person may sue or be sued as long as plaintiff is able to satisfy court that it has jurisdiction to hear matter. If plaintiff resides outside Singapore, he may be ordered by court to pay money into court as security for defendant's legal costs should plaintiff eventually fail to prove his claim.

Foreign Law.—Particulars of foreign law must be given if it is pleaded. Foreign law is to be proved as facts during trial. Experts can give oral evidence of foreign law. In absence of such evidence, Singapore law will be applied. Exception to this is that court takes judicial notice of all Acts passed by Parliament of Malaysia or Parliament of UK.

ADMINISTRATION:

See topic Executors and Administrators.

ADOPTION:

Regulated by Adoption of Children Act. (Cap. 4).

Requirements.—Before granting order under Act, court must be satisfied, inter alia, that infant is under age of 21 and is not married and both infant and petitioner are residents of Singapore. Consent of parent or parents or guardian of infant must be obtained or dispensed with by court.

Terms and Conditions of Adoption Order.—Court may impose such terms and conditions as court may think fit and in particular may require adopter by bond or otherwise to make such provision, if any, for such adopted child as in opinion of court is just and expedient.

Effect of Adoption Order.—All rights, duties, obligations and liabilities of parent or parents or guardian of adopted child are extinguished, and vest in and are exercisable by and enforceable against adopter.

Registration of Adopted Children.—Registrar of Births keeps record of children who have been legally adopted. Such registers and books are not open to public inspection or search except under court order.

ADVOCATES AND SOLICITORS:

See topic Attorneys and Counselors.

AFFIDAVITS AND STATUTORY DECLARATIONS:

Affidavit may contain such facts as deponent is able of his own knowledge to prove. Affidavit sworn for purpose of being used in interlocutory proceedings may contain statements of information or belief with sources and grounds thereof.

Affidavit purporting to have affixed seal or signature of court, judge, notary public or person having authority to administer oaths in Commonwealth country and in case of any other country, seal or signature of consular officer of Commonwealth country in testimony of affidavit being taken before it or him may be admitted in evidence without proof of seal or signature being seal or signature of that court, judge, notary public or person.

Statutory Declaration.—Verification of facts made under oath used for cases other than judicial proceedings. Form of declaration is as follows:

I, A.B., do solemnly and sincerely declare that ..., and I make this solemn declaration conscientiously believing the same to be true, and by virtue of the provisions of the Statutory Declarations Act, 1835.

Declared by the said A.B.)
at (address))
on (date))

Before me,

. . . .

(Signature of Commissioner
for Oaths or Notary Public)

See also topic Notaries Public.

AGENCY:

See topic Principal and Agent.

ALIENS:

See topic Immigration.

APPLICABLE LAW:

See topic Constitution and Government.

ARBITRATION AND AWARD:

Arbitration.—Arbitration Act (Cap. 10) regulates arbitration. Provisions of Act do not apply to international arbitration under International Arbitration Act ("IAA") (Cap. 143A) or to proceedings pursuant to Convention on Settlement of Investment Disputes between States and Nationals of Other States.

In arbitration conducted under Act, party may at any time after appearance, and before delivering any pleadings or taking any other steps in legal proceedings commenced by other party brought in breach of arbitration agreement, apply to court to stay proceedings. Court may stay proceedings if it is satisfied that: (a) there is no sufficient reason why matter should not be referred in accordance with arbitration agreement; and (b) applicant was, at time when proceedings were commenced and still remains, ready and willing to do all things necessary to proper conduct of arbitration.

Under IAA, court may stay legal proceedings commenced in breach of international arbitration agreement unless court is satisfied that arbitration agreement is null and void. Arbitration is international as provided under UNCITRAL rules. IAA applies UNCITRAL Model Law on International Commercial Arbitration adopted by United Nations Commission on International Trade Law on 21 June 1985 with exception of c. VIII. Relevant sections of IAA and UNCITRAL rules, however, will not apply if parties agree that any dispute that may arise between them is to be settled otherwise than in accordance with IAA or UNCITRAL rules.

Arbitral Awards.—Arbitration award under Act or pursuant to international arbitration agreement under IAA may by leave of court, be enforced in same manner as judgment or order to same effect and, where leave is so given, judgment may be entered in terms of award.

Arbitration (International Investment Disputes) Act (Cap. 11) implements Arts. 18, 19, 20, 21(a) (with Art. 22 as it applies to Art. 21[a]), 23(1) and 24 of International Convention on Settlement of Investment Disputes between States and Nationals of Other States. Award pursuant to Convention may be registered and be of same force and effect for purposes of execution as if it had been judgment of High Court.

Foreign Awards.—IAA gives effect to Convention on Recognition and Enforcement of Foreign Arbitral Awards 1958. Grounds for refusal of enforcement of convention award reflect provisions stated in Convention.

Convention award may be enforced in court by action or as judgment or order to same effect and, where leave is so given, judgment may be entered in terms of award in same manner as local arbitral award as stated above. Award may be relied upon by party by way of defence, set-off or otherwise in any legal proceedings in Singapore.

ASSIGNMENTS:

Assignment of debts and other choses in action are permitted under Singapore law. Assignment must be absolute in nature, embodied in written form duly signed by assignor and not be in nature of charge; express notice in writing must be given to debtor, trustee or other person from whom assignor would have been entitled to receive or claim such debt or chose in action. Assignment would, however, be subject to all equities which would have been entitled to priority over assignee's rights, i.e., those which were in existence prior to and down to time when express notice of assignment was given to debtor or other persons charged with making payment to assignor.

Noncompliance does not mean that assignment is ineffective, for assignment then becomes equitable one. From procedural point of view, equitable assignee will need to bring in assignor as party to any suit to enforce assigned debt and from substantive point of view, there may be issues on whether assignee must have provided consideration to assignor, particularly for assignments of future choses in action.

Generally, priorities between competing priorities are governed by time when notice in writing has been given to debtor. In case of equitable assignments, English common law rule in Dearle v. Hall (1828) 3 Russ. 1 applies, i.e., priority of claims will be determined by priority of notices of assignment given to debtor.

ASSOCIATIONS:

See topic Partnerships.

ATTACHMENT:

Attachment of debts after judgment possible through garnishment (see topic Executions) or stop notice.

Stop notice may be obtainable if person who is beneficially entitled to interest in any securities wishes to be notified of any proposed transfer or payment of those securities.

ATTORNEYS AND COUNSELORS:

Fused legal profession consisting of advocates and solicitors of Supreme Court and governed by Legal Profession Act. (Cap. 161).

Admission.—Regulated by Legal Profession Act. To qualify for admission to Bar, intending advocate and solicitor must satisfy one of following criteria:

Graduates from Singapore.—If admitted as candidate to read law at National University of Singapore ("NUS") on or after 1 May 1993, must pass final examinations with at least lower second class honours.

Graduates from U.K.—(1) If graduated from U.K. before 1 May 1993, must either be admitted as barrister or solicitor in U.K. or obtain Diploma in Singapore Law from NUS. (2) If admitted as candidate to read law in U.K. before 1 May 1993 and graduate after that date, must either be admitted as barrister or solicitor in U.K. or obtain

See Topical Index in front part of this volume.

ATTORNEYS AND COUNSELORS . . . *continued*
Diploma in Singapore Law from NUS. (3) If admitted as candidate to read law in U.K. on or after 1 May 1993 and commenced reading law in U.K. before 1 Jan. 1994 and graduate before 1 Jan. 1997, must either be admitted as barrister or solicitor in U.K. or obtain Diploma in Singapore Law from NUS. (4) If admitted as candidate to read law in U.K. on or after 1 May 1993 and commence reading law on or after 1 Jan. 1994 and graduate before 1 Jan. 1997, must be full-time internal student at recognised U.K. university, and must either be admitted as barrister or solicitor in U.K. or obtain Diploma in Singapore Law from NUS. (5) If admitted as candidate to read law in U.K. on or after 1 May 1993 and commence reading law on or after 1 Jan. 1994 and graduate on or after 1 Jan. 1997, must be full-time internal student and obtain at least upper second class from recognised U.K. university and obtain Diploma in Singapore Law from NUS.

Graduates from Recognised Commonwealth Universities.—Must have commenced reading law at recognised Commonwealth universities before 1 Jan. 1994 and must graduate and must obtain certificate from Board of Legal Education that intending advocate and solicitor is of sufficient standing.

External Graduates.—As general rule, no person who on or after 1 Jan. 1996 is conferred degree of Bachelor of Laws other than as full-time candidate in U.K., will be eligible for Bar.

Person who in 1996 is conferred degree of Bachelor of Laws other than as full-time internal candidate in U.K. is eligible for admission if he is: (a) admitted as candidate for that degree before 1 May 1993; and (b) admitted as barrister or solicitor in U.K. or obtained Diploma in Singapore Law from NUS.

Malayan Practitioners.—May be admitted if Malayan practitioner has been in active practice in any part of Malaysia for continuous period of at least three years in four years immediately preceding petition for admission or if not in active practice, has satisfied Board of Legal Education in such examination as may be prescribed by Board and therefore not required to serve pupillage in Singapore or attend any course of instruction.

Hong Kong Practitioners.—May be admitted if Hong Kong practitioner has been in active practice in Hong Kong for continuous period of at least three years immediately preceding petition for admission. Petition must have been filed before 1 Jan. 1995.

Special Category.—Persons with exceptional qualifications or expertise may be exempted from any of above criteria by Minister of Law after consultation with Board of Legal Education.

Other Requirements.—Unless exempted by Board of Legal Education, all intending advocates and solicitors must serve six months' pupillage and attend course of instruction (Practical Law Course) lasting about five months. At end of course, must sit for examinations.

Immigration Requirements.—Not necessary for non-Singapore citizens to seek clearance from immigration authorities to be admitted to the Bar. But non-Singapore citizens wishing to live and work or undergo training in Singapore are required to apply to Comptroller of Immigration: 95 South Bridge Road, #08-29, Pidemco Centre, Singapore 058717 for employment pass or training pass as case may be. Permanent residents of Singapore within meaning of Immigration Act (Cap. 133) are not required to seek permission from immigration authorities.

Professional Bodies.—

Law Society of Singapore.—1 Colombo Court, #08-29, Singapore 179742. Tel: 338 3615. Objectives are, inter alia, to: (a) further interests of legal profession and its members; (b) assist Government and courts in matters affecting legislation, administration and practice of law; and (c) assist public in matters concerning law.

Board of Legal Education: 9th Floor, Conference Room, Subordinate Courts, 1 Havelock Square, Singapore 059724. Tel: 534 1831. Responsible for registration of qualified persons seeking admission, training, education and examination of qualified persons and supervision over pupils.

Academy of Law: Third Level City Hall Building, St. Andrews Road, Singapore 178957. Tel: 332 4388. Responsible for promotion and maintenance of high standards of conduct, promotion of advancement and dissemination of knowledge of laws and legal system, promotion of research and scholarships and provision of continuing legal education.

Enquiries relating to Diploma in Singapore Law should be directed to NUS at 10 Kent Ridge Crescent, Singapore 119260.

Foreign law firms wishing to establish office may apply to Attorney General's Chambers: 1 Coleman Street, #10-00, Singapore 179803. Tel: 336 1411 for approval criteria.

AUTOMOBILES:

See topic Motor Vehicles.

BANKRUPTCY:

See topic Insolvency.

BANKS AND BANKING:

Monetary Authority of Singapore is responsible for promotion of monetary stability and credit and exchange conditions conducive to economic growth of Singapore (Monetary Authority of Singapore Act). (Cap. 186). It oversees licensing and regulation of all activities of banks and financial institutions in Singapore.

All banks operating in Singapore are required to obtain licences from Monetary Authority of Singapore under Banking Act (Cap. 19), and to comply with provisions of Act. Finance companies are regulated by same authority under Finance Companies Act. (Cap. 108).

BILLS AND NOTES:

Bills of Exchange Act (Cap. 23) is substantially similar to English Bills of Exchange Act 1882 and Cheques Act 1957. Common law applies except where inconsistent with Act. Conflicts rules are similar to those applicable in England.

BILLS OF SALE:

In general, chattel mortgages, other than mortgages and debentures registrable under Companies Act (Cap. 50) are governed by Bills of Sale Act (Cap. 24). Act is substantially similar to English Bills of Sale Acts of 1878 to 1891. Bills as defined in Act are void unless they are for S$100 or more, made in prescribed form and registered within three clear days of execution, and not partly or wholly given in consideration of preexisting debts. Registration has to be renewed every 12 months. Filed copies of bills are available for public inspection.

See also topic Chattel Mortgages.

CHATTEL MORTGAGES:

Mortgages of chattel, except mortgages and debentures registrable under Companies Act (Cap. 50), are registrable under Bills of Sale Act (Cap. 24). Floating charges over chattels, and any charge over any ship or aircraft, of company are registrable under Companies Act. This applies to property wherever situate for Singapore incorporated companies, and to property in Singapore for foreign companies registered in Singapore. Such charges must be registered within 30 days of execution (with extension of seven days for documents executed outside Singapore). Otherwise charge is void against liquidator and creditors of company.

Mortgages of Singapore ships are also registrable under Merchant Shipping Act. (Act No. 19 of 1995). No additional provisions for registration of aircraft mortgages.

See also topics Bills of Sale; Corporations.

COLLATERAL SECURITY:

See topic Pledges.

COMMERCIAL REGISTER:

Persons wishing to conduct business in Singapore must seek registration either under Business Registration Act (Cap. 32) or Companies Act (Cap. 50).

See also topics Corporations; Partnerships; Chattel Mortgages; Patents; Trademarks.

CONSTITUTION AND GOVERNMENT:

Singapore has been independent republic since 9 Aug. 1965. It has written constitution (Constitution of Republic of Singapore). Any law inconsistent with Constitution is to that extent void.

Executive authority is vested in President and exercisable by President or Cabinet in accordance with Constitution. President is popularly elected. Apart from being constitutional Head of State, he also has powers to prevent government from spending reserves accumulated by previous governments, and to veto key appointments to public service. Cabinet of Ministers, headed by Prime Minister, is made up of members of Parliament.

Legislature.—

Parliament.—Legislative power is vested in President and Parliament. Unicameral Parliament is elected legislature of Singapore. Proceedings are presided over by Speaker, who is member of Parliament. Bills in Parliament are read three times and passed by simple majority of members entitled to vote and present. Constitutional amendments require two-thirds majority of all members entitled to vote. Bills become law with President's assent, and come into force at date appointed in Act, or by default, upon gazetting of Act.

Nominated Members of Parliament.—Members are not elected, but appointed by parliamentary committee to sit in Parliament to participate in proceedings. Cannot vote on certain matters.

Presidential Council for Minority Rights.—Bills are screened by this appointed council for potential adverse effects on rights of minority races. Its objections must be considered but may be overruled by two-thirds of total voting members of Parliament.

Judiciary is made up of Supreme Court and Subordinate Courts. It is headed by Chief Justice. Supreme Court consists of Judges of Appeal and Judges of High Court. Judges are appointed until retirement at 65, by President on advice of Prime Minister, after consultation with Chief Justice. Senior members of Bar are occasionally appointed to sit as Judicial Commissioners for short terms. See also topic Courts.

CONTRACTS:

Contract laws based on and highly similar to contract laws of England.

Application of English Law Act.— Under Application of English Law Act (Cap. 7A), common law of England (including principles and rules of equity), so far as was part of law of Singapore immediately before 12 Nov. 1993, continues to be part of law of Singapore (subject to such modifications as required by circumstances of Singapore and its inhabitants). In addition, certain English statutes apply (with some modification) to Singapore, these include Misrepresentation Act 1967, Unfair Contract Terms Act 1977 (except certain portions), Sale of Goods Act 1979 (except certain portions) and Minors' Contracts Act 1987 (except certain portions).

Applicable Law.—General principles as under English Law.

Excuses for Non-Performance.—Principles as under English Law; see also topic Sales, subhead Unfair Contract Terms Act (Cap. 396).

Government Contracts.—Proceedings can be taken and enforced against Government; Government Proceedings Act. (Cap. 121).

COPYRIGHT AND REGISTERED DESIGN:

Copyright.—

Statute.—Copyright Act (Cap. 63), as amended by Copyright (Amendment) Act 1994. Changes to Act likely due to TRIPS (Trade Related Intellectual Property Rights under GATT).

Treaties.—Singapore is not yet member of Berne Convention but will probably become member since compliance with substantive provisions of Berne is requirement under GATT (TRIPS) rules. However, Singapore has bilateral treaties with U.S.A, U.K. and Australia; thus nationals and residents of these countries enjoy copyright protection in Singapore.

COPYRIGHT AND REGISTERED DESIGN . . . *continued*

Protection.—Works covered under Act comprise literary (which includes computer programmes), dramatic, musical and artistic works, sound recordings, cinematograph films, broadcasts, cable programmes and typographical format of published editions of work. No registration is required.

In respect of literary, dramatic, and musical works ("works"), copyright extends to: (a) making reproductions in material form; (b) publishing unpublished work in Singapore or any country to which Act applies; (c) broadcasting work; (d) performing work in public; (e) including work in cable programme; and (f) making adaptations of work.

In respect of artistic works, only (a) to (d) apply. For cinematographic films, copyright extends to copying film, causing film to be seen in public, broadcasting film and including work in cable programme. In case of television and sound broadcast, copyright extends to making cinematographic film of television broadcast or making copy of film, making sound recording of broadcast or copy of broadcast, causing broadcast to be seen or heard before paying audience and rebroadcasting or including it in cable programme. As for published editions of works, copyright is confined to right to make reproduction of edition.

For works, copyright has basic term of life of author and 50 years thereafter. Certain unpublished works can enjoy indefinite copyright term. For sound recording and cinematograph film—50 years from year of first publication. For television and sound broadcast—50 years from year broadcast was made. For cable programme—50 years from year in which programme was first included in cable service. For published editions of works—25 years from year of first publication.

Assignment.—Copyright can be assigned, but assignment must be in writing and signed by or on behalf of assignor.

Licence.—Copyright can be licensed either on exclusive or non-exclusive basis. Exclusive licence must be in writing. Licence binds every successor in title to copyright owner except for purchaser in good faith for value without notice (actual or constructive) of licence or person deriving from such purchaser.

Infringement of copyright takes place where, without permission of copyright owner, rights reserved exclusively to copyright owner (see supra) is exercised by someone other than copyright owner. Secondary infringement takes place where person sells, lets or hires or by way of trade offers or exposes article for sale or hire, distributes article for purpose of trade or exhibits article in public by way of trade and knows or reasonably ought to know that making of article was infringement or without consent of copyright owner. Similarly, infringement takes place if person imports article for above purposes.

Civil remedies include injuctions, damages or account of profits and delivery up of infringing copies and tools. Criminal sanctions are provided for under Act and include heavy fines and even imprisonment.

Registered Designs.—

Statute.—United Kingdom Designs (Protection) Act. (Cap. 339).

Procedure.—No registration or reregistration in Singapore is necessary. Registered proprietor of design registered in U.K. under Registered Designs Act 1949 enjoys in Singapore like privileges and rights as though certificate of registration in U.K. had been issued with extension to Singapore.

Registrability.—To be registrable, design must satisfy following: (a) it must be new; (b) it must have eye appeal; (c) features of shape or configuration of design of article must not be: (i) dictated solely by function which article has to perform, or (ii) dependent upon appearance of another article of which article is intended by author to form integral part; (d) appearance of article based on design must be material.

Rights.—Registered proprietor of design has monopoly over its use. No need to prove copying (*cf.* copyright). Registration gives proprietor exclusive right to: (a) make or import: (i) for sale or hire, or (ii) for use for purposes of trade or business; or (b) sell, hire or offer or expose for sale or hire, article in respect of which design is registered.

Duration.—Rights granted last for five years from date of registration but renewable for further periods of five years up to maximum of 25 years.

Infringement.—Person who does any of aforesaid acts reserved exclusively for registered proprietor without consent of proprietor is liable for design infringement. Defence of innocence is provided under Act, i.e., registered proprietor of design is not entitled to recover damages in respect of infringement of copyright in design from defendant who proves that at date of infringement, he was not aware nor had any reasonable means of making himself aware of existence of registration of design (however, this does not affect plaintiff's right to injunction).

Civil remedies include injunctions, damages, and delivery up of infringing copies and tools.

CORPORATIONS:

Companies Act (Cap. 50) regulates corporations. Companies Act is based on UK Companies Act 1948 and Australian Companies Acts.

Incorporation.—Two or more persons (including bodies corporate) may form limited companies. Apart from issuance of at least two shares, there is no prescribed minimum amount issued or authorised share capital, although in practice most companies have authorised capital of S$100,000.

Private company means company which by its Articles of Association restricts transfer of its shares, limits number of shareholders to 50 and prohibits invitation to public to subscribe for its shares or debentures. Company which does not impose such restrictions is public company. Public companies may invite public to subscribe for shares, usually by issue of prospectus. Name of limited company must end with word "Limited" or its abbreviation "Ltd". Private company must, additionally, have word "Private" or "Pte" as penultimate word.

Company may be formed as limited company (liability of members limited by shares or guarantee) or unlimited company (liability of members unlimited). Unlimited company can be converted to limited company, and vice versa; but company so converted may not be reconverted.

Public company may choose to be company listed on Stock Exchange of Singapore, if it meets listing criteria. Company listed on Stock Exchange of Singapore is also regulated by Listing Manual of Stock Exchange of Singapore.

Company must register its Memorandum of Association setting out its name, objects, statement of liability of members and amount of company's authorised share capital with number and value of shares into which such capital is divided, full names, addresses and occupations of subscribers and statement that such subscribers agree to take number of shares in capital of company as set opposite their respective names.

Objects of company are set out in its Memorandum, augmented by §23 and Third Schedule to Companies Act. Acts which do not come within scope of "objects clause" (or ancillary powers) are ultra vires.

Company must also file its Articles of Association which are rules governing internal regulation, duties of directors, rights of voting, etc. If Articles are not filed, statutory regulations known as "Table A" govern internal management. Applications for registrations of companies are made to Registrar of Companies, to whom proper set of Memorandum and Articles of Company is submitted.

Prospectus.—Public company may issue prospectus (or if applicable, statement in lieu of prospectus) setting out particulars specified in and complying with Companies Act requirements. Copy of every such prospectus (or statement) signed by every named director or proposed director or by his agent authorised in writing must be duly delivered to Registrar as required by Companies Act. No prospectus may be issued (or shares or debentures allotted) until this has been done. Every prospectus must be in English language. Registrar takes no responsibility as to contents of prospectus. Exemptions from prospectus requirements may, however, be invoked if offer is made in accordance with, and subject to, provisions of Division 5A, Part IV of Companies Act.

Reports.—Companies must file with Registrar annual return in requisite form signed by director containing specified information such as names of members, details of directors, etc. If company has share capital, return must give particulars of its share capital including extent to which it is paid up. All companies (other than private exempt companies) are required to file accounts. Foreign companies registered in Singapore must deliver to Registrar return of any alteration in prescribed particulars and annual audited accounts.

In addition to foregoing, company is required to lodge with Registrar changes in share capital of company, special resolutions, changes in directors, secretary, registered office, etc.

Directors.—Must be individuals. There must be at least two directors, at least one of whom must be ordinarily resident in Singapore.

Secretary.—Must be individual having certain qualifications and must ordinarily reside in Singapore.

Registration of Mortgages.—Mortgages and charges falling within categories specified in Companies Act are, in so far as any security is conferred thereby, void against liquidator and creditor of company unless prescribed particulars and relevant instrument (or certified copy thereof) are delivered to Registrar within 30 days after date of its creation.

Categories include charges to secure any issue of debentures; charges on uncalled share capital of company; charges on shares of subsidiary of company which are owned by company; charge or assignment created or evidenced by instrument which, if executed by individual, would require registration as bill of sale; charges on land or any interest therein; charges on book debts; floating charges on company's undertaking or property; charges on calls made but not paid; charges on ship or aircraft (or shares therein); and charges on goodwill, on patent, or licence under patent, on trade mark or on copyright or licence under copyright.

Winding up.—See topic Insolvency.

Foreign corporations establishing place of business or carrying on business in Singapore are required to register as foreign companies under Companies Act.

COURTS:

Supreme Court is superior court of record consisting of High Court and Court of Appeal.

Civil jurisdiction of Court of Appeal consists of power to hear and determine appeal against decision made by High Court, subject to provisions of Supreme Court of Judicature Act (Cap. 322) and other statutes which regulate terms and conditions under which appeals may be brought.

High Court has jurisdiction to hear and try action in personam where defendant is served with writ or other originating process in Singapore or outside Singapore in accordance with Rules of Court; or where defendant submits to jurisdiction of High Court.

High Court may, however, stay proceedings by reason of Singapore not being appropriate forum.

Subordinate Courts consist of, inter alia, District Courts and Magistrates' Courts. *District Court* has jurisdiction to determine matters where value of subject matter in dispute does not exceed S$100,000 and where, in respect of proceedings for administration of estate of deceased, value of estate does not exceed S$3 million. District Court has jurisdiction to grant injunction as sole relief in action, and make binding declarations of rights whether or not any consequential relief is or can be claimed.

Magistrates' Court has jurisdiction to determine matters where value of subject matter in dispute does not exceed S$30,000.

CURRENCY:

Monetary unit is Singapore dollar. Currency is issued by Board of Commissioners of Currency established under Currency Act. (Cap. 69).

There is general policy enforced by Monetary Authority of Singapore, which is established under Monetary Authority of Singapore Act (Cap. 186), against "internationalisation of the Singapore dollar". In general, amounts denominated in Singapore dollars may not be lent to nonresidents of Singapore or for purposes outside Singapore, without reference to Monetary Authority of Singapore, if such amounts are in excess of S$5 million.

CUSTOMS:

Customs duty is levied on certain categories of goods, including motor vehicles, tobacco, liquors and petroleum. Applicable rates of customs duty and types of dutiable goods are found in Customs Act (Cap. 70) and its regulations.

See also topic Foreign Trade Regulations.

DEATH:

Registration of Death.—All deaths must be registered with Registry of Death, Singapore.

Presumption of death of person may be judicially declared if man has not been heard of for seven years by those who would naturally have heard of him if he had been alive.

Presumption of Survivorship.—Where two or more persons die in circumstances rendering it uncertain which of them survived other or others, for purposes of affecting title to property, legal presumption is that younger died later than older.

Action for Causing Death.—Executor or administrator of deceased may on behalf and for benefit of dependents commence action in name of executor or administrator within three years of death against person who by reason of his wrongful act, neglect or default caused death to deceased. If there is no executor or administrator of deceased or no action is brought within six months after death by and in name of executor or administrator of deceased, action may be brought by and in name of all or any of persons for whose benefit executor or administrator could have brought it, which would include spouse, parent, grandparent, great-grandparent, child, grandchild or great-grandchild of deceased or any person who is, or is issue of, brother, sister, uncle or aunt of deceased. Damages that are recoverable would include pecuniary loss to estate, bereavement and funeral expenses.

DEEDS:

For individuals, every deed must be signed, sealed and delivered by party to be bound or by his attorney and attested by one witness.

For corporations, common seal must be used in accordance with company's Articles of Association. Usually affixing of common seal will be in presence of two directors or director and secretary. Person authorised by power of attorney to execute deeds on behalf of corporation may execute deed by signing his own name as attorney for corporation and affixing his seal thereto.

With respect to transactions involving land under Registration Of Deeds Act (Cap. 269), it is usual practice for deeds of conveyances and assignments to be certified in prescribed form by advocate and solicitor of Supreme Court of Singapore, consular officer or representative of Singapore; or notary public practising in country where execution takes place as otherwise Registry of Deeds may not accept registration of deed.

See also topic Seals.

DEPOSITIONS AND DISCOVERY:

Obtaining Evidence for Local Courts Before Trial.—Court may, in any cause or matter where it appears necessary for purposes of justice, make order for examination on oath before Judge or Registrar or some other person, at any place, of any person.

Where person to be examined on oath is out of jurisdiction, application may be made to High Court for issue of letter of request to judicial authorities of country in which that person is to be examined.

Subject to any directions contained in order for examination, any person ordered to be examined before examiner may be cross examined and reexamined.

Deposition may be received in evidence at trial of cause or matter if: (a) deposition was taken in pursuance of order of Court; (b) either party against whom evidence is offered consents or it is proved to satisfaction of Court that deponent is dead, or beyond jurisdiction of Court or unable from sickness or other infirmity to attend trial; and (c) notice of intention to use deposition is given to other party within reasonable time before trial.

Obtaining Evidence for Foreign Courts.—Under Evidence (Civil Proceedings in Other Jurisdictions) Act (Cap. 98), High Court may make orders for examination of witnesses, either orally or in writing for production of documents; for inspection, photocopying, preservation, custody or detention of property; for taking of samples of property and carrying out of experiments on or with property; for medical examination of person and for taking and testing of samples of blood from person. Order does not require person to state what documents relevant to proceedings to which application for order relates are or have been in his possession, custody or power; or to produce any documents other than particular documents specified in order as being documents appearing to be in his possession, custody or power. Person is not compelled to give evidence which he cannot be compelled to give in civil proceedings in Singapore High Court; or in civil proceedings in country or territory in which requesting court exercises jurisdiction.

Discovery.—During summons for directions after pleadings have closed, Court may order service of list of documents. List of documents enumerates documents in possession, custody or power of relevant party which he does not object to procure in Schedule I, Part I; documents relevant party objects to produce in Schedule I, Part II; documents which have been, but at date of service of list are not, in possession, custody or power of party in question in Schedule II. Court will also limit number of factual witnesses and expert witnesses. Evidence in chief of all witnesses is usually ordered to be in affidavit form and to be exchanged or disclosed. Witnesses may also give evidence through live video or live television link in any proceedings other than criminal proceedings in accordance with relevant provisions of Evidence Act.

DESCENT AND DISTRIBUTION:

In testacy, distribution of deceased's estate is governed by properly executed will. In intestate cases, distribution of movable property of deceased person is regulated by law of country in which he was domiciled at time of his death, while that of his immovable property is regulated by Intestate Succession Act. (Cap. 146).

In effecting distribution in intestacy, surviving spouse takes whole of estate absolutely if deceased leaves no issue and no parent. If deceased leaves issue, spouse is entitled to one-half of estate. Other half is to be distributed equally amongst children of deceased and in case any of those children is dead, descendants of children. If deceased leaves surviving spouse and no issue but parent or parents, spouse is entitled to one-half of estate and parent or parents to other half of estate. If deceased leaves no surviving spouse, descendants or parents, estate will be distributed equally amongst deceased's brothers and sisters, and in case any of them is dead, their descendants are entitled to share which he or she would have taken.

Grandparents may take whole of estate in equal portions if there are no surviving spouse, descendants, parents, brothers and sisters or children of such brothers and sisters. Uncles and aunts may take whole of estate in equal portions if there are no surviving spouse, descendants, parents, brothers and sisters or children of such brothers and sisters or grandparents.

Government is entitled to whole of estate in default of distribution under foregoing rules.

For purposes of distribution under Act, word "child" does not include illegitimate child.

Distribution provided for under Act may be affected by Inheritance (Family Provisions) Act (Cap. 138) which provides for maintenance of dependents in testacies and intestacies.

Law of Islamic Inheritance.—In case of Muslims, rules of intestate succession set out above do not apply. Distribution takes place only after legacies and debts, including funeral expenses, are paid out of property left behind by deceased.

If deceased is husband, and he leaves no issue and no parent, widow gets one-quarter. If deceased is wife and there are no issue and no parent, widower gets one-half. If deceased husband leaves issue and no parent, spouse is entitled to one-eighth of estate. On other hand, widower is entitled to one-half of his deceased wife's estate. Remaining share is to be distributed amongst children of deceased. Female children's share is generally half of male children's share.

If deceased leaves surviving spouse and no issue but parent or parents, widower is entitled to one-half of estate, and father and mother get two-thirds and one-third of remaining estate respectively. As for widow, she is entitled to one-quarter share of husband's estate and father and mother get two-thirds and one-third of remaining estate respectively.

If deceased leaves parents but no surviving spouse and children, mother will get one-third and father will get remaining two-thirds. If deceased leaves parents and children but no spouse, each parent takes one-sixth share while remaining share will be distributed among children.

DISPUTE RESOLUTION:

Mandatory Dispute Resolution.—It is practice of court to direct parties to attend pretrial conference personally, in addition to their solicitor, such that any matter including possibility of settlement of any or all issues in action or proceeding may be considered, with view to securing just, expeditious and economical disposal of proceeding. All facts disclosed and all matters considered in course of such pretrial conference are not to be communicated to court conducting trial of action or proceeding.

Voluntary Dispute Resolution.—Singapore International Arbitration Centre provides facilities for systematic conduct of arbitration hearings and conciliation. Conciliator may facilitate negotiations or may be empowered by parties to take evaluative role but without power to make any binding decision on parties. International Arbitration Act (Cap. 143A) recognizes existence of conciliation agreements independently of arbitration agreements. See also topic Arbitration and Award.

DIVORCE:

Jurisdiction.—Under Women's Charter ("Act") (Cap. 47) Court has jurisdiction to entertain proceedings for divorce, judicial separation and nullity of marriage only if: (a) marriage has been registered or is deemed to be registered under Act, or was solemnised under law which expressly or impliedly provides that marriage is to be monogamous; (b) either of parties to marriage is domiciled in Singapore at commencement of proceedings or habitually resident in Singapore for period of three years immediately preceding commencement of proceedings; (c) parties must have been married for at least three years unless case is one of exceptional depravity suffered by petitioner or of exceptional depravity on part of respondent.

Ground for Divorce.—Either party to marriage may petition for divorce on ground that marriage has irretrievably broken down by reason of one or more of following facts: (a) that respondent has committed adultery and petitioner finds it intolerable to live with respondent; (b) that respondent has behaved in such way that petitioner cannot reasonably be expected to live with respondent; (c) that respondent has deserted petitioner for continuous period of at least two years immediately preceding presentation of petition; (d) that parties to marriage have lived apart for continuous period of at least three years immediately preceding presentation of petition and respondent consents to decree being granted; (e) that parties to marriage have lived apart for continuous period of at least four years immediately preceding presentation of petition.

Judicial Separation.—Petition for judicial separation may be presented to Court by either party to marriage on ground and circumstances set out above. Where Court grants decree of judicial separation it is no longer obligatory for petitioner to cohabit with respondent. Judicial separation is no bar to petition for divorce.

Nullity of Marriage.—Either party to marriage can petition for decree of nullity on ground that marriage is void if either party was already lawfully married at date of marriage or if formal requirements relating to marriage under Act were not complied with or if parties are within prohibited degrees of consanguinity.

Where marriage was celebrated outside Singapore, marriage may be invalid for lack of capacity or by law of place in which it was celebrated.

Marriage may be voidable on grounds of non-consummation due to incapacity of either party or to wilful refusal of respondent or lack of consent of either party due to duress, mistake, unsoundness of mind or otherwise, or mental disorder of either party within meaning of Mental Disorders and Treatment Act (Cap. 178) or that respondent was suffering from venereal disease in communicable form or was pregnant by some person other than petitioner at time of marriage.

Dissolution of Marriage on Presumption of Death.—Any married person who alleges that reasonable grounds exist for supposing that other party to marriage is dead may present petition to Court to have it presumed that other party is dead and to have marriage dissolved, and Court, if satisfied that such reasonable grounds exist, may make decree nisi of presumption of death and of divorce. In such proceedings, fact that other party to marriage has been continually absent from petitioner for period of seven years

DIVORCE . . . *continued*
or upwards, and petitioner has no reason to believe that other party has been living within that time, is evidence that he or she is dead until contrary is proved.

Decree Nisi and Absolute.—If Court is satisfied that there is ground for divorce under Act, decree nisi will be granted which will not be made absolute before expiration of three months from its grant unless Court by general or special order from time to time fixes shorter period.

When granting decree of divorce, judicial separation or nullity of marriage, Court has power to order: (a) division of assets acquired by them during marriage; (b) payment of maintenance; and (c) custody of children of marriage.

Divorce in Islam.—Divorce in Islam, although permitted, is not encouraged. Divorce can be effected by Talak, Khu'lu or Fasakh.

Divorce by Talak may be effected once husband utters words of divorce.

Where husband does not agree to divorce wife but agrees to divorce by Khu'lu (redemption), Syariah Court may assess amount of payment to be made by wife according to her status and means. Husband will then have to pronounce divorce by redemption.

Married woman may apply for and obtain decree of Fasakh (divorce or rescision by judicial decree) on any ground which is recognised as valid for dissolution of marriage by Fasakh in Islamic law including defects in either spouse such as insanity (whether intermittent or permanent), leprosy, vitiligo and dangerous contagious disease or apostasy of either spouse.

When registering divorce, President of Syariah Court has power to order: (a) division of harta sepencarian (assets acquired by them during marriage); (b) payment of maintenance during Iddah (period of continence) and payment of mutaah (consolatory gift) which wife is entitled to in event of divorce by Talak and Fasakh; and (c) custody of children of marriage. See also topic Marriage, subhead Muslim Marriages.

EXCHANGE CONTROL:

Although there is Exchange Control Act (Cap. 99) on statute books, it has not been in operation as law in Singapore since 1 June 1978. In effect, there are no exchange control regulations applicable in Singapore. However, there is general policy against "internationalisation of the Singapore dollar". See also topic Currency.

EXECUTIONS:

Writ of execution may be issued to enforce judgment.

Commonest form of execution proceedings is issuance of writ of seizure and sale of movable property of judgment debtor. Seizure of immovable property is also available as form of execution of judgment. Seizure and sale of properties conducted by Bailiff appointed by Court.

Where judgment debtor is individual and judgment debt exceeds S$2,000, bankruptcy proceedings may be brought against judgment debtor. Where judgment debtor is company, winding up proceedings may be brought against judgment debtor on judgment debt if debt exceeds S$2,000. See topic Insolvency.

Debts due to be paid to judgment debtor may be garnished as form of execution proceedings. Debt must be due and owing at time of garnishment. Salaries of judgment debtor not due to be paid to judgment debtor may be garnished only after they become payable to judgment debtor.

Where judgment debtor's interest in immovable property takes form of interest under trust or where debt is not due to be paid to judgment debtor, Court may appoint receiver by way of equitable execution to receive debt or dividend when paid and hold amount for benefit of judgment creditor.

EXECUTORS AND ADMINISTRATORS:

Upon death of person, whole of his property, both real and personal, devolves to his personal representatives, i.e. executors, where he has left will; and administrators, where he has died intestate, and to whom letters of representation (grant of probate and letters of administration, as case may be), are granted by Subordinate Courts or Supreme Court. If value of estate is S$3 million or less, application for letters of representation may be made in Subordinate Courts. For estate worth more than S$3 million, application for letters of representation is to be made in Supreme Court.

Appointment.—Executors are normally appointed by will. Administrators are appointed by Court in cases of intestacy as well as testacy where executor is not named in will.

Authority of Administrator and Executor.—Administrator obtains his authority solely from grant of letters of administration. Until grant is obtained, administrator has no authority. Executor's authority stems from will. He obtains authority to conduct affairs of deceased, moment deceased dies. It is purely to lend authority and vest proper title that letters of probate are obtained.

Grant of Probate on Testacy.—Executors appointed under will can apply for Grant of Probate.

Letters of Administration on Intestacy.—Total number of administrators who may petition for letters of administration may not exceed four. If there is minority or life interest then law requires minimum of two persons to be administrators. If there is no such interest one administrator will suffice. If trust corporation applies for letters of administration then requirement of additional person is dispensed with.

Letters of administration are usually granted to next of kin in accordance with priorities to entitlement of estate under Intestate Succession Act. (Cap. 146). Public Trustee may also administer estate if no application for letters of administration has been made provided estate is worth less than S$50,000.

Muslims' Estates.—In case of petitions made to Court for letters of representation in respect of Muslim's estate, petitions have to be accompanied by advice on inheritance law in Islam given in form of certificate by President of Syariah Court.

Renunciation.—Executor or administrator may renounce his right to apply for letters of representation.

Grant of probate and letters of administration are normally given as matter of course once petition for letters of administration is filed. However, grant may not be extracted unless clearance is obtained from Commissioner of Estate Duties.

Domicile.—Before granting letters of representation, Court requires proof of domicile. Deceased's domicile would determine validity of his will or right of his personal representatives to apply for letters of representation and question of priorities between persons contending for letters of representation.

Security.—In intestate case, administration bond equivalent to value of estate is required before grant of letters of administration can be extracted. If value of estate exceeds S$250,000, security by way of two sureties up to value of estate has to be furnished to Court to guarantee proper administration of estate. Court may dispense with sureties if all creditors and beneficiaries, being of full age and capacity consent to dispensation.

In case of testacy, no security is required.

General Powers and Duties.—In addition to powers conferred by will, personal representative is also conferred certain powers in his capacity as trustee under Trustees Act. (Cap. 337). Duties of personal representatives revolve around tasks of calling in estate's assets, determining beneficiaries and shares they are entitled to, and thereafter distributing assets.

Assets and Liabilities.—Inventory of assets and liabilities of estate is first step to be taken by personal representatives of estate to determine amount of estate duty payable and for purposes of distribution.

Creditors.—After calling in all assets of deceased and payment of funeral and testamentary expenses and estate duty, executor or administrator must ensure that debts of deceased are paid. Where estate is large, executor or administrator must place advertisement in Gazette or newspapers to give notice to all creditors that they ought to submit their claims within period stipulated, after which distribution will be made. If claim is not presented within time limited in advertisement, personal representative may distribute estate without being personally liable for debts of which he had no knowledge, but creditor may follow assets.

Accounts.—Before executor or administrator winds up administration of estate, he must submit accounts for beneficiaries' perusal and approval before distribution.

Distribution.—Duty of administrator to distribute estate in accordance with laws on intestate succession. (Intestate Succession Act, Cap. 146). In case of testacy, it is duty of personal representative to carry out terms of will. There can be no distribution of estate until debts of estate are disposed of.

Resealing Letters of Representation.—Grant of probate or letters of administration by Commonwealth country may be resealed by High Court. Once grant is resealed, it is as of same effect as grant of probate or letters of administration of High Court.

FOREIGN CORPORATIONS:

See topic Corporations.

FOREIGN EXCHANGE:

There are no exchange control regulations applicable in Singapore although authorizing legislation remains on statute books. See topic Exchange Control.

Foreign exchange trading, however, is supervised generally by Monetary Authority of Singapore. Foreign exchange booking or advice on leveraged basis is (subject to certain exceptions) licensable under Futures Trading Act. (Cap. 116).

FOREIGN INVESTMENT:

Exchange Control.—No exchange restrictions on flow of capital in or out of Singapore.

Tax Incentives.—Singapore actively encourages foreign investment. Under Economic Expansion Incentive (Relief from Income Tax) Act (Cap. 86), various tax incentives are given to certain pioneer enterprises, pioneer service companies, established enterprises wanting to expand, and companies exporting goods or services. Tax incentives are also given to venture capital companies, countertrade companies, international oil traders, and for warehousing and servicing operations for certain products, international consultancy services, research and development activities, headquarters operations and product development activities. There are many tax incentives under Income Tax Act. (Cap. 134). Shipping profits are exempt from tax. Other incentives include concessions for approved headquarters companies, fund management companies, securities companies, and investment companies and for Asian Currency Unit (ACU) activities.

Real Property.—There are some restrictions on types of residential property that may be owned by foreigners. (Residential Property Act, Cap. 274).

FOREIGN TRADE REGULATIONS:

Port of Singapore is designated free trade zone. There is little regulation over goods in transit, but there are regulations applicable to imports into, and, to lesser extent, exports out of Singapore. Subject matter of regulation includes levying of customs duties including anti-dumping tariffs, requirement of import/export licences, control of products like certain animals, wildlife, drugs, poisons, petroleum and tobacco products, control of prices for some products, and prohibition of import of products containing certain drugs, counterfeit trademarks, pornography, indecency or other undesirable elements.

See also topic Foreign Investment.

FRAUDS, STATUTE OF:

No action may be brought in respect of contracts for sale of land or of interest in them or concerning them or for lease of land for more than three years, unless such contracts are in writing and signed by party transferring or leasing land or interests in land.

FRAUDULENT SALES AND PREFERENCE:

Individuals.—Bankruptcy Act 1995 contains provisions dealing with transactions at undervalue and unfair preferences. Transactions at undervalue within period of five years before person's bankruptcy may be set aside on Official Assignee's (government department) application to Court. Similarly for unfair preferences, these can be set

FRAUDULENT SALES AND PREFERENCE . . . *continued*
aside: for unfair preferences to any person, time period is six months, and to "associates" transaction is caught if it took place within two years before bankruptcy. There is also provision for setting aside extortionate credit transactions which occur within three years before bankruptcy. Extortionate credit transactions are those which require grossly exorbitant payments, or those which are harsh and unconscionable or substantially unfair.

Companies.— Companies Act (Cap. 50) contains provisions dealing with fraudulent sales and preferences.

Any transfer, mortgage, delivery of goods, payment, execution or other act relating to property carried out by company, which had it been undertaken by individual would be void or voidable under bankruptcy law, would otherwise be void or voidable in company's winding up.

Any transfer or assignment by company of all its property to trustees for benefit of creditors is void.

Floating charge on undertaking or property of company created within six months of commencement of winding up is void except to amount of cash paid to company at time of or subsequent to creation of floating charge with interest at 5% per annum. This is inapplicable where company was solvent at time floating charge was created.

GARNISHMENT:

See topic Executions.

HUSBAND AND WIFE:

Rights and Duties.—Under Women's Charter (Cap. 353) husband and wife are mutually bound to cooperate with each other in safeguarding interests of union and in caring and providing for children. Husband and wife have right separately to engage in trade or profession or in social activities and have equal rights in running of matrimonial household.

Wife has right to use her own surname and name separately. Wife may apply to Court for maintenance if husband neglects or refuses to provide her with reasonable maintenance.

Capacity of Married Woman.—Married woman can acquire, hold and dispose of, property and be liable for tort, contract, debt or obligation and can sue and be sued in her own name either in tort or in contract or otherwise and is entitled to all remedies and redress for all purposes and is subject to law relating to bankruptcy and to enforcement of judgments and orders.

IMMIGRATION:

Governed by Immigration Act. (Cap. 133).

General.—Non-Singapore citizen can enter Singapore if he has valid entry or reentry permit or if name endorsed on entry or reentry permit of accompanying husband/father, or if he has valid pass, or if specially exempted by Minister For Home Affairs. He must not be prohibited immigrant.

Passes entitle foreigner to enter and remain temporarily in Singapore:

Employment Pass.—Generally issued to professionals, technical personnel and skilled workers. For application to be considered, applicant must earn basic monthly salary of more than S$2,000, or hold acceptable educational qualifications.

Work Permit Pass.— Granted to holder of Work Permit issued under Employment of Foreign Workers Act. (Cap. 91A). "Foreign worker" means non-Singapore citizen employed at not more than S$2,000 per month. Also includes non-Singapore citizen earning more than S$2,000 per month but not holding Employment Pass. Generally, employer of foreign worker holding Work Permit is required to pay foreign worker levy of between S$200 and S$400 per month.

Dependent's Pass.—Wife and unmarried children below 21 years of Employment Pass or Work Permit Pass holder may apply for Dependent's Passes to enable them to remain with him in Singapore. Dependent's Pass holder is not allowed to work in Singapore without written consent of Controller of Immigration.

Visit Pass.—Issued to foreigner wishing to enter Singapore on social, business or professional visit or as tourist. Person on training visit in Singapore and who earns income of more than S$1,500 per month may apply for Training Visit Pass.

Professional Visit Pass.—Issued to foreign surgeons, Queen's Counsel, auctioneers, lecturers or speakers participating in seminar or conference, journalists, reporters, film crew, representatives of overseas schools or universities, participants in exhibition or trade fair, performing artistes and others.

Student's Pass.—Issued to foreigner who has been accepted as student by recognised university or approved educational institution in Singapore, or who possesses Minister For Education's Certificate that it is desirable he should be accepted as student at specified Singapore educational institution and that he has been so accepted.

Permanent Residence.—Controller of Immigration may issue entry permits to persons wishing to be Singapore Permanent Residents, and reentry permits to Singapore Permanent Residents wishing to reenter Singapore. Local sponsors are required for applications for entry permits. Five ways to acquire permanent residence as follows: (1) Wife or unmarried children below 21 years of Singapore citizen or Singapore Permanent Resident. (2) Aged parents above 55 years of Singapore citizen. (3) Professionals, technical personnel, skilled workers and their families. Applicant must be below 50 years. Applicant must have worked in Singapore for six months on Employment Pass or on three-year Skilled Work Permit, or must be officer in public service. (4) Foreign entrepreneurs under Permanent Residence Scheme for Entrepreneurs (Deposit Scheme). Administered by Economic Development Board ("EDB"). Applicant must deposit minimum S$1.5 million with Singapore Government. Deposited funds can be released for investment in approved business activity. Entire amount may be invested in project in Singapore approved by EDB. Alternatively, part of entire amount may be invested in approved regional project and remaining amount invested in Singapore. Applicant may utilise part of deposited funds to purchase commercial property (but not residential property) related to approved business activity. Investments have to be retained for at least five years. (5) Hong Kong Residents. Special scheme for Hong Kong residents who must not be above 50 years old. Applicant must possess, in general, acceptable educational or professional qualifications and/or relevant working experience.

Visas.—Required for entry into Singapore if person is holder of: (a) Hong Kong Document of Identity; (b) refugee travel documents; or (c) travel documents issued by following countries-Afghanistan, Algeria, Cambodia, India, Iraq, Jordan, Laos, Lebanon, Libya, People's Republic of China, former Soviet Union, Syria, Tunisia, Vietnam and Yemen. Visa applications may be made for social or business visits. Security deposit in form of banker's guarantee may be required from local sponsor.

Security Deposit.—Security by bond, guarantee, cash deposit or by other method, may have to be furnished as condition for issue of pass. Security provided is for purpose of ensuring compliance with immigration provisions, or conditions imposed in respect of pass.

INCOME TAX:

See topic Taxation.

INFANTS:

Age of majority is 21 years.

Actions By or Against Infant.—Can only be commenced by next friend and defended by guardian ad litem.

Contracts With Infants.—Following common law, generally unenforceable as against infant and voidable at option of infant, except contracts for necessaries (necessary goods and services supplied to infant) and contracts of apprenticeship, education and service. Such voidable contracts may be of two types: binding on infant unless repudiated during minority or within reasonable time of infant attaining majority, or not binding on infant unless and until ratified after attaining majority.

Infant is competent to enter into contract of service as employee under Employment Act (Cap. 91) but such contract is not enforceable as against infant unless it is for his benefit.

Wills.—Under Wills Act (Cap. 352), will made by infant is not valid unless privileged will, i.e. will made by soldier (including member of naval, marine or air forces) in actual military service or mariner or seaman at sea, even though below age of majority.

INHERITANCE TAX:

See topic Taxation.

INSOLVENCY:

Corporate Insolvency.—Companies incorporated in Singapore may be wound up voluntarily or compulsorily (by order of Court). Voluntary liquidation proceedings may be made by members of company (where company is solvent) or by creditors. Court may, at request of company, creditors or directors, place company under judicial management if Court is satisfied judicial management will bring about, inter alia, continued survival of company, or advantageous realisation of company's assets.

Receiver may be appointed if contract so provides or by way of court order.

Individual Insolvency.—Bankruptcy proceedings may be brought against individuals under various grounds, most commonly where judgment debtor has failed to pay debt exceeding bankruptcy level, currently S$2,000. Bankruptcy petition may not be presented to court if debtor was either not domiciled in Singapore or had no property in Singapore or was not resident within jurisdiction of Singapore for at least one year immediately preceding time of presentation of bankruptcy petition. Debtor may seek to have himself adjudicated bankrupt by filing bankruptcy petition. All assets of bankrupt vest in office of Official Assignee (government department).

INTEREST:

General.—Interest is payable only when allowed by statute or in accordance with contract. There is no general prohibition on rate of interest that can be charged. However, neither simple interest exceeding 12% or 18% per annum (for secured and unsecured loans respectively) nor compound interest may be charged by those carrying on business of moneylending. (Moneylenders Act, Cap. 188). Act does not apply to banks, and many finance companies have been exempted from application of Act.

Prejudgment.—Interest may be awarded by Court in respect of late payment of damages or debts. Interest may also be awarded for late payment of debts, even if debt is paid before commencement of proceedings. (Civil Law Act, Cap. 43; Supreme Court of Judicature Act, Cap. 322).

Post-judgment interest is, subject to agreement of parties, at rate to be determined at discretion of Court, subject to limit set by Chief Justice.

JUDGMENTS:

Judgments may be for liquidated claims or for declaration. Judgment in default may be entered against defendant if defendant fails to give notice of intention to defend proceedings, or does not file defence or fails to obey court order.

Foreign judgments for fixed sums enforceable as if obtained in Singapore Court if they are recognised as such by Reciprocal Enforcement of Commonwealth Judgments Act (Cap. 264) or Reciprocal Enforcement of Foreign Judgments Act (Cap. 265). Such foreign judgments must first be registered in Singapore Court.

Other judgments not so recognised may be enforceable by action, and underlying action giving rise to judgment will not normally be retried by Singapore Court.

LABOUR RELATIONS:

Trade unions established after commencement of Trade Unions Act (Cap. 333) have to be registered. Such trade unions also fall under Industrial Relations Act (Cap. 136), which governs relations between trade unions and employers. Trade unions may claim recognition by employers, and upon being accorded recognition, may negotiate for collective agreements. Industrial Arbitration Courts have power to deal with trade disputes under this Act.

Employment.—Governed by Employment Act ("Act") (Cap. 91) and common law principles.

Scope of Act.—Act affords protection for "employees", which includes "workmen" (both terms as defined in Act). Employee's rights are then governed by contract of

See Topical Index in front part of this volume.

LABOUR RELATIONS . . . *continued*
employment, collective agreement with relevant trade union (if applicable), and Act. Terms in Act are part of employment contract even if this is not expressly stated to be so in contract. Term in contract which is less favourable than that prescribed in Act will be regarded as illegal, null and void to extent that it is so less favourable.

However, Part IV of Act only applies to "employees" earning not more than S$1,600 per month (excluding overtime payments, bonus payments, annual wage supplements, productivity incentive payments and any allowance however described) and to all "workmen" regardless of salary.

"Employees" do not include inter alia seamen; domestic servants; or persons employed in managerial, executive or confidential positions. Where person is not protected by Act, he must look to contract of employment and collective agreement (if he is trade union member), for rights under employment.

Termination of Contracts.—Under Act, contract of service for unspecified period of time is deemed to run until terminated by either party by written notice. Period of notice required to be given is prescribed and varies depending on length of service with employer. If contract of service is terminated without notice or adequate notice, either party is entitled to salary in lieu of such notice.

In event of wilful breach of contract of service by party, other party may terminate contract without notice. Employer can dismiss employee without notice on grounds of misconduct only after due inquiry. Employer also has option of downgrading employee or suspending him from work without pay for up to one week.

If employee is not covered by Act and contract of employment is silent, termination is usually by reasonable notice according to common law.

Absence Without Reasonable Excuse.—Employee is deemed to have broken contract if he continuously absents himself for more than two days without employer's prior leave or without reasonable excuse or without informing or attempting to inform employer of excuse for such absence.

Payment of Salary.—Generally, salary must be paid within seven days after last day of relevant salary period. Overtime pay must be paid within 14 days after last day of salary period during which overtime work was performed. Employer is deemed to have broken contract of service if he fails to pay salary in accordance with Act.

Part IV of Act.—Applies only to all workmen regardless of how much they earn per month, and to other employees, as defined in Act, who earn S$1,600 per month or less. Part IV of Act relates to: (1) Hours of work. Generally, employee has: (a) right not to work for more than six consecutive hours without having period of leisure; and (b) right not to work for more than eight hours a day or more than 44 hours a week. This is subject to exceptions under Act. Legal limit of working hours may be exceeded in emergencies. Overtime work is not compulsory. If employee does overtime work at employer's request, he is entitled to overtime pay of at least 1.5 times his hourly rate of pay. Employer cannot require employee to do overtime for more than 72 hours a month. (2) Holidays. Employee is entitled to paid holiday at his ordinary rate of pay on gazetted public holidays. (3) Rest days. Employee is entitled to one rest day per week which need not be Sun., but if it is not Sun., employer must give roster informing employee of his rest days in that month. Employer may require employee to work on rest day in emergencies. Employee is entitled to be paid, at maximum, his ordinary rate of pay for voluntarily working on rest days. He is entitled to double pay if he works on rest days at employer's request. (4) Annual leave. Employee's entitlement to annual leave commensurates with length of service with employer, subject to maximum of 14 days of such leave. Employee who has not completed 12 months of continuous service in any year is entitled to prorated annual leave. (5) Sick leave. Generally, employee who has served employer for at least 12 months is entitled, upon medical examination by doctor appointed by employer, to paid sick leave not exceeding 14 days in each year if no hospitalisation is necessary, or 60 days in each year where hospitalisation is necessary. (6) Retrenchment benefit. Retrenchment compensation is available to employee if he has been in continuous service with employer for at least three years at time of termination of his service for reasons as specified in Act. Quantum is not stipulated. (7) Retirement benefit. If employee has been in continuous service with employer for less than five years, he is not entitled to any retirement benefit other than sums payable under Central Provident Fund Act. (Cap. 36).

Workmen's Compensation for Injury.—In general, Workmen's Compensation Act (Cap. 354) enables compensation to be claimed if workman (as defined therein) suffers prescribed physical injury by accident arising out of and in course of his employment; or contracts prescribed occupational disease either during his employment or within specified time frame after cessation of his employment, and incapacity or death of workman results from disease.

LAW REPORTS:

Singapore Law Reports and Malayan Law Journal are two main law reports covering local court cases. For period from 1930's to 1991, both Singapore and Malaysian cases are reported in Malayan Law Journal due to historical relationship between courts of both countries. Malayan Law Journal is published by company of same name. Since 1992, however, Singapore cases are reported in Singapore Law Reports published by Butterworths Asia under authority of Singapore Academy of Law.

LANDLORD AND TENANT:

Leases are generally governed by principles of contract. Parties can set out terms that should govern rights and duties of landlord and tenant.

Rights and duties are set out in contract. However, there are some implied terms on parts of both landlord and tenant.

Implied Terms on Landlord.—(1) Quiet enjoyment; (2) non-derogation from grant; and (3) fitness for human habitation.

Implied Terms on Tenant.—(1) To pay rent; (2) to maintain reasonable repairs; and (3) to permit landlord to view premises.

Some leases contain words "usual covenants". "Usual covenants" vary with prevailing practice of the times for area and kind of premises.

Four main "usual covenants" on part of tenant are: (1) to pay rent; (2) to pay taxes except those expressly payable by landlord; (3) to keep and deliver up premises in repair; and (4) to allow lessor to enter and view premises.

Two main "usual covenants" on part of landlord are: (1) reentry for nonpayment of rent; and (2) quiet enjoyment.

Creation of Lease.—Formalities are provided in Conveyancing and Law of Property Act. (Cap. 61). Lease of seven years and above must be by deed in English language. In regard to land under Land Titles Act (Cap. 157), lease of over seven years must be in prescribed form and must be registered.

Remedies for Breach of Covenant to Pay Rent.—Landlord has following remedies: (1) simply sue for money; (2) distress under Distress Act. (Cap. 84). Writ of distress is available when rent is at least 12 months in arrear. Writ authorises sheriff to seize and sell goods found on leased premises, except tenant's necessary clothes and bedding, tools of trade and goods "in actual use". Tenant is given five days from date of seizure in which to pay arrears or to obtain order restraining sale; and (3) forfeiture of lease. Normally takes form of action for possession and puts end to tenant's interest altogether. Right to reenter premises and forfeit lease for breach of covenant must be expressly provided for in lease.

Termination of Lease.—Lease may come to end by expiry, notice, forfeiture, surrender, frustration or merger.

LEGISLATURE:

See topic Constitution and Government.

LICENCES:

Licences are required for activities which include holding lottery draws, conducting remittance businesses, futures trading, stockbroking, carrying out finance business transactions, insurance, broadcasting, newspapers and printing, restaurants and entertainment, establishing massage and health centres, conducting import and export trade, selling and distributing liquor, conducting certain manufacturing activities, acting as travel agents, housing agents and auctioneers, driving motor vehicles, and conducting businesses as moneylenders or pawnbrokers.

See also topics Banks and Banking; Foreign Exchange.

LIENS:

Generally, liens may arise from common law, equitable, contractual or statutory sources.

Common Law Lien.—Legal lien is unassignable personal right of security exercisable by person in possession of goods against owner of goods, but with no power of sale. General lien entitles person in possession to retain goods until all claims or accounts against owner are satisfied. These liens arise only by general usage or by express agreement. Particular lien is right to retain chattels until owner pays charges incurred in respect of those chattels.

Equitable lien is equitable right to charge real or personal property of another until certain specific claims are satisfied. It does not depend on possession and holder of lien has power of sale. Equitable liens arise in particular relationships, e.g., partners, vendor and purchasers, or from course of conduct or express agreement of parties. Equitable liens arising from contract are registrable under Bills of Sale Act. (Cap. 24).

Contractual Lien.—It is matter of interpretation of contract what rights and obligations parties intended to arise from lien.

Statutory Lien.—It is question of statutory interpretation when such lien arises, what rights and obligations attach thereto. See, e.g., statutory unpaid seller's lien under Sale of Goods Act (Cap. 393), where there is limited power of sale.

Maritime Lien.—See topic Shipping.

LIMITATION OF ACTIONS:

Regulated by Limitation Act. (Cap. 163).

Three Years.—Action for damages for negligence, nuisance, or breach of duty where damages claimed consist of or include damages in respect of personal injuries to person from date on which cause of action accrued.

Six Years.—Actions founded on contract or on tort; action to enforce award; action for account.

12 Years.—Actions to recover land.

Disability.—Limitation period is extended for varying periods in case of disability.

Latent Injuries and Damages.—Limitation period is extended under certain circumstances.

Fresh Accrual of Action.—Fresh accrual of action to recover any debt or other liquidated pecuniary claims on acknowledgment or part payment of liquidated claim.

Fraud or Mistake.—Where action is based on fraud of defendant, or right of action is concealed by fraud of defendant or action is for relief from consequences of mistake, period of limitation does not begin to run until plaintiff has discovered fraud or mistake or could with reasonable diligence have discovered it.

Arbitration.—Limitation periods stated above apply to arbitration.

Maritime Actions.—Time limits for maritime collisions are laid down by Maritime Conventions Act made applicable in Singapore.

MARRIAGE:

All marriages contracted in Singapore must be monogamous and must comply with formalities laid down in Women's Charter ("Act"). (Cap. 353). Act does not, however, apply to marriage where both parties are Muslims.

Legal Requirements.—Requirements stated in Act must be satisfied before couples can get married under Act. Couples must be at least 21 years of age and must be residents of Singapore. If either party is below age of 18, special marriage licence from Minister must be obtained. Parties must not be within prohibited degrees of consanguinity unless approved by Minister.

MARRIAGE . . . *continued*

Procedure.—Registrar of Marriages will only issue marriage licence upon expiry of 21 days' notice of intended marriage. Marriage licence is valid for three months from date of notice.

Minister may, if he thinks fit, dispense with giving of notice and may grant special marriage licence authorising solemnisation of marriage between parties named in licence. However, Minister may only exercise his discretion if there is urgent need and good reason. Special licence is valid for one month from date of issue.

Solemnisation of marriage can take place after 21 days or within three months from date of notice, subject to availability of dates. Once marriage is solemnised, it must be registered.

Muslim Marriages.—For marriage to be valid in Islam, there must be offer of marriage by one party which offer must be accepted by other party. Words must indicate with reasonable certainty that marriage has been contracted. There must be two witnesses who are sane and adult male Muslims.

Each party must be at least 16 years old. Deputy Registrar of Muslim Marriages (Kathi) may however solemnise marriage of girl under 16 if she has attained puberty.

Parties must apply to marry by completing prescribed form and making statutory declaration declaring truth of particulars given. Marriage must be registered and marriage register signed by both bride and groom. Consent of bride is necessary.

Register of Muslim Marriages must include particulars of Mas-Kahwin and of any gifts given by husband. Mas-Kahwin is obligatory payment due under law to wife at time of marriage and may be paid in cash or in kind and can either be paid promptly or deferred. See also topic Divorce, subhead Divorce in Islam.

MORTGAGES:

Conveyancing and Law of Property Act (Cap. 61) stipulates that legal mortgages can only be created by way of deed in English language. Form of mortgage will be conveyance for freehold estates, or assignment for leasehold estates, by mortgagor of his interest in land to mortgagee with proviso for redemption when mortgage debt is repaid in future.

Equitable mortgages are also recognised, i.e., those which arise where mortgagor only has equitable interest in land or where mortgagor has deposited title deeds over land coupled with intention to create mortgage.

Act contains provisions conferring several rights and remedies to mortgagee which include foreclosure, sale, insurance, appointment of receiver and granting of leases over mortgaged property.

Registration is required for protection of legal mortgages under Registration of Deeds Act (Cap. 269) and Land Titles Act (Cap. 157), as priority of instruments under these Acts are determined according to time of registration. Equitable mortgages are protected by lodgement of caveats in relevant Registries. See topic Real Property, subhead Registration.

MOTOR VEHICLES:

Governed by Road Traffic Act (Cap. 276) and related subsidiary legislation.

Size and Weight Limits of Motor Vehicles.—(Unladen) weight limits of motor vehicles regulated by Act. Size limits regulated by subsidiary legislation.

Registration and Licensing of Motor Vehicles.—Motor vehicle which is kept or used in Singapore must be registered and licensed. Valid permit is required before motor vehicle can be registered. For registration of motor vehicles on or after 1 May 1990, certificate of entitlement, obtained via bidding process, must be produced before motor vehicle can be registered. Minister For Communications may prescribe number of certificates of entitlement available for bidding at any one time.

Licences issued are generally for six or 12 months. Motor vehicle registered as off-peak car will be issued with restricted licence. With restricted licence, motor vehicle may not be driven during specified hours on certain days, unless supplementary licence is in force.

Tax is also chargeable for first registration of every vehicle and for every vehicle used or kept on road in Singapore. Tax is payable upon licence taken out by person keeping vehicle.

Driving Licences.—Every driver of motor vehicle must have passed requisite driving tests and possess valid local driving licence. Non-resident may drive in Singapore with International Driving Permit issued under any International Convention on Road Traffic to which Singapore is party or if he has been licensed to drive by competent authority of country other than Singapore.

If driver has been awarded prescribed number of demerit points within specified time frame, then driving licence may be suspended for up to 36 months.

Person below 16 years is not allowed to drive motor vehicle on road. Person below 17 years is not allowed to drive any motor vehicle other than motorcycle or invalid carriage.

Use of Safety Helmets, Seat Belts and Child Restraints.—Drivers and pillion riders of motorcycles are required to wear protective helmets.

Seat belts must be fitted for drivers and front seat passengers. Motor cars and taxis registered on or after 1 Jan. 1993 must be fitted with seat belts for rear seat passengers. Driver and front seat passenger must wear seat belts. Rear seat passengers must wear seat belts if these are available for use. Child below eight years must wear approved child restraint if he is front seat passenger. If rear seat belt available for use, child below eight years must wear approved child restraint. Rules on use of approved child restraints do not apply to taxis.

Driving Under Influence of Drink or Drugs.—Driving while under influence of drink or drugs is offence.

Inspection of Motor Vehicles.—Motor vehicles are required to undergo inspection upon notification. Test certificate will be issued if motor vehicle passes requisite tests. It is offence to use, or cause or permit another to use, on road at any time, motor vehicle in respect of which there is no test certificate.

Third Party Insurance.—Compulsory to insure all motor vehicles in use with respect to third party risks in Singapore. Any person using, causing or permitting another to use motor vehicle without such insurance coverage commits offence. Third party victim although not privy to insurance contract, has direct claim against insurer after obtaining judgment against motorist, by virtue of rights conferred under Motor Insurance (Third-Party Risks and Compensation) Act. (Cap. 189).

NATIONALITY:

See topic Immigration.

NEGOTIABLE INSTRUMENTS:

See topic Bills and Notes.

NOTARIES PUBLIC:

Governed by Notaries Public Act. (Cap. 208).

Appointment.—Senate of Academy of Law is vested with power to appoint fit and proper persons to be notaries public. Such persons must be practising advocates and solicitors in Singapore, and must have so practised for at least seven years.

Functions.—In general, notaries public have and may exercise within Singapore all powers and functions ordinarily exercised by notaries public in England. But power of notary public to administer oaths or affirmations in connection with affidavits or statutory declarations, or to take or attest such affidavits or statutory declarations, is limited to certain situations as prescribed by Act.

PARTNERSHIPS:

Partnership subsists between persons carrying on business in common with view of profit and is regulated by Partnership Act. (Cap. 391). Common ownership or sharing of profits does not of itself create partnership. Act governs nature of partnership, relationship of persons dealing with partners, relations of partners to one another and dissolution of partnership and its consequences.

Formation of Partnership.—Partnership will have between two and 20 partners. Partnership which comprises more than 20 partners must be registered as company. Exception to above is partnership formed for purposes of carrying on profession or calling which under any written law may be exercised only by persons possessing stipulated qualifications.

Partner is agent of firm and has power to bind firm. Partners of firm are bound by acts done on behalf of firm unless otherwise agreed upon between all partners. Such acts will then not be binding on firm with respect to persons having notice of that agreement.

Liability of Partners.—Every partner is jointly liable with other partners of firm for all debts and obligations of firm incurred while he is partner; and after his death, his estate is also severally liable in due course of administration for such debts and obligations, so far as they remain unsatisfied but subject to prior payment of his separate debts.

Taxation for Partnership.—Partnership is not recognised in law as separate legal persona distinct from individuals who constitute it. Hence, for tax purposes, individual partners will be assessed on their respective share of income.

Common Law.—Although Act contains certain provisions relating to creation and liability of partners, rules of equity and common law continue to apply save where they are inconsistent with provisions of Act.

PATENTS:

Statute.—Governed by Patents Act 1994 and Patent Rules 1995. Changes may be made due to TRIPS (Trade Related Intellectual Property Rights under GATT).

Treaties.—Patent Cooperation Treaty 1970; Paris Convention.

Procedure.—For domestic application, there are four stages: (1) First stage involves filing application in requisite form with prescribed fee. Application must contain: (a) request for grant of patent; (b) specification containing description of invention; (c) claim or claims defining matter for which applicant seeks patent protection and any supporting drawings; and (d) abstract which provides technical information concerning invention. If application is in order, filing date is given to application. (2) At second stage, Registry conducts formalities examination to ensure compliance with all formal requirements specified in Rules. If necessary, Registrar will give applicant opportunity to make amendments. (3) At third stage, applicant files request for preparation of either search report or combined search and examination report in respect of invention. It is at this stage that invention will be published. (4) Finally, patent will be granted if all is well. Applicant must request issuance of Certificate of Grant and pay fee within 42 months from date of filing or priority date, whichever is earlier.

Alternatively, international application may be filed under Patent Cooperation Treaty at any one of world-wide Receiving Offices, designating Singapore as one of countries in which patent protection is sought. Registry in Singapore is also Receiving Office under Treaty.

Priority.—Patent application filed in Singapore may be based on earlier application made in Singapore or in another country up to 12 months earlier provided that country is party to Paris Convention. If this is done, filing date of earlier application becomes "priority" date of new application.

Duration of Protection.—Grant of patent confers on owner exclusive right to exploit invention for 20 years from date of filing provided that renewal fees are paid annually commencing from expiration of fourth year from date of filing.

Assignment/Licence.—Rights under patent or patent application may be assigned provided assignment is in writing and signed by or on behalf of parties to transaction. Licence may also be granted for working invention which is subject of patent.

Compulsory Licences.—Under certain circumstances, e.g., where there is abuse of patent monopoly rights as in case of failure to exploit invention sufficiently in Singapore or where invention relates to food and medicine, Act provides for grant of compulsory licences. There are also provisions touching on Use of Patented Inventions for Services of Government.

Infringement.—Patent is infringed if anyone without consent of proprietor makes, disposes of, offers to dispose of, uses or imports patented product or keeps it whether

PATENTS . . . *continued*

for disposal or otherwise. Same applies to patented process if unauthorised person uses it or does any of above acts in relation to product directly obtained by means of process.

Remedies include injunctions, damages, account of profits, and delivery up.

PERPETUITIES:

See topic Trusts.

PLEDGES:

Common Law.—Pledge (pawn) is delivery of chattel as security for debt by pledgor to pledgee who is entitled to retain possession until debt is discharged. Right of possession is coupled with power of sale upon default of payment. Contract of pledge, however, does not confer title on pledgee and general property in article remains in pledgor.

Pawnbrokers Act (Cap. 222).—Act applies where person taking pawn is pawnbroker defined as including person "who carries on business of taking goods and chattels in pawn". Person is deemed to be pawnbroker under Act where goods are taken or purchased by way of security for repayment of sum of money not exceeding S$1,000.

Mere delivery of possession is adequate under Act for creation of pledge if loan secured is in excess of S$100 and if rate of interest is 10% per annum or less. However, in all other transactions or pledges with pawnbroker, notwithstanding that loan advanced may exceed S$1,000 or that value of security exceeds S$1,000, Act requires that pawnbroker must give pawner pawn ticket on accepting pawn.

Realising Security.—Pawnee has power of sale upon default in payment at stipulated time. If no time of payment is fixed, pawnee may demand for payment and if there is default consequent thereon, he may realise pawn by sale upon service of proper notice as to its intention.

Under Act, pawn which is taken for S$50 or less, and is not redeemed within six months from date of pawning, becomes absolute property of pawnbroker.

Factors Act (Cap. 386).—Pledge of documents of title to goods is deemed to be pledge of goods. Where mercantile agent pledges goods as security for antecedent debt or liability due from pledgor to pledgee, pledgee acquires no further right to goods than could have been enforced by pledgor at time of pledge.

POWER OF ATTORNEY:

See topic Absentees.

PRINCIPAL AND AGENT:

Governed by common law. Generally principal is bound by his authorised agent. Agent may be authorised expressly, impliedly, or by estoppel or necessity. Agent acting outside his scope of authority may be liable for breach of warranty of authority. Agent acting for undisclosed principal is also personally liable.

See also topics Power of Attorney; Partnerships.

PROCESS:

Service of Process Within Jurisdiction.—Where defendant is individual, writ must be served personally on each defendant. Writ is deemed to have been duly served if defendant's solicitor indorses on writ, statement that he accepts service of writ on behalf of defendant or where defendant enters appearance in action.

Writ commencing action in respect of contract may also be served in accordance with terms of contract if contract provides that High Court has jurisdiction to hear and determine action in respect of contract or apart from such term, High Court has jurisdiction to hear and determine such action; and contract provides that, in event of action in respect of contract being begun, process by which it is begun may be served on defendant, or on such person on his behalf as may be specified in contract.

In certain cases, Court may on ex-parte application authorise service of writ to be effected on agent or manager instead of overseas principal.

Above rules generally apply with necessary modifications to originating summons, notice of originating motion and petition.

Where action is against corporation, document may be served by leaving it at or sending it by registered post to registered office of company.

If it appears to Court that it is impracticable for any reason to serve document personally on person, Court may make order for substituted service of that document.

Service of Process Out of Jurisdiction.—Service of originating process out of jurisdiction is permissible with leave of Court in many enumerated cases in accordance with Rules of Court, i.e., essentially where defendant or claim has some connection with forum.

Service of Foreign Process.—Service of process required in connection with foreign civil proceedings may be effected by letter of request from foreign court or tribunal requesting service on person in Singapore received by Minister and sent by him to High Court with intimation that it is desirable that effect should be given to request.

If civil proceedings are pending before court or tribunal of foreign country, being country with which there subsists Civil Procedure Convention providing for service in Singapore of process of tribunal of that country, letter of request may be from consular or other authority of that country requesting service on person in Singapore of any such process sent with letter which is received by Registrar. Letter of request must be accompanied by two copies in former case and one copy in latter case of English translation of process to be served.

REAL PROPERTY:

Generally, real property law in Singapore is similar to pre-1925 English law apart from registration system.

There are four types of land grants, namely estate in fee simple, estate in perpetuity, leases and temporary occupation licences, although in practice one deals mainly with first three types. English legal concepts and instruments such as licences, easements and profits, restrictive covenants, mortgages and charges are applicable.

Registration.—Two systems of registration, namely those governed by Registration of Deeds Act (Cap. 269) and those governed by Land Titles Act (Cap. 157).

Registration of Deeds Act.—This Act provides registration of deeds of conveyances, assignments, memorandum of charges and discharges, deeds of consent to discharge of trustee, private Acts, orders of court or certificates of appointment of trustee in bankruptcy. Leases of term in excess of seven years or assignments thereof have to be registered to be effective. Caveats can be filed in Registry Of Deeds by persons claiming estate or interest in land or by persons who have been granted estate or interest in land by proprietor of land. Caveat subsists for five years from date of registration unless withdrawn by caveator or cancelled by order of Court. Priorities of instruments registered or entitled to be registered under this system are given priority according to date of registration and not by date of instruments or of their execution.

Land Titles Act.—This system of registration is based on Torrens system in South Australia. System is similar in application to English Land Registration Act of 1925 but without many exceptions and pitfalls thereto.

Under this system, registration of instrument is required to protect one's legal interest in property. Instruments are ineffectual until registered. Person who becomes proprietor of registered land holds land free from all encumbrances, liens, estates and interests whatsoever except those notified in land-register. This is so notwithstanding person may not have dealt with proprietor or lack of good faith on part of person through whom he claims. There are exceptions, for example, fraud or forgery to which proprietor or his agent was party or which collusion exists. Persons dealing with proprietor are exonerated from effect of notice of matters like previous circumstances which led to current registered proprietor being registered, notice (actual or constructive) of bankruptcy proceedings, trusts or other unregistered interests.

Priority of instruments is accorded in order of their registration or notification irrespective of dates of instruments. Save for fraud, entering of caveat to protect unregistered interest in land will give priority over any other unregistered interest not so protected at time when caveat was entered.

Under this system any person claiming interest in land may lodge caveat forbidding registration of any dealing affecting interest which is protected by that caveat. Where instrument which is prohibited by caveat is entered, Registrar of Titles will serve notice on caveator that he will register instrument unless within 30 days caveator has obtained order of Court extending operation of caveat; or instrument is uplifted or withdrawn or otherwise becomes incapable of registration. Caveat lasts for five years from date of lodgement. Filing of caveats is particularly important in dealing with equitable interests under trusts because such interests are kept off land-register. Also, purchasers who deal with fiduciary proprietor are not concerned to enquire whether dealing is within latter's powers and can assume powers of disposition of beneficial owner and as absolute proprietor.

System provides for entry of instruments protecting mortgages and restrictive covenants. Leases in excess of seven years have to be registered to gain protection.

No title to land adverse or in derogation of proprietor of registered land can be acquired by any length of possession under Limitation Act (Cap. 163), i.e., there is no recognition of adverse possession claims under this system save for those entitled to lodge applications for possessory title and have done so before 1 Mar. 1994 or within six months thereafter.

Land Titles (Strata) Act (Cap. 158).—This deals with strata development in Singapore—registration of such titles follows Land Titles Act. Act provides, inter alia, for setting up of management corporations for strata estates and bye-laws for same, and has given extensive powers to management corporations. All strata properties under land titles registration system have to be governed in accordance with Act.

Public Housing.—Housing and Development Act (Cap. 129) deals with leases granted by Housing and Development Board in respect of flats built on land owned by it. These are usually 99-year leases and there is system of registration.

RECEIVERS:

See topics Executions; Insolvency.

SALES:

Governed by Sale of Goods Act (Cap. 393), other related statutes and common law. Principal Act is English Sale of Goods Act 1979 (c. 54) as received into Singapore on 12 Nov. 1993. Unlike England, there is no market overt in Singapore.

Notices Required.—Generally, notices not required under domestic sales law. Where contracts fall within United Nations Convention on Contracts for International Sale of Goods, then subject to agreement of parties, notices are required in many instances. For example, notice has to be given to avoid contract, except where other party has expressed intention not to perform, and notice of nonconformity of goods has to be given to seller in order for buyer to rely on rights based on nonconformity.

Applicable Law.—Generally, contract of sale is governed by law expressly or impliedly chosen by parties, whether such law is connected to contract or not, unless choice is illegal, not bona fide, or against public policy. In absence of choice, contract is governed by law having closest and most real connection with transaction. Governing law applies to most contractual issues, including validity, interpretation and effect of terms. Where United Nations Convention on Contracts for International Sale of Goods applies, issues relating to formation of contract and rights and obligations arising thereunder are subject to Convention rules.

Warranties.—Implied warranties are: (1) that seller has right to sell goods free from undisclosed encumbrances; (2) that goods sold are of merchantable quality, except if defect has been revealed to buyer or if buyer has examined goods and ought to have discovered it; (3) that goods are fit for buyer's purpose, provided that seller sells goods in course of business, and buyer makes known to seller particular purpose, unless buyer did not rely, or it was not reasonable for him to rely, on seller; (4) that in sale by description goods will correspond to description; and (5) that in sale by sample, goods will correspond to sample in description and quality, and that buyer will have reasonable opportunity to compare the two.

Supply of Goods Act (Cap. 394).—This is portion of English Supply of Goods and Services Act 1982 (c. 29) as received into Singapore on 12 Nov. 1993, dealing with supply and hire of goods. Warranties similar to that for sale of goods are implied.

Hire-Purchase Act (Cap. 125).—Act applies to hire-purchase of specified goods. Implied warranties are in respect of (1) title; (2) merchantability; and (3) fitness for

See Topical Index in front part of this volume.

SALES . . . *continued*

purpose. Latter two terms will not be implied if owner informs hirer that goods are secondhand, and that warranties are excluded.

Unfair Contract Terms Act (Cap. 396).—This is English Unfair Contract Terms Act 1977 (c. 50) as received into Singapore on 12 Nov. 1993. Liability for personal injury or death resulting from negligence cannot be excluded. Exclusion clauses for other damage are subject to test of reasonableness. Seller's warranty of title cannot be excluded. Other implied warranties cannot be excluded against consumer, and can only be excluded otherwise if reasonable in all circumstances. Similar protection is given with respect to corresponding warranties arising from contracts of supply, hire or hire-purchase of goods.

Misrepresentation Act (Cap. 390).—This is English Misrepresentation Act 1967 (c. 7) as received into Singapore on 12 Nov. 1993. Contract can be rescinded for misrepresentation even if representation has become term of contract, and even if contract is executed. Court has discretion to award damages in lieu of rescission where misrepresentation is innocent. Where misrepresentation is negligent, Court may award damages in addition to or instead of rescission. Exclusion of liability for misrepresentation is subject to test of reasonableness.

Consumer Protection (Trade Descriptions and Safety Requirements) Act (Cap. 53).—It is offence to apply false trade description to goods or to supply goods with false trade description. Certain goods are also required to carry certain information, e.g. expiry dates, or to comply with prescribed safety requirements.

Sale of Goods (United Nations Convention) Act (Cap. 283A). —This gives effect to United Nations Convention on Contracts for International Sale of Goods signed in Vienna on 11 Apr. 1980.

SEALS:

Contracts under Seal.—Governed by common law.

Corporate Bodies' Contracts Act (Cap. 385).—Contracts, which if made by private persons would be required under law to be in writing, signed by parties to be charged, may be made on behalf of body corporate in writing and signed by person acting under its express or implied authority; and contracts, which if made by private persons would be valid by parol and not reduced in writing, may be made by parol on behalf of body corporate by person acting under its express or implied authority. Such contracts are valid notwithstanding that they are not executed under seal.

Practice Relating to Company Seals and Seal Books.—Company secretary usually has custody of company common seal. Directors usually pass resolution each time common seal is to be affixed to document; usually, common seals are affixed and attested to by two directors, or director and company secretary, or director and another person authorised to attest such affixation. Name of company (whether or not it is carrying on business under business name) must appear on its seal.

Where seal is frequently used, particulars of documents sealed may be entered in Seal Book and book will be produced at each board meeting (or committee authorised by board of directors) and appropriate resolutions passed.

Singapore-incorporated company may also have official seal (which must be facsimile of common seal with addition of place in which it is to be used) for use outside Singapore, if company's objects require or comprise transactions of business outside Singapore and its articles authorise such use. See also topic Deeds.

SHIPPING:

Merchant Shipping.—Merchant Shipping Act as repealed and re-enacted by Merchant Shipping Act (Act No. 19 of 1995), regulates registration, mortgages, control of shipping, safety of shipping, construction, equipment and survey, manning, certification, masters and seamen, wreck and salvage. National Maritime Board Act (Cap. 198) regulates employment of seamen.

Towage.—Governed by private contract between parties.

Pilotage.—Regulated by Port of Singapore Authority Act. (Cap. 236).

Collisions.—Merchant Shipping (Prevention of Collisions at Sea) Regulations S96/83 give effect to International Regulations for Preventing Collisions at Sea 1972 as amended. United Kingdom Maritime Conventions Act 1911 applies in Singapore.

Liens.—Maritime liens governed by common law. Statutory liens for rent and expenses of wharfinger and warehouseman provided under Merchant Shipping Act. (Act No. 19 of 1995).

Pollution.—Civil liability for oil pollution by merchant ships regulated by Merchant Shipping (Oil Pollution) Act. (Cap. 180). International Convention for the Prevention of Pollution from Ships 1973 as modified is given effect by Prevention of Pollution of the Sea Act. (Cap. 243).

Carriage of Goods.—Carriage of Goods by Sea Act (Cap. 33, as am'd) gives effect to Hague Rules as amended by Brussels Protocol, Hague Visby Rules. Bills of Lading Act (Cap. 384) deals, inter alia with transfer of contractual rights to lawful holders of bills of lading, delivery orders and sea waybills.

Limitation and exclusion of liability of shipowners are regulated by Merchant Shipping Act and also by relevant provisions of Hague Visby Rules.

STATUTES:

Legislation enacted by Parliament is contained in Statutes of Singapore and subsidiary legislation made pursuant to statutes can be found in Subsidiary Legislation of Singapore. Both are published by Law Revision Commission under authority of Revised Edition of the Laws Act. (Cap. 275). Together, they make up principal source of written law in Singapore.

TAXATION:

Income Tax.—Payable by persons, including individuals, companies, trustees and bodies of persons, on income accruing in or derived from Singapore or remitted from overseas in respect of trade, business, profession, vocation or employment and dividends, interest, discounts, pension, charge, annuity, rents, royalties, premiums, profits arising from property and gains or profits of income nature. For nonresident individual, remittance of overseas income is exempted from tax.

Payment to nonresident in respect of royalties, rent for movable property and interest are subject to withholding tax of 15%.

Rate of income tax for resident company is 26%. Singapore adopts imputation system of taxation whereby tax paid on income of such company is imputed to its shareholders. Nonresident company is also taxed at same rate. There are no major differences in tax treatment for the two except that resident company is generally able to qualify for tax reliefs afforded by double taxation conventions. Tax rate of 27% also applies to income of trust, estate of deceased person, and non-resident unincorporated body. Approved institutions of public or charitable character are exempted from income tax.

Individual income tax rate for resident individuals is on progressive scale, with marginal rate from 2% to 28%. Various personal reliefs and rebates are available. Donations to approved charitable and public institutions are tax-deductible.

Nonresident employees are taxed at 15% or at resident's rate (whichever is higher). Nonresident partners, professionals, sole-proprietors and directors are taxed at flat rate of 27% whereas non-resident public entertainers are taxed at 15%. Nonresident employees exercising employment in Singapore for not more than 60 days are exempted from tax. Remittances of foreign-sourced income to nonresident individuals in Singapore are not subject to tax.

Income tax relief in respect of certain categories of income can be found in Income Tax Act (Cap. 134), and tax incentives for selected types of investment can be found in Economic Expansion Incentives (Relief from Income Tax) Act (Cap. 86).

Capital Gains Tax.—Not imposed in Singapore.

Goods and Services Tax.—Levied on supply of goods and services made in Singapore by registered person (including company). It must be collected by person making supply. Person is required to be registered if its annual turnover exceeds S$1 million. Current Goods and Services Tax rate is 3%.

Goods and Services Tax also applies to import of goods and services. However, tax on latter is currently suspended. Exemptions and zero-rating of tax are given to many categories of supply.

Property Tax.—Chargeable at rate of 12% on annual value of houses, buildings and land in Singapore unless exempted. Concessionary rate of 4% is given for owner-occupied residential premises.

Stamp Duty.—Imposed on specified classes of instruments and may be for fixed amount or on ad valorem basis. For conveyance of land, duty is payable at progressive rate up to 3% of value; for legal mortgage, up to maximum of S$500; on sale of stocks and shares, 0.2% of value; on stockbroker's contract note, 0.1%. Exemptions from stamp duty are given for various specified transactions.

Estate Duty.—Payable on estate of deceased person domiciled in Singapore in respect of its immovable properties situated in Singapore and movable properties situated in any part of world. Where deceased person is not domiciled in Singapore, only immovable property situated in Singapore is subject to duty. Gifts made within five years prior to death of deceased are still liable for estate duty. Where gifts are made for approved charitable or public purposes, period is reduced to 12 months.

Presently, exemption of S$9 million in respect of immovable residential properties and S$600,000 in respect of other properties, movable or immovable, is given. Central Provident Fund monies are wholly exempted from estate duty. If however, Central Provident Fund monies exceed S$600,000, S$600,000 exemption given for all other properties described above would have been fully utilised and such properties will then not be given exemption.

Rate of estate duty for value of estate up to S$12 million is 5%; for portion exceeding S$12 million, rate is 10%.

Double taxation agreements with 37 countries have been concluded and Singapore has limited agreements with another three. In addition, double taxation reliefs are available between Singapore and Commonwealth countries. For countries with which no such arrangements are in force, unilateral tax credits may be available upon certain prescribed conditions.

TRADEMARKS:

Statutes.—Governed by Trade Marks Act (Cap. 332) and Trade Marks Rules. These follow U.K. legislation closely. Registration is possible for services as well as goods. Changes may be made soon due to TRIPS (Trade Related Intellectual Property Rights under GATT).

Treaties.—Priority may be claimed for applications filed within six months from date of first application in approved countries set out in Schedule to Act. Singapore has also recently become member of Paris Convention.

Trademark is mark used or proposed to be used in relation to goods or services for purpose of indicating or so as to indicate, connection in course of trade between goods or services and person who has right, either as proprietor or as registered user, to use mark, whether with or without indication of identity of that person. Trademark may be device, brand, heading, label, ticket, signature, word, letter, numeral or combination of these.

Registrability.—Trade Marks Register is divided into Parts A and B. To qualify for registration in Part A, mark must be distinctive i.e. "adapted to distinguish" goods or services from that of others. Mark must have some intrinsic quality which makes it distinctive. To be registrable in Part A, mark must contain or consist of at least one of following: (1) name of company, individual or firm represented in special or particular manner; (2) signature of applicant or predecessor of his business; (3) invented word or words; (4) mark which does not have direct reference to character or quality of goods or services and which is not in its ordinary meaning, geographical name or surname; (5) any other distinctive mark.

Trademark which does not qualify for registration in Part A may qualify for registration in Part B. To qualify for Part B, mark need only be "capable of distinguishing" one's goods or services. It is less stringent test than that for Part A. Registrar of Trade Marks may have regard to extent to which trademark is inherently capable of distinguishing goods or services and/or by reason of use of mark or of any other circumstances, mark is in fact capable of distinguishing as aforesaid.

See Topical Index in front part of this volume.

TRADEMARKS . . . *continued*

Part A registration offers greater protection as original registration will, after seven years, be considered valid in all respects unless registration was obtained by fraud, mark consists of scandalous design or matter which is likely to deceive or cause confusion or would be disentitled to protection in court or would be contrary to law or morality. On other hand, Part B registration can never become conclusive as to validity as it can still be opposed to and removed from Register after seven years.

Protection.—Upon registration of mark, it remains valid for initial term of ten years from date of filing of application which may then be renewed for subsequent terms of ten years each.

Assignment.—Trademark may be assigned with or without goodwill of business. Under Act, all assignments must be registered with Trade Marks Registry. If one or more marks are associated, they must be assigned as whole and not separately.

Infringement.—Plaintiff has recourse to civil remedies in form of damages, injunction, seizure of goods and discovery. If his mark is registered under Part A, plaintiff need only show that his mark is registered and that defendant used mark identical or so nearly resembling it as to be likely to deceive or cause confusion. If his mark is registered in Part B, plaintiff gets no relief if defendant establishes that use of mark is not likely to deceive or cause confusion.

Common Law Rights.—Rights of action against person for tort of "passing off" or remedies in respect thereof have not been affected by provisions of Act. To succeed, plaintiff must show: (a) goodwill or reputation in his mark or business; (b) misrepresentation made by defendant in course of trade which is calculated to injure plaintiff's goodwill or business; and (c) damage has occurred or is likely to occur.

TREATIES:

Member, Association of South East Asian Nations (ASEAN), World Trade Organisation (WTO), Asia Pacific Economic Cooperation (APEC) and Asian Regional Forum (ARF). There are reciprocal trade arrangements with many countries, including Australia, Brunei, Hong Kong, Malaysia, New Zealand, U.K., Vietnam and Sri Lanka, providing for settlement of disputes, some by international arbitration. There are also various investment guarantee agreements with many countries, including U.S.A., U.K., ASEAN countries, Germany, France, Canada, Netherlands, Switzerland, Belgium, People's Republic of China, Vietnam and Sri Lanka. These agreements provide for protection for specified periods against unlawful expropriation. There are double taxation agreements with many countries (see topic Taxation).

See also Part VII of this volume for Selected Conventions to which U.S.A. and this country are parties.

TRUSTS:

Common law concept of trust and equitable interests behind them are recognised and applicable in Singapore. Trustees Act (Cap. 337) generally deals with matters like trustee investments, general powers of trustees and personal representatives, appointments and discharge of trustees, powers of court, charitable trusts and unit trust schemes.

One can appoint maximum of four trustees. Usually two are appointed for disposition in trust for sale of land or in settlement of net proceeds because Act requires that, save for trust corporation, two trustees are required to give good receipt for proceeds of sale or other capital monies. (Further exception is for sale of real property by sole personal representative.)

As in England, trusts of personal property can be created without any formalities at law. Trusts of immovable property i.e. land must be evidenced by some note or memorandum in writing, and grants and assignments of beneficial interests under existing trusts have to be in writing by virtue of Statue of Frauds. (29 Car 2, c. 3). These however do not apply to implied, resulting or constructive trusts. Common law rules relating to perpetuity i.e. those dealing with remoteness of vesting of trust property and creation of perpetual trusts are applicable.

WILLS:

Governed by Wills Act. (Cap. 352). Any person of sound mind may make will. Infant cannot make will, unless he is soldier being in actual military service, or mariner or seaman being at sea.

See also topic Infants.

Formalities of Execution.—Every will must be signed at its foot or end by testator, or by some other person in his presence and by his direction, and signature must be made or acknowledged by testator as signature to his will in presence of two or more witnesses present at same time, and those witnesses must subscribe will in presence of testator. Beneficiary or his spouse must not attest to execution of will.

Alterations, which include obliteration and interlineation, made prior to execution should be authenticated by being referred to specifically in body of will itself, or by signature or initials of testator and witnesses being placed on will.

Revocation.—Will or part thereof may be revoked otherwise by another will or codicil duly executed, or by declaring intention to revoke it and executed in same as will, or by burning, tearing, or otherwise destroying will by testator, or by some person in his presence and by his direction, with intention of revoking it.

Foreign Wills.—Will is treated as properly executed if its execution conformed to internal law in force in territory where it was executed or where testator was domiciled or habitually resident either at time of execution or at death or in state of which testator was national either at time of execution or at death.

Allowance for Maintenance of Dependents.—Any dependent of deceased person may apply to Court for share of deceased's net estate for maintenance of that dependant under Inheritance (Family Provision) Act. (Cap 138). If Court is satisfied that disposition of deceased's estate by his will is such that it fails to make reasonable provision for maintenance of that dependant, Court may order that such reasonable provision be made out of deceased's net estate for maintenance of that dependant as it thinks fit.

Act is not restricted to provisions in wills: application may be made in cases of intestacies as well. However, if surviving spouse had been provided for with not less than two-thirds of income of net estate and where only other dependents are children, then no application can be made.

Persons for whom provision may be made are spouse, unmarried daughter, infant son, or daughter or son who is, by reason of some mental or physical disability, incapable of maintaining herself or himself.

Court can have regard to any past, present or future capital or income from any source of dependant of deceased to whom application relates.

Any application under Act must be made within six months from date on which representation in regard to deceased's estate is first taken out. However, this is not rigid provision and Court will allow extension of time if Court feels that complying strictly with requirements of Act may prejudice interests of dependant.

Wills Made by Muslims.—In Islamic law, testator can make bequest of only a third of his property with consent of his lawful beneficiaries. No one however can make bequest in respect of any legal Quranic heir. In other words, one cannot increase or decrease portions of those relatives whose portions are fixed in Quran nor can one deprive legal heir through bequest.

See Topical Index in front part of this volume.

SLOVAK REPUBLIC LAW DIGEST

(The following is a list of all Topics, including cross-references, covered in this Digest.)

SLOVAK REPUBLIC LAW DIGEST

Prepared for the 1997 edition by

ČECHOVÁ, HRBEK, Bratislava, Slovak Republic.

Abbreviations used are: OSP, občiansky súdny poriadok (Civil Court Order, Act No. 99/1963 Coll., full wording No. 38/1995, as amended); OZ, občiansky zákonník (Civil Code, Act No. 40/1964 Coll., as amended); ObchZ, obchodný zákonník (Commercial Code, Act No. 513/1991 Coll., as amended); ZR, zákon o rodine (Family Act, Act No. 94/1963, as amended); ZMPSP, zákon o medzinárodnom práve súkromnom a procesnom (Act on International Private and Procedural Law, Act No. 97/1963 as amended); ZP, zákonník práce (Labor Code, Act No. 65/1965 Coll., full wording Act No. 451/1992 Coll., as amended); SR, Slovenská republika (the Slovak Republic); SKK, slovenská koruna (the Slovak Crown).

PRELIMINARY NOTE:

Slovak Republic (SR) declared its independence as sovereign state on Jan. 1, 1993 after taking all necessary political and legal steps at level of federate and national authorities for division of Czech and Slovak Federal Republic (C.S.F.R.). Both republics generally adopted federal laws, however, different needs and different ideas led immediately to number of legislative changes and caused differences in majority of acts and legal regulations. SR started to create its own legislation on particular subjects (e.g. competition, executors, privatization). Rapid changes represent one of most obvious features of Slovak legislation especially because of full transition to market economy and objective to become EU member.

SR became member of U.N. on 19th Jan., 1993 and of Council of Europe on 30th June, 1993. European Economic Community, European Atomic Energy Community, European Coal and Steel Community and their member countries entered into Europe Agreement with SR on 4th Oct., 1993, establishing Association between them. SR is member state of Central European Free Trade Association (CEFTA).

ABSENTEES:

In case of absence, any person may delegate authority to act on his/her behalf to (i) any other person, or (ii) lawyer, subject to provisions of law regarding power of attorney (see topic Principal and Agent).

Same position as for empowered attorney-at-law for whole Court proceedings is guaranteed by law to curator appointed by Court. Courts may appoint curator in cases where one cannot personally act in Court proceedings, there exists risk of delay and no other instruments are available, especially if one's domicile is unknown, or service of process on his/her known address abroad was unsuccessful, or he/she suffers from mental disease. (OSP, §29).

All documents of Court proceeding are delivered to attorney or curator.

ACKNOWLEDGMENTS:

Documents issued abroad for purposes of Court, administrative and other official use in SR are required to be legalized by Slovak consular officer, unless bilateral treaties on legal assistance or consular engagements stipulate otherwise. SR has entered into bilateral treaties with countries such as Belgium, France, Greece, Portugal, Austria, Spain, Tunisia, Cyprus and others. Unless bilateral treaties provide otherwise documents such as (i) birth, marriage, death certificates and other vital statistics issued by municipalities in SR are subject to verification by municipalities of higher level, and (ii) notarial and official translation authorizations and documents issued by Courts in SR are subject to legalization by Ministry of Justice of SR and then authentication by Ministry of Foreign Affairs of SR.

ACTIONS:

Commencement of Proceedings.—Trial shall commence upon petition which should contain name, employment, and residence of parties or their representatives, true description of material facts, identification of evidence claimed by petitioner and it should also show exactly what is claimed by petitioner. If party is legal person, petition should contain information required for identification of same, particularly its name or tradename and seat; in any disputes between entrepreneurs, it should also contain information about their incorporation in Commercial Register or any other register, petition should clearly identify Court to which it is addressed, person who files petition, matter to which it relates, and what is claimed by it, and it should be signed and dated. Petition should be filed in required number of copies with annexes attached so that one copy remains with Court and one copy is delivered to each party, if necessary.

Statement to Petition.—Court shall usually invite defending (respondent) party to make statement in respect of particular petition, containing clause that if party fails to give statement, Court may dispose of petition by judgment by default. (OSP, §153b).

Disposal of Petition.—Petitioner may, any time during trial, withdraw petition partially or fully. If respondent does not agree with withdrawal of petition due to serious reasons, Court proceeds with trial after resolution takes effect. Respondent's refusal to consent to withdrawal ineffective if petition is withdrawn prior to hearing. (OSP, §96).

Counterpetition.—Respondent may also, during trial, exercise rights against petitioner by counterpetition. Provisions on commencing trial, its change, and withdrawal (OSP, §97) shall apply accordingly to counterpetition for commencing trial.

Evidence.—Party and representative may produce evidence necessary to support their statements. This includes all evidence by which status of matter is disclosed, especially examination of witnesses, expert's opinions, reports and statements of authorities and legal entities, instruments, inspection and examination of parties. Unless manner of producing evidence is stipulated, it shall be determined by Court. (OSP, §§120-131).

Costs of trial include Court fees, lost income of participants, translation fees and expenses on evidence, and legal fees for representation by lawyer (advocate). Legal fees are stipulated by Decree of the Ministry of Justice of SR No. 240/1990 Coll., as amended (contractual, hourly rate, tariff, share remuneration). Court fees (Act No. 71/1992 Coll., as am'd) are payable simultaneously with submission of petition or upon Court request. Generally, Court fees represent 4% of price of requested recovery (minimum 200 SKK, maximum 100,000 SKK; in commercial matters minimum 500 SKK, maximum 500,000 SKK).

Application of Foreign Law.—In property and commercial matters Courts are obliged to apply foreign law if parties agree that their agreement will be governed by foreign law and as well as in cases directly determined to be governed by foreign law under conflict law rules (ZMPSP). ZMPSP permits Courts to ascertain foreign law through Ministry of Justice of SR. Ministry is entitled to issue opinion on foreign law. (ZMPSP, §53).

ADOPTION:

Adoption is regulated by ZR (Family Act). Slovak law recognizes violable and inviolable adoption. Courts, particularly district Court of adoptee's permanent residence, have exclusive power to decide on adoption. Adoption creates same relations between adopter and adoptee as relations between natural parents and children. Relationship also arises among adoptee and relatives of adopter. Adopter has same rights and duties as natural parents—e.g. duty to take systematic and consistent care of children's education and support. Court decides on adoption on basis of petition submitted by adopter. Natural parents are not participants in adoption proceedings if (i) they were deprived of parental rights, or (ii) they do not have full legal capacity, or (iii) their consent to adoption is not required (e.g. they were not interested in their child within period of six months, or they have already provided their consent to adoption on anonymous basis).

Violable adoption can be terminated by Court for important reasons, on basis of proposal of adoptee or adopter. If adoptee is major, adoption can be terminated also by agreement between adopter and adoptee recorded by Court. By termination of violable adoption, original relations between adoptee and his/her natural family are re-created. Adoptee also regains original surname and cannot inherit from adopter because of termination of relationship to adopter and renewal of relationship to natural parent.

Inviolable adoption cannot be terminated. In this case adopter is entered in birth register instead of natural parent of child.

In both cases by Court decision of adoption mutual relations between natural parents and adoptee are terminated, therefore adoptee has same position and rights as natural child as heir to adopter's estate. See also topic Descent and Distribution.

Conflict of Laws and Jurisdiction.—If adoptee is Slovak citizen, Slovak Courts have exclusive jurisdiction. Adoption is governed by law of state of adopter. If adopters are spouses of different citizenship, legal conditions of both states must be fulfilled. Permits and consents required for adoption by law of state of adoptee's citizenship must be taken into consideration.

ALIENS:

Aliens are deemed to be any persons not having Slovak citizenship enjoying same personal and property rights as Slovak citizens excluding political rights. (Constitution of SR and ZMPSP). Ownership of real property is limited by relevant provisions of Foreign Exchange Act. Residence permits are necessary for some stays of foreigners in SR (e.g. connected with entrepreneurial activities).

See topic Immigration.

Corporations Owned or Controlled by Aliens.—100% ownership and control of Slovak companies by aliens is allowed.

See topics Corporations, Foreign Investments.

ARBITRATION AND AWARD:

In disputes concerning commercial matters contracting parties may agree on domestic or foreign arbitration. In SR, Court of Arbitration of Slovak Chamber of Commerce and Industry is qualified as permanent independent arbitration body.

Domestic Arbitral Awards.—Act No. 218/1996 Coll. on arbitration stipulates conditions for domestic arbitration and for enforcement of foreign arbitral awards. Certain matters are excluded from arbitration e.g. disputes arising from bankruptcy procedure, disputes concerning real property rights. Certain legal entities may establish on basis of special law their own arbitration courts (e.g. Slovak Chamber of Commerce and Industry, Bratislava Stock Exchange). Arbitration is initiated by petition and defendant is obliged to present statement to petition within ten days. Arbitral award must solve all contentious matters of substance. Unless any party demands court, within 15 days from date of delivery of award, to cancel arbitral award, it would have same force as enforceable judgment.

Foreign Arbitral Awards.—SR is successor signatory of several international conventions concerning arbitrational matters, e.g. New York Convention on Recognition and Enforcement of Foreign Arbitral Awards, Geneva European Convention on International Commercial Arbitration, Geneva Protocol on Arbitration Clauses, Geneva Convention on Enforcement of Foreign Arbitral Awards. Any foreign arbitral award is enforceable in SR, if relevant Court in SR is satisfied that: (i) it was issued in matter substance of which excludes conclusion of arbitration agreement, or (ii) it was issued in matter, which was validly and effectively decided prior to its issue by court or other arbitration, or (iii) it is not valid or effective according to law of country in which it was issued, or (iv) there are reasons which make it contrary to public policy in Slovak Republic, or (v) arbitral award imposes obligation on losing party not allowed or impossible under Slovak law or contrary to proper morals.

See Topical Index in front part of this volume.

ASSIGNMENTS:

Slovak law expressly recognizes assignments of receivables; assignments of payables (or debt); fiduciary transfer of rights; fiduciary assignment of receivables.

Assignment of receivables may be made exclusively on basis of written agreement between creditor and assignee. No debtor's consent is required, however legal consequences of assignment are effective against debtor only from date when creditor notified debtor of assignment or assignee proves existence of assignment. Certain receivables may not be assigned, especially those which are linked to creditor's personality and expire upon creditor's death, or receivables substance of which would be changed, or receivables which cannot be enforced. Generally, all accessories, accruals and attached rights are transferred to assignee together with assigned receivable. If assignee pays for assignment, creditor may assume guarantee of payment by debtor, up to amount of compensation received in consideration of assigned receivable by creditor. (OZ, §§524-530).

Assignment of payables (debt) is created only by written agreement between (1) assignee and debtor (assignment of debt); or (2) assignee and creditor (accession to debt). Effects of any debt assignment are subject to creditor's approval. Otherwise, any assignment will be binding upon assignee only. Substance of assigned payable remains unaffected on assignment, however, security given by third parties continues to exist only if such parties approved assignment. Accession to debt makes assignee and debtor jointly and severally liable for payment to creditor. (OZ, §§531-534).

Fiduciary transfer of rights and fiduciary assignment of receivables, see topic Liens.

ASSOCIATIONS:

Basic regulation of associations is included in OZ (Civil Code). Unless special law provides otherwise, written agreement or foundation deed is required for establishment of any association. Association shall be established on day on which it is incorporated in register specified by law. Capacity of association to acquire rights and assume duties may be restricted only by law. Association may be dissolved by agreement, by lapse of time, by accomplishment of purposes for which it was established or by another means provided by special laws.

Associations of Citizens.—Act No. 83/1990 Coll. on association of citizens, as amended, provides for legal regulation of this kind of association. No permission is needed and association is formed on day of registration, following application of at least three citizens (one of them at least 18 years old) forming preparatory committee. Application is submitted to Ministry of Interior of SR and statutes of association containing (i) name, (ii) seat, (iii) purposes, (iv) procedure for creation of association's bodies, (v) basic principles for management of property, (vi) organizational parts with legal capacity. If Ministry refuses to register association, members of preparatory committee may appeal to Supreme Court of SR. If activities of association breach law, Ministry shall demand association refrain from prohibited activities. If association continues to do so, Ministry can dissolve association. Dissolution may be appealed to Supreme Court of SR.

Churches and Religious Associations.—Activities of churches and religious associations are regulated by Act No. 308/1991 Coll. on freedom of faith and status of churches and religious associations. Only churches and religious associations registered according to this law are deemed to be officially recognized. Application for registration shall be submitted to Ministry of the Interior of SR by at least three adult persons. Statute (or similar document) attached to application contains (i) name, (ii) seat of central office of church, (iii) bodies of church and procedure for their creation and their competencies, (iv) procedure for appointment of clergymen, (v) basic principles of faith, (vi) basic principles for management of property, (vii) procedure for approving statutes (or similar document), (viii) organizational parts with legal capacity. If Ministry refuses to register church, appeal may be taken to Supreme Court of SR. If activities of church breach law Ministry may cancel registration. Appeal of cancellation may be taken to Supreme Court.

Associations of Persons.—According to §§829-841 of OZ several persons (whether individual or legal entities) may associate themselves in order to endeavor jointly towards attainment of agreed purpose. However, this type of association does not have legal personality. Each of participants is obliged to engage in agreed activities and/or provide some money or other contributions to activities of association. Property provided or acquired through performance of their joint activities is considered to be in joint ownership of all participants. Participants are jointly and severally liable for obligations against third parties.

Interest Association of Legal Entities.—Legal entities may establish associations pursuing certain interests. Association is established by written agreement of founders or by constituent members' meeting (minutes of meeting must include list of members with their addresses and signatures) and statutes of association are to be attached. Association acquires its legal personality by entry into register of associations kept by relevant municipal office.

Associations with International Element.—This type of association is governed by Act No. 116/1985 Coll. on condition of activities of organizations with international element stipulating conditions for activity, for having seat in SR or for establishment of such organization in SR. International nongovernmental organizations and organizations of foreign citizens are deemed to be organizations with international element. Application for permission to establish above-mentioned organization is submitted to Ministry of the Interior of SR with document setting forth purposes of organization and its organization structure.

ATTACHMENT:

Role partially similar to attachment (not directly recognized by Slovak law) is played by injunctions used in trials. Injunction may be ordered both prior to (OSP, §74) and after commencing trial (OSP, §102) provided it is necessary to settle relations between parties for temporary period or provided there is threat that enforcement of Court's decision would be impaired. Court of competent jurisdiction for ordering injunction is Court having jurisdiction in matter. Parties to trial are same as in underlying matter.

In commercial dispute, Court may order any party to place specific financial amount or thing in deposit with Court, not to dispose of certain assets or rights, to do something, to refrain from something or to suffer something. Injunction is ordered by Court upon petition; no petition is required if injunction is ordered in trial which may be commenced by Court even without petition. Decision shall be rendered by Court without undue delay, no later than within 30 days from filing petition. Parties to trial need not be examined. Injunction shall cease in following cases: (a) if petitioner fails to file petition for commencing trial within time period determined by Court; (b) if petition in matter itself has been dismissed; (c) if petition in matter itself has been granted and 15 days have elapsed from enforceability of decision in matter; (d) if time period for which it had been ordered has elapsed.

Presiding Judge shall cancel injunction if grounds upon which it has been ordered no longer exist.

Injunction can never be justified if result will be intensive impairment of claims or if relations to be protected have not been sufficiently proved. Injunction is title for execution (similar to judgment). See topic Executions.

BANKRUPTCY:

Bankruptcy and Composition Act ("Act") No. 328/1991 Coll. came into force on 1st Oct., 1991 in former C.S.F.R. and it is this Act which continues to apply, with amendments, in SR.

Purpose of Act is to solve situation of debtor in bankruptcy. Any debtor is regarded bankrupt, if it has several creditors and is not able to meet its financial obligations for longer period of time, i.e. is insolvent. Additionally, each individual entrepreneur and each legal entity may become bankrupt if assets drop below liabilities. Bankruptcy proceedings fall under jurisdiction of regional Court of debtor.

Arbitration Procedures.—Slovak legislation requires that before any debtor may be formally declared bankrupt (i.e. before bankruptcy judgment is issued by Court), arbitration (or settlement) procedure is to commence, pend, and end. Whole procedure commences upon petition for bankruptcy judgment. Persons entitled to file application are: (1) debtor, (2) creditor, (3) liquidator, (4) other person if special legislation so stipulates. Arbitration (settlement) procedure must commence upon proposal either by debtor or any domestic creditor. If these persons fail to file proposal within ten days from delivery of application for bankruptcy judgment, Court shall commence procedure itself (ex officio).

If proposal is filed by debtor, debtor is required to attach list of creditors and sums due, to proposal. Should proposal be filed by creditor, copy of it must be delivered to debtor, who has three day deadline to provide Court with above-mentioned list. Debtor has duty to convene meeting of domestic creditors within 30 days from proposal filing, so that it can be held within 30 days from date of its convocation. It should be noted that Slovak Bankruptcy and Composition Act contains rather discriminating provisions, which limit participation of creditors in arbitration proceeding (especially election to board of domestic creditors) at this stage, to domestic creditors only. Meeting of domestic creditors further elects board of domestic creditors and has extensive powers concerning debtor's "recovery project". Fulfillment of aims of recovery project is main purpose of whole procedure preceding bankruptcy procedure. Commencement of arbitration procedure does not affect debtor's ability to continue in its ordinary business, however, there are several restrictions applicable from that moment.

If arbitration procedure is unsuccessful (usually at least three months are required for such determination) bankruptcy proceeding may start. Precondition of this start is that debtor owns assets sufficient to cover costs of proceedings.

Bankruptcy.—If Court is satisfied that all conditions for declaring bankruptcy (including compliance with requirements concerning arbitration procedures) have been met it renders judgment in form of resolution. Creditors then have 30 days from date of this resolution to file their claims. Bankruptcy has number of effects on bankrupt and creditors. In bankruptcy proceedings, whole control is transferred to administrator appointed by Court.

Law stipulates several consequences linked to commencement of bankruptcy proceedings (which is date of rendering bankruptcy judgment). Most relevant consequences are as follows: (1) nonpayable receivables and liabilities related to bankrupt's estate become mature, (2) bankrupt's instructions, powers of attorney and proposals for concluding contracts that have not been accepted until that time, shall cease to exist, (3) set-off is not allowed, if any of parties acquired receivable otherwise capable of being set-off, after bankruptcy proceedings commenced, (4) rights for separate satisfaction (priority claims based on pledges or liens) that originate on or later than date two months prior to date on which application for bankruptcy judgment was filed shall cease to exist. Additionally, either party to bilateral contract has right to repudiate contract in case contract on mutual performance was at moment of rendering bankruptcy judgment not performed by both bankrupt and other party, or in case it was fulfilled only partially.

Administrator prepares list of bankrupt's assets with bankrupt's assistance and it is reviewed by Court. Assets may be realized through sale and Court must approve realization of assets. After claims of creditors have been established by Court and administrator's report has been presented and reviewed by Court at one or more hearings, distribution schedule is prepared by administrator. Any claims made after bankruptcy judgment related to costs of administration and bankruptcy proceedings and employees claims are given priority and may be settled anytime during proceedings.

Following satisfaction of administrators' costs and employees' claims in full, other claims are satisfied in following order: (1) if issuer of mortgage bonds is bankrupt, claims of such bondholders; (2) any claims of bankrupt's employees arising from their employment in previous three years; (3) taxes, governmental fees, customs duties and social security contributions arising three years prior to declaration of bankruptcy proceedings; (4) if bank is bankrupt, claims of Deposit Protection Fund (if any); and (5) any other creditors' claims. If it is impossible to satisfy all claims in same class they are settled proportionally.

Compulsory and Voluntary Composition.—Bankrupt can propose compulsory composition prior to issue of distribution schedule. Court has discretion to reject such proposals in certain circumstances. Where composition has been proposed, Court will only confirm it if majority of creditors present or represented at hearings, who have filed claims, and whose total votes represent more than 3/4 of all filed claims, approve settlements. If Court confirms compulsory composition, bankrupt is able to manage his

See Topical Index in front part of this volume.

BANKRUPTCY . . . *continued*

property again and rights which were curtailed by declaration of bankruptcy are restored.

Voluntary composition can only be proposed by debtor prior to declaring bankruptcy proceedings. Debtor must provide details of composition offered and, if he is entrepreneur, he must include details of number of his employees and measures to be taken for reorganization and refinancing of company, details of creditors and details of any creditors who are connected to debtor in legal sense. Court has discretion to reject proposal under certain circumstances, such as if proposal does not provide for any unsecured creditors to be offered payment of at least 45% of their claims, including interest and other expenses, within two years from filing proposal.

If composition is approved, Court will appoint composition administrator and order hearings to take place no later than six weeks from date of resolution. Creditors have four weeks to file their claims from date of this resolution.

When composition has been approved (1) debtor is not allowed to take independent legal action which could restrict interests of creditors; (2) debtor is not allowed to propose declaration of bankruptcy proceedings while composition proceedings continue; (3) creditors cannot propose declaration of bankruptcy; (4) claims included in final composition are considered to be approved by debtors.

Court will confirm composition, if certain conditions are met. Resolution confirms that composition has become effective and debtor must fulfill obligations promptly and in full. Any obligations to creditors not covered by composition are extinct and court then issues further resolution declaring composition completed.

BILLS AND NOTES:

Although Czechoslovakia as legal predecessor of SR has never acceded to Geneva Convention on Bill of Exchange and Convention on Checks, principles of those Conventions have been incorporated and are generally recognized by Act No. 191/1950 Coll. on Bills of Exchange and Checks which is valid and effective without any amendments until recent time.

Bills of exchange and checks belong to securities generally and to extent not covered by Act No. 191/1950 Coll., they fall under Securities Act No. 600/1992 Coll., as amended. However, it should be noted that Act No. 191/1950 Coll. governance is so complex and detailed that there is not too much space for governance by Securities Act.

Act recognizes drawn bills of exchange as securities issued to order of party (not excluding issuer), contemplating acceptance for payment by another party (again not excluding issuer). These technical varieties in combination with legally recognized varieties of maturity (i) at sight, (ii) at certain time after sight, (iii) at certain time after date of issue, or (iv) on specific date, payment place and other details make bill of exchange rather flexible payment instrument, however only within scope permitted by Act No. 191/1950 Coll. Key feature of Act No. 191/1950 Coll. is that its provisions are generally of mandatory nature and that there is no space for modifications of contractual nature, unless Act No. 191/1950 Coll. expressly allows them.

Another type of bill of exchange called "note of hand" containing issuer's unconditional promise to pay relevant amount to authorized holder of note. Contrary to "drawn bill of exchange" containing unconditional instruction for payment by acceptor, "note of hand" contains promise. It makes this payment instrument very similar to Anglo-American promissory notes, and in practice, when translated it is often used to translate this type of bill of exchange as promissory note.

Each bill of exchange must contain designation "bill of exchange" incorporated into text, determination of beneficiary (bearer bills of exchange shall be invalid) and signature of issuer.

Other mandatory details are in case of "drawn bill of exchange": (i) above-mentioned unconditional instruction, (ii) name of acceptor, (iii) maturity details, (iv) payment place details, (v) date and place of issue. If some details are missing, there are certain legal assumptions that will apply, e.g. for missing maturity details, issue place and payment place.

Bill of exchange may be transferred through endorsements, unless this is prohibited by bill's text. In principle each endorser shall be liable for payment of amount of bill of exchange, unless its liability is expressly excluded in endorsement. Acceptor's liability cannot be excluded. Same shall apply to guarantor under bill of exchange ("aval").

Recourse rights against persons who are liable under bill of exchange (other than issuer's liability for payment) are usually contingent upon performance of certain procedural steps as protest by notary public and notifications.

Checks are governed by same rule as bills of exchange, i.e. Act No. 191/1950 Coll. Requirements for issue of this payment instrument are similar to those applicable to bills of exchange.

As substantial difference, it should be mentioned that check could be drawn without specifying its beneficiary and to be transferred as bearer security. Checks can be drawn on banks only, which will pay check amount either in cash or to account (or in case of specific checks only to another bank or to its own client).

Act No. 191/1950 Coll., especially part IV dealing with specific provisions of international law of bills of exchange, stipulates following rules for international legal relations established by bills of exchange: (1) capability of person to undertake under bill of exchange is governed by law of country of its incorporation; (2) form of declarations under bill of exchange is governed by law of country in which declaration was made, including formal essentials required for relevant security (bill of exchange or promissory note) to be validly issued; (3) consequences of binding declarations of relevant security issuer are governed by law of country of payment place. It should be noted that under Slovak law, if promissory note does not include payment place, it is irrefutably presumed that place of its issue is also payment place; (4) protest's form, deadlines related to protest and other applicable acts relating to maintaining or enforcement of rights under relevant security are governed by law of country in which protest or other legal act should be performed.

Conflict of laws provisions concerning checks generally follow same principles as mentioned above in connection with bills of exchange.

CHATTEL MORTGAGES:

See topics Mortgage, Pledges, Liens.

COMMERCIAL REGISTER:

For registration of all companies and cooperatives, Commercial Registers are kept at Courts in seats of Court districts (Bratislava, Banská Bystrica, Košice). Commercial Register (Obchodný register) is public list and any person can collect information or extracts from register. Any company which has to be registered in Commercial Register starts to exist effectively on day of entry to register. Data required to be in Commercial Register are stipulated by relevant provisions of ObchZ (Commercial Code, Obchodný zákonník): (i) business name, (ii) seat, (iii) identification number (identifikačné číslo—IČO assigned by Court), (iv) scope of business activities (in accordance with its foundation agreement/deed), (v) legal form, (vi) names of representatives, their addresses, and special number derived from birth dates, (vii) amount of registered capital, (viii) designation, address and scope of activities of entity branch, (ix) other facts required by law. Moreover, there are special further requirements for particular forms of legal entities. As far as foreign entities are concerned, information specified in par. (i), (ii), (iv) and (v) shall be added by location of branch of foreign person in Slovakia as well as name and address of its managing director. All changes to above-mentioned data should be announced to Court without undue delay.

Also liquidation of company (plus appointment of liquidator) and declaration of bankruptcy (plus identification of bankruptcy administrator) are subject to registration in Commercial Register.

According to Governmental Decree No. 100/1993 Coll. on Business Journal, relevant facts from Commercial Registries are published in Business Journal on basis of documents sent to publisher of journal by Courts keeping Commercial Register.

Procedure.—Registration procedure is governed by relevant provisions of ObchZ and OSP (Civil Court Order, Občiansky súdny poriadok). Documents proving authenticity of facts required to be registered in Commercial Register should be attached: foundation memorandum or foundation agreement, certification on contribution to registered capital, specimen signature of persons authorized to act on behalf of company, power of attorney (if applicable), trade license or concession (see topic Licenses), residence permit (if any foreign person will be registered as person authorized to act on behalf of company). All above-mentioned documents should be in original or in notarized copies and translated into Slovak language, if necessary. According to Law No. 71/1992 Coll. on Court fees and fee for extract from Criminal Register, Court fees are as follows: for first record in, or erasure from, Register in case of company limited by shares, 10,000 SKK and 3,000 SKK; in case of other legal entities or individuals; for application for record of changes in Commercial Register fees are 500 SKK per change.

CONSTITUTION AND GOVERNMENT:

Constitution of Slovak Republic dated Sept. 1, 1992 (No. 460/1992 Coll.) stipulates that SR is sovereign, democratic and law-abiding state. Guarantees of fundamental rights and freedoms incorporated into Constitution are inspired by International Covenant on Civil and Political Rights and by International Covenant on Economic, Social and Cultural Rights. These and other conventions on human rights and freedoms take precedence over Slovak laws if they guarantee greater extent of human rights and freedoms.

Parliament consisting of one chamber called National Council of SR is elected by means of general election every four years and has 150 members.

President with predominantly representative functions is head of state elected every five years by three-fifths majority of all deputies of National Council.

Government of SR is supreme body of executive power with members accountable for exercise of its function to National Council.

Constitutional Court of SR is independent judicial body protecting constitutionality consisting of ten judges selected from among 20 persons proposed by National Council and appointed by President for seven year term. Constitutional Court decides about conformity of generally binding legal regulations with Constitution and laws, jurisdictional disputes between governmental authorities, complaints against violation of fundamental rights and freedoms by authorities, indictment of President in matter of treason.

Impartial and independent judiciary power consists of Supreme Court of SR and other Courts as stipulated by laws.

Prosecutor's office is headed by Prosecutor-General appointed by President upon proposal of National Council. It safeguards compliance with laws and supervises bringing of criminals to justice.

Supreme Supervision Office of SR is independent body supervising management of budget means, state property, property rights and state debts.

Constitution stipulates municipality as independent territorial and administrative unit of SR entitled to create its own municipal bodies and to manage its own property and financial resources.

CONTRACTS:

OZ (Civil Code) sets forth most general outlines for contractual relations, ownership right related issues and general principles of performance in legal relations. Overall applicability of OZ is with respect to commercial contractual relations restricted by ObchZ which is key rule having impact on all existing relations in commerce generally. However, most fundamental and principal issues are still governed by OZ with specific adjustments included in ObchZ where rule applies that OZ applies, unless ObchZ refers to contrary, as far as contractual commercial relations are concerned. It is possible to state that principle of contractual freedom is leading principle of ObchZ's part dealing with contractual relations, however parties should be aware of several mandatory provisions, applicability of which cannot be avoided. Contractual relations are dealt with in ObchZ on general level applicable to all types of contracts and on specific level whereby ObchZ sets forth basic conditions of several types of contracts. Without prejudice to existence of these types, parties are allowed to agree on contract which is not mentioned on specific level provided parties were specific enough as to its contents.

CONTRACTS . . . *continued*

Excuses for nonperformance are regulated in principal by OZ; ObchZ completes provisions for excuses for subsequent nonperformance. If performance of obligation becomes impossible, liable party's duty to render performance shall be discharged, however, performance of obligation shall not be considered impossible if it can be performed under more difficult conditions, with greater expenditure or only after agreed time limit. If impossibility relates only to part of performance only that part of obligation shall be terminated. (OZ, §§575, 576).

After liable party has learned of certain circumstances which make it impossible to render performance, liable party is obliged to notify approved party accordingly without undue delay otherwise liable party shall be liable for damage suffered by approved party due to lack of notification of impossibility of rendering performance in time.

Performance of obligation shall be deemed unattainable if legal regulations passed after conclusion of contract and which have unlimited time validity prohibit conduct which liable party is bound to perform under concluded contract, or stipulate that certain license is required which, however, was not granted to liable party although liable party duly applied for it. Burden of proof concerning impossibility of performance shall rest with liable party. (ObchZ, §352). Liable party whose obligation was extinguished due to impossibility of performance shall be obliged to compensate damage caused to approved party unless impossibility of performance was caused by circumstances excluding responsibility. Such circumstances considered obstacles which occur regardless of liable party's will and which prevent such party from performing its obligation if it cannot be reasonably presumed that liable party could have prevented or overcome such obstacles or their effects and at outset of obligation could not have anticipated such obstacles.

Applicable Law.—According to ZMPSP (Act on International Private and Procedural Law, Zākon o medzinárodnom práve súkromnom a procesnom), parties may choose any law in property and commercial matters as governing law of agreement, provided such agreement comprises "foreign element". Foreign entity being party to agreement used to be most obvious example of fact that it constitutes foreign element in transaction and therefore choice of foreign law in such case would be recognized as valid according to Slovak law. Courts generally should uphold parties' choice of law and decide case in compliance with relevant rules of governing law. This opens question of choice of jurisdiction. ZMPSP allows parties to agreement to agree on jurisdiction of domestic as well as foreign Court.

There may also be cases in which choice of Slovak law would be more appropriate such as when party expects that it may be in need of prompt injunctive relief in Slovakia. In this case choice of foreign law may lead to lengthy procedures of expertise regarding foreign law.

Public Procurement.—Many contracts may be subject to applicable rules on public procurement, depending on nature of parties, or on origin of financial resources that should be paid for goods or services that are objective of contract.

Purpose of Act No. 263/1993 Coll. on Public Procurement, as amended is to stipulate standards and rules of procedure in connection with public provision of goods, services and public works paid from public means, in order to ensure that such public provision is carried out in efficient and transparent manner. Public means are understood as funds allocated from expenditures of State budget, State funds or municipalities' budgets. Framework created by Procurement Act is fairly similar to procurement rules in effect in many Western Europe countries and European Community. Procurement Act sets up system in which five forms of procurement are established: (1) public tender; (2) limited tender; (3) negotiation; (4) price offer; and (5) direct provision.

Public tender is broadest form of tender declared for unlimited number of applicants. Notice must be published in Business Journal of SR and in similar foreign journals containing terms and conditions of public tender for: (1) goods and services in amount exceeding 130,000 ECU; (2) for public works of building character in amount exceeding 5,000,000 ECU; and (3) for any other public works in amount exceeding 400,000 ECU. To be valid, at least three applicants must participate in public tender process.

Limited tender is invitation for submitting bids which is delivered to limited number of potential bidders, but no less than three. This form of tender may be used if: (1) declaration of public tender is not possible due to need to protect State secret; (2) organizing public tender would be, from perspective of time and money, unreasonable in view of advantages of value of required object of agreement; (3) previous public tender has not been successful; or (4) only limited number of applicants can reliably provide subject of procurement.

Under negotiation procedure, party calling for tender may benefit from flexibility in number of potential bidders (no less than three) and in manner in which contents of tender invitation and documentation are prepared. Negotiations are to take place with applicants on individual basis and afterwards bidders are to submit proposals. Following review of proposals, most suitable bid is identified and successful bidder is required to enter into agreement with party calling for tender. Negotiation procedure may be used where previous public tender or limited tender was not successful, where entity calling for tenders is unable to specify goods, services or public works, or unanticipated time pressure makes recourse to public tender or limited tender procedures impossible.

Price offer available for small quantities of mass produced goods readily available in market.

Direct provision by one applicant may be used if: (1) required goods, services or public works are available from one source only or applicant has exclusive rights relating to object of provision; (2) unanticipated time pressure makes recourse to public or limited tender procedures impossible; (3) required goods, services or work are additional to applicant's previous provision of goods, services or work, if such additional provision does not exceed 50% of price for previous provision and need for additional provision arises before former provision is fulfilled; (4) provision of required goods, services or works is subject to state secret protection; (5) need for provision is result of urgent natural disaster or emergency; or if (6) anticipated price of goods and services is less than 50,000 SKK.

Any failure to comply with Act will have consequence that budget rules of SR will be deemed to be violated, tender process will be deemed invalid and relevant competent officers will be subject to penalties up to 100,000 SKK.

Pursuant to Art. 1(2), Act will not apply in instances where: (1) security of country could be impaired by requiring that public procurement be carried out; (2) patent rights or copyrights might be infringed; (3) or such requirement would result in any liability arising from international treaties and agreements binding on SR; (4) or requirement would result in any change of public procurement procedures used abroad, if seat of entity calling for tenders is abroad.

COPYRIGHT:

Basic legal regulation in respect of copyright is Copyright Act 35/1965 Coll., as amended. At present, Copyright Act complies with standard world criteria of laws governing copyright.

Works protected by Copyright Act are deemed to be literary, scientific, and art works resulting from creative activities of authors, particularly literary, theater, music, and fine art works including architectural works and works of applied art, any film, photographic, and cartographic works, and computer programs (introduced in 1990). Copyright to any work arises at moment when work is expressed by words, script, drawing, sketch or in any perceptible form whatsoever.

Author has right to have copyright protected, particularly in respect to infringement of author's work, right to dispose of work, especially granting approval for using work, and has right to receive consideration for creative work. Work may be exploited, unless directly allowed by law, only upon author's consent. Lawful circumstances for exploiting any work without author's consent are strictly specified in copyright law and include, inter alia, e.g. quotations from author's work and attributing author, inclusions in any scientific or critic works, in textbooks or teaching aids, etc.

Copyright is not transferable in general and author may transfer only right to exploit work. Any transferee may transfer acquired right to any third person only upon author's consent. Copyright law also specifies essential types of copyright agreements which include Agreement on Work Dissemination, Agreement on Publishing, Agreement on Work Creation, Agreement on Work Public Performance. Copyright is valid for period of author's life, and after author's death for period of ten years in case of photographic works, journals, and magazines, and 50 years in case of literary, film, and any other works.

Basic protection of copyright is secured in territory of SR by specialized and professional authors' unions which procure, in addition to controlling compliance with copyright, collection of royalties for exploiting works. Unions actively cooperate with similar organizations worldwide.

In case of any infringement of copyright, author has right to claim infringement be prohibited, any consequences of infringement be removed and author receive reasonable satisfaction in cash or in kind. Further protection is provided to author by OZ allowing claim to liquidated damages caused by infringement of copyright. Criminal Code, by its last amendment in 1994, very precisely specifies wrongful acts regarding copyright and has materially extended imprisonment for such acts. For committing copyright crime, offender may be sentenced to imprisonment up to five years or fine up to 5 million SKK or forfeiture.

Software Protection.—Any computer program deemed to be author's work if it is result of author's creative work and is, in its essence, unrepeatable creation, its individuality arising from personal character of work. Computer program should be both expressed by any perceptible manner whatsoever and author's own work.

Upon complying with all terms and conditions for acknowledging computer program as object of copyright, author of work (natural person, team of natural persons—coauthors, legal entity) becomes holder of subjective copyright protected by Act. Permanency of copyright is secured by Act, unless stipulated otherwise, for period of author's life and 50 years after death.

According to Act, author may transfer only right to exploit work under specific conditions. Any other author's personal rights are deemed to be untransferable and are bound exclusively to author's person. Exception is any programs created in employment where presumption of Act is that employee-author of work has, by entering into employment contract with scope of activities including creation of computer programs, granted to employer general consent for exploiting work for its own internal purposes. However, any dissemination of work outside relevant organization requires consent of employee as author of work.

SR has gradually become participant in all international organizations for protection of software.

CORPORATIONS:

ObchZ (Commercial Code, Obchodný zákonnik) provides for five main forms of corporations which are understood as legal entities existing for purpose of undertaking business activities: (i) Company limited by shares (a.s.); (ii) limited liability company (s.r.o.); (iii) unlimited company (v.o.s.); (iv) limited partnership (k.s.); and (v) cooperative.

Company Limited by Shares—Akciová Spoločnost' (a.s.).—No shareholder in company limited by shares is liable for obligations of company. Shareholder is, however, liable to company to extent of any amounts unpaid on shares held. Company limited by shares must include designation "akciová spoločnost" or "a.s." in its name. Some companies limited by shares performing special activities (such as investment companies, investment funds, securities dealers) must include reference to these activities in legally recognized form into their company names.

Company limited by shares may be formed by private agreement to subscribe for shares or by public offer for subscription. Whichever method is chosen, company's registered capital must be at least 1,000,000 SKK (unless provided otherwise by special Acts) of which at least 30% of nominal value of any shares which are to be subscribed in cash must be paid up prior to constituent general meeting. Insurance companies must, in addition to share capital, give special bail in form of blocked deposit in amount stipulated by Ministry of Finance. Full nominal amount of share capital subscribed by each founder must be paid up within one year of registration in Commercial Register at latest. This does not apply to any employees' shares. Late

See Topical Index in front part of this volume.

CORPORATIONS . . . *continued*

payment bears interest at 20% per annum (unless otherwise specified in Articles of Association). Additional consequences of late payment are specified in ObchZ.

Company limited by shares must have two or more founders, unless sole founder is legal person (i.e. not individual). They must draw up and sign foundation agreement (foundation memorandum in case of sole founder) which contains, e.g., proposed share holding structure, as well as details relevant for public subscription of shares (if applicable). Founder's signatures must be notarized.

Constituent general meeting must be convened within 60 days of last subscription of shares. If it fails to be convened, subscription will be null and void and founders jointly and severally liable to return all subscription moneys received. Quorum required for this meeting is represented by subscribers holding at least 50% of total shares subscribed who have paid up their investment to amount due. Resolutions may be passed by simple majority of votes. Meeting deals with approval of formation of company, approval of Articles of Association and election of members of board of directors and supervisory board (unless Articles of Association provide otherwise). Articles of Association contain internal corporate and management rules, fundamental economic rules of company's operation, detailed rules for increases and reductions of share capital, rules for new shares and convertible bonds issues, and any other details founders or constituent general meeting (as case may be) consider fit and appropriate to include in Articles of Association. Company's officers' (directors and supervisory board members) details are not included in foundation memorandum. This is because they are elected by constituent general meeting or founders simultaneously with recording their approval of formation of company.

Course of meeting, resolutions passed, list of subscribers, nominal value of registered capital subscribed and amounts paid up by individual subscribers, together with names of persons elected to management board, must be notarially recorded.

Share may be issued in either registered or bearer form. Both types are generally transferable and Articles of Association cannot restrict transferability of publicly negotiable shares. It should be noted that Securities Act (Act No. 600/1992 Coll., as am'd) includes provision for compulsory dematerialisation of shares whether issued as publicly negotiable or not. Dematerialisation means registration in recognized Securities Center where share is represented by relevant record.

Furthermore, Securities Act imposes obligation to trade in shares exclusively on stock exchange or over-the-counter (called RM-System) markets, whether or not relevant shares are issued as publicly negotiable. Takeover regulations are included in Securities Act as well.

Voting and nonvoting preference shares are possible. However, nonvoting preference shareholders must acquire voting rights if company fails to pay dividend. Employees' shares which represent certain advantages attached thereto for their holders may be issued.

However, if advantage is based on exemption to pay full face value of share, aggregate of all parts of face values subject to such exemption must not exceed 5% of amount of registered capital. Any employees' shares may only be issued as registered shares and may only be transferred between employees of company (current or retired).

Corporation is managed by board of directors consisting of at least three members elected by general meeting. Powers of board of directors laid down in Articles of Association. Supervisory board elected by and reporting to, general meeting supervises activities of board of directors and if stipulated by Articles of Association it may elect and recall board of directors.

General meeting must be held at least once a year, although in addition it may be called at other times. Board of directors is obliged to convene general meeting if it is required to do so by qualified group of shareholders.

Quorum for general meeting is represented by shareholders holding over 30% of nominal value of registered capital, unless Articles of Association provide otherwise and subject to special quorum requirement related to capital reduction.

Decisions are generally taken by simple majority of votes cast, unless Articles of Association provide otherwise.

Limited Liability Company—Spoločnosť S Ručením Obmedzeným (s.r.o./spol. s r.o.).—Interests in s. r.o. are like percentage participation (referred to as "ownership interest"). Company does not issue shares and ownership relations are determined by constituent documents and reflected and evidenced by extracts from relevant Commercial Register. Generally, any participant holds only one ownership interest or share in s.r.o. One participant's share can be different size from another participant's and size of interest or share can be altered. Ownership interest represents member's participation in rights and obligations related to its membership in company including voting rights and rights to participate in profit distribution. Usually, proportions of members' ownership interests are equal to proportions of amounts of their contributions to registered capital, although constituent documentation may alter this rule. Amount of any participant's contribution to registered capital must be amount exceeding 20,000 SKK being multiple of 1,000 SKK, registered capital should be at least 100,000 SKK. Number of participants may not exceed 50.

Liability of participant in this type of company is limited to amount unpaid on participants' capital contributions.

S.r.o. may be founded by one person even if that person is individual. Foundation document of s.r.o is association agreement (or foundation memorandum if there is only one founder). ObchZ provides that association agreement may stipulate that participant may be required, in addition to its general duty to pay agreed amount of its contribution to registered capital, by general meeting to contribute to cover losses of up to 50% of registered capital held by it but without affecting size of its ownership interest. Generally, association agreement must include following: company's name and its registered office, objects of company at time of foundation, information on founders, amount of registered capital including details of each founder's contribution to registered capital, details of company's first directors, and details of company's first supervisory board members (if created). Signatures of founders must also be notarized and if there is sole founder, foundation memorandum must be executed in form of notarial record.

At least 50% of registered capital must be paid up before s.r.o. is registered in Commercial Register. If there is sole founder, total registered capital must be fully paid up before registration.

Generally, remaining unpaid capital must be paid up within five years of entry in Commercial Register. Interest of 20% is charged on any overdue contribution, with further sanction of possible expulsion from s.r.o.

Participants' rights can be set out in either Articles of Association or association agreement. Each participant has one vote per each 1,000 SKK of investment in s.r.o., unless Articles of Association or association agreement determine otherwise. Each participant has right to participate in supervising activities of s.r.o. through general meeting.

Participant is entitled to receive share of profit in same proportion as participant's paid up contribution to total registered capital, unless association agreement or Articles of Association provide for some other division.

S.r.o. can create reserve fund in first year it makes net profit.

As with joint stock company, general meeting is supreme governing body of s.r.o. It is authorized to make all major decisions, e.g. distributing profit, amending Articles of Association or association agreement, winding up company. In any event, general meeting is authorized to reserve right to decide any matter, whether falling within scope of its competencies or not.

Quorum for general meeting is satisfied when members holding more than one-half of all the votes are present.

Decisions are made by simple majority of votes of participants present except where association agreement or law requires higher number of votes. S.r.o. must hold general meeting at least once a year or at any time if reserve fund drops below half of its value as of day of last general meeting. Qualified participants are entitled to demand convocation of general meeting and should executives fail to do so, participants have right to convene general meeting themselves.

There must be at least one director in s.r.o. First directors appointed by association agreement, further directors appointed by decision of general meeting. Directors can act independently, unless constitutional documents provide otherwise. Decisions about management of s.r.o. must be taken by majority of directors.

It is not essential for s.r.o. to have supervisory board, unless association agreement requires; when required it must have at least three members.

Unlimited Company—Verejná Obchodná Spoločnosť (v.o.s./ver. obch. spol.).—V.o.s. is legal person in which at least two persons carry on business activities under common business name and bear joint and several liability for obligations of entity. Any legal persons or individuals may be partners.

V.o.s. fully liable for its obligations. If liabilities exceed assets, partners are jointly and severally liable for debts of firm to full extent of their property.

Business name should include designation "verejná obchodná spoločnosť" or either of abbreviations "ver. obch. spol." or "v.o.s." If at least one of partner's names is used in business name, only term "a spol" need be added.

Association agreement must specify main office and business name of v.o.s., names and addresses of all partners and scope of business activities or objects. Partners must all sign petition to enter v.o.s. in Commercial Register.

Constitution, rights and duties of parties are set out in ObchZ and in association agreement. Association agreement will typically cover such issues as specific rights and obligations of partners' profit and loss distribution, if not in equal shares, circumstances in which v.o.s. may be dissolved beyond those specified in ObchZ, etc. Where association agreement is silent, provisions of ObchZ will apply.

Any contribution made to v.o.s. becomes v.o.s. property. Association agreement should specify terms on which contributions of parties must be paid. If it does not, contributions must be paid within reasonable time of entry on Commercial Register. Interest of 20% is payable on late payment of contributions unless otherwise stipulated by association agreement. Obligations to contribute some capital may be agreed between partners in association agreement, although v.o.s. does not create registered capital.

Each partner has ostensible authority to bind v.o.s. as regards third parties. However, if this authority is restricted by association agreement and restriction is entered on Commercial Register it is effective against third parties.

As far as management of v.o.s. is concerned, each partner may act independently of others, unless association agreement provides that partners must act jointly. If association agreement allows management of all or part of affairs of v.o.s. to be delegated to managing partners, other partners relinquish their authority to manage v.o.s. to some extent. Managing partners must, however, be bound by decision of majority of partners.

Limited Partnership—Komanditná Spoločnosť (k.s./kom. spol.).—Limited partnership (or k.s.) is made up of limited partners, whose liability for obligations of k.s. is limited to amount of any unpaid part of that partner's investment, and general partners whose liability is unlimited.

Name of limited partnership must include designation "komanditná spoločnosť" or abbreviation "kom. spol." or "k.s." Business name should not include name of any limited partner.

Most of provisions relating to v.o.s. apply to k.s. and most of provisions relating to s.r.o. apply to legal position of limited partners. There are, however, some differences.

Association agreement establishing k.s. must be submitted with petition to appropriate Commercial Register.

In addition to containing similar terms to those included in association agreement for v.o.s., agreement must specifically state which of partners are to be general partners, and which limited partners, and amount of each limited partner's investment.

Only general partners are entitled to participate in management of business, although other matters are decided by simple majority vote on basis of one vote per partner, including those partners with limited liability. Alternative provisions in association agreement would, however, prevail unless affecting business management rights belonging to general partners.

Generally, only general partners can bind k.s., but if limited partner holds himself out as general partner limited partner will bear unlimited liability.

Profit is generally divided into two parts, each of which belongs to each class of partners, in proportion 1:1, unless association agreement stipulates otherwise. If not

CORPORATIONS . . . *continued*
agreed otherwise in association agreement, general partners share profits equally and limited partners in proportion to their paid up contributions.

Cooperative—Družstvo.—Cooperative is organization with unspecified number of members (at least five individuals or two legal entities) which is founded to undertake activities or to otherwise satisfy needs of its members. Its name must include designation "družstvo".

Minimum registered capital is 50,000 SKK. To become member (individual at least 15 years old or legal entity) of cooperative, member's basic investment or specific proportion of investment (stipulated by Articles of Association) shall be paid. In latter case, rest of member's basic investment must be paid within period of three years, unless otherwise provided by Articles of Association. Cooperative fully liable for its obligations. Members not personally liable for obligations of cooperative, however, Articles of Association may stipulate that in order to cover cooperative's losses, its members shall have compensation duty towards cooperative. It is possible to transfer member's rights and obligations (membership) to another cooperative's member unless Articles of Association provides otherwise. Transfer to any nonmember is possible only upon consent of Board of Directors (consent is not necessary in case of housing cooperatives).

Cooperative existence commences at constituent members' meeting which determines amount of registered basic capital, approves Articles of Association, elects Board of Directors and Supervisory Board. Record from this meeting takes form of notarial deed. Cooperative must be registered in Commercial Register. It is bound to create indivisible fund (which cannot be distributed among cooperative's members during existence of cooperative) equaling 50% of its registered capital.

Foreign Corporations.—According to ObchZ, foreign persons may conduct business activities in SR under same conditions as Slovak persons, unless law stipulates otherwise. Foreign person is authorized to conduct business (establishing own enterprise or branch) in SR only if registered in Commercial Register.

COURTS:

According to Art. 141 of Constitution of SR, judicial power is exercised by independent and impartial courts. Courts decide criminal and civil matters and review decisions of administrative bodies.

System of courts of general jurisdiction is composed by District Courts (Okresné súdy), Regional Courts (Krajské súdy) and Supreme Court (Najvyšší súd).

System of military courts consists of Military Local Courts (Vojenské obvodové súdy) and Higher Military Court (Vyšší vojenský súd) which is competent to decide criminal matters involving members of military forces.

District Courts hear all proceedings as court of first instance, except certain matters which are heard by Regional Courts. (OSP, §9). District Court decides in Senates or by single judge. Senates consist of one judge and two assessors who decide in labor matters and any other matters defined by law.

Regional Courts are appellate courts for decisions of District Courts in first instance. They are also competent to hear some proceedings in first instance. (OSP, §9). Decisions are made by single judge, except in matters defined in OSP, §36b which are decided by Senates consisting of (i) two judges (one of them being Presiding Judge) and three assessors if Senate decides in first instance criminal matters, or (ii) Presiding Judge and two judges in other matters.

For Supreme Court and Constitutional Court, see topic Constitution and Government.

CURRENCY:

Slovak Crown (SKK) divided into 100 hellers (singular "halier", plural "halierov") is lawful currency of SR. It was introduced shortly after split of former C.S.F.R. Exchange rates are approximately 30 SKK=US$1, 20 SKK=1 Deutschmark. According to Law No. 566/1992 Coll., National Bank of Slovakia is central bank of SR and among other functions it controls money supply, foreign currency reserves, issue of banknotes and coins, grants loans to commercial banks, accepts deposits from commercial banks, etc. It is also vested with authority to issue licenses for banking activities and some permits concerning foreign exchange regulations. Moreover, circulation of banknotes and coins, obligation to accept lawful currency, etc., is stipulated in Decree of the State Bank of Czechoslovakia No. 147/1992 Coll.

See also topic Foreign Exchange.

CUSTOMS DUTIES:

Customs duties are governed by Act No. 180/1996 Coll. and Act No. 44/1974 Coll., as amended (stipulating customs authorities). System consists of import duties, export duties, antidumping duties (and duties with similar effects).

As SR is member of GATT its system of import duties is based on GATT's internationally accepted list of tariffs. Customs tariffs are specified in Governmental Decree No. 300/1995 Coll. Tariff includes general rates, rates applicable according to bilateral or multilateral international treaties, rates applicable for imports from third world countries.

100% exemption from duties may be granted for goods imported for, e.g., purpose of processing and subsequent reexport. There is also another exemption applicable to imported machinery and technologies which are to be contributed as in kind contributions to commercial companies, provided that specific requirements stipulated by relevant decree of Ministry of Finance are complied with. SR and Czech Republic forms customs union and SR is also member of Central European Free Trade Agreement (CEFTA).

Customs declaration can be in written or oral form (including data transfer). Customs are administered by local customs authorities and General Directorate of Customs.

DEATH (PRESUMPTION OF AND ACTIONS FOR):

If death cannot be proved by inspection of corpse, Court shall pronounce certain natural person dead if person's death is proved in another manner (e.g. traffic accident). Court shall pronounce missing person dead if, taking into account all relevant circumstances, it may be assumed that person is not alive. If, taking into account all relevant circumstances, it is presumed that missing person is dead, Court shall summon missing person or any other person to produce any report about missing person. If no report is submitted within one year, Court shall pronounce person's death, stating date of death. If it is not possible to state exact sequence of death of several natural persons, it is presumed that they have died simultaneously. After person's death has been proved or pronounced by Court, inscription is made in register of deaths kept by municipalities.

In case of fatal injury, survivors of deceased to whom deceased person gave or was obliged to give support are entitled to receive compensation in form of pecuniary annuity from person responsible for death. (OZ, §448).

Human Organ Transplant.—Transplantation of human organs from dead persons regulated by Law No. 277/1994 Coll. It is presumed that person consents to organs being used for transplantation unless person disagreed with it in any written statement executed during life.

DEPOSITIONS:

According to Hague Convention on the Taking of Evidence Abroad in Civil or Commercial Matters (Mar. 18, 1970; No. 129/1976 Coll.), relevant foreign judicial authority may request taking of evidence or performance of another act of Court (Letter of Request). Ministry of Justice of SR is authority ensuring contacts between Slovak and foreign Courts. Detailed regulation is contained in Instruction of the Ministry of Justice of SR of Dec. 16, 1980 No. 100/1980-L/M-v. According to ZMPSP legal assistance is provided according to Slovak legal regulations; however, it is possible to proceed according to foreign procedure regulation, if requested by foreign authority unless this is contrary to public interest in SR. There are several bilateral treaties providing for international legal assistance.

DESCENT AND DISTRIBUTION:

According to OZ estate of any deceased person passes to heirs upon death. Any person may inherit by operation of law, under will, or in both ways. Since, according to OZ property of both spouses (unless provided otherwise by OZ) forms undivided coownership of spouses, after death of one of spouses property forming coownership is divided. Then, shares of relevant heirs are calculated from share of deceased spouse. There are four orders of succession. Intestate's children and spouse inherit in first order of succession, each of them in equal shares. Should descendants of decedent not inherit then decedent's spouse, decedent's parents and those who lived with decedent in common household for period of at least one year form second order of succession. Should neither decedent's spouse nor his/her parent inherit, decedent's siblings and person who lived with decedent in common household for period of at least one year form third order of succession. If one of decedent's siblings does not inherit, sibling's children acquire sibling's share of inheritance. Fourth order of succession is formed by grandparents of decedent or by their children. Any heir may disclaim inheritance within one month of day when heir was informed by Court of right to disclaim inheritance. Any estate which was not acquired by any heir shall escheat to State.

Probate proceeding are commenced ex officio by court of last domicile of deceased. If there is only single heir, Court shall confirm to heir that estate has passed to heir. If there are two or more heirs, heirs settle inheritance by agreement at relevant Court. If no agreement between heirs is reached Court shall confirm acquisition of inheritance to those heirs whose rights to inheritance have been duly proven.

DIVORCE:

Marriage can be dissolved exclusively upon Court decision if relations between spouses are unavoidably disrupted and marriage cannot fulfill its social purpose. (ZR, §24). In practice, disruption must be serious, intensive and surviving for long period. Court must take into consideration interests of minor children.

Action for divorce begins upon petition submitted to Court by one of spouses. Jurisdiction in district Court with seat in district of last common residence of spouses. This action also includes adjudication of rights and duties after divorce, of parents as to minor children born in marriage. Court shall especially assign which of parents will have custody of children, along with manner of contribution for support of children by both parents. Decision on rights and duties of parents as to children may be substituted by agreement of parents, approved by Court. Agreement on contact of parents with children does not require approval of court.

Aliens.—According to ZMPSP, §38 Slovak Court has power to dissolve marriage, if at least one spouse is citizen of SR. If neither spouse is Slovak citizen, Slovak Court has jurisdiction, if (a) at least one spouse is residing in SR and Court decision can be recognized in countries of domicile of both spouses, or (b) at least one spouse has residence in SR for significant period of time.

Court will apply law of state of which spouses are citizens. If spouses are citizens of different states, Court will apply law of SR. Slovak law will also be applied if foreign law, which normally should have applied, would not allow divorce, or allow it only under extremely difficult circumstances.

Unless bilateral international treaties provide otherwise, valid decisions of foreign courts are subject to declaration on enforcement by decision of Supreme Court of SR.

ENVIRONMENT:

Fundamental legal regulation is Act No. 17/1992 Coll. on environment which stipulates some basic obligations concerning protection of environment. Act No. 287/1994 Coll. on protection of nature and country stipulates scope of activities for exercise of which permission is necessary. Act also classifies those parts of country which are specially protected (national parks etc.). However, there is wide range of special legal regulations concerning particular parts of environment (soil, water, air, forests, waste etc.) and permission required for construction of buildings.

Water.—For use of water, fees are established which are paid by user of water in relation to amount of water used. Furthermore, there are fees for polluting water paid by polluter.

Air.—For pollution of air, special fees are set down based on quantity of emissions produced by relevant polluter.

See Topical Index in front part of this volume.

ENVIRONMENT . . . *continued*

Soil.—Act No. 307/1992 Coll. on protection of agricultural soil, as amended, stipulates obligations of users of agricultural soil. For change of agricultural soil to another type, special permission is necessary and payments to State are paid.

Forest.—Fundamental legal regulation in field of protection of forests is Act No. 61/1977 Coll. on forests, as amended. This regulation governs protection of forests, obligations of owners, classification of forests, fines imposed for violation of Act. Furthermore, special regulation stipulates payments, which are paid to state, if forest is replaced by another use.

Waste.—Act No. 238/1991 Coll., as amended, governs waste disposal (including radioactive waste). Any originator of waste is obliged to process waste as much as possible and to prevent it from polluting environment. Act also sets down sanctions for violation of Act. Relevant authority can decide on termination of activity, if originator of waste is not able to ensure appropriate liquidation of wastes. For deposition of waste special payments are paid according to character of waste. Only with permission obtained from relevant authority may waste be liquidated.

Construction Activities.—Act No. 50/1976 Coll., as amended, on territorial planning and construction rules stipulates basic principles and obligations concerning construction of buildings and connected activities. For purposes of further development of particular territory, territorial plans are adopted by relevant local State authorities. Further development of particular territory must be in compliance with these adopted plans. Furthermore, for any construction activity (excluding small buildings, repairs of buildings etc.) special permission is necessary, which is issued by local State authority following application of constructor. After construction is finished, State authority controls building from aspect of security requirements, compliance with construction plans. To engage in construction activities defined in Act, special qualification is necessary. Part of Act deals with expropriation procedure.

Environmental Impacts Assessment.—Act No. 127/1994 Coll. stipulates conditions for environmental impact assessment (EIA) which has to be produced before commencing any activity enumerated in annexes of Act. Proposal for intended activity is submitted to Ministry of the Environment of SR, which shall set down scope of information demanded for report. Report is prepared by entity which has submitted proposal. Ministry ensures production of final assessment and on basis of it issues final statement permitting or prohibiting activity.

EXCHANGE CONTROL:

See topic Foreign Exchange.

EXCHANGES:

Stock Exchange.—Stock Exchange Act No. 214/1992 Coll. ("Act") came into force on 21st Apr., 1992. This Act lays down basic framework for internal arrangements of stock exchange. Act allows any number of stock exchanges to be established in SR and lays down procedure for approval by Ministry of Finance of SR.

Under Act, any stock exchange must be company limited by shares and, as such, it is generally bound by provisions of ObchZ. It must be established by at least ten founders and its shares must be in registered form and cannot be subscribed in public. No priority or employees shares are allowed. It is anticipated that shareholders in exchange will also actively trade on it.

Foreign firms, or firms in which shareholding of 50% or more is in foreign hands, are not allowed to hold more than one-third of equity of exchange. Bratislava Stock Exchange (Burza cenných papierov v Bratislave, a.s.) is only stock exchange in Slovakia. Although Act does not limit number of stock exchanges that may operate within country, it is likely that Ministry of Finance, being supervisory and licensing authority in area of stock exchanges, would consider size of market, which is not considerably large, in deciding about approval to incorporate another stock exchange.

Governing bodies of stock exchange are general assembly of shareholders, stock exchange chamber and supervisory board. Each stock exchange has general assembly of shareholders which will approve regulations of that exchange and any amendments to them. It is also responsible for determining types of fees to be charged by exchange and how they are to be calculated. Furthermore, it creates stock exchange arbitration, approves its rules and executes standard powers of general assembly as usual with company limited by shares.

General assembly elects members of stock exchange chamber and also members of supervisory board. Voting is in proportion to nominal value of member's shares. However, to prevent domination by any one shareholder, no member may account for more than 20% of number of votes cast.

Stock exchange chamber creates several committees to perform its special activities. Day to day business of stock exchange managed by secretary general. Listing committee decides on securities listing. Act gives samples of criteria for listing as time of existence of issuer, its registered share capital, composition of its shareholders, volume of issue, etc.

Trading authorization belongs under Act either to shareholders of stock exchange or to persons authorized to trade in securities (securities dealers) that have been awarded such authorization by stock exchange chamber, being Stock Exchange members. There may be regular members of Stock Exchange whose membership is unlimited and temporary members, whose membership is limited to one year (with certain limits on rights and obligations such as nomination of representatives to Stock Exchange bodies and payment of acceptance fee). National Bank of Slovakia is automatically authorized to trade in securities on Stock Exchange. Those not entitled to trade on Stock Exchange may buy or sell securities on its floor only through persons admitted in one of ways mentioned above.

Commodity exchange is legal entity governed by Act No. 229/1992 Coll., as amended, organizing trades in goods. Legal form of commodity exchange is different from those generally governed by ObchZ. Only legal entities are allowed to be founders of commodity exchange which is founded by foundation deed. No profit may be distributed among founders or members of exchange. Whole profit may be used exclusively as reinvestment for further developments of exchange.

Licensing authorities are Ministry of Agriculture, if commodities traded on exchange are of agricultural or alimentary nature, and Ministry of Economy in all other cases.

Authorities are general assembly and exchange chamber. General assembly is supreme body of exchange, while exchange chamber is statutory and managing authority consisting of at least three members. Two-thirds of exchange chamber are elected by general assembly and one-third are nominated by relevant licensing authority.

Trades are concluded between exchange members (founders, commodity exchange brokers, members of exchange chamber and secretary general, and other members accepted by exchange chamber); other producers manufacturing or processing goods or trading license holders, provided they have been granted admission (and only through brokers); and entities created by law to regulate commodities markets.

EXECUTIONS:

Execution title is represented by enforceable Court decision adjudging right, determining liabilities or affecting property. Further, execution may also issue based on approved settlements, payment orders, assessments of delinquent payments, and agreements Court execution of which is permitted by law. Execution title is also represented by notarial deeds containing legal commitment and identifying person entitled and person liable, legal reason, subject and time of fulfillment provided person liable agreed with execution in notarial deed.

Currently, there is state of parallel existence of two institutional forms of enforcement of decision (enforcement of decisions is governed both by OSP and Act No. 233/1995 Coll. on Court executors and executing activities, "Execution Order"), and it is presumably temporary form which should serve for becoming familiar with enforcement of decisions by execution as only form of enforcement of resolution. Execution Order provides executor with more extensive scope of possibilities for collecting claims of persons entitled than OSP (Civil Court Order, Občiansky súdny poriadok).

For execution of foreign judgments see topic Judgments.

Executors.—By adoption of Execution Order, new institution has been introduced to fulfill function of liquidation of estate of debtor which previously was fulfilled by Courts pursuant to provisions of OSP §§251-559.

According to Execution Order, executor is independent (also economically) from State, being provided inevitable objectivity in performing activities. Executor is not governmental employee. Executor's activities exclude employment or any similar relation or any other activities performed for consideration. Only citizen fulfilling conditions stipulated by Execution Order (§10) may be appointed as executor. Executor is appointed by Minister of Justice upon proposal of Chamber of Executors. Executor may employ employees. Employees shall include executor's clerk preparing for future duties of executor who should also fulfill conditions stipulated by law for being admitted to bar of executor's clerks. Upon completing no less than a year executor's experience and passing professional examination, candidate may file application for entry into list of candidates. Term of so-called candidature is not limited by law. Candidate becomes executor upon appointment by Minister. Number of executor's offices shall be determined by Minister. Executor may also employ other employees representing administrative and technical set-up.

Execution Proceedings.—Execution proceedings shall commence upon petition of person entitled or upon petition of anyone proving that right from execution title has been transferred to him/her. Petition should clearly show executor to whom it is addressed, person by whom it has been filed, matter to which it relates, what is followed by it, and it should be signed and dated. In addition, it should contain exact identification of parties, i.e. person entitled (petitioner) and person liable (respondent). Petition should be accompanied by duplicate of execution title with confirmed enforceability.

Court Jurisdiction and Authorization to Perform Execution.—Person entitled may, regardless of seat of executor and jurisdiction of Court which issued execution title, elect which of executors shall perform execution. Executor having been served petition for execution shall immediately file such petition with Court, however, no later than within 15 days and shall apply for authorization to perform execution itself. Court shall, no later than within 15 days from delivery of petition, authorize executor in writing to perform execution. Upon authorization, executor and person entitled shall enter into written agreement on performing execution.

Notice of Commencement of Execution.—Executor shall notify both person entitled and person liable about commencing execution and shall invite person liable to satisfy claim of person entitled within 14 days of delivery of notice. At same time executor shall prohibit person liable to dispose of property.

Objections of Person Liable Against Execution.—Person liable may raise objections against execution within 14 days of delivery of notice. Objections shall represent defense of person liable against unlawful execution with purpose to declare execution inadmissible. Upon expiry of time period for raising objections or upon delivery to executor of decision dismissing objections of person liable against execution, executor shall render execution order for performing execution. Court may, under terms and conditions stipulated in law, adjourn or suspend execution.

Method of Execution.—Law precisely stipulates methods allowed for performing execution. If basis of execution is execution title imposing liability to pay any financial amount, execution may be performed by: (a) withholding payments from wage and other incomes; (b) notice of appropriation of receivable: (i) notice of appropriation of bank account, (ii) notice of appropriation of other receivables in money, (iii) affecting any other property rights; (c) sale of movable assets; (d) sale of securities; (e) sale of immovable assets; (f) sale of business. If execution title imposes any liability other than payment of financial amount, execution may be performed by: (i) clearance; (ii) distressing things; (iii) dividing common thing; (iv) realizing works and performances.

Other Executor's Activities.—Based on Power of Attorney executed by person entitled, executor may assist person entitled in collecting claims even prior to any Court's decision. Thus, he/she may influence person liable prior to proceedings or during proceedings to satisfy debt of person entitled. Executor may attend hearing in matter, if authorized by person entitled.

EXECUTIONS . . . *continued*

Executor may, in respect of Court or any other proceedings, receive money, instruments, and other movable assets to deposit. For performing execution activities, executor has right for consideration, reimbursement of out-of-pocket expenses, and compensation for waste of time. Person entitled and executor have right to be indemnified against fees and costs reasonably incurred in connection with making claim.

EXECUTORS AND ADMINISTRATORS:

Under Slovak law, functions of administering estate of decedent are performed by notaries public. See topic Notaries Public, subhead Role of Notaries in Estate Proceedings. Term "executor" refers to official who liquidates assets of debtor. See topic Executions.

FOREIGN EXCHANGE:

Slovak currency (Slovak Crown) is not freely convertible. Mechanism for regulating trade with freely convertible currencies for Slovak currency is set forth in Foreign Exchange Act No. 202/1995 Coll. ("Act").

There are several kinds of currency trading restrictions and obligations applicable to residents, defined as individuals and entities having their permanent residence or registered office within territory of SR. Restrictions imposed on nonresidents are not so extensive.

Obligations of residents are: (1) notification duty applicable especially to receivables and payables in connection with nonresidents, investments, loans, securities and financial operations; (2) duty to offer sale of foreign currency for Slovak currency to foreign exchange licensee, which has duty to offer National Bank of Slovakia; and (3) duty requiring resident to provide for transfer of funds acquired abroad to SR, with certain exemptions stated by Act.

Restrictions on residents relate particularly to (1) trade (sale/purchase) in foreign exchange values generally, funds in foreign currency, foreign securities, financial derivatives; (2) lending to and borrowing from, nonresidents; (3) acquiring real estate outside territory of SR; (4) acquiring shares or participation interests in foreign companies and corporations; and (5) securing liabilities of nonresidents. In above types of activities, foreign exchange permit generally required prior to any resident entering into transaction.

Foreign exchange licensees, usually licensed banks or licensed branches of foreign banks, generally exempt from above restrictions and are not required to apply for foreign exchange permit for each particular transaction. Licensees usually trade under scope of general foreign exchange license, to extent provided for in license. If licensees are counterparts to other residents in generally restricted transactions (e.g. financial derivatives), frequently their involvement relieves residents from obligation to get foreign exchange permit.

National Bank of Slovakia is licensing authority generally, issuing all types of licenses and foreign exchange permits, save for municipalities, state budget linked entities and certain other residents, which are under licensing authority of Ministry of Finance.

Nonresidents are also restricted, especially in foreign exchange values and currency sale/purchase deals, to concluding such deals with foreign exchange licensees. It is always advisable for nonresidents to determine whether they or their Slovak counterparts need foreign exchange permit prior to concluding transaction which may trigger applicability of Act. Nonresidents are strictly restricted in acquiring real estate in SR, with exemption of specific cases determined in Act. Local subsidiaries of nonresidents are under specific pricing regime in connection with acquiring of real estate. Each transfer to such entity could be effected only for professionally estimated price according to western standards accordingly applied. Such price is furthermore subject to approval by Ministry of Finance.

Import and exports of banknotes and coins in excess of specific limit are also restricted regardless of type of their import or export.

FOREIGN INVESTMENTS:

ObchZ (Commercial Code) provides foreign entities with same conditions for conducting business activities as Slovak entities, unless law stipulates otherwise. Foreign persons authorized to conduct business activities according to foreign law are considered entrepreneurs under ObchZ. Any foreign person may become founder of Slovak legal entity or become sole partner in any Slovak entity.

Any foreign person's property connected with business activities in SR may be expropriated or its ownership limited, only on basis of law or in public interest provided there is no other alternative. It is possible to appeal decision to Court. Foreign person shall receive compensation in foreign currency without undue delay in full value which is freely transferable abroad.

Pursuant to Decree of the Ministry of Finance of SR No. 261/1993 Coll., import customs are not paid for delivery of technology as in-kind contributions (excluding cars and things used for lotteries and similar activities) to registered capital of company having in its scope of business activities manufacturing activities. Share of foreign entity in registered capital must be at least 35%, in-kind contribution must be at least 10 million SKK and relevant technology may not be used and be older one year.

SR is part of Washington Convention on Resolving Disputes Arising from Investment between States and Citizens of other States (Mar. 18, 1965) and several bilateral treaties on foreign investment protection.

See also topics Foreign Exchange, Treaties.

FOREIGN TRADE REGULATIONS:

Companies, individual entrepreneurs and other entities registered in Commercial Register in SR may perform foreign trade activities to extent of business activities for which they are licensed. Interventions of State regulated by Act No. 42/1980 Coll. after several amendments, especially by Nos. 113/1990 Coll. and 513/1991 Coll. have substantially been reduced. Decree No. 302/1995 Coll. of Ministry of Economy on conditions of granting export and import licenses for goods and services as amended, stipulates duties of applicants for import and export of certain goods as defined in attachments to Act.

See also topics Customs Duties, Foreign Exchange, Foreign Investments, Treaties, Sales.

FRAUD:

No general statute requiring writing in transactions. See requirements for written documents in appropriate topics, e.g., Corporations, Labor Relations, Wills, Contracts, Real Property, etc.

FRAUDULENT SALES AND CONVEYANCES:

Under OZ (Civil Code), any legal act shall be deemed invalid if made by party acting in error based in fact which was decisive for party's decision to make legal act, provided that person being addressee of legal act either induced error or was aware of it. Decisive nature of relevant fact does not have to be proved, if error was deliberately induced by addressee of legal act. Decision whether legal act shall be invalid as consequence of error on side of acting party belongs to Courts (or arbitration if agreed by arbitration clause).

Generally under OZ (without it being necessary to wait for bankruptcy proceeding), creditor may demand that Court determine that legal acts adversely affecting satisfaction of its enforceable receivable shall not be effective against creditor. Only legal acts which have been made in intention to harm its creditors, if intention must have been known to counterparts in legal act, can be invalidated provided it was made not earlier than three years before affected creditor brings court proceeding. Also, legal acts made with relatives of debtor may be contested under similar conditions. Affected creditor who invalidates legal act may satisfy claim from debtor's assets or may claim compensation from party which benefited from contested legal act.

In connection with bankruptcy proceedings, any fraudulent sales and conveyances are subject to invalidation as well. Bankruptcy Act provides that creditor may apply to Court to annul acts performed by debtor within previous three years with intention of curtailing creditors' rights and if intention was known to other party, or acts which resulted in curtailment of creditors' rights and involve debtor and persons close to debtor in legal sense. This provision presents problem when creditor comes to agreement with debtor on repayment of its debts and then another creditor files petition for bankruptcy within three years, as agreement between debtor and original creditor may be set aside. If agreement is set aside, any benefit creditor had obtained would have to be paid back into bankrupt's estate and creditor would then rank as ordinary unsecured creditor in relation to proceeds.

GARNISHMENT:

Although "garnishment" is not expressly defined as term in Slovak law, it is used in some execution methods if basis of execution is execution title imposing liability to pay any financial amount. Such execution methods are: (a) withholding payments from wage and other incomes; (b) notice of appropriation of receivable. Notice of appropriation of receivable notice of appropriation of bank account, or notice of appropriation of other receivables in money can be used. In respect to withholding payments from wage according to Governmental Decree No. 16/1983 Coll. amount of 450 SKK per month cannot be subject to garnishment. Additional amounts of 150 SKK per person (if dependent on debtor for its subsistence) are excluded from garnishment.

See also topic Executions.

HOLIDAYS:

Holidays in SR are regulated by Act No. 241/1993 Coll. on State Holidays, Non-Business Days and Memorial Days, as amended.

According to Act, Legal State Holidays are: Jan. 1 (New Years Day, hereby Independence Day), July 5 (Holiday of Slavic Faith Messengers—St. Cyril and Methodius), Aug. 29 (Slovak National Uprising day), Sept. 1 (Day of Constitution).

Non-Business Days are following: Jan. 6 (Corpus Christi Day), Good Friday (last Fri. before Easter Monday), Easter Monday, May 1 (Labor Day), May 8 (Victory Day), Sept. 15 (Septuadolorous Virgin Mary), Nov. 1 (All Saints' Day), Dec. 24, 25, 26 (Christmas Days).

HUSBAND AND WIFE:

Rights, duties and powers of husband and wife are regulated by ZR (Family Act) and OZ (Civil Code).

Husband and wife have equal rights and duties in marriage. They have legal duty of common life, faithfulness, helping each other, creating healthy family environment, personal care of children, and other duties. Husband and wife decide about family matters jointly and if they disagree in essential matters, Court makes decision upon petition of either spouse.

Common matters concerning things jointly owned by spouses may be handled by either of spouses. In other matters, consent of both spouses is required, otherwise legal act is relatively invalid.

Anything acquired by either of spouses during their marriage which may be object of ownership is subject to undivided co-ownership of spouses except things acquired by one spouse before marriage or acquired during marriage by inheritance or gift, as well as things which by their nature serve personal needs or occupation purposes of one of spouses as well as things which on basis of restitution were returned to one of spouses.

Both spouses jointly entitled to use and enjoyment of all things in their undivided co-ownership; spouses also jointly cover expenses on those things or those connected with their use and maintenance. Spouses may by agreement recorded in form of notarial deed widen or restrict extent of their undivided co-ownership. Similarly, they can also make agreements on management of their joint property.

Dissolution of marriage also dissolves undivided co-ownership of spouses. For important reasons, upon petition of either spouse, Court may dissolve undivided co-ownership of spouses even during marriage. If co-ownership is dissolved, settlement of it shall be effected by agreement of spouses, or by Court upon petition of either spouse.

HUSBAND AND WIFE . . . *continued*

Conflict of Laws.—Court will apply law of State of which spouses are citizens in any disputes relating to personal and property relations of spouses. If spouses are citizens of different states, Slovak Court will apply law of SR.

IMMIGRATION:

Foreigners visiting and staying in SR must obtain visas. Visas granted by Slovak diplomatic missions or consular offices. Citizens from most Western European countries, U.S.A. and some other countries are exempt from visa requirement for period of 30 to 90 days according to relevant international agreements. Any foreigner may be permitted to stay in territory of SR for short term (maximum 180 days), long term (maximum one year) or permanent stay. For permission for long or permanent stay to be granted, foreigner is obliged to submit documents stating aim of stay, resources for stay, accommodation and documents stating that foreigner did not commit abroad or in territory of SR any willful crime, that foreigner has no infectious disease. Any foreigner required to have visa or if foreigner's stay will last longer than 30 days, or if permanent stay permitted, is obliged to report to police office beginning, address of stay and estimated period of stay in territory of SR. Local Police Department is responsible for agenda of foreigner's stay.

According to Act No. 283/1995 Coll. on refugees, foreigner is granted status of refugee if there are serious reasons to believe that foreigner is persecuted in foreigner's homeland because of religion, race, social status, etc. Refugees have same rights as Slovak citizens, unless stated otherwise in special regulations. Employment of foreigners and refugees is governed by special Act No. 1/1991 Coll. on employment, as amended. Acquisition of Slovak citizenship is governed by Act No. 40/1993 Coll. on citizenship of SR. Any foreigner may obtain Slovak citizenship following application provided that foreigner is permanent resident in territory of SR for no less than five years, foreigner was not sentenced for willful crime for period of five years, and knowledge of Slovak language is proved. Notwithstanding above-mentioned, Slovak citizenship can be granted to any person married to Slovak citizen. Any persons up to 18 years of age follow citizenship of their parents. Any Slovak citizen may have more foreign citizenships.

INDUSTRIAL PROPERTY RIGHTS AND PATENTS:

Issues of patents, inventions, industrial designs, and innovations are stipulated in Act No. 527/1990 Coll. covering also registration of industrial designs and innovations. Act also contains essential regulations governing proceedings before Industrial Property Right Office. SR has been, in standard way, engaged in international cooperation in field of registering and protecting patent rights. Slovakia is deemed to be party to Paris Convention for protection of industrial property, as amended by latest revisions, Strasbourg Agreement on international patent classification, Locarno Agreement on establishment of international classification of industrial designs and models, and Budapest Agreement on international recognition of depositing microorganisms for purposes of patent proceedings.

Patents are granted to any inventions which are new, are results of inventing activities, and are industrially exploitable. Any invention is new if it does not form part of state of technology. State of technology is everything which had existed prior to date from which innovator has priority right published in SR or in any other country. Patent owner has exclusive right to use invention, to grant approval to use invention to any third persons or to transfer patent to any third persons. Patent is valid for period of 20 years from filing application.

Industrial design is deemed to be any external layout of product which is new and industrially exploitable. Any industrial design is industrially exploitable if products can be repeatedly made according to design. Industrial design is registered in register of industrial designs. Industrial design owner has exclusive right to use industrial design, to grant approval for using industrial design to any third persons or to transfer industrial design to any third persons. Registration of industrial design is valid for period of five years from date of filing application and term may be extended for two additional five year terms.

Innovations are deemed to be any technical, manufacturing or operational developments as well as solutions of problems of labor safety and health protection and living environment which may be disposed by innovator. No rights from any innovation shall arise if prevented by any rights arising from patent or registered industrial design. Right to use any innovation shall arise by entering into agreement with innovator on accepting offer for innovation and receiving consideration for same.

Any foreign person has, in respect of patent law, same rights and liabilities as Slovak person under terms of reciprocity.

In Slovak law, patent rights' owner is protected by basic Act No. 527/1990 Coll. according to which owner may claim that any infringement of right be prohibited and that any consequences of infringement be removed. Owner has right to be indemnified against any actual damage and lost profit. He also has right to reasonable satisfaction both in cash and in kind. Additional protection is stipulated in ObchZ where unfair competition results from imitating any other products, their packings, or performances. Patent rights' owner has, according to ObchZ, right to demand that any infringer refrain from wrongful acts and to remove any wrongful condition. At same time, owner has right to receive reasonable satisfaction which may be claimed in money, liquidated damages, and recovery of any unjustifiable enrichment. Criminal Law specifies as criminal act any infringement of rights pertaining to protected invention, industrial design, applied design, or topography of semiconductor product. Any offender may be sentenced to imprisonment up to three years or fine up to 5 million SKK, and forfeiture.

INFANTS:

Both males and females reach majority at age of 18. Prior to this time, majority can only be attained by conclusion of marriage. Once majority is attained by conclusion of conclusion of marriage, person's majority is not lost by termination of marriage, or by its being pronounced invalid.

See also topic Marriage.

Minors possess capacity to perform only such legal acts which by their nature are suitable to intellectual and volitional maturity corresponding to their age. Minors under 15 do not have penal responsibility. Persons from 15 to 18 from penal point of view are juvenile delinquents.

Infant can be represented by either or both parents, provided parents have full legal capacity, or have not been deprived of their parental rights. Neither parent can represent children in legal acts involving conflict of interests (e.g. contractual property transfer) between parents and children or between children. If parents cannot represent child by reason of death, deprivation of parental rights, lack of legal capacity or conflict of interests Court will appoint curator of infant. Curator is responsible to Court and is subordinated to Court supervision. Any decision of curator concerning relevant matter of infant is subject to approval of Court.

Conflict of Laws.—According to Act No. 97/1963 Coll., relations between parents and children, including education and support of children, under conflict of laws are subject to law of state of which child is citizen. If child is living in SR, this relations can be regulated by Slovak law, if it is in interest of child.

Commencement and termination of curatorship are regulated by law of State of which infant is citizen. Duty to perform curatorship is regulated by law of curator's State. Relations between infant and curator are subject to law of State whose Court or competent body appointed curator.

INSOLVENCY:

See topic Bankruptcy.

JUDGMENTS:

Enforceability of Foreign Judgments.—In absence of international treaty which would provide otherwise, judgment duly obtained in Courts of jurisdiction other than SR ("other jurisdiction") will be enforceable in SR only if relevant Court in SR is satisfied that: (a) enforcement will be not contrary to public policy in SR; (b) judgment was not in respect of matter of which only Courts of SR could decide; (c) judgment was not in respect of matter of which Courts of SR have already decided; and (d) notice of process had been given to defendant in action and defendant had been given opportunity to appear before Courts of other jurisdiction.

LABOR RELATIONS:

ZP (Labor Code) was extensively modified to create better conditions for more practical, realistic labor relations after 1989. Prime effect of these changes was to restrict rights of employees which were extremely broad, however, ZP Code still contains concept of "the right to work", but it has been fundamentally weakened by changes.

Employment Contract.—Principal means of creating employment relationship under ZP is contract. There is no overall restriction on right to create employment relationship other than general prohibition on discrimination. Basic principle, as in other jurisdictions, is that employee will carry out lawful instructions of employer in return for wages. Parties to contract must agree upon job description, place of work and date on which employment commences. If contract is for fixed term, this term cannot exceed three years. Otherwise contract is deemed to be of indefinite duration, terminable on notice upon happening of limited range of termination events. It is also possible for there to be fixed probationary period of three months during which either party is free to terminate contract without giving reasons for doing so. Such period cannot normally be extended.

Where appropriate, contents of collective bargaining agreements are statutorily implied into individual contracts of employment. Therefore, simple written contract of employment is unlikely to contain complete terms of employment.

In SR, contract of employment can be amended by mutual consent. However, ZP heavily restricts ability of employer to require employees to cooperate with commercial imperative of flexibility. It would therefore appear that the clearer the job description, the less flexible employee will be.

Reassignment.—In certain circumstances, employer can reassign employee to new duties. This may arise where offer of alternative employment is made when employee's original job becomes redundant or where employee is incapacitated and unable to perform usual duties. Unilateral reassignment is also permitted in interests of disaster relief or "urgent operational necessity". However, no unilateral reassignment may last for more than 30 days. Employer may also be obliged to reassign employee, for example, where health of employee is threatened by nature of duties.

Hours of Work.—There are also restrictions on number of hours which may be worked per week. Working hours may not exceed 43 per week and in some particularly arduous or hazardous occupations, maximum figure may be lower. Overtime is permitted but may not exceed eight hours per week. Concept of compulsory overtime is frowned upon.

Holiday entitlements are also prescribed by law. Employees (save for employees in state sector having one more week and certain specific categories of employees) are entitled to four weeks of paid leave per annum increasing to five after 15 years' service.

Termination.—Employment contract may be terminated by mutual agreement in writing. Expiry of fixed term contract is also valid form of termination, as is expiry date of relevant work permit where foreigner is employed. Summary termination by employee allowed in case of serious health reasons of employee confirmed by medical statement or if employer did not pay salary within 15 days of its maturity. Summary termination by employer is only option in limited circumstances, i.e., where employee has committed serious criminal offense, is guilty of gross misconduct, or has failed to complete probationary period satisfactorily. Termination must take place within one month of date on which employer first became aware of misconduct or, in case of criminal offense, of sentence. Notwithstanding that, dismissal must take place within 12 months of event that triggers it. There is statutory minimum notice period of two months. Right to minimum notice accrues to employee on termination of probationary period. Notice takes effect by reference to complete calendar months only.

Employer may terminate contract by notice in cases defined by ZP. Main ones are: (1) where dismissal is necessitated by some urgent operational necessities; (2) where employee suffers from illness or disability which prevents employee from performing

LABOR RELATIONS . . . *continued*
duties; (3) where employee, having been warned within last 12 months that performance is deficient, fails to improve; (4) where employee, having been warned within last six months that conduct must improve, commits further acts of misconduct; and (5) where employer's undertaking is transferred to third party which has no work for employee to do.

There are, however, numerous conditions to be satisfied by employer before it can terminate by notice.

Additionally, employer may give notice if employee's post becomes redundant. Concept of redundancy is very narrowly defined in SR and principally describes situations where employer's undertaking ceases to exist or physically relocates. Employer is under obligation to attempt to find alternative work for employee within undertaking. Failing that, employer is obliged to assist State (through local employment office) to find new job for employee.

Where employee is single parent of child under age of three and employment is that household's only source of income, employer appears to be under absolute duty to ensure employee finds alternative employment and notice of termination is deemed not to have expired until that is achieved. Employee's right to wages continues until that time. In some circumstances, such employee will be entitled to redundancy payment of up to five months' pay, as well as to statutory minimum notice.

Foreign Workers.—Labor relations between workers and foreign employers on territory of SR, as well as labor relations between foreigners working in territory of SR and domestic employers are subject to ZP, ZMPSP does not stipulate otherwise. Labor relations of employees of international organization with headquarters in territory of SR established by international treaties, are subject to ZP, unless such treaties or other international conventions stipulate otherwise. Labor relations of employees of enterprises with foreign capital participation and organizations with international element with headquarters in territory of SR are subject to ZP, unless such employees work and reside in territory of same foreign country; in such case their labor relations are governed by governing law stipulated by provisions of ZMPSP.

Liability for Damage.—ZP regulates liability for damages and injury caused in connection with employment relationship. This liability can apply to both employer and employee. ZP also covers special kinds of liabilities, e.g. liability of employer for damage caused by employee carrying out duties. These responsibilities are controlled very strictly and are monitored by special State administrative bodies which can impose penalties when laws are broken.

Trade Unions.—Communist Revolutionary Trade Union Movement, which was arm of State and Communist Party, was dissolved in 1990. Elementary changes have been made in area of work of trade unions, not only those concerning organization of work, but also in program objectives. It has been replaced by pluralist movement which has developed from ground up. Amendments to ZP represent legal modification of status and position of trade unions and authorities, change in labor relations in case of private enterprises and in relations between trade unions and employers. One of basic roles of trade unions is to organize participation of workers in preparation, application and maintenance of labor law regulations. Trade unions also exercise control over maintenance of internal salary structures and over obligations under collective bargaining agreements which affect individual workers.

Social Security.—Employers must pay contributions to social security fund, health insurance fund and employment fund at rate of 38% of payroll, and employees must pay contributions at rate of 12% of their salaries. There are, however, certain caps over social security payments.

LAW REPORTS, CODES ETC.:

According to Act No. 1/1993 Coll., generally binding legal regulations, Constitution, constitutional laws, governmental decrees, decrees of ministries and other central governmental bodies, some decisions of Constitutional Court are published in Collection of Laws. Moreover, some central governmental bodies issue their own Bulletins including regulations from specific areas of their activities. Business Journal according to governmental Decree No. 100/1993 Coll. includes information which must be published according to ObchZ, information about bankruptcy procedures and other information if stipulated by particular laws (e.g. Act No. 21/1992 Coll. on banks).

Collection of Decisions of the Constitutional Court is issued every year. Moreover, Collection of Decisions and Statements of the Courts of SR is issued by Supreme Court. It should be noted that decisions of Courts (excluding Constitutional Court) are not source of Slovak law in common law sense.

LEGISLATURE:

National Council of SR is only constitutional legislative body of SR. Acts are adopted by absolute majority of deputies, provided absolute majority of all of deputies is present. Constitution and constitutional acts are adopted by at least three-fifths majority of all deputies. National Council is continually in session which is suspended by means of resolution for no longer than four months.

Referendum on important issues of public interest may be requested by National Council or petition of at least 350,000 citizens. Fundamental rights and freedoms, taxes, levies and state budget are not allowed to be subject of any referendum.

Generally binding acts are published in Collection of Laws, entering into force 15 days after date of publication, unless provided otherwise.

LICENSES:

For carrying on any trade activities, Trade License is required to be obtained according to Trade Licensing Act No. 455/1991 Coll., as amended. However, there are some activities excluded from Trade Licensing Act (see subhead Trade Licensing Procedure, infra).

Trade Licensing Procedure.—Trade Licensing Act classifies trades into two categories, notifiable trades and trades requiring concession. Which category trade falls into is set out in annex to Act. Notifiable trades are further split into categories as follows: (i) craftsmanship trades (whereby professional skills reached upon artisan training form is precondition to authorization to carry on this trade), (ii) trades requiring evidence of professional skills (whereby professional skills that do not relate to craftsmanship trades form are precondition to authorization to carry on this trade), (iii) free trades (whereby no professional skills are required). Where trade is notifiable, it must be notified to trade licensing office local to proposed place of business. If stipulated conditions are satisfied local trade licensing office issues trade license. In case of concession, local trade licensing office requires standpoint or approval of specific state bodies. Legal persons must appoint authorized representative, if they intend to perform any trade other than free trade. Authorized representative of physical person must be appointed, if physical person fails to meet conditions prescribed for desired trade, person is not Slovak resident or trade is performed in more than one workplace. Entrepreneur must report to local licensing office all changes concerning facts mentioned in trade license. Relevant Trade Licensing Authorities may impose sanctions for violation of this Act or for practicing any trades without license.

Special Licensing Procedures.—Governmental entrepreneurial activities excluded from Trade License Act require license granted by special state authority following satisfaction of special requirements such as technical (special facilities required), organizational and material, personal, financial (minimum required capital), documentary, and other. These activities include law, accountancy, translating and interpreting, professional appraising and medicine, mining, insurance, banking, operations of stock exchange, business of investment funds and companies, radio and television broadcasting. In some specific cases entrepreneur can carry out profession legally only as member of professional organization (e.g. advocates).

LIENS:

Slovak law recognizes number of instruments securing debtor's obligations. Although there is no overall definition or joint name, for ease of reference these may be all called liens. Following liens may be available to creditors in Slovak legal system: There are following types of security generally recognized in Slovak legal system: (1) Guarantees—(a) general, (b) bank and (c) state; (2) pledges—(a) immovables, (b) movables, (c) receivables and (d) securities; (3) fiduciary assignments of receivables; (4) fiduciary transfer of rights; (5) contractual penalty; and (6) retention right.

Guarantee is general instrument governed by OZ, taken in form of written declaration of guarantor upon which guarantor declares obligation to satisfy creditor's receivable should debtor fail to do so. Future or conditional obligation of debtor can be secured by guarantee. Generally, in nonbanking guarantees, accessory and subsidiary principle applies under which it is required that debtor fails to perform despite creditor's demand for such performance. Guarantor whose guarantee was called and used has right to require compensation from debtor. Bank guarantee is specific type of guarantee governed by ObchZ which can be given by bank as guarantor. Bank's obligation could be linked with either debtor's failure to fulfill certain obligation or occurrence of any predetermined condition. Confirmation of bank guarantee by another bank constitutes joint and several obligation of both banks. More flexible nature of bank guarantee allows various conditions of availability of guarantee. It is not necessary that debtor fail in fulfillment of duty prior to guarantee enforcement, so accessory and subsidiary principle is inapplicable in connection with bank guarantees. In certain circumstances governmental guarantees may be available to secure creditor's rights under loan agreements. Availability of governmental guarantees is limited by type of entity eligible to be guaranteed debtor and restricted by nature of project so that proceeds of loan must be used for project financing that is included in development program approved by governmental resolution. (OZ, §§546-550, ObchZ, §§303-322).

Pledges.—See topics Mortgage; Pledges.

Fiduciary Assignment of Receivables.—Fiduciary assignment of receivable is instrument based on assignment generally, with reservation that assignment is not definite because it only secures underlying receivable. Once such receivable is settled assignee must assign back receivable which was fiduciary-assigned. (OZ, §554).

Fiduciary Transfer of Rights.—Written agreement is required. OZ does not generally limit scope of rights that may be subject to fiduciary transfer. It is stipulated that only debtor may offer fiduciary transfer of rights and no third party is allowed to secure creditor's right against debtor, other than debtor. As transfer is of fiduciary nature, it ceases to exist upon fulfillment of underlying receivable. (OZ, §553).

Contractual Penalty.—Parties to contract are allowed to agree on contractual penalty. Generally, contractual penalty concept is governed by OZ. Under this arrangement party that breaches its contractual duty is obliged to pay penalty although breach did not result in damage to another party. However, compensation of damages could be claimed in addition to contractual penalty only if it was agreed between parties. Contractual penalty must be agreed in writing including its fixed amount or method of its calculation. Unless agreed otherwise, receipt of payment of contractual penalty does not mean waiver of obligation that was secured by contractual penalty arrangement. In commercial relations, certain provisions of ObchZ are applicable under which Court may in its discretion reduce amount of contractual penalty, if it finds penalty unreasonably high, taking into account volume and importance of secured obligation. (OZ, §§544-545, ObchZ, §§300-302).

Retention right is instrument recognized by OZ, applicable to persons who are under obligation to deliver movable asset to another party. Such movable delivery could be withheld as security over due receivable of person otherwise obliged to deliver movable. (OZ, §§151s-151v).

MARRIAGE:

According to ZR marriage is concluded on basis of voluntary consent to create harmonic, consistent and continual life union of man and woman. Declaration of consent of fiancées can be made before competent governmental authority or church authority recognized by State. Two witnesses are required for validity of marriage. Citizens concluding marriage are obliged to submit specified documents and declare that no circumstances are known to them which might exclude them from entering into marriage and that they are aware of health conditions of each other. They also must declare which of their surnames will be their joint surname, or to decide to use their original surnames.

See Topical Index in front part of this volume.

MARRIAGE . . . *continued*

There are some circumstances prohibiting conclusion of marriage. No marriage can be concluded by: (a) married man or married woman, (b) relatives of direct lineage, siblings, also relatives by adoption, if adoption still exists, (c) minors (citizens under 18 years), (d) any person whose mental defect could reduce legal capacity, as consequence. Court will pronounce any marriage under (a), (b) to be invalid. Court can permit marriage under (d), if health conditions of citizen comply with social purposes of marriage. Marriage between minors under 18, older than 16, can also be permitted by court due to important reasons (e.g. pregnancy of woman, etc.). Marriage between minors under 16 is void.

No limitations exist in respect of conclusion of marriage between any foreigner and any Slovak citizen.

See also topics Divorce; Husband and Wife.

MINES AND MINERALS:

According to Constitution of SR, raw materials (including oil and natural gas), underground waters, natural springs and water streams are property of SR. Act No. 44/1988 Coll., as amended on protection and use of mineral resources and Act No. 51/1988 Coll., as amended on mining activities, explosives and administration govern conditions for extraction and protection of mineral resources (excluding mineral waters, turf, sand). There are two main groups of minerals: (a) reserved, (b) unreserved. Unreserved minerals are part of land. For extraction of minerals license for mining activities must be issued by Local Mining Authority. Also, for any research activities permission is necessary. Permission for mining activities stipulates conditions for extraction and area of activities. There are royalty payments for extractions up to 10% of price of mineral or of mineral after initial proceeding set down by governmental decree. Person doing mining activities is responsible for all damages to other person caused by activity.

MONOPOLIES AND RESTRAINT OF TRADE:

Unfair business practices of entrepreneurs are prohibited in ObchZ and in Act No. 188/1994 Coll. on protection of economic competition ("Competition Act").

ObchZ prohibits any unauthorized use of business name, false advertising, deceptive labeling of goods and services, misuse of names and labelings, parasitic exploitation of company's reputation, bribery, discrediting, violation of business secrets, endangering health and environment. Consumer's rights impaired by unfair competition can also be defended by organizations protecting interests of consumers.

Competition Act stipulates other forms of unlawful restrictions of competition and concentration, which are as follows: (i) agreements restricting competition, (ii) abuse of dominant position in market, (iii) concentration. Antimonopoly Office of SR (hereinafter referred to as "Office") is governmental authority entitled to decide in relation to provisions of Competition Act.

Any agreements having as their object or effect restriction of competition are prohibited. They can involve direct or indirect fixing of prices, commitment to limit or control production, division of market, commitment by parties to agreement that different conditions of trade will be applied to individual entrepreneurs, conditions that conclusion of contracts will require acceptance of supplementary obligations. Abovementioned agreements are void. Agreements for transfer of rights or grant of licenses over inventions, trademarks, industrial designs, etc., can stipulate restrictions on competition if necessary for safeguarding of existence of these rights. Prohibition of agreements restricting competition do not apply if they contribute to improving production or distribution of goods or promoting technical progress, if they allow share of resulting benefits to users and if they do not impose on parties to agreement any restrictions not indispensable to attainment of above-mentioned objectives.

Dominant position in market is held by entrepreneur which is not subject to substantial competition. This position is presumed if entrepreneur's share in supply or purchase of identical goods in relevant market is at least 40%. Abuse of dominant position is in particular enforcement of disproportionate conditions in contracts, restricting production, sale or technological progress, applying different conditions for equal or comparable transactions to individual entrepreneurs resulting in competitive disadvantage, making conclusion of contract conditional upon another party accepting conditions unrelated to subject of contract.

Concentration (merger, amalgamation or acquiring control) is subject to control regime of Office, if turnover of participants of concentration is at least 300 million SKK and at least two of participants of concentration achieved turnover of at least 100 million SKK for previous accounting time period or if joint market share of participants of concentration exceeds 20% of total turnover in identical market in SR. Combined turnover or joint share as mentioned above shall be total of turnovers of (a) participants of concentration, (b) entrepreneurs, in which participant of concentration owns more than half capital, or has power to control or manage enterprise, (c) entrepreneur who owns or has rights described in part (b) in enterprise of participant of concentration, (d) all other entrepreneurs in which entrepreneur mentioned in part (c) owns or has rights described in part (b). On basis of notification of concentration, Office will issue decision prohibiting or permitting concentration. Concentration is prohibited if it impairs economic competition. Consumers whose rights have been violated by unlawful restriction of competition may require violating party to remedy breach. Office is entitled to fine entrepreneurs for breaching duties stipulated by Competition Act up to 10% of their turnover for previous accounting year and, if it is impossible to calculate turnover, up to 10 million SKK.

MORTGAGE:

Although "mortgage" is not expressly defined as term in Slovak legislation, some acts, in particular Banking Act No. 62/1996 Coll. and Bond Act No. 530/1990 Coll., as amended use mortgage as term specifying loans, banks, deals, bonds, always linked with security in real estate. Thus, mortgage may be defined, for purposes of comparison with other law, as lien on real estate.

General provisions on mortgages are laid down in OZ, in part dealing with liens generally, without specific definition, however with specific legally relevant details. Leading principle of mortgages, like all other liens, is to secure receivable and its accessories so that, should obligor fail to perform, creditor is entitled to be satisfied in rights from pledged asset, in case of mortgages from pledged real estate.

Instruments constituting mortgage are (i) written agreement, (ii) approved inheritance settlement; (iii) operation of law (e.g. decision of tax authority or customs authority to secure payments of taxes or custom duties). For purpose of effectiveness of any mortgage, registration with regionally competent land registry office is necessary. Land registry approves registration upon written application with all necessary enclosures including proof of title of mortgagor and pledge agreement. Relevant land registry should decide within 30 days of receiving complete application.

Agreement creating mortgage must be specific concerning subject of mortgage and secured receivable. Security in form of mortgage may be given for liability which will arise in future, or which is contingent.

In connection with ranking of two or more mortgages over one and same immovable, principle "first in time, first in right" applies, with priority always given to oldest registered mortgage, unless specific law stipulates otherwise. Example of such specific law may be found in Banking Act, according to which mortgages securing mortgage loans rank prior to any other mortgage or lien.

Mortgage loans are defined in Banking Act as long-term loans secured by mortgage, given by mortgage bank to borrowers for purposes of construction, reconstruction and maintenance of real estate, funded through issue and sale of mortgage bonds by mortgage bank. System is entirely new in Slovakia and is intended to work so that mortgage bonds are covered by receivables originating from mortgage loans, up to 60% of value of mortgaged immovables.

Mortgage exercise concept is based on sale of mortgaged assets and use of proceeds against debt. Potential positive balance of sale is paid to debtor.

MOTOR VEHICLES:

Driving license is required to drive motor vehicle in SR. Drivers must be sufficiently able-bodied and well-balanced, and minimum age of 18 years. They must also pass examination consisting of knowledge of road traffic regulations, knowledge of motor vehicles including their maintenance, and driving test. Licenses are issued by departments of police and are valid for lifetime.

Aliens may drive motor vehicles in SR on basis of valid home country license, if license of home country corresponds to form under Geneva Agreement on Road Traffic (1949) but for maximum of six months. In other cases, aliens may drive motor vehicle on basis of international driving license.

Only vehicles which satisfy technical operational standards required pursuant to valid legal regulation may be used in traffic in SR. Certificates of technical ability are issued by offices governed by Ministry of Transport, Posts and Telecommunications of SR. Vehicles driven in SR are subject to registration under state identification number which must be located in front and back parts of vehicle and may not be removed or damaged.

Insurance of motor vehicles for liability for injury or damages is mandatory and regulated by Decree of Ministry of Finance No. 423/1991 Coll.

See also topic Taxation.

NOTARIES PUBLIC:

Notaries and their activities are governed by Act No. 323/1992 Coll., as amended. Notaries are appointed by Minister of the Justice of SR following selection procedure for unlimited period of time. Notaries take oath administered by Minister, who also exercises state supervision over notaries. Notaries must be Slovak citizens, possess civil integrity, have university degree of law, complete five year apprentice period, and pass examination. There is obligatory membership in Chamber of Notaries, which is self-governed professional organization entitled to create its own bodies and to impose sanctions for violation of law of professional ethics. Notaries have seat in circuit of Court which appointed them.

Notaries exercise following activities: issue documents, perform property administration, verify authenticity of signatures and authenticity of copies of official documents, certify important facts, deposit documents and money, provide legal advice. Notaries can employ notarial candidates who are also registered at Chamber of Notaries. Some of above-mentioned activities may also be performed by notary employee or notarial candidate. Notarial fees are stipulated by decree of Ministry of Justice.

Role of Notaries in Estate Proceedings.—Activities of notaries as Court commissioners in estate proceedings are stipulated both in general provisions of OSP and special provisions of c. 5, part 3 of OSP. Notaries are authorized to do certain acts in estate proceedings according to schedule issued by chairman of Regional Court for each calendar year upon proposal of Notarial Chamber.

In cases stipulated by law, when there are no conflicts existing between heirs in respect of decedent's assets or manner of distributing estate, estate proceedings may be completed by executing certificate of heirship delivered to parties by notary acting in position of commissioner appointed by Court. Unless legal conditions for executing certificate are fulfilled, or unless notary has been authorized by Court to execute certificate of heirship, or unless agreement is reached among heirs as to distribution of estate, notary shall prepare all necessary documents for Court to issue resolution and proposal for Court's resolution.

PATENTS:

See topics Industrial Property Rights and Patents; Copyright.

PLEDGES:

Pledge can be established with written agreement. For validity and effectiveness of pledge, however, in most cases, further steps must be taken varying upon nature of pledged assets. General provisions on pledges are laid out in OZ (Civil Code). ObchZ (Commercial Code) applicable in commercial relations also includes provision enabling parties to agree upon faster enforcement procedure, which in practice is smoothly applicable only to movables.

Instruments constituting pledge may be (i) written agreement, (ii) approved inheritance settlement; (iii) operation of law (e.g. decision of tax authority or customs authority to secure payments of taxes or custom duties). Further legal act is always

PLEDGES . . . *continued*
necessary to make pledge fully effective, as follows: (1) in case of real estate, its registration of mortgage with regionally competent land registry office; (2) movable, delivery to pledgee or custodian; (3) pledged receivable, notification to debtor of pledge; and (4) security, registration of pledge in Securities Center (in case of book-entered securities) or delivery of security to pledgee or custodian (in case of documentary securities).

Agreement creating pledge must be specific concerning subject of pledge and secured receivable. Therefore, any creation of floating charge in respect of any asset which cannot be specified precisely in time of execution of agreement is impossible.

Exercise of immovable, movable and securities pledges based on sale of pledged assets and use of proceeds against debt. Potential positive balance of sale is paid to debtor.

See also topics Mortgage; Liens.

PRESCRIPTION:

According to OZ (Civil Code) legitimate possessor shall become owner of thing if possessor retains possession for continuous period of three years in case of movable thing and ten years in case of immovable thing (real estate). Possession is legitimate if possessor controls thing, has will to manage thing like possessor's own property and possessor keeps thing in good faith. Period during which legal predecessor held thing shall be counted as part of above-mentioned period. Period is interrupted if owner claims ownership of thing. It is also possible to apply above-mentioned regulation to easements. Principle of prescription introduced in 1983; no prescription principle previously since 1964.

PRINCIPAL AND AGENT:

Representation exists on basis of law, by decision of state authority or on basis of power of attorney. If legal act which is intended to be performed on basis of power of attorney by agent is in writing or if power of attorney relates to two or more legal acts it must be made in writing. If attorney acts on behalf of represented person, rights and duties are binding upon person who gave power of attorney, unless attorney acts beyond limits set out by power of attorney. Attorney may authorize another person to act in attorney's place on behalf of principal if attorney is expressly authorized to do so by principal or if latter is legal entity. Power of attorney expires (i) by performance of act to which it was limited, (ii) by principal's cancellation, (iii) by attorney's cancellation, (iv) by death of attorney.

Mandate.—Regulation of mandate is contained in OZ, §§724-732 and in ObchZ, §§566-576.

OZ Regulation.—Under mandate ("príkazná zmluva"), mandatory undertakes to look after certain matter or to accomplish some other activity on behalf of mandator. Mandatory may deviate from mandator's directions only if it is essential to mandator's interests and if mandatory cannot obtain mandator's consent in time. Mandatory must perform mandate personally; if mandatory entrusts another person with performance of mandate mandatory is liable as if mandatory had performed mandate. If mandator permitted mandatory to appoint representative, or if this was necessary, mandatory is liable only for fault with regard to choice of mandatory's representatives. Mandator is obliged to pay remuneration to mandatory only if it was agreed upon or when it is customary in mandatory profession (e. g. attorneys). Remuneration is to be paid even when there is no result of mandatory's activity, unless failure was caused by mandatory's breach of obligation.

ObchZ Regulation.—As far as mandate ("mandátna zmluva") according to ObchZ is concerned, mandator's undertaking to pay to mandatory certain remuneration is essential part of contract. If mandatory's professional activities include making such arrangements, it shall be presumed that some remuneration has been agreed upon. Mandatory is not bound to arrange matter personally, unless contract provides otherwise. However, mandatory is responsible for performance of mandate if it is performed by person authorized by mandatory.

PRIVATIZATION:

National Property Fund of SR ("NPF"), established as special purpose legal entity by Slovak Parliament in 1991, plays key role in privatization process. NPF is entity to which privatized property is transferred before it becomes private, and has extensive powers in privatization process.

Different methods of privatization are recognized under Privatization Act No. 92/1991 Coll., as amended.

Standard methods of privatization include: (i) direct sales to predetermined purchasers; (ii) sales in public tenders; and (iii) sales in public auction.

Agreements executed between NPF and transferees in process of privatization through standard methods other than public auctions must include specific provisions having generally protective nature of NPF's rights, e.g., maturity of whole purchase price and maturity of each installment thereof; conditions for repudiation of sale contract by NPF as consequence of breach of obligations by transferee of privatized assets; restriction on lease contracts regarding privatized assets until payment of whole purchase price, save for any short term lease for period shorter than one year with notice period shorter than three months; and others.

Further restrictions and liabilities can be imposed on transferee of privatized assets directly by Privatization Law. Transferee can be obliged to enable inspection of privatized assets and accounting documents by NPF, to ask NPF for approval of further transfer, contribution to company, pledge of privatized assets or to use proceeds from transfer of privatized assets for settlement of liabilities towards NPF.

Direct sales have been used rather widely in practice by NPF in 1995 and in beginning of 1996. Majority of direct sales were management buy outs whereby managements agreed with NPF payment conditions providing for deferred payment of purchase price. In some cases it was agreed that NPF would waive some part of its entitlement to be paid purchase price if transferee fulfills certain obligations with respect to reinvestment of profits and further investments to privatized assets.

Public tenders have been also used in privatization process. These were cases when NPF intended to provide for best sale conditions combining several criteria, especially purchase price, payment conditions, obligatory investments, expansions of production and employment.

Sale through public auction may be used if purchase price would be sole criterion of sale of privatized assets, however, this method is not extensively applied.

Nonstandard Methods.—Voucher scheme of privatization, applied in first wave in former C.S.F.R., was modified in Slovakia in 1995. Principle of modification is that holders of voucher books are not entitled to acquire directly shares of privatized enterprises or to assign this entitlement to investment funds against issue of shares of investment funds because this original entitlement was changed to entitlement to acquire bonds issued by NPF in nominal value of 10,000 SKK.

Coupon is determined at rate equal to discount rate of National Bank of Slovakia. Interest is due on date of maturity of bonds is 31st Dec., 2000. However, right of bondholders to claim payment of interest and principal of bonds begins only after 31st Dec., 2001. Before maturity date, bonds may be used only for purposes specified in Privatization Act and are transferable only to certain persons determined in Act. Bonds are not guaranteed by SR. NPF is entitled to exercise call option to bonds any time before their maturity.

Following persons are entitled to acquire bonds before their maturity: (i) persons having liabilities to NPF related to privatization of NPF's assets; (ii) owners of houses against transfer of title to flat, or persons claiming such transfer of title from their relatives for purpose of such transfer; (iii) entities providing additional pension insurance or additional medical insurance; (iv) banks determined for restructuralisation by special regulations; (v) other persons if stipulated by special act.

Foreign investors may participate in all standard methods of privatization process. Non-standard methods are available to Slovak citizens.

REAL PROPERTY:

Ownership and rights connected with real property are registered with land registry ("kataster nehnutel'ností") which are kept by appropriate land registry office ("katastrálny úrad"). Land registry is public registry, and extracts and information are available upon request. According to Act No. 162/1996 Coll., rights connected with real estate are acquired at time of relevant entry of such right in land registry. If right connected with relevant real estate is acquired on basis of written agreement or foundation deed of company, land registry office reviews validity of such document, particularly right of participants to dispose of real property.

Acquisition of domestic real property by foreigners is limited by Foreign Exchange Act No. 202/1995 Coll. Any foreigner may acquire real property located in territory of SR only (i) by inheritance, (ii) for diplomatic representation of foreign state, (iii) if property acquired is held in undivided coownership of spouses or if real estate is acquired from spouse, siblings, parents, grandparents, (iv) if real property is exchanged for another real property already owned by foreigner, (v) if foreigner has preemption right because of coownership of real estate, (vi) if real estate is building which was built on ground already owned by foreigner, (vii) if stipulated by special laws (restitution, privatization).

Any company with foreign participation (either joint venture or wholly-owned subsidiary) incorporated and registered in SR can acquire real estate. In such case, property should be valued using professionally estimated price according to western standards and price is to be approved by Ministry of Finance of SR.

In addition to above-mentioned legal regulation, there is special law concerning ownership of apartments and office premises. (Act No. 182/1993 Coll., as am'd). Act stipulates procedure for transfer of ownership of apartments and office premises from municipalities to private owners, requirements to be met by relevant contracts, principles of pricing. There are provisions concerning establishment and functions of association of apartments and office premises owners, which may be formed in house.

Real estate can be expropriated only by law for purposes stipulated by law (public interest, building of infrastructure, etc.) and for fair compensation. Expropriation procedure is regulated in Act No. 50/1976 Coll. on territorial planning and construction rules. Procedure is carried out by state construction authority.

SALES:

Principal provisions on sale of goods are determined by §§409-470 of ObchZ (Commercial Code). Buyer acquires title to goods at time of delivery, however, parties may agree in writing on different time of acquisition of title. Retail sale is governed by OZ. (§§612-627).

Consumer Protection.—OZ (Civil Code) stipulates general conditions for consumer protection, setting down liability of seller or service provider for quality of product. Furthermore, Act No. 634/1992 Coll. on consumer protection stipulates more precise obligations of seller and service provider in relation to consumer. Sellers and others are prohibited from misleading consumer, especially by giving false, unproved, incomplete, misleading, ambiguous information or failing to inform customer about real conditions of products. Provisions of Act impose obligations to seller as follows: (a) to inform about conditions of products, method of use and maintenance of products, any dangers or risks linked with incorrect use or maintenance (if necessary with respect to nature of product, in form of written operation manual); this obligation cannot be avoided by claim that correct or necessary information has not been made available by producer, importer or supplier; (b) to provide for visible labeling of products with information on: (i) producer and importer or supplier, (ii) quantity, quality, date of production, expiration time, or if it is not reasonable to provide for such label, to prove such information upon request of supervisory authority; (c) not to remove or change product's label or other information provided by producer, importer or supplier; if above-mentioned information is given in writing, it must be in Slovak or Czech language.

Fines for breach of above-mentioned obligations may be imposed up to 500,000 SKK (approx. 16,000 USD), in case of repetition of breach up to 1,000,000 SKK (approx. 32,000 USD).

Special governmental authority, Slovak Commercial Inspection (Slovenská obchodná inšpekcia—SOI) is entitled to control compliance with this and connected regulations. SOI is also entitled to impose sanctions if law is violated. Act No. 150/1995 Coll. on food relates to food, cosmetics and tobacco products and stipulates some specific obligations of producers and sellers of these products. According to Act No.

See Topical Index in front part of this volume.

SALES . . . *continued*
181/1994 Coll. on protection of economic competition, consumer whose rights have been violated by unlawful restriction of competition may bring lawsuit and require violating party to refrain from behavior or to remedy breach.

Prices.—Pricing Act No. 18/1996 Coll. governs process of agreeing, regulating and supervising pricing in Slovakia. Act recognizes several levels and methods of state intervention in contractual freedom in pricing formation process. Each seller or supplier subject to this Act (there are several exclusions) must prepare and prove calculation of its prices, costs and margins, upon request of supervising authorities.

Ministry of Finance is entitled to regulate prices, if (i) any extraordinary situation occurs in market, (ii) market could be impaired due to underdeveloped competitive environment, (iii) it is required by public interest, consumer or market protection, (iv) in cases of natural monopolies.

General and standard methods of intervention are (i) stipulating prices as fixed, maximum or minimum prices; (ii) stipulating thresholds of allowed increase or reduction of price in certain time period or maximum ratio in which inputs could be projected in prices; (iii) stipulating notice periods compulsory for each price increase, or other regulation based on certain time elapsed; (iv) price moratorium.

For natural monopolies specific mechanisms are applicable, such as stipulating prices, tariffs and tariff conditions; stipulating binding conditions of production, delivery and purchase; or stipulating justified costs and appropriate profit margin (including investments) being capable of incorporation into prices and tariffs.

Applicable Law.—See topic Contracts.

Advertisement.—Act No. 220/1996 Coll. stipulates general definitions and requirements for advertisement. Act prohibits some kinds of advertisement e.g. misleading, violating principles of proper morals, abusing beliefs of consumers, their lack of knowledge or their lack of experience, containing information promoting violence, advertising products damaging human health or environment, advertising tobacco, alcohol (excluding beer) in TV and radio broadcasting, audiovisual works, on billboards and in periodical press.

TAXATION:

Tax system as stipulated by Act No. 212/1992 Coll. on tax system is composed of following taxes: (a) income tax, (b) value added tax (V.A.T.), (c) consumers taxes, (d) road tax, (e) tax on transfer of ownership of real estate, (f) real estate tax, (g) gift tax and inheritance tax, (h) taxes for protection of environment (currently not applicable).

Income tax.—This tax is governed by Act No. 286/1992 Coll., as amended. Corporate income tax is charged at rate of 40% on worldwide profits, i.e., worldwide income including capital gains less allowable expenditure. This applies to Slovak entities and branch offices of foreign entities. Corporate income tax is assessable on calendar year basis. Tax is payable either monthly, quarterly or annually depending on level of tax paid in preceding fiscal year. Foreign entities with permanent establishments in SR are subject to Slovak corporate income tax calculated on basis of income of permanent establishment and any other Slovak source income. Foreign entities having no permanent establishment in SR may still become subject to tax on Slovak source income if, for example, they derive income from commercial, technical or other consultancy activities in SR for period exceeding six months.

Any individual resident in SR is taxed on both domestic and foreign source income. Income tax is charged on most types of income including salaries, directors' fees, income from business activities and income from capital investment. Where income is employment income, employer must deduct tax at source. Minimum rate is 15% on income up to 60,000 SKK. Maximum rate where income exceeds 1,080,000 SKK is 367,200 SKK plus 42% on excess income over 1,080,000 SKK. Any individuals not resident in SR are subject to tax on Slovak source income.

Payments of interests, dividends and royalties are subject to following withholding tax: interest and other income of loans 25%; royalties and consultancy fees 25%; dividends and interests on bonds 15%, however, for residents, interest and other income of loans form part of general income, and are not subject to withholding tax.

Rates of withholding taxes for nonresidents may be reduced upon existence of double taxation treaty between SR and income recipient's country. SR is party to or has succeeded to treaties with, inter alia, following countries: The Netherlands, France, Finland, Belgium, Japan, Austria, Norway, Sweden, Cyprus, Spain, Denmark, Germany, Italy, Greece, Brazil, U.K., Canada, Luxembourg, Czech Republic, U.S.A., Hungary, Poland.

Double taxation treaties may also provide for specific tax regime in other aspects.

Value Added Tax.—Slovak V.A.T. (Act No. 289/1995 Coll.) system is based on EU model and has following rates: (a) 23% for most goods, leases of movable property, certain services, etc.; (b) 6% for most services and certain items, including most food items, books and periodicals, medical products etc.

Business with turnover of more than 750,000 SKK in three preceding calendar months required to register for V.A.T., which is payable quarterly or monthly according to turnover of business.

Examples of exempt supplies include postal services, financial services and transfer and rental of land and buildings apart from residential letting services, insurance, radio and TV broadcasting, international transport and medical care.

Goods for export are free of V.A.T., but V.A.T. on costs attributable to them is nonetheless recoverable.

According to Decree of the Ministry of Finance of SR No. 55/1994 Coll. for proper levy of V.A.T., use of special record-keeping money-chests is mandatory for all entrepreneurs selling products or providing services, if price is paid in cash. Only certified money-chests can be used and paper tape produced by money-chest containing stipulated datas (tax identification number, turnovers etc.) for period of one day and one month must be kept for period of five years. Paper tape can be demanded by relevant tax authorities for control purposes.

Consumer Taxes.—Consumer tax is form of excise duty payable by producers and importers of certain goods such as oil, fuel and lubricants, spirits, liqueurs, beers, wine and tobacco products. (Act No. 316/1993 Coll., Act No. 229/1995 Coll., Act No. 310/1993 Coll., Act No. 309/1993 Coll., Act No. 312/1993 Coll.). Tax is payable monthly on basis of submitted tax return. For due payment of these taxes, special labels for liqueurs and tobacco products have been introduced which must be stuck on all such products sold in territory of SR.

Road tax (Act No. 87/1994 Coll.) is levied on vehicles used for business purposes (including foreign vehicles). Progressive scale of tax ranges from 1,200 SKK to 3,600 SKK (passenger cars) and from 1,800 SKK to 54,000 SKK (utility vehicles and buses) depending on type of vehicle. There are some tax incentives for ecological purposes.

Tax on transfer of ownership of real estate (as well as gift tax and inheritance tax) is governed by Act No. 318/1992 Coll. This tax is chargeable on any transfer of real estate for consideration. Tax rate depends on value of transferred assets and also on relationship of transferor and transferee (lower rates for family members).

Real Estate Tax.—This tax (Act No. 317/1992 Coll.) is computed annually and is payable by owners or occupiers of buildings and land according to type of land and building. Municipalities are entitled to change tax rate within limits stipulated by law according to local conditions.

Gift Tax and Inheritance Tax.—Tax rate in these cases depends on value of gift/inheritance and on relation between taxpayer to donor/deceased (charges are lower for family members).

Administration of Taxes.—Taxes are administered by local state tax authorities (Act No. 254/1993 Coll., as am'd) excluding real estate taxes which are governed by municipalities. Procedure for tax collection is governed by Act No. 511/1992 Coll., as amended on administration of taxes. According to this regulation, entity obtaining permission for entrepreneurial activities is obliged to register in period of 30 days at appropriate tax authority (if there is obligation to deduct taxes from employee's wages in period of 15 days). If tax is not paid properly, tax authority can subject taxpayer property to lien. If there is no other way to ensure payment of taxes, tax authority can decide on execution of taxpayer property.

For breaches of this Act fine up to 2 million SKK can be imposed and interest on amount of outstanding tax is 140% of discount rate of National Bank of Slovakia.

TRADEMARKS AND TRADENAMES:

Trademarks.—SR is signatory of all most important multilateral treaties concerning trademarks, e.g., Nice Agreement on international classification of products and services to which factory marks and trademarks apply, Madrid Agreement on registration of factory marks or trademarks, Madrid Agreement on suppressing any false or deceptive information of product origin and Lisbon Agreement on protection of marking origin and their international registration.

Basic law governing trademarks is Trademark Act 174/1988 Coll. and its supplementary decree of same year. Trademark, according to regulations, is deemed to be any brand name, picture, space or combined mark capable of differentiating products or services coming from various manufacturers or service providers and is registered in trademark register kept by Industrial Property Rights Office of SR with its seat in Banská Bystrica. Applicant acquires title to trademark on date of its registration in register.

Priority rights have been treated in standard manner, with priority determined from moment of filing application for trademark registration. Priority right provided according to international treaties should be shown by applicant in application for trademark registration and evidenced within three months from filing same.

Protection period of any registered trademark is ten years and commences on date of receiving application by Office. Protection period of any trademark may be extended upon request of trademark's owner always for period of next ten years.

Trademark's owner has exclusive right to mark by owner's trademark any products or services for which it is registered or to use in connection with such products or services. Rights to any trademark may be fully or partially transferred to any third person by written agreement. Transfer becomes effective on date of its registration in register.

Essential protection of trademark owner's rights is secured by Trademark Act according to which owner has right to demand that any infringement of rights be prohibited, that any wrongful condition be removed, and that owner be indemnified against any damage. ObchZ provides for protection of trademark owner in provision of unfair competition which is deemed to be using any deceptive mark of products and services and evoking danger of exchange. Owner has right to claim any infringer to refrain from any wrongful acts and to remove wrongful condition. Owner also has right to receive reasonable satisfaction which may be claimed in money, liquidated damages, and recovery of any unjustifiable enrichment. Removal of wrongful condition may also be claimed by relevant legal entity authorized to protect competitors' interests. Criminal Law protects rights pertaining to trademark in provision on infringement of rights to trademark, tradename, and protected mark of origin for which any offender may be sentenced to imprisonment up to one year, and may be fined up to 5 million SKK, and forfeiture.

Tradenames.—According to ObchZ tradename is designation which entrepreneur (either individual or legal entity) uses when conducting business activities. Tradename of individual is person's name and surname and (it may include addendum further specifying entrepreneur) under which entrepeneur is registered at local License Register or another register specified by relevant laws. Tradename of legal entity shall be name under which legal entity is incorporated in Commercial Register (or name under which it has been established if legal entity is not incorporated in Commercial Register). Entrepreneur must avoid tradename being confused with tradename of another entrepreneur. Tradename of legal entity is transferred with enterprise to its legal successor; transfer of tradename without simultaneous transfer of enterprise is ineffective.

TREATIES:

On Jan. 1, 1993, SR succeeded C.S.F.R. in all international obligations. During existence of independent SR, some new treaties and conventions have been entered into. Consequently SR is party to, inter alia, following treaties and conventions:

General.—Charter of the United Nations and Statutes of the International Court of Justice (June 26, 1945/Dec. 20, 1965); Vienna Convention on Diplomatic Relations

See Topical Index in front part of this volume.

TREATIES . . . *continued*
(Apr. 18, 1961); Vienna Convention on Consular Relations (Apr. 24, 1963); International Covenant on Civil and Political Rights (Dec. 19, 1966); International Covenant on Economic, Social and Cultural Rights (Dec. 19, 1966); Convention on the Law of Treaties (May 23, 1969); Vienna Convention on the Law of Treaties between States and International Organizations and between International Organizations (May 21, 1986); Convention on the Establishment of International Organization for Legal Metrology (Paris, May 28, 1958); Statutes of the International Atomic Energy Agency (Oct. 25, 1956); Constitution de l'Union Postale Universelle—UPC (Oct. 9, 1874); Convention on the Establishment of the International Civil Aviation Organization (Dec. 12, 1944); General Agreement on Tariffs and Trade—GATT (Oct. 30, 1947); Articles of Agreement of the International Finance Corporation (Nov. 3, 1955) Articles of Agreement of the International Development Association—IDA (Jan. 26, 1960); Convention Establishing the World Intellectual Property Organization (July 14, 1967); Convention on the Establishment of the Secretarial of the Conference on Security and Co-operation in Europe and on Privileges and Immunities of this Secretarial and Further Institutions of the CSCE (Paris, Dec. 11, 1991); Council for Customs Co-operation (Brusel, Dec. 15, 1950), Convention on Establishment Europe Agreement establishing an Association between the European Communities and their Member States of the one part, and SR, of the other part. (Luxembourg, Oct. 4, 1993); International Monetary Fund and International Bank for Reconstruction and Development—IMF (Bretton Woods, July 22, 1944); Agreement between the Slovak and Czech Republic on Creation of the Customs Union (Prague, Oct. 29, 1992).

Multilateral International Conventions on Legal Assistance and Enforcement of Judgments.—Hague Convention related to Court Procedure in Civil Matters (July 17, 1905); Hague Convention related to Procedure in Civil Matters (Mar. 1, 1954); Hague Convention on the Recognition and Enforcement of Decisions Relating to Maintenance Obligations in Respect of Children (Apr. 15, 1958); Hague Convention on the Service Abroad of Judicial and Extrajudicial Documents in Civil or Commercial Matters (Nov. 15, 1965); Hague Convention on the Taking of Evidence Abroad in Civil and Commercial Matters (Mar. 18, 1970); Hague Convention on Recognition of Divorces and Legal Separations (June 1, 1970); Hague Convention on the Recognition and Enforcement of Decisions Relating to Maintenance Obligations (Oct. 2, 1973).

Conventions Unifying Choice of Law Rules.—Hague Convention on the Law Applicable to Traffic Accidents (May 4, 1971).

Conventions Relating to Arbitration.—Geneva Convention on the Enforcement of Foreign Arbitral Awards (Sept. 26, 1927); New York Convention on the Recognition and Enforcement of Foreign Arbitral Awards (June 10, 1958).

Conventions Protecting Industrial and Copyright Rights.—Paris Convention for the Protection of Industrial Property Rights (Mar. 20, 1883); Strassbourg Agreement on International Patent Classification (Mar. 24, 1971); Patent Co-operation Treaty (Washington DC, June 17, 1970); Budapest Treaty on International Recognition of Deposit of Micro-organisms for Purpose of Patent Procedure (Apr. 28, 1977).

Conventions on Avoidance of Double Taxation with: The Netherlands, France, Finland, Belgium, Japan, Austria, Norway, Sweden, Cyprus, Spain, Italy, Denmark, Germany, Greece, India, Brazil, China (People's Republic of), Nigeria, U.K., Luxembourg, Yugoslavia, Algeria (income from international air transport), Tunisia, Canada, Czech Republic, U.S.A., Hungary, Poland, Romania.

Conventions on Protection of Investment with: France, Austria, Switzerland, Finland, Sweden, Canada, The Netherlands, Germany, Denmark, Czech Republic, Indonesia, Bulgaria, U.S.A. SR is also party to Convention on the Solution of Disputes Arising from Investments between States and Citizens of other States (Mar. 18, 1965).

Conventions Regulating only Various Fields of Legal Assistance with: Afghanistan, Albania, Algeria, Belgium, Bulgaria, Cyprus, Czech Republic, France, Greece, The Netherlands, Yemen (People's Republic of), Bosnia and Herzegovina, Croatia, Macedonia (FYROM), Yugoslavia (Serbia and Montenegro), North Korea, Cuba, Hungary, Mongolia, Poland, Portugal, Austria, Romania, Russia, Slovenia, U.S.A, Syria, Spain, Switzerland, Italy, Tunisia, Turkey, Uganda, Ukraine, U.K., Vietnam.

Conventions on Field of International Transport.—Convention on International Transport by Railway—COTIF (May 9, 1980); Convention on Transport Contract in International Road Cargo Transport—CMR (Geneva, May 16, 1956).

Conventions in Field of Criminal Law.—European Convention on Extradiction (Dec. 13, 1957), European Convention on Mutual Assistance in Criminal Matters (Apr. 20, 1959); European Convention on Transfer of Penal Proceedings (May 15, 1972); European Convention on Suppression of Terrorism (Jan. 27, 1977).

WILLS:

Testator's disposition of property is limited by provisions of OZ (Civil Code) which stipulate that descendants who are minors must receive at least as much as their intestate share in estate, adult descendants must receive at least as much as constitutes one half of their intestate share in estate. However, testator may disinherit descendant if there are reasons stipulated in OZ. Reasons must be specificated and disinheritance can be joined with will in single document. There are no limitations on amount which can be given to religious, charitable or social institutions. For holographic wills, attendance of witnesses is not necessary. If will is not written by testator, it must be signed in presence of two witnesses who also sign document. Nuncupative will can be produced by any person who cannot read and/or write in presence of three persons who also sign document. Will can be made in form of notarial deed. This form can only be used if testator is minor at least 15 years of age. If shares of descendants are not stipulated in will it is presumed that shares are equal. Testator can establish foundation, however, constituent documents establishing foundation must be included. Will is annulled by later executed will, by its revocation (in form prescribed in will) or by destruction of document containing will.

Testamentary capacity is governed by law of state of which testator was citizen at time when will was written. (ZMPSP).

See Topical Index in front part of this volume.

SOUTH AFRICA LAW DIGEST

(The following is a list of all Topics, including cross-references, covered in this Digest.)

SOUTH AFRICA LAW DIGEST

Revised for 1997 edition by

CLIFFE DEKKER & TODD Inc., Solicitors of the Supreme Court of South Africa, Johannesburg.

FINDLAY & TAIT INC., Cape Town, Contributor on the topic Shipping.

See topics Reports; Statutes.

ABSENTEES:

Generally speaking, persons who are absent from this country do not suffer any disabilities. Where a person having any property in South Africa is permanently absent from country, or his whereabouts are unknown, Master of Supreme Court (official in charge of estates belonging to people unable to administer them) may under §80 of Administration of Estates Act No. 66 of 1965, appoint a curator dative to administer absentee's property. Where a person is only temporarily absent, court may appoint a curator bonis for this purpose.

Where absence of a person results in his failing to perform any specific duty provision is made for an appropriate remedy; e.g., a debtor may be declared insolvent, if it is in interest of his creditors and he absents himself with intent by so doing to evade or delay payment of his debts.

Moneys due to a person whose whereabouts are unknown must be paid to Master of Supreme Court.

ACKNOWLEDGMENTS (Authentication):

(Rule 63 of Rules promulgated in terms of Supreme Court Act No. 59 of 1959).

(1) Any document executed outside Republic is deemed to be sufficiently authenticated for purpose of use inside Republic and South West Africa if it be duly authenticated at such foreign place by signature and seal of office: (a) Of head of South African diplomatic or consular mission or person in administrative or professional division of Public Service serving at South African diplomatic, consular or trade office abroad, or South African Foreign Service Officer Grade VI or Honorary South African Consul-General, Honorary Consul, Honorary Vice-Consul or Honorary Trade Commissioner; or (b) consul-general, consul, vice-consul or consular agent of U.K. or any other person acting in any of aforementioned capacities or pro-consul of U.K.; or (c) of any government authority of such foreign place charged with authentication of documents under law of that foreign country; or (d) of any notary public or other person in such foreign place who shall be shown by certificate of any person referred to in (1) (a), (b) and (c) or of any diplomatic or consular officer of such foreign country in Republic to be duly authorised to authenticate such document under law of that foreign country; or (e) of notary public in U.K. of Gt. Brit. and No. Ireland or in Zimbabwe, Lesotho, and Botswana or Swaziland; or (f) of commissioned officer of South African Defence Force as defined in Section One of Defence Act 1957 in case of document executed by any person on active service.

(2) If any person authenticating a document in terms of (1), above, has no seal of office, he shall certify that he possesses no such seal.

(3) Notwithstanding above, any court of law or public office may accept as sufficiently authenticated any document which is shown to satisfaction of such court or officer in charge of such public office, to have been actually signed by person purporting to have signed such document.

(4) No power of attorney executed in Lesotho, Botswana or Swaziland, and intended as authority to any person to take, defend or intervene in any legal proceedings in Magistrate's Court within Republic shall require authentication: Provided that any such power of attorney shall appear to have been duly signed and signature to have been attested by two competent witnesses.

ACTIONS:

(Supreme Court Act No. 59 of 1959; Magistrates Court Act No. 32 of 1944).

Actions for the enforcement of rights are usually by way of summons which is served upon any person or left at house or place of abode or business of any person, in order that such person may be affected thereby. In matters of urgency such as interdicts, sequestration proceedings, spoliation proceedings, etc., redress by way of application to Court on motion may be permitted. South African Law Commission has published working paper in which preliminary proposals are made regarding possible introduction of class actions and public interest actions. Commission recommends draft legislation to provide for aforementioned actions.

Power of attorney in favour of attorney is unnecessary in both Supreme Court and Magistrates Court. Power of attorney is required in Supreme Court if attorney's authority to act is challenged. Likewise power of attorney is not essential in applications by way of motion but applicant must have proper legal authority. Power of attorney must be properly authenticated. See topic Acknowledgments (Authentication); see also topic Courts.

Foreign Claims.—In regard to proof of foreign claims, questions relating to competency of witnesses, methods and sufficiency of proof are matters governed by South African statute and common law, consequently no action is maintainable on foreign claim if proof of such claim is wanting in South African Law. Generally speaking oral evidence is required and statements even if given under oath are not by themselves sufficient proof of any claim. Evidence of nonresident may be obtained on commission or in some other way sanctioned by court. The Law of Evidence Amendment Act No. 45 of 1988 empowers courts to take judicial notice of law of foreign state and indigenous law.

Death.—See topic Death.

Limitation of.—See topic Limitation of Actions.

ADMINISTRATION:

See topic Executors and Administrators.

ADOPTION:

Governed by Child Care Act No. 74/1983. Adoptions are dealt with on personal basis by Adoptions Magistrate. Act is well and sympathetically administered and great care is taken to see that all formalities and secrecy (where desired) are observed and that adoption is in best interests of child.

AFFIDAVITS:

Procedure and formalities are as in England. (See England Law Digest.) Affidavit should be headed:

Form

In the Supreme Court of South Africa,
(. . . . . . Division).

In re:

James Brown, Applicant,
versus
John Smith, Respondent.

Affidavit should begin:

I, Jack Roe do hereby make oath and say:—

. . . .

Affidavit should end:

. . . . .

Deponent's signature.

I CERTIFY THAT the deponent has acknowledged that he knows and understands the contents of this Affidavit, which was signed and sworn to before me at . . . . . . on the . . . . day of . . . . . ., 19. . .

. . . .
Commissioner of Oaths.

Commissioner of Oaths must furnish his full names, business address, designation and area for which he holds appointment or office held if appointment held ex officio, below his signature wherever he certifies.

AGENCY: See topic Principal and Agent.

ALIENS:

(Aliens Control Act No. 96 of 1991; South African Citizenship Act No. 88 of 1995).

An alien is subject to no disabilities and enjoys same privileges as a South African national, save that an alien wishing to immigrate to South Africa or to take up temporary employment in South Africa must apply for and obtain a permanent residence permit from immigration office in country of residence, or temporary work permit from Department of Home Affairs, Pretoria, as case may be, before proceeding to South Africa. Holiday, business and family visitors will be provided with temporary residence permits on being admitted. Aliens, unless naturalized, acquire no political rights.

No person shall acquire or lose South African citizenship merely by reason of marriage.

Naturalization may be granted to an alien who has resided in the Republic for a period of not less than one year and has in addition been resident in Republic for further period of not less than four years during eight years immediately preceding date of his/her application, is of good character and able to communicate in any official language of Republic, and intends to reside permanently in Republic. Naturalization is granted solely at discretion of Minister. Man or woman married to South African citizen may apply for naturalization after two years residence in Republic.

Immigration.—No alien may enter the Republic for the purpose of permanent residence unless he is in possession of a permit issued on application to the Immigrants Selection Board. The Board will issue permits only to persons who, in its entire discretion, are desirable immigrants, and will not do so unless the applicant is (a) of good character and (b) likely to become readily assimilated with inhabitants of Republic and be desirable inhabitant of Republic and (c) is not likely to be harmful to welfare of Republic and (d) not likely to pursue occupation in which sufficient persons are already engaged in Republic, or (e) spouse, dependent child or aged or indigent member of family of Republic resident who undertakes to maintain him or her.

All persons entering Republic must be in possession of a passport.

Corporations Owned or Controlled by Aliens.—There are no special requirements save that on all company catalogues, trade circulars or business letters bearing name of the company, the full names of the directors must be set out and where such a director is not a South African citizen, his nationality as well.

See also topic Corporations.

APPEAL AND ERROR: See topic Courts.

ARBITRATION AND AWARD:

Any matter in dispute between parties may by agreement be made the subject of arbitration except matters relating to personal status, matrimonial affairs, or to persons under a legal disability, or matters which are criminal or contrary to public policy. The form of arbitration may be decided upon by the parties otherwise the procedure laid down by legislation applies. The courts will enforce an arbitrator's award if satisfied that the arbitration was duly and fairly held.

See Topical Index in front part of this volume.

ARBITRATION AND AWARD . . . *continued*

Arbitration generally is governed by Act 42 of 1965 but parties may otherwise agree so as to exclude operation of Act in whole or in part.

Certain arbitrations are compulsory by statute for example in expropriation disputes.

ASSIGNMENTS:

There are no statutory restrictions, and these may be completed in any form that parties agree upon.

Assignments for Benefit of Creditors.—General provision for statutory assignments has been repealed. However under Land Bank Act No. 13/1944 farmer may obtain relief from his obligations under special procedure which permits assignment of his assets for benefit of his creditors.

Private Assignments.—A debtor may agree with creditors to release him of any portion of his debts or assign his assets to them upon any terms that he can get them to accept, but no creditor can be bound unless he joins in such arrangement. There are no restrictions upon such private assignments.

ASSOCIATIONS:

Non-trading associations such as clubs, sporting associations, etc., may be formed without restriction. Such associations may either be incorporated or not. Associations for trade must either consist of a partnership of persons or be incorporated. Under the Companies Act (Act 61 of 1973) more than 20 persons may not be associated for trade purposes without registration of a company. Exception is that certain professions including accountants, auditors, architects, attorneys, quantity surveyors, professional engineers and stockbrokers may now practice through medium of partnership and may have more than 20 members. In addition, no association of persons for gain or trade may now be body corporate unless it is registered as company under Companies Act as aforesaid or as close corporation in terms of Close Corporations Act (Act 69 of 1984).

Trade unions and employer organizations, in order to sue or be sued, must be registered under provisions of Labour Relations Act. (Act 28 of 1956 as am'd). Trade combinations for control of certain commodities are subject to government interference, but otherwise no restrictions are imposed by common law or statute law.

Unincorporated associations, since they have no separate legal personality, experience great difficulty in contracting or owning property and as to the form under which legal proceedings may be instituted or defended. Ordinarily, members do not incur any liability for obligations beyond unpaid subscriptions in the terms of the constitution.

See also topic Corporations.

ATTACHMENT:

(Supreme Court Act No. 59/1959; Magistrates Court Act No. 32/1944).

A creditor may, by order of court, attach the goods of his debtor in execution of a judgment. Civil process of provincial or local division against any judgment shall run through Republic and may be served or executed within jurisdiction of any division.

See also topics Exemptions; Garnishment.

Attachment to Found Jurisdiction.—If a claimant wishes to institute action in South African courts against a foreigner who has assets within Republic, he may obtain leave from courts to attach such assets to found jurisdiction. He is thereupon at liberty to institute proceedings in a South African court. Person of foreigner can be attached in similar manner to found jurisdiction.

ATTORNEYS AND ADVOCATES:

(Attorneys Act No. 53/1979; Admission of Advocates Act No. 74/1964).

South African legal profession is divided into two branches. Lawyers must accordingly elect whether to practice as attorneys or as advocates. They may not practice in dual capacity even if suitably qualified. Neither attorneys or advocates are allowed to accept work on contingent fee basis in strict sense of percentage of court award. They may charge according to amount of work they do either in accordance with tariff of fees if there is one or on reasonable basis if there is no such tariff. In Transvaal Province, attorneys and advocates are able, with effect from 18 May 1992, to enter into special fee arrangement in respect of claim for damages, provided that client is natural person and claim or counterclaim has not been acquired by transference of rights. Client is liable for payment of practitioner's fee only if claim or counterclaim is successful. Fee is however limited to 100% surcharge on lawyer's fees as calculated in terms of tariff. In principle other provinces have approved special fee arrangement although not yet implemented. South African Law Commission has published working paper in which desirability of speculative and contingency fee agreements is investigated. Working paper expounds various methods of determining extent of fee payable on success, disadvantages of contingency fee agreements as well as safeguards to ensure that client is not prejudiced.

The two professions are regulated in terms of two aforementioned Acts and by professional bodies—listed below—created in terms of Acts for protection and regulation of the two professions. The Rights of Appearance in Courts Act 62 of 1995 regulates by act of parliament right of advocates and attorneys to appear in courts in Republic. Provision is made for extension of existing right of attorneys to appear in court and for application by attorney to appear in Supreme Court. Subject to certain qualifications and requirements, it is possible for foreign lawyers to become members of different professional bodies and practice as lawyers or advocates in South Africa.

Representative professional body for lawyers is following: Association of Law Societies: The Association of Law Societies of the Republic of South Africa, Director-General: A. Jansen van Vuuren, Director of Professional Affairs: A. Botha, Education Officer: R. de Klerk, 304 Brooks Street, Menlo Park, 0102; P.O. Box 36636, Menlo Park, 0102; Tel (012) 342-3330, Fax (012) 342-3305, Telex 320486, Telegrams "Unionlaw", Docex 82.

Representative professional body for advocates is following: General Council of the Bar of South Africa, Secretary: D. F. Joubert, 1111 Schreiner Chambers, 94 Pritchard Street, Johannesburg, 2001; P.O. Box 2260, Johannesburg, 2000; Tel (011) 29-3976, Fax (011) 29-8970, Telex 48-6265 SA, Telegrams "Advolex".

BANKRUPTCY; INSOLVENCY:

The following forms of sequestration are recognized. (Act 24 of 1936).

(1) **Voluntary Surrender.**—This may be: (a) On application in writing of debtor or his duly authorized agent, setting forth that debtor is insolvent and tendering surrender of his estate for benefit of his creditors; (b) on like application of any person in whom is legally vested administration of estate of deceased debtor or debtor incapable of administering his estate; (c) on like application presented on behalf of partnership estate and made by all partners present or represented in Republic.

Notice of surrender must be published in the Government Gazette and in a newspaper circulating in the district concerned.

(2) **Compulsory Sequestration.**—Debtor may be declared insolvent if it is in interests of creditors and he is in fact insolvent or commits one of following acts: (a) If debtor absents himself with intent by so doing to evade or delay payment of his debts; (b) if, in answer to warrant of execution he renders return to effect that he has not sufficient disposable property to satisfy judgment obtained against him; (c) if he makes any disposition of any of his property which has effect of prejudicing his creditors or of preferring one creditor above another; (d) if he removes any of his property with intent to prejudice his creditors or to prefer one creditor above another; (e) if he makes or offers to make any arrangement with his creditors for releasing him wholly or partially from his debts; (f) if, having published notice of surrender, he omits to lodge his schedules as by law required, or fails to present his application to court on date mentioned in notice of surrender; (g) if he gives notice in writing to any of his creditors that he is unable to pay any of his debts; (h) if, being trader, he publishes notice of sale of any business or of goodwill, book debts, or assets of that business other than sales of stock in ordinary course of his trade and is unable to pay all his debts.

Compulsory sequestration of estate of a debtor may only be obtained at instance of a creditor who has a liquidated claim of not less than R100 or of creditors whose claims jointly amount to not less than R200.

Proof of Claims.—A creditor who desires to prove a claim in an estate must lodge with the officer presiding at meetings of creditors a detailed statement of account preferably on the creditor's letterhead together with an affidavit in undermentioned form. Where claim is in respect of payment of purchase price of goods sold on open account and delivered to insolvent, proof of such claim must contain statement showing detailed monthly account and brief description of purchases and payments for full period of trading or for period of 12 months immediately before date of sequestration, whichever is lesser. If creditor cannot appear in person he must authorize his agent by means of a duly authenticated power of attorney to appear on his behalf.

Form

Form.—Affidavit for Proof of Claim of

. . . .

Name of Creditor . . . .

Address in full . . . .

Total amount of claim R

I, (full name, stating relation of the deponent to the creditor as manager, secretary, general power holder, etc.) declare under oath:

(1) That . . . . . . whose estate has been sequestrated, was at the date of sequestration, and still is, indebted to . . . . . . in the sum of . . . . . . for . . . .

(2) That the said debt arose in the manner and at the time set forth in the account hereunto annexed.

(3) That no other person besides the said . . . . . . is liable (otherwise than as surety) for the said debt or any part thereof.

(4) That the said . . . . . . has not, nor has any other person, to my knowledge on my/his behalf received any security for the said debt or any part thereof, save and except (here insert nature, particulars and value of mortgage, pledge or other security if any).

(Signature of declarant) . . . . . .

I CERTIFY THAT the deponent has acknowledged that he knows and understands the contents of this Affidavit, which was signed and sworn to before me at . . . . . . on the . . . . day of . . . . . ., 19. . . . .

. . . .

Commissioner of Oaths.

If a creditor holds security against the assets of the debtor and there is a possibility of the debtor's total assets being insufficient on realization to pay the cost of administering the estate, the creditor so proving should declare that he relies entirely on his security for payment of his claim in order to avoid the possibility of paying into the estate a contribution towards the shortfall on the costs of administration.

"Security" above referred to relates only to property belonging to the insolvent and not guarantees received from third persons. Purchaser of land on instalments from seller who is made bankrupt after sale is protected to some extent in complicated manner by Alienation of Land Act No. 68 of 1981.

If the assets of the insolvent are insufficient to pay the costs of sequestration all creditors who have proved claims are liable to contribute proportionately to make up the shortfall. Creditors are therefore advised not to prove their claims until they have satisfied themselves that there are sufficient assets to pay a distribution.

A statement of insolvent's affairs must be lodged at office of Master of Supreme Court or at local Magistrate's Court, where it is available for public inspection.

Sales in execution of property in insolvent estate are prohibited after publication of a notice of surrender, an order of sequestration of insolvent or winding up of a company or appointment of a curator bonis.

Effects of Insolvency.—There are numerous effects of insolvency but main consequence is that all property of insolvent at date of sequestration and all property subsequently acquired by him during sequestration vest in trustee of his estate. During his insolvency insolvent accordingly may not dispose of any of his assets without his trustee's consent. Insolvent suffers disabilities and restrictions but may earn living. During insolvency he must keep accounts and pay to trustee any excess over his living expenses.

Rehabilitation of Insolvent.—Act provides that certain periods of time must elapse before insolvent can apply for his rehabilitation. Periods vary according to degree of

See Topical Index in front part of this volume.

BANKRUPTCY; INSOLVENCY . . . *continued*
severity of insolvency and vary from minimum of one year to five years and rehabilitation is in any event at discretion of court. Insolvent is deemed rehabilitated after ten years.

Liquidation of corporations unable to pay debts, see topic of Corporations, subhead Liquidation.

BILLS AND NOTES:

Generally speaking, in South Africa law of bills of exchange is same as that of England. Bills of Exchange Act is No. 34 of 1964, and does not vary to any great extent from English Act of 1882. Report by South African Law Commission has been completed recommending various changes in law. Developments in English law have also been considered. If recommendations are adopted, South African law will be more in line with modern legal thinking in South Africa and elsewhere on subject.

Negotiation of Bill.—To be able to negotiate bill, possessor of instrument must be a holder; where instrument is payable to bearer, delivery by holder is sufficient. If bill is payable to order, endorsement by holder is necessary prior to delivery. Where transferee takes delivery as holder in due course, he may enforce payment against all parties liable on bill. (See England Law Digest.) If transferee takes as mere holder, he may still sue on bill but subject to defects of title, which are either relative or absolute. Where an overdue bill is negotiated, it can only be negotiated subject to any defect of title affecting it at maturity. Where bill or note contains words prohibiting transfer, it is valid between parties thereto but transferee may not transfer it to any other person. Bill marked "nontransferable" is completely nontransferable but bill marked "not negotiable" and "a/c payee only" is transferable subject to equities. Possibility of delictual remedy against collecting bank in respect of these bills is not excluded.

Requirements of Form.—In order that instrument may be negotiated it must satisfy necessary requirements of form. Instrument must be an unconditional order or promise in writing addressed by one person to another signed by person giving it, requiring person to whom it was addressed to pay on demand or at fixed or determinable future date, sum certain in money to or to order of, specified person or to bearer. An instrument not complying with above is not a bill of exchange. Bill is not invalid because it has not an amount in figures, and/or it is not dated, and/or it does not specify value given, and/or that any value has been given therefor, and/or it does not specify place where it is drawn or payable. Stamp Duties Act 77 of 1968, as am'd requires stamping of negotiable instruments, effect of which is to prevent recovery at law until revenue authorities have been satisfied as to their claims but does not otherwise invalidate bill. Certain bills need not be stamped, notably cheques. If instrument is instrument of debt, it must comply with terms of Usury Act No. 73 of 1968, as am'd. Failure to comply therewith does not invalidate it, but any person knowingly dealing with such instrument remains liable to penalties prescribed therein. Under Administration of Estates Act, it is in certain cases necessary to state transaction which gave rise to instrument, and noncompliance therewith may entail criminal sanctions but does not invalidate instrument.

Notice and Protesting.—Except in case of maker of promissory note or an acceptor of bill and in certain circumstances drawer of cheque, then in order to make all parties to a note or bill liable, bill or note must be presented on due date and any notice of dishonour sent to all those affected also on due date. Also, foreign bill or note must be protested by notary public by not later than day following.

Special provisions of Act, which are too complex for inclusion herein exist in regard to liability of avals or sureties.

Conflict of Laws.—Where bill drawn in one country is negotiated, accepted or payable in another, rights, duties and liabilities of parties are determined as follows: (a) Act provides that formal validity of bill or note is determined by law of place of issue; validity of a supervening contract (i.e., acceptance or endorsement, etc.) is determined by law of place where contract was made; (b) interpretation of drawing, endorsing and acceptance is determined by law of place where contract was made; (c) where bill or note drawn or made in one country is payable in another, due date of instrument is determined according to law of place where it is payable; (d) prescription is governed by law of place where contract was made. See also England Law Digest.

Stamps.—See subhead Requirements of Form, supra.

CHATTEL MORTGAGES:

The usual form of pledge of movable assets if there is no delivery of the assets to the creditor is by means of a notarial bond, which is registered in the Deeds Office.

There is a subsidiary division of mortgages depending on whether the assets are specially indicated or not. If specified articles are mortgaged, such as stock in one particular warehouse, the bond is termed a special mortgage. On the other hand, a business may mortgage the whole of its assets, stock-in-trade, book debts, goodwill, etc., in which case the notarial bond is a general mortgage.

New legislation, security by means of movable property (Act No. 57 of 1993), provides that notarial bond hypothecating corporeal movable property, which is readily recognisable, although such property has not been delivered to mortgagee, will be deemed to have been pledged to mortgagee as if it had expressly been pledged and delivered to mortgagee.

Special notarial bonds over specified movable property confer preference over concurrent creditors in respect of free residue of insolvent estate.

Movable property hypothecated by notarial bond is not subject to landlord's tacit hypothec.

This Act referred to above has repealed Notarial Bonds (Natal) Act, Act No. 18 of 1932.

See also topic Pledges.

COMMERCIAL REGISTER:

There is no general requirement for registration of trades and businesses. However, most business undertakings require one or more of applicable trade licences. (See topic Licences.) As a rule, failure to obtain necessary licence will not preclude suit by businessman although it will render him liable for penalties in terms of provincial ordinances.

Business Names Act 27/1960 provides for control of business names but only in relation to their use and not to their registration. Registration of names of companies and close corporations are respectively regulated in terms of Companies Act (Act 61 of 1973) and Close Corporations Act (Act 69 of 1984). According to Business Names Act (which does not apply to corporations) stationery of business shall include certain particulars relating to business, such as name under which business is conducted, and name of person conducting it. It also states which names or titles may not be used in business and provides that Registrar of Companies may in writing order any person who is carrying on any business under any name to cease using such name if it is calculated to deceive or mislead public or gives offence to or is suggestive of blasphemy or indecency.

COMMISSIONS TO TAKE TESTIMONY:

See topic Depositions.

COMMUNITY PROPERTY:

See topic Husband and Wife.

CONDITIONAL SALES:

See topics Sales; Contracts.

CONSTITUTION AND GOVERNMENT:

Constitution of the Republic of South Africa Act, (No. 200 of 1993) came into force on Apr. 27, 1994. *Note:* Constitutional Assembly has drafted new Constitution of the Republic of South Africa in terms of interim Constitution. New Constitutional text must first be certified by Constitutional Court, before it can be promulgated. Constitutional Court refused to accept text which was presented to it; document is in process of being redrafted and is expected to be put before Constitutional Court for reexamination shortly.

Parliament consists of National Assembly and Senate. Legislative authority vests, subject to Constitution, in Parliament.

National Assembly consists of 400 members elected in accordance with system of proportional representation.

Senate is composed of ten Senators for each province, nominated by each party represented in National Assembly in accordance with system of proportional representation.

Executive authority vests in President, who is Head of State. Each party holding at least 80 seats in National Assembly is entitled to designate Executive Deputy President from among members of National Assembly.

Judicial authority of Republic vests in courts as established by Constitution.

Provincial Legislative Authority.—Each of the nine provinces has, subject to Constitution, it's own constitution and legislature. Legislative authority of province vests, subject to Constitution, in provincial legislature.

Members of provincial legislature are elected in accordance with system of proportional representation.

Provincial Executive Authority.—Executive authority of province vests in Premier of the Province.

Fundamental Rights.—Constitution, which is supreme law of Republic, includes Chapter of Fundamental Rights, which binds all legislative and executive organs of state at all levels of government.

CONTRACTS:

In general, common law rules govern. No formalities are required. Contract of sale of land must be signed by parties thereto or by their agents acting on written authority. Long lease of not less than ten years does not bind third parties unless in writing executed before notary public and registered against title deeds of property.

In addition there are three further Acts which require special formalities:

Credit Agreements Act No. 75 of 1980 effective as from Mar. 1, 1981, provides that certain material information must be given to credit receiver before contract is entered into. Also where contract is entered into outside credit grantor's premises, credit receiver may resile from contract within five days. Act replaces Hire Purchase Act and also includes instalment sales, lease lend transactions of movables, rendering of services on credit and certain other credit agreements where payment is to be made in future. Agreement must be in writing and contain certain essential information. Certain other provisions are not allowed and are invalid. In any event Act does not apply to transactions in excess of R500,000 and in certain other categories but it does apply in categories prescribed by regulation which include, amongst other things, various household, electrical, camping, electronic goods and motor vehicles. Sports goods are not included.

The Usury Act No. 73 of 1968 as am'd applies to money lending transactions in broadest sense, credit transactions and leasing transactions. It is most complicated and requires careful study when applicable. It was effective from Apr. 1, 1969 but does not apply to transactions involving principal debt of R500,000 or more, foreign loans, debentures on Stock Exchange, short-leasing transactions of movables and loans by Reserve Bank. Purpose of this Act is to limit and compel disclosure of finance charges when transaction is entered into. Transaction must be in writing and take form of instrument of debt as defined. No finance charges may be recovered if not disclosed in instrument of debt. Statute defines principal debt, finance charges and certain other charges relating to maintenance and legal costs which are recoverable. Maximum finance charge rates are laid down and borrower has right to anticipate due date of payment which right must be stated in instrument of debt. There are numerous other provisions covering variation of instalments, novation of debts and additional advances. Instrument of debt does not include covering bond insofar as it purports to convey security for future advances.

CONTRACTS . . . *continued*

Alienation of Land Act 68/1981.—This Act deals with sale of land (immovable property) by payment in instalments. Land in this connection includes land and all buildings and improvements thereon. It consolidates Contracts of Sale Act 71/1979 and Sale of Land by Instalments Act 72/1971.

Act includes various provisions in effort to protect rights of purchasers under sales by instalments. Act sets out numerous statutory requirements to be contained in instalment sale agreement and incidentally requires mortgagee on request from time to time to state amount then owing on any bond over property or amount of money required to release individual property if more than one mortgaged. It also provides for such agreements to be recorded in Deeds Office in order to give purchaser certain preference but not preference over mortgage bond registered over property prior to said registration. Provision is also made for certain payments to be held in trust until such time as it is legally possible to transfer immovable property sold and where there is instalment sale until said contract has been registered as above.

Excuses for Nonperformance.—Contracts are void and cannot be enforced in a court of law if they are unlawful, immoral, contrary to public policy or lacking in some legal formality.

Contracts are voidable at instance of grieved party for numerous reasons, inter alia being: (1) False representations (this can be either negligent, wilful and deliberate [fraud] or innocent); (2) party not having required legal capacity; (3) mistake (mistake of fact not of law); (4) force and fear; (5) undue influence; (6) mental disability; (7) impossibility of performance.

Conflict of Laws.—Intrinsic validity of a contract is determined by proper law of contract, namely law of country which has most real connection with contract. Law which governs formalities of contract is lex loci contractus (place where contract was entered into) even though contract may be totally unconnected with that system of law unless it can be shown that parties intended proper law to govern formalities. Mode of performance is determined by lex loci solutionis (place of performance) and rights and duties under contract by proper law with presumption in favour of lex loci solutionis, if choice of proper law proves indecisive. Interpretation of contract is determined by proper law unless parties clearly intend another system of law. Law governing capacity is not yet settled but party will be held to have capacity if capable by his domiciliary law or lex loci contractus.

Government Contracts.—There are no special formalities for government contracts.

Distributorships, Dealerships and Franchises—Franchise agreement is agreement between franchisor and franchisee whereby franchisee is granted license to operate business system devised by franchisor together with intellectual property rights such as trademarks, copyright, know-how, patents and designs which franchisor uses in his business system.

There are no special rules relating to formation and termination of these agreements. Franchisor and franchisee determine contents of their agreement including but not limited to following: (a) what intellectual property rights are applicable; (b) duties of franchisor; (c) obligations of franchisee; (d) under what circumstances agreement can be terminated; (e) what royalties are payable; (f) whether exclusive territory will be granted; and (g) whether or not franchisee will be affected by restraint covenant once franchise agreement has been terminated.

Terms "dealerships" and "distributorships" are interchangeably used for word franchise.

See also topics Copyright, Patents, Trademarks and Tradenames.

CONVEYANCES: See topic Deeds.

COPYRIGHT:

Law has been revised and consolidated in Copyright Act of 1978 as amended.

Nature of Copyright.—Copyright in any work vests in author or maker of that work, subject to various exceptions including work of employee in course of his business where it vests in his employer, provided author is qualified person, which means must be resident or domiciled in South Africa or South African Citizen or juristic body incorporated under South African law and in case of computer programmes, where copyright subsists in person who exercises control over making of programme. No registration of Copyright is required.

Where author is an unqualified person, he should ensure that his copyright is valid in one of countries of Berne Convention which has reciprocal arrangements with South Africa.

Copyright includes literary, musical and artistic works, cinematographic films, sound recordings, broadcasts, program carrying signals, computer programmes and published editions. There is also provision for copyright tribunal and advisory committee to determine disputes and recommend amendments to Act. Copyright in musical, literary and artistic works extends for life of artist and 50 years from date of death. Copyright in remaining items 50 years from making of work or first publication thereof.

Copyright Act makes provision for copyright holder to claim "reasonable royalty" in event of copyright infringement, amount being that which notional licensee could have been required to pay.

Industrial designs are covered by Designs Act of 1967. Artistic work may now be covered by both Copyright and Designs Act, but where three dimensional reproductions of artistic work were made available to public by or with consent of copyright owner, copyright will not be infringed if person without consent of owner makes three dimensional reproductions where authorised reproductions primarily have utilitarian purpose and are made by industrial process.

Infringement.—See England Law Digest.

Copyright Tribunal.—See England Law Digest.

Assignment.—See England Law Digest.

Reciprocal Arrangements.—Minister for Economic Affairs and Technology may extend protection afforded by Copyright Act, subject to any modifications as are thought necessary, to works of citizens of those countries whose laws give adequate protection to owners of copyright under South Africa Act. Similarly, Minister of Trade and Industry and Tourism may deny copyright to citizens of countries not giving adequate protection to work of South African citizens.

There are special reciprocal arrangements regarding copyright between U.S.A. and South Africa.

CORPORATIONS:

Registration of Companies is governed by statute, Companies Act 61 of 1973. Registrar of Companies with offices at Pretoria keeps a register of companies and attends to administration of Act.

Establishment of Company.—To establish a company it is necessary to obtain a name for company which is acceptable to Registrar of Companies and to file numerous forms and documents with Registrar. These include a power of attorney to an attorney to register company, which must be duly authenticated if signed outside South Africa. (See topic Acknowledgments.) Also a deed of incorporation, which consists of a memorandum and articles of association. Memorandum sets out powers or objects of company as against third parties and merely states main objects. Except where otherwise provided in its constitution every company has plenary powers but, as between directors and shareholders, its directors only have powers under main object and all ancillary objects. Articles correspond to regulations of American corporation and set out rules for internal workings of company. Certain of company forms must be signed personally by proposed directors of company.

There is also provision for registering company name in either official language of South Africa, namely, English or Afrikaans, as case may be, as well as shortened form of name of company. Provision is furthermore made for registering defensive name of business which may or may not be company. Purpose of registering defensive name is to prevent anyone else using it.

There are registration fees for various company forms. In addition, registration fee of company itself is basic amount of R350,00, plus additional amount of R5 for every R1,000 of nominal share capital.

Private companies are companies having share capital and by their Articles of Association: (a) Restrict right to transfer shares; (b) limit number of members to 50; (c) prohibit any offer to public for subscription of any shares or debentures of company. Such company must have one but not more than 50 shareholders, and have at least one director. Such company is not required to file annual balance sheet or profit and loss account with Registrar of Companies.

Public Companies.—All companies which are not private companies are public companies for purposes of Act. In addition companies limited by guarantee are deemed to be public companies. Any private company which fails to comply with provisions of its articles regarding restriction on transfer of shares, limitation of its membership or offers shares or debentures to public forthwith becomes subject to provisions of Act as if it were a public company. Public company must consist of not less than seven shareholders and have at least two directors. It must lodge with Registrar, under cover of prescribed form, a certified copy: (a) Of annual financial statements, group annual financial statements and group reports, if any; and (b) of annual financial statements of every private company controlled by that public company. Annual financial statements must be in conformity with generally accepted accounting practice, fairly present state of affairs of company and its business as at end of financial year concerned and profit and loss of company. There are no provisions which require that directors or shareholders of public or private companies must be South Africans.

Dividends paid by private or public company to South African shareholders are subject to taxation however, dividends are taxable in hands of company and not recipient. Tax is, however, levied on dividends paid to nonresident shareholders.

The Close Corporations Act No. 69 of 1984 became effective Jan. 2, 1985. Close corporation is separate legal entity with plenary powers. Its members have limited liability except in certain instances—those instances where elements of fraud may be involved or where corporation trades while it is de facto insolvent. Its members control it. Members must make contributions. There are no shares or share capital. Member's current interest is expressed as percentage which is recorded. It is established by registering founding statement. It has perpetual succession and it continues until deregistered or dissolved.

Membership is limited to natural persons. It may have between one and ten members.

Founding statement contains essential information and is only official public record. It is kept up-to-date by amending founding statements. Members may also have association agreement governing their relationship and corporation's internal administrative workings. Its name must be acceptable to Registrar with letters "CC" or "BK" and corporation's registered number added to name of close corporation.

Subject to certain requirements existing company may convert itself into close corporation or existing close corporation may convert itself into company.

New members may buy existing interests or join making additional contributions. Corporation itself may also buy existing interest. Total percentage interests of all members must always be 100 so that changes will result in adjustments. All members agree to changes. Member's contribution bears no relationship to his interest. Payments to members are as agreed by all members but in absence of agreement in proportion to their interests.

No audit is necessary.

Taxation of close corporation itself is similar to that of private company except with certain differences but its payments to members are not taxed. Nonresident shareholders' tax is payable. Assessed losses of company may be carried forward. Close corporations must make normal three provisional tax payments as company.

See also topic Taxation, subhead Business Taxes or Licences.

Liquidation.—A corporation unable to pay its debts may be liquidated under a compulsory winding up order issued by the Supreme Court at the instance of any creditor who has a direct or contingent claim. A foreign company must have established a place of business in the Republic of South Africa before it can be liquidated.

A company may be liquidated voluntarily by resolution in due form to that effect, with different procedure and consequences depending on whether creditors are to be paid in full or merely to receive a pro rata share of moneys available in the liquidation.

CORPORATIONS . . . *continued*

A moratorium can be procured by a company or a creditor thereof by obtaining a judicial management order against a company when it is proved to the Supreme Court that the company, if given time, can rehabilitate itself from temporary embarrassment.

The procedure for proving claims in bankruptcy (q. v.) applies to the proof of claims against a company under compulsory or voluntary liquidation but the forms should be modified to reflect that the subject matter is a company.

Foreign Companies.—Foreign company other than banking company or insurance company, which establishes "place of business" (which is defined as place where company transacts or holds itself out as transacting business and includes share transfer or share registration office) in Republic must, within 21 days after such establishment, lodge with Registrar following: (a) Certified copy of its memorandum (which is defined as charter, statutes, memorandum of association and articles, or other instrument constituting or defining constitution of company) and certified translation thereof in one of official languages if memorandum is not set out in such language; (b) notice of registered office and postal address of company; (c) consent of and name and address of auditor of company in Republic; (d) notice of financial year of company; (e) list in prescribed form containing: (i) particulars of each director's full names, former names, nationality, occupation, residential, business and postal addresses and date of appointment, distinguishing directors resident in Republic and nonresident directors, (ii) particulars of local manager and secretary (as in case of directors), (iii) name and address of auditor of company in Republic; (f) notice of name and address of person authorised to accept service of process and notices on behalf of company. Registrar must allocate registration number to foreign company. After registration foreign company must comply with provisions as to filing of information in terms of Act in same manner as domestic company.

Taxation of foreign company is same as for domestic company. Act provides for deregistration of foreign company which ceases to have place of business in Republic.

Name.—Companies must add distinctive last words or subjoined statements and registration numbers to their names: (a) Public company having share capital takes as last word, word "Limited"; (b) private company having share capital takes as last words, words "(Proprietary) Limited", but if its memorandum provides for its directors are jointly and severally liable for debts contracted during their period of office, last word is "Incorporated"; (c) company limited by guarantee takes as last word, word "Limited" and subjoins statement "(Limited by Guarantee)"; (d) an association not for gain subjoins statement "Incorporated Association not for Gain"; (e) an external company subjoins statement "Incorporated in . . . . (stating country concerned)".

Company names are protected by Companies Act which also protects other names associated with companies by registration of defensive names.

Every company and close corporation shall display its registration number after or immediately below its name in all letters, notices and other official documents.

See also topic Aliens, subhead Corporations Owned or Controlled by Aliens.

COURTS:

(Supreme Court Act No. 59/1959; Magistrates Court Act No. 39/1944).

Generally speaking, all claims for amounts up to R100,000 and all claims based on liquid documents, such as promissory notes and mortgage bonds, up to amount of R100,000 fall within jurisdiction of and should be instituted in magistrate's court. Unless parties consent to Magistrates Court jurisdiction all actions exceeding above in value must be brought in Supreme Court of South Africa which has, generally speaking, unlimited jurisdiction as to amount and subject matter.

There are provincial divisions of the Supreme Court in Pretoria, Capetown, Pietermaritzburg, Bloemfontein, Grahamstown and Kimberley and local divisions at Johannesburg, Durban and Port Elizabeth.

Provincial Divisions.—*Note:* In light of new Constitution (see topic Constitution and Government), provincial divisions have not yet been finalised.

Appellate Division may overrule all judgments of provincial divisions which do not fall within exclusive jurisdiction of Constitutional Court.

Constitutional Court has jurisdiction in Republic as Court of final instance over all matters relating to interpretation, protection and enforcement of Constitution.

See also topic Actions.

CURRENCY:

The Currency and Exchanges Act, No. 9 of 1933 as amended provides that notes issued by South African Reserve Bank be legal tender for any amount in repayment of any loans of money.

State President is also given power to make regulations in regard to any matter directly or indirectly affecting banking, currency or exchange.

Unit of currency is Rand (R), which is subdivided into 100 cents under a decimal system. Exchange control regulations restrict import and export of currency. Treasury certificate is required on imports and exports of currency. Regulations also prohibit direct transfer of funds through bank or exchange dealer, and also manipulations between private individuals such as acquiring debts or property in foreign country. Treasury may acquire from any resident in Republic, foreign currency held by him, existence of which must be disclosed to Treasury, and may also expropriate his securities in foreign countries. Normally payment to nonresidents of recent income and dividends and of debts resulting from commercial transactions are not restricted but other payments including capital in and out of country are governed by special regulations of Treasury.

Exchange Control Department of South African Reserve Bank, acting as agent for Treasury, together with authorised dealers (banks) control all foreign currency transactions.

See also topic Foreign Exchange, Foreign Trade and Investment.

CUSTOMS DUTIES:

Customs duties are levied on most imports. Different rates apply to various categories of goods. (See Customs and Excise Act 91/64.)

Trade agreements allowing for more favourable tariff between the parties exist between Republic and Zimbabwe and Malawi. In addition there is customs union agreement between Republic of South Africa, Botswana, Lesotho, Swaziland and Namibia which, broadly speaking, permits of free interchange of goods between these countries. Limited tariff preferences are given to certain imports from Mozambique. Republic is also member of G.A.T.T. By virtue of Republic's membership of G.A.T.T. and in terms of Uruguay Round of Multilateral Trade Negotiations, preliminary tariff offer on agricultural products has been compiled. For more detailed information it is suggested that one consult local S.A. Trade Commissioner.

See also topic Taxation.

DEATH:

The fact of death must be proved, and where there is no doubt, for example if the dead body has been identified, a death is registered with the Registrar of Deaths. Where the fact of death is not beyond doubt, for example in the case of a missing person, any interested party may apply to the Supreme Court for an order presuming death for a special purpose such as the administering of an estate. The Court acts in its discretion and may require security to be filed. There is no recognized period of absence giving rise to an automatic presumption of death. Similarly the Court may grant leave to one surviving spouse to remarry in justifiable circumstances.

Official death certificate may be obtained from Registrar of Births and Deaths, Union Buildings, Pretoria.

Survivorship.—In case of death of two or more persons about the same time in a common catastrophe or any like circumstance there is no presumption on account of age or sex that one died before the other.

Actions for Death.—Where a person is killed by intentional wrongdoing or through negligence his estate has no claim for damages. Each of his dependants such as wife, child or parent, however, has claim for compensation for pecuniary loss suffered as a result of such death. Amount of damages apportioned in accordance with extent to which deceased's negligence contributed to death. (Apportionment of Damages Act, No. 34 of 1956, as am'd.). Such loss is usually calculated on basis of annuity and on loss of support and maintenance. Ordinary laws regarding limitation of actions apply (see topic Limitation of Actions). There is also no special limit to amount claimable. Delictual responsibility must not be confused with obligation to indemnify dependants of workman under Workmen's Compensation Act where amount of indemnity is fixed but is due and owing independently of any fault or negligence on part of employer. Where person has committed wrong intentionally or negligently which in turn causes pecuniary loss, claim against his estate will lie to extent of such pecuniary loss. In case of contract, death of one party to contract normally does not discharge contract unless contract was personal to deceased, e.g., servant.

DECEDENTS' ESTATES:

See topics Descent and Distribution; Executors and Administrators; Wills.

DEEDS:

(Deeds Registries Act No. 47/1937).

Sales, exchanges and donations of immovable property must be in writing and signed by parties thereto to be of any force and effect. Ownership does not pass until property is registered in name of transferee in relevant deeds office. Save as is otherwise provided in any other law no deed of transfer, mortgage bond or certificate of title or registration of any kind shall be attested, executed or registered by registrar unless it has been prepared by conveyancer practising within province within which his registry is situated.

Leases need not be in writing to be valid but leases for ten years or more must be notarial and registered in relevant deeds office to be valid against third parties.

Mortgages of immovable property and notarial bonds over movable property as well as creation, transfer and cancellation of any real rights in immovable property also require registration in deeds office.

Acquisition or separation of mineral rights from land ownership may be by way of certificate of mineral rights, which is not notarial, or by way of notarial cession of mineral rights, which is also mode of acquiring mineral rights after first separation from land has occurred.

See also topic Sales.

DEPOSITIONS:

The Supreme Court of South Africa will recognize letters of request issued by foreign countries to take evidence within the Republic. Letters of request, instead of commissions to take evidence, should be issued in all cases where the witnesses to be examined must be compelled to appear.

Letters of request should be addressed by the responsible department of state to the Minister of Justice for South Africa, requesting the recognition of the commission to take evidence and the giving of effect thereto in the Republic of South Africa. It is advisable to designate an advocate as commissioner, with an alternate in case he cannot act. Law of Evidence Amendment Act No. 45 of 1988 provided that: (i) Rules relating to hearsay evidence be relaxed, (ii) courts take judicial notice of law of foreign states and indigenous law, (iii) communication between spouses during marriage can be admissable in certain circumstances.

See topic Acknowledgments.

DESCENT AND DISTRIBUTION:

Marriage under the common law, without contract, entitles the surviving spouse to one-half of the joint estate by reason of the community of property which such a marriage entails. See topic Husband and Wife.

By Intestate Succession Act No. 81 of 1987 surviving spouse inherits if no descendants, descendants inherit if no surviving spouse. If there is surviving spouse and descendants spouse takes greater of child's share or R125,000. In absence of spouse or descendants, estate is divided between relatives in ascendant and collateral lines according to formula too complicated to outline herein.

See Topical Index in front part of this volume.

DISPUTE RESOLUTION:

Mandatory Dispute Resolution.—§6 of Arbitration Act (No. 42 of 1965) provides that where there is agreement (in writing) between two or more parties that any dispute between them shall be referred to arbitration and one of parties initiates legal proceedings against another in respect of dispute, defendant in matter may apply to court for stay of proceedings provided he does so after having given notice of his intention to defend action, but before delivering any pleading or taking any other steps in proceedings, and if court is satisfied that there is no reason why dispute should not be referred to arbitration, court may make order staying such proceedings.

There are over 324 references to arbitration, mediation and conciliation under various Acts of Parliament under following headings: Agriculture, Fisheries, Forests & Water (15); Commercial Law (7); Constitutional Law (14); Education (7); Energy and Mining (9); Health and Welfare (2); Labour Law (148); Procedure (62); Property—Immovable (25); Trade and Industry (19); Transport (16).

Voluntary Dispute Resolution.—Various methods of voluntary dispute resolution include, amongst others, arbitration; commissions of enquiry; conciliation; facilitation; fact-finding; hybrid forms of dispute resolution; informal discussion and problem-solving; litigation; mediation; minitrial; negotiation and relationship-building initiatives.

Dispute Resolution Bodies.—The Association of Arbitrators (Southern Africa); Arbitration Foundation of Southern Africa ("AFSA"); Family Institute; Independent Mediation Service of South Africa ("IMSSA"); SA Association of Mediators.

See also topic Arbitration and Award.

DIVORCE:

(Divorce Act No. 70/1979).

Only grounds for divorce are: (1) Irretrievable breakdown of marriage which may be proved in various ways, (2) mental illness, and (3) continuous unconsciousness.

Court shall have jurisdiction in divorce action if: (1)(a) Parties to action are domiciled in area of jurisdiction of court on date on which action is instituted (domicile of married persons means domicile of husband), or (b) wife is plaintiff or applicant and she is ordinarily resident in area of jurisdiction of that court on date on which action is instituted and has been ordinarily resident in Republic for period of one year immediately prior to said date and: (i) is domiciled in Republic; or (ii) was domiciled in Republic immediately before cohabitation between her and her husband ceased; (iii) was South African citizen or was domiciled in Republic immediately prior to her marriage; (2) court which has jurisdiction in terms of subsection (1)(b) shall also have jurisdiction in respect of claim in reconvention or counter-application in divorce action concerned; (3) court which has jurisdiction in terms of this section in case where parties are not domiciled in Republic shall determine any issue in accordance with law which would have been applicable had parties been domiciled in area of jurisdiction of court concerned on date on which divorce action was instituted; (4) provisions of this Act shall not derogate from jurisdiction which court has in terms of any other law or common law.

On dissolution of marriage court may order spouse most responsible for breakdown to forfeit benefits of marriage in community of property if parties were married without executing ante-nuptial contract. (See topic Husband and Wife.) Court may in its discretion order either plaintiff or defendant to pay maintenance to other spouse. Factors taken into consideration are, inter alia, conduct of parties and financial circumstances.

Court considers welfare of children in matter of custody and has power to order either or both spouses to pay maintenance for children even after dissolution of marriage. The Mediation in Certain Divorce Matters Act, No. 24 of 1987, provides that reports and recommendations may be made by family advocate in divorces where minor or dependent children are involved, aim being to safeguard interests of such children.

There are no restrictions on the right of divorced persons to remarrying each other or third persons.

Separation.—Judicial separation has been abolished.

DOWER:

Dower as such does not exist in South African law.

The nearest approach in Roman Dutch law is termed "Douarie." This is a gift settled under antenuptial contract by a prospective husband on his intended spouse to take effect at the husband's death. It must be validated by marriage, when it becomes irrevocable, except in case of divorce, when court may rescind gift.

ENVIRONMENT:

Environmental legislation is of fragmented nature, having different government departments responsible for its enforcement.

Environmental rights were accorded fundamental rights status in The Constitution of the Republic of South Africa No. 200 of 1993—clause 29: "every person shall have the right to an environment which is not detrimental to his/her health or wellbeing."

1996 constitution details scope of such rights—clause 24 "Everyone has right (a) to an environment that is not harmful to their health or well being, and (b) to have the environment protected, for the benefit of present and future generations, through reasonable legislative and other measures that—(i) prevent pollution and ecological degradation; (ii) promote conservation; and (iii) secure ecologically sustainable development and use of natural resources while promoting justifiable economic and social development."

Environment Conservation Act No. 73 of 1989.—Provides for effective protection and controlled utilisation of environment. It enables Minister of Environmental Affairs to determine general policy to be applied to all aspects relating to conservation of environment. Act establishes council for environment and committee for environmental coordination, and board of investigation. Act enables Minister to make regulations regarding: (i) waste management; (ii) control of dumping of litter; (iii) noise and shock; (iv) environmental impact reports; (v) limited development areas.

Act creates offence and provides for penalties and forfeitures. Policy in terms of Act was published on 21 Jan. 1994—it makes every government department and institution accept full accountability for consequences that activities within its field of responsibility may have on environment. It gives guidelines regarding use, nature conservation, urban environment, pollution control, and calls for strategy for integrated waste control and integrated pollution control.

Pollution.—

Atmospheric Pollution Prevention Act No. 45 of 1965.—Provides for prevention of pollution of atmosphere and establishes National Air Pollution Advisory Committee. Act deals with: (i) noxious and offensive gases; (ii) smoke; (iii) dust; (iv) vehicular emissions.

Hazardous Substances Act No. 15 of 1975.—Provides for control of substances which may cause injury or ill health to or death of human beings; provides for division of such substances into groups in relation to degree of danger. Provides for prohibition and control of use, disposal, dumping of such substances and products.

Water Act No. 54 of 1956.—Controls most aspects of water pollution. Marine pollution is controlled in terms of The Dumping at Sea Control Act No. 73 of 1983; The Prevention and Combating of Pollution of the Sea by Oil Act No. 6 of 1981; The International Convention for the Prevention of Pollution from Ships Act No. 2 of 1986; The International Convention Relating to the Intervention on the High Seas in Cases of Oil Pollution Casualties Act No. 64 of 1987.

Solid Waste Pollution and Waste Management.—Dealt with in §19 of Environment Conservation Act of 1989—provides for prevention of littering. §24 of same act empowers Minister of Environmental Affairs to make regulations with regard to waste management concerning wide range of waste-related subjects such as: handling, storage, transport, disposal, reduction, reuse and processing of waste.

Minerals Act No. 50 of 1991.—Regulates orderly utilisation and rehabilitation of surface of land during and after prospecting and mining operations.

Conservation of Agricultural Resources Act No. 43 of 1993.—Provides for control over utilisation of natural agricultural resources of Republic to promote conservation of soil, water sources and vegetation, combating of weeds and invader plants.

Sea Fishery Act No. 12 of 1988.—Provides for conservation of marine ecosystems and orderly exploitation, fertilisation of certain marine resources and control of sea fishing.

Enforcement.—Almost all environmental statutes endow administrative officials and bodies with power to enforce their provisions by regulating procedures.

ESCHEAT: See topic Descent and Distribution.

EVIDENCE: See topic Depositions.

EXCHANGE CONTROL:

See topics Currency; Foreign Exchange, Foreign Trade and Investment.

EXECUTIONS:

See topics Attachment; Garnishment.

EXECUTORS AND ADMINISTRATORS:

(Administration of Estates Act No. 66/1965; Supreme Court Act No. 59/1959).

There are two classes of executors, namely, executors testamentary (appointed by will) and executors dative (appointed by the Supreme Court).

They have full power to administer and wind up deceased estates under the supervision of the Supreme Court. Security for the due administration must normally be given, and certain formalities must be complied with, such as publication of notice in Government Gazette and local newspaper, etc. It is duty of executors to file with Supreme Court death notice and inventory. Upon completion of liquidation they must render liquidation and distribution account.

All funds accruing to minors must be deposited in the Guardian's Fund of the Supreme Court until the minor reaches majority (21 years of age or marriage), unless the will provides otherwise.

In South Africa "administrator" to some extent corresponds to the English trustee.

Foreign executors wishing to administer assets within the Republic must have their letters of administration resealed by the Supreme Court of South Africa in order to become officially recognized and to enable them to realize South African assets.

Before foreign letters of administration will be recognized an executor is required to produce: (a) Official death certificate; (b) officially certified copy of letters of administration; (c) death notice giving particulars of the deceased as to age, parentage, marriage status, children, etc.; (d) inventory of South African assets; (e) power of attorney by foreign executor authorizing the Republic mandatory to apply for letters of administration in the latter's name; (f) certified copy of the will. Documents mentioned in (a), (b), (e) and (f) must be duly authenticated in terms of the Republic rules for authentication of documents. The Trust Property Control Act No. 57 of 1988 further regulates control of trust property. See topic Acknowledgments.

EXEMPTIONS:

(§39 of Supreme Court Act No. 59/1959; §67 of Magistrates Court Act No. 39/1944).

In respect of any process of execution issued out of any court the following property is protected from seizure and may not be attached or sold: (a) The necessary beds, bedding and wearing apparel of the person against whose property execution is levied and of his family; (b) the necessary furniture and household utensils, not exceeding R2,000 in value; (c) the supply of food and drink in the house sufficient for the needs of such person and of his family during one month; (d) tools and implements of trade, and tools necessarily used in the cultivation of land, not exceeding R2,000 in value; (e) professional books, documents, or instruments, necessarily used by such person in his profession, not exceeding R2,000 in value; (f) such arms and ammunition as person in respect of whose property execution has been issued is required by law, regulation or disciplinary order to have in his possession as part of his equipment.

Pensions and workmen's compensation payments are to a certain extent exempt from sale in execution and cannot be alienated by the beneficiary.

FOREIGN CORPORATIONS:

See topics Corporations; Aliens.

See Topical Index in front part of this volume.

FOREIGN EXCHANGE, FOREIGN TRADE AND INVESTMENT:

Finance.—Fairly strict exchange controls have existed in Republic since 1961, promulgated as Exchange Control Regulations, Orders and Rules, 1961 (as amended) in terms of Currency and Exchanges Act (Act 9 of 1933). Exchange Control Departments of South African Reserve Bank, acting as agent for Treasury, together with commercial banks as authorised dealers, control all foreign currency transactions. Dual-currency system whereby foreign companies and individuals had to invest in Republic through unit known as Financial Rand, was abolished on 10 Mar. 1995.

Government is committed to phasing out controls and all remaining exchange controls will be dismantled as soon as circumstances are favourable.

Following new measures will be promulgated: In terms of new regulations, wholly nonresident owned entity is able to borrow 100% of shareholders' equity; institutional investors, namely insurance companies, pension funds and unit trusts, may obtain foreign assets by way of asset swaps for up to 10% of their total assets, subject to stipulations of legal framework within which they operate; institutional investors will be allowed foreign currency transfers during 1996 of up to 3% of net inflow of funds during 1995 calendar year. Approval for such transfers will be subject to overall limit of 10%; corporate entities who operate in export field and also import goods from abroad, will be allowed to offset cost of imports against proceeds of exports, provided set-off takes place within period of 30 days.

Goods.—Control is vested in Director of Import and Export Control. Substantial tax and other privileges are given to anyone who carries on export trade as Government is most anxious to increase its foreign reserves. Present basis of import control was introduced in 1949 to stem drain on foreign exchange through excess of imports over exports. Certain goods may not be imported, certain goods require import permits and certain goods are exempt from this requirement. Foreign currency is made freely available for permissible imports.

Present Government has, however, acceded to, and is signing member of General Agreements on Tariffs and Trade (GATT) whereby import duties and controls will gradually be phased out.

See also topics Currency; Imports.

FRAUDS, STATUTE OF:

The Republic of South Africa has no Statute of Frauds, but certain contracts must be in writing, for instance, purchase and sale of land, leases exceeding ten years, transfer deeds, mortgage bonds, certain credit agreements, lease lend of movables, etc.

Bill of Exchange Act 34 of 1964 as amended also makes provisions regarding negotiable instruments in order to eliminate possibility of fraud.

FRAUDULENT SALES AND CONVEYANCES:

The Insolvency Act, No. 24 of 1936, renders void all dispositions made with intent to defraud creditors. They may be set aside at instance of trustee in insolvent estate only after bankruptcy proceedings. Various principles apply to "voidable preferences," "undue preferences" and "collusive dealings."

See also topic Sales.

GARNISHMENT:

(Supreme Court Act No. 59/1959; Magistrates Court Act No. 39/1944).

Provided the debtor is left sufficient for the living expenses of himself and his dependants the courts may normally order the attachment of any debt or wages due to such judgment debtor by any other person within its jurisdiction to satisfy the judgment. In addition the magistrate's courts may similarly attach not only debts due but also debts to become due.

HOLIDAYS:

Regulated by Public Holidays Act No. 36 of 1994 (commencement date: 1 Jan. 1995).

Following are statutory holidays in Republic of South Africa:

Calendar of public holidays: New Year's Day 1 Jan.; Human Rights Day 21 Mar.; Good Friday Fri. before Easter Sun.; Family Day Mon. after Easter Sun.; Freedom Day 27 Apr.; Worker's Day 1 May; Youth Day 16 June; National Women's Day 9 Aug.; Heritage Day 24 Sept.; Day of Reconciliation 16 Dec.; Christmas Day 25 Dec.; Day of Goodwill 26 Dec.

Note: Whenever any public holiday falls on Sun., following Mon. will be public holiday.

HOMESTEADS:

Before any private land is proclaimed as public digging, there shall be reserved to owner free and uninterrupted use of any homestead on land to be so dealt with.

Except as aforesaid, no special rules apply to protect homesteads, even in respect to creditors' claims or domestic rights.

HUSBAND AND WIFE:

Matrimonial Property Act No. 88 of 1984 became effective Nov. 1, 1984. Prior to introduction of Act there were three matrimonial property regimes, namely marriage in community of property with consequences that assets of both husband and wife fell into joint estate with husband having administrative control; marriage out of community of property without antenuptial contract with consequences that each of husband and wife retained their own estates and profit and loss as between them but with consequence that as against world marriage would be regarded as marriage in community of property, and marriage out of community of property with antenuptial contract.

Act has abolished marital power in all marriages concluded after Nov. 1, 1984 with consequences that in case of marriage in community of property both husband and wife have equal rights regarding administration of joint estate, but in certain instances contracting spouse will require consent of each other. Spouses who marry out of community of property and with antenuptial contract are now subject to accrual regime unless that regime is excluded, although regime itself can be modified.

Effect of accrual is, save for assets specifically excluded, that spouse whose estate shows no accrual or lesser accrual than estate of other spouse during marriage has claim against other spouse for one-half difference. Spouses married before Nov. 1, 1984 in community of property or with antenuptial contract may introduce accrual regime by jointly applying to Supreme Court for change of matrimonial property regime.

Regardless of where spouses are married if husband is then domiciled in South Africa, South African law applies.

Maintenance.—A wife can obtain maintenance during the existence of and on dissolution of marriage by civil process in Supreme Court. Enforcement of maintenance order can be achieved by criminal prosecution through magistrates' courts.

IMMIGRATION: See topic Aliens.

IMPORTS:

Due to special currency restrictions, some measures—promulgated in terms of Import and Export Control Act (Act 45 of 1963)—have restricted all imports into country except under permit granted by Department of Trade and Industry at Pretoria.

Certain goods may not be imported at all. Importation of some goods is exempt from requirements of import permit. In general, import surcharge is levied on most imports ranging from 10% to 60%, although Finance Minister recently abolished import surcharges on all capital and intermediate goods and has proposed that remaining surcharges be abolished in due course. See topics Currency; Foreign Exchange, Foreign Trade and Investment.

INFANCY AND MINORITY:

Infant is person under age of seven years. Minor is person under age of 21 years. Minors are under certain legal disabilities, for example, they cannot enter into any contract or incur any liability without consent or assistance of their parents or guardians. (See topics Contracts; Marriage.) Infant is irrebuttably presumed to be incapable of any wrongful act. Rebuttable presumption applies to minors between seven and 14 years. In terms of Age of Majority Act 57 of 1972, Supreme Court may grant express emancipation to minor who is at least 18 years of age, and who satisfies Court that he is fit and proper person to manage his own affairs. In such case Court decides on legal capacity of minor which is normally full legal capacity of major of 21 years or over. In addition, subject to marriage laws of South Africa, on marriage minor attains majority for all purposes and therefore has full legal capacity. (See topic Husband and Wife.)

Note: South African Law Commission is conducting investigation into granting of visitation rights to grandparents of minor children.

INSOLVENCY: See topic Bankruptcy; Insolvency.

INTEREST:

(Prescribed Rate of Interest Act No. 55/1975).

Where a debtor fails to pay a debt on due date and there has been no agreement regarding interest, the creditor is entitled to claim as compensation or damages interest at legal rate of 15.5% from such due date.

Maximum permissible interest rates on moneys owing and on leasing and hire purchase transactions fluctuate from time to time. (Usury Act No. 73 of 1968). There are various Acts controlling sales by instalments and hiring and leasing contracts which are most complicated and require various formalities.

Note: Prescribed Rate of Interest Amendment Bill has been tabled, principal object of which is to amend principal Act, so as to enable creditor to receive interest on unliquidated debt.

INTESTACY: See topic Descent and Distribution.

JOINT STOCK COMPANIES:

See topic Corporations.

JUDGMENTS:

(Supreme Court Act No. 59/1959; Magistrates Court Act No. 39/1944).

Apart from final judgment for plaintiff or defendant, courts may grant judgment known as absolution from instance, especially in cases where dispute turns on plaintiff's testimony against that of defendant, neither side being proved by any documentary or other verbal evidence. This judgment leaves matter open. It is not final and upon payment of defendant's costs, plaintiff is at liberty to issue fresh summons.

Prescription of Judgments.—See topic Limitation of Actions.

Foreign Judgments.—Action can be maintained on a foreign judgment but the defendant can plead a want of jurisdiction in the court which rendered the judgment or a defect in procedure or otherwise invalidating the judgment.

LABOUR RELATIONS:

There are agreements relating to various trades and industries, for example the building industry, which govern conditions of employment.

There is also legislation controlling workmen's compensation and trade unions, etc.

Employer organisations, trade unions and labour matters and disputes are normally controlled by Labour Relations Act 28 of 1956 as am'd. Act applies to every undertaking, industry, trade or occupation and also applies to persons employed as domestic servants, certain state employees and teachers. Unfair labour practices are restricted to employment situation and to those circumstances where adverse implications of relationships are considered unfair. Strikes and lockouts are excluded and not subject to consideration of fairness. Industrial Court may interdict illegal strikes and lockouts. Disputes fall under Industrial Court which runs parallel with Courts of Law and also is under jurisdiction of Manpower Board. Any decision, award, order or determination of Industrial Court may be executed as if same were made by Supreme Court. Decisions may be brought on appeal or review to Labour Appeal Court having jurisdiction. Appeals are heard by judge of Supreme Court and two assessors. Further appeals on questions of law lie to Appellate Division. Disputes may also be settled by Industrial Councils, Conciliation Boards, mediation, arbitration. There are also other special statutes relating to particular aspects of commerce and industry.

See Topical Index in front part of this volume.

LABOUR RELATIONS . . . *continued*

The Labour Relations Act 66 of 1995 was published on 5 Jan. 1996. Date of operation of this Act has not been promulgated although some of provisions came into effect on 1 Jan. 1996.

Most important changes in Act relate to institutions for collective bargaining, special needs of Public Service, essential services, employee participation at workplace, registration of trade unions and employer's associations, conciliation machinery and procedures, labour courts and unfair dismissal.

Note: Minister of Labour recently published policy proposals for new employment standards statute to replace Basic conditions of Employment Act and the Wage Act.

LAW REPORTS: See topic Reports.

LEGISLATURE:

See topic Constitution and Government.

LICENCES:

Licensing of trades and occupations are by ordinances in respective Provinces. Licence fees are payable in certain cases to Government or local authority.

LIENS:

Under common law, a lien is afforded to persons who are under obligation to render services to public or who expend money or moneys worth (such as labor) on improvement of another's property. Possession is essential requisite to retain effective lien and once possession is given up lien is destroyed and subsequent possession will not restore it.

A landlord has a special lien for unpaid rent on the tenant's goods, and also on a third person's goods brought on to the premises for use of the tenant excluding goods hypothecated in terms of Security by Means of Movable Property Act. Notice to landlord of ownership in third person defeats landlord's lien for rent accruing thereafter.

Carriers, hotelkeepers, boarding-house keepers, clearing agents, artificers and builders are amongst the class of persons who enjoy liens.

LIMITATION OF ACTIONS:

A consolidating measure (Act No. 68 of 1969) is now in force and enacts following periods of prescription:

Thirty years: In respect of (1) any debt secured by mortgage bond; (2) any judgment debt; (3) any debt in respect of any taxation imposed or levied by or under any law; (4) any debt owed to State in respect of any share of profits, royalties or any similar consideration payable in respect of right to mine minerals or other substances.

Fifteen years: In respect of any debt owed to State and arising out of an advance or loan of money or a sale or lease of land by State to debtor, unless a longer period applies in respect of debt in question as outlined in subhead Thirty Years, above.

Six years: In respect of a debt arising from a bill of exchange or other negotiable instrument or from a notarial contract, unless a longer period applied in respect of debt in question as outlined in subheads Thirty Years and Fifteen Years, above.

Three years: In respect of any other debt, but five years in respect of claims for personal injuries arising out of motor vehicle accident. Act sometimes provides otherwise for specific periods of prescription for claims against government and quasi-government bodies such as South African Railways and South African Police, provincial and local authorities.

When Prescription Begins to Run.—Generally, prescription shall commence to run as soon as debt is due. If, however, debtor wilfully prevents creditor from coming to know of existence of debt, prescription shall not commence to run until creditor becomes aware of existence of debt. Furthermore a debt shall not be deemed to be due until creditor has knowledge of identity of debtor and of facts from which debt arises (provided that creditor shall be deemed to have such knowledge if he could have acquired it by exercising reasonable care).

Completion of Prescription Delayed in Certain Circumstances.—(1) If (a) creditor is a minor or insane or a person under curatorship; or (b) creditor is prevented by vis major including any law, or any order of court from interrupting running of prescription by service of judicial process (see subhead Judicial Interruption of Prescription, infra) or (c) debtor is outside Republic; or (d) creditor and debtor are married to each other; or (e) creditor and debtor are partners and debt is a debt which arose out of partnership relationship; or (f) creditor is a juristic person and debtor is a member of governing body of such juristic person; or (g) debt is object of a dispute subjected to arbitration; or (h) debt is object of a claim filed against deceased or insolvent estate of debtor or against a company in liquidation or against an applicant under Agricultural Credit Act, 1966; or (i) creditor or debtor is deceased and an executor of estate in question has not yet been appointed; and in all such cases, if claim in question would have prescribed before or on or within one year after date of which relevant impediment has ceased to exist then period of prescription is extended for a year after day on which impediment has ceased to exist. (2) Debt which arises from a contract and which would become prescribed before a reciprocal debt which arises from same contract becomes prescribed, prescribes at same time as reciprocal debt. (3) Prescription of legal obligation of conscripts suspended during period of service in certain circumstances. Obligation to pay contractual debt and civil legal remedies against conscript similarly suspended. (Moratorium Act No. 25 of 1963).

Interruption of Prescription by Acknowledgment of Liability.—(1) Running of prescription is interrupted by an express or tacit acknowledgment of liability by debtor. (2) If running of prescription is interrupted as contemplated above prescription runs de novo from day on which acknowledgment takes place, or if debtor and creditor agree to postpone due date of debt, from date upon which debt again becomes due.

Judicial Interruption of Prescription.—Service of summons, or any judicial process claiming payment of any debt interrupts prescription. However, if creditor does not successfully prosecute his claim, such interruption shall lapse and period of prescription is deemed not to have been interrupted at all (subject to limitation that if debtor acknowledges liability, and as a result creditor does not prosecute his claim, prescription runs afresh from date of such acknowledgment.

LIMITED PARTNERSHIP: See topic Partnership.

MARRIAGE:

The parties must validly consent to marry and if under the age of 21 the consent of both parents if living or guardian or court is required. The marriage of a minor, provided it is not prohibited, is valid until set aside by parents in legal proceedings.

In case of marriage of a previously divorced person, a certified copy of order of court must be produced.

Prohibited Marriages.—Marriage is prohibited for: (a) Boys under the age of 18 and/or girls under the age of 15 unless with the permission of the Minister of Home Affairs; (b) mentally defective persons; (c) persons already married; (d) widowers or widows, unless they exhibit proof that portions left to minor children by deceased spouse have been suitably secured; (e) persons related within prohibited degrees of consanguinity or affinity or by virtue of adoption.

MARRIED WOMEN:

Marital power abolished in all marriages. See topic Husband and Wife.

See also topic Dower.

MONOPOLIES AND RESTRAINT OF TRADE:

Maintenance and Promotion of Competition Act 96 of 1979 as amended provides for establishment of Competition Board which recommends remedial recourse to Minister of Trade and Industry on questions of Economic Policy. Provision is made for exercising of control over "acquisitions", "restrictive practices" and "monopoly situations" not in public interest, after investigation instituted by Minister or Board itself. Matters which are liable for investigation are widely framed and include: Acquisition by holder of controlling interest in any business or undertaking involved in production, manufacture, supply or distribution of any commodity, also controlling interest in any arrangement, business or undertaking of any kind provided that in all cases interest restricts or is calculated to restrict competition. "Commodity" is defined very widely to include all goods and services; activities of State and professions are thus liable to investigation. Holder can be any person, firm, company or association of persons.

Activities excluded from scope of Act are: Exercise of rights regarding trade marks and patents; valid trade union agreements and distribution and production of unmanufactured agricultural products.

Board is empowered to make arrangement with any party under investigation, subject to Minister's control, and failing such arrangement, Minister may declare activity to be unlawful; may fix maximum selling price for affected commodity or may suspend import duty on commodities similar to those affected. His decisions are subject to appeal to special court.

Generally speaking restraint of trade is valid unless in circumstances it is unreasonable and not in public interest. Restraints are usually restricted in time and area. Minister may outlaw any restrictive practice which is not in public interest. In particular as result of general investigation Minister has declared following to be unlawful: (a) Resale price maintenance; (b) horizontal price collusion; (c) horizontal collusion on conditions of supply; (d) horizontal collusion on market sharing; or (e) collusive tendering.

There is no legislation corresponding to the Sherman Act of the United States.

Unfair Competition.—Under common law as matter of public policy there are various ways in which wrong can be committed by means of unfair trading. Normally proof of malice would be required. For example, it would be wrong for trader to injure rival trade by utilising information which latter having compiled by his own skill and labour has distributed to former, where former is aware of confidential nature of information. Also remedy would be available to party to contract who complains that third party has intentionally and without lawful justification induced another party to contract to commit breach thereof.

Trade Practices Act No. 76/1976.—This Act has been repealed but certain sections, in particular those dealing with false and misleading statements in advertising and promotions, remain in force until date fixed by Minister of Trade and Industry. At time of writing, such date has not yet been fixed. The Harmful Business Practices Act No. 71 of 1988, provides mechanism for regulation of business practices. Business Practices Committee was established by this Act to issue guidelines on current policy in relation to harmful business practices, to hear representations and to make investigations. Committee reports to Minister of Trade and Industry and makes recommendations upon which Minister may make ruling. This ruling may be appealed against. Full time member with legal and business skills is to be appointed to Committee and Committee will not only be responsible for investigating harmful business practises, but will also in cooperation with private sector, develop codes of conduct for consumer relations in wide range of business activities.

Takeovers and Mergers.—The Securities Regulation Code on Take-overs and Mergers eminates from Securities Regulation Panel which was established under provisions of 440B of Companies Act (No. 61 of 1973). Code is based to large extent on City Code on Take-overs and Mergers issued by London Panel on Take-overs and Mergers.

MORTGAGES: See topic Deeds.

MOTOR VEHICLES:

Motor vehicles are subject to certain taxes which vary according to the weight and power of the vehicle, whether required for private or business purposes. There is no Republic tax. The taxes in the various provinces differ considerably.

Motor Vehicle Carriers.—Conveyance of goods by motor service for hire or reward is controlled by Road Transportation Act, No. 74 of 1977. Transport Deregulation Act No. 80 of 1988 has repealed provisions in respect of conveyance of goods or persons in Act No. 74 of 1977 and has placed various powers and duties which originally vested in National Transport Commission into hands of South African Roads Board. The Road

MOTOR VEHICLES . . . *continued*
Traffic Act 29 of 1989 has consolidated and amended registration and licensing of vehicles and drivers, and regulates traffic on public roads.

NEGOTIABLE INSTRUMENTS:

See topic Bills and Notes.

NOTARIES PUBLIC:

Duties of notary public usually form adjunct to work of attorney, and no one can become notary public in South Africa unless he has qualified and is admitted as attorney.

The notary's work merely consists of noting bills of exchange and attesting certain deeds which must be executed before a notary, such as antenuptial contracts, leases of more than ten years' duration, etc.

PARTNERSHIP:

Companies' Act 61 of 1973 provides that no partnership may be formed of more than 20 persons, but such restriction does not apply to persons carrying on profession of public accountant, auditor, attorneys, architect, quantity surveyor, professional engineer or stockbroker.

A partnership may be constituted between two or more persons either orally or in writing. Each of the partners must contribute something, either capital or labor, for the joint benefit of the partnership and with the object of making a profit out of sharing the same. If any of these essentials are lacking, no partnership is constituted.

The liability of partners depends on terms of partnership agreement and each partner is liable in solidum for debts of partnership.

An act of insolvency by a partnership is deemed to be an act of insolvency of the individual partners, but it requires a special application to court against the individual partners to render their private estates administrable as insolvent.

Partnerships are extensively regulated by common law and there exists very little legislation dealing directly with partnerships.

PATENTS:

See Patents Act No. 57 of 1978.

Basis of statute originally modelled on English Law but now follows European Patent Conventions more closely. There are special procedures for applications for grants of patents for new inventions capable of being used in trade, industry or agriculture. Novelty is judged in terms of any matter made public anywhere in world prior to date of application. (§25[5] & [6]). There are also provisions for infringement actions and amendments. Patent must be novel but not obvious and contain "inventive step" of sufficient magnitude. Application must be made by inventor or his duly authorised representative. Patent must be kept secret until filed whereafter it may be used. Under 1978 Act patents run for 20 years with no extensions subject to payment of annual fees. There is provision for compulsory licences. Patents registered under Act 37 of 1952 are still governed by that Act. Republic of South Africa is signatory to International Patent Convention. In terms of International Convention if applicant for RSA patent files corresponding application in Convention country within a year effective date is date of filing of RSA application.

Reciprocal recognition of patents registered in numerous non-signatory countries has been established by proclamation of State President.

Patent law is complicated and patent matters must be dealt with by patent agent or expert.

PLEDGES:

Practically the only effective pledge of movables is by an agreement of pledge either verbal or in writing accompanied by delivery of the movables to the creditor and by retention of same by him. Corporeal and incorporeal property may be pledged. See also topic Chattel Mortgages.

PRESCRIPTION:

See topic Limitation of Actions.

PRINCIPAL AND AGENT:

The common law applies and the law is based on the English law.

If an agent acts within the scope of his authority and has disclosed his principal, only the principal is liable; but if the principal has not been disclosed, the third party has a right of action against either the principal or the agent.

A power of attorney is legally necessary only to enable an agent to transfer freehold property, to pass a mortgage bond over such property or to bring a law suit. But although not essential, a principal often arms his agent with a power of attorney clearly indicating the limits of the authority conferred on the agent.

REAL PROPERTY:

Apart from mining titles, this consists of freehold and leasehold property.

RECORDS: See topic Deeds.

REPLEVIN:

The true owner of property, movable as well as immovable, which has been alienated without his consent, by one who has stolen it, or to whom it has been lent or let or given in deposit, or by any other person not having a mandate to sell, may legally claim it from any one who is in possession of it, without making restitution of the price paid by the possessor.

REPORTS:

Until the end of 1946 decisions of each Provincial Division as well as the Appellate Division of the Supreme Court were published annually in separate volumes. Since the beginning of 1947 however all reports have been amalgamated into one set entitled the South African Law Reports. These reports contain selected decisions from all provincial and local divisions as well as the Appellate Division of the Supreme Court and each is published in quarterly volumes. Since 1990 criminal law decisions are published (though not exclusively) under title South African Criminal Law Reports. Decisions are published in quarterly volumes. Since July 1994, Constitutional law decisions are published under title Constitutional Law Reports. Decisions published every three months.

RESTRAINT OF TRADE:

See topic Monopolies and Restraint of Trade.

SALES:

Contract of sale is complete when buyer and seller have agreed that there is a sale of things sold and price to be paid. However, passing of ownership in thing sold requires both contract and delivery of kind of thing sold in pursuance of contract. Contract of sale alone is not enough to pass ownership. Contract, itself, may expressly provide any desired special conditions regarding sale, e.g., consignment contract or hire purchase contract.

Although ownership does not pass until thing sold is delivered, risk and benefit of thing sold does normally pass to purchaser on completion of contract. This can be varied by express agreement.

Movable property may normally be transferred without any written formality. Where there is contract to transfer ownership of movable property as well as delivery, ownership may pass although purchase price may not have been paid. However ownership may be retained by selling on suspensive condition better known as instalment sale transactions. See topic Contracts.

Sales of immovable property must be in writing and signed by parties to be of any force and effect. Ownership does not pass until property is registered in name of transferee in Deeds Office. (Deeds Registries Act No. 47/1937). There are special provisions for sale of land by instalments. (Alienation of Land Act No. 68/1981).

Warranties, Express and Implied.—Seller must deliver thing sold at proper time and place and take care of it until delivery. Seller is fully responsible for promises seriously made about quantity, quality, suitability and any other attributes of thing sold. Such promises are part of contract and are called "express warranties." Express warranties, however, must be distinguished from representations which induce a contract, but are not part of it. Purchaser is entitled on breach of warranty to be put into position as if warranty had been fulfilled. Purchaser, on a breach of a representation, is entitled to be put in position as if he had not been induced to contract. Even without express warranty, sale is presumed to be free of latent defects which render thing sold unfit for purpose for which it was bought. Manufacturers and merchants professing special knowledge are presumed to have knowledge of any latent defects and are therefore normally liable for consequential damages as well as other penalties for latent defects. Innocent seller, other than manufacturer and merchant, of article with latent defect is not liable for damages. Breach of express warranty by a seller always attracts damages. Rule of implied warranty against latent defects can be rebutted by express agreement that thing is sold as it stands, or "voetstoots" provided seller is innocent. Express warranty or serious representation must be distinguished from a mere invitation to buy. Normally buyer takes risk of thing sold. Where, however, there is a deliberate misrepresentation or breach of express warranty or a concealment of defect amounting to fraud, buyer can cancel sale and claim damages. In case of innocent seller of thing with latent defect, buyer cannot claim damages, but can claim rescission of contract against return of purchase price for serious defect and a reduction of purchase price, but no rescission if defect is minor.

Instalment Sale Transactions.—See Credit Agreements Act No. 75/1980, discussed in topic Contracts.

Price Control.—(Price Control Act No. 25/1964). Certain special items of merchandise are subject to price control. Also there are certain restrictive provisions regarding leasing of particular products which provisions are designed to supplement Credit Agreements Act.

Notices Required.—In terms of Insolvency Act No. 24 of 1936 §34(1) seller of a business or goodwill or any goods or property forming party thereof except in ordinary course of that business, is required to publish notices of sale in both official languages in certain newspapers and in Government Gazette within period of not less than 30 days and not more than 60 days before date of transfer. If seller of business does not publish notices of sale in both official languages in certain newspapers and in Government Gazette within time period, then sale is void as against his creditors for six months after sale, and void as against trustee of his estate if he is sequestrated within same period.

Applicable Law.—For rules regarding choice of law see topic Contracts.

SEALS:

Only public authorities, public corporations and notaries public carry seals and are supposed to affix them to their signatures. The use of a seal by a private person or corporation has no meaning in the legal sense.

SEQUESTRATION: See topics Bankruptcy; Insolvency.

SHIPPING:

Various statutes, which are to large extent based on English Law, have been enacted in South Africa dealing with question of control of shipping and matters incidental thereto.

Admiralty Jurisdiction Regulation Act 1983, provides for vesting of powers of admiralty courts of Republic of South Africa in Provincial and Local Divisions of Supreme Court of South Africa and law to be applied and procedure applicable in enforcement of "maritime claims" as defined in aforementioned Act.

Courts.—Jurisdiction is vested in Supreme Court in terms of Admirality Jurisdiction Regulation Act, 1983 for all maritime claims of whatever nature. Proceedings are commenced by arrest or attachment of ship or other property within jurisdiction. It is not ordinarily necessary to furnish security for damages. Property may be arrested for

See Topical Index in front part of this volume.

SHIPPING . . . *continued*
purposes of obtaining security for arbitration or legal proceedings in another jurisdiction. Sister ship arrests are possible, either of vessels in same ownership, or of ship owned by company controlled, when maritime claim arose, by person who then controlled company which owned ship in respect of which debt arose. Court has power to order examination, testing or inspection of any ship, cargo or documents for purposes of determining any maritime claim brought or to be brought or any defence thereto; these powers are not restricted to maritime claims being enforced in South Africa.

Limitation and Exclusion of Liability.—Tonnage limitation is governed by §261 of Merchant Shipping Act 1951 which entitles ship owner to limit his liability according to vessel's tonnage where loss results without his "actual fault or privity". In such case liability for loss of life or personal injury is limited to R552,000 per ton and liability for loss of or damage to property to R178,000 per ton.

Ranking of Claims.—This is regulated by §11 of Admirality Jurisdiction Regulation Act, 1983 which adopts in some measure relevant provisions of International Convention for the Unification of Certain Rules Relating to Maritime Liens and Mortgages (Brussels 1967).

Ships.—Ownership, mortgages, registration, construction, safety equipment, etc. are covered by Merchant Shipping Act, 1951.

Crew.—Merchant Shipping Act, 1951 provides for manning of ships, certification, authority, liability and welfare of Masters, Officers and Crew.

Safety.—This is governed by Chapter V of Merchant Shipping Act. International Convention for the Safety of Life at Sea, 1974 is incorporated into Merchant Shipping Act by second schedule thereto.

Carriage of Goods by Sea.—The Carriage of Goods by Sea Act, 1986 gives effect to "Hague Visby Rules".

STATUTES:

South African law is based on the common law of England, Roman-Dutch law and statutes.

Prior to the union, each of the four colonies had its own statutes, but since the union some of these have been repealed and replaced by Republic statutes.

Purely provincial matters are governed by provincial ordinances, and there is a tendency to unify the laws of the four provinces.

TAXATION:

Income Tax.—Basic act on income tax is The Income Tax Act, No. 58 of 1962. This act is amended year by year to provide for tax changes. A pay as you earn (P.A.Y.E.) system of taxation is included. Below is taxation for Mar. '96 to Feb. '97.

Employers have to deduct and pay employees' taxes from the latters' earnings. Standard Income Tax on Employees (S.I.T.E.) applies to all taxpayers whose net remuneration does not exceed R50,000 per annum. S.I.T.E. is final liability tax which is deducted by employers. No tax returns have to be submitted by persons subject only to S.I.T.E. Where employee's remuneration exceeds R50,000 per annum, P.A.Y.E. will be deducted in addition to S.I.T.E. Self-employed persons and persons who derive income which is not remuneration, for example, from profession, business, interest or dividends, directors and persons notified by Receiver of Revenue make two provisional tax payments per year based on estimated earnings. Persons over 65 years are exempted from submitting provisional returns if their taxable income does not exceed R50,000 per annum and will not be derived wholly or partly from carrying on of any business. Generally speaking Republic income tax is payable only on such income which has its source in Republic regardless of residence of taxpayer whether he is individual or company. Tax year normally ends at last day of Feb. each year.

By special agreements between Republic and various other countries, including U.K., relief is afforded in certain circumstances against double taxation in two countries of same commercial income. These agreements are complicated and vary in each case. See topic Treaties.

Tables in this topic are set out in Rand (R), South African currency.

Individuals.—In respect of persons other than companies normal tax is levied on all taxable income. Approximate rate of basic income tax is set out in Appendix A. In addition, there is system of tax rebates which are deductions from assessed amount of Income Tax (see catchline Rebates, infra). Certain special deductions are deductible from income and these are dealt with below.

Rebates.—There shall be deducted from normal tax payable by any person other than company or employee paying S.I.T.E. on rate of tax are as set out below. These rebates are allowed from tax as calculated by applying basic table, Appendix A. Any rebate to which taxpayer is entitled will effectively reduce amount of tax payable by him.

Following rebates are deductible from tax according to tax table:

	Natural Persons
Primary	R2,660
Persons 65 and over	R2,500

Deductions from Taxable Income.—

Medical Expenses.—Medical expenses actually incurred by persons under 65 years, so much as exceeds greater of R1,000 or 5% of taxable income as defined. There is no ceiling for persons over 65 years.

Donations.—Actual donations to educational institutions—greater of 2% of taxable income or R500. For companies, 5% of its taxable income prior to allowing deduction.

Physically Disabled.—Deduction from taxable income for expenditure actually incurred by physically disabled persons or their children, in respect of their physical disability, may be claimed to extent that that sum exceeds R500 per annum.

Dividends from companies located both inside and outside Republic of South Africa are exempt from tax.

Minimum standard deduction of R2,000 may be claimed on interest.

In assessing taxable income of individuals as well as corporations or companies there are certain other complicated additional and special deductions or allowances which apply in commerce and industry including in certain cases manufacturers, hotel keepers, exporters, industrialists in development areas, shipowners, aircraft owners, miners and farmers.

Fringe Benefits.—Special legislation was introduced with effect from Mar. 1, 1985. This is too lengthy and complicated to be included but basically actual or portion of actual costs or calculated cash value is placed on all benefits which now form part of individual's income.

Retirement Gratuities.—Maximum exemption from tax in respect of retirement gratuities paid to employee by reason of his retirement or impending retirement is R30,000. Exemption also granted to dismissed and retrenched employees but not to directors of companies who at any time held at least 5% of equity share capital of company. Lump sum benefits from pension, provident or retirement annuity fund are taxable, although certain deductions are permitted. Various formulae apply, depending on type of fund and whether payment is made upon retirement, death, resignation or withdrawal of member.

Retirement Fund Industry.—Monthly tax of 17% from 1 Mar. '96 on gross interest and net rental received by or accrued to pension, provident and retirement annuity funds.

Pension Fund Contributions.—Greater of R1,750 or 7.5% of pensionable income.

Retirement Annuity Fund Contributions.—Greater of 15% of non-pensionable taxable income or R3,500 less current contributions to pension funds or R1,750.

Normally tax year ends at end of Feb. but this can be altered with consent of Commissioner.

Rates.—See Appendix A.

Companies.—Rate of normal taxation for all companies, both public and private, other than certain mining companies, is 35%. Tax on distributed profits is also payable by company. Rates applicable are 15% on or after 17 Mar. 1993 and before 22 June 1994; and 25% on or after 22 June 1994; and 12.5% on or after 13 Mar. 1996. Companies are exempt from tax on dividends received from other companies. Public company for income tax purposes as distinct from private company is company in which general public is substantially interested. Commissioner of Inland Revenue decides when company is public company for tax purposes. Otherwise, it is private company.

Branch profits tax at rate of 40% of taxable income applicable from commencement of years of assessment ending on or after 1 Apr. 1996.

Close corporations are taxed at same rate as companies. See subheads Income Tax, catchline Individuals; Deductions from Taxable Income, catchline Dividends, supra.

Gold mining companies are taxed in varying degrees on special formula (or at rate of 48% from 31 Mar. '95 to 31 Mar. '96, and 42% from 1 Apr. '96) designed to encourage mines to work low grade ore and to prolong life of all gold mines. Diamond mining companies and base mineral companies have effective tax of 50.88%.

Dividends declared by companies on or after 1 Oct. 1995 are no longer subject to 15% nonresident shareholder's tax.

TABLES OF NORMAL TAX FOR THE YEAR ENDED 28 FEBRUARY 1997

Natural Persons

Taxable Income R	R	Rates of Tax R		R
0 -	15 000		17% of each R1	
15 000 -	20 000	2 550 +	19% of the amount over	15 000
20 000 -	30 000	3 500 +	21% of the amount over	20 000
30 000 -	40 000	5 600 +	30% of the amount over	30 000
40 000 -	60 000	8 600 +	41% of the amount over	40 000
60 000 -	80 000	16 800 +	43% of the amount over	60 000
80 000 -	100 000	25 400 +	44% of the amount over	80 000
100 000 +		34 200 +	45% of the amount over	100 000

Persons other than Natural Persons (e.g. Trusts)

Taxable Income R	R	Rates of Tax R		R
0 -	5 000		17% of each R1	
5 000 -	10 000	850 +	19% of the amount over	5 000
10 000 -	15 000	1 800 +	21% of the amount over	10 000
15 000 -	20 000	2 850 +	24% of the amount over	15 000
20 000 -	30 000	4 050 +	28% of the amount over	20 000
30 000 -	40 000	6 850 +	36% of the amount over	30 000
40 000 -	50 000	10 450 +	41% of the amount over	40 000
50 000 -	60 000	14 550 +	42% of the amount over	50 000
60 000 -	70 000	18 750 +	43% of the amount over	60 000
70 000 -	100 000	23 050 +	44% of the amount over	70 000
100 000 +		26 350 +	45% of the amount over	100 000

See Topical Index in front part of this volume.

Income Tax on Royalties or Similar Payments.—Where royalties or similar payments (including payment for use of patents, trademarks or designs and for "know-how") are payable to persons or companies not ordinarily resident or registered, managed or controlled in South Africa, payments are subject to withholding tax at rate of 12% unless royalty is subject to tax in recipient's hands in his country of residence.

Business Taxes or Licences.—In addition to income taxation there are various business taxes paid by way of trading licences, such as commercial traveller's tax. Close corporations initial registration fee of R100; no annual fee.

Foreign Exchange Gains and Losses.—Broadly speaking any gains are taxable and losses deductible.

Value Added Tax.—Indirect tax (VAT) is imposed on supplies and allied services and on professional services. Rate is 14% with certain basic foodstuffs and other items subject to zero rating (VAT at 0%).

Stamp Tax.—There is a stamp tax on most agreements, deeds, transfers of stocks and shares, policies of insurance, promissory notes, bills of exchange, contract notes, powers of attorney and checks. Documents from abroad must be stamped on arrival in South Africa otherwise penalties are imposed. Failure to stamp documents entails penalties but generally speaking does not invalidate document.

Customs Duties.—Customs duties are prescribed for various goods at various rates. Surcharge of between 10 and 60% charged at present on value of imports. The Customs and Excise Act 91 of 1964 provides for refunds, drawbacks and rebates of customs and excise duties paid on imports used in exported manufactured goods and in goods imported for re-export.

A donations tax is levied with certain exceptions on cumulative taxable value of all property gratuitously disposed of by a particular person. Tax is on donors who are persons ordinarily resident or companies controlled in Republic. Rate is 25% of taxable value of all property donated on or after 14 Mar. 1996. Exemptions include donations to charitable, educational or ecclesiastical institutions, donor's spouse, casual gifts to anybody not exceeding R25,000 per annum by natural persons and R5,000 per annum by non-natural persons. This relief refers only to Donation Tax but amount of gifts would be added back when calculating Estate Duty.

Death Duties.—Estate duty is payable in terms of Estate Duty Act No. 45 of 1955, as am'd, on net aggregate value of all property in Republic and property which passes or which is by statute deemed to pass on death after deducting liabilities, deductions and abatements. If deceased was ordinarily resident in Republic it is additionally payable on certain property outside Republic, with certain exceptions. Rate of estate duty and amounts of abatements are varied from time to time. At present there is flat rate of 25%. Allowable deductions include liabilities at time of death. At present basic abatement of Rlmillion applies in respect of all estates.

TRADEMARKS AND TRADENAMES:

South African law is contained in the Trade Marks Act No. 194 of 1993; which became operative on 1 May 1995 and replaces old Trade Marks Act No. 62 of 1963 in its entirety. 1993 Act sets out to streamline South African law relating to trademarks and to keep abreast of international developments. 1993 Act takes cognisanze of European Directive on Trade Marks (which requires member countries of European Union to adopt their national trademark laws in accordance with Directive's provisions) and furthermore closely resembles British Trade Marks Act 1994.

1963 Act will continue to apply to all applications and proceedings instituted before 1 May 1995. 1993 Act will apply to all new applications, oppositions, and cancellation and infringement proceedings commenced on or after aforementioned date. 1963 Act will determine validity of entry on register of trademarks existing at 1 May 1995.

Term "mark" is defined as "any sign capable of being represented graphically including a device, name, signature, word, letter, numeral, shape, configuration, pattern, ornamentation, colour or a container for goods or any combination of the aforementioned". Trademark is used in relation to goods or services for purpose of indicating connection in course of trade between goods or services and owner of trademark. 1993 Act defines trademark in terms of its distinguishing function only. This function is sufficiently wide to embrace not only traditional origin function of trademark but also its other socioeconomic functions, such as its quality and advertising functions. This facilitates more informal licensing system, inclusion of assignment and antidilution provisions, and protection of collective and certification marks.

To be registrable, trademark must be "capable of distinguishing" goods or services of proprietor of mark from goods or services of another person. Mark can be inherently capable of distinguishing, or it can be capable of distinguishing by reason of its prior use. Discretion which Registrar had in terms of 1963 Act no longer exists and 1993 Act lists 17 grounds for refusal of application to register trademark. Under 1993 Act one cannot register trademark defensively. (This could be done in terms of 1963 Act.) 1993 Act also provides for first time for registration of collective trademarks. Registration is initially for period of ten years but is renewable in perpetuity.

Apart from statute, common law protects against passing-off of activities which are calculated to mislead public.

TREATIES:

Numerous trade treaties exist with Commonwealth, European and South American Countries, particularly in relation to customs duties. (See topic Customs Duties.) These are too numerous to be detailed here and it is suggested that nearest South Africa Trade Commissioner or Consul be consulted.

Double Taxation Agreements.—South Africa has comprehensive double taxation agreements covering number of different types of income with following countries: Botswana; Fed. Rep. of Germany; Gambia; Nicaragua; Maesites; Seychelles; Sierra Leone; Israel; Italy; Lesotho; Malawi; Namibia; Netherlands; Swaziland; The U.K.; Zimbabwe; Denmark; Sweden; Finland; Romania; France; Korea.

South Africa has also restricted agreements, relating only to income derived from shipping and aircraft business concluded with: Belgium; Brazil; Denmark; Finland; France; Greece; Ireland; Japan; Norway; Portugal; Taiwan; Spain.

There are various agreements relating to death duties and avoidance of double taxation particularly in relation to following states: Zimbabwe; Lesotho, Botswana and Swaziland; Great Britain; U.S. and Sweden.

Foreign investment in South Africa is not liable to expropriation, but movements of money in and out of South Africa, into dollar and sterling exchange areas are subject to exchange control by Treasury. See topic Foreign Exchange, Foreign Trade and Investment.

See also Selected International Conventions section.

TRUSTS:

A trust may be created by last will or act inter vivos. A fideicommissum is a common provision in a will, i.e., there is a bequest to one person (the fiduciary) with a direction that on the happening of a certain event, usually the death of such person, the property vests in a third person (the fideicommissary).

Trusts are frequently entered into by persons during their lifetime so as to confer benefits through trustees on third persons. The Trust Property Control Act, No. 57 of 1988 regulates administration of trusts and prescribes certain formalities in respect of trusts.

USURY: See topics Interest; Contracts.

WILLS:

(Wills Act No. 7/1953; Administration of Estates Act No. 66/1965).

The only essential requirements are that every page of the will must be signed by the testator. This must be done in presence of two competent witnesses who need only sign at end of will. "Sign" includes initialing and, only as regards testator, making of mark. Witness to will, person signing on behalf of testator, and person writing out will may be declared competent by Court to receive benefit from will.

Every testator has the right to add one or more codicils to his will which require the same formalities as the will itself.

Under Law of Succession Act 43/1992 court is given wide powers to declare wills not executed in accordance with formalities valid if it is satisfied that no fraud is involved.

In event of death of testator, it is the duty of person discovering will to lodge it forthwith with Master of Supreme Court. The Trust Property Control Act, No. 57 of 1988 further regulates control of trust property.

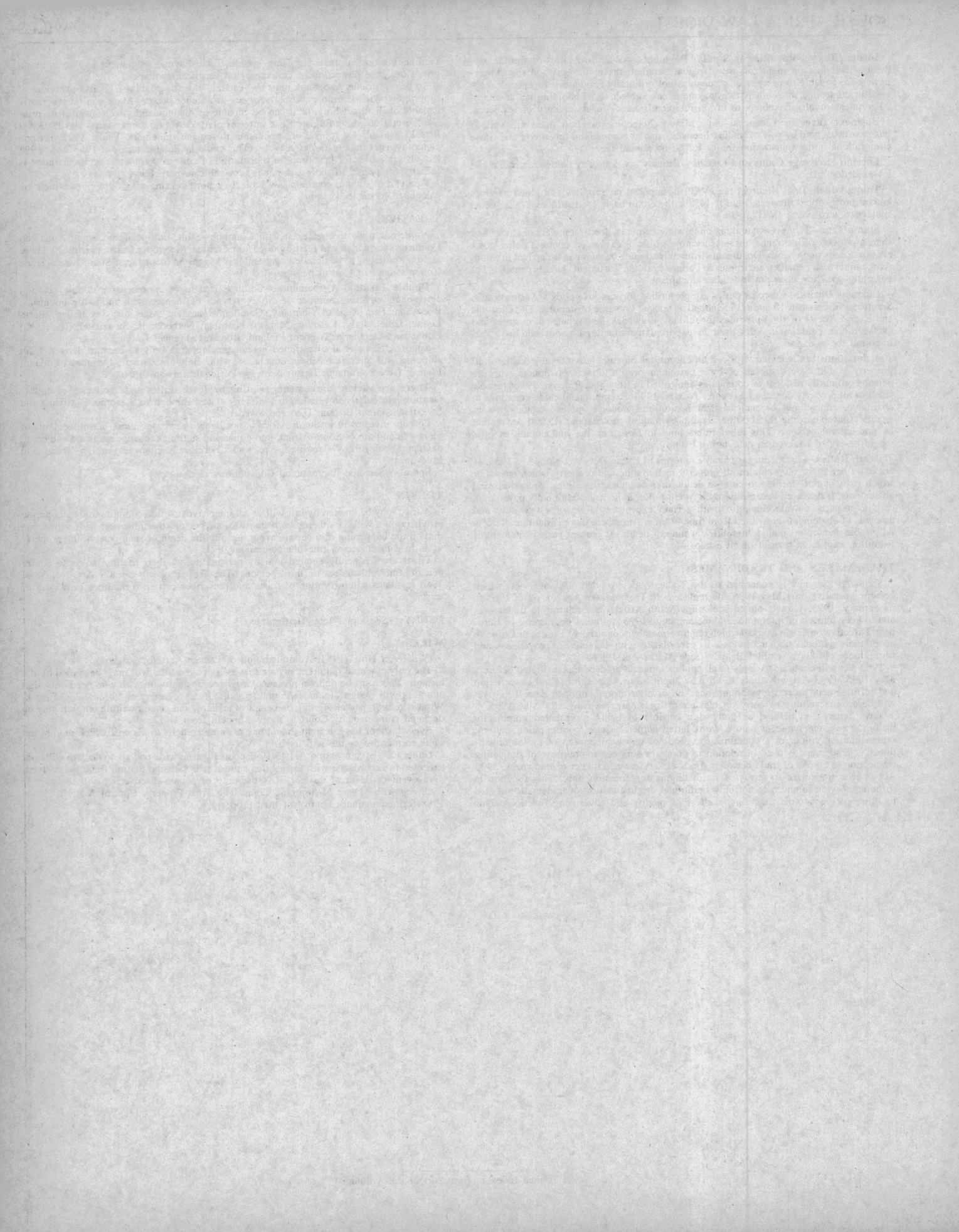

SPAIN LAW DIGEST REVISER

J. & A. Garrigues
José Abascal, 45
28003 Madrid, Spain
Telephone: 011 34 1 4569800
Fax: 011 34 1 3992408

Reviser Profile

The origins of the Firm go back to 1935, when the then Professor of Mercantile Law, Joaquín Garrigues Díaz-Cañavate, set up the office. Later, in 1942, his brother Antonio Garrigues Díaz-Cañavate joined the firm and it adopted the current name of J. & A. Garrigues. Antonio Garrigues was subsequently the Spanish Ambassador in the U.S. (1960-1963), the Spanish Ambassador at the Vatican (1964-1972) and later Minister of Justice (1976).

From its creation, the firm has specialized mainly in Company and Mercantile law, and among its members are personalities of recognised prestige in legal and university circles.

In 1966, the Firm was materially reorganized with the opening of an office in Barcelona and the creation of departments specializing in Litigation, Taxation and Labour Law. This reorganization has been furtherly developed in the last years and presently the Firm provides a wide array of legal services through nine departments specializing in the following practice areas: general corporate law, corporate finance, mergers and acquisitions, real estate and administrative law, labour, taxation, litigation, environmental and EU law.

In 1973, the J. & A. Garrigues office in New York was created. In January 1986, coinciding with Spain's accession to the Common Market, an office was set up in Brussels, and in January 1989, an office was set up in Marbella which, like the New York and the Barcelona offices, operate under the name of J. & A. Garrigues. The Firm has also set up offices in Sevilla, Oviedo, and in Lisbon.

The Firm, with 92 Lawyers at the present time is, because of its special nature and the volume of matters it handles, considered to be the leading firm in this country, and has among its numerous clients many of the companies with the largest trading volume and greatest prestige on the international market, in the various different industrial and financial sectors. Through a total of 8 offices, the Firm represents domestically and internationally a broad-spectrum of clients in the corporate, financial, industrial and government communities.

SPAIN LAW DIGEST

(The following is a list of all Topics, including cross-references, covered in this Digest.)

SPAIN LAW DIGEST

Revised for 1997 edition by

J. & A. GARRIGUES, of Madrid.

See topics Law Reports, Codes, Etc.; Statutes.

Spain is member of EU. See also European Union Law Digest.

ABSENTEES:

If a person leaves his domicile without leaving a duly appointed representative and nothing is heard from him, the court will, if requested by a third party or if his business is in imminent danger of loss, appoint an attorney to act in his behalf. After a period of one year since he was last heard of, if he left no proxy or attorney in fact, the court will appoint a trustee to administer his personal and real property to the extent provided for in the court order.

A declaration of death may be obtained in three instances: (1) after two years from the date of an event involving imminent risk of death in a disaster or act of violence likely to cause death if, in either case, nothing is heard from the victim-apparent; (2) after five years without hearing from the absentee, if at the end of the five years he would have been 75 years or older; or (3) after ten years without absolutely hearing from the absentee. If a declaration of death has been thus rendered, succession or inheritance of the absentee's estate, opening of his will, etc., will ensure as in the case of a person known to have actually died, and declaration, in itself, does allow absentee's spouse to remarry.

ACKNOWLEDGMENTS:

In Spain, documents requiring authentication by a public official must be executed before a notary public and recorded in his protocol file. Copies of the original deed are delivered upon application. If the notary discontinues his practice, the College of Notaries takes over his protocol file. In foreign countries, the Spanish consular officers act as notaries, and all documents to be recognized in Spain may be authenticated by them. Instruments executed before notary public of foreign country must have signature of notary duly authenticated by Spanish consular officer in foreign country, unless foreign country is party to 1961 The Hague Convention on legalization of documents, in which case affixment of apostille provided for in said Convention will be sufficient.

In the case of a corporation, the representative acting in its behalf must be fully empowered in writing to execute the deed in the name of the corporation. All contracts affecting real estate and instruments constituting profit-making corporations must be executed before a notary public before they can be recorded. See topic Corporations and Associations; also topic Notaries.

ACTIONS:

Civil actions may be brought before courts by any Spanish or foreign national. Courts will decide such actions in accordance with laws of Spain. Foreign laws may be taken into account, but are considered from legal standpoint as facts and must therefore be proved by those who adduce them before court itself. Rules governing legal procedure are set forth in Code of Civil Procedure (Ley de Enjuiciamiento Civil). There are different procedures according to amount and nature of action brought. Except in case of lawsuits involving small amounts, parties must be represented by a solicitor and defended by an attorney-at-law.

Limitation of.—See topic Statute of Limitations.

See also topic Courts.

ADMINISTRATION:

See topic Executors and Administrators.

AIRCRAFT:

Spain adheres to the following Conventions: Warsaw, on international transport; Rome, on attachment and liability, Chicago and Tokyo.

Decree of 22 Aug. 1970 defines Spanish air space.

As to domestic law, Aerial Navigation Act of June 21, 1960 and Aerial Navigation Criminal and Procedural Act of 1964 are applicable. In accordance with Aerial Navigation Act, various flight aspects are regulated, among others, sovereignty, administrative organization, aircraft, registration, airworthiness, airports, health, attachments, servitudes, traffic, liability, etc. Air navigation between Spain and other EEC countries is regulated by Decree of July 6, 1990.

Criminal and Procedural Act defines aeronautical offences and violations as classified therein and procedure for imposition of security measures.

Without prejudice to these laws, there are also international covenants with England, U.S.A., Switzerland, Argentina, Belgium, The Netherlands, Germany, France, Luxembourg and other countries.

Instrument of Ratification by Spain of Agreement between Republic of Gabon and Government of Spain (Official State Gazette, Dec. 23/1977) on Air Transport, signed in Libreville on May 3, 1976.

Agreement between Spanish Government and Government of Republic of Tunisia, on Air Transport; signed in Tunis on Jan. 11, 1977. (Official State Gazette July 21, 1977).

Agreement between Government of Spain and Government of U.S.S.R. (Official State Gazette, Dec. 15, 1977) on Air Transport, signed in Madrid on May 12, 1976.

Spain is a member of I.A.T.A. and its regular airline follows recommendations thereof regarding general contracting conditions.

ALIENS:

Rights and freedom of foreigners in Spain are governed by Organic Law 7/85 of July 1, 1985 as implemented by Royal Decree 155/1996 of Feb. 2, 1996 and Royal Decree of May 26, 1986. Administrative formalities for exercise of rights to enter, stay and work in Spain of citizens from European Community member States are also included in Royal Decree of May 26, 1986.

At present no visa is generally required to enter into Spain except for passports issued by few countries, i.e. Mongolia, Albania, Lebanon. Nonresidents willing to stay in Spain for periods exceeding 90 days must apply for special visa at Spanish Consulate in country where they reside prior to entering into Spain, said visa being required to file application for obtaining residence permit in Spain. Nonresidents may engage in business in Spain under conditions indicated below; if they wish to engage in remunerated activities or take employment they must apply simultaneously for residency and work permit except for work of less than 90 days duration for which granting of work permit will not require residence permit to be granted. Said application will have to be accompanied by employment contract when applicant wishes to be employed by third party. Political asylum and legal status of refugees is governed by Act 5/1984 of Mar. 26 and by Royal Decree 511/1985 of Feb. 20, as amended by Act 9/1994 of May 19 and implemented by Royal Decree of Feb. 10, 1995, establishing procedure for recognition of status of refugee, standards and guarantees to preside over procedures for nonadmission and effects of favourable or unfavourable rulings on applications for asylum. Specific legal coverage is created for displaced persons because of serious conflict or political, ethnic or religious disturbances, including access to structures of assistance contemplated for persons requesting asylum and refugees. Asylum related matters are coordinated by General Directorate of Foreigners and Asylum, a body created by Royal Decree of Dec. 29, 1993.

Nonresidents and foreign residents retain all civil rights under their national laws as regards inheritance provisions, etc. See topics Citizenship, subhead Dual Nationality; Foreign Investments in Spain; Husband and Wife.

ARBITRATION AND AWARD:

See topic Dispute Resolution.

ASSIGNMENTS:

Assignments of credits and rights are only effective, as regards debtor, as of date he is notified of action, and if he makes payment to creditor before being notified of assignment he is released from obligation. Assignor is responsible for legitimacy of credit and for capacity in which he made assignment. In some cases, he is responsible for solvency of debtor. Transfer of real estate and rights is valid as regards a third party as of date of record in Property Register. Principle of bona fide governs all relationships between assignor and assignee, former being responsible for any hidden defects during time specified by law.

ASSOCIATIONS:

See topic Corporations and Associations.

ATTACHMENT:

Attachments may be provisional or final. Latter are carried out upon obtaining an irrevocable decision by which a debtor is condemned to pay a certain amount. Object is to sell at public auction assets of debtor to extent required to pay creditor, after due appraisal by experts. Preventive attachments are carried out against persons who do not have their domicile or any real property in Spain, or who, though domiciled in Spain, have disappeared or may justifiably be deemed likely to go into hiding, if debt has been recognized in writing. See also topics Executions, Exemptions, and Homesteads.

ATTORNEYS AND COUNSELORS:

There are one or more Bar Associations in each province with authorities within that territorial scope and head office in provincial capital. Each Bar Association draws up its own by-laws governing its operation, and all Bar Associations are subject to General Statute of the Legal Profession, regulated in Royal Decree 2090 of July 24, 1982. General Council of Legal Profession is executive agency coordinate and represents Bar Associations.

General matters as to relation of attorney and client are governed by Ethical Standards of the Spanish Legal Profession (approved by Assembly of Deans on May 28 and 29, 1987).

Jurisdiction Over Admissions.—Board of Governors of each Bar Association decides on applications for membership. Application is formality and therefore no real discretionary power of Board of Governors is involved in deciding upon grant of membership.

Eligibility.—To practice legal profession, membership of respective Bar Association is required. To join Bar Association, candidate must produce evidence of following general conditions of aptitude: (1) that he is national of Spain or of European Union country; (2) that he is of legal age; (3) that he holds degree in law; (4) that he has no criminal record disqualifying him from professional practice; (5) he must pay respective membership fee; (6) he must join Mutual Aid Association for the Legal Profession; (7) he must register for tax licence where this is legally necessary.

In proposed new text for General Statute of the Legal Profession, General Council of Spanish Legal Profession plans to introduce system of single bar association membership through Mutual Qualification Agreement; accordingly, to practice in territory other than that of Bar Association of which lawyer is member, it is only necessary to obtain license to practice in city in question by payment of fee.

See Topical Index in front part of this volume.

ATTORNEYS AND COUNSELORS . . . *continued*

Registration as Law Student.—For membership of Bar Association, it is necessary to hold degree as bachelor at law.

Educational Requirements.—See subhead Registration as Law Student, supra.

Petition for Admission.—See subhead Eligibility, supra.

Examination.—Not applicable.

Clerkship.—Not applicable.

Admission without Examination.—See subhead Practice by Foreign Attorneys, infra.

Admission Pro Hac Vice.—Not applicable.

Licenses.—Not applicable.

Privileges.—Not applicable.

Prohibitions.—Attorneys are prohibited from advertising or publicising their services directly or through public media and from signing documents in matters entrusted to Business Agencies, Administrative Processing Agencies or firms of consultants and from issuing legal opinions free of charge in professional journals, press or public media without authorization from Board of Governors.

Liabilities.—Not applicable.

Compensation.—Attorneys receive their remuneration in form of fees and therefore it is not subject to tariff; Bar Associations may publish guidelines on fees. Contingent fee covenant is expressly prohibited.

Lien.—Not applicable.

Disbarment or Suspension.—Dean and Board of Governors of each Bar Association are authorized to impose discipline in cases of infringement by attorneys of their professional duties. General Statute of the Legal Profession provides following possible penalties for such cases: (a) written warning; (b) private reprehension; (c) suspension from legal practice for term not exceding two years; (d) expulsion from Bar Association. In addition to expulsion from Association, status of attorney may also be forfeited by firm judgment involving, as ancillary measure, disqualification from professional practice.

Unauthorized Practice.—Legal practice is incompatible with series of public offices laid down in General Statute for the Legal Profession; lawyer included in any event of incompatibility is obliged to notify his respective Association.

Following circumstances also determine incapacity for legal practice: (1) physical or mental disabilities which by their nature or degree make it impossible to comply with mission entrusted to attorneys of defending interests of others; (2) disqualification or express suspension from legal practice under firm judgment or court order; (3) disciplinary penalties involving suspension from professional practice or expulsion from respective Bar Association.

All these incapacities disappear when their causes have come to an end.

Mandatory Continuing Legal Education.—Not applicable.

Speciality Certification Requirements.—Not applicable.

Professional Association (or Corporation).—No statutory authorization for formation by lawyers.

Practice by Foreign Attorneys.—Under Royal Decree 607 of Mar. 21, 1986, national attorneys of EU member countries permanently established in those countries may render their services as lawyers freely in Spain on occasional basis; these services include consultation, legal advice and actions in court.

Contact Address.—Bar Association of Madrid, Serrano 9, 28001 Madrid, tlf: 4.35.78.10, fax: 5.76.29.91; Bar Association of Barcelona, Mallorca 283, 08205 Barcelona, tlf: 4.87.28.14, fax: 4.80.90.48.

AUTOMOBILES: See topic Motor Vehicles.

BANKRUPTCY AND/OR SUSPENSION OF PAYMENTS:

In Spain, there are two different legal institutions, as regards insolvency, both for private persons and business concerns.

Private parties are subject to procedure known as "creditors' meeting." Business concerns, including corporations, are subject to bankruptcy or suspension of payments. A suspension of payments occurs when, although debtor's assets exceed his liabilities, because of cash difficulties he cannot temporarily meet his current obligations. To obtain a declaration of suspension of payments, application must be submitted to judge, with an inventory of stock, a list of debts and an explanatory report on reasons for request attached to application. Suspension of payments will be considered as "provisional insolvency" when tradesman's assets exceed or equal his liabilities, and as "definite insolvency" if his liabilities exceed assets. Judge will convene creditors for consideration and approval of agreement, which may consist of a partial release, an extension, or both. During suspension of payments and until agreement is reached, debtor's business is controlled.

A declaration of bankruptcy is applicable when liabilities of debtor exceed his assets. In this case, either of two different legal procedures may be followed. Under one of them, creditors intervene to collect all credits of bankrupt and sell them, after due qualification, to determine their order of priority. Under other procedure possible liability of bankrupt is determined. Bankruptcy may be either fortuitous, guilty or fraudulent. In last case, criminal proceedings may be instituted against bankrupt.

Credit preference in event of bankruptcy is established in Arts. 912 to 919 of Commercial Code. For this purpose credits are divided into two groups. First group comprises those which are to be paid with proceeds of personal property. Second includes credits to be paid with proceeds of real property. Creditors belonging to first group are paid in following order: (a) Highly preferred creditors, such as creditors in respect of funeral, burial and estate expenses, dependants, and wage-earners; (b) creditors privileged under Commercial Code; this privilege is granted by Commercial Code to certain persons in connection with certain property, e.g., to a carrier in respect of the goods transported for payment of the price, to an insurer in respect of the property insured for payment of premiums, etc.; (c) creditors privileged under Civil Code; (d) creditors not enjoying privileges whose rights are recorded in a public instrument; (e) ordinary creditors in respect of commercial transactions; (f) ordinary civil law creditors. Creditors belonging to second group are paid in following order: (a) Jus in rem creditors pursuant to provisions of Mortgage Act: (b) other creditors in order set forth above.

At any stage of proceedings, after recognition of credits and classification of bankruptcy, bankrupt and his creditors may make any agreements they see fit. This right is not enjoyed by fraudulent bankrupts, or those absconding during bankruptcy proceedings.

Such agreements must be made at duly-assembled meeting of creditors, private agreements between bankrupt and any creditor being void.

Agreement approved with quorums provided in Art. 901 of Commercial Code is binding on debtor and creditors although latter may, if debtor defaults on agreement, request termination of agreement and resumption of bankruptcy proceedings for liquidation and distribution among creditors of bankrupt's assets.

BANKS AND BANKING:

Private Banks.—Regulations on access to banking activities differentiate between EU and non-EU applicants. As to EU credit institutions, Act 3/1994 implemented EU Directive 89/646 regulating rendering of banking services and set up of branches, both of Spanish credit institutions in EU member states and of EU credit institutions in Spain. Act provides swift procedures of notification to banking authorities prior to rendering of banking services or setting up branches, being applicant's member state banking authority one surveying and controlling applicant's solvency requirements. Additionally Royal Decree 1245/1995 regulates access to banking activities by setting up banking corporations. Access to banking activities through banking corporations is subject to nondiscretionary authorization from Ministry of Economy and Finance and opening of Representative Offices subject to authorization from Bank of Spain.

As to non-EU applicants, access to banking activities may be fulfilled through setting up of corporations, branches or representative offices, and in any case access to banking activities is subject to authorization from Ministry of Economy and Finance and compliance with reciprocity principle. Royal Decree 1245/1995 regulates matter, stating several limitations to expansion of banking activities during their first years of existence except opening of Representative Offices which is subject to Bank of Spain authorization.

Bank of Spain is public law entity acting with autonomy in relation with executive power and has, among others, following tasks: (i) definition and execution of monetary policy, (ii) management of currency and metal reserves, (iii) setting currency exchange rates, (iv) issuance of pesetas bills, and (v) surveillance of credit institutions. For performance of above tasks, Bank of Spain is entitled to issue regulations, its relations with third parties being governed by administrative law or private law depending on nature of specific transaction. According to Act 26/1988 (as amended) Bank of Spain is vested with broad powers over credit institutions which, in certain cases are shared with Ministry of Economy and Finance. Among such powers are power to impose monetary penalties, to replace board of directors and to intervene credit institutions. Legal procedure which must be observed by appropriate punitive authority in connection with administrative infringement affecting financial market is contemplated in Royal Decree 2119/1993 of Dec. 3.

Act 13/1992 of June 1 and Royal Decree 1343/1992 of Nov. 6 provide that credit entities must maintain, on consolidated basis, certain "own resources" ratio, as defined by said legislation. In addition credit entities must maintain certain other types of "ratios" as fixed by Ministry of Economy and Finance or by Bank of Spain such as liquidity ratio.

Interest Rates and Fees.—Banks may freely agree with their clients on interest rates and fees. Banks are obliged to comply with certain reporting requirements, informing their clients of effective rates.

BILLS, NOTES AND CHECKS:

Bills of exchange, promissory notes and checks are governed by Act 19/1985 of July 16.

Bills of exchange must show words "bill of exchange" inserted in text itself of security, in same language as text of same; pure and simple order to pay certain sum in pesetas or convertible foreign currency admitted for official listing; name of person who should pay, known as drawee; statement of date of maturity of bill; place at which payment should be made; name of person to whom payment should be made; date and place at which bill is drawn; signature of person issuing bill, known as drawer. Bills which do not comply with one or more of above requirements will only be considered as bills of exchange in following circumstances: (a) When maturity of bill of exchange is not stated it shall be considered as being payable at sight; (b) unless specially stated, place stated alongside name of drawee shall be considered as place of payment and, at same time, as domicile of drawee; (c) any bill of exchange that does not state its place of issue shall be considered as drawn at place stated alongside name of drawer.

Any person who signs bill of exchange as representative of someone else without powers of attorney to act on behalf of that person shall be obligated by bill. Should he pay said bill, he will have same rights as person supposedly represented by him would have had.

Above will also apply to representative who exceeds his powers.

Bill of exchange may be drawn: At fixed date; at term reckoned from date; at sight; at term reckoned from sight. Bills of exchange that state other maturity dates or successive maturity dates will be invalid. In bill of exchange payable at sight or at term from sight, drawer may have corresponding amount accrue interest, rate of interest per annum being stated on bill. Interest shall accrue from date on which bill of exchange is drawn should there be no other date stated for this purpose.

Payment of bill may be guaranteed either in full or for part of its amount, this guarantee being given by third party or also by person signing bill.

Bill of exchange at sight will be payable upon submission, and should be submitted for payment within one year from date thereof. Holder of bill of exchange payable on fixed date or at term to be reckoned from date or from sight should submit bill of exchange for payment on its maturity date, or on one of following working days. When it is question of bills of exchange which are domiciliated in account opened in

See Topical Index in front part of this volume.

BILLS, NOTES AND CHECKS . . . *continued*
credit entity, submission of such to clearing house or system of compensation would be equivalent to submission for payment.

Payment of bills of exchange drawn in convertible foreign currency admitted for official listing should be made in currency agreed, provided that obligation of payment in said currency is authorised or permitted in accordance with norms of exchange controls.

Transfer of bills of exchange is made by endorsement.

Notes.—Promissory notes should contain: Words "promissory note" inserted in text of security itself and in same language as that of text of said security; pure and simple promise to pay certain amount in pesetas or in convertible foreign currency admitted for official listing; statement of maturity date of security; place at which payment is to be made; name of person to whom payment is to be made or at whose order it is to be made; date and place at which promissory note is signed, signature of person issuing security, known as signatory. Any security that fails to fulfil any of above requirements shall not be considered as promissory note except in following circumstances: (a) When maturity of note is not stated it will be considered as payable at sight; (b) unless specifically stated, place of issue of security will be considered as place of payment and, at same time, as domicile of signatory; (c) when place of issue of bill is not stated it will be considered as signed at place stated alongside name of signatory.

Signatory of note will be obligated in same way as acceptor of bill of exchange and consequently, same provisions relating to bills of exchange are applicable to promissory note.

Checks.—Check should contain: Word "check" inserted in text of security itself, in same language as that of text of said security; pure and simple mandate to pay certain sum in pesetas or in convertible foreign currency admitted for official listing; name of person who is to pay, known as drawee, which should necessarily be bank; place of payment; date and place of issue of check; signature of person issuing check, known as drawer. Any check which fails to fulfil any of above requirements will not be considered as check except in following cases: (a) Unless specifically stated, place stated alongside name of drawee will be considered as place of payment. When various places are stated, check will be payable at first place stated; (b) failing these or any other statements check should be paid at place where it was issued or, should drawee have no establishment at said place, at place where drawee has his main establishment; (c) any check which has no statement of its place of issue will be considered as signed in place stated alongside name of drawer.

Check is payable at sight. Check submitted for payment before day stated as date of issue is payable on day on which it is submitted. Submission to clearing house or system of compensation is equivalent to submission for payment.

Any check issued and payable in Spain should be submitted for payment within term of 15 days. Any check issued abroad and payable in Spain should be submitted within term of 20 days, if issued in Europe, and 60 days if issued outside Europe.

Drawee who has funds which may be drawn on by drawer at moment of submitting his check, correctly issued, for payment, is obligated to pay. If he only has available partial provision, he will be obligated to deliver amount of such partial provision. Drawer who issues check without provision of funds in possession of drawee for amount stated in check, should pay to holder, in addition to this amount, 10% of amount outstanding, and compensation for loss and damage.

Check may not be accepted; however drawer or holder of check may apply to drawee bank for approval to be granted for same.

Check may be drawn for payment: (a) To particular person either with or without "by order" clause; (b) to particular person with "not by order" clause, or equivalent; (c) to bearer. Check to bearer is transferred by means of delivery or transfer. Check issued in favour of particular person with or without "by order" clause may be transferred by means of endorsement. Check issued in favour of particular person with "not by order" or equivalent clause, may only be transferred in form and with effects of ordinary assignment.

CHATTEL MORTGAGES:

In Spain property is divided into personal and real estate. Personal property is all property which can be moved to another place, either by the owner's or some other person's action; real estate is the land and all objects attached thereto (such as buildings, plant and equipment installed in such manner denoting that they are united to the building, trees when uncut, etc.). Real estate may be given as a guaranty for loans, through a mortgage. See topic Mortgages.

Law distinguishes between movable mortgage and pledge without removal. Both contracts must be executed before a notary public or an exchange broker in case of exchange negotiations, and must be recorded in the Registry of Deeds. There is a special Register for recording movable mortgages and pledges without removal. Failure to pay the insurance premium on the objects gives the creditor the right to recover the loan due. Merchandise of commercial companies, automobiles and other motor vehicles, airplanes, industrial equipment, intellectual and industrial property and railroad cars may be mortgaged. Crops, cattle and their products, machinery and agricultural implements may be pledged without removal. Chattel mortgages, may also be established in guarantte of current accounts of credit or bills of exchange. A pledge without removal may also be established on machinery for agricultural and forestry operations, animals and animal products, collections of objects of historic or artistic value, and so on. (Law of Dec. 16, 1954). See also topic Mortgages.

CITIZENSHIP:

Citizens include: (1) Children of Spanish father or mother; (2) children born in Spain of non-Spanish parents, provided at least one parent was born in Spain; (3) individuals born in Spain of non-Spanish parents, provided that both parents are stateless or if national law of either parent grants no citizenship to child; (4) children born in Spain of unknown parenthood; (5) after being resident of Spain for ten years, or after two years in case of nationals of Portugal, Philippines, some South American countries, Equatorial Guinea and Sefardies or after one year for individuals who either: (i) were born in Spain, (ii) were born out of Spain of father or mother having been originally Spanish, or (iii) have married Spanish spouse.

Children have nationality of their parents, but those (a) born abroad of foreign parents formerly Spaniards or (b) born in Spain of foreign parents may become Spaniards, if they notify official in charge of Registry of Vital Statistics of town in which they reside of their wish to choose Spanish nationality during year after age of majority.

Freedom is granted for proper names of persons to be recorded in their vernacular language, either one of languages of Spain or foreign language.

Foreign Marriage.—Spanish spouse marrying a foreigner loses his or her nationality only by voluntarily acquiring foreign one.

Foreign Residence.—Spaniards who have established their residence abroad must inform Spanish diplomatic or consular officers at their foreign place of residence of their intention to do so. They will be then entered in Register of Spanish Residents. Such a declaration is also necessary for their spouse, if married, and children.

Dual nationality may be enjoyed under the law of July 17, 1954, with respect to Spain and any Spanish-American country, Portugal, Brazil and the Philippine Islands, conditioned on the existence of a reciprocity law. Thus, Spaniards residing in said countries do not lose their rights as Spaniards if they adopt the nationality of the country of their residence. Dual nationality is governed by treaty between the two countries. Dual nationality agreements have been arranged with Bolivia, Chile, Costa Rica, Ecuador, Guatemala, Nicaragua, Paraguay, Peru and Dominican Republic, Argentina and most of Spanish-American countries.

Loss of Nationality.—In addition to general causes of loss of nationality by Spaniards, Decree of Dec. 28, 1967 considers as such army service by Spaniards on behalf of foreign countries.

COMMERCIAL REGISTRY:

Royal Decree 1597 of Dec. 29, 1989 approved Regulations governing Commercial (Mercantile) Registry. There is Commercial Registry for each province and Central Commercial Registry with offices in Madrid.

Registration on Commercial Registry is obligatory, under penalty of legal nonexistence, for individual shipper, commercial companies, credit and insurance cooperatives, investment funds, pension funds, savings banks and branches of foreign companies, among other entities; registration is optional for individual entrepreneur. Records are entered on Register of main acts and agreements of subjects susceptible of registration, such as increases and reductions of capital, changes to by-laws or articles of association, appointment of directors and attorneys in fact, mergers, issue of debentures, bankruptcies etc. Other functions of Commercial Registry are legalization of company books, appointment of independent experts (whose main task is to value property on occasion of incorporation or merger of companies) and of auditors (when companies obliged to have their accounts audited fail to appoint their auditors themselves) and finally deposit and making public of company accounts.

Contents of registration are assumed to be accurate and valid, and declaration of inaccuracy of entries on Register, which requires express court ruling, does not impair rights of third parties in good faith, acquired pursuant to Register. Acts and agreements susceptible of registration and not registered may not be opposed to third parties; those registered are assumed to be known by all and ignorance thereof cannot be alleged.

Register is public and acts or contracts recorded thereon are published in Official Commercial Registry Gazette, kept by Central Commercial Registry. All names of registered companies and entities are recorded at latter, and companies or entities may not adopt name that has already been entered.

CONFLICT OF LAWS:

Preliminary Title of Civil Code (arts. 8-12) establishes series of rules with respect to territorial and personal jurisdictions of law in Spain.

Spain has adhered to Treaty of Rome of June 19, 1980, on law applicable to contractual obligations.

See also topic Dispute Resolution.

CONSTITUTION AND GOVERNMENT:

Constitution.—New Constitution was approved by Parliament on Oct. 31, 1978, and ratified by referendum on Dec. 6, 1978. It enumerates Fundamental Rights of People, such as freedom of ideas, religious faith and worship, right to life and physical integrity, right to "habeaus corpus", and right of free association.

Basic Principles.—Spain is social and democratic State, pursuing as its supreme values freedom, justice, equality and political pluralism (art. 1.1); natural sovereignty belongs to Spanish people, source of all State powers (art. 1.2); State is organized as Monarchy (art. 1.3); Constitution is based upon indivisible unity of country, and recognizes to regions and nationalities right to be autonomous (art. 2); creation and activities of political parties and trade unions are free, provided they respect laws (arts. 6 and 7); all citizens and public entities are subject to Constitution (art. 9.1).

Crown.—King is head of State. Monitors and moderates operation of institutions; his person is inviolable and he may not be held responsible for his acts. (art. 56). Succession to throne is hereditary. (art. 57). King has following functions, among others: To give royal assent to laws, put forward candidate for President of the Government, appoint and dismiss ministers at suggestion of President of the Government, supreme command of armed forces and exercise right of pardon according to law. (art. 62).

Parliament has legislative power, represents Spanish people and is composed of two houses: Congress of Deputies and Senate. (art. 66).

Congress of Deputies has minimum 300 members, maximum 400, elected by universal, free, equal, direct and secret suffrage for term of four years. (art. 70).

Both houses meet yearly in two ordinary sessions; one running from Sept. to Dec. and other from Jan. to June. Houses may also hold special sessions at request of government, standing committee or absolute majority of members of either house. (art. 73).

Parliament has Legislative Power.—Following matters are of its exclusive competency: Basic conditions guaranteeing equality of all citizens before law; nationality,

See Topical Index in front part of this volume.

CONSTITUTION AND GOVERNMENT . . . *continued*
immigration, emigration, alienage and political asylum; international relations; defence and armed forces; justice; commercial, penal and penitentiary legislation; labor legislation, subject to execution thereof by autonomous communities; civil, copyright and patent trademark legislation; customs, excise and foreign trade regulations; currency system and basic regulations concerning credit, banking and insurance; legislation on weights and measures; general finances and State indebtedness; promotion and general coordination of scientific and technical research; external health measures, general coordination of and bases for health and legislation on pharmaceutical products; basic legislation and financial organization of Social Security System; maritime fisheries, merchant navy, coastal lights, general-purpose ports and airports, air transport and control of air space; railways and land transport passing through territory of more than one autonomous community; posts and telecommunications: hydraulic resources and developments whose waters flow through more than one autonomous community; basic environmental protection legislation; basic legislation on mines and energy; system of production, sale, possession and use of arms and explosives; basic rules relating to press, radio and television without prejudice to powers relative to development and implementation thereof vested in autonomous communities; public safety, without prejudice to possible creation of police forces by autonomous communities; conditions relating to obtaining, issuing and standardization of academic degrees and professional qualifications. (art. 149).

Parliament may delegate to government power to issue rules with standing of law in certain areas. Such delegation has to be given by basic law precisely defining purpose, scope and standards thereof. (art. 82).

Government.—Composed of President of the Government, Deputy President of the Government and Ministers. In charge of domestic and foreign policy, civil and military administration and defence. Exercises executive functions and statutory authority. (arts. 97 and 98).

After general elections to Congress of Deputies, King is to consult with delegates of political groups with parliamentary representation and put forward candidate for President of the Government. If absolute majority of members of Congress of Deputies give their vote of confidence, King formally appoints him President of the Government. If such majority is not obtained, there is second vote 48 hours later, simple majority then being sufficient. If two months elapse without vote of confidence by Congress of Deputies, King dissolves Parliament and calls general elections. (art. 99).

In cases of extraordinary and urgent necessity, government may issue interim legislative provisions in form of decree-laws which may not affect basic State institutions, rights, duties and liberties of citizenry, legal systems of autonomous communities or electoral law. Congress of Deputies must ratify or repeal such decree-laws within 30 days of their promulgation. (art. 86).

The Judiciary.—Justice emanates from people and is administered in name of King by judges who are required to be independent, irremovable, responsible and subject only to requirements of laws. Principle of jurisdictional unity is basis of organization and operation of courts. (art. 117).

Supreme Court is highest jurisdictional body in all branches of judicial system, except with regard to provisions concerning constitutional guarantees. (art. 123).

Constitutionality of Laws.—Constitutional Court is competent to hear and rule on unconstitutionality appeals against laws and regulations having force of law, conflicts of jurisdiction between State and autonomous communities or between any of latter, and other matters allotted to it by Constitution or by organic laws.

If in any action judicial body considers that law applicable to case may be unconstitutional, it may bring matter before Constitutional Court, but such referral may in no case have suspensive effects. (art. 163).

Local Administration.—Constitution acknowledges and guarantees existence of municipalities and provinces as local administrative entities with full legal personality. Government and administration of municipalities is vested in town councils, whose councillors are elected by presidents of municipality by universal, free, equal, direct and secret suffrage. Government and administration of provinces is vested in provincial councils. (arts. 140 and 141).

Autonomous Communities.—Constitution recognizes right of bordering provinces having common historical, cultural and economic characteristics to achieve self-government by forming autonomous communities. (art. 143).

Parliament authorizes formation of autonomous communities and approves their statutes of autonomy which constitute basic institutional norms thereof under Constitution. (arts. 144 and 147). Following matters are reserved to jurisdiction of autonomous communities: Organization of their self-governing institutions; town planning and housing; railways and roads lying entirely within territory thereof; agriculture and livestock breeding; woodlands and forestry; hunting and shooting; fluvial fishery; promotion and organization of tourism and sports.

Seventeen autonomous communities have already been formed: Catalunia, the Basque Country, Galicia, Andalucía, Asturias, Cantabria, La Rioja, Aragón, Canary Islands, Castilla-La Mancha, Valencia, Madrid, Murcia, Extremadura, Castilla-León, Navarra and Balearic Islands; each is governed by provisions of their respective Status of Autonomy.

Protection of Basic Rights.—A Law passed by Parliament on Dec. 26, 1978, provides for protection by Courts of following rights: Freedom of speech and of association, secrecy of correspondence, freedom of religion and domicile, protection against illegal arrests and freedom of movement within Spanish territory. Another Law, dated May 5, 1982 protects right of honour, personal and family privacy and self-esteem, to be measured by courts in accordance with laws and social standards/customs; use of recording/filming devices for registering private life of individuals are prohibited; damages will be awarded whenever court finds infringement of rights protected by Law and profits obtained by intruder will be taken into consideration when damages are computed; remedies under this Law are in addition to criminal remedies. Royal Decree of Mar. 26, 1993 has created Agency for Protection of Data, a body vested with power to implement provisions contained in Organic Law of Oct. 29, 1992 regarding Computerized Processing of Personal Data.

Ombudsman.—Designated by Parliament for period of five years, during which he cannot be prosecuted except for flagrant crimes. His function is defense of rights of individuals contained in Constitution, as well as supervision of activities of Autonomous Communities; he has access to any kind of governmental documents and may suggest appropriate remedies to any irregularity ascertained by him.

CONTRACTS:

Space does not permit giving detailed account of all types of contracts recognized under Spanish law. In general, for contract to exist there must be three basic requirements: consent of contracting parties, certain object, and reason for same. Any contract lacking one of these requirements is not valid. Contracts obtained by fraud or mistake are void. Several types of contracts require certain formalities.

As a rule, all pacts, clauses and conditions which the parties deem desirable to establish are valid, provided they are not contrary to law, morality or public order. However, at present there are several restrictions relative to contractual freedom for social reasons, as in rural or urban leases, etc.

Excuses for Nonperformance.—In addition to payment or fulfilment of relevant consideration, obligations are extinguished as a result of: (a) Loss of thing owed through no fault of debtor's, before debtor has defaulted; (b) conventional or tacit remission; (c) confusion of rights, i.e., concurrence in one and same person of both creditor and debtor; (d) compensation, which occurs when two persons, by their own right, are reciprocally creditors and debtors of each other; (e) objective or subjective novation.

Applicable Law.—By and large, and as regards their substance, contracts are interpreted and applied in accordance with Spanish Law. Parties may, however, stipulate that contract shall be governed by a foreign legislation, provided there exists a link with said legislation, as, e.g., nationality of the parties, place of performance, location of the property, etc. In addition, Spain is party to Rome Convention of June 19, 1980, regarding law applicable to international contracts and to United Nations Convention on Contracts for the International Sale of Goods, in force Aug. 1, 1991. See topic Treaties and Part VII, Selected International Conventions. Also lawful in Spain are contractual clauses entrusting foreign agencies or bodies with cognizance of differences which may arise in interpretation or performance of contracts, and their settlement through arbitration. Foreign Law is not, however, applied by judge as matter of course, but must be adduced and proved in court by interested party. See also topic Judgments, subhead Arbitration.

As regards their form, contracts are governed by law of country in which they are executed, but nevertheless when they have been authorized by Spanish diplomatic or consular officials abroad, the formalities prescribed by Spanish legislation must be observed.

Retail.—Act 7/1996 of Jan. 15 on Retail Trade has been passed. This Act provides basis for modernization of Spanish commercial structures, correcting disequilibrium between large and small traders and maintaining free and fair competition.

Act develops principle of free enterprise, while dealing more restrictively with opening of large commercial establishments, which is made subject to specific commercial licence. Requirements for establishment to meet status of "Large Establishment" will be stipulated by Autonomous Regional Communities; large establishments are those having useful sales area of over 2,500 m2. Licence is granted by Autonomous Authorities which will assess effect that opening of large establishment could have on commercial structure of area affected.

Act regulates sales promotions and what are known as "Special Sales", thus trying to create legal framework for series of contractual formulas which have arisen in recent years and which must always be carried on from standpoint of consumer protection, such as, seasonal bargain sales, special offers or promotions, closing sales, sales with gifts, offers of direct sales, sales at distance and sales by peddlers, under franchise system and at public auction.

Act contains regulations relating to infringements and penalties. Latter, which have to be imposed by Public Administrations, vary between at least 500,000 pesetas and at most 100 million pesetas; in extremely series cases, additional penalty is imposed consisting of temporary closure of infringing business for one year at most.

Organic Act 2/1996 of Jan. 15, supplementary to Retail Trade Act has been passed and provides full liberty of shopping hours throughout state territory. However, this full freedom will not be applicable until government so decides for each territory, together with respective agency of autonomous government and, in any event, not before Jan. 1, 2001.

Public Procurement Contracts.—Contracts made with Public Administration are governed by Act of May 18, 1995.

This Act is systematically implemented in general part which includes adminitrative organization of public procurement: competence and contracting agencies, subject matter and price of contracts; capacity and solvency of entrepreneurs; classification and registration of companies, guarantees for processing of procedures; contracting procedures: open, restricted and negotiated; forms of award: auction and public bidding; advertising, notice and terms of contract; nullity, effects of compliance and termination of contracts; assignment and subcontracts; price adjustments. Also has special part applicable to various contracts with independent regulations: works contracts, supply contracts, contracts for management of public services; consultancy and assistance contracts, service contracts and contracts for specific works not customarily performed by Administration.

Act is applicable to all contracts entered into by Public Administration and entities of public law with their own legal status, associated with or dependent on any of Public Administrations. Contracts entered into with Administration may be administrative or private.

Administrative contracts are those direct subject matter of which, jointly or separately, is performance of works, management of public services and performance of supplies, those of consultancy and assistance or services and those exceptionally entered into with individuals for performance of specific non-customary works. Contracts associated with specific trade of contracting administration are also of this kind, being of special administrative nature because they satisfy public purpose, directly or immediately. Other contracts are considered to be private. Administrative contracts are governed by Act and provisions implementing it and litigious administrative courts

See Topical Index in front part of this volume.

CONTRACTS . . . *continued*
have jurisdiction to resolve any dispute arising between parties. As for private contracts of Public Administration, their preparation and award are governed by this Act in absence of specific provisions, and their effects and termination are governed by rules of private law. Civil courts have jurisdiction to resolve any dispute arising between parties.

Contracts with Administration may be made by Spanish or foreign individuals or corporations with full capacity to act and evidencing their economic and financial solvency and technical or professional reputation. Act establishes means whereby economic and financial solvency and technical reputation may be evidenced. Act creates official registry of contractors, of public access, and dependent on Ministry of Economy and Finance.

Guaranty is contemplated as usual form for creating surety, and it is possible for global guaranty to secure all contracts entered into by one entrepreneur with single Public Administration or with one contracting agency.

Award may be made by open, restricted or negotiated procedure. In open procedure, any interested entrepreneur may file proposal. In restricted procedure, only those entrepreneurs which have been expressly selected by Administration at their request may file proposals.

In negotiated procedure, contract is awarded to entrepreneur selected in justified manner by Administration after consultation and negotiation of terms of contract with one or more entrepreneurs. Negotiated procedure is only applicable in events established by Act for each kind of contract.

Both in open and in restricted procedure, award may be made by auction or public bid. Auction is carried out on basis of upset price expressed in money, and it is awarded to bidder who offers lowest price without exceeding upset price. In public bid, award is made to bidder who makes most advantageous proposal as whole.

Act differentiates between several kinds of contracts: (a) works contract; (b) supply contract; (c) public service management contract; (d) consultancy and assistance contracts; (e) service contracts; (f) specific works not customarily of Administration.

For purposes of this Act, works contract is understood to be contract made between Administration and entrepreneur for building of real properties, performance of works to change form or substance of land or subsoil, or reform, repair, maintenance or demolition of those defined above.

Supplies contract is understood to be contract having as its subject purchase, lease or acquisition of movables or products, with exception of those relating to intangible assets and negotiable securities which are governed by legislation of patrimony of Public Administrations applicable to each case.

Public service management contracts are those whereby Public Administrations entrust management of public service to individual or company.

Consultancy and assistance contracts are those in which intellectual benefits are predominant such as: studies, preparation of reports, preparation of projects, introduction or organization systems, organization of public services, etc.

Service contracts are those having as their purpose, inter alia, preparation of computer programs developed specifically for Administration and to be freely used by it.

Contracts for specific works not customarily performed by Administration are those which are not included in above categories and which Administration enters into in exceptional cases when their purpose cannot be covered by ordinary tasks of Administrative agencies.

Each of above contracts receives independent treatment in Act, specific procedure and form of award being established for each type of contract.

Distributorships, Dealerships and Franchises.—On Feb. 21, 1992, Royal Decree 157/1992 exempted categories of distribution, franchising, licensing and R D agreements. Royal Decree authorizes agreements between two undertakings complying with EEC Block Exemption Regulations. Following art. 4 of Decree undertakings can apply for individual exemption according to art. 3 of Act 16/1989.

CONVEYANCES: See topic Deeds.

COPYRIGHTS:

Copyright of literary, artistic or scientific work belongs to author by virtue of mere fact of its creation and is governed by Royal Decree 1/1996 of Apr. 12. This act regulates on one hand, rights corresponding to author and those individuals or corporate bodies which must necessarily be involved in order to interpret, perform or make public work created by former and, on other hand it also governs actions and procedures necessary for protection of said rights. Exploitation rights of work shall remain in force throughout life of author and for 70 years after his death or declaration of death; if work is made public after death of author, exploitation rights shall remain in force for 50 years as from date of work's being made public provided that such takes place within 25 years following death of author, this term of 50 years likewise being applicable from moment when pseudonymous or anonymous works are made public. Copyright relating to works and other productions protected under Act 22/1987 may be subject to entry on General Copyrights Register, governed by Royal Decree 733/1993 of May 14. On Apr. 22, 1954, Spain ratified Universal Agreement of Geneva, of Sept. 6, 1952. Spain is also signatory to Berne Convention of 1948. Copyrights on films are regulated by Law of May 31, 1966, which grants author profit sharing on exhibition revenues. Copyright agreement with U.S.A. was signed in 1895 and renewed in 1902. Act 16/1993 of Dec. 23 provides framework for legal protection of copyrights deriving from software. This Act provides that duration of legal protection of copyright is 50 years if author is legal entity and throughout life of author and 50 years after his death if an individual.

CORPORATIONS AND ASSOCIATIONS:

Spain recognizes two classes of legal persons: public legal persons and private legal persons.

Public legal persons are the State, Autonomous Community, Province, Municipality and series of corporations created by special laws for developing certain objectives of State. These Corporations are governed by laws which created them and by complementary regulations.

Private legal persons may be of civil or mercantile law. Private legal persons of civil law are ruled by Civil Code, by Law on Associations of Dec. 24, 1964 and Regulation of May 20, 1965. Concept of legal persons of civil law, or associations, includes all private legal persons who do not join corporation for purpose of obtaining any profit, as in case of associations of cultural, sporting or charity nature, for medical care, pensions, co-operatives, etc. Right of association for such purpose is free, but association must draw by-laws or regulations by which it will be ruled and register them. As for religious congregations, Spanish State, in accordance with provisions of Concordate with Holy See, recognizes personalty granted to them under it. Pursuant to Act of July 5, 1980 on Religious Freedom, religious congregations or associations of any kind, are recognised as corporations existing under Spanish law, and are duly listed in record kept by Ministry of Justice; such listed congregations are able to practice any ritual activity as well as to exercise right of freedom of expression, demonstration, etc., provided that they do not break any law nor violate Public Order.

Profit-making companies are governed by the Code of Commerce, the Law on Joint Stock Corporations and the Law on Limited Liability Companies. The Code of Commerce governs the so-called Collective and Commandite Companies.

A general requirement for all mercantile companies is that they must be constituted by public deed subscribed before a notary public and entered in the Mercantile Registry. If the persons incorporating the company are aliens, they must present to the Registrar a certificate (issued by their consular officers) that they have the necessary legal capacity in accordance with the laws of their own countries to constitute the company.

The basic features of each of the above-mentioned companies are as follows:

(a) *Sociedad Regular Colectiva* (Regular Collective Company) is a personalized company with unlimited and joint liability of all the partners, to which it is possible to contribute capital or work, or both. Unless otherwise established, it is managed by all the partners. The agreement of all the other partners is required for the transfer of the rights of one of them.

(b) *Sociedad commanditaria* (Commandite Company). There are two classes of partners: collective and silent (or dormant). Former manage company and may contribute capital or work, or both. Their liability is unlimited. Silent partners contribute capital, but cannot intervene in management, and their liability is limited to capital contributed by them, but if they take part in management or their name appears in corporate style, they have unlimited liability for company's debts.

(c) *Sociedad de Responsabilidad Limitada* (Limited Liability Company). These companies are governed by Act of Mar. 23, 1995. Minimum capital is 500,000 pesetas, divided into portions which represent contributions made by partners to company and which must be fully paid up upon incorporation and upon each capital increase. General rule is that partner liability is limited to amount contributed to company. Portions are not represented by certificates nor by book entry.

Company may be incorporated by one or more partners and incorporation is by means of execution of public deed before notary public. Following items must be put on record at public deed: (1) Identification of partner or partners, either individuals or legal entities; (2) will of partners to form company; (3) contributions (cash or rights) made by each partner to company and portions received as consideration; (4) structure of initial management body and identification of persons upon which it is vested; (5) by-laws by which company is governed and which must at least indicate (a) name of company, (b) corporate purpose, (c) date of closing of fiscal year, (d) capital stock, (e) structure of management body.

Portions confer certain rights on partners. General principle is that transferability of portions to non-partners is restricted. By-laws may vary scope of restrictions but in any event provisions contained in by-laws which amount to complete freedom of transfer of portions are void. Company may not issue debentures or other debt securities.

Partners express at General Meetings maximum will of company and Act contains provisions regarding call, valid assembly, required majorities for adoption of resolutions, etc. By-laws may provide alternate management bodies/structure and General Meeting of Partners may opt for any of them. Representation and management of company is vested upon administrators (i.e., sole administrator, several administrators acting jointly or jointly and severally, Board of Directors, etc.), who may be elected for unlimited duration. Administrators prepare annual accounts and General Meeting of Partners approves accounts and resolves on allocation of profits.

Act contains provisions regarding capital increases and reductions, transformation, merger, spin-off, dissolution and liquidation.

(d) *Sociedad Anonima* (joint stock corporations). These companies are governed by Law of July 25, 1989 and by Royal Decree 1564 of Dec. 22, 1989. Minimum capital is 10,000,000 pesetas, divided into shares of stock and shareholders' liability is limited to amount of shares subscribed by them, provided that these have been fully paid. If they have not been fully paid, debtors and company itself may claim difference. Shares may be freely transferred, although certain restrictive covenants may be legally established. To form company of this kind, deed may be executed by only one person and must be executed before notary public, putting on record: (1) Family and given names and ages of incorporators, if they are individuals, or corporate name, in case of legal persons, and nationality and domicile in both cases; (2) will of incorporators to form joint stock corporation; (3) cash, merchandise and rights contributed by each partner, indicating title under which it is contributed and number of shares received in payment; (4) aggregate amount, at least approximate, of formation expenses; (5) by-laws by which corporation will be ruled, which must indicate: (a) company's name, (b) corporate purpose, (c) term for its existence, (d) date on which it will begin to operate, (e) corporate domicile and body competent to decide or resolve on creation, cancellation or transfer of branches, (f) corporate capital stating as appropriate unpaid part and form and maximum term in which to pay calls on capital, (g) number of shares into which capital stock is divided: their face value; their class and series if there are several, stating precise face value, number of shares and rights of each class; amount effectively paid in; and whether they are represented by share certificates or by book entry. When represented by share certificates, it should state whether these are in registered or bearer form and whether issue of multiple share certificates is contemplated, (h) structure of body entrusted with company's administration, determining directors to whom its representation is entrusted and their regime. Number of directors

CORPORATIONS AND ASSOCIATIONS . . . *continued*
is also stated, which in case of Board of Directors may not be less than three, or at least maximum and minimum number of directors, term of office and system for their remuneration, if any, (i) manner of deliberations and adoption of resolutions of company's bodies of management, (j) date of closing of fiscal year, (k) restrictions to free transferability of shares when this is stipulated, (l) system for supplementary services if such are established, expressly stating their contents, whether they are rendered gratuitously or for consideration, shares that include obligation to perform them and possible penalty clauses inherent in their default, (m) special rights reserved to founders or promoters, if any. Deed may also include any legal pacts and special conditions that incorporators may wish to insert provided that these are not contrary to law.

Shares may be represented by certificates or by book entry. Shares represented by certificates may be in registered or bearer form but are obligatorily registered until they have been fully paid up, when their transferability is subject to restrictions, when they include supplementary services or when so required by special provisions. Shares may have different rights as regards participation in profits but right to vote must be same on all shares of same face value. If they have different face values, right to vote must be proportional to their values. However, possibility is contemplated of company issuing nonvoting shares for face value not exceeding one-half of paid-in capital stock. Nonvoting shares confer, among others, right to receive minimum annual dividend which may not be under 5% of capital paid for each nonvoting share, in addition to ordinary dividend.

Company is managed by shareholders' meeting and by administrators (i.e., sole administrator, several administrators acting jointly or jointly and severally, Board of Directors, etc.) who are always dependent on will of shareholders as expressed at general meetings. Latter may remove some or all of members of board, no pact to contrary being valid. General shareholders' meeting must be held at least once a year to approve accounts submitted by board of directors. Annual accounts should be reviewed by auditors, with exceptions established by Law.

Board of directors may be elected for maximum period of five years and at its first meeting it elects chairman and secretary. Board may appoint one or more managing directors to manage daily business, to whom board may delegate any of its powers. Board may also elect executive committee formed by several directors. Dividend of at least 4% must be distributed to shareholders before directors may participate in company's profits, unless shareholders decide to allocate it to reserves.

Dividends may be freely distributed to extent that such distribution does not reduce net worth of company below capital figure.

See also topic Taxation.

Special Corporations and Entities.—

Sociedades de Inversión Mobiliaria (Securities Investment Companies).—Act 46 of Dec. 26, 1984 provides new rules on organization of companies, with fixed or variable capital stock, for acquisition, holding, enjoyment, management and sale of securities. These companies must be recorded at Commercial Registry and secure prior authorization from Ministry of Economy; their paid-in capital must exceed 400,000,000 pesetas and they are subject to strict disclosure and auditing requirements. If their shares are traded at Stock Exchange their profits are taxed at a special rate of 1%.

Fondos de Inversión Mobiliaria (Securities Investment Funds).—Act 46 of Dec. 26, 1984 states that their net worth must exceed 500,000,000 pesetas. They have to be recorded at Commercial Registry and secure prior authorization from Ministry of Economy. Management and representation must be vested upon special management corporation, whose paid-in capital must exceed 50,000,000 pesetas. If their quotas are traded at Stock Exchange their profits are taxed at special rate of 1%.

Real estate investment funds and companies are governed by Royal Decree 686/1993 of May 7.

Economical Interest Groups.—Act of Apr. 30, 1991 states that their corporate purpose must be limited to supporting activity of their members.

Branches.—Commercial Registry Regulations of Dec. 29, 1989, conceive branch to be any secondary establishment provided with permanent representation and degree of independence of management, through which some or all of main company's activities are carried on.

See also topic Taxation.

Corporations Whose Shares Are Traded in Stock Exchange.—Act 24 of July 28, 1988 which regulates Stock Exchange and Royal Decree 377/1991 of Mar. 15 and Order of Jan. 18, 1991, provide detailed rules concerning information to be provided to public by corporations whose shares are traded in Stock Exchange; they include periodic publication of financial position, disclosure of acquisitions/divestments concerning at least 25% of stock of company involved and publication of detailed information of any issuance of new shares/bonds.

Royal Decree 1197 of July 26, 1991 states new procedure to be followed whenever single entity wishes to acquire or control more than 25% of stock of company whose shares are traded in Stock Exchange: It basically consists of informing Stock Exchange authorities, who then have to publish conditions of offer; any acquisition of shares will have to be effected through Stock Exchange, by means of public offer. Royal Decree 291/1992 of Mar. 27 and Order of July 12, 1993, regulate issues and public offerings of securities, and set forth different types of financial prospectuses to be filed with "Comisión Nacional de Mercado de Valores" (Securities Exchange Comission).

"Comisión Nacional de Valores" is highest independent supervisory authority for Spanish securities markets.

Foreign Corporations.—Foreign companies setting up branch on Spanish territory must record it at Commercial Registry applicable to its domicile, for that purpose filing duly legalized documents evidencing existence of company, its by-laws in force and its directors, together with document setting up branch. Following should also be recorded: Any mention identifying branch; its domicile; activities entrusted to it, as appropriate; identity of representatives appointed permanently to branch, stating their authorities; and capital allocated to branch.

If foreign corporations operate in Spain through a permanent establishment or perform work contracts lasting more than 12 months, they are liable to corporation tax in respect of income they obtain in Spanish territory.

Foreign Investments in Spain.—See topic Foreign Investments in Spain; also topic Taxation.

See also topic Commercial Registry.

COURTS:

Organic Law 6/1985 of July 1 on Judiciary as amended by Organic Law 16/1994 of Nov. 8, governs organisation of judiciary, distribution of State into territories for judicial purposes, functioning of courts and tribunals, internal career-structure of judges and officials in service of administration of justice and state attorney's office, of lawyers and court solicitors and of judiciary police.

State is organised into territories for judicial purposes, into municipalities, provinces and autonomous communities, over which judicial power is exercised by Justices of Peace, Courts of First Instance and Instruction, Litigious-Administrative Courts, Social Courts, Penitentiary Supervision and Minor Courts, Provincial Courts and Higher Courts of Justice of Autonomous Communities. National Court and Supreme Court exercise judicial power over all of national territory. This latter is highest judicial body at all levels, except for provisions concerning matters of constitutional guarantees resting with Constitutional Court.

Act 38 of Dec. 28, 1988, and subsequent amendments, establishing boundaries of new judicial districts.

With regard to certain criminal cases Organic Law 5/1995 of May 22, (as am'd by Organic Law 8/1995 and Organic Law 10/1995) governs jury panel. It regulates scope of jurisdiction of jury, creation of jury panel and systems of selection and designation (requirements, events of incapacity or incompatibility, prohibitions, excuses and challenges), verdict (purpose, instructions, deliberations and ballot) and judgment.

See topic Constitution and Government.

CRIMINAL CODE:

In Criminal Law, legislation has been transformed in depth with passing of Organic Act 10/1995 of Nov. 23, approving new Criminal Code, which came into force on May 25, 1996.

Below is brief summary of its basic provisions:

System of penalties has been fully reformed, to achieve, to extent possible, aim of reincorporation of criminal in society. For this purpose, greater importance is given to penalties other than prison sentence, such as deprivation of rights and fines. "Accessory Penalties" are also dealt with in detail, including closing of commercial establishment, provided for certain offenses committed within business or industrial framework.

New forms of delinquency have been included which were either not statutory offenses or which were defined only briefly or insufficiently under previous Code. To this effect, special attention should be given to what are known as "Corporate Offenses", contemplating fraudulent conduct by administrators of companies, and "Offenses against the Public Treasury and the Social Security", in which list of types of fraud is extended and economic sum of fraud required to be guilty of tax offence is increased (15 million pesetas). New regulations of "Offenses against the workers' rights" should also be noted, providing truly exhaustive treament of these; as also those governing "Offenses Against Natural Resources and the Environment", "Offenses against Public Health", influence peddling and "Offenses against the Administration of Justice".

New Code also eliminates certain forms of offence, such as parricide and infanticide, which should be punished aside from social or moral connotations.

This in-depth reform of Criminal Law is supplemented, from procedural standpoint, by institution of jury for certain offenses (Basic Act 5/1995 of May 22, reformed by Basic Act 8/1995 of Nov. 16), and from penitentiary standpoint, with Royal Decree 190/1996 of Feb. 9, approving new Penitentiary Regulations.

CURRENCY:

National currency is peseta. Rate of exchange varies daily.

See topics Exchange Control; Foreign Exchange; and Foreign Investments in Spain.

CURTESY:

It does not exist in Spain. To know the rights of the survivor of the conjugal couple, see topic Descent and Distribution.

CUSTOMS:

Customs tariffs do not apply to import and export between Member States of European Union or European Economic Area. EU Common Custom Tariff fully applies to products coming from third States since Jan. 1, 1993.

Entry of goods into Spain is subject to two principal taxes: (a) custom duties on imports, according to rates established in Customs' Tariffs, (b) value added tax.

In general, entry of goods in Canary Islands, Ceuta and Melilla is subject to special taxes. In Canary Islands, goods imported from mainland are burdened with special tax, General Indirect Tax of Canary Islands. Act 20/1991 provides transitory period until Dec. 31, 2000, during which Spanish Administration may levy tax on all products either manufactured in or imported into Canary Islands. Common Custom Tariff will be progressively applied by Canary Islands to products imported from non-EU countries during period from July 1, 1991 until Dec. 31, 2000.

It is noteworthy that not only exemptions, reductions and suspensions recognized in Tariff Act shall apply but also those contained in international conventions ratified by Spain.

Smuggling.—Importation and exportation of goods without complying with customs or administrative requirements is smuggling offence, which is considered as criminal offence if amount smuggled exceeds 3,000,000 pesetas and administrative offence otherwise.

Penalties for criminal offences are prison terms of up to three years and fines of up to four times amount smuggled.

Administrative offences are punished with fines of up to three times value smuggled.

On Value Added Tax see topic Taxation.

DEATH:

Survivorship.—Should two or more persons, having a right to inherit from each other, die in same disaster, their death is presumed, under the law, to have happened at same time and no transfer of rights from the one to the other will take place. Anyone claiming the prior decease of one of those persons must submit evidence thereof.

Actions For Death.—Whoever causes, by action or omission, either wilfully or through his fault, the death of a person, must indemnify the heirs of the victim. Latter's heirs are entitled to a civil action against the author. They may, too, institute criminal proceedings in event of the death being a criminal offence. Amount of indemnities is not determined by law, and it is a matter left to the discretion of the court.

Death From A Work Accident.—Employees, even if foreigners, must be insured by employer against risks of sickness, injuries and death from a work accident. In the event of death, dependents, besides any other amounts they may receive from labor pension funds, are entitled to a life pension from 30% up to 100% of the salary subject to insurance.

Death During Travel.—Indemnities derived from a death which takes place while travelling in public transport facilities are, subject to actualization from time to time, as follows: (a) Ship and land transportation, up to maximum of 400,000 pesetas; (b) Air transport within the national territory (Spanish Law on Air Transportation), approximately 200,000 pesetas; (c) Air transportation in international flights (Warsaw Convention) approximately 450,000 pesetas.

Above indemnities do not preclude civil and criminal actions if applicable.

By virtue of resolution of Directorate General of Health, of July 13, 1976, number of provisions applying Regulation of Sanitary-Mortuary Rules are set forth. They include provision whereby it is obligatory to keep interments register for administrators of cemeteries in municipalities with more than 10,000 inhabitants. Likewise, there is provision calling for number of prior checks on health conditions in burial vaults constructed in cemeteries; and conditions and other indispensable requirements to remove corpses are regulated, certificate of approval thereof from physician who is qualified thanatologist being necessary; furthermore, coffin used must be of regulation type, equipped with device for absorption of gases, etc. Authorization to remove ashes of dead from Spain will be granted by Head of Provincial Health Office ("Jefe Provincial de Sanidad"). Non-embalmed corpses must be cremated for removal abroad.

By virtue of Order of July 28, 1976, maximum amount of life insurance which may be taken out without prior medical examination is 1,000,000 pesetas.

See also topic Absentees.

DEEDS:

Deeds are issued by notaries public to acknowledge transactions between contractual parties. Public deeds have direct and immediate effect against third parties, and formally acknowledge ownership of real estate, liens and encumbrances, etc.

DEPOSITIONS:

They must be made before judges or tribunals. If deponent lives in a distant place, the judge sends the inquiry, together with a rogatory letter to a judge in the place of residence of deponent, who interrogates him. Rogatory letters may also be sent to foreign tribunals through the Ministers of Justice and Foreign Affairs.

Where Spanish Courts must serve a summons or perform other court action in foreign country, they must address necessary letters requisitional to corresponding agency through diplomatic channel or through channel and in manner established in international treaties or, failing these, in §276 of Organic Act 6/1985 of July 1. In any case, art. 300 of Law of Civil Procedure provides that it is necessary to abide by principle of reciprocity. Same rules apply to comply in Spain with letters requisitional of foreign courts for performance of some court action. As a general rule, interested party must bear expenses caused by letters requisitional; although there are bilateral treaties which provide for free performance of certificates, legalizations and information rendered at request of public officials of other nation, whenever they refer to ex-officio matters.

DESCENT AND DISTRIBUTION:

An inheritance is transmitted to the heirs either by means of a will (see topic Wills) or according to law. The law establishes as obligatory heirs those who cannot be deprived of a part of the inheritance awarded through a will. The obligatory heirs are the descendants, and, in default of these, the ascendants and the spouse of decedent with special characteristics.

Children have a right to two thirds of the inheritance; one third must be distributed equally between them while the other third may be disposed of freely by the testator in favor of any of his children or grandchildren. Legitime of parents is one-half of inheritance. If both live, it must be divided in halves; if only one survives, he or she inherits it, even if grandparents of other branch survive. Grandparents have right to inherit in default of parents. Surviving consort has, in addition to one-half of property obtained during marriage (which may be considered as earnings of society constituted by both consorts, and in which each partner has equal share) usufruct of either: (1) One-third of inheritance, if he or she concurs with descendants; (2) one-half of inheritance, if he or she concurs with ascendants; or (3) two-thirds of inheritance if he or she concurs with heirs other than ascendants or descendants.

In case of intestate death, the inheritance goes (1) to the descendants; (2) in default of them, to the ascendants; (3) then to surviving spouse; (4) to brothers or sisters, who inherit by reason of their lineage; (5) to collaterals to fourth degree; and (6) in default of all these, to State.

Inheritance may be accepted pure and simple or to benefit for inventory. If accepted unconditionally, heir is responsible for debts of testator, not only to extent of estate, but also to that of his own property. If he accepts it conditionally, estate is responsible only for debts to extent of its value.

Under Art. 1011 of Civil Code, estate may be accepted with benefit to inventory even though testator has forbidden it. Heir may request inventory or list of property composing estate to be made within terms provided by law. Heir may likewise reserve a term to decide whether or not he will accept estate. Acceptance with benefit to inventory may be done either by notary or by writ of competent court. Benefit to inventory gives rise to following effects in heir's favour: he is responsible for debts and encumbrances on estate to extent of property thereof; private goods are not mixed in with those of estate; he continues to maintain against assets of estate all actions that he would have had against deceased.

DISPUTE RESOLUTION:

Arbitration and Award.—Act 36 of Dec. 5, 1988 on Arbitration permits individuals or corporations making agreement to submit to one or more arbitrators disputes in litigation that have arisen or may arise on matters which they are free to dispose of by law.

Following may not be subject of arbitration: (a) Questions on which firm and final court decision has been rendered, except for aspects arising from its enforcement; (b) matters inseparably united to others on which parties do not have power of disposal; (c) questions on which State Attorney is obliged to participate by law, representing and defending those who, lacking capacity to act or legal representation, are unable to act for themselves.

Arbitrations in labour law are excluded from scope of application of Arbitration Act.

Arbitrators decide on question in dispute in law or in equity, according to their best knowledge and understanding, at choice of parties. If parties have not expressly opted for arbitration in law, arbitrators decide in equity, unless adminstration of arbitration has been entrusted to corporation or association, in which case that body's regulations will be applicable. To be valid, arbitration must conform to provisions of Law.

When two or more persons, in a way different from that provided by Law, agree on decisive partcipation of one or more third parties, expressly or tacitly accepting their decision after its issuance, that agreement will be valid and binding for parties if it meets requirements necessary for validity of agreements.

If parties have not provided otherwise, arbitrators must render their award within six months reckoned from date on which last member of arbitration panel agreed to resolve dispute, or date on which he was replaced. This term may only be extended by agreement between parties, notified to arbitrators before initial term expires.

If term elapses without award being passed, arbitration agreement is rendered null and void and dispute may be raised before courts.

At any time before award is rendered, parties, in mutual agreement, may desist from arbitration or suspend it for specific period.

Award must be issued in writing and justified when arbitrators decide on matter in litigation in Law. It must also be executed before notary public and notified to parties by duly attested means.

Firm arbitration award has effect of res judicata, so that only appeal for reversal is possible against it, as provided in procedural legislation for firm court judgments.

Award may be annulled in following cases: (1) Where arbitration agreement is null; (2) where formalities and essential principles provided by Law have not been observed in appointment of arbitrators and development of arbitration procedure; (3) where award is rendered outside term; (4) where arbitrators have decided on items not submitted to their decision or on items that, while submitted for their decision, are not apt for arbitration. In these cases, annulment will only affect items not submitted for decision or not apt for arbitration, provided that these items have their own substance and are not indissolubly linked to main question; (5) where award is contrary to public policy.

Cognizance of appeal for annulment rests with Provincial Higher Court of place where award was rendered.

Arbitration awards are enforced in Spain in accordance with international treaties forming part of internal legislation and, in absence of treaty, in accordance with rules of Arbitration Act.

DIVORCE:

Law 30 of July 7, 1981 admits following causes of divorce: (1) Actual cessation of marital cohabitation for at least one year following lodging of separation petition by both spouses or by one spouse with consent of other; (2) actual cessation of marital cohabitation for at least two years following free acceptance by both spouses of their separation in fact or when one spouse can prove that other had committed action justifying separation at moment divorce petition was filed; (3) actual cessation of marital cohabitation for minimum of five years; and, (4) final court decision condemning one spouse for attempting against life of his ascendants, descendants or spouse.

Petitions of divorce requested by both spouses or with consent of other spouse have to be accompanied by proposal regarding custody of children, use of family home, liquidation of economic regime, alimony and each spouse's contribution to charges resulting from marriage. Alimony will be determined by court taking into consideration age and health, professional qualification, personal wealth and marriage duration, among other factors.

Spanish courts are competent to hear divorce cases when: (1) Both spouses have Spanish nationality; (2) both spouses are residents of Spain; (3) plaintiff is Spaniard and resident of Spain; or (4) defendant is resident of Spain.

DOWER:

Law of May 13, 1981 has repealed all provisions of Civil Code on dowry.

ENVIRONMENT:

General Environmental Protection.—Environmental legal protection is contained in art. 45 of Spanish Constitution of 1978. Right to environment and duty to preserve it are conceived as fundamental right and obligation in our Constitution. In addition, arts. 148 and 149 of Constitution lay down basic lines for distribution of competencies between central government and regional governments.

Environmental protection is also contained in Spanish Criminal Code, in arts. 325, et seq., which relate to offences against natural resources and environment.

Air Protection.—General provisions are contained in Act 38/1972 of Dec. 22, "Act for the Protection of the Atmosphere", implemented by Decree 833/1975 of Feb. 6.

See Topical Index in front part of this volume.

ENVIRONMENT . . . *continued*
Purpose of this Act is to prevent, supervise and correct situations of air pollution, regardless of causes for such pollution.

Procedure for protection established in Act is based on determination by Government of certain emission and absorption levels in order to prevent air pollution, which may not be exceeded. Notwithstanding, Government may establish more restricted emission levels when, according to circumstances, it considers that persons or goods located in influence area of emitting focus may be directly and seriously damaged; in such cases, individuals or entities responsible for emissions are bound to adopt corrective systems or measures which, in accordance with technical conditions, guarantee reduction of polluting emissions.

Water Protection.—Protection of continental and sea waters is contained in two texts, one on "Continental Water" (Inland water) and, another one on Coasts and Marine Waters.

Basic legislation on continental waters consists of Act 29/1985 of Aug. 2, "the Water Act" and its implementing regulations. This legislation provides for, among its basic aims, maintaining correct level of quality for waters, preventing accumulation of toxic or hazardous compounds and avoiding any other activity which may cause damage to waters.

Competence on continental waters rests with Hydrographic Confederations, agencies depending upon Ministry for the Environment. Nevertheless, in cases of intra-community river basins, responsibilities may be assumed by regional communities.

Basic rules currently in force regarding protection of coasts and sea are contained in Act 22/1988, Coast Act, and 1977 Act on marine pollution through dumping by vessels and aircraft. Basic aim of these rules is to determine, protect, use and police public land and sea areas and, in particular, sea coast.

As in case of continental waters, protection of sea waters is based on principle that discharges are subject to prior administative authorization and to payment of dumping fee. For this purpose, Act prohibits dumping of waste material both in sea and in protected area, except where it is previously duly authorised.

Marine Pollution Act, referring to dumping by vessels and aircraft, attempts to avoid direct or indirect tipping by man of substances, materials or forms of energy into sea, where such tipping may constitute danger to human health or damage tourism, landscape or biological resources and marine life.

Solid Waste.—Spanish legislation on waste is based on differentiation between toxic and hazardous waste, regulated by Act 20/86 and regulations implementing it, and urban solid waste, contemplated by Act 42/75, which governs not only household waste but also agricultural and construction waste and nontoxic industrial waste.

(a) Solid Urban Waste.—Under Act on Solid Urban Waste, monopoly and obligation to collect and treat solid urban waste rest with municipalities, laying down special provisions of treatment to be given to solid waste with characteristics making it toxic or hazardous.

(b) Toxic and Hazardous Waste.—All aspects relevant to hazardous waste are governed by Act 20/1986 of May 14, on Hazardous Waste, implemented by Regulations enacted through Royal Decree 833/1988, dated July 20. Purpose of Act is to set out basic legal regime intended to guarantee (a) protection of human health, (b) defense of environment and (c) preservation of natural resources in production and handling of hazardous waste.

Allocation of Environmental Administrative Authority in Spain.—At State level, authority responsible for environmental matters is Ministry for the Environment, set up in 1996.

At level of regional governments, administrative departments specializing in environmental matters within structure of respective executive government have been set up. In addition, extensive responsibilities for environmental matters rest with municipalities. These responsibilities are defined in local government legislation. (Act 7/1985 on Bases of Local Government).

EXCHANGE CONTROL:

According to Exchange Control Law of Dec. 10, 1979 (as am'd by Organic Law of Aug. 16, 1983) Government is given full powers in exchange control matters (except those governed by special Law). Government may subject any transactions giving right to payments abroad or from abroad to prior authorization, declaration, verification or to any other administrative control.

Royal Decree 1816/1991 of Dec. 20 establishes liberalization of foreign exchange control, affecting all payments of merchandise and services and movements of capital.

Following are liberalized: (a) Acts, business, transactions and operations which give rise to collections and payments between residents and nonresidents or transfers to or from abroad; (b) collections from and payments to foreign countries arising from transactions mentioned in (a) above. Exceptions are foreign investments in Spain and Spanish investments abroad, which shall continue to be governed by their specific norms. Royal Decree of Dec. 20, 1991 also contains two escape clauses for specific cases in which Government may prohibit or limit certain transactions with foreign countries. Export of bank notes, coins and bank drafts issued to bearer, for amounts exceeding 1 million pesetas or their equivalent in foreign currency, is subject to declaration to Directorate General of Foreign Transactions. Prior authorisation of Directorate is required when exports exceed amount of 5 million pesetas.

However, since entry into force of Treaty of Maastricht in Jan. 1, 1994, arts. 73 B et seq. have fully liberalised all movements of capital, not only between Member States of EU but also between EU countries and third States. Accordingly European Court of Justice declared that above mentioned requirement of prior authorisation for exports exceeding 5 million pesetas is contrary to EC rules, though Spanish authorities may still require declaration of exports of capital. Notwithstanding liberalisation carried on, aforesaid national rules have not been expressly derogated and export of bank notes, coins and bank drafts issued to bearer exceeding 5 million pesetas and lacking prior administrative authorisation are still penalised as being criminal offence. However, such rules may be deemed not to be applicable pursuant to European law, save for obligation to declare exports of capital exceeding 1 million pesetas.

Lastly, Act 19/93 on prevention of money laundering has created commission in charge of fight against this offence.

See topics Currency; Foreign Exchange; Foreign Investments in Spain; Foreign Trade Regulations.

EXECUTIONS:

Before a judgment is enforced, the debtor is requested to pay. If he does not and there is no property particularly affected by the debt, the recovery is pursued against the property of the debtor in the following order: cash, Government securities, securities listed on the Stock Exchange, jewels, short-range credits, commodities and profits, personal property and real estate, salaries and credits, long-range credits. Bonds which are quoted at Stock Exchange are sold under control of stockbroker; remaining assets are appraised and sold in public auction.

EXECUTORS AND ADMINISTRATORS:

Testator may appoint one or several executors, who must be of age. Heirs cannot be executors, except for widower. Executors may act jointly or severally and they may be appointed for special purpose or generally. Duty is voluntary but must be accepted or refused within six days from notification. Executorship is gratis but remuneration therefor may be provided by testator. It may not be delegated without specific authorisation of testator and executor must perform his duties within general term of one year from death of testator.

EXEMPTIONS:

The beds of the debtor and of his family, their clothes of daily use and working tools are exempt from seizure, also his wages or pension, according to a certain scale.

FOREIGN EXCHANGE:

By Decree Law of July 17, 1973, Spanish Institute of Foreign Exchange was abolished and its functions distributed by Decree of July 26, 1973, between Bank of Spain and Ministry of Economy and Finance through Directorate General of Foreign Transactions. For monetary purposes, consideration is paid to residence and not to citizenship. Consequently, same rules apply to Spaniards and foreigners resident in Spain, on one side, and to foreigners and Spaniards resident abroad, on other. Basic legislation is contained in Royal Decree 1816/91 of Dec. 20 (as am'd by Royal Decree 42/1993 of Jan. 15 in some aspects), and by several Circular letters of Bank of Spain.

Foreign Accounts.—Both residents and nonresidents may open bank accounts in pesetas or in foreign currency in Spain. Opening and holding of accounts in pesetas or in foreign currency abroad by residents in Spain has been liberalized by Royal Decree 1816/91 of Dec. 20, although holders of accounts must declare opening of accounts within 30 days from their opening and must report movements of such accounts in manner established by Bank of Spain. (Circular letter 24/92 of Bank of Spain, Dec. 18). This applies both to holders of accounts in bank or credit entities abroad, and to holders of accounts with nonresidents which are not bank nor credit entities. Cancellation of accounts must also be declared within 30 days.

License and Technical Assistance Agreements.—License agreements have been liberalized by Royal Decree of Dec. 20, 1991. There is no need, therefore, for prior filing of all license agreements.

Loans.—Royal Decree 1816/91, of Dec. 20 has liberalized loans of all kinds, including loans in foreign currency and loans granted by residents to nonresidents. However, before receiving loaned funds, borrower must notify Bank of Spain of main particulars of loan, and Bank of Spain must assign statistical number to loan. (Circular letter 23/92 of Bank of Spain Dec. 18). Loans of under 250,000,000 pesetas are excluded from prior declaration to Bank of Spain, (except when lender is resident in tax haven), but for statistical purposes they must be assigned number by Bank through which funds are received in Spain.

Travel.—Export of coins, bank notes and bank drafts issued to bearer (whether in pesetas or in foreign currency) have been liberalized by Royal Decree 1816/91 of Dec. 20 (as am'd by Royal Decree 42/93 of Jan. 15). Export is subject to declaration when amount exceeds 1,000,000 pesetas per person and trip. Existing prior authorization for amounts exceeding 5,000,000 pesetas per person and trip must be deemed not to be applicable following entry into force of Treaty of Maastricht, as interpreted by European Court of Justice (see also topic Exchange Control). Introduction in Spain of these means of payment is free (Royal Decree 42/93 of Jan. 15); however, introduction by nonresident travellers of such means of payment is subject to declaration before customs on entry, or before Directorate General for Foreign Transactions, when amount exceeds 1,000,000 pesetas in case travellers wish to carry out any transaction requiring justification of origin of referred means of payment (Order of Feb. 2, 1993).

See also topics Currency; Exchange Control; Foreign Investments in Spain; Foreign Trade Regulations.

FOREIGN INVESTMENTS IN SPAIN:

Basic legislation on foreign investments in Spain is contained in Royal Decree 671/1992 of July 2, as implemented by Resolution of the Directorate General for Foreign Transactions of July 6, 1992 as amended by Regulation of Oct. 26, 1992. Main point with regard to previous legislation is that amount of investments which do not require government verification is increased to 500,000,000 pesetas.

Such provisions distinguish between following means of investment and form thereof:

Classification of Investors.—Foreign investors are: (a) Individuals nonresident in Spain, whether Spanish or foreign; (b) private legal entities resident abroad; (c) Spanish companies with foreign participation in their capital, as well as branches and establishments in Spain of nonresidents in Spain, which incorporate other Spanish companies or acquire shares thereof; (d) foreign governments and public entities.

Means of Investment.—Foreign investments can be done by means of contribution of foreign or domestic capital. Following are considered as such: (a) Contribution of currency; (b) contribution of technical assistance, patents and licences; (c) contribution of capital equipment; (d) any other means.

Forms.—Foreign investments are classified for purpose of their regulation in: (a) Direct investments, which consist of holdings in Spanish companies allowing effective

See Topical Index in front part of this volume.

FOREIGN INVESTMENTS IN SPAIN . . . *continued*
influence over company's management or control (ownership of at least 10% of capital stock, active presence in decision-making bodies), creation in Spain of branches or establishments or granting to them of reimbursable cash advances, granting of loans with duration of over five years aimed at establishing lasting relations between lender and borrower; (b) portfolio investments consisting of purchase of securities, provided that they do not qualify as direct investment; (c) investments in real estate; (d) other forms of investment.

Administratives Approvals.—General rule is that foreign investments may be made freely, however, following investments are subject to prior verification by Directorate General for Foreign Transactions: (a) Direct investments, when foreign holding in Spanish company exceed 50% of its capital and more than 500,000,000 ptas are invested, and foreign holding in capital plus reserves exceeds 500,000,000 ptas; exception is made to investments by means of capitalization of reserves and reinvestment of non-distributed profits; (b) granting of loans exceeding 500,000,000 ptas; (c) creation of branches or establishments when amount exceeds 500,000,000 ptas; (d) portfolio investments consisting of issue or placing of shares in foreign markets; (e) investments in real estate and other forms of investments, when amount exceeds 500,000,000 ptas; (f) all foreign investments proceeding from countries or territories considered as Tax Havens, according to Royal Decree 1080/91 of July 5 except for direct investments where foreign holding in Spanish company does not exceed 50%, which follow general rule of freedom.

Profits.—Holders of foreign investments will enjoy right to transfer abroad, without any limitation as to amount of profits and dividends distributed and proceeds of sale of subscription rights of securities, and also capital invested and capital gains realized on sale thereof.

Specific Activities.—Foreign investments in following activities require express approval: Activities directly related to national defence (including exploitation of strategic minerals and telecommunications), television, gambling, radio and air transport. Such limitations are not applied to residents in EU Member States, except when they carry out certain activities related to national defence.

Investments by Foreign Governments and Legal Entities of Foreign Sovereignty.—Includes foreign companies and legal entities which are controlled in any manner by foreign government or by foreign public enterprise. Investments by foreign governments and official entities of foreign sovereignty, except those of EU countries, require approval by Spanish Government.

Areas to Which Access to Ownership by Foreigners is Restricted.—In areas next to Portuguese and French border and at Straits of Gibraltar and area of Cartagena and Coasts of Galicia, as well as in all Spanish islands, there are established certain maximum percentages of acquisition of real property by nonresidents which may reach up to 15% of total area in question. Acquisition of real property by nonresidents in such areas requires special military authorization. These limitations do not apply to residents in EU.

Registration of Investments.—Foreign investments must be executed in document certified by Spanish public attesting officer and registered at Foreign Investment Register in specific official forms. Public attesting officers must require from investors, apart from respective administrative approvals, certificate of their status of nonresident and means of contribution. Purchase of securities, transfer of which between residents may be made without intervention of public attesting officer, does not require such intervention provided transfer is made through security company or agency.

One of main novelties of new legislation is that foreign investments do not have to be domiciled at bank, neither do their certificates have to be deposited at Spanish banking entity.

Other Obligations.—Spanish companies with foreign participation exceeding 50% of their capital, capital of which plus reserves is more than 500,000,000 pesetas, have to present each year annual report before Directorate General for Foreign Transactions.

Spanish Investments Abroad.—Basic legislation on Spanish investments abroad is contained in Royal Decree 672/1992 of July 2, as implemented by Resolution of Directorate General for Foreign Transactions of July 7, 1992. Main point with regard to previous legislation is that amount of investments which do not require verification is increased to 250,000,000 ptas.

Spanish investments abroad are those made by: Individuals, whether Spanish or foreign, resident in Spain; private legal entities resident in Spain; branches and establishments in Spanish territory of nonresidents in Spain; companies resident abroad, when holding in them by residents in Spain exceeds 50% of their capital.

Spanish investments abroad are classified in four groups: (a) Direct investments. They may be effected through incorporation of company, acquisition of capital stock of existing company, creation of branches and agencies and grant of long-term (more than five years maturity) financial loans to foreign companies aimed at establishing lasting relations, in case of participation in foreign company. Effective influence on management of company is required (ownership of at least 10% of capital stock, active presence in decision making bodies). These investments are liberalized and may be made freely; however, such investments will require prior verification, when their amount exceeds 250,000,000 ptas, when main activity of foreign company is direct or indirect participation in capital stock of other companies, whatever amount of investment may be, and when destination of investment is country or territory considered as Tax Haven. (b) Portfolio investments are liberalized and do not need prior verification. (c) Investments in real estate are subject to prior verification, when amount exceeds 250,000,000 ptas. (d) Other forms of investment abroad are free, except when amount exceeds 250,000,000 ptas.

Spanish investments abroad may be made with any means of investments; when such means consist of contribution of real estate in Spain or of shares of capital stock of Spanish companies, prior verification is required when destination of investment is EEC country, and government approval when destination of investment is non-EEC country.

All Spanish investments abroad must be registered at Investments Registry of Ministry of Economy and Finance.

FOREIGN TRADE REGULATIONS:

Spanish foreign trade is entirely subject to EC Regulations since Jan. 1, 1993.

1. Imports.—System of importing goods is governed by Ministerial Order of Feb. 21, 1986 as am'd by Order of Apr. 6, 1994. Said Order establishes following systems for importing of goods, which varies according to countries and territories from which goods come and nature of goods in question.

(a) Imports under System of Free Trade.—This is general rule applicable to all imports of goods, except those which are subject to system of administrative approval for imports. System of free trade for imports includes some which are subject to statistical control prior to import. Goods subject to prior statistical control require issue of document known as "prior notice of import", which should be verified by Directorate General for Foreign Trade. For import of other types of goods it is sufficient to submit prior notice of import, import certificate or similar document for agricultural and fishing products, established by EC norms.

(b) System of Administrative Approval.—System of administrative approval is intended for small number of goods, import of which requires administrative approval for import to be issued by Directorate General for Foreign Trade. Imports of goods in which payment is offset by means of export of other goods also require administrative approval for import. Imports which do not give rise to payments are not subject to administrative approval anymore, as established by Order of Feb. 18, 1992, unless their commerce regime requires it.

(c) Payment and Domiciling.—Payments for imports are free, according to Royal Decree 1816/91 of Dec. 20, and can be done with only requirement of indicating to bank (through which payments should be done) main particulars of transaction; these are mainly name, address and Tax Identity Number of resident, name and address of nonresident, import, currency, amount in pesetas and concept of transaction. Declaration to bank must be done prior to payment, except in case of payments with bearer cheques against payer's bank account, in which case declaration must be done in term of 15 days from date payment is due at payer's account.

(d) Procedure for Investigation and Defence of Commercial Interests.—Directorate General for Foreign Trade may initiate, either officially or at request of significant part of sector, procedure for collection of information with view to adopting measures in defence of commercial interests in case that serious loss or threat of serious loss may arise out of development of import trade.

2. Exports.—System for exports is governed by Royal Decree 2701/1985 of Dec. 27, and by Orders of Feb. 21 and Feb. 26, 1986 (as am'd by Order of July 23, 1991). There are following systems for exports:

(a) Exports under System of Free Trade.—All exports of goods, except those which require administrative approval for export, will be carried out under system of free trade. Certain number of these goods are subject to prior statistical control, and in order to be exported require prior notice of export to be submitted, verification of which is responsibility of Directorate General for Foreign Trade. When submission of certain export document, export certificate or similar document for agricultural or fishing products established by EEC is required for export of certain products, said document will be issued by Directorate General for Foreign Trade. Outgoing goods not subject either to prior statistical control or to issue of document from EC require submission of customs declaration of export.

(b) Exports under System of Administrative Approval.—Exports of goods included in said system (which are minority) require "general administrative approval for export" or "administrative approval for export for a specific Operation" to be issued, responsibility for which lies with Directorate General for Foreign Trade.

(c) Collection and Domiciling.—Collections from exports are free, as established in Royal Decree 1816/91 of Dec. 20. Same requirements as regards payments for imports are applied to collections from exports. See subhead 1. Imports, catchline (c) Payment and Domiciling, supra.

(d) Procedure for Investigation and Defence of Commercial Interests.—Directorate General for Foreign Trade may initiate, either officially or at request of significant part of sector or sectors directly involved, procedure for collection of information for study of events affecting exports, for purpose of adopting appropriate measures for defence of commercial interests, when data available on evolution of export trade make such measures advisable.

See also topics Customs and Foreign Exchange.

FRAUDS, STATUTE OF:

Spain has no Statute of Frauds. See topic Contracts.

FRAUDULENT SALES AND CONVEYANCES:

Creditors have, under Spanish Law, possibility of exercising against debtor's fraudulent acts the subrogatory and revocatory or Paulien actions. By the first one, creditor may subrogate to rights and actions of debtor for purpose of obtaining satisfaction of debt. By the second action, creditor may annul such covenants as debtor may have executed with fraud of his rights. Both actions are regulated in art. 1111 of Civil Code which expressly provides that creditor, after having tried to attach property in possession of debtor to satisfy his debt, may exercise all rights and actions of latter for same purpose, except for such rights and actions inherent to his person; they may also impugn any acts which he may have performed with fraud of his right.

A prior requisite for exercise of both actions is previous prosecution of goods in possession of debtor in order thus to realise sum owed to creditors. Both actions thus have secondary character.

GARNISHMENT: See topic Attachment.

HOLIDAYS:

Public holidays may not exceed 14 days per year. Every year Official Gazette publishes calendar of working days; government of autonomous communities may substitute with local festivities up to two holidays. In addition, each municipality may establish up to two local feasts.

HOMESTEADS:

Certain items cannot be attached. Among them are the beds of the debtor and of his family, their clothes, worktools, and the debtor's salary, within certain limitations. (Law for Civil Procedure, Art. 1449 and following).

HUSBAND AND WIFE:

Contracting parties may establish pact for management of their estate, including separate management. Marriage contract may be amended after marriage. In absence of any specific stipulation their relations are governed by community of property system, where administration of community assets is entrusted jointly to husband and wife, each of them keeping full rights over their private or own assets.

Law of May 2, 1975 modifies Civil Code (Arts. 62, 63) to provide that marriage does not limit or restrain legal capacity of either husband or wife, and neither of them may freely represent each other without consent.

Consorts can sell any property to each other.

Marriage, either between foreigner and Spaniard and vice-versa does not determine by itself an alteration of previous nationality.

IMMIGRATION:

Foreigners may enter Spain furnished with passport except EU citizens who may enter with Identity Card. Non-EU foreigners wishing to work in Spain must apply for special permit from Ministry of Labor and for residence permit from civil government of province they intend to reside in. EU citizens may freely work in Spain, but must apply for residence card if anticipated that stay will exceed three months, this card being valid for all territory of Spain, with term of five years and subject to automatic extensions.

INFANTS:

Majority for both sexes is attained at age of 18. Minors may be emancipated at age of 16 by concession of parent exercising parental authority. Emancipation is automatically granted on marriage of minor.

INSOLVENCY:

See topic Bankruptcy and/or Suspension of Payments.

INTEREST:

Legal interest is approved yearly in General Budget Law prevailing on date as from which interest shall accrue.

JOINT STOCK COMPANIES:

See topic Corporations and Associations.

JUDGMENTS:

Judicial decisions in Spain may take three basic forms: (a) "Providencias," object of which is to expedite proceedings through their various stages; (b) "Auto," purpose of which is to canalize proceedings, settling any secondary questions which may arise therein; (c) "Sentencia," which is final judgment of the court or tribunal.

Judgments of foreign courts may be enforced in Spain when they fall under any of the three following cases: (1) *Treaties.*—That a treaty does exist on this matter between Spain and the foreign country. There is no such treaty with the United States. (2) *Reciprocity.*—That the foreign country enforces Spanish judgments. (3) *Conformance with certain requirements.*—That, short of treaties and reciprocity antecedents, the foreign judgments conform to certain requirements exacted by Spanish Laws.

Two fundamental requisites are that judgment not have been handed down in default of Spanish party and that it be final.

Enforcement order handed down by Spanish Supreme Court at instance of interested party is required.

Spain has adhered Treaty of Brussels of Sept. 27, 1968 on judicial competence and enforcement of judicial decisions on civil and commercial matters, when signing San Sebastián Convention. Spain has also adhered to Treaty of Lugano of Sept. 16, 1988, on judicial competence and enforcement of judicial decisions on civil and commercial matters.

Arbitration.—Act 36 of Dec. 5, 1988, regulates arbitrations taking place in Spain and amends Civil Procedure Act, making agreement between parties to submit question in litigation to arbitration reason for denial of cause for action. This Act also stipulates manner of implementing foreign arbitration awards, which will be enforced in accordance with provisions of international treaties or, in absence of these, in accordance with Arbitration Act itself.

Note: Instrument of Adhesion by Spain to Agreement on Recognition and Enforcement of Foreign Arbitratral Awards signed in New York June 10, 1958. (Official State Gazette July 11, 1977).

This instrument of adhesion is effective since Aug. 10, 1977 and it governs documents and necessary requirements for enforcement of foreign arbitration judgments. This Convention shall not affect validity of multilateral or bilateral agreements between different countries who are parties to Convention.

LABOUR RELATIONS:

Royal Legislative Decree 1/1995, of Mar. 24, approving Consolidated Text of the Workers' Statute, has substituted almost all applicable labour legislation and introduced new legal framework. All remunerated services rendered by individuals on behalf of third parties are within scope of labour law, except: (1) Civil servants and employees of public entities, (2) compulsory personal services, (3) services rendered as member of board of directors of companies, (4) services rendered within family, (5) services rendered in connection with commercial transactions, provided that all risks are assumed by agent.

Sources of labour law are: (1) Governmental regulations, (2) collective agreements, (3) individual employment agreements, (4) local and professional custom.

Basic rights of workers include: Effective occupation, free syndication, collective bargaining, assembly and strike.

Minimum working age is 16. Employment agreements need not, with some exceptions, be in writing, but any party may require execution of written agreement. Following must be in writing: part-time work contracts, home-work contracts, contracts for performance of specific job of work or service, contracts of workers engaged in Spain in service of Spanish companies abroad, contracts for specific time exceding four weeks, practical experience contracts and apprenticeship contracts.

Contracts may be entered into on permanent basis or for specific term, and after Act 11/1994 of May 19 they are no longer assumed to be permanent.

Act 10/1994 of May 19 on urgent measures to promote employment and Act 11/1994 of May 19, cited above, have made in-depth change to system of temporary engagements as measure to promote employment, and at present time contracts of this kind may only be arranged with workers from following groups: those over 45 years of age, disabled and those receiving unemployment benefit and who have been recorded at Labour Office as unemployed for at least one year.

Discrimination upon age, race, religion, politics and language is prohibited. Non-competition clauses after termination of agreement are valid if: (1) Employer has true commercial or industrial interest, (2) employee is given adequate economic compensation, and (3) duration does not exceed two years in case of technicians and six months for other employees.

Salary includes all consideration received by employees, whether in cash or in kind; taxes and social security contributions to be borne by employee may not be paid by employer and agreements providing otherwise are null and void.

Ordinary working time may not exceed 40 hours per week; minimum weekly rest period is set at 36 hours. Yearly remunerated vacations are set at minimum of 30 natural days.

As from Act 11/1994 of May 19, permission from Labour Authority is no longer required for geographical mobility, provided that economic, technical, organisational or production causes exist to justify mobility. Nevertheless "a posteriori" jurisdictional control of decision of transfer is possible in event of claim filed by workers affected who are not in agreement.

Temporary employment companies have been authorized by Act 14/1994 of June 1.

Employment agreements may be suspended by: Mutual agreement, temporary invalidism of worker, military service, worker's imprisonment, force majeure, economic or technological causes, strike and employer's lock-out, causes set out validly in contract, maternity of working woman, holding of representative public office, organizational or production causes and mandatory leave of absence. Suspension exonerates from working and paying salary and wages.

Employment agreements may be terminated by: Mutual agreement, expiry of duration, contractual reasons set forth in agreement, worker's resignation, death, permanent invalidism or retirement, force majeure, for economic, technical, organization or production causes. Authorization from Labour Authorities is only required when within one 90-day term termination affects at least: (a) ten workers, in companies with less than 100 workers; (b) 10% of number of workers of company in those with from 100 to 300 workers; (c) 30 workers in companies with 300 or more workers. In events of termination of contracts where these limits are not exceeded, no authorization is necessary, although subsequent control may be exerted by courts.

Employer may dismiss employee for: Repeated and unjustified lack of attendance, lack of discipline, oral or physical offenses, breach of bona fides and abuse of confidence, continued and voluntary reduction of worker's performance, customary use of drugs and alcohol. If court's judgment determines that dismissal was "due", agreement is terminated and employee is not entitled to any compensation. If dismissal is deemed "undue" employer may choose between readmission or payment of: (1) Compensation of 45 days of salary per year of employment, which compensation may not exceed salary of 42 months, and (2) salary from date of dismissal until date of mandatory prior conciliation hearing, provided that at this hearing employer recognizes dismissal to be unfair. When "undue" dismissal affects worker's representatives, option to be readmitted lies with worker, and employer is compelled to readmit worker if latter so chooses.

Regarding worker's representatives, they are elected by secret, direct and free voting, not exceeding number of three for business with less than 50 workers.

Collective agreements govern productivity and working conditions and may also stipulate conditions for "peace" in labour relationship. Their territorial scope may freely be determined by parties. They must be in writing and need not be approved by any governmental authority, although they have to be registered with labour authority.

Unemployment Benefits in General Social Security System.—Royal Decree 625 of Apr. 1, 1985, as modified by Act 22/1992, of July 30, which develops Act 31 of Aug. 2, 1984, provides as follows: Amount of unemployment benefit, whether due to dismissal or cancellation of work contract, is established during first 180 days at 70% of base amount, which will be quotient obtained by dividing 180 by sum of contributions made in six previous months; and as from day 181, at 60% of said base. Unemployment benefits cannot exceed 220% of Minimum Interprofessional Wage.

With regard to time during which unemployment benefit may be received: This will be in terms of periods of employment for which contributions were paid in six years prior to legal situation of unemployment, up to maximum of two years during which said benefit may be received. Once said two-year period has elapsed, unemployment subsidy may be received, which may be extended up to maximum of 18 months. However, there must exist justified legal grounds in judgment of competent authority in order for such subsidy to be received and amount of same will be equivalent to 75% of overall minimum salary in force for each year.

Worker in legal situation of unemployment who has not covered minimum term of contribution is entitled to unemployment subsidy when (i) he has contributed for at least three months and has family responsibilities; (ii) he has contributed for six months even when he has no family liabilities.

Unemployment benefits are only suspended in following events: for one month when, unless with justified cause, holder of right does not appear, having been required to do so, before "Entidad Gestora" or does not renew demand for employment within legally established terms; while he is rendering military service or substitute

See Topical Index in front part of this volume.

LABOUR RELATIONS . . . *continued*

social work; while he is serving prison sentence; while holder of post of work performs work for duration of less than 12 months.

Right to receive payments of basic unemployment benefit will be cancelled in following cases: Conclusion of maximum period for receiving such benefit; performance of work entailing inclusion in any Social Security System, provided that duration of said work exceeds 12 months and, in any case, should there be termination for causes attributable to employee; refusal of suitable offer of work or refusal, without good reason, to participate in professional endeavours for purpose of facilitating employment or training; commencement of receipt of retirement or disablement pension; change of residence in foreign country; obtaining or enjoying benefits by fraudulent means, etc.

Bases of Contribution to Social Security System.—Tariffed bases for contributions to General System of Social Security have been provided, being applicable to all situations and contingencies. Bases deriving from insurance for unemployment or occupational diseases are as follows: Different amounts or tariffed bases are provided, taking into account professional or labour classification of employees who are obligated to contribute.

Assessment and Collection of Amounts in General Social Security System.—Including compensation for work accidents and occupational diseases, together with assessment and collection of amounts in General Social Security System.

Accounts of Social Security System and those of Unemployment, Salary Guarantee Fund, Professional Training and Solidarity Fund for employment will be assessed and paid into collection offices by those responsible for contributions (employer) and bodies or agents authorised for collection during month after their becoming due, unless any other term is specially provided.

Employers will complete for this purpose relevant official forms (contribution forms) in accordance with legislation currently in force. In accordance with that established in Order of May 30, 1979 and additional provision of Order of Mar. 24, 1980, collection offices where said amounts may be collected are Beneficosocial Savings Banks, private banking establishments, official banking establishments expressly authorised by Directorate General for Social Security and Rural Credit Cooperative Banks. Also provided are number of interconnections between collection offices, Employees' Mutual Aid Societies, Employers' Mutual Aid Societies and Agencies of the National Institute for Provision. Likewise, subsequent to Spain's entry into European Economic Community, it will be necessary to abide, not only by provisions of Treaty of Rome of Mar. 25, 1957, but also by Directive 77/7 of Dec. 19, 1978 regarding equality of treatment between men and women in Social Security matters, and by Community Regulation 1,408 of June 14, 1971 regarding application of Social Security systems to salaried employees and their families who change residence within area of Community; also applicable is Coded Text of the Council of Europe of June 2, 1983.

Royal Decree of Dec. 28, 1995, establishing Minimum Wages.—Minimum wages are: workers of 18 years of age and over: 2,164 pesetas per day and 64,920 pesetas per month. Workers under 18 years of age: 1,674 pesetas per day and 50,220 pesetas per month.

Law 19 of Apr. 1, 1977 Concerning Regulation of Right of Trade Union Association.—Art. 1 provides that workers and employers may establish for each branch of activity, on territorial or national scale, such professional associations as they see fit for defence of their respective interest. By branch of activity is meant area of economic activity, profession or any other similar concept determined by employers or workers. Associations will establish their own by-laws, have full power to govern themselves and enjoy legal protection guaranteeing their independence vis-a-vis public Administration. By-laws must contain at least name of association, territorial and professional scope, representative bodies vis-a-vis Government and Administration, economic re-sources, system of admission of members, system of operation, etc. Art. 2 provides that workers and employers will be entitled to join said associations on sole condition that they respect by-laws. Art. 3 provides that associations formed under this Law will have full legal personality and capacity of action. They will be registered 20 days after filing their by-laws with Special Register, unless application is made to judicial authority for ruling that by-laws are not in accordance with Law. Art. 4 confirms that professional associations may set up federations and confederations for this purpose. Art. 5 provides that associations may only be suspended or dissolved by judicial decision based on conduct of activities implying unlawfulness, or other grounds contemplated in Law or by-laws.

Military personnel are excluded from scope of application of this Law. Exercise of rights of syndical association by civil servants, and civil personnel employed by military authority will be regulated in due course by specific provision.

Royal Decree-Law of Mar. 4, 1977, Concerning Labour Relations.—This Decree-Law expressly regulates strikes, collective disputes and agreements, lockout by employer and penalties.

Restructuring of personel (redundancy) is governed by Royal Decree 696/1980 of Apr. 14, regulating proceedings for substantial changes to working conditions and suspension and extinguishment of employment relations.

As regards strikes, these may be called either by majority resolution of representatives of workers (75% of workers is required), or directly by workers themselves at work centre, when a quarter of personnel decides that decision be put to secret vote and decision approved by simple majority. Declaration of strike must be notified to employer and to labour authority five days in advance, or ten days in case of companies furnishing public utilities. During continuance of strike worker shall not be entitled to payment of wages, and will be covered by special system of Social Security, while in all cases freedom to work of those employees who do not wish to take part in strike will be respected.

Strikes of political nature or called in sympathy or support of strikes intended to alter terms of collective agreement or award still in force, or which do not comply with requirements of this Decree, will be considered illegal.

As regards lock-outs, they may be declared where there is danger of serious violence to persons or property, where work centre has been illegally occupied or where nonattendance is so massive as to impede normal production activity.

In connection with collective agreements, it is provided that, during their continuance and until three months prior to their expiration, no parallel or substitute collective agreements may be negotiated.

Act 8 of Apr. 7, 1988 on Infringements and Sanctions in Field of Labour.—This Act develops administrative infringements in field of labour committed by employers and workers in following matters: Labour safety, hygiene and health at work, social security, employment and unemployment benefits, migratory movements and employment of foreigners. It also regulates sanctions imposed, consisting basically of fines. Act of Nov. 10, 1995 on Prevention of Labour Risks has been passed with purpose of fostering labour health and safety by adopting measures for prevention of labour related risks.

Act 8 of June 8, 1987 on Pension Plans and Funds; and Royal Decree 1307 of Sept. 30, 1988.—Both provisions regulate contractual conditions for creating pension-savings and instrument embodying such savings, known as Pension Plan. Pension Plans are conceived as voluntary and free social insurance institutions, private benefits of which may supplement obligatory Social Security system or otherwise, but which may never replace that system.

Act of Mar. 23, 1995, governs paternity and maternity leave permit.

Royal Legislative Decree of Apr. 7, 1995, on Labour Procedure.—Contemplates basic regulations on labour procedure: dismissal procedures, industrial disputes, appeals, rules on enforcement of judgments and rules on specific procedures.

LAW REPORTS, CODES, ETC.:

In Spain there is a Civil Code regulating civil matters, a Penal Code regulating criminal matters, and two Codes which regulate civil and criminal procedure respectively.

Boletín Oficial del Estado (Official State Bulletin) publishes daily all new legal provisions and "Colección Legislativa" publishes judgments of Supreme Court. There is one private collection, Aranzadi, which collects in separate volumes legislation and jurisprudence of Supreme Court.

See also topic Statutes.

LEGISLATURE:

See topic Constitution and Government, subhead Parliament.

LICENSES:

In Spain administrative authorization is necessary to carry on a number of operations of various kinds, among which may be mentioned opening of establishments and commercial premises, holding of firearms and utilization for industrial purposes of property of public domain, such as, e.g., waters and river beds.

LIENS:

Liens may be created by contract as in the case of pledges, mortgages and antichreses. They may also derive from law in following cases: (1) That of holder of a general storage warehouse receipt; (2) that of holder of mortgage bank bonds; (3) that of commission agent on goods shipped on consignment; (4) that of vendor as long as goods sold are in his possession; (5) liens deriving from a transportation contract in favour of carrier and loader; (6) liens deriving from a freight contract in favour of charterer and from a passage contract in favour of captain; (7) insurer's lien on movable property of insured; (8) insured's lien on legal reserves of insurance companies and on prior deposit; (9) captain's lien on salvaged goods in event of general average or shipwreck.

LIMITATIONS:

See topic Statute of Limitations.

MARRIAGE:

Spanish State recognizes only one kind of marriage, which may be contracted: (1) Before civil judge or substitute, (2) according to religious formalities, (3) before consular or diplomatic officer when marriage is to be contracted abroad; Spaniards, when abroad, may marry also pursuant to local formalities. Marriage of non-Spaniards in Spain may be contracted in accordance with Spanish law or with personal law of any contracting party.

Religious marriage has to be recorded at Civil Registry in order to be effective. Secret marriage may be authorized by Ministry of Justice.

Proof of birth, unmarried or widowed status and license or dispensation, if necessary, is required.

Before marriage, contracting parties may establish any conditions regarding administration and disposition of their respective estates. Such pact may be changed after marriage through public deed issued before notary public.

In absence of pact, economic conditions of marriage are governed by system of community of property which distinguishes: (1) Private property of each spouse, which includes property acquired by inheritance or legacy either before or after marriage and any property owned before marriage; (2) community property, which includes property acquired by any spouse after marriage resulting from personal work or industry and income from private and community property. In absence of any pact to contrary, community property is managed jointly by both spouses.

MARRIED WOMEN:

See topics Dower; Executors and Administrators; Husband and Wife; Marriage.

MINES AND MINERALS:

Law of July 19, 1944 has been replaced by Law 22 of July 21, 1973.

All mineral deposits and other geological resources are public property, exploration and utilization of which State may assume itself or may grant to public or private artificial or natural persons.

MINES AND MINERALS . . . *continued*

State may reserve any zones of special interest for national defense or economic development. Foreign companies may take part in exploration and exploitation of reserved zones.

Deposits are classified in following sections: (A) Those of little economic value and geographically restricted marketability, as well as infrastructure and construction materials; (B) mineral and thermal waters, principally; (C) those not included in foregoing sections; (D) coals, radioactive minerals, geothermic resources, bituminous rocks and geological resources of interest for energy purposes.

Within reserved zones, State may grant: Exploration permits, investigation permits and direct exploitation concessions concerning resources within section (C), or section (D) resources other than those which caused zone declared as reserved.

Utilization of resources of section (A) existing on private property, vests with owner of such property, with authorization of provincial Mining Office, and likewise owner has a preferential right over waters of section (B).

With regard to resources of section (C), State may grant: Exploration permits for one year, renewable for one more year, covering from 300 to 3,000 mining squares; exploration permits for three years, renewable for three more, and exceptionally, for further periods, covering from one to 300 mining squares; exploitation concessions for 30 years, renewable up to a maximum of 90 years, covering from one to 100 mining squares. Mining square has 20 seconds of a degree per side.

Companies holding permits and concessions pay surface royalty, those holding concessions also pay fiscal license, and they are all subject to general tax regulations. New Mines Law announces introduction of depletion allowance.

Law on Promotion of Mining (Jan. 4, 1977).—Object of this new law is to promote and develop both in and outside Spain, exploration, prospecting and exploitation of mines, with view to procuring supply of mineral raw materials for Spanish industry.

Ministry of Industry will be responsible for drawing up National Program for supply of mineral raw materials, which will be submitted for Government approval every two years. This Program will determine different mineral raw materials, directives to be followed and investment required in mining sector. Ministry of Industry will keep Mining Register, which will function as permanent up-to-date public archive.

Ch. II of this Law deals with marketing and supply of raw materials, and ch. III deals with financing and taxation, specifying tax benefits and "depletion factor" which it states may not exceed 30% of basis of Company Tax or Industrial Tax.

Hydrocarbons.—Law of Dec. 26, 1958 has been replaced by Law 21 of June 27, 1974.

All hydrocarbon deposits are public property, belonging to Nation. State may grant exploration and exploitation thereof to private or public artificial persons.

For purposes of Law, following three zones exist: (A) Peninsular and insular Spain, and Spanish territories in North Africa; (B) territory of Sahara; (C) subsoil of Spanish territorial waters and other marine depths.

Foreign companies may participate in hydrocarbons exploration and exploitation in Spain by means of any of following procedures: Without necessity for Government authorization, by incorporating a Spanish company whose capital is wholly foreign owned; with prior Government authorization, by directly establishing a branch. Onshore surface exploration does not need an administrative authorization.

Exploration permits are granted by Government at its discretion and allow exploration for six years, renewable.

Exploitation concessions allow exploitation of any deposit discovered for 30 years, renewable for two periods of ten years.

Exploitation concessionaries, provided they are Spanish companies, may refine and industrially handle such hydrocarbons as they obtain over and above quota for national consumption, which has preference.

Companies holding permits pay surface royalty and all their exploration expenses are amortizable. Companies holding concessions pay higher surface royalty and tax on profits at rate of 40%. Determination of net profits is carried out in accordance with general practice. Deduction is made for depletion allowance.

Spain signed instrument of ratification of International Convention of Brussels governing civil liability for damages from hydrocarbons contamination.

Hydrocarbons Regulations of July 30, 1976, as am'd by Royal Decree 1634/1993 of Sept. 17 (Complementing Law of June 27, 1974).—

Property of the Nation.—All deposits in Spanish territory and in subsoil of territorial waters, are public property, exploration of which may be undertaken by State or assigned to private parties in such manner as is established in laws.

Geographic Scope of Application of Law.—Zona A: Peninsular and insular territory and Spanish territories in North Africa. Zona C: Subsoil of territorial waters and sea beds are divided into: Atlantic seaboards; Mediterranean seaboards; Canary Islands.

Benefits Granted to Holders of Exploration and Exploitation Authorizations, Permits and Concessions: Compulsory expropriation; declaration of public utility of land.

Exploration Activities.—These may be carried out either by State directly, or by Spanish or foreign individuals or legal entities on conditions set forth below.

Exploitation Activities.—Only by means of concession, except in cases in which State undertakes activity directly.

Transportation, Storage and Refining Activities.—(A) Spanish companies: Their corporate purpose must include activities referred to. If they do not contain such provision, and as exception, Government may grant such permits providing companies in question proceed to amend their by-laws within term of six months from granting of authorization.

(B) Foreign companies: possibilities of operation. (1) By means of formation of Spanish corporation (subsidiary) they may carry out all above activities; (2) through branch: prior authorization of Council of Ministers is required, and once this has been granted for branch, it may only engage in exploration activities and exploitation concessions. It may also obtain authorization to conduct other activities outlined above.

In their establishment branches must comply with number of legal requirements.

(C) Channelling of foreign investment: Contribution of foreign currency; contribution of machinery, equipment and technical assistance, where this cannot be obtained in Spain in satisfactory conditions; by means of contribution of pesetas generated by profits or capital having status of transferable or convertible pesetas; by means of technical assistance.

Foreign Technical Personnel and Employees.—Staff of foreign technical personnel must always be fewer than Spanish personnel performing same functions. Staff of all foreign employees may not exceed 20% of total number of employees of firm.

For these purposes, Spanish technical personnel includes foreigners who have obtained validation in Spain of their respective qualifications.

Participation of Foreign States and Companies with State Interests.—Former cannot hold exploration permits or possess majority interest through individuals or legal entities acting as intermediaries (nominees) for this purpose.

Companies with foreign State participation may only conduct activities by forming Spanish corporation or participating in existing corporation.

Composition of Board.—In Spanish corporations ("sociedades anónimas") with foreign participation, number of directors may not exceed number proportional to amount of foreign capital. Powers of foreign directors must be held jointly and not severally. Chairman of board, managing directors or sole administrator must be Spanish nationals.

Differentiation of Activities: Authorizations.—No prior authorization is required for activities of earth's surface that are of merely geological nature (e.g., taking of samples, photogeological work, etc.).

Authorization from Ministry of Industry is required for all geophysical and geochemical methods of prospection, as well as for execution of other aerial, marine and terrestrial work or minor drillings (less than 300m).

Interested parties may request authorization for exploration to select areas which are of interest to them, in order to subsequently request relevant exploration permit, applications being addressed to Director General of Energy and processed in order of presentation.

Once exploration of surface has been carried out, interested parties must deliver copies of reports, maps, etc., which will be kept confidential for term of one year.

Exploration Permits: Duration.—(A) Zone (A), term of duration six years, which may be extended at request of interested party. Zone (C), eight years divided into periods of two and six years. This second period may be extended for further three year period. All extensions require approval of Administration. (B) Area of Exploration Permits: Zone A, minimum 10,000 hectares and maximum 40,000 hectares. Zone C, minimum 10,000 hectares and maximum 100,000 hectares. Deviations of up to 8% in maximum limits are allowed. Permits are defined by two meridians and two parallels, or by frontier lines, coasts, etc.

Exploitation Concessions.—Confer upon their holders right to carry out, on exclusive basis, exploitation of hydrocarbons deposits in areas awarded. Term of duration is 30 years, which may be extended for two further periods of ten years. Holders of exploration permits must submit application, accompanied by supplementary documents, requesting exploitation concession. Administration resolves upon applications within term of three months. Maximum term for commencement of activities by interested party will be three years as from date of authorization (save for exceptional reasons justifying need for longer term). Like holders of exploration permits, holders of concessions must submit full periodic information to Administration.

Activities of Transport, Storage, Purifying and Refining.—(1) Holders of exploitation concessions may refine and process industrially hydrocarbons they obtain in excess of those destined for national consumption, and may apply this surplus to export. Government exercises effective control or supervision over these activities, and requires holders to place at disposal of Petroleum Monopoly certain amounts of hydrocarbons obtained during period specified. (2) Holders may export, without tax, surplus hydrocarbons produced after satisfying needs of domestic market. To this end, they must address communication to Ministry of Commerce, after obtaining relevant certificate from Ministry of Industry, requesting exportation. (3) Formalities as regards applications for conduct of activities of this type are very similar to those which must be fulfilled in case of exploration permits and exploitation concessions.

Special Tax System.—(1) Holders of exploration permits and exploitation concessions must pay so-called surface royalty, in accordance with sliding scale based on hectares covered by permit and years of duration. (2) Tax exemptions: holders of permits and concessions are entitled to substantial exemptions and allowances in almost all taxes applicable under Spanish law. Activities relating to refining and any other activities distinct from exploration, exploitation, transport, storage, purifying and sale of hydrocarbons, will be subject to general tax system, i.e., without exemption. Companies whose corporate purpose does not exclusively provide for exploration and exploitation will be governed by different tax provisions from those granting tax exemptions referred to.

Extinction of Permits and Exploitation Concessions.—Generally speaking, they are extinguished as result of following causes: Lapsing, upon expiration of their respective terms; total or partial renunciation of holder, after complying with conditions on which they were granted; any other causes established by laws.

Law 21 of Apr. 1, 1977 Concerning Penalties for Marine Pollutions as Result of Dumping.—Concept of marine pollution includes dumping in sea, including estuaries, of substances, materials or forms of energy which may constitute hazard to human health, biological resources, landscape, marine life, etc. By "dumping" is meant deliberate emptying into sea of substances, materials or any form of energy. Liability is attributed to owners or representatives of Spanish and foreign vessels or aircraft, within any maritime zone subject to Spanish jurisdiction and sovereignty. Fines of up to 10,000,000 pesetas are established depending on type of substances dumped.

See topic Foreign Investments in Spain; also topic Taxation.

MONOPOLIES AND RESTRAINT OF TRADE:

Oil trade monopoly has been liberalized due to Spanish Accession to EC.

As far as tobacco monopoly is concerned Act 38/1985 and Royal Decree 2738/1986 liberalized import and wholesale trade coming from EC, maintaining monopoly for manufacturing and retail sales.

EC Directives relating to telephone systems have already been incorporated in Spanish law by Act 31/1987 and Act 32/1992. Acts provide that monopoly over cellular car radio telephone was ended on Jan. 1, 1994. Mobile telecommunications

MONOPOLIES AND RESTRAINT OF TRADE . . . *continued*
have been liberalized by means of award of licence to private operator to compete in field.

Act of July 17, 1989, prohibits, under penalty of invalidity, all express or tacit agreements that could or do have effect of impeding, restricting or distorting competition.

Exceptions to this general prohibition may be made: (i) by individual authorization granted by Court for Defense of Competition or (ii) by Ruling on exemption by categories of agreements, enacted by Government. In both cases, exemption may be grounded on fact that agreement improves production or marketing of goods and services or promotes technical or economic progress, provided that it benefits end consumer, does not impose essential restrictions and does not eliminate competition with regard to material part of products or services in question. Provided these circumstances do not occur, agreement may be authorized, with conditions and qualifications contemplated by Act, on individual or general basis if it favors general economic situation or is in public interest.

Act of July 17, 1989, prohibits, without exception, abusive exploitation by one or more companies of their dominant position and restrictive trade practices that distort competition and affect public interest.

Undertakings that adopt prohibited and unauthorized agreements, abuse their dominant position or carry out restrictive trade practices may, at instance of Court for the Defense of Competition, be penalized with fines that can amount to up to 10% of their annual turnover; they may also be obligated to remove effects caused and compensate injured parties.

Act of July 17, 1989 provides that Government, after opinion from Court for the Defence of Competition, may oppose concentrations of undertakings (and even order deconcentration) when they give rise to acquisition of market share of 25% or more or turnover of over 20,000,000,000 pesetas. Notification of mergers for prior authorisation by Government is not compulsory, but may be filed with competition authorities.

Finally Act grants authorities to Court for the Defence of Competition to investigate and propose elimination of public aids if so requested by Ministry of Economy.

Implementation of Act of July 19, 1989, is entrusted to Court for the Defence of Competition, administrative body assisted by Department for the Defense of Competition. Investigating or penalizing proceedings may be instituted officially by Department or at request of third party concerned, and they are resolved by Court after investigations carried out by Department. Court's rulings may be appealed before administrative-litigious jurisdiction.

Principle of Authenticity in Advertising Matters.—Art. 3 of Act of Nov. 11, 1988 prohibits deceptive advertising, this being advertising that could in any way, including its external aspects, mislead recipient, affecting latter's commercial conduct or cause damage to competitor. Law also considers advertising activity that fails to reveal any crucial item, misleading recipient as above, to be deceptive. Royal Decree 2160/1993 of Dec. 10, indicates means by which prices for products offered to users and consumers must be clearly displayed.

Unfair Competition Act of Jan. 10, 1991 prohibits deceptive, misleading or denigrating commercial activities.

MORTGAGES:

Real estate can be mortgaged. Real estate mortgage must be executed in public deed before notary public and recorded in Property Registry, this recording being legal requirement and of essence for existence of mortgage. Among property which may be mortgaged are crops, leases and insurance policies on property. Mortgage action becomes extinct after 20 years. There is special summary execution proceeding for mortgages. See also topic Chattel Mortgages.

Pursuant to Mortgage Law, in order to make transfer or burden of any property enforceable as regards third parties, contract must be executed before notary public and it must subsequently be recorded in Property Registry. Person acting in name of company or association must prove his right to represent it. Deed must describe property, state any liens on it and declare maximum amount by which such property can be used as collateral under such liens.

Royal Decree 2556/1977 of Aug. 27 (Official State Gazette Oct. 8, 1977) modifies certain articles of Mortgage Regulations.

Documents executed in foreign territory may be registered if they satisfy requirements laid down by rules of Private International Law, always providing they contain legalization and other prerequisites required for their authenticity in Spain.

Observance of foreign forms and solemnities with respect to legal aptitude and capacity necessary for act in question, may be evidenced, among other means, by affidavit or opinion of Notary or Spanish Consul, or of diplomat, consul or competent official of country of applicable legalization.

In same way, civil capacity of foreigners executing documents in Spanish territory susceptible of registration may be evidenced. Registrar, on his own responsibility may waive such evidence if he is sufficiently acquainted with foreign legislation in question, stating this fact in relevant entry.

MOTOR VEHICLES:

Motor vehicle traffic and highway safety are regulated by Royal Legislative Decree 339 of Mar. 2, 1990, and Royal Decree 13 of Jan. 17, 1992, developing Act of July 25, 1989, which lays down bases for this question. Vehicles must be registered and drivers must hold respective driving licence. Royal Decree of Oct. 14, 1994, governs technical inspections of vehicles. Infringements of traffic and highway safety regulations may be sanctioned with fine of up to 100,000 pesetas. Royal Decree 320/1994 of Feb. 25, sets forth punitive procedure for infringements of traffic and highway safety regulations.

Foreign motor cars may be temporarily or finally imported into Spain. Final import, subject to payment of customs duties, must be applied for to Ministry of Commerce, which may grant import licence. Temporary import can only be obtained by foreigners or by Spaniards permanently residing abroad who do not work in Spain. Temporary import remains in force during six months, if person making import resides in Europe, or Mediterranean country, and eight months if he resides overseas. Rights for temporary import are lost in event of acquiring residence in Spain or by engaging in any remunerative or lucrative activity in this country. However, Art. 9 of Act for Temporary Importation of Automobiles provides for exception authorising system of temporary importation for foreigners residing and working in Spain. Foreigners and Spanish nationals residing abroad may purchase and use in Spain within certain limitations, vehicles with special tourist registration.

As regards aviation, Spain adhered to the 1944 Chicago Convention. Foreign aviation companies may obtain landing and commercial permits from the Spanish Government.

NEGOTIABLE INSTRUMENTS:

See topic Bills, Notes and Checks.

NOTARIES:

Functions of notary public are very important in Spain. Many documents must be executed before notary to have full effect. Among these are deeds of constitution of all kinds of companies and all contracts affecting real estate, if they are to be entered in Mercantile and Property Registers, also affidavits and powers of attorney, to be effective in courts and before other authorities.

Requirements to be notary are: To be of Spanish nationality, and to have finished special studies determined by regulations. Notaries enter notarial body by competitive examination before deciding board.

PARTNERSHIP:

See topic Corporations and Associations.

PATENTS AND TRADEMARKS:

To be protected in Spain, a patent or trademark must be entered in Spanish office of Patents and Trademarks. Protection is granted to patents on inventions, trademarks and commercial names, useful designs and films. Spain is signatory of Agreements of The Hague of Nov. 6, 1925, for protection of industrial property, repression of false indications of origin of merchandise, international registry of trademarks and international deposit of industrial designs or models.

To register a particular designation as a trade name, it is necessary for such a designation to be name or style of person or company wishing to register it.

Patents are governed by Law 11/86 of Mar. 20 and Regulations of Oct. 10, 1986. Trademarks, trade names and commercial establishment signs are regulated by Act 32 of Nov. 10, 1988 and Regulations of May 18, 1990.

Taking effect as from Oct. 1, 1986, Spain has adhered to Convention on the granting of European Patents, made in Munich on Oct. 5, 1973.

PERPETUITIES:

The testator may stipulate that in case of death of the heir, the whole or part of the estate shall pass on to a third person, and so on, on condition that the second and third heirs survive the testator. Otherwise, the condition is void. Perpetual charges may be established, to be paid by the heirs, but the latter may redeem them by capitalization.

PLEDGES:

Pledge is a right ad rem which guarantees, by delivery of movable property, a certain debt. Pledge must be recorded in a public instrument before a notary public or, in case of securities, before a stockbroker. Pledge contract entitles creditor to retain thing pledged in his possession, or in that of third parties to whom it has been delivered, until his credit is paid. Creditor whose credit has not been paid may proceed, before a notary public, to dispose of pledge. Disposal must be carried out in a public auction, with summoning of debtor and owner of pledge, if any. If pledge is not disposed of at first auction, a second auction may be held with same formalities and if it still remains undisposed of, then creditor may take possession of pledge, giving debtor a receipt for whole of credit. In case of pledge of securities, special rules established by Code of Commerce are applicable.

PRESCRIPTION:

See topic Statute of Limitations.

PRINCIPAL AND AGENT:

Written or oral powers may be granted to an agent; acceptance by the agent may be expressed or implied from the fact that he makes use of the powers. Powers may be granted to one or more persons to act jointly or severally. If powers are granted for a transaction which must be recorded in the Mercantile or Property Registers (constitution of companies, purchase and sale of property, etc.) they must be executed through public deeds. The signatures of the notaries must be acknowledged by the Spanish consul in the district in which the notary is domiciled.

Powers to act in trials must be granted through public deeds before a notary public or a consular officer; they must be directed to one or more solicitors.

The powers may be revoked at any moment by the grantor, who may ask for the return of the document; there may be no pact to the contrary. The grantor must indemnify the agent for all expenses incurred in the discharge of his functions.

Together with basic rules on this question laid down in Spanish Civil Code, contractual relation between principal and agent is regulated by Act of May 27, 1992 on agency agreement. This Act defines agency agreement as relation in which individual or corporation called agency agrees with another, on continuous or stable basis and in exchange for remuneration, to promote commercial transactions on behalf of another or to promote and conclude such transactions on behalf of another, as independent intermediary and without assuming risk and venture of such transactions unless otherwise agreed.

REAL PROPERTY:

Art. 33 of Constitution recognizes right to own property and right to acquire property by inheritance, although said rights may be framed in accordance with their social role by laws. Confiscation is prohibited, but not expropriation on justified

REAL PROPERTY . . . *continued*
grounds of public utility or social interest. Civil Code requires courts to order restoration of property of persons who have been deprived of it. Limitations by reason of public interest are due to city planning, military needs, exploitation of mineral deposits, rights of vicinage, etc.

Property is acquired by law, occupation, contract, succession or possession and prescription in good faith during a certain time.

Act of June 26, 1992 establishes basic guidelines and principles of zoning law.

Leases on buildings are governed by Act 29/1994 of Nov. 24 on urban leases, providing different regulations according to whether buildings are intended as housing or for other uses. Act provides mandatory rules on question of deposits and legal proceedings. In case of leases for uses other than housing (business premises, offices, seasonal lets, etc.), legal system may be replaced by one agreed to by parties. In case of leases for housing, there is series of provisions that parties are unable to revoke of their own free will.

Particularly, lessee of dwelling is entitled to remain in it for five years even if shorter term was agreed; right of subrogation in favour of certain persons is established in event of lessee's death; and lessee has right of first refusal if lessor sells dwelling.

Given existence of lease agreements entered into under previous legislation, which, before 1985, recognised in lessee right to extend lease at his will, new Act provides interim system which declares this legislation to subsist to these effects, although it is changed on two essential aspects: (i) new system of cancellation and of subrogation in lease is established, more beneficial for lessor than system under previous legislation; and (ii) special system for rent adjustment is provided, in attempt to mitigate lack of updating in rents stipulated in many old agreements, adapting them to current situation of market.

RECORDS:

Following Registers exist in Spain: (1) Registry of Vital Statistics, in which are recorded births, marriages, deaths and naturalizations; (2) Wills and Testaments Register in which are recorded all testaments drawn before a notary public; (3) Property Register, in which are recorded estates, houses, etc., including their transfers, mortgages and other liens and seizures; mines are also recorded in this Register; (4) Commercial (Mercantile) Registry, in which are recorded all corporations with their by-laws and powers granted by their boards of directors to their managers to represent company, changes in by-laws, domicile, etc.; individual merchants and business men may also be recorded voluntarily; (5) Register of Convicts and Rebels, in which are recorded names of all persons convicted by courts for crimes committed; (6) Register of Patent and Trademarks, in which are recorded all patents, trademarks, tradenames and other forms of industrial property; (7) Literary Property Register on which are recorded original literary works and copyrights; (8) Register for classification of restrictive trade practices which are excepted from legal prohibition; (9) Special Register of Investment Companies and Funds; (10) Register of State Contractors, in which are recorded individual and legal entities classified as contractors; (11) Registrer of Vessels and Naval Corporations, in which are recorded vessels with Spanish flag and Spanish naval corporations; (12) Register of National Industrial Undertakings, where data regarding industrial products, power supply activities, minerals research and exploitation, nuclear power and agriculture and food-industry related facilties, etc. are recorded.

Note: Royal Decree 2573/1977 of June 17 (Official State Gazette Oct. 14, 1977 approving Organic Regulations of Autonomous Agency Known as Register of Industrial Property Matters): Official Authorities or court's request its organic structure is as follows: Management, Director General, Secretary General and Departments as follows: Patents and Models, Designs, Technological information, International Relations and Research.

REPLEVIN:

The owner of personal property may recover it from any holder not entitled to it, provided the right has not expired (see topic Statutes of Limitations). However, if the property has been sold in a public store, recovery is not possible but an indemnification may be requested from the seller. Securities sold at the Stock Exchange through an agent cannot be recovered. Owners of real estate that has been registered can claim its recovery through a special procedure.

SALES:

The sales contract becomes effective as soon as the contracting parties agree on the object to be sold and on its price, although neither the former or the latter have been handed over. The seller guarantees the buyer from eviction and as regards the integrity of the object sold. (C. C. 1445 to 1520). Sales of real estate are subject to a transfer tax of 6%; sales of personal property are also subject to same tax to extent of 2%. There are many exemptions among which are store sales. Installment sales are regulated by Law of Sept. 17, 1965 as supplemented by Royal Decree 604 of Feb. 8, 1984.

Spain has ratified United Nations Convention on Contracts for the International Sale of Goods.

Notices Required.—Spanish Law does not establish any special form in which purchaser is to notify vendor of his dissatisfaction with goods he has received therefrom on account of a defect in quantity or quality. A purchaser who examines goods upon receipt has no action for suing vendor on grounds of flaw or defect of quantity or quality in the goods. Purchaser is entitled to sue vendor for a defect of quantity or quality in goods received, provided he brings his action within four days following receipt of goods and damage is result of an act of God, a flaw in the goods or fraud. A purchaser who does not bring any claim based on hidden defects of object sold within 30 days following delivery loses all action and right of claim on these grounds against vendor.

Applicable Law.—See topic Contracts.

Warranties.—See subhead Notices Required, supra.

International Sale of Goods.—United Nations Convention on Contracts for the International Sale of Goods in force Aug. 1, 1991. See topic Treaties and Part VII, Selected International Conventions.

SEQUESTRATION:

The attachment of personal property belonging to the debtor is carried out by the judge upon the request of the creditor, who may propose a receiver. Otherwise, the judge will appoint one. As regards real estate, an authorization from the Registrar will suffice, but on some occasions the creditor is appointed as its administrator, or the creditor appoints one. See also Attachment; Exemptions.

SHIPPING:

Territorial Waters.—Spain has ratified 1958 Geneva Convention.

Law 10 of Jan. 4, 1977, on Territorial Sea.—Sovereignty of Spanish State extends beyond its territory from its interior waters to territorial waters adjoining its coasts.

Inward limit of territorial sea is defined by low-tide water line and, where applicable, by line of straight base-lines established by Government.

Outward territorial limit will be defined by line drawn in such a way that points forming same are located at distance of 12 nautical miles from nearest points baselines referred to in foregoing paragraph.

Law will not affect fishing rights recognized or granted to foreign vessels under international agreements.

Merchant Ships Construction.—Ships (Decree of Oct. 28, 1971), including among others certificates of maximum load lines in accordance with International Agreement of Apr. 5, 1966, technical conditions governing construction, inspection and seaworthiness of vessels are regulated.

Vessel mortgage is regulated supplementarily by Law of Aug. 21, 1893. On June 12, 1930, Spain ratified international agreement for unification of certain rules governing marine privileges and mortgages, signed in Brussels on Apr. 10, 1926. By an instrument of Sept. 11, 1953, Spain also ratified International Agreement on precautionary attachment of vessels, of May 10, 1952, which was incorporated in legislation by Law of Apr. 8, 1967.

Mortgage of vessels must be created in public instrument and entered on Commercial Register and on respective provincial License Register. Mortgage must be notified to Directorate General for the Merchant Navy. According to Royal Decree of July 28, 1989 exportation of mortgaged vessels to foreign country requires authorization of creditors.

Constructed Vessels; Purchase and Sale (Decree of July 28, 1989).—Vessels built have to be entered on Register of Vessels and Naval Corporations. Any transfer of title to vessel must be instrumented before notary public, entered on said register and notified to Directorate General for the Merchant Navy.

In case of purchase and sale of constructed vessels by a foreign individual or legal entity, Spanish law contemplates two different cases: (A) Purchase of a foreign vessel by a Spaniard; (B) purchase of a Spanish vessel by a foreigner.

Foreign vessels can be imported after compliance with technical and other regulatory controls.

Spanish law has liberalized exportation of Spanish vessels, except for mortgaged vessels, as explained above.

Flag and Marine Register.—Governed by law 27/1992 of Nov. 24. Thus, vessels may be protected by Spanish Marine legislation and obtain Spanish flag.

Marine Register keeps record of vessels with Spanish flag and Spanish naval corporations.

Charter Party.—Charter party is regulated by Code of Commerce Arts. 652 et seq. Likewise, 1949 Goods Transportation Act is in force as regards, fundamentally, relations between carrier, owner and consignee. This law is adaptation in Spain of rules of Hague. It is applicable only to goods transport contracts in which a bill of lading or similar document is issued relating to international transports between countries which have ratified Brussels agreement of 1924 and incorporated it in their national legislation (pursuant to Art. 24 of Law). Spanish doctrine, in accordance with principles of international law, is based on Art. 15 of Code of Commerce, which establishes principle "lex loci regit actum" in event of a dispute as to applicable law.

Bill of Lading.—This document is also regulated by Code of Commerce and Goods Transportation Act of 1949.

Average.—York-Antwerp rules are applied in Spain, although Code of Commerce continues, to some extent, to apply. (Arts. 806 et seq.).

Code of Civil Procedure also deals with determination of average (see Arts. 2131 to 2146, together with above-mentioned articles of Code of Commerce, namely, 665 and 666).

Towing.—Contract of towage is not regulated in Spanish law and is, therefore, a non-typical contract. In general, towage companies establish certain general conditions based on standard English forms. They are, therefore, subject to general law of contract.

Ports, Docks, Quays and Canals.—Regulated by Law 27/1992 of Nov. 24 of State Ports and Merchant Navy and Law of July 28, 1988 developed by Royal Decree of Dec. 1, 1989 referred to costs. Law 27/1992 classifies ports as commercial and non-commercial. Some ports are considered of general interest taking into consideration their importance in Spanish portuary system.

As regards liability for damage caused by vessels, there is a limitation of liability, since Spain has ratified Brussels convention of 1957. In case of ports owned by State, Law of July 26, 1957 (Art. 40) will be taken into account, which establishes liability of administration for any damage to property or rights of private parties, except in event of force majeure.

Administration of country's ports of general interest is carried out by Portuary Authorities.

Collision.—This subject is regulated in Spanish Code of Commerce (Arts. 826 to 839) to effect that, in event of negligence or unskillfulness of captain, owner of vessel that has collided shall indemnify damage and loss. If collision is attributable to both vessels, each shall bear its own damage and both shall be jointly and severally liable

SHIPPING . . . *continued*
for damage to cargoes. Same will apply in fortuitous event and force majeure: each vessel and its cargo shall bear its own damage. On Nov. 17, 1923, Spain ratified Brussels agreement of Sept. 23, 1910, for unification of rules on subject of collision. On Sept. 11, 1953, Brussels agreement of May 10, 1952, on civil jurisdiction in respect of collision, was ratified, and on same date same agreement was ratified on penal jurisdiction as regards collision.

International agreement on safety of human life at sea, of June 17, 1960, which also contains regulations for prevention of collisions as well as Instrument of Adhesion by Spain to Agreement on International Regulations for Avoidance of Collisions, executed in London on Oct. 20, 1972. (Official State Gazette, July 9, 1977).

Salvage.—This is governed in Spain by Law of Dec. 24, 1962, which incorporates text of Brussels agreement of Sept. 23, 1910. In includes assistance at sea to merchant ships, warships or vessels employed in a public service, as well as assistance at sea to aeroplanes. Law deals with removal of wreckage, and this subject is supplemented by Decree of Apr. 20, 1967. For general purposes of Law, and in accordance with Art. 2, any act of assistance or salvage that has led to a useful result will entitle fair remuneration. There will be no remuneration if there are no useful results and sum payable will not be value of goods salvaged. In general rule "no cure no pay" is applicable, and principle of English jurisprudence embodied in words "human life does not pay salvage" is also taken into account.

Findings are also regulated to effect that he who finds things abandoned at sea, without being produce thereof must place them at disposal of Naval Authority. This general principle does not extend to vessels abandoned on high sea, their cargoes or jettison, or non-commercial things.

In general, Commercial Code (Arts. 842 et seq.) regulates, to a certain extent, cases of salvage of goods. Law 27/1992 of Nov. 24 has created public service of Salvage and Maritime Safety.

Marine Insurance.—Apart from international custom, Code of Commerce is applicable in this respect. (Art. 737 et seq.). Provision is made regarding contract, risk, policy, special clauses, warranties, cargoes, value of goods, subrogation, etc. As regards nuclear marine insurance, reference must be made to Law of Apr. 29, 1964, particularly chapter 8, which deals with nuclear risk coverage.

Compulsory passenger insurance is regulated by Decree of Mar. 6, 1969.

Customs: Clearance of Vessels.—These subjects are regulated by Customs Ordinance by Decree of Oct. 17, 1947, as well as by General Agreement on Tariffs and Trade of Oct. 30, 1947. Protocol of ratification by Spain is dated July 29, 1963.

Customs Tariff was published by Decree of May 30, 1960. See topic Customs.

If there is no consignee of shipowner at a certain port, captain of ship will represent him and bind shipowner by his signature.

STATUTE OF LIMITATIONS:

Thirty years. Real actions on real estate.

Twenty years. Mortgages.

Fifteen years. All personal actions not included in other limitations.

Six years. Transfer tax on personal property.

Five years. Collection of rents of rural or urban property, any payments made by the year or shorter terms, collection of dividends from business firms.

Three years. Professional fees; actions on bills of exchange, promissory notes, checks, orders of payment, shareholders suits against corporations or vice-versa.

One year. Actions to recover the possession of property, responsibility derived from insults or slander and of culpa or negligence. Work done on, or goods delivered to ships; delivery of shipments by land or sea, indemnification for delays and damage to transported objects.

Six months. Collection of transportation fees, freight and damages.

STATUTES:

They are codified in Spain: the Civil Code, Commerce Code, the Law on Stock Corporations, Criminal Laws, Civil Prosecution Laws, Civil Register Law, Mercantile Register Law, etc.

TAXATION:

Direct taxes consist of income tax on companies, tax on income of individuals and tax on net worth of individuals. Indirect taxes consist, basically, of transfer tax and Valued Added Tax (VAT), both of which are entirely incompatible. There are also some special taxes (alcohol, petroleum, etc.) and customs duty.

Tax Laws have been codified.

Impuesto Sobre Bienes Inmuebles (Tax on Real Estate Assets).—It is local tax levied on value of rural and urban real property.

"Impuesto Sobre Actividades Económicas" (Tax on Commercial and Industrial Activities and on Revenue from Personal Work).—It is local tax and consists of fixed quota to be paid by artists, professionals and individuals conducting any kind of business activity.

"Impuesto sobre Sociedades".—Act 43/1995 of Dec. 27 on Corporate Tax has been passed, laying down new framework of legislation in harmony with opening uup of Spanish economy to capital movements and evolution of tax systems.

As regards taxable event, this Act eliminates classification of income as income from capital and from economic operations and capital gains and losses.

It eliminates minimum taxation for partially exempt entities (associations and foundations) and provides for these entities deduction for double taxation of dividends. Transparent companies become subject to provisions of this tax, although taxable base is attributed to partners.

Taxable base must be determined from results of accounts, in accordance with General Accountancy Plan and Commercial Code.

General tax rate of 35% is maintained and rate of 25% is established for insurance mutual aid companies, credit cooperatives and mutual guarantee companies.

As regards deductions, principles of Act 42/1994 on double taxation are included, so that for this purpose, both taxes levied at time profits are repatriated and tax on profit against which dividend was paid are considered.

Tax incentives are reduced to research and development activities and investments abroad intended to promote exports. Act also provides special incentive system companies with turnover of under 250 million pesetas in previous fiscal year.

From standpoint of international taxation, expenses payable in consideration for management support services are taxed at 25%, while tax on same expenses are eliminated when they are paid by branches.

Period for setting off negative taxable bases is extended to seven years.

Act also includes as special systems those previously regulated in diverse legislation, such as those relating to economic interest groupings, mergers and spin-offs and leasings, among others.

Corporate Tax Act came into force on Jan. 1, 1996 and is already applicable to transactions performed during 1996 calendar year, returns for which should be filed in Mar. 1997.

"Impuesto sobre la Renta de las Personas Físicas" (Tax on Income of Individuals).—Law 18/1991 of June 6. Tax is levied on all income, from whatever source, derived by individuals residing in Spain and on income derived by nonresidents from sources within Spain.

Taxable income consists of all income derived during fiscal year, particularly: (a) Proceeds from personal work, including indemnifications, pensions, salaries in kind; (b) proceeds derived from any capital assets not used by taxpayer in his profession or business. Personal dwelling of taxpayer will be deemed to produce income equal to 2% of value attributed to it on special tax on net worth of individuals; (c) profits derived from conduct of any kind business. Ordinary expenses and depreciation may be deducted, when applicable, as well as several other deductions; (d) capital gains derived from any onerous or lucrative transfer. Gain realized is difference between transfer price and acquisition price. Negative taxable basis may be carried forward for next five years.

Rates are progressive and vary from 20% to 56% and in no event may tax together with amount of net capital, exceed 70% of taxable base. Capital gains are taxed at general progressive rates. However gains derived from business or professional activities may not be taxed at rate higher than 35%. Capital gains obtained by nonresidents are taxed at fixed rate of 35%. Capital gain obtained is exempt from tax according to type of asset transferred and to period of time that transferred property remained in obligor's capital. Specifically, in case of real estate or interests in capital of companies over 50% of whose assets consist of real estate, capital gain is reduced, and therefore is not liable for tax, at rate of 5.26% for each year of possession in excess of two. In case of shares or interests in unlisted companies, reduction is 7.14% per year of possession in excess of two. Finally, in case of listed shares, reduction is 11.11% for each year in excess of two. Application of these percentages means that gains from disposal of real estate are no longer liable to tax at 20 years, those arising from unlisted companies at 15 years, and those from listed shares at ten years.

Main tax credits are as follows: (a) For each ascendant living with taxpayer: 15,500 pesetas. This tax credit is 31,000 pesetas if ascendant is aged 75 or over. (b) For each desendant living with taxpayer: 20,700 for first two children; and 25,000 and 30,000 pesetas for third and fourth children respectively. (c) For each taxpayer and, as may be case, for each disabled living with taxpayer: 54,000 pesetas, deductions (a) and (b) also being applicable. (d) For each taxpayer aged 65 or over: 15,500 pesetas. (e) 15% of expenses of sickness, including subscriptions to medical associations. (f) 10% of life insurance premium. (g) 15% of amounts paid for purchase, construction or reform of real estate which is usual dwelling. (h) 15% of expenses for maintenance and repair of property belonging to historic or artistic heritage or of cultural interest. (i) 15% of investment in property belonging to historical and artistic heritage. (Deductions under [f] to [i] have limit of 30% of taxable income.) (j) 10% of dividends received from corporations. (k) 15% of value of property belonging to historic and artistic heritage donated to state or autonomous community. (l) For receipt of earned income, amount of 26,000 pesetas is deductible. Under certain conditions, this deduction may be increased to 70,000 pesetas. (m) Investment and job creation tax credits for companies are also applicable to professional workers and businessmen.

Dividends, interest and other revenues derived from capital are subject to 25% withholding at source. Income derived from personal work is subject to withholding, determined in accordance with percentage table. Proceeds derived from professional and artistic activities are subject to 15% withholding. Proceeds derived by nonresidents from personal work, capital and professional and artistic activities are subject to withholding, at rate of 25%.

Profits and losses derived by following companies will be attributed to each shareholder, as if distributed: (a) Mutual funds, holding companies and companies not conducting any business, provided that: (i) more than 50% of stock belongs to members of family, and (ii) more than 50% of stock is owned by ten or less shareholders; (b) legal entities composed exclusively of professionals.

Inheritance Tax.—Inheritance and Gift Tax is governed by Act of Dec. 18, 1987. Acquisitions mortis causa, whether in respect of inheritance or legacy, are liable to tax, as also donations inter vivos. Tax rates are progressive, and are applied on net value of assets transferred, less certain amounts according to age of heir and his family relationship with deceased (this reduction not being applicable to donations). Tax amounts obtained is corrected by certain ratio according to family relationship of heir or donatee with respect to decedent or donator and his preexisting net worth; this last variable factor is most important new feature introduced by new Act. (Inheritances and donations to corporations or institutions are created for tax purposes as capital gains under Corporation Tax and are not liable to this tax.

"Impuesto sobre Transmisiones Patrimoniales y Actos Jurídicos Documentados" (Transfer Tax).—Assessed on three different concepts: (1) Transfer of assets inter vivos by individuals except for corporate sales which are taxed under VAT with certain exceptions in real estate transactions (second deliveries of real estate); (2) corporate activities such as incorporation, capital stock increase, merger/consolidation and liquidation; and (3) "actos jurídicos documentados" (legal acts recorded in private or public documents). Rates are: Transfer of real estate, 6%; transfer of personal property/chattels, 4%; creation, modification, transfer and extension of mortgages, pledges, loans or guarantees, 1%; corporate rates, 1%; rates on legal acts, 0.5%. Transfer Tax is governed by Royal Decree 1/1993 of Sept. 24.

See Topical Index in front part of this volume.

TAXATION . . . *continued*

Impuesto sobre el Valor Aĩnadido (IVA).—Valued Added Tax (VAT) is levied on deliveries of goods and supplies of services carried out by companies or professional persons, and also on imports. Rates are 16%, 7% and 4%. Removal of tax frontiers resulting from EEC Common Market prompted enactment of Act 37/1992 of Dec. 28, governing Value Added Tax. Common Market has also evidenced need to unify certain indirect taxes, such as tax on alcoholic drinks, on tobacco, on some means of transportation and on hydrocarbons, and consequently Act 38/1992 of Dec. 28, has been passed.

Wealth Tax.—This tax is levied on ownership of all kinds of property and economic rights. Residents of Spain are taxed on their worldwide assets; nonresidents are taxed on their assets located within Spain.

Taxable basis consists of: (a) Urban and rural properties: their taxable value will be highest of following: (1) Assigned value for purposes of "Impuesto sobre bienes inmuebles", (2) assessed value for purposes of any other tax (Impuesto sobre Transmisiones Patrimoniales), (3) price of acquisition. (b) Assets used by taxpayer in conduct of business activity, their value must be determined by difference between actual assets and liabilities contracted with third parties. (c) Deposits in checking, savings or term accounts must be computed by their ponderated balance. (d) Stocks traded in stock exchanges must be evaluated by average quotation of last quarter of year. (e) Non-traded stocks must be assessed in accordance with their book value, provided that balance sheet was certified by public accountant. Otherwise, value to be computed will be highest of following: (1) Nominal value, (2) book value, (3) value obtained by capitalizing at rate of 12.5% average of profits in last three years. (f) All other properties must be evaluated in accordance with market value. (g) Nominal amount of debts may be deducted.

Taxable base must be reduced in 15,000,000 pesetas.

Rates are progressive and vary from 0.2% (taxable base under 25,000,000 pesetas) to 2.5% (taxable basis above 1,600,000,000).

This tax has to be paid annually and is not deductible from any other tax. Companies and legal entities are not subjected to this tax.

Tax Incentives on Mergers.—Spin-offs and contributions of business activities. Tax incentives on parent-subsidiary relationship between companies residing at EU countries. According to Law 29/1991, mergers, spin-offs and contributions of business activities—whether to company or branch—can be made without any capital gain arising either in companies or in shareholders. This special treatment is applicable not only to companies residing in Spain but to foreign companies as well. There are also tax exemptions regarding VAT and transfer tax otherwise applicable in these kinds of transactions. In order to obtain tax incentives of Law 29/1991, companies must submit prior communication to tax authorities. Since Jan. 1st 1992, dividends paid by Spanish subsidiary to its parent company in EU country are not subject to any withholding tax. Sole exception to applicability of this rule refers to parent companies in which voting control is exercised by individuals or companies not residing in EU countries.

Tax Incentives for Regional Development.—(1) Act of July 26, 1984 granted following benefits to companies making investments in areas classified as industrial redevelopment areas by Government Decree: (a) Subsidies for investment, (b) preference in obtaining of official credit, (c) reduction in local taxes, (d) possibility of obtaining special depreciation plans; (2) Act of Dec. 23, 1985 provides that subsidies and benefits may be granted in employer's contribution to Social Security for investments made in areas determined by Government.

TRADEMARKS AND TRADENAMES:

See topic Patents and Trademarks.

TREATIES:

Spain has entered into a large number of international treaties of a commercial, labor and fiscal nature.

On Jan. 1, 1986 Spain became member of European Communities by Accession Treaty signed on June 12, 1985. Effective from July 1, 1987, Spain has ratified Sole European Act signed in Luxembourg on Feb. 17, 1986.

Tax Treaties: Double Taxation.—Spain has signed following conventions to avoid double taxation: Norway: Apr. 25, 1963; Switzerland: Apr. 26, 1966; Austria: Dec. 20, 1966; Germany: Dec. 5, 1966; Finland: Nov. 15, 1967; Portugal: May 29, 1968; Belgium: Sept. 24, 1970; Netherlands: June 16, 1971; Brazil: Nov. 14, 1974; France: June 27, 1973 as supplemented by complementary agreement of Dec. 6, 1977; Sweden: Apr. 25, 1963; on June 16, 1976 instrument of ratification of Spain was signed for Convention between Spain and Sweden to avoid double taxation in matters of income and capital taxes; Denmark: July 3, 1972, instrument of ratification of Convention between both countries to avoid double taxation in matters of income and assets taxes; Japan: Feb. 31, 1974, to avoid double taxation in matters of income tax; Great Britain and Northern Ireland: Oct. 21, 1975, and Instrument of Ratification of Oct. 28, 1976; Italy: Sept. 8, 1977; Roumania: May 24, 1979; Canada: Nov. 23, 1976, ratified by Spain on Apr. 10, 1981; Czechoslovakia: May 8, 1980, ratified by Spain on July 14, 1981; Poland: Nov. 15, 1979, ratified by Spain on June 15, 1982; USA: Feb. 22, 1990 ratified by Spain on Dec. 22, 1990. Since 1982, Spain has signed treaties with Luxembourg, Hungary, Tunez, Morocco, USSR, Bulgaria, Australia, Ecuador, U.S.A., Philippines, North Korea, India and Ireland.

See also: Order of Dec. 30, 1977 (Official State Gazette, Jan. 1, 1978) concerning application of Art. 12 of Agreement between Spain and Federal Republic of Germany for avoidance of double taxation in respect of income tax and capital (wealth) tax.

Great majority of these conventions follows OECD model prepared by that Organization's Tax Committee.

General rule or method to avoid double taxation followed by Spain in international conventions it has signed, dividends, interest and royalties excepted, consists of fact that foreign obligor of certain signatory country who is subject to Spanish tax sovereignty is exempt from paying tax in Spain for income of foreign origin, although such income is computed in Spain not for assessment purposes but only to calculate tax rate applicable to Spaniards. Once that rate has been calculated, it is only applicable to portion of income obtained in Spain.

Also, in general lines, all Conventions signed by Spain contain "tax sparing" clause, viz., Spain recognizes incentives which foreign country has afforded to investments in Spain.

Recently ratified treaties are: Agreement between Spain and Ireland on double taxation of income deriving from shipping and aerial navigation; Convention regarding Changes of Names and Surnames of Sept. 4, 1958 (Istanbul); Agreement Between Spanish Government and Federal Government of Austria on Personal Travel, Signed in Vienna on Feb. 1, 1978 (Official State Gazette Mar. 29, 1978); Cultural and Educational Co-Operation Agreement Between Governments of Spain and United States of Mexico, signed in Madrid on Oct. 14, 1977 (Official State Gazette Apr. 3, 1978); Instrument of Ratification by Spain of Treaty Between Government of People's Republic of Poland and Government of Spain on Cultural and Scientific Co-Operation, signed in Warsaw on May 27, 1978 (Official State Gazette Apr. 19, 1978); Instrument of Adhesion of Spain to Charter of Council of Europe, London May 5, 1949 (Official State Gazette Mar. 1, 1978). Instrument of Ratification by Spain of Supplementary Treaty on Extradition between Spain and U.S., Madrid Jan. 25, 1975; Chile: Dec. 8, 1976, to avoid double taxation of income derived from exploitation of aerial navigation; Instrument of Ratification by Spain of 1961 Hague Convention on legalization of public documents and deeds issued abroad (Convention Abolishing the Requirement of Legalisation for Foreign Public Documents); Instrument of Ratification by Spain of Second Amendment to Agreement Constituting the International Monetary Fund, of Apr. 30, 1976; Instrument of Ratification by Spain of 1957 Nice Convention on international classification of products and services for registration of trademarks; Instrument of Ratification by Spain of United Nations Convention on Recognition and Enforcement of Foreign Arbitral Awards, done at New York on June 10, 1958; Instrument of Adhesion by Spain to North Atlantic Treaty Organization (N.A.T.O.), signed in Washington on Apr. 4, 1949 (Official State Gazette May 31, 1982); Instrument of Ratification by Spain of European Convention on Extradition signed in Paris on Dec. 13, 1952.

See also topic Aircraft.

International Sale of Goods.—United Nations Convention on Contracts for the International Sale of Goods in force Aug. 1, 1991. See topic Sales and Part VII, Selected International Conventions.

WILLS:

There are three kinds of wills recognized in Spain: (a) The holograph, which must be entirely written in the testator's handwriting. It does not have to be certified by any officer and needs not be witnessed. After the death of the testator, it must be presented to a judge for authentication, upon which it comes into effect. (b) the "open will" is subscribed before a notary public, with certain formalities, the contents of the will being known to and guaranteed by the notary. (c) The "sealed will" is placed in an envelope by the testator, who appears before a notary public and states with certain formalities that it is his will, the notary certifying to it on the envelope. In foreign countries the Spanish consuls act as notaries for Spaniards residing there. Wills by members of the military and naval services executed under serious risk of death are recognized, and in certain regions of Spain some special types are also valid.

Any person may declare his will void and make a new one.

The testator may appoint an executor to administer his estate and distribute it among the heirs. He may also appoint guardians of his minor children and give directions as to their education, etc.

The heir may accept or refuse his inheritance. He may accept it either unconditionally or with the benefit to inventory. In the first case he is responsible with all his assets for all the debts of the testator. In the second case an inventory is made of all the inherited property and the heir is responsible for the testator's debts only to the extent of the property inherited, but the heir cannot take possession of the inheritance until the inventory is made.

See Topical Index in front part of this volume.

SWEDEN LAW DIGEST REVISER

Baker & McKenzie Advokatbyrå
Eriksbergsgatan 46
Post Office Box 26163
S-100 41 Stockholm, Sweden
Telephone: 46 8 676 7700
Fax: 46 8 24 8920

Reviser Profile

Baker & McKenzie was founded in 1949. Today, it is the largest law firm in the world with over 1,700 attorneys.

Baker & McKenzie is the world's only true multinational law firm with over 50 offices in more than 30 countries. Each office is staffed with attorneys admitted to practice in the local jurisdiction and capable of advising on local legal matters in a variety of domestic and international business transactions. Many of the attorneys have had multinational legal training and experience and a number are admitted to practice in more than one jurisdiction.

Baker & McKenzie attorneys are involved in legal matters relating to the international business of many countries, including transnational investment and tax planning, and international litigation, trade and finance.

Baker & McKenzie's Stockholm office, with 25 lawyers, was opened in 1991. As all Baker & McKenzie offices, the Stockholm office has from time to time on secondment lawyers from Baker & McKenzie's other offices. Thus, as well as having a strong Swedish practice, the firm is able to provide a valuable combination of Swedish and foreign expertise to its international clientele and is particularly well placed to advise on multijurisdictional transactions.

The following highlights some major areas of the Stockholm office's practice.

Corporate: The office acts for Swedish and non-Swedish companies. All types of corporate, partnership, commercial and financial work are dealt with.

Commercial: A substantial part of the practice includes drafting of commercial agreements, including agency, distribution and manufacturing agreements; advice in relation to joint ventures and franchising arrangements; general conditions in all commercial fields and advice on compliance with commercial legislation.

Litigation: Litigation services to commercial clients in Swedish courts and before arbitrators are provided.

Real Property: The office handles industrial, commercial and residential property transactions, including financing arrangements, sale, purchase and leasing of real property, landlord and tenant disputes, and construction agreements.

Intellectual Property: Advice is given on the law relating to the protection of intellectual property rights, including trademarks, copyright, and know-how on their exploitation by licensing etc.

Environment: The office handles matters regarding water and air pollution, waste disposal, control of toxic substances and environmental aspects of mergers and acquisitions.

Taxation: The office advises on taxation affecting corporations and individuals, partnerships and associations, including double taxation treaties, and conduct of tax appeals.

Insolvency: The office gives advice and assists creditors in cases of insolvency of their debtors, those anticipating their own insolvency and purchasers from or others dealing with an insolvent. The office acts as administrator in receiverships.

Maritime and Transport Law: The office handles maritime and transport law, including cargo claims, ship financing and other matters related to admiralty.

Aviation: The office handles financing arrangements, sale, purchase and leasing of aircraft.

Labor Law: Corporate clients are advised on aspects of the employer/employee relationship. Work includes litigation of labor disputes.

EU/EEA: European Union law and European Economic Area law.

SWEDEN LAW DIGEST

(The following is a list of all Topics, including cross-references, covered in this Digest.)

SWEDEN LAW DIGEST

Revised for 1997 edition by

BAKER & McKENZIE ADVOKATBYRA, of Stockholm.

Sweden is a member of EU. See also European Union Law Digest.

ABSENTEES:

Where an heir, a legatee or a beneficiary is missing, and where it is uncertain whether or not a decedent has left heirs, and generally in other cases of need of protection and administration of property of absentees, the court may appoint a trustee to represent the interest of the absentee during his absence. See also topic Death.

ACKNOWLEDGMENTS:

Documents acknowledged before a notary public which are intended for use in Sweden should have the signature of the notary public certified by the county clerk and the signature of the county clerk certified by a Swedish consular or diplomatic officer.

ACTIONS:

Limitation of.—See topics Limitation of Actions; Evidence.

ADMINISTRATION:

Administration (Inheritance Code of 1958) of estate of decedent may be handled by heirs informally. Administrator appointed by court is no legal requirement. However, on application of heir or creditor, court appoints administrator. If decedent has appointed executor of his will, he will as rule be appointed administrator.

Administrator's main duties are to prepare and register with court a statement of decedent's assets and liabilities, to collect assets and pay debts and to prepare estate for distribution among heirs. Administrator must before every Apr. 1 render account of his administration of estate for past year and render final account when estate is prepared for distribution.

See topic Descent and Distribution.

Estates of decedents, Swedish or alien, domiciled in Sweden at time of death, are administered according to Swedish law.

If the decedent was domiciled abroad, but left property in Sweden, as a rule an administrator must be appointed. If such decedent was a Swedish citizen, the administration includes property abroad; if an alien, only property in Sweden is included. (Act 1937:81).

ADOPTION:

A person of at least 25 years, jointly with his spouse if married, may petition the court for leave to adopt another person. No maximum age of adoptee is stipulated. (Parent Code of 1949).

Consent Required.—Consent of parents or guardian is required if adoptee is under 18, and of adoptee himself if over 12.

Conditions Precedent.—No decree of adoption may be entered unless the court finds that the adoption will be to the benefit of adoptee and applicant has brought up child, or will bring up child, or there is other specific reason in favor of adoption. Payment of compensation by natural parents to adopter or vice versa is not allowed.

Jurisdiction.—Court of first instance in district where adopter resides (City Court of Stockholm if a nonresident).

Proceedings.—Report by the Children Welfare Committee in the district where adoptee resides is required.

Name.—Adoptee takes adopter's name.

Effect of Adoption.—Gives adoptee all rights of natural child. See also topic Descent and Distribution.

Foreigners.—(Act 1971:796). Adoption is exclusively judged under Swedish law if applicant is Swedish citizen or domiciled in Sweden. If adoptee is under 18 it shall be carefully considered if it would be of great disadvantage to adoptee if adoption would not be valid in native country of adoptee.

Foreign decree of adoption is valid in Sweden if applicant was citizen of or domiciled in foreign country when leave was given and, if adoptee was Swedish citizen or domiciled in Sweden, adoption is approved by Government.

AFFIDAVITS:

Oath may be administered only by court for certain purposes. See topics Evidence; Notaries Public.

AGENCY: See topic Principal and Agent.

ALIENS:

In general foreign citizens enjoy the same civil rights as Swedish citizens. Aliens are expressly entitled to receive property by inheritance to the same extent as Swedish citizens. Generally, concept of nationality has been abandoned and concept of domicile has been adopted regarding civil capacity and family rights and other fields of law.

Exceptions.—Nonresident aliens may not without permit acquire real property rated as one or two family units or as agricultural unit. Permanent residence with or without exercise of gainful activity requires license. For citizens of U.S., Canada, Western European countries and increasing number of countries in other continents, no visa is required to enter Sweden; valid passport is sufficient.

Corporations Owned or Controlled by Aliens.—No disqualifications apply to such corporations. See also topics Real Property; Corporations, subhead Foreign Corporations and Economic Associations.

Citizenship.—Swedish citizenship through naturalization may be obtained by alien who: (a) Is over 18 years old; (b) has been domiciled in Sweden for five years and (c) is of good character.

See topic Immigration.

ARBITRATION AND AWARD:

(Arbitration Act 1929:145).

Any controversies amenable to out of court settlement may be submitted to decision of one or more arbitrators. Parties to a contract may in contract or special agreement, agree that any controversy arising from contract or otherwise shall be submitted to arbitration.

The Arbitration Act does not apply if the parties have reserved the right of appeal against the award.

If the arbitration agreement does not name the arbitrators or stipulate the number of arbitrators or prescribe the methods whereby they are to be chosen, then each one of the parties shall appoint one arbitrator, and those two arbitrators shall appoint a third arbitrator. If party fails to appoint arbitrator, or if arbitrators fail to agree on third arbitrator, such arbitrator may be appointed by court of first instance in district where arbitration shall take place. Arbitration clause may be supplemented, if parties so desire, by stipulations as to language of arbitration and applicable substantive law.

Each one of the parties may call for arbitration. The chairman of the arbitration tribunal shall decide on time and place of the meetings of the tribunal. The arbitration may then proceed as in regular court proceedings, except that depositions of witnesses may not be taken under oath before the arbitrators. However, at request of party arbitrators may decide that depositions under oath shall be taken in court. If parties have not chosen applicable substantive law or conflict of law rules arbitrators will make choice. Arbitrators will probably apply Swedish conflict of law rules even if not bound to do so unless otherwise agreed by parties.

Arbitrators have no means of effecting provisional measures without intervention of judicial authority.

Arbitrators shall render written and signed award within six months after arbitration was called for. Time may be extended by agreement of parties or by court of first instance. There is no time limit in international arbitration, i.e. when at least one of parties is resident outside Sweden. Parties are thus free to agree on time limit. Majority casts vote. If award is not rendered in time, arbitration agreement is null and void.

Arbitrators shall state amount of compensation to them in award. Award also contains decision on if and to what extent one party shall indemnify other for its costs. Basic rule in Swedish proceedings is that losing party pays all costs, reasonably necessary for conduct of winning party's case. Parties are vis-à-vis arbitrators jointly and severally liable to pay compensation to arbitrators.

There is no right of appeal against an arbitration award rendered under the stipulations of the Arbitration Act, except on the basis of deficiencies in form and proceedings.

An arbitration award can be enforced directly without any court confirmation or judgment. See also topics Attachment and Executions. Sweden is party both to New York Convention of 1958 and Geneva Convention of 1927.

Specific rules will apply if parties choose to provide for arbitration in Sweden under Rules of Arbitration Institute of Stockholm Chamber of Commerce. It can be noted that American Arbitration Association and USSR Chamber of Commerce and Industry 1977 prepared "Optional Arbitration Clause for Use in Contracts in USA-USSR Trade". If parties refer to that clause, arbitration shall be in accordance with UNCITRAL Arbitration Rules and arbitration takes place in Stockholm.

Foreign.—Arbitration is considered to be foreign if it takes place outside Sweden. (Act 1929:147, Concerning Foreign Arbitration Agreements and Awards).

A foreign arbitration award, i.e., an award rendered abroad, is valid in Sweden, except if deficient as to form or proceedings. Recognition for enforcement of a foreign arbitration award in Sweden may be obtained by application to Court of Appeal in Stockholm.

ASSIGNMENTS:

For transfer of negotiable documents see topics Bills and Notes; Corporations, subhead Shares. Assignment becomes effective as against assignor's creditors through delivery of instrument to assignee. Claims in general are treated as simple instruments (see topic Bills and Notes, subhead Instruments of Debt, last paragraph), and assignment becomes effective through notification of debtor. Assignment of incorporeal rights is made through contract.

ASSOCIATIONS: See topic Corporations.

ATTACHMENT:

There exist several types of provisional action intended to secure rights in anticipation of execution. (Code of Judicial Procedure, c. 15). Application is made to court. Protective measures may consist of having debtor's property covered by sequestration, or by order forbidding its sale or removal. Arbitrators cannot give interlocutory relief. If matter will be handled by arbitrators, application is made to court.

ATTORNEYS AND COUNSELORS:

Jurisdiction Over Admissions.—Admission to membership of national Swedish Bar Association is granted by its Board. Authority to grant admission is vested in Bar Association by law. Advocate is person who is member of Association.

See Topical Index in front part of this volume.

ATTORNEYS AND COUNSELORS . . . *continued*

Address: The Swedish Bar Association, P.O. Box 27321, S-102 54 Stockholm, Sweden. Telephone +46 8 459 03 00, telefax +46 8 660 07 79.

Eligibility.—Admission to membership of Bar Association may be granted to person who is citizen of and domiciled in Sweden or in another country within European Economic Area, has Swedish law degree (juris kandidat), has practised law for five years, of which three years under supervision of Advocate, or on his own, is known for his integrity, has shown that he is suitable for profession.

Examination.—No separate examination is required, but mandatory ethics seminar must be attended.

Admission Pro Hac Vice.—Advocates do not have monopoly. Consequently, lawyers who are not members of Association may practise as counselors, but may not use title Advocate. In order to appear in court counsel must have sufficient knowledge of Swedish language.

Privileges.—Members of Association are privileged in two respects: title of "Advocate" is reserved for them, and only member of Association can be assigned by court as defence counsel in criminal cases.

Disabilities.—Advocate may not be employed in service of government or municipality or by private person other than Advocate.

Compensation.—Fees charged shall be reasonable. Client who is dissatisfied with fee has right to call for arbitration under statute of Association at no cost to client.

Professional Ethics.—Association has issued guidelines on rules of conduct for Advocates, and exercises its disciplinary function by disciplinary committee, which may impose admonition, warning or disbarment.

AUTOMOBILES: See topic Motor Vehicles.

BANKRUPTCY:

(Bankruptcy Act 1987:672).

Bankruptcy proceedings may be initiated on the debtor's own application or on application of a creditor who, if the debtor does not admit insolvency, must prove some circumstance indicating insolvency. In both cases application is filed with the bankruptcy court.

Announcement is made in certain newspapers and written notice sent to all known creditors.

A complete and specific list of the assets and liabilities is sworn to by the bankrupt before the bankruptcy court. The estate comprises all property belonging to the bankrupt at the time bankruptcy proceedings commence and property acquired during bankruptcy proceedings which may be subject to execution. The estate also can recover through due process property which the bankrupt may have disposed of within certain periods prior to the bankruptcy to the detriment of creditors.

The bankrupt's assets are taken possession of, administered and disposed of by trustee in bankruptcy, or, in certain cases, several trustees. He shall be specialist, primarily a lawyer. His activities are controlled by commissioner's office.

Creditors must file written statements with bankruptcy court within time specified in bankruptcy order, varying from four to ten weeks thereafter. Domestic and foreign creditors have equal rights. The statements must be submitted in duplicate and be accompanied by documents (original or certified copies) on which the claims are founded. If a creditor claims priority, this must be set out in the statement. Creditor has normally full right to set off all claims against him.

Principal classes of priority claims are as follows, in this order (Act 1970:979): (a) Creditors holding pledged chattels or who according to law have right to retain chattels to cover their claims (e.g., craftsmen) and creditors holding mortgages on ships and aircraft; (b) creditors holding business mortgage duly registered by court, see topic Pledges; (c) creditors holding mortgage on real estate; (d) creditors who have obtained execution against chattels; (e) public taxes and charges; (f) employees' claims for wages, salaries, pensions, vacation and severance pay within certain limits.

Interest enjoys same priority as principal. Non-priority claims enjoy interest until date of bankruptcy.

After the expiration of the time set for filing of claims a creditor may still submit his statement, but he must pay expenses incurred by the delay.

After trustee has examined claims, he—as well as creditors who have filed claims—has right to make objections. Such disputed matters are taken up by so-called mediation meeting of creditors and if agreement cannot be reached there matters are referred to court for decision.

The money realized from the bankrupt's assets is used first of all to pay the costs of the bankruptcy and any debts incurred during the bankruptcy.

Ordinarily a bankruptcy is ended through the payment of dividends on claims filed. Discharge from bankruptcy does not absolve a debtor from the liability later to pay that portion of his debts not covered by the payments made to creditors during the bankruptcy. This, of course, only applies to bankrupts who are non-corporate bodies.

If a debtor has made written agreements for the payment of his debts with all creditors who have filed their claims in the bankruptcy, or if he submits other evidence that they have been satisfied, bankruptcy can be cancelled upon application to bankruptcy court. If such application is granted and if debtor is corporation, bankruptcy proceedings will be converted into corporate liquidation proceeding. In this case former board of directors of bankrupt corporation will regain its powers and complete dissolution of corporation by distribution of assets to shareholders.

If a bankrupt desires to offer composition, the question is submitted to a meeting of creditors where voting right is enjoyed principally by non-priority creditors. The composition is considered accepted only after a certain majority of the creditors present and entitled to vote have reached an agreement. To have legal effect the composition proposal must be approved by the bankruptcy court, which will refuse sanction if it is obviously not to the advantage of the creditors, or if it does not give all creditors equal rights and payment of at least 25% of amounts claimed within one year after approval of scheme by court.

A simpler method of procedure is prescribed when a bankrupt's resources are insufficient to meet the costs of bankruptcy proceedings, or when it can be assumed that administration of bankruptcy estate will be of less complicated nature. Trustee is appointed by court but creditor does not file written statements of claim with court.

State Guarantee.—(Act 1992:497). Payment of employee's claims for wages, salaries and pensions which enjoy priority is guaranteed by state up to a certain maximum.

Composition Without Bankruptcy.—(Act 1970:847). Under certain conditions, among which may be mentioned approval of qualified majority of creditors, it is possible under court supervision for debtor to reach binding composition without bankruptcy.

See also topics Mortgages; Pledges.

BILLS AND NOTES:

Bills of Exchange.—(Negotiable Instruments Act 1932:130).

A bill of exchange must include: (a) the designation "bill of exchange;" (b) an unconditional demand to pay a certain sum in money; (c) name of party who must pay the instrument (payer, drawee); (d) date of maturity; (e) name of place where it must be paid; (f) name of person to whom or to whose order payment must be made (payee); (g) date and place of drawing of instrument; (h) signature of party who draws the instrument (drawer). A bill of exchange must call for payment: (a) On a certain date; (b) upon presentation; (c) a certain time after presentation; or (d) a definite time after its making. If a bill of exchange is issued or accepted outside of Sweden, it is, in general, subject, as to its form, to the law of the place where the transaction took place.

Indorsement implies partly a transfer of ownership rights from the indorser to the indorsee and a demand to pay to the latter and partly also a liability in favor of the following indorsers. This liability always exists unless the indorsement indicates that it is made without recourse. Transfer is permitted without any special mention made thereof in the bill. If transfer is specifically prohibited but still takes place the new holder does not have any rights under the Negotiable Instruments Act. Both to order indorsements and merely signature of indorser are binding.

Only after acceptance does a drawee become liable. Acceptance must be written on the bill and can be accomplished merely by drawee writing his name on the face of the bill. If a bill of exchange is not accepted when presented the holder has the right of protest. A drawee to whom a bill of exchange is presented for acceptance has the right to demand one day of grace, and in such case the bill must be presented the following day. Neglect to present a bill for acceptance or failure to protest same in case of nonacceptance in certain circumstances may mean the loss of rights against drawer and indorsers.

If payment of a bill is refused, the holder, in order to protect his rights, must arrange to have it protested not later than the second week-day following the maturity date. In case a bill is not paid when presented for payment on or after its maturity, the acceptor is liable for payment of interest at the rate of 6% from the date of presentation and for any costs arising out of the delay. Rights against the acceptor are barred after three years from maturity. Holder of a protested bill is entitled to bring an action for payment against some or all of the previous indorsers at the same time or against any one of them separately. He has a right to receive the amount of the bill and, in addition, 6% interest from maturity, reimbursement for protest charges and other necessary expenses, as well as a commission amounting to one-third of 1% of the amount of the bill. The claim of the holder of a bill of exchange against indorser and drawer is barred one year from the date of protest or, in case provision has been made for recourse without protest, from the due date. Indorser's right against other indorser or against drawer is barred six months from the date the first-named paid the bill of exchange or from the date legal steps are instituted (such as court summons, claim in bankruptcy, etc.).

The negotiable instrument act also contains provisions for more rapid and effective court procedure than is the case with ordinary claims.

Checks.—(Act 1932:131). Check must contain: (a) Designation "check;" (b) unconditional demand to pay certain sum in money; (c) name of party by whom payment is to be made; (d) place of payment; (e) date and place of drawing; (f) signature of drawer. As medium of payment check must be payable only upon presentation. Check may be made payable to bearer but may, through indorsement, be made payable to specified person. When check has been paid or come into possession of drawee, it may not be circulated further. It must necessarily be payable by bank. Placing two parallel lines on face of check (crossing) indicates that payment can be made only to bank or customer of drawee bank. If name of bank is placed between parallel lines, payment must be made only to that bank, or if name of drawee bank itself appears, only to one of its customers.

If the drawee bank has placed its legal signature on the face of a check or through other notation thereon given reason to believe that the bank will honor the check, it is the duty of the bank to pay such check, when presented within the legal time limit.

The holder of a check, in order to preserve his right of recourse to the drawer or indorsers, must present same for payment within 20 days from its date or, if the check is drawn in a non-European country not bordering on the Mediterranean, 70 days.

The claim of a holder of a check against indorser, drawer and others is barred six months from the expiration of the proper presentation period. If a check debtor has paid same, his claims against other check debtors are barred six months from the date he paid the check.

In most respects the provisions of the negotiable instrument act with regard to indorsement, order of liability, payment, recourse, etc., also are applicable to checks.

Instruments of Debt.—(Act 1936:81). Debtor under instrument of debt can invoke defence based on underlying cause. If instrument is issued by several persons without limitation of liability they are jointly and severally liable. Any of them who has paid debt has recourse against co-debtors pro rata parte. Transferor of instrument is responsible for existence of debt but not for debtor's solvency.

A negotiable promissory note is an instrument issued either to bearer or to a specified person or order, as well as an instrument in which right to mortgage property has been granted. Debtor is not bound to honor a negotiable promissory note unless returned to him. Transferee to which a negotiable promissory note has been delivered is considered to have good title, provided, in case of an instrument payable to order, that he is able to rely on a chain of written transfers leading up to himself and

BILLS AND NOTES . . . *continued*

provided further that he has taken in good faith. Payment to such transferee is a valid discharge unless debtor knew that payee was not proper creditor or paid negligently.

A simple instrument is an instrument payable to a specified person, transfer of which is valid against transferor's creditors only when debtor is notified thereof. Defective title to a simple instrument cannot be remedied by transferee's good faith. Rules relating to simple instruments apply to debts in general.

CHATTEL MORTGAGES: See topic Pledges.

CITIZENSHIP: See topic Aliens.

COHABITATION: See topic Husband and Wife, subhead Cohabitation.

COLLATERAL SECURITY: See topic Pledges.

COMMERCIAL REGISTER:

Individuals and partnerships which are merchants are required to register name of firm and of those empowered to sign for it with county administration. (Act 1974:157).

Non-Swedish residents and enterprises, except European Economic Interest Groupings, are required to apply for registration in order to carry on business in Sweden. (Act 1992:160).

See also topic Corporations, subhead Foreign Corporations and Economic Associations.

CONDITIONAL SALES: See topic Sales.

CONSTITUTION AND GOVERNMENT:

Sweden is hereditary limited monarchy. Four fundamental statutes form constitution of Sweden: Instrument of Government of 1974, Act of Succession of 1810, Freedom of the Press Act of 1949, and Freedom of Speech Act of 1991.

Sweden is member of European Union (EU) and is obliged to follow laws of the Union.

The Executive Power.—Despite fact that Instrument of Government actually provides that King or Queen shall be Head of State, executive power has been transferred to government.

The Legislative Power is shared between government and Parliament. Parliament alone may levy taxes and controls national budget.

Members of Parliament number 349 and are elected by direct vote for four years. Every citizen who has reached 18 day of election is entitled to vote and is eligible.

Judicial Power is vested in courts (see topic Courts), which are independent of any other authority. Persons holding judicial office may not be removed by Government without due trial and judgment.

CONSUMER CREDIT:

Act (1992:830) provides protection for consumers when purchasing goods on credit. Creditor must disclose clearly conditions under which credit is offered, e.g. actual interest rate computed per annum. Consumer retains right under agreement with supplier against new holder of right to receive payment under agreement. Act is compatible with EEC directives concerning consumer credit and was adopted as part of Swedish harmonization process with EEC laws.

CONTRACTS: (Act 1915:218).

Unless time of grace is granted oral offer must be accepted immediately and offer made by mail or telephone must be accepted within such time as offeror could reasonably estimate as being required. Time of grace in offer by mail or telegram is to be calculated to run from day letter is dated or from the time of day telegram is handed in for transmission. Acceptance must reach offeror within time stated.

Prices in advertisements, price currents etc. do not represent a legally binding offer.

Contracts are as a rule valid regardless of their form, the most important exceptions being agreements to sell real property and marriage settlements which must be in writing. See also topics Husband and Wife; Records; Sales.

Excuses for Nonperformance.—Force majeure as an excuse for nonperformance is generally observed under Swedish law.

Debtor may allege invalidity as excuse for nonperformance if forced under duress or fraudulently induced to make contract. If obligee when concluding contract took advantage of situation where he could exercise undue influence on obligor, latter is excused from performance to obligee and any third party held to be cognizant of the circumstances.

Contract is not enforceable if circumstances at its conclusion were such that it would be incompatible with honor and good faith to enforce it and obligee was aware thereof.

Conditions which are unreasonable in consideration of content of contract or other circumstances whether at making of contract or occurring later, may be modified or set aside. Other conditions may be modified or entire contract may be set aside if unreasonable condition is of such significant importance that it cannot reasonably be demanded that contract shall be valid.

A sum certain agreed to be paid as estimated damages in case of nonperformance is considered as guarantee for performance and can be claimed regardless of debtor's negligence unless combined with a reservation. Such estimated damages may be reduced if exorbitant in relation to damage actually sustained. Normally they represent maximum of amount claimable by creditor.

Applicable Law.—Except as regards bills of exchange, checks, international sales of goods, and marriage settlements, there are no statutory rules governing conflicts of law in relation to contracts. Court cases are few and offer scant guidance. In general, courts will decide according to center-of-gravity method absent agreement. There is no interdiction of submission to foreign law or jurisdiction, except if contrary to Swedish public order.

Public Procurement.—(Act 1992:1528).

Act includes rules for public procurement of goods, services and constructions. It also contains rules regarding appeals and damages. Act is applicable when public is going to purchase something for more than certain amount. Purchases for public account are in principle made after call for tenders which must be presented in sealed envelope or, if made by telegram or telefax, so confirmed. Main rule is that public procurement shall be made in way using possibilities of competition at market.

Distributorships, Dealerships and Franchises.—There is no specific legislation re distributorship, dealership or franchise, but agreements relative thereto are generally governed by Act on Contracts and Sale of Goods Act. Subject to certain conditions, Competition Act (1993:20) exempts distributorships and franchises from prohibition set forth therein, by way of group exemptions. With regard to compensation upon termination of distributorship, analogies with Act on Commercial Agency may be made under certain circumstances.

See also topic Sales.

CONVEYANCES: See topic Deeds.

COPYRIGHT:

(Copyright Act 1960:729).

Scope.—Creator of literary or artistic work has copyright therein, whether it be in writing or speech, and whether musical, dramatic, cinematographic or photographic work, work of fine arts, architecture, works of utility art, or expressed in some other manner; maps, drawings and other works of descriptive nature, and computer programs are classified as literary works.

Stipulations re computer programs are also applicable to preparatory design material for computer programs. Copyright to computer program, including economical and moral right, may pass from employee to employer unless otherwise provided by contract.

Copyright includes exclusive right to control reproduction and publication of a literary or artistic work whether in its original or amended form, or whether translated or adapted.

Creator's personal interest (droit moral) is protected: name of creator must be stated when his work is reproduced or published, and his work may not be altered in any manner which is prejudicial to his literary or artistic reputation, or to his individuality.

A translator or adapter acquires copyright in his translation or adaptation, however not in conflict with copyright in original work.

Registration of copyright does not exist.

Limitations.—Exclusive copyright is subject to certain exceptions for religious, cultural or other social purposes, e.g. reproductions for private use; photographic reproductions in archives and libraries; quotations; reproduction of newspaper articles, or of works in anthologies for education; reproduction in Braille; performance for religious service or education; distribution or public exhibition of copies of published works. In some of these cases compensation must be paid to creator.

Transfer.—Copyright may be transferred, in whole or in part, by assignment, inheritance or will. Act contains regulations for public performance, publishing and film contracts, however applicable only in absence of other agreement.

Copyright is exempt from legal seizure as long as it remains with creator or his heirs.

Duration.—Copyright expires at end of 70th year after death of creator or, in case of photographic pictures at end of 50th year after production.

Performing Rights (Droits Voisins).—An artist's performance of literary or artistic works may not, without his consent, be broadcast, televised or recorded on phonograph records, films or other media. Sound recording by an artist may not be re-recorded without his consent until after 50 years. Phonograph record or other sound recording may not be copied or re-recorded without consent of producer until after 50 years. If sound recording is used in radio or television before end of 50 year period, compensation must be paid both to producer or recording and performing artist Radio or television broadcasts may not be rebroadcast or recorded without consent of broadcasting company, except for private use.

Liability.—Violation of copyright may entail damages and, if done wilfully or with gross negligence, punishment by fine or imprisonment.

Applicability of the Act.—Copyright Act applies to works of Swedish citizens and persons domiciled in Sweden, to works of stateless persons or refugees having residence in Sweden, to works first published in Sweden, and to works first published by certain international organizations. Sweden is party to Berne Convention and Universal Copyright Convention, to effect that Swedish Copyright Act is applicable also in relation to those other countries which have ratified said convention or conventions. However, Swedish Act does not provide protection for a work, if period of protection has expired in country of origin.

See topic Patents, subhead Design Patents.

CORPORATIONS:

Stock Corporation (company limited by shares, aktiebolag).—Act 1975:1385.

Introductory Provisions.—Swedish stock corporation is company carrying on activities with capital contributed by shareholders and divided into specific number of shares without personal liability of shareholders for obligations of company.

Companies may be public, offering shares or other securities to general public, or private.

Share capital shall be fixed in Swedish currency and may not be less than SEK 100,000 for private and SEK 500,000 for public companies. Share capital may be fixed in by-laws at minimum and maximum. Minimum may not be less than one-fourth of maximum.

Shares shall be issued at equal par value. Amount to be paid for share may not be less than par value. Payment shall be made in cash, unless otherwise provided in accordance with provisions of Act. Share certificates shall be issued in name of specific entities. Payment for shares in excess of par value to be transferred to premium fund.

CORPORATIONS . . . *continued*

Formation.—Company is formed by one or several founders, to be individual resident in European Economic Area or legal entity founded and with registered office within said area.

Founders shall prepare deed of formation, including draft of by-laws and subscription list. At constituent meeting decision to form company is reached and board of directors and auditors are elected. Company shall apply to Patent and Registration Office for registration not later than six months after signing of deed for formation. At registration share capital must have been paid.

Prior to registration company can neither acquire rights nor enter into obligation, nor can it sue, complain or defend in court or before any other authority. Persons acting in company's name before it is registered are personally liable for such action. At registration liability passes to company provided that obligation results from deed of formation or has arisen subsequent to formation of company.

By-laws shall specify: (a) Name of company, (b) municipality in Sweden where registered office of company is to be located, (c) objects of company, (d) share capital or minimum and maximum share capital, (e) par value of shares, (f) number, or minimum and maximum numbers, of directors, and auditors as well as deputy directors, if any, (g) manner for convening general meetings of shareholders, (h) matters to be dealt with at annual general meeting of shareholders, and (i) fiscal year.

By-laws may provide that shareholders or others shall have right of pre-emption where share has passed to new owner.

Shares.—Share certificates shall be signed by board of directors. Signatures may be printed. Certificate shall state name of company, serial number of shares, par value and date of issue. Share certificates may not be issued before full payment and registration.

Share certificate represents title to share. Bona fide holder of share certificate, who can prove his title by unbroken chain of transfers or endorsements in writing from duly registered shareholder to specific person or in blank, is protected as legitimate shareholder and is entitled to be registered as shareholder.

Board of directors shall keep share register in which all shares and shareholders shall be registered. This register, which is open to public, is basis for checking shareholders and their votes at general meeting of shareholders.

In order to simplify handling and trading of shares both for companies and individuals, Act 1987:623 allows recording functions to be entrusted to central body, Securities Register Center (VPC), which by using EDP, records all transfers, changes of share capital, etc.

Shares of different classes may be issued, e.g. preferred shares and common shares or classes of shares with different voting rights.

Shares must be fully paid not later than six months after signing of deed of formation. If payment is not made, board of directors may force subscriber by court action to fulfill his obligation or may declare his rights as subscriber forfeited.

Increase of Share Capital.—Share capital may be increased by subscription of new shares against payment (new issue) or by issue of shares or by increase of par value of existing shares without payment (bonus issue). Resolution to increase share capital shall be adopted at general meeting of shareholders. Act gives detailed provisions as to contents of resolution.

Increase of share capital by bonus issue may be effected by transfer to share capital of: (a) Such amounts as may be distributed as dividends, (b) amounts from revaluation reserve and statutory reserve, or (c) amounts of originating from revaluation of value of fixed assets.

Convertible Debt Instruments.—Company may for consideration issue convertible debt instruments, or debt instruments with right of option to subscribe to new shares, or similar instruments.

Reduction of Share Capital.—Share capital may be reduced for: (a) Transfer to statutory reserve or immediate coverage of loss, (b) repayment to shareholders, or (c) transfer to reserve for purposes to be decided by general meeting of shareholders.

Share capital may be reduced by: (a) Redemption or consolidation of shares, (b) withdrawal of shares without repayment, or (c) reduction in par value of shares with or without repayment.

Acquisition of Own Shares.—Company may not, except in very special cases, acquire its own shares or accept such shares as security. Agreement which violates this prohibition is invalid.

Management of Company.—Management is handled by board of directors and managing director.

Board of directors shall consist of at least three members. If share capital is less than SEK 1,000,000, board may consist of one or two members, provided that at least one deputy is appointed. Board of directors is normally elected by general meeting of shareholders.

In company where share capital amounts to at least SEK 1,000,000, board of directors shall appoint managing director. In other companies board of directors may appoint managing director. Managing director does not have to be member of board. Deputy managing director may also be appointed.

Managing director and at least half of members of board of directors, including employee representatives (see subhead Representation by Employees, infra), must reside in European Economic Area, unless exception is granted. One member of board is appointed chairman.

Board of directors shall represent and sign for company. Board of directors represents company in dealing with third parties, as well as before court and other authorities. Board of directors may authorize director, managing director or any other person to represent and sign for company, unless such delegation of authority is prohibited by by-laws. Managing director may always represent and sign for company with regard to measures which are within his duties.

Public Representation (Act 1987:618).—Government is entitled to appoint maximum five directors in bank companies. Public director shall specially protect public interest.

Representation by Employees (Act 1987:1245).—Local labor unions are entitled to appoint two directors and two deputies in companies or economic associations with at least 25 employees, or three directors and three deputies if 1,000 employees or more. Number of employees extends also to groups of companies.

Once employee directors have been appointed, right to board representation remains throughout mandate period, even if number of employees falls below 25.

General Meeting of Shareholders.—Shareholders' right to take decisions in company affairs is exercised at general meetings of shareholders. Shareholder may exercise his rights at general meeting of shareholders personally or by proxy. Nobody may vote for more than one-fifth of total number of votes attributable to shares represented at meeting, unless otherwise provided in by-laws.

Resolution of general meeting of shareholders shall be adopted by simple majority. In case of tie, chairman has casting vote except that election of directors and auditors shall be decided through drawing of lots. For certain important resolutions qualified majority is required. Annual general meeting of shareholders shall be held within six months from end of each fiscal year. At this general meeting resolutions shall be passed in respect to: (a) Adoption of income statement and balance sheet, (b) approbation of company's profit or loss according to balance sheet, (c) directors' and managing director's discharge from liability, (d) election of directors and auditors, and (e) other matters which according to Companies Act or by-laws shall be dealt with at this meeting.

Extraordinary general meeting of shareholders shall be held whenever board of directors may find it appropriate or when auditor or owners of one-tenth of all shares request this for special purpose.

Auditing.—General meeting of shareholders shall elect one or more auditors. Auditor may be individual or accounting firm, and must be approved by Board of Trade.

Auditor shall render report to general meeting of shareholders for every fiscal year. Auditor's report shall contain statement whether annual report has been prepared in conformity with Companies Act and Swedish GAAP, statement on directors' and managing director's discharge from liability, and statement on adoption of balance sheet, income statement and proposed allocation of company's profit or loss as made in directors' report. Auditor's report must be sent to registration authority within 15 months from fiscal year end.

Annual Report.—Annual report shall be prepared for each fiscal year. Report shall consist of income statement, balance sheet and directors' report.

Annual report shall be signed by directors and managing director.

Fiscal year shall be 12 months but may be extended up to maximum 18 months, as well as shortened to six months. Normally, calendar year is fiscal year. Fiscal year may also end on Apr. 30, June 30 or Aug. 31. When there are special reasons, National Tax Board may grant permission to use other closing date.

If annual report and auditor's report are not sent to registration authority within 15 months from fiscal year end, board members and general manager become liable for obligations of company.

Statutory Reserve and Dividends.—All companies earning profit must set up statutory reserve out of profits until statutory reserve plus premium fund amount to 20% of share capital or such higher amount as may be prescribed in by-laws. Annual amount transferred to statutory reserve may not be less than 10% of profit for year after deducting loss brought forward. Statutory reserve may not be distributed and may only be used to cover losses or to increase share capital through bonus issue.

Resolution to distribute dividend shall be adopted at general meeting of shareholders. Dividends may be distributed only out of equity in excess of share capital and statutory reserve. In group situations, maximum distribution is restricted to lesser of maximum distribution on parent company level or on group level. General meeting of shareholders may not distribute dividends which are higher than proposed or approved by board of directors. However, shareholders representing not less than 10% of share capital may, in certain circumstances, call for distribution of reasonable dividends.

Dividends may not be distributed to such extent that in view of company's or group's consolidation needs, cash needs or financial position in other respects distribution would be contrary to good business practices.

Company may not grant cash loans to shareholder, directors or managing director or to close relatives of such persons. This does not extend to parent company or shareholder with less than 1% of share capital. Foreign parent company is not considered as parent company in this respect.

Liquidation.—General meeting of shareholders may resolve that company shall be liquidated.

Where board of directors has reason to believe that company's equity capital is less than half of share capital, or if company upon seizure lacks seizable assets, board shall prepare control balance sheet and have it examined by auditors. If then it is found that equity is less than half of share capital, board shall refer as soon as possible to general meeting of shareholders question of liquidating company (technical bankruptcy). Unless balance sheet adopted at general meeting within eight months shows that equity capital is restored to share capital, board of directors shall, if general meeting does not resolve to liquidate company, apply to court to order liquidation of company.

General meeting of shareholders which resolves or court which orders that company shall be liquidated shall at same time appoint one or more liquidators. Liquidators shall replace board of directors and managing director and shall be responsible for carrying out liquidation.

Auditor's appointment does not terminate by fact that company enters into liquidation.

Act gives detailed provisions for administration of liquidation.

Name of Company and Division.—Name of company shall contain word "aktiebolag", or AB, and shall be clearly distinguishable from other names previously entered into Companies Register. Where name of company is to be registered in two or several languages, each version shall be mentioned in by-laws. Registered name of public company must contain word "publikt" (public) or be followed by designation "publ."

Stationery, invoices and order forms of all companies must list name of company, domicile of board of directors, and registration number of company.

Name of divisions or other business units may be registered in addition to name of company.

Miscellaneous.—Act contains detailed provisions regarding merger, compulsory transfer of minority shares in subsidiary, damages, penalties and registration.

See Topical Index in front part of this volume.

CORPORATIONS . . . *continued*

Insiders' Shareholdings.—(Act 1990:1342). Insiders as defined by law must give notice to public register of their shareholdings in companies listed on Stockholm Stock Exchange or quoted on list of Swedish Association of stockbrokers. Insider trading is criminal offence. Insider can be ordered to repay profits made.

Economic Associations (Ekonomiska Foreningar).—Act 1987:667.

The economic association is an incorporated association of an unrestricted number of individuals or corporate bodies or partnerships, created mainly for furthering or safeguarding by joint action certain economic interests of its members. It is entered upon its registration in special registers for economic associations kept by County Administrations (lansstyrelserna). Registration will be granted if: (1) There are at least five members, or at least three or four members, if three of them are registered associations or associations which are regarded as corporations without registration; (2) articles have been drawn up in written form and approved by members; (3) Board of Directors and Auditors have been elected.

The members of the association are not responsible for the liabilities of the association. The authority rests in the general meeting of the members, which has to pass or amend the articles, elect the Board of Directors and the Auditors, approve the operating accounts and balance sheet, distribute profits, grant release to the Board of Directors and exercise other powers provided by the Act or articles. Managing Director shall be appointed if average number of employees during last two years has exceeded 200. Managing Director and at least half of members of Board must reside within European Economic Area, unless exemption is granted. Auditors must examine conduct of business and yearly balance sheet. Members of Board, Auditors, liquidators, and members of association are liable for damage due to their activity on behalf of association in accordance with special rules given in Act.

New members may be admitted at any time, if no special reasons are referred to with respect to the character, the extent or the purpose of the activity of the association. If the articles do not provide otherwise the application for membership in written form will be examined by the Board of Directors. Members may give notice of withdrawal at any time. In the articles it may, however, be stipulated that such notice must not be given within two years from the admittance or within five years if such a stipulation has been approved by the county administration (lansstyrelsen). Liquidation takes place as provided for in the articles, or upon resolution of the general meeting of the members or in case of bankruptcy or in other cases in accordance with stipulations in the Act.

The stipulations of the Economic Associations Act regarding the content of the articles, the reserve fund, the surplus for dividend, the Board of Directors, the signing for the association, the annual rendering of accounts, the auditing, the general meeting of the members and liquidation and dissolution, are very similar to those of the Stock Corporation Act.

Foreign Corporations and Economic Associations.—For the reason of taxation and other circumstances it is generally advisable for a foreign enterprise, desirous of doing business in Sweden, to form a Swedish subsidiary corporation. However, under an Act 1992:160, enterprise which is legally established and registered as corporation or economic association in foreign country, and is duly engaged in business activities in that country, may do business in Sweden through branch office with independent administration.

Many of the requirements of a Swedish corporation are applicable to such branches, e.g., managing director, registration of firm, bookkeeping regulations, audit, and accounting. In all legal matters arising from business activities of Swedish branch, foreign enterprise shall be subject to Swedish law.

See also topics Partnership; Taxation.

CORRUPTION:

Any person who gives, promises or offers any bribe or improper remuneration whatever, to any employee or any person engaged in public service, whether within central or local governments, any person whose assignment is governed by any statutory regulation, any person serving in armed forces or other national defense units, any other person vested with public authority, any person acting as fiduciary in legal or economic matters, is guilty of bribery and shall be punished by fines or by imprisonment for not more than two years.

Any employee or any other person mentioned above who accepts or requests any bribe or improper remuneration or promise of any bribe or improper remuneration, in respect of his service, is guilty of bribe-taking and shall be punished by fines or by imprisonment for not more than two years. Same rule will apply if employee committed bribe-taking before taking up or after leaving service. If bribe-taking constitutes heinous crime, employee shall be punished by imprisonment of not more than six years. Any such remuneration given or taken with intention to violate lawful duty of bribee will constitute criminal offence. Criterion of impropriety will be decided on basis of all factors relevant to individual case. Improper transaction is meant to influence employee in respect of his service. (Penal Code c. 17, §7 and c. 20, §2).

COURTS:

First Instance.—There are some 90 courts of first instance. Court is composed of three or four judges except in criminal cases and matters of family law, where it consists of one judge and three or five lay assessors. In minor cases and at preliminary inquiries courts usually sit with one judge alone.

The courts of first instance have cognizance in all civil and criminal matters, irrespective of the amount claimed or of the gravity of the crime, with exception of matters which are assigned to special courts (see subhead Special Courts, infra). Courts of first instance handle all such matters as probate of wills, appointments of guardians and trustees, supervision of guardianships, registration and taxation of estates of decedents, registration of ownerships and encumbrances of real property and filing of private documents, such as marriage settlements.

An appeal lies to a court of appeal from any judgment or order of a court of first instance. However, if claimed amount is less than a certain amount, appeal may be obtained only under certain conditions.

Second Instance.—The courts of appeal (hovratterna) are six. They have appellate jurisdiction of civil and criminal appeals from courts of first instance within their territories. Court of appeal is in quorum with three or four judges in criminal cases supplemented with two lay assessors.

Mainly in cases of general interest as precedents, appeal may be obtained to Supreme Court against judgments and orders of a court of appeal.

Supreme Court sits in Stockholm and is composed of 20 judges. Court is in quorum with five judges but may in cases of special importance meet with 12 judges or in pleno.

Special Courts.—In addition to general courts described above there exist number of special courts, e.g. administrative courts primarily for tax matters, real estate courts handling matters such as expropriation, etc., and labor court.

CURRENCY:

Bank of Sweden (Sveriges Riksbank) holds monopoly on issue of paper money. As security for value of notes issued, exceeding total value of gold reserve, Bank of Sweden must hold easily negotiable assets. Name of currency is "Krona" (SEK), and "Ore" (1/100 Krona).

In 1931 Sweden joined Great Britain in leaving the gold standard.

See also topics Customs; Exchange Control; Foreign Trade Regulations.

CURTESY: See topic Husband and Wife.

CUSTOMS:

Sweden is member of European Union. Goods imported to Sweden from third countries are subject to Common Customs Tariff based on Harmonized System Nomenclature. See also European Union Law Digest and topics Exchange Control; Foreign Trade Regulations.

DAMAGES:

(Act 1972:207). Act refers to noncontractual claims (tort liability).

Anyone who deliberately or negligently causes damage shall pay full compensation. Children under 18 and mentally deficient have restricted liability.

Employer is, irrespective of own negligence, responsible for all damage, caused by fault or negligence, on part of his employees acting in his service. Employees are liable for damages in particular circumstance only. State and municipalities are liable for damage due to incorrect procedure; this liability being restricted in different respects.

See also topic Product Liability.

DEATH:

A petition to have a person declared legally dead may be presented ten years after the day he or she for the last time was known to be alive; or if he or she would be more than 75 years of age, then when five years have passed; or if the person was in mortal danger at the time of disappearance, then the petition may be presented after three years have passed.

The petition must be filed with the court. The court summons the person in question and his or her relatives to give notice to the court before a certain day, fixed at least one year after the summons has been published in the newspapers and as otherwise provided in the Act. If the court on the day appointed has no information that the person may be alive, the court will declare him or her dead. The day of death will be fixed at the end of the month when ten (or five) years have passed since the person was last known to be alive, or if he or she was in mortal danger, then on the day or at the end of the month on which the danger occurred.

Certificate of death may be obtained from local tax authority.

Action for Death.—If death has been caused wilfully or with negligence, wrongdoer, in discretion of court, may be liable to pay damages to such relatives of decedent who were legally entitled to support from decedent (surviving spouse, children, and, rarely, parents). Action on fatal accident occurring in transport by road, rail, sea or air must be brought within two years. See topic Limitation of Actions. In case of motor vehicle or aircraft accident, tort liability exists irrespective of negligence. These provisions apply to citizens and foreigners alike.

DECEDENTS' ESTATES:

See topics Descent and Distribution; Wills.

DEEDS:

Oral agreements, as a rule, are binding. However, the law requires written contracts in certain cases, for example contracts involving agreement to purchase real property, marriage settlements, etc.

See also topics Husband and Wife; Records.

DEPOSITIONS: See topic Evidence.

DESCENT AND DISTRIBUTION:

(Inheritance Code of 1958). Decedent's relatives are entitled to inherit in following order:

(1) Descendants receive equal shares. If one child is dead, his issue will take his place so that each line receives an equal share.

(2) If no descendants are alive the parents or their descendants inherit. If both parents are alive they each receive half of the residue estate. If either parent is dead, his or her share is divided among the decedent's brothers and sisters or their descendants, so that each line receives equal shares. Half brothers or half sisters or their descendants inherit on the same basis as other children the share that should have been received by their father or mother.

(3) If neither parent nor their descendants are alive, the grandparents, or, if there are no grandparents, the uncles and aunts, inherit.

Other relatives do not inherit.

DESCENT AND DISTRIBUTION . . . *continued*

When married person dies, residue estate goes to surviving spouse, except if decedent leaves direct heir, who is not also surviving spouse's direct heir. Upon surviving spouse's death residue estate goes to direct heirs in marriage between spouses or—if there are no such heirs—to spouses' parents, brothers or sisters or their descendants.

Surviving partner of same sex, in Registered Partnership, is treated as surviving spouse.

Illegitimate children or their descendants inherit and are inherited from as if they were born in wedlock.

Adopted children and their descendants inherit and are inherited from as if they were adopter's children in wedlock. Adoption cuts off the right of inheritance between the adopted child and its natural relatives, except that if one spouse adopts the child of the other spouse, then the right of inheritance is the same as if the child were the mutual child of the spouses.

If no heirs are found the estate goes to a so-called inheritance fund to promote the education and upbringing of children.

Estate inventory must be drawn up and signed within three months after death and filed with appropriate court within one month thereafter. In connection with registration, inheritance tax is levied on net assets of estate according to progressive scale ranging from 10% to 30%.

Distribution of estate may not take place until decedent's debts are paid or funds for payment have been allocated or settlement has been made to effect that debts will not fall upon heir. If estate is distributed before such measures have been taken, property distributed or part of it shall go back to estate. Heir can never be personally liable for decedent's debts unless heir causes damage to creditors.

See topic Administration.

DISPUTE RESOLUTION:

Mandatory Dispute Resolution.—Normal procedure for resolution of dispute is court action in accordance with Code of Court Procedure, except matter assigned to special courts. See topic Courts.

Fee Disputes.—See topic Attorneys and Counselors, subhead Compensation.

Voluntary Dispute Resolution.—

Arbitration.—Stipulation referring conflicts to be solved by arbitration is found in many national and international contracts, by application of Arbitration Act or to rules of arbitration of domestic or international arbitration institutes.

Arbitration Institute of Stockholm Chamber of Commerce has issued rules for expedited arbitration which is primarily recommended for minor disputes where parties desire speedy and inexpensive procedure.

Consumers.—Disputes between consumers and businesspersons regarding goods and services may be brought to Public Complaints Board (Allmänna Reklamationsnämnden), which issues recommendation on how dispute should be solved.

DIVORCE:

(Marriage Code of 1987). Either of spouses may obtain decree of divorce without cause upon joint or separate application. If only one of spouses wants divorce or if both or one of them has custody of child under 16, time for consideration must precede divorce. In such event either spouse has to file renewed request for divorce not less than six months but not more than one year after application was made. Otherwise, question of divorce is dropped. Separation is no requirement. Divorce is granted upon application forthwith if spouses have been separated for two years as well as in case of bigamy.

After divorce each spouse is responsible for his or her own support. In case of special need, reasonable alimony may be payable during transition period.

If spouses are separated while married, and on divorce, joint custody of children is normal but if parents disagree, court rules with regard to best interest of children.

Court decisions and agreements as to alimony payments or custody of children may be altered in case circumstances so justify. For effect of divorce on property interests, see topic Husband and Wife.

Foreign Divorce.—Cases of divorce between aliens may be tried in Sweden under Swedish law if defendant is domiciled in Sweden or if plaintiff is domiciled in Sweden for at least one year. (Act 1904:26).

DOWER: See topic Husband and Wife.

ENVIRONMENT:

Basic Statutes.—Basic statute for protection of environment is Environment Protection Act (1969:387), covering pollution of land, water and air and almost all other environmental nuisances. Act applies only to stationary sources of pollution, i.e. disturbances from use of real estate.

Act on Chemical Products (1985:426) applies to chemical substances and compounds. Ordinances under Act give special rules and standards for e.g. PCBs and pesticides.

Civil liability is stated in Environmental Damage Act (1986:225). Liability is mainly strict. Burden of proof is alleviated so that only predominant probability is required. Liability is imposed on those who own real estate or carry on activities there. Disturbances covered are same as according to Environment Protection Act. Even where public permission has been granted, compensation can be imposed. For disturbances not exceeding what is general usage, compensation is payable only when damage is caused willfully or through negligence.

Environment Protection Act contains special provisions for Environmental Damage Insurance. Indemnity is paid from this insurance to claimant for bodily injury or material damage covered by Environmental Damage Act, if claimant is entitled to indemnity but cannot get indemnity paid or if right to indemnity is statute-barred. Ordinance on Environmental Damage Insurance (1989:365) states size of annual amount payable by anyone carrying on certain environmentally hazardous activities.

Special provisions on environmental protection are to be found in Water Act (1983:291) and in forestry and agricultural legislation. The Nature Conservancy Act (1964:822) contains provisions for i.a. establishment of national parks and protection of plant and animal life.

Air and Water Quality.—Air and water preservation is based on Environment Protection Act. There are no general quality standards stated regarding air or water quality.

Special statutes are Automobile Exhaust Act (1986:1386) and attached ordinance (1991:1481), Act on Motor Gasoline (1985:838) and special statutes laying down limits to sulphur content of fuel oil (1976:1054, 1976:1055, 1990:587 and 1990:709).

Hazardous Waste.—Regulations are based on Environment Protection Act completed by Garbage Act (1979:596), Garbage Ordinance (1990:984) and Act on Environmentally Hazardous Waste (1991:1985:841).

Permit Procedures.—Environment Protection Ordinance (1989:346) lists most polluting and nuisance causing types of enterprise subject to examination procedures. For plant causing less nuisance, there is obligation to notify of planned activities. There is also free sector of activities, not subject to approval, but which must meet substantive standards of general application of law.

Environment Protection Act gives rules of conditions under which polluting activities may be carried on and provides general terms for balancing impact against benefit. It also contains rules on examination of applications.

Permit applications shall contain i.a. description of environmental effects that activity may cause, proposals for precautionary measures required to prevent detrimental effects and proposals as to how activity should be inspected.

Authorities and Supervision.—Permits under Environment Protection Act are issued by National Licensing Board for Environment Protection or by county administrations.

Under Act on Chemical Products Chemicals Inspectorate functions as central agency. National Environment Protection Board has primary responsibility as regards ambient environment, whereas Occupational Health Agency takes care of occupational hazards. At regional level, county administrations are supervisory bodies and issue licences under Act on Chemical Products. Locally, public health authorities are supervisors.

National Environment Protection Board is central supervisory authority. County administrations and municipal environment committees exercise supervision of individual environmentally hazardous activities.

Sanctions.—Anyone infringing regulations of Environment Protection Act or directives issued in pursuance of Act is liable to fine or maximum two years imprisonment. Any individual or legal entity disregarding regulations may also be liable to sanction charge or environment protection charge, corresponding to any profit derived from infringement.

EVIDENCE:

At request made through Ministry of Foreign Affairs a Swedish court will take evidence on behalf of a foreign court. Writs of subpoena may be issued in connection therewith. If a sworn statement is necessary to protect a lawful right abroad, oath may be administered by a Swedish court. A Swedish court may rule that evidence be taken by a foreign court and issue a corresponding letter rogatory which is forwarded by Ministry of Foreign Affairs. (Acts 1946:816, 817, 819).

As no forms of evidence are qualified by statute as conclusive, evidence taken abroad will be sifted in same manner as and together with evidence taken directly.

Although no action is pending, evidence can be taken by a court regarding circumstances which may eventually prove important for protection of a lawful right in case of risk that such evidence would otherwise get lost. (Act of Procedure, c. 41).

If foreign law is to be applied in a suit court may take advantage of own knowledge of such law and inform itself thereof. Court may also request either party to submit proof of applicable provisions of foreign law.

EXCHANGE CONTROL:

Exchange control regulations remain pro forma, but are de facto repealed for all commercial transactions, such as investment in Sweden, repatriation of capital from Sweden, and borrowing abroad. Restrictions remain for private persons with respect to keeping foreign accounts and foreign shares. Central Bank still requires notification of foreign exchange transactions for statistical and tax control purposes.

See also topics Currency; Customs; Foreign Trade Regulations.

EXECUTIONS:

(Execution Code of 1981). Matters subject to execution are: (1) Judgments of courts; (2) agreements confirmed by court; (3) arbitration awards; (4) certain alimony agreements; (5) orders of attachment.

Execution in order to secure payment of debts may be made on all assets of debtor with following exceptions: (1) Normal clothing and other purely personal belongings; (2) necessary furniture and household equipment; (3) necessary tools of trade; (4) lease of debtor's regular residence; (5) necessities of life required for one month or an equivalent sum of money. Execution may also be levied as garnishment. Execution must be made in such a manner that debtor suffers as little loss as possible. Real estate and taxes subject to execution only after formal application by creditor.

Property attached under execution must be listed, valued and sold at public auction, but not more may be sold than is necessary to meet debt and costs of execution. Sale of real estate under execution is subject to complicated rules based on principle that debts secured by mortgage having priority over execution may not be disturbed but must either be paid, if payment is accepted by such creditor, or be taken over by buyer.

Even though judgments of the court have not become legally effective they may be the basis of executive action. Such attached property, however, may not be sold until the court's decision is effective. The debtor may avoid such attachment by placing other security to cover the amount of the judgment and for the damage that may ensue on account of the delay.

EXECUTORS AND ADMINISTRATORS:

See topic Administration.

See Topical Index in front part of this volume.

EXEMPTIONS: See topic Executions.

FOREIGN ARBITRATION AWARDS:

See topic Arbitration and Award.

FOREIGN EXCHANGE:

See topics Currency; Exchange Control.

FOREIGN IMPORTS:

See topics Taxation; Foreign Trade Regulations.

FOREIGN INVESTMENT:

See topics Aliens; Corporations; Exchange Control.

FOREIGN JUDGMENTS: See topic Judgments.

FOREIGN TRADE REGULATIONS:

With exception of certain products of dangerous or other particular nature, e.g. explosives, weapons, pharmaceutical products, intoxicating liquors, poisons, narcotics, tobacco, living animals and plants, goods may in general be freely imported into Sweden. Licence is required for import of motor cars and agricultural products. Export of products from Sweden is free with very few exceptions, e.g. weapons and war materials including certain high-tech products which may be classified as parts/components in such material.

See also topics Currency; Customs; Exchange Control.

FOUNDATIONS:

(Act 1994:1220). Grantor may create foundation as legal entity. Foundations can be created in different ways. Most common is that grantor irreversibly transfers assets to be permanently and separately administered for specific purpose, such as scientific research, defence, or education of children. Fundraising foundation is created when grantor ordains all money raised, due to announcement by grantor, to promote permanent and specific purpose.

Foundations may conduct business.

Foundations with assets exceeding certain value, parent foundations and foundations conducting business must keep books and produce official annual accounts, inspected by qualified accountant. Liability of foundation is limited to extent of its assets.

Foundation directions may be changed or set aside with permission of Government Authority, unless grantor has stipulated that directions may be amended by trustee or council, but this is not possible as to foundation purpose. Otherwise, directions can generally be changed, repealed or set aside, only if—due to changed conditions—they cannot be met or if they are obviously ineffectual or incompatible with grantor's objective.

All foundations liable to produce annual accounts must be registered in County Foundation Register, as are other foundations, if prescribed by grantor. With few exceptions, foundations are supervised by County Administration.

FRAUDS, STATUTE OF:

Statute of Frauds concept is unknown to Swedish law. In general, very few contracts require writing to be enforceable, with notable exception of contracts for sale of real property.

GARNISHMENT: See topic Executions.

GUARANTEE:

(Commercial Code, c. 10). Contract of guarantee may be made either orally or written. Guarantee of simple nature involves only subsidiary responsibility: liability to pay occurs only after creditor has unsuccessfully tried to collect from principal debtor through all available legal means, including execution, bankruptcy, etc. Only when guarantee contract has been entered in special form of "proprieborgen" does primary responsibility occur: guarantor undertakes guaranteed debt as his own. In this case creditor can call upon either debtor or guarantor for payment.

In case several persons have entered into a guarantee and have not made themselves liable per capita, they are bound jointly and severally.

HOLIDAYS:

Legal holidays are: Jan. 1, Jan. 6, Good Friday, Easter Monday, May 1, Ascension Day, Whit Monday, All Saints Day, Dec. 25, Dec. 26. Due days falling on Sats., Suns., legal holidays as aforesaid, Midsummer Eve, Christmas Eve, and New Year's Eve are postponed until next weekday.

HUSBAND AND WIFE:

(Marriage Code of 1987). Basic principle underlying personal legal rights of husband and wife is that both stand as individuals enjoying equal freedom and right to decide on issues concerning family and home, including care of children, etc.

As rule, husband and wife remain owners of his or her respective property and earnings, but acquire undivided one-half interest in each other's property. Interest in such community property is realized when distributing property as result of divorce or death. Spouses are required to care for his/her community property during marriage to prevent that its value is not materially diminished to detriment of other spouse.

Marriage Code expressly provides that neither spouse may, without written consent of other party, dispose of or mortgage real estate which is community property.

Property may be deemed to be separate property of spouse, as opposed to community property, if property was declared separate by marriage settlement, or if property was acquired as gift from third party or if by inheritance on condition to be separate property of receiver.

Income from separate property will be considered as community property unless provided otherwise. Main effect of separate property is that spouse will not have dormant interest in separate property of other party.

Spouses may agree by marriage settlement that community property shall be considered separate, or vice versa. Marriage settlement may be entered into before or after wedding. In order for such settlement to be valid vis-á-vis third parties it must be registered with court and in National Marriage Settlement Register.

Spouses have general right to enter into contracts with each other. In order to protect creditors, gifts between spouses must be registered with court. This does not apply to ordinary gifts, value of which is not disproportionate to economic circumstances of donor.

As to debts, each spouse is responsible for his or her own debts, but spouses are jointly and severally liable for debts incurred jointly by them.

Cohabitation.—(Acts 1987:232 and 1993:1474). Cohabitation by unmarried man and unmarried woman living together in relationship as husband and wife, or by two unmarried people in homosexual relationship, is in many respects subject to rules comparable to those of marriage. If cohabitation is terminated, cohabitants are entitled to share of joint property, but only property which has been acquired in view of cohabitation will be included when determining each party's share of such property.

Registered Partnership.—(Act 1994:1117). Two persons of same sex may request registration of their partnership, provided that at least one of partners is Swedish citizen, domiciled in Sweden. Registered partnership has substantially same legal effect as marriage, except that partners may not adopt. Registered partnership is dissolved by death or by court decision.

IMMIGRATION:

Residence permit (Act 1989:529) by local police is required for residence in Sweden more than three months of foreign citizens, except Scandinavians, and must normally be obtained prior to entry into Sweden.

Work permit is required for employment in Sweden, or work in Sweden under foreign employment, of foreign citizens, except Scandinavians, and must normally be obtained prior to entry into country. Application forms available at Swedish consulates.

More liberal regulations apply to citizens within EEA.

INFANTS:

Age of majority, 18.

Infants over 16 may dispose of earnings from own work. Infants over 16 may, subject to guardian's permission, carry on business and make valid contracts within its scope. Otherwise infants' contracts made without consent are voidable by both guardian and opposite party.

In existing marriages, or when parents have custody jointly, both parents are guardians. In other cases parent having custody is guardian unless particular guardian has been appointed. Guardians' administration of minor's property is supervised by Chief Guardians.

See also topics Adoption; Divorce; Labor Relations; Marriage.

INTEREST:

(Interest Act 1975:635). Interest Act applies unless otherwise agreed or stipulated.

There is no liability to pay interest on debts before due date. If a definite date of payment is agreed in advance and payment is not made in due time, debtor becomes liable for interest from due date. If no date is agreed, interest is payable after 30 days have elapsed from day when creditor claimed payment and stated that claim includes interest. In case of damages, interest is payable 30 days from day when payee claimed damages and presented a statement of facts which reasonably enables payor to consider claim. Irrespective of 30 days period, interest is payable from date of service of lawsuit.

Rate of interest is current official discount of Bank of Sweden plus eight percentage points.

JOINT STOCK COMPANIES: See topic Corporations.

JUDGMENTS:

Foreign judgments cannot be enforced in Sweden unless expressly authorized by Swedish law, and such authorization exists only in a few cases. For example, certain judgments of Danish, Norwegian, Finnish and Icelandic courts can be enforced in Sweden in accordance with Act 1977:595. Foreign judgments based on rules of international conventions concerning merchandise transported by rail, etc. are enforceable in Sweden. (Act 1985:193). Sweden has ratified 1988 Lugano Convention enabling enforcement in Sweden of judgments from EU or EFTA countries. (Act 1992:794). Foreign arbitral awards are enforceable in Sweden pursuant to 1958 New York Convention. Application for recognition is submitted to Svea Court of Appeal.

LABOR RELATIONS:

Protection of Employment.—(Act 1982:80). Employee is granted a basic protection of his employment. Dismissal must be preceded by efforts of transferring employee to another job. Dismissal requires objective cause. Lack of jobs and personal misbehavior may be objective cause. Employee generally has right to remain at work until dispute about dismissal has been settled. Minimum period of notice is one month. Period increases with age of employee.

EC Directive on transfer of undertakings, business or parts of business, has been adopted. Buyer will assume seller's responsibilities in respect of employees transferred. Buyer is responsible also for obligations of seller with exception of pension claims.

Labor Unions Right to Co-determination.—(Act 1976:580).

Right of Negotiations.—(1) Employer bound by collective agreement to trade union: Before employer decides concerning important change of activity, employer must on his own initiative summon to negotiations with trade union. Same applies if employer wants to carry out important change of working or employment conditions for trade union members. At request of trade union, employer must also in other cases negotiate with union before issuing decision which affects members of union; (2) employer not bound by collective agreement: If employer's decision particularly concerns working

LABOR RELATIONS . . . *continued*
or employment conditions of employees who are trade union members, employer must negotiate with trade union to same extent as mentioned under (1).

Right of Information.—Employer shall keep trade union to which he is bound by collective agreement continuously informed of development of production and economy of his business and also of guidelines for his personnel policy.

European Works Council.—(Act 1996:359). Sweden has implemented EC Council Directive on purpose of informing and consulting employees of community-scale undertakings. (Council Directive 94/95/EC).

Hours of Labor.—Normal working week is legally fixed at maximum of 40 hours, subject however to exceptions under special circumstances, in certain occupations or agreed by collective agreements, etc. Overtime up to 200 hours annually is allowed.

Child Labor.—Children under 13 may not be employed at all, and special rules govern employment of children under 18.

Wages and salaries are preferred claims in case of bankruptcy and are guaranteed by state up to certain maximum. Setting off claims on employees against wages and salaries is prohibited without employee's consent, unless claim concerns compensation for deliberate damage caused in employer's service. Employee is granted full wage during notice period irrespective of reason of dismissal.

Vacation.—Twenty-five days, excluding Sats., Suns. and holidays, paid annual vacation is compulsory by law.

Workmen's compensation for accidental injuries and occupational diseases is legally prescribed, premiums to be paid by employers.

Health insurance providing free hospitalization, including cost of operations and other services, and doctors fees is legally prescribed, premiums to be paid partly by individual, partly by employers.

Pension.—Old age pension regardless of income (AFP) and supplementary pension based on earned income (ATP) are legally prescribed for everybody at age 65. These pension schemes include preretirement disability pension and survivors pension.

Group life insurance under private agreement is generally granted to industry employees, premiums paid by employers.

Unemployment insurance is voluntary and run by government-approved subsidized associations, initiated by labor unions, premiums included in union fees.

Labor Organizations.—Swedish labor is highly unionized, and labor unions are united into Confederation of Swedish Trade Unions (LO). Salaried employees are organized into Central Organization of Salaried Employees (TCO). Wages, salaries and other employment benefits are normally subject to industry-wide collective bargaining between said organizations and Swedish Employers Confederation (SAF).

Labor disputes concerning employment agreements are generally settled by Labor Court. Where no collective agreement applies, disputes shall be brought before District Court of first instance, with right of appeal to Labor Court.

There is no appeal against decree of Labor Court.

Foreign Employers' Obligation to Pay Social Security Charges.—In principle, foreign employers pay mandatory social security with 33.06% (1996) for employees performing services in Sweden. But obligation is conditional for employees sent to Sweden for restricted period. If employee shall stay in Sweden less than 12 months, there is no obligation to pay social security. If stay is intended to exceed 12 months, employer becomes liable to pay social security unless treaties reduce such liability. Sweden has treaties with several countries, including USA. Employees resident in Sweden taking employment with foreign employer may assume employer's liability to pay social security fees. See topic Taxation.

LAW REPORTS: See topic Reports.

LEGISLATURE:

See topic Constitution and Government.

LICENSES:

See topics Aliens; Exchange Control; Foreign Trade Regulations.

LIENS:

The principal cases involving liens are as follows:

(1) A seller has a lien on merchandise for any costs, for example, for storage arising because of buyer's delay. Similar right accrues to a buyer in case the purchase contract is cancelled and he is entitled to damages from the seller. (Sale of Goods Act 1990:931).

(2) Whoever has repaired goods has a lien thereon for remuneration.

(3) Commission merchants, commission agents and factors, and commercial travelers have lien as to goods, samples, patterns and similar property not intended for sale. (Act 1914:45 and 1991:351).

LIMITATION OF ACTIONS:

No action for collection of debts may be started ten years after the date the debt arose. However for consumer credits time limit is three years. These periods are prolonged by informal reminder to debtor, by debtor acknowledging debt, or by creditor commencing action against debtor, whereupon new period commences. (Act 1981:130).

Certain damage claims arising out of injury incurred in transport by (i) road or rail and (ii) sea or air, are in general barred after period of three and two years respectively (see topic Death, subhead Action for Death).

Shorter periods apply to complaints of legatees and taxation claims.

Agreement that claim shall not be barred by limitation, or that consumer credit limitation shall be extended over three years is invalid.

If a settlement of all of a person's debts may be desirable, for example in connection with a debtor's death, divorce, declaration of incapacity, liquidation of corporations, associations, etc., it is possible upon application to the court to secure an order addressed to unknown creditors. This is an order which is published by the court to unknown creditors that, unless they file their claims within six months, the claims will be barred. (Act 1981:131).

MARRIAGE:

(Marriage Code of 1987). Marriage before age of 18 requires permission by Provincial Government. Further obstacles to marriage are consanguinity or existing marriage.

Before marriage can take place nupturients have to apply to civil registry for an investigation to be made of obstacles to marriage. Application must be accompanied by nupturients' declaration in writing that no obstacles exist. Wedding must be performed by ministers, judges or person holding a license.

MONOPOLIES AND RESTRAINT OF TRADE:

Legislation regarding monopolies, antitrust and restraint of trade is contained in Competition Act (1993:20). Act mirrors EU competition rules and prohibits all agreements between undertakings, decisions by associations of undertakings and concerted practices which have as their object or effect prevention, restriction or distortion of competition in Swedish market. Act also prohibits abuse of dominant position. Agreements, decisions or provisions therein which are prohibited pursuant to aforesaid are automatically void. Act makes it possible to exempt either individually or by category certain agreements between undertakings, and for this purpose there are nine group exemptions, eight of which are more or less identical with those adopted under EU competition rules regarding exclusive distribution and purchasing agreements, specialization agreements, research and development agreements, patent license agreements, know-how license agreements, franchise agreements and motor vehicle distribution and servicing agreements. Ninth group exemption concerns chains in retail market for purpose of making it possible for them to cooperate with regard to joint purchase and marketing etc. Competent authorities under Act are Competition Authority, Market Court and Stockholm District Court.

Act provides for merger control and compulsory notification of all acquisitions of companies where parties (buyer's group and target) have aggregate worldwide annual turnover in excess of SEK 4 billion. Competition Authority can grant "negative clearance" for practices that do not infringe prohibitions. Competition Authority has extensive power of investigation, and Stockholm District Court may grant Competition Authority power to make on-the-spot investigations at undertakings. Certain decisions by Competition Authority may be appealed to Stockholm District Court, and certain awards and decisions by latter may be appealed to Market Court.

MORTGAGES:

Mortgages on real estate to secure payment of a claim are obtained upon owner's application to court in district where real estate is located. Court issues mortgage certificate of sum certain, which is used as security and pledged to mortgagee. Court maintains public register in which mortgages are recorded and anyone may obtain extract from this register regarding existing mortgages, involving any particular piece of real property. In general mortgage first applied for has a prior right to succeeding applications. If debt secured by mortgage is not paid when due, mortgagee may through intervention of appropriate officials have property sold at public auction and receive payment from proceeds. (Execution Code 1981, c. 12).

See also topic Bankruptcy.

Chattel Mortgages.—See topic Pledges.

MOTOR VEHICLES:

Motor vehicles must be officially examined and registered. Only persons over 18 years of age and who have passed certain tests may drive motor vehicles. Every motor vehicle owner is obliged to take out and maintain traffic insurance which grants right to indemnity from insurance compulsory to driver, passengers or third party for damages as result of vehicle's operation. (Act 1975:1410).

NEGOTIABLE INSTRUMENTS:

See topic Bills and Notes.

NOTARIES PUBLIC:

(Act 1981:1363).

Notaries public exist in most cities and may practice also elsewhere. Services of notaries public are not as commonly used in Sweden as in U.S. and some other countries. Notaries public do not administer oath.

See topic Evidence.

PARTNERSHIP:

General Partnership (Handelsbolag).—Act 1980:1102.

General partnership is at hand when two or more individuals or corporate bodies for purpose of conducting commercial business meet agreement of doing business in form of association. Partners are without limitation, jointly and severally liable for debts of partnership.

Formation.—No special form is required. Legal existence begins with conclusion of partnership agreement and entry into commercial register.

Firm Name.—The firm name of a general partnership must include either the names of all the partners or of one or more partners and indicate that a partnership exists.

Partners Inter Sese.—The relations between the partners are determined by the partnership agreement and by the Act.

The Relation of the Partnership and the Partners to Third Persons.—A general partnership may under its firm name acquire rights, incur liabilities, sue and be sued. The partnership is liable for damages caused by a partner when acting for the partnership.

In order to be valid with relation to third persons, restrictions as to the representation of the partnership must be entered in the commercial register. A partner may only be deprived of his right to represent the partnership for serious reasons.

The partners are personally and jointly liable with their entire property for the liabilities of the partnership. A new partner is liable for preexisting liabilities of the

See Topical Index in front part of this volume.

PARTNERSHIP . . . *continued*
partnership. Bankruptcy of the general partnership does not involve bankruptcy of the individual partners, nor vice versa. In order to receive satisfaction or security for their claims, the personal creditors of a partner may attach only his remuneration, share of the profit including interest on capital, and his share of the partnership assets. A partner is not responsible for liabilities of the partnership after his retirement, if the retirement was known to the creditor. The commercial register must be advised of the retirement of a partner, and the fact published in certain newspapers as laid down in the Act. When this has been done, third persons are presumed to know of the retirement.

Dissolution.—With certain exceptions, the partnership is dissolved when the time agreed for its duration is terminated or upon six months notice given by one of the partners. The partnership shall immediately be dissolved upon request of a partner, if another partner substantially does not fulfill his obligation according to partnership agreement or if there is any other important ground for dissolution. Partnership shall immediately be dissolved upon death of partner or if partner becomes bankrupt. Liquidation is attended to by partners having right to act for partnership; upon application by partner and existence of serious reasons, court may appoint special liquidators. Court may remove liquidator at any time, but the liquidator must be removed upon request of all partners.

General and limited partnership (kommanditbolag) is a contractual association of two or more individuals or corporate bodies for the purpose of conducting commercial, industrial or other business. In this form of partnership at least one of partners, however not foundation or nonprofitmaking association, is liable without limitation for debts of partnership, and one or more partners (limited partners, kommanditdelägare) are liable for debts of partnership up to agreed amount.

Formation.—Similar to general partnership.

Firm Name.—The firm name of a general and limited partnership must include the word "kommanditbolag." Otherwise the same rules as for the firm name of a general partnership are applicable.

Partners Inter Sese.—The relations between the partners are determined by the partnership agreement and as a complement to the agreement by the rules of the Act. As a rule the limited partners are not allowed to take part in the management of the partnership.

The Relation of the Partnership and the Partners to Third Persons.—The limited partners are not allowed to represent the partnership. An agreement is not binding for the partnership if the partnership was represented by a limited partner without power of attorney and the limitation was known to the contracting partner.

Dissolution.—Similar to general partnership.

Ordinary partnership (enkelt bolag) is at hand when two or more individuals or corporate bodies for purpose of conducting business meet agreement of doing business in form of association and it is not general partnership. Ordinary partnership may not have firm name under which it can acquire rights and assume obligations. It may as such not sue or be sued; partners may, however, apply for registration in commercial register and partnership is then to be considered as general partnership.

Formation.—No special form is required.

Partners Inter Sese.—All partners participate jointly in the management. Urgent measures may, however, be taken without the participation of all partners if a delay would cause damage.

The Relation of the Partnership and the Partners to Third Persons.—If the partnership agreement does not provide otherwise, the creditors of a partner can execute only his share of the partnership, but the partners are jointly liable for liabilities entered into by the partners or their representative.

Dissolution.—In principal, the dissolution of an ordinary partnership follows the same stipulations as for the dissolution of a general partnership.

PATENTS:

(Act 1967:837). Patent may be granted for invention which can be utilized in industry provided it is distinctly different from what is known on day of application. Patent may be secured only by inventor or by his heirs or assignees. Foreign inventors must have a representative resident in Sweden.

When patent is granted, it is registered and published by Patent Office in print with description of invention. Anyone may file written objections within nine months after patent is granted. As a rule, patents are granted for a period of 20 years from date of application if same has been filed after June 1, 1966. In addition to certain fees in connection with application, annual fees increasing successively are payable in order to maintain patent.

If patent is not exercised to a considerable extent within four years of application, or three years of its being granted, whichever occurs later, court may upon application by any other party grant a compulsory license for applicant to use patent on terms and conditions determined by court. Compulsory license under a patent may also be granted to holder of patent which cannot be utilized without such license. Compulsory license may further be granted for business use if warranted by important social reasons, and also to anybody who used an invention professionally when made object of patent application.

Sweden is a party to revised International Patent and Trademark Convention of June 2, 1934, Patent Cooperation Treaty of June 19, 1970 and European Patent Convention of Oct. 5, 1973. It is thus possible to apply for both national and European patent.

Design Patents.—(Act 1970:485). Design patent can be obtained through registration provided that design is new, i.e., not earlier published and essentially different from other designs known on day of application, and intended for industrial or handicraft manufacture. Protection is granted in different classes for a maximum of three periods of each five years. Effect of Design Patent is that copy or imitation of design for professional use in class where design has been registered is reserved to patentee.

Sweden is a party to revised Paris Union of 1883 regarding industrial copyright. See also topic Copyright.

PLEDGES:

Chattels are pledged through surrender by the proprietor of immediate possession through delivery to pledgee. As regards chattels in possession of a third party delivery is replaced by notification to third party either informally by pledger or by pledgee through service of a copy of the document of charge. To avoid cumbersome formalities such document should always provide that if debtor is in default pledgee is entitled to realize the pledge and satisfy his claim from proceeds. (Commerical Code, c. 10).

Ships and aircraft may be mortgaged through registration in court of a promissory note for a sum certain, containing a grant by registered owner of a specified ship or aircraft of right to treat it as security for note.

Related right—business mortgage (företagshypotek)—can be created by tradesmen or companies as floating charge. Business mortgage is created in assets of business comprising inventory, accounts receivable, goods in stock and other company assets; however not in cash, banking accounts, corporate stock or assets which can be subject to real estate mortgage, or mortgage in ships or aircraft, or such assets that cannot be subject to execution pursuant to Execution Act. Mortgage is obtained upon owner's application to central authority, mortgage certificate is issued of sum certain which certificate entitles to priority in case of distraint or bankruptcy. Holder of note may claim immediate payment if business is transferred or deteriorates. Business mortgage can be granted only in business conducted within Sweden.

A proviso that a pledge given for fulfilment of an obligation shall be forfeited if the obligation is not properly met is invalid.

See also topics Mortgages; Bankruptcy; Executions.

PRESCRIPTION:

See topic Limitation of Actions.

PRINCIPAL AND AGENT:

Power of Attorney.—(Act 1915:218).

Anyone who holds himself out as having a power of attorney is responsible for such a statement and is therefore liable to damages against a third party in case the principal is not liable. In principle a legal act is not binding for the principal against the third party after the latter knows or should have known that the holder of the power of attorney exceeded his authority.

If the principal dies, the power of attorney normally remains effective. If a principal is legally declared incapable of dealing with his affairs, any legal act by the agent has no more effect than if it had been done by the principal. If the principal is declared bankrupt, a third party is not entitled to any rights in the bankruptcy based on any legal act of the agent. (Act 1915:218).

A power of attorney authorizing legal proceedings may be made either orally before the court or by a written document. (Court Procedure Code, c. 12). Such power of attorney may, under certain circumstances, be given by telegram.

Written power of attorney is always required in cases of transferring or mortgaging real estate.

Commercial Agency.—(Act 1991:351). Commercial agent is defined as party who in business relationship has agreed with another party, principal, to effect sale or purchase of goods by procuring offers on behalf of principal or entering into agreements in name of principal.

Most of legal provisions are mandatory to benefit of agent, e.g. provision prohibiting evasion of protection of agent by choice of foreign law.

If rate of commission has not been agreed, agent is entitled to commission at rate customary in agent's area of operations, or else reasonable considering overall circumstances. In certain instances agent is entitled to subsequent commission on business deals concluded after termination of agency.

Minimum period of notice of termination of indefinite term agreement is one month if agency has lasted less than a year, extended by one month per commenced year, up to six months.

Agent is entitled to reasonable severances, maximum one year's commission, upon termination if agent has provided new customers or substantially increased business with existing customers.

Either party is entitled to damages in case of failure by other party to fulfil his contractual or legal obligations, unless he can prove that failure is not due to negligence.

Agent is not bound by noncompetition clause beyond two years after termination of agency.

Swedish law is in conformity with EC Directive on Commercial Agents of Dec. 18, 1986.

Commission Agency.—(Act 1914:45, as am'd). Commission agent is defined as party who has agreed to sell or purchase goods or securities or other personal property on behalf of another party, but in his own name. Act contains less mandatory provisions for protection of commission agent, as compared to Commercial Agency Act.

PRODUCT LIABILITY:

Product liability is governed by Product Liability Act (1992:18) ("PLA") which is based on 1985 EEC Directive (85/374) on product liability. PLA applies to personal injuries caused by all products that are defective, along with damages caused by defective product to property intended mainly for consumer use, but not to any other property.

PLA establishes presumption of liability for persons listed below of products which were defective when put into circulation. Liable under PLA are: manufacturer, producer or collector of defective product; person who has imported defective product to European Economic Area ("EEA"); subject to Brussels and Lugano conventions, person who for purpose of putting product into circulation has imported it from EFTA-state to EU or vice versa, or from EFTA-state to another EFTA state; person who has marketed product as his by putting his name or trademark or other characteristic on it.

Presumption of liability can only be overturned if person liable under PLA proves that he did not put product into circulation within framework of any business; makes it probable that defect which caused damage did not exist at time when product was put into circulation by him; proves that defect is due to compliance of product with

PRODUCT LIABILITY . . . *continued*
mandatory regulations issued by public authorities; or proves that scientific and technical knowledge at time when product was put into circulation was not such as to enable defect to be discovered.

Liability is strict, i.e. plaintiff need not show any fault on part of persons liable under PLA, nor any contractual relationship with these persons but only that product causing damage was not as safe as could reasonably have been expected. Where liability of persons liable under PLA cannot be established, each of them shall be liable unless any of them, within one month after claim or request for such identification has been put forward by injured person, identifies liable person. Same shall apply, in case of import to EEA and EFTA states as outlined above, if product does not indicate identity of importer.

PLA is mandatory to benefit of claimant. Standard provision limiting sellers liability for injuries or damages caused by product can therefore not prevent end-user from suing persons liable under PLA.

Statute of limitations on product liability claims is three years from time when claimant became aware or should have become aware of possibility of stating claim but not later than ten years after defective product was put into circulation by person liable under PLA.

See also topic Damages.

REAL PROPERTY:

Real property is the land and what pertains thereto, such as buildings, permanent improvements, fences, trees, manure, etc. To a building pertains in general anything necessary for continued use of building. To factory building pertains machinery and other equipment brought to property to be used in activity there. Vehicles, office equipment and hand tools do not, however, pertain to real property. If ground and building have different owners then latter is personal property. (Real Property Code 1970).

See also topics Aliens; Mortgages; Records.

RECORDS:

Every court of first instance maintains a register in which all transfers of ownerships, changes of mortgages, etc., are entered. Every transfer of real estate must be recorded in register. Fact of seller's registration combined with buyer's good faith generally gives buyer a good title, except in cases of grave irregularity, such as forgery, duress, etc. (Real Property Code 1970).

Land registers referred to above are public documents and correctness of entries are guaranteed by state. Certified abstracts from register can be obtained on application.

In addition to the land register mentioned above there are a number of other registers, for example, trade register, association register, corporation register, marriage register, ship register, patent register, trademark register, etc.

REPORTS:

Judgments of Supreme Court from year 1874 are to be found in "Nytt Juridiskt Arkiv," Section I, and of Supreme Administrative Court ("Regeringsrätten") from year 1909 in its yearbook "Regeringsrättens Arsbok." Complete records of decisions of lower courts do not exist, but certain important judgments of courts of second instance are published in "Svensk Juristtidning" and, since 1980, in "Rättsfall från Hovrätterna".

SALES:

(Sale of Goods Act 1990). Act applies to sale and exchange of chattels and to contracts for goods to be manufactured, unless otherwise agreed, or usage of trade or previous course of dealing between parties prevails. Stipulations below are non-mandatory.

Consideration is no prerequisite for validity of contract. Offer is binding. Buyer shall pay what is reasonable and when seller demands, but not until goods are delivered and examined. Delivery shall be made at seller's place of business or residence. if seller shall transport goods, delivery is made when buyer receives goods, or if transport to other place when left to carrier. Performance shall be made within reasonable time. Either party may withhold performance until performance by other party is tendered. Risk of loss passes on delivery.

Delay in performance by seller may entitle buyer to claim specific performance, if not unreasonable, or to cancel contract and, in both cases, claim damages. Cancellation applies only if breach is major or after expiration of additional period of time of reasonable length, fixed by demanding party. Buyer must notify seller of cancellation and claim damages within reasonable time.

Goods are defective if not in conformity with contract. Goods shall be fit for ordinary purpose, for particular purpose made known to seller, be in accordance with sample, and be ordinarily packaged. Goods are also defective if not in conformity with given information in advertisement or elsewhere before sale. If goods are sold "as is" they are considered defective if not in conformity with given information, seller has neglected to inform or goods are considerably worse than expected. Defective goods entitle buyer to claim reparation, delivery of substitute goods or price reduction, or to cancel contract. Buyer may also claim damages. Requirements for cancellation same as for delay. Buyer must give seller notice of defect when discovered or should have been discovered. If third party on reasonable grounds claims right to goods, buyer can exercise rights as if goods were defective. Buyer who prior to sale was offered opportunity to examine goods has no right of action in respect of discoverable defects. In all other cases buyer is liable to examine goods on receipt. Right of action in respect of defect expires two years after receipt of goods unless otherwise guaranteed.

If buyer does not pay or cooperate to fulfilment of contract, seller has right to perform or cancel contract. Seller must notify buyer of intention to perform without unreasonable delay. Right to cancel for late payment is contingent on buyer's major breach of contract or failure to fulfil payment after expiration of reasonable additional time fixed by seller. If goods are in buyer's possession, seller may not cancel for nonpayment.

Party is responsible for direct damages when delay or defect is not beyond his control. Consequential damages are rewarded only when party is negligent or guarantee is given.

If buyer fails to take delivery when tendered, seller is liable to keep goods but must re-sell perishable goods. Same applies to buyer in respect of rejected goods in his possession. Keeper of goods is entitled to reimbursement of expenses and has corresponding lien on goods. In case of buyer's insolvency, seller has right of stoppage in transit.

Warranties.—Sale implies warranty of freedom from defect and warranty of title to goods. Act is silent regarding warranty of freedom from charge in favor of third party arising from infringement of patent or other intangible right.

Conditional sales of goods are held valid vis-à-vis third parties without any further notice provided that seller has expressly reserved title to the goods. Conditional sale is generally combined with payment by instalments. (Acts of 1978:599 and 1992:830). Acts provide certain protection to buyer, even if agreed otherwise between parties, in connection with seller's right to take back goods in case buyer fails to fulfill his obligations.

Consumer Sales Act (1990:932) grants to consumers certain basic rights when buying goods for private use if goods are delayed or defective. Stipulations in act correspond to Sale of Goods Act with important difference that consumer cannot be deprived of these rights by contract.

Consumer Protection.—Marketing Practices Act (1995:450). Act applies to marketing of goods, services, real property and other objects of marketing including job opportunities. Act applies to measures to promote both sales and purchases. Marketing measures that violate good marketing practice are prohibited. Act imposes stringent requirement of truthfulness for advertising and other marketing. Court or Consumer Ombudsman may forbid tradesman to continue marketing measures that violates good marketing practice, and to continue marketing products for consumer use which are unfit for their purpose. Tradesman may be ordered to give information of importance to consumers. Tradesman that violates Act with intent or negligence may be imposed market disruption charge. Tradesman can also be ordered to pay damages to consumers or to other tradesmen.

Acts of unfair contract clauses (1994:1512 and 1984:292) prohibit traders to use contract clauses which are considered unfair to consumers or traders.

Door-to-door Sales Act (1981:1361) stipulates that such sales must be concluded in certain way. Consumer has unconditional right to withdraw from contract within one week unless purchase is below SEK 300. Act does not apply to sale of food or financial instruments such as shares and bonds.

Product Liability Act (1992:18) is aimed at compensation for damages caused by defective products. Act allows compensation for damage in cases of personal injury and damage to other property mainly used for personal purpose. Act does not cover compensation for damage on defective product itself.

International Sales.—(Act 1964:528, based on Haag Convention 1951 on Law Applicable to International Sales of Goods). Unless application of other law is agreed between parties, law of seller's country applies. But law of buyer's country applies if contract is concluded there. According to Act on International Sales (1987:822) arts. 1-13 and 25-88 on UN Convention 1980 on Contracts for the International Sale of Goods have been adopted as part of Swedish law.

In respect of examination of goods and consequential notices, as well as steps to be taken if goods are rejected, law of country where examination shall take place applies.

Act does not refer to sales of ships, aircraft or securities, nor to sales instrumental in enforcement of court decisions, and does not deal with parties' legal capacity, form of contract or contract's effect on third parties.

SEALS:

Swedish law contains no provisions concerning seals. They do not have any effect on the legality of documents.

SEQUESTRATION: See topic Attachment.

SHIPPING:

(Maritime Act 1994:1009). Ship is considered Swedish and entitled to carry national flag if it is at least half owned by Swedish citizen or by Swedish legal entity. Exemption may be granted by Government or by National Maritime Administration.

Vessel at least 12 meters long and four meters wide is defined as "ship" and is registered in Register of Ships kept by Stockholm City Court. Other vessels are defined as "boats" and are registered in Register of Boats also kept by Stockholm City Court, but only if used in professional trade.

Owner's liability is maximum 175,000 Special Drawing Rights (SDR) for personal injury per passenger or, in case of limited liability, 46,666 SDR per passenger, but maximum 25 MSDR. For cargo, maximum liability is 167,000 SDR for vessels under 500 tonnage plus 167 SDR for each tonnage up to 30,000 tonnage, 125 SDR for 30,001-70,000 tonnage and 83 SDR for tonnage over 70,000. Tonnage follows definition in convention for uniform system of tonnage measurement of ships.

Certain claims are secured by lien on ship and cargo, such as wages of officers and crew, salvage awards, damages for collision and debts incurred by master for protecting ship and continuing voyage.

Carrier is liable for damage for period goods is in carrier's custody. Bill of Lading issued by master is regarded as signed by carrier.

Sweden is party to International Convention on collissions between vessels (Brussels, 1910); International Convention on salvage (London, 1989); and Convention on Limitation of Liability for maritime claims (London, 1976); York-Antwerp Rules 1994; International Convention on Civil Liability for Oil Pollution Damage (London, 1992); and International Convention concerning Bills of Lading (1924) and Supplementary protocol of 1968 (Hague-Visby Rules).

Sweden is not party to 1978 UN Convention on Carriage of Goods by Sea (The Hamburg Rules). However, some of Hamburg Rules apply by law.

See Topical Index in front part of this volume.

STATUTES:

Swedish law is very largely based on a codification made in the year 1734. The greater part of this codified law has now been superseded by more modern laws, reference to the most important of which is made in this digest.

TAXATION:

Individuals are liable to income tax when resident in Sweden, on all income arising there or abroad (unrestricted tax liability), when nonresident in Sweden, on income of business activities in Sweden and employment performed in Sweden and paid by Swedish employer, and on profits from sale of real estate in Sweden and on profits from sale of Swedish securities (restricted tax liability).

There are three categories of income: income of employment, income of business and income of capital. Individuals are liable to tax derived from all three sources. Income from business and employment is subject to municipal and national income tax. Individuals' income from capital is subject to national income tax only.

Municipal income tax is proportional, ranging between 26 and 34%. National income tax is levied on income of individuals derived from employment, business and capital. This tax is payable on income from employment and business exceeding SEK 209,000 p.a. in total at rate of 25%.

Individuals' income from capital is taxable at flat rate of 30%. Capital gains and dividends related to closely held corporations are treated differently.

Corporations are subject only to national income tax, at flat rate of 28% on income from all sources. Corporations are, in principle, not subject to tax on dividends from subsidiaries, Swedish or foreign.

National Net Wealth Tax.—Following are liable to net wealth tax: (a) Individuals residing in Sweden, unsettled estates of decedents who at time of death were residents in Sweden, and legal entities whose members on account of their membership do not own share in property of legal entity; (b) individuals not residing in Sweden, unsettled estates of decedents who at time of death were not residents in Sweden, and foreign corporations to extent that they have capital invested in Sweden. Wealth tax is assessed at proportional rate of 1.5% on net assets exceeding SEK 800,000.

Coupon tax on dividends from shares in Swedish corporations is payable by individuals domiciled abroad and foreign legal entities; tax is levied at collection of dividend. Tax is reduced under tax treaties.

Swedish corporations do not pay national wealth tax. Partnerships are not subject to income or wealth tax, but partners are subject to tax on shares of partnership's income and net value.

Losses may be carried forward without any limitation in time. Loss must be utilized first year net surplus occurs. Right to loss carried forward is restricted in case of change of ownership of company with accrued loss.

Payment of Taxes.—Municipal and national income taxes and national wealth tax are payable on basis of preliminary assessment during income year. In subsequent year final assessment is raised on basis of tax return made by taxpayer at close of income year.

Value Added Tax.—VAT is payable on all commercial sales of goods and services, including rental, repair and maintenance. Tax paid is deductible until final consumption. Every seller or importer is liable taxpayer. Three tax rates apply, 6%, 12% and 25% depending on nature of goods and services.

Payroll Tax.—See subhead Social Security Taxes, infra.

Social Security Taxes.—Employer is charged social security taxes of 33.06% (1996) of gross salaries plus value of certain fringe benefits. Tax is deductible for income tax assessment. Social security taxes are charged also on foreign employers with employees performing services in Sweden. Social security conventions may reduce tax during limited period of time. Employee is charged with fee of 4.95% which is deductible for tax purposes. See topic Labor Relations.

International Tax Conventions.—Income tax conventions and death duty conventions exist between Sweden and Austria, Belgium, Denmark, Finland, France Germany, Great Britain and Northern Ireland, Hungary, Israel, Italy, The Netherlands, Norway, Spain, South Africa, Switzerland and USA.

Pure income tax conventions exist with Argentina, Australia, Bangladesh, Barbados, Belarussia, Belgium, Bolivia, Botswana, Brazil, Bulgaria, Canada, Cape Verde, China, Cyprus, Czech Republic, Egypt, Estonia, Gambia, Greece, Iceland, India, Indonesia, Ireland, Jamaica, Japan, Kenya, Latvia, Lithuania, Luxemburg, Malaysia, Malta, Mauritius, Mexico, Morocco, Namibia, New Zealand, Pakistan, Peru, The Philippines, Poland, Romania, The Russian Federation, Singapore, Slovakia, Sri Lanka, South Africa, South Korea, Tanzania, Thailand, Trinidad and Tobago, Tunisia, Turkey, Ukraine, Venezuela, Vietnam, Yugoslavia, Zambia and Zimbabwe.

Social security conventions exist between Sweden and Austria, Canada, Croatia, Denmark, Finland, France, Germany, Great Britain and Northern Ireland, Greece, Iceland, Israel, Italy, Luxemburg, Morocco, The Netherlands, Norway, Portugal, Slovania, Spain, Switzerland, Turkey, USA, and Yugoslavia.

TRADEMARKS:

(Act 1960:644). After written applications to competent authority, trademarks are protected by being registered in central register. Registration must be renewed every ten years. Exclusive right may also arise from use of trademark in manufacture, trade or other business in Sweden. Foreign owner of trademark must have representative resident in Sweden. Registered trademarks may be pledged by registration in central register.

1993 amendment of Trademark Act has extended possibilities of recognizing various devices as trademarks, protection of highly respected trademarks, and obligation to make use of trademarks.

Sweden is a party to the revised International Patent and Trademark Convention of June 2, 1934.

As EU member state, Sweden is also subject to Rules of Community Trademark Council Directive (EC) No. 40/94 of Dec. 20, 1993. These rules are added to Copyright Act.

TREATIES:

Sweden is party to Lugano Convention on Jurisdiction and Enforcement of Judgments in Civil and Commercial Matters, to Convention of Service Abroad of Judicial and Extrajudicial Documents in Civil or Commercial Matters, to Convention on the Recognition and Enforcement of Foreign Arbitral Awards, and to Convention on the Taking of Evidence Abroad in Civil or Commercial Matters. Act (1994:1500) on account of Sweden's membership EU law states treaties to which Sweden is party as member of EU. Sweden is not party to Convention Abolishing the Requirement of Legislation for Foreign Public Documents.

See also Selected International Conventions section for Selected Conventions to which U.S. and Sweden are parties.

International Sale of Goods.—United Nations Convention on Contracts for the International Sale of Goods, in force on Jan. 1, 1989. See topic Sales and Part VII, Selected International Conventions.

TRUSTS:

Trusts in meaning of law of equity are unknown to Swedish law, since there is no system of equity jurisprudence in Sweden. See topic Foundations.

WILLS:

(Inheritance Code of 1958). Person who is 18 years of age or over, or who is or has been married even though not 18 years of age may dispose of his or her property by will. Further person who has reached 16 years of age may dispose by will of his or her earned income.

To be valid a will must be made in writing and signed by the testator in the presence of two witnesses. If in case of emergency a will cannot be made in such a form, it is possible to make an oral disposition of property before two witnesses or a holograph document signed by the testator. Such emergency wills are not valid if during a succeeding period of three months the testator could have made a normal will. Alterations and codicils to wills must follow the rules set out above.

If a decedent, having direct heirs, gives away so much of his estate by will that amount which would be received by direct heirs is less than one-half of that to which they would be entitled under inheritance law, they are entitled to apply for alteration of will.

Only lives in being at testator's death and their heirs may take under will, latter to extent that legacy falls to them absolutely at death of ascendant or other legatee. Lives in being include child begotten at testator's death and born thereafter. No inequality may be stipulated between such children of same parent as are unborn or unbegotten at testator's death.

After death the legatees or the administrator or the executor, as case may be, must produce will to legal heirs. If legal heirs do not contest validity of will by starting legal proceedings against legatees within six months from date when will was produced to them terms of will become binding.

SWITZERLAND LAW DIGEST REVISER

Pestalozzi Gmuer & Patry
Loewenstrasse 1
Post Office Box 80 30 4
CH-8001 Zürich, Switzerland
Telephone: 41 1 217 91 11
Fax: 41 1 217 92 17
Email: pgpzh@access.ch
Geneva, Switzerland Office: 15, BD Des Philosophes, CH-1205. Telephone: 41 22 320 78 33. Fax: 41 22 320 43 41.
Brussels, Belgium Office: 165, Avenue Louise, B-1050. Telephone: 32 2 646 60 10. Fax: 32 2 646 75 34.

Reviser Profile

International commercial, corporate, tax and arbitration practice, industrial property and copyright. Fiscal, construction and administrative matters. Banking and financial law. Estate planning. Civil litigation, all Swiss Courts.

REVISERS OF THE SWITZERLAND LAW DIGEST FOR THIS DIRECTORY.

ZURICH
MEMBERS OF FIRM

Dr. Rudolf Heiz
Dr. Karl Arnold
Dr. Hans Bollmann
Dr. Pierre A. Karrer, LL.M.
Dr. Max Walter
Dr. Peter Pestalozzi
Dr. Urs Jordi
lic.iur. lic.oec. Christoph R. Ramstein
Dr. Marcus Desax, M.C.L.
Dr. Robert Furter
Dr. Silvia Zimmermann, LL.M.
Prof. Dr. Christian J. Meier-Schatz, LL.M.
Walter H. Boss, LL.M.
Dr. Silvan Hutter, LL.M.
Dr. Peter A. Straub, LL.M.
Dr. Jakob Höhn, LL.M.

OF COUNSEL

Dr. iur Dr. oec. Anton Pestalozzi
Dr. Paul Gmuer
Dr. Regula Pestalozzi
Prof. Dr. Markus Reich

ASSOCIATES

Dr. Thomas Meister
Dr. Christian A. Meyer
Dr. Thomas Rihm
lic.iur. Gerhard Niggli
lic.iur. Daniel Blättler

OF COUNSEL

Dr. Sibylle Pestalozzi-Früh
Dr. Anne-Catherine Imhoff-Scheier

GENEVA
MEMBERS OF FIRM

lic.iur. Jean Patry
lic.iur. Bernard Junet
lic.iur. Robert Simon
lic.iur. Alain Le Fort
lic.iur. Guy-Philippe Rubeli
lic.iur. François Dugast

ASSOCIATES

lic.iur. Christian Schilly
lic.iur. Denis Gobet
lic.iur. Cedric Aguet

SWITZERLAND LAW DIGEST

(The following is a list of all Topics, including cross-references, covered in this Digest.)

SWITZERLAND LAW DIGEST

Revised for 1997 edition by

PESTALOZZI GMUER & PATRY, of the Zurich and Geneva Bars.

(C.C. indicates Civil Code; C.O. indicates Code of Obligations.)

ABSENTEES:

If for reasons of absence a person of age (see topic Infants) cannot act in urgent matter nor designate representative, furthermore if property is not taken care of because person is continually absent with unknown abode or because of uncertainty as to heirs entitled to inheritance, curator (Beistand, curateur, curatore) is appointed by guardianship authority. (C.C. 392, point 1; 393, points 1 and 3; 548, subsection 1). See topics Death; Executors and Administrators, subhead Official Administrators of Estate.

Escheat.—Dividends subject to five years statute of limitations. Title to movables lost by abandonment only when coupled with intention to waive title. Estate passes to canton or municipality of last domicile of intestate decedent only if no grandparents or their issue survive.

ACKNOWLEDGMENTS AND OTHER PUBLIC AUTHENTICATIONS:

Publicly authenticated documents (Öffentliche Urkunde, acte authentique, atto pubblico) are of two kinds: (a) ordinary authentication, attestation or certification of facts by public officials, which include attestation of genuineness of a signature mostly based on acknowledgment by signing person (Beglaubigung, legalisation, autenticazione), and other certifications, e.g., as to conformity of copy with original, correctness of extract from document or register, etc., and (b) execution of publicly authenticated act or instrument by public official pertaining to legal relevant declarations of private persons.

Publicly authenticated documentations of all kinds provide full proof of facts evidenced but proof of incorrectness does not require special form. (C.C. 9).

Signature of blind person must be authenticated. (C.O. 14, 1085). All cantons have provisions for ordinary authentication of signatures or of other facts. Formal requirements of such ordinary authentications are within domain of cantonal law.

Form of publicly authenticated instrument is prescribed by federal law for validity of many legal acts of private law. (See topic Frauds, Statute of.) Inasmuch as federal law does not have pertinent provisions, as for matrimonial property contracts (C.C. 181), public wills (C.C. 499-503), inheritance pacts (C.C. 512), certain contracts of guaranty or of suretyship (C.O. 493), formal requirements for publicly authenticated instruments left to cantonal law (C.C. Final Title, 55). Authenticating person must make sure that instrument expresses true intention, and that it complies with formal requirements of federal or cantonal law.

Authenticating persons for ordinary authentications and/or publicly authenticated instruments are designated by cantonal law; in certain instances (e.g., civil status officers) within framework of federal law. These are notaries, judges, clerks of courts, mayors, clerks of municipalities or districts, special officials, sometimes private persons authorized to perform certain public authentications and insofar as to act as officials. See topic Notaries Public.

Signature of authenticating persons may be legalized, usually, but not always, directly by Chancellery of State of canton where person functions. Signature of that person may be superlegalized by Federal Chancellery in Berne, or by Swiss embassies or consulates abroad.

Switzerland is party to Convention for exemption of foreign public deeds from certification concluded in The Hague on Oct. 5, 1961, providing for "Apostille". See International Conventions section.

ACTIONS:

All actions must be brought before courts, with exception of summary, administrative procedures for collection of debts. See topic Collection of Debts and Bankruptcy.

Action is commenced in Switzerland when first procedural step is taken, such as conciliation procedure before justice of peace. Civil procedure is cantonal. Service of process is effectuated by courts, not by parties. Service of process for foreign proceedings must go through diplomatic channels and cannot be accomplished by Swiss lawyers. American lawyers may apply to local U.S. Consular Office in Switzerland for information. Brussels Convention applies, see topic Depositions and Discovery.

Swiss courts have judicial notice of foreign law but may in disputes of financial interest impose burden of proof on parties. If content of foreign law is unascertainable, Swiss law applies. Switzerland has joined European Convention July 7, 1968 on information on foreign law.

Limitation of.—See topic Limitation of Actions.

ADMINISTRATION:

See topic Executors and Administrators.

ADOPTION:

Adoption in Switzerland is governed by Swiss law unless to serious detriment of child it is not recognized in country of domicile or citizenship of adopting person or spouses.

Only a single person over 35 or spouses over 35 or whose marriage has lasted for more than five years may adopt another person who must be at least 16 years younger. (C.C. 264a-265). Adoptee, if capable of discernment, must consent and, if a minor or a person who has been placed under guardianship, parents or guardianship authorities must also consent. (C.C. 265-265d). Without consent of spouse no person can adopt or be adopted. Adoption is granted by competent authority at domicile of adopting person(s). (C.C. 268). Adoptee may take new name. Adoptee becomes adoptor's child and loses legal relationship to natural parents except to parent with whom adoptor is married. (C.C. 267). Only if adopted person is minor, does adoption by Swiss citizen convey Swiss citizenship. (C.C. 267a).

ADVOCATES AND COUNSELORS:

Admission to bar and regulation of profession is cantonal matter. Cantonal bar associations are private, but some exercise public function. Only persons called to Swiss bar may appear as lawyers in most court cases. Before Federal Supreme Court also professors of law at Swiss universities are admitted.

Generally, lawyers admitted to Swiss bar are called Avocats/Fürsprecher/Advokat/Rechtsanwalt/Avvocato. They are university graduates in law (licentiatus juris or doctor juris), have had at least one year's clerkship with court or apprenticeship in law firm and have taken cantonal bar examination.

Following bar associations will assist foreign attorney seeking local counsel: Swiss Federal Bar Association: Postfach 8321, 3001 Bern, Fax: 011 411 31 312 31 03; Bernischer Anwaltsverband, Beat Zürcher, Postfach 333, 3000 Bern 7, Fax: 011 411 31 312 28 20; Ordre des Avocats de Genève, Dr. Olivier Mach, Lenz & Staehelin, Case postale 429, 25, Grand-Rue, 1211 Genève 11, Fax: 011 411 22 319 06 00; Luzerner Anwaltsverband, Töpferstrasse 5, 6004 Luzern, Tel.: 011 411 41 52 93 73; Solothurnischer Anwaltsverband, lic. iur. Urs Meyer, Kirchstrassse 99, 2540 Grenchen, Fax: 011 411 65 52 60 44; St. Gallischer Anwaltsverband, Dr. Adrian Rüesch, Unterer Graben 1, 9000 St. Gallen, Fax: 011 411 71 23 63 51; Ordine degli Avvocati del Cantone Ticino, Corso San Gottardo 54 c, Casella postale 358, 6830 Chiasso, Fax: 011 411 91 41 25 62; Ordre des Avocats Vaudois, M. Olivier Freymond, Reymond, Bonnard, Maire, Freymond, Tschumy, Case Postale 3633, 5, Rue du Grand-Chêne, 1002 Lausanne, Fax: 011 411 21 320 82 49; Verein Zürcherischer Rechtsanwälte, lic. iur. Kurt Zollinger, Talstrasse 20, 8001 Zürich, Fax: 011 411 1 221 18 73.

Confidentiality obligation extends to names of clients. No contingency fees allowed. No advertising. In some cantons law firms may include some nonlawyers or foreign lawyers not admitted to bar in partnership.

Foreign lawyers may represent their clients freely in negotiation and arbitration in Switzerland. They may not take up residence or employment without permit, nor represent parties in Swiss courts.

AGENCY: See topic Principal and Agent.

ALIENS:

Conflicts.—International jurisdiction, private international law and recognition and enforcement of foreign decisions, to extent not covered by Lugano Convention Sept. 16, 1988 or other international treaties, are governed by Private International Law Statute. It covers also international bankruptcy and international arbitration.

Foreign Citizens need residence permit; for gainful activity, also work permit. Easier for intragroup transferees. Temporary personnel, such as technicians or industrial workers also need work permits, unless they only come for few days as consultants. Trainees need temporary permits. No tourist visa is necessary for nationals of many countries; for U.S. citizens, valid passport suffices. All foreigners must register with police after specified stay in Switzerland.

From Nov. 1, 1993 till Oct. 31, 1994 nationwide only 17,000 permits could be granted to new immigrant foreign workers to be employed by private or public employers with specific cantonal and federal quotas. Permits are usually granted for one-year periods. Normally, immigrant may not change employer, profession or canton during first year. Most work permits are granted by cantons with consent of federal administration in Berne. Applications concerning exceptional cases involving national interest, scientific research and professional qualifications not found in Switzerland are handled by federal administration directly. Special rules apply to seasonal workers, trainees, "au pair" maids and other short-term workers. Regulations are very detailed and subject to yearly renewal.

"Central register of foreigners" is kept. In exceptional cases, addresses of aliens may be disclosed to foreign authorities or persons, e.g., if it appears that alien is going into hiding in Switzerland.

Aliens may vote by mail in foreign elections if foreign law so provides.

Corporations Owned or Controlled by Aliens.—See topics Immovable Property, subhead Acquisition by Nonresidents; Corporations, subhead Share Corporation, catchline Alien Shareholders; and Foreign Investment.

ARBITRATION AND AWARD:

International arbitration (where one party is non-Swiss) commenced before or after Jan. 1, 1989 is governed by Federal Private International Law Statute. If parties have chosen arbitration rules, these govern appointment, challenge and removal of arbitrators exclusively. Arbitral Tribunal rules on its own jurisdiction. Parties or Arbitral Tribunal choose procedure and applicable law freely. Assistance of state courts available, also for interim measures. Challenges of award may be totally excluded if both parties are non-Swiss, otherwise challenge (at best) only as in New York Convention on the Recognition and Enforcement of Foreign Arbitral Awards of June 10, 1958.

ICC or ad hoc arbitration in Geneva or Zurich is frequent; so is Zurich Chamber of Commerce Arbitration. Zurich Chamber also has conciliation and Mini-Trial rules. Geneva Chamber offers arbitration, fast-trade arbitration and conciliation.

Domestic arbitration in all cantons is governed by Concordat of Mar. 27, 1969. Switzerland is party to New York Convention of 1958. No reservations.

See Topical Index in front part of this volume.

ASSIGNMENTS:

Applicable Law.—Law chosen by assignor and assignee, with respect to obligor only with obligor's assent, otherwise law applicable to obligation. Form of assignment governed by law applicable to contract providing for assignment.

Assignability.—Obligations are assignable without obligor's assent, unless not permissible by law, agreement, or nature of legal relationship. Obligor may not raise defense that assignment of obligation was excluded by agreement, if third person has become obligee in good faith based on written acknowledgment of indebtedness which does not mention its unassignability. (C.O. 164).

Instrument Transferring Title.—Assignment must be in writing; but promise to assign need not be in writing. (C.O. 165).

Notice.—Validity of assignment does not depend on notice to obligor. However, obligor in good faith without notice of assignment is validly discharged if obligor performs to former obligee. (C.O. 167).

Delivery of Evidence.—Assignor must deliver to assignee any document pertaining to obligation and other proof which assignor has. (C.O. 170).

Effect.—Rights connected with obligation pass ipso iure to assignee, unless inseparably connected with assignor's person. (C.O. 170).

Warranty.—In case of assignment for valuable consideration assignor warrants existence of claim at time of assignment, but warrants solvency of obligor only if so agreed. In case of assignment without valuable consideration, assignor is not even liable for existence of claim. (C.O. 171).

Defenses of Obligor.—In addition to special defenses against assignee, obligor has all defenses against assignor (and former assignors), provided such defenses existed at time obligor learned of assignment (C.O. 169); obligor has also defenses pertaining to validity of assignment or previous assignments.

ASSOCIATIONS:

Associations for noneconomic or economic purposes may be created in various forms either by agreement or incorporation.

Associations by agreement include various forms of partnerships. See topic Partnerships. Corporate bodies are legal entities (juristische Personen, personnes morales, persone giuridiche). Legal entities are entitled to all rights and subject to all liabilities, except those arising out of human nature, such as sex, age, family relationship. As general rule, corporate bodies for economic purposes acquire legal capacity upon their entry in Register of Commerce. Those not needing registration acquire legal capacity as soon as organized according to law. (C.C. 52-59).

Legal entities include membership association, foundation, share corporation, limited liability corporation, cooperative corporation, and corporate bodies under federal, cantonal or local public law. See topic Corporations.

ATTACHMENT:

Constitutes provisional security measure under Federal Statute on Collection of Debts and Bankruptcy of Dec. 16, 1994, as amended, in order to protect creditor before effectuation of seizure in collection proceedings or bankruptcy. See topic Collection of Debts and Bankruptcy.

Prerequisites.—Allowable for money claims of private law including establishment of security by deposit of money. In case of claim secured by pledge or mortgage attachment is only admissible for noncovered amount of claim. Creditor may be individual or legal entity, residing in Switzerland or abroad. Any movable or immovable property of debtor in Switzerland may be attached.

Grounds are: (1) Debtor has no fixed domicile; (2) is suspected of evading obligations by flight or removal of assets; (3) in transit or at fair or market, but attachment is only for debts payable forthwith; (4)(a) no other attachment ground is given, (b) debtor has no domicile in Switzerland, (c) there is either sufficient connection with Switzerland or enforceable judicial award or acknowledgment of debt signed by debtor; (5) creditor has "Certificate of Loss" against debtor. Claim must be payable, except in case of grounds (1) or (2). Particular rules apply to attachments for claims against foreign countries.

Order to Attach.—Creditor has to file petition with competent attachment court (not arbitral tribunal) at place where property is located. Provided existence of claim and ground for attachment appear to be credible, authority issues "Order to Attach" pursuant to which attachment will be effectuated similarly to seizure and recorded in document of attachment. Debtor may contest ground of attachment by action to be brought before competent attachment court at place of attachment within ten days after cognizance of document of attachment.

Indemnity.—Creditor is liable for damages resulting from unjustified attachment. Therefore attachment court usually orders bond when granting attachment or it does so later.

Validation.—If creditor, has not previously instituted court action or collection proceedings for claim, creditor must institute collection proceedings within ten days after receipt of document of attachment. Unless Lugano Convention applies or specific jurisdiction has been agreed upon by parties, attachment creates forum for claims against nonresidents where creditor can sue. "Opposition" of debtor must be removed by creditor within ten days after communication by court action, arbitration, or by petition for "removal of opposition"; denial of removal of opposition must be met by court action within ten days after communication.

Alleged rights of third persons to attached property must be notified to Collection Office within certain time after knowledge of attachment, otherwise they are deemed to be renounced for attachment procedure. If notified such rights will be dealt with in separate court procedure.

If "Opposition" has not been declared or has been removed, creditor must continue collection proceedings, either by way of seizure or by bankruptcy against debtor. In case of seizure, attaching creditor has some preferential rights with regard to other creditors of debtor, namely, (a) creditor participates in seizure of attached property effectuated by other creditors after issuance of order to attach but before attaching creditor could request seizure provided creditor makes such request within certain period of time, and (b) creditor is entitled to recover expenses of attachment from proceeds of attached property. In case of bankruptcy attached property belongs to bankrupt estate and attaching creditor has no special preferential rights.

Release of property from attachment will be granted to the debtor against security which may, inter alia, also be given by joint guaranty or by deposit.

BANKRUPTCY:

See topic Collection of Debts and Bankruptcy.

BANKS AND BANKING:

Banks, bank-like finance companies, underwriters, and finance companies that publicly offer their services as depositories of money must comply with Federal Banking Statute of Nov. 8, 1934, as amended, and are subject to supervision of Federal Banking Commission. They alone are entitled to use word "Bank" in their firm name, advertisements, etc.

Swiss National Bank has specific powers to regulate Swiss currency. It may, for instance, fix limits and set mandatory reserves, require foreign currency liabilities to be covered by foreign currency assets in specific percentages and make prescriptions on public issues of shares, bonds and the like. Presently no significant measures in place.

Bank secrecy is safeguarded by special provision of law. However, federal and cantonal regulations on securing evidence in criminal cases take precedence.

Federal Statute on International Judicial Assistance in Criminal Matters of Mar. 20, 1981 allows granting specific assistance (such as supplying information and obtaining evidence) in cases of tax fraud. Under tax treaty with U.S. Swiss Federal Tax Administration may under specific preconditions obtain information (also from Swiss banks) for U.S. Internal Revenue Service in case of U.S. tax fraud and the like. Under treaty with U.S. on assistance in criminal matters court hearing witness decides under specific preconditions whether or not bank secrecy should be lifted.

Under Agreement on Swiss bank's code of conduct with regard to exercise of due diligence convention of Oct. 1, 1992 between Swiss Banker's Association and member banks, signatory banks undertake: (i) To verify identity of their contracting partners and, in cases of doubt, to obtain from contracting partner declaration setting forth identity of beneficial owner of assets entrusted to bank; (ii) not to provide any active assistance in flight of capital; and (iii) not to provide any active assistance in cases of tax evasion or similar acts, by delivering incomplete or misleading attestations. Agreement does not modify obligation to observe banking secrecy, it lays down rules of good conduct in bank management.

Foreign Banks.—Ordinance of Mar. 22, 1984, applies to opening branch office of foreign bank. This is subject to license of Federal Banking Commission. Foreign bank's home country must grant reciprocity. Branch office must maintain 10% of its assets in Switzerland. Home country supervisory authorities must advise Federal Banking Commission of circumstances endangering creditors' positions. Majority of managers must be residents of Switzerland. License may be subject to specific conditions.

Representatives of foreign banks not engaged in banking business need license and must report to Federal Banking Commission.

Acquisition of majority of shares of existing bank with Swiss ownership, acquisition of substantial part of shares of bank with foreign ownership and creation of new bank by foreigners is also subject to license of Federal Banking Commission. Preconditions include proof of reciprocal right in respective foreign area, and undertaking to comply with credit and foreign exchange policies of Swiss National Bank.

Investment funds (Anlagefonds) whose funds are obtained by offers to public must comply with Federal Statute of Mar. 18, 1994. It is only type of investment fund that may be designated as "Anlagefonds" or similar.

Distribution of shares in foreign investment funds requires specific license from Federal Banking Commission.

BILLS AND NOTES:

See topic Negotiable Instruments.

CHATTEL MORTGAGES:

Known in Swiss law only in very limited sense of pledging cattle, ships and aircraft by registration. See topic Pledges.

CITIZENSHIP:

Swiss citizenship derives from citizenship of one or more Swiss cantons; cantonal citizenship is intrinsically connected with citizenship of one or more municipalities (cities or villages) within that canton. (Federal Constitution Arts. 43-44, 54, 68 and Federal Statute on Acquisition and Loss of Swiss citizenship, of Sept. 29, 1952 as am'd Mar. 23, 1990), to make men and women equal with respect to acquisition and loss of citizenship after marriage and to citizenship of their children.

Governing principles for acquisition and loss of Swiss citizenship are jus sanguinis, preservation of unity of family, and equality between men and women. There is no acquisition of Swiss citizenship by jus soli in Swiss law.

Acquisition.—Inter alia by (a) birth of child in wedlock, if father or mother is Swiss (except by former marriage), or out of wedlock if mother is Swiss or if father is Swiss and marries mother after birth of foreign minor child; (b) naturalization of aliens; (c) reinstatement into Swiss citizenship of certain former Swiss citizens; (d) adoption of foreign minor child by Swiss citizen or by spouses one of which is Swiss (except by former marriage).

Naturalization by ordinary procedure may be granted by Swiss canton and municipality within that canton with preceding authorization of federal authorities. Applicant must as a rule have been domiciled in Switzerland for total of 12 years, three of them during last five years preceding application. Years between tenth and 20th birthday of applicant count twice. If one spouse fulfils conditions other can also apply for Swiss citizenship, if spouse has lived in Switzerland for total of five years, including year

CITIZENSHIP . . . *continued*

preceding application. Same rule applies to spouse of person who has already been granted naturalization in Switzerland.

Naturalization by facilitated procedure may be granted free by federal authorities, as rule with consent of canton, (a) to alien spouse of Swiss citizen if spouse has lived in Switzerland for total of five years, including year preceding application, and has been married to Swiss for three years; (b) to alien spouse of Swiss citizen who lives or has lived abroad if spouse has been married to Swiss for six years and if spouse is closely related to Switzerland; (c) to child being born before July 1, 1985 in wedlock to mother, Swiss of origin, naturalization or adoption, and alien father, if child lives in Switzerland and application is made before child turns 32; if child older than 32, its father must have lived in Switzerland for total of five years, including year preceding application; (d) to child born in wedlock to mother, Swiss by previous marriage, and alien father, if mother is related closely to Switzerland or if child lives in Switzerland and has lived there for total of six years; (e) to alien child of Swiss father out of wedlock if application is made before child turns 22, if child has been living in Switzerland for one year or has been living with father for one year or child has permanent close relation to father or if child is stateless.

Reinstatement into Swiss citizenship may be granted by federal authorities, as a rule with consent of canton, to Swiss woman who lost Swiss citizenship when marrying alien, and to Swiss citizen born abroad who lost Swiss citizenship at age 22 because of omission to register. See infra, subhead Multiple Citizenship.

Loss.—(a) If parental relationship to parent who has given Swiss citizenship is annulled; (b) by release from Swiss citizenship; (c) by expatriation, admissible only for double or multiple citizens, see subhead Multiple Citizenship, infra; (d) by adoption of Swiss minor child by foreigner if child thereby acquires nationality of foreigner or already possesses foreign nationality of adopting person.

Release from Swiss Citizenship.—Prerequisite is that person in question possesses or has reliably been assured citizenship of another country, is not domicilied in Switzerland, and is at least 20 years old. Granted by canton or cantons of which applicant is citizen.

Minor child of applicant who is under parental power is included in release, provided such child also has no domicile in Switzerland; child over 16 must consent in writing.

Multiple Citizenship.—Subject to above exceptions, Swiss citizen who by virtue of foreign law or by naturalization acquires one or more citizenships of foreign countries does not lose thereby Swiss citizenship (multiple citizenship). However, Swiss multiple citizen born abroad loses citizenship upon becoming 22, unless registered with Swiss authority in Switzerland or abroad or written declaration to keep Swiss citizenship was filed. Reinstatement into Swiss citizenship is possible within ten years in case of excusable reasons for omission of such notification or declaration. Furthermore, Swiss multiple citizen who seriously impairs interests or reputation of Switzerland may be deprived of Swiss citizenship by federal authorities with consent of canton.

For jurisdiction of Swiss court at place of origin, Swiss citizenship suffices. For applicable law, citizenship with which person has closest connection counts. For recognition and enforcement of foreign decisions in Switzerland any citizenship will do. (Art. 23 Private International Law Statute).

Military Service.—See topic Treaties.

CLAIMS:

See topics Actions; Executors and Administrators.

COLLECTION OF DEBTS AND BANKRUPTCY:

Collection of Debts.—Collection of money claims including establishment of security by deposit of money is regulated by Federal Statute concerning Collection of Debts and Bankruptcy of Dec. 16, 1994, as amended. Enforcement of other kinds of claims is subject to procedural laws of cantons. Following explains summarily main features of collection under federal law. Periods of time are omitted; same may in certain instances be extended in favor of debtor residing outside of place of collection, especially outside of Switzerland.

Initial Procedure.—Collection of debts begins with "Order to Pay" (Zahlungsbefehl, Commandement de payer, Precetto esecutivo) transmitted upon mere request of creditor by enforcement office to debtor who can then declare "opposition" (Rechtsvorschlag, opposition, opposizione). If so, creditor must institute ordinary court action. However, by summary court procedure creditor may obtain decree to remove "opposition" (Rechtsoeffnung, mainlevee, rigetto), (1) finally, upon evidence of enforceable judgment or other decision, also foreign judgment or arbitral award, (2) provisionally, upon evidence of publicly authenticated deed or of acknowledgment of debt signed by debtor. Provisional "removal" becomes final if debtor within short period fails to bring ordinary court action for declaratory judgment that debt does not exist.

If "opposition" has not been declared or has been removed by ordinary judgment or "removal decree," enforcement continues at request of creditor in three possible ways: (1) Ordinarily, by seizure of specific property of debtor (Pfaendung, saisie, pigmoramento); or (2) for debts secured by pledge or mortgage, by realization of such property (Pfandverwertung, realisation du gage, realizzazione del pegno); (3) against merchants, by bankruptcy proceedings comprising all assets and liabilities of debtor (Konkurs, faillite, fallimento).

Seizure.—Property estimated sufficient to cover debt with interest and costs will be seized; property necessary for maintenance of livelihood and profession of debtor or debtor's family is not seizable. Other creditors who request seizure within period of time can participate in seizure (whereby additional property may be seized for additional coverage). All those creditors form "group of creditors". One or more groups formed later for other property seized on their behalf may be formed. Claims of third parties for liberation of property from seizure, e.g., because of ownership or creditorship thereon, are, if contested, adjudicated. Upon request of creditor, after certain time, seized property will be sold and proceeds distributed to creditors. Certain classes of claims are privileged, e.g., for salaries or family support payments. In cases of privileged creditors and of insufficient proceeds, schedule of creditors (collocations plan) is established before distribution. Schedule can be challenged in court. For unpaid claim, creditor receives "certificate of loss" (which does not bear interest and is not subject to statute of limitation during debtor's lifetime). This constitutes ground for attachment. See topic Attachment.

Realization of Pledge or Mortgage.—Procedure is roughly similar to procedure in case of seizure. For unpaid claim, creditor receives certificate evidencing that fact, but it does not have legal effects of "certificate of loss". See subhead Collection of Debts, catchline Seizure, supra.

Bankruptcy.—Not all debtors are subject to bankruptcy proceedings, only those recorded in Register of Commerce, further those whose whereabouts are unknown, or who have defrauded their creditors, etc. Debtor otherwise not subject to bankruptcy may voluntarily declare insolvency, thereby bringing about bankruptcy proceedings. Special rules apply if liabilities exceed assets of share or cooperative corporation (C.O. 725, 903), and to liquidation of estate of decedent by Bankruptcy Office; see topic Executors and Administrators.

Initial Procedure.—As outlined supra. If debt is evidenced by draft or check creditor can request special "draft collection". Periods of time are then shorter and "opposition" has to be granted by court order. There is no initial procedure in case of bankruptcy of debtor ordinarily not subject thereto.

Opening.—At creditor's request, debtor is notified and threatened with bankruptcy. Thereafter, bankruptcy court, unless certain permissible objections of debtor are sustained, declares bankruptcy opened.

Bankrupt Estate.—Comprises all property of bankrupt except certain property necessary for maintenance of livelihood and professional activity of debtor and debtor's family. All claims against debtor due except to extent secured by realty; nonmoney debts are converted into money debts. Dispositions of bankrupt with regard to property of estate are not valid with respect to creditors. Claims of third persons for separation from estate of tangible property (or securities) in (exclusive) possession of bankrupt, e.g., because of ownership, are adjudicated, if contested. Return of unpaid goods forwarded to bankrupt but not yet in bankrupt's possession when bankruptcy proceedings were opened may be demanded by seller (right of stoppage in transit).

Ordinary Procedure.—Bankruptcy office draws up inventory and publishes bankruptcy, ordering all creditors and debtors to file their claims and debts. Estate is administered by bankruptcy office, which may be replaced by one or more persons elected by creditors; they may also elect committee of creditors to supervise administrators and authorize them to take certain important measures. For such elections, and for other urgent matters, meeting of creditors is held. Administration must establish schedule of creditors (collocation plan). Thereafter, second creditor's meeting passes on all matters, including realization of assets by public auction or private sale; subsequent meetings may be held. After distribution of proceeds, Bankruptcy Court receives final accounting, and declares bankruptcy closed. Every creditor receives "certificate of loss" for unpaid balance of claim. See supra, subhead Collection of Debts, catchline Seizure.

Summary procedure may be ordered by bankruptcy court if assets do not warrant expenses of ordinary procedure. Bankruptcy office then proceeds to liquidations without participation of creditors. Any creditor can demand ordinary proceedings by advancing costs.

Closure for Lack of Assets.—If no assets are found, Bankruptcy Court orders bankruptcy closed. No "certificate of loss" is issued. However, within certain period of time creditor can institute execution of seizure against debtor, thereby obtaining such certificate.

Composition.—By agreement, debtor can conclude composition with all creditors.

By official procedure, three main kinds of composition (Nachlassvertrag, Concordat, Concordato) can be effectuated: (1) Stay of payment during certain time period; (2) payment of percentage of all non-privileged debts; (3) abandonment of all or part of debtor's assets to creditors (composition of liquidation). Such composition is possible for any debtor, even after execution procedure has started. Except in case of opened bankruptcy, debtor must petition for stay of payments with special "composition authority", submitting statement of assets and liabilities and draft of composition. If authority grants composition, commissioner is appointed. Debtor can, under supervision of commissioner, dispose of property, but not sell or encumber.

If composition liquidation is confirmed, creditor's meeting elects liquidators, and committee of creditors to supervise liquidators. Realization of assets and distribution of proceeds to creditors is similar to corresponding procedure in bankruptcy. No "certificate of loss" is issued; however, composition must provide whether or not unsatisfied claims may become effective subsequent to liquidation.

Special statutes apply inter alia to banks and savings institutions, hotels, and farms.

Foreign bankruptcy or composition has limited effect in Switzerland under Private International Law Statute, Art. 166 ff.

See topics Attachment; Treaties.

COMMERCIAL CODE:

Swiss Code of Obligations of Mar. 30, 1911 with amendments governs contracts and corporations. Separate statutes cover banking, insurance, unfair competition, etc.

COMMERCIAL REGISTER:

See topic Register of Commerce.

CONDITIONAL SALES:

See topic Sales.

CONSTITUTION AND GOVERNMENT:

Position within Europe: see topic Treaties.

(Federal Constitution of the Swiss Confederation of May 29, 1874, as am'd.)

Switzerland (Swiss Confederation) is federation of 26 states called cantons. Six cantons (called half cantons) send only one senator to Senate instead of two and have only one-half of vote in federal referenda requiring not only majority of voters but also

CONSTITUTION AND GOVERNMENT . . . *continued*
majority of cantons. Each canton has its own cantonal constitution. Cantons are competent in all matters not reserved by Federal Constitution to Confederation.

Every Swiss male and female over 18 years can participate in federal, cantonal and local elections and referenda. Some cantons and municipalities extend right to vote to foreign residents.

Total revisions of the Constitution and constitutional amendments must be submitted to popular referendum and require majority of voters and of cantons (mandatory constitutional referendum). With respect to popular referenda of federal statutes, etc. (optional and mandatory legislative referendum), see subhead Legislative Power, infra. One hundred thousand voters have right to request total revision of Constitution, or constitutional amendments (Initiative).

Human Rights.—Switzerland is party to European Convention on Human Rights. Basic rights of individual are set forth in Constitution. Governing principle is Art. 4: "All Swiss are equal before the law." Based on that provision Swiss Federal Supreme Court (see subhead Judicial Power, infra) has developed extensive practice for protection of individuals, including foreigners, against arbitrary measures by cantonal authorities which also execute most federal statutes. Men and women have equal rights and right to equal pay for equivalent work. *Note:* Implementing statute in force since July 1, 1996. Switzerland has joined international convention on elimination of all forms of racial discrimination (1965).

Constitution guarantees special freedoms of individuals: freedom of trade and industry; of settlement; of religion, conscience and religious cult; of marriage; of the press; of association; of petition to authorities. Various constitutional amendments since 1947 permit certain restrictions of freedom of trade and industry and State interventions for economic and social reasons by federal (and under some conditions also by cantonal) legislation, and federal legislation for peaceful labor relations.

Suits against solvent debtor must be brought before court at Swiss domicile (by 1999, this must be changed to comply with Lugano Convention). Court must have jurisdiction according to rules on conflict of jurisdiction. Court cannot accept or deny jurisdiction arbitrarily. Exceptional courts are not permitted.

German, French, Italian and Romansch are national languages. The first three are official languages in which all amendments to Federal Constitution, all federal statutes, and certain decrees of Federal Assembly, Federal Government and its departments, and Federal Supreme Court are published. Three published texts are equally authentic. International treaties concluded in one of three official languages are published with translations into two others; only original text is authentic, provided treaty itself does not stipulate otherwise.

As a general rule the organization of the federal authorities is built on the principle of separation of powers. The independence of courts is safeguarded by provisions of Constitution and statutes.

Legislative Power.—Legislative power is vested in Federal Assembly, consisting of two chambers: (a) House of Members (Nationalrat, Conseil National, Consiglio Nazionale) of 200 members and (b) Senate (Staenderat, Conseil des Etats, Consiglio degli Stati) of two members for each canton and one member for each half canton. There are four ordinary sessions per year, extraordinary sessions as necessary.

Certain matters, mainly elections, are deliberated and voted in joint session of both chambers. For all other matters separate approval of both chambers is required. Resolutions are passed in form of federal statutes or federal decrees.

Federal statutes and federal decrees must be submitted to popular referendum if requested by 50,000 voters or eight cantons. Majority of voters decide on acceptance or rejection. Same applies to federal decree approving certain International treaties, unless Federal Government concludes treaty based on prior authority by Federal Assembly. Federal decrees may be enacted at once for limited time by majority of members in each of two chambers. Such decrees, however, cease to be in force after one year, if not accepted by popular referendum if referendum was requested by 50,000 voters or eight cantons. If such decrees are not based on Constitution, popular referendum requiring majority of voters and of cantons is mandatory within one year, otherwise validity expires.

Executive Power.—Seven member Federal Government (Bundesrat, Conseil Fédéral, Consiglio Federale), elected for four years by House and Senate in joint session. Each member of Federal Government heads one department of federal administration. Every year another member acts as president and another as vice-president of Swiss Confederation with largely ceremonial powers.

Judicial Power.—The members of the Swiss Federal Supreme Court (Bundesgericht, Tribunal Fédéral, Tribunale Federale) are elected by House and Senate in joint session. See topic Courts.

CONSUMER PROTECTION:

Price supervision statute of Dec. 20, 1985 applies to goods and services.

Contracts with consumers are normally governed by law of habitual residence of consumer. (Art. 120 Private International Law Statute).

Statutes on product liability and on consumer credit and consumer information apply.

See also topic Sales, subhead Instalment and Prepayment Plan Purchases, and topic Product Liability.

CONTRACTS:

Applicable Law.—Contract is subject to law expressly agreed to by both parties. Otherwise, applicable law is that of country of habitual residence of party that under contract is required to perform obligation that is characteristic for type of contract in question. (Art. 117 Private International Law Statute). Special conflicts rules apply to contracts on immovables, with consumers, employment contracts and licence agreements. Same law is applied to contract formation. Different law may apply to specific questions such as form of contract, power of attorney, etc. See topic Sales.

Formation.—Contract requires: (a) Mutual agreement, express or implied; (b) "causa" only in certain cases, i.e., transfer of personal or immovable property; and (c) capacity of parties to contract. Every person who is of age (20) and sound mind has capacity. Minors of sound mind can validly accept only purely gratuitous benefits without their guardian's concurrence.

Consideration is not required.

Contracts are valid without any special form unless the law provides otherwise. If a form is legally prescribed, its observance is usually a condition of validity. Principal prescribed forms are written form and publicly authenticated instrument—usually notarial deed. Where parties, without requirement of law, have stipulated use of special form presumption is that they shall not be bound unless special form is complied with. Registration of contracts is as a rule necessary only in connection with immovables.

An offer including a time limit for acceptance binds offeror for period concerned. An offer with no time limit made in the presence of a prospective party or over the phone ceases to be binding if it is not accepted immediately. If made to a party at a different place it is binding until an answer should have been received if dispatched in due course and time. Where by reason of the special nature of the transaction or circumstances an express acceptance is not to be expected the contract is binding unless the offer is refused within reasonable time.

Excuses for nonperformance are: impossibility of performance by circumstances beyond debtor's control, force majeure, and clausula rebus sic stantibus.

Government Contracts.—As a rule there are no special requirements for contracting with governmental bodies.

See also topics Consumer Protection; Damages; Distributorships; Labor Relations; Landlord and Tenant; Mortgages; Pledges; Principal and Agent; Sales.

COPYRIGHT:

Revised Federal Statute in force since July 1, 1993.

Following are protected without registration or possibility of registration: works of literature, art, photography, collections and computer software. These terms are very broad and include: (1) literary, scientific and technical works by word and picture, also choreographical, cinematographical and similar works; (2) musical works; (3) works of fine art including architecture, graphic, applied art, etc.; (4) photographical works; (5) collections; (6) translations and reproductions of original works, rights of those on original work being reserved. Protection extends to works of Swiss citizens published in Switzerland or abroad and to unpublished works of Swiss citizens. Works of non-Swiss citizens are protected if first published in Switzerland; if first published abroad then only if country of publication grants reciprocity to Swiss citizens.

Exclusive right of reproduction includes right to changes, to translate work, to record and to film it. If author has permitted mechanical reproduction of musical work, residents of Switzerland are under certain conditions entitled to license for reproduction against compensation.

Reproductions for exclusively private use are permitted, except reproduction of architectural works, of musical compositions, and of pictorial arts. Law recognizes exceptions to exclusive rights of copyright owner (as newspaper articles not including novels, also small scientific or technical pictures and short literary works of smaller size for publication in schoolbooks).

Copyright may be transferred wholly or partly by assignment or inheritance, including rights to multiply, to dispose of, to reproduce and transmit, to expose and publish, to broadcast, televise, etc. However, personal copyright always remains vested in author, who may prevent alteration of work if it impairs integrity thereof, even if he has sold work. Duration of copyright protection for all materials, except software, is 70 years after author's death (50 years for software). Anonymous works are protected for 70 years from time of publication.

Violation of copyrights entails indemnification, and if intentional, possible punishment.

Semiconductor chips protected against copying under unfair competition rules. Statute for the Protection of Structures of Integrated Circuits of July 1, 1993, grants protection to uncommon three-dimensional structures of integrated circuits. Rarity required. Once registered with Federal Institute of Intellectual Property, protection lasts ten years from application. Two years only for structures not registered but simply circulated. (art. 9). Producer of structure has exclusive right to reproduce, circulate and exploit. Owner of structure benefits from same civil and criminal remedies against infringment as under Copyright Statute against copyright infringment.

Databases.—There exists no similar legislation in Switzerland to European Community's (EU) Regulation of Mar. 11, 1996, EC 96/9 on legal protection of databases. Database-provider in Switzerland is therefore referred to copyright protection and specific rules against unfair competition. Former grant protection against unlawful copying and exploitation of considerable contents of database within strict limits.

Conventions and Treaties.—Switzerland is party to Berne Convention of Nov. 13, 1908 for protection of literary and artistic works (Berlin Revision) Berne Convention of June 2, 1928 (Rome Revision), Berne Convention of June 26, 1948 (Brussels Revision), Universal Copyright Convention concluded at Geneva on Sept. 6, 1952. Declarations of reciprocity between Switzerland and U.S.A. issued by Switzerland on Sept. 26, 1924, by U.S.A. on Nov. 22, 1924, Rome Convention on Protection of Performers, Producers of Phonograms and Broadcasting Organizations of Oct. 26, 1961, Convention against Phonogram Piracy of Oct. 29, 1974, Satellite Convention.

Switzerland is member of World Intellectual Property Organisation (WIPO/OMPI) in Geneva and World Trade Organisation (WTO) included Trade Related Aspects of Intellectual Property Rights (TRIPS) of Jan. 1, 1995.

CORPORATIONS:

Share Corporation.—(Aktiengesellschaft, société anonyme, società anonima). Swiss Code of Obligations applies. Amended Share Corporation Title in force since July 1, 1992.

Legal entity with fixed capital divided into shares. No personal liability of shareholders beyond share capital. (C.O. 620).

Purpose.—Any defined lawful purpose, mostly business. (C.O. 620).

Corporate Name.—Chosen freely; must designate legal nature only if names of living persons are included. (C.O. 950).

See also topic Firm and Corporate Name.

CORPORATIONS . . . *continued*

Duration of Corporate Existence.—Perpetual (or limited if provided in articles).

Incorporators.—At time of incorporation there must be at least three shareholders. (C.O. 625). No restrictions as to nationality of shareholders, but see catchline Alien Shareholders, infra.

Capital.—Minimum capital SFr. 100,000. (C.O. 621).

If shareholder pays for shares in kind, or purchase of assets by corporation from shareholders or third parties is planned, details of transaction must be given in articles. Same for privileges granted to incorporators or other persons. (C.O. 628).

Articles must state corporate name, seat of registered office, purpose of enterprise, capital and contributions made thereto, par value and type of shares issued, manner of calling meetings, voting rights of shareholders, organization of management and internal auditing, and form of announcements by corporation. (C.O. 626).

Articles may provide for regulations (by-laws) specifying powers of different bodies in charge of management.

Incorporation.—Resolutions of organizing meeting must be embodied in publicly authenticated deed with basic documents attached. Same for any amendment of articles, especially any increase or reduction of capital, and for resolution of dissolution. (C.O. 637, 638, 647, 650, 736).

Following information must be recorded in Register of Commerce: Date when articles were passed, corporate name and seat of registered office, purpose, proposed length of existence, amount of capital, amount paid up, number and par value of shares, type of shares issued, transferability of shares, preferential rights of certain classes of shares, property received in payment of shares, privileges granted to certain classes of shareholders or to incorporators, number of profit sharing certificates indicating content of rights connected therewith, way in which directors and officers may act and sign for corporation, names, residences and nationality of directors and officers, name or corporate name of auditors and their seat or registered office, and manner in which corporate announcements will be made. (C.O. 641).

Corporation is incorporated upon its entry in Register of Commerce. Shares issued prior to registration are void. (C.O. 643-644).

Incorporation Tax or Fee.—Federal issuance stamp tax. (See topic Taxation.) Notary drawing up public deed of constituent meeting is entitled to fee, fixed by cantonal law.

License.—No license required to do business, except for purposes for which public concession is required, such as insurance, railroads; for banking, see topic Banks and Banking.

Paid-in Capital Requirements.—If capital consists of bearer shares, they must be paid-in fully. If there are registered shares, at time of constituent incorporators' meeting, at least 20% of capital must have been paid-in in cash or other assets, but not less than SFr. 50,000. (C.O. 632).

Amendment of articles must be approved by general meeting of shareholders or board of directors and embodied in publicly authenticated deed.

Amendments to change purpose, to create shares with privileged voting rights, to restrict transferability of registered shares, to increase capital authorized, subject to condition, out of equity, against contributions in kind, or for purpose of acquisition of assets and granting of special benefits, to limit or withdraw perceptive rights, to change domicile of company and to dissolve company without liquidation, require consent of at least two-thirds of votes represented and absolute majority of par value of shares represented. (C.O. 704).

Increase of Share Capital.—(a) Ordinary increase of share capital is resolved by general meeting and carried out by board of directors within three months (C.O. 650, 652-652h); (b) authorized increase of share capital: general meeting authorizes board of directors by amendment to articles to increase share capital within three years (C.O. 651, 651a, 652-652n); (c) increase of share capital subject to condition, if decided by general meeting to grant conversion or option rights to bondholders or employees (C.O. 653-653i).

Reduction of Share Capital.—Resolution of general meeting to reduce capital (without simultaneous increase to original amount by new fully paid-up capital) requires report by particularly qualified auditor stating that notwithstanding capital reduction claims of all creditors are covered. Resolution of general meeting must be published three times in Swiss Official Journal of Commerce and in manner of publication provided for in articles notifying creditors that, within two months after third publication, they may file their claims and demand satisfaction or surety. Publicly authenticated deed containing auditor's report must evidence that legal provisions were complied with. Notification is not required if capital is reduced exclusively to eliminate capital impairment caused by losses. (C.O. 732/35).

Acquisition of Own Shares.—Corporation may purchase its own shares if freely disposable equity in necessary amount is available and if total par value of these shares does not exceed 10% of share capital. Such shares cannot vote in shareholders' meeting. (C.O. 659/659b).

By-laws.—See supra, catchline Articles.

Shares may be issued in registered or bearer form. (C.O. 622). Corporation must keep register of owners of registered shares. (C.O. 685). Both types of shares may be issued in any proportion fixed by articles, which may also provide for subsequent changes between two types of shares and for issue of preferred shares. Minimum par value of share is SFr. 10, except in case of reorganization. Bearer shares may be issued only if fully paid-up. Registered shares may be issued for smaller amount than their nominal value, but shareholder remains liable for difference. (C.O. 622, 654, 656, 683, 687).

Articles may provide for participation capital, which shall not exceed twice amount of share capital. Participation certificates are issued against contribution, have par value and grant no voting rights. (C.O. 656a-656g).

Articles may provide for shares with preferential rights as to dividends, share in case of liquidation, subscription of newly issued shares (preferred shares); founder's share (Gründeranteilscheine, parts de fondateur), dividend-right certificates (Genussscheine, bons de jouissance) or bonds convertible into shares. (C.O. 627 No. 9, 628, 654-56, 657-58).

Share certificates must state corporate name, seat, nominal value, paid-up amounts, kind of shares (registered or bearer), kind of share in case there are different kinds. Document must be signed by at least one member of board of directors; if large number of issued shares facsimile signature is permissible. (C.O. 622).

If board so decides, shareholder may, as protective measure in case of international conflicts, request to be registered in special register to be kept abroad and that shareholder's share certificates be annulled.

Transfer of Shares.—Share certificates are negotiable instruments. Bearer shares are transferred by mere transfer of instrument; registered shares must also be endorsed or assigned, and with respect to corporation, shareholder must be entered in shareholders register. (C.O. 683-686a). There are special rules in case of restriction of transfer by articles. They differ between registered shares listed and not listed on stock exchange. (C.O. 685b-685g).

Shareholders have within provisions of law fundamental right to equal treatment, to vote, to contest resolutions of general meeting, to receive dividends, and to share in distribution of assets in case of liquidation. (C.O. 697a-697b).

Alien Shareholders.—Corporation law as rule does not prevent or limit formation of corporations by aliens or nonresidents. In few areas (e.g., vessels flying Swiss flag; enterprises for exploitation of Swiss oil wells) special provisions require specific majority of Swiss citizens as shareholders. There are no limitations regarding nonresident alien shareholders of domestic subsidiaries of foreign corporations, and no extraordinary accounting procedures. Alien shareholding, however, may be bar to double taxation treaty benefits. See also topic Immovable Property, subhead Acquisition by Nonresidents.

Shareholders' Liabilities.—Only capital of corporation is responsible for liabilities of corporation. Shareholder is liable only up to amount of his subscription. (C.O. 620, 680).

Shareholders' Meetings.—General shareholders' meeting is highest authority of corporation. It may amend articles, elect board of directors and internal auditors, and discharge them, approve balance sheet, profit-and-loss statement and declare dividends. It is called by directors ordinarily within six months after close of each business year and if necessary by auditors; shareholders representing at least one-tenth of all shares may demand that shareholders' meeting be called by stating purpose of meeting and motions of board of shareholders in writing. Notices of meetings must be given at least 20 days in advance, unless waived by all shareholders. (C.O. 698-701).

General meetings outside of Switzerland are possible. If general meeting has to make resolutions for which publicly authenticated deed is required, law of foreign place governing public authentications must be observed, which fact has to be certified by competent foreign authority. (Decree of Swiss Federal Government concerning Register of Commerce, as of June 7, 1937, art. 30).

Unless provided otherwise in articles, registered shareholder may issue written proxy to third party; in case of bearer shares possession gives right to vote. Representative shall comply with instructions of represented person. (C.O. 689-689e). For some purposes, number of votes may be made dependent on number of shares, rather than capital that they represent.

Directors and Officers.—Board of directors consists of one or more members who must be shareholders. (C.O. 707). Proposal for amendment of Constitution for introduction of so-called codetermination i.e., mandatory representation of employees on board of directors was rejected by public referendum in 1976. Majority of directors must be Swiss citizens residing in Switzerland. Federal Government may grant exceptions for holding corporations, in case majority of their holdings are in foreign countries. (C.O. 708).

If there are several groups of shareholders with different legal status, articles must provide for each group to elect at least one representative on board of directors. (C.O. 709). Articles may provide for representative of participants on board. (C.O. 656e).

Directors are elected and removed by general meeting. Articles specify term during which every director holds office, six years being maximum term. (C.O. 710). Vacancies are filled by general meeting only.

Directors must be shareholders. (C.O. 707).

At least one member of board of directors residing in Switzerland must be authorized to act and to sign for corporation. (C.O. 708). Unless articles or regulations provide otherwise all directors manage and act and sign for corporation individually. (C.O. 718). It follows that directors are actual officers of corporation, except in matters for which general meeting or other bodies are competent. (C.O. 716). Articles may empower board of directors to delegate in accordance with regulations management or any part thereof to one or more members of board (managing directors), or to third persons (managers). (C.O. 716b). Nontransferable and inalienable powers: ultimate management of corporation and giving of necessary directives, establishment of organization, structuring of accounting system and financial controls, appointment and removal of persons entrusted with management and representations, ultimate supervision of persons entrusted with management, preparation of business report and preparation of general meeting of shareholders and implementation of its resolutions, notification of court in case of overindebtedness. (C.O. 716a).

Persons with power to represent corporation may carry out in name of corporation all acts which purpose of corporation may require. Corporation is liable for all acts, including torts, that its directors and officers commit in business capacity. (C.O. 718a, 722).

Statutory Auditors.—General meeting of shareholders elects one or more statutory auditors to check balance sheet and profit-and-loss statement against books, and check whether result and financial position of corporation so represented comply with legal requirements as to accounting and any special provisions of articles. (C.O. 727, 728). At least one auditor must have domicile, seat or registered branch office in Switzerland. Auditors must be qualified to fulfil duties with corporation to be audited and must under some circumstances meet special professional qualifications, e.g. if corporation has outstanding bond issues or shares are listed on stock exchange. (C.O. 727a, 727b).

Auditors must be independent from board of directors and from shareholder with majority vote. (C.O. 727c). Statutory auditors must submit written report to general meeting recommending acceptance or rejection of annual accounts with or without reservation, and advising it with respect to annual accounts. (C.O. 729-729c).

Liability of Directors, Officers, Auditors and Liquidators.—Directors and other officers in charge of management, statutory auditors and liquidators of corporation are responsible to corporation and its shareholders for damage caused by their willful

See Topical Index in front part of this volume.

CORPORATIONS . . . *continued*
misconduct or negligence in performing their duties. Officer who rightfully delegates duties to another legal entity is liable for any damage caused by it unless officer proves that necessary care in selection, instruction and supervision was applied. (C.O. 752-754). Except for direct damages, shareholder can bring derivative suit only in case of bankruptcy of corporation. Creditors of corporation have similar claims in case corporation has been declared bankrupt. Direct and derivative personal liability under corporate, tax and social security laws has considerably increased under recent holdings by Swiss courts.

Claim of shareholder is barred if brought after six months after discharge by general meeting, or if shareholder has consented to discharge, or if shareholder has acquired shares with knowledge of discharge. (C.O. 756-758).

Dividends can be declared only from audited net earnings or reserves constituted for that purpose. (C.O. 675).

Books and Records.—Corporation must keep accurate books, as required by nature and extent of its business, establishing financial status, debits and credits connected with business and annual results. Annual financial status is composed of profit-and-loss statement, balance sheet and attachment. Attachment includes information required by law, e.g. total amount of guarantees, indemnity liabilities and pledges in favour of third parties, total amount of assets pledged or assigned for securing of own liabilities, liabilities to welfare institutions. Principles applying to balance sheet and profit-and-loss statement are set forth by statute. Inventory, profit-and-loss statement and balance sheet must be signed by management. Groups of corporations must prepare consolidated statement of accounts. Corporations whose shares are listed on stock exchange must include important shareholders and their participations in attachment to balance sheet. (C.O. 957-961, 662-674).

Merger and Consolidation.—Corporation may transfer all its assets and liabilities to another share corporation. In such case certain provisions for liquidation must be observed. (C.O. 748).

Several share corporations may be absorbed by newly formed share corporation in such manner that assets of existing corporations are taken over by new corporation. Rules on formation of share corporation and on transfer of all assets and liabilities to another corporation must be observed. (C.O. 749).

Dissolution.—Share corporation may be dissolved in accordance with its articles pursuant to resolution of general meeting of shareholders, in case of bankruptcy, or, with cause, by court at request of shareholders representing at least 10% of capital. (C.O. 736). As a rule, management attends to liquidation of corporation, but general meeting may elect other liquidators. At least one liquidator residing in Switzerland must have right to act and sign for corporation. Names of liquidators must be registered in Register of Commerce. Status of corporation as legal entity is not affected, but words "in liquidation" must be added to its corporate name. (C.O. 739, 740). When liquidation procedure is terminated, corporation is struck from Register of Commerce with consent of tax authorities. (C.O. 746).

Adaptation to New Law in Force Since July 1, 1992.—Share corporations already entered in Register of Commerce adapt articles within five years. Certain new provisions referring to participation certificates and dividend-right certificates are applicable to already existing companies even if inconsistent with articles or conditions of issuance. (Final Provisions of Federal Statute concerning amendment of Corporation Law 3, 4).

Transfer of Seat into and out of Switzerland.—Possible under certain conditions. (PIL Statute 161-164).

Protective Measures in Case of International Conflicts.—It is possible to register transfer of company's seat to another place in Switzerland, to any place abroad, or to possible future official seat of Swiss Federal Government, to become effective at future date fixed by Swiss Federal Government or at moment when it no longer exercises its power freely. In case of registration, authorities may require security for taxes due until transfer. When seat transfer becomes effective powers of official organs and of persons authorized to sign will be adapted to new situation.

Limited Partnership with Shares.—(Kommandit-Aktiengesellschaft; Société en commandite par actions; Società in accomandita per azioni). Limited partnership with shares is corporation with corporate name and capital divided into shares in which, in addition to corporate capital, one or more shareholders have joint unlimited personal liability in same way as partners of general partnership. (C.O. 764). This legal form is rarely used.

Unless specifically provided otherwise, provisions governing share corporations apply.

Corporate Name.—Same as for Limited Partnership.

Members Generally Liable.—Must be named in articles. They conduct business, act and sign for corporation, and form, by operation of law, board of directors. Majority of members generally liable must be Swiss citizens and residing in Switzerland. Swiss Federal Government may grant exceptions for holding corporations if majority of their holdings are located in foreign countries, but at least one member generally liable must be domiciled in Switzerland. (C.O. 765).

Consent of members generally liable is required for resolutions of general meeting for change of purpose, extension or restriction of scope of business or extension of duration beyond period fixed in articles. (C.O. 766).

Statutory auditors must be appointed by general meeting, in which members generally liable have no right to vote.

In cases of bad faith, this supervising body may sue directors, even if their liability has been discharged. (C.O. 768-69).

Dissolution.—The general and liimited partnership share corporation is dissolved by retirement, death, incapacity or bankruptcy of all members generally liable. In other respects provisions for dissolution of share corporations apply. (C.O. 770).

Member generally liable may withdraw from partnership upon notice to it like general partner, but, unless provided for otherwise by articles, partnership continues to exist if at least one or more members generally liable remains. (C.O. 771).

Limited Liability Corporation.—(Gesellschaft mit beschränkter Haftung; Société à responsabilité limitée; Societa a garanzia limitata). These are corporations of at least two natural persons or legal entities for commercial, industrial or other profit-making purpose with own corporate name and common capital fixed in advance. Every member participates in common capital with its capital contribution. (C.O. 772-827).

Corporate Name.—Limited liability corporation may freely choose its corporate name, which must disclose that it is limited liability corporation. (C.O. 949).

Capital.—Minimum capital is SFr. 20,000 and maximum SFr. 2,000,000. Capital contributions of members may be unequal in multiples of SFr. 1,000 with minimum of SFr. 1,000 for each member. Payment may be made in kind. Member may participate with only one capital contribution. At least 50% of each capital contribution must be paid-in at time of incorporation. (C.O. 773-774).

Articles of Incorporation.—Articles must state corporate name, seat, purpose, amount of common capital, capital contribution of each member, and form of notice given by corporation. There are no restrictions as to nationality of members. To be valid stipulations between members altering provisions of law must be mentioned in articles, e.g.: provision extending liability of members beyond amount of common capital, voting rights, prohibition or restrictions affecting assignment of capital parts. All members must execute publicly authenticated deed to effect that they incorporate limited liability corporation and abide by its articles, that they have subscribed all capital contributions, and that amount required by law or by articles has been paid-in. Corporation is incorporated upon its entry into Register of Commerce. Any amendment of articles must be publicly authenticated and entered in Register of Commerce. (C.O. 775-785).

Parts in Capital.—Capital contribution of member determines member's part. Document issued for part is not negotiable instrument but only documentary proof. All capital contributions and alterations thereof must be recorded in and communicated yearly to Register of Commerce. Assignment of part requires public deed and becomes effective with respect to corporation only after Register of Commerce has received notice and entered transfer in register of parts; subject to contrary provisions in articles, entry requires consent of at least three-fourths of all members and of common capital, except in case of transfer by death or marital property law. (C.O. 789-793).

Meeting of Members.—Is supreme body of corporation. Every member has one vote for each SFr. 1,000 contribution unless articles provide otherwise. Total exclusion of member from voting is prohibited. For certain measures, exclusive competence lies with members' meeting, e.g. change of articles, appointment and removal of managers and internal auditors, adoption of balance sheet and profit-and-loss statement, distribution of profits, discharge of managers. (C.O. 810).

Management and Representation.—All members participate jointly in management and representation, unless articles or resolution of corporation provide otherwise. Articles or resolution of corporation may confer management and representation upon nonmembers. At least one manager must reside in Switzerland. Managers sign for corporation by adding their names to corporate name. (C.O. 811-813, 815).

Provisions on share corporations apply with certain modification to scope of representation of Limited Partnership Corporation. (C.O. 814).

Liability of Members.—Members of Corporation are jointly liable for debts of corporation up to registered common capital. To extent that common capital has been paid-in and not been repaid in any form, liability of member is reduced. Articles may provide for limited additional contributions to eliminate losses shown on balance sheet. (C.O. 802-803).

Withdrawal.—Articles may grant right of withdrawal to members. Member may petition court to grant withdrawal or to dissolve corporation with cause. Corporation may, for same reason, request court to expel member, but only with consent of majority of members representing majority of common capital. (C.O. 822).

Dissolution and Liquidation.—Dissolution is effected according to articles by publicly authenticated resolution of at least three-fourths of members representing at least three-fourths of capital, in event of bankruptcy, or for other grounds provided in law. (C.O. 820, 822, 775).

For liquidation, provisions for share corporations apply. (C.O. 823).

Cooperative corporation (Genossenschaft, Société coopérative, Società cooperativa) is incorporated association of unrestricted number of legal entities or natural persons to further or safeguard certain economic interests by their joint action. (C.O. 823).

Corporate Name.—See subhead Share Corporation, supra.

Incorporation.—Cooperative corporation is incorporated by registration in Register of Commerce. Its articles (containing corporate name, seat, purpose, liabilities of members, if any, organization, and form of publication) must be in writing and approved by meeting of at least seven incorporators. (C.O. 830-838).

Capital.—Amount of cooperative corporation's capital cannot be determined beforehand. (C.O. 828).

Certificates of Membership.—Articles may provide for certificates of membership. Such certificates are made in member's name. They do not constitute documents of title but only documents of proof.

Transfer of certificate of membership confers membership rights to transferee if resolution of admittance is passed. (C.O. 852-853, 849).

General Meeting, Directors and Auditors.—Supreme authority rests in general meeting of members. It has following powers: Pass or amend articles, elect directors and internal auditors, approve operating accounts and balance sheet, distribute profits, grant release to directors and exercise other powers provided by law or articles. Majority of directors must be members and Swiss citizens residing in Switzerland. Auditors must examine conduct of business and yearly accounts. Directors, members of executive committee, auditors and liquidators are liable for damage due to willful violation of their duties or negligence. (C.O. 879-910, 916-920).

Admittance and Withdrawal of Members.—New members may be admitted at any time upon written application. For as long as termination of cooperative corporation has not been decided, members may withdraw at any time subject to restrictive conditions provided for in articles. (C.O. 839, 842).

Liability of Members.—Members are not responsible for liabilities of corporation, unless articles provide for limited responsibility of members for liabilities of corporation, or for unlimited or limited contributions of members to cover losses of corporation. (C.O. 868, 870, 871).

Dissolution takes place as provided for in articles, or upon resolution of general meeting of members, or in case of bankruptcy, or in other cases. (C.O. 911).

See Topical Index in front part of this volume.

CORPORATIONS . . . *continued*

Holding Corporations.—For such corporations regular law for share corporations or limited liability corporations applies, with some exceptions: (1) If majority of participations are outside Switzerland, with permission of Swiss Federal Government, majority of members of board of directors need not be Swiss citizens residing in Switzerland. (C.O. 711). However, one member of board entitled to represent corporation must reside in Switzerland. (2) Holding corporations are exempt from certain provisions concerning creation and use of legal reserves. (C.O. 671). Federal and many cantonal tax laws provide advantages for holding corporations.

Applicable Law.—Law of country of registration applies.

See also topics Register of Commerce; Firm and Corporate Name; Foundations; Membership Associations; Immovable Property, subhead Acquisition by Nonresidents; Taxation.

COURTS:

Cantonal Courts.—Most courts are cantonal courts.

Each canton has its own judicial organization, its own system of procedure.

There are special inferior courts, such as "Justice of the Peace", in some cantons mainly for conciliatory purposes before introduction of case to trial court.

Trial courts of general jurisdiction are variously called "District Court," "Circuit Court," "Court of First Instance," etc.

In many matters appeal is possible to intermediate appellate court, called "Superior Court," "Court of Appeal," "Cantonal Court," etc.

Commercial and industrial matters are often reserved to "Commercial Court". Other special courts are competent for labor, landlord and tenant, police matters, etc.

Swiss Federal Supreme Court (see topic Constitution and Government) in Lausanne has final review of decisions or measures taken by cantonal authorities under application of federal statutes, as in following matters: Complaints for violation of constitutional rights of individuals, recourses and complaints for violation of federal private or penal (not military penal) statutes, complaints against handling of specifically enumerated matters involving federal administrative statutes, such as Federal tax statutes. Swiss Federal Supreme Court also has final jurisdiction in matters concerning international treaties where such jurisdiction is not reserved to other federal authorities.

The question, however, whether or not federal statute, federal decree of general obligatory character (see topic Constitution and Government, subhead Legislative Power), or international treaty concluded by Confederation violates Federal Constitution is not subject to review by Swiss Federal Supreme Court.

Swiss Federal Supreme Court also acts as trial court in special matters, such as litigation involving Confederation or cantons, and special criminal matters.

Swiss Federal Supreme Court in Lucerne has final jurisdiction in matters concerning federal insurance for old age and survivors, disability insurance, federal military insurance.

Special Federal Military Criminal Courts have jurisdiction in matters involving federal military criminal law.

CRIMINAL LAW:

Federal Criminal Code of Dec. 21, 1937 with amendments governs crimes, offenses and main delinquencies. Cantonal and federal statutes govern criminal procedure.

Art. 161 Criminal Code forbids use or communication to third party by member of board, management or auditors of company or their agents of confidential information disclosure of which will considerably influence price of securities on stock exchange. Use of such information by tippee also falls under prohibition.

Art. 179 bis ff. forbids direct recording of nonpublic conversation of conference without consent of participants.

Art. 273 forbids under penalty of imprisonment or penitentiary, possibly combined with fine, to disclose business secrets to foreign state agency, organization or private enterprise. Direct or indirect interest worthy of protection must exist in Switzerland that fact of economic life remain secret. Waiver of secrecy by private persons or legal entities concerned is insufficient if third parties or Switzerland are involved.

For database transfer abroad permit required under Art. 6 Data Protection Statute.

Art. 271 forbids under same penalties to exercise on Swiss territory acts for foreign state which are reserved to public officers. Foreign tax officer may therefore not make inspections on Swiss territory, even though Swiss corporation concerned may have given its consent. Any persons furthering such acts fall under same penalties.

Art. 305 bis and 305 ter forbid money laundering and negligence in accepting money deposits.

Federal Statute on International Judicial Assistance in Criminal Matters of Mar. 20, 1981 defines preconditions and applicable measures.

Switzerland is party to European Convention on Assistance in Criminal Matters of Apr. 20, 1959 and to European Convention on Extradition of Dec. 13, 1957. It has concluded various similar agreements with various countries, including U.S. (Treaty, 1977).

See also topic Treaties.

CURRENCY:

Basic monetary unit is franc of 100 centimes. Bank notes are legal tender. See also topics Banks and Banking; Exchange Control.

Liechtenstein uses Swiss franc currency and subjects its banks to supervision of Swiss National Bank. See Currency Agreement of June 19, 1980.

CURTESY:

Unknown in Swiss law.

CUSTOMS:

Customs duties are levied by Confederation. Customs revenue goes to Federal Treasury. On average Switzerland levies rather low customs duties. Current Customs Tariff of 1959 is based on international customs nomenclature of Customs Council. It comprises only specific rates, mainly imposed on gross weight.

Since July 1, 1977 exemption from duties for industrial products exists in goods trade between EU and EFTA countries. It is granted upon application and against presentation of proof of origin ("Warenverkehrsbescheinigung"—or Form EUR. 2).

Switzerland grants preferential duties to developing countries in industrial sector and on certain agricultural products. Most-favored rates of Applicable Customs Tariff are in their majority required by WTO. Switzerland is party to Treaty on International Exhibitions of Nov. 22, 1928 and also to Customs Regulation concerned on Import of objects for international exhibition.

Value Added Tax on Imports (VAT).—See topic Taxation, subhead Indirect Federal Taxes, catchline Value Added Tax (VAT).

DAMAGES:

Party to contract is liable for damages in case of nonfulfillment unless party proves lack of fault.

If there is no contract general rule is that a person is liable for damage caused to another only if person has behaved unlawfully, be it willfully or by gross or slight negligence. This rule applies also to product liability.

There are special fields where liability results from causal relationship only and fault is not required, i.e., railways, motor vehicles, nuclear, water pollution, etc.

Statute concerning compensation to victims of violent crime provides for Government payments.

DEATH:

When exercising rights, whoever alleges death of person must prove it by Civil Status Records, or by other proof if such records are missing or proven to be incorrect. (Presumption of Life, C.C. 32, 33).

Survivorship.—When several persons die in a common disaster and it is impossible to prove which ones survived the others, their simultaneous death is presumed. (C.C. 32).

Disappearance.—In case of disappearance of person under circumstances indicating certain death, even if corpse is not seen, death may be assumed and entered in Civil Status Register by order of supervisory authority at request of any interested person. Nevertheless, any interested person may still request judicial determination of such death. (C.C. 34, 49).

Declaration of Absence.—If death of a person is highly probable, because person has either disappeared under great peril or has been absent for long time without having given any news, then at request of any person interested "Declaration of Absence" may be pronounced by competent court. Request can be presented only after one year following disappearance, and in case of absence after five years since last news. By appropriate publication court must call upon anyone in position to give information to report within stipulated time, in any case within one year after publication. If no report has been received within that time, court pronounces person to be absent and orders corresponding entry into Civil Status Register. Rights deriving from death of person declared absent may be exercised as if death were proven. (Presumption of Death, C.C. 35-38, 50). However, spouse of person declared absent must request dissolution of marriage, either together with request for declaration of absence or by special request. (C.C. 102).

Death certificate may be obtained, if death occurred in Switzerland, from Civil Status Office, where death was recorded in Register of Deaths.

Actions for Death.—Damages may be collected from person who caused death of another person for (a) funeral expenses, (b) cost of healing and inability to earn living if death did not occur immediately, (c) so-called "bread-winner-damage." Actions for (a) and (b) are as a rule limited to heirs. Claims for "tort-moral" may also be filed.

Amounts awarded are as a rule very low by American standards. In certain cases they are limited by specific statutes; e.g., Air Transport Regulation Art. 8 et seq.: SFr. 72,500 per dead person, but Swiss air carriers must cover each passenger with SFr. 200,000.

See topics Absentees; Records; Wills.

DECEDENTS' ESTATES:

See topics Descent and Distribution; Executors and Administrators; Wills.

DEEDS:

See topics Acknowledgments and other Public Authentications; Husband and Wife; Immovable Property.

DEPOSITIONS AND DISCOVERY:

Depositions in Switzerland are taken following court orders by special court procedure.

Letters rogatory addressed to particular court or generally to any court having jurisdiction will be executed by proper authorities. Written questionnaires must accompany letters rogatory, and should be drawn with special regard for difference between common law and civil law methods of taking testimony.

Attorneys or parties may not obatin depositions for foreign court procedure except with specific permit received from Police Division of Federal Department of Justice. Swiss Government will not permit commissions from foreign countries addressed to consuls, notaries, or any other individuals to be executed in Switzerland. U.S. Department of State has instructed American consular officials not to execute commissions addressed to them in Switzerland.

Depositions outside of Switzerland are obtained by courts through Swiss diplomatic channels with help either of competent foreign courts or of Swiss consular officers.

Switzerland is party to International Convention Concerning Civil Procedure, concluded in The Hague Mar. 1, 1954. No convention with U.S.

DESCENT AND DISTRIBUTION:

Applicable Law.—Swiss law applies if last domicile was in Switzerland, but non-Swiss may choose law of citizenship. Swiss law applies if Swiss with last domicile

DESCENT AND DISTRIBUTION . . . *continued*
abroad chooses Swiss law generally or for Swiss assets. Swiss law applies if foreign authorities do not deal with estate of Swiss citizen unless domicile law chosen. For non-Swiss with last domicile abroad, law applicable according to conflicts rules at domicile applies. Special rules for land.

Swiss inheritance law makes no distinction between immovable and personal property, with certain exceptions which are mainly with respect to farmland.

If decedent dies intestate, statutory heirs inherit. Same holds to extent that heirs appointed by disposition mortis causa (see topic Wills, subhead Testamentary Dispositions) do not inherit. Statutory heirs receive any property not disposed of by decedent. (C.C. 481 subs. 2). Thus appointed heirs and statutory heirs can inherit side by side: Expression "estate inherited intestate" used below may be entire estate or only part thereof not disposed of by decedent.

Statutory heirs: (1) Surviving spouse (after marital property allocation, see topic Husband and Wife) receives: (a) one-half if decedent leaves descendants; (b) three-fourths if decedent leaves no descendants, but leaves statutory heirs of line of decedent's parents; (c) whole estate if decedent leaves none of above. (C.C. 462).

(2) Children of decedent in equal shares: Predeceased child is replaced by child's descendants in all degrees per stirpes. (C.C. 457).

(3) If decedent leaves no descendants, parents of decedent each inherit one-half of estate; predeceased parent is replaced by his or her descendants in all degrees per stirpes. If predeceased parent leaves no descendants, whole estate inherited intestate goes to other parent or that parent's descendants. (C.C. 458).

(4) If decedent leaves no descendants and there are no descendants in either parental line, estate is inherited by grandparents equally on both sides. (C.C. 459).

(5) Public Body.—If decedent has no statutory heirs, estate escheats to canton in which decedent was last domiciled, or to municipality designated by that canton. (C.C. 466). As to restricted liability of public body for decedent's debts see topic Executors and Administrators, subhead Heirs.

Plural Relationship of Blood and Half Blood.—Relative of blood related several times to decedent is entitled within group according to each of relative's positions in main stems or lower stems; half blood is entitled within group only in main stem to which half blood belongs.

Determination of Statutory Heirs.—In absence of provision of code determination incumbent on cantons. In certain cantons certification as to statutory heirs is issued by notaries (e.g., Berne, Geneva). As to determination of heirs appointed by disposition mortis causa, see topic Wills.

Advance.—Statutory heirs are mutually bound to adjust among themselves any liberality received from decedent during lifetime, provided decedent when granting liberality intended advance against future inheritance of recipient. That intention is deemed to exist for liberalities granted by decedent to descendant as marriage portion, outfitting, transfer of property, release of debt, etc., unless decedent at any time clearly directed otherwise by disposition mortis causa, in written form or orally. (C.C. 626-633). If liberalities are not to be adjusted, they are subject to claim for reduction by an heir whose compulsory hereditary rights are thereby impaired. (C.C. 527 cipher 1). See topic Wills, subhead Testamentary Dispositions, catchline Compulsory Heirs; also subhead Contest, catchline Suit for Reduction.

Escheat.—The right of the public body to the estate inherited intestate (see subhead Statutory Heirs, supra) has legal character of hereditary right, not of occupancy right (escheat).

For compulsory heirs, appointed heirs by disposition mortis causa, and lawsuit for invalidity or for reduction, see topic Wills. For distinction between heirs and legatees, see topic Executors and Administrators, subhead Succession of Heirs and of Legatees. For liabilities of heirs, renunciation of inheritance, claims against decedent, administration by heirs, partition of estate, and lawsuit for inheritance, see topic Executors and Administrators.

DESERTION: See topic Divorce.

DISPUTE RESOLUTION:

Mandatory.—In most cantons, all cases first go to Justice of Peace for conciliation. All courts may, and frequently do promote amicable settlement.

Voluntary.—See topic Arbitration and Award.

DISTRIBUTORSHIPS:

Sole Distributorship.—Special contract type not covered by C.O.

Commercial Agency Agreement.—Noncompetition clause may be agreed, but gives agent mandatory claim for compensation in case of termination. If agent has by activity considerably enlarged circle of customers of principal and if after termination principal will enjoy considerable advantages thereby, then agent has claim for adequate compensation if principal terminates. This claim may not exceed average of agent's net profit during past five years.

According to case law, there is no such termination compensation claim if sole distributorship is terminated.

DIVORCE:

Applicable Law.—Swiss law applies if both parties have domicile in Switzerland, if defendant has domicile or plaintiff has had domicile for one year in Switzerland or is Swiss citizen. But if they have common foreign citizenship, that law applies unless divorce is impossible or highly impracticable under that law.

Grounds for Divorce.—Divorce may be granted for: (a) Adultery; action must be brought within six months after knowledge, in any case within five years and is precluded by consent or condonement; (b) attempt against other spouse's life, violence or grave insults; action must be brought within six months after knowledge, in any case within five years and is precluded by condonement; (c) infamous crime or gross misconduct; (d) malicious desertion or failure to return home without important reasons for over two years; action may be brought only if other spouse has not returned within six months after summons by court order; (e) incurable mental disease lasting three years which makes living together intolerable; (f) marital relations so seriously strained that living together has become intolerable; if this is due chiefly to one spouse, action may be brought only by other spouse. (C.C. 137-142).

Procedure is subject to cantonal law, but the following federal requirements must be complied with: (a) Court may not find facts unless convinced of their existence; (b) facts cannot be ascertained by oath; (c) court is not bound by declarations of parties; (d) court accepts proof at its discretion; (e) agreements concerning indirect consequences of divorce are valid only upon approval by court. (C.C. 158).

Court takes preliminary measures pertaining to residence and maintenance of wife, property rights and care of children. Divorced wife retains citizenship acquired by marriage. Spouse who changed name upon marriage keeps married name, unless request to regain old name is presented to Civil Status Official within six months of divorce. (C.C. 145, 149).

Alimony.—Innocent party whose financial situation is jeopardized because of divorce will receive from guilty party fair compensation; if seriously injured, such party may also receive compensation for moral wrongs. (C.C. 151). If innocent spouse would become destitute, other spouse, even if not guilty, may be obliged to pay alimony within limits of financial abilities. (C.C. 152).

Children.—Care and education of minor children, their maintenance and other related questions, are settled by court after consulting parties and, if necessary, Board of Orphans. (C.C. 156).

Separation.—Any ground for divorce applies also for separation. If action has been brought for separation, court cannot grant divorce. If action has been brought for divorce, separation can be granted only if reconciliation appears possible. Separation may be decreed for definite period lasting between one and three years or for unlimited period. Unless married life has been resumed, either spouse may ask divorce upon termination of separation decreed for definite period or when separation for unlimited period has lasted three years. (C.C. Arts. 143, 146-148).

Switzerland adheres to treaty of June 1, 1970 on recognition of divorces and separations.

DOWER:

Unknown in Switzerland.

ENFORCEMENT OF DEBTS AND BANKRUPTCY:

See topic Collection of Debts and Bankruptcy.

ENVIRONMENT:

Various federal, cantonal and local laws protect directly and indirectly environment, especially lakes and rivers, forests, air, etc. Federal Environmental Protection Statute of Oct. 7, 1983, in force since Jan. 1, 1985, will be followed by several implementing ordinances, in particular, setting strict limits to emission of harmful substances and defining content of environmental impact report to be submitted by owners of industrial plants.

EXCHANGE CONTROL:

Exchange Control.—See topics Banks and Banking; Foreign Investment.

Swiss National Bank has power to take measures for protection of Swiss currency including possibility to request banks to keep mandatory reserves and to control emissions.

There are no foreign exchange restrictions between U.S. and Switzerland.

EXECUTORS AND ADMINISTRATORS:

There are no special probate or surrogate's courts. Cantons must designate authorities competent for inheritance matters. No simplified procedures are available for small estates.

Succession of Heirs and of Legatees.—As general rule heir is distributee who succeeds to entire estate of decedent, (assets and liabilities) or to fraction of estate, statutory heir (see topic Descent and Distribution) and/or as heir appointed by dispositions mortis causa (see topic Wills, subhead Testamentary Dispositions). Upon decedent's death, immovable and movable property vests immediately by force of law as universal succession in statutory and/or appointed heirs. Several heirs constitute undivided community of heirs until distribution. Heirs become joint owners and creditors, of all of decedent's immovables, claims, and other inheritable rights; they become joint obligors of all of decedent's obligations under joint and several personal liability. (C.C. 560, 602-603).

A legatee receives a specific asset, including usufruct, by disposition mortis causa (C.C. 484) or by operation of law. Legatee is singular successor into asset and has merely personal claim against heir or heirs or legatee (sub-legacy) charged (C.C. 562 subd. 1); above-mentioned legal usufructs are however rights in rem (C.C. 563). Legatee is not liable for decedent's debts. See also topic Wills, subhead Legacies.

Capacity to Acquire.—In order to qualify as heir or as legatee person must survive decedent. Unworthy person lacks capacity to acquire from decedent's estate, e.g. if person wilfully caused or attempted to cause death of decedent, or committed certain fraudulent acts in connection with decedent's disposition mortis causa; such unworthiness is removed if forgiven by decedent. (C.C. 542, 543, 539-541).

Heirs.—If there is no testamentary executor (see subhead Testamentary Executors, infra) administration, liquidation and partition of estate is left to heirs. Competent authority at decedent's last domicile must order certain protective measures, as (1) sealing of estate if provided by cantonal law, (2) inventorization if heir is under guardianship or lastingly absent without representation or requests it, or (3) appointment of official administrator of estate (see subhead Official Administrators of Estate, infra). (C.C. 551-555).

Measures Limiting Liability of Heirs.—To avoid personal liability heir may either: (a) Renounce inheritance within three months, but renunciation is presumed, if deceased's insolvency was publicly known or officially established; or (b) demand public inventory and thereafter either accept inheritance unconditionally, or renounce it, or accept it subject to inventory, which means that heirs will be liable only for debts

EXECUTORS AND ADMINISTRATORS . . . *continued*

specified in inventory; or (c) demand official liquidation, but requests for official liquidation are not granted if another heir accepts inheritance. (C.C. 566-597). Public body inheriting as statutory heir is liable only for decedent's debts to extent of property received. (C.C. 592). See topic Descent and Distribution, subhead Statutory Heirs.

Presentation of Claims.—Claims against decedent should be promptly presented because in case of public inventory (see catchline Measures Limiting Liability of Heirs, supra) authority has to call on creditors and debtors by publication to file their claims and debts within period fixed in each case, but no less than one month from first day of publication. Claims and debts appearing in public records or in decedent's papers are included in inventory as matter of course. If unsecured creditors omitted to file claims, and their claims are not otherwise included in inventory, they forfeit personal liability of heirs with respect to assets in estate. If creditor omitted to file claim without fault or if filed claim was not included in inventory; heirs are liable inasmuch as enriched by inheritance. (C.C. 582-583, 590).

Determination of Heirs.—In case of intestacy, see topic Descent and Distribution; in case of heirs appointed by disposition mortis causa, see topic Wills.

Administration by Heirs.—If no testamentary executor or official administrator (see subheads Testamentary Executors and Official Administrators of Estate, infra) has been appointed, administration of estate is right and duty of heirs, who must act jointly, not severally. At request of co-heir competent authority may appoint representative of heirs up to distribution. (C.C. 602). Representative is solely entitled to act for heirs.

Distribution by Heirs.—Distribution of inheritance may be requested by any co-heir at any time, except when bound to continue community of heirs by agreement, and in certain cases provided by statute such as serious detriment to value of assets by distribution (in such case only temporary deferment is possible), and with regard to posthumous child. (C.C. 604-606).

All heirs have equal claim to assets of estate, except if statute or testator provides otherwise. If no executor is acting, heirs must establish as many portions out of estate assets as there are heirs or stems of heirs. If they do not agree, competent authority establishes portions at request of any one heir. Portions are allotted by agreement or by drawing lots among heirs. (C.C. 610-611). There are special provisions for distribution of immovable property, especially farm land. (C.C. 616-625bis). (See topic Immovable Property.) Distribution becomes binding upon heirs with acceptance of portions or with conclusion of distribution agreement in writing. (C.C. 634).

Performance of Legacies.—See topic Wills, subhead Legacies.

Testamentary executors may be appointed by (a) will or (b) inheritance pact, but provision in pact has nature of will and is, therefore, subject to unilateral revocation or amendment.

Eligibility.—Any legally capable natural person, resident or nonresident, citizen or noncitizen of Switzerland, including legal entity located inside or outside of Switzerland, is eligible.

Issuance of Letters.—Letters testamentary in sense of American practice are not executed. However, certificates containing appointment of executors are issued by judicial or administrative authorities.

Removal may be made by supervising authority on serious grounds.

Powers and Duties.—Executors derive their powers directly from will, which may grant unlimited powers or powers limited to certain executorial functions. Several executors act jointly, unless will provides otherwise. If will has no limitation as to powers of executor, executor has sole power and duty to administer estate, including making sales, paying decedent's debts, distributing legacies, and distributing to heirs according to will or statute. (C.C. 518).

Notice of Appointment.—Executor must be notified by authority opening will (see topic Wills). Within 14 days after receipt of this notice acceptance or refusal of office must be declared; silence means acceptance. (C.C. 517).

Actions.—Executor sues and is sued, as a rule, in executor's own name on behalf of estate.

Final Accounting.—After distribution executor must render final accounting to heirs.

Compensation.—Executors are entitled to proper compensation; no scale is fixed by Code. (C.C. 517). Contests on this are decided by competent authority.

Supervision.—Executors are subject to supervision by competent authority.

Official administrators of estate are appointed by competent authority under specific conditions only, mainly (1) if heir is lastingly absent and without representation, provided that heir's interests require it, (2) if none of claimants can prove right to inherit satisfactorily, or if it is uncertain whether there is heir (except public body), (3) if not all heirs are known, or (4) if opening authority (see topic Wills, subhead Probate) has special reasons. Executor appointed by will may but does not have to be appointed as official administrator. (C.C. 554, 556). See topic Absentees.

Evidence of appointment is by certified copy of appointing decree or special certification by appointing authority.

Powers and Duties.—Official administrator must administer estate as conservatory measure. Distribution is not a duty. During time for which official administrator is appointed, administrative powers of heirs or executor are suspended.

Supervision.—Official administrator is subject to supervision by appointing authority.

Official liquidation of estate is ordered by competent authority (1) at request of any heir if no other heir accepts inheritance unconditionally or subject to inventory (see subhead Heirs, supra), or (2) at request of creditors or legatees who have good reasons to fear that their claims will not be paid, unless security is given to them. (C.C. 593-594).

Procedure.—Official liquidation may be handled by authority itself or by one or several liquidating administrators appointed by authority. Property of decedent is sold, immovable property by public auction unless all heirs consent to another manner of sale; all debts must be paid, and legacies distributed after payment of all debts. Any surplus is distributed to heirs. (C.C. 595-596).

Supervision.—Competent authority supervises appointed official liquidators. Heirs may bring recourse against liquidation measures intended or already taken. (C.C. 595).

Liquidation of Estate by Bankruptcy Office.—If all next statutory heirs renounce inheritance, it is liquidated by bankruptcy office according to bankruptcy law. If ordinary or summary bankruptcy proceedings take place, any surplus, after performance of legacies, is distributed to statutory heirs. (C.C. 573).

Suit for Inheritance.—This special action is open to anyone who, as statutory or appointed heir, believes himself to have better right to inheritance or special property therein than actual possessor. Action must be based on title of inheritance, not on any other title. Court takes necessary measures of protection upon request of plaintiff. Limitation of such action: (1) against defendant in good faith, one year from time plaintiff learned of defendant's possession and plaintiff's own better right; in any case, after ten years from decedent's death or opening of will; (2) against defendant in bad faith, always 30 years. (C.C. 598-600). Before distribution, action against heir has to be brought by suit for distribution. See subhead Heirs, catchline Distribution by Heirs, supra. For other hereditary actions, see topic Wills.

Compulsory Heirship and Legacies.—See topic Wills.

Foreign Executors or Administrators and Foreign Probate.—Recognized under conditions of Arts. 92 and 96 Private International Law Statute.

EXEMPTIONS:

See topic Collection of Debts and Bankruptcy.

FIDUCIARIES:

Transfer of property to a fiduciary is recognized. Fiduciary becomes owner of tangible property and creditor of intangible property, and assumes obligation to retransfer to transferor or to transfer to third person under certain conditions. Case Law holds that fiduciary has status of full owner or full creditor; as a rule, fiduciary property falls into bankruptcy estate of fiduciary. Certain court decisions examine possible exceptions to this rule.

Transfer of property to fiduciary is also admissible in order to give security to claim. However, if tangible movable property remains with transferor on basis of special legal ground (e.g., lease) transfer does not become effective with respect to third persons if it was intended to harm them or to violate provisions of pledge. (See topic Pledges.) (C.C. 717).

See also topics Executors and Administrators; Foundations; Trusts.

FIRM AND CORPORATE NAME:

When doing business, any individual or association of persons must use firm or corporate name. (C.O. 944-956; Decree of Swiss Federal Government concerning Register of Commerce of June 7, 1937, Arts. 44-46; Federal Statute concerning penal provisions to Law of Register of Commerce and Firm and Corporate Names, of Oct. 6, 1924). No reservation of name is possible.

Selection of Firm and Corporate Names.—Meaning of name may not be deceptive or against public policy. Advertising claims may not be included in name. National or territorial designations, e.g., "International", "Europe", "Switzerland" may only be used by specific permission and, if nouns, must be put between brackets. (C.O. 944). Firm name of individual must mention individual's last name, with or without first name. (C.O. 945).

To determine availability and admissibility of name, inquiries should be addressed to Register of Commerce beforehand. However, clearance and actual registration by Registrar does not have binding legal effect. Aggrieved third parties may still sue for change of name.

Branch offices must use name of head office, possibly with additions valid only for branch office. Branch office of foreign enterprise must include place of business of head office and of branch office, and explicit designation as branch office. (C.O. 952).

Foreign Firm and Corporate Names.—If such names violate mandatory rules of Swiss law, they may not be used for Swiss branches of foreign enterprises.

Exclusiveness of Registered Firm and Corporate Name.—Two businesses in same relevant area may not have same name. (C.O. 946, 951).

FOREIGN EXCHANGE:

See topic Exchange Control.

FOREIGN INVESTMENT:

Flow of new foreign capital and funds into Switzerland or into Swiss currency may be subjected to specific restrictions and licensing. Investment in Swiss immovables requires license.

Switzerland is a party to Convention on Settlement of Investment Disputes between States and Nationals of other States concluded in Washington on Mar. 18, 1965.

See also topics Exchange Control; Immovable Property, subhead Acquisition by Nonresidents.

FOREIGN TRADE REGULATIONS:

Imports and exports are in principle subject to control of Swiss Federal Government, Department of Economics and its subsections. Licenses are presently required for goods relating to military and economic defense, protection of agriculture and of certain industries, and in connection with foreign trade or foreign exchange agreements. Particulars concerning these everchanging regulations should be sought from Swiss Consulates.

Switzerland is member of WTO.

Switzerland is member of European Free Trade Association. Duties on most imports from EFTA countries were reduced to nil.

On July 22, 1972 Switzerland entered into treaties with Common Market on foreign trade and European Community for Coal and Steel. Import customs duties and export duties have been reduced to nil.

See topic Treaties. See also topic Customs.

FOUNDATIONS:

Foundation (Stiftung, fondation, fondazione) is legal entity, created by dedication of assets for specific purpose which can be of public, charitable or private character. (C.C. 52-59, 80-89 bis).

Formation and Organization.—Dedication must be made by publicly authenticated deed, by will or inheritance pact. It must provide for organization of foundation, which consists in most cases of foundation council. Entry into Register of Commerce is mandatory except for family and ecclesiastical foundations. If not provided otherwise in deed, legal domicile of foundation is at its place of current administration, which must be in Switzerland.

Supervision.—Most foundations are subject to supervision to ensure that assets of foundation are used for intended purpose. Depending on scope of purpose, federal, cantonal or municipal authorities supervise.

Dissolution.—Foundations are lasting legal institutions. Foundation can be dissolved if purpose becomes unachievable or is or becomes illegal or immoral. General clause entitling founder, foundation council or any other person to dissolve it at will is not permissible.

Taxation.—See topic Taxation.

Family and ecclesiastical foundations are governed by special provisions. (C.O. 52, 87, 335). Family foundation may be created for benefit of particular family, with following purposes: Defraying expenses of education, endowments, support of family members or similar purposes. These purposes are narrowly interpreted. Swiss courts consider family foundations for general support as invalid. Family foundations and ecclesiastical foundations need not be entered in Register of Commerce, unless, incidentally to their purpose, they conduct business. They are not subject to official supervision, unless public law provides otherwise. See topic Trusts.

FRAUDS, STATUTE OF:

Unless law stipulates otherwise any legal act of private law including contract becomes valid, if intention was explicitly or conclusively expressed by party or parties. (C.O. 1; C.C. 7). If contested, proof by any means is admitted.

Formal Requirements.—

Written form may be mandatorily prescribed by statute or chosen by parties. (C.O. 13, 16). Document must be signed by all persons thereby obligated. Letter or original of telegram bearing signature of person or persons thereby obligating themselves fulfills requirements of written form.

Publicly authenticated instrument to extent that federal law does not have provisions, must follow form prescribed by cantonal law. (C.C. Final Title 55).

See topic Acknowledgements and Other Public Authentications.

Chosen Form.—Special form may be chosen by parties to contract which otherwise would need no special form in order to be valid; either (a) merely as means of proof, in which case parties are bound in ordinary way before execution of form but may enforce such execution, or (b) as condition for validity of contract, which intention is to be presumed (C.O. 16), but not for subsequent alterations of contract.

Mandatory Form.—For certain legal acts observance of special form is required. This is condition for validity unless law provides otherwise. (C.O. 11; C.C. 7). If form is prescribed for validity of legal act it must also be observed for any alterations, but supplementary nonessential clauses not in contradiction to act need not observe form. (C.O. 12).

Written form mandatory for: agreement for distribution of estate provided no new rights in rem are thereby created (see topics Executors and Administrators; Immovable Property); assignment of choses in action, but not promise to assign (see topic Assignments); promise of gift of movable property, i.e., all kinds of property except immovables and rights in rem on immovables (C.O. 243); covenant in restraint of trade (C.O. 358).

Publicly Authenticated Instrument Mandatory.—See topic Acknowledgments and Other Public Authentications. Mandatory for inter alia: matrimonial property contract (see topic Husband and Wife); public will and inheritance pact including promise of gift to be performed at death of donor (see topic Wills, and C.O. 245); most agreements for conveyance or incumbrance of immovable property (see topic Immovable Property); incorporation and certain legal acts pertaining to share corporations and to limited partnership corporations (see topic Corporations).

Contracts of guaranty (einfache Buergschaft, cautionnement simple, fideiussione semplice [C.O. 495]), or of suretyship (Solidarbuergschaft, cautionnement solidaire, fideiussione solidare [C.O. 496]), are subject to special provisions, inter alia to following: As a rule, written form is required; and maximum amount of liability of guarantor or of surety must be mentioned in instrument, in case of suretyship also several liability of surety. Special rules apply if guarantor or surety is natural person (with exception of guaranty or suretyship in favor of Swiss Confederation including its establishments or of canton for custom duties, taxes, etc.): if amount of liability of guarantor or of surety exceeds SFr. 2,000, publicly authenticated instrument containing also maximum amount of liability and signature of guarantor or surety is required; for lesser amount written form is sufficient, however with statement of maximum amount of liability in guarantor's or surety's own handwriting in instrument, in case of suretyship also solidarity clause (C.O. 493); if guarantor or surety is married and spouses not judicially separated, written consent of spouse required before or at entering of obligation, except if guarantor or surety is recorded in Register of Commerce (see topic Records) in certain capacities (C.O. 494). Special rules apply for subsequent alterations of such contract of guaranty or suretyship.

GARNISHMENT:

Any property of debtor in hands of third persons or claims against them may be reached by seizure for execution or attachment. See topic Attachment.

GUARDIAN AND WARD:

Hague Convention of Oct. 5, 1961 applies generally.

Children remain, as long as they are minors, under authority of their parents or surviving parent. Parents may not be arbitrarily deprived of parental authority. (C.C. 273).

During marriage both parents exercise parental power. When parents live separately or have been divorced child stands under parental authority of parent to whom custody has been awarded, or under guardianship. (C.C. 274).

Parents are, by statute, entrusted with representation of child as against third persons. They have also right and duty to manage all of child's assets, including bequests. As a rule parents are not required to account or to give security for faithful performance of their duties in this respect.

Guardians may be appointed officially when necessary and are under supervision of the guardianship authorities and must account at least once every two years. If competent and at least 16 years of age, ward is, if possible, consulted during accounting. (C.C. 413). Guardians and guardianship authorities are liable for losses caused willfully or by their negligence. If they are unable to pay damages, canton becomes liable. (C.C. 426, 427). As a rule, no bond is required from guardian.

See also topic Absentees.

HOLDING CORPORATIONS:

See topic Corporations.

HOLIDAYS:

Provisions for legal holidays are set by Confederation and by each individual canton. In Zürich, following are legal holidays: New Year's Day, Good Friday, Easter Monday, May 1, Ascension, Whitsun-Monday, Aug. 1, Christmas Day, and Dec. 26. If holiday falls on Sun., next day is usually not holiday. For legal purposes Sats. and Suns. are considered to be equal to legal holidays. Transactions on Sats., Suns. and holidays are legally valid.

Switzerland adheres to European Convention on the Calculation of Time Limits dated May 16, 1972.

HUSBAND AND WIFE:

Applicable law may be chosen by spouses among law of common (future) domicile and law of either spouse's citizenship, otherwise law of (last) common domicile applies.

Comprehensive revision came into force Jan. 1, 1989. Existing marital property contracts remain in effect. New law applies unless before Jan. 1, 1988 spouses wrote marital property register at their domicile that they wished to continue old marital combination of property system.

Swiss law provides three systems regulating property rights between spouses: Sharing of acquisitions (Errungenschaftsbeteiligung), community of property (Gütergemeinschaft) and separation of property (Gütertrennung). Sharing of acquisitions applies unless law or marriage property contract provides otherwise. (C.C. 181-184).

Sharing of Acquisitions.—Property earned during marriage, items for solely personal use and property owned before or inherited after marriage remains separate during marriage. Each spouse is responsible for administering his or her own property. Upon dissolution of marriage by death of spouse or divorce, personal use items and property owned before or inherited after marriage are retained by respective spouse (or, in case of death, his or her heirs). Gifts made to third parties within last five years and any other gifts made during marriage with intent of reducing other spouse's share are added to each spouse's property earned during marriage. Each spouse (or his or her heirs) receives one-half of all earned property. Other half is attributed to other spouse. (C.C. 196-220).

Community of Property.—Except as permitted to be modified by marital property contract, all property brought into marriage and all income earned during marriage is jointly owned by spouses. Only items for solely personal use are considered to belong to each spouse. Community property is administered jointly. Upon dissolution of marriage by divorce, each spouse receives items for solely personal use as well as property owned before or inherited after marriage. Remaining community property is split in half. Upon dissolution by death of spouse, surviving spouse and heirs of deceased spouse split community property in half. Marital property contract may determine different dispositions in case of divorce or death. (C.C. 221-246).

Separation of Property.—Each spouse retains and administers his or her property. (C.C. 247-251).

Special Provisions.—Each spouse may freely enter contracts and other legal relationships with third parties and with each other, but giving of security and installment or prepayment contract by one spouse requires consent of other spouse. (C.O. 226b, 228, 494).

If one spouse does not fulfill duty to provide maintenance to family, court may direct spouse's debtors to make payments to other spouse. (C.C. 177).

Property Arrangements Between Unmarried Persons.—In some cases ordinary partnership ("société simple") may exist. See topic Partnerships.

IMMIGRATION:

See topic Aliens.

IMMOVABLE PROPERTY:

Swiss law distinguishes between immovables (Grundstuecke, immeubles, fondi), tangible movable things, (bewegliche Sachen or Fahrnis, meubles, beni mobili), and intangibles (choses in action [Forderungen or Obligationen, creances or obligations, crediti or obbligazioni] negotiable instruments, and immaterial or industrial property rights, e.g., rights on patents, trademarks).

Following are immovables: (1) land with all buildings, plants and springs (C.C. 667), (2) independent and lasting rights entered in land register, e.g., specific building leases (right in rem), right to springs, (3) mines, (4) apartment ownership (condominium) (C.C. 655). Disposition of immovable made without reservations extends also to tangible movables which, according to local usage or intention of owner of immovable are permanently provided for its management, use or preservation, and brought in any way into relationship to immovable for its service (Zugehoer, accessories, accessori [C.C. 644-645]). Restricted rights in rem on immovables include: servitudes (C.C.

IMMOVABLE PROPERTY . . . *continued*
730-744), usufruct (C.C. 745-771), land charges (C.C. 782-792), mortgages (see topic Mortgages).

Acquisition.—Distinction made between underlying legal ground (causa) for acquisition of ownership or restricted rights in rem on immovables and acquisition itself. Underlying legal ground gives obligatory right of entry of ownership or of restricted right in rem into land register; only such entry brings right in rem into existence (principle of entry into land register). Certain exceptions of ipso jure acquisition of ownership or restricted rights in rem on immovables, e.g., in case of heirship, judgment, enforcement. In such cases entry is mere declaratory measure, which however is condition precedent for disposition of right. For mortgages principle of entry is as a rule fully applicable. (C.C. 656, 731, 746, 776, 783-784, 799, 971).

Entry in land register pertaining to ownership or to restricted right in rem is only valid, if underlying legal ground is valid (principle of legality or of causality [C.C. 974]). However, acquisition of ownership or of restricted right in rem on immovables by acquirer relying bona fide on entry in land register is protected (principle of public faith of land register [C.C. 973]).

Kind of effect of rights in rem can be given to certain obligatory rights pertaining to immovables by way of "annotation" in land register (C.C. 959), e.g., to right of first refusal, to purchase, to repurchase, ordinary lease, usufructuary lease (C.C. 681, 683; C.O. 216, 260, 282). Co-owners of immovable have, by virtue of law without entry in land register, right of first refusal against any third person who has acquired share in immovable. (C.C. 682).

Agreements to convey or encumber immovables to be valid agreements require in most cases public authentication (C.C. 657, 746, 776, 783, 799; C.O. 216, 243); written form suffices for certain agreements, e.g., for distribution of estate (including immovables) provided no new rights in rem are thereby created (C.C. 634; see topic Executors and Administrators), for servitudes (C.C. 732), for right of first refusal (C.O. 216, subdiv. 3). Recognition of publicly authenticated acts pertaining to immovables made outside of canton where immovable is located is left to laws of canton where immovable is situated. Certain cantons (e.g., Zurich, Berne) recognize only publicly authenticated acts made according to their own legislation by authenticating person authorized for district where immovable is located. Power of attorney for execution of publicly authenticated act duly executed at any locality is accepted.

Acquisition by Nonresidents.—Federal Statute on Acquisition of Immovables by Nonresidents of Dec. 16, 1983, in force since Jan. 1, 1985, applies (*Note*: amendments will not take effect before 1996). Acquisition of immovables (directly, or through purchase of shares in legal entity owning significant immovables) by nonresident aliens, or by legal entities dominated by such, requires license. 1995 and 1996 only 1,420 licenses available nationwide. No restrictions apply to alien persons who have lived in Switzerland without interruption for ten (or, in case of citizens of certain countries, five) years and have been granted permanent residence permit. Statutory heirs—as defined by Swiss law—do not need license. Other alien nonresident heirs must obtain one or otherwise sell property within two years. License may be granted only if federal requirements or special cantonal requirements have been met. License may be granted for immovables mainly serving as trading, manufacturing or other commercial establishment but only to persons already engaged in that business. Acquisition of personal vacation homes, vacation apartments and condominiums in apartment hotels is prohibited outside certain areas, and subject to quotas distributed yearly among cantons. No license can be obtained for farms and other establishments for agriculture and forestry, or for immovable property. Forbidden transactions are void. Persons participating in transactions for which no license was obtained can be imprisoned or fined and are barred from ever acquiring Swiss immovables. Competent public agency may sue for dissolution of legal entity violating law. Statute expected to become less discriminatory for resident aliens. Acquisition of real estate will be free of regulation except for vacation houses. Investment in alien dominated Swiss legal entities actually engaged in business in Switzerland will be free of regulation.

Rural Land Law.—Special rules apply. (Statute, Oct. 4, 1991).

Moratorium on resale within ten years after acquisition applies to agricultural land. Similar two year moratorium for nonagricultural land. Forbidden transactions are void. Exceptions may be granted by cantonal authority for partition of estate, etc. (C.O. 218, 218bis, 218ter, and Federal Decree of Oct. 6, 1989).

Construction of buildings is subject to regular licensing by local authorities.

Zoning and Planning.—Federal Law of June 22, 1979 limits use of immovable property in general and also further construction on borders of rivers and lakes, sites of special beauty or characteristics, etc. Details are or will be laid down by cantonal statutes. Entire territory must be divided into zones, in particular building and nonbuilding zones. Every construction requires permit.

See also topics Landlord and Tenant; Mortgages; Records, subhead Land Register; Acknowledgments and Other Public Authentications; Frauds, Statute of; Collection of Debts and Bankruptcy, subhead Composition.

INFANTS:

Law of habitual residence applies.

Person attains majority on completing 20th year, or by marrying, or on being declared of full age by proper authorities. To obtain this declaration, person must have parental consent and reached age 18.

See also topic Guardian and Ward.

Head of family is responsible for torts of child in household unless head of family can prove that care required by circumstances was observed.

INTEREST:

No interest is chargeable on money debts except when parties explicitly or implicitly agree to it, or if provided for by statute (e.g., in case of default of debtor, C.O. 104). However, in case of debts resulting from business transactions, e.g., commercial loan, interest is presumably owed. (C.O. 314).

Interest rate, unless agreed by parties, depends on custom, in case of loan presumably at rate customary for particular loan at time and place where it was made, frequently, with special cases excepted, rate is 5% (C.O. 73, 314); in case of recourse on draft or check rate is 6% (C.O. 1045/46, 1130). Stipulations for compound interest are not valid except when customary in business, as for current accounts and for savings bank accounts. (C.O. 314).

Federal law does not fix a maximum interest rate. However, it provides that, in case of manifest disproportion of mutual considerations of the parties caused by one party taking advantage of distress, inexperience, or carelessness of other party, prejudiced party can rescind contract and demand restitution within one year since conclusion of contract. (C.O. 21). Cantons may fix maximum interest rate for debts secured by immovable property. (C.C. 795). Legislation against abuses by agreed interest rates may be enacted by public law (C.O. 73), and exists in several cantons, e.g., Zurich, where lenders may charge monthly maximum 1% for interest and commission plus 0.5% for management cost and disbursements. Usury is punishable. (Swiss Criminal Code 157).

JUDGMENTS:

Judgments by courts in Switzerland in matters of private law relating to money claims or other kinds of claims must be recognized and enforced anywhere in Switzerland (Federal Constitution, art. 61), provided they are res judicata, rendered by competent court, and with due citation of defendant (who in case of incapacity must have been legally represented). Same holds for money claims for federal administrative decisions, also for certain cantonal administrative decisions, e.g., tax claims and for federal and cantonal penal judgments and decisions.

Foreign judgments in matters of private law are recognized and enforced: (a) under Lugano Convention of Feb. 21, 1990 on jurisdiction and enforcement with Finland, France, Germany, Ireland, Italy, Luxembourg, Netherlands, Norway, Portugal, Spain, Sweden, U.K. Other EU and EFTA countries expected to join; (b) under bilateral treaties, e.g. with Czech Republic, Liechtenstein, Slovakia; (c) otherwise, Private International Law Statute.

For procedure of enforcement, see topic Collection of Debts and Bankruptcy.

See topic Arbitration and Award.

LABOR RELATIONS:

Law of habitual place of work applies. Choice of law is limited. Sex discrimination statute in force since July 1, 1996.

Statutory termination period one to three months depending on length of employment. Reasons for terminating employment must be given on request. Damages if employment "abusively" terminated. (C.O. 335 to 336b).

Employers are required to grant long-time employees specific types of benefits. Special family allowances are compulsory.

Federal old age and disability insurance and unemployment insurance are compulsory state insurance (see topic Taxation, subhead Direct Federal Taxes, catchline Insurance: Old Age and Other), also specific Federal Accident Insurance for employees (Federal Statute of Mar. 20, 1981). Private pension plans and disability insurance compulsory (so called "Second Column") Federal Statute of June 25, 1982).

Work permits: see topic Aliens.

LANDLORD AND TENANT:

Leasing of apartments and business premises is subject to special Federal and Cantonal regulations and supervision in favor of lessees. In foreground are protective measures with regard to notice of termination and increase of rents. Lessee who has contracted new lease or renewed lease may apply thereafter within 30 days for reduction of rent. Leases are subject to judicial review on basis of building and capital cost and comparison with leases for similar properties.

Termination of Lease.—Lessee of residential or business premises may up to 60 days before end of fixed term of lease or within 30 days after having received notice of termination of indefinite lease apply to court for an extension of lease. Court may grant two extensions up to three years for residential and up to five years for business premises, if hardship suffered by lessee exceeds importance of interests of lessor. Application for a second extension must be submitted up to 60 days before end of first extension. Termination is valid only on special official form. On request reasons must be given. "Abusive" termination may be declared invalid by conciliation board or court.

LAW REPORTS:

Major decisions of Swiss Federal Supreme Court are published currently in its official collection "Entscheidungen des Schweizerischen Bundesgerichtes, Amtliche Sammlung", "Arrêts du Tribunal Fédéral Suisse, Receuil Officiel." Numerous, mostly unofficial reports and periodicals, publish court decisions, e.g.: "Praxis des Bundesgerichtes," "Blätter für Zürcherische Rechtssprechung," "Journal des Tribunaux," "Semaine judiciaire", "Zeitschrift des Bernischen Juristenvereins," "Basler Juristische Mitteilungen", "Repertorio di Giurisprudenza Patria".

LEGISLATURE:

See topic Constitution and Government.

LICENSES:

Applicable Law.—Law of habitual residence of licensor applies. Choice of law is permitted.

Manufacturing and Similar Licenses.—No specific requirements or forms have to be observed for license agreements. License agreements for patents can be entered in patent register.

Other Licenses and Restrictions.—Aliens must obtain residence and work permits to exercise gainful activity in Switzerland. (See topic Aliens.) Apart from this general provision and those concerning state monopolies, there are few restrictions for foreign enterprises or subsidiaries. Specific requirements apply to ownership, management and residence in connection with oil drilling and oil exploitation on lands in Switzerland (Concordat Sept. 24, 1955); pipelines (statute Oct. 3, 1963); nuclear power plants (statute Dec. 23, 1959); Swiss seagoing vessels (statute Sept. 23, 1953) (see topic Shipping); aircraft registered in Switzerland (statute Dec. 21, 1948). Acquisition of

LICENSES . . . *continued*
Swiss immovable property may not be refused if foreign enterprises will use it mainly for manufacturing, trading, or other commercial establishment. See topics Foreign Investment and Immovable Property.

LIENS:

Tangible movables and securities in hands of creditor with consent of debtor, may be retained until claim is paid, provided it is payable and connected property under lien. Among merchants connection of both with business suffices. (C.C. 895).

Commission merchants have lien on consigned goods or their proceeds for advances, disbursements, commissions and accrued charges. (C.O. 434). Forwarding agents have similar rights. Common carriers and warehousemen have liens on property in their hands to extent of their charges and disbursements. (C.O. 451, 485). Landlords have lien on furniture and equipment in rented business premises for past year's rent and current six months' rent. (C.O. 272). See topic Landlord and Tenant.

LIMITATION OF ACTIONS:

Under Swiss law statute of limitation for actions is part of substantive law, not of law of procedure.

Regular statute of limitation for claims is ten years, provided federal civil law does not specifically provide for shorter or longer period (C.O. 127), e.g., five years for rents, interests and other periodical payments, for food and board, for work done by craftsmen, for retail sales, for professional services of doctors, attorneys, law agents and notaries, for wages (C.O. 128), for right of borrower to receive loan and of lender for acceptance (C.O. 315). For claims based on responsibility against incorporators, directors and managers of corporations statute of limitation is five years, beginning with first knowledge of damage, at latest ten years from damaging act. (C.O. 760). If general meeting has granted release, dissenting shareholder must file claim for responsibility within six months. (C.O. 757). Claims for torts are barred after one year from time when damaged party has received knowledge of damage and of identity of person responsible therefor, but in any event in ten years after injury took place, except if criminal law provides for longer statute of limitation. (C.O. 60). Certain special statutes, such as federal statutes on liability of railways etc. of Mar. 28, 1905, and on road traffic etc. of Dec. 19, 1958, provide for two years. For statute of limitation of mortis causa dispositions, see topic Wills. Legal statutes of limitation may not be altered by previous agreement between parties. (C.O. 129).

Suspension or Interruption of Statutory Period.—Statute of limitation does not commence and, if it has begun to run, is suspended in cases of certain parental or marital relations, as between parent and child, guardian and ward, between spouses, in case usufruct on debt exists, also as long as claim cannot be brought before Swiss Court. (C.O. 134).

Statute of limitation is interrupted (1) by acknowledgment of debt by debtor, particularly by payment of interest and instalments, constitution of pledge or guaranty, (2) by commencement of proceedings for collection or court action by creditor. (C.O. 135).

See also topics Holidays; Sales, subhead Remedies of Buyers, catchline Statute of Limitations.

LIMITED PARTNERSHIP:

See topics Corporations; Partnerships.

MARRIAGE:

The right to marry is protected by Federal Constitution. (Art. 54; C.C. 90-136; Ordinance of Federal Government concerning Civil Status Matters [Civil Status Ordinance] of June 1, 1953).

Capacity to Marry.—Prerequisites: (1) age of 20 years for males, of 18 years for females; for important reasons cantonal government may permit males to marry at 18, females at 17; (2) capacity of judgment; (3) no mental illness; (4) consent for minors (see topic Infants) by both parents or of parent having parental power or of guardian. For persons of age under guardianship consent by guardian is required. If consent refused by guardian, complaint may be made with cantonal authorities. (C.C. 96-99).

Impediments to Marriage.—Include (1) relationship (a) by blood or by adoption between parent-child, brother-sister of whole or half blood, uncle-niece or aunt-nephew; (b) between parents-in-law and children-in-law, stepparents and stepchildren, even if marriage on which relationship is based has been terminated; (2) existing marriage of one of future spouses, unless proof is furnished of termination of former marriage by annulment, death or divorce (for absenteeism see topic Death, subhead Declaration of Absence); (3) prohibition of remarriage for woman, for 300 days after termination of marriage unless she gives birth prior to end of such period. Under special circumstances time limit may be shortened. (C.C. 100-104).

Aliens may marry in Switzerland if permitted under Swiss law or either spouse's law of citizenship if one has domicile in Switzerland, or marriage is recognized in country of domicile or citizenship of both, or would be if divorce decreed or recognized in Switzerland would be recognized. See topic Citizenship.

Publication and License.—Marriage to be celebrated in Switzerland requires prior publication of promise of marriage at Civil Status Offices of Swiss domicile and place of Swiss citizenship (see topic Citizenship) of each of future bridegroom and bride, except if both future spouses are aliens not domiciled in Switzerland. Among various participating Civil Status Officials, one is competent for direction of procedure in following order: Official at (1) Swiss domicile of bridegroom, (2) Swiss domicile of bride, (3) place of Swiss citizenship (see topic Citizenship) of bridegroom, (4) place of Swiss citizenship of bride. Promise of marriage must be declared personally or in writing with officially authenticated signatures, as rule to directing Civil Status Official to whom documentation as to domicile, civil status, capacity to marry, nonexistence of impediments must also be submitted. Persons living outside of Switzerland may file such promise with diplomatic or consular representative, or with competent foreign authority. If directing official finds incapacity or impediments to marriage, he refuses publication. Otherwise intended marriage will be published. If there are grounds for objection not clearly established by documents, directing official must communicate such grounds to cantonal supervisory authority for transmittal to authority competent to object.

Publication takes place for ten days at each of various Civil Status Offices mentioned above. Within time of publication any interested person may file in writing objections to marriage on grounds of incapacity or impediments. In case such grounds would warrant annulment of marriage for reason of nullity (see subhead Annulment, infra) objection must be filed ex officio by competent authority, also after publication up to celebration of marriage within ten days after having received actual knowledge of such grounds.

Objection will at once be communicated to future spouses who may contest it within ten days, in which case objector has to bring court action within ten days. If no objection was filed, or if contested and no court action was brought, or such action was dismissed, directing official, unless he sees pertinent ground for refusal of celebration of marriage, will inform future spouses that such celebration may take place. At request of future spouses "Certificate of Publication" (marriage license) is issued entitling future spouses to be married before any Civil Status Official in Switzerland within next six months. No such certificate is issued to alien bridegroom not domiciled in Switzerland because that marriage must be celebrated within canton where marriage permit (see subhead Aliens, supra) was granted. (C.C. 105-114; Ordinance of 1953, 148-162).

Marriage Ceremony.—Special circumstances excepted, marriage is celebrated publicly with participation of Civil Status Official at marriage hall in presence of two witnesses of age. Official asks bridegroom and bride separately whether each is willing to enter into marriage with other. After affirmative answers official declares that by such mutual consent marriage is concluded by force of law. Immediately afterwards marriage certificate is given to newlyweds. Religious marriage may optionally take place only after civil law marriage. (C.C. 116-118; Ordinance of 1953, 163-165).

Reports of Marriages.—After celebration marriage must immediately be entered in Marriage Register at place of official who performed celebration. Marriage of Swiss citizen celebrated abroad is entered in Marriage Register at place of Swiss citizenship. Marriage of Swiss citizen celebrated in Switzerland or abroad must also be entered in Family Register. See topic Records, subhead Civil Status Register.

Annulment.—Marriage is null and void if one of spouses was either: (1) Already married at time of celebration of marriage, (2) insane or experiencing lasting incapacity of judgment, (3) or if spouses are related in prohibited degree (see subhead Impediments to Marriage, clause [1], supra). Action must be brought by competent authority and may be brought by anybody having interest. (C.C. 120-122).

Marriage is voidable by one of spouses: (1) If spouse was incapable of judgment for transitory reason at time of celebration of marriage; (2) for error, if spouse declared consent to marriage but did not want to marry present spouse, or was induced to marriage by error as to qualities of other spouse of such importance that defect renders married life unbearable; (3) for fraud, if spouse was fraudulently deceived with respect to honorability of other spouse by other spouse or by third person with knowledge and consent of latter and thereby induced to marry, or if sickness apt to greatly endanger own or descendant's health was concealed; (4) for duress. Action lapses after six months from discovery of ground for avoidance or termination of duress, in any case after five years after celebration of marriage. Action for avoidance of marriage may also be brought by parents or guardians whose consent was required for marriage, unless in meantime respective spouse has become of age or if guardianship terminated or if woman has become pregnant. No action for avoidance is admissible in case of certain irregularities, such as violation of legal or judicial waiting period for woman whose former marriage has been terminated, or nonobservance of legal formalities with respect to marriage celebrated by Civil Status Official. (C.C. 123-128, 130, 131).

Marriage annulled on grounds of nullity or voidance has effect of valid marriage until annulment is declared by court. Spouse who changed name upon marriage may keep married name. Property rights between spouses, also relations between parents and children, are treated as in divorce. Same holds for jurisdiction and procedure. Right to bring action for annulment is not inheritable, but pending action may be continued by plaintiff's heirs. (C.C. 132-136). See also topic Names.

MEMBERSHIP ASSOCIATIONS:

Membership association (Verein, Association, Associazione) is legal entity organized for nonprofit purpose. It must have constitution with provisions as to its purpose, financing, organization, and name. It need not be entered in Register of Commerce, unless, incidentally to its purpose, it conducts business. (C.C. 60-79).

MINES AND MINERALS:

They are governed not by federal but by cantonal law. In most cantons, rights connected therewith are owned by state.

Concordat of Sept. 24, 1955 between certain cantons regulates granting of oil drilling and exploitation licenses.

Nuclear energy is regulated by federal statute. Procurement and use require federal license. Nuclear Liability Statute came into force Jan. 1, 1984.

MONOPOLIES AND RESTRAINT OF TRADE:

Unfair Competition.—Law of country of market applies. Federal Statute of Dec. 19, 1986 forbids unfair practices, especially incorrect misleading or unnecessarily sharp depreciation of goods or products of competitors or praise of one's own goods or products, unwarranted use of titles or professional distinctions, measures which may create or foster confusion with goods of competitors, using or copying competitor's work product, inducing employees or agents of competitor firms to take measures which are detrimental to their employer or to betray trade secrets, any surreptitious obtention of trade secrets, non-observance of labor conditions binding competitors.

Persons suffering from injury on account of above acts, whether as competitors or as customers, can apply for qualification of these acts as unfair trade practices, desistance from further practice, retraction of unwarranted claims, and indemnity for damage and under circumstances for "tort moral". If these acts have been committed by employees injured party can also proceed against employer. Upon request of injured party unfair

MONOPOLIES AND RESTRAINT OF TRADE . . . *continued*
trade practices can, if wilfully committed, be subject to criminal prosecution. If they have been committed by employee on behalf and with knowledge of employer, employer may also be criminally prosecuted.

Antitrust.—Law of country of market where direct damage is done applies. But in Switzerland no damages will be awarded beyond those under Swiss law. Federal Supreme Court in 1960 declared boycott illegal in principle, unless boycott is obviously and overwhelmingly in justified interests of cartel or similar organization. Federal Statute of Dec. 20, 1985 declares illegal certain collective measures against third parties, such as boycott, dumping, etc., and unreasonable internal obligations of cartel members. It permits investigations of cartels and under certain circumstances suits in public interest. *Note:* New Statute under discussion and might come into force mid-1996.

MORTGAGES:

Debts may be secured by immovables either as mortgage (Grundpfandverschreibung, Hypothèeque, Ipoteca), or as mortgage note (Schuldbrief, Cédules hypothécaires, Cartella ipotecaria). Third type, land charge certificate (Gült, Lettre de rente, Cartella di rendita), is not used. Mortgage may secure any, even future or contingent, debt. It secures payments due by whoever owns piece of immovables, regardless of any personal obligation on his part. Mortgage notes are negotiable instruments issued to name or to bearer, and may be transferred as such. Mortgage note is collateral security of determined and unconditional bond.

With certain exceptions, mortgages and mortgage notes become effective upon entry in Land Register. Maximum amount must be stated in Swiss currency. Entries, including amendments and cancellations, can be made only upon execution of publicly authenticated deed. Priority is established according to rank designated in Land Register, not according to date of registration. Stipulations to effect that upon cancellation of mortgage or mortgage note prior in rank subsequent mortgages or notes move up in rank are permitted.

When immovables are sold and buyer acknowledges his personal liability for debts secured by mortgage or mortgage note on such property, liability of original debtor ends unless creditor objects within one year.

Debts secured by mortgages or mortgage notes are not subject to statute of limitations. If debt is not paid in time, creditor may execute on property, including all accessories such as plant, hotel furniture and rent accrued after execution proceedings, unless expressly stipulated otherwise. Property gives security for principal, interest and expenses for execution of debt. If there is more than one creditor, proceeds of sale are distributed by rank.

Mortgages and mortgage notes are cancelled upon entry in Land Register or upon total destruction of immovables. Cancellation or return of instrument may be requested upon payment of debt. (C.C. 793-874).

MOTOR VEHICLES:

Switzerland is a party to the International Treaty concerning Motor Vehicles of Apr. 24, 1926 and to the Treaty Concerning Temporary Importation of Private Road Vehicles, dated New York, June 4, 1954. Under the latter, motor vehicles of nonresidents and registered abroad for personal use are free from taxes and levies for sojourns in Switzerland.

Foreigners domiciled abroad but staying temporarily in Switzerland can, under certain circumstances, obtain Swiss plates for a period up to two years without having to pay customs duties.

Insurance of motor vehicles for damages to third parties is mandatory. These may sue insurance company directly, which may claim indemnity from driver or holder under specific conditions.

NAMES:

Spouses select bride's or groom's family name as common family name, passed on to children. Bride can keep former family name as middle name.

See also topic Firm and Corporate Name.

NATURALIZATION:

See topic Citizenship.

NEGOTIABLE INSTRUMENTS:

Drafts.—(Wechsel, lettre de change et billet a ordre, cambiale e vaglia cambiario [paghero]; C.O. 991-1099). Switzerland adhered to three Geneva Conventions of 1930 and 1931 concerning uniform law of Drafts and Checks, on certain rules of conflicts of laws, and on stamp tax statutes connected therewith.

Requirements as to Content.—(1) Designation as draft or bill of exchange within text of document as drawn, (2) unconditional order to pay determined sum of money, (3) name of drawee, (4) maturity, (5) place of payment, (6) name of person to whom or to whose order payment is to be made, (7) date and place of drawing, (8) signature of drawer. (C.O. 991).

Maturity.—Draft not mentioning maturity is payable at sight. Draft not mentioning place of drawing is deemed to have been drawn at place indicated with name of drawer written on draft or on sheet attached to draft. (C.O. 1992).

Transfer.—Delivery of draft with unconditional endorsement on draft or on sheet attached, or with written assignment. If draft contains clause "not to order" or equivalent clause, transfer is effected only by delivery of draft with written assignment. (C.O. 1001-1003, 165).

Presentment and Acceptance.—Draft may be presented for written acceptance by drawee at drawee's place up to maturity unless prohibited in terms of draft; such prohibition is permissible only under certain conditions. Acceptance binds drawee for payment at maturity. Draft payable at sight must be presented within one year from date of drawing, unless otherwise stipulated. (C.O. 1011-1019, 1024).

Draft has to be presented by holder on date of payment or on one of two following working days.

Payment.—If draft calls for payment in currency other than legal tender at place of payment, amount may be converted into local currency at rate of exchange prevailing on date of maturity. If debtor delays payment, holder has option to demand payment either at rate of exchange in force on date of maturity or at rate prevailing on day of actual payment. Value of foreign currency is determined according to commercial custom at place of payment. Drawer may, however, in draft itself prescribe rate of exchange to be applied in converting foreign currency. (C.O. 1031).

Protest.—Drafts not accepted or not paid must be protested in usual manner, unless protest is waived. (C.O. 1034-1041, 1043).

Recourse in Default of Acceptance or Payment.—Holder may exact payment from endorsers, drawer and others liable on draft at maturity. This right also exists before maturity in case of nonacceptance, acceptor's insolvency or bankruptcy, or when execution on judgment against acceptor has been returned unsatisfied.

Any person paying draft has recourse against previous persons liable. (C.O. 1033-1052).

Days of Grace.—Not recognized, whether legal or judicial. (C.O. 1083).

Limitation of Actions.—Actions are barred by statute of limitations. Periods: Any entitled persons against acceptor, three years after date of maturity; holder against endorsers and drawer, one year after due protest or if protest is waived one year after maturity; endorser against other endorsers and drawer, six months after date of payment or judicial enforcement. (C.O. 1069).

Insofar as drawer and acceptor of draft are unjustly enriched at expense of holder, they remain liable to holder, even when their liability has become extinguished by statute of limitations or because some formal requirements have not been met. (C.O. 1052).

Negotiable Instruments, Revenue Stamps.—Confederation may levy stamp duties on negotiable instruments (Federal Constitution art. 41 bis); presently no stamp duties are levied.

Conflict of Laws.—Capacity of person to assume liability on draft is determined by law of country of citizenship. If competency is denied by that law, liability nevertheless exists if signature has been given within country according to laws of which person is competent. Form of contract on draft is governed by law of country where contract is signed. Form and time limits for protests and form of other acts necessary to exercise or preserve rights attaching to draft are governed by law of country in whose territory protest is to be made or where act is to be performed. Effect of contracts on draft of acceptor and maker of promissory note are governed by law of place of payment. Effects of other contracts on draft are governed by law of country where contracts were signed. Payment of draft on maturity, calculation of dates for maturity and payment and payment of draft made out in foreign currency are governed by law of country where draft is payable. See C.O. 1086-1095.

Checks.—Check must contain designation "check". Checks payable in Switzerland may be drawn only on banks. (C.O. 1102). Check cannot be accepted, it is payable on sight. Any provision to contrary is ineffective. (C.O. 1115, 1116). If check is "crossed," it may only be paid to bank or to customer of drawee. If check is "especially crossed", it may only be paid to especially designated bank or to bank's customer if bank is itself drawee. (C.O. 1123, 24). Check may contain phrase: "only for accounting" or "for deposit only", in this case payment of check in cash is excluded. (C.O. 1125).

Other Negotiable Instruments.—Law defines negotiable instrument (Wertpapier, papiervaleur, titolo di credito or cartavalore) as document to which right is connected in such way that right cannot be exercised against debtor nor transferred to third persons without document. (C.O. 965). Such instruments may be issued in name of specific creditor (C.O. 974-977) or payable to order of specifically named creditor (C.O. 1145-1152, 967-969) or to bearer (C.O. 978-989). Certain instruments are on order by operation of law, such as drafts, checks payable to specifically named person, registered shares, commercial paper (including warehouse receipts, warrants, bills of lading), mortgages issued on names. Instruments to bearer are frequently issued in Switzerland, especially for debentures and shares.

Transfer.—Full transfer may be effectuated only by delivery of instrument itself or of means procuring power over instrument. No further requirement for transfer of instruments to bearer. For instrument payable to named person written declaration of assignment by transferor either on document itself or separately is required; for instrument on order, either endorsement on instrument or sheet attached to it, or written assignment on instrument itself or separately.

Defenses.—In any kind of negotiable instrument debtor (obligor) has defenses (1) pertaining to validity and wording of instrument, (2) other defenses existing against immediate creditor.

In case of instruments to bearer or to order, other defenses of debtor based on legal relations between debtor and assignors are excluded, except in case of fraud. Defenses pertaining to validity of transfers are also excluded, but instrument to order must show uninterrupted chain of endorsements. (C.O. 979, 1007, 1146).

In case of instruments payable to named persons, additional defenses are possible based on legal relations between debtor and first creditor and all assignors; also defenses pertaining to validity of all transfers. (See topic Assignments.)

Special Kinds of Negotiable Instruments.—There are various forms of negotiable instruments showing only some of features described above. Instrument to order by law may be restricted as to transferability by endorsement, which gives it legal character of instrument payable to named person (so-called "recta-instrument", C.O. 1001); instrument payable to named person may have clause that debtor is entitled (but not bound) to perform to any holder of instrument (so-called "limping bearer instrument", C.O. 976). Instruments payable to named persons or to order may be subject to special restrictions of transfer (so-called "vinculation"), i.e., in case of registered shares condition subsequent of consent of legal entity according to articles. (C.O. 627 No. 8, 684-686a).

NOTARIES PUBLIC:

Legislation relating to notaries public pertains to domain of cantons. In most cantons notaries are public officials, e.g., Zurich, Berne, Ticino, Vaud, Geneva. In some cantons function of notary may be combined with other professions, as attorneys-at-law, e.g., Basle-City, Aargau. There are cantons without institution of special notaries,

NOTARIES PUBLIC . . . *continued*
but also those cantons have legislation relating to ordinary authentications and other certifications of facts and to execution of publicly authenticated instruments, e.g., Schaffhausen, St. Gall, Lucerne. In St. Gall and Lucerne attorneys-at-law domiciled in that canton are competent to execute public wills and inheritance pacts, but in Lucerne only if attorney-at-law has taken oath as authenticating person.

Notaries public and/or other authenticating persons, their functions, their fees, and keeping of their records, are subject to strict regulations and supervision.

See also topic Acknowledgments and Other Public Authentications.

PARTNERSHIPS:

Ordinary partnership (Einfache Gesellschaft, Société simple, Societá semplice) is contractual association of two or more natural or juridical persons to achieve common purpose by joint efforts. (C.O. 530-551). Ordinary partnership is not legal entity. It cannot, as such, acquire rights or assume obligations, and has no standing to sue or be sued; its rights and obligations pertain jointly and severally to all partners. (C.O. 544).

Formation.—No special form required.

Rights and Liabilities of Partners as Between Themselves.—Every partner must contribute equal share in capital (goods, credits) or labor, and has equal share in profits or losses. All partners participate jointly in management, unless they agree otherwise. (C.O. 531, 533, 535). No partner may frustrate purpose of partnership (in particular, he may not conduct business in competition with partnership).

Rights and Liabilities of Partners as to Third Persons.—If management has been conferred upon partner, third parties may assume that such partner may act for partnership (or all partners). If partnership agreement does not provide otherwise, creditors of one partner personally can execute only his share of liquidation of partnership. But partners are jointly and severally liable for liabilities entered into by partnership or its representative. (C.O. 543).

Dissolution.—Partnership can terminate by failure or achievement of purpose, by agreement, death, incapacitation or bankruptcy of partner, by judicial dissolution with cause, and, in some circumstances, by timely notice. Partners remain liable to third parties.

General or collective partnership (Kollektivgesellschaft, Société en nom collectif, Società in nome collettivo) is contractual association of two or more natural persons to conduct (commercial, industrial or other) business under joint firm name. All partners are jointly and severally responsible for liabilities of partnership. (C.O. 552-593).

Formation.—Entry into Register of Commerce is mandatory, unless purpose is not commercial; in any event, legal existence begins with conclusion of partnership contract. (C.O. 552, 553).

Firm name must include last names of at least one partner and indicate execution of partnership. (C.O. 947).

Rights and Liabilities of Partners as Between Themselves.—Relationship between partners is laid down by partnership agreement or, in absence of such agreement, by rules for ordinary partnerships, with certain modifications relating to accounting and profit distribution (financial items). (C.O. 557-561).

Rights and Liabilities of Partnership and Partners as to Third Persons.—General partnership is not corporation. However, it can, as such, acquire rights and assume liabilities, and it has standing to sue and be sued. Partnership is liable for torts committed and legal transactions carried out by partner when acting for partnership. (C.O. 562, 567).

In order to be valid against third persons, restrictions as to representation of partnership must be entered into Register of Commerce. Otherwise third parties in good faith may assume that each partner has right to act for partnership. With cause partner may be deprived of his right to represent partnership at any time. Third parties may only be appointed to act for partnership with consent of all partners. (C.O. 563-565).

Partners are jointly and severally liable with their entire assets for liabilities of partnership. New partner is liable for preexisting liabilities of partnership. Bankruptcy of general partnership does not entail bankruptcy of individual partners, nor vice versa. To receive satisfaction or security for their claims, personal creditors of partner may execute only from partner's partnership interest, remuneration, profits and share of liquidation. However, if partnership is bankrupt, has been dissolved or creditors have not been satisfied, partner can be rendered liable for claims against partnership, even if he has left partnership. This does not prejudice personal guarantee of partner.

Claims against individual partner for liabilities of partnership are unenforceable after five years after publication of partner's resignation or of dissolution of partnership in Swiss Official Journal of Commerce. (C.O. 591-593).

Dissolution.—With certain exceptions, rules governing dissolution of ordinary partnership also apply to general partnership. General partnership can also be dissolved by its filing for bankruptcy. Liquidation is attended to by partners having right to act for partnership. If partnership is dissolved, partners and, in some cases, competent court may appoint or remove special liquidators. Appointments must be entered into Register of Commerce.

After liquidation firm name must be cancelled in Register of Commerce. Books and documents must be deposited for ten years in some place determined by partners or, in case of disagreement, by Register of Commerce. (C.O. 574-590).

See also topic Register of Commerce.

Limited partnership (Kommanditgesellschaft, Société en commandite, Società in accomandita) is contract of two or more natural or juridical persons to conduct commercial, industrial or other business under joint firm name. At least one partner (general partner) has unlimited responsibility for liabilities of partnership and one or more partners (limited partners) are liable only up to fixed amount. Natural persons may be both general and limited partners, juridical persons may only be limited partners. (C.O. 594-619).

Formation.—Similar to General or Collective Partnership.

Firm Name.—Must name last name of at least one general partner and indicate existence of partnership. (C.O. 947). See also topic Firm and Corporate Name.

Rights and Liabilities of Partners as Between Themselves.—Relationship between partners is laid down by partnership agreement. In absence of such agreement, provisions for general partnership apply with following changes: General partners are in charge of managing partnership. Limited partner has no right or obligation in this respect. Partner cannot object to ordinary business transactions. Limited partner is entitled to copy of balance sheet and of profit-and-loss statement, which may be audited by partner or by independent expert. Limited partner shares in losses only up to fixed amount of partner's contribution. (C.O. 598-601).

Rights and Liabilities of Partners as to Third Parties.—Limited partnership may, as such, acquire rights and assume liabilities and has standing to sue and to be sued in same manner as general partnership. (C.O. 602).

Limited partner is responsible for liabilities of partnership up to amount of partner's contribution, as entered into Register of Commerce, unless partner, or partnership with partner's knowledge, has led others to believe that partner would be liable up to higher amount. Limited partner is liable without limitation: (1) For transactions concluded by partner for partnership without express statement that partner acted as agent or under power of attorney, (2) for liabilities incurred before registration of partner's partnership or of limitation of partner's contribution, unless creditor knew partner's actual status, or (3) if name of limited partners forms part of firm name of partnership. (C.O. 603-609). For general partners, generally, same provisions apply as for partners in general partnership.

Dissolution.—Provisions for dissolution and liquidation of general partnership are applicable, except that death of, or incapacity or establishment of guardianship for, limited partner does not cause dissolution of partnership. (C.O. 613-619).

Limited Partnership with Shares.—See topic Corporations.

Firm Name.—See topic Firm and Corporate Name.

PATENTS AND INDUSTRIAL DESIGNS:

Patents, including priority rights thereon, are regulated by Federal Statute of June 25, 1954, as am'd in 1976, 1994 and 1995, supplemented by Ordinance of Federal Government of Oct. 19, 1977 amended 1995. Patents in force on Jan. 1, 1978 remain in limited respects still subject to unamended Patent Statute of June 25, 1954. See also Art. 109 to 111 Private International Law Statute.

Switzerland has adhered to following treaties: Convention of Nov. 27, 1963 on unification of certain points of substantive law on patents for invention; Patent Cooperation Treaty of June 19, 1970 (PCT); Convention of Mar. 24, 1971 on international classification of patents; Convention of Oct. 5, 1973 on grant of European Patents (European Patent Convention). Patents can therefore be filed with European Patent Office in Munich. Convention with Liechtenstein of Dec. 22, 1978 on patent protection. Budapest Treaty on international recognition of deposit of microorganisms for patent procedures of Apr. 28, 1977, UPOV Convention for plant varieties of 1961 as amended in 1972 and 1978.

Grant of Patents.—Patents filed under local law in Switzerland are granted by Federal Institute of Intellectual Property (abbreviated FIIP), Eidgenössisches Institut für Geistiges Eigentum, Einsteinstrasse 2, Berne, for new inventions which may be used for industrial purposes. No such grant takes place if invention is either: (1) Contrary to public interest or immoral, (2) method of surgery, therapy or diagnostic applied to human or animal body, (3) subject to official preexamination and held not to be new (see infra). Species of, or procedure to breed, plants or animals, except microbiological procedures, protected under Federal Statute of June 1, 1977.

Applications must be filed with FIIP, together with accurate description of invention and summary thereof, designation of inventor, and registration fee. Applicants residing outside of Switzerland may file application only through representative residing in Switzerland. Grant, alteration or cancellation of patent is registered in Patent Register kept by FOIP, and thereafter published.

Patent is granted irrespective of whether or not FIIP holds invention to be new.

Assignment.—A patent is considered to be industrial property. As such it can be transferred by assignment or inheritance or be subject to a license for use. If in public interest, patent may be partly or fully expropriated upon decision of Federal Government.

Licenses.—Patentee may authorize another person to use invention (license).

Compulsory license, including determination of its duration and indemnity, may be granted judicially upon petition: (a) to patentee of patent which cannot be used without using former patent, provided later patent serves entirely different purpose or offers substantial technical progress; (b) to any interested person if indicated by public interest, provided patentee has rejected demand of license by petitioner without valid reasons; (c) to any interested person if patent has not been used in Switzerland during three consecutive years since its registration unless patentee starts to use patent before filing petition or has valuable reasons for not using it. In last case (c), if needs of Swiss economy are not satisfied by licenses within two years after grant of first forced license, any interested person may file complaint for judicial cancellation of patent. Such cancellation, however, does not take place with respect to citizens of countries granting reciprocity, existence of which is to be established by Federal Government and has been established with respect to U. S. A. on Jan. 28, 1908.

Infringement.—A patent excludes anyone not licensed from industrial use of the invention. Violation of patent rights entails indemnification; if intentional it is subject to punishment.

Expiration.—Patents expire (a) after 20 years from date on which application was filed, or (b) if patentee renounces patent in writing, or (c) in case of nonpayment of annual fee six months after due date. If payment is effected only during last three of these six months additional fee is due.

Drugs.—After application and preparation for market penetration, drugs and medicaments shall be protected for 15 years. Beyond original 20-year term for patent, certificate will be issued granting protection similar to patent protection for, at maximum, another five years to compensate for time spent on obtaining permission to market drugs.

Annulment.—Patents may be annulled by court if (1) there is no new invention for industrial use, or (2) subject matter cannot be covered by patent, or (3) invention is not sufficiently substantiated in its description in order that it can be carried out by expert, or (4) subject of patent goes beyond application which determined application date, or (5) patentee was not inventor or legal successor or otherwise entitled to patent. Such suit may be brought by any interested party, but in case of ground (5) only by party alleging title to patent, in which instance adjudication of patent instead of annulment may be demanded.

PATENTS AND INDUSTRIAL DESIGNS . . . *continued*

Industrial design and model protection (abbreviated design protection) is regulated by Federal Statute of Mar. 30, 1900, as amended, supplemented by Ordinance of Federal Government of July 27, 1900, as amended. Protection concerns forms, possibly combined with colors, which may serve as models for commercial manufacturing of articles. Design protection does not cover process of manufacturing, utility or technical effect of article produced by using design or model.

Switzerland is party to Paris Convention for protection of industrial property (Stockholm Revision of July 14, 1967). Hague Convention for International Deposit of Industrial Design and Models of Nov. 28, 1960; Locarno Convention for the International Clarification of Industrial Design of Oct. 8, 1968.

Application for design protection must be filed with FIIP by depositing design or model and paying fee. Deposit may be made in sealed envelope for first five years. Applications from persons outside of Switzerland must be made by authorized representative residing in Switzerland.

Design protection is granted for periods of five years and expires in any case after 15 years or by abandonment, or in case of failure to pay fee, three months after due date.

Owner of registered industrial models and designs (as well as copyright and trademark rights) upon request may be advised by Swiss custom during period of two years if consignment of goods to be imported or exported or in custom store appear conterfeited illegally. Custom authorities may block these goods up to 20 days.

Any interested party may sue for annulment of protection if (1) design or model was not new at time of application (it is new if not known to public), or (2) applicant was not originator nor legal successor, or (3) misrepresentations were furnished on behalf of design or model deposited in sealed envelope, or (4) it cannot be subject matter of design protection, or (5) it conflicts with provisions of other federal statutes or treaties, or (6) is immoral.

See also topic Copyright, subhead Semiconductor Chips.

PERPETUITIES:

Testator may charge an heir to pass on inheritance to another as a reversionary heir, but cannot impose similar obligation on heir.

Usufruct in favor of legal entity may not continue for more than 100 years. See also topic Immovable Property as to building leases.

PLEDGES:

Contract to pledge is governed by proper law; pledge as such by law of place of thing.

Movable property (with exception of cattle, aircraft and vessels) is pledged by delivery into possession of pledgee. If property is represented by document of title, delivery of title is sufficient. (C.C. 884-885). Claims are pledged by written agreement. Notification of debtor is optional, but debtor without notice may still pay pledgor and so discharge obligation. Negotiable bearer instruments may be pledged by being delivered into possession of pledgee. Negotiable instruments to name must also be endorsed or assigned in favor of pledgee. If, besides instrument representing title to merchandise, separate warrants have been issued in order to demonstrate existing pledge on merchandise, they must be given into possession of pledgee, and notice thereof must be made on any other instrument representing title to merchandise. Pledgor keeps voting right in pledged shares. (C.C. 899-902).

More than one pledge can be given on same property. Pledgor must notify first pledgee in writing and instruct pledgee to deliver, upon payment of debt by pledgor, property to second pledgee. Pledgee may pledge property only with consent of owner.

Pledge is not effective as long as property remains in exclusive power of pledgor; pledge is terminated when pledgee has lost possession or right to recover possession over property.

Pledgee must return property upon payment of debt. If debt is not paid in time, pledgee may start execution proceedings or sell property by private sale, if specifically so agreed. Pledge extends to accessories and, if claims have been pledged, as rule, to income derived therefrom. Pledges give security for principal, interest and costs of execution of debt. (C.C. 886-892). Similar provisions apply to statutory right of retention.

PRESCRIPTION:

See topic Limitation of Actions.

PRINCIPAL AND AGENT:

Swiss law makes distinction between power of attorney and its underlying legal basis. Power of attorney is unilateral authorization by principal to representative to perform legal acts on behalf of principal. (C.O. 32). Underlying legal basis of power of attorney may be ordinary mandate, or other contract.

Power of Attorney.—No special form is as a rule required; one exception is authorization to enter into surety (Buergschaft, cautionnement, fideiussione) on behalf of principal, which needs form prescribed for surety itself. (C.O. 493). Bona fide third person to whom power of attorney has been communicated by principal may rely on terms of communication; but representative may be held responsible by principal according to legal basis of power of attorney. Power of attorney can be revoked at any time by principal and, unless provided otherwise or implied by nature of business, expires in case of death, declaration of absence, loss of capacity or bankruptcy of principal and representative. Powers of attorney not expiring by death of principal are frequent in Switzerland. (C.O. 32-39).

There are two special kinds of commercial powers of attorney: (1) "Power of Procuration" for conduct of enterprise with right to sign "per procuram, par procuration". Such power must be entered in Commercial Register, but its existence does not depend on such entry. Holder of power is deemed to be authorized with respect to bona fide third persons to perform any legal act within purpose of business except sale and charge of immovable property, authority for which must be expressly granted. Power of procuration may be restricted to branch of business, or to effect that holder of power has to act together with one or more authorized persons (joint or collective procuration); other restrictions are not valid against bona fide third persons. (C.O. 458-461). (2) "Commercial Power" for conducting business or special transactions within its purpose, without right to sign "per procuram". This power cannot be entered in Register of Commerce. Holder of power is authorized to perform all legal acts which are usually connected with business or carrying out special transactions. Right to sign drafts, loan contracts, or to commence or conduct law suit requires express authorization. (C.O. 462). Power of procuration and commercial power does not expire at death or with incapacity of principal. (C.O. 465).

Ordinary Mandate.—Agent is responsible to principal to carry out mandate faithfully and carefully. Compensation is due if agreed or if customary. Principal is required to reimburse agent for outlays and expenses incurred in duly carrying out mandate, plus interest thereon, and to discharge agent from any obligations which agent contracted. Mandate may at any time be terminated by revocation or notice by any party. Where it is terminated at unreasonable time, terminating party is required to indemnify other party for damage caused. (C.O. 394-406).

Contracts kindred to mandate with partly special provisions are: Letters and Orders of Credit (C.O. 407-411); Brokerage (C.O. 412-418); Commercial Agency (C.O. 418a-418v); Commission (C.O. 425-439); Shipping Contract (C.O. 440-457).

PRODUCT LIABILITY:

Federal Statute in force since Jan. 1, 1994. Mainly based on EU Law. Strict liability of producer and importer for defective products. Compensation for death, personal injury and loss or damage to property in case of consumer goods.

PUBLIC REGISTERS:

See topic Records; also topic Register of Commerce.

REAL PROPERTY:

See topic Immovable Property.

RECORDS:

Federal law provides for certain public registers to be maintained by cantons under supervision of Confederation. Facts recorded therein are presumed to be true. (C.C. 9). Public registers are, with certain exceptions, open for public inspection and upon request authenticated copies of certain registered facts are issued. The most important public registers are as follows:

Register of Commerce (Handelsregister Registre de commerce, Registro di commercio).—See topic Register of Commerce.

Civil Status Register (Zivilstandsregister, Registre de l'état civil, Registro dello stato civile) for public recording of civil status of person. There are particular registers of birth, death, marriage, legitimization, recognition of illegitimate fatherhood. In addition Family Register is kept at Swiss place of citizenship (see topic Citizenship) containing all persons possessing citizenship of that place.

Registers are kept by Civil Status Officials appointed by respective cantons.

Register of Matrimonial Property Rights (Gueterrechtsregister, Registre des régimes matrimoniaux, Registro dei beni matrimoniali) retains information regarding spouses wishing to preserve marital property rights under pre-1988 law.

Land Register (Grundbuch, Registre foncier, Registro fondiario) for the public recording of all immovables in Switzerland with rights and charges thereon as provided for by law.

A right in rem on immovable property which by law has to be recorded in land register exists as in rem right only if it appears in land register. Whoever in good faith by relying upon ownership or other rights in rem, is protected in this acquisition. (C.C. 973).

Register of Reservation of Ownership (Eigentumsvorbehalts-Register, Registre des pactes de réserve de propriété, Registro della riserva della proprietà) for registration of movable property transferred under reservation of ownership. (C.C. 715).

REGISTER OF COMMERCE:

Anyone in trading, manufacturing or other business must register firm's name in Register of Commerce (Handelsregister, Registre de commerce, Registro di commercio) of canton or district where seat is located. Many legal entities, such as share corporations, limited liability corporations, cooperative corporation, etc., come into existence only when entered into Register of Commerce.

Registration of Swiss corporations is effected on basis of publicly authenticated deed.

Branch offices of Swiss corporations are registered in canton or district in which branch office has its place of business after registration of main office in its own district.

Branch offices of foreign corporations are registered in same way as branches of Swiss corporations. For such branches, agent residing in Switzerland and having power of representation must be appointed.

Nonregistered corporations etc. have no legal existence. Nonregistered branch offices may still do business in Switzerland.

Registrar of Register of Commerce may levy fines on persons and firms not complying with law. Articles, names of partners, board members and officers must be registered. Authenticated signatures of persons having signing power must be deposited. Any alterations must also be registered.

Certified copies and translations of foreign articles, extract of foreign Register of Commerce (or equivalent), board resolution creating branch office and appointing resident agent must be submitted.

Unless otherwise decreed, entries are published in Swiss Official Journal of Commerce (Schweizerisches Handelsamtsblatt, Feuille officielle suisse de commerce, Foglio ufficiale svizzero di commercio). Third parties have constructive notice of registration.

See also topics Corporations, Collection of Debts and Bankruptcy, Firm and Corporate Name, Foundations, Membership Associations, Partnerships, and Trademarks.

SALES:

International Sales.—Law of habitual residence of seller applies. Choice of law is permitted. For contracts made from Mar. 1, 1991 onwards Vienna Convention on Contracts for the International Sale of Goods applies. See Part VI.

Domestic Sales.—Sale of movable property is contract whereby seller agrees to deliver object of sale and to transfer ownership thereof to buyer, and whereby buyer agrees to pay purchase price to seller. (C.O. 184-215, 222-236).

In sales of movable property, unless otherwise provided by agreement or custom, delivery of property and payment of price are concurrent conditions. Price is considered as sufficiently determined if it is ascertainable. When contract for sale of personal property is entered into, benefit and risk of property pass to buyer, unless otherwise stipulated (C.O. 184, 185), but title remains in seller until transfer is effectuated.

In absence of contrary agreement or custom, seller must pay costs of delivery unless goods are to be shipped to place different from that of performance, in which case buyer has to bear costs of shipment. (C.O. 189).

Bills of Sale.—As a rule, no special instrument is mandatory for validity of sale of movable property. Sales agreement may be oral.

Transfer of Title.—Title to movable things passes by transfer of "possession" to buyer, either of thing itself or of means procuring power over thing. Bona fide tranferee of movable thing becomes its owner as soon as transferee's possession is protected according to rules of possession, even if transferor had no right to transfer ownership. (C.C. 714, 922-925).

When goods are sold on approval or subject to inspection, seller remains owner until approval. (C.O. 223).

Stoppage in Transitu.—Shipper may stop goods in hands of carrier, unless bill of lading has come into hands of consignee, or shipper is unable to return carrier's receipt, or consignee has been notified in writing to take delivery, or consignee has notified carrier after arrival of goods at place of destination that consignee is ready to take delivery. To exercise this right shipper need not specify any reasons. It is immaterial whether or not goods are actually in transit, provided they have not yet reached consignee. (C.O.443).

Warranties.—Seller warrants title, except if buyer knew risk of claim of third persons at time of contract. (C.O. 192-196). Seller warrants further by law for quality of object of sale and its fitness for intended use, even if seller has no knowledge of defects. Agreements excluding or limiting such warranties of seller are void where seller intentionally (in case of claims of third persons) or fraudulently (in case of defects) conceals claims of third persons or defects. (C.O. 197-200).

Remedies of Buyer.—Upon receipt of the goods buyer should promptly inspect them and notify seller of any deficiencies lest goods are deemed to be accepted. Deficiencies which cannot be detected by customary examination are excepted, but must be communicated immediately upon later discovery. (C.O. 201).

If seller's warranty for deficiencies is established, buyer may either rescind sale or claim difference resulting from deficiencies (reduction). Court at its discretion may grant reduction even if complaint asks for rescission. (C.O. 205).

In case of delivery of fixed quantity of fungible goods buyer is entitled to claim either rescission, or reduction, or goods of same kind. Unless goods are shipped from another place, seller may forestall any claim of buyer by delivering goods of same kind. (C.O. 206).

If sales agreement provides for fixed delivery date and seller defaults, it is assumed that buyer foregoes delivery and claims damages. Should buyer, however, elect to require delivery, buyer must notify seller immediately on default. Buyer's damages consist of difference between contract price and price at which buyer replaces goods in good faith. Where there is market price, or commodities exchange price, buyer may claim difference between that price and contract price on date of default, irrespective of whether substitute goods were purchased. (C.O. 190, 191).

Notices Required.—Notice of nonconforming delivery is preferably and customarily given in writing by registered letter.

Statute of Limitations.—Buyer's claim for warranties (C.O. 210) barred after one year of delivery to buyer even if buyer discovers deficiencies only later (unless seller has given warranty for longer period). Buyer has to file formal action in court within one year from delivery. Objections of buyer based on deficiencies do not prescribe if buyer has properly notified seller within one year. One year limitation cannot be invoked by seller, if seller's fraudulent behaviour can be proven.

Remedies of Seller.—If goods are sold only against prepayment or on terms providing for delivery against payment, seller may withdraw from contract on immediate notice if buyer has defaulted. If goods were delivered before payment and buyer defaults, seller may rescind sale and demand return of goods only if seller has explicitly reserved this right. (C.O. 214).

If buyer fails to pay in time, seller is entitled to damages which between merchants may be determined as difference between purchase price and price obtained by seller through bona fide resale of goods. If goods have market or exchange price, seller may abstain from resale and claim difference between sales price and market or exchange price at time of performance. (C.O. 215).

Instalment and Prepayment Plan Purchases are subject to restrictions. Instalment sales agreement can be revoked by buyer within five days after signature. As a rule 30% of purchase price has to be paid when goods received, instalments are not to exceed 24 months (furniture 25%, 30 months).

Conditional Sales.—Sale of movables with reservation of property rights by seller is recognized in Switzerland provided such transaction has been duly recorded in Register of Reservation of Ownership. (C.C. 715). See topic Records.

Price Supervision.—Federal Statute of Dec. 20, 1985 applies to goods and services. See also topic Distributorships.

SEALS:

Seals on private instruments including corporate documents are unknown.

SECURITIES:

Professional sale and purchase is subject to license in various cantons and to federal transfer tax.

Association of Swiss Stock Exchanges Take-over Code in force since Sept. 1, 1989 applies to public tender offers for securities quoted on Swiss stock exchanges. Take-over commission monitors takeovers. Code requires minimum disclosure by offeror, equal treatment of shareholders, buy-out vis-à-vis minority shareholders, minimum tender period of ten days, etc. Once offer has been made, target corporation must call shareholder's meeting if requested by offeror holding 10% of share capital regardless whether registered as shareholder.

See topics Criminal Law; Taxation, subhead Indirect Federal Taxes, catchline Stamp Taxes.

SHIPPING:

Federal Statute of Sept. 23, 1953 governs Swiss sea-going vessels and Swiss vessels on foreign inland waterways. Sea-going vessel can only be registered as Swiss ship and fly Swiss flag if owner is Swiss citizen or Swiss partnership or corporation of which all partners, shareholders, or members are Swiss citizens. Further special requirements in regard to Swiss domicile have to be fulfilled. Switzerland is party to series of international conventions concerning shipping. The York/Antwerp rules of 1950 apply to general average (Havarie Grosse).

STATUTE OF FRAUDS:

See topic Frauds, Statute of.

STATUTES:

All federal statutes are published in "Amtliche Sammlung der eidgenössischen Gesetze", "Receuil officiel des lois et ordonnance de la Confédération suisse" and in systematic looseleaf edition called "Systematische Sammlung des Bundesrechts", "Receuil systématigue du droit fédéral".

Each canton publishes its statutes in its own official cantonal collection.

TAXATION:

Federal Taxation.—Traditionally, direct taxes are levied by cantons and municipalities, and indirect taxes by Confederation (Federal constitution, Art. 42). But since 1915 (with exception of 1933), Confederation has also been levying direct taxes, and shares proceeds with cantons. Last amendment to Constitution continuing partly amended federal finance system, was approved by popular referendum in 1993. Its temporary features have been extended to 2006.

Direct Federal Taxes.—

Direct Federal Tax.—From 1995 onwards new statute applies to legal entities. Direct Federal Tax is levied yearly on profit and on capital (including reserves). Domestic partnerships are not taxable subjects, but foreign partnerships are. Legal entities are taxed based on yearly profit of current tax period. Tax period is same as business year. Tax on capital is levied on capital and reserves (after distribution of profit) at end of tax period. From individuals taxes are levied at canton's option based on current income of one year tax period (canton of Basel City) or based on average income of two preceding years (all other cantons). Generally capital gains are taxed as income or profit only when realized by business enterprises. Immovable property and business enterprises (permanent establishment) directly owned by Swiss taxpayers and operating outside of Switzerland are exempt from tax. Further exemptions are provided for Confederation, cantons and other bodies organized under public law, foreign countries and their diplomatic and professional consular representatives who are not Swiss citizens and legal entities which pursue public welfare or charitable objectives.

(1) Full tax is levied on: (a) Individuals and legal entities domiciled in Switzerland; (b) individuals involved in gainful activity in Switzerland and sojourning there for more than 30 days even if domiciled and taxable outside of Switzerland; (c) individuals not involved in gainful activity in Switzerland, but sojourning there for more than three months. Individuals domiciled or sojourning in Switzerland who are not and never were involved in gainful activity there may be taxed on basis of their living expenses, but such lump sum tax may not be lower than regular tax on income of individual derived from Swiss sources and foreign income for which individual claims exemption or reduction of foreign withholding taxes pursuant to double taxation agreements (students and patients in hospitals or similar institutions are exempt from full tax); (2) limited tax is levied on other individuals and corporate bodies, including foreign partnerships that own immovable property in Switzerland, or have claims secured by such immovable property or own Swiss business organizations or industrial plants (permanent establishment), and on individuals for remuneration that they receive as members of board of directors of Swiss legal entities. Non-Swiss members of foreign diplomatic and professional consular services, also charitable institutions, are exempt.

Tax rates are progressive. Husband and wife are taxed as unit. Income and property of minors is added to income and property of person who has parental power, except income from labor. Yearly marginal rates for individuals: 0.77-11.5%; highest rate for individuals applies to income over SFr. 659,000 for married couples living together, over SFr. 556,500 for others. Property of individuals is not taxed. For share corporations, limited partnerships with shares, limited liability partnership corporations and cooperative corporations yearly rates are 3.63-9.8% of net profit and 0.8 per mil of paid-in capital and reserves. Limited tax ([2] above) is levied only on income (or net profits) and assets (or capital and reserves) taxable in Switzerland, but, for individuals not domiciled in Switzerland and foreign commercial partnerships, rates are calculated on basis of total income, profits or capital and reserves. Corporations having participation in other corporations of at least 20%, or having taxable value of at least SFr. 2,000,000 receive tax reduction pro rata of such participation's income (holding privilege).

Withholding/Anticipatory Tax.—(Verrechnungssteuer, Impôt anticipé, Imposta preventiva). Confederation levies withholding tax at source on specific income from

TAXATION . . . *continued*
interest, annuities, dividends, profit distributions, etc., if debtor is resident of Switzerland. Rate is 35%. On life insurance annuities and capital payments to residents rate is 8% or 15%.

This tax is credited against cantonal and local taxes and excesses are refunded. Swiss legal entities also receive refund. Nonresidents subject to Swiss taxes may under specific conditions obtain credit. Owners, domiciled abroad, of Swiss bonds issued by Confederation, canton or municipality or instrumentality thereof under promise to be exempt from any Swiss taxes, and beneficiaries of income under Swiss trust certificates from foreign investments, are entitled to refund.

Further, nonresidents may, under conditions set forth in applicable double taxation treaties, obtain refunds. See subhead International Double Taxation, catchline International Treaties on Double Taxation, Income and Property Taxes, infra.

Regulation effective Jan. 1, 1967 authorizes Federal Tax Administration to request security to extent of potential withholding tax on liquidation profit of corporation: (a) If 80% of share capital is beneficially owned by nonresidents, (b) if assets consist mainly of assets located abroad or of claims against nonresidents, and (c) if corporation does not distribute every year adequate part of its net profit as dividends.

Military Exemption Levy (Militärpflichtersatz, Taxe d'exemption du service militaire Tassa d'esenzione dal servizio militare).—Every male Swiss citizen between age of 20 and 42 who is exempt from military service must pay tax on his income or minimum head tax. He is exempt from tax for any tax year in which he has been bona fide resident of foreign country for at least six months, provided he was granted appropriate military leave and provided further that one of following requirements is met: (a) He has been at beginning of year, bona fide resident of foreign country for uninterrupted period of at least three years; (b) during tax year in question he had to serve in armed forces of foreign country of residence or had to pay tax similar to military exemption tax for year in question to foreign country of residence; (c) he is also citizen of foreign country in which he resides and as such is subject to be called upon to perform military service after having served his regular term in armed forces of that country. Rates: Head tax SFr. 120, tax on income 3%. This tax is reduced according to age of taxpayer and time already served in Swiss army.

Insurance: Old Age and Other.—Federal law of Dec. 1946, as amended, applies. On average, contributions amount to 10.1% of income. Of this, employer bears roughly 50%, payroll deduction is made for remaining 50%. Contributions made over period of 40 years roughly add up to five times insured's annual salary.

Premiums that employee pays are credited to employee's individual account. Insurable wages and premiums fluctuate, hence it is not possible to determine end capital in advance. When beneficiary reaches retirement age, accumulated capital is translated into monthly pension according to rules in statute. As a rule of thumb, annual allowances correspond to 7.2% of accumulated capital. Payments are made until death. Benefits are regularly adjusted for inflation.

Mandatory employee benefits are paid to beneficiary monthly. Lump sum refund of accumulated capital is possible only under stringent circumstances. For instance, foreigner who definitively leaves Switzerland is entitled to refund if he or she paid premiums for more than nine months. (Art. 30 Occupational Pension Plan Statute).

While statute exhaustively regulates how premiums and benefits are processed and calculated, it does not require pension funds to adhere strictly to these regulations. If supervisory authorities are satisfied that employees receive at least statutory benefits, pension funds are relatively free to apply their own plans. Many corporate employers offer pension plans that set uniform premiums regardless of gender and age, or provide insurance coverage far beyond statutory maximum.

Cantonal levies for family allocations (children) are about 1.5% and federal contribution for farmers 2%. There is in addition federal unemployment insurance contribution of 3% on salaries up to SFr. 97,200 and of 1% on salary between SFr. 97,200 and cap of SFr. 243,000 both split equally between employee and employer. Further, compulsory and federal accident insurance of employees are borne by employer (on-the-job accidents) and employee (off-the-job accidents).

Indirect Federal Taxes.—

Stamp Taxes.—Federal Statute of June 27, 1973 applies, with amendments, effective Jan. 1, 1996.

(1) Issuance stamp tax of 3% on Swiss shares, parts of limited liability corporations and cooperative corporations, dividend-right certificates, money market papers. Tax is levied on par value and additional contributions given by shareholders without compensation. Provided that par value and additional contributions given by founders at incorporation of company are of market value less than SFr. 250,000, no stamp tax is levied. Stamp tax is reduced to nil in special cases such as merger, and seat transfer of foreign corporation into Switzerland. Stamp tax is SFr. 3 on dividend-right certificates without nominal value and 0.06% on money market papers. Former stamp taxes on bonds and on bills of exchange, checks and similar instruments were abolished.

(2) Transfer Stamp of 1.5 per mil on securities issued by resident and of 3 per mil on securities issued by nonresident. This tax is borne one half by each party, if banks, securities brokers, or corporations with more than Sfr. 10 million balance sheet assets in taxable securities are involved. No half tax on transfer of foreign securities for foreign bank or exchange agent. No tax if Swiss securities dealer acts as intermediary for transfer of foreign bonds between foreign parties.

(3) Stamp of 5% on cash premiums for insurance; 1.25% on liability insurance and full collision coverage of vehicles.

Value Added Tax (VAT).—Effective Jan. 1, 1995, replaced prior wholesale tax on goods. VAT is levied on supply of goods and services, own use, importation of goods and acquisition of services for consideration from foreign territory. Export of goods and services is exempt. Any person independently pursuing commercial or professional gainful activities must pay VAT provided its supplies of goods and services and own use exceed SFr. 75,000 a year. Normal rate: 6.5%. Reduced rate: 2% (applicable e.g. on supply of food and beverages, books and other printed matter). Input taxes may—as a rule—be deducted. VAT return due at end of each quarter. VAT on importation of goods is levied by Federal Customs Administration, all other VAT by Federal Tax Administration.

Special taxes are levied on certain manufactured goods (liquor, tobacco, cigarette paper), especially on tobacco products and cigarettes manufactured in Switzerland, for financing of federal insurance for old age and survivors.

Other indirect taxes are levied as custom duties (excises) (a) on barley, malt and beer, (b) on mineral oil and oil products, (c) and on cars and their components.

Cantonal Taxes.—Federal Statute on Harmonisation of Cantonal Taxes aims at partial harmonisation by 2001.

Income and Property Taxes.—Bulk of direct taxes is levied by cantons and municipalities. Tax laws of cantons differ, but most cantons (e.g. Zurich, Basel-City, Berne, Geneva) have system of tax on income and additional tax on property; few cantons (e.g., Vaud) still have old system of tax on earned income, and tax on property. In most cantons corporate bodies pay tax on net profits and on paid-in capital and reserves; some cantons assimilate corporate bodies to individuals (e.g. Appenzell I. Rh., Graubuenden). As rule, husband and wife and minor descendants living in same household as taxpayer are taxed as unit but should not be penalized as compared to nonmarried couples. Exemptions are provided for small incomes and property, also for dependents. Limited taxes are levied on nonresident individuals or foreign legal entities owning immovable property or doing business in canton.

Mostly, aggregate direct taxes levied by cantons and municipalities represent heavier burden than federal direct tax. Top rates in city of Zurich are about 32% (canton and city) and 11.5% (federal). To this, contribution to social security which is about 5.05% on entire earned income for employed person and about 9.5% for independent labor income must be added since these premiums are levied on gross income (without cap) and, presently, only premiums paid on first SFr. 69,840 actually entail social security benefits. Annual top rates on net worth wherever situated (except immovable property abroad) vary from canton to canton from 0.4% to 0.9% per year.

Certain cantons still offer specific statutory privileges to aliens who reside in canton without being engaged in business, but this becomes less frequent.

Cantons levy income tax on salaries of resident aliens with less than specified number of years of residence in Switzerland in form of withholding taxes.

Top effective (federal, cantonal and municipal) tax burden on corporations varies between 18% and 33% of profits before taxes, e.g., Zurich 29%; Geneva 32%; Zug 18%. In most cantons holding corporations are exempt from cantonal income taxes and subject only to capital tax at special (lower) rate, between 0.4 per mil and 7 per mil. Domiciliary, management, and service corporations are in some places treated similarly to holding corporations. In some cantons, corporations holding participations enjoy certain tax reductions. Family foundations created by persons domiciled outside of canton are in some cantons taxed as holding corporations.

Inheritance and Gift Taxes.—Are levied by most cantons (e.g. Zurich, Basel-City, Berne, Vaud, Geneva). Tax is levied by canton where decedent or donor is domiciled, but assessed against heirs, beneficiaries or donees, who are jointly liable for its payment. Rates vary with degree of relationship to decedent or donor, with amounts involved, and sometimes with private means of recipients. In some cantons, rate of taxes levied on transfers to nonrelated persons increases rapidly (e.g., Zurich 36% at approximately SFr. 1,000,000). (Graubuenden, Neuchatel and Solothurn assess tax on entire estate.)

Municipal Taxes.—Municipalities levy taxes mostly as percentage of cantonal tax, fixed yearly with statutory maximum. They also levy special taxes, mainly on immovables, or on capital gains derived from sales of immovables. Current taxes on immovables are negligible in comparison with real estate taxes in U.S. Immovables conveyance taxes can be as high as 4% of sales price. Taxes on capital gains resulting from sale of immovables may be as high as 60%.

Tax Agreements.—Cantons are parties to intercantonal treaty (Concordat) for prohibition of tax agreements, dated Dec. 10, 1949.

Intercantonal Double Taxation.—Federal Constitution (Art. 46) allows Federal Government to pass legislation for purpose of avoiding double taxation of same income subject to two or more cantons. To date no statute has been enacted, but Swiss Federal Supreme Court (see topic Courts), by extensive case law, established principles for prevention of double taxation by cantons.

International Double Taxation.—Principles of prohibition of intercantonal double taxation are not applicable to international double taxation. However, Swiss Federal Supreme Court has decided that foreign immovable property is not taxable in Switzerland if taxed at situs, or tax exempt there for public reasons.

International Treaties on Double Taxation, Income and Property Taxes.—Swiss Confederation has concluded treaties for avoidance of double taxation. More important ones are: (a) Regarding income and property: with Australia, Austria, Belgium, Canada, Denmark, Finland, France, Germany, Hungary, Ireland, Italy, Republic of Korea, Luxembourg, The Netherlands, Norway, Portugal, Spain, Sweden; (b) regarding income only: with U.S., U.K., South Africa, Pakistan, Japan, Trinidad and Tobago, Malaysia, New Zealand.

Treaties, with exception of those with U.S. and Pakistan follow pattern prepared by fiscal committee of League of Nations in 1928, and since 1965 certain features of pattern of Fiscal Committee of OECD. In treaties with continental European countries, country of residence or, in absence of residence, lasting sojourn is place of taxation, except if treaty rules differently. Treaty with U.S. determines place of taxation for each specifically mentioned source of income. Place of performance of labor or personal services becomes place of taxation, only after 183 days of temporary stay in this state, provided that compensation does not exceed $10,000 or compensation received for such labor is paid by employer of other state. U.S. citizens residing in Switzerland are not taxed in Switzerland for income derived from U.S. sources. Such income may, however, be relevant for rate of taxation on other income. All treaties provide that permanent establishment of enterprise in other country is taxed at place of establishment, with provisions, in some treaties, for apportionment. Immovables are taxed in country of situs.

Treaties grant relief from double taxation pursuant to withholdings at source by way of reductions (sometimes refund) or full exemption. Certain treaties provide further for limited tax credit for nonrefunded withholding taxes. Under treaty with U.S. withholding on dividends is reduced to 15%, on dividends of Swiss or American wholly (95%)—owned subsidiaries to 5%, on interests on bonds to 5%. Some treaties provide

TAXATION . . . *continued*
for exchange of information for correct application of treaty provisions. Treaty with U.S. additionally provides for exchange of information for prevention of fraud or the like in relation to taxes which are subject of treaty. Upon request of U.S. Internal Revenue Service, Swiss Federal Tax Administration obtains information and also supplies report on matters covered by Swiss banking secrecy in same manner as it can in internal Swiss tax fraud matter.

Effective Dec. 31, 1962 decree concerning misuse of Swiss double taxation treaties was issued. Swiss legal entities with nonresident beneficiaries may, as rule, enjoy reduction or refund of foreign taxes at source pursuant to double-taxation treaty only if: (a) 100% of receipts are entered into profit-and-loss statement, (b) not more than 50% are used for direct or indirect payments (in widest sense) to nonresidents, and (c) 25% are immediately distributed as dividends subject to 35% federal withholding tax.

Under decree of Aug. 22, 1967, Swiss resident taxpayers may under specific conditions request flat tax credit for taxes of certain foreign treaty countries levied on foreign dividends, interest and royalties. This applies to France, Germany, Ireland, Japan, The Netherlands, Portugal, South Africa, Spain, Sweden, U.K. etc., but not U.S.

Inheritance Tax.—Treaties regarding inheritance taxes with Germany, France, Sweden, Austria, The Netherlands, Denmark, Norway, and Finland are based on principle that state of last domicile has right to tax, also in regard to securities of corporations or debtors in another state, situs being of no importance. Immovables are taxable at situs. If, under specific conditions foreign state can levy its own tax, then it will, as rule, grant credit for Swiss tax.

Treaty with U.S. (1951) regarding inheritance taxes has following main features: It allows part of ordinary U.S. exemption to estate of Swiss citizen not domiciled in U.S., and also of alien domiciled in Switzerland. Further, it provides for certain tax credits for U.S. and Swiss taxes in regard to estates of U.S. citizens who were domiciled in Switzerland.

Treaty regarding inheritance taxes with U.K. (1956) permits state of last domicile to tax estate fully but limits rights of other state to tax only certain assets if deceased had no domicile there according to other state's law. Treaty permits U.K. to tax any right or interest passing under British will or title.

Special Tax Treaties.—Special treaties govern singular cases of taxation: Mainly on enterprises of ships and airlines, with Argentina, Liechtenstein, Italy, Greece, Brazil, Iran, Lebanon, Belgium, India, Poland, etc.

TRADEMARKS:

Trademarks and Tradenames.—Trademark statute provides for trademarks of goods, servicemarks, collective marks in force since Apr. 1, 1993.

Firm names must also be registered in Register of Commerce (see topic Firm and Corporate Name; also topic Register of Commerce) to be protected. So-called "famous trademarks" are protected in all categories of goods or services. Other trademarks to distinguish them from other products or to show their origin, may upon registration with Federal Institute of Intellectual Property (FIIP), be used exclusively. Right to exclude others from using same trademark is based on date of first registration, not first use. Service marks are now registrable.

Application.—Trademarks may be applied for by anybody, whether Swiss or foreign.

Trademarks of foreign organizations and corporations under foreign public law are protected only if they are protected in their own state and reciprocity is granted.

Registration.—Trademark must be deposited with FIIP. Conflict of trademark applied for with one already registered may be communicated by FIIP to applicant who may then decide whether to withdraw application. Registration is denied if trademark uses coats of arms or similar signs of Swiss Confederation or of canton, city, etc. and such signs of other countries granting reciprocity and international organizations. Registration is also denied if (a) filed by applicant not entitled to trademark, (b) registration fee has not been paid, (c) distinctive features of trademark are generally used or immoral, (d) there is more than one application for same trademark, or (e) trademark implies misrepresentation.

Assignment possible for part or all goods or services of registration even without transfer of respective business. Transfer of business entails transfer of trademarks.

Expiration.—Registration of trademark lasts for ten years from date of application. Unless extended, registration will be cancelled six months after its termination. It can be indefinitely extended for periods of ten years. If registered trademark has without valid reasons (illness, absence, difficulties of production) not been used for five consecutive years, court may cancel registration upon petition of any interested party.

Declarations of origin may be used, but only by manufacturers or producers residing at place of origin or by any party having bought such products there. Declarations of origin must be true. However, designations of goods by reference to locality or country having such general character as to designate kind and not origin of product are permissible.

Distinctions, prizes, and medals may be mentioned only by those entitled to them and on products, including packaging, directly connected with them.

Violations.—Illegal use of trademarks, declarations of origin, and commercial distinctions, etc., entails indemnification; if intentional punishment is also possible. Mechanism is provided for trademark owner to initiate post-registration opposition proceedings against similar or identical mark for same category of goods or services. Objection must be raised within three months from publication of registration in Gazette. After three months, objecting party may pursue legal remedies.

Conventions and Treaties.—Switzerland is a party to Madrid Convention for the prohibition of false designations of origin on goods (Stockholm Revision), Madrid Convention for international registration of trademarks (Stockholm Revision 1967). Treaty of Nice on International Classification of Goods and Services (Geneva Revision 1977) and Stockholm agreements of 1967. Switzerland has signed but not yet ratified Treaty on Trade Mark Rights (Geneva 1994) and will join Protocol to Madrid Convention for the international registration of Trademarks on Jan. 1, 1997.

See also exchange of notes with U.S. of May 14, 1883.

See also topics Copyright and Patents and Industrial Designs.

TRADE SECRETS:

Trade secrets and know-how may be protected under specific rules against unfair competition and under criminal law. There are no formalities required for protection of trade secret in Switzerland and time limits on protection vary depending solely on holder's own protective measures.

TREATIES:

International Sale of Goods.—United Nations Convention on Contracts for the International Sale of Goods, in force on Mar. 1, 1992. See topic Sales and Part VII, Selected International Conventions. Betton Woods—Treaty of Oct. 4, 1991 applies.

Europe.—Switzerland is member of Council of Europe (Strasbourg) and has adhered to certain of its treaties. On Oct. 3, 1974 Switzerland adhered to Convention for Protection of Human Rights and Basic Liberties.

Switzerland is member of European Free Trade Association but not of EU or EEA.

Switzerland joined Lugano Convention on recognition and enforcement of foreign judicial decisions with Finland, France, Germany, Iceland, Ireland, Italy, Luxembourg, Netherlands, Norway, Portugal, Spain, Sweden, U.K. All EFTA and European Union members may join.

Switzerland has concluded with most European countries and series of other countries treaties concerning residence and commerce. It is member of treaty on reciprocal recognition of inspections concerning manufacture of pharmaceutical products dated Oct. 8, 1970.

United States.—Treaty of Friendship, of Nov. 25, 1850, in force with alterations since Nov. 8, 1855, confers important rights on citizens of the two countries on basis of equal treatment of citizens of other country with her own citizens, e.g., right to free acquisition, possession and disposition inter vivos and per mortem of personal property (also of real property to extent that it may be held by foreigners) (Arts. I, V); free access to tribunals (Art. I). Treaty exempts citizens of one country from military service (not from military exemption taxes) in other country (Art. II); it also contains provisions relating to jurisdiction and applicable law in inheritance matters (Art. VI), and for consular services on basis of "most favored nation clause" (Art. VII).

Treaty of Nov. 11, 1937, regulates liability to military service and military exemption taxes of certain persons possessing citizenship of both countries, because born in one country of parents of other country. See topic Citizenship, subhead Multiple Citizenship.

Treaty concerning co-operation in field of peaceful use of atomic energy of Dec. 30, 1965 as am'd on Nov. 2, 1973 and treaty between International Atomic Energy Organization, U.S. and Switzerland of Feb. 28, 1972 on measures of control in regard to material and equipment.

Interim Agreement relating to Air Transport Services, of Aug. 3, 1945, as amended.

Exchange of notes with U.S., Oct. 13, 1961, as am'd on Jan. 7, 1977, regulates certification of air-worthiness. Switzerland and U.S. are parties to Convention of Dec. 16, 1970 to fight illegal occupation of aircraft.

Under Treaty on Social Security signed on July 18, 1979, two countries grant to citizens of other country benefits of their federal old age and dependents insurance and disability insurance.

Treaty of May 25, 1973 on assistance in criminal matters permits also to give assistance against organized crime and under certain conditions piercing of Swiss Bank Secret. Special statute of Oct. 3, 1975 regulates its application in Switzerland.

Treaty of Extradition, of May 14, 1900, as amended.

Hague Convention of Nov. 15, 1965 on Service Abroad in Civil and Commercial Matters applies (various reservations).

Switzerland and U.S. (on Dec. 24, 1980) have adhered to Treaty exempting foreign public deeds from legalization of Oct. 5, 1961 and U.S. has published list of Authorities competent to apply so-called "Apostille". See International Conventions section.

Memorandum of understanding was signed on May 3, 1980 by United States' Food and Drug Administration and Swiss Federal Office for Foreign Economic Affairs to develop standards or guidelines of good laboratory practices for laboratories conducting nonclinical experiments and to establish national programs of inspection.

See also topics Arbitration and Award; Copyright; Criminal Law; Foreign Trade Regulations; Judgments; Patents; Taxation, subhead International Double Taxation; Trademarks.

TRUSTS:

Creation of trust ownership in Anglo-American legal conception is not possible under Swiss law, but transfer of ownership or of claim to fiduciary is recognized by Swiss law.

The boards of legal entities are empowered to create foreign trusts as precautionary protective measure in case of international conflicts. General meeting must be notified.

See also topics Fiduciaries; Foundations.

WILLS:

Hague Convention of Oct. 5, 1961 on law applicable to form of last wills applies generally.

Individual may dispose of such part of property by disposition mortis causa (will or inheritance pact) to extent that law does not obligate individual to leave share of estate to certain statutory heirs (compulsory heirs). (C.C. 481).

Capacity to make Will.—Testator must be 18 years of age and capable of judgment. (C.C. 467).

Testamentary Dispositions.—

Appointed Heirs.—Testator may appoint one or more heirs. Whether disposition means appointment of heir or legacy depends on will of testator. To leave entire estate or fraction means to appoint heirs. (C.C. 483). To allot net estate or fraction is legacy. As to statutory heirs, see topic Descent and Distribution; as to distinction between heirs (statutory heirs and/or appointed heirs) and legatees, see topic Executors and Administrators, subhead Succession of Heirs and of Legatees; also see subhead Legacies, infra.

Compulsory Heirs.—Descendants, parents and surviving spouse have interest in decedent's estate not subject to will. This is calculated on basis of share which these

WILLS . . . *continued*

heirs would receive if decedent had died intestate. It is: (a) Three-fourths of such share for descendants, (b) one-half for each parent, (c) one-half for surviving spouse. (C.C. 470-471).

Testator may bequeath income deriving from share of common descendants and of uncommon descendants begetted during marriage to surviving spouse. This is reduced in case surviving spouse remarries. (C.C. 473).

Under certain circumstances (such as grave wrongs against testator, officially established insolvency of heir, etc.) testator may totally or partially disregard compulsory heirship (dishinherison). (C.C. 477-480).

Reversionary Heirs.—Testator may appoint preliminary heir (Vorerbe, grevé, erede gravato) with obligation to deliver inheritance to subsequent heir (Nacherbe, appelé, erede sostituito) upon happening of certain event. Reversionary heir cannot be charged with such duty. Same holds for legacy. (C.C. 488). Nondum conceptus may be designated as reversionary heir or as reversionary legatee. (C.C. 545). Preliminary heir acquires inheritance like any other appointed heir, subject to being divested thereof by happening of event provided for, in absence of such provision by death. Competent authority has to direct establishment of inventory. Preliminary heir has to give security unless relieved thereof by testator. (C.C. 490-492).

Replacement of Heirs.—Testator may designate in testamentary disposition one or more persons who shall receive inheritance in lieu of heir who does not acquire it for having died earlier, or renounced it (C.C. 487), or for other reasons. Similar dispositions are possible for replacement of legatee.

Legacies.—See subhead Legacies, infra.

Burdens and Conditions.—Testator may impose burdens or conditions to testamentary dispositions, performance of which can be demanded by anyone interested therein as soon as disposition becomes effective. (C.C. 482).

Above dispositions may also be made in inheritance pact. See subhead Inheritance Pacts, infra.

Forms of Wills.—Hague Convention of Oct. 5, 1961 applies, except that Swiss may not make will orally abroad save in extraordinary circumstances. In Switzerland wills may be made either in publicly authenticated form, in holographic form, or orally (nuncupative wills).

Public Wills.—These are publicly authenticated documents drawn up by officials designated by cantonal law. Document must be read and signed by testator and dated and signed by authenticating official. Immediately afterwards testator must declare before two qualifying witnesses in presence of official that testator has read document and that it contains testator's will. This declaration must be certified on document by two witnesses with their signatures, together with their statement that, to their observation, testator was legally capable. In case testator does not read and sign document, procedure is somewhat different. (C.C. 499-504).

Holographic wills must be written from beginning to end, including place of execution and year, month, and day of execution in testator's own handwriting, and signed by testator. (C.C. 505).

Nuncupative (Oral) Wills.—In certain cases of emergency testator may make oral will before two qualifying witnesses. Dispositions of testator must at once be written down by one witness with place, year, month and day of execution, be signed by both witnesses, and then deposited without delay by both witnesses with judicial authority, with declaration that testator, to observation of two witnesses, was legally capable and communicated to them this to be testator's last will under special prevailing circumstances. Instead of written record two witnesses may give oral record to judicial authority, with same declaration. Nuncupative will loses validity 14 days from time it becomes possible for testator to use one of other forms of wills. (C.C. 506-508).

Revocation.—Testator may alter or revoke will at any time. Alterations and revocations must be made by new will. Will may also be revoked by destroying original document. (C.C. 509).

Will in which previous will is not expressly revoked replaces previous will to extent that it does not doubtlessly merely complement it. (C.C. 511).

Testamentary dispositions are not avoided, if, subsequently, due to birth of issue, marriage of testator, legitimation of children or acquisition of compulsory right of heirship by others, testator's power to testamentary disposal is restricted; they are, however, subject to reduction. (C.C. 516). See infra, subhead Contest, catchline Suit for Reduction.

Revival.—A revoked will may revive by revocation of a subsequent will if such intention of testator appears from still more recent will expressing such revocation either specifically or by interpretation.

Probate.—Swiss law does not provide for probate proceedings such as known in American practice. Upon decedent's death all documents appearing to be wills must be delivered to authority of decedent's last domicile competent therefor. Within one month after delivery, decedent's will or wills must be "opened" by authority. Copy of entire will must be communicated to statutory heirs, appointed heirs, and executor with unlimited powers. Other persons interested receive copy to extent it concerns them. Persons with unknown abode are notified by publication. (C.C. 556-558).

Certificate of Inheritance.—If no objections have been filed by statutory heirs or by beneficiaries of prior disposition mortis causa within one month since communication to persons concerned, authority issues, upon request, certificate of inheritance to heirs appointed under will stating that they are recognized as such heirs, subject to suits contesting invalidity of will (see subhead Contest, infra), or of inheritance (see topic Executors and Administrators). (C.C. 559).

Contest.—

Suit for Invalidity.—Legal defects of a disposition mortis causa such as (1) incapacity of decedent at time when disposition was made, (2) dispositions made under influence of error, fraud, threats or duress, (3) immoral provisions or conditions, (4) defects of form, make disposition voidable, not null and void. Suit for invalidity or objection must be brought.

Statute of limitation for court action: (a) Against defendant in good faith, one year from time plaintiff receives notice of disposition mortis causa and ground of invalidity, and in any event ten years from day of opening of will. (b) Against defendant in bad faith, 30 years. Objections are not subject to any statute of limitation. (C.C. 519-521). Dispositions with defects as to (2) above become valid if decedent does not revoke them within one year after decedent has learned of error or of fraud or after influence of duress or threats has ceased. (C.C. 469).

Suit for Reduction.—Compulsory heirs who do not receive the value of their compulsory share by a disposition mortis causa may ask for reduction of disposition up to permitted extent by suit for reduction or by objection. Certain dispositions inter vivos, such as liberalities not subject to adjustment (see topic Descent and Distribution, subhead Advance), and gifts made within five years before decedent's death, are likewise subject to reduction. Statute of limitations: one year since heir has learned of violation of rights, in any event ten years to be computed in case of wills from day of opening, in case of other dispositions (inheritance pact or dispositions inter vivos) from death. If previous disposition mortis causa becomes valid because later disposition has been declared invalid, statute of limitations begins to run from date of invalidation. Objections are not subject to statute of limitations. (C.C. 522-533).

Suit for Inheritance.—See topic Executors and Administrators.

Legacies.—Person to whom specific property benefit has been bequeathed is not heir but legatee. Same legal position is held by person to whom usufruct of entire estate or fraction of estate has been bequeathed. (C.C. 484). Legacies may also be made to heirs; allotment of specific piece of property in estate to heir, however, has to be regarded as direction for distribution (see topic Executors and Administrators) and not as legacy, unless another intention of decedent appears from disposition mortis causa. (C.C. 608, subdivision 3).

Claim.—A legatee has a personal claim against the community of heirs, or against a single heir or a legatee (sub-legacy) charged with the legacy. If the legacies exceed the value of the estate, or if legacy exceeds inheritance or legacy of person charged with it or compulsory inheritance right, reduction can be claimed accordingly. (C.C. 486).

Performance.—Claims of creditors take precedence over legatees. If legacies are performed by heirs and if thereafter there are still debts of which heirs had no previous knowledge, heirs are entitled to claim proportionate restitution from legatees, as far as heirs could have claimed reduction of legacies, but only to extent legatees are still enriched at time when restitution is claimed. (C.C. 564-565).

Lapse.—In case a legatee predeceases decedent, legacy falls to person charged with it, unless another intention of decedent is shown from disposition per mortem. (C.C. 543).

Inheritance Pacts.—A person may undertake towards another person to leave entire estate or fraction of estate or legacy to other person or to third person, with or without compensation in return. Such undertakings do not have character of full obligations. Person bound by pact has, in principle, right to dispose freely inter vivos. However, dispositions mortis causa and gifts incompatible with undertakings in inheritance pact may be challenged. (C.C. 494). Inheritance pacts by which person foregoes heirship with or without compensation are also admissible. (C.C. 495-497).

Capacity to Make an Inheritance Pact.—Person making inheritance pact must have full legal capacity. (C.C. 468).

Form of Execution.—Same as for public wills. Parties have to declare their intention to official at same time and subscribe document before official and two witnesses. (C.C. 512).

Form of Revocation.—Pact may be revoked unilaterally by obligated person in one of forms of will, but only if, after execution of pact, heir or legatee has acted towards decedent in way giving ground to disinherit. (C.C. 513).

Probation.—Law does not provide for "opening" of inheritance pacts.

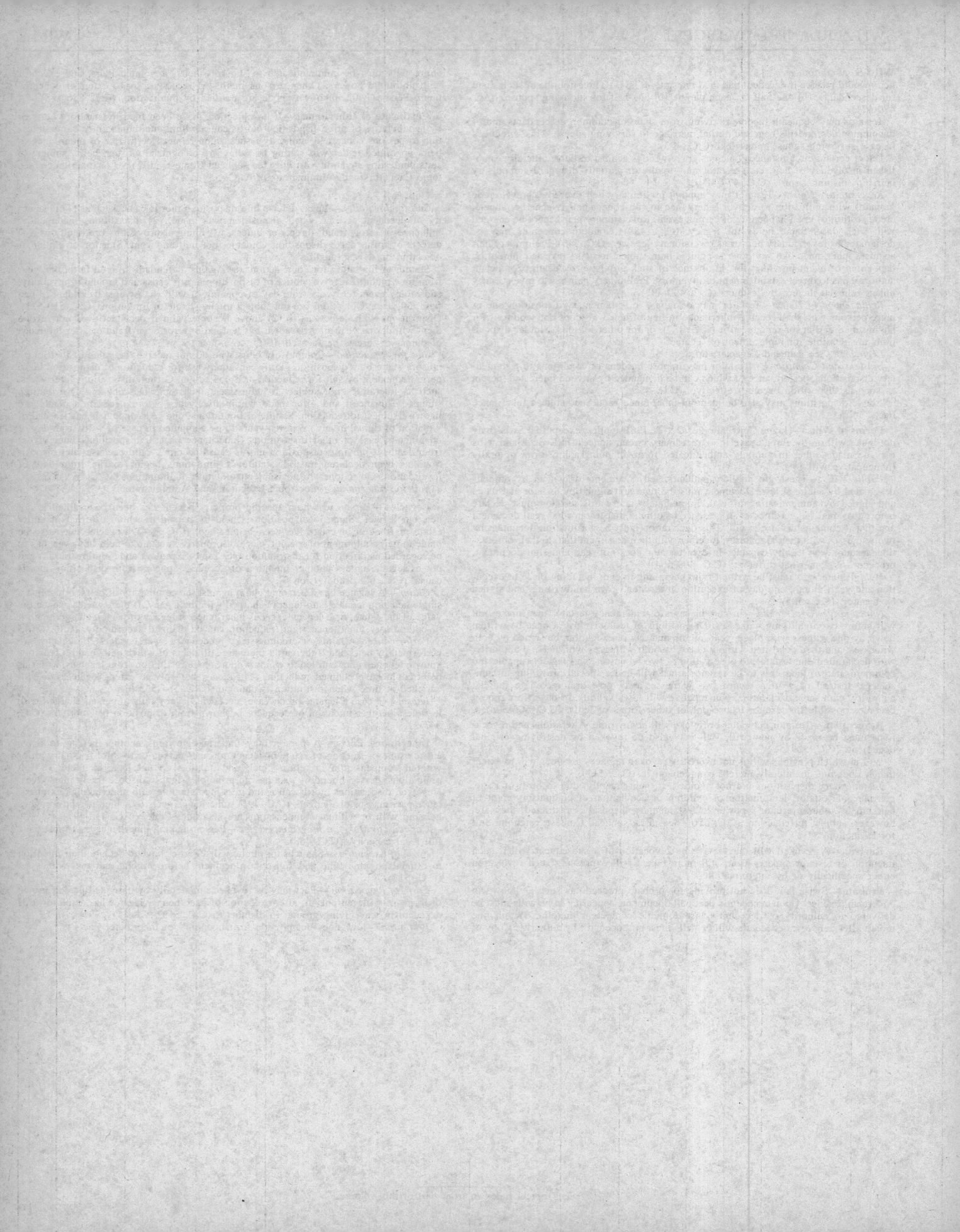

TAIWAN LAW DIGEST REVISER

Lee and Li
7th Floor, 201, Tun Hua North Road
Taipei 105, Taiwan, Republic of China
Telephone: 886 2 715 3300
Fax: 886 2 713 3966; 718 4389

Reviser Profile

History: Lee and Li began as the law office of Mr. James Lee. Mr. Lee began his law practice in Shanghai and formed his own firm in Taipei in 1953. He was joined by Dr. C.N. Li in 1965. In 1970, in memory of Mr. James Lee who passed away that year, Dr. Li named the office "Lee and Li", thus marking the formal establishment of the firm.

Growth and Areas of Emphasis: Keeping pace with the rapid economic development of the Republic of China (R.O.C), the firm has expanded steadily since its establishment. It is now the largest law firm in the R.O.C. and its scope of practice encompasses all areas of commercial law, with an emphasis on serving clientele of transnational nature. In addition to the legal services, Lee and Li is often called upon by the R.O.C. government to provide advice on various legislative and policy matters.

Structure: The firm is lead by C.V. Chen, Paul S.P. Hsu, Kwan-Tao Li, the executive partners, together with other partners. Lee and Li's main office in Taipei has more than 340 employees, with a legal and professional staff of 190. It also maintains an office in Kaohsiung, R.O.C.

Lee and Li has established correspondent relationships with foreign law firms throughout America, Europe, Asia and Africa to facilitate matters involving the legal systems of the other countries. Lee and Li also has well-established working relationships with major business consulting firms, accounting firms and banking facilities. These connections have proven to be valuable resource to clients, particularly for those who are less familiar with the R.O.C. business community.

Client Base: Among approximately 22,000 clients, most of them are multinational businesses. The leaders of modern industries including electronic, computer, petro-chemical, pharmaceutical, publication, trading, securities, insurance and banking industries, etc., of North America, Europe, Asia and other areas are mostly on Lee & Li's client list.

Scope of Practice: Lee and Li provides a full range of civil and commerical legal services. The specialization includes corporate & investment, banking, securities, insurance, international contracts, litigation, patent, trademark, copyright and industrial and intellectual property right planning and enforcement.

The Corporate & Investment Department handles incorporation procedures, tax planning, foreign investment, technical cooperation, know-how licensing, merger and acquisition, securities offerings, labor, management relations and other corporate matters.

The Banking and Financial Services Department handles legal matters in establishing on-shore and off-shore banking entities, commercial and investment banking, private banking, international financing, trade finance, foreign exchange, securities and related services.

The Patent and Trademark & Copyright Departments handle all aspects of intellectual property rights including patent, trademark and copyright registration, licensing and transfer for domestic and international clients. These Departments also support the other departments of the firm on the intellectual property protection aspects of corporate projects and enforcement action, where necessary.

The Litigation Department handles a variety of civil and commercial litigation, ranging from contract litigation, admiralty and trade disputes, to infringement litigation. The litigators not only attend to the substantive and procedural details in each case, but also bring an overall strategy into the dispute resolution setting.

The Industrial and Intellectual Property Right Planning and Enforcement Department assists domestic and international clients in their intensifying efforts to tackle patent, trademark, copyright, trade secret infringement in R.O.C. Together with the Litigation Department, it has handled several of the landmark cases in this area.

The Special Contracts Section assists clients not only in drafting and negotiation of contracts, but also actively participates in overall planning of the projects, including government procurement projects and bids of international contractors.

Case Handling Procedure: Lee and Li employs a unique team-work approach that provides the most comprehensive, efficient and cost-saving legal services to its clients. Moreover, a Data and Information Center is established to ensure quick access to up-to-date information on laws and related matters, so that services may be rendered in the most efficient manner.

TAIWAN LAW DIGEST

(The following is a list of all Topics, including cross-references, covered in this Digest.)

TAIWAN LAW DIGEST

Revised for 1997 edition by

LEE and LI, of Taipei, Taiwan (Formosa).

(Abbreviatons used are: C. C. for Civil Code; C. C. P. for Civil Code Procedure; L.S.L for Basic Labor Standards Law; Sup. Ct. for Supreme Court.)

PRELIMINARY NOTE:

Constitution of Republic of China (R.O.C.) took effect in 1947. Central government consists of five branches, Executive Yuan, Legislative Yuan, Judicial Yuan, Examination Yuan, and Control Yuan. Legislative Yuan exercises power to enact laws, while Executive Yuan exercises power to promulgate regulations for implementation of laws.

R.O.C. adopts civil law system. Many terms and expressions contained in texts of laws have no exact English equivalents. Most laws do not have official translation and different translations may exist.

In tandem with economic boom and efforts for liberalization and internationalization, many trade and investment related laws have been promulgated, which help to attract foreign investments. Such activities have placed foreign lawyers into increasing contact with R.O.C. law.

Laws digested below are in effect in all areas under control of government of R.O.C. on Taiwan, whose temporary capital is in Taipei.

ABSENTEES:

Generally speaking, an absentee may be represented by an attorney-in-fact. Yet, court may by ruling prohibit person other than lawyer from acting as agent ad litem. (C. C. P. 68). Courts may render default judgment against absentee upon request of parties who are present at hearing or by courts' discretion if absentee has been properly served. Action against absentee whose whereabouts are unknown may be effected by publication of service. (C. C. P. 149). If absentee's whereabouts are unknown and he fails to appoint administrator for his property, his properties are to be managed by person(s) in following order: (a) Spouse; (b) parents; (c) grandparents living with absentee; and (d) head of household. In case it is impossible for above-named person(s) to manage property, court may upon request of interested party appoint curator absent. (Law of Non-Litigious Matters 49).

ACKNOWLEDGMENTS:

Ordinarily the form of acknowledgment in country where it is taken may be employed. Occasionally, in practice, acknowledgment to be used in R.O.C. should be legalized by Chinese Consular or representative authorized by R.O.C. government offices in other countries. Acknowledgments to be used in U.S.A. may be taken before officials of American Institute in Taiwan. Same usually applies respecting other countries maintaining Consular or authorized representative offices in R.O.C. Office of notary public in R.O.C. is branch of court. All acknowledgments must be obtained before Chinese notary public in order to undergo subsequent official procedures.

ACTIONS:

Person capable of undertaking liabilities by his own juristic acts has capacity to sue. Entity without juristic personality has capacity to sue if it has appointed representative or administrator. Alien who has no capacity to sue under law of his own country shall be deemed to have such capacity if Chinese law so specifies. (C. C. P., 45, 46). Foreign corporation, whether officially recognized by R.O.C. government, may institute civil action as independent party. Except otherwise provided, service shall be effected ex officio by clerk of court and shall be served by process-server, post office or by publication. (C. C. P., 123, 124 & 149). Service on foreign juristic persons or corporate entities having business office establishments shall be executed by their representatives or managers residing in R.O.C. (C. C. P., 128). If person to be served on refuses to accept service without lawful grounds, service thereof shall be effected by leaving document at place of service. (C. C. P., 139). Burden of proof is on party who claims facts in his favor. Foreign law, if unknown to court shall be proved by party who cites it in his favor, yet court may ex officio investigate it. (C. C. P., 277 & 283). Evidence shall be proposed to courts before oral debate hearing.

ALIENS:

Regulations Governing Immigration and Residence of Foreigners in Domain of R.O.C. were promulgated on May 20, 1948, and last am'd on Jan. 6, 1989. Nationals of countries which confer privileges of immigration and residence to Chinese nationals will have similar privileges of immigration and residence in R.O.C. Aliens intending to work in R.O.C. must obtain employment permits. See topic Labor Relations, subhead The Employment Service Act. Aliens entering into R.O.C. on resident visa must register with local Police Bureau within 15 days of their arrival and obtain resident certificate. Changes of residence and all changes in personal status must be reported to Police within 15 days.

Any alien wishing to leave R.O.C. must report to Police at his place of residence three days before, to obtain multiple exit permit which is valid for six months. Aliens who want to do business in R.O.C. should obtain special permission. See topics Corporations; Partnership.

Acquisition of land rights by aliens may be enjoyed by aliens whose own countries have entered into equal and reciprocal treaty with R.O.C. such as treaty of Friendship, Commerce and Navigation between U.S. and R.O.C. For U.S. nationals, reciprocity is determined by laws of their State. Aliens may lease or purchase land for following purposes only: (1) Residence, (2) business premises or factories, (3) churches, (4) hospitals, (5) schools for foreign children, (6) diplomatic and consular establishments, premises for public welfare organizations, and (7) cemeteries. Ownership of and claims over real property located within domain of R.O.C. is solely governed by R.O.C. laws. Foreign company to acquire real property shall be further subject to approval of Ministry of Economic Affairs under Art. 376 of Company Law.

Alien enjoys in R.O.C. same civil rights as R.O.C. citizen. Alien's will must be in accordance with his national law. (Law Governing the Application of Laws of Civil Matters in Foreign Elements, Art. 24). Courts admit right of aliens to sue.

Naturalization of aliens is provided for by Nationality Law of Feb. 5, 1929, Articles 3, 4, 5, 6, 7, 8, and 9.

Marriage.—Alien woman who marries Chinese acquires Chinese nationality unless she retains her nationality in accordance with her national law. (Nationality Law, Art. 2, Para. 1). Chinese woman who marries foreign national loses her Chinese nationality only after having been granted permission by Ministry of Interior to renounce her nationality. (Nationality Law, Art. 10, par. 1).

Corporations Owned or Controlled by Aliens.—See topic Corporations.

ASSIGNMENTS:

Claim may be assigned unless: (1) Nature thereof prevents assignment; (2) there is agreement that claim shall not be assigned; or (3) claim is not subject to judicial attachment. Agreement mentioned in (2) cannot be asserted against bona fide third party. (C.C. Art. 294).

Collaterals and ancillary rights shall be transferred to assignee concurrently with assignment, except for those which are inseparable from and personal to assignor. Outstanding interest payment is transferred prima facie to assignee along with assignment of principal. (C.C. Art. 295).

Unless otherwise provided by law, assignment will not be binding on debtor unless and until he is notified of assignment by assignor or assignee. Tendering assignment document to debtor has same effect of notification. (C.C. Art. 297).

Upon notification of assignment or other conduct with equivalent effect, debtor may extend to assignee his defences which were originally enforceable against assignor. (C.C. Art. 299).

Ultra vires assignment refers to assignment in which assignment has not been concluded or effected but debtor has been informed of assignment by assignor. Debtor under ultra vires assignment may extend to original assignor his defences which were enforceable against assignee. (C.C. Art. 298).

Assignor should deliver to assignee upon assignment all documentation requisite to verify assigned claim and should provide assignee information with respect to enforcement of assigned claim. (C.C. Art. 296).

Delegation of obligation, if concluded between third party and obligee (creditor), becomes effective upon conclusion of delegation agreement and obligation in question transfers to third party immediately. (C.C. Art. 300).

Delegation, if concluded between third party and obligor (debtor), becomes binding on obligee (creditor) upon obligee's consent to delegation. Obligor or third party may ask obligee to respond within certain period to proposed delegation. Obligee's inaction or lack of response should be deemed as his refusal to accept delegation, which would allow either party to delegation right to withdraw their respective promises for delegation. (C.C. Arts. 301 and 302).

ASSOCIATIONS:

R.O.C. Civil Code (C. C. Arts. 45 and 46) distinguishes between associations whose object is to make profits and associations whose object is promotion of public welfare. Associations whose object is promotion of public welfare must, prior to legal entity registration, be approved by competent authorities.

Social affairs association, political associations and professional associations shall be formed for nonprofit objects and governed in accordance with "R.O.C. Private Associates Law" promulgated on Feb. 10, 1942 as last amended on Dec. 31, 1993. Civil Code shall also govern once such P.A.L. association is registered as legal entity.

In order to form association, articles of association must be drawn up. (P.A.L. Arts. 8 & 10 and C.C. Art. 47). Associations shall have three bodies, viz., assembly, board of directors and board of supervisors; and assembly is organ in which supreme power of association is vested. (C.C. Art. 50). Decisions of assembly for general matters are taken by simple majority. (P.A.L. Art. 27 and C.C. Art. 52). However, resolutions as to important matters, such as member dismissal, recall of director/supervisor, disposition of properties, amendment to articles of association, and dissolution of association, requires higher quorum and/or affirmative votes, as case may be applicable. (P.A.L. Art. 27 and C.C. Arts. 53 & 57). All changes in articles of association must be approved by competent authorities. (P.A.L. 54 and C.C. Art. 53).

Chambers of Commerce and Guilds are nonprofit associations in R.O.C.

Industrial guilds representing manufacturing concerns are governed by "The Industrial Association Law" promulgated on Dec. 28, 1974 and "The Union Law" promulgated on Oct. 21, 1929 as last am'd on May 21, 1975. Commercial guilds are governed by "Commercial Associations Law" promulgated on July 26, 1972 as last am'd on Dec. 15, 1982.

Most profit-seeking associations are termed "companies" and governed by Company Law (see topic Corporations).

ATTACHMENT:

Before judgment, an order for provisional seizure may be obtained. Property provisionally seized may not be transferred, sold or in any other way disposed of by debtor, except that movables may be sold by court upon request by debtor or creditor and money deposited with court if continued custody would lower their value or involve unreasonable expenses. (Compulsory Execution Law, Art. 134).

See Topical Index in front part of this volume.

ATTORNEYS AND COUNSELORS:

Description of R.O.C. Regulations Governing Attorneys.—Person may qualify to take R.O.C. bar examination by: (1) graduating from law school, equivalent to four years of undergraduate legal training; (2) passing qualification test; (3) passing court clerk examination and obtaining working experience in this position. Attorney is licensed to practice in R.O.C. upon passing bar examination and completion of six-month training program. Foreigners can be admitted to local bars only upon passing R.O.C. bar examination and receiving special approval from R.O.C. Ministry of Justice on basis of reciprocity.

Bar passing rate remained lower than 2% for most terms of past four decades, which was then lifted to around 5% to 15% for past seven years. Ministry of Justice is responsible for general governance of R.O.C. lawyers while local bar associations self-regulate in their districts.

Contact Addresses.—International Bar Association of the R.O.C., 5F, 130 Chungking S. Rd., Sec. 1, Taipei, Taiwan, Tel: (02) 331-2865, Fax: (02) 375-5594; Taipei Bar Association, 124 Chungking S. Rd., Sec. 1, Taipei, Taiwan, Tel: (02) 311-6247, (02) 381-7540, Fax: (02) 381-9022; Kaohsiung Bar Association, 2F, 1 Shih Chung Rd., No. 171, Kaohsiung, Taiwan, Tel: (07) 215-4892, (07) 215-4893, Fax: (07) 281-0228.

Foreign Attorneys in R.O.C.—Only R.O.C.-licensed lawyers are permitted to engage in courtroom representation, unless court approves otherwise. Lawyers without R.O.C. license are not allowed to provide litigation services. Licensed attorneys may affiliate themselves with foreign firm, and hire foreign attorneys. Foreign attorneys may provide non-litigation services, but are regarded as consultants, not lawyers. There has been recent trend of foreign attorneys, acting as consultants, rendering banking and investment services for overseas clients conducting business in R.O.C. There are very few R.O.C.-licensed foreign attorneys, primarily due to difficulty in mastering Chinese language to point sufficient for passing bar examination.

BANKRUPTCY:

R.O.C. Bankruptcy Law provides two proceedings applicable for situation under which debtor is unable to pay off his debts or debtor has ceased to make repayment, namely: (1) Composition through Court or Chamber of Commerce, and (2) bankruptcy. Both proceedings aim at distribution of debtor's properties among creditors.

Composition through Court or Chamber of Commerce is privilege offered to debtor who applies to court or Chamber of Commerce, subsequent to suspension of payment and prior to application for bankruptcy. (Bankruptcy Law, Arts. 6 and 41). Composition through Chamber of Commerce may be applied only by debtor who is merchant. It is similar to bankruptcy, except that only debtor can ask for it and control of debtor's property is not entirely divested. Proceedings must be carried out under supervision of court or local Chamber of Commerce and debtor's business may be continued. However, debtor, after applying for composition, may not perform any gratuitous act prejudicial to rights of creditors, nor any onerous acts beyond scope of normal managerial acts or of ordinary business. (Bankruptcy Law, Arts. 15, 16, and 49).

Bankruptcy proceedings may be commenced in case of insolvency or when application for composition or composition proposal is denied by court or when composition through court or Chamber of Commerce fails to reach result. Application for bankruptcy may be filed by debtor or his creditors. (Bankruptcy Law, Art. 58). Application for bankruptcy proceedings may be denied if it appears to court that composition is still possible or debtor has no property, or debtor only has one creditor. Provisions are made for meeting of creditors to pass resolution on certain matters. Bankrupt cannot leave his residence without court's permission and court may summon or detain bankrupt if this is deemed necessary. If bankrupt, within six months prior to bankruptcy, furnishes security on existing debts or makes payment of obligation not yet due, such transactions may be cancelled, and other acts prejudicial to creditors' rights which are cancellable under Civil Code may be cancelled on application to court. (Bankruptcy Law, Arts. 78 and 79).

Creditors must present claims within time fixed by published notice of court. Secured creditors may obtain satisfaction out of their security and if such is insufficient, they may participate with general creditors for balance.

Bankruptcy decree divests bankrupt of control of his present property and such as he may acquire during pendency of bankruptcy. (Bankruptcy Law, Art. 75).

Certain fraudulent acts of a bankrupt or debtor under composition aiming to prejudice creditors' rights, are punishable by imprisonment, detention and/or fines. (Bankruptcy Law, Arts. 155 and 156).

Composition or bankruptcy effected in a foreign country has no effect on the debtor's or bankrupt's property in R.O.C. (Bankruptcy Law, Art. 4).

BILLS AND NOTES:

Bills of exchange, promissory notes and checks are negotiable instruments within meaning of Negotiable Instruments Law of R.O.C., promulgated in 1929 and last am'd June 29, 1987. Person signing negotiable instrument is liable according to tenor thereof. Seal may be affixed to negotiable instrument in lieu of signature. In case of variation between words and figures with respect to amount of instrument, words prevail. Unless otherwise provided in Negotiable Instruments Law, instrument is invalid as negotiable instrument unless it contains following particulars required by said law.

Bills of exchange must be signed by drawer and contain: (1) Words indicating that instruments are promissory notes; (2) statement of certain sum of money; (3) unconditional order to pay; and (4) date of issue.

Promissory notes must be signed by maker and contain: (1) Words indicating that instrument is promissory note; (2) statement of certain sum of money; (3) unconditional promise to pay; and (4) date of issue; provided, however, that maker may authorize holder to insert date of maturity and other particulars which should have been completed prior to its issue and holder in due course will be fully protected as if such promissory note was legally issued and delivered on its date of issue.

Checks must be signed by drawer and contain: (1) Words indicating that instrument is check; (2) statement of certain sum of money; (3) name of payor; (4) unconditional order to pay; (5) date of issue; and (6) place of payment. Post-dated check is legally permitted. Holder of check may not present check for payment before date of issue stated thereon.

COMMERCIAL REGISTER:

Commercial Registration Act was promulgated and enforced as of June 28, 1937 and last am'd Oct. 23, 1989. Commercial Registration shall be handled in accordance with said Act and, if no applicable stipulation provided therein, shall be subject to regulations of other laws. Any firm including its branch in sole proprietorship or partnership shall not start operation before registration. (Art. 3 of Commercial Registration Act). As for company, it may not be formed until it is incorporated and has obtained certificate of incorporation pursuant to Company Law. Firm or company shall not engage in any business outside of scope of business for which it has been registered. (Art. 8 of Commercial Registration Act & Art. 15 of Company Law). If business of firm or company should require special permission or license of Government, such business can be registered only after such special permission or license is obtained. Businesses requiring special permission include but not limited to following: Banking, insurance, insurance brokerage, customs broker, construction, securities broker, dealer and underwriter, trust and investment company, venture capital company, securities investment consulting company, securities investment trust company, travel agent, shipping, shipping agent, transportation, publisher, drug dealer, air freight forwarder, pharmaceutical company, etc.

In addition, foreign company that desires to transact business and establish branch office within territory of R.O.C. shall apply for recognition pursuant to Company Law. See topic Corporations.

CONSTITUTION AND GOVERNMENT:

Constitution.—Constitution of R.O.C. adopted by National Government on Dec. 25, 1946, promulgated by National Government on Jan. 1, 1947, which came into force on Dec. 25, 1947, provides, among other things, that all citizens of R.O.C., irrespective of sex, religion, race, class and partisanship, shall be equal before law, that any citizen, arrested or seized shall be handed over to court within 24 hours after arrest, and that all citizens shall have freedom of domicile, liberty of religious belief, right of privacy in correspondence and in communication, freedom of association, speech and press. All citizens shall have right to vote for election, recall, initiative and referendum, and have right to take part in state examinations and to hold public offices. It is also provided that all citizens shall have duty of paying taxes, of performing military service in accordance with law and of receiving compulsory education. National Assembly, constituted of delegates elected from different areas, must, in accordance with provisions of Constitution, exercise political powers on behalf of people. Functions of National Assembly include recall of President and/or Vice President, amendment of Constitution and voting on proposed Constitutional amendments submitted by Legislative Yuan by way of referendum. Constitution also dictates government measures of improving living conditions of people and of developing economic resources of country, and specifies procedure by which it may be amended. Additional articles one through ten of Constitution of R.O.C. were adopted by Second National Assembly on July 29, 1994 and promulgated by President on Aug. 1, 1994.

Rights and obligations between people of mainland China area and those of free area, and disposition of other related affairs shall be specially regulated by law.

Effective from 1996 election for ninth-term President and Vice President, President and Vice President shall be elected by entire electorate in free area of R.O.C.

Government.—Government is known as Central Government of R.O.C. Pursuant to Art. 35 of Constitution, President is head of State representing R.O.C. in external relations. As to organization of Government, Constitution provides, among other things, for five yuans (departments or councils): Executive, Legislative, Judicial, Examination and Control.

Executive Yuan is highest administrative organ of Government and has power to establish or dissolve ministries and appoint commissions and other executive officers to take charge of specific executive matters. Executive Yuan is responsible to Legislative Yuan.

Legislative Yuan, being congress, is authorized to decide on legislation, budgets, state of emergency, amnesties, declarations of war, negotiations for peace treaties and other important matters of State. It is highest legislative organ of State, to be constituted of elected members who shall exercise power of legislation on behalf of people.

Judicial Yuan is highest judicial organ of State, and has duty of establishing courts for civil, criminal and administrative suits and is empowered to administer disciplinary measures over public functionaries, to exercise judicial review, to interpret Constitution, and to reconcile different constructions of laws and administrative orders.

Examination Yuan exercises powers of state examination, employment, qualifications for public office, registration and official grading, checking of records, scale of salaries, promotion and demotion, safeguarding of posts, commendation, retirement and pension.

Control Yuan exercises powers of impeachment, rectification and auditing over government books.

CONSUMER PROTECTION:

The Consumer Protection Law was passed on Jan. 11, 1994, and became effective on Jan. 13, 1994.

Products and services are required to be free from harm to safety, meet sanitary requirements, and contain proper warning/emergency handling labels. Designers, producers, manufacturers, importers of products, and providers of services are subject to strict product liability. Business operators are obligated to recall products or services which may endanger safety and health of consumers.

Standard contracts must be equal and reciprocal, interpretations should be in favor of consumers in case of ambiguity. Government may publish list of mandatory and prohibitory standard terms.

CONSUMER PROTECTION . . . *continued*

Consumers have right to terminate mail order and visitation sales contracts within seven days after receipt of products, and consumers are not responsible for keeping unsolicited goods mailed or delivered to them.

Installment sales must have written contracts which should set forth down payment, difference between cash price and total of installment payments, and interest rate.

Business operators are obligated to ensure accuracy of contents of their advertisements. Advertising media which knowingly advertise inaccurate advertisements are jointly and severally liable with business operator. Imported goods must have Chinese-language labels and instructions which should not contain less information than those used for place of origin.

Consumer protection groups are vested with power to conduct tests and surveys, to publicize reports, to provide consulting services to consumers, to assist consumers in consumer disputes, to initiate consumer litigation, and to advise government and business operators.

Enforcement responsibilities rest on both Central and local governments. Under Executive Yuan, Consumer Protection Commission was established, which is responsible for policy formation, analysis and review, and for supervising enforcement of such policies, but is not enforcement agency itself.

Consumers may file complaints with business operator, consumer protection groups, or consumer service center. If such complaint is not properly handled, consumer may request for mediation. Consumer litigation may be brought by consumer, representatives elected among consumers, consumer protection officials, or qualified consumer protection groups.

Punitive damages are allowed if injury to consumer by business operator is intentional or by negligence.

CONTRACTS:

Contracts are generally regulated by Civil Code. With few exceptions, most principles concerning contracts are consistent with Anglo-American law. Offer made during face-to-face negotiation ceases to be binding if not accepted at once. (C. C. Art. 156). Offer made inter absentee ceases to be binding if not accepted by offeree within reasonable period under ordinary circumstances. (C. C. Art. 157). If offeror specifies period for acceptance, acceptance must reach him within such period. (C. C. Art. 158).

Oral contracts are legally valid, with a few exceptions, such as real estate lease over a year (C. C. Art. 422); contract of mandate under which mandatory has to enter into juristic acts which are required by law to be in writing; transfer or creation of rights over immovables, and other special cases. (C. C. Art. 534).

Contracts creating third-party beneficiaries are legally enforceable unless beneficiaries express to either party to contracts their intention not to receive benefits so created under contracts. Moreover, parties to contracts may also modify or cancel contracts before third-party beneficiaries express their intention to receive such benefits. (C. C. Art. 269). Like creditor, third-party beneficiaries have right to enforce contracts against debtor.

Excuses for Nonperformance.—Party to contract may be relieved from performance if such performance becomes impossible due to cause for which he is not responsible, such as force majeure, due to nonperformance of other party who is obligated to perform first, or due to cause for which other party is responsible. (C. C. Art. 225).

Applicable Law.—Validity and effectiveness of contract involving foreign elements are determined by law agreed upon by parties to contract. Where parties intention is not ascertainable, applicable law shall be law of country of which both parties are nationals. If parties do not hold same nationality, applicable law shall be lex loci actus. If act is carried out at different places, place where offer is sent shall be deemed as place of act. If place where offer is sent is unknown to other party when making acceptance, domicile of offeror shall be deemed as place of act. If place of act spans more than two countries or does not belong to any country, lex loci solutionis shall apply. (6, Law Governing Choice of Law in Civil Cases involving Foreign Elements).

Government Contracts.—While law has not expressly specified status of government contracts, an established case law indicates that contracts made between government and any nationals involving private economic matters are governed by same body of law that regulates nongovernment contracts (see Appeal Case No. 1838, Sup. Ct. 1930).

Central government procurement is mainly governed by R.O.C. Law of Audit. In addition to Law of Audit, there are also administrative guidelines for centralized procurement of foreign goods. According to guidelines, overseas procurement with budget exceeding prescribed amount shall be entrusted to authority for handling in accordance with standard operating procedures. Overseas procurement below prescribed amount, or procurement over amount but with special permission granted by central government, can be conducted by end-user itself. There are also special projects, such as military procurements and computer equipment procurements, that are permitted to be handled by end-users. Government-owned enterprises may utilize and entrust authority for purchase if amount is above prescribed amount.

Under Law of Audit, central government procurement can be made by open tender call, restricted tender call or negotiation. If budget of purchase reaches amount prescribed by Ministry of Audit, purchase shall be conducted by open tender. Open tender requires at least three bidders participating while restricted tender requires two bidders. Where auditing agency has specifically given concurrence, purchase can be done by restricted tender or by negotiation.

Chronology of award process of central government procurement, if handled by authority, is as follows: (1) preparation of invitation-for-bids; (2) announcement of a tender (for open tenders); (3) submission of bids/tenders; (4) requirement for a bid bond; (5) tender opening & bid evaluation; (6) award of a contract; (7) signing of a contract; (8) requirement for a performance bond; (9) delivery of shipment & shipment documents; and (10) claims & disputes.

Note: As R.O.C. intends to become member of GATT, there will be major reforms in many areas of law including public procurement law. Reform is to unify numerous legislations and create new government procurement system including brand new Government Procurement Law. Goal is to make new government procurement procedure more systematic, fair and transparent.

Distributorship, Dealerships and Franchises.—

Distributorship, Dealerships.—Terms "distributor" and "dealer" are not defined in ROC law. There are no specific laws regulating such contracts. As such, rights and obligations of distributor or dealer are determined by provisions of contracts entered into by parties with reference to provisions in Civil Code pertaining to sales, entrustment, commercial agent, commission agent, etc. Antitrust and unfair competition provisions of Fair Trade Law also impose certain constraints on principal's control over local distributors and dealers, such as resale price maintenance or tying arrangements.

Franchises.—Term "franchises" is not defined in ROC law. In principle of freedom to contract, parties to franchise agreement may stipulate any terms and conditions in agreement so long as those do not violate any statutory or imperial provisions of ROC law or contravene ROC's public order or good morals. However, price fixing, division of markets, restriction on territory, business activities, or source of supply of raw materials which are often seen in franchise agreement may be viewed as unfair trade practices. Such practices are either restricted by Fair Trade Law or require prior approval from Fair Trade Commission in charge of implementing of Fair Trade Law.

COPYRIGHT:

R.O.C. Copyright Law was revised and effected on June 12, 1992. R.O.C. nationals will acquire copyright upon completion in respect of (1) oral and literary works; (2) musical works; (3) dramatic and choreographic works; (4) artistic works; (5) photographic works; (6) pictorial works; (7) audiovisual works; (8) sound recordings; (9) architectural works; (10) computer programs.

Contents of copyrights are divided into moral rights and property rights to work. Moral rights belong exclusively to author of work, which are unassignable and non-inheritable, in respect of: (1) releasing author's work; (2) indicating author's real name or alias or not to indicate author's name on original or reproduction of author's work or at time of releasing author's work; (3) maintaining integrity of contents, form and title of author's work. Property rights are exclusive to author in respect of: (1) reproducing author's work; (2) publicly reciting author's oral and/or literary work; (3) publicly broadcasting author's work; (4) publicly presenting author's audiovisual work; (5) publicly perform author's oral and/or literary work, musical work, dramatic and/or choreographic work; (6) publicly exhibiting original of author's artistic work or photographic work which has not been published; (7) adapting author's work to create derivative work or to edit author's work to create compilation; (8) leasing author's work to others.

Where work completed under employment or retained by patron, unless there is contrary agreement between parties concerned, copyright should be vested in author.

Copyright may be assigned in whole or in part and may be owned by co-owners. Assignment of property rights; restriction of disposal and exclusive license of property rights; and creation, assignment, alternation, extinguishment or restriction of disposal of pledge of property rights should be duly recorded, otherwise, such copyrights cannot be set up against others.

Property right to work is issued to author for duration of author's life from time of completion of intellectual work and it may be inherited by author's heir for 50 years. However, in each of following cases, term of property right to work is only for 50 years from time of public release of such work: (1) where work is copyrighted in name of juristic person; (2) where works are photographic work, audiovisual work, sound recording, or computer programs.

R.O.C. Copyright Law provides compulsory license clauses including literary works, musical works and sound recordings in respect to their translation and public broadcasting.

In case of infringement, copyright owner may prosecute penalty clause under R.O.C. Copyright Law and may also recover damages from such infringers. Unrecognized foreign juristic person in R.O.C. may still be qualified in filing criminal complaint or private prosecution against offenses stipulated in R.O.C. Copyright Law, provided that reciprocal rights exist in country of foreign juristic person. Remedies available to copyright owner of infringement include damages, removal of infringement and publication for final judgment. Copyright owner may claim damages equivalent to sum of profit obtained by infringer and loss suffered by copyright owner. If it is hard to prove actual damages, copyright owner may request court to determine amount of compensation within range from NT$10,000 to NT$1,000,000. Unrecorded intellectual works, printed with "recorded" or synonym thereof, shall be subject to fine not exceeding NT$30,000 and sale of said intellectual work will be prohibited. Offence regularly committed by person shall be prosecuted upon complaint by any party and sentence of imprisonment shall be raised to imprisonment of not more than seven years and not less than six months. Fines set further in R.O.C. Copyright Law. If case amounts to criminal offence, offender will be punished accordingly.

Copyright on Foreign Intellectual Works.—Protection of foreign works will be based upon creation rather than registration as under 1985 Law. It also provides translation rights to foreign authors/copyright owners, while 1985 Law reserves translation right to R.O.C. nationals. If unauthorized translation is made under 1985 Law, no reproduction of such translation will be allowed and remaining copies made previously can only be sold within two years after time of effective date and enforcement of R.O.C. Copyright Law.

Works of foreign national conforming to any of following conditions may be entitled to copyright protection under R.O.C. Copyright Law, unless otherwise provided in treaty or agreement which has been approved by resolution of Legislative Yuan: (1) Where work is first published in territory of Republic of China or in place outside territory of Republic of China and published simultaneously in territory of Republic of China within 30 days thereafter, provided that it has been duly verified, work of R.O.C. national is entitled to same protection under similar conditions in home country of said foreign national. (2) Where, according to treaty, agreement, laws, regulations, or customary practices in his/her home country, works produced by R.O.C. nationals are entitled to copyright protection in that country.

Parallel importation of copyrighted works is prohibited due to amendment of Arts. 87 and 87 bis of R.O.C. Copyright Law which became effective on 26 Apr. 1993. As a result, prior consent of copyright owner must be obtained before true copies of work can be imported by nonowner.

See Topical Index in front part of this volume.

CORPORATIONS:

Chinese Company Law provides for four kinds of companies: (1) unlimited company; (2) unlimited company with limited liability shareholders; (3) limited company; and (4) company limited by shares. Unlimited company is company organized by two or more shareholders who bear unlimited joint liability for obligations of company. Unlimited company with limited liability shareholders is one organized by one or more shareholders of unlimited liability and one or more shareholders of limited liability. In such company, shareholders of limited liability are liable only to extent of capital contributed or subscribed by them. Limited company is one organized by not less than five nor more than 21 shareholders who are liable to extent of capital subscribed by them. Company limited by shares is one organized by seven or more shareholders and capital of company is divided into shares and each shareholder is liable to extent of shares subscribed by him.

See also topic Commercial Register.

Special Permission.—If the business of a company should require special permission by Government, such business can be undertaken only after such special permission shall have been obtained. See topic Commercial Register.

Foreign corporations are governed by Company Law of R.O.C. as am'd Nov. 12, 1990, and references herein are to articles of this law.

Foreign corporations desiring to do business in R.O.C. through branch office must first be recognized by R.O.C. government as foreign corporate entity duly registered in country of its origin. Foreign company may or may not be recognized in case country of its origin does not recognize R.O.C. companies. After being recognized and certificate of recognition is issued, foreign corporation shall then apply for branch license in order to operate business within R.O.C. through branch. (Art. 371). Application for recognition is made to Ministry of Economic Affairs. Application for branch license is made to municipal or provincial government in district where branch is located.

Foreign company shall state following particulars and submit following documents when applying for recognition: (1) Name, class and nationality of company; (2) business of company and business to be undertaken within territory of R.O.C.; (3) total amount of capital and, in case shares are issued, total number of shares, kinds of shares, par value of each share and paid up amount; (4) amount of funds to be used for operation within territory of R.O.C.; (5) location of its head office and location of branch office to be established in territory of R.O.C.; (6) date of incorporation in its own country and date on which it began to operate business; (7) names, nationalities and domiciles of directors and other responsible persons of company; (8) names, nationalities and domiciles or residences of its representative in litigious and nonlitigious matters within territory of R.O.C. and his/her power of attorney; (9) names, nationalities and domiciles of all unlimited liability shareholders of unlimited company, unlimited company with limited liability shareholders or other companies, and number of shares subscribed to and amount paid on such shares by each of them; (10) copies or photostat copies of its articles of incorporation and other certificates of registration in its own country; in absence of articles of incorporation or other certificates of registration, documents issued by competent authority in its own country to prove that it is company; (11) copy or photostat copy of franchise granted by competent authority in its own country, if established under such franchise; (12) copy or photostat copy of franchise, if its business requires franchise according to law or ordinance of R.O.C.; (13) business plan for operation in R.O.C.; and (14) minutes of meeting of shareholders or board of directors relating to application for recognition. (Art. 435). In addition, information on introduction of parent company, annual revenue of parent company for past three years, estimated annual revenue of branch for next three years, number of employees and commencement date of fiscal year for branch should also be provided.

Upon issuance of certificate of recognition, foreign company must apply to local competent authorities for registration of its branch offices. (Arts. 436, 437). In case of any amendment in record of registration, application must be filed with local competent authority for change of record within 15 days after such amendment. Foreign corporation complying with legal formalities has same legal position as R.O.C. corporation. However, foreign company may not solicit shares from public or issue bonds in R.O.C. if laws of its mother state forbids R.O.C. company to solicit same in her territory, but sale or purchase of shares or bonds by its individual shareholders is permitted (Art. 383) so long as sale or purchase is conducted in accordance with R.O.C. laws.

Prior to any substitution or departure of its designated agent foreign company must designate another agent and file report with competent authority for record. (Art. 385).

Foreign company must keep copy of its articles of incorporation and register of shareholders of unlimited liability in its branch office or in office of its agent in litigious and non-litigious matters in R.O.C. (Art. 374).

Foreign company which does not wish to operate business in R.O.C. through branch but wishes to appoint representative in R.O.C. to do juristic acts related to its business may apply to government for establishment of representative office. (Art. 386).

COURTS:

Chinese courts, except administration court and military courts, consist of district courts, high courts, and supreme court.

District courts have been established in many cities of R.O.C., and branch district courts have been established in smaller cities. In each district court (and its branches), in addition to regular proceedings, there are summary divisions handling summary proceedings which are applicable to cases where sum involved does not exceed NT$300,000, certain other cases involving leases, employment agreements, bailments, etc., and other cases by mutual consent of parties. Such summary proceedings are also applicable to criminal cases specified in Art. 61 of Criminal Code and subject to application by Public Prosecutor. District courts for criminal cases may also render summary judgment if such judgment is regarded appropriate, with consent of both defendant and Public Prosecutor. District courts, other than summary divisions thereof, have general original jurisdiction, except for cases under jurisdiction of summary divisions and for certain cases which fall within original jurisdiction of high courts.

High courts are located in provincial and special districts and there are branch high courts in several large districts. National capital and special municipalities may install high courts. These courts have original jurisdiction in civil cases concerning certain election and recall litigation, and in criminal cases concerning internal or external security of nation. High courts also have jurisdiction over cases appealed to them from district courts.

Supreme Court sits at locality of national government and is court of final resort. However, in civil litigation, judgment of high court is final if sum involved is less than NT$300,000; in criminal litigation, judgment of high court is final if defendant is charged for crime specified in Art. 61 of Criminal Code.

CURRENCY:

Since June 15, 1949, New Taiwan Dollar is legal tender circulated in Taiwan. NT$1 = 100¢. Metal coins in denominations of 50¢, $1, $5, $10 and $50, and paper money in denominations of NT$50, 100, 500 and 1,000 are issued exclusively by Bank of Taiwan under constant supervision of Supervisory Committee composed of government officials and business leaders under jurisdiction of Central Bank of China. Bank notes are covered 100% by gold, silver, foreign exchange, qualified negotiable instruments and securities.

Conversion rates of foreign exchange float on daily basis against supply and demand.

DEATH:

Civil Code of R.O.C. (Arts. 8, 9, 11) provides that missing person may be declared dead by court upon application of procurator or any interested party if he has disappeared for seven years. If missing person was over 80 years of age he may be declared dead if he has disappeared for three years. If missing person was in special peril of his life he may be declared dead if he has disappeared for one year. In absence of proof to contrary, date of death specified in these instances is date of expiration of specified period of disappearance. If several persons have perished in common disaster and it is not possible to ascertain which of them perished first, they are presumed to have died simultaneously.

Actions for Death.—Civil action lies in favor of spouse, parents and children of victims, those who pay funeral expenses, and those to whom victims are statutorily obligated to furnish maintenance. Action must be brought within two years from date when injury and tortfeasor is known to those mentioned above, but in any case, within ten years from date when wrongful death was caused. (C. C. 197). Amount of damages recoverable covers funeral expenses, compensation for any damage arising therefrom and suffered by third party to whom victim was statutorily bound to furnish maintenance, and compensaton for mental anguish and non-pecuniary suffering to spouse, parents and children of victims. (C. C. 192, 194). Court will estimate and award damages according to circumstances of each case and financial situation of parties concerned.

DECEDENTS' ESTATES:

See topics Descent and Distribution; Wills.

DEPOSITIONS:

Depositions for use in U.S. courts may be taken in R.O.C. Instructions should be included in regard to signature of deposition, signature and endorsement of exhibits, if any, whether or not stenographer may be employed, use of interpreter if Chinese witness is to be examined, whether such witness should be sworn, whether form of oath should be included in deposition, form of final certificate or return, and method of wrapping and mailing, in order that deposition may fully comply with requirements of law in jurisdiction in which it is to be used.

DESCENT AND DISTRIBUTIONS:

Heirs, other than spouse, succeed to property in following order: (1) Lineal descendants; (2) parents; (3) brothers and sisters; and (4) grandparents. (C. C. 1138).

Surviving spouse inherits as follows: (1) Where decedent left lineal descendants, share equal to that of other heirs; (2) where decedent left no descendants but left parents, brother or sister, one-half of estate; (3) where decedent left only grandparents, two-thirds of estate; and (4) where decedent left none of aforementioned relatives, entire estate.

Limited Succession.—Heir may limit payment of deceased's debts to extent of property acquired by succession. Where there are several heirs and one of them asserts limited succession, other heirs are regarded as having come into limited succession also. (C.C. 1154).

Waiver of Inheritance.—Heir may waive his right of inheritance. Such waiver must be effected by written declaration to court, within two months from time when he had cognizance of succession. Notice shall also be given by heir, to extent it is practicable, to party who is entitled to inherit owing to heir's waiver of his right of inheritance.(C.C. 1174).

Unacknowledged Succession.—Where no heir acknowledges succession, on expiration of definite period as designated and announced by court, such part of property of deceased which remains after settlement of claims and delivery of legacies escheats to Treasury. (C.C. 1185).

DISPUTE RESOLUTION:

Litigation is primary dispute resolution mechanism. Civil procedures are governed by Code of Civil Procedures ("Code"). Court hearings are conducted in open court unless with statutory grounds. Code does not require mandatory representation by attorneys. Judge is responsible for directing proceeding, investigating evidence, finding facts and determining legal consequences (such as assessing damages). There is no jury trial.

Court of first instance (usually District Court) and second instance (usually High Court) conduct both factual and legal review. Appeals to Supreme Court may be made against judgments of second instance except where value of benefits of appeal do not exceed NT$300,000.

DISPUTE RESOLUTION . . . *continued*

Arbitration is recognized alternative for resolution of commercial disputes as authorized by Commercial Arbitration Act. Act, enacted in 1961 and amended in 1982 and 1986, provides for legal framework for arbitration and enforcement of arbitral awards.

Parties to dispute need to enter into written arbitration agreement, which can bar either party's right to litigation. Parties are free to designate procedural rules of arbitration and determine number of arbitrators (must be odd number) and their selection. Nomination for arbitrators may be rejected by other party on grounds enumerated in Act.

Unless otherwise provided in arbitration agreement, arbitrations conducted in Taiwan generally follow rules of ROC Commercial Arbitration Association, which provides necessary administrative support.

Arbitral award has same binding effect between parties as final judgment of court. In order to secure enforcement of award, Act authorizes granting of pre-litigation remedies, such as provisional seizure and preliminary injunction.

Awards can be enforced after court order for enforcement is obtained. Awards may be denied enforceability under enumerated statutory circumstances.

Noncommercial disputes may be subject to arbitration with special statutory authorization such as Law Governing Handling of Labor Disputes. Such arbitration is subject to special rules.

Mediation is also recognized dispute resolution mechanism, which is based on consensus. It can be conducted in court before initiation of litigation as authorized under Code, or out of court but under administration of local government as authorized by Statute Governing Mediation by Hsiang, Chen and Shih, or by Committee for Resolution of Public Nuisance Disputes as authorized by Statute Governing Handling of Public Nuisance Disputes.

DIVORCE:

Divorce is granted upon following grounds: (1) Bigamy; (2) adultery; (3) ill-treatment; (4) ill-treatment of lineal ascendants of one party by other or ill-treatment of one party by other party's lineal ascendants, so as to render living together intolerable; (5) malicious desertion, which still continues; (6) attempt on life of one party by other; (7) loathsome, incurable disease; (8) serious, incurable mental disease; (9) when for period of three years one party is uncertain whether other party is alive or not; (10) when other party has been sentenced to not less than three years imprisonment or has been sentenced for infamous crime; and (11) other serious reason causes marriage difficult to sustain; but if reason is caused by one party, only other party has right to request.

Husband and wife may effect divorce by written agreement signed before two witnesses and registration of it in Household Administration Authority. For aliens, divorce may be decreed for a ground which at time of its occurrence is by national law of husband, and law of R.O.C., considered as constituting ground for divorce. If either spouse is Chinese, then divorce should be governed by law of R.O.C.

Residence.—Chinese court will generally assume jurisdiction for divorce between aliens when husband is domiciled in R.O.C. There are no requirements as to length of residence necessary after domicile is acquired before proceedings are brought. Intention is a determining factor as to establishment of domicile.

Proceedings.—There must always be attempt at reconciliation. Simple confirmation is not admitted as proof for alleged ground of divorce.

Remarriage.—There are no restrictions on remarriage of divorced parties, except in following two cases: (1) person, who, on account of adultery, has been divorced or sentenced to criminal penalty may not marry other party to adultery; and (2) woman may not remarry until six months after divorce, unless she has given birth to child within such six months. See topic Marriage.

ENVIRONMENT:

Environment Authority.—In reaction to widespread, serious and steadily growing environmental degradation, Environmental Protection Administration (EPA) address at 41 Chunghwa Rd., Sec. 1, Taipei was founded under Executive Yuan on Aug. 22, 1987 in replacement of former Bureau of Environmental Protection under Department of Health. In provinces and metropolises, Environmental Protection Department and in counties and cities, Environmental Protection Agency is set up to assist EPA to enforce environmental protection laws and regulations.

Factories.—New factory falling in categories of industries governed by environmental protection laws and regulations is required to obtain pollution control approval or permit from environment authority before applying for factory construction permit. Factory license for operating factory will not be granted before discharge permit or operation permit is given by environment authority. Alteration or expansion having concern of increasing pollution requires discharge permit or operation permit of environment authority before granting alteration of factory registration. (Examination Guidelines for Factory Establishment Registration to Accommodate the Environmental Protection Laws and Regulations promulgated by Ministry of Economic Affairs on Feb. 15, 1994).

Same criteria applies to expansion projects of existing factories.

Water Pollution.—Water Pollution Control Statute (promulgated on July 11, 1974 and last amended on May 6, 1991) authorizes EPA to set forth standards for controlling effluent water. EPA promulgated Effluent Water Standards in three stages (last amended on Nov. 29, 1991), of which standards of initial stage will be enforced until Dec. 31, 1992, more strict standards for second stage will be enforced from Jan. 1, 1993 for period of six years and last stage's standards will be started on Jan. 1, 1998. Failure to meet with standards will be subject to penalty of up to NT$600,000, and failure to correct such default within period ordered by competent authority will be given same penalty for each day it is not correct, and, if event is substantially serious, competent authority may order postponement of business, or, if necessary, effluent permit may be cancelled or business may be forced to cease permanently. (Water Pollution Control Statute, Art. 38).

Permit will be required for discharging waste or (sewage) water in any manner, other than to sewerage system. (Water Pollution Control Statute, Arts. 14, 30).

Water Pollution Control Statute also regulates sewerage systems and deals with waste water containing hazardous substances and other substances harmful to humans, farming and fishing or drinking water resources, etc. (Water Pollution Control Statute, Arts. 26, 34).

Wastes Disposal.—Wastes Disposal Act (promulgated on July 26, 1974 and last amended on Nov. 11, 1988) defines solid wastes into general wastes, hazardous industrial wastes and nonhazardous industrial wastes. Industrial wastes shall be cleaned up and disposed of by industry itself or by contract to qualified public or private owned wastes clean-up and/or disposal entities. Under this Act, EPA has promulgated various regulations, guideline and rulings in governing recollecction, clean-up and disposal of specific kinds of wastes (such as containers, tires, batteries and automobiles, etc.).

Environmental Impact Assessment.—Environmental Impact Assessment Act was promulgated on Dec. 30, 1994. Any developments listed or announced by EPA should undertake environmental impact assessment in planning stage. Environmental impact statement must be submitted for examination in application for development permit. If environmental protection authorities deem necessary to conduct second stage of environmental impact assessment, environmental impact assessment report shall be provided subsequently following public hearing for review and comments by specialists, scholars, environmental protection organizations and local residents. Developments subject to environmental impact assessment includes namely, factory establishment, industrial district development, road, railway, public rapid transportation system, harbor and airport development, mining, resort facilities, golf course, cultural, educational or medical facilities, new urban area development, high rise buildings, old urban area redevelopment, environmental protection works, nuclear and other energies development and nuclear waste storage or disposal.

Public Nuisance Dispute Resolution.—On Feb. 1, 1992, Public Nuisance Dispute Resolution Law was promulgated thereby introducing alternative dispute resolution mechanism. Either party in public nuisance dispute may unilaterally request mediation and remediation to be conducted by Mediation Committee at county and state levels. Settlement proposals by majority votes of Mediation Committee will bind parties concerned if they fail to object to such proposals within certain period (not more than 14 days). Damage claim may be referred, by either party, to EPA adjudication committee after unsuccessful mediation at state level. Adjudication award rendered thereof will bind parties concerned if neither party initiates civil lawsuit within 20 days.

Others.—Various statutes, regulations, guidelines and requirements were implemented or are going to be implemented to regulate and control air pollution, noise, vibration, ocean pollution, waste disposal and recycling, soil pollution, public environmental sanitation, toxic chemicals, and drinking water, etc. and further, Soil Contamination Treatment Act, by adopting concept of current owner's responsibility to clean up contamination and Environmental Protection Basic Law (constitution of environmental protection) are going to be promulgated once they are enacted by legislators. Administrative and criminal punishment are or will be imposed on owners, responsible persons of industries and industries themselves.

EXCHANGE CONTROL:

See topic Foreign Exchange and Foreign Trade.

EXECUTIONS:

Generally, creditor may secure compulsory execution on any property of its debtor after favorable judgment, unless otherwise prohibited by relevant laws. Compulsory execution may also be obtained against debtor in respect of: (1) His money claims against third persons; (2) claims based on his rights to delivery of some movable or immovable property by third person; (3) claims other than those cited in (1) and (2) above, which debtor has over some property but constituting something other than ownership, such as claim for performance of some service. Court may issue necessary orders or restraining orders against debtor and/or against third persons to effect compulsory execution.

EXECUTORS AND ADMINISTRATORS:

There is no probate division of R.O.C. courts nor any procedure exactly corresponding to probate or grant of administration. Civil tribunals of R.O.C. courts have probate jurisdiction.

Estate vests directly in heirs. Where there is more than one heir, deceased's estate, as whole, is owned by its heirs in common before partition. (C. C. 1151). Heir may waive his right of inheritance by written declaration to court within two months from time when he had cognizance of succession. Notice shall also be given by heir to party who is entitled to inherit as result of heir's waiver of his right of inheritance. (C. C. 1174). Acceptance may be unconditional or subject to inventory, which means that heirs will, under no circumstances be liable over extent to which they are enriched by inheritance.

Administration is in hands of heirs. Testator may by will designate executor or third person to do so; but minor or interdicted person cannot act as executor. (C.C. 1210). Where will has not designated executor, nor designates third person to do so, family council may elect executor. Where such executor cannot be elected by family council he may be designated by court on application of interested party. (C. C. 1211). This article does not apply if the deceased died intestate.

Powers of executor are broad. He is charged with making inventory, administering and managing property. (C. C. 1214-1215). Implicitly he has power to sell property of estate in order to pay legacies and creditors.

Executor has no right to divide estate unless especially so charged by testator.

While executor is executing his duties, heir may not dispose of any of property covered by will or obstruct executor in execution of his duties.

Period of administration cannot be longer than is necessary for liquidation and division of estate.

Court or family council may remove executor for negligence or grave causes upon application of interested party.

FOREIGN EXCHANGE AND FOREIGN TRADE:

Foreign exchange and foreign trade are controlled by Government under Statute for Governing Foreign Exchange promulgated in 1949 as last am'd on Aug. 2, 1995 and other relevant regulations. Said Statute and regulations are presently enforced by Foreign Exchange Department of Central Bank of China (in respect of foreign exchange), Ministry of Finance (in respect of foreign exchange-related administration) and Board of Foreign Trade of Ministry of Economic Affairs (in respect of foreign trade). 1987 and 1995 amendments of Statute made major liberalization of foreign exchange control. Guiding principles thereof are to: (1) permit private sectors to freely own and use trade-related (i.e., non-capital transfer) foreign exchange, (2) properly regulate inward and outward remittance of funds not related to trade (i.e., capital transfer), (3) permit designated foreign exchange banks to freely set conversion rate of forward foreign exchange.

Current regulations favor trade-related foreign exchange transactions. Consequently, foreign currency earned from exports of merchandise and services may now be retained and used freely by same exporter, while all foreign currency needed for importation of merchandise and services may be purchased freely from designated foreign exchange banks.

Aside from trade-related foreign exchange transactions, R.O.C. companies and residents may, without foreign exchange approval, remit outward and inward R.O.C. foreign currencies of up to US$20 million and US$5 million respectively (or its equivalent) each calendar year. Above limits apply to remittances involving conversion between NT dollars and US dollars or other foreign currencies. In addition, foriegn persons may, subject to certain requirements, but without foreign exchange approval of Central Bank of China, remit outward and inward R.O.C. foreign currencies of up to US$100,000 (or its equivalent) for each remittance. Foreign financial institutions may not, however, make inward remittances for converting their foreign currency to NT dollars without approval of Central Bank of China. Above limit applies to remittances involving conversion between NT dollars and US dollars or other foreign currencies.

All private importers and exporters must register themselves before engaging in trading businesses and must have paid-in capital of no less than NT$5,000,000.

FOREIGN INVESTMENT:

(*Note:* R.O.C. Government is currently deregulating foreign investment. Relevant laws and regulations are also being amended. Please consult R.O.C. law firm for updated information in this regard.)

Government has adopted various measures to encourage foreign investment in R.O.C. and promulgated on July 14, 1954, Statute for Investment by Foreign Nationals, which was last am'd May 26, 1989. Under this Statute, foreign investment may consist of inward remittance of foreign exchange; machinery and supplies required for own use; technical know-how or patent rights, and such portions of principal, capital gain, net profit, interest or other income generated as result of transfer of investment, reduction of capital or dissolution/liquidation approved by Government. Forms of investment may be: (1) investing alone or in association with other foreign nationals or jointly with Government or with R.O.C. nationals or juristic persons, in establishing new enterprises or in expanding old ones; (2) purchasing stocks or debentures of existing enterprises, or extending loans of cash, machinery or supplies to same; (3) furnishing technical know-how or patent rights as capital stock for joint operation of enterprises with Government or with R.O.C. nationals or juristic persons.

Investments in following businesses, however, are prohibited: (1) businesses which are in conflict with public safety; (2) businesses which are in conflict with good morals; (3) businesses generating high rates of pollution; and (4) businesses in nature of monopoly or in which foreign investments are prohibited according to laws.

Investments in following businesses are subject to special approval from relevant authorities-in-charge: (1) public utilities; (2) financing and insurance; (3) news and publication; and (4) businesses in which foreign investment is restricted according to laws and regulations. Foreign investment in service industries is being allowed by Government, such as advertisement, department store, chain stores, financial consulting services, securities-related business (generally on joint venture basis) and export/import trading.

In 1988 R.O.C. Government also promulgated set of guidelines called "Negative Listings" (as last am'd on Sept. 6, 1995). These guidelines set forth sectors of R.O.C.'s economy in which foreign investment is either restricted or prohibited. Those sectors not on Negative List are then open to foreign investment without any restriction.

Technical know-how and patent rights to be recognized as items of foreign investments must be approved by R.O.C. Government. Foreign investors acquiring real property shall be further subject to approval of Ministry of Economic Affairs under Art. 376 of Company Law.

Foreign investor is entitled to remit entire annual profits of his investment. After one year from date when invested enterprise commences its business operation or when investor obtains title to stocks or debentures in existing investee enterprise, if investor transfers its investment upon Government approval, investor is legally permitted to repatriate 100% of his total equity investment. Privilege of remitting profits or repatriating capital is not transferable except to investor's heirs, or to transferee who has status of foreign national.

Enterprises in which foreign capital has been invested are treated on equal basis, with those of same nature, operated by R.O.C. nationals. Such enterprises, however, are exempt from certain restrictions including: (i) chairman and vice chairman of board of directors must be R.O.C. nationals and (ii) half of incorporators and at least one supervisor must be domiciled in R.O.C. Furthermore, if foreign investor's investment is 45% or more of total capital of duly qualified and approved investee enterprise, following restrictions are also exempt: (i) shares of enterprise invested must be publicly issued and (ii) 10% to 15% of newly issued shares must be reserved for subscription by employees of enterprise invested. Subject to Statute for Investment by Foreign Nationals, foreign investors may also be exempted from certain restrictions in Company Law, Mining Law, Land Law, Merchant Marine and Civil Aviation Law so that they can be treated on equal basis with R.O.C. investor.

Specific protection is accorded foreign investors against requisition, or expropriation for period of 20 years from commencement of business so long as foreign capital comprises 45% or more of total capital of enterprise.

Government's policy of encouraging local and foreign private investment and enterprise was evidenced by Statute for Encouragement of Investment which was promulgated on Sept. 10, 1960 and expired on Dec. 31, 1990 to provide qualified enterprises with certain tax incentives, such as five-year corporate income tax holiday, duty-free importation of machinery and equipment, investment credit on new machinery and equipment, etc. Statute for Encouragement of Investment has been superseded by new legislation, Statute for Upgrading Industries, took effect on Jan. 1, 1991 and am'd on Jan. 27, 1995 which provides companies with some investment incentives, such as five-year corporate income tax holiday and investment credit as well as accelerated depreciation of equipment and instruments for R & D, pollution control, energy conservation purposes, reduced withholding income tax rate on dividends received by foreign investors whose investments have been duly approved under Statute for Investment by Foreign Nationals, etc.

R.O.C. and U. S. Governments have concluded agreement whereby U. S. Government guarantees U. S. investors in R.O.C. against nonconvertibility in remittance of profits or repatriation of capital and against expropriation of investments.

R.O.C. Government has also promulgated a separate but similar law to the above affording encouragement, protection and privileges to Overseas Chinese investors.

FOREIGN TRADE REGULATIONS:

See topic Foreign Exchange and Foreign Trade.

FRAUDS, STATUTE OF:

Under Civil Law, there is no specific statute comparable to "Statute of Frauds", but certain agreements are required to be in written form, such as transfer of title of ownership of real property, lease of real property for period exceeding one year, and contractual regime of property of husband and wife.

FRAUDULENT SALES AND CONVEYANCES:

Based on general principle of Civil Law, fictitious declaration of intent made by declarant in collusion with other party is voidable, but fact of it being viod cannot be defence against bona fide third parties. If fictitious declaration of intent is to cover another juristic act, provisions of law with respect to such other juristic act shall apply.

Creditor or trustee in bankruptcy may apply to court for invalidation of debtor's gratuitous act if such act is detrimental to creditor's right; while non-gratuitous act of debtor may be invalidated only if party receiving benefits of act had knowledge of circumstances at time he received such benefits. If debtor, within six months prior to adjudication of bankruptcy, provides security laws were made prior to expiration of six month period before adjudication of bankruptcy or repays debts before their maturity, such act may be invalidated by trustee in bankruptcy.

GARNISHMENT: See topic Attachment.

HOLIDAYS:

National holidays are: Foundation Day, Jan. 1 and 2; Chinese New Year and the Eve, last day of Dec. and Jan. 1 through 3 (Lunar calendar); Youth Day, Mar. 29; Children's and Women's Day, Apr. 4; Tomb-Sweeping Day, Apr. 5; Dragon Boat Festival, May 5 (Lunar calendar); Mid-Autumn Festival, Aug. 15 (Lunar calendar); Birthday of Confucius, Sept. 28; Double Tenth National Day, Oct. 10; Taiwan's Retrocession Day, Oct. 25; Birthday of late President Chiang Kai-Shek, Oct. 31; Dr. Sun Yat Sen's Birthday, Nov. 12; Constitutional Day, Dec. 25. In addition, Annual Settlement Day, Jan. 3 and Semiannual Settlement Day, July 1 are banking holidays.

HUSBAND AND WIFE:

Husband and wife may hold property under statutory or contractual regime. (C. C. 1005 & 1016). Statutory regime prevails if spouses fail to adopt contractual regime. (C. C. 1005). Under statutory regimes, all property belonging to spouses at time of marriage as well as property acquired by them during continuance of marriage becomes their property in common. (C. C. 1016). Nevertheless, following property shall be vested in husband or wife respectively: (1) articles which are exclusively intended for personal use of husband or wife; (2) articles which are essential to occupation of husband or wife; (3) gifts acquired by husband or wife which donor has designated as separate property. (C. C. 1013). There are two types of contractual regimes: (1) common property regime; and (2) separation of property regime. (C. C. 1031 & 1044). Nevertheless, husband and wife may agree by contract that certain specific property shall be regarded as separate property. Contract, without being duly recorded, may not be held against third party.

Wife can choose to prefix to her surname that of husband by couple's mutual agreement, and "chui-fu" should prefix to his surname that of wife. (C. C. 1000). Wife takes husband's domicile as hers; "chui-fu" takes wife's domicile as his without mutual agreement to change principle. (C. C. 1002).

Husband and wife are agents to each other in daily household matters. If one of parties abuses right of agency, other party may restrict it. (C. C. 1003).

IMMIGRATION:

Regulations Governing Issuance of Visas of Foreign Passports were promulgated on Aug. 25, 1965, and last am'd on June 15, 1995.

Alien shall not be permitted to enter territory of R.O.C. without visa on his passport, travel certificate or provisional entry permit issued by R.O.C. consulate or designated agencies stationed overseas, and inspection by airport or harbor authority. Alien who wishes to make short stay or visit here shall apply for visitor visa. Validity of visitor visa shall be decided in accordance with alien whose government has reciprocal visa agreement with R.O.C. and normally visitor visa is valid for three months unless otherwise stipulated. Duration of stay for visitor visa varies from two weeks, 30 days to 60 days. Alien holder of visitor visa with duration of 60 days may, on good grounds and without "NO EXTENSION WILL BE GRANTED" restriction, apply at nearest

IMMIGRATION . . . *continued*

city/county police headquarters for maximum of two extensions, each for 60 days. No extension of stay will be granted to those who hold visitor visa with duration of stay restricted to two weeks or 30 days, except for situations caused by force majeure or matters of vital importance. Visitor visa holders are not permitted to assume employment in R.O.C. without authorization. (See topic Labor Relations.) Alien who desires to stay in R.O.C. for more than six months to engage in individual or social activities must apply for resident visa. In applying for resident visa, certificate outlining purpose of such stay and letter of guarantee issued by local resident regarding activities and means of living of applicant in R.O.C. is required. Resident visa for alien to take up employment in foreign investment enterprise or branch of foreign company in R.O.C., will most likely be approved. Any alien holding resident visa shall apply with local police bureau for resident certificate within 15 days after his arrival. Duration of stay for resident visa is indefinite and dependent on duration of stay granted in Alien Resident Certificate. See topic Aliens.

Key Points for Screening Applications for Issuance of Multi-Entry Resident and Visitor Visas to Foreign Nationals promulgated on Apr. 12, 1984 were abolished on July 31, 1995. "Regulations Governing Entry, Exit, Residence and Stay of Foreign Nationals" promulgated on Jan. 6, 1989 and last amended on Dec. 1, 1994 governs applications for and matters concerning entry, exit, residence and stay of foreigners.

Pursuant to July 3, 1995 letter of Ministry of Foreign Affairs ("MOEA") with Ref. No. Wai-84-Ling-Erh-Tzu-84315849, (1) only single-entry resident visa will be issued (after issuance of resident visa, multi-entry permit may be applied in accordance with Regulations Governing Entry, Exit, Residence and Stay of Foreign Nationals); (2) multi-entry visitor visa may be issued by MOFA at its discretion based on principle of reciprocity on case by case basis; (3) multi-entry visitor visa with effective period from three months to five years may be applied for with R.O.C. consulate or designated agencies overseas based on principle of reciprocity.

Foreigners or designated representatives of foreign juridical persons as listed below may apply for single-entry resident visas pursuant to following conditions: (1) Foreigner whose investment has been approved in territory of R.O.C. and in operation with paid-in capital reaching amount of US$200,000; (2) upon condition (1), for each increase of investment by amount of US$500,000, additional visa may be issued for one more person. However, such additional issuance shall be limited to four persons only. See ruling set forth in MOFA's letter of Aug. 11, 1995 with ref no. Wei-84-Ling-Erh-Tzu-84818488.

If foreigners who have been granted visas fail to pursue provisions of Art. 15 of "Regulations Governing Issuance of Visas of Foreign Passports", Ministry of Foreign Affairs may revoke their visas and inform visa holders to that effect.

INFANCY:

Majority begins with inception of 20th year of age. Minority ends when one reaches one's majority. (C. C. 12). Minor who has not attained his seventh year of age has no disposing capacity; who is at or over his seventh year of age has limited disposing capacity; and who marries acquires disposing capacity. (C. C. 13). Domicile of person having limited or no disposing capacity shall be domicile of his legal representative. (C. C. 21). Parents are legal representatives of their minor children. (C. C. 1086). Abandoning legal capacity as well as disposing capacity is void. (C. C. 16). For person lacking disposing capacity, making and receiving of declaration of intention shall be represented by his legal representative. (C. C. 76). Where person having limited disposing capacity makes or receives declaration of intention, approval of his legal representative(s) is necessary, unless declaration of intention relates to pure acquisition of legal benefit, or to necessity of his daily life according to his age and social status. (C. C. 77).

Without approval of his legal representative, unilateral act made by person having limited disposing capacity is void, and contract entered into by such person shall become effective only upon ratification of his legal representative. (C. C. 78 & 79). Juristic act done by person having limited disposing capacity is valid if such person has induced, through fraudulent means, opposing party to believe that he had disposing capacity or that he had obtained prior approval of his legal representative. (C. C. 83). In case where legal representative of person having limited disposing capacity has authorized latter to dispose of certain property, or to carry on business independently, person has capacity to dispose of such property or carry on such business. (C. C. 84 & 85).

INSOLVENCY: See topic Bankruptcy.

INTEREST:

Debtors and creditors may agree on interest rate, subject to maximum rate specified in Civil Code, i.e., 20% per annum. In absence of any interest rate being agreed upon, creditors may demand 5% per annum, unless otherwise stipulated by law. If interest rate agreed upon exceeds ceiling provided for by Civil Code, creditor is not entitled to claim portion of interest over ceiling. Agreement for interest on interest is, in principle, not permitted, except when it is made in writing with respect to accrued interest which has not been paid for period of over one year from due date or there shall be commercial usage that indicates otherwise.

INTESTACY:

See topic Descent and Distributions.

JOINT STOCK COMPANIES:

See topic Corporations.

JUDGMENTS:

Recognized foreign judgments of foreign courts have same force and effect as final judgments of R.O.C. courts. Such judgments will be considered void, however: (1) If foreign court would have no jurisdiction according to R.O.C. law; (2) if judgment was given by default against Chinese citizen without service on or notice to such Chinese citizen in country of foreign court or in R.O.C. through judicial assistance of R.O.C. court; (3) if judgment of foreign court is contrary to public order or good morals of R.O.C.; and (4) if there is no reciprocity as to recognition of judgments with country in court of which foreign judgment was rendered. (C. C. P. 402). Judgment of foreign court will be presumed genuine if it has been duly authenticated by appropriate Chinese diplomatic or consular officer.

LABOR RELATIONS:

Basic Labor Standard Law was promulgated on July 30, 1984 and effective on Aug. 1 of same year, which applies to following industries: (1) Agricultural, forestry, fishing and pasturage; (2) mining and quarrying; (3) manufacturing; (4) construction; (5) water, power and gas supplying; (6) transportation, warehousing and communication; (7) mass media; and (8) other industries designated by central authority-in-charge. Certain service industries (such as banks and financial institutions) are being considered by Government to be included within applicable scope. However, it is difficult to predict when this will become effective. Such basic working conditions as labor agreements, wages, work hours, rest periods and vacations, child and female workers, retirement and pension, compensation for occupational hazards, apprentices, work rules, etc. are included in Law.

Labor Agreements.—Job of temporary, short-term, seasonal or specific nature may be covered by fixed-term agreement. Job of on-going nature must be subject to non-fixed-term agreement. While fixed-term agreement can be terminated without advance notice and severance pay upon expiration of agreement, non-fixed-term agreement can be terminated only if any of following events occurs and advance notice and severance pay are granted: (1) Business is closed or transferred; (2) business suffers losses or retrenchment; (3) business is suspended for over a month due to force majeure; (4) reduction of workers becomes necessary because nature of business has changed and there is no appropriate job available for worker; or (5) it is ascertained that worker is not capable of performing work assigned by employer. Of course, worker who commits wrongdoing can be dismissed at any time without advance notice and severance pay being granted. (L.S.L. 9.11.12).

Hours of Work.—Adult workers' hours of work shall, in principle, be limited to an eight hour day. Under special circumstances, working hours may be extended to a 12 hour day, provided that total hours extended in a month shall not exceed 46 hours for male workers and 32 hours for female workers. (L.S.L. 30.32).

Statutory Basic Wage.—Prevailing minimum wage for adult worker is NT$14,880 per month.

As for child worker which refers to one who has reached his 15th but not 16th year of age, his work time shall not exceed an eight hour day, and he shall not be employed to work between hours of 8 p. m. and 6 a. m. in ensuing morning and shall not be employed to perform any heavy and/or dangerous work. (L.S.L. 44, 47, 48).

Female worker shall not be employed to work between hours of 10 p. m. and 6 a. m. in ensuing morning unless three-shift system is adopted and certain requirements are met. (L.S.L. 49).

Worker is entitled to take half hour break with pay after having worked for four consecutive hours and to have one day as holiday in every seven days. Worker shall be granted leave for rest with pay on all public holidays ordained by laws or regulations. In addition to official holidays, worker who has been employed continuously for specific period shall be entitled to special vacation (ranging from 7-30 days per year). If worker does not take his vacation he shall be paid additional wages due for period of such vacation. (L.S.L. 35-39).

In case of maternity, female laborer shall be given leave for rest before and after childbirth up to total of eight weeks; she shall receive full pay during such periods if she has been employed for six months or more. (L.S.L. 50).

Labor Insurance.—Labor Insurance Act specifies that all factories, mines and any enterprises having five or more employees are obligated to apply for insurance coverage with Labor Insurance Bureau (LIB) for their employees. 70% of insurance premium is to be paid up by employer and 20% by insured employee, leaving 10% to be borne by government.

Insured employee is entitled to receive following major beneifts: (a) Death payment; (b) old age retirement payment; and (c) disability payment.

Health Insurance.—Previously covered by labor insurance, medical care and sickness benefits (including maternity payment) are now included in national health insurance program since Mar. 1, 1995. Premiums will be shared by employer, insured and government at various percentages depending upon status of insured. Immediate dependants of insured are also subject to insurance coverage.

Layoff Notification.—At least seven days prior to termination of employment, employers must notify local competent authority and public employment agencies of such layoff, so that latter could assist in reemployment process of discharged employees. (E.S.A. 34).

Severance Pay.—Employees who are terminated according to Art. 11 or 13 of B.L.S.L. shall be given severance pay at rate of one month wage for one full year of service. (L.S.L. 17).

Retirement Benefits.—Employees who qualify for voluntary or compulsory retirement shall be granted retirement benefit at rate of two-month wage for one full year of service during initial 15 years and one-month wage for one full year of service in subsequent years, subject to maximum of 45-month wage. (L.S.L. 53, 54, 55).

Pension Fund Reservation.—Under Labor Standard Law, employer must set aside monthly amount equal to 2% to 15% of aggregate employee wages as pension fund, and deposit same into designated banks. Retirement plan and supervisory committee over pension fund must be established and registered with local government.

Employees' Welfare Fund Reservation.—Statute on the Employees' Welfare Fund, promulgated on Jan. 26, 1943, and last amended on Dec. 16, 1948, provides that all mines, factories or any other enterprises, privately or publicly owned, must set up Employees' Welfare Fund for conducting employees' welfare benefits. Term "any other enterprises" as specified in Enforcement Rules of the Statute, refers to all banks, corporations, business organizations and agricultural, fishing and animal husbandry enterprises which have 50 or more employees. Business entity operating factory or employing more than 50 persons, is subject to Statute for the Employees' Welfare

LABOR RELATIONS . . . *continued*
Fund. Statute also stipulates that enterprise must form Employees' Welfare Committee to manage utilization of employees' welfare fund.

Labor Unions.—According to Labor Union Law, industrial or craft union shall be organized when in one and same area, or when in one and same industry or workshop, number of workers above full 20 years of age in one and same factory or in one and same area is over 30. There are six national unions, viz., Chinese Federation of Labor Unions, National Union of Railway Workers, National Union of Seamen, National Union of Mailmen, National Union of Mine Workers and National Union of Salt Mine Workers. In addition, there exist many unions on provincial as well as municipal levels. Union organizations became very aggressive in past several years.

Labor Safety and Health Law.—In setting higher occupational safety standards to protect workers from exposure to toxic substances and hazardous working conditions, Labor Safety and Health Law, promulgated on Apr. 16, 1974 and amended on May 17, 1991, mandates installation of preventive measures in work places, subject to safety inspections.

Settlement of Labor Disputes Law provides for rights of workers to voice their grievances and resolve their disputes with management via mediation or arbitration.

The Employment Service Act ("E.S.A.") promulgated on May 8, 1992, addresses promotion of nationals' employment opportunities, management of employment service agencies and employment of foreign nationals in R.O.C. Foreigners qualified for work permits are confined, inter alia, to following categories: specialists and/or technical personnel; officers in enterprises invested by overseas Chinese or foreign nationals duly approved by R.O.C. Government; workers designated by central competent authority to meet requirements of important national construction projects or economic or social development projects; or other specialized personnel who are not available locally and have to be recruited from abroad with special approval of central competent authority. (E.S.A. 43). Employer must apply for permission before employing foreign national. After arrival of approved foreign national, employer applicant should submit employment contract and permission document for issuance of work permit. (E.S.A. 45).

LEGISLATURE:

See topic Constitution and Government.

LICENSES:

Practically, most of business activities, professions and means of transportation as well as all trademark and patent rights will need license or certificate from authority. (See topics Commercial Register, Corporations, Motor Vehicles, Patents, Shipping, and Trademarks.)

LIENS:

Law relative to liens is found under title "Right of Retention" in R.O.C. Civil Code. Creditor in possession of movable property belonging to his debtor may retain same provided that: (1) where debt has matured; (2) where there is specified connection between debt and movable property; and (3) where possession of movable property is legal. If debtor is insolvent, creditor may exercise his right of retention before debt matures. Creditor must exercise due care over property retained and may claim reimbursement for expenses incurred in connection with custody thereof. If debtor has given proper security for performance of debt, right of retention by creditor is extinguished. Right of retention is also extinguished by loss of possession of property. Lessor of real estate has right of retention over movable property of lessee in/on real estate, to cover damages which he is entitled to recover and rent in arrears.

Innkeeper may retain luggage or other property of guest pending payment for lodging, food or disbursements.

Carrier may retain sufficient goods to secure payment of freight and other expenses. Last carrier may exercise such right of retention for benefit of all.

Forwarding agent likewise has right of retention.

LIMITATION OF ACTIONS:

Claim is barred by limitation if not exercised within 15 years, unless shorter periods are provided by law.

Claims for each successive payment falling due at intervals of one year or less are barred by limitation if not exercised within five years.

Claims in respect of following are barred by limitation if not exercised within two years: charges for lodging, food, amusements, or for price of goods for consumption, and for disbursements made by inns, restaurants and places of amusement; cost of transportation and disbursements by carriers; rent due to person who carries on business of letting movables; fees, charges for medicine and remuneration of medical practitioners, druggists and nurses, and their disbursements; remuneration of attorneys, public accountants and notaries and their disbursements; restoration of things received from clients by attorneys, public accountants and notaries; remuneration of technical experts, contractors and their disbursements; claims of merchants, manufacturers and craftsmen for price of goods or products supplied.

Extinctive limitation begins to run from time when claim can be exercised, but is interrupted by: (1) Demand provided that legal action was taken within six months starting from service of demand; (2) recognition of claim; or (3) initiation of legal action. Limitation which has been interrupted recommences to run from moment when cause of interruption ceases. Interruption of limitation takes effect only as between parties and their successors and assignees.

Limitation of claim for which there is mortgage or pledge or right of retention does not prevent creditor from satisfying himself out of things mortgaged, pledged or retained.

Period of limitation cannot be altered by juristic acts.

Benefit of limitation cannot be waived beforehand.

MARRIAGE:

To contract a marriage, man must have completed his 18th year and woman must have completed her 16th year, and if either party is under 20 years of age, he or she must have consent from his or her guardian. Marriage must be held at public ceremony in presence of more than two witnesses. One is presumed to have married if any marriage registered under Census Law. Person who has spouse may not contract another marriage. Woman may not remarry until lapse of six months after dissolution of her prior marriage unless she has given birth to child within such six months. (C. C. 987).

MONOPOLIES AND RESTRAINT OF TRADE:

Fair Trade Law ("FTL") was promulgated on Feb. 4, 1991 and became effective on Feb. 4, 1992, which is administered by Fair Trade Commission ("FTC") under Executive Yuan.

Monopolization.—Monopoly is prohibited from unfairly excluding others from market, maintaining and/or modifying prices unjustifiably, requesting favored treatment unjustifiably, and otherwise abusing its dominant market position. Oligopolistic firms will be treated as monopolies on collective basis without need to prove any anticompetitive agreement. Conceivably, predatory and monopolistic pricing will constitute act of monopolization.

Merger.—Prior report to FTC and its approval will be required for combination of enterprises where (1) surviving enterprise will have one-third of market share; (2) one of constituent enterprises has one-fourth of market share; or (3) one of constituent enterprises has amount of sales for previous accounting year that exceeds sales criteria publicly announced by FTC.

"Combination" is broadly defined to include mergers, acquisitions of more than one-third of voting stock of or interest in another enterprise, transfer or lease in whole or major part of enterprise's business or property, exercise of effective control over personnel employment of another enterprise, and regular operation of another enterprise or joint operation. FTC has to determine whether combination approval should be granted under economic cost-benefit analysis. Failure to file for FTC's approval may result in divestiture, compulsory disposition of assets, cessation of business and fines.

Cartel.—Concerted actions to restrict prices, quantities, customers, territories or otherwise restrict each other's commercial activities are not allowed. Accordingly, enterprises in Taiwan would be prohibited from engaging in horizontal price-fixing, horizontal territorial allocation and output restrictions. Several exceptions will be approved if they are found to increase efficiency, unify standards, increase joint research and development, maintain orderly import and export, or avoid bankruptcy.

Restraint of Trade.—Resale price maintenance will be nullified, with exception of daily consumption goods as published by FTC. FTL will also prohibit certain exclusionary practices such as boycott, discrimination, unfair inducement, tying arrangements and breaches of confidence, if they are found to be unreasonable.

Unfair Practices.—FTL will also prohibit other means of unfair competition such as trademark infringement, passing off, intentional mislabeling and other acts that may confuse consumers, trade libel, misappropriation of trade secrets, and other deceptive and unfair practices. In addition, pyramid sales plan in which commissions, bonuses or other economic gains are principally derived from recruiting others to join plan is prohibited.

Liabilities and Remedies.—FTC will have power to investigate possible violations and to impose administrative sanctions. Any person injured by any anticompetitive act or unfair methods of competition could seek injunctive relief, and treble damages may be awarded at discretion of court. Court may use unfair advantage gained by such unlawful act as measure of compensation. Violation of FTL will result in criminal liability, including imprisonment up to three years and fine up to NT$1 million. Criminal sanctions also apply to individuals working for entities engaging in such anticompetitive activities. Importantly, unrecognized foreign legal persons and entities may bring action under FTL if reciprocity exists.

Exemptions from FTL.—FTL recognizes that patents, trademarks and copyright are legal monopolies granted by government, if such rights are exercised properly.

MORTGAGES:

Mortgage can be created over real property, vessel, aircraft and chattel specified in Art. 4, Chattel Secured Transactions Act. Mortgage on real property, unless otherwise provided in contract, secures principal debt, interest, interest for default, and expense of executing mortgage. Real property as mortgaged remains in possession of mortgagor. If several mortgages are created on same property to secure several claims, rank of each is determined by priority of registration. Transfer of property mortgaged by owner does not affect validity of mortgage. Mortgage may neither be transferred without transfer of claim nor made security for any other claim by separating it from claim. Injunction may be obtained to prevent any act of owner which would depreciate value of property mortgaged. On default, mortgagee may apply to court to have property mortgaged sold at auction and to satisfy his claim from proceeds. Agreement in mortgage that ownership shall be transferred to mortgagee on default is void, but after maturity of obligation, mortgagee may, by agreement with mortgagor, acquire ownership of property mortgaged in satisfaction of his claims. In obligations secured by mortgage, where its right of claim has been extinguished by limitation, mortgage is extinguished if not exercised by mortgagee within five years after completion of such limitation. Mortgage is extinguished due to destruction of property mortgaged but compensation which could be received from such destruction shall be distributed to mortgagees according to their rank of priority.

Rules on mortgage on real property apply to mortgage on vessel. However, priority of vessel mortgage is subsequent to maritime liens specified in Maritime Law.

Only items listed in Items of Articles of Chattel Secured Transactions prescribed by Executive Yuan can be objects of chattel mortgage, such as machinery, equipment, tools, raw materials, semifinished products, finished products and vehicles. On default, mortgagee may take possession of mortgaged chattel and sell it by court auction or private sale. If chattel mortgage agreement states that it is subject to direct compulsory

MORTGAGES . . . *continued*
execution upon any event of default which damages mortgagee's right, mortgagee may take possession of mortgaged chattel with court assistance through compulsory execution proceedings.

Provisions regarding chattel mortgage under Chattel Secured Transactions Act shall apply, mutatis mutandis, to aircraft mortgage.

MOTOR VEHICLES:

All motor vehicles must be licensed. Drivers licenses are required.

NEGOTIABLE INSTRUMENTS:

See topic Bills and Notes.

NOTARIES PUBLIC:

Regulations establishing notary public offices have been promulgated and applied in many localities with object of eventual uniform application throughout R.O.C. Such offices are established as special division of various local district courts, where notary public assigned to such duties may, on application of parties or other interested persons, issue notary public certificates concerning juristic acts or acts relating to private rights, or give authentication to private documents. Applicants must be properly identified. Fees vary in relation to values involved.

PARTNERSHIP:

R.O.C. Civil Code provides that partnership is contract whereby two or more persons agree to make contributions in common for collective purpose. Contributions of partners and all other properties of partnership are held in common by all partners. Unless otherwise provided for by contract, accounts of partnership must be settled and its profits distributed at end of each business year. If assets of partnership are not sufficient to cover liabilities, partners are liable as joint debtors for deficit.

Dissolution.—Partnership is dissolved in any of following cases: (1) Where period agreed upon for its duration has expired; (2) when partners unanimously decide to dissolve it; (3) when undertaking which forms its object is accomplished, or when it is impossible to accomplish it.

PATENTS:

R.O.C. Patent Law was first promulgated in 1944 and last amended on Jan. 21, 1994.

There are three kinds of patents: Invention, New Utility Model and New Design, with patent terms of 20, 12 and 10 years from filing date, respectively.

Based on reciprocity, priority dates can be claimed within 12 months from original filing date for invention and new utility model applications and six months for new design applications. Priority dates claimed must be later than Jan. 23, 1994.

R.O.C. adopts absolute novelty principle with six month grace period for publication and public use made for research or experimental purposes and for disclosure in government-recognized exhibition. Nonobviousness is also essential condition for patent.

Unpatentable items comprise new species of animal and plant; diagnostic, curing or operative methods for disease of human body or animals; scientific principles or art of mathematics; rules or methods of games and sports, methods or plans which can be carried out only by means of reasoning and memory of human beings; any article detrimental to public order, good morals, or public health and use of which is contrary to law; any article shape of which is identical or similar to party, national or military flag, national emblem, government medal, portrait of National Father Dr. Sun Yat-Sen or official seal.

New strains of microorganisms will be patentable only after R.O.C. has become member of GATT and one year after TRIPS Standards have become effective. However, this restriction does not apply to R.O.C. nationals or national of foreign country which has signed reciprocal treaty or agreement with R.O.C.

Employers in principle have rights to apply for patent and own patents for on-duty inventions made by employees.

Patent matters are administered by National Bureau of Standards under supervision of Ministry of Economic Affairs. Patent application should be filed by inventor, or his assignees or successors, by submitting written application, specification, drawings, oath, assignment (as case may be), and power of attorney.

Bureau voluntarily starts examination and normally issues first Office Action within eight months. Allowed patent applications are published in Patent Gazettes, which commences three-month opposition period. Patent rights commence from publication date.

Extension of two to five years of patent term may be obtained for pharmaceutical and agrichemical inventions to recoup time needed for obtaining permits for manufacture and sale. Extended term cannot exceed actual time, including time spent in foreign countries, required for obtaining permits. Such patent term extensions can be requested only for patent cases filed after Jan. 23, 1994.

Patent infringement constitutes both criminal and civil liabilities. Two-year imprisonment may be imposed for infringement of new utility model patent.

Patentees have exclusive rights to prevent unauthorized manufacture, sale, use and importation, subject to restrictions of "patent right exhaustion principle".

Although there is no working requirement for invention patents, compulsory licensing of invention patents may be granted under following conditions: (1) national emergency; (2) nonprofit use for public benefit; (3) failure to obtain licensing within considerable period of time under reasonable commercial terms; (4) patentee has committed unfair competition as determined by relevant government authorities; and (5) cross licensing arrangement cannot be made between two related patentees.

Patent marking is essential to claiming damages.

Patent annuity must be paid prior to anniversary of publication date. Late payment within six months can be made at double amount of original annuity.

Major amendments of R.O.C. Patent Law made in Jan. 1994 include: (1) allowing priority claims; (2) extending patent duration of pharmaceutical and agrichemical patents; (3) pledges on patents; (4) granting patents for microorganisms, foods and drinks; (5) cross licensing of patents; (6) reversal of burden-of-proof for imported products regarding process patents; and (7) deletion of imprisonment punishment for infringement on invention patents.

PLEDGES:

Pledge can be created on personal property and rights. Possession by pledgee of pledged property is required to create valid pledge. Endorsement will also be required to create valid pledge on securities exclusive of instrument to bearer. Pledge secures payments of principal debt, interest, default interest and expense of realizing pledge and any damages arising from latent defects in pledged property, except as otherwise provided for in pledge agreement. Pledgee must exercise due diligence to keep pledged property. Pledgee may make sub-pledge.

On default, pledgee may sell pledged property at auction by prior notice to pledgor personally or by court's enforcement of compulsory execution, and satisfy his claim from proceeds. Agreement that on default ownership of pledged property shall be transferred to pledgee is void; however, after maturity of obligation pledgee may, by agreement with pledgor, acquire ownership of pledged property in order to satisfy his claim.

Pledge is extinguished upon return of pledged property by pledgee to pledgor. Upon return of pledged property, any reservation made in regard to continuance of pledge is void. Pledge is extinguished when pledgee loses possession of pledged property and cannot demand return of it, or when pledged property is destroyed. If compensation can be obtained for destruction of pledged property, pledgee is entitled to such compensation to satisfy his claim.

PRESCRIPTION:

One who has, with intention of being owner, enjoyed open, peaceful and continuous possession, for five years of personal property of another or, for 20 years of real property of another which ownership has not been registered, acquires ownership of personal property, or can claim to be registered as owner of real property. In cases of bona fide possession of unregistered real property, period for prescription is ten years.

PRINCIPAL AND AGENT:

If any authority of agency is conferred by juristic act, act of conferring must be made by manifestation of intention to agent or to third party with whom business delegated is transacted. (C. C. 167). Manifestation of intention which agent makes in name of principal within scope of his delegated authority takes effect directly both in favor of or against principal. (C. C. Art. 103). No limitation or revocation of power conferred on agent can be asserted against bona fide third party, unless ignorance of third party is due to his fault. (C. C. Art. 107). At termination or revocation of power of agency agent has to return written power of agency to party who gave it; he has no right of retention to it. (C. C. Art. 109). Person, who by his own acts represents that he has conferred authority of agency to another person, or who knowing that another person declares himself to be his agent fails to express contrary intention, is liable to third parties in same way as person who confers that authority, unless third parties knew, or ought to have known of absence of authority. (C.C. Art. 169). Juristic act done by person having no authority to act as agent is ineffective against principal unless ratified by principal. (C.C. Art. 170).

REAL PROPERTY:

Real Property is governed primarily by Civil Code and Land Law, which are augmented, among others, by Statute for Equalization of Land Rights, Urban Plan Law and Area Plan Law for utilization of land.

Real property rights (such as ownership and mortgage, etc.), their transfer, amendment and/or cancellation are required to be registered in recording book kept in Land Office.

Farm land ownership can only be transferred to farmer. Lease requires no registration and, in principle, has full protection in case that landlord sells leased premises.

Law gives authorities rather large powers in restriction of utilization of real property.

Chapter III of Land Law regulates lease of houses and land. Law is rather favorable to the tenant as to termination of lease and rent, etc. See topic Aliens.

REPORTS:

No English translations of decisions of modern Chinese courts have been published. Pamphlet containing extracts from certain decisions of Chinese Supreme Court was published in 1923 by Commission on Extraterritoriality. Following are notable publications, among many others, published in Chinese by relevant judicial authorities: (1) Compilation of Interpretations of Judicial Yuan; (2) Compilation of Interpretations of Council of Grand Justices, Judicial Yuan; (3) Supreme Court Precedent Synopses; (4) Compilation of Selected Civil and Criminal Judgments of Supreme Court; (5) Compilation of Opinions and Conclusions of Symposia of Civil and Criminal Chamber of Supreme Court; (6) Compilation of Precedent Synopses of Administrative Court; (7) Compilation of Synopses of Administrative Court Judgments. First publication made in five volumes, including all interpretations made by Judicial Yuan during period from its establishment in 1928 to June, 1948 and all interpretations made by Supreme Court before 1928. Second publication refers to all interpretations made by Council of Grand Justice of Judicial Yuan from its establishment in 1948 to June 1994. Third in two volumes contains all extracts from binding precedents of Supreme Court in period of 1927 through 1988. Fourth publication contains 36 volumes which are part of decisions of Supreme Court from Jan., 1980 to Mar., 1990. Fifth contains summaries of resolutions adopted at plenary meeting of Civil and Criminal Chambers of Supreme Court in period of 1928 to 1984. Sixth publication contains all extracts from binding precedents of Administration Court for period of 1933 to 1989. Last one in 13 volumes contains part of decisions of Administration Court in period of Jan., 1978 to Dec., 1993.

SALES:

Contract of sale is consummated when parties mutually agree on object to be sold and price to be paid. Vendor is bound to deliver thing sold to buyer and to cause buyer to acquire its ownership. Vendor of claim or of right must warrant actual existence of claim or right, but not in respect of defect in right sold, existence of which was known to buyer at time of concluding contract. Vendor of claim does not warrant solvency of debtor unless otherwise provided by contract. Vendor warrants that thing sold is free from defect in quality which would render it unfit for ordinary purposes or for particular purpose under specific contract, or which would impair or destroy its value. If buyer declines to accept thing forwarded from another place because of defect he is bound to preserve it in his custody temporarily and to prove existence of defect immediately. He may also sell thing forwarded if it is perishable or easily deteriorates, having first acquired permission therefor of authorities, chamber of commerce, or notary of place where thing is. In case of nonperformance by vendor of his duties concerning defect of thing sold, buyer has option to rescind contract or to ask for reduction of price. However, if rescission of contract would apparently be unfair to transaction, buyer may only be entitled to reduced price. Rescission of contract on account of defect in principal thing extends to its accessory. Right of rescission of contract or reduction of price of thing sold in case of defect is extinguished if not exercised within six months after delivery, unless defect was intentionally concealed.

Unless otherwise provided by law, by contract or by custom, delivery of object sold and payment of price must take place simultaneously. Profits and risks of object sold pass to buyer at time of delivery, unless otherwise provided by contract. Right of redemption may be exercised if contract so provides, but period for exercising right cannot exceed five years. Cost of redemption must be borne by person who redeems.

Particular kinds of sales are: Sale on approval, sale by sample, sale by installments, and sale by auction. In sale by sample, vendor warrants that object sold will conform to sample.

Notices Required.—In case party to sales contract is in default, other party may specify reasonable period of time for him to perform. If party in default does not perform his obligation within such period, other party may rescind contract. In this connection, exercise of right of rescission will not affect right of party not in default to claim for damage. (C. C. 254 & 260). If according to nature of contract or expression of parties, object of contract cannot be fulfilled if performance is not effected within specific period of time, and if said period of time elapses without effectuation of performance by one party, other party may rescind contract without having to give notice required in C. C. Art. 254. (C. C. Art. 255). Yet notice of rescission must reach other party and is irrevocable. (C. C. 258).

Applicable Law.—See topic Contracts, subhead Applicable Law.

SECURITIES:

Unless otherwise stated, articles cited are those of Securities and Exchange Law ("SEL"), which was promulgated on Apr. 30, 1968 and last amended on Jan. 29, 1988.

Regulatory Powers of Supervising Authority.—Securities and Exchange Commission ("SEC") established under Ministry of Finance ("MOF") is authorized by SEL to administer within comprehensive regulatory framework provided by SEL. (Art. 3).

Definition of "Security" under SEL.—Under SEL, term "security" or "securities" shall include government bonds, corporate stocks and corporate bonds publicly offered or issued, and any other securities approved by MOF. In addition, any stock warrant certificate, any certificate of entitlement to new shares, any certificate of payment or any document of title to any of foregoing securities shall be deemed as securities. (Art. 6).

Catch-all wording of this article is intended to cover interim securities or other documents that would otherwise escape being governed by SEL. Under authority granted by Art. 6, MOF has ruled that beneficial certificates issued by securities investment trust enterprises are "Security".

In addition, MOF also ruled that "the offering and sale of foreign stocks, bonds, government bonds, beneficial certificates or other securities in the nature of investment vehicles shall be governed by relevant R.O.C. securities laws and regulations, without actually defining them as securities, and that conclusion of certain "investment contracts" by overseas Chinese or foreign nationals for purpose of raising funds in Taiwan is equivalent to issuance of securities. However, criteria for determining whether any such particular contract is investment contract has yet to be further defined under SEL. In Feb. 1996, MOF issued Guidelines Governing the Offering and Issuance of Securities by Foreign Issuers. Under Guidelines, "securities" refers to Taiwan Depositary Receipts and bonds issued by juristic persons organized under law of foreign jurisdiction.

Subscription, Issuance and Public Offering.—Offering and issuance of securities are subject to prior SEC registration or approval. (Art. 22). In addition to approval system, SEL adopted registration system whereby certain public offerings would become effective upon registration with SEC. Securities exempt from such approval or registration requirements include government bonds, and other securities specifically authorized by MOF.

SEL defines "Public Offering" to mean offering of corporate stocks or bonds to "nonspecific persons" by promoters prior to incorporation of company, or by issuer prior to issuance of securities. However, SEC has not yet defined and determined what would constitute "nonspecific persons".

Employees of companies limited by shares generally have preemptive rights on 10 to 15% of their company's new share issues. In addition, existing shareholders have preemptive rights over balance of newly issued shares after employees have exercised their preemptive rights in accordance with Art. 267 of Company Law. However, shareholders' preemptive rights are limited by SEL so that in cash offering of new shares by issuer whose stocks are either listed on Taiwan Stock Exchange ("TSE") or over-the-counter market ("OTC"), at least 10% of such new issuance must be set aside to be subscribed by public at same price offered to existing shareholders and employees. Public companies, whose shares are traded neither on TSE nor OTC but are subject to disclosure requirements under SEL must also set aside for public offering at least 10% of new shares offered for each, unless specific exemption from SEC is obtained. (Art. 28-1).

Disclosure and Reporting Requirements.—In application for registration to publicly offer and/or issue securities, issuer is required to submit prospectus in addition to those items required by Company Law. (Art. 30). Failure to tender prospectus to subscribers, making materially false statements, or omitting required material statements from prospectus will lead to liability of issuer, responsible person, officers signing on prospectus, related professionals, and underwriters. (Art. 31 and 32). In addition, "due diligence" defense to false or omitted statement in prospectus to related officers of issuer and underwriters involved in drafting prospectus is also specified in SEL. (Art. 32).

Public companies are required to report and publish audited annual and semi-annual financial reports as well as first and third quarter financial reports that have been reviewed by their respective independent certified auditors. Public companies are also required to report and publish monthly operating statement before tenth day of following month. In addition, Art. 36 of SEL provides that all public companies shall publish additional information which will keep reasonably current all statements filed with SEC. Events that may have significant impact on shareholders' interests or prices of securities of issuer also trigger financial reporting rquirement under 1988 SEL amendment.

Art. 25 of SEL imposes certain public disclosure and reporting requirements regarding share ownership of their managerial personnel, directors, supervisors and holders of more than 10% of shares of public companies. These reports must include class, number and par value of issuer's equity securities. Such shareholders must also report monthly with issuer itemizing changes in number of shares they held in preceding month. Issuer is required to consolidate such reports and file them with SEC. Calculation of such holdings includes shares held by shareholder's spouse, minor child and nominees.

Art. 22-2 of SEL also provides that transfer of shares by directors, supervisors, managers or holders of more than 10% of shares of issuer may only be effected in accordance with any of following methods: (1) by transfer to nonspecific person following approval by, or registration with, SEC; (2) by transfer of over 10,000 shares which are to be traded on TSE or in OTC within daily transfer allowance and which have been held for period prescribed by SEC, within three days following reporting to SEC; or (3) transfer within three days following reporting to SEC, by transfer to specific persons who meet certain qualifications prescribed by SEC.

Tender Offers.—Art. 43-1 of SEL requires any person acquiring, individually or jointly with other persons, more than 10% of the total issued and outstanding shares of public company to file with SEC report within ten days after such acquisition. Such report has to disclose purpose and funding source of share acquisition and any other matter as required by SEC. Unless otherwise approved by SEC, tender offers to public may not be made outside of TSE or OTC. SEL authorizes SEC to promulgate relevant regulations to govern and regulate tender offers.

Insider Trading.—Art. 157 of SEL is designed to prohibit corporate "insiders" from taking advantage of their access to information by engaging in short-term trading in securities held by them. This article permits issuer to claim for disgorgement of such profits within six months of trading from directors, managerial personnel, supervisors and 10% shareholders of issuer.

1988 amendment of SEL contains new Art. 157-1 which prohibits certain insiders, such as directors, supervisors and managers of issuer, or shareholders of more than 10% of equity shares, or any person who has learned information due to occupational or controlling relationship, or any person who has learned information from any of persons described above, to trade based on information which may materially affect price of issuer's securities on TSE or OTC prior to disclosure of such information to public. Persons violating above provisions will be liable for damages to third parties engaging in transactions on opposite side in good faith. Measure of damages will be limited by difference between purchase (or sale) price prior to disclosure and average of closing prices for ten business days after disclosure. In case of any egregious violation, court may award treble damages.

Anti-fraud Provisions and Civil Liabilities.—Art. 155 of SEL prohibits manipulative practices in securities trading and provides private remedy for investors injured by manipulative conduct prohibited by SEL. In effort to cover fraudulent and manipulative conduct that takes place in OTC, Art. 155 was amended in 1988 to encompass manipulative conducts on TSE and OTC. Amended article also modifies language of previous article in order to ensure effective enforcement. In contrast to previous article, which only provided criminal sanctions, new article provides civil remedies to bona fide purchasers or sellers of securities. Art. 155, as amended, prohibits "wash sales" or any transactions entered into simultaneously with purpose of creating misleading appearance of trading. This article also prohibits transactions entered into for purpose of depressing or raising prices of securities as well as spreading of rumors or misleading information for purpose of manipulating such prices. In addition, Art. 155 of SEL contains provision to prohibit any direct or indirect manipulative conduct aimed at affecting prices.

Under general anti-fraud provision contained in Art. 20 of SEL, fraudulent conduct in connection with offering and sale of securities is prohibited. In addition, misrepresentation or omission in financial reports or any other relevant documents filed or published by issuer is prohibited. Violation of either of these two prohibitions may result in both criminal and civil sanctions, which civil sanctions award damages to bona fide buyers or sellers.

Establishment of Securities Firms.—Criteria for the Establishment of Securities Firms ("Establishment Criteria") was promulgated on May 17, 1988 and last amended on May 30, 1995. Under Establishment Criteria, minimum paid-in capital for underwriting, dealing and brokerage operations is NT$400 million, NT$400 million, and NT$200 million, respectively. Therefore, integrated securities house operation will require total paid-in capital of NT$1 billion. Working capital requirement applicable to branches of foreign securities firms are different from capital requirements applicable to local securities firms.

Foreign access to securities firms can be made in any one of two following ways: First, any foreign investor or overseas Chinese may invest in securities operation by

See Topical Index in front part of this volume.

SECURITIES . . . *continued*
joint venturing with ROC investors. Second, foreign securities firms may set up branch operation; to date, SEC has only allowed foreign securities firms meeting certain requirements to set up branch offices in ROC to engage in securities brokerage business. SEC has discretion to limit number and business scope of foreign securities firms setting up branch operations or ROC branches of foreign banks setting up securities operations.

SHIPPING:

R.O.C. vessels are subject to provisions of Maritime Law promulgated on Dec. 30, 1929 and became effective on Jan. 1, 1931 as last am'd on July 25, 1962 and Vessel Law promulgated on Dec. 4, 1930 and became effective on July 1, 1931 as last am'd on Dec. 28, 1983. As provided in Art. 1 of Maritime Law, term "vessel", where used in this Law, refers to oceangoing vessels and vessels navigating on or in sea or waters intercommunicating with sea. Provisions of this Law are not applicable to following classes of vessel, save in case of collision: (1) motor driven vessels whose gross tonnage is less than 20 tons or nonmotor driven vessels whose gross tonnage is less than 50 tons, (2) military vessels, (3) vessels solely used on public affairs, (4) vessels not belonging to those defined in Art. 1 of Maritime Law.

Assignment of whole or part of vessel is void unless made in writing and in accordance with following provisions: (1) In R.O.C., application must be made to governing authority at place of assignment or place where vessel is lying, and such authority must seal and certify assignment; (2) abroad, application must be made to R.O.C. Consulate, which must seal and certify assignment.

Transfer of ownership of vessel may not be pleaded against third party unless it has been registered.

As provided in Art. 2 of Vessel Law, vessels owned by: (i) R.O.C. Government, (ii) R.O.C. nationals, (iii) R.O.C. companies, or (iv) R.O.C. juristic persons are R.O.C. flag vessels.

Foreign Shipping.—R.O.C. has not acceded to Hague Rules 1924 or to Visby Rules 1968. Nevertheless adoption in 1962 of main principles of Hague Rules resulted from adoption of American COGSA.

R.O.C. Maritime Law like American COGSA applies inward and outward. Law was also made to apply to internal carriage by water.

Per package or unit limitation is $9,000 in New Taiwan Currency. But if applicable law is foreign law, it is possible that foreign standard may apply.

There is no provision for punitive damages for breach of carriage contract, and responsibility for damage or loss of goods is calculated according to value at destination. Shipper may recover economic loss if damage or loss of goods results from intentional or gross negligence of carrier.

Himalaya clauses were discussed in 66 T.S. 458 and 66 T.S. 2549 (S.Ct. 1977). Regretfully, court did not consider arguments against this clause.

Jurisdiction clauses in bills of lading have been held invalid because there has been no real agreement by both parties.

Arbitration clauses have had no better fate in courts than jurisdiction clauses. In 63 S. 1336 (H.Ct. 1974), which is not COGSA case, defendant raised arbitration clauses as defense, and court upheld it on ground that there is no real agreement between carrier and holder of bill of lading. Although R.O.C. is not signatory state of New York Convention on Foreign Arbitral Awards 1958, in principle, foreign arbitral awards can be recognized and enforced in R.O.C., provided that there is real written arbitration agreement between parties and foreign court is possible to recognize R.O.C. arbitral award. However, courts may refuse to recognize those foreign arbitral awards which are in violation of R.O.C. coercive law, or of public order or good morals. Foreign shipping companies or their agents must register with Ministry of Transportation & Communications and Ministry of Economic Affairs. American ships are governed by Art. 22 of Treaty of Friendship, Commerce and Navigation between U.S.A. and R.O.C. which has been ratified by both parties. This treaty is based on reciprocity and thus duties, charges or conditions which are not imposed on R.O.C. ships will not be imposed on American ships.

Shipping Act, promulgated on June 3, 1981, governs all shipping enterprises and shipping industries including carriers, agents, sea cargo forwarders, vessel charters, ship leasing and charter operation, container terminals and leasing operations and employment of sailors. Foreign ships may not solicit or receive passengers or goods for transportation in R.O.C. unless R.O.C. shipping agent has been engaged to execute or handle matters related to carriage of passengers or goods. Such restriction is not applicable to foreign shipping carriers having branch office in R.O.C.

STATUTES:

Major codes promulgated by Chinese Government include Civil Code, Code of Civil Procedure, Criminal Code and Code of Criminal Procedure. In addition, laws have been promulgated on such subjects as companies, banking, negotiable instruments, patents, trademarks, copyrights, insurance, admiralty, securities, real estate, labor unions, labor standard, consumer protection, fair trade, nationality, taxation, etc.

TAXATION:

Income Tax Law was promulgated and enforced as of Jan. 29, 1963, and last am'd Jan. 27, 1995. It governs any income arising within territorial limits of R.O.C. except where enterprise has its head office in R.O.C. and branches outside of R.O.C., tax is collected on worldwide income, but with deductions of income tax already paid by branches outside of R.O.C. to resident countries.

Income of diplomatic and consular officials and other personnel who enjoy diplomatic privilege in foreign embassies, legations and consulates in R.O.C. acquired in course of their duties is tax free.

Income of other employees in foreign embassies, legations, consulates and their affiliated organizations in R.O.C., who are nationals of foreign country concerned but who do not enjoy diplomatic privileges, is also tax free if same privilege is accorded to Chinese employees in similar positions in country concerned.

Earnings of profit-seeking enterprises including corporations, partnerships or sole proprietorships are taxed on net income. Rates vary from 15% to 25%. Under Statute for Upgrading Industries revised on Jan. 27, 1995, any enterprises meeting government encouragement criteria and organized as companies are allowed accelerated depreciation on their fixed assets on an annual basis, and allowed tax credit for costs spent on investment in automotive production equipment or technology, acquisition of resources recovery or anti-pollution equipment or technology, engagement in research and development, personnel training or establishment of brand name in world market, and investment in energy conservation or waste water recycling. Investors of government prescribed important enterprise may credit their equity investment against their income tax. Five-year tax holiday is available to such important enterprise as alternative to investors' tax credit.

Income tax on all salaries, wages and emoluments is withheld at source at various rates (according to number of dependents of taxpayer) or at a flat rate of 10% for resident individuals, and at 20% for nonresident individuals.

For resident individuals, or business enterprise, with fixed office in R.O.C., income tax is withheld at source at 15% on dividends paid by corporations or cooperative associations to shareholders, rents and royalties and at 10% on commission and interest payment. In case of profit-seeking enterprise in form of company, where retained earnings have not been distributed and have accumulated to more than paid-up capital, procedure for increase of capital shall be effected in next fiscal year. Untouched retained earnings after capital increase shall not exceed paid-up capital after capital increase. If such procedure has not been effected, collecting authority shall compute amount of accumulated retained earnings distributable to each individual shareholder and collect from him consolidated income tax thereon according to tax rate of current year. Companies may pay 10% tax on retained earnings exceeding above limit to exempt capital increase or compulsory distribution procedures. This 10% surcharge tax is not refundable or offsetable. Limitation on paid-up capital is adjusted to amount not exceeding two times of paid-up capital for important industry as prescribed by Government.

For nonresident individuals, or business enterprises, without fixed office in R.O.C., income tax on dividend paid by corporation to shareholders is withheld at source at 20% in case investment project was approved according to Statute for Investment by Foreign Nationals or Statute for Investment by Overseas Chinese; or at 35% (for individuals) or 25% (for business enterprises) in case without approval according to same Statute, and on interest payments, commission, royalty and rents at 20%.

There is consolidated income tax on composite income of local individual residents, subject to various exemptions and deductions. Rates vary from 6% to 40% of different portions of net consolidated income according to progressive scale.

Income tax exemption is granted to specific items, e.g.: (1) Business income obtained from operation inside territory of R.O.C. by foreign enterprise engaged in international transportation, provided that reciprocal treatment is accorded by foreign country concerned to international transport enterprise of R.O.C. operating in its territory; (2) royalty earnings paid to foreign enterprise for use of patent rights, trademark and/or various kinds of special authorized rights under technical cooperation project certified by Industrial Development Bureau as used by important technological industries as well as payment to foreign enterprise for technical services in construction of factory of important technological industries or in production of products by designated important technological industries, all as prescribed by Government authorities; (3) interests accrued from loans extended or guaranteed by foreign government, financing institutions wholly or partly operated by foreign government and international economic development financing institutions to or for Government of R.O.C. and/or juristic persons within territory of R.O.C.; (4) interests accrued from credit facilities extended by foreign financing institutions to its branch office and/or other financing institutions within territory of R.O.C.; (5) interests accrued from loans extended by foreign financing institutions to juristic person within territory of R.O.C. for financing important economic construction projects as approved by Ministry of Finance.

If fund retained by company for use of expansion by way of declaring stock dividend, payment of income tax on such stock dividend will be deferred to time when such stock is transferred, if certain criteria are met.

Any business enterprise with head office outside territory of R.O.C., which is engaged in international transport, construction projects, technical services or machinery and equipment leasing and cost and expenses of which are difficult to calculate, may apply to Ministry of Finance for approval to consider 10% (for international transport business) or 15% (for construction projects, technical services or machinery and equipment leasing) of its total business revenue as its income derived from R.O.C. whether or not it has branch office or business agent in R.O.C. Withholding tax rate is 25% on this 10% or 15% income, i.e., 2.5% or 3.75% on total business revenue.

U.S. Government and R.O.C. Government concluded reciprocal agreement on exemption of transportation business income tax in May 1988. This agreement retroactively took effect on Jan. 1, 1987. R.O.C. Government has entered into tax treaty for avoidance of double taxation on income only with Singapore and Indonesia governments on Jan. 7, 1982 and Jan. 17, 1996 respectively.

Business Tax.—Business Tax Law was promulgated on Dec. 30, 1955 and last am'd Aug. 2, 1995. Except for banking, insurance, trust and investment, securities, short-term bills and commercial paper, and power enterprises which are still subject to gross business receipt tax ("GBRT") on their sales of goods or services, other business entities are governed by value-added tax ("VAT") system. GBRT is divided into several categories, i.e. 1% for reinsurance premium income of insurance business; 5% for banking, investment and trust, brokerage, stocks trading, insurance firms, short term bills and commercial paper enterprises and pawn enterprises; 15% for night clubs and restaurants with entertainment programs; 25% for liquor bars, tea houses, coffee shops and bars with attending hostesses. As to business other than above-mentioned, VAT rate is 5% currently.

Commodity Tax.—Commodity taxes are levied on some commodities, whether locally produced or imported. Tax rate ranges from 3% to 60% depending on goods involved. In case of imported commodities, total price comprised of duty-paying value (as defined in Customs Tax Law), import duty and harbor construction fee will be used to calculate commodity tax.

Government authorities have also adopted some criteria for determining commodity tax on certain products of which raw materials, components or parts are also subject to

See Topical Index in front part of this volume.

TAXATION . . . *continued*
commodity tax, such as air-conditioning systems (compressors thereof are taxable) and vehicles (audio/video system, including tape recorders, are taxable).

Stamp Tax.—Receipts of payment, contracts for purchase and sale of personal property, contracts for work and contracts for sale, transfer or separation of real property, which are made or produced in Taiwan, are subject to stamp tax at rates of 0.4%, NT$12, 0.1% and 0.1%, respectively. If receipts of payment are evidenced by "government uniform invoices", no separate stamp tax is leviable.

Customs Duty.—Unless otherwise exempted by law, all imported goods are subject to import duties. No duty is leviable on export goods. Import duty is calculated on basis of "duty-paying value" according to prescribed tariff rates which are classified into two categories, one applies to those goods imported from countries that give reciprocal treatment to R.O.C. goods and other is applicable to goods imported from non-reciprocal countries.

Term "duty-paying value" refers to transaction price of imported goods, which shall include commissions, handling charges and packaging costs to be borne by buyer, amount of reasonable value or discount given to buyer, royalty payments for patent or other licensing arrangements to be borne by buyer; and freight, processing and handling charges upon arrival at port of importation.

Under certain circumstances, customs offices are granted right to assess and recalculate true transaction price either based on available price of identical or similar goods imported or if that is not available, on domestic sales price of identical or similar goods imported.

Securities Tax.—Term "securities" is defined to include share certificates representing capital stock and debentures issued by company and any other securities approved by government to be issued to public. Transaction of securities, except for government bond, is subject to securities transaction tax at rate of 0.3% of transaction price. Securities transaction income tax (i.e., capital gains tax) will also be levied if transaction of securities would result in any income. However, capital gains tax is currently suspended.

Property taxes are leviable either on ownership or for transaction of real properties, and are calculated on value assigned and published from time to time by government.

Land value tax is imposed on land other than farm land that has been assigned value and is calculated at 1% if land value does not exceed starting cumulative value. If land value exceeds starting cumulative value, additional 0.5%, 1.5%, 2.5%, 3.5% and 4.5% will be levied for excessive portion on progressive basis. Privileged rates are available for land used for residence (0.2%) or for industries, mining, private part, zoos, etc. (1%). Land value tax shall be paid by land owner on yearly basis.

Housing tax is also paid by owner of house on yearly basis, and is calculated at different rates as follows: 1.38%-2% for residence; 3%-5% for business; and 1.5%-2.5% for nonprofit-making purposes.

Deed tax is leviable when person purchases, leases, exchanges, receives donation of, divides or takes possession of building, and is calculated at rate ranging from 2.5% (for exchange or division), 5% (for Dien which is equivalent to leasing), and 7.5% (for purchase, donation or possession).

Land value increment tax is levied on increased value of land as result of title transfer, and is calculated on progressive rate ranging from 40% to 50% to 60%, depending on value increment.

TRADEMARKS:

Any word, drawing, symbol, or combination thereof to be registered as trademark shall be distinctive and sufficient to cause of general buyers of goods to recognize it as mark identifying goods of certain manufacturer or merchant and distinguishing such goods from those manufactured or sold by others. Inherent nondistinctive mark, such as descriptive of goods, geographical names, surnames, and words, numerals, symbols or letters signifying product's grades or models, may acquire its distinctiveness for registration as trademark through use.

According to Trademark Law of R.O.C., trademark design having any one of following features may not be registered: (1) being identical with or similar to national flag, national emblem, national seal, military flags, military insignia, official seals, or medals of R.O.C. or national flag of any other nation; (2) being identical with or similar to image or name of late Dr. Sun Yat-Sen or of Chief of State; (3) being identical with or similar to red cross sign, or name, or emblem, or badge of domestic or famous international organization; (4) being identical with or similar to Chinese "Standard Quality" mark or any local or foreign mark of same nature; (5) being violative of public order or good morals; (6) being likely to lead public to misconceive or to form mistaken belief in nature, quality or place of origin of goods; (7) plagiarizing another person's trademark or any other mark, and thus likely to cause public to form mistaken belief; (8) being identical with or similar to mark which is customarily used on same goods; (9) being identical with or similar to mark used by government office of R.O.C. or by public show in nature of exhibition, or to medal awarded by such government office or public show; (10) using any word, drawing, symbol, or combination thereof, as description of goods designated for use of trademark sought for registration, or is customarily used to signify name, shape, quality or function of goods; (11) using image of another person, or name of another juristic person, organization, or nationally famous firm, or stage name, pen name or alias of another person without prior consent; provided, however, that this provision shall not apply if goods covered by scope of business of such firm or juristic person are not same or similar to those designated for use of trademark sought for registration; (12) being identical with or similar to another person's registered trademark which is designated for use on same goods or similar goods, or identical with or similar to registered trademark which has expired for less than two years; provided, that this provision shall not apply if registered trademark had not been used for three years immediately prior to its expiration; (13) using another person's registered trademark as part of applicant's own trademark proposed for use on same goods or similar goods.

All Chinese and foreigners of countries which have treaties with R.O.C. for mutual protection of trademarks have right to register trademarks and acquire right of exclusive use thereof for period of ten years commencing from date of registration. With regard to foreigners of countries which have no reciprocal treaties with R.O.C., they can obtain trademark protection through registration if their countries afford same trademark protection to R.O.C. applicant. Applicant may claim priority within six months from date of first application filed in foreign country that has treaty or agreement with R.O.C. for reciprocal protection of trademarks. Right of exclusive use shall be limited to exact goods as designated and registered. Period of exclusive use may, on application, be renewed indefinitely but only for ten years at one time. Applicants for registration must reside or have resident representatives in R.O.C. In case of dispute, first applicant in R.O.C. and not first user is entitled to registration. However, if first user can prove that his mark has attained well-known status worldwide prior to filing of mark in conflict, he may consider filing opposition or invalidation action against mark of first applicant based on clause of "plagiarizing another person's mark". If two or more such applications are filed on same date and there is no way of ascertaining who applied first, applicants shall come to agreement to let one of them enjoy exclusive use. If no agreement can be reached, it shall be determined by lot drawing.

Same person who designates use of same trademark device for similar goods or use of similar trademark devices for same goods or similar goods shall apply for registratin of associated trademark. Same person who designates use of same trademark for goods which are not same or similar but are of related nature may apply for registration of defensive trademark. However, famous trademark may apply for registration of defensive trademark designating goods of all kinds regardless of restriction of "goods of related nature". In addition to trademarks and service marks, collective marks distinguishing organizations and certification marks certifying quality or other characteristics of goods or services are also registrable. Assignment of right of exclusive use of trademark shall be recorded with Government Office in charge of trademark matters. Unrecorded assignment may not be set up as defense against third parties. Right of exclusive use of any associated trademark and defensive trademark which have not been assigned together with their principal trademark shall be extinguished. Where right of exclusive use of associated trademark or defensive trademark is separately assigned, such assignment shall be invalid. Trademark licensing shall be recorded with Trademark Authority and sublicensing requires recordaton as well. Unrecorded licensing may not be set up as defense against third parties.

Exclusive right of use of trademark may be cancelled at any time upon application by its owner. If any of following cases occurs after registration of trademark, Government Office in charge of trademark matters shall, on its own initiative or upon application by interested party, cancel registration: (1) where trademark with unauthorized alteration in its device or additional notes has been used whereby trademark is made similar to registered trademark of another person used on same or similar goods; (2) where without good cause, trademark has not been put into use for three years after registration, or has been continuously suspended from use for three years, except that associated trademark has been put in use for same goods or licensed user has used trademark and proof of such use has been produced; (3) where licensing of trademark to another person has not been recorded, or requirement for indicating trademark licensing is violated, and such violation is not corrected within time limit set in notice given to violator; or (4) where trademark has been adjudged by final judgment to have infringed upon copyright, new design patent or other rights of another person.

Penalty is provided in Trademark Law against malicious use of representations of written language in another person's registered trademark. Any person who maliciously uses word in another person's registered trademark as specific portion of name of his own company or firm for conducting business in respect of same goods or similar goods and has failed to stop such use after being requested by interested party to do so shall be punished with imprisonment for not more than one year, detention or fine of not more than NT$50,000. Above provisions shall not apply to cases where date of application for registration of name of company or firm precedes date of application for trademark registration. Infringers shall be punished with imprisonment for not more than three years, detention and, in addition thereto or in lieu thereof, fine of not more than NT$200,000 according to Art. 62. In addition to criminal liability, infringers are liable to pay for damages. Under Art. 66, trademark owner may claim against infringer any of following damages: (1) based on provisions of Art. 216 of Civil Code. However, in event that evidence cannot be presented to prove his damages, owner of right of exclusive use of trademark may take difference, as amount of damages, which is derived from subtracting profit gained after such infringement by use of registered trademark in question from profit that would have normally been gained from use of registered trademark; (2) based on profit gained by infringer of right of exclusive use of trademark as result of his infringing act, provided, however, that where infringer is unable to produce evidence to prove his costs and necessary expenses, total income derived from sale of counterfeit commodities shall be taken as his profit; (3) based on amount equal to 500 to 1,500 times unit retail price of seized commodities involved in infringement of right of exclusive use of trademark, provided, however, that if quantity of commodities under seizure exceeds 1,500 pieces, amount of compensation for damages shall be assessed based on total selling price thereof.

Arts. 62 and 63 of Trademark Law and Arts. 253, 254 and 255 of Criminal Code provide for punishments by fine and/or imprisonment for: counterfeiting or imitating registered trademark or tradename with intent to defraud; exporting, importing, selling or displaying for sale any goods known to bear counterfeit or imitative trademark or tradename; using false marking or other expression concerning quality or country of origin of goods; or knowingly exporting, importing, selling or displaying for sale any goods bearing false marks as to quality or country of origin. Under Art. 64 of Trademark Law, goods which are manufactured, sold, displayed, exported or imported in violation of any of provisions specified in Arts. 62 and 63 of Trademark Law are subject to confiscation, regardless of whether they belong to offender or not. The Fair Trade Law also protects trademarks, service marks, tradenames, corporate names, business symbols, product containers or packaging, product configuration that are commonly known to relevant public in Taiwan, as well as unregistered famous foreign trademarks. Any violator shall be punishable by imprisonment for not more than three years, detention, or in lieu thereof or in addition thereto fine of not more than NT$1,000,000. Injunctive and treble damages remedies are also available to aggrieved party, in addition to monetary damages.

Treaty of Friendship, Commerce and Navigation between U.S. and R.O.C. provides for reciprocal trademark privileges. According to FCN Treaty, nationals, corporations

See Topical Index in front part of this volume.

TRADEMARKS . . . *continued*
and associations of either country shall be accorded within territory of other country effective protection in exclusive use of trademarks and tradenames upon compliance with applicable laws and regulations, if any, respecting registration and other formalities which are or may hereafter be enforced by duly constituted authorities. Nevertheless, foreign juristic persons or entities, not limited to those recognized by government of R.O.C., may also file criminal complaint, initiate private prosecution or institute civil suit for trademark infringement under Art. 66-1 of Trademark Law.

National Bureau of Standards is authority in charge of trademark matters. All approved trademark applications and other trademark matters are published in Trademark Gazette of National Bureau of Standards.

TREATIES:

Generally speaking, thesis of primacy of treaties is recognized in Chinese legal system. Constitution clearly specifies that treaty must be respected. (The Constitution 141). Treaty is valid and enforceable in domestic court if it is ratified by R.O.C. In case of conflict between treaty and domestic law, treaty shall prevail where treaty is ratified after, or on same date of, promulgation of domestic law, and domestic enactment will not automatically overrule previous conflicting treaty but issue shall be presented for resolution on ad hoc basis. (See Decree of Judicial Yuan dated July 27, 1931, No. 459; Appeal case No. 1074, Sup. Ct. 1934.) Several cases indicate that court takes treaty prevalent to domestic laws. R.O.C. has ratified numerous treaties and international agreements. See also Selected International Conventions section.

USURY: See topic Interest.

WILLS:

Any person of over 16 years old may freely dispose of his or her property by will subject to provisions of Civil Code as long as he does not contravene provisions in regard to compulsory portions. Wills may be holographic, notarial, secret, dictated or oral. Will takes effect upon death of testator. Validity of will of alien shall be governed by national law of testator at time of its making.

THAILAND LAW DIGEST REVISER

Tilleke & Gibbins
Tilleke & Gibbins Building
64/1 Soi Tonson, Ploenchit Road
Bangkok 10330, Thailand
Telephone: 254 2640 58
Fax: 254 4304; 621 0172 73
Email: 4630672@mcimail.com
Library: beckyr@mozart.inet.co.th
Vietnam Offices: 51 Trieu Viet Vuong, Hai Ba Trung District, Hanoi. Telephone: 84 4 227-895/6; 268-860. Fax: 84 4 227-897. 2nd Floor, The Vietnam National Gold-Silver and Gemstones Corporation Building, 3-5 Ho Tung Mau, District 1, Ho Chi Minh. Telephone: 84 8 251-645; 251-695; 251-700. Fax: 84 8 242-226.
Cambodia Office: No. 56 Street Samdech Sothearos, Khan Duan Penh. Phnom Penh. Telephone: 855 23 62670. Fax: 855 23 62671. Email: Tilleke-Gibbins@uni.fi

Reviser Profile

History: Tilleke & Gibbins, the oldest and largest independent law firm in Thailand, was established in 1893 by William Alfred Tilleke, a Ceylonese, as a sole practitioner's office. In 1902, he was joined by an Englishman, Ralph Gibbins, to form Tilleke & Gibbins. Later partners, R. D. Atkinson, S. Brighouse and Victor Jacques, all British, carried on the firm from 1909 through 1941, retaining the original name. During World War II, Danish and Thai staff maintained the traditions of the firm, until the return in 1946 of Victor Jaques as the only remaining active partner. In 1951, Albert Lyman, an American lawyer, acquired the firm. Subsequently, he was joined by his wife, Freda Ring Lyman, also an American lawyer. The firm became a registered ordinary partnership in 1973 and is presently headed by Rojvit Periera, a Thai, and David Lyman, an American. Recognizing the expanding opportunities in Vietnam, Tilleke & Gibbins in 1989 established Tilleke & Gibbins Consultants Limited to provide investment and legal consulting services for businesses engaged in commercial activities in Vietnam. In 1992, Tilleke & Gibbins became the first foreign law firm to receive a license to establish a representative office in Vietnam. The office, situated in Ho Chi Minh City, was followed by the establishment in 1994 of a branch office in Hanoi. With the growing prominence of the Mekong subregion of Southeast Asia, the Firm expanded further by entering into a law firm partnership, Tilleke & Gibbins and Associates Ltd., in Phnom Penh, Cambodia, in January 1995.

Growing with the times, the firm has expanded in both number of staff and areas of service. From about six staff members in the early 1950s, the firm and its affiliates now boast a legal staff of almost 50 attorneys and a support staff of 168 people. To accommodate its need for more space, the firm constructed its own building which became its permanent home in 1987. Since then, another floor has been added to the existing three floors for further growth in its business.

Members of the Firm: The firm's lawyers are graduates of prestigious Thai universities, many of them holding graduate degrees in law from western institutions. Their education is supplemented by practical training in legal firms abroad to obtain international experience. They are active members of the Thai Bar Association, Law Society of Thailand, Lawyers Association of Thailand and many other local and international professional associations. In addition to Thai and English, many of our lawyers are fluent in other languages, including Japanese, Vietnamese, French, German and Spanish.

Services: Tilleke & Gibbins is a full service law firm comprised of different practice groups designed to provide specialist advice with optimum efficiency in the following areas of law: Banking and Finance, Corporate Services, Taxation, Intellectual Property, Commercial and International Trade, Dispute Resolution and Litigation, Property, Environment and Development, Transportation and Insurance, and Private Client Services. Two other groups, Japanese Client Development Group and Indochina Group, provide advice and assistance to Japanese clients and parties interested in the Indochina countries. Since its inception, Tilleke & Gibbins has been distinguished by its commitment to furnishing legal services of the highest quality. Its membership in worldwide associations of independent law firms such as Lex Mundi, and Multilaw enhances the firm's ability to serve the needs of clients.

Clients: The firm has an impressive roster of clients from over 75 countries, which include national government agencies; banks and other financial institutions; P&I clubs, shipping, freight-forwarding and courier companies; airlines, hotels and travel-related companies; construction and engineering companies; electrical, electronics, communications, computer manufacturers; software developers; pharmaceutical and chemical companies; cosmetics firms; garment manufacturers, fashion houses and retailers; food and beverage companies; jewelry, farm equipment, business equipment and other types of manufacturers, marketers and distributors; petroleum drilling and service companies; commercial and trading houses; advertising and other service firms; news bureaus; etc.

Significant Distinctions: William Alfred Tilleke was bestowed a peerage and given the title of Maha Ammart Tho Phraya Attakarn Prasiddhi by H.M. the King and was also Attorney General of Siam. Ralph Gibbins was a judge on the International Court (Appeals) in Bangkok. Victor Jaques, a highly decorated officer in World War I, was British Military Governor of Bangkok after World War II. Albert Lyman was a founder of the American Association of Thailand, now the American Chamber of Commerce, as well as a founder and Chairman of the Bangkok Stock Exchange, now the Stock Exchange of Thailand. Freda Ring Lyman, who received the Most Noble Order of the Crown of Thailand 5th Class in 1961, was the first foreign woman to be decorated by H.M. King Bhumibol Adulyadej. Rojvit Periera, one of Thailand's foremost trial lawyers, was Rotary Club's first District Governor for all of Thailand in 1982. David Lyman was a founding member of the Thai Prime Minister's

Foreign Investment Advisory Council and the Thailand Business Council for Sustainable Development; served as Director of the Thai Board of Trade, Director and Vice Chairman of the Asia Pacific Council of American Chambers of Commerce, Governor and President of the American Chamber of Commerce for many years; founder executive board member of Lex Mundi and Program Fellow of the World Economic Forum. Dr. Charoen Kanthawongse, elected Member of Parliament for many years, was Deputy Secretary General to the Prime Minister from 1980-1983; Deputy Minister of Agriculture from 1988-1990; Minister of Science, Technology and Energy in 1990; Deputy Ministry of Education, Feb.-June 1995. Suntorn Chantarasak was a career judge and retired as Senior Justice of the Supreme Court from 1986-1989. Junjiro Nishino, the senior Japanese in Thailand, was President of the Japanese Association of Thailand, Director of the Japanese Chamber of Commerce; in 1987, he received the decoration of Commander-Sacred Treasure of Japan from the Emperor of Japan.

The firm's Museum of Counterfeits has been featured on CNN, the BBC-TV, Australian and Danish television, and in various print media, and is used for education of police and government officials. Because of the firm's successes in anti-counterfeiting activities, it was invited to join the Counterforce Network of the Counterfeiting Intelligence Bureau of the International Chamber of Commerce. The Textile Collection of Tai and other mainland Southeast Asian native textiles is the largest private collection in Thailand open for viewing by the public. The firm also copublishes the leading investors' manual in Thailand, *Thailand Business Basics.*

THAILAND LAW DIGEST

(The following is a list of all Topics, including cross-references, covered in this Digest.)

THAILAND LAW DIGEST

Revised for 1997 Edition by

Tilleke & Gibbins, Thailand, Vietnam and Cambodia.

(Abbreviations used are: "A.A.", Arbitration Act, B.E. 2530 (A.D. 1987); "A.A.M.", Act for Adoption of Minor, B.E. 2522 (A.D. 1979); "A.B.L.", Alien Business Law (National Executive Council's Announcement No. 103, B.E. 2527 [A.D. 1994]; "A.O.L.", Act on Conflict of Laws, B.E. 2481 (A.D. 1938); "B.A.", Bankruptcy Act, B.E. 2483 (A.D. 1940); "B.E.", Buddhist Era; "C.A.", Copyright Act, B.E. 2521 (A.D. 1978); "C.C.C.", Civil and Commercial Code, B.E. 2535 (A.D. 1992) for Book I, B.E. 2468 (A.D. 1925) for Book II, B.E. 2472 (A.D. 1929) for Book III, B.E. 2475 (A.D. 1932) for Book IV, B.E. 2519 (A.D. 1976) and B.E. 2533 (A.D. 1990) for Book V, and B.E. 2477 (A.D. 1935) for Book VI; "C.H.S.", Committee on Hazardous Substances; "C.P.C.", Civil Procedure Code, B.E. 2477 (A.D. 1934); "C.R.A.", Commercial Registration Act, B.E. 2499 (A.D. 1956); "E.C.N.E.Q.A.", Enhancement and Conservation of National Environmental Quality Act; "E.I.A." Environmental Impact Assessments; "F.S.C.", Interest on Loan of Financial Institutions Act, B.E. 2523 (A.D. 1980); "H.S.A." Hazardous Substances Act B.E. 2535 (A.D. 1992); "L.A.", Practicing Lawyers Act, B.E. 2528 (A.D. 1985); "L.C.", Land Code, B.E. 2497 (A.D. 1954); "M.O.S.T.E.", Ministry of Science, Technology and Environment; "M.O.I.", Ministry of Industry; "M.V.S.P.R.A.", Mortgage of Vessels and Sea Preferential Rights Act, B.E. 2537 (A.D. 1994); "N.E.B.", National Environmental Board; "N.T.W.A.", Navigation in Thai Territorial Waters Act, B.E. 2456 (A.D. 1913); "P.C.A.", Pollution Control Area; "P.C.D.", Pollution Control Department; "P.L.C.A.", Public Limited Companies Act, B.E. 2522 (A.D. 1979); "S.E.C.", Securities and Exchange Commission.)

ABSENTEES:

Person who leaves his domicile may appoint agent with general authority to act for him. If person does not appoint agent and it is uncertain whether he is living or dead, any interested person or public prosecutor may apply to court for order for necessary management of his property. After one year has passed from day when person left his domicile or residence, if no news of him has been received, or from day when he was last seen or heard of, court may appoint manager for property. (C.C.C. 48). If person has left his domicile and it is not known whether he is living or dead for five years, court, upon application of any interested person or public prosecutor, may adjudge that person has disappeared; however, this period of time shall be reduced to two years from day person disappeared during battle or war; or when vehicle on which he had been traveling was lost or destroyed; or when he had been in other peril of his life. (C.C.C. 61). If person adjudged to have disappeared is living, he by himself, any interested person, or public prosecutor may apply to court to revoke order of disappearance. Nevertheless, all acts which had been done in good faith may not be affected by such revocation. (C.C.C. 63). See topic Principal and Agent.

Adjudication of disappearance and its revocation shall be published in Government Gazette. (C.C.C. 64).

ACTIONS:

Commencement of Actions.—Civil action by person whose rights under civil law are in dispute may be commenced by filing plaint (complaint) with Court of First Instance having territorial jurisdiction. (C.P.C. 55, 170). Plaint must clearly set forth plaintiff's claims, allegations on which claims are based and relief requested. (C.P.C. 172). Two or more persons may join in action as joint plaintiffs and may be joined as joint defendants where there are common interests in subject matter of suit. (C.P.C. 54). At time of filing plaint, plaintiff must deposit court fees in amount determined by nature of action and amount of relief requested. (C.P.C. Sched I). Lawyer representing plaintiff must file power of attorney signed by plaintiff authorizing representation. (C.P.C. 61). Court may examine any pleading for form, substance, compliance with law and payment of court fees and may accept pleading, reject pleading and order party to cure defects within time and on terms ordered. Failure to comply with order will cause pleading to be rejected. (C.P.C. 18). Upon acceptance, court issues summons to answer plaint. (C.P.C. 173).

Service of Process.—Within seven days from acceptance of plaint, plaintiff must request appropriate officer to serve summons to answer and copy of plaint on defendant. (C.P.C. 173). Service may be made on defendant at his domicile or place of business, in court or by defendant's acceptance of service. (C.P.C. 77). When service cannot be made, court may issue order for substituted service, by posting, advertisement or otherwise and service is effective 15 days after completion of such substituted service. (C.P.C. 79). In actions against non-domiciliary, service is made by sending process to defendant's foreign office or domicile. (C.P.C. 83 bis). Absent international treaty to which Thailand is party otherwise providing, plaintiff must provide translation of summons and plaint and other documents to be served into official language of country in which service is to be made or into English together with certification of accuracy of translation and deposit for expenses to be fixed by court. (C.P.C. 83 quarter). Absent international agreement otherwise providing (Thailand is not party to Hague Convention on the Service Abroad of Judicial and Extrajudicial Documents in Civil or Commercial Matters 1965), court will arrange service through Ministry of Justice and Ministry of Foreign Affairs. (C.P.C. 83 septum). Service will be effective 60 days after date of such service. (C.P.C. 83 octo). Where non-domiciliary conducts business in Thailand, directly or by agent, or by written agreement has designated agent for service in Thailand, service may be sent to defendant, his business or designated agent at location of business of defendant or agent's residence. (C.P.C. 83 bis). Service on non-domiciliary is effective 30 days after date of such service. (C.P.C. 83 sex).

Answer and Additional Pleadings.—Within 15 days from date of service, defendant must file written answer admitting or denying whole or part of plaintiff's allegations, reasons for denial and may, in answer, make counterclaim. (C.P.C. 177). If counterclaim relates to matters not connected to plaint, court will order defendant to file separate case. (C.P.C. 177). Within 15 days from date of service of answer, plaintiff must file answer to counterclaim. (C.P.C. 178). If date for settlement of issues has been set, parties may move to amend pleadings not less than seven days before date for settlement of issues, or seven days before commencement of trial if no date for settlement of issues has been set. (C.P.C. 180). No new claims or counterclaims may be added by amendment unless they are sufficiently related to original claims to justify joinder for trial. (C.P.C. 179). All pleadings and motions which raise issues are subject to court's examination, return for modification, acceptance or rejection in same manner as plaint. (C.P.C. 18).

Joinder of Additional Parties.—Third person not already party to pending action, by way of interpleading, may make application to court to become party where he has legal interest in result of case, or when necessary to protect his rights. Third person may, also by way of interpleading, be joined on application of existing party when existing party could sue or be sued by third party as result of outcome of pending action, or on order of court when joinder of third party is required by law or necessary in interest of justice. (C.P.C. 57).

Default Procedures.—When defendant fails to file answer, plaintiff may apply for default order. (C.P.C. 197). Should plaintiff fail to move for default within 15 days after date answer was due, court may order case stricken. (C.P.C. 198). Should defendant at or before commencement of trial, provide justification for failure to answer, court may permit answer to be filed. (C.P.C. 199). When court finds failure unjustified, court may order case to proceed without filing of answer. (C.P.C. 199). Should defendant fail to appear for trial, court will declare default and order case to be tried ex parte. (C.P.C. 202). Case will not be disposed of on mere ground of default and court will take such evidence and raise such points of law as court deems necessary to reach decision on merits. (C.P.C. 205). Such default procedures are equally applicable to plaintiff to whom counterclaim has been directed who fails to answer or appear for trial. (C.P.C. 197, 205).

Pretrial Dispositive Motions.—Dispositive pretrial motions, such as motions to dismiss, for judgment on pleadings and summary judgment are not available. However, when question of law is presented which would dispense with necessity for further trial of case or material issue therein, court in its discretion may determine such question and dispose of case or any issue therein by order or judgment. (C.P.C. 24).

Discovery.—Pretrial discovery procedures such as interrogatories, broad requests for document production and discovery depositions are generally not recognised. Any party may, however, not less than seven days before date for taking evidence, send to another party notice of facts on which he or she intends to rely and may request other party to admit such facts. (C.P.C. 100). If opposing party or third person possesses original of document which will be given as evidence at trial, court may order that original be filed with court. (C.P.C. 123). If evidence may be unavailable or difficult to produce at trial, court may, on application, take such evidence itself, or may appoint one of its judges or commission another court to do so on its behalf. (C.P.C. 101, 102). No evidence shall be taken without all parties having full opportunity to attend proceedings and exercise their rights. (C.P.C. 103). Where opposing party or third person is not domiciled in Thailand and has not yet been joined, court may order ex parte examination of witnesses. (C.P.C. 101). Commission of foreign court to take evidence on Thai court's behalf may be made by letters rogatory forwarded through Thai Ministry of Justice and Ministry of Foreign Affairs to relevant authorities in foreign court's country.

Prejudgment Remedies.—At any time before judgment, if court is of opinion that defendant intends to transfer property or remove property from court's jurisdiction to defraud plaintiff or obstruct execution of court order; intends to repeat wrongful act or breach of contract complained of; is likely to waste or damage property; will register or alter registration of property to plaintiff's detriment; is avoiding service of court orders and writs; or likely to remove himself from jurisdiction or conceal or destroy property; or for other good reason, court may, on plaintiff's ex parte application, order provisional seizure or attachment of property; temporary injunction; temporary withholding, amendment or revocation of property registration; or arrest and detention of plaintiff. (C.P.C. 254, 255). Court must be satisfied that suit is reasonably well grounded and there are sufficient grounds for granting protection order applied for. (C.P.C. 255). Provisional orders may be made on terms court deems appropriate, including requirement that plaintiff provide security for damages caused defendant by plaintiff's fault or negligence in securing provisional measure. (C.P.C. 257, 263). At any time after service of provisional order and before judgment, defendant may move to vacate or modify order. (C.P.C. 261, 262). In emergency cases, plaintiff may move for immediate order, subject to defendant's right to move for revocation. (C.P.C. 266, 267). Where there is reason to believe that if plaintiff is unsuccessful he or she will evade payment of court fees and expenses, or if plaintiff is not domiciled in Thailand, defendant may apply for court order requiring plaintiff to deposit security or provide guarantee for fees and expenses in amount and on terms court deems appropriate. (C.P.C. 253).

Settlement of Issues.—After plaint, answer and answer to counterclaim have been filed, court shall, except in prescribed circumstances, conduct settlement of issues (pretrial conference). (C.P.C. 182). Issues in dispute may be fixed according to parties' joint motion, but court will reject motion and conduct settlement of issues if it is of opinion that motion is incorrect. (C.P.C. 182). On date of settlement of issues, parties must appear and court, after examining pleadings, motions and responses to questions posed by court, will conclude issues of fact or law that are admitted, fix issues of fact or law in dispute and determine who bears burden of proof. (C.P.C. 183). Court also fixes date for taking evidence, which must be at least ten days after date for settlement of issues. (C.P.C. 184). Not less than seven days before date for taking evidence, parties must file with court list of witnesses, disclosing therein evidence on which they

See Topical Index in front part of this volume.

ACTIONS . . . *continued*
intend to rely at trial, and if intending to rely on court appointed expert or court inspection of evidence, must file application for appointment or inspection. (C.P.C. 88). If intending to rely on documentary evidence, party must, not less than seven days before date for taking evidence, file that document with court and send copies to other parties. (C.P.C. 90). Unless court permits otherwise, objections to admissibility of documents must be raised before documents are taken into evidence. (C.P.C. 125). If objection is made, party intending to rely on document must, if he or she possesses original, produce original on day for taking evidence. (C.P.C. 122).

Trial.—Jury trial is not available. All issues of law and fact are determined by one or more judges. Trials are conducted in open court in presence of attending parties. (C.P.C. 36). Burden of proof of fact falls on party alleging such fact in pleading. (C.P.C. 84). Witnesses are examined by direct, cross, and redirect examination (C.P.C. 117) and may be examined by court (C.P.C. 119). Relevant original documents may be admitted as evidence. (C.P.C. 87, 93). All proceedings are conducted in Thai language, and documents, if in foreign language, must be translated to Thai language. (C.P.C. 46). Translators provided by parties are permitted. (C.P.C. 46). After close of evidence, written or oral final arguments and rebuttal are presented. (C.P.C. 186). Judgments are rendered in writing, reciting particulars of case, decision of court and grounds therefor. (C.P.C. 141).

Proof of Foreign Laws.—Where foreign law is at issue, such law may be established by evidence thereof and party may offer proof by testimony of expert witness. (C.C.C. 98).

Foreign Judgments and Arbitration Awards.—Thailand is not party to any treaties or conventions on enforcement of foreign judgments and foreign judgments are not enforceable. Authenticated copies of foreign judgments may be received in evidence at trial. Thailand is party to New York Convention on the Recognition and Enforcement of Foreign Arbitral Awards (1958) and Geneva Convention for the Execution of Foreign Arbitral Awards (1927). Final foreign arbitration award rendered in proceeding wholly or mainly in foreign country, reciting all matters required by applicable convention, may be recognized and enforced if not contrary to public policy or morality. Court may refuse enforcement on proof of defenses such as: annulment, invalidity or lack of finality of award; lack of adequate notice during arbitration proceedings; award beyond scope of, or not disposing of issues submitted under arbitration agreement; or arbitration proceeding conducted other than in accordance with agreement of parties or law of country in which arbitration took place. (Arbitration Act, B.E. 2530 [A.D. 1987], 28-35).

Assessment for Costs and Fees.—Liability for costs of parties including lawyers' fees, witnesses' fees, costs of service of documents and other costs and fees provided for by law are borne by party losing case. Court may, however, in its discretion, order costs to be paid by prevailing party, to be apportioned between parties or to be borne by party incurring same. (C.P.C. 161). Amount of assessable court and lawyer fees is specified by law. (C.P.C. Sched II-VI).

ADMINISTRATION:

See topic Executors and Administrators.

ADOPTIONS:

Governed by C.C.C. and Act for Adoption of Minor, B.E. 2522 (A.D. 1979).

Conditions.—Person not less than 25 years of age may adopt another who is at least 15 years younger than him. (C.C.C. 1598/19). If minor is to be adopted, consent of his parents or, in case one of his parents died or has been deprived of parental power, of his living father or mother who has parental power is required. If there is no such person to give consent or such person cannot express consent or unreasonably refuses to give his consent, or has adversely affected health, progress and welfare of minor, court may, upon application of minor's legal representative, person intending to be adoptor, or public prosecutor, allow adoption. (C.C.C. 1598/21). Consent for adoption of minor having been deserted and having been taken care of by institution for child welfare under law on child welfare and protection must be obtained only from said institution, provided court may, upon application of public prosecutor based on such institution's unreasonable refusal to give consent, allow adoption. (C.C.C. 1598/22). In case person to be adopted is 15 years of age or over, his consent is also required. (C.C.C. 1598/20). Married person may adopt or be adopted provided consent of other spouse is obtained, but consent is not required if spouse cannot express consent or has been missing for no less than one year in which case, application for court's permission must be made. (C.C.C. 1598/25). Concurrent adoption by person other than spouse of adoptor of minor who is adopted child of adoptor is prohibited. (C.C.C. 1598/26). Unless permission of Minister of Ministry of Interior is obtained, it is offence to take or send minor out of Thailand for purpose of adoption abroad. (A.A.M. 18).

Proceedings.—Adoption is valid only upon registration with competent government official. (C.C.C. 1598/27). If minor is to be adopted, person to adopt must comply with all rules and procedures provided in Act. (A.A.M. 5). Official may give order denying registration of adoption of any minor on ground that person to adopt is not qualified. Person to adopt may, within 30 days from date of receiving order, file application by motion with Court of First Instance for court's order overruling order of official. Applicant may also request Court to allow child to stay under his care pending court proceedings. Order of Court of First Instance, whether or not in favor of person to adopt, is final and non-appealable. (A.A.M. 26, 28).

Effect of Adoption.—Adopted is deemed legitimate child of adoptor but his legal rights and duties toward his natural parents are not affected by adoption. After adoption, natural parents lose parental power, if any. (C.C.C. 1598/28). Being legitimate child, adopted has legal right of inheritance from adoptor. (C.C.C. 1627). However, adoptor has no legal right of inheritance from adopted. (C.C.C. 1598/29).

Dissolution.—Adoption may be dissolved upon mutual agreement of parties, if adopted is 20 years of age or over. (C.C.C. 1598/31). If adopted is minor, adoption may be dissolved: (a) by consent of adopted's natural parents, or (b) in case adoption was allowed by court, by court's permission upon application of interested person or public prosecutor. (C.C.C. 1598/31). Adoption is dissolved upon marriage between adoptor and adopted. (C.C.C. 1451, 1598/32). Under requirements provided by law, court may also dissolve adoption in action for dissolution of adoption brought by either adoptor or adopted. (C.C.C. 1598/33). Adopted who is under 15 years of age may not bring action for dissolution of adoption without consent of person whose consent is required for adoption. (C.C.C. 1598/35). After dissolution of adoption, all rights and duties between adopted and natural parents revive. (C.C.C. 1598/37).

AFFIDAVITS:

There are no provisions on affidavits under Thai law. However, in practice, affidavits are used in various legal procedures without specific forms.

ALIENS:

Major laws in this area are Nationality Act, B.E. 2508 (A.D. 1965), Alien Registration Act, B.E. 2493 (A.D. 1950), Alien Business Law (N.E.C. Announcement No. 281), B.E. 2515 (A.D. 1972), Alien Employment Act, B.E. 2521 (A.D. 1978) and Royal Decree Naming Occupations and Provisions Prohibited to Aliens, B.E. 2522 (A.D. 1979).

Alien is person not of Thai nationality. (N.A. 4; for definition of "alien" under A.B.L. see subhead Corporations Owned by Aliens, infra). Alien cannot hold any office and may not exercise any municipal, parliamentary or other franchises.

Actions by Aliens.—See topic Actions.

Actions Against Aliens.—See topic Actions.

Civil Rights.—Unless specifically restricted or denied by law, aliens enjoy same civil rights as Thai nationals. In general, certain restrictions in business and employment are imposed on aliens, that is, aliens are not allowed to engage in certain businesses (Alien Business Law [N.E.C. 281], B.E. 2515 [A.D. 1972]) or to perform certain occupations (Alien Employment Act, B.E. 2521 [A.D. 1978]).

Aliens are prohibited from owning land in Thailand. Condominium Act (No. 2), B.E. 2534 (A.D. 1991), however, entitles certain categories of foreigners to acquire condominium units in Thailand, provided that foreign ownership in condominium project does not exceed, in aggregate, 40% of total area of all condominium units in condominium building. Exemption to alien ownership rule applies to Board of Investment and Industrial Estate Authority of Thailand projects, wherein special privileges are granted to alien companies to buy land. In addition, alien oil companies which meet requirements of Petroleum Act may also own land.

Naturalization is governed by Nationality Act, B.E. 2508 (A.D. 1965). Alien may apply for naturalization provided he has reached age of majority both under Thai law and law of country of which he is national, is of good behavior, has sound occupation, has been domiciled in Thailand for consecutive period of not less than five years at date of submission of application, and has sufficient knowledge of Thai language as prescribed by ministerial regulations. (N.A. 10). Above requirements shall not apply to applicant who: (a) has rendered distinguished service to Thailand or performed acts beneficial to government as deemed appropriate by Minister of Interior; (b) is child or wife of person who has been naturalized as Thai or of person who has resumed Thai nationality; or (c) was former Thai national. Granting or rejecting application for naturalization is at discretion of Minister of Interior.

Corporations Owned or Controlled by Aliens.—Corporations 50% or more owned by aliens are regarded as aliens under A.B.L. As defined by A.B.L., "alien" is natural or juristic person not of Thai nationality and: (a) juristic person with half or more than half of capital belonging to aliens; (b) juristic person with half or more than half of number of its shareholders, partners or members being aliens, regardless of amount of capital invested by aliens; and (c) limited partnership or registered ordinary partnership where managing partner or manager is alien. A.B.L. prohibits or restricts operation of any specifically enumerated businesses by aliens. See also topics Companies, subhead Foreign Companies; Foreign Investment; Licenses.

ARBITRATION AND AWARD:

Arbitration and award are governed by Arbitration Act, B.E. 2530 (A.D. 1987).

Arbitration Agreement.—Parties may agree to submit existing or future civil dispute to arbitration. (A.A. 5). In order to be binding upon parties, such agreement must be evidenced by written document or mentioned in written correspondence between parties. (A.A. 6). Parties are free to agree upon arbitrators and procedures and in absence of agreed procedure, arbitral tribunal may conduct arbitration proceeding in any manner it thinks fit for justice purposes. (A.A. 17). Dispute which parties agree to submit to arbitration may not be litigated. (A.A. 10).

Enforcement of Domestic Arbitral Awards.—Arbitration award with which either party refuses to comply may be enforced only after court's judgment upholding such award is pronounced. Petition for enforcement of award must be filed with court within one year of date of delivery of copy of award to parties in dispute. (A.A. 23). Court may refuse enforcement of award only when it deems that award is unlawful under governing law, beyond purview of arbitration agreement or has arisen out of unlawful action or practice. (A.A. 24).

Enforcement of Foreign Arbitral Awards.—Arbitration is considered to be foreign if it takes place in whole or in part outside Thailand and either party in dispute is not Thai national. (A.A. 28). Foreign arbitral awards rendered in member countries of New York Convention on Recognition and Enforcement of Foreign Arbitral Awards, 1958 and of Geneva Protocol, 1923 are recognized and enforced in Thailand which is member of both conventions. (A.A. 29). Party wishing to enforce such award must file petition with court within one year of date of delivery of copy of award to parties in dispute. (A.A. 30). Court may not consider merits of case and may refuse enforcement of such award only on limited grounds as provided by Act. (A.A. 33, 34). Thus, arbitral awards are generally enforced wherever foreign judgments are not (see topic Actions, subhead Foreign Judgments and Arbitration Awards, topic Judgments, subhead Foreign Judgments).

See Topical Index in front part of this volume.

ASSIGNMENTS:

Transfer of Claims.—Claims are transferable unless otherwise agreed by parties or nature of claims does not permit it. Agreement between parties that claim is nontransferable cannot be set up against third person acting in good faith. (C.C.C. 303). Rights of mortgage or pledge existing on transferred claim and rights arising from suretyship established for such claim also pass to transferee as consequence of transfer of claim. (C.C.C. 305). Transfer of claim is effected by agreement between transferor and transferee. Transfer of obligation performance of which runs to specific creditor must be made in writing. Such transfer may not be asserted against debtor or third persons unless written notice thereof has been given to debtor or written consent has been obtained from debtor. (C.C.C. 306). Except where he has given consent without reservation, debtor may set up against transferee any defenses he had against transferor prior to receipt of transfer notice. (C.C.C. 308). Transfer of obligation performance of which runs to order or designated creditor with additional instruction that performance shall also be made to holder of instrument is not effective against debtor and third persons unless instrument is delivered to transferee with transfer endorsed thereon. (C.C.C. 309). If transferee acts in good faith in such transfer, debtor may set up against him only those defences as appear on face of instrument or result naturally from its character. (C.C.C. 312).

Assignment of Property.—Assignment of property right, whether real or personal property, may be made by means of valid declaration of intention on part of assignor. However, in order for assignment to be effective against third persons, assignment of immovables must be recorded, and those of movables must be accompanied by delivery. If referred to real property or other rights requiring recording in Registry of Property assignment must be made in public document.

Assignment of movable property is made by agreement between parties to that effect. Gift of movable property is generally valid only upon delivery of property given. (C.C.C. 523). Gift of property sale of which must be made in writing and registered with competent official, i.e. immovable property, ships or vessels (C.C.C. 456), is valid only when so made and registered, regardless of whether delivery of property given has been made (C.C.C. 525).

Title to personal property and rights may be transferred either by public or private instrument.

ASSOCIATIONS:

Association is created for conducting any activity which according to its nature is to be done continuously and collectively by persons other than that of sharing profits or incomes earned. (C.C.C. 78). Association must be registered and upon registration becomes juristic person. (C.C.C. 83). Directors of association carry on activities of association under supervision of general meetings. (C.C.C. 86). General meeting shall be called by directors of association at least once a year. (C.C.C. 93).

Dissolution of Association.—Association is dissolved: (a) In cases provided for in its regulations; (b) by expiration of time fixed for its duration; (c) upon achievement of its purposes; (d) by resolution of general meeting; (e) by its bankruptcy adjudication; (f) by name struck off; and (g) by court order. (C.C.C. 101). After liquidation, remaining assets shall be transferred to other association or foundation or any juristic person whose object is for charity purposes as designated in regulations, or be vested in State. (C.C.C. 107).

ATTACHMENT:

Seizure or attachment before judgment of whole or part of defendant's property including money or property due to defendant by third person is provided for by C.P.C. as one of provisional protective measures before judgment in any action other than petty cases. Property so seized or attached must be delivered to and retained by executing officer or other official as ordered by court. (C.P.C. 254).

Grounds and Procedure.—Plaintiff may apply ex parte for provisional seizure or attachment at time of filing of complaint or at any time before judgment. (C.P.C. 254). Court may only grant application upon proof to its satisfaction that: (a) complaint and application, at time of filing, are reasonably grounded; and (b) defendant, in order to delay or obstruct execution of any decree which may be made against him or in order to defraud plaintiff, intends to transfer, sell or dispose of whole or part of his property, or to remove it from jurisdiction of court or there are, in court's opinion, other just and reasonable grounds for seizure or attachment. (C.P.C. 255).

Indemnity and Security.—Plaintiff is liable for damages which defendant may sustain from unjustified seizure or attachment based on plaintiff's fault or carelessness. (C.P.C. 263). Court may, before issuing writ of seizure or attachment, require plain tiff to deposit with court such sum of money as court thinks fit as security for indemnity. (C.P.C. 257).

Withdrawal of Writ of Seizure or Attachment.—On application by defendant or another who suffers damage because of seizure or attachment, court may withdraw writ of seizure or attachment if it is of opinion that there is insufficient grounds for issuance of writ, or for other reasonable cause. Court may make such other order it sees fit in interests of justice. (C.P.C. 261). When facts or circumstances on which provisional seizure or attachment was ordered change, court may, on its own motion or on application as described above, amend or withdraw writ of seizure or attachment. (C.P.C. 262). Writ of seizure or attachment is automatically cancelled seven days after judgment is entered in favour of defendant, subject to plaintiff moving court to continue provisional measures pending appeal. (C.P.C. 260).

ATTORNEYS AND COUNSELORS:

The profession is limited in Thailand to Thai nationals. However, those foreign attorneys who have obtained lifetime work permits before first Alien Employment Act was passed in 1972 are allowed to give legal advice, i.e. act as legal consultants.

Authority to regulate admission to practice law in Thailand and to discipline and supervise practicing lawyers is vested in Law Society of Thailand under Lawyers Act, B.E. 2528 (A.D. 1985). Lawyers may practice law in Thailand only upon registering and obtaining license to practice law from Law Society of Thailand, (L.A. 6, 33, 34). There is only one class of practicing lawyers in Thailand, that is, attorney-at-law; distinctions between solicitors, advocates, pledgers, etc., do not exist. In order to register and obtain license to practice law, applicant must be Thai national of at least 20 years of age who meets all other requirements more important ones of which are: (a) being graduate with Bachelor of Law Degree or Associate Degree in Law or Certificate in Law equivalent to Bachelor's Degree or Associate Degree from one of institutions recognized by Law Society; (b) being member of Thai Bar Association; and (c) having successfully completed practical training program of Law Society. (L.A. 35, 38). Practical training program of Law Society is arranged by Institute of Law Practice Training at least once a year. Program is divided into two parts, i.e. (1) theoretical training of at least 90 hours, and (2) practical training in law firms of at least six months. After completion of both parts, lawyer is entitled to register and receive license to practice. Requirement for completion of training program is waived for applicant who was attorney-at-law, judge, public prosecutor, judge in court-martial, military prosecutor or attorney under laws concerning organization of courts-martial or who has at least one year apprenticeship in law office. (L.A. 38). Once lawyers are registered and licensed to practice law, they enjoy right to practice law throughout country and are automatically accepted as members of Law Society. (L.A. 37).

Law school graduates of institutions recognized by Thai Bar Association are not required to pass bar examination in order to be irregular member of Thai Bar Association. Bar examination is given yearly by Institute of Legal Education of Thai Bar Association for law school graduates who enroll in its one-year professional course. Lawyers passing bar examination receive title of barrister-at-law and are eligible for regular membership in Thai Bar Association and for sitting in competitive examination to become public prosecutor or judge trainees. Being barrister-at-law, although not requirement for practicing lawyers, is considered to be prestigious since only approximately 10% of about 5,000 candidates pass bar examination each year.

BILLS AND NOTES:

Bills are governed by C.C.C.

Classification of Bills.—Within meaning of C.C.C., bills are of three kinds: (1) bills of exchange; (2) promissory notes; and (3) checks. (C.C.C. 898).

Bill of exchange must contain: (a) statement that it is bill of exchange; (b) unconditional order to pay certain sum of money; (c) name or trade name of drawee; (d) maturity date; (e) place of payment; (f) name or trade name of payee who may be drawer or bearer; (g) date and place of issuance; and (h) signature of drawer. (C.C.C. 909, 912). If any of above particulars is missing, instrument is invalid as bill of exchange except that: (i) it will be deemed to be bill of exchange payable at sight, if no maturity date is specified; (ii) if no place of payment is designated, domicile of drawee will be considered place of payment; (iii) domicile of drawer is deemed to be place at which bill of exchange was issued, if not shown; and (iv) if date of issuance is not provided, any lawful holder acting in good faith may fill in true date. (C.C.C. 910). Bill of exchange may be drawn on either drawer himself or on account of third person. (C.C.C. 912).

Promissory note must contain: (a) statement that it is promissory note; (b) unconditional promise to pay certain sum of money; (c) maturity date; (d) place of payment; (e) name or trade name of payee; (f) date and place of issuance; and (g) signature of maker. (C.C.C. 983). Similar to bill or exchange, instrument lacking any of these particulars is invalid as promissory note save in exceptional cases similar to those of bill of exchange. (C.C.C. 984). Rights and obligations of maker of promissory note are same as those of acceptor of bill of exchange. (C.C.C. 986).

Check must contain: (a) statement that it is check; (b) unconditional order to pay certain sum of money; (c) name or trade name and address of banker; (d) name or trade name of payee or mention that it is payable to bearer; (e) place of payment; (f) date and place of issuance; and (g) signature of drawer. (C.C.C. 988). Lack of any of these particulars renders instrument invalid as check, except in instances similar to those of bill of exchange. (C.C.C. 910).

Several provisions of C.C.C. governing bills of exchange, except, among others, those dealing with acceptance, are applicable to promissory notes and checks in so far as they are not inconsistent with nature of these instruments. (C.C.C. 985, 989).

Endorsements.—Transfer of bill with words "not negotiable" or any equivalent expression appearing on its face may be effected only in accordance with provisions of C.C.C. governing transfer of claims. (C.C.C. 917, 985, 989; see also topic Assignments). Bills of exchange and checks which are payable to bearer may be transferred by mere delivery. (C.C.C. 918, 989). Any other bill may be transferred by endorsement and delivery. (C.C.C. 917, 985, 989). Endorsements must be unconditional and partial endorsement is void. (C.C.C. 922. 985. 989). Endorsement may specify beneficiary or be in blank; however, it must be signed by endorser. (C.C.C. 919, 985, 989). Holder may fill up endorsement in blank either with his name or third person's name or endorse bill again either in blank or to third person or transfer bill to third person without endorsing it or filling up blank. Endorsement transfers all rights arising out of bill. (C.C.C. 920, 985, 989). Endorsements of bill of exchange and check which are payable to bearer operate only as guarantees (avals) for drawers. (C.C.C. 921, 989).

Acceptance is not applicable to promissory notes and checks. (C.C.C. 985, 989). Unless presentment for acceptance is prohibited by drawer (such prohibition not being allowed in case of bill of exchange drawn payable at particular place other than drawee's domicile or at certain time after sight) holder or possessor may, at any time before maturity, present bill of exchange to drawee at his residence for acceptance. (C.C.C. 927). Holder of bill of exchange payable at end of fixed period after sight, presentment for acceptance of which cannot be prohibited by drawer, must present it for acceptance within six months from its date of issuance or within such time as specified by drawer. (C.C.C. 927, 928); or if payable at particular place other than drawee's domicile, at such place specified by drawer. Mere signature of drawee on face of bill of exchange constitutes acceptance. (C.C.C. 931). By acceptance of bill of exchange, drawee becomes bound to pay amount accepted according to tenor of his acceptance. (C.C.C. 937).

Aval is guarantee given by third person or any party to bill for whole or part of payment of bill. (C.C.C. 938, 985, 989). Aval is given by having such words as "good as aval" or any equivalent expression written on bill itself or on allonge and signature of giver of aval affixed to bill. Except in case of signature of drawee or drawer, mere

See Topical Index in front part of this volume.

BILLS AND NOTES . . . *continued*
signature of giver of aval on front of bill constitutes aval. (C.C.C. 939, 985, 989). If party for whom aval is given is not specified, aval is deemed to be given for drawer. Giver of aval is bound in same manner as person whom he guarantees and will, upon his payment of bill, have rights of recourse against said person and all persons responsible for said person. (C.C.C. 940).

Payment.—Holder of bill of exchange or promissory note must present it for payment on its maturity date. (C.C.C. 941, 985). Holder of bill of exchange or promissory note cannot be compelled to receive payment thereof before maturity. Drawee or maker who pays before maturity does so at his own risk and peril. (C.C.C. 942, 985). Maturity date of bill of exchange and promissory note may be on demand or at sight; at end of fixed period after sight; on fixed day; or at end of fixed period after date of bill. (C.C.C. 913, 985). Bills of exchange and promissory notes which are payable on demand or at sight; at end of fixed period after sight; will be payable upon presentment and their holders must present them for payment within six months from their dates of issuance, or within such time as otherwise specified by drawer or maker. (C.C.C. 928, 944, 985). Maturity of bill of exchange payable at end of fixed period after sight is determined by date of acceptance or date of protest, as case may be. (C.C.C. 943). Promissory note payable at end of fixed period after sight must be presented for visa of maker within six months from its date of issuance, or within such time as specified by maker. (C.C.C. 986, 928). Its maturity is determined by date of visa, signed by maker of promissory note, or date of protest, which is required as evidence, for maker's refusal to give his visa. (C.C.C. 986). Check is payable on demand or to order of payee. (C.C.C. 987). In order to preserve right of recourse against endorsers and certain rights against drawer (to extent of any injury caused to drawer by failure of presentment), holder of check must present it for payment to banker within one month after date of issuance, if payable in same town of issuance, or within three months, if payable elsewhere. (C.C.C. 990). If check is presented for payment later than six months after date of issuance, or money to credit of account of customer is insufficient to meet payment under check, or notice is given that check has been lost or stolen, banker is not bound to pay it. (C.C.C. 991). Payment of crossed check must be made only to banker. (C.C.C. 994).

Protest.—Nonacceptance or nonpayment of bill of exchange must be evidenced by formal document called protest made by district officer or his deputy or attorney having license for that purpose. (C.C.C. 960, 961). There is no requirement for protest for nonacceptance of promissory note or check since acceptance is not applicable to promissory notes or checks. For promissory notes and checks, protest of nonpayment is only required in cases of nonpayment of foreign promissory notes and nonpayment of foreign check. (C.C.C. 960, 985, 989). Protest may be waived if drawer or maker (in case of foreign promissory note) or endorser stipulates in bill "without protest", "protest not necessary" or any other equivalent expression. (C.C.C. 964, 985, 989). Protest must be made within three days following expiration of time fixed for presentment for acceptance in case of protest for nonacceptance of bill of exchange or within three days following maturity date in case of protest for nonpayment of bill of exchange or foreign promissory note or foreign check. (C.C.C. 960, 985, 989). Officer or attorney making protest shall deliver protest to person at whose request it is made, and shall also forthwith give notice thereof to person against whom it is made. (C.C.C. 962, 985, 989).

Notice of Nonacceptance or Nonpayment.—Holder of bill of exchange or foreign promissory note or foreign check, as case may be, must give notice of nonacceptance or nonpayment to his immediate endorser and drawer or maker, as case may be, within four days following day of protest, or day of presentment if protest is waived. Every endorser must within two days from receipt thereof give notice of receipt to his immediate endorser and so on through series until drawer is reached. Notice of nonpayment is also required in cases of foreign promissory note and foreign check. If any person fails to give notice within prescribed period, he is liable for any injury caused by his negligence, compensation of which is limited to amount of bill, but he does not lose his rights of recourse. (C.C.C. 963, 985, 989).

Rights of Recourse.—Holder of bill is entitled to rights of recourse against endorsers, drawers and other persons liable under bill if payment has not been made at maturity. Even before maturity, holder is also entitled to rights of recourse against such persons if: (a) drawee, drawer of check, maker of promissory note or drawer of bill of exchange which needs not be accepted has become bankrupt; (b) drawee has suspended payment, even if suspension is not authenticated by judgment, or (c) execution has been levied against drawee's property without result. (C.C.C. 959, 985, 989). Holder of bill of exchange also has same rights of recourse before maturity when acceptance has been refused. (C.C.C. 959). Holder loses his rights of recourse against endorsers, drawer and other persons liable under bill but not against acceptor if: (a) he fails to present bill of exchange payable at sight or at end of fixed period after sight within prescribed period; (b) he fails to present bill of exchange for acceptance within prescribed period, in which case he loses both his rights of recourse for nonpayment and for nonacceptance unless it appears from terms of stipulation that drawer meant only to release himself from guarantee of acceptance; (c) he fails to have protest for nonacceptance of bill of exchange or protest for nonpayment of bill of exchange, foreign promissory note or foreign check made within prescribed period; and (d) he fails to present bill of exchange, protest of which has been waived, for payment within prescribed period. (C.C.C. 973, 985, 989). Holder who fails to present check for payment within prescribed period loses his right of recourse against endorsers and his right against drawer to extent of any injury caused to drawer by his failure of such presentment. (C.C.C. 990).

CHATTEL MORTGAGES:

Under Thai law, mortgages may be constituted on certain movable property. Provisions of C.C.C. governing general mortgages apply to chattel mortgages.

Mortgages may only be taken on following movable property: (a) Ships or vessels of six tons and over; steam launches or motorboats of five tons and over; (b) floating houses; (c) beasts of burden; and (d) any other movables with regard to which law may provide registration for that purpose. (C.C.C. 703).

However, mortgage of vessel 60 tons gross or more, powered by machine or machines, for use on sea by virtue of Thai Navigation Act is controlled under new Mortgage of Vessels and Sea Preferential Rights Act, B.E. 2537 (A.D. 1994) (M.V.S.P.R.A.). Provisions in C.C.C. shall be applied to mortgage of vessels under M.V.S.P.R.A. to extent that they are not in conflict with provisions in M.V.S.P.R.A. Coverage of vessels shall extend to equipment on board vessel and other things which are prescribed by law as being mandatory on board vessel, regardless of whether said items were present at time of registration of mortgage or acquired afterwards. (M.V.S.P.R.A. 9).

According to Registration of Machinery Act B.E. 2514 (A.D. 1971), owner of machine must first register with Ministry of Industry to establish ownership. After any machinery is registered, it shall be regarded as movable and can be mortgaged according to §703(4) of C.C.C. Mortgagor must produce for registrar mortgagee's letter of consent to remove registered mortgaged machinery removed in course of normal operation. Right of mortgage in removed machinery shall be regarded as continuing to exist.

Aircraft may not be mortgaged. Although Thailand is signatory to Geneva Convention on the International Recognition of Rights in Aircraft, it has not yet adopted system of registering aircraft mortgages; nor does Thailand have any domestic legislation dealing specifically with creation of security interest in aircrafts.

COMMERCIAL REGISTER:

Compulsory Registration.—According to Commercial Registration Act, B.E. 2499 (A.D. 1956), commercial registration with Ministry of Commerce of natural persons, branch offices of foreign companies, unregistered partnerships and sole proprietorships engaged in certain businesses specified in Act is compulsory. (C.R.A. 5, 6, 11). Companies, registered partnerships and other juristic persons duly organized and registered with Registrar of Partnerships and Companies of Ministry of Commerce under C.C.C. after Nov. 14, 1972 are exempted from commercial registration requirement. (C.R.A. 7, Announcement of Ministry of Commerce dated Nov. 14, 1972). If commercial registration is required, it must be applied for at Commercial Registration Division where business is located within 30 days of commencing business. (C.R.A. 10, 11).

Disclosures.—Commercial registration records information of registered business concerning capital, nature of business, trade name, name of owner (in case of individual), corporate name (in case of company), partnership name (in case of partnership), shareholders and their shareholdings (in case of company), partners and their contributions (in case of partnership), locations of principal office, branch offices, warehouses and agents, date of commencing business in Thailand and trade name of transferor of business, if applicable. (C.R.A. 12). Upon registration, commercial registration certificate which must be prominently displayed in business's premises will be issued by Commercial Registrar. (C.R.A. 14).

Penalties.—Any person failing to carry out commercial registration within specified period or wilfully submitting false information is guilty of offence and liable to fine not exceeding Baht 2,000 and, in case of failure to carry out commercial registration, further fine not exceeding Baht 100 per day for continued default. (C.R.A. 19). Any person failing to prominently display commercial registration certificate in business' premise is guilty of offence and liable to fine not exceeding Baht 200 and further fine not exceeding Baht 20 per day for continued failure. (C.R.A. 20).

COMPANIES:

Under Thai law, there are two types of company: (a) Private limited company; and (b) public limited company. C.C.C. provides for private limited company; public limited company is governed by Public Limited Companies Act, B.E. 2535 (A.D. 1992).

Private Limited Companies.—Private limited company is juristic person, that is, legal entity distinct from its shareholders. (C.C.C. 70). As juristic person, it can sue or be sued or hold title to properties, and so forth, in its name. (C.C.C. 66, 67). See also topic Juristic Persons.) Capital of private limited company is divided into equal shares of designated nominal amount (par value) not less than Baht 5. (C.C.C. 1096, 1117). Company may not issue shares for price below their par value. If authorized by memorandum, shares, may be issued at price higher than their par value. (C.C.C. 1105). Shares may be common or preferred. Nature and extent of preferential rights accruing to preferred shares must be fixed by statutory meeting. (C.C.C. 1108). All shareholders have preemptive right concerning all subsequent shares issued. (C.C.C. 1222).

Shares may be issued in registered form or to bearer. (C.C.C. 1127). There is no minimum registered capital requirement, but registered capital should reasonably reflect nature of company's business. Upon formation of company, capital shares must be totally subscribed or alloted and at least 25% of registered capital must be paid. (C.C.C. 1104, 1105). Private limited company is prohibited from holding its own shares or taking them in pledge. (C.C.C. 1143). Private limited company that is not authorized by Securities and Exchange Commission (S.E.C.) may neither issue debentures nor offer its shares to public. (C.C.C. 1102, 1229).

Private limited company must have minimum of seven promoters who must each subscribe at least one share. (C.C.C. 1097, 1100). It is required to have at least seven shareholders, including juristic persons (if any), provided that there be no similar limitation on total number of shareholders in private limited company organized before Dec. 26, 1978. (C.C.C. 1096, 1237 and Civil and Commercial Code Amendment Act, B.E. 2521 [A.D. 1978], 12).

Liability of shareholders is limited to any unpaid amount on shares held. (C.C.C. 1096). Accordingly, if shareholder has fully paid for his shares, he is not subject to further liability; if he has not fully paid up, his maximum liability is amount outstanding on those shares.

Shares are freely transferable. Restraints may, however, be placed on transfer of registered shares if restriction is done pursuant to company's regulations. (C.C.C. 1129). Shares issued to bearer are transferred by mere delivery of certificate. (C.C.C. 1135). Transfer of registered shares is void unless made in writing with numbers of shares stated and signatures of transferor and transferee and at least one witness

COMPANIES . . . *continued*
affixed therein. Such transfer is invalid as against company and third persons until fact of transfer and name and address of transferee are entered in register of shareholders. (C.C.C. 1129).

Private limited company is managed by one or more directors, whether or not shareholders of company, elected by general meeting of shareholders. (C.C.C. 1144, 1151). Directors may be reelected and are subject to removal by general meeting at any time. (C.C.C. 1151, 1153).

Ordinary meeting which is statutory general meeting of shareholders must be held at least once a year. (C.C.C. 1171). Board of directors may call other general meetings of shareholders which are known as extraordinary meetings whenever they think fit or upon written request of shareholders holding at least one-fifth of shares of company. (C.C.C. 1172, 1173). Unless otherwise provided in by-laws, quorum for general meeting is one-fourth of capital. (C.C.C. 1177, 1178). In case quorum is not present, general meeting, if called upon shareholders' request, must be dissolved, if not, another general meeting at which no quorum is required must be called within 14 days. (C.C.C. 1179). All shareholders may vote, either in person or by proxy, unless they have special interest in resolutions. (C.C.C. 1176, 1184, 1187). Save in exceptional cases prescribed by law or unless otherwise provided in by-laws, majority vote is required in order to pass resolution in general meeting.

Dividend may, upon resolution passed in general meeting, be distributed from company's profits. No dividend may, however, be distributed until prior losses are covered. Interim dividends may be distributed out of company's profits by decision of board of directors. (C.C.C. 1201). At each distribution of dividend, company must appropriate at least 5% of profits to reserve fund until such fund amounts to 10% of registered capital or such higher proportion thereof as stipulated in by-laws. (C.C.C. 1202).

Private limited company is dissolved: (a) In cases provided for in by-laws; (b) by expiration of time fixed for its duration; (c) upon achievement of purposes; (d) by special resolution of general meeting; and (e) by bankruptcy adjudication. (C.C.C. 1236). Private limited company may also be dissolved by court on grounds prescribed by law. (C.C.C. 1237). After dissolution, company is liquidated but it is deemed to continue for such period necessary for liquidation. (C.C.C. 1249).

C.C.C. provides for consolidation of private limited companies which is called "amalgamation", that is, when two or more private limited companies integrate new one. Amalgamation requires special resolutions of general meetings from all companies involved. (C.C.C. 1238). If creditor objects to amalgamation, company may not proceed with its plan unless it has satisfied creditor's claim or given security for it. (C.C.C. 1240). By amalgamation, new company whose share capital is equivalent to total share capital of amalgamated companies is formed. (C.C.C. 1242). New company acquires all rights and duties of amalgamated companies. (C.C.C. 1243).

Public Company Limited.—Public company limited is designed for wide public shareholding. It is company established for purpose of offering shares for sale to public and liability of shareholders is limited to amount paid on shares. (P.L.C.A. 15). Fifteen or more natural persons as promoters, not less than half of whom must be residing in Thailand and whose subscription is at least 5% of shares in capital, are required. (P.L.C.A. 16, 17). Offering of shares for sale to public shall require prior permission from Securities and Exchange Commission under Securities and Exchange Commission Act. Once registrar accepts registration, public company limited shall become juristic person. (P.L.C.A. 41). Shares of company shall be equal in value and shall have par value of not less than Baht 5. (P.L.C.A. 50). Share is indivisible; all shares must be fully paid up. (P.L.C.A. 53, 54). Shares may be common or preferred. Preferred share cannot be converted into ordinary share unless otherwise stipulated in Articles of Association. (P.L.C.A. 65). Company cannot own its shares or take them in pledge. (P.L.C.A. 66). Transfer of shares is effected by delivery of certificate endorsed by signatures of transferor and transferee with name of transferee stated therein. Such transfer binds company upon receipt of request for registration thereof and after registration has been effected, binds all third persons. (P.L.C.A. 58).

Public company limited is managed by board of directors consisting of no less than five directors, half of whom must be residents of Thailand. (P.L.C.A. 67). Directors shall be natural persons but may or may not be shareholders. (P.L.C.A. 68, 69). Directors are elected annually by general meeting of shareholders. Directors may be reelected. (P.L.C.A. 71).

Annual ordinary general meeting will be called by board of directors within four months of last day of fiscal year of company. (P.L.C.A. 98). Extraordinary general meeting will be called by board of directors whenever they think fit or upon request of shareholders holding at least one-fifth of shares sold or shareholders numbering not less than 25 persons holding shares not less than one-tenth of total number of shares sold. (P.L.C.A. 99, 100). Unless otherwise prescribed by this Act, quorum for general meeting requires presence of at least 25 persons or not less than one-half of total number of shareholders holding shares amounting to not less than one-third of total number of shares sold. (P.L.C.A. 103). Resolution of general meeting requires majority vote of shareholders who attend meeting in ordinary event, and not less than three-quarters of total number of votes of shareholders who attend meeting in event of sale of business, purchase of business, making or terminating contracts of lease of business or amalgamation of business. (P.L.C.A. 107).

Dividend, upon resolution passed in general meeting, may be distributed from company profits. Interim dividend may be distributed out of company profits by decision of board of directors. (P.L.C.A. 115). Company must appropriate at least 5% of its annual net profits after deduction of prior losses, if any, to reserve fund until such fund amounts to at least 10% of registered capital or such higher proportion thereof as stipulated by its Articles of Association or by other laws. (P.L.C.A. 116).

Balance sheet and statement of profit and loss account of company need to be prepared once a year and submitted after examination by auditor to annual general meeting for approval. (P.L.C.A. 112).

Public company limited is dissolved: (a) by resolution of general meeting; (b) by bankruptcy; or (c) by court order. (P.L.C.A. 154). After dissolution, company is liquidated but it is deemed to continue for such period necessary for liquidation. (P.L.C.A. 158).

Foreign Companies.—Foreign company that wishes to do business in Thailand may set up branch office from which to operate. In order to establish branch office, foreign company must appoint branch manager and submit certain documents to Ministry of Commerce such as its certificate of incorporation, by-laws, articles of incorporation, power of attorney appointing branch manager, and so forth.

Under Thai law, branch office is not distinct legal entity separate from its parent company. Therefore, branch office is itself treated as foreign company, and parent company can be held liable for losses and liabilities of its branch in Thailand. No Thai law specifically governs rights and powers of foreign company. Generally, foreign company enjoys same rights and powers as Thai company unless any specific legislation provides otherwise; for example, under Land Code, foreign company cannot own land in Thailand.

Foreign company and its branch office may not engage in prohibited or restricted businesses enumerated in A.B.L. However, A.B.L. does not apply to foreign companies which engage in business with Thai government's permission or whose activities are covered by agreements between their home countries and Thailand which exclude application of A.B.L. Treaty of Amity and Economic Relations between Thailand and U.S. is only agreement of this type. Treaty guarantees that American nationals and companies that establish or acquire interest in commercial, industrial, financial and other business enterprises in Thailand will receive all rights and privileges afforded to Thai nationals. Treaty does not cover businesses in fields of communications, transport, fiduciary functions, banking involving depositary functions, exploitation of land or other natural resources, or domestic trade in indigenous agricultural products. In these fields, American investors receive most favored nation treatment.

Besides A.B.L., there are also several other less important statutes that prohibit operation of specific businesses by foreign companies and impose conditions regarding majority ownership and management by Thai nationals in companies engaging in those businesses such as Commercial Banking Act B.E. 2505 (A.D. 1962), Finance, Securities and Credit Foncier Businesses Act B.E. 2522 (A.D. 1979) and Thai Vessel Act B.E. 2481 (A.D. 1938).

Representative Office.—Regulations of the Office of the Prime Minister Governing Application for Establishment of Representative Office of Foreign Juristic Person Respecting International Trading Business, B.E. 2529 (A.D. 1986) defines representative office ("rep office") as office in Thailand of foreign company engaged in business of international trading. This definition excludes regional offices and other business-related trading activities. Rep office in Thailand cannot engage in any profit-seeking or profit-making enterprise. Rep offices are considered operation of services under Annex C, c. 3(1) of A.B.L.

In Thailand, representative or liaison offices of overseas companies can: (a) find suppliers of goods or services in Thailand for head office (H.O.) abroad; (b) check and control quality and quantity of goods purchased or hired by H.O. for manufacturing purposes in Thailand; (c) provide advice on various aspects of goods sold by H.O. to agents, distributors and/or customers in Thailand; (d) provide information to interested persons in Thailand concerning goods or services of H.O.; and (e) report to H.O. on movements of business in Thailand.

Activities of rep offices are restricted; it cannot earn income as business enterprise in Thailand. Scope must be limited to those mentioned above, or significant Thai tax liabilities can arise, i.e. income of parent or affiliated companies may be deemed earned in Thailand and subject to taxation.

If rep office engages in other non-permitted activities, such as buying or selling goods on behalf of H.O., it will be regarded as doing business in Thailand and may be subject to Thai taxation on all income received from Thailand. Also, rep office may not act on behalf of third persons. Any such business or income-earning activities could amount to violation of conditions of license to establish and operate rep office which could result in revocation of license.

Rep office undertaking in Thailand any activities specified previously without rendering any other services and refrains from prohibited activities is not subject to Thai taxation. Such rep office is deemed to receive subsidy from H.O. to meet its expenses in Thailand. Gross receipts or revenues, which rep office operating in Thailand receives from H.O., are not characterized as revenue included in computation of juristic person income tax or VAT. All rep offices are required to obtain Corporate Tax Identification number and to submit juristic person income tax returns to Revenue Department, even though not taxed in Thailand.

Rep office must obtain Alien Business Permit under Annex C, c. 3(1) of A.B.L. prior to starting its activities. Alien Business Permit serves as permission/license to establish rep office. Application for permit to establish rep office, together with supporting documents, must be filed with Department of Commercial Registration, Ministry of Comerce.

To work in rep office, alien must apply for work permit with proper authority upon obtaining rep office permission/license. Up to five aliens may be granted permission to work in rep office, depending on necessity, nature and volume of work involved.

Over five-year initial life of permit, at least Baht 5 million must be remitted to Thailand for operational expenses of rep office, with Baht 2 million in first operational year, and at least Baht 1 million in each of three following operational years. To qualify, remittances can be made only after permit is granted.

Regional Office.—Regulations of the Office of the Prime Minister Governing Application for Establishment of Regional Office of Transnational Corporation, B.E. 2535 (A.D. 1992) controls regional offices of multinational companies in Thailand.

Regional offices do not have to be registered as partnerships or companies in accordance with C.C.C. Regional offices are permitted to: contact, coordinate work of and supervise operations of branches or affiliated companies located in same region on behalf of H.O.; and provide advisory services and management services; personnel training and development; financial management; marketing supervision and sales promotion planning; and product development and research and development services, provided no income is earned.

Regional offices have no authority to accept purchase orders, make sales offers or conduct business negotiations with other persons or juristic entities. Operational expenses of regional office must be remitted into Thailand from H.O.

Regional office must obtain Alien Business Permit under Annex C, c. 3(1) of A.B.L. Permits are valid for period of five years under following conditions: (a) Total amount

COMPANIES . . . *continued*
of loans used in operation of permitted business must not exceed seven times capital owned by shareholders or proprietors of business. (b) During five-year period, at least Baht 5 million must be remitted into Thailand for operational expenses of regional office. At least Baht 2 million should be remitted in first operational year. In any event, however, not less than Baht 1 million must be brought in within first six months and not less than Baht 1 million in each subsequent year until required amount is fully paid in. (c) At least one of persons responsible for operation of permitted business must be domiciled in Thailand.

Applications to establish regional office, as well as related work permits, must be filed with Department of Commercial Registration, Ministry of Commerce. Work permits for aliens employed by regional office may be granted to extent necessary, but may not exceed five persons. Regional offices need not submit balance sheets to Department of Commercial Registration.

CONSTITUTION AND GOVERNMENT:

Constitution.—Thailand is democratic, constitutional monarchy. Written Constitution of Thailand B.E. 2534 (A.D. 1991), with four amendments in B.E. 2535 (A.D. 1992) and one in B.E. 2538 (A.D. 1995), provides that King is head of State and has no political responsibility. King exercises sovereignty which is derived from Thai people through National Assembly, Council of Ministers (or government) and Courts in accordance with provisions of Constitution. Equality before law and other basic rights such as freedom of speech, association, religion and domicile are guaranteed by Constitution.

Legislative power is vested in National Assembly composed of Senate and House of Representatives. Senators are appointed by King upon government's recommendation and hold office for four year term. Representatives are elected in general, popular elections every four years. Senators and Representatives may be reappointed or re-elected as case may be. Proposed bill becomes Act after adoption of both House of Representatives and Senate, receipt of King's royal assent and being promulgated in Government Gazette. House of Representatives may pass motion of no-confidence against government and may be, on other hand, dissolved by King upon government's advice.

Executive power is vested in Council of Ministers composed of Prime Minister and other Ministers appointed by King. Prime Minister must be member of House of Representatives but Ministers need not be members. Prime Minister is appointed by King upon recommendation of President of House of Representatives. Ministers may be recalled by King upon advice of Prime Minister.

Judicial power for adjudication of cases is vested in courts. Judiciary is independent from control of executive. Judges are appointed and removed by King upon recommendation of judicial commission. Constitutional Tribunal, not Courts, is empowered to interpret Constitution. See also topic Courts.

Government administrative structure is divided into three parts by virtue of Government Administration Act B.E. 2534 (1991).

Central government consists of offices of Prime Minister and 14 ministries. Central government includes all departments, divisions and sections within each individual ministry. Prime Minister's Office is also officially considered ministry, explaining why reference to 15 ministries is often made.

Provincial government is set up in each of 75 provinces outside of Bangkok. Bangkok Metropolis is governed under special act, namely Bangkok Metropolitan Administration Act, B.E. 2528 (A.D. 1985), am'd B.E. 2534 (A.D. 1991). There is provincial governor and one or two deputy governors that have authority over personnel and provincial issues which are within domain of Ministry of Interior. Provincial governors do not have direct authority outside of Interior Ministry or in any other ministry. Within province, there are districts (amphur), townships (tambol) and villages (muban).

Local governments in any form are created and operated from Ministry of Interior. Some local government units include provincial administrative organizations, municipalities, sanitation districts and tambol administrative bodies. These local level groups are comprised of elected individuals and operate on government grants and loans from central government. New Tambol Assembly and Tambol Administrative Organization Act B.E. 2537 (A.D. 1994) decentralizes more power and duty to local authority in relation to public affairs and taxation in that tambol (township).

CONTRACTS:

Formation of contract, effect of contract, rescission of contract and all other basic legal aspects of contract are governed by C.C.C. Conflict of laws rules are provided in Act on Conflict of Laws, B.E. 2481 (A.D. 1938). According to C.C.C., contract is one source of obligation. Other sources of obligation are management of affairs without mandate, unjust enrichment and tortious acts (wrongful acts). C.C.C. also provides for provisions relating to formation of and rights and obligations of parties to 23 specific contracts such as sale, carriage, loan, etc. By virtue of principle of freedom of contract underlying C.C.C., parties may create contract which is not provided for by C.C.C. Moreover, provisions of C.C.C. which are not deemed to be within law of public order or good morals are subject to contrary agreement of parties. (C.C.C. 150).

Formation.—Contract is created by acceptance of offer. Both offers and acceptances made to person in his presence take effect from time intention becomes known to receiver. (C.C.C. 168). Offers and acceptances made to person not in his presence take effect from time they reach other parties and are ineffective if revocation is received by such other parties previously or simultaneously. (C.C.C. 169). After offer or acceptance has been sent, death or incapacity of offeror or offeree does not impair validity of offer or acceptance as case may be except that offer in such case is invalid if offeror has declared contrary intention or if offeree knew of offeror's death or incapacity prior to acceptance. (C.C.C. 169, 360). Offer specifying period of acceptance cannot be revoked before termination of such period. (C.C.C. 354). Offer must be accepted within period of acceptance specified therein. (C.C.C. 357). Offer with no specified period of acceptance, if made to person present or by telephone, must be accepted immediately or, if made to person at distance, must be accepted within reasonable period of time during which time it cannot be revoked. (C.C.C. 355, 356). Acceptance of offer which arrives out of time constitutes new offer. Conditional acceptance constitutes both refusal and counter-offer. (C.C.C. 359). Any act which can be deemed declaration of intention to accept may give rise to contract between persons at distance at time of its occurrence if according to declared intention of offeror or ordinary usage no notice of acceptance is required. In other cases, contract between persons at distance comes into existence at time notice of acceptance reaches offeror. (C.C.C. 361).

Except for contracts which C.C.C. explicitly requires be made in writing and registered with competent official or be in compliance with other specified forms, such as sale of immovable property, mortgage, company formation, etc., contracts may be concluded orally. Contract which is not in form prescribed by law is void. (C.C.C. 152).

Contract may be void if its object is expressly prohibited by law, impossible or contrary to public order or good morals. (C.C.C. 150).

Void contract cannot be ratified. Nullity of void contract may be alleged at any time by any interested person. (C.C.C. 172).

Both juristic and natural persons having legal capacity may be parties to contract. Contract entered into by incapacitated person is voidable but only incapacitated person himself after he has recovered his capacity, his legal representative, guardian, curator or heir may have contract nullified on incapacity grounds. (C.C.C. 175). Such person may also ratify voidable contract but ratification is invalid unless it is made after ground of voidability has ceased to exist. (C.C.C. 179). Voidable contract which has been ratified is deemed to have been valid from beginning but rights of third persons are not affected thereby. (C.C.C. 177).

Concept of "consideration" requirement does not exist under C.C.C.

Excuses for Nonperformance.—If specified property under bilateral contract for creation or transfer of real right therein is lost or damaged by cause not attributable to debtor, loss or damage falls on creditor. (C.C.C. 370). If bilateral contract is subject to condition precedent and property forming its subject is lost or damaged by cause not attributable to creditor while condition is pending, creditor has option, when condition is fulfilled, either to demand performance with reduction of his counter-performance or to rescind contract provided he is also entitled to compensation if cause of loss or damage is attributable to debtor. (C.C.C. 371). In other cases, impossibility of performance of obligation by cause not attributable to either party such as force majeure is excuse for nonperformance for both parties. If performance becomes impossible by cause attributable to creditor, debtor is entitled to counter-performance. (C.C.C. 372). According to C.C.C., force majeure is event which its happening or pernicious results could not be prevented with appropriate care. (C.C.C. 8).

Effect.—Except where obligation of other party is not yet due, party to reciprocal contract may refuse performance of his obligation unless other party performs or tenders performance of his obligation. (C.C.C. 369). Contracts in favor of third persons are permissible and such third persons may demand performance directly from debtors. (C.C.C. 374). After right of third person is created, it cannot be changed or extinguished by original parties to contract. (C.C.C. 375).

Rescission.—Right of rescission is provided by C.C.C. and may also be created by contract. Rescission is irrevocable and effected by declaration of intention to other party. (C.C.C. 386). Notice demanding performance is required before rescission unless object of contract according to its nature or declared intention of parties can be accomplished only by performance at stipulated time or within fixed period. (C.C.C. 387, 388). If performance is wholly or partly impossible because of fault of debtor, creditor may rescind contract. (C.C.C. 389). Rescission binds each party to restore other party to his condition prior to formation of contract. Rights of third persons are not impaired by rescission. Rescission does not preclude claims for damages. (C.C.C. 391).

Government Contracts.—Provisions of C.C.C. applicable to ordinary contracts also apply to government contracts. Nevertheless, special procedures concerning method of procurement set forth in Regulations of Office of Prime Minister on Procurement, B.E. 2535 (A.D. 1992), or certain relevant Cabinet Resolutions must be complied with. Generally, government contracts are awarded on basis of competitive bidding and performance bonds must be posted. Most government contracts must be finally approved by Department of Public Prosecution. State enterprises have their own rules of procurement which are similar to those applicable to government agencies.

Privatization.—Enormous responsibilities associated with Thailand's demand for infrastructure (in transport, electricity and other public utilities) cannot be borne by government alone. Act Governing Permission to Allow Private Bodies to Join or Operate State Businesses, B.E. 2535 (A.D. 1992) ("Concessions Act") requires all state units to get National Economic and Social Development Board's approval for concessions on government/private sector joint venture projects worth Baht 1 billion or more. If project is worth more than Baht 5 billion, proposing agency must commission feasibility studies and detailed project analyses conducted by independent consultants. Also, projects must be endorsed by committee comprised of other agencies concerned.

Applicable Law.—Unless otherwise provided by law, form of contract is governed by law of country where contract is made. (C.O.L. 9). Formation and effect of contract is governed by law of country expressly or implicitly chosen by parties. In event that chosen law cannot be ascertained, applicable law is law of their nationality if parties are of same nationality or, if not of same nationality, law of country where contract has been made. (C.O.L. 13). Capacity or incapacity of person is governed by law of his nationality except that capacity of person to enter into contract relating to immovable property is governed by law of country where immovable property is situated. Alien entering into contract not involving family law or law of succession in Thailand is deemed to have capacity for it insofar as he would be capable under Thai law notwithstanding fact that he would have no capacity or limited capacity under law of his nationality. (C.O.L. 10).

COPYRIGHT:

Copyright is regulated by Copyright Act, B.E. 2537 (A.D. 1994).

See Topical Index in front part of this volume.

COPYRIGHT . . . *continued*

Nature of Copyright.—Copyright subsists in every original work of literature, drama, art, music, audiovisual materials, sound recordings, cinematographic materials, sound and video broadcasting, computer programs, disseminated sound or picture or other works in fields of literature, science, and the arts. "Literary works" has been defined to include specifically computer programs by act itself. Copyright subsists in every original work if: (a) Author was at time of making work, in case of unpublished work, or when work was first published, in case of published work, Thai citizen or person resident, at all times or most of time, in Thailand, or national or resident of member country of Berne Convention or (b) work was first published within Thailand or member country of Berne Convention. (C.A. 4, 8).

No copyright protection extended to ideas, steps, processor systems, methods of use or operation, concepts, principles, discoveries or scientific or mathematical theories. (C.A. 6). Author of work is owner of copyright subsisting in work. Copyright owner processes exclusive right to take any action concerning work in which copyright subsists, including reproduction, adaptation, or dissemination to public. (C.A. 15). Copyright subsists automatically without any registration. However, copyrighted work and information concerning creation and publication of such work can be recorded with Department of Intellectual Property, Ministry of Commerce. When work is created in capacity of officer or employee under hire of service, officer or employee is entitled to copyright, unless otherwise agreed in writing. (C.A. 9). When work is created by contractor for commission, employer is entitled to copyright unless otherwise agreed by parties. (C.A. 10).

Performers' Rights.—Exclusive rights to sound and video broadcasting or dissemination to public of performances, except when performance used in broadcasting or dissemination to public was recorded; recordings of their unrecorded performance, reproduction of performances, recorded without their permission. (C.A. 44). Performer shall have right to receive compensation provided that performer is resident or citizen of Thailand or substantial portion of performance occurred in Thailand or in member country of international convention on protection of performer's rights of which Thailand is also member. (C.A. 48). Performer's rights are protected for term of 50 years from last day of calendar year of performance or recording of performance. (C.A. 49). Assignment of performer's rights must be in writing, can be made both wholly and in part and, other than inheritance, if there is no period of time specified in assignment contract, it shall be deemed that assignment is for period of three years. (C.A. 51).

Assignment/License.—Copyright is transferrable. (C.A. 17). Copyright owner may grant to another person license for reproduction, adaptation, dissemination to public of its copyrighted work or renting original or copy of computer program, audiovisual work, cinematographic work and sound recording with or without conditions. (C.A. 15[5]).

Term.—In general, copyright subsists for life of author and for additional period of 50 years after his death. If author is juristic person, copyright subsists for period of 50 years after work is first published or, if unpublished, after its creation. (C.A. 19).

Infringement.—Reproduction, adaptation, dissemination to public, rental of original or copy of work, publication of work by person who is not owner of copyright and without license of owner constitute infringement. (C.A. 15, 27, 28). Computer programs are infringed upon if reproduced, adapted, disseminated to public, or rented. (C.A. 30). Prescription period for action on copyright infringement is three years from date copyright owner became aware of infringement or not more than ten years from date of infringement. (C.A. 63).

Penalties.—In general, penalties for infringement are fines up to Baht 200,000. (C.A. 69). Commercial infringement results in higher penalty of fine up to Baht 800,000 or four years imprisonment, or both. (C.A. 69). One half of fine paid by offender for infringement according to court judgment is paid to copyright owner who is then also entitled to bring civil action against infringer for other damages. (C.A. 76).

Protection of Foreign Copyrights.—Thailand has adhered to Berne Convention for the Protection of Literary and Artistic Works since 1931. Copyrighted work of creator of member country of Berne Convention shall enjoy protection under Thai Copyright Act of 1994. (C.A. 61).

COURTS:

Judicial system is administered under Law for Organization of Courts of Justice, B.E. 2477 (A.D. 1934). Courts consist of following: (a) Courts of First Instance, which are trial courts having original and general jurisdiction of all civil, criminal, labor, tax and juvenile and family matters (see topic Actions); (b) Courts of Appeal, which determine questions of law, and under certain circumstances, questions of fact on appeals from Courts of First Instance (C.P.C. 224, 225, 230); and (c) Dika Court (Supreme Court), which determines questions of law and unless otherwise provided, questions of fact which were raised in Courts of First Instance and Courts of Appeal on appeal from Courts of Appeal and, if appeal is based only on questions of law, may determine such questions on direct appeal from Court of First Instance (C.P.C. 248, 249, 223 bis). House of Representatives has initiated procedures to establish two additional courts, Intellectual Property Court and Administrative Court. Former will be added to Court of First Instance, and will consider both international trade and intellectual property disputes such as trademarks, patents and copyrights. Latter will also be added as First Instance Court, and will settle disputes arising from unjust or illegal government administration.

CURRENCY:

Monetary unit is Baht which is divided into 100 stangs. Bank of Thailand has exclusive right to issue bank notes which are legal tender. Obligations governed by Thai law which are payable in foreign currency may be paid in Thai currency at exchange rate prevailing in place of payment at time of payment. (C.C.C. 196).

DEATH:

Notification of Death.—Under Private Person Registration Act, B.E. 2534 (A.D. 1991), if death takes place in house, owner of house must notify area registrar of death within 24 hours. If house where death occurred has no owner, person who discovers body must notify registrar wthin 24 hours.

If death takes place outside house, person in company of deceased or person who discovers deceased must notify area registrar or other authority within 24 hours from time of death or discovering deceased. Alternatively, administrative official or police can be notified.

Due to problems of transportation and communication, director of Central Registration Office may extend time period to give notification of death as appropriate, but such period shall not be more than seven days from date of death or date body was discovered. Late report is subject to fine. In cases where person dies under unusual circumstances, nearest police station and/or coroner should be notified. Autopsy is usually performed to determine cause of death.

Death of foreign national in Thailand should be reported immediately to consular section of deceased person's embassy and to police. Consular section should also be notified if and when remains of body are to be sent overseas. Consular officials will advise about undertakers, cremation, burial or shipment of body abroad. In absence of anyone locally to look after personal effects of deceased, consular officials are usually authorized to act on temporary basis as administrators of deceased's estate in order to preserve and protect it.

Death certificate may be obtained from area registrar where death was recorded. In foreign country, Thai embassy or consular office is area registrar for any Thai or alien having residence in Thailand under Thai immigration laws out of Thailand. Evidence of such registration shall be recognized as death certificate. If there is no Thai embassy or consular office, official certificate issued by competent authority of that country, certified and translated by Ministry of Foreign Affairs of Thailand can be used as death certificate. (Private Person Registration Act, §28).

Presumption of Absence.—Person adjudicated by court to have disappeared is deemed to have died at completion of two or five years as case may be. (C.C.C. 62). See also topic Absentees.

Presumption as to Survivorship.—When several persons have perished in common peril and it is not possible to determine who died first, law presumes that they died simultaneously. (C.C.C. 17).

Action for Death.—Person, by wrongful act, causing death to another person is bound to make compensation including funeral and other necessary expenses. If death did not occur immediately, compensation shall include cost of medical expenses and damages for loss of earning. Any person who has been deprived of deceased person's support (spouse, descendants, parents, etc.) is entitled to compensation from liable person. (C.C.C. 443). If deceased person was bound by law to perform service in favor of third party in his household or industry, liable person shall be bound to make compensation to third person for loss of such service. (C.C.C. 445).

In case of criminal act, public prosecutor and ascendant or descendant, husband or wife of deceased person are entitled to institute criminal prosecution in court for wrongful death. (C.P.C. §2[4], §5[2], §28).

Anatomical Gift.—There is no special statutory provision for anatomical gift. Any person may make his will concerning arrangement of his properties or other matters after his death. (C.C.C. 1646).

Living will does not exist in Thailand because it is against law and public morality.

DEPOSITIONS:

For Use in Foreign Court.—Thailand is not party to Hague Convention on Taking of Evidence Abroad in Civil and Commercial Matters (1970). As matter of comity, Court of First Instance may compel attendance of witness to respond to questions submitted by foreign court through Letters Rogatory issued by foreign court and transmitted through diplomatic authorities of nation of foreign court to Thai Ministry of Foreign Affairs. Examination is conducted by judge. Lawyers for parties may be present and may request judge to ask supplemental questions. Judge's record of witness' answers are returned to foreign court through diplomatic channels. Deposition of witness voluntarily submitting to deposition without necessity for issuance of subpoena by Court of First Instance may be conducted in Thailand.

For Use in Thai Court.—See topic Actions, subhead Discovery.

DESCENT AND DISTRIBUTION:

Estate and Statutory Heirs.—From moment of decedent's death, his estate which includes properties of every kind, as well as rights, duties and liabilities, except those which by law or their nature are purely personal to him, passes either to legatees by will or to his statutory heirs by operations of law. (C.C.C. 1599, 1603). Acceptance of inheritance is not required. Both legatees and statutory heirs are not liable in excess of shares of inheritance received by them. (C.C.C. 1601). Whole of decedent's property may be freely disposed of by will. (C.C.C. 1646). If decedent made no will or made invalid will, his whole estate must be distributed among his statutory heirs. If only certain part of decedent's estate has been disposed of by will, part of estate not disposed of by will must be distributed among his statutory heirs. (C.C.C. 1620). Unless otherwise provided in will, statutory heir who has received property under will still has normal statutory right of inheritance in part of estate not disposed of by will. (C.C.C. 1621). If decedent was married, surviving spouse, although not statutory heir, is also entitled to share of inheritance as prescribed by law in estate which has not been disposed of by will. (C.C.C. 1635). If there is no statutory heir or legatee or creation of foundation under will of surviving spouse, estate devolves on State. (C.C.C. 1635, 1753).

Statutory Rights of Inheritance.—There are six classes of statutory heirs and presence of heirs or their representatives in one class excludes inheritance rights of statutory heirs in all lower classes: (a) Descendants, provided that only decedent's children which include adopted children and illegitimate children who have been legitimated by decedent, if any, are entitled to inherit (C.C.C. 1627, 1631); (b) parents, provided no representation is allowed for this class of statutory heir; (c) brothers and sisters of full blood; (d) brothers and sisters of half blood; (e) grandfathers and grandmothers, provided no representation is allowed for this class of statutory heir; and (f) uncles and aunts. (C.C.C. 1629). Only exception to this rule is that presence of

DESCENT AND DISTRIBUTION . . . *continued*
descendants does not exclude inheritance rights of surviving parent or parents. In such case each parent is entitled to same share as each child. (C.C.C. 1630). Statutory heirs of class to which estate of decedent passes are entitled to equal shares. If there is only one statutory heir in such class, he is entitled to whole estate. (C.C.C. 1633).

Surviving spouse is entitled to following shares of inheritance: (i) Same share as each child in case descendants inherit; (ii) one-half of inheritance in case parents or brothers and sisters of full blood inherit; and (iii) two-thirds of inheritance in case brothers and sisters of half blood, grandfathers and grandmothers or uncles and aunts inherit. If there exists no statutory heir, surviving spouse is entitled to whole inheritance. (C.C.C. 1635).

Renunciation.—Statutory heir may renounce whole, but not part of, inheritance by express written declaration of intention which must be deposited with competent official or by entering into compromise agreement. Renunciation of inheritance is irrevocable and cannot be made subject to condition or time clause. (C.C.C. 1612, 1613).

Foreign Decedents.—Thai law applies to succession concerning immovable property of foreign decedent in Thailand, but law of his last domicile governs succession concerning his movable property. (C.O.L. 37, 38).

DIVORCE:

Marriage may be terminated by death, divorce, or annulment by court. Divorce can be effected either by mutual consent or court judgment. (C.C.C. 1501, 1514).

Divorce by mutual consent must be made in writing and certified by signatures of at least two witnesses and except for marriage effected according to form prescribed by law of foreign countries, must also be registered with competent official by spouses. (C.C.C. 1514, 1515).

Divorce by Judgment of Court.—Court may, on application by either spouse, grant divorce on following grounds: (a) Maintenance or recognition of another woman as his wife by husband, or adultery by wife; (b) misconduct; (c) cruelty or gross insult to other spouse or his or her ascendants; (d) desertion for more than one year; (e) final court sentence of more than one year imprisonment for offence without other spouse's participation, consent or knowledge; (f) spouses voluntarily live separately for more than three years; (g) adjudication of disappearance by court or spouse having left domicile for more than three years and it is not known whether he or she is alive; (h) acts seriously adverse to relationship of spouses or failure to give proper maintenance and support to extent that other has been in excessive trouble; (i) serious and hardly curable insanity for over three years; (j) breaking of bond of good behavior executed by him or her; (k) serious incurable contagious disease; and (l) physical disadvantage so as to be permanently unable to cohabit as husband and wife. (C.C.C. 1516). Right to institute action for divorce is waived by act of spouse entitled thereto showing forgiveness to ground of action for divorce. (C.C.C. 1518).

Divorce Involving Aliens.—Divorce by mutual consent is valid if permitted by laws of nationalities of spouses. (C.O.L. 26). Divorce may be effected by judgment of Thai court only when laws of nationalities of spouses permit termination of marriage by divorce. Grounds of action for divorce are those provided by Thai law. (C.O.L. 27).

Custody of Children.—Divorce agreement should contain provisions concerning custody of children and amount of contribution which either spouse or both spouses will make to support children. (C.C.C. 1520, 1522). In absence of such provisions or if agreement on such provisions cannot be reached, court is empowered to decide matters. (C.C.C. 1520). Man or woman who does not obtain custody of child still has right to continue such personal relations with child as may be reasonable according to circumstances. If there is change of circumstance or it appears that person having custody of any child behaves himself or herself improperly, court may, after taking into consideration happiness and interest of child, appoint new guardian. (C.C.C. 1521).

Corollary Relief.—If one spouse is found to have been solely responsible for ground of action for divorce and divorce results in other spouse's insufficient income to support himself or herself, court may, upon application made by such spouse in complaint or counterclaim in action for divorce, require that spouse against whom finding of responsibility for divorce has been rendered make payment of support to other spouse. (C.C.C. 1526). If cruelty or gross insult, desertion, acts seriously adverse to relationship of spouses or failure to give proper maintenance and support which is ground of particular action for divorce is intentionally created by responsible spouse in such action such that action for divorce is inevitable, other spouse is entitled to compensation. (C.C.C. 1524).

Division of Property.—Upon divorce, man and woman must be equally liable for common debts and their properties must be divided equally between them. (C.C.C. 1533, 1535). Following properties are not subject to division: (a) property acquired before marriage; (b) property for personal use, dress or ornament suitable for station in life, or tools necessary for carrying on profession; (c) property acquired by man or woman during marriage through will or gift; and (d) property given by man to woman as evidence of betrothal (e.g., ring or ceremonial money). (C.C.C. 1471, 1533).

DOWER AND CURTESY:

Dower and curtesy rights do not exist in Thai law.

ENVIRONMENT:

For two decades, industrializing nation of Thailand has had one of world's highest continuous rates of economic growth. Concurrently, and probably as price thereof, Thailand has become environmental disaster. Both Government and general public are aware of these problems and attempts are being made to prevent further deterioration as result of future economic development.

Public pressure for environmental regulation is particularly strong in Thailand and there have been numerous demonstrations against developments and facilities which are seen to be potentially damaging to environment. In addition, Crown takes keen interest in environmental matters and has strong persuasive ability.

Effective execution of Thailand's Seventh Economic and Social Development Plan (1991-1996) mandated necessity for updated environmental legislation and regulatory agency with proper scope and empowerment to achieve such objectives. Although Thailand had (and still has) uncoordinated, often overlapping, hodgepodge of some 70-plus laws and regulations of some environmental concern, legislature base required extensive revamping to carry out specific objectives of Seventh Plan. As result, in 1992, government passed six of most comprehensive pieces of environmental legislation to date and also strengthened state regulatory bodies which administer them. New legislation included Enhancement and Conservation of National Environmental Quality Act (N.E.Q.A.), revamped Factories Act, Hazardous Substances Act, new Public Health Act, Energy Conservation Promotion Act and revised Cleanliness and Orderliness of Country Act. Of these, first three pieces of legislation are most important in terms of their scope and impact on commerce and industry.

Administration and Enforcement of Environment Legislation (General Supervision).—Art. 74 of 1991 Constitution requires government to "conserve and maintain the environment, the balance of natural resources and substitutes, and prevent and eliminate pollution and plan appropriate soil and water use".

Thailand in last decade has become party to several international treaties including: Convention on International Trade in Endangered Species of Wild Flora and Fauna, ratified Mar. 21, 1983, effective Apr. 21, 1983, as amended in 1993; Vienna Convention for the Protection of the Ozone Layer, accession on July 7, 1985; UNESCO Convention Concerning the Protection of the World Cultural and Natural Heritage, accession on Sept. 17, 1987; The Montreal Protocol on Substances that Deplete the Ozone Layer, signed on Sept. 15, 1988, ratified on July 7, 1989; Basel Convention for the Control of Transboundary Movements of Hazardous Wastes and their Disposal, signed on Mar. 22, 1990, not yet ratified by National Assembly; United Nations Convention on Biological Diversity, Rio de Janeiro, signed June 12, 1992, not yet ratified by National Assembly; United Nations Framework Convention on Climate Change, Rio de Janeiro, signed June 12, 1992, not yet ratified by National Assembly.

New Enhancement and Conservation of National Environmental Quality Act B.E. 2535 (A.D. 1992) ("E.C.N.E.Q.A.") has recently been enacted, repealing National Environmental Quality Act. Under new Act, National Environment Board ("N.E.B."), which was established in 1975 under old law, has been reorganized but still serves as central agency for environmental matters. N.E.B. is responsible for providing policies and opinions on environmental and conservation issues to Council of Ministers. N.E.B. is also concerned with recommending environmental quality standards and coordinating environment-related work of other government agencies.

E.C.N.E.Q.A. contains provisions giving government officials authority to enforce environmental quality legislation. New Act adopts "polluter pays" principle and provides public with legal right to information in relation to environmental matters and right to compensation from State in case of damage caused by project or business managed or supported by Government or state enterprise, including right to make complaint.

Under Act, recognized nongovernmental organizations may be allowed to register as private organizations for protection of environment and conservation of natural resources, with authority to bring court action on behalf of victims of environmental damage or pollution. E.C.N.E.Q.A. also decentralizes to local authorities power to manage environmental quality in their areas.

Ministry of Science, Technology and Environment (M.O.S.T.E.) generally oversees environmental concerns of Thailand. Other governmental agencies, national and local, are also authorized to regulate in their respective fields. Since scope of powers and duties of many governmental authorities may overlap, inconsistencies in environmental standards set forth by each agency are bound to occur. In event of such inconsistencies, M.O.S.T.E.'s standards prevail unless inconsistency is expressly authorized by E.C.N.E.Q.A. and its subsequent regulations.

One of M.O.S.T.E.'s primary duties concerning pollution control is to prescribe emission and effluent standards for control of discharge or emission of waste water, air pollution, and other waste products or pollutants from point sources into environment. In event that there are other standards which have been determined by another environmental agency, M.O.S.T.E.'s standards shall prevail over any inconsistent standard for same type of emission.

In areas deemed by N.E.B. to have aggravated pollution problem, it may designate such areas as pollution control area (P.C.A.). In this event, each provincial governor in P.C.A. is authorized to prescribe more stringent set of emission or effluent standards for their area in order to control and reduce pollution. Designated P.C.A.s under this legislation are Pattaya (Cholburi Province), Amphoe Hat Yai, Amphoe Muang (Songkhla Province), Pee Pee Islands (Krabi Province), and complete provinces of Phuket, Samut Prakan, Nonthaburi, Samut Sakhon, Nakhon Pathom and Pathum Thani.

E.C.N.E.Q.A. established Environmental Fund with aim of assisting government agencies, local authorities, individuals or recognized private organizations to set up systems for remediation of pollution.

Violators of E.C.N.E.Q.A. are subject to strict civil liability except on three occasions: (1) force majeure or war, (2) acts done with government approval, or (3) damages resulting from act or omission by victim or third party who is either directly or indirectly responsible for damages. Violator is liable for all damages resulting from contamination, including any expenses incurred for clean-up and value of any natural resources destroyed or damaged in process. Criminal liabilities for violations of E.C.N.E.Q.A. range from one month to five years imprisonment and/or fines of US$400-20,000 (Baht 10,000-500,000).

In case of company, directors or managers of such company shall also be liable for such offenses unless it can be proved that they have no part to play in commission of such offence.

Party who owns or possesses point source of pollution planning to install on-site treatment facility, whether or not required to do so by law, is entitled to request assistance from government regarding import duties of necessary machinery, equipment and materials for facility which are not available in Thailand, and permission to bring in foreign experts and specialists concerning construction and operation of facility if such qualified persons are not available in Thailand. Foreign specialists may also qualify for exemption from taxation of their income earned in Thailand for purposes of construction and operation of facility. Applications for these perquisites

See Topical Index in front part of this volume.

ENVIRONMENT . . . *continued*
under E.C.N.E.Q.A. are to be made to N.E.B. in accordance with its rules and regulations.

Addresses.—Office of Environment Policy and Planning, Ministry of Science, Technology and Environment, 60/1 Soi Phibulwatana 7, Rama VI Road, Bangkok 10400, Tel: 279-7180-9, Fax: (662) 271-3226; Department of Pollution Control, Ministry of Science, Technology and Environment, 404 Phaholyothin Center Building, Phaholyothin Road, Samsen Nai, Phyathai, Bangkok 10400, Tel: 619-2299-2304, Fax: (662) 619-2285; Department of Environmental Quality Promotion, Ministry of Science, Technology and Environment, 60/1 Soi Phibulwattana 7, Rama VI Road, Bangkok 10400, Tel: 279-7180-9, 272-3033, Fax: (662) 272-3032; Industrial Environmental Division, Department of Industrial Works, Ministry of Industry, 75/6 Rama VI Road, Bangkok 10400, Tel: 202-4162, 202-4171, Fax: (66-2) 202-4162, Toxic and Hazardous Substances Control Division, Food and Drug Administration, Ministry of Public Health, Tivanont Road, Nonthaburi 11000, Tel: 591-8482-3, Fax: (662) 591-8483.

Environmental Legislation.—Range of environmental legislation has been enacted in Thailand in recent decades. Legislation to control all major pollutants and pollutable media is in existence. In additon to E.C.N.E.Q.A. discussed above, 1992 legislation includes revamped Factories Act, Hazardous Substances Act, Energy Conservation Promotion Act, new Public Health Act, and revised Cleanliness and Orderliness of the Country Act. Of these, first three pieces of legislation are most important in terms of their scope and impact on commerce and industry.

New Factories Act B.E. 2535 (A.D. 1992) has tremendous impact on business and individual polluters. Implementation of this Act is under supervision of Ministry of Industry (M.O.I.). Factories Act empowers Minister to regulate factories for prevention of disturbances, damages and danger to public or environment.

Pursuant to 1992 Factories Act, Ministry of Industry has promulgated several new ministerial regulations and notifcations regulating activities in business operations of factories which impact environment. One of regulations prescribes actions to be followed in disposal of waste water and waste products by factory, while one of notifications sets limits on discharge of air pollutants by factory. Measurements of value of contaminants in air are taken from air discharged from chimney during operation of factory, if appropriate, or from location determined by competent authority.

Air Pollution.—Under E.C.N.E.Q.A. "polluted air" means waste in state of exhaust, odor, smoke, gas, soot, dust, ash, or other polluting substance being so fine and light that it can collect in atmosphere.

National ambient air quality objectives have been established for number of air pollutants including sulphur dioxide, nitrogen oxides, particulates, carbon monoxide, photochemical oxidants and lead. Industrial Environmental Division of Ministry of Industry has proposed emission standards for range of pollutants including heavy metals, ammonia, chlorine and arsenic. These standards will apply to new facilities, existing facilities wishing to expand and existing facilities which are subject of air pollution complaints. Standards are also in existence for emissions from motor vehicles.

Water Pollution.—Under E.C.N.E.Q.A., "waste water" means waste in liquid state, including pollutant contained or contaminated in such liquid.

Discharge standards have been set for industrial and domestic effluents entering water. Among industrial effluents regulated in this way are chlorine, oil, grease, heavy metals and suspended and dissolved solids. Certain types of industrial facility are required to employ suitably qualified personnel to have responsibility for pollution control measures at installation. Reporting system has been established whereby facilities must provide results of analysis of discharges at regular intervals.

Water quality standards exist for drinking water and groundwater. Coastal waters and number of surface waters are subject to quality classifications and quality objectives.

E.C.N.E.Q.A. authorizes N.E.B., with advice of Pollution Control Department (P.C.D.), to set service fees for any central waste water treatment plant or central waste disposal facility that is constructed and brought into operation with governmentally related funding, including grants from Environmental Fund.

Waste.—Under E.C.N.E.Q.A., "waste" means solid waste, refuse, waste water, polluted air, pollutant, or other harmful object discharged or derived from pollutant sources, including sludge, sediment, or residue thereof, which is in solid, liquid, or gaseous state. Facility operators are required to provide management plan for treatment and disposal of hazardous waste.

Disposal of waste at landfill sites is also regulated. Specific preventative measures such as use of impermeable liners are required and operators must establish regular programme of groundwater monitoring and retain system of records giving details of waste treated at site.

Hazardous Substances.—Under Hazardous Substances Act B.E. 2535 (A.D. 1992) (H.S.A.) hazardous substances means explosives, flammable substance, oxidizing agent and peroxide, toxic substances and substance causing diseases, radioactive substance, mutant causing substance, corrosive substance, irritating substance and other substance either chemicals or otherwise which may cause injury to persons, animals, plants, property, or environments.

Hazardous Substance Act is under direct authority of Minister of Industry, with cooperation of Minister of Defense, Minister of Agriculture and Cooperatives, Minister of Interior, Minister of Public Health, and Minister of Science, Technology and Environment. Committee on Hazardous Substances (C.H.S.), was established under this Act and chaired by Minister of Industry with powers and duties to supervise works and activities in relation to hazardous substances.

Minister of Industry, with advice of C.H.S., is responsible for prescribing names or qualifications of hazardous substances, types of hazardous substances, periods of application and responsible agencies for control of hazardous substances. Appropriate ministry then administers all other regulations concerning safety precautions to prevent danger in handling, treatment and use of hazardous substances, and procedures for registration of hazardous substance. Hazardous substances are grouped into four classifications, ranging from those types which are banned outright to others that must simply comply with HSA prior to production, import, export or possession by party.

Apart from H.S.A. hazardous substances are regulated by number of statutes such as Fertilizers Act B.E. 2518 (A.D. 1975), Drugs Act B.E. 2510 (A.D. 1967) and Consumer Protection Act B.E. 2522 (A.D. 1979). Range of standards exist which control manufacture, storage, disposal, transport, use and exposure of workers to hazardous materials. Production of hazardous substances is closely controlled. Operators are required to maintain documentation giving information on manufacture of each substance and toxic nature of such materials must be clearly shown on labels of containers. Importation, manufacture and sale of number of hazardous substances has been completely prohibited. These include pesticides DDT and dieldrin.

Under H.S.A., injuries caused by hazardous substance will subject producer, importer, carrier or possessor of said substance to civil liability without regard to knowledge so long as injuries were sustained without force majeure or fault of injured party. Same liability is imposed upon seller of substance, or one who delivers it. Criminal penalties range from one month to ten years imprisonment and/or fines of US$400-40,000 (Baht 10,000-1,000,000), the heftiest under any environmental law in Thailand. All these legal provisions cause a lot of concern among industry and business as heavy financial liability, civil or criminal, may be put upon them in near future.

Environmental Impact Assessment.—Environmental impact assessments (E.I.A.) must be carried out prior to commencement of certain developments. To further environmental quality promotion and conservation, Minister of M.O.S.T.E., with approval of N.E.B., also determines types and sizes of projects or activities which are likely to have environmental impact and consequently, are required to prepare E.I.A. reports of their proposed projects or activities in seeking approval.

Types of projects which will require formal assessment include petrochemical plants, oil refinery, natural gas separation or processing, thermal power plant, mining, mass transit system, commercial port, industrial estate commercial airport, iron and/or steel industry, cement industry, smelting industry other than iron or steel, pulp industry, chemical fertilizer industry using chemical process in production, pesticide industry or industry producing active ingredients by chemical process, land allocation for residential or commercial purposes, residential condominium, hotels and tourist facilities developed in close proximity to sensitive areas such as beaches and rivers, etc.

E.I.A.s may only be conducted by appropriately trained individuals who are licensed by N.E.B. On completion, assessment will be submitted to N.E.B. for approval. N.E.B. has authority to insist on alteration of aspects of project if it is felt that it will have adverse effect on environment.

EXCHANGE CONTROL:

Exchange control restrictions are set forth in Exchange Control Act, B.E. 2485 (A.D. 1942) as am'd and are administered by Bank of Thailand under supervision of Ministry of Finance.

As general rule, all matters involving foreign currency are regulated by and require permission of Bank of Thailand. In particular, except for sale of foreign exchange by authorized dealers (i.e. authorized banks, companies or persons) which have been authorized and delegated certain powers to approve certain foreign exchange transactions on behalf of Bank of Thailand, no person other than such authorized dealers may buy, sell, exchange or transfer any foreign exchange without permission of Bank of Thailand.

However, since May 22, 1990 foreign exchange control has been considerably relaxed because of its major liberalization by Bank of Thailand by which Thailand's international financial position was elevated to Art. 8 status under International Monetary Fund Agreement. Subsequently, further regulations announced by Bank of Thailand have also extended scope of liberalization to include bank deposits, trade and other related transactions. At present, several transactions in foreign currency are under less strict control and can be performed merely upon obtaining approval of authorized commercial banks which are normally granted if applicants provide reasonable grounds for remittance and properly follow required procedures.

Permitted Transactions.—Unlimited amounts of Thai Baht or foreign currency may be brought into Thailand; however, as general rule, such foreign currency must be sold or converted into Thai Baht, or deposited into foreign currency account, with authorized commercial banks in Thailand within 15 days from inward remittance thereof. Thai Baht may be taken out of Thailand (i) into countries immediately bordering Thailand, i.e. Laos, Cambodia, Malaysia, Myanmar and Vietnam up to Baht 500,000 per trip; or (ii) into other countries up to Baht 50,000 per trip. Foreign currency accounts and Baht accounts may be opened at authorized commercial banks under specified conditions set forth by Bank of Thailand by anyone domiciled in Thailand.

Transactions to be Approved by Authorized Commercial Banks.—Commercial banks are authorized by Bank of Thailand to approve certain foreign exchange transactions, in its name, including: (a) Remittance of unlimited amount in payment of imported goods; however, importer importing goods valued at more than Baht 500,000 or its equivalent per transaction must submit application (Form Thor. Tor. 2) to customs official when submitting bill of lading; (b) remittance of up to US$10 million or its equivalent per year per remittee for direct foreign investment (investor must have management control) or for lending to subsidiaries in foreign countries (i.e. subsidiary in which at least 25% of shares owned by parent company resident in Thailand); (c) remittance of up to US$100,000 or its equivalent per year per remittee to relatives or family members permanently living abroad; (d) remittance of up to US$1 million or its equivalent belonging to Thai national permanently living abroad per year; (e) remittance of inherited money to heir living permanently abroad up to US$1 million or its equivalent per year per remittee; (f) remittance of unlimited amount in repayment of foreign loan and payments of accrued interest and other related fees and cost, having proper documentary evidence; (g) unlimited remittance of proceeds from sale of shares having required documentary evidence; (h) remittance of unlimited amount in payment of certain types of service fees, including transport and communication, having appropriate documentary evidence; and (i) sale of unlimited amount of foreign currency to any buyer for traveling purposes. When purchasing foreign curreny for one of aforesaid purposes in amount exceeding US$5,000 or its equivalent, application Form Thor. Tor. 4 must be submitted to authorized banks, together with appropriate supporting documentary evidence.

EXCHANGE CONTROL . . . *continued*

Transactions to be Approved by Bank of Thailand.—Foreign exchange transactions involving amounts in excess of above limitations, or for purposes other than those mentioned above, require approval of Bank of Thailand. Remittance of foreign currency for investment in foreign securities or immovable property also requires Bank of Thailand approval.

EXECUTIONS:

Means of Execution.—Property belonging to judgment debtor may be seized or attached and sold by public auction if he fails to comply in whole or in part with judgment or order of court. (C.P.C. 271, 278). Execution is carried out by executing officer after court's issuance of writ of execution at request of creditor. (C.P.C. 275, 278).

Rights of Other Judgment Creditors.—Property seized or attached by executing officer on behalf of one judgment creditor may not later be seized or attached on behalf of other judgment creditors. Other judgment creditors may be allowed by court to share proceeds of sale of such property if it deems that they cannot be paid out of other property of judgment debtor. (C.P.C. 290).

Arrest and Detention of Judgment Debtor.—Judgment creditor may, at any time, file application for arrest of judgment debtor for wilful disobedience of judgment or order of court. If court is satisfied that judgment debtor could have complied with judgment or order by acting in good faith and that there is no alternative form of execution suitable, judgment debtor may be arrested and detained until security for compliance is posted. (C.P.C. 297, 300).

EXECUTORS AND ADMINISTRATORS:

Appointment, Resignation and Removal.—Testator may appoint one or more executors. (C.C.C. 1715). If person dies intestate or no executor is appointed by testator, heirs jointly carry on administration and distribution of estate and may distribute estate by severally taking possession of property or by selling estate and dividing proceeds of sale among themselves. (C.C.C. 1745, 1750). If executor or heirs are unwilling or unable to carry on or are impeded in carrying on administration or distribution of estate, court may, upon application by any heir or any other interested person or public prosecutor, appoint administrator of estate. Administrator may also be appointed by court upon application by any interested person or public prosecutor if testator's appointment of executor is, for any reason, ineffective or where there is no executor and statutory heirs or legatees are missing or are abroad or are minors. (C.C.C. 1713). Offices of executor and administrator are voluntary but executor or administrator who has accepted office may, subject to court's permission, resign only for reasonable cause. (C.C.C. 1727). Court may remove executor or administrator who has not completed inventory of estate in form prescribed by law in due time or whose inventory is unsatisfactory to court because of negligence, dishonesty or obvious incapability. (C.C.C. 1731). Executor or administrator may also be removed by court upon application, prior to completion of distribution of estate, by any interested person because of his neglect of duties or any other reasonable cause. (C.C.C. 1727).

Qualification.—Minors, bankrupts or persons of unsound mind or adjudged quasi-incompetent cannot be executors or administrators. (C.C.C. 1718).

Powers, Duties and Liabilities.—Executor and administrator have powers and duties to do all acts necessary for general administration or distribution of estate and for bringing about effect intended by express or implied order in will. (C.C.C. 1719). Executor and administrator may not execute functions through agents unless expressly or impliedly authorized by will or by order of court or required by circumstances for benefit of estate. (C.C.C. 1723). Unless otherwise provided by will, several executors or administrators of one estate must exercise powers and perform duties on majority vote. In case of tie, decision shall be made by court on application of any interested person. (C.C.C. 1726). Executor and administrator must complete distribution of estate, account of management and other work within one year or within period fixed by testator, court or majority of heirs. (C.C.C. 1732). No remuneration may be paid from estate to executor or administrator unless permitted by will or majority of heirs. (C.C.C. 1721). Executor and administrator are liable to heirs for any damage resulting from their negligence or non-execution of duties, or from act done in absence of or in excess of authority. (C.C.C. 1720).

Creditors.—Advertisement for or notices to creditors are not required by law. Prior to partition of estate, executor or administrator must have paid all known debts of estate. (C.C.C. 1736). Creditors of estate are entitled to be paid only out of property in estate. (C.C.C. 1734). Creditor of estate may enforce his claim against any heir provided executor or administrator, if any, be summoned by creditor to appear in action or may, prior to division of estate, enforce full payment of his claim from estate. (C.C.C. 1737, 1738). Heir is liable to creditor of estate only up to value of property inherited by him and has right of recourse against other heirs for amount in excess of his proportionate share in obligation and may, if claim is enforced against him before division of estate, require that performance be made out of estate or secured therefrom. (C.C.C. 1738).

FOREIGN EXCHANGE:

See topic Exchange Control.

FOREIGN INVESTMENT:

Forms of Business Organization.—Any form of business organization may be utilized by foreign investors. Nonetheless, because of restrictions on alien participation in certain business activities in Thailand, joint venture with local partners may in some cases be required for foreign investor and will have effect of limiting percentage of his investment in prospective project. (See topic Aliens, subhead Corporations Owned or Controlled by Aliens.) Under Thai law, joint venture can be organized in five different forms, as follows: (a) ordinary partnership; (b) registered ordinary partnership; (c) limited partnership; (d) private limited company; and (e) public limited company. Joint venture has, except for corporate income tax purposes, no defined legal meaning under Thai law. It is not recognized by law as distinct form of business organization and is merely general term used in describing agreement or contractual relationship between two or more parties (usually from two or more countries) for conduct of business or particular project which in order to carry on its business must take form of business organization recognized by law as mentioned above.

Investment Incentives.—Investment Promotion Act, B.E. 2520 (A.D. 1977), as am'd by Investment Promotion Act (No. 2), B.E. 2534 (A.D. 1991), offers various investment incentives to foreign and domestic investment considered important and useful to social and economic development of Thailand. Act is administered by Board of Investment (B.O.I.). B.O.I.'s general objective is to encourage both Thai and foreign investors to locate their projects in Thai provincial areas. Incentives for projects in provinces are more lucrative than incentives for projects in developed areas. Some incentives are not available for certain types of projects in developed areas; and certain types of projects in developed areas cannot qualify for any incentives. Incentives are subject to various conditions stipulated by B.O.I., such as amount and source of capital, Thai shareholders' participation, export requirements, usage of local raw materials, efficiency and capacity of production processes, and environmental protection systems; in addition, special criteria are utilized for projects which are wholly or partially foreign owned. These special criteria govern, among other things, maximum percentage of share capital that can be owned by foreigners. Major incentives available under Act include: (a) guarantees against nationalization, against price control, against competition of new state enterprises; (b) permission to own land necessary for operation notwithstanding other laws to contrary, and to bring into Thailand foreign experts and skilled workers to work on promoted projects (see topics Aliens and Immigration); (c) exemption from corporate income tax for period of three to eight years; and reduction thereof by 50% for five years after exemption period; (d) whole or partial exemption from import duties on machinery and raw or essential materials used in export products for period of from one to five years; and (e) protections such as import ban on competitive products. Additional incentives from other government organizations under other laws are available for goods produced for export.

In addition, certain activities are eligible to receive nontax incentives; included among such activities are trade and investment support offices, whose activities are permitted to go beyond activities permissible for regional offices (see topic Companies, subhead Regional Office) to end that Thailand will be regional center for trade and investment, and range from engineering, testing and training services to consulting and software design. Approved projects in this activity must be limited companies established under Thai law with minimal annual operation expenses of Baht 10,000,000.

Industrial Estate Authority.—In order to alleviate strain on Bangkok's infrastructure and to spread benefits of development to countryside, Industrial Estate Authority of Thailand Act, B.E. 2522 (A.D. 1979) provides assistance and special incentives for investors who operate within industrial estate. Permit to operate business in industrial estate must be obtained from governor of Industrial Estate Authority of Thailand. Major incentives available under Act include: (a) right to own land in industrial estate; (b) exemption from import duties on necessary machinery and equipment, raw materials, or other items used in manufacture of goods; (c) exemption from, and refund of, taxes on any goods sent into export industrial zone for use within export industrial zone. Location of industrial estate will determine how lucrative incentives will be. If company is promoted by B.O.I., additional incentives can be obtained under Investment Promotion Acts cited and described above.

FOREIGN TRADE REGULATIONS:

Foreign trade is essentially regulated by Act Controlling Importation and Exportation of Goods, B.E. 2522 (A.D. 1979). As general rule, imports and exports are free from external regulation, subject to controls by Ministry of Commerce in form of licensing requirements. Controls of imports and exports also exist in several other laws such as Merchant Marine Promotion Act, B.E. 2521 (A.D. 1978), Export Standards Act, B.E. 2503 (A.D. 1960), and No. 2 B.E. 2522 (A.D. 1979) etc. Violators of regulations may be subject to criminal penalties.

Import Controls.—Minister of Commerce, with approval of Cabinet, has authority to specify classes of goods which are subject to import controls under Act Controlling Importation and Exportation of Goods, B.E. 2522 (A.D. 1979). Goods subject to control require import licenses from Ministry of Commerce.

Export Controls.—Minister of Commerce, with approval of Cabinet, has authority to specify classes of goods which are subject to export controls under Act Controlling Importation and Exportation of Goods, B.E. 2522 (A.D. 1979). Goods subject to control require export licenses from Ministry of Commerce. Export Standards Act, B.E. 2503 (A.D. 1960) and No. 2 B.E. 2522 (A.D. 1979) further subjects certain classes of goods to export license from Commodity Standards Office of Ministry of Commerce. The ASEAN Free Trade Area negotiations, together with the successful conclusion of GATT Uruguay Round in 1994 and Thailand's accession to World Trade Organization in 1995 have brought about many changes in Thailand's tariff regime. Number of goods subject to control, as well as ad valorem tariff schedule rates, have fallen considerably in past few years.

FRAUDS, STATUTE OF:

There is no statute of frauds in Thailand. However, C.C.C. provides that: (a) Sale, contract of exchange and gift of immovable property, ships or vessels of six tons and over, steam launches or motor boats of five tons and over, floating houses, or beasts of burden are void unless made in writing and registered by competent official (C.C.C. 456, 525); (b) contract of hire-purchase is void unless made in writing (C.C.C. 572); (c) hire of immovable property for more than three years is enforceable only for three years unless made in writing and registered by competent official (C.C.C. 538); (d) acquisition by juristic act of immovable property or of real right appertaining thereto is incomplete unless such juristic act is made in writing and registered by competent official (C.C.C. 1299); (e) divorce by mutual consent must be made in writing and certified by signatures of at least two witnesses (C.C.C. 1514); (f) will may be made by public document according to procedures set forth by C.C.C. or made in writing dated at time of making of will and certified by signatures of at least two witnesses

FRAUDS, STATUTE OF . . . *continued*
present at time of execution (C.C.C. 1655, 1656); and (g) oral testimony is not sufficient and some written evidence of agreement signed by party liable is required to prove following contracts: (1) unless earnest money is given or there is part performance, agreement to sell or buy property sale of which must be made in writing and registered by competent official (C.C.C. 456); (2) unless earnest money is given or there is part performance, sale of movable property where agreed price is Baht 500 or more (C.C.C. 456); (3) hire of immovable property for three years or less (C.C.C. 538); (4) loan of sum exceeding Baht 50 (C.C.C. 653); (5) contract of suretyship (C.C.C. 680); (6) contract of compromise (C.C.C. 851); and (7) contract of insurance (C.C.C. 867).

All other contracts for which C.C.C. does not specifically provide forms may be executed orally.

FRAUDULENT SALES AND CONVEYANCES:

Court may, upon application by affected creditor, cancel: (a) Any gratuitous conveyance of debtor's property done with debtor's knowledge that it would prejudice said creditor; and (b) any other juristic act whose subject is property right done by debtor with knowledge that it would prejudice said creditor provided that third person enriched by such act was, at time of act, aware of facts which would make it prejudicial to creditor. (C.C.C. 237). Claim for cancellation cannot be brought later than one year from time when creditor knew of cause of cancellation, or later than ten years since act was done. (C.C.C. 240).

In case of bankruptcy, such rights of actions are vested in government receiver. (B.A. 113). Debtor who made any transfer of or allowed any charge on his property which may, if he becomes bankrupt, be deemed act of giving preference is considered to be insolvent and his creditor may petition court for his bankruptcy adjudication if other requirements are met. (B.A. 8, 9). Upon application by government receiver in bankruptcy action, court may also cancel: (a) any act involving or any conveyance of debtor's property performed by debtor or with debtor's consent within three years before commencement of bankruptcy proceeding or within three years thereafter, unless person enriched by such act or transferee can prove to court's satisfaction that such act or such conveyance was performed for value and in good faith; and (b) any act involving or any conveyance of debtor's property performed by debtor or with debtor's consent within three months before commencement of bankruptcy proceeding or within three months thereafter in order to give preference to one or some of his creditors. (B.A. 114, 115).

GARNISHMENT:

See topics Attachment and Executions.

HOLIDAYS:

Jan 1. (New Year's Day); Feb. 9 (Makha Bucha Day); Apr. 6 (Chakri Memorial Day); Apr. 13 (Songkran Festival Day); May 1 (Labor Day); May 5 (Coronation Day); May 8 (Wisaka Bucha Day); July 7 (Asarnha Bucha Day); July 8 (Buddhist Lent Day); Aug. 12 (H.M. the Queen's Birthday); Oct. 23 (Chulalongkorn Day); Dec. 5 (H.M. the King's Birthday); Dec. 10 (Constitution Day); and Dec. 31 (New Year's Eve).

HOMESTEADS:

There is no homestead exemption law in Thailand.

HUSBAND AND WIFE:

Husband and wife are obliged to live together, unless authorized to live apart by court on grounds set forth by law, and mutually maintain and support each other according to their ability and station in life. (C.C.C. 1461).

Both husband and wife may freely engage in business or follow profession or employment without permission or consent of each other. However, debts incurred before or during marriage for which either spouse is held personally liable must be first paid out of his or her individual property not included in community property acquired after marriage and, if not enough, then paid out of his or her portion of community property ("sin somros"). (C.C.C. 1488).

Community Property.—Antenuptial agreement concerning ownership and administration of property of husband and wife executed prior to their marriage is enforceable if recorded in Marriage Register at time of marriage registration or made in writing signed by them and at least two witnesses and attached to Marriage Register which mentions its attachment. (C.C.C. 1466). Any particular clause in antenuptial agreement which is contrary to public order or good morals or provides that relations between parties regarding their property are to be governed by foreign law is void. (C.C.C. 1465).

Unless otherwise agreed in antenuptial agreement, community property ("sin somros"), as regulated by law, includes property acquired after time of marriage. (C.C.C. 1465). Following properties (called "sin suan tua") are excluded from community property: (a) property of either spouse before marriage; (b) property for personal use, dress or ornament suitable for station in life, or tools necessary for carrying on profession of either spouse; (c) property acquired by either spouse during marriage through gift or inheritance, either by will or operation of law; and (d) property given by husband to wife as evidence of betrothal. (C.C.C. 1470, 1471). Each spouse may freely administer his or her individual property ("sin suan tua"). (C.C.C. 1473). Community property belongs to both husband and wife equally. If not otherwise agreed to in agreement before marriage, either husband or wife can manage community property without other spouse's consent. However, husband and wife must jointly manage following transactions, otherwise, spouse doing these transactions has to get other spouse's consent (§1476): (1) selling, exchanging, selling with right of redemption, engaging in hire-purchase, mortgaging, releasing mortgage or transferring right of mortgage on immovable property or mortgageable movable property; (2) creating or terminating whole or part of servitude, right of habitation, superficies, usufruct, or encumbrance of immovable property; (3) letting immovable property for more than three years; (4) lending money; (5) making gift, unless it is gift for charitable, social or moral purposes and is suitable to family condition; (6) making compromise; (7) submitting dispute to arbitration; (8) putting up property as guarantee or security with government official or court.

Neither spouse has right to dispose by will of more than his or her portion of community property. (C.C.C. 1481). Debts for which both spouses are jointly liable, such as (a) debts incurred in connection with business carried on by both spouses in common; (b) debts incurred in connection with management of affairs necessary for family, such as maintenance and medical expenses of household, proper education of children, etc.; or (c) debts incurred by either spouse only for his or her own benefit but ratified by other, may be paid out of both community property and their individual property. (C.C.C. 1489, 1490). Upon death or bankruptcy adjudication of either spouse or divorce, community property will be equally divided between spouses. (C.C.C. 1491, 1533, 1625).

IMMIGRATION:

Visa.—Immigration into Thailand is governed by Immigration Act, B.E. 2522 (A.D. 1979) and is administered by Immigration Bureau of Royal Thai Police Department, Ministry of Interior. Unless otherwise exempted, foreigners must obtain proper visa from Thai embassy or consulate prior to entering Thailand. Foreigners in transit and tourists from over 100 countries, including U.S.A. and Canada, which have agreements with Thailand concerning visits of not more than 15 or 30 days depending upon countries, are not required to obtain visas before entering Thailand. However, entry permission must be obtained at airport, seaport or land border checkpoint of entry.

Permissible duration of stay is always entered in passport. There are various types of visas, with each category restricted to purpose for which visa was issued. Foreigners wishing to apply for work permit in Thailand must obtain nonimmigrant visa, which will generally be granted for 90 days, from Thai embassy or consulate. Multiple entry permit should be requested while submitting application if foreigner expects to travel out of Thailand frequently during 90-day period, or reentry permit can be obtained from Immigration Division in Bangkok, otherwise visa will be automatically cancelled. Reentry permit must be used within validity period of visa, otherwise it will be void.

Thai consulates nearest to Thailand are in Singapore, Malaysia (Kuala Lumpur and Penang), Vietnam, Laos and Hong Kong. Tourist and nonimmigrant visas usually take one day for issuance depending on number of applications processed by consulate.

Work Permit.—Foreigners working in Thailand are subject to Alien Employment Act, B.E. 2521 (A.D. 1978). Foreigners who intend to work in Thailand must obtain valid work permit, issued principally by Department of Employment. Unless individual or work performed falls within exception of Act, foreigner cannot perform any act of work or service unless work permit has been obtained. Certain foreigners exempt from work permit requirements include members of diplomatic or consular missions, representatives or officials of United Nations, persons performing duties or missions under agreement between government of Thailand and another foreign government or international organization, persons with special permission from government of Thailand to enter and perform duties or missions in Thailand, etc. Exceptions to Act permit foreigners to perform work deemed necessary and urgent which can be completed within 15 days. However, Department of Employment must be informed before work begins. Team "work" is defined very broadly, i.e. "working by exerting one's physical energy or employing one's knowledge, whether or not for wages or other benefits".

There are 39 occupations solely reserved for Thais which are closed to foreigners. These include labor work; agriculture, forestry or fishery; brokerage or agency, except brokerage or agency in international trading; accountancy; civil engineering; architectural work; and legal sevice, among others.

Applicant for work permit must either hold nonimmigrant visa or residence permit. Nonimmigrant visa must be obtained from Thai embassy or consulate prior to entering Thailand. Application for residence permit may be made only after foreigner has resided in Thailand for at least three consecutive years under nonimmigrant visa. Employer or potential employer may file application for advance permission for foreigner to work before he enters Thailand. However, work permit itself will not be issued until foreigner enters Thailand on valid nonimmigrant visa. Regardless of length of time approved in work permit, it is valid only as long as foreigner's visa permits him to remain in Thailand. Also, work permit is good only for particular job for which it was issued and within geographic limitations specified in work permit.

Penalties for working without work permit or doing work not specified in permit include imprisonment not exceeding three months or fine of up to Baht 5,000, or both. Foreigners who perform work reserved solely for Thais are liable to imprisonment of up to five years or fine from Baht 2,000 to Baht 100,000, or both.

INFANTS:

Age of majority for both sexes is 20 but upon marriage, minor of at least 17 years of age (which is legal age for marriage) is automatically emancipated. (C.C.C. 19, 20, 1448).

Capacity.—Juristic acts other than those strictly personal, or suitable to his condition in life and actually required for his reasonable needs, or merely entitle him to certain rights or free him from certain duties performed by minors without consent of his legal representative (parents or guardian) are voidable. (C.C.C. 21—24). Consent of legal representative is not required for making of will by minor of at least 15 years of age. (C.C.C. 25). Minor who has been permitted to carry on one or more businesses has full capacity in relation to such businesses. (C.C.C. 27).

Avoidance and Ratification.—Voidable acts of minor may be either avoided by minor himself or his legal representative or ratified by his legal representative or, after he attains majority, by minor himself. (C.C.C. 175, 177). Voidable act may not be avoided after one year since minor attains majority or after ten years since act is done. (C.C.C. 181).

INTEREST:

General Interest Rate.—Wherever interest is to be paid, interest rate of 7.5% per annum shall apply, unless otherwise fixed by juristic act or determined by express provision of law. (C.C.C. 7). Interest on loan of money may not exceed 15% per annum. If higher interest is fixed by contract, only interest rate of 15% per annum may

INTEREST . . . *continued*
be charged. (C.C.C. 654). Compound interest is prohibited except that parties to particular loan agreement may agree in writing to have interest due for one year or more added to principal amount and whole shall bear interest. (C.C.C. 655).

Interest rate chargeable by banks or financial institutions is regulated by Interest on Loan of Financial Institutions Act, B.E. 2523 (A.D. 1980) (I.F.A.) and relevant notifications of Bank of Thailand issued by virtue of Commercial Banking Act, B.E. 2505 (A.D. 1962), as am'd, or Act on the Undertaking of Finance Business, Securities Business and Credit Foncier Business, B.E. 2522 (A.D. 1979), as am'd. Under I.F.A., maximum interest rates chargeable by financial institutions, which may exceed 15% per annum, are published from time to time by Announcements of Ministry of Finance as empowered by Act. (I.F.A. 4). At present, commercial banks and finance companies are, by virtue of relevant notifications, allowed to set interest rates as they see fit, provided that said banks or finance companies post announcements respecting their interest rates in conspicuous places at all of their offices and send such announcements to Bank of Thailand within prescribed period from date of announcements.

JUDGMENTS:

Judgment or order must be rendered upon completion of trial. (C.P.C. 133). Judgment or order of court disposing of case must decide on every claim in complaint and may not, with few exceptions, grant relief not applied for therein. (C.P.C. 142). Judgment or order must be in writing and state clearly decision of court on issues of case and decision as to costs and ground for all decisions. (C.P.C. 141). Court may not render judgment or order disposing of case in favor of any party on mere ground that opposing party fails to appear. (C.P.C. 205). Judgment or order of court, if not complied with, is enforceable by way of execution. (See topic Executions.)

Foreign Judgments.—Thailand is not party to any multilateral or bilateral treaties for enforcement of foreign judgments. Foreign judgment is not enforceable, however, authenticated foreign judgment may be submitted as evidence and may be considered as persuasive authority by court. Person in whose favor foreign judgment has been pronounced must institute suit in Thai court having jurisdiction over it based on same cause of action in order to obtain Thai court's judgment. See topic Actions.

JURISTIC PERSONS:

In Thai law, juristic person refers to organization created or registered according to law which is distinct legal entity separate and apart from parties composing it. Juristic persons under Thai law include governmental ministries, monasteries, private and public limited companies, limited partnerships, registered ordinary partnerships, associations, and authorized foundations. Juristic person enjoys same rights and is subject to same duties as natural person, except those which, by reason of their very nature, may be enjoyed or incurred only by natural person. Will of juristic person is declared through its representatives. (C.C.C. 65-70).

See topics Associations; Companies; Partnership.

LABOR RELATIONS:

Labor relations are governed by Labor Relations Act, B.E. 2518 (A.D. 1975), Labor Relations Act (No. 2), B.E. 2534 (A.D. 1991), Compensation Fund Act B.E. 2537 (A.D. 1994), Act Establishing the Labor Court Procedure, B.E. 2522 (A.D. 1979), Announcement of the National Executive Council No. 103 and Notifications of the Ministry of Interior thereunder, and C.C.C.

Working Conditions, Wages and Notice.—Employer must provide working conditions which are not less than those minimum standards set by law and must pay compensation in amount not less than minimum wage periodically established by Notification of Ministry of Interior. Employer having ten or more employees must submit written work regulations to Department of Labor Protection and Welfare and must post copy at place of work. Regulations must cover working days, regular hours and rest periods; holidays and rules for taking holiday; rules on overtime and holiday work; date and place of payment of wages, overtime pay and holiday pay; leave and rules for taking leave; disciplinary measures and punishment; procedures for submission of grievances; and procedures for termination of employment.

Hours of Work.—Standard work hours are as follows: industrial work, not more than 48 hours per week; transport work not more than eight hours per day; work which may be detrimental to health, as determined by Ministry of Interior, not more than 42 hours per week; commercial or otherwise unclassified work not more than 54 hours per week. Work performed in excess of such hours shall be paid at rate of one and one-half times regular hourly rate. After five hours of work, employer must provide a one-hour rest period. Employer and employee may agree to rest periods of less than an hour, but not less than 20 minutes each, provided total rest periods are not less than one hour per day.

Holidays and Vacations.—Employer must grant one day holiday for each week of work and 13 additional holidays per year, one of which must be National Labor Day. After one year of service, employees are entitled to paid annual vacation of not less than six working days.

Maternity and Sick Leave.—Employer must grant 30 working days of paid sick leave per year and must grant female employee 90 days of maternity leave with full pay for each day of leave taken, but not to exceed 45 days including holidays.

Termination.—Employee may be dismissed for cause without notice or compensation for: dishonestly performing duty or intentionally committing criminal offense against employer; intentionally causing damage to employer; violating work regulations or rules or lawful orders of employer after written warning has been given by employer, other than in cases when employer is not required to give warning has been given by employer, other than in cases when employer is not required to give warning; neglecting duty for three consecutive working days without justifiable reason; negligently causing serious damage to employer; imprisonment by final judgment of imprisonment. When termination is without cause, employer must give notice of termination not less than one pay period before date of termination, or in lieu of such notice, may terminate employee immediately by paying wages for one pay period. Employer must pay severance in amount determined by length of employee's service as follows: 120 days, but less than one year, 30 days wages; one year, but less than three years, 90 days wages; three years and over, 180 days wages.

As of 13 Oct. 1994, special provision has been made for employees terminated for redundancy when companies bring in new technology to upgrade working units, manufacturing process, distribution or services. Employers are required to notify employees and Labor Inspector of termination date, reasons for such termination and list of such terminated employees, at least 60 days prior to termination. Failure in rendering proper notice or rendering less than required advance notice will cause employer to be liable for severance pay in lieu of advance notice equal to 60 days at employee's last wage rate. Where such severance pay has been paid, it is considered that employer makes payment in lieu of advance notice to employees as provided by CCC. In addition to usual six-months severance pay entitlement, terminated employees employed by company for at least six years are also entitled to be paid special severance pay of 15 days per year of service for portion which exceeds six years, but not exceeding 360 days, at their last rate of wages. Period of work exceeding 180 days in any year is considered as one year.

Labor Unions.—Employees working for same employer or doing same type of work may establish labor union having objective of protecting employees' interest in conditions of employment, promoting better relationships between employers and employees and among employees themselves. Labor unions must be registered with registrar of Department of Labor Protection and Welfare and can operate only upon issuance of license. License is issued after investigation is made by registrar to confirm that regulations of union are not contrary to law and public order and do not constitute threat to national security or economy.

Workmen's Compensation.—Under Compensation Fund Act B.E. 2537 (A.D. 1994), employers must pay compensation if employees suffer injury, sickness, or death in course of employment, but not if injury or illness is based upon consuming intoxicants or drugs beyond self-control or intentional self inflicted injury or allowing others to inflict injury. Employer must provide immediate medical care and treatment in amount as specified by ministerial regulation for employee injury or sickness. If rehabilitation is necessary, employer must pay actual rehabilitation costs in accordance with rules prescribed by ministerial regulation. If death occurs, employer must pay funeral expenses equal to 100 times prevailing maximum daily minimum wage. Sick or injured employee (or his legal beneficiaries i.e., parents, spouse, children etc.) is entitled to apply for compensation fund benefits from local social security office within 180 days from date of incident. Compensation payment requirements are contained in separate notification of Ministry of Interior. Said rates differ with nature of injury, disability, disappearance or death. Act provides for Compensation Fund in Social Security Office, Ministry of Labor and Social Welfare, to which all employers are required to contribute. (Compensation fund program has been in force in Bangkok since 1973, in five other provinces surrounding Bangkok since 1976, in most other areas of Kingdom since Dec. 1978 and throughout Kingdom as of June 1993.) All employers, with labor force of ten employees or more, must contribute annually to Workmen's Compensation Fund. Applicable rates depend upon type of business and nature of work performed. Contribution rates range between 0.2% and 2% of total wages paid to employees up to maximum of Baht 240,000 (approximately USD 10,000).

LANDLORD AND TENANT:

Laws regarding lease of property or buildings fall under Hire of Property—General Provisions of C.C.C. Land, houses, condominium units and other buildings may be leased for up to 30 years, with optional renewal for up to 30 more years. (C.C.C. 540). However, renewal option might not be enforceable against one purchasing property from lessor. Lease contract of immovable property for three years or less is not enforceable unless made in writing and signed by liable party. Leases of more than three years need to be registered with land office, otherwise they will be valid for only three years. (C.C.C. 538).

Amendment to C.C.C. extending leasing terms to 99 years, proposed by private sector, is being considered by government.

If lease is extinguished before end of agreed lease period, innocent party has number of recourse options. If taken to court, verdict can vary depending on specifics of case and actual damage plaintiff is able to prove to court.

At end of agreed lease period, if tenant retains possession of leased property and landlord does not object, it is deemed that lease is extended for indefinite period. (C.C.C. 570). However, if no period is agreed upon, at end of each rental period either party may terminate lease contract by providing other party notice of at least one rental period (or not more than two months' notice in case of yearly rental periods). (C.C.C. 566). Lessee cannot transfer rights to third person unless otherwise provided in contract. (C.C.C. 544).

LICENSES:

Exercise of most professions as well as operation of factories and certain businesses such as banking, insurance, etc. are subject to licenses. Certain businesses can be operated with majority foreign ownership only with permission of Commercial Registration Department (which permission is difficult to obtain) or promotion by Board of Investment. See also topics Aliens; Companies, subhead Foreign Companies; and Foreign Investment.

LIENS:

Preferential rights entitling obligee to right to receive performance of obligation out of certain property of obligee in preference to other creditors; rights of retention: and rights of retention and sale; arise by operation of law on land and things permanently affixed (immovable property) and on all other property, both corporeal and incorporeal (movable property) as follows:

Seller's Right of Retention and Sale.—When buyer of property impairs or reduces security given for payment of purchase price, becomes bankrupt before delivery, or, without seller's knowledge, was bankrupt at time of sale, seller is entitled to retain property sold, unless buyer gives proper security. Where contract of sale did not provide date for payment of purchase price, seller may retain property until purchase

See Topical Index in front part of this volume.

LIENS . . . *continued*
price is paid. (C.C.C. 468, 469). When buyer is in default, seller may, by written notice, demand payment of purchase price and incidental charges within reasonable time. (C.C.C. 470). Upon buyer's failure to comply with notice, seller may sell property by public auction and apply proceeds to amounts due, forthwith delivering any surplus to buyer. (C.C.C. 470, 471). See also subheads Right of Retention, Special Preferential Rights in Immovable Property, Special Preferential Rights in Movable Property, infra.

Innkeeper's Right of Retention and Sale.—Innkeeper and hotelier may retain property of guest or traveller located in inn or hotel until receipt of payment for lodging and other services, including disbursements. (C.C.C. 679). Property which has been left for six weeks without payment of debt may be sold at public auction after at least one month notice of intended sale, giving short description of property to be sold and name of owner (if known), is advertised in local newspaper. (C.C.C. 679). Proceeds of sale may be applied to amounts due and surplus (if any) must be paid to owner of property or deposited at Deposit Office according to provisions of C.C.C. (C.C.C. 679). See also subheads Right of Retention, Special Preferential Rights in Movable Property, infra.

Carrier of Goods Right of Retention and Sale.—Carrier of goods may retain goods necessary to secure payment of freight and other charges. (C.C.C. 630). When consignee cannot be found or refuses delivery, carrier must give notice thereof and request instruction from sender. When giving of notice is impracticable, timely instruction not received, or sender's instructions cannot be carried out, transported goods may be deposited in Deposit Office by carrier, or in case of goods which are perishable or whose value appears insufficient to satisfy costs of carriage, may be sold at public auction. Carrier must, unless impracticable, give notice to sender or consignee of sale without delay. Net proceeds of sale may be applied to amounts due, and surplus (if any) must be forthwith delivered to person entitled to it. (C.C.C. 631, 632). See also subheads Right of Retention, Special Preferential Rights in Movable Property, infra.

Carrier of Passengers Right of Retention and Sale.—Luggage, of which passenger does not take delivery within one month after its arrival, entrusted to carrier of passengers, may be thereafter sold at public auction, and if of perishable nature, may be sold by public auction within 24 hours of its arrival. Proceeds of sale may be applied to sums due, surplus being returned to person entitled thereto. (C.C.C. 636). See also subheads Right of Retention, Special Preferential Rights in Movable Property, infra.

Right of Retention.—Obligee in lawful possession of property of obligor may, unless inconsistent with obligee's duties, contrary to instruction of obligor given before or at time of delivery of property or against public order, retain property as security for performance of obligation then due relating to property possessed. (C.C.C. 241, 242). Upon obligor's insolvency, property may be retained for performance of obligation not yet due; upon insolvency occurring or made known to obligee after obtaining possession, property may be retained notwithstanding contrary duty of obligee or instruction of obligor. (C.C.C. 243). Holder of right of retention may appropriate products and proceeds of retained property to performance of obligation in preference to other creditors. (C.C.C. 245). Loss of possession extinguishes right of retention, except in case where retained property is let or pledged with consent of obligor. (C.C.C. 250).

General Preferential Rights.—Obligee of duty or obligation arising out of: expenditures incurred for preservation, liquidation or distribution of debtor's property for common benefit of creditors; funeral expenses; taxes and rates due for current and preceding years; certain wages of clerk, servant and workman; daily necessaries provided to debtor, family members and servants for period of six months; has right of preference in all property of debtor. (C.C.C. 253-258).

Special Preferential Rights in Immovable Property.—Obligee of obligation arising out of preservation of immovable for expense of preservation, has preferential right in immovable. (C.C.C. 274). Such right retains its effect upon being registered immediately after completion of act of preservation. (C.C.C. 285). Architect, builder or contractor performing work upon immovable, has preferential right in such immovable for charges for work done and is limited to increase in value of immovable created by such work. (C.C.C. 275). Such right retains its effect by provisional estimate of cost being registered before commencement of work to extent that actual cost does not exceed provisional estimate. (C.C.C. 286). Seller of immovable, for sales price and interest, has preferential right in immovable sold. (C.C.C. 276). Right retains its effect by registration of both contract of sale and declaration of default in payment of price or interest at same time. (C.C.C. 288).

Special Preferential Rights in Movable Property.—Lessor of immovable property, for rent and other obligations of lessee, has right of preference in lessee's movable property in or on leased property; and in case of lease of land, in such movable property brought by lessee upon leased land or into buildings subservient to use of such land; in such movables destined to use of leased land and in such fruits of land as are in possession of lessee. (C.C.C. 260, 261). Innkeeper or hotelier, for lodging and other services, including disbursements, has right of preference in luggage or property of guest or traveller which is located in hotel or inn. (C.C.C. 265). Lessor of immovable, innkeeper and hotelier may enforce right of preference in same manner as pledgee. C.C.C. provisions on enforcement of pledge apply. (C.C.C. 266). See topic Pledges. Carrier of goods, or passengers for charges of carriage and expenses, has right of preference in all property in possession of carrier. (C.C.C. 267). Obligee of obligation arising out of preservation of movable for expense of preservation of such movable and for necessary expenses incurred for having right relating to such movable preserved, acknowledged or enforced, has preferential right in such movable. (C.C.C. 269). Seller of movable for sales price and interest has right of preference in property sold. (C.C.C. 270). Supplier of seeds, young plants and fertilizers, for sales price and interest, has preferential right on products grown on land for which those things have been used within one year of use. (C.C.C. 271). Provider of agricultural services, for one year's wages, and provider of industrial services, for three month's wages, have right of preference in all products resulting from such service. (C.C.C. 272).

Priority of Holders of Preferential Rights.—When rights of holders of general preferential rights, holders of special preferential rights, pledgees and mortgagees are in conflict, their relative rights to subject property and their rank of precedence are governed by C.C.C. 277-289.

LIMITATION OF ACTIONS:

See topic Prescription.

MARRIAGE:

Registration of Marriage.—Marriage shall be effected only upon registration in person (not by attorney-in-fact) at any amphur (district office) in Thailand. (C.C.C. 1457, 1458). Each spouse is given marriage certificate by registrar. Common law marriage is not recognized under Thai law.

Marriage can take place only when both man and woman are 17 years of age. However, court may, for appropriate reasons, allow them to marry before attaining such age. (C.C.C. 1448).

Consent Required.—In case of marriage of minor, consent of following persons is required: (1) both parents, if they are still alive; (2) only one parent, if other is no longer living, or is unable to give consent; (3) adoptive parent, if minor is adopted child; (4) guardian, if there is no person to give consent under (1), (2) and (3) or such person is deprived of parental power.

Giving consent to marriage may be made verbally before two witnesses or in writing. Once consent has been given, it cannot be revoked. (C.C.C. 1455).

Minor may file application with court for its consent to marriage if there is no authorized person to give consent or such person refuses or is unable to give consent. (C.C.C. 1456).

Prohibited Marriages.—Marriage is prohibited if: (1) man or woman is insane or adjudged incompetent (C.C.C. 1449); (2) they are blood relations in direct ascendant or descendant line, or brother or sister of full or half blood, without regard as to legitimacy of relationship (C.C.C. 1450); (3) between adopter and adoptee (C.C.C. 1451); and (4) man or woman is already spouse of another person (C.C.C. 1452).

Widow or divorced woman cannot register new marriage within 310 days after termination of previous marriage, unless: child has been born during such period; divorced couple remarry; there is valid doctor's certificate declaring that she is not pregnant; or court order allows marriage. (C.C.C. 1453).

Child born of parents who are not married is deemed to be legitimate child of mother. (C.C.C. 1546). Father may legitimize child by marrying mother, or with consent of child and mother, register child as his legal child or request court order. (C.C.C. 1547).

Foreign Marriages.—Marriage in foreign countries between Thais and foreigners may be effected according to form prescribed by Thai law at Thai embassies or consulates, or by law of country where marriage takes place.

MINES AND MINERALS:

Exploration and extraction of minerals in Thailand is under jurisdiction of Department of Mineral Resources (DMR), Ministry of Industry. Mining industry is regulated by Minerals Act, B.E. 2510 (A.D. 1967) as am'd by Minerals Act No. 2, B.E. 2516 (A.D. 1973), Minerals Act No. 3, B.E. 2522 (A.D. 1979), and Minerals Act No. 4, B.E. 2534 (A.D. 1991). Royal Proclamation, B.E. 2526 (A.D. 1983) amending Minerals Act, B.E. 2510 (A.D. 1967) and Royal Proclamation No. 2, B.E. 2528 (A.D. 1985) amending Minerals Act, B.E. 2510 (A.D. 1967) give further guidance to mining companies. Because mining activity is covered by annex C of Alien Business Law, aliens must obtain specific permission to conduct mining business from Director-General of Dept. of Commercial Registration, Ministry of Commerce. (See also topic Aliens.)

Operation of Mines.—

Exploration.—Mining companies must obtain license before conducting exploration and operation. There are three types of prospecting licenses: General License (GPL), Exclusive License (EPL), and Special License (SPL). GPL grants non-exclusive right to explore for minerals by way of geophysical exploration over specific area. EPL grants exclusive right to explore for minerals in specific area. SPL, which also grants exclusive prospecting right, is issued only in circumstances where proposed exploration project requires considerable investment and special technical skills. Applicant for SPL must specify yearly prospecting expenses during term of SPL and may offer special benefits to government when SPL is granted. Licenses for exploration are not transferable. (M.A. §§25-40, as am'd in 1979). Upon receiving approval for exploration or mining, companies must have consent of owners or possessors of surface rights to land being prospected before commencing exploration.

Under Environment Protection and Conservation Act, B.E. 2535 (A.D. 1992), mining businesses are required to submit environmental impact assessment reports to Office of Environmental Policy and Planning of Ministry of Science, Technology and Environment.

Mining.—Mining license is required to exploit ore deposits. Mining license is granted for maximum of 300 rai (2.5 rai = 1 acre) onshore and 50,000 rai offshore. (M.A. §44, as am'd in 1979). Minister, with Cabinet's concurrence, may increase offshore area to more than 50,000 rai. (M.A. §45). Both types of mining license will not be granted for period exceeding 25 years. (M.A. §54). In case of pending mining license, provisional mining license which is valid for one year shall be issued. Mining license may be transferred only upon approval of Minister of Industry. (M.A. §78).

Safety of Employees.—Companies are required to arrange first aid free of charge for employees and other people in case of emergency. Any accident must be reported to local geologist in that area within 72 hours. Companies shall provide fire fighting equipment at site, arrange first aid and safety training for personnel, keep site in good condition and safe from failure or collapse, and arrange to have foreman or his representative to supervise during operations.

Petroleum and Natural Gas.—Petroleum Act, B.E. 2514 (A.D. 1971) am'd by Petroleum Act (Nos. 1-5), governs exploration, production, storage, transport, sale and disposal of petroleum, including natural gas onshore and offshore. Petroleum business

MINES AND MINERALS . . . *continued*
is also under jurisdiction of Department of Mineral Resources (DMR), Ministry of Industry.

Petroleum Concessions.—Petroleum concession is required for exploration, production, storage, transport, sale and disposal of petroleum including natural gas in concession area. Petroleum concession may be awarded to company which has assets, plans and expertise adequate to exploit petroleum or to applicant guaranteed by such company. Concessions are awarded on sealed bid basis to applicant who offers most favorable terms to government.

Petroleum Exploration and Production.—Exploration period under concession is up to six years which can be extended for another three years. Concession expires at end of exploration period unless concessionaire shows that "commercial" well has been found or determines production area. Production period under concession is not more than 20 years commencing from end of exploration period.

Taxes and Royalties.—If actual mining is initiated, mining companies must pay royalties under Mineral Royalty Rates Act, B.E. 2509 (A.D. 1966) and its amendments, and are subject to Revenue Code taxes.

Royalties on petroleum concessions are paid on sliding scale according to production volumes, with higher marginal rates for higher levels of production as prescribed in Petroleum Act No. 4, B.E. 2532 (A.D. 1989). Taxation on petroleum operation income is imposed by Petroleum Income Tax Act, B.E. 2514 (A.D. 1971) and its amendments, and is exempted from Revenue Code and other laws.

MONOPOLIES AND RESTRAINT OF TRADE:

The Price Control and Anti-Monopoly Act B.E. 2522 (A.D. 1979) protects consumers from businesses establishing price-fixing control measures and prohibits monopolies that hinder free trade. The Central Price Control and Anti-Monopoly Board has power to declare goods as controlled or declare controlled businesses monopolies, and may regulate sales prices of goods where unregulated prices would result in unreasonably high profit margins.

MORTGAGES:

It is required under Thai law that contract of mortgage be made in writing, and that registration of mortgage over mortgaged property be made with competent authority in Thailand. In regard to mortgages of machineries competent authority is Ministry of Industry. With respect to mortgage of land, competent authority is Land Department.

Properties than can be mortgaged are (i) immovable properties of any kind, and (ii) certain types of movable properties which have been registered in accordance with Thai law. Machineries must therefore be registered with Ministry of Industry first before they can be mortgaged as security under Thai law.

Contract of mortgage must contain, in Thai currency (i.e. Thai Baht), either sum certain or maximum amount for which mortgaged property is assigned as security. In any event, only owner of mortgaged property can create mortgage.

Under Thai law, when one and same property is mortgaged to several mortgagees, they rank according to respective dates and hours of registration, and earlier mortgagee shall be satisfied before later one. Accordingly, later mortgagee cannot enforce his right to injury of earlier one.

Enforcement of mortgage under Thai law can be carried out by two methods. First method of enforcement can only be handled by taking court action to obtain judgment to have mortgaged property seized and sold at public auction. In order to obtain judgment, mortgagee must have notified debtor in writing to perform obligation within reasonable time, and debtor failed to comply with said notice. In case of enforcement of mortgage wherein net proceeds from sale in public auction are less than amount due, debtor is not liable for difference unless agreement has been made otherwise.

Second remedy is for mortgagee to claim foreclosure of mortgage, subject to following conditions: (1) if debtor failed to pay interest for at least five years; (2) mortgagor has not satisfied court that value of property is greater than amount due; and (3) there are no other registered mortgages or preferential rights on same property.

It should be noted, that under Thai law, agreement made before obligation becomes due to effect that mortgagee shall, in case of nonperformance, become owner of mortgaged property or dispose of it otherwise than in accordance with provisions concerning Enforcement of Mortgage under Civil and Commercial Code of Thailand, shall be invalid.

After enforcement/execution of mortgage mortgagee entitled to receive payment out of net proceeds of auction to extinction of obligation secured.

As mortgage is legally considered secondary obligation, it can be validly created or given only as security for valid primary obligation. Thus, it is essential that primary obligation, which is to be secured by mortgage, is legal and valid obligation under applicable laws enforceable against primary debtor.

MOTOR VEHICLES:

Car ownership is allowed for foreigners but it is expensive. Car rental, with or without driver, is available. However, both alternatives are expensive solutions to long-term transportation needs.

Thai driver's license is needed to drive in Thailand. Although international driving licenses are recognized in Thailand, they are of limited validity and may not be acknowledged by local insurance policies. To obtain Thai license, foreigner will need: (1) interpreter; (2) medical certificate; (3) two small photos; (4) passport (both original and copy); and (5) certifying residence letter from his embassy. Compulsory third-party automobile insurance is now mandated by law in Thailand. This includes proof of insurance for vehicles registered in other countries being driven in Thailand.

Anyone involved in vehicular accident may be subject to both criminal and civil penalties for negligent driving. If one is involved in accident which is not his fault, he is entitled to compensation if other party is capable of payment. If, on the other hand, he is at fault, he could be liable for cost of compensation and subject to impoundment of his vehicle, as well as fine or imprisonment. In case of serious bodily injury, immediate imprisonment or high cash bail is usually imposed until matter is disposed of in criminal court. On-the-spot or out-of-court settlements after accident which does not result in grievous bodily harm to another person are common and acceptable alternative in resolving incident. Foreigners usually try to reach settlement through their insurance companies. Police will often act as intermediaries to effect compromises.

PARTNERSHIP:

Partnerships are governed by C.C.C. Three types of partnership are recognized by C.C.C.: (a) Ordinary partnership; (b) registered ordinary partnership; and (c) limited partnership. (C.C.C. 1013).

Ordinary Partnerships.—Ordinary partnership resembles American partnership. Of three partnership forms provided for by C.C.C., only ordinary partnership is not juristic person, that is, legal entity distinct from partners composing it. (See also topic Juristic Persons.) Therefore, even though ordinary partnership can conduct business under its name, it may not sue, be sued, or acquire rights and obligations in its name.

All partners in ordinary partnership are jointly and without limit liable for all obligations of partnership. (C.C.C. 1025). Creditor is entitled to seek performance of mature obligations due from ordinary partnership from any of its partners, who are then left with right to take legal action against other partners. Former partner is still liable for obligations partnership incurred while he was partner; this liability is for unlimited time provided that claims are not barred by prescription. (C.C.C. 1051).

Partnership creates general mutual agency among partners whereby acts of each partner, made within scope of partnership business, bind partnership. (C.C.C. 1050). No restriction on power of any partner can be used as defense against claim by third party against partnership.

Person may not become partner of ordinary partnership without unanimous consent of existing partners unless there is agreement providing otherwise. (C.C.C. 1040). In absence of agreement covering management, all partners have management rights and power to represent partnership as its agent but may not enter into contract to which another partner objects. (C.C.C. 1033). Without consent of other partners, no partner may, either on his own or another person's behalf, carry on competing business of same nature as that of partnership. (C.C.C 1038).

If there is no agreement to contrary, partners share profits and losses in proportion to their contributions. (C.C.C. 1044). Contributions may be in cash, property or services. (C.C.C. 1026). In case of doubt, contributions are presumed to be of equal value. (C.C.C. 1027). If partner's contribution consists only of his personal services and partnership agreement does not fix value of such services, then said partner's share of profits and losses is equivalent to average of shares of partners whose contributions are in money or other properties. (C.C.C. 1028).

Establishing ordinary partnership is simple: no filings or other public formalities are required. Ordinary partnership is deemed to be voluntary association which may arise by agreement of partners, which may be either express, as where they sign agreement, or implied, as where they simply commence business without having formally discussed terms of their partnership.

Registered Ordinary Partnerships.—Ordinary partnership may be registered with Ministry of Commerce. (C.C.C. 1064). Upon registration, it becomes registered ordinary partnership, which is juristic person. As juristic person, it is legal entity separate from its partners and can sue or be sued or hold title to properties, and so forth, in its name. (See also topic Juristic Persons.)

Like partners in ordinary partnership, all partners in registered ordinary partnership are jointly and without limit liable for all partnership's obligations. Nevertheless, their liability is, in certain aspects, totally different from that of partners in ordinary partnership.

Ordinary partnership's creditors are entitled to seek performance of mature partnership obligations from any partner, while registered ordinary partnership's creditors are entitled to demand performance of partnership obligations from any partner only when partnership is in default. (C.C.C 1070). Even then, this right is not absolute. If creditor brings suit against partner demanding performance of partnership obligation in default, it is within court's discretion to order creditor to enforce obligation first against partnership's assets if partner being sued proves that such assets are sufficient to satisfy all or part of obligation and that enforcement against partnership would not be difficult. (C.C.C. 1071). Thus, partners in registered ordinary partnership may be considered as sureties of partnership.

Former partner in registered ordinary partnership is liable for obligations partnership incurred while he was still partner; this liability ends two years after he ceases being partner. (C.C.C. 1068).

Public limited company may not be partner in registered ordinary partnership. (P.C.A. 12).

Limited Partnerships.—Major difference between limited partnership and both registered and unregistered ordinary partnerships is that former has two separate groups of partners: (a) One or more partners whose liability for partnership's obligations is limited to capital contributed, and (b) one or more partners who are jointly and without limit liable for all partnership's obligations. (C.C.C. 1077).

Limited partnership must be registered with Ministry of Commerce and, upon registration, becomes juristic person distinct from its partners. (C.C.C. 1078. See also topic Juristic Persons.) Until registration, it is deemed to be ordinary partnership, and all partners have joint and unlimited liability for all partnership obligations. (C.C.C. 1079).

Contributions from unlimited partners may be in form of cash, property, or services, but those from limited partners must be in form of cash or property (not services). (C.C.C. 1083).

Only unlimited partner can be managing partner. (C.C.C. 1087). In other words, limited partner cannot participate in management of partnership. If limited partner interferes with such management, he becomes jointly and without limit liable for all partnership's obligations, along with other unlimited partners. Opinions, advice and votes cast for appointment or dismissal of managers under partnership contract are not considered interference and would not cause limited partner to lose his status. (C.C.C. 1088).

Limited, but not unlimited, partner may transfer his share without consent of other partners. (C.C.C. 1091). Transfer of unlimited partner's share without other partners' consent does not render third-person transferee partner. (However, transfer of any partner's share in ordinary or registered ordinary partnerships without consent of other partners would not render third-person transferee partner.)

See Topical Index in front part of this volume.

PARTNERSHIP . . . *continued*

If limited partnership has several unlimited partners, their relations with each other and with partnership are governed by same rules as apply to relationships between partners in ordinary partnership. Moreover, general provisions applicable to ordinary partnership also apply to limited partnership insofar as they are not excluded or modified by provisions specifically governing latter. (C.C.C. 1080). Creditor of limited partnership may not bring action against any limited partner unless partnership has been dissolved. (C.C.C. 1095).

Public limited company may be limited, but not unlimited, partner in limited partnership. (P.C.A. 12).

Dissolution of Partnerships.—Partnership, regardless of type, is dissolved: (a) In cases provided for in partnership contract; (b) by expiration of time fixed for its duration; (c) upon achievement of its purposes; (d) by due notice of any partner given to other partners in manner prescribed by law, and (e) by death, bankruptcy or incapacity adjudication of any partner, provided in cases under (d) and (e), subsisting partners may buy shares of departing partner and, as consequence, partnership contract continues between subsisting partners. (C.C.C. 1055, 1060). Partnership may also be dissolved by court on grounds prescribed by law. (C.C.C. 1057). Registered ordinary partnership and limited partnership are dissolved if they become bankrupt. (C.C.C. 1069, 1080). After its dissolution, partnership is liquidated. (C.C.C. 1061, 1249). Registered ordinary partnership and limited partnership are deemed to continue for such period necessary for liquidation. (C.C.C. 1249).

PATENTS:

Thai Patent Act, B.E. 2522 (A.D. 1979) as am'd by Patent Act (No. 2), B.E. 2535 (A.D. 1992) provides protection for inventions and designs.

Patentable invention must be: (1) novel; (2) inventive (nonobvious); and (3) industrially applicable. Following inventions are not patentable: (a) invention for which patent application is pending in foreign country for more than 12 months prior to date of Thai application; (b) invention design which has been disclosed to public and/or patented or registered elsewhere prior to filing of Thai application; (c) microorganisms which naturally exist and their components, animals and plants or extracts from animals and plants; (d) computer programs; (e) scientific or mathematical rules or theories; and (f) method for diagnosing, treating or curing human or animal diseases.

Term of patent is 20 years from filing date for invention and ten years for design. Thailand is not party to any international convention but priority may be claimed from basic patent application if country of which applicant is national accords same right to Thai national. Thus far, only Japan, Spain, Switzerland, DPR of Korea and United Kingdom have officially confirmed reciprocal treatment of applications filed by Thai nationals. However, Switzerland and DPR of Korea will grant priority rights to Thai citizens only for inventions. Although no other countries have at this date confirmed reciprocal treatment of applications filed by Thai nationals, applicants of other nationalities may nevertheless express desire on application form to claim priority.

Thailand has early publication system which can be deferred on request. Pre-grant opposition exists and must be filed within 90 days from publication date. Examination as to novelty and obviousness is not automatic and must be requested within five years from publication date. Annuities are payable after grant and beginning from fifth year of term of patent and annually thereafter.

Licensing agreement must be registered with and approved by Department of Intellectual Property. Compulsory license may be obtained if after three years from grant of patent or four years from date of application, whichever is later, patent has not been worked.

In case of process patent infringement, for civil case, burden of proof will be on defendant.

Assignment of patent must be in writing and signed by assignor and assignee.

PLEDGES:

Pledge is contract whereby pledgor delivers to pledgee movable property as security for performance of obligation. Accordingly, delivery of pledged property, by owner thereof, as pledgor, to pledgee is essential and legally required for creation of valid pledge under Thai law. However, parties to pledge may agree to have pledged property kept by third person. With respect to pledge of shares, shares pledged can be set up against company and/or any third person only if creation of pledge is recorded/entered in company's book.

In event pledged property is right represented by written instrument, pledge shall be valid only if instrument is delivered to pledgee, and debtor of right is notified in writing about pledge. Accordingly, if instrument to order is pledged, creation of pledge must be endorsed upon instrument, otherwise pledge cannot be set up against third person. Furthermore, in case of pledge of instrument issued to named person and not transferable by endorsement, pledge must be stated on such instrument. However, it cannot be set up against debtor thereunder or any third person, unless pledge is notified to debtor.

Pledgor is entitled to receive performance of obligation due to him from pledged property in preference to other creditors. However, any agreement made before obligation becomes due to effect that pledgee shall, in case of nonperformance, become owner of pledged property or dispose of it otherwise than in accordance with provisions concerning Enforcement of Pledge under C.C.C., shall be invalid.

Enforcement of pledge under Thai law can be carried out by pledgee even without having to first take court action. On enforcement of pledge in case where debtor has failed to perform obligations, pledgee must first notify debtor in writing to perform obligation and accessories within reasonable time to be fixed in notice. If debtor fails to comply with notice, pledgee is entitled to sell pledged property, but only by public auction. Pledgee must also notify pledgor in writing of place and time of auction. If notification is impracticable, however, pledgee may sell pledged property by public auction after one month from time obligation became due. If several properties are pledged as security for one obligation, pledgee may sell any of such properties pledged as it may select, but pledgee may not sell more than is necessary for satisfaction of its right.

After enforcement of pledge, pledgee must appropriate net proceeds to extinction of obligation and accessories, and accordingly, must return surplus to pledgor or any person entitled thereto. If proceeds derived from enforcement of pledge are less than amount due, debtor of obligation still remains liable for difference.

Pledge is extinguished (1) when obligation secured is extinguished otherwise than by prescription; or (2) when pledgee allows pledged property to return into possession of pledgor.

PRESCRIPTION:

Claim is barred by prescription (limitation of action) after expiration of following periods, unless such period has been interrupted. (C.C.C. 193/9, /10, /14). Periods of prescription begin to run, unless otherwise provided, from date claim can be enforced. (C.C.C. 193/12).

Ten years: Claim of government for taxes (C.C.C. 193/31); claim established by final judgment (C.C.C. 193/32).

Five years: Interest in arrears; installment payments of principal; arrears of rent due to other than lessor in business of leasing chattels; arrears of salaries, annuities, pensions, maintenance and other periodic payments; claims of merchants, manufacturers and artisans for goods delivered or work rendered for debtor's business; claims of those engaged in agriculture or forestry for delivery of products thereof for other than debtor's domestic use. (C.C.C. 193/33).

Three years: Claim against maker of promissory note or acceptor of bill of exchange, from date of maturity. (C.C.C. 1001).

Two years: Claims of merchants, manufacturers and artisans for goods delivered and work rendered other than for business of debtor; claims of those engaged in agriculture or forestry for delivery of products for domestic use; claims of carriers for fare, freight, fees and costs; claims of innkeepers, hoteliers, providers of food and drink and entertainment services for food, lodging services and costs; claims of those in business of leasing chattels; claims of employees and those in private service for expenses, wages or other compensation; claims of employers for advances; claims of masters of apprentices for contracted compensation and expenses; claims of educational institutions or nursing homes for fees and expenses; claims of persons providing education and maintenance for compensation and expenses; claims of those providing maintenance or training to animals for compensation and expenses; claims of practitioners of medicine, dentistry, nursing, veterinary surgeons and related fields, lawyers and expert witnesses, engineers, architects, auditors or other independent professions for compensation and expenses (C. P. C. 193/34); claims for compensation on contract of insurance, from date of loss (C.C.C. 882); claim for payment or refund of premium on insurance contract, from date due (C.C.C. 882); claims against liquidated companies and partnerships, partners, shareholders and liquidators thereof, from end of liquidation (C.C.C. 1272); claim against transferor of share of company for unpaid sums due on share, from date of entry of transfer in shareholder register (C.C.C. 1133).

One year: Avoidance of voidable act, from date notification could have been made, but not later than ten years from act (C.C.C. 181); cancellation of rights procured by fraud or prejudicial act, from date creditor knew of fraud or prejudicial act, but not later than ten years from act (C.C.C. 240); claim based on undue enrichment, from date party became aware of right of restitution, but not later than ten years from accrual of right (C.C.C. 419); claim based on wilful or negligent damage to person, property or right, from date wrongful act and identity of actor becomes known to injured party, but not later than ten years from date of act, provided if such act is punishable under criminal law for which longer period of prescription is provided, longer period shall apply (C.C.C. 448); claim for excess or deficiency in quantity or area of property purchased, from date of delivery (C.C.C. 467); claim based on failure of purchased property to conform to sample or description, from date of delivery (C.C.C. 504); claim based on defect in property purchased, from date of discovery of defect (C.C.C. 474); claim against contractor for defect in work, from date of appearance of defect (C.C.C. 601); claim against carrier for loss, damage or delay, from, except in cases of bad faith, date of delivery or when delivery should have been made (C.C.C. 624); claim by holder of warehouse warrant against prior endorsers after timely public auction, from date of auction (C.C.C. 794); claim by holder against drawer and endorsers of bill of exchange, from date of timely protest, or if protest unnecessary, from date of maturity (C.C.C. 1002); claim for disturbance to or deprivation of possession of property, from date of disturbance or loss of possession (C.C.C. 1374, 1375); claim arising out of usufruct, from date of end of usufruct or if owner could not have known of end of usufruct, from date owner knew or should have known (C.C.C. 1428); claim of registered partnership against partner for competition against partnership, from date of competition (C.C.C. 1067); application for cancellation of marriage on ground of duress, from date spouse is free from duress (C.C.C. 1507); application for cancellation of marriage by party whose consent to marriage is required by C.C.C. 1436, from date marriage is known (C.C.C. 1510); actions for divorce and other rights of action arising from grounds specified in C.C.C. 1516 (1), (2), (3), (6), 1523, from date such grounds are or should have been known (C.C.C. 1529); claims between spouses which would, by prescription, have expired before or within one year after dissolution of marriage, from date of dissolution of marriage (C.C.C. 193/22); actions for repudiation of child, from date of birth of child but not later than ten years after date of birth (C.C.C. 1542); actions concerning inheritance, from date of death of de cujus, or date heir knows or should have known of death; actions concerning legacies, from date legatee knows or should have known of his rights under will; claim of creditor against de cujus which is subject to prescription longer than one year, from date creditor knows or should have known of death of de cujus; but not later than ten years after date of death (C.C.C. 1754); claims in favor of or against descendant which would be prescription, have expired within one year from date of death, from date of death (C.C.C. 193/23).

Six months: Claims of lessor of property based on lease contract, from date of return of leased property (C.C.C. 563); claim of grantor of right of habitation in building, from date of return (C.C.C. 1409); claim arising out of loan for use of property, from date of ending of contract (C.C.C. 649); claim arising out of deposit of property, from date of ending of contract (C.C.C. 671); claim against innkeeper or hotelier for damage to property of guest or traveller, from date of departure of guest or traveller (C.C.C. 678); claim for damage to pledged property caused by pledgee; claim

PRESCRIPTION . . . *continued*
for expenses incurred in maintaining pledged property; claim for injury to pledgee arising out of latent defect in pledged property; from return or auction sale of pledged property (C.C.C. 763); claim for recourse by endorser of bill of exchange against drawer and endorsers, from date of payment of bill of exchange or date of commencement of suit against claiming endorser (C.C.C. 1003); claim of disapproving shareholders based on acts of directors causing injury to company which were approved by general meeting of shareholders, from date of general meeting (C.C.C. 1170).

Three months: Action for cancellation of testamentary disposition, if ground for cancellation was known to applicant during life of testator, from date of death of testator; if ground not known during life of testator, from date applicant acquired knowledge of ground; if ground known but testamentary disposition affecting claimants interest unknown, from date applicant knew or should have known of testamentary disposition; but not later than ten years from date of death of testator. (C.C.C. 1710).

90 days: Application for cancellation of marriage on ground of fraud, from date spouse knew or should have known of fraud or one year from date of marriage. (C.C.C. 1506).

Actions Not Specifically Provided For.—Period of prescription for which no other period is provided is ten years. (C.C.C. 193/30).

Interruption of Period of Prescription.—Prescription is interrupted by: debtor's acknowledgment of claim by part payment; payment of interest; giving of security or other unequivocal act of acknowledgment; creditor's commencement of action on claim, or performance of act having equal effect; creditor's application for debt in bankruptcy; creditor's submission of claim to arbitration. (C.C.C. 193/14). Commencement of action, performance of act having equivalent effect, filing of application in bankruptcy, or submission to arbitration which is terminated and disposed of on grounds of withdrawal or abandonment or entry of final judgment of dismissal does not constitute interruption. (C.C.C. 193/17, 193/18). When interruption occurs, time which has elapsed does not count for prescription purposes and new period of prescription begins to run from date interruption ceases. (C.C.C. 193/15).

New Actions.—Where court refuses to accept, returns or dismisses creditor's action, application in bankruptcy or submission to arbitration for lack of jurisdiction, or dismisses with leave to refile, and period of prescription expired pending proceedings or period would have expired within 60 days from date of final judgment or order, creditor may commence action again within 60 days from date of judgment or order of court. (C.C.C. 193/17, 193/18).

Disabilities of Plaintiff.—When claims of minors or incompetents, including claims against his guardian, curator or legal representative would be prescribed during period of minority, or incompetency, or within one year from period minor or incompetent was without guardian or legal representative, prescription shall not be completed until one year after majority, restoration to competency or existence of guardian or legal representative. If period of otherwise applicable prescription would have been less than one year, such shorter period shall apply. (C.C.C. 193/20, 193/21). If at time prescription would end, creditor is prevented by force majeure from effecting interruption, prescription is not completed until 30 days after date of cessation of force majeure. (C.C.C. 193/19).

Contractual Limitations.—Periods of prescription fixed by law cannot be waived, extended or reduced. (C.C.C. 193/11).

Pleading.—Unless raised as defense, claim will not be dismissed on ground of prescription. (C.C.C. 193/29).

PRINCIPAL AND AGENT:

Agency may be express or implied. (C.C.C. 797). Agent is not entitled to receive remuneration unless it is provided by contract or implied from conduct between parties that remuneration shall be paid or by common practice. (C.C.C. 803). Principal is bound to third party by acts done by his agent or subagent within scope of authority. (C.C.C. 820). Agent without authorization from principal cannot enter into any juristic act in name of his principal with himself or as agent of third party except for performance of obligation only. (C.C.C. 805).

Person who holds out another person as his agent or knowingly allows another person to hold himself out as his agent is liable to any third person acting in good faith. (C.C.C. 821). Principal is not liable to any act of his agent without authority or beyond scope of his authority unless principal ratifies such action. Agent who makes contract on behalf of principal being and having domicile abroad is personally liable on contract though name of principal has been disclosed, unless terms of contract are inconsistent with his authority. (C.C.C. 823, 824).

Express Agent.—Agent who has special authority may do on behalf of his principal whatever is necessary to perform work entrusted to him. (C.C.C. 800). Agent who has general authority may do all acts of management on behalf of his principal except: (1) selling or mortgaging immovable property; (2) letting immovable property for more than three years; (3) making gift; (4) making compromise; (5) entering action in Court; and (6) submitting dispute to arbitration. (C.C.C. 801).

Implied Agent.—Undisclosed principal may declare himself and accept any contract entered into on his behalf. Principal cannot prejudice rights of third party for any acts of agent done before agency becomes known by such party. (C.C.C. 806).

Appointment of Agent.—Law requires written appointment of agent only where transaction is required to be made in writing or if transaction is required to be evidenced by writing. (C.C.C. 798). Appointment of agent shall be evidenced by writing for cases such as sale of immovable property, vessel over six tons, etc. (C.C.C. 456). If several agents have been appointed by same principal for same matter in one contract, it is presumed that they cannot act separately. (C.C.C. 804).

Subagent.—Agent cannot appoint subagent without authorization by principal. Subagent is directly liable to principal and vice versa. (C.C.C. 814). Agent shall be liable to principal only in case where he knows of unfitness or untrustworthiness of subagent and fails to inform principal or revoke subagency. (C.C.C. 813).

Duties and Liabilities of Agent and Principal.—Agent is liable for any injury resulting from his negligence or nonexecution of agency, or from act done without or in excess of authority. (C.C.C. 812). Agent must give information of matters entrusted to him at reasonable time if requested by principal. Agent must surrender all monies and other properties received in connection with agency to principal as well as rights acquired in his own name but on behalf of principal. (C.C.C. 809, 810).

If required, principal must advance necessary sums to agent in order to perform matters entrusted to him. If agent has made advances or expenses as necessary, he can claim reimbursement from principal of such money with interest from day when payment was made. In case it is necessary if agent has assumed obligation, he may require principal to perform in his place or to give proper security if time of maturity of such has not yet arrived. Agent may also claim compensation from principal if he has suffered any damages from performance of agency. (C.C.C. 815, 816). However, if agent has used for his own benefit monies which he ought to have handed over to principal or to have used for principal, he must pay interest to principal from day such sums were used for his own benefit. (C.C.C. 811).

Agent is entitled to retain any property of principal in his possession by reason of agency until he has been paid all that becomes due to him on account of agency. (C.C.C. 819).

Revocation and Extinction of Agency.—Revocation of agency can be made by either party at any time. (C.C.C. 826, 827). Agency for special authority is terminated after authorized events have been concluded. (C.C.C. 800). Agency also ceases when either of parties dies or becomes incapacitated or bankrupt except where it is contrary to terms of contract or nature of business. (C.C.C. 826). Agent must give account to principal after agency has ended. (C.C.C. 809). Upon extinction of agency, principal is entitled to demand submission of any power of attorney given to agent. (C.C.C. 832).

However, causes for extinction of agency resulting from either principal or agent cannot be raised against other contractual party until such extinction is informed to or becomes known by that party. (C.C.C. 830). Extinction of agency cannot be raised against third party acting in good faith, unless third party is ignorant of fact by his own negligence. (C.C.C. 831).

Commission Agency.—Commission agent is person who undertakes to buy or sell property or undertakes any other commercial transaction in his own name in course of his business on account of principal. (C.C.C. 833). Commission agent is entitled to remuneration at usual rate on every transaction concluded by him. (C.C.C. 834). Transaction concluded by commission agent shall have same effect as if it had been concluded directly in name of principal.

Brokerage.—Broker is presumed to have no authority to receive on behalf of parties payment or other performances due under contract. (C.C.C. 844).

REAL PROPERTY:

Land ownership by Thai nationals may be individual or shared. Any Thai national may purchase land in Kingdom unless he/she is married to foreigner. Thai law on community property under marriage provisions of C.C.C. results in Thais relinquishing their right to buy land upon registration of marriage to foreigner. Land issues are governed primarily by Land Code, B.E. 2497 (A.D. 1954), Land Reform for Agriculture, Act B.E. 2518 (A.D. 1975), National Executive Council Announcement No. 286, B.E. 2515 (A.D. 1972) (Housing Estates), City Planning Act, B.E. 2518 (A.D. 1975), Condominium Act, B.E. 2522 (A.D. 1979) and (No. 2) B.E. 2534 (A.D. 1991), Rules Relating to Land Allocation, B.E. 2535 (A.D. 1992) and C.C.C. Land regulations are determined by Ministry of Interior.

Restrictions on Ownership by Foreigners.—In general, foreign individuals and foreign companies are prohibited from owning land in Thailand. Companies incorporated in Thailand which are more than 50% Thai-owned may legally own land. If company has significant foreign equity, it will be investigated by Land Department to determine whether or not foreigner is true owner of land before company is allowed to register purchase of land.

Exception to foreign ownership rule applies to Board of Investment and Industrial Estate Authority of Thailand projects. Under these projects, special privileges are given to some companies to buy land. In addition, foreign oil companies meeting requirements of Petroleum Act may also own land.

Foreigners may own building on leased land because there are no restrictions on building ownership. Foreigners can lease land, construct building, office tower, apartment or house on leased land and own structure.

Condominium Ownership.—Formerly, foreigners could not legally own condominiums because of issue concerning common ownership of land on which condominium was situated. Condominium Act (No. 2), B.E. 2534 (A.D. 1991) now entitles certain groups of foreigners (both individuals and juristic persons) to acquire condominium units in Thailand, provided that foreign ownership in condominium project does not exceed, in aggregate, 40% of total area of all units in condominium building, and foreigners present required documentation. See also topic Aliens, subhead Civil Rights.

Documentation.—

Registration.—Land transactions in provinces are registered in land office in province where land is located. Transactions for land located in Bangkok area are registered at district land offices. All land transactions should be recorded in written document, have title deed and be registered. Since unsurveyed land is not registered, other documents are used to show ownership.

Land Documents.—Following documents evidence land ownership or possession rights.

Title Deed or "chanote" purest form of land ownership. It ensures easy transfer and is issued mainly in urban areas. One original set is kept in district land office where registration of land transfer takes place and other original set is given to land owner.

Confirmed Certificate of Use or "ngor sor saam gor" certifies right to use land and is often issued pending title deed. Transfer of certificate is mainly completed at district land office or branch district level, as case may be.

Certificate of Use or "ngor sor saam" is similar to confirmed certificate of use, but lacks completion of formalities, such as provision of aerial photo of land. Transfer of certificate requires posting of intent at provincial land office or branch land office,

REAL PROPERTY . . . *continued*
district land office or branch district office, house of village headman, location of land, and municipal office (if land is in municipality). There is 30-day waiting period before transfer is registered.

Certificate of Possession or "sor kor neung" only recognizes possession and does not imply ownership rights with possession. The certificate is nontransferable; however, person in possession may transfer physical possession. This certificate is required for issuance of Certificate of Use and is most common in rural areas. Tax receipt is evidence of possession but does not confer ownership rights with possession. It is useful when applying for Certificate of Possession.

Condominium unit title deed or "nangsue kammasit hong-chut" is evidence of ownership of condominium unit. It is of similar importance to land title deed. Administrative procedures relating to registration and issuance of land title deed are applicable to registration and issuance of condominium unit title deed.

SALES:

Contract of Sale.—Sale is contract whereby seller transfers ownership of property to buyer, and buyer agrees to pay to seller price therefor. (C.C.C. 453).

Sale of immovable property, as well as sale of certain movables, i.e. ships or vessels of six tons and over, steam launches or motorboats of five tons and over, floating houses and beasts of burden, is void if not made in writing and registered with competent official. Agreement to sell or to buy any of aforesaid property or promise to sell such property is enforceable by action if there is written evidence signed by party liable or deposit is given or there is partial performance. (C.C.C. 456).

Contract of sale of movable property with agreed price of Baht 500 or more is under same requirement. (C.C.C. 456). Fees for contract of sale, if any, shall be borne equally by both parties. (C.C.C. 457).

Transfer of Title.—Generally, title to property sold is transferred to buyer at time of execution of contract. (C.C.C. 458). If contract of sale is subject to condition or to time clause, title of property is not transferred until condition is fulfilled or time has arrived. (C.C.C. 459). For sale of unascertained property, title is not transferred until property has been marked, counted, weighed, measured or selected, or its identity has otherwise been rendered certain. (C.C.C. 460).

Delivery.—Seller is bound to deliver property sold to buyer. (C.C.C. 461). If contract of sale provides that property sold shall be sent from one place to another, delivery takes place at moment when property is delivered to carrier. (C.C.C. 463). Costs of transportation of property sold to place other than place of performance are to be borne by buyer. (C.C.C. 464). Buyer is bound to take delivery of property sold and to pay price in accordance with terms of contract sale. (C.C.C. 486). If time is fixed for delivery of property sold, it is presumed that same time is fixed for payment of price. (C.C.C. 490). Action for liability for deficiency or excess in delivery must be taken within one year from date of delivery. (C.C.C. 467). When there is no stipulation of time for payment, seller is entitled to retain property sold until price is paid (C.C.C. 468) and other than using ordinary remedies for nonperformance, seller can notify buyer who is in default, in writing, to pay price and expenses within reasonable time, then if buyer does not comply with notice, seller can sell property by public auction (C.C.C. 470). Seller shall deduct from net proceeds of public auction what is due to him for price and expenses and deliver forthwith any surplus to buyer. (C.C.C. 471).

Liability for Defect.—Seller is liable for any defect of property sold which impairs either its value or its fitness for ordinary purposes, or for purpose of contract (C.C.C. 472) except where buyer knew of defect at time of sale or would have known if such care as might be expected from person of ordinary prudence had been exercised, or if defect was apparent at time of delivery and buyer accepted property without reservation, or if property was sold by auction (C.C.C. 473). If buyer has discovered defects in property sold, he is entitled to withhold price or part thereof unless seller provides proper security. (C.C.C. 488). Buyer is also entitled to withhold price in whole or in part, if he is threatened or has good reason to believe that he is about to be threatened, with action by mortgagee or by person claiming property sold, until seller causes such threat to cease or gives proper security. (C.C.C. 489). Action for liability for defect must be taken within one year after delivery of defective property. (C.C.C. 474).

Liability for Interference With Right of Peaceful Possession.—Seller is liable for consequences of any interference with right of peaceful possession of buyer by any person having right over property sold, except where buyer knew at time of sale that right of person causing disturbance existed. (C.C.C. 475, 476).

Agreement for exemption of liability for defects or disturbance is enforceable. (C.C.C. 483).

SHIPPING:

In 1991, Thailand enacted Carriage of Goods by Sea Act, B.E. 2534 (A.D. 1991). Previously, Thai court applied Civil and Commercial Code by analogy to matter concerned. Other laws controlling maritime matters include Navigation in Thai Territorial Waters Act, B.E. 2456 (A.D. 1913) (N.T.W.A.) as am'd, Thai Vessels Act, B.E. 2481 (A.D. 1938) as am'd, Mercantile Marine Promotion Act, B.E. 2521 (A.D. 1978), Prevention of Ship Collision Act, B.E. 2522 (A.D. 1979), Arrest of Vessels Act, B.E. 2534 (A.D. 1991), and Mortgage of Vessel and Sea Preferential Rights Act, B.E. 2537 (A.D. 1994) (M.V.S.P.R.A.). The three newest acts are detailed below.

Carriage of Goods by Sea Act, B.E. 2534 (A.D. 1991).—Based on terms from Hague Rules, Hague-Visby Rules and Hamburg Rules, Act became effective in Feb. 1992. Act covers definitions of terms related to maritime industry, scope of application, duties and rights of carrier and shipper when goods are carried by sea, liabilities of carrier, exclusion of liability of carrier, limitation of liability of carrier, period of prescription, bills of landing, etc.

Scope of Application.—Generally, Act applies to carriage of goods by sea from within Thai waters to outside Thai waters, and vice versa. Bill of lading may provide that law of another jurisdiction applies; however, if one of parties is Thai natural or juristic person, Act will automatically apply.

Duties and Rights of Carrier.—Under Act, carrier has duties to make vessel seaworthy, to take care of cargo, to issue bill of lading, and to notify consignee of arrival of goods at destination. Carrier is entitled to carry goods on deck where there is agreement with shipper to that effect, or there is usage of trade entitling such carriage, or there are laws or regulations entitling it. Carrier has right to freight or accessories of freight when goods have been carried to port of destination or to place agreed upon to be destination and is ready to deliver goods unless there is term in bill of lading or agreement set forth in contract for carriage of goods by sea. Carrier is also empowered to retain goods until he has been paid both freight and accessories of freight or until consignee has given reasonable security.

Liabilities of Carrier.—Generally, carrier shall be liable for damage resulting from loss of or damage to goods which have been handed over to him by shipper and from any delay in delivery while goods were in his custody. However, carrier shall not be liable for loss, damage or delay in delivery if it can be proved that such loss, damage or delay in delivery arose or resulted from exclusion of liability of carrier similar to catalogue of exceptions under Hague-Visby Rules. In addition, carrier shall not be liable for loss, damage or delay in delivery caused by or resulting from: (a) fire, unless claimant can prove that fire arose from fault or neglect on part of carrier or servant or agent of carrier; (b) carrier's taking measures that could reasonably be required of him to put out fire and to avoid or to mitigate consequences thereof, unless such loss is proved by claimant to have resulted from fault of or neglect by carrier, his servants or agents in taking such measures; (c) carrier's taking measures to save human life or taking reasonable measures to save property at sea; and (d) any special risks usually inherent in carriage of live animals, or from special nature of animals which did not result from fault or neglect on part of carrier or his servant or agents.

Limitation of Liability of Carrier.—Liability of carrier for damage resulting from loss of or damage to goods is limited to Baht 10,000 per unit of carriage or Baht 30 per kilogram of net weight of goods, whichever amount is larger. Liability of carrier for delay in delivery of goods is limited to amount equivalent to two and a half times freight payable for delayed goods, but sum must not exceed total freight payable under contract of carriage of goods by sea.

Period of Prescription.—Any right to claim for damages arising from loss of or damage to goods, or for delay in delivery of goods carried under contract of carriage of goods by sea is time barred if judicial or arbitral proceeding has not been instituted within period of one year from date on which carrier delivered goods or, where no delivery was made, from date on which goods were stipulated to have been delivered or after date on which it would have been reasonable to require delivery.

Bill of Lading means document which carrier issues to shipper under contract for carriage of goods by sea as evidence that carrier has taken goods specified in bill of lading into his custody or has loaded goods and undertakes to deliver goods to person entitled to receive them upon surrender of bill of lading. Therefore, bill of lading functions as (a) receipt for goods shipped; (b) evidence of contract of carriage; and (c) document of title.

Arrest of Vessels Act, B.E. 2534 (A.D. 1991).—Enacted in 1991, this Act provides legal means for Thai creditor to bring successful action against foreign shipowner or, at least, have subject vessel arrested until merits of claim are decided. There are several grounds on which creditor can request that court issue warrant for arrest of vessel, including contracts for use of vessel, contracts for carriage of goods by sea, charges for port facilities and mortgage of vessel. In order to seek arrest of vessel in Thailand, complainant must be domiciled in Thailand and vessel must either be already in Thai waters or about to enter Thai waters.

Application for arrest of vessel is brought by ex parte motion. This allows for timely arrest of vessel, often same day motion is filed. Arrest procedure provides creditor with some security for his claim while case is argued on its merits and provides creditor something to collect on if his complaint is found valid. When ordering arrest of vessel, court is required to stipulate amount shipowner can pledge in lieu of having vessel arrested. Vessel can be released against bond issued by Bank of Thailand or bank guarantee. Court may require that complainant post funds as well, to guard against frivolous actions.

Mortgage of Vessel and Sea Preferential Rights Act, B.E. 2537 (A.D. 1994).—This is newest law relating to maritime. It became effective in June 1994. Act deals with two main issues: (1) mortgage of vessel; and (2) sea preferential right.

Mortgage of vessel deals with general provisions, execution of contract and registration of mortgage of vessel, and effects and enforcement of mortgages. Act requires that contract for mortgage of vessel be made in writing and registered in accordance with criteria and procedures prescribed in ministerial regulations. M.V.S.P.R.A. defines vessel as vessel of size of 60 tons gross or more powered by machine or machines, regardless of whether it uses other forms of power or not, and has characteristics for seagoing use in accordance with laws controlling vessel inspection issued under law governing navigation of vessels in Thai territorial waters. Provisions of M.V.S.P.R.A. extent to enforcement of mortgage on non-Thai vessels. Act provides that contract in which owner of non-Thai vessel has committed his vessel to another person as guarantee for payment of debts shall be held to be mortgage which may be enforced in accordance with this Act if it is subject to following conditions: (a) contract made with full validity under laws of country in which vessel is registered; (b) contract has been registered in register which general public is permitted to inspect at office of state which has duty to register such contracts; and (c) it is case where plaintiff may present plaint to court in accordance with C.P.C., law governing detention of vessel, or other laws. Therefore, mortgage of vessel under foreign flag registered outside Thailand but subject to M.V.S.P.R.A. may be enforced in Thailand by mortgagee. Thai court may order mortgagor or mortgagee to sell vessel or order public auction. If mortgaged vessel is lost or damaged, coverage extends to include: compensation for tort resulting in loss of or damage to vessel or items covered by vessel mortgage rights; general average for proportion which shipowner is entitled to claim for it; salvage cost; and compensation from insurance coverage. Mortgagee possesses right to receive payment for debts from mortgaged ship before preferential creditors under C.C.C. and other creditors of owner of vessel.

Holder of sea preferential rights has right to receive outstanding amounts due to him from vessel, if subject to enforcement of sea preferential rights, before other creditors, regardless of whether or not debtor of right to claim is owner of vessel. Sea preferential right shall be valid without any registration and shall take priority over mortgage rights under this Act as well as preferential rights under C.C.C. Sea preferential rights

See Topical Index in front part of this volume.

SHIPPING . . . *continued*
include: claim for crew's wages; compensation for loss of life or injury to any person arising from work operations of ship; claim for vessel salvage; claim for tortious act arising from work operations of vessel, etc. Where sea preferential rights are transferred, transferee shall have same sea preferential rights as those of transferor. Where sea preferential rights have arisen before any transfer of ownership of vessel, such sea preferential rights are not extinguished by such transfer, unless transferee has notified sea preferential rights creditors to submit their claims to transferee within prescribed period, but not less than 60 days from date of notification. If sea preferential rights creditors file to submit their claims to transferee within prescribed period, sea preferential rights shall have ended.

TAXATION:

Taxes are imposed both at national and local levels, with central government being main taxing authority. Ministry of Finance administers majority of tax collections through its three departments: Customs Department which is responsible for collection of import and export duties; Revenue Department which is in charge of collection of income tax, value added tax, specific business tax and stamp duty; and Excise Department which collects excise tax. Property tax and municipal tax are collected by local governments. In general, tax administration follows self-assessment system. Taxpayer has legal duty to declare his income and pay tax to authorities. Declaration and tax payment are regarded to be correct; however, additional assessments may be made by authorities in case of failure to file tax returns or filing of false or inadequate tax returns. Appeal against additional assessments is allowed.

Personal Income Tax.—Individual, whether Thai citizen or alien, who lives in Thailand for one or more periods totaling 180 days or more in any tax year (calendar year) is, for tax purposes, deemed resident of Thailand and subject to tax on all assessable income derived from sources within Thailand, whether such income is paid within or outside Thailand, and on assessable income derived from foreign sources to extent that such income is brought into Thailand in year in which income is received. Nonresident individual is subject to tax only on assessable income from Thai sources (regardless of place of payment). Non-juristic partnerships (unregistered ordinary partnerships) and non-juristic body of persons are also subject to personal income tax.

Capital gains arising from transfer of assets are treated as ordinary income and must be included in assessable income except for those exempt from personal income tax such as proceeds of sale of movable property acquired by bequest or acquired with no intention to trade or make profit and capital gains from sale of securities, not in form of debenture or bonds, in Stock Exchange of Thailand.

Exclusions from assessable income are certain types of income such as moving expenses received by employee to assume employment for first time or to return to his place of origin at termination of employment, per diem or transportation expenses spent by employee exclusively and wholly for carrying out his duties, inheritance, scholarships, etc.

Deductions are: (a) for income from employment or service rendered, standard deduction of 40% but not exceeding Baht 60,000; (b) for other categories of income, taxpayer may elect between standard deductions which range from 10% to 85% depending on nature of income and actual expenditure incurred in deriving such income.

Allowances, among others, are: (a) Baht 30,000 for taxpayer; (b) Baht 30,000 for taxpayer's spouse; (c) Baht 15,000 for each child (who is not over 25 years of age and is still studying) plus Baht 2,000 for each child's education (in Thailand), provided if there is more than one child and any of children was born on or after Jan 1, 1979, exemptions may be claimed for no more than three children; (d) insurance premiums for taxpayer's life insurance policy covering period of at least ten years taken from insurance company in Thailand, not exceeding Baht 10,000; (e) interest paid on loan granted for acquiring houses, not exceeding Baht 10,000; (f) contributions to provident fund, not exceeding Baht 10,000.

Personal income tax rates are at progressive rate ranging from 5% on net income not exceeding Baht 100,000 to 37% on net income exceeding Baht 4,000,000. Net income is arrived at by deducting all applicable deductions and allowances from assessable income. Tax payable of taxpayer having assessable income, other than employment income, amounting to Baht 60,000 or more must be minimum of 0.5% of total amount of assessable income.

Tax credit in respect of dividend is permitted for individual domiciled in Thailand and receiving dividend from any company organized under Thai law. Credit is three-sevenths of dividend. Such credit shall be first included as assessable income and then deducted from total amount of tax.

Corporate Income Tax.—Companies and juristic partnerships organized under Thai law (hereinafter "Thai companies") are subject to taxation on their worldwide income, both from sources within Thailand and from foreign sources (see also topic Juristic Persons). Companies and juristic partnerships organized under foreign laws (hereinafter "foreign companies") are subject to taxation only on income from sources within Thailand. Revenue Code takes view that if foreign companies carry on business in Thailand, their income arising from or in consequence of that business constitutes Thai source income. Foreign company is deemed to be carrying on business in Thailand if it has employee, representative, or go-between in Thailand to carry on its business and thereby derives income or gains in Thailand. Therefore, foreign company that establishes branch office and derives income or gains in Thailand therefrom is deemed to be carrying on business in Thailand and subject to corporate income tax for its branch office's net profits in Thailand. Wholly-owned subsidiaries of foreign companies established as companies or juristic partnerships under Thai law are deemed Thai, not foreign, companies and subject to corporate income tax. Joint venture, defined by Revenue Code as business or profit-seeking enterprise carried on jointly by company and another company, by company and juristic partnership, or by company and/or juristic partnership on one hand, and individual, non-juristic body of persons, ordinary partnership or another juristic person on other hand, is also subject to corporate income tax. Foreign companies engaged in international transportation fall within scope of corporate income tax but have special provisions attached to them.

Corporate income tax rate of 30% is, with few exceptions, imposed on worldwide net profits received by Thai companies and on Thai source net profits received by foreign companies during given tax year (accounting period). Foreign companies engaged in international transportation are subject to tax at rate of 3% of gross ticket receipts collected in Thailand for transportation of passengers and 3% of gross freight charges collected anywhere for transportation of goods from Thailand in lieu of tax on net profits.

Dividends received by Thai companies or foreign companies carrying on business in Thailand are taxable as ordinary income. However, Thai company is entitled to include in its taxable income only one-half of dividends received from another Thai company, provided that shares have been held for period of at least three months before and three months after receipt of such dividends ("holding period"). Thai company will be exempt from taxation on all dividends received from another Thai company if recipient company holds at least 25% of total shares with voting rights in payer company and has so held shares in complying with holding period, and payer does not hold any share in recipient company whether directly or indirectly. Thai company listed on Stock Exchange of Thailand is exempt from taxation on all dividends received from another Thai company if they comply with just holding period.

Business expenses and depreciation allowances generally incurred by nature of business are allowed at rates ranging from 5% to 100% per annum as deductions from gross income in order to determine net profits. However, reserves not required by law, private expenses, gifts to charitable institutions exceeding 2% of net profits, donation for education or athletics exceeding 2% of net profits, non-maintenance capital expenditure, penalties or fines are not allowed as deductions.

Net losses may be carried forward for five accounting periods to offset against future profits. Loss carrybacks are not allowed.

Income Tax on Foreign Companies Not Carrying on Business in Thailand.—Foreign companies which are not deemed to be carrying on business in Thailand but deriving assessable income in Thailand such as interest, dividends, royalties, professional fees, etc. are subject to income tax in form of withholding tax based on gross income. Applicable tax rate is 15% except for dividends which are subject to withholding tax at rate of 10%. Tax must be withheld at source and at time of payment by payer of such assessable income. See also topic Treaties, subhead Avoidance of Double Taxation Treaties.

Additional Taxes on Remittance of Branch's Profits.—In addition to 30% corporate income tax on net profits, branch's remittance of profit abroad to its head office is subject to taxation at rate of 10% of amount actually or deemed remitted. This amount of tax must be withheld by branch.

Inheritance Tax.—None.

Estate Tax.—None.

Gift Tax.—None.

Business Tax.—Such tax has been replaced by value added tax and specific business tax since Jan. 1, 1992.

Value Added Tax (VAT).—Tax is generally imposed at single rate of 7% (this 7% tax already includes municipal tax which is charged at rate of one-ninth of VAT rate) and applies, with few exceptions, to goods and services supplied in, or imported into, Thailand. Trader will charge VAT on sale of goods or provision of services to consumer (output tax). VAT paid by such trader itself to other traders for purchase of goods or services (input tax) is then deducted and balance remitted to Revenue Department. Thus, tax will accrue at each stage only on "value added" to goods or services in that stage. Under VAT system, tax will be eventually borne by ultimate consumer and trader is regarded as collector of tax on behalf of Revenue Department. Exclusions from VAT are business subject to specific business tax, business necessary for maintenance of life and social welfare (i.e. health care services, educational services, domestic transportation, sale of unprocessed agricultural products), cultural services, religious and charitable services. Small-scale traders whose annual turnover does not exceed Baht 600,000 are exempt from VAT. However, those traders whose annual turnover exceeds Baht 600,000 but not Baht 1,200,000 may select to pay 1.5% tax on gross receipts or pay 7% VAT. If traders select to pay 1.5% tax on gross receipts, they are not entitled to offset this tax against their VAT paid for purchase of goods or services and their customers will not be able to claim any tax credit (input tax) in respect of purchase of goods or services from such traders. Traders whose annual turnover exceeds Baht 1,200,000 are subject to 7% VAT. Zero percent rate applies to certain businesses such as export of goods or services, international transportation by sea or air, sale of goods and services to United Nations-related organizations or embassies, etc. Traders who do only zero-rated supply business will not be required to collect VAT on their supplies, but can refund all VAT paid for purchase of goods and services from other traders. Services provided by traders residing abroad and utilized in Thailand are regarded as being rendered in Thailand and subject to 7% VAT. Recipient of such service must remit VAT to Revenue Department when paying service fees to overseas traders.

Specific Business Tax.—This tax is imposed on certain types of businesses whose "value added" is difficult to define such as banking, finance, credit foncier, insurance, pawnshop, real estate, etc. Such businesses are considered to be outside VAT system and not subject to VAT. Specific business tax is computed on monthly gross receipt at rates varying from 0.1% to 3% (rates do not include municipal tax). Traders liable to specific business tax may have to pay VAT on business activities that are not directly related to specific businesses and on business activities that are directly related to specific businesses but are prescribed by law as business subject to VAT (i.e. provision of credit card services, consultancy services, securities brokerage and agency services, securities underwriting services, letting out movable properties on hire, etc.). Traders residing outside Thailand may be liable to specific business tax if they carry on business through place of business, agent or representative, or employee in Thailand.

Municipal Tax.—When specific business tax is paid, municipal tax at rate of 10% of specific business tax is imposed on taxpayer. When VAT is paid, rate already includes municipal tax which is charged at rate of one-ninth of VAT rate (1/9 of 6.3%).

Petroleum Income Tax.—Income derived from petroleum operation of company owning interest in petroleum concession granted by Thai government and of company purchasing oil for export from concession holder are subject to income tax imposed by Petroleum Income Tax Act, B.E. 2514 (A.D. 1971) as am'd. Taxes levied by Revenue

See Topical Index in front part of this volume.

TAXATION . . . *continued*
Code including tax on remittance of profits and dividends are not applicable to such income. Income from petroleum operation includes gross income from sale or disposal of petroleum, gross income arising from transfer of any property or right related to petroleum business and any other income arising from conducting petroleum business. Value of petroleum delivered as payment of royalty to government must also be included in company's income from petroleum operation. Deductions, among others, are royalties, both in cash and in kind, paid to Thai government and head office expenditure reasonably allocatable to petroleum business of company. Petroleum income tax is chargeable on net profits at rate of 50%. Net profits for petroleum income tax is computed in same manner as corporate income tax but net losses may be carried forward for ten accounting periods.

Stamp duty is levied on 28 classes of documents and transactions listed in Stamp Duty Schedule of Revenue Code such as promissory notes, bills of exchange, leases, powers of attorney, letters of credit, checks, bills of lading, etc. Rates vary according to classification of transaction contained in instrument.

Excise Tax.—Tax is imposed on selected goods (mainly luxury goods) such as gasoline and petroleum products, tobacco, liquor, soft drinks, playing cards, crystal glasses, perfume and cosmetic products, vessels, air conditioners not over 72,000 BTU, passenger cars with less than ten seats, etc. Excise tax will be computed according to Excise Tax Tariff on ad valorem basis or at specific rate, whichever is greater. All goods subject to excise tax remain subject to VAT.

Customs duty is mainly imposed on imported and selected export goods specified by Law on Customs Tariff. Most tariffs are ad valorem. In general, invoice price is basis for computation of duty and duty is normally applied to C.I.F. value.

Property Tax.—There are two kinds of property tax in Thailand: house and land tax and local development tax. Under House and Land Tax Act, B.E. 2475 (A.D. 1932) as am'd, tax is imposed on owners of house, building, structure or land which is rented or otherwise put to commercial use. Taxable property under house and land tax includes houses not occupied by owner, industrial and commercial buildings and land used in connection therewith. Tax rate is 12.5% of actual or assessed annual rental value of property. Under Local Development Tax Act, B.E. 2508 (A.D. 1965) as am'd, tax is imposed upon person who either owns land or is in possession of land. Tax rates vary according to assessed value of land. Allowances are granted for land utilized for personal dwellings, raising of livestock and cultivation of crops by owner. Extent of allowances differs according to location of land.

Signboard Tax.—Under Signboard Tax Act, B.E. 2510 (A.D. 1967) as am'd, tax is levied on signboards showing names, symbols or marks of business or advertisement. Rates specified in Signboard Tax Act are computed on signboard size ranging from Baht 1 to Baht 40 per 500 square centimeters.

TRADEMARKS AND TRADENAMES:

Trademarks were first regulated under Trademark Act, B.E. 2474 (A.D. 1931), which was replaced by Trademark Act, B.E. 2534 (A.D. 1991). Act provides legal protection through registration of trademark, service mark, certification mark, collective mark, and trademark/service mark license/registered user.

Any interested person or juristic person who is proprietor of mark can file application for registration with Department of Intellectual Property.

Registrable Marks.—Marks shall include photograph, drawing, picture, brand, name, word, letter, numeral, signature or any combination thereof but not product design which is registrable under Patent Act.

Registrable mark must: (1) be distinctive and contain or consist of at least one of following particulars: (a) name of juristic person, first name and surname (except well-known surname) of individual, or tradename presented in special manner, (b) signature of applicant for registration or some predecessor in his business or of another (used with permission), (c) invented letter, numeral or word, (d) word or clause having no direct reference to character or quality of goods and not being geographical name, (e) photograph of applicant or another person (used with permission), (f) invented device, and (g) any other distinctive mark; (2) not be forbidden under Act; and (3) not be identical or so similar to another trademark as to be confusing or misleading to public. Certain items such as royal names and royal monograms, official and national flags, etc., are prohibited for use as trademarks. Marks which do not fall within descriptions in (a) to (g) above may become registrable through prior long and extensive use.

Registration.—Application for registration of trademark may be made for particular kind of goods which must be clearly declared. International Classification of Goods and Services was adopted to replace Thailand's national classification of goods. Full class heading of International Classification of Goods and Services cannot be used, i.e. application for "whole class" cannot be filed. Goods must individually be specified. Separate application must be made for each class of goods.

Trademark shall be registrable only if proprietor or his representative has office or any place of business in Thailand which registrar can contact. After registration is deemed acceptable by registrar, notice is sent to applicant for payment of publication fee within 30 days of receipt of notice. After application proceeds to publication, interested parties have 90 days from date of publication to oppose registration of mark. If no opposition is filed within this time, mark may proceed to registration. Notice is then sent to applicant for payment of registration fee within 30 days from date of receipt of notice. Registration of trademark is valid for ten years from date application was filed. Registration of trademark may be renewed for further period of ten years within 90 days before date of expiration of original registration, or of latest renewal of registration, as case may be. Process may be repeated indefinitely.

Assignment.—Rights to trademark application or registered trademark are transferable and inheritable. Proprietor of registered trademark may grant license to other persons to use his trademark for any or all of goods for which it was registered. Trademark license agreement must be in writing and registered with Department of Intellectual Property.

Protection Afforded.—When trademark is registered, proprietor of trademark shall have exclusive right to its use with goods for which registration was granted.

Infringement.—Act imposes penalties on person who forges or imitates any other person's trademark, service mark, certification mark or collective mark already registered in Thailand. Punishment includes both imprisonment of maximum four years and fine. However, civil action for damages for trademark infringement is based on law of tort under C.C.C. Action for damages for trademark infringement cannot be taken if trademark is not registered in Thailand.

Unregistered Trademark.—According to Act, owner of unregistered trademark is not entitled to institute any legal proceedings in court to prevent use or to recover damages for infringement. Certain protection for owner of unregistered trademark is also afforded by Penal Code which imposes penalties on use of name, figure, artificial mark or wording in carrying on trade of another person or causes same to appear on merchandise, packing covering, advertisement, price list, commercial letter or like in order to make public believe that it is merchandise or trade of such person. However, under C.C.C. owner of unregistered trademark has right to institute court case against any person for passing-off goods as those of true proprietor.

Owner of trademark cannot use letter "R" in circle on imported goods if trademark is not registered in Thailand. Importer is subject to punishment of both imprisonment and fine.

Tradenames.—Although there is no law which specifically governs tradenames, Penal Code provides that it is offence to use other person's name, figure, artificial mark or any wording used in carrying on trade in order to deceive public that one's trade is that of such other person. One's imitation of sign-board or the like of other person's trading premise situated nearby which is likely to make public believe that his trading premise is that of such other person is also offence under Penal Code. Unauthorized use of other person's tradename may also be considered intentional tort under C.C.C. and entitles owner of said tradename to civil action for damages.

TREATIES:

Thailand is signatory to several multilateral treaties, conventions and agreements; following are among those concerning commerce, trade and foreign investment:

General Treaties.—(1) Berne Convention for the Protection of Literary and Artistic works, Sept. 9, 1886; (2) Convention for the Pacific Settlement of International Disputes, Oct. 18, 1907; (3) International Air Services Transit Agreement, Dec. 7, 1944; (4) Convention on International Civil Aviation, Dec. 7, 1944; (5) Charter of the United Nations and Statute of the International Court of Justice, June 26, 1945; (6) Constitution of the United Nations Food and Agriculture Organization, Oct. 16, 1945; (7) Articles of Agreement of the International Bank for Reconstruction and Development, Dec. 27, 1945; (8) Articles of Agreement of the International Monetary Fund, Dec. 27, 1945; (9) General Agreement on Tariffs and Trade (GATT), Oct. 30, 1947; (10) Convention on the International Recognition of Rights in Aircraft, June 19, 1948; (11) Convention Establishing a Customs Co-Operation Council, Dec. 15, 1950; (12) Articles of Agreement of the International Finance Corporation, May 25, 1955; (13) Convention on Fishing and Conservation of Living Resources of the High Seas, Apr. 29, 1958; (14) Convention on the High Seas, Apr. 29, 1958; (15) Convention on the Continental Shelf, Apr. 29, 1958; (16) Convention on the Territorial Sea and Contiguous Zone, Apr. 29, 1958; (17) Convention on the Recognition and Enforcement of Foreign Arbitral Awards, June 10, 1958; (18) Articles of Agreement of the International Development Association, Jan. 26, 1960; (19) Articles of Agreement Establishing the Asian Development Bank, Dec. 4, 1965; (20) Operating Agreement Relating to the International Telecommunications Satellite Organization (INTELSAT), Aug. 20, 1971; (21) Agreement Regarding International Trade in Textiles, Dec. 20, 1973; (22) General Agreement on Tariffs and Trade (GATT), Oct. 20, 1982; (23) Protocol Extending Arrangement Regarding International Trade in Textiles of Dec. 20, 1973, July 31, 1986; (24) Agreement Establishing the International Fund for Agricultural Development, June 13, 1976; (25) Constitution of the United Nations Industrial Development Organization, Apr. 8, 1979; (26) International Coffee Agreement, Sept. 16, 1982; (27) International Telecommunications Convention, Nov. 6, 1982; (28) Convention on the Law of the Sea 1982; (29) International Sugar Agreement 1987, Sept. 11, 1987; (30) Basel Convention for the Control of Transboundary Movements of Hazardous Wastes and their Disposal, Mar. 22, 1990; (31) Agreement on the Common Effective Preferential Tariff (CEPT) Scheme for the ASEAN Free Trade Area (AFTA), Jan. 28, 1992; (32) Framework Agreement on Enhancing ASEAN Economic Cooperation, Jan. 28, 1992; (33) United Nations Framework Convention on Climate Change, May 9, 1992; (34) Convention on Biological Diversity, June 5, 1992, (signed but not ratified); (35) Agreement on Judicial Assistance in Civil and Commercial Matters and Cooperation in Arbitration between Thailand and People's Republic of China, Mar. 16, 1994; (36) WTO Agreement, Apr. 15, 1994 of which following agreements are integral parts of it: Annex A: Multilateral. General Agreement on Tariffs and Trade 1994, Agreement on Agriculture, Agreement on the Application of Sanitary and Phytosanitary Measures, Agreement on Textiles and Clothing, Agreement on Technical Barriers to Trade, Agreement on Trade-Related Investment Measures, Agreement on Implementation of Article VI of the General Agreement on Tariffs and Trade 1994, Agreement on Implementation of Article VII of the General Agreement on Tariffs and Trade 1994, Agreement on Reshipment Inspection, Agreement on Rules of Origin, Agreement on Import Licensing Procedures, Agreement on Subsidies and Countervailing Measures, Agreement on Safeguards, Annex B: General Agreement on Trade in Services, Annex C: Agreement on Trade-Related Aspects of Intellectual Property Rights; (37) Convention and Operating Agreement on International Maritime Satellite Organization (INMARSAT), Dec. 14, 1994; and (38) Protocol Amendment to Memorandum of Understanding Brand-to-Brand Complementation on the Automotive Industry Under the Basic Agreement on ASEAN Industrial Complementation, Mar. 1995; (39) The International Natural Rubber Agreement 1995; (40) The ASEAN Framework Agreement on Intellectual Property Cooperation, Dec. 1995; (41) The Southeast Asia Nuclear Weapon Free Zone Treaty, Dec. 1995.

See also Selected International Conventions section, for text of Convention on the Recognition and Enforcement of Foreign Arbitral Awards, June 10, 1958.

Trade and Investment Agreements.—(1) Thailand has international trade agreements with numerous countries, including Argentina, Australia, Austria, Bangladesh, Brazil, Bulgaria, Cambodia, Canada, Chile, China, Czech Republic, Egypt, France,

TREATIES . . . *continued*
Hungary, India, Iran, Iraq, Japan, Kuwait, Laos, Myanmar, the Netherlands, New Zealand, North Korea, Pakistan, Poland, Romania, Senegal, South Korea, Spain, Taiwan, Tunisia, Turkey, Uruguay, Vietnam and Yugoslavia. (2) Thailand has signed investment treaties with several countries, including Bangladesh, Belgium, Brunei, Cambodia, People's Republic of China, Finland, Germany, Hungary, Indonesia, Italy, Laos, Luxembourg, Malaysia, the Netherlands, Peru, Philippines, Poland, Romania, Singapore, South Korea, Sri Lanka, Taiwan, the U.K. and Vietnam. (3) The Treaty of Amity and Economic Relations between the United States and Thailand, signed on May 29, 1966 and ratified at Washington D.C. on May 8, 1968, allows U.S. nationals and companies to establish companies or branch offices in Thailand for trade and investment. See topic Companies, subhead Foreign Companies.

Avoidance of Double Taxation Treaties.—Thailand has signed bilateral agreements concerning double taxation with number of other countries to eliminate or mitigate double taxation of income. These countries are Australia, Austria, Belgium, Canada, China, Czech Republic, Denmark, Finland, France, Germany, Hungary, India, Indonesia, Italy, Japan, South Korea, Malaysia, the Netherlands, Norway, Pakistan, the Philippines, Poland, Singapore, Sri Lanka, Sweden, the U.K., and Vietnam. Thailand has signed (but not yet ratified) double taxation with following countries: (1) Israel, (2) Luxembourg, (3) Switzerland, (4) Tunisia, (5) USA. Thailand is currently negotiating double taxation agreements with Bangladesh, Cyprus, Greece, Kuwait, Laos, Malta, Mexico, New Zealand, Romania, Spain, United Arab Emirates.

TRUSTS:

Testamentary trusts and trusts effective during lifetime of settlor are prohibited and may not be created, whether directly or indirectly, by will or juristic act. (C.C.C. 1686). Other kinds of trusts and trustees are unknown in Thailand.

WILLS:

Wills may be made by persons of at least 15 years of age. (C.C.C. 25). Testator who is married may not dispose by will of more than his or her portion of community property. (C.C.C. 1481).

Forms.—Will made by Thai national in foreign country may be made either in any of hereinafter prescribed forms in which case Thai Diplomatic or Consular Officer will have same powers and duties as competent official (nai amphoe) or in forms prescribed by law of such foreign country. (C.C.C. 1667). According to C.C.C., will may be made in any of the following forms:

Allograph will is will made in writing and dated and affixed with signatures of testator and at least two witnesses. (C.C.C. 1656).

Holograph will is will entirely written, dated and signed by hand of testator himself. (C.C.C. 1657).

Open will is will made by testator's declaration of his will to competent official (nai amphoe) in presence of at least two witnesses. Such declaration must be written down and read aloud by said official to testator and witnesses. Will so written must be signed by testator who confirms that it corresponds with his declaration and by witnesses and countersigned, dated and affixed with his seal by said official. (C.C.C. 1658).

Closed will is will privately prepared and signed by testator and states name and domicile of writer, if not entirely written by testator. Will must be enclosed in sealed envelope signed by testator across place of closure and testator must, in presence of competent official (nai amphoe) and at least two witnesses, declare that enclosed document contains his testamentary dispositions. Said official must make minute of such declaration, state date thereof and affix his seal and signature on such envelope which must also be signed by testator and witnesses. (C.C.C. 1660).

Oral will is will made orally in presence of at least two witnesses by testator who is prevented from making his will in any of above forms by exceptional circumstance such as imminent danger of death, epidemic or war. Oral will is not valid if not reduced to writing by competent official (nai amphoe) from statement of said witnesses who, without delay after oral will was made, appear before him. Official's statement of will must be signed by said witnesses. (C.C.C. 1663). However, whenever testator is again able to make will in any other form, oral will so made becomes null and void one month after he has regained such capacity. (C.C.C. 1664).

Military will is will which may be made in Thailand and foreign countries at time when state of war exists in Thailand, by military men or persons acting in connection with armed forces. Military will must take form of open will, closed will or oral will and military officer or official of commissioned rank will have same powers and duties, if will is made in Thailand, as those of competent official (nai amphoe) or, if will is made in foreign country, as those of Thai Diplomatic or Consular Officer. (C.C.C. 1669).

Witnesses.—Following cannot be witnesses to wills: minors, persons of unsound mind, persons adjudged quasi-incompetent and persons who are blind, deaf or dumb. (C.C.C. 1670).

Revocation.—Testator may at any time revoke his will. Revocation may be total or partial. (C.C.C. 1693). Unless otherwise declared in will by testator, all provisions of former will which are in conflict with latter will are deemed to have been revoked but those not in conflict will still remain in force. (C.C.C. 1697). If property which is subject of will has been intentionally transferred to third person or destroyed by testator, testamentary disposition of such property is deemed to have been revoked. (C.C.C. 1696).

Foreign Wills.—Will made by foreigner in Thailand is valid if made in form prescribed by C.C.C. or in form prescribed by his law of nationality. (C.O.L. 40).

See Topical Index in front part of this volume.

TURKEY LAW DIGEST

(The following is a list of all Topics, including cross-references, covered in this Digest.)

TURKEY LAW DIGEST

Revised for 1997 edition by

YILMAZ ÖZ, of the Ankara Bar.

(Con. indicates Constitution; C. C. indicates Civil Code; C. C. P. indicates Code of Civil Procedure; C. Obl. indicates Code of Obligations; Com. C. indicates Commercial Code; C. E. and B. indicates Code on Execution of Debts and Bankruptcy. See also topic Statutes.)

ABSENTEES:

If, for reasons of illness, absence or similar reasons, a major cannot act in an urgent matter, nor designate a representative and in case property is not taken care of because a person is continuously absent and his whereabouts is unknown and also in case of uncertainty as to the heirs entitled to an estate, a curator is appointed by Peace Court. (C. C. 376 cipher 1; 377 ciphers 1 and 3; 528 paragraph 1).

ACKNOWLEDGMENTS:

Acknowledgments made before a notary public are prima facie evidence in courts. Documents acknowledged before a notary public in foreign countries and intended for use in Turkey, should be made in accordance with lex loci and legalized by Turkish consular officers or other political representatives. Such documents also are accepted as prima facie evidence. (C. C. P. 296).

Turkey has ratified (Law No. 3028, Decree 84/8373—Sept. 16, 1984) The Hague Convention of Oct. 5, 1961, on Abolishing the Requirement of Legalisation for Foreign Public Documents. "Apostille" issued by competent authority of State from which document emanates should be sufficient.

ACTIONS:

All actions must be brought before law courts. There is however a summary procedure for collection of debts before special authorities (i.e., "Execution Office") if claimant can produce written proof (like enforceable judgment; promissory notes or acknowledgment of debt signed by debtor, etc.).

Rules governing procedure of civil actions are set forth in Code of Civil Procedure. Parties are not required to be represented by an attorney-at-law and may handle their cases personally.

See topics Aliens, subhead Actions by Aliens; Courts.

Limitation of.—See topic Limitation of Actions.

ALIENS:

Status of aliens in Turkey is based upon Convention signed at Lausanne (July 24, 1923) and on special conventions and treaties made with different countries and Law No. 5683, dated July 15, 1950. Aliens, on condition of reciprocity, have access to courts of justice, may own, transfer, bequeath, sell or exchange all kinds of personal property and also real estate, except that they are not allowed to own real estate situated within village boundaries. They are not subject to any heavier taxation than that borne by Turkish citizens.

In matters of personal status such as marriage, divorce, matrimony, capacity, inheritance of personal property, etc., only national courts of the aliens have jurisdiction. In case both parties to the case sign a written statement accepting the jurisdiction of Turkish courts, the latter decide the case according to the national law of the parties.

Residence.—Registration is required and residence permit is issued upon application. If, however, resident intends to work in Turkey, work permit should also be obtained. It is recommended that this permit be obtained before entry into country. This permit is issued by Director General of Petroleum Affairs for those who work in Petroleum operations, by Foreign Capital Department for those who work in enterprises benefiting from Foreign Capital Encouragement Law No. 6224 and by police authorities in other cases.

Civil Rights.—Aliens on Turkish soil have same protection as Turkish citizens both for themselves and their belongings; except that rights and liberties granted to Turkish citizens by Constitution may be limited by legislation and in conformity with rules of international law in case of aliens. (Con. 16). Practically speaking, position of aliens in civil matters is nearly same as that of Turkish citizens.

Actions by Aliens.—Aliens suing in Turkey may be required, at request of defending party to give such guaranty as court may fix, considering costs of suit and damages to which alien plaintiff might be sentenced. (C. C. P. 97). However, treaty arrangements are reserved. Since, under Law No. 1574 (1972), Turkey ratified The Hague Convention on Civil Procedures (Mar. 1, 1954), alien should be able to request court to set aside request for guaranty. (Art. 17 of said Convention).

Actions Against Aliens.—Where an alien is resident in Turkey civil and/or penal actions may be commenced against him. There are cases where alien not resident in Turkey may be summoned before Turkish courts. These cases are those concerning real estate situate in Turkey, contracts entered into or to be performed in Turkey, debts attached in Turkey, bankruptcy declared in Turkey and sea accidents.

Corporations Owned or Controlled by Aliens.—There are no disqualifications applying to corporations owned or controlled by aliens in Turkey.

See also topics Bankruptcy; Copyright; Shipping; Trademarks and Tradenames; Foreign Investment.

ALIMONY: See topic Divorce.

ANTI-DUMPING LAWS:

Law No. 3577 of June 14, 1989 (as supplemented by set of Regulations published in Official Journal of Sept. 27, 1989) contains some rules aiming at prevention of dumping and unfair competition in import of goods.

ANTIQUITY:

Unauthorized collection, purchase or export of antiquities is illegal and punishable by stiff penalties (both imprisonment and fines). (Law No. 2863 of July 21, 1983).

ARBITRATION:

All disputes may be submitted to arbitration. Parties may enter into separate agreement, or submission to arbitration is provided for in main contract. (C. C. P. 516). No particular form of submission is required except that it must be in writing. (C. C. P. 517). Unless otherwise provided by agreement, three arbitrators are appointed by judge who is competent to try case. (C. C. P. 520).

Arbitrators are obliged to give award within six months after their first meeting. (C. C. P. 529). Decision of majority is binding (C. C. P. 531). Arbitrators' award can only be appealed: (a) When it is delivered after lapse of prescribed period; (b) if it contains provision which was not asked for by parties; (c) when it has decisions beyond authority of arbitrators; (d) in case where award does not take up and decide each point raised by parties.

When award is ready it is submitted by arbitrators to court and recorded. Copies are given to parties. (C. C. P. 532). After award becomes final it is certified by court and can be executed. (C. C. P. 536).

Arbitration awards given in foreign countries and certified by foreign court may be executed in Turkey under one of following conditions: (a) There must exist agreement of reciprocity between Republic of Turkey and state where award is given or (b) there must exist, in state where award is given, legal provision whereby execution is possible of judgment awarded by Turkish arbitrator or court, or (c) in absence of legal provision under para. b, there must exist precedent of such execution. Foreign arbitration awards whose execution has been granted "exequatur" by competent Turkish court shall be executed as if awarded by Turkish courts. (Law dated May 20, 1982, No. 2675).

By Laws Nos. 3730 and 3731 (May 8, 1991), Turkey has ratified European Convention on International Commercial Arbitration, signed in Geneva, Apr. 21, 1961, as well as, New York Convention of June 10, 1958, on Recognition and Enforcement of Foreign Arbitral Awards (in commercial matters and on condition of reciprocity).

See also topics Dispute Resolution; Judgments.

ASSIGNMENTS:

The consent of the debtor is not necessary for the assignment of a claim by the creditor to a third person, except in cases where the law or agreement prohibits the assignment or where the claim is unassignable by nature. (C. Obl. 162). An assignment must be in writing. If the debtor pays the claim to the assignor or to one of the previous assignees (in case there are several) before any of the assignees or assignors notify him, he is discharged. (C. Obl. 165). When a dispute arises as to who should be paid the debtor may refuse to pay, or may discharge himself by depositing the amount in a court. (C. Obl. 166). If the assignment of a claim is made for consideration the assignor impliedly warrants the existence of a claim at the time of the assignment. Unless expressly so stipulated, he is not liable for the insolvency of the debtor. (C. Obl. 169). The assignee acquires all the rights and privileges of the assignor excepting those that are personal. In addition to special defenses vis-a-vis assignee, debtor has all defenses against assignor (and former assignees) provided such defenses existed at time debtor was informed of assignment. (C. Obl. 167).

ASSOCIATIONS:

Nature.—Legal personality or legal person is used in Turkey, as in other civil law countries, in contrast to natural person or human being. When individuals bring their capital or skill together to achieve a common purpose they may fulfill certain formalities required by law and obtain a legal personality. If founders do not intend to make and share profits, organization is a society (such as Society for the Prevention of Cruelty to Animals). If, on other hand, intention is to share profits it is an association (such as commercial company or corporation).

Ordinary partnership is simplest form of association. It does not have legal personality separate from partners and is administered by partners themselves. All partners are jointly liable towards third persons because of transactions and their liability is unlimited. See topic Partnership.

Societies are legal persons formed by seven or more persons to bring together continuously their knowledge and activities for a nonprofit sharing purpose. Societies may be organized for a charitable, political, scientific and artistic purpose and for any other purpose which is not profit sharing and are regulated generally by provisions of Civil Code, Art. 53-72 and specifically by those of Law of Societies. (2908, Oct. 6, 1983).

Formation.—When seven or more persons prepare by-laws and sign and submit them with other pertinent documents to authorities, society acquires legal personality. (Law of Societies Art. 9). No prior authorization nor any registration or publication are prerequisite. However, after its formation each society must submit statement to highest civil authority of locality attaching four copies of its by-laws. (Law of Societies Art. 9). Furthermore, by-laws of society should be published in newspaper. (Law of Societies Art. 13).

No society can be formed against basic principles cited in preamble of Constitution. It is prohibited among others to form certain societies such as: (a) Those aiming to break national and political unity and integrity of state; (b) those based on religious and sectarian principles; (c) those based on family or race; (d) secret societies and those whose aims are concealed; (e) societies organized for regional purposes, etc.

See Topical Index in front part of this volume.

ASSOCIATIONS . . . *continued*
(Law of Societies Art. 5). International societies cannot be formed (Art. 7) and Art. 11 brings certain restrictions to international activities of societies.

Capacity of Societies.—Societies may enter into transactions, acquire and alienate all kinds of property and generally may do everything which a real person may do except those things which are peculiar to human beings. However, capacity of a society is limited by purposes enumerated in its by-laws.

Business Associations.—Certain types of associations are classified in Commercial Code as business associations. All such associations have legal personality. See topics Corporations; Partnership.

ATTACHMENT:

This remedy constitutes provisional security measure provided for by Law No. 2004 on Execution of Debts and Bankruptcy (June 9, 1932, as last am'd by Law No. 3494, Nov. 25, 1988) in order to protect creditor before effectuation of seizure or bankruptcy in execution proceedings.

Attachment of the property of the debtor is allowed where an unsecured debt is due; and even though the debt has not matured the writ may be issued where the debtor (1) has no fixed domicile or (2) is suspected of trying to evade his obligations by flight or removal of assets. (C. E. and B. 257).

Writ is issued by court on ex parte application of creditor. (C. E. and B. 258). Creditor is liable for any damages that may arise due to attachment, and may be required to give a bond. (C. E. and B. 259). Attachment gives no prior lien on goods. Creditor must begin suit within seven days after writ of attachment is communicated to him. See also topic Sequestration.

ATTORNEYS AND COUNSELLORS:

Pursuant to the Act on the Legal Profession (No. 1136 of Mar. 19, 1969, as am'd) practice of law is deemed liberal profession having nature of public service.

Requirements as to eligibility are: (a) being graduate of law school in Turkish university (or, if graduate of foreign law school, having passed exam in such courses not taken that are included in curriculum of Turkish law schools), (b) having successfully concluded apprenticeship for one year (first six months in court system, and balance with established lawyer), (c) maintaining domicile within area of bar with which candidate desires to be listed, (d) not having any impediments to practice (e.g., not having been condemned for any felonies, or, declared bankrupt, or, serving as someone's employee, etc.).

Turkey does not have barrister/solicitor distinction of Anglo-Saxon practice. Licensed attorney can plead before every level of courts anywhere in Turkey, even outside of local bar. Somewhat resembling professional firms or associations in some Western countries, lawyers in Turkey are permitted to join together to form "Joint Attorneys Bureau".

Offenses against attorneys are treated some as those against judges.

Foreign lawyers cannot directly represent their clients in Turkish jurisdiction, unless they meet criteria listed above. Representation and practice may be arranged only through association with Turkish attorneys already qualified and registered with local bar.

Two bar associations that could assist foreign lawyers seeking local counsel are: (1) Turkiye Barolar Birligi, (Turkish Union of Bar Associations), Karanfil s. 5/62, 06650 Kizilay, Ankara. President: Onder SAV. Phone: 90-312-418 0512. Telecopier: 90-312-418 7857. (2) Ankara Barosu, (Bar Association of Ankara), Adliye Sarayi, Kat-5, Sihhiye, Ankara. President: Erdal MERDOL. Phone: 90-312-312 4500. Telecopier: 90-312-311 2560.

BANKRUPTCY:

Only traders (including legal entities such as partnerships and corporations) are subject to law of bankruptcy. (Com. C. 20). In all cases declaration of bankruptcy is made by a commercial court. A previous notification through Execution Department is necessary, except that a declaration of bankruptcy may be made without such previous notification: (1) Where debtor has no residence, or absconds, makes fraudulent transactions to prejudice his creditors, or hides his property while execution is taking place; (2) where a trader stops payments on his debts; (3) where a corporation is insolvent; (4) where debtor himself applies to court to be declared bankrupt.

The bankruptcy decree divests the bankrupt of the control of his property. All his property subject to execution forms a "masse" (estate). Such property as he may acquire during bankruptcy is also included. All debts of the bankrupt except those secured by a real estate mortgage become due. Interest keeps accruing even after initiation of bankruptcy. Preferential payments can be made to creditors whose claims are secured by pledge or mortgage. Proceeds of sale from such properties are paid directly to those creditors, after deduction of outstanding customs duties, land taxes, etc. Ordinary, or non-preferential creditors are combined within six specific groups. Creditors of same group receive equal payments. Creditors with claims for wages, funeral expenses; debtor's minor children and his wife are combined within group one.

As soon as bankruptcy is declared a list of all the property belonging to the debtor is prepared by the Execution Department. Notices are put in the newspapers calling all creditors to a meeting. They elect a bankruptcy commission. The judicial liquidation then takes place. This must be terminated within six months.

Foreigners in Turkey are subject to bankruptcy upon the same basis as Turkish citizens. (C.E. and B. 154-256).

In general a foreign adjudication of bankruptcy may be enforced in Turkey only after being submitted to, and approved by a Turkish court.

BANKS AND BANKING:

Banking in Turkey is governed by Law No. 3182, Apr. 25, 1985.

Organization.—Banks must be organized as corporations (Societés Anonymes). Foreign banks wishing to engage in banking operations in Turkey must have corporate or equivalent status under law of countries of origin. Permission of Council of Ministers must be obtained to found bank. Same requirement exists for foreign banks wishing to set up branches.

Capital.—Minimum amount of capital is TL one trillion. Foreign banks desiring to operate in Turkey must also allocate same amount to Turkey.

BILLS AND NOTES:

All actions in respect of bills of exchange, promissory notes and checks are brought before the tribunals of commerce.

Bill of exchange must contain: (1) The word "bill of exchange," in the language in which it is written; (2) an unconditional order to pay a certain sum of money; (3) the name of the drawee; (4) term; (5) place of payment; (6) name of the payee; (7) place where it is made and date; (8) signature of the drawer. No statement of consideration is necessary. (Com. C. 583).

There are no days of grace. Bills falling due on a holiday are payable on the succeeding business day. The holder must present the bill for payment on the due date or within two business days thereafter. The endorsers and the guarantors of a bill of exchange are jointly and severally liable to the holder for its payment. Bills may be prepared in several copies. Each copy must contain a serial number; otherwise each is considered a separate bill.

Promissory note must contain: (1) The words "promissory note" in the language in which it is written; (2) an unconditional promise to pay a certain sum of money; (3) term; (4) place of payment; (5) name of the payee; (6) place where it is made and date; (7) signature. Notes are subject to the rules relating to bills of exchange, in so far as these concern maturity, endorsement, joint and several liability, payment, payment for honor, protest, rights and duties of the holder, conflict of laws and limitation.

Check must contain: (1) The word "check" in the language in which it is written; (2) an unconditional order to pay a certain sum of money; (3) name of the drawee; (4) place of payment; (5) place where it is made and date; (6) signature. A check must be payable at sight. The rules governing the liability of endorsers and drawer and protests are the same as those for bills of exchange. Crossed checks, with the same general principles, are used in Turkey. Banks are required to notify Central Bank as to holders of checking accounts, in order that register thereof be maintained. Severe penalties (including prison terms) are provided, along with civil liability, for issuers of bad checks. (Law No. 3167, Mar. 19, 1985).

In the matter of conflict of laws the following rules prevail: Capacity to assume obligations under a bill of exchange is governed by the law of the state of which a person is a citizen; the form of the obligation is governed by the law of the state where it is made; rules concerning protest and all other steps to safeguard the interests of the parties concerned are governed by the laws of the country where such steps are to be taken.

CHATTEL MORTGAGES:

Movable property can be mortgaged (pledged) only by delivery to another to hold as security for a debt or performance of an obligation (dead pledge). (C. C. 853). Animals may be pledged whereby animal remains in holding of owner by registering in special official register. (C. C. 854).

COLLATERAL SECURITY: See topic Pledges.

COMMERCIAL REGISTER:

Attached to each basic court trying commercial cases and subject to supervision of this court there is organized an office of Commercial Register. (Com. C. 26). Matters relating to traders and to commercial companies and all other matters required by law to be registered in a Commercial Register must be so registered. Failure to register a matter or refusal to do so when notified by Commercial Registrar, may entail a fine. (Com. C. 35). Those who make false statements in bad faith to Registrar for registration are both fined and imprisoned.

Commercial Registers are open to public and all entries, unless otherwise provided by law are published in full in official Commercial Register Gazette. (Com. C. 37). Any person may examine records and documents in a Commercial Register and may obtain certified copies. (Com. C. 37).

Those who make untrue statements in Commercial Register are liable for damages caused to third parties. (Com. C. 40). For records in Register responsibility of state is definitely established; that is, state may be sued for damages in case a third party suffers because of a statement in Commercial Register.

See also topics Corporations; Limited Companies; Partnership; Records.

COMMUNITY PROPERTY:

See topic Husband and Wife.

CONSTITUTION AND GOVERNMENT:

Constitution as adopted by Constituent Assembly on Sept. 24, 1982 has been approved by referendum held on Nov. 7, 1982.

General Principles.—Turkish State is a republic (Con. 1) based on the principles of human rights and is a national, democratic secular and social (i.e. welfare) state bound by the rule of law (Con. 2). Sovereignty, is unconditionally vested in the nation. No exclusive person, group or class can, under any circumstances, be entrusted with the exercise of sovereign power. No person or organ can exercise any public authority which does not emanate from Constitution. (Con. 6). No law can be contrary to provisions of Constitution. (Con. 11).

Fundamental Rights.—Constitution provides practically for all democratic and civil liberties, rights and obligations. (Con. 12 to 65). Personal liberty and domicile are inviolable, except where provided by law and authorized by judiciary. (Con. 17, 21, 26). Freedom of speech and writing (Con. 25), press (Con. 28) movement (Con. 23) meeting (Con. 34) and association (Con. 33) are safeguarded. Every person may act as claimant or defendant in lawsuit for protection of his rights and interests. (Con. 36). No one can be punished for act which at time it was committed was not punishable by specific stipulation of law.

See Topical Index in front part of this volume.

CONSTITUTION AND GOVERNMENT . . . *continued*

Criminal liability is personal. No one can be forced to make a statement or to bring evidence incriminating himself or his near relations. (Con. 38). Elementary education is compulsory and free. (Con. 42).

Social and Economic Rights.—Right of private property is recognized. This can be limited only by law. Its use can not be contrary to public interest. (Con. 35). Expropriation for public interest by paying real value is possible. (Con. 46). State is authorized to nationalize private enterprises by paying their real value. This payment, when allowed by law, can be made in ten equal installments over five years, with interest. (Con. 46). Every worker is entitled to have proper working conditions (Con. 48) and rest with pay (Con. 50). State is required to take measures to assure that workers receive wages in proportion to their work and in every case to assure them dignified standard of living. Organization of unions is free. (Con. 51). Right of collective bargaining and to strike are recognized. (Con. 53, 54).

Political Rights.—All citizens of age 18 are electors. Ballot is personal, equal, free, secret and direct. Political parties can be founded without prior approval. All political parties have to adhere to principles of human rights and to those underlying Constitution. (Con. 68, 69).

Legislature.—Turkish Parliament is named "The Turkish Grand National Assembly". Enacting, amending or repealing laws, approving State Budget are among prerogatives of Turkish Grand National Assembly. (Con. 87).

Turkish Grand National Assembly is composed of 550 representatives elected by direct universal ballot. (Con. 75). All citizens who have reached age of 30 can be elected. (Con. 76). Elections for National Assembly take place every five years. (Con. 77).

Executive.—President of Republic is elected by Grand National Assembly by secret ballot from among its own members for term of seven years. President is not eligible for second term. (Con. 101). President is head of state. (Con. 104). Council of Ministers is composed of Prime Minister and ministers. Prime Minister is directly appointed by President of Republic from among members of Grand National Assembly. Ministers are selected by Prime Minister from among members of Grand National Assembly of Turkey or from outside. (Con. 109). Complete budgetary system is provided for. (Con. 161).

For administrative purposes country is divided into provinces (ils) and these in turn into minor divisions (ilce, bucak, koy). (Con. 126).

Judiciary.—Justice is administered by independent courts in the name of Turkish People. (Con. 9). See also topic Courts.

Constitutional Court decides on controversies relating to constitutionality of laws and of internal regulations of Grand National Assembly. It also tries, as a high court, the President of the Republic, ministers and some other high officials. (Con. 148).

Council of State "Danistay" is highest administrative and consultative court composed of several departments. It is established by constitution and is subject to Law No. 2575 dated Jan. 6, 1982. Council of State acts as court of first instance or as court of appeals in administrative and tax cases referred to it by law. In both cases its decisions are final and binding. It also gives opinion on draft laws and regulations prepared by Council of Ministers.

Special-purpose courts such as State Security Courts, Administrative Courts, Tax Courts (as well as Regional Administrative Courts, for appellate review of certain judgments issuing from latter two) handle special matters prescribed under their appropriate laws.

CONSUMER PROTECTION:

Law No. 4077 (Feb. 23, 1995) provides for protection of consumers against fraud and deceptive trade practices. It contains detailed rules as to accurate advertising, proper labelling, buyers' right to return and demand free repairs or replacement within specified time following purchase, payment on basis of instalment-plan, door-to-door sales, warranty, consumer credits and Consumers' Council, etc. No "plain language" statute exists.

CONTRACTS:

Contracts are governed by Code of Obligations of 1926 (taken almost verbatim from Swiss Federal Code).

A contract requires: (a) Mutual agreement, express or implied; (b) a "causa", only in certain cases such as transfer of personal or real property; and (c) capacity of parties to contract. Every person who has reached age of majority which is 18 and is discriminating has legal capacity. Discriminating minors can validly accept only purely gratuitous benefits without concurrence of their guardians.

Unless otherwise provided by law, contracts are valid without any special form. In cases where a form is prescribed it is usually a condition of validity. Principal forms prescribed for validity are written form and publicly authenticated instrument such as notarial deed and title registration for real estate. Where parties, without requirement of law, have stipulated use of a special form, contract entered into does not become binding unless such form is complied with. (C. Obl. 16). Contracts concerning real estate must be executed before land registrar and registered in Title Deeds Office.

If offer is made with a time limit offerer is bound with his offer until end of this limit. If no acceptance is expressed within time prescribed offer ceases to be binding. (C. Obl. 3). An offer with no time limit, made in presence of other party or by phone ceases to be binding if it is not accepted immediately. (C. Obl. 4). When an offer without fixing a time limit has been made to a person not present, offerer is bound until moment when he can expect a reply dispatched in due course and time. (C. Obl. 5). Where, by reason of special nature of transaction or circumstances, an express acceptance is not to be expected the contract is presumed to have been concluded unless offer is rejected within a reasonable time. (C. Obl. 6).

Excuses for Nonperformance.—Impossibility of performance by circumstances beyond debtor's control, force majeure, clausula rebus sic stantibus and nonperformance on part of other contracting party.

Applicable Law.—Formal validity of contract is determined by laws of place of contracting (locus regit actum). Under reservation of public policy, parties to contract are free to determine and to choose applicable law. If such determination is not made, as a rule, law of place of performance will apply.

Government Contracts.—As a rule government enters into contracts for economic purpose only on basis of acceptance of bids (Law 2886, Sept. 8, 1983), with specifically negotiated contracts being exception. Conditions and specifications of bids are published and constitute part of contract. In order to participate at bid contractors must submit preliminary bond. Successful contractor who is awarded bid has to submit performance bond. Advance payments must be made against bank letters of guarantee. For all disputes arising out of such contracts jurisdiction lies with ordinary courts.

See also topic Frauds, Statute of.

COPYRIGHT:

Copyright issues from provisions of Law No. 5846 of 1951 (as am'd by Law-4110 in June 1995) on Works of Intellect and Art. Copyrightable items include works of fine arts, scientific, literary and musical works, motion pictures and computer programs.

Rights of copyright holders (including aliens whose works are first published in Turkey, or, whose works are first published abroad and covered by international treaties to which Turkey is party) cover wide range from authorship to publication, reproduction, rearrangements, stage productions, translations, broadcasting, etc. Copyright belongs to author during his/her lifetime and to his/her heirs for period of 70 years following death. Copyright infringements could result in both civil claims and criminal prosecution.

Turkey has joined Rome Convention on Protection of Performing Artists, Phonogram Producers and Broadcasting Entities (Law-4115, July 1995), as well as, Berne Convention on Protection of Literary and Artistic Works, as am'd in Paris (1979), with reservation as provided in Art. 31 thereof (Law-4117, July 1995).

CORPORATIONS:

Term "corporation" under this heading is akin to "joint stock company" or "societe anonyme" in European law.

Corporations are legal entities. In order to form corporation there must be at least five founders executing Articles of Incorporation before notary. Articles, inter alia, must contain name, object, amount of capital (minimum TL five billion), investment in kind (if any). (Com. C. 277, 279). If "gradual formation" mode is used, founders must put up at least 10% of capital and seek authorization of Ministry of Industry and Commerce prior to any public offering. Upon receipt of such authorization public may be invited to subscribe. When capital is fully subscribed to and 25% thereof is paid in, Formative General Meeting of Shareholders is held, in order to approve actions taken by founders and to elect or ratify election of board and auditors. Thereafter application is made to local commercial tribunal for ratification of formation. Tribunal so ratifies and directs commercial registrar to register corporation and publicize its formation in Commercial Registry Journal.

Corporations whose shareholders exceed 100 are deemed "open to the public" and are subject to additional special requirements (e.g., closer supervision by Capital Market Council as formed under Law No. 2499, July 30, 1981).

Corporation may also be organized "instantaneously", if at least five founders subscribe to all shares and pay in 25% of capital. In this mode, authorization from Ministry is sought forthwith upon execution of Articles before notary, and, based on such authorization, ratification by commercial tribunal and subsequent registry and publication could follow. (Com. C. 303).

Face value of shares must be TL 500 or higher multiples of 100. While preferred shares are possible, stock with no par value is not allowed. Corporation may issue bonds but outstanding amount thereof cannot exceed paid-in capital. Shares may be issued at premium but not at discount. Liability of shareholders is limited to amount subscribed for.

Each share entitles holder to at least one vote. Provided this rule is observed, weighted voting rights may be granted to specified classes of shares. (Com. C. 373, 401).

Administration and representation of corporation vests with Board of Directors composed of minimum of three members, as elected by shareholders. Corporation is required to have one to five auditors, similarly elected.

Unless higher quorum is required under law or Articles of Incorporation, at least one-fourth of capital must be represented at regular shareholders' meetings. If this is not obtained at first meeting, second meeting is held wherein resolutions may be adopted without regard to amount of capital represented. (Com. C. 372). Quorum of two-thirds is required for decisions regarding any amendments to articles relative to objectives and fields of endeavor, or, increase or decrease of capital, or, dissolution. (Com. C. 388).

Setting aside of reserves is required at 5% of each year's profits, until it reaches 20% of capital. (Com. C. 466).

See also topic Limited Companies.

Foundations.—Foundation is a corporate body created by dedication of property for a specific purpose. Whole of a property or its realised or realisable income as well as rights which have economic value may be subject of a foundation. (Arts. 73-81 of C.C. as am'd by Law No. 903; dated July 13, 1967).

Formation and Organization.—Foundation is established either by authenticated deed or by will and assumes legal entity by being registered at local court which notifies General Direction of Foundations, of creation of a foundation.

Supervision.—Foundations are subject to supervision of General Direction of Foundations. Supervising authority takes care that provisions of deed of foundation are carried out and property of foundation is used for purpose to which it has been dedicated.

Dissolution.—Foundation is a lasting legal entity but can be dissolved under certain conditions. Foundation of which purpose has become unobtainable is automatically dissolved. Also foundation whose purposes become illegal or immoral is dissolved by competent court on application of supervising authority.

COURTS:

There are different categories of courts exercising jurisdiction over civil, criminal, commercial, executionary, labor, military, administrative and tax matters. Competence and jurisdiction of each are determined under law. There is no jury trial.

In both civil and criminal matters, composition of courts ranges from single Justice of Peace, to single-judge Executionary and/or Labor Courts, to Courts (civil and/or criminal) of First Instance (of either one-judge or panel of three), to Central Criminal Tribunals, as well as, Commercial Tribunals. There are no appellate courts, per se, except that Court of Cassation ("Yargitay"), with its several specialized Chambers (composed of five-judge panel), sits as highest appellate court in civil and criminal matters, while Council of State ("Danistay") with its special Chambers, sits as final review authority on administrative, governmental and tax matters. There is also separate Military Court of Cassation.

See also topic Constitution and Government, subhead Judiciary.

CURRENCY:

Issue of banknotes is under monopoly of "Türkiye Cumhuriyeti Merkez Bankasi" (Central Bank of Republic of Turkey), organized under Law 1211, Jan. 26, 1970. Coins are also issued, at various denominations, under authority of Undersecretariat for Treasury and Foreign Trade. (Law 1264, June 6, 1970).

Although monetary system is legally based on gold, paper money is issued by Central Bank, having same legal tender privileges. These notes are not yet convertible and may be issued against such items as gold, foreign exchange, securities and negotiable instruments.

Exchange rate of TL is readjusted daily according to fluctuation of foreign exchange currencies in world market.

By "Law for Protection of Value of Turkish Currency" (Law No. 1567), Feb. 20, 1930, special powers have been bestowed on Council of Ministers to regulate by decree foreign exchange transactions. With decrees (mainly, Decree No. 32, Aug. 7, 1989) and circulars so far promulgated under this law, exchange controls have largely been abolished. Most important provisions of the current system may be summarized as follows: (1) Import and export of Turkish currency as well as of negotiable instruments in Turkish currency is substantially liberalized. Persons entering Turkey are free to bring any amount in TL currency or negotiable instruments in Turkish currency and those leaving country may have maximum of $5,000 equivalent to TL; (2) foreign exchange may be freely imported to country, and is not subject to any restriction and its origin is not investigated; (3) foreigners who come to Turkey can export foreign currency in amount that they have declared at their entrance when this amount is over $5,000. No declaration is required for sums below $5,000 (N.B.: Similar rules and limits apply to precious metals [i.e. gold and platinum] and precious stones and/or jewelry containing same, as brought in and out by travelers); (4) foreigners may repurchase foreign exchange from banks in Turkey against TL, provided that sum does not exceed foreign exchange that they have converted into TL in Turkey; (5) investments and engagements in commercial activities in Turkey by persons domiciled abroad and activities of same nature abroad by persons domiciled in Turkey are subject to provisions of relevant laws and agreements; (6) investments, participations in corporations, setting-up branches, buying shares, establishing offices, representations and agencies in Turkey by persons domiciled abroad are permitted provided that capital required for such business is brought in foreign exchange in amount of minimum $50,000 and that permission is obtained from Department of Foreign Capital and operations are carried out within framework of this permission. Import of intangible rights such as patent, license and know-how into Turkey must be subject to same provisions; (7) persons domiciled abroad investing or engaging in commercial activities in Turkey must register cash capital that they have brought with Department of Foreign Capital; (8) provisions governing matters cited under (6) above, transfer of profits, dividends, proceeds of sales and liquidation and amounts payable in return of use of intangible rights or use or blocking thereof in TL in Turkey must be regulated by Department of Foreign Capital. These provisions, however, do not apply to concerns operating under Foreign Investment and Petroleum Laws and to activities undertaken in accordance with agreements concerning International Monetary Fund and International Bank for Reconstruction and Development or with laws conferring special powers on Central Bank.

CUSTOMS DUTIES:

See topic Foreign Trade Regulations.

DEATH:

In case two or more persons die under circumstances which make it impossible to determine the order in which death has occurred, all of them are presumed to have died at the same time. (C. C. 28).

If a person, whose body cannot be found, has disappeared under circumstances which necessarily indicate his death, he is presumed dead. (C. C. 30).

In case a person disappears while in danger of death or in case the death of a person, from whom no news has been received for a long time, appears to be probable, the judge, on request of parties whose rights depend upon his death, may decide on the absence of the person concerned. (C. C. 31). In order that a judge may be requested to render this decision, at least one year from the danger of death or five years from the last news must have elapsed. Then an announcement is made and, at least a year from this announcement must elapse. (C. C. 32). In case the person in question does not appear or no news is received from him by the end of this term, the judge decides on "absence" and all rights dependent upon death are acquired as if the person had actually died. (C. C. 34).

Actions for Death.—No special statutory procedure for wrongful death. Relatives of deceased can collect damages from person who has caused wrongful death under general provisions governing damages for wrongful acts.

Official death certificates are issued by the Population Bureaux. Only courts can issue presumption of death decrees. Interested parties should apply to the Bureaux or to the courts having jurisdiction in the matter. There is no central office.

DECEDENTS' ESTATES:

See topics Descent and Distribution; Wills.

DEPOSITIONS:

In principle, testimony is taken by competent court, with witness appearing personally. Rogatory commissions, both within and from outside of Turkey are allowed. (C. C. P. Arts. 253-257). When Turkish courts take evidence on behalf of foreign courts, Turkish procedural rules apply. Turkey has ratified The Hague Convention on Civil Procedures (Law-1574, Mar. 1954), as well as, The Hague Convention Abolishing the Requirement of Legalisation for Foreign Public Documents (Law-3028, June 1984).

See topic Acknowledgments.

DESCENT AND DISTRIBUTION:

No distinction is made between real and personal property. Distribution among heirs takes place as follows: (1) Heirs of the first degree are the descendants of the decedent, children receive equal shares, children of deceased children take their parents' share. (C. C. 439). (2) If there be no descendants the decedent's property is divided between his father and mother, or if they are deceased, the property goes to the descendants of his parents. (C. C. 440). (3) If there be none of the above mentioned heirs, the property of the decedent goes to the grandparents, and in case they are deceased, to their descendants. (C. C. 441). (4) If there be no nearer heirs the decedent's property ascends to his great-grandparents, but for life only, and in the form of a right of usufruct. (C. C. 442).

Illegitimate children inherit as though legitimate. (C. C. 443).

Surviving Spouse.—If the decedent left issue, the surviving spouse takes one-fourth of estate. If decedent left no issue, but left parents or descendants of parents, surviving spouse takes one-half of estate. If decedent left neither issue, parents nor descendants of parents, but left grandparents or descendants of grandparents, surviving spouse takes three-fourths of estate. If decedent left none of relatives mentioned above, surviving spouse takes entire estate. (C. C. 444).

Escheat.—If there be no persons entitled to take a decedent's estate, the property escheats to the state.

DESERTION: See topic Divorce.

DISPUTE RESOLUTION:

Mandatory Dispute Resolution.—This is provided for in some rare instances. Where required, modes and procedures of selection of mediators and/or arbiters are shown in their special laws.

According to Law No. 2822 (May 5, 1983) on Collective Bargaining, Strikes and Lockouts, in case of deadlocked negotiations in collective bargaining, dispute may be referred to "mediator" who would be appointed either jointly by parties or selected from among "official list" by draw of names, or, similarly appointed by court. Mediator would be asked to render opinion in 15 days, strictly in advisory capacity. If mediator fails to get parties to agree, strike and/or lockout could be announced. Invoking public health and safety or national security grounds, Government has authority to decree deferral thereof for 60 days, during which parties and/or Minister of Labor could demand referral of dispute for final resolution by High Arbitration Board (eight-person body headed by President of that Division of High Appeals Court charged with review of labor disputes). Same Board would also resolve similar disputes in such areas of endeavor or work sites wherein strikes and lockouts are prohibited by law.

Law No. 3533 (June 29, 1938) requires mandatory settlement of disputes between government agencies, as follows: If dispute is between two agencies whose budgets are contained in national budget, member of cabinet is to act as final arbiter. Where dispute involves agencies whose budgets are treated only as adjunct to national budget, one of heads of divisions of High Court of Appeals, or, in disputes between municipalities and other government agencies or entities wholly-owned by government, highest local court official would act as final arbiter.

Voluntary Dispute Resolution.—Voluntary Arbitration, per se, is recognized mode of dispute resolution. Code of Civil Litigation Procedures contains detailed rules relevant to arbitration in Turkey. (Arts. 516-536).

See also topic Arbitration.

DIVORCE:

Grounds.—Separation or divorce is grantable in cases of adultery; attempt against life of spouse and cruelty; committing of crime; leading infamous life; desertion; insanity lasting for three or more years and rendering common life intolerable; marital union undergoing severe shock and inability to resume common life. Right to action is forfeited if guilty spouse is pardoned by other, in cases of attempt to life or cruelty, or, of leading infamous life.

Jurisdiction.—Court at plaintiff's domicile has jurisdiction. Aliens residing in Turkey may sue for separation or divorce. Grounds therefor and legal consequences thereof are to be decided upon in accordance with laws of country which is common to both parties (provided same is not against public morals or order of Turkey). When parties are of different nationality, laws of their common domicile, or lacking same, laws of their common residence, and lacking that, Turkish law would govern.

Name.—The divorced wife reacquires the surname which she had before the marriage. If it is determined that she has vested interest therein and that it would not harm ex-husband, court may permit divorcee to continue using her ex-husband's surname.

Alimony.—If the spouse who is not guilty falls into poverty on account of the divorce, the other party, even if not guilty, may be ordered to pay alimony to such spouse for a period not exceeding one year.

Remarriage.—If one of the parties is guilty he or she may be forbidden to remarry for a period not less than one and not more than two years. A divorced wife cannot remarry for 300 days, but this term may be shortened by court order.

Annulment of Marriage.—See topic Marriage.

ENVIRONMENT:

Notable pieces of relevant laws and regulations include: Environmental Protection Act (No. 2872, Aug. 9, 1983); Law No. 3086 (1984) on Coastal Strips; Law No. 1380 (1971) Concerning Marine Life; Regulations regarding (payments into) the Fund to Prevent Environmental Pollution (May 17, 1985); Regulations on Protection of Air Quality (Nov. 2, 1986), re Controls on Water Pollution (Sept. 4, 1988), re Environmental Impact Assessment of (proposed) Investments (Feb. 7, 1993), re Controls on Imports of Dangerous and Deleterious Substances (June 5, 1986).

Ministry of Environment ("Cevre Bakanligi") in Ankara is agency entrusted with authority to oversee environmental matters.

ESCHEAT: See topic Descent and Distribution.

EXCHANGE CONTROL:

See topics Currency; Foreign Investment; and Foreign Trade Regulations.

EXECUTIONS:

Execution is granted in respect of judgments as well as of acknowledgments made before a notary and settlements made in a court. In case of ordinary and commercial debts the creditor, before going to the court, may serve a payment order on the debtor. If no objection is brought against this order within seven days (this term is five days for negotiable instruments) the claim is assumed to have been admitted and is executed.

The debtor is obliged to make a declaration giving a detailed account of his property sufficient to pay his debt. Moveable goods are seized and real estate is attached by registration on official record. All property must be sold by auction through the execution department. In exceptional cases movables may be sold by private agreement.

EXPROPRIATION:

See topic Constitution and Government, subhead Social and Economic Rights.

EXTRADITION:

Turkey has adhered to European Convention of Dec. 13, 1957, on "Extradition". (Law No. 7376, Nov. 18, 1959). Additionally, Turkey has extradition treaties with several (17) countries.

FOREIGN EXCHANGE:

See topics Currency; Foreign Investment; and Foreign Trade Regulations.

FOREIGN INVESTMENT:

Foreign capital, which is considered useful for economic development of country by competent department of government, receives special treatment in connection with transfer of profits, dividends and principal capital. (Law No. 6224, dated Jan. 18, 1954 entitled "The Law for the Encouragement of Foreign Capital"). This Law applies to foreign capital imported into Turkey and to loans made from abroad. In order that investment may come under this law, it must (a) tend to promote economic development of country, (b) operate in field of activity open to Turkish private enterprise, (c) entail no monopoly or special privilege.

Decree 95/6990 of June 7, 1995 names Directorate General of Foreign Capital of the Treasury Undersecretariat as body authorized to regulate inflow of foreign capital, as well as, formation of or participation in local companies, and engaging in commercial activities, setting up of branches or liaison offices in Turkey, and licensing, technical assistance, technology transfer and/or management, and financing arrangements.

"Foreign capital base," as envisaged by this law, may consist of (a) capital in form of foreign exchange, (b) machinery, equipment, materials and other items approved by competent department, (c) intangible rights, such as licenses, patent rights, trademarks and services, (d) profits converted into capital through reinvestment.

Profits realized on investment, as well as proceeds of sale or liquidation, are entitled to transfer abroad in currency of country from which foreign capital base originated and at prevailing official rate of exchange. Same law authorizes Treasury Undersecretariat, subject to decision of Council of Ministers, to guaranty, against security, payment in TL (not in foreign currency) of principal and interest on foreign loan to enterprise fulfilling above-mentioned requirements. Principal and interest of such loans also are transferable similar to invested risk capital and profits.

All rights, immunities and facilities granted to domestic capital and enterprise are available, on equal terms, to foreign capital and enterprise engaged in same field.

Turkey adhered to Oct. 11, 1985 and June 24, 1987 Conventions (Washington D.C.) regarding Multilateral Investments Guarantee Association, as well as, the submission to the International Centre for Settlement of Investment Disputes (ICSID) of any disputes (excepting those concerning "real property" located in Turkey) arising from foreign investments authorized under current legislation and on which investment activities have actually commenced. (Laws No. 3453 and 3460, June 2, 1988).

See also topic Currency.

FOREIGN JUDGMENTS: See topic Judgments.

FOREIGN TRADE REGULATIONS:

Import-export regimens are usually announced for each calendar year by Government decrees. Currently, these have largely been liberalized. Import-export may be effected by using Turkish currency, as well.

Imports (except on no-charge basis) are effected under Importer's Certificates. License along with payment of relative fee is required. Advance posting of bond is not required anymore. In addition to customs duties and related taxes, all imports are subject to payment of VAT, as well as, certain premiums into special "Fund" created for financing of low-cost Mass Housing Projects.

Exports are effected under Exporter's Certificates. No license required (except prerecordation on certain items). Export transactions are exempt from all taxes, fees and charges. Certain portions of export revenues are held tax-exempt and some of proceeds obtained from exports, in foreign exchange, may be kept by exporter for his own needs.

Customs-Union Agreement signed with E.U. in Mar. 1995 went into effect on Jan. 1, 1996.

Free Trade Zones.—Several are established per Law No. 3218 (June 6, 1985).

FRAUDS, STATUTE OF:

Turkey has no special statutes of fraud. However, where party to contract has been induced to enter into contract by wilful fraud of other party, defrauded party is not bound by contract, even though misrepresentation was not material. Where party to contract was wilfully defrauded by third person, such party is bound by contract unless other contracting party had or should have had knowledge of fraud when entering into contract. (C. Obl. 28). Right of defrauded party to sue is forfeited within one year from time he obtains knowledge about fraud. (C. Obl. 31).

See, however, topic Contracts, as to formal requirements.

GARNISHMENT:

Any property of debtor, in his possession or in hands of third persons or claims against them may be reached by seizure for execution, up to amount of creditor's claim. (C. E. and B. Art. 85).

GUARDIANSHIP:

See topic Infancy.

HOLIDAYS:

Following are general holidays in Turkey: Sundays, and for banks and government offices also Saturdays; Oct. 28th noon to evening of Oct. 30th, Declaration of Republic; Aug. 30th, Victory Day; Apr. 23rd, National Sovereignty Day; May 19th, Youth and Sports Day; two Mohammedan religious holidays, namely three and a half days of Sheker Bayram, falling on 1st, 2nd and 3rd of Shevval, lunar month, four and a half days of Kurban Bayram, falling on 10th, 11th, 12th and 13th of Zilhidja, also lunar month; Dec. 31st from noon and Jan. 1st, New Year's Day. In case last day of holiday falls on Fri. whole of Sat. following becomes holiday also.

HUSBAND AND WIFE:

It is not customary to fix marital property rights by contract. The parties are obliged to adopt one of the régimes mentioned by the law. If no régime is mentioned in the marriage contract or no such contract is made, the parties are assumed to have adopted "separation of property." (C. C. 170-71).

In order to have capacity to make a marriage contract or to rescind or to amend it, one must be discriminating. Minors and interdicted persons must be authorized by their "legal representatives." (C. C. 172). A marriage contract must be prepared in the authentic form and signed by the parties or by their legal representatives. (C. C. 173).

In the régime of the separation of property, both the husband and the wife continue to keep the ownership of their property and can manage the same. In case the wife leaves the management of her property in the hands of her husband, the income of her property is deemed to have been given to the husband for household expenses. Both husband and wife enjoy their present earnings and incomes received from their property. Husband can demand that wife contribute to household expenses.

The parties may adopt the régime of the "combination of property." Under this régime all property possessed by the spouses at the time of marriage and all property acquired during the marriage, except property expressly excluded by the marriage contract, are included in the combination. The property acquired by gift inter vivos is also included unless the donor expresses a contrary intention. Under this régime the property remains separate, but is administered by the husband, who is entitled to the income.

The third régime that the parties may accept is that of "community of property." Under this régime all property is owned and administered jointly by the spouses. The community is liable for the debts of either and upon the death of one is divided as follows: one-half to the survivor and the balance to the heirs (including the surviving spouse).

IMMIGRATION:

Residence of foreigners in Turkey is subject to issuance of residence permits. Certain jobs are reserved for Turkish citizens. Exceptions may be granted under Petroleum Law and Law for Encouragement of Foreign Capital. In general, technicians and industrial personnel may be admitted with prior approval of government.

INCOME TAX: See topic Taxation.

INDUSTRIAL PROPERTY:

Protection is available for such property (including industrial designs and geographical signs of origin).

See topics Patents; Trademarks and Tradenames; Unfair Competition.

INFANCY:

Children remain, as long as they are minors, under authority of their parents. Parents may not be arbitrarily deprived of such authority. (C. C. Art. 274). During existence of marriage relationship both parents exercise parental power. When parents cannot agree, father's determination is decisive. When parents have been divorced child stands under parental authority of spouse to whom its custody has been awarded by court. (C. C. Art. 148).

Guardians may be appointed officially when necessary (i.e., loss of parents, etc.) and are under supervision of guardianship authorities (i.e., courts) and must account to authorities.

INHERITANCE TAX: See topic Taxation.

INTELLECTUAL PROPERTY:

See topic Copyright.

INTEREST:

In commercial matters, parties are free to fix rate of interest. (Com. C. 8). If contract stipulates for interest but is silent about rate, or if interest is required by law, rate is 30% for commercial matters. In civil matters parties are free to fix rate not to exceed limits prescribed under Law; when no rate is mentioned it is 30%.

In current accounts it is possible to compound interest for periods not less than three months. (Com. C. 94). In case of default in commercial obligations rate of interest is 30% per annum. Council of Ministers has authority to revise this rate upward or downward by 80%.

Special Decree-Law 90, Oct. 6, 1983, and amendments thereto, provide for procedure of fixing interest rates to be received and paid by those who are engaged in loan transactions, including banks.

JUDGMENTS:

Foreign judgments are enforced in Turkey by decision of Turkish court to that effect under one of conditions set forth under topic Arbitration, supra.

LABOR LEGISLATION:

Scope of Legislation.—Main pieces are: (a) Labor Law (Law 1475, Aug. 25, 1971, as am'd); (b) Trade Unions Law (Law 2821, May 5, 1983, as am'd); (c) Collective Bargaining, Strike and Lockout Law (Law 2822, May 5, 1983, as am'd); (d) Social Security Act (Law 506, July 17, 1964).

Main Features.—Contracts for individual employment for specified period in excess of one year must be in writing. Continuous employment contracts for indefinite period may be terminated by either party by advance notice of two to eight weeks, depending on length of service.

Minimum wages, as redetermined every second year, by special commission comprising of representatives of unions and government, do apply.

Normal work week is 45 hours per week on basis of maximum 7.5 hours a day (for blue collar) and up to 40 hours per week for white collar workers. Regular (non-sporadic) overtime for maximum of three hours per day (maximum 90 days/year) requires permission from labor authorities, as well as, consent of worker. Unless higher rate is provided in union contracts, overtime requires 50% more pay in addition to regular wages.

Workers are entitled to paid weekly holiday, which, as rule, is Sun. (for white-collar workers, Sat. and Sun.). Those working on Suns. are given weekly holiday on another day of week. For general holidays, they are entitled to full day's wage for each holiday on which no work is done. For actual work on any such day, workers receive double wage. They are also entitled to paid annual vacation from 12 to 24 days, depending on length of service with employer. Union contracts may provide for longer vacation periods.

Workers are entitled to seniority compensation equal to one month's pay for each year of service (not to exceed similar benefit to which highest civil servant may be entitled upon retirement, calculated per coefficients ordained each year in national budget), in case of pensioning due to retirement or disability or of being dismissed by employer.

Strike and Lockout.—Workers of age 16 and over (excepting military personnel, civil servants in government and high-echelon administrators of state-owned enterprises) are free to join any union of their choice within job classification of their worksite. Unions have right, under certain conditions, to negotiate collective labor contracts with employers. Upon request of one fourth of workers in jobsite vote must be taken for strike, which would go into effect unless simple majority votes it down.

Employers also have the right to form their unions. Lockout is permitted under certain conditions.

Strikes and lockouts may be deferred for 60 days maximum, per decree by Council of Ministers, on grounds of public health or national security.

Social Security.—Sophisticated system is in effect. Per Social Security Act, as amended, all workers (excepting civil servants who are covered under separate Pension Fund rules) are subject to social security for following coverages: (a) work accidents and professional sickness; (b) maternity; (c) sickness; (d) old age and disability. Both employer and employee contribute their respective shares of premiums, subject to wage-salary ceiling determined by Government semi-annually. These premiums are collected and deposited through payroll deductions.

Retirement benefits are payable after meeting age and other requirements. Death benefits too are payable to survivors. Self-employed people are also covered under similar schemes. They are required to pay their premiums for similar benefits, into agencies specifically created therefor.

LAW REPORTS, CODES, ETC.:

See topics Reports; Statutes.

LEASING:

Arrangements for minimum period of four years are allowed on financial leasing arrangements regarding capital goods. (Law No. 3226, June 10, 1985).

LEGISLATURE:

See topic Constitution and Government.

LICENCES:

See topic Monopolies and Trade Restrictions.

LICENSING:

See topic Foreign Investment.

LIENS:

Creditor who with consent of debtor is in possession of personal property or securities of latter has right to retain them until claim is paid, provided claim is due and has a natural connection with property retained.

In case of merchants this connection is deemed to exist when possession of property and claim result from their commercial relations. (C. C. 864).

A warehouseman has a lien for the warehousing fees on the goods stored. (C. Obl. 476). A common carrier has a lien for freight, etc., on the goods transported. (C. Obl. 442). Landlords (C. Obl. 267) and hotel keepers (C. Obl. 482) have liens for rent and charges on the goods of tenants and guests.

LIMITATION OF ACTIONS:

All claims, unless otherwise stipulated in the law, are barred after ten years. (C. Obl. 125). The following are subject to a five-year period: Rent, interest, professional fees, wages, and retail trade debts. (C. Obl. 126). The above mentioned periods cannot be changed by agreement. All actions for damages due to torts are barred after one year. Different periods running from six months to five years are applied in special cases of civil and commercial law.

Running of limitations is interrupted by: (1) Admission of the claim by the debtor; (2) commencement of legal proceedings; (3) application of the creditor to the receivers in bankruptcy. (C. Obl. 133).

The fact that a claim is secured by a pledge does not prevent the running of limitation; provided, however, that the creditor reserves the right to collect his claim by sale of the pledge. (C. Obl. 138).

All letters of guaranties issued for certain period of time shall be valid within duration indicated in said letter of guaranty. It is permissible for guarantor (e.g., bank) to stipulate in its letter that if beneficiary does not submit claim in writing, prior to stated expiry thereof, "the guarantee shall become null and void." (C. Obl. 110 as am'd in July 1981).

LIMITED COMPANIES:

A limited company is a form of commercial association in which liability of all partners is limited to amount invested and capital is not divided into shares represented by share certificates. Transfer of a share in company is valid only if this fact is notified to company and recorded in share register. For this purpose it is necessary that at least three-fourths of shareholders give their consent to transfer and consenting shareholders own at least three-fourths of capital. Limited companies can deal in any business except insurance and banking. They are organized by a notarized contract which among other points must contain name, main office, purpose, total capital and amount undertaken by each partner, procedure of announcements to be made and term of company. This contract is submitted for authorization of Ministry of Industries and Commerce. After authorization is obtained company is registered at Commercial Register and this fact, with text of contract, is published in Commercial Register Gazette of Turkey. This authorization is not granted unless all capital is subscribed for and 25% paid. Minimum number of partners is two and maximum 50. Minimum amount of capital is TL 500 million. Limited companies with more than 20 partners have partners' meetings held according to rules governing those of corporations. (Com. C. 503-556).

MARRIAGE:

The minimum age at which marriage may lawfully be contracted is 17 in case of males and 15 in case of females. In exceptional cases, however, the court may allow marriage of a male at 15 or a female at 14, the parents and guardian being consulted. (C. C. 88). Only discriminating persons may marry. The consent of guardian or parents is necessary in case of minors. (C. C. 90).

Licenses are issued by municipalities. Except when allowed by the court the license cannot be given before the publication of banns. The ceremony may be performed by municipal authorities only. No religious ceremony can take place unless a certificate of marriage is received from the officer of civil status.

Prohibited Marriages.—Intermarriage among the following is forbidden: Parents and descendants, whether parenthood is legitimate or not; brothers and sisters; uncles and nieces; aunts and nephews; a man and parents or descendants of his wife; a woman and parents or descendants of her husband; adopted children or their spouses and adopting parents. (C. C. 92).

Annulment.—Any interested person or the attorney-general directly may petition to annul a marriage. A marriage is void where one of the parties is already married, where one of the parties was not discriminating at the time of the ceremony, or where intermarriage was legally forbidden. Either spouse may petition for an annulment when he or she was not of sound mind at the time the marriage took place, or was deceived about a material fact the non-existence of which would make married life unbearable, or where one of the parties was led into marriage by fraud or duress.

Common law marriages are not recognized.

MARRIED WOMEN:

See topics Descent and Distribution; Divorce; Husband and Wife; Marriage.

MONOPOLIES AND TRADE RESTRICTIONS:

There are two kinds of "monopolies": Production or import and sale of certain consumer goods, and, performance of certain public services.

Production or import and sale of certain consumer goods is under monopoly of Directorate General of Monopolies, attached to Ministry of Finance and Customs, e.g.: Spirits and alcoholic drinks, with exception of wine and beer; salt; playing cards, etc.; public services like railroads; gas and (with minor exceptions) electricity, etc.

Special permits and licenses are required for certain business activities, i.e., in field of banking, insurance, aviation, chemistry, pharmacy, private hospitals and clinics, etc. To obtain such permit, necessary qualification or financial potency to conduct such business generally must be proven.

See Topical Index in front part of this volume.

MORTGAGES:

A mortgage contract can only be made before land registrar and in authentic form. Mortgage does not take effect until registered. No limitation runs on a debt that is secured by mortgage. Contracts allowing creditor to declare a forfeiture of property in case of nonpayment are void.

MOTOR VEHICLES:

Traffic is controlled by Law 2918, Oct. 13, 1983. Car owners must register their vehicles and obtain license plate and pay yearly taxes. Import of motor vehicles into Turkey is subject to certain restrictions and to customs duties, motor vehicles of nonresidents and registered abroad for personal use are free from taxes and levies for sojourns in Turkey in accordance with provisions of related international treaties.

Foreigners domiciled abroad but staying in Turkey because of special employments can, under certain conditions, obtain special Turkish plates for period up to two years without having to pay customs duties. This period may be extended for additional three years. (Law of Customs. Art. 119).

Insurance of motor vehicles for damages to third parties is mandatory.

NEGOTIABLE INSTRUMENTS:

See topic Bills and Notes.

NOTARIES PUBLIC:

Notaries are public servants. They are appointed by Ministry of Justice from among holders of law degrees who have successfully completed novitiate of one year (lawyers, judges and prosecutors excepted). They must post bond, amount of which varies according to their gross annual notarial income. Papers and documents of legal nature as made and acknowledged before and authenticated by notaries are deemed official and held as prima facie evidence before courts. Notaries keep copies of all transactions authenticated by them. (Law on Notaries Public, No. 1512, dated Jan. 18, 1972).

PARTNERSHIP:

All commercial partnerships in Turkey are legal entities. They are registered at the Commercial Register and this fact with the text of contract is published in the Commercial Register Gazette of Turkey. The following can be invested as capital: Personal property, such as money, chattels, etc.; intangible property such as patents, trademarks, and good will; all kinds of real estate; usufruct; work; commercial credit. Each partner is obliged to exercise the same care and diligence in the affairs of the partnership as that he would in his own business. When the contract is silent as to the distribution of profits and losses the partners share equally. In case only distribution of profits or losses is mentioned the others also are distributed according to the same ratio. Conditions giving all profits to one of the partners or excluding one from losses are void, except that a partner who brings in his labor only can stipulate not to be liable for losses.

A general partnership ("kolektif sirketi") is formed by a written contract, a copy of which must be filed with the commercial register at the place of its organization. Signatures on this document must be authenticated by a notary. Announcement should be made in the newspapers. The business is carried under a firm name containing the names of all or at least of one of the partners and indicating the kind of partnership. In the latter case the words "and Co." are added to the firm name. The liability of the partners is unlimited. Unless otherwise stated in the contract all partners represent the partnership. A general partnership exists as to third persons only from the date of its registration and announcement. Partners are jointly and severally liable for the debts of the partnership with all their property.

A special partnership ("komandit sirketi") is composed of two kinds of partners. General partners or ("komandite") have unlimited liability; special partners ("komanditer") are liable only to the amount that they have agreed to contribute to the partnership. A special partner who permits his name to appear on the firm name becomes liable as a general partner. Special partners cannot participate in the affairs of business; if they do, they become liable with all their property.

A special partnership with shares is organized under a notarial act signed by all founders and "komandite." The business is carried on by the general partners. This form of partnership occupies a middle position between the general partnership and corporation. The limited part of the capital is divided into shares owned by special partners. Rules governing shares and meetings of corporations are applicable in this kind of partnership.

Limited Companies.—See topic Limited Companies.

PATENTS:

Patent matters are governed under Law/Decree No. 551 (O.J. June 27, 1995), as am'd by Law/Decree No. 566 (O.J. Sept. 22, 1995) and Law No. 4128 (O.J. Nov. 7, 1995), and by Regulations issued by Ministry of Industry and Commerce (O.J. Nov. 5, 1995). Per Law-4115 (O.J. July 12, 1995) Turkey also became party to several treaties and conventions (The Paris Convention of 1883 on the Protection of Industrial Property, as am'd under London and Stockholm texts, respectively, in 1934 and 1967; The Washington Convention of June 19, 1970, on Cooperation on Patents, as am'd on Oct. 2, 1979 and Feb. 3, 1994).

Applications through duly authorized agents must be filed with and publicized in Official Bulletin by Turkish Patents Institute (TPE). For those who have already filed for registry in country signatory to Paris Convention, preferential right is accorded, if application is made in Turkey within 12 months of such filing abroad. Protection is accorded unto applicant from date of application. However, rights emanating from patents and/or applications therefor are assertable vis-à-vis third parties only after registry in Patents Register. Approved patents are registered for 20 years (if granted with search duly conducted), and for seven years (if granted without due search). (For so-called "Useful Models" period of protection is limited to ten years.) Patents must be in use within three years of registry. Patent infringements could give rise to both civil claims and criminal prosecution.

Duly observing relevant procedures, patents may be assigned and/or licensed on exclusive or non-exclusive basis.

Protection is available to all private individuals or corporate persons domiciled or doing business in Turkey as well as to persons who are qualified therefor under Paris Convention of 1883 (as am'd), and to private or corporate citizens of such foreign countries as have accorded similar protection to Turks. (Patents for pharmaceutical production procedures and products shall be available only from Jan. 1, 1999 onwards.)

Protection similar to patents is also available for industrial designs (and geographical signs of origin).

See also topic Unfair Competition.

PETROLEUM LEGISLATION:

Petroleum Law dated Mar. 16, 1954 (No. 6326, as am'd by Laws No. 6558, 6987, 1702 and 2808), and Petroleum Regulations dated May 11, 1989, provide for exploitation of oil resources under certain conditions. As general principle, oil resources of country are under rule and domain of State. Under incentive-oriented legal framework (including rights to export certain portion of oil produced, and to remit invested capital and earnings), qualifying corporations (Turkish and foreign alike) may be granted rights to exploration, production, transport and refining.

PLEDGES:

Movable objects and assignable rights and claims may be pledged. The pledge is not complete until the pledgee takes possession of the goods pledged. (C. C. 853). Goods in transit and in warehouses may be pledged by the endorsement of securities. The pledgee is liable for any damage of the pledged articles unless he proves that the damage has been caused without his fault. All stipulations to the effect that the creditor shall forfeit the goods pledged in case of nonpayment are void. The pledged goods can only be sold through the Execution Department.

See also topic Bankruptcy.

PRESCRIPTION:

See topic Limitation of Actions.

PRINCIPAL AND AGENT:

No special form is required for a power of attorney. Powers given to conduct business must be recorded at the register of commerce. Power of attorney may be revoked any time. The agent is free to resign; but if he resigns at a time which is not proper and causes damage to the principal, he is liable. All bona fide transactions made with the agent are binding on the principal until the latter announces to the public the revocation of the power of attorney. Power of attorney given to commercial representative must be general in nature. But it can be limited to specific branch of business or by requiring two or more persons to act together. No commercial representative can, without special authority, sell or mortgage real property. (C. Obl. 450, 451).

REAL PROPERTY:

In civil law, rights are classified as real rights and personal rights. Personal right is a right which exists only against a certain person or persons. Real right, on other hand, is a right in property which may be claimed against any person. Ownership is broadest real right. Other real rights are mainly servitudes, usufruct and mortgage.

Property.—In Turkish Law, word "property" has different meanings. In first place, it indicates the thing subject to real rights. Property also means the real right involved.

Property may be classified as movable and immovable.

Immovable Property.—Property which cannot be moved such as land and buildings is called immovable property. Mines, too, are immovable property. Rights which are registered in title-deed registry as independent and permanent rights are also considered immovable property. (C. C. 632).

Movable Property.—Property which can be carried from one place to another is movable property. Such things as electricity, gas and steam which are not considered as immovable are movable property. (C. C. 686).

Title-deed registry has been established for purpose of evidencing transfer of possession and ownership of real property as well as rights, such as mortgages. Title-deed registries are kept by state in accordance with provisions of Regulation on Title-deed Registry. (C. C. 910). There are separate registries for various districts in cities, towns and rural areas. Certain principles govern operation of title-deed registry: (a) No real right in immovable property may be acquired without registration of such right (C. C. 633 and 910); (b) in addition to entry in register, parties must conclude an agreement to effect that disposition has to come into force. Other facts such as court judgment or prescription may take place of such agreement; (c) registration together with good faith gives presumption of ownership; (d) all interested parties may inspect title-deed registry; (e) when a damage results because of improper registration, state is liable (C. C. 917); (f) only certain real rights may be registered.

Ownership of land carries with it exclusive ownership of ground under land and air space above it to reasonable limits. (C. C. 644). All buildings on land are considered as part of land and registered in title-deed registry together with land itself. However, a special law has been issued providing for separate ownership of parts of a building such as flats or shops. (Law No. 634, dated June 23, 1965, am'd by Law 2814, Apr. 13, 1983).

Acquisition of Immovable Property.—(a) Transfer of title to real property should be recorded in title-deed registry (C. C. 634); (b) real property may also be acquired by filling space from sea (C. C. 636); (c) land not previously registered in register, may, if occupied by a person as owner for 20 years without dispute, be claimed as property of occupant and registration in his own name may be requested from competent court (C. C. 639).

RECORDS:

The Commercial Code requires the establishment of a commercial register at each district. This register is under the control of the commercial court of the district. The

See Topical Index in front part of this volume.

RECORDS . . . *continued*
names of all traders, partnerships, corporations and agents, with information concerning their activities are recorded.

Personal status, marriages, divorces, births, deaths, changes of name, etc., are recorded by a government department.

REPLEVIN:

The action most similar to replevin in Turkish law is an action to recover property wrongfully acquired, in which both the return of property and damages may be ordered by the court. Temporary measures for the protection of property thus disputed may be taken. This action must be brought within a year from the time the owner learns that he has the right to recover.

REPORTS:

Constitutional Court and State Council reports are being published regularly.

SALES:

A contract of sale may be made by notarial act or in the form of a private agreement which may be oral or written.

A sale may be proved by documents signed by the parties or by witnesses and by means of other satisfactory evidences. The sale is complete when the agreement is concluded and, unless the contrary is specifically provided for in the contract or understood from the circumstances, the risk falls on the buyer from this moment. In the following cases, however, the risk falls on the seller even after the conclusion of the sale: (1) Where the property sold is designated in kind but not separated; (2) when goods have to be shipped and seller has not yet given up his hold on such goods; (3) where the contract is conditional and such conditions have not yet been fulfilled.

If no price is mentioned and goods are sold and delivered the buyer pays the market price current at the time and place of the contract. (C. Obl. 209).

Obligations of the seller are the following: (1) Delivery, all expenses of delivery being borne by the seller in the absence of contrary stipulation or custom; (2) warranty against dispossession, any stipulation to be free from such responsibility being void in case the seller is aware of rights of third persons; (3) warranty of conformity of the thing sold to description or to sample and against defects that render the thing sold unfit for the purpose for which it was bought or which reduce its value greatly. Liability for latent defects exists even if the seller was unaware of them. (C. Obl. 194).

When defects in the thing sold are discovered or when it is found not to have the qualities mentioned in the contract, the buyer is free either to rescind the contract or to have the price reduced. (C. Obl. 204).

Obligations of the buyer are: (1) To pay the price; and (2) to receive the goods. When the buyer refuses to pay the price, in sales where the delivery is to be made after the payment, the seller can rescind the sale. (C. Obl. 211). In commercial sales, however, the seller may serve a notice on the buyer and fix a delay after which he has the right to request the court to have the goods sold for the account of the buyer.

F. O. B. and C. I. F. Sales.—Legal provisions concerning these two types of commercial sale are almost identical with generally accepted rules in world trade.

Conditional Sales.—A sale of personal property with a reservation of ownership by seller is possible, provided such transaction is authenticated by Notary Public of domicile of buyer and duly recorded in special Register of Reservation of Ownership. Reservation of Ownership in case of sale of animals is prohibited. (C. C. 688).

Notices Required.—If one of parties does not fulfill its obligations properly, for example buyer does not make payment accordingly or seller does not deliver in time or delivered goods are defective, notice must be given to other party. In general, orally given notice is sufficient. However, for sake of proof it is advisable to give notice through notary public or by registered letter. In commercial transactions, in order to put other party in default, this notice must be given either through notary public or by registered letter or by cable. (Com. C. Art. 20).

Buyer is under obligation to examine delivered goods with such dispatch as is reasonable and in case of defect notify seller. In case of defects which were not patent on customary examination and are found later, notice must be given forthwith upon their discovery. (C. Obl. Art. 198). In cases of commercial transactions, if defect is obvious, notice must be given within two days from date of delivery. If defect was not obvious, buyer must have goods examined within eight days, and, in case of defects, give notice within that term. (Com. C. Art. 25).

Applicable Law.—See topic Contracts.

SEALS:

Public authorities and commercial corporations have seals, but such seals have no value unless accompanied by the signature of the person in authority. Signatures of private persons must be in their own handwriting; only those who cannot write may use a seal or a sign legalized by a notary.

SEQUESTRATION:

In case of litigation about the ownership of movable property or real estate, courts may order it to be attached or taken into legal custody, and provisional measures for the safekeeping of such property may be decreed.

SHIPPING:

Only ships totally owned by Turkish citizens can fly Turkish flag. Aliens cannot own part in Turkish ship. Turkish corporation in which Turkish citizens have voting majority in General Assembly and Board can own Turkish flag vessel. (Com. C. 823). In many instances liability of owner of vessel is restricted to vessel and freight.

The owner of a vessel is liable for the negligence and the fault of the crew. If he is also faulty, he is personally liable. Suits for damages are brought against the ship owners or against masters even in cases where they are not personally liable.

Liens, due to such claims as averages, salvage fees, wages, port expenses, etc., peculiar to maritime law, do not require actual possession of the vessel.

Vessels are registered by special bureaus. Purchase and sale of ships must be recorded.

Cabotage.—Coastal trade and maritime services (piloting, salvage etc.) are reserved for Turkish-flag carriers and citizens. (Law No. 815, Apr. 19, 1926).

SOCIAL SECURITY:

See topic Labor Legislation.

STATUTES:

Turkish legal system is part of continental European legal system. Turkish Civil Code (C. C.) and Code of Obligations (C. Obl.) are translations of Swiss Civil Code and Code of Obligations. Commercial Code (Com. C) is based on German, Swiss and French laws. Central European legal publications, like text books, commentaries, law journals and court decisions, are common sources frequently used for interpretation and application of Turkish laws. Thus, Turkish legal system is not a strange or different one for those familiar with European continental laws.

Legislation.—Legislative power is vested in Turkish Grand National Assembly. This power cannot be delegated. (Con. 7).

Constitution is supreme law of country. No law can be contrary to any of its provisions. (Con. 11). Constitutional Court renders rulings as to constitutionality of laws and internal regulations of Grand National Assembly. (Con. 148).

Codes and Statutes.—Some important codes are: Civil Code; Code of Obligations; Criminal Code; Code of Commerce: Code of Civil Procedure; Code of Criminal Procedure, etc.

International Treaties.—See topic Treaties.

Regulations are issued by Council of Ministers providing for mode of application of statutes. Regulations cannot be in conflict with laws and must be reviewed and approved by Council of State. They must be signed by President and promulgated in same manner as statutes. (Con. 111).

Instructions or Communiqués are directives issued by ministries and public corporate bodies with purpose of assuring application of statutes and regulations related to their particular field of activity and in conformity with such statutes and regulations. Instructions must be published in Official Gazette.

Decrees or ordinances are legal provisions issued by Council of Ministers which do not require approval of Parliament and have same sanctions as laws. They are issued by Executive on basis of authority granted by Parliament.

See also topic Constitution and Government.

TAXATION:

Note: Tax legislation is subject to frequent changes. The summary information below reflects the status as of May 31, 1996.

I. Direct Taxes.—

Corporation Tax.—Following are subject to this tax: Companies, that is: (a) Corporation (sociétés anonymes), special partnerships with shares, limited companies and foreign firms of same type; (b) cooperatives; (c) public economic organizations (enterprises owned and/or operated by state, provincial administrations or municipalities and engaged in commercial, industrial and agricultural activities); (d) economic organizations owned and operated by associations and foundations; (e) business partnerships.

Economic organizations and firms owned by foreign states or associations are subject to corporation tax under the same conditions as Turkish public organizations.

Some Government-owned organizations and firms and profits of certain types of others are exempted from the tax.

Corporations domiciled in Turkey pay this tax on all of their corporate earnings, whether in Turkey or outside. Corporations not domiciled in Turkey pay tax only on their earnings in Turkey.

Corporation tax is assessed on basis of statement submitted during month of Apr. following closing of fiscal year. Fiscal year starts on first of Jan.

Rate of Tax.—25% of net profit is subject to corporate tax (final tax burden is required to be not less than 20% before taking of deductions and exemptions, if any). Also withholding tax of 20% is to apply (effective Jan. 1, 1995) on balance remaining after calculation of corporation tax (except that lower rates may apply for corporations which are nationals of countries with which treaties of avoidance of double-taxation exist). Turkish entities doing business with foreign companies with limited Turkish tax liability must withhold 25% on their gross payment (except that lower rates are prescribed per decree for certain types of earnings). Those foreign companies with limited tax liabilities rendering service in Turkey who have profits and earnings in type of: (i) Remunerations; (ii) professional profits; (iii) earnings from immovable capital; (iv) earnings from movable capital; (v) proceeds from sale, transfer, assignment of incorporeal rights such as copyrights, concessions, patents, exploitations, trade names, trademarks and like are not forced to file annual or special tax return for such income or to include such profits and earnings on returns (except that interest income from bonds, stocks and deposit accounts must be included in return). (Corp. Tax Law, Art. 24).

Income Tax.—Income of real persons is subject to progressive income tax (maximum 55%). Net sum total of all earnings and/or income accruing during calendar year is considered as income of person.

Real persons who are residents in Turkey or who live in this country more than six months during a calendar year pay income tax on all their income accrued in Turkey or outside (full tax liability). Those who are not residents in Turkey or live six months or less during calendar year or visit country for business, treatment or rest, pay this tax only on their income accrued in Turkey (limited tax liability).

Foreign diplomats, consular employees as well as employees of non-domiciled corporations doing business in Turkey, being paid in foreign exchange and out of employer's non-Turkish income are also exempted from this tax under certain conditions.

There are also some other exemptions in case of certain types of income tax.

Corporate taxpayers, individual merchants and professionals must pay "Temporary Tax" against income for current year. This tax is calculable to 50% for individuals and 70% for corporations (which, at Government's discretion, may be raised to 100% or

See Topical Index in front part of this volume.

TAXATION . . . *continued*

reduced to 25%) of corporation and/or income taxes reported for previous calendar year, and is payable by being divided into 12 equal monthly instalments (nevertheless reduced by withholding taxes, if any, being applied to current income).

Withholding.—In certain cases income tax is withheld at the source and in some instances the tax payer is allowed to deduct these amounts from his total yearly tax.

Foreign Taxes.—Persons resident in Turkey and paying similar taxes on their incomes in foreign countries are allowed to deduct from their income tax an amount proportionate to the income earned in those countries.

Land and building taxes paid are assessed based upon value declared by owners and are entered as expenses from yearly income. Rates vary between three to six per mille for land and four to five per mille for buildings.

Tax Procedure.—A special law provides for procedure to be followed in case of evaluation, assessment, collection of and objection against all state taxes. Special rules have been established with regard to the computation of net income and valuation of assets.

Inheritance and Transfer Tax.—All personal and real property inherited by, or bequeathed or donated to real or juridical persons is subject to inheritance tax, unless exempted. All property escheating to state or bequeathed or donated to state, municipalities and villages, personal property bequeathed or donated to places of worship, charitable hospitals and asylums, all house chattels inherited and all personal property inherited from descendants, father, mother, wife or husband and small portion of value of all presents and gifts customarily exchanged among friends and relatives are exempted from this tax.

In all cases inheritance tax (varying from 4% to 30%) is ascending one both as regards to amount inherited or received and to proximity between beneficiary and donor or testator. Exempted amounts which are readjusted upwards each year according to revaluation ratios announced by government are available for each surviving spouse and descendant (correspondingly higher for spouses when there are no descendants).

II. Other Taxes and Charges.—There are variety of these: Value Added Tax (V.A.T.) on all deliveries of goods and services (with minor exceptions) at basic rate of 15% (but variable from 1% to 23% on selected items and even higher for liquor and tobacco); Expenditure Tax in banking and insurance transactions at basic rate of 3% (but per decree 5% until Dec. 31, 1996, thereafter 1%); 85% gasoline consumption tax; motor vehicle taxes (applicable at variable rates, both during purchase and use thereof); various municipal taxes and levies; various and sundry fees; customs duties (at variable rates, at time of import of dutiable goods, along with ancillary taxes and levies); stamp tax (collected at variable rates—for example, 6 per mille on contracts specifying sum—, in form of cash and/or stamps to be affixed to certain papers—some of which are printed by Government under label "valuable papers"); housing assistance (mandatory for employers who employ ten plus workers).

Apart from above, both income (except on salaries and wages) and corporate taxpayers are required to pay three surcharges which are calculated as percentage of income and corporation taxes themselves. These are: "Fund for the Support of the Defense Industry" (Law No. 3238, Nov. 13, 1985); "Fund for the Support of Social Assistance and Solidarity" (Law No. 3294, May 29, 1986), and "Fund for the Development and Dissemination of Vocational, Technical and Apprenticeship Training" (Law No. 3308, June 19, 1986). All of these Funds have been combined and are payable at flat 10% of income and corporation taxes as calculated on basis of annual returns.

III. Avoidance of Double-Taxation.—Turkey has treaties (ratified) with: Austria, Belgium, Britain, Denmark, France, Finland, Federal Republic of Germany, Hungary, Italy, Japan, Jordan, Republic of Korea, the Netherlands, Norway, Pakistan, Romania, Russia, Sweden, Tunisia, Turkish Republic of Northern Cyprus, as well as, with Saudi Arabia, Switzerland, Israel and UAE (for certain transport incomes only). Treaties (as yet unratified) have also been signed with Canada and U.S.

TRADEMARKS AND TRADENAMES:

Trademarks (including service marks, warranty marks, marks held jointly in name of group of companies) and tradenames are protected under provisions of Law/Decree No. 556 (O.J. June 27, 1995) as am'd (by Law No. 4128 of Nov. 3, 1995) and by Regulations issued by Ministry of Industry and Commerce (O.J. Nov. 5, 1995).

Applications through duly authorized agents must be filed with, approved and publicized in Official Bulletin, by Turkish Patents Institute (TPE). For those who have already filed for registry of their mark in country signatory to Paris Convention, preferential right is accorded, if application is made in Turkey, within six months of such filing abroad. No right of action against infringement exists until such filing is effected. Approved marks are registered for ten years and may be renewed as often as desired. Trademark infringements could give rise to both civil claims (including compensation for damages, confiscation and destruction of counterfeit items, corrective advertisements), as well as, criminal prosecution.

Duly observing relevant procedures, trademarks may be assigned, fully or in part, and may be licensed on exclusive or non-exclusive basis. Protection is available to all private individuals or corporate persons domiciled or doing business in Turkey as well as to persons who are qualified therefor under Paris Convention of Mar. 20, 1883 on Protection of Industrial Property, and to private or corporate citizens of such foreign countries as have accorded similar protection to Turks.

See also topics Industrial Property and Unfair Competition.

TREATIES:

Ratification and Force of International Treaties.—Ratification of treaties entered into with foreign states and international organizations in behalf of Turkish Republic is dependent upon approval of Turkish Grand National Assembly through enactment of a law.

Treaties which regulate economic, commercial and technical relations and which are to be in force for period not to exceed one year may be put into effect on publication, provided they do not entail any financial commitment for state and provided they do not infringe upon status of individuals and upon ownership rights of Turkish citizens in foreign countries. Such treaties, within two months after their publication, must be submitted to Grand National Assembly for information.

Agreements concluded in connection with implementation of an international treaty and economic, commercial, technical and administrative treaties concluded pursuant to authority provided by laws are not required to be approved by Grand National Assembly. Economic and commercial treaties or treaties affecting rights of individuals cannot go into effect unless published.

All treaties involving amendments in Turkish legislation must be ratified by Grand National Assembly through enactment of a law. International treaties duly put into effect carry force of law. No recourse to constitutional court may be made in regard to these treaties.

"Treaties on Reciprocal Promotion and Protection of Investments" have been concluded with Albania, Argentina, Austria, Bangladesh, the Benelux Countries, China, Denmark, Finland, Georgia, Great Britain, Hungary, Japan, Jordan, Kazakhstan, Kirghizistan, Kuwait, Ozbekhistan, Poland, Romania, South Korea, Switzerland, Tunisia, Turkmenistan, Turkish Republic of Northern Cyprus and U.S.

See also Selected International Conventions section.

UNFAIR COMPETITION:

Main body of rules governing fair competition are in Law No. 4054 (O.J. Dec. 13, 1994) which contains elaborate provisions parallel to those being applied in European Union. Independent board of broad powers has been created to monitor and intercept market developments detrimental to competition and issue heavy fines to violators wherever indicated.

There are also complementary rules in Code of Obligations (Art. 48) taken almost verbatim from Swiss Federal Code of 1926, with further elaborations in Commercial Code (Arts. 56-65).

See also topics Anti-Dumping Laws; Patents; Trademarks and Tradenames.

WILLS:

All persons above 15 and who are discriminating are capable of making wills disposing of their property. In order to make a contract of heirship one must have attained the age of majority.

Any condition not immoral or unlawful may be attached to the will or to a contract of heirship. (C. C. 462).

Wills may be made in one of the following ways: (1) Formal wills are drawn by notaries or similar officials, who are obliged to keep originals or legalized copies on file. (C. C. 479-484). Such wills must be signed by the testator and by the officials in charge. (2) A will may be prepared by the testator himself. In this case the entire will, including the date and the place of execution, must be written in the testator's own handwriting. No witnesses are required. Such wills are deposited with the justice of peace or with a notary public to be kept either open or in a sealed envelope. (3) In cases of emergency, such as impending death, war, etc., when the testator cannot make a will in any other way he may declare his desires to two witnesses whom he requests to have such desires written at their earliest convenience.

Reserved Portions.—The part of the property which can be disposed by will or contract of heirship is limited to that which the law does not obligate a person to leave to his lawful heirs. Descendants, parents, brothers and sisters, husband or wife have certain interests in the estate of the decedent of which they cannot be deprived by will. (C. C. 452). The shares of these heirs are the following portions of the shares which they would take in case of intestacy: For a descendant three-fourths; for each parent one-half; for each brother or sister one-fourth; for the surviving spouse the whole share, if congregating with descendants, and one-half thereof if he or she is congregating with heirs other than descendants. (C. C. 453).

Any of the heirs may be deprived of inheritance by the will of the decedent if he has been guilty of a great wrong against the testator or against one of his near relatives or if he is gravely negligent of his duties towards the testator.

See Topical Index in front part of this volume.

UKRAINE LAW DIGEST REVISER

Altheimer & Gray
Suite 4000
10 South Wacker Drive
Chicago, Illinois 60606
Telephone: 312-715-4000
Fax: 312-715-4800
Kyiv, Ukraine Office: Altheimer & Gray Kyiv, 42/4 Pushkinska Street, 252004 Kyiv, Ukraine.
Telephone: 7 044 230-2534. Fax: 7 044 230-2535.

Reviser Profile

History and General Description: Altheimer & Gray, founded in 1915, is a Chicago-based multinational law firm focusing on business transactions worldwide.

More than 200 attorneys serve both publicly and privately owned companies, including firms listed on the New York, London, Warsaw, Prague and American Stock Exchanges and traded on NASDAQ. Clients include large manufacturing, service, distribution, retail, real estate development, hotel and financial organizations, emerging and mid-size businesses, and the governments of several Central and Eastern European countries. In many instances the firm's relationships with clients date back more than 50 years.

The firm's attorneys are experienced in a variety of international practice areas and have assisted foreign clients in connection with investment in the United States, and American and foreign clients in their direct investments and licensing of technology outside the United States, including international joint ventures, eurocurrency/eurodollar financing transactions, international arbitrations, taxation, complex financing, real estate and construction projects, acquisitions and divestitures, finance and banking, securities, antitrust, environmental matters, patents, licensing, intellectual property, insurance and counseling emerging governments.

Attorneys in the firm have significant contacts and relationships with foreign governments, lawyers, banks and corporations in Eastern and Western Europe; Canada; Latin America; and the Far East, including Japan and the People's Republic of China.

Eastern and Southern European Experience: Altheimer & Gray has represented clients in connection with Central and Eastern European matters for over twenty years and Southern Europe for over ten years. In September, 1990 we became the first American law firm to open an office in Poland. Then, in December of 1991, we opened an office in Prague, Czech Republic, in July of 1993 we expanded once more with the opening of offices in Kyiv, Ukraine and in December, 1993 Bratislava, Slovakia. In April 1994, we opened an office in Istanbul, Turkey. The majority of our attorneys in the European offices are multilingual Nationals, fluent in English. Several American lawyers are resident in those offices, while a large core group of American attorneys divide their time between Chicago and European assignments.

The firm's practice in Central, Eastern and Southern Europe, serviced from our Warsaw, Prague, Kyiv, Bratislava and Istanbul offices, concentrates in the following areas:

Privatizations: The privatization of Polish, Czech, Slovak, Ukrainian and Turkish companies represents a major segment of the firm's current practice.

In Ukraine, Altheimer & Gray is active in privatizations and joint ventures. Recently, Altheimer & Gray Kyiv concluded two acquisitions for tobacco and food processing clients. The Kyiv office also assists its clients in establishing and maintaining relations with Ukrainian government and parliamentary officials. Our attorneys counsel both the foreign companies and the government from initial structuring to negotiations to the completion of a successful business transaction. Clients include multinational companies in the agro-chemical, food processing, consumer products, oil exploration and refining, construction equipment, telecommunications and hotel industries. This year the Director of Altheimer & Gray Kyiv was appointed by President Clinton to the Board of Directors of the Western NIS Enterprise Fund.

In Poland, Altheimer & Gray represented the acquiror in the first privatization in which a Western firm was permitted to purchase a controlling interest in a state-owned enterprise. Virtually every aspect of this transaction created precedents which have had an impact on subsequent privatizations. In numerous privatizations, the firm has represented either the purchasers, the Ministry of Privatization, the Ministry of Industry or the acquired company, including the first bank privatization in Poland.

In the Czech Republic, Altheimer & Gray has been involved in numerous privatizations representing the acquiring company and also acted as a Senior Advisor to the Czech Republic Ministry of Privatization during the initial period of the first wave of large-scale privatization. In this position, the firm reviewed and negotiated many significant privatization projects involving foreign participation presented to the Ministry. The firm also provided assistance in connection with the establishment of uniform procedures to increase the efficiency of the privatization process, including preparation of the original form purchase agreements which were accepted by the Fund of National Property for use in privatization transactions involving foreign participation. These form agreements represent the Ministry's institutional position on numerous issues arising in the acquisition process.

In Slovakia, Altheimer & Gray is involved in matters similar to those we address in the Czech Republic.

In Istanbul, Altheimer & Gray is active in acquisitions, privatizations and joint ventures. Our attorneys counsel western businesses entering Turkey's emerging markets as state-owned enterprises are converted in private concerns. Clients include multinational companies in the banking, consumer products, construction, petroleum, pharmaceutical and textile industries.

During the last three years in Central and Eastern Europe the firm has been involved in more than 50 privatization transactions.

Joint Ventures and Foreign Investment: The firm is representing numerous multinational corporations, real estate developers, hotel chains, investors and others in structuring joint ventures with Polish, Czech, Slovak, Ukrainian and Turkish enterprises.

Real Estate Development: The firm is representing clients in major commercial, industrial and hotel real estate development projects. Advice is provided in a wide range of legal matters, including tax planning, structuring and documentation, leasing, financing, management and construction arrangements.

Banking and Finance: The firm has represented major U.S. and European money-center financial institutions and a consortium of European banks and Scandinavian banking firms in their respective establishments of banking, financing and leasing operations. The firm also represents major international multilateral financial institutions, investment funds and merchant banks in connection with their financing and investment activities in Central, Eastern and Southern Europe.

Insurance: The firm advises clients on foreign and domestic business and insurance requirements and risk management matters and counsels insurers and reinsurers on the area's evolving statutory mandates.

Taxation: Altheimer & Gray serves as tax counsel to numerous local and multinational clients, providing advice on all aspects of local tax law with respect to both transaction matters and on-going operations.

Altheimer & Gray's Support Systems: We offer clients direct communication links via modem with our Kyiv, Prague, Warsaw, Bratislava, Istanbul and Chicago offices. Our network system in the Chicago office allows us to offer 24-hour service. Altheimer & Gray's multilingual support staff is equipped with the latest technology.

UKRAINE LAW DIGEST

(The following is a list of all Topics, including cross-references, covered in this Digest.)

UKRAINE LAW DIGEST

Revised for 1997 edition by

ALTHEIMER & GRAY, of the Illinois Bar, and Kyiv, Ukraine.

ABSENTEES:

Personal Representative.—If individual cannot personally realize his rights and duties for legal or actual reasons, then he may delegate authority to representative as means to realize rights and duties. Legal reasons for incapacity include: individual under age 18; limited or complete capacity of individual; lack of status of organization as legal entity. Actual reasons include circumstances which hamper individual to realize his rights and duties: disease, absence in residential area, legal illiteracy, etc.

Representation shall mean agreement made by representative on behalf of represented individual on basis of power of attorney, law or enactment, which creates, alters or terminates civil rights and duties of represented individual. Representative may not make agreement on behalf of represented individual neither with respect to himself nor to other individual, whose interests he represents simultaneously.

Agreement by representative prohibited which, by its character, may be realized only personally. Representative cannot sign will nor register marriage on behalf of person represented.

Power of Attorney.—Voluntary representation shall be based on agreement or power of attorney (contrary to legal representation which is based on law or enactment). Power of attorney may be issued only by capable individuals and legal entities within limits of their charter rights and obligations. Minor citizens (15-18 years old) may independently issue powers of attorney within limits of rights they may realize personally (disposition by their grants, wages, copyright). Legal entity may be submitted with power of attorney only to make agreements which are not in contravention of its charter. Power of attorney is executed in written form and may be (i) simple or (ii) certified by notary. When absentee issues power of attorney for receiving his salary or other payment and his correspondence, then his power of attorney may be certified by officials of organization where trustee is employed or by administration of hospital where trustee is patient. Powers of attorney to make agreements which must be made in notary form and those for proceedings related to state and public organizations must be certified by notary. Following kinds of powers of attorney shall be equivalent to certification by notary: powers of attorney of military personnel and other individuals who are patients in hospitals, sanatoriums and other military medical institutions, which are certified by directors, their deputies and doctors of these institutions; powers of attorney of military personnel, as well as employees, workers, and members of families thereof located at military institutions and organizations, where there are no state notary offices, which are certified by commanders of areas thereof; powers of attorney of individuals who are in penal institutions, which are certified by heads thereof.

Agreement made by individual, who is not authorized to make such agreement or who acts in excess of his authority on behalf of other individual, shall create, alter and terminate civil rights and duties of represented individual only in event of future approval of agreement by represented individual.

Term of power of attorney shall not exceed three years. Power of attorney shall be effective during one year from day of its execution if term of effectiveness thereof is not specified. If power of attorney certified by state notary, is executed for legal acts outside Ukraine and does not include term of effectiveness thereof, it shall be in force till revocation thereof by individual who issued it.

Power of attorney without indication of term of effectiveness shall be deemed invalid.

According to content and extent of authorities which are delegated to representative, following three kinds of powers of attorney may be distinguished: general powers of attorney shall be issued for execution of various agreements and other legal proceedings during certain period of time; special powers of attorney shall be issued for execution of number of similar agreements or other; single powers of attorney shall be granted for execution of definite agreement or other legal proceedings.

Individual who issued power of attorney may at any time revoke it and individual who acts on basis of power of attorney may reject it. (Arts. 62-70, Civil Code of Ukraine).

Citizens may plead their causes personally or through their representatives. Representation as act of civil right must be distinguished from proceeding representation: on civil matters in court, arbitration court, or in criminal proceedings.

In event individual, deemed absentee in established manner, must take part in proceedings, trustee appointed for protection and disposition of property of absentee, shall be representative thereof.

If inheritance not adopted and if successor of deceased individual takes part in proceedings, trustee appointed for protection and disposition of inherited property shall be representative of successor.

Before courts, absentee may be represented by advocate or by person who is joint party to absentee in proceedings.

Documents which confirm powers of representatives shall be power of attorney or oral statement of truster included in protocol of court proceedings and order of association bar (for advocates).

Following individuals cannot be representatives in court: individuals under 18; individuals under wardship; judges, investigators and prosecutors except where they act as parents and trustees. (Part 12, Civil Legal Code of Ukraine).

ACKNOWLEDGMENTS:

In accordance with general rule, documents executed abroad shall become effective in Ukraine upon legalization (acknowledgment) in established manner. Similarly, official documents executed in Ukraine shall be duly legalized (acknowledged) for use abroad.

In Ukraine, "consular legalization" shall mean procedure which includes confirmation of authenticity of documents or trustworthiness of seals, stamps, etc. by diplomatic and consular officers. Consular legalization shall confirm competence of documents for international communication.

Functions related to consular legalization shall be carried out: abroad by embassies or consular agencies of Ukraine; in Ukraine by Consular Department of Ministry of Foreign Relations of Ukraine, representative offices of Ministry of Foreign Economic Relations of Ukraine.

Several means of legalization exist for various types of documents: (1) In event of legalization of documents concerning registration of acts of civil status (certificates of birth, death, marriage, documents on education and academic level), documents shall be submitted for legalization by Consular Department of Ministry of Foreign Relations of Ukraine or consular agencies of Ukraine abroad in original only. (2) Documents issued by ministries, agencies, institutions, organizations and enterprises, may be submitted for legalization as printed copies to be confirmed by First State Notary Agencies (in oblasts and city in Kyiv and Sevastopol). Signatures of notaries shall be confirmed by respective entries in Ministry of Justice of Ukraine, and further, signatures of officers of Ministry of Justice shall be confirmed by Consular Department of Ministry of Foreign Relations of Ukraine. Documents so executed shall be recognized by foreign diplomatic representative offices in Ukraine as legally effective. (3) Documents executed abroad and intended for use in Ukraine, upon notary confirmation by notary of respective country and government agencies of consular area, may be legalized by consular agency of Ukraine in such country. Ukraine is not member of 1961 Hague Convention.

Legalization of documents shall be subject to payment by concerned individuals and legal entities of consular fee and actual costs connected with carrying out of such actions.

ACTIONS:

In accordance with Civil Proceedings Code of Ukraine which regulates proceedings of civil actions, any person may sue or be sued in court in established manner. Adult persons and legal entities may appeal to court personally or entrust commencement of action in court to representative. Rights of minors and fully or partially incapable persons are represented in court by parents, adopters or trustees thereof. (See topic Absentees.) Actions of legal entities are brought to court by agents, heads or representatives thereof which act within competence granted to them by charter. Civil Proceedings Code laws in effect on day action commenced govern.

Proceedings against state of type which have been developed in U.S., have not yet been legally established in Ukraine. Civil Proceedings Code regulates only procedure of submitting claim against actions of: (i) state executive agencies and officers thereof; (ii) bodies of self-governance and officers thereof; (iii) heads of enterprises and associations thereof; (iv) organizations and institutions irrespective of their ownership forms; (v) governing bodies and heads of associations of citizens; (vi) officials who fulfill organizational and managerial, administrative and business obligations or those who are specifically authorized to fulfill such obligations; (vii) officials in connection with complaints on decisions regarding religious organizations; (viii) upon prosecutor's claim on recognition of legal action as unlawful. Status of law in this area is influenced by fact that during Soviet rule, complaints against any agency were submitted by citizens to local councils of people's deputies or other higher agencies (local radas) which were authorized to consider and decide all issues. As state management has been modified, claim to court to commence action against state is now permitted and is effectuated according to principle that "everything is allowed which is not prohibited by law". Such claims sometimes occur but they are aimed mainly against officer or agency. Such actions are commenced according to general procedures with some exceptions and amendments anticipated by cc. 30-32 of Civil Proceedings Code.

Ukraine law, like other laws of continental European states, does not include action in equity. Legal proceedings in courts of Ukraine may take form of: (i) litigation proceedings—main subjects of which are disputes arising from civil, family, labor and cooperative legal relations; (ii) legal proceedings of cases arising from administrative and legal relations—Civil Proceedings Code of Ukraine includes list of such cases (part III-B; see also topic Courts); (iii) independent legal proceedings—main characteristic of which is non-litigation. List of such cases is also given in Civil Proceedings Code of Ukraine (part III-C) (1) on recognition of person as fully or partially incapable; (2) on recognition of person as absentee or deceased; (3) on recognition of entry in state documents as incorrect; (4) on identification of legally important facts; (5) on renewal of rights for lost bearer securities; (6) on appeal of notarial actions or refusal to carry out such actions.

Jurisdiction.—In its broadest sense, jurisdiction means all civil cases which are subject to consideration and decision at any level of court system. There are two kinds of jurisdiction: common—distribution of civil cases among separate levels of court system—and territorial—distribution of cases among separate courts depending on territory of such courts. (See also topic Courts.)

Costs include duty and expenses connected with consideration of case, namely: (i) amounts which must be paid to experts and witnesses; (ii) expenses to be paid for examination at place of case; (iii) expenses to search for defendant; (iv) expenses connected with performance of decision. Court or judge, on basis of property status of citizen, may release such citizen from payment of state court fees. Every petition on commencement of action, primary or supplementary, petition on contract disputes, petition of third party who independently appeals to court on subject of dispute, complaints, issuance of second copy of court decision, is subject to court fee in amount specified by Decree of the Cabinet of Ministers of Ukraine No. 7-93 Jan. 21, 1993 "On State Duty" with its amendments and modifications.

Some categories of claimants are exempted from payment of court expenses, for example: (i) claimants-employees on claims arising from labor relations; (ii) claimants on claims arising from copyright, patent right, etc.; (iii) claimants on claims of alimony; (iv) claimants on claims on compensation of damage caused by disability or

See Topical Index in front part of this volume.

ACTIONS . . . *continued*
health injury; (v) state insurance and state security agencies for claims on compensation by person who caused damage. (Detailed list is contained in art. 70 of Civil Proceedings Code of Ukraine.)

Prevailing party must be compensated for all court expenses by other party, even if this party is exempted from court expenses in favor of state. If claim is partially allowed, share of allowed claim is paid by defendant, and share of abandoned (disallowed) claim is paid to state budget by claimant. Court expenses must be paid by each party in proportion to part of claim which was abandoned. If winning party is exempted from court fees then court fees must be paid by other party to state budget. If claim of claimant exempted from court fees is abandoned, then expenses are paid by state. In case of termination of matter as result of cancellation thereof by claimant, expenses are paid according to decision of court. Upon cancellation of claim by claimant, his expenses are not compensated by defendant, except for instances when claimant cancels claim as result of defendant's voluntary satisfaction of claimant's requirements.

Security for Costs.—There is no special provision in Ukrainian Code of Civil Procedure concerning liability for aliens commencing civil actions before Ukrainian courts to post security for defendant's costs. C.C.P., art. 73, provides general rules requiring party commencing action before court to pay, in advance, costs necessary for legal proceedings.

See also topics Courts; Foreign Law; Limitation of Actions.

ADOPTION:

Adoption of children is permitted exclusively in their interests.

Children, given up by parents at maternity house, may be adopted upon reaching age of two months under written consent of parents.

Adoption is performed upon application of individual willing to adopt child, in accordance with court procedures.

Any capable adult may adopt. Age difference between adopter and adoptee must be not less than 15 years; if adoption is by relatives, age is not factor.

Adopters cannot be (i) individuals without paternity rights; (ii) individuals who submitted adoption documents known to be untrustworthy; (iii) individuals willing to perform adoption for purposes of obtaining material or other benefits; (iv) individuals who do not earn regular wages, etc.

Notarized consent of parents is required for adoption.

Such consent is not required if (i) parents are unknown; (ii) parents are deprived of paternity rights; (iii) parents are recognized incapable or missing; (iv) parents (or one of them) have not lived with child for over six months and without serious reasons do not support or show parental interest in child.

Application for adoption by foreign individuals is submitted to Child Adoption Center. Confidentiality of adoption does not extend to instances of adoption by foreign individuals.

Adoption of child who is citizen of Ukraine is performed if such child has been registered with Child Adoption Center for not less than one year. In instances when foreign individuals are relatives of such child or if such child is ill, adoption is performed without compliance with established periods.

Adopted children reserve their citizenship until they reach age 18.

Adoption arises from date of effectiveness of court decision on adoption.

Priority right for adoption is granted to citizens of countries which participate in international adoption treaties.

In accordance with resolution of Mar. 30, 1996, Child Adoption Center was established at Ministry of Education. Such Center assists in settling orphans in families of Ukrainian and foreign individuals by means of adoption; creates database on children who lost parents; provides necessary information to Ukrainian and foreign individuals about adoptable children; issues permits to custody and care agencies for adoption in established manner of children by foreign individuals.

AFFIDAVITS:

Statements or declarations reduced to writing and sworn to or affirmed before officer who has authority to administer oath or affirmation is unknown as item of special evidence in Ukrainian Law.

AGENCY:

Under Ukrainian civil law, relations which in U.S. are regulated by agency agreements, are regulated by (i) mandate agreement and (ii) commission agreement.

In accordance with mandate agreement, agent is obligated to take certain legal actions on behalf of principal and at principal's expense. Parties to any mandate agreement may be competent individuals and legal entities. Legal entities may act only as permitted under articles of incorporation thereof. Individuals, who make and carry out mandate agreements for purpose of commercial intermediation, must be registered as entrepreneurs. In accordance with general provisions on form of agreements, mandate agreements may be verbal or written. Under mandate agreement, principal as rule issues power of attorney in favor of agent. Term of mandate agreement is established in accordance with nature thereof, but cannot exceed effective term of power of attorney.

Transformation of Ukraine to market economy considerably broadened sphere of application of mandate agreements, as this is useful and profitable legal form of carrying out various middleman services with participation of such commercial structures as broker offices, sales agents, etc.

In commission agreement, commission agent is obligated on principal's instruction and with compensation to carry out one or several agreements for principal in his own name and at principal's expense.

Commission agreements regulate representative relations mainly for trade and intermediary transactions.

Commission agreements are used in such new areas of commercial activity as trade on stock exchange; often trade and intermediary transactions under such agreements are combined with additional services, such as insurance, transportation of goods, etc. Parties to commission agreements may be individuals and legal entities. Agreements must be executed in written form.

Both mandate agreements and commission agreements are based on representation relations; but with respect to former direct representation is meant, while latter is realized on basis of indirect representation.

In addition, mandate agreements may be made with or without indemnity, while commission agreements are always made with indemnity.

For commission agreement subject is agreement only, and for mandate agreement it is "certain legal actions", (Civil Code of Ukraine, cc. 34, 35; Laws of Ukraine "On Stock Exchange", "On Entrepreneurial Activity").

ALIENS:

Law of Ukraine "On the Legal Status of Foreigners" as of Feb. 4, 1994 defines foreign individuals as those, who have citizenship of foreign states and who are not citizens of Ukraine, and stateless individuals, namely persons who do not belong to citizenship of any state.

Foreigners enjoy rights equal with Ukrainians and have duties equal with Ukrainians unless otherwise provided by Constitution, by this or other laws of Ukraine and international agreements of Ukraine.

On territory of Ukraine, foreigners are entitled to conduct investment, foreign economic and other kinds of entrepreneurial activity stipulated by legislation of Ukraine. While conducting these kinds of activities they will enjoy rights equal with Ukrainian citizens and fulfil duties equal with Ukrainian citizens unless otherwise provided by Constitution and effective legislation of Ukraine.

Foreigners, who regularly reside in territory of Ukraine, enjoy medical care equal to that of its citizens. Any foreigner enjoys medical care in manner specified by Cabinet of Ministers of Ukraine.

Foreigners enjoy right for social security, including right to receive pension and other forms of social assistance in accordance with effective legislation and international agreements of Ukraine. In case definite period of work is required for pension to be obtained, foreigner's period of work abroad may also be included into his total period of work in manner and on grounds established by effective legislation and international agreements of Ukraine.

Foreigners who regularly reside in Ukraine, enjoy right to housing on conditions and in manner, established for citizens of Ukraine, unless otherwise provided by legislation of Ukraine. Foreigners may acquire ownership rights to housing in accordance with legislation of Ukraine. (See also topic Real Property.)

Foreigners who regularly reside in Ukraine, enjoy rights to education equal with Ukrainians. All foreigners pay for education, unless otherwise provided by legislation of Ukraine and other International Agreements of Ukraine.

Foreigners, who permanently reside in Ukraine, shall have right to join, on grounds equal with Ukrainian citizens, legally recognized societies of citizens unless otherwise provided by effective legislation of Ukraine and if not otherwise specified by charters of these societies. Foreigners cannot be members of political parties of Ukraine.

Foreigners may get married and divorced with Ukrainian citizens and other individuals, in accordance with legislation of Ukraine. Foreigners have rights and duties regarding marriage and family relations equal with Ukrainians.

Entering, leaving and transit through territory of Ukraine by foreigners (foreign individuals and persons without citizenship) is regulated by provisions approved by Cabinet of Ministers of Ukraine. Foreigners may enter or leave Ukraine with their effective national passports or documents for such passports. Foreigners entering Ukraine should obtain entrance visas at consular offices, Ukraine's Embassies and consulates abroad unless otherwise provided by legislation of Ukraine.

Legal entities or individuals which host foreigners are responsible for due execution of documents regarding right of foreigners to stay in Ukraine, traveling in territory of Ukraine and leaving Ukraine after expiration of specified term of stay. Ukrainian enterprises (institutions, organizations) joint ventures or foreign enterprises (institutions, organizations) registered in established manner as well as individuals which reside or temporarily stay in Ukraine in connection with studying, training, etc. may host foreigners.

Agencies of internal affairs, jointly with Ministry of Foreign Affairs, State Security Service and Frontier Troops, upon written petition of hosts, register foreigners. National passport must be submitted for registration to appropriate agencies within three days. Registration is also conducted in hotels where foreigners stay.

Following persons are relieved from registration: heads of countries, representatives of governmental delegations and members of families thereof; persons under 18; foreigners who came to Ukraine for not more than three days, etc. Following persons are registered with Ministry of Foreign Affairs: employees of diplomatic organizations and services, members of their families and guests thereof; employees of international organizations; foreign journalists and reporters; passports of representatives of state and public organizations and members of their families who came on unofficial visit are registered at request of diplomatic services.

Term of effectiveness for registration of national passport of foreigner is extended pursuant to same procedure as registration. In event of visa entrance to Ukraine, registration of passport is conducted after extension by agency of internal affairs of term of effectiveness for exit visa.

Extension of term of stay on private matters is conducted on basis of written petition of foreigner and under consent of hosts; this term cannot exceed one year. Extension of term of stay may be refused in event of unavailability of resources to pay costs or termination of reasons for stay.

Restrictions on traveling and choice of residential location are permitted if needed for security of Ukraine, safeguard of public order, protection of health, protection of rights and public interests of citizens and other individuals who reside in Ukraine.

Foreigner is not allowed to leave Ukraine in following cases: when foreigner is under juridical or preliminary investigation, or in case action has been already commenced, upon expiration of term of action's conduct; before expiration of term of his punishment or his release from punishment, if foreigner was sentenced by court for crime; when foreigner's departure is in contravention of security interests of Ukraine.

Foreigner's departure from Ukraine can be postponed upon execution on his property in order to resolve liabilities by such foreigner to individuals and legal entities of Ukraine.

ALIENS . . . *continued*

In event of visit of foreigner to Ukraine or person without citizenship for purpose of employment, employer must receive permission for such foreigner to be employed in Republican Center of Employment of Ministry of Labor of Ukraine. Permission for employment is basis for issuance of entry visa to Ukraine to foreigner. Permission for employment is not required: for foreign citizens who have permission (certificate, card) for residence (green card); for heads of joint ventures and subjects of entrepreneurial activity; employees of foreign mass media, accredited to work in Ukraine, etc. Permission for employment is given for one year. Persons who came to Ukraine on private affairs and stay in Ukraine temporarily do not have right for employment and permission for employment is not issued to them.

Foreigners are taxed in accordance with effective legislation and international agreements of Ukraine. (See also topic Taxation.)

Foreigners have right to appeal to court and other state bodies for protection of their personal, property and other rights.

Foreigners as participants of legal process enjoy legal rights equal with Ukrainian citizens. Foreigners may not vote in elections nor be elected to state government bodies and self-government bodies or participate in referenda.

Foreigners, who commit crime, violate their competence or other infringements, bear responsibility on common grounds.

Foreigners are not subject to general military duty; they do not serve in Army of Ukraine or in other army troops, formed in accordance with effective legislation of Ukraine.

If international agreements of Ukraine establish standards other than these which are specified in domestic Ukrainian Law, standards of international agreements will apply.

(Resolution "On Rules of Entrance of Foreigners to Ukraine, Their Leaving of Ukraine and Transit through Territory of Ukraine," dated Dec. 29, 1995. Order of Ministry of Labor of Ukraine "On Approval of Temporary Regulation on Conditions and Manner of Execution of Permissions for Employment in Ukraine," dated Mar. 24, 1995).

See topics Foreign Investment; Immigration.

ALIMONY:

See topic Divorce.

ANTITRUST LAWS:

See topic Monopolies and Trade Restraints.

APPEAL AND ERROR:

See topics Arbitration and Award; Courts.

ARBITRATION AND AWARD:

Art. 6 of Civil Code of Ukraine stipulates that along with regular courts and courts of arbitrazh (commercial courts) protection of civil rights may be also exercised by arbitration tribunals. Art. 25 of Civil Proceedings Code of Ukraine also provides that civil cases may be considered by arbitration tribunal in compliance with Regulations on Arbitration Tribunal. Term "arbitration tribunal" (in Ukrainian "tretejskiy sud") as used in Ukrainian legislative acts refers to sole arbitrator or panel of arbitrators. Generally speaking Ukrainian legislation provides insufficient regulatory framework with respect to arbitration except for arbitration of commercial disputes involving foreign parties.

Disputes of Individuals.—Currently effective Regulations on Arbitration Tribunal ("Regulations") apply only to arbitration of disputes among individuals. They set forth that Ukrainian individuals based upon their respective written agreement may submit to arbitration tribunal any dispute except for disputes arising from labor and family relations. Arbitration tribunal is formed only ad hoc and may consist of one or more arbitrators as agreed upon by parties. Regulations also provide certain rules of arbitral proceedings as well as mandatory requirements regarding form of arbitration agreement and arbitral award. Arbitral award can be submitted for enforcement to regular court of district where arbitral proceedings took place. As matter of fact above mentioned legislative provisions do not work and there are no precedents of settlement of disputes between Ukrainian individuals through arbitration.

Disputes of Legal Entities.—

General Regulations.—In addition to few provisions of Civil Code and Civil Proceedings Code which generally stipulate possibility of referring civil disputes to arbitration tribunal, Art. 12 of Arbitrazh Proceedings Code also sets forth that Ukrainian enterprises and organizations may submit disputes falling within competence of arbitrazh courts (economic disputes) to arbitration tribunals, except disputes concerning (i) matters involving claim of legal invalidity and (ii) disputes relating to conclusion, alteration, cancellation, termination and performance of economic contracts based on state order. There are no detailed legislative regulations of arbitral proceedings for legal entities like above-mentioned Regulations on Arbitration Tribunal for disputes among individuals or for institutional arbitration bodies in Ukraine except arbitration institutions for settlement of disputes arising from foreign economic contracts or those involving in certain manner foreign entities as discussed below. Moreover, along with general declarations of possibility to resort to arbitration, Ukrainian law contains certain provisions which substantially impede or reduce effectiveness of arbitration between legal entities. For instance, Art. 1 of Arbitrazh Proceedings Code stipulates that contractual waiver to apply to court of arbitration has no legal effect. Art. 91 of that Code provides that arbitral decision at application of any disputing party may be revised, changed or canceled by court of arbitrazh by way of court supervision. Thus, it is not clear whether arbitration tribunal chosen by agreement of parties may be regarded as exclusive and final forum for resolution of disputes. In practice Ukrainian legal entities never resort to arbitral settlement of their purely domestic economic disputes, all such matters are submitted to courts of arbitrazh.

Arbitral settlement of disputes involving foreign parties is based on specific and more clear legal rules and therefore is practically workable. Art. 26 of Law of Ukraine "On Regime of Foreign Investments", Mar. 19, 1996, No. 93/96-BP, provides that disputes between foreign investors and state of Ukraine relating to state regulation of foreign investments and activity of enterprises with foreign investments are subject to rèsolution by Ukranian regular courts unless otherwise provided by international treaties of Ukraine. All other disputes are subject to resolution by regular courts, courts of arbitrazh or, pursuant to agreement of disputing parties, by arbitration tribunals either within or outside of Ukraine. According to Art. 38 of Law of Ukraine "On Foreign Economic Activity", Apr. 16, 1991, No. 959-XII, disputes between Ukrainian and foreign parties arising from or in connection with their foreign economic activity may be subjected to resolution by Ukrainian regular courts, courts of arbitrazh or, pursuant to agreements of disputing parties, by International Commercial Arbitration Court and Maritime Arbitration Commission of Chamber of Commerce and Industry of Ukraine or by any other forum for dispute resolution provided that that is not in contravention with effective laws of Ukraine or is envisaged by international treaties of Ukraine.

Law of Ukraine "On International Commercial Arbitration", Feb. 1994, provides most detailed regulation concerning settlement of disputes arising in international trade, and takes into account arbitration provisions specified in international treaties of Ukraine and substantially follows model law adopted in 1985 by UNCITRAL and recommended by UN General Assembly of UN for use by member states in their legislation.

Law "On International Commercial Arbitration" applies to international commercial arbitration if place of arbitration is in Ukraine. However, certain provisions of this Law also apply in cases when arbitration takes place abroad.

According to Law following disputes may be submitted upon agreement of parties to International Commercial Arbitration: (i) disputes relating to contractual or other civil relations arising in course of international economic activity provided that commercial enterprise of at least one of parties is located outside of Ukraine and (ii) disputes between enterprises with foreign investments and between international associations and organizations set up in Ukraine, disputes between their participants and their disputes with other Ukrainian legal entities. Term "commercial" should be given wide interpretation so as to cover matters arising from all relationships of commercial nature, whether contractual or not. Relationships of commercial nature include, but are not limited to, following transactions: any trade transaction for supply or exchange of goods or services; distribution agreements; commercial representation or agency; factoring; leasing; construction; works; consulting; engineering; licensing; investment; financing; banking; insurance; exploitation agreement or concession; joint venture and other forms of business cooperation; carriage of goods or passengers by air, sea, rail or road. Parties are free to determine number of arbitrators, manner of their appointment and their nationality. Parties are also free to choose law which is to govern their relations, giving parties freedom to choose more than one legal system.

Law does not allow any regular or other court intervention in matters which are subject to International Commercial Arbitration except as in few cases expressly set forth by that Law, for example, parties prior to or during arbitration proceedings may appeal not only to arbitral tribunal but also to regular court with request to take interim protective measures.

Arbitral decision and award, irrespective of country in which it was made shall be recognized as final and binding upon parties and is enforceable upon written application of relevant party to respective regular court of Ukraine. Recognition or enforcement of arbitral award, irrespective of country in which it was made, may be refused only at request of party against which it is invoked, if that party furnishes to competent court where recognition or enforcement is sought proof that: (i) party to arbitration agreement was under some incapacity or agreement is not valid under law to which parties have subjected it; or (ii) party against which award is invoked was not given proper notice on appointment of arbitrators or on arbitration proceedings or for other grounded reasons it was not allowed to present its case; or (iii) award deals with dispute not contemplated by or not in conformity with arbitration agreement or contains decisions on matters beyond scope of arbitration agreement; or (iv) composition of arbitral panel or arbitral procedure did not conform with agreement of parties or failing such agreement was not in accordance with law of country where arbitration proceedings took place; or (v) award has not become binding upon parties or has been set aside or suspended by court of country in which or under law of which that award was made; or (vi) court finds that (a) subject-matter of dispute is not capable of being settled by arbitration under Ukrainian law; or (b) award is in conflict with public policy of Ukraine.

In accordance with this Law, International Commercial Arbitration Court is independent permanently operating arbitration agency of Chamber of Commerce and Industry of Ukraine. Chamber of Commerce and Industry of Ukraine approves Regulations of International Commercial Arbitration Court procedure of computing arbitration duties, arbitrator's fees and other arbital expenses, and facilitates its activity.

In addition, in accordance with Law, Maritime Arbitration Commission is created in Ukraine, which is also independent permanently operating arbitration agency of Chamber of Commerce and Industry of Ukraine.

Maritime Arbitration Commission provides arbitration on disputes arising from contractual and other civil relations resulting from commercial navigation irrespective of whether parties thereof are subjects of Ukrainian or foreign, or only Ukrainian, or only foreign law. In particular, Maritime Arbitration Commission will settle issues arising from relations connected with: (1) freight of vessels, maritime transportation of shipments, transportation of shipments through mixed navigation (rivers and seas); (2) maritime insurance and reinsurance; (3) purchase-sale, lien and repair of vessels and other floating means; (4) salvage of maritime vessels or by navy vessels; (5) hoisting of vessels and other property lost at sea; (6) collision of vessels, and with damage of port premises, means of navigation, other objects, etc. caused by vessels.

Maritime Arbitration Commission will also deal with other disputes, provided that parties thereof agree on transfer of case for its settlement. Commission will also settle disputes transferred by parties for settlement in accordance with international treaties.

Detailed provisions of Law "On International Commercial Arbitration", when taken together with 1958 New York Convention on Recognition and Enforcement of Foreign Arbitral Awards to which Ukraine is signatory, provide comprehensive framework for resolution of disputes arising under international commercial transactions.

ASSIGNMENTS:

Assignment of claims and transfer of debt are regulated by Civil Code of Ukraine. (par. 17). Under some instances while obligations are still in effect, original creditor or debtor may be substituted.

Assignment of Claim.—Creditors may assign their rights to other persons. Agreements on assignment of rights must comply with all requirements set forth by Civil Code of Ukraine. Art. 44 of Civil Code of Ukraine establishes indispensable written format for such agreements. Noncompliance with written format of agreement raises consequences anticipated by Art. 46 of Civil Code of Ukraine and agreement is regarded as ineffective. Assignment of claims personal to creditor, alimonies, wages, recovery of losses caused by injury or death is prohibited.

Transfer of Debt.—In some instances creditors are required to transfer claims to other persons. For instance, creditor to whom debt is paid by trustee, is obligated to transfer his rights to latter, for use by him for retroactive claim against debtor.

As result of assignment of claim to new creditor, whole complex of rights, including all rights which provide for realization of such claims (e.g. right to impose forfeit), are also transferred from original creditor. Original creditor is obligated to transfer all documents which confirm transfer of claim (e.g. receipt) to new creditor. Creditor assigning claim to another creditor, is not liable to such creditor for commitments which were not fulfilled by debtor within period established by agreement.

Consent is not required for assignment of claim to be effective, but debtor should be notified about assignment of claim to new creditor.

Debt may be transferred to new debtor only with creditor's consent, otherwise such transfer is ineffective. Person assuming debt may assert all defenses of original debtor against creditor (e.g. to ask for delay of realization) if such right was given by creditors to original debtor.

If debt is transferred to new debtor, then bond given earlier and mortgage established by third person to assure fulfillment of obligations becomes ineffective.

Assignment of claim and transfer of debt should be executed in same form as was established for agreement on which claim or debt is based.

ASSIGNMENTS FOR BENEFIT OF CREDITOR:

See topic Assignments.

ASSOCIATIONS:

Individual freedom of association is guaranteed by Constitution and legislation of Ukraine, in particular by Law of Ukraine "On Associations", June 16, 1992.

Association is voluntary nongovernmental (public) union of persons established on basis of common interests in order to carry out jointly their rights and freedoms.

Association of persons, regardless of name (rukh, congress, associations, etc.) is recognized as political party or public organization.

Association activity aimed against economic and political state system (e.g. forcible replacement of constitutional system and illegal changing of territorial integrity of country; undermining of security of country through carrying out activity in favor of foreign countries; propaganda of war, violence or cruelty, fascism or new-fascism) is prohibited in Ukraine.

Associations are created and operate on basis of voluntariness, equality of rights of members, self-government, legality and publicity. Associations are free to choose directions of activity thereof. Associations of Ukrainian persons may have status of all-Ukrainian, local and international.

Associations with activity involving whole of Ukraine with local centers in majority of oblasts have status of all-Ukrainian associations. Political parties are created and operate in Ukraine as all-Ukrainian associations.

Associations with activity involving particular administrative-territorial unit or region, have status of local associations. Territory may be specified by association independently.

Association is international if its activity involves Ukraine and at least one foreign country.

Establishment and Termination of Associations.—

Political parties are established at initiative of any Ukrainian person over 18 years old, whose competence is not limited by court, and who is not kept incarcerated. Members of political parties may only be citizens of Ukraine who are over 18.

Political parties and international public organizations must be registered with Ministry of Justice. Petition for registration of political party must be confirmed (supported) by not less than 1,000 citizens of Ukraine who have right to vote, and must include charter (by-laws), protocol of constituent assembly (congress) or general meeting, information on structure of central charter bodies, data on local centers, documents confirming payment of registration fee. Political parties should also attach their program (strategy) documents.

Political parties also may obtain ownership of property received as result of distribution of public and political literature, other propaganda materials, products with symbols of such party, maintenance of festivals, holidays, exhibitions, lectures, and other political arrangements.

Political parties, institutions and organizations established by them, may not set up enterprises (except for mass media) nor engage in economic and other commercial activity, except for distribution of public and political literature, other propaganda materials, products with symbols of such parties, maintenance of festivals, holidays, exhibitions, lectures, and other political arrangements.

Political parties have right to establish or join international unions, provided that their charters anticipate creation of consultative or coordinating central agencies only.

Other Associations.—Founders of associations may be citizens of Ukraine, citizens of other countries, persons without citizenship over 18 years old, or over 15 years old for youth/children's organizations.

Decision to establish association is taken by Constituent Assembly (Conference) or General Meeting.

Members of associations (except for youth/children's organizations) may be persons over 14 years old. Age qualification for membership in youth and children organizations is established by charter thereof.

Association operates on basis of its charter, which must include name of association, its status and legal address, goal and purposes, conditions and membership procedure, rights and duties of members, and some other provisions.

Legalization (acknowledgment) of association is obligatory and is carried out through registration or notice of establishment thereof, otherwise activity of associations not legalized (acknowledged) or forcibly dissolved by court is illegal.

Association acquires status of legal entity upon its registration. Legalization of public organization is carried out by Ministry of Justice of Ukraine, local agencies of state executive power, executive committees of rural, municipal or city Radas respectively. Government agency legalizing association, is required to publish such information in newspapers.

Founders of any association must submit application for registration thereof which must include charter (by-laws), protocol of constituent assembly (congress) or general meeting, information on structure of central charter bodies, data on local centers, documents confirming payment of registration fee.

Public organization and unions thereof may be legalized (acknowledged) by notifying in writing Ministry of Justice of Ukraine, local agencies of state executive power, executive committees of rural, municipal or city Radas respectively. Associations may have funds and other property needed for carrying out their charter activity.

Associations may obtain ownership of funds and other property transferred by founders, members (participants) or state, acquired as result of entrance and membership fee, individual donations, enterprises, institutions and organizations, and ownership right for property purchased with associations' funds, or on other terms which are not prohibited by law.

Public organizations may obtain ownership of property and funds obtained as result of economic and other commercial activity of self-financing institutions, organizations and enterprises established by these public organizations.

In order to realize charter goals and purposes, associations may carry out required economic and other commercial activity by creating self-financing institutions and organizations with status of legal entities, and establishing enterprises in manner established by legislation.

In case of law violation by association, following penalties may be incurred: fine, warning, temporary prohibition of some activities, temporary prohibition of all activity, and, forced dissolution.

Public organizations and unions thereof may in accordance with their charters establish or join international public (nongovernmental) organizations, create international unions of associations, maintain direct international contacts and relations, make respective agreements, and participate in taking measures which are not in contravention of international obligations of Ukraine.

International public organizations, branches, sections, representative offices, and other structural units of public (nongovernmental) organizations of foreign countries operate in Ukraine in accordance with Ukrainian law.

AUTOMOBILE:

See topic Motor Vehicles.

BANKRUPTCY:

Issues of bankruptcy are governed by laws of Ukraine "On Bankruptcy", May 14, 1992; and "On Banks and Banking Activity", May 20, 1991 and by Arbitrazh Procedure Code of Ukraine.

Under this Law, subjects of bankruptcy may be legal entities, which are subjects of entrepreneurial activity, unable to fulfil their obligations to creditors and budget. Written petition of any creditor, debtor agency, of state tax service or audit inspection to Arbitration Court is basis for bankruptcy case. Creditor may file bankruptcy petition of legal entity if during one month legal entity has been unable to comply with its acknowledged claims or pay its debt in accordance with execution documents. Debtor, on its own initiative, may petition to Arbitration Court in case of financial insolvency or threat thereof.

Creditor shall be individual or legal entity possessing proper documents confirming property claims against creditor, except for creditors whose property claims are fully guaranteed by mortgage. If two or more creditors have property claims against same debtor, latter must convene meeting of creditors.

Not later than one month from day of commencement of bankruptcy case, Court of Arbitration has preliminary meeting and obligates petitioner to submit announcement on commencement of bankruptcy case to edition of Supreme Rada or Cabinet of Ministers of Ukraine. Within one month from moment of publishing announcement on commencement of bankruptcy case, creditors submit to debtor written petition with property claims. According to results of this investigation, Arbitration Court shall by its resolution either approve or reject these claims.

Arbitration Court may pass resolution on bailout of debtor if there are proposals from entities willing to satisfy requirements of creditors to debtor and fulfil budget obligations on conditions of consent of Creditors' Meeting to transfer debt. Individuals and legal entities willing to take part in bailout of debtor, must, within one month, submit to Court of Arbitration written obligation to transfer debt to them and indicate terms and conditions of bailout of legal entity-debtor.

Arbitration Court shall adjudge debtor as bankrupt either in absence of bailout proposals, or where there is disagreement among creditors with conditions and terms of debtor's bailout.

From moment of recognition of debtor as bankrupt: entrepreneurial activity of debtor is suspended; right to dispose bankrupt's property and all its proprietary rights and commitments is transferred to liquidation committee; time limits of all debt obligations of debtor are deemed expired; charging of penalties and interests for all types of indebtedness of debtor is suspended.

Liquidators, appointed by Arbitration Court, establish Liquidation Committee. Liquidation Committee disposes of debtor's property; carries out inventory and evaluation of bankrupt's property; distributes debtor's property and takes other measures to satisfy claims of creditors.

Arbitration Court may recognize as invalid some agreements concerning sale of property by debtor, executed within certain period of time before commencement of case on bankruptcy.

BANKRUPTCY . . . *continued*

Funds obtained from sale of bankrupt's property, are used to satisfy creditors' claims. Initially expenses for conduct of claim in Arbitration Court, operation of Liquidation Committee, work of executor of property and creditors' claims, covered by mortgage, are covered.

Priority of satisfying creditors' claims is established by law. If no property remains after satisfaction of all claims of creditors in accordance with results of liquidation balance, Arbitration Court shall pass resolution on liquidation of legal entity-bankrupt. If bankrupt possesses sufficient property to satisfy creditors' claims, bankrupt shall be deemed free from debt and may continue entrepreneurial activity thereof.

BANKS AND BANKING:

Banking system in Ukraine exists at two levels: National Bank of Ukraine and commercial banks of different kinds and forms of ownership. Banks are economically independent and make their own decisions regarding economic activity.

Employees of state administrative agencies are prohibited from participating in statutory bodies of banks' management.

Law contains list of transactions to be carried out by banks. All transactions are carried out according to procedures established by National Bank of Ukraine. Banks carry out transactions within limits specified by their respective charters.

National Bank of Ukraine is owned by State of Ukraine. National Bank's statutes must be approved by Presidium of Supreme Rada of Ukraine.

National Bank of Ukraine is central bank of country. National Bank conducts state policy in areas of money circulation, credit, promotion of monetary unit, interbank accounts, banking system activities in general, and exchange rates of establishment as against other currencies.

National Bank of Ukraine organizes state deposits of country, preserves reserve funds of banknotes, precious metals and gold and currency reserves. National Bank of Ukraine represents interests of Ukraine in relations with central banks of other countries, at international banks and other financial and credit organizations, where interstate cooperation is stipulated at central bank level.

National Bank issues instructions and regulations setting forth norms on matters within limits of its authority. Instructions of National Bank of Ukraine, adopted within limits of its authorities, are obligatory for all legal entities and individuals.

National Bank of Ukraine issues permission to organize commercial banks in country by registration thereof. National Bank of Ukraine maintains Republican Book of Registration of Banks, currency exchanges and other financial and credit institutions. Commercial banks acquire status of legal entity upon registration in this book. Foreign banks may conduct banking transactions only upon registration in Republican Book of Registration.

Commercial banks of different kinds and forms of ownership are organized on stock or share basis. Legal entities and individuals (except for councils of people's deputies of all levels, executive bodies thereof, political and trade union organizations, societies and parties, public foundations and commercial banks) may be founders and shareholders of commercial banks.

Contribution to charter fund shall be paid in national currency of Ukraine. Legal entities transfer contributions from their operational accounts, individuals from personal accounts or pay cash. To register commercial bank following documents must be submitted: (a) application on registration; (b) founding documents; (c) economic feasibility report; (d) report of audit firm on financial standing of bank founders; (e) information on professional competence of bank leadership recommended by founders. To register foreign banks and/or banks with foreign capital additional documents are required: (a) from foreign legal entities: resolution of foreign founder on creation of bank in Ukraine and written consent of supervising agency of country where bank is located, if required by laws of respective country; (b) from foreign individuals: confirmation of first class of bank financial solvency of individual, recommendations of two legal entities or individuals with good financial standing. Board of Directors of National Bank of Ukraine decides on registration of bank with foreign capital. National Bank of Ukraine approves provision on licensing of banks in Ukraine. Registration fee and fee for introduction of amendments and modifications into founding documents is 100 untaxable minimums which is equivalent of $900; license fee—50 untaxable minimums or $450. Registration is conducted within one month upon receipt of application and other documents required for registration.

Minimum amount of charter fund for commercial banks is established in amount of one million ECU at official exchange rate of Ukrainian currency unit. Minimum amount of charter fund for commercial banks with foreign capital is established in amount of three million ECU at official exchange rate of Ukrainian currency unit; for commercial banks with 100% foreign capital—not less than five million ECU. Commercial bank may own real estate, total value of which does not exceed 10% of its charter fund with premises used by bank departments not included in this restriction.

Commercial bank may organize leagues, associations and other unions for coordination of its activity and protection of interests. Banks are prohibited from making written and oral agreements for purpose of restricting competition in banking activity and monopolization of services related to credits, interest rates, etc.

Individual anonymous account is opened exclusively in hard currency without presentation of identity card of owner of account.

Authorized banks must obtain general license of National Bank of Ukraine for right to operate with hard currency and have required software for opening of anonymous accounts.

Anonymous account is opened for determined or undetermined period of time on basis of application by individual of desire to open account.

Maximum amount of cash which may be put to account within one working day must not exceed ten thousand US dollars; in cashless form amount is not limited.

Information on anonymous account may be disclosed only upon request of owner of account or on basis of court decision.

In event of loss of access code, money which is on account is not given to owner but is transferred to state budget after expiration of limitation period which commences on date of submission of application on loss of code or in three years after expiration of term of agreement.

Anonymous accounts are subject to other requirements: (i) for deposit of cash into account, registration with customs agencies is not required; (ii) when money is withdrawn from account, it is not permitted to transfer money abroad, or to any accounts of nonresidents in banks of Ukraine (except for comparable anonymous accounts of nonresidents).

Pursuant to effective legislation, hard currency accounts are not subject to taxation.

Pursuant to Decree of President of Ukraine as of Aug. 1, 1995, authorized banks may open anonymous currency accounts for individual (residents and nonresidents). National Bank of Ukraine prepares Procedure for Opening and Operation of Anonymous Currency Accounts of Individuals as of Aug. 16, 1995. (According to amended and modified Law of Ukraine "On Banks and Banking Activity").

BROKERS (COMMODITY):

Concept of "broker" is term of recent usage in Ukraine; brokers did not exist under prior political regime. Term "broker" as intermediary is found only in Law of Ukraine "On Commodity Exchange" as of Dec. 10, 1991. Thus, broker is individual registered at exchange in conformity with charter thereof, whose obligations are to act on behalf of founders, Ukrainian and foreign legal entities and individuals, members of exchange. Brokers represent members of exchange and conduct exchange transactions by seeking contracts and submitting of transactions for registration at exchange; only brokers and members of exchange are permitted to conduct exchange transactions. Number of brokers on any commodity exchange are determined by exchange committee (council). Brokers are entitled to ascertain availability and quality of goods, as well as solvency (paying capacity) of buyer, to propose alternative terms and conditions of contracts and to undertake any other actions which do not contradict clients' interests. Brokers are prohibited to disclose commercial secrets concerning clients' transactions conducted at exchange with their participation and to serve two or more clients simultaneously, if there is conflict of their interests.

Ukrainian law also contains term "intermediary activity", essence of which is "brokerage". Law of Ukraine "On Securities and Stock Exchange" regulates intermediary activity on issuance and turnover of securities. Such activity is conducted by banks and other associations (hereinafter referred to as stock brokers) and it is exclusive kind of their activity. Stock brokers are entitled to conduct activities such as: (i) activity on issuance of securities; (ii) commission activity on securities; (iii) commercial activity on securities. Activity on issuance of securities means organization of subscription for securities on behalf of and at expense of issuer or other distribution thereof by stock broker. Upon agreement with issuer, in event of incomplete distribution of securities, stock broker may obligate itself to buy undistributed securities from issuer. Commercial activity on securities means purchase and sale of securities by stock broker on its own behalf and at its expenses.

Instruction of the State Property Fund of Ukraine No. 514 of Nov. 25, 1993 contains concept of "representative activity", which can also be viewed as form of brokerage. This instruction concerns trust company activity in servicing owners of privatization papers, i.e. exchange of privatization papers to shares, which is conducted at expense and on behalf of owners by representatives. State Property Fund of Ukraine issues license to conduct representative activity with privatization papers. Such licenses are issued to legal entities established as companies with additional liability. (Decree of the Cabinet of Ministers of Ukraine "On Trust Companies" No. 23-93 of Mar. 17, 1993). State Property Fund may suspend license in event of: financial violations connected with expenses of trustees; repeated untimely fulfillment of trust company obligations to trustees; refusal of trustees to submit documents required by State Property Fund; determination that fraudulent documents were purposefully submitted to Fund by trustees on basis of which license was issued; failure to inform Fund within established term on modifications in founding documents which must be included into state register. Decision on suspension of effectiveness of license or cancellation thereof may be contested by trust company in Court of Arbitration.

See also topics Agency; Securities.

BUSINESS ASSOCIATIONS:

Law of Ukraine "On Economic Associations", Sept. 19, 1991, as amended, establishes five types of business associations: joint-stock associations; limited liability associations; additional liability associations; full liability associations; and limited partnership associations.

Although names of these five types of business associations are presented here in literal translation into English language, on closer comparison entities bear some similarity to American entities such as corporations, partnerships and associations. Generally, business associations are defined as enterprises, organizations and institutions established on basis of agreement by legal entities and individuals by joining of property and entrepreneurial activity for purpose of earning profit. Business associations are legal entities which may conduct all legal entrepreneurial activity, enjoy property and personal non-property rights, make commitments, and act in court and Court of Arbitration on their own behalf. Founders of business associations may be Ukrainian and foreign individuals and legal entities and persons without citizenship. Enterprises, organizations and institutions which are participants of associations, do not lose their status as legal entity.

Joint-stock, limited and additional liability associations are established and operate on basis of founding agreement and charter; complete and limited associations are established and operate on basis of founding agreement. Name of association identifies kind of activity thereof; names of participants identify kind of activity for complete and limited associations. Association acquires status of legal entity from day of its state registration. Association is entitled to establish affiliates, subsidiaries and representative offices in and outside Ukraine. Founder's contribution to authorized capital may be made in cash (including hard currency) and in kind of: buildings, premises, equipment and other material valuables, securities, land use rights, water and other natural resources as well as rights to use buildings and premises. Use of state budget funds, funds obtained as credit and collateral may not be used for formation of charter fund. Activity of association is terminated through its reorganization (merging, joining, division and apportionment) or liquidation.

Joint-Stock Association (Joint-Stock Company).—Joint-stock association has charter fund, divided into certain number of common shares of definite equal nominal

BUSINESS ASSOCIATIONS . . . *continued*

value. Joint-stock association carries responsibility for its obligation only to limits of its property. Shareholders are liable for association only within limits of shares they own. Charter fund of joint-stock association cannot be less than sum equivalent to 1,250 karbovanets minimal wages, based on minimal wage rates effective at moment of creation. Currently, minimum wage is equal to 60,000 karbovantsi. Joint-stock associations may be of two forms: open joint-stock association, shares thereof are distributed through open subscription and trading at stock exchanges; and, closed joint-stock association, its shares are distributed only among the founders and cannot be distributed by open subscription and trading at stock exchange.

Joint-stock associations have following structure: (a) highest body—General Meeting of Shareholders; (b) Supervisory Council, which may be appointed by General Meeting of Shareholders and which controls activity of management; (c) executive bodies: management board, which directs joint-stock association activity, and Audit Committee, which controls financial and economic activity of management board.

Limited liability association has its authorized capital divided into equal parts, as determined by founding documents. Participants of limited liability association are liable only within limits of their contributions. Authorized capital of limited liability association may not be less than equivalent of 625 karbovanets minimal wages, based on minimal wage rate in effect at moment of creation. Participant of association is obligated to contribute its share of authorized capital within one year from state registration. Participant of limited liability association may relinquish its share of authorized capital. Participant's withdrawing from limited liability association will be paid value of share of association's property pro rata to participant's share in authorized capital.

Shareholder's meeting shall be highest body of limited liability association. Board of directors is highest executive body of association. Audit committtee controls activity of board of directors.

Additional liability association is treated under Ukrainian Law as limited liability association with several differences. Thus, additional liability association has authorized capital, divided into parts whose size is determined by founding documents. Participants of such association shall be responsible for its obligations, with their contributions into authorized capital; in cases of insufficiency of those sums, additional property belonging to them shall be reapportioned on pro rata basis as each participant's contribution. Limits of responsibility of participants is provided in founding documents.

Full liability association is created by persons who take up common association activity and carry joint responsibility for association's obligation with all of their property. Constituent agreement of full liability association describes size, kind and order of contribution and manner in which participants take part in activity of complete association. Management of full liability association may be carried out either by all participants or by one or several of them who act on association's behalf and is conducted by joint consent of all participants. Participants of full liablility associations are forbidden to conduct any kind of activity on their own of activity undertaken by association or to participate in any other associations (except for joint-stock associations in capacity as shareholders) which have same aim of their own complete association. Participant is responsible for association's debts without regard to whether they were incurred after or before joining association. Participant who completely paid association's debts may seek pro rata contribution from other participants who share responsibility in proportion to their shares in association's property.

Limited partnership association is association where at least one participant (partner) is responsible without limitation and responsibility of at least one participant (limited partner) is limited. Legal status of such association is equal to complete association but management of limited association is carried out by participants (partners) with complete responsibility. If two or more participants take full responsibility in operation of limited association, they are jointly responsible for debts of association. Limited association shall terminate its activity when all of participants with full responsibility withdraw from association. In event of liquidation of association, funds remaining after all payments, are distributed among partners, and then among limited partners.

CARTEL LAW:

See topic Monopolies and Trade Restraints.

CHATTEL MORTGAGES:

Chattel mortgage is means of securing obligations of debtor under which creditor is entitled to obtain pledged movables or their value preferentially over other creditors in event of default by debtor. Concept of "chattel mortgage" is recent development of Ukrainian law. Chattel mortgages are regulated by Law of Ukraine "On Mortgage", Oct. 2, 1992. Mortgage relationships are not fully developed in Ukraine.

Pledged movables may be owned by pledger, creditor or third person. Chattel mortgage is subject to concept of "pledge". According to agreement between creditor and pledger, object of chattel mortgage may be left with pledger under lock and seal of creditor (firm mortgage). Specific object may be left with pledger with signs or marks certifying "mortgage/lien".

In accordance with agreement, creditor may be obligated to: take measures necessary for object of chattel mortgage to be preserved; insure object of chattel mortgage in amount of its value at expense and in favor of pledger, etc. Creditor may use object of chattel mortgage as specified by agreement. Creditor may demand replacement of object of chattel mortgage in case of its destruction, damage or diminution of its value, not caused by creditor. Upon refusal of pledger to satisfy this requirement, creditor may demand immediate payment of obligation.

Parties to mortgage agreement may specify their own rules on basis of Law of Ukraine "On Mortgage".

COMMERCIAL LAW:

Under Soviet legal system, economic law was designated as branch of legislation which regulated economic activity of socialist enterprises. Legal norms, creating economic laws were not codified in universal code. Most important legislative provisions were "Provisions on Socialist State Manufacturing Enterprises", "Provisions on Deliveries", "Provisions on Contractual Agreements for Capital Construction", etc. Many men of science held view that economic relations were regulated by state, civil, administrative or other laws, thus it was not correct to regard economic relations as separate branch of law. Actually, many provisions which regulated economic relations, were contained in Civil Code and Code on Violations of Competence.

First Ukrainian law aimed at regulating business in new economic environment, Law "On Entrepreneurial Activity" was signed on Feb. 7, 1991. In particular, it specified (i) subjects of economic activity; (ii) list of activities which cannot be carried out without special license (manufacturing and sale of pharmaceuticals and chemicals; manufacturing of alcohol, beer and wine; wholesale or retail trade; public catering; non-foodstuff; distribution and public sale of alcohol beverages; prospecting and use of mineral resources; manufacturing, repair and sale of sport and hunting weapons; medical practice, etc.); (iii) procedures for entrepreneurial activity; and (iv) general principles for relations between entrepreneurs and state.

Activity connected with circulation of drugs, manufacture and sale of military weapons and supplies, explosives, extraction of amber, protection of certain state-owned objects of great importance, list of which is specified in manner established by Cabinet of Ministers of Ukraine, may be carried out only by state enterprises and organizations.

On Mar. 27, 1991 Law "On Enterprises" was published. This law specified types and structures of enterprises as well as provisions for organization, registration, reorganization and liquidation thereof. Law designates enterprise as main independently operating structural unit of Ukrainian economy, with all rights of legal entity, engaged in production, scientific-research and commercial activity in order to obtain profit (income).

Enterprise maintains its own financial existence, bank accounts, and corporate seal with name; and also trademark for products (goods) and services.

In accordance with forms of ownership established by Laws "On Ownership" and "On Enterprises", following types of enterprises are established: individual enterprise based on personal property and labor of individual; family enterprise, based on property of Ukrainian citizens who are members of one family and reside together; private enterprise which is established on basis of property of certain citizen of Ukraine who may employ workers; collective enterprise which is established on basis of property of labor collective of enterprise, or cooperative, or other statutory association, public or religious organization; state communal enterprise which is established on basis of state (republican) property; state enterprise based on state/republican property; joint venture which is established on basis of property of different owners (mixed ownership). In accordance with laws of Ukraine, founders of joint venture may be legal entities and individuals of Ukraine and other countries.

Law "On Economic Associations", Sept. 19, 1991 sets forth terms and types of economic associations, provisions for their organization and operation, and rights and obligations of participants and founders thereof.

Under this law, economic associations are enterprises, organizations and institutions, established by agreement of legal entities and individuals to join their property and entrepreneurial activity in order to obtain profit.

Law recognizes following economic associations: joint-stock, limited liability, additional responsibility, full liability and limited partnership associations.

Economic associations are legal entities, they may undertake any entrepreneurial activity which is not in contravention of Ukrainian laws. They may acquire property and individual non-property rights, enter into obligations, act in court or arbitrate in their own name.

Economic associations acquire all rights of legal entity from date of their state registration. Economic associations may create affiliates and representative offices and subsidiaries in Ukraine and abroad in accordance with effective legislation of Ukraine.

Economic associations are owners of: property transferred by founders and participants thereof; products made as result of their economic activity; profits; other property obtained by means which are not prohibited by law.

Law on Economic Associations also clarifies term of each of above mentioned associations, and particulars of charter, formation of charter fund, administration and control bodies, and liquidation procedures.

See topic Business Associations.

COMMERCIAL REGISTER:

See topic State Register (Commercial Register).

CONSTITUTION:

On June 28, 1996, only under Presidential threat of disbandment, Ukrainian Parliament-Narodna Rada of Ukraine-accepted new Basic Law, in spite of conflict on major articles between communists and democrats. Date of enactment is effective date.

Preamble states: "We, the Ukrainian people, expressing sovereign will, as supported by a many-century history of creation of Ukrainian state and on the basis of the right for self-determination exercised by the Ukrainian nation, exercising care for providing all human rights and freedoms, adequate conditons for life, and for development and strengthening of a democratic, social, legal state, being fully aware of responsibility before God, previous, current and future generations, proclaim this Constitution as Basic Law of Ukraine."

Ukraine had three prior Constitutions. 1710 Constitution of Pylyp Orlyk declared integrity and inviolability of borders and ratified principles of separation of power and independence of Ukraine. Ukrainska Narodna Respublika adopted second Ukrainian Constitution in 1918, declaring Ukraine sovereign and independent state in which all power in country belonged to people. Unfortunately, because of numerous external and internal reasons, both of above-named state documents which declared Ukraine's independent were of short-lived effectiveness. From 1922 and beginning of Soviet period of Ukrainian history, Constitution of Ukraine was created in accordance with Constitution of Soviet Union. Latest Soviet Constitution of 1978 with modifications and amendments was in effect until June 28, 1996.

Separation of Powers.—In accordance with new Constitution, Ukraine is republic. All power in Ukraine belongs to people. Ukrainian people constitute all citizens of Ukraine of all nationalities and are bearers of sovereignty and only source of power.

CONSTITUTION . . . *continued*
People realize state power directly through elections, referenda and other forms of democracy, and through agencies of state power and local self-governance.

State power is carried out by three branches: legislative, executive and judicial.

In Ukraine, principle of supremacy of law is in effect. Constitution is highest law of land and constitutional norms may be applied directly. Laws and other legal acts must not be in contravention of Constitution and constitutional laws of Ukraine. Applying to court for protection of constitutional rights and freedoms directly on basis of Constitution of Ukraine is guaranteed. Individuals are equal in rights and freedoms and are equal under law.

State guarantees equality of protection of all forms of ownership and ecomony. In Ukraine, right of private ownership for land is proclaimed.

Parliament.—Exclusive body of legislative power in Ukraine is Narodna Rada of Ukraine which is competent to legislate on any issues of state and social life of Ukraine, except for those which are settled exclusively by All-Ukrainian Referendum, or are within competence of President of Ukraine, executive and judicial power, oblasts, Autonomous Republic of Crimea, and agencies of local self-governance.

Narodna Rada consists of 450 deputies of Ukraine elected directly by people for four years. Any citizen of Ukraine, eligible to vote, not younger than 21 on day of election, and resident of UKraine for not less than five years, may be deputy of Ukraine. Deputies of Ukraine fulfill their duties on full-time basis; while holding deputy mandate, deputies may not pursue other activities except for those stipulated by laws.

Legislative immunity is guaranteed. Deputies cannot be detained or arrested without consent of Narodna Rada, unless appropriate decision is made by court.

Following activities are within competence of Narodna Rada: (i) introduction of modifications and amendments to Constitution; (ii) assignment of all-Ukrainian referendum; (iii) approval of State budget; (iv) preparation and enactment of laws; (v) approval and election to positions stipulated by Constitution (one third of Constitution Court, Ombudsman on Human Rights, etc.); (vi) confirming, entering into and renouncing of international agreements, and other authorities stipulated by Constitution.

Narodna Rada approves list of Committees of Narodna Rada which conduct legislative drafting work.

Right of legislative initiative in Narodna Rada belongs to deputies, President of Ukraine, Cabinet of Ministers of Ukraine and National Bank of Ukraine. Upon review in committees and discussion at session of Narodna Rada, law must be signed by President of Narodna Rada and immediately given to President. President affixes his signature to law and makes it available to public within 15 days or vetoes it and sends it back to Narodna Rada with reasons for veto and proposals for second review. If in course of such review Law is adopted by two thirds of Narodna Rada, President will be obligated to sign it and make available to public within ten days. Law comes into effect in ten days from date of official publication, unless otherwise provided by law itself.

State budget of Ukraine is approved annually by Narodna Rada at submission of Cabinet of Ministers. Control over use of funds is carried out by Accounting Office. Ukrainian currency is hryvna. (Temporary currency—karbovanets—is currently in circulation).

Parliamentary control over compliance with constitutional rights of people is carried out by Ombudsman of Narodna Rada of Ukraine on human rights.

President of Ukraine is head of state and acts on its behalf. President of Ukraine is elected by Ukrainian citizens on basis of common, equal and direct electoral right by secret ballot for period of five years.

Any citizen of Ukraine eligible to vote, 35 years or older, who resides in Ukraine and speaks state language may be elected President. One person cannot be President for more than two consecutive terms.

President, on basis of and in enforcement of Constitution and laws of Ukraine, issues resolutions and decrees which are binding in Ukraine.

President has right to call for all-Ukrainian referendum on issue of no-confidence in Narodna Rada of Ukraine. President forms Cabinet of Ministers, appoints, with consent of Narodna Rada, Prime Minister, General Prosecutor, Head of Anti-Monopoly Committee and Head of State Property Fund.

President announces state awards, issues pardons, supervises Council of National Security and Defense.

Title of President is protected by law and belongs to holder of office forever if President was not impeached.

Next election of President of Ukraine will take place on last Sun. of Oct., 1999 and on that date every five years thereafter.

During three years from effective date of Constitution of Ukraine, President is entitled to issue Decrees approved by Cabinet of Ministers on subjects not regulated by existing law with simultaneous submission of appropriate draft law to Narodna Rada of Ukraine. Such Decree shall be effective only if within 30 days Narodna Rada does not approve appropriate law or does not reject submitted draft law. This Decree is effective until adoption of appropriate law.

Government.—Cabinet of Ministers of Ukraine is highest body of state executive power of Ukraine. Cabinet of Ministers of Ukraine is responsible to President and reports to Narodna Rada.

Cabinet of Ministers along with other powers conducts financial, monetary, investment, price, credit, custom and tax policy of Ukraine, develops and ensures compliance with state budget, coordinates activities of ministries, regional state administrations and other bodies of executive power subordinated to Cabinet of Ministers, etc.

Executive power in regions and districts is executed by local state administrations. Heads of local state administrations are appointed by President of Ukraine upon submission by Cabinet of Ministers of Ukraine.

Judiciary.—

(a) Prosecutor's Office.—General Prosecutor, and prosecutors subordinated to him, have following obligations: initiation of government actions in court; supervision of compliance with laws by agencies which conduct investigation/search activities; investigation of crimes on issues within competence of prosecutor's office; representation of interests of individual or state in court.

General Prosecutor of Ukraine is appointed and dismissed by President of Ukraine with consent of Narodna Rada of Ukraine for five years. Prosecutors of regions (lands), districts and cities are appointed by General Prosecutor of Ukraine.

(b) Courts.—Judiciary system of Ukraine consists of Constitutional Court and courts of general jurisdiction.

People of Ukraine directly participate in operation of justice system through people's representative to court and juries.

System of courts is built on territorial and specialty principles. Supreme Court of Ukraine is highest court.

Constitution guarantees judicial independence and immunity; influence on judges of general jurisdiction is impermissible. Judges may be in office for unlimited period. Individual who is older than 25, has higher education in law and was employed in law for not less than three years may be recommended for position of judge. First appointment for position of professional judge for period of five years is fulfilled by President, all other judges except for judges of Constitutional Court of Ukraine are elected for unlimited period by Narodna Rada.

Vyscha Rada of Justice functions as court supervision and administration of justice system in Ukraine. Vyscha Rada submits proposals on appointment and dismissal of judges, supervises and controls activity of judges of all levels. Vyscha Rada consists of 21 members: three representatives of Narodna Rada of Ukraine, three representatives of President of Ukraine, three representatives of Judges' Congress, three representatives of Lawyers' Congress (Bar Association), three representatives of highest educational establishments in law (law schools) and two representatives of Vyscha Rada of Justice; such officers as Head of Supreme Court, Minister of Justice and General Prosecutor are also members of Vyscha Rada of Justice, Vyscha Rada is headed by President of Ukraine.

(c) Constitutional Court of Ukraine decides on questions of constitutionality of other laws and other legal issues under Constitution of Ukraine and officially interprets Constitution and laws of Ukraine, supervises legitimacy of dismissal of President according to impeachment procedure.

Constitutional Court consists of 18 judges. President of Ukraine, Narodna Rada and Judges' Congress each appoint six judges of Constitutional Court of Ukraine. Judges are appointed for nine year period without right of reappointment. Head of Constitutional Court is elected from its judges for three year period by secret ballot.

Regional Administration and Territorial Self-Governance.—System of territorial order of Ukraine consists of Republic of Crimea, regions (oblasts), cities, districts, towns and villages.

Laws and enactments of Verkhovna Rada of Autonomous Republic of Crimea and resolutions of Council of Ministers of Autonomous Republic of Crimea must be in compliance with Constitution and laws of Ukraine. Verkhovna Rada of Autonomous Republic of Crimea, within limits of its power, approves resolutions and decisions, creates and determines procedure for activity of its agencies of legislative and executive power and local self-governance. Head of Rada of Ministers of Republic of Crimea is appointed by Verkhovna Rada of Republic of Crimea with approval of President of Ukraine.

Local self-governance is conducted by territorial communities of village, town and city residents directly or through agencies elected by them. Village, town, district and city radas and executive bodies thereof are agencies of self-governance. Local rada may consist of counselors elected by residents of this territory for four year period. Head of executive rada is elected for four year period by secret ballot.

District rada is established by village, town and city radas of district; regional rada—by district, city or town (which are of regional subordination) radas of region. Heads of district and regional radas are elected by respective radas and head their executive branches. Self-governance radas function within limits of powers established by Constitution and laws: they manage communal property, approve and control budgets of respective administrative units, establish local taxes and fees, ensure conduct of local referenda, etc.

Regulations on Amendments to Constitution.—Draft law on introduction of amendments and modifications to Constitution may be submitted to Narodna Rada by President of Ukraine and one-third of constitutional membership of Narodna Rada. Law on introduction of amendments and modifications to Constitution as parliamentary initiative is approved by Narodna Rada by not less than two-thirds of votes of its membership as determined by Constitution. Amendments and modifications to such parts as General Principles, Elections, Referendum and On Introduction of Amendments and Modifications to Constitution must be additionally approved by All-Ukrainian Referendum. Issue of change of territory must be decided exclusively by All-Ukrainian Referendum.

Amendments and modifications to Constitution which are aimed at liquidation of independence and territorial integrity of Ukraine or intend to change constitutional regime, restrict or cancel forms of ownership, rights and freedoms of people guaranteed by Constitution may not be introduced. Under circumstances of state of emergency, introduction of amendments and modifications to Constitution are not permitted.

Second submission of amendments and modifications which were adopted earlier is permitted only after one year. Draft law is reviewed only upon availability of Constitutional Court of Ukraine.

CONTRACTS:

General provisions regarding obligations arising from contracts, are regulated by Civil Code of Ukraine, Part III.

Conclusion of Contracts.—Contracts are deemed executed if parties thereto agreed on all significant conditions and terms thereof. Significant are conditions and terms recognized as such by law or required for particular agreements, and all conditions and terms agreed to by parties thereto (e.g. price—in purchase-sale agreements).

If parties agree to conclude contract in certain form, then such contract is recognized as executed from date of execution. If offer of contract indicates period within which acceptance should be given, then contract is deemed executed provided that acceptance was made within such period. If offer of contract is made without fixed period for reply, then contract is deemed executed on condition that acceptance by

See Topical Index in front part of this volume.

CONTRACTS . . . *continued*
other party was immediate if offer was verbal, or within commonly required period if offer was written.

If delay in return of acceptance to offer is not acceptor's fault, then such offer is deemed delayed only on condition that offerer immediately notifies acceptor of delay in acceptance. In this event acceptance is regarded as counteroffer, as well as any acceptance and offer to conclude contract on conditions other than originally proposed.

By agreement of parties, difference arising between enterprises and organizations in course of concluding contract may be referred for review by regular or special court of arbitration.

In event that party to contract anticipated that contractual obligations are to be performed in favor of third person, then such performance of obligations may be required by both parties to contract or third party, unless otherwise provided by agreements or results from its content.

Conditions of Effectiveness.—In accordance with Civil Code (Civil Code, c. 2), individual civil competence (individual competence to acquire civil rights and create civil obligations as result of individual's actions) begins at age of 18. In event that person under 18 years gets married, then such person is deemed competent from date of marriage.

Minors at age of 15 through 18 may enter into contracts with consent of their parents or trustees. They may conclude contracts for retail trade, disposal of their wages, stipends, carry out copyrights for their works and/or inventions. Contracts of minors under 15 are concluded in their names by their parents/trustees, except for contracts for retail trade.

Trustees make contracts in name of persons recognized by court proceedings as incompetent as result of mental illness, or mental defect. Individual whose competence is limited by court proceedings as result of alcohol abuse or drugs, and individual who is under trusteeship, may carry out contracts on disposal of property only under trustee's written consent.

Contracts may be both verbal and written (simple or notarial). Under general rule, contracts which are carried out while being concluded, may be verbal. Written contract (simple or notarial) is required in certain transactions: contract for purchase-sale of house must be certified by notary; contracts of enterprises, institutions, organizations between themselves or with individuals, except for contracts which are carried out while being concluded; contracts between individuals, if such contracts are in excess of 100 karbovantsi (this sum was established by Civil Code, 1985, and has not been changed yet; this sum is specified in proportion to untaxed minimum).

Contracts concluded abroad should be executed in accordance with form accepted in foreign country. Noncompliance with form required by law will result in recognizing contracts as invalid only in instances when form is directly anticipated by special law regulating such contracts. Noncompliance with form of foreign trade contracts and procedure of signing thereof will result in recognizing such contracts as invalid. Noncompliance with simple written form of contracts results in depriving parties thereto of witnesses' evidence in case of dispute.

Following contracts are invalid: contracts which are contrary to law, in particular those encroaching property rights of minors; contracts concluded by minors under 15, and minors of 15 through 18 without parents' (trustees') consent, except for consumer contracts; contracts concluded by individuals recognized as incompetent, or with limited competence, or unable to understand meaning of their actions; contracts concluded as result of significant mistakes, or fraud, or violence, or threat, or coincidence of difficult circumstances; contracts concluded only pro forma, without intent to create legal consequences, or contracts concluded in order to hide other contracts (simulated contracts).

Such contracts are deemed invalid from date of conclusion thereof.

Execution of Contracts.—Obligations should be executed duly and within established period. Unilateral refusal to carry out obligations and unilateral modification of contractual provisions are not permitted. If period of fulfilling obligations is not established by contract, then creditor may demand fulfillment thereof at any time, and debtor must fulfil obligations within seven days upon submittance of demand, unless immediate fulfillment anticipated by contract. Individual debtor may fulfil obligations ahead of time, unless otherwise provided by contract or law. Premature fulfillment of obligations between enterprises and organizations is permitted only if such provision is anticipated by law or contract, or under creditor's consent.

If place of execution of obligation is not specified by contract or law, then obligation may be fulfilled: for obligation to transfer buildings, at location thereof; for financial obligations (except for obligations of enterprises and organizations), at creditor's residence; for any other obligations, at debtor's residence, if debtor is legal entity, at location thereof.

Payments under financial obligations between enterprises and organizations are effected through financial institutions.

Financial obligations may be expressed and are subject to payment in Ukrainian currency. In accordance with Decree of the Cabinet of Ministers "On Regime (System) of Currency Regulation and Currency Control", Feb. 19, 1993, residents trading in products (work, services), rights of intellectual property and other property rights for foreign currency in Ukraine are obligated to obtain individual licenses in manner and within period established by National Bank of Ukraine.

If several creditors/debtors are parties to contract, then each creditor may request execution and each debtor must fulfill obligations on pro rata basis, provided that respective obligations or demands are not joint. Joint obligations or demands arise if they are anticipated by contract or established by law, in particular when objects cannot be divided. Under joint obligations, each creditor may demand realization of obligations in full amount, and, respectively, each debtor is fully responsible for fulfillment of such obligations.

Assurance of Execution of Obligations.—Execution of obligations may be ensured in accordance with law of contract by forfeit (penalty, fine), mortgage or guarantee.

Forfeit (penalty, fine) is sum of money established by law or contract which should be paid by debtor to creditor in event of failure to fulfill or timely fulfill obligation. Forfeit contract should be executed in written form. Breach of such contracts result in recognizing such contracts as ineffective.

Under mortgage, in event that debtor fails to fulfill obligations secured by mortgage, creditor (mortgagee) may get satisfaction from value of mortgaged property, which is his privilege as against other creditors. Mortgage arises by contract or by law (see topic Mortgages).

Under contract of guarantee, guarantors are liable for other persons' obligations to creditors of these persons. Guarantee contracts should be executed in written form.

Responsibility for Breach of Contracts.—In event of breach or timely fulfillment by debtor of obligation, debtor must compensate creditor's losses resulting from such breach or nonfulfillment. Losses mean creditor's expenses, loss or damage of property, or profit lost as result of debtor's nonfulfillment of obligations.

If forfeit (penalty, fine) for nonfulfillment of obligations is established, then losses are compensated in part which was not covered by forfeit. Debtor is released from responsibility if nonfulfillment or unduly fulfillment of his obligations resulted from creditor's malice prepense or negligence. If obligation is not fulfilled as result of both parties' fault, then debtor's obligations will be reduced for respective sum.

Termination of Obligations.—Obligations may be terminated: if carried out in timely manner; if extinguished by comparable conditions whose term expired; with parties' agreement; as result of debtor's death if obligation must be fulfilled by debtor only; as result of creditor's death, if obligation was fulfilled personally for creditor; as result of liquidation of legal entity (debtor or creditor).

COPYRIGHT:

Copyrights are regulated by Law of Ukraine "On Copyright and Related Rights" of Dec. 23, 1993, and by Arts. 472 through 513 of Civil Code of Ukraine.

Works of science, literature, arts, regardless of form, designation, value and means of creation (written and verbal works, musical, choreographic, dramatic works, computer programs, photos, works of art) are subject to copyright.

Protection is granted to authors, regardless of citizenship and permanent residence, whose works are published for first time, or are not published but exist in some form in Ukraine; authors whose works were published for first time abroad, and within next 30 days were published in Ukraine, regardless of author's citizenship and permanent residence; and, authors who are citizens of Ukraine or permanently reside in Ukraine, regardless of territory where their works were published for first time.

Person whose name is indicated on sample of work made available to public, or on manuscript, or on original work of art, is author, unless otherwise proved in court proceedings.

Authors have following moral rights: to be recognized as author, and identified by name in connection with use of work; to prohibit use of his name, if author wants to remain anonymous; to choose pseudonym (pen name) in connection with use of work; to oppose any distortion, deterioration, any other change or other infringement on work which may be harmful to author's honor and reputation; to promulgate work.

Author has following property rights: exclusive use of work in any form and by any means; to permit or prohibit use of work by any means, including reproduction of works; performance of works in public; demonstration in public; any repeated performance on air or by wares of works by another organization; translation of works; alteration, adaptation, arrangement or other similar changes of works; distribution of works by sale, alienation by other means or through rent or lease or other transfer prior to first sale; rent after first sale, other alienation of copies of audiovisual works, musical works, and works in form of phonogram or readable by machines; import of copies of works, etc.

Exclusive copyrights for works of architecture, bridge building, landscaping also include right to participate in actual execution of project.

Individual holding copyright may ask for reimbursement for any use of his work, except that following uses are permitted without consent of author or other person who has copyright, provided that author's name and source are mentioned for use of quotation of published work, including quotations of newspaper and magazine articles in press surveys; free use of quotations in form of short excerpts from performances and works; use of works of literature and art in scope which is proved by purpose of its use; as illustration in publications; in copying sound or depiction of original; reproduction of works for court and administrative proceedings, scope of which is proved by this purpose; performance of musical works in public in course of official or religious ceremonies or funeral, scope of which is proved by nature of such ceremonies.

Compensation may be as onetime payment, or as percent of sale price for each copy, or each use of work, or as combination of such payments.

Copyrights are effective during author's life and 50 years thereafter, except in instances anticipated by Art. 24 of Law "On Copyright and Related Rights". Author's ownership rights may be inherited, may be transferred (assigned) by author or any other owner to other person. Authors have such rights as right to make works available to public, right to get reimbursement for use of his work, etc.

Ukraine as one of successor states of former USSR, is party to Universal Convention On Copyright of 1952.

CORPORATIONS:

Activity of enterprises in Ukraine is regulated by some laws, including Law of Ukraine "On Enterprises in Ukraine", Mar. 27, 1991; Law of Ukraine "Foreign Economic Activity", Apr. 16, 1991; Law of Ukraine "On Entrepreneurial Activity", Feb. 7, 1991; Law of Ukraine "On Economic Associations", Sept. 19, 1991.

Law determines following types of economic associations: joint-stock companies; limited liability companies; additional liability companies; full liability associations; limited partnership associations.

Economic associations are legal entities and may undertake any kind of entrepreneurial activity which is not in contravention of Ukrainian legislation. Enterprises, organizations, institutions, Ukrainian citizens, foreign citizens, individuals without citizenship, foreign legal entities and international organizations may be founders or participants in economic associations, except where prohibited by law. Economic associations may acquire proprietary and personal nonproprietary rights, make commitments, and act in court and court of arbitration on their own behalf. Economic associations acquire rights of legal entity from day of its state registration.

See Topical Index in front part of this volume.

CORPORATIONS . . . *continued*
Joint-stock, limited and additional liability associations are established and operate on basis of founding agreement and charter; full liability and limited partnership associations operate on basis of founding agreement.

Joint-stock association is one that has charter fund, divided into certain number of shares of definite equal nominal value and carries liability for association obligations only to limits of its property. Shareholders are liable for association only for shares they own. Joint-stock associations may be of two forms: open or closed to new investment.

Limited liability association is such that has charter fund divided into parts, amount of which is determined by founding documents. Participants of limited liability association are liable only within limits of their contributions.

Additional liability association has charter fund, divided into parts whose size is determined by founding documents. Participants of such association are responsible for its commitments, with their contributions into charter fund; in cases of insufficiency of those sums, property additionally belonging to them shall be reapportioned on pro rata basis to each participant's contribution. Limits of responsibility of participants is provided by founding documents.

Full liability association means such association where all persons take up common entrepreneurial activity and carry joint responsibility for association's commitment regarding all of its property.

Limited partnership association is association in which one or more participants are responsible with all their property for association's commitments and one or more participants have responsibility which is limited by their share in association's property. If two or more participants take full responsibility in operation of limited association, they are jointly responsible for debts of association.

Activity of association is terminated through its reorganization (merging, joining, division and apportionment) or liquidation. Association is reorganized by decision of its highest body.

COURTS:

Court system of Ukraine consists of Constitutional Court, regular courts and courts of arbitrazh (commercial courts).

Structure, procedure, and operation of Ukrainian courts is established by Laws of Ukraine "On Judicial System", as revised on June 17, 1992; "On Constitutional Court", Feb. 4, 1993; "On Court of Arbitrazh", June 30, 1993, Civil Procedure Code, Feb. 2, 1994 (hereinafter CPC); Criminal Procedure Code, Feb. 25, 1994 (hereinafter CrPC); and Arbitrazh Procedure Code, June 30, 1993 (hereinafter APC).

Constitutional Court of Ukraine is independent agency of judicial system. Its task is to ensure compliance of respective laws, other normative acts of legislative and executive power with Constitution of Ukraine, and to protect individual rights and freedoms provided by Constitution.

Constitutional Court of Ukraine consists of president, two vice-presidents, and 12 members. Judges are elected by Parliament for ten year term. At expiration of such term, judges continue with their duties until replacement judges are elected. Reelection of judges is not permitted.

Judicial candidates are nominated by Chairman of Parliament and President of Ukraine, on pro rata basis; six candidates each.

Constitutional Court hears cases on constitutional issues; and changes to effective laws of Ukraine and other acts adopted by Parliament; unimplemented laws and other acts adopted by Parliament; decrees and orders of President; resolutions of Presidium of Parliament of Ukraine; laws and other acts adopted by Parliament of Republic of Crimea and its Presidium; and resolutions and orders of Cabinet of Ministers of Ukraine and Cabinet of Ministers of Republic of Crimea.

Constitutional Court of Ukraine also reviews cases arising from alleged violation by state agencies and state officials of their authority; violation of authority of local Radas of different levels established by Constitutions of Ukraine and Republic of Crimea respectively, or violation of authority by local Radas and agencies of state executive power; and lawfulness of organization of elections and referenda.

Constitutional Court may review cases challenging normative acts adopted by agencies of legislative and executive power, specified in Constitution of Ukraine, if procedure of adopting thereof, as anticipated by Constitution of Ukraine, was violated.

Constitutional Court also has authority to review cases of challenges to constitutionality of any law or other normative document infringing individual rights and freedoms provided by Constitution or international treaty.

Constitutional Court of Ukraine also settles disputes between national-local governmental levels on issues regulated by Constitutions of Ukraine and Republic of Crimea respectively. Upon request of Parliament, Constitutional Court also decides whether President, Prime-Minister and other members of government, President of Supreme Court, President of Supreme Court of Arbitrazh, General Prosecutor of Ukraine, diplomatic and other representatives of Ukraine acted in accordance with Constitution and laws of Ukraine, when issue of premature termination of authority of such persons is raised. Constitutional Court decides on constitutionality of international treaties and agreements submitted for ratification by Parliament. Constitutional Court resolves issues of constitutionality of activity and forcible dissolution (liquidation) of political parties, international and all-Ukrainian public organizations.

Decisions, sentences, verdicts and resolutions of judicial agencies, and resolutions of agencies which conducted preceding investigation of case, and prosecuting magistracy are not within competence of Constitutional Court of Ukraine.

Decisions of Constitutional Court of Ukraine are binding for all state agencies, agencies of local and regional self-government, institutions, organizations, enterprises, officers thereof, associations and individuals. In case of unconstitutionality of laws, other normative acts or particular provisions thereof, or in event that international treaties and/or agreements are not duly executed or ratified, then Constitutional Court regards them as ineffective from date of introduction thereof.

Currently, Constitutional Court is not operating as result of presently lasting debates on its structure. President of Constitutional Court of Ukraine has been elected.

Also see topics Constitution; Law Reports, Codes, Etc.

Regular courts of Ukraine are courts of general jurisdiction. Their competence includes both civil and criminal cases, and in certain instances also cases arising from administrative legal relations. System of regular courts consists of Supreme Court of Ukraine, Supreme Court of Republic of Crimea, oblast courts, inter-oblast court, courts of cities of Kyiv and Sevastopol, inter-rayon courts, rayon courts, military courts of regions, Army and Navy Forces and garrisons. Highest control and supervision of judicial activity of regular courts is carried out by Supreme Court of Ukraine, particularly by following bodies thereof: Plenum of Supreme Court, Judicial Board of Supreme Court on Civil Cases, Judicial Board of Supreme Court on Criminal Cases and Presidium of Supreme Court.

Civil cases subject to settlement by regular courts are: disputes arising from civil, family, labor and cooperative relations, provided that at least one of parties thereto is individual; disputes arising from transportation agreements connected with direct international railroad or air transportation between state enterprises, institutions, organizations on one part, and agencies of railroad or air transport on other part, provided that such agreements arise from respective international agreements; cases on recognition of person as fully or partially incompetent, or missing, or dead; cases on recognition of entry to state documents as incorrect, on identification of legally important facts, on renewal of rights in lost securities issued in favor of bearer thereof, on appeal of notarial actions or refusal to carry out such actions; cases in which foreign persons, persons without citizenship, foreign enterprises and organizations participate; cases arising from administrative/legal relations, namely: (a) complaints for incorrectness of electorate lists, complaints concerning decisions and actions of local election committees for election of deputies and heads of local Radas, cases on petitions for cancellation of decisions of election committees regarding registration of candidate, (b) complaints challenging decisions and actions of Central and local Presidential election committees, and for cancellation of decisions of Central election committee, (c) complaints challenging conduct of agencies and offices in connection with imposition of administrative penalty, (d) complaint challenging unlawfulness of official conduct as encroaching upon individual rights; (e) prosecutor's petition for recognition of legal act as unlawful. (Art. 236, Civil Proceedings Code of Ukraine).

All cases subject to hearing in accordance with civil judicial procedure, are reviewed by rayon (city) courts which are courts of first level. Civil cases where one of parties thereto is rayon (city) court, are reviewed by oblast court or courts of cities of Kiev and Sevastopol. Jurisdiction of civil cases in which one of parties thereto is oblast court or court of Kiev/Sevastopol, is established by Supreme Court of Ukraine.

Lawsuits are filed in court at place of respondent's residence. Lawsuits against legal entities are submitted to courts at location of managing agency thereof. Lawsuits for imposition of alimonies, identification of paternity, suits arising from labor relations, copyrights or ownership for inventions are filed at place of plaintiff's residence. Lawsuits for compensation of losses caused by injury or loss of bread-winner are filed at place of plaintiff's residence or injury. Lawsuits for rights for buildings and procedure of use of land parcels should be submitted at location of party.

Complaints challenging decisions of local election committees (i) on refusal to register candidates for deputies or heads of rural, municipal, rayon, oblast or city Radas, (ii) on cancellation of decisions on registration of candidates or issues of preelection campaign, (iii) on recognition of elections as invalid are reviewed by local courts at location of respective election committee. Petitions for cancellation of decisions of district election committees regarding registration of candidates to deputies of Parliament are reviewed by Supreme Court of Ukraine. Decisions of Central Election Committee regarding election of deputies on recognition of elections as invalid may be appealed to Supreme Court of Ukraine.

Complaints challenging decisions of Central Election Committee for (i) refusing to register participation of party (electoral block) in election of President of Ukraine, for refusal of this committee to register candidate for president as such, (ii) recognition of elections as invalid and (iii) cancellation of decisions of Central Election Committee regarding registration of candidates to President, are reviewed by Supreme Court of Ukraine.

Individuals may appeal to court imposition of administrative penalty, or resolution of official regarding issue of administrative infringement at location of agency itself or place where such officer works. (CPC, cc. 3, 15, 29 through 39).

Criminal Cases Reviewed by Regular Courts.—All criminal cases are reviewed by local court as court of first instance, except in cases within competence of higher courts or military courts.

Supreme Court of Autonomous Republic of Crimea, oblast courts, Kiev and Sevastopol city courts, inter-oblast court as courts of first instance hear following cases: on dangerous national crimes; on other national crimes, including violation of equal rights of people regarding race, nationality or religion, divulging state secrets, loss of documents containing state secrets, transfer of state secret data to foreign organizations, banditry, mass riots, airline hijacking, forgery of currency, coins or securities, hiding of currency gains; theft of state or collective property in large amounts, premeditated murder under aggravating circumstances by dangerous recidivist, raping of juveniles, taking bribe.

Cases of particularly complicated issues or of exceptional public significance are reviewed by Supreme Court as court of first instance. Supreme Court of Ukraine may hear any case triable to court of lower level, or to transfer case for review of other respective court of Ukraine.

Crime committed by individuals with military rank, including colonel or captain of second rank, except for cases under competence of highest ranking courts martial, are under jurisdiction of courts martial of garrisons as courts of first instance.

Cases within competence of courts martial of regions and Army and Navy Forces as courts of first instance include cases: (a) on crimes committed by colonels or captains of second rank; (b) on crimes committed by commanders of regiments, ship commander of first and higher ranks, and persons with equal rank; (3) on all crimes which, during peaceful time, may be punishable by sentence to death.

Military board of Supreme Court of Ukraine resolves cases of particular significance, cases on crimes committed by military men with rank of general or admiral, or have positions of commander of unit or higher, or equivalent rank. Court martial of region, or Army and Navy Forces, or military board of Supreme Court of Ukraine may act as court of first instance and accept for review any case under competence of garrison's court.

COURTS . . . *continued*

Criminal cases are tried in court in territory where crime was committed. If place of crime cannot be identified, then case is resolved by court on territory of which inquest or preliminary investigation was carried out. (CrPC, c. 2).

Appeals.—Ukrainian law anticipates review of decisions and sentences of courts of first instance in civil and criminal cases which did not yet become effective. Ukraine, unlike other countries, has no separate courts of appeal, and issues on appeal and judicial supervision are reviewed by courts of higher ranks.

Thus, appeals from sentences and decisions of rayon (city) courts are submitted to Supreme Court of Republic of Crimea, oblast courts, courts of cities of Kiev and Sevastopol, while appeals from decisions and sentences of judicial board on criminal Supreme Court are submitted to Supreme Court. Any court's decision may be appealed by parties and other participants of civil case, and in criminal cases by condemned, or defense counsel, or legal representative, and, in criminal cases, by victim or his representative. Prosecutor or deputy-prosecutor presents appeal regardless of his participation in civil or criminal case. Period for appeal is seven days from date of adjudication for criminal cases, and ten days from date of decision on civil case. Supreme Court of Ukraine can decide all categories of cases, decisions of rayon (city) courts regarding complaints for incorrectness of electoral lists or complaints for actions of agencies and officers thereof in connection with infliction of administrative penalties.

Appeal should be executed in writing and submitted through court of first instance which heard case. Upon review of appeal in its content, court of appeal may (i) leave decision or sentences unchanged; (ii) cancel decision or sentences or part thereof and remand case for rehearing by court of first instance, or conclude case; (iii) enter new decision or sentence. (CPC, cc. 40, 41; CrPC, cc. 29, 30).

Judicial Supervision.—Lower court's final decisions may be retried by supervision as follows: Presidium of Parliament of Republic of Crimea, oblast court or Kyiv city court upon protest of President of Supreme Court of Ukraine, General Prosecutor of Ukraine and deputies thereof, chairman of oblast courts or city courts of Kiev and Sevastopol, President of Supreme Court of Republic of Crimea, prosecutor of Republic of Crimea, oblasts, Kyiv, and Sevastopol and deputies thereof, concerning decisions, sentences and verdicts of oblast courts and city courts of Kyiv and Sevastopol; judicial board for civil cases of Supreme Court of Ukraine, and judicial board for criminal cases and military board of Supreme Court of Ukraine upon protest of President of Supreme Court of Ukraine, General Prosecutor of Ukraine and deputies thereof against decisions, sentences and verdicts of rayon (city) peoples' courts, inter-rayon (district) courts, oblast courts, city courts, courts martial of garrisons, regions, Army and Navy Forces, and against resolutions of Supreme Court of Republic of Crimea, oblast court, courts of Kyiv and Sevastopol, and against resolution of courts; Plenum of Supreme Court of Ukraine, upon protest of President of Supreme Court of Ukraine, General Prosecutor of Ukraine and deputies thereof against decision and verdicts of judicial board for civil cases of Supreme Court of Ukraine, against verdicts and sentences of judicial board for criminal cases of Supreme Court of Ukraine, and against decisions of judges of this court; military court of region or Army and Navy Forces—upon protests of President of Supreme Court of Ukraine, General Prosecutor of Ukraine, deputies thereof, chairman of military court of region or Army and Navy Forces, military prosecutor (who has right of oblast prosecutor) against sentences, verdicts and resolutions of garrison's court martial.

Decision of court may be appealed only by persons mentioned above.

As result of review of case, court may: leave decision, adjudication or verdict unchanged; cancel decision or adjudication and all further court's verdicts and decisions, and close case or transfer it for new investigation or retrial; cancel verdict, further court's verdicts and resolutions, provided that they were made on appeal, and to leave as effective, changed or unchanged, court's decision or verdict; introduce changes to any sentence, verdict or resolution of court. (CPC, c. 41, CrPC, c. 31).

Conduct of Case in Connection with New Evidence.—Final decisions, verdicts, resolutions and sentences of court may be retried as result of new evidence unknown when decision was rendered, and such facts themselves or in connection with fact revealed earlier prove error of court's decision. Decisions of courts of first instance, on appeal or on supervision may be retried on grounds of new evidence.

Decisions for civil cases may be reviewed on grounds of new evidence. In criminal cases, issues on protest to presidium of oblast or city court must be raised by prosecutor of Republic of Crimea, oblast prosecutor, or prosecutor of Kyiv or Sevastopol.

Prosecutor of Republic of Crimea, oblast prosecutor or prosecutor of Kyiv or Sevastopol send cases where sentences were entered by oblast or city court to General Prosecutor of Ukraine who decides on submitting protest to Supreme Court of Ukraine. (CPC, c. 43, CrPC, c. 32).

Courts of Arbitrazh are commercial courts which settle all economic disputes arising between legal entities, state and other agencies.

Organization and activity of courts of arbitrazh is specified by Constitution of Ukraine, Law "On the Court of Arbitrazh", Arbitrazh Procedure Code of Ukraine and other enactments of Ukraine. System of courts of arbitrazh consists of Supreme Court of Arbitrazh of Ukraine, Court of Arbitrazh of Republic of Crimea, courts of arbitrazh of oblasts, and cities of Kyiv and Sevastopol. Each of these institutions is legal entity.

Any legal entity of Ukraine and foreign countries as well as Ukrainian state bodies and international organizations may apply to court of arbitrazh in accordance with competence thereof. Disputes involving natural persons are not subject to this court. Waiver of right to apply to court of arbitrazh is null and void. Competence of court of arbitrazh basically includes: (i) disputes relating to conclusion, alteration, termination and performance of economic contracts and (ii) bankruptcy cases.

Supreme Court of Arbitrazh of Ukraine is highest agency settling economic disputes and supervising realization of decisions and operation of courts of arbitrazh of Ukraine.

Court of Arbitrazh of Republic of Crimea, courts of arbitrazh of oblasts, and cities of Kyiv and Sevastopol review all cases which are within competence of courts of arbitrazh, except for instances which are within competence of Supreme Court of Arbitrazh.

Supreme Court of Arbitrazh hears: (1) disputes arising from economic agreements for amount exceeding 100,000 minimal wages (currently minimal wage is equal to 60,000 karbovantsi without cost-of-living indexation), and when carrying out agreements and other commitments in amount exceeding 10,000 minimal wages (without indexation), when agreements exceeding 100,000 minimal wages (without indexation) are recognized invalid, except for disputes between parties thereto located in Republic of Crimea, within one oblast, cities of Kyiv and Sevastopol; (2) disputes invalidating documents of non-lawful origin, issued by central agencies of state executive power and other all Ukrainian agencies, associations and unions; (3) disputes invalidating documents of non-lawful origin, issued by oblast, Kyiv and Sevastopol City Radas, representatives of President of Ukraine in oblasts and cities of Kyiv and Sevastopol, oblast and local state administration of Kyiv and Sevastopol; (4) disputes on documents containing state secrets; (5) disputes which are within competence of Supreme Court of Arbitrazh under laws of Ukraine, intergovernmental treaties and agreements.

Supreme Court of Arbitrazh may also settle any issue which is subject to settlement by courts of arbitrazh of Ukraine.

Regarding territorial subordination of various courts of arbitrazh, in accordance with general rule, disputes are settled by court of arbitrazh at place of location of party obligated under agreement, to carry out actual actions (to transfer property, to perform works, etc.) in favor of another party, or at respondent's place of residence or location. Disputes in which respondents participate will be reviewed by court of arbitrazh at place of residence or location of one of respondents at plaintiff's choice.

Economic disputes in which one of parties is court of arbitrazh of Republic of Crimea, or arbitrazh courts of oblasts, and cities of Kyiv or Sevastopol, will be settled at place specified by Supreme Court of Arbitrazh.

Bankruptcy cases shall be settled by court of arbitrazh at bankrupt's residence or location.

Disputes arising from transportation agreements in which one of respondents is transportation agency, will be settled by court of arbitrazh at place of residence or location of such transportation agency.

Enterprises, institutions, organizations, individual and joint ventures, international associations of Ukrainian organizations and organizations of other countries, and other legal entities, regardless of ownership form and structure, have right to appeal to court of arbitrazh for protection of their rights and interests. Main purpose of court of arbitrazh is to provide agreement between parties. In instances where it is impossible to come to agreement, decision shall be made by sole arbitrator or majority of arbitrators' votes.

Dispute may be transferred for settlement by court of arbitrazh, provided that prior to arbitrazh, this dispute was settled by parties thereto in accordance with procedure established for this category of disputes. In order to settle disputes directly with person violating rights or legitimate interests of enterprises or organizations, these enterprises or organizations will appeal directly to infringer with written petition. Such petition should contain (i) information on circumstances causing claim; (ii) information which is sufficient proof of such circumstances; (iii) references to appropriate enactments; (iv) applicant's demands. Documents confirming applicant's demands should be attached in original or in copy, duly certified by notary. Claim is subject to review within a month term computed from day of receipt of application.

Response to appeal is executed in writing and sent to applicant. If appeal is fully or partially rejected, applicant may appeal to court of arbitrazh for settlement of dispute.

Claim to be submitted to court of arbitrazh should be executed in writing and signed by director/deputy director of enterprise or organization, by prosecutor and it should contain following information: (i) name of court of arbitrazh to which claim is addressed; (ii) names of parties, their addresses; (iii) amount of claim, if claim is valued in money; (iv) amount of agreement (for disputes arising from economic agreements); (v) content of claim; (vi) if claim is addressed to some respondents, content of claim to each of them; (vii) information on circumstances on which claim is based; (viii) confirmation of facts which caused claim; (ix) substantiation of amount to be recovered; (x) law on which claim is based; (xi) information on measures taken to settle dispute before transfer thereof to court of arbitrazh; (xii) list of documents and proofs to be attached to petition. Other data may be given in petition if it is required to facilitate settlement of dispute.

Issues of acceptance of claim are settled by arbitrator.

Arbitrators reject petitions for claims if: petition is not subject to settlement by courts of arbitrazh of Ukraine; in proceedings of court of arbitrazh or other agency which is settling dispute within its competence, there is dispute between same parties, on same issue, on same grounds, or decision of this agency on this issue is available; claim is addressed to liquidated enterprise or organization.

Within five days upon receipt of petition with claim, arbitrator notifies parties or prosecutor (if applicable) on commencing actions.

Legitimacy and reasonableness of decisions made by court of arbitrazh may be checked by review, at request of parties, prosecutor's protest, or at initiative of court of arbitrazh. Court of arbitrazh may reconsider its earlier decisions which are essential for this case but which were not and could not be known by applicant.

Decisions and awards of courts of arbitrazh are enforceable in Ukraine and also in very limited number of foreign countries such as CIS countries, Lithuania and Poland with which Ukraine entered into respective international treaties. These decisions and awards do not fall under UN Convention on Recognition and Enforcement of Foreign Arbitral Awards (New York, 1958).

Courts of arbitrazh which are in fact type of commercial court should not be confused with institutional or ad hoc arbitration. (Also see topic Arbitration and Award.)

International Treaties.—Foreign individuals, enterprises and organizations may apply to Ukrainian courts and enjoy rights equal with those of Ukrainian citizens, enterprises, and organizations.

Ukrainian courts carry out matters and judgments transferred to them in established manner by foreign courts, when executing particular procedural acts (distribution of written notifications, other documents, interrogation of parties and witnesses, conduct of expert examination, etc.), except for instances when: (i) such actions are in contravention of sovereignty or threaten security of Ukraine; (ii) such actions are not within competence of court.

Performance of requests for actions of foreign courts is carried out on basis of Ukrainian laws. Procedure of executing decisions of foreign regular courts and courts of arbitration in Ukraine is established by respective international treaties of Ukraine.

See Topical Index in front part of this volume.

CURRENCY:

Ukraine's present monetary unit is coupon-karbovanets. This temporary currency is expected to be substituted by Hryvna. Resolution of Presidium of Parliament of Ukraine "On National Currency of Ukraine", Nov. 1991, anticipated measures for introduction of new local currency.

The National Bank of Ukraine has already issued 500,000, 200,000, 100,000, 50,000, 20,000, 10,000, 5,000, 2,000, 1,000, and 500 karbovantsi banknotes. Banknotes of one through 200 karbovantsi are no longer in use because of their insignificant purchase value.

National Bank of Ukraine has exclusive right for issuance of money in Ukraine. In Ukraine there are no coins. National Bank of Ukraine together with Ministry of Finance establishes system of protection of banknotes, value thereof, etc. Main principles of circulation, creation and application of main standards of exchange of coupon-karbovanets for foreign currencies are established by Cabinet of Ministers of Ukraine. Official rates of currency exchange are established and made available to public through mass media by National Bank of Ukraine.

CUSTOMS:

Ukraine has exclusive customs jurisdiction over territory of Ukraine including territory of artificial islands, equipment and premises created in maritime zone of Ukraine. Customs border of Ukraine, also referred to as "unified customs territory of Ukraine", coincides with its state border with exception of boundaries of special customs zones.

Three types of customs duty exist in Ukraine: ad valorem, which is assessed in percent to customs value of commodities and other items which are subject to customs duty; specific, assessed in specific money amount for unit of commodities and other items subject to customs duty; combined, which combines these two types of customs duty.

Common Customs Tariff of Ukraine means systematized list of customs duty rates which are applied to products/goods which are imported to or exported outside customs territory of Ukraine.

Law of Ukraine "On the Common Customs Tariff of Ukraine" of Feb. 5, 1992 (with amendments and modifications made by Decree No. 4-93 as of Jan. 11, 1993 and No. 36-93 as of Apr. 23, 1993) specifies procedure of formation and application of common customs tariff of Ukraine upon import of products/goods to territory of Ukraine. Duty is paid in national currency of Ukraine.

Customs duty rates are set and modified by Cabinet of Ministers of Ukraine.

Import duty on products/goods is levied upon import thereof into Ukraine. Preferential rates of import duty specified by Common Customs Tariffs apply to products/ goods imported from countries which, along with Ukraine, are members of customs alliances, which have specific customs zones with Ukraine, according to specific preferential customs rules pursuant to international agreements in which Ukraine participates, and from developing countries; customs privileges and preferential rates of import duty, specified by Common Customs Tariff of Ukraine, apply to products/ goods imported from countries or economic communities, with respect to which Ukraine has policy of facilitating trade and import. Full (general) customs duty rates are applied to other commodities.

Duty is not paid upon import of products/goods acquired for State Hard Currency Fund, republican (Republic of Crimea), local hard currency funds or foreign credits, guaranteed by Cabinet of Ministers. Duty is not paid upon import of means of plant and animal protection, potash and phosphate fertilizers and humanitarian and technical aid, as determined by Cabinet of Ministers. Duty is reduced by 50% on import of products/goods for children.

Import duty rates may be altered by Cabinet of Ministers of Ukraine. Customs duty rates set forth by Common Customs Tariff of Ukraine are changed by Cabinet of Ministers, except for import duty rates for exercisable goods. Cabinet of Ministers is entitled to change rates of customs duties only for objects of customs taxation—goods and other things which are transported through customs border of Ukraine. Import duty rates for exercisable goods are established and changed by Supreme Rada of Ukraine (Parliament).

Imported products/goods are subject not only to customs but to sanitary, veterinary, radiological and ecological control as well. Transit of products/goods through Ukraine's customs border are subject to compulsory customs duty. Vehicles, commodities and other things of international foreign organizations and representations must be declared by customs offices of Ukraine by submitting application with precise information on commodities and purpose of transfer thereof.

Customs Code of Ukraine determines exemptions for diplomatic and consular representative offices, representatives and members of delegations of foreign countries, international organizations, representations of foreign states. Joint ventures with participation of Ukrainian and foreign legal entities and individuals, foreign enterprises, organizations and representations thereof, foreign employees of these organizations and representations and members of their families are also extended certain exemptions from import/export duties.

According to law, excise duty, VAT, import duty and customs fees are levied on excisable goods which are imported to customs territory of Ukraine by subjects of entrepreneurial activity of all ownership forms irrespective of quantity of customs value of such goods. Law "On Some Issues of Taxation of Excisable Goods" as of Nov. 16, 1995 cancelled all privileges regarding payment of customs fees irrespective of fact whether these goods are imported for further sale or for consumption.

Untaxable private import of excisable goods is limited to 200 ECU (approximately $140) or single thing value of which does not exceed 300 ECU (approximately $285).

According to new law there are peculiarities regarding stamping of alcohol beverages and tobacco products in course of import to Ukraine. Changes were introduced also regarding VAT for imported goods. See topic Taxation.

Customs fees are levied for customs legalization of goods and is 0.15% of total value of products/goods.

Export duty is assessed on products/goods upon export thereof outside Ukraine and is paid in national currency. To determine customs duty value, currency of contract is converted into national currency of Ukraine according to current rate of exchange of National Bank of Ukraine as of day of customs declaration submission.

Products/goods, works, services exported by subjects of entrepreneurial activity within export quota limits, and commodities manufactured of imported raw materials, are exempted from export duty.

Export of goods (works, services) for repaying of indebtedness on foreign credits provided under guarantee of Cabinet of Ministers of Ukraine or on foreign credits received under individual licenses of National Bank of Ukraine, is not subject to export customs duty. (Decree of Cabinet of Ministers 6-93).

Subject of entrepreneurial activity may postpone payment of export duty by issuing promissory note to pay export duty at later date, in accordance with Instruction of Ministry of Finance of Ukraine No. 95 as of Nov. 23, 1993 "On approval of the procedure of issuance, accounting and submitting for payment of promissory notes while paying export duty".

Some products/goods may be subject to seasonal import/export duty for period not exceeding four months.

According to new procedure of transportation of imported and exported goods through customs border of Ukraine, customs clearance and transit of such goods, subject of entrepreneurial activity must receive permission for import, export and transit of goods and, if required, specification of goods must be attached.

Specific duty applies in some specific events upon import/export of products/goods, i.e.: specific customs duty; anti-dumping customs duty; compensation duty. Specific duty applies: (i) in order to protect domestic manufacturers, if goods similar to or competitive with domestic are imported to Ukraine in quantities and on conditions, which may cause damage; (ii) in order to prevent violation of state interests by participants of foreign economic activity or from unfair competition; (iii) as response to discrimination and/or unfriendly actions of some countries and communities thereof, restricting legal rights and interests of Ukrainian business. Specific duty rate is specified in every separate case.

Anti-dumping duty applies in event of: (i) import to Ukraine of goods at substantially lower than their competitive price in country of export at moment of export if such export causes damage to domestic manufacturers producing similar or competitive goods or prevents organization or expansion of manufacturing of similar goods in Ukraine; (ii) export out of Ukraine of goods at substantially lower prices than prices of other exports of similar or competitive goods at moment of export, if such export causes damage to state interests. Anti-dumping duty rate must not exceed difference between existing wholesale price of product in country of export and price declaring under import into Ukraine or difference between price of goods exported from Ukraine at dumping prices and average price of Ukrainian export of similar or competitive goods at that time.

Compensation duty applies in event: (i) import into Ukraine of goods, in manufacturing and export of which subsidies were used, if such export causes damages to domestic manufacturers of similar or competitive goods or prevents organization and/ or expansion of manufacturing of such goods in Ukraine; (ii) import into Ukraine of goods, in manufacturing and export of which subsidies were used, if such export causes damages to state interests of Ukraine. Compensation duty rate must not exceed amount of subsidies. Examination will be conducted on initiative of Customs Tariff Board or interested Ukrainian or foreign government agencies, enterprises and organizations to determine whether facts exist for implementation of either special, anti-dumping or compensatory duties by Ministry of Foreign Relations. As consequence of such examination, special, anti-dumping or compensatory duty may be imposed.

Products/goods which are exported from territory of Ukraine by citizens of Ukraine, and products/goods acquired by Ukrainian citizens, foreign individuals and persons without citizenship in Ukraine, are subject to customs duty in amount of 50% of retail price thereof established in Ukraine upon payment of duty.

Exemptions.—Following categories of products/goods are exempted from customs duty: vehicles, which regularly deliver international shipments as well as fuel, food and other property necessary for normal operation of vehicle during trip; material and technical equipment as well as fuel, raw material for industrial processing, food and other property, exported from Ukraine to ensure manufacturing activity of Ukrainian-owned and Ukrainian leased enterprises and organizations, fishing ships, production which is later imported to Ukraine; currency of Ukraine, foreign currency and securities; products/goods damaged before crossing border and cannot be used as materials or products/goods; products/goods imported into Ukraine for official and individual use or are exported from Ukraine by organizations and individuals, enjoying right, pursuant to international agreements of Ukraine, to be exempted from paying import and export duty; products/goods originally from Ukraine but reimported to Ukraine without refining or processing as well as foreign products/goods which are reexported from Ukraine without refining and processing; other goods and products/goods specified by Cabinet of Ministers of Ukraine.

Rates of import and export duty for some products/goods may also be reduced.

Exemption from duty or preferential duty applies to certain products/goods: products/goods imported in specific customs zones of Ukraine for final consumption in these zones; products/goods exported from specific customs zones for consumption outside Ukraine and originally from these zones; products/goods exported from specific customs zones to customs territory of Ukraine and originally from these zones.

Special duty rates established for subjects of entrepreneurial activity apply to import of products/goods by lots.

No customs duty is assessed on sums of money which Ukrainian citizens receive on postal orders from abroad.

If international agreement of Ukraine establishes rules which differ from those of customs legislation of Ukraine, then rules of international agreement will apply.

In 1992 Ukraine joined 1950 Convention on Establishment of Council of Customs Cooperation.

DEATH:

Missing person may be declared dead by court proceedings. Absence of information on missing person at his domicile for three years shall be sufficient ground for such court decision.

DEATH . . . *continued*

If missing person disappeared under life threatening circumstances (for example, flood, earthquake, etc.) or other circumstances raising presumption of person's accidental death (for example, shipwreck), then above mentioned period may be reduced to six months.

Military person or any other person who disappeared without trace during course of military action may be declared dead by court proceedings not earlier than two years from day of termination of such military action.

Where missing person is adjudicated dead by court proceedings, date of death is date of such court decision. If person disappeared under life threatening circumstances or circumstances raising presumption that such person is dead by accident, then date of presumed death of such person may be declared by court as date of death thereof.

If person declared dead reappears, or place of his presence becomes known, respective decision will be cancelled by court.

DEPOSITIONS:

See topic Courts.

DESCENT AND DISTRIBUTION:

Descent is realized by law and by will. Descent is realized by law when and if such descent was not changed by will.

Descendants may be persons who were alive on date of decedent's death, and decedent's children who were conceived during lifetime but born after decedent's death.

Any persons taking life of decedent or his descendants on purpose or making attempt on life thereof, have no right of inheritance, either by law or by will.

Parents have no right to inherit from children after parental rights terminated, provided that such rights were not reinstated as of date of inheritance. Persons, who persistently avoided support obligations to decedent, have no right to inherit after him, provided that such circumstances were confirmed by court proceedings.

First Level of Descendants.—In course of descent by law, decedent's children (including adopted), spouse, and parents (adoptee) inherit in equal parts. After born child of decedent is also first level descendent.

Decedent's grandchildren and great-grandchildren are descendants by law, provided that on date of decedent's death parent who would have been descendent is dead; they inherit in equal parts share which would have been inherited by their deceased parent by law.

Second Level of Descendants by Law.—In absence of decedent's descendants of first level or in event such descendants do not accept inheritance, decedent's brothers and sisters, and his grandmothers and grandfathers inherit in equal parts.

Inheritance by Dependents.—Disabled persons who were dependent on decedent within not less than year prior to his death, inherit by law. Should other descendants also exist, they will inherit in equal parts with descendants of level involved in inheritance.

Inheritance by Adopted Persons.—Adopted persons and heirs thereof inherit from adoptive parent and/or his relatives, and as descendants are equal with adoptive parent's natural children or heirs thereof. Adopted persons do not inherit from their parents and other blood relatives in line of ascent, or their brothers and sisters.

In inheriting after death of adopted person or his heirs, adoptive parents and their relatives are equal to parents and other blood relatives of adopted person. Natural parents or other blood relatives in line of ascent, and his brothers and sisters do not inherit, by law, after death of adopted person or his heirs.

By will every individual may leave all property or part of it to one or several persons, both included and not included in group of descendants by law, and to state or firms, institutions, organizations.

Regardless of will provisions, however, disabled children, spouse or parents of deceased inherit certain part of property.

Remainder of property which is not inherited, is divided among descendants by law to whom another part of property was left by will, unless otherwise provided by will.

Also see topic Wills.

DISPUTE RESOLUTION:

General.—Practically, Ukraine has only judicial proceedings for dispute resolution (see topic Courts) and arbitration (see topic Arbitration and Award); latter topic also covers arbitration in foreign business context. No statutes or court rules for non-arbitral procedures such as mediation, factfinding, minitrials, etc.

Mandatory Dispute Resolution.—See general comment above. But for certain types of individual labor disputes, parties must submit claim to labor dispute committee before filing court suit. Such committees are special bodies elected by employees of companies with over 15 employees.

Voluntary Dispute Resolution.—See general comment above. Enforceability of agreement on nonjudicial dispute resolution procedure other than arbitration is doubtful.

DIVORCE:

Marriage may be dissolved only by divorce upon petition of one or both parties.

Husband, however, does not have right to commence divorce action without wife's consent during wife's pregnancy and for one year after child's birth.

Divorce may be obtained by court judgment; or by grant of state registration agencies in event of mutual consent and when husband and wife are without minor children.

Disputes concerning jointly owned property or alimony, custody of common child or alimony for disabled spouse are decided by court upon petition of either party. In issuing divorce decree, court takes measures to protect interests of minor children and disabled spouse.

Divorce from persons: who are recognized as absentees; who are recognized as incapable as result of disease or mental defect; and, who are incarcerated for period not less than three years is granted by state registration agencies.

In event when spouse who was incarcerated or trustee of incompetent spouse commences dispute on child custody, or joint property or child support in favor of incompetent spouse, then divorce is issued by court.

Marriage is deemed dissolved upon registration of divorce with state registration agencies.

In event of divorce, parent (who does not have custody of minor child) provides material support for minor children in amount of: (i) 1/4 of salary (income) for one child; (ii) 1/3 of salary (income) for two children; and, (iii) 1/2 of salary (income) for three or more children.

When spouse obligated by court to provide material support refuses to voluntarily do so, other spouse may appeal to court with support petition.

Divorce of Ukrainian citizens from foreign citizens and between foreign citizens is effectuated in accordance with current legislation of Ukraine.

ENFORCEMENT OF JUDGMENT AND ATTACHMENT:

When court decides in favor of plaintiff after trial, plaintiff may request court for certain guarantees that defendant, though unwilling, will be forced to fulfil decision of court. Court or court of arbitration, at request of parties or on its own initiative, may take steps to guarantee actual fulfillment of its judgment. Securing claim is permitted at any stage of civil or arbitration court case, if failure to take measures may make enforcement of judgment decision more difficult or impossible. Civil Procedure Code of Ukraine, Feb. 2, 1994, and Arbitration Procedure Code, June 30, 1993, which regulate issue of securing of claim, does not contain list of circumstances when application of securing measures is appropriate; issue of securing claim is decided on case-by-case basis by judge or arbitrator. For example, in civil matters such as payment of alimony, salary, and compensation of losses caused by damage to health or bereavement of breadwinner, judge may on own initiative decide on need to secure claim or judgment. Depending on circumstances court may decide on complete or partial securing of claim/judgment. Claim may be secured by: attachment of property or pecuniary sums belonging to defendant; prohibition of certain conduct by defendant; prohibition of other persons from taking certain conduct regarding claim; suspension of collecting on basis of documents according to which recovery is executed in undisputed manner; suspension of sale of contested property. (Art. 152 of Civil Procedure Code and Art. 67 of Arbitration Procedure Code).

Concept of "securing a claim/judgment" also exists in Criminal Procedure Code of Ukraine. In this context, civil claim is considered by court along with criminal case and is raised against defendant or persons materially responsible for actions of defendant for material damages as result of crime. Criminal Procedure Code, Dec. 28, 1960 specifies obligations of investigating agency, investigator, prosecutor and court in securing civil claim when information is available that crime caused material damages to victim or necessitated health care expenses for treatment of victim. (art. 29). In all other instances Civil Procedure Code applies.

Certain actions to secure claims are restricted by law. Securing claim is not permitted by: attachment of wages, pension, stipend/scholarship, financial aid or social security. But these restrictions are not applicable to claims on alimony, compensation for damages, damage to health and damage from loss of breadwinner.

In deciding to secure claim, court must take into consideration interests of both plaintiff and defendant. For example, upon petition of one party and considering explanations of other party, court may permit substitution of one method of securing claim by another or permit several means of securing claim. If plaintiff loses claim, defendant may after decision is final demand from plaintiff compensation for losses caused defendant by securing plaintiff's claim.

Court may cancel decision of judge on securing claim. Decisions on securing claim may be appealed, but petition on protest does not suspend decision on securing claim and does not prevent case from further consideration.

ENVIRONMENT:

Basic Laws on Protection of Environment.—Area of protection of environment in Ukraine is regulated by Law "On Environmental Protection", June 25, 1991, which applies to land, water, forests, minerals, air, and by other specific laws developed in accordance with above Law.

Law "On Environmental Protection" sets forth legal, economic and social basis for environmental protection. This Law regulates protection, replenishment and use of natural resources, provision of ecological safety, minimization of negative influence of economic and other activities on environment, maintenance of natural resources, genetic fund, scenery and other natural complexes. Law includes provisions on authorities of managing agencies in area of environmental protection, ecological rights of individuals, economic arrangements for providing environmental protection, issues of natural reserve fund, responsibilities for infringement of laws on environmental protection.

Specific Legislation.—

Air.—Law "On Protection of Atmospheric Air", Oct. 16, 1992 is basic legislation in this area; it establishes following: (a) norms of ecological safety of air; (b) marginal norms of acceptable discharge of wastes into air and other harmful influence of physical and biological factors by stationary sources; (c) marginal norms for contaminating substances released into air in course of operation of technological and other equipment, premises and objects; (d) norms for use of air as raw material of basic production application; (e) norms of content of contaminating substances in waste gases of transferrable sources and harmful influence of their physical factors. Norms are developed and/or approved by Ministry of Health of Ukraine and Ministry of Environmental Protection of Ukraine.

Enterprises, institutions and organizations whose activity is connected with discharge of contaminating substances into air are obligated to assure ongoing effective work and maintenance in good standing of premises, equipment and devices including equipment used for cleanup and reduction of levels of other harmful influence, to control scope and structure of contaminants which are discharged into air, to have contingency plans on environmental protection for events such as accidents and unfavorable meteorological conditions, and to take measures for elimination of reasons for and consequences of contamination of environment.

See Topical Index in front part of this volume.

ENVIRONMENT . . . *continued*

Organizational and economic arrangements should exist to provide protection and effective use of air. These arrangements anticipate following: (a) establishing limits of contamination and other harmful discharges into air; (b) establishing limits for use of air as raw material of basic production application; (c) establishing norms and amounts of fees for discharge of contaminants into atmospheric air and other harmful influence on it; (d) establishing norms of payment for exceeding discharge limits, other harmful influence, and issuing permits for use of air; (e) providing enterprises, institutions, organizations and individuals with tax credit and other exemptions in course of introduction by them of technological processes resulting in minimal or no waste, or for energy or resource saving technological processes, performance of other environmental protective arrangements in accordance with laws.

Procedure for establishing discharge limits, levels of harmful influence of physical and biological factors, and normative fees for contamination of air, shall be established by Cabinet of Ministers of Ukraine.

Any infringement of air protection laws shall result in administrative or criminal responsibilities in accordance with Ukrainian laws.

Water.—Water Code of Ukraine is basic document in area of water protection. This Code anticipates conditions of placement, design, construction and operation of enterprises, premises and other objects which influence condition of water; prohibition of discharges of wastes and harmful substances for which marginal levels of concentration in water are not established; protection of surface of water and ice surface of reservoirs and water piping, protection of water from contamination and trash; establishing of protective sanitation areas and zones; arrangements for protection of waters from exhaustion.

Any infringement of water protection laws shall result in administrative or criminal responsibilities in accordance with Ukrainian laws.

Land, Forest, Resources.—Land Code of Ukraine, Forest Code of Ukraine and Code of Ukraine on Resources regulate procedure for use and protection of lands, forests and resources. These laws specify environmental, sanitary and technical standards, competence of agencies which conduct state control over use and protection of lands, forests and resources as well as responsibility for violation of legislation in these spheres.

Contamination from Industrial, Household and Other Waste.—Legislation of Ukraine does not contain separate enactment which regulates procedure of utilization of waste. Law "On Environmental Protection" anticipates obligation of enterprises, institutions, organizations and individuals to take effective steps in order to reduce amounts of waste and to decontaminate, process, safely store and bury waste. Storage, conservation or placement of waste shall be permitted in areas defined by local councils of people's deputies within limits specified by these councils with observance of sanitary and environmental norms only on condition that special permit is available; storage, conservation or placement of wastes shall be conducted by method which ensures possibility of further economic use thereof and safety for environment and people's health.

Environmental Safety of Vehicles.—Manufacturing and maintenance of vehicles and other transportation equipment whose exhausts and discharges contain contaminants exceeding established norms shall be prohibited in accordance with previously mentioned Law "On Environmental Protection". Heads of transport organizations and owners of vehicles shall be responsible for observance of norms of discharge and exhaust limits and limits of permitted levels of physical influence on environment which have been established for respective type of vehicles.

Environmental Examination.—Law "On Environmental Examination", Feb. 9, 1995 determines list of objects which are subject to this examination. This list includes draft laws, documents on introduction of new techniques, technologies, materials, substances which may negatively affect environment. Examination shall be carried out by Ministry of Environmental Protection and Nuclear Security of Ukraine, its local agencies, specialized committees and institutions established by them, agencies of Ministry of Health, public environmental organizations. Conclusions of state environmental examination are mandatory for fulfillment.

Law regulates grounds, conditions and terms and procedures for environmental examination, content and period of effectiveness of results and procedures for appealing of these conclusions. Persons whose fault in violation of legislation in sphere of environmental examination is evident shall be held responsible according to Administrative, Disciplinary, Civil or Criminal Code.

General Supervision.—Environmental protection shall be governed by Cabinet of Ministers of Ukraine, Councils of People's Deputies, executive agencies thereof, and authorized state agencies on environmental protection: Ministry of Environmental Protection and Nuclear Security, Ministry of Health, Governmental Committee on Issues of Environmental Security and Extraordinary Situations, Presidential Committee on Issues of Nuclear Policy and Environmental Security, Parliament Committee on Issues of Environmental Policy, State Committee of Ukraine on Land Resources.

Public control shall be conducted by public inspectors on environmental protection in accordance with Regulations approved by Ministry of Environmental Protection.

Settlement of Disputes in Sphere of Environmental Protection.—Disputes in sphere of environmental protection shall be settled by general court, arbitration court, councils of peoples' deputies or agencies established by them within limits of their competence and according to procedure established by effective legislation of Ukraine.

Responsibility for Violation of Legislation on Environmental Protection.—Grounds and conditions and terms of this responsibility are anticipated by Law of Ukraine "On Environmental Protection" and special enactments—Water, Forest, Land Codes, Law of Ukraine "On Protection of Atmospheric Air", etc. as well as by Administrative Code, Civil Code and Criminal Code.

Damage caused as result of violation of legislation on environmental protection shall be subject to compensation regardless of other penalties.

EXCHANGE CONTROL:

See topics Foreign Exchange; Banks and Banking.

EXECUTION OF COURT DECISIONS:

Execution of court decisions and resolutions is carried out by court executive officers, and, in cases directly anticipated by law, execution activities are carried out by bank agencies, Ministry of Finance, etc. Main agent of execution activities is court executive officer. Officer is official of court.

Demands of court executive officer (regarding executions of court decisions) must be complied with by all enterprises, institutions, organizations, authorities and individuals.

Execution of particular decision is carried out by executive officer of court within jurisdiction in which debtor's property is located, or where debtor resides or works.

If debtor is legal entity, then execution is carried out at location of its agency or property.

Executive letter is issued upon any effective court decision and should include name of court which issued letter, matter, date of decision, effective date of decision, date of issuance of executive letter, full names and addresses of claimant (person in favor of whom debtor must carry out certain actions) and debtor.

Court executive officer commences execution activities at request of claimant, or prosecutor, or persons who may apply to court with claims for protection of rights of other persons (trustees, parents, etc.). Letters regarding exaction of alimonies, compensation of losses resulting from crime, compensation of damage, confiscation of property, are transferred by court directly to court executive officer and claimant is notified.

Court decisions regarding cases in which at least one party is individual, may be presented for forced execution within three years from effective date thereof, and in other cases within one year.

Decisions on execution of periodic payments may be presented for execution within whole period for which such payments were adjudged.

Time period which was missed for valid reasons may be renewed by court.

Court executive officer cannot participate in execution of decision if officer, spouse of officer, or close relatives have any interest in execution of decision.

When commencing execution of decision, court executive officer sends writ to debtor offering voluntary execution. If period of realization was not established by court decision, then executive officer establishes following periods for voluntary execution: in matters of expulsion from lodgings this period is ten days, in other matter it is not more than five days.

Court executive officer proceeds to forcible execution if debtor does not execute court decision within established period. Following forcible means of execution are recognized in law: exaction of debtor's property by arrest of sale thereof; exaction of debtor's property and sums of money which are kept by other persons; exaction of debtor's wages, other earnings, or pensions, or stipends; alienation from debtor and transfer to claimant of certain items specified in court decision; other measures anticipated by court's decision.

These measures are taken no later than ten days from expiration of period of voluntary execution.

With court approval, executive officer may delay execution or divide it into parts.

Court is obligated to terminate or suspend execution of decisions: in case of debtor's death or termination of legal entity, in claims for which inheritance of rights is permitted by law; if debtor lost his capability; if debtor serves in operating Army; if debtor disputes notary's executive resolution; in case of submittance of claim for exclusion of property; in case of claims for actions of administrative agencies.

Execution of decisions is terminated in instances of: acceptance by court of claimant's written refusal from execution; cancellation of acts on which execution was based; approval by court of amicable agreements between debtor and claimant; debtor's or claimant's death, provided that rights or obligations anticipated by decision are not transferable to successor of deceased; expiration of prescriptive period specified by law.

In event of termination or suspension of execution, all measures taken by court executive officer for forcible execution (distraint or arrest of property, etc.) are cancelled. Termination of executive proceedings cannot be recommenced.

Within five days of any action under claim, debtor or claimant may raise claims regarding actions of court executive officers in connection with execution of decisions or refusal to carry out such actions. Claim is presented to court where court executive officer serves.

Sums exacted by court executive officer from debtor are used to compensate execution costs and remaining sums are used for satisfaction of claimant's demands. Any amount remaining after satisfaction of claimant's demands is given back to debtor.

FAMILY LAW:

Husband and Wife.—Marriage is regulated by Code of Ukraine on Marriage. Ukrainian law considers marriage as equal and voluntary union of man and woman. Marriage requires voluntary consent of parties who must be at least minimum marriage age: 17 years for women and 18 for men. Only under extenuating circumstances may minimum marriage age be reduced. Marriage may not be contracted by any person already married, between relatives in direct line, between siblings or kin in direct line, between adopter and adoptee, or between disabled as result of mental disease. Law anticipates that parties in marriage are required to know about state of health of each other but medical examination is not required.

Parties intending to get married personally submit established application form to state registration agency at place of residence of one of parties or one of parents. They must show documents certifying their identity. Party who was previously married must also submit document which confirms termination of previous marriage. After receipt of application, state registration agency appoints date and time of marriage registration taking into account that period between submission of application and state registration of marriage must not be shorter than one month. Under valid circumstances, this period may be shortened. It is permitted to conclude marriage contract which specifies property and non-property rights of spouses, procedure of division of property in case of divorce, etc. Marriage contract must not be in contravention of effective legislation.

Fictious marriage (marriage without intention to create family) is deemed invalid. Marriage is terminated as result of death of spouse or declaration of spouse as deceased or on basis of court judgment. During life of spouses, marriage may be

FAMILY LAW . . . *continued*
dissolved only by divorce upon petition of one or both parties, prosecutor or trustee of incapable spouse. According to general rule, divorce may be obtained by court judgment; or by grant of state registration agencies in event of mutual consent and when husband and wife are without minor children. Upon registration of divorce, spouse may demand last name which spouse had before marriage.

Property obtained by parties during marriage is joint property. Every spouse has equal rights in joint property irrespective of availability of independent income or salary and amounts thereof. All issues concerning property are decided jointly. Every spouse may require division of property obtained during marriage or within three years after divorce. In addition to joint property, each spouse may own personal property.

FOREIGN CORPORATIONS:

See topics Corporations; Foreign Investment.

FOREIGN EXCHANGE:

Currency exchange is governed by Law "On Procedure of Settling Foreign Currency Accounts", Sept. 23, 1994 and decrees of Cabinet of Ministers "On Temporary Procedure of Use of Incomes in Foreign Currency", "On Regime of Currency Accounts of Citizens in the Authorized Banks of Ukraine", "On the System of Currency Regulation and Currency Control" which establish regime of currency transactions, determine general principles of currency regulation, authority of state agencies, functions of banks and other financial institutions in regulation of currency transactions, rights and obligations of subjects of currency relations, procedure of currency control, responsibility for violation of currency legislation.

Currency transactions are transactions connected with transfer of ownership right for currency, except for transactions which are conducted between Ukrainian residents in Ukrainian currency; transactions connected with use of currency in international turnover as means of payment, with transfer of debts and other liabilities subject of which is currency; transactions connected with import, export, transfer and shipping of currency to and from Ukraine.

Subjects of currency regulations are divided into two categories: residents and nonresidents. "Residents" are individuals (citizens of Ukraine, persons without citizenship) who permanently reside in Ukraine including those who temporarily live abroad; legal entities, subjects of entrepreneurial activity, which do not have status of legal entity (subsidiaries, representative offices, etc.) with their place of business in Ukraine, which operate in Ukraine on basis of Ukraine law; diplomatic, consular, trade and other official representative offices of Ukraine abroad which have immunity and diplomatic privileges as well as subsidiaries and representative offices of enterprises and organizations of Ukraine abroad, which do not undertake entrepreneurial activity. "Nonresidents" are individuals (foreign individuals, citizens of Ukraine, persons without citizenship) who reside out of Ukraine including those who temporarily live in Ukraine; legal entities, subjects of entrepreneurial activity, which do not have status of legal entity (subsidiaries, representative offices, etc.) with principal place of business outside Ukraine, which are established and operate in accordance with laws of foreign state, including legal entities and other subjects of entrepreneurial activity with participation of legal entities and other subjects of entrepreneurial activity of Ukraine; foreign diplomatic, consular, trade and other official representative offices, international organizations and their subsidiaries located in Ukraine which have immunity and diplomatic privileges as well as representative offices of other organizations and firms which do not conduct entrepreneurial activity on basis of Ukrainian law. Residents and nonresidents have right to own currency. Residents have right also to own currency outside Ukraine, except for instances specified by laws. Residents and nonresidents have right to conduct currency transactions taking into consideration restrictions established by legislative enactments on currency. Only method of payment of conditions and obligations without any limitations in Ukraine is currency of Ukraine. All foreign currency revenue to residents is subject to sale by authorized banks at interbank currency exchange except: hard currency acquired at interbank currency exchange through authorized banks and other financial institutions, which are licensed by National Bank of Ukraine to conduct currency transactions for settling accounts with nonresidents, residents who buy foreign currency through authorized banks in order to ensure fulfillment of obligations to nonresidents, must transfer such amounts within five working days from date of entry of these amounts into currency accounts of residents. In event of violation of this term by residents, purchased currency may be sold by authorized banks within five working days at interbank currency market of Ukraine. Positive exchange rate from such transaction is included to State budget every three months, while negative exchange rate is ascribed to results of economic activity of resident; foreign currency obtained by individuals-residents, including salary, except for funds obtained as result of entrepreneurial activity; foreign currency owned by authorized banks and other financial institutions, which are licensed by National Bank of Ukraine for conduct of currency transactions; funds in international clearing units, used in trade turnover with foreign countries and funds in nonconvertible foreign currency used in non-trade turnover with foreign countries on basis of international agreements of Ukraine; foreign currency, from privatization of state-owned property.

National Bank of Ukraine issues individual and general licenses for currency transactions, subject to regime of licensing specified in Decree "On the System of Currency Regulation and Currency Control". General licenses are issued to commercial banks and other financial and credit institutions of Ukraine for conduct of currency transactions, which do not require individual licenses. Individual licenses which retail trade and servicing enterprises had prior to Aug. 1, 1995 remain effective and are used only for on account payments in following events: (i) in retail trade and service enterprises on condition of payment for services with plastic cards or checks; (ii) between legal entities—residents of Ukraine on condition that recipient has reregistered license for conduct of wholesale and retail trade and provision of services for hard currency or individual license of National Bank of Ukraine for settling accounts with resident of Ukraine in foreign currency; (iii) to individuals-residents and nonresidents of Ukraine upon provison of powers of attorney to authorized banks for transfer of currency from private account to account of trade and servicing enterprises. Simultaneously it should be noted that new licenses are not being issued by National Bank of Ukraine. Authorized banks and other financial institutions with general license are entitled to open currency exchange points on basis of agent agreements with other legal entities or residents. Authorized banks are obliged to sell 50% of foreign currency incomes to residents at interbank currency exchange within five banking days from receipt of such revenues in their correspondent accounts. Ukrainian currency obtained by authorized banks from these transactions is subject to transfer to residents within two banking days from time these funds are included on balances of these banks. Individual licenses are issued to residents and nonresidents to conduct single currency transaction. Individual licenses are required for following transactions: (a) export, transfer and shipping of currency outside Ukraine except for: export, transfer and shipping of foreign currency for amount specified by National Bank of Ukraine by individual residents outside Ukraine, export, transfer and shipping by resident and nonresident individuals of foreign currency earlier legally imported by them outside Ukraine, payments in foreign currency paid by residents outside Ukraine to fulfil commitments to nonresidents as payment for production, services, works, rights of intellectual property and other ownership rights, except payment for currency, payments of interest for credits, income or profit from foreign investment in foreign currency outside Ukraine, export of foreign investment conducted earlier in foreign currency in event of termination of investment activity; (b) import, transfer and shipping of Ukrainian currency outside Ukraine; (c) credits for residents in foreign currency if terms and amounts of such credits do not exceed norms established by Ukrainian law; (d) use of hard currency as means of payment or collateral in Ukraine; (e) transfer of currency at accounts outside Ukraine except: opening by individual—residents of accounts in foreign currency for period they stay abroad, opening by authorized banks of correspondent accounts, opening of accounts in foreign currency by residents; (f) investment abroad, including acquisition of securities, except for securities or other corporate rights, obtained by individual-residents as gift or inheritance.

Receipt of license for currency transaction by one party automatically grants permission to other parties to transaction or third persons thereof, unless otherwise provided by terms and conditions of individual license.

In Nov. 1994, National Bank of Ukraine issued Order under which issuance of licenses for trading and providing services for hard currency is suspended starting Nov. 18, 1994. According to Resolution of National Bank of Apr. 4, 1995, individual licenses for trading and providing services for hard currency, which were issued earlier, were terminated starting May 16, 1995. Since this date, use of foreign currency as payment instrument is permitted in Ukraine only under reregistered individual licenses of NBU for trading and providing services for hard currency.

Residents and nonresidents are permitted to settle accounts in foreign currency in following events: (i) purchase of fuels and lubricants, food and provision of services at territory of international ports, airports, railway stations of Ukraine, servicing to foreign vehicles, planes, ships, buses, passengers and members of crews—accounts are settled pursuant to contract concluded with legal entities which anticipates payment in cash in hard currency; (ii) payment of insurance installments; (iii) payment for hotel services; (iv) purchase of tickets and vouchers for international passenger and tourist flights and tours on territory of international airports and railway stations.

Basis for acceptance by authorized banks of foreign currency is available account of tourist or insurance company and customs declaration which shows that payer legally imported currency into Ukraine or availability of receipt on obtaining of cash for plastic accounting card.

Resolution of National Bank of Ukraine, dated Sep. 27, 1995 approved Procedure on Issuance of Licenses for Conduct of Operations with Currency Valuables by commercial banks which operate in Ukraine not less than one year. License permits following operations: (1) maintenance of currency accounts of clients; (2) non-trade operations; (3) establishment of correspondent relations with foreign banks; (4) operations with international trade accounts; (5) operations on trade, attraction and placement of foreign currency in domestic and international currency market; (6) operations with monetary metals at domestic and international markets.

National Bank of Ukraine is also developing new procedure for currency licensing of commercial banks. In this connection, starting Mar. 15, 1995, review of documents of Ukrainian commercial banks for providing these banks with right to transact in currrency valuables is temporarily suspended. New license for right to transact in currency valuables may be obtained by commercial banks only if charter funds of such banks registered with NBU as of Mar. 1, 1995, and actually paid for in foreign or local currency, is not less than amount equivalent to 200,000 ECU.

Residents and nonresident individuals may sell foreign currency to authorized banks and other financial institutions, licensed by National Bank of Ukraine or through such banks as intermediaries to other individual residents.

Individual residents may purchase foreign currency from authorized banks and other financial institutions, licensed by National Bank of Ukraine or through such banks as intermediaries from other individual residents and nonresidents.

Letter of National Bank of Ukraine as of Apr. 17, 1996 established terms and conditions for purchase and use of foreign currency on interbank market.

General grounds for purchase of currency are: (i) duly executed contract on import of goods, work. services, except for supplied raw materials; (ii) documents confirming legitimacy of transfer abroad of income received by foreign investors as result of investment in Ukraine and documents regarding license by National Bank of Ukraine of currency operations on circulation of capital; (iv) documents confirming legitimacy of purchase of foreign currency for payment and servicing of foreign credit.

Currency purchased and entered to specific account of client must be used in full conformity to contract within five days.

Foreign currency is used as means of payment in settling accounts between residents and nonresidents through authorized banks. According to Decree of Cabinet of Ministers "On Regime (System) of Currency Regulation and Currency Control", amended as of Apr. 11, 1995, nonresident employers are deprived of right to pay wages to employees in foreign currency. Settlement of accounts in Ukrainian currency between residents and nonresidents in trade turnover is permitted on condition that individual licensed by National Bank of Ukraine. Hard currency gains of residents must be transferred from abroad within terms required for payment of contractual debt, but not later than 90 days from time exported production crosses Ukrainian border; or in case

See Topical Index in front part of this volume.

FOREIGN EXCHANGE . . . *continued*
of export of works or services, from time act or other document, confirming performance of works or services is signed. Residents of Ukraine, who purchase foreign currency through authorized banks at interbank currency exchange for fulfillment of their obligations to nonresidents are obligated to transfer acquired sums within five banking days from time such sums are entered in balance of residents currency accounts. On basis of President's Decree "On Measures Stimulating Foreign Economic Activity" of Mar. 19, 1992, residents trading products (work or service), intellectual property rights and other ownership rights for hard currency in Ukraine are obligated to obtain individual license.

Currency and other property of residents which is outside Ukraine is subject to mandatory declaration to National Bank of Ukraine. Currency transactions of residents and nonresidents are subject to currency control. Obligations to declare currency and other property are also subject to currency control. National Bank of Ukraine is main agency of currency control. Authorized banks control currency transactions which are conducted by residents and nonresidents in these banks. State Tax Inspection conducts financial control of currency transactions of residents and nonresidents in Ukraine. Ministry of Communications controls enforcement of rules for shipping currency outside Ukraine. State Customs Committee of Ukraine controls enforcement of rules for transferring of currency through customs border of Ukraine.

Violation of currency laws is subject to civil, administrative and criminal penalty. Sanctions are applied to residents and nonresidents: if commercial bank conducts currency transactions without general license, such bank will pay penalty in amount equal to value of transaction converted into Ukrainian currency according to official exchange rate as of transaction day and this bank may be excluded from Republican bank register; if commercial bank conducts currency transactions, without individual license, such bank will pay penalty in amount equal to value of transaction converted into Ukranian currency according to official exchange rate for transaction day; if commercial bank or other financial institution trades currency without license and/or violates terms and conditions of trading currency at interbank currency exchange of Ukraine, such institution will pay penalty in amount equivalent to value of transaction converted into Ukrainian currency according to official exchange rate as of transaction day and this institution may be excluded from Republican bank register; if resident does not observe procedure of settling accounts established by law, such resident will pay penalty in amount equivalent to value of transaction converted into Ukrainian currency according to official exchange rate as of transaction day. Penalty is also levied in wrong accounting on currency transactions, and for nonobservance by residents of currency declaration rules. Sanctions and penalties specified by this provision are applied by National Bank of Ukraine or institutions authorized by it. Actions on penalties may be plead in accordance with court procedure.

FOREIGN INVESTMENT:

Basic legal acts governing business activity of foreign entities in Ukraine are: Law "On Regime of Foreign Investment" as of May 20, 1993; "State Program of Encouraging of Foreign Investments in Ukraine" as of Dec. 17, 1993; and, "Temporary Procedure of Providing Foreign Investors with Privileges" as of Mar. 31, 1994.

Foreign investors may be: legal entities, established in accordance with legislation other than Ukrainian; individuals who are not residents of Ukraine; foreign states, international governmental and nongovernmental organizations; and, other subjects of investment activity, that are deemed as such according to legislation of Ukraine. Foreign investment may involve contributions of hard currency, movable property and real estate, equipment, securities, right to intellectual property, etc.

Foreign investments in Ukraine may be carried out in following form: as share participation in enterprises which are established together with Ukrainian individuals and legal entities, or acquisition of share of existing enterprises; as establishment of enterprises owned by foreign investors, affiliates and other separate subdivisions of foreign legal entities, or full acquisition of operating enterprises; as acquisition of movable property and real estate not directly prohibited by legislation of Ukraine; as acquisition, independently or with participation of Ukrainian legal entities or individuals, of rights to use land and concessions, to use natural resources in Ukraine; as acquisition of other ownership rights; and, as investments in other forms not directly prohibited by legislation of Ukraine, including forms established without creating legal entities under agreements with subjects of economic activity.

Enterprise with foreign investment is enterprise of any organizational form created in accordance with Ukranian legislation, provided that foreign investment in its charter fund constitutes not less than 10%.

Foreign investments in Ukraine may be carried out in: any foreign currency which is recognized by National Bank of Ukraine; Ukrainian currency in event of reinvestment in object of initial investment or any other objects of investment, provided that profit tax is paid; acquisition of movables or real property and associated property rights; securities, including corporate rights (ownership of share in charter fund of foreign or Ukrainian legal entity) expressed in foreign currency; monetary claims and right of claim for performance of contractual obligations which are guaranteed by banks and have value in convertible currency; any rights of intellectual property value of which is verified by laws of investor's country or international traditions and expert evaluation in Ukraine; rights for conduct of economic activity including rights for use of natural resources provided in accordance with laws or agreements whose value in convertible currency is verified in accordance with investor's country or international traditions; other valuables not prohibited by law.

State registration of foreign investments is executed by Executive Committee of city, district (in cities), district Councils of People's Deputies within three days from date of actual contribution of investment.

Order putting law into effect indicates modifications of this law do not apply to foreign investments contributed prior to putting this law into effect. (Decree of Cabinet of Ministers "On Regime of Foreign Investment" as of May 20, 1993).

See also topics Foreign Trade and Foreign Investment; State Register (Commercial Register); Investment Protection.

Ukrainian government has identified priority spheres for foreign investments: agro-industrial complex, light industry, wood industry, machine building, medical industry, metallurgical complex and manufacturing of metals, fuel and energy complex, transport infrastructure, communications, chemical and petrochemical industries and social infrastructure. Foreign investments in priority spheres are provided special privileges and exemptions, such as accelerated depreciation of machines and equipment.

Profits of enterprises with foreign investments, which were registered prior to putting into effect Law "On Taxation of Profits of Enterprises", Dec. 28, 1994, are not subject to taxation within five years from date of qualified investment, except for profits from activities taxed under specific tariffs (intermediary activity, gambling business, etc.). Tax holidays anticipated in this section are extended to enterprises with foreign investments, provided that qualified foreign investment is not alienated within tax holiday period.

In instances of alienation of qualified foreign investment before established terms, such enterprises pay tax in full amount for tax holiday year during which such tax was not paid.

See also topic Foreign Trade and Foreign Investment.

FOREIGN LAW:

Foreigners and persons without citizenship are subject to national law with respect to their legal capacity. Some exceptions may be specified by Ukrainian law. With respect to competence of foreigners, law of country of his citizenship will apply. Civil competence of persons without citizenship is determined by law of country of their permanent residence. Civil competence of foreigners and persons without citizenship with respect to agreements made by them in Ukraine and obligations resulting from damage caused in Ukraine, is determined by Ukrainian law. Recognition of foreigners and persons without citizenship incompetent or partially competent is executed in accordance with Ukrainian law. Form of agreement made abroad must correspond to requirements of law in country where it is made. Rights and obligations of parties of foreign economic agreement are determined by law in place of agreement unless otherwise provided by agreement of parties.

Form and term of effectiveness of power of attorney are specified by law of country where power of attorney was issued. Limitation period is determined pursuant to law of country which is applied to determine rights and obligations of parties. Right to own property is determined by law of country where such property is located. Inheritance relationships are determined by law of country where testator had last resided.

If international agreement establishes rules different from those of Ukrainian law, then rules of international agreement will apply.

FOREIGN TRADE AND FOREIGN INVESTMENT:

Foreign economic activity is regulated by Law of Ukraine "On Foreign Economic Activity", Mar. 17, 1993; by Decrees of Cabinet of Ministers of Ukraine "On the Common Customs Tariff of Ukraine", Jan. 11, 1993, "On Quotation and Licensing of Export of Goods (Works, Services)", Jan. 12, 1993, and "On State Guarantees for Foreign Credits, in Ukraine according to International Agreements", Mar. 17, 1993.

Subjects of foreign economic activity are: (i) individuals—residents of Ukraine, foreign citizens and persons without citizenship who are competent in accordance with Ukrainian legislation and permanently reside in Ukraine; (ii) legal entities that are permanently located in Ukraine (enterprises, organizations and associations of all kinds, including joint-stock and other kinds of economic associations, societies, concerns, consortia, trade houses, intermediary and consulting companies, cooperatives, financing institutions, international associations, organizations, etc.) including legal entities, property and/or assets which are fully owned by foreign subjects of economic activity; (iii) associations of individuals, legal entities, legal entities and individuals, which, in accordance with law of Ukraine, are not legal entities but are permanently located in Ukraine and in accordance with civil law; (iv) structural units of foreign subjects of economic activity, which are, according to Ukrainian law, not legal entities but are permanently located in Ukraine (departments, subsidiaries, etc.); (v) joint ventures with participation of Ukrainian and foreign subjects of economic activity registered and permanently located in Ukraine; and, (vi) other subjects of economic activity as specified by Ukrainian law.

Ukraine, as well as other countries taking part in economic activity in Ukraine, may participate in foreign economic activity represented by government agencies, local government agencies and administration, and act as legal entities.

Subjects of foreign economic activity regardless of forms of ownerships and other characteristics may conduct activities on equal basis.

Individuals may conduct foreign economic activity from moment of acquiring civil competence. Individual permanent residents of Ukraine acquire this right if they are registered as entrepreneurs in accordance with Law of Ukraine "On Entrepreneurial Activity". Individual non-permanent residents of Ukraine enjoy this right if they are subjects of economic activity in accordance with law of country of their residence or citizenship. Legal entities have right to conduct foreign economic activity according to founding documents thereof from moment of registration. Foreign economic activity of subjects may be suspended as result of their violation of Ukrainian law as foreign economic activity.

Representative Offices.—Foreign subjects conducting foreign economic activity in Ukraine may open representative offices in Ukraine.

Representative office of subject of economic activity is not legal entity and does not perform independent commercial activity; in any and all instances it acts on behalf of and under power of attorney of foreign subject of economic activity specified in registration certificate and performs its functions in accordance with effective legislation of Ukraine.

According to law, foreign representative offices are not subjects of foreign economic activity and conduct their businesses upon state registration. Registration is performed by Ministry of Foreign Economic Activity in accordance with Instruction. To perform registration, following documents must be submitted: (1) Application, which specifies: name of firm; county of location of firm; address of firm; phone and fax numbers; place in which representative office will be opened and its future address; if branches are opened, specify places; number of foreign individuals who will work in representative office; date of establishment of firm; legal status; name of bank and account

See Topical Index in front part of this volume.

FOREIGN TRADE AND FOREIGN INVESTMENT . . . *continued*

number; sphere of business; purpose of establishing and sphere of business of representative office, information on business relations with Ukrainian partners and prospective of development of cooperation. (2) Excerpt from trade (bank) register of country of location of officially registered chief management agency of foreign subject of economic activity. (3) Certificate of bank institution in which foreign subject of economic activity officially set up its account. (4) Power of attorney for conduct of representative functions in Ukraine executed in accordance with laws of country in which office of foreign subject is registered.

All documents must be notarized, duly legalized in consular institutions which represent interests of Ukraine and be accompanied by translation into Ukrainian confirmed by seal of official translator.

Documents must be submitted to Ministry of Foreign Economic Relations and Trade of Ukraine not less than in six months from date of issuance thereof.

Upon submission of documents for registration, applicant shall be advised of account number to which state fee in amount of $2,500 must be transferred.

Certificate of registration of representative office is issued upon submission of documents, not later than in 60 business days from date of payment of state fee.

Failure to permit registration within established period or decision to reject registraton may be appealed to court of arbitrazh of Ukraine.

Upon registration, certificate is issued to applicant.

Registration is entered on register of representative offices maintained by Ministry of Foreign Economic Relations and Trade of Ukraine.

Registration certificate should contain following information: official name of representative office; number of foreign individuals who are employees of foreign subject and are employees of representative office; registration number of representative office; location of representative offices and branches thereof.

Registration certificate issued by Ministry of Foreign Economic Relations and Trade of Ukraine is basis for: application: (a) to agencies of Visa Department and registration of Internal Ministry of Ukraine for registration of passports and obtaining visas for foreign employees; (b) to Ministry of Labor of Ukraine for permit to work for foreign employees of representative office in Ukraine during operation of representative office; setting up operational accounts in banks of Ukraine; duty-free transportation of equipment temporarily imported into Ukraine and required for equipping office and operation of representative office; registration and obtaining from State Auto Inspection agencies of Internal Ministry of Ukraine of appropriate license plates for cars owned by representative office.

Within one month from date of obtaining certificate, representative office is obligated to register with tax inspector at location thereof.

Director of representative office acts under power of attorney issued by foreign subject of economic activity and confirmed in accordance with requirements of effective legislation.

Representative office is obligated to notify Ministry of Foreign Economic Relations and Trade about changes in management, location of representative office, structure of foreign employees within month of occurence.

Representative office operating in Ukraine must notify Ministry of Foreign Economic Relations and Trade of Ukraine of changes of name, legal status, legal address or recognition of subject insolvent or bankrupt within seven days.

Activity of representative office is terminated: in event of liquidation of foreign subject represented by such subject; in event of termination of agreement under which representative office opened or operated; under decision of foreign subject which opened representative office; under decision of court. (Instruction on Procedure of Registration of Representative Offices of Foreign Subjects of Economic Activity in Ukraine approved by order of Ministry of Foreign Economic Relations and Trade of Ukraine of Jan. 18, 1996). State agencies are prohibited from demanding reregistration of already registered representative office in Ukraine of foreign subject of economic activity. Economic activity, including foreign economic activity and foreign investment, is regulated by laws of Ukraine.

Foreign Economic Agreements; Choice of Law.—Subjects of foreign economic activity may conclude any kinds of international agreements or contracts except those which are directly and exclusively prohibited by Ukrainian laws. Foreign economic agreement may be deemed invalid by court or court of arbitration if it is not in conformity with requirements of Ukrainian or international laws. Form of foreign economic contract is determined by place of making thereof. Agreement made abroad may not be deemed invalid as result of violation of form if it is made in accordance with requirements of Ukrainian laws. Form of agreement regarding real estate located in Ukraine is determined by Ukrainian laws. Rights and obligations of parties of foreign economic agreements or contracts are defined by place of its conclusion unless otherwise agreed by parties. Place of agreement is determined by Ukrainian laws. Rights and obligations of parties of foreign economic agreements or contracts are defined by law of country chosen by them or upon further consent. Where parties of foreign economic agreements have not made a choice of law by consent, then applicable law is of country of residence or location of: seller in sale-purchase agreement; lessee in property lease agreement; licenser in license agreement on application of exclusive or non-exclusive rights; bailor in bailment agreement; consignor in consignment agreement; trustee in trustee agreement; haulage contractor in transportation agreement; expeditor shipper in expedition shipment agreement; insurer in insurance agreement; creditor in credit agreement; donor in gift agreement; guarantor in guarantee agreement; mortgagee in mortgage agreement.

Law of country where foreign economic activity is carried out is applied to foreign economic agreements or contracts on manufacturing cooperation, specialization and conduct of construction and assembling operations, unless otherwise agreed by parties. Law of country where joint venture is established and registered applies to foreign economic agreement on establishment of joint venture. Law of country where auction, tender or exchange is located, applies to foreign economic agreements made at auction, tender or exchange. All subjects of foreign economic activity have right to freely choose banking and financial for opening currency accounts for settling their foreign economic activity accounts.

For purpose of specifying details of provisions of Art. 6 of Law "On Foreign Economic Activity", Resolution on Form of Foreign Economic Agreements was developed. This Resolution applies in course of executing purchase-sale agreements for goods (services, work) and barter agreements between Ukrainian and foreign subjects of entrepreneurial activity irrespective of ownership forms and businesses.

Such agreements must stipulate following terms: (i) name, number of agreement, date and place of execution; (ii) preamble which specifies full names of parties to agreement, country of registration, and documents used by parties in course of making agreement; (iii) subject matter of agreement, which sets forth actions to be performed by each party; (iv) amount and quality of goods (work, services), and amount of work and period for performance thereof; (v) basic terms of delivery of goods (acceptance of work or services); (vi) price and aggregate value of agreement; (vii) payment terms (manner, procedure and period for financial settlements and guaranteed of performance of mutual obligations); (viii) terms of acceptance of goods (work, services); (ix) packaging and marking; (x) force majeure; (xi) sanctions and complaints; (xii) place of arbitration (country and applicable law); (xiii) legal addresses, mail and payment requisites.

Under agreement additional terms and conditions may apply, such as insurance quality guarantees, terms of attracting agents, transporters, protection of trademarks, procedure of payment of taxes, duties, procedure of introducing changes and amendments to agreement, etc.

List of legal and normative acts of Ukraine which regulate issues of form, procedure of execution and performance of foreign economic agreements (contracts): Civil Code of Ukraine; Law of Ukraine "On Foreign Economic Activity", Apr. 16, 1991; Law of Ukraine "On Procedure of Settling Accounts in Foreign Currency", Sept. 29, 1994; Law of Ukraine "On Transactions with Supplied Raw Materials in Foreign Economic Relations"; Decree of Cabinet of Ministers of Ukraine "On System of Currency Regulation and Currency Control"; Decree of President of Ukraine "On Indicative Prices on Goods in Course of Performance of Export-Import Transactions in Foreign Economic Activity by Ukrainian Subjects"; Decree of President of Ukraine "On Measures regarding Maintenance of Accounts under Agreement made by Ukrainian Subjects of Entrepreneurial Activity"; Decree of President of Ukraine "On Use of International Rules of Interpreting Commercial Terms"; Decree of President of Ukraine "On Regulation of Barter Transaction in Foreign Economic Activity"; Order of Cabinet of Ministers of Ukraine and National Bank of Ukraine #444 of 06.21.1995 "On Typical Payment Terms of Foreign Economic Agreements (Contracts) and Typical Forms of Protective Restrictions in Respect of Foreign Economic Agreements (Contracts) which Stipulate Settlement of Accounts on Foreign Currency".

Taxation of Foreign Economic Activity.—All foreign economic activity is taxed at equal rates, depending on commodity involved. Tax rates are established by Cabinet of Ministers of Ukraine with Parliamentary ratification. Special tax holidays are granted to subjects of foreign economic activity export exceeding import for fiscal year; value for export which is not less than 5% of value of distributed goods; export of scientific goods, and goods where value includes not less than 30% of VAT. Tax privileges in form of depreciation of fixed manufacturing assets are also granted in form of: accelerated depreciation standards used for manufacturing of export goods; preferential depreciation standards of fixed assets established with new investments and used for manufacturing of export goods; depreciation standards for imported equipment, used for manufacturing of export goods, but not less than in country manufacturing this equipment.

Customs regulation of foreign economic activity is conducted in accordance with Law of Ukraine "On Foreign Economic Activity", Customs Code of Ukraine, Common Customs Tariff of Ukraine and international agreements of Ukraine. Conduct of foreign economic activity by Ukrainian entrepreneurs does not require registration thereof as participants of foreign economic activity. But Cabinet of Ministers of Ukraine, at request of Ministry of Economy, may decide on introduction of licensing and quotation of export or import and determines herewith list of goods (works or services) which are subject to licensing and quotation and terms of effectiveness of this regime. Export or import quota is amount (in units or in value) of certain category of goods which are permitted to be exported from or imported to Ukraine within definite period. Export or import license is duly executed right, within definite term, to export or import goods or currency for purpose of investment and credit. Goods (works or services) exported by subjects of entrepreneurial activity within limits of their quotas or according to governmental agreements, state contracts or state orders in amount approved by Cabinet of Ministers of Ukraine are exempted from customs duty. Quotas for export of goods (works or services) are approved by Cabinet of Ministers of Ukraine. Quotas and export licenses are sold by Ministry of Foreign Economic Relations of Ukraine. Licenses are issued to subjects of entrepreneurial activity on basis of quotas obtained by them or confirmation of their payment of export duty.

Disputes between Ukrainian subjects of foreign economic activity and foreign subjects of economic activity may be reviewed by regular courts or courts of arbitration of Ukraine and such other institutions chosen by parties if not against Ukrainian law or specified by international agreements of Ukraine.

See topics Customs; Foreign Investment; Taxation.

FOREIGN TRADE REGULATIONS:

See topics Foreign Exchange; Foreign Investment; Foreign Trade and Foreign Investment.

FOUNDATIONS:

Parliament Committee on Youth, and Cabinet of Ministers of Ukraine have been given task of developing draft of Law of Ukraine on charitable funds and submitting it for review of Parliament. Cabinet of Ministers is to specify procedure of payment and amounts of fees for registration of charitable funds.

Prior to adoption of law which would regulate procedure of establishment and operation of charitable funds and prior to adoption of law on charitable funds, state registration of international, Ukrainian and local charitable funds established by legal entities and individuals is carried out by Ministry of Justice of Ukraine, Cabinet of Ministers of Republic of Crimea and local agencies of state executive power.

FOUNDATIONS . . . *continued*

Majority of currently existing and operating funds of Ukraine were established in accordance with Resolutions of the Parliament of Ukraine regarding each such fund. These funds operate under special provisions developed by Parliament committees.

Such provisions include information regarding applicability of fund, sources at expense of which funds are created, procedure of use of funds, structure of Fund's Board, etc.

In Ukraine, following funds are operating: Fund of "State Independence of Ukraine"; Fund for Assistance to Establishing and Developing of Local and Regional Self-government in Ukraine; Fund for Cultural Development of National Minorities in Ukraine; State Fund for Fundamental Research; Fund for Development of Culture and Arts (by Ministry of Culture); Ukrainian National Fund for Mutual Understanding and Reconciliation; State Fund for Assistance to Development of Youth; Fund for Social Protection of Ukrainian Population; "Mutual Understanding and Reconciliation"; "Independent Press of Ukraine".

FRAUDULENT SALES AND CONVEYANCES:

See topic Contracts.

GARNISHMENT:

See topics Execution of Court Decisions; Labor Relations.

HOLIDAYS:

In accordance with Labor Code of Ukraine such holidays are established: (1) Jan. 1—New Year; (2) Jan. 7—Christmas; (3) Mar. 8—International Women's Day; (4) May 1, 2—International Day of Peoples' Solidarity; (5) May 9—Victory Day; (6) Aug. 24—Independence Day; Nov. 7, 8—Anniversary of Great October Socialist Revolution.

Three religious days also provide days off: (1) Christmas (but if Sat. or Sun., then following Mon.), (2) Mon. after Easter and (3) Mon. after Witsunday (Pentecost). All per Julian calendar, not Gregorian.

At request of nonorthodox religious societies registered in Ukraine, enterprises, institutions, and organizations give to individuals, who profess such religions, three days off in order to celebrate important holidays. Those who celebrate such holidays are to work at any three other days during the year.

Should holiday/nonworking day coincide with day-off, then day-off will be shifted to day following holiday/nonworking day.

HUSBAND AND WIFE:

See topics Descent and Distribution; Divorce; Infants.

IMMIGRATION:

Foreigners, i.e. individuals who have citizenship of foreign countries and who are not citizens of Ukraine and persons without citizenship, may immigrate to Ukraine for permanent residence or employment for definite period of time or may temporarily be in Ukraine. Foreigners may enter Ukraine with valid national passports or documents which substitute for passport, and visa. Foreigner may obtain permission for immigration and immigrate for permanent residence if he: has legal source of existence in Ukraine; has close relatives (father, mother, brother, sister, children, spouse, grandfather, grandmother, grandchildren) in Ukraine; is supported by citizen of Ukraine; supports citizen of Ukraine.

Foreigners who immigrate for permanent residence or temporary employment must obtain special certificates. Foreigners who are in Ukraine according to other legal grounds, are deemed to have entered Ukraine temporarily. They must register passports or documents which substitute for passports and must leave Ukraine after expiration of designated term. When changing residences, they must notify respective agencies of internal affairs where their passports are registered.

Foreigner may obtain status of refugee on grounds and in manner specified by law of Ukraine "On Refugees".

Pursuant to Constitution and Law of Ukraine "On Ukrainian Citizenship" foreigners may obtain Ukrainian citizenship.

Permission to be employed in Ukraine is issued to foreigner on condition that there is lack of employees who may do this kind of work in region, or other grounds to employ foreigners. Permission to be employed is basis for issuance of visa for entrance into Ukraine by foreigner. Permission is issued by Republican Center of Employment of Ministry of Labor of Ukraine. Employer must submit application, copy of draft of contract, list of foreign employees and receipt on payment of fee for application to be considered.

Following categories of foreigners do not need permission for employment in Ukraine: foreigners who have certificate for residence in Ukraine; refugees; heads of joint ventures and foreign subjects of business activity; employees of foreign mass media accredited for work in Ukraine; representatives of foreign maritime fleet and foreign air companies, who grant services in Ukraine; actors and art workers who work in Ukraine according to their profession; employees of emergency and rescuing services. Last two categories are entitled to work without permission for term of two months. Permission for employment is issued for term not exceeding one year but this term may be extended; to do so, employer must address Republican Center of Employment of Ministry of Labor of Ukraine one month before expiration of previous term. Maximum period of time of foreigner's employment in Ukraine must not exceed four years. After absence for not less than six months, foreigner may obtain permission for employment in Ukraine again.

INFANTS:

Basic provisions of legal standing of infant are specified by Marriage and Family Code of Ukraine, Law of Ukraine "On State Pension to Families with Infants" Nov. 21, 1992, "Provision on Procedure of Appointing and Payment of State Allowance to Families with Infants" Mar. 19, 1993 and decrees of Plenum of Supreme Court of Ukraine.

Mutual rights and obligations of parents and infants are based on origin of children certified in established manner. If child was born in registered marriage then his origin is certified by entry on parents' marriage. If parents are not in registered marriage, then origin of child is established by submission of joint application of parents to state registration agencies. It is assumed that husband of child's mother is father of child. Entry on paternity may be subject to dispute. If person who has registered as mother or father of child did not dispute this fact during his or her life then this fact cannot be subject to dispute.

Paternity may be established upon petition of one of parents as trustee of child, person who supports child or child at reaching age of 18, according to court procedure. Child gets name under parents' consent, patronymic which is granted to child, is father's first name, in case when mother is not in registered marriage with father of child, and there is no recognition of paternity, then patronymic is determined by first name of person who is registered as child's father. Child receives last name of one of parents or their joint last name. Parents have equal rights and duties concerning child even if marriage is dissolved. Parents may be deprived of paternity under certain circumstances.

Parents protect rights and interests of minor children (except for minor children who contracted marriage) and are their legal representatives. Parents are obligated to support their minor and disabled adult children who need material support. If parents refuse to do so, then expenses for material support may be exacted by court procedure. Children may be adopted and trustees for children may be established.

INTEREST:

Term "interest" means income from debt claims of every kind whether or not secured by mortgage and whether or not carrying right to participate in debtor's profits, and in particular, income from bonds and debentures, including premiums or prices attaching to such securities, bonds, or debentures as well as all other income that is treated as income from money lent by taxation law of Ukraine.

INTERNATIONAL TREATIES:

See topic Treaties.

INTESTACY:

See topics Descent and Distribution; Wills.

INVESTMENT PROTECTION:

There are five principal Ukrainian government guarantees for protection of foreign investments: (1) reimbursement and compensation of damages to foreign investors (including lost profit and moral damage) caused by actions or passivity of state agencies of Ukraine or its officers, which are in contravention of effective legislation of Ukraine; (2) guarantees in event of termination of investment activity: in this event foreign investor has right to be repaid for its investments in kind or in currency of investment in amount of actual contribution and income from this investment by no later than six months from day of termination of activity thereof; (3) guarantees of transfer of incomes, profits and other amounts connected with foreign investments: foreign investor is guaranteed free transfer of its profits, incomes and other costs in foreign currency, obtained on legal basis in connection with foreign investments abroad after payment of taxes, duties and other indispensable fees; (4) guarantees against forced deductions as well as illegal actions of state authorities and officers thereof: foreign investments in Ukraine shall not be subject to nationalization. Only in special cases such as disaster, natural catastrophes etc. may they be requisitioned with compensation. (5) Guarantees against modifications of legislation: in event new specific law of Ukraine on foreign investments modifies terms and conditions of protection of foreign investments, specific legislation which was in force at moment of registration of investment will apply to foreign investments during ten years from day of effectiveness of this new legislation.

Related enactments: Laws of Ukraine "On Protection of Foreign Investment in Ukraine" of Sept. 10, 1991; and "On Regime of Foreign Investment" of Mar. 19, 1996.

See also topics: Foreign Investment; Foreign Trade and Foreign Investment; Taxation; Customs.

JUDGMENTS:

Generally, judgments of foreign courts are valid and executed in territory of Ukraine on basis of international or bilateral agreements of Ukraine on legal assistance in criminal and civil cases. Recognition of foreign court decisions means permission by state to enforce foreign country decision on territory of Ukraine and recognition by domestic court of juridical act of foreign country. In this connection, domestic court makes decision which is act of recognition of decision of foreign court and provides grounds for execution thereof. (Art. 348 of Civil Proceedings Code). Foreign court decisions in countries party to bilateral agreement on legal assistance, which are not subject to compulsory execution, are recognized, if, within one month, there are no objections of interested parties or persons.

When making decision whether to accept foreign court judgment, court must, initially, ascertain if decision corresponds to effective international agreement because only decisions within scope of agreement and arising after effectiveness of agreement are subject to execution. Then, court determines if decision is still effective or if limitation period established by Art. 427 of Civil Proceedings Code has expired. Pursuant to this article, decision of foreign court may be subject to compulsory execution within three years from moment of its effectiveness. If decision relates to compensation of periodic payments then such decision may be subject to execution within entire time period of such payments. Consideration of petition on recognition of decision related to compensation for payments is carried out by court in open meeting in presence of debtor. Court after hearing debtor's explanations, makes decision whether or not to accept compulsory execution of decision of foreign court.

See Topical Index in front part of this volume.

LABOR RELATIONS:

General Provisions.—Basic law of Ukraine on labor is Code of Laws of Ukraine on Labor, Dec. 15, 1993, and laws on related topics, in particular: Laws of Ukraine "On Collective Contracts and Agreements", July 1, 1993; "On Labor Protection", Oct. 14, 1992; "On Basic Principles of Social Protection of Labor Verterans and Other Elderly People in Ukraine", Dec. 16, 1993; "On State Service", Dec. 16, 1993; Law "On Wages", May 1, 1995.

Labor legislation of Ukraine regulates labor relations of employees of all enterprises, institutions and organizations irrespective of their forms of property, kinds of activities and branch operations. Particulars regarding employment of members of cooperative societies, collective farms, rental organizations and joint ventures are determined by charters thereof and current legislation. If international contract or agreement in which Ukraine participates, provides other than Ukrainian labor legislation, then rules of international agreement or contract will apply. Labor relations of foreigners in Ukraine are regulated by Law of Ukraine "On Legal Status of Foreigners", Feb. 4, 1994. Law indicates that foreigners have rights and duties in labor relations equal to Ukrainians; unless otherwise provided by special labor legislation, this provision is effective. Foreigners permanently residing in Ukraine have right to be employed at enterprises, institutions and organizations or to undertake other activity on basis and in manner which is established for Ukrainian citizens. Foreigners immigrating to Ukraine for purpose of employment for definite period of time may undertake labor activity in accordance with permission to be employed obtained in established manner. Foreigners may not be appointed to certain positions or involved in certain types of labor activity if pursuant to Ukrainian law only Ukrainian citizens may occupy such posts or be involved in such activity.

Arising of Labor Relations.—Labor contract is indisputable basis for establishment of labor relations. Some positions, however, may require additional basis. For example, certain state officers must be appointed or elected.

Content of labor agreement includes essential provisions (on salary, position, place, conditions, amount of work; term and form of agreement) and additional provisions (on probation period) determining rights and obligations of parties. Conditions and terms of contract are established by agreement of parties. Contract is deemed concluded at moment of agreement of parties on all issues. Labor contract may be established for undetermined period of time, for certain term, or for time required to accomplish designated task. Early labor contracts were often made orally in Ukraine. Today, such contracts are often concluded in writing. Ukrainian law requires labor contract to be in writing if: employees are hired for special purpose; temporary labor contracts are concluded for work in regions with specific environmental, geographical and geological conditions and high risks for health; temporary labor contract is made with minor citizens; employee insists on execution of contract in written form.

Recently in Ukraine form of labor agreement was introduced. Originally, contract in labor law meant labor agreement for certain period of time, which was compiled irrespective of law and only under parties' consent. But currently pursuant to Resolution of the Cabinet of Ministers "On Regulation of Contract Form of Labor Agreement", Mar. 19, 1994, contract must meet certain requirements: (i) employer cannot include provisions on full material liability of employee if such liability is not anticipated by law; (ii) it is prohibited to establish by contract procedure for deciding labor disputes other than anticipated by law; (iii) contracts must be made in conformity with form of contract developed by Ministry of Labor of Ukraine. So, contract may not include provisions on agreeing upon labor conditions violative of law. Currently contractual form is established by legislation for such groups of employees as: (i) heads of state enterprises and structural subdivisions thereof; (ii) officers of state administrations except for those who are appointed; (iii) heads of institutions of higher education and structural subdivisions thereof, subordinated to Ministry of Education of Ukraine. Formally employee is deemed employed upon issuance of order of head of enterprise or organization. Within five days employee must have all required entries in his labor book which is main document on labor activity of employee. Information on job, incentives and awards for work at enterprise, institution or organization are included in labor book. Entries on dismissal are made in conformity with exact wording of effective legislation and with reference to respective article or paragraph of law.

Upon establishing labor contract, probation period may be established for employee. Probation period cannot exceed three months—for officers; one month—for workers. Probation period cannot be established for minor citizens, for young specialists after graduation from colleges, technical and vocational schools, disabled, etc.

Termination of Labor Relations.—General grounds for termination of labor contract are specified in Art. 36 of Labor Code of Ukraine and they are: (1) agreement between parties (for labor contracts for unspecified period of time); (2) expiration of period of contract if no party intends to continue contract (for labor contracts which determine period of contract). Upon expiration of period of contract and on condition of actual continuation of labor relations, labor contract is automatically transformed into contract with undefined time frame; (3) induction of employee into military or alternative service; in this case employee is paid dismissal allowance in amount not less than employee's average salary for two months and employee has right to continue his work after demobilization; (4) termination of temporary labor contract (i) on employee's initiative—contract for unspecified period may be terminated with obligatory written notification of employer at least two weeks in advance; in event of violation of labor legislation or terms and conditions of collective labor agreement on this issue by employer—within period determined by employee; contract concluded for definite period is subject to termination, at employee's request, in event of disease, disability thereof or violation of labor legislation, collective or labor agreement by employer. When terminating labor contract as result of violation by employer of labor legislation or terms and conditions of collective and labor agreement employee is paid dismissal allowance in amount not less than one month's salary; in event of violation of legislation in provision of labor, employee is paid not less than three average monthly salaries; (ii) on employer's (or authorized body's) initiative—labor contract concluded for definite period as well as labor contract for unspecified period may be terminated on employer's initiative only on grounds specified by legislation or agreement of parties. Guarantee against groundless dismissal of employee exists because employer must approve such dismissal in each particular case, except for some events, with trade union. Owner must appeal with written petition indicating reasons and grounds for dismissal to trade union agency, which must within ten day period inform employer on its decision. If employer does not receive decision of trade union agency employer may dismiss employee. Decision of trade union agency is effective for one month term. Terms and conditions as well as grounds of termination of labor agreement on employer's initiative are specified by Arts. 40, 41 of Labor Code of Ukraine: (a) changes in organization of manufacturing and labor process, including reorganization and change of profile of enterprise, institution or organization, and reduction of staff thereof; (b) nonconformity of employee to job or position for reason of insufficient qualification thereof or bad health preventing work performance; (c) systematic failure to fulfill employee's duties, specified by labor contract or regulations of labor schedule, for invalid reasons, if earlier this employee has been subjected to penalties or chastisement; (d) absence at enterprise and neglect of duty (including absence at enterprise during any period exceeding three hours) for invalid reasons; (e) absence at enterprise and neglect of duty, in course of period exceeding four months running, for reason of temporary disability to work, except for leave for pregnancy and child delivery as well as other particular diseases in course of which job is preserved for employee for longer period, i.e. tuberculosis—12 months, etc. Employees disabled as result of professional disease or labor disablement have right to continue their job after rehabilitation of ability to work or establishment of official disability; (f) readmission to enterprise of employee who was involved in job before; (g) attendance at enterprise, institution or organization in intoxicated or narcotic state; (h) depredation at enterprise, institution, organization (including petty larceny) of property, established by effective sentence of court or other body, which is competent to penalize; (i) inappropriate actions of employee whose job is connected with monetary means and other material valuables, resulting in distrust by employer; (j) in case of administrative official, if such official even once violates his/her duties; (k) inappropriate behavior of employee which is incompatible with continuation of his work. Consent of trade union bodies is not obligatory upon dismissal under grounds indicated in provision (a) only in case of liquidation of enterprise; in provisions (f), (h) and (i) as well as upon dismissal of employee who is not member of trade union organization or dismissal from enterprise where there is no trade union organization. It is not permitted to dismiss employee in course of his temporary disability or vacations (except for instances specified by provision [e] or complete liquidation of enterprise). Dismissal allowance is paid to employee who is dismissed in accordance with provisions (a) and (f) in amount not less than employee's average monthly salary. Dismissal at trade union agency request: trade union agency which was entrusted by collective to sign collective agreement, may demand cancellation of labor agreement (contract) with officer who violates labor legislation and does not fulfill duties on collective agreement. (5) Transfer of employee, upon his consent, to another enterprise or transfer to elective post: upon expiration of term of elective post, employees who transferred to elective posts have right to be employed in their former position; (6) refusal of employee to be transferred to another location together with enterprise, institution or organization and his refusal to continue work for reason of considerable changes in labor conditions, i.e. position, job, etc., in this event employee is paid dismissal allowance not less than average monthly salary; (7) effectiveness of court sentence, under which employee was incarcerated (except for cases of probationary sentence or suspended sentence), penitentiary works, outside location of employee's enterprise, and other punishments, which exclude further continuation of previous job; (8) grounds, provided by contract.

Working Hours.—Duration of working time of employees in Ukraine cannot exceed 40 hours per week. Shortened working time is 36 hours for minor citizens and for those who are employed at enterprises with harmful labor conditions. Enterprises may determine shortened working hours for women having minor children in collective agreement of enterprise. All employees have annual vacations (with preservation of job) paid at average salary.

Salary.—Salaries of employees of enterprises cannot be less than minimal amount established by state (minimum wage) and are subject to indexation in manner specified by Ukrainian law.

In Law "On Wages" "minimum wage" is defined as "statutorily established minimally tolerable level of monthly wages for simple, unqualified work". Minimum wage does not include bonuses, awards or other incentives and compensatory payments.

For current year, minimum wage will be established by Parliament in conjunction with renegotiation of various labor agreements. In subsequent year, minimum wage will be established annually by Parliament on petition of Cabinet of Ministers contermінously with approval of state budget.

Contractual wages are to be determined by negotiated labor agreement between employer and workers at national, regional or manufacturing (collective) levels, in accordance with effective legislation. Forms and systems of payments, labor standards, tariffs, rates, conditions of establishment and amounts of raises, additional charges, bonuses and other incentives and compensatory payments are to be determined by enterprise in labor agreement which observes norms and guarantees of effective legislation.

Wages in Ukraine must be paid in currency legally circulating in Ukraine, by checks in manner established by Cabinet of Ministers, with approval of National Bank of Ukraine in bank-to-bank nonmonetary transfers (only with written authorization of employee), or in kind. However, payment of wages with debt instruments or other script is prohibited.

Guarantees, Privileges and Compensations.—Labor Code of Ukraine establishes following kinds of guarantees, compensations and privileges: guarantees against deductions from salaries—such may be executed only in instances specified by legislation (child support, etc.); deductions from dismissal allowances and other compensations are not permitted; privileges for women—opportunity to grant leave on pregnancy and child delivery, leaves with preservation of partial salary on taking care of children; prohibition against dismissal of pregnant women; privileges for young people—prohibition against employment of minors in some kinds of jobs, restrictions on dismissal.

Labor Disputes.—(Part 15 of Labor Code).

Labor disputes are considered by committees on labor disputes and courts.

See Topical Index in front part of this volume.

LABOR RELATIONS . . . *continued*

Committees on labor disputes are elected among employees at general meeting of enterprise with number of employees not less than 15. Committees on labor disputes are primary organs of investigation of labor disputes arising at enterprises except for labor disputes of judges, investigators, employees of prosecutor's office, employees of educational, scientific and other institutions of prosecutor's office (particulars of investigation of such disputes are determined by specific legislation on such categories of employees) and labor disputes which are subject to investigation in court. Employee may appeal to committee on labor disputes within three month period from day when employee learned of violation of his rights. Committee on labor disputes must within ten day period from day of submission of petition, investigate dispute. Dispute is investigated in presence of appealing employee and representatives of employer. In case of disagreement with decision of committee on labor disputes, employee or employer may appeal this decision in court within ten day period upon receipt of entry of protocol of committee's meeting. Decision of committee on labor disputes is subject to fulfillment by employer within three day period upon expiration of ten day period required for appeal. Decision on restoring employee to his/her post must be fulfilled outright.

Local (city and district) courts consider labor disputes upon petitions of: (a) employee or employer, if they do not agree with decision of committee on labor disputes; (b) prosecutor if he thinks that committee's decision is in contravention of current legislation. Such courts also consider disputes upon petitions of: (a) employees of enterprises with no committee on labor disputes; (b) employees on restoring their posts irrespective of grounds of termination of labor contract, on change of date and reason for dismissal, on payment of forced absence at enterprise, except for disputes on dismissal of employees of elective paid posts of public and other associations upon decision of bodies which elected these employees; employer on compensation of damage caused to enterprise by employees; as well as disputes on refusal to employ such categories of employees as: employees who were invited by transfer from other enterprise, young specialists having graduated from higher educational institutions and receiving recommendation to this enterprise, pregnant women, women having children under three years old or disabled child, single mothers having children under 14, elective employees upon expiration of period of their authority.

Trade Unions.—In accordance with Constitution of Ukraine and Labor Code of Ukraine, employees are entitled to join trade unions. Trade unions act according to their charters.

LAND:

In Ukraine land relations are governed by Land Code of Ukraine, adopted on Mar. 13, 1992. Form of state act for right of perpetual use of land is specified by respective Decrees of Supreme Rada of Ukraine dated Mar. 13, 1992.

Ownership of land exists in following forms: state, collective, private. Use of land in Ukraine may be permanent (period of use is not established) and temporary (within three years or from three to 25 years). Use of land for rent for agricultural purposes must be long-term.

State-owned land may be given by local (appropriate) councils of people's deputies for permanent use to: citizens of Ukraine for purpose of farming and development of personal subsidiary businesses; agricultural enterprises and organizations; public associations; religious organizations; non-agricultural enterprises, institutions and organizations; specialized enterprises for forestry; housing, housing-construction, garage and dacha-construction cooperatives; joint ventures, international associations and organizations with participation of Ukrainian and foreign legal entities and individuals; enterprises completely owned by foreign investors.

Land is given for temporary use by councils of people's deputies from state-owned lands to same subjects listed above except for enterprises fully owned by foreign investors.

Land is given for temporary use on condition of rent to citizens of Ukraine for purpose of farming and development of personal subsidiary businesses; agricultural enterprises and organizations; public associations; religious organizations; non-agricultural enterprises, institutions and organizations; specialized enterprises for keeping forestry; housing, housing-construction, garage and dacha-construction cooperatives; joint ventures, international associations and organizations with participation of Ukrainian and foreign legal entities and individuals; enterprises completely owned by foreign investors as well as to foreign countries, international organizations, foreign legal entities and individuals without citizenship.

Land lessors may be local councils of people's deputies and owners of land. Term of land lease may be up to 50 years with opportunity to renew this term. Terms and conditions as well as value of lease are determined by parties' agreement and are specified in contract.

Land parcels are transferred to collective and private ownership by councils of people's deputies on territory of which such parcels are located. Ownership right or right to perpetual use of land is certified by state acts issued and registered with local councils of people's deputies.

Enterprises, institutions, organizations and individuals which are interested in receiving land parcels appeal with respective petition or application to local council of people's deputies entitled to provide land parcels. Documents which must be attached to petition include: copy of general plan of construction or other graphic materials which describe and explain amount of land, certificate on financing of construction, etc.

LAW REPORTS, CODES, ETC.:

Ukraine is country of code law. General sources of Ukrainian law are laws and agreements and, in some branches of law, customs and usage approved and codified by state such as Air Code and Maritime Code. Unlike countries of common law, doctrine of court and administrative precedent is not widely applied, but it would be wrong to state that judicial and administrative precedent is completely unusual for Ukraine. Constitutional Court of Ukraine is only state agency which may establish precedent, as its decisions are generally binding and assume force of law. Presently, Constitutional Court membership is not complete and it does not operate.

Ukrainian laws are hierarchically organized with Constitution of Ukraine at top. Present Constitution, adopted by Ukrainian S.S.R. in 1978, has numerous amendments and modifications; draft of new post-Soviet Constitution of Ukraine, based on principle of priority of common human rights, is being developed by group of government specialists and lawyers. Parliamentary action as well as national referendum may be needed to approve new Constitution. Next level in this hierarchy consists of Constitutional laws: which either amend and modify Constitution or are anticipated by Constitution (those on issue of Ukrainian citizenship, on referendum and election, on status of deputy of Ukraine, on Cabinet of Ministers, on status of judges, on legal status of oblasts, etc.). Next level consists of current laws, which constitute bulk of legislation of Ukraine. Lowest stage in legislative system are decrees and orders of government branches and divisions, i.e.: decrees and instructions of President of Ukraine; resolutions of Supreme Rada of Ukraine; resolutions and instructions of Cabinet of Ministers; enactments of ministries and agencies (orders, instructions, etc.); instructions of representatives of President of Ukraine; resolutions of local Radas; and, local enactments, i.e. those which are intended for certain group of citizens, for example: students, servicemen, etc. Such decrees and orders are issued on basis of existing enabling laws and must correspond to them.

Currently Ukrainian legislation is being codified. Essentially, every branch of Ukrainian law is regulated by respective Code (Civil Code, 1961; Dwelling Code, 1983; Code of Arbitration Procedure, 1991; Land Code, 1992; etc.). But numerous amendments and modifications must be included into Codes as consequence of changes in economy and policy of Ukraine.

Supreme Rada of Ukraine (Parliament) consisting of 450 deputies is only legislative body in Ukraine. Supreme Rada is authorized to consider and decide any issue which, according to Constitution of Ukraine, is not within competence of state executive or juridical authorities and which must not be decided exclusively by national referendum. Supreme Rada of Ukraine may enact five types of legislative acts: laws, appeals, resolutions, statements, and, declarations.

Law of Ukraine "On Effectiveness of International Agreements in Ukraine" as of Dec. 10, 1991, establishes that international agreements duly made and ratified by Ukraine shall be integral part of national legislation of Ukraine and shall apply in manner specified for standards of national legislation. On basis of internal Ukrainian legislation there is priority of international law. In event when provisions of Ukrainian and international laws contradict each other, provisions of international laws apply.

Ukraine has three official journals for publication of laws and other legislative and government enactments: newspaper "Holos Ukrainy" and magazine "Vidomosti Verkhovnoyi Radi Ukrayini" are editions of Supreme Rada, and newspaper "Uryadoviy Kuryer" is publication of executive branch of Ukrainian government.

LEGISLATURE:

See topics Constitution; Law Reports, Codes, Etc.

LICENSES:

Licensing is system of issuing permissions for conduct of certain types of activity. Following types of licensing exist in Ukraine: (i) general licensing of certain kinds of entrepreneurial activity; (ii) licensing (certification) of trade activity; (iii) permits for certain kinds of entrepreneurial activity as specific type of licensing; (iv) licensing of export and import of goods (work, services); (v) licensing of manufacturing and trade in ethyl, cognac and fruit spirits; (vi) licensing of manufacturing alcoholic beverages and tobacco products; (vii) licensing of right to use broadcasting channels; (viii) licensing of foreign property investment by Ukrainian residents.

Licensing of Entrepreneurial Activity.—Law on "On Entrepreneurial Activity" and Resolution of Cabinet of Ministers of Ukraine specifies list of activities which are subject to licensing and agencies which are authorized to issue such licenses: (i) Ministry of Construction and Architecture—for prospecting mineral deposits, conducting of engineering and prospecting; (ii) State Committee on Geology—for use of mineral deposits; (iii) Ministry of Internal Affairs—manufacturing, repair and sale of sport, hunters' firearms and ammunition for such arms; cold steel, professional arms and gas pistols; aerosol cans with Mace or gases of similar action; maintenance of shooting galleries, shooting grounds; provision of security services and services connected with protection of collective and private property; assembly, repair and maintenance of security means; making of seals and stamps; activity connected with sale of vehicles which are subject to registration with agencies of internal affairs; (iv) Ministry of Justice—conduct of law practice, provision of special expert consulting to courts (except for forensic medicine and psychiatric consulting expertise); (v) State Committee on Gardens and Wine Manufacturing—for manufacturing of wine and cognac products; (vi) State Committee on Food—for manufacturing of beer, spirits, hard liquors and tobacco products; (vii) Ministry of Finance—for extraction of precious metals and precious stones and for manufacturing and sale of goods with precious metals and stones; (viii) Ministry of Finance upon agreement with National Bank of Ukraine—for production of securities, money orders and other signs of mail payment; (ix) Ministry of Communications—for payment and receipt of postal money orders; construction and servicing stations of satellite communications, state networks of transmission of information, networks of telecommunications, mobile communications networks, TV and radio broadcasting networks, processing of mail, use of radio frequencies; (x) Ministry of Transport—for domestic and international transportation of passengers, repair and maintenance of vehicles; (xi) Ministry of Health—for conduct of doctor's (medical) practice, retail trade in pharmaceuticals; (xii) Ministry of Environmental (Ecological) Security—for construction and maintenance of nuclear equipment; (xiii) Ministry of Industry—for manufacturing and sale of chemicals, collection, processing, purchase and sale of scrap metal and wastes of metal; (xiv) city, town and district executive committees—for creation and maintenance of gambling enterprises; trade activity in sphere of retail trade in food, personal hygiene items, alcoholic beverages and tobacco products, products of household chemistry, region executive committees, government of Autonomous Republic of Crimea and Kyiv and Sevastopol city executive committees—for wholesale trade in aforementioned products; (xv) State Property Fund of Ukraine—for conduct of intermediary activity with privatization papers; (xvi) State Committee on Tourism—for conduct of activity connected with tourist services; (xvii) Audit Chamber of Ukraine—for conduct of audit

LICENSES . . . *continued*
activity; (xviii) Committee on Supervision of Insurance Activity—for conduct of insurance activity and some other kinds of activity.

Decision on issuance of license or refusal to issue license must be adopted within 30 days from date of receipt of required documents.

Licensing of Trade Activity.—From Oct. 1, 1995, trade activity is conducted by subjects of entrepreneurial activity on condition that they have certificates entitling them to conduct wholesale and retail trade in goods, except for those trade activities requiring license.

Certificate to conduct wholesale trade is issued by trade department of regional, Kyiv and Sevastopol city state administrations, Ministry of Trade and Foreign Economic Relations of Autonomous Republic of Crimea; to conduct retail sale—by trade departments of district state administrations and executive committees of city councils on basis of documents specified by Regulation of Cabinet of Ministers of Ukraine.

Permits for Certain Kinds of Entrepreneurial Activity.—Actually this is additional type of licensing in sphere of retail trade, trade in foreign currency and provision of services in gambling business.

Trade permit is issued by agencies of Central State Tax Inspection of Ukraine at location of subjects of entrepreneurial activity on basis of application to acquire trade permit; such permit entitles holder to conduct aforementioned entrepreneurial activity.

However, trade permit does not certify right to intellectual property.

Following businesses are subject to permitting: (i) retail trade which is conducted by retail trade locations. According to legislation objects of retail trade are shops which are located in separate premises, total square of which does not exceed 20 sq. meters, kiosks, tents, automobile stores, vendors' tables, etc. Value of trade permit is equal to 160 ECU per calendar month. Trade by Ukrainian producers in their own products is not subject to this law. Trade permit is issued free of charge to those subjects of entrepreneurial activity which conduct retail trade exclusively in goods of national production, such as: bread, wheat and rye flour, salt, sugar, vegetable oil, beef and pork, potato, fruits, vegetables and berries, periodicals, monthly tickets, coal, illuminating and condensed gas, peat briquettes, peat in pieces for heating, children's food products; (ii) trade in foreign currency cash: trade operations with foreign currency cash which are carried out by subjects of entrepreneurial activity or structural (separate) subdivisions thereof at exchange points are subject to permit requirement, except for operations with foreign currency cash which are carried out by banking institutions in their own operational offices. Price of such permit is 160 ECU for calendar month and term of its effectiveness is 36 calendar months; (iii) activity in sphere of gambling business: use of slot machine with monetary award or prize (350 ECU for one year); use of gambling table with roulette wheel (8,000 ECU for one year); bowling lane (1,000 ECU for one year for each track); use of table for billiards (300 ECU for one year). Term of effectiveness of permit is 60 calendar months, payment is made every quarter of year.

Subjects of entrepreneurial activity are responsible for violation of requirements of this law in following way: (i) in event of delay of payment—fine in amount of one value of trade permit and cancellation thereof; (ii) for violation of procedure of use of trade permit—fine in amount of one month value of trade permit; (ii) for carrying out operation which is subject to this law without obtaining permit—fine in double amount of value trade permit for complete term of effectiveness thereof.

Licensing of Export and Import of Goods.—Regional departments of foreign economic relations obtain right to issue one-time licenses for export and import of goods, which are subject to quoting and licensing, if value of goods does not exceed $100,000. Decision on issuance of license is made within 15 days after submission of appropriate documents. General licenses are obtained only by enterprises authorized by government. All other subjects of entrepreneurial activity obtain one-time licenses for each separate contract. To obtain license for import of goods, it is required to submit certificate of experitse of imported goods issued by Chamber of Commerce and Industry of Ukraine. Resolution of Cabinet of Ministers of Ukraine specifies that import to Ukraine of slag and other wastes of manufacturing of steel and cast iron, plant-protecting chemicals, pharmaceuticals, veterinary preparations and cosmetic means is subject to licensing. Export quotas in Ukraine still exist for precious and semiprecious stones, precious and non-ferrous metals, concentrate.

Licensing of Manufacturing and Trade in Ethyl, Cognac and Fruit Spirits; Licensing of Manufacturing of Alcoholic Beverages and Tobacco Products.—Following types of activity are subject to licensing: (i) manufacturing and trade in ethyl spirits. Such trade may be carried out exclusively by state enterprises; (ii) manufacturing of cognac and fruit spirits. Such trade may be conducted at state enterprises and wine-producing enterprises irrespective of ownership forms on condition that such enterprises upon enactment of this law had appropriate license and such products are intended for their own manufacturing demands without right of sale; (iii) manufacturing of alcoholic beverages and tobacco products is conducted by subjects of entrepreneurial activity irrespective of their ownership forms on condition of obtaining license.

License is issued upon submission of application by subject of entrepreneurial activity and on basis of copy of certificate which confirms status of entrepreneur—for individuals; and copies of founders' documents—for legal entities.

License is issued for five years, yearly license fee is: (i) for manufacturing of ethyl, cognac and fruit spirits and alcoholic beverages—500 untaxable minimum incomes of citizens (approximately $4,570); (ii) for manufacturing of tobacco products—300 untaxable minimum incomes of citizens (approximately $2,742).

License for import, export and wholesale trade in ethyl, cognac and fruit spirits is issued only to state enterprises which are authorized by Cabinet of Ministers of Ukraine. Annual license for export or wholesale trade is 5,000 untaxable minimum incomes of citizens (approximately $45,700), for import—10,000 untaxable minimum incomes of citizens (approximately $91,400).

Annual license for import, export and wholesale trade in alcoholic beverages and tobacco products is issued to subjects of entrepreneurial activity irrespective of their ownership forms in following amounts: (i) import—10,000 untaxable minimum incomes of citizens (approximately $91,400); (ii) export and wholesale trade—100 untaxable minimum incomes of citizens (approximately $914).

Participants in entrepreneurial activity shall be subject to financial sanctions in form of fines in event of: undue registration as excise duty payer; manufacturing, wholesale (including export and import) and retail sale of ethyl, cognac and fruit spirits, alcoholic beverages and tobacco products without license or with violation of rules established for trade thereof; retail trade in alcoholic beverages and tobacco products without quality certificate.

Licensing of Right to Use TV and Radio Broadcasting Channels.—National TV and Radio Council is authorized to issue licenses for right to use broadcasting channels to TV and radio organizations including those which broadcast using their own technical and communications means.

Established amounts of license fees are reduced: (i) by 90% if TV or radio organization is supported by state budget; (ii) by 30% if TV or radio organization, irrespective of ownership form, broadcasts educational or children's programs. Amounts are increased: (i) by two times if broadcasting of foreign programs exceeds 20% of total amount of broadcasting time; (ii) by five tmes if broadcasting of foreign programs exceeds 35% of total amount of broadcasting time.

Individual Licenses for Conduct by Residents of Property Investments Outside Ukraine are issued by Ministry of Foreign Economic Relations and Trade on basis of documents set forth by law and for appropriate fee.

Unified License Register was created in order to register all agencies which issue licenses to subjects of entrepreneurial activity which obtain licenses and types of licenses.

Register is maintained by License Chamber at Ministry of Economy.

See also Laws of Ukraine "On Entrepreneurial Activity" as of Feb. 26, 1991, "On Permitting of Certain Kinds of Entrepreneurial Activity" as of Mar. 23, 1996, "On State Regulation of Manufacturing and Trade in Ethyl, Cognac, Fruit Spirits, Alcoholic Beverages and Tobacco Products" as of Dec. 19, 1995; Provision on procedure of issuance to subjects of entrepreneurial activity of special permits to conduct certain kinds of activity as of May 17, 1994; Provision of Cabinet of Ministers of Ukraine "On Unified License Register" as of Mar. 27, 1996 and "On Manner of Issuance of Individual Licenses for Conduct by Residents of Property Investments Outside Ukraine" as of Feb. 19, 1996, "Provision on manner of licensing of export of goods in 1996" as of Feb. 26, 1996.

See also topics Brokers (Commodity); Commercial Law; Foreign Exchange; Foreign Trade and Foreign Investment; Foreign Investment; State Register (Commercial Register).

LIMITATION OF ACTIONS:

General period within which action must be brought to assert legal right is three years for individuals; and one year for claims of state organizations, collective farms and other cooperative and public organizations against each other.

Six month limitation period applies to actions involving: penalties; defaults in sold goods; supply of products of bad quality; untimely fulfillment of contract work; defaults in work fulfilled according to contract. Claims on concealed defects in contract works are subject to shortened one year limitation, except for instances when one of parties to contract for construction of houses and premises is individual; in this event usual three year limitation applies.

Limitation period begins from date when right to claim arises. Right to claim arises from date when individual finds out or should have found out about violation of rights.

Limitation period may be terminated or cancelled: (i) if extraordinary and inevitable circumstances prevent party from raising claim; (ii) for reason of delay in fulfillment of obligations specified by legislation (moratorium); (iii) if claimant or defendant serves in Army which is under military alert. Limitation period is terminated if such circumstances arose or existed for last six months of claim; if limitation period does not exceed six months, limitation period is terminated during its course. Limitation period is continued from day of cessation of circumstance which was basis for termination. For claims concerning compensation for damages, connected with harm caused to health or death, limitation period is suspended, upon petition of victim or victim's dependent with request to provide pension or allowance support until decision on providing pension support or refusal is made.

Expiration of limitation period for claim before claim is raised is ground for refusal of claim. Court, court of arbitration or third party arbitration may enforce expired claim if it finds valid reason for so doing.

Limitation of action does not apply to: claims arising from breach of personal nonproperty rights, except for instances provided by legislation; claims of state organizations for refunding of property by cooperative and other public organizations or individuals; in other events specified by law.

MINES AND MINERALS:

Use of resources is regulated by Code of Ukraine on Resources, Law of Ukraine "On Protection of Environment" and certain other enactments.

All resources belong to one state fund of resources. Enterprises, institutions and citizens, including foreign entities, may be users of resources. Citizens have right to freely use these resources for satisfaction of their everyday life demands without ownership of these resources by separate individuals.

Subjects of entrepreneurial activity must obtain license to: search or prospect for deposits of minerals, develop deposits of minerals, fulfill engineering and prospecting works for objects of energy, develop state communication systems, defense complexes, gas pipes, main pipelines, bridges, tunnels, electric power stations, airports, and city ports in unstable seismic zones. Separate license is issued for every kind of activity. To obtain license application must be submitted. License issued for development of geological prospecting works at mine does not include right to its exploitation, but holder of such license has priority right to obtain license for exploitation.

Issuance of licenses to exploit mines is executed only after expert evaluation of deposits of minerals in established manner and transfer of mine to entrepreneur. License holder has exclusive right to fulfill activity according to license within limits of territory described in license. Other legal entities or individuals may work at this parcel only upon consent of main user and upon receipt of additional license.

MONOPOLIES AND TRADE RESTRAINTS:

Law of Ukraine "On Restriction of Monopoly and Prohibition of Unfair Competition in Entrepreneurial Activity", Feb. 18, 1992 regulates legal principles restricting monopoly and prohibiting unfair competition in entrepreneurial activity.

According to provisions of this Law, following actions are deemed as violations of antimonopoly law: (i) imposition of onerous contract terms, giving commercial enterprise which imposes such terms unjustifiable profits or terms which are not related to subject of contract; (ii) limitation or termination of manufacturing and withdrawal of goods from trade for purpose of establishing or supporting deficits in market or establishment of monopolistic prices; (iii) partial or complete refusal to distribute or purchase goods if there are no alternative sources of supply or distribution, for purpose of establishing or supporting deficits in market or establishment of monopolistic prices; and other actions undertaken for purpose of creation of barriers to availability of market to other entrepreneurs; (iv) formation of discriminatory prices or tariffs restricting rights of some consumers; (v) establishment of monopolistically high prices (tariffs, rates) for goods which result in violation of consumers' rights; (vi) establishment of monopolistically low prices (tariffs, rates) for goods which result in restriction of competition.

Unfair competition means: (i) illegal use of trademark, firm name or marking of goods, as well as copying of form, packaging or appearance of goods; imitation or copying of goods of another entrepreneur, unauthorized use of name; (ii) intentional spreading of information which may cause damage to business reputation or property interests of another entrepreneur; (iii) receiving, using and divulging secrets or confidential information for purpose of causing damage to business reputation or property interests of another entrepreneur; (iv) order, production, placement or distribution by legal entities or individuals of advertisement which does not comply with requirements of effective legislation of Ukraine and may cause harm to citizens, institutions, organizations or state.

Following are deemed to be discrimination of entrepreneurs by state agency and administration: Prohibition to create new enterprises or other organizatonal forms of entrepreneurship in any sphere of activity and restrictions on conduct of certain kinds of activity and for production of certain kinds of products in order to restrict competition; pressure on entrepreneurs to join associations, concerns, interbranch, regional and other associations of enterprises and to make priority agreements, privileged supplies of goods to certain groups of consumers (par. 3, provision 1, art. 6 in wording of Law #258/95-BP as of July 5, 1995); deciding on centralized distribution of goods which results in monopoly position in market; prohibition on sale of goods from one region of republic to another; provision of certain entrepreneurs with tax holidays and other privileges resulting in their privileged position regarding other entrepreneurs and monopolization of market of certain goods; restriction of rights of entrepreneurs regarding acquisition and sale of goods; prohibition or restrictions regarding certain entrepreneurs or groups of entrepreneurs.

Discrimination of entrepreneurs is also making agreements between state agencies, creation of structures of state governance or provision of existing ministries, state committees and other structures of state governance with authority to fulfill actions which are discriminatory according to law.

Laws and enactments of Ukraine may establish exceptions from provisions of this article for purpose of ensuring national security, defense, public interests.

Pursuant to this Law state policy restricting monopoly may be carried out by authorized agencies and may include financial, material and technical, informational, consulting and other support to entrepreneurs, which assist development of competition. Demonopolization of economy and development of competition in Ukraine are guaranteed according to specific program which is developed by Cabinet of Ministers of Ukraine and approved by Supreme Rada of Ukraine (Parliament).

Antimonopoly Committee of Ukraine within limits of its competence supervises observance of antimonopoly legislation, protection of entrepreneurs' and consumers' interests as result of such violations, including abuse of monopoly position and unfair competition.

Antimonopoly Committee of Ukraine is established by Supreme Rada of Ukraine and includes Head of Antimonopoly Committee and ten state officers.

Antimonopoly Committee of Ukraine is subordinate to Cabinet of Ministers of Ukraine and accountable to Supreme Rada of Ukraine.

Antimonopoly Committee of Ukraine establishes regional departments and determines their competence. Antimonopoly Committee of Ukraine and its regional departments constitute system of agencies of Antimonopoly Committee of Ukraine, headed by Head of Committee.

Antimonopoly Committee of Ukraine acts on basis of Constitution of Ukraine, Law of Ukraine "On Antimonopoly Committee of Ukraine", other law and enactments of Ukraine and international agreements in which Ukraine participates.

In order to prevent monopoly position of certain entrepreneurs in market, creation, reorganization (merger, joining), acquisiton of assets, liquidation of economic subjects, creation of associations, concerns, interbranch, regional and other organizations, transformation of governing agencies into aforementioned associations in events specified by effective legislation is performed on condition of obtaining consent of Antimonopoly Committee of Ukraine.

Officers of state agencies, heads (disposers of credits) of enterprises (organizations, economic associations, etc.) and individuals who undertake entrepreneurial activity without creation of legal entity shall be responsible according to Administrative Code and effective legislation for: abuse of monopoly position; unfair competition; discrimination of enterprises by state agencies; non-provision, undue provision of information or provision of inaccurate information to Antimonopoly Committee of Ukraine and its regional departments; misfeasance or malfeasance of decision of Antimonopoly Committee and its regional departments. Fines are recovered according to court procedure.

If entrepreneurs, agencies and other interested persons do not agree with decisions of Antimonopoly Committee of Ukraine and territorial administrations thereof, they may appeal to court, or Court of Arbitration with petition for cancellation or modification, partially or completely, of decisions of Antimonopoly Committee and territorial administrations thereof. Submission of petition does not suspend decisions for time of consideration if court or Court of Arbitration does not decide to suspend or terminate effectiveness of such decisions. Damages caused by Antimonopoly Committee and territorial administrations thereof, are compensated at expense of state budget irrespective of faults of officers of Antimonopoly Committee and territorial administrations thereof.

MORTGAGES:

In Ukraine legal relations connected to mortgages are regulated by Law "On Mortgages", of Oct. 2, 1992. In accordance with this Law, mortgage is used to secure obligations.

Mortgagee (creditor) has right for satisfaction before other creditors in event of mortgagor's failure to realize obligations secured by mortgage.

Mortgage results from agreement or law. Mortgage secures any obligations arising from credit (bank credits), purchase-sale, rent, transportation and other agreements.

Mortgage may secure potential future obligations, provided that there is agreement of parties specifying amount of such mortgage. Real estate in Ukraine is used for mortgage. Other property and property rights may also be used as collateral for mortgage. Certain property by virtue of specific character, or law may not be mortgaged. State owned national cultural and historical valuables which are registered or are subject to registration in State Register of National Cultural Property, however, cannot be objects of mortgage.

In Ukraine following forms of mortgage are distinguished: (1) Hypothecation or mortgage of land, real estate under which land and/or property which is object of mortgage is kept by mortgagor or third person. Object of hypothecation may be property connected with land, namely buildings, premises, flat, enterprise (its structural subdivision) as entire property complex, and other property regarded by legislation as real property. Under Ukrainian law, object of hypothecation may also be land parcels and perennial plants owned by individuals as private property. (2) Mortgage of turnover goods or processing. Objects of such mortgage may be raw materials, partially assembled products, assembly parts, etc. (3) Pawn, which means mortgage of movables transferred by mortgagor for mortgagee's ownership. Under agreement between mortgagee and mortgagor, object of mortgage may be left with mortgagor, provided it is locked and sealed by mortgagee (hard mortgage). If object of mortgage is of particular importance, mortgagor must confirm existence of mortgage by marks on object. (4) Mortgage of property right means mortgage of right for claims on obligations in which mortgagor is creditor of present and future claims. (5) Mortgage of securities is carried out by transfer of entry (endorsement) and transference of endorsed security to mortgagee.

Object of mortgage may be substituted only with mortgagee's consent.

Collectively (jointly) owned property may be mortgaged only under consent of all co-owners.

Mortgage agreement must be executed in writing. With parties' consent, mortgage agreement may be certified by notary where required by one of parties thereto, even though not required by Ukrainian law. Mortgage agreement should include name (name, patronymic and last name) and location (residence) of parties thereto, nature of claim secured by mortgage, its amount, period of realization of obligations, description, value, location of property, and any other terms. If object of mortgage is real estate, transportation means, space object, turnover goods or goods under processing, then agreement must be certified by notary on basis of respective legislative documents. Notary certification of mortgage agreement is carried out at place of registration of transportation means and space objects, or at place of location of enterprise (for agreements on turnover goods or under processing).

If parties to mortgage agreement fail to meet requirement as to form and notary certification thereof, then agreement is recognized as ineffective.

Mortgage right arises from date of making mortgage agreement, or, if agreement is certified by notary, from date of notary certification thereof. If object of mortgage is to be kept by mortgagee in accordance with agreement or law, then mortgage right arises from date of transfer of object to mortgagee. If such transfer was carried out prior to making agreement, then mortgage right arises from date of making such agreement.

Mortgage of goods may be carried out through transfer of document for disposition of goods (as security) to mortgagee. Securities transferred for mortgage may be kept in notary office or in bank.

Mortgagee has right to satisfy fully his claims at expense of mortgaged property, as of date of actual satisfaction, including interest, recovery of losses (or forfeit) resulting from delay, costs for maintenance of mortgaged property, and costs for satisfaction of obligations secured by this mortgage, unless otherwise provided by mortgage agreement.

Imposition of fine against mortgaged property is carried out under decision of court, Court of Arbitration, and in uncontested manner on basis of instructions of notary agencies.

If mortgage is used for international circulation, form of any agreement is specified by law of country where such agreement is made. Mortgage agreement rights and obligations of parties thereto are set forth by law of country in which agreement is made, unless otherwise provided by parties' agreement.

Form of mortgage agreement for buildings, premises and other real property located in Ukraine, ownership right for such property, and form of mortgage agreement for turnover property made by mortgagor established, residing/located and operating in Ukraine, is established by Ukrainian law.

Ukrainian laws regulating ownership rights for property and relations on which particular right is based, set forth whether such property may be object of mortgage.

Means, conditions and terms, and procedure of protection of mortgagee's and mortgagor's ownership rights for mortgaged property and property rights from violation thereof by third parties, are specified in laws regulating ownership right for such property and relations on which such right is based. In event when, according to such law, notary certification of mortgage agreement is obligatory, then it should be carried out in manner established by this law, provided that object of mortgage is real estate located in Ukraine; object of mortgage is ownership right to real estate located in Ukraine; object of mortgage is real estate which is subject to registration, in accordance with law of Ukraine; object of agreement is property which is in circulation or under processing, on condition that mortgagor is established, resides/is located or whose principal place of business is in Ukraine; object of mortgage is marine buildings, premises, artificial islands (and ownership rights for them), which are outside

See Topical Index in front part of this volume.

MORTGAGES . . . *continued*
territorial waters of Ukraine or other countries, provided they are objects of ownership or rent by individuals or legal entities of Ukraine or foreign legal entity with participation of Ukrainian party, or international intergovernmental organizations whose headquarters are in Ukraine.

Notary certification or registration of mortgage agreements by agencies of foreign countries, are recognized in Ukraine, provided they are duly certified by notary in accordance with this law.

In making mortgage agreement or as result of further agreement, parties to foreign trade mortgage agreement may set forth that mortgaged property may be sold at auctions outside Ukraine if not against law of Ukraine. Procedure for sale of mortgaged property at auctions, is specified by law of country in which auction is held.

If mortgaged property located in Ukraine is subject to sale at auction outside Ukraine, then requirements of customs legislation of Ukraine should apply to such sale.

If international treaties in which Ukraine participates establish mortgage provisions other than those set forth in this Law, then provisions of international treaty will apply.

MOTOR VEHICLES:

Operator's license is required for operating motor vehicle in Ukraine. Minimal age varies according to type of vehicle to be driven: citizens over 16 may operate motor vehicles and motor side-cars; citizens over 18 may operate all categories and types of cars, and trams and trolley buses; citizens over 19 may operate buses and trucks equipped for transportation of more than eight passengers.

Citizens of Ukraine, aliens and persons without citizenship are permitted to operate motor vehicles of certain category provided they have operators' licenses of appropriate category.

Local and international operator's licenses executed in accordance with International Convention on Traffic, are effective in Ukraine. Procedure for issuance of such licenses is established by Cabinet of Ministers.

Person seeking to obtain license to operate motor vehicles is required to have special training course at specialized driving school, provided that such institution is licensed for driver training.

Driver may lose his motor vehicle license (i) if subsequent health condition hampers safe operation of vehicle, or (ii) if driver fails to carry out established obligations anticipated by legislation.

Loss of right to operate motor vehicles shall be realized by removal of operator's license by authorized officers of State Auto Inspection of the Ministry of Internal Affairs of Ukraine; list of such officers shall be specified by legislation of Ukraine.

Alien operator's licenses (for tourists, business travelers and diplomats) which meet requirements of International Convention on Traffic of 1968 shall be effective in Ukraine only if operated during tourist trips, international transportation of cargo, business trips, term of which is not more than a year.

If alien comes to Ukraine for permanent residence, operator's license must be exchanged for Ukrainian license upon medical examination of this person. Operator's licenses of aliens who have operated motor vehicles for 12 months or more will be exchanged without tests. Operator's licenses of persons who have not operated motor vehicles for 12 months will be exchanged upon passing written and driving exams. Employees of foreign diplomatic and consulate representative offices in Ukraine, permanent representatives of mass media and other foreign organizations will be issued Ukrainian operator's licenses without exams/tests and medical examinations, provided such persons have effective international operator's licenses or licenses of their country, on condition that countries of their residence are parties to International Convention of Traffic.

If foreign persons and persons without citizenship have no national or international operator's licenses, Ukrainian operator's licenses shall be issued for them in accordance with Ukrainian domestic requirements. International operator's licenses obtained by Ukrainian drivers abroad will be subject to exchange for national documents in accordance with Ukrainian domestic requirements.

Registration is required for automobiles and other motor vehicles. State registration shall be carried out by agencies of State Auto Inspection of the Ministry of Internal Affairs of Ukraine in accordance with procedure of registration which shall be established by Cabinet of Ministers of Ukraine.

In accordance with Decree of President of Ukraine "On Mandatory Insurance of Civil Responsibility of Owners of Motor Vehicles", owners of motor vehicles are required to have mandatory insurance in order to protect rights of victims of traffic accidents.

Beginning in 1995, Decree on Mandatory Insurance of Civil Responsibility of Owners of Motor Vehicles was suspended. Decree may be renewed upon conformance of legislative enactments, which are currently effective in area of insurance, and analysis of activity of insurance companies.

Rule of the road in Ukraine is to drive on right side of road. International road signs are used.

If international treaty of Ukraine establishes rules other than provisions of legislation of Ukraine on traffic, then provisions of international treaty will apply.

NEGOTIABLE INSTRUMENTS:

Negotiable instruments are not used in Ukraine.

See topic Securities.

NOTARIES PUBLIC:

Legal position of notary in Ukraine is established by Law of Ukraine "On Notaries" and Code of Civil Procedure of Ukraine.

"Notaries of Ukraine" means system of agencies and officers appointed to certify rights and facts of legal importance, and to perform other notarial acts in order to make them trustworthy. In Ukraine notary acts are performed by state or private notaries. Documents executed by state and private notaries have equal legal effectiveness.

In foreign countries notarial acts are performed by consular agencies of Ukraine, or, in specified cases, by diplomatic representative offices of Ukraine.

Notary may be citizen of Ukraine with legal training (University, Academy, Institute) and six months of practical training in state notary office or at private notary office, who passed qualification exam and obtained certificate confirming right for notary activity. Person previously convicted of crime cannot be notary.

State notary offices are established and terminated by Ministry of Justice of Ukraine. State notary office is legal entity and is headed by manager.

State notary is also appointed and dismissed by agencies of justice of Cabinet of Ministers of Republic of Crimea, oblasts, and administrations of Kiev and Sevastopol.

State notary office may certify agreements (for example, contracts, wills, powers of attorney, marriage contracts, etc.), issue certificates for right of inheritance; issue certificates on acquisition of housing at public auction; confirm compliance of copies and excerpts with submitted documents; confirm authenticity of signatures on documents and translation of documents; confirm existence of person or residence in definite place; take money and securities for escrow; issue executive resolutions, etc.

Performance of notarial acts is compensated by state-set fee.

Private Notary Activity.—Registration of private notary activity is carried out by departments of justice of Rada of Ministers of Republic of Crimea, oblasts, and administrations of Kiev and Sevastopol on petition of person entitled for notary activity. Upon receipt of registration certificate, private notary is required to start notarial activity within three months.

Private notary performs same notarial acts as state notary, except for imposition and removal of prohibition to deprive someone of housing, flat, country house, garage, land parcel, other real estate; issuing ownership certificate for share in joint property of couple in event of spouse's death; issuing inheritance certificate; taking measures for protection of inheritable property; certifying agreements of lifelong support; certifying authenticity of powers of attorneys and signatures on documents to be used abroad.

Private notary is compensated for performance of notarial acts by agreement between notary and individual or legal entity.

Notarial acts are performed in state notary offices, in state notary archives, in private notary's office, or premises of executive committees of village, municipal or city Radas. If person cannot appear in above mentioned places, or if it is required by specific features of agreement to be certified, then notarial acts may be performed outside above mentioned places. Notarial acts are performed upon payment on date when all required documents are submitted. Performance of notarial acts may be suspended, if officers of enterprises, institutions and organizations are required to submit additional information or documents, or if, in accordance with law, notary questions absence of persons interested in matter.

In course of notarial act notary and other officials must identify person, his representative or representative of enterprise, institution, or organization which requested such notarial act. Such person is identified under his passport or other documents which exclude any doubts regarding person requesting notarial acts.

Notary or official performing notarial act, shall refuse to perform such act if such acts are in contravention of law; such acts are performed by another notary or officer; petition for performance of notary acts is given by incompetent person or representative within required authority; agreement to be made on behalf of legal entity is in contravention of purposes specified in charter or provisions thereof.

Interested person who considers performance or refusal to perform notarial act as incorrect, may appeal to rayon (city) people's court at place of location of respective state notary office, state notary archive, executive committees of village, municipal or city Rada, or private notary's office.

Documents compiled abroad with participation of foreign authorities or issued by them shall be accepted by notaries, provided that such documents were acknowledged by Ministry of Foreign Relations of Ukraine. Documents which were not acknowledged shall be accepted by notaries in instances anticipated by law of Ukraine or international treaties in which Ukraine participates. If provisions on notarial acts specified by international treaties differs from Ukrainian law, then provisions of international treaties will apply. If notarial acts which were not anticipated by law of Ukraine are related by international treaties to sphere of notary's competence, then notary will perform this act in manner established by Ministry of Justice of Ukraine.

PATENTS:

Relations which arise in connection with acquisition and realization of ownership right for inventions, useful (applicable) models, industrial samples and trademarks of goods and services in Ukraine, are regulated by Laws of Ukraine "On Protection of Rights for Inventions and Valuable Models" of Dec. 15, 1993, "On Protection of Rights for Trademarks of Goods and Services" of Dec. 15, 1993, and by Stockholm edition of Paris Convention of Protection of Industrial Ownership of 1967 ("Basic Provisions Concerning International Relations in the Sphere of Legal Protection of Industrial Ownership").

Patent is certificate (verification) which is issued by competent state agency—State Committee of Ukraine on Issues of Intellectual Ownership (common name—State Patent Agency of Ukraine) and confirms ownership right for invention, valuable model, industrial sample or trademark of goods/services. Effective term of such certificate is computed from date of application to State Patent Agency, and is: (i) for invention—20 years; (ii) for useful (applicable) model—five years; (iii) for industrial sample and trademarks of goods/services—ten years.

Patentable invention may be either product or means. Patent issued for means of producing product, shall extend to resulting product by such means as well.

Patentable useful (applicable) model may be design execution of device.

Patentable industrial sample may be form (shape), picture (pattern), color execution, or combination thereof, which are used to distinguish product and to meet aesthetic and ergonomic needs.

Patentable trademark may be verbal, pictorial, volumetrical and other symbols and combinations thereof executed in any color or combination of colors.

Legal protection is provided to any invention, useful (applicable) model, industrial sample or trademark which is not in contravention of public interests, principles of humanism and morality, and are competitive, namely: (i) invention should be new, with level of originality and applicable for industrial needs; (ii) useful (applicable)

PATENTS . . . *continued*
model should be new and applicable for industry; (iii) industrial sample should be new and applicable for industry.

Right of patent for inventions, useful (applicable) models, industrial samples is to: inventor (author) or successors thereof. Inventor (author) shall be owner of copyright which is unalienable private right, and protection of which is not limited in term; employer, provided that invention, useful (applicable) model or industrial sample is created in connection with realization of professional obligation or at employer's order; successor of inventor (author) or employer; first applicant, whose application to State Patent Agency of Ukraine is dated earlier, provided that invention, useful (applicable) model or industrial sample were created as result of separate work.

Applicant whose date of application to State Patent Agency of Ukraine is earlier, shall have right to patent.

Individual willing and entitled to obtain patent, shall apply to State Patent Agency of Ukraine, through patent agent. After that State Patent Agency shall conduct examination in accordance with provisions established by legislation.

Patent shall be issued within one month after registration by state agencies. If group of persons have collective right to obtain patent, one patent only shall be given to all of them.

Rights and obligations arising from patent, become effective from date of publication of information concerning issuance of patent, provided that annual fee for effectiveness of patent is paid. At request of patent owner, violation of his rights must be terminated, and person which violated such rights shall compensate losses caused to patent owner.

PLEDGES:

See topic Chattel Mortgages.

PRESCRIPTION:

See topic Limitation of Actions.

PRINCIPAL AND AGENT:

Ukrainian agency law recognizes three participants (i) agent, (ii) principal, and (iii) third persons.

Principal is individual or legal entity, on whose behalf agent takes legally significant actions. Principal may be (i) any individual from moment of birth, or (ii) any legal entity from date of commencement of activity thereof.

Agent is individual or legal entity authorized to realize legally significant actions on behalf of and in interests of principal. Individuals acting as agents are fully competent, and have no statutory restrictions. Legal entities may represent individuals or other legal entities, provided such activity is in accordance with articles of incorporation thereof.

Third persons are individuals or legal entities with which principal's subjective rights and obligations are established, modified or terminated as result of agent's actions.

Authority of agent may be based on power of attorney, law or regulation. Agent cannot make agreements on behalf of principal neither on his own behalf, nor on behalf of any other person simultaneously represented by him.

Any agreement made on behalf of principal by agent unauthorized to make such agreement, or exceeding his authority, creates, modifies or terminates civil rights and obligations of principal only if such agreement is approved by such principal.

Agent must personally carry out appropriate actions. Agent may delegate his actions to another person only if authorized by principal, or if forced by circumstances to do so in order to protect interests of principal.

Agent who delegated his authority to another individual, is obligated to notify principal, and provide principal with all necessary information regarding individual to whom authority was delegated. Failure to carry out this obligation will result in agent's continuing responsibility for actions of individual to whom such authority was delegated.

Power of attorney shall be terminated at: expiration of its effective term; cancellation of power of attorney by principal; rejection by agent of power of attorney; termination of legal entity on behalf of whom power of attorney was issued; termination of legal entity to which power of attorney was issued; death of principal who issued power of attorney, recognition of such person as incompetent or with restricted competence or disappearance thereof; death of person for whom power of attorney was issued, recognition of such person as incompetent or with restricted competence or disappearance thereof.

Power of attorney may at any time be canceled by principal, or rejected by agent to whom it was issued.

PRIVATIZATION:

Legal, economic and organizational bases for privatization of state owned, republican (Republic of Crimea) and communal ownership enterprises are regulated by Law "On Privatization of Property of State Owned Enterprises", Mar. 4, 1992; Law "On Privatization of Small State Enterprises (Small Privatization)", Mar. 6, 1992; Law "On Lease of Property of State Enterprises and Organizations", Apr. 10, 1992; State Privatization Program (prepared annually); Law "On Privatization Certificates", Mar. 6, 1992 and other laws and enactments of President of Ukraine, Supreme Rada (Parliament) and Cabinet of Ministers.

In three and a half years of privatization in Ukraine approximately 28,000 enterprises have changed ownership of business form. 85% of such objects are objects of small scale privatization. Share of state fixed assets reduced from 90% to 62%. Over 52% of Ukrainian citizens received their property privatization certificates.

Privatization Objects, Purchasers, and Supervision Agencies.—State owned objects which are subject to privatization include: (a) property of enterprises, sections or other subdivisions which divide into independent enterprises and form integral property complexes; (b) uncompleted construction; (c) state owned shares (quotas) in property of economic and other associations.

Privatization shall not extend to state owned objects required for performance by state of its respective functions: property of agencies of state power and administration, Military Forces of Ukraine, National Guards, Security Services, Border Service, justice and customs agencies; gold and currency reserves; enterprises which provide printing of securities and money, etc.

List of objects which are not subject to privatization is approved by Parliament at submission of Cabinet of Ministers.

Governmental policy in area of privatization shall be carried out by State Property Fund of Ukraine, its regional branches and representative offices in districts and cities.

Purchasers of privatization objects may be Ukrainian citizens, foreigners, individuals without citizenship, Ukrainian and foreign legal entities, except for some instances anticipated by Law.

Incentives for privatization may come from State Property Fund, its regional branches and representative offices in districts and cities.

Decisions on privatization of any object shall be made by State Property Fund or appropriate state privatization agency.

Ways of Privatization.—Privatization of state property may be performed by one of following means: (a) sale of privatization objects at auction, by bid, which means direct transfer of ownership right to purchaser who offered best price; (b) sale of shares in property of enterprises at auction, by bid, at stock exchange, or other means performed by converting state enterprises into joint stock companies; (c) buy-out of leased property of state enterprise; (d) buy-out of small privatization objects by purchasers' associations created by employees of such objects.

Privatization of property of state enterprise as integral property complex shall be by appropriate purchase-sale agreement between purchaser and seller. Such agreement may include obligations on (1) maintenance of effective output volume of certain products (services); (2) compensation of debts of state enterprise; (3) maintenance of objects of social and consumer application; (4) arrangements for safe labor conditions and protection of environment; (5) other obligations of purchaser and seller, provided they are anticipated by privatization plan. Owners of privatized objects shall have priority right for long-term lease of land parcels occupied by such objects with further rights of buy out of these parcels according to effective legislation of Ukraine.

Financial Conditions in Privatization.—State property may be acquired with purchasers' own and/or borrowed funds. In process of privatization, foreign investors, purchasers and enterprises with foreign investments shall pay value of state property in hard currency.

According to Decree of President of Ukraine #809/94, Dec. 27, 1994, payments for privatization objects which are subject to free transfer in process of privatization of property of state enterprises to Ukrainian citizens, shall be made from deposit accounts of citizens or with privatization certificates. Privatization certificates shall be effective until Dec. 31, 1996. From Jan. 2, 1995 Ukrainian citizens received their privatization certificates at branches of savings bank at their places of residence. Certificates may be obtained by June 1, 1996.

In order to sell privatization objects, Centers of Certificate Auctions, nonprofit organizations, are established in Ukraine. These centers shall sell shares and privatization objects, get applications from citizens and financial intermediaries for acquisition of shares at certificate auctions, keep privatization certificates, register privatization certificates and transactions with them, inform population on sale of shares, provide consultant services. National network of centers consists of Ukrainian Center of Certificate Auctions, regional centers in Republic of Crimea, regions and cities of Kyiv and Sevastopol and branch offices thereof.

From Dec. 1, 1995, registered housing checks equivalent to cash have been introduced for circulation. Such registered housing checks are used by Ukrainian individuals in course of privatization of state housing resources, and may also be used for privatization of property of state owned enterprises or land resources. (Decree of President of Ukraine #713/95 of 08.08.1995). Housing checks will be effective until Dec. 31, 1996. Conversion coefficient of property certificates and housing checks is one, which means that 1KBV of value of certificate is equal to 1KBV of value of housing check.

Small Privatization.—Privatization of property of small enterprises (small privatization) shall be carried out in compliance with Law of Ukraine "On Privatization of Small State Enterprises (small privatization)", (July 1992). This Law shall apply to industrial sectors which are subject to first priority privatization: processing industry, manufacturing of construction materials, light and food industries, construction, some types of transport, trade and public nutrition, consumer services, housing maintenance and repair industries.

Objects of state land and housing funds shall be privatized according to specific procedure—see topic Real Property.

PROMISSORY NOTES:

Ukraine has been participant to Geneva Convention on promissory notes since 1930. New legislation of Ukraine on promissory notes as well as legislation of former Soviet Union which is not in contravention to Ukrainian legislation is effective in Ukraine.

Promissory note is security certifying absolute monetary commitment of drawer to pay definite sum of money to drawee at fixed term.

Following types of promissory notes are issued: ordinary and endorsement. Ordinary promissory note is signed by debtor and is commitment of debtor to pay definite sum of money to any individual. Endorsement promissory note is drawn and signed by creditor and is order of creditor to debtor to pay out indicated sum to third person. Promissory note with term of payment not fixed shall be regarded as liable to payment when produced.

Promissory note may be endorsed. In this case person who endorses promissory note acquires all rights of demand on promissory note. Endorsement must not contain any limitations in its effectiveness. All limitation terms and conditions included in promissory note, are deemed invalid.

Upon expiration of its term, promissory note must be presented to payer. Refusal of payer to pay or present promissory note for acceptance must be certified by special document. Bearer of promissory note may commence action when payment was not duly paid. In specific cases specified by law (for example under bankruptcy) such action may be commenced earlier.

REAL PROPERTY:

"Real estate" consists of land, buildings located on land, or parts of such buildings.

Land.—Ukraine has no specific law concerning real estate. Land rights are established by Land Code of Ukraine as amended by Law of Ukraine #2196-12 as of Mar. 13, 1992, Law #3179 as of May 5, 1993, and Decree of the Cabinet of Ministers #15092 as of Dec. 26, 1992.

In accordance with Land Code, there are three forms of land ownership: (i) state, (ii) collective, and (iii) private. These three forms are equal under law.

State ownership of land rests with Parliament of Ukraine; Parliament of Republic of Crimea which has land rights within its territory, except for state owned lands; and oblast, rayon, city, settlement, and rural Radas, which have land rights within their territories, except for state owned lands.

Currently land rights in Ukraine are being restructured and Ukrainian land laws are not fully developed, especially concerning private ownership.

Under Soviet Union, land was not transferrable to private ownership. Thus, normative regulation of relations of private land ownership rights in Ukraine needs to be considerably developed. Ownership right, and private ownership right in particular, includes three elements: right to own, right to use, and right to dispose. In accordance with Land Code, disposal of lands is within competence of Radas of different levels which may transfer lands for ownership, or use, or remove lands from use. Land may be removed from use in event of inappropriate use of land plot; systematic failure to pay land tax or rental fee within established periods; such use of land which causes fall of fertility of soils or pollutes them with chemical or radioactive elements; failure to use land parcel for original purpose, etc. Under this provision, individual private owner of lands has no right to dispose of lands, which is confirmed by Decree of Cabinet of Ministers of Ukraine #15-92 "On Privatization of Land Parcels" as of Dec. 26, 1992. In accordance with this Decree, any agreement on purchase-sale or other exclusion of land parcels is to be notarized and registered by rural, municipal or city Rada where land parcel is located. Final decision whether to recognize agreement on exclusion of land parcel as effective or invalid is made by respective Rada.

Land Code establishes another restriction regarding disposal of land, e.g. land parcel transferred for individual ownership, may be used as collateral for mortgage only under obligation and participation of credit institution.

Individual land parcel owner has right to rent such parcel for three year period without changing purpose of its use, or for five year period, if individual is temporarily disabled, or serves in Army of Ukraine, or enters educational institution.

Citizens of Ukraine have right to sell land parcels transferred to them by rural, municipal or city Radas, without changing purpose of land use. Art. 6 of Land Code of Ukraine limits individual right. Citizens of Ukraine may receive ownership of land parcels for: farming; private small-scale farming; construction and servicing of housing and industrial premises; orchards; construction of country houses and garages.

Private ownership of land in Ukraine is restricted.

Individuals acquire ownership as result of heritage; as part of marital property; and as result of purchase-sale, gift or exchange.

Land may be transferred by local Radas to individual ownership free of charge for following purposes: farming within average land parcel, defined as follows: total territory of arable lands used by enterprise, institution, organization or individuals (except for enterprises, institutions and organizations whose lands are not subject of privatization) is divided by number of persons who work in agriculture, pensioners who worked in agriculture and live in villages, and individuals who work in rural consumer service; private small-scale farming; construction and servicing of housing and industrial premises, provided that territory thereof is not in excess of 0.25 hectares in villages, 0.15 hectares in municipal, and 0.1 hectare in cities respectively; orchards; construction of country houses (within 0.1 hectare) and garages (within 0.01 hectare).

Land parcels in excess of average standard are transferred to individuals' ownership on paid basis.

Individuals and legal entities of Ukraine who do not own shares of state-owned property have right to privatization of land parcels not intended for agriculture in order to conduct entrepreneurial activity, except for: lands of general municipal use (squares, streets, pastures, hay-making parcels, embankments, parks, town forests, boulevards, cemeteries, waste reprocessing centers) and land parcels intended for state agency buildings; land parcels of mining industry, unified energy and space systems, transport, communications, defense; parcels of land used for environmental protection, resorts, recreation zones, lands intended for historical and cultural purposes; forest lands of country, except for small (not exceeding five hectares) parcels of forests included in agricultural lands of enterprises, individual farms; waterways and reservoirs, alluvial plains of country, except for small (not exceeding three hectares) ponds, lakes or marshes included in agricultural lands of enterprises, individual (farmer) farms; lands of agricultural research development organizations and training institutions and research farms thereof, training farms of educational establishments, state plant breeding stations and departments, elite seed growing and seed growing farms, stock breeding farms and plants, horse breeding plants, farms growing hops, essential-oil plants, herbs, fruits and grapes.

Privatization of land parcels not intended for agriculture for purposes of entrepreneurial activity is carried out by appropriate state administrations, executive committees of local Radas by sale of such land parcels. Land parcels not intended for agriculture included in objects which are privatized according to legislation of Ukraine may be privatized or leased together with such objects.

Individuals and legal entities of Ukraine which are purchasers according to legislation of Ukraine on privatization may privatize land parcels included in objects which are privatized. In such events privatization of land parcels is carried out according to same procedure as privatization of objects which are located on land parcels.

Privatization of land parcels on which privatized enterprises are located is carried out at initiative of owners thereof. (Decree of President of Ukraine #608/95, July 12, 1995).

Lands are not transferred for ownership by foreign citizens and persons without citizenship.

Peculiarities of transformation period account for existence of distinctive right of land ownership from right of land use. Under Land Code, permanent use, temporary use and use on rental terms are distinguished. Term "land ownership" appears only in latest Land Code, while in previous term "perpetual inheritance control" was used instead, and had same element of ownership: use—with limiting restrictions. In accordance with latest Land Code, use of land which is not limited by previously established term, shall be deemed permanent.

Local Radas transfer land chosen from state owned lands for permanent use to: citizens of Ukraine for farming and private small-scale farming; agricultural enterprises and organizations; public association; religious organizations; industrial, transport and other nonagricultural enterprises, institutions and other organizations; military units, military educational establishments, enterprises and organizations of Ukrainian Army, other military units for purposes of defense; cultivation of forests by specialized enterprises; cooperatives for construction of houses, garages, country houses, or housing; and joint ventures, international associations and organizations with participation of legal entities and individuals, enterprises fully owned by foreign investors.

Temporary use of land may be short term (up to three years) and long term (from three up to 25 years).

Local Radas transfer land chosen from state owned lands for temporary use to citizens of Ukraine for gardening, hay-mowing, pastures and farming; industrial, transportation and other nonagricultural enterprises, institutions and organizations; public associations; religious organizations; military units, military educational establishments, enterprises and organizations of Ukrainian Army, other military units for purposes of defense; agricultural enterprises and organizations; cooperatives for construction of houses, garages, country houses, or housing; joint ventures, international associations and organizations with participation of Ukrainian/foreign legal entities and individuals.

Land may be rented for temporary use to citizens of Ukraine, enterprises, institutions and organizations, public associations and religious organizations, joint ventures, international associations and organizations with participation of Ukrainian legal entities and individuals, to enterprises fully owned by foreign investors and by foreign states, international organizations, foreign legal entities and individuals without citizenship.

Lessors of land may be rural, settlement, city, and rayon Radas, and land owners.

Land may be rented for short-term use (up to three years—for pasturage of cattle, hay-mowing, truck farming, for state and public necessities), and for long-term use (up to 50 years). Conditions and terms of rent, and amount of rental fee specified in agreement between parties.

In 1994 first auctions on sale of leasehold rights for city land parcels were held in Ukraine. Under effective laws, lease period is 50 years with option to prolong lease for next 50 years. Should laws change, leasehold purchased at auction will automatically convert into ownership rights. Leasehold should be recorded by resolution of Executive Committee of City Council of People's Deputies.

Land relations in Ukraine are realized through specific Rada, in which particular land parcel is located. Enterprises, establishments, organizations and citizens interested in receiving land parcels, must address petition to local Rada. Petitions for land parcels, which are within authority of Parliament, are dispatched to oblast Radas or city Radas of Kiev and Sevastopol.

Land ownership right or right for use of land arises after survey of borders of land parcel in nature, and after receipt of certificate. Right of temporary use of land, including use on rental terms, is arranged by agreement.

Lands in Ukraine are used on paid basis. Land owners and land users annually pay for land in form of land tax or rental fee established in accordance with quality and location of land parcel based on its Cadastre valuation. Right of land use may be suspended under resolution of respective Rada or by court proceeding, in event there is violation of land use, use of land not for intended purpose, failure to pay land tax, etc.

Rights of owners of land parcels and land users may be renewed.

Renewal of rights of land owners or land users is carried out by Rada in accordance with competence thereof, or by court, court of arbitration or treaty court.

For last two years, Ukrainian laws were supplemented only by three progressive normative acts on private ownership of land. Decree of the President of Ukraine "On Privatization of Objects of Uncompleted Construction" permits ownership of (i) objects of uncompleted construction, whose construction period is twice as long as the standard, or only 50% of which have been constructed, or (ii) conserved structures (uncompleted construction) which were financed from state, republican (for Republic of Crimea) or local budgets, and for costs of enterprises and associations thereof, are privatized together with land parcels which were allocated in established manner for construction of such objects.

Pursuant to Decree of the President of Ukraine #612/93 "On Privatization of Gasoline Stations that Sell Fuel and Lubricating Materials Exceptionally to the Population", Dec. 29, 1993, land where stations are located are to be privatized simultaneously with privatization of gasoline stations that are selling fuel and lubricating materials exceptionally to population.

Right for privatization of uncompleted construction and land allocated (rented) for such purpose, and gasoline stations and attached parcels is granted to: citizens of Ukraine, foreign citizens, persons without citizenship; any legal entity registered in Ukraine, under condition no part of its statutory fund is state property; and any legal entity of any foreign country.

Decision on privatization of uncompleted construction and gasoline stations is made by State Property Fund of Ukraine, privatization agencies of Republic of Crimea and other administrative-territorial units. These decisions are made at same time as decisions on privatization (rent) of land parcels. Privatization of uncompleted construction and gasoline stations is carried out through sale at auctions or on competitive basis.

Purchaser's land ownership right of uncompleted construction or gasoline station is effective from date of registration of certificate on ownership right for uncompleted construction/gasoline stations by local body of State Committee of Ukraine on Land Resources. Appropriate entry shall be made in land-cadastre documents and this shall be certified by State Act on right of ownership for land.

If land parcel is not privatized, then respective local rada is obligated to make agreement on rent of such land parcel within month from date of purchaser's receipt of certificate on ownership right for uncompleted construction/gasoline station. New owner is obligated to preserve profile of gasoline station within ten years from date of executing purchase-sale agreement.

See Topical Index in front part of this volume.

REAL PROPERTY . . . *continued*

Presidential Decree #666/94 of Nov. 10, 1994 "On Urgent Measures for Expediting Land Reform in Area of Agricultural Production" introduces privatization of land parcels which are used by agricultural enterprises and organizations. According to this Decree, certificate of private ownership for land parcel is issued for each member of agricultural enterprise. Decree establishes that right for land parcel may be object of purchase-sale, donation, exchange or pledge. However, this Decree extends only to land parcels which are subject to agricultural turnover. Decree emphasizes that only owner of share in agricultural enterprise may be owner of land parcel. Size of land parcel is limited by effective land laws to 50 hectares for farming.

This Decree instructs introduction of changes to Land Code, Civil Code, other enactments, and to develop provisions which regulate process of transfer of land parcels to private ownership. As of now this Decree is still in contravention of Land and Civil Codes of Ukraine.

Buildings.—Apartments in multi-apartment buildings and single dwelling houses, which were privatized by tenants as provided by law, are also recognized as real estate. Privatization of state housing fund is carried out through sale, or transfer of apartments to individuals free of charge.

Apartments or houses are transferred to individuals free of charge on following basis: 21 square meters of total area per lessee of apartment and each member of family who lives in apartment or house together with lessee, or who has right for this housing as of July 1, 1992, plus additional ten square meters for family. Square meters in excess of such norms are subject of sale to tenants of apartment.

Privatization is carried out by authorized agencies established by local administration, and agencies of self-management, state enterprises, organizations, and institutions to which state housing fund is subordinated.

Transfer of apartments or houses to individual ownership is registered with privatization agencies and ownership certificate for apartment or house is issued; such certificate is not subject to notary acknowledgment. Privatization agencies have no right to reject tenants' request for privatization, except for instances when apartment or house is not subject to privatization by law.

Disputes which arise in connection with privatization of state housing fund are settled by court or court of arbitration in accordance with competence thereof.

Owner of privatized housing has right at his own discretion to sell housing, transfer it as gift, rent, exchange, pledge or carry out other agreements which are not prohibited by law. Procedure of realization of such right by owner of housing is regulated by Civil Code of Ukraine.

In accordance with Law of Ukraine "On Ownership" as of May 5, 1993, objects of private ownership right may be houses, apartments, garden houses, land parcels and plants on them, which is real estate. Structure, quantity and value of real estate which may be owned by individuals, is not limited, except for instances anticipated by law.

RECORDS:

See topics Acknowledgments; Associations; Chattel Mortgages; Contracts; Corporations; Death; Execution of Court Decisions; Foundations; Mortgages; Motor Vehicles; Notaries Public; Patents; Real Property; Sales; State Register (Commercial Register); Trademarks.

REPORTS:

See topics Law Reports, Codes, Etc.

REPRIVATIZATION AND RESTITUTION:

Law on reprivatization does not exist in Ukraine.

SALES:

Sale-purchase agreements are contracts, pursuant to which seller obliges himself to transfer ownership of particular object and buyer obliges himself to accept such object at seller's price. Objects can be movable or immovable if law does not prohibit acquisition of such objects. Law may specify procedure of object's acquisition (for example specific procedure for purchase of foreign currency). Sale-purchase agreement is effective from moment it is signed by parties. Price is essential provision of agreement. While making agreement, seller is obligated to notify buyer of all rights of third parties in connection with object which is subject of sale. Nonobservance of this requirement entitles buyer to demand lower price or to cancel agreement and receive compensation for damages. If seller violates agreement and does not transfer goods which are sold to buyer, buyer is entitled to demand transfer of goods and to receive compensation for losses caused by delay of transfer, or to cancel agreement and demand compensation for losses. If buyer violates agreement and refuses to accept goods or to pay established price, seller is entitled to demand acceptance of goods and payment by buyer of price as well as to receive compensation of losses caused by delay in acceptance of goods or, cancel agreement and demand compensation of losses.

Quality of goods must correspond to agreement's provisions; if there are no provisions on quality in agreement, then quality of goods must correspond to requirements generally commercially established. If seller sells goods of inferior quality (if buyer was not informed on this issue and did not agree to such inferior quality), buyer is entitled to demand either to substitute goods for higher quality goods or to reduce sale price, or to improve quality of goods and receive compensation for improvement of quality by buyer, or to cancel agreement with compensation of losses to buyer.

Buyer is entitled, within six months, to make claim on quality of goods to seller if seller did not inform buyer about defects in quality before transfer to buyer. If object of sale agreement is house or building, such claim may be made within one year after transfer thereof to buyer; if day of transfer is impossible to determine or buyer owned this building prior to making sale-purchase agreement, then within one year period after date of registration of sale-purchase agreement in established manner.

If third party, on grounds which arose before sale of goods, commences action against buyer on confiscation of goods, then buyer is obliged to notify seller of this action and seller is obliged to participate in such action on buyer's behalf. If buyer does not notify seller of such action, then seller is exempted from responsibility. If, pursuant to decision of regular court or Court of Arbitration, object sold to buyer is confiscated from buyer, seller must compensate losses to buyer.

Goods may be sold on credit. In this event, value of object is paid in installments within established period. In event seller sells article with warranty, seller is obliged, within warranty period, to remedy defects in object or substitute object for object of proper quality.

SECURITIES:

Law of June 18, 1991, as amended on Oct. 14, 1992, "On Securities and Stock Exchange" sets forth conditions, and procedure for issuance of securities, and regulates intermediary activity in organizing trade in securities in Ukraine.

In accordance with this law, following types of securities can be issued and traded in Ukraine: shares; bonds issued by Republican and local bodies; bonds issued by enterprises; treasurer liabilities of Republic; saving certificates; promissory notes.

Procedure for issuance of securities is established by Cabinet of Ministers of Ukraine, or, under instruction thereof, by Ministry of Finance of Ukraine.

In accordance with Procedure of Issuance of Permits for Conduct of Activity on Issuance and Circulation of Securities as Exclusive Activity, approved by Ministry of Finance on July 20, 1995, traders in securities have right to perform following activities provided they have permits of Securities and Financial Market Department of Ministry of Finance: (a) activity on issuance of securities; (b) commission activity on securities; (c) commercial activity on securities.

Permit may be obtained by joint stock companies charter fund of which is made exclusively of registered shares, limited liability companies, additional liability companies, general partnerships, limited partnerships for which transactions with securities constitute exclusive activity.

To obtain permit, applicant must submit to Ministry of Finance list of documents, including copies of founding and registration documents; list of all founders of companies who have up to 5% of shares in charter fund; list of all founders who have from 5% to 10% of shares in charter fund; list of all founders who have more than 10% of shares in charter fund; list of all enterprises and organizations in which applicant is founder; auditor's report on payment of charter fund, etc. provided, however, that any and all lists, information, reports submitted by company were executed not later than month before submission and are duly signed by director and sealed with company's seal.

Intermediary activity on issuance of and trading in securities may be carried out by banks or joint stock companies, whose statutory fund established exclusively at expense of named shares, or any other companies (hereinafter—dealers of), for which transactions with securities are exclusive activity.

Permission to conduct any kind of activity on issuance of and trading in securities will not be granted to dealers of securities, which directly or indirectly own property of other dealers of securities value of which exceeds 10% of statutory fund, including indirectly value in excess of 5% of statutory fund of other dealer. If share of any legal entity which does not have permission for conduct of activity on use of securities, or share of any person in statutory fund of some dealers of securities exceeds 5% for each dealer, these dealers will not trade securities with each other.

Dealer will not trade with: securities of its own issuance; shares of issuer, if dealer owns, directly or indirectly, property in amount of 5% or more of statutory fund of issuer.

Anti-Monopoly Committee of Ukraine exercises control over adherence to requirements of antimonopoly laws in course of securities circulation.

Stock Exchange.—In accordance with Law of June 18, 1991 stock exchange may be formed by not less than 20 founders which are dealers of securities and have permission to conduct commercial and commission activity related to securities, on condition they contributed not less than 50 million karbovantsi into statutory fund.

Should number of members of stock exchange drop to less than ten members, activity of stock exchange will be terminated. Should only ten members remain in stock exchange and new members are not accepted within six months, activity of stock exchange will also be terminated.

Activity of stock exchange shall be terminated in accordance with law of Ukraine on Economic Associations.

In event of violation of terms and conditions specified in permissions for conduct of activity on issuance of and trading in securities as well as in charter and by-laws of stock exchange, state financial agencies may apply following sanctions: (a) to forewarn; (b) to suspend subscription and sale of securities for period of one year or less; (c) to suspend for definite period making of deals for certain activities on issuance of and trading in securities; (d) to annul permissions for activity on issuance of and trading in securities in event sanctions contained in paragraphs (a), (b), (c) of this Art. are applied for second time.

In case stock exchange violates its statutory authority, Ministry of Finance of Ukraine may suspend activity of stock exchange and demand this activity to be corrected according to charter and rules of stock exchange.

Any claims against actions of state financial agencies which resulted from conduct by state financial agencies of control for issuance of and trading in securities was investigated by higher state financial agency. Any decision made by state financial agency may be appealed in regular court or Court of Arbitration. Should international agreements of Ukraine set forth rules different from those set forth by Law of Ukraine on securities and stock exchange, provisions of international agreement will be applied.

SECURITY FOR COSTS:

See topic Actions.

SEQUESTRATION:

See topics Actions; Bankruptcy; Execution of Court Decisions.

SHIPPING:

See topics Brokers (Commodity); Chattel Mortgages; Customs; Foreign Trade Regulations; State Register (Commercial Register).

STATE REGISTER (COMMERCIAL REGISTER):

Under Ukrainian law, enterprises of all ownership forms must be registered by executive committee of local state administration at location of enterprise. Upon registration local state administration must include enterprise on state register of Ukraine.

Enterprise will acquire rights of legal entity upon such registration.

Where any changes to founding documents of enterprise are done by founders, such changes shall be submitted to local state authority for registration within ten days.

State Register consists of following chapters: Identification number of enterprise; full name of enterprise; structuring of enterprise; divisions and affiliates; and, director of enterprise.

Application should include exact data required to fill in each chapter of register.

STATUTE OF FRAUDS:

See topic Contracts.

STATUTES:

See topics Law Reports, Codes, Etc.; State Register (Commercial Register).

SUPPORT:

See topic Divorce.

SYSTEM OF GOVERNMENT:

See topic Constitution.

TAXATION:

Law "On System of Taxation", June 25, 1991, Law "On State Budget of Ukraine", which is adopted annually, Law "On Taxation of Profits of Enterprises", Dec. 28, 1994 and other enactments determine principles of taxation system in Ukraine, taxes, duties, and other obligatory fees to budgets and contributions to state special funds as well as rights and obligations of payers.

In keeping with requirements imposed on Ukraine by IMF and approved by Parliament in Oct. 1994, Ukrainian Parliament undertook review of existing economic legislation deemed to be impediment to economic reform. Present tax laws with their punitive tax rates which discourage business were first on list for change.

In fall of 1994, new tax policy was developed by Cabinet of Ministers and presented for consideration by Parliament. Main goals of this new tax policy are simplification of Ukraine's tax system, reduction of tax rates and elimination of tax privileges. To date only new Laws "On Taxation of Profits of Enterprises" and "On Excise Tax for Tobacco Products and Alcoholic Beverages" were fully enacted. Laws "On Individual Income Tax" and "On Value Added Tax" are currently being studied by parliamentary committees. Draft laws "On Taxation of Property of Enterprises", "On Individual Real Estate Tax", and "On Taxation of Objects of Uncompleted Construction" and "On Excise Tax for Tobacco Products" are expected to be dicussed in Parliament in near future.

According to effective tax system, Ukrainian government levies following taxes and charges: (a) value added tax; (b) excise tax; (c) tax profits of enterprises and organizations; (d) individuals income tax; (e) customs duty; (f) fees for court, marriage, divorce etc.; (g) property tax of enterprises; (h) real estate tax; (i) land tax; (j) tax on automobiles and other vehicles and mechanisms; (k) tax on handcrafts; (l) payment for mineral-exploration rights; (m) tax on specific use of natural resources; (n) tax on pollution of environment; (o) user charges for maintenance, construction and repair of highways; (p) payment to Chernobyl Fund for purpose of liquidation of consequences of Chernobyl accident; (q) payment to Employment Fund; (r) payment to Social Insurance Fund; (s) payment to Pension Fund.

Two new taxes which were not anticipated in Law "On System of Taxation" were introduced by Law "On State Budget of Ukraine for 1994", Feb. 2, 1994. They are: (a) value added tax for imported goods; (b) excise duty for imported goods.

Local taxes and fees include: (a) hotel registration fee; (b) parking fee; (c) fee for trading at market; (d) fee for issuance of warrant for apartment; (e) resort fee; (f) fee for participation in race at hippodrome; (g) tax on winnings at racecourse; (h) tax paid by individuals playing totalizator; (i) advertising tax; (j) fee for right to use local symbols; (k) fee for right to make films and other TV and movie programs; (l) fee for right to conduct local auctions, contest sales and lotteries; (m) fee for communal services; (n) border toll which is established by local agency; (o) retail trade fee.

Value Added Tax (VAT).—This tax is established and regulated by Decree of Cabinet of Ministers "On Value Added Tax", Dec. 26, 1992, Instruction of Central State Tax Inspection on Procedure of Computation and Payment of Value Added Tax of Oct. 2, 1993, Instruction of Ministry of Finance and Central State Tax Inspection "On Procedure of Calculation and Payment of Value Added Tax and Excise Duty for Goods, Imported to Ukraine and on Goods, Exported from Ukraine", May 31, 1994, Instruction of State Customs Committee "On Procedure of Imposition of Value Added Tax and Excise Duty upon Import of Goods to Ukraine", July 7, 1994. From Jan. 1, 1995 according to Instruction of Ministry of Finance, Jan. 10, 1995 VAT rate is 20% of taxable turnover. Subjects of entrepreneurial activity located in Ukraine, international associations, and foreign legal entities and individuals conducting manufacturing or other entrepreneurial activity in their own name are taxpayers. Revenues from sale of goods (works, services), except sale thereof for hard currency, are subject to VAT tax. Imported goods are subject to taxation at difference between sale price of imported goods for national currency of Ukraine and customs (purchase) value, converted at official exchange rate of National Bank of Ukraine effective on day declaration submitted (acquisition of goods, carrying out of works, granting services).

For enterprises engaged in trade, state purchase, wholesale, supply and distribution, and for other enterprises operating as intermediaries, VAT is calculated on difference between sale prices of goods (works, services) and purchase prices as settled with suppliers, including sum of VAT. Report on VAT due is executed by submitting VAT declaration. Penalties for untimely payment of VAT are 50% of amount of payment, and fine is 0.03% of amount for every day of delay. Any and all privileges existing earlier with respect to payment of VAT upon import (sending) to Ukrainian customs territory of excisable goods for either further distribution thereof or for use by Ukrainian individuals, foreign individuals, individuals without citizenship or subjects of entrepreneurial activity of any and all ownership forms, including charitable funds, associations of individuals, religious organizations, institutions of National Bank of Ukraine, enterprises with foreign investments have been cancelled under Law "On Some Issues of Taxation of Excisable Goods" commencing Jan. 1, 1996.

Value Added Tax for Imported Goods.—Object of taxation of goods imported into Ukraine, with exception of confiscated goods, inherited property, undeclared goods, treasures and other valuables inherited by State, and goods in transit across Ukraine's territory, is their declared customs value (DCV) calculated in Ukrainian currency according to National Bank of Ukraine rate on date customs declaration is submitted to Customs (including actual customs duty paid and duty and/or excise tax on excisable goods). Tax rate is 20% of taxable turnover in accordance with Instruction of Ministry of Finance, Jan. 10, 1995.

Payers of this tax are same entities and persons who pay VAT tax. Value added tax for imported goods is paid simultaneously with customs duty. Also in accordance with Law "On Some Issues of Taxation of Excisable Goods" of 11.16.1995, payers of VAT upon import are Ukrainian individuals, foreign individuals and individuals without citizenship who import (send) items (goods) to territory of Ukraine in amounts taxable in accordance with legislation. Subject to taxation are excisable goods in amounts exceeding 200 ECU (or single items in excess of 300 ECU). However, four categories constitute substantial exceptions of indexable margin of 200-300 ECU: (i) tobacco goods; (ii) alcohol beverages; (iii) video equipment; (iv) vehicles. These groups are taxable commencing with value of $1. (Letter of Cabinet of Ministers of Ukraine #2232/96 of 02.01.1996).

Excise Tax is regulated by Decree of Cabinet of Ministers "On Excise Duty", Dec. 26, 1992, Instruction "On Procedure of Calculation and Payment of Excise Duty" No. 24, June 22, 1993, Instruction of Ministry of Finance and Central State Tax Inspection of Ukraine "On Procedure of Calculation and Payment of Value Added Tax and Excise Duty for Goods Imported to Ukraine and Goods (Works, Services) Exported from Ukraine", May 31, 1994, Instruction of State Customs Committee of Ukraine "On Procedure of Imposition of Value Added Tax and Excise Duty upon Import of Goods to Ukraine", July 7, 1994 and Resolution of Parliament of Ukraine "On Introduction of Changes to List of Excisable Goods (Products) and Rates Thereof", Aug. 5, 1994. Subjects of entrepreneurial activity which manufacture excisable goods (products) and subjects of entrepreneurial activity which import excised goods (products) pay excise tax. Excise tax is calculated on revenues from sale of excised goods (products) less VAT. Rates of this tax range from 10%-300% of sale price. Excise tax is not imposed on sale of excised goods (products) exported for hard convertible currency (CIS currencies not included). Penalties for timely payment of excise tax are similar to those for timely payment of VAT.

Excise Duty on Imported Goods.—This new tax was introduced by Law "On State Budget for 1994". Customs value of excisable goods taking into account actually paid customs duties shall be subject to taxation. Subjects of entrepreneurial activity which manufacture excisable goods (products) and subjects of entrepreneurial activity which import excised goods (products) pay excise tax. Also goods imported by Ukrainian individuals, foreign individuals or individuals without citizenship, value of which exceeds 200 ECU (see par. VAT for imported goods), are subject to excise tax in accordance with Law "On Some Issues of Taxation of Excisable Goods". Rates of excise duty on imported goods are same as rates of excise duty. Excise duty on imported goods shall be paid simultaneously with customs duties. Any and all privileges existing earlier with respect to payment of excise duty have been cancelled under Law "On Some Issues of Taxation of Excisable Goods" (also see par. VAT for imported goods).

Excise Duty For Alcohol Beverages and Tobacco Goods.—In accordance with Law approved by Supreme Rada of Ukraine on Sept. 15, 1995, excise tax stamps were introduced. Such stanps are used to mark alcohol beverages and tobacco goods. Import of tobacco goods and alcohol beverages to Ukraine without such stamps is prohibited. Payment of excise tax is mandatory for (a) Ukrainian manufacturers of alcohol beverages and tobacco goods; (b) customers at request of which such products are manufactured under give and take terms; (c) subjects of entrepreneurial activity, including enterprises with foreign investments irrespective of data of registration hereof, which import alcohol beverages and tobacco goods to Ukraine for use by them or for production needs of for purpose of sale; (d) individuals who import to customs territory of Ukraine alcohol beverages and tobacco goods in amount subject to import duty; (e) legal entities and individuals, international organizations and branches thereof which sell alcohol beverages and tobacco goods in customs territory of Ukraine.

Revenues from selling of alcohol beverages and tobacco goods, value of alcohol beverages and tobacco goods manufactured by Ukrainian manufacturers with supplied raw materials; customs value of alcohol beverages and tobacco goods imported into Ukraine are subject to taxation.

Rules of manufacturing, storage and sale of excise tax stamps and marking of alcohol beverages and tobacco goods were approved by Cabinet of Ministers of Ukraine on Dec. 11, 1995.

Local enterprises pay excise duty to state budget on third business day upon turnover, and manufacturers of tobacco goods pay it by 16th day of month after reporting period. Individuals pay excise tax in course of customs registration.

Tax on Profits of Enterprises.—First law enacted under new tax policy is Law On Taxation of Profits of Enterprises, Dec. 28, 1994. In connection with some inadequacies of Law, Supreme Rada of Ukraine issued "Provisions on Application of Law On Taxation of Profits of Enterprises", 06.27.1995 which constitutes additionally developed text of Law. This new law applies to domestic and foreign business and for first time in Ukraine taxes "profit" as opposed to "gross income". Additionally, as compared to previous legislation, new law presents simpler taxation mechanism. Under new law, entrepreneurial profit is taxed at base tax rate of 30%, intermediary activity at 45% of profit, and 60% of profit for casinos and gambling houses.

Passive profits of nonresidents which do not conduct entrepreneurial activity in Ukraine through permanent branch office in case of repatriation thereof outside

TAXATION . . . *continued*
Ukraine shall be taxed at rate of 15%. Profits of nonresidents received in connection with their entrepreneurial activity in Ukraine through permanent branch office shall be taxed at basic rate. Profits from freight which are paid by Ukrainian enterprises to nonresidents in connection with international transportation shall be taxed at rate of 6%.

New law contains certain pro-business features: (a) newly created enterprises may carry forward their first three years' losses to future profits and may offset such losses against new income for up to five years. Same loss-carry-forward benefit is provided for privatized enterprises; (b) any applicable income tax may be reduced by additional 20% if profit is used for reconstruction and expansion of enterprise's manufacture; (c) any applicable income tax may also be reduced by additional 50% if profit is used for installation of special equipment for handicapped workers; (d) enterprise is also not subject to taxation if more than 50% of its workers are invalids and profit is used for their rehabilitation; (e) profit of off-shore companies located in Ukraine, and of agricultural enterprises is totally exempt from tax.

For Ukrainian resident businesses, this new law presents simplified quarterly tax payment system. Nonresident businesses continue to submit their year-end tax reports (by no later than Feb. 5 of following year) and pay tax due after closing of books for prior year and audit.

Strict enforcement mechanism is included in this Law. Failure to submit necessary reports or to pay tax will result in penalty of 110% on tax due. Additional 10% penalty will be levied where taxpayer fails to submit tax declarations, accounts, audit reports and other documents required of calculation of tax or fails to instruct banks to pay due tax. Underdeclaration (concealment of income) will result in payment of tax due plus penalty of twice that amount.

Law prospectively cancels all tax holidays and privileges available to foreign investors. All subjects of entrepreneurial activity, whether domestic or foreign, are treated equally. However, foreign investment enterprises which received five-year tax holiday prior to adoption of new law, can continue to benefit from such holiday.

Tax on Owners of Motor Vehicles, Other Movable Machines and Mechanisms.—Motor vehicle tax is levied on enterprises, associations and organizations, legal entities, foreign legal entities, citizens of Ukraine, foreign citizens and persons without citizenship, which have motor vehicles. Public transportation enterprises, institutions and organizations which are financed from state budget, and disabled are exempt from tax. Tax is paid prior to registration, reregistration or annual inspection of vehicles. Tax rates are computed in proportion to minimal untaxed income and are: for passenger cars according to power of engine—from 0.01 to 0.05 for each horsepower; for motor trucks with up to seven ton capacity in respect to power of engine—0.015 for each horsepower; for trucks with capacity exceeding seven tons and other vehicles, mechanisms and buses—0.02 for each horsepower.

Individual Income Tax.—Citizens of Ukraine, foreign citizens and persons without citizenship, both residents and nonresidents of Ukraine, pay income tax. Residents of Ukraine are Ukrainian citizens, foreign citizens and persons without citizenship who reside in Ukraine not less than 183 days in calendar year. Citizens who permanently reside in Ukraine pay tax on total taxable income for calendar year obtained from different sources either in Ukraine or abroad. Income obtained from Ukrainian sources is taxed for citizens who do not permanently reside in Ukraine. When total taxable income is calculated, then incomes obtained both in kind and cash in local or foreign currency are taken into account.

Tax on income obtained in foreign currency, is paid in Ukrainian karbovantsi. Income obtained in foreign currency is converted into Ukrainian karbovantsi at exchange rate established by National Bank of Ukraine as of date of obtaining thereof.

Total taxable income obtained for taxable period does not include following: allowance established in accordance with state social insurance and state social security, except for allowance for temporary disability, including support for custody of child; pension; monetary security, monetary bonuses and other payments received by military people, persons who serve in units of domestic security institutions in connection with fulfillment of their duties; sums received as result of alienation of individual-owned property, notary certificate which is subject to state fee, except for income received from distribution of products and other property as result of realization of entrepreneurial and other activity in order to receive income; income received as result of sale of products cultivated in private land plots, products of vegetation, cattle-breeding and beekeeping; sums received as result of inheritance and gift, except for royalties received by heirs (successors) of authors of work of science, literature, art, inventions, discoveries and industrial samples; profits gained for state bonds and lotteries, interest and profit on deposits in banking institutions, saving certificates and state treasury liabilities; sums received as result of mandatory and voluntary state insurance (except for instances when contributions for insurance are made at expense of enterprises, institutions and organizations); allowance in cash and/or kind, regardless of amounts thereof, on condition such material assistance is provided on basis of decisions of Ukrainian Government in connection with calamities, natural disasters, accidents and catastrophes; sums received as result of allocation of persons' savings in current deposit accounts of Ukrainian banks, including accounts in foreign currency; income for purchase of shares, and sums invested in reconstruction and improvement of facilities of subjects of entrepreneurial activity; sums, not in excess of 20 minimal wages per year, transferred, at request of persons (including individuals who are subjects of entrepreneurial activity) to any branches of charitable and ecological funds, enterprises, institutions, organizations and establishments of culture, education, science, health and social security which are financed from state budget; sums received by employees for compensation of damages resulted from any job-related disability, and in connection with loss of breadwinner.

Income tax is calculated, deducted and transferred to state budget by enterprises, institutions, organizations of any property forms and individuals which pay income. Citizens receiving income from enterprises, institutions, organizations and individuals not at place of principle employment, are obligated to submit declaration on income to state tax inspection.

Taxable income obtained by individual during course of one year from entrepreneurial activity not organized as legal entity, is total net income: difference between gross income (proceeds in cash and kind) and expenses directly connected with receipt of income and confirmed by documents.

Taxable income of foreign citizens and persons without citizenship which have permanent residence in Ukraine is calculated in same manner as taxable incomes of citizens of Ukraine. Taxable income of foreign citizens includes: (a) additional sums paid in connection with their stay in Ukraine; (b) sums paid to reimburse costs for education of children at schools, for catering, trip of taxpayer's families to vacations, and other similar purposes. Taxable income of foreign citizens does not include: (a) sums deducted by employer of foreign citizens to funds of state social security and pensions; (b) sums paid as compensation of expenses for rent of housing and maintenance of car for official needs; (c) allowances for business trips.

Foreigners who permanently reside in Ukraine and earn incomes both in Ukraine and abroad must submit declaration on income received to respective tax agency where they conduct their activity in Ukraine. Within one month after day of their arrival in Ukraine, must submit declaration on expected potential income in current year regardless of source of income. Further declaration on earned income shall be submitted within 15 days after expiration of each three month period. At year end, declaration on income actually received, where total sums of earned incomes, expenses and paid tax are mentioned, must be submitted by Feb. 1, of next reporting year. In case of termination of activity or departure from Ukraine within calendar year, foreigners must submit declaration on income actually received within one month prior to departure.

Foreigners enjoy tax exemptions equal with Ukrainins, in same amounts and similar conditions. When submitting declaration to tax agency, foreigners who are entitled child dependent exemptions must submit corresponding documents, confirming existence of dependents.

Imposition of tax on foreigners may be terminated or limited by corresponding international agreements.

In anticipation of new Law "On Individual Income Tax" which is still in drafting process, Decree of President of Ukraine, Sept. 13, 1994 (with modifications introduced according to Presidential Decrees dated Oct. 1, 1995) establishes new income tax rates for citizens. Applicable tax rates are determined on basis of number of untaxed minimum monthly wages ("UMMW").

Monthly taxable aggregate income	*Rates and amounts of tax*
up to 1,700,000.00KBV (from income in amount of one indexable minimum)	is not taxable
1,700,001.00–8,500,000.00KBV (from 1 to 5 indexable minimums)	10% of income in excess of amount of one indexable minimum
8,500,001.00–17,000,000.00KBV (from 5 to 10 indexable minimums)	680,000.00KBV + 15% of amount in excess of 8,500,000.00KBV
17,000,001.00–102,000,000.00KBV (from 10 to 60 indexable minimums)	1,955,000.00KBV + 20% of amount in excess of 17,000,000.00KBV
102,000,001.00–170,000,000.00KBV (from 60 to 100 indexable minimums)	18,955,000.00KBV + 30% of amount in excess of 102,000,000.00KBV
170,000,001.00 and more (over 100 indexable minimums)	39,355,000.00KBV + 40% of amount in excess of 170,000,000.00KBV

Law "On State Register of Individual Payers of Tax and Other Mandatory Payments" (Dec. 22, 1994) was put into effect on Jan. 1, 1996. In accordance with Law, each individual residing in Ukraine and obligated to pay taxes and other mandatory payments, or individual not residing in Ukraine but in accordance with effective legislation obligated to pay taxes in Ukraine is given identification number. Appropriate data on income and paid taxes should be entered under such identification number with tax inspection agency.

Structure of State Tax Service in Ukraine.—State Tax Service of Ukraine is created as agency of Ministry of Finance of Ukraine, and includes Central State Tax Inspection of Ukraine and State Tax Inspections of Republic of Crimea, oblasts, regions, cities and regions of cities.

Inspections of higher level may cancel resolutions of subordinated inspections, in case of their noncompliance with effective legislation.

Resolution of Central State Tax Inspection may be canceled by court. Complaints against actions of State Tax Inspections officials must be submitted to those State Tax Inspections to which they are directly subordinated.

If international agreements of Ukraine establish provisions other than those of Ukrainian tax law, then provisions of international agreement will apply.

Also see topics Customs; Foreign Investment.

TRADEMARKS:

Law "On Protection of Rights for Goods and Services Trademarks", Dec. 15, 1993, governs legal protection of trademarks.

Regulations of Cabinet of Ministers of Ukraine approved by Resolution of Cabinet of Ministers #701, Oct. 10, 1994 establishes procedure for payment of fees for actions connected with protection of rights for inventions, effective models, industrial samples, and trademarks for goods and services.

Regulations approved by Resolution of Ukrainian Parliament, Jan. 19, 1995 establishes procedure for registration and use of rights for inventions, effective models and industrial samples which are state secrets.

Trademark is mark by which goods and services of enterprises are distinguished from similar goods and services of other enterprises. Mark is recognized trademark exclusively by State Committee of Ukraine on intellectual property (hereinafter referred to as "State Patent Office"). Mark presented as trademark must be new, easy to mark goods with and meet requirements of industrial ethics. In particular, trademark may be word, design, ornament, sound signal or combination of such elements. Legal protection is acquired upon registration. Registered mark receives "protection certificate", which is issued to its owner. Owner of trademark, personally or through patent agent, submits application for registration to State Patent Office of Ukraine. Application relates to one mark only and contains such information: written request on registration of trademark; design of trademark, list of goods and services, subject to

See Topical Index in front part of this volume.

TRADEMARKS . . . *continued*

trademark, compiled in accordance with international classification of goods and services for registration of trademark; name of applicant and its legal address. Applicant must pay fee for application to be submitted. Date of application is date of receipt by State Patent Office of such materials as: petition for registration of trademark executed in Ukrainian language in free form; information on applicant and applicant's address executed in Ukrainian language; element, which looks like sign which can be trademark; information on list of goods or services, for which trademark is applied for.

Applicant given two months to introduce modifications. If discrepancy is not eliminated within this period, application is deemed invalid. Otherwise date of application shall be date of receipt by State Patent Office of corrected materials. If, according to results of examination conducted by State Patent Office, mark meets all requirements for trademark to be legally protected, then State Patent Office forwards to applicant decision on registration of trademark. Otherwise application is rejected. On basis of decision on registration of trademark and on condition registration fee is paid, State Patent Office publishes information on issuance of certificate in official bulletin and in state register of trademarks for goods and services. Within one month after state registration State Patent Office issues certificate on trademark of goods and services. Certificate is effective within ten years from date of submission of application to State Patent Office and may be continued by State Patent Office for ten years upon petition of owner, submitted during last year of effectiveness of certificate.

Applicant, within three months upon date of receipt of decision, may contest any decision of State Patent Office on application to Board of Appeal of State Patent Office.

Certificate grants its owner exclusive right to use and dispose trademark at its own discretion, to prohibit other persons and entities to use trademark without owner's permission, except for instances when use of trademark is not deemed as violation of owner's rights under this law. Owner of certificate may transfer ownership right for trademark to any person, who is its successor. Owner may make license agreement for use of trademark with any person. Such agreements are effective only upon their registration with State Patent Office. If trademark is not used or used insufficiently in Ukraine for three years from date of publishing information on issuance of certificate, any person may appeal to court or court of arbitration with petition to terminate certificate before trademark expires. Certificate is not effective when owner does not timely pay fee for continuation of its effectiveness. Certificate may be terminated on basis of decision of court or court of arbitration when trademark is transformed into mark which is generally used for goods and services of definite kind after date of submission of application. No person, besides owner, has right to reregister trademark within three years after termination of certificate. Any person may register trademark in foreign countries. Pursuant to Madrid Agreement On Registration of Trademarks, application for registration of trademarks in foreign countries is submitted to State Patent Office. Applicant or other person under applicant's consent bears expenses for registration of trademark in foreign countries.

Foreigners and persons without citizenship have rights equal with Ukrainian citizens, anticipated by law "On Protection of Rights for Trademarks for Goods and Services", pursuant to international laws of Ukraine or on basis of principle of reciprocity. Foreigners or persons without citizenship who reside or are located outside Ukraine realize their rights in relations with State Patent Office through representatives, registered in accordance with Instruction on representatives on intellectual property, approved by Cabinet of Ministers of Ukraine.

See also topics Copyright; Patents.

TREATIES:

This issue in Ukrainian law is regulated by Law of Ukraine "On International Treaties of Ukraine", dated Dec. 22, 1993.

Law establishes procedure of signing, implementation and denunciation of international treaties of Ukraine with purpose of most appropriately ensuring protection of national interests, and most appropriately achieving aims, tasks and principles of foreign policy of Ukraine in accordance with Constitution of Ukraine.

Law is applied to all international treaties of Ukraine—interstate and intergovernmental treaties—which have been regulated by international law, regardless of their name and form of signing (i.e. Treaty, Agreement, Pact, Protocol, Exchange Letters, etc.).

Generally, provisions of Law correspond to provisions of Vienna Convention on the Law of Treaties of May 23, 1969, to which Ukraine has been party since June 13, 1986.

Law provides that signed and ratified treaties of Ukraine are integral part of Ukrainian legislation, and if norms of international treaties of Ukraine contradict Ukrainian domestic legislation, norms of international treaties prevail because of supremacy of international law.

At present, Ukraine is party to 178 multilateral international conventions and has signed more than 500 bilateral treaties or agreements with 130 countries of the world.

TRUSTS:

See topics Bankruptcy; Wills.

WILLS:

Wills and relations arising from inheritance are governed by arts. 534-564 of Civil Code of Ukraine.

Wills in General.—Individual may dispose of his property at death by will (testament) and may leave all property to other individuals, legal entities or state. Will (testament) must be made by testator personally, it cannot be drawn up by representative or agent. Only person with full capacity to enter into legal transaction may draw up will; otherwise will (testament) will be invalid. Will is deemed invalid if it was executed as result of fraud, violence, threat or was drawn up by individual in absence of conscious or free decision-making or expression of intention.

Ordinary Wills.—Last will and testament must: be written, indicate place and date of its execution; be signed by testator, and be certified by notary. In areas where there are no notary offices, local agency of state power certifies testament. Will may be signed by individual other than testator only when testator cannot sign will as result of physical defects, disease or other reason. Then, at testator's request, will may be signed by another individual other than heir in presence of notary or other officers, as specified in Code, with reason for lack of testator's signature indicated on document.

In Ukraine notary certification of testament is executed by notary in presence of testator only, without witnesses. Notary is authorized to certify testator's will, authenticity of his signature, and capacity thereof by notary stamp. Testament is executed on stamped paper of Form No. 11 which is unique for Ukraine; it must be handwritten by notary according to testator's words in his presence. Information of testament is confidential and is protected by law.

Emergency Wills.—Civil Code of Ukraine (art. 542) specifies instances when wills which are not certified by notary are equal to certified wills drawn up by citizens sailing on Ukrainian ships that are certified during navigation by captains thereof; and wills made by individuals who are in hospitals, sanatoriums, special homes for disabled or old people that are certified by medical personnel thereof, etc.

Modification and Revocation of Will.—Testator may at any time alter or revoke will. Modification or revocation of will may be done either by submitting petition to respective agency where will is executed or by testator's drawing up new will. New will cancels previous one either entirely or in particular provisions thereof which contradict previous will.

Legitimate Portions of Inheritance.—Civil Code of Ukraine (art. 535) specifies persons who inherit certain part of property of deceased irrespective of content of will. They are: disabled or minor descendants (children), natural and adopted, disabled spouse, disabled parents or adopters and dependents, who were supported by deceased for not less than a year before his death. By Ukrainian law, these persons inherit not less than two-thirds of value of inheritance which would have passed to them according to legal procedure. Heirs of second level and grandchildren are not subject to this rule even when there are no heirs of first level. Law establishes specific category of heirs, disabled dependents who were supported by testator for not less than a year. Family relationship is of no importance in such cases; on condition that there are other heirs, dependents will inherit on equal terms with heirs of level that is in process of inheritance; on condition that there are no heirs of first or second level dependents will inherit independently. Dependents are entitled to inherit on two conditions: they must be disabled and supported by testator for not less than a year. Women of 55 and older, men of 60 and older, invalids irrespective of fact that they get pension, persons under age 16 and students under 18 are disabled persons. Disabled person is deemed supported if fully supported by testator or got material aid which was main and permanent source of existence for disabled. Fact that dependent got pension or aid from testator (irrespective of fact whether testator was obligated to provide dependent with this aid or did voluntarily) as well as place of residence (whether dependent resided with testator or separately) is of no importance. Civil Code of Ukraine anticipates right of individual to disinherit either according to current law or by will of those persons who committed intentional crime against his life or life of any heirs.

Foreign Wills.—Validity of will and other legal actions to inheritance are determined by national law of country of testator's latest residence. Capacity of individual to draw up or revoke will, as well as contracts of inheritance, are specified by national law of testator at day of execution thereof. Will and revocation thereof shall not be deemed invalid as result of nonobservance of its form if it is in conformity with requirements of such documents provided by law of Ukraine. If property to be transferred by will is building located in Ukraine, then form of this will, and capacity of individual to draw up or revoke it, is determined by law of Ukraine.

See also topic Notaries Public.

URUGUAY LAW DIGEST REVISER

Curtis, Mallet-Prevost, Colt & Mosle
101 Park Avenue
New York, New York 10178-0061
Telephone: 212-696-6141
Fax: 212-697-1559
Email: CMP-NY@mcimail.com

Reviser Profile

The Firm began in 1830 when two practicing lawyers started a long line of lawyers and law firms extending in an unbroken chain up to the present time. In 1897, the firm name became Curtis, Mallet-Prevost & Colt; in 1925 it was changed to Curtis, Mallet-Prevost, Colt & Mosle. The Firm is now made up of approximately 120 lawyers, including experts who have published extensively on such diverse subjects as international money management, transnational contracts, state contracts, litigation against foreign states, sovereign immunity and the act of state doctrine, and the International Court of Justice. Its principal offices are in New York City. There are branch offices in Paris, London, Frankfurt Am Main, Hong Kong, Washington, D.C., Houston, Texas, Newark, N.J., and Mexico City. The Firm has five departments: Corporate and International; Litigation; Real Estate; Tax; and Trusts and Estates. The corporate and international department acts as general counsel to various public and private corporations and individual entrepreneurs. Clients are in the banking, insurance, securities, manufacturing, real estate and oil and gas industries. In addition, the corporate and international department frequently acts as special counsel to domestic and foreign clients, providing assistance in financing, know-how licensing, the negotiation and drafting of all types of contracts and instruments, counselling on all aspects of corporate law, and establishing the vehicles necessary to enable clients to conduct their domestic and foreign business activities. The Firm's international work permeates all areas of its practice and involves questions of private international law, foreign law and an unusual amount of public and quasi-public international law. Traditionally, much of the Firm's international practice has been concerned with Latin America. The Firm maintains its excellence in that area, with its Mexican affiliate, and also through the expertise of Latin American lawyers based in the New York office. The Firm's international practice has undergone a major expansion beyond Latin America to Europe, Africa and the Near and Far East. The Firm's litigation practice includes commercial litigation and arbitration, and white-collar criminal defense. It has substantial experience in civil aviation matters; it also has represented foreign States in transnational litigation and international arbitration arising out of acts of nationalization and alleged breach of economic development or natural resource supply contracts. Among the Firm's clients in real estate matters are institutional lenders and investors, real estate developers, both individual and corporate, foreign and domestic investors and syndicators. The tax department has substantial experience in all aspects of domestic and international business tax matters and real estate taxation. The matters the tax department deals with on a regular basis include: Taxation of foreign investments; the structuring of corporate transactions, including mergers, acquisitions, liquidations and reorganization; federal and state tax litigation; and tax planning for U.S. and foreign individuals. The trusts and estates department engages in general domestic trusts and estates practice and in tax planning for foreign persons wishing to invest in U.S. assets through offshore trusts and corporations. It represents individuals, trust companies, and banks acting as fiduciaries. It works for various charitable organizations located both in the United States and abroad including private foundations, museums, universities and hospitals. A group of fiduciary accountants with vast experience in the field assists the lawyers of the trusts and estates department. Curtis, Mallet-Prevost, Colt & Mosle has served as a Reviser for most of Latin American Law Digests since 1930.

URUGUAY LAW DIGEST

(The following is a list of all Topics, including cross-references, covered in this Digest.)

URUGUAY LAW DIGEST

Revised for 1997 edition by

CURTIS, MALLET-PREVOST, COLT & MOSLE, of the New York Bar.

(Abbreviations used are: C. C., Civil Code; C. Com., Code of Commerce; C. C. P., Code of Civil Procedure; C. M., Code of Minors. Numbers refer to the articles of these codes.)

ABSENTEES: See topic Death.

ACKNOWLEDGMENTS:

Documents which require authentication are executed before a notary public, who in the instrument itself certifies to its execution. He retains the original and issues certified copies. (Notarial Law 1421 of Dec. 31, 1878 as am'd).

Documents executed abroad are accepted as valid if executed in accordance with the laws of the respective country and duly legalized to be effective in Uruguay. (C. C. 6, 1574-1580). Customary procedure with respect to documents executed in U.S. is to have signature of American notary certified by county clerk or other competent official and signature of latter certified by Uruguayan diplomatic or consular representative. (C. C. P. 72). Powers of attorney granted abroad must also be translated and notarized in Uruguay. (Decree 155 of Feb. 22, 1968 as am'd by Decree 175/992 of May 5, 1992).

ACTIONS:

Actions for Death.—See topic Death, subhead Actions for Death.

Limitation of.—See topic Prescription, subhead Limitation of Actions.

ADMINISTRATION:

See topic Executors and Administrators.

ADOPTION:

C.C. arts. 243-251, C.M. arts. 156-172; Law 10674 of Nov. 20, 1945, as am'd.

ADVERSE POSSESSION: See topic Prescription.

AGENCY: See topic Principal and Agent.

ALIENS:

In general aliens enjoy the same civil rights and have the same civil obligations as citizens. They may acquire property and carry on business and industries. When they own local property or carry on personal activities, they can acquire Uruguayan citizenship after five years of residence, this term is reduced to three years if they have settled family. (Const., art. 78; Resolution of Apr. 8, 1926; C. C. 22; Immigration Decree of Feb. 28, 1947 as am'd; Decrees of Oct. 25, 1949; Nov. 5, 1959 and 104 of Feb. 21, 1967 which grants special benefits to technicians and skilled workers).

ALIMONY: See topic Divorce.

ASSIGNMENTS:

As towards third persons an assignee of a credit is not considered as owner until the debtor is notified. The notification is effected by exhibiting the credit document, which must bear a note signed by the assignor and designate the assignee. The assignment is ineffective as towards the debtor so long as he is not notified and does not consent to the assignment or renew his obligation toward the new creditor; when it becomes effective the debtor is bound to pay the new creditor and no one else. If the debtor does not wish to acknowledge the assignee as creditor he must declare his refusal within three days after being notified; after this period he is considered to have consented. If he refuses his consent he may make use of all defenses against the assignee which he might have alleged against the assignor.

The assignment of a credit comprises all accessory rights such as guarantees, pledges and mortgages. An assignor in good faith is liable for the existence and legality of the credit unless he assigns it as doubtful; but he is not liable for the solvency of the debtor or guarantors unless otherwise agreed or unless the insolvency was publicly known and occurred prior to the assignment. When the solvency of the debtor is guaranteed by agreement, such guarantee refers to present solvency and not to future solvency, unless otherwise agreed. An assignor in bad faith is liable for the solvency of the debtor and for all expenses and damages. (C. C. 1757-1766; C. Com. 563-571).

The foregoing provisions are not applicable to bills of exchange, promissory notes, bearer shares and other mercantile credit documents which are governed by the Code of Commerce or special laws. See topic Bills and Notes.

An assignment of credits must be recorded when it involves rights on real property. See topic Records.

ASSIGNMENTS FOR BENEFIT OF CREDITORS:

An assignment for benefit of creditors may be made by a debtor who in consequence of inevitable accident is unable to pay his debts. The debtor may request it notwithstanding stipulations to the contrary, and the judge must admit it upon a hearing. Any creditor may demand that the debtor prove that he is without fault. Creditors must accept the assignment unless the debtor: (a) Has been convicted of theft, forgery or fraudulent bankruptcy; (b) has obtained deductions or extensions from his creditors; (c) has squandered his property; (d) has not truthfully set forth the condition of his business or has resorted to fraudulent practices. Property not subject to attachment need not be included in the assignment. After the assignment has been offered and while it is under advisement by the judge the assignor cannot be sued by any creditor. Upon the admission of the assignment the creditors may dispose of the property and its revenues until their credits are paid, but the assignment does not convey the ownership of the property to the creditors, and the credits are extinguished only up to the amount realized from the property. With respect to property acquired after the assignment, the debtor may retain what is necessary for a modest subsistence, according to his class and circumstances, and is obliged to pay any balance when his fortune improves. After an assignment the creditors may by majority vote leave the administration of the property to the debtor and make such agreements with him as they consider advisable, without prejudice to the rights of the preferred creditors. (C. C. 1494, 2359-2367).

ASSOCIATIONS:

The law grants legal personalty to the state, the treasury, the municipalities and the Catholic Church. Other institutions and associations which are recognized by the authorities are also considered as legal entities with civil rights and obligations. (C. C. 21).

In order to be recognized as a legal entity a resolution must be obtained from Ministry of Culture and Education. For that purpose articles of association and by-laws must be submitted and recorded in special registry called "registry of juridical persons." Record must state name and object of association, its domicile, date of resolution acknowledging it, its duration or that it is founded for indeterminate time, its property or capital, extensions, modifications of by-laws and dates of respective approvals, etc. (Decree Apr. 13, 1925).

ATTACHMENT:

(C.C.P. 260, 311-317, 335, 336, 353-362, 377 et seq.).

Provisional attachment may be issued when court considers it is necessary for protection of creditor's right when satisfaction of credit may be otherwise lost. Creditor must give bond to secure costs and damages.

Attachments will also be issued in summary actions. Such actions may be brought on certain documents when they carry obligations of paying specific and past due sums. Such documents are: (a) Public instruments; (b) acknowledged private documents; (c) bank checks, bills of exchange or promissory notes; (d) acknowledged merchandise invoices; (e) final judgments and arbitration awards; (f) credits guaranteed by mortgage or pledge; (g) settlements; (h) agreements executed in conciliation proceedings.

A third person may intervene in the attachment alleging ownership of the property attached. The proceeding which follows depends on whether or not the property is recorded at Public Registry.

BANKRUPTCY:

A merchant who ceases in the current payment of his mercantile obligations is considered in a state of bankruptcy. A merchant debtor or a mercantile company, except corporations, may avoid a declaration of bankruptcy by making an agreement with creditors, which may be extrajudicial or judicial.

For the purpose of making an extrajudicial agreement the debtor must apply to the court and file: (1) A draft settlement signed by (a) the majority of creditors representing at least three-fourths the total liabilities, and (b) the majority of persons representing at least three-fourths the mercantile liabilities; (2) explanation of the causes of the suspension of payments; (3) a statement of the assets and liabilities. The majority of the creditors holding mercantile credits may appoint one or more supervisors to watch over the business of the debtor. The judge orders the publication of the agreement and grants the debtor a provisional moratorium which suspends the execution of personal judgments. Other suits may continue to judgment but merchandise belonging to the business of the debtor cannot be attached in executions for personal credits. Suits may be brought and attachments issued on privileged credits. The agreement is approved by the court unless there is opposition from creditors. (C. Com. 1524-1530).

For the purpose of making a judicial agreement the debtor files his petition with the same documents required for an extrajudicial agreement except that in place of the draft agreement signed by the creditors he submits the bases on which he proposes a settlement. The judge grants a provisional delay, designates an accountant to watch over the business and make a report, and calls a meeting of creditors. Such meeting is held, presided over by the judge. The creditors vote on the debtor's proposition; if they accept, the judge approves it; if they reject, a declaration of bankruptcy follows.

During the pendency of the proceedings relating to the creditors' agreement the debtor cannot sell, encumber or lease his real property or sell or pledge his personal property without permission of the judge nor can he leave the country without such permission. Privileged creditors cannot vote on the settlement unless they waive their preferences; the waiver is without effect if the settlement is not approved by the judge.

A declaration of bankruptcy may be made on the petition of a debtor or of one or more creditors or by the judge of his own motion. Upon the declaration of bankruptcy the business of the bankrupt must be liquidated.

The bankruptcy of a partnership carries with it the bankruptcy of the general partners, but the bankruptcy of a partner does not involve the bankruptcy of the partnership. A bankruptcy declared in a foreign country does not prejudice creditors in Uruguay with respect to their rights as to the property situated in Uruguay or with respect to settlements they may have made with the bankrupt. When a bankruptcy has been declared in Uruguay the creditors appearing in a bankruptcy abroad are entitled only to what remains after the creditors of the Uruguayan bankruptcy have been paid.

A merchant who ceases payments must within five days file with the judge a statement of the condition of his business, setting forth the reasons for his failure. Creditors may request the declaration of bankruptcy if they present documents on which execution might issue and against which the debtor alleged no valid defense when payment was demanded. A bankruptcy may be (a) Casual; (b) culpable; (c) fraudulent.

BANKRUPTCY . . . *continued*

From the time of the declaration of bankruptcy the bankrupt loses the administration of his property. Suits cannot be prosecuted against him but must be directed against the receiver. All his unmatured debts fall due. (C. Com. 1531-1597).

The following acts of the bankrupt within sixty days before the declaration of bankruptcy are void: (a) Gratuitous gifts and alienations; (b) conveyances of real estate in payment of unmatured debts. The following acts may be annulled if performed in fraud of creditors: (a) Mercantile contracts or operations within ten days before the bankruptcy; (b) loans within six months before the bankruptcy if actual delivery is not proved; (c) alienations of real estate in the month preceding the bankruptcy; (d) all contracts made within two years before the bankruptcy in which fraudulent simulation is proved. All sums paid by the bankrupt within fifteen days prior to the bankruptcy, for obligations maturing later, must be returned to the estate. (C. Com. 1602-1612).

A receiver is appointed and a meeting of creditors called to discuss and approve the credits. The creditors appoint a vigilance committee. Propositions between the bankrupt and the creditors may be made with the approval of two-thirds the creditors representing three-fourths the approved credits or three-fourths the creditors representing two-thirds the approved credits.

The personal credits are divided into four grades; the first three representing preferred credits which are paid in their order, and any balance is used for the payment of credits of the fourth class. The property of the bankrupt is sold by the receiver.

A bankrupt may be discharged: (a) If the bankruptcy was casual; (b) if, in the case of a culpable or fraudulent bankruptcy, the bankrupt has served his punishment or the same has prescribed; (c) if he pays all his debts or is released by creditors representing three-fourths of the total liabilities; (d) upon the elapsing of five years after the bankruptcy, if it is proved that no estate remains, that he has no further property and that at least 50% of the creditors who appeared have been paid. (C. Com. 1613-1781).

As to priorities in case of bankruptcy, see topic Liens.

BILLS AND NOTES:

Law 14.701 of Sept. 12, 1977 as am'd, which regulates existing provisions of Commercial Code governing this subject, supersedes such provisions as follows:

Bills and notes must contain: (a) Name of type of instrument; (b) place and date of issue; (c) right evidenced by instrument; (d) place and date to exercise such right; (e) signature of maker. Payment of bills and notes may be guaranteed, absolutely or partially, by guarantee called "aval", which must appear in writing on instrument or on document annexed thereto, and must bear signature of person granting same (avalista). Powers of representation to bind oneself in instrument may be granted by power of attorney (mandato) or by letter addressed to presumptive holder. Instruments may be nominative (to order of given person), which are presumed to be to order, or to bearer. Order instruments are transferred by endorsements and delivery.

Endorsement of bills and notes must contain following in order to be valid: (a) Name of endorsee; (b) type of endorsement; (c) place and date; (d) signature of endorser or his representative. Blank endorsements must bear endorser's signature. Endorsements may transfer title, right to prosecute action or be by way of guarantee. Transfer of bearer instruments is effected by mere delivery thereof.

Bills of exchange must contain, in addition to aforementioned requirements: (a) Unconditional order to pay sum certain; (b) name of drawee; (c) maturity date; (d) name of payee. Bills without indication of maturity date will be considered drawn at sight. Bill may be drawn: (a) To order of drawer; (b) against drawer himself; or (c) to order of third party. Drawer guarantees payment and may guarantee acceptance.

Endorsement transfers title to instrument, and can be made in favor of drawee, drawer or of third party. It must be written on draft or on document attached thereto, and signed by endorser, and may fail to designate beneficiary, in which case it is blank endorsement. Holder of blank endorsement may: (a) Fill in blank space with its name or name of another person; (b) reendorse bill of exchange in blank or in favor of another person, (c) deliver bill to third party, without endorsing it.

Acceptance must be written on draft with word "acepto" and must be signed by drawee. It may be limited to part of amount. By acceptance, drawee assumes obligation to pay bill of exchange at maturity. Bill may be drawn: (a) At signt; (b) at certain time after signt; (c) at certain time after its date of issue; (d) at fixed date. Payment of bill at sight must be made when it is presented. Period for drafts drawn at certain time after sight is counted from date of acceptance or protest. Holder of bill payable at fixed date, or at certain date or at sight must be presented for payment on day on which bill must be paid, or on one of two immediately succeeding working days. Payment of bill which matures on nonworking day must be made on first working day succeeding same.

Protest for failure to accept or pay must be made before notary. Protest for failure to accept does not exempt holder of bill from obligation to protest it again if not paid. Draft to be protested must be presented to notary within two days following date on which it was to hve been accepted or paid, and must be protested within two immediately succeeding working days from submission to notary.

Actions for nonacceptance and for nonpayment are set forth in Arts. 99-108 of this law.

Cancellation by judge may occur in case of loss, theft or destruction of bill. Bond must be posted to safeguard rights of holder.

Prescription for actions will be: (a) Three years against acceptor; (b) one year against endorsers and drawer; (c) six months for action of one endorser against other endorsers and drawer. Prescription for action for recovery of money is one year.

Promissory notes and similar documents must contain in addition: (a) Words promissory note (note) in text thereof; (b) unconditional promise to pay sum certain. Only clauses which may be included are: Payment of current or moratorium interest in event of default due to expiration of maturity date; designation of domicile; choice of forum. Installment payments may be agreed upon. Maturity clauses other than those indicated in Art. 78 of this law, are void. There is refutable presumption that promissory notes are authentic and will be entitled to executive action without protest or judicial recognition of signature. They are subject to same provisions as those governing bills of exchange, to extent applicable.

Checks are subject to general provisions of this law and to those relating to bills of exchange, as well as to Law 14,412 of July 27, 1975 and its regulations, to extent that they are not opposed to it.

CHATTEL MORTGAGES:

In addition to the system of "rural pledge" or "industrial pledge" an extension of existing laws to cover chattel mortgages on automobiles or on machinery or equipment of an identifiable nature is allowed by Law 12367 of Jan. 8, 1957. Aircraft may be mortgaged. (Law 14305 of Nov. 29, 1974). Contracts of rural and industrial pledge may be made by owners of urban or rural industries, or factories, shops or agrarian establishments. Creditors in such case can be only Bank of the Republic, credit institutions, commercial institutions keeping books in proper form, rural banks, and vendors of personal property used in any of industries above mentioned, for unpaid purchase price. Following may be encumbered under these contracts: (a) Live stock and its products; (b) personal property used in rural exploitation of industrial establishments; (c) fruits of any kind produced in the agricultural year in which contract is made, timber, raw material, products of mines and of industries; (d) machinery and agricultural implements; (e) implements of industrial or manual labor but only in favor of vendor; (f) trademarks, patents, privileges, exemptions, insurance and other rights considered industrial property; (g) things which gradually substitute or complement original articles. Debtor continues to hold property in name of creditor but in some cases custody can be delivered to third person. Object encumbered is liable for loan, interest and costs.

The contract must be made in writing and does not take effect either between the contracting parties or towards third persons until it is recorded in the registry office at the place where the property is situated.

A debtor cannot make a new contract regarding the encumbered property without the consent of the creditor nor can such property be transferred without notifying the creditor. If the debtor alienates or further encumbers such property he is liable to punishment. Abandonment of the encumbered property causes the debt to mature and gives rise to punishment.

Upon the registration of the pledge the registrar issues a certificate stating the names of the parties, the amount and maturity of the debt, conditions of the same, kind, amount and location of the articles pledged, date of recording and name of the person to whom the certificate is issued. These certificates are transmissible by endorsement and can be used as the basis of a summary action against the property of the insurance thereon.

Registration must be renewed every five years counted from date of registration if contract is not renewed. Debtor may pay at any time. (Laws 5649 of Mar. 21, 1918, regulations Decree of Aug. 20, 1918, 8292 of Sept. 24, 1928; Regulations Nov. 29, 1928; Law 12367 of Jan. 8, 1957).

COLLATERAL SECURITY:

See topic Pledges.

COMMERCIAL REGISTER:

See topic Records.

COMMUNITY PROPERTY:

See topic Husband and Wife.

CONSTITUTION AND GOVERNMENT:

Uruguay is democratic republic with representative form of government. Legislative power is vested in General Assembly which has two Chambers with members elected by direct popular vote for five years. Executive power is vested in President acting with ministers or with council of ministers. President is elected by direct popular vote for five years. To hold these offices for new term, five years must elapse from expiration date of first term. Judicial power is vested in Supreme Court of Justice created to regulate administration of Justice. Government and administration of each of departments in which Republic is divided is vested in "intendente" (executive), and Junta (legislative board). Semi-autonomous administrative agencies provide services for and regulate various industrial and commercial activities, their degree of decentralization being determined by law. (Constitution of 1967 as am'd).

CONTRACTS:

(Civil Code, Book IV, Commercial Code Arts. 191-298; 935-1028; 299-934; 1159-1432. Law 8888; Sept. 28, 1932 on computation of contractual periods and terms.)

For existence of contract, law requires following: Capable parties, valid consent, licit object, lawful cause and licit form. Legal capacity is acquired at 21 years of age. (See topic Infancy.) Contracts obtained by fraud are void. Contracts are binding with respect to terms stated therein. Contracts may be made on future objects, provided they are determinable but, they cannot be made on right to inherit from living person even with his consent. Cause of onerous contract is advantage or benefit that one party receives from other. In gratuitous contracts it is liberality of giver. Consent must be obtained without violence, mistake or fraud. Oral proposal is without effect if not accepted immediately unless offeror wishes to maintain offer. Contract made by correspondence is perfected at place and at moment acceptance reaches offeror. Until that time, offeror may withdraw his offer unless he has agreed to await answer or to maintain offer for fixed time. Conditional acceptance is binding when party who proposed condition receives reply from other party advising that he agrees to condition. If no time was fixed, offeror who has agreed to await answer and who receives acceptance within 24 hours, when residing in same city, or within 30 days plus time necessary for communications when residing elsewhere, is bound by contract if he does not notify acceptor of change of intention. If contract, in order to exist, requires additional legal formality, delivery of object or compliance with formalities are necessary. Either party may freely withdraw if formality is not fulfilled unless previous contract compels it to make formal contract.

In computing period of time by number of days, date of contract is not counted. For periods computed by months, months are counted without taking into account different

See Topical Index in front part of this volume.

CONTRACTS . . . *continued*
number of days they have. If due date falls on holiday, time is extended to first business day thereafter. If no period of time is stipulated and no period is fixed by law, fulfillment of obligation is due ten days after its date. Mercantile contracts are governed by Commercial Code and by uses and traditions of trade. These rules are supplemented by Civil Code. Commercial character of contract does not depend on whether contracting parties are merchants, but on its object or purpose. Commercial Code defines under each kind of contract features which make it commercial. In contract of sale transfer of ownership is effected by actual or implied delivery of object only; as long as this transfer has not happened, vendor continues as owner.

Valid contracts bind parties to comply with obligations expressly contracted. Terms of contract may be modified only by mutual agreement. Contract must be fulfilled in good faith and obligates parties to perform not only what is expressly stated therein but anything else in its nature required by equity, usage or law. Contract that is relatively void is extinguished by judicial declaration of its nullity. Relative nullity occurs whenever there is defect in consent or when one contracting party has relative incapacity. Relative incapacity may be invoked only by party who contracted without necessary capacity or whose consent was defective. Nullity produced by unlawful object or cause or resulting from omission of necessary formality is absolute. Absolute nullity must be declared by judge and it may be invoked by any person having interest, except one who benefited from invalid payment. Contracts do not have consequences as to third parties unless certain formalities have been met, e.g. recording in appropriate register. Stipulation in contract in favor of third party is legal.

Applicable Law.—Parties may stipulate that contracts shall be governed by foreign legislation and jurisdiction, provided there exists link with said legislation. However, said stipulation is not valid if contracts refer to matters of exclusive jurisdiction of Uruguayan courts, e.g. contracts to be performed in Uruguay.

Public Contracts.—(Law 15637 of Sept. 28, 1984 and Law 15903 of Nov. 10, 1987, Decree 108/992 of Mar. 16, 1992). Contracts executed with Government, State agencies and State enterprises are subject to special rules.

CONVEYANCES:

See topics Deeds; Public Instruments.

COPYRIGHT:

Copyright may cover any literary, scientific or artistic creation, including software, books, pictures, maps, music, theatrical works, moving picture scripts, paintings, drawings, sculptures, etc. It comprises right to alienate, publish, reproduce, translate, execute and circulate in any manner. It is obtained by inscription in copyright registry and filing two copies, photographs or reproductions in National Library; copyright is granted after announcement is made in official newspaper. Inscription must be requested within two years after publication of work in Uruguay, or within three years if work is published abroad and author is Uruguayan. Assignments are recorded in same registry. Imprisonment is provided for illegal edition or reproduction of intellectual works.

The author preserves his right during his life and his heirs or legatees keep it for 40 years thereafter. An assignment is effective until 15 years after the author's death, whereupon the right reverts to his heirs. In case of successive assignments the author is entitled to 25% of the increased value of his work. (Copyright Law 9739 of Dec. 17, 1937, as am'd by Law 9769 of Feb. 25, 1938 and Law 15913 of Nov. 27, 1987; Regulation by Decree of Apr. 21, 1938 as am'd by Decree 154 of Apr. 11, 1989).

CORPORATIONS:

(Law 16060 of Sept. 4, 1989).

Corporations are designated by name accompanied by words "Sociedad Anónima" or abbreviation "S.A." At least two shareholders are required for organization and continued legal existence of corporation.

Corporate capital is divided into shares. Responsibility of shareholders is limited to their shares. 50% of capital shall be subscribed and 25% paid in on incorporation. Minimum capital in local currency is required by law.

There are "open" and "closed" corporations. "Open" corporations are: (1) Those which have their shares traded on Stock Exchange; (2) those established by public subscription; or (3) those which issue debentures. "Closed" corporations are those which do not fulfill any of above requirements. Corporations may be established by private or public subscriptions. Corporate documents may be private or public documents. In any case they should contain: (1) Name of shareholders; (2) name and domicile of corporation; (3) purpose; (4) duration; (5) capital, kind, number, value of shares, manner and time of payment; (6) organization, administration and control by stockholders; (7) distribution of dividends; and (8) any other agreement such as stockholders' meetings, etc.

Corporate documents require administrative authorization. Corporate documents and respective authorization must be recorded in Public Register of Commerce and extract of such documents published. Any amendment of by-laws must be filed and published in like manner.

When corporation is established by public subscription, promoters draw up prospectus. It must be approved by administrative authority and recorded at Register of Commerce. Organization meeting must be called after subscription period, to decide on incorporation; approval of deed of incorporation, report of promoters, evaluation of contribution other than money, and other matters.

Management.—Corporation may be managed by administrator or by board of directors appointed by stockholders' meeting for one year period. Directors may be reelected and need not be shareholders. Open corporations must be managed by board of directors. Stockholders' meetings are ordinary, extraordinary or special. Ordinary meetings are held at least once a year in order to approve financial statements, distribution of profits, appointment of members of board of directors and comptroller (síndico).

Extraordinary meetings may be held at any time to decide matters especially enumerated by law such as modification of articles of incorporation, dissolution, issuance of bonds, etc. Stockholders may be represented by proxies.

Open corporations are subject to government supervision.

Stock.—Capital, number of shares and par value must be specified. Shares may be common, preferred or "de goce" according to rights granted to shareholders. Shares may be nominative or bearer shares. Shares may be represented by certificates, but so long as they are not fully paid up they must be nominative. Amount of corporate capital and value of shares may be increased or reduced by modification of articles of incorporation. Corporations are authorized to issue debentures which may be converted into shares.

Dissolution.—Corporations are dissolved by expiration of term, when all shares are owned by one person, resolution of stockholders, conclusion of purpose for which it was constituted, bankruptcy, or loss of more than 75% of its capital.

Foreign corporations must comply with same requisites as local companies with regard to registration and publication of corporate documents. Their acts and operations are subject to local laws.

Corporations, limited partnerships issuing shares of stock can own or exploit land in rural areas, provided stock of owner company is represented by nominative shares and their stockholders are physical persons; unless corporation has industrial purpose or land is used for reforestation for energy purpose. (Law 13,608 of Sept. 8, 1967 as am'd by Law 13,892 of Oct. 19, 1970; Law 14,095 of Nov. 17, 1972; Law 14,252 of Aug. 22, 1974; art. 494 of Law 16230 of Nov. 1, 1992 and Decree 59/993 of Feb. 2, 1993).

COURTS:

Justice is administered by: (a) Supreme Court of Justice and for Contentious-Administrative Matters which reviews decisions of courts of appeals totally or partially revoking judgments of lower courts and has various additional functions; (b) courts of appeals which hear appeals from law judges, in civil, criminal and labor cases; (c) judges of first instance (juzgados letrados) for labor, civil, criminal, family, customs, and contentious-administrative matters over certain amount; (d) departmental judges with jurisdiction in civil and contentious-administrative matters; (e) court of misdemeanors; and (f) justices of peace with jurisdiction in certain minor civil, commercial, contentious-administrative and fiscal matters in rural areas. (Const., arts. 233-261, 307-321, Laws 15750 of June 24, 1985 as am'd by Law 15860 of Apr. 4, 1987 and 15524 of Jan. 9, 1984 as am'd).

CURRENCY:

Monetary unit is Peso Uruguayo ($) divided into 100 centésimos. (Law 16226 of Oct. 26, 1991 and Decree 636/992 of Dec. 22, 1992).

See also topic Exchange Control.

CURTESY:

No estate by curtesy. As to rights of surviving husband see topics Descent and Distribution; Husband and Wife; Wills.

CUSTOMS:

Common External Tariff approved by member countries of southern common market (MERCOSUR) is in effect; each member country has list of goods excluded from common external tariff and subject to their own duty rates. Most goods traded among member countries are not subject to tariff or quota restrictions.

DEATH:

Where a person has disappeared for a period of four years, or six years if he left an attorney in fact, he may be judicially declared an absentee. The declaration may not be made until one year after publication in a newspaper. Administration of his estate may then be provisionally granted. If the absence continues for 15 years thereafter, or if 80 years elapse from the date of the absentee's birth, an interested party may petition for definitive administration of the absentee's property and any security given for the provisionsl administration is released. (C. C. arts. 55-80).

All deaths must be recorded in the Civil Register of the place where death occurs. Application for death certificates must be made to the Chief of the Civil Registry. A nominal fee is charged.

Actions for Death.—There is no statute creating wrongful death action, although this could be supported by the general provision of Civil Code (arts. 1319 et seq.) on torts. Tort actions are limited to four years.

DECEDENTS' ESTATES:

See topics Descent and Distribution; Executors and Administrators; Wills.

DEEDS:

Instruments executed before a public notary are written in his protocol; they may be written by hand with indelible ink or by typewriter. They begin by stating date and place. No abbreviations or initials may be used to designate names or places and all amounts must be written out. Parties are identified by stating their business, their residence, whether they are single, married or widowed and in latter cases name of spouse, and other data. Amendments and corrections in body of instrument are not permitted but must be indicated by notary before signature. Notary retains original signed copy in his protocol and delivers certified copy to parties requesting same. For further certified copies judicial order is required. Certified copies may be typewritten or printed but indelible ink must be used. In court notarial copies have effect of originals. (Law 1421 of Dec. 31, 1878, as am'd, Resolution 4716 of 1971).

See also topics Husband and Wife; Records.

DEPOSITIONS:

All testimony of witnesses is by deposition. The party desiring the examination of witnesses must make a petition to the court stating the name and residence of the witness and indicating facts on which witnesses are to be examined. Each witness must be examined separately and contrary party may cross-examine. Deposition is written out and signed by witness, with counter-signature of judge. When witness resides

See Topical Index in front part of this volume.

DEPOSITIONS . . . *continued*
away from place of trial, deposition is taken by judge of his residence under letters rogatory. (C. C. P. 142, 154-164).

DESCENT AND DISTRIBUTION:

In case of intestate succession the estate of the decedent goes to his legitimate or natural descendants, without prejudice to the marital portion pertaining to the surviving spouse. If there are no legitimate or natural descendants estate goes to legitimate ascendants of nearest degree and to spouse; in this case it is divided into two parts. If there is only one of said classes of heirs, such class receives entire estate.

In case of lack of classes of heirs above mentioned, estate goes one-half to legitimate or natural brothers and sisters and one-half to adopted children; if one or other of these two classes is lacking, other receives entire estate.

In case of the lack of two classes of heirs above considered, estate goes to adopting father or mother and to legitimate or natural collaterals from third and fourth degree.

The right of representation exists, and a deceased heir, or an heir who cannot or will not accept the inheritance, are represented by their descendants. The legitimate descendants and the natural descendants acknowledged or declared as such have the right of representation.

The marital portion is one-fourth of the estate, unless there are legitimate descendants or natural descendants acknowledged or declared as such, in which case it is equal to share of each child as obligatory heir. (See topic Wills.) If spouse is left more by will than amount of marital portion, excess is considered as testamentary inheritance.

If there is a total lack of legal heirs, the estate goes to the public treasury. (C. C. 36, 881-895, 1011-1036).

DIVORCE:

Divorce dissolves marriage bond. It may be demanded in following cases: (a) Adultery of either spouse; (b) conviction of attempted murder of spouse; (c) grave cruelty or insults; (d) proposal of husband to prostitute wife; (e) attempt of either spouse to prostitute children or connivance in such prostitution; (f) continual quarrels and disputes which make married life impossible; (g) when one of spouses is sentenced to penitentiary for over ten years; (h) abandonment for over three years; (i) after three years of uninterrupted separation provided one of spouses consents; (j) incapacity of one spouse due to permanent illness declared by court; (k) mutual consent; (l) will of wife alone.

After decreed sentence of divorce, former spouse must help to maintain economic status of incapacitated party jointly with other persons obliged to provide support.

In any case provisional separation of spouses is decreed by court. Husband may demand that house be specified where wife is to live during proceedings. Temporary situation of minor children is determined by court, as well as amounts to be paid for alimony of wife and maintenance of children and for wife's expenses in proceedings. After provisional separation is decreed spouses may make agreements as to definitive custody of children, except when cause of divorce is attempt to prostitute children. If there is no agreement or until one is made, children below five years of age are confided to mother; with respect to those over five, judge decides after hearing parents.

A divorce by will of wife alone can be decreed only after two years of marriage.

In the case of a divorce by mutual consent, the spouses must personally appear before the judge who endeavors to reconcile them. If there is no reconciliation, judge will decree provisional separation and judge specifies period of three months after which spouses again appear to reaffirm their desire to be divorced. If at such hearing spouses persist in their desire to be divorced, divorce is decreed but if spouses do not appear case is closed.

For the divorce by the will of the wife alone she must appear before the judge, who summons the parties for a hearing for the purpose of endeavoring to reconcile them. If the husband does not appear and if no reconciliation is effected, the judge designates a new hearing to be held after six months, at which the wife must again appear to reiterate her petition. At the second hearing the judge designates a third hearing to be held after one year, when the wife must again reaffirm her petition. At such final hearing the judge once more summons the spouses to endeavor to reconcile them. If the husband does not appear or if there is no reconciliation, the divorce is decreed.

The competent court is the court of the husband's domicile, except for divorce by the will of the wife alone, in which case it is the court of the wife's domicile. Domicile is considered to mean the permanent residence or establishment.

Divorce dissolves marital community. If cause was adultery guilty party loses property rights in marriage community. (See topic Husband and Wife.)

A separation may be granted for the same causes which are causes for divorce except mutual consent and the sole desire of the wife. Three years after the judgment of separation either of the spouses may request that it be converted into a divorce. In such case the divorce is granted as a matter of course and the other spouse is notified. (C. C. 145-197).

DOWER:

No dower estate as in American law. For rights of widow, see topics Descent and Distribution; Husband and Wife; Wills.

ENVIRONMENT:

(Law 16466 of Jan. 26, 1994).

Environmental impact statements are mandatory for projects having environmental impact, such as, mining, petroleum, oil and gas pipelines, energy generating plants, ports, airports, railroads, roads, manufacturing plants, disposal of hazardous waste and dams, among others in order to obtain authorization to start projects. Failure to comply with obligation to prevent damage to environment, clean-up plans and with legal provisions are sanctioned with temporary suspension of projects. Environmental liability is regulated by general principles of Civil Code which creates obligation to indemnify for damages caused or to restore environment to previous state. Environmental protection for areas such as water pollution and handling and treatment of hazardous waste are regulated by specific legislation.

EXCHANGE CONTROL:

Law 12670 of Dec. 17, 1959 constitutes enabling legislation for current provisions of foreign exchange regulation. Currency transactions are made only through Central Bank or for its account and order. Purchase and sale of foreign currency is governed by supply and demand. Central Bank administers fund for stabilization and protection of currency, which through intervention in free market prevents speculation and variations in currency quotations. There are no import restrictions, but imports are subject to minimum surtax of 10% collected by Central Bank, some imports are exempted. (Decree 125 of Mar. 2, 1977).

Law 14,629 of Jan. 5, 1977 as am'd, and its regulations established single tax applied to imports with basic rate of 25% based on value in customs as defined by Brussels Council for Customs Corporation except when official c.i.f. prices exist. This rate may be increased, reduced or eliminated by Executive Power.

EXECUTIONS:

(C.C.P. 387-396).

When attachment has been levied and order of execution is issued, attached property is appraised and thereupon offered for public auction. Sale is made on basis of two thirds of appraised value, unless parties had agreed by contract that it may be made to highest bidder. If there is no bidder, new auction is called on basis of 50% of appraisement. If there is no bidder, property is adjudicated to plaintiff unless he decides to waive this right and keep his credit.

EXECUTORS AND ADMINISTRATORS:

A testator may appoint one or more executors. If there is no executor appointed or the appointee does not qualify, the execution of the last will of the testator pertains to the heirs.

Minors cannot act as executors. Executor may decline to accept office, but after acceptance he must discharge it, except in cases where attorney in fact is permitted to resign. See topic Principal and Agent.

The office of executor cannot be delegated, but the executor may appoint agents for whose acts he is liable. When there are several executors, they are jointly liable unless their powers were divided by the testator or the judge and they restricted themselves to their respective duties.

An executor must make a formal inventory of the estate unless the heirs are all persons capable of administering their property and unanimously determine that no inventory be made. He must also summon the creditors of the estate by newspaper advertisements. The powers and obligations given by the law to executors cannot be amplified nor waived by the testator.

An executor may be removed on the petition of the heirs for his fault or fraud. If no compensation was designated by the testator the judge determines it, taking into consideration the value of the estate and the amount of work involved. The office continues during the time designated by the testator. If no time was designated, the period is one year, subject to extension. Upon terminating his office the executor must render accounts. (C. C. 964-997).

EXEMPTIONS:

The following earnings and property are not subject to attachment or execution: (a) All wages and salaries of private and public employees and retirement payments, but one-third of rights may be attached for alimony debts and one half for child support debts; (b) articles of personal use of debtor and his family and household articles except parlor furniture which may be attached if debt is for price of furniture or for rental of house; (c) professional books; (d) machinery and instruments used by debtor to teach science or art except if debt is for their price; (e) foodstuffs and combustibles in possession of debtor sufficient for consumption of his family for three months; (f) purely personal rights such as that of habitation; (g) real property given to debtor with declaration that it is not subject to attachment, provided its value was judicially appraised at time of delivery, but any additional value may be attached; (h) national or municipal taxes and revenues; (i) public properties; (j) religious articles; (k) private property in cemeteries; (l) uniforms and military equipment; (m) author's copyrights. (C. C. P. 381; C. C. 1180; Laws of June 25, 1908, 10052 of Sept. 19, 1941 and 12417 of Oct. 8, 1957).

Homestead Exemption.—See topic Homesteads.

FORECLOSURE: See topic Mortgages.

FOREIGN CORPORATIONS: See topic Corporations.

FOREIGN EXCHANGE:

See topic Exchange Control.

FOREIGN INVESTMENT:

Decree 808 of Oct. 10, 1974 governs foreign investments. Any capital coming from abroad in any form, such as foreign exchange, machinery, etc., shall be considered as foreign investment. Any corporation with more than 50% foreign capital shall be considered as Foreign Capital Corporation. It is incumbent upon Executive Branch to authorize foreign investments, by means of Investment Contract, except where investment is for less than $100,000, in which case it shall be authorized by Ministry of Economy. Foreign investment in areas which requires express executive authorization are: Electricity, hydrocarbons, basic petrochemicals, atomic energy, exploitation of strategic minerals, livestock, cold storage industries, financial operations, railways, telecommunication, press and those activities reserved by law to state enterprises. State guarantees remittance of profits and repatriation of capital and Central Bank of Uruguay guarantees convertibility and transfer of remittances.

Invested capital may not be repatriated until three years after investment contract is in force, except in cases where special contracts with government covering specific terms or benefits fix longer repatriation terms and, in event of reinvestment of profits, not until one year has elapsed since last capitalization. If profits are not remitted within

FOREIGN INVESTMENT . . . *continued*
two years, they shall be considered as capitalized. (Law 14,179 of Mar. 28, 1974 as am'd, Law 14,244 of July 26, 1974).

FOREIGN TRADE REGULATIONS:

See topic Exchange Control.

FRAUDS, STATUTE OF:

See topic Public Instruments.

FRAUDULENT SALES AND CONVEYANCES:

Contracts having a false or illicit consideration are of no effect.

As to void and voidable acts of a bankrupt, see topic Bankruptcy.

HOLIDAYS:

Jan. 1 (New Year's); Jan. 6 (Epiphany); Mon. and Tues. Carnival*; Holy Week*; Apr. 19 (Crusade of the 33 Liberators); May 1 (Labor Day); May 18 (Battle of Las Piedras); June 19 (Artigas Birthday); July 18 (Constitution Day); Aug. 25 (Independence Day); Oct. 12 (Columbus Day); Nov. 2 (All Souls' Day); Dec. 8 (Immaculate Conception); Dec. 25 (Christmas). (Law 14,977 of Dec. 14, 1979).

*These are movable holidays.

HOMESTEADS:

Homestead exempt from attachment and execution may comprise a dwelling house or an occupied or cultivated rural property, including in the latter case the necessary machinery and utensils, and working animals. Maximum value of homestead exemption is fixed every year by government. (Law 15597 of July 10, 1984).

HUSBAND AND WIFE:

Husband and wife have equal civil capacity. The marriage domicile is determined by mutual agreement and the spouses contribute to the expenses of the home in proportion to their economic situation. The wife may freely administer and dispose of her private property.

Before marriage, the spouses may make agreements regarding property they then own or which they may later acquire, and the administration of the same; such agreements must state the property of each spouse and its value and the debts of each.

Community Property.—If there is no agreement on subject, marriage creates marriage community with respect to property of spouses. They retain as their private property what each one brings to marriage or receives during marriage as gift or by inheritance. Following property belongs to marriage community: (a) Property acquired for valuable consideration during marriage at cost of common property; (b) whatever is acquired by industry, profession, employment or work of either spouse; (c) property acquired by chance; (d) fruits, revenues and interest obtained from common property and from separate property of spouses; (e) whatever is received by either spouse on account of usufruct of property of children of former marriage; (f) increase in value of separate property of either spouse. Whatever is owned by either spouse at dissolution of marriage is considered as marriage community property unless it be proved that it was owned by such spouse before marriage or was acquired by inheritance, legacy or gift.

Each spouse has administration of his/her own assets and those of community which are under his/her name or were brought by him or her to community. Any real estate, business or agricultural enterprise, belonging to community, whether in name of either or both spouses, may be alienated or encumbered only with consent of both.

Either spouse may, at any time, request the termination of the marriage community, the liquidation of its assets and their distribution among the spouses. In case of such separation the spouses must contribute to the support of the home and the education and support of the children in proportion to their respective property.

The marriage community is dissolved by: (a) annulment of the marriage; (b) dissolution of the marriage; (c) judgment of separation; (d) judicial dissolution at the request of either spouse; (e) declaration of absence of either spouse. (C. C. 33, 127-130, 1938-2018; Law 10783 of Sept. 18, 1946).

INFANCY:

(C. C. arts. 252-430, 1278-1280; C.M. arts. 204-252).

The age of majority is 18. Contracts by males under 14 and females under 12 are void and contracts of minors over those ages are voidable except those permitted to emancipated minors. Ordinarily, infants of the marriage or acknowledged as natural by father are subject to parental authority of both parents and illegitimate ones to the mother's. Parental authority includes custody, legal representation and administration plus enjoyment of the usufruct of the minor's real and personal property, with certain exceptions. Parents granting emancipation may reserve one-half of such usufruct until majority. In the absence or incapacity of parents a guardian is appointed. Parents and guardians have restricted powers of disposition.

INSOLVENCY: See topic Bankruptcy.

INTEREST:

In order that a loan may produce interest an express written agreement is necessary; an oral agreement produces no effects in court.

Legal interest is 12%. (C. C. art. 2207).

Interest, compensation or commissions above 75% of average normal market rate prevailing for similar operations during preceding quarter are considered criminal usury and punishable with imprisonment from six months to four years. (Law 14,095 of Nov. 17, 1972 as am'd; Law 14,887 of Apr. 27, 1979).

JUDGMENTS:

(C. C. P. 195-202, 527, 537-543).

Judgments are classified as: (a) Interlocutory, when they render an incidental decision which does not terminate the litigation; and (b) definitive, when they relate to the principal object of the suit. There are also mere orders or decrees relating to procedure. Judgments must contain express and precise decisions and declare the rights of the parties. They must set forth the findings of fact and the considerations of law.

Foreign judgments may only be enforced if: (a) Document containing it complies with all formalities required for its authenticity in country of origin; it is duly legalized and translated into Spanish; (b) judgment was rendered by court with subject matter jurisdiction, it is final judgment, and it is not in conflict with public policy; (c) defendant was legally summoned and due process of law has been followed. Supreme Court of Justice decides whether or not foreign judgment should be executed by local courts after hearing defendant and attorney general. If execution is granted, papers are sent to respective court and judgment is executed according to procedure of executory action.

LAW REPORTS, CODES, ETC.:

See topics Reports; Statutes.

LEGISLATURE:

The General Assembly convenes Mar. 15 in each year and continues in session until Dec. 15, except that the first annual meeting of each new general assembly begins Feb. 15. (Const., art. 104).

LIENS:

The Law divides personal privileged credits in bankruptcy and insolvency matters into three classes of which the second may be regarded as comprising liens. The first class comprises: (a) Costs and expenses for the common benefit of the creditors and costs of administration during insolvency proceedings; (b) funeral expenses in certain cases; (c) expenses of last illness; (d) doctor's and attorney's fees, salaries and wages of employees, workmen and servants during one year before bankruptcy; (e) articles for maintenance of bankrupt and his family during one year before bankruptcy; (f) public or municipal taxes; (g) sums paid to custom house by customs agents for duties on merchandise dispatched and other expenses for forwarding merchandise.

The second class comprises: (a) Transportation costs, with respect to the objects transported; (b) credits of innkeepers, with respect to property of the debtor in the inn; (c) cost of seeds and cost of cultivation and harvest, with respect to the crop of the last year; (d) rentals, with respect to personal property of the tenant on the property, and in case of rural property also with respect to the crop of that year; (e) the purchase price with respect to the object purchased, so long as such object is in the possession of the vendor; (f) costs of construction, improvement or preservation of a thing while the same is in possession of the debtor; (g) salvage costs with respect to the thing salvaged and its products; (h) salaries of captain and crew for the last voyage, with respect to the vessel and freight earnings; (i) amounts lent for the purchase, repair or provisioning of a vessel, with respect to such vessel or its sales price; (j) expenses of general average with respect to the freight; (k) credits of the shipper for the articles shipped, with respect to wagons, boats and other accessories of the transport; (l) maritime loans with respect to the object for which they were made.

The third class comprises: (a) Credits of the treasury against revenue collectors and administrators; (b) credits of national establishments of charity or education and credits of municipalities, churches and religious communities against collectors and administrators of their funds; (c) claims of child against property of parent for child's property which was administered by parent and no longer exists in kind; (d) claims of persons under guardianship against their guardians, curators or guarantors of such persons.

With respect to certain properties the law considers that a claim is not a privileged credit but a property claim, as in the case of claims for property given in deposit, pledge, rental bailment, etc. (C. Com. 1732-1760; C. C. 2368-2371).

LIMITATION OF ACTIONS: See topic Prescription.

LIMITED PARTNERSHIP: See topic Partnership.

MARRIAGE:

(C. C. 83-115, Regulations June 2, 1885).

Only marriages having civil effects are marriages performed before official of civil status.

Persons under age of 18 cannot marry without express consent of their parents, ascendant in nearest degree or guardian.

Before marriage is performed a proceeding must be had before a justice of peace to show that no impendiments exist. Justice issues publications in a newspaper and by edict calling on those who know of any impediment to state same. If none are reported official of civil status and contracting parties determine on a time for marriage and ceremony is performed before four witnesses.

Following causes are bars to marriage: (a) Fact that male is less than 14 or female less than 12 years of age; (b) lack of consent; (c) an undissolved previous marriage; (d) relationship in direct line by consanguinity or affinity; (e) relationship between brothers and sisters; (f) homicide, attempted homicide, or complicity of homicide of a spouse, with respect to other; (g) failure to perform a religious marriage when same was stipulated as a condition and compliance thereof is demanded on same day of civil ceremony.

Foreign Marriages. — Marriages performed abroad in accordance with foreign laws or in accordance with Uruguayan laws have the same effects in Uruguay as if performed in that country. If a Uruguayan marries abroad in violation of Uruguayan laws, the violation has the same effect as if committed in the country. A marriage legally dissolved abroad but which could not have been dissolved under Uruguayan laws does not enable a spouse to marry again in Uruguay so long as the other spouse is living. A marriage, however it might have been disolved according to the laws of the foreign country where it was contracted, can be dissolved in Uruguay only in accordance with Uruguayan laws.

MARRIED WOMEN:

See topics Dower; Executors and Administrators; Husband and Wife; Marriage.

MINES AND MINERALS:

(Mining Code, Law 15242 of Jan. 8, 1982 as am'd and its regulation, Decree 110/ 982 of Mar. 26, 1982; Law 14,181 of Mar. 29, 1974 as am'd).

Mines in General.—State is owner of all mineral and fossil substances, whoever may be owner of surface. Mining activity is regarded as of public interest. Mines constitute real property distinct from surface, although both may be possessed by same owner. They may be alienated and encumbered in accordance with rules of Civil Code, but ownership is not considered as transferred nor is mortgage effective for third persons until recorded in Mining Registry. Law classifies mineral deposits, whether beneath or on surface, at sea or on land, into: (1) Deposits of fossil fuels, which includes petroleum, natural gas, coking coal, lignite, peat, bituminous rocks, petroleum sands and other deposits of mineral substances or other elements that may be used to generate energy industrially; (2) those mineral deposits included in Mining Reserve or in Registry of Vacant Mines; (3) all deposits of mineral substances, both metallic and non-metallic, which are not included in foregoing classes. It includes also those deposits of class (4) when mineral substance is used as raw material for industry or it is subject to certain exploitation requirements for better economical results in exploitation of mine; (4) deposits of non-metallic mineral substances that are directly used as construction materials, without previous industrial process that determines physical or chemical transformation of mineral substance. Mining titles are granted to following parties: On mineral deposits under class (1) above only on behalf of state and state agencies and companies; and on mineral deposits under classes (2), (3) and (4) above, on behalf of any party in accordance with rules and requirements under Mining Code and regulations thereof. State may contract, under its responsibility, carrying out of prospecting, exploration or exploitation by third parties.

State as owner of mineral and fossil substances may grant mining titles that are transferable. Any national or foreign natural or juridical person, whether of private or public nature may be beneficiary of mining title. All mining activities and disputes are subject to Uruguayan law and jurisdiction, and any agreement to contrary is null and void. Law classifies mining rights into: (1) Prospecting, (2) exploration, and (3) exploitation. (1) Prospecting rights are granted for term that goes from 12 to 24 months. This term may be extended for additional 12 months but 50% of original area allocated must be released. Maximum area allocated for each prospecting title is 100,000 hectares and 200,000 hectares to any one individual or legal entity. (2) Exploration rights are granted for two years, which may be extended twice for periods of one year each; in such case 50% of area allocated must be released. Maximum area allocated for each exploration title is 1,000 hectares and 2,000 hectares to any one individual or legal entity. (3) Exploitation rights are granted for term of 30 years, which may be extended for successive periods of 15 years each, as long as mineral is being exploited. Each exploitation title covers maximum of 500 hectares and 1,000 hectares for specific mineral to any one individual or legal entity, which may be increased by governmental authorization. Law establishes causes for expiration and cancellation of mining titles; in such cases mining deposits will become vacancies, available to direct request by any person.

Mining Tax.—Mining rights are subject to tax as follows: (1) Prospecting right N$100 pesos for each 100 hectares or fraction thereof for original term, and N$200 pesos for each extension of such term for each remaining 100 hectares or fraction thereof; (2) exploration right: for first year N$200 pesos per hectare or fraction thereof, for second year N$400 pesos per hectare or fraction thereof and for third year and any subsequent year N$600 pesos per hectare or fraction thereof (increased by Decree 571/ 985 of Oct. 24, 1985); (3) exploitation right: as from moment of use of concession percentage of market value of gross product extracted from mine. For first five years of exploitation 5% (2% to state and 3% to owner of surface) and for following years of exploitation 8% (3% to state and 5% to owner of surface). Beneficiaries of deposits of class (4) will compute their tax from beginning of exploitation at rate of 10% (5% to state and 5% to owner of surface).

Law 15294 of June 23, 1982 establishes special tax on hydrocarbons.

Exemption of import duties of machinery, equipment, tools and their parts used for mining activities related to metallic minerals is granted by Decree 609/986 of Sept. 10, 1986.

MONOPOLIES AND RESTRAINT OF TRADE:

Right of industrial monopoly may be granted to persons wishing to establish new industries beneficial to country's economy, under certain conditions. Initial capital must be at least of 20,000 pesos and a bond of 5% of the capital must be deposited as guarantee which will be forfeited in specific cases of failure to fulfill certain conditions. Objection to granting of an industrial monopoly may be made by persons proving that they are exploiting or implanting in country an industry for which privilege is requested. Government may abolish concession if it becomes prejudicial to general interest and other industrialists wish to exploit said industry under system of free competition. In such case, interested industrialists must indemnify owner of privilege.

Industrial monopoly lasts for nonrenewable period of nine years. It cannot be granted for production of combustible liquids, drugs or chemicals used in pharmacy, etc. Besides end of term of concession, law provides additional grounds for termination of monopoly. (Law 10079 of Nov. 14, 1941 as am'd by Law 10281 of Nov. 20, 1942).

Local production is protected from unfair practices of international trade by imposition of countervailing duties on import of foreign goods. Dumping and subvention are considered unfair practices. Dumping is defined as import of foreign goods at lower price than normal value of similar or same product in origin or export place in normal commercial transactions. Normal value is determined according to method indicated by law. Subvention is defined as financial assistance from government or public organization in country of origin or exporting country to producer or exporter, such as direct or indirect incentives, premiums, repayment or similar advantages in order to make them more competitive on international market.

Restrictive covenants may be issued to temporarily protect local production from massive import of same or similar products that may cause pecuniary loss to local producers. (Decree 142/996 of Apr. 23, 1996).

MORTGAGES:

Uruguayan legislation considers a mortgage as a pledge of real property which remains in possession of the debtor. Mortgages are created by agreement of the parties and must always appear in a public instrument and be recorded in the mortgage registry. Without these requisites they have no effect. Their date is counted only from the day of record. The record of a mortgage must contain: (a) The name and domicile of the creditor and of the debtor and of their representatives who ask for the record; (b) date and nature of the contract guaranteed by the mortgage and designation of the archive where it is to be found; (c) description of the property; (d) amount; (e) date of the record and signature of the registrar.

A mortgage can only be placed on real property, whether owned in fee or for life, ships and aircraft; never on future interests. The mortgage covers all accessories and inprovements added to the property; it also covers the insurance of the mortgaged property and the fruits pending at the time of foreclosure. In case of nonpayment and creditor may cause the property to be sold in judicial proceedings at public sale, and if there is no legal bid, to have it adjudicated to him for the minimum price at which a third person could legally have bought it. (See topic Executions.) Stipulations that the creditor may take over the mortgaged object or privately dispose of the same are void, as are also stipulations which would deprive the creditor of the power to demand the sale of the property when the credit becomes demandable.

If the property is lost or deteriorates so as to become insufficient to secure the debt, the creditor is entitled to ask that additional property be subjected to the mortgage, unless he consents to receive different security; or he is entitled to demand immediate payment of the debt, although it may not have matured. In the foreclosure proceedings the creditor may have the property sold, whoever may possess it and under whatever title; the only exception is, when a third person has acquired the property in a public sale after personal summons of the mortgage creditors.

It is allowable to stipulate the upset price of the property for the case of foreclosure. The usual proceedings of the executive action may also be waived; in such case, the judge immediately orders the sale; if the waiver did not also contain a designation of the price, such price is determined by appraisement. See topic Executions.

A mortgage is extinguished: (a) By extinction of the principal obligation and by all other usual means by which obligations are extinguished; (b) by termination of the right of the person who constituted it; (c) by the expiration of the term for which it was constituted; (d) by cancellation by the creditor. Mortgages prescribe in 30 years. (C. C. 2322-2348).

NEGOTIABLE INSTRUMENTS:

See topic Bills and Notes.

NOTARIES PUBLIC:

In order to be a notary it is necessary: (a) To pass special law course; (b) to be citizen and if naturalized to have been so naturalized at least three years; (c) to be 23 years of age; (d) to be honest and of good habits; (e) to take necessary oath before high court of justice, which grants authorization.

A notary must register his signature and notarial scroll. The following cannot be notaries: (a) Persons below 23 years of age; (b) deaf and dumb persons; (c) blind persons; (d) persons criminally prosecuted; (e) convicts or exconvicts; (f) members of the clergy or of the army.

Notaries keep a protocol or register containing all documents executed before them. (Law July 13, 1897; Resolution Sept. 10, 1897; Law Dec. 15, 1916; Decree-Law 1421 of Dec. 31, 1878; Order June 28, 1865; Resolution 4716 of 1971).

PARTNERSHIP:

(Law 16060 of Sept. 4, 1989).

General partnership (sociedad colectiva) requires partnership articles appearing in a public or private document. Such articles must contain: (a) Names and domicile of founders; (b) firm name; (c) administration of partnership; (d) business in which partnership is to engage and capital contributed by each partner in money, credits or effects, stating value given to latter or basis on which appraisement is to be made; (e) participation of each partner in profits and losses; (f) duration of partnership and manner of liquidation; (g) any other clauses necessary to determine rights and obligations of partners among themselves or towards third persons. Partnership articles are recorded in Registry of Commerce.

Partners are jointly and severally liable for the operations of the partnership to an unlimited degree. If partnership is engaged in specific business, prohibition of partners to engage in business relates only to business of same kind.

Unless otherwise stipulated profits are distributed in proportion to the interest of each partner. An industrial partner, unless otherwise agreed, receives a share equal to that of the capitalist partner having the smallest participation and in his relations with his copartners does not participate in losses.

If there are several managing partners and no specific functions are assigned to them and it is not stipulated that they must act together, any one of them may perform all acts of management. If it was stipulated that neither can act for the other, joint action is necessary. If nothing is stated as to the form of management, each partner has the right to act for the others. Unless otherwise stipulated, the partnership articles cannot be changed to allow operations foreign to the original object of the partnership without unanimous consent; in other cases a majority vote decides and votes are computed in proportion to the capital invested, the smallest capital being entitled to one vote and the number of votes of the others being ascertained in comparison with the smallest vote.

Partnership may be entirely dissolved: (a) By expiration of its term or by termination of business for which it was constituted; (b) by accord of all partners; (c) by entire loss of capital; (d) by bankruptcy of partnership or of any partner.

PARTNERSHIP . . . *continued*

Upon the dissolution of the partnership its business must be liquidated by the managing partners, adding to the firm name the words "in liquidation," unless the partnership articles provide otherwise or the partners entrust the liquidation to one of the partners or to a third person. Private property of the partners cannot be levied upon for payment of the partnership debts until all the partnership property has been attached. Liquidators cannot make compromises regarding the partnership interests without the special written authorization of the partners.

Limited partnership (sociedad en comandita) is composed of "comanditados" who are jointly liable without limitation for partnership debts and "comanditarios" whose liability is limited to amount of their contribution. Requisites as to constitution and registration of these partnerships are same as for general partnerships.

The name of "comanditarios" cannot appear in firm name under penalty of making him jointly liable, nor can he have any intervention in management of partnership even as attorney-in-fact of managing partners. Rules regulating management and liquidation of general partnerships are also applicable to limited partnerships.

Limited liability companies, for their formation, require minimum of two partners and maximum of 50.

Contract of formation may be private or public document, in any case it should contain: (1) Name of partners; (2) name and domicile of company; (3) purpose; (4) duration; (5) capital, value and number of quotas, manner and time of payment; (6) administration; and (7) distribution of profits, supervision, transfer of quotas.

Liability of partners is limited to amount of their contribution. Capital is divided into quotas of equal value, indivisible and may not be represented by negotiable certificates. Minimum and maximum amount of capital is fixed by law. 50% of contribution per partner paid in cash must be paid upon formation and balance within two years. Contribution in kind must be fully paid upon formation. Shares may not be transferred to third persons except with consent of majority of members representing three-fourths of capital. Legal reserve of 20% of capital must be formed by setting aside 5% of annual profits.

PATENTS:

The law considers as new discoveries or inventions, new industrial products, new means to obtain an industrial result or product, and new applications of known means. Patents cannot be granted for: (a) discoveries or inventions for which applications have already been made or which are sufficiently known in or out of the country in printed works of any kind; (b) purely theoretical inventions not of an industrial character, financial or publicity plans; (c) pharmaceutical and chemical compositions; (d) matters contrary to law or good customs.

Patents are granted for a term of 15 years which cannot be extended. Annual payments must be made. Patent must be exploited within three years or within extension of two years granted by Executive for good reasons, otherwise any interested person may obtain license to exploit same with payment to inventor of compensation determined by committee of experts. Terms of such license may be modified every three years. When exploitation is begun, government must be notified.

Foreign patents not exploited in the Republic may be revalidated in Uruguay within three years after being granted in the country of origin. Whoever improves a patented discovery or invention may obtain a patent for such improvement, but in order to exploit it, he requires an agreement with the owner of the principal patent, or if such agreement cannot be obtained, he may exploit the improved patent, paying the owner of the principal patent a compensation determined by experts.

Patents are void: (a) when granted in violation of law; (b) when the alleged invention is not new; (c) when obtained by others than the true owners; (d) when the drawing or description is inaccurate or incomplete; (e) when obtained by false evidence; (f) when illegally obtained by revalidation.

Patents expire: (a) on termination of the period for which they were granted; (b) for failure to pay annuities; (c) if the owner of a patent as to which an exploitation license has been requested fails to comply with the legal requisites. Patent can be revalidated if payment of annuities is made within six months of date of due payment.

Nullity of a patent is declared by court judgment after a summary procedure. (Law 10,089 of Dec. 12, 1941).

An industrial privilege for the exclusive exploitation of new industries may be obtained for a period of nine years, except with respect to combustible liquids, medicinal products or simple procedures or products which might supplant articles used in the country. (Law 10,079 of Nov. 14, 1941, Decree 712 of Dec. 26, 1991 as am'd by Decree 226/993 of May 20, 1993).

PERPETUITIES:

A testator may designate a second person to receive an inheritance if the first person appointed fails to accept it, but no further limitation is allowed. Specifically the following provisions are forbidden: (a) those declaring all or part of the estate inalienable; (b) those designating a remainderman after the death of the heir; (c) those leaving property to an individual to be applied in accordance with instructions left by the testator. (C. C. 858-869).

PLEDGES:

The contract of pledge consists in the delivery of personal property to secure a credit and gives the creditor the right to be paid preferentially from the object pledged. A credit may be given in pledge by delivering the credit document, but the debtor must be advised not to pay any one other than the pledge creditor.

The creditor must carefully keep the pledge and is liable for damages suffered by it through his fault, having the same obligations as a depositary. Any clause depriving the creditor of the right to ask for the sale of the pledged article is void.

In case of nonpayment of the debt at maturity the creditor may request sale of the pledged property at public auction or its adjudication to himself for the minimum price which would be accepted from another; when there is no period stipulated the creditor may request such sale when ten days have elapsed from the time he formally demanded that the debtor comply with the obligation. It may be agreed that the pledge be sold extrajudicially, in which case if it consists in a quoted security it is delivered to a broker for sale, otherwise it is delivered to a public auctioneer. The creditor is paid from the proceeds of the sale and the balance is delivered to the debtor. If upon the sale of the pledge the price is insufficient to cover entire debt it is applied first to the interest and expenses and the balance to the principal.

If the debtor pays the secured credit the creditor must restore the pledge; but he may retain it if he holds other credits against the debtor which have the following requisites: (a) That they are liquid and certain; (b) that they were contracted subsequent to the obligation secured by the pledge; and (c) that they became demandable before the payment of such obligation. (C. C. 2292-2321).

As to rural and industrial pledges, see topic Chattel Mortgages.

PRESCRIPTION:

Prescription is a method of acquiring property by virtue of possession or extinguishing rights of action by failure to enforce them.

By acquisitive prescription real and personal property may be acquired belonging to individuals, companies, the state and public establishments and corporations. Real estate and real estate rights are acquired by possession for ten years among present persons and twenty years among absent persons, with good faith and just title. Good faith consists in believing that the person from whom the article was received is the owner and is authorized to alienate it; just title is understood to mean a title derived from an act executed with the legal formalities and capable of transferring ownership. Real property and real rights may also be acquired by prescription without just title and without good faith, but in such case possession must continue for thirty years. Personal property may be acquired by possession for three yeras with just title and good faith whether between present or absent persons; but if the possessor of stolen property purchases the same in a public fair, market or sale or from a person who usually sells similar property, the owner cannot demand its delivery without reimbursing the possessor. Personal property may also be acquired by prescription without just title or good faith by possession for six years, but this rule does not apply to the thief who stole the article or to his accomplices.

The period of prescription for extinguishing rights of action depends upon the nature of the action. The most important are: (a) Real estate actions not otherwise limited, thirty years; (b) personal actions not otherwise limited, twenty years; (c) summary actions (see topic Attachment), ten years; (d) liability actions against judges and lawyers, suits for construction or repair of party walls, suits for paving taxes, five years; (e) actions for aliments, royalties, interest and amounts payable annually or in shorter periods, four years; (f) actions of lawyers and notaries for their fees, actions of physicians and druggists for their fees and medicines furnished, actions of teachers or keepers of boarding schools for tuition and board, actions of merchants and artisans for goods sold if the debtor lives in the country (if he lives abroad the period is four years), actions of teachers of science and arts for fees payable to them monthly, two years; (g) actions for salaries and wages to servants and workmen with whom annual contracts are made, one year; (h) actions of innkeepers for rooms or board, six months.

Limitation of Actions.—Commercial actions are limited by the following prescriptive periods: (a) Actions derived from commercial obligations whether contracted in public or private instruments and not otherwise limited, twenty years; (b) actions derived from endorseable paper, if there has been no judgment or if the date was not acknowledged in a separate document; actions of third parties against partners, actions on accounts current, delivered and accepted, actions for interest on money lent, actions for annulment or rescission, four years; (c) actions for merchandise furnished, if the debtor is nonresident, four years, and if he is resident, two years; (d) actions to enforce a commercial obligation proved only by witnesses, two years; (e) actions based on insurance policies, one year if the obligation was contracted in the country, or three years if contracted abroad; (f) actions of artisans and laborers whose compensation is adjusted per annum, actions for common average, for delivery of freight, for damage to freight, for freight charges and demurrage, for salaries of crews and for supplies to vessels, one year; (g) actions of brokers, of innkeepers and of employees whose pay is adjusted per month, six months. (C. C. 1188-1244; C. Com. 1013-1029).

See also topic Death, subhead Actions for Death.

PRINCIPAL AND AGENT:

An agency may be express or tacit. It is express when it appears in a public or private instrument or is given by letter or correspondence or even orally. It is tacit when the owner of the business is present or knows the action taken by the other person and makes no objection. Instruments containing revocation, substitution, limitation, suspension or renunciation of agency must be recorded in general registry for powers of attorney. Agency may be gratuitous or for remuneration; it is presumed gratuitous when no remuneration is stipulated, unless it refers to powers conferred by law or to work pertaining to profession or business of agent.

An agency is general when given for all business of the principal or for all business with one or two specific exceptions, and special when it relates only to one or more specified matters A special agency may be absolute, allowing the agent to act according to his discretion, or limited if rules are prescribed which are to cover his action.

A general agency comprises only acts of administration. In order to make compromises, alienate, mortgage or perform any act affecting ownership, a special power of attorney is required. The power to compromise does not include the power to submit to arbitration.

An agency is perfected by the acceptance of the agent, which may be tacit, as when the agent begins to act under the agency. There may be one or more principals or one or more agents; in the latter case if the business was not distributed the agents may divide it among themselves unless specifically forbidden to do so.

An agent is liable for failure to carry out the agency. He must abstain from carrying it out when its execution would clearly be injurious to the principal. He may appoint a substitute if not forbidden to do so, but he is liable for the acts of the substitute if he was not expressly empowered to appoint one or if, having been so empowered, he chooses a notoriously incompetent or insolvent person. An agent cannot purchase for himself objects belonging to the principal or sell his property to the principal, unless expressly authorized to do so. If instructed to borrow money at interest he may himself make the loan at the current rate of interest, but he cannot without authorization

See Topical Index in front part of this volume.

PRINCIPAL AND AGENT . . . *continued*
borrow for himself money belonging to the principal. An Agent must give accounts of his administration.

The principal is liable for the actions of the agent within the limits of the agency but he is not liable for what the agent may do beyond such limits unless he expressly or tacitly ratifies the same. He must advance to the agent the sums required for the execution of the agency and must reimburse the agent for all expenses and losses incurred in connection with the agency.

The agency is terminated by: (a) The termination of the business for which it was given; (b) the expiration of its period or the occurence of the condition upon which its termination depended; (c) revocation; (d) renunciation by the agent; (e) death of the principal or agent; (f) bankruptcy or insolvency; (g) marriage of a woman agent; (h) cessation of the functions of the principal if the agency was given in the exercise of such functions. (C. C. 2051-2101).

Representative of foreign firm is any individual or juridical person locally domiciled who in autonomous and habitual manner renders his services to promote or prepare, sale of goods or services offered by foreign firms by payment of commission or percentage by foreign firm. Representatives of foreign firms must be registered at National Registry of Representatives of Foreign Firms. (Law 16497 of June 15, 1994 and Decree 369/994 of Aug. 22, 1994).

PUBLIC INSTRUMENTS:

The following are public instruments: (a) Instruments executed before a notary and entered in a public protocol or registry; (b) instruments executed before any functionary authorized by law to certify them; (c) instruments of an official character issued by a competent official in accordance with required forms and within the limits of his powers. Others are private instruments. Instruments executed abroad must come with the legalization of a legation, consulate or vice-consulate of Uruguay.

Public instruments are conclusive evidence of the fact of their execution and of their date. With respect to the parties they are proof of the obligations and discharges declared therein. Numerous contracts must necessarily appear in a public instrument, among them being contracts of sale and exchange of real property, mortgages, contracts relating to easements, articles of marriage, etc. The lack of a public instrument cannot be supplied by other evidence.

Private instruments judicially acknowledged by the party against whom they are alleged, or declared acknowledged in the manner provided by law, have the same effect as public instruments with respect to the parties. The date of a private instrument cannot be alleged against a third person except as of the date: (1) When the document was exhibited in court or in a public office and remained on file; (2) when one of the signers died; (3) when it was recorded in a public registry.

A writing, either public or private, is required for obligations involving over 100 readjustable units exclusive of interest. (C. C. 1574-1599; C. C. P. 165-176).

REAL PROPERTY:

Trees and plants are considered real property so long as they are attached to the soil by their roots; also pending fruits of such plants. Articles permanently devoted to the use, cultivation and benefit of a parcel of real property are considered as real property although they might without detriment be separated therefrom, as for example paving tiles, water pipes, agricultural and mining implements, animals used on the farm and placed thereon by the owner, fertilizers, presses, machinery, etc. The products of real property and its accessories, such as grass, timber, fruits, soil or sand, metals, etc., are considered personalty even before being separated, for the purpose of conceding a right in favor of a third person. (C. C. 463-470).

RECORDS:

There are registries of various kinds, among them: (a) Registry of transfers of ownership, for documents constituting, modifying, transferring or extinguishing rights in real property; (b) registry of mortgages, for mortgages and construction liens on real property and vessels; (c) registry of prohibitions, for attachments of real and personal property and vessels, complaints in rescission suits and paternity actions, and sales of real estate on installments; (d) registry of leases and antichresis. Registry of powers of attorney is for recording renewals, substitutions, extensions, revocations, limitations, suspensions or renunciations of powers of attorney. (C. C. 2053; Law 10793 of Sept. 25, 1946; Decree 188 of Apr. 4, 1978).

In the registry of commerce are recorded: (a) The petition required from each merchant, to be considered as such merchant; (b) dowry settlements and matrimonial agreements made by merchants; (c) company agreements of all kinds; (d) powers of attorney granted by merchants to their factors and employees; (e) authorizations to married women and minors; (f) other documents whose registration is required by Code of Commerce. (C. Com. 32, 34, 35, 38, 39, 46-48, 50-53).

Registration of vessels is kept in an office called "Escribanía de Marina." Documents relating to ownership of vessels of over six tons are recorded therein. (Law 3130 of Nov. 20, 1906). Registration of aircraft and encumbrances thereon is made in National Registry of Airships. (Law 14305 of Nov. 29, 1974).

REPORTS:

Uruguay judicial decisions need be followed only in the case in which they were given, and are not necessarily regarded as precedents for other cases. (C. C. 12).

SALES (Realty and Personalty):

A sale is perfected from the moment when the parties agree on the article sold and on the price, except: (a) In case of real property, easements, or estates of decedents, as the sale of such property is perfected only by the execution of a public instrument; (b) if the contracting parties stipulate that the sale shall not be considered perfected until the execution of a public or private instrument.

A sale may be made on instalments or under a condition precedent or subsequent. The sale of the property of another is valid, without prejudice to the rights of the owner so long as they are not extinguished by prescription. The purchase of property already belonging to the purchaser is not valid and the purchaser is entitled to the restoration of any amount he may have paid.

The following sales are prohibited: (a) Parents cannot buy the property of their children under their parental authority; (b) guardians cannot buy property of their wards; (c) public employees cannot buy property sold through their intervention; (d) judges, notaries and court officials cannot buy property sold in a litigation in which they intervened.

The principal obligations of the vendor are delivery and warranty of the thing sold. By virtue of warranty the vendor guarantees the quiet possession of the thing sold and that it has no hidden defects; nevertheless it may be stipulated that the vendor does not warrant.

The principal obligation of the purchaser is to pay the price at the place and time designated in the contract; if there is no agreement on this point payment must be made at the place and time of delivery of the thing sold; if the sale is on credit or usage allows time for payment, the price is payable at the domicile of the purchaser. The purchaser must pay interest on the purchase price: (a) If so agreed; (b) if the article sold produces fruits or revenues; (c) if he is in default.

It may be agreed that in case the price is not paid at the time stipulated the sale shall be void. It may also be agreed that if within a period not exceeding six months another person should offer a better price the sale will be void; but in such case the first purchaser may keep the article if he pays the excess price comprised in the new offer. Likewise it may be stipulated that the vendor may within a period not exceeding three years recover the property sold, by reimbursing to the purchaser either a specific amount or the purchase price; in such case the purchaser is entitled to 90 days notice in the case of real property or 15 days notice in the case of personalty, and if the property is of a kind which bears fruit from time to time in consequence of work or money investment the restoration cannot be required until after the collection of the fruits. (C. C. 1661-1756).

A special law provides specific conditions for the contract of "promise of alienation of real property on instalment payments." (Law June 17, 1931).

SEQUESTRATION: See topics Attachment; Executions.

SHIPPING:

Uruguayan flag may be used by merchant vessels holding permanent or temporary registry. Application for permanent registry must be made within four months of date of provisional registry. Applicant may be individual or juridical person locally domiciled. Registered vessels are not required to travel to local ports but in case they do travel to port of registration, they are required to transport Uruguayan mail to and from local port, and deserting or surviving mariners of Uruguayan nationality. All acts related to registered vessels must be registered at National Vessels Registry. At least 75% of crew of Uruguayan vessels must be Uruguayan citizens. (Law 10945 of Oct. 10, 1947 as am'd, Decree 14365 of Aug. 31, 1949, Law 16387 of June 27, 1993 regulated by Decree 426/994 of Sept. 20, 1994).

Coastwise trade reserved to national vessels is enforced at third party request against those foreign flag vessels of countries enforcing coastwise trade reserve.(Laws 12091 of Jan. 23, 1954, Law 14650 of May 12, 1977 as am'd and Decree 31/994 of Jan. 25, 1994).

Territorial waters include zone of six miles from coast plus six miles for police purposes. For purposes of regulating foreign fishing vessels, Uruguayan sovereignty extends 200 nautical miles from coast. (Decree of Feb. 21, 1963; Decree 604/969 of Dec. 3, 1969). Foreign vessels fishing in Uruguayan territorial waters are extensively regulated, requirements being laid down concerning exploitation of sea resources in general, as well as definitions given with regard to fishing and hunting sea life. (Law 13833 of Dec. 23, 1969; Decree 540/971 of Aug. 26, 1971; Decree 711/971 of Oct. 28, 1971; Decree 77/973 of Jan. 18, 1973).

STATUTE OF FRAUDS:

See topic Public Instruments.

STATUTES:

Uruguayan laws are published in a daily Government paper called "Diario Oficial." Another official publication called "Registro Nacional de Leyes, Decretos y Otros Documentos" appears annually with indices.

TAXATION:

(Law 14306 of Nov. 19, 1974, [Fiscal Code] containing procedural regulations applicable to all taxes and numerous regulations; Decree 388 of Aug. 17, 1992; Decree 534 of Sept. 30, 1991 as am'd).

Most important taxes are: (1) Tax on agricultural income; (2) tax on income from industry and commerce (IRIC); (3) value added tax (IVA); (4) real property tax to which, in case of nonresidents, absentee owner tax is added; (5) tax on patrimony; (6) internal specific tax (IMESI).

Tax on Patrimony.—(Decree 534 of Sept. 30, 1991 and its regulations, Decree 600 of Sept. 21, 1988 as am'd). This tax is levied on net worth of natural persons, family units, undivided estates, numbered bank accounts, as well as domestic and foreign legal entities. Tax is applied to difference between assets and liabilities adjusted in accordance with law and its regulations.

For natural persons, family units and undivided estates, tax is applied exceeding untaxable minimums established from time to time in accordance with following scale: Up to one time nontaxable minimum, 0.7%; from one time to two times nontaxable minimum, 1.1%; from two times to four times minimum 1.4%; from four times to six times minimum, 1.9%; from six times to nine times minimum, 2.2%; from nine times to 14 times minimum, 2.7%; for excess over 14 times minimum, 3%. For banks and financial institutions 2.8%, for other juridical persons, rate is 1.5% for property used on income generating activities and 2% on other property; for numbered bank accounts, debentures, savings certificates or other similar assets, rate is 3.5%; for companies regulated by Law 11073 of June 24, 1948 as am'd, rate is 3%.

Law 15294 of June 23, 1982 establishes tax on salaries and pensions. Employee pays 1% on salaries and pensions below three-month minimum wage and 2% on salaries and pensions above that benchmark. Employers pay 1% of monthly payroll regardless of salary levels.

See Topical Index in front part of this volume.

TAXATION . . . *continued*

Tax on Income from Industry and Commerce.—(Decree 534 of Sept. 30, 1991 as am'd regulated by Decree 840 of Dec. 14, 1988 as am'd by Decree 237 of June 1, 1992). Tax on income from industry and commerce is assessed on net Uruguayan source income derived from industrial, commercial or similar activities earned or received by taxpayers during fiscal year.

Taxable income is that derived from capital and labor applied to regular industrial, commercial or similar activities performed on profit basis.

Following taxpayers are taxed on their total adjusted income from Uruguayan source, except income from rural activities which are subject to tax on agricultural activities or tax on agricultural income: (1) Corporations; (2) specific limited partnerships (Sociedades en Comandita por Acciones) on income from limited partners' share capital; (3) local branches of foreign corporation; (4) government enterprises.

Taxpayers are all types of legal entities and business enterprises, however organized, that carry out activities subject to tax. Law defines business enterprise as productive unit performing regular operations through use of capital and labor on profit basis through circulation of goods or rendering services.

Income is considered derived from Uruguayan sources when derived from activities performed in, or from property located in, or rights used in, Uruguay, independently of nationality, domicile or residence of participants in transactions and place where these are agreed upon.

Gross income is obtained by deducting costs of acquisition or production from total net sales. Other nonoperating items are considered as forming part of gross income. In general, any increase in net worth is taken as gross income, including exchange differences arising from transactions in foreign currency when transactions are subject to tax.

Inventories can be valued at cost or at their market value at year-end, at option of taxpayer, but on consistent basis.

Exempt from this tax are commissions and income from exempt activities or income earned by airlines and shipping companies. Income of companies engaged in activities related to fishing industry are exempt on gradually declining basis.

Income derived from activities of cultural and educational institutions, sports associations and nonprofit organizations, international organizations of which Uruguay is member, dividends paid or credited to individuals or legal entities domiciled abroad unless they are taxed in recipient country and credit is granted there for tax locally paid, exchange losses on debts on foreign exchange income received by banks or financial institutions constituted abroad and not having branches in Uruguay derived from loans or advances to local banks are all tax exempt.

In order to determine net income all expenses necessary to obtain and maintain taxable income are deductible from gross income.

Fixed assets, excluding those located abroad may be amortized at annual rates based on their useful life.

Net income applied to improvement or extension of plant equipment up to maximum of 50% of net imcome for year (after deduction of nontaxable income) is exempted.

Other deductions expressly authorized are: Extraordinary losses not covered by insurance; fiscal losses for previous three years adjusted for inflation; donations to public entities; justifiable bad debts; amortization of organization expenses; and contributions for workers' welfare.

Rates.—Rate of 30% is levied on net taxable income. Executive Power may reduce it.

Income from agriculture and stock raising is subject to ordinary agricultural income tax computed on actual income (Impuesto a las Rentas Agropecuarias, Decree 534 of Sept. 30, 1991 as am'd and its regulations, Decree 599 of Sept. 21, 1988) or to special agricultural income tax computed on presumed income (Impuesto a las Actividades Agropecuarias, Decree 534 of Sept. 30, 1991 and its regulations, Decree 598 of Sept. 21, 1988). Taxpayers can choose either two systems when taxable income does not exceed certain amount.

Tax on Agricultural Income.—(Decree 534 of Sept. 30, 1991 and its regulations, Decree 599 of Sept. 21, 1988). Tax rate of 30% applicable to net income of Uruguayan source from agriculture, stock raising, grazing contracts, renting of rural land, agricultural partnerships, and similar activities. Tax is levied on individuals, associations and foundations from agricultural and stock raising activities, joint proprietorships, companies and de facto companies.

Tax on Transfer of Agricultural Products.—(Decree 534 of Sept. 30, 1991 as am'd and its regulations, Decree 681 of Nov. 28, 1985 as am'd). Tax is levied on some transfers of some agricultural and cattle raising products. Maximum rate is 4% calculated on price of products. Tax paid is creditable against tax on agricultural activities and tax on agricultural income. Same products are also subject to 2 per mil tax calculated on sales price as indicated by Decree 534 of Sept. 30, 1991 and its regulations, Decree 242 of Apr. 30, 1986.

Tax on Transfer of Real Property.—(Decree 534 of Sept. 30, 1991 as am'd and its regulations of Jan. 3, 1993). Transfer of rights on real property is taxed at 2% to be paid by transferee and transferor, at 4% to be paid by beneficiaries when transfer is free, and at 3% to be paid by heirs and legatees.

Tax on Exploration or Exploitation of Hydrocarbons.—Tax rate of 15% applicable to 50% of obtained income will be paid by contractor under exploration or exploitation contract. Taxpayer may choose to pay said tax in kind, at rate of 7.5% of his corresponding total amount of hydrocarbons. Executive Power may grant exemption of this tax. (Decree 534 of Sept. 30, 1991).

Tax on Commission.—(Decree 534 of Sept. 30, 1991 regulated by Decree 691 of Dec. 21, 1990 as am'd). Commissions paid to agents, brokers and similars are taxed at 9% rate on gross income when such income is more than 50% of their total gross income. Net income corresponding to commissions is exempt of tax on income from industry and commerce.

Tax on Establishment and Capital Increase of Corporation.—(Decree 534 of Sept. 30, 1991 regulated by Decree 164 of Mar. 20, 1991). Establishment of corporation and increase of capital is taxed at rate of 1% on capital stock except in case of compulsory increase of capital.

Investment companies are taxed at rate of 3% upon their capital and surplus; insurance companies with domicile and subscribed capital established outside country are taxed on their gross income at rate of 7%, 4% for sea insurances and 2% on life insurances; if they are established inside country rate is 5%, 2% on sea insurances and 1/2% on life insurances. (Decree 534 of Sept. 30, 1991).

Banks and financial companies are taxed on certain assets. Tax is calculated on taxable assets at end of each month at one-twelfth of annual rates. General rate is 2%. (Decree 534 of Sept. 30, 1991 as am'd regulated by Decree 791 of Dec. 30, 1987 as am'd; Decree 136 of Mar. 31, 1992 as am'd).

Value Added Tax.—(Decree 534 of Sept. 30, 1991 regulated by Decree 158 of Apr. 28, 1995).

Tax is applied to: (a) Goods circulated within country; (b) services rendered within country and exportation of services; and (c) importation of goods into country.

Basic tax rate is 23%, while minimum is 14%. Minimum tax is applicable to such things as medications, and other items. There are several items and services which are totally exempted.

Internal Specific Tax.—(Decree 534 of Sept. 30, 1991, Decree 597 of Sept. 21, 1988). First sale of automobiles and vehicles, are taxed at rate of 22%; motorcycles and others are taxed at rates of 3% and 13%; petroleum products at rate from 5% to 102%, liquors and tobaccos from 15% to 85%.

Free Zones.—(Law 15921 of Dec. 17, 1987 regulated by Decree 454 of July 8, 1988 as am'd). Free zones can be publicly or privately owned and are administrated by "Dirección de Zonas Francas". All types of industries, trading centers and services are allowed to operate there. They are exempted from all Uruguayan present and future taxes, except contributions to state social security. Enterprises operating in free zones must employ 75% Uruguayan nationals. Authorization for lower percentage may be obtained in some cases. Dividends or profits paid or credited to nonresident individuals or juridical persons are not exempted if they are taxed in their country of domicile and get credit of tax paid in Uruguay. No restrictions exist for entering to and exit from free zones of goods, negotiable instruments, Uruguayan and foreign currencies and precious metals.

Tax Incentives.—Law 14178 of Mar. 28, 1974 as am'd, regulated by Decree 703 of Sept. 5, 1979, grants tax incentives for promotion of industrial activities.

See also topic Exchange Control.

TRADEMARKS AND TRADENAMES:

Trademarks may comprise: The names of objects or the names of persons in a particular form, emblems, monograms, engravings, seals, vignettes, reliefs, stripes, fanciful words or names, letters and numbers in special design, and any sign to distinguish the product of a factory, the objects of a business or the products of industry. However, the law contains a long list of exceptions which cannot be used as trademarks.

The applicant for a trademark or commercial or agricultural mark must address himself to National Center of Industrial Property, indicating if mark to be registered is Uruguayan or foreign. To obtain registration of foreign mark it is necessary to present certificate of inscription in country of origin. Petition must be accompanied also by: (a) Eight copies of mark; (b) description and statement of objects for which mark is to be used; (c) receipt showing that tax has been deposited; (d) power of attorney if petition is made by agent. Publications are made and if there is no objection mark is granted. Ownership of trademark passes to heirs of owner and may be transferred by contract or inheritance; all transfers must be recorded and transfer tax must be paid. Owner of unregistered mark may object to petition of third party for registration of such mark; or have such registration annulled if already made; such right of annulment expires in two years. Proof of notorious use of mark, in country or abroad, is admissible in opposition proceedings to registration as well as in cancellation proceedings of registered mark. Registration confers exclusive right to mark for ten years, which can be extended for periods of ten years indefinitely.

The ownership of a trademark is extinguished: (a) By petition of the interested party; and (b) when the mark is declared void by competent authority. (Decree 106 of Feb. 16, 1979 as am'd by Decree 559 of Dec. 12, 1984).

The name of a merchant or industrialist, the company name, and the title or designation of a firm or establishment doing business in certain articles, constitute industrial property. A merchant or industrialist desiring to carry on an industry already exploited by another person must adopt a name distinct from that used by the earlier establishment. Damages may be claimed for improper use of a factory or trade name; the action expires in two years. The registration of such name is not required unless it forms part of a trademark. (Law 9956 of Oct. 4, 1940 as am'd, regulated by Decree of Nov. 29, 1940; Decree 51/993 of Jan. 27, 1993).

Uruguay has been party to Paris Convention for the Protection of Industrial Property since 1967. (Decree 967 of Sept. 7, 1967).

TREATIES:

Multilateral Treaties.—Multilateral Trade Negotiations, The Uruguay Round, Final Act, Marrakesh, Apr. 15, 1994 and Agreement Establishing the World Trade Organization, Marrakesh, Apr. 15, 1994. International Convention for the Unification of Certain Rules relating to Maritime Liens and Mortgages, International Convention for the Prevention of Pollution of the Sea by Oil, International Convention on Telecommunications, International Convention on Facilitation of International Waterborne Transportation (Convention of Mar del Plata), and treaty creating Latin American Integration Association (LAIA), Asunción Treaty, signed on Mar. 26, 1991 creating southern common market "MERCOSUR". Uruguay is party to following Pan-American conventions of June 19, 1935, approved by Law 9529 of Dec. 18, 1935: Convention on the Repression of Smuggling (with Brazil, Chile and Ecuador); Convention Relative to Creation of Pan-American Tourist Passport and of Transit Passport for Vehicles (with Paraguay); Convention Relating to Transit of Airplanes (with Chile, Ecuador, and Mexico); Convention for Creation of Pan American Commercial Committees (with Dominican Republic).

See Topical Index in front part of this volume.

TRUSTS:

In view of the freedom of contract it would be possible to establish relations similar to the American trust, but such contractual trusts are practically unknown. Testamentary trusts are specifically prohibited. (C. C. 865-867).

USURY: See topic Interest.

WILLS:

(C. C. 779-1010).

The following cannot make wills: (a) Males below 14 years of age and females below 12; (b) persons who have been declared mentally unsound; (c) persons who although they have not been declared mentally unsound are not at the time in their sound mind, by reason of insanity, intoxication or otherwise; (d) persons who cannot clearly express their will by word or in writing. The following cannot inherit: (a) Persons not conceived at the time the estate vests or who were not born alive or did not live 24 hours; (b) associations or corporations which by law are prohibited from inheriting; (c) the father confessor of the testator in his last illness, also the relatives of such father confessor within the fourth degree and the persons who live with him, also his church or community, unless the father confessor is a relative of the testator within the fourth degree, but this impediment refers only to the will made during the illness during which the confession was given; (d) the notary before whom the will is made, his wife, his relatives within the fourth degree, his employees and the witnesses to the will; (e) persons convicted of an attempt or crime of homicide against the decendent or against the spouse or descendants of the testator; (f) a male heir who is of age and who knowing of the violent death of the decedent does not notify the authorities within 60 days; (g) persons who voluntarily accused the decendent of a serious crime; (h) relatives who did not have an insane testator taken care of; (i) persons who by force or fraud interfered with the making of the will.

A will may be either: (a) Solemn; or (b) less solemn or special. A solemn will is one in which all solemnities required by law are observed; a less solemn or special will is one in which some of the solemnities may be omitted by virtue of special circumstances. A solemn will may be open or closed: it is open when the testator communicates his will to the notary and witnesses, and it is closed when the notary and witnesses have no knowledge of its provisions. A will must always be in writing.

Solemn open will must be executed before a notary and three witnesses. The notary must know the testator or assure himself as to his identity and so state in the instrument. He must read the instrument to the testator in the presence of the witnesses; during the reading all the witnesses must be present at one time; the will must be signed by the testator, the notary and the witnesses. If the testator cannot sign, this must be stated, as well as his request that one of the witnesses sign for him; such witness signs for the testator and must also sign as witness. If any of the witnesses cannot sign another one signs for him but in any case at least two must sign. A will thus executed is effective without need of any judicial action.

Solemn closed will requires a notary and five witnesses, of whom at least three must know how to write. The testator must sign the will whether it was written by himself or by another at his request, but if for any reason he cannot sign it, he must declare before the notary and witnesses that he has read it and state the reason why he does not sign. Persons who cannot read may not execute a closed will. The testator closes and seals the paper or the envelope and gives it to the notary and witnesses, declaring that it contains his last will, written and signed by him. The notary writes a statement on the envelope and the same is signed by the testator, the notary and all the witnesses who are able to write, not to be less than three in number. If the testator cannot sign, this must be stated and a witness signs for him. In order that a closed will may be effective it must be submitted to a competent judge, who opens it following the procedure established by law.

Less solemn or special wills are allowed in certain special cases, such as sudden attack or accident, imminent danger of death, being a soldier or prisoner or hostage in times of war, being on a vessel at sea, etc.

Testamentary Disposition.—A testator may fully dispose of his property only in so far as the law does not oblige him to make provision for the following: (a) Aliments owing to certain persons; (b) the marital portion to which an indigent spouse is entitled and which is one-fourth of the estate, unless there are legitimate descendants, in which event the spouse shares equally with the children; (c) the legal portions which the law assigns to certain classes of heirs, namely, legitimate and natural descendants and legitimate ascendants. The total amount of such legal portions ranges from one-half to three-fourths of the estate, depending on the number and relationship of the heirs. Such obligatory heirs may be disinherited for specified grave reasons. (C. C. 779-1010).

Foreign Wills.—A will made abroad by a Uruguayan citizen can be made by public instrument in accordance with the foreign law or before a diplomatic or consular official of Uruguay. In the latter case the witnesses must be at least two, preferably Uruguayans or foreigners domiciled in Uruguay or at the place of execution; furthermore the rules applicable to solemn open wills must be observed, the instrument must bear the seal of the legation or consular office and the rubric of the respective official at the beginning and end of each page; and a certified copy must be sent to the Department of Foreign Affairs of the Republic, which after legalizing the signature of the diplomatic or consular agent forwards the document to the proper judge.

See Topical Index in front part of this volume.

VENEZUELA LAW DIGEST REVISER

Curtis, Mallet-Prevost, Colt & Mosle
101 Park Avenue
New York, New York 10178-0061
Telephone: 212-696-6141
Fax: 212-697-1559
Email: CMP-NY@mcimail.com

Reviser Profile

The Firm began in 1830 when two practicing lawyers started a long line of lawyers and law firms extending in an unbroken chain up to the present time. In 1897, the firm name became Curtis, Mallet-Prevost & Colt; in 1925 it was changed to Curtis, Mallet, Prevost, Colt & Mosle. The Firm is now made up of approximately 120 lawyers, including experts who have published extensively on such diverse subjects as international money management, transnational contracts, state contracts, litigation against foreign states, sovereign immunity and the act of state doctrine, and the International Court of Justice. Its principal offices are in New York City. There are branch offices in Paris, London, Hong Kong, Frankfurt Am Main, Washington, D.C., Houston, Texas, Newark, N.J., and Mexico City. The Firm has five departments: Corporate and International; Litigation; Real Estate; Tax; and Trusts and Estates. The corporate and international department acts as general counsel to various public and private corporations and individual entrepreneurs. Clients are in the banking, insurance, securities, manufacturing, real estate and oil and gas industries. In addition, the corporate and international department frequently acts as special counsel to domestic and foreign clients, providing assistance in financing, know-how licensing, the negotiation and drafting of all types of contracts and instruments, counselling on all aspects of corporate law, and establishing the vehicles necessary to enable clients to conduct their domestic and foreign business activities. The Firm's international work permeates all areas of its practice and involves questions of private international law, foreign law and an unusual amount of public and quasi-public international law. Traditionally, much of the Firm's international practice has been concerned with Latin America. The Firm maintains its excellence in that area, with its Mexican affiliate, and also through the expertise of Latin American lawyers based in the New York office. The Firm's international practice has undergone a major expansion beyond Latin America to Europe, Africa and the Near and Far East. The Firm's litigation practice includes commercial litigation and arbitration, and white-collar criminal defense. It has substantial experience in civil aviation matters; it also has represented foreign States in transnational litigation and international arbitration arising out of acts of nationalization and alleged breach of economic development or natural resource supply contracts. Among the Firm's clients in real estate matters are institutional lenders and investors, real estate developers, both individual and corporate, foreign and domestic investors and syndicators. The tax department has substantial experience in all aspects of domestic and international business tax matters and real estate taxation. The matters the tax department deals with on a regular basis include: Taxation of foreign investments; the structuring of corporate transactions, including mergers, acquisitions, liquidations and reorganization; federal and state tax litigation; and tax planning for U.S. and foreign individuals. The trusts and estates department engages in general domestic trusts and estates practice and tax planning for foreign persons wishing to invest in U.S. assets through offshore trusts and corporations. It represents individuals, trust companies, and banks acting as fiduciaries. It works for various charitable organizations located both in the United States and abroad including private foundations, museums, universities and hospitals. A group of fiduciary accountants with vast experience in the field assists the lawyers of the trusts and estates department. Curtis, Mallet-Prevost, Colt & Mosle has served as a Reviser for most of Latin American Law Digests since 1930.

VENEZUELA LAW DIGEST

(The following is a list of all Topics, including cross-references, covered in this Digest.)

VENEZUELA LAW DIGEST

Revised for 1997 edition by

CURTIS, MALLET-PREVOST, COLT & MOSLE, of the New York Bar.

(Abbreviations: C. C.—Civil Code; C. Com.—Code of Commerce; C. C. P.—Code of Civil Procedure.)

ABSENTEES: See topic Death.

ACKNOWLEDGMENTS:

Acknowledgments are made before registrars and in certain cases before judicial officers. Usually two witnesses are required, of legal age, able to write Spanish and known to the maker of the document. If the registrar does not know the maker of the document two additional witnesses, known to him, are required to identify such maker. Relatives of the registrar within the fourth degree cannot be witnesses. Public acknowledgments of private documents are made before judicial officers. (Public Registry Law of Feb. 6, 1978).

ACTIONS:

Actions for Death.—See topic Death, subhead Actions for Death.

Limitation of.—See topic Prescription, subhead Limitation of Actions.

ADMINISTRATION:

See topic Executors and Administrators.

ADOPTION:

Law of Aug. 18, 1983 entitled "Law on Adoption" creates two modes of adoption: Full adoption ("adopción plena") and partial adoption ("adopción simple"). Full adoption gives adopted child identical status with that of child, creating lines of kinship between adopted child and adoptive parents' family, as well as between adopted child's spouse and issue and adoptive parents' family. Adoption extinguishes legal bonds between adopted child and his natural parents. Partial adoption permits adopted child to inherit equally in same proportions as child from adoptive parent, and prevents adoptive parent from inheriting from adopted child (unless such child has no heirs or devisees).

AGENCY: See topic Principal and Agent.

AIRCRAFT: See topic Motor Vehicles.

ALIENS:

Aliens in general have the same civil rights and duties as citizens, both with respect to persons and property. Aliens cannot hold public office, except certain positions such as teachers, engineers, etc. Aliens who violate laws or whose presence may disturb public order may be refused admission or expelled from territory. Foreign nations can hold no property in Republic except buildings for their embassies or legations. No contract of public interest made by Federal Government, States or Municipalities can be assigned to foreign Government, and all such contracts must contain clause stating that all controversies arising from contract are subject to decision by Venezuelan Courts and cannot give rise to foreign claims. (Alien Law of July 31, 1937, and Regulations of May 7, 1942; Tourist Law of Dec. 18, 1992; Law of June 29, 1942; Const., Arts. 1, 107, 108).

See also topic Immigration.

ALIMONY: See topic Divorce.

ASSIGNMENTS:

The assignment of a credit, right or action is perfect from the moment there is agreement as to the thing assigned and the price, even before there is tradition. Tradition is effected by delivering the document proving the debt or right. The assignee has no rights against third persons until the debtor has been notified of the assignment or has accepted it. The assignment of a credit carries with it the accessories thereof, such as securities. The assignor of a credit guarantees its existence unless the assignment is made without guaranty, but he is not responsible for the solvency of the debtor unless expressly stipulated. (C. C. Arts. 1549-1557).

ASSIGNMENTS FOR BENEFIT OF CREDITORS:

An assignment for the benefit of creditors may be made in good faith by a debtor who, as a consequence of unavoidable misfortunes, is unable to pay his creditors. It may be made by agreement with the creditors or under judicial order. The court will not allow the assignment if the debtor has: (1) Alienated part of his assets in the previous six months without leaving sufficient to pay all his debts; (2) paid a creditor within the preceding six months to the damage of the other creditors; (3) wasted his assets or is himself responsible for his difficulties; (4) obtained an extension from his creditors; (5) failed to repay amounts administered by him for the government; (6) hidden part of his assets; (7) inserted fictitious items in his list of debts. By unanimous approval of creditors the court may allow the assignment in the first four cases but under no circumstances in the last three.

The following acts of the debtor effected after the assignment or within 20 days previous thereto are void: (1) Alienation of property without valuable consideration; (2) giving of special security for debts contracted before the said period; (3) payments of unmatured debts; (4) payments of matured debts made otherwise than in money or negotiable paper.

The results of the assignment are: (1) Interest ceases on all debts except those especially secured; (2) unmatured debts fall due; (3) debts are extinguished up to the amount covered by the assignment; (4) if the assignment is insufficient to pay all debts and the debtor afterwards acquires further property, he must complete payment with such property.

The creditors may permit the debtor to continue administering the property and make any agreement they consider advisable, with the approval of two-thirds of the creditors present holding three-quarters of the credits, or three-quarters of the creditors present holding two-thirds of the credits. (C. C. Arts. 1934-1949).

ASSOCIATIONS:

Associations legally established acquire a juridical personality through the recording of their articles of association, which must contain the name, domicile and object of the association and the manner of administration. The by-laws of the association must also be filed. (C. C. Art. 19).

ATTACHMENT:

In any state of a litigation either of the parties upon producing evidence constituting a grave presumption in favor of the right demanded, may ask for: (1) Prohibition of the alienation or encumbrance of real property; (2) sequestration of specific property; (3) attachment of personal property. The order for attachment may also be granted, even though the legal requirements are not covered, if the petitioning party gives bond. All such preliminary orders must be vacated if the other party gives bond.

After judgment an attachment is issued against real and personal property belonging to the debtor and designated by the creditor, for an amount equal to double the judgment.

If a third party intervenes before judgment and claims the property in dispute or under attachment, the judgment in the principal suit will not be executed unless bond be given, but if the intervention is based upon a document authorizing a summary action, no bond will be admitted and the principal action is continued and intervention is decided separately unless its decision is fundamental for decision of principal action. If objection be made to attachment issued by virtue of judgment, it is decided by court in brief summary proceeding. (C. C. P. Arts. 523-607).

AUTOMOBILES: See topic Motor Vehicles.

BANKRUPTCY:

A merchant whose assets exceed his liabilities, but who is obliged to suspend payments, may apply to the Court of Commerce for authorization to liquidate his business in a period not exceeding twelve months. The court appoints a receiver and calls a meeting of creditors, and after hearing their report gives its decision. During the period of liquidation no ordinary actions can be brought against the debtor for collection of debts and the debtor may make any agreements with the creditors.

If not covered by the foregoing provisions a merchant who ceases payments is considered in bankruptcy. Bankruptcy may be of three kinds: (1) Fortuitous, if arising from fortuitous causes or force majeure; (2) culpable, if occasioned by imprudent or dissipated conduct of the bankrupt; (3) fraudulent, if it involves fraudulent acts of the bankrupt to the damage of his creditors. In the last two cases the debtor is subject to punishment under the Penal Code. If a corporation falls into culpable or fraudulent bankruptcy its promoters and directors are subject to punishment if they have not complied with the law.

Within three days after ceasing payments the debtor must advise the court and file his balance and a statement of the reasons for the bankruptcy. Creditors may demand a declaration of bankruptcy although their credits have not matured. The court appoints a receiver and thereafter the administration of the estate belongs to the creditors through the receivers. An inventory is made and a general meeting of creditors called, at which the creditors may propose that instead of the court bankruptcy proceedings, the liquidation be effected by the creditors, for which purpose a liquidator may be appointed by the court and a committee of three creditors elected to assist him.

As a result of the declaration of bankruptcy all debts of the bankrupt mature. The following may be recovered: (1) Bills of exchange and other documents of credit given to the bankrupt or to a third person for him, if remitted merely for collection; (2) merchandise consigned for sale for account of the owner or deposited with the bankrupt, while unchanged in kind and capable of identification, also the unpaid part of the purchase money for such merchandise; (3) merchandise shipped to the bankrupt, if not yet delivered in his warehouses or any other warehouses at his disposal, but recovery cannot take place if the bankrupt sold the merchandise, without fraud, before its arrival.

The receivers make a list of debts and preferences and the creditors' meeting passes on their report, disagreements being decided by the court. The debtor may at any time make settlements with the creditors if they accept unanimously. If unanimity cannot be obtained, a meeting of creditors is called and propositions are accepted which secure the vote of two-thirds of the creditors representing three-fourths of the credits, or three-fourths of the creditors representing two-thirds of the credits. A fraudulent bankrupt cannot make agreements with the creditors. If no agreement is made the property is sold and distributed. Sales of personal property are public but the judge may authorize private sales. Real property must be sold with the formalities observed in the sale of real property of minors. (C. Com. Arts. 898-1081).

See also topic Fraudulent Sales and Conveyances.

BANKS AND BANKING:

(General Banking Law Decree 3228 of Oct. 28, 1993, and its regulations, Decree 651 of June 3, 1985).

Credit operations which are typical banking operations are reserved to banks and credit institutions. They are governed by General Banking Law. Activities of banks and credit institutions must be carried out in accordance with abovementioned law,

BANKS AND BANKING . . . *continued*
Commercial Code, regulations issued by national Executive and resolutions issued by Central Bank of Venezuela or national Executive through Superintendency of Banks.

Central Bank purpose is to create and maintain monetary credit and exchange conditions favorable to monetary stability, to economic equilibrium of country and to orderly development of economy.

Inspection, supervision and control of banks and credit institutions is responsibility of Superintendency of Banks.

Financial leasing operations are subject to supervision of Superintendency of Banks.

BILLS AND NOTES:

A bill of exchange must contain: (1) Statement that it is a bill of exchange; (2) order to pay a specific sum; (3) name of drawee; (4) maturity date, the bill being considered a sight draft if no date is stated; (5) place of payment; (6) name of person to whom or to whose order payment is to be made; (7) date and place of issue; (8) signature of drawer. A bill drawn at sight, or at a certain time after sight, may bear interest, which, unless otherwise expressed, is 5%. The drawer guarantees acceptance and payment. He may exempt himself from guaranteeing acceptance, but not from guaranteeing payment.

Endorsements must be unconditional. Endorsements to bearer are invalid but blank endorsements are allowed. Unless otherwise stated, the endorser guarantees acceptance and payment. An endorsement after maturity has the same effect as if made before maturity, but after protest, or the time allowed for protest, it has merely the effect of an assignment.

Bills of exchange must be presented for acceptance before maturity or at the time indicated in the bill. Those drawn at a certain period after sight must be presented within six months from their date unless a different time is stipulated by the drawer, but the endorsements may reduce such time limits. The drawee may demand that the bill be presented to him a second time on the day after the first presentation. Acceptance may be partial, but cannot be otherwise modified.

There are no days of grace. Failure to pay or accept must be evidenced by protest. Protest for failure to pay must be made on the day of maturity or on one of the following two working days. Protest for failure to accept must be made before the end of the period for acceptance. The holder must, within four working days, notify his endorser and the drawer of the failure to accept or pay and each endorser must notify the previous endorser within two days. In suing on the bill the holder may claim: (1) The amount of the bill with interest if stipulated; (2) interest at 5% from maturity; (3) the cost of the protest and other expenses; (4) a commission of 1/6% of the amount of the bill, unless a smaller amount was stipulated. In case of failure to present a bill at the proper time or to protest it for lack of acceptance or payment, the holder loses his rights against all persons except the acceptor. In case the presentation of the bill or the making of the protest are impeded by force majeure the respective periods are extended, but the holder must advise his endorser and attach a statement of such advice to the bill. If the force majeure continues over 30 days from maturity all actions may be exercised without presentation or protest.

Promissory notes must state: (1) Date; (2) amount in words and figures; (3) maturity; (4) person to whom or to whose order payment shall be made; (5) whether for value received and in what manner or for what account. Most of the rules covering bills of exchange are applicable to promissory notes.

Checks must state the amount payable and date. They may be drawn to bearer. They may be payable at sight or within a period not exceeding six days after presentation. Many of the rules relating to bills of exchange apply to checks, including the protest requirements. Checks must be presented within eight days after the date of issue, if payable in the same place where issued, and within fifteen days if drawn elsewhere. The holder who fails to present a check within these periods, or to demand payment at maturity, loses his rights against the endorsers and also against the drawer, if the amount of the check is no longer available through acts of the drawee. (C. Com. Arts. 410-502).

CHATTEL MORTGAGES:

Chattel mortgage may be placed on: (1) Business enterprises or stock in trade; (2) motorcycles, automobiles, passenger vehicles, freight vehicles, locomotives, railroad cars and other equipment; (3) aircraft; (4) industrial machinery; (5) intellectual property rights (copyrights, literary property, patents and industrial property); and (6) vessels. (Law of Chattel Mortgages and Pledges without Delivery of Dec. 20, 1972, Law of Aug. 24, 1983).

CLAIMS: See topic Executors and Administrators.

COLLATERAL SECURITY: See topic Pledges.

COMMERCIAL REGISTER:

See topic Records.

COMMISSIONS TO TAKE TESTIMONY:

See topic Depositions.

COMMUNITY PROPERTY:

See topic Husband and Wife.

CONDITIONAL SALES: See topic Sales (of Realty and Personalty).

CONSTITUTION AND GOVERNMENT:

Constitution promulgated on Jan. 23, 1961 as am'd.

The official name of the country is Republic of Venezuela. In form it is a union of twenty states, each of which has its legislative assembly. Caracas, the national capital, is located in a Federal District and there are two Federal territories.

The executive power is exercised by a President and the Ministers of State. President is elected by popular vote for five year term and may serve again as president ten years after completion of his term in office. Legislative power lies in Congress which consists of Senate and Chamber of Deputies. Members of Congress are elected by popular vote for term of five years. Judicial power resides in Supreme Court of Justice and other courts and tribunals established by law.

The powers reserved to the Federal Government are very broad, including power to legislate regarding civil, mercantile and penal matters, procedure, mining, waters, sanitation, labor, banking, trademarks, elections, etc.

CONTRACTS:

(Civil Code art. 1133 et seq.).

A contract is closed with offeror's knowledge of acceptance. Essential requirements for existence of a contract are: (a) Consent (b) a licit object (c) a licit consideration.

All civil contracts for an amount in excess of 2,000 Bolivares must be in written form. Parol evidence of their existence is not admissible.

Formalities of contracts are governed by law of place of execution. However, it shall be necessary to comply with Venezuelan law when latter requires that contracts be executed by means of either public or private instruments.

Art. 107 et seq. of Commercial Code, governs commercial contracts, which are those executed among merchants or with a merchant. Contracts executed abroad to be performed in Venezuela shall be governed by Venezuelan law unless otherwise provided by parties.

CONVEYANCES: See topic Deeds.

COPYRIGHT:

Copyrights include all kinds of intellectual (including software), scientific, literary and artistic creations reproduced by any means. Law also protects translations, adaptions, musical arrangements and other transformation of private intellectual works; to protect these copyright works written authorization from original owner of work is necessary. Performers' rights are also protected. Literary and artistic works, performances and other productions are protected by law without requiring registration. Work is deemed created by sole fact of realization of thought of author, even if unfinished.

Author has moral and property rights which terminate 50 years after his death. Upon death the rights pass pursuant to rules of descent or provisions of will. An inter vivos or testamentary trust may be created. If forced heirs' rights are not respected, these may have some claims over royalties or periodic proceeds. Upon marriage, copyrights already existing continue being separate property of author during his life even if a pre-nuptial agreement is executed to the contrary, but if community property system prevails the rights are considered to belong one-half to surviving spouse. Author rights on works created during the marriage which is under community are community rights. Producer of motion picture is protected for 50 years from first projection.

Assignment of exploitation rights must be made for a royalty measured in proportion to proceeds of the assignee, unless the calculation or supervision are impracticable or expenses therefor excessive or if nature or conditions of exploitation make it impossible; in such cases, or when author resides abroad lump sum may be agreed upon. A life annuity may be agreed in lieu of royalty. Assignment of publication rights of certain limited kinds of books may be made for a lump sum. Author has right to revoke assignment at any time during his life, regardless of agreement to the contrary, upon indemnifying assignee. There are special provisions for assignment of rights of representation of works, edition, publication of newspaper or magazine articles.

Author rights must be recorded in a special registry and a deposit of a copy of the work must be made in Registrar's office. However, lack of said deposit does not prejudice protection of rights. Assignments, use rights, and similar acts may be recorded.

An author may obtain an injunction to prevent violation of his rights. He may have the illegal objects or copies and tools for their making destroyed or sequestered under certain circumstances. Violation of author rights constitutes a crime.

This law applies when author or one of co-authors, if several, is Venezuelan national or domiciliary or a refugee or stateless person, or if the work is first published in Venezuela or republished there within 30 days after first publication. Other works are protected pursuant to international treaties or, in absence thereof, by applying reciprocity rule. (Law of Dec. 12, 1962 and Decision 351 of Dec. 17, 1993 of Cartagena Commission regulated by Decree 618 of Apr. 11, 1995).

Venezuela ratified Universal Copyright Convention on Apr. 27, 1966.

CORPORATIONS:

(C. Com. Arts. 202-226, 242-352 and Law of Apr. 29, 1975, "Ley de Mercado de Capitales").

Incorporation.—Articles of incorporation must state: (1) The name and domicile of the company, of its establishments and of its representatives; (2) object; (3) amount of capital subscribed and amount paid in; (4) name and domicile of the shareholders or number or nominal value of the shares, whether the latter are registered or to bearer, whether registered shares can be converted into bearer shares and vice versa, and when and for what amounts payments are to be made by the shareholders; (5) value of credits and other properties assigned to the company by the incorporators; (6) rules relating to balances and distribution of profits; (7) special rights reserved to promoters; (8) number of directors and their rights and obligations, stating who can sign for the company; (9) number of financial inspectors; (10) rights of stockholders meetings and any special rules relating to votes; (11) when company is to begin and end.

Corporations may be formed by an instrument executed by all the subscribers of the capital stock and stating who are to be the directors and financial inspectors until the first stockholders meeting. They may also be constituted by public subscription in which case the promoters publish a prospectus inviting subscriptions. For the definitive constitution of the company the entire amount of the capital must be subscribed and each shareholder must have paid in at least one-fifth of the amount of the shares subscribed by him, unless a larger sum is required by the articles of incorporation. If property other than money is assigned to the company, the shareholders must approve the same and the value given thereto. No special privilege in shares or bonds can be

CORPORATIONS . . . *continued*
reserved to the promoters but they can be granted not exceeding one-tenth of the profits for a period not exceeding five years.

Stockholders meetings, unless otherwise provided in the by-laws, require the presence of holders of shares representing more than one-half of the corporate capital. If a sufficient number do not appear at the regular meeting, another is attempted three days later and if a sufficient number is still lacking, another call issues for a period of five days for a meeting at which any number of stockholders suffices for a quorum. Calls for meetings are issued by the directors and published in a newspaper. Directors must issue calls if required by stockholders representing one-fifth of the capital. Unless otherwise provided by the by-laws, the presence of stockholders representing three-fourths of the capital and the vote of stockholders representing at least one-half the capital, is required for: (1) Dissolution of the company before the period specified; (2) extension of the company; (3) fusion with another company; (4) sale of corporate property; (5) reimbursement or increase of capital; (6) reduction of capital; (7) change of object; (8) revision of the by-laws with respect to aforesaid matters. If a sufficient number of stockholders does not attend, another call is issued for a meeting at which any number of stockholders may be present, but the decisions of such meeting must be published and must be ratified by another meeting called in the regular manner at which any number of stockholders may be present. Stockholders may be represented by proxies, but neither directors, financial inspectors nor managers can be proxies.

Directors of a corporation may be one or more in number and need not be stockholders. They are elected by the stockholders. As security for their actions they must deposit in the treasury of the company such number of shares as may be determined in the by-laws. When there are several directors one-half of the number constitutes a quorum unless the by-laws provide otherwise. Unless otherwise provided in the by-laws, the directors continue in office for two years and may be re-elected. Directors cannot intervene in matters in which they have a personal interest. Every six months they must prepare a summary account of the company's assets and liabilities. They are also required to prepare financial statements, with vouchers, showing the status of the corporate capital, the amounts paid in and those owing, the profits obtained and losses suffered. Within ten days after the approval of the statement by the stockholders, a copy of such statement and of the report of the financial inspectors must be filed with the judge of commerce.

Financial inspectors, one or more in number, who need not be stockholders, are elected by the stockholders to inspect the accounts of the directors and report thereon to the stockholders meetings. Art. 8 of Law of Aug. 26, 1982 establishes that financial inspectors must have university degree in administration, economy or public accounting. They may examine books, correspondence and all other documents of company. Any stockholder may complain to these inspectors regarding acts of directors which he considers improper and inspectors must refer to such complaints in their report to stockholders. If complaint is made by stockholders representing one-tenth of capital inspectors must report as to matters complained of. If they consider complaints well founded and urgent they may call meeting of stockholders.

Ordinary management of the business may be confided to managers or other agents, whether stockholders or not, whose appointment and powers are regulated by the by-laws.

Shares of stock must all be of the same value and they carry the same rights unless otherwise provided by the by-laws. Stock certificates must state: (1) Name of the company, its domicile, the place where the by-laws are registered, mentioning the date and number of the registration; (2) amount of the capital, the value of the share and if there are several kinds of shares, a statement as to their preferences and the amount of the different classes; (3) date when the regular annual meeting of stockholders is held according to the by-laws; (4) duration of the company. Shares which are not fully paid must be registered shares. A company cannot purchase its own shares except when authorized by the stockholders' assembly and when the purchase is made with the profits of the company. A company cannot make loans with the guarantee of its own shares. Shares of stock cannot bear interest and dividends can be paid only from liquidated and collected profits.

Reserve.—Annually at least 5% of the profits must be set aside to form a reserve fund until an amount is reached as designated in the by-laws and which cannot be less than 10% of the capital.

Obligations, whether bearer or registered, cannot be issued for an amount exceeding the capital paid in and still subsisting according to the latest balance. This prohibition does not apply to bills of exchange or books of deposit or other documents arising from a specific business. Issues of obligations require the same majority of shareholders as is required for dissolution of the company and other special resolutions.

Dissolution.—If it should become apparent that the capital has diminished by one-third, the shareholders must decide whether they will make up the loss, or limit the capital to the smaller sum, or place the company in liquidation. Commercial companies are dissolved by: (1) Expiration of their term; (2) failure or cessation of the purpose of the company; (3) final accomplishment of such purpose; (4) bankruptcy; (5) loss of capital; (6) resolution of the shareholders; (7) incorporation with another company. The shareholders' meeting which decides upon the dissolution appoints the liquidators.

Corporate Fees and Taxes.—Corporations are required to pay an annual municipal license tax depending on the importance of their business, but never very large. A tax of one per mil on the corporate capital is paid once upon organization and on further capital increases (Judicial Tariff). Bearer shares are subject besides to a special tax. (See topic Taxation, subhead Inheritance Tax.) Assignments of these securities are subject to a similar tax.

Cooperative companies have a variable capital, indefinite duration and an unlimited number of members, not less than seven. Each member has one vote, whatever the number of his shares. They are subject to special regulation of the Government and are governed in general by the rules relating to corporations. (Law of July 11, 1966 as am'd).

Insurance companies (Law of Dec. 8, 1994) are subject to strict regulations and supervision. Among other requirements, they have to be organized as corporations, by at least five shareholders who may be natural or juridical persons, with minimum capital indicated by law and with nominative shares all of one class. Also required is deposit in Banco Central to operate.

Limited liability companies have some characteristics of a corporation and some of a partnership. Capital is divided into quotas of equal par value of Bs. 1,000 or a multiple thereof. Liability of quotaholders is limited to amount of their respective quotas. The company is administered by one or more persons who need not be quotaholders. Company must have financial inspectors if its capital exceeds certain amount. Unless otherwise provided, limited liability companies are governed by provisions of the Code of Commerce relating to corporations and partnerships insofar as applicable. (C. Com. Arts. 312-336).

Foreign Companies.—Companies constituted abroad which have their principal seat of business in Venezuela are considered Venezuelan companies. Those constituted abroad and having only branches in the Republic, or business which does not constitute their principal object, preserve their nationality but are considered domiciled in Venezuela. Foreign corporations must register in the registry of commerce of the place where they have their agency and must publish in a local paper their articles of incorporation and a duly legalized copy of the respective articles of the laws of their nationality. They must also file a copy of their by-laws. All foreign companies must have a representative in Venezuela enjoying full powers except the power to alienate the enterprise or concession, unless such power is also given to him expressly.

Foreign companies which have no branches or exploitations in Venezuela may nevertheless do business in the country and appear in court. All persons contracting in the name of companies constituted abroad and not duly registered in Venezuela are personally and jointly liable for obligations contracted in the country and the company itself may also be sued. See also subhead Insurance Companies, supra.

Public Corporations.—Law of Aug. 10, 1990 regulated by Decree 1906 of Oct. 17, 1991; and Decree 1821 of Aug. 30, 1991 regulate contracts of services and purchase of goods by public entities and state corporations, giving preference to contracting of services and purchase of goods locally before resorting to foreign sources. By Organic Law of Public Credit, of Oct. 26, 1992, public institutions require special authorization to engage in credit negotiations.

COURTS:

There is national judiciary system composed of inferior courts and Supreme Court of Justice which is highest tribunal of Republic. Federal Court has jurisdiction in various criminal and civil matters involving government or high officials.

Courts are: (a) Parish courts for minor civil and criminal matters; (b) committing magistrate courts for investigation of criminal offenses; (c) departmental courts for class of civil matters of greater importance than those confided to parish courts; (d) criminal courts; (e) court of commerce; (f) courts of first instance for decision of civil matters in general and for appeals from lower courts; (g) superior court which hears appeals from court of first instance, criminal court and court of commerce; (h) Supreme Court which can, in certain cases, review decisions of superior court, exercises various special functions and has administrative supervision over courts. There are similar courts in various states. Labor matters are under jurisdiction of Labor Tribunals of First Instance and Labor Superior Courts. (See topic Labor Relations.) (Const. Arts. 129-135; Organic Law of the Judicial Power of July 28, 1987; Organic Law of Supreme Court of July 26, 1976).

CURRENCY:

Monetary unit is bolívar, divided in 100 cents. Banco Central is only bank which may issue bank notes. Accounts in Venezuela must be in bolívares and international transactions contracted in foreign money may be entered in that currency but must also show bolívar equivalent. Obligations in foreign money may be paid in national currency at exchange rate prevailing at time of payment, or in agreed currency. (Central Bank Law of Dec. 4, 1992, Arts. 67, 68, 94 and 95).

CURTESY:

There is no estate by curtesy. See topics Descent and Distribution; Husband and Wife; Wills.

CUSTOMS DUTIES:

See topic Taxation.

DEATH:

A person who disappears is presumed an absentee if the absence is for two years, or three years if he left an agent to administer his property. The presumptive heirs may petition to have him judicially declared an absentee. Ten years thereafter, or if 100 years elapse from the date of the absentee's birth, he may be judicially presumed dead and definitive possession of his property may be decreed. (C. C. Arts. 418-444).

Deaths are recorded in the Civil Register. Death certificates may be obtained from the Registrar of the district where death occurred. Nominal fees are fixed by local regulation.

Actions for Death.—Within the few provisions of Civil Code dealing with torts, art. 1196 provides that a wrongdoer is liable for material and moral damages resulting from his tortious act and that the court may grant an indemnity to relatives, including in-laws, and spouse of a decedent for their suffering resulting from the wrongful death. Automobile insurance is compulsory. See topic Motor Vehicles.

DECEDENTS' ESTATES:

See topics Descent and Distribution; Executors and Administrators; Wills.

DEEDS:

Deeds must state the name, age, profession and domicile of the parties, and the date of the instruments in words, give a clear description of the property, and if real estate is involved they must refer to the deed by which the grantor acquired his rights. Two witnesses are required and the deed must be acknowledged before the registrar. Deeds

DEEDS . . . *continued*
must be written by hand, but typewritten documents from abroad will be recorded, having first been recopied by hand. Real consideration must be stated; if fair consideration does not appear registrar may designate value for tax purposes. Recording fee varies from 1/4% of consideration to 3/4% plus minor sums depending on length of document. (C. C. Arts. 1913-1924; Public Registry Law of Apr. 6, 1978 as am'd; Fiscal Stamp Law of Dec. 17, 1987 as am'd).

DEPOSITIONS:

Testimony is usually taken in civil cases on written interrogatories with the right to the other party to ask questions orally or in writing. Judges may commission other judges to take such interrogatories. Orders of foreign courts regarding the examination of witnesses and similar matters will be executed by decree of the judge of first instance of the respective locality, provided they come together with letters rogatory of the judge who issued them and are legalized by a diplomatic or consular officer of Venezuela or go through diplomatic channels, and provided that some person has been designated to pay the expenses. (C.C.P. Arts. 477-510, 857, 858).

DESCENT AND DISTRIBUTION:

In the case of intestacy the rule of succession is as follows: (1) Ascendants are succeeded by their legitimate children and the legitimate descendants of the latter whose filiation is proved legally. Surviving spouse has share equal to that of child whose filiation is proved legally. (2) If deceased has no children or descendant whose filiation is legally proved, his estate is divided as follows: (a) If there are ascendants and surviving spouse, inheritance is divided in half; (b) if there are no ascendants, inheritance is shared by surviving spouse and brothers and sisters of deceased, and their children. (3) If none of foregoing rules can be applied, estate goes to nearest collaterals, but not beyond sixth degree, collaterals of half blood having same rights as collaterals of whole blood. (4) If there is lack of heirs estate goes to nation. Persons guilty of certain criminal or dishonorable acts towards decedent cannot inherit. (C. C. Arts. 807-832).

Adopted Children.—See topic Adoption.

DIVORCE:

Following are causes for absolute divorce: (1) Adultery of wife; (2) voluntary abandonment; (3) cruelty, making life in common impossible; (4) attempt of either spouse to corrupt children or connivance in such corruption; (5) penitentiary sentence; (6) habitual drunkenness or drug addiction; (7) legal separation for more than one year without reconciliation or separation in fact for more than five years. In last case divorce is granted on mere petition of either party upon notice to other; (8) interdiction of either spouse for serious psychical disturbances that make life in common impossible, but previously assuring that ill spouse has financial support and is under medical treatment.

The grounds for legal separation are the same as the first six causes for divorce, and, in addition, mutual consent of the spouses.

No particular length of residence is required but domicile within the jurisdiction is a prerequisite.

Upon the institution of an action of divorce or separation, the judge may: (1) provide who is to have charge of children during litigation; (2) order inventory of all common assets.

In all divorce and separation cases the Department of Public Prosecution is a party to assure good faith. Children are definitely awarded to the innocent party and if both are at fault, the court determines who is to have charge of them, but up to the age of seven years children may remain with their mother unless court, for serious reasons, determines otherwise.

After a divorce the parties may freely remarry, except that the woman cannot remarry for ten months after dissolution of the marriage, unless a child is born within that period or medical certificate is issued stating that she is not pregnant. (C. C. Arts. 185-196).

DOWER:

There is no provision for dower. See topics Descent and Distribution; Husband and Wife; Wills.

ENVIRONMENT:

(Organic Environmental Law of June 15, 1976 and its regulations, Criminal Environmental Law of Jan. 2, 1992). Organic Environmental Law establishes general rules for conservation, protection and improvement of environment to benefit quality of life; deals with environmental planning and administration; and contains list of activities which are considered to potentially damage environment; creates National Council on Environment whose main function is environmental policy formulation. Conservation, protection and improvement of environment are declared to be of public utility. Criminal Environmental Law defines crimes against environment, establishes its sanctions and preventive, punitive and corrective measures to repair damages caused. Within environmental protection are air, water, hazardous waste and noise pollution.

Air.—Stationary and mobile sources of emissions of pollutant elements must control emissions to maintain them within maximum permissible levels. Facilities with stationary source of emission must obtain operating license, which contains mandatory conditions.

Water.—Handling, treatment and disposal of waste water is regulated. Special permit is required to discharge pollutants to any body of water including municipal sewer system. Mandatory conditions include discharge limits, sampling and analysis.

Hazardous Waste.—Waste is considered hazardous when it is explosive, ignitable, corrosive, reactive and toxic among others. List of hazardous materials and waste is published in official gazette. Registration must be obtained before generating or handling hazardous waste. Generator is responsible for its elimination, including final treatment. There are requirements for locations and containers for storing hazardous waste and recycling. Importation of hazardous waste is sanctioned with imprisonment from three to six years.

Noise.—Stationary and mobile sources of noise must control production to maintain them within maximum permissible levels. Permissible levels vary within each zone. Facilities with stationary source of noise must comply with operating schedule within zone.

Environmental impact statements are required for activities such as mining, metallurgy, chemical industry, energy production, construction materials and infrastructure construction. Regulations which implement law set forth requirements, procedures, conditions and limits that must be complied with. Administrative or criminal penalties are imposed for violations of laws. Sanctions include fines and imprisonment, depending on whether hazardous material or waste, air pollution, or water pollution is involved; temporary or permanent closure of facility, arrest of company officials and revocation of permits, depending on gravity of offense and prior violations.

ESCHEAT: See topic Descent and Distribution.

EVIDENCE: See topic Depositions.

EXCHANGE CONTROL:

(Law on Foreign Exchange Regime of May 17, 1995, Decree 1292 of Apr. 17, 1996).

Foreign exchange market is controlled completely by Central Bank. Currency transactions are made only through Banco Central de Venezuela or for its account at single floating rate of exchange based on supply and demand. By foreign exchange agreements between Minister of Finance and Central Bank of Venezuela single exchange rate is fixed and terms and conditions for purchase and sale of foreign currency are established. Exporters are required to sell export revenues to Central Bank.

Exportation and importation of metal coins, bank notes, bank checks payable to bearer, gold coins or bullion with value over fixed amount must be declared.

EXECUTIONS:

After a final judgment the court, upon the petition of a party, issues an order for the attachment of property of twice the amount of the judgment. The sale of the property is announced by posters and advertisements. The value of the property is assessed by a commission of three persons appointed, one by each party and the third by the parties or the court. The property is offered at public sale but no bid of less than one-half of such assessed valuation is accepted. If no admissible bid is received the property is again advertised for a brief period and in such second offer the lowest bid must be two-fifths of the valuation, unless the parties agree otherwise. If there is still no bid the property is again offered, this time in rental for the purpose of paying the debt out of the rents. The creditor may in such case agree to take it in antichresis, i.e., to administer it and pay himself out of the income. If at such third offer there is no bid the property is put up a fourth time at which the lowest bid is one-third the valuation, unless the valuation commission considers such offer inadvisable by reason of market conditions, in which event the property remains in deposit and the sale is postponed for six months or until one of the parties asks for a new valuation. In case of personal property the third offer is made on a basis of one-third of the assessed valuation. Once a sale is made there is right of replevin. (C. C. P. Arts. 523-584).

EXECUTORS AND ADMINISTRATORS:

Minors and persons incapable of obligating themselves cannot be executors. It is the executor's duty to provide for the funeral, pay legacies, carry out the provisions of the will and pay debts, if under the will he is in possession of the entire estate. He must conclude his duties within the time designated by the testator or, if no time was designated, within a year, which period may be extended by the judge. The office of executor is voluntary, but once accepted cannot be resigned without the court's approval, and carries no remuneration unless one was designated by the testator.

Immediately upon the death of a person the ownership and right of possession of his estate pass to his heirs. Heirs may accept their share of the estate unconditionally or subject to inventory. Unconditional acceptance may be express or implied and involves the assumption of the payment of debts and legacies. Acceptance subject to inventory must be given in writing to the competent court and the inventory must be formally made before a judicial authority. The heir in actual possession of the estate must make an inventory within three months or such further time as may be allowed by the court, otherwise he is considered to have accepted unconditionally. Within forty days after the inventory is terminated, the heirs must state whether they accept the inheritance, but heirs in possession of the estate and who had no intervention in its administration may make their decision within ten years, unless an action is meanwhile brought against them by an interested party, and with respect to minors and incapacitated persons, the period runs for a year counting from the time when the incapacity ends. During the time of deliberation the estate is in charge of a curator who is either the heir or a person appointed by the court. The effect of acceptance subject to inventory is that the heir need pay debts and legacies only to the extent of the value of the property received by him and not out of his personal property, and that he may relieve himself of all obligations by abandoning the estate to the creditors and legatees. Unless otherwise determined by the testator the heirs who accept unconditionally are jointly liable for the payment of the debts of the estate, the portion of an insolvent heir being distributed among the others. An heir who pays more than his portion may proceed against the other heirs for the difference. (C. C. Arts. 967-1125).

EXEMPTIONS:

The following are not subject to attachment or sale under execution: (1) The bed of the debtor, his wife and his children; (2) clothing of the same persons and furniture and utensils strictly necessary for the debtor and his family; (3) books, tools and instruments necessary for the exercise of the debtor's profession or trade; (4) salaries or pensions of less than Bs. 400 except for claims of support, and four-fifths of salaries or pensions between Bs. 400 and Bs. 1,200; (5) homesteads (q.v.); (6) cemetery lots

EXEMPTIONS . . . *continued*

and their accessories; (7) participations in profits by laborers under Labor Code or contractual provision or similar benefits, including Christmas bonus, except that 50% thereof may be attached for support of family or payments upon dissolution of community property in marriages or de facto unions. (C.C. Art. 1929; Laws Apr. 9, 1946 as am'd and of Dec. 20, 1990).

FIDUCIARIES:

See topics Executors and Administrators; and Trusts.

FILING FEES:

See topics Corporations; Deeds.

FORECLOSURE: See topic Mortgages.

FOREIGN CORPORATIONS: See topic Corporations.

FOREIGN EXCHANGE:

See topics Exchange Control; Currency.

FOREIGN INVESTMENT:

(Decree 2095 of Feb. 13, 1992, Decision 291 and 292 of Mar. 21, 1991 of Commission of Cartagena Agreement).

Foreign investment is defined as foreign source contributions made by foreign individuals or juridical entities in freely convertible currency, tangible property or in intangible technological contributions such as mark, industrial models, technical assistance, patented or unpatented technical know-how in form of physical goods, technical documents and instructions. Reinvestments made by foreign individuals or entities in local currency originating from profits, capital gains, interest, amortization of loans, liquidation of companies and sale of shares, participations and any other funds which foreigners are entitled to remit abroad, as well as investments made with funds resulting from debt-equity swaps, are regarded as foreign investment. Foreign investors have same rights and duties as national investors, except as expressly indicated in special laws and Decree 2095.

Superintendencia de Inversiones Extranjeras ("SIEX"), which is attached to Ministerio de Hacienda, has jurisdiction over foreign investment in all areas except domestic banking, insurance, petrochemicals, coal, mining and external public credits. Latter areas are under jurisdiction of other agencies.

Except when foreign investment is made contrary to rules limiting foreign investment in certain areas, no prior authorization is required for foreign investment to participate in national, mixed or foreign companies (as such companies are defined below). However, foreign investment must be registered with SIEX within 60 days following date of registration with Commercial Registry. Value of foreign investment, of reinvestments and of increases of capital must be evidenced through SIEX.

For foreign investment purposes, companies are classified as follows: (a) "National company", one in which more than 80% of capital belongs to national investors, provided SIEX considers that technical, financial and commercial management is 80% or more in hands of national investors; (b) "mixed company", one whose capital belongs to national investors in proportion which may fluctuate between 51% and 80% provided SIEX considers that management is controlled by national investors 51% to 80%; (c) "foreign company", one whose capital in hands of national investors amounts to less than 51%, or if national investors hold more equity, when SIEX nevertheless considers that management control in hands of national investors is less than 51%.

National investors are State, national individuals, nonprofit juridical local entities, national companies and foreign individuals who reside in country for at least one year (or less if approved by SIEX) with appropriate visas and waive repatriation rights and rights for remittance of profits abroad.

Foreign companies are authorized to establish or incorporate branches or subsidiaries, provided that they notify SIEX of such establishment or incorporation. Solution of conflicts and disputes arising from direct foreign investment or transfer of technology may be subject to arbitration.

Decree permits foreign investment in all economic activities. However, following limitations apply as to participation percentage of foreign investment: Television, radio, newspapers published in Spanish language, companies providing professional services regulated by domestic laws are reserved to national companies.

There are also limitations as to participation of foreign investors with regard to concessions related to hydrocarbons, iron ore; and investments related to national defense.

Foreign investors may acquire shares, participations or rights held by other foreign investors in national, mixed or foreign companies without prior authorization provided they notify SIEX within 60 days following acquisition. They also may acquire shares in local stock markets with no further limitations than those set forth in regulations governing stock markets. However, at end of each year foreign investor must notify SIEX of such investments still in his hands.

Foreign investors may reinvest profits of registered foreign investment without prior approval, provided SIEX is notified.

Except for profits from investments deriving from debt-equity swaps, there is no legal limitation on profit amounts foreign investors may remit abroad, provided: (i) Applicable taxes have been paid; and (ii) profits are computed at end of fiscal year. Profits or dividends from investments deriving from debt-equity swaps are limited to 10% of investment annually during three years as from registration thereof. Special fund was established according to exchange control legislation to guaranty foreign investors their right to purchase foreign exchange to remit dividends abroad, profits and payments, but they must register before SIEX and comply with procedural requirements set forth in Decree 714 of June 14, 1995.

Foreign investors are generally entitled to repatriate their original investments plus any capital gains. Nevertheless, there are limitations on capital repatriation of investments deriving from debt-equity swaps under Art. 9 of Decree 86 of Mar. 15, 1989, namely, that investors may not repatriate any capital during first five years of investment and repatriation is limited to 12.5% of investment annually during eight subsequent years.

License agreements on transfer of technology and use and exploitation of foreign patents and trademarks do not require prior authorization. All transfer of technology agreements must be registered with SIEX.

FOREIGN TRADE REGULATIONS:

See topic Exchange Control.

FRAUDS, STATUTE OF:

See topic Public Instruments.

FRAUDULENT SALES AND CONVEYANCES:

Conveyances of property without valuable consideration made after suspension of payments or within a period of ten days before such suspension, are null and void with respect to creditors, and likewise mortgages, pledges, etc., given for debts contracted before said period of ten days. Other conveyances and contracts executed after suspension of payments and before bankruptcy proceedings may be annulled if the person contracting with the debtor was aware of his situation. Creditors may attack any acts of the debtor executed in fraud of their rights. Acts executed without valuable consideration by the debtor when insolvent or which cause him to become insolvent are considered executed in fraud of creditors; likewise acts executed by him when his insolvency was notorious, also guarantees given by insolvent debtor to secure unmatured debts. Actions to set aside such acts may be brought within five years from the date on which the creditors had notice of the same; if they relate to acts of a bankrupt they must be brought within a year after it appears that there is no agreement with the creditors. Acts simulated by the debtor to defraud his creditors may also be set aside within five years from the time they have notice thereof. (C. Com. Arts. 945, 946; C. C. Arts. 1279-1281).

See also topic Assignments for Benefit of Creditors.

GARNISHMENT:

The proportion of salaries and pensions attached cannot exceed one-fifth of their amount. (C. C. Art. 1929). Attachments can be issued against property of the debtor in the hands of third persons.

HOLIDAYS:

Jan. 1 (New Year's); Jan. 6 (Epiphany); Mon. and Tues. Carnival*; Ash Wednesday (half holiday)*; Maundy Thursday*; Good Friday*; Holy Saturday*; April 19 (Declaration of Independence); May 1 (Labor Day); Corpus Christi*; June 24 (Battle of Carabobo); July 5 (Independence Day); July 24 (Bolivar's Birthday); Aug. 15 (Assumption); Oct. 12 (Columbus Day); Nov. 1 (All Saints' Day); Dec. 24 (Christmas Eve); Dec. 25 (Christmas); Dec. 31, New Year's Eve (half holiday).

* These are movable holidays.

Regional holidays: Feb. 3 (Sucre's Birthday), Cumana, State of Sucre; Mar. 10 (Vargas' Day), port of La Guaira; Mar. 19 (St. Joseph), port of Puerto Cabello, State of Carabobo; Sept. 8 (Cocomoto), Las Piedras port, State of Falcon; Oct. 24 (Urdancia's Birthday), Maracaibo, State of Zulia; Nov. 14 (General Anzoategui's Birthday), Puerto La Cruz, State of Anzoategui; Nov. 18 (Chiquinquira Day), Maracaibo, State of Zulia.

HOMESTEADS:

A person may constitute a homestead for himself and family. The homestead may consist of a house alone or a house and lands. Homestead is constituted by writing filed with judge of first instance designating persons in whose favor it is constituted and property. It is exempted from attachments by creditors and cannot be alienated or encumbered without hearing persons for whose benefit it was established and without judicial authorization. When last participating person dies or ceases to have interest, property returns to heirs of persons constituting homestead. (C. C. Arts. 632-643).

HUSBAND AND WIFE:

Husband and wife have same rights and duties; they should live together and owe each other fidelity and assistance. In special cases, they can live separately, with authorization of judge; in such cases conjugal domicile is last common residence. Both must contribute reciprocally to each other's needs, in proportion to their respective resources and incomes. Both have right of decision with respect to matters relating to their joint married life.

Unless otherwise provided by an antenuptial agreement property of marriage partnership is considered community property. Separate property of spouses is composed of property each brings to marriage and of additional property acquired during marriage by gift, inheritance, legacy, or otherwise by gratuitous transfer. Each spouse may freely administer and dispose of separate property, but may not give it away or renounce inheritance without consent of other spouse. Acts of administration by either spouse for other, with toleration of other, are valid. There can be no sale of property between husband and wife.

The community property comprises: (1) all property acquired during the marriage at the cost of the community capital; (2) everything obtained through the industry, profession, salaries or wages of the husband or the wife; (3) the fruits and revenues of the common property and of the separate property of each spouse. All the property is presumed to belong to the community so long as it is not proved to be separate property. The community property is liable for: (1) debts and obligations contracted by either spouse in cases where each spouse has the right of administration; (2) rents and interest payable for the community property and the separate property of the spouses; (3) minor repairs to separate property; (4) all expenses of administration of the community; (5) maintenance of the family and education of the children; (6) support of ascendants of either spouses if the income from the separate property of such spouse is insufficient. Liability for illicit acts of either spouse does not affect the other's separate property or interest in the community.

See Topical Index in front part of this volume.

HUSBAND AND WIFE . . . *continued*

Neither spouse may alienate community property without consent of other. If either spouse dissipates property so administered, other spouse may appeal to court for protection or request separation of property. Marriage community is extinguished by dissolution of marriage, by absence declared by court and by judicial separation of property of the spouses. There is then liquidation; separate property of each spouse is set apart and balance is divided. (C. C. Arts. 137-183, 1481).

IMMIGRATION:

Law of Immigration and Colonization of July 11, 1966 regulated by Decree 2620 of Nov. 5, 1992 purports to stimulate immigration. Immigrants are not required to effect any payment or deposit upon entering country, and tax exemptions and other benefits are given to them under certain conditions. Executive may grant land to private companies for colonization projects.

INFANCY:

(C. C. Arts. 18, 46, 261-281, 301-412, 1144, 1347-1349).

The age of majority is 18. Contracts of minor are voidable; if entered into by his fraud in concealing his age he cannot contest them, but mere misrepresentation of age is not enough. Minors are subject to parental authority of their parents, which includes custody, legal representation and administration and enjoyment of infant's not excepted real and personal property's usufruct; but father who acknowledged his illegitimate child as natural after birth was recorded gets no usufruct. In absence of parents guardian is appointed. Parents and guardians have restricted powers of disposition.

INHERITANCE TAX: See topic Taxation.

INSOLVENCY: See topic Bankruptcy.

INTEREST:

The legal civil rate of interest is 3% but the parties may agree on any other rate not exceeding the current rate by one-half and in no case over 12%. Mercantile debts bear interest at the rate current in the market, not exceeding 12%. Usury is punishable by fine and imprisonment. (C. C. Arts. 1745-1748; C. Com. Art. 108; Law 247 of Apr. 9, 1946 as am'd).

INTESTACY: See topic Descent and Distribution.

JUDGMENTS:

Judgments must state the reasons on which they are founded. A judgment is considered to impose a judicial mortgage on the judgment debtor's property, but the lien is not effective until recorded in the registry with respect to such property. See topic Mortgages.

Foreign judgments will be executed in Venezuela if they fulfil the following conditions: (1) That it was given by competent authority and not in derogation of Venezuelan jurisdiction; (2) that it has force of res judicata in State where rendered; (3) that it was rendered in personal actions, civil or mercantile; (4) that defendant was legally summoned and given sufficient time to answer complaint; (5) that it does not interfere with local judgment; (6) that judgment is not in conflict with public policy or Venezuelan public law. (C. C. P. 242-254, 850-858).

LABOR RELATIONS:

Rights of employees and laborers are regulated principally by Constitution (Arts. 61-64); Labor Law of Dec. 20, 1990 regulated by Decree 1965 of Dec. 5, 1991, Decree 2483 of Aug. 13, 1992 as am'd, Decree 2506 of Aug. 26, 1992 and Decree 2528 of Sept. 10, 1992.

Labor Relations.—Law protects any labor relationship which exists between provider and receiver of personal services in exchange of monetary compensation. In any company or establishment at least 90% of workers must be Venezuelans, no more than 10% foreigners and remunerations paid to them cannot exceed 20% of total remunerations paid by employer. In contracts for indeterminate period, advance notice of termination must be given, varying from one week to one month according to length of service.

Eight-hour day is in effect with a maximum of 44 hours per week, for day shift and seven hours per day with maximum of 40 hours per week for night shift.

Paid Vacations.—Vacation period is 15 working days plus one additional day for each year worked, up to maximum 15 additional days. Workers also receive vacation allowance equal to minimum seven days' salary plus one day's salary per year of employment after first year, up to total of 21 days' salary.

Wages must be paid in money. Executive power may appoint commissions to designate minimum wages. Workers are entitled to a participation of 15% in net profits of establishments where they render services, in amounts equal to 15 days' salary to four months' salary. In certain cases Executive may issue resolution ordering distribution in form of bonuses when profits failed to materialize.

Profit Sharing.—Employer must distribute no less than 15% of net profit among all employees calculated according to law.

Day Care Centers.—Employers with more than 20 employees must have day care centers for infants and children up to six years of age. Employer may also comply with this obligation by payment of day care center fee to any public or private institution, or sharing expenses of day care center with various companies.

Women and Minors.—Children under 14 may not be employed in industrial, commercial or mining work. Minors under 18 and women may not be employed for night work, except for certain services, nor in mines, nor in certain other establishments. There are special provisions to protect pregnant women.

Workmen's compensation is payable in the case of labor accidents and occupational diseases in the amounts specified in the law.

Conciliation boards and labor tribunals endeavor to settle collective conflicts and insure the proper enforcement of the Labor Law.

Labor exchanges under the supervision of a national employment agency attempt to coordinate labor supply and demand.

Decree 1178 of July 16, 1986 creates national salary-grant program for companies or cooperatives with more than ten workers consisting of on job training.

LAW REPORTS, CODES, ETC.:

See topics Reports; Statutes.

LEGISLATURE:

Congress meets at Caracas from Mar. 2d to July 6th, and from Oct. 1st to Nov. 30th every year. Special sessions may be called to consider matters designated in the call. (Const., Arts. 154-155).

LIENS:

The following credits enjoy general liens on all the personal property of the debtor; (1) Legal expenses incurred to preserve the property; (2) funeral expenses; (3) expenses of the last illness not exceeding three months; (4) domestic wages not exceeding three months; (5) maintenance of debtor and family for the last six months; (6) national and municipal taxes during the current year and the previous year.

The following credits enjoy liens on specific personal property: (1) Credits secured by pledge, with regard to the property pledged; (2) credits for the construction, preservation or improvement of an article, while that article is in the hands of the creditor; (3) debts for seeds and for work of cultivation and collection of crops, with respect to the respective fruits; (4) rents of real property for not exceeding two years, with respect to the crops obtained during the year and to everything used for cultivating the property or required for the object to which it is devoted; (5) debts to innkeepers with respect to the effects of the guest; (6) transportation expenses, with respect to the articles transported while they are in possession of the carrier or within three days thereafter if in possession of the person to whom delivered; (7) credits for pensions or rents, with regard to the products of the estate charged therewith; (8) amounts due by public employees, with regard to salaries owing to them; (9) salaries of employees of a commercial or industrial concern, for a period of three months prior to the date of bankruptcy or assignment to creditors, with respect to the personal property belonging to the establishment.

The following are liens on real property: (1) Expenses incurred for the benefit of creditors in the attachment, deposit or public sale of the property; (2) taxes for the current and preceding year, recording fees and inheritance taxes. (C. C. 1863-1876). Due debts from merchant to merchant give a right of retention of the debtor's chattels in the creditor's possession. The same right arises regarding non-matured debts in case of the debtor's insolvency. (C. Com. 122-123).

LIMITATION OF ACTIONS: See topic Prescription.

LIMITED PARTNERSHIP: See topic Partnership.

MARRIAGE:

Following marriages are invalid: (a) those of males under 16 years and females under 14 except in cases established by Law; (b) those of persons manifestly and permanently impotent; (c) those of persons non compos mentis; (d) those of persons already married; (e) those of ministers of religion which forbids their marrying; (f) between ascendants and descendants by consanguinity or affinity; (g) between brothers and sisters; (h) between spouse and person guilty of killing or attempting to kill other spouse.

The following marriages are forbidden: (a) Between uncles and nieces and descendants of nieces and between aunts and nephews and descendants of nephews; (b) between brothers-in-law and sisters-in-law when the former marriage was dissolved by divorce; (c) between a person and the adopted child of that person or the spouse or descendants of the adopted child or between an adopted child and the spouse of the person adopting; (d) between guardian and ward until the accounts of the guardianship are proved. The impediments of cases (a), (b) and (d) may be waived by the competent judge.

The following marriages are likewise forbidden: (a) Those of women formerly married until ten months after the termination of the former marriage, unless a child was born in meantime or medical certificate of nonpregnancy is issued; (b) those of males or females under 18 years unless consent of parents or authorization of judge has been obtained.

Persons intending to marry must advise an official authorized to perform the ceremony, who posts an announcement for eight days in a public place of the domicile of each party. The marriage may be performed by the civil chief of the district, or the first civil authority or the judge of the parish or municipality, or the president of the municipal council or of the communal board, and a record is inscribed in the civil registry. After such civil marriage the parties may, if they choose, have a religious ceremony, but a religious ceremony without a previous civil ceremony is prohibited.

Venezuelans marrying abroad must, within six months, notify the first civil authority of the parish or municipality of their last domicile in Venezuela so that the proper entry may be made in the civil registry. An alien marrying in Venezuela must file evidence that he is not married and is able to contract marriage under the law of his nationality. Alien married couples who become domiciled in Venezuela must, within one year after arriving in the country, have a record of their marriage inscribed in the civil registry.

Invalid marriages may be annulled, but if contracted in good faith they produce civil effects with regard to the parties and the children. Marriages contracted in violation of legal prohibitions are not subject to annulment but the parties are liable to punishment. (C. C. Arts. 41-136).

MARRIED WOMEN:

See topics Husband and Wife; Marriage.

See Topical Index in front part of this volume.

MINES AND MINERALS:

(Mining Law of Dec. 28, 1944, Dec. 2039 of Feb. 15, 1977, Res. 115 of Mar. 20, 1990 and Res. 429 of Nov. 11, 1982).

The law distinguishes between soil and subsoil; the former is considered to extend only to the depth required for the works or buildings of the owner of the soil.

Mineral substances do not belong to the owner of the soil and their extraction is governed by specific laws. The Mining Law governs mineral substances in general, and there is a special law for petroleum and other hydrocarbons and another law for salt mines.

Mining Law relates specifically to minerals, precious stones and similar deposits. Right of exploiting such substances is obtained through concessions granted by Federal Executive. If concessionaire cannot reach agreement with owner of soil he may obtain expropriation of such part of soil as he may require. Concessionaires have right to exploit all minerals found within boundary of concession.

Prospecting rights are granted for one year. This term may be extended for additional year. Maximum area allocated for each prospecting title is 2,000 hectares. Rights conferred by prospecting title are not transferable. Complete report of result of survey must be filed at Ministry of Energy in order to obtain priority over other applications for concession under same technical conditions and economic capacity.

Mining concessions are granted by Ministry of Energy and Mines to individuals, private entities, local or foreign, with exception of certain government officials, in accordance with regulations of Mar. 20, 1990 on mining concessions and Decree 2518 of Oct. 27, 1988 on foreign investment in mining sector. Foreign states or sovereigns may have no mining rights or concessions nor be members or shareholders of mining corporations.

Mining concessions are granted up to 40 years, depending on type of deposits. Decree 2039 establishes minimum requirements to be taken into account by Government in order to grant mining concessions: (1) Technical and economic capacity; (2) agreement to manufacture or refine mineral locally; (3) favorable tax regime for Government; (4) supply and transfer of technology to local mining industry; (5) agreement to turn over to Government all equipment and installation at termination of concession; (6) any other special advantage considered convenient for protection of national mining interests. Applicants for mining concession may offer additional prerogatives to Government in order to obtain favorable decision; such prerogatives may include agreement to pay other taxes besides those established by Mining Law, to encourage local research to improve or develop techniques and methods to be used in concession; to implement program of technical and administrative instructions; to reduce term of concession to 20 years to be renewed for additional periods of ten years. Mining taxes vary according to nature of deposit, area concerned, and value of mineral extracted.

Exploitation of iron ore is regulated by Decree 580 of Sept. 26, 1974 and its regulations.

Exploration and exploitation of minerals is subject to rules on environmental protection in Decree 1739 of July 25, 1991.

Petroleum.—(Law of Aug. 12, 1971; Law of May 28, 1973; Law of Aug. 29, 1975 and its Regulations, Decrees 1307 of Dec. 2, 1975, 1369 of Dec. 30, 1976, 1404 of Jan. 20, 1976, and 1419 of Feb. 3, 1976; Decree 1123 of Aug. 30, 1975 as am'd; Leg. Accord of July 7, 1995).

Petroleum industry is public utility and of social interest enjoying preferential right to utilize surface with right to expropriation on payment of compensation. Government has right to explore or exploit petroleum, asphalt and other hydrocarbons, manufacture, refining, transportation and storage, domestic and foreign trade of substances exploited or refined. These activities are carried out by Petroleos de Venezuela, S.A., state owned corporation or by its subsidiaries. Such public corporations may enter into agreements with private entities for certain period of time and under control of Government; authorization of Congress is required to enter into such agreements. Association agreements may be entered into for up to 39 years with assumption of risks for exploration and exploitation and commercialization of light and medium crude deposits under profit-sharing plan.

MONOPOLIES AND RESTRAINT OF TRADE:

(Const. Jan. 26, 1961, Arts. 32, 96, 98, Anti-Trust Law of Dec. 30, 1991 regulated by Decrees 2775 of Jan. 21, 1993 and 1311 of May 2, 1996; Decree 230 of June 1, 1955; Decree 3303; Law on Consumer Protection of May 17, 1995, regulated by Decrees 2270 and 2271 of May 21, 1992, 2755, 2756 of Jan. 14, 1993 and 3072 of July 15, 1993; Law on Unfair Foreign Trade Practices of June 18, 1992 regulated by Decree 2883 of Apr. 5, 1993; Law on Rent Control of Aug. 1, 1960, Customs Law, Sept. 18, 1978).

The constitution guarantees freedom of work and industry with such limitations as are required by public order and good customs. Monopolies for the exclusive exercise of any industry are therefore prohibited. Temporary privileges may be granted only with regard to copyrights, patents and trademarks and for the establishment and exploitation of railroads, canalization systems, telephone and telegraph lines and other communication systems.

Constitution authorizes State to enact rules for preventing undue rise in prices and maneuvers tending to obstruct or restrict economic freedom. Law empowers Executive to prohibit importation of certain merchandise or to subject it to granting of special licenses. Executive is empowered to fix wholesale prices and retail prices for articles that are of prime necessity. Rental of urban and suburban buildings of commercial or industrial sites is subject to regulation and control.

Anti-trust law promotes and protects free competition, prohibits monopolistic and oligopolistic practices and any other unfair practice that may limit economic freedom. Law is applied to individuals and to public or private juridical persons and nonprofit organizations engaged in economic activities.

Law prohibits any practices, arrangements or agreements that limit or restrict free competition such as manipulation of production or distribution of goods, of technological development or investment; economic concentration leading to domination of part or whole market; abuse of dominant position in market; unfair competition, especially misleading or false advertising, promotion of goods and services based on false statements, commercial bribery, infringement of industrial secrets and counterfeiting of products. Government may allow some monopolistic practices as exception. "Superintendencia para la Promoción y Protección de la Libre Competencia" is in charge of enforcing this law, and it is empowered to impose fines in case of infringement.

Law on consumer protection regulates organization, management, inspection, coordination and execution of measures, plans and programs adopted in country for legal protection of consumers; investigation of consumer services and consumer products, their price structure and education, promotion and reporting of needs, interests and problems of consumers. It also regulates adhesion contracts, sales on credit contracts, warranties, profiteering, hoarding and usury advertisements, credit sales. Noncompliance with law is considered administrative offense or crime and penalties include imposition of fines and imprisonment up to six years. Law protects local production from unfair practices of international trade, imposing countervailing duties on import of foreign goods. Dumping and subvention are considered unfair practices. Dumping is defined as import of foreign goods at lower price than normal value in place of origin. Normal value is determined according to method indicated by law. Subvention is defined as direct or indirect incentives, subsidies, premiums or assistance of any kind, including preferential exchange rate granted by foreign governments to producers, manufacturers, transporters or exporters of goods in order to make them more competitive on international market. Anti-dumping and Subsidies Commission is in charge of enforcing this law.

See also topic Foreign Investment.

MORTGAGES:

Mortgages have no effect unless recorded. They cover real property and all its improvements and accessories. They are of three kinds: legal, judicial and conventional.

Legal mortgages are various mortgages granted by act of law: (1) the vendor has a legal mortgage on the real estate sold for the unpaid part of the selling price; (2) coheirs and partners have a mortgage on the common property; (3) wards have a mortgage on designated property of their guardians.

Judicial mortgages are judgment liens. A judgment creates a lien equal to double the amount of the judgment. The judgment creditor designates the property of the debtor on which this mortgage should be filed.

Conventional mortgages are the usual mortgages created by act of the parties. They rank according to the date of recording. They are subject to recording fees that vary according to amount of capital plus minor dues. In case of foreclosure owner of property is given four days to pay, after which proceedings continue as in case of execution of judgment. If mortgage debtor or owner of property files opposition, sale is suspended unless creditor gives bond. There is right of replevin. (C. C. Arts. 1877-1912; C. C. P. Arts. 660-665).

MOTOR VEHICLES:

Motor vehicles must be registered and covered by a guarantee to secure liability for property damages and personal injuries, for minimum amounts. Owners are liable for driver's liability. (Laws of Land Traffic of Oct. 9, 1986; Regulations by Decree of Jan. 20, 1976 as am'd).

Aircraft.—The State reserves the right to regulate all matters pertaining to aerial navigation. National aircraft must be registered in the aerial register. In order to obtain Venezuelan registry, it is necessary that the craft belong to a Venezuelan individual or company and have a certificate of navigation. Aircraft must enter and leave the country by way of the zones designated by the Executive, and may not fly over prohibited zones. (Aviation Law, Apr. 12, 1955). Acquisition and leasing of aircraft require prior government authorization in order that aircraft may be registered in official aviation registry. (Decree 898 of Aug. 8, 1967).

On June 15, 1955, Venezuela became a party of the Warsaw Convention of 1929, and ratified the International Convention on Civil Aviation signed at Chicago Dec. 7, 1944.

NEGOTIABLE INSTRUMENTS:

See topic Bills and Notes.

NOTARIES PUBLIC:

(Decree 1393 of Jan. 6, 1976).

Notaries are public officials whose functions are more important than those of notaries under American law. They must be lawyers, have the same qualifications required for judges, and give bond before taking office. They keep books in which contracts, deeds, powers of attorney and other documents are inscribed and signed. Such books are preserved as public records. Notaries also register protests of negotiable instruments and intervene in the opening of wills. They supply certified copies of the documents as executed in their records. In some jurisdictions the notaries are replaced by the registrars in charge of the record offices, before whom the parties appear to acknowledge deeds, mortgages, etc., and in certain cases by judicial officers.

PARTNERSHIP:

(C. Com. Arts. 200-358; C. C. 1649-1683).

General partnership (compañía en nombre colectivo) is one in which all the partners are liable jointly and to an unlimited extent for the partnership obligations. They are considered as legal entities in the same manner as corporations. The firm name can contain only names of partners unless the partnership is a successor of another and so describes itself. Partnership must file with the court of commerce an extract from the partnership agreement, stating: (1) Names and domicile of the partners; (2) name of the partnership and its object; (3) name of the partners authorized to sign for the partnership; (4) period during which the partnership will continue. This extract is also published in a newspaper of the locality or, if there is none, by posters. The liability of the partners cannot be limited by any clause of their contract but creditors cannot bring suit against them without first having brought suit against the partnership. The partnership can be obligated only by the partners authorized to appear, but any partner whose name appear in the firm name may act for the firm.

PARTNERSHIP . . . *continued*
Partners cannot be interested in other firms having the same object except with the consent of their associates, nor can they do business of the same kind for their own account or for a third person. Partnerships are dissolved by: (1) Expiration of their term; (2) failure or cessation of their object; (3) full attainment of their object; (4) bankruptcy; (5) loss of their capital; (6) decision of the members; (7) incorporation with another firm.

Limited partnership (compañía en comandita) is one in which social liabilities are guaranteed by unlimited and solidary responsibility of one or more partners, so called solidary partners or special partners, and for limited responsibility up to certain amount of one or more partners called silent partners. Capital of so called silent partners may be divided into shares. They constitute legal entities. Name of limited partner cannot appear in firm name; if it does, he is liable for firm's obligations. Limited partners cannot perform any act of administration or be general agents of firm but they may be special agents if this is clearly expressed. Interest of special partners may be represented by shares.

Temporary partnership (asociación en participación) arises when a person gives to one or more persons a participation in some or all of his commercial operations. In such cases third persons have rights and obligations only with respect to the person with whom they contracted. The participants have no property rights in the object of the association, their rights being limited to receiving an accounting of the funds contracted by them.

Civil partnership may be formed by any two or more persons who contribute something in order to divide the resulting profits. If there is no agreement as to its duration it is considered contracted for an unlimited time, but in such cases it may be dissolved at the option of any of the parties. When two or more associates have been entrusted with the administration of the partnership without a further determination of their attributes, each can act alone. If it was stipulated that they must act by unanimous consent or majority vote, such agreement must be observed unless the case is an urgent one where failure to act might produce irreparable injury. If there has been no special stipulation as to the method of administration, it is presumed that the associates have reciprocally given each other the power to administer and each associate may make use of the property of the association in a reasonable manner and may obligate the others to contribute to the expenses of the association, but he cannot make innovations in the real estate of the association if the others do not consent.

Foreign Partnerships.—See topic Corporations.

PATENTS:

Any invention of products or proceedings in any technology field which are novel, represent inventive step and are susceptible of industrial application. Invention is novel when it is not within state of art.

Discoveries, scientific theories and mathematical methods; scientific, literary and artistic works; therapeutic, surgical and diagnostic methods among others are not considered inventions. Inventions contrary to public policy, morals and against life or health of people or animals and environment; on animal species and races and biological procedures to obtain them; inventions related to nuclear substances, to pharmaceutical products listed by World Health Organization as essential medicines; and related to substances composing human body are not patentable. Patents are granted for 20 years from application date. Patents are subject to annual tax according to their classification and registration fee is payable for their assignment. Persons desiring patent apply to Registry of Industrial Property which causes application to be published and, if there is no opposition, issues certificate. Patent owner must exploit it, directly or by granting license in any member country of Andean Pact. Industrial production or importation, distribution and commercialization of patented product, are considered exploitation of patent. Utility models for new forms of objects or mechanism, provided they have practical use may be registered. Registration term is ten years from filing date.

Industrial designs, any new design which may be applied to industrial object may be registered as ownership of author if no publicity thereof in any form has been made before filing application. Registration is granted for eight years.

Law also protects trade secrets and considers them as any confidential information that is valuable and provides competitive or economic advantages to owner. Information considered trade secret must be expressed in tangible form such as documents, microfilm films, laser discs or any other similar means.

Vegetal species are protected when they are novel, homogeneous, distinguishible and stable and generic designation has been assigned to them. When registered certificate of holder is issued for 15 to 25 years, depending on type of vegetal variety.

Provisions regarding patents are applicable to utility models and industrial designs. Venezuela approved Convention for the Protection of Industrial Property, Paris, Mar. 21, 1883, Stockholm Revision of July 14, 1967 as am'd on Sept. 28, 1979. (Decisions 344 and 345 of Oct. 29, 1993 of Commission of Cartagena Agreement, Decree 2887 of Apr. 15, 1993).

PERPETUITIES:

Property may be left by will to various persons successively but they must be persons in being at the time of the death of the testator. (C. C. Art. 963).

PLEDGES:

By the contract of pledge the debtor delivers an article to the creditor as security for a debt. The pledge must be delivered into the physical possession of the creditor or a third person designated by the parties. If the article is worth over Bs. 2,000 the transaction must be set forth in writing. If the debt is not paid at maturity the creditor may have the pledged article sold at a judicial sale. (C. C. Arts. 1837-1854).

Pledges without delivery are permissible under certain circumstances. See topic Chattel Mortgages.

PRESCRIPTION:

Prescription is a method of acquiring a right or extinguishing an obligation through lapse of time. In default of provisions designating a shorter time, actions pertaining to real estate are barred by prescription in 20 years and personal actions in ten years, even in the absence of just title and good faith. When real property is acquired by an instrument duly recorded, title by prescription arises in ten years from the date of recording.

Limitation of Actions.—The following actions are barred in the periods designated:

Twenty years: Actions on judgments.

Five years: Actions to set aside conveyances in fraud of creditors; to oblige partners to pay firm debts; actions in connection with maritime obligations where no other period is provided by law.

Three years: Actions to recover rentals; to recover interest or amounts payable in one year or shorter periods; to require attorneys to account for papers or other matters; actions on bills of exchange against the acceptor.

Two years: Actions to recover amounts due for support; to recover lawyers' fees, registrars' fees, agents' salaries, fees of physicians, surgeons and druggists, compensation of teachers, engineers, architects and surveyors, hotel and board bills, the value of merchandise sold by merchants to others who are not merchants, fees of judges, court clerks and bailiffs, wages of servants, laborers and mechanics; actions to recover personal property lost or stolen.

One year: Actions against the maker and endorsers of bills of exchange and promissory notes; for supplies for vessels and wages in connection with the construction and repair of vessels; for wages of crews and for delivery of merchandise transported.

Six months: Actions of endorsers against each other and against the maker; actions for the recovery of freight and passenger charges and contributions for gross average.

Prescription is interrupted by a judicial demand, by a recognition of the obligation and, in case of credits, by extrajudicial demand. (C. C. Arts. 1346, 1952-1988; C. Com. Arts. 371-375, 479-480, 889-897).

PRINCIPAL AND AGENT:

An agency may be express or tacit and may be accepted expressly or tacitly. It may be general or special.

A general agency comprises only acts of administration; in order to compromise, alienate, mortgage or execute other than ordinary administrative acts, the power must be expressly conferred. The agent must render accounts to the principal and in case he acts through another he is liable to the principal if he had no right to substitute or if he wrongfully selected the substitute or gave him instructions. The principal is obliged to reimburse the agent for losses suffered through the agency if through no fault of the agent and must pay him interest on advances.

The agency is terminated by: (1) Revocation; (2) resignation of the agent; (3) death or insolvency of the principal or agent; (4) incapacity of the principal or agent if the acts to be done require the approval of a curator. The principal may freely revoke the agency but such revocation does not affect third persons who in ignorance thereof contracted in good faith with the agent. The appointment of a new agent for the same business causes the revocation of the former agency from the day the appointment is announced. The agent may resign by notifying the principal, and if such resignation causes damage to the principal he must indemnify the damage unless he could not continue exercising the agency without suffering serious damage himself. Action taken by an agent who does not know that his powers have been revoked is valid if the parties acted in good faith. (C. C. Arts. 1684-1712, C. Com. arts. 376-409).

PUBLIC INSTRUMENTS:

The evidence of witnesses is not admissible to prove the establishment or extinction of an obligation when the amount involved exceeds Bs. 2,000, nor is such evidence admissible to vary the terms of a written instrument. There are two kinds of written instruments: Public and private. Public instruments are those acknowledged before a registrar or other public officer and may be used as evidence against third persons. Private instruments merely obligate the parties and have no specific date with respect to third persons except from the date when one of the signers dies or becomes unable to write or when the instrument is filed in a public registry or presented in court. (C. C. Arts. 1355-1393).

REAL PROPERTY:

Real property may be such either by nature, by destination or by reason of the object to which it refers. Real property by nature consists of lands, mines, buildings, waters, ungathered crops, herds of cattle or sheep while in their pasture, etc. Real property by destination consists of objects placed on the estate for service and cultivation, such as farming animals and implements, fertilizers, machinery, etc. Real property because of the object with which it is connected consists of easements, mortgages, usufruct, etc. When property belongs to more than one owner, the vote of the majority decides as to its administration. Any co-owner may demand the partition of the property unless there is an agreement not to divide, but no such agreement can be made for a longer term than five years. (C. C. Arts. 526-530, 759-770). Law of Aug. 17, 1983 regulates co-operative apartments.

RECORDS:

Among the principal documents which must be recorded are the following: Mortgages; instruments of conveyance of real estate; instruments creating or canceling easements and other rights in real estate; leases for more than six years; contracts of association for over six years when involving the enjoyment of real estate; instruments and judgments assigning or terminating future rentals for periods of over one year; attachments on real estate; certain actions for the recovery of real estate.

In the capital of the Republic and in each state there is a principal registry office and throughout the country there are numerous subordinate registry offices. The principal registry offices are depositaries of the duplicate records from subordinate offices and of numerous other administrative and judicial archives and keep books for the recording of certain documents of a general nature, such as degrees of physicians, engineers, lawyers, and druggists, appointments of various employees, etc. The subordinate offices keep four principal registry books: (1) For the recording of instruments relating to the conveyance and encumbrance of real estate, leasing of property, creation of corporations and partnerships, mining etc.; (2) for recording of documents relating to

See Topical Index in front part of this volume.

RECORDS . . . *continued*

matrimonial affairs and property, judgments of divorce and separation, adoption, guardianship matters, etc.; (3) for recording of powers of attorney and commercial matters; (4) for recording of intestacy and probate matters. They also keep book of prohibitions and attachments and special mortgage book.

There is a special registry for industrial enterprises (Decree 502 of Dec. 30, 1958); and there is also a special civil registry for births, deaths and marriages (C. C. Arts. 445-524, 1913-1928; Public Registry Law of Feb. 6, 1978 as am'd). See topic Wills.

REDEMPTION: See topics Executions; Mortgages.

REPORTS:

The decisions of the Supreme Court of Justice are published in Official Gazette. They are also published in annual memorial submitted by court to Congress.

RESTRAINT OF TRADE:

See topic Monopolies and Restraint of Trade.

SALES (OF REALTY AND PERSONALTY):

A sale is perfect between the parties and the title passes to the purchaser from the moment the parties manifest their consent in legal manner. The article sold remains at the risk of the buyer although there has been no delivery, except that, if the sale was by weight, count or measure, it is not perfect until these acts have been realized. A sale may be absolute or subject to a condition precedent or subsequent. The price of a sale must be determined by the parties or may be left to be determined by a third person. The costs of the instrument of sale and other accessories are payable by the purchaser. Parents cannot purchase property of the children under their care, nor guardians the property of persons under their guardianship, nor agents the property entrusted to them for sale, nor can attorneys make contracts of sale with their clients regarding matters handled by them.

The principal obligations of the vendor are delivery and warranty of the object sold. The object sold must be delivered as described in the contract. If real estate is sold at a fixed price per unit and the area is found to differ from that stated in the contract there is an adjustment in the price, but the purchaser may withdraw if the excess is more than one-twentieth. Where the object is sold as a whole and is found to vary more than one-twentieth from the size stated in the contract an adjustment of the price may be demanded unless otherwise stipulated.

Warranty covers defects which were not apparent but does not cover those which could be seen. The parties may by agreement increase or limit the usual warranty of the vendor.

Options to repurchase are valid but cannot be stipulated for a longer period than five years, although this period may be extended from time to time. (C. C. Arts. 1161, 1197-1200, 1474-1557).

Conditional sales on installments are governed by Law 491 of Dec. 26, 1958.

SEALS:

Seals are used by the government departments, registry offices and courts but not by private persons. Documents issued by public officials must bear their official seal. For private persons documents executed as public instruments take the place of sealed instruments. See topic Public Instruments.

SEQUESTRATION:

Sequestration will be allowed with regard to: (1) Personal property which is the object of the litigation, when the defendant is irresponsible or it is feared that he may hide, alienate or deteriorate it; (2) the matter in litigation when its possession is doubtful; (3) community property or spouse's property equivalent in amount to community property, when said spouse is administrating community property and dissipating it; (4) parts of decedent's estate when they are claimed as legal portion of heir; (5) real property which defendant has purchased and is enjoying without having paid purchase price; (6) matter in litigation when after judgment against possessor he appeals without giving bond; (7) leased property when defendant has failed to pay rental or is allowing property to deteriorate or is not making agreed improvements or lease expires, if date of expiration is set by contract in public or private document. In order to obtain order of sequestration it is necessary to submit proof to court showing grave presumption that remedy should be granted. Sequestration may be raised by giving bond. (C. C. P. Arts. 585-590, 599).

SHIPPING:

Admiralty matters are governed principally by the Navigation Law and Regulations (Law Aug. 9, 1944 as am'd; Decree Oct. 24, 1944; Decrees 242 to 246, all of July 20, 1951, 49 of Oct. 31, 1953 and Law of Dec. 6, 1985); Code of Commerce and Customs Law. Venezuelan registry will be granted to native or foreign vessels provided they belong to Venezuelan individuals or companies. Captain, pilot, master and engineer must obtain necessary license and be Venezuelan citizens, but in exceptional cases alien may obtain license. Except for transportation of passengers, coastwise trade is restricted to Venezuelan vessels.

STATUTES:

The laws of Venezuela are published in the official newspaper, the "Gaceta Oficial," which appears daily except on holidays, and also in an annual publication called Compilation of the Laws and Decrees of Venezuela. Official editions of important codes and other laws are also occasionally issued. Among the principal codes and laws are the following: National Constitution; Civil Code; Code of Civil Procedure; Penal Code; Code of Criminal Procedure; Code of Commerce; Customs Law; Treasury Law; Mining Law; Law governing Hydrocarbons and other Combustible Minerals; Labor Law; Organic Law of Public Credit; Law of Administrative Procedures.

TAXATION:

Organic Taxation Code (Law of Sept. 11, 1992 as am'd) comprises provisions for tax exonerations, surcharges on delinquent payments, penalties, collection procedures, appeals, statute of limitations and other regulations applicable to all national taxes, except to customs taxes and state and municipal taxes, in which cases applicable only as supplement. It overrules provisions of previous special tax laws.

The income of the Government is derived principally from: (a) Customs revenues; (b) taxes collected under the petroleum and mining laws (see topic Mines and Minerals); (c) income tax; (d) stamp taxes; (e) inheritance taxes; (f) registry fees.

Stamp Taxes and Stamped Paper.—A tax stamp is applied on certain documents such as personal identity cards, passports, certificates of registration of trademarks, patents, professional diplomas, passenger transport tickets going abroad, wherever purchased, etc. Also, practically every document addressed to or issued by judicial or administrative authorities must be on stamped paper. (Stamp Tax Law of May 25, 1994 regulated by Decree 2269 of May 21, 1992 as am'd).

Consumer's Tax on Luxury Goods Wholesale.—(Law-Decree 187 of May 25, 1994 as am'd regulated by Decree 449 of Dec. 7, 1994). Tax is levied on sales of goods, rendering of services, on import of goods and services. General tax rate is 16.5%, luxury goods are taxed at additional rate of 10% or 20%.

Income Tax.—(Law of May 25, 1994 as am'd regulated by Decrees 1028 of Jan. 17, 1996 and 1344 of May 29, 1996).

Natural persons (including decedents' estates) and juridical persons are subject to different tax rates on net income derived from economic activities realized or property located in Venezuela as indicated by law.

Exemptions and Exonerations.—Venezuelan public entities, Venezuelan Investment Fund, charitable institutions, workmen's compensation for accidents, some insurance compensation, and gifts and inheritance, among others, are tax exempt.

Tax structure is based not only on nature of recipient of income, individual or juridical person, but also on type of activity producing income. Income is classified, for practical purposes, in three major categories: (1) Corporate and business income derived from all industrial or commercial activities except mining and oil; (2) income derived from mining or petroleum activity, and from related activities such as refining and transportation of minerals, by individuals, corporations and other juridical persons. Business income from buying and exporting minerals, and royalties derived from all above activities are also included; (3) income other than that classified in categories 1 and 2 received by individuals and decedents' estates, e.g., wages, salaries, professional fees, rents from leasing real property, etc.

Deductions follow same principle that applies to determine taxable income; only those costs and expenses incurred in Venezuela can be deducted. In general, deductions are allowed only for disbursements actually made during taxable year. Different deductions are allowed in computing taxable income corresponding to above income categories.

Category 1.—Gross income, for purpose of tax under this category, is computed by deducting from gross receipts: cost of goods destined for sale or for processing in Venezuela, or of goods necessary to raise income; commissions, if based on normal percentages; freight and insurance. Cost of goods acquired by barter (exchange swap) or in performance of obligation is fair market value thereof at date of transaction. Insurance companies are permitted to deduct indemnifications, payments on policies which have terminated, and other similar disbursements. Net income is finally established by deducting from gross income salaries, wages and other remuneration for services to taxpayer, interest on loans, taxes paid on goods from which income is derived, and taxes on commercial operations other than this tax, depreciation, losses not covered by insurance, royalties, etc. Total deduction for salaries or other payments for services to directors or managers of corporations cannot exceed 15% of gross income. In case of juridical persons other than corporations, above are not allowed if directors or managers share profits and losses of concern. Tax Office may reduce deductions for salaries and other payments for services if dividend payment may be reasonably presumed when compared to salaries which are normally paid by similar companies.

Net income of certain activities is established in the law in terms of fixed percentages of gross income; foreign moving picture producers, 25%; international news agencies, 15%; foreign technical assistance, 30% and technological services, 50%; foreign concerns exporting goods to Venezuela on consignment, 25%; international airlines, 10%; insurance companies, 30%; royalties or similar passive income, 90% of gross receipts. This rule is only for those who are not domiciled in Venezuela. Entities engaged in noncommercial professions and which are not domiciled in Venezuela; net income is set at 90% of gross receipts. Income from foreign sources not specifically taxed in law earned by national individuals or Venezuelan "comunidades" or "comunidades" domiciled in Venezuela is subject to proportional 40% tax on 35% of gross income.

Category 2.—Gross income is computed by deducting from gross receipts corresponding to this income category cost of products sold and services rendered within Venezuela, and which correspond to those described above in Category 1. Net income, under this category, is also computed by deducting from gross income deductions allowed in Category 1. Special rules apply for allowable amount of certain deductions. In case of royalties deduction allowed for administrative expenses actually paid is limited to maximum of 5% of income realized.

Category 3.—Net income is computed by deducting from gross income corresponding to this category,750 UTs. (tributary units) or obligatory social security payments not otherwise deductible, medical and dental expenses actually paid, interest paid in connection with acquisition of home, rent on dwelling used as home, amounts for education of children under 25, hospitalization insurance premiums, paid to companies domiciled in country. Amount for transfer of main house shall not be taken into account for purposes of gross income under certain conditions. Additionally, tax reduction is granted in amount of 10 UTs. (tributary units) for taxpayer himself, for his spouse, and for each of his dependents.

Losses must be calculated separately for each of categories. Net losses in one category may be deducted from net profits on another of taxpayer's income categories. Total net losses may be carried forward three years.

TAXATION . . . *continued*

Rates.—Corporate tax rates are 15% on net yearly income up to 2,000 UTs. (tributary units); on excess up to 3,000 UTs., 22%, and 34% on excess of latter sum. Mining and petroleum companies must pay 20% and 67.7% rates, respectively. Rates for personal income taxes range from 6% on amounts over 1,000 UTs. (tributary units), increasing progressively until it becomes 34% on excess over 6,000 UTs. (tributary units), for individuals locally domiciled; same rates apply to decedents' estates. For individuals nonresident rate is 34% on all taxable income. Late payment of taxes is subject to 18% annual interest. Income arising from lottery games, and track betting is taxed at flat rate of 16%.

Returns.—Natural persons and decedents' estates with net income in excess of equivalent to 1,000 UTs. (tributary units) or gross income of more than 1,500 UTs. (tributary units) must file annual sworn return. All juridical persons established in Venezuela or foreign corporations and individuals nonresident must file return regardless of amount of income.

Husband and wife must file joint return except when under system of separation of property. However, wife may file separate return for her own professional fees and salaries or pensions. When filing separately there is no deduction for other spouse.

Withholding.—Payment of salaries, pensions, lottery prizes, etc., are subject to withholding. Commissions to brokers in real estate transactions, interest from capital loans, payments for rights to exhibit movies and for television rights, insurance premiums and royalties paid to nonresidents are also subject to withholding. Withholding rate varies.

Failure to withhold taxes carries a penalty of 100% of amount to be withheld.

Fixed assets revaluation with adjustment for inflation based on consumer price index for taxpayers that carry out business activities is regulated by law.

Tax deduction of 10% is granted for five years to new investments in mining, forestry activities, tourist, and telecommunications.

Tax on Assets.—(Decree-Law 3266 of Nov. 26, 1993 regulated by Decree 504 of Dec. 28, 1994). Tax at annual rate of 1% of value of assets is assessed on all legal entities and individuals engaged in commercial and industrial activities or exploitation of mines and hydrocarbon and related activities according to law.

Inheritance tax depends on the amount of the inheritance and the degree of relationship. It ranges from 1% in cases where the amount received by ascendants, descendants or spouse does not exceed 15 UTs (tributary units) to 55% in cases where amount received by collaterals beyond fourth degree, relatives by affinity, or unrelated persons exceeds 4,000 UTs (tributary units). Inheritance of shares of registered open capital corporation with market value up to Bs. 5,000,000 is exempted. (Law of Aug. 13, 1982, Decree 1481 of Feb. 25, 1987, Regulations of Dec. 30, 1939).

State Taxes.—The states derive their revenues principally from: (a) appropriations in the national budget; (b) stamped paper; (c) other taxes imposed by the state legislatures. (Const., Art. 17, §3).

Municipal Taxes.—The municipalities receive their income largely from municipal licenses and permits and from house taxes.

Franchise Taxes.—See topic Corporations, subhead Corporate Fees and Taxes.

Customs Law.—(Law of Sept. 18, 1978, Decree 1595 of May 16, 1991). Base for import duties is "normal" value of merchandise. "Normal" value is understood as free market value of imported merchandise; this must appear in customs declaration. Official import prices are fixed in cases of suspected dumping. Law determines that normal price of merchandise must reflect usual price of competition defined as prevailing between independent buyer and seller in free market. Law establishes three types of import duties: Ad valorem, specific and mixed, which will be applied to particular case according to customs tariff regulations.

Free Zones.—(Law of Aug. 4, 1991). Activities in free zones are: industrial when dedicated to assembling, producing or to any other economic process of goods to be exported or reexported; for services when dedicated to performing any service related to foreign trade; and commercial when dedicated to commercialization of national or foreign goods to be exported or reexported. Free zones can be publicly or privately administrated, installation and operation is authorized by "Ministerio de Hacienda". Importation of raw material and capital goods are exempted from duties and taxes, and income arising from export of goods in exempted from income tax for ten years. Income arising from other activities is exempted from income tax.

TRADEMARKS AND TRADENAMES:

(Decision 344 of Oct. 29, 1993 of Commission of Cartagena Agreement, Decree 2887 of Apr. 15, 1993; Industrial Norms Decree 1,043 of June 25, 1963).

Those signs visible and sufficiently distinctive and susceptible of graphic representation can be registered as marks. Trademark is any sign used to distinguish products or services produced or commercialized by one person from same or similar products or services produced or commercialized by another person. Slogans are words, sentences or captions used as supplement to trademark.

Following, among others, cannot be used as trademarks (1) forms and color of product; (2) generic terms; (3) local common names used to describe products; (4) immoral expression or designs; (5) geographical names; (6) letters, names, words, coat of arms and emblems used by national or international organizations; (6) trademarks similar to others, protecting articles of same kind; (7) name or picture of person without consent; (8) title of literary, artistic or scientific works protected by copyright without permission of owner; (9) marks contrary to law, those against public policy, denomination of protected vegetal varieties, those identical or similar to registered trade slogans and tradenames provided under circumstances public may be confused; those that are reproduction, imitation, translation or total or partial transcription of distinctive signs, locally or internationally, well known, without taking into consideration classification of goods or services concerned; or because of similarly to well-known trademarks causes confusion to public independent of classification of goods and services for which registration is applied for. Persons desiring trademark apply to Registry of Industrial Property which causes application to be published and if it considers it in order and there is no opposition, issues certificate. Term of registration is ten years subject to renewal for period of ten years. Renewal application can be filed during six months after expiration of ten-year period. Trademarks can be cancelled for nonuse for consecutive three years by owner or licensee in any member country of Andean Pact.

Tradenames may be registered under the same formalities as trademarks.

Use of word NORVEN or N.V. is restricted to industrial products satisfying standards of Commission of Industrial Norms which will authorize it.

Producers or traders associations may register collective marks. Origin denominations belong to State who may grant right to use them for ten years, renewable.

Venezuela approved Convention for the Protection of Industrial Property, Paris, Mar. 21, 1883, Stockholm Revision of July 14, 1967 as am'd on Sept. 28, 1979.

TREATIES:

Convention on petroleum policy and formation of organization of petroleum exporting countries, signed at Bagdad on Sept. 14, 1960 by Venezuela and Iraq, Iran, Kuwait, and Saudi Arabia; Convention on Private International Law (Bustamante Code) Havana 1928; Universal Copyright Convention, Apr. 27, 1966; Andean Pact Treaty (Mar. 1973); Latin American Economic System (SELA) Treaty of Panama 1975; Montevideo Treaty 1980 (Latin American Integration Association [LAIA]); Inter-American Conventions: On conflicts of laws concerning checks, on extraterritorial validity of foreign judgments and arbitral awards, on conflicts of laws concerning commercial companies, on proof of and information on foreign law, additional protocol to Inter-American convention on letters rogatory, and on general rules of private international law, signed at Montevideo on May 8, 1979; on international commercial arbitration, on taking evidence abroad and on legal regime of powers of attorney to be used abroad, signed at Panama on Jan. 30, 1975; Convention on the Recognition and Enforcement of Foreign Arbitral Awards, New York, 1958; Convention on the settlement of investment disputes between states and nationals of other states, Washington, Aug. 18, 1993; Convention for the Protection of Performers, Producers of Phonograms and Broadcasting Organization (Rome, 1961), Universal Copyright Convention (Geneva, 1952) Revised 1971.

TRUSTS:

Trusts may be created in a will or by an inter vivos act and may comprise personal or real property. A trust of real property must be recorded in the Registry of Real Property in order to be valid against third persons. A trust may be created for benefit of several persons successively provided all were living at time the trust enured to first beneficiary. A trust in favor of a juridical person may not exceed 30 years. Only banks and insurance companies organized in Venezuela and authorized by the government may act as trustees. A trust is terminated: (a) Upon realization of purpose for which it was created or if said realization becomes impossible; (b) upon termination of its duration or the occurrence of condition subsequent; (c) upon renouncement of all beneficiaries; (d) upon revocation by creator of the trust if so provided in the instrument; and (e) in the absence of beneficiary, if no substitution is possible. (Law of July 26, 1956).

VITAL STATISTICS: See topic Records.

WILLS:

All persons may make wills except: (1) Minors below 16 years of age unless they have been married; (2) persons declared incapacitated for intellectual defects; (3) persons non compos mentis; (4) deaf and dumb persons and dumb persons who cannot write.

Persons guilty of serious offenses against the testator are incapable of inheriting from him. The following are also incapable of inheriting: (1) Churches and mortmain institutions; (2) clerics and ministers of religion, unless such person be a spouse, ascendant, descendant or blood relative within the fourth degree of the testator. Legacies in favor of the registrar or witnesses who intervene in the making of the will are invalid.

Witnesses to wills must be of age, able to read and write, and know the testator. The following cannot be witnesses; Blind persons; deaf and dumb persons; those who do not know Spanish; relatives within the fourth degree of consanguinity or second of affinity of the registrar before whom the will is made; heirs and legatees mentioned in the will and their relatives in the said degrees in case of an open will; any one who could not act as witness in court.

There are two classes of wills: Ordinary and special. The ordinary will is open or closed.

An open will is one declared by the testator before witnesses, who thus learn of its contents. It may be executed; (a) in accordance with the provisions of the public registry law, before a registrar and three witnesses, recording the document in the public registry; (b) without recording, before a registrar and three witnesses; (c) before five witnesses, in which event it must be acknowledged in court within six months by at least two of the witnesses and also by the testator if he still lives. If executed before a registrar, the will may be submitted to him in complete form or may be drawn up under his supervision, but in any case it must be read before the witnesses.

A closed will is one enclosed in an envelope which is closed and sealed in the presence of a registrar and five witnesses. In delivering the same to the registrar the testator must declare that the enclosed document is his will and state whether or not it is written and signed by him. A minute of the delivery is written on the envelope and signed by the testator and witnesses and registrar. Persons unable to read cannot make a closed will.

Special wills are: (1) Those made in case of epidemics before a registrar or judicial authority in the presence of two witnesses who may be of either sex but must be at least 18 years old. Such wills lapse within two months after the epidemic ceases or the testator re-moves elsewhere. (2) Maritime wills, which may be made during a voyage before the captain and two witnesses. Such wills are effective only until the lapse of two months from the time the testator reaches a point where he might make another will. (3) Military wills, which may be made before certain military officers during a campaign.

Foreign wills are valid if made in accordance with the laws of the place where executed, but they must be in authentic form and may not be oral or holographic, nor can they be joint wills of several persons. They may also be made in accordance with

See Topical Index in front part of this volume.

WILLS . . . *continued*

Venezuelan laws and executed before a representative of Venezuela at the place of execution.

A testator cannot dispose of the legal portion of his estate which by law must be set aside for his descendants, ascendants and surviving spouse. Such legal portion is one-half the participation which those persons would have in case of intestacy. (See topic Descent and Distribution). The balance of the property may be freely disposed of. (C. C. Arts. 833-992).

A report of the execution of any will must be filed with the Registry of Wills. (Decree 601 of Sept. 20, 1957).

VIETNAM LAW DIGEST REVISER

Tilleke & Gibbins Consultants Limited
Tilleke & Gibbins Building
64/1 Soi Tonson, Ploenchit Road
Bangkok 10330, Thailand
Telephone: 254 2640 58
Fax: 254 4304; 621 0172 73
Email: 4630672@mcimail.com
Library: beckyr@mozart.inet.co.th
Vietnam Offices: 51 Trieu Viet Vuong, Hai Ba Trung District, Hanoi. Telephone: 84 4 227-895/6; 268-860. Fax: 84 4 227-897. 2nd Floor, The Vietnam National Gold-Silver and Gemstones Corporation Building, 3-5 Ho Tung Mau, District 1, Ho Chi Minh. Telephone: 84 8 251-645; 251-695; 251-700. Fax: 84 8 242-226.
Cambodia Office: No. 56 Street Samdech.Sothearos, Khan Duan Penh. Phnom Penh. Telephone 855 23 62670. Fax: 855 23 62671. Email: Tilleke-Gibbins@uni.fi

Reviser Profile

History: Tilleke & Gibbins, the oldest and largest independent law firm in Thailand, recognizing the business potential in Vietnam, in 1989 established Tilleke & Gibbins Consultants Limited (TGCL) to provide investment and legal consulting services for businesses engaged in commercial activities in Vietnam. In July 1992, Tilleke & Gibbins became the first foreign law firm to be granted a license to establish a representative office in Vietnam. The office, located in Ho Chi Minh City, Vietnam's commercial center, was followed by the establishment in January 1994 of a branch office in Hanoi.

Members of the Firm: The Firm has professional staff and attorneys with personal experience in the Vietnamese business environment. They also have extensive experience in dealing with government and quasi-government agencies and private businesses in Vietnam. The foreign and Vietnamese attorneys of Tilleke & Gibbins Consultants Limited are complemented by the expertise of the attorneys and support staff as well as the resources of Tilleke & Gibbins in Thailand. In addition to Vietnamese and English, the Firm has significant German, French, Spanish, and Japanese language capabilities.

Services: Tilleke & Gibbins Consultants Limited sees its relationships with clients as proactive, long-term and based upon a fundamental understanding of each client's business activities and objectives. TGCL also works closely with local Vietnamese legal firms to ensure that each client receives the best possible service. The Firm provides legal advice and assistance in the following areas: banking and finance, commercial and international trade, communications and telecommunications; corporate services and establishing representative offices, dispute resolution, environment, foreign investment, human resources, intellectual property, maritime, property and construction, transportation and taxation. The Firm is the member for Vietnam of Lex Mundi and Multilaw, worldwide associations of independent law firms, enhancing the Firm's ability to serve its clients.

Clients: The Firm's clients include pharmaceutical and chemical companies; cosmetic firms; garment manufacturers; banks and financial institutions; food and beverage companies; petroleum drilling and service companies; commercial and trading houses; computer manufacturers and software developers; electrical, electronics and communications companies; hotels and travel-related industries.

VIETNAM LAW DIGEST

(The following is a list of all Topics, including cross-references, covered in this Digest.)

VIETNAM LAW DIGEST

Prepared for 1997 edition by

TILLEKE & GIBBINS CONSULTANTS LIMITED of the Bangkok, Thailand, Hanoi and Ho Chi Minh City, Vietnam and Phnom Penh, Cambodia Bars

INTRODUCTION:

Vietnam is 1,750 km long, with coastline of 3,250 km, and total land area of 330,000 square km. Two cities dominate country: Hanoi and Ho Chi Minh City. Hanoi, in north, is government seat and has population of 3 million. Ho Chi Minh City, in south, is commercial center and has population of 4.3 million. Other major urban centers are Haiphong, population of 1.7 million; Da Nang, 600,000; Nha Trang, 300,000; and Hue, 300,000.

Total population is between 72-74 million, making it world's twelfth and Asia's fifth most populous country, second only to Indonesia in South East Asia. Vietnam has diverse population. Eighty-four percent are etho-Vietnamese, 2% ethnic Chinese and remainder consists of about 60 ethno-linguistic groups called "Montagnards", or "highlanders" in French; Khmers; and Chams (descendants of Champa Kingdom). Seventy-five percent of population lives in rural areas. Sixty percent is under 25 years old (of which 40% is under 15 years old). 35 million are in labor force. Ninety percent of adult populace is literate.

Language.—Vietnamese language (kinh) is spoken throughout country and is combination of Mon-Khmer, Tai and Chinese. Some ethnic minority groups do not speak it fluently. There are minor differences between the way it is spoken in North and South. It is tonal language and meaning of word changes depending on how pronounced. There are six tones in north and five in south.

Main Western languages spoken are French, English and Russian. English has become very important in professional and commercial dealings. Since reunification teaching of Russian has been stressed throughout country.

Office Hours and Time Zone.—Vietnam is seven hours ahead of Greenwich Mean Time and because of proximity to equator has no daylight saving time (summer time). Office hours are usually from 7 to 8 am to 11 or 11:30 am, when they close for lunch; then from 1 or 2 pm to 4 or 5 pm. Almost all government offices and businesses are closed on Suns. Museums are generally closed on Mon. as well.

ARBITRATION AND AWARD:

There is currently no legislation governing enforcement of arbitration adjudicated by Vietnamese arbitrators in Vietnam. However, Vietnam recently acceded to New York Convention on the Recognition and Enforcement of Foreign Arbitral Awards on Aug. 31, 1995, effective Nov. 1995 ("The Convention"). This accession followed adoption of Ordinance on the Recognition and Enforcement of Foreign Arbitral Awards in Vietnam ("The Ordinance") which became effective Jan. 1, 1996. This Ordinance enables arbitrations held both outside and within Vietnam by foreign arbitrators, which are according to Vietnamese law as adjudged by Vietnamese judges, to be enforceable in Vietnam.

Arbitration in Vietnam may take place at nongovernmental economic arbitration centers or Vietnam International Arbitration Center ("VIAC"), part of Vietnam Chamber of Commerce in Hanoi, Vietnam. Five or more Vietnamese arbitrators are needed to establish economic arbitration center according to Government Decree No. 116/CP on the Organisation and Operation of the Economic Arbitration Center. (Art. 7). Foreign arbitrators cannot hear arbitration disputes within this Economic Arbitration Center. Since there is no legal mechanism for enforcing arbitration adjudicated by Vietnamese arbitrators, arbitration held by Economic Arbitration Centers in Vietnam are not capable of being enforced in Vietnam other than by voluntary process. There is currently no provision in Vietnamese law providing for Vietnamese arbitration award to be enforceable in same manner as Vietnamese civil judgment. However, under Ordinance, foreign arbitrage awards, defined as both arbitral awards heard by arbitrators located outside Vietnam and foreign arbitrators located in Vietnam, recognized by Vietnamese Court, would be enforced in same manner as civil Vietnamese judgments.

Arbitration held at VIAC may be heard by Vietnamese arbitrators or foreign arbitrators. If arbitration is heard by foreign arbitrators, it may be recognized and enforced in Vietnam as foreign arbitrage award according to The Ordinance.

As in China, arbitration, after amicable conciliation, is favorable means of resolving international commercial disputes. Prior to 1987, international commercial disputes were settled by Vietnam Foreign Arbitration Council, which has now been merged with Vietnamese Maritime Arbitration Council and is known as Vietnam International Arbitration Centre (VIAC). VIAC, nongovernmental organization, is attached to Vietnam Chamber of Commerce and Industry, quasi-governmental and powerful business organization. VIAC has no compulsory jurisdiction and may only act where parties agree to refer disputes to it. Awards issued by VIAC are final and binding upon parties and are not reviewable by domestic courts. Parties to dispute may select their own arbiter from panel of both Vietnamese and foreign law experts. If parties cannot agree on arbiter, Chairman of VIAC may name presiding arbiter.

As previously stated, foreign arbitration may be enforced in Vietnam under 1958 New York Convention on Recognition and Enforcement of Foreign Arbitral Awards and Ordinance on Recognising and Implementing in Vietnam Awards of Foreign Arbitrators dated Sept. 14, 1995 and effective on Jan. 1, 1996 ("The Ordinance"). The Ordinance gives Vietnamese courts power to recognize and implement in Vietnam foreign arbitrage awards from countries with which Vietnam has signed international convention or on basis of reciprocal interest. (Art. 2). Successful party to foreign award ("claimant") must pay court fee and may only file written request for recognition and implementation to competent Vietnamese court via Vietnamese Ministry of Justice only if unsuccessful party ("respondent") has business operation or resides in Vietnam or if property being subject of dispute is in Vietnam at time of request. (Art. 3).

Written request must include full name and address of both parties and legal representative of successful party in Vietnam, if any, or address of relevant property in Vietnam. (Art. 10). Documents to be enclosed with request include documents provided under Convention. If international convention does not specify documents to be attached or there is no convention relating to matter, then Vietnamese original or notarized and certified copy of foreign arbitrage award in accordance with Vietnamese laws should be attached to request. (Art. 11).

Panel of Vietnamese judges will not retry substantive issues already determined by foreign arbitrators. However, respondent could request panel of judges to set aside award if respondent could affirmatively prove that parties to arbitration agreement do not have capacity to sign agreement; arbitration agreement has no legal effect in country law of which parties have elected to apply or under law of country where arbitration was held if no governing law was chosen; claimant did not receive timely notice of appointment of arbiters, procedure to be followed or for some other reason party was prevented from exercising its rights; award was based on issues which party did not agree to arbitrate. If arbitrable issues are severable, those may be recognized and enforceable; composition of arbiters or arbitration proceedings do not conform to arbitration agreement or laws of country where arbitration was held; foreign arbitrage award has been dismissed or suspended by competent authority of country where award was made. In addition, foreign arbitrage award will not be recognized and enforced in Vietnam where court decides that dispute should not have been settled by arbitration, or recognition and enforcement is contrary to basic Vietnamese principles. (Art. 16).

In contrast, foreign arbitrage award which is recognized and enforceable has same legal effect as legally effective decision issued by Vietnamese court and its enforcement by appropriate enforcement agency is treated like civil Vietnamese judgment. (Art. 20).

Appellant wishing to appeal to Supreme People's Court in Vietnam for nonrecognition and nonenforcement of foreign arbitrage award must file appeal with such Court within 15 days from date Provincial People's Court's issuance of any court decision. (Art. 18).

ATTORNEYS AND COUNSELORS:

Introduction.—Substantial economic reforms have been implemented in Vietnam in last decade. With industrialization and modernization, both local and foreign lawyers and consultants have been presented with numerous challenges and opportunities and their services have become indispensable. With increased importance of these professions, need for regulation has arisen.

The Provisional Decree 1945.—Law practice in Vietnam is very different from that of western world due primarily to fact that Vietnamese lawyers are under administrative and political restraint. Besides having obligations to his client, Vietnamese lawyer also has obligations to state. Thus, in pursuing his client's interests, he must also ensure that these interests conform with those of State.

In 1945, after Vietnam regained its independence, Democratic Republic of Vietnam (now referred to as Socialist Republic of Vietnam) was established. Before 1945 Constitution, Provisional Decree continued to recognize bar associations formed during former regime and introduced changes regarding conditions for practicing law in Vietnam, one significant change being that lawyers had to be Vietnamese nationals. Decree also specified certain rights granted only to lawyers. One such right enabled Vietnamese lawyers to represent clients in all Vietnamese courts, including military courts.

In practical application, Decree was not strictly adhered to. Despite reaffirmation by Constitutions of 1959 and 1980 and Criminal Code of person's right to legal defense, large gap existed between what was stipulated by Constitution and what was implemented due to lack of government attention in enforcment, war, and lack of training available for law graduates. All these factors eventually led to dissolution of lawyers' associations.

Lawyers' associations reemerged from 1989 decision of People's Committee in Ho Chi Minh City and both lawyers' associations and bar associations now exist in Vietnam.

Lawyers' associations began to form in Hanoi in 1955 and are open to all Vietnamese citizens working in legal fields including lawyers, court clerks, prosecutors, judges, and even policemen. Associations' activities are both social and professional. These associations also have political tone as they were formed soon after French withdrawal from Vietnam. The government expects members to work for Vietnamese benefit, to be instruments of communist/socialist government, and to act as role models.

Bar Associations.—No bar associations were formed until 1987, when State Council (now Standing Committee of National Assembly) adopted Ordinance on Bar Associations (the Ordinance) which provides that bar associations may be established in provinces, cities or in special administrative units. The Ordinance places bar associations and their members under control of Ministry of Justice, People's Council, and People's Committee of city or province where located. It also stipulates that People's Committees (administrative and political organizations) in city or province monitor activities of bar association and members. Nevertheless, as bar association membership rights are limited to lawyers (although it is neither mandatory nor a right for lawyers) and do not apply to members of state agencies unless they are law researchers or professors, bar associations maintain more of legal focus than lawyers' associations. For example, bar associations contribute significantly to drafting laws and act as informal body of legal advisors to government.

Bar Association Membership Requirements.—Ordinance on Bar Associations stipulates membership requirements of bar associations. To join, applicant must be Vietnamese citizen; have graduated from law university or possess legal knowledge equivalent to that obtained in law university; have good qualities and morals; have personal data approved by general conference of local bar association or by supervisor at applicant's office; be elected at member's meeting of bar association; and be on probation for two years (this period may be reduced depending on applicant's prior legal experience). Despite these requirements, there is also certain amount of subjectivity involved in admission of lawyers to bar associations. Applicants qualified as

See Topical Index in front part of this volume.

ATTORNEYS AND COUNSELORS . . . *continued*
lawyers in South Vietnam under pre-1975 government and lawyers who graduated from socialist university abroad can become members of bar association by either having practiced law for five years or by taking one year course in socialist law. (No practical difference exists between lawyers who were licensed to practice in south before unification of country in 1975 and those qualified since.) One can also receive membership by serving as apprentice in government legal office for five years. Furthermore, if membership application is rejected, applicant can appeal first to People's Committee of city or province and then to Ministry of Justice.

Rights and Obligations of Vietnamese Lawyers.—Lawyers may practice in any court in Vietnam, regardless of locality of bar association membership. Furthermore, under Ordinance and 1989 Decree of the Government which promulgates regulations of bar associations, Vietnamese lawyers may represent parties in civil cases (including marriage, family and labor cases); represent parties in criminal cases or in any other legal matter; represent cases which fall within competence of military court; represent and provide legal consultation to individual, State, collective and private economic organizations or any other entity in commercial or other matter including foreign business enterprises. Furthermore, Art. 17 of Ordinance stipulates that, when providing legal consultation, lawyers have right to represent economic enterprises in disputes brought to arbitration or other judicial forums; provide any other legal services to citizens and organizations; receive fees in accordance with bar association rules.

In representing clients, lawyers must review files and insist that all public files be accurate and updated; treat all parties equally; request removal of party to action if there is conflict of interest or for other just cause; participate in all procedures before court; make comments or corrections to court's minutes of proceedings; appeal court's judgment and keep client confidences. Lawyer's participation in matter may be challenged if he has acted as investigator, prosecutor, judge, people's accuser, witness, legal expert or translator in matter, or if he is related to client.

Types of Vietnamese Lawyers.—Presently, there are two types of Vietnamese lawyers. Luat gia are eligible for membership only in lawyers' associations. Luat su, of higher status, are eligible to apply to bar associations.

To qualify as luat gia, applicant must be Vietnamese national and law university graduate or hold equivalent level of legal knowledge. Applicant must have good character, and be recommended by two lawyers' association members. There is no period of probation to qualify as luat gia. Most work in Office of Juridical Services and provide legal services only to government and/or to public pursuant to local justice administration control. To represent client before court, luat gia is required to have power of attorney from client and approval by either head of Office of Investigations, prosecutor, chief judge or court's council (comprised of judge and two jurors).

To qualify as luat su, applicant must be Vietnamese national and law university graduate or hold equivalent level of legal knowledge. Applicant must have good character. He cannot be simultaneously employed by courts, prosecutor's office or police. Board of Management of bar associations reviews and approves applications. Once qualified, luat su, unlike luat gia, requires only letter of introduction from bar association in order to appear before court.

Apart from above two clearly defined types of lawyers exists third category: persons not qualified as either luat su or luat gia, but who hold law degree. Persons in this category may still perform same tasks as luat gia if client specifically requests and appropriate certificates issued.

Offices.—Apart from few lawyers using clients' offices, most bar association members are government employees who share one office from which they represent private clients. Private offices are not allowed unless two lawyers and two additional lawyers under probation request permission from Board of Management of bar association to set up bar association branch.

Fees.—All arrangements engaging lawyers' services must be in writing and placed on file in bar association office. Fees are set by bar association and approved by respective People's Committee. Fees are paid directly to bar association. Approximately 80% are returned to lawyer.

1987 Ordinance and 1989 Government Decree played significant role in revival of legal profession in Vietnam during period of great economic and political change. Vietnamese lawyers now are supporters of public and business community and profession is growing rapidly. As of 1995, there were 700 lawyers and 51 bar associations in Vietnam. As provided by 1987 Ordinance, lawyers are principally involved with criminal cases, not civil cases. Thus, foreign and domestic businesses as well as economic enterprises still have nowhere to go for legal representation.

Legal Consulting Firms.—Resulting from 1987 Foreign Investment Law of Vietnam and increased development, new legal profession, lying outside regulating scope of Ordinance developed. Vietnamese lawyers working for consultation firms and companies, formed pursuant to Vietnamese Company law or under lines of state agencies or social organizations, provide legal advice mainly to foreign and domestic business enterprises. Presently, amount of legal advice rendered through consultation firms has surpassed that rendered through government offices. As most of these consultation firms are not members of bar associations, their lawyers are not qualified to participate in litigation. They may provide legal representation only on Vietnamese laws, usually in investment and business areas.

Vietnamese government is greatly concerned that no laws currently regulate these consultation firms' conduct and professional liability.

Foreign Lawyers Practicing in Vietnam.—With increased foreign investment came many foreign lawyers. Vietnamese government responded by allowing foreign legal firms to open representative offices in Vietnam. (Having representative office status does not allow foreign lawyers to practice law in Vietnam.) On July 8, 1995, government enacted Decree 42/CP on Regulations Concerning Legal Consulting of Foreign Lawyers' Organization in Vietnam (Decree 42). Government also instructed Ministry of Justice to research into and draft laws on foreign legal practice in Vietnam.

Decree 42 states that foreign law firms or lawyers' organizations that want to establish legal consultation offices in Vietnam must apply for branch offices. Each foreign entity can establish two branches in Vietnam. Term of branch is five years with each renewal not exceeding three years. Foreign lawyers working in branch offices must have at least five years of legal consultation experience. Foreign lawyers are limited in what they can do in Vietnam. For example, they cannot participate in judicial procedures of Vietnamese courts as representatives and may only practice international law, not Vietnamese law.

Legal Education in Vietnam.—In order for there to be standard of legal professionalism in Vietnam, all Vietnamese lawyers must have Bachelor of Law degree and complete training course before being accepted as trainee lawyer.

Teaching of contemporary law is still new in Vietnam. Hanoi University of Law, established in 1979, and its branch in Ho Chi Minh City, are only designated law schools. Recently, General University of Ho Chi Minh City also introduced law course offered for either two or four years. Classes are taught mainly by professors trained in Vietnam or other socialist countries.

Typical law curriculum covers subjects in both law and politics. As there is very limited teaching of law and free market economy concepts, curriculum changes needed to assist law students to handle changing political and legal environment in Vietnam are presently underway.

Legal Training in Vietnam.—Vietnamese government is establishing legal training program for holders of Bachelor of Law degree. No legal training schools currently exist in Vietnam, so all training on substantive law and professional skills is being provided through bar associations or law firms and offices, inevitably producing lawyers of varying degrees of capability. In order to bring more consistency to profession, Vietnamese government, in addition to establishment of judge training school, plans to organize one-year training courses for those who hold Bachelor of Law degrees and who want to become lawyers.

CIVIL ACTION:

Legislation.—Civil Code, promulgated by National Assembly, on Nov. 28, 1995 and effective July 1, 1996 (CCV); Ordinance on Procedures of Settlement of Civil Lawsuits, issued by State Council (Standing Committee of National Assembly), on Jan. 1, 1990 (OPSC); Ordinance on Procedures of Settlement of Economic Lawsuits, issued by Standing Committee of National Assembly on Mar. 16, 1994 (OPSE).

Current court system in Vietnam consists of criminal courts, civil courts (including family and intellectual property courts), economic courts (including maritime courts), labor courts, and administrative courts. Administrative courts and labor courts have only been established since July 1, 1996.

Deposition.—With respect to civil and economic lawsuits, litigants are each obligated to provide evidence to substantiate their case. (OPSC, Art. 3; OPSE, Arts. 3 and 4). Court may, in its discretion, collect more evidence, or question genuineness of evidence litigants provide. (OPSE, Art. 35). Admissible evidence must be legal, objective, and relevant. Types of evidence obtained before trial admissible in Vietnamese courts are documentary evidence including, but not limited to, tangible items, related documents, laboratory results and evaluation.

Litigant may also provide written interrogatories to court at pretrial level for other litigant to answer if some issues are still unclear. Witnesses are only summoned to attend trial and need not give oral depositions at pretrial. (OPSC, Art. 20; OPSE, Arts. 47 and 48).

In both civil and economic courts, presiding judge within one jurisdiction may ask another Vietnamese court located outside his jurisdiction to collect or verify certain evidence for his use. (OPSC, Art. 39).

Judgments.—Civil court trial panel consists of presiding judge and two jurors. Final judgment by such court is determined by majority vote as in economic court cases. Decision must state: date and place of court hearing; full name of trial panel including that of prosecutor and of court's secretary; full name and address of litigants and their legal representatives; claims and defenses; facts alleged and proven; court holding and its legal basis; duties of each litigant with respect to court fees; and right of litigants to appeal. (OPSE, Art. 52).

Copy of judgment must be delivered to litigants and prosecutor within seven days, or at most 15 days, from judgment issuance date. (OPSC, Art. 57; OPSE, Art. 57).

At appeal level, panel, consisting of three judges, will determine whether to reverse or maintain lower court judgment by majority vote. Decision of appeal court is final and binding on litigants. (OPSC, Art. 70; OPSE, Art. 72).

Statute of Limitations.—For economic lawsuits, plaintiff must file suit within six months from date dispute giving rise to action arises, unless other laws provide otherwise. (OPSE, Art. 31). (Currently other laws do not provide for other statute of limitations to apply.)

For civil lawsuits, OPSC does not explicitly provide for any statute of limitation. Under Civil Code, however, three kinds of statute of limitations are mentioned: limitation for enjoying civil rights; limitations for release from civil obligation; and limitation of action for initiating legal action. (CCV, Art. 164). No statute of limitation exists for request to return assets owned collectively by the people; request to protect violation of personal rights, unless law provides otherwise; and other circumstances stipulated by law. (CCV, Art. 169).

Replevin action is available in Vietnam as in other jurisdictions.

Sequestration.—In both economic and civil courts, judge may order sequestration of witnesses at request of either party or their lawyers in order to insure that in-court testimony of each witness is not colored by what another witness said. (OPSC, Art. 49[4]; OPSE, Art. 46[4]).

COMMERCIAL REGISTER:

Commercial registration under Vietnamese laws means business registration and registration of other commercial or noncommercial activities necessary for company business operations.

Business Registration.—Vietnamese enterprises including state-run companies and foreign-invested companies (hereinafter called, "company") must first obtain business permit from competent State authorities of Vietnam in order to operate their business in Vietnam. This business permit is certificate evidencing legal status of company.

Vietnamese companies also need to obtain business license, issued by Provincial Planning Committee, in order to conduct business activities. This Committee will determine whether or not to grant business license, within 6-12 months of filing of

See Topical Index in front part of this volume.

COMMERCIAL REGISTER . . . *continued*
company's business permit and legitimate documents evidencing company's legal address, such as office lease agreement, with them.

If Vietnamese company wishes to open branch offices in other provinces, or to amend scope of permitted activities, to amend registered capital, or to move legal office, a reregistration application must be filed with same Committee and contain original copy of business license, board of director's resolution on amendments to be made, bank certificate showing capital increasing (in case of capital increase), and house leasing agreement or housing certificate (if company is moving office location).

For companies with foreign invested capital, including wholly foreign-owned companies and joint venture companies, business license issued by MPI is sufficient form of business registration.

Other Types of Registration.—

Registration for Patent, Trademark, and Copyright Protection.—All organizations and individuals, domestic or foreign, are entitled to submit applications for obtaining protection of their industrial properties in Vietnam.

National Office for Industrial Property (NOIP) is authorized agency to receive, consider applications, and issue certificates for protection of trademark, and patents.

Department for Copyright is authorized agency to receive, consider and grant copyright certificates.

Registration for Export-Import Rights of Companies with Foreign Invested Capital in Vietnam.—In order to directly or indirectly import necessary raw materials or equipment to contribute in kind by foreign party in joint venture company in Vietnam, joint venture company must obtain import-export license registration from Ministry of Trade. Documents to be submitted to Ministry of Trade for consideration include: application for import-export license, copy of joint venture investment license, and company's specific, detailed import plan for year.

Registration of Licensing Contracts and Transfer of Technology Contracts.—Under Vietnamese laws, licensing contracts and transfer of technology contracts between foreign organizations or individuals and Vietnamese organizations or individuals must be approved by Ministry of Science, Technology and Environment and registered with NOIP.

Business Registration of Foreign Legal Consultancy Companies.—Foreign law firms, permitted by Ministry of Justice to establish branch offices in Vietnam in accordance with Decree No. 42-CP dated July 8, 1995 (see topic Attorneys and Counselors) must register business activities with Department of Justice in Hanoi or Ho Chi Minh City.

Registration of Pharmaceutical Companies or Products.—Foreign pharmaceutical companies, wishing to distribute their products in Vietnam must register their respective companies and products with Ministry of Health of Vietnam.

Registration of Mortgaged or Pledged Properties.—Moveable and immovable properties may be mortgaged or pledged to creditors to secure their interests. Registration takes place when pledge or mortgage contract is executed. Vietnam Committee for Civil Aviation is entitled to certify mortgaging contracts for planes, while Maritime Department certifies ship mortgage contracts.

Registration of Foreign Representative Office Activities.—Ministry of Trade issues business licenses for establishment of foreign representative offices in Vietnam. However, representative office must register office address, business activities and number of staff with respective Provincial People's Committee where office is to be located. Documents to be submitted with registration application include certified copy of lease agreement, and list of names of Vietnamese staff and foreign staff to be employed. Similar procedures are applied when office sets up branch offices in other locations within Vietnam.

Registration of Labor Contracts of Enterprises with Foreign Invested Capital.—Enterprises with foreign invested capital looking for Vietnamese staff to hire may seek assistance of Labor Department or local service agencies. Once company wants to hire Vietnamese staff, it must register labor contract with same Department of Labor or local service agencies.

CONSTITUTION AND GOVERNMENT:

Vietnam is committed socialist state where communist party is dominant. Country is ruled by Cabinet of Ministers through Prime Minister's Office. 395-seat lawmaking National Assembly is highest state organ. Laws, including Civil Code and Criminal Code, are passed by National Assembly. There have been four constitutions. Most recent was passed in 1992. Permanent Standing Committee acts on behalf of National Assembly when it is not in session, including passing Ordinances. Decrees are passed by government and generally implement laws or ordinances. Decrees are often accompanied by more detailed "Regulations". Circulars are issued by individual ministries and usually provide guidance as to how particular ministry will administer law, ordinance, or decree. Guidelines are not legal instruments, but are policy outlines issued by Prime Minister indicating that governmental committees should be set up to deal with issues. Recital of each legal instrument normally sets out other legal instrument to which it is subordinate. If one instrument is intended to replace previous one, that fact is normally mentioned at end of instrument.

In 1986, Vietnam instituted its "Doi Moi", or "renovation", reform program to move from centrally-planned Marxist economy to state-regulated market economy. Key elements of this program include: promotion of private sector; phase-out of most price controls; reform of industrial policy to give State-owned entities greater autonomy; restructure of banking system; adjustment of foreign exchange rates; replacement of farm collectives with privatized family farming; and new foreign investment law. This foreign investment law (FIL) is centerpiece of "Doi Moi" and was passed in 1987 along with companion legislation covering matters such as taxation, banking, foreign exchange, labor, import and export, technology transfer, and corporate governance. FIL guarantees that invested capital and assets of foreign investors may not be requisitioned or expropriated and enterprise with foreign investment capital may not be nationalized. Hanoi-based State Committee for Cooperation and Investment ("SCCI") has authority to issue licenses for qualifying investment projects. Foreign investors may implement investments through joint venture enterprises, foreign wholly owned enterprises, business cooperation contracts, and build-operate transfer arrangements.

CONTRACTS:

With establishment of Democratic Republic of Vietnam (in 1945) and then reunification in 1975, contract laws have developed gradually under Socialist Republic of Vietnam regime.

In first legal document on contracts, Decree No. 97-SL issued by President Ho Chi Minh on May 22, 1950, basic principles of Vietnamese civil laws were first discussed. Second significant legal document was Decree No. 735/TTg on Apr. 10, 1957 (issued with Temporary Regulation on Business Contracts). This decree covered provisions governing contractual relationship between economic units such as state-owned enterprises, cooperatives, and private sector. All contracts are governed by principles of free will, equality, honesty, and are for mutual benefit of parties and for benefit of national economy development.

Until 1960, no clear distinction between civil contracts and economic/business contracts existed. After 1960, socialist economy was initiated and new laws on economic contracts were issued separating laws on contracts from laws on civil contracts. These new laws assisted State to better manage socialist economy. However, economic contracts during this period did not correctly reflect demand and supply relationship of market, and were simply a tool to execute State's economic goals. Execution of economic contracts was not based on mutual agreements between contractual parties, but instead was compulsory obligation of economic units vis-à-vis the State. Scope of economic contracts was limited to State-owned and collective sectors.

Not until 1986, with new economic policy, was Vietnamese contract law really developed, with several types of contract becoming available for growing economy including economic, civil, and commercial contracts. All are based on four main principles: it must be valid, voluntary contract, made between parties with equal bargaining power, for mutual benefit.

Civil Contract.—

Legislation.—1992 Constitution of Vietnam (c. II "The economic regime" and c. V, "Basic rights and responsibilities of citizens"); Civil Code, adopted by National Assembly, on Oct. 28, 1995, effective July 1, 1996; Ordinance on Procedure for Settlement of Civil Cases, Council of Ministers (Government), on Oct. 29, 1989.

Parties of Civil Contract.—Civil Code (CC) has replaced Ordinance on Civil Contract, issued by Standing Committee of National Assembly, on July 1, 1991. Under CC, parties to civil contract are: (1) Individuals having legal capacity to engage in civil acts (See CC, Arts. 16–22); (2) legal entities established or permitted to establish as private companies by competent authorities; legally permitted to own and be responsible for properties on which companies are established; and able to file civil actions or be sued; (3) households and cooperatives (CC, Arts. 116 and 120); (4) foreign organizations and individuals (CC, Art. 826).

Formation.—Civil contracts may be formed in writing, verbally, or by performance of specific activity when law does not otherwise prohibit. (CC, Art. 400[1]). If law provides that contract be formed in writing, certified by Notary Public, and registered, then these provisions must be complied with. (CC, Art. 400[2]). Pledge, mortgage or third-party guarantee is executed to guarantee performance of civil contract.

Execution.—Civil contracts must be executed with principles of honesty, mutual benefit and trust kept in mind. Quality, quantity, and category must be ensured and contract must be executed in time and in accordance with agreements of parties. It must also not infringe upon interest of State, public interest, or legal rights and interests of third parties. (CC, Art. 409). CC further provides for execution of both unilateral and bilateral contracts as well as execution of contracts for benefit of third parties. CC also provides for means to amend or to terminate unilaterally such contracts.

Types of civil contracts discussed throughout CC include contracts for sale and purchase of moveable properties (Arts. 421 to 442); contracts for sale and purchase of house (Arts. 443 to 451); moveable property exchange contracts (Arts. 459 to 466); property loan contracts (Arts. 467-514); property leasing contracts (Arts. 476 to 514); property borrowing contracts (Arts. 515 to 520); service contracts (Arts. 521 to 529); transport contracts (Arts. 530 to 549); processing contracts (Arts. 550 to 561); bailment contracts (Arts. 562 to 570); insurance contracts (Arts. 571 to 584); and power-of-attorney contracts (Arts. 585-594).

Dispute Settlement.—Any disputes arising from civil contract must first be resolved by direct negotiations between parties.

Economic Contract.—

Legislation.—Ordinance on Economic Contract, on Sept. 25, 1989 (OOEC); Decree No. 17/CP dated Jan. 16, 1990 providing in detail implementation of Ordinance on Economic Contract, issued by Council of Ministers (Government), on Jan. 16, 1990 (Decree No. 17/CP); Ordinance on Procedure for Settlement of Economic Cases, issued by Standing Committee of National Assembly, on Mar. 16, 1994.

Economic contract defined as agreement in writing or exchange of documents between contracting parties on execution of production, exchange of goods, services, research, and application of scientific and technical know-how and other business agreements which clearly set out parties' rights and responsibilities. (OOEC, Art. 1).

Economic contract may be signed between Vietnamese juridical persons. (OOEC, Art. 2). This term covers state-owned entities, entities incorporated under Companies Law, and Vietnamese citizens licensed under Law on Private Enterprises. Although joint venture companies and wholly foreign-owned companies are considered to be Vietnamese juridical entities for this purpose, only Vietnamese party to business co-operation contract recognized as Vietnamese juridical entity.

Economic contract must be in writing and may be inferred from official letters, telegrams, offer letters and purchase orders made. (OOEC, Art. 11).

Some characteristics which distinguish economic contract from civil contract include its business aim, parties involved, and contract form. Economic contract must be made for commercial purpose, be in writing, and be made between parties where at least one is legal entity; while civil contract may be between individuals, may be in writing or in verbal form, and may be for noncommercial purpose.

Economic contract will be void in its entirety if purpose prohibited by law; if one of contracting parties has not legally registered its business; or if it was signed by incompetent State authority or was fraudulently made. (OOEC, Art. 39).

Where provisions of invalid contract are severable, provisions which are valid may be severable and unaffected.

See Topical Index in front part of this volume.

CONTRACTS . . . *continued*

Party held to have breached economic contract will be fined and must pay damages to other contractual party. Fine ranges from to 2 to 12% of value of part of economic contract breached. (OOEC, Art. 29 and Decree No. 17/CP).

Before July 1, 1994, general economic disputes were adjudicated by now dissolved State Economic Arbitration body. At present, litigants of economic disputes may settle such disputes at economic courts, at Vietnam International Arbitration Center, or at nongovernmental economic arbitration centers to be established.

Commercial Contract.—Currently, no commercial code exists. National Assembly is expected to promulgate this code in near future. Now, commercial contracts such as import-export contracts to be signed between foreign party and Vietnamese party are governed by local import-export laws, as well as international trade treaties and customs.

Foreign Investment Contract.—Under Law on Foreign Investment in Vietnam, four forms of investment vehicles exist: joint venture, business cooperation, build-operate-transfer, and wholly foreign-owned entity. Contract to establish first three types of investment vehicles are executed between Vietnamese party and foreign party in accordance with above Foreign Investment Law.

COPYRIGHT:

Introduction.—Before July 1, 1996, copyright protection in Vietnam was governed by Ordinance on Copyright Protection of Standing Committee of National Assembly, Dec. 2, 1994. Copyright protection is now also regulated by Civil Code, enacted Nov. 28, 1995 and effective on July 1, 1996.

Legislation.—Civil Code (CC) promulgated by National Assembly on Nov. 28, 1995, effective July 1, 1996; Ordinance on Copyright Protection (Copyright Ordinance) promulgated in Hanoi on Dec. 2, 1994 by Standing Committee of National Assembly.

Nature of Copyright.—Copyright protection promotes creation of literary, artistic, scientific and technical works; develops national, modern, and human culture; and extends cooperation and exchange of culture, science and technology with other nations. In Vietnam, copyrights consist of moral and economic rights of proprietor to his work. (Art. 750).

Vietnam is not party to either Berne Convention for the Protection of Literary and Artistic Works or Universal Copyright Convention. Should Vietnam join either convention in future, its copyright laws will need to be amended to be consistent with those Conventions. Also, copyright protection in Vietnam will be extended to all other convention signatories if Vietnam joins either convention.

Responsibility for copyright protection and lawmaking in Vietnam rests with Ministry of Culture and Information in conjunction with other ministries and branches that are given such responsibility. These responsibilities include drafting and submitting legal bills and ordinances on copyrights; registering and managing protection of copyrights; inspecting, controlling and solving infringements of copyrights; and implementing international control of copyrights.

Who is Covered.—In Vietnam, different types of copyright protection are extended to creators who are also owners of their work (proprietor of work), owners who acquired legal rights over literary work due to such contract as employment (assignee), and creators who created work to be copyrighted but who must assign such right to another based on such contracts as employment (assignor). (Arts. 751, 752, and 753). Previously, Copyright Ordinance explicitly stated who could obtain copyright protection: work produced by any Vietnamese person, organization, or collection of individuals, using real name or pseudonym, whether produced in Vietnam or abroad, may be protected in Vietnam. CC, however, is silent about who in Vietnam could obtain copyright protection in Vietnam. Implementing regulations of CC, expected to be promulgated soon, should address this issue.

CC, however, does state that foreigners may gain copyright protection in Vietnam if their copyrightable works were first published in Vietnam or if their copyrightable works were first created and fixed expressions formed in Vietnam. In those cases, term of protection will be according to Vietnamese laws and applicable treaties to which Vietnam is signatory party. (Art. 836).

Scope of Protection.—CC extends copyright protection to original literary, artistic, scientific, and technical works, which include writings, oral works, theater and performance, cinema, audiovisual works, photographs, music, computer software, architecture and other technical works, scientific works, and translations, adaptations, compilations, modifications and transformations, and other works to be copyrighted by laws. (Art. 747). Works copyrighted by law (which were previously not protected under Copyright Ordinance) include current news published, folkloric works, and official texts of state bodies, political, economic or social institutions, and any translations. (Art. 748).

In contrast, any work characterized as going against Vietnamese people, or destroying solidarity; that propagandizes violence or aggressive wars; causes hatred among nations, depravity and debauchery, criminal behavior, social evils, superstitions, or which sabotages good morals and customs cannot be copyrighted. Any work disclosing secrets of State, Party, economy, personal life of citizens and any other secret protected by law; any work distorting history, rejecting revolutionary achievements, offending national heroes, slandering or hurting prestige, honor and dignity of organizations or citizens, cannot be copyrighted. (Art. 749).

Copyright Registration.—Copyright arises on creation of copyrightable work, but registration creates presumption of ownership. It is registerable with National Office of Industrial Property (NOIP).

CC designates different types of moral rights and economic rights to different types of parties claiming copyright over work. First, creators who are also proprietors of work (proprietor) have moral right to claim authorship of any part of work they created; have their name or pseudonym indicated on their portion of work; have publishing right of work; have their name cited when such work is used by others; have claims for protection of integrity of their work and from any modifications made thereto by others, as well as have control over who may obtain license to use work. Same proprietors have economic right to receive royalties, remuneration, material benefits for assigning use of their work to other users, and to receive awards or prizes deriving from copyrightable work. (Art. 752).

Creator's rights also exist in work produced in course of employment, in artistic performances, in phonographs and work resulting from modifications to existing work. Distinction of rights is made between that of assignee (i.e. employer who paid employee to produce such work), and assignor (i.e. employee who creates work but must assign it to employer based on contract). Assignor may have all moral rights of proprietor as previously mentioned, except right to publish or to permit others to publish or use such work. Similarly, assignor may have all economic rights of proprietor as mentioned, except right to receive material benefits derived from license contract. (Art. 752).

Assignee, on other hand, receives all moral and economic rights of proprietor not given to assignor as aforementioned. (Art. 753). If there are joint proprietors, each coproprietor is joint owner of work and has all rights as that of proprietor as mentioned. If work is to benefit co-assignors, then all rights attached to assignor apply as mentioned. (Art. 755).

CC further provides for rights and duties of artistic performers, producers of phonograms, and broadcasting organizations. Artistic performers are entitled to have names indicated when performance takes place; to have performances protected from distortion; to control whether or not performances may be copied and disseminated; to receive remuneration for performances, and unless that work contains some aspect of current news or serves educational purposes, to control whether work is broadcast or not; to receive remuneration from license contract, or to require infringer to stop infringement. (Art. 775).

Performers must, however, pay remuneration to anyone whose work they utilize or must pay damages if they have caused infringement. Permission from creator is not necessary if it is published work, but must be sought if work has not been published. (Art. 774).

In cases of audiovisual work, whether solo or joint performance, directors, scenario writers, camera operators, music composers and painters are entitled to same copyright protection as those of proprietor mentioned earlier. (Art. 758).

When using work of others to produce programs, producer of phonograms must sign contract with proprietor, or assignee of work used, or sign contract with performers in case of audio-visual work. (Art. 776). Name of proprietor, assignee, or performer must be indicated on work and remuneration must be paid. (Art. 776).

Term of Protection.—Copyright protection term differs with respect to moral rights versus economic rights of proprietors, assignors, and assignees of literary work or artistic work. All moral rights of proprietor and assignor, except for right to publish or to permit others to publish or use such work, are protected in perpetuity. (Art. 766[1]). Moral rights of proprietor, joint-proprietor, or assignor, which are not protected in perpetuity, are protected for life of such proprietor or joint-proprietor or assignor plus 50 years. Similarly, all economic rights associated with such proprietor, joint-proprietor, or assignor also protected under same term. (Art. 766[2] and [3]). Audiovisual, broadcasting, television, video, or posthumous manuscript work is protected for 50 years from date of first publication. Protection covers moral rights such as right to publish or to permit others to publish or use such work, and all economic rights associated with proprietor or assignor as mentioned earlier. (Art. 766[4]). Moreover, all rights granted to producers of phonograms as aforementioned are also protected for 50 years. (Art. 777[2]).

Transfer of Copyright Protection.—Only certain moral rights of proprietor are transferrable; i.e. right to publish or to permit others to publish or use such work. (Art. 763[1]). But all economic rights of proprietors, assignors, or assignees are transferable in part or in entirety by assignment contract or according to inheritance law. (Art. 763[2]).

Licensing.—Any person or organization seeking to use copyrighted work must sign written contract with proprietor or assignee of work, unless laws provide otherwise or parties to such contract agree otherwise. (Art. 767[2]). License contract should specify form of use of work; scope and period for which work is licensed; amount of royalty to be paid and when payable; and responsibility of each party in event of breach, as well as any other terms parties desire to include. (Art. 768). Licensee may unilaterally terminate agreement, and may request for damage if work is not delivered by licensor as stipulated. (Art. 772[3]). Licensor, on other hand, cannot transfer work to third party during existence of current license contract unless consent given by licensee, and must pay damages to user-licensee if transfer did not conform with contract terms. (Art. 769).

Infringement occurs when goods are reproduced for commercial purpose without remuneration to author, if source of work is not indicated, and if use harms normal exploitation of work and author's legitimate interests. Copyright holder has legal recourse for unauthorized use, manufacture, reproduction, copying or sale of work. Copyright owner may require infringer to stop all infringing actions, apologize for conduct, rectify any wrongs committed, and pay compensation for any harm resulting therefrom; require responsible State authority to solve problem as stipulated by law; and file suit in court.

Situations exist in which what appears to be infringement is permissible. It is acceptable to make reproductions for private use (except for architectural works, graphic works, or computer software reproduction); to quote from work for comments and illustrations in another work; to take extracts from work for articles, periodicals, audiovisual programs and documentaries; to take extracts from work for teaching and examination purposes; for archival purposes and in libraries; for translations into languages of ethnic minorities; for performance of theatrical works, songs, and musical compositions done in public places for motivational purposes; to make live recordings or televising performances as stipulated for current news or teaching work; to take photographs or videos of graphic, architectural, photographic works, and works of applied arts displayed in public places for sake of introduction thereof; or transformation of works into embossed scripts for the blind. (Art. 761).

Industrial Property Rights of Foreign Organizations and Individuals.—Copyright of foreign individuals and/or juridical persons, in respect to any work which is first publicized or disseminated in Vietnam or which is created and takes definite form in Vietnam, shall be protected in accordance with law of Socialist

See Topical Index in front part of this volume.

COPYRIGHT . . . *continued*
Republic of Vietnam and international treaties which Vietnam has signed or acceded to. (CC, Art. 836).

Implementing regulations of CC, when promulgated, should give more detailed guidelines concerning scope of industrial property protection granted to foreign organizations and individuals under Vietnamese laws.

CORPORATIONS:

Legislation.—Law on Companies promulgated by National Assembly, on Dec. 21, 1990, and amended July 1, 1995 (LCE).

Companies Law.—Any Vietnamese individuals over 18 may establish company under Companies Law (see also topic Private Enterprise, subhead Law on Enterprises). Under this law, company may be established as shareholding company (SC) or as private limited liability company (LLC). (LCE, Art. 2). LLC may not issue shares while SC may. LLC and SC are enterprises where all members contribute capital, share profits, and bear losses and liabilities in proportion to capital contributed. (LCE, Art. 2). Members of both types have right to own entire assets of company, proportionate to capital contributed; participate in general meetings of shareholders; vote in proportion to capital contributed on business matters within power of general meetings; require board of management or directors to convene shareholders meeting to consider and resolve business matters not attended to by board of management or directors, provided that members requiring such meeting own at least one-fourth of company's charter capital. Meeting must be convened by board of management or directors within 30 days of request. (LCE, Art. 8). Capital contribution by each member may be in gold, Vietnamese or foreign currency, assets of any kind, or industrial property rights. (LCE, Art. 9).

Company's charter should include form, objectives, name, head office, and duration of company; full names of company's founding members; charter capital; capital contributed by each member in case of LLC or value and number of issued shares in case of SC; formalities for conducting shareholders' general meetings; management structure of company; company financial policies; rules for accounting and profit-sharing; provisions relating to merger, change of company formation, dissolution and formalities for liquidation of company's assets. (LCE, Art. 10).

People's Committees issue company licenses to Vietnamese businesses. However, approval by Prime Minister is required for businesses which manufacture and distribute explosives, poisons and toxic chemicals; mine certain precious metals; production and supply of electricity and water on large scale; manufacture of information transmitting facilities, postal and telecommunication services, broadcasting, television, and publication; ocean shipping and air transportation; specialist export and import business; and international tourism. (LCE, Art. 11). Each company may manage its own business including right to select location of branch office, to determine scope and scale of business activities; to determine method and form of raising capital; to enter into direct contract with its customers; to recruit and hire labor; to spend foreign currency earned; and to make decisions on use of remaining revenue. (LCE, Art. 12).

To establish company, founding members must submit application to People's Committee where head office is to be based, and must state on application names, ages, and permanent addresses of founding members; name and address of proposed head office; objectives, branches, and areas of business of company; charter capital and method of contributing capital; measures to be taken for environmental protection; and development program for such company. (LCE, Art. 14).

Each new company must also be registered at relevant planning committee. Documents to be submitted include business license, company charter, and certificate acknowledging existence of its business office. (LCE, Art. 17). For LLC, business registration must be completed within 180 days from issuance date of business license. For SC, same must be completed within one year from issuance date of business license. (LCE, Art. 17). When company is registered, same planning committee will send copy of certificate and company profile to taxation, financial and technical branches or equivalent. (LCE, Art. 18).

Limited liability company is private company established with capital paid in full by all members. Name of company may be descriptive or be that of member; and words "limited liability" must be added to name and stated on all signs, vouchers, advertisements, reports, documents, and other company business documents. (LCE, Art. 26). LLC may not issue shares of any kind. Capital may be transferred among partners without restriction, but transfers between persons not already members requires unanimous approval from members representing at least three quarters of charter capital of company. (LCE, Art. 25[2]).

Procedures for conducting company's business vary depending on total number of existing members and such procedures must be stipulated in company's charter. Less than 11 members will meet as group and vote on all business actions of LLC together. (LCE, Art. 27). If more than 11 members, company will be managed by board of management elected by members at members' general meeting. (LCE, Art. 28).

LLC may increase charter capital in three ways: by increasing capital contributed by each existing member, admitting new members; or drawing on reserve fund. (LCE, Art. 29).

Any individuals or State authorities who breach this law will be subject to administrative or criminal penalties, depending on seriousness of charge.

Shareholding company must have at least seven shareholders. Any name may be adopted by such company, but must include "shareholding company", and be stated on all signs, vouchers, advertisements, reports, transaction documents, and other company documents. (LCE, Art. 31). In addition, company's charter capital is divided into equal parts called shares, each with share value. Each shareholder may purchase one or more shares. All founding members must own at least 20% of shares planned to be issued by company. Rest may be offered to public. (LCE, Art. 32). Members of public interested in buying company shares must file application following set procedure. Founding members and members of board of management may carry "named shares" which are not freely transferrable with some exceptions. "Named shares" of board members may be transferred after two years when such member has ceased to be on board of management. (LCE, Art. 39). "Bearer shares", in contrast, are held by rest of shareholders, and may be freely transferred without board's approval when such transfer does not damage company. (LCE, Art. 30).

Company may also issue new shares if certain conditions are met. It must apply to local People's Committee for new issuance of shares or stocks; all previous issuance of shares must have been fully paid-in; all business activities under good and effective management; assistance of bank retained to provide fund management and accountancy services relating to shares issuance; proper prospectus established for issuing shares to public. (LCE, Art. 35).

Vietnamese individuals who manage company without license, or carry out prohibited business activities, are considered to have breached this law. Depending on seriousness of breach, breaching party may be liable for administrative penalty or criminal prosecution. (LCE, Art. 44). Likewise, any State authorities who take advantage of their position and authority to issue, or fail to issue, business license or registration certificate to one otherwise not qualified or qualified, is also subject to administrative penalty or criminal prosecution. (LCE, Art. 45).

CURRENCY:

Currency of Vietnam is the dong. Banknotes circulate in denominations of 20d, 50d, 100d, 200d, 500d, 1,000d, 2,000d, and 5,000d. No coins are used in Vietnam. Vietnamese Dong is hedged to US Dollar and exchange rate is approximately 10,000 Vietnamese Dong to 1 US Dollar.

CUSTOMS:

Legislation.—Ordinance on Customs, issued by Government, on 20 Feb. 1991; Decree No. 114/HDBT on State Administration of Export and Import, issued by Government, on 7 Apr., 1992 (Decree No. 114/HDBT); Law on Export and Import Duties, promulgated by National Assembly, on 26 Dec. 1991, amended 16 Jan. 1992 and 5 July 1993 (Law); Decree No. 54-CP on Export and Import Duties, issued by Government, on 28 Aug. 1993 (Decree No. 54-CP); Circular No. 20-TC-TCT on Import and Export Duties, issued by Ministry of Finance, on 16 Mar. 1995 (Circular No. 20-TC-TCT); Circular No. 72A-TC-TCT on Export and Import Duties, issued by Ministry of Finance, on 30 Aug. 1993 (Circular No. 72A-TC-TCT).

Introduction.—Vietnam customs is centralized and organized under Government. Stated purpose of custom ordinance is to create favorable conditions for export and import activity and exit and entry across borders of Vietnam in accordance with law of Vietnam and international treaties relating to customs activities. (Ordinance on Customs, Arts. 1 and 5).

Custom Duties.—Vietnamese Government strongly encourages export, and provides guidance for efficient use of imports in manufacturing and general consumption, to protect and develop domestic production, increase effectiveness of export and import activities, expand foreign economic and trade relations, and contribute towards achieving national social and economic goals. (Decree No. 114/HDBT, preamble).

General Department of Customs (GDC) is responsible for organizing collection of duties for imports and exports. People's Committees of border provinces coordinate with tax and customs offices for collection of duties. Organizations and individuals who import or export goods are required to make declaration and pay appropriate duty. Tax office examines declaration and carries out procedures for collection of duty. (Law, Arts. 15 and 16).

Goods liable for payment of duty include: imports and exports of Vietnamese and foreign economic organizations; products from enterprises in export processing zones ("EPZ") which are not exported; goods for samples, advertising, or exhibition; refundable or nonrefundable humanitarian goods from aid programs; personal belongings of Vietnamese or foreigners exceeding exemption of duty quantity; gifts or presents exceed exemption from duty quantity of foreign organizations, individuals, or foreign nationals of Vietnamese origin, brought or sent back to organizations or individuals in Vietnam or vice versa; imports or exports which exceed exemption from duty of Vietnamese citizens appointed by State to assignments, work, and studies overseas, of international organizations and foreign diplomatic agencies in Vietnam, and of foreigners working in any organizations referred to or in any forms of foreign investment in Vietnam; and movable assets exceeding exemption from duty quantity of foreign organizations or individuals which are exported across Vietnamese border at end of residency or work in Vietnam, or of Vietnamese citizens permitted to emigrate by Government. (Decree No. 54-CP, Art. 1). Also not exempt are any machinery, equipment, materials or means of transportation exceeding quota stated in feasibility study and technical design statement; and when enterprise with foreign owned capital wishes to reinvest in new equipment or means of transportation by replacing existing fixed assets which, when first imported, were exempt from import duty. (Circular No. 20-TC-TCT, c. 1).

Ministry of Trade (MoT) is responsible for approval of import plans determining quantity and type of goods exempted from import duty and is responsible for directing and guiding customs offices to verify quantity of goods and amount of import duty exempted. Enterprises with foreign owned capital must, on annual basis or upon completion of first investment project or each investment phase of project, prepare and submit reports to responsible tax authority, MoT and GDC, on import and use of goods exempted from import duty. (Circular No. 20-TC-TCT, c. II).

Goods exempt from duty payment, provided that all customs formalities are carried out, include: goods in transit, including goods transported on roads crossing Vietnamese borders on basis of treaty signed between two governments, imported from foreign countries into EPZs, goods exported to foreign countries' governments from EPZs, and goods transported from one EPZ to another EPZ within Vietnam; goods in transit including goods transported directly from port of exporting country to port of importing country without transiting through Vietnam, goods transported to Vietnamese port and then to port of importing country without being subject to Vietnamese import procedures, and goods put into bonded warehouses and then transported to another country in accordance with administrative regulations of bonded warehouse without being subject to Vietnamese import procedures; and humanitarian aid including goods supplied by United Nations organizations, goods supplied by State in accordance with agreed aid programs and projects, and other aid from Government in event of unforeseen circumstances, or from foreign organizations assisting in case of natural disasters or epidemics. (Decree No. 54-CP, Art. 3). Other exempt goods include materials imported for purpose of processing for export; temporary imports and reexports; goods

See Topical Index in front part of this volume.

CUSTOMS . . . *continued*

of organizations and individuals having diplomatic immunity as stipulated by Government; goods imported for purposes of security, national defense, scientific research, education and training; imports and exports of enterprise with foreign owned capital and of capital parties to encourage investment; gifts from foreign organizations and individuals to Vietnamese organizations and individuals; and duty-free goods. (Circular No. 72A-TC-TCT, c. V, Art. 1). Other goods, entities, and conditions to be considered for customs exemption include: enterprises with foreign owned capital and parties to business cooperation contracts and petroleum production sharing contracts; equipment, machinery, spare parts, business and production facilities and materials imported into Vietnam for purpose of capital constructions of enterprise or as fixed assets for implementation of business cooperation contract (quantity and value of goods to be exempted from import duty at time of first import must be specified in original feasibility study of project and approved by Ministry of Trade); goods and equipment imported for petroleum activities under petroleum exploration contracts; means of transportation, subject to government quotas on importation of cars with foreign owned capital. (Circular No. 20-TC-TCT, c. I).

Customs Duty Calculation.—Basis for calculating amount of import and export duty is: (1) quantity of each item listed on declaration form, (2) dutiable value (as defined below), and (3) rates of duty applicable to each item (explained below). Duty will be paid in Vietnamese currency, or freely convertible foreign currency. Amount of duty equals quantity of each item actually exported or imported multiplied by dutiable value and by rate of duty applicable to each item. (Decree No. 54-CP, Arts. 6, 8 and 9).

Dutiable value is determined for (1) exports: by contract selling price at border gate excluding insurance and transportation costs, and (2) imports: by contract purchasing price at port of destination including transportation and insurance costs. For goods imported or exported pursuant to sale or purchase contracts, dutiable value is determined by contract provisions. Ministries of Trade and Finance are responsible for determining dutiable value basis pursuant to sales or purchase contract. If conditions for determining dutiable value are not satisfied, or contract price is low compared to market price, or goods exported or imported by means other than selling, purchasing, or settlement through banks, dutiable value is actual minimum selling or purchase price at border gates. (Decree No. 54-CP, Art. 7). If sales or purchase contract contains provisions for deferred payment and stated purchase or sale price includes interest payable, dutiable value is difference between purchase or sales price and interest payable under contract. For exports or imports applicable for Vietnamese EPZs, dutiable value is actual price paid or sold at border gates. (Circular No. 72A-TC-TCT, c. II).

Rates of duty include standard and preferential rates. Standing Committee of National Assembly determines rates of duty for each separate group of goods, and Government determines rate of duty applicable for each separate item of goods. (Law, Arts. 8 and 9). Preferential rate is equal to 70% of standard rate. (Decree No. 54-CP, Art. 11[2][b]). Preferential rate is granted for goods that are: exported and imported under trade agreements between Vietnamese government and foreign government including terms for preferential treatment; exports with certified documentation that they are manufactured in Vietnam; and imports of foreign country with certified documentations that such foreign country has signed agreements for preferential commercial trading with Vietnam. (Circular No. 72A-TC-TCT, Art. 11[2].

Organization of Implementation.—Ministry of Finance (MoF) delegates to General Department of Taxation power to inspect collection and payment of export and import duties carried out by GDC. (Circular No. 72A-TC-TCT, c. X). Organizations or individuals make declaration at customs offices or with agencies authorized by GDC for each consignment of goods permitted to be exported or imported. Customs office has eight business hours, after lodging of declaration concerning exports or imports, to officially notify liable person of amount to be paid. Payment must be made in full within specified time frame ranging from 15-90 days, or before goods are exported from or imported into Vietnam. (Decree No. 54-CP, Arts. 17 and 21). Within 15 days of trading exports, and within 30 days for trading imports, from date that customs office confirms lodging of declaration, if individual or organization does not actually have goods for export or import, both lodged declaration and notification of duty payable will no longer be valid. (Decree No. 54-CP, Art. 21).

Dealing with Breaches.—When payment is overdue, organizations and individuals liable for duty must pay fine of 1/5 of 1% of overdue payment for each day's delay. When payment is delayed more than 90 days from date of official notification from tax office, customs office will suspend processing of next consignment of that person, and at same time, notify Ministry of Trade. MoT will suspend issuance of licenses for export or import of goods to that person until all outstanding duty is paid.

Any person liable for duty committing fraud regarding duty payment will be fined between two to five times amount of duty subject to fraud. Any person continuing to evade payment after notification of fine, which is administrative punishment, or who evades payment of large amount of duty, or commits serious breach will be prosecuted for criminal responsibility under Art. 169 of Criminal Code. When person disagrees with fine imposed by tax office, he must pay fine and immediately lodge claim for review with Minister of Finance. Within 30 days, Minister of Finance must fully resolve matter and his decision is final. Entities engaging in fraudulent conduct are liable for penalties as follows: (1) if entity does not declare exported or imported goods: first offense: two times amount of duty owed subject to fraud; second offense: three times; third offense and thereafter: five times; (2) where entity made false declaration as to actual goods to be imported or exported, or regarding quantity, type, quality, etc.: first offense: two times amount of duty owed subject to fraud; second offense: three times; third offense and thereafter: five times; (3) where breach is serious, or breach was result of abuse of power or position, or of taking advantage of natural disasters, epidemic, or war, or where entity tries to avoid law and cover up breach that has already occurred, entity will be fined amount up to three times amount of duty owed subject to breach. Upon discovery of fraudulent conduct by entity liable for duty, customs office has power to fine and to collect such fines. (Circular No. 72A-TC-TCT, c. VIII).

FOREIGN ENTERPRISE EXCHANGE CONTROL:

Legislation.—Circular No. 01-TT-NH7 on Foreign Exchange Control, issued by State Bank of Vietnam, on 20 Jan. 1992 (Circular No. 01-TT-NH7); Decree No. 18-CP Providing Regulations on Foreign Investment in Vietnam, issued by the Government, on 16 Apr. 1993 (Decree No. 18-CP).

Enterprises with foreign owned capital includes joint venture enterprises and enterprises with 100% foreign owned capital. Above regulations also govern rights and duties of business cooperation contracts and foreigners who work for enterprises with foreign owned capital. (Circular No. 01-TT-NH7, Art. 1).

After receiving investment license from MPI, each enterprise with foreign owned capital may open bank accounts in both foreign currency and Vietnamese Dong at: (1) any Vietnamese bank permitted to deal in foreign currency, (2) any joint venture bank, or (3) any foreign bank branch in Vietnam approved by SBV. Enterprise with foreign owned capital may open only one main account at bank, but may open auxiliary accounts at branch offices of bank to conduct business. (Circular No. 01-TT-NH7, Art. 2).

Receipts of foreign currency must cover foreign currency expenditures including profits transferred overseas. Profit may only be transferred overseas in year enterprise posts profit and following fulfillment of all financial obligations to Vietnam including payment of profits tax.

Enterprise with foreign owned capital producing import substitutes or building infrastructure must use Vietnamese Dong for payments of utilities and rent; purchase of goods for export; and purchase of foreign currency. Foreign currency may be used for business production such as purchases of machinery, equipment, spare parts, raw materials, fuel, and other materials; loan repayments; and other proper business expenditures. (Circular No. 01-TT-NH7, c. III).

Enterprise may sell products for foreign currency to all local economic organizations which purchase import substitutes, while foreign currency paid into accounts by foreigners may be used for payment for services or commodities purchases where foreign currency is accepted; sale of foreign currency; transfer abroad according to laws on foreign exchange control. (Circular No. 01-TT-NH7, c. III).

Upon liquidation or dissolution of business, foreign investor or organization may transfer abroad its share of capital, if any remains, after discharging all financial obligations in Vietnam and after completion of all liquidation procedures required by Vietnamese financial authorities. Transfer abroad will normally take place over three years with following exceptions for shorter time period: when amount to be remitted is one million U.S. dollars or less; where at least 80% of budgeted business is achieved; or if such enterprise established within five years of implementation of Law on Foreign Investment in Vietnam. (Circular No. 01-TT-NH7, c. V).

Upon expiry of business cooperation contract, foreign party to contract may transfer total amount of its capital abroad, provided that all financial obligations in Vietnam have been fulfilled. When amount to be transferred is greater than original investment, foreign investor must apply to MPI for approval of transfer. That decision may take form of either conversion of Dong into foreign currency or payment in kind of equivalent value. Foreigners working in enterprises with foreign owned capital may transfer salaries and other legitimate revenues abroad after payment of taxes and other living expenses in Vietnam. (Circular No. 01-TT-NH7, c. VI).

Foreign economic organizations and foreigners investing in Vietnam may transfer abroad: business profits; any revenue from provision of services and transfer of technology principal amount and interest of loans made during operations; invested capital; and any other sums of money and assets owned by them. (Decree No. 18-CP, Art. 83).

FOREIGN EXCHANGE:

Legislation.—Ordinance on the State Bank of Vietnam, promulgated by Government, on 23 May 1990 (SB Ordinance); Government Decision No. 337-HDBT on Foreign Exchange Control, on 25 Oct. 1991 (Decision No. 337-HDBT); Government Decision No. 396/TTg on Amendments of and Additions to Foreign Currency Control in the Prevailing Circumstances, on 4 Aug. 1994 (Decision No. 396/TTg); Decision No. 257-QD-NH7 on Foreign Currency, issued by State Bank, on 21 Oct. 1994 (Decision No. 257-QD-NH7); Circular No. 12-TT-NH7 on Foreign Currency Control, issued by State Bank, on 5 Sept. 1994 (Circular No. 12-TT-NH7).

Introduction.—Vietnamese currency is the dong and is issued by State Bank of Vietnam ("SBV"). SBV is responsible for management of foreign exchange and regularly issues rules and regulations controlling foreign exchange. It is also responsible for licenses to organizations and private persons for foreign exchange transactions. All acts of import, export, purchase, sale, transfer, and payment of foreign exchange are subject to State regulations on management of foreign exchange. (SB Ordinance, Arts. 50 and 51).

General Principles.—All foreign currency earnings from export of goods and services can only be transferred abroad through bank authorized by SBV. Vietnamese organizations and citizens are not permitted to open accounts and deposit foreign currency in foreign countries, except when permitted by SBV. All purchases and sales made and services provided will be made in dong except where SBV has licensed entity to conduct business in foreign currencies. All organizations in Vietnam having foreign currency must sell all such currency, apart from amount permitted to be retained according to foreign exchange regulations, to banks permitted to engage in business of foreign exchange. When required, organizations in Vietnam may purchase foreign currency at bank or in domestic foreign exchange market. Vietnamese citizens having foreign currency must sell it to bank permitted to engage in business of foreign exchange. When required, they may purchase foreign currency at bank according to regulations of State on management of foreign exchange. All operations of borrowing, debt servicing, lending, recovering of debt carried out with foreign countries will take place through banks licensed by SBV. (SB Ordinance, Art. 51).

Exchange rate between Vietnamese dong and foreign currencies are published by SBV. Ministry of Commerce and Tourism closely controls issue of import licenses which are basis for purchase and sale of foreign currency. SBV closely controls use of foreign currency by all entities and properly organizes foreign exchange centers to facilitate purchase and sale of foreign currency. (Decision No. 337-HDBT, Arts. 3, 4, and 5).

See Topical Index in front part of this volume.

FOREIGN EXCHANGE . . . *continued*

All foreign currency received from export of goods and provision of services to foreign countries, sale of goods and provision of services in Vietnam and other revenue of organizations and units, must be deposited in accounts at banks permitted to conduct business in foreign currency. Sums deposited in foreign currency in banks will bear interest in relevant foreign currency. Foreign currency of organizations and units deposited into banks may be used for: payment of goods imported pursuant to license issued by Ministry of Commerce and Tourism; payment of services provided by foreign countries; payment of loans made by banks and of loans borrowed from foreign countries; contributions to capital of joint venture enterprises; payment of other expenses to foreign countries according to law; and sale to banks permitted to conduct business in foreign currency or sale at foreign exchange centers.

No units except banks, permitted to engage in business in foreign currency, may lend, pay, purchase, sell, or assign foreign currency. (Decision No. 337-HDBT, Art. 1).

Certain organizations and units are permitted to open foreign currency accounts overseas to meet requirements of their business and production activities: Banks and financial companies meeting conditions stipulated by SBV; units in aviation, maritime, postal, and insurance fields to make payments, receive foreign currency and clear payments for their operations according to international practice; enterprises with foreign-owned capital to obtain foreign loans; and Vietnamese economic units permitted by Prime Minister to establish offices in foreign countries to conduct business and production activities.

SBV issues permits for opening foreign currency accounts overseas and monitoring operations of such accounts. Organizations and units are permitted to retain part of foreign currency deposited into their accounts to maintain their business and production activities. Remaining foreign currency not used in each quarter must be sold to banks authorized to deal in foreign currency. SBV, in conjunction with organizations and units which earn large amounts of foreign currency, determines amount of foreign currency to be retained quarterly for immediate use of units and amount of foreign currency to be sold to banks.

Use of foreign currency by organizations and units must be for purposes of making payments for imported goods and for services provided by foreigners, or repaying loans to local and foreign creditors. Domestic units will only make payments in foreign currency to domestic units in following areas: where payments are made between agent and principal through foreign currency accounts for exports or imports; or where payments are made to organizations acting as agents for foreign companies for expenditures and services such as ticket sales, airfreight, seafreight, foreign insurance and reinsurance, international postal fees and where payments are made to foreign agents.

Organizations and units operating shops which formerly were permitted to sell goods and services for foreign currency within country may now only receive Vietnamese currency. (Decision No. 396/TTg, Art. 4).

When entering or exiting Vietnam, Vietnamese citizens and foreigners with foreign currency up to US$5,000 in cash or equivalent amount in other foreign currency are not required to declare amount to customs offices. Any amount greater than US$5,000 must be declared at customs office at border. Vietnamese citizens or foreigners exiting or entering Vietnam with more than US$5,000 in cash must carry with them permits issued by SBV or commercial bank authorized by SBV, except those who, upon their departure from Vietnam, carry unspent currency declared upon entry into Vietnam. (Decision No. 257-QD-NH7, Arts. 1 and 2).

Organizations and units must deposit all foreign currency obtained within or outside country into foreign currency accounts opened at banks authorized to deal in foreign currency in Vietnam according to following stipulations: organizations and units authorized to conduct import-export businesses and provide services to foreigners must deposit foreign currency revenue in their foreign currency accounts; organizations and units issued permits from SBV to receive foreign currency for sale of goods and provision of services, and organizations and units receiving foreign currency from other sources either within country, such as aid, gifts, advertisements, exhibitions, etc., or outside country, must deposit such foreign currency in their foreign currency accounts. (Circular No. 12-TT-NH7, Art. 1).

Procedures.—To open foreign accounts overseas (off-shore accounts), requirements for banks and financial companies are as follows: must have permit to deal in foreign currency issued by Governor of SBV; have charter capital equivalent to at least 50 billion Vietnamese dong; be in efficient operation for at least two years; be in agency relationship with foreign bank; have qualified staff able to conduct international business transactions. (Circular No. 12-TT-NH7, Art. 1, §1.1).

Documents needed include application to open foreign currency account overseas; board of management decision for establishing foreign account overseas and operating license of bank; certificate of business registration; annual report on operations of bank from most recent year, with written comments of Director of local branch of SBV concerning bank's capacity to conduct foreign exchange professional services and business. (Circular No. 12-TT-NH7, Art. 1, §1.2).

For units in aviation, maritime, postal, and insurance industries, there are no specific conditions. Documents required for submission to SBV include: application to open foreign currency account overseas; decision for establishment of enterprise; certificate of business registration; documents of competent agency in foreign country permitting Vietnamese agency to sell tickets directly or transport goods in foreign country (for aviation and maritime industries); contract signed with foreign partner regarding payment settlements (for postal and insurance industries). (Circular No. 12-TT-NH7, Art. 1, §1.2).

Vietnamese economic units permitted by Prime Minister to open business offices abroad are not subject to any specific conditions. Documents needed are: application to open foreign currency account overseas; decision for establishment of enterprise; certificate of business registration; Government decision permitting establishment of business offices overseas. (Circular No. 12-TT-NH7, Art. 1, §1.4).

SBV may request additional documents. Banks and financial companies, and organizations and units permitted by SBV to open off-shore accounts must comply fully with stipulations in permit and are responsible for submission of periodic reports to SBV on foreign currency made through and deposited into such overseas accounts. (Circular No. 12-TT-NH7, Arts. 1.1, 1.2, and 1.4).

Allowable Uses of Foreign Currency.—Foreign currency may be used for: making payments to foreign countries for imported goods and services; repaying loans to banks or foreign lenders; making capital contributions to joint venture enterprises; selling to banks and financial companies authorized to deal in foreign currency; purchasing bank bonds in foreign currency; remitting foreign currency abroad for investment; withdrawing foreign currency for employees of such organizations or units who sent overseas for business, study, research, seminars, etc., or for payments of salaries, bonuses, etc., to foreign and Vietnamese personnel of foreign organizations and offices or of enterprises with foreign owned capital.

Organizations and units, excluding banks and financial companies are not permitted in any way to purchase, sell, make payments in, assign, or make loans in foreign currency to each other. (Circular No. 12-TT-NH7, Art. 3). Exceptions to general rule allowing payments to be made in foreign currency are: making payments for goods, and paying commissions between import and export agents and principals; transferring foreign currency between legal entity and its independent accounting subsidiaries and vice versa; paying for insurance of import and export goods, air freight, sea freight, oil and gas, foreign investment projects, and for foreign organizations and individuals; making payments for international tickets, freight for goods, and luggage to organizations and units acting as ticket sales agents for foreign aviation and maritime agencies; and making payments for international postal fees to organizations and units authorized to provide international postal and telecommunications services. (Circular No. 12-TT-NH7, Art. 3).

Organizations and units are not permitted to accept foreign currency domestically. As of 1 Oct. 1994, organizations and units which previously had been issued permits to provide services and sell goods to foreigners for foreign currency had to change to Vietnamese dong. Exceptions to this rule are duty-free shops and shops providing services to foreigners at seaports, airports, bordergates, and such other places as permitted by Prime Minister. (Circular No. 12-TT-NH7, Art. 4).

FOREIGN INVESTMENT:

Legislation.—Law on Foreign Investment in Vietnam, promulgated by National Assembly, on 29 Dec. 1987, amended 30 June 1990, and 23 Dec. 1992 (Law); Government Decree No. 18-CP Providing Regulations on Foreign Investment in Vietnam, on 16 Apr. 1993 (Decree No. 18-CP); Build-Operate-Transfer Contracts Regulation of the Government, (issued with Government Decree No. 87-CP) on 23 Nov. 1993 (BOT Regulation [23 Nov. 93]); MPI Circular No. 215-UB-LXT on Guidelines of Foreign Investment in Vietnam, on 8 Feb. 1995 (Circular No. 215-UB-LXT); MPI Circular No. 333 UB/LXT on Build-Operate-Transfer, on 28 Feb. 1994 (Circular No. 333 UB/LXT); Ministry of Finance Circular No. 47-TC-TCDN on The Collection of Application Fees Paid in Respect of Foreign Owned Capital, on 21 Oct. 1989 (Circular No. 47-TC-TCDN); Government Regulations on Formulation, Evaluation and Implementation of Foreign Direct Investment Projects, on 28 Dec. 1994 (FDI Regulations [28 Dec 94]); Regulations on Establishment and Operation of Representative Offices of Foreign Economic Organizations in Vietnam, on 2 Aug. 1994, amended 2 Nov. 1994 (Regulations/Rep Offices); Government Decree No. 179-CP on Representative Offices, on 2 Nov. 1994 (Decree No. 179-CP); Ministry of Trade Circular No. 3-TM-PC on Establishment and Operation of Representative Offices of Foreign Economic Organizations in Vietnam, on 10 Feb. 1995 (Circular No. 3-TM-PC).

Introduction.—Vietnam allows investment by foreigners in many sectors, but encourages investment in export production; import substitution; use of high technology and skilled labor to better utilize resources and increase capacity of existing enterprises; use of Vietnamese natural resources and Vietnamese raw materials through labor intensive production; infrastructure building; foreign currency earning services such as tourism, ship repair, airports and sea ports. (Law, Art. 3). Government determines duration of enterprise with foreign owned capital, but cannot exceed 50 years, with some exceptions of 70 years. (Law, Art. 15).

Main Business Forms.—

Joint Venture Enterprise (JVE).—JVE is enterprise set up in Vietnam pursuant to joint venture contract, or new enterprise set up by existing joint venture enterprise and foreign individual or organization. (Law, Art. 2[7]). JVE is established as limited liability company and as Vietnamese legal entity. Liability of each party is limited to amount of capital contributed. Formal establishment occurs when Ministry of Planning and Investment (MPI) issues investment license and certificate of registration. (Decree No. 18-CP, Art. 19).

Foreign party may make its contribution of capital in: foreign currency; plant, buildings, equipment, tools, machinery, etc.; or patents, technological services and processes. Vietnamese party to JVE may make its contribution of capital in: Vietnamese currency (Vietnamese Dong) or foreign currency; natural resources; building materials, fixtures, and furnishings; value of right to use land, water, or sea; plant, other buildings, equipment, machinery, tools, etc.; or supervision of construction and commissioning of plant, patents, and technology. (Law, Art. 7).

Business Cooperation Contracts (BCC).—BCC is established by document signed by two or more parties to jointly conduct one or more business operations in Vietnam. BCC has mutual allocation of responsibilities, and sharing of profits and losses, without creating legal entity. Parties will agree to duration, nature, and objectives of business and get approval from MPI. (Decree No. 18-CP, Art. 8).

Enterprises with 100% Foreign Owned Capital (EFOC).—EFOC consists of enterprise in which foreign organizations or individuals own 100% percent of capital. It is established as limited liability company, fully responsible for own management, and is Vietnamese legal entity. (Decree No. 18-CP, Arts. 43, 44).

Build-Operate-Transfer Project (BOT).—BOT is any project approved by Vietnamese government to construct and operate infrastructure projects. (Regulations [23 Nov. 93], Art. 1). Business can take form of any of three above enterprises. Investors have responsibility to organize and manage project within time period of sufficient length to recover their invested capital and reasonable profit; after which they have obligation to transfer project, without compensation, to Vietnamese Government. (Decree No. 18-CP, Art. 55).

FOREIGN INVESTMENT . . . *continued*

Ancillary contractors are any foreign or Vietnamese contractors who contract with BOT company to construct, supply, finance, advise, insure, or invest in BOT project. (BOT Regulation [23 Nov. 93], Art. 1). BOT company may enter into following ancillary contracts: (1) contracts for right to use land, (2) contracts for construction, (3) contracts for consultancy and valuation services, (4) contracts for supply of goods and provision of technical services, (5) contracts for loan capital and other forms of capital finance, (6) mortgage contracts, and (7) labor contracts. (BOT Regulation [23 Nov. 93], Art. 14).

Government encourages these types of enterprises and will grant preferential treatment to BOT companies and foreign ancillary contractors (see subhead Incentives for Foreign Investment, infra). (BOT Regulation [23 Nov. 93], Art. 2). BOT company is permitted to open bank accounts in foreign countries if lender requests and such account is used for, among other things, repayment of loans. (BOT Regulation, Art. 4).

Alternative Business Forms.—

(a) Representative Offices.—Any foreign economic organization satisfying conditions below could be considered for representative office license. (Regulations/Rep Office, Art. 1). Such entity may apply for: (1) establishment of various independent rep offices; or (2) establishment of one rep office and establishment of various branch offices of that representative office. (Circular No. 3-TM-PC, Art. 2). Scope of activities of rep office may include: formulation of projects on economic, scientific, and technical cooperation with Vietnamese parties; and supervision and control of implementation of economic, scientific, and technical contracts with authorized Vietnamese parties. Rep office is not permitted to operate business directly, provide services, or collect money in any form in Vietnam (Regulations/Rep Office, Art. 3); or to represent other companies in Vietnam, sublet its office, or sign commercial contracts without legal authority (Circular 3-TM-PC, Art. 20).

Approval Process.—Conditions to be satisfied before issuance of license are: (1) foreign economic organization be established according to laws of own country, (2) organization has been in operation for at least five years; (3) organization has feasible investment or commercial projects with Vietnamese parties which will assist economic and commercial development of Vietnam. (Circular No. 3-TM-PC, Art. 2). Such projects include investment projects licensed by competent Vietnamese bodies; economic, scientific, and/or technology transfer contracts; and contracts to import Vietnamese goods exist. Condition (2) above may be reduced if investment is for more than $10 million USD, or is to implement contracts relating to import of goods produced or processed in Vietnam. (Circular No. 3-TM-PC, c. II, Art. 2).

Ministry of Trade is responsible for administration of licensing of rep offices. (Decree No. 179-CP, Art. 1). To obtain license, organization must submit application with: (1) application for establishment of rep office; (2) certificate of incorporation; (3) brief profile of company; (4) certificate of financial status of company by auditor; and (5) investment license issued by MPI, or commercial contract if investment project has not been licensed. (Circular No. 3-TM-PC, c. III). Ministry of Trade has 30 days to notify organization of its decision to grant license. (Regulations/Rep Office, Art. 6).

(b) Branches.—Only certain categories of foreign economic organizations are eligible to open branch offices: (1) companies that produce goods through cooperation or joint venture, (2) companies that export Vietnamese goods without importing to Vietnam, (3) companies specializing in certain services (i.e. airlines, banking, legal consultancy, insurance), and (4) companies trading in goods essential for development of Vietnam's economy and trade. Conditions to be met before branch office can be established: (1) foreign company must be established and operating in its home country for at least five years; (2) must comply with Vietnamese laws, and goods or services provided must be essential to Vietnam's economy and trade development; and (3) branch must have working capital of at least $US600,000.

Licensing procedure similar to procedure for rep offices. Successful applicant must pay fee equal to 1% of capital allocated to branch, and fee must be at least $US10,000.

Branch has different rights from rep office, chiefly right to earn profit from its business activities. Plus, branch may open settlement accounts in both Vietnamese Dong and foreign currency at Vietnamese banks. Head of branch office may also sign contracts with Vietnamese enterprises. Among obligations of branch offices is 10% profit remittance tax for profits remitted abroad.

Approval Process For Main Business Forms.—Evaluation of foreign investment projects includes: (1) legal status and financial capacity of foreign and Vietnamese investors, (2) conformity of proposed project with government's plan for socio-economic development, (3) interests of Vietnam and Vietnamese party ability to create new production capabilities, professions, products, and expand market; ability to create employment for working class; and sources of financial revenue, (4) technical skills and technology to be applied, reasonable use and protection of resources, and protection of environment, (5) reasonable land use, compensation plan for site clearance, and valuation of assets to be contributed as capital by Vietnamese party (if any), and (6) tax rates; land, sea, and water rents; and any preferential treatment. (FDI Regulation [28 Dec. 94], Art. 5). Consideration and approval of projects (1) Prime Minister decides on Group A projects: (a) construction of infrastructure for industrial zones, EPZs and BOT projects; (b) projects with invested capital of 40 million US dollars or more in fields of electricity, mining, oil and gas, metallurgy, cement, chemicals, engineering, electronics, seaports, airports, telecommunications, trade centers, cultural and tourist areas, and real estate businesses; (c) cultural, press, and publishing projects; (d) national defense and security projects; (e) projects using five or more hectares of urban land, or 50 or more hectares of other land. (2) Chairman of MPI decides on Group B projects (all projects not in Group A). Land leases considered simultaneously in evaluation of project. (FDI Regulation [28 Dec. 94], Art. 6).

Joint Venture Enterprises.—Application for investment license, signed by parties, must be submitted to MPI with following documents: (1) joint venture contract; (2) JVE charter; (3) information on legal capacity and financial standing of parties; and (4) feasibility study. (Decree No. 18-CP, Art. 20).

Joint venture contract should contain: (1) nationalities, addresses, and authorized representatives of JVE parties; (2) name, address, and business activities of JVE; (3) details on capital (proportion, timetable, form, etc.); (4) description of main equipment and materials required, products of JVE and anticipated market, and proportion of revenue; (5) duration of JVE; (6) resolution of disputes plan; (7) responsibilities of parties; and (8) effectiveness of contract. (Decree No. 18-CP, Art. 21).

Charter should include: (1) nationalities, addresses, and authorized representatives of JVE parties; (2) name, address, and business activities of JVE; (3) capital details; (4) details of board of management (number, rights, obligations, duration); (5) legal representatives (i.e. appear before Vietnamese courts); (6) financial management plan; (7) ratio of distribution of profits and losses; (8) duration of JVE, and events giving rise to termination and dissolution; (9) labor relations; (10) training plan for executives and employees; and (11) procedure for amending charter. (Decree No. 18-CP, Art. 22).

Feasibility study is detailed discussion of economic and technical aspects of project. MPI will notify parties to JVE of its decision within three months from date of receipt of application. If approved, MPI issues investment license and certificate of registration. MPI may require additional documents and will issue request within one month of application. JVE parties have 45 days to respond to MPI, and if they do not, application will be deemed invalid. (Decree No. 18-CP, Art. 23).

Business Cooperation Contracts.—Application to MPI for issue of business license, signed by contracting parties, will include: (1) business cooperation contract; (2) necessary info such as parties' financial standing, legal capacity, charter in case of company, etc., and (3) economic-technical statement of contract. MPI will notify parties of its decision within three months. (Decree No. 18-CP, Art. 11).

Contract will include: (1) nationalities, addresses, and names of authorized representatives of contracting parties; (2) description of intended business activities; (3) list of main equipment and materials, quantity and quality, product specifications, proportion of product to be sold domestically and internationally, and proportion of revenue to be received in Vietnamese Dong and foreign currency; (4) rights and obligations of contracting parties; (5) duration of contract; (6) procedures for resolution of disputes; and (7) effectiveness of contract. (Decree No. 18-CP, Art. 10).

Foreign party shall delegate task of applying for registration to Vietnamese contracting party.

Enterprises with 100% Foreign Owned Capital.—Signed application for business license must be submitted to MPI with: (1) charter of enterprise; (2) all necessary information on legal capacity and financial standing of foreign investor; and (3) feasibility study. (Decree No. 18-CP, Art. 46). MPI will evaluate economic importance of project, suggesting investor to state consent to Vietnamese enterprise purchasing share of enterprise, thus converting into JVE. Prescribed capital will constitute at least 30% of invested capital of enterprise, with possible exceptions for less than 30%, on MPI approval. (Decree No. 18-CP, Art. 47).

Charter of EFOC must include: (1) nationality, address, and authorized representative of foreign investor; (2) name of EFOC, its address, and activities; (3) invested capital, prescribed capital, timetable for capital distribution, and any construction project; (4) legal representative;, (5) principles on financial matters; (6) duration, termination and dissolution procedures; (7) labor relations; (8) training plans for executives and employees; and (9) procedures for amending charter. (Decree No. 18-CP, Art. 48).

MPI will issue business license upon approval. Within 30 days of issuance of business license, EFOC will publish in central or local newspaper: (1) name and address of foreign investors; (2) name, address, and business activities of EFOC; (3) invested capital and prescribed capital of EFOC; (4) legal representative; and (5) duration of operation and date of issue of investment license. (Decree No. 18-CP, Art. 49).

BOT Companies and Ancillary Contractors.—Approval will come from office of Prime Minister and MPI, who keep list of potential BOT projects, and contract will be evaluated by government committee. (BOT Regulation [23 Nov. 93], Art. 11). Contract must be in writing and include: (1) matters on design of project; (2) procedures for submitting and checking designs; (3) responsibility for timely construction; (4) right to use land, roads, and other necessary supporting facilities; (5) rights and obligations of parties; (6) provisions on tolls, fees, and other applicable charges; (7) obligation to maintain normal operation of project; (8) duration of project; (9) consultancy, inspection of design, equipment, and implementation, completion, operation, maintenance, and transfer of project; (10) allocation of risks between BOT company and Government; (11) measures if BOT project ceases prior to expiry; and (12) provisions on assignment of contract. (BOT Regulation [23 Nov. 93], Art. 14).

Upon approval, MPI will issue investment license for BOT project which will include: (1) main terms of contract; (2) commitments of Government and other relevant State bodies; (3) duration of project; (4) tax and financial obligations; (5) right to use land and other supporting facilities; (6) tolls, fees, and other charges applicable to BOT company; (7) provisions on conversion of Vietnamese currency into foreign currency; (8) provisions on export and import of equipment, machinery, and goods (BOT Regulation [23 Nov. 93], Art. 16); (9) approval of BOT contract between State body and investor; (10) any other provisions deemed necessary by MPI; and (11) approval of establishment and charter of BOT company.

BOT company will be legal entity and permitted to operate after issuance of investment license and certificate of registration of its charter by MPI. Charter will include: (1) capital structure and contributions by parties; (2) legal capital and invested capital; (3) provisions on sale, purchase, and assignment of capital; (4) organization and management of BOT company; (5) power and responsibilities of board of management and board of directors; (6) procedures and meetings of board of management; (7) circumstances of and procedures for dissolution and liquidation, (8) dispute settlement, (9) rights and obligations of BOT company and investor; and (10) procedures for amending charter. (Circular No. 333 UB/LXT, c. III, §4.2).

Application Fees.—All foreign individuals and organizations, must pay application fee in US dollars to establish these enterprises. If invested capital is not in convertible foreign currency, fee may be paid in Vietnamese dong. Application for foreign investment is not complete until fee paid in full. (Circular No. 47-TC-TCDN, c. I). Amount of fee is 0.01 of 1% of total invested capital or, for BCC's, of total capital contributed

See Topical Index in front part of this volume.

FOREIGN INVESTMENT . . . *continued*
by both parties as long as fee is no less than US$50 and no more than US$10,000. (Circular No. 47-TC-TCDN, c. II).

Organization and Management of Enterprises.—
Joint Venture Enterprises.—Highest body in charge is board of management. Each party appoints members to board in proportion to capital contribution but Vietnamese party must have at least two members on board. If new JVE is product of existing JVE and one or more foreign parties, existing JVE will have at least two members, and one must be Vietnamese. (Law, Art. 12). Board is responsible for management of assets and operations of JVE. (Decree No. 18-CP, Art. 33). Board meets at least once a year. Meetings are at request of chairman or two thirds of members. (Decree No. 18-CP, Art. 32). Unanimous vote of members is required for all important matters such as: (1) long term and annual production and business plans of JVE, its budget, and borrowings; (2) any amendment of or addition to charter of JVE; and (3) appointment or dismissal of chairman of board of management, general director, first deputy director, or chief accountant. (Decree 18-CP: Art. 33). Others matters only require two thirds majority of board members present (two thirds of members must be present). (Decree 18-CP, Art. 33).

Board of management appoints general director and first deputy director who are responsible for daily operation of JVE. (Law, Art. 12). Either general director or first deputy general director must be Vietnamese citizen. (Law, Art. 12). General director has right to make final decision on daily operation of enterprise. General director will hold discussions with first deputy director on matters having direct effect on board decisions and other matters such as organizational structure, salaries, and bonuses; appointment and dismissal of division executives; financial statements; and contracts with other economic entities. (Circular No. 215-UB-LXT, §2.3).

Business Cooperation Contract Parties and Enterprises with Foreign Owned Capital.—Parties to business cooperation contract and enterprises with foreign owned capital are fully entitled to determine own business programs and plans. They will be permitted to conduct business according to operational objectives stipulated in investment or business license, and may export their products directly or sell them directly to Vietnamese domestic market. (Decree No. 18-CP, Arts. 62 and 64).

Incentives for Foreign Investment.—See also topic Taxation, subhead Corporate Profit Tax.

JVE's and EFOC's.—Profit tax rates are determined for each individual project: (1) best rate for infrastructure construction projects, information, communication, and telecommunication projects in mountainous regions or other unfavorable areas; commercial afforestation; and projects of significant importance as determined by MPI; (2) next best rate for infrastructure construction projects in favorable areas; exploitation of natural resources (except for petroleum or rare and precious resources); projects in heavy industry; cultivation of perennial industrial trees; investment in mountainous regions or other unfavorable areas; and projects where foreign party plans to transfer all assets, without compensation, to Vietnam upon expiry of operation; (3) third best rate for investments where 500 or more Vietnamese workers are employed; some technology transfer projects; where at least 80% of produced products are exported; and where prescribed capital is at least ten million US dollars; (4) highest rate will apply to investment projects in areas of finance, insurance, banking, consultancy, accounting, auditing, and commercial and hotel services. (Decree No. 18-CP, Art. 67).

BOT will be subject to preferential tax treatment (i.e. lower tax rates, tax exemption or reduction). Foreign ancillary contractors may be subject to same preferential tax treatment as BOT. (BOT Regulation [23 Nov. 93], Art. 2[2]). For BOT projects in mountainous regions and areas where natural, social, and economic conditions are unfavorable, BOT company may enjoy other preferential treatment which will be stipulated in investment license. (Circular No. 333 UB/LXT, c. II, Art. 1).

BOT company and foreign ancillary contractors will be exempt from import duty for goods (equipment, machinery, accessories, materials, and supplies) imported for investigating, designing, implementing, constructing, and operating BOT projects. Where local commercial conditions are comparable, preference will be given for local purchase in Vietnam instead of importation. When imported goods are sold or transferred in Vietnam, approval of Ministry of Trade is needed, and import duty and turnover tax will be collected. (Circular No. 333 UB/LXT, c. II, Art. 1, §1.3).

Government will guarantee that revenue received by BOT company can be converted from Vietnamese Dong to foreign currency to be used for loan payments, business expenditures requiring foreign currency, and paying foreign investors their share of profits. If BOT company wishes to remit abroad profits exceeding those stated in contract, and Vietnam faces difficulties with foreign exchange, MPI may consider possibility of remitting such profits in form of goods of equivalent value and/or purchasing export goods and/or permitting payment of expenses incurred in Vietnam in Vietnamese currency which otherwise must be paid in foreign currency. (Circular No. 333 UB/LXT, c. II, Art. 2, §2.2).

BOT company may be allowed, contingent on government approval, to mortgage (1) factories, equipment, buildings, and real estate of BOT company; (2) other assets; (3) right to use land; and (4) other contractual rights that have economic value. (BOT Regulation [23 Nov. 93], Art. 6).

Government will grant preferential treatment to BOT company for rights to use land, roads, and other supporting public facilities needed for project. Right to use land will be exempt from rent payments. (BOT Regulation [23 Nov. 93], Art. 7).

Tax Incentives.—Law on foreign investment provides for lowest corporate income tax rate of 10%, with up to eight years of tax exemptions and reductions for major investment projects in areas of export earning, high technology, import substitution, infrastructure projects employing more than 500 persons, heavy industry, and afforestation.

Vietnam law further provides for tax refund to FIEs meeting certain criteria in reinvesting profits to increase their legal or investment capital in current or other Vietnam-based projects. Criteria include reinvestment of profits in areas where State promotes investment; reinvested capital will be used for at least three years; and legal capital recorded in investment license of original project has been contributed in full.

Government also encourages export-oriented and import substitution projects. To encourage such activities, Government may exempt from tax liability those enterprises which export at least 80% of their total production and or produce import substitutes.

Additional incentives are available to FIEs operating in export processing zones in Vietnam. Investors in these zones are eligible for duty-free import of raw materials and equipment, duty-free export of finished products, extended income tax holidays, some corporate income tax reductions over limited period, and preferential rates for corporate income and profit remittance taxes.

Lastly, signing of bilateral taxation treaties with many industrialized nations, granting tax credits in respect of certain taxes paid abroad, indicate other types of tax incentives available in Vietnam.

FOREIGN TRADE REGULATIONS:

Legislation.—Government Decree 33/CP on State Administration of Export/Import Activities on 19 Apr. 1994. (Decree 33/CP).

Vietnam remains one of poorest nations in the world even after launching economic liberalization reform in 1986. Since demise of Soviet bloc, Vietnam has had to rely on other foreign investors, in particular, its Asian neighbors Hong Kong, Singapore, Taiwan, Korea, and Japan, to assist in economic development.

Extensive government regulation of import/export activities exists; import levels are fixed by powerful State Planning Committee, through both tariff and nontariff means, such as production subsidies, quotas, and prohibited imports. State-owned enterprises had virtual monopoly over import business licenses before 1994. Under Decree 33/CP, joint venture companies and 100% foreign owned Vietnamese companies are now also eligible for import business licenses.

Tariff rates are calculated to encourage imports of capital goods and raw materials and intermediate goods for domestic processing and reexport and to discourage import of most consumer goods. Ministry of Finance sets minimum price levels based on quality of goods and estimated price for such goods in region adjacent to where goods are imported to prevent importer fraud.

To encourage foreign investment, both foreign invested enterprises and foreign parties to business cooperation contracts (see topic Foreign Investment) are exempted from import duties on equipment, machinery, parts, and means of production or business, and other material contributed as capital. Import duties are also exempted for raw materials, components, parts, and other materials imported to produce exports. MPI may also grant tariff reductions or exemptions in cases where encouragement of investment is needed.

Government also promotes export production and discourages consumer goods imports through nontariff measures such as quotas and import limits. Ministry of Trade also publishes list of prohibited items for import.

State subsidizes production of strategic raw materials to meet annual production targets set by State Planning Committee. This practice insulates domestic industry from foreign competition and boosts exports.

HOLIDAYS:

Vietnam follows both Gregorian (solar) and Chinese (lunar) calendars. Different holidays fall on dates from each calendar. Lunar calendar begins in 2637 B.C. and has 29 or 30 days each month, with 355 days in a year. Every three years, a month is added between third and fourth months so pace between calendars is maintained.

Tet (Tet Nguyen Dan), or Vietnamese New Year, is most important annual festival. It marks new lunar year as well as advent of spring and falls in late Jan. or early Feb. Liberation Day is commemorated on Apr. 30, and celebrates date on which Saigon surrendered to Hanoi backed forces. Other major holidays are International Labour Day, May 1, and Vietnam National Day, Sept. 2, commemorating establishment of nation by Ho Chi Minh in 1945.

INTEREST:

State Bank (SBV) determines and then announces discount rate, minimum interest on deposit for financial institutions, and maximum interest on loans. Interest takes two forms. (1) Earned interest occurs when investor deposits his money with bank and bank pays interest to investor. Current interest rates: (a) Demand Saving Deposit: 0.7% per month; (b) Three Month Deposit: 1.2% per month; (c) Six Month Deposit: 1.4% per month. (2) Interest on loans occurs when banks lend money, and interest accrues at higher rate than earned interest. Current interest rates: (a) Loan for Export Assistance: 1.2% per month; (b) Medium and Long Term Loan: 1.6% per month: (c) Short Term Loan: no more than 1.75% per month.

If loan is overdue, interest rate will change to 150% of original loan interest. In addition, CC provides that where debtor is late in making payment, interest must be paid on unpaid balance at rate equivalent to rate for overdue loans as set by SBV of Vietnam, unless otherwise agreed upon or stipulated by other laws. (CC, Art. 313[2]).

SBV can vary earned interest rate on bank deposits depending on vagaries of economy. If interest rate is set too low or too high, there can be negative economic consequences. If too low, investors will not deposit funds, leaving banks with no liquid assets to make investments. If too high, investors will deposit in banks rather than invest in business.

LICENSES:

Many kinds of licenses-permits-approvals are granted under Vietnamese law by relevant State authorities (hereinafter called "licensing"). Licenses discussed below include, but are not limited to, those issued to domestic organizations and individuals, or to foreign organizations and individuals.

Licenses Issued to Domestic Organizations and Individuals.—
Business Establishment License.—See topic Commercial Register.
Permit for Company's Dissolution.—Vietnamese company wishing to terminate its business operation must submit application for dissolution to same agency which granted business license. Application must clearly state duration and procedures for liquidation of assets, and time limit for payment of all outstanding debts and satisfying all contracts.

Other Licensing.—Vietnamese shareholding company which wants to issue shares or bonds must obtain license from People's Committee of province or city where company's principal place of business is located. (Company Law, Art. 34).

LICENSES . . . *continued*

National Office for Industrial Property (NOIP) issues licenses for protection of trademark, patent, and copyright.

Lastly, provincial Housing Department is authority that considers and issues housing lease licenses to foreigners residing in Vietnam.

License Issued to Foreign Organizations and Individuals.—Foreign investors doing business in Vietnam must obtain business license from Ministry of Planning and Investment (MPI). Ministry must also approve changes in company including proposals extending business duration, increasing registered capital or terminating business operations earlier than business expiry date.

Once investor obtains business license, it must then obtain land leasing license evidenced by land-use certificate issued by Provincial People's Committee where principal place of office is located. Joint venture companies, however, may obtain this land leasing license through Vietnamese party, who may have contributed it as part of capital contribution in kind.

After investment license is issued, company may need to obtain construction license from Ministry of Construction or by respective Provincial People's Committee depending on nature of project.

In addition, company may apply for import-export license from Ministry of Trade. This license will stipulate volume of imported goods to be exempted from import tax. Company may also fulfill procedures obtaining exemption for import tax license issued by central or provincial Customs Department.

If technology transfer contract is executed, its approval is granted by Ministry of Science, Technology and Environment.

Other Licenses Issued to Foreign Organizations and Individuals.—Chief of Vietnam Civil Aviation Agency is responsible for granting licenses to foreign, commercial airlines wishing to fly in and out of Vietnam; while application for foreign, noncommercial planes must be submitted to chief of Vietnam Civil Aviation Agency together with Vietnam Ministry of Foreign Affairs for consideration.

MINES AND MINERALS:

Legislation.—Mineral Resources Law (Law) promulgated by National Assembly on Mar. 20, 1996 and effective Sept. 1, 1996.

Law replaces Ordinance on Mineral Resources issued on Aug. 7, 1989 and states that provisions of all previous mineral legislation remain except for provisions contrary to current Law. For entities and individuals granted licenses under previous legislation, conditions stated in unexpired license still apply, unless contrary to Law or unless licensee elects to apply provisions of Law. Foreign enterprises and individuals investing in mining activities in Vietnam are subject to Law unless international convention to which Vietnam is party stipulates otherwise.

Under Law, minerals are defined as resources found underground, on land surface in form of natural accumulations of useful minerals, and mineral substances in solid, liquid or gaseous states, which are exploitable. (Law, Art. 1).

"Mining activities" not expressly defined under Law. However, mining activities appear to encompass: (1) basic geological investigation activities; (2) basic geological investigation of mineral resources; (3) mineral prospecting; (4) mineral exploration; and (5) mineral exploitation. Basic geological investigation involves research and study of structure and development history of earth's crust and related mineralization thereof. Basic geological investigation of mineral resources involves overall evaluation of mineral resources potential on basis of basic geological investigation, to serve as scientific basis for orientation of mineral prospecting and exploration activities. Mineral prospecting involves study of geological documentation on mineral resources and actual field surveys aimed at identifying prospective areas for mineral exploration. Mineral exploration covers searching for and discovering reserves of minerals, determining their quality and establishing technical requirements of extraction including collection and testing of bulk samples and preparing feasibility studies on mineral exploration. Mineral exploitation requires basic construction of mines, excavation and production and other activities directly related to mineral extraction. Mineral processing involves classification and value adding of minerals. (Law, Art. 3).

Mining activities may be carried out in three areas: "restricted areas", "bidding areas", and "common areas". Restrictive areas are subject to restrictive conditions stated in bidding results. Common areas involve mineral activities carried out without restrictions applicable to restricted areas or bidding areas. (Law, Art. 13). Government will list restricted areas and bidding areas in implementing legislation.

Licenses.—Law provides for five types of licenses: mineral prospecting, mineral exploration, mining, secondary mining, and processing licenses. Rights and obligations differ for each license. Duration of exploration license cannot exceed two years with maximum extension of two more years. Prospecting license cannot exceed one year with maximum extension not exceeding another year. (Law, Art. 21[2]). Mining license may be granted for maximum of 30 years with maximum extension of another 20 years. (Law, Art. 31[3]).

Mining Authorities.—Industry regulates mining activities and must report to Government. Mineral Reserves Assessment Council assists Government in appraisal and approval of mineral reserves.

Entities engaged in mining activities must pay mineral resource tax based on actual commercial mining quantity and selling price. Mining activities are also subject to royalty tax under Ordinance on Royalties, Mar. 30, 1990.

Mining activities must also comply with Environmental Protection Law and Land Law. All permanent mineral prospecting and exploration activities affecting land surface require land lease contracts signed with Government. Exploitation of underground minerals not requiring use of land surface or temporary mineral prospecting and exploration activities not affecting land surface do not require foreign investor to take out land lease.

MORTGAGES:

Real Property.—

Mortgage of Real Estate.—Ownership of buildings and residential houses is possible in Vietnam but not land ownership. Mortgage of real estate is defined as use of real property, including land, houses and buildings on land, by owner to ensure performance of obligation. (CC, Art. 346). Mortgage of real estate must distinguish mortgage of buildings and houses from land. Each type of mortgage is governed by different set of regulations.

Mortgage of buildings and residential houses is currently governed by three regulations. Most recent CC provisions on mortgages supersede any provisions in earlier regulations that contradict those in CC. Mortgage laws on real estate are mentioned in 1989 Ordinance on Economic Contracts issued by Government on Sept. 25, 1989; Regulation on Security Against Bank Loans issued by Governor of State Bank, on Nov. 18, 1989; and CC promulgated by National Assembly effective July 1, 1996.

Mortgage of buildings or houses is governed by all regulations mentioned above and by Arts. 346 through 362 of CC. CC requires all mortgages to be in writing, notarized by State notary officer or certified by People's Committee official, and registered with appropriate People's Committee at provincial or district level. (CC, Arts. 346 and 347). To perfect registration, mortgagor must register mortgage contract with aforementioned authority, deliver mortgage documents to mortgagee and inform mortgagee of list of prior secured creditors of same property. (CC, Art. 351). Mortgaged property may be used to secure performance of more than one obligation if parties agree or if stipulated by law. (CC, Art. 352[2]). Mortgaged property will be retained for use by mortgagor unless parties agree otherwise to transfer it to mortgagee or to third party until performance of obligation is satisfied. (CC, Art. 346[2]).

If mortgagor retains possession of property, such party is entitled to use property, but must maintain and repair it and is prohibited from selling, exchanging or donating it to third party, unless such third party, who becomes buyer, gift recipient, or is willing to exchange such mortgaged property with another equivalent valued property, agrees with mortgagee to become guarantor to pay off obligation due, in case mortgagor fails to perform obligation. (CC, Arts. 351[4] and 358).

If mortgagee holds property and title deed, such party could use and exploit property for economic benefits subject to certain limitations. (CC, Art. 354). Mortgagee is required to maintain and repair property to avoid depreciation in value. If depreciation is caused by mortgagee's activities, such party is liable to pay damages to mortgagor. (CC, Art. 353). Mortgagee is required to return property and all relevant documents to mortgagor upon mortgagor's fulfillment of obligation or if such mortgage is replaced by another security. (CC, Art. 353[2]).

In contrast to western principles, mortgage contract in Vietnam only represents single transaction guaranteeing performance of obligation and does not convey to creditor all incidents of legal ownership, for under CC, mortgagee does not have legal right to sell off encumbered property when term to perform obligation becomes due and mortgagor fails to perform it or performs it at variance with mortgaged agreement. Mortgagee may demand that mortgaged property be auctioned off and net sale proceeds to be applied to pay off unperformed obligation or improperly performed obligation, after deducting maintenance and auction expenses. (CC, Arts. 359 and 360). When mortgaged property must be auctioned off to satisfy obligation due, right of all secured creditors of same mortgaged property will be determined together and according to their order of mortgage registration filing. (CC, Art. 360[2]).

Mortgage is extinguished when (1) obligation secured by mortgage performed; (2) mortgaged property cancelled or substituted by another security; or (3) mortgaged property disposed of to settle nonperformance of obligation or performance in variance to mortgage contract. To effect termination of mortgage contract, same State authority who registered contract must certify termination. (CC, Art. 362).

Upon termination of mortgage contract when obligation has been performed, mortgaged property replaced by another security, or mortgaged property auctioned off, authority with whom mortgaged property was registered must certify termination of mortgage. (CC, Art. 360[2]).

Mortgage of Land-Use Right Certificate.—Land mortgage is governed by Arts. 727-737 of Civil Code (CC) and Land Law issued by National Assembly on July 14, 1993 ("Land Law 1993") and its implementing regulations. These regulations include Ordinance on Rights and Obligations of Foreign Individuals and Organizations Leasing Land in Vietnam issued by National Assembly and effective Jan. 1, 1995 ("Foreign Land Leasing Ordinance"); Decree No. 11-CP on Implementation of the Ordinance on Rights and Obligations of Foreign Individuals and Organizations Leasing Land in Vietnam issued by Government on Jan. 24, 1995 ("Decree 11"); and Decree No. 18-CP on Implementation of the Ordinance on the Rights and Obligations of Vietnamese Domestic Entities Who Have Been Granted a Land License or a Land Lease by the State issued by the Government on Feb. 13, 1995 ("Decree 18").

Land in Vietnam is collectively owned by Vietnamese people and is administered by State. Company or person may receive at most right to use allocated plot of land for stated purpose over prescribed duration. User, Vietnamese or foreigner, may acquire land-use right evidenced by land-use certificate.

Vietnamese land user may acquire land-use right either by free-of-charge grant from government ("land license") or under lease agreement with government or Vietnamese person or entity ("land lease"). Foreign entity or individuals may obtain land lease but not land license from Government. (Land Law 1993, Art. 80).

Government issues land license only to Vietnamese individuals and entities. Holder of land license may be Vietnamese individual or household using land for residential purposes or for any of four major economic uses such as agriculture, forestry, aquaculture or salt production. (Land Law 1993, Art. 22). Government also issues land license to government entities and Vietnamese State enterprises for public use, such as development of infrastructure projects including transport and irrigation projects, and building government offices, schools, hospitals and parks. (Decree 18, Art. 2[1]).

Decree 18 governing Vietnamese entity as land lessee: If Government grants land-use right to Vietnamese state enterprises, joint stock companies, limited companies and cooperatives for same four economic uses as aforementioned, then land license is free of charge. (Decree 18, Art. 1). If same Vietnamese entity decides to enter into joint venture with Vietnamese entity or individual and uses land for any one of four economic uses aforementioned, land license remains and land value, which may be contributed to such joint venture as determined by respective People's Committee of city or province under central authority and as stipulated by Ministry of Finance, may also be mortgaged at bank to guarantee repayment of loan. (Decree 18, Arts. 6 and 7).

Although mortgaged object is land-use right certificate, mortgage value as determined by lending bank is based on value of property attached to land. Lending bank

See Topical Index in front part of this volume.

MORTGAGES . . . *continued*
must restrict its mortgage contract amount to current property value attached to land. (Decree 18, Art. 7[1]). If mortgagee defaults on loan repayment, lending bank may request Vietnamese State Auction Committee to auction property attached to land to repay principal and interest due. Buyer of such property may then receive transfer of land-use right for continued use of land. (Decree 18, Art. 7[2]). Land mortgagor is responsible for registering commencement and termination of aforementioned land mortgaging contract at Land Administration Department of province or city under central authority. (CC, Art. 733; Decree 18, Art. 7[3]).

As of Jan. 1, 1995, if same Vietnamese entity decides to enter into joint venture with Vietnamese entity or individual and purpose of land use is not for agriculture, forestry, aquaculture or salt production, then such entity must convert land license into land lease by relinquishing land license to government and entering into lease agreement with government as lessor. (Land Law 1993, Art. 22; Decree 18, Art. 5). Total rental payment for land lease can be contributed as capital to joint venture. (Decree 18, Art. 6[1][b]). If joint venture decides to obtain loan and use rental value of land lease as guarantee for repayment of loan, such mortgage is permitted only at Vietnamese Bank according to Decree 18. (Decree 18, Art. 9). Maximum total value of mortgage contract based on total value of property attached to land at time of loan contract plus rental payment already made. (Decree 18, Art. 9[1]). This criterion of mortgage contract valuation is inconsistent with subsequent legal provision providing that upon default of payment by borrower, Vietnamese lender may request same State Auction Committee to sell off property attached to land for satisfying amount of principal and interest due. (Decree 18, Art. 9[2]). Since land cannot be sold, its incorporated valuation in original mortgage contract is incomprehensible.

Decree 11 governing foreign entity or individual as land lessee: Also on Jan. 1, 1995, Decree 11 implemented in detail Ordinance of the Rights and Obligations of Foreign Entities and Individuals as Land Lessee. If joint venture is paying land rental, then its legal representative is designated by law as lessee. If Vietnamese party to joint venture contributed value of land-use right to joint venture, then land lessee is ironically in name of Vietnamese party. (Decree 11, Art. 3). In either case, land lessee may obtain loan from Vietnamese bank and mortgage value of property attached to land. Upon default of loan, Vietnamese lending institution may request same State Auction Committee to sell property attached to land at auction to satisfy repayment of principal and interest due. Buyer of property must continue to use transferred land for same purpose. (Decree 11, Art. 13).

Effective as of July 1, 1996, Arts. 727-737 of CC outline in detail terms and conditions of land mortgage contracts. Code specifies inter alia that registration and termination of land mortgage is to be executed by both land mortgagor and mortgagee. (CC, Art. 735).

NOTARIES PUBLIC:

Legislation.—Decree No. 31/CP on the Organizations and Operations of Public Notaries, issued by Government, on May 18, 1996 (Decree No. 31/CP).

Public notary is defined in Decree No. 31/CP as person who may certify legality of contracts and documents prescribed by laws, in order to protect lawful rights and interests of citizens, state bodies, economic organizations, and social organizations. (Art. 1). Public notary is not allowed to certify certain documents not specified in scope of public notary's responsibility; those considered invalid under Vietnamese laws; or those relating to such public notary or his family.

Public notary office, under Justice Department and provincial People's Committees, is empowered to notarize certain legal documents and certain documents are only valid if notarized by public notary office. Such documents include: immovable property auction contracts; civil contracts with foreign element; translations of applications; written property appraisals of appraisal council for properties contributed in kind by owners of private enterprises; civil decisions of foreign court; foreign arbitral awards concerning Vietnamese individual or organization to be enforced in Vietnam; foreign marriage certificate involving Vietnamese marrying foreigners; adoption papers of Vietnamese children; documents recognizing illegitimate Vietnamese children; translation of wills from foreign language into Vietnamese; and other legal documents required by law to be notarized such as driver's license or university diploma. (Art. 18). People's Committees of provinces and cities may certify as true copies certain original legal documents but not those documents mentioned above which may only be notarized by public notary office (Art. 19[1]) while People's Committees at village level may witness (1) document whereby heir denies property given by will, or (2) signing of wills or other documents as prescribed by laws (Art. 19[2]). Certification of documents by provincial People's Committees are executed by its permanent Deputy Chairman or Chief Official. In addition, diplomatic offices and Vietnamese consulate offices abroad may certify papers or documents of Vietnamese citizens residing in those locations.

Copy or translation of original document may also be legalized. In latter case, all documents submitted to Vietnamese authorities must be in Vietnamese. Therefore, documents in foreign language must be translated into Vietnamese and said translation should be certified. Certification of copy or translation results in assurance that said copy or translation is exact duplicate or contains same information as original copy. In case translation is certified, State official in that case only assumes responsibility for correctness of translation and not content.

More than one public notary office may exist in province. Public notaries within provincial People's Committee are appointed and dismissed by Chairman, or by Director of provincial Department of Justice as in case of a public notary under supervision of Department of Justice. Public notary must have graduated from law university with five or more years of legal experience and have good political record.

PATENT LAW:

Legislation.—Civil Code promulgated by National Assembly on Nov. 28, 1995 and effective July 1, 1996 (CC); Decree on the Protection of Industrial Property Rights promulgated by Order No. 13 LCT/HDNN8 on Feb. 12, 1989 (IP Decree); Ordinance No. 31-CP on Innovations To Effect Technical Improvement and Rationalization in Production and on Inventions promulgated by Government on Jan. 23, 1981, as amended by Government Decree No. 84-HDBT on Mar. 20, 1990 (Ordinance on Inventions); Ordinance on Utility Solution promulgated by Government on Jan. 23, 1981, as amended by Government Decree No. 84-HDBT on Mar. 20, 1990 (Ordinance on Utility Solution); Ordinance on Industrial Design, promulgated by Government, on Jan. 23, 1981 and as amended by Government Decree No. 84-HDBT, on Mar. 20, 1990 (Ordinance on Industrial Design).

Implementing decrees are being drafted but have not yet been published to implement Civil Code (CC), including more detailed regulations of industrial property laws expected to conform with TRIPs.

Introduction.—Vietnam's new CC became effective July 1, 1996. CC replaced some existing intellectual property laws including Ordinance on the Protection of Industrial Property of Jan. 28, 1989. CC amended some criteria regarding patent inventions, utility solutions and industrial designs, including revised definitions for utility solutions and inventions, and determination date of prior users of patents.

Treaties.—Vietnam is member of Paris Convention for the Protection of Industrial Property and World Intellectual Property Organization (WIPO), established by Stockholm Convention on July 14, 1967. WIPO provides registration services for intellectual property and facilitates transfer of intellectual property from developed countries to less developed countries.

Vietnam is also member of Patent Cooperation Treaty. Thus, Vietnamese patent laws must conform to these intellectual property treaties.

Registration of Patents.—Vietnam's patent law provides protection for inventions, utility solutions (utility models and petty patents), and industrial designs. Invention is defined as "a technical solution which presents worldwide novelty, an inventive step, and applicability in socio-economic fields". (CC, Art. 782). Utility solution is defined as technical solution which presents worldwide novelty and is applicable in socio-economic areas. Utility solution need not include inventive step; however, technical solution has to be substance, process or product in order to be protected. (CC, Art. 783). As criterion of novelty required for registering utility solution is of lesser degree than for invention, it is possible to convert invention application into utility solution application. Industrial design is defined as specific appearance of product embodied by lines, three-dimensional forms, colors or combination of these, which has absolute novelty and is capable of serving as pattern for industrial product or handicraft. (CC, Art. 784).

Patent Application Filing.—Right to file patent application in Vietnam belongs to creator proprietor of invention, utility solution, or design, unless his right to industrial property has been assigned to another party, such as his employer. Furthermore, right to file patent application may also belong to invention's successor in title.

For service invention, service utility solution, or service industrial design, right to file application for protection belongs to organization or unit. (IP Decree, Art. 8[3]). If within two months following date of receipt of notification given by proprietor, organization or unit has not undertaken filing of application for protection, proprietor will have right to file application himself.

For invention, utility solution, or industrial design made during execution of scientific-technological research and development contract, right to file application for protection belongs to employing party, except if otherwise provided for in contract.

For invention, utility solution or industrial design made in basic unit under labor contract, right to file application for protection belongs to that basic unit unless otherwise provided for in contract.

For invention, utility solution or industrial design, right to file application for protection may be transferred to another organization or person through Deed of Assignment.

Filing Principle.—In Vietnam, first-to-file principle applies, making filing date of patent application of crucial significance in protecting one's patent rights.

Filing Requirements.—Applications for patents, utility models and industrial designs are submitted to National Office of Industrial Property (NOIP). Application may be filed covering two or more inventions, provided they serve single purpose and can be used commonly up to filing date. In order to file patent, utility solution or industrial design application, following documents must be submitted: application form, notarized Power of Attorney, notarized Deed of Assignment from inventor(s) to applicant(s), and certain other documents listed in detail below. Specifically, application form is prescribed by NOIP and contains following information: name, address, and nationality of applicant(s); name, address, place of work, and nationality of inventor(s); date, place, and number of first filing date and place of exhibition (if documents certifying convention priority are to be filed later). Original copy of notarized Power of Attorney may be filed with NOIP within one month of filing date. Three extensions of one month each are available.

Further, notarized Deed of Assignment from inventor(s) to applicant(s) should be submitted. Original may be filed with NOIP within one month of filing date. Again, three extensions of one month each are available. Also, original notarized Deed of Assignment of priority may also be filed with NOIP within one month of filing date, with three extensions of one month each available. In addition, specification of invention, utility solution or industrial design, with claims and abstract in English, French or Russian, has to be submitted in time for translation into Vietnamese. Two copies of specification, claims and abstract need to be submitted. Also, drawings, diagrams, calculations, and other illustrations, illustrating alleged invention, utility solution or industrial design, may also be submitted with application, if necessary. For invention or utility solution application, four copies are submitted to NOIP, whereas only two copies are submitted for industrial design applications. Lastly, certified copies of first filed original application, or certificate of exhibition organizers to claim convention priority, if priority is to be claimed, must be submitted. Original certified copy must be submitted to NOIP within one month of filing date.

Filing Procedures.—

Invention.—Application should be filed with NOIP which will review application within three months of filing date to ensure that all formalities have been complied with. If application is accepted, it will make its priority date effective. If unacceptable because application form has not been filled out properly, it will be returned to applicant and process must be re-initiated. Substantive examination of subject application as to its registrability will be conducted within 18 months. If application is accepted for registration, it will be registered with NOIP and registration certificate

See Topical Index in front part of this volume.

PATENT LAW . . . *continued*
will be granted. If application is rejected by NOIP, applicant has possibility of appealing or changing application to one for utility solution. If NOIP decides to refuse registration, it is required to notify applicant of reason for decision. If patent is granted, it will be registered with NOIP and registration certificate is issued to applicant(s). Patent is subsequently published within three months from granting date in Industrial Property Gazette. (Ordinance on Inventions, Arts. 28-34).

Utility solution applications are also filed with NOIP which has three months, following receipt of application, to review application to ensure it conforms with formalities. Substantive examination of utility solution's registrability will be conducted within nine months. If NOIP approves utility solution application, it issues registration certificate to applicant(s) and publishes that information in Industrial Property Gazette. (Ordinance on Utility Solution, Arts. 20-24).

Industrial design applications must be filed with NOIP which reviews application for compliance with formalities within 15 days from receipt of application. Substantive examination of industrial design's registrability will be conducted within six months. Industrial design is then published in Industrial Property Gazette after publication fee paid. Within three months following publication date, any organization or person may file notice of opposition to grant certificate of industrial design with NOIP. Within term prescribed, if no opposition filed, NOIP grants certificate of industrial design to applicant. It is then entered into NOIP Register of Industrial Designs and published in official Industrial Property Gazette. (Ordinance on Industrial Design, Arts. 10-21).

In contrast, if opposition is filed, NOIP will immediately inform applicant(s) and will request that applicant submit response to opposition within three months. If NOIP decides that opposition is not well founded, industrial design is granted registration. If NOIP decides that opposition is justified, NOIP will reject applicant's registration and will inform applicant.

Rejection and Appeal.—If NOIP rejects invention, utility solution or industrial design, it notifies applicant(s) immediately, either directly or through official agents. NOIP is obliged to state reason for rejecting application.

Applicant(s) may then file appeal within three months of rejection and NOIP is required to respond to appeal within one month from receipt of appeal. If NOIP refuses to register invention, utility solution or industrial design even after appeal, second appeal may be lodged with Chairman of State Committee for Sciences (SCS) whose final decision will be passed within one month of filing appeal. (IP Decree, Art. 28).

Opposition and Cancellation Actions.—Opposition actions are not provided for against inventions and utility solutions; however, opposition period is provided for industrial designs after publication. Opposition must be filed with NOIP and decision as to registration is made by NOIP within one month after opposition received.

Title of protection for invention, utility solution or industrial design may lapse before expiration of its term of validity in certain cases, such as owner of title of protection files written surrender to NOIP; or patent invention or utility solution has not paid prescribed annuity fee.

Cancellation of title of protection before expiration of term of validity is recorded in Register at NOIP, and published in Official Gazette of Industrial Property. (Art. 24 of Decree). CC further provides wider range of grounds for cancellation or suspension of patent registration. (CC, Arts. 792 and 793). Certificate of protection may be cancelled where, at time of issuance of such certificate, subjects stated therein do not meet criteria required by law; certificate of protection is issued to person who does not have right to submit application; and other circumstances stipulated by law. (CC, Art. 792). Effectiveness of protection certificate may be suspended if patent owner fails to pay fees for maintaining effectiveness of such certificate within prescribed time; and other circumstances stipulated by law. (CC, Art. 793[1][a] and [d]).

Term of Protection.—Currently, registration for patent of invention is valid for 15 years from either application date or priority date. Newly registered utility solution is protected for six years from application date or priority date. Term of protection for industrial design is five years from application date or priority date.

No renewal is available for inventions or utility solutions. Registered industrial design with maximum protection of 15 years may be extended for two successive five-year periods. (Ordinance on Industrial Design, Art. 23).

Inheritance Rights.—Rights of invention, utility solution, or industrial design are inheritable. (CC, Art. 796).

Infringement.—Patent proprietor of invention, utility solution, or industrial design owns exclusive rights to patent, including right to possess, use, and transfer rights. Third party use without proprietor's consent considered infringement and is actionable. Proprietor is responsible for initiating action against infringer's and determining amount of compensation due him, based on economic benefits gained by infringers, use of his invention, utility solution or industrial design.

Remedies.—Proprietor of infringed intellectual property can demand that competent State authority stop infringement. Another option is relief through Vietnamese courts. Generally, proprietors of patented inventions, utility solutions, or industrial designs may receive better results from negotiating with infringer before going to respective governmental agency or court such as People's Court for relief, as judicial avenues for relief are rarely best first step. In addition to being of questionable efficiency, patent laws are relatively new and untested.

Industrial Property Rights of Foreign Organizations and Individuals.—Industrial property rights of foreign individuals and juridical persons for which State has issued certificate of protection will be protected in accordance with Vietnamese laws and international treaties in which Vietnam is signatory party. (CC, Art. 837).

Implementing regulations of CC will give more detailed guidelines concerning scope of industrial property protection granted to foreign organizations and individuals under Vietnamese laws.

PLEDGES:

Pledge is written contract whereby pledgor delivers to pledgee movable property as security to ensure performance of obligation. Pledge contract, which must be in writing, must state nature of pledged property, quantity, quality and value of said property, duration of pledge and manner for disposing of pledged property, and must either be notarized by State notary official or certified by a competent People's Committee. (CC, Art. 330). Accordingly, delivery of pledged property by owner thereof, as pledgor, to pledgee is essential and legally required to create valid pledge under Vietnamese law. (CC, Art. 329[1]). However, parties to pledge may agree to have registered pledged property kept by pledgor or by third person. (CC, Art. 329[1]). If pledged property is kept by either pledgor or third person, neither may sell, exchange, donate, lease or lend out pledged property. (CC, Arts. 332[5] and 337). Furthermore, neither pledgee nor third party may enjoy fruits or benefits generated from such property without prior consent from pledgor. (CC, Art. 334[3] and 337[2]). Third party who is asked to hold pledged property may receive remuneration and indemnification for property maintenance expenses. (CC, Art. 337[1]).

In event pledged property right is represented by written instrument, for example stocks, pledge shall be valid only if instrument is delivered to pledgee, and debtor of such right is notified about such pledge. Movable property may be used to effect several pledges as long as total sum of values of guaranteed obligations does not exceed that property's value. (Civil Code, Art. 329[2]).

Pledgee is entitled to receive payment for nonperformance of obligation due to him from pledged property. Pledged property may be applied to ensure performance of several obligations. In such case, each pledge contract must be in writing and registered. (Civil Code, Art. 342[1]). Nonperformance of one obligation will trigger settlement of all other obligations at which time order of priority in payment due to different pledgees will be determined based on policy of "first-register, first-payment". (Civil Code, Art. 342[2]). Civil Code also recognizes written agreement among parties to pledge contract to satisfy nonperformance of obligation in accordance to agreement. (Civil Code, Art. 341). If no agreement exists as to disposal of pledged property in case of nonperformance, then pledged property may be auctioned off. (Civil Code, Art. 341).

Pledge is extinguished when (1) civil obligation secured by pledge has been terminated; (2) pledge has been cancelled or substituted by another security; or (3) pledged property has been disposed of to settle nonperformance of obligation or performance in variance to pledge contract. (Civil Code, Art. 343).

PRIVATE ENTERPRISES:

Legislation.—Law of Private Enterprises promulgated by National Assembly, dated Dec. 21, 1990 and as amended July 1, 1994 (LPE).

Law on Enterprises.—Vietnamese companies may be governed by law of LPE or Companies Law (see topic corporations, subhead Companies Law). "Private Vietnamese enterprise" is business unit with level of capital no less than that of its legal capital, owned by individual who shall, to extent of his total assets, be responsible for its business activities. (LPE, Art. 2). Any Vietnamese over 18 may establish private enterprise. (LPE, Art. 1).

People's Committees have authority to supervise licensing of Vietnamese companies. Approval of Prime Minister, however, is required for establishment of private enterprises in manufacturing and distribution of explosives, poison and toxic chemicals; mining of certain precious metals; production and supply of electricity and water on large scale; manufacture of information transmission facilities, postal and telecommunication services, broadcasting, television, and publication; ocean shipping and air transportation; specialist export and import business; and international tourism. (LPE, Art. 5).

Applications to establish private enterprise must include: name, age and permanent address of owners of enterprise; proposed head office; objectives, specific branches, and areas of business; initial investment capital, and whether capitalized in Vietnamese or foreign currency, gold or any other asset; and what environmental protection measures are to be taken. (LPE, Art. 8). Within 30 days of issuance of license, owner-grantee must publish in local or central newspaper full name of enterprise and owner; address of head office; objectives, branches, and areas of business of enterprise; initial invested capital; date license granted issuance number and date of business registration certificate; commencement date business operations. (LPE, Art. 13).

Enterprise owner may employ another to manage business operations, but remains personally responsible for all activities. (LPE, Art. 19). Owner of private enterprise may manage own business including selecting branch offices (if any), selecting area of activities, and scale of business; selecting form and method of raising funds; selecting customers and entering into direct contracts with them; recruiting and hiring labor; spending earned foreign currencies; making business decisions regarding use of remaining revenue; and taking initiatives in all registered business activities. (LPE, Art. 22). Owner may lease enterprise, but must first report in writing to People's Committee which issued certificate of business registration. (LPE, Art. 23). He may also sell or merge enterprise with another, but must first submit application requesting permission from same People's Committee that granted license. (LPE, Art. 24). Owner of private enterprise is obliged to make correct declarations of his business's invested capital; carry on business's activities in accordance with business license; give priority to use of local labor, and follow local labor laws and respect rights of trade union organizations under Law on Trade Unions; guarantee quality of goods in accordance with standards stated in business registration; observe all environmental protection regulations; keep books of account and cost accounting in accordance with accountancy law and be subject to audit by State financial authorities; and pay taxes and fulfil other obligations stipulated under Vietnamese laws. (LPE, Art. 25).

Private enterprise may be dissolved only if owner guarantees full payment of all debts and complete settlement of all signed contracts. Enterprise must submit application of dissolution to same People's Committee that granted license, and must publish information concerning dissolution in local or central newspaper. Application must explain in detail enterprise's procedure of liquidating of assets; time limit for all debt payments and settlement of all contracts. Committee will grant this dissolution only where no claim has been made after 15 days from expiry of time limit for payment of debts and settlement of all contracts as stated in dissolution application. (LPE, Art. 16).

See Topical Index in front part of this volume.

PROPERTY:

Real Property.—Law on Land, adopted by National Assembly on July 14, 1993 ("Land Law 1993"), provides that land in Vietnam is to be owned by all people. (Art. 1). State, through National Assembly, manages land on peoples' behalf. (Art. 7). National Assembly in turn delegates to executive government, and national and local People's Committees power to manage land on its behalf. State through its executive arm, Government, issues land-use rights, free of charge ("land license"), or at subsidized rent to Vietnamese individuals and institutions ("land lease"). (Art. 1). State may for national defense or public interest purposes, recover land allocated. (Art. 27). State may also recover land-use rights if (1) organization allocated land dissolves, becomes bankrupt, moves away, or individual user dies without heirs; (2) user voluntarily returns allocated land to State; (3) user leaves land unused for 12 consecutive months without permission from competent land authority to do so; (4) land user does not intend to perform its State obligations; (5) land is used for purpose other than allocated; and (6) land was issued by unauthorized authority. (Art. 26).

No organization or individual may buy, sell, or appropriate land by unlawful means. (Art. 6). Vietnamese individuals may transfer, exchange, lease, leave by inheritance, or mortgage land-use right pursuant to Land Law 1993 and implementing regulations (Art. 3[2]).

Land is categorized based on purpose of use: agricultural, forestry, residential, urban, specialized, or virgin-unused land. (Art. 11).

Government is preparing comprehensive survey, mapping and zoning of entire country. (Art. 16). Based on land survey and mapping, government will draw up national land-use plan to submit to National Assembly for review and adoption. (Art. 18). It is also issuing land-use certificates, registering them and managing land-use contracts. (Art. 13[5]). Implementation of land-use plan is, however, local government's responsibility, that is, the 53 Vietnamese provincial People's Committees. These People's Committees have broad executive power over land-use within their respective jurisdictions. They allot land, enter into land agreements, determine value of land-use rights, issue land-use certificates, register land-use rights, and cancel land licenses not used in accordance with registered purpose. (Art. 32).

Current land administration practice in Vietnam is characterized by multilayered bureaucracy. Local land management administration is scattered among local Department of Land Administration, Department of Construction, Department of Administration of Agricultural Land, and Office of Chief Architect. Further, local land management decisions are reviewed by central Government authorities and in some cases by Prime Minister.

If in any year, land reserved for agriculture and/or forestry purposes is to be diverted to other uses, Government must seek permission from Standing Committee of National Assembly. (Art. 23[1] and [2]).

Duration of land allocation is determined based on purpose of use: (1) for agricultural activities: 20 years for planting annual trees and aquaculture activites; 50 years for planting perennial trees. Duration of both uses is renewable. (2) Land allocated to Vietnamese households and individuals for residential purposes is for indefinite and long-term usage. Such land shall only revert to State if user violates Land Law 1993 or if such land is recovered for national security or defense purposes. (3) Land allocated for other purposes shall be stipulated by Government in separate regulations. (Art. 20). Land allocated to foreign investors corresponds to duration of their business licenses.

Land use transfer may be effected in all cases except where (1) land used is without any legal documents; (2) land allocated to organizations, such as state enterprises, is prohibited from being transferred; or (3) such land is subject of dispute. (Art. 30).

State authorities in charge of resolving land disputes are also divided among different authorities. State encourages all land disputes to be resolved by amicable conciliation (Art. 38[1]). Failing such conciliation, land dispute is settled by respective People's Committee or court of law depending on whether land user has been issued land-use certificate. For land users who have not yet received certificate, land disputes in such cases are resolved either by (1) People's Committee of districts, provincial districts and provincial cities if disputes involve individuals and households (Art. 38[2][a]), individuals or households and organizations, or between organizations under their authority; or by (2) People's Committee of provinces and cities under central authority for disputes between organizations, or between organizations and households or individuals under central authority. (Art. 38[2][b]). Land disputes involving users with land-use certificates shall be resolved by Vietnamese court of law. (Art. 38[3]).

SALES:

Legislation.—Civil Code (CC), promulgated by National Assembly, on Oct. 28, 1995.

Sale contract may be civil contract, economic contract or commercial contract. Currently, no uniform commercial law exists regulating all types of contracts in Vietnam. CC regulates formation of civil contract, and is applicable to formation of economic and commercial contracts. Sale contract is agreement by which property is transferred from seller to buyer ("the parties") for fixed price in money, paid or agreed to be paid by buyer. (Art. 421).

Sale contract should specify object of sale contract, quantity, quality, agreed price, and place of delivery. If any of these terms are not specified in contract between parties, then CC will provide default rules. Seller must own and be legally able to transfer to buyer goods to be sold. (Art. 422). Goods may be moveable or immoveable property. If moveable property, value, type, quantity and quality must be specified. If immoveable property, seller must have documents of ownership available. Parties should negotiate and agree on purchase price and mode of payment. If price is set by State, parties should agree to set price within regulated price list. (Art. 424). Delivery place is also determined by parties. If parties contract is silent about delivery place, then for sale of real property, designated delivery place is location of real property itself. For sale of moveable properties, delivery place is buyer's residence or office. (Art. 426). Seller should deliver goods to buyer at stipulated delivery date, or at earlier date if buyer approves.

CC also provides for contract remedies. If seller delivers goods in excess of ordered amount, buyer may refuse or accept excess goods delivered. If buyer accepts additional goods, he must pay seller for excess amount at agreed price. (Art. 428 [1]). If seller delivers lesser amount than what was ordered, buyer may cancel or accept goods delivered. In either case, buyer may ask for damages and for rest of goods to be delivered or just accept lesser amount. (Art. 428[2]). Similarly, if incomplete set of goods are delivered such that buyer is unable to make use of such goods, he may repudiate or accept goods delivered. In either case, he may request for damage payment and ask for rest of set to be delivered. If buyer has paid for such goods in advance, he may request seller to pay him damage compensation as well as interest at rate of overdue loans stipulated by State Bank, from delivery date of incomplete set until full set is delivered. (Art. 429).

Buyer may repudiate nonconforming goods and ask for damage payment, accept goods at agreed price, or request for conforming goods to be delivered and request for damage payment. (Art. 430).

Above contract rules apply to all contracts. In addition, each type of contract is also governed by specific rules stipulated in CC.

Ownership of goods is transferred from buyer to seller on date buyer receives goods sold, except otherwise agreed by parties or as stipulated by law. If sale goods are registered goods, ownership transfers on date property registration is complete. (Art. 433).

Sale of certain types of properties must be certified by public notary and registered with competent State bodies. This includes house purchasing contracts, transfer of land-use right certificates, sale transport contracts and sale contracts for aircraft or ships.

SEALS:

Legislation.—Decree No. 62/CP On the Management and Use of Official Seals, issued by Government, on Sept. 22, 1993 (Decree No. 62/CP).

Official seals are used by State, economic, social and military organizations, hereinafter referred to as "organizations". (Art. 1). Any exchange of documents made between these organizations or between organization and individual are considered valid only if official seal is affixed.

Ministry of Interior has standard application for applicants interested in making official seal. In order to certify legal existence of organization, appropriate Vietnamese company license and business registration certificate must be submitted to provincial police department. Once seal application approved, certificate of seal registration will be granted. $10 dollar fee is charged for seal production, which must be manufactured to conform to standard size and shape determined by Ministry of Interior. (Art. 5).

Foreign economic organizations must also apply for seal from Ministry of Interior. Existing seal of foreign economic organization must be approved by same Ministry. (Art. 7). Foreign diplomatic offices must notify Ministry of Foreign Affairs of Vietnam of seals used. (Art. 7). Red is only color of ink permitted to be used with seal.

TAXATION:

Introduction.—Foreigners doing business in Vietnam will encounter one or more of following main taxes depending on form of business adopted and level of involvement in Vietnam. Taxes examined are corporate profit tax; personal income tax for persons with high incomes; turnover tax; special sales tax; import and export duties; profit remittance tax; royalty tax on exploitation of natural resources; tax on incomes generated from royalties; and value-added tax.

Corporate Profit Tax.—

Legislation.—Law on Corporate Income Tax passed on June 30, 1990 and effective Oct. 10, 1990 (CPT Law); Law on Amendment of and Addition to some Articles of the Law on Corporate Income Tax passed on July 6, 1993 and effective Sept. 1, 1993 (CPT Amended Law); Law on Foreign Investment in Vietnam adopted by National Assembly on Dec. 29, 1987, amended and supplemented on June 30, 1990 and Dec. 23, 1992 (LFI); Decree No. 18/CP of the Vietnamese Government on Apr. 16, 1993 Providing in Detail the LFI (Decree No. 18); Circular No. 48/TC-TCDN Guiding the Implementation of Certain Provisions of Decree 18/CP on Business Organisation of Enterprises Which Have Foreign Invested Capital issued by Ministry of Finance on June 30, 1993 (Decree No. 48); Circular No. 51-TC/TCT Guiding the Implementation of the Tax Provisions Applicable to Foreign Investment in Vietnam issued by Ministry of Finance on July 3, 1993 (Circular No. 51-TC/TCT).

Taxpayers.—Foreign Investment Enterprises (FIE), including joint venture companies, enterprises with 100% foreign-owned capital, and foreign parties to business cooperation contracts are subject to corporate income tax (CPT). CPT Law requires economic organizations and individuals earning income from manufacturing, construction, transportation, commerce and trade, food and dining, services, and other economic activities in Vietnam to pay CPT. (CPT Law, Art. 1).

Taxable Income Calculation.—CPT payable is amount of taxable income earned in tax year multiplied by tax rate stipulated in investment license issued by Ministry of Planning and Investment (MPI) to FIEs or to foreign parties to business cooperation contracts. (Circular No. 51-TC/TCT, Part II, §A, Art. 3). Tax year is financial accounting year of each FIE. Taxable income is difference between total revenues and total expenditures of enterprise, including additional incomes (e.g., income from subsidiaries) received during tax year. (CPI Law, Art. 7). FIE's revenues include revenue from sale of goods or from any other activity of enterprise during tax year. (CPT Law, Art. 8).

Additional incomes include income from real estate leasing, liquidation proceeds or transfer of assets, transfer of shares, profits earned from joint venture operations with third parties, and other profits from financial dealings. (CPT Law, Art. 8; Circular No. 51-TC/TCT, Part II, §A, Art. 7).

Deductible expenditures are: (1) Expenditure on materials and energy used in production of main-products or by-products or for provision of services; (2) salaries, wages, and other allowances paid to all employees, both Vietnamese and foreign; (3) depreciation of fixed assets used for business production; (4) purchase of or payment for right to use technical data, invention certificates, technology licenses, and technical services; (5) enterprise administration expenditures, including expenditure such as labour protection, fire protection, and security (CPT Law, Art. 9); (6) taxes, charges, and fees in form of tax paid (except CPT); (7) interest on loans; (8) losses carried forward from previous years. Joint venture enterprises and enterprises with 100% foreign-owned capital are permitted to carry losses of any financial year forward to subsequent years and set them off against profits of those years, for period of up to five

See Topical Index in front part of this volume.

TAXATION . . . *continued*
years commencing year after that in which loss was suffered; and (9) other expenditures not included in above list provided that expenditure does not exceed 5% of total expenditures claimed above. (Circular No. 51-TC/TCT, Part II, §A, Art. 11).

Tax Rate.—CPT rate for each investment project must be negotiated and stated in investment license issued by MPI, and is effective for project's entire term. Tax rates for FIE business income range from 10% to 25%, with standard rate of 25% applying to most manufacturing, real estate, and service-oriented FIEs. Oil and gas exploitation projects are taxed at rate in excess of 25% standard. (Decree 18, Art. 66). Projects subject to 25% rate may be exempted from CPT for one year after enterprise becomes profitable, and 50% tax reduction for up to two years after that. (Decree No. 18, Art. 69).

Flat rate of 20% applies to investments meeting two of following four criteria: enterprise employs 500 or more workers; it uses advanced technology; it exports at least 80% of production; and foreign party's registered capital is at least US$10 million. (Decree No. 18, Art. 67[1]). Flat rate of 15% applies to some infrastructure and natural resource projects under which foreign party pledges to transfer all assets without compensation to Vietnamese party upon expiration of project term. These projects are eligible for two-year tax holiday, followed by four-year 50% reduction in profit tax, beginning in their first profit-making year. (Decree No. 18, Art. 69[3]). Other infrastructure projects in mountainous regions, afforestation, and projects of "significant importance" will be taxed at 10% rate. (Decree No. 18, Art. 67[3]). Such projects are eligible for four-year tax holiday and further four-year 50% profit tax reduction, beginning in first profit-making year. (Decree No. 18, Art. 69[4]).

Investment projects subject to standard 25% rate will pay this rate for entire project term. Preferential tax rates between 15% and 20% are valid for only five to seven years starting from date of issuance of investment license. (Circular No. 48, Part II, Art. 1). Projects taxed at 10% may enjoy this rate for eight to ten years. (Circular No. 48, Part II, Art. 2). In all cases, preferential tax rate period may be extended, but may not exceed 15 years. (Circular No. 48, Part II, Art. 2).

Avoidance of International Double Taxation.—By end of May 1996, Vietnam had concluded bilateral tax agreements with 28 countries to facilitate its open door policy and avoid international double taxation. Where taxpayer obtains income outside Vietnam, credit for taxes paid abroad on that income may be set off against Vietnamese taxation of same income. Tax credit may not, however, exceed tax payable on that part of income sourced abroad, as calculated according to Vietnam Tax Law.

Personal Income Tax.—

Legislation.—Ordinance On Personal Income Tax Applicable To Persons With High Incomes issued by Standing Committee of National Assembly on May 19, 1994 (Amended Ordinance on PIT); Decree No. 5-CP Implementing the Amended Ordinance on PIT issued by Government on Jan. 20, 1995 (Decree No. 5); Circular No. 27-TC-TCT Providing Guidelines for the Implementation Of Decree No. 5 issued by Ministry of Finance on Mar. 30, 1995 (Circular No. 27).

Taxpayers.—Personal income tax (PIT) is assessed on worldwide income of Vietnamese citizens, foreigners working in Vietnam, and individuals who reside in Vietnam for more than 183 days within calendar year period or for indefinite term. (Amended Ordinance on PIT, Arts. 1 and 9; Decree No. 5, Art. 6).

Taxable Income.—PIT applies to both regular and irregular incomes earned. Tax rates differ between Vietnamese citizens and expatriate employees.

Regular taxable income is total income earned by each individual calculated as monthly average throughout year. (Circular No. 27, Art. 1.1). Regular income includes salaries, wages, allowances, wage-like bonuses, and income other than salaries or wages arising from participation in business production activities or service activities not subject to corporate profit tax. (Amended Ordinance on PIT, Art. 2[1]). It includes income received from participation in business associations and boards of management. (Circular No. 27, Art. 2.1.3).

Irregular taxable income of individual is based on payments received from time to time. (Circular No. 27, Art. 2.1). Irregular income includes gifts or donations, in cash or in kind, received from anywhere in world; lottery prizes; technology transfer fees; or consulting fees for technical construction design. (Amended Ordinance on PIT, Art. 2[2]). It also includes income derived from royalties earned for literary or artistic works. (Decree No. 27, Art. 2.2.3).

Income Tax Basis.—Basis for income tax payment is individual's taxable income multiplied by applicable tax rate. (Amended Ordinance on PIT, Art. 8).

Tax Rate.—Tax rates for PIT vary according to both type of individual subject to tax who has to pay such tax and form of income considered. Specifically, tax rates vary from 10% to 50% for regular income of expatriate employees and Vietnamese employees with income earned from overseas; and from 10% to 30% for irregular income of all individuals. (Amended Ordinance on PIT, Art. 10[2]). Tax rates for Vietnamese citizens range from 10% to 60%. (Amended Ordinance on PIT, Art. 10[1]).

Tax Exemption.—Interest on capital gains-type income derived from sources such as bank deposits, bonds, and shares are temporarily exempt from PIT. (Amended Ordinance on PIT, Art. 3[1]). Sixteen other types of personal income exempt from PIT include insurance compensation payments under personal and property insurance policies, profits of private business already subject to corporate profit tax, and regular income of foreigners who reside in Vietnam for less than 30 days within consecutive 12-month period. (Circular No. 27, Art. 4).

Tax Treaties.—Personal income taxes paid in other countries may be applied as credit and deducted from income tax payable in Vietnam. In event of any inconsistency between tax treaty in force and domestic tax provisions, treaty will prevail. (Amended Ordinance on PIT, Art. 4).

Tax on Income in Form of Royalties.—

Legislation.—Circular No. 08-TC-TCT on Taxation of Royalties issued by Ministry of Finance on Feb. 5, 1994 (Circular No. 8).

Taxpayers.—Any individual or organizations, domestic or foreign, earning royalty income from transfer of technology and training; provision of support, technical and consulting services; or copyright licensing must pay royalty tax. (Circular No. 8, §1, Art. I and §2, Art. 1).

Tax Calculation.—Tax levied on royalties is based on amount of royalty income received multiplied by tax rate. (Circular No. 8, §3, Art. 2).

Tax Rate.—Tax rates range from 5% to 15% depending on amount of income generated, term of technology transfer contract, and whether parties involved are individuals or economic organizations. Rate of 5% applies if transferor or licensor is domestic or foreign individual and income generated is over 1.8 million Vietnamese dong. (Circular No. 8, §3, Art. 1[a]). Rate is 10% if transferor or licensor is domestic or foreign legal entity and transfer contract term less than five years. Rate climbs to 15% for similar contracts of five years or more. (Circular No. 8, §3, Art. 1[a]).

Any royalties paid for technology transfer by foreign party as part of its legal contribution to joint venture or business cooperation contract is exempted from royalty tax. (Circular No. 8, §3, Art. 4).

Avoidance of Double Taxation.—Circular No. 8 prescribes measure by which transferor or licensor may avoid payment of double taxation on royalty income earned.

Tax on Remittance of Profit Abroad.—

Legislation.—Law on Foreign Investment adopted by National Assembly on Dec. 29, 1987, as amended and supplemented on June 30, 1990 and Dec. 23, 1992 (LFI); Decree on 18/CP of the Vietnamese Government on Apr. 16, 1993 providing in Detail the LFI (Decree 18); Circular No. 51-TC/TCT Guiding the Implementation of the Tax Provisions Applicable to Foreign Investment in Vietnam issued by Ministry of Finance on July 3, 1993 (Circular No. 51-TC/TCT).

Taxpayers.—Foreign Investment Enterprises (FIE) or individuals transferring profits abroad must pay withholding tax. (LFI, Art. 33).

Tax Rate.—One of three levels of tax (5%, 7%, or 10%) will apply to amount of profits remitted abroad. (LIF, Art. 33). 5%, 7%, and 10% rates apply respectively to FIE projects in which foreign party contributes at least US$10 million, US$5 million, or some other amount to company's legal capital. (Decree No. 18, Art. 10). Tax rate on remittances should be stipulated in investment license issued by MPI.

Tax Calculation.—Amount of profit remittance tax (PRT) payable is amount of profit transferred abroad multiplied by PRT rate stipulated in investment license. (Circular No. 51-TC/TCT, Part B, Art. 2).

If foreign party to production-sharing contract transfers profits abroad in form of products, then PRT amount is determined by multiplying quantity of products exported by free-on-board (FOB) sale price, and then by PRT rate. (Circular No. 51-TC/TCT, Part B, Art. 2).

Reductions and Exemptions.—In special cases where investment encouragement is needed, exemption or reduction of PRT tax may be granted by MPI. (LFI, Art. 3).

Royalty Tax on Natural Resource Exploitation.—

Legislation.—Ordinance on Royalties issued by Government on Mar. 30, 1990; Implementing Decree No. 6-HDBT issued by Government on Jan. 1, 1991 (Decree No. 6); Circular No. 7-TC-TCT Making Detailed Provisions for the Implementation of Decree No. 6 issued by Ministry of Finance on Feb. 7, 1991 (Circular No. 7).

Taxpayers.—All Foreign Investment Enterprises (FIE) and foreign parties to business cooperation contracts who exploit natural resources in Vietnam must pay natural resource tax on profits derived from such activities. (Circular No. 7, Art. 1).

Tax Calculation.—Tax liability is calculated by multiplying quantity of resources exploited by taxable value of each unit exploited, and then by royalty rate. (Circular No. 7, §2, Art. 1). Quantity of resources exploited is total output of each resource type that is periodically exploited, regardless of whether actually sold. (Circular No. 7, §2, Art. 1). Taxable value of each unit exploited is average selling price of raw resource at time royalty tax calculated. (Circular No. 7, §2, Art. 2). Royalty tax rates vary from 1% to 40% depending on resource exploited. (Circular No. 7, §2, Art. 3).

Taxable Product.—Groups of products subject to royalty tax are: (a) metallic and nonmetallic mineral resources; (b) timber, wood, and other natural forest products; and (c) fish and other marine products.

Reduction.—Current legislation provides for reduction in natural resource tax for Vietnamese individuals or organizations meeting certain economic criteria, but not for FIEs. Maximum reduction for eligible taxpayers is 50% of tax payable. (Circular No. 7, §4, Art. 12).

Special Sales Tax.—

Legislation.—Law on Special Sales Tax issued by National Assembly on June 30, 1990; as amended July 5, 1993; Decree No. 97/CP on Special Sales Tax issued by Government in Jan. 1996 (Decree No. 97).

Taxpayers.—Individuals and organizations who manufacture luxury goods such as liquor, cigarettes, beer, firecrackers, vehicles that carry less than 24 people, or petroleum products must pay special sales tax (SST). (Decree No. 97, Art. 7).

Tax Calculation.—SST is calculated by first multiplying quantity of taxable goods sold by their taxable value, and then by applicable tax rate. (Decree No. 97, Art. 4). For domestic goods, quantity of goods taxable is total amount to be sold, exchanged, given away, or consumed internally by manufacturing entity. (Decree No. 97, Art. 5[1]). For imported goods, quantity of goods taxable is total amount declared on import customs form. (Decree No. 97, Art. 5[2]). Taxable value of goods produced locally is selling price as determined by producer at place of manufacture where no SST is levied. (Decree No. 97, Art. 6[1]). Taxable value of processing goods or goods to be given away or used internally is selling price of similar goods. (Decree No. 97, Art. 6[1]). Taxable value of imported goods is adjusted upwards by applicable import tax. (Decree No. 97, Art. 6[2]).

Rate.—SST rates vary from 15% to 100% depending on luxury goods concerned. For example, petroleum products and medicinal liquor are taxed at 15%, while cars with less than five seats and firecrackers are taxed at 100%.

Exemption.—FIEs producing goods subject to SST may, in certain circumstances, receive exemption or reduction in SST liability.

Reduction may be available if taxable goods of enterprise are adversely affected by natural disaster, war, or other contingencies. Such reduction may not exceed 50% of SST otherwise payable nor 30% of total value of goods so affected within 180 days of incident of damage.

If enterprise is newly established or, in applying new manufacturing technology, faces loss because of SST payment, reduction (if any) will be determined year by year. Any reduction may not exceed 30% of SST payable within two-year period. (Decree No. 97, Art. 15).

Exemption from SST liability is available where goods otherwise subject to SST are: (a) manufactured for export; (b) commissioned to import/export companies for

See Topical Index in front part of this volume.

TAXATION . . . *continued*
export; (c) element of nonrefundable foreign aid; (d) exempted under treaty to which Vietnam is signatory; (e) in transit from Vietnam; (f) imported for reexport; (g) imported to be used as input in goods manufactured for export; or (h) accompanied by persons entering or exiting Vietnam.

Turnover Tax.—

Legislation.—Turnover tax is levied on enterprise's gross sales revenue at rates ranging from 1% to 40%, depending on product or service involved. Primary legislation on turnover tax is: Law on Turnover Tax adopted by National Assembly on June 30, 1990, amended on July 5, 1993. (Law on Turnover Tax).

Tariff for turnover tax rates is periodically revised. Recent revisions are found in: Decree No. 55-CP on the Turnover Tax Tariff Rates issued by Government on Aug. 28, 1993 (Decree No. 55); Circular No. 73A-TCT on Turnover Tax, Providing Guidelines on the Implementation of Decree No. 55 issued by Ministry of Finance on Aug. 30, 1993 (Implementation Regulation - Circular No. 73A-TCT); Circular No. 40-TC/TCT Giving Guidance on the Amendments and Supplements to Implementing Regulation Circular No. 73A-TCT (Circular No. 40-TC/TCT); Resolution No. 216-NQ-UBTVQ H9 Amending and Supplementing the Tariff of Turnover Tax Rates issued by Standing Committee of National Assembly on Aug. 30, 1994 (Resolution No. 216); Decree No. 182-CP Stipulating in Detail the Implementation of Resolution No. 216 issued by Government on Nov. 10, 1994 (Decree No. 182); Circular No. 20-TC-TCT issued by Ministry of Finance on Mar. 12, 1994 (Circular No. 20); Circular No. 07-TC/TCT Providing Additional Guidelines for Implementing Circular No. 20-TC-TCT issued by Ministry of Finance on Jan. 7, 1995 (Circular No. 7); Decree No. 96/CP Regulating Detailed Implementation of the Law on Turnover Tax and the Law on Amendments and Supplements of the Law on Turnover Tax issued by Government on Dec. 27, 1995 (Decree No. 96); Law on Amendments and Supplements to a Number of Articles of the Law on Turnover Tax issued by National Assembly on Oct. 28, 1995 (Law on Amendments of Turnover Tax of Oct. 28, 1995).

Taxpayers.—Vietnamese and foreign organizations and individuals carrying on business production or business operations such as construction, transportation, commerce, services, and other activities in Vietnam and which experience turnover in cash or in kind must pay turnover tax. (Law on Turnover Tax, Art. 1).

Turnover Tax Basis.—Amount of turnover on which tax is imposed is total revenue earned from sales/commissions on sales or services provided. (Law on Turnover Tax, Art. 8).

Business establishment conducting multiple economic activities will pay different rates of turnover tax for each activity conducted. (Law on Turnover Tax, Art. 12).

Tax Rate.—There are currently 18 different turnover tax rates, ranging from 0% to 40% depending on product or service involved. (Decree No. 182, Art. 1).

Exemption.—Turnover tax does not apply to agricultural production, which is already subject to agricultural tax; commodities production, which is subject to special sales tax; production of goods for export; or credit activities of banks. (Law on Amendments of Turnover Tax of Oct. 28, 1995, Art. 2).

Taxpayers exempt from turnover tax payments include elderly, disabled people, and small-scale traders with minimal monthly turnover revenue and who maintain subsistence-level standard of living. (Law on Turnover Tax, Art. 18; Decree No. 55, Art. 12).

Reductions.—Business establishments which suffer losses due to natural disasters, war, or other contingencies may receive reduction in turnover tax liability. Reduction of up to 50% is possible for businesses facing losses in any economic sector and which have operated in highland or mountainous areas for up to three years. (Law on Turnover Tax, Art. 18; Decree No. 55, Art. 12).

Value-Added Tax.—

Legislation.—Decision No. 468-TC-TCT Concerning Trial Collection of Value Added Tax issued by Ministry of Finance on July 5, 1993 (Decision No. 468); Implementing Regualtion of Decision No. 468 (Implementing Regulation).

Scope of VAT.—Value Added Tax (VAT) is intended to eventually replace turnover tax. Law on Value Added Tax is currently being drafted; meanwhile, turnover tax expected to remain in place.

Since Aug. 1993, Ministry of Finance (MoF) has, on trial basis, authorized 11 enterprises to pay VAT instead of turnover tax provided they meet criteria stipulated in Decision No. 468. Specifically, these enterprises must obtain written permission from MoF and adopt accounting system conforming to State's accounting principles and reflecting enterprise's turnover and costs. (Implementing Regualtion, Art. 2).

VAT Tax Calculation.—VAT calculation is based on value added to product during subsequent transactions and VAT rate, which ranges from 5 to 15%. (Implementing Regualtion, §2, Art. 4).

Two methods of calculating VAT are: (a) deductive method; and (b) difference method. (Implementing Regulation, §2, Art. 5).

Under deductive method, taxable turnover is multiplied by applicable rate; VAT already paid on materials and goods purchased are then deducted. (Implementation Regulation, §2, Art. 5[1]). Difference method, which may only be used by businesses involved in precious metals, trading, and commercial banking activities, deducts taxable turnover from cost of materials and goods purchased. This amount is then multiplied by applicable tax rate to determine VAT payable. (Implementation Regulation §2, Art. 5[2]).

Reduction.—No VAT exemptions are contemplated. Reductions, however, may be granted if business is harmed by incidents of natural disaster or force majeure, or otherwise incurs loss if VAT liability exceeds turnover tax otherwise payable. (Implementation Regulation, §4, Art. 13).

Import and Export Duties.—See topics on Foreign Exchange; Customs.

TRADEMARK LAW:

Legislation.—Civil Code (CC) enacted by National Assembly on Nov. 28, 1995 and effective July 1, 1996; Ordinance No. 197-HDBT on Trademarks issued by Government on Dec. 14, 1982, as amended Mar. 20, 1990 (Ordinance on Trademarks); Implementing Regulations on Trademarks issued by Government on Mar. 20, 1990 (IROT).

Introduction.—Before July 1, 1996, trademarks were protected under Ordinance on the Protection of Industrial Property, Jan. 28, 1989, and Ordinance on Trademark Protection and its implementing regulations. CC repealed Ordinance on the Protection of Industrial Property and codified other trademarks regulations. Regulations to implement CC will provide further clarification.

Treaties and Conventions.—Vietnam has acceded to Paris Convention for the Protection of Industrial Property of Mar. 20, 1883, and its revision in Stockholm on July 14, 1967. Vietnam has also signed Madrid Agreement of Apr. 14, 1891, also revised in Stockholm in 1967. Vietnam is member of WIPO and has adopted International Classification of Goods and Services system which divides goods and services into 42 classes. Trademark laws in Vietnam must conform to above treaties.

Industrial Protection Authority.—National Office of Industrial Property (NOIP), under administrative control of Ministry of Science, Technology, and the Environment (MSTE), is responsible for registration and protection of trademarks (as well as other industrial properties). Once trademark is registered, protection from infringement may be sought through Market Management Department under Ministry of Trade, or through People's Court.

Scope of Protection.—Trademarks, symbols used to distinguish same category of products or services from various business or production facilities, may be in form of words, images or combination of these elements, and in one or more colors. (CC, Art. 785).

Certain trademarks may be denied registration prima facie including: signs that do not possess distinctive characteristics, consisting of assembly of simple geometric shapes, figures, or letters that cannot be pronounced (except where widely used and recognized over long period of time); conventional signs and usual figures and denominations for goods that are widely used and matter of public knowledge; signs expressing time, place, manufacturing process, type, quality, quantity, nature, composition, purpose, value, or that have descriptive character in relation to product; signs liable to mislead public as to origin, nature or purpose of product, or signs likely to deceive consumer; signs identical or similar to official initials indicating control, quality, warranty, and so forth, of national or international organizations; signs representing state flags, armorial bearings or emblems, portraits of national leaders or heroes, geographical denominations relating to Vietnam or other countries, names or emblems of international organizations, except where use of such signs has been authorized by competent authorities; signs contrary to law, to public policy and to socialist morality; in case of goods of same type, signs identical or similar to marks previously registered in Vietnam or protected by international convention to which Vietnam is signatory party. (IROT, Art. 2[2]).

Trademark Protection Applicants.—State, collective, or private organizations having status of juridical person, and natural persons engaged in lawful manufacturing, commercial, or service activities, are entitled and obliged to register and use trademarks and service marks to designate their products or services, pursuant to provisions of Ordinance. (IROT, Art. 1[1]).

Under CC, industrial property rights of foreign individuals and/or legal persons granted certificates of protection for their industrial property by Vietnam are protected by Vietnamese laws as well as industrial property treaties to which Vietnam is signatory party. (CC, Art. 837). Natural persons or legal entities with no residence, headquarters, or representative offices in Vietnam must apply for trademark protection through authorized industrial property agent in Vietnam. (IROT, Art. 1[4]).

Application Filing Requirements.—Application must be filed for each class of trademark registration. Complete application must include full name, address, and line of business of applicant, types of mark, colors claimed (if any), description of mark briefly indicating significance of elements constituting mark and its structure, priority date claimed (if applicable), country, and date priority sought. Accompanying documents include notarized copy of applicant's business license or equivalent; notarized power of attorney; list of goods which will bear mark; and 18 representations of mark (including word marks), no smaller than 5 cm. by 5 cm. and no larger than 8 cm. by 8 cm. in size (except for purely nominative marks). Further, depending on specific circumstances, it may be advisable to submit supporting information designed to demonstrate legitimacy of mark and its owner.

Complete application filed must be in Vietnamese. In practice, application may be forwarded to official agent in English, French, German, or Russian, and agent will submit Vietnamese translation of application materials within one month of filing date. As Vietnamese language is romanized, applicants not required to register Vietnamese translation of mark, although advisable, as such registration will protect owner from would be infringers capitalizing on goodwill of mark simply by adopting Vietnamese equivalent. In practice, only marks in Chinese require romanized translation of mark and its meaning.

Filing Procedure.—Prior to filing trademark application with NOIP, applicant should conduct trademark search of trademark he plans to register. Search may be conducted by one of Vietnam's authorized trademark agents. Information produced by search may provide applicant with better chance to protect his trademark by anticipating avoidable objections. Search will also indicate whether similar or identical mark has already been registered or applied for. If similar mark has been registered, then chances of rejection are higher.

Once search has been successfully conducted, applicant files application with NOIP and pays application fee. As Vietnam follows "first to file" rule, date on which NOIP receives application is crucial. If trademark seeking protection is already protected by registration in treaty country, then priority date is date of original application. If products bearing trademark are exhibited in official exhibition in Vietnam, then date of exhibition serves as priority date if application is filed within six months of exhibition.

If application is complete and accepted by NOIP, its priority date will be recognized and effective with respect to any conflicting applications. If application is deemed incomplete, it is returned to applicant and process must be reinitiated. Only in cases where applicant is deemed to have disclosed substance of trademark in original, albeit incomplete application, will applicant receive priority right of original application. NOIP has six months to complete review of trademark application for its acceptance to registration. Implementing regulations of CC are expected to extend this period to nine months or a year.

See Topical Index in front part of this volume.

TRADEMARK LAW . . . *continued*

Once mark is registered, registration certificate is issued to proprietor and mark is entered into National Register of Marks. Registered mark will then be published in official Bulletin of Inventions and Marks, issued by National Office of Inventions. (IROT, Art. 5).

Appeals.—If trademark registration is denied by Registrar, written explanation must accompany rejection letter. Applicant has three months (or time period stipulated in rejection letter) to file appeal with NOIP. NOIP is required to respond to appeal within two months of receipt. If NOIP denies appeal, second and final appeal may be made to MSTE. (IROT, Art. 13).

Term of Protection.—Registered mark is protected for term of ten years commencing from priority date. Use of mark is compulsory and subject to termination and cancellation as provided by Ordinance on Trademarks and CC. Mark registration may be renewed indefinitely in ten year increments, provided that renewal application is filed six months prior to expiry date of previous term of protection. (IROT, Art. 8).

Cancellation.—Vietnamese laws do not provide for formal opposition to particular mark. Instead, opposition requests take form of cancellation action. Cancellation action may be brought at any time during period of registration. As matter of practice, cancellation action may be brought before mark is registered, such as during review period. Where true owner of mark discovers that spurious or potentially conflicting mark has been applied for, he may file under circular dated Mar. 19, 1993, where requirements of such action are set forth.

Interested party may also cancel registered trademarks, and MSTE circular states that in order to proceed with action against registered mark, third party must have widely and continuously used mark with respect to goods or services identical (or confusingly similar) to those which disputed mark is registered for, prior to disputed mark's registration. Mark must be "well known" among consumers due to products being sold bearing mark; or advertised using mark; or be mark which has gained recognition in international market; mark for which substantial sales figures can be substantiated; mark used over long period of time; or mark which has obtained registrations worldwide.

Registered mark may also be cancelled if not used for period of five consecutive years from decision date for granting certificate of registration without adequate legal reason; it may also be terminated if manufacturing or commercial establishment owning mark no longer carries on activities.

Furthermore, §12 of Trademark Ordinance provides that throughout term of validity of mark's registration certificate, any organization or person who discovers that mark was registered in manner contrary to provisions of this Ordinance has right to file declaration with NOIP requesting cancellation of legal protection of mark concerned.

CC codifies grounds for cancellation and termination of right to protection of marks in §§792, 793(1)(b) and 793(1)(c).

Assignments and Licenses.—Proprietor of protected mark may assign or license his rights to another person. License or assignment must be registered with NOIP within one month of executing agreement and following documents must accompany registration: two copies of original license contract or assignment; original registration certificate of mark concerned; notarized power of attorney; and copy of royalty payments.

Assignee may transfer rights to another person if he wishes; however licensee, in contrast, may not transfer right to use mark to third party. (CC, Art. 821[1]).

Enforcement.—While trademark registration is valid, owner of trademark or transferee under license contract has exclusive use of mark in relation to goods or services for which it is registered. Trademark violations are more easily detected than patent or copyright violations. Trademark infringer may face civil or criminal sanctions in Vietnam.

Enforcement of registered mark can take several forms. If owner of registered trademark or his/her empowered authorized agent discovers infringement has occurred, he/she or agent must inform NOIP which will issue written order instructing infringer to cease infringing activities. In practice, however, owner of registered trademark usually contacts Market Management Department in order to stop infringement, as one of its functions is to oversee market activities, including trademark use.

Civil action, though not most pragmatic method of enforcement, is only option available if civil damages are sought from infringer. Civil complaint is filed in People's Court of Hanoi, Ho Chi Minh City, or Quang Nam-Danang Province. It may take long time before decision is handed down and, though court decides on relief given, it is NOIP's responsibility to assess severity of trademark violation. Some remedies available are interim injunction; permanent injunction damages calculated by lost profit to trademark holder due to infringing activities; destruction of infringing or counterfeit goods; or public apology at infringer's expense.

Trademark owner may seek criminal action by filing complaint with public prosecutor, and must supply evidence of infringement to support such case. Case is heard by local People's Court. In case of foreign complainant, People's Courts of either Hanoi or Ho Chi Minh City will adjudicate case. Criminal remedies available are seizure and destruction of infringing goods; fines (maximum being one to three times value of genuine goods per infringing product and minimum being one to three times illegal profits, or 10% to 50% of infringing goods' value); jail sentence (maximum of up to 20 years or minimum ranging from four to seven years). Death sentence may be ordered for severe cases.

Bureau for protection of customers' interests, in response to complaint filed by trademark owner, is empowered to temporarily seize infringing goods while awaiting outcome of case, provided sufficient evidence exists to support infringement claim. However, list of registered trademarks available at most other countries' Customs Departments is not yet available in Vietnam; it is therefore difficult for Customs personnel to detect counterfeit trademarks and take effective action against infringers.

Most practical method by far of enforcing trademark rights is through informal action. Many foreign trademark owners have successfully sought assistance of Vietnamese authorities in stopping trademark infringements, and such practice has become their protocol. Foreign company may empower authorized agents to act on its behalf. Authorized agent would then contact local authorities and enlist their aid in stopping infringement activities, and/or send cease-and-desist letters to infringers. Letters, signed by local attorney, warn infringers that activity is in violation of Vietnamese law, and warn of civil and criminal actions which might be taken if infringing activity does not stop. They may also publish warnings to consumers in local newspapers that infringing products are on market. Such warnings are accompanied by educational information on how consumer may recognize genuine articles from counterfeit ones.

Industrial Property Rights of Foreign Organizations and Individuals.—Industrial property rights of foreign individuals and juridical persons to industrial property for which State of Socialist Republic of Vietnam has issued certificate of protection, will be protected in accordance with Vietnamese laws and international treaties in which Vietnam is signatory party. (CC, Art. 837).

Implementing regulations of CC, when issued, will give more detailed guidelines concerning scope of industrial property protection granted to foreign organizations and individuals under Vietnamese laws.

See Topical Index in front part of this volume.

Part VI

Selected International Conventions to Which The United States is a Party

---

SELECTED INTERNATIONAL CONVENTIONS

Note: Abbreviations for International Conventions page numbers appears as “IC”.

SELECTED INTERNATIONAL CONVENTIONS

Annotations provided by U.S. Department of State. Current information on the status of these conventions is always available from the Treaty Affairs Section of the Office of the Legal Adviser, Department of State, Washington, D. C. 20520.

Note: This Revision includes information as of 8/1/96.

CONVENTION OF THE SERVICE ABROAD OF JUDICIAL AND EXTRAJUDICIAL DOCUMENTS IN CIVIL OR COMMERCIAL MATTERS

The States signatory to the present Convention,

Desiring to create appropriate means to ensure that judicial and extrajudicial documents to be served abroad shall be brought to the notice of the addressee in sufficient time,

Desiring to improve the organisation of mutual judicial assistance for that purpose by simplifying and expediting the procedure,

Have resolved to conclude a Convention to this effect and have agreed upon the following provisions:

Article 1

The present Convention shall apply in all cases, in civil or commercial matters, where there is occasion to transmit a judicial or extrajudicial document for service abroad.

This Convention shall not apply where the address of the person to be served with the document is not known.

CHAPTER I—JUDICIAL DOCUMENTS

Article 2

Each contracting State shall designate a Central Authority which will undertake to receive requests for service coming from other contracting States and to proceed in conformity with the provisions of articles 3 to 6.

Each State shall organise the Central Authority in conformity with its own law.

Article 3

The authority or judicial officer competent under the law of the State in which the documents originate shall forward to the Central Authority of the State addressed a request conforming to the model annexed to the present Convention, without any requirement of legalisation or other equivalent formality.

The document to be served or a copy thereof shall be annexed to the request. The request and the document shall both be furnished in duplicate.

Article 4

If the Central Authority considers that the request does not comply with the provisions of the present Convention it shall promptly inform the applicant and specify its objections to the request.

Article 5

The Central Authority of the State addressed shall itself serve the document or shall arrange to have it served by an appropriate agency, either—

(a) by a method prescribed by its internal law for the service of documents in domestic actions upon persons who are within its territory, or

(b) by a particular method requested by the applicant, unless such a method is incompatible with the law of the State addressed.

Subject to sub-paragraph (b) of the first paragraph of this article, the document may always be served by delivery to an addressee who accepts it voluntarily.

If the document is to be served under the first paragraph above, the Central Authority may require the document to be written in, or translated into, the official language or one of the official languages of the State addressed.

That part of the request, in the form attached to the present Convention, which contains a summary of the document to be served, shall be served with the document.

Article 6

The Central Authority of the State addressed or any authority which it may have designated for that purpose, shall complete a certificate in the form of the model annexed to the present Convention.

The certificate shall state that the document has been served and shall include the method, the place and the date of service and the person to whom the document was delivered. If the document has not been served, the certificate shall set out the reasons which have prevented service.

The applicant may require that a certificate not completed by a Central Authority or by a judicial authority shall be countersigned by one of these authorities.

The certificate shall be forwarded directly to the applicant.

Article 7

The standard terms in the model annexed to the present Convention shall in all cases be written either in French or in English. They may also be written in the official language, or in one of the official languages, of the State in which the documents originate.

The corresponding blanks shall be completed either in the language of the State addressed or in French or in English.

Article 8

Each contracting State shall be free to effect service of judicial documents upon persons abroad, without application of any compulsion, directly through its diplomatic or consular agents.

Any State may declare that it is opposed to such service within its territory, unless the document is to be served upon a national of the State in which the documents originate.

Article 9

Each contracting State shall be free, in addition, to use consular channels to forward documents, for the purpose of service, to those authorities of another contracting State which are designated by the latter for this purpose.

Each contracting State may, if exceptional circumstances so require, use diplomatic channels for the same purpose.

Article 10

Provided the State of destination does not object, the present Convention shall not interfere with—

(a) the freedom to send judicial documents, by postal channels, directly to persons abroad,

(b) the freedom of judicial officers, officials or other competent persons of the State of origin to effect service of judicial documents directly through the judicial officers, officials or other competent persons of the State of destination,

(c) the freedom of any person interested in a judicial proceeding to effect service of judicial documents directly through the judicial officers, officials or other competent persons of the State of destination.

Article 11

The present Convention shall not prevent two or more contracting States from agreeing to permit, for the purpose of service of judicial documents, channels of transmission other than those provided for in the preceding articles and, in particular, direct communication between their respective authorities.

Article 12

The service of judicial documents coming from a contracting State shall not give rise to any payment or reimbursement of taxes or costs for the services rendered by the State addressed.

The applicant shall pay or reimburse the costs occasioned by—

(a) the employment of a judicial officer or of a person competent under the law of the State of destination,

(b) the use of a particular method of service.

Article 13

Where a request for service complies with the terms of the present Convention, the State addressed may refuse to comply therewith only if it deems that compliance would infringe its sovereignty or security.

It may not refuse to comply solely on the ground that, under its internal law, it claims exclusive jurisdiction over the subject-matter of the action or that its internal law would not permit the action upon which the application is based.

The Central Authority shall, in case of refusal, promptly inform the applicant and state the reasons for the refusal.

Article 14

Difficulties which may arise in connection with the transmission of judicial documents for service shall be settled through diplomatic channels.

Article 15

Where a writ of summons or an equivalent document had to be transmitted abroad for the purpose of service, under the provisions of the present Convention, and the defendant has not appeared, judgment shall not be given until it is established that—

(a) the document was served by a method prescribed by the internal law of the State addressed for the service of documents in domestic actions upon persons who are within its territory, or

(b) the document was actually delivered to the defendant or to his residence by another method provided for by this Convention,

and that in either of these cases the service or the delivery was effected in sufficient time to enable the defendant to defend.

Each contracting State shall be free to declare that the judge, notwithstanding the provisions of the first paragraph of this article, may give judgment even if no certificate of service or delivery has been received, if all the following conditions are fulfilled—

(a) the document was transmitted by one of the methods provided for in this Convention,

(b) a period of time of not less than six months, considered adequate by the judge in the particular case, has elapsed since the date of the transmission of the document,

(c) no certificate of any kind has been received, even though every reasonable effort has been made to obtain it through the competent authorities of the State addressed.

Notwithstanding the provisions of the preceding paragraphs the judge may order, in case of urgency, any provisional or protective measures.

Article 16

When a writ of summons or an equivalent document had to be transmitted abroad for the purpose of service, under the provisions of the present Convention, and a judgment has been entered against a defendant who has not appeared, the judge shall have the power to relieve the defendant from the effects of the expiration of the time for appeal from the judgment if the following conditions are fulfilled—

(a) the defendant, without any fault on his part, did not have knowledge of the document in sufficient time to defend, or knowledge of the judgment in sufficient time to appeal, and

(b) the defendant has disclosed a *prima facie* defence to the action on the merits.

An application for relief may be filed only within a reasonable time after the defendant has knowledge of the judgment.

Each contracting State may declare that the application will not be entertained if it is filed after the expiration of a time to be stated in the declaration, but which shall in no case be less than one year following the date of the judgment.

This article shall not apply to judgments concerning status or capacity of persons.

CHAPTER II—EXTRAJUDICIAL DOCUMENTS

Article 17

Extrajudicial documents emanating from authorities and judicial officers of a contracting State may be transmitted for the purpose of service in another contracting State by the methods and under the provisions of the present Convention.

CHAPTER III—GENERAL CLAUSES

Article 18

Each contracting State may designate other authorities in addition to the Central Authority and shall determine the extent of their competence.

The applicant shall, however, in all cases, have the right to address a request directly to the Central Authority.

Federal States shall be free to designate more than one Central Authority.

Article 19

To the extent that the internal law of a contracting State permits methods of transmission, other than those provided for in the preceding articles, of documents coming from abroad, for service within its territory, the present Convention shall not affect such provisions.

Article 20

The present Convention shall not prevent an agreement between any two or more contracting States to dispense with—

(a) the necessity for duplicate copies of transmitted documents as required by the second paragraph of article 3,

(b) the language requirements of the third paragraph of article 5 and article 7,

(c) the provisions of the fourth paragraph of article 5,

(d) the provisions of the second paragraph of article 12.

Article 21

Each contracting State shall, at the time of the deposit of its instrument of ratification or accession, or at a later date, inform the Ministry of Foreign Affairs of the Netherlands of the following—

(a) the designation of authorities, pursuant to articles 2 and 18,

(b) the designation of the authority competent to complete the certificate pursuant to article 6,

(c) the designation of the authority competent to receive documents transmitted by consular channels, pursuant to article 9.

Each contracting State shall similarly inform the Ministry, where appropriate, of—

(a) opposition to the use of methods of transmission pursuant to articles 8 and 10,

(b) declarations pursuant to the second paragraph of article 15 and the third paragraph of article 16,

(c) all modifications of the above designations, oppositions and declarations.

Article 22

Where Parties to the present Convention are also Parties to one or both of the Conventions on civil procedure signed at The Hague on 17th July 1905,[1] and on 1st March 1954,[2] this Convention shall replace as between them articles 1 to 7 of the earlier Conventions.

[1] 99 BFSP 990

[2] 286 UNTS 265

Article 23

The present Convention shall not affect the application of article 23 of the Convention on civil procedure signed at The Hague on 17th July 1905, or of article 24 of the Convention on civil procedure signed at The Hague on 1st March 1954.

These articles shall, however, apply only if methods of communication, identical to those provided for in these Conventions, are used.

Article 24

Supplementary agreements between parties to the Conventions of 1905 and 1954 shall be considered as equally applicable to the present Convention, unless the Parties have otherwise agreed.

Article 25

Without prejudice to the provisions of articles 22 and 24, the present Convention shall not derogate from Conventions containing provisions on the matters governed by this Convention to which the contracting States are, or shall become, Parties.

Article 26

The present Convention shall be open for signature by the States represented at the Tenth Session of the Hague Conference on Private International Law.

It shall be ratified, and the instruments of ratification shall be deposited with the Ministry of Foreign Affairs of the Netherlands.

Article 27

The present Convention shall enter into force on the sixtieth day after the deposit of the third instrument of ratification referred to in the second paragraph of article 26.

The Convention shall enter into force for each signatory State which ratifies subsequently on the sixtieth day after the deposit of its instrument of ratification.

Article 28

Any State not represented at the Tenth Session of the Hague Conference on Private International Law may accede to the present Convention after it has entered into force in accordance with the first paragraph of article 27. The instrument of accession shall be deposited with the Ministry of Foreign Affairs of the Netherlands.

The Convention shall enter into force for such a State in the absence of any objection from a State, which has ratified the Convention before such deposit, notified to the Ministry of Foreign Affairs of the Netherlands within a period of six months after the date on which the said Ministry has notified it of such accession.

In the absence of any such objection, the Convention shall enter into force for the acceding State on the first day of the month following the expiration of the last of the periods referred to in the preceding paragraph.

Article 29

Any State may, at the time of signature, ratification or accession, declare that the present Convention shall extend to all the territories for the international relations of which it is responsible, or to one or more of them. Such a declaration shall take effect on the date of entry into force of the Convention for the State concerned.

At any time thereafter, such extensions shall be notified to the Ministry of Foreign Affairs of the Netherlands.

The Convention shall enter into force for the territories mentioned in such an extention on the sixtieth day after the notification referred to in the preceding paragraph.

Article 30

The present Convention shall remain in force for five years from the date of its entry into force in accordance with the first paragraph of article 27, even for States which have ratified it or acceded to it subsequently.

If there has been no denunciation, it shall be renewed tacitly every five years.

Any denunciation shall be notified to the Ministry of Foreign Affairs of the Netherlands at least six months before the end of the five year period.

It may be limited to certain of the territories to which the Convention applies.

The denunciation shall have effect only as regards the State which has notified it. The Convention shall remain in force for the other contracting States.

Article 31

The Ministry of Foreign Affairs of the Netherlands shall give notice to the States referred to in article 26, and to the States which have acceded in accordance with article 28, of the following—

(a) the signatures and ratifications referred to in article 26;

(b) the date on which the present Convention enters into force in accordance with the first paragraph of article 27;

(c) the accessions referred to in article 28 and the dates on which they take effect;

(d) the extensions referred to in article 29 and the dates on which they take effect;

(e) the designations, oppositions and declarations referred to in article 21;

(f) the denunciations referred to in the third paragraph of article 30.

IN WITNESS WHEREOF the undersigned, being duly authorised thereto, have signed the present Convention.

DONE at The Hague, on the 15th day of November, 1965, in the English and French languages, both texts being equally authentic, in a single copy which shall be deposited in the archives of the Government of the Netherlands, and of which a certified copy shall be sent, through the diplomatic channel, to each of The States represented at the Tenth Session of the Hague Conference on Private International Law.

[Signatures omitted. Annex containing Forms printed at pp. 9, 10.]

Convention on the service abroad of judicial and extrajudicial documents in civil or commercial matters. Done at The Hague November 15, 1965; entered into force for the United States February 10, 1969. 20 UST 361; TIAS 6638; 658 UNTS 163. States which are parties:

Antigua and Barbuda[1]
Barbados[1a]
Belgium[2]
Botswana[2a2]
Canada[3]
China[3a]
Cyprus[3b]
Czech Republic[3c]
Denmark[4]
Egypt[5]
Estonia[5a]
Finland[6]
France[7]
Federal Republic of Germany[7a]
Greece[7b]
Ireland[7c]
Israel[8]
Italy[8a]
Japan[9]
Latvia
Luxembourg[9a]
Malawi[10]
Netherlands[10a]
Norway[11]
Pakistan[11a]
Poland[11b]
Portugal[11c]
Seychelles[11d]
Slovak Republic[11e]
Spain[11f]
Sweden[12]
Switzerland[12a]
Turkey[13]
United Kingdom[14]
United States[15]
Venezuela[16]

---

[1] *Notification in conformity with Article 31 of the Convention*

By note of 1 May 1985, received at the Ministry of Foreign Affairs of the Kingdom of the Netherlands on 17 May 1985, the Government of Antigua and Barbuda informed the Ministry of Foreign Affairs it does consider itself bound by the abovementioned Convention, declared applicable to Antigua by the Government of the United Kingdom of Great Britain and Northern Ireland on 20 May 1970.

Notification in conformity with Article 31, letter e, of the Convention

The Government of Antigua and Barbuda informed the Ministry of Foreign Affairs of the Kingdom of the Netherlands by Note of 2 May 1986 that as the authority referred to in Article 21 has been designated:

The Registrar—Eastern Caribbean Supreme Court.

Notification in conformity with Article 31, letter e, of the Convention

Rectification of the Notifications *Judicial and Extrajudicial Documents Nos. 2 and 3/ 1987* of 14 July 1987 and 28 August 1987.

The competent authorities under Article 21 of the above-mentioned Convention, designated by the Government of Antigua and Barbuda, are:

a) The Governor-General, Antigua and Barbuda;

b) The Registrar of the High Court of Antigua and Barbuda, St. John's, Antigua.

The Hague, 18 November 1987

Notification in conformity with Article 31, paragraph e, of the Convention

Referring to the extension of the Convention in 1970 to Hong Kong and the designation of the Central Authority for Hong Kong the Government of the United Kingdom of Great Britain and Northern Ireland informed the Ministry of Foreign Affairs of the Kingdom of the Netherlands by letter of 3 May 1984 that "the Colonial Secretary of

Hong Kong" has been re-designated as "the Chief Secretary of Hong Kong". Requests for documents to be served in Hong Kong should be addressed accordingly.

[1a]With the following declaration:

"The Government of Barbados has designated the Registrar of the Supreme Court of Barbados as the Central Authority for the purposes of Articles 2 and 18, in accordance with the provisions of Article 21 of the Convention."

[2]With the following declaration:

1. In conformity with the first paragraph of Article 2 of the Convention, the Ministry of Justice, Administration de la Législation, Place Poelaert, 4, 1.000 Brussels is designated as the Central Authority;
2. The Ministry of Justice is also designated as the competent authority to receive documents forwarded by the channels provided for in the first paragraph of Article 9 of the Convention;
3. The Belgian Government is opposed to use being made within its territory of the freedom to effect service provided for in the first paragraph of Article 8;
4. The Belgian Government declares that it will avail itself of the provision contained in the second paragraph of Article 15;
5. In conformity with the third paragraph of Article 16, the Belgian Government declares that the applications mentioned in the second paragraph of Article 16 will not be entertained if they are filed after the expiration of a period of one year following the date of the judgment;
6. The Belgian Government believes it should draw attention to the fact that any request for the service of documents made under sections a) or b) of the first paragraph of Article 5 requires the agency of a process-server (huissier de justice) and that the resulting costs should be reimbursed in conformity with Article 12 of the Convention.

[2a]With the following declaration:

"1. Pursuant to the first paragraph of Article 2 of the Convention the Minister of State in the Office of the President of the Republic of Botswana has been designated the Central Authority to receive requests for service from other contracting states.
2. The Registrar of the High Court of Botswana is designated as the authority competent to complete the certificate in the form of the Model annexed to the Convention pursuant to the first paragraph of Article 6.
3. In accordance with the provisions of Article 9 of the Convention the Minister of State in the Office of the President is designated as the receiver of process sent through Consular channels.
4. It is declared that the Government of Botswana objects to the method of service referred to in sub-paragraphs (b) and (c) of Article 10.
5. It is declared that a judge of the High Court of Botswana may give judgment if all the conditions specified in paragraph 2 of Article 15 are fulfilled."

All documents forwarded for service must be in duplicate and written in or translated into the English language.

[3]*Notification in conformity with Article 31, paragraph c, of the Convention*

Canada deposited its instrument of accession to the above-mentioned Convention with the Ministry of Foreign Affairs of the Kingdom of the Netherlands on 26 September 1988 in accordance with Article 28, paragraph 1.

The States which have ratified the Convention were notified by the Dutch Government of the accession on 29 September 1988. Since none of these States raised an objection to the accession within the period of six months specified in Article 28, paragraph 2, the said accession became perfect on 10 April 1989.

In accordance with Article 28, paragraph 3, the provisions of the Convention will enter into force for Canada on 1 May 1989.

A copy of a document transmitted by Canada and containing the designations and declarations referred to in Article 21 of the Convention is attached to this Notification.

CANADA

A. *Transmission and execution of requests for service*

1. Central Authority
(Article 2 and Article 18, paragraph 3)

comment: To save time, requests should be forwarded directly to the Central Authority of the province or territory concerned. They may, however, also be forwarded to the Federal Central Authority which will transmit them to the relevant Central Authority.

Alberta
name: Attorney-General for Alberta
Att: Executive Director—Court Services
address: 9833-109th Street
Edmonton, Alberta
Canada T5K 2E8
telephone: (403) 427-4992

British Columbia
name: Ministry of the Attorney-General
for British Columbia
Office of the Deputy Minister
address: Fifth Floor, 910 Government Street
Victoria, British Columbia
Canada V8V 1X4
telephone: (604) 387-5211

Manitoba
name: Attorney-General for Manitoba
c/o Director—Civil Legal Services
address: Woodsworth Building
6th Floor
405 Broadway
Winnipeg, Manitoba
Canada, R3C 0V8
telephone: (204) 945-2847

New Brunswick
name: Attorney-General for New Brunswick
address: P.O. Box 6000
Fredericton, New Brunswick
Canada, E3B 5H1
telephone: (506) 453-2208

Newfoundland
name: Department of Justice
address: Confederation Building
St. John's, Newfoundland
Canada A1C 5T7
telephone: (709) 576-2869

Nova Scotia
name: Attorney General of Nova Scotia
Legal Services Division
address: P.O. Box 7
Halifax, Nova Scotia
B3J 2L6
telephone: (902) 424-4024

Ontario
name: Ministry of the Attorney General for Ontario
Reciprocity Office: Civil Law Division
address: 18 King Street East
Toronto, Ontario
Canada M5C 1C5
telephone: (416) 965-2570

Prince Edward Island
name: Attorney General of Prince Edward Island
Office of the Deputy Minister
address: P.O. Box 2000
Charlottetown, Prince Edward Island
Canada C1A 7N8
telephone: (902) 368-4570

Québec
name: Ministre de la Justice du Québec
a/s Le service juridique
address: 1200 route de l'Église
5ème étage
Ste-Foy, Québec
Canada G1V 4M1
telephone: (418) 643-1436

Saskatchewan
name: Minister of Justice for Saskatchewan
Att. of Director of Sheriff Services
address: 1874 Scarth St., 10th Floor
Regina, Saskatchewan
Canada S4P 3V7
telephone: (306) 787-5488

Yukon
name: Director of Court Services
address: Department of Justice,
Box 2703
Whitehorse, Yukon Y1A 2C6
telephone: (403) 667-5942

Northwest Territories
name: Deputy Minister of Justice
Government of the Northwest Territories
address: Box 1320
Yellowknife, Northwest Territories
Canada X1A 2L9
telephone: (613) 995-0119

Canada
name: Director, Legal Advisory Division
Department of External Affairs
address: 125 Sussex Drive
Ottawa, Ontario
Canada K1A 0G2
telephone: (613) 995-0119

Payment of Service Costs:

The payment of Service costs should be made to:

Alberta:	Provincial Treasurer of Alberta
British Columbia:	Minister of Finance of British Columbia
Prince Edward Island:	Minister of Finance of Prince Edward Island
Manitoba:	Minister of Finance of Manitoba
New Brunswick:	Minister of Finance of New Brunswick
Nova Scotia:	Minister of Finance of Nova Scotia
Ontario:	Treasurer of Ontario
Quebec:	"Ministre des Finances du Québec"
Saskatchewan:	Department of Justice of Saskatchewan—Sheriff Services
Newfoundland:	Newfoundland Exchequer Account
Yukon:	Territorial Treasurer of the Government of Yukon
Northwest Territories:	Government of the Northwest Territories

2. Methods of service employed by the Central Authority (Article 5)

2.1 Formal service
(Article 5, paragraph 1, sub-paragraph a)

In Canada, service will be effected according to the methods of service prescribed by the laws in force in each province and territory.

The normal procedure that will be used by central authorities in Canada is personal service made by a sheriff or deputy sheriff or a *huissier* in Quebec, on an individual or on a corporation by handing a copy of the document to the defendant in person, wherever he may be, or to the President, Chairman or other Chief Officer of a corporation at the place of business.

Service may also be effected by leaving a copy of the document with a person of a reasonable age at the defendant's domicile or residence.

Where service is made on a corporation, provincial laws usually provide for service on a director or senior officer of the corporation or, in some cases, on a registered agent or on a responsible person at the registered office of the corporation.

2.2 Informal delivery (Article 5, paragraph 2)

The practice of informal delivery ("par simple remise") of judicial or extra-judicial documents is not known in Canada.

2.3 Service by a particular method (Article 5, paragraph 1, sub-paragraph b)

In Alberta, New Brunswick and Ontario, service will be made by certified mail at the option of the requesting party. In Ontario, the Central Authority will serve by any form of mail, at the option of the requesting party.

2.4 Translation requirements (Article 5, paragraph 3)

For both Formal service and Service by a particular method, translation requirements will depend on the province or territory concerned.

For Alberta, British Columbia, Newfoundland, Nova Scotia, Prince Edward Island, Saskatchewan, all documents must be written in or translated into English.

For Ontario, Manitoba, and the Northwest Territories, all documents must be written in or translated into English or French.

For New Brunswick and the Yukon, all documents must be written in or translated into English or French. The Central Authority of New Brunswick or the Yukon may reserve the right to require documents to be translated into English or French depending on the language understood by the addresse.

For Quebec, translation will be required in all cases where the recipient does not understand the language in which the document is written. All documents which commence actions must be translated. Summary translation of all other documents is acceptable if the recipient agrees. Translation is to be done into the French language; however, the Quebec central authority may, upon request, allow a translation in English at the condition that the recipient understands this language.

Costs (Article 12, paragraph 2, sub-paragraph a)

Costs for execution of service will be of $50.-Can.

3. Authority competent to complete the certificate of service (Article 6)

In addition to the Central Authorities, the sheriffs, deputy-sheriffs, sub-sheriffs, clerk of the court or his/her deputy for the judicial district (except in Manitoba where there are no judicial districts) in which the person is to be served or the *huissiers* (only in Quebec) are competent to complete the certificate of service.

B. *Forwarding of requests for service to the Central Authority of another Contracting State*

Forwarding Authorities (Article 3)

Requests for service to Central Authorities of other States may be transmitted by:

— The Attorney General for Canada
— The Attorneys General or the Ministry of Attorney General or Minister of Justice of a province or a territory—as the case may be.
— Clerks of the courts and their deputies for a judicial or a court district
— The members of the law societies of all provinces and territories
— The member of the Board of Notaries of the Province of Quebec (for non-litigious matters only).
— Local registrars
— The huissiers and sheriffs
— The prothonotaries and deputy prothonotaries
— The "Percepteur des pensions alimentaires" in Québec

CANADA

I *Transmission through consular or diplomatic channels (Articles 8 and 9)*

A Acceptance

On accession, Canada has not declared that it objects to service by consular or diplomatic channels on its territory.

Receiving authority (Article 9, paragraph 1)

The Central Authorities in Canada designated in accordance with Articles 2 and 18 of the *Convention* are competent to receive requests for service transmitted by a foreign consul within Canada.

B Forwarding to the Contracting States

Canada does not object to service by consular channels of Canadian documents abroad providing that the recipient accepts this method of service.

II *Transmission through postal channels (Article 10, sub-paragraph a)*

A Acceptance

Canada does not object to service by postal channels.

B Forwarding to other contracting States

Canadian law allows the use of postal channels to serve Canadian documents to persons abroad.

III *Service through judicial officers, notably "huissiers", etc. of the requested State (Article 10, sub-paragraphs b) and c))*

On accession, Canada has not declared to object to methods of service of Article 10, sub-paragraphs b) and c).

IV *Other direct channels (Article 11); special agreements (Articles 24 and 25)*

Canada is party to bilateral conventions on civil procedure with the following States:

Austria	Canada Treaty Series, 1935, n° 16
Belgium	Canada Treaty Series, 1928, n° 16
Czechoslovakia	Canada Treaty Series, 1928, n° 17
Denmark	Canada Treaty Series, 1936, n° 4
Finland	Canada Treaty Series, 1936, n° 5
France	Canada Treaty Series, 1928, n° 15
Germany	Canada Treaty Series, 1935, n° 11
Greece	Canada Treaty Series, 1938, n° 11
Hungary	Canada Treaty Series, 1939, n° 6
Iraq	Canada Treaty Series, 1938, n° 12
Italy	Canada Treaty Series, 1938, n° 14
Netherlands	Canada Treaty Series, 1936, n° 2
Norway	Canada Treaty Series, 1935, n° 15
Poland	Canada Treaty Series, 1935, n° 18
Portugal	Canada Treaty Series, 1935, n° 17
Spain	Canada Treaty Series, 1935, n° 12
Sweden	Canada Treaty Series, 1935, n° 13
Turkey	Canada Treaty Series, 1935, n° 19
Yugoslavia	Canada Treaty Series, 1939, n° 4

CANADA

GUARANTEES UNDER THE CONVENTION

Declarations made pursuant to Articles 15, paragraph 1 or 16, paragraph 3.

1. *Stays of entry* (Article 15, paragraph 2)

Canada declares that the judges may give judgment under the conditions stated in Article 15 of the Convention.

2. *Relief from expiration of the period of time for appeal* (Article 16, paragraph 3)

Canada declares that an application filed under Article 16 of the Convention will not be entertained if it is filed after the expiration of one year following the date of the judgment, except in exceptional cases determined by the rules of the Court seized of the matter.

3a The People's Republic of China deposited its instrument of accession with the Ministry of Foreign Affairs of the Kingdom of the Netherlands on May 6, 1991, in accordance with Article 28, paragraph 1, of the Convention.

The instrument of accession contains the following declarations:

"1. to designate according to Article 2 and Article 9 of the Convention the Ministry of Justice of the People's Republic of China as the Central Authority and the authority competent to receive documents transmitted by foreign States through consular channels.

The communication address is:

Bureau of International Judicial Assistance
Ministry of Justice of the People's Republic of China
No 11, Xiaguangli
Niuwangmiao, Chaoyang district
BEIJING, 100016
People's Republic of China

2. to declare according to the second paragraph of Article 8 that the means of service stipulated in the first paragraph of that Article may be used within the territory of the People's Republic of China only when the document is to be served upon a national of the State in which the documents originate.

3. to oppose the service of documents in the territory of the People's Republic of China by the methods provided by Article 10 of the Convention.

4. to declare in accordance with the second paragraph of Article 15 of the Convention that if all the conditions provided in that paragraph are fulfilled, the judge, notwithstanding the provisions of the first paragraph of that Article, may give judgment even if no certificate of service or delivery has been received.

5. to declare in accordance with the third paragraph of Article 16 of the Convention that the application for relief from the effects of the expiration of the time for appeal shall not be entertained except that it is filed within one year following the date of the judgment."

(courtesy translation)

In accordance with the terms of Article 28, paragraph 1, of the Convention any State not represented at the Tenth Session of the Hague Conference on private international law may accede to the present Convention after it has entered into force in accordance with the first paragraph of Article 27 (viz.: 10 February 1969).

In accordance with Article 28, paragraph 2, the Convention shall enter into force for the People's Republic of China in the absence of any objection from a State which has ratified the Convention (at present: Belgium, Denmark, Egypt, Finland, France, the Federal Republic of Germany, Greece, Israel, Italy, Japan, Luxembourg, the Kingdom of the Netherlands, Norway, Portugal, Spain, Sweden, Turkey, the United Kingdom of Great Britain and Northern Ireland and the United States of America) before such deposit, notified to the Ministry of Foreign Affairs of the Kingdom of the Netherlands within a period of six months after the date on which the said Ministry has notified it of such accession. For practical reasons this six months' period in this case is running from *1 June 1991 till 1 December 1991.*

Notification in conformity with Article 31 of the Convention

The People's Republic of China deposited its instrument of accession to the above-mentioned Convention with the Ministry of Foreign Affairs of the Kingdom of the Netherlands on 6 May 1991 in accordance with Article 28, paragraph 1.

The instrument of accession contains the following declarations:

Courtesy translation

1. to designate according to Article 2 and Article 9 of the Convention the Ministry of Justice of the People's Republic of China as the Central Authority and the authority competent to receive documents transmitted by foreign states through consular channels.
   The communication address is:
   Bureau of International Judicial Assistance
   Ministry of Justice of the People's Republic of China
   N°11, Xiaguangli
   Niuwangmiao, Chaoyang District
   Beijing, 100016
   The People's Republic of China
2. to declare according to the second paragraph of Article 8 that the means of service stipulated in the first paragraph of that Article may be used within the territory of the People's Republic of China only when the document is to be served upon a national of the State in which the documents originate.
3. to oppose the service of documents in the territory of the People's Republic of China by the methods provided by Article 10 of the Convention.
4. to declare in accordance with the second paragraph of Article 15 of the Convention that if all the conditions provided in that paragraph are fulfilled, the judge, notwithstanding the provisions of the first paragraph of that Article, may give judgment even if no certificate of service or delivery has been received.
5. to declare in accordance with the third paragraph of Article 16 of the Convention that the application for relief from the effects of the expiration of the time for

appeal shall not be entertained except that it is filed within one year following the date of the judgement.

The States which ratified the Convention were notified of the accession by the Dutch Government on 17 May 1991. Since none of these States raised an objection to the accession within the period of six months specified in Article 28, paragraph 2, the said accession became perfect on 1 December 1991.

The provisions of the Convention will enter into force for the People's Republic of China on 1 January 1992 in accordance with Article 28, paragraph 3.

[3b] *Notification in conformity with Article 31, paragraph c, of the Convention*

The Republic of Cyprus deposited its instrument of accession with the Ministry of Foreign Affairs of the Kingdom of the Netherlands on 26 October 1982 in accordance with Article 28, paragraph 1, of the Convention.

In accordance with Article 28, paragraph 3, the provisions of the Convention will enter into force for the Republic of Cyprus on 1 June 1983.

The States which have ratified the Convention were notified by the Netherlands Government of the accession on 3 November 1982. Since none of these States raised an objection to the accession within the period of six months specified in Article 28, paragraph 2, the said accession became perfect on 15 May 1983.

Referring to the accession of Cyprus to the above-mentioned Convention the Embassy of Turkey at The Hague addressed a Note dated 6 April 1983 to the Ministry of Foreign Affairs of the Kingdom of the Netherlands. [See note 13.]

Notification in conformity with Article 31, paragraph e, of the Convention

In conformity with Article 21 of the Convention the Government of Cyprus informed the Ministry of Foreign Affairs of the Kingdom of the Netherlands by Note dated 5 January 1984 of the designation of the following authorities and made the following declarations:

"(a) *Article 2:*
Designation of Central Authority which will undertake to receive requests for service:—Ministry of Justice.

(b) *Article 6:*
Designation of the authority competent to complete the certificate of Service:—Ministry of Justice.

(c) *Article 9:*
Designation of the authority competent to receive documents transmitted by Consular Channels:—Ministry of Justice.

(d) *Articles 8 and 10:*
No opposition to the methods of transmission of documents provided by these articles.

(e) *Article 15:*
Declaration that judgement may be given if all conditions laid down in paragraph 2 are fulfilled.

(f) *Article 16:*
Declaration pursuant to paragraph 3 that the application will not be entertained if it is filed after the expiration of one year from the date of the judgement.

(g) *Article 18:*
Designation of other authorities in addition to the Central Authorities.
The Courts of the Republic. Competence:
Service of documents through their Registries.".

[3c] *Notification in conformity with Article 31, paragraphs c and e, of the Convention*

By notification dated January 28, 1993 the Czech Republic communicated the following: "In accordance with the valid principles of international law and to the extent defined by it, the Czech Republic, as a successor state created as a result of the division of the Czech and Slovak Federal Republic, considers itself bound, as of January 1, 1993, i.e. the date of the division of the Czechoslovak federation, by multilateral international treaties to which the Czech and Slovak Federal Republic was a party on that date, including reservations and declarations to their provisions made earlier by Czechoslovakia", which are as follows:

Translation

—in accordance with Article 8 of the Convention, within the territory of the Socialist Republic of Czechoslovakia judicial documents may not be served directly through the diplomatic or consular agents of another contracting State unless the document is to be served upon a national of the State in which the documents originate;

—in accordance with Article 10 of the Convention, within the territory of the Socialist Republic of Czechoslovakia judicial documents may not be served by another contracting State through postal channels nor through the judicial officers, officials or other competent persons;

—in accordance with Article 15, paragraph 2 of the Convention, Czechoslovakian judges may give judgement even if the conditions pursuant to Article 15, paragraph 1, have not been fulfilled;

—the provisions of Article 29 of the Convention concerning the extension of the Convention to territories for the international relations of which the contracting States are responsible are at variance with the Declaration of the United Nations General Assembly on the Granting of Independence to Colonial Countries and Peoples of 14 December 1960, and for this reason the Socialist Republic of Czechoslovakia does not consider itself to be bound by these provisions.

A copy of the original text of the declaration is attached.

By Note dated 31 March 1982 and received at the Ministry of Foreign Affairs on 1 April 1982, the Embassy of the Czechoslovak Socialist Republic communicated the following with regard to the above-cited declaration concerning Article 29 of the Convention:

"This declaration cannot be considered a reserve in view of the fact that it does not follow other purposes than a similar declaration made at the ratification of the Convention on the Taking of Evidence Aboard in Civil or Commercial Matters, though a different formulation was used.

By this declaration the Czechoslovak Socialist Republic expresses its disagreement of principle with the status of colonies and other dependent territories which is in contradiction with the Declaration of the United Nations General Assembly on the Granting of Independence to Colonial Countries and Peoples of December 14, 1960. The Czechoslovak Socialist Republic, however, has no intention to exclude the application of the Convention on the relations with the territories on which the use of the Convention has been extended in accordance with its Art. 29.".

The States which have ratified the Convention were notified by the Netherlands Government of the accession on 26 October 1981. Since none of these States raised an objection to the accession within the period of six months specified in Article 28, paragraph 2, the said accession became perfect on 9 May 1982.

The provisions of the Convention will enter into force for the Czechoslovak Socialist Republic on 1 June 1982.

The Czechoslovak Government has designated the following authorities as the authorities referred to in Articles 2, 6 and 9 of the Convention;

competent for the Czech Socialist Republic:

Ministerstvo spravedlnosti České socialistické republiky/Ministry of Justice of the Czech Socialist Republic 128 10 Praha 2, Vyšehradská 16;

competent for the Slovak Socialist Republic:

Ministerstvo spravodlivosti Slovenskej socialistickej republiky/Ministry of Justice of the Slovak Socialist Republic 883 11 Bratislava, Suvorovova 12.

[4]With the following declarations:

re Art. 2 and 18
The Ministry of Justice is designated as the Central Authority.

re Art. 6
The Danish court of law that has asked for the service to be made is designated as competent to complete the certificate in accordance with Article 6.

re Art. 9
The local judge of first instance—though, as regards the court of first instance at Copenhagen and the court of first instance of the city and of the canton of Arhus, the president of the court—is designated as competent to receive documents forwarded through consular channels in accordance with Art. 9.

re Art. 10
Denmark is unable to recognize the method of effecting service set out in Art. 10, para. c.

re Art. 15
Denmark avails itself of the power, provided for in Art. 15, second paragraph, to declare that the judge may give judgment in a matter even if the provisions of Art. 15, first paragraph, are not fulfilled.

re Art. 16
Denmark avails itself of the power, provided for in Art. 16, third paragraph, to declare that an application will not be entertained if it is made after the expiration of a period of one year following the date of judgment. The question of the re-hearing of a matter in which a person has been judged by default shall be decided in accordance with the rules of the code of procedure, Art. 373 and Art. 374, cf. Art. 434. According to these rules, any person against whom judgment is given by default in an action, in first instance may apply for a re-hearing of the matter if he can prove that the default cannot be imputed to him. The application for a re-hearing should be filed as soon as possible and may not be submitted after the expiration of a period of one year following the date of judgment.

[5]With a declaration that the signing of the Agreement "does not mean in any way a recognition of Israel" by the Arab Republic of Egypt and that "no treaty relation will arise between" the two countries.

The Arab Republic of Egypt also declared that it "opposes the use of the methods of transmitting abroad the judicial and extrajudicial documents according to Articles 8 and 10 of the Convention."

In conformity with article 21 of the Convention the Arab Republic of Egypt has designated the Ministry of Justice as the central authority as provided for in Articles 2 and 18.

First paragraph of declaration withdrawn effective Jan. 25, 1980.

[5a] *Notification in conformity with Article 31, paragraph c, of the Convention*

The Republic of Estonia deposited its instrument of accession to the above-mentioned Convention with the Ministry of Foreign Affairs of the Kingdom of the Netherlands on 2 February 1996, in accordance with Article 28, paragraph 1, of the Convention.

The instrument of accession of the Republic of Estonia contains the following declarations:

"1) the Republic of Estonia is against the way of forwarding referred to in point c of Article 10;
2) on the basis of Article 15 the judge may give judgment under the said conditions;
3) on the basis of paragraph 3 of Article 16 for a period of three years;"

In accordance with the terms of Article 28, paragraph 1, of the Convention any State not represented at the Tenth Session of the Hague Conference on Private International Law may accede to the present Convention after it has entered into force in accordance with the first paragraph of Article 27 (viz: 10 February 1969).

In accordance with Article 28, paragraph 2, the Convention shall enter into force for such a State in the absence of any objection from a State, which has ratified the Convention (at present: Belgium, Denmark, Egypt, Germany, Finland, France, Greece, Ireland, Israel, Japan, the Kingdom of the Netherlands, Luxemburg, Norway, Portugal, Spain, Sweden, Switzerland, Turkey, the United Kingdom of Great Britain and Northern Ireland and the United States of America) before such deposit, notified to the Ministry of Foreign Affairs of the Kingdom of the Netherlands within a period of six months after the date on which the said Ministry has notified it of such accession. For practical reasons this six months' period will in this case run from 15 March 1996 to 15 September 1996.

[6]With the following declarations:

"1. The Ministry of Justice has been designated Central Authority, pursuant to the first paragraph of article 2 of the Convention.
2. The Central Authority (The Ministry of Justice) is acting as the authority presupposed in art. 9 of the Convention.
3. Finnish authorities are not obliged to assist in serving documents transmitted by using any of the methods referred to in sub-paragraphs (b) and (c) of art. 10 of the Convention."

(Ministry of Justice was substituted for Ministry of Foreign Affairs as Central Authority by Note dated 31 March 1982, effective 1 June 1982.)

[7]With the following declarations:

"1. In conformity with Articles 2 and 18 of the Convention, the Ministry of Justice, Civil Division of International Judicial Assistance (Ministàere de la Justice, Service Civil de l'Entraide judiciaire internationale), 13 Place Vendôme, Paris (1er), is designated as the Central Authority to the exclusion of all other authorities.
2. The authority competent to complete the certificate referred to in Article 6 is the Public Prosecutor of the Republic (Procureur de la République) in whose district the addressee of the document to be served resides.
3. The Public Prosecutor of the Republic (Procureur de la République) is likewise authorized to receive documents forwarded through consular channels in accordance with Article 9.
4. The Government of the French Republic declares that it is opposed, as has been provided for in Article 8, to the direct service, through diplomatic and consular agents of the contracting States, of documents upon persons who are not nationals of those States.
5. The Government of the French Republic declares that the provisions of the second paragraph of Article 15 have its approval. It furthermore declares, with reference to Article 16, paragraph 3, that an application for relief from the effects of the expiration of the time for appeal from a judgment will not be entertained if it is filed more than twelve months following the date of the judgment."

[7a]On October 3, 1990 the German Democratic Republic acceded to the Federal Republic of Germany.

With the following declarations:

"(1) Requests for service shall be addressed to the Central Authority of the Land where the request is to be complied with. The Central Authority pursuant to Article 2 and paragraph 3 of Article 18 of the Convention shall be for

Baden-Württemberg	das Justizministerium Baden-Württemberg (The Ministry of Justice of Baden-Wëurttemberg), D 7000 Stuttgart
Bavaria	das Bayerische Staatsministerium der Justiz (The Bavarian State Ministry of Justice), D 8000 Mëunchen
Berlin	der Senator für Justiz (The Senator of Justice), D 1000 Berlin

By Note of 29 September 1992 the following central authorities were designated pursuant to Articles 2 and 18

in Brandenburg:	Das Ministerium der Justiz des Landes Brandenburg D-O-1561 Potsdam;
Bremen	der Prësident des Landgerichts Bremen (The President of the Regional Court of Bremen), D 2800 Bremen
Hamburg	der Prësident des Amtsgerichts Hamburg (The President of the Local Court of Hamburg), D 2000 Hamburg
Hesse	der Hessische Minister der Justiz (The Hessian Minister of Justice), D 6200 Wiesbaden
Lower Saxony	der Niedersëchsische Minister der Justiz (The Minister of Justice of Lower Saxony), D 3000 Hannover

By Note of 29 September 1992 the following central authority was designated

in Mecklenburg-Western Pomerania:	Der Minister für Justiz, Bundes-und Europaangelegenheiten D-O-2754 Schwerin
Northrhine-Westphalia	Pursuant to Article 21 of the Convention, the Government of the Federal Republic of Germany notified the Ministry of Foreign Affairs of the Kingdom of the Netherlands by note dated February 19, 1991, that with effect from April 1, 1991, the designated authority for the Land Northrhine-Westphalia will no longer be "der Justizminister des Landes Nordrhein-Westfalen" but "der Präsident des Oberlandesgerichts Düsseldorf". D 4000 Düsseldorf
Rhineland-Palatinate	das Ministerium der Justiz (The Ministry of Justice), D 6500 Mainz
Saarland	der Minister für Rechtspflege (The Minister of Justice), D 6600 Saarbrücken

By Note of 29 September 1992 the following central authority was designated

in Saxe:	Das Sächsische Staatsministerium der Justiz D-O 8060 Dresden

By Note of 29 September 1992 the following central authority was designated

in Saxe-Anhalt:	Das Ministerium der Justiz des Landes Sachsen-Anhalt D-O 3037 Magdeburg
Schleswig-Holstein	der Justizminister des Landes Schleswig-Holstein (The Minister of Justice of the Land Schleswig-Holstein), D 2300 Kiel

By Note of 29 September 1992 the following central authority was designated

in Thuringe:	Das Justizministerium Thüringen D-O-5082 Erfurt

The Central Authorities are empowered to have requests for service complied with directly by postal channels if the conditions for service in accordance with paragraph 1(a) of Article 5 of the Convention have been fulfilled. In that case the competent Central Authority will hand over the document to the postal authorities for service. In all other cases the local court (Amtsgericht) in whose district the documents are to be served shall be competent to comply with requests for service. Service shall be effected by the registry of the local court. Formal service (paragraph 1 of Article 5 of the Convention) shall be permissible only if the document to be served is written in, or translated into, the German language.

(2) The Central Authority shall complete the certificate (paragraphs 1 and 2 of Article 6 of the Convention) if it has itself arranged for the request for service to be complied with directly by postal channels; in all other cases this shall be done by the registry of the local court.

(3) The Central Authority of the Land where the documents are to be served and the authorities competent under Section 1 of the Act of 18th December 1958 implementing the Convention on Civil Procedure, signed at The Hague on 1st March 1954, to receive requests from consuls of foreign States, shall be competent to receive requests for service transmitted by a foreign consul within the Federal Republic of Germany (paragraph 1 of Article 9 of the Convention). Under that Act the president of the regional court (Landgericht) in whose district the documents are to be served shall be competent; in his place the president of the local court shall be competent if the request for service is to be complied with in the district of the local court which is subject to his administrative supervision.

(4) In accordance with paragraph 2(a) of Article 21 of the Convention, the Government of the Federal Republic of Germany objects to the use of methods of transmission pursuant to Articles 8 and 10. Service through diplomatic or consular agents (Article 8 of the Convention) is therefore only permissible if the document is to be served upon a national of the State sending the document. Service pursuant to Article 10 of the Convention shall not be effected." At the time of the deposit of its instrument of ratification the Federal Republic of Germany declared that the said Convention shall also apply to Land Berlin with effect from the date on which it enters into force for the Federal Republic of Germany.

By a Note dated November 19, 1992 addressed to the Ministry of Foreign Affairs of the Kingdom of the Netherlands, the Government of the Federal Republic of Germany made in conformity with Article 21, second paragraph, letter b, of the above-mentioned Convention the following declaration:

1. Notwithstanding the provisions of the first paragraph of Article 15, a German judge may give judgement even if no certificate of service or delivery has been received, if all the following conditions are fulfilled:
- *the document was transmitted by one of the methods provided for in this Convention,*
- *a period of time of not less than six months, considered adequate by the judge in the particular case, has elapsed since the date of the transmission of the document,*
- *no certificate of any kind has been received, even though every reasonable effort has been made to obtain it through the competent authorities of the State addressed.*

2. An application for relief in accordance with Article 16 will not be entertained if it is filed after the expiration of one year following the termination of the time-limit which has not been observed.".

[7b]*Notification in conformity with Article 31 of the Convention*

In accordance with Article 26 of the Convention the Ambassador of Greece at The Hague signed on 20 July 1983 for the Hellenic Republic the above-mentioned Convention as follows:

P. ECONOMOU 20 juillet 1983

and deposited on the same date the instrument of ratification by the Hellenic Republic of the Convention.

In conformity with its Article 27, paragraph 2, the Convention will enter into force for the Hellenic Republic on 18 September 1983.

The Greek Government designated the Department of Administrative and Judicial Affairs of the Ministry of Foreign Affairs of the Hellenic Republic as the Central Authority pursuant to Article 2 of the Convention.

The Permanent Bureau of the Hague Conference on private international law presents its compliments to the Diplomatic Missions of the Member States and to the National Organs and has the honour to inform them that, by a Note dated 23 November 1989 addressed to the Ministry of Foreign Affairs of the Kingdom of the Netherlands, the Government of

the *Hellenic Republic*

made in conformity with Article 15, second paragraph, and Article 21, second paragraph, of the above-mentioned Convention the following declaration:

The judges of the Hellenic Republic may give judgment if all the conditions in Article 15, paragraph 2, letters (a), (b), and (c) of the Convention are fulfilled even if no certificate of service or delivery has been received.

[Translation]

[7c]*Notification in conformity with Article 31*

Ireland deposited, in accordance with Article 26, paragraph 2, of the above-mentioned Convention, its instrument of ratification with the Ministry of Foreign Affairs of the Kingdom of the Netherlands on 5 April 1994.

The instrument of ratification contains the following declarations:

"Article 3

The authority or judicial officer competent under the laws of Ireland for the purpose of Article 3 of the Convention are the Central Authority, a practising Solicitor, a Country Registrar or a District Court Clerk.

Article 15

Pursuant to the Second paragraph of Article 15 a Judge in Ireland may give judgment even if no certificate of service or delivery has been received, if the conditions set out in the second part of Article 15 of the Convention are fulfilled.

and the following objections:

Article 10

In accordance with the provision in Article 10 of the Convention the Government of Ireland objects to

(i) the freedom under Article 10(b) of judicial officers, officials or other competent persons of the State of origin to effect service in Ireland of judicial documents directly to judicial officers, officials or other competent persons and
(ii) the freedom under Article 10(c) of any person interested in a judicial proceeding to effect service in Ireland of judicial documents directly through judicial officers, officials or other competent persons
but this is not intended to preclude any person in another contracting State who is interested in a judicial proceeding (including his lawyer) from effecting service in Ireland directly through a solicitor in Ireland."

The Master of the High Court is designated as the Central Authority for Ireland in accordance with Article 2 and shall be the appropriate authority for completion of certificates in the form of the model annexed to the Convention.

The Convention will enter into force for Ireland on 4 June 1994.

By Note, received at the Ministry of Foreign Affairs of the Kingdom of the Netherlands on 31 March 1994, the Government of the United States of America declared that in accordance with Article 29, paragraph 2, of the above-mentioned Convention, in addition to the territorial extensions made upon deposit of the U.S. instrument of ratification (November 19, 1970), the Government of the United States of America hereby declares that the Convention shall also be extended to the Commonwealth of the Northern Mariana Islands (which became a U.S. Commonwealth on November 3, 1986).

The authorities currently designated by the Government of the United States of America to perform certain functions under the Treaty shall also be the authorities designated to perform those functions for the Commonwealth of the Northern Mariana Islands.

The Convention will enter into force for the Commonwealth of the Northern Mariana Island on 30 May 1994.

[8]With the following declarations and reservations:

"a) The Central Authority in Israel within the meaning of Articles 2, 6 and 18 of the Convention is: The Director of Courts, Directorate of Courts, Russian Compound, Jerusalem;
b) The State of Israel, in its quality as State of destination, will, in what concerns Article 10, paragraphs b) and c), of the Convention, effect the service of judicial documents only through the Directorate of Courts, and only where an application for such service emanates from a judicial authority or from the diplomatic or consular representation of a Contracting State;
c) An application to relieve a defendant from the effects of the expiration of the time of appeal from a judgment within the meaning of Article 16 of the Convention will be entertained only if filed within one year from the date of the judgment in question."

[8a] *Notification in conformity with Article 31, paragraph a and e of the Convention*
In accordance with Article 26, paragraph 2, the Italian Republic deposited its instrument of ratification of the Convention with the Ministry of Foreign Affairs of the Kingdom of the Netherlands on 25 November 1981.
On the occasion of the deposit of the instrument of ratification the Italian Government notified of the following:
Translation

"a) pursuant to Articles 2 and 18, "l'Ufficio unico degli ufficiali giudiziari presso la corte d'appello di Roma" (the registry of the court of appeal in Rome) is designated as the Central Authority for the purpose of Article 5;
b) "gli uffici unici degli ufficiali giudiziari costituiti presso le corti di appello e i tribunali e gli ufficiali giudiziari addetti alle preture" (the registries of the courts of appeal and other courts, and the bailiffs appointed to the courts of first instance) are competent to issue the certificate pursuant to Article 6;
c) "gli uffici unici degli ufficiali giudiziari presso le corti di appello e i tribunali e gli ufficiali giudiziari addetti alle preture" (the registries of the courts of appeal and other courts, and the bailiffs appointed to the courts of first instance) are competent to receive for the purpose of service, documents forwarded by consular or diplomatic authorities pursuant to Article 9;
d) the costs proceeding from each request for service in accordance with Article 5, first paragraph, under a and b, which requires the employment of a bailiff, have to be paid in advance in the size of 6,000 lire, except adjustment at the time of restitution of the notified document.
However, the costs in relation to the notified document pursuant to Article 12, paragraph 2, of the Convention, can be paid after the restitution in a way specifically fixed by the bailiff.
The Italian State shall not require any advance or repayment of costs for service of documents requested by the Contracting States in so far as those States for their parts shall not require the payment or repayment of costs for documents originated from Italy.".

In accordance with Article 27, paragraph 2, the Convention shall enter into force for the Italian Republic on 24 January 1982.

[9]With the following declarations and reservations:

"(1) The Minister for Foreign Affairs is designated as the Central Authority which receives requests for service from other contracting States, pursuant to the first paragraph of Article 2.
(2) The District Court which has rendered judicial aid with respect to the service is designated as the authority competent to complete the certificate in the form of the model annexed to the Convention, pursuant to the first paragraph of Article 6.
(3) The Minister for Foreign Affairs is designated as the authority competent to receive documents transmitted through consular channels, pursuant to the first paragraph of Article 9.
(4) It is declared that the Government of Japan objects to the use of the methods of service referred to in subparagraphs (b) and (c) of Article 10.
(5) It is declared that Japanese courts may give judgment if all the conditions specified in the second paragraph of Article 15 are fulfilled."

[9a]With the following declarations:

"1. The Public Prosecutor at the Superior Court of Justice has been designated as the Central Authority within the meaning of Article 2 of the Convention. He is also competent to receive the documents forwarded through the channels referred to in Article 9, para. 1, of the Convention.
2. In accordance with Article 8, the Luxembourg Government is opposed to diplomatic and consular agents directly serving within its territory judicial documents on persons other than nationals of their own country.
3. (Withdrawn by Note dated June 2, 1978.)
4. When foreign judicial documents are served, in connection with Articles 5(a) and 10(b) and (c), through the intermediary of a Luxembourg official, they must be drawn up in French or German or accompanied by a translation into one of those languages.
5. The Luxembourg Government declares that notwithstanding the provisions of Article 15, para. 1, of the Convention, its judges can enter judgment if the conditions set out in para. 2 of the said Article are fulfilled.
6. In accordance with Article 16, para. 3, of the Convention, the Luxembourg Government declares that the applications referred to in para. 2 of the said Article will not be entertained if they are filed after the expiration of a period of one year following the date of the judgment."

[10]With a declaration designating the Registrar of the High Court of Malawi, P.O. Box 30244, Chichiri, Blantyre 3, Malawi, as the Central Authority referred to in Article 2.

[10a]With the following declarations:

"1. The Public Prosecutor at the District Court of The Hague is designated for the Netherlands as the Central Authority referred to in Article 2 of the Convention. The office of the Public prosecutor is situated at Juliana van Stolberglaan 2-4, The Hague.
2. Pursuant to Article 18, paragraph 1, of the Convention, the Public Prosecutor at a District Court other than that of The Hague is likewise competent to receive requests and serve documents in accordance with Articles 3 to 6 of the Convention within the area of jurisdiction of such other Court.
3. The Public Prosecutor at the District Court in the area of jurisdiction where service of the document has been requested is competent to complete a certificate as referred to under Article 6 of the Convention.
4. The Public Prosecutor at the District Court in the area of jurisdiction where service of the document is requested has been designated for the Netherlands as the authority referred to in Article 9, paragraph 1, of the Convention which is competent to serve documents forwarded through consular channels.
5. Notwithstanding the provisions of Article 15, paragraph 1, of the Convention, the Netherlands Court may give judgment, even if no certificate of service or delivery has been received, if all the following conditions are fulfilled:
a) the document was transmitted by one of the methods provided for in this Convention;
b) a period of time of not less than six months, considered adequate by the judge in the particular case, has elapsed since the date of the transmission of the document;
c) no certificate, either of service or of delivery, has been received even though every reasonable effort has been made to obtain it through the competent authorities.
6. An application for relief from the effects of the expiration of the time for appeal as provided for in Article 16 is only admissible, if it is submitted within a year, to be calculated from the date on which the judgment is given."

In accordance with Article 27, paragraph 2, the Convention shall enter into force for the Kingdom of the Netherlands (for the Kingdom in Europe) on January 2, 1976.

In accordance with Article 29, paragraph 2, the Kingdom of the Netherlands declared on 28 May 1986 that the above-mentioned Convention shall extend to Aruba.
In conformity with Article 29, paragraph 3, the Convention will enter into force for Aruba on 27 July 1986.

Notification in conformity with Article 31, letter e, of the Convention
The Ministry of Foreign Affairs of the Kingdom of the Netherlands notifies hereby the designation of the

Head, Central Office for General
Legal Affairs
L.G. Smith Boulevard 76
Oranjestad
Aruba

as the authority for Aruba referred to in Article 21 of the Convention.

[11]With the following declarations:

"1. In accordance with Article 2, the Ministry of Justice, Oslo/Dep, is designated as the Central Authority.
2. In accordance with Article 6, the County or Town Court in whose district the document has been served is designated for the purpose of completing the certificate in the form annexed to the Convention.
3. In accordance with Article 9 first paragraph, the County or Town Court in whose district the person to be served is a resident or is staying, is designated as receiver of documents forwarded through consular channels.
4. The Government of Norway is opposed to the use of such methods of service or transmission of documents on its territory as mentioned in Articles 8 and 10 of the Convention.
5. Norwegian courts may give judgment when all the conditions specified in the second paragraph of Article 15 are fulfilled.
6. In accordance with the third paragraph of Article 16, applications for relief according to Article 16 will not be entertained if they are delivered to the competent Norwegian authorities after the expiration of three years following the date of the judgment."

[11a]*Notification in conformity with Article 31, paragraph c, of the Convention*
Pakistan deposited its instrument of accession to the above-mentioned Convention with the Ministry of Foreign Affairs of the Kingdom of the Netherlands on 7 December 1988 in accordance with Article 28, paragraph 1.
The States which have ratified the Convention were notified by the Dutch Government of the accession on 19 December 1988. Since none of these States raised an objection to the accession within the period of six months specified in Article 28, paragraph 2, the said accession became perfect on 6 July 1989.

The provisions of the Convention will enter into force for Pakistan on 1 August 1989 in accordance with Article 28, paragraph 3.

The Permanent Bureau of the Hague Conference on private international law presents its compliments to the Diplomatic Missions of the Member States and to the National Organs and has the honour to inform them that, by a Note dated 1 February 1990, the Government of

Pakistan

informed the Ministry of Foreign Affairs of the Kingdom of the Netherlands of the designation of authorities, in conformity with Article 21 of the above-mentioned convention, and made declarations. The text of the communication is as follows:

"the Government of Pakistan has designated the Solicitor, Ministry of Law and Justice to the Government of Pakistan in Islamabad, as the central authority, for receiving requests for service coming from other Contracting States and Registrars of Lahore High Court Lahore, Peshawar High Court Peshawar, Baluchistan High Court Quetta, and the High Court of Sind, Karachi, 'other authorities' in addition to the Central Authority, within their respective territorial jurisdictions.

The certificate prescribed by Article 6 of the Convention if not completed by a judicial authority shall be completed or countersigned by the Registrars of the High Courts.

For the purposes of Article 8 of the Convention it is hereby declared that the Government of Pakistan is opposed to service of Judicial Documents upon persons, other than nationals of the requesting States, residing in Pakistan, directly through the Diplomatic and Consular agents of the requesting States. However, it has no objection to such service by postal channels directly to the persons concerned [Article 10(a)] or directly through the judicial officers of Pakistan in terms of Article 10(b) of the Convention if such service is recognised by the law of the requesting State.

In terms of the second paragraph of Article 15 of the Convention, it is hereby declared that notwithstanding the provision of the first paragraph there-of the judge may give judgement even if no certificate of service or delivery has been received, if the following conditions are fulfilled:—

a) the document was transmitted by one of the methods provided for in the Convention;

b) the period of time of not less than 6 months, considered adequate by the Judge in the particular case, has elapsed since the date of transmission of the document; and

c) no certificate of any kind has been received even though every reasonable effort has been made to obtain it through the competent authorities of the State addressed.

As regards Article 16, paragraph 3, of the Convention it is hereby declared that in case of ex-parte decisions, an application for setting it aside will not be entertained if it is filed after the expiration of the period of limitation prescribed by law of Pakistan."

11b*Notification in conformity with Article 31, paragraph c, of the Convention*

The Republic of *Poland* deposited with the Ministry of Foreign Affairs of the Kingdom of the Netherlands its instrument of accession to the above-mentioned Convention on 13 February 1996, in accordance with Article 28, paragraph 1, of the Convention.

The instrument of accession of the Republic of Poland contains a declaration the text of which is attached and the translation of which is as follows:

Translation

— The Republic of Poland has decided to join the Convention, declaring that it is opposed to the modes of service specified in Articles 8 and 10 within its territory;

The instrument of accession was accompanied by a declaration the text of which is also attached and the translation of which is as follows:

In compliance with Article 21, the following actions are undertaken:

Article 2, Paragraph 1—the Central Authority designated to receive requests for service coming from another contracting State shall be the Ministry of Justice.

Article 18—other authorities (in addition to the Central Authority) designated to received requests for service are Presidents of the voivodship courts.

Article 6—the authority designated to complete a certificate of service in the Republic of Poland shall be the court that has performed such service.

Article 9, Paragraph 1—the authorities designated for that purpose shall be the voivodship courts.

Articles 8 and 10—the Republic of Poland declares that it is opposed to the modes of service specified in Articles 8 and 10 within its territory.

In accordance with the terms of Article 28, paragraph 1, of the Convention any State not represented at the Tenth Session of the Hague Conference on Private International Law may accede to the present Convention after it has entered into force in accordance with the first paragraph of Article 27 (viz: 10 February 1969).

In accordance with Article 28, paragraph 2, the Convention shall enter into force for such a State in the absence of any objection from a State, which has ratified the Convention (at present: Belgium, Denmark, Egypt, Germany, Finland, France, Greece, Ireland, Israel, Japan, the Kingdom of the Netherlands, Luxemburg, Norway, Portugal, Spain, Sweden, Switzerland, Turkey, the United Kingdom of Great Britain and Northern Ireland and the United States of America) before such deposit, notified to the Ministry of Foreign Affairs of the Kingdom of the Netherlands within a period of six months after the date on which the said Ministry has notified it of such accession. For practical reasons this six months' period will in this case run from 29 February 1996 to 29 August 1996.

11c*Declaration of Portugal.*—Legal Affairs Department of Ministry of Justice has been designated as Central Authority, in accordance with Art. 2, paragraph 1, of Convention. Justice Department officials: court clerks (escrivães) and process-servers (officiais de diligências) have been designated as persons competent to prepare certificate referred to in Article 6 of Convention. In accordance with Art. 8, paragraph 2, of Convention, the Portuguese government grants diplomatic and consular agents power to serve documents on their own nationals only. Portuguese government declares that, notwithstanding provisions of first paragraph of Art. 15 of Convention its judges may give judgment if conditions listed in paragraph 2 of said Art. are fulfilled. In accordance with Art. 16, paragraph 3 of Convention, Portuguese government states that applications referred to in Art. 16, paragraph 2, will not be considered if they are made after expiration of a period of one year from date of judgment.

11d*Notification in conformity with Article 31, paragraph e of the Convention*

By Note dated 4 June 1981 and received at The Ministry of Foreign Affairs of the Kingdom of the Netherlands on 14 July 1981 the Republic of Seychelles informed the Ministry in accordance with Article 21 of the Convention of the following:

"Article 2

The Central Authority designated is:
The Registrar
Supreme Court,
Victoria,
Mahé,
Republic of Seychelles.

Article 8

The Government of the Republic of Seychelles declares that it is opposed to service by a contracting state of judicial documents upon persons abroad, without application of any compulsion, directly through the diplomatic or consular agents of that contracting state unless the document is to be served upon a national of the state in which the documents originate.

Article 10

The Government of the Republic of Seychelles declares that it objects to paragraph (b) and (c) of this Article, is so far as they permit service of judicial documents through officials or persons *other than* judicial officers.

Article 15

The Government of the Republic of Seychelles declares that notwithstanding the provisions of the first paragraph of this Article, the judge may give judgement even if no certificate of service or delivery has been received, if all the following conditions are fulfilled.

a) the document was transmitted by one of the methods provided for in this Convention,

b) a period of time of not less than six months, considered adequate by the judge in the particular case, has elapsed since the date of the transmission of the document,

c) no certificate of any kind has been received, even though every reasonable effort has been made to obtain it through the competent authorities of the State addressed.

Article 16

The Government of the Republic of Seychelles declares that it will not entertain an application for relief if filed later than one year following the date of the judgement."

11eBy notification dated March 15, 1993 the Slovak Republic communicated the following: "In accordance with relevant principles and norms of international law and to extent defined by it, the Slovak Republic, as a successor State, born from the division of the Czech and Slovak Federal Republic, considers itself bound, as of January 1, 1993, i.e. the date of the division of the Czechoslovak Federation, by multilateral international treaties to which the Czech and Slovak Federal Republic was a party at that date, including reservations and declarations in respect of provisions made earlier by Czechoslovakia, as well as objections by Czechoslovakia in respect of reservations made by other treaty parties", which are as follows: [Same declarations and reservations, *mutatis mutandis,* under Czech Republic, see footnote 3c].

11fThe Permanent Bureau of the Hague Conference on private international law presents its compliments to the Diplomatic Missions of the Member States and to the National Organs and has the honour to inform them that, by instrument deposited on 4 June 1987 with the Ministry of Foreign Affairs of the Kingdom of the Netherlands,

Spain

ratified the above-mentioned Convention.

In accordance with Article 27, paragraph 2, the Convention will enter into force for *Spain* on *3 August 1987.*

The instrument of ratification contains the following declarations:

"1) The Spanish State declares that its judges, notwithstanding the provisions of Article 15, may give judgment even if no certificate of service or delivery of documents has been received, if all the conditions enumerated in the said Article 15, paragraph 2, are fulfilled.

2) The Spanish State declares that the time of expiration, referred to in Article 16, is sixteen months from the date of the judgment.

3) The Spanish State designates as the Central Authority to issue the certificates in the form of the model annexed to the Convention: Secretaría General Técnica,
Subdirección de Cooperación Jurídica Internacional,
Ministerio de Justicia,
San Bernardo, 45,
28015 MADRID." (Translation)

12With the following declarations:

"a) The Ministry for Foreign Affairs (address: Utrikesdepartementet, Juridiska bryån, Box 16121, S-103 23 Stockholm 16, Sweden) has been designated Central Authority.

b) The Central Authority (the Ministry for Foreign Affairs) has been designated to receive documents transmitted through consular channels, pursuant to art. 9.

c) Swedish authorities are not obliged to assist in serving documents transmitted by using any of the methods referred to in sub-paragraphs (b) and (c) of art. 10.

By virtue of the third paragraph of art. 5 of the Convention the Central Authority requires that any document to be served under the first paragraph of the same article must be written in or translated into Swedish."

12aThe Permanent Bureau of the Hague Conference on private international law presents its compliments to the Diplomatic Missions of the Member States and to the National Organs and has the honour to inform them that, by instrument deposited on 2 November 1994 with the Ministry of Foreign Affairs of the Kingdom of the Netherlands,

Switzerland

ratified the above-mentioned Convention.

In accordance with Article 27, paragraph 2, the Convention will enter into force for *Switzerland* on *1 January 1995.*

The instrument of ratification contains the following reservations and declarations:

Translation:

"Re Article 1

1. With regard to Article 1, Switzerland takes the view that the Convention applies exclusively to the Contracting States. In particular, it believes that documents which are effectively addressed to a person resident abroad cannot be served on a legal entity who is not authorized to receive them in the country in which they were drawn up without derogating from Articles 1 and 15, first paragraph, of the Convention.

Re Articles 2 and 18

2. In accordance with Article 21, first paragraph (a), Switzerland designates the cantonal authorities listed in the annex as Central Authorities as referred to in Articles 2 and 18 of the Convention. Requests for the service of documents may also be addressed to the Federal Justice and Police Department in Bern, which will forward them to the appropriate Central Authority.

Re Article 5, third paragraph

3. Switzerland declares that in cases where the addressee does not voluntarily accept a document, it cannot officially be served on him or her in accordance with Article 5, first paragraph, unless it is in the language of the authority address, *i.e.* in German, French or Italian, or accompanied by a translation into one of these languages, depending on the part of Switzerland in which the document is to be served (*cf.* annex).

Re Article 6

4. In accordance with Article 21, first paragraph (b), Switzerland designates the competent cantonal court or the cantonal Central Authority as the body responsible for completing the certificate referred to in Article 6.

Re Articles 8 and 10

5. In accordance with Article 21, second paragraph (a), Switzerland declares that it is opposed to the use in its territory of the methods of transmission provided for in Articles 8 and 10.

Re Article 9

6. In accordance with Article 21, first paragraph (c), Switzerland designates the cantonal Central Authorities as the authorities competent to receive documents transmitted by consular channels pursuant to Article 9 of the Convention".

The list of Central Authorities for the Cantons is attached.

Cantonal Central Authorities — *Annex*

Cantons	Official language(s) (G=German) (F=French) (I=Italian)	Addresses	Telephone numbers
Appenzell Ausserrhoden	G	Kantonsgericht Appenzell A.Rh., 9043 Trogen	071/ 94 24 61
Appenzell Innerrhoden	G	Kantonsgericht Appenzell I.Rh., 9050 Appenzell	071/ 87 95 51
Aargau	G	Obergericht des Kantons Aargau, 5000 Aarau	064/ 21 19 40
Basel-Landschaft	G	Obergericht des Kantons Basel-Landschaft, 4410 Liestal	061/925 51 11
Basel-Stadt	G	Appellationsgericht Basel-Stadt, 4054 Basel	061/267 81 81
Bern	G/F	Justizdirektion des Kantons Bern, 3011 Bern	031/633 76 76
Fribourg	F/G	Tribunal cantonal, 1700 Fribourg	037/ 25 39 10
Genève	F	Parquet du Procureur général, 1211 Genève 3	022/319 21 11
Glarus	G	Obergericht des Kantons Glarus, 8750 Glarus	058/ 61 15 32
Graubünden	G	Justiz-, Polizei- und Sanitätsdepartement Graubünden, 7001 Chur	081/ 21 21 21
Jura	F	Département de la Justice, 2800 Delémont	066/ 21 51 11
Luzern	G	Obergericht des Kantons Luzern, 6002 Luzern	041/ 24 51 11
Neuchâtel	F	Département de Justice, 2001 Neuchâtel	038/ 22 31 11
Nidwalden	G	Kantonsgericht Nidwalden, 6370 Stans	041/ 63 79 50
Obwalden	G	Kantonsgericht des Kantons Obwalden, 6060 Sarnen	041/ 66 92 22
St. Gallen	G	Kantonsgericht St. Gallen, 9001 St. Gallen	071/ 21 31 11
Schaffhausen	G	Obergericht des Kantons Schaffhausen, 8201 Schaffhausen	053/ 82 74 22
Schwyz	G	Kantonsgericht Schwyz, 6430 Schwyz	043/ 24 11 24
Solothurn	G	Obergericht des Kantons Solothurn, 4500 Solothurn	065/ 21 73 11
Tessin	I	Tribunale di appello, 6901 Lugano	091/ 21 51 11
Thurgau	G	Obergericht des Kantons Thurgau, 8500 Frauenfeld	054/ 22 31 21
Uri	G	Gerichtskanzlei Uri, 6460 Altdorf	044/ 4 22 44
Valais	F/G	Tribunal cantonal, 1950 Sion	027/ 22 93 93
Vaud	F	Tribunal cantonal, 1014 Lausanne	021/313 15 11
Zug	G	Obergericht des Kantons Zug, Rechtshilfe, 6300 Zug	042/ 25 33 11
Zürich	G	Obergericht des Kantons Zürich, Rechtshilfe, 8023 Zürich	01/257 91 91

Autorités centrales cantonales — *Annexe*

Cantons	Langue(s) officielle(s) (a=allemand) (F=français) (i=italien)	Adresses	Numéros de téléphone
Appenzell Ausserrhoden	a	Kantonsgericht Appenzell A.Rh., 9043 Trogen	071/ 94 24 61
Appenzell Innerrhoden	a	Kantonsgericht Appenzell I.Rh., 9050 Appenzell	071/ 87 95 51
Aargau	a	Obergericht des Kantons Aargau, 5000 Aarau	064/ 21 19 40
Basel-Landschaft	a	Obergericht des Kantons Basel-Landschaft, 4410 Liestal	061/925 51 11
Basel-Stadt	a	Appellationsgericht Basel-Stadt, 4054 Basel	061/267 81 81
Bern	a/f	Justizdirektion des Kantons Bern, 3011 Bern	031/633 76 76
Fribourg	f/a	Tribunal cantonal, 1700 Fribourg	037/ 25 39 10
Genève	f	Parquet du Procureur général, 1211 Genève 3	022/319 21 11
Glarus	a	Obergericht des Kantons Glarus, 8750 Glarus	058/ 61 15 32
Graubünden	a	Justiz-, Polizei- und Sanitätsdepartement Graubünden, 7001 Chur	081/ 21 21 21
Jura	f	Département de la Justice, 2800 Delémont	066/ 21 51 11
Luzern	a	Obergericht des Kantons Luzern, 6002 Luzern	041/ 24 51 11
Neuchâtel	f	Départment de Justice, 2001 Neuchâtel	038/ 22 31 11
Nidwalden	a	Kantonsgericht Nidwalden, 6370 Stans	041/ 63 79 50
Obwalden	a	Kantonsgericht des Kantons Obwalden, 6060 Sarnen	041/ 66 92 22
St. Gallen	a	Kantonsgericht St. Gallen, 9001 St. Gallen	071/ 21 31 11
Schaffhausen	a	Obergericht des Kantons Schaffhausen, 8201 Schaffhausen	053/ 82 74 22
Schwyz	a	Kantonsgericht Schwyz, 6430 Schwyz	043/ 24 11 24
Solothurn	a	Obergericht des Kantons Solothurn, 4500 Solothurn	065/ 21 73 11
Tessin	i	Tribunale di appello, 6901 Lugano	091/ 21 51 11
Thurgau	a	Obergericht des Kantons Thurgau, 8500 Frauenfeld	054/ 22 31 21
Uri	a	Gerichtskanzlei Uri, 6460 Altdorf	044/ 4 22 44
Valais	f/a	Tribunal cantonal, 1950 Sion	027/ 22 93 93
Vaud	f	Tribunal cantonal, 1014 Lausanne	021/313 15 11
Zug	a	Obergericht des Kantons Zug, Rechtshilfe, 6300 Zug	042/ 25 33 11
Zürich	a	Obergericht des Kantons Zürich, Rechtshilfe, 8023 Zürich	01/257 91 91

[13]With the following declaration:

"1. Pursuant to Article 2, paragraph 1 of the Convention, the Directorate General of Civil Affairs of the Ministry of Justice (Adalet Bakanliği Hukuk Isleri Genel Müdürlüğü, Ankara) is designated as the Central Authority.

2. The Directorate General of Civil Affairs of the Ministry of Justice is also competent to complete certificates as referred to in Article 6 of the Convention.

3. The Directorate General of Civil Affairs is also designated as the authority competent to receive documents forwarded through the channels specified in Article 9, paragraph 1 of the Convention.

4. Pursuant to Article 8 of the Convention, the Government of the Republic of Turkey acknowledges the freedom of diplomatic and consular agents to serve judicial documents upon their own nationals only.

5. The Government of the Republic of Turkey declares that it is opposed to the use of the methods of serving judicial documents listed in Article 10 of the Convention.

6. The Government of the Republic of Turkey declares that its judges, notwithstanding the provisions of the first paragraph of Article 15, may give judgment if all the conditions set out in the second paragraph of the said Article are fulfilled.

7. Pursuant to Article 16, paragraph 3, the Government of the Republic of Turkey declares that applications for relief as referred to in Article 16, paragraph 2, will not be entertained if they are filed after the expiration of a period of one year following the date of the judgment."

Embassy of the Republic of Turkey [at The Hague]
No. 18313/328-78

The Embassy of Turkey presents its compliments to the Ministry of Foreign Affairs, the depositary of the Convention on the service abroad of judicial and extrajudicial documents in civil or commercial matters, and has the honor to inform it of the text of

the declaration of the Turkish Government regarding the accession to the aforementioned Convention by the Greek Cypriot Government:
Quote:
The Republic of Turkey, although not exercising its right of opposition as set forth in Article 28(2) of the Convention, declares that it does not consider itself bound to apply the provisions of the Convention with respect to the Greek Cypriot Government which, in constitutional terms, is not authorized to represent the "Republic of Cyprus" as a whole.
The Embassy of Turkey avails itself of this opportunity to renew to the Ministry of Foreign Affairs the assurances of its highest consideration.
The Hague, April 6, 1983
[Initialed]
[Official stamp]

14With the following declarations:

(1) "(a) In accordance with the provisions of Articles 2 and 18 of the Convention, Her Majesty's Principal Secretary of State for Foreign Affairs is designated as the Central Authority; and the Senior Master of the Supreme Court, Royal Courts of Justice, Strand, London W.C. 2, the Crown Agent for Scotland, Lord Advocate's Department, Crown Office, 9 Parliament Square, Edinburgh 1, and [as per letter dated 10 June 1980] the Master (Queen's Bench and Appeals), Royal Courts of Justice, Belfast 1, are designated as additional authorities for England and Wales, Scotland, and Northern Ireland respectively.

(b) The authorities competent under Article 6 of the Convention to complete the Certificate of Service are the authorities designated under Articles 2 and 18.

(c) In accordance with the provisions of Article 9 of the Convention, the United Kingdom designates as receivers of process through consular channels the same authorities as those designated under Articles 2 and 18.

(d) With reference to the provisions of paragraphs (b) and (c) of Article 10 of the Convention, documents for service through official channels will be accepted in the United Kingdom only by the central or additional authorities and only from judicial, consular or diplomatic officers of other Contracting States.

(e) The United Kingdom declares its acceptance of the provisions of the second paragraph of Article 15 of the Convention.

(f) In accordance with the provisions of the third paragraph of Article 16 of the Convention, the United Kingdom declares, in relation to Scotland only, that applications for setting aside judgments on the grounds that the defendant did not have knowledge of the proceedings in sufficient time to defend the action will not be entertained if filed more than one year after the date of judgment.

The authorities designated by the United Kingdom will require all documents forwarded to them for service under the provisions of the Convention to be in duplicate and, pursuant to the third paragraph of Article 5 of the Convention, will require the documents to be written in, or translated into, the English language.

A notification under the second and third paragraphs of Article 29 regarding the extension of the Convention to the territories for the international relations of which the United Kingdom is responsible will be addressed to the Royal Netherlands Government in due course."

(2) "(a) In accordance with Article 18 of the Convention the Chief Secretary of Hong Kong is designated as the Authority competent to receive requests for service in accordance with Article 2 of the Convention.

(b) The authority competent under Article 6 of the Convention to complete the Certificate of Service is the Registrar of the Supreme Court of Hong Kong.

(c) In accordance with the provisions of Article 9 of the Convention the Registrar of the Supreme Court of Hong Kong is designated as the receiver of process sent through consular channels.

(d) With reference to the provisions of paragraph (b) and (c) of Article 10 of the Convention, documents sent for service through official channels will be accepted in Hong Kong only by the central or additional authority and only from judicial, consular or diplomatic officers of other Contracting States.

(e) The acceptance by the United Kingdom of the provisions of the second paragraph of Article 15 of the Convention shall equally apply to Hong Kong.

The authorities designated above will require all documents forwarded to them for service under the provisions of the Convention to be in duplicate and, pursuant to the third paragraph of Article 5 of the Convention, will require the documents to be written in, or translated into, the English language."

(3) "(a) In accordance with Article 18 of the Convention the authority shown against the name of each territory in the Annex (hereinafter severally called "the designated authority") is designated as the authority in that territory competent to receive requests for service in accordance with Article 2 of the Convention.

(b) The authority in each territory competent under Article 6 of the Convention to complete the Certificate of Service is the designated authority.

(c) In accordance with the provisions of Article 9 of the Convention, the designated Authority shall receive process sent through consular channels.

(d) With reference to the provisions of paragraphs (b) and (c) of Article 10 of the Convention, documents sent for service through official channels will be accepted in a territory listed in the Annex by the designated authority and only from judicial, consular or diplomatic officers of other Contracting States.

(e) The acceptance by the United Kingdom of the provisions of the second paragraph of Article 15 of the Convention shall equally apply to the territories named in the Annex.

The authorities designated in the Annex will require all documents forwarded to them for service under the provisions of the Convention to be in duplicate and, pursuant to the third paragraph of Article 5 of the Convention, will require the documents to be written in, or translated into, the English language."

ANNEX

Antigua and Barbuda*	The Governor General, Antigua and Barbuda The Registrar of the High Court of Antigua and Barbuda, St. John's, Antigua
Bermuda	The Registrar of the Supreme Court, Bermuda.
British Honduras	The Supreme Court Registry, British Honduras.
British Solomon Islands Protectorate	The Registrar of the High Court, Honiara, British Solomon Islands Protectorate.
British Virgin Islands	The Registrar of the Supreme Court, British Virgin Islands.
Cayman Islands	The Clerk of the Courts, Grand Cayman, Cayman Islands
Central and Southern Line Islands	The Registrar of the High Court, Honiara, British Solomon Islands Protectorate.
Falkland Islands and Dependencies	The Registrar of the Supreme Court, Stanley, Falkland Islands.
Fiji	The Registrar of the Supreme Court, Fiji.
Gibraltar	The Registrar of the Supreme Court, Gibraltar.
Gilbert and Ellice Islands Colony	The Registrar of the High Court, Tarawa, Gilbert and Ellice Islands Colony.
Guernsey	The Bailiff, Bailiff's Office, Royal Court House, Guernsey, Channel Islands.
Isle of Man	The First Deemster and Clerk of the Rolls, Rolls Office, Douglas, Isle of Man.
Jersey	The Attorney General, Jersey, Channel Islands.
Montserrat	The Registrar of the High Court, Montserrat.
Pitcairn	The Governor and Commander-in-Chief, Pitcairn.
St. Helena and Dependencies	The Supreme Court, St. Helena.
St. Lucia	The Registrar of the High Court of Justice, St. Lucia.
St. Vincent	The Registrar of the Supreme Court, St. Vincent.
Seychelles*	The Supreme Court, Seychelles.
Turks and Caicos Islands	The Registrar of the Supreme Court, Turks and Caicos Islands.

* Ed. note—Now independent parties to the Convention. See also country footnote.

Extension to Anguilla.—

Notification in conformity with Article 31, paragraphs d and e, of the Convention

In accordance with Article 29, paragraph 2, of the Convention the Ambassador of the United Kingdom of Great Britain and Northern Ireland at The Hague notified the Minister of Foreign Affairs of the Kingdom of the Netherlands, by a Letter dated 30 July 1982 and received on 3 August 1982, the extension of the Convention to Anguilla.

In accordance with Article 29, paragraph 3, the Convention will enter into force for Anguilla on 28 September 1982.

The extension was accompanied by the following declarations:

(a) in accordance with Article 18 of the Convention the Registrar of the Supreme Court of Anguilla (hereinafter called the designated authority) is designated as the authority competent to receive requests for service in accordance with Article 2 of the Convention.

(b) the authority competent under Article 6 of the Convention to complete the Certificate of Service is the designated authority.

(c) in accordance with the provisions of Article 9 of the Convention the designated authority shall receive process sent through consular channels.

(d) with reference to the provisions of paragraphs (b) and (c) of Article 10 of the Convention, documents sent for service through official channels will be accepted by the designated authority and only from judicial, consular or diplomatic officers of other contracting states.

(e) the acceptance by the United Kingdom of the provisions of the second paragraph of Article 15 of the Convention shall apply to Anguilla.

The designated authority will require all documents forwarded to it for service under the provisions of the Convention to be in duplicate and, pursuant to the third paragraph of Article 5 of the Convention, will require the documents to be written in, or translated into, the English language.

Extension to the Associated State of Saint Christopher and Nevis.

Notification in conformity with Article 31, paragraphs d and e, of the Convention

In accordance with Article 29, paragraph 2, of the Convention the Ambassador of the United Kingdom of Great Britain and Northern Ireland at The Hague notified the Minister of Foreign Affairs of the Kingdom of the Netherlands by Letter dated 1 March 1983 and received on 2 March 1983 of the extension of the Convention to the Associated State of Saint Christopher and Nevis.

In accordance with Article 29, paragraph 3, the Convention will enter into force for Saint Christopher and Nevis on 1 May 1983.

The Letter contains the following declarations:

"a) in accordance with Article 18 of the Convention the Registrar of the West Indies Associated State Supreme Court, Saint Christopher and Nevis circuit (hereinafter called the designated authority) is designated as the authority competent to receive requests for service in accordance with Article 2 of the Convention;

b) the authority competent under Article 6 of the Convention to complete the Certificate of Service is the designated authority;

c) in accordance with the provisions of Article 9 of the Convention the designated authority shall receive process sent through consular channels;

d) with reference to the provisions of paragraphs (b) and (c) of Article 10 of the Convention, documents sent for service through official channels will be accepted by the designated authority and only from judicial, consular or diplomatic officers of other contracting states;

e) the acceptance by the United Kingdom of the provisions of the second paragraph of Article 15 of the Convention shall apply to Saint Christopher and Nevis.

The designated authority will require all documents forwarded to it for service under the provisions of the Convention to be in duplicate and, pursuant to the third paragraph of Article 5 of the Convention, will require the documents to be written in, or translated into, the English language."

15With the following declarations:

"1. In accordance with Article 2, the United States Department of Justice is designated as the Central Authority to receive requests for service from other Contracting States and to proceed in conformity with Articles 3 to 6.

2. In accordance with Article 6, in addition to the United States Department of Justice, the United States Marshal or Deputy Marshal for the judicial district in which service is made are designated for the purpose of completing the certificate in the form annexed to the Convention.

3. In accordance with the second paragraph of Article 15, it is declared that the judge may, notwithstanding the provisions of the first paragraph of Article 15, give judgment even if no certificate of service or delivery has been received, if all the conditions specified in subdivisions (a), (b) and (c) of the second paragraph of Article 15 are fulfilled.

4. In accordance with the third paragraph of Article 16, it is declared that an application under Article 16 will not be entertained if it is filed (a) after the expiration of the period within which the same may be filed under the procedural regulations of the court in which the judgment has been entered, or (b) after the expiration of one year following the date of the judgment, whichever is later.

5. In accordance with Article 29, it is declared that the Convention shall extend to all the States of the United States, the District of Columbia, Guam, Puerto Rico, and the Virgin Islands.

6. By Note, received at the Ministry of Foreign Affairs of the Kingdom of the Netherlands on 31 March 1994, the Government of the United States of America declared that in accordance with Article 29, paragraph 2, of the above-mentioned Convention, in addition to the territorial extensions made upon deposit of the U.S. instrument of ratification (November 19, 1970), the Government of the United States of America hereby declares that the Convention shall also be extended to the Commonwealth of the Northern Mariana Islands (which became a U.S. Commonwealth on November 3, 1986).

The authorities currently designated by the Government of the United States of America to perform certain functions under the Treaty shall also be the authorities designated to perform those functions for the Commonwealth of the Northern Mariana Islands.

The Convention will enter into force for the Commonwealth of the Northern Mariana Islands on 30 May 1994."

Each request for service should be accompanied by an international money order (not 'postal' money order) made payable to the 'Treasurer of the United States' in the sum of $15.00. No fee will be charged for a request for service from any State party to the Convention which does not impose a charge for the service of documents sent from the United States for service under the Convention.

(The address of the U.S. Central Authority for purposes of service under the Convention is: Office of International Judicial Assistance, Department of Justice, Washington, D.C. 20530.)

[16] The Permanent Bureau of the Hague Conference on private international law presents its compliments to the Diplomatic Missions of the Member States and to the National Organs and has the honour to inform them that, by instrument deposited on 29 October 1993 with the Ministry of Foreign Affairs of the Kingdom of the Netherlands,

the *Republic of Venezuela*

acceded to the above-mentioned Convention.

The instrument of accession contains the following declarations:

Translation

1.–With regard to Article 5, paragraph 3:
"The Republic of Venezuela declares that notices and documents and other items annexed to the notices will be accepted only when they are properly translated into the Spanish language".

2.–With regard to Article 8:
"The Republic of Venezuela does not agree to the exercise of the faculty provided for in the first paragraph of this Article within its territory, in respect of other persons who are not nationals of the country of origin".

3.–With regard to Article 10 (a):
"The Republic of Venezuela does not agree to the transmission of documents through postal channels".

4.–With regard to Article 15 (a), (b) and (c):
"The Republic of Venezuela declares that 'Venezuelan judges shall be empowered to decide when the conditions contained in sections (a), (b) and (c) of this Article are fulfilled, even though they have not received any communication evidencing either the notice or transfer, or delivery of the document'".

5.–With regard to Article 16:
"The Republic of Venezuela declares that the request allowed by the third paragraph of this Article shall not be admissible if it is made after the expiration of the period specified in Venezuelan law".

The States which ratified the Convention were notified of the accession by the Netherlands Government on 30 November 1993. Since none of these States raised an objection to the accession within the period of six months specified in Article 28, paragraph 2, the said accession became perfect on 15 June 1994.

In accordance with Article 28, paragraph 3, the Convention entered into force for the *Republic of Venezuela* on *1 July 1994*.

Notification in conformity with Article 31

The Ministry of Foreign Affairs of the Kingdom of the Netherlands, depositary of the Convention on the service abroad of judicial and extrajudicial documents in civil or commercial matters of 15 November 1965, has the honour to inform the Member States of the Hague Conference on Private International and the States having acceded to the Convention that in accordance with Article 2 Venezuela has designated the "Ministry of Foreign Affairs" as the Central Authority.

Service of Documents Convention
ANNEX TO THE CONVENTION
*Forms**

REQUEST
FOR SERVICE ABROAD OF JUDICIAL OR EXTRAJUDICIAL DOCUMENTS

Convention on the service abroad of judicial and extrajudicial documents in civil or commercial matters, signed at The Hague, November 15, 1965.

Identity and address of the applicant	Address of receiving authority

The undersigned applicant has the honour to transmit—in duplicate—the documents listed below and, in conformity with article 5 of the above-mentioned Convention, requests prompt service of one copy thereof on the addressee, i.e.,
(identity and address) . . . .
. . . .

(a) in accordance with the provisions of sub-paragraph (a) of the first paragraph of article 5 of the Convention *.
(b) in accordance with the following particular method (sub-paragraph (b) of the first paragraph of article 5) *: . . . .
. . . .
. . . .

(c) by delivery to the addressee, if he accepts it voluntarily (second paragraph of article 5) *.
The authority is requested to return or to have returned to the applicant a copy of the documents—and of the annexes *—with a certificate as provided on the reverse side.

List of documents
. . . .
. . . .
. . . .
. . . .
. . . .
. . . .
. . . .
. . . .

Done at . . . . , the . . . .

Signature and/or stamp.

* Delete if inappropriate.

Reverse of the request

CERTIFICATE

The undersigned authority has the honour to certify, in conformity with article 6 of the Convention,
1) that the document has been served *
—the (date) . . . .
—at (place, street, number) . . . .
. . . .

—in one of the following methods authorised by article 5—
(a) in accordance with the provisions of sub-paragraph (a) of the first paragraph of article 5 of the Convention *.
(b) in accordance with the following particular method *: . . . .
. . . .

(c) by delivery to the addressee, who accepted it voluntarily *.
The documents referred to in the request have been delivered to:
—(identity and description of person) . . . .
. . . .

—relationship to the addressee (family, business or other) . . . .
. . . .

2) that the document has not been served, by reason of the following facts *:
. . . .
. . . .
. . . .
. . . .

In conformity with the second paragraph of article 12 of the Convention, the applicant is requested to pay or reimburse the expenses detailed in the attached statement *.

Annexes

Documents returned: . . . .
. . . .
. . . .

In appropriate cases, documents establishing the service: . .
. . . .
. . . .

Done at . . . . , the . . . .

Signature and/or stamp.

* Delete if inappropriate.

* These forms may be obtained from the Offices of United States Marshals.

SUMMARY OF THE DOCUMENT TO BE SERVED

Convention on the service abroad of judicial and extrajudicial documents in civil or commercial matters, signed at The Hague, the 15th of November 1965.

(article 5, fourth paragraph)

Name and address of the requesting authority: ....

Particulars of the parties *: ....

JUDICIAL DOCUMENT **

Nature and purpose of the document: ....

Nature and purpose of the proceedings and, where appropriate, the amount in dispute: ....

Date and place for entering appearance **: ....

Court which has given judgment **: ....

Date of judgment **: ....

Time limits stated in the document **: ....

EXTRAJUDICIAL DOCUMENT **

Nature and purpose of the document: ....

Time limits stated in the document **: ....

* If appropriate, identity and address of the person interested in the transmission of the document.
** Delete if inappropriate.

CONVENTION ON THE RECOGNITION AND ENFORCEMENT OF FOREIGN ARBITRAL AWARDS

Article I

1. This Convention shall apply to the recognition and enforcement of arbitral awards made in the territory of a State other than the State where the recognition and enforcement of such awards are sought, and arising out of differences between persons, whether physical or legal. It shall also apply to arbitral awards not considered as domestic awards in the State where their recognition and enforcement are sought.

2. The term "arbitral awards" shall include not only awards made by arbitrators appointed for each case but also those made by permanent arbitral bodies to which the parties have submitted.

3. When signing, ratifying or acceding to this Convention, or notifying extension under article X hereof, any State may on the basis of reciprocity declare that it will apply the Convention to the recognition and enforcement of awards made only in the territory of another Contracting State. It may also declare that it will apply the Convention only to differences arising out of legal relationships, whether contractual or not, which are considered as commercial under the national law of the State making such declaration.

Article II

1. Each Contracting State shall recognize an agreement in writing under which the parties undertake to submit to arbitration all or any differences which have arisen or which may arise between them in respect of a defined legal relationship, whether contractual or not, concerning a subject matter capable of settlement by arbitration.

2. The term "agreement in writing" shall include an arbitral clause in a contract or an arbitration agreement, signed by the parties or contained in an exchange of letters or telegrams.

3. The court of a Contracting State, when seized of an action in a matter in respect to which the parties have made an agreement within the meaning of this article, shall, at the request of one of the parties, refer the parties to arbitration, unless it finds that the said agreement is null and void, inoperative or incapable of being performed.

Article III

Each Contracting State shall recognize arbitral awards as binding and enforce them in accordance with the rules of procedure of the territory where the award is relied upon, under the conditions laid down in the following articles. There shall not be imposed substantially more onerous conditions or higher fees or charges on the recognition or enforcement of arbitral awards to which this Convention applies than are imposed on the recognition or enforcement of domestic arbitral awards.

Article IV

1. To obtain the recognition and enforcement mentioned in the preceding article, the party applying for recognition and enforcement shall, at the time of the application, supply:

(*a*) The duly authenticated original award or a duly certified copy thereof;

(*b*) The original agreement referred to in article II or a duly certified copy thereof.

2. If the said award or agreement is not made in an official language of the country in which the award is relied upon, the party applying for recognition and enforcement of the award shall produce a translation of these documents into such language. The translation shall be certified by an official or sworn translator or by a diplomatic or consular agent.

Article V

1. Recognition and enforcement of the award may be refused, at the request of the party against whom it is invoked, only if that party furnishes to the competent authority where the recognition and enforcement is sought, proof that:

(*a*) The parties to the agreement referred to in article II were, under the law applicable to them, under some incapacity, or the said agreement is not valid under the law to which the parties have subjected it or, failing any indication thereon, under the law of the country where the award was made; or

(*b*) The party against whom the award is invoked was not given proper notice of the appointment of the arbitrator or of the arbitration proceedings or was otherwise unable to present his case; or

(*c*) The award deals with a difference not contemplated by or not falling within the terms of the submission to arbitration, or it contains decisions on matters beyond the scope of the submission to arbitration, provided that, if the decisions on matters submitted to arbitration can be separated from those not so submitted, that part of the award which contains decisions on matters submitted to arbitration may be recognized and enforced; or

(*d*) The composition of the arbitral authority or the arbitral procedure was not in accordance with the agreement of the parties, or, failing such agreement, was not in accordance with the law of the country where the arbitration took place; or

(*e*) The award has not yet become binding on the parties, or has been set aside or suspended by a competent authority of the country in which, or under the law of which, that award was made.

2. Recognition and enforcement of an arbitral award may also be refused if the competent authority in the country where recognition and enforcement in sought finds that:

(*a*) The subject matter of the difference is not capable of settlement by arbitration under the law of that country; or

(*b*) The recognition or enforcement of the award would be contrary to the public policy of that country.

Article VI

If an application for the setting aside or suspension of the award has been made to a competent authority referred to in article V(1)(e), the authority before which the award is sought to be relied upon may, if it considers it proper, adjourn the decision on the enforcement of the award and may also, on the application of the party claiming enforcement of the award, order the other party to give suitable security.

Article VII

1. The provisions of the present Convention shall not affect the validity of multilateral or bilateral agreements concerning the recognition and enforcement of arbitral awards entered into by the Contracting States nor deprive any interest party of any right he may have to avail himself of an arbitral award in the manner and to the extent allowed by the law or the treaties of the country where such award is sought to be relied upon.

2. The Geneva Protocol on Arbitration Clauses of 1923 and the Geneva Convention on the Execution of Foreign Arbitral Awards of 1927[1] shall cease to have effect between Contracting States on their becoming bound and to the extent that they become bound, by this Convention.

[1] 27 LNTS 157; 92 LNTS 301.

Article VIII

1. This Convention shall be open until 31 December 1958 for signature on behalf of any Member of the United Nations and also on behalf of any other State which is or hereafter becomes a member of any specialized agency of the United Nations, or which

is or hereafter becomes a party to the Statute of the International Court of Justice,[2] or any other State to which an invitation has been addressed by the General Assembly of the United Nations.

2. This Convention shall be ratified and the instrument of ratification shall be deposited with the Secretary-General of the United Nations.

[2] TS 993; 59 Stat. 1055.

Article IX

1. This Convention shall be open for accession to all States referred to in article VIII.

2. Accession shall be effected by the deposit of an instrument of accession with the Secretary-General of the United Nations.

Article X

1. Any State may, at the time of signature, ratification or accession, declare that this Convention shall extend to all or any of the territories for the international relations of which it is responsible. Such a declaration shall take effect when the Convention enters into force for the State concerned.

2. At any time thereafter any such extension shall be made by notification addressed to the Secretary-General of the United Nations and shall take effect as from the ninetieth day after the day of receipt by the Secretary-General of the United Nations of this notification, or as from the date of entry into force of the Convention for the State concerned, whichever is the later.

3. With respect to those territories to which this Convention is not extended at the time of signature, ratification or accession, each State concerned shall consider the possibility of taking the necessary steps in order to extend the application of this Convention to such territories, subject, where necessary for constitutional reasons, to the consent of the Governments of such territories.

Article XI

In the case of a federal or non-unitary State the following provisions shall apply:

(*a*) With respect to those articles of this Convention that come within the legislative jurisdiction of the federal authority, the obligations of the federal Government shall to the extent be the same as those of Contracting States which are not federal States;

(*b*) With respect to those articles of this Convention that come within the legislative jurisdiction of constituent states of provinces which are not, under the constitutional system of the federation, bound to take legislative action, the federal Government shall bring such articles with a favourable recommendation to the notice of the appropriate authorities of constituent states or provinces at the earliest possible moment;

(*c*) A federal State Party to this Convention shall, at the request of any other Contracting State transmitted through the Secretary-General of the United Nations, supply a statement of the law and practice of the federation and its constituent units in regard to any particular provision of this Convention, showing the extent to which effect has been given to that provision by legislative or other action.

Article XII

1. This Convention shall come into force on the ninetieth day following the date of deposit of the third instrument of ratification or accession.

2. For each State ratifying or acceding to this Convention after the deposit of the third instrument of ratification or accession, this Convention shall enter into force on the ninetieth day after deposit by such State of its instrument of ratification or accession.

Article XIII

1. Any Contracting State may denounce this Convention by a written notification to the Secretary-General of the United Nations. Denunciation shall take effect one year after the date of receipt of the notification by the Secretary-General.

2. Any State which has made a declaration or notification under article X may, at any time thereafter, by notification to the Secretary-General of the United Nations, declare that this Convention shall cease to extend to the territory concerned one year after the date of the receipt of the notification by the Secretary-General.

3. This Convention shall continue to be applicable to arbitral awards in respect of which recognition or enforcement proceedings have been instituted before the denunciation takes effect.

Article XIV

A Contracting State shall not be entitled to avail itself of the present Convention against other Contracting States except to the extent that it is itself bound to apply the Convention.

Article XV

The Secretary-General of the United Nations shall notify the States contemplated in article VIII of the following:

(*a*) Signatures and ratifications in accordance with article VIII;

(*b*) Accessions in accordance with article IX;

(*c*) Declarations and notifications under articles I, X and XI;

(*d*) The date upon which this Convention enters into force in acordance with article XII;

(*e*) Denunciations and notifications in accordance with article XIII.

Article XVI

1. This Convention, of which the Chinese, English, French, Russian and Spanish texts shall be equally authentic, shall be deposited in the archives of the United Nations.

2. The Secretary-General of the United Nations shall transmit a certified copy of this Convention to the States contemplated in article VIII.

Convention on the Recognition and Enforcement of Foreign Arbitral Awards. Done at New York June 10, 1958; entered into force for the United States December 29, 1970, subject to declarations.

21 UST 2517: TIAS 6997; 330 UNTS 3.

Implementing Legislation Pub. L. 91-368, 84 Stat 692, 9 USC 201-208

States which are parties:

Algeria[1]
Antigua and Barbuda[1a]
Argentina[1b]
Australia[1c]
Austria[1d]
Bahrain[1e]
Bangladesh
Barbados[1f]
Belarus[1g]
Belgium[2]
Bolivia
Bosnia and Herzegovina[2a]
Botswana[2b]
Bulgaria[3]
Burkina Faso
Cambodia
Cameroon
Canada[4]
Central African Republic[5]
Chile
China[5a]
Colombia
Costa Rica
Cote d'Ivoire
Croatia
Cuba[5b]
Cyprus[5c]
Czech Republic[6]
Dahomey
Denmark[7]
Djibouti
Dominica
Ecuador[8]
Egypt
Estonia
Finland
France[9]
Georgia
German Democratic Republic[9a]
Germany, Fed. Rep.[10]
Ghana
Greece[10a]
Guatemala[10b]
Guinea
Haiti
Holy See[10c]
Hungary[11]
India[12]
Indonesia[12a]
Ireland[12b]
Israel
Italy
Japan[13]
Jordan[13a]
Kazakstan
Kenya[13b]
Korea[14]
Kuwait[14a]
Latvia
Lesotho
Lithuania[14b]
Luxembourg[14c]
Former Yugoslav Republic of Macedonia
Madagascar[15]
Malaysia[15a]
Mali
Mauritius
Mexico
Monaco[15b]
Mongolia[15c]
Morocco[16]
Netherlands[17]
New Zealand[17a]
Niger
Nigeria[18]
Norway[19]
Panama
Peru
Philippines[20]
Poland[21]
Portugal[21a]
Romania[21b]
Russian Federation[22]
San Marino
Saudi Arabia[22a]
Senegal
Singapore[22b]
Slovakia[22c]
Slovenia
South Africa
Spain
Sri Lanka (Ceylon)
Sweden
Switzerland[23]
Syrian Arab Rep.
Tanzania[24]
Thailand
Trinidad and Tobago[25]
Tunisia[25a]
Turkey[26]
Uganda[26a]
Ukraine[27]
United Kingdom[28]
United States[29]
Uruguay
Uzbekistan
Venezuela[29a]
Vietnam[29b]
Yugoslavia[30]
Zimbabwe

---

[1] On February 7, 1989, an instrument of accession was deposited with the Secretary General of the United Nations by Algeria.

Referring to the possibility offered by article I, paragraph 3, of the Convention, the People's Democratic Republic of Algeria declares that it will apply the Convention, on the basis of reciprocity, to the recognition and enforcements of arbitral awards made only in the territory of another Contracting State and only where such awards have been made with respect to differences arising out of legal relationships, whether contractual or not, which are considered as commercial under Algerian law.

In accordance with Article XII (2), the Convention will enter into force for Algeria on May 8, 1989.

[1a] On February 2, 1989, an instrument of accession was deposited with the Secretary General of the United Nations by Antigua and Barbuda.

"In accordance with Article I, the Government of Antigua and Barbuda declares that it will apply the Convention on the basis of reciprocity only to the recognition and enforcement of awards made in the territory of another contracting state.

The Government of Antigua and Barbuda also declares that it will apply the Convention only to differences arising out of legal relationships, whether contractual or not, which are considered as commercial under the laws of Antigua and Barbuda."

In accordance with Article XII (2), the Convention will enter into force for Antigua and Barbuda on May 3, 1989.

[1b] On 14 March 1989, the instrument of ratification by the Government of Argentina of the above-mentioned Convention was deposited with the Secretary-General.

The instrument of ratification contains the following declaration:

On the basis of reciprocity, the Republic of Argentina will apply the Convention only to the recognition and enforcement of foreign arbitral awards made in the territory of another Contracting State. It will also apply the Convention only to differences arising out of legal relationships, whether contractual or not, which are considered as commercial under its national law.

The Convention will be interpreted in accordance with the principles and clauses of the National Constitution in force or those resulting from modification made by virtue of the Constitution.

In accordance with Article XII (2), the Convention will enter into force for Argentina on 12 June 1989, i.e. the ninetieth day after the date of the deposit of its instrument.

[1c] With the following declaration in accordance with the provisions of article X (1): ". . . the Convention shall extend to all the external Territories for the international relations of which it"—Australia—"is responsible other than Papua New Guinea."

[1d] Subject to the following reservations and declarations:

The Republic of Austria will apply the Convention, in accordance with the first sentence of article I(3) thereof, only to the recognition and enforcement of arbitral awards made in the territory of another Contracting State.

In a communication received on 25 February 1988, the Government of Austria notified the Secretary-General of its decision to withdraw the following reservation, made upon accession to the above-mentioned Convention:

(Translation) (Original: German)

The Republic of Austria will apply the Convention, in accordance with the first sentence of article I (3), thereof, only to the recognition and enforcement of arbitral awards made in the territory of another Contracting State.

The said withdrawal took effect on 25 February 1988, the date of receipt of the notification.

12 May 1988

[1e] On 6 April 1988, the instrument of accession by the Government of Bahrain to the above-mentioned Convention was deposited with the Secretary-General.

The instrument of accession contains the following declarations:

(Original: English)

"1. The accession by the State of Bahrain to the Convention on the Recognition and Enforcement of Foreign Arbitral Awards, 1958 shall in no way constitute recognition of Israel or be a cause for the establishment of any relations of any kind therewith.

2. In accordance with Article 1 (3) of the Convention, the State of Bahrain will apply the Convention, on the basis of reciprocity, to the recognition and enforcement of only those awards made in the territory of another Contracting State party to the Convention.

3. In accordance with Article 1 (3) of the Convention, the State of Bahrain will apply the Convention only to differences arising out of legal relationships, whether contractual or not, which are considered as commercial under the national law of the State of Bahrain."

In accordance with Article XII (2), the Convention will enter into force for Bahrain on 5 July 1988, i.e. the ninetieth day after the date of the deposit of its instrument.

[1f] On March 16, 1993, the instrument of accession by the Government of Barbados to the above-mentioned Convention was deposited with the Secretary-General.

The instrument of accession contains the following declarations:

(Original: English)

"(i) In accordance with Article 1(3) of the Convention, the Government of Barbados declares that it will apply the Convention on the basis of reciprocity to the recognition and enforcement of awards made only in the territory of another Contracting State.

(ii) The Government of Barbados will also apply the Convention only to differences arising out of legal relationships, whether contractual or not which are considered as commercial under the laws of Barbados."

In accordance with paragraph 2 of its article XII, the Convention will enter into force for Barbados on the ninetieth day after the date of deposit of the instrument, i.e., on 14 June 1993.

26 May 1988

[1g] [Belarus] will apply the provisions of this Convention in respect to arbitral awards made in the territories of non-contracting States only to the extent to which they grant reciprocal treatment.

[2] (Translation) In accordance with article I, paragraph 3, the Government of the Kingdom of Belgium declares that it will apply the Convention to the recognition and enforcement of arbitral awards made only in the territory of a Contracting State.

[2a] DECLARATION:

"The Convention will be applied to the Republic of Bosnia and Herzegovina only relating [to] those arbitral awards that have been brought after entering into force of the Convention.

The Republic of Bosnia and Herzegovina will apply the Convention, on the basis of reciprocity, to the recognition and enforcement of only those awards made in the territory of another Contracting State.

The Republic of Bosnia and Herzegovina will apply the Convention only to differences arising out of legal relationships, whether contractual or not, which are considered as commercial under the national law of the Republic of Bosnia and Herzegovina."

[2b] "The Republic of Botswana will apply the Convention only to differences arising out of legal relationship, whether contractual or not, which are considered commercial under Botswana law.

The Republic of Botswana will apply the Convention to the Recognition and Enforcement of Awards made in the territory of another Contracting State."

[3] Bulgaria will apply the Convention to recognition and enforcement of awards made in the territory of a contracting State. With regard to awards made in the territory of non-contracting States, it will apply the Convention only to the extent to which these States grant reciprocal treatment . . .

[4] (Dictated): The Government of Canada declares with respect to the Province of Alberta, that it will apply the Convention only to the recognition and enforcement of awards made in the territory of another Contracting State. The Government of Canada declares that it will apply the Convention only to differences arising out of legal relationships whether contractual or not which are considered as commercial under the National Law of Canada.

On 20 May 1987, the Secretary-General received from the Government of Canada, in respect of the above declaration, the following revised declaration:

(Original: English and French)

"The Government of Canada declares, with respect to the Province of Saskatchewan, that it will apply the Convention only to the recognition and enforcement of awards made in the territory of another Contracting State.

The Government of Canada declares that it will apply the Convention only to differences arising out of legal relationships, whether contractual or not, which are considered as commercial under the laws of Canada, except in the case of the Province of Quebec where the law does not provide for such limitation."

In light of the depositary practice followed in similar cases, the Secretary-General proposes to receive the declaration in question for deposit in the absence of any objection on the part of any of the Contracting Parties, either to the deposit itself or to the procedure envisaged, within a period of 90 days from the date of the present depositary notification. In the absence of any such objection, the said declaration will take effect upon the expiration of the above-stipulated 90-day period, and will then replace the previous declaration.

22 July 1987

The Secretary-General of the United Nations, acting in his capacity as depositary, and referring to depositary notification C.N.111.1987.TREATIES-3 of 22 July 1987 concerning the declaration made by the Government of Canada communicates the following:

In the absence of any objection on the part of any of the Contracting Parties, either to the declaration or to the procedure applied, within 90 days from the date of the above-mentioned depositary notification, the said declaration is deemed to have been accepted.

The declaration took effect on 20 October 1987, i.e. upon the expiration of the above-mentioned 90-day period, and has accordingly replaced the previous declaration made upon accession.

The Secretary-General of the United Nations, acting in his capacity as depositary, and referring to depositary notification C.N.111.1987.TREATIES-3 of 22 July 1987 concerning the declaration made by the Government of Canada, communicates the following:

In a communication received on 25 November 1988, the Government of Canada notified the Secretary-General of its decision to withdraw the following part of its revised declaration deposited on 20 May 1987:

(Original: English and French)

"The Government of Canada declares, with respect to the Province of Saskatchewan, that it will apply the Convention only to the recognition and enforcement of awards made in the territory of another Contracting State."

The said withdrawal took effect on 25 November 1988, the date of receipt of the notification.

24 November 1987

[5] . . .the Central African Republic declares that it will apply the Convention on the basis of reciprocity, to the recognition and enforcement of awards made only in the territory of another contracting State; it further declares that it will apply the Convention only to differences arising out of legal relationships, whether contractual or not, which are considered as commercial under its national law.

[5a] The Secretary-General of the United Nations, acting in his capacity as depositary, communicates the following:

"On 22 January 1987, the instrument of accession by the Government of China to the above-mentioned Convention was deposited with the Secretary-General.

The instrument of accession contains the following declaration made in accordance with paragraph 3 of article I of the Convention:

(Courtesy translation) (Original: Chinese)

1. The People's Republic of China will apply the Convention, only on the basis of reciprocity, to the recognition and enforcement of arbitral awards made in the territory of another Contracting State;

2. The People's Republic of China will apply the Convention only to differences arising out of legal relationships, whether contractual or not, which are considered as commercial under the national law of the People's Republic of China.

In accordance with article XII (2), the Convention will enter into force for China on 22 April 1987, i.e. the ninetieth day after the deposit of its instrument."

[5b] *Declaration of Cuba.*—Republic of Cuba will apply Convention to recognition and enforcement of arbitral awards made in territory of another contracting State. With respect to arbitral awards made by other noncontracting States, it will apply Convention only in so far as those States grant reciprocal treatment as established by mutual agreement between parties. Moreover, it will apply Convention only to differences arising out of legal relationships, whether contractual or not, which are considered as commercial under Cuban legislation.

[5c] *With the following declaration:* "The Republic of Cyprus will apply the Convention, on the basis of reciprocity, to the recognition and enforcement of awards made only in the territory of another Contracting State; furthermore it will apply the Convention only to differences arising out of legal relationships, whether contractual or not, which are considered as commercial under its national law."

[6] "[Czech Republic] will apply the Convention to recognition and enforcement of awards made in the territory of another contracting State. With regard to awards made in the territory of non-contracting States it will apply the Convention only to the extent to which these States grant reciprocal treatment."

[7] ". . . the Government of Denmark has withdrawn its reservation pursuant to Article X, paragraph 1 of the Convention with respect to the applicability of the Convention to the Faroe Islands and Greenland with effect from 1 January, 1976."

[8] Ecuador, on the basis of reciprocity, will apply the Convention to the recognition and enforcement of arbitral awards made in the territory of another contracting State only if such awards have been made with respect to differences arising out of legal relationships which are regarded as commercial under Ecuadorean law.

[9] (1) Referring to the possibility offered by paragraph 3 of Article I of the Convention, France declares that it will apply the Convention on the basis of reciprocity, to the recognition and enforcement of awards made only in the territory of another contracting State; (2) Referring to paragraphs 1 and 2 of Article X of the Convention, France declares that this Convention will extend to all the territories of the French Republic.

In a communication received on 27 November 1989, the Government of France notified the Secretary-General of its decision to withdraw the following declaration, made upon ratification of the said Convention:

(Translation) (Original: French)

France declares that it will apply the Convention only to differences arising out of legal relationships, whether contractual or not, which are considered as commercial under its national law.

The said withdrawal took effect on 27 November 1989, the date of receipt of the notification.

[9a] On October 3, 1990 the German Democratic Republic acceded to the Federal Republic of Germany.

With the following declarations:

In respect of article I:

(Translation) The German Democratic Republic will apply the Convention to the recognition and enforcement of arbitral awards made in the territory of another Contracting State. To arbitral awards made in the territories of non-contracting States, the Convention will be applied only to such extent as those States grant reciprocity. Furthermore, the German Democratic Republic will apply the Convention only to differences arising out of contractual or non-contractual legal relationships which are considered as commercial under the national law of the German Democratic Republic.

In respect of articles VIII and IX:

(Translation) The German Democratic Republic considers that the provisions of Articles VIII and IX of the Convention are inconsistent with the principle that all States pursuing their policies in accordance with the purposes and principles of the Charter of the United Nations shall have the right to become parties to conventions affecting the interests of all States.

In respect of article X:

(Translation) The position of the German Democratic Republic on Article X of the Convention, as far as the application of the Convention to colonial and other dependent territories is concerned, is governed by the provisions of the United Nations Declaration on the Granting of Independence to Colonial Countries and Peoples (Res. 1514 (XV) of 14 December 1960) proclaiming the necessity of bringing to a speedy and unconditional end colonialism in all its forms and manifestations.

The instrument of accession to the European Convention on International Commercial Arbitration, done at Geneva on 21 April 1961, contains the following declaration in respect of article X, paragraph 6:

(Translation) The functions conferred by virtue of Article IV of the Convention on the President of the competent Chamber of Commerce will be exercised in the German Democratic Republic by the President of the Chamber of Foreign Trade of the German Democratic Republic.

In a note accompanying the instruments of accession, the Ministry of Foreign Affairs made the following declaration on behalf of the German Democratic Republic, as regards the application of the said conventions to Berlin (West):

(Transaction) . . . Pursuant to the Quadripartite Agreement of 3 September 1971 between the Governments of the Union of Soviet Socialist Republics, the United Kingdom of Great Britain and Northern Ireland, the United States of America and the French Republic, that Berlin (West) is not a constituent part of the Federal Republic of Germany and not to be governed by it. The statements by the Federal Republic of Germany to the effect that these Conventions also apply to "*Land* Berlin" are therefore contrary to the Quadripartite Agreement, which states further that treaties affecting matters of security and status may not be extended to Berlin (West) by the Federal Republic of Germany. The statements by the Federal Republic of Germany cannot therefore have legal effects.

Pursuant to paragraph 2 of article XII, and paragraph 8 of article X, respectively, the above-mentioned Conventions will enter into force for the German Democratic Republic on the ninetieth day after the deposit of its instruments of accession, that is to say, on 21 May 1975.

[10] On October 3, 1990 the German Democratic Republic acceded to the Federal Republic of Germany. "(1) The Convention on the Recognition and Enforcement of Foreign Arbitral Awards, done at New York on 10 June 1958, will also apply to Land Berlin as from the day on which the Convention enters into force for the Federal Republic of Germany; (2) With respect to paragraph 1 of article I, and in accordance with paragraph 3 of article I of the Convention, the Federal Republic of Germany will apply the Convention only to the recognition and enforcement of awards made in the territory of another contracting State.

[10a] By communication received by the U.N. Secretary-General on Apr. 18, 1980 the Government of Greece stated that upon accession it had been the intention to formulate the following declaration included in the enactment approving the Convention:

(Translation) The present Convention is approved on condition of the two limitations set forth in article 1(3) of the Convention.

[10b] The Secretary-General of the United Nations, acting in his capacity as depositary, communicates the following:

On 21 March 1984, the instrument of accession by the Government of Guatemala to the above-mentioned Convention was deposited with the Secretary-General.

The instrument of accession contains the following declaration made in accordance with paragraph 3 of article I of the Convention:

(Translation) (Original: Spanish)

On the basis of reciprocity, the Republic of Guatemala will apply the above Convention to the recognition and enforcement of arbitral awards made only in the territory of another contracting State; and will apply it only to differences arising out of legal relationships, whether contractual or not, which are considered as commercial under its national law.

In accordance with article XII (2), the Convention will enter into force for Guatemala on 19 June 1984, i.e., on the ninetieth day after the deposit of its instrument.

[10c] The instrument of accession contains a declaration pursuant to article 1, paragraph 3, to the effect that the State of Vactican City will apply the said Convention on the basis of reciprocity, in one hand, to the recognition and enforcement of awards made only in the territory of another Contracting State, and on the other hand, only to differences arising out of legal relationships, whether contractual or not, which are considered as commercial under Vactican law.

[11] ". . . the Hungarian People's Republic shall apply the Convention to the recognition and enforcement of such awards only as have been made in the territory of one of the other Contracting States and are dealing with differences arising in respect of a legal relationship considered by the Hungarian law as a commercial relationship."

[12] "In accordance with Article I of the Convention, the Government of India declare that they will apply the Convention to the recognition and enforcement of awards made only in the territory of a State, party to this Convention. They further declare that they will apply the Convention only to differences arising out of legal relationships, whether contractual or not, which are considered as commercial under the Law of India."

[12a] The Secretary-General of the United Nations, acting in his capacity as depositary of the Convention on the Recognition and Enforcement of Foreign Arbitral Awards, done at New York on 10 June 1958, communicates the following:

On 7 October 1981, the instrument of accession by the Government of Indonesia to the above-mentioned Convention was deposited with the Secretary-General.

The instrument of accession contains the following declaration:

"Pursuant to the provision of article I (3) of the Convention, the Government of the Republic of Indonesia declares that it will apply the Convention on the basis of reciprocity, to the recognition and enforcement of awards made only in the territory of another Contracting State, and that it will apply the Convention only to differences arising out of legal relationships, whether contractual or not, which are considered as commercial under the Indonesian Law".

In accordance with its article XII (2), the Convention will enter into force for Indonesia on the ninetieth day after the deposit of its instrument of accession, that is to say, on 5 January 1982.

[12b] *With the following declaration:* "In accordance with article I (3) of the said Convention the Government of Ireland declares that it will apply the Convention to the recognition and enforcement of arbitral awards made only in the territory of another Contracting State."

[13] ". . . it will apply the Convention to the recognition and enforcement of awards made only in the territory of another Contracting State."

[13a] The instrument of ratification contains a reservation to the effect that

(translation) [the Government of Jordan] shall not be bound by any awards which are made by Israel or to which an Israeli is a party.

In accordance with its article XII (2), the Convention will enter into force for Jordan on the ninetieth day after the deposit of its instrument of ratification, that is to say, on 13 February 1980, subject to the legal effects which each Party might wish to draw from the above-mentioned reservation as regards the application of the said Convention.

[13b] On February 10, 1989, an instrument of accession was deposited with the Secretary-General of the United Nations by Kenya.

"In accordance with Article I (3) of the said Convention the Government of Kenya declares that it will apply the Convention to the recognition and enforcement of arbitral awards made only in the territory of another contracting state."

In accordance with Article XII (2), the Convention will enter into force for Kenya on May 11, 1989.

[14] "By virtue of paragraph 3 of Article 1 of the present Convention, the Government of the Republic of Korea declares that it will apply the Convention to the recognition and enforcement of arbitral awards made only in the territory of another Contracting State. It further declares that it will apply the Convention only to differences arising out of legal relationships, whether contractual or not, which are considered as commercial under its national law."

[14a] The instrument of accession contains the following declaration under article 1 of the Convention:

(Translation) The State of Kuwait will apply the Convention to the recognition and enforcement of awards made only in the territory of another Contracting State.

The instrument of accession is accompanied by an understanding which reads as follows:

(Translation) It is understood that the accession of the State of Kuwait to the Convention on the Recognition and Enforcement of Foreign Arbitral Awards, done at New York, on the 10th of June 1958, does not mean in any way recognition of Israel or entering with it into relations governed by the Convention thereto acceded by the State of Kuwait.

[14b] DECLARATION:

"[The Republic of Lithuania] will apply the provisions of the said Convention to the recognition of arbitral awards made in the territories of the Non-Contracting States, only on the basis of reciprocity."

[14c] On 9 September 1983, the instrument of ratification by the Government of Luxembourg of the above-mentioned Convention was deposited with the Secretary-General.

In a note accompanying the said instrument, the Government of Luxembourg made the following declaration:

(Translation) (Original: French)

The Convention is applied on the basis of reciprocity to the recognition and enforcement of only those arbitral awards made in the territory of another Contracting State.

In accordance with article XII(2), the Convention will enter into force for Luxembourg on 8 December 1983, i.e., on the ninetieth day after the deposit of its instrument.

[15] [Madagascar] will apply the Convention on the basis of reciprocity, to the recognition and enforcement of awards made only in the territory of another Contracting State; it further declares that it will apply the Convention only to differences arising out of legal relationships, whether contractual or not, which are considered as commercial under its national law.

[15a] *Accession by Malaysia—*

The Secretary-General of the United Nations, acting in his capacity as depositary, communicates the following:

On 5 November 1985, the instrument of accession by the Government of Malaysia to the above-mentioned Convention was deposited with the Secretary-General.

The instrument of accession contains the following declaration made in accordance with paragraph 3 of article I of the Convention:

(Original: English)

". . . the government of Malaysia, in accordance with the provision of Article 1(3) of the Convention, declares that it will apply the Convention on the basis of reciprocity, to the recognition and enforcement of awards made only in the territory of another Contracting State. Malaysia further declares that it will apply the Convention only to differences arising out of legal relationships, whether contractual or not, which are considered as commercial under Malaysian law."

In accordance with article XII (2), the Convention will enter into force for Malaysia on 3 February 1986, i.e., on the ninetieth day after the deposit of its instrument.

[15b] The instrument of ratification contains the following declarations:

(Translation) (Original: French)

Referring to the possibility offered by article I(3) of the Convention, the Principality of Monaco will apply the Convention, on the basis of reciprocity, to the recognition of and enforcement of awards made only in the territory of another contracting State; furthermore, it will apply the Convention only to differences arising out of legal relationship, whether contractual or not, which are considered as commercial under its national law.

In accordance with article XII(2), the Convention will enter into force for Monaco on the ninetieth day after the deposit of its instrument of ratification, that is to say, on 31 August 1982.

[15c] DECLARATION:

"1. Mongolia will apply the Convention, on the basis of reciprocity, to the recognition and enforcement of arbitral awards made only in the territory of another Contracting State.

2. Mongolia will apply the Convention only to differences arising out of legal relationships, whether contractual or not, which are considered as commercial under the national law of Mongolia."

[16] The Government of His Majesty the King of Morocco will only apply the Convention to the recognition and enforcement of awards made only in the territory of another contracting State.

[17] [Instrument of ratification stipulates that the Convention is ratified for the Kingdom in Europe, Surinam and the Netherlands Antilles.] "Referring to paragraph 3 of article I of the Convention on the Recognition and Enforcement of Foreign Arbitral Awards, the Government of the Kingdom declares that it will apply the Convention to the recognition and enforcement of awards made only in the territory of another Contracting State."

Statement of Dec. 24, 1985:

"The island of Aruba, which is at present still part of the Netherlands Antilles, will obtain internal autonomy as a country within the Kingdom of the Netherlands as of 1 January 1986. Consequently the Kingdom will from then on no longer consist of two countries, namely the Netherlands (the Kingdom in Europe) and the Netherlands Antilles (situated in the Caribbean region) but will consist of three countries, namely the said two countries and the country Aruba.

As the change (sic) being made on 1 January 1986 concern a shift only in the internal consitutional relations within the Kingdom of the Netherlands, and as the Kingdom as such will remain subject under international law with which treaties are concluded, the said changes will have no consequences in international law regarding to treaties concluded by the Kingdom which already apply to the Netherlands Antilles, including Aruba. These treaties will remain in force for Aruba in its new capacity of country within the Kingdom. Therefore these treaties will as of 1 January 1986, as concerns the Kingdom of the Netherlands, apply to the Netherlands Antilles (without Aruba) and Aruba.

Consequently the treaties referred to in the annex, to which the Kingdom of the Netherlands is a Party and which apply to the Netherlands Antilles, will as of January 1986 as concerns the Kingdom of the Netherlands apply to the Netherlands Antilles and Aruba."

[17a] The instrument of accession contains the following declarations:

(Original: English)

"In accordance with paragraph 3 of article 1 of the Convention, the Government of New Zealand declares that it will apply the Convention, on the basis of reciprocity, to the recognition and enforcement of awards made only in the territory of another Contracting State."

"Accession to the Convention by the Government of New Zealand shall not extend for the time being, pursuant to article X of the Convention, to the Cook Islands and Niue."

In accordance with article XII(2), the Convention will enter into force for New Zealand on 6 April 1983, i.e., on the ninetieth day after the deposit of its instrument of accession.

[18] "In accordance with paragraph 3 of article I of the Convention, the Federal Military Government of the Federal Republic of Nigeria declares that it will apply the Convention on the basis of reciprocity to the recognition and enforcement of awards made only in the territory of a State party to this Convention and to differences arising out of legal relationships, whether contractual or not, which are considered as commercial under the Laws of the Federal Republic of Nigeria."

[19] "1. We will apply the Convention only to the recognition and enforcement of awards made in the territory of one of the Contracting States.

"2. We will not apply the Convention to differences where the subject matter of the proceedings is immovable property situated in Norway, or a right in or to such property."

[20] ". . . the Philippines, on the basis of reciprocity, will apply the Convention to the recognition and enforcement of awards made only in the territory of another Contracting State and only to differences arising out of legal relationships, whether contractual or not, which are considered as commercial under the national law of the State making such declaration."

[21] "With reservations as mentioned in Article I, par. 3."

[21a] DECLARATION:

Within the scope of the principle of reciprocity, Portugal will restrict the application of the Convention to arbitral awards pronounced in the territory of a State bound by the said Convention.

[21b] The Romanian People's Republic will apply the Convention only to differences arising out of legal relationships, whether contractual or not, which are considered as commercial under its legislation.

The Romanian People's Republic will apply the Convention to the recognition and enforcement of awards made in the territory of another Contracting State. As regards awards made in the territory of certain non-contracting States, the Romanian People's Republic will apply the Convention only on the basis of reciprocity established by joint agreement between the parties.

[22] [The Russian Federation] will apply the provisions of this Convention in respect to arbitral awards made in the territories of noncontracting States only to the extent to which they grant reciprocal treatment.

[22a] On 19 April 1994, the instrument of accession by the Government of Saudi Arabia to the above-mentioned Convention was deposited with the Secretary-General.

The instrument of accession contains the following declaration:

(Translation) (Original: Arabic)

"On the basis of reciprocity, the Kingdom declares that it shall restrict the application of the Convention to the recognition and enforcement of arbitral awards made in the territory of a Contracting State."

In accordance with paragraph 2 of its article XII, the Convention will enter into force for Saudi Arabia on the ninetieth day after the date of deposit of the instrument, i.e. on 18 July 1994.

[22b] The Secretary-General of the United Nations, acting in his capacity as depositary, communicates the following:

On 21 August 1986, the instrument of accession by the Government of Singapore to the above-mentioned Convention was deposited with the Secretary-General.

The instrument of accession contains the following declaration made in accordance with paragraph 3 of article I of the Convention:

(Original: English)

"The Republic of Singapore will on the basis of reciprocity apply the said Convention to the recognition and enforcement of only those awards which are made in the territory of another Contracting State."

In accordance with article XII (2), the Convention will enter into force for Singapore on 19 November 1986, i.e. the ninetieth day after the deposit of its instrument.

[22c] "[Slovakia] will apply the Convention to recognition and enforcement of awards made in the territory of another contracting State. With regard to awards made in the territory of non-contracting States it will apply the Convention only to the extent to which these States grant reciprocal treatment."

[23] On April 29, 1993, the Government of Switzerland notified the Secretary-General its decision to withdraw the declaration it had made upon ratification, on June 1, 1965, which reads as follows: Referring to the possibility offered by paragraph 3 of article I, Switzerland will apply the Convention to the recognition and enforcement of awards made only in the territory of another Contracting State.

[24] [Tanzania] "will apply the Convention, in accordance with the first sentence of articles I(3) thereof, only to the recognition and enforcement of awards made in the territory of another Contracting State."

[25] "In accordance with Article I of the Convention, the Government of Trinidad and Tobago declares that it will apply the Convention to the recognition and enforcement of awards made only in the territory of another Contracting State. The Government of Trinidad and Tobago further declares that it will apply the Convention only to differences arising out of legal relationships, whether contracted or not, which are considered as commercial under the Law of Trinidad and Tobago."

[25a] ". . . with the reservations provided for in article I, paragraph 3, of the Convention, that is to say, the Tunisian State will apply the Convention to the recognition and enforcement of awards made only in the territory of another Contracting State and only to differences arising out of legal relationships, whether contractual or not, which are considered as commercial under Tunisian law."

[26] On 2 July 1992, the instrument of accession by the Government of Turkey to the above-mentioned Convention was deposited with the Secretary-General.

The said instrument contains the following declaration:

(Original: Turkish and English)

"In accordance with the Article I paragraph 3 of the Convention, the Republic of Turkey declares that it will apply the Convention, on the basis of reciprocity, to the recognition and enforcement of awards made only in the territory of another contracting State. It further declares that it will apply the Convention only to differences arising out of legal relationships, whether contractual or not, which are considered as commercial under its national law".

In accordance with its article XII (2), the Convention entered into force for Turkey on the ninetieth day after the date of deposit of the instrument, i.e. on 30 September 1992.

[26a] On 12 February 1992, the instrument of accession by the Government of Uganda to the above-mentioned Convention was deposited with the Secretary-General.

Upon accession, the Government of Uganda made the following declaration with respect to article 1 of the Convention:

(Original: English)

"The Republic of Uganda will only apply the Convention to recognition and enforcement of awards made in the territory of another Contracting State."

In accordance with paragraph 2 of its article XII, the Convention will enter into force for Uganda on the ninetieth day after the date of deposit of the instrument, i.e. on 12 May 1992.

[27] [Ukraine] will apply the provisions of this Convention, as regards arbitral awards made in the territory of States not parties to the Convention, only on the basis of reciprocity.

[28] In a communication accompanying the instrument of accession, the Government of the United Kingdom declared that in accordance with article X of the Convention the latter shall extend to Gibraltar, for the international relations of which the Government of the United Kingdom is responsible. (Extended to Hong Kong, effective Apr. 21, 1977, and to the Isle of Man, effective May 23, 1979.)

Extended to Bermuda, effective Feb. 12, 1980, with the following declaration:

". . . The Government of Bermuda will apply the Convention, in accordance with article I, paragraph 3 thereof, only to the recognition and enforcement of awards made in the territory of another Contracting State."

In a communication received on May 5, 1980, the Government of the United Kingdom of Great Britain and Northern Ireland notified the Secretary-General that its instrument of accession to the said Convention (letter C.N.261.1975-TREATIES-8 of Oct. 1, 1975) should have specified that the United Kingdom would apply the Convention only to the recognition and enforcement of awards made in the territory of another Contracting State and that this declaration should also have been made on behalf of Gibraltar, Hong Kong and the Isle of Man to which the Convention had been subsequently extended (letters C.N.27.1977.TREATIES-1 of Feb. 25, 1977 and C.N.39.1979.TREATIES-1 of Mar. 12, 1979).

Extended to Belize and the Cayman Islands, effective February 24, 1981, with the following declaration:

". . . The Government of the Cayman Islands and the Government of Belize will apply the Convention, in accordance with article I, paragraph 3 thereof, only to the recognition and enforcement of awards made in the territory of another Contracting State."

Extended to Guernsey, effective July 18, 1985, with the following declaration:

"[. . .] the Convention will be applied in respect of Guernsey, in accordance with Article I, paragraph 3 thereof, only to the recognition and enforcement of awards made in the territory of another Contracting State."

[29] "The United States of America will apply the Convention, on the basis of reciprocity, to the recognition and enforcement of only those awards made in the territory of another Contracting State."

"The United States of America will apply the Convention only to differences arising out of legal relationships, whether contractual or not, which are considered as commercial under the national law of the United States."

The Convention applies to all of the territories for the international relations of which the United States of America is responsible.

[29a] DECLARATIONS:

(a) The Republic of Venezuela will apply the Convention only to the recognition and enforcement of foreign arbitral awards made in the territory of another Contracting State.

(b) The Republic of Venezuela will apply the present Convention only to differences arising out of legal relationships, whether contractual or not, which are considered as commercial under its national law.

[29b] DECLARATIONS:

1. [The Socialist Republic of Viet Nam] considers the Convention to be applicable to the recognition and enforcement of arbitral awards made only in the territory of another Contracting State. With respect to arbitral awards made in the territories of non-contracting States, it will apply the Convention on the basis of reciprocity.

2. The Convention will be applied only to differences arising out of legal relationships which are considered as commercial under the laws of Viet Nam.

3. Interpretation of the Convention before the Vietnamese Courts or competent authorities should be made in accordance with the Constitution and the law of Viet Nam.

Ed. Note—The U.S. view is that the Socialist Federal Republic of Yugoslavia has dissolved and no successor state represents its continuation.

[30] With the following reservations:

"1. The Convention is applied in regard to the Socialist Federal Republic of Yugoslavia only to those arbitral awards which were adopted after the coming of the Convention into effect.

2. The Socialist Federal Republic of Yugoslavia will apply the Convention on a reciprocal basis only to those arbitral awards which were adopted on the territory of the other State Party to the Convention.

3. The Socialist Federal Republic of Yugoslavia will apply the Convention [only] with respect to the disputes arising from the legal relations, contractual and non-contractual, which, according to its national legislation, are considered as economic."

CONVENTION ON THE TAKING OF EVIDENCE ABROAD IN CIVIL OR COMMERCIAL MATTERS

The States signatory to the present Convention,

Desiring to facilitate the transmission and execution of Letters of Request and to further the accommodation of the different methods which they use for this purpose.

Desiring to improve mutual judicial co-operation in civil or commercial matters,

Have resolved to conclude a Convention to this effect and have agreed upon the following provisions—

CHAPTER I—LETTERS OF REQUEST

Article 1

In civil or commercial matters a judicial authority of a Contracting State may, in accordance with the provisions of the law of that State, request the competent authority of another Contracting State, by means of a Letter of Request, to obtain evidence, or to perform some other judicial act.

A Letter shall not be used to obtain evidence which is not intended for use in judicial proceedings, commenced or contemplated.

The expression 'other judicial act' does not cover the service of judicial documents or the issuance of any process by which judgments or orders are executed or enforced, or orders for provisional or protective measures.

Article 2

A Contracting State shall designate a Central Authority which will undertake to receive Letters of Request coming from a judicial authority of another Contracting State and to transmit them to the authority competent to execute them. Each State shall organize the Central Authority in accordance with its own law.

Letters shall be sent to the Central Authority of the State of execution without being transmitted through any other authority of that State.

Article 3

A Letter of Request shall specify—

(a) the authority requesting its execution and the authority requested to execute it, if known to the requesting authority;

(b) the names and addresses of the parties to the proceedings and their representatives, if any;

(c) the nature of the proceedings for which the evidence is required, giving all necessary information in regard thereto;

(d) the evidence to be obtained or other judicial act to be performed.

Where appropriate, the Letter shall specify, inter alia—

(e) the names and addresses of the persons to be examined;

(f) the questions to be put to the persons to be examined or a statement of the subject-matter about which they are to be examined;

(g) the documents or other property, real or personal, to be inspected;

(h) any requirement that the evidence is to be given on oath or affirmation, and any special form to be used;

(i) any special method or procedure to be followed under Article 9.

A Letter may also mention any information necessary for the application of Article 11.

No legalization or other like formality may be required.

Article 4

A Letter of Request shall be in the language of the authority requested to execute it or be accompanied by a translation into that language.

Nevertheless, a Contracting State shall accept a Letter in either English or French, or a translation into one of these lanaguages, unless it has made the reservation authorized by Article 33.

A Contracting State which has more than one official languge and cannot, for reasons of internal law, accept Letters in one of these languages for the whole of its territory, shall, by declaration, specify the language in which the Letter or translation thereof shall be expressed for execution in the specified parts of its territory. In case of failure to comply with this declaration, without justifiable excuse, the costs of translation into the required language shall be borne by the State of origin.

A Contracting State may, by declaration, specify the language or languages other than those referred to in the preceding paragraphs, in which a Letter may be sent to its Central Authority.

Any translation accompanying a Letter shall be certified as correct, either by a diplomatic officer or consular agent or by a sworn translator or by any other person so authorized in either State.

Article 5

If the Central Authority considers that the request does not comply with the provisions of the present Convention, it shall promptly inform the authority of the State of origin which transmitted the Letter of Request, specifying the objections to the Letter.

Article 6

If the authority to whom a Letter of Request has been transmitted is not competent to execute it, the Letter shall be sent forthwith to the authority in the same State which is competent to execute it in accordance with the provisions of its own law.

Article 7

The requesting authority shall, if it so desires, be informed of the time when, and the place where, the proceedings will take place, in order that the parties concerned, and their representatives, if any, may be present. This information shall be sent directly to the parties or their representatives when the authority of the State of origin so requests.

Article 8

A Contracting State may declare that members of the judicial personnel of the requesting authority of another Contracting State may be present at the execution of a Letter of Request. Prior authorization by the competent authority designated by the declaring State may be required.

Article 9

The judicial authority which executes a Letter of Request shall apply its own law as to the methods and procedures to be followed.

However, it will follow a request of the requesting authority that a special method or procedure be followed, unless this is incompatible with the internal law of the State of execution or is impossible of performance by reason of its internal practice and procedure or by reason of practical difficulties.

A Letter of Request shall be executed expeditiously.

Article 10

In executing a Letter of Request the requested authority shall apply the appropriate measures of compulsion in the instances and to the same extent as are provided by its internal law for the execution of orders issued by the authorities of its own country or of requests made by parties in internal proceedings.

Article 11

In the execution of a Letter of Request the person concerned may refuse to give evidence in so far as he has a privilege or duty to refuse to give the evidence—

(a) under the law of the State of execution; or

(b) under the law of the State of origin, and the privilege or duty has been specified in the Letter, or, at the instance of the requested authority, has been otherwise confirmed to that authority by the requesting authority.

A Contracting State may declare that, in addition, it will respect privileges and duties existing under the law of States other than the State of origin and the State of execution, to the extent specified in that declaration.

Article 12

The execution of a Letter of Request may be refused only to the extent that—

(a) in the State of execution the execution of the Letter does not fall within the functions of the judiciary; or

(b) the State addressed considers that its sovereignty or security would be prejudiced thereby.

Execution may not be refused solely on the ground that under its internal law the State of execution claims exclusive jurisdiction over the subject-matter of the action or that its internal law would not admit a right of action on it.

Article 13

The documents establishing the execution of the Letter of Request shall be sent by the requested authority to the requesting authority by the same channel which was used by the latter.

In every instance where the Letter is not executed in whole or in part, the requesting authority shall be informed immediately through the same channel and advised of the reasons.

Article 14

The execution of the Letter of Request shall not give rise to any reimbursement of taxes or costs of any nature.

Nevertheless, the State of execution has the right to require the State of origin to reimburse the fees paid to experts and interpreters and the costs occasioned by the use of a special procedure requested by the State of origin under Article 9, paragraph 2.

The requested authority whose law obliges the parties themselves to secure evidence, and which is not able itself to execute the Letter, may, after having obtained the consent of the requesting authority, appoint a suitable person to do so. When seeking this consent the requested authority shall indicate the approximate costs which would result from this procedure. If the requesting authority gives its consent it shall reimburse any costs incurred; without such consent the requesting authority shall not be liable for the costs.

CHAPTER II—TAKING OF EVIDENCE BY DIPLOMATIC OFFICERS, CONSULAR AGENTS AND COMMISSIONERS

Article 15

In a civil or commercial matter, a diplomatic officer or consular agent of a Contracting State may, in the territory of another Contracting State and within the area where he exercises his functions, take the evidence without compulsion of nationals of a State which he represents in aid of proceedings commenced in the courts of a State which he represents.

A Contracting State may declare that evidence may be taken by a diplomatic officer or consular agent only if permission to that effect is given upon application made by him or on his behalf to the appropriate authority designated by the declaring State.

Article 16

A diplomatic officer or consular agent of a Contracting State may, in the territory of another Contracting State and within the area where he exercises his functions, also take the evidence, without compulsion, of nationals of the State in which he exercises his functions or of a third State, in aid of proceedings commenced in the courts of a State which he represents, if—

(a) a competent authority designated by the State in which he exercises his functions has given its permission either generally or in the particular case, and

(b) he complies with the conditions which the competent authority has specified in the permission.

A Contracting State may declare that evidence may be taken under this Article without its prior permission.

Article 17

In a civil or commercial matter, a person duly appointed as a commissioner for the purpose may, without compulsion, take evidence in the territory of a Contracting State in aid of proceedings commenced in the courts of another Contracting State if—

(a) a competent authority designated by the State where the evidence is to be taken has given its permission either generally or in the particular case; and

(b) he complies with the conditions which the competent authority has specified in the permission.

A Contracting State may declare that evidence may be taken under this Article without its prior permission.

Article 18

A Contracting State may declare that a diplomatic officer, consular agent or commissioner authorized to take evidence under Articles 15, 16 or 17, may apply to the competent authority designated by the declaring State for appropriate assistance to obtain the evidence by compulsion. The declaration may contain such conditions as the declaring State may see fit to impose.

If the authority grants the application it shall apply any measures of compulsion which are appropriate and are prescribed by its law for use in internal proceedings.

Article 19

The competent authority, in giving the permission referred to in Articles 15, 16 or 17, or in granting the application referred to in Article 18, may lay down such conditions as it deems fit, *inter alia,* as to the time and place of the taking of the evidence. Similarly it may require that it be given reasonable advance notice of the time, date and place of the taking of the evidence; in such a case a representative of the authority shall be entitled to be present at the taking of the evidence.

Article 20

In the taking of evidence under any Article of this Chapter persons concerned may be legally represented.

Article 21

Where a diplomatic officer, consular agent or commisioner is authorized under Articles 15, 16 or 17 to take evidence—

(a) he may take all kinds of evidence which are not incompatible with the law of the State where the evidence is taken or contrary to any permission granted pursuant to the above Articles, and shall have power within such limits to administer an oath or take an affirmation;

(b) a request to a person to appear or to give evidence shall unless the recipient is a national of the State where the action is pending, be drawn up in the language of the place where the evidence is taken or be accompanied by a translation into such language;

(c) the request shall inform the person that he may be legally represented and, in any State that has not filed a declaration under Article 18, shall also inform him that he is not compelled to appear or to give evidence;

(d) the evidence may be taken in the manner provided by the law applicable to the court in which the action is pending provided that such manner is not forbidden by the law of the State where the evidence is taken;

(e) a person requested to give evidence may invoke the privileges and duties to refuse to give the evidence contained in Article 11.

Article 22

The fact that an attempt to take evidence under the procedure laid down in this Chapter has failed, owing to the refusal of a person to give evidence, shall not prevent an application being subsequently made to take the evidence in accordance with Chapter I.

CHAPTER III—GENERAL CLAUSES

Article 23

A Contracting State may at the time of signature, ratification or accession, declare that it will not execute Letters of Request issued for the purpose of obtaining pre-trial discovery of documents as known in Common Law countries.

Article 24

A Contracting State may designate other authorities in addition to the Central Authority and shall determine the extent of their competence. However, Letters of Request may in all cases be sent to the Central Authority.

Federal States shall be free to designate more than one Central Authority.

Article 25

A Contracting State which has more than one legal system may designate the authorities of one of such systems, which shall have exclusive competence to execute Letters of Request pursuant to this Convention.

Article 26

A Contracting State, if required to do so because of constitutional limitations, may request the reimbursement by the State of origin of fees and costs, in connection with the execution of Letters of Request, for the service of process necessary to compel the appearance of a person to give evidence, the costs of attendance of such persons, and the cost of any transcript of the evidence.

Where a State has made a request pursuant to the above paragraph, any other Contracting State may request from that State the reimbursement of similar fees and costs.

Article 27

The provisions of the present Convention shall not prevent a Contracting State from—

(a) declaring that Letters of Request may be transmitted to its judicial authorities through channels other than those provided for in Article 2;

(b) permitting, by internal law or practice, any act provided for in this Convention to be performed upon less restrictive conditions;

(c) permitting, by internal law or practice, methods of taking evidence other than those provided for in this Convention.

Article 28

The present Convention shall not prevent an agreement between any two or more Contracting States to derogate from—

(a) the provisions of Article 2 with respect to methods of transmitting Letters of Request;

(b) the provisions of Article 4 with respect to the languages which may be used;

(c) the provisions of Article 8 with respect to the presence of judicial personnel at the execution of Letters;

(d) the provisions of Article 11 with respect to the privileges and duties of witnesses to refuse to give evidence;

(e) the provisions of Article 13 with respect to the methods of returning executed Letters to the requesting authority;

(f) the provisions of Article 14 with respect to fees and costs;

(g) the provisions of Chapter II.

Article 29

Between Parties to the present Convention who are also Parties to one or both of the Conventions on Civil Procedure signed at the Hague on the 17th of July 1905[1] and the 1st of March 1954,[2] this Convention shall replace Articles 8-16 of the earlier Conventions.

Article 30

The present Convention shall not affect the application of Article 23 of the Convention of 1905, or of Article 24 of the Convention of 1954.

Article 31

Supplementary Agreements between Parties to the Conventions of 1905 and 1954 shall be considered as equally applicable to the present Convention unless the Parties have otherwise agreed.

Article 32

Without prejudice to the provisions of Articles 29 and 31, the present Convention shall not derogate from conventions containing provisions on the matters covered by this Convention to which the Contracting States are, or shall become Parties.

Article 33

A State may, at the time of signature, ratification or accession exclude, in whole or in part, the application of the provisions of paragraph 2 of Article 4 and of Chapter II. No other reservation shall be permitted.

Each Contracting State may at any time withdraw a reservation it has made; the reservation shall cease to have effect on the sixtieth day after notification of the withdrawal.

When a State has made a reservation, any other State affected thereby may apply the same rule against the reserving State.

Article 34

A State may at any time withdraw or modify a declaration.

Article 35

A Contracting State shall, at the time of the deposit of its instrument of ratification or accession, or at a later date, inform the Ministry of Foreign Affairs of the Netherlands of the designation of authorities, pursuant to Articles 2, 8, 24 and 25.

A Contracting State shall likewise inform the Ministry, where appropriate, of the following—

(a) the designation of the authorities to whom notice must be given, whose permission may be required, and whose assistance may be invoked in the taking of evidence by diplomatic officers and consular agents, pursuant to Articles 15, 16 and 18 respectively;

(b) the designation of the authorities whose permission may be required in the taking of evidence by commissioners pursuant to Article 17 and of those who may grant the assistance provided for in Article 18;

(c) declarations pursuant to Articles 4, 8, 11, 15, 16, 17, 18, 23 and 27;

(d) any withdrawal or modification of the above designations and declarations;

(e) the withdrawal of any reservation.

Article 36

Any difficulties which may arise between Contracting States in connection with the operation of this Convention shall be settled through diplomatic channels.

Article 37

The present Convention shall be open for signature by the States represented at the Eleventh Session of the Hague Conference on Private International Law.

It shall be ratified, and the instruments of ratification shall be deposited with the Ministry of Foreign Affairs of the Netherlands.

Article 38

The present Convention shall enter into force on the sixtieth day after the deposit of the third instrument of ratification referred to in the second paragraph of Article 37.

The Convention shall enter into force for each signatory State which ratifies subsequently on the sixtieth day after the deposit of its instrument of ratification.

Article 39

Any State not represented at the Eleventh Session of the Hague Conference on Private International Law which is a Member of this Conference or of the United Nations or of a specialized agency of that Organization, or a Party to the Statute of the International Court of Justice[1] may accede to the present Convention after it has entered into force in accordance with the first paragraph of Article 38.

The instrument of accession shall be deposited with the Ministry of Foreign Affairs of the Netherlands.

The Convention shall enter into force for a State acceding to it on the sixtieth day after the deposit of its instrument of accession.

The accession will have effect only as regards the relations between the acceding State and such Contracting States as will have declared their acceptance of the accession. Such declaration shall be deposited at the Ministry of Foreign Affairs of the Netherlands; this Ministry shall forward, through diplomatic channels, a certified copy to each of the Contracting States.

The Convention will enter into force as between the acceding State and the State that has declared its acceptance of the accession on the sixtieth day after the deposit of the declaration of acceptance.

Article 40

Any State may, at the time of signature, ratification or accession, declare that the present Convention shall extend to all the territories for the international relations of which it is responsible, or to one or more of them. Such a declaration shall take effect on the date of entry into force of the Convention for the State concerned.

At any time thereafter, such extensions shall be notified to the Ministry of Foreign Affairs of the Netherlands.

The Convention shall enter into force for the territories mentioned in such an extension on the sixtieth day after the notification indicated in the preceding paragraph.

Article 41

The present Convention shall remain in force for five years from the date of its entry into force in accordance with the first paragraph of Article 38, even for States which have ratified it or acceded to it subsequently.

If there has been no denunciation, it shall be renewed tacitly every five years.

Any denunciation shall be notified to the Ministry of Foreign Affairs of the Netherlands at least six months before the end of the five year period.

It may be limited to certain of the territories to which the Convention applies.

The denunciation shall have effect only as regards the State which has notified it. The Convention shall remain in force for the other Contracting States.

Article 42

The Ministry of Foreign Affairs of the Netherlands shall give notice to the States referred to in Article 37, and to the States which have acceded in accordance with Article 39, of the following—

(a) the signatures and ratifications referred to in Article 37;

(b) the date on which the present Convention enters into force in accordance with the first paragraph of Article 38;

(c) the accessions referred to in Article 39 and the dates on which they take effect;

(d) the extensions referred to in Article 40 and the dates on which they take effect;

(e) the designations, reservations and declarations referred to in Articles 33 and 35;

(f) the denunciations referred to in the third paragraph of Article 41.

IN WITNESS WHEREOF the undersigned, being duly authorized thereto, have signed the present Convention.

DONE at The Hague, on the 18th day of March 1970, in the English and French languages, both texts being equally authentic, in a single copy which shall be deposited in the archives of the Government of the Netherlands, and of which a certified copy shall be sent, through the diplomatic channel, to each of the States represented at the Eleventh Session of the Hague Conference [Signatures omitted.]

Convention on the taking of evidence abroad in civil or commercial matters. Done at The Hague March 18, 1970; entered into force for the United States October 7, 1972. TIAS 7444; 23 UST 2555

States which are parties:

Argentina[1]
Australia[1a]
Barbados[1b]
Cyprus[1c]
Czech Republic[1d]
Denmark[1e]
Estonia[1f]
Finland[2]
France[2a]
Federal Republic of Germany[2b]
Israel[2c]
Italy[2d]
Latvia[2e]
Luxemburg[2f]
Mexico[2g]
Monaco[2h]
Netherlands[2i]
Norway[3]
Poland[3a]
Portugal[3b]
Singapore[3c]
Slovak Republic[3d]
Spain[3e]
Sweden[3f]
Switzerland[3g]
United Kingdom[3h]
United States[4]
Venezuela

---

[1] *Notification pursuant to Article 42 of the Convention*

In conformity with Article 39, paragraph 2, the instrument of accession by the Argentine Republic to the above-mentioned Convention was deposited with the Ministry of Foreign Affairs of the Kingdom of the Netherlands on 8 May 1987.

The instrument of accession of the Argentine Republic contains the following reservation, referred to in Article 33, first paragraph, of the Convention:

> "La República Argentina excluye totalmente la applicación de las dfsposiciones del párrafo 2º del artículo *4*º, así como las del capítulo II."
>
> (Translation)
>
> The Argentine Republic totally excludes the application of the provisions of paragraph 2 of Article *4*, as well as those of Chapter II.;

and the following declaration regarding Article 23 of the Convention:

> "La República Argentina no cumplirá los exhortos que tengan por objeto un procedimiento conocido en los Estados del "Common Law", por el nombre de "pre-trial discovery of documents (exhibicion de documentos antes del juicio)."
>
> (Translation)
>
> The Argentine Republic will not execute Letters of Request issued for the purpose of obtaining pre-trial discovery of documents as known in the Common Law Countries.

Furthermore, the instrument contains the declaration annexed to this notification.

In accordance with paragraph 3 of Article 39, the Convention will enter into force for the Argentine Republic on 7 July 1987.

According to Article 39, paragraph 4 of the Convention, the accession will have effect only as regards the relations between the Argentine Republic and such Contracting States as will have declared their acceptance of the accession. Such declarations shall be deposited at the Ministry of Foreign Affairs of the Kingdom of the Netherlands.

The Hague 20, May 1987

"The Argentine Republic excludes the extension of the application of the Convention on the taking of evidence abroad in civil or commercial matters, adopted at The Hague on March 18, 1970, to the Malvinas, South Georgia, and South Sandwich Islands, which was notified by the United Kingdom of Great Britain and Northern Ireland to the Ministry of Foreign Affairs of the Kingdom of the Netherlands on November 23, 1979, and reaffirms its rights of sovereignty over the Malvinas, South Georgia and South Sandwich Islands, which form an integral part of its national territory."

The General Assembly of the United Nations has adopted resolutions 2065 (XX), 3160 (XXVIII), 31/49, 37/9, 38/12, 39/6, 40/21 and 41/40 in which the existence of a dispute of sovereignty is recognized in reference to the Malvinas Islands, and it urges the Argentine Republic and the United Kingdom of Great Britain and Northern Ireland to maintain negotiations with the purpose of finding a peaceful and definitive solution to the dispute as soon as possible, with the good offices of the Secretary General of the United Nations, who will inform the General Assembly of the progress that has been accomplished.

In like manner, "the Argentine Republic excludes the June 19, 1986 approval formulated by the United Kingdom of Great Britain and Northern Ireland for the Malvinas, South Georgia and South Sandwich Islands with respect to the accession of the Principality of Monaco to the aforementioned Convention." (Translation provided by the Division of Language Services, Department of State)

In accordance with Article 35 of the Convention the Government of the Argentine Republic designated the following competent authority:

Ministerio de Relaciones Exteriores y Culto
Reconquista 1088
Buenos Aires.

In accordance with Article 39 the Convention will enter into force between Argentina and

the United States of America	January 30, 1988
Finland	6 April 1990
Sweden	20 November 1987
Israel	23 November 1987
Denmark	7 December 1987
France	11 January 1988
Norway	18 January 1988
United Kingdom of Great Britain and Northern Ireland also for Anguilla, the Cayman Islands, the Falklands, Gibraltar, Guernsey, Hong Kong, the Isle of Man, South Georgia and South Sandwich Islands and the Sovereign Base Areas of Akrotiri and Dhekelia in the islands of Cyprus	11 April 1988
Czechoslovakia	11 April 1988
Federal Republic of Germany	21 June 1988
Jersey	9 September 1988
Spain	28 August 1994
Switzerland	13 January 1995

1a *Notification pursuant to Article 42 of the Convention.*—In conformity with Article 39, paragraph 2, the instrument of accession by Australia to the above-mentioned Convention was deposited with the Ministry of Foreign Affairs of the Kingdom of the Netherlands on 23 October 1992.

The instrument of accession of Australia contains the following reservation and declarations:

Pursuant to Article 33, it excludes the operation of paragraph 2 of Article 4.

The Government of Australia hereby declares, for and on behalf of Australia, that:

— pursuant to Article 2, the Secretary to the Attorney-General's Department of the Commonwealth of Australia will be its Central Authority;

— pursuant to Article 8, members of the judicial personnel of the requesting authority of another Contracting State may be present at the execution of a Letter of Request, subject to prior authorisation by the judicial executing the Letter of Request;

— pursuant to Article 15, evidence may be taken by a diplomatic officer or consular agent only if permission to that effect is given upon application to the Secretary of the Attorney-General's Department of the Commonwealth of Australia;

— pursuant to Article 16, the Secretary to the Attorney-General's Department of the Commonwealth of Australia will be its competent authority for the purposes of that Article and is empowered to specify conditions with respect to any permission given under that Article; and

— pursuant to Article 23, it will not execute Letters of Request issued for the purpose of obtaining pre-trial discovery of documents as known in Common Law Countries.

— pursuant to Article 24, it designates the Registrars of the State and Territory Supreme Courts as additional authorities.

— pursuant to Article 40, the Convention extends to all the territories for the international relations of which it is responsible.

In accordance with paragraph 3 of Article 39, the Convention will enter into force for Australia on 22 December 1992.

According to Article 39, paragraph 4, of the Convention the accession will have effect only as regards the relations between Australia and such Contracting States as will have declared their acceptance of the accession. Such declarations shall be deposited at the Ministry of Foreign Affairs of the Kingdom of the Netherlands.

The following States have declared their acceptance of Australia's accession to the Convention: Aruba, Cyprus, Finland, France, the Federal Republic of Germany, Luxembourg, the Kingdom of the Netherlands (for the Kingdom in Europe), Norway, Switzerland, the United States of America.

In accordance with Article 39 the Convention will enter into force between Australia and

the United States of America . . . . 22 August 1993
France . . . . 27 March 1993
Denmark . . . . 12 April 1993
the United Kingdom of Great Britain and Northern Ireland . . . . . 20 April 1993
Cyprus . . . . 19 June 1993
the Federal Republic of Germany . . . . 3 July 1993
Luxembourg . . . . 9 February 1993
the Kingdom of the Netherlands . . . . 14 February 1993
(for the Kingdom in Europe)
Aruba . . . . 19 July 1993
Finland . . . . 23 July 1993
Sweden . . . . 1 March 1994
Norway . . . . 18 June 1994
Spain . . . . 28 August 1994
Italy . . . . 16 January 1996
Slovak Republic . . . . 20 May 1996

1b *Notification in conformity with Article 42, sub e, of the Convention.*—By a Letter of 2 September 1982, received at The Ministry of Foreign Affairs of the Kingdom of the Netherlands on 29 September 1982, Barbados informed the Depositary in accordance with Article 35 of the abovementioned Convention of the following: ". . . . for the purpose of the said Convention, the Central Authority is the Registrar of the Supreme Court of Barbados."

In accordance with Article 39 the Convention will enter into force between Barbados and

Spain . . . . 28 August 1994
Switzerland . . . . 13 January 1995

1c Notification in conformity with Article 42, sub e, of the Convention.—After having designated the Central Authority on 3 May 1984 (see Notification No. 2/1984) the Government of Cyprus informed the Ministry of Foreign Affairs of the Kingdom of the Netherlands of the following on 15 May 1984:

"The Republic of Cyprus makes the following declarations:

1. Under Article 2 the Ministry of Justice is designated as the Competent Authority.
2. Under Article 16 the Ministry of Justice is designated as the Competent Authority.
3. Under Article 17 the Ministry of Justice is designated as the Competent Authority.
4. In accordance with Article 18 the Republic of Cyprus declares that a diplomatic officer, consular agent or commissioner authorised to take evidence under Articles 15, 16 or 17 may apply to the Competent Authority for appropriate assistance to obtain such evidence by compulsion as prescribed by the law for internal proceedings, provided that the requesting Contracting State has made a declaration affording reciprocal facilities under Article 18.
   Under Article 18 the Supreme Court is designated as the Competent Authority.
5. In accordance with Article 23, the Government of the Republic of Cyprus declares that the Republic of Cyprus will not execute Letters of Request issued for the purpose of obtaining pre-trial discovery of documents. The Government of the Republic of Cyprus further declares that the Republic of Cyprus understands 'Letters of Request issued for the purpose of obtaining pre-trial discovery of documents' for the purposes of the foregoing declaration as including any Letter of Request which requires a person:
   a. to state what documents relevant to the proceedings to which the Letter of Request relates are, or have been, in his possession, custody or power; or
   b. to produce any documents other than particular documents specified in the Letter of Request as being documents appearing to the requested court to be, or likely to be, in his possession, custody or power.

The Republic of Cyprus makes the following reservations:

1. In accordance with Article 8 the Republic of Cyprus declares that members of the judicial personnel of the requesting authority may be present at the execution of a Letter of Request.
2. In accordance with the provisions of article 33 the Republic of Cyprus will not accept a Letter of Request in French."

According to the depositary the declaration under 5 and the reservation under 2 should have been made at the time of accession. The States which have declared to accept Cyprus' accession to the Convention, namely: the Federal Republic of Germany, Finland, France, Israel, Italy, the Kingdom of the Netherlands, Luxembourg, Portugal, the United Kingdom of Great Britain and Northern Ireland, Sweden and Czechoslovakia, are requested to inform the Ministry of Foreign Affairs of the Kingdom of the Netherlands whether they accept the declaration and the reservation concerned.

Notification pursuant to Article 42 of the Convention

The following State declared its acceptance of the accession of Cyprus to the above-mentioned Convention:

the United States of America . . . . 1 December 1987

In accordance with Article 39 the Convention will enter into force between Cyprus and

the United States of America . . . . 30 January 1988
Spain . . . . 10 July 1994
Switzerland . . . . 13 January 1995

1d By notification dated January 28, 1993 the Czech Republic communicated the following: "In accordance with the valid principles of international law and to the extent defined by it, the Czech Republic, as a successor state created as a result of the division of the Czech and Slovak Federal Republic, considers itself bound, as of January 1, 1993, i.e. the date of the division of the Czechoslovak federation, by multilateral international treaties to which the Czech and Slovak Federal Republic was a party on that date, including reservations and declarations to their provisions made earlier by Czechoslovakia", which are as follow:

(Translation)

"The Socialist Republic of Czechoslovakia declares, with reference to Article 16 of the Convention on the taking of evidence abroad in civil or commercial matters, concluded at The Hague on 18 March 1970, that evidence may be taken in accordance with Chapter II without its prior permission provided the principal of reciprocity is applied.

The Socialist Republic of Czechoslovakia also declares, in connection with Article 18 of the said Convention, that a diplomatic officer, consular agent or commissioner authorized to take evidence under Articles 15, 16 and 17, may request the competent Czechoslovak court or the Czechoslovak state notary to carry out procedural action and that such a diplomatic officer, consular agent or commissioner will transmit the dossier to that court or notary through the intermediary of the Minister of Justice of the Czech Socialist Republic in Prague or the Minister of Justice of the Slovak Socialist Republic in Bratislava, provided the principal of reciprocity is applied.

The Socialist Republic of Czechoslovakia wishes to state, in connection with Article 40 of the Convention according to all states the right to declare that the convention shall be applicable to all territories for the international relations of which it is responsible, that keeping certain countries in a state of dependence is in its opinion contrary to the spirit and objectives of the United Nations Declaration of 14 December 1960 on the granting of independence to colonial countries and peoples, which declares the necessity for a speedy and unconditional end to colonialism in all its forms.".

By notification contained in Note dated May 28, 1978, the Minister of Justice of the Czech Socialist Republic and the Minister of Justice of the Slovak Socialist Republic have been designated as central authorities in accordance with Articles 2 and 24 of the Convention.

1e With the following reservations:

"1)Availing itself of the provisions laid down in Article 33, the Danish Government hereby declares, in accordance with Article 4, that Denmark will not accept Letters of Request which are sent in French.

2) Availing itself of the provisions laid down in Article 33, the Danish Government hereby declares, in accordance with Article 17, that Denmark will not accept the taking of evidence by commissioners."

And with the following declarations in accordance with Article 35:

"Article 2

The Ministry of Justice is hereby designated as Central Authority.

Article 4

Letters of Request may be sent in Norwegian and Swedish, and Denmark accepts no obligation to return evidence taken in other languages than Danish.

Article 8

Members of the judicial personnel of the requesting authority of another contracting State may be present at the execution of a Letter of Request if they have obtained prior authorization from the competent Danish authority.

Article 15

A diplomatic officer or consular agent may take evidence if he has been authorized to do so by the Ministry of Justice.

Article 16

The Ministry of Justice will issue authorizations to take evidence.

Article 23

Letters of Requests issued for the purpose of obtaining pre-trial discovery of documents may not be executed in Denmark.

Article 27 a

As has been the case hitherto, Letters of Request may be transmitted directly to the competent Danish court by the consular agents of foreign States."

Additional declaration of July 23, 1980:

"The declaration made by the Kingdom of Denmark in accordance with article 23 concerning 'Letters of Request issued for the purpose of obtaining pre-trial discovery of documents' shall apply to any Letter of Request which requires a person:

a) to state what documents relevant to the proceedings to which the Letter of Request relates are, or have been, in his possession, other than particular documents specified in the Letter of Request;

or

b) to produce any documents other than particular documents which are specified in the Letter of Request, and which are likely to be in his possession."

1f The Permanent Bureau of the Hague Conference on private international law presents its compliments to the Diplomatic Missions of the Member States and to the National Organs and has the honour to inform them that, by instrument deposited on 2 February 1996 with the Ministry of Foreign Affairs of the Kingdom of the Netherlands.

the *Republic of Estonia*

acceded to the above-mentioned Convention.

The instrument of accession contains the following declarations:

"1) on the basis of Article 8 the judges of the pursuing state have the right to participate in the process operation subject to the preceding consent of the Ministry of Justice of the Republic of Estonia;

2) on the basis of Article 11, a person may refuse to participate in the taking of evidence or process operation, in case he has the right or commitment to it in accordance with the laws of his home-state;

3) on the basis of Article 23 the Republic of Estonia fulfills a requisition where the producing of the documents or its copy is requested if it corresponds to the following requirements:

a) process has been launched;

b) documents have been reasonably identified according to the dates, the contents or other information;

c) circumstances have been indicated giving ground to presume that the documents are in the property, possession of the person or known to him."

According to Articles 16 and 17 of the Convention the competent authority designated to give its permission is the *Ministry of Justice of the Republic of Estonia.*

In accordance with the terms of Article 39, paragraph 3, the Convention will enter into force for the *Republic of Estonia* on *2 April 1996.*

According to Article 39, paragraph 4, of the Convention the accession will have effect only as regards the relations between the Republic of Estonia and such Contracting States as will have declared their acceptance of the accession. Such declaration shall be deposited with the Ministry of Foreign Affairs of the Kingdom of the Netherlands.

In accordance with Article 39 the Convention entered into force between Estonia and

Luxembourg	18 June 1996
Denmark	22 June 1996
Slovak Republic	25 June 1996
Israel	30 June 1996
Germany	2 July 1996
Italy	6 July 1996
Finland	5 August 1996
Netherlands (for the Kingdom in Europe and Aruba)	16 August 1996
Poland	14 September 1996

2 With the following reservation and declaration:

Reservation:

"In conformity with Article 33, Finland enters a reservation to paragraph 2 of Article 4 to the effect that Letters of Request in the English or French languages will not be accepted."

Declaration:

"1. In Finland the Ministry of Justice (as of 6/1/82) shall be the Central Authority referred to in Article 2.

2. Swedish is the second official language of Finland. Finland will therefore in accordance with paragraph 1 of Article 4 accept Letters of Request in the Swedish language. The answer shall be given in the Swedish language if in connection with the Letter of Request this has been specifically requested.

3. A member of the judicial personnel of the requesting authority may in accordance with Article 8 be present at the execution of a Letter of Request, provided that the Finnish Ministry of Justice has given its consent.

4. The evidence referred to in Articles 16 and 17 of the Convention may be taken without the prior permission of the Finnish authorities.

5. Finland is not going to execute Letters of Request referred to in Article 23 issued for the purpose of obtaining pre-trial discovery of documents as known in Common Law countries."

Notification in conformity with Article 42, paragraph e, of the Convention

By note dated 11 December 1980 and received at the Ministry of Foreign Affairs of the Kingdom of the Netherlands on 12 December 1980 the Government of Finland informed the Ministry of the withdrawal in part of the reservation to Article 4, paragraph 2, of the above-mentioned Convention made at the time of ratification and declared that it hereafter accepts the Letters of Request done in or translated into the English language. In accordance with Article 35, sub c, the Government of Finland made the following declaration:

"By accepting Letters of Request in English, the Republic of Finland does not undertake to execute the request, or transmit the evidence thus obtained in the English language; nor to have translated the documents which establish the execution of the Letter of Request.".

Furthermore the Government of Finland modified the declaration concerning Article 23 of the above-mentioned Convention made at the time of ratification. The modified declaration is worded as follows:

"The declaration made by the Republic of Finland in accordance with Article 23 concerning "Letters of Request issued for the purpose of obtaining pre-trial discovery of documents" shall apply only to Letters of Request which require a person:

a) to state what documents relevant to the proceedings to which the Letter of Request relates are, or have been, in his possession, custody or power;

b) to produce any documents other than particular documents specified in the Letter of Request, which are likely to be in his possession, custody or power.".

2a With the following declarations:

With respect to the first paragraph of Article 40 of the Convention, France declares that the Convention shall apply to all the Territory of the French Republic.

In conformity with the provisions of Article 33, the French Government declares:

That, in application of the second paragraph of Article 4, it will execute only Letters in French or accompanied by a translation in French.

That, in application of Article 23, it will not execute Letters of Request issued for the purpose of obtaining pre-trial discovery of documents as known in Common Law countries;

In conformity with the provisions of Article 2, the Ministry of Justice, Civil Division of International Judicial Assistance, 13 Place Vendôme, Paris (1er), is designated as the Central Authority to the exclusion of any other authority.

In conformity with the provisions of Article 16, the Ministry of Justice, Civil Division of International Judicial Assistance, 13 Place Vendôme, Paris (1er), is designated as the competent authority to give permission to diplomatic officers or consular agents of a Contracting State to take the evidence, without compulson, of persons other than nationals of that State in aid of proceedings commenced in the courts of a State which they represent.

That permission, which shall be given for each specific case and shall be accompanied by special conditions when appropriate, shall be granted under the following general conditions:

1. Evidence shall be taken only within the confines of the Embassies or Consulates;
2. The date and time of taking the evidence shall be notified in due time to the Civil Division of International Judicial Assistance so that it may have the opportunity to be represented at the proceedings;
3. Evidence shall be taken in premises accessible to the public:
4. Persons requested to give evidence shall be served with an official instrument in French or accompanied by a translation into French, and that instrument shall mention:

a. That evidence is being taken in conformity with the provisions of The Hague Convention of March 18, 1970 on the Taking of Evidence Abroad in Civil or Commercial Matters and relates to legal proceedings pending before a jurisdiction specifically designated by a Contracting State;

b. That appearance is voluntary and failure to appear will not give rise to criminal proceedings in the State of origin;

c. That the parties to the trial are consenting or, if not, the grounds of their objections;

d. That in the taking of evidence the person concerned may be legally represented;

e. That a person requested to give evidence may invoke a privilege or duty to refuse to give evidence.

A copy of these requests shall be transmitted to the Ministry of Justice.

5. The Civil Division of International Judicial Assistance shall be kept informed of any difficulty.

In conformity with the provisions of Article 17, the Ministry of Justice, Civil Division of International Judicial Assistance, 13 Place Vendôme, Paris (1er), is appointed as the competent authority to give permission to persons duly appointed as commissioners to proceed, without compulsion, to take any evidence in aid of proceedings commenced in the courts of a Contracting State.

This permission, which shall be given for each specific case and shall be accompanied by special conditions when appropriate, shall be granted under the following general conditions:

1. Evidence shall be taken only within the Embassy confines;
2. The date and time of taking the evidence shall be notified in due time to the Civil Division of International Judicial Assistance so that it may have the opportunity to be represented at the proceedings;
3. Evidence shall be taken in premises accessible to the public;
4. Persons requested to give evidence shall be served with an official instrument in French or accompanied by a translation in French, and that instrument shall mention:

a. That evidence is being taken in conformity with the provisions of The Hague Convention of March 18, 1970 on the Taking of Evidence Abroad in Civil or Commercial Matters and relates to legal proceedings pending before a jurisdiction specifically designated by a Contracting State;

b. That appearance is voluntary and failure to appear will not give rise to criminal proceedings in the State of origin;

c. That the parties to the trial are consenting and, if not, the grounds of their objections;

d. That in the taking of evidence the person concerned may be legally represented;

e. That a person requested to give evidence may invoke the privilege and duty to refuse to give evidence.

A copy of these requests shall be transmitted to the Ministry of Justice.

5. The Civil Division of International Judicial Assistance shall be kept informed of any difficulty.

The request for permission transmitted by the requesting authority to the Ministry of Justice shall specify:

1. The motives that led to choosing this method of taking evidence of preference to that of a Letter of Request, considering the judiciary costs incurred;
2. The criteria for appointing commissioners when the person appointed does not reside in France.

The French Government declares that, in application of the provisions of Article 8, members of the judicial personnel of the requesting authority of a Contracting State may be present at the execution of a Letter of Request.

The Permanent Bureau of the Hague Conference on private international law presents its compliments to the Diplomatic Missions of the Member States and to the National Organs and has the honour to inform them that, by a letter received at the Ministry of Foreign Affairs of the Kingdom of the Netherlands on 19 January 1987, in accordance with Article 34 of the Convention, *France* has modified its declaration regarding Article 23 as follows:

The declaration made by the French Republic in accordance with Article 23 relating to Letters of Request issued for the purpose of obtaining pre-trial discovery of documents does not apply when the requested documents are enumerated limitatively in the Letter of Request and have a direct and precise link with the object of the procedure. (Translation)

The Permanent Bureau avails itself of this opportunity to renew to the Diplomatic Missions of the Member States and to the National Organs an assurance of its highest consideration and esteem.

2b "A. The Government of the Federal Republic of Germany makes the following declarations in accordance with paragraph 1 of Article 33 of the Convention of 18th March 1970:

The Federal Republic of Germany makes the reservation provided for in the first sentence of paragraph 1 of Article 33 of the Convention excluding the application of the provisions of paragraph 2 of Article 4 of the Convention. Letters of Request to be executed under Chapter 1 of the Convention must, in accordance with paragraphs 1 and 5 of Article 4 of the Convention, be in the German language or be accompanied by a translation into that language. The Federal Republic of Germany declares in accordance with the option provided for in the first sentence of paragraph 1 of Article 33 of the Convention to make a reservation excluding the application of the provisions of Chapter II of the Convention that the taking of evidence by diplomatic officers or consular agents is not permissible in its territory if German nationals are involved.

B. The Government of the Federal Republic of Germany makes the following declarations pursuant to Article 35 of the Convention of 18th of March 1970:

(1) The authority competent to execute a Letter of Request shall be the local court (Amtsgericht) in whose district the official act is to be performed. Letters of Request shall be addressed to the Central Authority of the Land in which the respective request is to be executed. Germany has deposited the following revised list of Central Authorities designated in accordance with Article 2 of the Convention:

Baden-Württemberg	Justizministerium Baden-Württemberg Schillerplatz 4 70173 Stuttgart
Bavaria	Bayerisches Staatsministerium der Justiz Justizpalast Prielmayerstrasse 7 80335 München
Berlin	Senatsverwaltung für Justiz von Berlin Salzburger Strasse 21-25 10825 Berlin
Brandenburg	Ministerium der Justiz des Landes Brandenburg Heinrich-Mann-Allee 107 14460 Potsdam
Bremen	Der Präsident des Landsgerichts Domsheide 16 28195 Bremen
Hamburg	Präsident des Amtsgerichts Hamburg Sievekingplatz 1 20335 Hamburg
Hesse	Hessisches Ministerium der Justiz Luisenstrasse 13 65185 Wiesbaden
Lower Saxony	Niedersächisches Justiz- ministerium Am Waterlooplatz 1 30169 Hannover
Mecklenburg-Western Pomerania	Ministerium für Justiz, Bundes- und Europaangelegen- heiten des Landes Mecklenburg- Vorpommern Demmlerplatz 14 19053 Schwering
Northrhine-Westphalia	Präsident des Oberlandes- gerichts Düsseldorf Cecilienallee 3 40474 Düsseldorf
Rhineland-Palatinate	Ministerium der Justiz Ernst-Ludwig-Strasse 3 55116 Mainz
Saarland	Ministerium der Justiz des Saarlandes Zähringerstrasse 12 66119 Saarbrücken
Saxe	Sächisches Staatsministerium der Justiz Archivstrasse 1 01097 Dresden
Saxe-Anhalt	Ministerium des Justiz des Landes Sachsen-Anhalt Wilhelm-Höpfner-Ring 6 39116 Magdeburg
Schleswig-Holstein	Der Justizminister des Landes Schleswig-Holstein Lorentzdamm 35 24103 Kiel
Thuringe	Thüringer Justizministerium Alfred-Hess-Strasse 8 99094 Erfurt

(2) Pursuant to Article 8 of the Convention, the Government of the Federal Republic of Germany declares that members of the requesting court of another Contracting State may be present at the execution of a Letter of Request by the local court if prior authorization has been given by the Central Authority of the Land where the request is to be executed.

(3) The taking of evidence by diplomatic officers or consular agents pursuant to paragraph 1 of Article 16 of the Convention which involves nationals of a third State or stateless persons shall be subject to permission from the Central Authority of the Land where the evidence is to be taken. Pursuant to paragraph 2 of Article 16 of the Convention, permission shall not be required if the national of the third State is also a national of the State of the requesting court.

(4) A commissioner of the requesting court may not take evidence pursuant to Article 17 of the Convention unless the Central Authority of the Land where the evidence is to be taken has given its permission. Such permission may be made subject to conditions. The local court in whose district official acts would have to be performed by virtue of a Letter of Request in the same matter shall be entitled to control the preparation and the actual taking of the evidence. Under the second sentence of Article 19 of the Convention, a member of the court may be present at the taking of the evidence.

(5) The Federal Republic of Germany declares in pursuance of Article 23 of the Convention that it will not, in its territory, execute Letters of Request issued for the purpose of obtaining pre-trial discovery of documents as known in Common Law countries."

2c *Notification in conformity with Article 42, paragraph e, of the Convention*

In accordance with Article 35 of the Convention Israel notified by a Note dated April 17, 1980 and received at the Ministry of Foreign Affairs of the Kingdom of the Netherlands on April 25, 1980, that the Central Authority designated by the State of Israel in accordance with Article 2 of the above-mentioned Convention, is the Director of Courts, 19 Jaffa Road, Jerusalem.

2d *Notification in conformity with Article 42, sub a and e, of the Convention*

The Italian Republic deposited its instrument of ratification of the above-mentioned Convention with the Ministry of Foreign Affairs of the Kingdom of the Netherlands on 22 June 1982, in accordance with Article 37, paragraph 2, of the Convention.

In accordance with Article 38, paragraph 2, the Convention will enter into force for Italy on 21 August 1982.

At the time of the deposit of the instrument of ratification the Italian Government notified the Ministry of Foreign Affairs of the following:

Translation

(1) The Italian Government declares, in accordance with Article 8, that members of the judicial personnel of the requesting authority of another Contracting State may be present at the execution of a Letter of Request, subject to prior authorization by the competent authority designated by the Italian State under (4) paragraph 2 below.

(2) The Italian Government declares, in accordance with Article 18, that a diplomatic officer, consular agent or commissioner who is taking evidence under Article 15, 16 or 17, may apply to Authority designated by the Italian State under (4) paragraph 2 below, for appropriate assistance to obtain the evidence by compulsion.

(3) The Italian Government declares, in accordance with Article 23, that it will not execute Letters of Request issued for the purpose of obtaining pre-trial discovery of documents as known in Common Law countries.

(4) In accordance with Article 35 the Italian Government designates the Ministry of Foreign Affairs pursuant to Article 2 as the Central Authority which will undertake to receive Letters of Request coming from a judicial authority of another Contracting State and to transmit them to the authority competent to execute them.

In accordance with the abovementioned Article the Italian Government designates the Court of Appeal within whose jurisdiction proceedings are to take place as the authority competent to:

—authorize foreign judicial personnel to be present at the execution of a Letter of Request, pursuant to Article 8;

—authorize foreign diplomatic officers, consular agents or commissioners to take evidence under Article 16 or 17;

—grant the judicial assistance provided for in Article 18.

2e In accordance with Article 2 the following Central Authority has been designated by Latvia:

Ministry of Justice
Brivibas Boulevard 34
LV-1536, Riga
Tel: 282607
Fax: 285575

In accordance with Article 39, paragraph 5, the Convention will enter into force between Latvia and

Luxembourg	15 July 1995
Finland	21 August 1995
United Kingdom of Great Britain and Northern Ireland	12 September 1995
United States	24 October 1995
Germany	11 November 1995
Italy	16 January 1996
Australia	20 January 1996
Norway	27 January 1996
Israel	27 February 1996
Slovak Republic	20 May 1996
Denmark	22 June 1996
Netherlands (for the Kingdom in Europe and Aruba)	16 August 1996

2f *Notification in accordance with Article 42, sub a and e, of the Convention*

In accordance with Article 37, paragraph 2, Luxemburg deposited on 26 July 1977 its instrument of ratification of the Convention with the Ministry of Foreign Affairs of the Kingdom of the Netherlands.

In conformity with Article 38, paragraph 2, the Convention shall enter into force for Luxemburg on 24 September 1977.

On the occasion of the deposit of the said instrument of ratification the Government of Luxemburg made the following declarations and reservations (translation):

"—In accordance with Article 2 the Parquet Général is designated as the Central Authority.

—In pursuance of Article 4, paragraph 4, Letters of Request in German shall also be accepted.

—In pursuance of Article 23, Letters of Request issued for the purpose of obtaining pre-trial discovery of documents as know in Common Law countries shall not be executed.

—In accordance with the provisions of Article 16, the Parquet Général is designated as the authority competent to authorise the diplomatic officers or consular agents of a Contracting State to take, without compulsion, the evidence of persons other than the nationals of the State in aid of proceedings commenced in the courts of the State which they represent.

This authorisation, which is given in each specific case and to which specific conditions, where appropriate, are attached, is granted under the following general conditions:

1—The evidence shall be taken only within the precincts of an Embassy or Consultate.

2—The Parquet Général shall be given reasonable advance notice of the time, date and place of the taking of evidence so that it can, if it wishes, be represented.

3—A request to a person to appear shall, in accordance with the regulations, be in the form of an official document in French or German or accompanied by an (sic) translation into one of these languages stating:

a) that the evidence is to be taken in accordance with the provisions of the Convention on the taking of evidence abroad in civil or commercial matters concluded at The Hague on 18 March 1970, and in the framework of a judicial procedure followed in a jurisdiction designated by a Contracting State;

b) that the appearance is voluntary and that no prosecution in the requesting State will result from failure to appear;

c) that the parties to the action, where appropriate, consent to the taking of the evidence or are opposed to it for reasons to be given;

d) that the person requested to appear may be legally represented;

e) that the person requested to appear may invoke a privilege or a duty to refuse to give evidence.

—In accordance with the provisions of Article 17, the Parquet Général is designated as the authority competent to authorise persons designated in accordance with the regulations as commissioners to take evidence, without compulsion, in aid of proceedings commenced in the courts of another Contracting State.

This authorisation, which is given in the particular case and to which specific conditions, where appropriate, are attached, is granted under the following general conditions:

1—The Parquet Général shall be given reasonable advance notice of the time, date and place of the taking of evidence so that it can, if it wishes, be represented.

2—A request to a person to appear shall, in accordance with the regulations, be in the form of an official document in French or German or accompanied by a translation into one of these languages stating:

a) that the evidence is to be taken in accordance with the provisions of the Convention on the taking of evidence abroad in civil or commercial matters concluded at The Hague on 18 March 1970, and in the framework of a judicial procedure followed in a jurisdiction designated by a Contracting State;

b) that the appearance is voluntary and that no prosecution in the requesting State will result from failure to appear;

c) that the parties to the action, where appropriate, consent to the taking of the evidence or are opposed to it for reasons to be given;

d) that the person requested to appear may be legally represented;

e) that the person requested to appear may invoke a privilege or a duty to refuse to give evidence.

—In pursuance of Article 8, members of the judicial personnel of the requesting authority of a Contracting State may be present at the execution of a Letter of Request."

[2g] In conformity with Article 39, paragraph 2, the instrument of accession by the United Mexican States to the above-mentioned Convention was deposited with the Ministry of Foreign Affairs of the Kingdom of the Netherlands on 27 July 1989.

The instrument of accession of the United Mexican States contains the declarations and reservations the text of which together with a translation in English is annexed to this notification.

In accordance with paragraph 3 of Article 39, the Convention will enter into force for the United Mexican States on 25 September 1989.

According to Article 39, paragraph 4, of the Convention the accession will have effect only as regards the relations between the United Mexican States and such Contracting States as will have declared their acceptance of the accession. Such declarations shall be deposited at the Ministry of Foreign Affairs of the Kingdom of the Netherlands.

Unofficial translation

A) TRANSMISSION AND EXECUTION OF LETTERS OF REQUEST

1. *Central Authority (Article 2)*

Name: Secretaría de Relaciones Exteriores, Dirección General de Asuntos Jurídicos.
Address: Ricardo Flores Magón No. 1
Telephone: 782-34-40
Telex: 01762090

2. *Language requirements (Article 4)*

2.1 The United Mexican States does hereby make a special reservation related to the provisions of paragraph 2 of Article 4, and declares in accordance with paragraph 4 of the same Article, that letters of request sent to its Central Authority or judicial authorities shall be written in the spanish language or shall otherwise be accompanied by a translation into said language.

B) TAKING OF EVIDENCE ABROAD BY DIPLOMATIC OFFICERS, CONSULAR AGENTS AND COMMISSIONS (CHAPTER II)

3. The United Mexican States makes a special and complete reservation concerning the provisions contained in Articles 17 and 18 of this Chapter in relation to the "commissioners" and the use of measures to compulsion by diplomatic officers and consular agents.

C) FORMULATION OF PRE-TRIAL DISCOVERY OF DOCUMENTS

4. With reference to Article 23 of the Convention, the United Mexican States declares that according to Mexican law, it shall only be able to comply with letters of request issued for the purpose of obtaining the production and transcription of documents when the following requirements are met:

a) that the judicial proceeding has been commenced;

b) that the documents are reasonably identifiable as to date, subject and other relevant information and that the request specifies those facts and circumstances that lead the requesting party to reasonable believe that the requested documents are known to the person from whom they are requested or that they are in his possession or under his control or custody;

c) that the direct relationship between the evidence or information sought and the pending proceeding be identified.

D) OTHER TRANSMISSION CHANNEL TO THE JUDICIAL AUTHORITIES DIFFERENT FROM THOSE PROVIDED FOR IN ARTICLE 2

5. In regard to Article 27, paragraph a) of the Convention, the United Mexican States does hereby declare that the letters of request may be transmitted to its judicial authorities not only through the Central Authority but also through diplomatic or consular channels or through judicial channels (directly sent from the foreign court to the Mexican Court), providing that in the latter case all requirements relating to legalization of signatures are fulfilled.

6. In regard to Article 32 of the Convention, the United Mexican States informs that it is a State Party to the Interamerican Convention on the Taking of Evidence Abroad, signed in Panama on January the thirtieth, nineteen hundred and seventy-five, as well as to its Additional Protocol signed in La Paz, Bolivia, on May the twenty-fourth, nineteen hundred and eighty-four.

In accordance with Article 39 the Convention will enter into force between the United Mexican States and

Norway	20 November 1989
Israel	17 December 1989
the United States of America	24 December 1989
Argentina	25 December 1989
Finland	16 January 1990
Denmark	22 January 1990
the United Kingdom of Great Britain and Northern Ireland	16 March 1990
(also for Anguilla, the Cayman Islands, the Falkland Islands, Gibraltar, Guernsey, Hong Kong, the Isle of Man, Jersey, South Georgia and the South Sandwich Islands and the Sovereign Base Areas of Akrotiri and Dhekelia in the Island of Cyprus)	
the Federal Republic of Germany	23 March 1990
Czechoslovakia	2 April 1990
the Kingdom of the Netherlands (for the Kingdom in Europe)	16 April 1990
Aruba	18 May 1991
Sweden	17 April 1990
Portugal	14 October 1991
Spain	29 June 1994
Switzerland	13 January 1995
Italy	25 May 1996

[2h] *Notification in conformity with Article 42, sub c and e, of the Convention*

In accordance with Article 39, paragraph 2, the Principality of Monaco deposited its instrument of accession to the above-mentioned Convention with the Ministry of Foreign Affairs of the Kingdom of the Netherlands on 17 January 1986, with the following declarations and reservations:

Translation

1. In accordance with article 2, the Directorate of Judicial Services, MC 98025 MONACO CEDEX, is designated as the Central Authority.

2. Under article 4, paragraph 2, only Letters of Request drawn up in French or accompanied by a translation in that language shall be accepted.

3. Under article 23, Letters of Request issued for the purpose of obtaining pre-trial discovery of documents shall not be executed.

4. In accordance with articles 16 and 17, the Directorate of Judicial Services is designated as a competent authority for the purpose of authorising, as appropriate:

—the consular authorities of a Contracting State to take the evidence without compulsion of persons other than nationals of that State and in aid of proceedings commenced in a court of the State which they represent, or

—persons duly designated as commissioners to take evidence without compulsion in aid of proceedings commenced in a court of the Contracting State.

Such authorisation, which shall be granted for each particular case and may contain specific conditions, shall be subject to the following general conditions:

a) evidence shall be taken solely on the premises of consulates when the latter are situated within the Principality, and in other cases in the Palais de Justice of Monaco;

b) the Directorate of Judicial Services shall be informed of the date and time of the taking of the evidence in time to permit the Directorate to be represented, and, if necessary, to provide courtroom accommodation at the Palais de Justice of Monaco;

c) the persons concerned in the taking of evidence shall be duly summoned by an official document drawn up in French or accompanied by a translation in that language; this document shall indicate:

—that the taking of the evidence in question is being conducted in accordance with the provisions of the Hague Convention of 18 March 1970 on the Taking of Evidence Abroad in Civil or Commercial Matters, and that the procedure constitutes part of legal proceedings pursued under the specially designated jurisdiction of a Contracting State;

—that appearance is voluntary and non-appearance would not entail legal proceedings in the requesting State;

—that the person concerned in the taking of evidence may be represented by a lawyer of defense counsel;

—that the parties in the proceedings, should they be instituted, give their consent, and if not the document shall state the reason for their opposition;

—that the person concerned in the taking of evidence may apply to be exempted or barred from testifying.

A copy of the summonses shall be sent to the Directorate of Judicial Services, which is also to be kept informed of any difficulties.

Pursuant to Article 39, paragraph 3, the Convention will enter into force for the Principality of Monaco on 18 March 1986.

The accession will have effect only as regards the relations between Monaco and such Contracting States as will have declared their acceptance of the accession.

Notification pursuant to Article 42 of the Convention

In accordance with Article 39 the Convention will enter into force between Monaco and

the United States of America	January 30, 1988
The Kingdom of the Netherlands (Kingdom in Europe)	14 July 1986
Portugal	14 October, 1991
Spain	29 June 1994
Switzerland	13 January 1995

[2i] *Notification in conformity with Article 42, sub a and e, of the Convention.*

"The Kingdom of the Netherlands deposited on 8 April 1981, in accordance with Article 37, paragraph 2, of the Convention its instrument of ratification for the Kingdom in Europe of the above-mentioned Convention.

Upon the deposit of the instrument of ratification the Government of the Kingdom of the Netherlands has made the following declaration:

Translation

In the Netherlands the Convention shall be applied as follows:

Article 2

The Public Prosecutor at The Hague district Court is designated as the Central Authority.

Article 4

Letters of Request will be accepted in Dutch, German, English or French, or if they are accompanied by a translation into one of these languages.

The Netherlands does not undertake to translate documents for the execution of a Letter of Request.

Article 8

Members of the judicial personnel of another Contracting State may be present at the execution of a Letter of Request provided that the court which is responsible for execution authorises this and provided that any conditions which the court may impose are respected.

Article 11

Only the court which is responsible for executing the Letter of Request shall be competent to decide whether any person concerned by the execution has a privilege or duty to refuse to give evidence under the law of a State other than the State or origin; no such privilege or duty exists under Dutch law.

Article 14

Fees paid to experts and interpreters and costs occasioned by the use of a special procedure requested by the State of origin under Article 9, paragraph 2 of the Convention shall be borne by the State or origin.

Article 16

In the Netherlands, no prior permission is required for the taking of evidence as provided for in Article 16.

Article 17

The permission referred to in Article 17 must be requested from the President of the District Court in the area in which evidence is to be taken. If evidence is to be taken from witnesses or experts, the area in question will be that in which the witnesses or experts, or the majority of them reside. If the President gives permission, he may impose any conditions which he considers necessary to ensure that the evidence is taken in proper manner. He may decide that the evidence should be taken at the court, under the supervision of a judge designated by him. Permission will only be granted if the following conditions are met:

a) the witness or expert concerned must have been duly summoned; the summons must be in Dutch or must be accompanied by a Dutch translation and must contain;

—the facts of the case and a summary of the proceedings in connection with which the evidence is to be taken, and details of the court which has requested the evidence;

—a statement to the effect that there is no obligation for the witness or expert to appear, and that if he refuses to appear, to take an oath, to give his word of honour or to give evidence, he will not incur any penalty or measure of any kind, either in the Netherlands or in the State where the proceedings have been instituted;

—a statement to the effect that the person concerned may be legally represented;

—a statement to the effect that in so far as the person concerned has a privilege or duty to refuse to give evidence, he may do so;

—a statement to the effect that the commissioner will reimburse expenses incurred by the witness or expert in connection with his appearance to give evidence.

b) A copy of the summons must be forwarded to the President.

c) The request for permission must state the reasons why the taking of evidence has been entrusted to a commissioner and it must state the commissioner's official status unless he is a lawyer competent to practise in the Netherlands.

d) The costs of taking the evidence, i.e. the expenses of the witnesses, experts or interpreters, must be reimbursed in full.

Article 23

The Netherlands will not execute Letters of Request issued for the purpose of obtaining pre-trial discovery of documents as known in Common Law countries.

For the purposes of Article 23 of the Convention, "Letters of Request issued for the purpose of obtaining pre-trial discovery of documents as known in Common Law countries", which the Netherlands will not execute, are defined by the Government of the Kingdom of the Netherlands as being any Letters of Request which require a person:

a. to state which of the documents which are of relevance to the proceedings to which the Letter of Request relates have been in his possession, custody or power; or

b. to produce any document other than particular documents specified in the Letter of Request as being documents which the court which is conducting the proceedings believes to be in his possession, custody or power.

Article 26

The Netherlands will request that any State of origin which has made a request pursuant to paragraph 1 of Article 26 should reimburse the fees and costs to which this paragraph refers.

In accordance with Article 38, paragraph 2, the Convention will enter into force for the Kingdom of the Netherlands (the Kingdom in Europe) on 7 June 1981."

In accordance with Article 40, paragraph 2, the Kingdom of the Netherlands declared on 28 May 1986 that the Convention shall extend to Aruba.

In conformity with Article 40, paragraph 3, the Convention will enter into force for Aruba on 27 July 1986.

The Permanent Bureau of the Hague Conference on private international law presents its compliments to the Diplomatic Missions of the Member States and to the National Organs and has the honour to inform them that, in accordance with Article 2 of the above-mentioned Convention, the

Kingdom of the Netherlands

has designated the *"Procureur-Generaal in Aruba van het Gemeenschappelijk Hof van Justitie van de Nederlandse Antillen en Aruba"* (the Attorney-General in Aruba of the joint Court of Justice of the Netherlands Antilles and of Aruba) as Central Authority for *Aruba.*

The Convention is being applied in Aruba subject to the same declarations as made upon ratification of the Convention on 8 April 1981 by the Kingdom of the Netherlands for the Kingdom in Europe. In addition, in conformity with Article 4, paragraphs 3 and 4, Aruba will not accept Letters of Request in French, unless accompanied by a translation into Dutch, English or Spanish.

The Permanent Bureau avails itself of this opportunity to renew to the Diplomatic Missions of the Members States and to the National Organs an assurance of its highest consideration and esteem.

[3] With the following reservation:

"In conformity with article 33, Norway enters a reservation to paragraph 2 of article 4 to the effect that Letters of Request in the French language will not be accepted."

And with the following declarations:

"I. The Royal Ministry of Justice and Police is designated as the Central Authority with reference to article 2 and as the Competent Authority with reference to articles 15, 16 and 17.

II. With reference to article 4, paragraph 3, the Kingdom of Norway declares that letters in the Danish or Swedish languages can be sent to the Central Authority.

III. By accepting Letters of Request in another language than the Norwegian, the Kingdom of Norway does not undertake to execute the request, or transmit the evidence thus obtained in this other language; nor to have translated the documents which establish the execution of the Letter of Request.

IV. By virtue of article 15, evidence can be taken by diplomatic officers or consular agents only if, upon application, prior permission to that effect has been granted.

V. By virtue of article 23, the Kingdom of Norway declares that it will not execute Letters of Request issued for the purpose of obtaining pre-trial discovery of documents as known in Common Law countries."

The declaration made by the Kingdom of Norway in accordance with article 23 concerning "Letters of Request issued for the purpose of obtaining pre-trial discovery of documents" shall apply only to Letters of Request which require a person

a) to state what documents relevant to the proceedings to which the Letter of Request relates, are, or have been, in his possession, other than particular documents specified in the Letter of Request; or

b) to produce any documents other than particular documents which are specified in the Letter of Request, and which are likely to be in his possession.

[3a] The Permanent Bureau of the Hague Conference on private international law presents its compliments to the Diplomatic Missions of the Member States and to the National Organs and has the honour to inform them that, by instrument deposited on 13 February 1996 with the Ministry of Foreign Affairs of the Kingdom of the Netherlands,

the *Republic of Poland*

acceded to the above-mentioned Convention.

./. The instrument of accession contains a reservation, the text of which is attached.

Translation

Articles 23 et 33 will not be applicable within the territory of the Republic of Poland.

./. The instrument of accession was accompanied by the following declarations and reservations, the text of which is also attached.

Translation

Declarations

Article 2, Paragraph 1—the Central Authority designated to receive requests for service coming from another Contracting State shall be the Ministry of Justice.

Article 8—the Authority designated to complete a certificate of service in the republic of Poland shall be the Ministry of Justice.

Article 24 and Article 27, sub-paragraph a—other authorities (in addition to the Central Authority) designated to receive requests for service shall be the voivodship courts.

Reservations

Article 23—the Republic of Poland declares, that it will not execute Letters of Request issued for the purpose of obtaining "pre-trial discovery of documents" as known in common law countries.

Article 33—the Republic of Poland excludes the application on its territory:

—the provisions of Article 4, paragraph 2,

—the provisions of Chapter II, excluding provisions of Article 15.

In accordance with paragraph 3 of Article 39, the Convention will enter into force for the *Republic of Poland* on *13 April 1996.*

According to Article 39, paragraph 4, of the Convention the accession will have effect only as regards the relations between the Republic of Poland and such Contracting States as will have declared their acceptance of the accession. Such declarations shall be deposited with the Ministry of Foreign Affairs of the Kingdom of the Netherlands.

In accordance with Article 39, paragraph 5, the Convention will enter into force between Poland and

Luxembourg . . . 2 June 1996
Denmark . . . 22 June 1996
Slovak Republic . . . 25 June 1996
Israel . . . 30 June 1996
Finland . . . 5 August 1996
Netherlands (for the Kingdom in Europe and Aruba) . . . 16 August 1996

3b With the following reservations and declarations:

(Translation)

"a) In accordance with Article 33 of the Convention, the Portuguese State makes the following reservations:
1. exclusion of the application of paragraph 2 of Article 4;
2. exclusion of the application of Chapter II, with the exception of Article 15.

b) In accordance with Articles 15 and 23 of the Convention, the Portuguese State makes the following declarations:
1. The Portuguese State declares that the evidence as referred to in Article 15, can only be taken if permission to that effect is given by the appropriate authority designated by it upon application made by the diplomatic or consular agent;
2. The Portuguese State declares that it will not execute Letters of Request issued for the purpose of obtaining pre-trial discovery of documents as known in Common Law Countries.

c) With regard to Articles 2 and 15 of the Convention, the competent Portuguese authority will be the Director-General of the Judiciary Department ("Direccào-Geral dos Serviços Judiciários") of the Ministry of Justice.".

3c In accordance with Article 39, paragraph 3, the Convention shall enter into force for the Republic of Singapore on December 26, 1978.

Notification in accordance with Convention Article 42(c) and (e):

On October 27, 1978, the Ministry of Foreign Affairs of the Kingdom of the Netherlands received the instrument of accession of the Republic of Singapore to the Convention on the Taking of Evidence Abroad in Civil and Commercial Matters in accordance with Article 39, Paragraph 2, of the aforesaid Convention.

At the time of its accession the Government of the Republic of Singapore made the following reservations:

"(i) The entire Chapter II of the Convention is not applicable to the Republic of Singapore; and

"(ii) With regard to Article 4, paragraph 2, the Republic of Singapore will not accept a Letter of Request in a language other than English, since this language is the one used by the judicial personnel in Singapore."

In accordance with Article 23 the Government of the Republic of Singapore has declared that the Republic of Singapore will not execute Letters of Request issued for the purpose of obtaining pre-trial discovery of documents as known in Common Law countries.

The Government of the Republic of Singapore has further declared that it understands "Letters of Request issued for the purpose of obtaining pre-trial discovery of documents" for the purposes of the foregoing declaration as including any Letter of Request which requires a person:

(a) to state what documents relevant to the proceedings to which the Letter of Request relates are, or have been, in his possession, custody or power; or

(b) to produce any documents other than particular documents specified in the Letter of Request as being documents appearing to the requested court to be, or likely to be, in his possession, custody or power. It is also understood that the reference to civil or commercial actions in the Convention does not include tax matters for the Republic of Singapore.

In accordance with Article 39, paragraph 3, the Convention shall enter into force for the Republic of Singapore on December 26, 1978.

The accession shall be effective only for relations between the Republic of Singapore and contracting States that declare that they accept this accession.

Notification in conformity with Article 42, paragraph e, of the Convention:

In accordance with Article 35 of the Convention Singapore notified the Ministry of Foreign Affairs of the Kingdom of the Netherlands by a Note dated August 4, 1979, that the Central Authority which will undertake to receive Letters of Request referred to in Article 2 of the Convention, is the Registrar of the Supreme Court.

In accordance with Article 39, paragraph 5, the Convention will enter into force between Singapore and

Spain . . . 28 August 1994
Switzerland . . . 13 January 1995
United States . . . 24 October 1995

3d By notification dated March 15, 1993 the Slovak Republic communicated the following: "In accordance with relevant principles and norms of international law and to extent defined by it, the Slovak Republic, as a successor State, born from the division of the Czech and Slovak Federal Republic, considers itself bound, as of January 1, 1993, i.e. the date of the division of the Czechoslovak Federation, by multilateral international treaties to which the Czech and Slovak Federal Republic was a party at that date, including reservations and declarations in respect of provisions made earlier by Czechoslovakia, as well as objections by Czechoslovakia in respect of reservations made by other treaty parties", which are as follows: [Same declarations and reservations, *mutatis mutandis*, under Czech Republic, see footnote 1d].

The Slovak Republic has designated in accordance with Articles 2 and 8 [of the Convention] the following Central Authority:

Ministerstvo spravodlivosti Slovenskej republiky
Zupne namestie 13, 813 11 Bratislava
Slovak Republic
fax: (00427) 5316035

3e *Notification pursuant to Article 42 of the Convention*

In accordance with Article 37, paragraph 2, of the above-mentioned Convention Spain deposited its instrument of ratification with the Ministry of Foreign Affairs of the Kingdom of the Netherlands on 22 May 1987.

The instrument of ratification contains the following reservation:

"De conformidad con el artículo 33 en relacíon con el artículo 4.º, párrafo 2, Espãna no aceptará comisiones rogatorias que no estén redactadas en español o acompañadas de una traducción.

Translation

In accordance with Article 33 in relation with Article 4, paragraph 2, Spain will not accept Letters of Request which are not drawn up in Spanish or accompanied by a translation.

and the following declarations:

"a) La Autoridad Central española a que se refiere el artículo 2 será: El Ministerio de Justicia.-Secretaría General Técnica.-(San Bernardo, 45. 28015 MADRID), con exclusíon de cualquier otra Autoridad.

b) Previa autorización del Ministerio de Justicia espaõnol, un Juez del Estado requirente podrá intervenir en el cumplimiento de una comisíon rogatoria, de conformidad con el artículo 8.

c) De conformidad con los artículos 16 y 17, la prueba podrá ser practicada, sin necesidad de autorización previa de la Autoridad española, en los locales de la Representacíon diplomática o consular del Estado requirente.

d) A tenor del artículo 23, España no acepta las comisiones rogatorias derivadas del procedimiento "pre-trial discovery of documents" conocido en los países del "Common Law".".

Translation

a) The Spanish Central Authority is:

"La Direccion General de Codificacion y Cooperacion Juridica Internacional, Ministerio de Justicia e Interior", with exclusion of any other Authority.

b) With prior authorization of the Spanish Ministry of Justice, a Judge of the requesting State may intervene in the execution of a Letter of Request, in accordance with Article 8.

c) In accordance with Articles 16 and 17, the evidence may be taken, without prior permission of the Spanish Authority, in the premises of the diplomatic or consular representation of the requesting State.

d) Pursuant to Article 23 Spain does not accept Letters of Request derived from the "pre-trial discovery of documents" procedure known in Common Law countries.

The Convention will enter into force for Spain on 21 July 1987.

3f With the following declarations:

(Translation)

—That, in pursuance of Article 4, para. 4, Letters of Request in the Danish and Norwegian languages will be accepted;

—That, in pursuance of Article 8, members of the judicial personnel of the requesting authority of another Contracting State may be present at the execution of a Letter of Request without prior authorisation;

—That, in pursuance of Article 15, para. 2, a diplomatic officer or consular agent may only take evidence if permission to do so has been granted by the competent Swedish authority;

—That, in pursuance of Article 23, Letters of Request issued for the purpose of obtaining pre-trial discovery of documents as known in Common Law countries will not be executed;

—That documents provided by Sweden which establish that a Letter of Request has been executed will be in the Swedish language only.

Ministry of Foreign Affairs, Stockholm, has been designated as the Central Authority referred to in Article 2 and also as the Competent Authority referred to in Article 15-17.

Additional declaration of July 11, 1980:

"The Swedish Government understands 'Letters of Request issued for the purpose of pre-trial discovery of documents' for the purposes of the foregoing Declaration as including any Letter of Request which requires a person:

a) to state what documents relevant to the proceedings to which the Letter of Request relates are, or have been, in his possession, custody or power; or

b) to produce any documents other than particular documents specified in the Letter of Request, which are likely to be in his possession, custody or power."

3g *Notification pursuant to Article 42 of the Convention*

In accordance with Article 37, paragraph 2, of the above-mentioned Convention *Switzerland* deposited its instrument of ratification with the Ministry of Foreign Affairs of the Kingdom of the Netherlands on 2 November 1994.

The instrument of ratification contains the following reservation and declarations:

Translation

"Re Article 1

1. With regard to Article 1, Switzerland takes the view that the Convention applies exclusively to the Contracting States. Moreover, regarding the conclusions of the Special Commission which met in The Hague in April 1989, Switzerland believes that, whatever the opinion of the Contracting States on the exclusive application of the Convention, priority should in any event be given to the procedures provided for in the Convention regarding requests for the taking of evidence abroad.

Re Articles 2 and 24

2. In accordance with Article 35, first paragraph, Switzerland designates the cantonal authorities listed in the annex as Central Authorities as referred to in Articles 2 and 24 of the Convention. Requests for the taking of evidence or the execution of any other judicial act may also be addressed to the Federal Justice and Police Department in Bern, which will forward them to the appropriate Central Authority.

Re Article 4, second and third paragraphs

3. In accordance with Articles 33 and 35, Switzerland declares, with regard to Article 4, second and third paragraphs, that Letters of Request and any accompanying documents must be in the language of the authority requested to execute them, *i.e.* in German, French or Italian, or accompanied by a translation into one of these languages, depending on the part of Switzerland in which the documents are to be

executed. The documents confirming execution will be drawn up in the official language of the requested authority (*cf.* annex).

Re Article 8

4. In accordance with Article 35, second paragraph, Switzerland declares, with regard to Article 8, that members of the judicial personnel of the requesting authority of another Contracting State may be present at the execution of a Letter of Request provided they have obtained prior authorization from the executing authority.

Re Articles 15, 16 and 17

5. In accordance with Article 35, Switzerland declares that evidence may be taken according to Articles 15, 16 and 17 subject to prior authorization by the Federal Justice and Police Department. A request for authorization must be addressed to the Central Authority in the canton where the evidence is to be taken.

Re Article 23

6. In accordance with Article 23, Switzerland declares that Letters of Request issued for the purpose of obtaining pre-trial discovery of documents will not be executed if:
   a. the request has no direct and necessary link with the proceedings in question; or
   b. a person is required to indicate what documents relating to the case are or were in his/her possession or keeping or at his/her disposal; or
   c. a person is required to produce documents other than those mentioned in the request for legal assistance, which are probably in his/her possession or keeping or at his/her disposal; or
   d. interests worthy of protection of the concerned persons are endangered".

The list of Central Authorities for the Cantons is attached.

Autorités centrales cantonales — *Annexe*

Cantons	Langue(s) officielle(s) (a=allemand) (f=français) (i=italien)	Adresses	Numéros de téléphone
Appenzell Ausserrhoden	a	Kantonsgericht Appenzell A.Rh., 9043 Trogen	071/ 94 24 61
Appenzell Innerrhoden	a	Kantonsgericht Appenzell I.Rh., 9050 Appenzell	071/ 87 95 51
Aargau	a	Obergericht des Kantons Aargau, 5000 Aarau	064/ 21 19 40
Basel-Landschaft	a	Obergericht des Kantons Basel-Landschaft, 4410 Liestal	061/925 51 11
Basel-Stadt	a	Appellationsgericht Basel-Stadt, 4054 Basel	061/267 81 81
Bern	a/f	Justizdirektion des Kantons Bern, 3011 Bern	031/633 76 76
Fribourg	f/a	Tribunal cantonal, 1700 Fribourg	037/ 25 39 10
Genève	f	Parquet du Procureur général, 1211 Genève 3	022/319 21 11
Glarus	a	Obergericht des Kantons Glarus, 8750 Glarus	058/ 61 15 32
Graubünden	a	Justiz-, Polizei- und Sanitäts-departement Graubünden, 7001 Chur	081/ 21 21 21
Jura	f	Département de la Justice, 2800 Delémont	066/ 21 51 11
Luzern	a	Obergericht des Kantons Luzern, 6002 Luzern	041/ 24 51 11
Neuchâtel	f	Département de Justice, 2001 Neuchâtel	038/ 22 31 11
Nidwalden	a	Kantonsgericht Nidwalden, 6370 Stans	041/ 63 79 50
Obwalden	a	Kantonsgericht des Kantons Obwalden, 6060 Sarnen	041/ 66 92 22
St. Gallen	a	Kantonsgericht St. Gallen, 9001 St. Gallen	071/ 21 31 11
Schaffhausen	a	Obergericht des Kantons Schaffhausen, 8201 Schaffhausen	053/ 82 74 22
Schwyz	a	Kantonsgericht Schwyz, 6430 Schwyz	043/ 24 11 24
Solothurn	a	Obergericht des Kantons Solothurn, 4500 Solothurn	065/ 21 73 11
Tessin	i	Tribunale di appello, 6901 Lugano	091/ 21 51 11
Thurgau	a	Obergericht des Kantons Thurgau, 8500 Frauenfeld	054/ 22 31 21
Uri	a	Gerichtskanzlei Uri, 6460 Altdorf	044/ 4 22 44
Valais	f/a	Tribunal cantonal, 1950 Sion	027/ 22 93 93
Vaud	f	Tribunal cantonal, 1014 Lausanne	021/313 15 11
Zug	a	Obergericht des Kantons Zug, Rechtshilfe, 6300 Zug	042/ 25 33 11
Zürich	a	Obergericht des Kantons Zürich, Rechtshilfe, 8023 Zürich	01/257 91 91

3h *Notification in conformity with Article 42, under a and e, of the Convention:*

In accordance with Article 37, paragraph 2, the United Kingdom of Great Britain and Northern Ireland deposited on July 16, 1976 its instrument of ratification with the Ministry of Foreign Affairs of the Netherlands.

In conformity with Article 38, paragraph 2, the Convention shall enter into force for the United Kingdom on September 14, 1976.

The instrument of ratification mentioned above, contains the following reservation: ". . . . in accordance with the provisions of Article 33 the United Kingdom will not accept a Letter of Request in French."

On the occasion of the deposit of the said instrument of ratification the Government of the United Kingdom of Great Britain and Northern Ireland made the following declarations:

"1. In accordance with Article 8 Her Majesty's Government declare that members of the judicial personnel of the requesting authority may be present at the execution of a Letter of Request.
2. In accordance with Article 18 Her Majesty's Government declare that a diplomatic officer, consular agent or commissioner authorised to take evidence under Articles 15, 16 and 17 may apply to the competent authority designated hereinbefore for appropriate assistance to obtain such evidence by compulsion provided that the Contracting State whose diplomatic officer, consular agent or commissioner makes the application has made a declaration affording reciprocal facilities under Article 18.
3. In accordance with Article 23 Her Majesty's Government declare that the United Kingdom will not execute Letters of Request issued for the purpose of obtaining pre-trial discovery of documents. Her Majesty's Government further declare that Her Majesty's Government understand "Letters of Request issued for the purpose of obtaining pre-trial discovery of documents" for the purposes of the foregoing Declaration as including any Letter of Request which requires a person:—
   a. to state what documents relevant to the proceedings to which the Letter of Request relates are, or have been, in his possession, custody, or power; or
   b. to produce any documents other than particular documents specified in the Letter of Request as being documents appearing to the requested court to be, or to be likely to be, in his possession, custody or powers.
4. In accordance with Article 27 Her Majesty's Government declare that by the law and practice of the United Kingdom the prior permission referred to in Articles 16 and 17 is not required in respect of diplomatic officers, consular agents or commissioners of a Contracting State which does not require permission to be obtained for the purposes of taking evidence under Articles 16 and 17."

In accordance with Article 35 of the Convention, the Government of the United Kingdom made the following designations:

1. Under Article 2: the Foreign and Commonwealth Office.
2. Under Article 16: the Foreign and Commonwealth Office.
3. Under Article 17: the Foreign and Commonwealth Office.
4. Under Article 18: the Senior Master of the Supreme Court (Queen's Bench Division) for England and Wales; the Crown Agent for Scotland, for Scotland; the Master (Queen's Bench and Appeals). The address of the Master (Queen's Bench and Appeals) is Royal Courts of Justice, Belfast 1.
5. Under Article 24: the Senior Master of the Supreme Court (Queen's Bench Division) in England and Wales; the Crown Agent for Scotland, for Scotland; the Master (Queen's Bench and Appeals). The address of the Master (Queen's Bench and Appeals) is Royal Courts of Justice, Belfast 1.

By notification received on June 23, 1978 by the Ministry of Foreign Affairs of the Netherlands, the Convention was extended to Hong Kong effective Aug. 22, 1978, with the following declaration:

"(a) In accordance with the provisions of article 4 and article 33 of the Convention, Hong Kong will not accept a Letter of Request in French.

(b) In accordance with article 35 and article 24 of the Convention, the Registrar of the Supreme Court of Hong Kong is designated as an additional authority competent to receive Letters of Request for execution in Hong Kong.

(c) In accordance with article 35 and articles 16 and 17 of the Convention, the Chief Secretary is designated as the competent authority of Hong Kong."

Extension to Gibraltar.—

In accordance with Article 40, Paragraph 3, the Convention shall enter into force for Gibraltar on January 20, 1979.

The extension declaration contains the following reservation: "In accordance with the provisions of Article 4 and Article 33 of the Convention, Gibraltar will not accept a Letter of Request in French."

In accordance with Article 35 of the Convention the following designations have been made;

"(a) Under Articles 16 and 17 of the Convention, the Deputy Governor is designated as the competent authority for Gibraltar;

"(b) Under Article 18 of the Convention, the Registrar of the Supreme Court of Gibraltar is designated as the competent authority;

"(c) Under Article 24 of the Convention, the Deputy Governor is designated as an additional authority competent to receive Letters of Request for execution in Gibraltar."

[For declarations see the original note.]

Notification in conformity with article 42, sub d and e, of the Convention

By a letter dated November 20, 1978, and received at the Ministry of Foreign Affairs of the Kingdom of the Netherlands on November 21, 1978, the Ambassador of the United Kingdom of Great Britain and Northern Ireland at The Hague, referring to the deposit on July 16, 1976 of the instrument of ratification of the above-mentioned Convention by the United Kingdom of Great Britain and Northern Ireland, declared in accordance with article 40 that the Convention shall extend to Gibraltar. The Convention shall enter into force for Gibraltar on January 20, 1979.

The declaration of extension contains the following reservation:

". . . . in accordance with the provisions of Article 4 and Article 33 of the Convention, Gibraltar will not accept a Letter of Request in French."

In accordance with Article 35 of the Convention the following designations have been made:

a) under Articles 16 and 17 of the Convention the Deputy governor is designated as the competent authority for Gibraltar;
b) under Article 18 of the Convention, the Registrar of the Supreme Court of Gibraltar is designated as the competent authority;
c) under Article 24 of the Convention, the Deputy Governor is designated as an additional authority competent to receive Letters of Request for execution in Gibraltar, and the following declarations:

1. In accordance with Article 8, members of the judicial personnel of the requesting authority may be present at the execution of a Letter of Request in Gibraltar.

2. In accordance with Article 18, a diplomatic officer, consular agent or commissioner authorised to take evidence under Articles 15, 16 and 17 of the Convention may apply to the competent authority in Gibraltar designated hereinbefore for appropriate assistance to obtain such evidence by compulsion provided that the Contracting State whose diplomatic officer, consular agent or commissioner makes the application has made a declaration affording reciprocal facilities under Article 18.
3. In accordance with Article 23, Gibraltar will not execute Letters of Request issued for the purpose of obtaining pre-trial discovery of documents. The Government of Gibraltar understands "Letters of Request issued for the purpose of obtaining pre-trial discovery of documents" for the purposes of the foregoing Declaration as including any Letter of Request which requires a person:
   a) to state what documents relevant to the proceedings to which the Letter of Request relates are, or have been, in his possession, custody or power; or
   b) to produce any documents other than particular documents specified in the Letter of Request as being documents appearing to the requested court to be, or likely to be, in his possession, custody or power.
4. In accordance with Article 27, by the law and practice of Gibraltar the prior permission referred to in Articles 16 and 17 of the Convention is not required in respect of diplomatic officers, consular agents or commissioners of a Contracting State which does not require permission to be obtained for the purposes of taking evidence under Articles 16 or 17.

Extension to Sovereign Base Areas of Akrotiri and Dhekalia in the Island of Cyprus.—

"The Convention shall enter into force for the Sovereign Base Areas of Akrotiri and Dhekelia in the Island of Cyprus on August 24, 1979.

The declaration of extension contains the following reservation:

". . . in accordance with the provisions of Article 4 and Article 33 of the Convention, the Sovereign Base Areas will not accept a Letter of Request in French.".

In accordance with Article 35 of the Convention the following designations have been made:

a) under Articles 16 and 17 of the Convention the Chief Officer, Sovereign Base Areas, is designated as the competent authority for the Sovereign Base Areas;
b) under Article 18 of the Convention, the Senior Registrar of the Judge's Court of the Sovereign Base Areas of Akrotiri and Dhekelia is designated as the competent authority;
c) under Article 24 of the Convention, the Senior Registrar of the Judge's Court of the Sovereign Base Areas of Akrotiri and Dhekelia is designated as an additional authority competent to receive Letters of Request for execution in the Sovereign Base Areas.

and the following declarations:

1. In accordance with Article 8, members of the judicial personnel of the requesting authority may be present at the execution of a Letter of Request in the Sovereign Base Areas.
2. In accordance with Article 18, a diplomatic officer, consular agent or commissioner authorised to take evidence under Article 15, 16 and 17 of the Convention may apply to the competent authority in the Sovereign Base Areas designated hereinbefore for appropriate assistance to obtain such evidence by compulsion provided that the Contracting State whose diplomatic officer, consular agent or commissioner makes the application has made a declaration affording reciprocal facilities under Article 18.
3. In accordance with Article 23, the Sovereign Base Areas will not execute Letters of Request issued for the purpose of obtaining pre-trial discovery of documents. The Administration of the Sovereign Base Areas understands "Letters of Request issued for the purpose of obtaining pre-trial discovery of documents" for the purposes of the foregoing Declaration as including any Letter of Request which requires a person:
   a) to state what documents relevant to the proceedings to which the Letter of Request relates are, or have been, in his possession, custody or power; or
   b) to produce any documents other than particular documents specified in the Letter of Request as being documents appearing to the requested court to be, or likely to be, in his possession, custody or power.
4. In accordance with Article 27, by the law and practice of the Sovereign Base Areas the prior permission referred to in Articles 16 and 17 of the Convention is not required in respect of diplomatic officers, consular agents or commissioners of a Contracting State which does not require permission to be obtained for the purposes of taking evidence under Articles 16 or 17."

Extension to Falkland Islands and Dependencies.—

Notification in conformity with Article 42, sub d and e, of the Convention

By a letter dated November 23, 1979, and received at the Ministry of Foreign Affairs of the Kingdom of the Netherlands on November 26, 1979, the Ambassador of the United Kingdom of Great Britain and Northern Ireland at The Hague, referring to the deposit on July 16, 1976 of the instrument of ratification of the above-mentioned Convention by the United Kingdom of Great Britain and Northern Ireland, declared in accordance with Article 40 that the Convention shall extend to the Falkland Islands and Dependencies.

The Convention shall enter into force for the Falkland Islands and Dependencies on January 25, 1980.

The declaration of extension contains the following reservation:

". . . . in accordance with the provisions of Article 4 and Article 33 of the Convention, the Falkland Islands and Dependencies will not accept a Letter of Request in French." In accordance with Article 35 of the Convention the following designations have been made:

a) under Articles 16, 17 and 18 of the Convention the Judge of the Supreme Court of the Falkland Islands, is designated as the competent authority for the Falkland Islands and Dependencies;
b) under Article 24 of the Convention, the Governor of the Falkland Islands and its dependencies is designated as an additional authority competent to receive Letters of Request for execution in the Falkland Islands and Dependencies.

and the following declarations:

1. In accordance with Article 8, members of the judicial personnel of the requesting authority may be present at the execution of a Letter of Request in the Falkland Islands and Dependencies.
2. In accordance with Article 18, a diplomatic officer, consular agent or commissioner authorised to take evidence under Article 15, 16, and 17 of the Convention may apply to the competent authority in the Falkland Islands and Dependencies designated hereinbefore for appropriate assistance to obtain such evidence by compulsion provided that the Contracting State whose diplomatic officer, consular agent or commissioner makes the application has made a declaration affording reciprocal facilities under Article 18.
3. In accordance with Article 23, the Falkland Islands and Dependencies will not execute Letters of Request issued for the purpose of obtaining pre-trial discovery of documents.
   The Governor of the Falkland Islands and its dependencies understands "Letters of Request issued for the purposes of obtaining pre-trial discovery of documents" for the purposes of the foregoing declaration as including any Letter of Request which requires a person:
   a) to state what documents relevant to the proceedings to which the Letter of Request relates are, or have been, in his possession, custody or power; or
   b) to produce any documents other than particular documents specified in the Letter of Request as being documents appearing to the requested court to be, or likely to be, in his possession, custody or power.
4. In accordance with Article 27, by the law and practice of the Falkland Islands and Dependencies the prior permission referred to in Articles 16 and 17 of the Convention is not required in respect of diplomatic officers, consular agents or commissioners of a Contracting State which does not require permission to be obtained for the purposes of taking evidence under Articles 16 or 17.

Extension to Isle of Man.—

Notification is conformity with article 42, sub d and e, of the Convention

By a letter dated April 16, 1980, and received at the Ministry of Foreign Affairs of the Kingdom of the Netherlands on April 16, 1980, the Ambassador of the United Kingdom of Great Britain and Northern Ireland at The Hague, referring to the deposit on July 16, 1976 of the instrument of ratification of the above-mentioned Convention by the United Kingdom of Great Britain and Northern Ireland, declared in accordance with article 40 that the Convention shall extend to the Isle of Man.

The Convention shall enter into force for the Isle of Man on June 15, 1980.

The declaration of extension contains the following reservation:

". . . . in accordance with the provisions of Article 4 and Article 33 of the Convention, the Isle of Man will not accept a Letter of Request in French."

In accordance with Article 35 of the Convention the following designations have been made:

a) under Articles 16, 17 and 18 of the Convention Her Majesty's First Deemster and Clerk of the Rolls is designated as the competent authority for the Isle of Man;
b) under Article 24 of the Convention, Her Majesty's First Deemster and Clerk of the Rolls is designated as an additional authority competent to receive Letters of Request for execution in the Isle of Man.

and the following declarations:

1. In accordance with Article 8, members of the judicial personnel of the requesting authority may be present at the execution of a Letter of Request in the Isle of Man.
2. In accordance with Article 18, a diplomatic officer, consular agent or commissioner authorised to take evidence under Article 15, 16 and 17 of the Convention may apply to the competent authority in the Isle of Man designated hereinbefore for appropriate assistance to obtain such evidence by compulsion provided that the Contracting State whose diplomatic officer, consul-ar agent or commissioner makes the application has made a declaration affording reciprocal facilities under Article 18.
3. In accordance with Article 23, the Isle of Man will not execute Letters of Request issued for the purpose of obtaining pre-trial discovery of documents.
   The Government of the Isle of Man understands "Letters of Request issued for the purpose of obtaining pre-trial discovery of documents" for the purposes of the foregoing declaration as including any Letter of Request which requires a person:
   a) to state what documents relevant to the proceedings to which the Letter of Request relates are, or have been, in his possession, custody or power; or
   b) to produce any documents other than particular documents specified in the Letter of Request as being documents appearing to the requested court to be, or likely to be, in his possession, custody or power.
4. In accordance with Article 27, by the law and practice of the Isle of Man the prior permission referred to in Articles 16 and 17 of the Convention is not required in respect of diplomatic officers, consular agents or commissioners of a Contracting State which does not require permission to be obtained for the purposes of taking evidence under Articles 16 or 17.

Extension to Cayman Islands.—

Notification in conformity with Article 42, sub d and e, of the Convention

By letter dated 16 September 1980 and received at the Ministry of Foreign Affairs of the Kingdom of the Netherlands on that same date, the Ambassador of the United Kingdom of Great Britain and Northern Ireland at The Hague referring to the deposit on 16 July 1976 of the instrument of ratification of the above-mentioned Convention by the United Kingdom of Great Britain and Northern Ireland declared in accordance with Article 40 that the Convention shall extend to the Cayman Islands.

The Convention will enter into force for the Cayman Islands on 15 November 1980.

The declaration of extension contains the following reservation:

". . . in accordance with the provisions of Article 4 and Article 33 of the Convention, . . . the Cayman Islands will not accept a Letter of Request in French".

In accordance with Article 35 of the Convention the following designations have been made:

a) Under Articles 16 and 17 of the Convention, the Attorney General is designated as the competent authority for the Cayman Islands;
b) Under Article 18 of the Convention, the Clerk of the Grand Court is designated as the competent authority;
c) Under Article 24 of the Convention, His Excellency the Governor is designated as an additional authority competent to receive Letters of Request for execution in the Cayman Islands.

and the following declarations:

1. In accordance with Article 8, members of the judicial personnel of the requesting authority may be present at the execution of a Letter of Request in the Cayman Islands.
2. In accordance with Article 18, a diplomatic officer, consular agent or commissioner authorised to take evidence under Article 15, 16 and 17 of the Convention may apply to the competent authority in the Cayman Islands designated hereinbefore for appropriate assistance to obtain such evidence by compulsion provided that the Contracting State whose diplomatic officer, consular agent or commissioner makes the application has made a declaration affording reciprocal facilities under Article 18.
3. In accordance with Article 23, the Cayman Islands will not execute Letters of Request issued for the purpose of obtaining pre-trial discovery of documents. The Government of the Cayman Islands understand "Letters of Request issued for the purpose of obtaining pre-trial discovery of documents" for the purposes of the foregoing declaration as including any Letter of Request which requires a person:
   a) to state what documents relevant to the proceedings to which the Letter of Request relates are, or have been, in his possession, custody or power; or
   b) to produce any documents other than particular documents specified in the Letter of Request as being documents appearing to the requested court to be, or likely to be, in his possession, custody or power.
4. In accordance with Article 27, by the law and practice of the Cayman Islands the prior permission referred to in Article 16 and 17 of the Convention is not required in respect of diplomatic officers, consular agents or commissioners of a Contracting State which does not require permission to be obtained for the purposes of taking evidence under Articles 16 or 17.

Extension to Guernsey.—

Notification in accordance with Article 42, sub d and e, of the Convention

With reference to the deposit of its instrument of ratification of the above-mentioned Convention on 16 July 1985 the Government of the United Kingdom of Great Britain and Northern Ireland declared by letter of 13 November 1985 which was received by the Ministry of Foreign Affairs of the Kingdom of the Netherlands on 19 November 1985, in accordance with Article 40, second paragraph, that the Convention shall extend to Guernsey.

In accordance with Article 35 the Government of the United Kingdom furthermore declared that:

"(a) under Articles 8 and 25 of the Convention, the Bailiff, Deputy Bailiff, any Jurat of the Royal Court of Guernsey, the Chairman or a Jurat of the Court of Alderney and the Seneschal (or Deputy) of the Court of the Seneschal of Sark are designated as the competent authorities for Guernsey;

(b) under Article 23 of the Convention, Guernsey will not execute Letters of Request issued for the purpose of obtaining pre-trial discovery of documents.".

In accordance with Article 40, third paragraph, the Convention will enter into force for Guernsey on 18 January 1986.

Extension to Anguilla.—

Notification pursuant to Article 42, paragraph c, d and e, of the Convention

In accordance with Article 40, paragraph 2, the Kingdom of Great Britain and Northern Ireland declared, by a Letter dated 1 July 1986, received at the Ministry of Foreign Affairs on 3 July 1986, that the present Convention shall extend to Anguilla.

In accordance with Article 35, of the Convention, the following designations have been made:

"a. Under Articles 16, 17 and 18 of the Convention the Registrar of the East Caribbean Supreme Court is designated as the competent authority for Anguilla.

b. Under Article 24 of the Convention, the Governor of Anguilla is designated as an additional authority competent to receive Letters of Request for execution in Anguilla."

and the following declarations:

". . . . . . . in accordance with the provisions of Articles 4 and 33 of the Convention, Anguilla will not accept a Letter of Request in French.

In accordance with Article 8, members of the juridical personnel of the requesting authority may be present at the execution of a Letter of Request in Anguilla.

In accordance with Article 18, a diplomatic officer, consular agent or commissioner authorized to take evidence under Articles 15, 16 and 17 of the Convention may apply to the competent authority in Anguilla designated above for appropriate assistance to obtain such evidence by compulsion provided that the contracting State whose diplomatic officer, consular agent or commissioner makes (sic) the application has made a declaration affording reciprocal facilities under Article 18.

In accordance with Article 23, Anguilla will not execute Letters of Request issued for the purpose of obtaining pre-trial discovery of documents. Anguilla understands "Letters of Request issued for the purpose of obtaining pre-trial discovery of documents" for the purposes of the foregoing declaration as including any Letter of Request which requires a person:

i. to state what documents relevant to the proceedings to which the Letter of Request relates are, or have been, in his possession, custody or power; or

ii. to produce any documents other than particular documents specified in the Letter of Request as being documents appearing to the requested court to be, or likely to be, in his possession, custody or power.

In accordance with Article 27, by the law and practice of Anguilla the prior permission referred to in Articles 16 and 17 of the Convention is not required in respect of diplomatic officers, consular agents or commissioners of a Contracting State which does not require permission to be obtained for the purposes of taking evidence under Articles 16 or 17."

In accordance with Article 40, the Convention entered into force for Anguilla on 1 September 1986.

[4] With the following designations and declarations:

The United States Department of Justice, Washington, D.C., 20530, is designated as the Central Authority referred to in Article 2 of the Convention.

Under paragraph 2 of Article 4 of the United States has agreed to accept a Letter of Request in or translated into French. The United States wishes to point out that owing to the necessity of translating such documents into English it will take the Central Authority longer to comply with a Letter of Request in or translated into French than with a similar request received in English.

In accordance with paragraph 3 of Article 4 the United States declares that it will also accept Letters of Request in Spanish for execution in the Commonwealth of Puerto Rico.

In accordance with Article 8 the United States declares that subject to prior authorization members of the judicial personnel of the requesting authority of another Contracting State may be present at the execution of a Letter of Request. The Department of Justice is the competent authority for the purposes of this Article.

The United States declares that evidence may be taken in the United States under Articles 16 and 17 without its prior permission.

In accordance with Article 18 the United States declares that a diplomatic or consular officer or a commissioner authorized to take evidence under Articles 15, 16 or 17 may apply for appropriate assistance to obtain the evidence by compulsion. The competent authority for the purposes of Article 18 is the United States district court of the district in which a person resides or is found. Such court may order him to give his testimony or statement or to produce a document or thing for use in a proceeding in a foreign tribunal. The order may direct that the testimony or statement be given, or the document or other thing be produced, before a person appointed by the court.

In accordance with Article 40 the United States declares that the Convention shall extend to Guam, Puerto Rico and the Virgin Islands.

In accordance with the provisions of Article 39 of the Convention, the United States declared its acceptance of the accessions by Argentina, Barbados, Cyprus, Monaco, and Singapore.

[5] In accordance with Article 2 [of the Convention] Venezuela designated the following Central Authority: el ministerio de Relaciones Exteriores.

In accordance with Article 39, paragraph 5, the Convention will enter into force between Venezuela and

Cyprus . . . . 29 April 1994
United Kingdom of Great Britain and Northern Ireland . . . . . . 15 August 1994*
Sweden . . . . 3 September 1994
Germany . . . . 21 October 1994
Denmark . . . . 27 November 1994
Spain . . . . 6 February 1995
Finland . . . . 11 March 1995
Italy . . . . 16 January 1996
Australia . . . . 20 January 1996
Israel . . . . 19 March 1996
Slovakia . . . . 20 May 1996

* The Permanent Bureau of the Hague Conference on private international law presents its compliments to the Diplomatic Missions of the Member States and to the National Organs and has the honour to inform them that, by a Note dated 9 February 1995 and received on 21 February 1995, the Embassy of the United Kingdom of Great Britain and Northern Ireland informed the Ministry of Foreign Affairs of the Kingdom of the Netherlands that the acceptance of Venezuela's accession to the Convention, set out in the Embassy's Note of 14 June 1994 (see L.c. A No 51/L.c. ON No 47 dated 26 July 1994) was also in respect of the territories for the international relations of which the United Kingdom is responsible and to which the application of the Convention has been extended.

The Embassy also informed that, unless otherwise stated, in future the acceptance by the United Kingdom of the accession of any State to the Convention shall also be acceptance in respect of all the territories for the international relations of which the United Kingdom is responsible and to which the application of the Convention has been extended.

MODEL FOR LETTERS OR REQUEST RECOMMENDED FOR USE IN APPLYING THE HAGUE CONVENTION OF 18 MARCH 1970 ON THE TAKING OF EVIDENCE ABROAD IN CIVIL OR COMMERCIAL MATTERS

REQUEST FOR INTERNATIONAL JUDICIAL ASSISTANCE PURSUANT TO THE HAGUE CONVENTION OF 18 MARCH 1970 ON THE TAKING OF EVIDENCE IN CIVIL OR COMMERCIAL MATTERS

N.B. Under the first paragraph of article 4, the Letter of Request shall be in the language of the authority requested to execute it or be accompanied by a translation into that language. However, the provisions of the second and third paragraphs may permit use of other languages.

In order to avoid confusion, please spell out the name of the month in each date.

I *(Items to be included in all Letters of Request.)*

1 Sender —*(identity and address)*— ______________________

2 Central Authority of the Requested State —*(identity and address)*— ______________________

3 Person to whom the executed request is to be returned —*(identity and address)*— ______________________

II *(Items to be included in all Letters of Request.)*

4 In conformity with article 3 of the Convention, the undersigned applicant has the honour to submit the following request:

5 *a* Requesting judicial authority (article 3, *a)* —*(identity and address)*—

b To the competent authority of (article 3, *a*) —*(the requested State)*—

6 Names and addresses of the parties and their representatives (article 3, *b*)
a Plaintiff

b Defendant

c Other parties

7 Nature and purpose of the proceedings and summary of the facts (article 3, *c*)

8 Evidence to be obtained or other judicial act to be performed (article 3, *d*)

III *(Items to be completed where applicable.)*
9 Identity and address of any person to be examined (article 3, *e*)

10 Questions to be put to the persons to be examined or statement of the subject-matter about which they are to be examined (article 3, *f*) —*(or see attached list)*—

11 Documents or other property to be inspected (article 3, *g*) —*(specify whether it is to be produced, copied, valued, etc.)*

12 Any requirement that the evidence be given on oath or affirmation and any special form to be used (article 3, *h*) —*(In the event that the evidence cannot be taken in the manner requested, specify whether it is to be taken in such manner as provided by local law for the formal taking of evidence.)*

13 Special methods or procedure to be followed (articles 3, *i*) and 9)
14 Request for notification of the time and place for the execution of the Request and identity and address of any person to be notified (article 7)
15 Request for attendance of participation of judicial personnel of the requesting authority at the execution of the Letter of Request
16 Specification of privilege or duty to refuse to give evidence under the law of the State of origin (article 11, *b*)

17 The fees and costs incurred which are reimbursable under the second paragraph of article 14 or under article 26 of the Convention will be borne by —*(identity and address)*—

IV *(Items to be included in all Letters of Request.)*
18 Date of request
19 Signature and seal of the requesting authority

CONVENTION ABOLISHING THE REQUIREMENT OF LEGALISATION FOR FOREIGN PUBLIC DOCUMENTS

The States signatory to the present Convention,

Desiring to abolish the requirement of diplomatic or consular legalisation for foreign public documents,

Have resolved to conclude a Convention to this effect and have agreed upon the following provisions:

Article 1

The present Convention shall apply to public documents which have been executed in the territory of one contracting State and which have to be produced in the territory of another contracting State.

For the purposes of the present Convention, the following are deemed to be public documents:

(a) Documents emanating from an authority or an official connected with the courts or tribunals of the State, including those emanating from a public prosecutor, a clerk of a court or a process server ("huissier de justice");

(b) Administrative documents;

(c) Notarial acts;

(d) Official certificates which are placed on documents signed by persons in their private capacity, such as official certificates recording the registration of a document or the fact that it was in existence on a certain date and official and notarial authentications of signatures.

However, the present Convention shall not apply:

(a) To documents executed by diplomatic or consular agents;

(b) To administrative documents dealing directly with commercial or customs operations.

Article 2

Each contracting State shall exempt from legalisation documents to which the present Convention applies and which have to be produced in its territory. For the purposes of the present Convention, legalisation means only the formality by which the diplomatic or consular agents of the country in which the document has to be produced certify the authenticity of the signature, the capacity in which the person signing the document has acted and, where appropriate, the identity of the seal or stamp which it bears.

Article 3

The only formality that may be required in order to certify the authenticity of the signature, the capacity in which the person signing the document has acted and, where appropriate, the identity of the seal or stamp which it bears, is the addition of the certificate described in Article 4, issued by the competent authority of the State from which the document emanates.

However, the formality mentioned in the preceding paragraph cannot be required when either the laws, regulations, or practice in force in the State where the document is produced or an agreement between two or more contracting States have abolished or simplified it, or exempt the document itself from legalisation.

Article 4

The certificate referred to in the first paragraph of Article 3 shall be placed on the document itself or on an "allonge"; it shall be in the form of the model annexed to the present Convention.

It may, however, be drawn up in the official language of the authority which issues it. The standard terms appearing therein may be in a second language also. The title "Apostille (Convention de La Haye du 5 octobre 1961)" shall be in the French language.

Article 5

The certificate shall be issued at the request of the person who has signed the document or of any bearer.

When properly filled in, it will certify the authenticity of the signature, the capacity in which the person signing the document has acted and, where appropriate, the identity of the seal or stamp which the document bears.

The signature, seal and stamp on the certificate are exempt from all certification.

Article 6

Each contracting State shall designate by reference to their official function, the authorities who are competent to issue the certificate referred to in the first paragraph of Article 3.

It shall give notice of such designation to the Ministry of Foreign Affairs of the Netherlands at the time it deposits its instrument of ratification or of accession or its declaration of extension. It shall also give notice of any change in the designated authorities.

Article 7

Each of the authorities designated in accordance with Article 6 shall keep a register or card index in which it shall record the certificates issued, specifying:

(a) The number and date of the certificate,

(b) The name of the person signing the public document and the capacity in which he has acted, or in the case of unsigned documents, the name of the authority which has affixed the seal or stamp.

At the request of any interested person, the authority which has issued the certificate shall verify whether the particulars in the certificate correspond with those in the register or card index.

Article 8

When a treaty, convention or agreement between two or more contracting States contains provisions which subject the certification of a signature, seal or stamp to certain formalities, the present Convention will only override such provisions if those formalities are more rigorous than the formality referred to in Articles 3 and 4.

Article 9

Each contracting State shall take the necessary steps to prevent the performance of legalisations by its diplomatic or consular agents in cases where the present Convention provides for exemption.

Article 10

The present Convention shall be open for signature by the States represented at the Ninth session of the Hague Conference on Private International Law and Iceland, Ireland, Liechtenstein and Turkey.

It shall be ratified, and the instruments of ratification shall be deposited with the Ministry of Foreign Affairs of the Netherlands.

Article 11

The present Convention shall enter into force on the sixtieth day after the deposit of the third instrument of ratification referred to in the second paragraph of Article 10.

The Convention shall enter into force for each signatory State which ratifies subsequently on the sixtieth day after the deposit of its instrument of ratification.

Article 12

Any State not referred to in Article 10 may accede to the present Convention after it has entered into force in accordance with the first paragraph of Article 11. The instrument of accession shall be deposited with the Ministry of Foreign Affairs of the Netherlands.

Such accession shall have effect only as regards the relations between the acceding State and those contracting States which have not raised an objection to its accession in the six months after the receipt of the notification referred to in sub-paragraph d) of Article 15. Any such objection shall be notified to the Ministry of Foreign Affairs of the Netherlands.

The Convention shall enter into force as between the acceding State and the States which have raised no objection to its accession on the sixtieth day after the expiry of the period of six months mentioned in the preceding paragraph.

Article 13

Any State may, at the time of signature, ratification or accession, declare that the present Convention shall extend to all the territories for the international relations of which it is responsible, or to one or more of them. Such a declaration shall take effect on the date of entry into force of the Convention for the State concerned.

At any time thereafter, such extension shall be notified to the Ministry of Foreign Affairs of the Netherlands.

When the declaration of extension is made by a State which has signed and ratified, the Convention shall enter into force for the territories concerned in accordance with Article 11. When the declaration of extension is made by a State which has acceded, the Convention shall enter into force for the territories concerned in accordance with Article 12.

Article 14

The present Convention shall remain in force for five years from the date of its entry into force in accordance with the first paragraph of Article 11, even for States which have ratified it or acceded to it subsequently.

If there has been no denunciation, the Convention shall be renewed tacitly every five years.

Any denunciation shall be notified to the Ministry of Foreign Affairs of the Netherlands at least six months before the end of the five year period.

It may be limited to certain of the territories to which the Convention applies.

The denunciation will only have effect as regards the State which has notified it. The Convention shall remain in force for the other contracting States.

Article 15

The Ministry of Foreign Affairs of the Netherlands shall give notice to the States referred to in Article 10, and to the States which have acceded in accordance with Article 12, of the following:

(a) The notifications referred to in the second paragraph of Article 6;
(b) The signatures and ratifications referred to in Article 10;
(c) The date on which the present Convention enters into force in accordance with the first paragraph of Article 11;
(d) The accessions and objections referred to in Article 12 and the date on which such accessions take effect;
(e) The extensions referred to in Article 13 and the date on which they take effect;
(f) The denunciations referred to in the third paragraph of Article 14.

In witness whereof the undersigned, being duly authorised thereto, have signed the present Convention.

Done at The Hague the 5th October 1961, in French and in English, the French text prevailing in case of divergence between the two texts, in a single copy which shall be deposited in the archives of the Government of the Netherlands, and of which a certified copy shall be sent, through the diplomatic channel, to each of the States represented at the Ninth session of the Hague Conference on Private International Law and also to Iceland, Ireland, Liechtenstein and Turkey.

[Signatures omitted.]

ANNEX TO THE CONVENTION

Model of certificate

The certificate will be in the form of a square
with sides at least 9 centimetres long

APOSTILLE
(Convention de La Haye du 5 octobre 1961)

1. Country: . . . .
This public document
2. has been signed by . . . .
3. acting in the capacity of . . . .
4. bears the seal/stamp of . . . .
. . . .

Certified

5. at . . . . 6. the . . . .
7. by . . . .
8. N° . . . .
9. Seal/stamp: 10. Signature:
. . . .

Convention abolishing the requirement of legalization for foreign public documents, with annex. Done at The Hague October 5, 1961; entered into force for the United States October 15, 1981. (TIAS 10072; 527 UNTS 189).

Parties to the Convention

In addition to the United States, the following are parties to the Convention:

Contracting State	Territories to which Extended
Andorra[1]	
Antigua and Barbuda	
Argentina[1a]	
Armenia	
Australia[1b]	All the territories for the international relations of which it is responsible
Austria	
Bahamas	
Barbados	
Belarus[1c]	
Belgium	
Belize[1d]	
Bosnia-Herzegovina	
Botswana	
Brunei	
Croatia	
Cyprus	
El Salvador	
Fiji	
Finland	
France	Entire territory of the French Republic Anglo-French Condominium of the New Hebrides (Vanuatu)*
Germany, Federal Republic of[1e]	
Greece	
Hungary	
Israel	
Italy	
Japan	
Latvia	
Lesotho	
Liberia[1f]	
Liechtenstein	
Luxembourg	
Macedonia, former Yugoslav Republic of	
Malawi	
Malta	
Marshall Islands[2]	
Mauritius	
Mexico	
Netherlands	the Kingdom in Europe Netherlands Antilles and Aruba
Norway	
Panama	
Portugal	Angola* Mozambique* and other overseas departments
Russian Federation[3]	
San Marino	
Seychelles	
Slovenia	
South Africa	
Spain	
St. Kitts & Nevis	
Suriname	
Swaziland	
Switzerland	
Tonga	
Turkey	
United Kingdom of Great Britain and Northern Ireland	Anguilla the Bailiwick of Guernsey Barbados* Bermuda British Antarctic Territory British Guiana (Guyana)* British Solomon Islands Protectorate (Solomon Islands)* Cayman Islands Dominica* Falkland Islands Gibraltar Gilbert and Ellice Islands (Kiribati/Tuvalu)* Grenada* Hong Kong the Isle of Man Jersey Montserrat New Hebrides (Vanuatu)* St. Helena Saint Christopher and Nevis* Saint Lucia* Saint Vincent* Southern Rhodesia (Zimbabwe)* Turks and Caicos Islands British Virgin Islands
United States	Those territories for the foreign relations of which the United States is responsible
Yugoslavia[4]	

* Now independent and no confirmation issued by the newly independent country that the Convention is deemed to apply.

[1] *Notification in conformity with Article 15 of the Convention*

On 15 April 1996 the Ministry of Foreign Affairs of the Kingdom of the Netherlands received the instrument of accession of the Principality of Andorra to the above-mentioned Convention in accordance with Article 12, first paragraph, of the Convention.

In accordance with the terms of Article 12, paragraph 1, of the Convention any State not mentioned in Article 10 may accede to this Convention. In accordance with Article 12, paragraph 2, such accession shall have effect only as regards the relations between the

Principality of Andorra and those contracting States (at present: Antigua and Barbuda, Argentina, Armenia, Australia, Austria, Bahamas, Barbados, Belgium, Belize, Byelorus, Bosnia and Herzegovina, Botswana, Brunei, Darussalam, Croatia, Cyprus, El Salvador, Fiji, Finland, France, Germany, Greece, Hungary, Israel, Italy, Japan, the Kingdom of the Netherlands, Lesotho, Liechtenstein, Luxembourg, The former Yugoslav Republic of Macedonia, Malawi, Malta, Marshall Islands, Mauritius, Mexico, Norway, Panama, Portugal, Russia, Saint Kitts and Nevis, San Marino, Seychelles, Slovenia, South Africa, Spain, Surinam, Swaziland, Switzerland, Tonga, Turkey, the United Kingdom of Great Britain and Northern Ireland and the United States of America) which have not raised an objection to its accession in the six months after receipt of this notification. For practical reasons this six months' period will run from 1 May 1996 till 1 November 1996.

[1a] In accordance with Article 12, paragraph 1, the instrument of accession by the Argentine Republic to the above-mentioned Convention was deposited with the Ministry of Foreign Affairs of the Kingdom of the Netherlands on 8 May 1987. The instrument of accession contains the declaration annexed to this notification.

"In accordance with the terms of Article 12, paragraph 1, of the Convention any State not mentioned in Article 10 may accede to this Convention. In accordance with Article 12, paragraph 2, such accession shall have effect only as regards the relations between the Argentine Republic and those contracting States (at present: Antigua and Barbuda, Austria, Bahamas, Belgium, Botswana, Brunei Darussalam, Cyprus, Fiji, Finland, France, the Federal Republic of Germany, Greece, Hungary, Israel, Italy, Japan, Lesotho, Liechtenstein, Luxembourg, Malawi, Malta, Mauritius, the Kingdom of the Netherlands, Norway, Portugal, Seychelles, Spain, Surinam, Swaziland, Switzerland, Tonga, Turkey, the United Kingdom of Great Britain and Northern Ireland, the United States of America and Yugoslavia) which have not raised an objection to its accession in the six months after the receipt of this notification. For practical reasons this six months' period will extend from 20 June 1987 till 20 December 1987."

"The Argentine Republic rejects the extension of the application of the Convention Abolishing the Requirement of Legalization for Foreign Public Documents, concluded at The Hague on October 5, 1961, to the Malvinas, South Georgia, and South Sandwich Islands, as notified by the United Kingdom of Great Britain and Northern Ireland to the Ministry of Foreign Affairs of the Kingdom of the Netherlands on February 24, 1965, and reaffirms its sovereign rights over the Malvinas, South Georgia, and South Sandwich Islands, which form an integral part of its national territory.

"The United Nations General Assembly has adopted resolutions 2065(XX), 3160(XXVIII), 31/49, 37/9, 38/12, 39/6, 40/21, and 41/40, acknowledging the existence of a sovereignty dispute with respect to the question of the Malvinas Islands, and urging the Argentine Republic and the United Kingdom of Great Britain and Northern Ireland to continue negotiating in order to reach a peaceful and definitive solution to the dispute as soon as possible, through the good offices of the United Nations Secretary General, who is to inform the General Assembly of the progress achieved.

"The Argentine Republic also rejects the extension of the Convention, notified on the same date as above, to the so-called "British Antarctic Territory," and thereby reaffirms the rights of the Republic to the Argentine Antarctic Sector, including those relating to its corresponding maritime sovereignty or jurisdiction. It further recalls the safeguards on claims of territorial sovereignty in Antarctica set forth in Article IV of the Antartic Treaty, done at Washington on December 1, 1959, to which the Argentine Republic and the United Kingdom of Great Britain and Northern Ireland are parties." (Translation provided by the Division of Language Services, Department of State)

[1b] *Notification in conformity with Article 15 of the Convention*

On 11 July 1994 Australia deposited its instrument of accession at the Ministry of Foreign Affairs of the Kingdom of the Netherlands to the above-mentioned Convention in accordance with Article 12, first paragraph, of the Convention.

Australia made the following declarations:

"—pursuant to the second paragraph of Article 6, the Secretary to the Department of Foreign Affairs and Trade of the Commonwealth will be its competent authority for the purpose of that Article; and

—pursuant to Article 13, the Convention shall extend to all the territories for the international relations of which it is responsible."

In accordance with the terms of Article 12, paragraph 1, of the Convention any State not mentioned in Article 10 may accede to this Convention. In accordance with Article 12, paragraph 2, such accession shall have effect only as regards the relations between Australia and those contracting States (at present: Antigua and Barbuda, Argentina, Armenia, Austria, Bahamas, Belgium, Belize, Byelorus, Bosnia and Herzegovina, Botswana, Brunei Darussalam, Croatia, Cyprus, Fiji, Finland, France, Germany, Greece, Hungary, Israel, Italy, Japan, the Kingdom of the Netherlands, Lesotho, Liechtenstein, Luxemburg, The former Yugoslav Republic of Macedonia, Malawi, Malta, Marshall Islands, Mauritius, Norway, Panama, Portugal, Russia, Seychelles, Slovenia, Spain, Surinam, Swaziland, Switzerland, Tonga, Turkey, the United Kingdom of Great Britain and Northern Ireland and the United States of America) which have not raised an objection to its accession in the six months after receipt of this notification. For practical reasons this six months' period will run from 15 July 1994 till 15 January 1995.

[1c] The Ministry of Foreign Affairs of the Byelorussian Republic communicated the following by Note of 8 February 1993:

Translation

....the Ministry would advise that in accordance with Article 6 of the Convention and in accordance with the Decree issued by the Government of the Byelorussian Republic on 1 January 1993, offcial documents issued by government agencies of the Byelorussian Republic for use in the territories of contracting States of the Hague Convention, repealing the necessity of legalisation of foreign official documents, are now authorised only by an apostille written on these documents.

[1d] *Notification in conformity with Article 15 of the Convention*

On 17 July 1992 the Ministry of Foreign Affairs of the Kingdom of the Netherlands received the instrument of accession by Belize to the above-mentioned Convention in accordance with Article 12, first paragraph, of the Convention.

In accordance with the terms of Article 12, paragraph 1, of the Convention any State not mentioned in Article 10 may accede to this Convention. In accordance with Article 12, paragraph 2, such accession shall have effect only as regards the relations between Belize and those contracting States (at present Antigua and Barbuda, Argentina, Austria, Bahamas, Belgium, Botswana, Brunei Darussalam, Cyprus, Fiji, Finland, France, the Federal Republic of Germany, Greece, Hungary, Israel, Italy, Japan, Lesotho, Liechtenstein, Luxembourg, Malawi, Malta, Marshall Islands, Mauritius, the Kingdom of the Netherlands, Norway, Panama, Portugal, Russia, Seychelles, Spain, Surinam, Swaziland, Switzerland, Tonga, Turkey, the United Kingdom of Great Britain and Northern Ireland, the United States of America and Yugoslavia) which have not raised an objection to its accession in the six months after the receipt of this notification. For practical reasons this six months' period will extend from 10 August 1992 till 10 February 1993.

The Contracting States were notified by the depositary of the accession on 10 August 1992. None of these States raised an objection to the accession within the period of six months specified in Article 12, paragraph 2, which period expired on 10 February 1993.

The provisions of the Convention will enter into force between Belize and the Contracting States on 11 April 1993.

[1e] On October 3, 1990 the German Democratic Republic acceded to the Federal Republic of Germany.

[1f] *Ed. Note*—The Government of the United States of America does not accept the accession of the Government of Liberia to the Convention. The Convention is not in force between the Government of the United States of America and the Government of Liberia.

[2] *Notification in conformity with Article 15 of the Convention*

The Government of the Marshall Islands deposited its instrument of accession to the Convention with the Ministry of Foreign Affairs of the Kingdom of the Netherlands on 18 November 1991 in accordance with Article 12, first paragraph, of the Convention.

The Contracting States were notified by the depositary of the accession on 25 November 1991. None of these States raised an objection to the accession within the period of six months specified in Article 12, paragraph 2, which period expired on 15 June 1992.

The provisions of the Convention entered into force between the Marshall Islands and the Contracting States on 14 August 1992.

[3] . . . the Convention entered into force between the Russian Federation and the Contracting States on 31 May 1992. The status of the Republics with respect to this Convention is under review by the Depositary.

Authorities in the United States of America Competent to Issue the Certificate Referred to in Article 3 of the Convention

I. Authentication Officer and Acting Authentication Officer, United States Department of State

II. Clerks and deputy clerks of the following: The Supreme Court of the United States, the Courts of Appeals for the First through the Eleventh Circuits, the District of Columbia Circuit and the Federal Circuit; the United States District Courts; the United States Court of International Trade; the United States Claims Court; the District Court of Guam, the District Court of the Virgin Islands, and the District Court for the Northern Mariana Islands.

The District Court for the District of the Canal Zone ceased to exist on Mar. 31, 1982. Its records have been transferred to the National Archives which will certify those records.

III. Officers of the individual States and other subdivisions as indicated:

States:

Alabama: Secretary of State
Alaska: Lieutenant Governor; Attorney General; Clerk of the Appellate Court.
Arizona: Secretary of State; Assistant Secretary of State
Arkansas: Secretary of State; Chief Deputy Secretary of State
California: Secretary of State; any Assistant Secretary of State; any Deputy Secretary of State
Colorado: Secretary of State; Deputy Secretary of State
Connecticut: Secretary of the State; Deputy Secretary of the State
Delaware: Secretary of State; Acting Secretary of State
Florida: Secretary of State
Georgia: Secretary of State; Notary Public Division Director
Hawaii: Lieutenant Governor of the State of Hawaii
Idaho: Secretary of State; Chief Deputy Secretary of State; Deputy Secretary of State; Notary Public Clerk
Illinois: Secretary of State; Assistant Secretary of State; Deputy Secretary of State
Indiana: Secretary of State; Deputy Secretary of State
Iowa: Secretary of State; Deputy Secretary of State
Kansas: Secretary of State; Assistant Secretary of State; any Deputy Assistant Secretary of State
Kentucky: Secretary of State; Assistant Secretary of State
Louisiana: Secretary of State
Maine: Secretary of State; Deputy Secretary of State
Maryland: Secretary of State
Massachusetts: Deputy Secretary of the Commonwealth of Massachusetts for Public Records (beginning in 1981 through January 13, 1995); Deputy Secretary of State of the Commonwealth of Massachusetts (beginning January 16, 1995, through November 16, 1995); Secretary of the Commonwealth of Massachusetts (from November 17, 1995)
Michigan: Secretary of State; Deputy Secretary of State
Minnesota: Secretary of State; Deputy Secretary of State
Mississippi: Secretary of State; any Assistant Secretary of State
Missouri: Secretary of State; Deputy Secretary of State
Montana: Secretary of State; Chief Deputy Secretary of State; Government Affairs Bureau Chief
Nebraska: Secretary of State; Deputy Secretary of State
Nevada: Secretary of State; Chief Deputy Secretary of State; Deputy Secretary of State

New Hampshire: Secretary of State; Deputy Secretary of State
New Jersey: Secretary of State; Assistant Secretary of State
New Mexico: Secretary of State
New York: Secretary of State; Executive Deputy Secretary of State; any Deputy Secretary of State; any Special Deputy Secretary of State
North Carolina: Secretary of State; Deputy Secretary of State
North Dakota: Secretary of State; Deputy Secretary of State
Ohio: Secretary of State; Assistant Secretary of State
Oklahoma: Secretary of State; Assistant Secretary of State; Budget Officer of the Secretary of State
Oregon: Secretary of State; Deputy Secretary of State; Acting Secretary of State; Assistant to the Secretary of State
Pennsylvania: Secretary of the Commonwealth; Executive Deputy Secretary of the Commonwealth
Rhode Island: Secretary of State; First Deputy Secretary of State; Second Deputy Secretary of State
South Carolina: Secretary of State
South Dakota: Secretary of State; Deputy Secretary of State
Tennessee: Secretary of State
Texas: Secretary of State; Assistant Secretary of State
Utah: Lieutenant Governor; Deputy Lieutenant Governor; Administrative Assistant
Vermont: Secretary of State; Deputy Secretary of State
Virginia: Secretary of the Commonwealth; Chief Clerk, Office of the Secretary of the Commonwealth
Washington (State): Secretary of State; Assistant Secretary of State; Director, Department of Licensing
West Virginia: Secretary of State; Under Secretary of State; any Deputy Secretary of State
Wisconsin: Secretary of State; Assistant Secretary of State
Wyoming: Secretary of State; Deputy Secretary of State
Other Subdivisions:
American Samoa: Secretary of American Samoa; Attorney General of American Samoa
District of Columbia (Washington, D.C.): Executive Secretary; Assistant Executive Secretary; Mayor's Special Assistant and Assistant to the Executive Secretary; Secretary of the District of Columbia
Guam (Territory of): Director, Department of Administration; Acting Director, Department of Administration; Deputy Director, Department of Administration; Acting Deputy Director, Department of Administration
Northern Mariana Islands (Commonwealth of the): Attorney General; Acting Attorney General; Clerk of the Court, Commonwealth Trial Court; Deputy Clerk, Commonwealth Trial Court
Puerto Rico (Commonwealth of): Under Secretary of State; Assistant Secretary of State for External Affairs; Assistant Secretary of State; Chief, Certifications Office; Director, Office of Protocol; Assistant Secretary of State for International Affairs; Chief, Certification Office
Virgin Islands of the United States: no authority designated

[4] *Ed. Note*—The U.S. view is that the Socialist Federal Republic of Yugoslavia has dissolved and no successor state represents its continuation.

UNITED NATIONS CONVENTION ON CONTRACTS FOR THE INTERNATIONAL SALE OF GOODS

THE STATES PARTIES TO THIS CONVENTION,

BEARING IN MIND the broad objectives in the resolutions adopted by the sixth special session of the General Assembly of the United Nations on the establishment of a New International Economic Order,

CONSIDERING that the development of international trade on the basis of equality and mutual benefit is an important element in promoting friendly relations among States,

BEING OF THE OPINION that the adoption of uniform rules which govern contracts for the international sale of goods and take into account the different social, economic and legal systems would contribute to the removal of legal barriers in international trade and promote the development of international trade,

HAVE AGREED as follows:

PART I

SPHERE OF APPLICATION AND GENERAL PROVISIONS

Chapter I

SPHERE OF APPLICATION

Article 1

(1) This Convention applies to contracts of sale of goods between parties whose places of business are in different States:

(a) when the States are Contracting States; or

(b) when the rules of private international law lead to the application of the law of a Contracting State.

(2) The fact that the parties have their places of business in different States is to be disregarded whenever this fact does not appear either from the contract or from any dealings between, or from information disclosed by, the parties at any time before or at the conclusion of the contract.

(3) Neither the nationality of the parties nor the civil or commercial character of the parties or of the contract is to be taken into consideration in determining the application of this Convention.

Article 2

This Convention does not apply to sales:

(a) of goods bought for personal, family or household use, unless the seller, at any time before or at the conclusion of the contract, neither knew nor ought to have known that the goods were bought for any such use;

(b) by auction;

(c) on execution or otherwise by authority of law;

(d) of stocks, shares, investment securities, negotiable instruments or money;

(e) of ships, vessels, hovercraft or aircraft;

(f) of electricity.

Article 3

(1) Contracts for the supply of goods to be manufactured or produced are to be considered sales unless the party who orders the goods undertakes to supply a substantial part of the materials necessary for such manufacture or production.

(2) This Convention does not apply to contracts in which the preponderant part of the obligations of the party who furnishes the goods consists in the supply of labour or other services.

Article 4

This Convention governs only the formation of the contract of sale and the rights and obligations of the seller and the buyer arising from such a contract. In particular, except as otherwise expressly provided in this Convention, it is not concerned with:

(a) the validity of the contract or of any of its provisions or of any usage;

(b) the effect which the contract may have on the property in the goods sold.

Article 5

This Convention does not apply to the liability of the seller for death or personal injury caused by the goods to any person.

Article 6

The parties may exclude the application of this Convention or, subject to article 12, derogate from or vary the effect of any of its provisions.

Chapter II

GENERAL PROVISIONS

Article 7

(1) In the interpretation of this Convention, regard is to be had to its international character and to the need to promote uniformity in its application and the observance of good faith in international trade.

(2) Questions concerning matters governed by this Convention which are not expressly settled in it are to be settled in conformity with the general principles on which it is based or, in the absence of such principles, in conformity with the law applicable by virtue of the rules of private international law.

Article 8

(1) For the purposes of this Convention statements made by and other conduct of a party are to be interpreted according to his intent where the other party knew or could not have been unaware what that intent was.

(2) If the preceding paragraph is not applicable, statements made by and other conduct of a party are to be interpreted according to the understanding that a reasonable person of the same kind as the other party would have had in the same circumstances.

(3) In determining the intent of a party or the understanding a reasonable person would have had, due consideration is to be given to all relevant circumstances of the case including the negotiations, any practices which the parties have established between themselves, usages and any subsequent conduct of the parties.

Article 9

(1) The parties are bound by any usage to which they have agreed and by any practices which they have established between themselves.

(2) The parties are considered, unless otherwise agreed, to have impliedly made applicable to their contract or its formation a usage of which the parties knew or ought to have known and which in international trade is widely known to, and regularly observed by, parties to contracts of the type involved in the particular trade concerned.

Article 10

For the purposes of this Convention:

(a) if a party has more than one place of business, the place of business is that which has the closest relationship to the contract and its performance, having regard to the circumstances known to or contemplated by the parties at any time before or at the conclusion of the contract;

(b) if a party does not have a place of business, reference is to be made to his habitual residence.

Article 11

A contract of sale need not be concluded in or evidence by writing and is not subject to any other requirement as to form. It may be proved by any means, including witnesses.

Article 12

Any provision of article 11, article 29 or Part II of this Convention that allows a contract of sale or its modification or termination by agreement or any offer, acceptance or other indication of intention to be made in any form other than in writing does not apply where any party has his place of business in a Contracting State which has made a declaration under article 96 of this Convention. The parties may not derogate from or vary the effect of this article.

Article 13

For the purposes of this Convention "writing" includes telegram and telex.

PART II

FORMATION OF THE CONTRACT

Article 14

(1) A proposal for concluding a contract addressed to one or more specific persons constitutes an offer if it is sufficiently definite and indicates the intention of the offeror to be bound in case of acceptance. A proposal is sufficiently definite if it indicates the goods and expressly or implicitly fixes or makes provision for determining the quantity and the price.

(2) A proposal other than one addressed to one or more specific persons is to be considered merely as an invitation to make offers, unless the contrary is clearly indicated by the person making the proposal.

Article 15

(1) An offer becomes effective when it reaches the offeree.

(2) An offer, even if it is irrevocable, may be withdrawn if the withdrawal reaches the offeree before or at the same time as the offer.

Article 16

(1) Until a contract is concluded an offer may be revoked if the revocation reaches the offeree before he has dispatched an acceptance.

(2) However, an offer cannot be revoked:

(a) if it indicates, whether by stating a fixed time for acceptance or otherwise, that it is irrevocable; or

(b) if it was reasonable for the offeree to rely on the offer as being irrevocable and the offeree has acted in reliance on the offer.

Article 17

An offer, even if it is irrevocable, is terminated when a rejection reaches the offeror.

Article 18

(1) A statement made by or other conduct of the offeree indicating assent to an offer is an acceptance. Silence or inactivity does not in itself amount to acceptance.

(2) An acceptance of an offer becomes effective at the moment the indication of assent reaches the offeror. An acceptance is not effective if the indication of assent does not reach the offeror within the time he has fixed or, if no time is fixed, within a reasonable time, due account being taken of the circumstances of the transaction, including the rapidity of the means of communication employed by the offeror. An oral offer must be accepted immediately unless the circumstances indicate otherwise.

(3) However, if, by virtue of the offer or as a result of practices which the parties have established between themselves or of usage, the offeree may indicate assent by performing an act, such as one relating to the dispatch of the goods or payment of the price, without notice to the offeror, the acceptance is effective at the moment the act is performed, provided that the act is performed within the period of time laid down in the preceding paragraph.

Article 19

(1) A reply to an offer which purports to be an acceptance but contains additions, limitations or other modifications is a rejection of the offer and constitutes a counter-offer.

(2) However, a reply to an offer which purports to be an acceptance but contains additional or different terms which do not materially alter the terms of the offer constitutes an acceptance, unless the offeror, without undue delay, objects orally to the discrepancy or dispatches a notice to that effect. If he does not so object, the terms of the contract are the terms of the offer with the modificatons contained in the acceptance.

(3) Additional or different terms relating, among other things, to the price, payment, quality and quantity of the goods, place and time of delivery, extent of one party's liability to the other or the settlement of disputes are considered to alter the terms of the offer materially.

Article 20

(1) A period of time for acceptance fixed by the offeror in a telegram or a letter begins to run from the moment the telegram is handed in for dispatch or from the date shown on the letter or, if no such date is shown, from the date shown on the envelope. A period of time for acceptance fixed by the offeror by telephone, telex or other means of instantaneous communication, begins to run from the moment that the offer reaches the offeree.

(2) Official holidays or non-business days occurring during the period for acceptance are included in calculating the period. However, if a notice of acceptance cannot be delivered at the address of the offeror on the last day of the period because that day falls on an official holiday or a non-business day at the place of business of the offeror, the period is extended until the first business day which follows.

Article 21

(1) A late acceptance is nevertheless effective as an acceptance if without delay the offeror orally so informs the offeree or dispatches a notice to that effect.

(2) If a letter or other writing containing a late acceptance shows that it has been sent in such circumstances that if its transmission had been normal it would have reached the offeror in due time, the late acceptance is effective as an acceptance unless, without delay, the offeror orally informs the offeree that he considers his offer as having lapsed or dispatches a notice to that effect.

Article 22

An acceptance may be withdrawn if the withdrawal reaches the offeror before or at the same time as the acceptance would have become effective.

Article 23

A contract is concluded at the moment when an acceptance of an offer becomes effective in accordance with the provisions of this Convention.

Article 24

For the purposes of this Part of the Convention, an offer, declaration of acceptance or any other indication of intention "reaches" the addressee when it is made orally to him or delivered by any other means to him personally, to his place of business or mailing address or, if he does not have a place of business or mailing address, to his habitual residence.

PART III

SALE OF GOODS

Chapter I

GENERAL PROVISIONS

Article 25

A breach of contract committed by one of the parties is fundamental if it results in such detriment to the other party as substantially to deprive him of what he is entitled to expect under the contract, unless the party in breach did not foresee and a reasonable person of the same kind in the same circumstances would not have foreseen such a result.

Article 26

A declaration of avoidance of the contract is effective only if made by notice to the other party.

Article 27

Unless otherwise expressly provided in this Part of the Convention, if any notice, request or other communication is given or made by a party in accordance with this Part and by means appropriate in the circumstances, a delay or error in the transmission of the communication or its failure to arrive does not deprive that party of the right to rely on the communication.

Article 28

If, in accordance with the provisions of this Convention, one party is entitled to require performance of any obligation by the other party, a court is not bound to enter a judgement for specific performance unless the court would do so under its own law in respect of similar contracts of sale not governed by this Convention.

Article 29

(1) A contract may be modified or terminated by the mere agreement of the parties.

(2) A contract in writing which contains a provision requiring any modification or termination by agreement to be in writing may not be otherwise modified or terminated by agreement. However, a party may be precluded by his conduct from asserting such a provision to the extent that the other party has relied on that conduct.

Chapter II

OBLIGATIONS OF THE SELLER

Article 30

The seller must deliver the goods, hand over any documents relating to them and transfer the property in the goods, as required by the contract and this Convention.

Section I. *Delivery of the goods and handing over of documents.*

Article 31

If the seller is not bound to deliver the goods at any other particular place, his obligation to deliver consists:

(a) if the contract of sale involves carriage of the goods—in handing the goods over to the first carrier for transmission to the buyer;

(b) if, in cases not within the preceding subparagraph, the contract relates to specific goods, or unidentified goods to be drawn from a specific stock or to be manufactured or produced, and at the time of the conclusion of the contract the parties knew that the goods were at, or were to be manufactured or produced at, a particular place—in placing the goods at the buyer's disposal at that place;

(c) in other cases—in placing the goods at the buyer's disposal at the place where the seller had his place of business at the time of the conclusion of the contract.

Article 32

(1) If the seller, in accordance with the contract or this Convention, hands the goods over to a carrier and if the goods are not clearly identified to the contract by markings on the goods, by shipping documents or otherwise, the seller must give the buyer notice of the consignment specifying the goods.

(2) If the seller is bound to arrange for carriage of the goods, he must make such contracts as are necessary for carriage to the place fixed by means of transportation appropriate in the circumstances and according to the usual terms for such transportation.

(3) If the seller is not bound to effect insurance in respect of the carriage of the goods, he must, at the buyer's request, provide him with all available information necessary to enable him to effect such insurance.

Article 33

The seller must deliver the goods:

(a) if a date is fixed by or determinable from the contract, on that date;

(b) if a period of time is fixed by or determinable from the contract, at any time within that period unless circumstances indicate that the buyer is to choose a date; or

(c) in any other case, within a reasonable time after the conclusion of the contract.

Article 34

If the seller is bound to hand over documents relating to the goods, he must hand them over at the time and place and in the form required by the contract. If the seller has handed over documents before that time, he may, up to that time, cure any lack of conformity in the documents, if the exercise of this right does not cause the buyer unreasonable inconvenience or unreasonable expense. However, the buyer retains any right to claim damages as provided for in this Convention.

Section II. *Conformity of the goods and third party claims*

Article 35

(1) The seller must deliver goods which are of the quantity, quality and description required by the contract and which are contained or packaged in the manner required by the contract.

(2) Except where the parties have agreed otherwise, the goods do not conform with the contract unless they:

(a) are fit for the purposes for which goods of the same description would ordinarily be used;
(b) are fit for any particular purpose expressly or impliedly made known to the seller at the time of the conclusion of the contract, except where the circumstances show that the buyer did not rely, or that it was unreasonable for him to rely, on the seller's skill and judgement;
(c) possess the qualities of goods which the seller has held out to the buyer as a sample or model;
(d) are contained or packaged in the manner usual for such goods or, where there is no such manner, in a manner adequate to preserve and protect the goods.

(3) The seller is not liable under subparagraphs (a) to (d) of the preceding paragraph for any lack of conformity of the goods if at the time of the conclusion of the contract the buyer knew or could not have been unaware of such lack of conformity.

Article 36

(1) The seller is liable in accordance with the contract and this Convention for any lack of conformity which exists at the time when the risk passes to the buyer, even though the lack of conformity becomes apparent only after that time.

(2) The seller is also liable for any lack of conformity which occurs after the time indicated in the preceding paragraph and which is due to a breach of any of his obligations, including a breach of any guarantee that for a period of time the goods will remain fit for their ordinary purpose or for some particular purpose or will retain specified qualities or characteristics.

Article 37

If the seller has delivered goods before the date for delivery, he may, up to that date, deliver any missing part or make up any deficiency in the quantity of the goods delivered, or deliver goods in replacement of any non-conforming goods delivered or remedy any lack of conformity in the goods delivered, provided that the exercise of this right does not cause the buyer unreasonable inconvenience or unreasonable expense. However, the buyer retains any right to claim damages as provided for in this Convention.

Article 38

(1) The buyer must examine the goods, or cause them to be examined, within as short a period as is practicable in the circumstances.

(2) If the contract involves carriage of the goods, examination may be deferred until after the goods have arrived at their destination.

(3) If the goods are redirected in transit or redispatched by the buyer without a reasonable opportunity for examination by him and at the time of the conclusion of the contract the seller knew or ought to have known of the possibility of such redirection or redispatch, examination may be deferred until after the goods have arrived at the new destination.

Article 39

(1) The buyer loses the right to rely on a lack of conformity of the goods if he does not give notice to the seller specifying the nature of the lack of conformity within a reasonable time after he has discovered it or ought to have discovered it.

(2) In any event, the buyer loses the right to rely on a lack of conformity of the goods if he does not give the seller notice thereof at the latest within a period of two years from the date on which the goods were actually handed over to the buyer, unless this time-limit is inconsistent with a contractual period of guarantee.

Article 40

The seller is not entitled to rely on the provisions of articles 38 and 39 if the lack of conformity relates to facts of which he knew or could not have been unaware and which he did not disclose to the buyer.

Article 41

The seller must deliver goods which are free from any right or claim of a third party, unless the buyer agreed to take the goods subject to that right or claim. However, if such right or claim is based on industrial property or other intellectual property, the seller's obligation is governed by article 42.

Article 42

(1) The seller must deliver goods which are free from any right or claim of a third party based on industrial property or other intellectual property, of which at the time of the conclusion of the contract the seller knew or could not have been unaware, provided that the right or claim is based on industrial property or other intellectual property:
(a) under the law of the State where the goods will be resold or otherwise used, if it was contemplated by the parties at the time of the conclusion of the contract that the goods would be resold or otherwise used in that State; or
(b) in any other case, under the law of the State where the buyer has his place of business.

(2) The obligation of the seller under the preceding paragraph does not extend to cases where:
(a) at the time of the conclusion of the contract the buyer knew or could not have been unaware of the right or claim; or
(b) the right or claim results from the seller's compliance with technical drawings, designs, formulae or other such specifications furnished by the buyer.

Article 43

(1) The buyer loses the right to rely on the provisions of article 41 or article 42 if he does not give notice to the seller specifying the nature of the right or claim of the third party within a reasonable time after he has become aware or ought to have become aware of the right or claim.

(2) The seller is not entitled to rely on the provisions of the preceding paragraph if he knew of the right or claim of the third party and the nature of it.

Article 44

Notwithstanding the provisions of paragraph (1) of article 39 and paragraph (1) of article 43, the buyer may reduce the price in accordance with article 50 or claim damages, except for loss of profit, if he has a reasonable excuse for his failure to give the required notice.

Section III. *Remedies for breach of contract by the seller*

Article 45

(1) If the seller fails to perform any of his obligations under the contract or this Convention, the buyer may:
(a) exercise the rights provided in articles 46 to 52;
(b) claim damages as provided in articles 74 to 77.

(2) The buyer is not deprived of any right he may have to claim damages by exercising his right to other remedies.

(3) No period of grace may be granted to the seller by a court or arbitral tribunal when the buyer resorts to a remedy for breach of contract.

Article 46

(1) The buyer may require performance by the seller of his obligations unless the buyer has resorted to a remedy which is inconsistent with this requirement.

(2) If the goods do not conform with the contract, the buyer may require delivery of substitute goods only if the lack of conformity constitutes a fundamental breach of contract and a request for substitute goods is made either in conjunction with notice given under article 39 or within a reasonable time thereafter.

(3) If the goods do not conform with the contract, the buyer may require the seller to remedy the lack of conformity by repair, unless this is unreasonable having regard to all the circumstances. A request for repair must be made either in conjunction with notice given under article 39 or within a reasonable time thereafter.

Article 47

(1) The buyer may fix an additional period of time of reasonable length for performance by the seller of his obligations.

(2) Unless the buyer has received notice from the seller that he will not perform within the period so fixed, the buyer may not, during that period, resort to any remedy for breach of contract. However, the buyer is not deprived thereby of any right he may have to claim damages for delay in performance.

Article 48

(1) Subject to article 49, the seller may, even after the date for delivery, remedy at his own expense any failure to perform his obligations, if he can do so without unreasonable delay and without causing the buyer unreasonable inconvenience or uncertainty of reimbursement by the seller of expenses advanced by the buyer. However, the buyer retains any right to claim damages as provided for in this Convention.

(2) If the seller requests the buyer to make known whether he will accept performance and the buyer does not comply with the request within a reasonable time, the seller may perform within the time indicated in his request. The buyer may not, during that period of time, resort to any remedy which is inconsistent with performance by the seller.

(3) A notice by the seller that he will perform within a specified period of time is assumed to include a request, under the preceding paragraph, that the buyer make known his decision.

(4) A request or notice by the seller under paragraph (2) or (3) of this article is not effective unless received by the buyer.

Article 49

(1) The buyer may declare the contract avoided:
(a) if the failure by the seller to perform any of his obligations under the contract or this Convention amounts to a fundamental breach of contract; or
(b) in case of non-delivery, if the seller does not deliver the goods within the additional period of time fixed by the buyer in accordance with paragraph (1) of article 47 or declares that he will not deliver within the period so fixed.

(2) However, in cases where the seller has delivered the goods, the buyer loses the right to declare the contract avoided unless he does so:
(a) in respect of late delivery, within a reasonable time after he has become aware that delivery has been made;
(b) in respect of any breach other than late delivery, within a reasonable time:
  (i) after he knew or ought to have known of the breach;
  (ii) after the expiration of any additional period of time fixed by the buyer in accordance with paragraph (1) of article 47, or after the seller has declared that he will not perform his obligations within such an additional period; or
  (iii) after the expiration of any additional period of time indicated by the seller in accordance with paragraph (3) of article 48, or after the buyer has declared that he will not accept performance.

Article 50

If the goods do not conform with the contract and whether or not the price has already been paid, the buyer may reduce the price in the same proportion as the value that the goods actually delivered had at the time of the delivery bears to the value that conforming goods would have had at that time. However, if the seller remedies any failure to perform his obligations in accordance with article 37 or article 48 or if the buyer refuses to accept performance by the seller in accordance with those articles, the buyer may not reduce the price.

Article 51

(1) If the seller delivers only a part of the goods or if only a part of the goods delivered is in conformity with the contract, articles 46 to 50 apply in respect of the part which is missing or which does not conform.

(2) The buyer may declare the contract avoided in its entirety only if the failure to make delivery completely or in conformity with the contract amounts to a fundamental breach of contract.

Article 52

(1) If the seller delivers the goods before the date fixed, the buyer may take delivery or refuse to take delivery.

(2) If the seller delivers a quantity of goods greater than that provided for in the contract, the buyer may take delivery or refuse to take delivery of the excess quantity. If the buyer takes delivery of all or part of the excess quantity, he must pay for it at the contract rate.

Chapter III

OBLIGATIONS OF THE BUYER

Article 53

The buyer must pay the price for the goods and take delivery of them as required by the contract and this Convention.

Section I. *Payment of the price*

Article 54

The buyer's obligation to pay the price includes taking such steps and complying with such formalities as may be required under the contract or any laws and regulations to enable payment to be made.

Article 55

Where a contract has been validly concluded but does not expressly or implicitly fix or make provision for determining the price, the parties are considered, in the absence of any indication to the contrary, to have impliedly made reference to the price generally charged at the time of the conclusion of the contract for such goods sold under comparable circumstances in the trade concerned.

Article 56

If the price is fixed according to the weight of the goods, in case of doubt it is to be determined by the net weight.

Article 57

(1) If the buyer is not bound to pay the price at any other particular place, he must pay it to the seller:
(a) at the seller's place of business; or
(b) if the payment is to be made against the handing over of the goods or of documents, at the place where the handing over takes place.

(2) The seller must bear any increase in the expenses incidental to payment which is caused by a change in his place of business subsequent to the conclusion of the contract.

Article 58

(1) If the buyer is not bound to pay the price at any other specific time, he must pay it when the seller places either the goods or documents controlling their disposition at the buyer's disposal in accordance with the contract and this Convention. The seller may make such payment a condition for handing over the goods or documents.

(2) If the contract involves carriage of the goods, the seller may dispatch the goods on terms whereby the goods, or documents controlling their disposition, will not be handed over to the buyer except against payment of the price.

(3) The buyer is not bound to pay the price until he has had an opportunity to examine the goods, unless the procedures for delivery or payment agreed upon by the parties are inconsistent with his having such an opportunity.

Article 59

The buyer must pay the price on the date fixed by or determinable from the contract and this Convention without the need for any request or compliance with any formality on the part of the seller.

Section II. *Taking delivery*

Article 60

The buyer's obligation to take delivery consists:
(a) in doing all the acts which could reasonably be expected of him in order to enable the seller to make delivery; and
(b) in taking over the goods.

Section III. *Remedies for breach of contract by the buyer*

Article 61

(1) If the buyer fails to perform any of his obligations under the contract or this Convention, the seller may:
(a) exercise the rights provided in articles 62 to 65;
(b) claim damages as provided in articles 74 to 77.

(2) The seller is not deprived of any right he may have to claim damages by exercising his right to other remedies.

(3) No period of grace may be granted to the buyer by a court or arbitral tribunal when the seller resorts to a remedy for breach of contract.

Article 62

The seller may require the buyer to pay the price, take delivery or perform his other obligations, unless the seller has resorted to a remedy which is inconsistent with this requirement.

Article 63

(1) The seller may fix an additional period of time of reasonable length for performance by the buyer of his obligations.

(2) Unless the seller has received notice from the buyer that he will not perform within the period so fixed, the seller may not, during that period, resort to any remedy for breach of contract. However, the seller is not deprived thereby of any right he may have to claim damages for delay in performance.

Article 64

(1) The seller may declare the contract avoided:
(a) if the failure by the buyer to perform any of his obligations under the contract or this Convention amounts to a fundamental breach of contract; or
(b) if the buyer does not, within the additional period of time fixed by the seller in accordance with paragraph (1) of article 63, perform his obligation to pay the price or take delivery of the goods, or if he declares that he will not do so within the period so fixed.

(2) However, in cases where the buyer has paid the price, the seller loses the right to declare the contract avoided unless he does so:
(a) in respect of late performance by the buyer, before the seller has become aware that performance has been rendered; or
(b) in respect of any breach other than late performance by the buyer, within a reasonable time:
(i) after the seller knew or ought to have known of the breach; or
(ii) after the expiration of any additional period of time fixed by the seller in accordance with paragraph (1) of article 63, or after the buyer has declared that he will not perform his obligations within such an additional period.

Article 65

(1) If under the contract the buyer is to specify the form, measurement or other features of the goods and he fails to make such specification either on the date agreed upon or within a reasonable time after receipt of a request from the seller, the seller may, without prejudice to any other rights he may have, make the specification himself in accordance with the requirements of the buyer that may be known to him.

(2) If the seller makes the specification himself, he must inform the buyer of the details thereof and must fix a reasonable time within which the buyer may make a different specification. If, after receipt of such a communication, the buyer fails to do so within the time so fixed, the specification made by the seller is binding.

Chapter IV

PASSING OF RISK

Article 66

Loss of or damage to the goods after the risk has passed to the buyer does not discharge him from his obligation to pay the price, unless the loss or damage is due to an act or omission of the seller.

Article 67

(1) If the contract of sale involves carriage of the goods and the seller is not bound to hand them over at a particular place, the risk passes to the buyer when the goods are handed over to the first carrier for transmission to the buyer in accordance with the contract of sale. If the seller is bound to hand the goods over to a carrier at a particular place, the risk does not pass to the buyer until the goods are handed over to the carrier at that place. The fact that the seller is authorized to retain documents controlling the disposition of the goods does not affect the passage of the risk.

(2) Nevertheless, the risk does not pass to the buyer until the goods are clearly identified to the contract, whether by markings on the goods, by shipping documents, by notice given to the buyer or otherwise.

Article 68

The risk in respect of goods sold in transit passes to the buyer from the time of the conclusion of the contract. However, if the circumstances so indicate, the risk is assumed by the buyer from the time the goods were handed over to the carrier who issued the documents embodying the contract of carriage. Nevertheless, if at the time of the conclusion of the contract of sale the seller knew or ought to have known that the goods had been lost or damaged and did not disclose this to the buyer, the loss or damage is at the risk of the seller.

Article 69

(1) In cases not within articles 67 and 68, the risk passes to the buyer when he takes over the goods or, if he does not do so in due time, from the time when the goods are placed at his disposal and he commits a breach of contract by failing to take delivery.

(2) However, if the buyer is bound to take over the goods at a place other than a place of business of the seller, the risk passes when delivery is due and the buyer is aware of the fact that the goods are placed at his disposal at that place.

(3) If the contract relates to goods not then identified, the goods are considered not to be placed at the disposal of the buyer until they are clearly identified to the contract.

Article 70

If the seller has committed a fundamental breach of contract, articles 67, 68 and 69 do not impair the remedies available to the buyer on account of the breach.

Chapter V

PROVISIONS COMMON TO THE OBLIGATIONS OF THE SELLER AND OF THE BUYER

Section I. *Anticipatory breach and instalment contracts*

Article 71

(1) A party may suspend the performance of his obligations if, after the conclusion of the contract, it becomes apparent that the other party will not perform a substantial part of his obligations as a result of:
(a) a serious deficiency in his ability to perform or in his creditworthiness; or
(b) his conduct in preparing to perform or in performing the contract.

(2) If the seller has already dispatched the goods before the grounds described in the preceding paragraph become evident, he may prevent the handing over of the goods to the buyer even though the buyer holds a document which entitles him to obtain them. The present paragraph relates only to the rights in the goods as between the buyer and the seller.

(3) A party suspending performance, whether before or after dispatch of the goods, must immediately give notice of the suspension to the other party and must continue with performance if the other party provides adequate assurance of his performance.

Article 72

(1) If prior to the date for performance of the contract it is clear that one of the parties will commit a fundamental breach of contract, the other party may declare the contract avoided.

(2) If time allows, the party intending to declare the contract avoided must give reasonable notice to the other party in order to permit him to provide adequate assurance of his performance.

(3) The requirements of the preceding paragraph do not apply if the other party has declared that he will not perform his obligations.

Article 73

(1) In the case of a contract for delivery of goods by instalments, if the failure of one party to perform any of his obligations in respect of any instalment constitutes a fundamental breach of contract with respect to that instalment, the other party may declare the contract avoided with respect to that instalment.

(2) If one party's failure to perform any of his obligations in respect of any instalment gives the other party good grounds to conclude that a fundamental breach of contract will occur with respect to future instalments, he may declare the contract avoided for the future, provided that he does so within a reasonable time.

(3) A buyer who declares the contract avoided in respect of any delivery may, at the same time, declare it avoided in respect of deliveries already made or of future deliveries if, by reason of their interdependence, those deliveries could not be used for the purpose contemplated by the parties at the time of the conclusion of the contract.

Section II. *Damages*

Article 74

Damages for breach of contract by one party consist of a sum equal to the loss, including loss of profit, suffered by the other party as a consequence of the breach. Such damages may not exceed the loss which the party in breach foresaw or ought to have foreseen at the time of the conclusion of the contract, in the light of the facts and matters of which he then knew or ought to have known, as a possible consequence of the breach of contract.

Article 75

If the contract is avoided and if, in a reasonable manner and within a reasonable time after avoidance, the buyer has bought goods in replacement or the seller has resold the goods, the party claiming damages may recover the difference between the contract price and the price in the substitute transaction as well as any further damages recoverable under article 74.

Article 76

(1) If the contract is avoided and there is a current price for the goods, the party claiming damages may, if he has not made a purchase or resale under article 75, recover the difference between the price fixed by the contract and the current price at the time of avoidance as well as any further damages recoverable under article 74. If, however, the party claiming damages has avoided the contract after taking over the goods, the current price at the time of such taking over shall be applied instead of the current price at the time of avoidance.

(2) For the purposes of the preceding paragraph, the current price is the price prevailing at the place where delivery of the goods should have been made or, if there is no current price at that place, the price at such other place as serves as a reasonable substitute, making due allowance for differences in the cost of transporting the goods.

Article 77

A party who relies on a breach of contract must take such measures as are reasonable in the circumstances to mitigate the loss, including loss of profit, resulting from the breach. If he fails to take such measures, the party in breach may claim a reduction in the damages in the amount by which the loss should have been mitigated.

Section III. *Interest*

Article 78

If a party fails to pay the price or any other sum that is in arrears, the other party is entitled to interest on it, without prejudice to any claim for damages recoverable under article 74.

Section IV. *Exemptions*

Article 79

(1) A party is not liable for a failure to perform any of his obligations if he proves that the failure was due to an impediment beyond his control and that he could not reasonably be expected to have taken the impediment into account at the time of the conclusion of the contract or to have avoided or overcome it, or its consequences.

(2) If the party's failure is due to the failure by a third person whom he has engaged to perform the whole or a part of the contract, that party is exempt from liability only if:

(a) he is exempt under the preceding paragraph; and

(b) the person whom he has so engaged would be so exempt if the provisions of that paragraph were applied to him.

(3) The exemption provided by this article has effect for the period during which the impediment exists.

(4) The party who fails to perform must give notice to the other party of the impediment and its effect on his ability to perform. If the notice is not received by the other party within a reasonable time after the party who fails to perform knew or ought to have known of the impediment, he is liable for damages resulting from such non-receipt.

(5) Nothing in this article prevents either party from exercising any right other than to claim damages under this Convention.

Article 80

A party may not rely on a failure of the other party to perform, to the extent that such failure was caused by the first party's act or omission.

Section V. *Effects of avoidance*

Article 81

(1) Avoidance of the contract releases both parties from their obligations under it, subject to any damages which may be due. Avoidance does not affect any provision of the contract for the settlement of disputes or any other provision of the contract governing the rights and obligations of the parties consequent upon the avoidance of the contract.

(2) A party who has performed the contract either wholly or in part may claim restitution from the other party of whatever the first party has supplied or paid under the contract. If both parties are bound to make restitution, they must do so concurrently.

Article 82

(1) The buyer loses the right to declare the contract avoided or to require the seller to deliver substitute goods if it is impossible for him to make restitution of the goods substantially in the condition in which he received them.

(2) the preceding paragraph does not apply:

(a) if the impossibility of making restitution of the goods or of making restitution of the goods substantially in the condition in which the buyer received them is not due to his act or omission;

(b) if the goods or part of the goods have perished or deteriorated as a result of the examination provided for in article 38; or

(c) if the goods or part of the goods have been sold in the normal course of business or have been consumed or transformed by the buyer in the course of normal use before he discoverd or ought to have discovered the lack of conformity.

Article 83

A buyer who has lost the right to declare the contract avoided or to require the seller to deliver substitute goods in accordance with article 82 retains all other remedies under the contract and this Convention.

Article 84

(1) If the seller is bound to refund the price, he must also pay interest on it, from the date on which the price was paid.

(2) The buyer must account to the seller for all benefits which he has derived from the goods or part of them:

(a) if he must make restitution of the goods or part of them; or

(b) if it is impossible for him to make restitution of all or part of the goods or to make restitution of all or part of the goods substantially in the condition in which he received them, but he has nevertheless declared the contract avoided or required the seller to deliver substitute goods.

Section VI. *Preservation of the goods*

Article 85

If the buyer is in delay in taking delivery of the goods or, where payment of the price and delivery of the goods are to be made concurrently, if he fails to pay the price, and the seller is either in possession of the goods or otherwise able to control their disposition, the seller must take such steps as are reasonable in the circumstances to preserve them. He is entitled to retain them until he has been reimbursed his reasonable expenses by the buyer.

Article 86

(1) If the buyer has received the goods and intends to exercise any right under the contract or this Convention to reject them, he must take such steps to preserve them as are reasonable in the circumstances. He is entitled to retain them until he has been reimbursed his reasonable expenses by the seller.

(2) If goods dispatched to the buyer have been placed at his disposal at their destination and he exercises the right to reject them, he must take possession of them on behalf of the seller, provided that this can be done without payment of the price and without unreasonable inconvenience or unreasonable expense. This provision does not apply if the seller or a person authorized to take charge of the goods on his behalf is present at the destination. If the buyer takes possession of the goods under this paragraph, his rights and obligations are governed by the preceding paragraph.

Article 87

A party who is bound to take steps to preserve the goods may deposit them in a warehouse of a third person at the expense of the other party provided that the expense incurred is not unreasonable.

Article 88

(1) A party who is bound to preserve the goods in accordance with article 85 or 86 may sell them by any appropriate means if there has been an unreasonable delay by the other party in taking possession of the goods or in taking them back or in paying the price or the cost of preservation, provided that reasonable notice of the intention to sell has been given to the other party.

(2) If the goods are subject to rapid deterioration or their preservation would involve unreasonable expense, a party who is bound to preserve the goods in accordance with article 85 or 86 must take reasonable measures to sell them. To the extent possible he must give notice to the other party of his intention to sell.

(3) A party selling the goods has the right to retain out of the proceeds of sale an amount equal to the reasonable expenses of preserving the goods and of selling them. He must account to the other party for the balance.

PART IV

FINAL PROVISIONS

Article 89

The Secretary-General of the United Nations is hereby designated as the depositary for this Convention.

Article 90

This Convention does not prevail over any international agreement which has already been or may be entered into and which contains provisions concerning the matters governed by this Convention, provided that the parties have their places of business in States parties to such agreement.

Article 91

(1) This Convention is open for signature at the concluding meeting of the United Nations Conference on Contracts for the International Sale of Goods and will remain open for signature by all States at the Headquarters of the United Nations, New York until 30 September 1981.

(2) This Convention is subject to ratification, acceptance or approval by the signatory States.

(3) This Convention is open for accession by all States which are not signatory States as from the date it is open for signature.

(4) Instruments of ratification, acceptance, approval and accession are to be deposited with the Secretary-General of the United Nations.

Article 92

(1) A Contracting State may declare at the time of signature, ratification, acceptance, approval or accession that it will not be bound by Part II of this Convention or that it will not be bound by Part III of this Convention.

(2) A Contracting State which makes a declaration in accordance with the preceding paragraph in respect of Part II or Part III of this Convention is not to be considered a Contracting State within paragraph (1) of article 1 of this Convention in respect of matters governed by the Part to which the declaration applies.

Article 93

(1) If a Contracting State has two or more territorial units in which, according to its constitution, different systems of law are applicable in relation to the matters dealt with in this Convention, it may, at the time of signature, ratification, acceptance, approval or accession, declare that this Convention is to extend to all its territorial units or only to one or more of them, and may amend its declaration by submitting another declaration at any time.

(2) These declarations are to be notified to the depositary and are to state expressly the territorial units to which the Convention extends.

(3) If, by virtue of a declaration under this article, this Convention extends to one or more but not all of the territorial units of a Contracting State, and if the place of business of a party is located in that State, this place of business, for the purposes of this Convention, is considered not to be in a Contracting State, unless it is in a territorial unit to which the Convention extends.

(4) If a Contracting State makes no declaration under paragraph (1) of this article, the Convention is to extend to all territorial units of that State.

Article 94

(1) Two or more Contracting States which have the same or closely related legal rules on matters governed by this Convention may at any time declare that the Convention is not to apply to contracts of sale or to their formation where the parties have their places of business in those States. Such declarations may be made jointly or by reciprocal unilateral declarations.

(2) A Contracting State which has the same or closely related legal rules on matters governed by this Convention as one or more non-Contracting States may at any time declare that the Convention is not to apply to contracts of sale or to their formation where the parties have their places of business in those States.

(3) If a State which is the object of a declaration under the preceding paragraph subsequently becomes a Contracting State, the declaration made will, as from the date on which the Convention enters into force in respect of the new Contracting State, have the effect of a declaration made under paragraph (1), provided that the new Contracting State joins in such declaration or makes a reciprocal unilateral declaration.

Article 95

Any State may declare at the time of the deposit of its instrument of ratification, acceptance, approval or accession that it will not be bound by subparagraph (1)(b) of article 1 of this Convention.

Article 96

A Contracting State whose legislation requires contracts of sale to be concluded in or evidenced by writing may at any time make a declaration in accordance with article 12 that any provision of article 11, article 29, or Part II of this Convention, that allows a contract of sale or its modification or termination by agreement or any offer, acceptance, or other indication of intention to be made in any form other than in writing, does not apply where any party has his place of business in that State.

Article 97

(1) Declarations made under this Convention at the time of signature are subject to confirmation under ratification, acceptance or approval.

(2) Declarations and confirmations of declarations are to be in writing and be formally notified to the depositary.

(3) A declaration takes effect simultaneously with the entry into force of this Convention in respect of the State concerned. However, a declaration of which the depositary receives formal notification after such entry into force takes effect on the first day of the month following the expiration of six months after the date of its receipt by the depositary. Reciprocal unilateral declarations under article 94 take effect on the first day of the month following the expiration of six months after the receipt of the latest declaration by the depositary.

(4) Any State which makes a declaration under this Convention may withdraw it at any time by a formal notification in writing addressed to the depositary. Such withdrawal is to take effect on the first day of the month following the expiration of six months after the date of the receipt of the notification by the depositary.

(5) A withdrawal of a declaration made under article 94 renders inoperative, as from the date on which the withdrawal takes effect, any reciprocal declaration made by another State under that article.

Article 98

No reservations are permitted except those expressly authorized in this Convention.

Article 99

(1) This Convention enters into force, subject to the provisions of paragraph (6) of this article, on the first day of the month following the expiration of twelve months after the date of deposit of the tenth instrument of ratification, acceptance, approval or accession, including an instrument which contains a declaration made under article 92.

(2) When a State ratifies, accepts, approves or accedes to this Convention after the deposit of the tenth instrument of ratification, acceptance, approval or accession, this Convention, with the exception of the Part excluded, enters into force in respect of that State, subject to the provisions of paragraph (6) of this article, on the first day of the month following the expiration of twelve months after the date of the deposit of its instrument of ratification, acceptance, approval or accession.

(3) A State which ratifies, accepts, approves or accedes to this Convention and is a party to either or both the Convention relating to a Uniform Law on the Formation of Contracts for the International Sale of Goods done at The Hague on 1 July 1964 (1964 Hague Formation Convention) and the Convention relating to a Uniform Law on the International Sale of Goods done at The Hague on 1 July 1964 (1964 Hague Sales Convention) shall at the same time denounce, as the case may be, either or both the 1964 Hague Sales Convention and the 1964 Hague Formation Convention by notifying the Government of the Netherlands to that effect.

(4) A State party to the 1964 Hague Sales Convention which ratifies, accepts, approves or accedes to the present Convention and declares or has declared under article 92 that it will not be bound by Part II of this Convention shall at the time of ratification, acceptance, approval or accession denounce the 1964 Hague Sales Convention by notifying the Government of the Netherlands to that effect.

(5) A State party to the 1964 Hague Formation Convention which ratifies, accepts, approves or accedes to the present Convention and declares or has declared under article 92 that it will not be bound by Part III of this Convention shall at the time of ratification, acceptance, approval or accession denounce the 1964 Hague Formation Convention by notifying the Government of the Netherlands to that effect.

(6) For the purpose of this article, ratifications, acceptances, approvals and accessions in respect of this Convention by States parties to the 1964 Hague Formation Convention or to the 1964 Hague Sales Convention shall not be effective until such denunciations as may be required on the part of those States in respect of the latter two Conventions have themselves become effective. The depositary of this Convention shall consult with the Government of the Netherlands, as the depositary of the 1964 Conventions, so as to ensure necessary co-ordination in this respect.

Article 100

(1) This Convention applies to the formation of the contract only when the proposal for concluding the contract is made on or after the date when the Convention enters into force in respect of the Contracting States referred to in subparagraph (1)(a) or the Contracting State referred to in subparagraph (1)(b) of article 1.

(2) This Convention applies only to contracts concluded on or after the date when the Convention enters into force in respect of the Contracting States referred to in subparagraph (1)(a) or the Contracting State referred to in subparagraph (1)(b) of article 1.

Article 101

(1) A Contracting State may denounce this Convention, or Part II or Part III of the Convention, by a formal notification in writing addressed to the depositary.

(2) The denunciation takes effect on the first day of the month following the expiration of twelve months after the notification is received by the depositary. Where a longer period for the denunciation to take effect is specified in the notification, the denunciation takes effect upon the expiration of such longer period after the notification is received by the depositary.

DONE at Vienna, this day of eleventh day of April*, one thousand nine hundred and eighty, in a single original, of which the Arabic, Chinese, English, French, Russian and Spanish texts are equally authentic.

IN WITNESS WHEREOF the undersigned plenipotentiaries, being duly authorized by their respective Governments, have signed this Convention. [Signatures omitted]

---

* Editor's note: Thus in U.N.-certified text.

United Nations convention on contracts for the international sale of goods. Done at Vienna April 11, 1980; entry into force for the United States January 1, 1988.

States which are parties:

Argentina[1]
Australia[2]
Austria
Belarus[3]
Bosnia and Herzegovina
Bulgaria
Canada[3a]
Chile[4]
China[5]
Cuba
Czech Republic[6]
Denmark[7]
Ecuador
Egypt
Estonia[7a]
Finland[8]
France
Georgia
Germany, Federal Republic of[9]
Guinea
Hungary[10]
Iraq
Italy
Lesotho
Lithuania[10a]
Mexico
Moldova
Netherlands[10b]
New Zealand[10c]
Norway[11]
Poland
Romania
Russian Federation[11a]
Singapore[11b]
Slovakia[11c]
Slovenia
Spain
Sweden[12]
Switzerland
Syrian Arab Republic
Uganda
Ukraine[13]
United States[14]
Yugoslavia[15]
Zambia

[1] The instrument of accession by the Government of Argentina contains the following declaration:

(Translation) (Original: Spanish)

In accordance with articles 96 and 12 of the United Nations Convention on Contracts for the International Sale of Goods, any provision of article 11, article 29 or Part II of the Convention that allows a contract of sale or its modification or termination by agreement or any offer, acceptance or other indication of intention to be made in any form other than in writing does not apply where any party has his place of business in the Argentine Republic.

[2] The instrument of accession by the Government of Australia contains the following declaration:

(Original: English)

"The Convention shall apply to all Australian States and mainland territories and to all external territories except the territories of Christmas Island, the Cocos (Keeling) Islands and the Ashmore and Cartier Islands."

[3] The instrument of accession by the Government of [Belarus] contains the following declaration:

(Translation) (Original: Russian)

"[Belarus], in accordance with articles 12 and 96 of the Convention declares that any provision of article 11, article 29 or Part II of this Convention that allows a contract of sale or its modification or termination by agreement or any offer, acceptance or other indication of intention to be made in any form other than in writing does not apply where any party has his place of business in [Belarus]."

[3a] The instrument of accession by the Government of Canada contains the following declaration:

"The Government of Canada declares, in accordance with Article 93 of the Convention, that the Convention will extend to Alberta, British Columbia, Manitoba, New Brunswick, Newfoundland, Nova Scotia, Ontario, Prince Edward Island and the Northwest Territories."

Subsequently the Government of Canada declared that "the Convention shall also extend to Quebec and Saskatchewan" (9 April 1992) and "applies also to the Territory of the Yukon" (29 June 1992).

[4] The instrument of ratification by the Government of Chile contains the following declaration:

(Translation) (Original: Spanish)

"The State of Chile declares, in accordance with articles 12 and 96 of the Convention, that any provision of article 11, article 29 or Part II of the Convention that allows a contract of sale or its modification or termination by mutual agreement or any offer, acceptance or other indication of intention to be made in any other form than in writing, does not apply where any party has its place of business in Chile."

[5] The instrument of approval by the Government of China contains the following declaration:

(Courtesy translation) (Original: Chinese)

The People's Republic of China does not consider itself to be bound by subparagraph (b) of paragraph 1 of Article 1 and Article 11 as well as the provisions in the Convention relating to the content of Article 11.

[6] Subject to the following declaration:

(Courtesy Translation) (Original: Czechoslovak)

"Pursuant to Article 95, the [Czech Republic] declares that it shall not consider itself bound by the provision of Article 1, paragraph 1, item b), of the Convention."

[7] The instrument of ratification by the Government of Denmark was accompanied by the following declarations:

(Original: English)

"Upon ratifying the Convention, the Kingdom of Denmark declares:

1) under paragraph 1 of Article 92 that Denmark will not be bound by Part II of the Convention,

2) under paragraph 1 of Article 93 that the Convention shall not apply to the Faroe Islands and Greenland,

3) under paragraph 1 cf. paragraph 3 of Article 94 that the Convention shall not apply to contracts of sale where one of the parties has his place of business in Denmark, Finland, Norway or Sweden and the other party has his place of business in another of the said states,

4) under paragraph 2 of Article 94 that the Convention is not to apply to contracts of sale where one of the parties has his place of business in Denmark, Finland, Norway or Sweden and the other party has his place of business in Iceland".

[7a] The instrument of accession by the Government of Estonia contains the following declaration:

"In accordance with Articles 12 and 96 of the United Nations Convention on Contracts for the International Sale of Goods any provision of Article 11, Article 29 or Part II of the Convention that allows a contract of sale or its modification or termination by agreement or any offer, acceptance or other indication of intention to be made in any form other than in writing does not apply where any party has his place of business in the Republic of Estonia."

[8] The instrument of ratification by the Government of Finland contains the following declarations:

(Original: English)

"1. With reference to Article 92, Finland will not be bound by Part II of this Convention (Formation of the Contract).

2. With reference to Article 94, in respect of Sweden in accordance with paragraph (1) and otherwise in accordance with paragraph (2) the Convention will not apply to contracts of sale where the parties have their places of business in Finland, Sweden, Denmark, Iceland or Norway."

[9] On October 3, 1990 the German Democratic Republic acceded to the Federal Republic of Germany.

The instrument of ratification by the Government of the Federal Republic of Germany contains the following declaration:

(Courtesy Translation) (Original: German)

"The Government of the Federal Republic of Germany holds the view that Parties to the Convention that have made a declaration under article 95 of the Convention are not considered Contracting States within the meaning of subparagraph (1) (b) of article 1 of the Convention. Accordingly, there is no obligation to apply—and the Federal Republic of Germany assumes no obligation to apply—this provision when the rules of private international law lead to the application of the law of a Party that has made a declaration to the effect that it will not be bound by subparagraph (1) (b) of article 1 of the Convention. Subject to this observation the Government of the Federal Republic of Germany makes no declaration under article 95 of the Convention."

In a note accompanying the instrument of ratification the Government of the Federal Republic of Germany stated that the said Convention shall also apply to Berlin (West) with effect from the date on which it enters into force for the Federal Republic of Germany.

The Federal Republic of Germany denounced, on 1 January 1990, the Conventions relating to the formation of contracts for the international sale of goods and the international sale of such goods, both done at The Hague on 1 July 1964. These denunciations shall take effect on 31 December 1990, and the present Convention will therefore enter into force for the Federal Republic of Germany on 1 January 1991, in accordance with paragraph 2 and 6 of article 99.

[10] In a note accompanying its instrument of ratification, the Government of Hungary made the following declarations:

— "It [Hungary] considers the General Conditions of Delivery of Goods between Organizations of the Member Countries of the Council for Mutual Economic Assistance/GCD CMEA, 1968/1975, version of 1979/ to be subject to the provisions of article 90 of the Convention;

— It states, in accordance with articles 12 and 96 of the Convention, that any provision of article 11, article 29 or part II of the Convention that allows a contract of sale or its modification or termination by agreement or any offer, acceptance or other indication of intention to be made in any form other than in writing, does not apply where any party has his place of business in the Hungarian People's Republic."

[10a] The instrument of accession by the Government of Lithuania contains the following declaration:

In accordance with articles 96 and 12 of the said Convention, the Republic of Lithuania declares that any provisions of article 11, article 29 or Part II of the Convention that allows a contract of sale or its modification or termination by agreement or any offer, acceptance or other indication of intention to be made in any form other than in written does not apply where any party has his place of business in the Republic of Lithuania.

[10b] For the Kingdom in Europe and Aruba.

[11] The instrument of ratification by the Government of Norway contains the following declarations:

(Original: English)

"1. In accordance with Article 92, paragraph (1), the Government of the Kingdom of Norway declares that Norway will not be bound by Part II of this Convention. (Formation of the Contract).

2. With reference to Article 94, in respect of Finland and Sweden in accordance with paragraph (1) and otherwise in accordance with paragraph (2), the Government of the Kingdom of Norway declares that the Convention will not apply to contracts of sale where the parties have their places of business in Norway, Denmark, Finland, Iceland or Sweden."

[11a] The instrument of accession by the Government of the [Russian Federation] contains the following declaration:

(Translation) (Original: Russian)

"In accordance with articles 12 and 96 of the Convention, the [Russian Federation] declares that any provision of article 11, article 29 or Part II of the Convention that allows a contract of sale or its modification or termination by agreement or any offer, acceptance or other indication of intention to be made in any form other than in writing does not apply where any party has his place of business in the [Russian Federation]."

[11b] The instrument of ratification by the Government of Singapore contains the following declaration:

In accordance with article 95 of the said Convention, the Government of the Republic of Singapore will not be bound by sub-paragraph (1)(b) of article 1 of the Convention and will apply the Convention to the Contracts of Sale of Goods only between those parties whose places of business are in different States when the States are Contracting States.

[11c] Subject to the following declaration:

(Courtesy Translation) (Original: Czechoslovak)

"Pursuant to Article 95, [Slovakia] declares that it shall not consider itself bound by the provision of Article 1, paragraph 1, item b), of the Convention."

[12] The instrument of ratification by the Government of Sweden contains the following declarations:

(Original: English)

"1. With reference to Article 92, Sweden will not be bound by Part II of this Convention (Formation of the Contract).

2. With reference to Article 94, in respect of Finland in accordance with paragraph (1) and otherwise in accordance with paragraph (2) the Convention will not apply to contracts of sale where the parties have their places of business in Sweden, Finland, Denmark, Iceland or Norway."

[13] The instrument of accession by the Government of [Ukraine] contains the following declaration:

(Translation) (Original: Russian)

"In accordance with articles 12 and 96 of the Convention, [Ukraine] declares that any provision of article 11, article 29 or Part II of the Convention that allows a contract of sale or its modification or termination by agreement or any offer, acceptance or other indication of intention to be made in any form other than in writing does not apply where any party has his place of business in [Ukraine]."

[14] The instrument of ratification by the Government of the United States contains the following declaration:

"Pursuant to article 95 the United States will not be bound by subparagraph (1)(b) of Article 1."

[15] *Ed. note*—The U.S. view is that the Socialist Federal Republic of Yugoslavia has dissolved and no successor state represents its continuation.

CONVENTION ON THE LIMITATION PERIOD IN THE INTERNATIONAL SALE OF GOODS AS AMENDED BY THE PROTOCOL AMENDING THE CONVENTION ON THE LIMITATION PERIOD IN THE INTERNATIONAL SALE OF GOODS

PREAMBLE

The States Parties to the present Convention,

Considering that international trade is an important factor in the promotion of friendly relations amongst States,

Believing that the adoption of uniform rules governing the limitation period in the international sale of goods would facilitate the development of world trade,

Have agreed as follows:

PART I. SUBSTANTIVE PROVISIONS

SPHERE OF APPLICATION

Article 1

1. This Convention shall determine when claims of a buyer and a seller against each other arising from a contract of international sale of goods or relating to its breach, termination or invalidity can no longer be exercised by reason of the expiration of a period of time. Such a period of time is hereinafter referred to as "the limitation period".

2. This Convention shall not affect a particular time-limit within which one party is required, as a condition for the acquisition or exercise of his claim, to give notice to the other party or perform any act other than the institution of legal proceedings.

3. In this Convention:

(a) "buyer", "seller" and "party" mean persons who buy or sell, or agree to buy or sell, goods, and the successors to and assigns of their rights or obligations under the contract of sale;

(b) "creditor" means a party who asserts a claim, whether or not such a claim is for a sum of money;

(c) "debtor" means a party against whom a creditor asserts a claim;

(d) "breach of contract" means the failure of a party to perform the contract or any performance not in conformity with the contract;

(e) "legal proceedings" includes judicial, arbitral and administrative proceedings;

(f) "person" includes corporation, company, partnership, association or entity, whether private or public, which can sue or be sued;

(g) "writing" includes telegram and telex;

(h) "year" means a year according to the Gregorian calendar.

Article 2

For the purposes of this Convention:

(a) a contract of sale of goods shall be considered international if, at the time of the conclusion of the contract, the buyer and the seller have their places of business in different States;

(b) the fact that the parties have their places of business in different States shall be disregarded whenever this fact does not appear either from the contract or from any dealings between, or from information disclosed by, the parties at any time before or at the conclusion of the contract;

(c) where a party to a contract of sale of goods has places of business in more than one State, the place of business shall be that which has the closest relationship to the contract and its performance, having regard to the circumstances known to or contemplated by the parties at the time of the conclusion of the contract;

(d) where a party does not have a place of business, reference shall be made to his habitual residence;

(e) neither the nationality of the parties nor the civil or commercial character of the parties or of the contract shall be taken into consideration.

*Article 3**

1. This Convention shall apply only

(a) if, at the time of the conclusion of the contract, the places of business of the parties to a contract of international sale of goods are in Contracting States; or

(b) if the rules of private international law make the law of a Contracting State applicable to the contract of sale.

2. This Convention shall not apply when the parties have expressly excluded its application.

* Text as amended in accordance with article I of the 1980 Protocol. States that make a declaration under article 36 bis (article XII of the 1980 Protocol) will be bound by article 3 as originally adopted in the Limitation Convention, 1974. Article 3 as originally adopted reads as follows:

"*Article 3*

1. This Convention shall apply only if, at the time of the conclusion of the contract, the places of business of the parties to a contract of international sale of goods are in Contracting States.

2. Unless this Convention provides otherwise, it shall apply irrespective of the law which would otherwise be applicable by virtue of the rules of private international law.

3. This Convention shall not apply when the parties have expressly excluded its application."

*Article 4**

This Convention shall not apply to sales:

(a) of goods bought for personal, family or household use, unless the seller, at any time before or at the conclusion of the contract, neither knew nor ought to have known that the goods were bought for any such use;

(b) by auction;

(c) on execution or otherwise by authority of law;

(d) of stocks, shares, investment securities, negotiable instruments or money;

(e) of ships, vessels, hovercraft or aircraft;

(f) of electricity.

* Text of paragraphs (a) and (e) as amended in accordance with article II of the 1980 Protocol. Paragraphs (a) and (e) of article 4 as originally adopted in the Limitation Convention, 1974, prior to its amendment under the 1980 Protocol, read as follows:
"(a) of goods bought for personal, family or household use;
(e) of ships, vessels, or aircraft;".

Article 5

This Convention shall not apply to claims based upon:

(a) death of, or personal injury to, any person;

(b) nuclear damage caused by the goods sold;

(c) a lien, mortgage or other security interest in property;

(d) a judgement or award made in legal proceedings;

(e) a document on which direct enforcement or execution can be obtained in accordance with the law of the place where such enforcement or execution is sought;

(f) a bill of exchange, cheque or promissory note.

Article 6

1. This Convention shall not apply to contracts in which the preponderant part of the obligations of the seller consists in the supply of labour or other services.

2. Contracts for the supply of goods to be manufactured or produced shall be considered to be sales, unless the party who orders the goods undertakes to supply a substantial part of the materials necessary for such manufacture or production.

Article 7

In the interpretation and application of the provisions of this Convention, regard shall be had to its international character and to the need to promote uniformity.

THE DURATION AND COMMENCEMENT OF THE LIMITATION PERIOD

Article 8

The limitation period shall be four years.

Article 9

1. Subject to the provisions of articles 10, 11 and 12 the limitation period shall commence on the date of which the claim accrues.

2. The commencement of the limitation period shall not be postponed by:

(a) a requirement that the party be given a notice as described in paragraph 2 of article 1, or

(b) a provision in an arbitration agreement that no right shall arise until an arbitration award has been made.

Article 10

1. A claim arising from a breach of contract shall accrue on the date on which such breach occurs.

2. A claim arising from a defect or other lack of conformity shall accrue on the date on which the goods are actually handed over to, or their tender is refused by, the buyer.

3. A claim based on fraud committed before or at the time of the conclusion of the contract or during its performance shall accrue on the date on which the fraud was or reasonably could have been discovered.

Article 11

If the seller has given an express undertaking relating to the goods which is stated to have effect for a certain period of time, whether expressed in terms of a specific period of time or otherwise, the limitation period in respect of any claim arising from the undertaking shall commence on the date on which the buyer notifies the seller of the fact on which the claim is based, but not later than on the date of the expiration of the period of the undertaking.

Article 12

1. If, in circumstances provided for by the law applicable to the contract, one party is entitled to declare the contract terminated before the time for performance is due, and exercises this right, the limitation period in respect of a claim based on any such circumstances shall commence on the date on which the declaration is made to the other party. If the contract is not declared to be terminated before performance becomes due, the limitation period shall commence on the date on which performance is due.

2. The limitation period in respect of a claim arising out of a breach by one party of a contract for the delivery of or payment for goods by instalments shall, in relation to each separate instalment, commence on the date on which the particular breach occurs. If, under the law applicable to the contract, one party is entitled to declare the contract terminated by reason of such breach, and exercises this right, the limitation period in respect of all relevant instalments shall commence on the date on which the declaration is made to the other party.

CESSATION AND EXTENSION OF THE LIMITATION PERIOD

Article 13

The limitation period shall cease to run when the creditor performs any act which, under the law of the court where the proceedings are instituted, is recognized as commencing judicial proceedings against the debtor or as asserting his claim in such proceedings already instituted against the debtor, for the purpose of obtaining satisfaction or recognition of his claim.

Article 14

1. Where the parties have agreed to submit to arbitration, the limitation period shall cease to run when either party commences arbitral proceedings in the manner provided for in the arbitration agreement or by the law applicable to such proceedings.

2. In the absence of any such provision, arbitral proceedings shall be deemed to commence on the date on which a request that the claim in dispute be referred to

arbitration is delivered at the habitual residence or place of business of the other party or, if he has no such residence or place of business, then at his last known residence or place of business.

Article 15

In any legal proceedings other than those mentioned in articles 13 and 14, including legal proceedings commenced upon the occurrence of:

(a) the death or incapacity of the debtor,

(b) the bankruptcy or any state of insolvency affecting the whole of the property of the debtor, or

(c) the dissolution or liquidation of a corporation, company, partnership, association or entity when it is the debtor,

the limitation period shall cease to run when the creditor asserts his claim in such proceedings for the purpose of obtaining satisfaction or recognition of the claim, subject to the law governing the proceedings.

Article 16

For the purposes of articles 13, 14 and 15, any act performed by way of counterclaim shall be deemed to have been performed on the same date as the act performed in relation to the claim against which the counterclaim is raised, provided that both the claim and the counterclaim relate to the same contract or to several contracts concluded in the course of the same transaction.

Article 17

1. Where a claim has been asserted in legal proceedings within the limitation period in accordance with article 13, 14, 15 or 16, but such legal proceedings have ended without a decision binding on the merits of the claim, the limitation period shall be deemed to have continued to run.

2. If, at the time such legal proceedings ended, the limitation period has expired or has less than one year to run, the creditor shall be entitled to a period of one year from the date on which the legal proceedings ended.

Article 18

1. Where legal proceedings have been commenced against one debtor, the limitation period prescribed in this Convention shall cease to run against any other party jointly and severally liable with the debtor, provided that the creditor informs such party in writing within that period that the proceedings have been commenced.

2. Where legal proceedings have been commenced by a subpurchaser against the buyer, the limitation period prescribed in this Convention shall cease to run in relation to the buyer's claim over against the seller, if the buyer informs the seller in writing within that period that the proceedings have been commenced.

3. Where the legal proceedings referred to in paragraphs 1 and 2 of this article have ended, the limitation period in respect of the claim of the creditor or the buyer against the party jointly and severally liable or against the seller shall be deemed not to have ceased running by virtue of paragraphs 1 and 2 of this article, but the creditor or the buyer shall be entitled to an additional year from the date on which the legal proceedings ended, if at that time the limitation period had expired or had less than one year to run.

Article 19

Where the creditor performs, in the State in which the debtor has his place of business and before the expiration of the limitation period, any act, other than the acts described in articles 13, 14, 15 and 16, which under the law of that State has the effect of recommencing a limitation period, a new limitation period of four years shall commence on the date prescribed by that law.

Article 20

1. Where the debtor, before the expiration of the limitation period, acknowledges in writing his obligation to the creditor, a new limitation period of four years shall commence to run from the date of such acknowledgement.

2. Payment of interest or partial performance of an obligation by the debtor shall have the same effect as an acknowledgement under paragraph 1 of this article if it can reasonably be inferred from such payment or performance that the debtor acknowledges that obligation.

Article 21

Where, as a result of a circumstance which is beyond the control of the creditor and which he could neither avoid nor overcome, the creditor has been prevented from causing the limitation period to cease to run, the limitation period shall be extended so as not to expire before the expiration of one year from the date on which the relevant circumstance ceased to exist.

MODIFICATION OF THE LIMITATION PERIOD BY THE PARTIES

Article 22

1. The limitation period cannot be modified or affected by any declaration or agreement between the parties, except in the cases provided for in paragraph 2 of this article.

2. The debtor may at any time during the running of the limitation period extend the period by a declaration in writing to the creditor. This declaration may be renewed.

3. The provisions of this article shall not affect the validity of a clause in the contract of sale which stipulates that arbitral proceedings shall be commenced within a shorter period of limitation than that prescribed by this Convention, provided that such clause is valid under the law applicable to the contract of sale.

GENERAL LIMIT OF THE LIMITATION PERIOD

Article 23

Notwithstanding the provisions of this Convention, a limitation period shall in any event expire not later than ten years from the date on which it commenced to run under articles 9, 10, 11 and 12 of this Convention.

CONSEQUENCES OF THE EXPIRATION OF THE LIMITATION PERIOD

Article 24

Expiration of the limitation period shall be taken into consideration in any legal proceedings only if invoked by a party to such proceedings.

Article 25

1. Subject to the provisions of paragraph 2 of this article and of article 24, no claim shall be recognized or enforced in any legal proceedings commenced after the expiration of the limitation period.

2. Notwithstanding the expiration of the limitation period, one party may rely on his claim as a defence or for the purpose of set-off against a claim asserted by the other party, provided that in the latter case this may only be done:

(a) if both claims relate to the same contract or to several contracts concluded in the course of the same transaction; or

(b) if the claims could have been set-off at any time before the expiration of the limitation period.

Article 26

Where the debtor performs his obligation after the expiration of the limitation period, he shall not on that ground be entitled in any way to claim restitution even if he did not know at the time when he performed his obligation that the limitation period had expired.

Article 27

The expiration of the limitation period with respect to a principal debt shall have the same effect with respect to an obligation to pay interest on that debt.

CALCULATION OF THE PERIOD

Article 28

1. The limitation period shall be calculated in such a way that it shall expire at the end of the day which corresponds to the date on which the period commenced to run. If there is no such corresponding date, the period shall expire at the end of the last day of the last month of the limitation period.

2. The limitation period shall be calculated by reference to the date of the place where the legal proceedings are instituted.

Article 29

Where the last day of the limitation period falls on an official holiday or other *dies non juridicus* precluding the appropriate legal action in the jurisdiction where the creditor institutes legal proceedings or asserts a claim as envisaged in article 13, 14 or 15, the limitation period shall be extended so as not to expire until the end of the first day following that official holiday or *dies non juridicus* on which such proceedings could be instituted or on which such a claim could be asserted in that jurisdiction.

INTERNATIONAL EFFECT

Article 30

The acts and circumstances referred to in articles 13 through 19 which have taken place in one Contracting State shall have effect for the purposes of this Convention in another Contracting State, provided that the creditor has taken all reasonable steps to ensure that the debtor is informed of the relevant act or circumstances as soon as possible.

PART II. IMPLEMENTATION

Article 31

1. If a Contracting State has two or more territorial units in which, according to its constitution, different systems of law are applicable in relation to the matters dealt with in this Convention, it may, at the time of signature, ratification or accession, declare that this Convention shall extend to all its territorial units or only to one or more of them, and may amend its declaration by submitting another declaration at any time.

2. These declarations shall be notified to the Secretary-General of the United Nations and shall state expressly the territorial units to which the Convention applies.

3. If a Contracting State described in paragraph 1 of this article makes no declaration at the time of signature, ratification or accession, the Convention shall have effect within all territorial units of that State.

* 4. If, by virtue of a declaration under this article, this Convention extends to one or more but not all of the territorial units of a Contracting State, and if the place of business of a party to a contract is located in that State, this place of business shall, for the purposes of this Convention, be considered not to be in a Contracting State, unless it is in a territorial unit to which the Convention extends.

* New paragraph 4, added in accordance with article III of the 1980 Protocol.

Article 32

Where in this Convention reference is made to the law of a State in which different systems of law apply, such reference shall be construed to mean the law of the particular legal system concerned.

Article 33

Each Contracting State shall apply the provisions of this Convention to contracts concluded on or after the date of the entry into force of this Convention.

PART III. DECLARATIONS AND RESERVATIONS

*Article 34**

1. Two or more Contracting States which have the same or closely related legal rules on matters governed by this Convention may at any time declare that the Convention shall not apply to contracts of international sale of goods where the parties have their places of business in those States. Such declarations may be made jointly or by reciprocal unilateral declarations.

* Text as amended in accordance with article IV of the 1980 Protocol. Article 34 as originally adopted in the Limitation Convention, 1974, prior to its amendment under the 1980 Protocol, read as follows:

"*Article 34*

Two or more Contracting States may at any time declare that contracts of sale between a seller having a place of business in one of these States and a buyer having a place of business in another of these States shall not be governed by this

Convention, because they apply to the matters governed by this Convention the same or closely related legal rules."

2. A Contracting State which has the same or closely related legal rules on matters governed by this Convention as one or more non-Contracting States may at any time declare that the Convention shall not apply to contracts of international sale of goods where the parties have their places of business in those States.

3. If a State which is the object of a declaration under paragraph 2 of this article subsequently becomes a Contracting State, the declaration made shall, as from the date on which this Convention enters into force in respect of the new Contracting State, have the effect of a declaration made under paragraph 1, provided that the new Contracting State joins in such declaration or makes a reciprocal unilateral declaration.

Article 35

A Contracting State may declare, at the time of the deposit of its instrument of ratification or accession, that it will not apply the provision of this Convention to actions for annulment of the contract.

Article 36

Any State may declare, at the time of the deposit of its instrument of ratification or accession, that it shall not be compelled to apply the provisions of article 24 of this Convention.

Article 36 bis (Article XII of the Protocol)

Any State may declare at the time of the deposit of its instrument of accession or its notification under article 43 bis that it will not be bound by the amendments to article 3 made by article I of the 1980 Protocol*. A declaration made under this article shall be in writing and be formally notified to the depositary.

* Such a State will then be bound by article 3 of the unamended Convention. For its text, see footnote under article 3.

*Article 37**

This Convention shall not prevail over any international agreement which has already been or may be entered into and which contains provisions concerning the matters governed by this Convention, provided that the seller and buyer have their places of business in States parties to such agreement.

* Text as amended in accordance with article V of the Protocol. Article 37 as originally adopted in the Limitation Convention, 1974, prior to its amendment under the 1980 Protocol, read as follows:

> "*Article 37*
>
> This Convention shall not prevail over conventions already entered into or which may be entered into, and which contain provisions concerning the matters covered by this Convention, provided that the seller and buyer have their places of business in States parties to such a convention."

Article 38

1. A Contracting State which is a party to an existing convention relating to the international sale of goods may declare, at the time of the deposit of its instrument of ratification or accession, that it will apply to this Convention exclusively to contracts of international sale of goods as defined in such existing convention.

2. Such declaration shall cease to be effective on the first day of the month following the expiration of twelve months after a new convention on the international sale of goods, concluded under the auspices of the United Nations, shall have entered into force.

Article 39

No reservation other than those made in accordance with articles 34, 35, 36, 36 bis and 38 shall be permitted.

Article 40

1. Declarations made under this Convention shall be addressed to the Secretary-General of the United Nations and shall take effect simultaneously with the entry of this Convention into force in respect of the State concerned, except declarations made thereafter. The latter declarations shall take effect on the first day of the month following the expiration of six months after the date of their receipt by the Secretary-General of the United Nations. *Reciprocal unilateral declarations under article 34 shall take effect on the first day of the month following the expiration of six months after the receipt of the latest declaration by the Secretary-General of the United Nations.*

2. Any State which has made a declaration under this Convention may withdraw it at any time by a notification addressed to the Secretary-General of the United Nations. Such withdrawal shall take effect on the first day of the month following the expiration of six months after the date of the receipt of the notification by the Secretary-General of the United Nations. In the case of a declaration made under article 34 of this Convention, such withdrawal shall also render inoperative, as from the date on which the withdrawal takes effect, any reciprocal declaration made by another State under that article.

* Last sentence of paragraph 1 of article 40 (between asterisks) added in accordance with article VI of the 1980 Protocol.

PART IV. FINAL CLAUSES

Article 41

This Convention* shall be open until 31 December 1975 for signature by all States at the Headquarters of the United Nations.

* Refers to the 1974 Limitation Convention.

Article 42

This Convention* is subject to ratification. The instruments of ratification shall be deposited with the Secretary-General of the United Nations.

* Refers to the 1974 Limitation Convention.

Article 43

This Convention* shall remain open for accession by any State. The instruments of accession shall be deposited with the Secretary-General of the United Nations.

* Refers to the 1974 Limitation Convention.

Article 43 bis (Article X of the Protocol)

If a State ratifies or accedes to the 1974 Limitation Convention after the entry into force of the 1980 Protocol, the ratification or accession shall also constitute a ratification of or an accession to the Convention as amended by the 1980 Protocol if the State notifies the depositary accordingly.

Article 43 ter (Article VIII (2) of the Protocol)

Accession to the 1980 Protocol by any State which is not a Contracting Party to the 1974 Limitation Convention shall have the effect of accession to that Convention as amended by the Protocol, subject to the provisions of article 44 bis.

Article 44

1. This Convention shall enter into force on the first day of the month following the expiration of six months after the date of the deposit of the tenth instrument of ratification or accession.

2. For each State ratifying or acceding to this Convention after the deposit of the tenth instrument of ratification or accession, this Convention shall enter into force on the first day of the month following the expiration of six months after the date of the deposit of its instrument of ratification or accession.

Article 44 bis (Article XI of the Protocol)

Any State which becomes a Contracting Party to the 1974 Limitation Convention, as amended by the 1980 Protocol, shall, unless it notifies the depositary to the contrary, be considered to be also a Contracting Party to the Convention, unamended, in relation to any Contracting Party to the Convention not yet a Contracting Party to the 1980 Protocol.

Article 45

1. Any Contracting State may denounce this Convention by notifying the Secretary-General of the United Nations to that effect.

2. The denunciation shall take effect on the first day of the month following the expiration of twelve months after receipt of the notification by the Secretary-General of the United Nations.

Article 45 bis (Article XIII (3) of the Protocol)

Any Contracting State in respect of which the 1980 Protocol ceases to have effect by the application of paragraphs (1) and (2)* of article XIII of the 1980 Protocol shall remain a Contracting Party to the 1974 Limitation Convention, unamended, unless it denounces the unamended Convention in accordance with article 45 of that Convention.

* Paragraphs (1) and (2) of article XIII of the Protocol read as follows:
"(1) A Contracting State may denounce this Protocol by notifying the depositary to that effect.
(2) The denunciation shall take effect on the first day of the month following the expiration of twelve months after receipt of the notification by the depositary."

Article 46

The original of this Convention, of which the Chinese, English, French, Russian and Spanish texts are equally authentic, shall be deposited with the Secretary-General of the United Nations.

Convention on the limitation period in the international sale of goods done at New York June 4, 1974, as amended by the Protocol amending the Convention on the limitation period in the international sale of goods done at Vienna April 11, 1980; entered into force for the United States December 1, 1994. States which are parties:

Argentina
Cuba
Czech Republic*
Egypt
Guinea
Hungary
Mexico
Poland
Romania
Slovakia*
Slovenia
Uganda
United States*
Zambia

States which are parties only to the 1974 Convention:
[*Ed. note*—The provisions of the original 1974 Convention will apply as between the United States and these states.]
Bosnia and Herzegovina
Dominican Republic
Ghana
Norway[1]
Ukraine
Yugoslavia[2]

* Pursuant to article XII of the Protocol (article 36 *bis* of the Convention), this State has declared it will not be bound by article I of the Protocol. Thus, it is bound by article 3 as originally adopted in the 1974 Convention (see note at article 3 *ante*).

[1]Declaration made upon signature and confirmed upon ratification:

> In accordance with article 34 the Government of the Kingdom of Norway declares that the Convention shall not govern contracts of sale where the seller and the buyer both have their relevant places of business within the territories of the Nordic States (i.e. Norway, Denmark, Finland, Iceland and Sweden).

[2]*Ed. note*—The U.S. view is that the Socialist Federal Republic of Yugoslavia has dissolved and no successor state represents its continuation.

CONVENTION ON THE CIVIL ASPECTS OF INTERNATIONAL CHILD ABDUCTION

The States signatory to the present Convention.

Firmly convinced that the interests of children are of paramount importance in matters relating to their custody.

Desiring to protect children internationally from the harmful effects of their wrongful removal or retention and to establish procedures to ensure their prompt return to the State of their habitual residence, as well as to secure protection for rights of access.

Have resolved to conclude a Convention to this effect, and have agreed upon the following provisions—

CHAPTER I

SCOPE OF THE CONVENTION

Article 1

The objects of the present Convention are—

a to secure the prompt return of children wrongfully removed to or retained in any Contracting State; and

b to ensure that rights of custody and of access under the law of one Contracting State are effectively respected in the other Contracting States.

Article 2

Contracting States shall take all appropriate measures to secure within their territories the implementation of the objects of the Convention. For this purpose they shall use the most expeditious procedures available.

Article 3

The removal or the retention of a child is to be considered wrongful where—

a it is in breach of rights of custody attributed to a person, an institution or any other body, either jointly or alone, under the law of the State in which the child was habitually resident immediately before the removal or retention; and

b at the time of removal or retention those rights were actually exercised, either jointly or alone, or would have been so exercised but for the removal or retention.

The rights of custody mentioned in sub-paragraph *a* above, may arise in particular by operation of law or by reason of a judicial or administrative decision, or by reason of an agreement having legal effect under the law of that State.

Article 4

The Convention shall apply to any child who was habitually resident in a Contracting State immediately before any breach of custody or access rights. The Convention shall cease to apply when the child attains the age of 16 years.

Article 5

For the purposes of this Convention—

a 'rights of custody' shall include rights relating to the care of the person of the child and, in particular, the right to determine the child's place of residence;

b 'rights of access' shall include the right to take a child for a limited period of time to a place other than the child's habitual residence.

CHAPTER II

CENTRAL AUTHORITIES

Article 6

A Contracting State shall designate a Central Authority to discharge the duties which are imposed by the Convention upon such authorities.

Federal States, States with more than one system of law or States having autonomous territorial organizations shall be free to appoint more than one Central Authority and to specify the territorial extent of their powers. Where a State has appointed more than one Central Authority, it shall designate the Central Authority to which applications may be addressed for transmission to the appropriate Central Authority within that State.

Article 7

Central Authorities shall co-operate with each other and promote co-operation amongst the competent authorities in their respective States to secure the prompt return of children and to achieve the other objects of this Convention.

In particular, either directly or through any intermediary, they shall take all appropriate measures—

a to discover the whereabouts of a child who has been wrongfully removed or retained;

b to prevent further harm to the child or prejudice to interested parties by taking or causing to be taken provisional measures;

c to secure the voluntary return of the child or to bring about an amicable resolution of the issues;

d to exchange, where desirable, information relating to the social background of the child;

e to provide information of a general character as to the law of their State in connection with the application of the Convention;

f to initiate or facilitate the institution of judicial or administrative proceedings with a view to obtaining the return of the child and, in a proper case, to make arrangements for organizing or securing the effective exercise of rights of access;

g where the circumstances so require, to provide or facilitate the provision of legal aid and advice, including the participation of legal counsel and advisers;

h to provide such administrative arrangements as may be necessary and appropriate to secure the safe return of the child;

i to keep each other informed with respect to the operation of this Convention and, as far as possible, to eliminate any obstacles to its application.

CHAPTER III

RETURN OF CHILDREN

Article 8

Any person, institution or other body claiming that a child has been removed or retained in breach of custody rights may apply either to the Central Authority of the child's habitual residence or to the Central Authority of any other Contracting State for assistance in securing the return of the child.

The application shall contain—

a information concerning the identity of the applicant, of the child and of the person alleged to have removed or retained the child;

b where available, the date of birth of the child;

c the grounds on which the applicant's claim for return of the child is based;

d all available information relating to the whereabouts of the child and the identity of the person with whom the child is presumed to be. The application may be accompanied or supplemented by—

e an authenticated copy of any relevant decision or agreement;

f a certificate or an affidavit emanating from a Central Authority, or other competent authority of the State of the child's habitual residence, or from a qualified person, concerning the relevant law of that State;

g any other relevant document.

Article 9

If the Central Authority which receives an application referred to in Article 8 has reason to believe that the child is in another Contracting State, it shall directly and without delay transmit the application to the Central Authority of that Contracting State and inform the requesting Central Authority, or the applicant, as the case may be.

Article 10

The Central Authority of the State where the child is shall take or cause to be taken all appropriate measures in order to obtain the voluntary return of the child.

Article 11

The judicial or administrative authorities of Contracting States shall act expeditiously in proceedings for the return of children.

If the judicial or administrative authority concerned has not reached a decision within six weeks from the date of commencement of the proceedings, the applicant or the Central Authority of the requested State, on its own initiative or if asked by the Central Authority of the requesting State, shall have the right to request a statement of the reasons for the delay. If a reply is received by the Central Authority of the requested State, that Authority shall transmit the reply to the Central Authority of the requesting State, or to the applicant, as the case may be.

Article 12

Where a child has been wrongfully removed or retained in terms of Article 3 and, at the date of the commencement of the proceedings before the judicial or administrative authority of the Contracting State where the child is, a period of less than one year has elapsed from the date of the wrongful removal or retention, the authority concerned shall order the return of the child forthwith.

The judicial or administrative authority, even where the proceedings have been commenced after the expiration of the period of one year referred to in the preceding paragraph, shall also order the return of the child, unless is demonstrated that the child is now settled in its new environment.

Where the judicial or administrative authority in the requested State has reason to believe that the child has been taken to another State, it may stay the proceedings or dismiss the application for the return of the child.

Article 13

Notwithstanding the provisions of the preceding Article, the judicial or administrative authority of the requested State is not bound to order the return of the child if the person, institution or other body which opposes its return establishes that—

a the person, institution or other body having the care of the person of the child was not actually exercising the custody rights at the time of removal or retention, or had consented to or subsequently acquiesced in the removal or retention; or

b there is a grave risk that his or her return would expose the child to physical or psychological harm or otherwise place the child in an intolerable situation.

The judicial or administrative authority may also refuse to order the return of the child if it finds that the child objects to being returned and has attained an age and degree of maturity at which it is appropriate to take account of its views.

In considering the circumstances referred to in this Article, the judicial and administrative authorities shall take into account the information relating to the social background of the child provided by the Central Authority or other competent authority of the child's habitual residence.

Article 14

In ascertaining whether there has been a wrongful removal or retention within the meaning of Article 3, the judicial or administrative authorities of the requested State may take notice directly of the law of, and of judicial or administrative decisions, formally recognized or not in the State of the habitual residence of the child, without recourse to the specific procedures for the proof of that law or for the recognition of foreign decisions which would otherwise be applicable.

Article 15

The judicial or administrative authorities of a Contracting State may, prior to the making of an order for the return of the child, request that the applicant obtain from the authorities of the State of the habitual residence of the child a decision or other determination that the removal or retention was wrongful within the meaning of Article 3 of the Convention, where such a decision or determination may be obtained in that State. The Central Authorities of the Contracting States shall so far as practicable assist applicants to obtain such a decision or determination.

Article 16

After receiving notice of a wrongful removal or retention of a child in the sense of Article 3, the judicial or administrative authorities of the Contracting State to which the child has been removed or in which it has been retained shall not decide on the merits of rights of custody until it has been determined that the child is not to be returned under this Convention or unless an application under this Convention is not lodged within a reasonable time following receipt of the notice.

Article 17

The sole fact that a decision relating to custody has been given in or is entitled to recognition in the requested State shall not be a ground for refusing to return a child under this Convention, but the judicial or administrative authorities of the requested State may take account of the reasons for that decision in applying this Convention.

Article 18

The provisions of this Chapter do not limit the power of a judicial or administrative authority to order the return of the child at any time.

Article 19

A decision under this Convention concerning the return of the child shall not be taken to be a determination on the merits of any custody issue.

Article 20

The return of the child under the provisions of Article 12 may be refused if this would not be permitted by the fundamental principles of the requested State relating to the protection of human rights and fundamental freedoms.

CHAPTER IV

RIGHTS OF ACCESS

Article 21

An application to make arrangements for organizing or securing the effective exercise of rights of access may be presented to the Central Authorities of the Contracting States in the same way as an application for the return of a child.

The Central Authorities are bound by the obligations of co-operation which are set forth in Article 7 to promote the peaceful enjoyment of access rights and the fulfilment of any conditions to which the exercise of those rights may be subject. The Central Authorities shall take steps to remove, as far as possible, all obstacles to the exercise of such rights.

The Central Authorities, either directly or through intermediaries, may initiate or assist in the institution of proceedings with a view to organizing or protecting these rights and securing respect for the conditions to which the exercise of these rights may be subject.

CHAPTER V

GENERAL PROVISIONS

Article 22

No security, bond or deposit, however described, shall be required to guarantee the payment of costs and expenses in the judicial or administrative proceedings falling within the scope of this Convention.

Article 23

No legalization or similar formality may be required in the context of this Convention.

Article 24

Any application, communication or other document sent to the Central Authority of the requested State shall be in the original language, and shall be accompanied by a translation into the official language or one of the official languages of the requested State or, where that is not feasible, a translation into French or English.

However, a Contracting State may, by making a reservation in accordance with Article 42, object to the use of either French or English, but not both, in any application, communication or other document sent to its Central Authority.

Article 25

Nationals of the Contracting States and persons who are habitually resident within those States shall be entitled in matters concerned with the application of this Convention to legal aid and advice in any other Contracting State on the same conditions as if they themselves were nationals of and habitually resident in that State.

Article 26

Each Central Authority shall bear its own costs in applying this Convention.

Central Authorities and other public services of Contracting States shall not impose any charges in relation to applications submitted under this Convention. In particular, they may not require any payment from the applicant towards the costs and expenses of the proceedings or, where applicable, those arising from the participation of legal counsel or advisers. However, they may require the payment of the expenses incurred or to be incurred in implementing the return of the child.

However, a Contracting State may, by making a reservation in accordance with Article 42, declare that it shall not be bound to assume any costs referred to in the preceding paragraph resulting from the participation of legal counsel or advisers or from court proceedings, except insofar as those costs may be covered by its system of legal aid and advice.

Upon ordering the return of a child or issuing an order concerning rights of access under this Convention, the judicial or administrative authorities may, where appropriate, direct the person who removed or retained the child, or who prevented the exercise of rights of access, to pay necessary expenses incurred by or on behalf of the applicant, including travel expenses, any costs incurred or payments made for locating the child, the costs of legal representation of the applicant, and those of returning the child.

Article 27

When it is manifest that the requirements of this Convention are not fulfilled or that the application is otherwise not well founded, a Central Authority is not bound to accept the application. In that case, the Central Authority shall forthwith inform the applicant or the Central Authority through which the application was submitted, as the case may be, of its reasons.

Article 28

A Central Authority may require that the application be accompanied by a written authorization empowering it to act on behalf of the applicant, or to designate a representative so to act.

Article 29

This Convention shall not preclude any person, institution or body who claims that there has been a breach of custody or access rights within the meaning of Article 3 or 21 from applying directly to the judicial or administrative authorities of a Contracting State, whether or not under the provisions of this Convention.

Article 30

Any application submitted to the Central Authorities or directly to the judicial or administrative authorities of a Contracting State in accordance with the terms of this Convention, together with documents and any other information appended thereto or provided by a Central Authority, shall be admissible in the courts or administrative authorities of the Contracting States.

Article 31

In relation to a State which in matters of custody of children has two or more systems of law applicable in different territorial units—

a any reference to habitual residence in that State shall be construed as referring to habitual residence in a territorial unit of that State;

b any reference to the law of the State of habitual residence shall be construed as referring to the law of the territorial unit in that State where the child habitually resides.

Article 32

In relation to a State which in matters of custody of children has two or more systems of law applicable to different categories of persons, any reference to the law of that State shall be construed as referring to the legal system specified by the law of that State.

Article 33

A State within which different territorial units have their own rules of law in respect of custody of children shall not be bound to apply this Convention where a State with a unified system of law would not be bound to do so.

Article 34

This Convention shall take priority in matters within its scope over the *Convention of 5 October 1961 concerning the powers of authorities and the law applicable in respect of the protection of minors,* as between Parties to both Conventions. Otherwise the present Convention shall not restrict the application of an international instrument in force between the State of origin and the State addressed or other law of the State addressed for the purposes of obtaining the return of a child who has been wrongfully removed or retained or of organizing access rights.

Article 35

This Convention shall apply as between Contracting States only to wrongful removals or retentions occurring after its entry into force in those States.

Where a declaration has been made under Article 39 or 40, the reference in the preceding paragraph to a Contracting State shall be taken to refer to the territorial unit or units in relation to which this Convention applies.

Article 36

Nothing in this Convention shall prevent two or more Contracting States, in order to limit the restrictions to which the return of the child may be subject, from agreeing among themselves to derogate from any provisions of this Convention which may imply such a restriction.

CHAPTER VI

FINAL CLAUSES

Article 37

The Convention shall be open for signature by the States which were Members of the Hague Conference on Private International Law at the time of its Fourteenth Session.

It shall be ratified, accepted or approved and the instruments of ratification, acceptance or approval shall be deposited with the Ministry of Foreign Affairs of the Kingdom of the Netherlands.

Article 38

Any other State may accede to the Convention.

The instrument of accession shall be deposited with the Ministry of Foreign Affairs of the Kingdom of the Netherlands.

The Convention shall enter into force for a State acceding to it on the first day of the third calendar month after the deposit of its instrument of accession.

The accession will have effect only as regards the relations between the acceding State and such Contracting States as will have declared their acceptance of the accession. Such a declaration will also have to be made by any Member State ratifying, accepting or approving the Convention after an accession. Such declaration shall be deposited at the Ministry of Foreign Affairs of the Kingdom of the Netherlands; this Ministry shall forward, through diplomatic channels, a certified copy to each of the Contracting States.

The Convention will enter into force as between the acceding State and the State that has declared its acceptance of the accession on the first day of the third calendar month after the deposit of the declaration of acceptance.

Article 39

Any State may, at the time of signature, ratification, acceptance, approval or accession, declare that the Convention shall extend to all the territories for the international relations of which it is responsible, or to one or more of them. Such a declaration shall take effect at the time the Convention enters into force for that State.

Such declaration, as well as any subsequent extension, shall be notified to the Ministry of Foreign Affairs of the Kingdom of the Netherlands.

Article 40

If a Contracting State has two or more territorial units in which different systems of law are applicable in relation to matters dealt with in this Convention, it may at the time of signature, ratification, acceptance, approval or accession declare that this Convention shall extend to all its territorial units or only to one or more of them and may modify this declaration by submitting another declaration at any time.

Any such declaration shall be notified to the Ministry of Foreign Affairs of the Kingdom of the Netherlands and shall state expressly the territorial units to which the Convention applies.

Article 41

Where a Contracting State has a system of government under which executive, judicial and legislative powers are distributed between central and other authorities within that State, its signature or ratification, acceptance or approval of, or accession to this Convention, or its making of any declaration in terms of Article 40 shall carry no implication as to the internal distribution of powers within that State.

Article 42

Any State may, not later than the time of ratification, acceptance, approval or accession, or at the time of making a declaration in terms of Article 39 or 40, make one or both of the reservations provided for in Article 24 and Article 26, third paragraph. No other reservation shall be permitted.

Any State may at any time withdraw a reservation it has made. The withdrawal shall be notified to the Ministry of Foreign Affairs of the Kingdom of the Netherlands.

The reservation shall cease to have effect on the first day of the third calendar month after the notification referred to in the preceding paragraph.

Article 43

The Convention shall enter into force on the first day of the third calendar month after the deposit of the third instrument of ratification, acceptance, approval or accession referred to in Articles 37 and 38.

Thereafter the Convention shall enter into force—

1 for each State ratifying, accepting, approving or acceding to it subsequently, on the first day of the third calendar month after the deposit of its instrument of ratification, acceptance, approval or accession;

2 for any territory or territorial unit to which the Convention has been extended in conformity with Article 39 or 40, on the first day of the third calendar month after the notification referred to in that Article.

Article 44

The Convention shall remain in force for five years from the date of its entry into force in accordance with the first paragraph of Article 43 even for States which subsequently have ratified, accepted, approved it or acceded to it. If there has been no denunciation, it shall be renewed tacitly every five years.

Any denunciation shall be notified to the Ministry of Foreign Affairs of the Kingdom of the Netherlands at least six months before the expiry of the five year period. It may be limited to certain of the territories or territorial units to which the Convention applies. The denunciation shall have effect only as regards the State which has notified it. The Convention shall remain in force for the other Contracting States.

Article 45

The Ministry of Foreign Affairs of the Kingdom of the Netherlands shall notify the States Members of the Conference, and the States which have acceded in accordance with Article 38, of the following—

1 the signatures and ratifications, acceptances and approvals referred to in Article 37;
2 the accessions referred to in Article 38;
3 the date on which the Convention enters into force in accordance with Article 43;
4 the extensions referred to in Article 39;
5 the declarations referred to in Articles 38 and 40;
6 the reservations referred to in Article 24 and Article 26, third paragraph, and the withdrawals referred to in Article 42;
7 the denunciations referred to in Article 44.

IN WITNESS WHEREOF the undersigned, being duly authorized thereto, have signed this Convention.

DONE at The Hague, on the 25th day of October 1980 in the English and French languages, both texts being equally authentic, in a single copy which shall be deposited in the archives of the Government of the Kingdom of the Netherlands, and of which a certified copy shall be sent, through diplomatic channels, to each of the States Members of the Hague Conference on Private International Law at the date of its Fourteenth Session.

[Signatures omitted.]

Convention on the civil aspects of international child abduction. Done at The Hague October 25, 1980; entered into force for the United States July 1, 1988. States which are parties:

Argentina[1]
Australia[1a]
Austria[1b]
Bahamas[1c]
Belize[1d]
Bosnia and Herzegovina
Burkina Faso[1e]
Canada[2]
Chile[2a]
Colombia[2b]
Croatia[2c]
Cyprus[2d]
Denmark[2e]
Ecuador[2f]
Finland[2g]
France[3]
Germany, Fed. Rep.[3a]
Greece[3b]
Honduras[3c]
Hungary[4]
Iceland[4a]
Ireland[4b]
Israel[4c]
Italy
Luxembourg[5]
Macedonia, Former Yugoslav Republic of
Mauritius[5a]
Mexico[5b]
Monaco[5c]
Netherlands[6]
New Zealand[6a]
Norway[6b]
Panama
Poland[6c]
Portugal[7]
Romania[7a]
Slovenia[7b]
Spain[8]
St. Kitts & Nevis[7c]
Sweden[8a]
Switzerland[9]
United Kingdom[10]
United States[11]
Yugoslavia[12]
Zimbabwe[13]

---

[1] *Notification pursuant to Article 45, first paragraph, of the Convention*

In conformity with Article 37, first paragraph, the Chargé d'Affaires a.i. of the Argentine Republic signed the above-mentioned Convention for the Argentine Republic as follows on 28 January 1991:

GASIÓ

28 JAN 91

In accordance with Article 37, paragraph 2, Argentina deposited its instrument of ratification of the abovementioned Convention with the Ministry of Foreign Affairs on 19 March 1991.

In accordance with Article 6, paragraph 1, of the Convention Argentina has designated as the Central Authority:

the Ministry of Foreign Relations—Legal Affairs Department—.
(Ministerio de Relaciones Exteriores y Culto—Dirección de Asuntos Jurídicos—.)

In accordance with Article 43 the Convention will enter into force for Argentina on 1 June 1991.

Central Authority designated under the *Hague Convention of 25 October 1980 on the civil aspects of international child abduction.*

adresse/address:	Ministry of Foreign Relations Legal Affairs Department (Ministerio de Relaciones Exteriores y Culto Direción de Asuntos Jurídicos) Reconquista 1088—3rd floor BUENOS AIRES (c.p. 1003) Argentina
numéro de téléphone/telephone number:	(54)-1-311-6815
numéro de télex/telex number:	—
numéro de télécopie/telefax number:	(54)-1-315-3813 (54)-1-311-3539 (54)-1-311-6815
personnes à contacter/persons to contact:	M./Mr Mariano MACIEL Director General de Asuntos Jurídicos tél./tel.: (54)-1-311-6815 Mme/Mrs Maria SEONAE DE CHIODI Directora de Asistencia Judicial Internacional tél./tel.: (54)-1-311-0071 ext. 162 M./Mr Ignacio GOICOECHEA (languages of communication: Spanish/English tél./tel.: (54)-1-311-0071 ext. 166

[1a] *Notification pursuant to Article 45 of the Convention*

In conformity with Article 37, first paragraph, the above-mentioned Convention was signed for Australia on 29 October 1986 as follows:

"GEOFFREY PRICE
29 October 1986."

In conformity with Article 37, paragraph 2, Australia deposited on the same date its instrument of ratification of the Convention with the Ministry of Foreign Affairs of the Kingdom of the Netherlands.

The Government of Australia declared in accordance with Article 40 that the Convention extends to the legal system applicable only in the Australian States and mainland Territories.

In accordance with Article 43, paragraph 1, the Convention will enter into force for Australia on 1 January 1987.

The Australian Embassy informed the Ministry of Foreign Affairs of the Kingdom of the Netherlands by Note of 23 December 1986 of the designation of the following Central Authorities by Australia in accordance with Article 6 of the above-mentioned Convention:

A. Commonwealth Central Authority
The Secretary,
Attorney-General's Department,
National Circuit,
Barton A.C.T. 2600.

B. State Central Authorities
(i) Director,
Department of Children's Services,
Queensland
(ii) Secretary,
Department of Community Development,
Northern Territory.

(iii) Director-General,
Department of Community Services,
Victoria.
(iv) Director-General
Department of Youth and Community Services,
New South Wales.
(v) Director for Community Welfare,
Department for Community Welfare,
Tasmania.
(vi) Commissioner,
Western Australian Police Department,
Western Australia.
(vii) Commissioner,
South Australian Police Department,
South Australia.
(viii) Director of Welfare,
Department of Territories,
Australian Capital Territory.

The Embassy furthermore advised that applications should be forwarded to The Secretary of the Attorney-General's Department

[1b] *Notification pursuant to Article 45 of the Convention*

In accordance with Article 37, paragraph 2, Austria deposited on 14 July 1988 its instrument of ratification of the above-mentioned Convention with the Ministry of Foreign Affairs of the Kingdom of the Netherlands.

The Convention will enter into force for Austria in accordance with Article 43 on 1 October 1988.

Austria designated as the Central Authority mentioned in Article 6 of the Convention:

adresse/address:	Bundesministerium für Justiz Abteilung I 10 Postfach 63 A-1016 Vienna Austria
numéro de téléphone/telephone number:	Secrétariat/Secretariat: (222) 52152 147
numéro de télex/telex number:	13/1264
numéro de télécopie/telefax number:	(222) 52152 727
personnes à contacter/persons to contact:	M/Mr Werner SCHÜTZ (langues de communication/languages of communication: anglais et allemand/English and German) tél./tel.: (222) 52152 134 ou/or (en cas d'absence/in his absence) M/Mr Ihor TARKO (langues de communication/languages of communication: anglais et allemand/English and German) tél./tel.: (222) 52152 116 M/Mr Wolfgang REISHOFER (langues de communication/languages of communication: anglais, français, allemand/English, French, German) tél./tel.: (222) 52152 282

[1c] In accordance with Article 38, paragraph 5, the Convention is in force between the Bahamas and the following States:

United States of America (EIF: 1 January 1994); *Netherlands (for the Kingdom in Europe)* (EIF: 1 February 1994); *Luxembourg* (EIF: 1 March 1994); *United Kingdom of Great Britain and Northern Ireland* (EIF: 1 March 1994)*; *Germany* (EIF: 1 May 1994); *Finland* (EIF: 1 August 1994); *Australia* (EIF: 1 September 1994); *Switzerland* (EIF: 1 October 1994); *Ireland* (EIF: 1 December 1994); *Sweden* (EIF: 1 January 1995); *Spain* (EIF: 1 March 1995); *Argentina* (EIF: 1 May 1995); *Canada* (EIF: 1 August 1995); *New Zealand* (EIF: 1 November 1995); *Mexico* (EIF: 1 December 1995); *Israel* (EIF: 1 January 1996).

* The United Kingdom made the following declaration with regard to the accession of the Bahamas to the Convention:

"Notwithstanding the provisions of the said Article 38 regarding entry into force of the Convention as between the acceding State and the State declaring its acceptance of the accession, amendments will have been made to the United Kingdom municipal law in order to give effect to the Convention between it and the Bahamas as of 1 January 1994 when the Convention enters into force for the Bahamas." The Ministry of Foreign Affairs of the Kingdom of the Netherlands has not yet received any communication from the Government of the Bahamas concerning the date of entry into force proposed by the United Kingdom.

[1d] *Notification pursuant to Article 45 of the Convention*

In accordance with Article 38, paragraph 2, of the above-mentioned Convention Belize deposited its instrument of accession to the Convention with the Ministry of Foreign Affairs of the Kingdom of the Netherlands on 22 June 1989.

The instrument of accession contains the following reservations:

"1) any application or other documents transmitted to the Central Authority under the Convention must be accompanied by a translation in English and not in French and

"2) Belize will not be bound to assume any costs relating to applications under the Convention resulting from the participation of legal counsel or advisers, or from court proceedings, except insofar as these costs may be covered by its system of legal aid and advice.".

The Convention will enter into force for Belize in accordance with Article 38, paragraph 3, on 1 September 1989.

The accession will have effect only as regards the relations between the acceding State and such Contracting States as will have declared their acceptance of the accession.

In accordance with Article 6, paragraph 1, of the Convention, on July 13, 1990 Belize has designated the following as Central Authority:

adresse/address:	Ministry of Social Services and Community Development Delmopan Belize
numéro de télex/telex number:	
numéro de télécopie/telefax number:	
personnes à contacter/persons to contact:	M./Mr H. REMIJIO MONTEJO tél./tel.: (08) 22248 ou/or (en cas d'absence/in his absence) M./Mr Patrick BERNARD tél./tel.: (08) 22246

In accordance with Article 38, paragraph 5, the Convention is in force between Belize and the following States:

United Kingdom of Great Britain and *Northern Ireland* (1 October 1989); *United States of America* (1 November 1989); *Australia* (1 March 1990); *Portugal* (1 May 1990); *the Netherlands (for the Kingdom in Europe)* (1 September 1990); *Federal Republic of Germany* (1 December 1990); *Luxembourg* (1 January 1991); *Sweden* (1 April 1991); *Canada* (1 September 1991); *Ireland* (1 October 1991); *New Zealand* (1 December 1991); *France* (1 January 1992); *Israel* (1 February 1992); *Spain* (1 July 1992); *Switzerland* (1 September 1992); *Norway* (1 October 1992); *Finland* (EIF: 1 August 1994).

[1e]The Permanent Bureau of the Hague Conference on private international law presents its compliments to the Diplomatic Missions of the Member States and to the National Organs and has the honour to inform them that, by instrument deposited on 25 May 1992 with the Ministry of Foreign Affairs of the Kingdom of the Netherlands,

Burkina Faso

acceded to the above-mentioned Convention.

In conformity with Article 38, paragraph 3, the Convention will enter into force for *Burkina Faso* on 1 August 1992.

According to Article 38, paragraph 4, the accession will have effect only as regards Burkina Faso and such Contracting States as will have declared their acceptance of the accession.

In accordance with Article 38, paragraph 5, the Convention entered into force between Burkina Faso and: *the Kingdom of the Netherlands, for the Kingdom in Europe,* (1 September 1992); *the United Kingdom of Great Britain and Northern Ireland* (1 November 1992); *the United States of America* (November 1, 1992); *Luxembourg* (EIF: 1 November 1992); *France* (EIF: 1 January 1993); *Germany* (EIF: 1 January 1993); *Ireland* (EIF: 1 April 1993); *Australia* (EIF: 1 April 1993); *Argentina* (EIF: 1 August 1993); *Canada* (EIF: 1 October 1993); *Israel* (EIF: 1 November 1993); *Sweden* (EIF: 1 December 1993); *Finland* (EIF: 1 August 1994); *Switzerland* (EIF: 1 October 1994); *Spain* (EIF: 1 December 1994); *New Zealand* (EIF: 1 November 1995); *Mexico* (EIF: 1 December 1995).

The Permanent Bureau of the Hague Conference on private international law presents its compliments to the Diplomatic Missions of the Member States and to the National Organs and has the honour to inform them that, in accordance with Article 6, paragraph 1, of the above-mentioned Convention, *Burkina Faso* has designated as Central Authority:

"Le Ministère délégué chargé de l'Action Sociale et de la Famille du Burkina Faso."

[2] *Notification in accordance with Article 45, paragraphs 1, 5 and 6 of the Convention*

In conformity with Article 37, paragraph 2, Canada deposited its instrument of ratification of the above-mentioned Convention with the Ministry of Foreign Affairs of the Kingdom of the Netherlands on 2 June 1983. Canada made the following declarations and reservations.

"Extension of the Convention

1. In accordance with the provisions of Article 40, the Government of Canada declares that the Convention shall extend to the Provinces of Ontario, New Brunswick, British Columbia and Manitoba.

Central Authorities

2. In accordance with the provisions of Article 6, paragraph 2, the Minister of Justice and Attorney General of Canada, as represented by the Domestic Legal Services in the Department of External Affairs, is designated as the Central Authority to which applications may be addressed for transmission to the appropriate Central Authority within Canada.

3. In accordance with the provisions of Article 6, paragraph 2, the Ministry of the Attorney General of Ontario is designated as the Central Authority for the Province of Ontario.

4. In accordance with the provisions of Article 6, paragraph 2, the Attorney General of New Brunswick is designated as the Central Authority for the Province of New Brunswick.

5. In accordance with the provisions of Article 6, paragraph 2, the Attorney General of British Columbia is designated as the Central Authority for the Province of British Columbia.

6. In accordance with the provisions of Article 6, paragraph 2, the Attorney General of Manitoba is designated as the Central Authority for the Province of Manitoba.

Reservations

7. In accordance with the provisions of Article 42 and pursuant to Article 26, paragraph 3, the Government of Canada declares that, with respect to applications submitted under the Convention concerning the Provinces of Ontario, New Brunswick and British Columbia, Canada will assume the costs referred to in paragraph 2 of Article 26 only insofar as these costs are covered by the system of legal aid of the Province concerned.

Other declarations and reservations

8. The Government of Canada further declares that it may at any time submit other declarations or reservations, pursuant to Articles 6, 40 and 42 of the Convention, with respect to other territorial units.".

Notification in accordance with Article 45, paragraphs 3 and 5, of the Convention

In conformity with Article 40 the Government of Canada extended the above-mentioned Convention to the Province of Nova Scotia by Note dated 24 February 1984 and received at the Ministry of Foreign Affairs of the Kingdom of the Netherlands on 27 February 1984.

The Canadian declaration extending the Convention to the Province of Nova Scotia contains the following declarations and reservations:

"Central Authority
In accordance with the provisions of Article 6, paragraph 2, the Attorney General of Nova Scotia is designated as the Central Authority for the Province of Nova Scotia.
Reservation
In accordance with the provisions of Article 42 and pursuant to Article 26, paragraph 3, the Government of Canada declares that, with respect to applications submitted under the Convention concerning the Province of Nova Scotia, Canada will assume the costs referred to in paragraph 2 of Article 26 only insofar as these costs are covered by the system of legal aid of the Province of Nova Scotia.
Other declarations and reservations
The Government of Canada further declares that it may at any time submit other declarations or reservations, pursuant to Articles 6, 40 and 42 of the Convention, with respect to other territorial units.".
In conformity with Article 43, paragraph 2, the Convention will enter into force for the Province of Nova Scotia on 1 May 1984.
Federal Government:

Ministre de la Justice et Procureur général du Canada représenté par:	*Minister of Justice and Attorney General of Canada as represented by:*
Le Service de droit interne *Ministère des Affaires extérieures (JDS)* *Tour C, 7e étage* *Imm. Lester B. Pearson* *125 Promenade Sussex* *OTTAWA, Ontario K1A OG2* Canada	
	Domestic Legal Services Department of External Affairs (JDS) Tower C, 7th Floor Lester B. Pearson Building 125 Sussex Drive OTTAWA, Ontario K1A OG2 Canada
numéro de téléphone/telephone number:	(613) 992 6299
numéro de télex/telex number:	053 3745
numéro de télécopie/telefax number:	(613) 992 2467
personnes à contacter/persons to contact:	Me/Mr Richard FIUTOWSKI tél./tel.: (613) 992 8608 ou/or Me/Ms Nora O'BRIEN tél./tel.: (613) 992 6299
British Columbia:	Attorney General of British Columbia, Parliament Buildings, VICTORIA, British Columbia, V8V 1X4 Contact: Bob Adamson, Assistant Deputy Attorney General, Policy Planning, telephone: (604) 384-4435
Ontario:	
adresse/address:	Reciprocity Office Ministry of the Attorney General 720 Bay Street, 4th Floor TORONTO, Ontario Canada M5G 2K1
numéro de téléphone/telephone number:	(1)-416-326-2556
numéro de télex/telex number:	—
numéro de télécopie/telefax number:	(1)-416-326-2568
personne à contacter/person to contact:	Mlle/Ms Mary Anne KELLY (langues de communication/languages of communication: anglais et français/English and French)
Manitoba:	
adresse/address:	Department of Justice Family Law Branch 4th Floor, 405 Broadway WINNIPEG, Manitoba R3C 3L6 Canada
numéro de téléphone/telephone number:	(204) 945 2841
numéro de télex/telex number:	075 7346
numéro de télécopie/telefax number:	(204) 945 0053
personnes à contacter/persons to contact:	Me/Ms Joan MacPHAIL
New Brunswick:	Attorney General of New Brunswick, P.O. Box 6000, Room 551, Centennial Building, FREDERICTON, New Brunswick, E3B 5H1 Contact: Director of Public Prosecutions Branch telephone: (173) 453-2583
Nova Scotia:	Attorney General of Nova Scotia, 1723, Hollis Street, HALIFAX, Nova Scotia, B3J 2L6 Contact: Mr R. Gerald Conrad, Q.C. Director (Civil) Department of the Attorney General telephone: (902) 424-4041

Pour la Province du Québec/For the Province of Quebec

adresse/address:	Direction générale des affaires juridiques Ministère de la Justice du Québec 1200 route de l'Eglise 5e étage SAINTE-FOY, Québec G1V 4M1 Canada
numéro de téléphone/telephone number:	(418) 644 7152
numéro de télex/telex number:	0513 1650
numéro de télécopie/telefax number:	(418) 646 1696
personnes à contacter/persons to contact:	Me Jean-Marc NEAULT (langues de communication/languages of communication: français, anglais/French, English)

Notification in accordance with Article 45, paragraphs 3 and 5, of the Convention
In conformity with Article 40 the Government of Canada extended the above-mentioned Convention to the Province of Newfoundland by Note dated 5 July 1984 and received at the Ministry of Foreign Affairs of the Kingdom of the Netherlands on 6 July 1984. The Canadian declaration extending the Convention to the Province of Newfoundland contains the following declarations and reservations:
"Central Authority
In accordance with the provisions of Article 6, paragraph 2, the Attorney General of Newfoundland is designated as the Central Authority for the Province of Newfoundland.
Reservation
In accordance with the provisions of Article 42 and pursuant to Article 26, paragraph 3, the Government of Canada declares that, with respect to applications submitted under the Convention concerning the Province of Newfoundland, Canada will assume the costs referred to in paragraph 2 of Article 26 only insofar as these costs are covered by the system of legal aid of the Province of Newfoundland.
Other declarations and reservations
The Government of Canada further declares that it may at any time submit other declarations or reservations, pursuant to Articles 6, 40 and 42 of the Convention, with respect to other territorial units.".
In conformity with Article 43, paragraph 2, the Convention will enter into force for the Province of Newfoundland on 1 October 1984.

The Permanent Bureau of the Hague Conference on private international law presents its compliments to the Diplomatic Missions of the Member States and to the National Organs and has the honour to inform them that, by a letter received at the Ministry of Foreign Affairs of the Kingdom of the Netherlands on 11 October 1984, the Government of *Canada* declared, in accordance with Article 40, that the above-mentioned Convention shall extend to the Province of *Quebec.*

The Convention shall enter into force for the Province of Quebec on *1 January 1985.*

The declaration of extension contains the following declarations and reservations:
"Central Authority
In accordance with the provisions of Article 6, paragraph 2, the Department of Justice of Quebec is designated as the Central Authority for the Province of Quebec.
Reservations
In accordance with the provisions of Article 42 and pursuant to Article 24, paragraph 2, translation in the French language will be required for any application, communication or other document concerning the Province of Quebec when the original language is neither French nor English.
In accordance with the provisions of Article 42 and pursuant to Article 26, paragraph 3, the Government of Canada declares that, with respect to applications submitted under the Convention concerning the Province of Quebec, Canada will assume the costs referred to in paragraph 2 of Article 26 only insofar as these costs are covered by the system of legal aid of the Province of Quebec.
Other declarations and reservations
The Government of Canada further declares that it may at any time submit other declarations or reservations, pursuant to Articles 6, 40 and 42 of the Convention, with respect to other territorial units.".
Notification in accordance with Article 45, paragraphs 3 and 5, of the Convention
In conformity with Article 40 the Government of Canada extended the above-mentioned Convention to the Yukon Territory by Note dated 15 November 1984 and received at the Ministry of Foreign Affairs of the Kingdom of the Netherlands on 16 November 1984. The Canadian declaration extending the Convention to the Yukon Territory contains the following declarations and reservation:
"CENTRAL AUTHORITY
In accordance with the provisions of Article 6, paragraph 2, the Minister of Justice of the Yukon Territory is designated as the Central Authority for the Yukon Territory.
RESERVATION
In accordance with the provisions of Article 42, and pursuant to Article 26, paragraph 3, the Government of Canada declares that, with respect to applications submitted under the Convention concerning the Yukon Territory, Canada will assume the costs referred to in paragraph 2 of Article 26 only insofar as these costs are covered by the system of legal aid of the Yukon Territory.
OTHER DECLARATIONS AND RESERVATIONS
The Government of Canada further declares that it may at any time submit other declarations or reservations, pursuant to Articles 6, 40 and 42 of the Convention, with respect to other territorial units.".
In conformity with Article 43, paragraph 2, the Convention will enter into force for the Yukon Territory on 1 February 1985.

Notification in accordance with Article 45, paragraphs 3 and 5, of the Convention

In conformity with Article 40 the Government of Canada extended the above-mentioned Convention to the Province of Prince Edward Island by Note dated 11 February 1986 and received at the Ministry of Foreign Affairs on 12 February 1986.

The Canadian declaration extending the Convention to the Province of Prince Edward Island contains the following declarations and reservation:

"CENTRAL AUTHORITY

In accordance with the provisions of Article 6, paragraph 2, the Department of Justice and Attorney General of Prince Edward Island is designated as the Central Authority for the Province of Prince Edward Island.

RESERVATION

In accordance with the provisions of Article 42, and pursuant to Article 26, paragraph 3, the Government of Canada declares that, with respect to applications submitted under the Convention concerning the Province of Prince Edward Island, Canada will assume the costs referred to in paragraph 2 of Article 26 only insofar as these costs are covered by the system of legal aid of the Province of Prince Edward Island.

The Government of Canada further declares that it may at any time submit other declarations or reservations, pursuant to Articles 6, 40 and 42 of the Convention, with respect to other territorial units.".

In conformity with Article 43, paragraph 2, the Convention will enter into force for the Province of Prince Edward Island on 1st May 1986.

In accordance with Article 40, paragraph 2, Canada has declared, by a Note dated 7 August 1986, received at the Ministry of Foreign Affairs on 11 August 1986, that this Convention shall extend to the Province of Saskatchewan, under the following reservation:

"In accordance with the provisions of Article 42, and pursuant to Article 26, paragraph 3, the Government of Canada declares that, with respect to applications submitted under the Convention concerning the Province of Saskatchewan, Canada will assume the costs referred to in paragraph 2 of Article 26 only insofar as these costs are covered by the system of legal aid of the Province of Saskatchewan.",

and the following declaration:

"The Government of Canada further declares that it may at any time submit other declarations or reservations, pursuant to Articles 6, 40 and 42 of the Convention, with respect to other territorial units.".

In conformity with Article 43, paragraph 2, the Convention shall enter into force for the Province of Saskatchewan on 1 November 1986.

In conformity with Article 6, paragraph 2, of the Convention Canada has designated as Central Authority for the Province of Saskatchewan:

the Minister of Justice of Saskatchewan.

Notification pursuant to Article 45 of the Convention

In conformity with Article 40 of the above-mentioned Convention Canada declared, by a Note dated 4 November 1986, received at the Ministry of Foreign Affairs on the same date, that the Convention shall extend to the Province of Alberta, under the following reservation:

"In accordance with the provisions of Article 42, and pursuant to Article 26, paragraph 3, the Government of Canada declares that, with respect to applications submitted under the Convention concerning the Province of Alberta, Canada will assume the costs referred to in paragraph 2 of Article 26 only insofar as these costs are covered by the system of legal aid of the Province of Alberta.";

and the following declarations:

"In accordance with the provisions of Article 6, paragraph 2, the Attorney General of Alberta is designated as the Central Authority for the Province of Alberta.

The Government of Canada further declares that it may at any time submit other declarations or reservations, pursuant to Articles 6, 40 and 42 of the Convention, with respect to other territorial units.".

In accordance with Article 43, paragraph 2, the Convention will enter into force for the Province of Alberta on 1 February 1987.

The Permanent Bureau of the Hague Conference on private international law presents its compliments to the Diplomatic Missions of the Member States and to the National Organs and has the honour to inform them that, by a letter received at the Ministry of Foreign Affairs of the Kingdom of the Netherlands on 26 January 1988, the Government of *Canada* declared, in accordance with Article 40, that the above-mentioned Convention shall extend to the *Northwest Territories.*

The Convention now extends to all the territorial units of Canada.

In conformity with Article 43, paragraph 2, the Convention shall enter into force for the *Northwest Territories* on *1 April 1988.*

The declaration of extension contains the following declaration and reservation:

"Central Authority

In accordance with the provisions of Article 6, paragraph 2, the Minister of Justice of the Northwest Territories is designated as the Central Authority for the Northwest Territories.

Reservation

In accordance with the provisions of Article 42, and pursuant to Article 26, paragraph 3, the Government of Canada declares that, with respect to applications submitted under the Convention concerning the Northwest Territories, Canada will assume the costs referred to in paragraph 2 of Article 26 only insofar as these costs are covered by the system of legal aid of the Northwest Territories."

The instrument of accession from Chile contained the following declaration (in Spanish): "Chile understands Article 3 of the Convention on the Civil Aspects of International Child Abduction in the sense that it is not inconsistent with the national legislation which provides that the right to guardianship and custody is exercised until the age of 18." (Translation)

[2a] In accordance with Article 38, paragraph 4,

—the following States declared their acceptance of the accession of *Chile* to the above-mentioned Convention: the United States of America 8 April 1994, the Kingdom of the Netherlands (for the Kingdom in Europe) 20 April 1994, the United Kingdom of Great Britain and Northern Ireland* 29 April 1994, Luxembourg 9 May 1994, Finland 25 May 1994.

* with the following declaration:

"Notwithstanding the provisions of the said Article 38 regarding entry into force of the Convention as between the acceding State and the State declaring its acceptance of the accession, amendments will have been made to the United Kingdom municipal law in order to give effect to the Convention between it and Chile as of 1 May 1994 when the Convention enters into force for Chile."

In accordance with Article 38, paragraph 5, the Convention will enter into force —between *Chile* and

the *United States of America* . . . . *1 July 1994; United Kingdom of Great Britain and Northern Ireland* (EIF: 1 July 1994)*; *Netherlands (for the Kingdom in Europe)* (EIF: 1 July 1994); *Finland* (EIF: 1 August 1994); *Luxembourg* (EIF: 1 August 1994); *Switzerland* (EIF: 1 October 1994); *Australia* (EIF: 1 November 1994); *Ireland* (EIF: 1 December 1994); *Sweden* (EIF: 1 January 1995); *Panama* (EIF: 1 March 1995); *Argentina* (EIF: 1 May 1995); *Germany* (EIF: 1 June 1995); *Canada* (EIF: 1 August 1995); *Spain* (EIF: 1 September 1995); *New Zealand* (EIF: 1 November 1995); *Mexico* (EIF: 1 December 1995); *Israel* (EIF: 1 January 1996); *France* (EIF: 1 February 1996); *Cyprus* (EIF: 1 May 1996); *Saint Kitts and Nevis* (EIF: 1 May 1996); *Slovenia* (EIF: 1 May 1996); *Zimbabwe* (EIF: 1 May 1996); *Chile and Italy* (EIF: 1 August 1996).

* The United Kingdom made the following declaration with regard to the accession of Chile to the Convention: "Notwithstanding the provisions of the said Article 38 regarding entry into force of the Convention as between the acceding State and the State declaring its acceptance of the accession, amendments will have been made to the United Kingdom municipal law in order to give effect to the Convention between it and Chile as of 1 May 1994 when the Convention enters into force for Chile." The Ministry of Foreign Affairs of the Kingdom of the Netherlands has not yet received any communication from the Government of Chile concerning the date of entry into force proposed by the United Kingdom.

[2b]Central Authority designated under the *Hague Convention of 25 October 1980 on the Civil Aspects of International Child Abduction.*

adresse/address:	Instituto Colombiano de Bienestar Familiar Sede Nacional Avenida 68 No 64-01 Santafé de Bogotá, DC Colombia
numéro de téléphone/telephone number:	—
numéro de télex/telex number:	—
numéro de télécopie/telefax number:	(57)-1-231-4558
personnes à contacter/persons to contact:	Mme/Ms Carmen Elena TAMARA Subdirectora de Protección

In accordance with Article 38, paragraph 5, the Convention entered into force between Colombia and the following States:

Luxembourg . . . . 1 April 1996
Panama . . . . 1 May 1996
Israel . . . . 1 June 1996
United States . . . . 1 June 1996
Cyprus . . . . 1 August 1996
Netherlands (for the Kingdom in Europe) . . . . 1 September 1996

[2c] *In conformity with Article 6 Para. 1 of the Convention, the Executive Authority is the Ministry of Labour and Welfare and Executive Authority to which applications may be submitted to be forwarded to the Central Executive Authority from Article 6 Para. 1 of the Convention is the Ministry of Justice and Administration.*

[2d]In accordance with Article 38, paragraph 5, the Convention entered into force between Cyprus and the following States:

United Kingdom of Great Britain and Northern Ireland (EIF: 1 February 1995); *Netherlands (for the Kingdom in Europe)* (EIF: 1 March 1995); *United States of America* (EIF: 1 March 1995); *Luxembourg* (EIF: 1 April 1995); *Germany* (EIF: 1 May 1995); *Panama* EIF: 1 June 1995); *Sweden* (EIF: 1 October 1995); *France* (EIF: 1 October 1995); *Australia* (EIF: 1 November 1995); *New Zealand* (EIF: 1 November 1995); *Mexico* (EIF: 1 December 1995); *Israel* (EIF: 1 January 1996); *Chile* (EIF: 1 May 1996); *Colombia* (1 August 1996); *Greece* (1 August 1996); *Zimbabwe* (1 August 1996).

[2e] *Notification pursuant to Article 45 of the Convention*

In accordance with Article 37, paragraph 1, the Ambassador of the Kingdom of Denmark at The Hague signed the above-mentioned Convention for Denmark on 17 April 1991 as follows:

PER GROOT

17th April, 1991

In accordance with Article 37, paragraph 2, the Ambassador deposited the instrument of ratification of Denmark of the above-mentioned Convention with the Ministry of Foreign Affairs of the Kingdom of the Netherlands on 17 April 1991.

Upon the ratification Denmark declared that:

"1) pursuant to the provisions of Article 39, paragraph 1, the Convention shall not be applicable to the territories of the Faroe islands and Greenland;

2) pursuant to the provisions of Article 42, paragraph 1,

a) the Kingdom of Denmark objects to the use of French in any application, communication or other document sent to its Central Authority (cf. Article 24, paragraph 2); and

b) it shall not be bound to assume any costs resulting from the participation of legal counsel or advisers or from court proceedings, except insofar as those costs may be covered by its system of legal aid and advice (cf. Article 26, paragraph 3);

3) Central Authority designated under the *Hague Convention of 25 October 1980 on the Civil Aspects of International Child Abduction.*

adresse/address:	Ministry of Justice (Justitsministeriet) Department of Private Law (Civilretsdirektoratet) Æbeløgade 1 2100 COPENHAGEN Ø Denmark
numéro de téléphone/telephone number:	(45)-33923302 (from 10.00 till 14.30)

numéro de télex/telex number: —
numéro de télécopie/telefax number: (45)-39271889
personnes à contacter/persons to contact:

M./Mr Ole GRÆSBØLL OLESEN, Head of Secretariat
(langues de communication/languages of communication: danois, anglais/Danish, English)
tél./tel.: (45)-33922869 or (45)-39275605 (direct lines)

Mme/Mrs Rie THOUSTRUP SØRENSEN, Head of Section
(langues de communication/languages of communication: danois, anglais/Danish, English)
tél./tel.: (45)-33922859 (direct line)

Mme/Mrs Anne Marie VON LÜTTICHAU, Head of Section
(langues de communication/languages of communication: danois, anglais/Danish, English)
tél./tel.: (45)-33922827 (direct line)

M./Mr Henning LARSEN, Head of Section
(langues de communication/languages of communication: danois, anglais/Danish, English)
tél./tel.: (45)-33922904 (direct line)

Note: La Convention ne s'applique pas aux territoires de Iles Féroé et du Groenland. The Convention does not apply to the territories of the Faroe Islands and Greenland.

In accordance with Article 43 the Convention will enter into force for Denmark on 1 July 1991.

The Operation of the Central Authority for Denmark.

1. *Rules.*

A. The International Child Abduction Act, no 793 of November 27th, 1990.
The International Child Abduction Act incorporates the Conventions into the Danish legal system and thus enables the courts to enforce decisions about rights of custody etc. of the other contracting states.
The Act also outlines the duties of the Central Authority and authorizes the Minister of Justice to appoint the Central Authority. (Section 3 of the Act)

B. Government Order no. 453 of June 18th, 1990, on International Child Abduction. By this Government Order the Minister of Justice has appointed the Department of Private Law as Central Authority.

2. *Accommodation.*

The Central Authority for Denmark is the Department of Private Law. This Department is part of the Ministry of Justice. All correspondance should be directed to "Ministry of Justice, Department of Private Law, (Civilretsdirektoratet), AEbeløgade 1, DK-2100 København Ø. The Fax no. of the Department is -45- 3927 1889". The cases will be dealt with by a younger member of the legal staff of the Division of Family Law (a head of section) under the supervision of the head of the Division or one of his 2 deputies, whose names and telephone nos have been communicated to the other parties to the conventions.

3. *Case management.*

In its file each case has a sheet recording all relevant information such as the facts of the case (including letters, telefonecalls, action taken etc.) and the considerations of the officers who have dealt with the case. The file will be marked in a way which indicates its urgent nature. Until the case is closed, the file will be kept on the desk of the officer who deals with the case.

4. *Applications forwarded to Denmark.*

A. Procedures when the application reaches the Central Authority.

When an application reaches the Central Authority, it will immediately be examined in order to establish whether it meets the requirements of the convention under which it has been made. If further information or documents are necessary they will be requested.

If it is manifest that the requirements are not fulfilled or that the application is otherwise not well founded, the Central Authority will immediately inform the applicant or the Central Authority through which the application has been submitted that the application cannot be accepted and of the reasons for this. (See art. 27 of the Hague Convention and Article 4, paragraph 4 of the European Convention) All other applications will be translated into Danish and sent by facsimile and letter to the bailiff's court of the town where the abductor resides.

If it is thought to be expedient the Central Authority will ask the local administrative authority (statsamt) to summon the abductor and, if possible, the applicant to an interview in order to seek a solution on a voluntary basis. (See article 10 of the Hague Convention)

If the whereabouts of the child are unknown the Central Authority will request the police (Politiets Eftersøgningstjeneste) to find the child (see Article 7 litra a of the Hague Convention and Article 5, la, of the European Convention). All available information that may help the police to find the child will immediately be forwarded to the police.

B. The procedure in the court.

When the court has received the application it will automatically assign a lawyer for the applicant. (See Section 18, 2nd paragraph of the International Child Abduction Act) (If the applicant has already hired a Danish lawyer, this lawyer may be assigned to the case, if he is willing to accept the rules of legal aid.) The lawyer will act on behalf of the applicant and will see to it that all relevant information is put before the court. The Department of Private Law will offer to supply the court and the lawyer with information concerning the application of the convention.

According to Section 15 in the International Child Abduction Act the courts shall act expeditiously in these cases. To meet this requirement the application should contain all relevant information and be accompanied by all relevant documents. The defendant parent will then be ordered to appear before the court according to Sections 493 and 494 of the Danish Administration of Justice Act.

If it is found to be necessary the court can decide that the child should stay with one of the parents or in a place chosen by the local social security authority until the court has reached a final decision (See Section 17 of the International Child Abduction Act).

C. Costs of the application.

The costs of the application are covered by Denmark only insofar as those costs may be covered by the Danish system of legal aid and advice.

However the Central Authority does not have to apply for legal aid, because the Danish Child Abduction Act establishes a right for the applicant to get legal aid when the bailiff has assigned a lawyer to the case, cf. 5 B.

5. *Cases where a Danish decision on custody or visitation is necessary.*

A. Where recognition or enforcement is refused and the applicant requests that the Central Authority brings proceedings concerning the substance of the case, the Central Authority will consider whether it should comply with the request. (This only applies where the European Convention is applicable) (See Article 5, paragraph 4 in the European Convention)

If the Central Authority complies with the request it will apply for legal aid on behalf of the applicant. Further information about the financial circumstances of the applicant may be neccesary to decide whether legal aid can be granted. However the Department of Private Law can decide that legal aid may be provided regardless of this, for instance due to the general interest of the matter or to the special significance of the case for the applicant. (See the Danish Administration of Justice Act, sections 330-331 a). Foreign citizens have the same right to legal aid as Danish citizens. The local court will assign lawyer to the case cf. 5 B.

B. If the Central Authority receives an application to make arrangements for organizing or securing the effective exercise of rights of access, it will forward the application to the local administrative authority (statsamt). (See Article 21 in the Hague Convention) The local administrative authority will try to settle any disputes between the two parties. If this is not possible a decision will be made on the matter according to the Danish rules on access rights. In such cases the way that access has been exercised earlier—whether on the basis of an agreement or on a foreign decision—will be taken into account.

Either party may appeal the decision of the local administrative authority to the Department of Private Law.

[2f] By instrument deposited on 22 January 1992 with the Ministry of Foreign Affairs of the Kingdom of the Netherlands, Ecuador acceded to the Convention. In conformity with Article 38, paragraph 3, the Convention will enter into force for Ecuador on 1 April 1992. According to Article 38, paragraph 4, the accession will have effect only as regards Ecuador and such Contracting States as will have declared their acceptance of the accession.

In accordance with Article 38, paragraph 5, the Convention entered into force between Ecuador and: *the United States* (1 April 1992); *Netherlands, for the Kingdom in Europe* (1 May 1992); *Israel, Luxembourg, United Kingdom of Great Britain and Northern Ireland* (1 June 1992); *Spain* (1 July 1992); *Argentina, the Federal Republic of Germany and Switzerland* (1 September 1992); *Ireland* (EIF: 1 April 1993); *Australia* (EIF: 1 April 1993); *Canada* (EIF: 1 December 1993); *Sweden* (EIF: 1 December 1993); *Finland* (EIF: 1 August 1994); *New Zealand* (EIF: 1 November 1995); *Mexico* (EIF: 1 December 1995).

[2g] In accordance with Article 43, paragraph 2, the Convention will enter into force for *Finland* on *1 August 1994.*

The instrument of acceptance contains the following declarations:

"1. Finland declares, according to Article 42 and Article 24, paragraph 2, of the Convention, that it accepts only the use of English in applications, communications and other documents sent to its Central Authority.

2. Finland declares, according to Article 42 and Article 26, paragraph 3, of the Convention, that it shall not be bound to assume any costs referred to in Article 26, paragraph 2, resulting from the participation of legal counsel or advisers or from court proceedings, except insofar as those costs may be covered by its system of legal aid and advice."

In accordance with Article 6, first paragraph, of the Convention Finland has designated as the Central Authority:

Ministry of Justice
Eteläesplanadi 10
P.O. Box 1
FIN-00131 HELSINKI — Tel: 358-0-18251
FINLAND — Telefax: 358-0-1825224
Liaison Officers: Senior Ministerial Secretary
Mr. Hannu Taimisto Tel. 358-0-1825327
Senior Ministerial Secretary
Ms. Mirja Kurkinen Tel. 358-0-1825321

[3] *Notification in accordance with Article 45, paragraphs 4 and 6, of the Convention*

On the occasion of the approval by France of the above-mentioned Convention the French Government made the following reservations and declarations:

Translation

1) In accordance with the provisions of Article 42 and pursuant to Article 24, paragraph 2, the Government will consider only those applications which are drawn up in French, or are accompanied by a translation into French, and will require a translation into French of any communication or document sent to its Central Authority.
2) In accordance with the provisions of Article 42 and pursuant to Article 26, paragraph 3, the Government declares that it will assume the costs referred to in paragraph 2 of Article 26 only insofar as these costs are covered by the French system of legal aid.
3) In accordance with the provisions of Article 39, the Government declares that the Convention shall extend to the whole of the territory of the French Republic.

Autorité centrale française:

1Le Ministère de la Justice

Bureau de l'Entaide Judiciaire Internationale

adresse/address — Le Ministère de la Justice

Bureau de l'Entraide Judiciaire Internationale
13, Place Vendôme
75001 PARIS France

numéro de téléphone/telephone number: (1) 42.61.80.22
numéro de télex/telex number: 211802
télécopieur (*nouveau*)/telecopier (*new*): (1) 44 77 60 70
personnes à contacter/persons to contact:

M/Mr B. STURLESE, magistrat (Chef du Bureau de l'Entraide Judiciaire Internationale) langues de communication/ languages of communication: français, anglais/French, English

tél./tel.: (1) 44 77 65 80

Mme/Mrs D. LAVAU, magistrat (Chef adjoint du Bureau de l'Entraide Judiciaire Internationale) langues de communication/languages of communication: français, anglais/ French, English

tél./tel.: (1) 44 77 63 84

Mme/Mrs PRIVE

tél./tel.: (1) 44 77 63 89

(The effective date of this information is *3 July 1990*)
The instrument of approval by France was deposited on 16 September 1982.
[3a] On October 3, 1990 the German Democratic Republic acceded to the Federal Republic of Germany.

Notification pursuant to Article 45 of the Convention

In accordance with Article 37, paragraph 2, the Federal Republic of Germany deposited its instrument of ratification of the above-mentioned Convention on 27 September 1990

with the declaration that the Convention shall also apply to Berlin (West) with effect from the date on which it enters into force for the Federal Republic of Germany,

with the following reservation:

[Die Bundesrepublik Deutschland]"erklärt in Übereinstimmung mit Artikel 26 Abs. 3, daB sie nur insoweit gebunden ist, die sich aus der Beiordnung eines Rechtsanwalts oder aus einem Gerichtsverfahren ergebenden Kosten im Sinn des Artikels 26 Abs. 2 zu übernehmen, als diese Kosten durch ihre Vorschriften über die ProzeBkosten und Beratungshilfe gedeckt sind."

courtesy translation

[The Federal Republic of Germany] declares in accordance with the third paragraph of Article 26 that it is not bound to assume any costs referred to in the second paragraph of Article 26 resulting from the participation of legal counsel or advisers or from court proceedings, except insofar as those costs may be covered by its regulations concerning legal aid and advice.

and stating the following:

"Die Bundesrepublik Deutschland geht davon aus, daB Ersuchen aus anderen Vertragsstaaten gemäB Artikel 24 Abs. 1 regelmäBig von einer deutschen Übersetzung begleitet sein werden."

courtesy translation

The Federal Republic of Germany assumes that, in accordance with the first paragraph of Article 24, applications from other Contracting States shall regularly be accompanied by a translation into German.

In accordance with Article 6, paragraph 1, of the Convention the Federal Republic of Germany has designated as Central Authority:

Der Generalbundesanwalt beim Bundesgerichtshof —zentrale Behörde nach dem Sorgerechtsübereinkommens—Ausführungsgesetz—(the Public Prosecutor General of the Federal Court of Justice—Central Authority pursuant to the statute implementing the Convention on the Custody of Children—)

Postfach 11 06 29
D-1000 Berlin 11
Federal Republic of Germany

Telephone number: (030) 2596-1
Telex number: 185 505 bzrb d
Telefax number: (030) 2596-391.
Persons to contact: Ms. Renate Seier
tel.: (030) 2596-344

languages of communication: English and German

or (in her absence):
Ms. Gisela Hennig
tel.: (030) 2596-277

languages of communication: English and German.

The Convention will enter into force for the Republic of Germany on 1 December 1990.

[3b] *Notification pursuant to Article 45 of the Convention.*

In accordance with Article 37, paragraph 2, Greece deposited its instrument of ratification of the above-mentioned Convention with the Ministry of Foreign Affairs of the Kingdom of the Netherlands on 19 March 1993.

Upon ratification Greece made the following reservations and declaration:

Translation

1. In accordance with Article 42 of the Convention on the Civil Aspects of International Child Abduction Greece declares that is shall not be bound to assume any costs referred to in the second paragraph of Article 26 resulting from the participation of legal counsel or advisers or from court proceedings, except insofar as those costs concern cases of free legal aid.
2. In accordance with Article 42 of the above-mentioned Convention Greece declares that it objects to the use of the French language in any application, communication or other document sent to its Central Authority.
3. In accordance with Article 6, first paragraph, of the Convention the Ministry of Justice (Direction de l'élaboration des lois, 4ème section) is designated as the Central Authority of Greece.

In accordance with Article 43 the Convention will enter into force for Greece on 1 June 1993.

[3c] In accordance with Article 38, paragraph 2, of the above-mentioned Convention the Republic of Honduras deposited its instrument of accession with the Ministry of Foreign Affairs of the Kingdom of the Netherlands on 20 December 1993. The Republic of Honduras acceded to the Convention subject to the reservation provided for in its Article 26, third paragraph.

The Convention will enter into force for the Republic of Honduras on 1 March 1994 in accordance with Article 38, paragraph 3.

The accession will have effect only as regards the relations between the Republic of Honduras and such Contracting States as will have declared their acceptance of the accession.

Central Authority designated under the *Hague Convention of 25 October 1980 on the Civil Aspects of International Child Abduction.*

adresse/address: Junta Nacional de Bienestar Social
Frente Emisoras Unidas
Contiguo a Leche 2 Pinos
Boulevard Suyapa
Tegucigalpa, M.D.C.
Honduras

numéro de téléphone/telephone number: (504)-39-1020 ou/or 39-1004 ou/or 37-9302
numéro de télécopie/telefax number: (504)-39-1011
personnes à contacter/persons to contact: Yamileth MEJIA (General Secretary)

The Convention is in force between *Honduras* and the following States: *United Kingdom of Great Britain and Northern Ireland* (EIF: 1 May 1994)*; *Luxembourg* (EIF: 1 May 1994); *United States of America* (EIF: 1 June 1994); *Netherlands (for the Kingdom in Europe)* (EIF: 1 June 1994); *Finland* (EIF: 1 August 1994); *Germany* (EIF: 1 August 1994); *Australia* (EIF: 1 September 1994); *Switzerland* (EIF: 1 October 1994); *Ireland* (EIF: 1 December 1994); *Sweden* (EIF: 1 January 1995); *Canada* (EIF: 1 August 1995); *New Zealand* (EIF: 1 November 1995); *Mexico* (EIF: 1 December 1995); *Israel* (EIF: 1 January 1996).

* The United Kingdom made the following declaration with regard to the accession of Honduras to the Convention: "Notwithstanding the provisions of the said Article 38 regarding entry into force of the Convention as between the acceding State and the State declaring its acceptance of the accession, amendments will have been made to the United Kingdom municipal law in order to give effect to the Convention between it and Honduras as of 1 March 1994 when the Convention enters into force for Honduras."

The Ministry of Foreign Affairs of the Kingdom of the Netherlands has not yet received any communication from the Government of Honduras concerning the date of entry into force proposed by the United Kingdom.

[4] *Notification in accordance with Article 45, paragraphs 2 and 3, of the Convention*

In conformity with Article 38, paragraphs 1 and 2, the Hungarian People's Republic deposited its instrument of accession to the above-mentioned Convention with the Ministry of Foreign Affairs of the Kingdom of the Netherlands on 7 April 1986.

In conformity with Article 43, paragraph 2, the Convention will enter into force for the Hungarian People's Republic on 1 July 1986.

According to Article 38, paragraph 4, the accession will have effect only as regards the Hungarian People's Republic and such Contracting States as will have declared their acceptance of the accession.

In conformity with Article 6, paragraph 1, of the Convention, the Hungarian Peoples Republic designated as Central Authority to discharge the duties which are imposed by the Convention:

Bureau compétent auprès du Ministère de la Justice: Bureau du droit international et des relations internationales./Competent unit within the Ministry of Justice: Department of International Law and International Relations.

Directeur/Director: Dr Tamas BÁN (langues de communication/languages of communication: anglais et français/English and French)

Directeur adjoint/Deputy Director: Mme/Mrs Dr Klara NÉMETH (langues de communication/languages of communication: allemand et français/German and French)

adresse/address: "The Ministry of Justice
Szalay utca 16
PO Box 54
1363 BUDAPEST
Hongrie/Hungary

numéro de téléphone/telephone number: 36 1 1 318 188 ou/or 36 1 1 114 015
numéro de télex/telex number: 224998
numéro de télécopie/telefax number: 36 1 1 114 015

personnes à contacter/persons to contact: Mme/Mrs Dr Katalin BENEDEK (langue de communication/language of communication: anglais/English)

(heures de bureau: lundi à vendredi 8 à 16 h.)

Mme/Mrs Dr Éva HORVATH (langues de communication/languages of communication: français, russe/ French, Russian)

(working hours: Monday to Friday 8-16 hours)

Mlle/Miss Dr Marianna SZÉKELY (langue de communication/language of communication: anglais/English)

M./Mr Dr Jozsef GEHÉR (langues de communication/languages of communication: allemand, français, anglais/German, French, English)

M./Mr Dr Gabor HIDASI (langues de communication/languages of communication: allemand, anglais, italien/German, English, Italian)

In accordance with Article 43, paragraph 2, the Convention is in force between Hungary and the following States:

the United Kingdom of Great Britain and Northern Ireland (entered into force: 1 September 1986); Luxembourg (entered into force: 1 January 1987); France (entered into force: 1 February 1987); Australia (entered into force: 1 March 1988); Canada (entered into force: 1 April 1988); United States of America (entered into force: 1 July 1988); Sweden (entered into force: 1 July 1990); the Netherlands (for the Kingdom in Europe) (entered into force: 1 September 1990); Austria (entered into force: 1 November 1990); Federal Republic of Germany (entered into force: 1 December 1990); Norway (entered into force: 1 February 1991); New Zealand (1 December 1991); Israel (1 February 1992); Denmark (1 March 1992); Australia (1 June 1992); Spain (1 July 1992); Portugal (1 August 1992); Switzerland (1 September 1992) Ireland (1 October 1991); Israel (EIF: 1 February 1992); Denmark (EIF: 1 March 1992); Spain (EIF: 1 July 1992); Portugal (EIF: 1 August 1992); Switzerland (EIF: 1 September 1992); Finland (EIF: 1 August 1994).

[4a] *Notification pursuant to Article 45 of the Convention*
The Ministry of Foreign Affairs of the Kingdom of the Netherlands, depositary of the above-mentioned Convention, has the honour to inform the Member States of the Hague Conference on Private International Law and States having acceded to the Convention that in accordance with Article 38, paragraph 2, Iceland deposited its Instrument of accession with the Ministry of Foreign Affairs of the Kingdom of the Netherlands on 14 August 1996.
The instrument of accession contains the following reservations:
"1. In accordance with Article 42, paragraph 1, and Article 24, paragraph 2, of the Convention, Iceland makes a reservation with regard to Article 24, paragraph 1, and objects to the use of French in any application, communication or other document sent to its Central Authority.
2. In accordance with Article 42, paragraph 1, and Article 26, paragraph 3, of the Convention, Iceland makes a reservation that it shall not be bound to assume any costs referred to in Article 26, paragraph 2, resulting from the participation of legal counsel or advisers or from court proceedings, except insofar as those costs may be covered by its system of legal aid and advice.
The other provisions of the Convention shall be inviolably observed."
The Convention will enter into force for Iceland on 1 November 1996 in accordance with Article 38, paragraph 3.
The accession will have effect only as regards the relations between Iceland and such Contracting States as will have declared their acceptance of the accession.

[4b] The Permanent Bureau of the Hague Conference on private international law presents its compliments to the Diplomatic Missions of the Member States and to the National Organs and has the honour to inform them that, by instrument deposited on 16 July 1991 with the Ministry of Foreign Affairs of the Kingdom of the Netherlands, Ireland ratified the above-mentioned Convention.
In accordance with Article 6, paragraph 1, Ireland has designated as Central Authority:

"The Minister for Justice
Department of Justice
St. Stephen's Green
Dublin 2
Ireland
Telephone: 01–789711
Telefax: 01–615461
Communication Language: *English*
Contact Persons: *Mr Ken O'Leary*
Ms Mary Dardis
Ms Breda Walshe"

In accordance with Article 43, paragraph 2, the Convention will enter into force for Ireland on 1 October 1991.

[4c] *Notification pursuant to Article 45 of the Convention*
The Ambassador Extraordinary and Plenipotentiary of Israel at The Hague signed on 4 September 1991, in accordance with Article 37, paragraph 1, the above mentioned Convention for the State of Israel as follows:

M.N. Bawly
4 septembre 1991

In accordance with Article 37, paragraph 2, Israel deposited its instrument of ratification of the above mentioned Convention with the Ministry of Foreign Affairs on 4 September 1991. The instrument of ratification contains the following reservation:
"In accordance with Articles 26 and 42 of the Convention, the State of Israel hereby declares that, in proceedings under the Convention, it shall not be bound to assume any costs resulting from the participation of legal counsel or advisers or from court proceedings, except insofar as those costs may be covered by its system of legal aid and advice."
In accordance with Article 43 the Convention will enter into force for the State of Israel on 1 December 1991.
Denmark has modified, as from 15 August 1991, the Central Authority referred to in Article 6 of the Convention:

Ministry of Justice
Department of Private Law
(Civilretsdirektorat)
AEbeløgade 1
DK2100 Copenhagen Ø

[5] *Notification pursuant to Article 45 of the Convention*
In conformity with Article 37, paragraph 2, the Grand-Duchy of Luxemburg deposited its instrument of ratification of the above-mentioned Convention with the Ministry of Foreign Affairs of the Kingdom of the Netherlands on 8 October 1986.
At the time of ratification the following declarations were made:
Translation
The Grand-Duchy of Luxemburg declares that it shall not be bound to assume any costs referred to in Article 26, paragraph 2, of the Convention, namely the costs resulting from the participation of legal counsel or advisers or from court proceedings, except insofar as those costs are covered by the Luxemburg system of legal aid and advice.
The "procureur général d'Etat" is designated as the Central Authority referred to in Article 6 of the Convention.

adresse/address:	Le Procureur Général d'Etat Palais de Justice Boîte postale 15 L-2010 LUXEMBOURG Luxembourg
numéro de téléphone/telephone number:	Secrétariat/Secretariat: 273- 94 ou/or 475981-336
numéro de télex/telex number:	
numéro de télécopie/telefax number:	470550
personnes à contacter/persons to contact:	M./Mr Claude NICOLAY tél./tel. 475981-278 ou/or (en case d'absence/in his absence) M./Mr Edmond GERARD tél/tel.: 475981-332

In accordance with Article 43, paragraph 1, the Convention will enter into force for Luxemburg on 1 January 1987.

[5a] *Notification pursuant to Article 45 of the Convention.—*
In accordance with Article 38, paragraph 2, of the above-mentioned Convention the Republic of Mauritius deposited its instrument of accession with the Ministry of Foregin Affairs of the Kingdom of the Netherlands on 23 March 1993.
The Convention will enter into force for the Republic of Mauritius on 1 June 1993 in accordance with Article 38, paragraph 3.
The accession will have effect only as regards the relations between the Republic of Mauritius and such Contracting States as will have declared their acceptance of the accession.

The Ministry of Foreign Affairs of the Kingdom of the Netherlands, in its notification No. 3/1993 of 19 April 1993 concerning the accession by the Republic of Mauritius to the abovementioned Convention, omitted to state that the Republic of Mauritius made the following reservation:
"The Republic of Mauritius declares that is shall not be bound to assume any costs referred to in paragraph 2 of article 26 resulting from the participation of legal counsel or advisers or from court proceedings, except insofar as those costs may be covered by its system of legal aid and advice."

Notification pursuant to Article 45 of the Convention
The Ministry of Foreign Affairs of the Kingdom of the Netherlands, depositary of the Convention on the Civil Aspects of International Child Abduction of 25 October 1980, has the honour, to inform the Member States of the Hague Conference on Private International Law and the States having acceded to the abovementioned Convention that in accordance with Article 6, first paragraph, of the Convention the Attorney General's Office is designated as the Central Authority of Mauritius.
In accordance with Article 38, paragraph 5, the Convention entered into force between Mauritius and the following States: *the Kingdom of the Netherlands (for the Kingdom in Europe)* (1 August 1993); *the United Kingdom of Great Britain and Northern Ireland* (1 September 1993); *Luxembourg* (1 September 1993); *United States of America* (EIF: 1 October 1993); *Germany* (EIF: 1 December 1993); *Sweden* (EIF: 1 December 1993); *Israel* (EIF: 1 December 1993); *Australia* (EIF: 1 January 1994); *Argentina* (EIF: 1 February 1994); *Finland* (EIF: 1 August 1994); *Switzerland* (EIF: 1 October 1994); *Ireland* (EIF: 1 December 1994); *Spain* (EIF: 1 December 1994); *France* (EIF: 1 July 1995); *Canada* (EIF: 1 August 1995); *New Zealand* (EIF: 1 November 1995).

[5b] The Permanent Bureau of the Hague Conference on private international law presents its compliments to the Diplomatic Missions of the Member States and to the National Organs and has the honour to inform them that, by instrument deposited on 20 June 1991 with the Ministry of Foreign Affairs of the Kingdom of the Netherlands,

Mexico

acceded to the above-mentioned Convention.
In conformity with Article 38, paragraph 3, the Convention will enter into force for *Mexico* on *1 September 1991.*
According to Article 38, paragraph 4, the accession will have effect only as regards Mexico and such Contracting States as will have declared their acceptance of the accession.
In accordance with Article 38, paragraph 5, the Convention is in force between Mexico and the following States:

Ireland (1 October 1991); *United Kingdom of Great Britain and Northern Ireland* (1 October 1991); *the Netherlands (for the Kingdom in Europe)* (1 October 1991); *United States of America* (1 October 1991); *Argentina* (1 October 1991); *Luxembourg* (1 November 1991); *New Zealand* (1 December 1991); *France* (1 January

1992); *Israel, Federal Republic of Germany* (1 February 1992); *Norway* (1 March 1992); *Canada, Spain* (1 July 1992); *Portugal, Sweden* (1 August 1992); *Switzerland* (1 September 1992); *Denmark* (EIF: 1 December 1992); *Finland* (EIF: 1 August 1994); *Austria* (EIF: 1 November 1994); Bahamas (EIF: 1 December 1995); *Burkina Faso* (EIF: 1 December 1995); *Chile* (EIF: 1 December 1995); *Cyprus* (EIF: 1 December 1995); *Ecuador* (EIF: 1 December 1995); *Honduras* (EIF: 1 December 1995); *Monaco* (EIF: 1 December 1995); *Panama* (EIF: 1 December 1995); *Poland* (EIF: 1 December 1995); *Romania* (EIF: 1 December 1995); *Saint Kitts and Nevis* (EIF: 1 December 1995); *Slovenia* (EIF: 1 December 1995); *Zimbabwe* (EIF: 1 December 1995).

Notification pursuant to Article 45 of the Convention

Mexico has designated as the Central Authority referred to in Article 6 of the Convention:

"Ministry of Foreign Affairs
Juridical Consultancy

Address:	Homero 213, 16th floor, Colonia Chapultepec-Morales, Mexico City 11570.
Telephone:	254-7306 254-7318
Fax:	254-7316
Telex:	176-3479 (SREME)"

The following officials can be contacted:

"Dr. Carlos Pujalte Pineiro, Adjunct Juridical Consultant; Dr. Eduardo Pena Haller, Coördinator of the Adviser's and Defense Office for Mexicans Abroad."

5c In accordance with Article 38, paragraph 5, the Convention entered into force between Monaco and the following States:

France (EIF: 1 March 1993); *Netherlands (for the Kingdom in Europe)* (EIF: 1 March 1993); *Luxembourg* (EIF: 1 April 1993); *United Kingdom of Great Britain and Northern Ireland* (EIF: 1 April 1993); *Ireland* (EIF: 1 April 1993); *United States of America* (EIF: 1 June 1993); *Germany* (EIF: 1 July 1993); *Argentina* (EIF: 1 August 1993); *Israel* (EIF: 1 November 1993); *Sweden* (EIF: 1 December 1993); *Australia* (EIF: 1 January 1994); *Finland* (EIF: 1 August 1994); *Switzerland* (EIF: 1 October 1994); *Austria* (EIF: 1 November 1994); *Spain* (EIF: 1 December 1994); *Denmark* (EIF: 1 May 1995); *Canada* (EIF: 1 June 1995); *New Zealand* (EIF: 1 November 1995); *Mexico* (EIF: 1 December 1995).

6 The Permanent Bureau of the Hague Conference on private international law presents its compliments to the Diplomatic Missions of the Member States and to the National Organs and has the honour to inform them that, in accordance with Article 37, paragraph 2,

the *Kingdom of the Netherlands*

deposited on *12 June 1990 for the Kingdom in Europe* the instrument of acceptance of the above-mentioned Convention. The instrument of acceptance contains the following reservation:

The Kingdom of the Netherlands shall not be bound to assume any costs referred to in the second paragraph of Article 26 of the Convention on the Civil Aspects of International Child Abduction, done at The Hague on 25 October 1980, resulting from the participation of legal counsel or advisers or from court proceedings, except insofar as those costs may be covered by its system of legal aid and advice.

In accordance with Article 43, paragraph 2, the Convention will enter into force for the *Kingdom of the Netherlands (the Kingdom in Europe)* on *1 September 1990.*

In accordance with the provisions of Article 6 of the Convention, the Central Authority designated is:

for the *Kingdom in Europe*: the *Ministry of Justice at The Hague.*

adresse/address:	Ministerie van Justitie Hoofd Afdeling Staats- en Strafrecht Afdeling Internationale Rechtshulp Schedeldoekshaven 100 Postbus 20301 2500 EH THE HAGUE Netherlands
numéro de téléphone/telephone number:	31/70 3707911
numéro de télex/telex number:	
numéro de télécopie/telefax number:	31/70 3647504
personnes à contacter/persons to contact:	Mme/Ms M.T.E. FORD-CLAASEN (langues de communication/ languages of communication: anglais, allemand, (français)/ English, German (French)) tél./tel.: 31/70 3706916

6a *Notification pursuant to Article 45 of the Convention*

In accordance with Article 38, paragraph 2, New Zealand deposited its instrument of accession to the above-mentioned Convention with the Ministry of Foreign Affairs of the Kingdom of the Netherlands on 31 May 1991.

The instrument of accession contains the following declarations:

"the Government of New Zealand hereby declares in accordance with Article 24 and Article 42 of the Convention that any application, communication or other document sent to its Central Authority should either be in the English language or accompanied by a translation thereof in the English language;

And the Government of New Zealand hereby further declares in accordance with Article 26 and Article 42 of the Convention that it reserves the right not to be bound to assume the costs referred to in Article 26 resulting from the participation of legal counsel or advisers or from Court proceedings, except insofar as those costs may be covered by its system of legal aid and advice."

In accordance with Article 38, paragraph 3, the Convention will enter into force for New Zealand on 1 August 1991. The accession will have effect only as regards the relations between New Zealand and such Contracting States as will have declared their acceptance of the accession. Such declaration shall be deposited at the Ministry of Foreign Affairs of the Kingdom of the Netherlands.

New Zealand designated as the Central Authority under Article 6, paragraph 2:

adresse/address:	The Secretary Department of Justice Private Box 180 Wellington New Zealand
numéro de téléphone/telephone number:	(04) 725-980
numéro de télex/telex number:	
numéro de télécopie/telefax number:	(04) 732-362
personnes à contacter/persons to contact:	Mme/Ms Heather TAVASSOLI (langues de communication/ language of communication: allemand/German) Mme/Mrs Virginia LYNCH Mme/Mrs Ellen FRANCE

In accordance with Article 38, paragraph 5, the Convention is in force between New Zealand and the following States:

the Netherlands (for the Kingdom in Europe) (1 September 1991); *Argentina, Denmark, Ireland, Luxembourg, United Kingdom of Great Britain, Northern Ireland and United States* (1 October 1991); *France* (1 January 1992); *Federal Republic of Germany, Israel* (1 February 1992); *Australia* (1 June 1992); *Canada, Spain* (1 July 1992); *Portugal, Sweden* (1 August 1992); *Switzerland* (1 September 1992); *Norway* (1 October 1992); *Finland* (EIF: 1 August 1994); *Austria* (EIF: 1 November 1994); *Bahamas* (EIF: 1 November 1995); *Burkina Faso* (EIF: 1 November 1995); *Chile* (EIF: 1 November 1995); *Cyprus* (EIF: 1 November 1995); *Ecuador* (EIF: 1 November 1995); *Honduras* (EIF: 1 November 1995); *Mauritius* (EIF: 1 November 1995); *Monaco* (EIF: 1 November 1995); *Panama* (EIF: 1 November 1995); *Poland* (EIF: 1 November 1995); *Romania* (EIF: 1 November 1995); *Slovenia* (EIF: 1 November 1995); *Zimbabwe* (EIF: 1 November 1995).

6b *Notification pursuant to Article 45 of the Convention*

In accordance with its Article 37, paragraph 1, the above-mentioned Convention was signed for Norway on 9 January 1989 as follows:

(sd.) BJØRN BLAKSTAD
9th January 1989
subject to ratification and to the reservations
set out in the full powers to sign.

The text of those reservations is worded as follows:

"1. In accordance with Articles 24 and 42, the Norwegian Government reserves the right not to accept applications, communications or other documents sent to the General Authority in French.

2. In accordance with Articles 26 and 42, Norway makes the reservation that it shall not be bound to assume any costs resulting from the participation of legal counsel or advisers or from court proceedings, except insofar as those costs may be covered by Act of 13 June 1980 relating to free legal aid."

In accordance with Article 37, paragraph 2, Norway deposited on 9 January 1989 also its instrument of ratification of the said Convention with the Ministry of Foreign Affairs of the Kingdom of the Netherlands. The instrument of ratification contains the same reservations as the full powers to sign the Convention.

The Convention will enter into force for Norway in accordance with Article 43 of 1 April 1989.

In accordance with Article 6, paragraph 1, Norway has designated as Central Authority:

Justisdepartementet
Rettshjelpskontor
Postboks 8005 dep
0030 Oslo 1
tel. 02-349090

The Convention is in force between *Panama* and the following States: *United States of America* (EIF: 1 June 1994); *Netherlands (for the Kingdom in Europe)* (EIF: 1 June 1994); *Luxembourg* (EIF: 1 June 1994); *United Kingdom of Great Britain and Northern Ireland* (EIF: 1 July 1994)*; *Finland* (EIF: 1 August 1994); *Australia* (EIF: 1 September 1994); *Switzerland* (EIF: 1 October 1994); *Ireland* (EIF: 1 December 1994); *Sweden* (EIF: 1 January 1995); *Chile* (EIF: 1 March 1995); *Argentina* (EIF: 1 May 1995); *Germany* (EIF: 1 June 1995); *Cyprus* (EIF: 1 June 1995); *Saint Kitts and Nevis* (EIF: 1 June 1995); *Slovenia* (EIF: 1 June 1995); *Canada* (EIF: 1 August 1995); *Spain* (EIF: 1 September 1995); *New Zealand* (EIF: 1 November 1995); *Mexico* (EIF: 1 December 1995); Israel (EIF: 1 January 1996); *Colombia* (EIF: 1 May 1996).

* with the following declaration:

"Notwithstanding the provisions of the said Article 38 regarding entry into force of the Convention as between the acceding State and the State declaring its acceptance of the accession, amendments will have been made to the United Kingdom municipal law in order to give effect to the Convention between it and Panama as of 1 May 1994 when the Convention enters into force for Panama. I would be grateful for confirmation of the date of 1 May 1994 as the date on which the Convention will enter into force between the United Kingdom and Panama."

6c In accordance with Article 38, paragraph 2, of the above-mentioned Convention the Republic of Poland deposited its instrument of accession to the Convention with the Ministry of Foreign Affairs of the Kingdom of the Netherlands on 10 August 1992. The instrument of accession contains the following reservation:

Translation

In accordance with Article 42 the Republic of Poland makes the reservation pursuant to Article 26, paragraph 3, of the Convention and declares that it shall not be bound to assume any costs referred to in the preceding paragraph, resulting from court proceedings, except insofar as those costs may be covered by its system of legal aid and advice. The Convention will enter into force for the Republic of Poland in accordance with Article 38, paragraph 3, on 1 November 1992.

The accession will have effect only as regards the relations between the Republic of Poland and such Contracting States as will have declared their acceptance of the accession.

In accordance with Article 38, paragraph 5, the Convention will enter into force between Poland and the following States: *United States of America, Kingdom of the Netherlands* (1 November 1992); *Luxembourg* (1 January 1993); *Germany, United Kingdom of Great Britain and Northern Ireland* (1 February 1993); *Ireland* (1 April 1993); *Norway* (1 July 1993); *Israel* (EIF: 1 November 1993); *Sweden* (EIF: 1 December 1993); *Australia* (EIF: 1 January 1994); *Argentina* (EIF: 1 February 1994); *Canada* (EIF: 1 February 1994); *Finland* (EIF: 1 August 1994); *Switzerland* (EIF: 1 October 1994); *Austria* (EIF: 1 November 1994); *Spain* (EIF: 1 December 1994); *Denmark* (EIF: 1 May 1995); *New Zealand* (EIF: 1 November 1995); *Mexico* (EIF: 1 December 1995); *Italy* (EIF: 1 February 1996).

[7] *Notification in accordance with Article 45, paragraphs 1 and 3 of the Convention*

In conformity with Article 37, paragraph 2, Portugal deposited its instrument of ratification of the above-mentioned Convention with the Ministry of Foreign Affairs of the Kingdom of the Netherlands on 29 September 1983.

The Portugese Government notified that the Portugese Central Authority as provided for in Article 6 of the Convention is: "Direcção-Geral dos Serviços Tutelares de Menores do Ministério da Justiça".

adresse/address:	Direcçao-Geral dos Serviços Tutelares de Menores Ministério da Justiça Avenida Almirante Reis, 101 1197 LISBOA CODEX Portugal
numéro de téléphone/telephone number:	352 47 09 352 26 60 54 81 50
numéro de télex/telex number:	
numéro de télécopie/telefax number:	52 69 85
personnes à contacter/persons to contact:	M./Mr MIRANDA PEREIRA, Directeur-Général (langues de communication/ languages of communication: portugais, anglais, français/ Portuguese, English, French) Mme/Mrs BAPTISTA-LOPES (langues de communication/ languages of communication: portugais, français/Portuguese, French) Mme/Mrs TRIGO DE SOUSA (langues de communication/ languages of communication: portugais, anglais, français/ Portuguese, English, French)

In accordance with Article 43 the Convention shall enter into force the first December 1983 for Canada, France and Portugal.

[7a] In accordance with Article 38, paragraph 5, the Convention entered into force between Romania and the following States: *the United States of America* (June 1, 1993); *the Federal Republic of Germany* (1 July 1993); *Argentina* (1 August 1993); *Israel* (EIF: 1 November 1993); *Sweden* (EIF: 1 December 1993); *Australia* (EIF: 1 January 1994); *Finland* (EIF: 1 August 1994); *Switzerland* (EIF: 1 October 1994); *Austria* (EIF: 1 November 1994); *Spain* (EIF: 1 December 1994); *Denmark* (EIF: 1 May 1995); *Canada* (EIF: 1 June 1995); *New Zealand* (EIF: 1 November 1995); *Mexico* (EIF: 1 December 1995).

[7b] The instrument of accession contains the following declaration:

"Saint Kitts and Nevis is not bound to assume any costs resulting under the Convention from the participation of legal counsel or advisers [or] from court proceedings in terms of paragraph 3 of Article 26 of the Convention."

In accordance with Article 38, paragraph 3, the Convention will enter into force for *Saint Kitts and Nevis* on *1 August 1994.*

According to Article 38, paragraph 4, the accession will have effect only as regards Saint Kitts and Nevis and such Contracting States as will have declared their acceptance of the accession.

The Convention is in force between *Saint Kitts and Nevis* and the following States: *United Kingdom of Great Britain and Northern Ireland* (EIF: 1 August 1994); *Netherlands (for the Kingdom in Europe)* (EIF: 1 October 1994); *Luxembourg* (EIF: 1 November 1994); *Ireland* (EIF: 1 December 1994); *Sweden* (EIF: 1 January 1995); *Germany* (EIF: 1 May 1995)*; *United States of America* (EIF: 1 June 1995); *Panama* (EFI: 1 June 1995); *Canada* (EIF: 1 August 1995); *Australia* (EIF: 1 November 1995); *Mexico* (EIF: 1 December 1995); *Israel* (EIF: 1 January 1996); *Chile* (EIF: 1 May 1996).

* The Note of the Embassy of Germany contains the following declaration: "The reservation under Article 26, paragraph 3, of the Convention made by Saint Kitts and Nevis on its accession is believed by the competent German judicial authorities to be connected with the fact that Saint Kitts and Nevis does not have a system of legal aid. Introduction of such a system would, however, render the reservation in its present form inadmissible. A possible solution would be for Saint Kitts and Nevis to supplement its reservation under Article 26, paragraph 3, accordingly." (Translation)

[7c] In accordance with Article 6, paragraph 1, of the above-mentioned Convention, the *Republic of Slovenia* has designated as Central Authority:

"The Ministry of Labour, Family and Social Affairs of the Republic of Slovenia
Section for Social Affairs
61000 Ljubljana
Kotnikova 5
tel: 386 61 171 33 86
fax: 386 61 171 33 77
Contact person: Mrs Tatjana PETRIČEK
Counsellor to the Government
communication languages:
English, Croatian."

The Convention is in force between *Slovenia* and the following States: *United Kingdom of Great Britain and Northern Ireland* (EIF: 1 June 1994); *Netherlands (for the Kingdom in Europe)* (EIF: 1 July 1994); *Luxembourg* (EIF: 1 August 1994); *Switzerland* (EIF: 1 October 1994); *Australia* (EIF: 1 November 1994); *Austria* (EIF: 1 November 1994); *Ireland* (EIF: 1 December 1994); *Sweden* (EIF: 1 January 1995); *United States of America* (EIF: 1 April 1995); *Argentina* (EIF: 1 May 1995); *Panama* (EIF: 1 June 1995); *Germany* (EIF: 1 June 1995); *Canada* (EIF: 1 August 1995); *Spain* (EIF: 1 September 1995); *New Zealand* (EIF: 1 November 1995); *Mexico* (EIF: 1 December 1995); *Israel* (EIF: 1 January 1996); *Chile* (EIF: 1 May 1996).

Central Authority designated under the *Hague Convention of 25 October 1980 on the civil aspects of international child abduction.*

adresse/address:	Attorney General's Chambers Government Headquarters Basseterre PO Box 164 St. Kitts and Nevis West Indies
numéro de téléphone/telephone number:	(809)-465-2521
numéro de télex/telex number:	(809)465-5040
numéro de télécopie/telefax number:	—
personnes à contacter/persons to contact:	Mr. Delano Bart, Attorney General

[8] *Notification pursuant to Article 45 of the Convention*

In accordance with Article 37, paragraph 2, Spain deposited on 16 June 1987 its instrument of ratification of the above-mentioned Convention with the Ministry of Foreign Affairs of the Kingdom of the Netherlands.

Spain designated as the Central Authority mentioned in Article 6 of the Convention: "La Secretaría General Técnica del Ministerio de Justicia, San Bernardo, 45.-28015 Madrid".

address:	Secretaria General Técnica del Ministerio de Justicia San Bernardo, 45 28015 MADRID Espagne
telephone number:	For telephone calls made within Spain, the access code for Madrid is (091)
telefax number:	(1) 522 1539
telex number:	22545
person to contact:	M./Mr A. LAGUIA ARRAZOLA tél./tel. (1) 521 7046 (langues de communication/languages of communication: espagnol, français anglais/Spanish, French, English)

The Convention will enter into force for Spain in accordance with its Article 43 on 1 September 1987.

[8a] The Permanent Bureau of the Hague Conference on private international law presents its compliments to the Diplomatic Missions of the Member States and to the National Organs and has the honour to inform them that on 22 March 1989 the above-mentioned Convention was signed and ratified by

Sweden.

In accordance with article 43, paragraph 2, the Convention will enter into force for *Sweden* on *1 June 1989.*

The instrument of ratification contains the following reservation:

In accordance with the provisions of article 42 and pursuant to article 42 and pursuant to article 26, Sweden declares that it shall not be bound to assume any costs referred to in article 26, paragraph 2, resulting from the participation of legal counsel or advisers or from court proceedings, except insofar as those costs may be covered by the Swedish system of legal aid.

In accordance with the provisions of article 6, the *Ministry of Foreign Affairs* is designated as the Central Authority.

[9] *Notification in accordance with Article 45, paragraphs 1 and 3 of the Convention*

In conformity with Article 37, paragraph 2, Switzerland deposited its instrument of ratification of the above-mentioned Convention with the Ministry of Foreign Affairs of the Kingdom of the Netherlands on 11 October 1983.

The Swiss Government notified that the Central Authority as provided for in Article 6 of the Convention is:

"L'Office fédéral de Justice du Département fédéral de Justice et Police".

Office fédéral de la Justice,
Autorité centrale en matière
d'enlèvement international
d'enfants,
3003 BERNE
Chef: Bernard Deschenaux, avocat
Téléphone: 031-61 41 18

In accordance with Article 43 the Convention shall enter into force for Switzerland on 1 January 1984.

[10] *Notification in pursuance of Article 45, paragraphs 1 and 3, of the Convention*

In conformity with Article 37, paragraph 2, the United Kingdom of Great Britain and Northern Ireland deposited its instrument of ratification of the above-mentioned Convention with the Ministry of Foreign Affairs of the Kingdom of the Netherlands on 20 May 1986.

The instrument of ratification contains the following reservation:

"...., in accordance with the provisions of Article 42 of the Convention, the United Kingdom declares that it shall not be bound to assume any costs referred to in the second paragraph of Article 26 of the Convention resulting from the participation of legal counsel or advisers or from court proceedings, except insofar as those costs may be covered by its system of legal aid and advice."

The Government of the United Kingdom declared, that, in accordance with Article 6 of the Convention, it has designated the following Central Authorities:

"(i) for England and Wales,

(Central Authority for England and Wales and the Central Authority to which applications may be addressed for transmission to the appropriate Central Authority within the United Kingdom.)

adresse/address: The Child Abduction Unit
Official Solicitors Department
4th Floor
81 Chancery Lane
LONDON WC2A 1DD
United Kingdom

numéro de téléphone/telephone number: (44)-71-911-7127 (renseignements/enquiries)

numéro de télex/telex number: —

numéro de télécopie/telefax number: (44)-71-911-7248

personnes à contacter/persons to contact: Mlle/Miss Andrea DYE
tél./tel.: (44)-71-911-7047
Mlle/Miss Wendy DUNBAR (langues de communication/languages of communication: espagnol, français/Spanish, French)
tél./tel.: (44)-71-911-7094

(ii) for Northern Ireland,
Northern Ireland Court Service
Windsor House,
9/15 Bedford Street,
Belfast BT 7LT.;
Northern Ireland
telephone number: (0232) 228 594
persons to contact: M./Mr J.W. BAILIE
(remplace Mme Bowers/replaced Mrs Bowers)

(iii) Office of the Secretary of State
for Scotland
The Scottish Courts Administration
26/27 Royal Terrace
EDINBURGH EH7 5AH
Scotland U.K.
numéro de téléphone/telephone number: (031) 556 0755
personnes à contacter/persons to contact: M./Mr ROBERTSON

In conformity with Article 6, paragraph 2, of the Convention, the United Kingdom of Great Britain and Northern Ireland designated as Central Authority to which applications may be addressed for transmission to the appropriate Central Authority:

the Lord Chancellor's Department,
House of Lords,
London SW1A 0PW

The Convention is ratified in respect of the United Kingdom of Great Britain and Northern Ireland only. The Government of the United Kingdom declared, that, in accordance with Article 39 of the Convention, it will notify the depositary in due course of the territories for the international relations of which it is responsible, to which the Convention is to be extended.

In accordance with Article 43, paragraph 1, the Convention will enter into force for the United Kingdom of Great Britain and Northern Ireland on 1 August 1986.

Notification pursuant to Article 45 of the Convention

On 28 June 1991 the United Kingdom of Great Britain and Northern Ireland declared in accordance with Article 39 that the Convention shall extend to the Isle of Man.

The Convention will enter into force for the Isle of Man on 1 September 1991 in accordance with Article 43, paragraph 2.

[11] *Notification pursuant to Article 45 of the Convention*

In accordance with Article 37, paragraph 2, the United States of America deposited on 29 April 1988 its instrument of ratification of the above-mentioned Convention with the Ministry of Foreign Affairs of the Kingdom of the Netherlands.

The instrument of ratification contains the following reservations:

"(1) Pursuant to the second paragraph of Article 24, and Article 42, the United States makes the following reservation: All applications, communications and other documents sent to the U.S. Central Authority should be accompanied by their translation into English.

(2) Pursuant to the third paragraph of Article 26, the United States declares that it will not be bound to assume any costs or expenses resulting from the participation of legal counsel or advisers or from court and legal proceedings in connection with efforts to return children from the United States pursuant to the Convention except insofar as those costs or expenses are covered by a legal aid program."

The United States of America designated as the Central Authority mentioned in Article 6 of the Convention: Central Authority designated under the *Hague Convention of 25 October 1980 on the civil aspects of international child abduction.*

adresse/address: Office of Children's Issues (CA/OCS/CI)
Room 4800
US Department of State
2201 C Street, N.W.
WASHINGTON, DC 20520
United States of America

numéro de téléphone/telephone number: (1)-202-647-2688

numéro de télex/telex number: —

numéro de télécopie/telefax number: (1)-202-647-2835

personnes à contacter/persons to contact: M./Mr James L. SCHULER, Acting Director
Mme/Ms Anita D. BANKS
Mme/Ms Barbara M. DEROSA
Mme/Ms Elizabeth M. WADIUM
Mme/Ms Judy ROUSE
Mme/Ms Charisse PHILLIPS

In accordance with Article 43, the Convention entered into force for the United States of America on July 1, 1988.

P.L. 100-300 (International Child Abduction Remedies Act) was enacted to facilitate implementation of the Convention. Pertinent regulations may be found at 22 CFR 94; pertinent forms may be obtained from the Office of Citizens Consular Services (CA/OCS/CCS), Room 4817, Department of State, Washington, D.C. 20520; phone number (202) 647-3666.

[12] *Notification pursuant to Article 45 of the Convention*

The First Secretary of the Embassy of Yugoslavia at The Hague signed on 27 September 1991, in accordance with Article 37, paragraph 1, the above-mentioned Convention for the Socialist Federal Republic of Yugoslavia as follows:

27.09.1991
R. JANKOVIĆ

In accordance with Article 37, paragraph 2, Yugoslavia deposited its instrument of ratification of the above-mentioned Convention with the Ministry of Foreign Affairs of the Kingdom of the Netherlands on 27 September 1991.

In accordance with Article 43 the Convention will enter into force for the Socialist Federal Republic of Yugoslavia on 1 December 1991.

Ed. Note—The U.S. view is that the Socialist Federal Republic of Yugoslavia has dissolved and no successor state represents its continuation.

[13] In accordance with Article 6, paragraph 1, Zimbabwe has designated as Central Authority: "the Secretary for the Ministry of Justice, Legal and Parliamentary Affairs".

In accordance with article 38, paragraph 5, the Convention entered into force between Zimbabwe and the following States: *United States of America* (EIF: 1 August 1995); *United Kingdom of Great Britain and Northern Ireland* (EIF: 1 October 1995)*; *Luxembourg* (EIF: 1 October 1995); *Netherlands (for the Kingdom in Europe)* (EIF: 1 November 1995); *New Zealand* (EIF: 1 November 1995); *Mexico* (EIF: 1 December 1995); *Australia* (EIF: 1 April 1996); *Chile* (EIF: 1 May 1996); *Zimbabwe* and *Cyprus* (EIF: 1 August 1996).

* The Note of the Embassy of the United Kingdom contains the following declaration with regard to the accession of Zimbabwe to the Convention: "Notwithstanding the provisions of the said Article 38 regarding entry into force of the Convention as between the acceding State and the State that has declared its acceptance of the accession, the municipal law of the United Kingdom will be amended with effect from 1 July 1995 to give effect to the provisions of the Convention between it and Zimbabwe from the date when the Convention enters into force for Zimbabwe. I should be grateful for confirmation of the date of 1 July 1995 as the date on which the Convention will enter into force between the United Kingdom and Zimbabwe." The Ministry of Foreign Affairs of the Kingdom of the Netherlands has not yet received any communication from the Government of Zimbabwe concerning the date of entry into force proposed by the United Kingdom.

INTER-AMERICAN CONVENTION ON LETTERS ROGATORY

The Governments of the Member States of the Organization of American States, desirous of concluding a convention on letters rogatory, have agreed as follows:

I. USE OF TERMS

Article 1

For the purposes of this Convention the terms "exhortos" and "cartas rogatorias" are synonymous in the Spanish text. The terms "letters rogatory", "commissions rogatoires", and "cartas rogatórias" used in the English, French and Portuguese texts, respectively, cover both "exhortos" and "cartas rogatorias".

II. SCOPE OF THE CONVENTION

Article 2

This Convention shall apply to letters rogatory, issued in conjunction with proceedings in civil and commercial matters held before the appropriate judicial or other adjudicatory authority of one of the States Parties to this Convention, that have as their purpose:

a. The performance of procedural acts of a merely formal nature, such as service of process, summonses or subpoenas abroad;
b. The taking of evidence and the obtaining of information abroad, unless a reservation is made in this respect.

Article 3

This Convention shall not apply to letters rogatory relating to procedural acts other than those specified in the preceding article; and in particular it shall not apply to acts involving measures of compulsion.

III. TRANSMISSION OF LETTERS ROGATORY

Article 4

Letters rogatory may be transmitted to the authority to which they are addressed by the interested parties, through judicial channels, diplomatic or consular agents, or the Central Authority of the State of origin or of the State of destination, as the case may be.

Each State Party shall inform the General Secretariat of the Organization of American States of the Central Authority competent to receive and distribute letters rogatory.

IV. REQUIREMENTS FOR EXECUTION

Article 5

Letters rogatory shall be executed in the States Parties provided they meet the following requirements:

a. The letter rogatory is legalized, except as provided for in Articles 6 and 7 of this Convention. The letter rogatory shall be presumed to be duly legalized in the State of origin when legalized by the competent consular or diplomatic agent;
b. The letter rogatory and the appended documentation are duly translated into the official language of the State of destination.

Article 6

Whenever letters rogatory are transmitted through consular or diplomatic channels or through the Central Authority, legalization shall not be required.

Article 7

Courts in border areas of the States Parties may directly execute the letters rogatory contemplated in this Convention and such letters shall not require legalization.

Article 8

Letters rogatory shall be accompanied by the following documents to be delivered to the person on whom process, summons or subpoena is being served:

a. An authenticated copy of the complaint with its supporting documents, and of other exhibits or rulings that serve as the basis for the measure requested;
b. Written information identifying the judicial or other adjudicatory authority issuing the letter, indicating the time-limits allowed the person affected to act upon the request, and warning of the consequences of failure to do so;
c. Where appropriate, information on the existence and address of the court-appointed defense counsel or of competent legal-aid societies in the State of origin.

Article 9

Execution of letters rogatory shall not imply ultimate recognition of the jurisdiction of the judicial or other adjudicatory authority issuing the letter rogatory or a commitment to recognize the validity of the judgment it may render or to execute it.

V. EXECUTION

Article 10

Letters rogatory shall be executed in accordance with the laws and procedural rules of the State of destination.

At the request of the judicial or other adjudicatory authority issuing the letter rogatory, the authority of the State of destination may execute the letter through a special procedure, or accept the observance of additional formalities in performing the act requested, provided this procedure or the observance of those formalities is not contrary to the law of the State of destination.

Article 11

The authority of the State of destination shall have jurisdiction to determine any issue arising as a result of the execution of the measure requested in the letter rogatory.

Should such authority find that it lacks jurisdiction to execute the letter rogatory, it shall *ex officio* forward the documents and antecedents of the case to the authority of the State which has jurisdiction.

Article 12

The costs and other expenses involved in the processing and execution of letters rogatory shall be borne by the interested parties.

The State of destination may, in its discretion, execute a letter rogatory that does not indicate the person to be held responsible for costs and other expenses when incurred. The identity of the person empowered to represent the applicant for legal purposes may be indicated in the letter rogatory or in the documents relating to its execution.

The effects of a declaration *in forma pauperis* shall be regulated by the law of the State of destination.

Article 13

Consular or diplomatic agents of the States Parties to this Convention may perform the acts referred to in Article 2 in the State in which they are accredited, provided the performance of such acts is not contrary to the laws of that State. In so doing, they shall not perform any acts involving measures of compulsion.

VI. GENERAL PROVISIONS

Article 14

States Parties belonging to economic integration systems may agree directly between themselves upon special methods and procedures more expeditious than those provided for in this Convention. These agreements may be extended to include other States in the manner in which the parties may agree.

Article 15

This Convention shall not limit any provisions regarding letters rogatory in bilateral or multilateral agreements that may have been signed or may be signed in the future by the States Parties or preclude the continuation of more favorable practices in this regard that may be followed by these States.

Article 16

The States Parties to this Convention may declare that its provisions cover the execution of letters rogatory in criminal, labor, and "contentious-administrative" cases, as well as in arbitrations and other matters within the jurisdiction of special courts. Such declarations shall be transmitted to the General Secretariat of the Organization of American States.

Article 17

The State of destination may refuse to execute a letter rogatory that is manifestly contrary to its public policy ("ordre public").

Article 18

The States Parties shall inform the General Secretariat of the Organization of American States of the requirements stipulated in their laws for the legalization and the translation of letters rogatory.

VII. FINAL PROVISIONS

Article 19

This Convention shall be open for signature by the Member States of the Organization of American States.

Article 20

This Convention is subject to ratification. The instruments of ratification shall be deposited with the General Secretariat of the Organization of American States.

Article 21

This Convention shall remain open for accession by any other State. The instrument of accession shall be deposited with the General Secretariat of the Organization of American States.

Article 22

This Convention shall enter into force on the thirtieth day following the date of deposit of the second instrument of ratification.

For each state ratifying or acceding to the Convention after the deposit of the second instrument of ratification, the Convention shall enter into force on the thirtieth day after deposit by such State of its instrument of ratification or accession.

Article 23

If a State Party has two or more territorial units in which different systems of law apply in relation to the matters dealt with in this Convention, it may, at the time of signature, ratification or accession, declare that this Convention shall extend to all its territorial units or only to one or more of them.

Such declaration may be modified by subsequent declarations, which shall expressly indicate the territorial unit or units to which the Convention applies. Such subsequent declarations shall be transmitted to the General Secretariat of the Organization of American States, and shall become effective thirty days after the date of their receipt.

Article 24

This Convention shall remain in force indefinitely, but any of the States Parties may denounce it. The instrument of denunciation shall be deposited with the General Secretariat of the Organization of American States. After one year from the date of deposit of the instrument of denunciation, the Convention shall no longer be in effect for the denouncing State, but shall remain in effect for the other States Parties.

Article 25

The original instrument of this Convention, the English, French, Portuguese and Spanish texts of which are equally authentic, shall be deposited with the General Secretariat of the Organization of American States. The Secretariat shall notify the Member States of the Organization of American States and the States that have acceded to the Convention of the signatures, deposits of instruments of ratification, accession, and denunciation as well as of reservations, if any. It shall also transmit the information mentioned in the second paragraph of Article 4 and in Article 18 and the declarations referred to in Articles 16 and 23 of this Convention.

IN WITNESS WHEREOF the undersigned Plenipotentiaries, being duly authorized thereto by their respective Governments, have signed this Convention.

DONE AT PANAMA CITY, Republic of Panama, this thirtieth day of January one thousand nine hundred and seventy-five.

[Signatures omitted]

Inter-American Convention on Letters Rogatory.
Done at Panama January 30, 1975; entered into force for the United States August 27, 1988.
States which are parties:
Argentina*
Brazil*
Chile[1],*
Colombia*
Costa Rica
Ecuador[2],*
El Salvador[3]
Guatemala[4],*
Honduras
Mexico[5],*
Panama*
Paraguay*
Peru*
Spain[6]
United States[7]
Uruguay[8],*
Venezuela[9]*

* The United States has a treaty relationship only with those countries, which are a party to the Convention and the Additional Protocol.

---

[1] (Declaration made at the time of ratification, according to Article 16 of the Convention)

The instrument of ratification corresponding to this Convention contains the declaration "that its provisions cover the execution of letters rogatory in criminal, labor, and contentious-administrative cases, as well as in arbitrations and other matters within the jurisdiction of special courts".

(Provided information in accordance with Article 4)
The Central Authority to receive and distribute letters rogatory is the Ministry of Foreign Affairs of the Republic of Chile (May 7, 1987).

[2] On 23 April 1984 sent information (Note No. 89-OEA/84), appointing the Asesoría Técnico-Jurídica of the Ministry of Foreign Affairs of Ecuador as the "Central Authority, to carry out the functions entrusted to it in the Inter-American Convention on Letters Rogatory."

[3] Reservation to application of Article 7.
(Provided information in accordance with Articles 4 and 18)
In El Salvador the Supreme Court of Justice is the competent central authority for receiving and distributing Letters Rogatory. The requirements exacted for legalization and translation of Letters Rogatory are those prescribed in Article 261 of the Code of Civil Procedures and Articles 388, 389, 391 and 392 of the Bustamente Code . . . (The text of the articles is omitted).

[4] (Provided information in accordance with Article 4)
The Central Authority competent to transmit, receive and distribute letters rogatory is the Supreme Court of Justice (October 21, 1987)

[5] With the interpretative declaration made at the time of signature.
"It is the interpretation of the Government of Mexico that Article 9 of this Convention refers to the international validity of foreign judgments."
(Provided information in accordance with Article 4)
The Central Authority competent to receive and distribute letters rogatory is the Secretariat of Foreign Affairs of Mexico.

[6] (Provided information in accordance with Article 4)
The Central Authority competent to receive and distribute letters rogatory is the General Technical Secretariat of the Ministry of Justice (Secretaría General Técnica), whose address is: San Bernardo 47, Madrid 28015, Spain (April 14, 1988).

[7] (Reservations made at the time of ratification)
"1. Pursuant to Article 2(b) of the Inter-American Convention on Letters Rogatory, letters rogatory that have as their purpose the taking of evidence shall be excluded from the rights, obligations and operation of this Convention between the United States and another State Party.
2. In ratifying the Inter-American Convention on Letters Rogatory, the United States accepts entry into force and undertakes treaty relations only with respect to States which have ratified or acceded to the Additional Protocol as well as the Inter-American Convention, and not with respect to States which have ratified or acceded to the Inter-American Convention alone."
(Provided information in accordance with Articles 4 and 18)
Pursuant to Article 4 of the Convention and Article 2 of the Additional Protocol, the Government of the United States wishes to inform the Secretary General that the Department of Justice is the Central Authority competent to receive and distribute letters rogatory. The mailing address for these purposes is:
Office of International Judicial Assistance
Civil Division
Department of Justice
Todd Building Room 1234
550 11th Street, N.W.
Washington, D.C. 20530 (*)
Pursuant to Article 18 of the Convention, the Government of the United States wishes to inform the Secretary General that letters rogatory to be executed in the United States must be translated into the English language.
(*) Phone: (202) 724-7455

[8] (Provided information in accordance with Article 4)
On 30 August 1985 sent information (Note No. 961/85) appointing the Ministry of Education and Culture "Asesoría Autoridad Central de Cooperación Jurídica Internacional" as the "Central Authority" provided for in Article 4 of the Convention.

[9] (Reservation made at the time of ratification)
With reservation to letter b) of Article 2 of the Convention.
(Provided information in accordance with Article 4)
The Central Authority competent to receive and distribute letters rogatory is the Ministry of Foreign Affairs of the Republic of Venezuela (11 December 1984).

ADDITIONAL PROTOCOL TO THE INTER-AMERICAN CONVENTION ON LETTERS ROGATORY

The Governments of the Member States of the Organization of American States, desirous of strengthening and facilitating international cooperation in judicial procedures as provided for in the Inter-American Convention on Letters Rogatory, done in Panama on January 30, 1975, have agreed as follows:

I. SCOPE OF PROTOCOL

Article 1

This Protocol shall apply only to those procedural acts set forth in Article 2(a) of the Inter-American Convention on Letters Rogatory, hereinafter referred to as "the Convention". For the purposes of this Protocol, such acts shall be understood to mean procedural acts (pleadings, motions, orders, and subpoenas) that are served and requests for information that are made by a judicial or other adjudicatory authority of a State Party to a judicial or administrative authority of another State Party and are transmitted by a letter rogatory from the Central Authority of the State of origin to the Central Authority of the State of destination.

II. CENTRAL AUTHORITY

Article 2

Each State Party shall designate a central authority that shall perform the functions assigned to it in the Convention and in this Protocol. At the time of deposit of their instruments of ratification or accession to this Protocol, the States Parties shall communicate the designations to the General Secretariat of the Organization of American States, which shall distribute to the States Parties to the Convention a list containing the designations received. The Central Authority designated by a State Party in accordance with Article 4 of the Convention may be changed at any time. The State Party shall inform the above-mentioned Secretariat of such change as promptly as possible.

III. PREPARATION OF LETTERS ROGATORY

Article 3

Letters rogatory shall be prepared on forms that are printed in the four official languages of the Organization of American States or in the languages of the State of origin and of the State of destination and conform to Form A contained in the Annex to this Protocol.

Letters regatory shall be accompanied by the following:

a. Copy of the complaint or pleading that initiated the action in which the letter rogatory was issued, as well as a translation thereof into the language of the State of destination;
b. Untranslated copy of the documents attached to the complaint or pleading;
c. Untranslated copy of any rulings ordering issuance of the letter rogatory;
d. Form conforming to Form B annexed to this Protocol and containing essential information for the person to be served or the authority to receive the documents; and
e. Certificate conforming to Form C annexed to this Protocol on which the Central Authority of the State of destination shall attest to execution or non-execution of the letter rogatory.

The copies shall be regarded as authenticated for the purposes of Article 8 (a) of the Convention if they bear the seal of the judicial or other adjudicatory authority that issued the letter rogatory.

A copy of the letter rogatory together with Form B and the copies referred to in items a, b, and c of this Article shall be delivered to the person notified or to the authority to which the request is addressed. One of the copies of the letter rogatory and the documents attached to it shall remain in the possession of the State of destination; the untranslated original, the certificate of execution and the documents attached to them shall be returned to the Central Authority of the State of origin through appropriate channels.

If a State Party has more than one official language, it shall, at the time of signature, ratification or accession to this Protocol, declare which language or languages shall be considered official for the purposes of the Convention and of this Protocol. If a State Party comprises territorial units that have different official languages, it shall, at the time of signature, ratification or accession to this Protocol, declare which language or languages in each territorial unit shall be considered official for the purposes of the Convention and of this Protocol. The General Secretariat of the Organization of American States shall distribute to the States Parties to this Protocol the information contained in such declarations.

IV. TRANSMISSION AND PROCESSING OF LETTERS ROGATORY

Article 4

Upon receipt of a letter rogatory from the Central Authority in another State Party, the Central Authority in the State of destination shall transmit the letter rogatory to the appropriate judicial or administrative authority for processing in accordance with the applicable local law.

Upon execution of the letter rogatory, the judicial or administrative authority or authorities that processed it shall attest to the execution thereof in the manner prescribed in their local law, and shall transmit it with the relevant documents to the Central Authority. The Central Authority of the State Party of destination shall certify execution of the letter rogatory to the Central Authority of the State Party of origin on a form conforming to Form C of the Annex, which shall not require legalization. In addition, the Central Authority of the State of destination shall return the letter rogatory and attached documents to the Central Authority of the State of origin for delivery to the judicial or other adjudicatory authority that issued it.

V. COSTS AND EXPENSES

Article 5

The processing of letters rogatory by the Central Authority of the State Party of destination and its judicial or administrative authorities shall be free of charge. However, this State Party may seek payment by parties requesting execution of letters rogatory for those services which, in accordance with its local law, are required to be paid for directly by those parties.

The party requesting the execution of a letter rogatory shall, at its election, either select and indicate in the letter rogatory the person who is responsible in the State of destination for the cost of such services or, alternatively, shall attach to the letter rogatory a check for the fixed amount that is specified in Article 6 of this Protocol for its processing by the State of destination and will cover the cost of such services or a document proving that such amount has been transferred by some other means to the Central Authority of the State of destination.

The fact that the cost of such services ultimately exceeds the fixed amount shall not delay or prevent the processing or execution of the letter rogatory by the Central Authority or the judicial or administrative authorities of the State of destination. Should the cost exceed that amount, the Central Authority of the State of destination may, when returning the executed letter rogatory, seek payment of the outstanding amount due from the party requesting execution of the letter rogatory.

Article 6

At the time of deposit of its instrument of ratification or accession to this Protocol with the General Secretariat of the Organization of American States, each State Party shall attach a schedule of the services and the costs and other expenses that, in accordance with its local law, shall be paid directly by the party requesting execution of the letter rogatory. In addition, each State Party shall specify in the above-mentioned schedule the single amount which it considers will reasonably cover the cost of such services, regardless of the number or nature thereof. This amount shall be paid when the person requesting execution of the letter rogatory has not designated a person responsible for the payment of such services in the State of destination but has decided to pay for them directly in the manner provided for in Article 5 of this Protocol.

The General Secretariat of the Organization of American States shall distribute the information received to the States Parties to this Protocol. A State Party may at any time notify the General Secretariat of the Organization of American States of changes in the above-mentioned schedules, which shall be communicated by the General Secretariat to the other States Parties to this Protocol.

Article 7

States Parties may declare in the schedules mentioned in the foregoing articles that, provided there is reciprocity, they will not charge parties requesting execution of letters rogatory for the services necessary for executing them, or will accept in complete satisfaction of the cost of such services either the single fixed amount specified in Article 6 or another specified amount.

Article 8

This Protocol shall be open for signature and subject to ratification or accession by those Member States of the Organization of American States that have signed, ratified, or acceded to the Inter-American Convention on Letters Rogatory signed in Panama on January 30, 1975.

This Protocol shall remain open for accession by any other State that accedes or has acceded to the Inter-American Convention on Letters Rogatory, under the conditions set forth in this article.

The instruments of ratification and accession shall be deposited with the General Secretariat of the Organization of American States.

Article 9

This Protocol shall enter into force on the thirtieth day following the date on which two States Parties to the Convention have deposited their instruments of ratification or accession to this Protocol.

For each State ratifying or acceding to the Protocol after its entry into force, the Protocol shall enter into force on the thirtieth day following deposit by such State of its instrument of ratification or accession, provided that such State is a Party to the Convention.

Article 10

If a State Party has two or more territorial units in which different systems of law apply in relation to matters dealt with in this Protocol, it may, at the time of signature, ratification or accession, declare that this Protocol shall extend to all its territorial units or only to one or more of them.

Such declaration may be modified by subsequent declarations that shall expressly indicate the territorial unit or units to which this Protocol applies. Such subsequent declarations shall be transmitted to the General Secretariat of the Organization of American States, and shall become effective thirty days after the date of their receipt.

Article 11

This Protocol shall remain in force indefinitely, but any of the States Parties may denounce it. The instrument of denunciation shall be deposited with the General Secretariat of the Organization of American States. After one year from the date of deposit of the instrument of denunciation, the Protocol shall no longer be in effect for the denouncing State, but shall remain in effect for the other States Parties.

Article 12

The original instrument of this Protocol and its Annex (Forms A, B and C), the English, French, Portuguese and Spanish texts of which are equally authentic, shall be deposited with the General Secretariat of the Organization of American States, which will forward an authenticated copy of the text to the Secretariat of the United Nations for registration and publication in accordance with Article 102 of its Charter. The General Secretariat of the Organization of American States shall notify the Member States of that Organization and the States that have acceded to the Protocol of the signatures, deposits of instruments of ratification, accession and denunciation, as well as of reservations, if any. It shall also transmit to them the information mentioned in Article 2, the last paragraph of Article 3, and Article 6 and the declarations referred to in Article 10 of this Protocol.

IN WITNESS WHEREOF the undersigned Plenipotentiaries, being duly authorized thereto by their respective Governments, have signed this Protocol.

DONE AT MONTEVIDEO, Republic of Uruguay, this eighth day of May, one thousand nine hundred and seventy-nine.

[Signatures omitted]

ANNEX TO THE ADDITIONAL PROTOCOL TO THE INTER-AMERICAN CONVENTION ON LETTERS ROGATORY

FORM A

LETTER ROGATORY[1]

1	2
REQUESTING JUDICIAL OR OTHER ADJUDICATORY AUTHORITY Name Address	CASE: DOCKET No.:
3	4
CENTRAL AUTHORITY OF THE STATE OF ORIGIN Name Address	CENTRAL AUTHORITY OF THE STATE OF DESTINATION Name Address
5	6
REQUESTING PARTY Name Address	COUNSEL TO THE REQUESTING PARTY Name Address

PERSON DESIGNATED TO ACT IN CONNECTION WITH THE LETTER ROGATORY

Name

Address

Is this person responsible for costs and expenses?
YES h NO h
* If not, check in the amount of __________ is attached
* Or proof of payment is attached

[1] Complete the original and two copies of this form; if A(1) is applicable, attach the original and two copies of the translation of this item in the language of the State of destination.
* Delete if inapplicable.

The Central Authority signing this letter rogatory has the honor to transmit to you in triplicate the documents listed below and, in conformity with the Protocol to the Inter-American Convention on Letters Rogatory:

*A. requests their prompt service on:

____

____

____

The undersigned authority requests that service be carried out in the following manner:

*(1). In accordance with the special procedure or additional formalities that are described below, as provided for in the second paragraph of Article 10 of the above-mentioned Convention; or

____

____

____

____

*(2). By service personally on the identified addressee or, in the case of a legal entity, on its authorized agent; or

*(3). If the person or the authorized agent of the entity to be served is not found, service shall be made in accordance with the law of the State of destination.

*B. Requests the delivery of the documents listed below to the following judicial or administrative authority:

Authority______________________________

____

____

*C. Requests the Central Authority of the State of destination to return to the Central Authority of the state of origin one copy of the documents listed below and attached to this letter rogatory, and an executed Certificate on the attached Form C.

Done at __________ this ________ date of __________, 19 __.

______________________________	______________________________
Signature and stamp of the judicial or other adjudicatory authority of the State of origin	Signature and stamp of the Central Authority of the State of origin

Title or other identification of each document to be delivered:

____

____

(Attach additional pages, if necessary.)

* Delete if inapplicable.

ANNEX TO THE ADDITIONAL PROTOCOL TO THE INTER-AMERICAN CONVENTION ON LETTERS ROGATORY

FORM B

ESSENTIAL INFORMATION FOR THE ADDRESSEE[1]

To (Name and address of the person being served)

____

____

You are hereby informed that (Brief statement of nature of service) ____________

A copy of the letter rogatory that gives rise to the service or delivery of these documents is attached to this document. This copy also contains essential information for you. Also attached are copies of the complaint or pleading initiating the action in which the letter rogatory was issued, of the documents attached to the complaint or pleading, and of any rulings that ordered the issuance of the letter rogatory.

ADDITIONAL INFORMATION

I *

FOR SERVICE

A. The document being served on you (original or copy) concerns the following:

B. The remedies sought or the amount in dispute is as follows:

C. By this service, you are requested:

D. * In case of service on you as a defendant you can answer the complaint before the judicial or other adjudicatory authority specified in Form A, Box 1 (State place, date and hour):

* You are being summoned to appear as:

* If some other action is being requested of the person served, please describe:

[1] Complete the original and two copies of this form in the language of the State of origin and two copies in the language of the State of destination.

* Delete if inapplicable.

E. If you fail to comply, the consequences might be:

F. You are hereby informed that a defense counsel appointed by the Court or the following legal aid societies are available to you at the place where the proceeding is pending.

Name:

Address:

The documents listed in Part III are being furnished to you so that you may better understand and defend your interests.

II*

FOR INFORMATION FROM JUDICIAL OR ADMINISTRATIVE AUTHORITY

To:

(Name and address of the judicial or administrative authority)

You are respectfully requested to furnish the undersigned authority with the following information:

The documents listed in Part III are being furnished to you to facilitate your reply.

* Delete if inapplicable.

III

LIST OF ATTACHED DOCUMENTS

(Attach additional pages if necessary.)

Done at ______ this ______ day of ______, 19__

Signature and stamp of the judicial or other adjudicatory authority of the State of origin	Signature and stamp of the Central Authority of the State of Origin

ANNEX TO THE ADDITIONAL PROTOCOL TO THE INTER-AMERICAN CONVENTION ON LETTERS ROGATORY

FORM C

CERTIFICATE OF EXECUTION[1]

To: ______________________________

____

____

(Name and address of judicial or other adjudicatory authority that issued the letter rogatory)

In conformity with the Additional Protocol to the Inter-American Convention on Letters Rogatory, signed at Montevideo on May 8, 1979, and in accordance with the attached original letter rogatory, the undersigned Central Authority has the honor to certify the following:

*A. That one copy of the documents attached to this Certificate has been served or delivered as follows:

Date: ______________________________

At (Address) ______________________________

By one of the following methods authorized by the Convention.

*(1) In accordance with the special procedure or additional formalities that are described below, as provided for in the second paragraph of Article 10 of the above-mentioned Convention, or

____

____

____

*(2) By service personally on the identified addressee or, in the case of a legal entity, on its authorized agent, or

*(3) If the person or the authorized agent of the entity to be served was not found, in accordance with the law of the State of destination: (Specify method used)

____

____

____

____

*B. That the documents referred to in the letter rogatory have been delivered to:

Identity of person ______________________________

____

____

Relationship to the addressee ______________________________

(family, business or other)

____

*C. That the documents attached to the Certificate have not been served or delivered for the following reason(s):

____

____

____

____

*D. In conformity with the Protocol, the party requesting execution of the letter rogatory is requested to pay the outstanding balance of costs in the amount indicated in the attached statement.

Done at ____________ the ____________ day of ____________ 19__

____

Signature and stamp of Central Authority of the State of destination

Where appropriate, attach originals or copies of any additional documents proving service or delivery, and identify them.

---

[1] Complete the original and one copy in the language of the State of destination.

* Delete if inapplicable.

Additional Protocol to the Inter-American Convention on Letters Rogatory, with Annex. Done at Montevideo May 8, 1979; entered into force for the United States August 27, 1988. States which are parties:

Argentina*
Brazil*
Chile*
Colombia*
Ecuador[1]*
Guatemala*
Mexico[2]*
Panama[2a]*
Paraguay*
Peru*
United States[3]
Uruguay[4]*
Venezuela*

* The United States has a treaty relationship only with those countries which are a party to the Convention and the Additional Protocol

---

[1] On 23 April 1984 sent information (Note No. 89-OEA/84), appointing the Asesoría Técnico-Jurídica of the Ministry of Foreign Affairs of Ecuador as the "Central Authority", to carry out the functions entrusted to it in the Additional Protocol to the Inter-American Convention on Letters Rogatory.

[2] In accordance with the provisions stipulated in Article 2 of the Additional Protocol to the Inter-American Convention on Letters Rogatory relative to the designation of a centeral authority, I notify Your Excellency that this shall be the Secretariat of Foreign Affairs of Mexico (9 March 1983).

[2a] (Provided information in accordance with Article 2 of the Protocol)

On October 4, 1991, Panama designated the Ministry of Foreign Affairs as the Central Authority competent pursuant to the functions of article 2 of the Protocol.

[3] (Reservations made at the time of ratification)

"1. Pursuant to Article 2(b) of the Inter-American Convention on Letters Rogatory, letters rogatory that have as their purpose the taking of evidence shall be excluded from the rights, obligations and operation of this Convention between the United States and another State Party.

2. In ratifying the Inter-American Convention on Letters Rogatory, the United States accepts entry into force and undertakes treaty relations only with respect to States which have ratified or acceded to the Additional Protocol as well as the Inter-American Convention, and not with respect to States which have ratified or acceded to the Inter-American Convention alone."

(Provided information in accordance with Article 2)

Pursuant to Article 4 of the Convention and Article 2 of the Additional Protocol, the Government of the United States wishes to inform the Secretary General that the Department of Justice is the Central Authority competent to receive and distribute letters rogatory. The mailing address for these purpose is:

Office of International Judicial Assistance
Civil Division
Department of Justice
Todd Building Room 1234
550 11th Street, N.W.
Washington, D.C. 20530
Phone: (202) 724-7455

(Declarations made at the time of ratification)

Pursuant to Article 6 of the Additional Protocol, the Government of the United States declares that the United States reserves the right to charge a total of twenty-five dollars for performance of the services referred to therein.

Pursuant to Article 7 of the Additional Protocol, the Government of the United States declares that the aforementioned charge shall be waived on a reciprocal basis for the execution of a letter rogatory emanating from any State Party to both the Convention and Additional Protocol and may be otherwise waived as appropriate.

[4] (Declaration made at the time of ratification)

With the declaration made at the time of signature.

The scope of public order:

Uruguay wishes to state that it expressly ratifies the line of thought enunciated in Panama at CIDIP-I, reaffirming its genuine Pan American spirit and its clear and positive decision to contribute with its ideas and endorsement to the successful development of the legal community.

This line of thinking and conduct has been evidenced in undoubtable form by the unreserved ratification by Uruguay of all the Conventions of Panama, approved by law number 14,534 in 1976.

In line with the foregoing, Uruguay gives its affirmative vote to the formula regarding public order. Nevertheless, Uruguay wishes to state expressly and clearly that, in accordance with the position it maintained in Panama, its interpretation of the aforementioned exception refers to international public order as an individual juridical institution, not necessarily identifiable with the internal public order of each state.

Therefore, in the opinion of Uruguay, the approved formula conveys an exceptional authorization to the various States Parties to declare in a nondiscretionary and well-founded manner that the precepts of foreign law are inapplicable whenever these concretely and in a serious and open manner offend the standards and principles essential to the international public order on which each individual state bases its legal individuality.

(Provided information in accordance with Articles 2, 6 and 7)

For the purposes indicated in articles six and seven of the above-cited Protocol, I wish to state that the single fixed amount of the cost of the services necessary for execution of the letter rogatory will be twenty readjustable units or its equivalent in currency. Also the schedule of the services that must be paid directly by the interested party will be limited to the possibility of resorting to the need for the services of appraisers, experts and other assistants in the case affected.

On 30 August 1985 sent information (Note No. 961/85) appointing the Ministry of Education and Culture "Asesoría Autoridad Central de Cooperación Jurídica Internacional" as the "Central Authority" provided for in Article 2 of the Protocol.

INTER-AMERICAN CONVENTION
ON INTERNATIONAL COMMERCIAL ARBITRATION

The Governments of the Member States of the Organization of American States, desirous of concluding a convention on international commercial arbitration, have agreed as follows:

Article 1

An agreement in which the parties undertake to submit to arbitral decision any differences that may arise or have arisen between them with respect to a commercial transaction is valid. The agreement shall be set forth in an instrument signed by the parties, or in the form of an exchange of letters, telegrams, or telex communications.

Article 2

Arbitrators shall be appointed in the manner agreed upon by the parties. Their appointment may be delegated to a third party, whether a natural or juridical person.

Arbitrators may be nationals or foreigners.

Article 3

In the absence of an express agreement between the parties, the arbitration shall be conducted in accordance with the rules of procedure of the Inter-American Commercial Arbitration Commission.

Article 4

An arbitral decision or award that is not appealable under the applicable law or procedural rules shall have the force of a final judicial judgment. Its execution or recognition may be ordered in the same manner as that of decisions handed down by national or foreign ordinary courts, in accordance with the procedural laws of the country where it is to be executed and the provisions of international treaties.

Article 5

1. The recognition and execution of the decision may be refused, at the request of the party against which it is made, only if such party is able to prove to the competent authority of the State in which recognition and execution are requested:

a. That the parties to the agreement were subject to some incapacity under the applicable law or that the agreement is not valid under the law to which the parties have submitted it, or, if such law is not specified, under the law of the State in which the decision was made; or

b. That the party against which the arbitral decision has been made was not duly notified of the appointment of the arbitrator or of the arbitration procedure to be followed, or was unable, for any other reason, to present his defense; or

c. That the decision concerns a dispute not envisaged in the agreement between the parties to submit to arbitration; nevertheless, if the provisions of the decision that refer to issues submitted to arbitration can be separated from those not submitted to arbitration, the former may be recognized and executed; or

d. That the constitution of the arbitral tribunal or the arbitration procedure has not been carried out in accordance with the terms of the agreement signed by the parties or, in the absence of such agreement, that the constitution of the arbitral tribunal or the arbitration procedure has not been carried out in accordance with the law of the State where the arbitration took place; or

e. That the decision is not yet binding on the parties or has been annulled or suspended by a competent authority of the State in which, or according to the law of which, the decision has been made.

2. The recognition and execution of an arbitral decision may also be refused if the competent authority of the State in which the recognition and execution is requested finds:

a. That the subject of the dispute cannot be settled by arbitration under the law of that State; or

b. That the recognition or execution of the decision would be contrary to the public policy ("ordre public") of that State.

Article 6

If the competent authority mentioned in Article 5.1.e has been requested to annul or suspend the arbitral decision, the authority before which such decision is invoked may, if it deems it appropriate, postpone a decision on the execution of the arbitral decision and, at the request of the party requesting execution, may also instruct the other party to provide appropriate guaranties.

Article 7

This Convention shall be open for signature by the Member States of the Organization of American States.

Article 8

This Convention is subject to ratification. The instruments of ratification shall be deposited with the General Secretariat of the Organization of American States.

Article 9

This Convention shall remain open for accession by any other State. The instruments of accession shall be deposited with the General Secretariat of the Organization of American States.

Article 10

This Convention shall enter into force on the thirtieth day following the date of deposit of the second instrument of ratification.

For each State ratifying or acceding to the Convention after the deposit of the second instrument of ratification, the Convention shall enter into force on the thirtieth day after deposit by such State of its instrument of ratification or accession.

Article 11

If a State Party has two or more territorial units in which different systems of law apply in relation to the matters dealt with in this Convention, it may, at the time of signature, ratification or accession, declare that this Convention shall extend to all its territorial units or only to one or more of them.

Such declaration may be modified by subsequent declarations, which shall expressly indicate the territorial unit or units to which the Convention applies. Such subsequent declarations shall be transmitted to the General Secretariat of the Organization of American States, and shall become effective thirty days after the date of their receipt.

Article 12

This Convention shall remain in force indefinitely, but any of the States Parties may denounce it. The instrument of denunciation shall be deposited with the General Secretariat of the Organization of American States. After one year from the date of deposit of the instrument of denunciation, the Convention shall no longer be in effect for the denouncing State, but shall remain in effect for the other States Parties.

Article 13

The original instrument of this Convention, the English, French, Portuguese and Spanish texts of which are equally authentic, shall be deposited with the General Secretariat of the Organization of American States. The Secretariat shall notify the Member States of the Organization of American States and the States that have acceded to the Convention of the signatures, deposits of instruments of ratification, accession, and denunciation as well as of reservations, if any. It shall also transmit the declarations referred to in Article 11 of this Convention.

IN WITNESS WHEREOF the undersigned Plenipotentiaries, being duly authorized thereto by their respective Governments, have signed this Convention.

DONE AT PANAMA CITY, Republic of Panama, this thirtieth day of January one thousand nine hundred and seventy-five.

[Signatures omitted]

Inter-American Convention on International Commercial Arbitration. Done at Panama City January 30, 1975; entered into force for the United States October 27, 1990.

States which are parties:

Argentina
Brazil
Chile
Colombia
Costa Rica
Ecuador
El Salvador
Guatemala
Honduras
Mexico
Panama
Paraguay
Peru
United States[1]
Uruguay
Venezuela

---

[1] In accordance with Article 8 of the Convention, the Instrument of Ratification of the Government of the United States of America was deposited with the Secretary General of the Organization of American States on September 27, 1990.

In ratifying the aforesaid Convention, the Government of the United States of America made the following reservations:

"1. Unless there is an express agreement among the parties to an arbitration agreement to the contrary, where the requirements for application of both the Inter-American Convention on International Commercial Arbitration and the Convention on the Recognition and Enforcement of Foreign Arbitral Awards are met, if a majority of such parties are citizens of a state or states that have ratified or acceded to the Inter-American Convention and are member states of the Organization of American States, the Inter-American Convention shall apply. In all other cases, the Convention on the Recognition and Enforcement of Foreign Arbitral Awards shall apply.

2. The United States of America will apply the rules of procedure of the Inter-American Commercial Arbitration Commission which are in effect on the date that the United States of America deposits its instrument of ratification, unless the United States of America makes a later official determination to adopt and apply subsequent amendments to such rules.

3. The United States of America will apply the Convention, on the basis of reciprocity, to the recognition and enforcement of only those awards made in the territory of another Contracting State".